2015
STANDARD POSTAGE STAMP CATALOGUE

ONE HUNDRED AND SEVENTY-FIRST EDITION IN SIX VOLUMES

VOLUME 1

UNITED STATES AND AFFILIATED TERRITORIES
UNITED NATIONS

COUNTRIES OF THE WORLD
A-B

EDITOR	Charles Snee
MANAGING EDITOR	Donna Houseman
EDITOR EMERITUS	James E. Kloetzel
SENIOR EDITOR /NEW ISSUES & VALUING	Martin J. Frankevicz
SENIOR EDITOR	David Akin
SENIOR VALUING ANALYST	Steven R. Myers
ADMINISTRATIVE ASSISTANT/CATALOGUE LAYOUT	Eric Wiessinger
PRINTING AND IMAGE COORDINATOR	Stacey Mahan
CREATIVE DIRECTOR	Mark Potter
ADVERTISING	Angela Nolte
CIRCULATION / PRODUCT PROMOTION MANAGER	Tim Wagner
VICE PRESIDENT/OPERATIONS	Steve Collins
VICE PRESIDENT/PRODUCT DEVELOPMENT	Dean Horowitz
PRESIDENT	Jeff Greisch

Released April 2014
Includes New Stamp Listings through the February 2014 *Linn's Stamp News Monthly* Catalogue Update

Scott Publishing Co.

911 Vandemark Road, Sidney, OH 45365-0828
A division of AMOS PRESS, INC., publishers of *Linn's Stamp News, Linn's Stamp News Monthly, Coin World* and *Coin World Monthly.*

Table of Contents

See Volume 2 through 6 for Countries of the World, C-Z

Volume 2: C-F
Volume 3: G-I
Volume 4: J-M
Volume 5: N-Sam
Volume 6: San-Z

Scott Publishing Mission Statement

The Scott Publishing Team exists to serve the recreational, educational and commercial hobby needs of stamp collectors and dealers.

We strive to set the industry standard for philatelic information and products by developing and providing goods that help collectors identify, value, organize and present their collections.

Quality customer service is, and will continue to be, our highest priority. We aspire toward achieving total customer satisfaction.

ISBN 0-89487-488-8

Library of Congress Card No. 2-3301

Scott Publishing Co.

SCOTT 911 VANDEMARK ROAD, SIDNEY, OHIO 45365 937-498-0802

Greetings, Fellow Scott Catalogue User:

Here come the 2015 Scott catalogues.

Although we are just a few weeks into 2014 as I write, the 2015 Scott catalogue season has been underway in earnest since October 2013.

Almost 12,000 value changes are recorded in Vol. 1 of the 2014 Scott *Standard Postage Stamp Catalogue*, which provides listings for the United States, United Nations and countries of the world, A-B. Almost 2,600 of these changes are recorded for the U.S. and U.N. listings.

Let's take a look at the U.S. scene.

Up front, in the Postage section, there are scattered changes, both up and down. Values for the 1¢ through 90¢ special printings of 1880 (Scott 192-202) are down modestly. There are a few bright spots. The 1857 3¢ rose Washington stamps, Scott 25 and 25A, each rise in value unused, a reflection of the challenge finding these stamps in very fine condition. In the modern era, values are holding steady. Two noticeable exceptions are the 9¢ Capitol Dome stamps that come from booklet panes, Scott 1590 (from booklet pane No. 1623a) and 1590A (from No. 1623Bc). These stamps are now valued used at $20 and $50, respectively. The values apply only to stamps with contemporaneous cancels.

In the Air Post section, values for the iconic Jenny Invert airmail error, Scott C3a, have been lowered. In unused condition, the value drops to $400,000, from $450,000 in 2014. A larger drop is seen in never-hinged condition: from $1,100,000 to $850,000. These decreases are based on rather lackluster sales of several examples during the past couple of years.

The bulk of the value changes are concentrated in the Postal Stationery and United Nations sections. Values for cut squares continue to drop, a trend that began in earnest last year. Collectors appear to be gravitating toward envelope entires, with action concentrated in used entires. Of the 1,200 value changes seen in the UN listings, we see increases concentrated in the modern issues.

Among the small number of new error listings, perhaps the most unusual is a die-cutting-omitted error of the 23¢ Wilma Rudolph booklet pane of 10, Scott 3436c. The plate number, P44, and the product number on the back of the pane indicate that the new error comes from the printing used to produce the folded booklet without the peel strip in the middle, Scott BK279A. On the error, the peel strip is intact.

The design-type descriptions, headlines and illustrations for the 1871-74 Proprietary revenue stamps have been reworked to bring them in line with the listings as presented in the Scott *Specialized Catalogue of United States Stamps and Covers*. These changes make the Vol. 1 listings much easier to understand.

There are new listings for the imperforate pairs of the 1940 Stock Transfer stamps, Scott RD67a-RD85a. The pairs are valued without gum at $250 each.

A new Confederate postmaster's provisional has been added for Fort Valley, Georgia, as Scott 148XU1.

In United Nations (New York), a new printing variety has been added to the listings for the UN Emblem stamp of 1965. Produced using a new plate/cylinder for the dark blue color, the new stamp is Scott 149a. The tagged variety from the Berlin printing has been changed from Scott 149a to 149b.

Finally, numerous footnotes have been added, expanded or corrected for clarity.

As for the A-B countries, it's quiet out there.

The listings for Bahamas were reviewed in their entirety, resulting in more than 900 value changes. With the exception of a small number of increases among the classic-era issue, values are down modestly.

Ready availability of stamps from the beginning of the reign of Queen Elizabeth II through the early 1990s also has kept values steady or slightly declining. Among the handful of increases are the minor varieties of the 1996 Shells definitives that are inscribed 1997, 1999, 2000 and 2001. Each of these sets rises about 10 percent.

The almost 1,500 value changes recorded for Benin reflect moderate decreases in the Postage and Air Post sections. The various surcharged stamps and stamps of Dahomey surcharged for use in Benin increase in value. The surcharged 2008 200-franc-on-250fr Benin Coat of Arms, Scott 1461, rockets from $4.25 mint, never hinged and used in 2014, to $60 mint and $35 used this year.

There are substantial increases among the surcharged air post stamps of 2005-09, Scott C544-C653. Good news: a number of these stamps are now valued for the first time. For example, Scott 915-923 are valued beginning this year, as are Scott C363-C373, C374-C387, C394-C402 and Q12-Q27. Market data for these stamps is scant, so many of the values are listed in italics.

A front-to-back review of Bermuda results in almost 700 value adjustments. Leading the way are substantial increases for the Postmaster stamps of 1848-56. The 1-penny red on bluish paper, dated 1854 (Scott X2a), soars 135 percent, from $275,000 in the 2014 catalog to $375,000 this year. Among the early classic issues, there are notable jumps for selected errors. The 1875 1p-on-1-shilling surcharge without period, Scott 15b, rises $5,000 in unused condition, from $35,000 to $40,000.

Used examples of the various King George V issues of 1920-35 show healthy gains. The 1sh Silver Jubilee, Scott 103, is now valued at $50 used — double its value in 2014.

The editors sometimes have difficulty obtaining an accurate picture of the market for certain countries. This was the case this year for Bolivia. While some dealer price lists track Scott values for Bolivia rather closely, other sellers' retail prices are noticeably higher than Scott. When a mixed picture such as this presents itself, our practice is to proceed with caution. As such, just under 200 value changes were made; these are concentrated almost exclusively among stamps issued during 2007-12.

The editors also cast their eyes over some of the more obscure countries in the 2014 Vol. 1. For example, all but four values for the French protectorate of Annam and Tonkin have been adjusted. The 1-centime-on-10c claret on lavender paper, Scott 9, rises from $575 used to $675 this year. Similar increases are seen for the French colony Anjouan.

For a summary of these and other listing-related changes, it is highly recommended that you look over the Number Additions, Deletions & Changes listing, located on page 1542 in this volume. Please note that many of these changes are carried over from the 2014 Scott *Classic Specialized Catalogue of Stamps and Covers 1840-1940*.

Black-and-white images almost banished from the catalogues.

Among the hundreds of thousands of stamps illustrated in six volumes of the Scott Standard catalogue, about 150 are still showing in black and white, instead of color.

For the past three years, Scott printing and image coordinator Stacey Mahan has spearheaded the effort to have 100 percent color in the catalogues. She searches myriad websites and works with numerous dealers and collectors to find stamps suitable for gracing our pages. If you have a stamp that would aid in our quest, please contact me at csnee@amospress.com.

Now grab your stamp album, pick up your tongs, settle in with your copy of the Scott catalogue, and bask in the pleasures of the world's greatest hobby. Cheers!

Charles Snee/Catalogue Editor

Acknowledgments

Our appreciation and gratitude go to the following individuals who have assisted us in preparing information included in this year's Scott Catalogues. Some helpers prefer anonymity. These individuals have generously shared their stamp knowledge with others through the medium of the Scott Catalogue.

Those who follow provided information that is in addition to the hundreds of dealer price lists and advertisements and scores of auction catalogues and realizations that were used in producing the catalogue values. It is from those noted here that we have been able to obtain information on items not normally seen in published lists and advertisements. Support from these people goes beyond data leading to catalogue values, for they also are key to editorial changes.

A special acknowledgment to Liane and Sergio Sismondo of The Classic Collector for their assistance and knowledge sharing that have aided in the preparation of this year's Standard and Classic Specialized Catalogues.

Roland Austin
Robert Ausubel (Great Britain Collectors Club)
Jack Hagop Barsoumian (International Stamp Co.)
John Birkinbine II
Brian M. Bleckwenn
Roger S. Brody
Keith & Margie Brown
Tina & John Carlson (JET Stamps)
Henry Chlanda
Frank D. Correl
Tony L. Crumbley (Carolina Coin & Stamp, Inc.)
Stephen R. Datz
Charles Deaton
Ubaldo Del Toro
Bob & Rita Dumaine (Sam Houston Duck Co.)
Sister Theresa Durand
Mark Eastzer (Markest Stamp Co.)
Paul G. Eckman
Mehdi Esmaili
George Eveleth (Spink Shreves Galleries)
Henry Fisher
Jeffrey M. Forster
Ernest E. Fricks (France & Colonies Philatelic Society)
Richard Friedberg
Frank Geiger (Worldstamps.com)
Bob Genisol (Sultan Stamp Center)
Stan Goldfarb
Allan Grant (Rushstamps, Ltd.)
Daniel E. Grau
Grosvenor Auctions
Chris Harmer (Harmer-Schau Auctions)
Bruce Hecht (Bruce L. Hecht Co.)
Clifford O. Herrick (Fidelity Trading Co.)
Peter Hoffman
Armen Hovsepian (Armenstamp)
Philip J. Hughes
John Jamieson (Saskatoon Stamp and Coin)
Peter Jeannopoulos
Stephen Joe (International Stamp Service)
William A. Jones
Allan Katz (Ventura Stamp Co.)
Stanford M. Katz
Patricia A. Kaufmann (Confederate Stamp Alliance)
George Krieger
Ingert Kuzych
John R. Lewis (The William Henry Stamp Co.)
Ulf Lindahl
Ignacio Llach (Filatelia Llach S.L.)
Robert L. Markovits (Quality Investors, Ltd.)
Larry Martin (Crown Colony Stamp Co.)
Marilyn R. Mattke
William K. McDaniel
Gary N. McLean
Mark S. Miller
Allen Mintz
William E. Mooz
Gary Morris (Pacific Midwest Co.)
Bruce M. Moyer (Moyer Stamps & Collectibles)
Richard H. Muller
Behruz Nassre
Robert P. Odenweller
Nik & Lisa Oquist
Dr. Everett Parker
Donald J. Peterson (International Philippine Philatelic Society)
Stanley M. Piller (Stanley M. Piller & Associates)
Todor Drumev Popov
Philippe & Guido Poppe (Poppe Stamps, Inc.)
Peter W. W. Powell
Siddique Mahmudur Rahman
Ghassan D. Riachi
Eric Roberts
Robert G. Rufe
Mehrdad Sadri (Persiphila)
Theodosios Sampson
Alex Schauss (Schauss Philatelics)
Jacques C. Schiff, Jr. (Jacques C. Schiff, Jr., Inc.)
Guy Shaw
Jeff Siddiqui
Sergio & Liane Sismondo (The Classic Collector)
Jay Smith
Merle Spencer (The Stamp Gallery)
Frank J. Stanley, III
Peter Thy
Scott R. Trepel (Siegel Auction Galleries)
Dan Undersander (United Postal Stationery Society)
Philip T. Wall
Kristian Wang
Daniel C. Warren
Giana Wayman
William R. Weiss, Jr. (Weiss Expertizing)
Kirk Wolford (Kirk's Stamp Company)
Ralph Yorio
Val Zabijaka
Alfonso G. Zulueta

Addresses, Telephone Numbers, Web Sites, E-Mail Addresses of General & Specialized Philatelic Societies

Collectors can contact the following groups for information about the philately of the areas within the scope of these societies, or inquire about membership in these groups. Aside from the general societies, we limit this list to groups that specialize in particular fields of philately, particular areas covered by the Scott Standard Postage Stamp Catalogue, and topical groups. Many more specialized philatelic society exist than those listed below. These addresses are updated yearly, and they are, to the best of our knowledge, correct and current. Groups should inform the editors of address changes whenever they occur. The editors also want to hear from other such specialized groups not listed. Unless otherwise noted all website addresses begin with http://

American Philatelic Society
100 Match Factory Place
Bellefonte PA 16823-1367
Ph: (814) 933-3803
www.stamps.org
E-mail: apsinfo@stamps.org

American Stamp Dealers Association, Inc.
P.O. Box 692
Leesport PA 19553
Ph: (800) 369-8207
www.americanstampdealer.com
E-mail: asda@americanstampdealer.com

National Stamp Dealers Association
Dick Keiser, President
2916 NW Bucklin Hill Road #136
Silverdale WA 98383-8514
Ph: (800) 875-6633
www.nsdainc.org
E-mail: gail@nsdainc.org

International Society of Worldwide Stamp Collectors
Joanne Berkowitz, MD
P.O. Box 19006
Sacramento CA 95819
www.iswsc.org
E-mail: executivedirector@iswsc.org

Royal Philatelic Society
41 Devonshire Place
London, W1G 6JY
UNITED KINGDOM
www.rpsl.org.uk
E-mail: secretary@rpsl.org.uk

Royal Philatelic Society of Canada
P.O. Box 929, Station Q
Toronto, ON, M4T 2P1
CANADA
Ph: (888) 285-4143
www.rpsc.org
E-mail: info@rpsc.org

Young Stamp Collectors of America
Janet Houser
100 Match Factory Place
Bellefonte PA 16823-1367
Ph: (814) 933-3820
www.stamps.org/ysca/intro.htm
E-mail: ysca@stamps.org

Philatelic Research Resources

(The Scott editors encourage any additional research organizations to submit data for inclusion in this listing category)

American Philatelic Research Library
Tara Murray
100 Match Factory Place
Bellefonte PA 16823
Ph: (814) 933-3803
www.stamplibrary.org
E-mail: aprl@stamps.org

Institute for Analytical Philately, Inc.
P.O. Box 8035
Holland MI 49422-8035
Ph: (616) 399-9299
www.analyticalphilately.org
E-mail: info@analyticalphilately.org

The Western Philatelic Library
P.O. Box 2219
1500 Partridge Ave.
Sunnyvale CA 94087
Ph: (408) 733-0336
www.fwpf.org

Groups focusing on fields or aspects found in worldwide philately (some might cover U.S. area only)

American Air Mail Society
Stephen Reinhard
P.O. Box 110
Mineola NY 11501
www.americanairmailsociety.org
E-mail: sreinhard1@optonline.net

American First Day Cover Society
Douglas Kelsey
P.O. Box 16277
Tucson AZ 85732-6277
Ph: (520) 321-0880
www.afdcs.org
E-mail: afdcs@afdcs.org

American Revenue Association
Eric Jackson
P.O. Box 728
Leesport PA 19533-0728
Ph: (610) 926-6200
www.revenuer.org
E-mail: eric@revenuer.com

American Topical Association
Vera Felts
P.O. Box 8
Carterville IL 62918-0008
Ph: (618) 985-5100
www.americantopicalassn.org
E-mail: americantopical@msn.com

Christmas Seal & Charity Stamp Society
John Denune
234 E. Broadway
Granville OH 43023
Ph: (740) 587-0276
www.seal-society.org
E-mail: jdenune@roadrunner.com

Errors, Freaks and Oddities Collectors Club
Scott Shaulis
P.O. Box 549
Murrysville PA 15668-0549
Ph: (724) 733-4134
www.efocc.org

First Issues Collectors Club
Kurt Streepy, Secretary
3128 E. Mattatha Drive
Bloomington IN 47401
www.firstissues.org
E-mail: secretary@firstissues.org

International Society of Reply Coupon Collectors
Peter Robin
P.O. Box 353
Bala Cynwyd PA 19004
E-mail: peterrobin@verizon.net

The Joint Stamp Issues Society
Richard Zimmermann
124, Avenue Guy de Coubertin
Saint Remy Les Chevreuse, F-78470
FRANCE
www.jointstampissues.net
E-mail: contact@jointstampissues.net

National Duck Stamp Collectors Society
Anthony J. Monico
P.O. Box 43
Harleysville PA 19438-0043
www.ndscs.org
E-mail: ndscs@ndscs.org

No Value Identified Club
Albert Sauvanet
Le Clos Royal B, Boulevard des Pas Enchantes
St. Sebastien-sur Loire, 44230
FRANCE
E-mail: alain.vailly@irin.univ nantes.fr

The Perfins Club
Jerry Hejduk
P.O. Box 490450
Leesburg FL 34749-0450
Ph: (352) 326-2117
E-mail: flprepers@comcast.net

Postage Due Mail Study Group
John Rawlins
13, Longacre
Chelmsford, CM1 3BJ
UNITED KINGDOM
E-mail: john.rawlins2@ukonline.co.uk.

Post Mark Collectors Club
Beverly Proulx
7629 Homestead Drive
Baldwinsville NY 13027
Ph: (315) 638-0532
www.postmarks.org
E-mail: stampdance@yahoo.com

Postal History Society
Joseph F. Frasch, Jr.
P.O. Box 20387
Columbus OH 43220-0387
www.stampclubs.com
E-mail: jfrasch@ix.netcom.com

Precancel Stamp Society
Rick Podwell
P.O. Box 85
Fawn Grove PA 17321
Ph: (717) 817-8807
www.precancels.com
E-mail: psspromosec@comcast.net

United Postal Stationery Society
Stuart Leven
P.O. Box 24764
San Jose CA 95154-4764
www.upss.org
E-mail: poststat@gmail.com

United States Possessions Philatelic Society
Daniel F. Ring
P.O. Box 113
Woodstock IL 60098
www.uspps.net
E-mail: danielfring@hotmail.com

Groups focusing on U.S. area philately as covered in the Standard Catalogue

Canal Zone Study Group
Tom Brougham
737 Neilson St.
Berkeley CA 94707
www.CanalZoneStudyGroup.com
E-mail: czsgsecretary@gmail.com

Carriers and Locals Society
Martin Richardson
P.O. Box 74
Grosse Ile MI 48138
www.pennypost.org
E-mail: martinr362@aol.com

Confederate Stamp Alliance
Patricia A. Kaufmann
10194 N. Old State Road
Lincoln DE 19960
Ph. (302) 422-2656
www.csalliance.org
E-mail: trishkauf@comcast.net

Hawaiian Philatelic Society
Kay H. Hoke
P.O. Box 10115
Honolulu HI 96816-0115
Ph: (808) 521-5721

Plate Number Coil Collectors Club
Gene Trinks
16415 W. Desert Wren Court
Surprise AZ 85374
Ph: (623) 322-4619
www.pnc3.org
E-mail: gctrinks@cox.net

Ryukyu Philatelic Specialist Society
Laura Edmonds, Secy.
P.O. Box 240177
Charlotte NC 28224-0177
Ph: (336) 509-3739
www.ryukyustamps.org
E-mail: secretary@ryukyustamps.org

United Nations Philatelists
Blanton Clement, Jr.
P.O. Box 146
Morrisville PA 19067-0146
www.unpi.com
E-mail: bclemjr@yahoo.com

United States Stamp Society
Executive Secretary
P.O. Box 6634
Katy TX 77491-6631
www.usstamps.org
E-mail: webmaster@usstamps.org

U.S. Cancellation Club
Arden Callender
Houston TX 77077
Ph: (281) 589-1075
bob.trachimowicz.org/uscchome.htm
E-mail: callenderardy@secglobal.net

U.S. Philatelic Classics Society
Rob Lund
2913 Fulton St.
Everett WA 98201-3733
www.uspcs.org
E-mail: membershipchairman@uspcs.org

Groups focusing on philately of foreign countries or regions

Aden & Somaliland Study Group
Gary Brown
P.O. Box 106
Briar Hill, Victoria, 3088
AUSTRALIA
E-mail: garyjohn951@optushome.com.au

American Society of Polar Philatelists (Antarctic areas)
Alan Warren
P.O. Box 39
Exton PA 19341-0039
www.polarphilatelists.org

Andorran Philatelic Study Circle
D. Hope
17 Hawthorn Drive
Stalybridge, Cheshire, SK15 1UE
UNITED KINGDOM
apsc.free.fr
E-mail: apsc@free.fr

Australian States Study Circle of The Royal Sydney Philatelic Club
Ben Palmer
GPO 1751
Sydney, N.S.W., 2001
AUSTRALIA
www.philas.org.au/states

Austria Philatelic Society
Ralph Schneider
P.O. Box 23049
Belleville IL 62223
Ph: (618) 277-6152
www.austriaphilatelicsociety.com
E-mail: rschneiderstamps@att.net

Baltic States Philatelic Society
Anatoly Chlenov
5719 Drysdale Court
San Jose CA 95124
Ph: (650) 863-1552
www.baltic-philately.com
E-mail: achlenov@localstamps.com

American Belgian Philatelic Society
Edward de Bary
11 Wakefield Drive Apt. 2105
Asheville NC 28803

Bechuanalands and Botswana Society
Neville Midwood
69 Porlock Lane
Furzton, Milton Keynes, MK4 1JY
UNITED KINGDOM
www.nevsoft.com
E-mail: bbsoc@nevsoft.com

Bermuda Collectors Society
John Pare
405 Perimeter Road
Mount Horeb WI 53572
www.bermudacollectorssociety.org
E-mail: science29@comcast.net

Brazil Philatelic Association
William V. Kriebel
1923 Manning St.
Philadelphia PA 19103-5728
Ph: (215) 735-3697
www.brazilphilatelic.org
E-mail: info@brazilphilatelic.org

British Caribbean Philatelic Study Group
Dr. Reuben Ramkissoon
11075 Benton St. #236
Loma Linda CA 92354-3812
Ph: (909) 796-6409
www.bcpsg.com
E-mail: rramkissoon@juno.com

The King George VI Collectors Society (British Commonwealth)
Brian Livingstone
21 York Mansions, Prince of Wales Drive
London, SW11 4DL
UNITED KINGDOM
www.kg6.info
E-mail: livingstone484@btinternet.com

British North America Philatelic Society (Canada & Provinces)
David G. Jones
184 Larkin Drive
Nepean, ON, K2J 1H9
CANADA
www.bnaps.org
E-mail: shibumi.management@gmail.com

British West Indies Study Circle
John Seidl
4324 Granby Way
Marietta GA 30062
Ph: (770) 642-6424
www.bwisc.org
E-mail: john.seidl@gmail.com

Burma Philatelic Study Circle
Michael Whittaker
1, Ecton Leys, Hillside
Rugby, Warwickshire, CV22 5SL
UNITED KINGDOM
www.burmastamps.homecall.co.uk
E-mail: manningham8@mypostoffice.co.uk

Cape and Natal Study Circle
Dr. Guy Dillaway
P.O. Box 181
Weston MA 02493
www.nzsc.demon.co.uk

Ceylon Study Circle
R. W. P. Frost
42 Lonsdale Road, Cannington
Bridgewater, Somerset, TA5 2JS
UNITED KINGDOM
www.ceylonsc.org
E-mail: rodney.frost@tiscali.co.uk

Channel Islands Specialists Society
Moira Edwards
86, Hall Lane, Sandon
Chelmsford, Essex, CM2 7RQ
UNITED KINGDOM
www.ciss1950.org.uk
E-mail: membership@ciss1950.org.uk

China Stamp Society
Paul H. Gault
P.O. Box 20711
Columbus OH 43220
www.chinastampsociety.org
E-mail: secretary@chinastampsociety.org

Colombia/Panama Philatelic Study Group (COPAPHIL)
Thomas P. Myers
P.O. Box 522
Gordonsville VA 22942
www.copaphil.org
E-mail: tpmphil@hotmail.com

Association Filatelic de Costa Rica
Giana Wayman
c/o Interlink 102, P.O. Box 52-6770
Miami FL 33152
E-mail: scotland@racsa.co.cr

Society for Costa Rica Collectors
Dr. Hector R. Mena
P.O. Box 14831
Baton Rouge LA 70808
www.socorico.org
E-mail: hrmena@aol.com

International Cuban Philatelic Society
Ernesto Cuesta
P.O. Box 34434
Bethesda MD 20827
www.cubafil.org
E-mail: ecuesta@philat.com

Cuban Philatelic Society of America®
P.O. Box 141656
Coral Gables FL 33114-1656
www.cubapsa.com
E-mail: cpsa.usa@gmail.com

Cyprus Study Circle
Colin Dear
10 Marne Close, Wem
Shropshire, SY4 5YE
UNITED KINGDOM
www.cyprusstudycircle.org/index.htm
E-mail: colindear@talktalk.net

Society for Czechoslovak Philately
Tom Cassaboom
P.O. Box 4124
Prescott AZ 86302
www.csphilately.org
E-mail: klfck1@aol.com

Danish West Indies Study Unit of the Scandinavian Collectors Club
Arnold Sorensen
7666 Edgedale Drive
Newburgh IN 47630
Ph: (812) 480-6532
www.scc-online.org
E-mail: valbydwi@hotmail.com

East Africa Study Circle
Michael Vesey-Fitzgerald
Vernalls Orchard, Gosport Lane
Lyndhurst, SO43 7BP
UNITED KINGDOM
www.easc.org.uk
E-mail: secretary@easc.org.uk

Egypt Study Circle
Mike Murphy
109 Chadwick Road
London, SE15 4PY
UNITED KINGDOM
Trent Ruebush: North American Agent
E-mail: truebrush@usaid.gov
egyptstudycircle.org.uk
E-mail: egyptstudycircle@hotmail.com

Estonian Philatelic Society
Juri Kirsimagi
29 Clifford Ave.
Pelham NY 10803
Ph: (914) 738-3713

Ethiopian Philatelic Society
Ulf Lindahl
21 Westview Place
Riverside CT 06878
Ph: (203) 866-3540
home.comcast.net/~fbheiser/ethiopia5.htm
E-mail: ulindahl@optonline.net

Falkland Islands Philatelic Study Group
Carl J. Faulkner
Williams Inn, On-the-Green
Williamstown MA 01267-2620
Ph: (413) 458-9371
www.fipsg.org.uk

Faroe Islands Study Circle
Norman Hudson
40 Queenís Road, Vicarís Cross
Chester, CH3 5HB
UNITED KINGDOM
www.faroeislandssc.org
E-mail: jntropics@hotmail.com

Former French Colonies Specialist Society
COLFRA
BP 628
75367 Paris, Cedex 08
FRANCE
www.colfra.com
E-mail: clubcolfra@aol.com

France & Colonies Philatelic Society
Edward Grabowski
111 Prospect St., 4C
Westfield NJ 07090
E-mail: edjjg@alum.mit.edu

Germany Philatelic Society
P.O. Box 6547
Chesterfield MO 63006
www.germanyphilatelicusa.org

Gibraltar Study Circle
David R. Stirrups
152 The Rowans, Milton
Cambridge, CB24 6YX
UNITED KINGDOM
www.gibraltarstudycircle.wordpress.com
E-mail: beggloops@gmail.com

Great Britain Collectors Club
Steve McGill
10309 Brookhollow Circle
Highlands Ranch CO 80129
www.gbstamps.com/gbcc
E-mail: steve.mcgill@comcast.net

International Society of Guatemala Collectors
Jaime Marckwordt
449 St. Francis Blvd.
Daly City CA 94015-2136
www.guatemalastamps.com

Haiti Philatelic Society
Ubaldo Del Toro
5709 Marble Archway
Alexandria VA 22315
www.haitiphilately.org
E-mail: u007ubi@aol.com

Hong Kong Stamp Society
Ming W. Tsang
P.O. Box 206
Glenside PA 19038
www.hkss.org
E-mail: hkstamps@yahoo.com

Society for Hungarian Philately
Robert Morgan
2201 Roscomare Road
Los Angeles CA 90077-2222
Ph; (253) 759-4078
www.hungarianphilately.org
E-mail: ruthandlyman@nventure.com

India Study Circle
John Warren
P.O. Box 7326
Washington DC 20044
Ph: (202) 564-6876
www.indiastudycircle.org
E-mail: warren.john@epa.gov

Indian Ocean Study Circle
E. S. Hutton
29 Patermoster Close
Waltham Abby, Essex, EN9 3JU
UNITED KINGDOM
www.indianoceanstudycircle.com
E-mail:
secretary@indianoceanstudycircle.com

Society of Indo-China Philatelists
Ron Bentley
2600 N. 24th St.
Arlington VA 22207
www.sicp-online.org
E-mail: ron.bentley@verizon.net

Iran Philatelic Study Circle
Mehdi Esmaili
P.O. Box 750096
Forest Hills NY 11375
www.iranphilatelic.org
E-mail: m.esmaili@earthlink.net

Eire Philatelic Association (Ireland)
David J. Brennan
P.O. Box 704
Bernardsville NJ 07924
www.eirephilatelicassoc.org
E-mail: brennan704@aol.com

Society of Israel Philatelists
Edwin Kroft
P.O. Box 507
Northfield OH 44067
www.israelstamps.com
E-mail: israelstamps@gmail.com

Italy and Colonies Study Circle
Richard Harlow
7 Duncombe House, 8 Manor Road
Teddington, TW11 8BE
UNITED KINGDOM
www.icsc.pwp.blueyonder.co.uk
E-mail: harlowr@gmail.com

International Society for Japanese Philately
William Eisenhauer
P.O. Box 230462
Tigard OR 97281
www.isjp.org
E-mail: secretary@isjp.org

Korea Stamp Society
John E. Talmage
P.O. Box 6889
Oak Ridge TN 37831
www.pennfamily.org/KSS-USA
E-mail: jtalmage@usit.net

Latin American Philatelic Society
Jules K. Beck
30½ St. #209
St. Louis Park MN 55426-3551

Liberian Philatelic Society
William Thomas Lockard
P.O. Box 106
Wellston OH 45692
Ph: (740) 384-2020
E-mail: tlockard@zoomnet.net

Liechtenstudy USA (Liechtenstein)
Paul Tremaine
410 SW Ninth St.
Dundee OR 97115
Ph: (503) 538-4500
www.liechtenstudy.org
E-mail: editor@liechtenstudy.org

Lithuania Philatelic Society
John Variakojis
8472 Carlisle Court.
Burr Ridge IL 60527
Ph: (630) 974-6525
lithuanianphilately.com/lps
E-mail: variakojis@sbcglobal.net

Luxembourg Collectors Club
Gary B. Little
7319 Beau Road
Sechelt, BC, V0N 3A8
CANADA
lcc.luxcentral.com
E-mail: gary@luxcentral.com

Malaya Study Group
David Tett
P.O. Box 34
Wheathampstead, Herts, AL4 8JY
UNITED KINGDOM
www.m-s-g.org.uk
E-mail: davidtett@aol.com

Malta Study Circle
Alec Webster
50 Worcester Road
Sutton, Surrey, SM2 6QB
UNITED KINGDOM
E-mail: alecwebster50@hotmail.com

Mexico-Elmhurst Philatelic Society International
Thurston Bland
50 Regato
Rancho Santa Margarita CA 92688-3003
www.mepsi.org

Asociacion Mexicana de Filatelia
AMEXFIL
Jose Maria Rico, 129, Col. Del Valle
Mexico City DF, 03100
MEXICO
www.amexfil.mx
E-mail: alejandro.grossmann@gmail.com

Society for Moroccan and Tunisian Philately
206, bld. Pereire
75017 Paris
FRANCE
members.aol.com/Jhaik5814
E-mail: splm206@aol.com

Nepal & Tibet Philatelic Study Group
Roger D. Skinner
1020 Covington Road
Los Altos CA 94024-5003
Ph: (650) 968-4163
www.fuchs-online.com/ntpsc/
E-mail: colinhepper@hotmail.co.uk

American Society for Netherlands Philately
Hans Kremer
50 Rockport Court
Danville CA 94526
Ph: (925) 820-5841
www.asnp1975.com
E-mail: hkremer@usa.net

New Zealand Society of Great Britain
Michael J. Wilkinson
121 London Road
Sevenoaks, Kent, TN13 1BH
UNITED KINGDOM
www.cs.stir.ac.uk/~rgc/nzsgb
E-mail: mwilk799@aol.com

Nicaragua Study Group
Erick Rodriguez
11817 SW 11th St.
Miami FL 33184-2501
clubs.yahoo.com/clubs/
nicaraguastudygroup
E-mail: nsgsec@yahoo.com

Society of Australasian Specialists/ Oceania
David McNamee
P.O. Box 37
Alamo CA 94507
www.sasoceania.org
E-mail: dmcnamee@aol.com

Orange Free State Study Circle
J. R. Stroud
24 Hooper Close
Burnham-on-sea, Somerset, TA8 1JQ
UNITED KINGDOM
orangefreestatephilately.org.uk
E-mail: richardstroudph@gofast.co.uk

Pacific Islands Study Circle
John Ray
24 Woodvale Ave.
London, SE25 4AE
UNITED KINGDOM
www.pisc.org.uk
E-mail: info@pisc.org.uk

Pakistan Philatelic Study Circle
Jeff Siddiqui
P.O. Box 7002
Lynnwood WA 98046
E-mail: jeffsiddiqui@msn.com

Centro de Filatelistas Independientes de Panama
Vladimir Berrio-Lemm
Apartado 0823-02748
Plaza Concordia Panama
PANAMA
E-mail: panahistoria@gmail.com

Papuan Philatelic Society
Steven Zirinsky
P.O. Box 49, Ansonia Station
New York NY 10023
Ph: (718) 706-0616
www.communigate.co.uk/york/pps
E-mail: szirinsky@cs.com

International Philippine Philatelic Society
Donald J. Peterson
7408 Alaska Ave., NW
Washington DC 20012
Ph: (202) 291-6229
www.theipps.info
E-mail: dpeterson@comcast.net

Pitcairn Islands Study Group
Dr. Everett L. Parker
249 NW Live Oak Place
Lake City FL 32055-8906
Ph: (386) 754-8524
www.pisg.net
E-mail: eparker@hughes.net

Polonus Philatelic Society (Poland)
Robert Ogrodnik
P.O. Box 240428
Ballwin MO 63024-0428
Ph: (314) 821-6130
www.polonus.org
E-mail: rvo1937@gmail.com

International Society for Portuguese Philately
Clyde Homen
1491 Bonnie View Road
Hollister CA 95023-5117
www.portugalstamps.com
E-mail: cjh1491@sbcglobal.net

Rhodesian Study Circle
William R. Wallace
P.O. Box 16381
San Francisco CA 94116
www.rhodesianstudycircle.org.uk
E-mail: bwall8rscr@earthlink.net

Rossica Society of Russian Philately
Alexander Kolchinsky
1506 Country Lake Drive
Champaign IL 6821-6428
www.rossica.org
E-mail: alexander.kolchinsky@rossica.org

St. Helena, Ascension & Tristan Da Cunha Philatelic Society
Dr. Everett L. Parker
249 NW Live Oak Place
Lake City FL 32055-8906
Ph: (386) 754-8524
www.atlanticislands.org
E-mail: eparker@hughes.net

St. Pierre & Miquelon Philatelic Society
James R. (Jim) Taylor
2335 Paliswood Road SW
Calgary, AB, T2V 3P6
CANADA

Associated Collectors of El Salvador
Joseph D. Hahn
1015 Old Boalsburg Road Apt G-5
State College PA 16801-6149
www.elsalvadorphilately.org
E-mail: jdhahn2@gmail.com

Fellowship of Samoa Specialists
Donald Mee
23 Leo St.
Christchurch, 8051
NEW ZEALAND
www.samoaexpress.org
E-mail: donanm@xtra.co.nz

Sarawak Specialists' Society
Stu Leven
P.O. Box 24764
San Jose CA 95154-4764
Ph: (408) 978-0193
www.britborneostamps.org.uk
E-mail: stulev@ix.netcom.com

Scandinavian Collectors Club
Steve Lund
P.O. Box 16213
St. Paul MN 55116
www.scc-online.org
E-mail: steve88h@aol.com

Slovakia Stamp Society
Jack Benchik
P.O. Box 555
Notre Dame IN 46556

Philatelic Society for Greater Southern Africa
Alan Hanks
34 Seaton Drive
Aurora, ON, L4G 2KI
CANADA
Ph: (905) 727-6993
www.psgsa.thestampweb.com
Email: alan.hanks@sympatico.ca

South Sudan Philatelic Society
William Barclay
134A Spring Hill Road
South Londonerry VT 05155
E-mail: bill.barclay@wfp.org

Spanish Philatelic Society
Robert H. Penn
1108 Walnut Drive
Danielsville PA 18038
Ph: (610) 760-8711
E-mail: roberthpenn@aol.com

Sudan Study Group
David Sher
5 Ellis Park Road
Toronto, ON, M6S 2V2
CANADA
www.sudanstamps.org

American Helvetia Philatelic Society (Switzerland, Liechtenstein)
Richard T. Hall
P.O. Box 15053
Asheville NC 28813-0053
www.swiss-stamps.org
E-mail: secretary2@swiss-stamps.org

Tannu Tuva Collectors Society
Ken R. Simon
P.O. Box 385
Lake Worth FL 33460-0385
Ph: (561) 588-5954
www.tuva.tk
E-mail: yurttuva@yahoo.com

Society for Thai Philately
H. R. Blakeney
P.O. Box 25644
Oklahoma City OK 73125
E-mail: HRBlakeney@aol.com

Transvaal Study Circle
Jeff Woolgar
c/o 9 Meadow Road
Gravesend, DA11 7LR
UNITED KINGDOM
www.transvaal.org.uk

Ottoman and Near East Philatelic Society (Turkey and related areas)
Bob Stuchell
193 Valley Stream Lane
Wayne PA 19087
www.oneps.org
E-mail: rstuchell@msn.com

Ukrainian Philatelic & Numismatic Society
Michael G. Matus
157 Lucinda Lane
Wyomissing PA 19610-1026
Ph: (610) 927 3838
www.upns.org
E-mail: michael.matus@verizon.net

Vatican Philatelic Society
Sal Quinonez
1 Aldersgate, Apt. 1002
Riverhead NY 11901-1830
Ph: (516) 727-6426
www.vaticanphilately.org

British Virgin Islands Philatelic Society
Giorgio Migliavacca
P.O. Box 7007
St. Thomas VI 00801-0007
www.islandsun.com/FEATURES/bviphil9198.html
E-mail: issun@candwbvi.net

West Africa Study Circle
Martin Bratzel
1233 Virginia Ave.
Windsor, ON, N8S 2Z1
CANADA
www.wasc.org.uk/
E-mail: marty_bratzel@yahoo.ca

Western Australia Study Group
Brian Pope
P.O. Box 423
Claremont, Western Australia, 6910
AUSTRALIA
www.wastudygroup.com
E-mail: black5swan@yahoo.com.au

Yugoslavia Study Group of the Croatian Philatelic Society
Michael Lenard
1514 N. Third Ave.
Wausau WI 54401
Ph: (715) 675-2833
E-mail: mjlenard@aol.com

Topical Groups

Americana Unit
Dennis Dengel
17 Peckham Road
Poughkeepsie NY 12603-2018
www.americanaunit.org
E-mail: info@americanaunit.org

Astronomy Study Unit
John W. G. Budd
29203 Coharie Loop
San Antonio FL 33576-4643
Ph: (352) 588-4706
www.astronomystudyunit.com
E-mail: jwgbudd@earthlink.net

Bicycle Stamp Club
Tony Teideman
P.O. Box 90
Baulkham Hills, NSW, 1755
AUSTRALIA
members.tripod.com/~bicyclestamps
E-mail: tonimaur@bigpond.com

Biology Unit
Alan Hanks
34 Seaton Drive
Aurora, ON, L4G 2K1
CANADA
Ph: (905) 727-6993

Bird Stamp Society
S. A. H. (Tony) Statham
Ashlyns Lodge, Chesham Road,
Berkhamsted, Hertfordshire HP4 2ST
UNITED KINGDOM
www.bird-stamps.org/bss
E-mail: tony.statham@sky.com

Canadiana Study Unit
Robert Haslewood
5140 Cumberland Ave.
Montreal, Quebec, H4V 2N8
CANADA
E-mail: robert.haslewood058@sympatico.ca

Captain Cook Society
Brian P. Sandford
173 Minuteman Drive
Concord MA 01742-1923
www.captaincooksociety.com
E-mail: US@captaincooksociety.com

Casey Jones Railroad Unit
Roy W. Menninger MD
85 SW Pepper Tree Lane
Topeka KS 66611-2072
www.uqp.de/cjr/index.htm
E-mail: roymenn@sbcglobal.net

Cats on Stamps Study Unit
Mary Ann Brown
3006 Wade Road
Durham NC 27705
www.catsonstamps.org
E-mail: mabrown@nc.rr.com

Chemistry & Physics on Stamps Study Unit
Dr. Roland Hirsch
20458 Water Point Lane
Germantown MD 20874
www.cpossu.org
E-mail: rfhirsch@cpossu.org

Chess on Stamps Study Unit
Ray C. Alexis
608 Emery St.
Longmont CO 80501
E-mail: chessstuff911459@aol.com

Christmas Philatelic Club
Jim Balog
P.O. Box 774
Geneva OH 44041
www.web.295.ca/cpc/
E-mail: jpbstamps@windstream.net

Christopher Columbus Philatelic Society
Donald R. Ager
P.O. Box 71
Hillsboro NH 03244-0071
Ph: (603) 464-5379
ccps.maphist.nl/
E-mail: meganddon@tds.net

Collectors of Religion on Stamps
James Bailey
P.O. Box 937
Brownwood TX 76804
www.coros-society.org
E-mail: corosec@directtv.net

Dogs on Stamps Study Unit
Morris Raskin
202A Newport Road
Monroe Township NJ 08831
Ph: (609) 655-7411
www.dossu.org
E-mail: mraskin@cellurian.com

Earth's Physical Features Study Group
Fred Klein
515 Magdalena Ave.
Los Altos CA 94024
epfsu.jeffhayward.com

Ebony Society of Philatelic Events and Reflections, Inc. (African-American topicals)
Manuel Gilyard
800 Riverside Drive, Suite 4H
New York NY 10032-7412
www.esperstamps.org
E-mail: gilyardmani@aol.com

Europa Study Unit
Tonny E. Van Loij
3002 S. Xanthia St.
Denver CO 80231-4237
www.europastudyunit.org/
E-mail: tvanloij@gmail.com

Fine & Performing Arts
Deborah L. Washington
6922 S. Jeffery Blvd., #7 - North
Chicago IL 60649
E-mail: brasslady@comcast.net

Fire Service in Philately
John Zaranek
81 Hillpine Road
Cheektowaga NY 14227-2259
Ph: (716) 668-3352
E-mail: jczaranek@roadrunner.com

Gay & Lesbian History on Stamps Club
Joe Petronie
P.O. Box 190842
Dallas TX 75219-0842
www.glhsc.org
E-mail: glhsc@aol.com

Gems, Minerals & Jewelry Study Unit
Mrs. Gilberte Proteau
138 Lafontaine
Beloeil QC J3G 2G7
CANADA
Ph: (978) 851-8283
E-mail: gilberte.ferland@sympatico.ca

Graphics Philately Association
Mark H. Winnegrad
P.O. Box 380
Bronx NY 10462-0380
www.graphics-stamps.org
E-mail: indybruce1@yahoo.com

Journalists, Authors & Poets on Stamps
Ms. Lee Straayer
P.O. Box 6808
Champaign IL 61826
E-mail: lstraayer@dcbnet.com

Lighthouse Stamp Society
Dalene Thomas
8612 W. Warren Lane
Lakewood CO 80227-2352
Ph: (303) 986-6620
www.lighthousestampsociety.org
E-mail: dalene@lighthousestampsociety.org

Lions International Stamp Club
John Bargus
108-2777 Barry Road RR 2
Mill Bay, BC, V0R 2P2
CANADA
Ph: (250) 743-5782

Mahatma Gandhi On Stamps Study Circle
Pramod Shivagunde
Pratik Clinic, Akluj
Solapur, Maharashtra, 413101
INDIA
E-mail: drnanda@bom6.vsnl.net.in

Masonic Study Unit
Stanley R. Longenecker
930 Wood St.
Mount Joy PA 17552-1926
Ph: (717) 669-9094
E-mail: natsco@usa.net

Mathematical Study Unit
Monty J. Strauss
4209 88th St.
Lubbock TX 79423-2041
www.math.ttu.edu/msu/
E-mail: m.strauss@ttu.edu

Medical Subjects Unit
Dr. Frederick C. Skvara
P.O. Box 6228
Bridgewater NJ 08807
E-mail: fcskvara@optonline.net

Military Postal History Society
Ed Dubin
1 S. Wacker Drive, Suite 3500
Chicago IL 60606
www.militaryPHS.org
E-mail: dubine@comcast.net

Mourning Stamps and Covers Club
James Bailey, Jr.
P.O. Box 937
Brownwood TX 76804
E-mail: jfbailey238@directv.net

Napoleonic Age Philatelists
Ken Berry
4117 NW 146th St.
Oklahoma City OK 73134-1746
Ph: (405) 748-8646
www.nap-stamps.org
E-mail: krb4117@att.net

Old World Archeological Study Unit
Caroline Scannell
11 Dawn Drive
Smithtown NY 11787-1761
www.owasu.org
E-mail: editor@owasu.org

Petroleum Philatelic Society International
Dr. Chris Coggins
174 Old Bedford Road
Luton, England, LU2 7HW
UNITED KINGDOM
E-mail: WAMTECH@Luton174.fsnet.co.uk

Rotary on Stamps Unit
Gerald L. Fitzsimmons
105 Calla Ricardo
Victoria TX 77904
rotaryonstamps.org
E-mail: glfitz@suddenlink.net

Scouts on Stamps Society International
Lawrence Clay
P.O. Box 6228
Kennewick WA 99336
Ph: (509) 735-3731
www.sossi.org
E-mail: lclay3731@charter.net

Ships on Stamps Unit
Les Smith
302 Conklin Ave.
Penticton, BC, V2A 2T4
CANADA
Ph: (250) 493-7486
www.shipsonstamps.org
E-mail: lessmith440@shaw.ca

Space Unit
Carmine Torrisi
P.O. Box 780241
Maspeth NY 11378
Ph: (917) 620-5687
stargate.1usa.com/stamps/
E-mail: ctorrisi1@nyc.rr.com

Sports Philatelists International
Mark Maestrone
2824 Curie Place
San Diego CA 92122-4110
www.sportstamps.org
Email: president@sportstamps.org

Stamps on Stamps Collectors Club
Alf Jordan
156 W. Elm St.
Yarmouth ME 04096
www.stampsonstamps.org
E-mail: ajordan1@maine.rr.com

Windmill Study Unit
Walter J. Hollien
607 N. Porter St.
Watkins Glenn NY 14891-1345
Ph: (862) 812-0030
E-mail: whollien@earthlink.net

Wine On Stamps Study Unit
Bruce L. Johnson
115 Raintree Drive
Zionsville IN 46077
www.wine-on-stamps.org
E-mail: indybruce@yahoo.com

Women on Stamps Study Unit
Hugh Gottfried
2232 26th St.
Santa Monica CA 90405-1902
E-mail: hgottfried@adelphia.net

Expertizing Services

The following organizations will, for a fee, provide expert opinions about stamps submitted to them. Collectors should contact these organizations to find out about their fees and requirements before submiting philatelic material to them. The listing of these groups here is not intended as an endorsement by Scott Publishing Co.

General Expertizing Services

American Philatelic Expertizing Service (a service of the American Philatelic Society)
100 Match Factory Place
Bellefonte PA 16823-1367
Ph: (814) 237-3803
Fax: (814) 237-6128
www.stamps.org
E-mail: ambristo@stamps.org
Areas of Expertise: Worldwide

B. P. A. Expertising, Ltd.
P.O. Box 1141
Guildford, Surrey, GU5 0WR
UNITED KINGDOM
E-mail: sec@bpaexpertising.org
Areas of Expertise: British Commonwealth, Great Britain, Classics of Europe, South America and the Far East

Philatelic Foundation
70 W. 40th St., 15th Floor
New York NY 10018
Ph: (212) 221-6555
Fax: (212) 221-6208
www.philatelicfoundation.org
E-mail: philatelicfoundation@verizon.net
Areas of Expertise: U.S. & Worldwide

Philatelic Stamp Authentication and Grading, Inc.
P.O. Box 37-2460
Satellite Beach FL 32937
Customer Service: (305) 345-9864
www.psaginc.com
E-mail: info@psaginc.com
Areas of Expertise: U.S., Canal Zone, Hawaii, Philippines, Canada & Provinces

Professional Stamp Experts
P.O. Box 6170
Newport Beach CA 92658
Ph: (877) STAMP-88
Fax: (949) 833-7955
www.collectors.com/pse
E-mail: pseinfo@collectors.com
Areas of Expertise: Stamps and covers of U.S., U.S. Possessions, British Commonwealth

Royal Philatelic Society Expert Committee
41 Devonshire Place
London, W1N 1PE
UNITED KINGDOM
www.rpsl.org.uk/experts.html
E-mail: experts@rpsl.org.uk
Areas of Expertise: Worldwide

Expertizing Services Covering Specific Fields Or Countries

China Stamp Society Expertizing Service
1050 W. Blue Ridge Blvd.
Kansas City MO 64145
Ph: (816) 942-6300
E-mail: hjmesq@aol.com
Areas of Expertise: China

Confederate Stamp Alliance Authentication Service
Gen. Frank Crown, Jr.
P.O. Box 278
Capshaw AL 35742-0396
Ph: (302) 422-2656
Fax: (302) 424-1990
www.csalliance.org
E-mail: csaas@knology.net
Areas of Expertise: Confederate stamps and postal history

Errors, Freaks and Oddities Collectors Club Expertizing Service
138 East Lakemont Drive
Kingsland GA 31548
Ph: (912) 729-1573
Areas of Expertise: U.S. errors, freaks and oddities

Estonian Philatelic Society Expertizing Service
39 Clafford Lane
Melville NY 11747
Ph: (516) 421-2078
E-mail: esto4@aol.com
Areas of Expertise: Estonia

Hawaiian Philatelic Society Expertizing Service
P.O. Box 10115
Honolulu HI 96816-0115
Areas of Expertise: Hawaii

Hong Kong Stamp Society Expertizing Service
P.O. Box 206
Glenside PA 19038
Fax: (215) 576-6850
Areas of Expertise: Hong Kong

International Association of Philatelic Experts United States Associate members:

Paul Buchsbayew
119 W. 57th St.
New York NY 10019
Ph: (212) 977-7734
Fax: (212) 977-8653
Areas of Expertise: Russia, Soviet Union

William T. Crowe
P.O. Box 2090
Danbury CT 06813-2090
E-mail: wtcrowe@aol.com
Areas of Expertise: United States

John Lievsay
(see American Philatelic Expertizing Service and Philatelic Foundation)
Areas of Expertise: France

Robert W. Lyman
P.O. Box 348
Irvington on Hudson NY 10533
Ph and Fax: (914) 591-6937
Areas of Expertise: British North America, New Zealand

Robert Odenweller
P.O. Box 401
Bernardsville NJ 07924-0401
Ph and Fax: (908) 766-5460
Areas of Expertise: New Zealand, Samoa to 1900

Sergio Sismondo
The Regency Tower, Suite 1109
770 James Street
Syracuse NY 13203
Ph: (315) 422-2331
Fax: (315) 422-2956
Areas of Expertise: British East Africa, Camerouns, Cape of Good Hope, Canada, British North America

International Society for Japanese Philately Expertizing Committee
132 North Pine Terrace
Staten Island NY 10312-4052
Ph: (718) 227-5229
Areas of Expertise: Japan and related areas, except WWII Japanese Occupation issues

International Society for Portuguese Philately Expertizing Service
P.O. Box 43146
Philadelphia PA 19129-3146
Ph and Fax: (215) 843-2106
E-mail: s.s.washburne@worldnet.att.net
Areas of Expertise: Portugal and Colonies

Mexico-Elmhurst Philatelic Society International Expert Committee
P.O. Box 1133
West Covina CA 91793
Areas of Expertise: Mexico

Ukrainian Philatelic & Numismatic Society Expertizing Service
30552 Dell Lane
Warren MI 48092-1862
Areas of Expertise: Ukraine, Western Ukraine

V. G. Greene Philatelic Research Foundation
P.O. Box 204, Station Q
Toronto, ON, M4T 2M1
CANADA
Ph: (416) 921-2073
Fax: (416) 921-1282
www.greenefoundation.ca
E-mail: vggfoundation@on.aibn.com
Areas of Expertise: British North America

Information on Catalogue Values, Grade and Condition

Catalogue Value

The Scott Catalogue value is a retail value; that is, an amount you could expect to pay for a stamp in the grade of Very Fine with no faults. Any exceptions to the grade valued will be noted in the text. The general introduction on the following pages and the individual section introductions further explain the type of material that is valued. The value listed for any given stamp is a reference that reflects recent actual dealer selling prices for that item.

Dealer retail price lists, public auction results, published prices in advertising and individual solicitation of retail prices from dealers, collectors and specialty organizations have been used in establishing the values found in this catalogue. Scott Publishing Co. values stamps, but Scott is not a company engaged in the business of buying and selling stamps as a dealer.

Use this catalogue as a guide for buying and selling. The actual price you pay for a stamp may be higher or lower than the catalogue value because of many different factors, including the amount of personal service a dealer offers, or increased or decreased interest in the country or topic represented by a stamp or set. An item may occasionally be offered at a lower price as a "loss leader," or as part of a special sale. You also may obtain an item inexpensively at public auction because of little interest at that time or as part of a large lot.

Stamps that are of a lesser grade than Very Fine, or those with condition problems, generally trade at lower prices than those given in this catalogue. Stamps of exceptional quality in both grade and condition often command higher prices than those listed.

Values for pre-1900 unused issues are for stamps with approximately half or more of their original gum. Stamps with most or all of their original gum may be expected to sell for more, and stamps with less than half of their original gum may be expected to sell for somewhat less than the values listed. On rarer stamps, it may be expected that the original gum will be somewhat more disturbed than it will be on more common issues. Post-1900 unused issues are assumed to have full original gum. From breakpoints in most countries' listings, stamps are valued as never hinged, due to the wide availability of stamps in that condition. These notations are prominently placed in the listings and in the country information preceding the listings. Some countries also feature listings with dual values for hinged and never-hinged stamps.

Grade

A stamp's grade and condition are crucial to its value. The accompanying illustrations show examples of Very Fine stamps from different time periods, along with examples of stamps in Fine to Very Fine and Extremely Fine grades as points of reference. When a stamp seller offers a stamp in any grade from fine to superb without further qualifying statements, that stamp should not only have the centering grade as defined, but it also should be free of faults or other condition problems.

FINE stamps (illustrations not shown) have designs that are quite off center, with the perforations on one or two sides very close to the design but not quite touching it. There is white space between the perforations and the design that is minimal but evident to the unaided eye. Imperforate stamps may have small margins, and earlier issues may show the design just touching one edge of the stamp design. Very early perforated issues normally will have the perforations slightly cutting into the design. Used stamps may have heavier than usual cancellations.

FINE-VERY FINE stamps will be somewhat off center on one side, or slightly off center on two sides. Imperforate stamps will have two margins of at least normal size, and the design will not touch any edge. For perforated stamps, the perfs are well clear of the design, but are still noticeably off center. *However, early issues of a country may be printed in such a way that the design naturally is very close to the edges. In these cases, the perforations may cut into the design very slightly.* Used stamps will not have a cancellation that detracts from the design.

VERY FINE stamps will be just slightly off center on one or two sides, but the design will be well clear of the edge. The stamp will present a nice, balanced appearance. Imperforate stamps will be well centered within normal-sized margins. *However, early issues of many countries may be printed in such a way that the perforations may touch the design on one or more sides. Where this is the case, a boxed note will be found defining the centering and margins of the stamps being valued.* Used stamps will have light or otherwise neat cancellations. This is the grade used to establish Scott Catalogue values.

EXTREMELY FINE stamps are close to being perfectly centered. Imperforate stamps will have even margins that are slightly larger than normal. Even the earliest perforated issues will have perforations clear of the design on all sides.

Scott Publishing Co. recognizes that there is no formally enforced grading scheme for postage stamps, and that the final price you pay or obtain for a stamp will be determined by individual agreement at the time of transaction.

Condition

Grade addresses only centering and (for used stamps) cancellation. *Condition* refers to factors other than grade that affect a stamp's desirability.

Factors that can increase the value of a stamp include exceptionally wide margins, particularly fresh color, the presence of selvage, and plate or die varieties. Unusual cancels on used stamps (particularly those of the 19th century) can greatly enhance their value as well.

Factors other than faults that decrease the value of a stamp include loss of original gum, regumming, a hinge remnant or foreign object adhering to the gum, natural inclusions, straight edges, and markings or notations applied by collectors or dealers.

Faults include missing pieces, tears, pin or other holes, surface scuffs, thin spots, creases, toning, short or pulled perforations, clipped perforations, oxidation or other forms of color changelings, soiling, stains, and such man-made changes as reperforations or the chemical removal or lightening of a cancellation.

Grading Illustrations

On the following two pages are illustrations of various stamps from countries appearing in this volume. These stamps are arranged by country, and they represent early or important issues that are often found in widely different grades in the marketplace. The editors believe the illustrations will prove useful in showing the margin size and centering that will be seen on the various issues.

In addition to the matters of margin size and centering, collectors are reminded that the very fine stamps valued in the Scott catalogues also will possess fresh color and intact perforations, and they will be free from defects.

Examples shown are computer-manipulated images made from single digitized master illustrations.

Stamp Illustrations Used in the Catalogue

It is important to note that the stamp images used for identification purposes in this catlaogue may not be indicative of the grade of stamp being valued. Refer to the written discussion of grades on this page and to the grading illustrations on the following two pages for grading information.

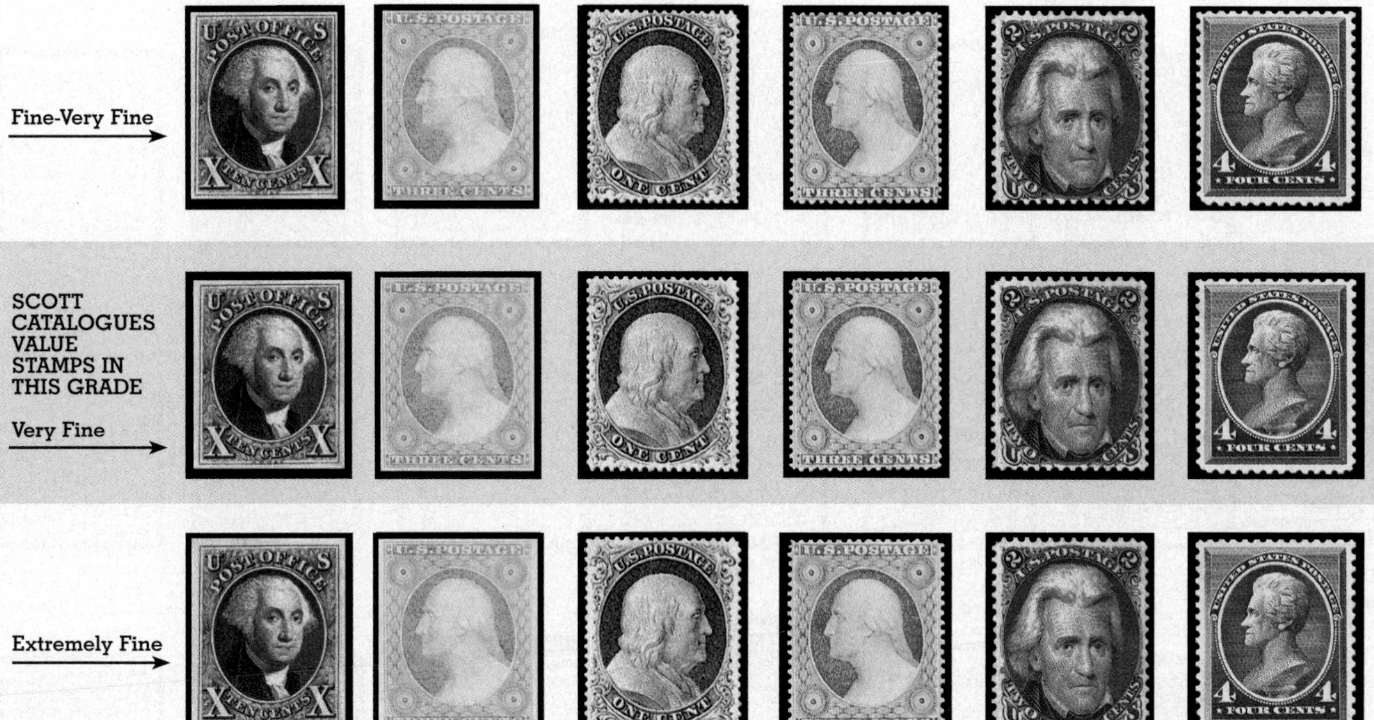

Fine-Very Fine →

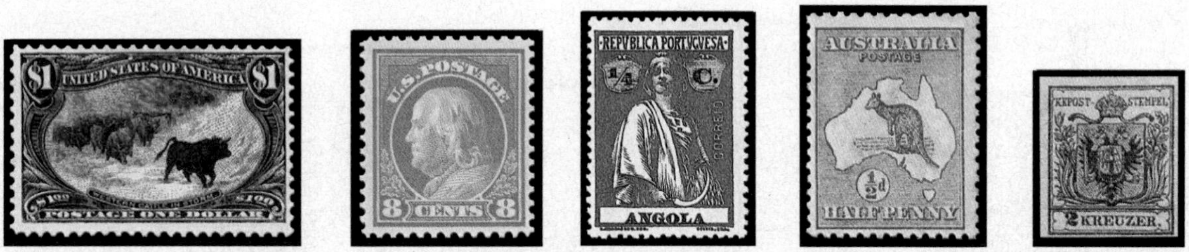

SCOTT CATALOGUES VALUE STAMPS IN THIS GRADE

Very Fine →

Extremely Fine →

Fine-Very Fine →

SCOTT CATALOGUES VALUE STAMPS IN THIS GRADE

Very Fine →

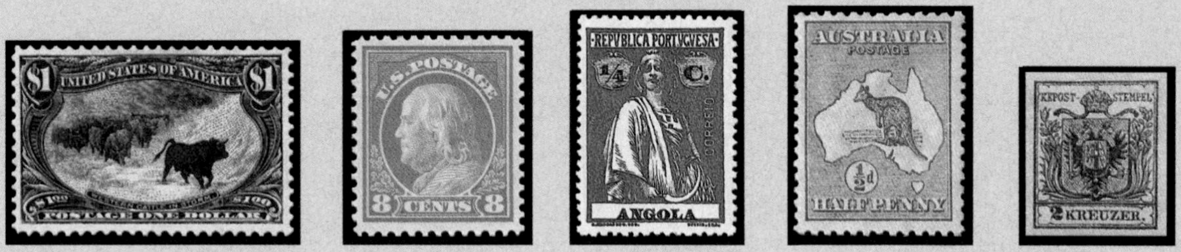

Extremely Fine →

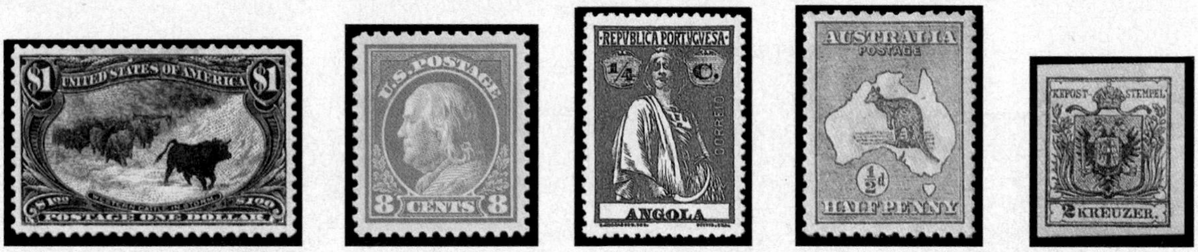

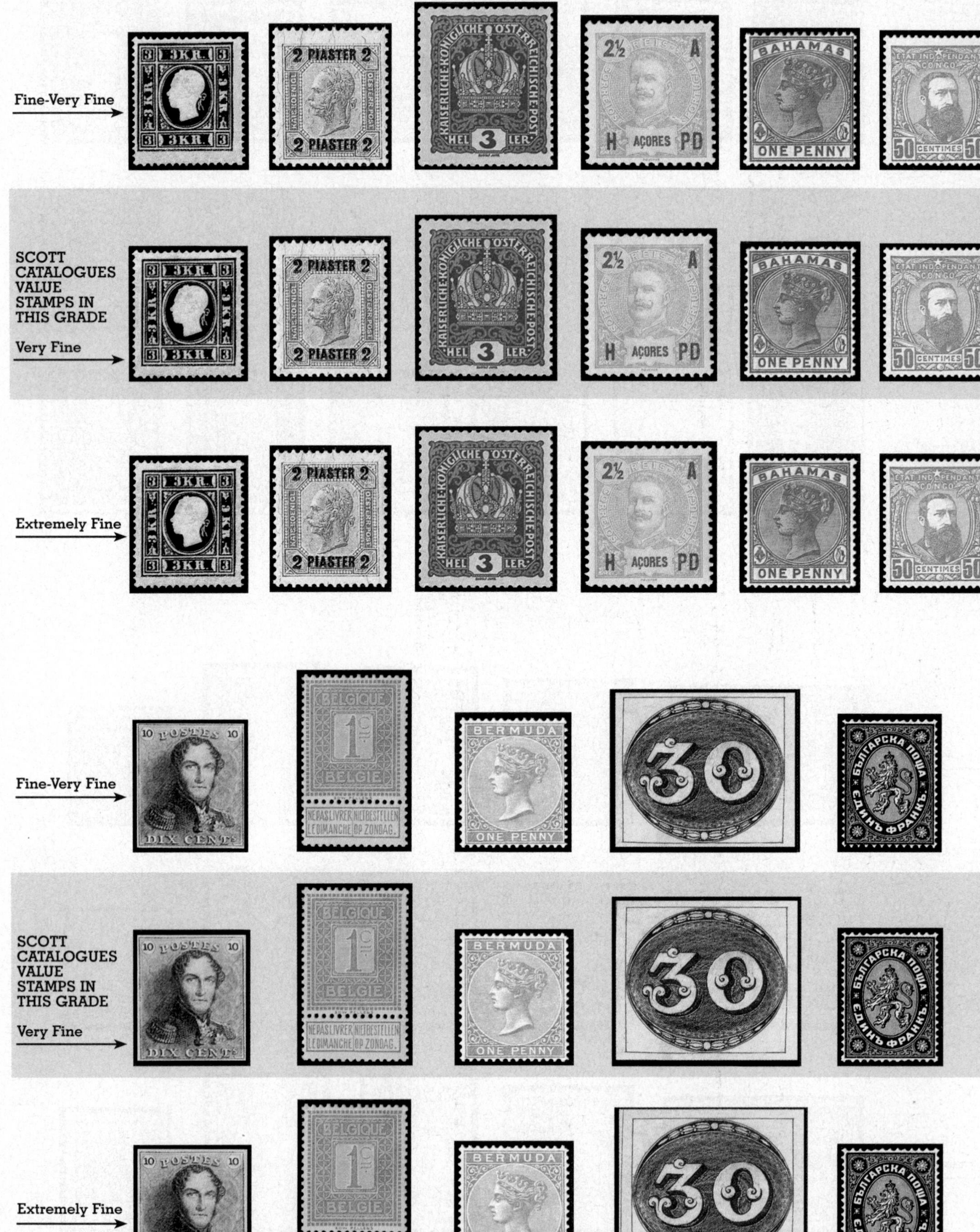
Fine-Very Fine
SCOTT CATALOGUES VALUE STAMPS IN THIS GRADE
Very Fine
Extremely Fine
Fine-Very Fine
SCOTT CATALOGUES VALUE STAMPS IN THIS GRADE
Very Fine
Extremely Fine

For purposes of helping to determine the gum condition and value of an unused stamp, Scott Publishing Co. presents the following chart which details different gum conditions and indicates how the conditions correlate with the Scott values for unused stamps. Used together, the Illustrated Grading Chart on the previous pages and this Illustrated Gum Chart should allow catalogue users to better understand the grade and gum condition of stamps valued in the Scott catalogues.

Gum Categories:	MINT N.H.	ORIGINAL GUM (O.G.)				NO GUM
	 **Mint Never Hinged** *Free from any disturbance*	 **Lightly Hinged** *Faint impression of a removed hinge over a small area*	 **Hinge Mark or Remnant** *Prominent hinged spot with part or all of the hinge remaining*	 **Large part o.g.** *Approximately half or more of the gum intact*	 **Small part o.g.** *Approximately less than half of the gum intact*	 **No gum** *Only if issued with gum*
Commonly Used Symbol:	★★	★	★	★	★	(★)
Pre-1900 Issues (Pre-1881 for U.S.)	*Very fine pre-1900 stamps in these categories trade at a premium over Scott value*			Scott Value for "Unused"		Scott "No Gum" listings for selected unused classic stamps
From 1900 to break-points for listings of never-hinged stamps	Scott "Never Hinged" listings for selected unused stamps	Scott Value for "Unused" (Actual value will be affected by the degree of hinging of the full o.g.)				
From breakpoints noted for many countries	Scott Value for "Unused"					

Never Hinged (NH; ★★): A never-hinged stamp will have full original gum that will have no hinge mark or disturbance. The presence of an expertizer's mark does not disqualify a stamp from this designation.

Original Gum (OG; ★): Pre-1900 stamps should have approximately half or more of their original gum. On rarer stamps, it may be expected that the original gum will be somewhat more disturbed than it will be on more common issues. Post-1900 stamps should have full original gum. Original gum will show some disturbance caused by a previous hinge(s) which may be present or entirely removed. The actual value of a post-1900 stamp will be affected by the degree of hinging of the full original gum.

Disturbed Original Gum: Gum showing noticeable effects of humidity, climate or hinging over more than half of the gum. The significance of gum disturbance in valuing a stamp in any of the Original Gum categories depends on the degree of disturbance, the rarity and normal gum condition of the issue and other variables affecting quality.

Regummed (RG; (★)): A regummed stamp is a stamp without gum that has had some type of gum privately applied at a time after it was issued. This normally is done to deceive collectors and/or dealers into thinking that the stamp has original gum and therefore has a higher value. A regummed stamp is considered the same as a stamp with none of its original gum for purposes of grading.

Understanding the Listings

On the opposite page is an enlarged "typical" listing from this catalogue. Below are detailed explanations of each of the highlighted parts of the listing.

1 Scott number — Scott catalogue numbers are used to identify specific items when buying, selling or trading stamps. Each listed postage stamp from every country has a unique Scott catalogue number. Therefore, Germany Scott 99, for example, can only refer to a single stamp. Although the Scott catalogue usually lists stamps in chronological order by date of issue, there are exceptions. When a country has issued a set of stamps over a period of time, those stamps within the set are kept together without regard to date of issue. This follows the normal collecting approach of keeping stamps in their natural sets.

When a country issues a set of stamps over a period of time, a group of consecutive catalogue numbers is reserved for the stamps in that set, as issued. If that group of numbers proves to be too few, capital-letter suffixes, such as "A" or "B," may be added to existing numbers to create enough catalogue numbers to cover all items in the set. A capital-letter suffix indicates a major Scott catalogue number listing. Scott generally uses a suffix letter only once. Therefore, a catalogue number listing with a capital-letter suffix will seldom be found with the same letter (lower case) used as a minor-letter listing. If there is a Scott 16A in a set, for example, there will seldom be a Scott 16a. However, a minor-letter "a" listing may be added to a major number containing an "A" suffix (Scott 16Aa, for example).

Suffix letters are cumulative. A minor "b" variety of Scott 16A would be Scott 16Ab, not Scott 16b.

There are times when a reserved block of Scott catalogue numbers is too large for a set, leaving some numbers unused. Such gaps in the numbering sequence also occur when the catalogue editors move an item's listing elsewhere or have removed it entirely from the catalogue. Scott does not attempt to account for every possible number, but rather attempts to assure that each stamp is assigned its own number.

Scott numbers designating regular postage normally are only numerals. Scott numbers for other types of stamps, such as air post, semi-postal, postal tax, postage due, occupation and others have a prefix consisting of one or more capital letters or a combination of numerals and capital letters.

2 Illustration number — Illustration or design-type numbers are used to identify each catalogue illustration. For most sets, the lowest face-value stamp is shown. It then serves as an example of the basic design approach for other stamps not illustrated. Where more than one stamp use the same illustration number, but have differences in design, the design paragraph or the description line clearly indicates the design on each stamp not illustrated. Where there are both vertical and horizontal designs in a set, a single illustration may be used, with the exceptions noted in the design paragraph or description line.

When an illustration is followed by a lower-case letter in parentheses, such as "A2(b)," the trailing letter indicates which overprint or surcharge illustration applies.

Illustrations normally are 70 percent of the original size of the stamp. Oversized stamps, blocks and souvenir sheets are reduced even more. Overprints and surcharges are shown at 100 percent of their original size if shown alone, but are 70 percent of original size if shown on stamps. In some cases, the illustration will be placed above the set, between listings or omitted completely. Overprint and surcharge illustrations are not placed in this catalogue for purposes of expertizing stamps.

3 Paper color — The color of a stamp's paper is noted in italic type when the paper used is not white.

4 Listing styles — There are two principal types of catalogue listings: major and minor.

Major listings are in a larger type style than minor listings. The catalogue number is a numeral that can be found with or without a capital-letter suffix, and with or without a prefix.

Minor listings are in a smaller type style and have a small-letter suffix or (if the listing immediately follows that of the major number) may show only the letter. These listings identify a variety of the major item. Examples include perforation and shade differences, multiples (some souvenir sheets, booklet panes and se-tenant combinations), and singles of multiples.

Examples of major number listings include 16, 28A, B97, C13A, 10N5, and 10N6A. Examples of minor numbers are 16a and C13Ab.

5 Basic information about a stamp or set — Introducing each stamp issue is a small section (usually a line listing) of basic information about a stamp or set. This section normally includes the date of issue, method of printing, perforation, watermark and, sometimes, some additional information of note. *Printing method, perforation and watermark apply to the following sets until a change is noted.* Stamps created by overprinting or surcharging previous issues are assumed to have the same perforation, watermark, printing method and other production characteristics as the original. Dates of issue are as precise as Scott is able to confirm and often reflect the dates on first-day covers, rather than the actual date of release.

6 Denomination — This normally refers to the face value of the stamp; that is, the cost of the unused stamp at the post office at the time of issue. When a denomination is shown in parentheses, it does not appear on the stamp. This includes the non-denominated stamps of the United States, Brazil and Great Britain, for example.

7 Color or other description — This area provides information to solidify identification of a stamp. In many recent cases, a description of the stamp design appears in this space, rather than a listing of colors.

8 Year of issue — In stamp sets that have been released in a period that spans more than a year, the number shown in parentheses is the year that stamp first appeared. Stamps without a date appeared during the first year of the issue. Dates are not always given for minor varieties.

9 Value unused and Value used — The Scott catalogue values are based on stamps that are in a grade of Very Fine unless stated otherwise. Unused values refer to items that have not seen postal, revenue or any other duty for which they were intended. Pre-1900 unused stamps that were issued with gum must have at least most of their original gum. Later issues are assumed to have full original gum. From breakpoints specified in most countries' listings, stamps are valued as never hinged. Stamps issued without gum are noted. Modern issues with PVA or other synthetic adhesives may appear ungummed. Unused self-adhesive stamps are valued as appearing undisturbed on their original backing paper. Values for used self-adhesive stamps are for examples either on piece or off piece. For a more detailed explanation of these values, please see the "Catalogue Value," "Condition" and "Understanding Valuing Notations" sections elsewhere in this introduction.

In some cases, where used stamps are more valuable than unused stamps, the value is for an example with a contemporaneous cancel, rather than a modern cancel or a smudge or other unclear marking. For those stamps that were released for postal and fiscal purposes, the used value represents a postally used stamp. Stamps with revenue cancels generally sell for less.

Stamps separated from a complete se-tenant multiple usually will be worth less than a pro-rated portion of the se-tenant multiple, and stamps lacking the attached labels that are noted in the listings will be worth less than the values shown.

10 Changes in basic set information — Bold type is used to show any changes in the basic data given for a set of stamps. These basic data categories include perforation gauge measurement, paper type, printing method and watermark.

11 Total value of a set — The total value of sets of three or more stamps issued after 1900 are shown. The set line also notes the range of Scott numbers and total number of stamps included in the grouping. The actual value of a set consisting predominantly of stamps having the minimum value of 25 cents may be less than the total value shown. Similarly, the actual value or catalogue value of se-tenant pairs or of blocks consisting of stamps having the minimum value of 25 cents may be less than the catalogue values of the component parts.

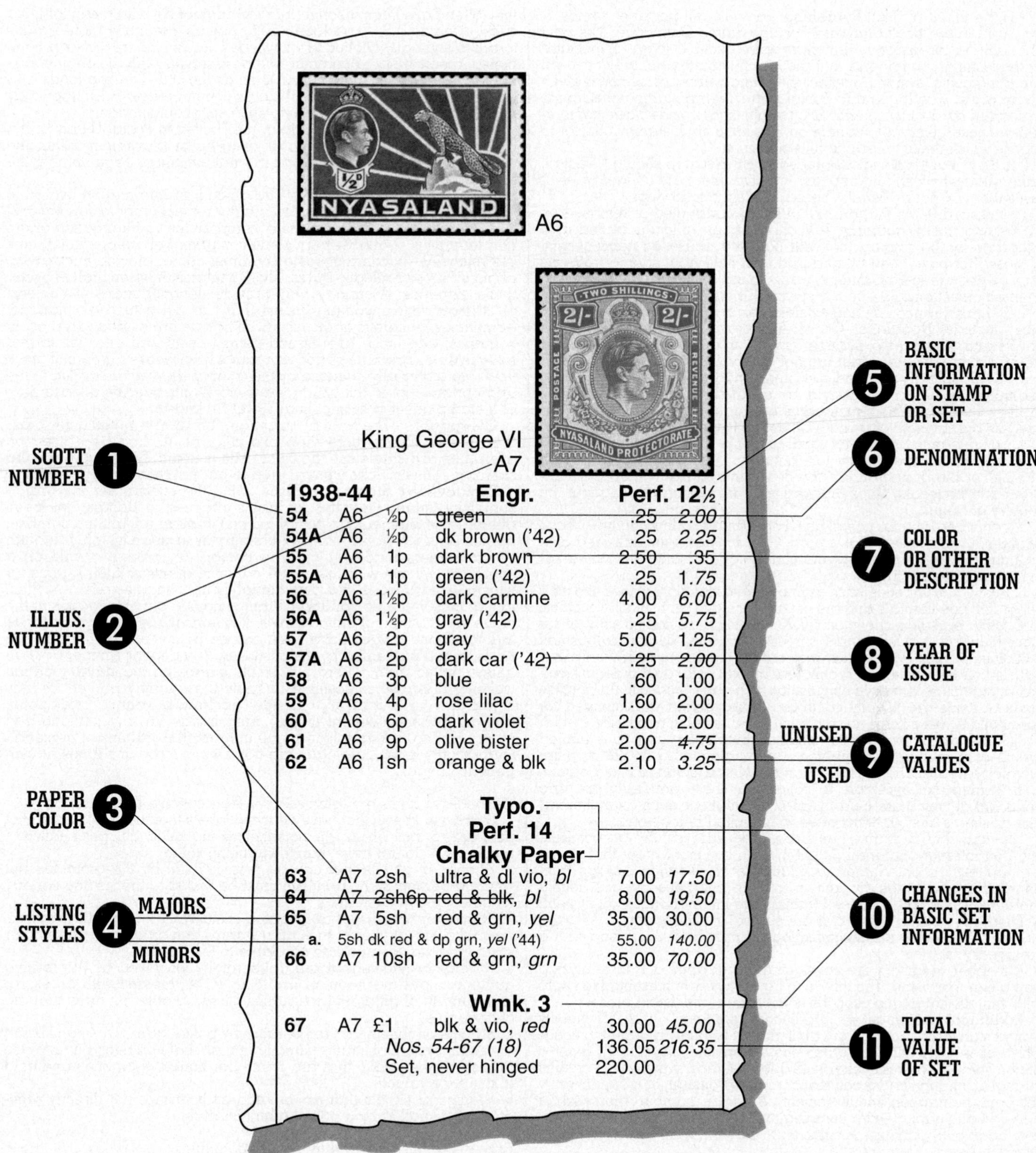
NYASALAND
A6
TWO SHILLINGS
2/-
2/-
POSTAGE
REVENUE
NYASALAND PROTECTORATE
King George VI
A7
1938-44 Engr. Perf. 12½
54 A6 ½p green .25 2.00
54A A6 ½p dk brown ('42) .25 2.25
55 A6 1p dark brown 2.50 .35
55A A6 1p green ('42) .25 1.75
56 A6 1½p dark carmine 4.00 6.00
56A A6 1½p gray ('42) .25 5.75
57 A6 2p gray 5.00 1.25
57A A6 2p dark car ('42) .25 2.00
58 A6 3p blue .60 1.00
59 A6 4p rose lilac 1.60 2.00
60 A6 6p dark violet 2.00 2.00
61 A6 9p olive bister 2.00 4.75
62 A6 1sh orange & blk 2.10 3.25
Typo.
Perf. 14
Chalky Paper
63 A7 2sh ultra & dl vio, bl 7.00 17.50
64 A7 2sh6p red & blk, bl 8.00 19.50
65 A7 5sh red & grn, yel 35.00 30.00
a. 5sh dk red & dp grn, yel ('44) 55.00 140.00
66 A7 10sh red & grn, grn 35.00 70.00
Wmk. 3
67 A7 £1 blk & vio, red 30.00 45.00
Nos. 54-67 (18) 136.05 216.35
Set, never hinged 220.00
1 SCOTT NUMBER
2 ILLUS. NUMBER
3 PAPER COLOR
4 LISTING STYLES
MAJORS
MINORS
5 BASIC INFORMATION ON STAMP OR SET
6 DENOMINATION
7 COLOR OR OTHER DESCRIPTION
8 YEAR OF ISSUE
UNUSED
USED
9 CATALOGUE VALUES
10 CHANGES IN BASIC SET INFORMATION
11 TOTAL VALUE OF SET

Catalogue Listing Policy

It is the intent of Scott Publishing Co. to list all postage stamps of the world in the *Scott Standard Postage Stamp Catalogue*. The only strict criteria for listing is that stamps be decreed legal for postage by the issuing country and that the issuing country actually have an operating postal system. Whether the primary intent of issuing a given stamp or set was for sale to postal patrons or to stamp collectors is not part of our listing criteria. Scott's role is to provide basic comprehensive postage stamp information. It is up to each stamp collector to choose which items to include in a collection.

It is Scott's objective to seek reasons why a stamp should be listed, rather than why it should not. Nevertheless, there are certain types of items that will not be listed. These include the following:

1. Unissued items that are not officially distributed or released by the issuing postal authority. If such items are officially issued at a later date by the country, they will be listed. Unissued items consist of those that have been printed and then held from sale for reasons such as change in government, errors found on stamps or something deemed objectionable about a stamp subject or design.
2. Stamps "issued" by non-existent postal entities or fantasy countries, such as Nagaland, Occusi-Ambeno, Staffa, Sedang, Torres Straits and others. Also, stamps "issued" in the names of legitimate, stamp-issuing countries that are not authorized by those countries.
3. Semi-official or unofficial items not required for postage. Examples include items issued by private agencies for their own express services. When such items are required for delivery, or are valid as prepayment of postage, they are listed.
4. Local stamps issued for local use only. Postage stamps issued by governments specifically for "domestic" use, such as Haiti Scott 219-228, or the United States non-denominated stamps, are not considered to be locals, since they are valid for postage throughout the country of origin.
5. Items not valid for postal use. For example, a few countries have issued souvenir sheets that are not valid for postage. This area also includes a number of worldwide charity labels (some denominated) that do not pay postage.
6. Intentional varieties, such as imperforate stamps that look like their perforated counterparts and are usually issued in very small quantities. Also, other egregiously exploitative issues such as stamps sold for far more than face value, stamps purposefully issued in artificially small quantities or only against advance orders, stamps awarded only to a selected audience such as a philatelic bureau's standing order customers, or stamps sold only in conjunction with other products. All of these kinds of items are usually controlled issues and/or are intended for speculation. These items normally will be included in a footnote.
7. Items distributed by the issuing government only to a limited group, club, philatelic exhibition or a single stamp dealer or other private company. These items normally will be included in a footnote.
8. Stamps not available to collectors. These generally are rare items, all of which are held by public institutions such as museums. The existence of such items often will be cited in footnotes.

The fact that a stamp has been used successfully as postage, even on international mail, is not in itself sufficient proof that it was legitimately issued. Numerous examples of so-called stamps from non-existent countries are known to have been used to post letters that have successfully passed through the international mail system.

There are certain items that are subject to interpretation. When a stamp falls outside our specifications, it may be listed along with a cautionary footnote.

A number of factors are considered in our approach to analyzing how a stamp is listed. The following list of factors is presented to share with you, the catalogue user, the complexity of the listing process.

Additional printings — "Additional printings" of a previously issued stamp may range from an item that is totally different to cases where it is impossible to differentiate from the original. At least a minor number (a small-letter suffix) is assigned if there is a distinct change in stamp shade, noticeably redrawn design, or a significantly different perforation measurement. A major number (numeral or numeral and capital-letter combination) is assigned if the editors feel the "additional printing" is sufficiently different from the original that it constitutes a different issue.

Commemoratives — Where practical, commemoratives with the same theme are placed in a set. For example, the U.S. Civil War Centennial set of 1961-65 and the Constitution Bicentennial series of 1989-90 appear as sets. Countries such as Japan and Korea issue such material on a regular basis, with an announced, or at least predictable, number of stamps known in advance. Occasionally, however, stamp sets that were released over a period of years have been separated. Appropriately placed footnotes will guide you to each set's continuation.

Definitive sets — Blocks of numbers generally have been reserved for definitive sets, based on previous experience with any given country. If a few more stamps were issued in a set than originally expected, they often have been inserted into the original set with a capital-letter suffix, such as U.S. Scott 1059A. If it appears that many more stamps than the originally allotted block will be released before the set is completed, a new block of numbers will be reserved, with the original one being closed off. In some cases, such as the U.S. Transportation and Great Americans series, several blocks of numbers exist. Appropriately placed footnotes will guide you to each set's continuation.

New country — Membership in the Universal Postal Union is not a consideration for listing status or order of placement within the catalogue. The index will tell you in what volume or page number the listings begin.

"No release date" items — The amount of information available for any given stamp issue varies greatly from country to country and even from time to time. Extremely comprehensive information about new stamps is available from some countries well before the stamps are released. By contrast some countries do not provide information about stamps or release dates. Most countries, however, fall between these extremes. A country may provide denominations or subjects of stamps from upcoming issues that are not issued as planned. Sometimes, philatelic agencies, those private firms hired to represent countries, add these later-issued items to sets well after the formal release date. This time period can range from weeks to years. If these items were officially released by the country, they will be added to the appropriate spot in the set. In many cases, the specific release date of a stamp or set of stamps may never be known.

Overprints — The color of an overprint is always noted if it is other than black. Where more than one color of ink has been used on overprints of a single set, the color used is noted. Early overprint and surcharge illustrations were altered to prevent their use by forgers.

Personalized Stamps — Since 1999, the special service of personalizing stamp vignettes, or labels attached to stamps, has been offered to customers by postal administrations of many countries. Sheets of these stamps are sold, singly or in quantity, only through special orders made by mail, in person, or through a sale on a computer website with the postal administrations or their agents for which an extra fee is charged, though some countries offer to collectors at face value personalized stamps having generic images in the vignettes or on the attached labels. It is impossible for any catalogue to know what images have been chosen by customers. Images can be 1) owned or created by the customer, 2) a generic image, or 3) an image pulled from a library of stock images on the stamp creation website. It is also impossible to know the quantity printed for any stamp having a particular image. So from a valuing standpoint, any image is equivalent to any other image for any personalized stamp having the same catalogue number. Illustrations of personalized stamps in the catalogue are not always those of stamps having generic images.

Personalized items are listed with some exceptions. These include:

1. Stamps or sheets that have attached labels that the customer cannot personalize, but which are nonetheless marketed as "personalized," and are sold for far more than the franking value.
2. Stamps or sheets that can be personalized by the customer, but where a portion of the print run must be ceded to the issuing country for sale to other customers.
3. Stamps or sheets that are created exclusively for a particular commercial client, or clients, including stamps that differ from any similar stamp that has been made available to the public.
4. Stamps or sheets that are deliberately conceived by the issuing authority that have been, or are likely to be, created with an excessive number of different face values, sizes, or other features that are changeable.
5. Stamps or sheets that are created by postal administrations using the same system of stamp personalization that has been put in place for use by the public that are printed in limited quantities and sold above face value.
6. Stamps or sheets that are created by licensees not directly affiliated or controlled by a postal administration.

Excluded items may or may not be footnoted.

Se-tenants — Connected stamps of differing features (se-tenants) will be listed in the format most commonly collected. This includes pairs, blocks or larger multiples. Se-tenant units are not always symmetrical. An example is Australia Scott 508, which is a block of seven stamps. If the stamps are primarily collected as a unit, the major number may be assigned to the multiple, with minors going to each component stamp. In cases where continuous-design or other unit se-tenants will receive significant postal use, each stamp is given a major Scott number listing. This includes issues from the United States, Canada, Germany and Great Britain, for example.

Special Notices

Classification of stamps

The *Scott Standard Postage Stamp Catalogue* lists stamps by country of issue. The next level of organization is a listing by section on the basis of the function of the stamps. The principal sections cover regular postage, semi-postal, air post, special delivery, registration, postage due and other categories. Except for regular postage, catalogue numbers for all sections include a prefix letter (or number-letter combination) denoting the class to which a given stamp belongs. When some countries issue sets containing stamps from more than one category, the catalogue will at times list all of the stamps in one category (such as air post stamps listed as part of a postage set).

The following is a listing of the most commonly used catalogue prefixes.

Prefix ....Category
C.........Air Post
M........Military
P.........Newspaper
N.........Occupation - Regular Issues
O........Official
Q........Parcel Post
J..........Postage Due
RA......Postal Tax
B.........Semi-Postal
E.........Special Delivery
MR......War Tax

Other prefixes used by more than one country include the following:
H.........Acknowledgment of Receipt
I..........Late Fee
CO......Air Post Official
CQ......Air Post Parcel Post
RAC....Air Post Postal Tax
CF......Air Post Registration
CB......Air Post Semi-Postal
CBO...Air Post Semi-Postal Official
CE......Air Post Special Delivery
EY.......Authorized Delivery
S.........Franchise
G........Insured Letter
GY......Marine Insurance
MC.....Military Air Post
MQ.....Military Parcel Post
NC......Occupation - Air Post
NO......Occupation - Official
NJ........Occupation - Postage Due
NRA....Occupation - Postal Tax
NB......Occupation - Semi-Postal
NE......Occupation - Special Delivery
QY......Parcel Post Authorized Delivery
AR......Postal-fiscal
RAJ.....Postal Tax Due
RAB....Postal Tax Semi-Postal
F.........Registration
EB.......Semi-Postal Special Delivery
EO......Special Delivery Official
QE......Special Handling

New issue listings

Updates to this catalogue appear each month in the *Linn's Stamp News Special Edition* magazine. Included in this update are additions to the listings of countries found in the *Scott Standard Postage Stamp Catalogue* and the *Specialized Catalogue of United States Stamps and Covers*, as well as corrections and updates to current editions of this catalogue.

From time to time there will be changes in the final listings of stamps from the *Linn's Stamp News Special Edition* to the next edition of the catalogue. This occurs as more information about certain stamps or sets becomes available.

The catalogue update section of the *Linn's Stamp News Special Edition* is the most timely presentation of this material available. Annual subscriptions to *Linn's Stamp News* are available from Linn's Stamp News, Box 926, Sidney, OH 45365-0926.

Number additions, deletions & changes

A listing of catalogue number additions, deletions and changes from the previous edition of the catalogue appears in each volume. See Catalogue Number Additions, Deletions & Changes in the table of contents for the location of this list.

Understanding valuing notations

The *minimum catalogue value* of an individual stamp or set is 25 cents. This represents a portion of the cost incurred by a dealer when he prepares an individual stamp for resale. As a point of philatelic-economic fact, the lower the value shown for an item in this catalogue, the greater the percentage of that value is attributed to dealer mark up and profit margin. In many cases, such as the 25-cent minimum value, that price does not cover the labor or other costs involved with stocking it as an individual stamp. The sum of minimum values in a set does not properly represent the value of a complete set primarily composed of a number of minimum-value stamps, nor does the sum represent the actual value of a packet made up of minimum-value stamps. Thus a packet of 1,000 different common stamps — each of which has a catalogue value of 25 cents — normally sells for considerably less than 250 dollars!

The *absence of a retail value* for a stamp does not necessarily suggest that a stamp is scarce or rare. A dash in the value column means that the stamp is known in a stated form or variety, but information is either lacking or insufficient for purposes of establishing a usable catalogue value.

Stamp values in *italics* generally refer to items that are difficult to value accurately. For expensive items, such as those priced at $1,000 or higher, a value in italics indicates that the affected item trades very seldom. For inexpensive items, a value in italics represents a warning. One example is a "blocked" issue where the issuing postal administration may have controlled one stamp in a set in an attempt to make the whole set more valuable. Another example is an item that sold at an extreme multiple of face value in the marketplace at the time of its issue.

One type of warning to collectors that appears in the catalogue is illustrated by a stamp that is valued considerably higher in used condition than it is as unused. In this case, collectors are cautioned to be certain the used version has a genuine and contemporaneous cancellation. The type of cancellation on a stamp can be an important factor in determining its sale price. Catalogue values do not apply to fiscal, telegraph or non-contemporaneous postal cancels, unless otherwise noted.

Some countries have released back issues of stamps in canceled-to-order form, sometimes covering as much as a 10-year period. The Scott Catalogue values for used stamps reflect canceled-to-order material when such stamps are found to predominate in the marketplace for the issue involved. Notes frequently appear in the stamp listings to specify which items are valued as canceled-to-order, or if there is a premium for postally used examples.

Many countries sell canceled-to-order stamps at a marked reduction of face value. Countries that sell or have sold canceled-to-order stamps at *full* face value include United Nations, Australia, Netherlands, France and Switzerland. It may be almost impossible to identify such stamps if the gum has been removed, because official government canceling devices are used. Postally used examples of these items on cover, however, are usually worth more than the canceled-to-order stamps with original gum.

Abbreviations

Scott Publishing Co. uses a consistent set of abbreviations throughout this catalogue to conserve space, while still providing necessary information.

COLOR ABBREVIATIONS

amb. amber	crim. crimson	ol ..... olive
anil.. aniline	cr ..... cream	olvn . olivine
ap.... apple	dk .... dark	org... orange
aqua aquamarine	dl ..... dull	pck .. peacock
az .... azure	dp.... deep	pnksh pinkish
bis ... bister	db.... drab	Prus . Prussian
bl..... blue	emer emerald	pur... purple
bld... blood	gldn. golden	redsh reddish
blk ... black	gryshgrayish	res ... reseda
bril... brilliant	grn... green	ros ... rosine
brn... brown	grnsh greenish	ryl.... royal
brnsh brownish	hel ... heliotrope	sal ... salmon
brnz. bronze	hn.... henna	saph sapphire
brt.... bright	ind... indigo	scar . scarlet
brnt . burnt	int .... intense	sep .. sepia
car ... carmine	lav ... lavender	sien . sienna
cer ... cerise	lem .. lemon	sil..... silver
chlky chalky	lil ..... lilac	sl...... slate
chamchamois	lt ...... light	stl .... steel
chnt . chestnut	mag. magenta	turq.. turquoise
choc chocolate	man. manila	ultra ultramarine
chr ... chrome	mar.. maroon	Ven .. Venetian
cit .... citron	mv ... mauve	ver ... vermilion
cl...... claret	multi multicolored	vio ... violet
cob .. cobalt	mlky milky	yel ... yellow
cop .. copper	myr .. myrtle	yelsh yellowish

When no color is given for an overprint or surcharge, black is the color used. Abbreviations for colors used for overprints and surcharges include: "(B)" or "(Blk)," black; "(Bl)," blue; "(R)," red; and "(G)," green.

Additional abbreviations in this catalogue are shown below:

Adm. ....Administration
AFL...............American Federation of Labor
Anniv............Anniversary
APS ....American Philatelic Society
Assoc. ....Association
ASSR. ....Autonomous Soviet Socialist Republic
b. ....Born
BEP...............Bureau of Engraving and Printing
Bicent............Bicentennial
Bklt...............Booklet
Brit................British
btwn. ....Between
Bur................Bureau
c. or ca..........Circa
Cat. ....Catalogue
Cent. ....Centennial, century, centenary
CIO ....Congress of Industrial Organizations
Conf. ....Conference
Cong.............Congress
Cpl. ....Corporal
CTO ....Canceled to order
d. ....Died
Dbl. ....Double
EDU..............Earliest documented use
Engr. ....Engraved
Exhib............Exhibition
Expo.............Exposition
Fed. ....Federation
GB ....Great Britain
Gen. ....General
GPO ....General post office
Horiz. ....Horizontal
Imperf. ....Imperforate
Impt..............Imprint
Intl. ....International
Invtd.............Inverted
L ....Left
Lieut., lt.........Lieutenant
Litho.............Lithographed
LL ....Lower left
LR.................Lower right
mm ....Millimeter
Ms. ....Manuscript
Natl. ....National
No.................Number
NY ....New York
NYC ....New York City
Ovpt. ....Overprint
Ovptd...........Overprinted
P ....Plate number
Perf...............Perforated, perforation
Phil. ....Philatelic
Photo............Photogravure
PO ....Post office
Pr. ....Pair
P.R................Puerto Rico
Prec. ....Precancel, precanceled
Pres. ....President
PTT...............Post, Telephone and Telegraph
R ....Right
Rio................Rio de Janeiro
Sgt................Sergeant
Soc. ....Society
Souv. ....Souvenir
SSR..............Soviet Socialist Republic, see ASSR
St..................Saint, street
Surch. ....Surcharge
Typo. ....Typographed
UL.................Upper left
Unwmkd. ......Unwatermarked
UPU..............Universal Postal Union
UR ....Upper Right
US ....United States
USPOD ....United States Post Office Department
USSR ....Union of Soviet Socialist Republics
Vert...............Vertical
VP.................Vice president
Wmk.............Watermark
Wmkd. ....Watermarked
WWI ....World War I
WWII ....World War II

Examination

Scott Publishing Co. will not comment upon the genuineness, grade or condition of stamps, because of the time and responsibility involved. Rather, there are several expertizing groups that undertake this work for both collectors and dealers. Neither will Scott Publishing Co. appraise or identify philatelic material. The company cannot take responsibility for unsolicited stamps or covers sent by individuals.

All letters, E-mails, etc. are read attentively, but they are not always answered due to time considerations.

How to order from your dealer

When ordering stamps from a dealer, it is not necessary to write the full description of a stamp as listed in this catalogue. All you need is the name of the country, the Scott catalogue number and whether the desired item is unused or used. For example, "Japan Scott 422 unused" is sufficient to identify the unused stamp of Japan listed as "422 A206 5y brown."

Basic Stamp Information

A stamp collector's knowledge of the combined elements that make a given stamp issue unique determines his or her ability to identify stamps. These elements include paper, watermark, method of separation, printing, design and gum. On the following pages each of these important areas is briefly described.

Paper

Paper is an organic material composed of a compacted weave of cellulose fibers and generally formed into sheets. Paper used to print stamps may be manufactured in sheets, or it may have been part of a large roll (called a web) before being cut to size. The fibers most often used to create paper on which stamps are printed include bark, wood, straw and certain grasses. In many cases, linen or cotton rags have been added for greater strength and durability. Grinding, bleaching, cooking and rinsing these raw fibers reduces them to a slushy pulp, referred to by paper makers as "stuff." Sizing and, sometimes, coloring matter is added to the pulp to make different types of finished paper.

After the stuff is prepared, it is poured onto sieve-like frames that allow the water to run off, while retaining the matted pulp. As fibers fall onto the screen and are held by gravity, they form a natural weave that will later hold the paper together. If the screen has metal bits that are formed into letters or images attached, it leaves slightly thinned areas on the paper. These are called watermarks.

When the stuff is almost dry, it is passed under pressure through smooth or engraved rollers - dandy rolls - or placed between cloth in a press to be flattened and dried.

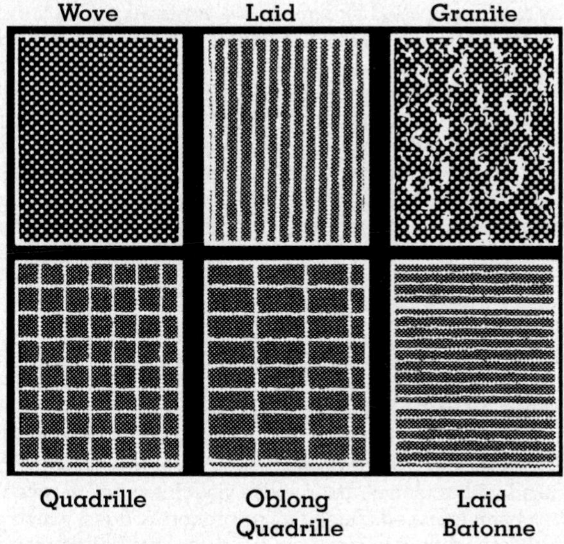

Stamp paper falls broadly into two types: wove and laid. The nature of the surface of the frame onto which the pulp is first deposited causes the differences in appearance between the two. If the surface is smooth and even, the paper will be of fairly uniform texture throughout. This is known as *wove paper*. Early papermaking machines poured the pulp onto a continuously circulating web of felt, but modern machines feed the pulp onto a cloth-like screen made of closely interwoven fine wires. This paper, when held to a light, will show little dots or points very close together. The proper name for this is "wire wove," but the type is still considered wove. Any U.S. or British stamp printed after 1880 will serve as an example of wire wove paper.

Closely spaced parallel wires, with cross wires at wider intervals, make up the frames used for what is known as *laid paper*. A greater thickness of the pulp will settle between the wires. The paper, when held to a light, will show alternate light and dark lines. The spacing and the thickness of the lines may vary, but on any one sheet of paper they are all alike. See Russia Scott 31-38 for examples of laid paper.

Batonne, from the French word meaning "a staff," is a term used if the lines in the paper are spaced quite far apart, like the printed ruling on a writing tablet. Batonne paper may be either wove or laid. If laid, fine laid lines can be seen between the batons.

Quadrille is the term used when the lines in the paper form little squares. *Oblong quadrille* is the term used when rectangles, rather than squares, are formed. Grid patterns vary from distinct to extremely faint. See Mexico-Guadalajara Scott 35-37 for examples of oblong quadrille paper.

Paper also is classified as thick or thin, hard or soft, and by color. Such colors may include yellowish, greenish, bluish and reddish.

Brief explanations of other types of paper used for printing stamps, as well as examples, follow.

Colored — Colored paper is created by the addition of dye in the paper-making process. Such colors may include shades of yellow, green, blue and red. *Surface-colored papers*, most commonly used for British colonial issues in 1913-14, are created when coloring is added only to the surface during the finishing process. Stamps printed on surface-colored paper have white or uncolored backs, while true colored papers are colored through. See Jamaica Scott 71-73.

Pelure — Pelure paper is a very thin, hard and often brittle paper that is sometimes bluish or grayish in appearance. See Serbia Scott 169-170.

Native — This is a term applied to handmade papers used to produce some of the early stamps of the Indian states. Stamps printed on native paper may be expected to display various natural inclusions that are normal and do not negatively affect value. Japanese paper, originally made of mulberry fibers and rice flour, is part of this group. See Japan Scott 1-18.

Manila — This type of paper is often used to make stamped envelopes and wrappers. It is a coarse-textured stock, usually smooth on one side and rough on the other. A variety of colors of manila paper exist, but the most common range is yellowish-brown.

Silk — Introduced by the British in 1847 as a safeguard against counterfeiting, silk paper contains bits of colored silk thread scattered throughout. The density of these fibers varies greatly and can include as few as one fiber per stamp or hundreds. U.S. revenue Scott R152 is a good example of an easy-to-identify silk paper stamp.

Silk-thread paper has uninterrupted threads of colored silk arranged so that one or more threads run through the stamp or postal stationery. See Great Britain Scott 5-6 and Switzerland Scott 14-19.

Granite — Filled with minute cloth or colored paper fibers of various colors and lengths, granite paper should not be confused with either type of silk paper. Austria Scott 172-175 and a number of Swiss stamps are examples of granite paper.

Chalky — A chalk-like substance coats the surface of chalky paper to discourage the cleaning and reuse of canceled stamps, as well as to provide a smoother, more acceptable printing surface. Because the designs of stamps printed on chalky paper are imprinted on what is often a water-soluble coating, any attempt to remove a cancellation will destroy the stamp. *Do not soak these stamps in any fluid.* To remove a stamp printed on chalky paper from an envelope, wet the paper from underneath the stamp until the gum dissolves enough to release the stamp from the paper. See St. Kitts-Nevis Scott 89-90 for examples of stamps printed on this type of chalky paper.

India — Another name for this paper, originally introduced from China about 1750, is "China Paper." It is a thin, opaque paper often used for plate and die proofs by many countries.

Double — In philately, the term double paper has two distinct meanings. The first is a two-ply paper, usually a combination of a thick and a thin sheet, joined during manufacture. This type was used experimentally as a means to discourage the reuse of stamps.

The design is printed on the thin paper. Any attempt to remove a cancellation would destroy the design. U.S. Scott 158 and other Banknote-era stamps exist on this form of double paper.

The second type of double paper occurs on a rotary press, when the end of one paper roll, or web, is affixed to the next roll to save time feeding the paper through the press. Stamp designs are printed over the joined paper and, if overlooked by inspectors, may get into post office stocks.

Goldbeater's Skin — This type of paper was used for the 1866 issue of Prussia, and was a tough, translucent paper. The design was printed in reverse on the back of the stamp, and the gum applied over the printing. It is impossible to remove stamps printed on this type of paper from the paper to which they are affixed without destroying the design.

Ribbed — Ribbed paper has an uneven, corrugated surface made by passing the paper through ridged rollers. This type exists on some copies of U.S. Scott 156-165.

Various other substances, or substrates, have been used for stamp manufacture, including wood, aluminum, copper, silver and gold foil, plastic, and silk and cotton fabrics.

Watermarks

Watermarks are an integral part of some papers. They are formed in the process of paper manufacture. Watermarks consist of small designs, formed of wire or cut from metal and soldered to the surface of the mold or, sometimes, on the dandy roll. The designs may be in the form of crowns, stars, anchors, letters or other characters or symbols. These pieces of metal - known in the paper-making industry as "bits" - impress a design into the paper. The design sometimes may be seen by holding the stamp to the light. Some are more easily seen with a watermark detector. This important tool is a small black tray into which a stamp is placed face down and dampened with a fast-evaporating watermark detection fluid that brings up the watermark image in the form of dark lines against a lighter background. These dark lines are the thinner areas of the paper known as the watermark. Some watermarks are extremely difficult to locate, due to either a faint impression, watermark location or the color of the stamp. There also are electric watermark detectors that come with plastic filter disks of various colors. The disks neutralize the color of the stamp, permitting the watermark to be seen more easily.

Multiple watermarks of Crown Agents and Burma

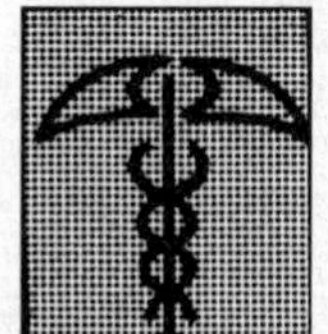

Watermarks of Uruguay, Vatican City and Jamaica

WARNING: Some inks used in the photogravure process dissolve in watermark fluids (Please see the section on Soluble Printing Inks). Also, see "chalky paper."

Watermarks may be found normal, reversed, inverted, reversed and inverted, sideways or diagonal, as seen from the back of the stamp. The relationship of watermark to stamp design depends on the position of the printing plates or how paper is fed through the press. On machine-made paper, watermarks normally are read from right to left. The design is repeated closely throughout the sheet in a "multiple-watermark design." In a "sheet watermark," the design appears only once on the sheet, but extends over many stamps. Individual stamps may carry only a small fraction or none of the watermark.

"Marginal watermarks" occur in the margins of sheets or panes of stamps. They occur on the outside border of paper (ostensibly outside the area where stamps are to be printed). A large row of letters may spell the name of the country or the manufacturer of the paper, or a border of lines may appear. Careless press feeding may cause parts of these letters and/or lines to show on stamps of the outer row of a pane.

Soluble Printing Inks

WARNING: Most stamp colors are permanent; that is, they are not seriously affected by short-term exposure to light or water. Many colors, especially of modern inks, fade from excessive exposure to light. There are stamps printed with inks that dissolve easily in water or in fluids used to detect watermarks. Use of these inks was intentional to prevent the removal of cancellations. Water affects all aniline inks, those on so-called safety paper and some photogravure printings - all such inks are known as fugitive colors. *Removal from paper of such stamps requires care and alternatives to traditional soaking.*

Separation

"Separation" is the general term used to describe methods used to separate stamps. The three standard forms currently in use are perforating, rouletting and die-cutting. These methods are done during the stamp production process, after printing. Sometimes these methods are done on-press or sometimes as a separate step. The earliest issues, such as the 1840 Penny Black of Great Britain (Scott 1), did not have any means provided for separation. It was expected the stamps would be cut apart with scissors or folded and torn. These are examples of imperforate stamps. Many stamps were first issued in imperforate formats and were later issued with perforations. Therefore, care must be observed in buying single imperforate stamps to be certain they were issued imperforate and are not perforated copies that have been altered by having the perforations trimmed away. Stamps issued imperforate usually are valued as singles. However, imperforate varieties of normally perforated stamps should be collected in pairs or larger pieces as indisputable evidence of their imperforate character.

PERFORATION

The chief style of separation of stamps, and the one that is in almost universal use today, is perforating. By this process, paper between the stamps is cut away in a line of holes, usually round, leaving little bridges of paper between the stamps to hold them together. Some types of perforation, such as hyphen-hole perfs, can be confused with roulettes, but a close visual inspection reveals that paper has been removed. The little perforation bridges, which project from the stamp when it is torn from the pane, are called the teeth of the perforation.

As the size of the perforation is sometimes the only way to differentiate between two otherwise identical stamps, it is necessary to be able to accurately measure and describe them. This is done with a perforation gauge, usually a ruler-like device that has dots or graduated lines to show how many perforations may be counted in the space of two centimeters. Two centimeters is the space universally adopted in which to measure perforations.

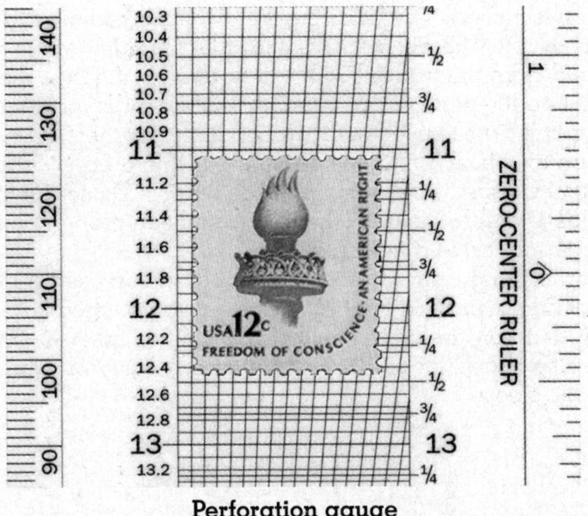

Perforation gauge

To measure a stamp, run it along the gauge until the dots on it fit exactly into the perforations of the stamp. If you are using a graduated-line perforation gauge, simply slide the stamp along the surface until the lines on the gauge perfectly project from the center of the bridges or holes. The number to the side of the line of dots or lines that fit the stamp's perforation is the measurement. For example, an "11" means that 11 perforations fit between two centimeters. The description of the stamp therefore is "perf. 11." If the gauge of the perforations on the top and bottom of a stamp differs from that on the sides, the result is what is known as *compound perforations*. In measuring compound perforations, the gauge at top and bottom is always given first, then the sides. Thus, a stamp that measures 11 at top and bottom and 10½ at the sides is "perf. 11 x 10½." See U.S. Scott 632-642 for examples of compound perforations.

Stamps also are known with perforations different on three or all four sides. Descriptions of such items are clockwise, beginning with the top of the stamp.

A perforation with small holes and teeth close together is a "fine perforation." One with large holes and teeth far apart is a "coarse perforation." Holes that are jagged, rather than clean-cut, are "rough perforations." *Blind perforations* are the slight impressions left by the perforating pins if they fail to puncture the paper. Multiples of stamps showing blind perforations may command a slight premium over normally perforated stamps.

The term *syncopated perfs* describes intentional irregularities in the perforations. The earliest form was used by the Netherlands from 1925-33, where holes were omitted to create distinctive patterns. Beginning in 1992, Great Britain has used an oval perforation to help prevent counterfeiting. Several other countries have started using the oval perfs or other syncopated perf patterns.

A new type of perforation, still primarily used for postal stationery, is known as microperfs. Microperfs are tiny perforations (in some cases hundreds of holes per two centimeters) that allows items to be intentionally separated very easily, while not accidentally breaking apart as easily as standard perforations. These are not currently measured or differentiated by size, as are standard perforations.

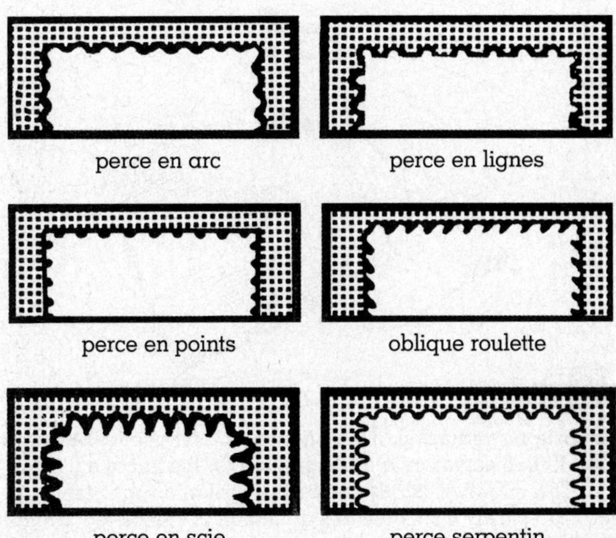

ROULETTING

In rouletting, the stamp paper is cut partly or wholly through, with no paper removed. In perforating, some paper is removed. Rouletting derives its name from the French roulette, a spur-like wheel. As the wheel is rolled over the paper, each point makes a small cut. The number of cuts made in a two-centimeter space determines the gauge of the roulette, just as the number of perforations in two centimeters determines the gauge of the perforation.

The shape and arrangement of the teeth on the wheels varies. Various roulette types generally carry French names:

Perce en lignes - rouletted in lines. The paper receives short, straight cuts in lines. This is the most common type of rouletting. See Mexico Scott 500.

Perce en points - pin-rouletted or pin-perfed. This differs from a small perforation because no paper is removed, although round, equidistant holes are pricked through the paper. See Mexico Scott 242-256.

Perce en arc and *perce en scie* - pierced in an arc or saw-toothed designs, forming half circles or small triangles. See Hanover (German States) Scott 25-29.

Perce en serpentin - serpentine roulettes. The cuts form a serpentine or wavy line. See Brunswick (German States) Scott 13-18.

Once again, no paper is removed by these processes, leaving the stamps easily separated, but closely attached.

DIE-CUTTING

The third major form of stamp separation is die-cutting. This is a method where a die in the pattern of separation is created that later cuts the stamp paper in a stroke motion. Although some standard stamps bear die-cut perforations, this process is primarily used for self-adhesive postage stamps. Die-cutting can appear in straight lines, such as U.S. Scott 2522, shapes, such as U.S. Scott 1551, or imitating the appearance of perforations, such as New Zealand Scott 935A and 935B.

Printing Processes

ENGRAVING (Intaglio, Line-engraving, Etching)

Master die — The initial operation in the process of line engraving is making the master die. The die is a small, flat block of softened steel upon which the stamp design is recess engraved in reverse.

Master die

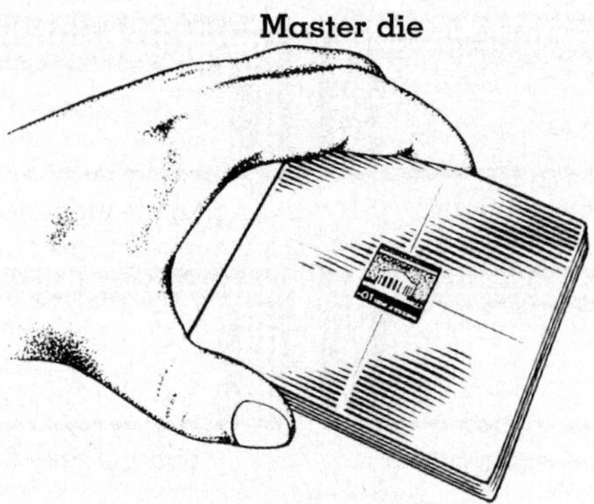

Photographic reduction of the original art is made to the appropriate size. It then serves as a tracing guide for the initial outline of the design. The engraver lightly traces the design on the steel with his graver, then slowly works the design until it is completed. At various points during the engraving process, the engraver hand-inks the die and makes an impression to check his progress. These are known as progressive die proofs. After completion of the engraving, the die is hardened to withstand the stress and pressures of later transfer operations.

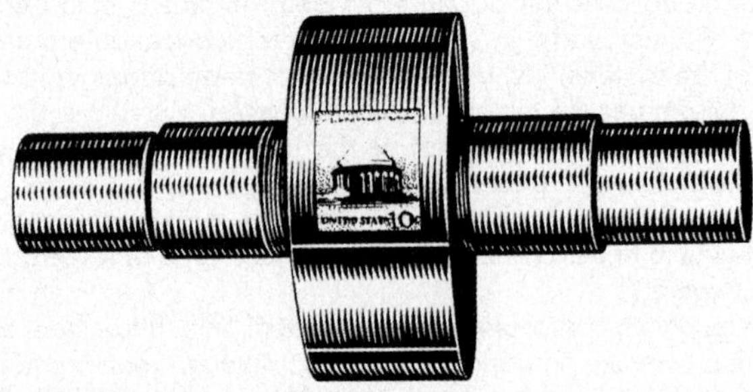

Transfer roll

Transfer roll — Next is production of the transfer roll that, as the name implies, is the medium used to transfer the subject from the master die to the printing plate. A blank roll of soft steel, mounted on a mandrel, is placed under the bearers of the transfer press to allow it to roll freely on its axis. The hardened die is placed on the bed of the press and the face of the transfer roll is applied to the die, under pressure. The bed or the roll is then rocked back and forth under increasing pressure, until the soft steel of the roll is forced into every engraved line of the die. The resulting impression on the roll is known as a "relief" or a "relief transfer." The engraved image is now positive in appearance and stands out from the steel. After the required number of reliefs are "rocked in," the soft steel transfer roll is hardened.

Different flaws may occur during the relief process. A defective relief may occur during the rocking in process because of a minute piece of foreign material lodging on the die, or some other cause. Imperfections in the steel of the transfer roll may result in a breaking away of parts of the design. This is known as a relief break, which will show up on finished stamps as small, unprinted areas. If a damaged relief remains in use, it will transfer a repeating defect to the plate. Deliberate alterations of reliefs sometimes occur. "Altered reliefs" designate these changed conditions.

Plate — The final step in pre-printing production is the making of the printing plate. A flat piece of soft steel replaces the die on the bed of the transfer press. One of the reliefs on the transfer roll is positioned over this soft steel. Position, or layout, dots determine the correct position on the plate. The dots have been lightly marked on the plate in advance. After the correct position of the relief is determined, the design is rocked in by following the same method used in making the transfer roll. The difference is that this time the image is being transferred from the transfer roll, rather than to it. Once the design is entered on the plate, it appears in reverse and is recessed. There are as many transfers entered on the plate as there are subjects printed on the sheet of stamps. It is during this process that double and shifted transfers occur, as well as re-entries. These are the result of improperly entered images that have not been properly burnished out prior to rocking in a new image.

Modern siderography processes, such as those used by the U.S. Bureau of Engraving and Printing, involve an automated form of rocking designs in on preformed cylindrical printing sleeves. The same process also allows for easier removal and re-entry of worn images right on the sleeve.

Transferring the design to the plate

Following the entering of the required transfers on the plate, the position dots, layout dots and lines, scratches and other markings generally are burnished out. Added at this time by the siderographer are any required *guide lines, plate numbers* or other *marginal markings.* The plate is then hand-inked and a proof impression is taken. This is known as a plate proof. If the impression is approved, the plate is machined for fitting onto the press, is hardened and sent to the plate vault ready for use.

On press, the plate is inked and the surface is automatically wiped clean, leaving ink only in the recessed lines. Paper is then forced under pressure into the engraved recessed lines, thereby receiving the ink. Thus, the ink lines on engraved stamps are slightly raised, and slight depressions (debossing) occur on the back of the stamp. Prior to the advent of modern high-speed presses and more advanced ink formulations, paper had to be dampened before receiving the ink. This sometimes led to uneven shrinkage by the time the stamps were perforated, resulting in improperly perforated stamps, or misperfs. Newer presses use drier paper, thus both *wet* and *dry printings* exist on some stamps.

Rotary Press — Until 1914, only flat plates were used to print engraved stamps. Rotary press printing was introduced in 1914, and slowly spread. Some countries still use flat-plate printing.

After approval of the plate proof, older *rotary press plates* require additional machining. They are curved to fit the press cylinder. "Gripper slots" are cut into the back of each plate to receive the "grippers," which hold the plate securely on the press. The plate is then hardened. Stamps printed from these bent rotary press plates are longer or wider than the same stamps printed from flat-plate presses. The stretching of the plate during the curving process is what causes this distortion.

Re-entry — To execute a re-entry on a flat plate, the transfer roll is re-applied to the plate, often at some time after its first use on the press. Worn-out designs can be resharpened by carefully burnishing out the original image and re-entering it from the transfer roll. If the original impression has not been sufficiently removed and the transfer roll is not precisely in line with the remaining impression, the resulting double transfer will make the re-entry obvious. If the registration is true, a re-entry may be difficult or impossible to distinguish. Sometimes a stamp printed from a successful re-entry is identified by having a much sharper and clearer impression than its neighbors. With the advent of rotary presses, post-press re-entries were not possible. After a plate was curved for the rotary press, it was impossible to make a re-entry. This is because the plate had already been bent once (with the design distorted).

However, with the introduction of the previously mentioned modern-style siderography machines, entries are made to the preformed cylindrical printing sleeve. Such sleeves are dechromed and softened. This allows individual images to be burnished out and re-entered on the curved sleeve. The sleeve is then rechromed, resulting in longer press life.

Double Transfer — This is a description of the condition of a transfer on a plate that shows evidence of a duplication of all, or a portion of the design. It usually is the result of the changing of the registration between the transfer roll and the plate during the rocking in of the original entry. Double transfers also occur when only a portion of the design has been rocked in and improper positioning is noted. If the worker elected not to burnish out the partial or completed design, a strong double transfer will occur for part or all of the design.

It sometimes is necessary to remove the original transfer from a plate and repeat the process a second time. If the finished re-worked image shows traces of the original impression, attributable to incomplete burnishing, the result is a partial double transfer.

With the modern automatic machines mentioned previously, double transfers are all but impossible to create. Those partially doubled images on stamps printed from such sleeves are more than likely re-entries, rather than true double transfers.

Re-engraved — Alterations to a stamp design are sometimes necessary after some stamps have been printed. In some cases, either the original die or the actual printing plate may have its "temper" drawn (softened), and the design will be re-cut. The resulting impressions from such a re-engraved die or plate may differ slightly from the original issue, and are known as "re-engraved." If the alteration was made to the master die, all future printings will be consistently different from the original. If alterations were made to the printing plate, each altered stamp on the plate will be slightly different from each other, allowing specialists to reconstruct a complete printing plate.

Dropped Transfers — If an impression from the transfer roll has not been properly placed, a dropped transfer may occur. The final stamp image will appear obviously out of line with its neighbors.

Short Transfer — Sometimes a transfer roll is not rocked its entire length when entering a transfer onto a plate. As a result, the finished transfer on the plate fails to show the complete design, and the finished stamp will have an incomplete design printed. This is known as a "short transfer." U.S. Scott No. 8 is a good example of a short transfer.

TYPOGRAPHY (Letterpress, Surface Printing, Flexography, Dry Offset, High Etch)

Although the word "Typography" is obsolete as a term describing a printing method, it was the accepted term throughout the first century of postage stamps. Therefore, appropriate Scott listings in this catalogue refer to typographed stamps. The current term for this form of printing, however, is "letterpress."

As it relates to the production of postage stamps, letterpress printing is the reverse of engraving. Rather than having recessed areas trap the ink and deposit it on paper, only the raised areas of the design are inked. This is comparable to the type of printing seen by inking and using an ordinary rubber stamp. Letterpress includes all printing where the design is above the surface area, whether it is wood, metal or, in some instances, hardened rubber or polymer plastic.

For most letterpress-printed stamps, the engraved master is made in much the same manner as for engraved stamps. In this instance, however, an additional step is needed. The design is transferred to another surface before being transferred to the transfer roll. In this way, the transfer roll has a recessed stamp design, rather than one done in relief. This makes the printing areas on the final plate raised, or relief areas.

For less-detailed stamps of the 19th century, the area on the die not used as a printing surface was cut away, leaving the surface area raised. The original die was then reproduced by stereotyping or electrotyping. The resulting electrotypes were assembled in the required number and format of the desired sheet of stamps. The plate used in printing the stamps was an electroplate of these assembled electrotypes.

Once the final letterpress plates are created, ink is applied to the raised surface and the pressure of the press transfers the ink impression to the paper. In contrast to engraving, the fine lines of letterpress are impressed on the surface of the stamp, leaving a debossed surface. When viewed from the back (as on a typewritten page), the corresponding line work on the stamp will be raised slightly (embossed) above the surface.

PHOTOGRAVURE (Gravure, Rotogravure, Heliogravure)

In this process, the basic principles of photography are applied to a chemically sensitized metal plate, rather than photographic paper. The design is transferred photographically to the plate through a halftone, or dot-matrix screen, breaking the reproduction into tiny dots. The plate is treated chemically and the dots form depressions, called cells, of varying depths and diameters, depending on the degrees of shade in the design. Then, like engraving, ink is applied to the plate and the surface is wiped clean. This leaves ink in the tiny cells that is lifted out and deposited on the paper when it is pressed against the plate.

Gravure is most often used for multicolored stamps, generally using the three primary colors (red, yellow and blue) and black. By varying the dot matrix pattern and density of these colors, virtually any color can be reproduced. A typical full-color gravure stamp will be created from four printing cylinders (one for each color). The original multicolored image will have been photographically separated into its component colors.

Modern gravure printing may use computer-generated dot-matrix screens, and modern plates may be of various types including metal-coated plastic. The catalogue designation of Photogravure (or "Photo") covers any of these older and more modern gravure methods of printing.

For examples of the first photogravure stamps printed (1914), see Bavaria Scott 94-114.

LITHOGRAPHY (Offset Lithography, Stone Lithography, Dilitho, Planography, Collotype)

The principle that oil and water do not mix is the basis for lithography. The stamp design is drawn by hand or transferred from engraving to the surface of a lithographic stone or metal plate in a greasy (oily) substance. This oily substance holds the ink, which will later be transferred to the paper. The stone (or plate) is wet with an acid fluid, causing it to repel the printing ink in all areas not covered by the greasy substance.

Transfer paper is used to transfer the design from the original stone or plate. A series of duplicate transfers are grouped and, in turn, transferred to the final printing plate.

Photolithography — The application of photographic processes to lithography. This process allows greater flexibility of design, related to use of halftone screens combined with line work. Unlike photogravure or engraving, this process can allow large, solid areas to be printed.

Offset — A refinement of the lithographic process. A rubber-covered blanket cylinder takes the impression from the inked lithographic plate. From the "blanket" the impression is *offset* or transferred to the paper. Greater flexibility and speed are the principal reasons offset printing has largely displaced lithography. The term "lithography" covers both processes, and results are almost identical.

EMBOSSED (Relief) Printing

Embossing, not considered one of the four main printing types, is a method in which the design first is sunk into the metal of the die. Printing is done against a yielding platen, such as leather or linoleum. The platen is forced into the depression of the die, thus forming the design on the paper in relief. This process is often used for metallic inks.

Embossing may be done without color (see Sardinia Scott 4-6); with color printed around the embossed area (see Great Britain Scott 5 and most U.S. envelopes); and with color in exact registration with the embossed subject (see Canada Scott 656-657).

HOLOGRAMS

For objects to appear as holograms on stamps, a model exactly the same size as it is to appear on the hologram must be created. Rather than using photographic film to capture the image, holography records an image on a photoresist material. In processing, chemicals eat away at certain exposed areas, leaving a pattern of constructive and destructive interference. When the phororesist is developed, the result is a pattern of uneven ridges that acts as a mold. This mold is then coated with metal, and the resulting form is used to press copies in much the same way phonograph records are produced.

A typical reflective hologram used for stamps consists of a reproduction of the uneven patterns on a plastic film that is applied to a reflective background, usually a silver or gold foil. Light is reflected off the background through the film, making the pattern present on the film visible. Because of the uneven pattern of the film, the viewer will perceive the objects in their proper three-dimensional relationships with appropriate brightness.

The first hologram on a stamp was produced by Austria in 1988 (Scott 1441).

FOIL APPLICATION

A modern technique of applying color to stamps involves the application of metallic foil to the stamp paper. A pattern of foil is applied to the stamp paper by use of a stamping die. The foil usually is flat, but it may be textured. Canada Scott 1735 has three different foil applications in pearl, bronze and gold. The gold foil was textured using a chemical-etch copper embossing die. The printing of this stamp also involved two-color offset lithography plus embossing.

THERMOGRAPHY

In the 1990s stamps began to be enhanced with thermographic printing. In this process, a powdered polymer is applied over a sheet that has just been printed. The powder adheres to ink that lacks drying or hardening agents and does not adhere to areas where the ink has these agents. The excess powder is removed and the sheet is briefly heated to melt the powder. The melted powder solidifies after cooling, producing a raised, shiny effect on the stamps. See Scott New Caledonia C239-C240.

COMBINATION PRINTINGS

Sometimes two or even three printing methods are combined in producing stamps. In these cases, such as Austria Scott 933 or Canada 1735 (described in the preceding paragraph), the multiple-printing technique can be determined by studying the individual characteristics of each printing type. A few stamps, such as Singapore Scott 684-684A, combine as many as three of the four major printing types (lithography, engraving and typography). When this is done it often indicates the incorporation of security devices against counterfeiting.

INK COLORS

Inks or colored papers used in stamp printing often are of mineral origin, although there are numerous examples of organic-based pigments. As a general rule, organic-based pigments are far more subject to varieties and change than those of mineral-based origin.

The appearance of any given color on a stamp may be affected by many aspects, including printing variations, light, color of paper, aging and chemical alterations.

Numerous printing variations may be observed. Heavier pressure or inking will cause a more intense color, while slight interruptions in the ink feed or lighter impressions will cause a lighter appearance. Stamps printed in the same color by water-based and solvent-based inks can differ significantly in appearance. This affects several stamps in the U.S. Prominent Americans series. Hand-mixed ink formulas (primarily from the 19th century) produced under different conditions (humidity and temperature) account for notable color variations in early printings of the same stamp (see U.S. Scott 248-250, 279B, for example). Different sources of pigment can also result in significant differences in color.

Light exposure and aging are closely related in the way they affect stamp color. Both eventually break down the ink and fade colors, so that a carefully kept stamp may differ significantly in color from an identical copy that has been exposed to light. If stamps are exposed to light either intentionally or accidentally, their colors can be faded or completely changed in some cases.

Papers of different quality and consistency used for the same stamp printing may affect color appearance. Most pelure papers, for example, show a richer color when compared with wove or laid papers. See Russia Scott 181a, for an example of this effect.

The very nature of the printing processes can cause a variety of differences in shades or hues of the same stamp. Some of these shades are scarcer than others, and are of particular interest to the advanced collector.

Luminescence

All forms of tagged stamps fall under the general category of luminescence. Within this broad category is fluorescence, dealing with forms of tagging visible under longwave ultraviolet light, and phosphorescence, which deals with tagging visible only under shortwave light. Phosphorescence leaves an afterglow and fluorescence does not. These treated stamps show up in a range of different colors when exposed to UV light. The differing wavelengths of the light activates the tagging material, making it glow in various colors that usually serve different mail processing purposes.

Intentional tagging is a post-World War II phenomenon, brought about by the increased literacy rate and rapidly growing mail volume. It was one of several answers to the problem of the need for more automated mail processes. Early tagged stamps served the purpose of triggering machines to separate different types of mail. A natural outgrowth was to also use the signal to trigger machines that faced all envelopes the same way and canceled them.

Tagged stamps come in many different forms. Some tagged stamps have luminescent shapes or images imprinted on them as a form of security device. Others have blocks (United States), stripes, frames (South Africa and Canada), overall coatings (United States), bars (Great Britain and Canada) and many other types. Some types of tagging are even mixed in with the pigmented printing ink (Australia Scott 366, Netherlands Scott 478 and U.S. Scott 1359 and 2443).

The means of applying taggant to stamps differs as much as the intended purposes for the stamps. The most common form of tagging is a coating applied to the surface of the printed stamp. Since the taggant ink is frequently invisible except under UV light, it does not interfere with the appearance of the stamp. Another common application is the use of phosphored papers. In this case the paper itself either has a coating of taggant applied before the stamp is printed, has taggant applied during the papermaking process (incorporating it into the fibers), or has the taggant mixed into the coating of the paper. The latter method, among others, is currently in use in the United States.

Many countries now use tagging in various forms to either expedite mail handling or to serve as a printing security device against counterfeiting. Following the introduction of tagged stamps for public use in 1959 by Great Britain, other countries have steadily joined the parade. Among those are Germany (1961); Canada and Denmark (1962); United States, Australia, France and Switzerland (1963); Belgium and Japan (1966); Sweden and Norway (1967); Italy (1968); and Russia (1969). Since then, many other countries have begun using forms of tagging, including Brazil, China, Czechoslovakia, Hong Kong, Guatemala, Indonesia, Israel, Lithuania, Luxembourg, Netherlands, Penrhyn Islands, Portugal, St. Vincent, Singapore, South Africa, Spain and Sweden to name a few.

In some cases, including United States, Canada, Great Britain and Switzerland, stamps were released both with and without tagging. Many of these were released during each country's experimental period. Tagged and untagged versions are listed for the aforementioned countries and are noted in some other countries' listings. For at least a few stamps, the experimentally tagged version is worth far more than its untagged counterpart, such as the 1963 experimental tagged version of France Scott 1024.

In some cases, luminescent varieties of stamps were inadvertently created. Several Russian stamps, for example, sport highly fluorescent ink that was not intended as a form of tagging. Older stamps, such as early U.S. postage dues, can be positively identified by the use of UV light, since the organic ink used has become slightly fluorescent over time. Other stamps, such as Austria Scott 70a-82a (varnish bars) and Obock Scott 46-64 (printed quadrille lines), have become fluorescent over time.

Various fluorescent substances have been added to paper to make it appear brighter. These optical brightners, as they are known, greatly affect the appearance of the stamp under UV light. The brightest of these is known as Hi-Brite paper. These paper varieties are beyond the scope of the Scott Catalogue.

Shortwave UV light also is used extensively in expertizing, since each form of paper has its own fluorescent characteristics that are impossible to perfectly match. It is therefore a simple matter to detect filled thins, added perforation teeth and other alterations that involve the addition of paper. UV light also is used to examine stamps that have had cancels chemically removed and for other purposes as well.

Gum

The Illustrated Gum Chart in the first part of this introduction shows and defines various types of gum condition. Because gum condition has an important impact on the value of unused stamps, we recommend studying this chart and the accompanying text carefully.

The gum on the back of a stamp may be shiny, dull, smooth, rough, dark, white, colored or tinted. Most stamp gumming adhesives use gum arabic or dextrine as a base. Certain polymers such as polyvinyl alcohol (PVA) have been used extensively since World War II.

The *Scott Standard Postage Stamp Catalogue* does not list items by types of gum. The *Scott Specialized Catalogue of United States Stamps and Covers* does differentiate among some types of gum for certain issues.

Reprints of stamps may have gum differing from the original issues. In addition, some countries have used different gum formulas for different seasons. These adhesives have different properties that may become more apparent over time.

Many stamps have been issued without gum, and the catalogue will note this fact. See, for example, United States Scott 40-47. Sometimes, gum may have been removed to preserve the stamp. Germany Scott B68, for example, has a highly acidic gum that eventually destroys the stamps. This item is valued in the catalogue with gum removed.

Reprints and Reissues

These are impressions of stamps (usually obsolete) made from the original plates or stones. If they are valid for postage and reproduce obsolete issues (such as U.S. Scott 102-111), the stamps are *reissues.* If they are from current issues, they are designated as *second, third,* etc., *printing.* If designated for a particular purpose, they are called *special printings.*

When special printings are not valid for postage, but are made from original dies and plates by authorized persons, they are *official reprints. Private reprints* are made from the original plates and dies by private hands. An example of a private reprint is that of the 1871-1932 reprints made from the original die of the 1845 New Haven, Conn., postmaster's provisional. *Official reproductions* or imitations are made from new dies and plates by government authorization. Scott will list those reissues that are valid for postage if they differ significantly from the original printing.

The U.S. government made special printings of its first postage stamps in 1875. Produced were official imitations of the first two stamps (listed as Scott 3-4), reprints of the demonetized pre-1861 issues (Scott 40-47) and reissues of the 1861 stamps, the 1869 stamps and the then-current 1875 denominations. Even though the official imitations and the reprints were not valid for postage, Scott lists all of these U.S. special printings.

Most reprints or reissues differ slightly from the original stamp in some characteristic, such as gum, paper, perforation, color or watermark. Sometimes the details are followed so meticulously that only a student of that specific stamp is able to distinguish the reprint or reissue from the original.

Remainders and Canceled to Order

Some countries sell their stock of old stamps when a new issue replaces them. To avoid postal use, the *remainders* usually are canceled with a punch hole, a heavy line or bar, or a more-or-less regular-looking cancellation. The most famous merchant of remainders was Nicholas F. Seebeck. In the 1880s and 1890s, he arranged printing contracts between the Hamilton Bank Note Co., of which he was a director, and several Central and South American countries. The contracts provided that the plates and all remainders of the yearly issues became the property of Hamilton. Seebeck saw to it that ample stock remained. The "Seebecks," both remainders and reprints, were standard packet fillers for decades.

Some countries also issue stamps *canceled-to-order (CTO),* either in sheets with original gum or stuck onto pieces of paper or envelopes and canceled. Such CTO items generally are worth less than postally used stamps. In cases where the CTO material is far more prevalent in the marketplace than postally used examples, the catalogue value relates to the CTO examples, with postally used examples noted as premium items. Most CTOs can be detected by the presence of gum. However, as the CTO practice goes back at least to 1885, the gum inevitably has been soaked off some stamps so they could pass as postally used. The normally applied postmarks usually differ slightly from standard postmarks, and specialists are able to tell the difference. When applied individually to envelopes by philatelically minded persons, CTO material is known as *favor canceled* and generally sells at large discounts.

Cinderellas and Facsimiles

Cinderella is a catch-all term used by stamp collectors to describe phantoms, fantasies, bogus items, municipal issues, exhibition seals, local revenues, transportation stamps, labels, poster stamps and many other types of items. Some cinderella collectors include in their collections local postage issues, telegraph stamps, essays and proofs, forgeries and counterfeits.

A *fantasy* is an adhesive created for a nonexistent stamp-issuing authority. Fantasy items range from imaginary countries (Occusi-Ambeno, Kingdom of Sedang, Principality of Trinidad or Torres Straits), to non-existent locals (Winans City Post), or nonexistent transportation lines (McRobish & Co.'s Acapulco-San Francisco Line).

On the other hand, if the entity exists and could have issued stamps (but did not) or was known to have issued other stamps, the items are considered *bogus* stamps. These would include the Mormon postage stamps of Utah, S. Allan Taylor's Guatemala and Paraguay inventions, the propaganda issues for the South Moluccas and the adhesives of the Page & Keyes local post of Boston.

Phantoms is another term for both fantasy and bogus issues.

Facsimiles are copies or imitations made to represent original stamps, but which do not pretend to be originals. A catalogue illustration is such a facsimile. Illustrations from the Moens catalogue of the last century were occasionally colored and passed off as stamps. Since the beginning of stamp collecting, facsimiles have been made for collectors as space fillers or for reference. They often carry the word "facsimile," "falsch" (German), "sanko" or "mozo" (Japanese), or "faux" (French) overprinted on the face or stamped on the back. Unfortunately, over the years a number of these items have had fake cancels applied over the facsimile notation and have been passed off as genuine.

Forgeries and Counterfeits

Forgeries and counterfeits have been with philately virtually from the beginning of stamp production. Over time, the terminology for the two has been used interchangeably. Although both forgeries and counterfeits are reproductions of stamps, the purposes behind their creation differ considerably.

Among specialists there is an increasing movement to more specifically define such items. Although there is no universally accepted terminology, we feel the following definitions most closely mirror the items and their purposes as they are currently defined.

Forgeries (also often referred to as *Counterfeits*) are reproductions of genuine stamps that have been created to defraud collectors. Such spurious items first appeared on the market around 1860, and most old-time collections contain one or more. Many are crude and easily spotted, but some can deceive experts.

An important supplier of these early philatelic forgeries was the Hamburg printer Gebruder Spiro. Many others with reputations in this craft included S. Allan Taylor, George Hussey, James Chute, George Forune, Benjamin & Sarpy, Julius Goldner, E. Oneglia and L.H. Mercier. Among the noted 20th-century forgers were Francois Fournier, Jean Sperati and the prolific Raoul DeThuin.

Forgeries may be complete replications, or they may be genuine stamps altered to resemble a scarcer (and more valuable) type. Most forgeries, particularly those of rare stamps, are worth only a small fraction of the value of a genuine example, but a few types, created by some of the most notable forgers, such as Sperati, can be worth as much or more than the genuine. Fraudulently produced copies are known of most classic rarities and many medium-priced stamps.

In addition to rare stamps, large numbers of common 19th- and early 20th-century stamps were forged to supply stamps to the early packet trade. Many can still be easily found. Few new philatelic forgeries have appeared in recent decades. Successful imitation of well-engraved work is virtually impossible. It has proven far easier to produce a fake by altering a genuine stamp than to duplicate a stamp completely.

Counterfeit (also often referred to as *Postal Counterfeit* or *Postal Forgery*) is the term generally applied to reproductions of stamps that have been created to defraud the government of revenue. Such items usually are created at the time a stamp is current and, in some cases, are hard to detect. Because most counterfeits are seized when the perpetrator is captured, postal counterfeits, particularly used on cover, are usually worth much more than a genuine example to specialists. The first postal counterfeit was of Spain's 4-cuarto carmine of 1854 (the real one is Scott 25). Apparently, the counterfeiters were not satisfied with their first version, which is now very scarce, and they soon created an engraved counterfeit, which is common. Postal counterfeits quickly followed in Austria, Naples, Sardinia and the Roman States. They have since been created in many other countries as well, including the United States.

An infamous counterfeit to defraud the government is the 1-shilling Great Britain "Stock Exchange" forgery of 1872, used on telegraph forms at the exchange that year. The stamp escaped detection until a stamp dealer noticed it in 1898.

Fakes

Fakes are genuine stamps altered in some way to make them more desirable. One student of this part of stamp collecting has estimated that by the 1950s more than 30,000 varieties of fakes were known. That number has grown greatly since then. The widespread existence of fakes makes it important for stamp collectors to study their philatelic holdings and use relevant literature. Likewise, collectors should buy from reputable dealers who guarantee their stamps and make full and prompt refunds should a purchased item be declared faked or altered by some mutually agreed-upon authority. Because fakes always have some genuine characteristics, it is not always possible to obtain unanimous agreement among experts regarding specific items. These students may change their opinions as philatelic knowledge increases. More than 80 percent of all fakes on the philatelic market today are regummed, reperforated (or perforated for the first time), or bear forged overprints, surcharges or cancellations.

Stamps can be chemically treated to alter or eliminate colors. For example, a pale rose stamp can be re-colored to resemble a blue shade of high market value. In other cases, treated stamps can be made to resemble missing color varieties. Designs may be changed by painting, or a stroke or a dot added or bleached out to turn an ordinary variety into a seemingly scarcer stamp. Part of a stamp can be bleached and reprinted in a different version, achieving an inverted center or frame. Margins can be added or repairs done so deceptively that the stamps move from the "repaired" into the "fake" category.

Fakers have not left the backs of the stamps untouched either. They may create false watermarks, add fake grills or press out genuine grills. A thin India paper proof may be glued onto a thicker backing to create the appearance an issued stamp, or a proof printed on cardboard may be shaved down and perforated to resemble a stamp. Silk threads are impressed into paper and stamps have been split so that a rare paper variety is added to an otherwise inexpensive stamp. The most common treatment to the back of a stamp, however, is regumming.

Some in the business of faking stamps have openly advertised fool-proof application of "original gum" to stamps that lack it, although most publications now ban such ads from their pages. It is believed that very few early stamps have survived without being hinged. The large number of never-hinged examples of such earlier material offered for sale thus suggests the widespread extent of regumming activity. Regumming also may be used to hide repairs or thin spots. Dipping the stamp into watermark fluid, or examining it under longwave ultraviolet light often will reveal these flaws.

Fakers also tamper with separations. Ingenious ways to add margins are known. Perforated wide-margin stamps may be falsely represented as imperforate when trimmed. Reperforating is commonly done to create scarce coil or perforation varieties, and to eliminate the naturally occurring straight-edge stamps found in sheet margin positions of many earlier issues. Custom has made straight-edged stamps less desirable. Fakers have obliged by perforating straight-edged stamps so that many are now uncommon, if not rare.

Another fertile field for the faker is that of overprints, surcharges and cancellations. The forging of rare surcharges or overprints began in the 1880s or 1890s. These forgeries are sometimes difficult to detect, but experts have identified almost all. Occasionally, overprints or cancellations are removed to create non-overprinted stamps or seemingly unused items. This is most commonly done by removing a manuscript cancel to make a stamp resemble an unused example. "SPECIMEN" overprints may be removed by scraping and repainting to create non-overprinted varieties. Fakers use inexpensive revenues or pen-canceled stamps to generate unused stamps for further faking by adding other markings. The quartz lamp or UV lamp and a high-powered magnifying glass help to easily detect removed cancellations.

The bigger problem, however, is the addition of overprints, surcharges or cancellations - many with such precision that they are very difficult to ascertain. Plating of the stamps or the overprint can be an important method of detection.

Fake postmarks may range from many spurious fancy cancellations to a host of markings applied to transatlantic covers, to adding normally appearing postmarks to definitives of some countries with stamps that are valued far higher used than unused. With the increased popularity of cover collecting, and the widespread interest in postal history, a fertile new field for fakers has come about. Some have tried to create entire covers. Others specialize in adding stamps, tied by fake cancellations, to genuine stampless covers, or replacing less expensive or damaged stamps with more valuable ones. Detailed study of postal rates in effect at the time a cover in question was mailed, including the analysis of each handstamp used during the period, ink analysis and similar techniques, usually will unmask the fraud.

Restoration and Repairs

Scott Publishing Co. bases its catalogue values on stamps that are free of defects and otherwise meet the standards set forth earlier in this introduction. Most stamp collectors desire to have the finest copy of an item possible. Even within given grading categories there are variances. This leads to a controversial practice that is not defined in any universal manner: stamp *restoration*.

There are broad differences of opinion about what is permissible when it comes to restoration. Carefully applying a soft eraser to a stamp or cover to remove light soiling is one form of restoration, as is washing a stamp in mild soap and water to clean it. These are fairly accepted forms of restoration. More severe forms of restoration include pressing out creases or removing stains caused by tape. To what degree each of these is acceptable is dependent upon the individual situation. Further along the spectrum is the freshening of a stamp's color by removing oxide build-up or the effects of wax paper left next to stamps shipped to the tropics.

At some point in this spectrum the concept of *repair* replaces that of restoration. Repairs include filling thin spots, mending tears by reweaving or adding a missing perforation tooth. Regumming stamps may have been acceptable as a restoration or repair technique many decades ago, but today it is considered a form of fakery.

Restored stamps may or may not sell at a discount, and it is possible that the value of individual restored items may be enhanced over that of their pre-restoration state. Specific situations dictate the resultant value of such an item. Repaired stamps sell at substantial discounts from the value of sound stamps.

Terminology

Booklets — Many countries have issued stamps in small booklets for the convenience of users. This idea continues to become increasingly popular in many countries. Booklets have been issued in many sizes and forms, often with advertising on the covers, the panes of stamps or on the interleaving.

The panes used in booklets may be printed from special plates or made from regular sheets. All panes from booklets issued by the United States and many from those of other countries contain stamps that are straight edged on the sides, but perforated between. Others are distinguished by orientation of watermark or other identifying features. Any stamp-like unit in the pane, either printed or blank, that is not a postage stamp, is considered to be a *label* in the catalogue listings.

Scott lists and values booklet panes. Modern complete booklets also are listed and valued. Individual booklet panes are listed only when they are not fashioned from existing sheet stamps and, therefore, are identifiable from their sheet stamp counterparts.

Panes usually do not have a used value assigned to them because there is little market activity for used booklet panes, even though many exist used and there is some demand for them.

Cancellations — The marks or obliterations put on stamps by postal authorities to show that they have performed service and to prevent their reuse are known as cancellations. If the marking is made with a pen, it is considered a "pen cancel." When the location of the post office appears in the marking, it is a "town cancellation." A "postmark" is technically any postal marking, but in practice the term generally is applied to a town cancellation with a date. When calling attention to a cause or celebration, the marking is known as a "slogan cancellation." Many other types and styles of cancellations exist, such as duplex, numerals, targets, fancy and others. See also "precancels," below.

Coil Stamps — These are stamps that are issued in rolls for use in dispensers, affixing and vending machines. Those coils of the United States, Canada, Sweden and some other countries are perforated horizontally or vertically only, with the outer edges imperforate. Coil stamps of some countries, such as Great Britain and Germany, are perforated on all four sides and may in some cases be distinguished from their sheet stamp counterparts by watermarks, counting numbers on the reverse or other means.

Covers — Entire envelopes, with or without adhesive postage stamps, that have passed through the mail and bear postal or other markings of philatelic interest are known as covers. Before the introduction of envelopes in about 1840, people folded letters and wrote the address on the outside. Some people covered their letters with an extra sheet of paper on the outside for the address, producing the term "cover." Used airletter sheets, stamped envelopes and other items of postal stationery also are considered covers.

Errors — Stamps that have some major, consistent, unintentional deviation from the normal are considered errors. Errors include, but are not limited to, missing or wrong colors, wrong paper, wrong watermarks, inverted centers or frames on multicolor printing, inverted or missing surcharges or overprints, double impressions, missing perforations, unintentionally omitted tagging and others. Factually wrong or misspelled information, if it appears on all examples of a stamp, are not considered errors in the true sense of the word. They are errors of design. Inconsistent or randomly appearing items, such as misperfs or color shifts, are classified as freaks.

Color-Omitted Errors — This term refers to stamps where a missing color is caused by the complete failure of the printing plate to deliver ink to the stamp paper or any other paper. Generally, this is caused by the printing plate not being engaged on the press or the ink station running dry of ink during printing.

Color-Missing Errors — This term refers to stamps where a color or colors were printed somewhere but do not appear on the finished stamp. There are four different classes of color-missing errors, and the catalog indicates with a two-letter code appended to each such listing what caused the color to be missing. These codes are used only for the United States' color-missing error listings.

FO = A *foldover* of the stamp sheet during printing may block ink from appearing on a stamp. Instead, the color will appear on the back of the foldover (where it might fall on the back of the selvage or perhaps on the back of the stamp or another stamp). FO also will be used in the case of foldunders, where the paper may fold underneath the other stamp paper and the color will print on the platen.

EP = A piece of *extraneous paper* falling across the plate or stamp paper will receive the printed ink. When the extraneous paper is removed, an unprinted portion of stamp paper remains and shows partially or totally missing colors.

CM = A misregistration of the printing plates during printing will result in a *color misregistration*, and such a misregistraion may result in a color not appearing on the finished stamp.

PS = *A perforation shift* after printing may remove a color from the finished stamp. Normally, this will occur on a row of stamps at the edge of the stamp pane.

Measurements – When measurements are given in the Scott catalogues for stamp size, grill size or any other reason, the first measurement given is always for the top and bottom dimension, while the second measurement will be for the sides (just as perforation gauges are measured). Thus, a stamp size of 15mm x 21mm will indicate a vertically oriented stamp 15mm wide at top and bottom, and 21mm tall at the sides. The same principle holds for measuring or counting items such as U.S. grills. A grill count of 22x18 points (B grill) indicates that there are 22 grill points across by 18 grill points down.

Overprints and Surcharges — Overprinting involves applying wording or design elements over an already existing stamp. Overprints can be used to alter the place of use (such as "Canal Zone" on U.S. stamps), to adapt them for a special purpose ("Porto" on Denmark's 1913-20 regular issues for use as postage due stamps, Scott J1-J7) or to commemorate a special occasion (United States Scott 647-648).

A *surcharge* is a form of overprint that changes or restates the face value of a stamp or piece of postal stationery.

Surcharges and overprints may be handstamped, typeset or, occasionally, lithographed or engraved. A few hand-written overprints and surcharges are known.

Personalized Stamps — In 1999, Australia issued stamps with se-tenant labels that could be personalized with pictures of the customer's choice. Other countries quickly followed suit, with some offering to print the selected picture on the stamp itself within a frame that was used exclusively for personalized issues. As the picture used on these stamps or labels vary, listings for such stamps are for any picture within the common frame (or any picture on a se-tenant label), be it a "generic" image or one produced especially for a customer, almost invariably at a premium price.

Precancels — Stamps that are canceled before they are placed in the mail are known as precancels. Precanceling usually is done to expedite the handling of large mailings and generally allow the affected mail pieces to skip certain phases of mail handling.

In the United States, precancellations generally identified the point of origin; that is, the city and state. This information appeared across the face of the stamp, usually centered between parallel lines. More recently, bureau precancels retained the parallel lines, but the city and state designations were dropped. Recent coils have a service inscription that is present on the original printing plate. These show the mail service paid for by the stamp. Since these stamps are not intended to receive further cancellations when used as intended, they are considered precancels. Such items often do not have parallel lines as part of the precancellation.

In France, the abbreviation *Affranchts* in a semicircle together with the word *Postes* is the general form of precancel in use. Belgian precancellations usually appear in a box in which the name of the city appears. Netherlands precancels have the name of the city enclosed between concentric circles, sometimes called a "lifesaver." Precancellations of other countries usually follow these patterns, but may be any arrangement of bars, boxes and city names.

Precancels are listed in the Scott catalogues only if the precancel changes the denomination (Belgium Scott 477-478); if the precanceled stamp is different from the non-precanceled version (such as untagged U.S. precancels); or if the stamp exists only precanceled (France Scott 1096-1099, U.S. Scott 2265).

Proofs and Essays — Proofs are impressions taken from an approved die, plate or stone in which the design and color are the same as the stamp issued to the public. Trial color proofs are impressions taken from approved dies, plates or stones in colors that vary from the final version. An essay is the impression of a design that differs in some way from the issued stamp. "Progressive die proofs" generally are considered to be essays.

Provisionals — These are stamps that are issued on short notice and intended for temporary use pending the arrival of regular issues. They usually are issued to meet such contingencies as changes in government or currency, shortage of necessary postage values or military occupation.

During the 1840s, postmasters in certain American cities issued stamps that were valid only at specific post offices. In 1861, postmasters of the Confederate States also issued stamps with limited validity. Both of these examples are known as "postmaster's provisionals."

Se-tenant — This term refers to an unsevered pair, strip or block of stamps that differ in design, denomination or overprint.

Unless the se-tenant item has a continuous design (see U.S. Scott 1451a, 1694a) the stamps do not have to be in the same order as shown in the catalogue (see U.S. Scott 2158a).

Specimens — The Universal Postal Union required member nations to send samples of all stamps they released into service to the International Bureau in Switzerland. Member nations of the UPU received these specimens as samples of what stamps were valid for postage. Many are overprinted, handstamped or initial-perforated "Specimen," "Canceled" or "Muestra." Some are marked with bars across the denominations (China-Taiwan), punched holes (Czechoslovakia) or back inscriptions (Mongolia).

Stamps distributed to government officials or for publicity purposes, and stamps submitted by private security printers for official approval, also may receive such defacements.

The previously described defacement markings prevent postal use, and all such items generally are known as "specimens."

Tete Beche — This term describes a pair of stamps in which one is upside down in relation to the other. Some of these are the result of intentional sheet arrangements, such as Morocco Scott B10-B11. Others occurred when one or more electrotypes accidentally were placed upside down on the plate, such as Colombia Scott 57a. Separation of the tete-beche stamps, of course, destroys the tete beche variety.

Pronunciation Symbols

ə .... banana, collide, abut

ˈə, ˌə .... humdrum, abut

ᵊ .... immediately preceding \l\, \n\, \m\, \ŋ\, as in battle, mitten, eaten, and sometimes open \ˈō-pᵊm\, lock and key \-ᵊŋ-\; immediately following \l\, \m\, \r\, as often in French table, prisme, titre

ər .... further, merger, bird

ˈər-, ˈə-r .... as in two different pronunciations of hurry \ˈhər-ē, ˈhə-rē\

a .... mat, map, mad, gag, snap, patch

ā .... day, fade, date, aorta, drape, cape

ä .... bother, cot, and, with most American speakers, father, cart

ȧ .... father as pronounced by speakers who do not rhyme it with *bother*; French patte

aů .... now, loud, out

b .... baby, rib

ch .... chin, nature \ˈnā-chər\

d .... did, adder

e .... bet, bed, peck

ˈē, ˌē .... beat, nosebleed, evenly, easy

ē .... easy, mealy

f .... fifty, cuff

g .... go, big, gift

h .... hat, ahead

hw .... whale as pronounced by those who do not have the same pronunciation for both *whale* and *wail*

i .... tip, banish, active

ī .... site, side, buy, tripe

j .... job, gem, edge, join, judge

k .... kin, cook, ache

k̲ .... German ich, Buch; one pronunciation of loch

l .... lily, pool

m .... murmur, dim, nymph

n .... no, own

ⁿ .... indicates that a preceding vowel or diphthong is pronounced with the nasal passages open, as in French *un bon vin blanc* \œⁿ-bōⁿ-vaⁿ-bläⁿ\

ŋ .... sing \ˈsiŋ\, singer \ˈsiŋ-ər\, finger \ˈfiŋ-gər\, ink \ˈiŋk\

ō .... bone, know, beau

ȯ .... saw, all, gnaw, caught

œ .... French boeuf, German Hölle

œ̄ .... French feu, German Höhle

ȯi .... coin, destroy

p .... pepper, lip

r .... red, car, rarity

s .... source, less

sh .... as in shy, mission, machine, special (actually, this is a single sound, not two); with a hyphen between, two sounds as in *grasshopper* \ˈgras-ˌhä-pər\

t .... tie, attack, late, later, latter

th .... as in thin, ether (actually, this is a single sound, not two); with a hyphen between, two sounds as in *knighthood* \ˈnīt-ˌhu̇d\

t̲h̲ .... then, either, this (actually, this is a single sound, not two)

ü .... rule, youth, union \ˈyün-yən\, few \ˈfyü\

u̇ .... pull, wood, book, curable \ˈkyu̇r-ə-bəl\, fury \ˈfyu̇r-ē\

ue .... German füllen, hübsch

ue̅ .... French rue, German fühlen

v .... vivid, give

w .... we, away

y .... yard, young, cue \ˈkyü\, mute \ˈmyüt\, union \ˈyün-yən\

ʸ .... indicates that during the articulation of the sound represented by the preceding character the front of the tongue has substantially the position it has for the articulation of the first sound of *yard*, as in French *digne* \dēnʸ\

z .... zone, raise

zh .... as in vision, azure \ˈa-zhər\ (actually, this is a single sound, not two); with a hyphen between, two sounds as in *hogshead* \ˈhȯgz-ˌhed, ˈhägz-\

\ .... slant line used in pairs to mark the beginning and end of a transcription: \ˈpen\

ˈ .... mark preceding a syllable with primary (strongest) stress: \ˈpen-mən-ˌship\

ˌ .... mark preceding a syllable with secondary (medium) stress: \ˈpen-mən-ˌship\

- .... mark of syllable division

( ) .... indicate that what is symbolized between is present in some utterances but not in others: *factory* \ˈfak-t(ə-)rē\

÷ .... indicates that many regard as unacceptable the pronunciation variant immediately following: *cupola* \ˈkyü-pə-lə, ÷-ˌlō\

COMMON DESIGN TYPES

Pictured in this section are issues where one illustration has been used for a number of countries in the Catalogue. Not included in this section are overprinted stamps or those issues which are illustrated in each country. Because the location of Never Hinged breakpoints varies from country to country, some of the values in the listings below will be for unused stamps that were previously hinged.

EUROPA

Europa, 1956

The design symbolizing the cooperation among the six countries comprising the Coal and Steel Community is illustrated in each country.

Belgium....................................496-497
France......................................805-806
Germany..................................748-749
Italy..715-716
Luxembourg.............................318-320
Netherlands.............................368-369

Nos. 496-497 (2)	9.00	.70
Nos. 805-806 (2)	6.80	1.10
Nos. 748-749 (2)	7.00	1.20
Nos. 715-716 (2)	11.50	1.25
Nos. 318-320 (3)	74.25	21.50
Nos. 368-369 (2)	72.50	1.75
Set total (13) Stamps	181.05	27.50

Europa, 1958

"E" and Dove — CD1

European Postal Union at the service of European integration.

1958, Sept. 13

Belgium....................................527-528
France......................................889-890
Germany..................................790-791
Italy..750-751
Luxembourg.............................341-343
Netherlands.............................375-376
Saar...317-318

Nos. 527-528 (2)	4.25	.60
Nos. 889-890 (2)	1.65	.55
Nos. 790-791 (2)	3.35	.60
Nos. 750-751 (2)	1.85	.60
Nos. 341-343 (3)	2.40	1.15
Nos. 375-376 (2)	2.50	.75
Nos. 317-318 (2)	1.05	2.30
Set total (15) Stamps	17.05	6.55

Europa, 1959

6-Link Enless Chain — CD2

1959, Sept. 19

Belgium....................................536-537
France......................................929-930
Germany..................................805-806
Italy..791-792
Luxembourg.............................354-355
Netherlands.............................379-380

Nos. 536-537 (2)	1.55	.60
Nos. 929-930 (2)	1.85	.90
Nos. 805-806 (2)	1.90	.65
Nos. 791-792 (2)	.80	.50
Nos. 354-355 (2)	5.00	2.20
Nos. 379-380 (2)	9.90	1.25
Set total (12) Stamps	21.00	6.10

Europa, 1960

19-Spoke Wheel CD3

First anniverary of the establishment of C.E.P.T. (Conference Europeenne des Administrations des Postes et des Telecommunications.) The spokes symbolize the 19 founding members of the Conference.

1960, Sept.

Belgium....................................553-554
Denmark..379
Finland......................................376-377
France......................................970-971
Germany..................................818-820
Great Britain............................377-378
Greece..688
Iceland......................................327-328
Ireland......................................175-176
Italy..809-810
Luxembourg.............................374-375
Netherlands.............................385-386
Norway..387
Portugal...................................866-867
Spain..941-942
Sweden.....................................562-563
Switzerland..............................400-401
Turkey...................................1493-1494

Nos. 553-554 (2)	1.25	.55
No. 379 (1)	.65	.65
Nos. 376-377 (2)	1.70	1.80
Nos. 970-971 (2)	.55	.50
Nos. 818-820 (3)	2.25	1.25
Nos. 377-378 (2)	9.75	5.00
No. 688 (1)	5.00	2.00
Nos. 327-328 (2)	1.30	1.30
Nos. 175-176 (2)	75.00	14.00
Nos. 809-810 (2)	.70	.50
Nos. 374-375 (2)	1.50	.80
Nos. 385-386 (2)	3.65	1.50
No. 387 (1)	1.25	1.25
Nos. 866-867 (2)	2.25	1.25
Nos. 941-942 (2)	1.50	.75
Nos. 562-563 (2)	1.05	.55
Nos. 400-401 (2)	1.25	.65
Nos. 1493-1494 (2)	2.10	1.35
Set total (34) Stamps	112.70	35.65

Europa, 1961

19 Doves Flying as One — CD4

The 19 doves represent the 19 members of the Conference of European Postal and Telecommunications Administrations C.E.P.T.

1961-62

Belgium....................................572-573
Cyprus......................................201-203
France....................................1005-1006
Germany..................................844-845
Great Britain............................382-384
Greece......................................718-719
Iceland......................................340-341
Italy..845-846
Luxembourg.............................382-383
Netherlands.............................387-388
Spain......................................1010-1011
Switzerland..............................410-411
Turkey...................................1518-1520

Nos. 572-573 (2)	.75	.50
Nos. 201-203 (3)	*2.10*	*1.20*
Nos. 1005-1006 (2)	.50	.50
Nos. 844-845 (2)	.60	.75
Nos. 382-384 (3)	.75	.90
Nos. 718-719 (2)	.80	.50
Nos. 340-341 (2)	.90	.90
Nos. 845-846 (2)	.55	.50
Nos. 382-383 (2)	.60	.55
Nos. 387-388 (2)	.55	.50
Nos. 1010-1011 (2)	.70	.55
Nos. 410-411 (2)	1.25	.60
Nos. 1518-1520 (3)	2.45	1.30
Set total (29) Stamps	12.50	9.25

Europa, 1962

Young Tree with 19 Leaves CD5

The 19 leaves represent the 19 original members of C.E.P.T.

1962-63

Belgium....................................582-583
Cyprus......................................219-221
France....................................1045-1046
Germany..................................852-853
Greece......................................739-740
Iceland......................................348-349
Ireland......................................184-185
Italy..860-861
Luxembourg.............................386-387
Netherlands.............................394-395
Norway.....................................414-415
Switzerland..............................416-417
Turkey...................................1553-1555

Nos. 582-583 (2)	.65	.65
Nos. 219-221 (3)	*76.25*	*4.40*
Nos. 1045-1046 (2)	.60	.50
Nos. 852-853 (2)	.65	.60
Nos. 739-740 (2)	2.25	1.15
Nos. 348-349 (2)	.85	.85
Nos. 184-185 (2)	2.00	1.50
Nos. 860-861 (2)	1.35	.55
Nos. 386-387 (2)	.85	.70
Nos. 394-395 (2)	1.40	.75
Nos. 414-415 (2)	2.25	2.25
Nos. 416-417 (2)	1.65	1.00
Nos. 1553-1555 (3)	*3.00*	1.55
Set total (28) Stamps	93.75	16.45

Europa, 1963

Stylized Links, Symbolizing Unity — CD6

1963, Sept.

Belgium....................................598-599
Cyprus......................................229-231
Finland..419
France....................................1074-1075
Germany..................................867-868
Greece......................................768-769
Iceland......................................357-358
Ireland......................................188-189
Italy..880-881
Luxembourg.............................403-404
Netherlands.............................416-417
Norway.....................................441-442
Switzerland.....................................429
Turkey...................................1602-1603

Nos. 598-599 (2)	1.60	.55
Nos. 229-231 (3)	*54.75*	*5.15*
No. 419 (1)	1.60	.80
Nos. 1074-1075 (2)	.60	.50
Nos. 867-868 (2)	.50	.55
Nos. 768-769 (2)	5.25	1.90
Nos. 357-358 (2)	1.50	1.50
Nos. 188-189 (2)	4.75	3.25
Nos. 880-881 (2)	.65	.50
Nos. 403-404 (2)	1.00	.75
Nos. 416-417 (2)	2.25	1.00
Nos. 441-442 (2)	4.75	3.00
No. 429 (1)	.90	.60
Nos. 1602-1603 (2)	1.40	.60
Set total (27) Stamps	81.50	20.65

Europa, 1964

Symbolic Daisy — CD7

5th anniversary of the establishment of C.E.P.T. The 22 petals of the flower symbolize the 22 members of the Conference.

1964, Sept.

Austria..738
Belgium....................................614-615
Cyprus......................................244-246
France....................................1109-1110
Germany..................................897-898
Greece......................................801-802
Iceland......................................367-368
Ireland......................................196-197
Italy..894-895
Luxembourg.............................411-412
Monaco.....................................590-591
Netherlands.............................428-429
Norway..458
Portugal...................................931-933
Spain......................................1262-1263
Switzerland..............................438-439
Turkey...................................1628-1629

No. 738 (1)	1.20	.80
Nos. 614-615 (2)	1.40	.60
Nos. 244-246 (3)	*35.75*	*3.45*
Nos. 1109-1110 (2)	.50	.50
Nos. 897-898 (2)	.50	.50
Nos. 801-802 (2)	5.00	1.90
Nos. 367-368 (2)	2.00	1.65
Nos. 196-197 (2)	20.00	4.25
Nos. 894-895 (2)	.55	.50
Nos. 411-412 (2)	.90	.55
Nos. 590-591 (2)	2.50	.70
Nos. 428-429 (2)	1.80	.60
No. 458 (1)	4.50	4.50
Nos. 931-933 (3)	*10.00*	*2.00*
Nos. 1262-1263 (2)	1.30	.80
Nos. 438-439 (2)	1.60	.50
Nos. 1628-1629 (2)	2.65	1.35
Set total (34) Stamps	92.15	25.15

Europa, 1965

Leaves and "Fruit" CD8

1965

Belgium....................................636-637
Cyprus......................................262-264
Finland..437
France....................................1131-1132
Germany..................................934-935
Greece......................................833-834
Iceland......................................375-376
Ireland......................................204-205
Italy..915-916
Luxembourg.............................432-433
Monaco.....................................616-617
Netherlands.............................438-439
Norway.....................................475-476
Portugal...................................958-960
Switzerland.....................................469
Turkey...................................1665-1666

Nos. 636-637 (2)	.50	.50
Nos. 262-264 (3)	*25.35*	*3.80*
No. 437 (1)	1.50	.65
Nos. 1131-1132 (2)	.75	.80
Nos. 934-935 (2)	.50	.50
Nos. 833-834 (2)	2.25	1.15
Nos. 375-376 (2)	2.50	1.75
Nos. 204-205 (2)	20.00	3.35
Nos. 915-916 (2)	.50	.50
Nos. 432-433 (2)	.90	.75
Nos. 616-617 (2)	3.25	1.65
Nos. 438-439 (2)	.75	.55
Nos. 475-476 (2)	4.00	3.10
Nos. 958-960 (3)	*10.00*	*2.75*
No. 469 (1)	1.15	.25
Nos. 1665-1666 (2)	3.50	2.10
Set total (32) Stamps	77.40	24.15

Europa, 1966

Symbolic Sailboat — CD9

1966, Sept.

Andorra, French...............................172
Belgium....................................675-676
Cyprus......................................275-277
France....................................1163-1164
Germany..................................963-964

Greece 862-863
Iceland 384-385
Ireland 216-217
Italy 942-943
Liechtenstein 415
Luxembourg 440-441
Monaco 639-640
Netherlands 441-442
Norway 496-497
Portugal 980-982
Switzerland 477-478
Turkey 1718-1719

No. 172 (1)	3.00	3.00
Nos. 675-676 (2)	.80	.50
Nos. 275-277 (3)	*4.75*	*1.90*
Nos. 1163-1164 (2)	.60	.50
Nos. 963-964 (2)	.50	.55
Nos. 862-863 (2)	2.25	1.05
Nos. 384-385 (2)	5.00	3.80
Nos. 216-217 (2)	7.00	2.00
Nos. 942-943 (2)	.50	.50
No. 415 (1)	.40	.35
Nos. 440-441 (2)	1.10	.80
Nos. 639-640 (2)	2.00	.65
Nos. 441-442 (2)	1.50	.65
Nos. 496-497 (2)	5.00	3.00
Nos. 980-982 (3)	*9.75*	2.25
Nos. 477-478 (2)	1.60	.60
Nos. 1718-1719 (2)	3.35	1.75
Set total (34) Stamps	49.10	23.85

Europa, 1967

Cogwheels
CD10

1967

Andorra, French 174-175
Belgium 688-689
Cyprus 297-299
France 1178-1179
Germany 969-970
Greece 891-892
Iceland 389-390
Ireland 232-233
Italy 951-952
Liechtenstein 420
Luxembourg 449-450
Monaco 669-670
Netherlands 444-447
Norway 504-505
Portugal 994-996
Spain 1465-1466
Switzerland 482
Turkey B120-B121

Nos. 174-175 (2)	10.75	6.25
Nos. 688-689 (2)	1.05	.55
Nos. 297-299 (3)	*4.25*	*1.75*
Nos. 1178-1179 (2)	.80	.70
Nos. 969-970 (2)	.55	.55
Nos. 891-892 (2)	3.75	1.00
Nos. 389-390 (2)	3.00	2.00
Nos. 232-233 (2)	6.15	2.30
Nos. 951-952 (2)	.60	.50
No. 420 (1)	.45	.40
Nos. 449-450 (2)	1.25	.85
Nos. 669-670 (2)	2.75	.70
Nos. 444-447 (4)	5.00	1.85
Nos. 504-505 (2)	3.25	2.75
Nos. 994-996 (3)	*9.50*	1.85
Nos. 1465-1466 (2)	.50	.50
No. 482 (1)	.70	.25
Nos. B120-B121 (2)	3.50	2.75
Set total (38) Stamps	57.80	27.50

Europa, 1968

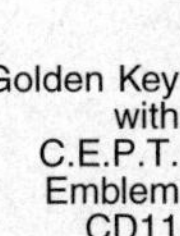

Golden Key
with
C.E.P.T.
Emblem
CD11

1968

Andorra, French 182-183
Belgium 705-706
Cyprus 314-316
France 1209-1210
Germany 983-984
Greece 916-917
Iceland 395-396
Ireland 242-243
Italy 979-980
Liechtenstein 442
Luxembourg 466-467
Monaco 689-691
Netherlands 452-453
Portugal 1019-1021
San Marino 687
Spain 1526
Switzerland 488
Turkey 1775-1776

Nos. 182-183 (2)	16.50	10.00
Nos. 705-706 (2)	1.25	.50
Nos. 314-316 (3)	*2.90*	*1.75*
Nos. 1209-1210 (2)	.90	.55
Nos. 983-984 (2)	.50	.55
Nos. 916-917 (2)	3.75	1.65
Nos. 395-396 (2)	3.00	2.50
Nos. 242-243 (2)	3.75	3.00
Nos. 979-980 (2)	.50	.50
No. 442 (1)	.45	.40
Nos. 466-467 (2)	1.10	.85
Nos. 689-691 (3)	*5.40*	.95
Nos. 452-453 (2)	2.10	.70
Nos. 1019-1021 (3)	*9.75*	2.10
No. 687 (1)	.55	.35
No. 1526 (1)	.25	.25
No. 488 (1)	.45	.25
Nos. 1775-1776 (2)	5.00	2.00
Set total (35) Stamps	58.10	28.85

Europa, 1969

"EUROPA"
and "CEPT"
CD12

Tenth anniversary of C.E.P.T.

1969

Andorra, French 188-189
Austria 837
Belgium 718-719
Cyprus 326-328
Denmark 458
Finland 483
France 1245-1246
Germany 996-997
Great Britain 585
Greece 947-948
Iceland 406-407
Ireland 270-271
Italy 1000-1001
Liechtenstein 453
Luxembourg 475-476
Monaco 722-724
Netherlands 475-476
Norway 533-534
Portugal 1038-1040
San Marino 701-702
Spain 1567
Sweden 814-816
Switzerland 500-501
Turkey 1799-1800
Vatican 470-472
Yugoslavia 1003-1004

Nos. 188-189 (2)	18.50	12.00
No. 837 (1)	.65	.30
Nos. 718-719 (2)	.75	.50
Nos. 326-328 (3)	*3.00*	*1.35*
No. 458 (1)	1.10	.75
No. 483 (1)	4.50	1.00
Nos. 1245-1246 (2)	.55	.50
Nos. 996-997 (2)	.65	.50
No. 585 (1)	.25	.25
Nos. 947-948 (2)	5.00	1.50
Nos. 406-407 (2)	4.20	2.40
Nos. 270-271 (2)	4.00	2.00
Nos. 1000-1001 (2)	.70	.50
No. 453 (1)	.45	.45
Nos. 475-476 (2)	1.10	.70
Nos. 722-724 (3)	*10.50*	2.00
Nos. 475-476 (2)	2.60	1.15
Nos. 533-534 (2)	3.75	2.35
Nos. 1038-1040 (3)	17.85	2.40
Nos. 701-702 (2)	.90	.90
No. 1567 (1)	.25	.25
Nos. 814-816 (3)	4.00	2.85
Nos. 500-501 (2)	1.85	.60
Nos. 1799-1800 (2)	3.85	2.25
Nos. 470-472 (3)	.75	.75
Nos. 1003-1004 (2)	4.00	4.00
Set total (51) Stamps	95.70	44.20

Europa, 1970

Interwoven
Threads
CD13

1970

Andorra, French 196-197
Belgium 741-742
Cyprus 340-342
France 1271-1272
Germany 1018-1019
Greece 985, 987
Iceland 420-421
Ireland 279-281
Italy 1013-1014
Liechtenstein 470
Luxembourg 489-490
Monaco 768-770
Netherlands 483-484
Portugal 1060-1062
San Marino 729-730
Spain 1607
Switzerland 515-516
Turkey 1848-1849
Yugoslavia 1024-1025

Nos. 196-197 (2)	20.00	8.50
Nos. 741-742 (2)	1.10	.55
Nos. 340-342 (3)	*2.70*	*1.90*
Nos. 1271-1272 (2)	.65	.50
Nos. 1018-1019 (2)	.65	.50
Nos. 985,987 (2)	7.75	2.00
Nos. 420-421 (2)	6.00	4.00
Nos. 279-281 (3)	9.50	3.30
Nos. 1013-1014 (2)	.65	.50
No. 470 (1)	.45	.45
Nos. 489-490 (2)	1.25	.75
Nos. 768-770 (3)	*6.35*	2.10
Nos. 483-484 (2)	2.50	1.15
Nos. 1060-1062 (3)	*9.85*	2.35
Nos. 729-730 (2)	.90	.55
No. 1607 (1)	.25	.25
Nos. 515-516 (2)	1.85	.60
Nos. 1848-1849 (2)	5.00	2.25
Nos. 1024-1025 (2)	.80	.80
Set total (40) Stamps	78.20	33.00

Europa, 1971

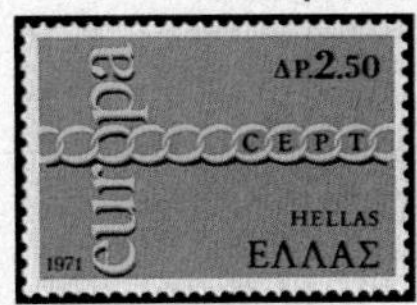

"Fraternity,
Cooperation,
Common
Effort"
CD14

1971

Andorra, French 205-206
Belgium 803-804
Cyprus 365-367
Finland 504
France 1304
Germany 1064-1065
Greece 1029-1030
Iceland 429-430
Ireland 305-306
Italy 1038-1039
Liechtenstein 485
Luxembourg 500-501
Malta 425-427
Monaco 797-799
Netherlands 488-489
Portugal 1094-1096
San Marino 749-750
Spain 1675-1676
Switzerland 531-532
Turkey 1876-1877
Yugoslavia 1052-1053

Nos. 205-206 (2)	20.00	7.75
Nos. 803-804 (2)	1.30	.55
Nos. 365-367 (3)	*2.60*	*1.75*
No. 504 (1)	5.00	.75
No. 1304 (1)	.45	.40
Nos. 1064-1065 (2)	.60	.50
Nos. 1029-1030 (2)	4.00	1.80
Nos. 429-430 (2)	5.00	3.75
Nos. 305-306 (2)	5.00	1.50
Nos. 1038-1039 (2)	.65	.50
No. 485 (1)	.45	.45
Nos. 500-501 (2)	1.35	.95
Nos. 425-427 (3)	*.80*	*.80*
Nos. 797-799 (3)	*15.00*	2.80
Nos. 488-489 (2)	2.50	1.15
Nos. 1094-1096 (3)	*9.75*	1.75
Nos. 749-750 (2)	.65	.55
Nos. 1675-1676 (2)	.75	.55
Nos. 531-532 (2)	1.85	.65
Nos. 1876-1877 (2)	5.60	2.50
Nos. 1052-1053 (2)	.50	.50
Set total (43) Stamps	83.80	31.90

Europa, 1972

Sparkles, Symbolic
of Communications
CD15

1972

Andorra, French 210-211
Andorra, Spanish 62
Belgium 825-826
Cyprus 380-382
Finland 512-513
France 1341
Germany 1089-1090
Greece 1049-1050
Iceland 439-440
Ireland 316-317
Italy 1065-1066
Liechtenstein 504
Luxembourg 512-513
Malta 450-453
Monaco 831-832
Netherlands 494-495
Portugal 1141-1143
San Marino 771-772
Spain 1718
Switzerland 544-545
Turkey 1907-1908
Yugoslavia 1100-1101

Nos. 210-211 (2)	21.00	7.00
No. 62 (1)	65.00	45.00
Nos. 825-826 (2)	.95	.55
Nos. 380-382 (3)	*5.95*	*2.45*
Nos. 512-513 (2)	8.50	1.40
No. 1341 (1)	.50	.35
Nos. 1089-1090 (2)	.85	.50
Nos. 1049-1050 (2)	2.00	1.55
Nos. 439-440 (2)	2.90	2.65
Nos. 316-317 (2)	13.00	4.50
Nos. 1065-1066 (2)	.65	.50
No. 504 (1)	.45	.45
Nos. 512-513 (2)	1.80	.85
Nos. 450-453 (4)	1.05	1.40
Nos. 831-832 (2)	5.00	1.40
Nos. 494-495 (2)	3.25	1.15
Nos. 1141-1143 (3)	*9.85*	1.50
Nos. 771-772 (2)	.70	.50
No. 1718 (1)	.50	.40
Nos. 544-545 (2)	1.65	.60
Nos. 1907-1908 (2)	7.50	3.00
Nos. 1100-1101 (2)	1.20	1.20
Set total (44) Stamps	154.25	78.90

Europa, 1973

Post Horn
and Arrows
CD16

1973

Andorra, French 219-220
Andorra, Spanish 76
Belgium 839-840
Cyprus 396-398
Finland 526
France 1367
Germany 1114-1115
Greece 1090-1092
Iceland 447-448
Ireland 329-330
Italy 1108-1109
Liechtenstein 528-529
Luxembourg 523-524
Malta 469-471
Monaco 866-867
Netherlands 504-505
Norway 604-605
Portugal 1170-1172
San Marino 802-803
Spain 1753
Switzerland 580-581
Turkey 1935-1936
Yugoslavia 1138-1139

Nos. 219-220 (2)	20.00	11.00
No. 76 (1)	.65	.55
Nos. 839-840 (2)	1.00	.65
Nos. 396-398 (3)	*4.25*	*2.10*
No. 526 (1)	1.40	1.25
No. 1367 (1)	1.60	.75
Nos. 1114-1115 (2)	.85	.50
Nos. 1090-1092 (3)	2.10	1.40
Nos. 447-448 (2)	7.00	4.05

Nos. 329-330 (2)	5.25	2.00
Nos. 1108-1109 (2)	.65	.50
Nos. 528-529 (2)	.60	.60
Nos. 523-524 (2)	2.35	1.05
Nos. 469-471 (3)	.90	1.20
Nos. 866-867 (2)	15.00	2.40
Nos. 504-505 (2)	2.85	1.10
Nos. 604-605 (2)	6.25	2.40
Nos. 1170-1172 (3)	13.00	2.15
Nos. 802-803 (2)	1.00	.60
No. 1753 (1)	.35	.25
Nos. 580-581 (2)	1.55	.60
Nos. 1935-1936 (2)	10.00	4.50
Nos. 1138-1139 (2)	1.15	1.10
Set total (46) Stamps	99.75	42.70

Europa, 2000

CD17

2000

Albania 2621-2622
Andorra, French 522
Andorra, Spanish 262
Armenia 610-611
Austria 1814
Azerbaijan 698-699
Belarus 350
Belgium 1818
Bosnia & Herzegovina (Moslem) 358
Bosnia & Herzegovina (Serb) 111-112
Croatia 428-429
Cyprus 959
Czech Republic 3120
Denmark 1189
Estonia 394
Faroe Islands 376
Finland 1129
Aland Islands 166
France 2771
Georgia 228-229
Germany 2086-2087
Gibraltar 837-840
Great Britain (Jersey) 935-936
Great Britain (Isle of Man) 883
Greece 1959
Greenland 363
Hungary 3699-3700
Iceland 910
Ireland 1230-1231
Italy 2349
Latvia 504
Liechtenstein 1178
Lithuania 668
Luxembourg 1035
Macedonia 187
Malta 1011-1012
Moldova 355
Monaco 2161-2162
Poland 3519
Portugal 2358
Portugal (Azores) 455
Portugal (Madeira) 208
Romania 4370
Russia 6589
San Marino 1480
Slovakia 355
Slovenia 424
Spain 3036
Sweden 2394
Switzerland 1074
Turkey 2762
Turkish Rep. of Northern Cyprus 500
Ukraine 379
Vatican City 1152

Nos. 2621-2622 (2)	13.00	13.00
No. 522 (1)	2.00	1.00
No. 262 (1)	1.60	.70
Nos. 610-611 (2)	9.00	9.00
No. 1814 (1)	1.40	1.40
Nos. 698-699 (2)	8.00	8.00
No. 350 (1)	2.00	2.00
No. 1818 (1)	1.75	.75
No. 358 (1)	4.75	4.75
Nos. 111-112 (2)	135.00	135.00
Nos. 428-429 (2)	4.40	3.50
No. 959 (1)	2.10	1.40
No. 3120 (1)	1.00	.40
No. 1189 (1)	3.50	2.25
No. 394 (1)	1.25	1.25
No. 376 (1)	3.00	3.00
No. 1129 (1)	2.00	.90
No. 166 (1)	1.75	1.50
No. 2771 (1)	1.40	.40
No. 228-229 (1)	9.00	9.00
Nos. 2086-2087 (2)	2.90	2.05
Nos. 837-840 (4)	6.25	6.25
Nos. 935-936 (2)	2.40	2.40
No. 883 (1)	1.50	1.50
No. 1959 (1)	3.00	3.00
No. 363 (1)	1.90	1.90
Nos. 3699-3700 (2)	6.50	2.50
No. 910 (1)	2.00	2.00
Nos. 1230-1231 (2)	4.75	4.75
No. 2349 (1)	1.50	.40
No. 504 (1)	5.00	2.40
No. 1178 (1)	2.25	1.75
No. 668 (1)	1.50	1.50
No. 1035 (1)	2.00	1.00
No. 187 (1)	3.50	3.50
Nos. 1011-1012 (2)	4.35	4.35
No. 355 (1)	3.50	3.50
Nos. 2161-2162 (2)	2.80	1.40
No. 3519 (1)	1.10	.50
No. 2358 (1)	1.25	.65
No. 455 (1)	1.25	.50
No. 208 (1)	1.25	.50
No. 4370 (1)	2.50	1.25
No. 6589 (1)	1.75	.85
No. 1480 (1)	1.00	1.00
No. 355 (1)	1.10	.55
No. 424 (1)	3.25	1.60
No. 3036 (1)	.75	.40
No. 2394 (1)	3.00	2.25
No. 1074 (1)	2.10	.75
No. 2762 (1)	2.00	2.00
No. 500 (1)	1.90	1.90
No. 379 (1)	4.50	3.00
No. 1152 (1)	1.25	1.25
Set total (68) Stamps	295.45	264.30

The Gibraltar stamps are similar to the stamp illustrated, but none have the design shown above. All other sets listed above include at least one stamp with the design shown, but some include stamps with entirely different designs. Bulgaria Nos. 4131-4132, Guernsey Nos. 802-803 and Yugoslavia Nos. 2485-2486 are Europa stamps with completely different designs.

PORTUGAL & COLONIES
Vasco da Gama

Fleet Departing CD20

Fleet Arriving at Calicut — CD21

Embarking at Rastello CD22

Muse of History CD23

San Gabriel, da Gama and Camoens CD24

Archangel Gabriel, the Patron Saint CD25

Flagship San Gabriel — CD26

Vasco da Gama — CD27

Fourth centenary of Vasco da Gama's discovery of the route to India.

1898

Azores 93-100
Macao 67-74
Madeira 37-44
Portugal 147-154
Port. Africa 1-8
Port. Congo 75-98
Port. India 189-196
St. Thomas & Prince Islands 170-193
Timor 45-52

Nos. 93-100 (8)	122.00	76.25
Nos. 67-74 (8)	136.00	96.75
Nos. 37-44 (8)	44.55	34.00
Nos. 147-154 (8)	169.30	43.45
Nos. 1-8 (8)	23.95	21.70
Nos. 75-98 (24)	34.45	34.45
Nos. 189-196 (8)	20.25	12.95
Nos. 170-193 (24)	37.85	34.30
Nos. 45-52 (8)	21.50	10.45
Set total (104) Stamps	609.85	364.30

Pombal
POSTAL TAX
POSTAL TAX DUES

Marquis de Pombal — CD28

Planning Reconstruction of Lisbon, 1755 — CD29

Pombal Monument, Lisbon — CD30

Sebastiao Jose de Carvalho e Mello, Marquis de Pombal (1699-1782), statesman, rebuilt Lisbon after earthquake of 1755. Tax was for the erection of Pombal monument. Obligatory on all mail on certain days throughout the year. Postal Tax Dues are inscribed "Multa."

1925

Angola RA1-RA3, RAJ1-RAJ3
Azores RA9-RA11, RAJ2-RAJ4
Cape Verde RA1-RA3, RAJ1-RAJ3
Macao RA1-RA3, RAJ1-RAJ3
Madeira RA1-RA3, RAJ1-RAJ3
Mozambique RA1-RA3, RAJ1-RAJ3
Nyassa RA1-RA3, RAJ1-RAJ3
Portugal RA11-RA13, RAJ2-RAJ4
Port. Guinea RA1-RA3, RAJ1-RAJ3
Port. India RA1-RA3, RAJ1-RAJ3
St. Thomas & Prince Islands RA1-RA3, RAJ1-RAJ3
Timor RA1-RA3, RAJ1-RAJ3

Nos. RA1-RA3,RAJ1-RAJ3 (6)	7.50	6.00
Nos. RA9-RA11,RAJ2-RAJ4 (6)	6.60	9.30
Nos. RA1-RA3,RAJ1-RAJ3 (6)	6.00	5.40
Nos. RA1-RA3,RAJ1-RAJ3 (6)	19.50	4.20
Nos. RA1-RA3,RAJ1-RAJ3 (6)	4.35	12.45
Nos. RA1-RA3,RAJ1-RAJ3 (6)	2.55	2.70
Nos. RA1-RA3,RAJ1-RAJ3 (6)	52.50	38.25
Nos. RA11-RA13,RAJ2-RAJ4 (6)	5.80	5.20
Nos. RA1-RA3,RAJ1-RAJ3 (6)	3.30	2.70
Nos. RA1-RA3,RAJ1-RAJ3 (6)	3.45	3.45
Nos. RA1-RA3,RAJ1-RAJ3 (6)	3.60	3.60
Nos. RA1-RA3,RAJ1-RAJ3 (6)	2.10	3.90
Set total (72) Stamps	117.25	97.15

Vasco da Gama CD34

Mousinho de Albuquerque CD35

Dam CD36

Prince Henry the Navigator CD37

Affonso de Albuquerque CD38

Plane over Globe CD39

1938-39

Angola 274-291, C1-C9
Cape Verde 234-251, C1-C9
Macao 289-305, C7-C15
Mozambique 270-287, C1-C9
Port. Guinea 233-250. C1-C9
Port. India 439-453, C1-C8
St. Thomas & Prince Islands ... 302-319, 323-340, C1-C18
Timor 223-239, C1-C9

Nos. 274-291,C1-C9 (27)	141.35	22.25
Nos. 234-251,C1-C9 (27)	100.00	31.20
Nos. 289-305,C7-C15 (26)	701.70	135.60
Nos. 270-287,C1-C9 (27)	60.95	11.20
Nos. 233-250,C1-C9 (27)	86.05	30.70
Nos. 439-453,C1-C8 (23)	74.75	25.50
Nos. 302-319,323-340,C1-C18 (54)	319.25	190.35
Nos. 223-239,C1-C9 (26)	149.25	73.15
Set total (237) Stamps	1,633.	519.95

Lady of Fatima

Our Lady of the Rosary, Fatima, Portugal — CD40

1948-49

Angola 315-318
Cape Verde 266
Macao 336
Mozambique 325-328
Port. Guinea 271
Port. India 480
St. Thomas & Prince Islands 351
Timor 254

Nos. 315-318 (4)	88.50	17.90
No. 266 (1)	8.50	4.50
No. 336 (1)	40.00	12.00
Nos. 325-328 (4)	20.00	4.50
No. 271 (1)	3.25	3.00
No. 480 (1)	2.50	2.25
No. 351 (1)	7.25	6.50
No. 254 (1)	3.00	3.00
Set total (14) Stamps	173.00	53.65

A souvenir sheet of 9 stamps was issued in 1951 to mark the extension of the 1950 Holy Year. The sheet contains: Angola No. 316, Cape Verde No. 266, Macao No. 336, Mozambique No. 325, Portuguese Guinea No. 271, Portuguese India Nos. 480, 485, St. Thomas & Prince Islands No. 351, Timor No. 254. The sheet also contains a portrait of Pope Pius XII and is inscribed "Encerramento do

Ano Santo, Fatima 1951." It was sold for 11 escudos.

Holy Year

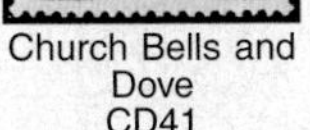

Church Bells and Dove CD41

Angel Holding Candelabra CD42

Holy Year, 1950.

1950-51

Angola	331-332
Cape Verde	268-269
Macao	339-340
Mozambique	330-331
Port. Guinea	273-274
Port. India	490-491, 496-503
St. Thomas & Prince Islands	353-354
Timor	258-259

Nos. 331-332 (2)	7.60	1.35
Nos. 268-269 (2)	4.75	2.20
Nos. 339-340 (2)	55.00	12.50
Nos. 330-331 (2)	1.75	.85
Nos. 273-274 (2)	3.50	2.60
Nos. 490-491,496-503 (10)	12.80	5.40
Nos. 353-354 (2)	7.50	4.40
Nos. 258-259 (2)	3.75	3.25
Set total (24) Stamps	96.65	32.55

A souvenir sheet of 8 stamps was issued in 1951 to mark the extension of the Holy Year. The sheet contains: Angola No. 331, Cape Verde No. 269, Macao No. 340, Mozambique No. 331, Portuguese Guinea No. 275, Portuguese India No. 490, St. Thomas & Prince Islands No. 354, Timor No. 258, some with colors changed. The sheet contains doves and is inscribed 'Encerramento do Ano Santo, Fatima 1951.' It was sold for 17 escudos.

Holy Year Conclusion

Our Lady of Fatima — CD43

Conclusion of Holy Year. Sheets contain alternate vertical rows of stamps and labels bearing quotation from Pope Pius XII, different for each colony.

1951

Angola	357
Cape Verde	270
Macao	352
Mozambique	356
Port. Guinea	275
Port. India	506
St. Thomas & Prince Islands	355
Timor	270

No. 357 (1)	5.25	1.50
No. 270 (1)	1.50	1.25
No. 352 (1)	35.00	9.00
No. 356 (1)	2.25	1.00
No. 275 (1)	1.00	.65
No. 506 (1)	1.60	1.00
No. 355 (1)	2.50	2.00
No. 270 (1)	2.00	1.75
Set total (8) Stamps	51.10	18.15

Medical Congress

CD44

First National Congress of Tropical Medicine, Lisbon, 1952. Each stamp has a different design.

1952

Angola	358
Cape Verde	287
Macao	364
Mozambique	359
Port. Guinea	276
Port. India	516
St. Thomas & Prince Islands	356
Timor	271

No. 358 (1)	1.25	.45
No. 287 (1)	.70	.50
No. 364 (1)	9.75	3.50
No. 359 (1)	1.10	.55
No. 276 (1)	.45	.35
No. 516 (1)	4.75	2.00
No. 356 (1)	.30	.30
No. 271 (1)	1.00	1.00
Set total (8) Stamps	19.30	8.65

Postage Due Stamps

CD45

1952

Angola	J37-J42
Cape Verde	J31-J36
Macao	J53-J58
Mozambique	J51-J56
Port. Guinea	J40-J45
Port. India	J47-J52
St. Thomas & Prince Islands	J52-J57
Timor	J31-J36

Nos. J37-J42 (6)	4.05	3.15
Nos. J31-J36 (6)	2.80	2.30
Nos. J53-J58 (6)	20.50	3.15
Nos. J51-J56 (6)	1.80	1.55
Nos. J40-J45 (6)	2.55	2.55
Nos. J47-J52 (6)	6.10	6.10
Nos. J52-J57 (6)	4.15	4.15
Nos. J31-J36 (6)	3.50	3.50
Set total (48) Stamps	45.45	26.45

Sao Paulo

Father Manuel da Nobrega and View of Sao Paulo — CD46

Founding of Sao Paulo, Brazil, 400th anniv.

1954

Angola	385
Cape Verde	297
Macao	382
Mozambique	395
Port. Guinea	291
Port. India	530
St. Thomas & Prince Islands	369
Timor	279

No. 385 (1)	.80	.50
No. 297 (1)	.70	.60
No. 382 (1)	14.00	2.75
No. 395 (1)	.40	.30
No. 291 (1)	.35	.25
No. 530 (1)	.80	.40
No. 369 (1)	.80	.60
No. 279 (1)	.85	.70
Set total (8) Stamps	18.70	6.10

Tropical Medicine Congress

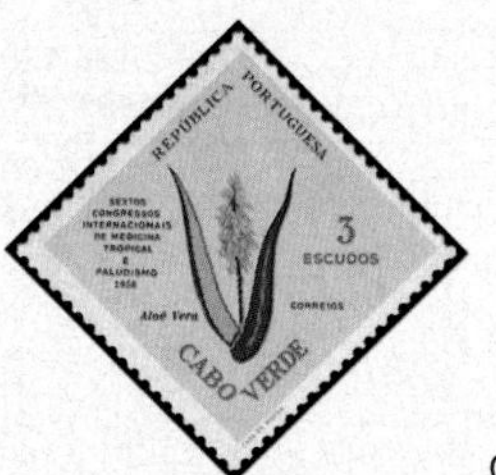

CD47

Sixth International Congress for Tropical Medicine and Malaria, Lisbon, Sept. 1958. Each stamp shows a different plant.

1958

Angola	409
Cape Verde	303
Macao	392
Mozambique	404
Port. Guinea	295
Port. India	569
St. Thomas & Prince Islands	371
Timor	289

No. 409 (1)	3.50	1.10
No. 303 (1)	5.50	2.10
No. 392 (1)	8.00	2.50
No. 404 (1)	4.00	.85
No. 295 (1)	2.75	1.10
No. 569 (1)	1.75	.75
No. 371 (1)	2.75	2.25
No. 289 (1)	3.00	2.75
Set total (8) Stamps	31.25	13.40

Sports

CD48

Each stamp shows a different sport.

1962

Angola	433-438
Cape Verde	320-325
Macao	394-399
Mozambique	424-429
Port. Guinea	299-304
St. Thomas & Prince Islands	374-379
Timor	313-318

Nos. 433-438 (6)	6.50	3.20
Nos. 320-325 (6)	12.25	5.20
Nos. 394-399 (6)	74.00	11.60
Nos. 424-429 (6)	5.00	2.45
Nos. 299-304 (6)	4.95	2.15
Nos. 374-379 (6)	6.75	3.20
Nos. 313-318 (6)	6.40	3.70
Set total (42) Stamps	115.85	31.50

Anti-Malaria

Anopheles Funestus and Malaria Eradication Symbol — CD49

World Health Organization drive to eradicate malaria.

1962

Angola	439
Cape Verde	326
Macao	400
Mozambique	430
Port. Guinea	305
St. Thomas & Prince Islands	380
Timor	319

No. 439 (1)	2.00	.90
No. 326 (1)	1.40	.90
No. 400 (1)	7.00	2.00
No. 430 (1)	1.40	.40
No. 305 (1)	1.25	.45
No. 380 (1)	2.00	1.50
No. 319 (1)	.75	.60
Set total (7) Stamps	15.80	6.75

Airline Anniversary

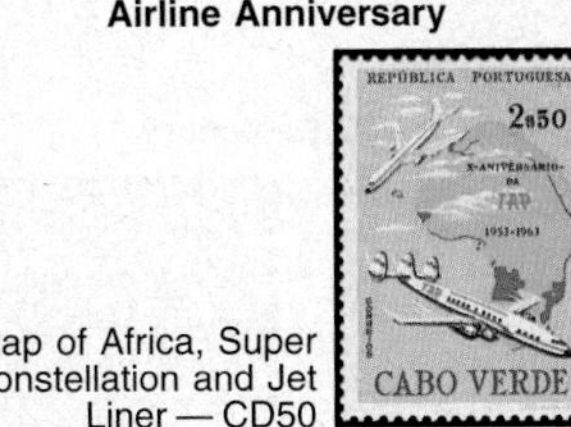

Map of Africa, Super Constellation and Jet Liner — CD50

Tenth anniversary of Transportes Aereos Portugueses (TAP).

1963

Angola	490
Cape Verde	327
Mozambique	434
Port. Guinea	318
St. Thomas & Prince Islands	381

No. 490 (1)	1.25	.50
No. 327 (1)	1.10	.70
No. 434 (1)	.40	.25
No. 318 (1)	.65	.35
No. 381 (1)	.70	.60
Set total (5) Stamps	4.10	2.40

National Overseas Bank

Antonio Teixeira de Sousa — CD51

Centenary of the National Overseas Bank of Portugal.

1964, May 16

Angola	509
Cape Verde	328
Port. Guinea	319
St. Thomas & Prince Islands	382
Timor	320

No. 509 (1)	.90	.30
No. 328 (1)	1.10	.75
No. 319 (1)	.65	.40
No. 382 (1)	.70	.50
No. 320 (1)	.75	.60
Set total (5) Stamps	4.10	2.55

ITU

ITU Emblem and the Archangel Gabriel — CD52

International Communications Union, Cent.

1965, May 17

Angola	511
Cape Verde	329
Macao	402
Mozambique	464
Port. Guinea	320
St. Thomas & Prince Islands	383
Timor	321

No. 511 (1)	1.25	.65
No. 329 (1)	2.10	1.40
No. 402 (1)	5.50	1.50
No. 464 (1)	.40	.25
No. 320 (1)	1.90	.75
No. 383 (1)	1.50	1.00
No. 321 (1)	1.50	.90
Set total (7) Stamps	14.15	6.45

National Revolution

CD53

40th anniv. of the National Revolution. Different buildings on each stamp.

1966, May 28

Angola	525
Cape Verde	338
Macao	403
Mozambique	465
Port. Guinea	329
St. Thomas & Prince Islands	392
Timor	322

No. 525 (1)	.45	.25
No. 338 (1)	.60	.45
No. 403 (1)	5.00	1.50
No. 465 (1)	.50	.30
No. 329 (1)	.55	.35
No. 392 (1)	.75	.50
No. 322 (1)	1.50	.90
Set total (7) Stamps	9.35	4.25

Navy Club

CD54

Centenary of Portugal's Navy Club. Each stamp has a different design.

1967, Jan. 31

Angola 527-528
Cape Verde 339-340
Macao 412-413
Mozambique 478-479
Port. Guinea 330-331
St. Thomas & Prince Islands ...393-394
Timor 323-324

Nos. 527-528 (2) 2.25 1.00
Nos. 339-340 (2) 2.00 1.40
Nos. 412-413 (2) 9.50 3.75
Nos. 478-479 (2) 1.20 .65
Nos. 330-331 (2) 1.20 .90
Nos. 393-394 (2) 3.20 1.25
Nos. 323-324 (2) 4.00 2.00
Set total (14) Stamps 23.35 10.95

Admiral Coutinho

CD55

Centenary of the birth of Admiral Carlos Viegas Gago Coutinho (1869-1959), explorer and aviation pioneer. Each stamp has a different design.

1969, Feb. 17

Angola 547
Cape Verde 355
Macao 417
Mozambique 484
Port. Guinea 335
St. Thomas & Prince Islands 397
Timor 335

No. 547 (1) 1.00 .35
No. 355 (1) .35 .25
No. 417 (1) 3.75 1.50
No. 484 (1) .25 .25
No. 335 (1) .35 .25
No. 397 (1) .50 .35
No. 335 (1) 1.10 .85
Set total (7) Stamps 7.30 3.80

Administration Reform

Luiz Augusto Rebello da Silva — CD56

Centenary of the administration reforms of the overseas territories.

1969, Sept. 25

Angola 549
Cape Verde 357
Macao 419
Mozambique 491
Port. Guinea 337
St. Thomas & Prince Islands 399
Timor 338

No. 549 (1) .25 .25
No. 357 (1) .35 .25
No. 419 (1) 5.00 1.00
No. 491 (1) .25 .25
No. 337 (1) .25 .25
No. 399 (1) .45 .45
No. 338 (1) .40 .25
Set total (7) Stamps 6.95 2.70

Marshal Carmona

CD57

Birth centenary of Marshal Antonio Oscar Carmona de Fragoso (1869-1951), President of Portugal. Each stamp has a different design.

1970, Nov. 15

Angola 563
Cape Verde 359
Macao 422
Mozambique 493
Port. Guinea 340
St. Thomas & Prince Islands 403
Timor 341

No. 563 (1) .45 .25
No. 359 (1) .55 .35
No. 422 (1) 1.50 .75
No. 493 (1) .40 .25
No. 340 (1) .35 .25
No. 403 (1) .75 .45
No. 341 (1) .25 .25
Set total (7) Stamps 4.25 2.55

Olympic Games

CD59

20th Olympic Games, Munich, Aug. 26-Sept. 11. Each stamp shows a different sport.

1972, June 20

Angola 569
Cape Verde 361
Macao 426
Mozambique 504
Port. Guinea 342
St. Thomas & Prince Islands 408
Timor 343

No. 569 (1) .65 .25
No. 361 (1) .65 .30
No. 426 (1) 3.50 1.00
No. 504 (1) .30 .25
No. 342 (1) .45 .25
No. 408 (1) .35 .25
No. 343 (1) .50 .50
Set total (7) Stamps 6.40 2.80

Lisbon-Rio de Janeiro Flight

CD60

50th anniversary of the Lisbon to Rio de Janeiro flight by Arturo de Sacadura and Coutinho, March 30-June 5, 1922. Each stamp shows a different stage of the flight.

1972, Sept. 20

Angola 570
Cape Verde 362
Macao 427
Mozambique 505
Port. Guinea 343
St. Thomas & Prince Islands 409
Timor 344

No. 570 (1) .35 .25
No. 362 (1) 1.50 .30
No. 427 (1) 22.50 7.50
No. 505 (1) .25 .25
No. 343 (1) .25 .25
No. 409 (1) .35 .25
No. 344 (1) .25 .40
Set total (7) Stamps 25.45 9.20

WMO Centenary

WMO Emblem — CD61

Centenary of international meterological cooperation.

1973, Dec. 15

Angola 571
Cape Verde 363
Macao 429
Mozambique 509
Port. Guinea 344
St. Thomas & Prince Islands 410
Timor 345

No. 571 (1) .45 .25
No. 363 (1) .65 .30
No. 429 (1) 6.25 1.00
No. 509 (1) .30 .25
No. 344 (1) .45 .35
No. 410 (1) .60 .50
No. 345 (1) 1.75 2.00
Set total (7) Stamps 10.45 4.65

FRENCH COMMUNITY

Upper Volta can be found under Burkina Faso in Vol. 1
Madagascar can be found under Malagasy in Vol. 3

Colonial Exposition

People of French Empire CD70

Women's Heads CD71

France Showing Way to Civilization CD72

"Colonial Commerce" CD73

International Colonial Exposition, Paris.

1931

Cameroun 213-216
Chad 60-63
Dahomey 97-100
Fr. Guiana 152-155
Fr. Guinea 116-119
Fr. India 100-103
Fr. Polynesia 76-79
Fr. Sudan 102-105
Gabon 120-123
Guadeloupe 138-141
Indo-China 140-142
Ivory Coast 92-95
Madagascar 169-172
Martinique 129-132
Mauritania 65-68
Middle Congo 61-64
New Caledonia 176-179
Niger 73-76
Reunion 122-125
St. Pierre & Miquelon 132-135
Senegal 138-141
Somali Coast 135-138
Togo 254-257
Ubangi-Shari 82-85
Upper Volta 66-69
Wallis & Futuna Isls. 85-88

Nos. 213-216 (4) 23.00 18.25
Nos. 60-63 (4) 22.00 22.00
Nos. 97-100 (4) 25.00 25.00
Nos. 152-155 (4) 22.00 22.00
Nos. 116-119 (4) 20.00 20.00
Nos. 100-103 (4) 18.00 18.00
Nos. 76-79 (4) 30.00 30.00
Nos. 102-105 (4) 19.00 19.00
Nos. 120-123 (4) 17.50 17.50
Nos. 138-141 (4) 19.00 19.00
Nos. 140-142 (3) 11.50 11.50
Nos. 92-95 (4) 22.50 22.50
Nos. 169-172 (4) 7.90 5.00
Nos. 129-132 (4) 21.00 21.00
Nos. 65-68 (4) 24.50 24.50
Nos. 61-64 (4) 18.50 18.50
Nos. 176-179 (4) 24.00 24.00
Nos. 73-76 (4) 22.50 22.50
Nos. 122-125 (4) 22.00 22.00
Nos. 132-135 (4) 24.00 24.00
Nos. 138-141 (4) 18.00 18.00
Nos. 135-138 (4) 26.00 26.00
Nos. 254-257 (4) 26.00 26.00
Nos. 82-85 (4) 22.00 22.00
Nos. 66-69 (4) 19.00 19.00
Nos. 85-88 (4) 35.00 35.00
Set total (103) Stamps 559.90 552.25

Paris International Exposition
Colonial Arts Exposition

"Colonial Resources"
CD74 CD77

Overseas Commerce CD75

Exposition Building and Women CD76

"France and the Empire" CD78

Cultural Treasures of the Colonies CD79

Souvenir sheets contain one imperf. stamp.

1937

Cameroun 217-222A
Dahomey 101-107
Fr. Equatorial Africa 27-32, 73
Fr. Guiana 162-168
Fr. Guinea 120-126
Fr. India 104-110
Fr. Polynesia 117-123
Fr. Sudan 106-112
Guadeloupe 148-154
Indo-China 193-199
Inini 41
Ivory Coast 152-158
Kwangchowan 132
Madagascar 191-197
Martinique 179-185
Mauritania 69-75
New Caledonia 208-214
Niger 73-83
Reunion 167-173
St. Pierre & Miquelon 165-171
Senegal 172-178
Somali Coast 139-145
Togo 258-264
Wallis & Futuna Isls. 89

Nos. 217-222A (7) 18.95 20.45
Nos. 101-107 (7) 19.95 21.20
Nos. 27-32, 73 (7) 25.60 26.60
Nos. 162-168 (7) 22.50 24.50
Nos. 120-126 (7) 22.55 23.55
Nos. 104-110 (7) 21.15 24.40
Nos. 117-123 (7) 58.50 75.00
Nos. 106-112 (7) 19.95 21.70
Nos. 148-154 (7) 19.55 21.05
Nos. 193-199 (7) 17.70 19.70
No. 41 (1) 19.00 22.50
Nos. 152-158 (7) 19.95 21.20
No. 132 (1) 9.25 11.00
Nos. 191-197 (7) 17.55 18.30
Nos. 179-185 (7) 19.95 21.70
Nos. 69-75 (7) 19.95 21.70
Nos. 208-214 (7) 39.00 50.50
Nos. 73-83 (11) 42.70 44.20
Nos. 167-173 (7) 21.70 23.20
Nos. 165-171 (7) 49.60 64.00
Nos. 172-178 (7) 19.95 21.70
Nos. 139-145 (7) 25.95 27.95
Nos. 258-264 (7) 19.40 20.90
No. 89 (1) 28.50 37.50
Set total (154) Stamps 598.85 684.50

Curie

Pierre and Marie Curie CD80

40th anniversary of the discovery of radium. The surtax was for the benefit of the Intl. Union for the Control of Cancer.

1938

Cameroun B1
Cuba B1-B2
Dahomey B2
France B76
Fr. Equatorial Africa B1
Fr. Guiana B3
Fr. Guinea B2
Fr. India B6
Fr. Polynesia B5
Fr. Sudan B1
Guadeloupe B3
Indo-China B14
Ivory Coast B2
Madagascar B2
Martinique B2
Mauritania B3
New Caledonia B4
Niger B1
Reunion B4
St. Pierre & Miquelon B3
Senegal B3
Somali Coast B2
Togo B1

No. B1 (1)	10.00	10.00
Nos. B1-B2 (2)	8.50	2.40
No. B2 (1)	9.50	9.50
No. B76 (1)	21.00	12.50
No. B1 (1)	24.00	24.00
No. B3 (1)	13.50	13.50
No. B2 (1)	9.00	9.00
No. B6 (1)	10.00	10.00
No. B5 (1)	20.00	20.00
No. B1 (1)	12.50	12.50
No. B3 (1)	11.00	10.50
No. B14 (1)	12.00	12.00
No. B2 (1)	11.00	9.50
No. B2 (1)	11.00	11.00
No. B2 (1)	13.00	13.00
No. B3 (1)	8.75	8.75
No. B4 (1)	16.50	16.50
No. B1 (1)	17.00	17.00
No. B4 (1)	14.00	14.00
No. B3 (1)	21.00	22.50
No. B3 (1)	13.00	13.00
No. B2 (1)	8.75	8.75
No. B1 (1)	20.00	20.00
Set total (24) Stamps	315.00	299.90

Caillie

Rene Caillie and Map of Northwestern Africa — CD81

Death centenary of Rene Caillie (1799-1838), French explorer. All three denominations exist with colony name omitted.

1939

Dahomey 108-110
Fr. Guinea 161-163
Fr. Sudan 113-115
Ivory Coast 160-162
Mauritania 109-111
Niger 84-86
Senegal 188-190
Togo 265-267

Nos. 108-110 (3)	3.90	3.90
Nos. 161-163 (3)	3.20	3.20
Nos. 113-115 (3)	3.15	3.15
Nos. 160-162 (3)	3.20	3.20
Nos. 109-111 (3)	3.90	3.90
Nos. 84-86 (3)	3.20	3.20
Nos. 188-190 (3)	3.20	3.20
Nos. 265-267 (3)	3.15	3.15
Set total (24) Stamps	26.90	26.90

New York World's Fair

Natives and New York Skyline CD82

1939

Cameroun 223-224
Dahomey 111-112
Fr. Equatorial Africa 78-79
Fr. Guiana 169-170
Fr. Guinea 164-165
Fr. India 111-112
Fr. Polynesia 124-125
Fr. Sudan 116-117
Guadeloupe 155-156
Indo-China 203-204
Inini 42-43
Ivory Coast 163-164
Kwangchowan 133-134
Madagascar 209-210
Martinique 186-187
Mauritania 112-113
New Caledonia 215-216
Niger 87-88
Reunion 174-175
St. Pierre & Miquelon 205-206
Senegal 191-192
Somali Coast 179-180
Togo 268-269
Wallis & Futuna Isls. 90-91

Nos. 223-224 (2)	2.80	2.40
Nos. 111-112 (2)	2.40	2.40
Nos. 78-79 (2)	3.65	3.65
Nos. 169-170 (2)	2.60	2.60
Nos. 164-165 (2)	2.80	2.80
Nos. 111-112 (2)	3.00	3.00
Nos. 124-125 (2)	4.80	4.80
Nos. 116-117 (2)	2.40	2.40
Nos. 155-156 (2)	2.50	2.50
Nos. 203-204 (2)	2.05	2.05
Nos. 42-43 (2)	7.50	9.00
Nos. 163-164 (2)	3.00	3.00
Nos. 133-134 (2)	2.50	2.50
Nos. 209-210 (2)	3.75	3.75
Nos. 186-187 (2)	2.35	2.35
Nos. 112-113 (2)	1.60	1.60
Nos. 215-216 (2)	3.35	3.35
Nos. 87-88 (2)	2.40	2.40
Nos. 174-175 (2)	2.80	2.80
Nos. 205-206 (2)	4.80	6.00
Nos. 191-192 (2)	2.00	2.00
Nos. 179-180 (2)	2.90	2.90
Nos. 268-269 (2)	2.50	2.50
Nos. 90-91 (2)	6.00	6.00
Set total (48) Stamps	76.45	78.75

French Revolution

Storming of the Bastille CD83

French Revolution, 150th anniv. The surtax was for the defense of the colonies.

1939

Cameroun B2-B6
Dahomey B3-B7
Fr. Equatorial Africa B4-B8, CB1
Fr. Guiana B4-B8, CB1
Fr. Guinea B3-B7
Fr. India B7-B11
Fr. Polynesia B6-B10, CB1
Fr. Sudan B2-B6
Guadeloupe B4-B8
Indo-China B15-B19, CB1
Inini B1-B5
Ivory Coast B3-B7
Kwangchowan B1-B5
Madagascar B3-B7, CB1
Martinique B3-B7
Mauritania B4-B8
New Caledonia B5-B9, CB1
Niger B2-B6
Reunion B5-B9, CB1
St. Pierre & Miquelon B4-B8
Senegal B4-B8, CB1
Somali Coast B3-B7
Togo B2-B6
Wallis & Futuna Isls. B1-B5

Nos. B2-B6 (5)	60.00	60.00
Nos. B3-B7 (5)	47.50	47.50
Nos. B4-B8,CB1 (6)	107.50	107.50
Nos. B4-B8,CB1 (6)	79.50	79.50
Nos. B3-B7 (5)	48.75	48.75
Nos. B7-B11 (5)	45.00	45.00
Nos. B6-B10,CB1 (6)	122.50	122.50
Nos. B2-B6 (5)	50.00	50.00
Nos. B4-B8 (5)	50.00	50.00
Nos. B15-B19,CB1 (6)	85.00	85.00
Nos. B1-B5 (5)	80.00	87.50
Nos. B3-B7 (5)	43.75	43.75
Nos. B1-B5 (5)	46.25	46.25
Nos. B3-B7,CB1 (6)	65.50	65.50
Nos. B3-B7 (5)	52.50	52.50
Nos. B4-B8 (5)	47.50	47.50
Nos. B5-B9,CB1 (6)	101.50	101.50
Nos. B2-B6 (5)	60.00	60.00
Nos. B5-B9,CB1 (6)	87.50	87.50
Nos. B4-B8 (5)	67.50	72.50
Nos. B4-B8,CB1 (6)	63.00	63.00
Nos. B3-B7 (5)	52.50	52.50
Nos. B2-B6 (5)	47.50	47.50
Nos. B1-B5 (5)	95.00	95.00
Set total (128) Stamps	1,606.	1,618.

Plane over Coastal Area CD85

All five denominations exist with colony name omitted.

1940

Dahomey C1-C5
Fr. Guinea C1-C5
Fr. Sudan C1-C5
Ivory Coast C1-C5
Mauritania C1-C5
Niger C1-C5
Senegal C12-C16
Togo C1-C5

Nos. C1-C5 (5)	4.00	4.00
Nos. C1-C5 (5)	4.90	4.90
Nos. C1-C5 (5)	3.95	3.95
Nos. C1-C5 (5)	4.05	4.05
Nos. C1-C5 (5)	3.90	3.90
Nos. C1-C5 (5)	4.00	4.00
Nos. C12-C16 (5)	4.00	4.00
Nos. C1-C5 (5)	4.05	4.05
Set total (40) Stamps	32.85	32.85

Defense of the Empire

Colonial Infantryman — CD86

1941

Cameroun B13B
Dahomey B13
Fr. Equatorial Africa B8B
Fr. Guiana B10
Fr. Guinea B13
Fr. India B13
Fr. Polynesia B12
Fr. Sudan B12
Guadeloupe B10
Indo-China B19B
Inini B7
Ivory Coast B13
Kwangchowan B7
Madagascar B9
Martinique B9
Mauritania B14
New Caledonia B11
Niger B12
Reunion B11
St. Pierre & Miquelon B8B
Senegal B14
Somali Coast B9
Togo B10B
Wallis & Futuna Isls. B7

No. B13B (1)	1.60
No. B13 (1)	1.20
No. B8B (1)	3.50
No. B10 (1)	1.40
No. B13 (1)	1.40
No. B13 (1)	1.25
No. B12 (1)	3.50
No. B12 (1)	1.40
No. B10 (1)	1.00
No. B19B (1)	1.60
No. B7 (1)	1.75
No. B13 (1)	1.25
No. B7 (1)	.85
No. B9 (1)	1.50
No. B9 (1)	1.40
No. B14 (1)	.95
No. B11 (1)	1.60
No. B12 (1)	1.40
No. B11 (1)	1.60
No. B8B (1)	3.75
No. B14 (1)	1.25
No. B9 (1)	1.60
No. B10B (1)	1.25
No. B7 (1)	2.40
Set total (24) Stamps	40.40

Each of the CD86 stamps listed above is part of a set of three stamps. The designs of the other two stamps in the set vary from country to country. Only the values of the Common Design stamps are listed here.

Colonial Education Fund

CD86a

1942

Cameroun CB3
Dahomey CB4
Fr. Equatorial Africa CB5
Fr. Guiana CB4
Fr. Guinea CB4
Fr. India CB3
Fr. Polynesia CB4
Fr. Sudan CB4
Guadeloupe CB3
Indo-China CB5
Inini CB3
Ivory Coast CB4
Kwangchowan CB4
Malagasy CB5
Martinique CB3
Mauritania CB4
New Caledonia CB4
Niger CB4
Reunion CB4
St. Pierre & Miquelon CB3
Senegal CB5
Somali Coast CB3
Togo CB3
Wallis & Futuna CB3

No. CB3 (1)	1.10	
No. CB4 (1)	.80	5.50
No. CB5 (1)	1.50	
No. CB4 (1)	1.10	
No. CB4 (1)	.80	5.50
No. CB3 (1)	.90	
No. CB4 (1)	2.00	
No. CB4 (1)	.80	5.50
No. CB3 (1)	1.10	
No. CB5 (1)	1.10	
No. CB3 (1)	1.25	
No. CB4 (1)	1.00	5.50
No. CB4 (1)	1.00	
No. CB5 (1)	.65	
No. CB3 (1)	1.00	
No. CB4 (1)	.80	
No. CB4 (1)	1.60	
No. CB4 (1)	.80	
No. CB4 (1)	.90	
No. CB3 (1)	5.25	
No. CB5 (1)	.80	6.50
No. CB3 (1)	1.75	
No. CB3 (1)	.70	
No. CB3 (1)	2.25	
Set total (24) Stamps	30.95	28.50

Cross of Lorraine & Four-motor Plane CD87

1941-5

Cameroun C1-C7
Fr. Equatorial Africa C17-C23
Fr. Guiana C9-C10
Fr. India C1-C6
Fr. Polynesia C3-C9
Fr. West Africa C1-C3
Guadeloupe C1-C2
Madagascar C37-C43

Martinique C1-C2
New Caledonia C7-C13
Reunion C18-C24
St. Pierre & Miquelon C1-C7
Somali Coast C1-C7

Nos. C1-C7 (7)	6.30	6.30
Nos. C17-C23 (7)	11.35	6.35
Nos. C9-C10 (2)	3.80	3.10
Nos. C1-C6 (6)	9.30	9.30
Nos. C3-C9 (7)	13.75	10.00
Nos. C1-C3 (3)	9.50	3.90
Nos. C1-C2 (2)	3.75	2.50
Nos. C37-C43 (7)	5.60	3.80
Nos. C1-C2 (2)	3.00	1.60
Nos. C7-C13 (7)	8.35	8.35
Nos. C18-C24 (7)	7.05	5.00
Nos. C1-C7 (7)	11.60	9.40
Nos. C1-C7 (7)	16.80	12.75
Set total (71) Stamps	110.15	82.35

Transport Plane CD88

Caravan and Plane CD89

1942

Dahomey C6-C13
Fr. Guinea C6-C13
Fr. Sudan C6-C13
Ivory Coast C6-C13
Mauritania C6-C13
Niger C6-C13
Senegal C17-C25
Togo C6-C13

Nos. C6-C13 (8)	7.15
Nos. C6-C13 (8)	6.00
Nos. C6-C13 (8)	7.95
Nos. C6-C13 (8)	7.95
Nos. C6-C13 (8)	6.30
Nos. C6-C13 (8)	6.25
Nos. C17-C25 (9)	9.45
Nos. C6-C13 (8)	6.55
Set total (65) Stamps	57.60

Red Cross

Marianne CD90

The surtax was for the French Red Cross and national relief.

1944

Cameroun B28
Fr. Equatorial Africa B38
Fr. Guiana B12
Fr. India B14
Fr. Polynesia B13
Fr. West Africa B1
Guadeloupe B12
Madagascar B15
Martinique B11
New Caledonia B13
Reunion B15
St. Pierre & Miquelon B13
Somali Coast B13
Wallis & Futuna Isls. B9

No. B28 (1)	2.00	1.60
No. B38 (1)	1.60	1.20
No. B12 (1)	1.75	1.25
No. B14 (1)	1.50	1.25
No. B13 (1)	2.00	1.60
No. B1 (1)	6.50	4.75
No. B12 (1)	1.40	1.00
No. B15 (1)	.90	.90
No. B11 (1)	1.20	1.20
No. B13 (1)	1.50	1.50
No. B15 (1)	1.60	1.10
No. B13 (1)	2.75	2.40
No. B13 (1)	2.40	2.00
No. B9 (1)	4.50	3.25
Set total (14) Stamps	31.60	25.00

Eboue

CD91

Felix Eboue, first French colonial administrator to proclaim resistance to Germany after French surrender in World War II.

1945

Cameroun 296-297
Fr. Equatorial Africa 156-157
Fr. Guiana 171-172
Fr. India 210-211
Fr. Polynesia 150-151
Fr. West Africa 15-16
Guadeloupe 187-188
Madagascar 259-260
Martinique 196-197
New Caledonia 274-275
Reunion 238-239
St. Pierre & Miquelon 322-323
Somali Coast 238-239

Nos. 296-297 (2)	2.55	1.95
Nos. 156-157 (2)	2.55	2.00
Nos. 171-172 (2)	2.45	2.00
Nos. 210-211 (2)	2.20	1.95
Nos. 150-151 (2)	3.60	2.85
Nos. 15-16 (2)	3.20	2.30
Nos. 187-188 (2)	2.05	1.60
Nos. 259-260 (2)	1.70	1.45
Nos. 196-197 (2)	2.05	1.55
Nos. 274-275 (2)	3.40	3.00
Nos. 238-239 (2)	2.40	2.00
Nos. 322-323 (2)	4.40	3.45
Nos. 238-239 (2)	3.25	3.25
Set total (26) Stamps	35.80	29.35

Victory

Victory — CD92

European victory of the Allied Nations in World War II.

1946, May 8

Cameroun C8
Fr. Equatorial Africa C24
Fr. Guiana C11
Fr. India C7
Fr. Polynesia C10
Fr. West Africa C4
Guadeloupe C3
Indo-China C19
Madagascar C44
Martinique C3
New Caledonia C14
Reunion C25
St. Pierre & Miquelon C8
Somali Coast C8
Wallis & Futuna Isls. C1

No. C8 (1)	1.60	1.20
No. C24 (1)	1.60	1.25
No. C11 (1)	1.75	1.25
No. C7 (1)	1.00	.95
No. C10 (1)	2.75	2.00
No. C4 (1)	1.60	1.20
No. C3 (1)	1.25	1.00
No. C19 (1)	1.00	.55
No. C44 (1)	.90	.35
No. C3 (1)	1.30	1.00
No. C14 (1)	2.25	1.25
No. C25 (1)	1.10	.90
No. C8 (1)	2.10	1.75
No. C8 (1)	2.00	1.60
No. C1 (1)	2.50	1.90
Set total (15) Stamps	24.70	18.15

Chad to Rhine

Leclerc's Departure from Chad — CD93

Battle at Cufra Oasis — CD94

Tanks in Action, Mareth — CD95

Normandy Invasion — CD96

Entering Paris — CD97

Liberation of Strasbourg — CD98

"Chad to the Rhine" march, 1942-44, by Gen. Jacques Leclerc's column, later French 2nd Armored Division.

1946, June 6

Cameroun C9-C14
Fr. Equatorial Africa C25-C30
Fr. Guiana C12-C17
Fr. India C8-C13
Fr. Polynesia C11-C16
Fr. West Africa C5-C10
Guadeloupe C4-C9
Indo-China C20-C25
Madagascar C45-C50
Martinique C4-C9
New Caledonia C15-C20
Reunion C26-C31
St. Pierre & Miquelon C9-C14
Somali Coast C9-C14
Wallis & Futuna Isls. C2-C7

Nos. C9-C14 (6)	12.05	9.70
Nos. C25-C30 (6)	13.40	10.25
Nos. C12-C17 (6)	12.65	10.35
Nos. C8-C13 (6)	12.80	9.20
Nos. C11-C16 (6)	17.55	13.40
Nos. C5-C10 (6)	14.40	11.30
Nos. C4-C9 (6)	12.00	9.60
Nos. C20-C25 (6)	6.40	6.40
Nos. C45-C50 (6)	10.30	8.40
Nos. C4-C9 (6)	8.85	7.30
Nos. C15-C20 (6)	13.40	11.90
Nos. C26-C31 (6)	10.25	6.55
Nos. C9-C14 (6)	17.30	14.35
Nos. C9-C14 (6)	19.35	14.60
Nos. C2-C7 (6)	13.75	10.45
Set total (90) Stamps	194.45	153.75

UPU

French Colonials, Globe and Plane — CD99

Universal Postal Union, 75th anniv.

1949, July 4

Cameroun C29
Fr. Equatorial Africa C34
Fr. India C17
Fr. Polynesia C20
Fr. West Africa C15
Indo-China C26
Madagascar C55
New Caledonia C24
St. Pierre & Miquelon C18
Somali Coast C18
Togo C18
Wallis & Futuna Isls. C10

No. C29 (1)	8.00	4.75
No. C34 (1)	14.50	11.00
No. C17 (1)	11.50	8.75
No. C20 (1)	20.00	15.00
No. C15 (1)	12.50	8.75
No. C26 (1)	4.75	4.00
No. C55 (1)	4.00	2.75
No. C24 (1)	8.25	5.25
No. C18 (1)	20.00	12.00
No. C18 (1)	13.50	11.00
No. C18 (1)	8.75	7.25
No. C10 (1)	12.50	8.25
Set total (12) Stamps	138.25	98.75

Tropical Medicine

Doctor Treating Infant CD100

The surtax was for charitable work.

1950

Cameroun B29
Fr. Equatorial Africa B39
Fr. India B15
Fr. Polynesia B14
Fr. West Africa B3
Madagascar B17
New Caledonia B14
St. Pierre & Miquelon B14
Somali Coast B14
Togo B11

No. B29 (1)	7.25	5.50
No. B39 (1)	7.25	5.50
No. B15 (1)	6.00	4.00
No. B14 (1)	10.50	8.00
No. B3 (1)	9.50	7.25
No. B17 (1)	5.50	5.50
No. B14 (1)	6.75	5.25
No. B14 (1)	17.00	13.00
No. B14 (1)	8.75	7.25
No. B11 (1)	5.50	4.00
Set total (10) Stamps	84.00	65.25

Military Medal

Medal, Early Marine and Colonial Soldier — CD101

Centenary of the creation of the French Military Medal.

1952

Cameroun 322
Comoro Isls. 39
Fr. Equatorial Africa 186

Fr. India 233
Fr. Polynesia 179
Fr. West Africa 57
Madagascar 286
New Caledonia 295
St. Pierre & Miquelon 345
Somali Coast 267
Togo 327
Wallis & Futuna Isls. 149

No. 322 (1)	7.25	3.25
No. 39 (1)	52.50	40.00
No. 186 (1)	7.25	5.50
No. 233 (1)	7.00	4.75
No. 179 (1)	13.50	10.00
No. 57 (1)	8.75	6.50
No. 286 (1)	3.75	2.50
No. 295 (1)	7.50	6.00
No. 345 (1)	17.00	13.00
No. 267 (1)	10.50	8.75
No. 327 (1)	6.50	4.75
No. 149 (1)	9.50	7.00
Set total (12) Stamps	151.00	112.00

Liberation

Allied Landing, Victory Sign and Cross of Lorraine — CD102

Liberation of France, 10th anniv.

1954, June 6

Cameroun C32
Comoro Isls. C4
Fr. Equatorial Africa C38
Fr. India C18
Fr. Polynesia C22
Fr. West Africa C17
Madagascar C57
New Caledonia C25
St. Pierre & Miquelon C19
Somali Coast C19
Togo C19
Wallis & Futuna Isls. C11

No. C32 (1)	7.25	4.75
No. C4 (1)	47.50	24.00
No. C38 (1)	9.50	7.25
No. C18 (1)	11.00	8.00
No. C22 (1)	10.00	8.00
No. C17 (1)	9.50	5.50
No. C57 (1)	3.25	2.00
No. C25 (1)	8.25	5.00
No. C19 (1)	18.00	12.00
No. C19 (1)	12.00	9.50
No. C19 (1)	8.00	6.50
No. C11 (1)	12.50	8.25
Set total (12) Stamps	156.75	100.75

FIDES

Plowmen CD103

Efforts of FIDES, the Economic and Social Development Fund for Overseas Possessions (Fonds d' Investissement pour le Developpement Economique et Social). Each stamp has a different design.

1956

Cameroun 326-329
Comoro Isls. 43
Fr. Equatorial Africa 189-192
Fr. Polynesia 181
Fr. West Africa 65-72
Madagascar 292-295
New Caledonia 303
St. Pierre & Miquelon 350
Somali Coast 268-269
Togo 331

Nos. 326-329 (4)	6.90	3.20
No. 43 (1)	2.75	1.60
Nos. 189-192 (4)	3.35	1.75
No. 181 (1)	4.00	2.00
Nos. 65-72 (8)	13.55	6.35
Nos. 292-295 (4)	2.25	1.20
No. 303 (1)	1.90	1.10
No. 350 (1)	6.50	3.50
Nos. 268-269 (2)	5.90	3.60
No. 331 (1)	4.75	2.40
Set total (27) Stamps	51.85	26.70

Flower

CD104

Each stamp shows a different flower.

1958-9

Cameroun 333
Comoro Isls. 45
Fr. Equatorial Africa 200-201
Fr. Polynesia 192
Fr. So. & Antarctic Terr. 11
Fr. West Africa 79-83
Madagascar 301-302
New Caledonia 304-305
St. Pierre & Miquelon 357
Somali Coast 270
Togo 348-349
Wallis & Futuna Isls. 152

No. 333 (1)	1.60	.80
No. 45 (1)	6.50	4.50
Nos. 200-201 (2)	3.30	1.60
No. 192 (1)	6.50	4.00
No. 11 (1)	10.00	8.00
Nos. 79-83 (5)	8.85	4.75
Nos. 301-302 (2)	1.50	.55
Nos. 304-305 (2)	9.25	3.00
No. 357 (1)	4.50	2.40
No. 270 (1)	4.00	1.60
Nos. 348-349 (2)	1.00	.50
No. 152 (1)	4.50	2.50
Set total (20) Stamps	61.50	34.20

Human Rights

Sun, Dove and U.N. Emblem CD105

10th anniversary of the signing of the Universal Declaration of Human Rights.

1958

Comoro Isls. 44
Fr. Equatorial Africa 202
Fr. Polynesia 191
Fr. West Africa 85
Madagascar 300
New Caledonia 306
St. Pierre & Miquelon 356
Somali Coast 274
Wallis & Futuna Isls. 153

No. 44 (1)	15.00	11.00
No. 202 (1)	2.40	1.25
No. 191 (1)	13.00	8.75
No. 85 (1)	2.40	2.00
No. 300 (1)	.80	.40
No. 306 (1)	3.00	1.50
No. 356 (1)	3.50	2.50
No. 274 (1)	3.25	2.40
No. 53 (1)	5.75	4.00
Set total (9) Stamps	49.10	33.80

C.C.T.A.

CD106

Commission for Technical Cooperation in Africa south of the Sahara, 10th anniv.

1960

Cameroun 339
Cent. Africa 3
Chad 66
Congo, P.R. 90
Dahomey 138
Gabon 150
Ivory Coast 180
Madagascar 317
Mali 9
Mauritania 117
Niger 104
Upper Volta 89

No. 339 (1)	1.60	.40
No. 3 (1)	1.90	.65
No. 66 (1)	1.75	.35
No. 90 (1)	1.00	1.00
No. 138 (1)	.50	.25
No. 150 (1)	1.10	1.10
No. 180 (1)	1.10	.50
No. 317 (1)	.60	.30
No. 9 (1)	1.40	.50
No. 117 (1)	.75	.40
No. 104 (1)	.85	.45
No. 89 (1)	.45	.40
Set total (12) Stamps	13.00	6.30

Air Afrique, 1961

Modern and Ancient Africa, Map and Planes — CD107

Founding of Air Afrique (African Airlines).

1961-62

Cameroun C37
Cent. Africa C5
Chad C7
Congo, P.R. C5
Dahomey C17
Gabon C5
Ivory Coast C18
Mauritania C17
Niger C22
Senegal C31
Upper Volta C4

No. C37 (1)	1.00	.50
No. C5 (1)	1.00	.55
No. C7 (1)	1.00	.25
No. C5 (1)	1.75	.90
No. C17 (1)	.80	.40
No. C7 (1)	.75	.25
No. C18 (1)	2.00	1.25
No. C17 (1)	2.50	1.25
No. C22 (1)	1.75	.90
No. C31 (1)	.80	.30
No. C4 (1)	.65	.45
Set total (11) Stamps	14.00	7.00

Anti-Malaria

CD108

World Health Organization drive to eradicate malaria.

1962, Apr. 7

Cameroun B36
Cent. Africa B1
Chad B1
Comoro Isls. B1
Congo, P.R. B3
Dahomey B15
Gabon B4
Ivory Coast B15
Madagascar B19
Mali B1
Mauritania B16
Niger B14
Senegal B16
Somali Coast B15
Upper Volta B1

No. B36 (1)	1.00	.45
No. B1 (1)	1.40	1.40
No. B1 (1)	1.00	.45
No. B1 (1)	4.00	4.00
No. B3 (1)	1.00	1.00
No. B15 (1)	.75	.75
No. B4 (1)	1.00	1.00
No. B15 (1)	1.25	1.25
No. B19 (1)	.90	.50
No. B1 (1)	1.25	.60
No. B16 (1)	.80	.80
No. B14 (1)	.60	.60
No. B16 (1)	1.10	.65
No. B15 (1)	7.25	7.25
No. B1 (1)	.95	.95
Set total (15) Stamps	24.25	21.65

Abidjan Games

CD109

Abidjan Games, Ivory Coast, Dec. 24-31, 1961. Each stamp shows a different sport.

1962

Cent. Africa 19-20, C6
Chad 83-84, C8
Congo, P.R. 103-104, C7
Gabon 163-164, C6
Niger 109-111
Upper Volta 103-105

Nos. 19-20,C6 (3)	3.90	2.60
Nos. 83-84,C8 (3)	6.30	1.30
Nos. 103-104,C7 (3)	3.85	1.80
Nos. 163-164,C6 (3)	5.75	3.75
Nos. 109-111 (3)	2.60	1.10
Nos. 103-105 (3)	3.15	1.80
Set total (18) Stamps	25.55	12.35

African and Malagasy Union

Flag of Union CD110

First anniversary of the Union.

1962, Sept. 8

Cameroun 373
Cent. Africa 21
Chad 85
Congo, P.R. 105
Dahomey 155
Gabon 165
Ivory Coast 198
Madagascar 332
Mauritania 170
Niger 112
Senegal 211
Upper Volta 106

No. 373 (1)	2.00	.45
No. 21 (1)	1.25	.60
No. 85 (1)	1.25	.25
No. 105 (1)	1.20	.40
No. 155 (1)	1.25	.90
No. 165 (1)	1.60	1.25
No. 198 (1)	2.10	.75
No. 332 (1)	.80	.80
No. 170 (1)	.75	.50
No. 112 (1)	.80	.40
No. 211 (1)	.80	.50
No. 106 (1)	1.50	.90
Set total (12) Stamps	15.30	7.70

Telstar

Telstar and Globe Showing Andover and Pleumeur-Bodou — CD111

First television connection of the United States and Europe through the Telstar satellite, July 11-12, 1962.

1962-63

Andorra, French 154
Comoro Isls. C7
Fr. Polynesia C29
Fr. So. & Antarctic Terr. C5
New Caledonia C33
St. Pierre & Miquelon C26
Somali Coast C31
Wallis & Futuna Isls. C17

No. 154 (1)	2.00	1.60
No. C7 (1)	6.50	4.75
No. C29 (1)	11.50	8.00

No. C5 (1)	29.00	21.00
No. C33 (1)	30.00	18.50
No. C26 (1)	7.25	5.50
No. C31 (1)	1.00	1.00
No. C17 (1)	3.50	3.50
Set total (8) Stamps	90.75	63.85

Freedom From Hunger

World Map and Wheat Emblem CD112

U.N. Food and Agriculture Organization's "Freedom from Hunger" campaign.

1963, Mar. 21

Cameroun	B37-B38
Cent. Africa	B2
Chad	B2
Congo, P.R.	B4
Dahomey	B16
Gabon	B5
Ivory Coast	B16
Madagascar	B21
Mauritania	B17
Niger	B15
Senegal	B17
Upper Volta	B2

Nos. B37-B38 (2)	2.25	.75
No. B2 (1)	1.25	1.25
No. B2 (1)	1.00	.45
No. B4 (1)	1.25	1.00
No. B16 (1)	.80	.80
No. B5 (1)	1.00	1.00
No. B16 (1)	1.50	1.50
No. B21 (1)	.70	.45
No. B17 (1)	.80	.80
No. B15 (1)	.60	.60
No. B17 (1)	.80	.50
No. B2 (1)	.95	.95
Set total (13) Stamps	12.90	10.05

Red Cross Centenary

CD113

Centenary of the International Red Cross.

1963, Sept. 2

Comoro Isls.	55
Fr. Polynesia	205
New Caledonia	328
St. Pierre & Miquelon	367
Somali Coast	297
Wallis & Futuna Isls.	165

No. 55 (1)	9.50	8.00
No. 205 (1)	15.00	12.00
No. 328 (1)	9.00	6.75
No. 367 (1)	12.00	6.75
No. 297 (1)	7.25	7.25
No. 165 (1)	4.00	3.50
Set total (6) Stamps	56.75	44.25

African Postal Union, 1963

UAMPT Emblem, Radio Masts, Plane and Mail CD114

Establishment of the African and Malagasy Posts and Telecommunications Union.

1963, Sept. 8

Cameroun	C47
Cent. Africa	C10
Chad	C9
Congo, P.R.	C13
Dahomey	C19
Gabon	C13
Ivory Coast	C25
Madagascar	C75
Mauritania	C22
Niger	C27
Rwanda	36
Senegal	C32
Upper Volta	C9

No. C47 (1)	2.25	1.00
No. C10 (1)	1.90	.85
No. C9 (1)	2.40	.40
No. C13 (1)	1.25	.75
No. C19 (1)	.75	.25
No. C13 (1)	1.90	.80
No. C25 (1)	2.50	1.50
No. C75 (1)	1.25	.80
No. C22 (1)	1.75	.60
No. C27 (1)	1.25	.60
No. 36 (1)	.75	.55
No. C32 (1)	1.75	.50
No. C9 (1)	1.50	.75
Set total (13) Stamps	21.20	9.35

Air Afrique, 1963

Symbols of Flight — CD115

First anniversary of Air Afrique and inauguration of DC-8 service.

1963, Nov. 19

Cameroun	C48
Chad	C10
Congo, P.R.	C14
Gabon	C18
Ivory Coast	C26
Mauritania	C26
Niger	C35
Senegal	C33

No. C48 (1)	1.25	.40
No. C10 (1)	2.40	.40
No. C14 (1)	.85	.50
No. C18 (1)	1.25	.65
No. C26 (1)	1.00	.50
No. C26 (1)	.70	.25
No. C35 (1)	.90	.50
No. C33 (1)	2.00	.65
Set total (8) Stamps	10.35	3.85

Europafrica

Europe and Africa Linked — CD116

Signing of an economic agreement between the European Economic Community and the African and Malagasy Union, Yaounde, Cameroun, July 20, 1963.

1963-64

Cameroun	402
Cent. Africa	C12
Chad	C11
Congo, P.R.	C16
Gabon	C19
Ivory Coast	217
Niger	C43
Upper Volta	C11

No. 402 (1)	2.25	.60
No. C12 (1)	2.50	1.75
No. C11 (1)	1.75	.40
No. C16 (1)	1.50	1.00
No. C19 (1)	1.60	.75
No. 217 (1)	1.10	.35
No. C43 (1)	.85	.50
No. C11 (1)	1.50	.80
Set total (8) Stamps	13.05	6.15

Human Rights

Scales of Justice and Globe CD117

15th anniversary of the Universal Declaration of Human Rights.

1963, Dec. 10

Comoro Isls.	56
Fr. Polynesia	206
New Caledonia	329
St. Pierre & Miquelon	368
Somali Coast	300
Wallis & Futuna Isls.	166

No. 56 (1)	9.50	8.00
No. 206 (1)	15.00	10.00
No. 329 (1)	8.00	6.00
No. 368 (1)	6.50	3.50
No. 300 (1)	9.50	9.50
No. 166 (1)	8.00	7.50
Set total (6) Stamps	56.50	44.50

PHILATEC

Stamp Album, Champs Elysees Palace and Horses of Marly CD118

Intl. Philatelic and Postal Techniques Exhibition, Paris, June 5-21, 1964.

1963-64

Comoro Isls.	60
France	1078
Fr. Polynesia	207
New Caledonia	341
St. Pierre & Miquelon	369
Somali Coast	301
Wallis & Futuna Isls.	167

No. 60 (1)	4.75	4.75
No. 1078 (1)	.25	.25
No. 207 (1)	18.00	12.50
No. 341 (1)	8.50	6.75
No. 369 (1)	11.00	8.00
No. 301 (1)	8.75	8.75
No. 167 (1)	3.50	3.50
Set total (7) Stamps	54.75	44.50

Cooperation

CD119

Cooperation between France and the French-speaking countries of Africa and Madagascar.

1964

Cameroun	409-410
Cent. Africa	39
Chad	103
Congo, P.R.	121
Dahomey	193
France	1111
Gabon	175
Ivory Coast	221
Madagascar	360
Mauritania	181
Niger	143
Senegal	236
Togo	495

Nos. 409-410 (2)	2.50	.50
No. 39 (1)	1.00	.55
No. 103 (1)	1.00	.25
No. 121 (1)	.60	.35
No. 193 (1)	.80	.35
No. 1111 (1)	.25	.25
No. 175 (1)	.90	.60
No. 221 (1)	1.10	.35
No. 360 (1)	.60	.25
No. 181 (1)	.60	.35
No. 143 (1)	.80	.40
No. 236 (1)	1.60	.85
No. 495 (1)	.80	.25
Set total (14) Stamps	12.55	5.30

ITU

Telegraph, Syncom Satellite and ITU Emblem CD120

Intl. Telecommunication Union, Cent.

1965, May 17

Comoro Isls.	C14
Fr. Polynesia	C33
Fr. So. & Antarctic Terr.	C8
New Caledonia	C40
New Hebrides	124-125
St. Pierre & Miquelon	C29
Somali Coast	C36
Wallis & Futuna Isls.	C20

No. C14 (1)	24.00	17.50
No. C33 (1)	80.00	52.50
No. C8 (1)	200.00	160.00
No. C40 (1)	12.00	9.00
Nos. 124-125 (2)	40.50	34.00
No. C29 (1)	24.00	11.00
No. C36 (1)	17.50	10.50
No. C20 (1)	21.00	15.00
Set total (9) Stamps	419.00	309.50

French Satellite A-1

Diamant Rocket and Launching Installation — CD121

Launching of France's first satellite, Nov. 26, 1965.

1965-66

Comoro Isls.	C16a
France	1138a
Reunion	359a
Fr. Polynesia	C41a
Fr. So. & Antarctic Terr.	C10a
New Caledonia	C45a
St. Pierre & Miquelon	C31a
Somali Coast	C40a
Wallis & Futuna Isls.	C23a

No. C16a (1)	11.00	11.00
No. 1138a (1)	.65	.65
No. 359a (1)	3.50	3.00
No. C41a (1)	14.00	14.00
No. C10a (1)	29.00	24.00
No. C45a (1)	8.25	7.00
No. C31a (1)	15.00	15.00
No. C40a (1)	9.00	9.00
No. C23a (1)	9.25	9.25
Set total (9) Stamps	99.65	92.90

French Satellite D-1

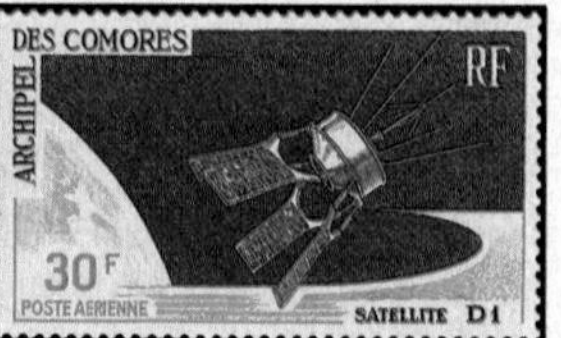

D-1 Satellite in Orbit — CD122

Launching of the D-1 satellite at Hammaguir, Algeria, Feb. 17, 1966.

1966

Comoro Isls.	C17
France	1148

Fr. Polynesia C42
Fr. So. & Antarctic Terr. C11
New Caledonia C46
St. Pierre & Miquelon C32
Somali Coast C49
Wallis & Futuna Isls. C24

No. C17 (1)	4.00	4.00
No. 1148 (1)	.25	.25
No. C42 (1)	7.00	4.75
No. C11 (1)	57.50	40.00
No. C46 (1)	3.00	2.00
No. C32 (1)	10.50	6.50
No. C49 (1)	4.75	3.25
No. C24 (1)	3.50	3.50
Set total (8) Stamps	90.50	64.25

Air Afrique, 1966

Planes and Air Afrique Emblem — CD123

Introduction of DC-8F planes by Air Afrique.

1966

Cameroun C79
Cent. Africa C35
Chad C26
Congo, P.R. C42
Dahomey C42
Gabon C47
Ivory Coast C32
Mauritania C57
Niger C63
Senegal C47
Togo C54
Upper Volta C31

No. C79 (1)	.80	.25
No. C35 (1)	1.00	.40
No. C26 (1)	.75	.25
No. C42 (1)	.60	.25
No. C42 (1)	.75	.25
No. C47 (1)	1.00	.60
No. C32 (1)	1.00	.60
No. C57 (1)	.80	.30
No. C63 (1)	.60	.35
No. C47 (1)	.80	.30
No. C54 (1)	.80	.25
No. C31 (1)	.75	.50
Set total (12) Stamps	9.65	4.30

African Postal Union, 1967

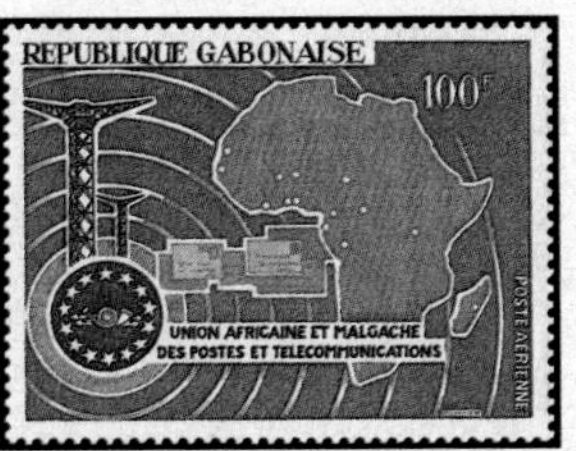

Telecommunications Symbols and Map of Africa — CD124

Fifth anniversary of the establishment of the African and Malagasy Union of Posts and Telecommunications, UAMPT.

1967

Cameroun C90
Cent. Africa C46
Chad C37
Congo, P.R. C57
Dahomey C61
Gabon C58
Ivory Coast C34
Madagascar C85
Mauritania C65
Niger C75
Rwanda C1-C3
Senegal C60
Togo C81
Upper Volta C50

No. C90 (1)	2.40	.65
No. C46 (1)	2.25	.85
No. C37 (1)	1.90	.40
No. C57 (1)	1.25	.60
No. C61 (1)	1.75	.95
No. C58 (1)	2.25	.95
No. C34 (1)	3.50	1.50
No. C85 (1)	1.25	.60
No. C65 (1)	1.25	.60
No. C75 (1)	1.40	.60

Nos. C1-C3 (3)	2.30	1.25
No. C60 (1)	1.75	.50
No. C81 (1)	1.90	.30
No. C50 (1)	1.80	.70
Set total (16) Stamps	26.95	10.45

Monetary Union

Gold Token of the Ashantis, 17-18th Centuries — CD125

West African Monetary Union, 5th anniv.

1967, Nov. 4

Dahomey 244
Ivory Coast 259
Mauritania 238
Niger 204
Senegal 294
Togo 623
Upper Volta 181

No. 244 (1)	.65	.65
No. 259 (1)	.85	.40
No. 238 (1)	.45	.25
No. 204 (1)	.45	.25
No. 294 (1)	.60	.25
No. 623 (1)	.60	.25
No. 181 (1)	.70	.35
Set total (7) Stamps	4.30	2.40

WHO Anniversary

Sun, Flowers and WHO Emblem CD126

World Health Organization, 20th anniv.

1968, May 4

Afars & Issas 317
Comoro Isls. 73
Fr. Polynesia 241-242
Fr. So. & Antarctic Terr. 31
New Caledonia 367
St. Pierre & Miquelon 377
Wallis & Futuna Isls. 169

No. 317 (1)	3.25	2.25
No. 73 (1)	3.25	3.25
Nos. 241-242 (2)	22.00	12.75
No. 31 (1)	65.00	45.00
No. 367 (1)	4.50	2.25
No. 377 (1)	12.00	8.00
No. 169 (1)	6.50	4.50
Set total (8) Stamps	116.50	78.00

Human Rights Year

Human Rights Flame — CD127

1968, Aug. 10

Afars & Issas 322-323
Comoro Isls. 76
Fr. Polynesia 243-244
Fr. So. & Antarctic Terr. 32
New Caledonia 369
St. Pierre & Miquelon 382
Wallis & Futuna Isls. 170

Nos. 322-323 (2)	7.00	4.25
No. 76 (1)	4.00	4.00
Nos. 243-244 (2)	24.00	14.00
No. 31 (1)	65.00	45.00
No. 369 (1)	3.00	1.50
No. 382 (1)	10.00	5.50
No. 170 (1)	3.75	3.75
Set total (9) Stamps	116.75	78.00

2nd PHILEXAFRIQUE

CD128

Opening of PHILEXAFRIQUE, Abidjan, Feb. 14. Each stamp shows a local scene and stamp.

1969, Feb. 14

Cameroun C118
Cent. Africa C65
Chad C48
Congo, P.R. C77
Dahomey C94
Gabon C82
Ivory Coast C38-C40
Madagascar C92
Mali C65
Mauritania C80
Niger C104
Senegal C68
Togo C104
Upper Volta C62

No. C118 (1)	3.25	.55
No. C65 (1)	1.90	1.90
No. C48 (1)	2.25	1.25
No. C77 (1)	1.75	1.75
No. C94 (1)	2.25	2.25
No. C82 (1)	2.25	2.25
Nos. C38-C40 (3)	14.50	14.50
No. C92 (1)	1.75	.85
No. C65 (1)	2.00	1.00
No. C80 (1)	1.90	.75
No. C104 (1)	2.75	1.90
No. C68 (1)	2.00	1.40
No. C104 (1)	2.25	.45
No. C62 (1)	4.00	3.75
Set total (16) Stamps	44.80	34.55

Concorde

Concorde in Flight CD129

First flight of the prototype Concorde supersonic plane at Toulouse, Mar. 1, 1969.

1969

Afars & Issas C56
Comoro Isls. C29
France C42
Fr. Polynesia C50
Fr. So. & Antarctic Terr. C18
New Caledonia C63
St. Pierre & Miquelon C40
Wallis & Futuna Isls. C30

No. C56 (1)	30.00	18.00
No. C29 (1)	24.00	16.00
No. C42 (1)	1.00	.35
No. C50 (1)	55.00	35.00
No. C18 (1)	55.00	37.50
No. C63 (1)	35.00	20.00
No. C40 (1)	32.50	12.00
No. C30 (1)	15.00	10.00
Set total (8) Stamps	247.50	148.85

Development Bank

Bank Emblem — CD130

African Development Bank, fifth anniv.

1969

Cameroun 499
Chad 217
Congo, P.R. 181-182
Ivory Coast 281
Mali 127-128
Mauritania 267
Niger 220
Senegal 317-318
Upper Volta 201

No. 499 (1)	.80	.25
No. 217 (1)	.70	.25
Nos. 181-182 (2)	.70	.50
No. 281 (1)	.70	.40
Nos. 127-128 (2)	1.25	.50
No. 267 (1)	.60	.25
No. 220 (1)	.60	.30
Nos. 317-318 (2)	1.55	.50
No. 201 (1)	.70	.30
Set total (12) Stamps	7.60	3.25

ILO

ILO Headquarters, Geneva, and Emblem — CD131

Intl. Labor Organization, 50th anniv.

1969-70

Afars & Issas 337
Comoro Isls. 83
Fr. Polynesia 251-252
Fr. So. & Antarctic Terr. 35
New Caledonia 379
St. Pierre & Miquelon 396
Wallis & Futuna Isls. 172

No. 337 (1)	3.00	2.25
No. 83 (1)	1.60	1.20
Nos. 251-252 (2)	24.00	12.50
No. 35 (1)	18.50	11.00
No. 379 (1)	2.25	1.10
No. 396 (1)	10.00	5.50
No. 172 (1)	3.00	2.90
Set total (8) Stamps	62.35	36.45

ASECNA

Map of Africa, Plane and Airport CD132

10th anniversary of the Agency for the Security of Aerial Navigation in Africa and Madagascar (ASECNA, Agence pour la Securite de la Navigation Aerienne en Afrique et a Madagascar).

1969-70

Cameroun 500
Cent. Africa 119
Chad 222
Congo, P.R. 197
Dahomey 269
Gabon 260
Ivory Coast 287
Mali 130
Niger 221
Senegal 321
Upper Volta 204

No. 500 (1)	2.00	.60
No. 119 (1)	2.25	.80
No. 222 (1)	.75	.25
No. 197 (1)	2.00	.40
No. 269 (1)	.90	.55
No. 260 (1)	2.00	.95
No. 287 (1)	.90	.40
No. 130 (1)	1.00	.40
No. 221 (1)	1.25	.70
No. 321 (1)	1.60	.50
No. 204 (1)	1.75	1.00
Set total (11) Stamps	16.40	6.55

U.P.U. Headquarters

CD133

New Universal Postal Union headquarters, Bern, Switzerland.

1970

Afars & Issas 342
Algeria 443
Cameroun 503-504
Cent. Africa 125
Chad 225
Comoro Isls. 84
Congo, P.R. 216
Fr. Polynesia 261-262
Fr. So. & Antarctic Terr. 36
Gabon 258
Ivory Coast 295
Madagascar 444
Mali 134-135
Mauritania 283
New Caledonia 382
Niger 231-232
St. Pierre & Miquelon 397-398
Senegal 328-329
Tunisia 535
Wallis & Futuna Isls. 173

No. 342 (1)	3.25	1.75
Nos. 503-504 (2)	2.60	.55
No. 125 (1)	1.90	.70
No. 225 (1)	.75	.25
No. 84 (1)	5.50	2.75
No. 216 (1)	.70	.25
Nos. 261-262 (2)	20.00	10.00
No. 36 (1)	45.00	29.00
No. 258 (1)	.90	.55
No. 295 (1)	1.10	.50
No. 444 (1)	.55	.25
Nos. 134-135 (2)	1.25	.50
No. 283 (1)	.60	.30
No. 382 (1)	3.00	1.50
Nos. 231-232 (2)	1.10	.60
Nos. 397-398 (2)	34.00	17.50
Nos. 328-329 (2)	1.55	.55
No. 535 (1)	.50	.25
No. 173 (1)	4.00	4.00
Set total (25) Stamps	128.25	71.75

De Gaulle

CD134

First anniversary of the death of Charles de Gaulle, (1890-1970), President of France.

1971-72

Afars & Issas 356-357
Comoro Isls. 104-105
France 1325a
Fr. Polynesia 270-271
Fr. So. & Antarctic Terr. 52-53
New Caledonia 393-394
Reunion 380a
St. Pierre & Miquelon 417-418
Wallis & Futuna Isls. 177-178

Nos. 356-357 (2)	16.00	9.50
Nos. 104-105 (2)	10.25	8.75
No. 1325a (1)	4.50	4.00
Nos. 270-271 (2)	51.50	29.50
Nos. 52-53 (2)	47.00	33.50
Nos. 393-394 (2)	25.00	11.75
No. 380a (1)	9.25	8.00
Nos. 417-418 (2)	57.50	30.00
Nos. 177-178 (2)	24.00	16.25
Set total (16) Stamps	245.00	151.25

African Postal Union, 1971

UAMPT Building, Brazzaville, Congo — CD135

10th anniversary of the establishment of the African and Malagasy Posts and Telecommunications Union, UAMPT. Each stamp has a different native design.

1971, Nov. 13

Cameroun C177
Cent. Africa C89
Chad C94
Congo, P.R. C136
Dahomey C146
Gabon C120
Ivory Coast C47
Mauritania C113
Niger C164
Rwanda C8
Senegal C105
Togo C166
Upper Volta C97

No. C177 (1)	2.00	.40
No. C89 (1)	2.25	.85
No. C94 (1)	1.50	.25
No. C136 (1)	1.40	.75
No. C146 (1)	1.75	.80
No. C120 (1)	2.00	.70
No. C47 (1)	2.00	1.00
No. C113 (1)	1.10	.65
No. C164 (1)	1.25	.60
No. C8 (1)	3.75	2.00
No. C105 (1)	1.60	.50
No. C166 (1)	1.25	.40
No. C97 (1)	1.50	.70
Set total (13) Stamps	23.35	9.60

West African Monetary Union

African Couple, City, Village and Commemorative Coin — CD136

West African Monetary Union, 10th anniv.

1972, Nov. 2

Dahomey 300
Ivory Coast 331
Mauritania 299
Niger 258
Senegal 374
Togo 825
Upper Volta 280

No. 300 (1)	.65	.25
No. 331 (1)	1.00	.50
No. 299 (1)	.75	.25
No. 258 (1)	.55	.30
No. 374 (1)	.50	.30
No. 825 (1)	.60	.25
No. 280 (1)	.60	.25
Set total (7) Stamps	4.65	2.10

African Postal Union, 1973

Telecommunications Symbols and Map of Africa — CD137

11th anniversary of the African and Malagasy Posts and Telecommunications Union (UAMPT).

1973, Sept. 12

Cameroun 574
Cent. Africa 194
Chad 294
Congo, P.R. 289
Dahomey 311
Gabon 320
Ivory Coast 361
Madagascar 500
Mauritania 304
Niger 287
Rwanda 540
Senegal 393
Togo 849
Upper Volta 297

No. 574 (1)	1.75	.40
No. 194 (1)	1.25	.75
No. 294 (1)	1.75	.40
No. 289 (1)	1.50	.45
No. 311 (1)	1.25	.55
No. 320 (1)	1.25	.75
No. 361 (1)	2.50	1.00
No. 500 (1)	1.00	.35
No. 304 (1)	1.10	.40
No. 287 (1)	.90	.60
No. 540 (1)	4.00	1.75
No. 393 (1)	1.60	.50
No. 849 (1)	1.25	.35
No. 297 (1)	1.25	.70
Set total (14) Stamps	22.35	8.95

Philexafrique II — Essen

CD138

CD139

Designs: Indigenous fauna, local and German stamps. Types CD138-CD139 printed horizontally and vertically se-tenant in sheets of 10 (2x5). Label between horizontal pairs alternately commemoratives Philexafrique II, Libreville, Gabon, June 1978, and 2nd International Stamp Fair, Essen, Germany, Nov. 1-5.

1978-1979

Benin C286a
Central Africa C201a
Chad C239a
Congo Republic C246a
Djibouti C122a
Gabon C216a
Ivory Coast C65a
Mali C357a
Mauritania C186a
Niger C292a
Rwanda C13a
Senegal C141a
Togo C364a

No. C286a (1)	10.00	10.00
No. C201a (1)	7.50	7.50
No. C239a (1)	8.00	4.00
No. C246a (1)	5.25	5.25
No. C122a (1)	8.50	8.50
No. C216a (1)	9.00	5.00
No. C65a (1)	9.00	9.00
No. C357a (1)	7.50	3.00
No. C186a (1)	4.50	4.00
No. C292a (1)	6.00	5.00
No. C13a (1)	4.00	4.00
No. C147a (1)	10.00	4.00
No. C364a (1)	5.00	5.00
Set total (13) Stamps	94.25	74.25

BRITISH COMMONWEALTH OF NATIONS

The listings follow established trade practices when these issues are offered as units by dealers. The Peace issue, for example, includes only one stamp from the Indian state of Hyderabad. The U.P.U. issue includes the Egypt set. Pairs are included for those varieties issued with bilingual designs se-tenant.

Silver Jubilee

Windsor Castle and King George V CD301

Reign of King George V, 25th anniv.

1935

Antigua 77-80
Ascension 33-36
Bahamas 92-95
Barbados 186-189
Basutoland 11-14
Bechuanaland Protectorate 117-120
Bermuda 100-103
British Guiana 223-226
British Honduras 108-111
Cayman Islands 81-84
Ceylon 260-263
Cyprus 136-139
Dominica 90-93
Falkland Islands 77-80
Fiji 110-113
Gambia 125-128
Gibraltar 100-103
Gilbert & Ellice Islands 33-36
Gold Coast 108-111
Grenada 124-127
Hong Kong 147-150
Jamaica 109-112
Kenya, Uganda, Tanzania 42-45
Leeward Islands 96-99
Malta 184-187
Mauritius 204-207
Montserrat 85-88
Newfoundland 226-229
Nigeria 34-37
Northern Rhodesia 18-21
Nyasaland Protectorate 47-50
St. Helena 111-114
St. Kitts-Nevis 72-75
St. Lucia 91-94
St. Vincent 134-137
Seychelles 118-121
Sierra Leone 166-169
Solomon Islands 60-63
Somaliland Protectorate 77-80
Straits Settlements 213-216
Swaziland 20-23
Trinidad & Tobago 43-46
Turks & Caicos Islands 71-74
Virgin Islands 69-72

The following have different designs but are included in the omnibus set:

Great Britain 226-229
Offices in Morocco (Sp. Curr.) 67-70
Offices in Morocco (Br. Curr.) 226-229
Offices in Morocco (Fr. Curr.) 422-425
Offices in Morocco (Tangier) 508-510
Australia 152-154
Canada 211-216
Cook Islands 98-100
India 142-148
Nauru 31-34
New Guinea 46-47
New Zealand 199-201
Niue 67-69
Papua 114-117
Samoa 163-165
South Africa 68-71
Southern Rhodesia 33-36
South-West Africa 121-124

Nos. 77-80 (4)	21.50	*22.75*
Nos. 33-36 (4)	61.00	*113.00*
Nos. 92-95 (4)	25.00	*43.00*
Nos. 186-189 (4)	35.75	54.60
Nos. 11-14 (4)	13.35	*20.00*
Nos. 117-120 (4)	13.75	23.00
Nos. 100-103 (4)	18.00	*58.25*
Nos. 223-226 (4)	18.35	35.50
Nos. 108-111 (4)	15.25	*15.35*
Nos. 81-84 (4)	16.95	17.75
Nos. 260-263 (4)	12.60	23.35
Nos. 136-139 (4)	39.75	*34.40*
Nos. 90-93 (4)	18.85	19.85
Nos. 77-80 (4)	50.00	13.35
Nos. 110-113 (4)	15.25	29.00
Nos. 125-128 (4)	18.55	*26.90*
Nos. 100-103 (4)	28.90	41.00
Nos. 33-36 (4)	39.50	*53.50*
Nos. 108-111 (4)	26.75	*62.85*
Nos. 124-127 (4)	16.60	*39.50*
Nos. 147-150 (4)	76.50	21.00
Nos. 109-112 (4)	19.80	34.50
Nos. 42-45 (4)	8.25	*10.75*
Nos. 96-99 (4)	28.50	32.10
Nos. 184-187 (4)	25.00	34.70
Nos. 204-207 (4)	47.60	58.25
Nos. 85-88 (4)	10.25	*30.25*
Nos. 226-229 (4)	17.00	12.05
Nos. 34-37 (4)	12.55	*59.75*
Nos. 18-21 (4)	15.75	16.25
Nos. 47-50 (4)	37.25	*80.25*
Nos. 111-114 (4)	31.15	*33.25*
Nos. 72-75 (4)	11.55	*18.50*
Nos. 91-94 (4)	16.00	*20.80*
Nos. 134-137 (4)	9.45	*21.25*
Nos. 118-121 (4)	17.50	*31.00*
Nos. 166-169 (4)	18.50	*55.00*
Nos. 60-63 (4)	27.50	38.00
Nos. 77-80 (4)	17.75	*46.00*
Nos. 213-216 (4)	15.00	*25.10*
Nos. 20-23 (4)	4.20	13.00
Nos. 43-46 (4)	12.30	27.75
Nos. 71-74 (4)	8.60	16.25
Nos. 69-72 (4)	22.20	47.50
Nos. 226-229 (4)	7.25	*7.45*
Nos. 67-70 (4)	14.35	*26.10*
Nos. 226-229 (4)	8.20	*28.90*
Nos. 422-425 (4)	3.90	2.00
Nos. 508-510 (3)	18.80	*23.85*
Nos. 152-154 (3)	45.75	60.35

Nos. 211-216 (6) 27.85 13.35
Nos. 98-100 (3) 6.75 14.00
Nos. 142-148 (7) 23.25 11.80
Nos. 31-34 (4) 12.60 13.85
Nos. 46-47 (2) 4.10 1.70
Nos. 199-201 (3) 21.75 31.75
Nos. 67-69 (3) 7.80 22.50
Nos. 114-117 (4) 9.20 17.00
Nos. 163-165 (3) 4.40 5.00
Nos. 68-71 (4) 62.50 167.00
Nos. 33-36 (4) 29.00 45.25
Nos. 121-124 (4) 14.50 36.10
Set total (245) Stamps 1,338. 2,058.

Coronation

Queen Elizabeth and King George VI CD302

1937

Aden....13-15
Antigua....81-83
Ascension....37-39
Bahamas....97-99
Barbados....190-192
Basutoland....15-17
Bechuanaland Protectorate....121-123
Bermuda....115-117
British Guiana....227-229
British Honduras....112-114
Cayman Islands....97-99
Ceylon....275-277
Cyprus....140-142
Dominica....94-96
Falkland Islands....81-83
Fiji....114-116
Gambia....129-131
Gibraltar....104-106
Gilbert & Ellice Islands....37-39
Gold Coast....112-114
Grenada....128-130
Hong Kong....151-153
Jamaica....113-115
Kenya, Uganda, Tanzania....60-62
Leeward Islands....100-102
Malta....188-190
Mauritius....208-210
Montserrat....89-91
Newfoundland....230-232
Nigeria....50-52
Northern Rhodesia....22-24
Nyasaland Protectorate....51-53
St. Helena....115-117
St. Kitts-Nevis....76-78
St. Lucia....107-109
St. Vincent....138-140
Seychelles....122-124
Sierra Leone....170-172
Solomon Islands....64-66
Somaliland Protectorate....81-83
Straits Settlements....235-237
Swaziland....24-26
Trinidad & Tobago....47-49
Turks & Caicos Islands....75-77
Virgin Islands....73-75

The following have different designs but are included in the omnibus set:

Great Britain....234
Offices in Morocco (Sp. Curr.)....82
Offices in Morocco (Fr. Curr.)....439
Offices in Morocco (Tangier)....514
Canada....237
Cook Islands....109-111
Nauru....35-38
Newfoundland....233-243
New Guinea....48-51
New Zealand....223-225
Niue....70-72
Papua....118-121
South Africa....74-78
Southern Rhodesia....38-41
South-West Africa....125-132

Nos. 13-15 (3) 3.00 6.10
Nos. 81-83 (3) 2.00 4.50
Nos. 37-39 (3) 2.75 2.75
Nos. 97-99 (3) 1.15 3.05
Nos. 190-192 (3) 1.10 1.95
Nos. 15-17 (3) 1.25 3.00
Nos. 121-123 (3) .95 3.35
Nos. 115-117 (3) 1.25 5.00
Nos. 227-229 (3) .80 3.05
Nos. 112-114 (3) 1.20 2.35
Nos. 97-99 (3) 1.10 2.30
Nos. 275-277 (3) 8.25 10.35
Nos. 140-142 (3) 3.75 6.50
Nos. 94-96 (3) .85 2.40
Nos. 81-83 (3) 2.90 2.30
Nos. 114-116 (3) 1.35 5.75
Nos. 129-131 (3) 1.00 4.70
Nos. 104-106 (3) 2.60 6.45
Nos. 37-39 (3) .95 2.00
Nos. 112-114 (3) 3.10 10.00
Nos. 128-130 (3) 1.00 .85
Nos. 151-153 (3) 27.00 12.50
Nos. 113-115 (3) 1.25 1.25
Nos. 60-62 (3) 1.05 1.60
Nos. 100-102 (3) 1.55 3.90
Nos. 188-190 (3) 1.35 1.65
Nos. 208-210 (3) 2.05 3.75
Nos. 89-91 (3) 1.00 3.35
Nos. 230-232 (3) 7.00 2.80
Nos. 50-52 (3) 3.25 8.50
Nos. 22-24 (3) 1.35 2.00
Nos. 51-53 (3) 1.05 1.30
Nos. 115-117 (3) 1.45 2.05
Nos. 76-78 (3) .95 2.05
Nos. 107-109 (3) 1.05 2.05
Nos. 138-140 (3) .80 4.75
Nos. 122-124 (3) 1.20 1.90
Nos. 170-172 (3) 1.95 5.65
Nos. 64-66 (3) .90 2.00
Nos. 81-83 (3) 1.10 3.40
Nos. 235-237 (3) 3.25 1.60
Nos. 24-26 (3) 1.05 1.35
Nos. 47-49 (3) 1.00 1.00
Nos. 75-77 (3) 1.30 1.55
Nos. 73-75 (3) 1.20 5.00

No. 234 (1) .25 .25
No. 82 (1) .80 .80
No. 439 (1) .35 .25
No. 514 (1) .55 .55
No. 237 (1) .30 .25
Nos. 109-111 (3) .85 .80
Nos. 35-38 (4) 1.15 5.50
Nos. 233-243 (11) 33.20 29.90
Nos. 48-51 (4) 1.40 7.90
Nos. 223-225 (3) 1.40 2.75
Nos. 70-72 (3) .80 2.05
Nos. 118-121 (4) 1.60 5.25
Nos. 74-78 (5) 9.25 11.05
Nos. 38-41 (4) 4.00 16.25
Nos. 125-132 (8) 5.50 8.45
Set total (189) Stamps 168.80 257.65

Peace

King George VI and Parliament Buildings, London CD303

Return to peace at the close of World War II.

1945-46

Aden....28-29
Antigua....96-97
Ascension....50-51
Bahamas....130-131
Barbados....207-208
Bermuda....131-132
British Guiana....242-243
British Honduras....127-128
Cayman Islands....112-113
Ceylon....293-294
Cyprus....156-157
Dominica....112-113
Falkland Islands....97-98
Falkland Islands Dep....1L9-1L10
Fiji....137-138
Gambia....144-145
Gibraltar....119-120
Gilbert & Ellice Islands....52-53
Gold Coast....128-129
Grenada....143-144
Jamaica....136-137
Kenya, Uganda, Tanzania....90-91
Leeward Islands....116-117
Malta....206-207
Mauritius....223-224
Montserrat....104-105
Nigeria....71-72
Northern Rhodesia....46-47
Nyasaland Protectorate....82-83
Pitcairn Islands....9-10
St. Helena....128-129
St. Kitts-Nevis....91-92
St. Lucia....127-128
St. Vincent....152-153
Seychelles....149-150
Sierra Leone....186-187
Solomon Islands....80-81
Somaliland Protectorate....108-109
Trinidad & Tobago....62-63
Turks & Caicos Islands....90-91
Virgin Islands....88-89

The following have different designs but are included in the omnibus set:

Great Britain....264-265
Offices in Morocco (Tangier)....523-524
Aden
Kathiri State of Seiyun....12-13
Qu'aiti State of Shihr and Mukalla....12-13
Australia....200-202
Basutoland....29-31
Bechuanaland Protectorate....137-139
Burma....66-69
Cook Islands....127-130
Hong Kong....174-175
India....195-198
Hyderabad....51-53
New Zealand....247-257
Niue....90-93
Pakistan-Bahawalpur....O16
Samoa....191-194
South Africa....100-102
Southern Rhodesia....67-70
South-West Africa....153-155
Swaziland....38-40
Zanzibar....222-223

Nos. 28-29 (2) .70 2.30
Nos. 96-97 (2) .50 .80
Nos. 50-51 (2) .90 1.75
Nos. 130-131 (2) .50 1.40
Nos. 207-208 (2) .50 1.10
Nos. 131-132 (2) .55 .55
Nos. 242-243 (2) 1.05 1.40
Nos. 127-128 (2) .50 .50
Nos. 112-113 (2) .60 .80
Nos. 293-294 (2) .60 2.10
Nos. 156-157 (2) 1.00 .70
Nos. 112-113 (2) .50 .50
Nos. 97-98 (2) .90 1.35
Nos. 1L9-1L10 (2) 1.40 1.00
Nos. 137-138 (2) .50 1.75
Nos. 144-145 (2) .50 .95
Nos. 119-120 (2) .75 1.00
Nos. 52-53 (2) .50 .50
Nos. 128-129 (2) 1.85 3.75
Nos. 143-144 (2) .50 .95
Nos. 136-137 (2) 5.55 7.50
Nos. 90-91 (2) .65 .65
Nos. 116-117 (2) .50 .50
Nos. 206-207 (2) .65 2.00
Nos. 223-224 (2) .50 1.05
Nos. 104-105 (2) .50 .50
Nos. 71-72 (2) .70 2.25
Nos. 46-47 (2) 1.25 2.00
Nos. 82-83 (2) .50 .50
Nos. 9-10 (2) 1.40 1.40
Nos. 128-129 (2) .65 .70
Nos. 91-92 (2) .50 .50
Nos. 127-128 (2) .50 .60
Nos. 152-153 (2) .50 .50
Nos. 149-150 (2) .55 .50
Nos. 186-187 (2) .50 .50
Nos. 80-81 (2) .50 1.30
Nos. 108-109 (2) .50 .50
Nos. 62-63 (2) .50 .50
Nos. 90-91 (2) .50 .50
Nos. 88-89 (2) .50 .50

Nos. 264-265 (2) .50 .70
Nos. 523-524 (2) 1.50 3.00
Nos. 12-13 (2) .50 .90
Nos. 12-13 (2) .50 1.05
Nos. 200-202 (3) 1.60 3.00
Nos. 29-31 (3) 2.10 2.60
Nos. 137-139 (3) 2.05 4.75
Nos. 66-69 (4) 1.60 1.30
Nos. 127-130 (4) 2.20 2.00
Nos. 174-175 (2) 10.25 3.00
Nos. 195-198 (4) 4.75 3.60
Nos. 51-53 (3) 1.50 1.70
Nos. 247-257 (11) 3.95 3.90
Nos. 90-93 (4) 1.70 2.20
No. O16 (1) 5.50 7.00
Nos. 191-194 (4) 1.80 1.00
Nos. 100-102 (3) 1.20 4.00
Nos. 67-70 (4) 1.40 1.75
Nos. 153-155 (3) 2.55 3.50
Nos. 38-40 (3) 2.40 6.50
Nos. 222-223 (2) .65 1.00
Set total (151) Stamps 82.90 108.55

Silver Wedding

King George VI and Queen Elizabeth
CD304 CD305

1948-49

Aden....30-31
Kathiri State of Seiyun....14-15
Qu'aiti State of Shihr and Mukalla....14-15
Antigua....98-99
Ascension....52-53
Bahamas....148-149
Barbados....210-211
Basutoland....39-40
Bechuanaland Protectorate....147-148
Bermuda....133-134
British Guiana....244-245
British Honduras....129-130
Cayman Islands....116-117
Cyprus....158-159
Dominica....114-115
Falkland Islands....99-100
Falkland Islands Dep....1L11-1L12
Fiji....139-140
Gambia....146-147
Gibraltar....121-122
Gilbert & Ellice Islands....54-55
Gold Coast....142-143
Grenada....145-146
Hong Kong....178-179
Jamaica....138-139
Kenya, Uganda, Tanzania....92-93
Leeward Islands....118-119
Malaya
Johore....128-129
Kedah....55-56
Kelantan....44-45
Malacca....1-2
Negri Sembilan....36-37
Pahang....44-45
Penang....1-2
Perak....99-100
Perlis....1-2
Selangor....74-75
Trengganu....47-48
Malta....223-224
Mauritius....229-230
Montserrat....106-107
Nigeria....73-74
North Borneo....238-239
Northern Rhodesia....48-49
Nyasaland Protectorate....85-86
Pitcairn Islands....11-12
St. Helena....130-131
St. Kitts-Nevis....93-94
St. Lucia....129-130
St. Vincent....154-155
Sarawak....174-175
Seychelles....151-152
Sierra Leone....188-189
Singapore....21-22
Solomon Islands....82-83
Somaliland Protectorate....110-111
Swaziland....48-49
Trinidad & Tobago....64-65
Turks & Caicos Islands....92-93
Virgin Islands....90-91
Zanzibar....224-225

The following have different designs but are included in the omnibus set:

Great Britain....267-268
Offices in Morocco (Sp. Curr.)....93-94
Offices in Morocco (Tangier)....525-526
Bahrain....62-63
Kuwait....82-83
Oman....25-26
South Africa....106
South-West Africa....159

Nos. 30-31 (2) 37.90 47.50
Nos. 14-15 (2) 21.50 16.00
Nos. 14-15 (2) 22.00 18.50
Nos. 98-99 (2) 15.00 14.25
Nos. 52-53 (2) 58.15 60.60
Nos. 148-149 (2) 45.25 40.30
Nos. 210-211 (2) 18.35 13.05
Nos. 39-40 (2) 50.30 50.25
Nos. 147-148 (2) 42.85 47.75
Nos. 133-134 (2) 47.75 55.25
Nos. 244-245 (2) 24.25 28.45
Nos. 129-130 (2) 22.75 53.20
Nos. 116-117 (2) 22.75 28.50
Nos. 158-159 (2) 58.50 78.05
Nos. 114-115 (2) 25.25 32.75
Nos. 99-100 (2) 112.10 83.60
Nos. 1L11-1L12 (2) 4.25 6.00
Nos. 139-140 (2) 18.20 10.75
Nos. 146-147 (2) 22.25 21.25
Nos. 121-122 (2) 71.00 90.50
Nos. 54-55 (2) 15.25 24.25
Nos. 142-143 (2) 29.25 29.25
Nos. 145-146 (2) 20.25 20.25
Nos. 178-179 (2) 403.50 111.00
Nos. 138-139 (2) 30.35 70.25
Nos. 92-93 (2) 45.25 70.25
Nos. 118-119 (2) 6.75 6.75
Nos. 128-129 (2) 29.25 53.25
Nos. 55-56 (2) 35.25 50.25
Nos. 44-45 (2) 35.75 62.75
Nos. 1-2 (2) 35.40 49.75
Nos. 36-37 (2) 28.10 38.20
Nos. 44-45 (2) 28.00 38.05
Nos. 1-2 (2) 40.50 37.80
Nos. 99-100 (2) 27.80 37.75
Nos. 1-2 (2) 33.50 58.00
Nos. 74-75 (2) 30.25 25.30

Nos. 47-48 (2)	35.25	*62.75*
Nos. 223-224 (2)	40.55	45.25
Nos. 229-230 (2)	17.75	*45.25*
Nos. 106-107 (2)	9.25	*18.25*
Nos. 73-74 (2)	13.85	*20.30*
Nos. 238-239 (2)	35.30	*45.75*
Nos. 48-49 (2)	92.80	80.25
Nos. 85-86 (2)	19.25	*32.75*
Nos. 11-12 (2)	56.75	53.50
Nos. 130-131 (2)	32.80	*42.80*
Nos. 93-94 (2)	11.25	7.25
Nos. 129-130 (2)	22.25	*45.25*
Nos. 154-155 (2)	27.75	*30.25*
Nos. 174-175 (2)	52.90	*55.40*
Nos. 151-152 (2)	16.25	*45.75*
Nos. 188-189 (2)	24.75	*26.25*
Nos. 21-22 (2)	146.25	55.40
Nos. 82-83 (2)	13.40	13.40
Nos. 110-111 (2)	7.00	*8.25*
Nos. 48-49 (2)	30.30	*40.25*
Nos. 64-65 (2)	32.75	*38.25*
Nos. 92-93 (2)	14.25	*19.30*
Nos. 90-91 (2)	18.85	21.35
Nos. 224-225 (2)	29.60	38.00
Nos. 267-268 (2)	40.40	40.25
Nos. 93-94 (2)	20.10	25.35
Nos. 525-526 (2)	23.10	29.25
Nos. 62-63 (2)	38.45	*72.50*
Nos. 82-83 (2)	45.50	45.50
Nos. 25-26 (2)	40.50	*47.50*
No. 106 (1)	.70	1.25
No. 159 (1)	1.25	.35
Set total (136) Stamps	2,626.	2,733.

U.P.U.

Mercury and Symbols of Communications — CD306

Plane, Ship and Hemispheres — CD307

Mercury Scattering Letters over Globe CD308

U.P.U. Monument, Bern CD309

Universal Postal Union, 75th anniversary.

1949

Aden 32-35
Kathiri State of Seiyun....16-19
Qu'aiti State of Shihr and Mukalla 16-19
Antigua 100-103
Ascension 57-60
Bahamas 150-153
Barbados 212-215
Basutoland....41-44
Bechuanaland Protectorate....149-152
Bermuda....138-141
British Guiana....246-249
British Honduras....137-140
Brunei....79-82
Cayman Islands....118-121
Cyprus....160-163
Dominica....116-119
Falkland Islands 103-106
Falkland Islands Dep....1L14-1L17
Fiji....141-144
Gambia....148-151
Gibraltar....123-126
Gilbert & Ellice Islands....56-59
Gold Coast....144-147
Grenada....147-150
Hong Kong 180-183
Jamaica 142-145
Kenya, Uganda, Tanzania 94-97
Leeward Islands 126-129
Malaya
Johore 151-154
Kedah....57-60
Kelantan....46-49
Malacca....18-21
Negri Sembilan 59-62
Pahang....46-49
Penang....23-26
Perak....101-104
Perlis 3-6
Selangor....76-79
Trengganu 49-52
Malta....225-228
Mauritius....231-234
Montserrat 108-111
New Hebrides, British 62-65
New Hebrides, French 79-82
Nigeria 75-78
North Borneo....240-243
Northern Rhodesia....50-53
Nyasaland Protectorate....87-90
Pitcairn Islands....13-16
St. Helena 132-135
St. Kitts-Nevis....95-98
St. Lucia 131-134
St. Vincent....170-173
Sarawak....176-179
Seychelles 153-156
Sierra Leone....190-193
Singapore 23-26
Solomon Islands....84-87
Somaliland Protectorate....112-115
Southern Rhodesia 71-72
Swaziland 50-53
Tonga....87-90
Trinidad & Tobago 66-69
Turks & Caicos Islands 101-104
Virgin Islands....92-95
Zanzibar....226-229

The following have different designs but are included in the omnibus set:

Great Britain 276-279
Offices in Morocco (Tangier) 546-549
Australia....223
Bahrain 68-71
Burma....116-121
Ceylon 304-306
Egypt 281-283
India....223-226
Kuwait....89-92
Oman....31-34
Pakistan-Bahawalpur 26-29, O25-O28
South Africa....109-111
South-West Africa 160-162

Nos. 32-35 (4)	6.60	*8.95*
Nos. 16-19 (4)	2.40	*6.80*
Nos. 16-19 (4)	2.55	3.25
Nos. 100-103 (4)	3.95	*6.60*
Nos. 57-60 (4)	10.90	7.75
Nos. 150-153 (4)	5.60	9.55
Nos. 212-215 (4)	4.40	14.15
Nos. 41-44 (4)	4.75	*10.00*
Nos. 149-152 (4)	3.35	*7.25*
Nos. 138-141 (4)	4.75	5.55
Nos. 246-249 (4)	2.65	4.20
Nos. 137-140 (4)	3.35	4.75
Nos. 79-82 (4)	7.75	6.75
Nos. 118-121 (4)	4.00	6.40
Nos. 160-163 (4)	4.60	8.30
Nos. 116-119 (4)	2.30	5.65
Nos. 103-106 (4)	15.65	18.10
Nos. 1L14-1L17 (4)	15.50	14.00
Nos. 141-144 (4)	3.35	14.00
Nos. 148-151 (4)	3.50	7.85
Nos. 123-126 (4)	6.75	9.50
Nos. 56-59 (4)	4.85	*8.75*
Nos. 144-147 (4)	3.05	*6.95*
Nos. 147-150 (4)	2.30	3.55
Nos. 180-183 (4)	72.25	19.75
Nos. 142-145 (4)	2.65	6.00
Nos. 94-97 (4)	2.90	3.40
Nos. 126-129 (4)	3.65	*3.75*
Nos. 151-154 (4)	4.70	8.90
Nos. 57-60 (4)	4.80	10.25
Nos. 46-49 (4)	4.25	11.15
Nos. 18-21 (4)	4.25	*17.30*
Nos. 59-62 (4)	3.50	10.75
Nos. 46-49 (4)	3.00	7.25
Nos. 23-26 (4)	5.10	11.75
Nos. 101-104 (4)	3.65	10.75
Nos. 3-6 (4)	3.95	14.25
Nos. 76-79 (4)	4.90	12.30
Nos. 49-52 (4)	4.95	9.75
Nos. 225-228 (4)	4.50	5.35
Nos. 231-234 (4)	4.35	6.70
Nos. 108-111 (4)	3.40	3.85
Nos. 62-65 (4)	1.60	*4.10*
Nos. 79-82 (4)	21.75	21.75
Nos. 75-78 (4)	2.80	*9.25*
Nos. 240-243 (4)	7.15	6.50
Nos. 50-53 (4)	5.00	*6.50*
Nos. 87-90 (4)	4.05	4.05
Nos. 13-16 (4)	27.00	18.75
Nos. 132-135 (4)	4.85	7.10
Nos. 95-98 (4)	3.35	4.70
Nos. 131-134 (4)	2.55	*3.85*
Nos. 170-173 (4)	2.20	*5.05*
Nos. 176-179 (4)	9.00	11.10
Nos. 153-156 (4)	3.25	4.10
Nos. 190-193 (4)	3.00	5.10
Nos. 23-26 (4)	24.25	14.20
Nos. 84-87 (4)	4.35	4.90
Nos. 112-115 (4)	2.45	7.95
Nos. 71-72 (2)	1.95	*2.25*
Nos. 50-53 (4)	3.00	2.20
Nos. 87-90 (4)	3.25	*5.25*
Nos. 66-69 (4)	3.15	3.15
Nos. 101-104 (4)	3.65	4.00
Nos. 92-95 (4)	2.60	4.60
Nos. 226-229 (4)	6.25	13.50
Nos. 276-279 (4)	1.85	2.40
Nos. 546-549 (4)	3.20	*10.15*
No. 223 (1)	.60	.55
Nos. 68-71 (4)	5.00	*16.75*
Nos. 116-121 (6)	7.15	5.30
Nos. 304-306 (3)	3.35	4.25
Nos. 281-283 (3)	5.75	2.70
Nos. 223-226 (4)	35.50	10.50
Nos. 89-92 (4)	8.75	10.00
Nos. 31-34 (4)	5.00	15.75
Nos. 26-29,O25-O28 (8)	2.00	*42.00*
Nos. 109-111 (3)	3.00	3.00
Nos. 160-162 (3)	3.95	6.00
Set total (313) Stamps	507.15	675.05

University

Arms of University College CD310

Alice, Princess of Athlone CD311

1948 opening of University College of the West Indies at Jamaica.

1951

Antigua 104-105
Barbados 228-229
British Guiana....250-251
British Honduras....141-142
Dominica....120-121
Grenada....164-165
Jamaica 146-147
Leeward Islands 130-131
Montserrat 112-113
St. Kitts-Nevis....105-106
St. Lucia 149-150
St. Vincent....174-175
Trinidad & Tobago 70-71
Virgin Islands....96-97

Nos. 104-105 (2)	1.35	*3.25*
Nos. 228-229 (2)	1.85	1.55
Nos. 250-251 (2)	1.10	*1.25*
Nos. 141-142 (2)	1.40	2.15
Nos. 120-121 (2)	1.40	*1.75*
Nos. 164-165 (2)	1.20	*1.60*
Nos. 146-147 (2)	.95	.85
Nos. 130-131 (2)	1.35	*2.00*
Nos. 112-113 (2)	.85	*1.50*
Nos. 105-106 (2)	.90	1.50
Nos. 149-150 (2)	1.40	1.50
Nos. 174-175 (2)	1.00	*2.15*
Nos. 70-71 (2)	.75	.75
Nos. 96-97 (2)	1.50	*3.40*
Set total (28) Stamps	17.00	25.20

Coronation

Queen Elizabeth II — CD312

1953

Aden 47
Kathiri State of Seiyun....28
Qu'aiti State of Shihr and Mukalla 28
Antigua 106
Ascension 61
Bahamas 157
Barbados....234
Basutoland....45
Bechuanaland Protectorate....153
Bermuda....142
British Guiana....252
British Honduras....143
Cayman Islands....150
Cyprus....167
Dominica....141
Falkland Islands 121
Falkland Islands Dependencies 1L18
Fiji....145
Gambia....152
Gibraltar....131
Gilbert & Ellice Islands....60
Gold Coast 160
Grenada....170
Hong Kong 184
Jamaica 153
Kenya, Uganda, Tanzania 101
Leeward Islands 132
Malaya
Johore 155
Kedah....82
Kelantan....71
Malacca....27
Negri Sembilan 63
Pahang....71
Penang....27
Perak....126
Perlis 28
Selangor....101
Trengganu 74
Malta....241
Mauritius....250
Montserrat 127
New Hebrides, British 77
Nigeria 79
North Borneo....260
Northern Rhodesia....60
Nyasaland Protectorate....96
Pitcairn Islands....19
St. Helena 139
St. Kitts-Nevis....119
St. Lucia 156
St. Vincent....185
Sarawak....196
Seychelles 172
Sierra Leone....194
Singapore 27
Solomon Islands....88
Somaliland Protectorate....127
Swaziland 54
Trinidad & Tobago 84
Tristan da Cunha....13
Turks & Caicos Islands 118
Virgin Islands....114

The following have different designs but are included in the omnibus set:

Great Britain....313-316
Offices in Morocco (Tangier) 579-582
Australia....259-261
Bahrain 92-95
Canada....330
Ceylon 317
Cook Islands 145-146
Kuwait....113-116
New Zealand 280-284
Niue 104-105
Oman....52-55
Samoa 214-215
South Africa....192
Southern Rhodesia 80
South-West Africa 244-248
Tokelau Islands....4

No. 47 (1)	1.25	1.25
No. 28 (1)	.40	*1.50*
No. 28 (1)	1.10	.60
No. 106 (1)	.50	*.75*
No. 61 (1)	1.25	1.25
No. 157 (1)	1.25	.75
No. 234 (1)	1.00	.25
No. 45 (1)	.50	*.60*
No. 153 (1)	.75	.35
No. 142 (1)	.85	.40
No. 252 (1)	.45	.25
No. 143 (1)	.55	.40
No. 150 (1)	.40	*1.00*
No. 167 (1)	1.50	1.00
No. 141 (1)	.40	.40
No. 121 (1)	.90	1.50
No. 1L18 (1)	1.50	1.50
No. 145 (1)	1.75	.60
No. 152 (1)	.45	.40
No. 131 (1)	.50	.50
No. 60 (1)	.65	2.25
No. 160 (1)	.95	.25
No. 170 (1)	.30	.25
No. 184 (1)	7.00	.35
No. 153 (1)	1.50	.25
No. 101 (1)	.40	.25
No. 132 (1)	1.00	*2.25*

No. 155 (1)	1.40	.30
No. 82 (1)	2.25	.60
No. 71 (1)	1.60	1.60
No. 27 (1)	1.10	1.50
No. 63 (1)	1.40	.65
No. 71 (1)	2.25	.25
No. 27 (1)	1.75	.30
No. 126 (1)	1.60	.25
No. 28 (1)	1.75	4.00
No. 101 (1)	1.75	.25
No. 74 (1)	1.50	1.00
No. 241 (1)	.55	.25
No. 250 (1)	1.00	.25
No. 127 (1)	.65	.50
No. 77 (1)	.75	.60
No. 79 (1)	.45	.25
No. 260 (1)	2.00	1.00
No. 60 (1)	.70	.25
No. 96 (1)	.75	.75
No. 19 (1)	2.50	2.50
No. 139 (1)	1.25	1.25
No. 119 (1)	.35	.25
No. 156 (1)	.70	.35
No. 185 (1)	.50	.30
No. 196 (1)	2.00	2.25
No. 172 (1)	.80	.80
No. 194 (1)	.40	.40
No. 27 (1)	2.75	.40
No. 88 (1)	1.10	1.10
No. 127 (1)	.40	.25
No. 54 (1)	.30	.25
No. 84 (1)	.25	.25
No. 13 (1)	1.10	1.75
No. 118 (1)	.40	1.10
No. 114 (1)	.40	1.00
Nos. 313-316 (4)	15.30	8.75
Nos. 579-582 (4)	7.40	5.20
Nos. 259-261 (3)	4.60	3.25
Nos. 92-95 (4)	15.25	12.75
No. 330 (1)	.25	.25
No. 317 (1)	1.50	.25
Nos. 145-146 (2)	2.90	2.90
Nos. 113-116 (4)	16.00	8.50
Nos. 280-284 (5)	5.65	6.85
Nos. 104-105 (2)	1.75	1.75
Nos. 52-55 (4)	13.75	6.50
Nos. 214-215 (2)	1.75	1.75
No. 192 (1)	.30	.25
No. 80 (1)	7.25	7.25
Nos. 244-248 (5)	4.90	3.50
No. 4 (1)	4.00	2.75
Set total (106) Stamps	172.00	122.30

Separate designs for each country for the visit of Queen Elizabeth II and the Duke of Edinburgh.

Royal Visit 1953

1953

Aden 62
Australia 267-269
Bermuda 163
Ceylon 318
Fiji 146
Gibraltar 146
Jamaica 154
Kenya, Uganda, Tanzania 102
Malta 242
New Zealand 286-287

No. 62 (1)	.65	.60
Nos. 267-269 (3)	2.35	1.90
No. 163 (1)	.50	.25
No. 318 (1)	1.25	.25
No. 146 (1)	.65	.35
No. 146 (1)	.50	.35
No. 154 (1)	.55	.25
No. 102 (1)	.50	.25
No. 242 (1)	.35	.25
Nos. 286-287 (2)	.50	.50
Set total (13) Stamps	7.80	4.95

West Indies Federation

Map of the Caribbean CD313

Federation of the West Indies, April 22, 1958.

1958

Antigua 122-124
Barbados 248-250
Dominica 161-163
Grenada 184-186
Jamaica 175-177
Montserrat 143-145
St. Kitts-Nevis 136-138
St. Lucia 170-172
St. Vincent 198-200
Trinidad & Tobago 86-88

Nos. 122-124 (3)	5.80	3.80
Nos. 248-250 (3)	1.70	2.90
Nos. 161-163 (3)	2.00	2.00
Nos. 184-186 (3)	1.50	1.20
Nos. 175-177 (3)	3.10	4.20
Nos. 143-145 (3)	2.35	1.35
Nos. 136-138 (3)	2.90	2.90
Nos. 170-172 (3)	2.05	2.80
Nos. 198-200 (3)	1.50	1.75
Nos. 86-88 (3)	.75	.90
Set total (30) Stamps	23.65	23.80

Freedom from Hunger

Protein Food CD314

U.N. Food and Agricultural Organization's "Freedom from Hunger" campaign.

1963

Aden 65
Antigua 133
Ascension 89
Bahamas 180
Basutoland 83
Bechuanaland Protectorate 194
Bermuda 192
British Guiana 271
British Honduras 179
Brunei 100
Cayman Islands 168
Dominica 181
Falkland Islands 146
Fiji 198
Gambia 172
Gibraltar 161
Gilbert & Ellice Islands 76
Grenada 190
Hong Kong 218
Malta 291
Mauritius 270
Montserrat 150
New Hebrides, British 93
North Borneo 296
Pitcairn Islands 35
St. Helena 173
St. Lucia 179
St. Vincent 201
Sarawak 212
Seychelles 213
Solomon Islands 109
Swaziland 108
Tonga 127
Tristan da Cunha 68
Turks & Caicos Islands 138
Virgin Islands 140
Zanzibar 280

No. 65 (1)	1.75	1.75
No. 133 (1)	.35	.35
No. 89 (1)	1.00	1.00
No. 180 (1)	.65	.65
No. 83 (1)	.50	.25
No. 194 (1)	.50	.50
No. 192 (1)	1.00	.50
No. 271 (1)	.45	.25
No. 179 (1)	.65	.25
No. 100 (1)	3.25	2.25
No. 168 (1)	.50	.30
No. 181 (1)	.30	.30
No. 146 (1)	12.00	3.50
No. 198 (1)	5.25	2.75
No. 172 (1)	.50	.25
No. 161 (1)	4.00	2.25
No. 76 (1)	1.40	.40
No. 190 (1)	.30	.25
No. 218 (1)	57.50	8.75
No. 291 (1)	2.25	2.75
No. 270 (1)	.50	.50
No. 150 (1)	.55	.45
No. 93 (1)	.60	.25
No. 296 (1)	1.90	.75
No. 35 (1)	17.50	7.00
No. 173 (1)	2.25	1.10
No. 179 (1)	.40	.40
No. 201 (1)	.90	.50
No. 212 (1)	1.60	1.75
No. 213 (1)	.85	.35
No. 109 (1)	2.00	.85
No. 108 (1)	.50	.50
No. 127 (1)	.70	.35
No. 68 (1)	1.00	.40
No. 138 (1)	.50	.50
No. 140 (1)	.50	.50
No. 280 (1)	1.50	.80
Set total (37) Stamps	127.85	46.20

Red Cross Centenary

Red Cross and Elizabeth II CD315

1963

Antigua 134-135
Ascension 90-91
Bahamas 183-184
Basutoland 84-85
Bechuanaland Protectorate 195-196
Bermuda 193-194
British Guiana 272-273
British Honduras 180-181
Cayman Islands 169-170
Dominica 182-183
Falkland Islands 147-148
Fiji 203-204
Gambia 173-174
Gibraltar 162-163
Gilbert & Ellice Islands 77-78
Grenada 191-192
Hong Kong 219-220
Jamaica 203-204
Malta 292-293
Mauritius 271-272
Montserrat 151-152
New Hebrides, British 94-95
Pitcairn Islands 36-37
St. Helena 174-175
St. Kitts-Nevis 143-144
St. Lucia 180-181
St. Vincent 202-203
Seychelles 214-215
Solomon Islands 110-111
South Arabia 1-2
Swaziland 109-110
Tonga 134-135
Tristan da Cunha 69-70
Turks & Caicos Islands 139-140
Virgin Islands 141-142

Nos. 134-135 (2)	1.10	1.50
Nos. 90-91 (2)	8.25	2.70
Nos. 183-184 (2)	2.30	2.55
Nos. 84-85 (2)	1.20	.90
Nos. 195-196 (2)	1.05	1.05
Nos. 193-194 (2)	2.75	2.55
Nos. 272-273 (2)	1.05	.80
Nos. 180-181 (2)	1.00	2.25
Nos. 169-170 (2)	.95	2.00
Nos. 182-183 (2)	.70	1.05
Nos. 147-148 (2)	20.25	6.50
Nos. 203-204 (2)	4.00	3.55
Nos. 173-174 (2)	.85	.85
Nos. 162-163 (2)	7.05	5.40
Nos. 77-78 (2)	2.25	3.25
Nos. 191-192 (2)	.80	.50
Nos. 219-220 (2)	39.50	8.85
Nos. 203-204 (2)	.75	1.65
Nos. 292-293 (2)	3.25	5.00
Nos. 271-272 (2)	.90	.90
Nos. 151-152 (2)	1.00	.80
Nos. 94-95 (2)	1.00	.50
Nos. 36-37 (2)	12.40	7.00
Nos. 174-175 (2)	1.70	2.30
Nos. 143-144 (2)	.90	.90
Nos. 180-181 (2)	1.25	1.25
Nos. 202-203 (2)	.90	.90
Nos. 214-215 (2)	1.10	.90
Nos. 110-111 (2)	1.25	1.15
Nos. 1-2 (2)	1.25	1.25
Nos. 109-110 (2)	1.10	1.10
Nos. 134-135 (2)	1.00	1.25
Nos. 69-70 (2)	2.00	1.00
Nos. 139-140 (2)	.95	1.10
Nos. 141-142 (2)	.80	.80
Set total (70) Stamps	128.55	76.00

Shakespeare

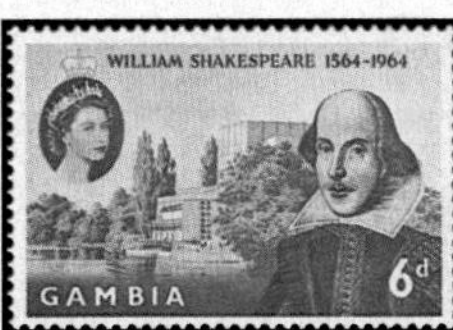

Shakespeare Memorial Theatre, Stratford-on-Avon — CD316

400th anniversary of the birth of William Shakespeare.

1964

Antigua 151
Bahamas 201
Bechuanaland Protectorate 197
Cayman Islands 171
Dominica 184
Falkland Islands 149
Gambia 192
Gibraltar 164
Montserrat 153
St. Lucia 196
Turks & Caicos Islands 141
Virgin Islands 143

No. 151 (1)	.40	.25
No. 201 (1)	.60	.35
No. 197 (1)	.35	.35
No. 171 (1)	.35	.30
No. 184 (1)	.35	.35
No. 149 (1)	1.75	.50
No. 192 (1)	.35	.25
No. 164 (1)	.65	.55
No. 153 (1)	.35	.25
No. 196 (1)	.45	.25
No. 141 (1)	.40	.40
No. 143 (1)	.45	.45
Set total (12) Stamps	6.45	4.25

ITU

ITU Emblem CD317

Intl. Telecommunication Union, cent.

1965

Antigua 153-154
Ascension 92-93
Bahamas 219-220
Barbados 265-266
Basutoland 101-102
Bechuanaland Protectorate 202-203
Bermuda 196-197
British Guiana 293-294
British Honduras 187-188
Brunei 116-117
Cayman Islands 172-173
Dominica 185-186
Falkland Islands 154-155
Fiji 211-212
Gibraltar 167-168
Gilbert & Ellice Islands 87-88
Grenada 205-206
Hong Kong 221-222
Mauritius 291-292
Montserrat 157-158
New Hebrides, British 108-109
Pitcairn Islands 52-53
St. Helena 180-181
St. Kitts-Nevis 163-164
St. Lucia 197-198
St. Vincent 224-225
Seychelles 218-219
Solomon Islands 126-127
Swaziland 115-116
Tristan da Cunha 85-86
Turks & Caicos Islands 142-143
Virgin Islands 159-160

Nos. 153-154 (2)	1.65	1.35
Nos. 92-93 (2)	1.90	1.50
Nos. 219-220 (2)	1.35	1.35
Nos. 265-266 (2)	1.50	1.25
Nos. 101-102 (2)	.85	.65
Nos. 202-203 (2)	1.20	.75
Nos. 196-197 (2)	2.15	2.25
Nos. 293-294 (2)	.60	.55
Nos. 187-188 (2)	.85	.85
Nos. 116-117 (2)	1.75	1.75
Nos. 172-173 (2)	1.00	1.00
Nos. 185-186 (2)	.55	.55
Nos. 154-155 (2)	8.00	3.65
Nos. 211-212 (2)	2.70	2.70
Nos. 167-168 (2)	11.25	5.95
Nos. 87-88 (2)	.95	.75
Nos. 205-206 (2)	.50	.50
Nos. 221-222 (2)	32.00	4.55
Nos. 291-292 (2)	1.20	.65
Nos. 157-158 (2)	1.25	1.15
Nos. 108-109 (2)	.65	.50
Nos. 52-53 (2)	14.50	8.55
Nos. 180-181 (2)	.80	.60
Nos. 163-164 (2)	.60	.60
Nos. 197-198 (2)	1.25	1.25
Nos. 224-225 (2)	.80	.90
Nos. 218-219 (2)	.90	.60
Nos. 126-127 (2)	.70	.55
Nos. 115-116 (2)	.75	.75
Nos. 85-86 (2)	1.50	.65
Nos. 142-143 (2)	.90	.90
Nos. 159-160 (2)	.95	.95
Set total (64) Stamps	97.50	50.50

Intl. Cooperation Year

ICY Emblem CD318

1965

Antigua	155-156
Ascension	94-95
Bahamas	222-223
Basutoland	103-104
Bechuanaland Protectorate	204-205
Bermuda	199-200
British Guiana	295-296
British Honduras	189-190
Brunei	118-119
Cayman Islands	174-175
Dominica	187-188
Falkland Islands	156-157
Fiji	213-214
Gibraltar	169-170
Gilbert & Ellice Islands	104-105
Grenada	207-208
Hong Kong	223-224
Mauritius	293-294
Montserrat	176-177
New Hebrides, British	110-111
New Hebrides, French	126-127
Pitcairn Islands	54-55
St. Helena	182-183
St. Kitts-Nevis	165-166
St. Lucia	199-200
Seychelles	220-221
Solomon Islands	143-144
South Arabia	17-18
Swaziland	117-118
Tristan da Cunha	87-88
Turks & Caicos Islands	144-145
Virgin Islands	161-162

Nos. 155-156 (2)	.60	.50
Nos. 94-95 (2)	1.30	1.50
Nos. 222-223 (2)	.65	1.40
Nos. 103-104 (2)	.75	.85
Nos. 204-205 (2)	1.00	1.15
Nos. 199-200 (2)	2.25	1.25
Nos. 295-296 (2)	.65	.60
Nos. 189-190 (2)	.60	.55
Nos. 118-119 (2)	.85	.85
Nos. 174-175 (2)	1.00	.95
Nos. 187-188 (2)	.55	.55
Nos. 156-157 (2)	7.10	2.00
Nos. 213-214 (2)	2.60	2.35
Nos. 169-170 (2)	1.35	*3.00*
Nos. 104-105 (2)	.95	.60
Nos. 207-208 (2)	.50	.50
Nos. 223-224 (2)	26.00	4.10
Nos. 293-294 (2)	.70	.70
Nos. 176-177 (2)	.80	.65
Nos. 110-111 (2)	.50	.50
Nos. 126-127 (2)	12.00	12.00
Nos. 54-55 (2)	14.35	6.75
Nos. 182-183 (2)	.95	.50
Nos. 165-166 (2)	.70	.60
Nos. 199-200 (2)	.55	.55
Nos. 220-221 (2)	.90	.65
Nos. 143-144 (2)	.70	.60
Nos. 17-18 (2)	1.20	.50
Nos. 117-118 (2)	.75	.75
Nos. 87-88 (2)	1.65	.75
Nos. 144-145 (2)	.85	.85
Nos. 161-162 (2)	.80	.80
Set total (64) Stamps	86.10	49.85

Churchill Memorial

Winston Churchill and St. Paul's, London, During Air Attack CD319

1966

Antigua	157-160
Ascension	96-99
Bahamas	224-227
Barbados	281-284
Basutoland	105-108
Bechuanaland Protectorate	206-209
Bermuda	201-204
British Antarctic Territory	16-19
British Honduras	191-194
Brunei	120-123
Cayman Islands	176-179
Dominica	189-192
Falkland Islands	158-161
Fiji	215-218
Gibraltar	171-174
Gilbert & Ellice Islands	106-109
Grenada	209-212
Hong Kong	225-228
Mauritius	295-298
Montserrat	178-181
New Hebrides, British	112-115
New Hebrides, French	128-131
Pitcairn Islands	56-59
St. Helena	184-187
St. Kitts-Nevis	167-170
St. Lucia	201-204
St. Vincent	241-244
Seychelles	222-225
Solomon Islands	145-148
South Arabia	19-22
Swaziland	119-122
Tristan da Cunha	89-92
Turks & Caicos Islands	146-149
Virgin Islands	163-166

Nos. 157-160 (4)	3.05	2.55
Nos. 96-99 (4)	10.00	7.15
Nos. 224-227 (4)	2.30	*3.20*
Nos. 281-284 (4)	3.00	4.45
Nos. 105-108 (4)	2.80	2.75
Nos. 206-209 (4)	2.80	2.30
Nos. 201-204 (4)	4.00	4.00
Nos. 16-19 (4)	46.35	20.00
Nos. 191-194 (4)	2.55	1.80
Nos. 120-123 (4)	8.00	7.25
Nos. 176-179 (4)	3.40	3.55
Nos. 189-192 (4)	1.15	1.15
Nos. 158-161 (4)	13.00	6.55
Nos. 215-218 (4)	5.15	3.45
Nos. 171-174 (4)	3.80	5.45
Nos. 106-109 (4)	1.75	1.30
Nos. 209-212 (4)	1.10	1.10
Nos. 225-228 (4)	68.00	12.15
Nos. 295-298 (4)	4.05	4.05
Nos. 178-181 (4)	1.60	1.55
Nos. 112-115 (4)	2.30	1.00
Nos. 128-131 (4)	10.25	10.25
Nos. 56-59 (4)	19.75	12.90
Nos. 184-187 (4)	1.85	1.95
Nos. 167-170 (4)	1.60	1.55
Nos. 201-204 (4)	1.50	1.50
Nos. 241-244 (4)	1.50	1.75
Nos. 222-225 (4)	3.20	3.60
Nos. 145-148 (4)	1.75	1.75
Nos. 19-22 (4)	3.80	2.50
Nos. 119-122 (4)	1.80	1.95
Nos. 89-92 (4)	7.00	2.70
Nos. 146-149 (4)	1.60	1.75
Nos. 163-166 (4)	1.90	1.90
Set total (136) Stamps	247.65	142.80

Royal Visit, 1966

Queen Elizabeth II and Prince Philip CD320

Caribbean visit, Feb. 4 - Mar. 6, 1966.

1966

Antigua	161-162
Bahamas	228-229
Barbados	285-286
British Guiana	299-300
Cayman Islands	180-181
Dominica	193-194
Grenada	213-214
Montserrat	182-183
St. Kitts-Nevis	171-172
St. Lucia	205-206
St. Vincent	245-246
Turks & Caicos Islands	150-151
Virgin Islands	167-168

Nos. 161-162 (2)	3.80	2.60
Nos. 228-229 (2)	3.05	3.05
Nos. 285-286 (2)	3.00	2.00
Nos. 299-300 (2)	3.35	1.60
Nos. 180-181 (2)	3.45	1.80
Nos. 193-194 (2)	3.00	.60
Nos. 213-214 (2)	.90	.50
Nos. 182-183 (2)	1.70	1.00
Nos. 171-172 (2)	.80	.75
Nos. 205-206 (2)	1.50	1.35
Nos. 245-246 (2)	2.75	1.35
Nos. 150-151 (2)	1.20	.70
Nos. 167-168 (2)	2.25	2.25
Set total (26) Stamps	30.75	19.55

World Cup Soccer

Soccer Player and Jules Rimet Cup CD321

World Cup Soccer Championship, Wembley, England, July 11-30.

1966

Antigua	163-164
Ascension	100-101
Bahamas	245-246
Bermuda	205-206
Brunei	124-125
Cayman Islands	182-183
Dominica	195-196
Fiji	219-220
Gibraltar	175-176
Gilbert & Ellice Islands	125-126
Grenada	230-231
New Hebrides, British	116-117
New Hebrides, French	132-133
Pitcairn Islands	60-61
St. Helena	188-189
St. Kitts-Nevis	173-174
St. Lucia	207-208
Seychelles	226-227
Solomon Islands	167-168
South Arabia	23-24
Tristan da Cunha	93-94

Nos. 163-164 (2)	.85	.50
Nos. 100-101 (2)	2.50	1.80
Nos. 245-246 (2)	.65	.65
Nos. 205-206 (2)	1.75	1.75
Nos. 124-125 (2)	1.40	1.00
Nos. 182-183 (2)	.75	.75
Nos. 195-196 (2)	1.20	.75
Nos. 219-220 (2)	2.00	1.20
Nos. 175-176 (2)	2.00	1.80
Nos. 125-126 (2)	.80	.60
Nos. 230-231 (2)	.65	*.95*
Nos. 116-117 (2)	1.00	1.00
Nos. 132-133 (2)	7.00	7.00
Nos. 60-61 (2)	8.00	4.75
Nos. 188-189 (2)	1.25	.60
Nos. 173-174 (2)	.85	.80
Nos. 207-208 (2)	1.15	.90
Nos. 226-227 (2)	.85	.85
Nos. 167-168 (2)	.70	.70
Nos. 23-24 (2)	1.90	.55
Nos. 93-94 (2)	1.50	.80
Set total (42) Stamps	38.75	29.70

WHO Headquarters

World Health Organization Headquarters, Geneva — CD322

1966

Antigua	165-166
Ascension	102-103
Bahamas	247-248
Brunei	126-127
Cayman Islands	184-185
Dominica	197-198
Fiji	224-225
Gibraltar	180-181
Gilbert & Ellice Islands	127-128
Grenada	232-233
Hong Kong	229-230
Montserrat	184-185
New Hebrides, British	118-119
New Hebrides, French	134-135
Pitcairn Islands	62-63
St. Helena	190-191
St. Kitts-Nevis	177-178
St. Lucia	209-210
St. Vincent	247-248
Seychelles	228-229
Solomon Islands	169-170
South Arabia	25-26
Tristan da Cunha	99-100

Nos. 165-166 (2)	1.05	.55
Nos. 102-103 (2)	6.60	3.50
Nos. 247-248 (2)	.80	.80
Nos. 126-127 (2)	1.35	1.00
Nos. 184-185 (2)	2.25	1.40
Nos. 197-198 (2)	.75	.75
Nos. 224-225 (2)	5.10	3.90
Nos. 180-181 (2)	7.50	4.75
Nos. 127-128 (2)	.80	.70
Nos. 232-233 (2)	.80	.50
Nos. 229-230 (2)	14.25	2.30
Nos. 184-185 (2)	1.00	1.00
Nos. 118-119 (2)	.75	.50
Nos. 134-135 (2)	8.75	8.75
Nos. 62-63 (2)	13.00	7.00
Nos. 190-191 (2)	3.50	1.50
Nos. 177-178 (2)	.65	.65
Nos. 209-210 (2)	.80	.80
Nos. 247-248 (2)	1.15	1.05
Nos. 228-229 (2)	1.25	.75
Nos. 169-170 (2)	.80	.80
Nos. 25-26 (2)	2.10	.70
Nos. 99-100 (2)	2.25	1.25
Set total (46) Stamps	77.25	44.90

UNESCO Anniversary

"Education" — CD323

"Science" (Wheat ears & flask enclosing globe). "Culture" (lyre & columns). 20th anniversary of the UNESCO.

1966-67

Antigua	183-185
Ascension	108-110
Bahamas	249-251
Barbados	287-289
Bermuda	207-209
Brunei	128-130
Cayman Islands	186-188
Dominica	199-201
Gibraltar	183-185
Gilbert & Ellice Islands	129-131
Grenada	234-236
Hong Kong	231-233
Mauritius	299-301
Montserrat	186-188
New Hebrides, British	120-122
New Hebrides, French	136-138
Pitcairn Islands	64-66
St. Helena	192-194
St. Kitts-Nevis	179-181
St. Lucia	211-213
St. Vincent	249-251
Seychelles	230-232
Solomon Islands	171-173
South Arabia	27-29
Swaziland	123-125
Tristan da Cunha	101-103
Turks & Caicos Islands	155-157
Virgin Islands	176-178

Nos. 183-185 (3)	1.90	*2.50*
Nos. 108-110 (3)	11.00	6.15
Nos. 249-251 (3)	2.35	2.35
Nos. 287-289 (3)	2.50	2.15
Nos. 207-209 (3)	4.30	3.90
Nos. 128-130 (3)	5.00	*7.40*
Nos. 186-188 (3)	2.50	1.70
Nos. 199-201 (3)	1.60	.75
Nos. 183-185 (3)	7.50	3.75
Nos. 129-131 (3)	2.50	1.65
Nos. 234-236 (3)	1.10	1.20
Nos. 231-233 (3)	89.00	20.00
Nos. 299-301 (3)	2.10	1.50
Nos. 186-188 (3)	2.40	2.40
Nos. 120-122 (3)	1.90	1.90
Nos. 136-138 (3)	7.75	7.75
Nos. 64-66 (3)	12.85	7.10
Nos. 192-194 (3)	5.25	3.65
Nos. 179-181 (3)	.90	.90
Nos. 211-213 (3)	1.15	1.15
Nos. 249-251 (3)	2.30	1.35
Nos. 230-232 (3)	2.40	2.40
Nos. 171-173 (3)	2.00	1.50
Nos. 27-29 (3)	5.65	6.30
Nos. 123-125 (3)	1.45	1.45
Nos. 101-103 (3)	2.50	1.40
Nos. 155-157 (3)	1.05	1.05
Nos. 176-178 (3)	1.30	1.30
Set total (84) Stamps	184.20	96.60

Silver Wedding, 1972

Queen Elizabeth II and Prince Philip — CD324

Designs: borders differ for each country.

1972

Anguilla	161-162
Antigua	295-296
Ascension	164-165
Bahamas	344-345
Bermuda	296-297
British Antarctic Territory	43-44
British Honduras	306-307
British Indian Ocean Territory	48-49

Brunei 186-187
Cayman Islands 304-305
Dominica 352-353
Falkland Islands 223-224
Fiji 328-329
Gibraltar 292-293
Gilbert & Ellice Islands 206-207
Grenada 466-467
Hong Kong 271-272
Montserrat 286-287
New Hebrides, British 169-170
Pitcairn Islands 127-128
St. Helena 271-272
St. Kitts-Nevis 257-258
St. Lucia 328-329
St.Vincent 344-345
Seychelles 309-310
Solomon Islands 248-249
South Georgia 35-36
Tristan da Cunha 178-179
Turks & Caicos Islands 257-258
Virgin Islands 241-242

Nos. 161-162 (2) 2.00 1.50
Nos. 295-296 (2) .50 .50
Nos. 164-165 (2) .80 .80
Nos. 344-345 (2) .60 .60
Nos. 296-297 (2) .50 .50
Nos. 43-44 (2) 7.75 6.10
Nos. 306-307 (2) .90 .90
Nos. 48-49 (2) 2.50 1.00
Nos. 186-187 (2) .65 .85
Nos. 304-305 (2) .75 .75
Nos. 352-353 (2) .65 .65
Nos. 223-224 (2) 1.10 1.10
Nos. 328-329 (2) 1.00 1.00
Nos. 292-293 (2) .50 .50
Nos. 206-207 (2) .50 .50
Nos. 466-467 (2) .70 .70
Nos. 271-272 (2) 2.10 1.75
Nos. 286-287 (2) .55 .55
Nos. 169-170 (2) .50 .50
Nos. 127-128 (2) 1.15 .80
Nos. 271-272 (2) .70 1.20
Nos. 257-258 (2) .55 .50
Nos. 328-329 (2) .75 .75
Nos. 344-345 (2) .55 .55
Nos. 309-310 (2) .95 .95
Nos. 248-249 (2) .60 .60
Nos. 35-36 (2) 1.40 1.40
Nos. 178-179 (2) .75 .70
Nos. 257-258 (2) .50 .50
Nos. 241-242 (2) .50 .50
Set total (60) Stamps 32.95 29.20

Princess Anne's Wedding

Princess Anne and Mark Phillips — CD325

Wedding of Princess Anne and Mark Phillips, Nov. 14, 1973.

1973

Anguilla 179-180
Ascension 177-178
Belize 325-326
Bermuda 302-303
British Antarctic Territory 60-61
Cayman Islands 320-321
Falkland Islands 225-226
Gibraltar 305-306
Gilbert & Ellice Islands 216-217
Hong Kong 289-290
Montserrat 300-301
Pitcairn Islands 135-136
St. Helena 277-278
St. Kitts-Nevis 274-275
St. Lucia 349-350
St. Vincent 358-359
St. Vincent Grenadines 1-2
Seychelles 311-312
Solomon Islands 259-260
South Georgia 37-38
Tristan da Cunha 189-190
Turks & Caicos Islands 286-287
Virgin Islands 260-261

Nos. 179-180 (2) .65 .55
Nos. 177-178 (2) .65 .65
Nos. 325-326 (2) .50 .50
Nos. 302-303 (2) .50 .50
Nos. 60-61 (2) 1.25 1.10
Nos. 320-321 (2) .55 .55
Nos. 225-226 (2) .85 .85
Nos. 305-306 (2) .70 .70
Nos. 216-217 (2) .50 .50
Nos. 289-290 (2) 3.25 2.25
Nos. 300-301 (2) .65 .65
Nos. 135-136 (2) .90 .60
Nos. 277-278 (2) .50 .50
Nos. 274-275 (2) .50 .50
Nos. 349-350 (2) .50 .50
Nos. 358-359 (2) .50 .50
Nos. 1-2 (2) .65 .65
Nos. 311-312 (2) .70 .70
Nos. 259-260 (2) .70 .70
Nos. 37-38 (2) .75 .75
Nos. 189-190 (2) .50 .50
Nos. 286-287 (2) .50 .50
Nos. 260-261 (2) .50 .50
Set total (46) Stamps 17.25 15.70

Elizabeth II Coronation Anniv.

CD326

CD327

CD328

Designs: Royal and local beasts in heraldic form and simulated stonework. Portrait of Elizabeth II by Peter Grugeon. 25th anniversary of coronation of Queen Elizabeth II.

1978

Ascension 229
Barbados 474
Belize 397
British Antarctic Territory 71
Cayman Islands 404
Christmas Island 87
Falkland Islands 275
Fiji 384
Gambia 380
Gilbert Islands 312
Mauritius 464
New Hebrides, British 258
St. Helena 317
St. Kitts-Nevis 354
Samoa 472
Solomon Islands 368
South Georgia 51
Swaziland 302
Tristan da Cunha 238
Virgin Islands 337

No. 229 (1) 2.50 2.50
No. 474 (1) 1.35 1.35
No. 397 (1) 1.75 1.75
No. 71 (1) 6.00 6.00
No. 404 (1) 2.00 2.50
No. 87 (1) 3.75 *4.25*
No. 275 (1) 4.00 4.00
No. 384 (1) 2.75 2.75
No. 380 (1) 1.50 1.50
No. 312 (1) 1.40 1.40
No. 464 (1) 2.75 2.75
No. 258 (1) 1.75 1.75
No. 317 (1) 1.75 1.75
No. 354 (1) 1.00 1.00
No. 472 (1) 3.00 3.00
No. 368 (1) 3.00 3.00
No. 51 (1) 3.00 3.00
No. 302 (1) 2.50 2.50
No. 238 (1) 1.60 1.60
No. 337 (1) 2.25 2.25
Set total (20) Stamps 49.60 50.60

Queen Mother Elizabeth's 80th Birthday

CD330

Designs: Photographs of Queen Mother Elizabeth. Falkland Islands issued in sheets of 50; others in sheets of 9.

1980

Ascension 261
Bermuda 401
Cayman Islands 443
Falkland Islands 305
Gambia 412
Gibraltar 393
Hong Kong 364
Pitcairn Islands 193
St. Helena 341
Samoa 532
Solomon Islands 426
Tristan da Cunha 277

No. 261 (1) .50 .50
No. 401 (1) .45 .45
No. 443 (1) .45 .45
No. 305 (1) .40 .40
No. 412 (1) .40 .50
No. 393 (1) .35 .35
No. 364 (1) 1.10 1.00
No. 193 (1) .70 .70
No. 341 (1) .50 .50
No. 532 (1) .70 .70
No. 426 (1) .50 .50
No. 277 (1) .45 .45
Set total (12) Stamps 6.50 6.50

Royal Wedding, 1981

Prince Charles and Lady Diana — CD331

CD331a

Wedding of Charles, Prince of Wales, and Lady Diana Spencer, St. Paul's Cathedral, London, July 29, 1981.

1981

Antigua 623-627
Ascension 294-296
Barbados 547-549
Barbuda 497-501
Bermuda 412-414
Brunei 268-270
Cayman Islands 471-473
Dominica 701-705
Falkland Islands 324-326
Falkland Islands Dep. 1L59-1L61
Fiji 442-444
Gambia 426-428
Ghana 759-764
Grenada 1051-1055
Grenada Grenadines 440-443
Hong Kong 373-375
Jamaica 500-503
Lesotho 335-337
Maldive Islands 906-909
Mauritius 520-522
Norfolk Island 280-282
Pitcairn Islands 206-208
St. Helena 353-355
St. Lucia 543-549
Samoa 558-560
Sierra Leone 509-518
Solomon Islands 450-452
Swaziland 382-384
Tristan da Cunha 294-296
Turks & Caicos Islands 486-489
Caicos Island 8-11
Uganda 314-317
Vanuatu 308-310
Virgin Islands 406-408

Nos. 623-627 (5) 7.55 2.55
Nos. 294-296 (3) 1.30 1.30
Nos. 547-549 (3) .90 .90
Nos. 497-501 (5) 10.95 10.95
Nos. 412-414 (3) 2.00 2.00
Nos. 268-270 (3) 2.15 *4.50*
Nos. 471-473 (3) 1.35 1.35
Nos. 701-705 (5) 10.15 3.15
Nos. 324-326 (3) 2.00 2.00
Nos. 1L59-1L61 (3) 1.45 1.45
Nos. 442-444 (3) 1.70 1.70
Nos. 426-428 (3) .90 .90
Nos. 759-764 (9) 5.00 5.00
Nos. 1051-1055 (5) 9.85 1.85
Nos. 440-443 (4) 2.35 2.35
Nos. 373-375 (3) 3.30 3.10
Nos. 500-503 (4) 1.55 1.25
Nos. 335-337 (3) 1.10 1.10
Nos. 906-909 (4) 1.70 1.80
Nos. 520-522 (3) 2.75 2.75
Nos. 280-282 (3) 1.35 1.35
Nos. 206-208 (3) 1.35 1.35
Nos. 353-355 (3) .85 .85
Nos. 543-549 (5) 8.50 8.50
Nos. 558-560 (3) 1.15 1.15
Nos. 509-518 (10) 15.50 15.50
Nos. 450-452 (3) 1.05 1.05
Nos. 382-384 (3) 2.15 2.15
Nos. 294-296 (3) .95 .95
Nos. 486-489 (4) 2.20 2.20
Nos. 8-11 (4) 6.25 6.25
Nos. 314-317 (4) 3.30 3.00
Nos. 308-310 (3) 1.60 1.60
Nos. 406-408 (3) 1.30 1.30
Set total (131) Stamps 117.50 99.15

Princess Diana

CD332

CD333

Designs: Photographs and portrait of Princess Diana, wedding or honeymoon photographs, royal residences, arms of issuing country. Portrait photograph by Clive Friend. Souvenir sheet margins show family tree, various people related to the princess. 21st birthday of Princess Diana of Wales, July 1.

1982

Antigua 663-666
Ascension 313-316
Bahamas 510-513
Barbados 585-588
Barbuda 544-547
British Antarctic Territory 92-95
Cayman Islands 486-489
Dominica 773-776
Falkland Islands 348-351
Falkland Islands Dep. 1L72-1L75
Fiji 470-473
Gambia 447-450
Grenada 1101A-1105
Grenada Grenadines 485-491
Lesotho 372-375
Maldive Islands 952-955
Mauritius 548-551
Pitcairn Islands 213-216
St. Helena 372-375
St. Lucia 591-594
Sierra Leone 531-534
Solomon Islands 471-474
Swaziland 406-409
Tristan da Cunha 310-313
Turks and Caicos Islands 531-534
Virgin Islands 430-433

Nos. 663-666 (4) 9.70 9.70
Nos. 313-316 (4) 3.95 3.95
Nos. 510-513 (4) 6.00 3.85
Nos. 585-588 (4) 3.40 3.25
Nos. 544-547 (4) 9.75 7.70
Nos. 92-95 (4) 5.30 3.45
Nos. 486-489 (4) *5.40* *2.70*
Nos. 773-776 (4) 7.80 7.80
Nos. 348-351 (4) 3.30 3.15
Nos. 1L72-1L75 (4) 3.20 4.00
Nos. 470-473 (4) 4.50 4.50
Nos. 447-450 (4) 3.25 3.25
Nos. 1101A-1105 (7) 16.05 15.55
Nos. 485-491 (7) 17.65 17.65
Nos. 372-375 (4) 4.00 4.00
Nos. 952-955 (4) 7.25 7.25
Nos. 548-551 (4) 5.50 5.50
Nos. 213-216 (4) 3.40 3.40
Nos. 372-375 (4) 2.95 2.95
Nos. 591-594 (4) 9.90 9.90
Nos. 531-534 (4) 7.60 7.60
Nos. 471-474 (4) 2.90 2.90
Nos. 406-409 (4) 5.00 5.00
Nos. 310-313 (4) 4.75 1.45
Nos. 531-534 (4) 10.75 7.75
Nos. 430-433 (4) 3.55 3.55
Set total (110) Stamps 166.80 151.75

250th anniv. of first edition of Lloyd's List (shipping news publication) & of Lloyd's marine insurance.

CD335

Designs: First page of early edition of the list; historical ships, modern transportation or harbor scenes.

1984

Ascension	351-354
Bahamas	555-558
Barbados	627-630
Cayes of Belize	10-13
Cayman Islands	522-526
Falkland Islands	404-407
Fiji	509-512
Gambia	519-522
Mauritius	587-590
Nauru	280-283
St. Helena	412-415
Samoa	624-627
Seychelles	538-541
Solomon Islands	521-524
Vanuatu	368-371
Virgin Islands	466-469

Nos. 351-354 (4)	3.30	2.55
Nos. 555-558 (4)	4.55	2.95
Nos. 627-630 (4)	6.10	5.15
Nos. 10-13 (4)	3.05	3.05
Nos. 522-526 (5)	9.30	8.45
Nos. 404-407 (4)	3.70	3.70
Nos. 509-512 (4)	6.15	6.15
Nos. 519-522 (4)	4.85	4.50
Nos. 587-590 (4)	8.95	8.95
Nos. 280-283 (4)	2.90	2.85
Nos. 412-415 (4)	2.40	2.40
Nos. 624-627 (4)	2.65	2.65
Nos. 538-541 (4)	5.25	5.25
Nos. 521-524 (4)	4.65	3.95
Nos. 368-371 (4)	2.90	2.90
Nos. 466-469 (4)	5.00	5.00
Set total (65) Stamps	75.70	70.45

Queen Mother 85th Birthday

CD336

Designs: Photographs tracing the life of the Queen Mother, Elizabeth. The high value in each set pictures the same photograph taken of the Queen Mother holding the infant Prince Henry.

1985

Ascension	372-376
Bahamas	580-584
Barbados	660-664
Bermuda	469-473
Falkland Islands	420-424
Falkland Islands Dep	1L92-1L96
Fiji	531-535
Hong Kong	447-450
Jamaica	599-603
Mauritius	604-608
Norfolk Island	364-368
Pitcairn Islands	253-257
St. Helena	428-432
Samoa	649-653
Seychelles	567-571
Zil Elwannyen Sesel	101-105
Solomon Islands	543-547
Swaziland	476-480
Tristan da Cunha	372-376
Vanuatu	392-396

Nos. 372-376 (5)	5.35	5.35
Nos. 580-584 (5)	7.95	6.45
Nos. 660-664 (5)	8.00	6.70
Nos. 469-473 (5)	9.90	9.90
Nos. 420-424 (5)	8.80	8.80
Nos. 1L92-1L96 (5)	8.25	8.25
Nos. 531-535 (5)	7.05	7.05
Nos. 447-450 (4)	10.25	8.50
Nos. 599-603 (5)	7.50	8.00
Nos. 604-608 (5)	11.80	11.80
Nos. 364-368 (5)	5.05	5.05
Nos. 253-257 (5)	6.00	6.15
Nos. 428-432 (5)	5.25	5.25
Nos. 649-653 (5)	7.75	7.75
Nos. 567-571 (5)	8.70	8.70
Nos. 101-105 (5)	7.15	7.15
Nos. 543-547 (5)	4.45	4.45
Nos. 476-480 (5)	7.65	7.00
Nos. 372-376 (5)	5.40	5.40
Nos. 392-396 (5)	6.15	6.15
Set total (99) Stamps	148.40	143.85

Queen Elizabeth II, 60th Birthday

CD337

1986, April 21

Ascension	389-393
Bahamas	592-596
Barbados	675-679
Bermuda	499-503
Cayman Islands	555-559
Falkland Islands	441-445
Fiji	544-548
Hong Kong	465-469
Jamaica	620-624
Kiribati	470-474
Mauritius	629-633
Papua New Guinea	640-644
Pitcairn Islands	270-274
St. Helena	451-455
Samoa	670-674
Seychelles	592-596
Zil Elwannyen Sesel	114-118
Solomon Islands	562-566
South Georgia	101-105
Swaziland	490-494
Tristan da Cunha	388-392
Vanuatu	414-418
Zambia	343-347

Nos. 389-393 (5)	2.80	2.80
Nos. 592-596 (5)	2.75	3.70
Nos. 675-679 (5)	3.35	3.20
Nos. 499-503 (5)	4.90	4.90
Nos. 555-559 (5)	4.55	4.45
Nos. 441-445 (5)	4.95	4.95
Nos. 544-548 (5)	4.05	4.05
Nos. 465-469 (5)	9.60	6.85
Nos. 620-624 (5)	2.85	3.00
Nos. 470-474 (5)	2.10	2.10
Nos. 629-633 (5)	3.70	3.70
Nos. 640-644 (5)	4.50	4.50
Nos. 270-274 (5)	3.85	3.85
Nos. 451-455 (5)	3.05	3.05
Nos. 670-674 (5)	3.55	3.55
Nos. 592-596 (5)	2.70	2.70
Nos. 114-118 (5)	2.25	2.25
Nos. 562-566 (5)	2.50	2.50
Nos. 101-105 (5)	3.55	3.55
Nos. 490-494 (5)	3.95	3.95
Nos. 388-392 (5)	3.60	3.60
Nos. 414-418 (5)	4.80	4.80
Nos. 343-347 (5)	2.25	2.25
Set total (115) Stamps	86.15	84.25

Royal Wedding

Marriage of Prince Andrew and Sarah Ferguson CD338

1986, July 23

Ascension	399-400
Bahamas	602-603
Barbados	687-688
Cayman Islands	560-561
Jamaica	629-630
Pitcairn Islands	275-276
St. Helena	460-461
St. Kitts	181-182
Seychelles	602-603
Zil Elwannyen Sesel	119-120
Solomon Islands	567-568
Tristan da Cunha	397-398
Zambia	348-349

Nos. 399-400 (2)	1.45	1.45
Nos. 602-603 (2)	2.75	2.75
Nos. 687-688 (2)	2.00	1.25
Nos. 560-561 (2)	1.50	2.15
Nos. 629-630 (2)	1.75	1.75
Nos. 275-276 (2)	2.75	2.75
Nos. 460-461 (2)	1.05	1.05
Nos. 181-182 (2)	1.75	1.75
Nos. 602-603 (2)	2.50	2.50
Nos. 119-120 (2)	2.30	2.30
Nos. 567-568 (2)	1.00	1.00
Nos. 397-398 (2)	1.50	1.50
Nos. 348-349 (2)	1.30	1.45
Set total (26) Stamps	23.60	23.65

Queen Elizabeth II, 60th Birthday

Queen Elizabeth II & Prince Philip, 1947 Wedding Portrait — CD339

Designs: Photographs tracing the life of Queen Elizabeth II.

1986

Anguilla	674-677
Antigua	925-928
Barbuda	783-786
Dominica	950-953
Gambia	611-614
Grenada	1371-1374
Grenada Grenadines	749-752
Lesotho	531-534
Maldive Islands	1172-1175
Sierra Leone	760-763
Uganda	495-498

Nos. 674-677 (4)	9.00	9.00
Nos. 925-928 (4)	6.75	6.75
Nos. 783-786 (4)	25.60	25.60
Nos. 950-953 (4)	7.15	7.15
Nos. 611-614 (4)	8.25	7.90
Nos. 1371-1374 (4)	6.80	6.80
Nos. 749-752 (4)	6.75	6.75
Nos. 531-534 (4)	5.50	5.50
Nos. 1172-1175 (4)	7.00	7.00
Nos. 760-763 (4)	6.30	6.30
Nos. 495-498 (4)	8.50	8.50
Set total (44) Stamps	97.60	97.25

Royal Wedding, 1986

CD340

Designs: Photographs of Prince Andrew and Sarah Ferguson during courtship, engagement and marriage.

1986

Antigua	939-942
Barbuda	809-812
Dominica	970-973
Gambia	635-638
Grenada	1385-1388
Grenada Grenadines	758-761
Lesotho	545-548
Maldive Islands	1181-1184
Sierra Leone	769-772
Uganda	510-513

Nos. 939-942 (4)	8.25	8.25
Nos. 809-812 (4)	15.90	15.80
Nos. 970-973 (4)	8.50	8.50
Nos. 635-638 (4)	9.25	9.25
Nos. 1385-1388 (4)	8.30	8.30
Nos. 758-761 (4)	9.00	9.00
Nos. 545-548 (4)	7.95	7.95
Nos. 1181-1184 (4)	10.20	10.20
Nos. 769-772 (4)	5.55	5.55
Nos. 510-513 (4)	9.50	10.25
Set total (40) Stamps	92.40	93.05

Lloyds of London, 300th Anniv.

CD341

Designs: 17th century aspects of Lloyds, representations of each country's individual connections with Lloyds and publicized disasters insured by the organization.

1986

Ascension	454-457
Bahamas	655-658
Barbados	731-734
Bermuda	541-544
Falkland Islands	481-484
Liberia	1101-1104
Malawi	534-537
Nevis	571-574
St. Helena	501-504
St. Lucia	923-926
Seychelles	649-652
Zil Elwannyen Sesel	146-149
Solomon Islands	627-630
South Georgia	131-134
Trinidad & Tobago	484-487
Tristan da Cunha	439-442
Vanuatu	485-488

Nos. 454-457 (4)	5.00	5.00
Nos. 655-658 (4)	8.90	4.95
Nos. 731-734 (4)	11.50	7.70
Nos. 541-544 (4)	8.25	5.60
Nos. 481-484 (4)	5.25	5.25
Nos. 1101-1104 (4)	5.25	5.25
Nos. 534-537 (4)	11.00	7.85
Nos. 571-574 (4)	8.35	8.35
Nos. 501-504 (4)	8.70	7.15
Nos. 923-926 (4)	9.40	9.40
Nos. 649-652 (4)	13.10	13.10
Nos. 146-149 (4)	11.25	11.25
Nos. 627-630 (4)	7.90	4.45
Nos. 131-134 (4)	6.30	3.70
Nos. 484-487 (4)	11.85	8.50
Nos. 439-442 (4)	6.75	6.75
Nos. 485-488 (4)	7.20	7.20
Set total (68) Stamps	145.95	121.45

Moon Landing, 20th Anniv.

CD342

Designs: Equipment, crew photographs, spacecraft, official emblems and report profiles created for the Apollo Missions. Two stamps in each set are square in format rather than like the stamp shown; see individual country listings for more information.

1989

Ascension	468-472
Bahamas	674-678
Belize	916-920
Kiribati	517-521
Liberia	1125-1129
Nevis	586-590
St. Kitts	248-252
Samoa	760-764
Seychelles	676-680
Zil Elwannyen Sesel	154-158
Solomon Islands	643-647
Vanuatu	507-511

Nos. 468-472 (5)	9.15	8.35
Nos. 674-678 (5)	23.00	19.70
Nos. 916-920 (5)	27.40	23.50
Nos. 517-521 (5)	13.25	13.25
Nos. 1125-1129 (5)	10.65	10.65
Nos. 586-590 (5)	7.50	7.50
Nos. 248-252 (5)	8.75	8.75
Nos. 760-764 (5)	10.25	10.25
Nos. 676-680 (5)	16.65	16.65
Nos. 154-158 (5)	26.85	26.85

Nos. 643-647 (5) 12.75 11.60
Nos. 507-511 (5) 12.25 12.25
Set total (60) Stamps 178.45 169.30

Queen Mother, 90th Birthday

CD343

CD344

Designs: Portraits of Queen Elizabeth, the Queen Mother. See individual country listings for more information.

1990

Ascension 491-492
Bahamas 698-699
Barbados 782-783
British Antarctic Territory 170-171
British Indian Ocean Territory 106-107
Cayman Islands 622-623
Falkland Islands 524-525
Kenya 527-528
Kiribati 555-556
Liberia 1145-1146
Pitcairn Islands 336-337
St. Helena 532-533
St. Lucia 969-970
Seychelles 710-711
Zil Elwannyen Sesel 171-172
Solomon Islands 671-672
South Georgia 143-144
Swaziland 565-566
Tristan da Cunha 480-481

Nos. 491-492 (2) 4.75 5.65
Nos. 698-699 (2) 5.65 5.65
Nos. 782-783 (2) 4.00 3.70
Nos. 170-171 (2) 6.75 6.75
Nos. 106-107 (2) 20.75 21.25
Nos. 622-623 (2) 5.10 *6.75*
Nos. 524-525 (2) 5.25 5.25
Nos. 527-528 (2) 7.00 7.00
Nos. 555-556 (2) 5.60 5.60
Nos. 1145-1146 (2) 4.25 4.25
Nos. 336-337 (2) 5.25 5.25
Nos. 532-533 (2) 5.25 5.25
Nos. 969-970 (2) 5.25 5.25
Nos. 710-711 (2) 6.60 6.60
Nos. 171-172 (2) 8.25 8.25
Nos. 671-672 (2) 6.50 *6.40*
Nos. 143-144 (2) 5.75 5.75
Nos. 565-566 (2) 4.20 4.10
Nos. 480-481 (2) 6.25 5.60
Set total (38) Stamps 122.40 124.30

Queen Elizabeth II, 65th Birthday, and Prince Philip, 70th Birthday

CD345

CD346

Designs: Portraits of Queen Elizabeth II and Prince Philip differ for each country. Printed in sheets of 10 + 5 labels (3 different) between. Stamps alternate, producing 5 different triptychs.

1991

Ascension 506a
Bahamas 731a
Belize 970a
Bermuda 618a
Kiribati 572a
Mauritius 734a
Pitcairn Islands 349a
St. Helena 555a
St. Kitts 319a
Samoa 791a
Seychelles 724a
Zil Elwannyen Sesel 178a
Solomon Islands 689a
South Georgia 150a
Swaziland 587a
Vanuatu 541a

No. 506a (1) 3.50 3.75
No. 731a (1) 4.00 4.00
No. 970a (1) 3.75 3.75
No. 618a (1) 4.00 4.00
No. 572a (1) 4.00 4.00
No. 734a (1) 3.75 3.75
No. 349a (1) 3.50 3.50
No. 555a (1) 2.75 2.75
No. 319a (1) 2.75 2.75
No. 791a (1) 4.50 4.50
No. 724a (1) 5.00 5.00
No. 178a (1) 6.50 6.50
No. 689a (1) 4.50 4.50
No. 150a (1) 7.00 7.00
No. 587a (1) 4.25 4.25
No. 541a (1) 3.00 3.00
Set total (16) Stamps 66.75 67.00

Royal Family Birthday, Anniversary

CD347

Queen Elizabeth II, 65th birthday, Charles and Diana, 10th wedding anniversary: Various photographs of Queen Elizabeth II, Prince Philip, Prince Charles, Princess Diana and their sons William and Henry.

1991

Antigua 1446-1455
Barbuda 1229-1238
Dominica 1328-1337
Gambia 1080-1089
Grenada 2006-2015
Grenada Grenadines 1331-1340
Guyana 2440-2451
Lesotho 871-875
Maldive Islands 1533-1542
Nevis 666-675
St. Vincent 1485-1494
St. Vincent Grenadines 769-778
Sierra Leone 1387-1396
Turks & Caicos Islands 913-922
Uganda 918-927

Nos. 1446-1455 (10) 21.95 20.30
Nos. 1229-1238 (10) 146.25 139.90
Nos. 1328-1337 (10) 29.85 29.85
Nos. 1080-1089 (10) 24.65 24.40
Nos. 2006-2015 (10) 25.45 22.10
Nos. 1331-1340 (10) 23.85 23.35
Nos. 2440-2451 (12) 37.05 36.70
Nos. 871-875 (5) 13.55 13.55
Nos. 1533-1542 (10) 29.60 29.60
Nos. 666-675 (10) 25.65 25.65
Nos. 1485-1494 (10) 26.75 25.90
Nos. 769-778 (10) 27.10 27.10
Nos. 1387-1396 (10) 26.55 26.55
Nos. 913-922 (10) 31.65 30.00
Nos. 918-927 (10) 26.60 26.60
Set total (147) Stamps 516.50 501.55

Queen Elizabeth II's Accession to the Throne, 40th Anniv.

CD348

CD349

Various photographs of Queen Elizabeth II with local Scenes.

1992 - CD348

Antigua 1513-1518
Barbuda 1306-1311
Dominica 1414-1419
Gambia 1172-1177
Grenada 2047-2052
Grenada Grenadines 1368-1373
Lesotho 881-885
Maldive Islands 1637-1642
Nevis 702-707
St. Vincent 1582-1587
St. Vincent Grenadines 829-834
Sierra Leone 1482-1487
Turks and Caicos Islands 978-987
Uganda 990-995
Virgin Islands 742-746

Nos. 1513-1518 (6) 16.00 14.10
Nos. 1306-1311 (6) 144.50 98.75
Nos. 1414-1419 (6) 12.50 12.50
Nos. 1172-1177 (6) 17.10 16.85
Nos. 2047-2052 (6) 15.95 15.95
Nos. 1368-1373 (6) 17.00 15.35
Nos. 881-885 (5) 11.90 11.90
Nos. 1637-1642 (6) 17.55 17.55
Nos. 702-707 (6) 13.80 13.80
Nos. 1582-1587 (6) 14.40 14.40
Nos. 829-834 (6) 20.55 20.55
Nos. 1482-1487 (6) 22.50 22.50
Nos. 978-987 (10) 31.10 31.10
Nos. 990-995 (6) 19.50 19.50
Nos. 742-746 (5) 15.50 15.50
Set total (92) Stamps 389.85 340.30

1992 - CD349

Ascension 531-535
Bahamas 744-748
Bermuda 623-627
British Indian Ocean Territory 119-123
Cayman Islands 648-652
Falkland Islands 549-553
Gibraltar 605-609
Hong Kong 619-623
Kenya 563-567
Kiribati 582-586
Pitcairn Islands 362-366
St. Helena 570-574
St. Kitts 332-336
Samoa 805-809
Seychelles 734-738
Zil Elwannyen Sesel 183-187
Solomon Islands 708-712
South Georgia 157-161
Tristan da Cunha 508-512
Vanuatu 555-559
Zambia 561-565

Nos. 531-535 (5) 6.35 6.35
Nos. 744-748 (5) 6.90 4.70
Nos. 623-627 (5) 8.20 7.30
Nos. 119-123 (5) 24.75 *21.00*
Nos. 648-652 (5) 7.60 7.10
Nos. 549-553 (5) 7.40 7.40
Nos. 605-609 (5) 6.55 *7.00*
Nos. 619-623 (5) 5.65 2.65
Nos. 563-567 (5) 9.10 9.10
Nos. 582-586 (5) 3.85 3.85
Nos. 362-366 (5) 6.55 6.55
Nos. 570-574 (5) 5.70 5.70
Nos. 332-336 (5) 7.00 7.00
Nos. 805-809 (5) 8.60 8.60
Nos. 734-738 (5) 10.80 10.80
Nos. 183-187 (5) 9.40 9.40
Nos. 708-712 (5) 7.95 7.30
Nos. 157-161 (5) 5.85 5.75
Nos. 508-512 (5) 9.45 8.30
Nos. 555-559 (5) 4.50 4.50
Nos. 561-565 (5) 6.40 6.40
Set total (105) Stamps 168.55 156.75

Royal Air Force, 75th Anniversary

CD350

1993

Ascension 557-561
Bahamas 771-775
Barbados 842-846
Belize 1003-1008
Bermuda 648-651
British Indian Ocean Territory 136-140
Falkland Is. 573-577
Fiji 687-691
Montserrat 830-834
St. Kitts 351-355

Nos. 557-561 (5) 15.55 14.05
Nos. 771-775 (5) 26.00 22.20
Nos. 842-846 (5) 12.90 11.60
Nos. 1003-1008 (6) 19.40 18.70
Nos. 648-651 (4) 10.50 9.95
Nos. 136-140 (5) 17.50 17.50
Nos. 573-577 (5) 11.50 11.50
Nos. 687-691 (5) 18.95 18.95
Nos. 830-834 (5) 14.35 14.35
Nos. 351-355 (5) 23.70 23.70
Set total (50) Stamps 170.35 162.50

Royal Air Force, 80th Anniv.

Design CD350 Re-inscribed

1998

Ascension 697-701
Bahamas 907-911
British Indian Ocean Terr 198-202
Cayman Islands 754-758
Fiji 814-818
Gibraltar 755-759
Samoa 957-961
Turks & Caicos Islands 1258-1265
Tuvalu 763-767
Virgin Islands 879-883

Nos. 697-701 (5) 17.35 17.35
Nos. 907-911 (5) 14.25 13.55
Nos. 198-202 (5) 21.00 21.00
Nos. 754-758 (5) 15.75 15.75
Nos. 814-818 (5) 15.50 15.50
Nos. 755-759 (5) 12.20 12.20
Nos. 957-961 (5) 18.00 18.00
Nos. 1258-1265 (2) 32.00 32.00
Nos. 763-767 (5) 9.75 9.75
Nos. 879-883 (5) 17.00 17.00
Set total (47) Stamps 172.80 172.10

End of World War II, 50th Anniv.

CD351

CD352

1995

Ascension 613-617
Bahamas 824-828
Barbados 891-895
Belize 1047-1050
British Indian Ocean Territory 163-167
Cayman Islands 704-708
Falkland Islands 634-638
Fiji 720-724
Kiribati 662-668
Liberia 1175-1179
Mauritius 803-805
St. Helena 646-654
St. Kitts 389-393
St. Lucia 1018-1022
Samoa 890-894
Solomon Islands 799-803
South Georgia 198-200
Tristan da Cunha 562-566

Nos. 613-617 (5) 19.75 19.50
Nos. 824-828 (5) 22.00 18.70
Nos. 891-895 (5) 12.85 10.75
Nos. 1047-1050 (4) 6.50 5.90
Nos. 163-167 (5) 16.25 16.25
Nos. 704-708 (5) 18.15 14.45
Nos. 634-638 (5) 16.35 16.35
Nos. 720-724 (5) 21.35 21.35
Nos. 662-668 (7) 16.30 16.30
Nos. 1175-1179 (5) 19.60 19.60
Nos. 803-805 (3) 7.50 7.50

Nos. 646-654 (9)	26.10	26.10
Nos. 389-393 (5)	20.90	20.90
Nos. 1018-1022 (5)	14.25	11.15
Nos. 890-894 (5)	18.00	18.00
Nos. 799-803 (5)	17.50	17.50
Nos. 198-200 (3)	14.00	14.00
Nos. 562-566 (5)	22.85	22.85
Set total (91) Stamps	310.20	297.15

UN, 50th Anniv.

CD353

1995

Bahamas 839-842
Barbados 901-904
Belize 1055-1058
Jamaica 847-851
Liberia 1187-1190
Mauritius 813-816
Pitcairn Islands 436-439
St. Kitts 398-401
St. Lucia 1023-1026
Samoa 900-903
Tristan da Cunha 568-571
Virgin Islands 807-810

Nos. 839-842 (4)	8.00	7.05
Nos. 901-904 (4)	6.55	5.45
Nos. 1055-1058 (4)	5.70	5.60
Nos. 847-851 (5)	6.30	5.85
Nos. 1187-1190 (4)	15.00	15.00
Nos. 813-816 (4)	3.90	3.90
Nos. 436-439 (4)	11.25	11.25
Nos. 398-401 (4)	6.40	6.40
Nos. 1023-1026 (4)	7.50	7.25
Nos. 900-903 (4)	10.50	10.50
Nos. 568-571 (4)	14.90	14.90
Nos. 807-810 (4)	9.45	9.45
Set total (49) Stamps	105.45	102.60

Queen Elizabeth, 70th Birthday

CD354

1996

Ascension 632-635
British Antarctic Territory 240-243
British Indian Ocean Territory 176-180
Falkland Islands 653-657
Pitcairn Islands 446-449
St. Helena 672-676
Samoa 912-916
Tokelau 223-227
Tristan da Cunha 576-579
Virgin Islands 824-828

Nos. 632-635 (4)	5.90	5.90
Nos. 240-243 (4)	10.50	8.90
Nos. 176-180 (5)	11.25	11.25
Nos. 653-657 (5)	13.75	13.75
Nos. 446-449 (4)	10.50	10.50
Nos. 672-676 (5)	12.70	12.70
Nos. 912-916 (5)	12.00	12.00
Nos. 223-227 (5)	11.35	11.35
Nos. 576-579 (4)	9.15	9.15
Nos. 824-828 (5)	11.80	11.80
Set total (46) Stamps	108.90	107.30

Diana, Princess of Wales (1961-97)

CD355

1998

Ascension 696
Bahamas 901A-902
Barbados 950
Belize 1091
Bermuda 753
Botswana 659-663
British Antarctic Territory 258
British Indian Ocean Terr. 197
Cayman Islands 752A-753
Falkland Islands 694
Fiji 819-820
Gibraltar 754
Kiribati 719A-720
Namibia 909
Niue 706
Norfolk Island 644-645
Papua New Guinea 937
Pitcairn Islands 487
St. Helena 711
St. Kitts 437A-438
Samoa 955A-956
Seycelles 802
Solomon Islands 866-867
South Georgia 220
Tokelau 252B-253
Tonga 980
  Niuafo'ou 201
Tristan da Cunha 618
Tuvalu 762
Vanuatu 718A-719
Virgin Islands 878

No. 696 (1)	5.50	5.50
Nos. 901A-902 (2)	5.30	5.30
No. 950 (1)	5.00	5.00
No. 1091 (1)	5.50	5.50
No. 753 (1)	5.50	5.50
Nos. 659-663 (5)	10.25	10.10
No. 258 (1)	6.25	6.25
No. 197 (1)	6.50	6.50
Nos. 752A-753 (3)	7.75	7.75
No. 694 (1)	6.25	6.25
Nos. 819-820 (2)	6.00	6.00
No. 754 (1)	5.50	5.50
Nos. 719A-720 (2)	4.85	4.85
No. 909 (1)	1.90	1.90
No. 706 (1)	5.50	5.50
Nos. 644-645 (2)	5.25	5.25
No. 937 (1)	6.50	6.50
No. 487 (1)	5.25	5.25
No. 711 (1)	4.25	4.25
Nos. 437A-438 (2)	6.15	6.15
Nos. 955A-956 (2)	14.50	14.50
No. 802 (1)	6.25	6.25
Nos. 866-867 (2)	6.90	6.90
No. 220 (1)	5.25	5.25
Nos. 252B-253 (2)	6.75	6.75
No. 980 (1)	5.75	5.75
No. 201 (1)	7.75	7.75
No. 618 (1)	6.00	6.00
No. 762 (1)	4.00	4.00
Nos. 718A-719 (2)	11.50	11.50
No. 878 (1)	5.50	5.50
Set total (46) Stamps	195.10	194.95

Wedding of Prince Edward and Sophie Rhys-Jones

CD356

1999

Ascension 729-730
Cayman Islands 775-776
Falkland Islands 729-730
Pitcairn Islands 505-506
St. Helena 733-734
Samoa 971-972
Tristan da Cunha 636-637
Virgin Islands 908-909

Nos. 729-730 (2)	5.90	5.90
Nos. 775-776 (2)	5.50	5.50
Nos. 729-730 (2)	13.50	13.50
Nos. 505-506 (2)	9.00	9.00
Nos. 733-734 (2)	5.00	5.00
Nos. 971-972 (2)	6.00	6.00
Nos. 636-637 (2)	8.00	8.00
Nos. 908-909 (2)	8.30	8.30
Set total (16) Stamps	61.20	61.20

1st Manned Moon Landing, 30th Anniv.

CD357

1999

Ascension 731-735
Bahamas 942-946
Barbados 967-971
Bermuda 778
Cayman Islands 777-781
Fiji 853-857
Jamaica 889-893
Kirbati 746-750
Nauru 465-469
St. Kitts 460-464
Samoa 973-977
Solomon Islands 875-879
Tuvalu 800-804
Virgin Islands 910-914

Nos. 731-735 (5)	13.90	13.90
Nos. 942-946 (5)	14.10	14.10
Nos. 967-971 (5)	8.40	7.50
No. 778 (1)	8.00	8.00
Nos. 777-781 (5)	10.30	10.30
Nos. 853-857 (5)	10.40	10.40
Nos. 889-893 (5)	10.20	10.00
Nos. 746-750 (5)	8.85	8.85
Nos. 465-469 (5)	10.25	9.75
Nos. 460-464 (5)	13.90	13.90
Nos. 973-977 (5)	16.50	16.50
Nos. 875-879 (5)	10.00	9.85
Nos. 800-804 (5)	7.45	7.45
Nos. 910-914 (5)	15.00	15.00
Set total (66) Stamps	157.25	155.50

Queen Mother's Century

CD358

1999

Ascension 736-740
Bahamas 951-955
Cayman Islands 782-786
Falkland Islands 734-738
Fiji 858-862
Norfolk Island 688-692
St. Helena 740-744
Samoa 978-982
Solomon Islands 880-884
South Georgia 231-235
Tristan da Cunha 638-642
Tuvalu 805-809

Nos. 736-740 (5)	17.00	17.00
Nos. 951-955 (5)	14.00	12.90
Nos. 782-786 (5)	9.15	9.15
Nos. 734-738 (5)	29.85	29.85
Nos. 858-862 (5)	15.00	15.00
Nos. 688-692 (5)	10.30	10.30
Nos. 740-744 (5)	16.15	16.15
Nos. 978-982 (5)	13.25	13.25
Nos. 880-884 (5)	10.00	9.45
Nos. 231-235 (5)	30.25	29.75
Nos. 638-642 (5)	20.00	20.00
Nos. 805-809 (5)	8.65	8.65
Set total (60) Stamps	193.60	191.45

Prince William, 18th Birthday

CD359

2000

Ascension 755-759
Cayman Islands 797-801
Falkland Islands 762-766
Fiji 889-893
South Georgia 257-261
Tristan da Cunha 664-668
Virgin Islands 925-929

Nos. 755-759 (5)	17.75	17.75
Nos. 797-801 (5)	13.05	12.75
Nos. 762-766 (5)	20.50	20.50
Nos. 889-893 (5)	14.00	14.00
Nos. 257-261 (5)	29.00	29.00
Nos. 664-668 (5)	21.00	21.00
Nos. 925-929 (5)	14.75	14.75
Set total (35) Stamps	130.05	129.75

Reign of Queen Elizabeth II, 50th Anniv.

CD360

2002

Ascension 790-794
Bahamas 1033-1037
Barbados 1019-1023
Belize 1152-1156
Bermuda 822-826
British Antarctic Territory 307-311
British Indian Ocean Territory 239-243
Cayman Islands 844-848
Falkland Islands 804-808
Gibraltar 896-900
Jamaica 952-956
Nauru 491-495
Norfolk Island 758-762
Papua New Guinea 1019-1023
Pitcairn Islands 552
St. Helena 788-792
St. Lucia 1146-1150
Solomon Islands 931-935
South Georgia 274-278
Swaziland 706-710
Tokelau 302-306
Tonga 1059
  Niuafo'ou 239
Tristan da Cunha 706-710
Virgin Islands 967-971

Nos. 790-794 (5)	17.25	17.25
Nos. 1033-1037 (5)	15.75	15.75
Nos. 1019-1023 (5)	12.25	12.25
Nos. 1152-1156 (5)	15.50	15.15
Nos. 822-826 (5)	18.50	18.50
Nos. 307-311 (5)	25.00	25.00
Nos. 239-243 (5)	22.00	22.00
Nos. 844-848 (5)	14.25	14.25
Nos. 804-808 (5)	23.50	23.50
Nos. 896-900 (5)	8.00	8.00
Nos. 952-956 (5)	18.00	18.00
Nos. 491-495 (5)	19.75	19.75
Nos. 758-762 (5)	19.50	19.50
Nos. 1019-1023 (5)	14.50	14.50
No. 552 (1)	11.50	11.50
Nos. 788-792 (5)	19.75	19.75
Nos. 1146-1150 (5)	12.25	12.25
Nos. 931-935 (5)	16.00	16.00
Nos. 274-278 (5)	28.50	28.50
Nos. 706-710 (5)	12.50	12.50
Nos. 302-306 (5)	17.00	17.00
No. 1059 (1)	8.00	8.00
No. 239 (1)	7.00	7.00
Nos. 706-710 (5)	19.00	19.00
Nos. 967-971 (5)	19.00	19.00
Set total (113) Stamps	414.25	413.90

Queen Mother Elizabeth (1900-2002)

CD361

2002

Ascension 799-801
Bahamas 1044-1046
Bermuda 834-836
British Antarctic Territory 312-314

British Indian Ocean Territory........245-247
Cayman Islands........................857-861
Falkland Islands.......................812-816
Nauru.......................................499-501
Pitcairn Islands........................561-565
St. Helena................................808-812
St. Lucia..............................1155-1159
Seychelles......................................830
Solomon Islands......................945-947
South Georgia..........................281-285
Tokelau....................................312-314
Tristan da Cunha.....................715-717
Virgin Islands...........................979-983

Nos. 799-801 (3)	9.75	9.75
Nos. 1044-1046 (3)	9.35	9.35
Nos. 834-836 (3)	12.50	12.50
Nos. 312-314 (3)	19.25	19.25
Nos. 245-247 (3)	19.50	19.50
Nos. 857-861 (5)	15.00	15.00
Nos. 812-816 (5)	32.00	32.00
Nos. 499-501 (3)	17.25	17.25
Nos. 561-565 (5)	18.50	18.50
Nos. 808-812 (5)	12.00	12.00
Nos. 1155-1159 (5)	13.00	13.00
No. 830 (1)	6.50	6.50
Nos. 945-947 (3)	11.00	11.00
Nos. 281-285 (5)	20.00	20.00
Nos. 312-314 (3)	14.25	13.75
Nos. 715-717 (3)	16.00	16.00
Nos. 979-983 (5)	26.50	26.50
Set total (63) Stamps	272.35	271.85

Head of Queen Elizabeth II

CD362

2003

Ascension.......................................822
Bermuda...865
British Antarctic Territory.................322
British Indian Ocean Territory.........261
Cayman Islands..............................878
Falkland Islands.............................828
St. Helena......................................820
South Georgia.................................294
Tristan da Cunha............................731
Virgin Islands................................1003

No. 822 (1)	13.50	13.50
No. 865 (1)	55.00	55.00
No. 322 (1)	10.00	10.00
No. 261 (1)	12.50	12.50
No. 878 (1)	17.00	17.00
No. 828 (1)	10.00	10.00
No. 820 (1)	9.00	9.00
No. 294 (1)	9.00	9.00
No. 731 (1)	11.00	11.00
No. 1003 (1)	10.00	10.00
Set total (10) Stamps	157.00	157.00

Coronation of Queen Elizabeth II, 50th Anniv.

CD363

2003

Ascension................................823-825
Bahamas..............................1073-1075
Bermuda..................................866-868
British Antarctic Territory..........323-325
British Indian Ocean Territory........262-264
Cayman Islands........................879-881
Jamaica...................................970-972
Kiribati....................................825-827
Pitcairn Islands........................577-581
St. Helena...............................821-823
St. Lucia..............................1171-1173
Tokelau....................................320-322
Tristan da Cunha......................732-734
Virgin Islands........................1004-1006

Nos. 823-825 (3)	13.50	13.50
Nos. 1073-1075 (3)	13.00	13.00
Nos. 866-868 (3)	14.25	14.25
Nos. 323-325 (3)	22.00	22.00
Nos. 262-264 (3)	31.00	31.00
Nos. 879-881 (3)	20.25	20.25
Nos. 970-972 (3)	12.25	12.25
Nos. 825-827 (3)	13.50	13.50
Nos. 577-581 (5)	18.50	18.50
Nos. 821-823 (3)	7.25	7.25
Nos. 1171-1173 (3)	8.75	8.75
Nos. 320-322 (3)	20.00	20.00
Nos. 732-734 (3)	17.00	17.00
Nos. 1004-1006 (3)	25.00	25.00
Set total (44) Stamps	236.25	236.25

Prince William, 21st Birthday

CD364

2003

Ascension.......................................826
British Indian Ocean Territory.........265
Cayman Islands........................882-884
Falkland Islands.............................829
South Georgia.................................295
Tokelau...323
Tristan da Cunha............................735
Virgin Islands........................1007-1009

No. 826 (1)	7.50	7.50
No. 265 (1)	9.00	9.00
Nos. 882-884 (3)	7.65	7.65
No. 829 (1)	12.00	12.00
No. 295 (1)	9.00	9.00
No. 323 (1)	7.25	7.25
No. 735 (1)	7.00	7.00
Nos. 1007-1009 (3)	10.00	10.00
Set total (12) Stamps	69.40	69.40

British Commonwealth of Nations

Dominions, Colonies, Territories, Offices and Independent Members

Comprising stamps of the British Commonwealth and associated nations.

A strict observance of technicalities would bar some or all of the stamps listed under Burma, Ireland, Kuwait, Nepal, New Republic, Orange Free State, Samoa, South Africa, South-West Africa, Stellaland, Sudan, Swaziland, the two Transvaal Republics and others but these are included for the convenience of collectors.

1. Great Britain

Great Britain: Including England, Scotland, Wales and Northern Ireland.

2. The Dominions, Present and Past

AUSTRALIA

The Commonwealth of Australia was proclaimed on January 1, 1901. It consists of six former colonies as follows:

New South Wales
Queensland
South Australia
Victoria
Tasmania
Western Australia

The following islands and territories are, or have been, administered by Australia: Australian Antarctic Territory, Christmas Island, Cocos (Keeling) Islands, Nauru, New Guinea, Norfolk Island, Papua.

CANADA

The Dominion of Canada was created by the British North America Act in 1867. The following provinces were former sepa- rate colonies and issued postage stamps:

British Columbia and Vancouver Island
New Brunswick
Newfoundland
Nova Scotia
Prince Edward Island

FIJI

The colony of Fiji became an independent nation with dominion status on Oct. 10, 1970.

GHANA

This state came into existence Mar. 6, 1957, with dominion status. It consists of the former colony of the Gold Coast and the Trusteeship Territory of Togoland. Ghana became a republic July 1, 1960.

INDIA

The Republic of India was inaugurated on January 26, 1950. It succeeded the Dominion of India which was proclaimed August 15, 1947, when the former Empire of India was divided into Pakistan and the Union of India. The Republic is composed of about 40 predominantly Hindu states of three classes: governor's provinces, chief commissioner's provinces and princely states. India also has various territories, such as the Andaman and Nicobar Islands.

The old Empire of India was a federation of British India and the native states. The more important princely states were autonomous. Of the more than 700 Indian states, these 43 are familiar names to philatelists because of their postage stamps.

CONVENTION STATES

Chamba
Faridkot
Gwalior
Jhind
Nabha
Patiala

FEUDATORY STATES

Alwar
Bahawalpur
Bamra
Barwani
Bhopal
Bhor
Bijawar
Bundi
Bussahir
Charkhari
Cochin
Dhar
Dungarpur
Duttia
Faridkot (1879-85)
Hyderabad
Idar
Indore
Jaipur
Jammu
Jammu and Kashmir
Jasdan
Jhalawar
Jhind (1875-76)
Kashmir
Kishangarh
Kotah
Las Bela
Morvi
Nandgaon
Nowanuggur
Orchha
Poonch
Rajasthan
Rajpeepla
Sirmur
Soruth
Tonk
Travancore
Wadhwan

NEW ZEALAND

Became a dominion on September 26, 1907. The following islands and territories are, or have been, administered by New Zealand:

Aitutaki
Cook Islands (Rarotonga)
Niue
Penrhyn
Ross Dependency
Samoa (Western Samoa)
Tokelau Islands

PAKISTAN

The Republic of Pakistan was proclaimed March 23, 1956. It succeeded the Dominion which was proclaimed August 15, 1947. It is made up of all or part of several Moslem provinces and various districts of the former Empire of India, including Bahawalpur and Las Bela. Pakistan withdrew from the Commonwealth in 1972.

SOUTH AFRICA

Under the terms of the South African Act (1909) the self-governing colonies of Cape of Good Hope, Natal, Orange River Colony and Transvaal united on May 31, 1910, to form the Union of South Africa. It became an independent republic May 3, 1961.

Under the terms of the Treaty of Versailles, South-West Africa, formerly German South-West Africa, was mandated to the Union of South Africa.

SRI LANKA (CEYLON)

The Dominion of Ceylon was proclaimed February 4, 1948. The island had been a Crown Colony from 1802 until then. On May 22, 1972, Ceylon became the Republic of Sri Lanka.

3. Colonies, Past and Present; Controlled Territory and Independent Members of the Commonwealth

Aden
Aitutaki
Antigua
Ascension
Bahamas
Bahrain
Bangladesh
Barbados
Barbuda
Basutoland
Batum
Bechuanaland
Bechuanaland Prot.
Belize
Bermuda
Botswana
British Antarctic Territory
British Central Africa
British Columbia and Vancouver Island
British East Africa
British Guiana

British Honduras
British Indian Ocean Territory
British New Guinea
British Solomon Islands
British Somaliland
Brunei
Burma
Bushire
Cameroons
Cape of Good Hope
Cayman Islands
Christmas Island
Cocos (Keeling) Islands
Cook Islands
Crete,
  British Administration
Cyprus
Dominica
East Africa & Uganda
  Protectorates
Egypt
Falkland Islands
Fiji
Gambia
German East Africa
Gibraltar
Gilbert Islands
Gilbert & Ellice Islands
Gold Coast
Grenada
Griqualand West
Guernsey
Guyana
Heligoland
Hong Kong
Indian Native States
  (see India)
Ionian Islands
Jamaica
Jersey
Kenya
Kenya, Uganda & Tanzania
Kuwait
Labuan
Lagos
Leeward Islands
Lesotho
Madagascar
Malawi
Malaya
  Federated Malay States
  Johore
  Kedah
  Kelantan
  Malacca
  Negri Sembilan
  Pahang
  Penang
  Perak
  Perlis
  Selangor
  Singapore
  Sungei Ujong
  Trengganu
Malaysia
Maldive Islands
Malta
Man, Isle of
Mauritius
Mesopotamia
Montserrat
Muscat
Namibia
Natal
Nauru
Nevis
New Britain
New Brunswick
Newfoundland
New Guinea
New Hebrides
New Republic
New South Wales
Niger Coast Protectorate
Nigeria
Niue
Norfolk Island
North Borneo
Northern Nigeria
Northern Rhodesia
North West Pacific Islands
Nova Scotia
Nyasaland Protectorate
Oman
Orange River Colony
Palestine
Papua New Guinea
Penrhyn Island
Pitcairn Islands
Prince Edward Island
Queensland
Rhodesia
Rhodesia & Nyasaland
Ross Dependency
Sabah
St. Christopher
St. Helena
St. Kitts
St. Kitts-Nevis-Anguilla
St. Lucia
St. Vincent
Samoa
Sarawak
Seychelles
Sierra Leone
Solomon Islands
Somaliland Protectorate
South Arabia
South Australia
South Georgia
Southern Nigeria
Southern Rhodesia
South-West Africa
Stellaland
Straits Settlements
Sudan
Swaziland
Tanganyika
Tanzania
Tasmania
Tobago
Togo
Tokelau Islands
Tonga
Transvaal
Trinidad
Trinidad and Tobago
Tristan da Cunha
Trucial States
Turks and Caicos
Turks Islands
Tuvalu
Uganda
United Arab Emirates
Victoria
Virgin Islands
Western Australia
Zambia
Zanzibar
Zululand

POST OFFICES IN FOREIGN COUNTRIES

Africa
  East Africa Forces
  Middle East Forces
Bangkok
China
Morocco
Turkish Empire

Colonies, Former Colonies, Offices, Territories Controlled by Parent States

Belgium

Belgian Congo
Ruanda-Urundi

Denmark

Danish West Indies
Faroe Islands
Greenland
Iceland

Finland

Aland Islands

France

COLONIES PAST AND PRESENT, CONTROLLED TERRITORIES

Afars & Issas, Territory of
Alaouites
Alexandretta
Algeria
Alsace & Lorraine
Anjouan
Annam & Tonkin
Benin
Cambodia (Khmer)
Cameroun
Castellorizo
Chad
Cilicia
Cochin China
Comoro Islands
Dahomey
Diego Suarez
Djibouti (Somali Coast)
Fezzan
French Congo
French Equatorial Africa
French Guiana
French Guinea
French India
French Morocco
French Polynesia (Oceania)
French Southern & Antarctic Territories
French Sudan
French West Africa
Gabon
Germany
Ghadames
Grand Comoro
Guadeloupe
Indo-China
Inini
Ivory Coast
Laos
Latakia
Lebanon
Madagascar
Martinique
Mauritania
Mayotte
Memel
Middle Congo
Moheli
New Caledonia
New Hebrides
Niger Territory
Nossi-Be
Obock
Reunion
Rouad, Ile
Ste.-Marie de Madagascar
St. Pierre & Miquelon
Senegal
Senegambia & Niger
Somali Coast
Syria
Tahiti
Togo
Tunisia
Ubangi-Shari
Upper Senegal & Niger
Upper Volta
Viet Nam
Wallis & Futuna Islands

POST OFFICES IN FOREIGN COUNTRIES

China
Crete
Egypt
Turkish Empire
Zanzibar

Germany

EARLY STATES

Baden
Bavaria
Bergedorf
Bremen
Brunswick
Hamburg
Hanover
Lubeck
Mecklenburg-Schwerin
Mecklenburg-Strelitz
Oldenburg
Prussia
Saxony
Schleswig-Holstein
Wurttemberg

FORMER COLONIES

Cameroun (Kamerun)
Caroline Islands
German East Africa
German New Guinea
German South-West Africa
Kiauchau
Mariana Islands
Marshall Islands
Samoa
Togo

Italy

EARLY STATES

Modena
Parma
Romagna
Roman States
Sardinia
Tuscany
Two Sicilies
  Naples
  Neapolitan Provinces
  Sicily

FORMER COLONIES, CONTROLLED TERRITORIES, OCCUPATION AREAS

Aegean Islands
  Calimno (Calino)
  Caso
  Cos (Coo)
  Karki (Carchi)
  Leros (Lero)
  Lipso
  Nisiros (Nisiro)
  Patmos (Patmo)
  Piscopi
  Rodi (Rhodes)
  Scarpanto
  Simi
  Stampalia
Castellorizo
Corfu
Cyrenaica
Eritrea
Ethiopia (Abyssinia)
Fiume
Ionian Islands
  Cephalonia
  Ithaca
  Paxos
Italian East Africa
Libya
Oltre Giuba
Saseno
Somalia (Italian Somaliland)
Tripolitania

POST OFFICES IN FOREIGN COUNTRIES

"ESTERO"*
Austria
China
  Peking
  Tientsin
Crete
Tripoli
Turkish Empire
  Constantinople
  Durazzo
  Janina
Jerusalem
Salonika
Scutari
Smyrna
Valona

*Stamps overprinted "ESTERO" were used in various parts of the world.

Netherlands

Aruba
Netherlands Antilles (Curacao)
Netherlands Indies
Netherlands New Guinea
Surinam (Dutch Guiana)

Portugal

COLONIES PAST AND PRESENT, CONTROLLED TERRITORIES

Angola
Angra
Azores
Cape Verde
Funchal
Horta
Inhambane
Kionga
Lourenco Marques
Macao
Madeira
Mozambique
Mozambique Co.
Nyassa
Ponta Delgada
Portuguese Africa
Portuguese Congo
Portuguese Guinea
Portuguese India
Quelimane
St. Thomas & Prince Islands
Tete
Timor
Zambezia

Russia

ALLIED TERRITORIES AND REPUBLICS, OCCUPATION AREAS

Armenia
Aunus (Olonets)
Azerbaijan
Batum
Estonia
Far Eastern Republic
Georgia
Karelia
Latvia
Lithuania
North Ingermanland
Ostland
Russian Turkestan
Siberia
South Russia
Tannu Tuva
Transcaucasian Fed. Republics
Ukraine
Wenden (Livonia)
Western Ukraine

Spain

COLONIES PAST AND PRESENT, CONTROLLED TERRITORIES

Aguera, La
Cape Juby
Cuba
Elobey, Annobon & Corisco
Fernando Po
Ifni
Mariana Islands
Philippines
Puerto Rico
Rio de Oro
Rio Muni
Spanish Guinea
Spanish Morocco
Spanish Sahara
Spanish West Africa

POST OFFICES IN FOREIGN COUNTRIES

Morocco
Tangier
Tetuan

Dies of British Colonial Stamps

DIE A:

1. The lines in the groundwork vary in thickness and are not uniformly straight.

2. The seventh and eighth lines from the top, in the groundwork, converge where they meet the head.

3. There is a small dash in the upper part of the second jewel in the band of the crown.

4. The vertical color line in front of the throat stops at the sixth line of shading on the neck.

DIE B:

1. The lines in the groundwork are all thin and straight.

2. All the lines of the background are parallel.

3. There is no dash in the upper part of the second jewel in the band of the crown.

4. The vertical color line in front of the throat stops at the eighth line of shading on the neck.

DIE I:

1. The base of the crown is well below the level of the inner white line around the vignette.

2. The labels inscribed "POSTAGE" and "REVENUE" are cut square at the top.

3. There is a white "bud" on the outer side of the main stem of the curved ornaments in each lower corner.

4. The second (thick) line below the country name has the ends next to the crown cut diagonally.

DIE Ia.	DIE Ib.
1 as die II.	1 and 3 as die II.
2 and 3 as die I.	2 as die I.

DIE II:

1. The base of the crown is aligned with the underside of the white line around the vignette.

2. The labels curve inward at the top inner corners.

3. The "bud" has been removed from the outer curve of the ornaments in each corner.

4. The second line below the country name has the ends next to the crown cut vertically.

Wmk. 1
Crown and C C

Wmk. 2
Crown and C A

Wmk. 3
Multiple Crown and C A

Wmk. 4
Multiple Crown and Script C A

Wmk. 4a

Wmk. 314
St. Edward's Crown and C A Multiple

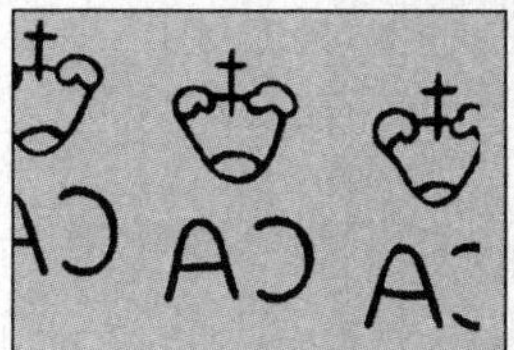

Wmk. 373

Wmk. 384

Wmk. 406

British Colonial and Crown Agents Watermarks

Watermarks 1 to 4, 314, 373, 384 and 406, common to many British territories, are illustrated here to avoid duplication.

The letters "CC" of Wmk. 1 identify the paper as having been made for the use of the Crown Colonies, while the letters "CA" of the others stand for "Crown Agents." Both Wmks. 1 and 2 were used on stamps printed by De La Rue & Co.

Wmk. 3 was adopted in 1904; Wmk. 4 in 1921; Wmk. 314 in 1957; Wmk. 373 in 1974; Wmk. 384 in 1985; Wmk 406 in 2008.

In Wmk. 4a, a non-matching crown of the general St. Edwards type (bulging on both sides at top) was substituted for one of the Wmk. 4 crowns which fell off the dandy roll. The non-matching crown occurs in 1950-52 printings in a horizontal row of crowns on certain regular stamps of Johore and Seychelles, and on various postage due stamps of Barbados, Basutoland, British Guiana, Gold Coast, Grenada, Northern Rhodesia, St. Lucia, Swaziland and Trinidad and Tobago. A variation of Wmk. 4a, with the non-matching crown in a horizontal row of crown-CA-crown, occurs on regular stamps of Bahamas, St. Kitts-Nevis and Singapore.

Wmk. 314 was intentionally used sideways, starting in 1966. When a stamp was issued with Wmk. 314 both upright and sideways, the sideways varieties usually are listed also – with minor numbers. In many of the later issues, Wmk. 314 is slightly visible.

Wmk. 373 is usually only faintly visible.

UNITED STATES

yu-ˌnī-təd 'stāts

GOVT. — Republic
AREA — 3,615,211 sq. mi.
POP. — 308,745,538 (2010)
CAPITAL — Washington, DC

In addition to the 50 States and the District of Columbia, the Republic includes Guam, the Commonwealth of Puerto Rico, the Virgin Islands, American Samoa, Wake, Midway, and a number of small islands in the Pacific Ocean, all of which use stamps of the United States.

100 Cents = 1 Dollar

Catalogue values for unused stamps in this country are for Never Hinged items, beginning with Scott 772 in the regular postage section, Scott C19 in the air post section, Scott E17 in the special delivery section, Scott FA1 in the certified mail section, Scott O127 in officials section, Scott J88 in the postage due section, Scott RW1 in the hunting permit stamps section.

Watermarks

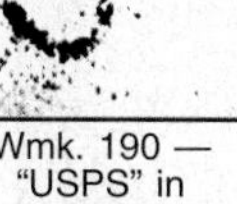

Wmk. 190 — "USPS" in Single-lined Capitals

Wmk. 191 — Double-lined "USPS" in Capitals

Watermark 191 has 9 letters for each horizontal row of 10 stamps. Watermark 190 has 8 to 9 letters for each horizontal row. Each watermark has 9 letters for each vertical row of 10 stamps This results in a number of stamps in each pane showing only a small portion of 1 or more watermark letters. This is especialy true of watermark 190.

Wmk. 190PI — PIPS, used in the Philippines
Wmk. 191PI — PIPS, used in the Philippines
Wmk. 191C — US-C, used for Cuba
Wmk. 191R — USIR

PROVISIONAL ISSUES BY POSTMASTERS

Values for Envelopes are for entires.

ALEXANDRIA, VA.

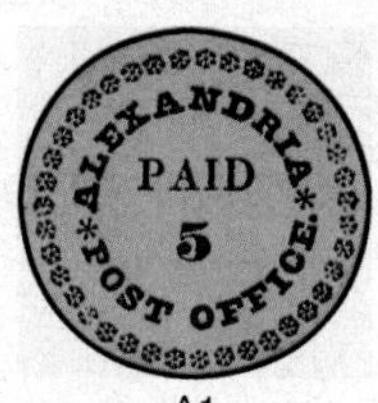

A1

All known examples are cut to shape.
Type I — 40 asterisks in circle.
Type II — 39 asterisks in circle.

1846 **Typeset** ***Imperf.***

1X1 A1 5c black, *buff,* type I 325,000.
a. 5c black, *buff,* type II 625,000.
1X2 A1 5c black, *blue,* type I, on cover —

ANNAPOLIS, MD.

E1

1846

2XU1 E1 5c carmine red, *white* 600,000.

Handstamped impressions of the circular design with "2" in blue or red exist on envelopes and letter sheets. Values: blue $7,500, red $11,000.

A letter sheet exists with circular design and "5" handstamped in red. Values: blue $10,000, red $12,500.

A similar circular design in blue was used as a postmark.

BALTIMORE, MD.

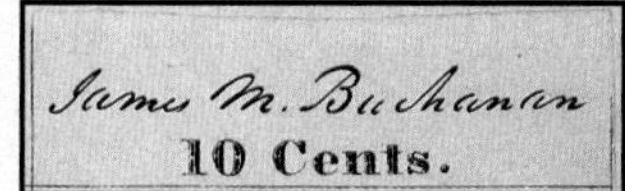

Signature of Postmaster — A1

Printed from a plate of 12 (2x6) containing nine 5c stamps and three 10c.

1845 **Engr.** ***Imperf.***

3X1 A1 5c black 6,000.
3X2 A1 10c black, on cover 80,000.
3X3 A1 5c black, *bluish* 65,000. 6,000.
3X4 A1 10c black, *bluish* 50,000.

Nos. 3X1-3X4 were printed from a plate of 12 (2x6) containing nine 5c and three 10c.

Envelopes

E1

The color given is that of the "PAID 5" and oval. "James M. Buchanan" is handstamped in black, blue or red. The paper is manila, buff, white, salmon or grayish.

1845 **Handstamped**
Various Papers

3XU1 E1 5c blue 6,500.
3XU2 E1 5c red 10,000.
3XU3 E1 10c blue 20,000.
3XU4 E1 10c red 20,000.

On the formerly listed "5+5" envelopes, the second "5" in oval is believed not to be part of the basic prepaid marking.

BOSCAWEN, N. H.

A1

1846 (?) **Typeset** ***Imperf.***

4X1 A1 5c dull blue, *yellowish,* on cover 300,000.

BRATTLEBORO, VT.

Initials of Postmaster (FNP) — A1

Plate of 10 (5x2).

1846 ***Imperf.***
Thick Softwove Paper Colored Through

5X1 A1 5c black, *buff* 9,000.

LOCKPORT, N. Y.

A1

"Lockport, N.Y." oval and "PAID" separately handstamped in red, "5" in black ms.

1846 ***Imperf.***

6X1 A1 5c red, *buff,* on cover 300,000.

MILLBURY, Mass.

George Washington — A1

Printed from a woodcut, singly, on a hand press.

1846 ***Imperf.***

7X1 A1 5c black, *bluish* — 50,000.

NEW HAVEN, CONN.

ENVELOPES

E1

Impressed from a brass handstamp at upper right of envelope.

Signed in blue, black or magenta ms., as indicated in parentheses.

1845

8XU1 E1 5c red (M) 100,000.
8XU2 E1 5c red, *light bluish* (Bk) 125,000.
8XU3 E1 5c dull blue, *buff* (Bl) 75,000.
8XU4 E1 5c dull blue (Bl) 60,000.

Values of Nos. 8XU1-8XU4 are a guide to value. They are based on auction realizations and other sales, and take condition into consideration. All New Haven envelopes are of equal rarity (each is unique), with the exception of No. 8XU2, of which two exist. An entire of No. 8XU2 is the finest example known, and this is reflected in the value shown. The other envelopes are valued according to condition, and cut squares also are valued according to condition as much as rarity.

Reprints were made at various times between 1871 and 1932. They can be distinguished from the originals, primarily due to differences in paper. See the Scott Specialized Catalogue of United States Stamps and Covers for more detail and values.

NEW YORK, N. Y.

George Washington — A1

Plate of 40 (5x8). Nos. 9X1-9X3 and varieties unused are valued without gum. Examples with original gum are extremely scarce and will command higher prices.

9X1 A1 5c black, signed ACM, connected, *1846* 1,500. 500.
a. Signed ACM, AC connected 1,750. 575.
b. Signed A.C.M. 4,500. 700.
c. Signed MMJr 10,000.
d. Signed RHM 13,000. 3,500.
e. Without signature 3,750. 950.

These stamps were usually initialed "ACM" in magenta ink, as a control, before being sold or passed through the mails.

A plate of 9 (3x3) was made from which proofs were printed in black on white and deep blue papers; also in blue, green, brown and red on white bond paper. Stamps from this plate were not issued, and it is possible that it is an essay, as the design differs slightly from the issued stamps from the sheet of 40. No examples from the plate of nine are known used.

1847 **Engr.** ***Imperf.***
Blue Wove Paper

9X2 A1 5c black, signed ACM connected 6,500. 3,500.
a. Signed RHM —
b. Signed ACM, AC connected 8,000.
d. Without signature 11,000. 7,250.

On the only example known of No. 9X2a the "R" is illegible and does not match those of the other "RHM" signatures.

No. 9X2b is unique.

1847 **Engr.** ***Imperf.***
Gray Wove Paper

9X3 A1 5c black, signed ACM connected 5,250. 2,250.
a. Signed RHM 7,000.
b. Without signature 13,000.

PROVIDENCE, R. I.

A1 & A2

10X1 A1 5c gray black 350. *1,900.*
10X2 A2 10c gray black 1,150. *16,500.*
a. Se-tenant with 5c 2,000.

Plate of 12 (3x4) contains 11-5c and 1-10c.

Reprints were made in 1898. Each stamp bears one of the following letters on the back: B. O. G. E. R. T. D. U. R. B. I. N. Value of 5c, $65; 10c, $160; sheet, $1,000.

Reprint singles or sheets without back print sell for more.

ST. LOUIS, MO.

A1

A2

A3

Missouri Coat of Arms

Nos. 11X1-11X8 unused are valued without gum.

Wove Paper Colored Through

1845, Nov.-1846 ***Imperf.***

11X1	A1	5c black, *greenish*	*50,000.*	*8,000.*
11X2	A2	10c black, *greenish*	*50,000.*	*8,000.*
11X3	A3	20c black, *greenish*		*160,000.*

Printed from Plate 1 (3 varieties each of the 5c and 10c) and Plate 2 (1 variety of the 5c, 3 of the 10c, 2 of the 20c).

1846

11X4	A1	5c black, (III), *gray lilac*	—	*55,000.*
11X5	A2	10c black, *gray lilac*	*50,000.*	*10,000.*
11X6	A3	20c black, *gray lilac*	*100,000.*	*55,000.*

One variety of 5c, 3 of 10c, 2 of 20c.
No. 11X6 unused is unique. It is in the grade of fine and valued thus.

1847 **Pelure Paper**

11X7	A1	5c black, *bluish*	—	*11,000.*
11X8	A2	10c black, *bluish*	*17,500.*	*15,000.*
a.		Impression of 5c on back		*77,500.*

Three varieties of 5c, 3 of 10c.
Values of Nos. 11X7-11X8 reflect the usual poor condition of these stamps, which were printed on fragile pelure paper. Attractive examples with minor defects sell for considerably more.
Used values are for pen-canceled stamps.
No. 11X8a is unique.

Please Note:
Stamps are valued in the grade of very fine unless otherwise indicated.
Values for early and valuable stamps are for examples with certificates of authenticity from acknowledged expert committees, or examples sold with the buyer having the right of certification. This applies to examples with original gum as well as examples without gum. Beware of stamps offered "as is," as the gum on some unused stamps offered with "original gum" may be fraudulent, and stamps offered as unused without gum may in some cases be altered or faintly canceled used stamps.

Manuscript Cancels on Used Stamps

Manuscript (pen) cancels reduce the value of used stamps by about 50%. See the Scott U.S. Specialized Catalogue for individual valuations.

GENERAL ISSUES
All Issues from 1847 through 1894 are unwatermarked.

Benjamin Franklin — A1

1847, July 1 **Engr.** ***Imperf.***
Thin Bluish Wove Paper

1	A1	5c red brown	6,750.	425.
		No gum	2,400.	
		Pen Cancel		230.
a.		5c dark brown	8,750.	800.
		No gum	3,250.	
b.		5c orange brown	10,000.	900.
		No gum	3,500.	
c.		5c red orange	*25,000.*	*9,500.*
		No gum	*9,500.*	
d.		5c brown orange	—	1,100.
		No gum	*4,500.*	

George Washington — A2

2	A2	10c black	*35,000.*	1,000.
		No gum	*15,000.*	
		Pen Cancel		575.
a.		Diagonal half used as 5c on cover		*12,500.*
b.		Vertical half used as 5c on cover		*30,000.*
c.		Horizontal half used as 5c on cover		—

A3

A4

REPRODUCTIONS of 1847 ISSUE
Actually, official imitations made from new plates of 50 subjects made by the Bureau of Engraving and Printing by order of the Post Office Department. These were not valid for postal use.

5c. On the originals the left side of the white shirt frill touches the oval on a level with the top of the "F" of "Five." On the reproductions it touches the oval about on a level with the top of the figure "5." On the originals, the bottom of the right leg of the "N" in "CENTS" is blunt. On the reproductions, the "N" comes to a point at the bottom.

10c. On the reproductions, line of coat at left points to right tip of "X" and line of coat at right points to center of "S" of CENTS. On the originals, line of coat points to "T" of TEN and between "T" and "S" of CENTS. The bottom of the right leg of the "N" of "CENTS" shows the same difference as on the 5c originals and reproductions. On the reproductions, the gap between the bottom legs of the left "X" is noticeably wider than the gap on the right "X." On the originals, the gaps are of equal width. On the reproductions, the eyes have a sleepy look, the line of the mouth is straighter, and in the curl of hair near the left cheek is a strong black dot, while the originals have only a faint one.

(See Nos. 948a and 948b for 1947 reproductions—5c blue and 10c brown orange in larger size.)

1875 ***Imperf.***
Bluish paper, without gum

3	A3	5c red brown	825.
4	A4	10c black	1,000.

Numbers in parentheses are quantities sold.

In Nos. 5-17, the 1¢, 3¢ and 12¢ have very small margins between the stamps. The 5¢ and 10¢ have moderate size margins. The values of these stamps take the margin size into consideration.

Values for Nos. 5A, 6b and 19b are for the less distinct positions. Best examples sell for more.

Values for No. 16 are for outer line recut at top. Other recuts sell for more.

Franklin — A5

Type I

Type Ib

ONE CENT. Issued July 1, 1851.
Type I. Has complete curved lines outside the labels with "U. S. Postage" and "One Cent." The scrolls below the lower label are turned under, forming little balls. The ornaments at top are substantially complete.
Type Ib. As type I, but balls below bottom label are not as clear. Plume-like scrolls at bottom are incomplete.

1851-57 ***Imperf.***

5	A5	1c blue, type I (7R1E)	*225,000.*	*75,000.*
5A	A5	1c blue, type 1b	*32,500.*	*9,250.*
		No gum	*12,000.*	

A6

Type Ic

Type Ia. Same as type I at bottom, but top ornaments and outer line at top are partly cut away.
Type Ic. Same as type Ia, but bottom right plume and ball ornament incomplete. Bottom left plume is complete or nearly complete.

6	A6	1c blue, type 1a ('57)	*45,000.*	*11,000.*
		No gum	*20,000.*	
6b	A6	1c blue, type 1c	*7,000.*	*3,250.*
		No gum	*3,000.*	

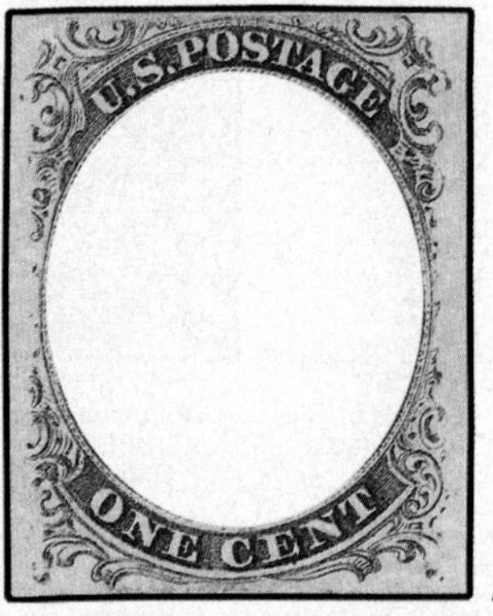

A7

Type II — Same as Type I at top, but the little balls of the bottom scrolls and the bottoms of the lower plume ornaments are missing. The side ornaments are substantially complete.

7	A7	1c blue, type II	1,050.	145.
		No gum	400.	

A8

Newbury 1961

Lilly 1967

Kapiloff 1992

Honolulu Advertiser 1995

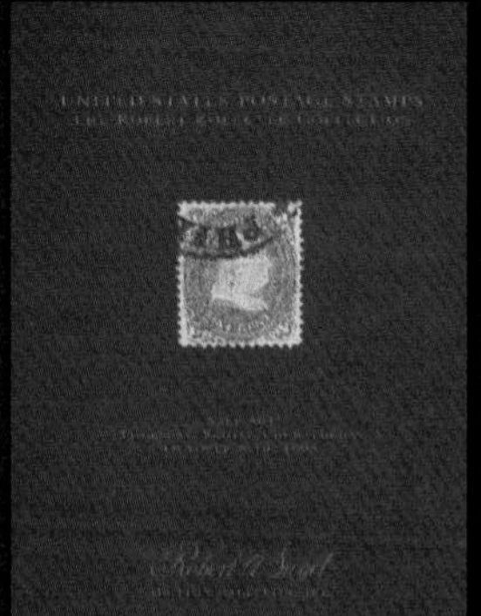

Zoellner 1998

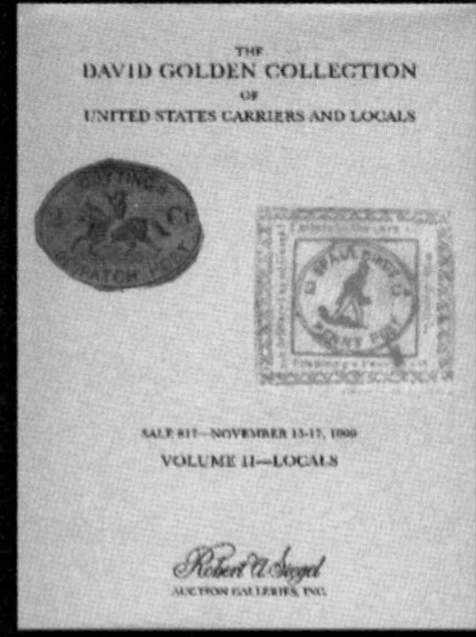

Golden 1999

Islander 2008

Whitman 2009

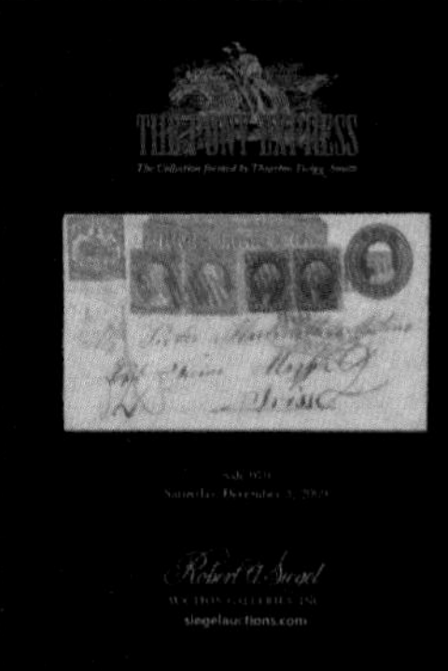

Twigg-Smith 2009

Frelinghuysen 2012

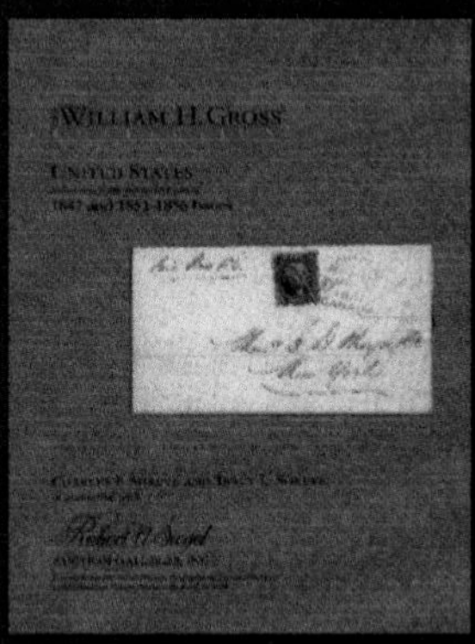

Gross 2013

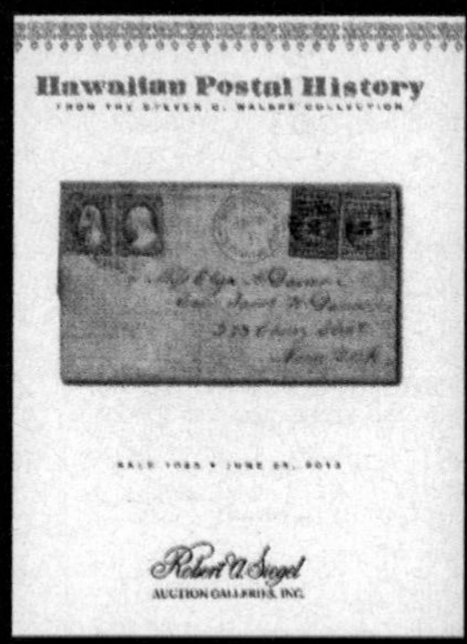

Walske 2013

Type IIIa

Type III. The top and bottom curved lines outside the labels are broken in the middle. The side ornaments are substantially complete.

Type IIIa. Similar to type III with the outer line broken at top or bottom but not both.

8 A8 1c blue, type III *25,000.* 2,250.
No gum *7,500.*

Values for type III are for at least a 2mm break in each outer line. Examples of type III with wider breaks in outer lines command higher prices; those with smaller breaks sell for much less.

8A A8 1c blue, type IIIa 6,000. 900.
No gum 2,250.

Stamps of type IIIa with bottom line broken command higher prices than those with top line broken. See note after No. 8 on width of break of outer lines.

A9

Type IV. Similar to type II, but with the curved lines outside the labels recut at top or bottom or both.

9 A9 1c blue, type IV ('52) 750.00 95.00
No gum 275.00
a. Printed on both sides, reverse inverted *50,000.*
b. Diagonal half used as ½c on cover *60,000.*

No. 9a is unique.

The No. 9b cover, a printed-matter circular mailed in 1853, is unique. The circular likely should have been sent at the 1c rate for printed matter in effect at the time. However, both the sending (New Haven, Conn.) and receiving (Hartford, Conn.) post offices treated it as fully prepaid with ½c postage applied. Value is based on 2013 auction realization.

Washington — A10

All of the 3c stamps of the 1851 and 1857 issues were recut at least to the extent of the outer frame lines, sometimes the inner lines at the sides (type II stamps), and often other lines in triangles, diamond blocks, label blocks and/or top/bottom frame lines. Some of the most prominent varieties are listed below each major listing (others are described in "The 3c Stamp of U.S. 1851-57 Issue," by Carroll Chase).

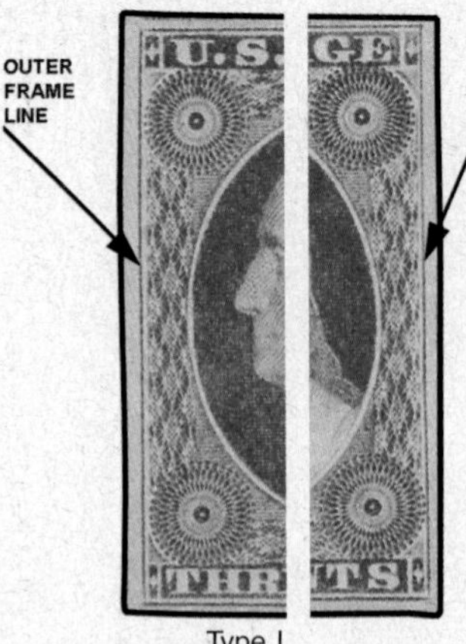

Type I

THREE CENTS.

Type I — There is an outer frame line on all four sides. The outer frame lines at the sides are always recut, but the inner lines at the sides are not.

10 A10 3c org brown, type I 4,000. 200.00
No gum 1,500.

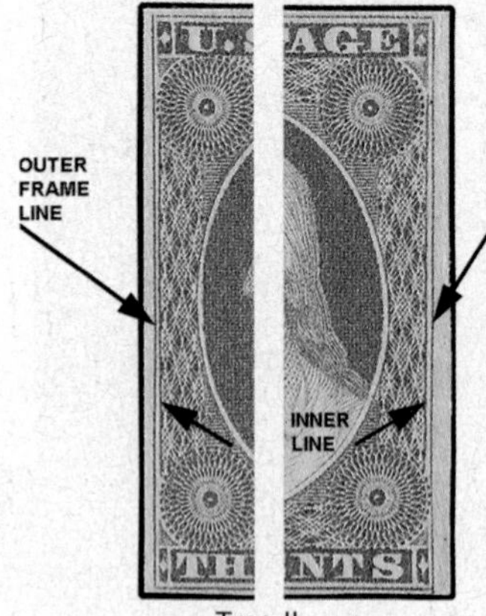

Type II

Type II — As type I, but with the inner lines at the sides also recut.

10A A10 3c org brown, type II 3,250. 160.00
No gum 1,250.
b. Printed on both sides *55,000.*

Only one example of No. 10Ab is recorded.

11 A10 3c dull red, type I ('55) 275.00 15.00
No gum 85.00

11A A10 3c dull red, type II ('53-'55) 275.00 15.00
No gum 85.00
c. Vertical half used as 1c on cover *5,000.*
d. Diagonal half used as 1c on cover *5,000.*
e. Double impression *30,000.*

Thomas Jefferson — A11

FIVE CENTS.

Type I — Projections on all four sides.

12 A11 5c red brown, type I ('56) *30,000.* 700.
No gum *11,000.*

Washington — A12

TEN CENTS

Type I — The "shells" at the lower corners are practically complete. The outer line below the label is very nearly complete. The outer lines are broken above the middle of the top label and the "X" in each upper corner.

13 A12 10c green, type I ('55) *19,000.* 925.
No gum *8,500.*

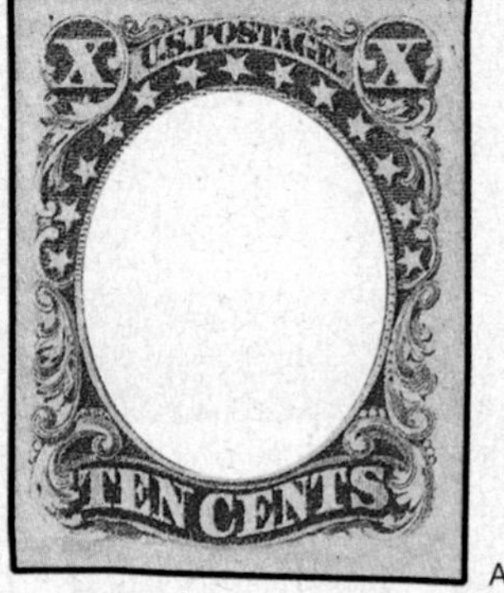

A13

Type II — The design is complete at the top. The outer line at the bottom is broken in the middle. The shells are partly cut away, as shown.

14 A13 10c green, type II ('55) 5,000. 160.
No gum 1,800.

A14

Type III — The outer lines are broken above the top label and the "X" numerals. The outer line at the bottom and the shells are partly cut away, as shown, similar to type II.

15 A14 10c green, type III ('55) 5,000. 160.
No gum 1,800.

A15

Type IV. The outer lines have been recut at top or bottom or both.

Types I, II, III and IV have complete ornaments at the sides of the stamps and three pearls at each outer edge of the bottom panel.

16 A15 10c green, type IV ('55) *35,000.* 1,650.
No gum *15,000.*

Washington — A16

17 A16 12c gray black 6,250. 250.
No gum 2,200.
a. Diagonal half used as 6c on cover *2,500.*
b. Vertical half used as 6c on cover *8,500.*
c. Printed on both sides *40,000.*

SAME DESIGNS AS 1851-57 ISSUES

Nos. 18-39 have small or very small margins. The values take into account the margin size.

1857-61 ***Perf. 15½***

18 A5 1c blue, type I ('61) 2,100. 550.
No gum 800.

19 A6 1c blue, type Ia *42,500.* *9,000.*
No gum *20,000.*
b. blue, type Ic 4,250. 2,500.
No gum *1,750.*

20 A7 1c blue, type II 900. 275.
No gum 375.

21 A8 1c blue, type III *17,500.* 2,000.
No gum *7,000.*
a. Horiz. pair, imperf between *23,000.*

22 A8 1c blue, type IIIa 2,400. 500.
No gum 850.
b. Horizontal pair, imperf. between *10,000.*

One pair of No. 22b is reported. Beware of numerous pairs that have blind perforations. These are not to be confused with No. 22b.

23 A9 1c blue, type IV 10,000. 900.
No gum 4,250.

Franklin — A20

Type V — Similar to type III of 1851-57 but with side ornaments partly cut away. About one-half of all positions have side scratches. Wide breaks in top and bottom framelines.

Type Va — Stamps from Plate 5 with almost complete ornaments at right side and no side scratches. Many, but not all, stamps from Plate 5 are Type Va, the remainder being Type V.

24 A20 1c blue, type V 140.00 40.00
No gum 55.00
b. Laid paper *7,500.*

Albums! Albums! and more Albums!

SUBWAY STAMP SHOP, INC.

Cover Album

- Complete album with 25 pages (page size 8⅞x9") Available in: **Blue, Black, Wine Red**
- Black-back two-sided 2 pocket pages (holds 100 180x108mm covers)
  ZGK-838A $31.17, **$23.38**
- Same with all-clear pages (holds 100 covers or 50 viewed from both sides)
  ZGK-838AC $31.17, **$23.38**
- Binder Size 10x9½x2¼"
  ZGK-830B $19.27, **$14.45**

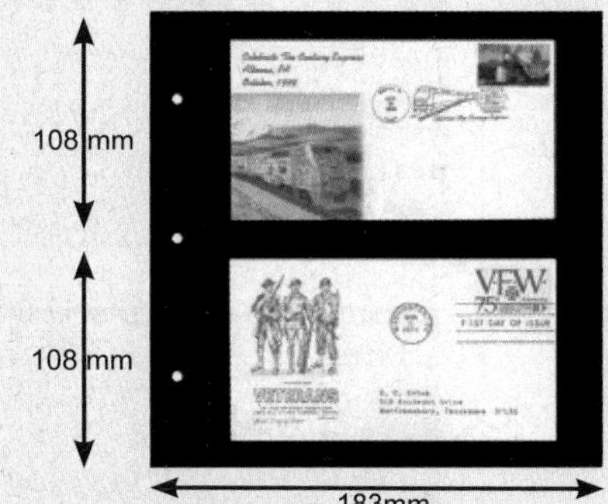

Euro Cover Album

- Complete album with 25 pages (page size 9x11⅛") Available in: **Blue, Black, Wine Red**
- Black-back two-sided 2 pocket pages (holds 100 202x135mm covers)
  ZGK-850A $37.25, **$27.94**
- Same with all-clear pages (holds 100 covers or 50 viewed from both sides)
  ZGK-850AC $37.25, **$27.94**
- Binder Size 10x11⅞x2⅜"
  ZGK-850B $21.82, **$16.37**

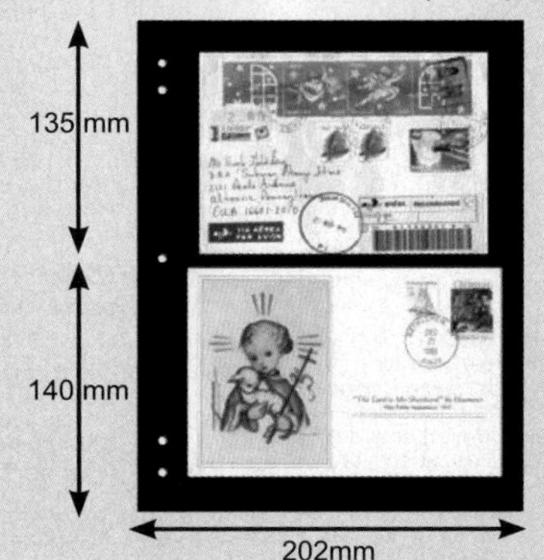

Postcard Album

- Complete album with 25 pages (page size 8⅞x9") Available in: **Blue, Black, Wine Red**
- Black-back two-sided 2 pocket pages (holds 100 154x108mm cards)
  ZGK-836A $31.17, **$23.38**
- Same with all-clear pages (holds 100 cards or 50 viewed from both sides) **ZGK-836AC** $31.17, **$23.38**
- Binder Size 10x9½x2¼"
  ZGK-830B $19.27, **$14.45**

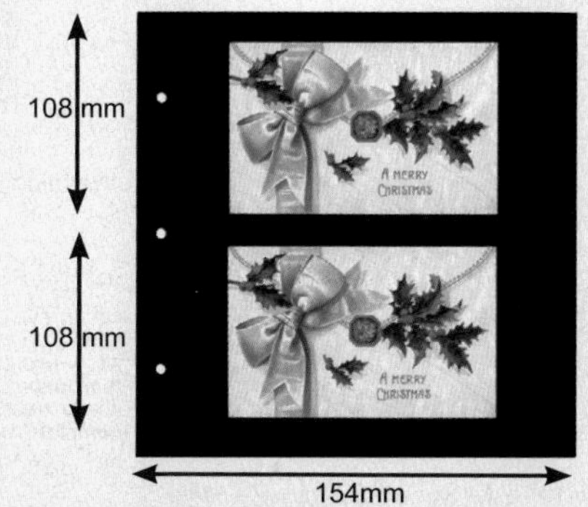

#10 Cover Album

- Complete album with 25 pages (Page Size 10½x11½") Available in: **Blue, Black, Wine Red**
- Black-back two-sided 2 pocket pages (holds 100 248x140mm covers)
  ZGK-822A $47.59, **$33.31**
- Same with all-clear pages (holds 100 covers or 50 viewed from both sides)
  ZGK-822AC $47.59, **$33.31**
- Binder Size 11¾x12¼x2⅜"
  ZGK-821B $26.01, **$19.51**

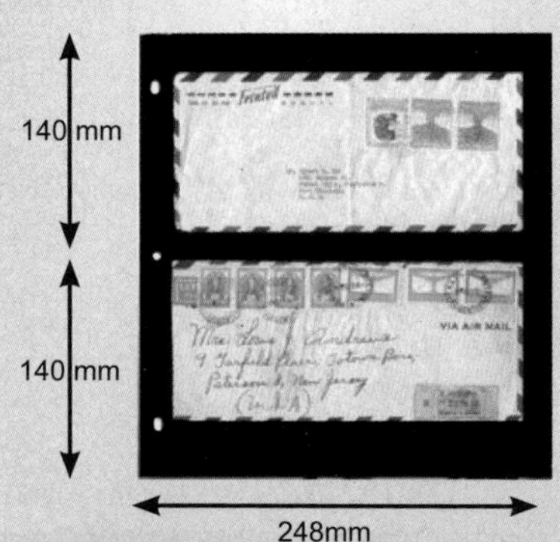

U.S. Full Sheet Album

- Complete album with 50 pages (Page Size 10¾x11⅜") Available in: **Blue, Black, Wine Red**
- Open top and right side for easy insertion of sheets
- Black-Back two-sided pages (hold 100 250x283mm sheets)
  ZGK-820A $69.16, **$48.41**
- Same with all-clear lightweight pages
  ZGK-820AC $69.16, **$48.41**
- Binder Size 11¾x12¼x 2⅜"
  ZGK-821B $26.01, **$19.51**

283mm

250mm

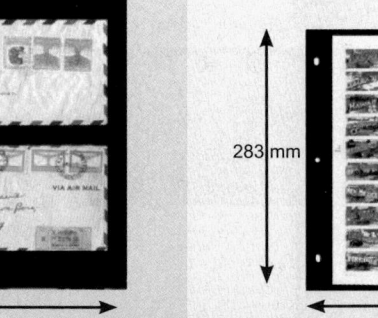

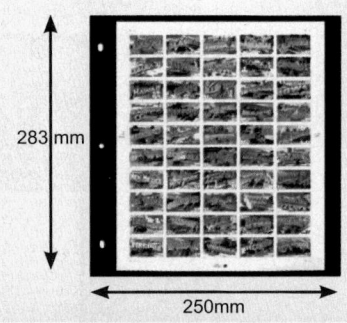

Small Pane Album

- Complete album with 25 pages (Page Size 8¾x9"") Available in: **Blue, Black, Wine Red**
- Black-back two-sided 1 pocket pages (holds 50 190x223mm panes)
  ZGK-840A $31.17, **$23.38**
- Same with all-clear pages (holds 25 viewed from both sides)
  ZGK-836AC $31.17, **$23.38**
- Binder Size 10x9½x2¼"
  ZGK-830B $19.27, **$14.45**

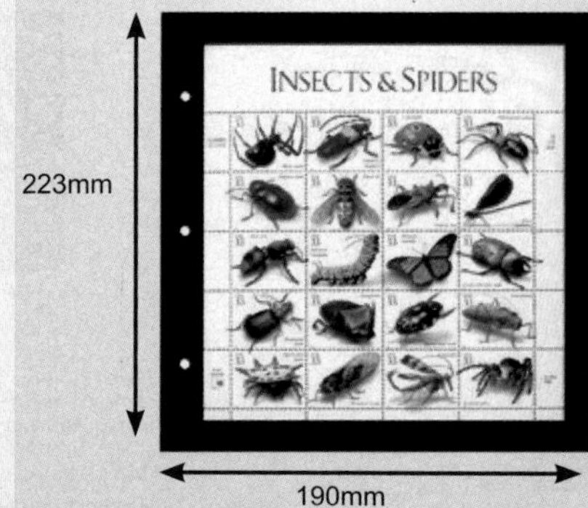

America's (and the World's) Largest Stamp Collecting Supply Company

SHIPPING CHARGES

By MAIL/UPS *: $7.50 Min. Orders over $54 ADD 12%,
Over $100 ADD 10%, Over $250 ADD 8%
* Some Remote Areas Carry Higher Shipping charges.
PA Residents: ADD 6% Sales Tax
ADD $5/$10 Per Parcel on high weight/low cost orders shipped to the 11 Western States & TX
Ask for Shipping Charges to AK, HI, P.R., APO's, FPO's, Foreign

Phone: 1-800-221-9960 Fax: 1-888-221-9960
Email: custserv@subwaystamp.com Phone: 814-946-1000 Fax: 814-946-9997

2121 Beale Ave, Altoona, Pa 16601 - Scott Vol. I
www.subwaystamp.com/
Prices subject to change without notice
Not Responsible For Typographical Errors

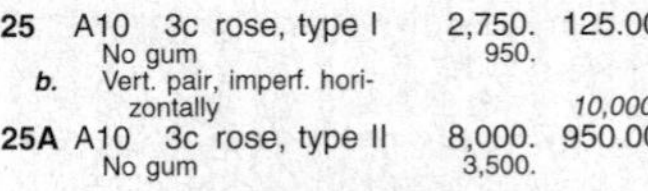

25 A10 3c rose, type I 2,750. 125.00
No gum 950.
b. Vert. pair, imperf. horizontally *10,000.*

25A A10 3c rose, type II 8,000. 950.00
No gum 3,500.

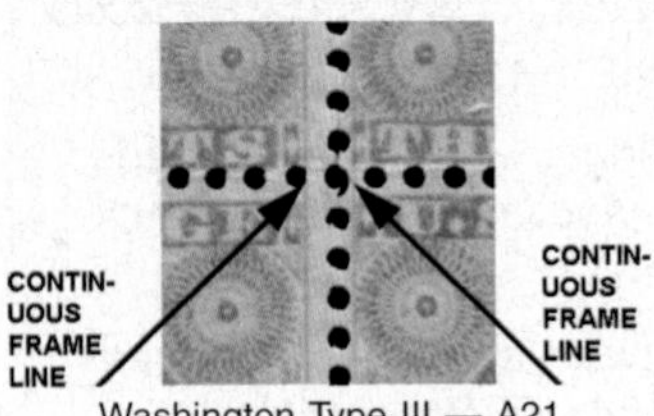

Washington Type III — A21

Type III — There are no outer frame lines at top and bottom. The side frame lines were recut so as to be continuous from the top to the bottom of the plate. Stamps from the top or bottom rows show the ends of the side frame lines and may be mistaken for Type IV.

26 A21 3c dull red, type III 65.00 9.00
No gum 22.50
b. Horiz. pair, imperf. vertically *14,000.* —
c. Vert. pair, imperf. horizontally *16,000.*
d. Horizontal pair, imperf. between —
e. Double impression *15,000.*

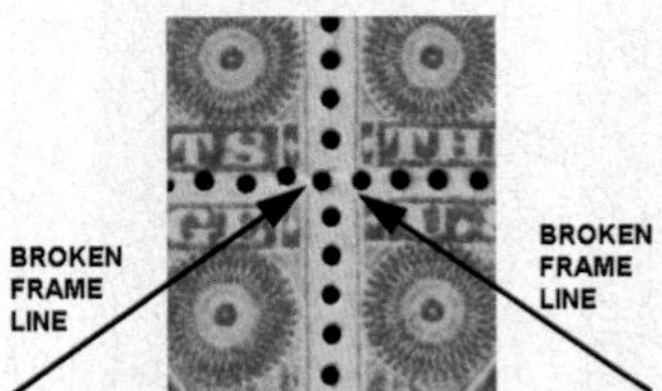

Washington Type IV — A21a

Type IV — As type III, but the side frame lines extend only to the top and bottom of the stamp design. All Type IV stamps are from plates 10 and 11 (each of which exists in three states), and these plates produced only Type IV. The side frame lines were recut individually for each stamp, thus being broken between the stamps vertically.

Beware of type III stamps with frame lines that stop at the top of the design (from top row of plate) or bottom of the design (from bottom row of plate). These are often mistakenly offered as No. 26A.

26A A21a 3c dull red, type IV 600.00 150.00
No gum 225.00
f. Horiz. strip of 3, imperf. vert., on cover *14,500.*

No. 26Af is unique.

27 A11 5c brick red, type I ('58) *80,000.* 1,700.
No gum *20,000.*

28 A11 5c red brown, type I *60,000.* 1,200.
No gum 15,000.
b. Bright red brown 70,000. 2,500.
No gum 20,000.

28A A11 5c Indian red, type I ('58) *175,000.* 3,500.
No gum *40,000.*

No. 28A unused is valued in the grade of fine. Only four examples are recorded with any amount of gum.

29 A11 5c brown, type I ('59) 5,500. 400.
No gum 1,750.

Jefferson — A22

FIVE CENTS.
Type II — The projections at top and bottom are partly cut away.

30 A22 5c orange brown, type II ('61) 1,250. *1,400.*
No gum 500.

30A A22 5c brown, type II ('60) 2,200. 300.
No gum 825.
b. Printed on both sides *45,000.*

31 A12 10c green, type I *35,000.* 1,250.
No gum *11,500.*

32 A13 10c green, type II 6,000. 200.
No gum 2,150.

33 A14 10c green, type III 6,000. 200.
No gum 2,150.

34 A15 10c green, type IV *50,000.* 2,250.
No gum *20,000.*

Example I Example II

Washington (Two typical examples) — A23

TEN CENTS
Type V — The side ornaments are slightly cut away. Usually only one pearl remains at each end of the lower label, but some copies show two or three pearls at the right side. At the bottom the outer line is complete and the shells nearly so. The outer lines at top are complete except over the right "X."

35 A23 10c green, type V ('59) 225.00 65.00
No gum 85.00

No. 36 outer frame lines recut on plate

TWELVE CENTS. Printed from two plates.
Plate 1 (No. 36) — Outer frame lines were recut on the plate and are complete. Very narrow spacing of stamps on the plate.

36 A16 12c black (Plate 1) 1,900. 350.
No gum 575.
a. Diagonal half used as 6c on cover *17,500.*
c. Horizontal pair, imperf. between *12,500.*

Typical No. 36B, outer frame lines not recut

Plate III (No. 36B) — Weak outer frame lines from the die were not recut and are noticeably uneven or broken, sometimes partly missing. Somewhat wider spacing of stamps on the plate.

36B A16 12c black, plate III ('59) 700. 275.
No gum 325.

Washington A17

Franklin A18

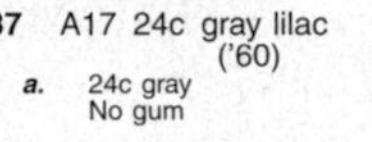

37 A17 24c gray lilac ('60) 1,400. 375.
a. 24c gray 1,400. 375.
No gum 525.

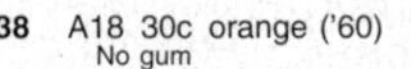

38 A18 30c orange ('60) 2,150. 425.
No gum 800.

Washington — A19

39 A19 90c blue ('60) 3,000. *11,000.*
No gum 1,100.

See Die and Plate proofs in the Scott United States Specialized Catalogue for imperfs. of the 12c, 24c, 30c, 90c.

Genuine cancellations on the 90c are rare. Used examples must be accompanied by certificates of authenticity issued by recognized expertizing committees.

REPRINTS OF 1857-60 ISSUE
White paper, without gum.

1875 ***Perf. 12***

40	A5	1c bright blue	*575.*	
41	A10	3c scarlet	*3,000.*	
42	A22	5c orange brown	*1,200.*	
43	A12	10c blue green	*2,500.*	13,000.
44	A16	12c greenish black	*2,750.*	
45	A17	24c blackish violet	*3,000.*	10,000.
46	A18	30c yellow orange	*3,000.*	
47	A19	90c deep blue	*4,000.*	

Nos. 41-46 are valued in the grade of fine.

Nos. 40-47 exist imperforate. Very infrequent sales preclude establishing a value at this time. One set of imperforate pairs is recorded and it sold for $110,000 in a 2009 auction.

Essays-Trial Color Proofs

The paper of former Nos. 55-62 (Nos. 63E11e, 65-E15h, 67-E9e, 69-E6e, 72-E7h, Essay section, Nos. 70eTC, 71bTC, Trial Color Proof section, Scott U.S. Specialized) is thin and semitransparent. That of the postage issues is thicker and more opaque, except Nos. 62B, 70c and 70d.

Franklin — A24

A24

Washington — A25

A25

Jefferson — A26

A26

Washington — A27

A27

A27a

Washington — A28

A28

Washington A29

Franklin A30

Washington — A31

A31

1c — There is a dash under the tip of the ornament at right of the numeral in upper left corner.

3c — Ornaments at corners end in a small ball.

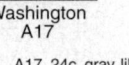

5c — There is a leaflet in the foliated ornaments at each corner.

10c (A27a) — A heavy curved line has been cut below the stars and an outer line added to the ornaments above them.

12c — There are corner ornaments consisting of ovals and scrolls.

90c — Parallel lines form an angle above the ribbon with "U. S. Postage"; between these lines there is a row of dashes and a point of color at the apex of the lower line.

1861 ***Perf. 12***

62B A27a 10c dark green *8,000.* 1,600.
No gum *3,250.*

1861-62 ***Perf. 12***

63 A24 1c blue 300.00 50.00
No gum 100.00
a. 1c ultramarine *2,500.* *800.00*
No gum *1,000.*
b. 1c dark blue 800.00 800.00
No gum 300.00
c. Laid paper, horiz. or vert. *8,500.* *5,000.*
d. Vertical pair, imperf. horiz. —
e. Printed on both sides, reverse inverted — *50,000.*
64 A25 3c pink *14,000.* 800.00
No gum *5,000.*
a. 3c pigeon blood pink *50,000.* *5,000.*
No gum *15,000.*
b. 3c rose pink, *Aug. 17, 1861* 600.00 150.00
No gum 230.00
65 A25 3c rose 125.00 3.00
No gum 40.00
b. Laid paper, horiz. or vert. — *1,250.*
d. Vertical pair, imperf. horiz. *15,000.* *1,500.*
e. Printed on both sides, reverse inverted *40,000.* *8,000.*
f. Double impression *15,000.*

The 3c lake can be found under No. 66 in the Trial Color Proofs section of the Scott U.S. Specialized Catalogue. The imperf 3c lake under No. 66P in the same section. The imperf 3c rose can be found in the Die and Plate Proofs section of the Specialized.

67 A26 5c buff *27,500.* 950.
No gum *10,500.*
a. 5c brown yellow *30,000.* 1,200.
No gum *11,500.*
b. 5c olive yellow — 4,000.

Values of Nos. 67, 67a, 67b reflect the normal small margins.

68 A27 10c green 1,100. 60.00
No gum 400.
a. 10c dark green 1,400. 85.00
No gum 525.
b. Vertical pair, imperf. horiz. *30,000.*
69 A28 12c black 1,800. 100.00
No gum 725.
70 A29 24c red lilac ('62) 3,000. 300.00
No gum 1,150.
a. 24c brown lilac 3,250. 325.00
No gum 1,250.
b. 24c steel blue ('61) *16,500.* 900.00
No gum *6,250.*
c. 24c violet, thin paper, *Aug. 20, 1861* *35,000.* 2,250.
No gum *13,500.*
d. 24c pale gray violet, thin paper *25,000.* 3,000.
No gum *6,000.*

There are numerous shades of the 24c stamp in this and the following issue.

Color changelings, especially of No. 78, are frequently offered as No. 70b. Obtaining a certificate from an acknowledged expert committee is strongly advised.

Nos. 70c and 70d are on a thinner, harder and more transparent paper than Nos. 70, 70a, 70b or the latter Nos. 78, 78a, 78b and 78c.

71 A30 30c orange 2,600. 190.
No gum 1,000.
a. Printed on both sides —

Values for No. 71 are for examples with small margins, especially at sides. Large-margined examples sell for much more.

72 A31 90c blue 3,250. 600.
No gum 1,300.
a. 90c pale blue 3,250. 650.
No gum 1,300.
b. 90c dark blue 4,000. 1,000.
No gum 1,600.

Please Note:

Stamps are valued in the grade of very fine unless otherwise indicated.

Values for early and valuable stamps are for examples with certificates of authenticity from acknowledged expert committees, or examples sold with the buyer having the right of certification.

This applies to examples with original gum as well as examples without gum.

Beware of stamps offered "as is," as the gum on some unused stamps offered with "original gum" may be fraudulent, and stamps offered as unused without gum may in some cases be altered or faintly canceled used stamps.

DESIGNS AS 1861 ISSUE

Andrew Jackson
A32

Abraham Lincoln
A33

1861-66 ***Perf. 12***

73 A32 2c black ('63) 375.00 65.00
No gum 140.00
a. Diagonal half used as 1c as part of 3c rate on cover 1,500.
b. Diagonal half used alone as 1c on cover *3,000.*
c. Horiz. half used as 1c as part of 3c rate on cover *3,500.*
d. Vert. half used as 1c as part of 3c rate on cover 2,000.
e. Vert. half used alone as 1c on cover *4,000.*
f. Printed on both sides, reverse not inverted *30,000.*
g. Laid paper — *12,500.*

No. 73f unused is unique. It has perfs cut off on two sides and is valued thus.

The 3c scarlet can be found under No. 74 in the Scott U.S. Specialized Catalogue Trial Color Proofs section.

75 A26 5c red brown ('62) 5,750. 475.
No gum 2,200.

Values for No. 75 reflect the normal small margins.

76 A26 5c brown ('63) 1,400. 120.
No gum 525.
a. 5c black brown 2,250. 400.
No gum 850.
b. Laid paper —

Values of Nos. 76, 76a reflect the normal small margins.

77 A33 15c black ('66) 4,750. 180.
No gum 1,850.
78 A29 24c lilac ('62) 2,750. 350.
No gum 950.
a. 24c grayish lilac 2,900. 425.
No gum 1,000.
b. 24c gray 2,900. 450.
No gum 1,000.
c. 24c blackish violet *100,000.* *22,500.*
No gum *30,000.*

Only three examples are recorded of No. 78c unused with original gum. No. 78c unused with and without gum are valued in the grade of fine-very fine.

d. Printed on both sides, reverse inverted *22,500.*

SAME DESIGNS AS 1861-66 ISSUES

Grill

Embossed with grills of various sizes. Some authorities believe that more than one size of grill probably existed on one of the grill rolls.

A peculiarity of the United States issues from 1867 to 1870 is the grill or embossing. The object was to break the fiber of the paper so that the ink of the canceling stamp would soak in and make washing for a second using impossible. The exact date at which grilled stamps came into use is unsettled. Luff's "Postage Stamps of the United States" places the date as probably August 8, 1867.

Horizontal measurements are given first.

GRILL WITH POINTS UP

Grills A and C were made by a roller covered with ridges shaped like an inverted V. Pressing the ridges into the stamp paper forced the paper into the pyramidal pits between the ridges, causing irregular breaks in the paper. Grill B was made by a roller with raised bosses.

A. GRILL COVERING THE ENTIRE STAMP

1867 ***Perf. 12***

79 A25 3c rose 8,500. 1,500.
No gum 2,750.
b. Printed on both sides —

Nos. 79, 79b, are valued for fine-very fine centering but with minor perforation faults.

An essay which is often mistaken for No. 79 (#79-E15) shows the points of the grill as small squares faintly impressed in the paper, but not cutting through it.

On No. 79 the grill breaks through the paper. Examples free from defects are rare.

80 A26 5c brown *260,000.*
a. 5c dark brown *260,000.*
81 A30 30c orange *210,000.*

Four examples of Nos. 80 and 80a (two of each shade), and eight examples of No. 81 (one in the New York Public Library Miller collection and not available to collectors) are known. All are more or less faulty and/or off center. Values are for off-center examples with small perforation faults.

B. GRILL ABOUT 18x15mm (22x18 POINTS)

82 A25 3c rose *1,000,000.*

The four known examples of No. 82 are valued in the grade of fine.

Earliest documented use: Feb. 1?, 1869 (dated cancel on off-cover stamp).

C. GRILL ABOUT 13x16mm (16 TO 17 BY 18 TO 21 POINTS)

The grilled area on each of four C grills in the sheet may total about 18x15mm when a normal C grill adjoins a fainter grill extending to the right or left edge of the stamp.

This is caused by a partial erasure on the grill roller when it was changed to produce C grills instead of the all-over A grill.

The imperf. can be found in the *Scott U.S. Specialized Catalogue* Die and Plate Proofs section.

83 A25 3c rose 6,000. 1,100.
No gum 2,150.

GRILL WITH POINTS DOWN

The grills were produced by rollers with the surface covered, or partly covered, by pyramidal bosses. On the D, E and F grills the tips of the pyramids are vertical ridges. On the Z grill the ridges are horizontal.

D. GRILL ABOUT 12x14mm (15 BY 17 TO 18 POINTS)

84 A32 2c black *16,000.* 4,500.
No gum *6,500.*

No. 84 is valued in the grade of fine.

85 A25 3c rose 6,000. 1,100.
No gum 2,150.

Z. GRILL ABOUT 11x14mm (13 TO 14 BY 18 POINTS)

85A A24 1c blue *3,000,000.*

Two examples of No. 85A are known. One is contained in the New York Public Library collection, which is on long-term loan to the Smithsonian National Postal Museum.

85B A32 2c black 17,500. 1,300.
No gum 6,750.
85C A25 3c rose *25,000.* 3,500.
No gum *9,000.*
85D A27 10c green *650,000.*

Six examples of No. 85D are known. One is contained in the New York Public Library collection. Value is for a well-centered example with small faults.

85E A28 12c intense black *17,500.* 2,500.
No gum *6,500.*
85F A33 15c black *2,000,000.*

Two examples of No. 85F are documented, one in the grade of very good, the other extremely fine. Value is for the extremely fine example.

E. GRILL ABOUT 11x13mm (14 BY 15 TO 17 POINTS)

86 A24 1c blue 3,250. 475.
No gum 1,250.
a. 1c dull blue 3,250. 450.
No gum 1,250.
87 A32 2c black 1,750. 200.
No gum 675.
a. Diagonal half used as 1c on cover *2,000.*
b. Vertical half used as 1c on cover *2,000.*
88 A25 3c rose 1,000. 27.50
No gum 375.
a. 3c lake red 1,250. 50.00
No gum 475.
b. Two diagonal halves from different stamps used as 3c stamp (fraudulent use), one half having grill with points up, on cover —
89 A27 10c green 5,250. 350.
No gum 2,100.
90 A28 12c black 4,750. 400.
No gum 1,900.
91 A33 15c black 12,500. 650.
No gum 4,500.

F. GRILL ABOUT 9x13mm (11 TO 12 BY 15 TO 17 POINTS)

92 A24 1c blue 3,000. 475.
No gum 1,000.
a. 1c pale blue 2,500. 425.
No gum 750.
93 A32 2c black 450. 60.00
No gum 170.
a. Vertical half used as 1c as part of 3c rate on cover *1,250.*
b. Diagonal half used as 1c as part of 3c rate on cover *1,250.*
c. Horizontal half used alone as 1c on cover *2,500.*
d. Diagonal half used alone as 1c on cover *2,500.*
94 A25 3c red 350. 10.00
a. 3c rose 350. 10.00
No gum 140.
c. Vertical pair, imperf. horiz. *15,000.*
d. Printed on both sides *9,000.*

The imperf. 3c can be found in the Scott U.S. Specialized Catalogue Die and Plate Proofs section.

95 A26 5c brown 3,500. 900.
No gum 1,300.
a. 5c black brown 4,750. 2,250.
No gum 1,800.

Values of Nos. 95, 95a reflect the normal small margins.

96 A27 10c yel grn 2,750. 250.
No gum 900.
97 A28 12c black 3,000. 260.
No gum 1,100.
98 A33 15c black 4,250. 300.
No gum 1,600.
99 A29 24c gray lilac 8,500. 1,600.
No gum 3,250.
100 A30 30c orange 8,500. 950.
No gum 3,250.

Values for No. 100 are for examples with small margins, especially at sides. Large-margined examples sell for much more.

101 A31 90c blue 14,500. 2,250.
No gum 5,500.

RE-ISSUE OF 1861-66 ISSUES
Without Grill, Hard White Paper
White Crackly Gum

1875 ***Perf. 12***

102 A24 1c blue *850.* *1,500.*
No gum *375.*
103 A32 2c black *3,750.* *15,000.*
No gum *1,750.*
104 A25 3c brown red *4,250.* *17,500.*
No gum *2,000.*
105 A26 5c brown *2,750.* *8,000.*
No gum *1,350.*
106 A27 10c green *3,500.* *125,000.*
No gum *1,650.*
107 A28 12c black *4,250.* *15,000.*
No gum *2,100.*
108 A33 15c black *4,750.* *35,000.*
No gum *2,350.*
109 A29 24c deep violet *6,000.* *20,000.*
No gum *2,750.*
110 A30 30c brownish org *6,250.* *25,000.*
No gum *3,000.*
111 A31 90c blue *6,750.* *225,000.*
No gum *3,250.*

These stamps can be distinguished from the 1861-66 issues by the shades and the paper which is hard and very white instead of yellowish. The gum is white and crackly.

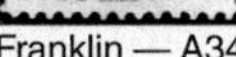
Franklin — A34

Post Horse and Rider — A35

G. Grill measuring 9½x9mm (12 by 11 to 11½ points)

1869 Hard Wove Paper ***Perf. 12***

112 A34 1c buff 650. 150.
No gum 225.
b. Without grill *35,000.*
113 A35 2c brown 550. 85.
No gum 200.
b. Without grill *7,500.*
c. Half used as 1c on cover, diagonal, vertical or horizontal *6,000.*
d. Printed on both sides *9,000.*

Locomotive A36

Washington A37

114 A36 3c ultramarine 250. 17.50
No gum 80.
a. Without grill *10,000.* *18,000.*
Without grill, gray paper 3,750.
b. Vert. one-third used as 1c on cover —
c. Vert. two-thirds used as 2c on cover *10,000.*
d. Double impression *15,000.*
e. Printed on both sides, reverse inverted *100,000.*

No. 114a used on normal paper and 114a used on gray paper are each unique. No. 114a was lifted from a cover, original gum adhering, examined, and placed back. With 2011 Philatelic Foundation certificate. No. 114a on gray paper is a strip of three on piece, mostly detached from piece, with full gum. It is very good to fine and has 1978 and 2006 Philatelic Foundation certificates.

Nos. 114d and 114e each are unique. No. 114d has a pre-printing paper fold.

115 A37 6c ultramarine 2,750. 225.
No gum 950.
b. Vertical half used as 3c on cover *50,000.*

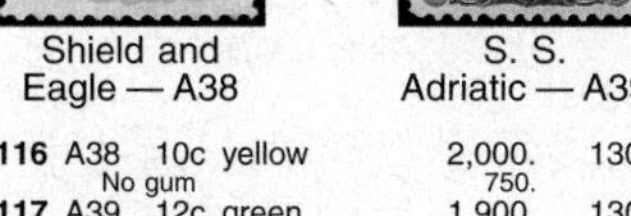
Shield and Eagle — A38

S. S. Adriatic — A39

116 A38 10c yellow 2,000. 130.
No gum 750.
117 A39 12c green 1,900. 130.
No gum 700.

Landing of Columbus — A40

Type I. Picture unframed.

No. 118 has horizontal shading lines at the left and right sides of the vignette.

118 A40 15c brn & bl, type I 9,500. 800.
No gum 3,250.
a. Without grill *13,000.*

A40a

Type II. Picture framed.

No. 119 has diagonal shading lines at the left and right sides of the vignette.

119 A40a 15c brn & bl, type II 3,250. 225.
No gum 1,150.
b. Center inverted *1,100,000.* *22,500.*
No gum *750,000.*
c. Center double, one inverted *80,000.*

Declaration of Independence — A41

120 A41 24c green & violet 8,000. 675.
No gum 2,800.
a. Without grill *15,000.*
b. Center inverted *750,000.* *37,500.*

Shield, Eagle and Flags — A42

Lincoln — A43

121 A42 30c ultra & carmine 5,500. 450.
No gum 2,000.
a. Without grill *11,000.*
b. Flags inverted *900,000.* *105,000.*
No gum *250,000.*

Seven examples of No. 121b unused are recorded. Only one has part of its original gum.

122 A43 90c carmine & black 12,000. 2,100.
No gum 4,500.
a. Without grill *24,000.*

Values of varieties of Nos. 112-122 without grill are for examples with original gum.

Most examples of Nos. 119b, 120b are faulty. Values are for stamps with fine centering and only minimal faults. No. 120b unused is valued without gum, as all of the three examples available to collectors are without gum.

RE-ISSUE OF 1869 ISSUE
Without grill, hard white paper, with white crackly gum.

The gum is almost always somewhat yellowed with age, and unused stamps with original gum are valued with such gum.

A new plate of 150 subjects was made for the 1c. The plate for the frame of the 15c was made using the same die as that used to make the type I frame for No. 118. For No. 118, the lines on each side of the vignette area were entered onto the plate itself, one position at a time. Upon close examination, each stamp position will be found to exhibit minute differences in these horizontal fringe lines.

1875 ***Perf. 12***

123 A34 1c buff 550. 400.
No gum 230.
124 A35 2c brown 650. 800.
No gum 260.
125 A36 3c blue *5,000.* *27,500.*
No gum 2,500.

Used value for No. 125 is for an attractive fine to very fine example with minimal faults.

126 A37 6c blue 1,650. *3,250.*
No gum 725.
127 A38 10c yellow 1,650. 2,000.
No gum 725.
128 A39 12c green 2,250. *3,250.*
No gum 1,025.
129 A40 15c brn & bl, Type III 1,350. 1,250.
No gum 600.
a. Imperf. horizontally, single *14,000.* *20,000.*
No gum *5,000.*

Two used examples of No. 129a are recorded. Both have faults and are valued thus.

130 A41 24c grn & violet 2,100. 1,750.
No gum 900.
131 A42 30c ultra & car 2,500. 3,000.
No gum 1,100.
132 A43 90c car & blk 3,750. *6,500.*
No gum 1,500.

Soft Porous Paper

1880-82

133 A34 1c buff, issued with gum 325. *450.*
No gum 140.
a. 1c brown orange, issued without gum ('81 and '82) 250. *350.*

PRODUCED BY THE NATIONAL BANK NOTE COMPANY

Franklin — A44

A44

Jackson — A45

A45

Washington — A46

A46

Lincoln — A47

A47

Edwin M. Stanton — A48

A48

Jefferson — A49

A49

Henry Clay — A50

A50

Daniel Webster — A51

A51

Gen. Winfield Scott
A52

Alexander Hamilton
A53

Commodore O.H. Perry — A54

H. GRILL ABOUT 10x12mm (11 TO 13 BY 14 TO 16 POINTS)

The "H" grills can be separated into early state and late state, based on the shape of the tip of the grill. Early-state grills show a point or very small vertical line at the tip of the pyramid, while late-state grills show the pyramid tips truncated and flat.

Early-state "H" grills tend to be on vertical-mesh wove paper, while later printings and all late-state grills were printed on horizontal-mesh wove paper, resulting in stamp designs being approximately ¼mm shorter than the designs printed on vertical-mesh wove paper. The late-stage "H" grills virtually all seem to have been used only after Jan. 1873.

Poor printing quality often resulted in grills that show only a few grill points or a very few rows of points. This is especially true of the "H" grills. When there are not enough grill points to clearly identify whether the grill is an "H" or an "I," it must be assumed it is the lower-valued "H" grill variety. Authentication is advised for these stamps with high catalogue values.

White Wove Paper, Thin to Medium Thick.

1870-71 ***Perf. 12***

134 A44 1c ultramarine 2,000. 200.00
No gum 700.
b. Pair, one without grill —
135 A45 2c red brown 1,000. 80.00
No gum 360.
b. Diagonal half used as 1c on cover —
c. Vertical half used as 1c on cover —
136 A46 3c green 575. 32.50
No gum 190.
b. Printed on both sides —

The imperf. 3c can be found in the Scott U.S. Specialized Catalogue Die and Plate Proofs section.

137 A47 6c carmine 5,000. 575.00
No gum 1,750.
b. Pair, one without grill —
138 A48 7c vermilion 4,250. 550.
No gum 1,550.
139 A49 10c brown 7,000. 850.
No gum 2,550.
b. Pair, one without grill, one with split grill, on cover —
140 A50 12c dull violet *27,500.* 3,750.
No gum *13,000.*
141 A51 15c orange 7,500. 1,400.
No gum 2,500.
142 A52 24c purple — 7,250.
143 A53 30c black 20,000. 4,000.
No gum 7,500.
144 A54 90c carmine 25,000. 2,500.
No gum 10,000.

I. GRILL ABOUT 8½x10mm (10 TO 11 BY 10 TO 13 POINTS)

The "I" grills can be separated into early state and late state, based on the shape of the tip of the grill. Early state grills show small tips of the pyramid, while late state grills show the pyramid tips truncated and flat.

Early state "I" grills tend to be on vertical-mesh wove paper, while later printings and all late-state grills were printed on horizontal-mesh wove paper, resulting in stamp designs being approximately ¼mm shorter than the designs printed on vertical-mesh wove paper. The late-stage "I" grills all seem to have been used only after Jan. 1873.

Values are for stamps with grills that are clearly identifiable. Poor printing quality often resulted in grills that show only a few grill points or a very few rows of points. When there are not enough grill points to clearly identify whether the grill is an "H" or an "I," it must be assumed it is the lower-valued "H" grill variety. Authentication is advised for these stamps with high catalogue values.

134A A44 1c ultramarine *2,750.* *275.00*
No gum *800.00*
135A A45 2c red brown *2,500.* *225.00*
136A A46 3c green *1,000.* *100.00*
a. Pair, one without grill, on cover —
137A A47 6c carmine *7,000.* *900.00*
138A A48 7c vermilion ('71) *6,500.* *1,200.*
No gum *2,400.*
139A A49 10c brown *15,000.* *7,500.*

The unused No. 139A is unique, and it is valued in the grade of fine.

140A A50 12c dull violet *30,000.*

The unused No. 140A is unique, and it is valued in the grade of fine.

141A A51 15c orange *17,500.* *8,000.*
143A A53 30c black
144A A54 90c carmine — *15,000.*

The unused No. 144A has a vertically split grill and is unique.

White Wove Paper Without Grill.

1870-71 ***Perf. 12***

145 A44 1c ultra 675. 25.00
No gum 250.
146 A45 2c red brown 325. 20.00
No gum 115.
a. Diagonal half used as 1c on cover *700.00*
b. Vertical half used as 1c on cover *800.00*
c. Horiz. half used as 1c on cover *800.00*
d. Double impression *9,000.*
147 A46 3c green 225. 2.00
No gum 80.
a. Printed on both sides, reverse inverted *17,500.*
b. Double impression *30,000.*

Nos. 147a and 147b are valued in the grade of fine.

The imperf. 3c can be found in the Scott U.S. Specialized Catalogue Die and Plate Proofs section.

148 A47 6c carmine 1,000. 25.00
No gum 320.
a. Vertical half used as 3c on cover *6,500.*
b. Double impression, on cover *20,000.*
c. Double paper — *100.00*

No. 148b is unique.

149 A48 7c vermilion ('71) 1,000. 100.00
No gum 320.
150 A49 10c brown 2,250. 35.00
No gum 850.
151 A50 12c dull violet 2,750. 220.00
No gum 1,000.
152 A51 15c brt org 3,000. 220.00
No gum 1,100.
a. Double impression *11,000.*

No. 152a is unique.

153 A52 24c purple 1,800. 230.00
No gum 625.
a. Double paper — —
154 A53 30c black 7,500. 300.00
No gum 2,750.
155 A54 90c carmine 5,000. 350.00
No gum 1,900.

PRINTED BY THE CONTINENTAL BANK NOTE COMPANY

Designs of the 1870-71 Issue with secret marks on the values from 1c to 15c, as described and illustrated:

The object of secret marks was to provide a simple and positive proof that these stamps were produced by the Continental Bank Note Company and not by their predecessors.

Almost all of the stamps of the Continental Bank Note Co. printing including the Department stamps and some of the Newspaper stamps may be found upon a paper that shows more or less the characteristics of a ribbed paper.

Franklin — A44a

1c. In the pearl at the left of the numeral "1" there is a small crescent.

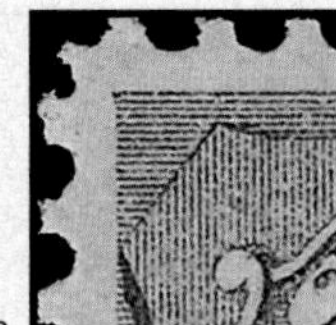

Jackson — A45a

2c. Under the scroll at the left of "U. S." there is a small diagonal line. This mark seldom shows clearly. The stamp, No. 157, can be distinguished by its color.

Washington — A46a

3c. The under part of the upper tail of the left ribbon is heavily shaded.

Lincoln — A47a

6c. The first four vertical lines of the shading in the lower part of the left ribbon have been strengthened.

Stanton — A48a

7c. Two small semi-circles are drawn around the ends of the lines that outline the ball in the lower right hand corner.

Jefferson — A49a

10c. There is a small semi-circle in the scroll at the right end of the upper label.

Clay — A50a

12c. The balls of the figure "2" are crescent shaped.

Webster — A51a

15c. In the lower part of the triangle in the upper left corner two lines have been made heavier forming a "V." This mark can be found on some of the Continental and American (1879) printings, but not all stamps show it.

Secret marks were added to the dies of the 24c, 30c and 90c but new plates were not made from them. The various printings of the 30c and 90c can be distinguished only by the shades and paper.

Experimental J. Grill about 7x9½mm exists on all values except 24c and 90c. Grill was composed of truncated pyramids and was so strongly impressed that some points often broke through the paper.

White Wove Paper, Thin to Thick Without Grill

1873, July (?) ***Perf. 12***

156 A44a 1c ultra 225. 6.00
No gum 85.
e. With grill *2,000.*
f. Imperf., pair — *1,500.*
157 A45a 2c brown 350. 25.00
No gum 125.
c. With grill *1,850.* *750.00*
d. Double impression *16,500.*
e. Vertical half used as 1c on cover *1,000.*

No. 157d is unique.

158 A46a 3c green 110. 1.00
No gum 30.
a. Double paper 600. 100.00
e. With grill *550.*
h. Horizontal pair, imperf. vert. —
i. Horizontal pair, imperf. between *1,300.*
j. Double impression *7,500.*
k. Printed on both sides *20,000.*

Nos. 158j and 158k are valued in the grade of fine.

The imperf 3c, with and without grill, can be found in the Scott U.S. Specialized Catalogue Die and Plate Proofs section.

159 A47a 6c dull pink 400. 20.00
No gum 130.
a. Diagonal half used as 3c on cover *7,250.*
b. With grill *1,800.*
160 A48a 7c orange vermilion 1,150. 90.00
No gum 400.
a. With grill *3,500.*
161 A49a 10c brown 1,000. 27.50
No gum 300.
a. Double paper —
c. With grill *3,750.*
d. Horizontal pair, imperf. between *25,000.*
162 A50a 12c blackish violet 2,400. 145.00
No gum 800.
a. With grill *5,500.*
163 A51a 15c yellow orange 2,500. 160.00
No gum 800.
a. With grill *5,750.*
164 A52 24c purple *357,500.*

The Philatelic Foundation has certified as genuine a 24c on vertically ribbed paper, and that is the unique stamp listed as No. 164. Specialists believe that only Continental used ribbed paper. It is not known for sure whether or not Continental also printed the 24c value on regular paper; if it did, specialists currently are not able to distinguish these from No. 153. The catalogue value represents a 2004 auction sale price realized.

165 A53 30c gray black 4,000. 140.
No gum 1,300.
a. Double paper —
c. With grill *22,500.*
166 A54 90c rose carmine 2,250. 300.00
No gum 750.

Special Printing of the 1873 Issue

Hard, White Wove Paper Without Gum

1875 ***Perf. 12***

167 A44a 1c ultramarine *16,500.*
168 A45a 2c dark brown *7,750.*
169 A46a 3c blue green *26,000.* —
170 A47a 6c dull rose *22,500.*
171 A48a 7c reddish vermilion *5,000.*
172 A49a 10c pale brown *21,000.*
173 A50a 12c dark violet *7,000.*
174 A51a 15c bright orange *19,000.*
175 A52 24c dull purple *4,250.* *22,500.*
176 A53 30c greenish black *15,000.*
177 A54 90c violet carmine *22,500.*

Although perforated, these stamps were usually cut apart with scissors. As a result, the perforations are often much mutilated and the design is frequently damaged.

These can be distinguished from the 1873 issue by the shades; also by the paper, which is very white instead of yellowish.

These and the subsequent issues listed under the heading of "Special Printings" are special printings of stamps then in current use which, together with the reprints and re-issues, were made for sale to collectors. They were available for postage except for the Officials, Newspaper and Periodical, and demonetized issues.

Only three examples of No. 175 used have been certified. They all have small faults and are valued thus.

Yellowish Wove Paper

1875 *Perf. 12*

178 A45a 2c vermilion 350. 15.00
No gum 110.
b. Half used as 1c on cover *750.00*
c. With grill 900. *2,750.*

The imperf 2c can be found in the Scott U.S. Specialized Catalogue Die and Plate Proofs section.

Zachary Taylor — A55

179 A55 5c blue 700. 25.00
No gum 225.
c. With grill 4,500.

SPECIAL PRINTING OF 1875 ISSUE

Hard, White Wove Paper
Without Gum

1875

180 A45a 2c carmine ver *75,000.*
181 A55 5c bright blue *500,000.*

Unlike Nos. 167-177, Nos. 180-181 were not cut apart with scissors.

Please Note:

Stamps are valued in the grade of very fine unless otherwise indicated.

Values for early and valuable stamps are for examples with certificates of authenticity from acknowledged expert committees, or examples sold with the buyer having the right of certification.

This applies to examples with original gum as well as examples without gum.

Beware of stamps offered "as is," as the gum on some unused stamps offered with "original gum" may be fraudulent, and stamps offered as unused without gum may in some cases be altered or faintly canceled used stamps.

IMPORTANT INFORMATION REGARDING VALUES FOR NEVER-HINGED STAMPS

Collectors should be aware that the values given for never-hinged stamps from No. 182 on are for stamps in the grade of very fine, just as the values for all stamps in the catalogue are for very fine stamps unless indicated otherwise. The never-hinged premium as a percentage of value will be larger for stamps in extremely fine or superb grades, and the premium will be smaller for fine-very fine, fine or poor examples. This is particularly true of the issues of the late-19th and early-20th centuries. For example, in the grade of very fine, an unused stamp from this time period may be valued at $100 hinged and $200 never hinged. The never-hinged premium is thus 100%. But in a grade of extremely fine, this same stamp will not only sell for more hinged, but the never-hinged premium will increase, perhaps to 200%-400% or more over the higher extremely fine value. In the grade of superb, a hinged stamp will sell for much more than a very fine stamp, and additionally the never-hinged premium will be much larger, perhaps as large as 500%-1,000%. On the other hand, the same stamp in a grade of fine or fine-very fine not only will sell for less than a very fine stamp in hinged condition, but additionally the never-hinged premium will be smaller than the never-hinged premium on a very fine stamp, perhaps as small as 40%-60%.

Please note that the above statements and percentages are NOT a formula for arriving at the values of stamps in hinged or never-hinged condition in the grades of very good, fine, fine to very fine, extremely fine or superb. The percentages given apply only to the size of the premium for never-hinged condition that might be added to the stamp value for hinged condition. Further, the percentages given are only generalized estimates. Some stamps or grades may have percentages for never-hinged condition that are higher or lower than the ranges given.

VALUES FOR NEVER-HINGED STAMPS PRIOR TO SCOTT 182

This catalogue does not value pre-1879 stamps in never-hinged condition. Premiums for never-hinged condition in the classic era invariably are even larger than those premiums listed for the 1879 and later issues. Generally speaking, the earlier the stamp is listed in the catalogue, the larger will be the never-hinged premium. On some early classics, the premium will be several multiples of the unused, hinged values given in the catalogue.

Values given for never-hinged plate blocks are for blocks in which all stamps have original gum that has never been hinged and has no disturbances, and all selvage, whether gummed or ungummed, has never been hinged.

For values of the most popular U.S. stamps in the grades of very good, fine, fine to very fine, very fine, very fine to extremely fine, extremely fine, extremely fine to superb, and superb, see the *Scott Stamp Values U.S. Specialized by Grade*, updated and issued each year as part of the U.S. specialized catalogue.

PRINTED BY THE AMERICAN BANK NOTE COMPANY

SAME AS 1870-75 ISSUES
Soft Porous Paper
Varying from Thin to Thick

1879 *Perf. 12*

182 A44a 1c dark ultra 225. 6.00
Never hinged 775.
No gum 75.
183 A45a 2c vermilion 100. 5.00
Never hinged 370.
No gum 35.
a. Double impression — *5,500.*
b. Half used as 1c on cover *750.00*

No. 183a is valued in the grade of fine.

184 A46a 3c green 90. 1.00
Never hinged 330.
No gum 28.
b. Double impression *5,000.*

No. 184b is valued in the grade of fine.

The imperf 3c can be found in the Scott U.S. Specialized Catalogue Die and Plate Proofs section.

185 A55 5c blue 450. 17.50
Never hinged *1,500.*
No gum 140.
186 A47a 6c pink 900. 30.00
Never hinged *3,100.*
No gum 275.
187 A49 10c brown, without secret mark 3,250. 42.50
Never hinged *11,000.*
No gum 1,100.
188 A49a 10c brown, with secret mark 1,800. 32.50
Never hinged *6,500.*
No gum 625.
189 A51a 15c red orange 200. 30.00
Never hinged 675.
No gum 80.
190 A53 30c full black 900. 95.00
Never hinged *3,000.*
No gum 325.
191 A54 90c carmine 2,000. 360.00
Never hinged *7,000.*
No gum 650.

The Continental Bank Note Co. was consolidated with the American Bank Note Co. on February 4, 1879. The American Bank Note Company used many plates of the Continental Bank Note Company to print the ordinary postage, Departmental and Newspaper stamps. Therefore, stamps bearing the Continental Company's imprint were not always its product.

The A. B. N. Co. also used the 30c and 90c plates of the N. B. N. Co. Some of No. 190 and all of No. 217 were from A. B. N. Co. plate 405.

Early printings of No. 188 were from Continental plates 302 and 303 which contained the normal secret mark of 1873. After those plates were re-entered by the A. B. N. Co. in 1880, pairs or multiple pieces contained combinations of normal, hairline or missing marks. The pairs or other multiples usually found contain at least one hairline mark which tended to disappear as the plate wore.

A. B. N. Co. plates 377 and 378 were made in 1881 from the National transfer roll of 1870. No. 187 from these plates has no secret mark.

The imperf. 90c can be found in the Scott U.S. Specialized Catalogue Die and Plate Proofs section.

Special Printing of the 1879 Issue

Soft Porous Paper
Without Gum

1880 *Perf. 12*

192 A44a 1c dark ultra *67,500.*
193 A45a 2c black brown *21,000.*
194 A46a 3c blue green *120,000.*
195 A47a 6c dull rose *80,000.*
196 A48a 7c scarlet vermilion *8,250.*
197 A49a 10c deep brown *42,500.*
198 A50a 12c blackish purple *12,000.*
199 A51a 15c orange *35,000.*
200 A52 24c dark violet *11,000.*
201 A53 30c greenish black *24,000.*
202 A54 90c dull carmine *35,000.*
203 A45a 2c scarlet vermilion *120,000.*
204 A55 5c deep blue *300,000.*

Nos. 192 and 194 are valued in the grade of fine.

No. 197 was printed from Continental plate 302 (or 303) after plate was re-entered. Therefore, the stamp may show normal, hairline or missing secret mark.

The Post Office Department did not keep separate records of the 1875 and 1880 Special Printings of the 1873 and 1879 issues, but the total quantity sold of both is recorded.

Unlike the 1875 hard-paper Special Printings (Nos. 167-177), the 1880 soft-paper Special Printings were never cut apart with scissors.

James A. Garfield — A56

1882

205 A56 5c yellow brown 240. 12.00
Never hinged 775.
No gum 80.

Special Printing

1882 *Perf. 12*

Soft porous paper, without gum

205C A56 5c gray brown *70,000.*

DESIGNS OF 1873 RE-ENGRAVED

Franklin — A44b

1c — The vertical lines in the upper part of the stamp have been so deepened that the background often appears to be solid. Lines of shading have been added to the upper arabesques.

1881-82

206 A44b 1c gray blue 70.00 1.00
Never hinged 225.00
No gum 21.00
a. Double impression —

No. 206a is a partial double impression, with "ONE 1 CENT," etc. at bottom doubled.

Earliest documented use: Oct. 11, 1881.

Washington — A46b

3c. The shading at the sides of the central oval appears only about one-half the previous width. A short horizontal dash has been cut about 1mm below the "TS" of "CENTS."

207 A46b 3c blue green 70.00 .80
Never hinged 225.00
No gum 20.00
c. Double impression *5,000.*

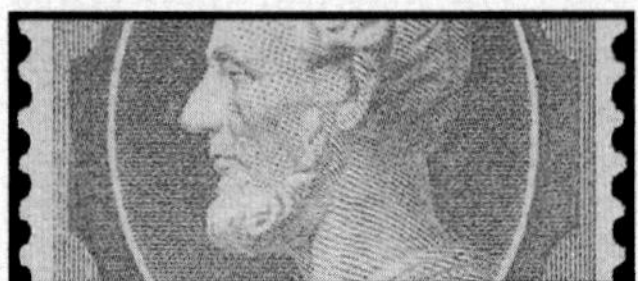

Lincoln — A47b

6c. On the original stamps four vertical lines can be counted from the edge of the panel to the outside of the stamp. On the re-engraved stamps there are but three lines in the same place.

208 A47b 6c rose 775. 110.00
 Never hinged 2,400.
 No gum 225.
 a. 6c deep brown red 550. 175.00
 Never hinged 1,600.
 No gum 150.

Jefferson — A49b

10c. On the original stamps there are five vertical lines between the left side of the oval and the edge of the shield. There are only four lines on the re-engraved stamps. In the lower part of the latter, also, the horizontal lines of the background have been strengthened.

209 A49b 10c brown 160. 6.00
 Never hinged 475.
 No gum 50.
 b. 10c black brown 3,000. 350.00
 Never hinged 6,000.
 No gum 950.
 c. Double impression —

Specimen stamps (usually overprinted "Sample") without overprint exist in a brown shade that differs from No. 209. The unoverprinted brown specimen is cheaper than No. 209. Expertization is recommended.

Washington
A57

Jackson
A58

Nos. 210-211 were issued to meet the reduced first class rate of 2 cents for each half ounce, and the double rate, which Congress approved Mar. 3, 1883, effective Oct. 1, 1883.

1883, Oct. 1 ***Perf. 12***

210 A57 2c red brown 42.50 .75
 Never hinged 130.00
 No gum 12.50
211 A58 4c blue green 250. 27.50
 Never hinged 900.
 No gum 80.

Imperfs can be found in the Scott U.S. Specialized Catalogue Die and Plate Proofs section.

Special Printing

1883-85 Soft porous paper ***Perf. 12***

211B A57 2c pale red brown, with gum ('85) 375. —
 Never hinged 1,000.
 No gum 130.
 c. Horizontal pair, imperf. between *2,000.*
 Never hinged *3,000.*
211D A58 4c deep blue grn *60,000.*

No. 211D is without gum.

Franklin — A59

1887 ***Perf. 12***

212 A59 1c ultramarine 90.00 2.50
 Never hinged 290.00
 No gum 30.00
213 A57 2c green 40.00 .60
 Never hinged 120.00
 No gum 12.00
 b. Printed on both sides —

Imperf 1c, 2c can be found in the Scott U.S. Specialized Catalogue Die and Plate Proofs section.

214 A46b 3c vermilion 60.00 55.00
 Never hinged 180.00
 No gum 20.00
 Nos. 212-214 (3) 190.00 58.10

1888 ***Perf. 12***

215 A58 4c carmine 190. 27.50
 Never hinged 550.
 No gum 55.
216 A56 5c indigo 225. 17.50
 Never hinged 700.
 No gum 75.
217 A53 30c orange brn 250. 100.00
 Never hinged 900.
 No gum 80.
218 A54 90c purple 900. 250.00
 Never hinged 2,750.
 No gum 275.
 Nos. 215-218 (4) 1,565. 395.00

Imperfs can be found in the Scott U.S. Specialized Catalogue Die and Plate Proofs section.

Franklin
A60

Washington
A61

Jackson
A62

Lincoln
A63

Ulysses S. Grant
A64

Garfield
A65

William T. Sherman
A66

Daniel Webster
A67

Henry Clay
A68

Jefferson
A69

Perry — A70

1890-93 ***Perf. 12***

219 A60 1c dull blue 20.00 .75
 Never hinged 65.00
219D A61 2c lake 190.00 5.50
 Never hinged 600.00
220 A61 2c carmine 20.00 .70
 Never hinged 60.00
 a. Cap on left "2" 150.00 12.50
 Never hinged 425.00
 c. Cap on both "2's" 650.00 35.00
 Never hinged 1,800.
221 A62 3c purple 65.00 9.00
 Never hinged 200.00
222 A63 4c dark brown 90.00 4.75
 Never hinged 275.00
223 A64 5c chocolate 70.00 4.75
 Never hinged 220.00
224 A65 6c brown red 65.00 25.00
 Never hinged 200.00
225 A66 8c lilac ('93) 50.00 17.00
 Never hinged 150.00
226 A67 10c green 175.00 5.00
 Never hinged 525.00
227 A68 15c indigo 225.00 27.50
 Never hinged 675.00
228 A69 30c black 325.00 35.00
 Never hinged 975.00
229 A70 90c orange 475.00 150.00
 Never hinged 1,450.
 Nos. 219-229 (12) 1,770. 284.95

The No. 220 with "cap on right 2" variety is due to imperfect inking, not a plate defect.

Imperfs. can be found in the *Scott U.S. Specialized Catalogue* Die and Plate Proofs section.

COLUMBIAN EXPOSITION ISSUE

Columbus in Sight of Land — A71

Landing of Columbus
A72

Flagship of Columbus
A73

Fleet of Columbus
A74

Columbus Soliciting Aid from Isabella
A75

Columbus Welcomed at Barcelona
A76

Columbus Restored to Favor — A77

Columbus Presenting Natives
A78

Columbus Announcing his Discovery
A79

Columbus at La Rábida
A80

Recall of Columbus
A81

Isabella Pledging her Jewels
A82

Columbus in Chains
A83

Columbus Describing his Third Voyage
A84

Isabella & Columbus
A85

Columbus
A86

1893 ***Perf. 12***

No.	Type	Description	Unused	Used
230	A71	1c deep blue	14.00	.40
		Never hinged	35.00	
231	A72	2c brown violet	14.00	.30
		Never hinged	35.00	
232	A73	3c green	37.50	17.50
		Never hinged	105.00	
233	A74	4c ultra	55.00	9.00
		Never hinged	160.00	
a.		4c blue (error)	*17,500.*	*16,500.*
		Never hinged	*32,500.*	

No. 233a exists in two shades. No. 233a used is valued with small faults, as almost all examples come thus.

No.	Type	Description	Unused	Used
234	A75	5c chocolate	55.00	9.50
		Never hinged	160.00	
235	A76	6c purple	55.00	25.00
		Never hinged	160.00	
a.		6c red violet	55.00	25.00
		Never hinged	160.00	
236	A77	8c magenta	52.50	12.00
		Never hinged	160.00	
237	A78	10c black brown	100.00	9.00
		Never hinged	285.00	
238	A79	15c dark green	225.00	82.50
		Never hinged	675.00	
239	A80	30c orange brown	240.00	100.00
		Never hinged	725.00	
240	A81	50c slate blue	500.00	200.00
		Never hinged	1,450.	
		No gum	225.	
241	A82	$1 salmon	1,100.	650.
		Never hinged	3,750.	
		No gum	500.	
242	A83	$2 brown red	1,150.	650.
		Never hinged	3,800.	
		No gum	525.	
243	A84	$3 yellow green	1,600.	900.
		Never hinged	5,000.	
		No gum	750.	
a.		$3 olive green	1,600.	900.
		Never hinged	5,000.	
		No gum	750.	
244	A85	$4 crimson lake	2,100.	1,150.
		Never hinged	7,250.	
		No gum	1,000.	
a.		$4 rose carmine	2,100.	1,150.
		Never hinged	7,250.	
		No gum	1,000.	
245	A86	$5 black	2,500.	1,300.
		Never hinged	10,500.	
		No gum	1,200.	

World's Columbia Expo., Chicago, May 1-Oct. 30, 1893.

Nos. 230-245 are known imperf., but were not regularly issues.

See Scott U.S. Specialized Catalogue Die and Plate Proofs section for the 2c.

Never-Hinged Stamps

See note before No. 182 regarding premiums for never-hinged stamps.

Bureau Issues

Starting in 1894, the Bureau of Engraving and Printing at Washington produced most U.S. postage stamps.

Until 1965 Bureau-printed stamps were engraved except Nos. 525-536 which were offset.

The combination of lithography and engraving (see #1253) was first used in 1964, and photogravure (see #1426) in 1971.

Franklin
A87

Washington
A88

Jackson
A89

Lincoln
A90

Grant
A91

Garfield
A92

Sherman
A93

Webster
A94

Clay
A95

Jefferson
A96

Perry
A97

James Madison
A98

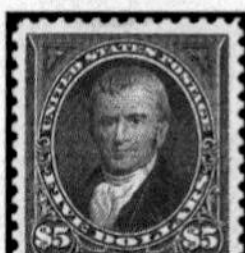

John Marshall — A99

1894 **Unwmk.** ***Perf. 12***

No.	Type	Description	Unused	Used
246	A87	1c ultramarine	30.00	7.00
		Never hinged	90.00	
247	A87	1c blue	65.00	4.00
		Never hinged	190.00	

TWO CENTS:

Triangle A (Type I)

Type I (Triangle A). The horizontal lines of the ground work run across the triangle and are of the same thickness within it as without.

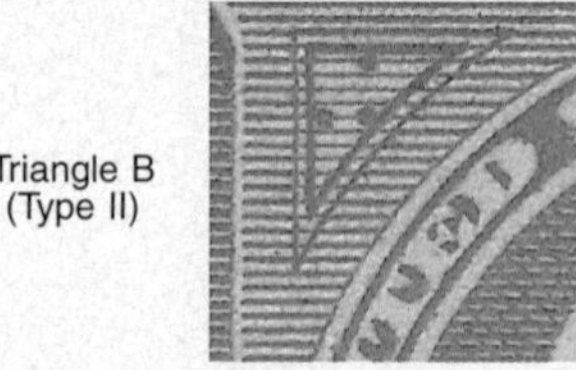

Triangle B (Type II)

Type II (Triangle B). The horizontal lines cross the triangle but are thinner within it than without. Other minor design differences exist, but the change to Triangle B is a sufficient determinant.

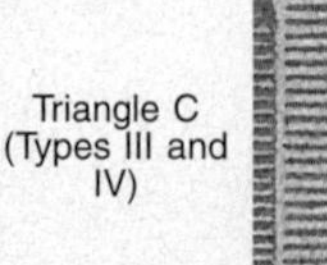

Triangle C (Types III and IV)

Type III (Triangle C). The horizontal lines do not cross the double lines of the triangle. The lines within the triangle are thin, as in Type II. The rest of the design is the same as Type II, except that most of the designs had the dot in the "S" of "CENTS" removed. Stamps with this dot present are listed; some specialists refer to them as "Type IIIa" varieties.

Type IV

Type IV (Triangle C). See No. 279B and its varieties. Type IV is from a new die with many major and minor design variations including, (1) re-cutting and lengthening of hairline, (2) shaded toga button, (3) strengthening of lines on sleeve, (4) additional dots on ear, (5) "T" of "TWO" straight at right, (6) background lines extend into white oval opposite "U" of "UNITED." Many other differences exist.

For further information concerning type IV, see also George Brett's article in the Sept. 1993 issue of the "The United States Specialist" and the 23-part article by Kenneth Diehl in the Dec. 1994 through Aug. 1997 issues of the "The United States Specialist."

No.	Type	Description	Unused	Used
248	A88	2c pink, type I	30.00	9.00
		Never hinged	90.00	
a.		Vert. pair, imperf horiz.	*5,500.*	
249	A88	2c carmine lake, type I	150.00	7.00
		Never hinged	450.00	
a.		Double impression		—
250	A88	2c carmine, type I	30.00	3.00
		Never hinged	90.00	
a.		2c rose, type I	37.50	6.00
		Never hinged	110.00	
b.		2c scarlet, type I	27.50	3.00
		Never hinged	82.50	
d.		Horizontal pair, imperf. between	*2,000.*	
251	A88	2c carmine, type II	375.00	15.00
		Never hinged	1,100.	
a.		2c scarlet, type II	350.00	14.00
		Never hinged	1,050.	
252	A88	2c carmine, type III	125.00	14.00
		Never hinged	375.00	
		On cover		22.50
a.		2c scarlet, type III	110.00	16.00
		Never hinged	325.00	
b.		Horiz. pair, imperf. vert.	*5,000.*	
c.		Horiz. pair, imperf. between	*5,500.*	
253	A89	3c purple	110.00	13.00
		Never hinged	325.00	
254	A90	4c dark brown	175.00	10.00
		Never hinged	525.00	
255	A91	5c chocolate	110.00	10.00
		Never hinged	325.00	
c.		Vert. pair, imperf. horiz.	*4,000.*	
256	A92	6c dull brown	160.00	30.00
		Never hinged	475.00	
a.		Vert. pair, imperf. horiz.	*3,000.*	
257	A93	8c violet brown	160.00	22.50
		Never hinged	475.00	
258	A94	10c dark green	300.00	22.50
		Never hinged	900.00	
259	A95	15c dark blue	300.00	70.00
		Never hinged	900.00	
260	A96	50c orange	500.	160.
		Never hinged	1,500.	

Type I

Type II

ONE DOLLAR

Type I. The circles enclosing "$1" are broken where they meet the curved line below "One Dollar."

Type II. The circles are complete.

No.	Type	Description	Unused	Used
261	A97	$1 black, type I	1,000.	375.
		Never hinged	3,150.	
		No gum	325.	
261A	A97	$1 black, type II	2,100.	825.
		Never hinged	6,500.	
		No gum	675.	
262	A98	$2 bright blue	2,750.	1,250.
		Never hinged	8,750.	
		No gum	1,000.	
263	A99	$5 dark green	4,500.	2,750.
		Never hinged	15,000.	
		No gum	2,000.	

For imperfs. and the 2c pink, vert. pair, imperf. hoirz., see Scott U.S. Specialized Catalogue Die and plate Proofs.

Same as 1894 Issue

Wmk. 191 Horizontally or Vertically

1895 ***Perf. 12***

No.	Type	Description	Unused	Used
264	A87	1c blue	6.00	.60
		Never hinged	17.50	
265	A88	2c car, type I	27.50	3.50
		Never hinged	82.50	
266	A88	2c car, type II	32.50	5.50
		Never hinged	100.00	
267	A88	2c car, type III	5.50	.50
		Never hinged	16.00	
a.		2c pink, type III	20.00	5.00
		Never hinged	60.00	
b.		2c vermilion, type III	*50.00*	15.00
c.		2c rose carmine, type III	—	—

The three left vertical rows from plate 170 are type II, the balance being type III.

No.	Type	Description	Unused	Used
268	A89	3c purple	37.50	2.25
		Never hinged	115.00	
269	A90	4c dark brown	42.50	3.50
		Never hinged	125.00	
270	A91	5c chocolate	35.00	3.50
		Never hinged	105.00	
271	A92	6c dull brown	120.00	8.50
		Never hinged	360.00	
a.		Wmkd. USIR	*15,000.*	*8,500.*
272	A93	8c violet brown	70.00	2.75
		Never hinged	210.00	
a.		Wmkd. USIR	*6,000.*	1,000.
273	A94	10c dark green	95.00	2.25
		Never hinged	280.00	
274	A95	15c dark blue	210.00	17.50
		Never hinged	625.00	
275	A96	50c orange	260.	40.00
		Never hinged	775.	
a.		50c red orange	350.	47.50
		Never hinged	1,050.	
276	A97	$1 black, type I	600.	100.
		Never hinged	1,800.	
		No gum	175.	
276A	A97	$1 black, type II	1,250.	210.
		Never hinged	3,750.	
		No gum	375.	
277	A98	$2 bright blue	900.	425.
		Never hinged	2,900.	
		No gum	260.	
a.		$2 dark blue	900.	425.
		Never hinged	2,900.	
		No gum	260.	
278	A99	$5 dark green	2,000.	625.
		Never hinged	6,250.	
		No gum	625.	

For imperfs. and the 1c horiz. pair, imperf. vert., see Scott U.S. Specialized Catalogue Die and Plate Proofs.

For "I.R." overprints see Nos. R155, R156-R158.

No. 271a unused is valued in the grade of fine.

Wmk. 191 Horizontally or Vertically

1897-1903 ***Perf. 12***

No.	Type	Description	Unused	Used
279	A87	1c deep green, horiz. wmk ('98)	9.00	.50
		Never hinged	25.00	
a.		Vert. wmk (error)	*50.00*	*7.50*
		Never hinged	*150.00*	
279B	A88	2c red, type IV ('99)	9.00	.40
		Never hinged	25.00	
c.		2c rose carmine, type IV ('99)	275.00	200.00
		Never hinged	850.00	
d.		2c orange red, type IV, horiz. wmk. ('00)	11.50	2.00
		Never hinged	32.50	
e.		2c orange red, type IV, vert. wmk.	*35.00*	*10.00*
		Never hinged	*110.00*	
f.		2c carmine, type IV	10.00	2.00
		Never hinged	27.50	
g.		2c pink, type IV	50.00	5.00
		Never hinged	150.00	
h.		2c vermilion, type IV ('99)	11.00	3.00
		Never hinged	30.00	
i.		2c brown org, type IV ('99)	*250.00*	*50.00*
		Never hinged	*675.00*	
j.		Booklet pane of 6, red, type IV, horiz. wmk. ('00)	500.00	*3,000.*
		Never hinged	1,000.	
k.		Booklet pane of 6, red, type IV, vertical watermark ('02)	500.00	—
		Never hinged	1,000.	
l.		As No. 279B, all color missing (FO)	*500.00*	

No. 279Bl must be collected se-tenant with a partially printed stamp.

280 A90 4c rose brn ('98) 25.00 3.25
Never hinged 75.00
a. 4c lilac brown 25.00 3.25
Never hinged 75.00
b. 4c orange brown 25.00 3.00
Never hinged 75.00
281 A91 5c dk blue ('98) 32.50 2.25
Never hinged 100.00
282 A92 6c lake ('98) 45.00 6.50
Never hinged 140.00
a. 6c purple lake 70.00 15.00
Never hinged 210.00

Type I. The tips of the foliate ornaments do not impinge on the white curved line below "ten cents."

282C A94 10c brown, type I ('98) 175.00 6.50
Never hinged 525.00

Type II. The tips of the ornaments break the curved line below the "e" of "ten" and the "t" of "cents."

283 A94 10c org brn, type II, horiz. wmk. 150.00 6.00
Never hinged 450.00
a. Vert. wmk. ('00) *225.00* *12.50*
Never hinged *700.00*
284 A95 15c olive grn ('98) 160.00 13.00
Never hinged 500.00
Nos. 279-284 (8) 605.50 38.40

For "I.R." overprints, see Nos. R153-R155A.

VALUES FOR VERY FINE STAMPS
Please note: Stamps are valued in the grade of Very Fine unless otherwise indicated.

TRANS-MISSISSIPPI EXPOSITION ISSUE

Marquette on the Mississippi A100

Farming in the West — A101

Indian Hunting Buffalo A102

Frémont on the Rocky Mountains A103

Troops Guarding Wagon Train — A104

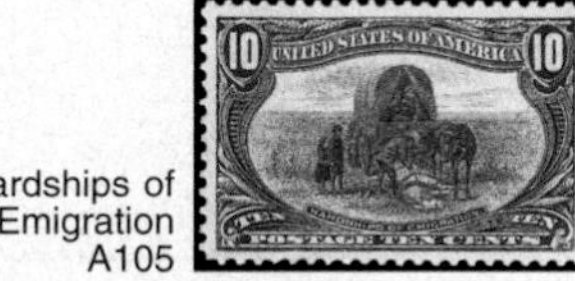
Hardships of Emigration A105

Western Mining Prospector A106

Western Cattle in Storm A107

Mississippi River Bridge A108

1898, June 17 Wmk. 191 *Perf. 12*

285 A100 1c dark yellow green 25.00 7.00
Never hinged 67.50
286 A101 2c copper red 25.00 2.75
Never hinged 67.50
287 A102 4c orange 110.00 27.50
Never hinged 300.00
288 A103 5c dull blue 100.00 25.00
Never hinged 275.00
289 A104 8c violet brown 150.00 50.00
Never hinged 425.00
a. Vert. pair, imperf. horiz. *27,500.*
290 A105 10c gray vio 150.00 35.00
Never hinged 425.00
291 A106 50c sage grn 600.00 200.00
Never hinged 1,800.
292 A107 $1 black 1,200. 725.
Never hinged 3,500.
No gum 600.
293 A108 $2 org brn 1,900. 1,100.
Never hinged 6,000.
No gum 875.
Nos. 285-293 (9) 4,260. 2,172.

Trans-Mississippi Exposition, Omaha, Neb., June 1 to Nov. 1, 1898.
For "I.R" overprints see #R158A-R158B.

Never-Hinged Stamps
See note before No. 182 regarding premiums for never-hinged stamps.

PAN-AMERICAN EXPOSITION ISSUE

Fast Lake Navigation A109

"Empire State" Express A110

Electric Automobile A111

Bridge at Niagara Falls — A112

Canal Locks at Sault Ste. Marie — A113

Fast Ocean Navigation — A114

1901, May 1 Wmk. 191 *Perf. 12*

294 A109 1c grn & blk 16.50 3.00
Never hinged 42.50
a. Center inverted *12,500.* *20,000.*
Never hinged *22,500.*
295 A110 2c car & blk 15.50 1.00
Never hinged 40.00
a. Center inverted *55,000.* *60,000.*
296 A111 4c dp red brn & blk 70.00 19.00
Never hinged 170.00
a. Center inverted *75,000.* —
297 A112 5c ultra & black 75.00 18.00
Never hinged 180.00
298 A113 8c brn vio & blk 95.00 55.00
Never hinged 240.00
299 A114 10c yel brn & blk 125.00 32.50
Never hinged 300.00
Nos. 294-299 (6) 397.00 128.50
Nos. 294-299, never hinged 1,032.

No. 296a was a special printing.
Almost all unused examples of Nos. 295a and 296a have partial or disturbed gum. Values are for examples with full original gum that is slightly disturbed.

Franklin A115

Washington A116

Jackson A117

Grant A118

Lincoln A119

Garfield A120

Martha Washington A121

Webster A122

Benjamin Harrison A123

Clay A124

Jefferson A125

David G. Farragut A126

Madison A127

Marshall A128

1902-03 Wmk. 191 *Perf. 12*

300 A115 1c blue grn ('03) 11.00 .25
Never hinged 27.50
b. Booklet pane of 6 600.00 *11,500.*
Never hinged 1,150.
Wmk. horiz. —
301 A116 2c car ('03) 15.00 .50
Never hinged 37.50
c. Booklet pane of 6 500.00 *6,000.*
Never hinged 950.00
302 A117 3c brt vio ('03) 50.00 4.00
Never hinged 130.00
303 A118 4c brn ('03) 55.00 2.50
Never hinged 140.00
304 A119 5c blue ('03) 60.00 2.25
Never hinged 150.00
305 A120 6c claret ('03) 60.00 5.75
Never hinged 150.00
306 A121 8c vio black 40.00 3.50
Never hinged 100.00
307 A122 10c pale red brn ('03) 60.00 3.25
Never hinged 150.00
308 A123 13c purple blk 40.00 11.00
Never hinged 100.00
309 A124 15c ol grn ('03) 180.00 14.00
Never hinged 475.00
310 A125 50c org ('03) 400. 37.50
Never hinged 1,200.
311 A126 $1 black ('03) 625.00 95.00
Never hinged 1,900.
No gum 130.00
312 A127 $2 dk bl ('03) 875.00 225.00
Never hinged 2,750.
No gum 200.00
313 A128 $5 dk grn ('03) 2,250. 750.00
Never hinged *6,500.*
No gum 500.00
Nos. 300-313 (14) 4,721. 1,154.

For listings of designs A127 and A128 with Perf. 10 see Nos. 479 and 480.

1906-08 *Imperf.*

314 A115 1c blue green 15.00 20.00
Never hinged 32.50
314A A118 4c brn ('08) *100,000.* *52,500.*
Never hinged *200,000.*
315 A119 5c blue ('08) 325.00 *1,250.*
Never hinged 600.00

No. 314A was issued imperforate but all examples were privately perforated with large oblong perforations at the sides (Schermack type III).
Beware of examples of No. 303 with trimmed perforations and fake private perfs added.
Used examples of Nos. 314 and 315 must have contemporaneous cancels.

COIL STAMPS

Warning! Imperforate stamps are known fraudulently perforated to resemble coil stamps and part-perforate varieties. Fully perforated stamps and booklet stamps also are known with perforations fraudulently trimmed off to resemble coil stamps.

1908 *Perf. 12 Horizontally*

316 A115 1c blue green *115,000.*
317 A119 5c blue *6,000.* —
Never hinged *12,500.*

Perf. 12 Vertically

318 A115 1c blue green *4,500.*
Never hinged *9,500.*

Coil stamps for use in vending and affixing machines are perforated on two sides only, either horizontally or vertically.
They were first issued in 1908, using perf. 12. This was changed to 8 ½ in 1910, and to 10 in 1914.
Imperforate sheets of certain denominations were sold to the vending machine companies which applied a variety of private perforations and separations.
Several values of the 1902 and later issues are found on an apparently coarse ribbed paper caused by worn blankets on the printing press and are not true paper varieties.
All examples of Nos. 316-318 must be accompanied by certificates of authenticity issued by recognized expertizing committees.
No. 318 mint never hinged is valued in the grade of fine.

Washington — A129

Type I

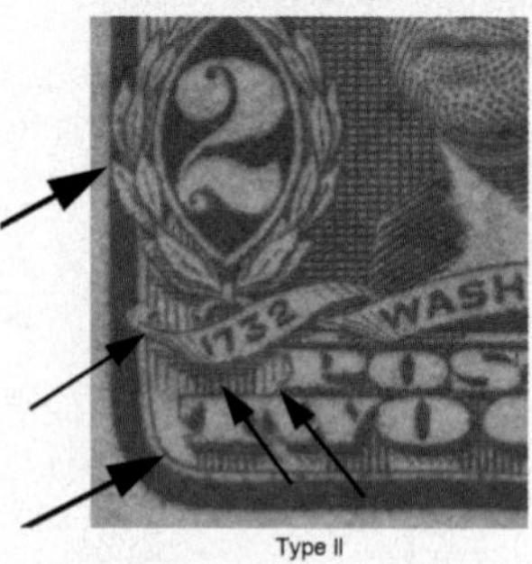

Type II

The two large arrows in the illustrations highlight the two major differences of the type II stamps: closing of the thin left border line next to the laurel leaf, and strengthening of the inner frame line at the lower left corner. The small arrows point out three minor differences that are not always easily discernible: strengthening of shading lines under the ribbon just above the "T" of "TWO," a shorter shading line to the left of the "P" in "POSTAGE," and shortening of a shading line in the left side ribbon.

Type I

1903, Nov. 12 Wmk. 191 ***Perf. 12***

No.	Description	Unused	Used
319	A129 2c carmine, type I	6.00	.25
	Never hinged	15.00	
a.	2c lake	—	
b.	2c carmine rose	15.00	.40
	Never hinged	45.00	
c.	2c scarlet	10.00	.30
	Never hinged	25.00	
d.	Vert. pair, imperf. horiz., No. 319	*7,500.*	
	Never hinged	*17,500.*	
e.	Vert. pair, imperf. between	—	
r.	Vert. pair, rouletted between	*3,250.*	

During the use of No. 319, the postmaster of San Francisco discovered in his stock panes that had the perforations missing between the top two rows of stamps. To facilitate their separation, the imperf rows were rouletted, and the stamps were sold over the counter. These vertical pairs with regular perfs all around and rouletted between are No. 319r. No 319e is from a different source. One example has been authenticated, and collectors are warned that other pairs exist with faint blind perfs or indentations from the perforating machine.

No.	Description	Unused	Used
g.	Booklet pane of 6, carmine	125.00	*450.00*
	Never hinged	240.00	
n.	Booklet pane of 6, carmine rose	275.00	*700.00*
	Never hinged	500.00	
p.	Booklet pane of 6, scarlet	185.00	*625.00*
	Never hinged	350.00	

Type II

1908 Wmk. 191 ***Perf. 12***

No.	Description	Unused	Used
319F	A129 2c lake	10.00	.30
	Never hinged	25.00	
i.	2c carmine	65.00	*50.00*
	Never hinged	150.00	
j.	2c carmine rose	85.00	1.75
	Never hinged	185.00	
k.	2c scarlet	70.00	2.00
	Never hinged	160.00	
q.	Booklet pane of 6, lake	300.00	*800.00*
	Never hinged	575.00	

Type I

1906, Oct. 2 Wmk. 191 ***Imperf.***

No.	Description	Unused	Used
320	A129 2c carmine	15.00	*19.00*
	Never hinged	32.50	
c.	2c carmine rose	75.00	42.50
	Never hinged	150.00	

Type II

1908 Wmk. 191 ***Imperf.***

No.	Description	Unused	Used
320A	A129 2c lake	45.00	50.00
	Never hinged	100.00	
d.	2c carmine	*120.00*	*2,500.*
	Never hinged	*175.00*	

No. 320Ad was issued imperforate, but all examples were privately perforated with large oblong perforations at the sides (Schermack type III).

COIL STAMPS

1908 ***Perf. 12 Horizontally***

No.	Description	Unused	Used
321	A129 2c carmine, type I, pair	*450,000.*	*250,000.*

Four authenticated unused pairs of No. 321 are known and available to collectors. A fifth, unauthenticated pair is in the New York Public Library Miller collection, which is on long-term loan to the Smithsonian National Postal Museum. The value for an unused pair is for a fine-very fine example. Two fine pairs are recorded and one very fine pair.

There are no authenticated unused single stamps recorded. The used value is for a single on cover, of which two authenticated examples are known, both used from Indianapolis in 1908.

Numerous counterfeits exist.

No.	Description	Unused	Used
322	A129 2c carmine, type II	*7,000.*	—
	Never hinged	*15,000.*	

This Government Coil Stamp should not be confused with those of the International Vending Machine Co., which are perforated 12½.

All examples of Nos. 321-322 must be accompanied by certificates of authenticity issued by recognized expertizing committees.

VALUES FOR VERY FINE STAMPS

Please note: Stamps are valued in the grade of Very Fine unless otherwise indicated.

LOUISIANA PURCHASE EXPOSITION ISSUE

Robert R. Livingston A130

Thomas Jefferson A131

James Monroe A132

William McKinley A133

Map of Louisiana Purchase A134

1904, Apr. 30 Wmk. 191 ***Perf. 12***

No.	Description	Unused	Used
323	A130 1c green	25.00	5.00
	Never hinged	65.00	
324	A131 2c carmine	25.00	2.00
	Never hinged	65.00	
a.	Vertical pair, imperf. horiz.	*25,000.*	
325	A132 3c violet	70.00	30.00
	Never hinged	185.00	
326	A133 5c dark blue	75.00	25.00
	Never hinged	200.00	
327	A134 10c red brown	130.00	30.00
	Never hinged	330.00	
	Nos. 323-327 (5)	325.00	92.00
	Nos. 323-327, never hinged	845.00	

JAMESTOWN EXPOSITION ISSUE

Captain John Smith — A135

Founding of Jamestown A136

Pocahontas A137

1907 Wmk. 191 ***Perf. 12***

No.	Description	Unused	Used
328	A135 1c green	22.50	5.00
	Never hinged	60.00	
329	A136 2c carmine	25.00	4.50
	Never hinged	70.00	
a.	2c carmine lake	—	
330	A137 5c blue	120.00	32.50
	Never hinged	300.00	
	Nos. 328-330 (3)	167.50	42.00
	Nos. 328-330, never hinged	450.00	

Franklin A138

Washington A139

There are several types of some of the 2c and 3c stamps of this and succeeding issues. These types are described under the dates at which they first appeared.

Illustrations of Types I-VII of the 2c (A140) and Types I-IV of the 3c (A140) are reproduced by permission of H. L. Lindquist.

1908-09 Wmk. 191 ***Perf. 12***

No.	Description	Unused	Used
331	A138 1c green	6.75	.40
	Never hinged	17.00	
a.	Booklet pane of 6	150.00	*700.00*
	Never hinged	300.00	

No. 331 exists in horizontal pair, imperforate between, a variety resulting from booklet experiments. Not regularly issued. Value in the grade of fine, $3,750.

No. 331a used is valued with a contemporaneous cancel. A certificate of authenticity is advised.

No.	Description	Unused	Used
332	A139 2c carmine	6.25	.35
	Never hinged	15.00	
a.	Booklet pane of 6	135.00	*500.00*
	Never hinged	240.00	
b.	2c lake	*4,250.*	

No. 332a used is valued with a contemporaneous cancel. A certificate of authenticity is advised.

No. 332b is valued in the grade of fine.

Washington — A140

TYPE I

THREE CENTS.

Type I. The top line of the toga rope is weak and the rope shading lines are thin. The 5th line from the left is missing. The line between the lips is thin. (For descriptions of 3c types II, III and IV, see notes and illustrations preceding Nos. 484, 529-530.)

Used on both flat plate and rotary press printings.

No.	Description	Unused	Used
333	A140 3c deep violet, type I	30.00	3.00
	Never hinged	75.00	
334	A140 4c orange brown	37.50	1.50
	Never hinged	92.50	
335	A140 5c blue	50.00	2.50
	Never hinged	120.00	
336	A140 6c red orange	65.00	6.50
	Never hinged	150.00	
337	A140 8c olive green	45.00	3.00
	Never hinged	105.00	
338	A140 10c yellow ('09)	67.50	2.00
	Never hinged	160.00	
339	A140 13c bl green ('09)	37.50	19.00
	Never hinged	90.00	
340	A140 15c pale ultra ('09)	65.00	6.50
	Never hinged	150.00	
341	A140 50c violet ('09)	300.00	22.50
	Never hinged	700.00	
342	A140 $1 violet brn ('09)	500.00	100.00
	Never hinged	1,150.	
	Nos. 331-342 (12)	1,210.	167.25

For listings of other perforated sheet stamps of A138, A139 and A140 see:

Nos. 357-366 Bluish paper

Nos. 374-382, 405-407 Single line wmk. Perf. 12

Nos. 423A-423C Single line wmk. Perf 12x10

Nos. 423D-423E Single line wmk. Perf 10x12

Nos. 424-430 Single line wmk. Perf. 10

Nos. 461 Single line wmk. Perf. 11

Nos. 462-469 unwmk. Perf. 10

Nos. 498-507 unwmk. Perf. 11

Nos. 519 Double line wmk. Perf. 11

Nos. 525-530 and 536 Offset printing

Nos. 538-546 Rotary press printing

Imperf

No.	Description	Unused	Used
343	A138 1c green	4.00	*5.50*
	Never hinged	8.50	
344	A139 2c carmine	4.75	3.25
	Never hinged	10.00	
345	A140 3c dp violet, type I	9.00	*22.50*
	Never hinged	19.00	
346	A140 4c org brn ('09)	13.50	*25.00*
	Never hinged	29.00	
347	A140 5c blue ('09)	27.50	*37.50*
	Never hinged	60.00	
	Nos. 343-347 (5)	58.75	*93.75*
	Nos. 343-347, never hinged	126.50	

For listings of other imperforate stamps of designs A138, A139 and A140 see Nos. 383, 384, 408, 409 and 459 Single line wmk.

Nos. 481-485 unwmk.

Nos. 531-535 Offset printing

COIL STAMPS

1908-10 *Perf. 12 Horizontally*

348 A138 1c green 35.00 *50.00*
Never hinged 75.00
349 A139 2c carmine ('09) 90.00 *100.00*
Never hinged 210.00
350 A140 4c org brn ('10) 140.00 *210.00*
Never hinged 325.00
351 A140 5c blue ('09) 140.00 *300.00*
Never hinged 325.00
Nos. 348-351 (4) 405.00 660.00

1909 *Perf. 12 Vertically*

352 A138 1c green 95.00 *190.00*
Never hinged 220.00
353 A139 2c carmine 90.00 *220.00*
Never hinged 200.00
354 A140 4c org brn 190.00 *275.00*
Never hinged 400.00
355 A140 5c blue 210.00 *300.00*
Never hinged 475.00
356 A140 10c yellow 3,500. *4,500.*
Never hinged 8,500.

For listings of other coil stamps of designs A138, A139 and A140, see #385-396, 410-413, 441-458 (single line wmk.), #486-496 (unwatermarked).

Beware of stamps offered as No. 356 which may be examples of No. 338 with perfs. trimmed at top and/or bottom. Beware also of plentiful fakes in the marketplace of Nos. 348-355, made by fraudulently perforating imperforate stamps or by fraudulently trimming perforations off fully perforated stamps. Authentication of all these coils is advised.

BLUISH PAPER

This was made with 35 percent rag stock instead of all wood pulp. The "bluish" color (actually grayish blue) goes through the paper showing clearly on the back as well as on the face.

1909 *Perf. 12*

357 A138 1c green 85.00 *150.00*
Never hinged 180.00
358 A139 2c carmine 80.00 *150.00*
Never hinged 170.00
359 A140 3c dp violet, type I 1,800. *9,000.*
Never hinged 4,000.
360 A140 4c org brn *27,500.*
361 A140 5c blue 5,750. *17,500.*
Never hinged *14,500.*
362 A140 6c red org 1,250. *12,500.*
Never hinged 3,000.
363 A140 8c olive green *30,000.*
Never hinged *85,000.*
364 A140 10c yellow 1,600. *10,000.*
Never hinged 4,000.
365 A140 13c blue green 2,600. *4,000.*
Never hinged 6,000.
366 A140 15c pale ultra 1,250. *12,500.*
Never hinged 3,000.

Nos. 360 and 363 were not regularly issued.

Used examples of Nos. 357-366 must bear contemporaneous cancels, and Nos. 359-366 used must be accompanied by certificates of authenticity issued by recognized expertizing committees.

LINCOLN CENTENARY OF BIRTH ISSUE

Lincoln — A141

1909, Feb. 12 **Wmk. 191** *Perf. 12*

367 A141 2c carmine 5.00 2.00
Never hinged 10.50

Imperf

368 A141 2c carmine 14.00 22.50
Never hinged 25.00

BLUISH PAPER

Perf. 12

369 A141 2c carmine 150.00 *250.00*
Never hinged 320.00

ALASKA-YUKON-PACIFIC EXPOSITION ISSUE

William H. Seward — A142

1909, June 1 **Wmk. 191** *Perf. 12*

370 A142 2c carmine 7.50 2.25
Never hinged 16.00

Imperf

371 A142 2c carmine 16.00 24.00
Never hinged 32.50

Seattle, Wash., June 1 to Oct. 16.

HUDSON-FULTON CELEBRATION ISSUE

"Half Moon" and Steamship A143

1909, Sept. 25 **Wmk. 191** *Perf. 12*

372 A143 2c carmine 10.00 4.75
Never hinged 21.00

Imperf

373 A143 2c carmine 20.00 27.50
Never hinged 40.00

Tercentenary of the discovery of the Hudson River and Centenary of Robert Fulton's steamship.

DESIGNS OF 1908-09 ISSUES

1910-11 **Wmk. 190** *Perf. 12*

374 A138 1c green 6.50 .25
Never hinged 15.00
a. Booklet pane of 6 225.00 *400.00*
Never hinged 375.00
375 A139 2c carmine 6.50 .25
Never hinged 15.00
a. Booklet pane of 6 125.00 *300.00*
Never hinged 200.00
b. 2c lake *800.00*
Never hinged *1,750.*
c. As "b," booklet pane of 6 *10,000.*
d. Double impression *750.00* —
Never hinged *1,500.*
376 A140 3c deep violet, type I ('11) 20.00 2.00
Never hinged 45.00
377 A140 4c brown ('11) 30.00 1.00
Never hinged 70.00
378 A140 5c blue ('11) 30.00 .75
Never hinged 70.00
379 A140 6c red org ('11) 40.00 1.25
Never hinged 90.00
380 A140 8c ol grn ('11) 100.00 15.00
Never hinged 225.00
381 A140 10c yellow ('11) 95.00 6.00
Never hinged 220.00
382 A140 15c pale ultra ('11) 240.00 22.50
Never hinged 550.00
Nos. 374-382 (9) 568.00 49.00

1910, Dec. *Imperf.*

383 A138 1c green 2.00 *2.25*
Never hinged 4.25
384 A139 2c carmine 3.25 2.75
Never hinged 7.00

COIL STAMPS

1910, Nov. 1 *Perf. 12 Horizontally*

385 A138 1c green 45.00 45.00
Never hinged 100.00
386 A139 2c carmine 130.00 100.00
Never hinged 280.00

1910-11 *Perf. 12 Vertically*

387 A138 1c green 190.00 140.00
Never hinged 400.00
388 A139 2c carmine 1,300. *2,250.*
Never hinged 3,250.

Stamps offered as No. 388 frequently are privately perforated examples of No. 384, or examples of No. 375 with top and/or bottom perfs trimmed.

389 A140 3c dp violet, type I ('11) *110,000.* *10,500.*
Never hinged *240,000.*

No. 389 is valued in the grade of fine.

Stamps offered as No. 389 sometimes are examples of No. 376 with top and/or bottom perfs trimmed.

Beware also of plentiful fakes in the marketplace of Nos. 385-387.

Expertization by competent authorities is recommended.

1910 *Perf. 8½ Horizontally*

390 A138 1c green 4.50 *14.00*
Never hinged 10.00
391 A139 2c carmine 42.50 *50.00*
Never hinged 90.00

1910-13 *Perf. 8½ Vertically*

392 A138 1c green 27.50 *55.00*
Never hinged 60.00
393 A139 2c carmine 45.00 45.00
Never hinged 105.00
394 A140 3c dp violet, type I ('11) 60.00 *67.50*
Never hinged 135.00
395 A140 4c brown ('12) 60.00 *70.00*
Never hinged 135.00
396 A140 5c blue ('13) 60.00 67.50
Never hinged 135.00
Nos. 392-396 (5) 252.50 305.00

Beware also of plentiful fakes in the marketplace of Nos. 390-393.

PANAMA-PACIFIC EXPOSITION ISSUE

Vasco Nunez de Balboa — A144

Pedro Miguel Locks, Panama Canal — A145

Golden Gate — A146

Discovery of San Francisco Bay — A147

1913 **Wmk. 190** *Perf. 12*

397 A144 1c green 16.50 2.00
Never hinged 40.00
398 A145 2c carmine 18.00 1.00
Never hinged 40.00
a. 2c carmine lake *1,500.*
Never hinged *2,500.*
b. 2c lake *5,000.*
Never hinged *8,500.*
399 A146 5c blue 70.00 10.00
Never hinged 160.00
400 A147 10c orange yel 120.00 22.50
Never hinged 270.00
400A A147 10c orange 180.00 20.00
Never hinged 400.00
Nos. 397-400A (5) 404.50 55.50
Nos. 397-400A, never hinged 910.00

1914-15 *Perf. 10*

401 A144 1c green 25.00 7.00
Never hinged 60.00
402 A145 2c car ('15) 70.00 2.75
Never hinged 170.00
403 A146 5c blue ('15) 160.00 20.00
Never hinged 390.00
404 A147 10c orange ('15) 725.00 75.00
Never hinged 1,700.
Nos. 401-404 (4) 980.00 104.75
Nos. 401-404, never hinged 2,320.

1912-14 **Wmk. 190** *Perf. 12*

405 A140 1c green 6.50 .25
Never hinged 15.00
a. Vert. pair, imperf. horiz. *2,000.* —
b. Booklet pane of 6 65.00 *75.00*
Never hinged 110.00
c. Double impression *6,000.*

TYPE I

TWO CENTS

Type I. There is one shading line in the first curve of the ribbon above the left "2" and one in the second curve of the ribbon above the right "2."

The button of the toga has only a faint outline.

The top line of the toga rope, from the button to the front of the throat, is also very faint.

The shading lines of the face terminate in front of the ear with little or no joining, to form a lock of hair.

Used on both flat plate and rotary press printings.

406 A140 2c car, type I 6.50 .25
Never hinged 15.00
a. Booklet pane of 6 65.00 *90.00*
Never hinged 110.00
b. Double impression *1,250.*
c. 2c lake, type I *2,000.* *6,000.*
Never hinged *4,500.*
407 A140 7c black ('14) 70.00 14.00
Never hinged 160.00
Nos. 405-407 (3) 83.00 14.50

1912 *Imperf.*

408 A140 1c green 1.00 1.00
Never hinged 2.00
409 A140 2c car, type I 1.20 1.20
Never hinged 2.40

COIL STAMPS

1912 *Perf. 8½ Horizontally*

410 A140 1c green 6.00 *12.50*
Never hinged 13.00
411 A140 2c carmine, type I 10.00 *15.00*
Never hinged 22.50

Perf. 8½ Vertically

412 A140 1c green 25.00 25.00
Never hinged 55.00
413 A140 2c carmine, type I 50.00 25.00
Never hinged 110.00
Nos. 410-413 (4) 91.00 77.50

Beware also of plentiful fakes in the marketplace of Nos. 410-413.

Franklin — A148

1912-14 Wmk. 190 *Perf. 12*

414 A148 8c pale ol grn 42.50 2.00
Never hinged 100.00
415 A148 9c sal red ('14) 52.50 14.00
Never hinged 120.00
416 A148 10c orange yellow 42.50 .80
Never hinged 100.00
a. 10c brown yellow *1,250.*
Never hinged *2,750.*
417 A148 12c cl brn ('14) 42.50 5.00
Never hinged 100.00
418 A148 15c gray 85.00 4.50
Never hinged 190.00
419 A148 20c ultra ('14) 190.00 19.00
Never hinged 400.00
420 A148 30c org red ('14) 115.00 19.00
Never hinged 250.00
421 A148 50c violet ('14) 350.00 30.00
Never hinged 800.00
Nos. 414-421 (8) 920.00 94.30

No. 421 almost always has an offset of the frame lines on the back under the gum. No. 422 does not have this offset.

VALUES FOR VERY FINE STAMPS

Please note: Stamps are valued in the grade of Very Fine unless otherwise indicated.

1912, Feb. 12 Wmk. 191 *Perf. 12*

422 A148 50c violet 225.00 25.00
Never hinged 525.00
423 A148 $1 violet brown 475.00 80.00
Never hinged 1,050.

Perforated sheet stamps of type A148: #431-440 (single line wmk., perf. 10), #460 (double line wmk. perf. 10), #470-478 (unwmkd., perf. 10), #508-518 (unwmkd., perf. 11).

1914 Wmk. 190 *Perf. 12x10*

423A A140 1c green *15,000.* *6,000.*
Never hinged —
423B A140 2c rose red, type I *175,000.* *17,500.*
423C A140 5c blue *20,000.*

Nos. 423A-423C formerly were Nos. 424a, 425d and 428a, respectively.

No. 423A unused is valued in the grade of fine. Values for 423A used and 423B-423C are for fine-very fine examples.

1914 Wmk. 190 *Perf. 10x12*

423D A140 1c green *12,500.*
423E A140 2c rose red, type I —

Nos. 423D and 423E formerly were Nos. 424b and 425c, respectively. Only one example is recorded of No. 423E.

No. 423D is valued in the grade of fine-very fine.

1913-15 Wmk. 190 *Perf. 10*

424 A140 1c green ('14) 2.50 .25
Never hinged 5.25
c. Vert. pair, imperf. horiz. *3,000.* *2,500.*
Never hinged *4,500.*
d. Booklet pane of 6 ('13) 5.25 *7.50*
Never hinged 8.75
e. As "d," imperf. *1,650.*
f. Vert. pair, imperf. between and with straight edge at top *13,000.*

All known examples of No. 424e are without gum.

425 A140 2c rose red, type I ('14) 2.30 .25
Never hinged 4.75
e. Booklet pane of 6 ('13) 17.50 *25.00*
Never hinged 30.00

For former Nos. 425c and 425d, see Nos. 423A and 423D.

426 A140 3c dp vio, type I ('14) 14.00 1.50
Never hinged 32.50
427 A140 4c brown ('14) 32.50 1.00
Never hinged 75.00
428 A140 5c blue ('14) 32.50 1.00
Never hinged 75.00

For former No. 428a, see No. 423C.

429 A140 6c red orange ('14) 45.00 2.00
Never hinged 105.00
430 A140 7c black ('14) 90.00 5.00
Never hinged 200.00
431 A148 8c pale olive grn ('14) 35.00 3.00
Never hinged 82.50
a. Double impression —
432 A148 9c salmon red ('14) 45.00 9.00
Never hinged 105.00
433 A148 10c org yellow ('14) 45.00 1.00
Never hinged 105.00
434 A148 11c dk grn ('15) 22.50 8.50
Never hinged 55.00
435 A148 12c claret brown ('14) 25.00 6.00
Never hinged 60.00
a. 12c copper red 30.00 7.00
Never hinged 72.50
437 A148 15c gray ('14) 125.00 7.25
Never hinged 280.00
438 A148 20c ultra ('14) 190.00 6.00
Never hinged 430.00
439 A148 30c orange red ('14) 220.00 20.00
Never hinged 500.00
440 A148 50c violet ('15) 450.00 20.00
Never hinged 1,050.
Nos. 424-440 (16) 1,376. 91.75

COIL STAMPS

1914 *Perf. 10 Horizontally*

441 A140 1c green 1.00 *1.50*
Never hinged 2.00
442 A140 2c carmine, type I 10.00 *45.00*
Never hinged 22.50

1914 *Perf. 10 Vertically*

443 A140 1c green 30.00 *45.00*
Never hinged 65.00
444 A140 2c carmine, type I 45.00 35.00
Never hinged 110.00
a. 2c lake *2,000.*
445 A140 3c violet, type I 225.00 *250.00*
Never hinged 525.00
446 A140 4c brown 130.00 *150.00*
Never hinged 300.00
447 A140 5c blue 45.00 *115.00*
Never hinged 100.00
Nos. 443-447 (5) 475.00 595.00

Beware also of plentiful fakes in the marketplace of Nos. 441-447.

ROTARY PRESS STAMPS

The Rotary Press Stamps are printed from plates that are curved to fit around a cylinder. This curvature produces stamps that are slightly larger, either horizontally or vertically, than those printed from flat plates. Designs of stamps from flat plates measure about 18½-19mm wide by 22mm high.

When the impressions are placed sidewise on the curved plates the designs are 19½-20mm wide; when they are placed vertically the designs are 22½ to 23mm high. A line of color (not a guide line) shows where the curved plates meet or join on the press.

ROTARY PRESS COIL STAMPS
Stamp designs: 18½-19x22½mm

1915-16 *Perf. 10 Horizontally*

448 A140 1c green 7.50 *17.50*
Never hinged 16.00

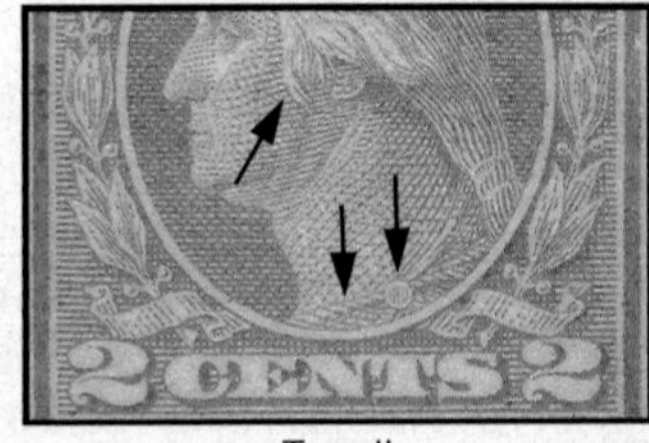

Type II

TWO CENTS.
Type II. Shading lines in ribbons as on type I.
The toga button, rope and rope shading lines are heavy.
The shading lines of the face at the lock of hair end in a strong vertical curved line.
Used on rotary press printings only.

Type III

Type III. Two lines of shading in the curves of the ribbons.
Other characteristics similar to type II.
Used on rotary press printings only.

Fraudulently altered examples of type III (Nos. 455, 488, 492 and 540) have had one line of shading scraped off to make them resemble type II (Nos. 454, 487, 491 and 539).

449 A140 2c red, type I 2,500. 600.00
Never hinged 5,500.
450 A140 2c carmine, type III ('16) 12.50 *22.50*
Never hinged 27.50

Stamp designs: 19½-20x22mm

1914-16 *Perf. 10 Vertically*

452 A140 1c green 10.00 *17.50*
Never hinged 21.00
453 A140 2c carmine rose, type I 140.00 17.50
Never hinged 300.00
454 A140 2c red, type II 70.00 22.50
Never hinged 160.00
455 A140 2c carmine, type III 8.00 3.50
Never hinged 18.00
456 A140 3c vio, type I ('16) 225.00 170.00
Never hinged 475.00
457 A140 4c brown ('16) 25.00 30.00
Never hinged 55.00
458 A140 5c blue ('16) 27.50 30.00
Never hinged 60.00
Nos. 452-458 (7) 505.50 291.00

Horizontal Coil

1914, June 30 *Imperf.*

459 A140 2c carmine, type I 175. *1,300.*
Never hinged 275.

When the value for a used stamp is higher than the unused value, the stamp must have a contemporaneous cancel. Valuable stamps of this type should be accompanied by certificates of authenticity issued by recognized expertizing committees. The used value for No. 459 is for an example with such a certificate.

Beware of examples of No. 453 with perforations fraudulently trimmed to resemble single examples of No. 459.

FLAT PLATE PRINTINGS

1915, Feb. 8 Wmk. 191 *Perf. 10*

460 A148 $1 violet black 675. 140.
Never hinged 1,500.

1915, June 17 Wmk. 190 *Perf. 11*

461 A140 2c pale carmine red, type I 125. *360.*
Never hinged 325.

Beware of fraudulently perforated examples of No. 409 being offered as No. 461.
See note on used stamps following No. 459.

Unwatermarked

From 1916 onward all postage stamps except Nos. 519 and 832b are on unwatermarked paper.

1916-17 Unwmk. *Perf. 10*

462 A140 1c green 7.00 .35
Never hinged 16.00
a. Booklet pane of 6 9.50 *12.50*
Never hinged 16.00
463 A140 2c carmine, type I 4.50 .40
Never hinged 10.00 .45
a. Booklet pane of 6 110.00 *110.00*
Never hinged 180.00

See No. 467 for P# block of 6 from plate 7942.

464 A140 3c violet, type I 70.00 19.00
Never hinged 175.00

Beware of fraudulently perforated examples of No. 483 being offered as No. 464.

465 A140 4c org brn 40.00 2.50
Never hinged 90.00
466 A140 5c blue 70.00 2.50
Never hinged 160.00
467 A140 5c car (error in plate of 2c, '17) 450.00 *1,500.*
Never hinged 850.00

No. 467 is an error caused by using a 5c transfer roll in re-entering three subjects: 7942 UL 74, 7942 UL 84, 7942 LR 18; the balance of the subjects on the plate being normal 2c entries. No. 467 imperf. is listed as No. 485. The error perf 11 on unwatermarked paper is No. 505.

468 A140 6c red orange 85.00 9.00
Never hinged 190.00
469 A140 7c black 120.00 15.00
Never hinged 270.00
470 A148 8c olive green 55.00 8.00
Never hinged 125.00
471 A148 9c salmon red 55.00 18.50
Never hinged 125.00
472 A148 10c orange yel 100.00 2.50
Never hinged 230.00
473 A148 11c dark green 40.00 18.50
Never hinged 90.00
474 A148 12c claret brn 50.00 7.50
Never hinged 115.00
475 A148 15c gray 180.00 16.00
Never hinged 400.00
476 A148 20c lt ultra 225.00 20.00
Never hinged 525.00
476A A148 30c orange red *2,500.*
Never hinged *4,750.*

No. 476A is valued in the grade of fine.

477 A148 50c lt violet ('17) 900. 85.00
Never hinged 2,000.
478 A148 $1 violet black 625.00 30.00
Never hinged 1,450.
Nos. 462-466,468-476,477-478 (16) 2,626. 254.75

TYPES OF 1903 ISSUE

1917, Mar. 22 Unwmk. *Perf. 10*

479 A127 $2 dark blue 210.00 40.00
Never hinged 475.00
480 A128 $5 light green 170.00 35.00
Never hinged 375.00

1916-17 *Imperf.*

481 A140 1c green .95 .95
Never hinged 1.90

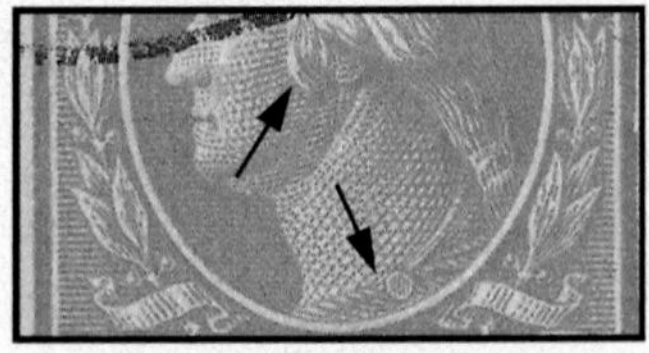

Type Ia

TWO CENTS
Type Ia. The design characteristics are similar to type I except that all of the lines of the design are stronger.
The toga button, toga rope and rope shading lines are heavy.
The latter characteristics are those of type II, which, however, occur only on impressions from rotary plates.
Used only on flat plates 10208 and 10209.

482 A140 2c carmine, type I 1.30 1.30
Never hinged 2.60
482A A140 2c deep rose, type Ia — *65,000.*

No. 482A was issued imperforate but all examples were privately perforated with large oblong perforations at the sides (Schermack type III).

Type II

THREE CENTS
Type II. The top line of the toga rope is strong and the rope shading lines are heavy and complete.
The line between the lips is heavy.
Used on both flat plate and rotary press printings.

483 A140 3c violet, type I ('17) 10.00 10.00
Never hinged 22.00
484 A140 3c violet, type II 8.00 8.00
Never hinged 18.00

485 A140 5c car (error in plate of 2c) ('17) *9,000.*
Never hinged *16,000.*

Although No. 485 is valued as a single stamp, such examples are seldom seen in the marketplace.

No. 485 usually is seen as the center stamp in a block of 9 with 8 No. 482 (value with No. 485 never hinged, $22,500) or as two center stamps in a block of 12 (value with both No. 485 never hinged, $42,500).

ROTARY PRESS COIL STAMPS
(See note over No. 448)

1916-18 ***Perf. 10 Horizontally***

Stamp designs: 18½-19x22½mm

486 A140 1c green ('18) .85 .85
Never hinged 1.75
487 A140 2c carmine, type II 12.50 14.00
Never hinged 27.50
488 A140 2c carmine, type III 3.00 *5.00*
Never hinged 6.50
489 A140 3c vio, type I ('17) 4.50 2.25
Never hinged 10.00
Nos. 486-489 (4) 20.85 22.10

1916-22 ***Perf. 10 Vertically***

Stamp designs: 19½-20x22mm

490 A140 1c green .50 *.60*
Never hinged 1.05
491 A140 2c carmine, type II 2,500. 800.00
Never hinged 5,250.
492 A140 2c carmine, type III 9.00 1.00
Never hinged 19.00
493 A140 3c vio, type I ('17) 14.00 4.50
Never hinged 30.00
494 A140 3c vio, type II ('18) 10.00 2.50
Never hinged 21.50
495 A140 4c org brn ('17) 10.00 7.00
Never hinged 21.50
496 A140 5c blue ('19) 3.25 2.50
Never hinged 7.00
497 A148 10c org yel ('22) 17.50 17.50
Never hinged 37.50

Blind Perfs

Listings of imperforate-between varieties are for examples which show no trace of "blind perfs," traces of impressions from the perforating pins which do not cut into the paper.

Some unused stamps have had the gum removed to eliminate the impressions from the perforating pins. These stamps do not qualify as the listed varieties.

FLAT PLATE PRINTINGS
TYPES OF 1913-15 ISSUE

1917-19 **Unwmk.** ***Perf. 11***

498 A140 1c green .35 .25
Never hinged .75
a. Vertical pair, imperf. horiz. 800.00
Never hinged *1,600.*
b. Horizontal pair, imperf. between 700.00
Never hinged *1,600.*
c. Vertical pair, imperf. between *700.00* —
d. Double impression 250.00 *3,750.*
e. Booklet pane of 6 2.50 *2.00*
Never hinged 4.25
f. Booklet pane of 30 *1,050.* *12,500.*
Never hinged *1,700.*
g. Perf. 10 at top or bottom *17,500.* *20,000.*
Never hinged *27,500.*

No. 498g used is valued in the grade of fine.

499 A140 2c rose, type I .35 .25
Never hinged .75
a. Vertical pair, imperf. horiz., type I 1,000.
Never hinged 2,000.
b. Horiz. pair, imperf. vert., type I *550.00* *225.00*
Never hinged *1,100.*
c. Vert. pair, imperf. btwn., type I *900.00* *300.00*
e. Booklet pane of 6, type I 4.00 *2.50*
Never hinged 6.75
f. Booklet pane of 30, type I *22,500.* —
Never hinged *32,500.*
g. Double impression, type I 200.00 *2,000.*
Never hinged *400.00*
h. 2c lake, type I 500.00 800.00
Never hinged *1,000.*

No. 499b is valued in the grade of fine. No 499g used is valued in the grade of fine.

500 A140 2c deep rose, type Ia 250.00 240.00
Never hinged 550.00
501 A140 3c lt vio, type I 10.00 .40
Never hinged 23.00
b. Booklet pane of 6, type I 75.00 *80.00*
Never hinged 125.00
c. Vert. pair, imper. horiz., type I *2,500.*
Never hinged *4,000.*
d. Double impression *3,500.* *3,500.*
Never hinged *5,000.*

No. 501d is valued in the grade of fine.

502 A140 3c dark violet, type II 13.00 .75
Never hinged 30.00
b. Bklt. pane of 6, type II 60.00 *75.00*
Never hinged 100.00
c. Vert. pair, imperf. horiz., type II *1,400.* *750.00*
Never hinged *2,750.*
d. Double impression 800.00 *1,000.*
Never hinged 1,600.
e. Perf. 10 at top or bottom *15,000.* *30,000.*
Never hinged *21,500.*
503 A140 4c brown 9.00 .40
Never hinged 20.00
b. Double impression —
504 A140 5c blue 8.00 .35
Never hinged 18.00
a. Horizontal pair, imperf. between *20,000.* —
b. Double impression *2,000.* *1,600.*
505 A140 5c rose (error in plate of 2c) 300.00 *600.00*
Never hinged 625.00
506 A140 6c red orange 12.00 .40
Never hinged 27.50
a. Perf. 10 at top or bottom *30,000.* *8,000.*
b. Double impression, never hinged —

No. 506a also exists as a transitional stamp gauging partly perf 10 and partly perf 11 at top. Value thus the same as normal 506a.

No. 506b is a partial double impression. Two authenticated examples are documented.

507 A140 7c black 26.00 1.25
Never hinged 60.00
508 A148 8c olive bister 12.00 .65
Never hinged 27.50
b. Vertical pair, imperf. between — —
c. Perf. 10 at top or bottom *10,000.*
509 A148 9c salmon red 12.00 1.75
Never hinged 27.50
a. Perf. 10 at top or bottom *7,500.*
Never hinged *37,500.*

No. 509a also exists as a transitional stamp gauging partly perf 10 and partly perf 11 at top or bottom. Value thus the same as normal 509a.

510 A148 10c orange yellow 16.00 .25
Never hinged 36.00
a. 10c brown yellow *1,400.*
Never hinged *3,250.*
511 A148 11c lt green 8.00 2.50
Never hinged 18.00
a. Perf. 10 at top or bottom *4,000.* *3,750.*
Never hinged *7,500.*

No. 511a also exists as a transitional stamp gauging partly perf 10 and partly perf 11 at top or bottom. Value thus the same as normal 511a.

512 A148 12c claret brown 8.00 .40
Never hinged 18.00
a. 12c brown carmine 9.00 .50
Never hinged 20.00
b. Perf. 10 at top or bottom *27,500.* *15,000.*
513 A148 13c apple grn ('19) 10.00 6.00
Never hinged 22.00
514 A148 15c gray 35.00 1.50
Never hinged 80.00
a. Perf. 10 at bottom *10,000.*
515 A148 20c lt ultra 42.50 .45
Never hinged 90.00
b. Vertical pair, imperf. between *4,000.* *3,250.*
c. Double impression *1,250.*
d. Perf. 10 at top or bottom — *12,500.*

No. 515b is valued in the grade of fine.

Beware of pairs with blind perforations inside the design of the top stamp that are offered as No. 515b.

No. 515c is a partial double impression.

516 A148 30c orange red 30.00 1.50
Never hinged 70.00
a. Perf. 10 at top or bottom *20,000.* *8,500.*
Never hinged *37,500.*
b. Double impression —

No. 516a used is valued in the grade of fine.

517 A148 50c red violet 47.50 .75
Never hinged 115.00
b. Vertical pair, imperf. between & with natural straight edge at bottom *6,000.*
c. Perf. 10 at top or bottom *17,500.*

No. 517b is valued in average condition and may be a unique used pair (precanceled). The editors would like to see authenticated evidence of an unused pair.

518 A148 $1 violet brown 37.50 1.50
Never hinged 95.00
b. $1 deep brown *1,900.* *1,250.*
Never hinged *4,000.*
Nos. 498-504,506-518 (20) 587.20 261.30

No. 518b is valued in the grade of fine to very fine.

TYPE OF 1908-09 ISSUE

1917, Oct. 10 **Wmk. 191** ***Perf. 11***

519 A139 2c carmine 400.00 *1,750.*
Never hinged 850.00

Beware of examples of No. 344 fraudulently perforated and offered as No. 519. Obtaining a certificate from a recognized expertizing committee is strongly recommended.

Warning: See note following No. 459 regarding used stamps.

Franklin — A149

1918, Aug. **Unwmk.** ***Perf. 11***

523 A149 $2 org red & blk 525. 250.
Never hinged 1,150.
524 A149 $5 dp grn & blk 170. 35.00
Never hinged 360.

See No. 547 for $2 carmine & black.

TYPES OF 1917-19 ISSUE
OFFSET PRINTING

1918-20 **Unwmk.** ***Perf. 11***

525 A140 1c gray green 2.50 .90
Never hinged 6.00
a. 1c dark green 10.00 1.75
Never hinged 25.00
c. Horizontal pair, imperf. between *500.00* *650.00*
d. Double impression *40.00* *750.00*
Never hinged 90.00

No. 525c is valued in the grade of fine and with natural straight edge at right, as all recorded examples come thus. No. 525d used is valued in the grade of very good.

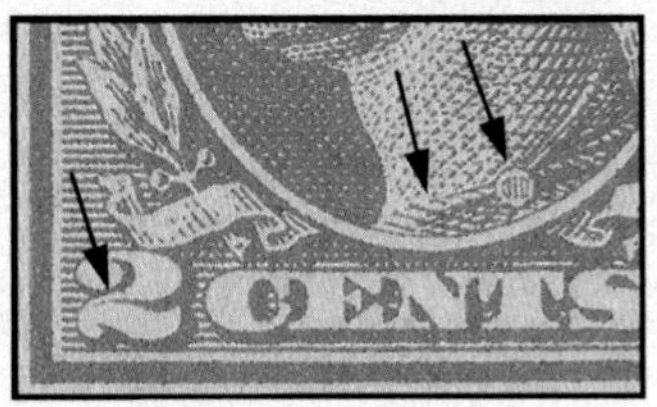

Type IV

TWO CENTS

Type IV — Top line of the toga rope is broken.

The shading lines in the toga button are so arranged that the curving of the first and last form "D (reversed) ID."

The line of color in the left "2" is very thin and usually broken.

Used on offset printings only.

Type V

Type V — Top line of the toga is complete.

There are five vertical shading lines in the toga button.

The line of color in the left "2" is very thin and usually broken.

The shading dots on the nose are as shown on the diagram.

Used on offset printings only.

Type Va

Type Va — Characteristics are the same as type V except in the shading dots of the nose. The third row of dots from the bottom has four dots instead of six. The overall height is ⅓mm shorter than the other types.

Used on offset printings only.

Type VI

Type VI — General characteristics the same as type V except that the line of color in the left "2" is very heavy.

Used on offset printings only.

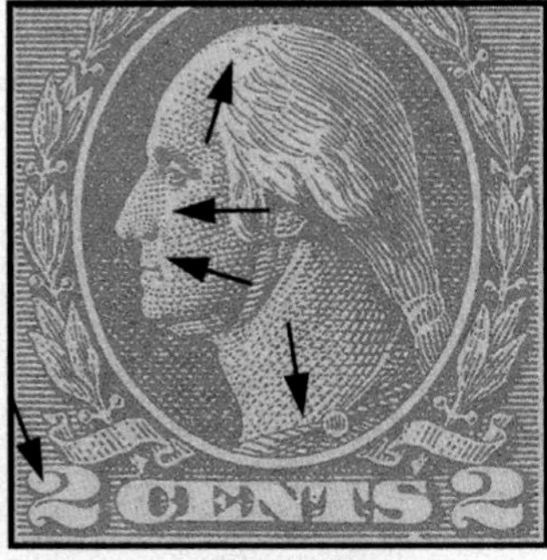

TYPE VII

Type VII — The line of color in the left "2" is invariably continuous, clearly defined and heavier than in type V or Va but not as heavy as type VI.

An additional vertical row of dots has been added to the upper lip.

Numerous additional dots have been added to the hair on top of the head.

Used on offset printings only.

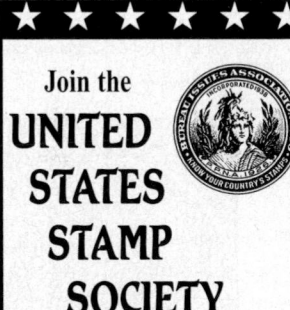

526 A140 2c car, type IV ('20) 25.00 4.00
Never hinged 57.50
527 A140 2c car, type V ('20) 18.00 1.25
Never hinged 40.00
a. Double impression 75.00 —
Never hinged 160.00
b. Vert. pair, imperf. horiz. *850.00*
c. Horiz. pair, imperf. vert. *1,000.* —
528 A140 2c car, type Va ('20) 8.00 .40
Never hinged 20.00
c. Double impression 55.00
Never hinged 125.00
g. Vert. pair, imperf. between *3,500.*
528A A140 2c car, type VI ('20) 47.50 2.00
Never hinged 115.00
d. Double impression 180.00 *900.00*
Never hinged 400.00
f. Vert. pair, imperf. horiz. —
h. Vert. pair, imperf. between *5,000.*
528B A140 2c car, type VII ('20) 20.00 .75
Never hinged 50.00
e. Double impression 77.50 *400.00*

No. 528Be used is valued in the grade of very good to fine.

TYPE III

THREE CENTS

Type III — The top line of the toga rope is strong but the 5th shading line is missing as in type I.

Center shading line of the toga button consists of two dashes with a central dot.

The "P" and "O" of "POSTAGE" are separated by a line of color.

The frame line at the bottom of the vignette is complete.

Used on offset printings only.

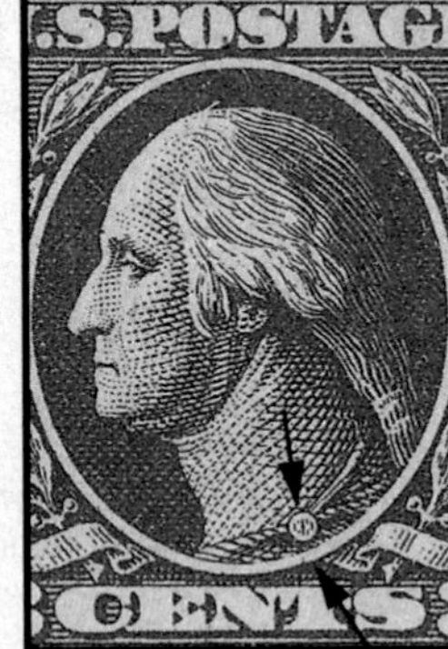

TYPE IV

Type IV — The shading lines of the toga rope are complete.

The second and fourth shading lines in the toga button are broken in the middle and the third line is continuous with a dot in the center.

The "P" and "O" of "POSTAGE" are joined.

The frame line at the bottom of the vignette is broken.

Used on offset printings only.

529 A140 3c vio, type III 3.50 .50
Never hinged 7.75
a. Double impression 45.00 *800.00*
Never hinged 100.00
b. Printed on both sides *2,500.*

No. 529a used is valued in the grade of very good.

530 A140 3c pur, type IV 2.00 .30
Never hinged 4.50
a. Double impression 35.00 *750.00*
b. Printed on both sides *350.00*
Never hinged *650.00*
c. Triple impression *1,750.* —
Nos. 525-530 (8) 126.50 10.10

No. 530a used is valued in the grade of fine.

1918-20 ***Imperf.***

531 A140 1c green ('19) 10.00 12.00
Never hinged 21.00
532 A140 2c car rose, type IV ('20) 32.50 35.00
Never hinged 70.00
533 A140 2c car, type V ('20) 85.00 100.00
Never hinged 180.00
534 A140 2c car, type Va ('20) 12.00 11.00
Never hinged 26.00
534A A140 2c car, type VI ('20) 35.00 32.50
Never hinged 75.00
534B A140 2c car, type VII ('20) 1,750. 1,250.
Never hinged 3,250.
535 A140 3c vio, type IV 8.00 5.00
Never hinged 18.00
a. Double impression 95.00 —
Never hinged 200.00
Nos. 531-534A,535 (6) 182.50 195.50

1919, Aug. 15 ***Perf. 12½***

536 A140 1c gray green 20.00 *35.00*
Never hinged 45.00
a. Horiz. pair, imperf. vert. *1,200.*

VICTORY ISSUE

"Victory" and Flags of the Allies — A150

FLAT PLATE PRINTING

1919, Mar. 3 **Engr.** ***Perf. 11***

537 A150 3c violet 10.00 3.25
Never hinged 20.00
a. 3c deep red violet *1,250.* *1,750.*
Never hinged *2,300.*
b. 3c light reddish violet 150.00 50.00
Never hinged 300.00
c. 3c red violet 200.00 60.00
Never hinged 400.00

Victory of the Allies in World War I.
No. 537a is valued in the grade of fine.

ROTARY PRESS PRINTINGS

1919 ***Perf. 11x10***

Stamp designs: 19½-20x22-22¼mm

538 A140 1c green 10.00 9.00
Never hinged 23.00
a. Vert. pair, imperf. horiz. 60.00 *125.00*
Never hinged 125.00
539 A140 2c carmine rose, type II 2,750. *17,500.*
Never hinged 4,000.
540 A140 2c car rose, type III 12.00 9.50
Never hinged 27.50
a. Vert. pair, imperf horiz. 60.00 *140.00*
Never hinged 125.00
b. Horiz. pair, imperf. vert. *1,750.*
541 A140 3c vio, type II 40.00 32.50
Never hinged 100.00

The part perforate varieties of Nos. 538a and 540a were issued in sheets and may be had in blocks; similar part perforate varieties, Nos. 490 and 492, are from coils and are found only in strips.

See note over No. 448 regarding No. 539.
No. 539 is valued in the grade of fine.
No. 540b is valued in the grade of fine.

1920, May 26 ***Perf. 10x11***

Stamp design: 19x22½-22¾mm

542 A140 1c green 12.50 1.50
Never hinged 30.00

1921 ***Perf. 10***

Stamp design: 19x22½mm

543 A140 1c green .70 .40
Never hinged 1.75
a. Horizontal pair, imperf. between *5,000.*

1922 ***Perf. 11***

Stamp design: 19x22½mm

544 A140 1c green *22,500.* *3,750.*
Never hinged *35,000.*

No. 544 is valued in the grade of fine.

1921

Stamp designs: 19½-20x22mm

545 A140 1c green 170.00 200.00
Never hinged 400.00
546 A140 2c carmine rose, type III 105.00 *190.00*
Never hinged 230.00
a. Perf. 10 on left side *7,500.* *17,500.*

No. 546a used is valued in the grade of very good. It is unique used.

FLAT PLATE PRINTING

1920, Nov. 1 ***Perf. 11***

547 A149 $2 carmine & black 125. 40.
Never hinged 270.
a. $2 lake & black 200. 40.
Never hinged 425.

PILGRIM TERCENTENARY ISSUE

"Mayflower" A151

Landing of the Pilgrims — A152

Signing of the Compact — A153

1920, Dec. 21 ***Perf. 11***

548 A151 1c green 4.00 2.25
Never hinged 10.00
549 A152 2c carmine rose 5.25 1.60
Never hinged 12.50
550 A153 5c deep blue 35.00 14.00
Never hinged 85.00
Nos. 548-550 (3) 44.25 17.85
Nos. 548-550, never hinged 107.50

Tercentenary of the landing of the Pilgrims at Plymouth, Mass.

Nathan Hale A154

Franklin A155

Harding A156

Washington A157

Lincoln A158

Martha Washington A159

Theodore Roosevelt A160

Garfield A161

McKinley A162

Grant A163

Jefferson A164

Monroe A165

Rutherford B. Hayes A166

Grover Cleveland A167

American Indian A168

Statue of Liberty A169

Golden Gate — A170

Niagara Falls — A171

American Buffalo A172

Arlington Amphitheater A173

Lincoln Memorial A174

U.S. Capitol A175

Head of Freedom Statue, Capitol Dome — A176

FLAT PLATE PRINTINGS

1922-25 **Unwmk.** ***Perf. 11***

551 A154 ½c olive brown ('25) .25 .25
Never hinged .50
552 A155 1c dp green ('23) 1.40 .25
Never hinged 3.00
a. Booklet pane of 6 7.50 *4.00*
Never hinged 12.50
553 A156 1½c yel brn ('25) 2.25 .25
Never hinged 4.60
554 A157 2c carmine ('23) 1.30 .25
Never hinged 3.00
a. Horiz. pair, imperf. vert. *275.00*
b. Vert. pair, imperf. horiz. *6,000.*
Never hinged *10,000.*
c. Booklet pane of 6 7.00 *3.00*
Never hinged 12.00
d. Perf. 10 at top or bottom *17,500.* *10,000.*
555 A158 3c violet ('23) 14.00 1.20
Never hinged 30.00
556 A159 4c yel brn ('23) 17.50 .50
Never hinged 37.50
a. Vert. pair, imperf. horiz. *12,500.*
b. Perf. 10 at top or bottom *3,500.* *22,500.*

No. 556a is unique. It resulted from a sheet that was damaged and patched during production.

No. 556b used also exists as a transitional stamp gauging 10 at left top and 11 at right top. Value the same.

557 A160 5c dark blue 17.50 .30
Never hinged 37.50
a. Imperf., pair *2,000.*
Never hinged *3,750.*

b. Horiz. pair, imperf. vert. —
c. Perf. 10 at top or bottom — *9,500.*
558 A161 6c red orange 32.50 1.00
Never hinged 70.00
559 A162 7c black ('23) 7.75 .75
Never hinged 16.50
560 A163 8c olive grn ('23) 40.00 1.00
Never hinged 90.00
561 A164 9c rose ('23) 12.50 1.25
Never hinged 27.00
562 A165 10c orange ('23) 15.00 .35
Never hinged 32.50
a. Vert. pair, imperf. horiz. *2,250.*
Never hinged *3,500.*
b. Imperf., pair *2,500.*
c. Perf. 10 at top or bottom *70,000. 15,000.*

No. 562a is valued in the grade of fine, with gum and without blue defacing lines. No. 562b is valued without gum and without blue pencil defacing lines. No. 562c is valued in the grade of fine.

563 A166 11c greenish blue 1.40 .60
Never hinged 3.00
a. 11c light bluish green 1.40 .60
Never hinged 3.00
d. Imperf., pair *20,000.*

Many other intermediate shades exist for Nos. 563 and 563a, all falling within the blue or green color families.

564 A167 12c brn vio ('23) 5.25 .35
Never hinged 11.50
a. Horiz. pair, imperf. vert. *4,250.*
565 A168 14c blue ('23) 4.75 .90
Never hinged 10.50
566 A169 15c gray 17.50 .30
Never hinged 37.50
567 A170 20c car rose ('23) 17.50 .30
Never hinged 37.50
a. Horiz. pair, imperf. vert. *2,750.*
Never hinged *5,250.*

No. 567a is valued in the grade of fine.

568 A171 25c yel grn 15.00 .75
Never hinged 32.50
b. Vert. pair, imperf. horiz. *3,250.*
c. Perf. 10 at one side *5,000. 11,000.*
Never hinged *7,500.*

No. 568b is valued in the grade of fine. No. 568c used is valued in the grade of fine.

569 A172 30c ol brn ('23) 25.00 .60
Never hinged 55.00
570 A173 50c lilac 35.00 .40
Never hinged 75.00
571 A174 $1 vio brn ('23) 37.50 .75
Never hinged 80.00
572 A175 $2 dp blue ('23) 70.00 9.00
Never hinged 150.00
573 A176 $5 car & bl ('23) 110.00 15.00
Never hinged 230.00
a. $5 car lake & dk bl 190.00 30.00
Never hinged 350.00
Nos. 551-573 (23) 500.85 36.30
Nos. 551-573, never hinged 1,075.

No. 556a is unique. No. 554b is valued in the grade of fine. No. 562b is valued without gum and without blue pencil defacing lines. No. 568b is valued in the grade of fine.

For other listings of perforated stamps of designs A154 to A173 see:
Nos. 578 & 579, Perf. 11x10
Nos. 581-591, Perf. 10
Nos. 594-596, Perf. 11
Nos. 632-642, 653, 692-696, Perf. 11x10½
Nos. 697-701, Perf. 10½x11

This series also includes #622-623 (perf. 11), 684-687 & 720-723.

1923-25 ***Imperf.***
Stamp design 19¼x22¼mm

575 A155 1c green 5.00 5.00
Never hinged 11.00
576 A156 1½c yel brn ('25) 1.25 *1.50*
Never hinged 2.70

The 1½c A156 Rotary press imperforate is listed as No. 631.

577 A157 2c carmine 1.30 1.25
Never hinged 2.90
a. 2c carmine lake —
Nos. 575-577 (3) 7.55 7.75
Nos. 575-577, never hinged 16.60

ROTARY PRESS PRINTINGS
(See note over No. 448)

1923 ***Perf. 11x10***
578 A155 1c green 75.00 *160.00*
Never hinged 170.00
579 A157 2c carmine 70.00 *140.00*
Never hinged 160.00

Nos. 578-579 were made from coil waste of Nos. 597, 599 and measure approximately 19¾x22¼mm.

1923-26 ***Perf. 10***
581 A155 1c green 10.00 .75
Never hinged 22.50
582 A156 1½c brown ('25) 6.00 .65
Never hinged 13.50
583 A157 2c car ('24) 3.00 .30
Never hinged 6.50
a. Booklet pane of 6 110.00 *150.00*
Never hinged 200.00
584 A158 3c violet ('25) 27.50 3.00
Never hinged 62.50
585 A159 4c yel brn ('25) 17.50 .65
Never hinged 37.50
586 A160 5c blue ('25) 17.50 .40
Never hinged 37.50
a. Horizontal pair, imperf. vertically *8,000.*

No. 586a is unique, precanceled, with average centering and small faults, and it is valued as such.

587 A161 6c red org ('25) 9.25 .60
Never hinged 21.00
588 A162 7c black ('26) 12.50 6.25
Never hinged 27.50
589 A163 8c ol grn ('26) 27.50 4.50
Never hinged 60.00
590 A164 9c rose ('26) 6.00 2.50
Never hinged 13.50
591 A165 10c orange ('25) 45.00 .50
Never hinged 100.00
Nos. 581-591 (11) 181.75 20.10
Nos. 581-591, never hinged 402.00

1923 ***Perf. 11***
594 A155 1c green *35,000. 10,500.*
With gum *65,000.*

The main listing for No. 594 unused is for an example without gum; both unused and used are valued with perforations just touching frameline on one side.

595 A157 2c carmine 250.00 *375.00*
Never hinged 500.00

Nos. 594-595 were made from coil waste of Nos. 597 and 599, and measure approximately 19¾x22¼mm.

596 A155 1c green *150,000.*
Precanceled *100,000.*

No. 596 was made from rotary press sheet waste and measures approximately 19¼x22½mm. A majority of the examples carry the Bureau precancel "Kansas City, Mo." No. 596 is valued in the grade of fine.

COIL STAMPS
ROTARY PRESS

1923-29 ***Perf. 10 Vertically***
Stamp designs approximately 19¾x22¼mm

597 A155 1c green .30 .25
Never hinged .60
598 A156 1½c brown ('25) .90 .25
Never hinged 1.80

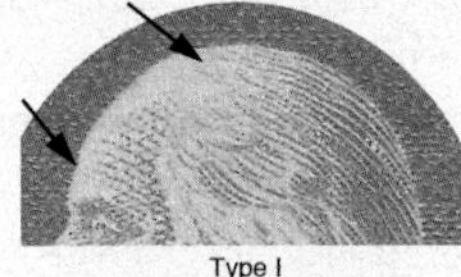

Type I

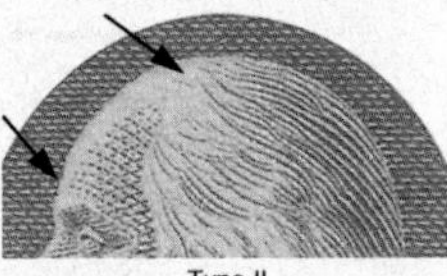

Type II

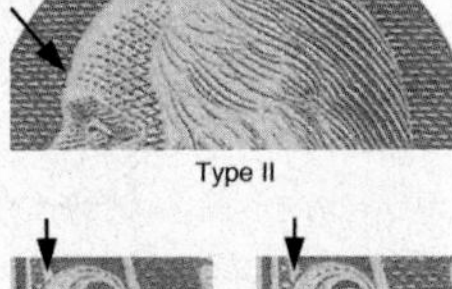

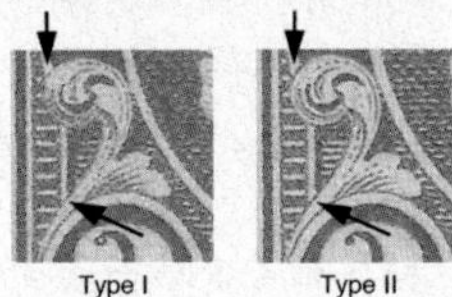

Type I Type II

TYPE I. No heavy hair lines at top center of head. Outline of left acanthus scroll generally faint at top and toward base at left side.

TYPE II. Three heavy hair lines at top center of head; two being outstanding in the white area. Outline of left acanthus scroll very strong and clearly defined at top (under left edge of lettered panel) and at lower curve (above and to left of numeral oval). This type appears only on Nos. 599A and 634A.

599 A157 2c car, type I .35 .25
Never hinged .70
b. 2c carmine lake, type I, never hinged *200.00* —
599A A157 2c car, type II ('29) 115.00 17.50
Never hinged 225.00
600 A158 3c violet ('24) 6.25 .25
Never hinged 12.50
601 A159 4c yel brn 3.75 .35
Never hinged 7.50
602 A160 5c dk blue ('24) 1.75 .25
Never hinged 3.50
603 A165 10c orange ('24) 3.50 .25
Never hinged 7.00

The 6c design A161 coil stamp is listed as No. 723.

1923-25 ***Perf. 10 Horizontally***
Stamp designs: 19¼x22½mm

604 A155 1c green ('24) .40 .25
Never hinged .80
605 A156 1½c yel brn ('25) .40 .25
Never hinged .80
606 A157 2c carmine .40 .25
Never hinged .80
a. 2c carmine lake *45.00*
Never hinged *90.00*
Nos. 597-599,600-606 (10) 18.00 2.60
Nos. 597-599, 600-606, never hinged 36.00

HARDING MEMORIAL ISSUE

Warren G. Harding — A177

FLAT PLATE PRINTING
Stamp designs: 19¼x22¼mm

1923 ***Perf. 11***
610 A177 2c black .55 .25
Never hinged 1.10
a. Horiz. pair, imperf. vert. *1,750.*
b. Imperf, P#14870 block of 6 *25,000.*

No. 610a is valued in the grade of fine.

No. 610b comes from left side error panes found in a normal pad of No. 610 stamps before No. 611 was issued. Two left side plate blocks and one top position plate block are recorded. Plate #14870 was not used to print No. 611. Loose stamps separated from the top and left plate blocks are indistinguishable from No. 611.

Imperf

611 A177 2c black 4.75 4.00
Never hinged 9.50

ROTARY PRESS PRINTING
Stamp designs: 19¼x22½mm
Perf. 10

612 A177 2c black 15.00 1.75
Never hinged 32.50

Perf. 11

613 A177 2c black *40,000.*

Tribute to President Warren G. Harding, who died August 2, 1923.

No. 613 was produced from rotary press sheet waste. It is valued in the grade of fine.

HUGUENOT-WALLOON TERCENTENARY ISSUE

"New Netherland" A178

Landing at Fort Orange A179

Monument to Jan Ribault at Duvall County, Fla. — A180

FLAT PLATE PRINTINGS

1924, May 1 ***Perf. 11***
614 A178 1c dark green 2.40 *3.25*
Never hinged 4.75
615 A179 2c carmine rose 4.00 2.25
Never hinged 8.00
616 A180 5c dark blue 16.00 13.00
Never hinged 32.50
Nos. 614-616 (3) 22.40 18.50
Nos. 614-616, never hinged 45.25

Tercentenary of the settling of the Walloons and in honor of the Huguenots.

LEXINGTON-CONCORD ISSUE

Washington at Cambridge A181

"Birth of Liberty," by Henry Sandham A182

The Minute Man, by Daniel Chester French A183

1925, Apr. 4 ***Perf. 11***
617 A181 1c deep green 2.10 2.50
Never hinged 4.25
618 A182 2c carmine rose 3.75 4.00
Never hinged 7.50
619 A183 5c dark blue 15.00 13.00
Never hinged 30.00
Nos. 617-619 (3) 20.85 19.50
Nos. 617-619, never hinged 41.75

150th anniv. of the Battle of Lexington-Concord.

NORSE-AMERICAN ISSUE

A184

A185

1925, May 18 ***Perf. 11***
620 A184 2c carmine & black 3.25 3.00
Never hinged 6.50
621 A185 5c dark blue & black 10.00 10.00
Never hinged 20.00

100th anniv. of the arrival in NY on Oct. 9, 1825, of the sloop "Restaurationen" with the first group of immigrants from Norway to the U.S.

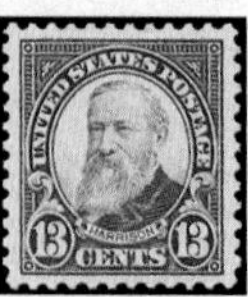
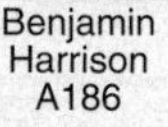
Benjamin Harrison A186

Woodrow Wilson A187

1925-26 ***Perf. 11***
622 A186 13c green ('26) 10.00 .75
Never hinged 20.00
623 A187 17c black 10.00 .30
Never hinged 20.00

SESQUICENTENNIAL EXPOSITION ISSUE

Liberty Bell — A188

1926, May 10 ***Perf. 11***
627 A188 2c carmine rose 2.25 .50
Never hinged 4.25

150th anniv. of the Declaration of Independence, Philadelphia, June 1-Dec. 1.

ERICSSON MEMORIAL ISSUE

Statue of John Ericsson — A189

1926, May 29 ***Perf. 11***
628 A189 5c gray lilac 5.25 3.25
Never hinged 9.00

John Ericsson, builder of the "Monitor."

BATTLE OF WHITE PLAINS ISSUE

Alexander Hamilton's Battery — A190

1926, Oct. 18 ***Perf. 11***
629 A190 2c carmine rose 1.75 1.70
Never hinged 3.00

Battle of White Plains, NY, 150th anniv.

INTERNATIONAL PHILATELIC EXHIBITION ISSUE

Souvenir Sheet

A190a

Condition valued:

Centering: Overall centering will average very fine, but individual stamps may be better or worse.
Perforations: No folds along rows of perforations.
Gum: There may be some light gum bends but no gum creases.
Hinging: There may be hinge marks in the selvage and on up to two or three stamps, but no heavy hinging or hinge remnants (except in the ungummed portion of the wide selvage.
Margins: Top panes should have about ½ inch bottom margin and 1 inch top margin.
Bottom panes should have about ½ inch top margin and just under ¾ inch bottom margin. Both will have one wide side (usually 1 inch plus) and one narrow (½ inch) side margin. The wide margin corner will have a small diagonal notch on top panes.

1926, Oct. 18 ***Perf. 11***
630 A190a 2c carmine rose, pane of 25 350.00 *475.00*
Never hinged 600.00

Issued in panes measuring 158-160¼x136-146½mm containing 25 stamps with inscription "International Philatelic Exhibition, Oct. 16th to 23rd, 1926" in top margin.

VALUES FOR VERY FINE STAMPS
Please note: Stamps are valued in the grade of Very Fine unless otherwise indicated.

TYPES OF 1922-26
ROTARY PRESS PRINTINGS
(See note over No. 448.)

1926, Aug. 27 ***Imperf.***
631 A156 1½c yellow brown 2.00 1.70
Never hinged 3.00

1926-34 ***Perf. 11x10½***
632 A155 1c green ('27) .25 .25
Never hinged .35
a. Booklet pane of 6 5.00 *4.00*
Never hinged 8.00
b. Vertical pair, imperf. between *3,000.* —
Never hinged *5,500.*
c. Horiz. pair, imperf. between *5,000.*

No. 632b is valued in the grade of fine. No. 632c is valued in the grade of fine and never hinged. It is possibly unique.

633 A156 1½c yel brn ('27) 1.70 .25
Never hinged 2.60
634 A157 2c car, type I .25 .25
Never hinged .30
b. 2c carmine lake *190.00* *500.00*
Never hinged *400.00*
c. Horiz. pair, imperf. btwn. *6,000.*
d. Booklet pane of 6, carmine 1.50 1.50
Never hinged 2.50
e. As "d," carmine lake *500.00* *1,250.*
Never hinged *1,000.*

Shades of the carmine exist.
No. 634c is valued in the grade of fine.

634A A157 2c car, type II ('28) 325.00 13.50
Never hinged 650.00
635 A158 3c violet ('27) .60 .25
Never hinged .90
a. 3c bright violet ('34) .25 .25
Never hinged .30
636 A159 4c yel brn ('27) 1.90 .25
Never hinged 3.00
637 A160 5c dk blue ('27) 1.90 .25
Never hinged 3.00
638 A161 6c red org ('27) 2.00 .25
Never hinged 3.20
639 A162 7c black ('27) 2.00 .25
Never hinged 3.20
a. Vertical pair, imperf. between 600.00 250.00
Never hinged 1,000.
640 A163 8c ol grn ('27) 2.00 .25
Never hinged 3.20
641 A164 9c rose ('27) 1.90 .25
Never hinged 3.00
642 A165 10c org ('27) 3.25 .25
Never hinged 5.50
Nos. 632-634,635-642 (11) 17.75 2.75
Nos. 632-634, 635-642 never hinged 28.00

The 1½c, 2c, 4c, 5c, 6c, 8c imperf. (dry print) are printer's waste.
For ½c, 11c-50c see Nos. 653, 692-701.

VERMONT SESQUICENTENNIAL ISSUE

Battle of Bennington, 150th anniv. and State independence.

Green Mountain Boy — A191

FLAT PLATE PRINTING

1927, Aug. 3 ***Perf. 11***
643 A191 2c carmine rose 1.20 .80
Never hinged 2.00

BURGOYNE CAMPAIGN ISSUE

Battles of Bennington, Oriskany, Fort Stanwix and Saratoga.

"The Surrender of General Burgoyne at Saratoga," by John Trumbull A192

1927, Aug. 3 ***Perf. 11***
644 A192 2c carmine rose 3.10 2.10
Never hinged 5.50

VALLEY FORGE ISSUE

150th anniversary of Washington's encampment at Valley Forge, Pa.

Washington at Prayer — A193

1928, May 26 ***Perf. 11***
645 A193 2c carmine rose 1.20 .50
Never hinged 1.90
a. 2c lake —
Never hinged —

BATTLE OF MONMOUTH ISSUE

150th anniv. of the Battle of Monmouth, N.J., and "Molly Pitcher" (Mary Ludwig Hayes), the heroine of the battle.

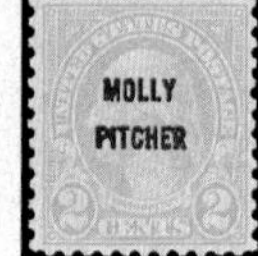

No. 634 Overprinted

ROTARY PRESS PRINTING

1928, Oct. 20 ***Perf. 11x10½***
646 A157 2c carmine 1.00 1.00
Never hinged 1.60
a. "Pitcher" only *675.00*
b. 2c carmine lake *2,500.*

No. 646a is valued in the grade of fine.
Normally the overprints were placed 18mm apart vertically, but pairs exist with a space of 28mm between the overprints.

HAWAII SESQUICENTENNIAL ISSUE

Sesquicentennial Celebration of the discovery of the Hawaiian Islands.

Nos. 634 and 637 Overprinted

ROTARY PRESS PRINTING

1928, Aug. 13 ***Perf. 11x10½***
647 A157 2c carmine 4.00 4.00
Never hinged 7.25
648 A160 5c dark blue 11.00 12.50
Never hinged 21.50

Nos. 647-648 were sold at post offices in Hawaii and at the Postal Agency in Washington, D.C. They were valid throughout the nation.
Normally the overprints were placed 18mm apart vertically, but pairs exist with a space of 28mm between the overprints.

AERONAUTICS CONFERENCE ISSUE

Intl. Civil Aeronautics Conf., Washington, D.C., Dec. 12 - 14, 1928, and 25th anniv. of the 1st airplane flight by the Wright Brothers, Dec. 17, 1903.

Wright Airplane A194

Globe and Airplane A195

FLAT PLATE PRINTING

1928, Dec. 12 ***Perf. 11***
649 A194 2c carmine rose 1.10 .80
Never hinged 1.75
650 A195 5c blue 4.50 3.25
Never hinged 7.25

GEORGE ROGERS CLARK ISSUE

150th anniv. of the surrender of Fort Sackville, the present site of Vincennes, Ind., to Clark.

Surrender of Fort Sackville A196

1929, Feb. 25 ***Perf. 11***
651 A196 2c carmine & black .75 .50
Never hinged 1.20

Type of 1922-26 Issue
ROTARY PRESS PRINTING

1929, May 25 ***Perf. 11x10½***
653 A154 ½c olive brown .25 .25
Never hinged .35

Edison's First Lamp A197

Maj. Gen. John Sullivan A198

ELECTRIC LIGHT'S GOLDEN JUBILEE ISSUE

Invention of the 1st incandescent electric lamp by Thomas Alva Edison, Oct. 21, 1879, 50th anniv.

FLAT PLATE PRINTING

1929 ***Perf. 11***
654 A197 2c carmine rose .70 .65
Never hinged 1.20
a. 2c lake —

ROTARY PRESS PRINTING
Perf. 11x10½

655 A197 2c carmine rose .65 .25
Never hinged 1.10

ROTARY PRESS COIL STAMP
Perf. 10 Vertically

656 A197 2c carmine rose 11.00 1.75
Never hinged 21.00

SULLIVAN EXPEDITION ISSUE

150th anniversary of the Sullivan Expedition in New York State during the Revolutionary War.

FLAT PLATE PRINTING

1929, June 17 ***Perf. 11***
657 A198 2c carmine rose .60 .60
Never hinged 1.00
a. 2c lake 350.00 250.00
Never hinged 575.00
b. Vert. pair, imperf. btwn. *4,000.*

The unique No. 657b resulted from a paper foldover before perfing, and it has angled errant perfs from another row of horiz. perfs through the left side of the stamps.

Nos. 632-634, 635-642 Overprinted

This special issue was authorized as a measure of preventing losses from post office burglaries. Approximately a year's supply was printed and issued to postmasters. The P.O. Dept. found it desirable to discontinue the State overprinted stamps after the initial supply was used.

ROTARY PRESS PRINTING

1929, May 1 ***Perf. 11x10½***

658 A155 1c green 2.50 2.00
Never hinged 5.00
a. Vertical pair, one without ovpt. *300.00*
Never hinged *500.00*
659 A156 1½c brown 3.25 2.90
Never hinged 6.50
a. Vertical pair, one without ovpt. *475.00*
660 A157 2c carmine 4.00 1.00
Never hinged 7.50
661 A158 3c violet 17.50 15.00
Never hinged 35.00
a. Vertical pair, one without ovpt. *600.00*
Never hinged *775.00*
662 A159 4c yellow brown 17.50 9.00
Never hinged 35.00
a. Vertical pair, one without ovpt. *500.00*
663 A160 5c deep blue 12.50 9.75
Never hinged 25.00
664 A161 6c red orange 25.00 18.00
Never hinged 50.00
665 A162 7c black 25.00 27.50
Never hinged 50.00
666 A163 8c olive green 72.50 65.00
Never hinged 145.00
667 A164 9c light rose 14.00 11.50
Never hinged 27.50
668 A165 10c org yel 22.50 12.50
Never hinged 45.00
Nos. 658-668 (11) 216.25 174.15
Nos. 658-668, never hinged 431.50

See notes following No. 679.

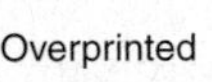

Overprinted

1929, May 1

669 A155 1c green 3.25 2.25
Never hinged 6.50
b. No period after "Nebr." (19338, 19339 UR 26, 36) 50.00
670 A156 1½c brown 3.00 2.50
Never hinged 6.00
671 A157 2c carmine 3.00 1.30
Never hinged 6.00
672 A158 3c violet 11.00 12.00
Never hinged 22.00
a. Vertical pair, one without ovpt. *500.00*
673 A159 4c yellow brown 17.50 15.00
Never hinged 35.00
674 A160 5c deep blue 15.00 15.00
Never hinged 30.00
675 A161 6c red orange 35.00 24.00
Never hinged 70.00
676 A162 7c black 22.50 18.00
Never hinged 45.00
677 A163 8c olive green 30.00 25.00
Never hinged 60.00
678 A164 9c light rose 35.00 27.50
Never hinged 70.00
a. Vertical pair, one without ovpt. *750.00*
679 A165 10c org yel 90.00 22.50
Never hinged 180.00
Nos. 669-679 (11) 265.25 165.05
Nos. 669-679, never hinged 530.50

Nos. 658-661, 669-673, 677-678 are known with the overprints on vertical pairs spaced 32mm apart instead of the normal 22mm.

Important: Nos. 658-679 with original gum have either one horizontal gum breaker ridge per stamp or portions of two at the extreme top and bottom of the stamps, 21mm apart. Multiple complete gum breaker ridges indicate a fake overprint. Absence of the gum breaker ridge indicates either regumming or regumming and a fake overprint.

Gen. Anthony Wayne Memorial
A199

Lock No. 5, Monongahela River
A200

BATTLE OF FALLEN TIMBERS ISSUE

Memorial to Gen. Anthony Wayne and for 135th anniv. of the Battle of Fallen Timbers, Ohio.

FLAT PLATE PRINTING

1929, Sept. 14 ***Perf. 11***

680 A199 2c carmine rose .70 .70
Never hinged 1.10

OHIO RIVER CANALIZATION ISSUE

Completion of the Ohio River Canalization Project, between Cairo, Ill. and Pittsburgh, Pa.

1929, Oct. 19 ***Perf. 11***

681 A200 2c carmine rose .60 .60
Never hinged .95
a. 2c lake *425.00* —
Never hinged *650.00*
b. 2c carmine lake, never hinged —

Mass. Bay Colony Seal — A201

Gov. Joseph West & Chief Shadoo, a Kiowa — A202

MASSACHUSETTS BAY COLONY ISSUE

300th anniversary of the founding of the Massachusetts Bay Colony.

1930, Apr. 8 ***Perf. 11***

682 A201 2c carmine rose .70 .50
Never hinged 1.00

CAROLINA-CHARLESTON ISSUE

260th anniv. of the founding of the Province of Carolina and the 250th anniv. of the city of Charleston, S.C.

1930, Apr. 10 ***Perf. 11***

683 A202 2c carmine rose 1.05 1.05
Never hinged 1.65

Warren G. Harding
A203

William H. Taft
A204

Type of 1922-26 Issue
ROTARY PRESS PRINTING

1930 ***Perf. 11x10½***

684 A203 1½c brown .40 .25
Never hinged .55
685 A204 4c brown .80 .25
Never hinged 1.25

ROTARY PRESS COIL STAMPS
Perf. 10 Vertically

686 A203 1½c brown 1.75 .25
Never hinged 2.60
687 A204 4c brown 3.00 .45
Never hinged 4.50

Statue of Col. George Washington
A205

General von Steuben
A206

BRADDOCK'S FIELD ISSUE

175th anniversary of the Battle of Braddock's Field, otherwise the Battle of Monongahela.

FLAT PLATE PRINTING

1930, July 9 ***Perf. 11***

688 A205 2c carmine rose .90 .85
Never hinged 1.40

VON STEUBEN ISSUE

Baron Friedrich Wilhelm von Steuben (1730-1794), participant in the American Revolution.

FLAT PLATE PRINTING

1930, Sept. 17 ***Perf. 11***

689 A206 2c carmine rose .50 .50
Never hinged .75
a. Imperf., pair *2,750.*
Never hinged *3,500.*

General Casimir Pulaski
A207

"The Greatest Mother"
A208

PULASKI ISSUE

150th anniversary (in 1929) of the death of Gen. Casimir Pulaski, Polish patriot and hero of the American Revolutionary War.

1931, Jan. 16 ***Perf. 11***

690 A207 2c carmine rose .30 .25
Never hinged .40

TYPE OF 1922-26 ISSUES
ROTARY PRESS PRINTING

1931 ***Perf. 11x10½***

692 A166 11c light blue 2.50 .25
Never hinged 3.75
693 A167 12c brown violet 5.00 .25
Never hinged 8.00
694 A186 13c yellow green 2.25 .25
Never hinged 3.50
695 A168 14c dark blue 4.00 .60
Never hinged 6.25
696 A169 15c gray 7.75 .25
Never hinged 12.00

Perf. 10½x11

697 A187 17c black 4.75 .25
Never hinged 7.25
698 A170 20c carmine rose 7.75 .25
Never hinged 12.50
699 A171 25c blue green 8.00 .25
Never hinged 13.00
700 A172 30c brown 13.00 .25
Never hinged 22.50
701 A173 50c lilac 30.00 .25
Never hinged 52.50
Nos. 692-701 (10) 85.00 2.85
Nos. 692-701, never hinged 141.25

RED CROSS ISSUE

50th anniversary of the founding of the American Red Cross Society.

FLAT PLATE PRINTING

1931, May 21 ***Perf. 11***

702 A208 2c black & red .25 .25
Never hinged .35
a. Red cross missing (FO) *40,000.*

One example of No. 702a is documented; believed to be unique. Value reflects most recent sale price at auction in 1994.

YORKTOWN ISSUE

Surrender of Cornwallis at Yorktown, 1781.

Count de Rochambeau, Washington, Count de Grasse — A209

1931, Oct. 19 ***Perf. 11***

703 A209 2c carmine rose & black .35 .25
Never hinged .50
a. 2c lake & black 4.50 .75
Never hinged 6.25
b. 2c dark lake & black *400.00*
Never hinged *750.00*
c. Horiz. pair, imperf. vertically *7,000.*
Never hinged *8,500.*

No. 703c is valued in the grade of fine.

WASHINGTON BICENTENNIAL ISSUE

200th anniversary of the birth of George Washington. Various Portraits of George Washington.

A210

A211

A212

A213

A214

A215

A216

A217

A218

A219

A220 A221

ROTARY PRESS PRINTINGS

1932, Jan. 1 ***Perf. 11x10½***

704 A210 ½c olive brown .25 .25
Never hinged .35
705 A211 1c green .25 .25
Never hinged .35
706 A212 1½c brown .45 .25
Never hinged .60
707 A213 2c carmine rose .30 .25
Never hinged .45
708 A214 3c deep violet .55 .25
Never hinged .80
709 A215 4c light brown .60 .25
Never hinged .85
710 A216 5c blue 1.50 .25
Never hinged 2.25
711 A217 6c red orange 3.00 .25
Never hinged 4.50
712 A218 7c black .60 .25
Never hinged .85

713 A219 8c olive bister 2.75 .50
Never hinged 4.00
714 A220 9c pale red 2.25 .25
Never hinged 3.25
715 A221 10c orange yellow 10.00 .25
Never hinged 15.00
Nos. 704-715 (12) 22.50 3.25
Nos. 704-715, never hinged 33.25

Skier — A222

Boy and Girl Planting Tree — A223

OLYMPIC WINTER GAMES ISSUE

3rd Olympic Winter Games, held at Lake Placid, N.Y., Feb. 4-13, 1932.

FLAT PLATE PRINTING

1932, Jan. 25 ***Perf. 11***
716 A222 2c carmine rose .40 .25
Never hinged .55
a. 2c lake *500.00*
Never hinged *1,000.*

ARBOR DAY ISSUE

ROTARY PRESS PRINTING

1932, Apr. 22 ***Perf. 11x10½***
717 A223 2c carmine rose .25 .25
Never hinged .35

60th anniv. of the 1st observance of Arbor Day in Nebr., April, 1872.
Birth centenary of Julius Sterling Morton, who conceived the plan and the name "Arbor Day," while a member of the Nebr. State Board of Agriculture.

OLYMPIC GAMES ISSUE

Issued in honor of the 10th Olympic Games, held at Los Angeles, Calif., July 30 to Aug. 14, 1932.

Runner at Starting Mark A224

Myron's Discobolus A225

ROTARY PRESS PRINTING

1932, June 15 ***Perf. 11x10½***
718 A224 3c violet 1.50 .25
Never hinged 2.00
719 A225 5c blue 2.25 .25
Never hinged 2.90

Washington — A226

ROTARY PRESS PRINTING

1932, June 16 ***Perf. 11x10½***
720 A226 3c deep violet .25 .25
Never hinged .30
b. Booklet pane of 6 35.00 *12.50*
Never hinged 60.00
c. Vertical pair, imperf. between *700.00* *1,350.*
Never hinged *1,400.*

ROTARY PRESS COIL STAMPS

1932 ***Perf. 10 Vertically***
721 A226 3c deep violet 2.75 .25
Never hinged 3.50

Perf. 10 Horizontally
722 A226 3c deep violet 1.50 .35
Never hinged 2.00

Issued: #721, 6/24; #722, 10/12.

TYPE OF 1922-26 ISSUES

1932, Aug. 18 ***Perf. 10 Vertically***
723 A161 6c deep orange 11.00 .30
Never hinged 15.00

William Penn A227

Daniel Webster A228

WILLIAM PENN ISSUE

250th anniv. of the arrival in America of Penn (1644-1718), English Quaker and founder of Pennsylvania.

FLAT PLATE PRINTING

1932, Oct. 24 ***Perf. 11***
724 A227 3c violet .45 .25
Never hinged .60
a. Vert. pair, imperf. horiz. —

DANIEL WEBSTER ISSUE

FLAT PLATE PRINTING

1932, Oct. 24 ***Perf. 11***
725 A228 3c violet .45 .25
Never hinged .60

Daniel Webster (1782-1852), statesman.

Gen. James Edward Oglethorpe — A229

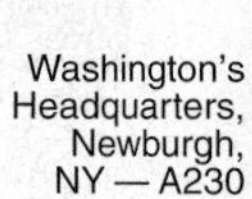

Washington's Headquarters, Newburgh, NY — A230

GEORGIA BICENTENNIAL ISSUE

200th anniv. of the founding of the Colony of Georgia, and honoring Oglethorpe, who landed from England, Feb. 12, 1733, and personally supervised the establishing of the colony.

FLAT PLATE PRINTING

1933, Feb. 12 ***Perf. 11***
726 A229 3c violet .50 .25
Never hinged .65

PEACE OF 1783 ISSUE

150th anniv. of the issuance by George Washington of the official order containing the Proclamation of Peace marking officially the ending of hostilities in the War for Independence.

ROTARY PRESS PRINTING

1933, Apr. 19 ***Perf. 10½x11***
727 A230 3c violet .25 .25
Never hinged .30

See No. 752.

CENTURY OF PROGRESS ISSUES

"Century of Progress" Intl. Exhibition, Chicago, which opened June 1, 1933, and centenary of the incorporation of Chicago as a city.

Restoration of Fort Dearborn A231

Federal Building at Chicago, 1933 A232

ROTARY PRESS PRINTING

1933, May 25 ***Perf. 10½x11***
728 A231 1c yellow green .25 .25
Never hinged .30
729 A232 3c violet .25 .25
Never hinged .35

AMERICAN PHILATELIC SOCIETY ISSUE

SOUVENIR SHEETS

Restoration of Fort Dearborn — A231a

Federal Building at Chicago, 1933 — A232a

FLAT PLATE PRINTING

1933, Aug. 25 ***Imperf.***

Without Gum

730 A231a 1c deep yellow green, pane of 25 25.00 25.00
a. Single stamp .75 .50
731 A232a 3c deep violet, pane of 25 22.50 22.50
a. Single stamp .65 .50

Issued in panes measuring 134x120mm.
See Nos. 766-767.

NATIONAL RECOVERY ACT ISSUE

Issued to direct attention to and arouse the support of the nation for the National Recovery Act.

Group of Workers — A233

ROTARY PRESS PRINTING

1933, Aug. 15 ***Perf. 10½x11***
732 A233 3c violet .25 .25
Never hinged .30

BYRD ANTARCTIC ISSUE

Issued in connection with the Byrd Antarctic Expedition of 1933 and for use on letters mailed through the Little America Post Office established at the Base Camp of the Expedition in the territory of the South Pole.

World Map on van der Grinten's Projection — A234

FLAT PLATE PRINTING

1933, Oct. 9 ***Perf. 11***
733 A234 3c dark blue .50 .50
Never hinged .60

See Nos. 735, 753.

KOSCIUSZKO ISSUE

Kosciuszko (1746-1807), Polish soldier and statesman served in the American Revolution, on the 150th anniv. of the granting to him of American citizenship.

Statue of Gen. Tadeusz Kosciuszko — A235

FLAT PLATE PRINTING

1933, Oct. 13 ***Perf. 11***
734 A235 5c blue .55 .25
Never hinged .65
a. Horiz. pair, imperf. vert. *2,000.*
Never hinged *2,800.*

NATIONAL STAMP EXHIBITION ISSUE

SOUVENIR SHEET

A235a

1934, Feb. 10 ***Imperf.***

Without Gum

735 A235a 3c dark blue, pane of 6 11.00 9.00
a. Single stamp 1.75 1.25

Issued in panes measuring 87x93mm.
See No. 768.

MARYLAND TERCENTENARY ISSUE

300th anniversary of the founding of Maryland.

"The Ark" and "The Dove" — A236

FLAT PLATE PRINTING

1934, Mar. 23 ***Perf. 11***
736 A236 3c carmine rose .30 .25
Never hinged .40
a. Horizontal pair, imperf between *6,500.*
b. 3c lake — —
c. 3c carmine lake, never hinged —

The unique No. 736a resulted from a paper foldover before perfing, and it has angled errant perfs from another column of vert. perfs through the upper-left corner of the left stamp.

MOTHERS OF AMERICA ISSUE

Issued to commemorate Mother's Day.

Adaptation of Whistler's Portrait of his Mother A237

ROTARY PRESS PRINTING

1934, May 2 ***Perf. 11x10½***
737 A237 3c deep violet .25 .25
Never hinged .30

FLAT PLATE PRINTING
Perf. 11

738 A237 3c deep violet .25 .25
Never hinged .30

See No. 754.

WISCONSIN TERCENTENARY ISSUE

Arrival of Jean Nicolet, French explorer, on the shores of Green Bay, 300th anniv. According to historical records, Nicolet was the 1st white man to reach the territory now comprising the State of Wisconsin.

Nicolet's Landing A238

FLAT PLATE PRINTING

1934. July 7 *Perf. 11*

739 A238 3c deep violet .25 .25
Never hinged .40
a. Vert. pair, imperf. horiz. *600.00*
Never hinged *1,100.*
b. Horiz. pair, imperf. vert. *1,000.*
Never hinged *1,850.*

See No. 755.

NATIONAL PARKS YEAR ISSUE

El Capitan, Yosemite (California) A239

Old Faithful, Yellowstone (Wyoming) A243

Grand Canyon (Arizona) A240

Mt. Rainier and Mirror Lake (Washington) — A241

Mesa Verde (Colorado) A242

Crater Lake (Oregon) A244

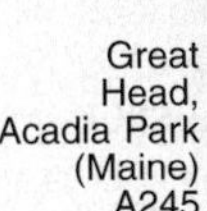

Great Head, Acadia Park (Maine) A245

Great White Throne, Zion Park (Utah) A246

Great Smoky Mts. (North Carolina) A248

Mt. Rockwell (Mt. Sinopah) and Two Medicine Lake, Glacier Natl. Park (Montana) A247

FLAT PLATE PRINTING

1934 Unwmk. *Perf. 11*

740 A239 1c green .30 .25
Never hinged .40
a. Vert. pair, imperf. horiz., with gum *1,750.*
Never hinged *3,250.*
741 A240 2c red .30 .25
Never hinged .40
a. Vert. pair, imperf. horiz., with gum *900.00*
Never hinged *1,600.*
b. Horiz. pair, imperf. vert., with gum *1,000.*
Never hinged *1,850.*
742 A241 3c deep violet .40 .25
Never hinged .50
a. Vert. pair, imperf. horiz., with gum *1,000.*
Never hinged *1,850.*
743 A242 4c brown .50 .40
Never hinged .70
a. Vert. pair, imperf. horiz., with gum *1,500.*
Never hinged *3,000.*
744 A243 5c blue .80 .65
Never hinged 1.10
a. Horiz. pair, imperf. vert., with gum *1,500.*
Never hinged *3,000.*
745 A244 6c dark blue 1.20 .85
Never hinged 1.65
746 A245 7c black .80 .75
Never hinged 1.10
a. Horiz. pair, imperf. vert., with gum *1,000.*
Never hinged *1,850.*
747 A246 8c sage green 1.75 1.50
Never hinged 2.70
748 A247 9c red orange 1.60 .65
Never hinged 2.40
749 A248 10c gray black 3.25 1.25
Never hinged 5.00
Nos. 740-749 (10) 10.90 6.80
Nos. 740-749, never hinged 15.95

Beware of fakes of the part-perforate errors of Nos. 740-749, including those with gum (see "without gum" note before No. 752).
See Nos. 750-751, 756-765, 769-770, 797.

AMERICAN PHILATELIC SOCIETY ISSUE

SOUVENIR SHEET

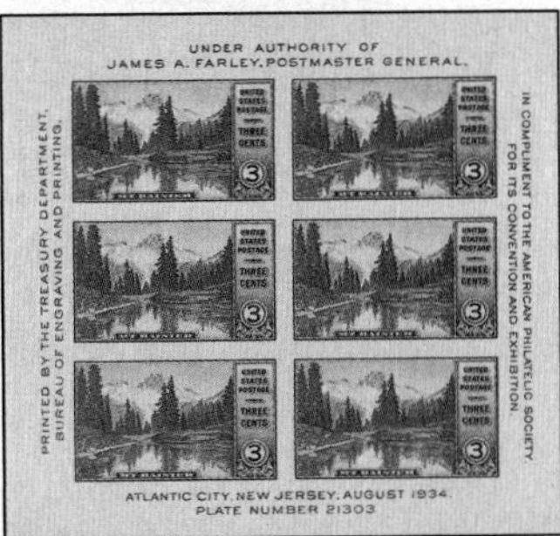

A248a

1934, Aug. 28 *Imperf.*

750 A248a 3c deep violet, pane of 6 30.00 27.50
Never hinged 37.50
a. Single stamp 3.75 3.25
Never hinged 4.75

Issued in panes measuring approximately 98x93mm.
See No. 770.

TRANS-MISSISSIPPI PHILATELIC EXPOSITION ISSUE

SOUVENIR SHEET

A248b

1934, Oct. 10 *Imperf.*

751 A248b 1c green, pane of 6 12.50 12.50
Never hinged 16.00
a. Single stamp 2.00 1.60
Never hinged 2.60

Issued in panes measuring approximately 92x99mm.
See No. 769.

SPECIAL PRINTING
(Nos. 752-771 inclusive)

"Issued for a limited time in full sheets as printed, and in blocks thereof, to meet the requirements of collectors and others who may be interested." — From Postal Bulletin No. 16614.

Issuance of the following 20 stamps in complete sheets resulted from the protest of collectors and others at the practice of presenting, to certain government officials, complete sheets of unsevered panes, imperforate (except Nos. 752 and 753) and generally ungummed.

Designs of Commemorative Issues
Without Gum

NOTE: In 1940 the P.O. Department offered to and did gum full sheets of Nos. 756-765 and 769-770 sent in by owners. No other Special Printings were accepted for gumming.

TYPE OF PEACE ISSUE
Issued in sheets of 400
ROTARY PRESS PRINTING
Perf. 10½x11

1935, Mar. 15 Unwmk.

752 A230 3c violet .25 .25

TYPE OF BYRD ISSUE
Issued in sheets of 200
FLAT PLATE PRINTING
Perf. 11

753 A234 3c dark blue .50 .45

No. 753 is similar to No. 733. Positive identification is by blocks or pairs showing guide line between stamps. These lines between stamps are found only on No. 753.

TYPE OF MOTHERS OF AMERICA ISSUE
Issued in sheets of 200
FLAT PLATE PRINTING
Imperf

754 A237 3c deep violet .60 .60

TYPE OF WISCONSIN ISSUE
Issued in sheets of 200
FLAT PLATE PRINTING
Imperf

755 A238 3c deep violet .60 .60

TYPES OF NATIONAL PARKS ISSUE
Issued in sheets of 200
FLAT PLATE PRINTING
Imperf

756 A239 1c green .25 .25
757 A240 2c red .25 .25
758 A241 3c deep violet .50 .45
759 A242 4c brown 1.00 .95
760 A243 5c blue 1.60 1.40
761 A244 6c dark blue 2.40 2.25
762 A245 7c black 1.60 1.40
763 A246 8c sage green 1.90 1.50
764 A247 9c red orange 2.00 1.75
765 A248 10c gray black 4.00 3.50
Nos. 756-765 (10) 15.50 13.70
Nos. 756-765, with original gum, never hinged 136.25
Nos. 756-765, P# blocks of 6 274.25

SOUVENIR SHEETS

Note: Single items from these sheets are identical with other varieties, 766 and 730, 766a and 730a, 767 and 731, 767a and 731a, 768 and 735, 768a and 735a, 769a and 756, 770a and 758.

Positive identification is by blocks or pairs showing wide gutters between stamps. These wide gutters occur only on Nos. 766-770 and measure, horizontally, 13mm on Nos. 766-767; 16mm on No. 768, and 23mm on Nos. 769-770.

TYPE OF CENTURY OF PROGRESS ISSUE
Issued in sheets of 9 panes of 25 stamps each
FLAT PLATE PRINTING
Imperf

766 A231a 1c yellow green, pane of 25 25.00 25.00
a. Single stamp .70 .50
767 A232a 3c violet, pane of 25 23.50 23.50
a. Single stamp .60 .50

NATIONAL EXHIBITION ISSUE
TYPE OF BYRD ISSUE
Issued in sheets of 25 panes of 6 stamps each
FLAT PLATE PRINTING
Imperf

768 A235a 3c dark blue, pane of six 20.00 15.00
a. Single stamp 2.80 2.40

TYPES OF NATIONAL PARKS ISSUE
Issued in sheets of 20 panes of 6 stamps each
FLAT PLATE PRINTING
Imperf

769 A248b 1c green, pane of six 12.50 11.00
a. Single stamp 1.85 1.80
770 A248a 3c deep violet, pane of six 30.00 24.00
a. Single stamp 3.25 3.10

Hinged examples of Nos. 769-770 with original gum sell for approximately half the values shown for never-hinged stamps.

TYPE OF AIR POST SPECIAL DELIVERY
Issued in sheets of 200
FLAT PLATE PRINTING
Imperf

771 APSD1 16c dark blue 2.75 2.60

Catalogue values for unused stamps in this section, from this point to the end, are for Never Hinged items.

VALUES FOR HINGED STAMPS AFTER NO. 771

This catalogue does not value unused stamps after No. 771 in hinged condition. Hinged unused stamps from No. 772 to the present are worth considerably less than the values given for unused stamps, which are for never-hinged examples.

CONNECTICUT TERCENTENARY ISSUE

300th anniv. of the settlement of Connecticut.

Charter Oak A249

ROTARY PRESS PRINTING
Perf. 11x10½

1935, Apr. 26 Unwmk.

772 A249 3c violet .35 .25

CALIFORNIA PACIFIC EXPOSITION ISSUE

California Pacific Exposition at San Diego.

View of San Diego Exposition A250

1935, May 29 **Unwmk.**

773	A250	3c purple	.35	.25

BOULDER DAM ISSUE

Dedication of Boulder Dam.

Boulder Dam — A251

FLAT PLATE PRINTING

1935, Sept. 30 **Unwmk.** ***Perf. 11***

774	A251	3c purple	.35	.25

MICHIGAN CENTENARY ISSUE

Advance celebration of Michigan Statehood centenary.

Michigan State Seal A252

ROTARY PRESS PRINTING

1935, Nov. 1 **Unwmk.** ***Perf. 11x10½***

775	A252	3c purple	.35	.25

TEXAS CENTENNIAL ISSUE

Centennial of Texas independence.

Sam Houston, Stephen F. Austin and the Alamo A253

1936, Mar. 2 **Unwmk.**

776	A253	3c purple	.35	.25

RHODE ISLAND TERCENTENARY ISSUE

300th anniv. of the settlement of Rhode Island.

Statue of Roger Williams — A254

1936, May 4 **Unwmk.** ***Perf. 10½x11***

777	A254	3c purple	.35	.25

THIRD INTERNATIONAL PHILATELIC EXHIBITION ISSUE

SOUVENIR SHEET

A254a

FLAT PLATE PRINTING

1936, May 9 **Unwmk.** ***Imperf.***

778	A254a	violet, pane of 4	1.75	1.25
a.		3c Type A249	.40	.30
b.		3c Type A250	.40	.30
c.		3c Type A252	.40	.30
d.		3c Type A253	.40	.30

Issued in panes measuring 98x66mm containing four stamps, inscribed in the margins: "Printed by the Treasury Department, Bureau of Engraving and Printing, under authority of James A. Farley, Postmaster General, in compliment to the third International Philatelic Exhibition of 1936. New York, N. Y., May 9-17, 1936. Plate No. 21557 (or 21558)."

ARKANSAS CENTENNIAL ISSUE

100th anniv. of the State of Arkansas.

Arkansas Post, Old and New State Houses A255

ROTARY PRESS PRINTING

Perf. 11x10½

1936, June 15 **Unwmk.**

782	A255	3c purple	.35	.25

OREGON TERRITORY ISSUE

Opening of the Oregon Territory, 1836, 100th anniv.

Map of Oregon Territory A256

1936, July 14 **Unwmk.**

783	A256	3c purple	.35	.25

SUSAN B. ANTHONY ISSUE

Susan Brownell Anthony (1820-1906), woman-suffrage advocate, and 16th anniv. of the ratification of the 19th Amendment which grants American women the right to vote.

Susan B. Anthony — A257

1936, Aug. 26 **Unwmk.**

784	A257	3c violet	.25	.25

ARMY ISSUE

Issued in honor of the United States Army.

George Washington, Nathanael Greene and Mount Vernon — A258

Andrew Jackson, Winfield Scott and the Hermitage A259

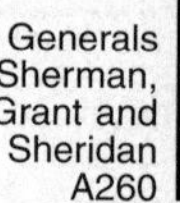

Generals Sherman, Grant and Sheridan A260

Generals Robert E. Lee, "Stonewall" Jackson and Stratford Hall A261

U.S. Military Academy, West Point A262

1936-37 **Unwmk.**

785	A258	1c green	.30	.25
786	A259	2c carmine ('37)	.30	.25
787	A260	3c purple ('37)	.40	.25
788	A261	4c gray ('37)	.60	.25
789	A262	5c ultra ('37)	.75	.25
		Nos. 785-789 (5)	2.35	1.25

NAVY ISSUE

Issued in honor of the United States Navy.

John Paul Jones and John Barry A263

Stephen Decatur and Thomas MacDonough — A264

Admirals David G. Farragut and David D. Porter A265

Admirals William T. Sampson, George Dewey and Winfield S. Schley A266

Seal of U.S. Naval Academy and Naval Midshipmen — A267

1936-37 **Unwmk.**

790	A263	1c green	.30	.25
791	A264	2c carmine ('37)	.30	.25
792	A265	3c purple ('37)	.40	.25
793	A266	4c gray ('37)	.60	.25
794	A267	5c ultra ('37)	.75	.25
		Nos. 790-794 (5)	2.35	1.25

ORDINANCE OF 1787 SESQUICENTENNIAL ISSUE

150th anniv. of the adoption of the Ordinance of 1787 and the creation of the Northwest Territory.

Manasseh Cutler, Rufus Putnam and Map of Northwest Territory A268

1937, July 13 **Unwmk.**

795	A268	3c red violet	.30	.25

VIRGINIA DARE ISSUE

350th anniv. of the birth of Virginia Dare, 1st child born in America of English parents (Aug. 18, 1587), and the settlement at Roanoke Island.

Virginia Dare and Parents — A269

FLAT PLATE PRINTING

1937, Aug. 18 **Unwmk.** ***Perf. 11***

796	A269	5c gray blue	.35	.25

SOCIETY OF PHILATELIC AMERICANS ISSUE

SOUVENIR SHEET

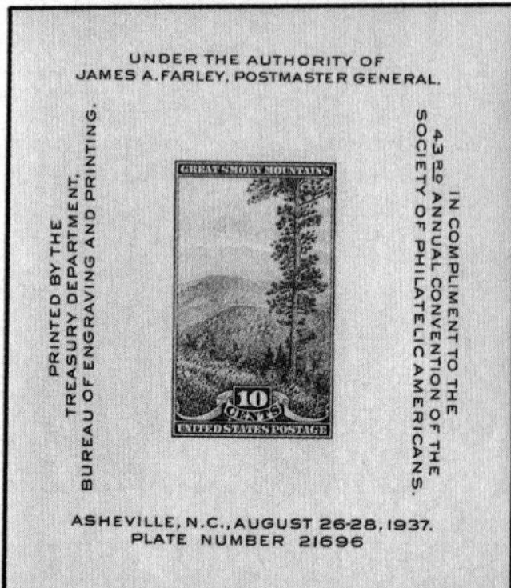

A269a

TYPE OF NATIONAL PARKS ISSUE

1937, Aug. 26 **Unwmk.** ***Imperf.***

797	A269a	10c blue green	.60	.40

Issued in panes measuring 67x78mm.

CONSTITUTION SESQUICENTENNIAL ISSUE

150th anniversary of the signing of the Constitution on September 17, 1787.

Signing of the Constitution A270

Perf. 11x10½

1937, Sept. 17 **Unwmk.**

798	A270	3c bright red violet	.40	.25

TERRITORIAL ISSUES

Hawaii

Statue of Kamehameha I, Honolulu — A271

Alaska

Landscape with Mt. McKinley A272

Puerto Rico

La Fortaleza, San Juan A273

Virgin Islands

Charlotte Amalie A274

1937	**Unwmk.**	***Perf. 10½x11***	
799 A271 3c violet		.35	.25
	Perf. 11x10½		
800 A272 3c violet		.40	.25
801 A273 3c bright violet		.40	.25
802 A274 3c light violet		.40	.25
Nos. 799-802 (4)		1.55	1.00

PRESIDENTIAL ISSUE

Benjamin Franklin A275

George Washington A276

Martha Washington A277

John Adams A278

Thomas Jefferson A279

James Madison A280

White House A281

James Monroe A282

John Q. Adams A283

Andrew Jackson A284

Martin Van Buren A285

William H. Harrison A286

John Tyler — A287

James K. Polk — A288

Zachary Taylor A289

Millard Fillmore A290

Franklin Pierce A291

James Buchanan A292

Abraham Lincoln A293

Andrew Johnson A294

Ulysses S. Grant A295

Rutherford B. Hayes A296

James A. Garfield A297

Chester A. Arthur A298

Grover Cleveland A299

Benjamin Harrison A300

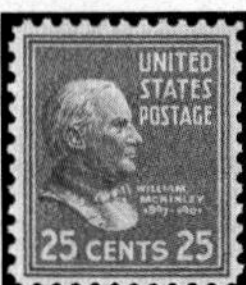

William McKinley A301

Theodore Roosevelt A302

William Howard Taft A303

Woodrow Wilson A304

Warren G. Harding A305

Calvin Coolidge A306

1938		**Unwmk.**
803 A275 ½c deep orange	.25	.25
804 A276 1c green	.25	.25
b. Booklet pane of 6	2.00	*.50*
c. Horiz. pair, imperf between (from booklet pane)		—
805 A277 1½c bister brown	.25	.25
b. Horiz. pair, imperf. between	125.00	20.00

No. 805b unused is not precanceled. Precanceled examples are considered used and are valued in the used column. They are valued with gum; pairs without gum are worth less.

806 A278 2c rose carmine	.25	.25
b. Booklet pane of 6	5.50	*1.00*
807 A279 3c deep violet	.25	.25
a. Booklet pane of 6	8.50	*2.00*
b. Horiz. pair, imperf. between	*2,000.*	—
c. Imperf., pair	—	
d. As "a," imperf between vert.		—

No. 807c is believed to be unique and has two certificates of authentication. Some specialists question the existence of No. 807c as a genuine error and believe the documented pair to be a counterfeit. The editors would like to examine the pair and would like to see documented evidence of the pair's existence, to include a new certificate of authenticity from a recognized expertizing body.

808 A280 4c red violet	.75	.25
809 A281 4½c dark gray	.40	.25
810 A282 5c bright blue	.35	.25
811 A283 6c red orange	.40	.25
812 A284 7c sepia	.40	.25
813 A285 8c olive green	.40	.25
814 A286 9c rose pink	.45	.25
815 A287 10c brown red	.45	.25
816 A288 11c ultramarine	.75	.25
817 A289 12c bright violet	1.00	.25
818 A290 13c blue green	1.30	.25
819 A291 14c blue	1.00	.25
820 A292 15c blue gray	.90	.25
821 A293 16c black	1.50	.25
822 A294 17c rose red	1.00	.25
823 A295 18c brown carmine	2.25	.25
824 A296 19c bright violet	1.30	.35
825 A297 20c bright blue green	1.20	.25
826 A298 21c dull blue	1.30	.25
827 A299 22c vermilion	1.20	.40
828 A300 24c gray black	3.50	.25
829 A301 25c deep red lilac	1.20	.25
830 A302 30c deep ultramarine	4.00	.25
a. 30c blue	15.00	—
b. 30c deep blue	*240.00*	—
831 A303 50c light red violet	5.50	.25

FLAT PLATE PRINTING

1938		***Perf. 11***
832 A304 $1 purple & black	7.00	.25
a. Vert. pair, imperf. horiz.	*1,250.*	
b. Watermarked USIR ('51)	200.00	65.00
c. $1 red violet & black ('54)	6.00	.25
d. As "c," vert. pair, imperf. horiz.	*1,000.*	
e. Vert. pair, imperf. btwn.	*2,750.*	
f. As "c," vert. pair, imperf. btwn.	*8,500.*	
g. As "c," bright magenta & black	*75.00*	—
h. As No. 832, red violet & black	—	—

No. 832c is dry printed from 400-subject flat plates on thick white paper with smooth, colorless gum.

No. 832g is the far end of the color spectrum for the No. 832c stamp, trending toward a more pinkish shade, but the shade is not pink. No. 832g is known in bright magenta and in deep bright magenta; both shades qualify as No. 832g. No. 832h is the wet-printed first printing, but the shade essentially matches the red violet normally seen on No. 832c.

833 A305 $2 yellow green & black	17.50	3.75
834 A306 $5 carmine & black	85.00	3.00
a. $5 red brown & black	*3,000.*	*7,000.*
Nos. 803-834 (32)	143.25	14.50

No. 834 can be chemically altered to resemble Scott 834a. No. 834a should be purchased only with competent expert certification.

Watermarks

All stamps from No. 835 on are unwatermarked.

CONSTITUTION RATIFICATION ISSUE

150th anniversary of the ratification of the United States Constitution.

Old Court House, Williamsburg, Va. — A307

ROTARY PRESS PRINTING

1938, June 21	***Perf. 11x10½***	
835 A307 3c deep violet	.45	.25

SWEDISH-FINNISH TERCENTENARY ISSUE

Tercentenary of the founding of the Swedish and Finnish Settlement at Wilmington, Delaware.

Landing of the Swedes and Finns — A308

FLAT PLATE PRINTING

1938, June 27	***Perf. 11***	
836 A308 3c red violet	.35	.25

NORTHWEST TERRITORY SESQUICENTENNIAL

Statue Symbolizing Colonization of the West — A309

ROTARY PRESS PRINTING

1938, July 15	***Perf. 11x10½***	
837 A309 3c bright violet	.30	.25

IOWA TERRITORY CENTENNIAL ISSUE

Old Capitol, Iowa City A310

1938, Aug. 24		
838 A310 3c violet	.40	.25

ROTARY PRESS COIL STAMPS
Types of 1938

1939, Jan. 20 ***Perf. 10 Vertically***

839	A276	1c	green	.30	.25
840	A277	1½c	bister brown	.30	.25
841	A278	2c	rose carmine	.40	.25
842	A279	3c	deep violet	.50	.25
843	A280	4c	red violet	7.50	.40
844	A281	4½c	dark gray	.70	.40
845	A282	5c	bright blue	5.00	.35
846	A283	6c	red orange	1.10	.25
847	A287	10c	brown red	11.00	1.00

1939, Jan. 27 ***Perf. 10 Horizontally***

848	A276	1c	green	.85	.25
849	A277	1½c	bister brown	1.25	.30
850	A278	2c	rose carmine	2.50	.40
851	A279	3c	deep violet	2.50	.40
			Nos. 839-851 (13)	33.90	4.75

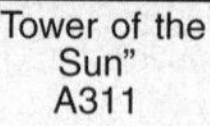

"Tower of the Sun" A311

Trylon and Perisphere A312

GOLDEN GATE INTL. EXPOSITION, SAN FRANCISCO

ROTARY PRESS PRINTING

1939, Feb. 18 ***Perf. 10½x11***

852 A311 3c bright purple .30 .25

NEW YORK WORLD'S FAIR ISSUE

1939, Apr. 1

853 A312 3c deep purple .30 .25

WASHINGTON INAUGURATION ISSUE

Sesquicentennial of the inauguration of George Washington as First President.

George Washington Taking Oath of Office — A313

FLAT PLATE PRINTING

1939, Apr. 30 ***Perf. 11***

854 A313 3c bright red violet .60 .25

BASEBALL CENTENNIAL ISSUE

Sand-lot Baseball Game A314

ROTARY PRESS PRINTING

1939, June 12 ***Perf. 11x10½***

855 A314 3c violet 1.75 .25

PANAMA CANAL ISSUE

25th anniv. of the opening of the Panama Canal.

Theodore Roosevelt, Gen. George W. Goethals and Gaillard Cut — A315

FLAT PLATE PRINTING

1939, Aug. 15 ***Perf. 11***

856 A315 3c deep red violet .40 .25

PRINTING TERCENTENARY ISSUE

Issued in commemoration of the 300th anniversary of printing in Colonial America. The Stephen Daye press is in the Harvard University Museum.

Stephen Daye Press — A316

ROTARY PRESS PRINTING

1939, Sept. 25 ***Perf. 10½x11***

857 A316 3c violet .25 .25

50th ANNIVERSARY OF STATEHOOD ISSUE

Map of North and South Dakota, Montana and Washington A317

1939, Nov. 2 ***Perf. 11x10½***

858 A317 3c rose violet .35 .25

FAMOUS AMERICANS ISSUES AMERICAN AUTHORS

Washington Irving — A318

James Fenimore Cooper — A319

Ralph Waldo Emerson A320

Louisa May Alcott A321

Samuel L. Clemens (Mark Twain) — A322

1940 ***Perf. 10½x11***

859	A318	1c	bright blue green	.25	.25
860	A319	2c	rose carmine	.25	.25
861	A320	3c	bright red violet	.25	.25
862	A321	5c	ultramarine	.35	.25
863	A322	10c	dark brown	1.75	1.20
			Nos. 859-863 (5)	2.85	2.20

AMERICAN POETS

Henry W. Longfellow A323

John Greenleaf Whittier A324

James Russell Lowell A325

Walt Whitman A326

James Whitcomb Riley — A327

864	A323	1c	bright blue green	.25	.25
865	A324	2c	rose carmine	.25	.25
866	A325	3c	bright red violet	.25	.25
867	A326	5c	ultramarine	.50	.25
868	A327	10c	dark brown	1.75	1.25
			Nos. 864-868 (5)	3.00	2.25

AMERICAN EDUCATORS

Horace Mann — A328

Mark Hopkins — A329

Charles W. Eliot — A330

Frances E. Willard — A331

Booker T. Washington — A332

869	A328	1c	bright blue green	.25	.25
870	A329	2c	rose carmine	.25	.25
871	A330	3c	bright red violet	.25	.25
872	A331	5c	ultramarine	.50	.25
873	A332	10c	dark brown	2.25	1.10
			Nos. 869-873 (5)	3.50	2.10

AMERICAN SCIENTISTS

John James Audubon A333

Dr. Crawford W. Long A334

Luther Burbank — A335

Dr. Walter Reed — A336

Jane Addams — A337

874	A333	1c	bright blue green	.25	.25
875	A334	2c	rose carmine	.25	.25
876	A335	3c	bright red violet	.25	.25
877	A336	5c	ultramarine	.50	.25
878	A337	10c	dark brown	1.50	.85
			Nos. 874-878 (5)	2.75	1.85

AMERICAN COMPOSERS

Stephen Collins Foster — A338

John Philip Sousa — A339

Victor Herbert A340

Edward MacDowell A341

Ethelbert Nevin — A342

879	A338	1c	bright blue green	.25	.25
880	A339	2c	rose carmine	.25	.25
881	A340	3c	bright red violet	.25	.25
882	A341	5c	ultramarine	.50	.25
883	A342	10c	dark brown	3.75	1.35
			Nos. 879-883 (5)	5.00	2.35

AMERICAN ARTISTS

Gilbert Charles Stuart — A343

James A. McNeill Whistler — A344

Augustus Saint-Gaudens A345

Daniel Chester French A346

Frederic Remington — A347

884	A343	1c	bright blue green	.25	.25
885	A344	2c	rose carmine	.25	.25
886	A345	3c	bright red violet	.30	.25
887	A346	5c	ultramarine	.50	.25
888	A347	10c	dark brown	1.75	1.25
			Nos. 884-888 (5)	3.05	2.25

AMERICAN INVENTORS

Eli Whitney — A348

Samuel F. B. Morse — A349

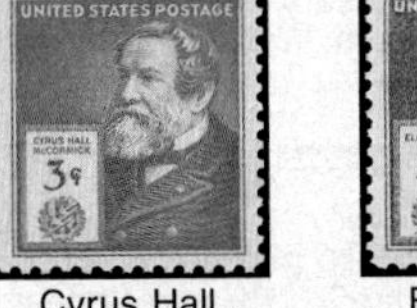

Cyrus Hall McCormick A350

Elias Howe A351

Alexander Graham Bell — A352

889 A348 1c bright blue green .25 .25
890 A349 2c rose carmine .30 .25
891 A350 3c bright red violet .30 .25
892 A351 5c ultramarine 1.10 .30
893 A352 10c dark brown 11.00 2.00
Nos. 889-893 (5) 12.95 3.05
Nos. 859-893 (35) 33.10 16.05

PONY EXPRESS, 80th ANNIV. ISSUE

Pony Express Rider A353

1940, Apr. 3 ***Perf. 11x10½***
894 A353 3c henna brown .50 .25

PAN AMERICAN UNION ISSUE

Founding of the Pan American Union, 50th anniv.

The Three Graces from Botticelli's "Spring" — A354

1940, Apr. 14 ***Perf. 10½x11***
895 A354 3c light violet .30 .25

IDAHO STATEHOOD, 50th ANNIV.

Idaho Capitol, Boise A355

1940, July 3 ***Perf. 11x10½***
896 A355 3c bright violet .35 .25

WYOMING STATEHOOD, 50th ANNIV.

Wyoming State Seal — A356

1940, July 10 ***Perf. 10½x11***
897 A356 3c brown violet .35 .25

CORONADO EXPEDITION, 400th ANNIV.

"Coronado and His Captains," painted by Gerald Cassidy A357

1940, Sept. 7 ***Perf. 11x10½***
898 A357 3c violet .35 .25

NATIONAL DEFENSE ISSUE

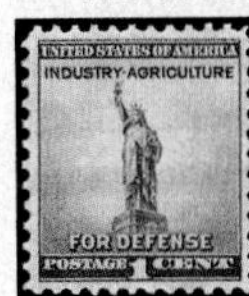

Statue of Liberty — A358

90-millimeter Anti-aircraft Gun — A359

Torch of Enlightenment — A360

1940, Oct. 16
899 A358 1c bright blue green .25 .25
a. Vertical pair, imperf. between 600.00 —
b. Horizontal pair, imperf. between 32.50 —
900 A359 2c rose carmine .25 .25
a. Horizontal pair, imperf. between 37.50 —
901 A360 3c bright violet .25 .25
a. Horizontal pair, imperf. between 22.50 —
Nos. 899-901 (3) .75 .75

THIRTEENTH AMENDMENT ISSUE

75th anniv. of the 13th Amendment to the Constitution abolishing slavery.

"Emancipation," Statue of Lincoln and Slave, by Thomas Ball — A361

1940, Oct. 20 ***Perf. 10½x11***
902 A361 3c deep violet .50 .25

VERMONT STATEHOOD, 150th ANNIV.

Vermont Capitol, Montpelier A362

1941, Mar. 4 ***Perf. 11x10½***
903 A362 3c light violet .45 .25

KENTUCKY STATEHOOD, 150th ANNIV.

Daniel Boone and Three Frontiersmen, from mural by Gilbert White — A363

1942, June 1
904 A363 3c violet .30 .25

WIN THE WAR ISSUE

American Eagle — A364

1942, July 4
905 A364 3c violet .25 .25
b. 3c reddish violet 750.00 350.00

All examples of No. 905b are precanceled either Los Angeles, Calif., or Fremont, Ohio. Value is for Los Angeles, which is the more common. Value of Fremont, unused $1,750.

CHINESE RESISTANCE ISSUE

Issued to commemorate the Chinese people's five years of resistance to Japanese aggression.

Lincoln, Sun Yat-sen & Map A365

1942, July 7
906 A365 5c bright blue 2.25 .35

ALLIED NATIONS ISSUE

Allegory of Victory — A366

1943, Jan. 14
907 A366 2c rose carmine .25 .25

Bureau Precancels: Denver, Baltimore.

FOUR FREEDOMS ISSUE

A367

1943, Feb. 12
908 A367 1c bright blue green .25 .25

OVERRUN COUNTRIES ISSUE

Printed by the American Bank Note Co.

FRAMES ENGRAVED, CENTERS OFFSET LETTERPRESS
ROTARY PRESS PRINTING

Flag of Poland A368

1943-44 ***Perf. 12***
909 A368 5c Poland .25 .25
a. Double impression of "Poland" 175.00
b. Double impression of black flag color and red "Poland" —
910 A368a 5c Czechoslovakia .25 .25
a. Double impression of "Czechoslovakia" 650.00
911 A368b 5c Norway .25 .25
a. Double impression of "Norway" 225.00
912 A368c 5c Luxembourg .25 .25
a. Double impression of "Luxembourg" —
913 A368d 5c Netherlands .25 .25
914 A368e 5c Belgium .25 .25
a. Double impression of "Belgium" 275.00
915 A368f 5c France .25 .25
916 A368g 5c Greece .50 .25
917 A368h 5c Yugoslavia .40 .25
b. Double impression of black — 200.00
918 A368i 5c Albania .25 .25
a. Double impression of "Albania" — 600.00
919 A368j 5c Austria .30 .25
a. Double impression of "Austria" —
c. Double impression of black —
920 A368k 5c Denmark (blue violet, red and black) .30 .25
b. 5c blue violet, red & gray .30 .25
921 A368m 5c Korea .25 .25
a. Double impression of "Korea" —
c. Double impression of red — —
Nos. 909-921 (13) 3.75 3.25

TRANSCONTINENTAL RAILROAD ISSUE

Completion of the 1st transcontinental railroad, 75th anniv.

"Golden Spike Ceremony" Painting by John McQuarrie A369

ENGRAVED
ROTARY PRESS PRINTING

1944, May 10 ***Perf. 11x10½***
922 A369 3c violet .25 .25

STEAMSHIP ISSUE

1st steamship to cross the Atlantic, 125th anniv.

"Savannah" A370

1944, May 22
923 A370 3c violet .25 .25

TELEGRAPH ISSUE

1st message transmitted by telegraph, cent.

Telegraph Wires & the First Transmitted Words "What Hath God Wrought"
A371

1944, May 24
924 A371 3c bright red violet .25 .25

PHILIPPINE ISSUE

Final resistance of the US and Philippine defenders on Corregidor to the Japanese invaders in 1942.

View of Corregidor
A372

1944, Sept. 27
925 A372 3c deep violet .25 .25

MOTION PICTURE, 50th ANNIV.

Motion Picture Showing for the Armed Forces in South Pacific
A373

1944, Oct. 31
926 A373 3c deep violet .25 .25

FLORIDA STATEHOOD, CENTENARY

Old Florida Seal, St. Augustine Gates and State Capitol
A374

1945, Mar. 3
927 A374 3c bright red violet .25 .25

UNITED NATIONS CONFERENCE ISSUE

United Nations Conference, San Francisco, Calif.

A375

1945, Apr. 25
928 A375 5c ultramarine .25 .25

IWO JIMA (MARINES) ISSUE

Battle of Iwo Jima and honoring the achievements of the US Marines.

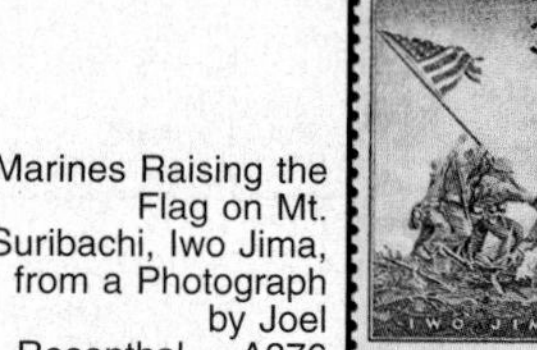
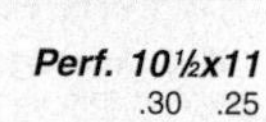

Marines Raising the Flag on Mt. Suribachi, Iwo Jima, from a Photograph by Joel Rosenthal — A376

1945, July 11 *Perf. 10½x11*
929 A376 3c yellow green .30 .25

FRANKLIN D. ROOSEVELT ISSUE

Franklin Delano Roosevelt (1882-1945).

Roosevelt and Hyde Park Home
A377

Roosevelt and "Little White House," Warm Springs, Georgia
A378

Roosevelt and White House
A379

Roosevelt, Globe and Four Freedoms
A380

1945-46 *Perf. 11x10½*

930	A377	1c blue green	.25	.25
931	A378	2c carmine rose	.25	.25
932	A379	3c purple	.25	.25
933	A380	5c bright blue	.25	.25
		Nos. 930-933 (4)	1.00	1.00

ARMY ISSUE

Achievements of the US Army in World War II.

U.S. Troops Passing Arch of Triumph, Paris
A381

1945, Sept. 28
934 A381 3c olive .25 .25

NAVY ISSUE

Achievements of the U.S. Navy in World War II.

U.S. Sailors
A382

1945, Oct. 27
935 A382 3c blue .25 .25

COAST GUARD ISSUE

Achievements of the US Coast Guard in World War II.

Coast Guard Landing Craft and Supply Ship
A383

1945, Nov. 10
936 A383 3c bright blue green .25 .25

ALFRED E. SMITH ISSUE

Alfred E. Smith — A384

1945, Nov. 26
937 A384 3c purple .25 .25

TEXAS STATEHOOD, 100th ANNIV.

U.S. and Texas State Flags
A385

1945, Dec. 29
938 A385 3c dark blue .25 .25

MERCHANT MARINE ISSUE

Achievements of the US Merchant Marine in World War II.

Liberty Ship Unloading Cargo
A386

1946, Feb. 26
939 A386 3c blue green .25 .25

VETERANS OF WORLD WAR II ISSUE

Issued to honor all veterans of World War II.

Honorable Discharge Emblem — A387

1946, May 9
940 A387 3c dark violet .25 .25

TENNESSEE STATEHOOD, 150th ANNIV.

Andrew Jackson, John Sevier & Tennessee Capitol
A388

1946, June 1
941 A388 3c dark violet .25 .25

IOWA STATEHOOD, 100th ANNIV.

Iowa State Flag & Map
A389

1946, Aug. 3
942 A389 3c deep blue .25 .25

SMITHSONIAN INSTITUTION ISSUE

100th anniversary of the establishment of the Smithsonian Institution, Washington, D.C.

Smithsonian Institution
A390

1946, Aug. 10
943 A390 3c violet brown .25 .25

KEARNY EXPEDITION ISSUE

100th anniversary of the entry of General Stephen Watts Kearny into Santa Fe.

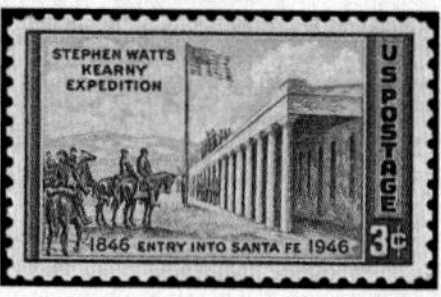

"Capture of Santa Fe" by Kenneth M. Chapman
A391

1946, Oct. 16
944 A391 3c brown violet .25 .25

THOMAS A. EDISON ISSUE

Thomas A. Edison, Birth Centenary — A392

1947, Feb. 11 *Perf. 10½x11*
945 A392 3c bright red violet .25 .25

JOSEPH PULITZER ISSUE

Joseph Pulitzer & Statue of Liberty
A393

1947, Apr. 10 *Perf. 11x10½*
946 A393 3c purple .25 .25

POSTAGE STAMP CENTENARY ISSUE

Centenary of the first postage stamps issued by the United States Government

Washington & Franklin; Early and Modern Mail-carrying Vehicles — A394

1947, May 17
947 A394 3c deep blue .25 .25

CENTENARY INTERNATIONAL PHILATELIC EXHIBITION ISSUE

SOUVENIR SHEET

A395

FLAT PLATE PRINTING

1947, May 19 *Imperf.*

948	A395	Pane of 2	.55	.45
a.		5c blue, type A1	.25	.25
b.		10c brown orange, type A2	.25	.25

Pane size varies: 96-98x66-68mm.

DOCTORS ISSUE

Issued to honor the physicians of America.

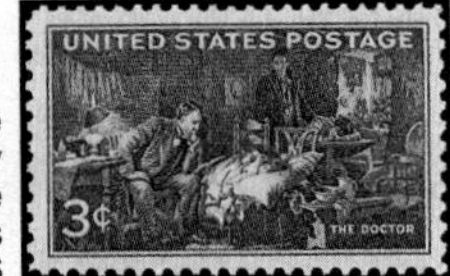

"The Doctor," by Sir Luke Fildes
A396

ROTARY PRESS PRINTING

1947, June 9 *Perf. 11x10½*
949 A396 3c brown violet .25 .25

UTAH ISSUE

Centenary of the settlement of Utah.

Pioneers Entering the Valley of Great Salt Lake
A397

1947, July 24
950 A397 3c dark violet .25 .25

U.S. FRIGATE CONSTITUTION ISSUE

150th anniversary of the launching of the U.S. frigate Constitution ("Old Ironsides").

Naval Architect's Drawing of Frigate Constitution
A398

1947, Oct. 21
951 A398 3c blue green .25 .25

Great White Heron and Map of Florida — A399

Dr. George Washington Carver — A400

EVERGLADES NATIONAL PARK ISSUE

Dedication of the Everglades National Park, Florida, Dec. 6, 1947.

1947, Dec. 5 *Perf. 10½x11*
952 A399 3c bright green .25 .25

GEORGE WASHINGTON CARVER ISSUE

5th anniversary of the death of Dr. George Washington Carver, (1864-1943), botanist.

1948, Jan. 5
953 A400 3c bright red violet .25 .25

CALIFORNIA GOLD CENTENNIAL ISSUE

Sutter's Mill, Coloma, California
A401

1948, Jan. 24 *Perf. 11x10½*
954 A401 3c dark violet .25 .25

MISSISSIPPI TERRITORY ISSUE

Mississippi Territory establishment, 150th anniv.

Map, Seal and Gov. Winthrop Sargent
A402

1948, Apr. 7
955 A402 3c brown violet .25 .25

FOUR CHAPLAINS ISSUE

George L. Fox, Clark V. Poling, John P. Washington and Alexander D. Goode, the 4 chaplains who sacrificed their lives in the sinking of the S.S. Dorchester, Feb. 3, 1943.

Four Chaplains and Sinking S.S. Dorchester
A403

1948, May 28
956 A403 3c gray black .25 .25

WISCONSIN STATEHOOD, 100th ANNIV.

Map on Scroll & State Capitol
A404

1948, May 29
957 A404 3c dark violet .25 .25

SWEDISH PIONEER ISSUE

Centenary of the coming of the Swedish pioneers to the Middle West.

Swedish Pioneer with Covered Wagon Moving Westward — A405

1948, June 4
958 A405 5c deep blue .25 .25

PROGRESS OF WOMEN ISSUE

Century of progress of American Women.

Elizabeth Stanton, Carrie C. Catt & Lucretia Mott
A406

1948, July 19
959 A406 3c dark violet .25 .25

WILLIAM ALLEN WHITE ISSUE

William Allen White, Editor and Author — A407

1948, July 31 *Perf. 10½x11*
960 A407 3c bright red violet .25 .25

UNITED STATES-CANADA FRIENDSHIP ISSUE

Century of friendship between the US and Canada.

Niagara Railway Suspension Bridge
A408

1948, Aug. 2 *Perf. 11x10½*
961 A408 3c blue .25 .25

FRANCIS SCOTT KEY ISSUE

Francis Scott Key (1779-1843), Maryland lawyer and author of "The Star-Spangled Banner" (1813).

Key and American Flags of 1814 and 1948
A409

1948, Aug. 9
962 A409 3c rose pink .25 .25

SALUTE TO YOUTH ISSUE

Issued to honor the Youth of America and to publicize "Youth Month," September, 1948.

Girl and Boy Carrying Books
A410

1948, Aug. 11
963 A410 3c deep blue .25 .25

OREGON TERRITORY ISSUE

Centenary of the establishment of Oregon Territory.

John McLoughlin, Jason Lee & Wagon on Oregon Trail
A411

1948, Aug. 14
964 A411 3c brown red .25 .25

HARLAN F. STONE ISSUE

Chief Justice Harlan Fiske Stone — A412

1948, Aug. 25 *Perf. 10½x11*
965 A412 3c bright violet .25 .25

PALOMAR MOUNTAIN OBSERVATORY ISSUE

Dedication, August 30, 1948.

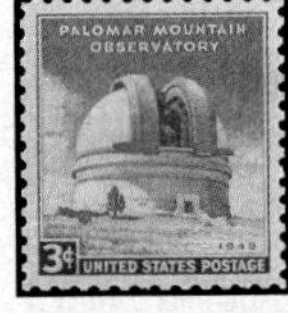

Observatory, Palomar Mt., Cal. — A413

1948, Aug. 30
966 A413 3c blue .25 .25
a. Vert. pair, imperf. between *300.00*

CLARA BARTON ISSUE

Founder of the American Red Cross (1882)
A414

Designed by Charles R. Chickering.

1948, Sept. 7 *Perf. 11x10½*
967 A414 3c rose pink .25 .25

POULTRY INDUSTRY CENTENNIAL ISSUE

Light Brahma Rooster
A415

1948, Sept. 9
968 A415 3c sepia .25 .25

GOLD STAR MOTHERS ISSUE

Issued to honor the mothers of deceased members of the United States armed forces.

Star and Palm Frond — A416

1948, Sept. 21 *Perf. 10½x11*
969 A416 3c orange yellow .25 .25

FORT KEARNY ISSUE

Establishment of Fort Kearny, Neb., centenary.

Fort Kearny and Pioneer Group
A417

1948, Sept. 22 *Perf. 11x10½*
970 A417 3c violet .25 .25

VOLUNTEER FIREMEN ISSUE

300th anniv. of the organization of the 1st volunteer firemen in America by Peter Stuyvesant.

Peter Stuyvesant; Early and Modern Fire Engines
A418

1948, Oct. 4
971 A418 3c bright rose carmine .25 .25

INDIAN CENTENNIAL ISSUE

Centenary of the arrival in Indian Territory, later Oklahoma, of the Five Civilized Indian Tribes: Cherokee, Chickasaw, Choctaw, Muscogee and Seminole.

Map of Indian Territory & Seals of Five Tribes
A419

1948, Oct. 15
972 A419 3c dark brown .25 .25

ROUGH RIDERS ISSUE

50th anniversary of the organization of the Rough Riders of the Spanish-American War.

Statue of Capt. William O. (Bucky) O'Neill A420

1948, Oct. 27
973 A420 3c violet brown .25 .25

JULIETTE LOW ISSUE

Low (1860-1927), founder of the Girl Scouts of America. Mrs. Low organized the 1st Girl Guides troop in 1912 at Savannah. The name was changed to Girl Scouts in 1913 and headquarters moved to New York.

Low and Girl Scout Emblem A421

1948, Oct. 29
974 A421 3c blue green .25 .25

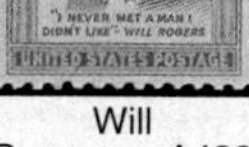

Will Rogers — A422 Fort Bliss and Rocket — A423

WILL ROGERS ISSUE

1948, Nov. 4 ***Perf. 10½x11***
975 A422 3c bright red violet .25 .25

Will Rogers, 1879-1935, humorist and political commentator.

FORT BLISS CENTENNIAL ISSUE

1948, Nov. 5
976 A423 3c henna brown .25 .25

MOINA MICHAEL ISSUE

Moina Michael (1870-1944), educator who originated (1918) the Flanders Field Poppy Day idea as a memorial to the war dead.

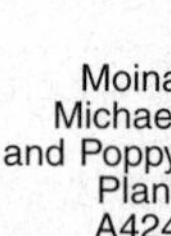

Moina Michael and Poppy Plant A424

1948, Nov. 9 ***Perf. 11x10½***
977 A424 3c rose pink .25 .25

GETTYSBURG ADDRESS ISSUE

85th anniversary of Abraham Lincoln's address at Gettysburg, Pennsylvania.

Lincoln and Quotation from Gettysburg Address A425

1948, Nov. 19
978 A425 3c bright blue .25 .25

Torch and American Turners' Emblem — A426

Joel Chandler Harris — A427

AMERICAN TURNERS ISSUE

Formation of the American Turners Soc., cent.

1948, Nov. 20 ***Perf. 10½x11***
979 A426 3c carmine .25 .25

JOEL CHANDLER HARRIS ISSUE

1948, Dec. 9
980 A427 3c bright red violet .25 .25

Harris (1848-1908), editor and author.

MINNESOTA TERRITORY ISSUE

Establishment of Minnesota Territory, cent.

Pioneer and Red River Oxcart A428

1949, Mar. 3 ***Perf. 11x10½***
981 A428 3c blue green .25 .25

WASHINGTON AND LEE UNIVERSITY ISSUE

Bicentenary of Washington and Lee University.

George Washington, Robert E. Lee and University Building — A429

1949, Apr. 12
982 A429 3c ultramarine .25 .25

PUERTO RICO ELECTION ISSUE

First gubernatorial election in the Territory of Puerto Rico, Nov. 2, 1948.

Puerto Rican Farmer Holding Cogwheel and Ballot Box A430

1949, Apr. 27
983 A430 3c green .25 .25

ANNAPOLIS TERCENTENARY ISSUE

Founding of Annapolis, Maryland, 300th anniv.

Stoddert's 1718 Map of Regions about Annapolis, Redrawn A431

1949, May 23
984 A431 3c aquamarine .25 .25

G.A.R. ISSUE

Final encampment of the Grand Army of the Republic, Indianapolis, Aug. 28 - Sept. 1, 1949.

Union Soldier and GAR Veteran of 1949 A432

1949, Aug. 29
985 A432 3c bright rose carmine .25 .25

EDGAR ALLAN POE ISSUE

Edgar Allan Poe (1809-1849), Poet, Story Writer and Editor — A433

1949, Oct. 7 ***Perf. 10½x11***
986 A433 3c bright red violet .25 .25

AMERICAN BANKERS ASSOCIATION ISSUE

75th anniv. of the formation of the Association.

Coin, Symbolizing Fields of Banking Service — A434

1950, Jan. 3 ***Perf. 11x10½***
987 A434 3c yellow green .25 .25

SAMUEL GOMPERS ISSUE

Samuel Gompers (1850-1924), Labor Leader — A435

1950, Jan. 27 ***Perf. 10½x11***
988 A435 3c bright red violet .25 .25

NATIONAL CAPITAL SESQUICENTENNIAL ISSUE

150th anniversary of the establishment of the National Capital, Washington, D.C.

Statue of Freedom on Capitol Dome — A436

Executive Mansion A437

Supreme Court Building A438

United States Capitol A439

1950 ***Perf. 10½x11, 11x10½***
989 A436 3c bright blue .25 .25
990 A437 3c deep green .25 .25
991 A438 3c light violet .25 .25
992 A439 3c bright red violet .25 .25
Nos. 989-992 (4) 1.00 1.00

RAILROAD ENGINEERS ISSUE

Issued to honor the Railroad Engineers of America. Stamp portrays John Luther (Casey) Jones (1864-1900), locomotive engineer killed in train wreck near Vaughn, Miss.

"Casey" Jones and Locomotives of 1900 and 1950 — A440

1950, Apr. 29 ***Perf. 11x10½***
993 A440 3c violet brown .25 .25

KANSAS CITY, MISSOURI, CENTENARY ISSUE

Kansas City, Missouri, incorporation.

Kansas City Skyline, 1950 and Westport Landing, 1850 A441

1950, June 3
994 A441 3c violet .25 .25

BOY SCOUTS ISSUE

Honoring the Boy Scouts of America on the occasion of the 2nd National Jamboree, Valley Forge, Pa.

Three Boys, Statue of Liberty and Scout Badge A442

1950, June 30
995 A442 3c sepia .25 .25

INDIANA TERRITORY ISSUE

Establishment of Indiana Territory, 150th anniv.

Gov. William Henry Harrison & First Indiana Capitol, Vincennes A443

1950, July 4
996 A443 3c bright blue .25 .25

CALIFORNIA STATEHOOD ISSUE

Gold Miner, Pioneers and S.S. Oregon A444

1950, Sept. 9
997 A444 3c yellow orange .25 .25

UNITED CONFEDERATE VETERANS FINAL REUNION ISSUE

Final reunion of the United Confederate Veterans, Norfolk, Virginia, May 30, 1951.

Confederate Soldier & United Confederate Veteran A445

1951, May 30
998 A445 3c gray .25 .25

NEVADA CENTENNIAL ISSUE

Centenary of the settlement of Nevada.

Carson Valley, c. 1851 A446

Designed by Charles R. Chickering.

1951, July 14
999 A446 3c light olive green .25 .25

LANDING OF CADILLAC ISSUE

250th anniversary of the landing of Antoine de la Mothe Cadillac at Detroit.

Detroit Skyline and Cadillac Landing A447

1951, July 24
1000 A447 3c blue .25 .25

COLORADO STATEHOOD, 75th ANNIV.

Colorado Capitol and Mount of the Holy Cross A448

1951, Aug. 1
1001 A448 3c blue violet .25 .25

AMERICAN CHEMICAL SOCIETY ISSUE

75th anniv. of the formation of the Society.

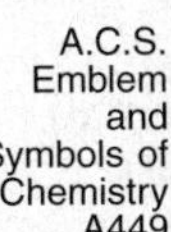

A.C.S. Emblem and Symbols of Chemistry A449

1951, Sept. 4
1002 A449 3c violet brown .25 .25

BATTLE OF BROOKLYN, 175th ANNIV.

Gen. George Washington Evacuating Army A450

1951, Dec. 10
1003 A450 3c violet .25 .25

BETSY ROSS ISSUE

200th anniv. of the birth of Betsy Ross, maker of the first American flag.

Betsy Ross Showing Flag to Gen. George Washington, Robert Morris & George Ross — A451

1952, Jan. 2
1004 A451 3c carmine rose .25 .25

4-H CLUB ISSUE

Farm, Club Emblem, Boy and Girl — A452

1952, Jan. 15
1005 A452 3c blue green .25 .25

B. & O. RAILROAD ISSUE

125th anniv. of the granting of a charter to the Baltimore and Ohio Railroad Company by the Maryland Legislature.

Charter and Three Stages of Rail Transportation — A453

1952, Feb. 28
1006 A453 3c bright blue .25 .25

A. A. A. ISSUE

50th anniversary of the formation of the American Automobile Association.

School Girls and Safety Patrolman, Automobiles of 1902 and 1952 — A454

1952, Mar. 4
1007 A454 3c deep blue .25 .25

NATO ISSUE

Signing of the North Atlantic Treaty, 3rd anniv.

Torch of Liberty and Globe — A455

1952, Apr. 4
1008 A455 3c deep violet .25 .25

GRAND COULEE DAM ISSUE

50 years of Federal cooperation in developing the resources of rivers and streams in the West.

Spillway, Grand Coulee Dam A456

1952, May 15
1009 A456 3c blue green .25 .25

LAFAYETTE ISSUE

175th anniversary of the arrival of Marquis de Lafayette in America.

Marquis de Lafayette, Flags, Cannon and Landing Party A457

1952, June 13
1010 A457 3c bright blue .25 .25

MT. RUSHMORE MEMORIAL ISSUE

Dedication of the Mt. Rushmore National Memorial in the Black Hills of South Dakota, 25th anniv.

Sculptured Heads on Mt. Rushmore — A458

1952, Aug. 11 *Perf. 10½x11*
1011 A458 3c blue green .25 .25

ENGINEERING CENTENNIAL ISSUE

American Society of Civil Engineers founding.

George Washington Bridge & Covered Bridge of 1850s A459

1952, Sept. 6 *Perf. 11x10½*
1012 A459 3c violet blue .25 .25

SERVICE WOMEN ISSUE

Women in the United States Armed Services.

Women of the Marine Corps, Army, Navy and Air Force A460

1952, Sept. 11
1013 A460 3c deep blue .25 .25

GUTENBERG BIBLE ISSUE

Printing of the 1st book, the Holy Bible, from movable type, by Johann Gutenberg, 500th anniv.

Gutenberg Showing Proof to the Elector of Mainz A461

1952, Sept. 30
1014 A461 3c violet .25 .25

NEWSPAPER BOYS ISSUE

Newspaper Boy, Torch and Group of Homes A462

1952, Oct. 4
1015 A462 3c violet .25 .25

RED CROSS ISSUE

Globe, Sun and Cross A463

1952, Nov. 21
1016 A463 3c deep blue & carmine .25 .25

NATIONAL GUARD ISSUE

National Guardsman and Amphibious Landing A464

1953, Feb. 23
1017 A464 3c bright blue .25 .25

OHIO STATEHOOD, 150th ANNIV.

Map and Ohio State Seal — A465

1953, Mar. 2
1018 A465 3c chocolate .25 .25

WASHINGTON TERRITORY ISSUE

Organization of Washington Territory, cent.

Medallion, Pioneers and Washington Scene A466

1953, Mar. 2
1019 A466 3c green .25 .25

LOUISIANA PURCHASE, 150th ANNIV.

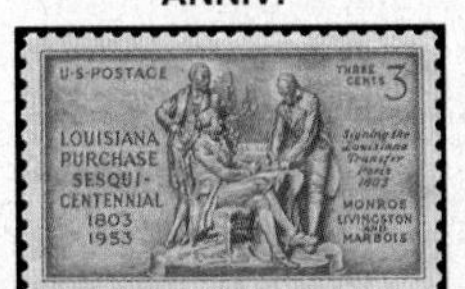

Monroe, Livingston and Barbé-Marbois — A467

1953, Apr. 30
1020 A467 3c violet brown .25 .25

OPENING OF JAPAN CENTENNIAL ISSUE

Centenary of Commodore Matthew Calbraith Perry's negotiations with

Japan, which opened her doors to foreign trade.

Commodore Perry and 1st Anchorage off Tokyo Bay — A468

1953, July 14

1021 A468 5c green .25 .25

AMERICAN BAR ASSOCIATION, 75th ANNIV.

Section of Frieze, Supreme Court Room A469

1953, Aug. 24

1022 A469 3c rose violet .25 .25

SAGAMORE HILL ISSUE

Opening of Sagamore Hill, Theodore Roosevelt's home, as a national shrine.

Home of Theodore Roosevelt A470

1953, Sept. 14

1023 A470 3c yellow green .25 .25

FUTURE FARMERS ISSUE

25th anniversary of the organization of Future Farmers of America.

Agricultural Scene and Future Farmer A471

1953, Oct. 13

1024 A471 3c deep blue .25 .25

TRUCKING INDUSTRY ISSUE

50th anniv. of the Trucking Industry in the US.

Truck, Farm and Distant City A472

1953, Oct. 27

1025 A472 3c violet .25 .25

GENERAL PATTON ISSUE

Honoring Gen. George S. Patton, Jr. (1885-1945), and the armored forces of the US Army.

Gen. George S. Patton, Jr., and Tank in Action A473

1953, Nov. 11

1026 A473 3c blue violet .25 .25

NEW YORK CITY, 300th ANNIV.

Dutch Ship in New Amsterdam Harbor A474

1953, Nov. 20

1027 A474 3c bright red violet .25 .25

GADSDEN PURCHASE ISSUE

Centenary of James Gadsden's purchase of territory from Mexico to adjust the US-Mexico boundary.

Map and Pioneer Group A475

1953, Dec. 30

1028 A475 3c copper brown .25 .25

COLUMBIA UNIVERSITY, 200th ANNIV.

Low Memorial Library A476

1954, Jan. 4

1029 A476 3c blue .25 .25

Wet and Dry Printings

In 1953 the Bureau of Engraving and Printing began experiments in printing on "dry" paper (moisture content 5-10 per cent). In previous "wet" printings the paper had a moisture content of 13-35 per cent.

The new process required a thicker, stiffer paper, special types of inks and greater pressure to force the paper into the recessed plates. The "dry" printings show whiter paper, a higher sheen on the surface, feel thicker and stiffer, and the designs stand out more clearly than on the "wet" printings.

Nos. 832c and 1041 (flat plate) were the first "dry" printings to be issued of flat-plate, regular-issue stamps. No. 1063 was the first rotary-press stamp to be produced entirely by "dry" printing. Nos. QE1a, QE2a and QE3a, RF26A and RW21 (all flat plate) were the first "dry" printings of back-of-the-book issue stamps.

All postage stamps have been printed by the "dry" process since the late 1950's.

See the Scott *Specialized Catalogue of United States Stamps* for listings of the wet and dry printings and for No. 1033 on Silkote paper.

LIBERTY ISSUE

Franklin A477

Washington A478

Palace of the Governors, Santa Fe — A478a — 1031A

Mount Vernon — A479

Thomas Jefferson A480

Bunker Hill Monument, Mass. Flag, 1776 A481

Statue of Liberty A482

Abraham Lincoln A483

The Hermitage A484

James Monroe A485

Theodore Roosevelt A486

Woodrow Wilson A487

A488

Statue of Liberty A489

The Alamo A490

Independence Hall — A491

Statue of Liberty — A491a

Benjamin Harrison A492

John Jay A493

Monticello A494

Paul Revere A495

Robert E. Lee A496

John Marshall A497

Susan B. Anthony A498

Patrick Henry A499

Alexander Hamilton — A500

ROTARY PRESS PRINTING

1954-68 ***Perf. 11x10½, 10½x11***

1030 A477 ½c red orange ('55) .25 .25

1031 A478 1c dark green .25 .25

1031A A478a 1¼c turquoise ('60) .25 .25

1032 A479 1½c brn car ('56) .25 .25

1033 A480 2c car rose .25 .25

1034 A481 2½c gray blue ('59) .25 .25

1035 A482 3c deep violet .25 .25

a. Booklet pane of 6, *June 30, 1954* 4.00 *1.25*

b. Horiz. pair, imperf. btwn in #1035a with foldover (one pair recorded) or miscut (three pairs recorded) *2,000.*

e. Tagged ('66) .35 .25

f. Imperf., pair *2,400.*

g. Horiz. pair, imperf. between *1,500.*

No. 1057b measures about 19½x22mm; No. 1035f, about 18¾x22½mm.

1036 A483 4c red violet .25 .25

b. Booklet pane of 6 ('58) 2.75 *1.25*

c. As "b," imperf. horiz. *10,000.*

d. Horiz. pair, imperf between *4,750.*

e. Tagged ('63) .65 .40

1037 A484 4½c blue green ('59) .25 .25

1038 A485 5c deep blue .25 .25

1039 A486 6c carmine ('55) .40 .25

b. Imperf, block of 4 (unique) *23,000.*

1040 A487 7c rose car ('56) .25 .25

a. dk rose car .25 .25

FLAT PLATE PRINTING

Size: 22.7mm high

Perf. 11

1041 A488 8c dk vio blue & car .25 .25

a. Double impression of carmine *575.00* —

ROTARY PRESS PRINTING

Size: 22.9mm high

1041B A488 8c dk vio blue & car .40 .25

GIORI PRESS PRINTING

Redrawn design

1042 A489 8c dk vio bl & car rose ('58) .25 .25

The 8c John J. Pershing stamp, formerly No. 1042A, is now included with the regular issue of 1961-66. See No. 1214.

ROTARY PRESS PRINTING

Perf. 10½x11

1043 A490 9c rose lilac ('56) .30 .25
a. 9c dark rose lilac .30 .25

1044 A491 10c rose lake ('56) .30 .25
b. 10c dark rose lake .25 .25
d. Tagged 2.00 1.00

GIORI PRESS PRINTING

Perf. 11

1044A A491a 11c car & dk vio bl ('61) .30 .25
c. Tagged 2.50 1.60

Perf. 11x10½, 10½x11

1045 A492 12c red ('59) .35 .25
a. Tagged ('68) .35 .25

1046 A493 15c rose lake ('58) .60 .25
a. Tagged 1.10 .80

1047 A494 20c ultra ('56) .50 .25
a. deep bright ultra .50 .25

1048 A495 25c green ('58) 1.10 .75

1049 A496 30c black ('55) 1.20 .75
b. 30c intense black .80 .25

No. 1049b is from later printings and is on a harder, whiter paper than No. 1049.

1050 A497 40c brown red ('55) 1.75 .25

1051 A498 50c brt pur ('55) 1.75 .25

1052 A499 $1 purple ('55) 5.25 1.00

FLAT PLATE PRINTING

Perf. 11

1053 A500 $5 black 55.00 6.75
Nos. 1030-1053 (27) 72.45 15.00

Luminescence

During 1963 quantities of certain issues (Nos. C64a, 1213b, 1213c and 1229a) were overprinted with phosphorescent coating, "tagged," for use in testing automated facing and canceling machines. Listings for tagged varieties of stamps previously issued without tagging start with Nos. 1035b and C59a.

The entire printings of Nos. 1238, 1278, 1280-1281, 1283B, 1286-1288, 1298-1305, 1323-1340, 1342-1362, 1364, and C69-C75 and all following listings, unless otherwise noted, were tagged.

Stamps tagged with zinc orthosilicate glow yellow green. Airmail stamps with calcium silicate overprint glow orange red. Both tagging overprints are activated only by shortwave ultraviolet light.

ROTARY PRESS COIL STAMPS

Perf. 10 Vert., Horiz. (1¼c, 4½c)

1954-80

1054 A478 1c dark green .60 .25
c. Imperf., pair 3,000. —

1054A A478a 1¼c turquoise ('60) .25 .25
d. Imperf., pair —

All examples of No. 1054Ad are precanceled "SEATTLE/WASH."

1055 A480 2c car rose .60 .25
b. Tagged ('68) .25 .25
c. Imperf. pair, (Bureau precanceled) 375.00
d. As "b," Imperf. pair 450.00

1056 A481 2½c gray blue ('59) .30 .25

1057 A482 3c deep violet .35 .25
b. Imperf., pair 1,750. 800.00
d. Tagged ('66) 1.00 .50

No. 1057b measures about 19½x22mm; No. 1035f, about 18¾x22½mm.

1058 A483 4c red violet ('58) 22.50 .50
b. Imperf., pair 75.00 70.00

Collectors should note that a 1958 second printing of No. 1058 was made using the "dry printing" method. These dry printings, without Bureau precancels (No. 1058a in the Scott U.S. Specialized catalogue), are considerably less expensive: unused 75 cents, used 25 cents. For most general collectors, the less expensive variety should be used to fill the album space for the 4c coil. See the Scott U.S. Specialized catalogue for more details.

1059 A484 4½c blue green ('59) 1.50 1.00

1059A A495 25c green ('65) .50 .30
b. Tagged .80 .25
d. Imperf., pair, tagged 30.00

Value for No. 1059Ad is for fine centering.

NEBRASKA TERRITORY ISSUE

Establishment of the Nebraska Territory, centenary.

Mitchell Pass, Scotts Bluff & "The Sower," by Lee Lawrie
A507

ROTARY PRESS PRINTING

1954, May 7 *Perf. 11x10½*
1060 A507 3c violet .25 .25

KANSAS TERRITORY ISSUE

Establishment of the Kansas Territory, centenary

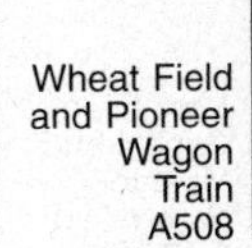

Wheat Field and Pioneer Wagon Train
A508

1954, May 31
1061 A508 3c brown orange .25 .25

GEORGE EASTMAN ISSUE

George Eastman (1854-1932), Inventor & Philanthropist
A509

1954, July 12 *Perf. 10½x11*
1062 A509 3c violet brown .25 .25

LEWIS AND CLARK EXPEDITION

150th anniv. of the Lewis and Clark expedition.

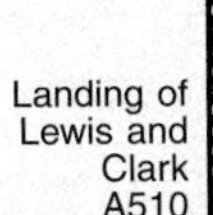

Landing of Lewis and Clark
A510

1954, July 28 *Perf. 11x10½*
1063 A510 3c violet brown .25 .25

PENNSYLVANIA ACADEMY OF THE FINE ARTS ISSUE

150th anniversary of the founding of the Pennsylvania Academy of the Fine Arts, Philadelphia.

Charles Willson Peale in his Museum, Self-portrait — A511

1955, Jan. 15 *Perf. 10½x11*
1064 A511 3c rose brown .25 .25

LAND GRANT COLLEGES ISSUE

Centenary of the founding of Michigan State College and Pennsylvania State University, first of the land grant institutions.

Open Book and Symbols of Subjects Taught
A512

1955, Feb. 12 *Perf. 11x10½*
1065 A512 3c green .25 .25

ROTARY INTERNATIONAL, 50th ANNIV.

Torch, Globe and Rotary Emblem
A513

1955, Feb. 23
1066 A513 8c deep blue .25 .25

ARMED FORCES RESERVE ISSUE

Marine, Coast Guard, Army, Navy, & Air Force Personnel
A514

1955, May 21
1067 A514 3c purple .25 .25

NEW HAMPSHIRE ISSUE

Sesquicentennial of the discovery of the "Old Man of the Mountains."

Great Stone Face — A515

1955, June 21 *Perf. 10½x11*
1068 A515 3c green .25 .25

SOO LOCKS ISSUE

Centenary of the opening of the Soo Locks.

Map of Great Lakes and Two Steamers
A516

1955, June 28 *Perf. 11x10½*
1069 A516 3c blue .25 .25

ATOMS FOR PEACE ISSUE

Issued to promote an Atoms for Peace policy.

Atomic Energy Encircling the Hemispheres — A517

1955, July 28
1070 A517 3c deep blue .25 .25

FORT TICONDEROGA ISSUE

Bicentenary of Fort Ticonderoga, New York.

Map of the Fort, Ethan Allen and Artillery
A518

1955, Sept. 18
1071 A518 3c light brown .25 .25

Andrew W. Mellon — A519

"Franklin Taking Electricity from the Sky," by Benjamin West — A520

ANDREW W. MELLON ISSUE

1955, Dec. 20 *Perf. 10½x11*
1072 A519 3c rose carmine .25 .25

Mellon, U.S. Sec. of the Treasury (1921-32), financier and art collector.

BENJAMIN FRANKLIN ISSUE

250th anniv. of the birth of Benjamin Franklin.

1956, Jan. 17
1073 A520 3c bright carmine .25 .25

BOOKER T. WASHINGTON ISSUE

Washington (1856-1915), black educator, founder and head of Tuskegee Institute in Alabama.

Log Cabin
A521

1956, Apr. 5 *Perf. 11x10½*
1074 A521 3c deep blue .25 .25

FIFTH INTERNATIONAL PHILATELIC EXHIBITION ISSUES

FIPEX, New York City, Apr. 28 - May 6, 1956.

SOUVENIR SHEET

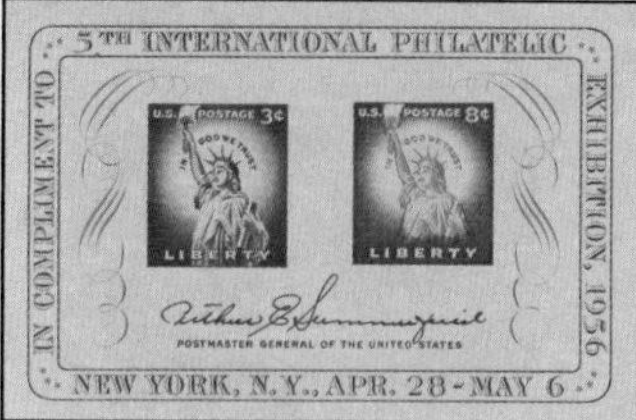

A522

FLAT PLATE PRINTING

1956, Apr. 28 ***Imperf.***

1075 A522 Pane of 2 1.20 1.50
  a. A482 3c deep violet .75 .60
  b. A488 8c dark violet blue & carmine .85 .75

No. 1075 measures 108x73mm. Nos. 1075a and 1075b measure 24x28mm.

Inscriptions printed in dark violet blue; scrolls and stars in carmine.

New York Coliseum & Columbus Monument A523

ROTARY PRESS PRINTING

1956, Apr. 30 ***Perf. 11x10½***

1076 A523 3c deep violet .25 .25

WILDLIFE CONSERVATION ISSUE

Issued to emphasize the importance of Wildlife Conservation in America.

Wild Turkey A524

Pronghorn Antelope A525

King Salmon A526

1956

1077 A524 3c rose lake .25 .25
1078 A525 3c brown .25 .25
1079 A526 3c blue green .25 .25
  Nos. 1077-1079 (3) .75 .75

PURE FOOD AND DRUG LAWS, 50th ANNIV.

Harvey W. Wiley — A527

1956, June 27 ***Perf. 10½x11***

1080 A527 3c dark blue green .25 .25

WHEATLAND ISSUE

President Buchanan's Home, "Wheatland," Lancaster, PA — A528

1956, Aug. 5

1081 A528 3c black brown .25 .25

LABOR DAY ISSUE

Mosaic, AFL-CIO Headquarters A529

1956, Sept. 3 ***Perf. 10½x11***

1082 A529 3c deep blue .25 .25

NASSAU HALL ISSUE

200th anniv. of Nassau Hall, Princeton University.

Nassau Hall, Princeton, NJ — A530

1956, Sept. 22

1083 A530 3c black, *orange* .25 .25

DEVILS TOWER ISSUE

Issued to commemorate the 50th anniversary of the Federal law providing for protection of American natural antiquities. Devils Tower National Monument, Wyoming, is an outstanding example.

Devils Tower — A531

1956, Sept. 24 ***Perf. 10½x11***

1084 A531 3c violet .25 .25

CHILDREN'S ISSUE

Issued to promote friendship among the children of the world.

Children of the World A532

1956, Dec. 15 ***Perf. 11x10½***

1085 A532 3c dark blue .25 .25

ALEXANDER HAMILTON (1755-1804)

Alexander Hamilton (1757-1804) and Federal Hall A533

1957, Jan. 11

1086 A533 3c rose red .25 .25

POLIO ISSUE

Honoring "those who helped fight polio," and on for 20th anniv. of the Natl. Foundation for Infantile Paralysis and the March of Dimes.

Allegory — A534

1957, Jan. 15 ***Perf. 10½x11***

1087 A534 3c red lilac .25 .25

COAST AND GEODETIC SURVEY ISSUE

150th anniversary of the establishment of the Coast and Geodetic Survey.

Flag of Coast and Geodetic Survey and Ships at Sea A535

1957, Feb. 11 ***Perf. 11x10½***

1088 A535 3c dark blue .25 .25

ARCHITECTS ISSUE

American Institute of Architects, centenary.

Corinthian Capital and Mushroom Type Head & Shaft A536

1957, Feb. 23

1089 A536 3c red lilac .25 .25

STEEL INDUSTRY ISSUE

Centenary of the steel industry in America.

American Eagle and Pouring Ladle — A537

1957, May 22 ***Perf. 10½x11***

1090 A537 3c bright ultramarine .25 .25

INTERNATIONAL NAVAL REVIEW ISSUE

Issued to commemorate the International Naval Review and the Jamestown Festival.

Aircraft Carrier and Jamestown Festival Emblem A538

1957, June 10 ***Perf. 11x10½***

1091 A538 3c blue green .25 .25

OKLAHOMA STATEHOOD, 50th ANNIV.

Map of Oklahoma, Arrow and Atom Diagram A539

1957, June 14

1092 A539 3c dark blue .25 .25

SCHOOL TEACHERS ISSUE

Teacher and Pupils A540

1957, July 1

1093 A540 3c rose lake .25 .25

FLAG ISSUE

"Old Glory" (48 Stars) A541

GIORI PRESS PRINTING

1957, July 4 ***Perf. 11***

1094 A541 4c dark blue & deep carmine .25 .25

"Virginia of Sagadahock" and Seal of Maine — A542

Ramon Magsaysay, (1907-1957), Philippines President — A543

SHIPBUILDING ISSUE

350th anniversary of shipbuilding in America.

ROTARY PRESS PRINTING

1957, Aug. 15 ***Perf. 10½x11***

1095 A542 3c deep violet .25 .25

CHAMPION OF LIBERTY ISSUE

Magsaysay (1907-57), Pres. of the Philippines.

GIORI PRESS PRINTING

1957, Aug. 31 ***Perf. 11***

1096 A543 8c car, ultra & ocher .25 .25

For other Champion of Liberty issues, see Nos. 1110-1111, 1117-1118, 1125-1126, 1136-1137, 1147-1148, 1159-1160, 1165-1166, 1168-1169, 1174-1175.

Marquis de Lafayette A544

Whooping Cranes A545

LAFAYETTE BICENTENARY ISSUE

1957. Sept. 6 ***Perf. 10½x11***

1097 A544 3c rose lake .25 .25

WILDLIFE CONSERVATION ISSUE

Issued to emphasize the importance of Wildlife Conservation in America.

GIORI PRESS PRINTING

1957, Nov. 22 ***Perf. 11***

1098 A545 3c blue, ocher & green .25 .25

Bible, Hat and Quill Pen — A546

"Bountiful Earth" — A547

RELIGIOUS FREEDOM ISSUE

300th anniv. of the Flushing Remonstrance.

ROTARY PRESS PRINTING

1957, Dec. 27 ***Perf. 10½x11***

1099 A546 3c black .25 .25

GARDENING HORTICULTURE ISSUE

Issued to honor the garden clubs of America and in connection with the centenary of the birth of Liberty Hyde Bailey, horticulturist.

1958, Mar. 15

1100 A547 3c green .25 .25

BRUSSELS EXHIBITION ISSUE

Issued in honor of the opening of the Universal and International Exhibition at Brussels, April 17.

U.S. Pavilion at Brussels A551

1958, Apr. 17 ***Perf. 11x10½***

1104 A551 3c deep claret .25 .25

JAMES MONROE ISSUE

James Monroe, by Gilbert Stuart — A552

1958, Apr. 28

1105 A552 3c purple .25 .25

MINNESOTA STATEHOOD, 100th ANNIV.

Minnesota Lakes and Pines A553

1958, May 11

1106 A553 3c green .25 .25

GEOPHYSICAL YEAR ISSUE

International Geophysical Year, 1957-58.

Solar Disc and Hands from Michelangelo's "Creation of Adam" — A554

GIORI PRESS PRINTING

1958, May 31 ***Perf. 11***

1107 A554 3c black & red orange .25 .25

GUNSTON HALL ISSUE

Issued for the bicentenary of Gunston Hall and to honor George Mason, author of the Constitution of Virginia and the Virginia Bill of Rights.

Gunston Hall, Virginia A555

ROTARY PRESS PRINTING

1958, June 12 ***Perf. 11x10½***

1108 A555 3c light green .25 .25

Mackinac Bridge — A556

Simon Bolivar — A557

MACKINAC BRIDGE ISSUE

Dedication of Mackinac Bridge, Michigan.

1958, June 25 ***Perf. 10½x11***

1109 A556 3c brt greenish blue .25 .25

CHAMPION OF LIBERTY ISSUE

Simon Bolívar, South American freedom fighter.

1958, July 24

1110 A557 4c olive bister .25 .25

GIORI PRESS PRINTING
Perf. 11

1111 A557 8c car, ultra & ocher .25 .25

ATLANTIC CABLE CENTENNIAL ISSUE

Centenary of the Atlantic Cable, linking the Eastern and Western hemispheres.

Neptune, Globe and Mermaid A558

ROTARY PRESS PRINTING

1958, Aug. 15 ***Perf. 11x10½***

1112 A558 4c reddish purple .25 .25

LINCOLN SESQUICENTENNIAL ISSUE

Sesquicentennial of the birth of Abraham Lincoln. No. 1114 also for the centenary of the founding of Cooper Union, New York City. No. 1115 marks the centenary of the Lincoln-Douglas Debates.

Lincoln, by George Healy — A559

Lincoln, by Gutzon Borglum — A560

Abraham Lincoln and Stephen A. Douglas Debating A561

Lincoln, by Daniel Chester French A562

1958-59 ***Perf. 10½x11***

1113 A559 1c green ('59) .25 .25

1114 A560 3c dark rose ('59) .25 .25

Perf. 11x10½

1115 A561 4c sepia .25 .25

1116 A562 4c dark blue ('59) .25 .25

Nos. 1113-1116 (4) 1.00 1.00

Lajos Kossuth, (1802-1892) A563

Early Press and Hand Holding Quill A564

CHAMPION OF LIBERTY ISSUE

Lajos Kossuth, Hungarian freedom fighter.

1958, Sept. 19 ***Perf. 10½x11***

1117 A563 4c green .25 .25

GIORI PRESS PRINTING
Perf. 11

1118 A563 8c car, ultra & ocher .25 .25

FREEDOM OF PRESS ISSUE

Honoring Journalism and freedom of the press in connection with the 50th anniv. of the 1st School of Journalism at the University of Missouri.

ROTARY PRESS PRINTING

1958, Sept. 22 ***Perf. 10½x11***

1119 A564 4c black .25 .25

OVERLAND MAIL ISSUE

Centenary of Overland Mail Service.

Mail Coach and Map of Southwest U.S. A565

1958, Oct. 10 ***Perf. 11x10½***

1120 A565 4c crimson rose .25 .25

Noah Webster — A566

Forest Scene — A567

NOAH WEBSTER ISSUE

Webster (1758-1843), lexicographer and author.

1958, Oct. 16 ***Perf. 10½x11***

1121 A566 4c dark carmine rose .25 .25

FOREST CONSERVATION ISSUE

Issued to publicize forest conservation and the protection of natural resources and to honor Theodore Roosevelt, a leading forest conservationist, on the centenary of his birth.

GIORI PRESS PRINTING

1958, Oct. 27 ***Perf. 11***

1122 A567 4c green, yellow & brown .25 .25

FORT DUQUESNE ISSUE

Bicentennial of Fort Duquesne (Fort Pitt) at future site of Pittsburgh.

Occupation of Fort Duquesne A568

ROTARY PRESS PRINTING

1958, Nov. 25 ***Perf. 11x10½***

1123 A568 4c blue .25 .25

OREGON STATEHOOD, 100th ANNIV.

Covered Wagon and Mt. Hood A569

1959, Feb. 14

1124 A569 4c blue green .25 .25

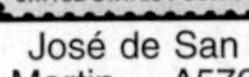

José de San Martin — A570

NATO Emblem — A571

CHAMPION OF LIBERTY ISSUE

San Martin, So. American soldier and statesman.

1959, Feb. 25 ***Perf. 10½x11***

1125 A570 4c blue .25 .25

a. Horiz. pair, imperf. between *900.00*

GIORI PRESS PRINTING
Perf. 11

1126 A570 8c car, ultra & ocher .25 .25

NATO ISSUE

North Atlantic Treaty Organization, 10th anniv.

ROTARY PRESS PRINTING

1959, Apr. 1 ***Perf. 10½x11***

1127 A571 4c blue .25 .25

ARCTIC EXPLORATIONS ISSUE

Conquest of the Arctic by land by Rear Admiral Robert Edwin Peary in

1909 and by sea by the submarine "Nautilus" in 1958.

North Pole, Dog Sled and "Nautilus"
A572

1959, Apr. 6 ***Perf. 11x10½***
1128 A572 4c bright greenish blue .25 .25

WORLD PEACE THROUGH WORLD TRADE ISSUE

Issued in conjunction with the 17th Congress of the International Chamber of Commerce, Washington, D.C., April 19-25.

Globe and Laurel
A573

1959, Apr. 20
1129 A573 8c rose lake .25 .25

SILVER CENTENNIAL ISSUE

Discovery of silver at the Comstock Lode, Nevada.

Henry Comstock at Mount Davidson Site
A574

1959, June 8
1130 A574 4c black .25 .25

ST. LAWRENCE SEAWAY ISSUE

Opening of the St. Lawrence Seaway.

Great Lakes, Maple Leaf and Eagle Emblems
A575

GIORI PRESS PRINTING

1959, June 26 ***Perf. 11***
1131 A575 4c red & dark blue .25 .25

See Canada No. 387.

49-STAR FLAG ISSUE

U.S. Flag, 1959
A576

1959, July 4
1132 A576 4c ocher, dark blue & deep carmine .25 .25

SOIL CONSERVATION ISSUE

Issued as a tribute to farmers and ranchers who use soil and water conservation measures.

Modern Farm
A577

1959, Aug. 26
1133 A577 4c blue, green & ocher .25 .25

PETROLEUM INDUSTRY ISSUE

Centenary of the completion of the nation's first oil well at Titusville, Pa.

Oil Derrick — A578

ROTARY PRESS PRINTING

1959, Aug. 27 ***Perf. 10½x11***
1134 A578 4c brown .25 .25

DENTAL HEALTH ISSUE

Issued to publicize Dental Health and for the centenary of the American Dental Association.

Children
A579

1959, Sept. 14 ***Perf. 11x10½***
1135 A579 4c green .25 .25

Ernst Reuter
A580

Dr. Ephraim McDowell
A581

CHAMPION OF LIBERTY ISSUE

Ernst Reuter, Mayor of Berlin, 1948-53.

1959, Sept. 29 ***Perf. 10½x11***
1136 A580 4c gray .25 .25

GIORI PRESS PRINTING
Perf. 11

1137 A580 8c car, ultra & ocher .25 .25
a. Ocher missing (EP) *3,250.*
b. Ultramarine missing (EP) *4,000.*
c. Ocher & ultramarine missing (EP) *4,250.*
d. All colors missing (EP) *2,250.*

DR. EPHRAIM McDOWELL ISSUE

Honoring McDowell (1771-1830) on the 150th anniv. of the 1st successful ovarian operation in the US, performed at Danville, Ky., 1809.

ROTARY PRESS PRINTING

1959, Dec. 3 ***Perf. 10½x11***
1138 A581 4c rose lake .25 .25
a. Vert. pair, imperf. btwn. *375.00*
b. Vert. pair, imperf. horiz. *225.00*

AMERICAN CREDO ISSUE

Issued to re-emphasize the ideals upon which America was founded and to honor those great Americans who wrote or uttered the credos.

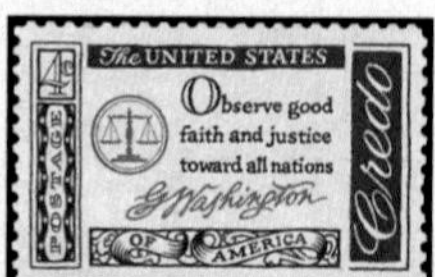

Quotation from Washington's Farewell Address, 1796 — A582

Benjamin Franklin Quotation
A583

Thomas Jefferson Quotation
A584

Francis Scott Key Quotation
A585

Abraham Lincoln Quotation
A586

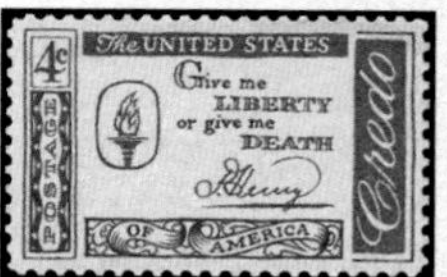

Patrick Henry Quotation
A587

Designed by Frank Conley.

GIORI PRESS PRINTING

Plates of 200 subjects in four panes of 50.

1960-61				***Perf. 11***	
1139	A582	4c	dk vio bl & car	.25	.25
1140	A583	4c	ol bister & grn	.25	.25
1141	A584	4c	gray & vermilion	.25	.25
1142	A585	4c	car & dark blue	.25	.25
1143	A586	4c	magenta & green	.25	.25
1144	A587	4c	green & brown	.25	.25
			Nos. 1139-1144 (6)	1.50	1.50

Issued: 1/20; 3/31; 5/8; 9/14; 11/19; 1/11/61.

BOY SCOUT JUBILEE ISSUE

50th anniv. of the Boy Scouts of America.

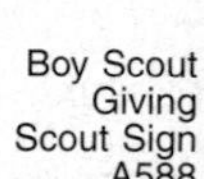

Boy Scout Giving Scout Sign
A588

1960, Feb. 8
1145 A588 4c red, dark blue & dark bister .25 .25

Olympic Rings and Snowflake
A589

Thomas G. Masaryk
A590

OLYMPIC WINTER GAMES ISSUE

Opening of the 8th Olympic Winter Games, Squaw Valley, Feb. 18-29, 1960.

ROTARY PRESS PRINTING

1960, Feb. 18 ***Perf. 10½x11***
1146 A589 4c dull blue .25 .25

CHAMPION OF LIBERTY ISSUE

Issued to honor Thomas G. Masaryk, founder and president of Czechoslovakia (1918-35), on the 110th anniversary of his birth.

1960, Mar. 7
1147 A590 4c blue .25 .25
a. Vert. pair, imperf. between *2,250.*

GIORI PRESS PRINTING
Perf. 11

1148 A590 8c car, ultra & ocher .25 .25
a. Horiz. pair, imperf. between —

WORLD REFUGEE YEAR ISSUE

World Refugee Year, July 1, 1959-June 30, 1960.

Refugee Family Walking Toward New Life
A591

ROTARY PRESS PRINTING

1960, Apr. 7 ***Perf. 11x10½***
1149 A591 4c gray black .25 .25

WATER CONSERVATION ISSUE

Issued to stress the importance of water conservation and to commemorate the 7th Watershed Congress, Washington, D.C.

Water, from Watershed to Consumer
A592

GIORI PRESS PRINTING

1960, Apr. 18 ***Perf. 11***
1150 A592 4c dk bl, brn org & grn .25 .25
a. Brown orange missing (EP) *2,250.*

SEATO ISSUE

South-East Asia Treaty Organization and for the SEATO Conf., Washington, D.C., May 31-June 3.

SEATO Emblem — A593

ROTARY PRESS PRINTING

1960, May 31 ***Perf. 10½x11***
1151 A593 4c blue .25 .25
a. Vertical pair, imperf. between *125.00*

AMERICAN WOMAN ISSUE

Issued to pay tribute to American women and their accomplishments in civic affairs, education, arts and industry.

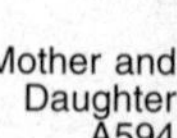

Mother and Daughter
A594

1960, June 2 ***Perf. 11x10½***
1152 A594 4c deep violet .25 .25

50-STAR FLAG ISSUE

U.S. Flag, 1960 — A595

GIORI PRESS PRINTING

1960, July 4 *Perf. 11*
1153 A595 4c dark blue & red .25 .25

PONY EXPRESS CENTENNIAL ISSUE

Pony Express Rider A596

ROTARY PRESS PRINTING

1960, July 19 *Perf. 11x10½*
1154 A596 4c sepia .25 .25

Man in Wheelchair Operating Drill Press — A597

5th World Forestry Congress Seal — A598

EMPLOY THE HANDICAPPED ISSUE

Promoting the employment of the physically handicapped and publicizing the 8th World Congress of the Intl. Soc. for the Welfare of Cripples, New York City.

1960, Aug. 28 *Perf. 10½x11*
1155 A597 4c dark blue .25 .25

WORLD FORESTRY CONGRESS ISSUE

5th World Forestry Cong., Seattle, Wash., Aug. 29-Sept. 10.

1960, Aug. 29
1156 A598 4c green .25 .25

A599

A600

MEXICAN INDEPENDENCE, 150th ANNIV.

GIORI PRESS PRINTING

1960, Sept. 16 *Perf. 11*
1157 A599 4c green & rose red .25 .25

See Mexico No. 910.

US-JAPAN TREATY ISSUE

Centenary of the United States-Japan Treaty of Amity and Commerce.

1960, Sept. 28
1158 A600 4c blue & pink .25 .25

Ignacy Jan Paderewski A601

Robert A. Taft A602

CHAMPION OF LIBERTY ISSUE

Jan Paderewski, Polish statesman and musician.

ROTARY PRESS PRINTING

1960, Oct. 8 *Perf. 10½x11*
1159 A601 4c blue .25 .25

GIORI PRESS PRINTING
Perf. 11

1160 A601 8c car, ultra & ocher .25 .25

SENATOR TAFT MEMORIAL ISSUE

Senator Robert A. Taft (1889-1953) of Ohio.

ROTARY PRESS PRINTING

1960, Oct. 10 *Perf. 10½x11*
1161 A602 4c dull violet .25 .25

WHEELS OF FREEDOM ISSUE

Issued to honor the automotive industry and in connection with the National Automobile Show, Detroit, Oct. 15-23.

Globe and Steering Wheel with Tractor, Car and Truck A603

1960, Oct. 15 *Perf. 11x10½*
1162 A603 4c dark blue .25 .25

BOYS' CLUBS OF AMERICA ISSUE

Boys' Clubs of America movement, centenary.

Profile of a Boy — A604

GIORI PRESS PRINTING

1960, Oct. 18 *Perf. 11*
1163 A604 4c indigo, slate & rose red .25 .25

FIRST AUTOMATED POST OFFICE IN THE US ISSUE

Publicizing the opening of the 1st automated post office in the US at Providence, R.I.

Architect's Sketch of New Post Office, Providence, RI — A605

1960, Oct. 20
1164 A605 4c dark blue & carmine .25 .25
a. Red missing (PS) *250.00*

Baron Gustaf Emil Mannerheim A606

Camp Fire Girls Emblem A607

CHAMPION OF LIBERTY ISSUE

Baron Karl Gustaf Emil Mannerheim (1867-1951), Marshal and President of Finland.

ROTARY PRESS PRINTING

1960, Oct. 26 *Perf. 10½x11*
1165 A606 4c blue .25 .25

GIORI PRESS PRINTING

Plates of 288 subjects in four panes of 72 each.
Perf. 11

1166 A606 8c car, ultra & ocher .25 .25

CAMP FIRE GIRLS ISSUE

50th anniv. of the Camp Fire Girls' movement and in connection with the Golden Jubilee Convention celebration of the Camp Fire Girls.

GIORI PRESS PRINTING

1960, Nov. 1 *Perf. 11*
1167 A607 4c dark blue & bright red .25 .25

Giuseppe Garibaldi (1807-1882) A608

Walter F. George (1878-1957) A609

CHAMPION OF LIBERTY ISSUE

Giuseppe Garibaldi (1807-1882), Italian patriot and freedom fighter.

ROTARY PRESS PRINTING

1960, Nov. 2 *Perf. 10½x11*
1168 A608 4c green .25 .25

GIORI PRESS PRINTING
Perf. 11

1169 A608 8c car, ultra & ocher .25 .25

SENATOR GEORGE MEMORIAL ISSUE

Walter F. George (1878-1957) of Georgia.

ROTARY PRESS PRINTING

1960, Nov. 5 *Perf. 10½x11*
1170 A609 4c dull violet .25 .25

Andrew Carnegie A610

John Foster Dulles A611

ANDREW CARNEGIE ISSUE

Carnegie (1835-1919), industrialist & philanthropist.

1960, Nov. 25
1171 A610 4c deep claret .25 .25

JOHN FOSTER DULLES MEMORIAL ISSUE

Dulles (1888-1959), Secretary of State (1953-59).

1960, Dec. 6
1172 A611 4c dull violet .25 .25

ECHO I — COMMUNICATIONS FOR PEACE ISSUE

World's 1st communications satellite, Echo I, placed in orbit by the Natl. Aeronautics and Space Admin., Aug. 12, 1960.

Radio Waves Connecting Echo I and Earth A612

1960, Dec. 15 *Perf. 11x10½*
1173 A612 4c deep violet .25 .25

CHAMPION OF LIBERTY ISSUE

Mohandas K. Gandhi, leader in India's struggle for independence.

Mahatma Gandhi — A613

1961, Jan. 26 *Perf. 10½x11*
1174 A613 4c red orange .25 .25

GIORI PRESS PRINTING
Perf. 11

1175 A613 8c car, ultra & ocher .25 .25

RANGE CONSERVATION ISSUE

Issued to stress the importance of range conservation and to commemorate the meeting of the American Society of Range Management. "The Trail Boss" from a drawing by Charles M. Russell is the Society's emblem.

The Trail Boss and Modern Range A614

1961, Feb. 2 *Perf. 11*
1176 A614 4c blue, slate & brown orange .25 .25

HORACE GREELEY ISSUE

Horace Greeley (1811-1872), Publisher and Editor — A615

ROTARY PRESS PRINTING

1961, Feb. 3 *Perf. 10½x11*
1177 A615 4c dull violet .25 .25

CIVIL WAR CENTENNIAL ISSUE

Centenaries of the firing on Fort Sumter (No. 1178), the Battle of Shiloh (No. 1179), the Battle of Gettysburg (No. 1180), the Battle of the Wilderness (No. 1181) and the surrender at Appomattox (No. 1182).

Sea Coast Gun of 1861 A616

Rifleman at Shiloh, 1862 A617

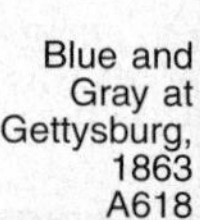

Blue and Gray at Gettysburg, 1863 A618

Battle of the Wilderness, 1864 A619

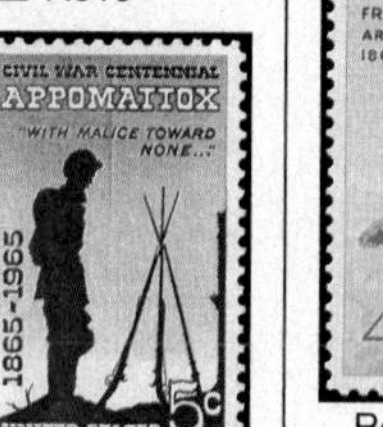

Appomattox, 1865 — A620

1961-65 ***Perf. 11x10½***

1178 A616 4c light green .25 .25
1179 A617 4c black, *peach blossom* .25 .25

GIORI PRESS PRINTING

Plates of 200 subjects in four panes of 50.

Perf. 11

1180 A618 5c gray & blue .25 .25
1181 A619 5c dk red & black .25 .25
1182 A620 5c Prus. blue & blk .30 .25
a. Horiz. pair, imperf. vert. *4,500.*
Nos. 1178-1182 (5) 1.30 1.25

Issued: #1178-1182, 4/12; 4/7/62; 7/1/63; 5/5/64; 4/9/65.

KANSAS STATEHOOD, 100th ANNIV.

Sunflower, Pioneer Couple and Stockade A621

1961, May 10 ***Perf. 11***

1183 A621 4c brown, dark red & green, *yellow* .25 .25

SENATOR NORRIS ISSUE

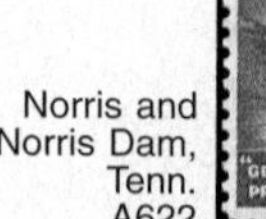

Norris and Norris Dam, Tenn. A622

ROTARY PRESS PRINTING

1961, July 11 ***Perf. 11x10½***

1184 A622 4c blue green .25 .25

NAVAL AVIATION, 50th ANNIV.

Navy's First Plane (Curtiss A-1 of 1911) and Naval Air Wings A623

1961, Aug. 20

1185 A623 4c blue .25 .25

WORKMEN'S COMPENSATION ISSUE

50th anniv. of the 1st successful Workmen's Compensation Law, enacted by the Wisconsin legislature.

Scales of Justice, Factory, Worker and Family — A624

1961, Sept. 4 ***Perf. 10½x11***

1186 A624 4c ultramarine, *grayish* .25 .25

Remington's "Smoke Signal" — A625

Sun Yat-sen — A626

FREDERIC REMINGTON ISSUE

Remington (1861-1909), artist of the West. The design is from an oil painting, Amon Carter Museum of Western Art, Fort Worth, Texas.

GIORI PRESS PRINTING

1961, Oct. 4 ***Perf. 11***

1187 A625 4c multicolored .25 .25

REPUBLIC OF CHINA ISSUE

50th anniversary of the Republic of China.

ROTARY PRESS PRINTING

1961, Oct. 10 ***Perf. 10½x11***

1188 A626 4c blue .25 .25

Basketball A627

Student Nurse Lighting Candle A628

NAISMITH — BASKETBALL ISSUE

Honoring basketball and James Naismith (1861-1939), Canada-born director of physical education, who invented the game in 1891 at Y.M.C.A. College, Springfield, Mass.

1961, Nov. 6

1189 A627 4c brown .25 .25

NURSING ISSUE

Issued to honor the nursing profession.

GIORI PRESS PRINTING

1961, Dec. 28 ***Perf. 11***

1190 A628 4c bl, grn, org & blk .25 .25

NEW MEXICO STATEHOOD, 50th ANNIV.

Shiprock A629

1962, Jan. 6

1191 A629 4c lt. blue, maroon & bister .25 .25

ARIZONA STATEHOOD, 50th ANNIV.

Giant Saguaro Cactus — A630

1962, Feb. 14

1192 A630 4c carmine, violet blue & green .25 .25

PROJECT MERCURY ISSUE

1st orbital flight of a US astronaut, Lt. Col. John H. Glenn, Jr., Feb. 20, 1962.

"Friendship 7" Capsule and Globe A631

1962, Feb. 20

1193 A631 4c dark blue & yellow .25 .25

Imperfs. are printers waste.

MALARIA ERADICATION ISSUE

World Health Organization's drive to eradicate malaria.

Great Seal of U.S. and WHO Symbol A632

1962, Mar. 30

1194 A632 4c blue & bister .25 .25

Charles Evans Hughes A633

Space Needle and Monorail A634

CHARLES EVANS HUGHES ISSUE

Hughes (1862-1948), Governor of New York, Chief Justice of the US.

ROTARY PRESS PRINTING

1962, Apr. 11 ***Perf. 10½x11***

1195 A633 4c black, *buff* .25 .25

SEATTLE WORLD'S FAIR ISSUE

"Century 21" International Exposition, Seattle, Wash., Apr. 21-Oct. 21.

GIORI PRESS PRINTING

1962, Apr. 25 ***Perf. 11***

1196 A634 4c red & dark blue .25 .25

LOUISIANA STATEHOOD, 150th ANNIV.

Riverboat on the Mississippi A635

1962, Apr. 30

1197 A635 4c blue, dark slate green & red .25 .25

HOMESTEAD ACT, CENTENARY

Sod Hut and Settlers A636

ROTARY PRESS PRINTING

1962, May 20 ***Perf. 11x10½***

1198 A636 4c slate .25 .25

GIRL SCOUTS ISSUE

50th anniversary of the Girl Scouts of America.

Senior Girl Scout & Flag A637

1962, July 24

1199 A637 4c rose red .25 .25

SENATOR BRIEN McMAHON ISSUE

McMahon (1903-52) of Connecticut had a role in opening the way to peaceful uses of atomic energy through the Atomic Energy Act establishing the Atomic Energy Commission.

Brien McMahon & Atomic Diagram A638

1962, July 28

1200 A638 4c purple .25 .25

APPRENTICESHIP ISSUE

National Apprenticeship Program and 25th anniv. of the National Apprenticeship Act.

Machinist Handing Micrometer to Apprentice A639

1962, Aug. 31

1201 A639 4c blk, *yellow bister* .25 .25

SAM RAYBURN ISSUE

Sam Rayburn and Capitol — A640

GIORI PRESS PRINTING

1962, Sept. 16 ***Perf. 11***

1202 A640 4c dark blue & red brown .25 .25

DAG HAMMARSKJOLD ISSUE

UN Headquarters & Dag Hammarskjold, U.N. Sec. Gen., 1953-61 — A641

1962, Oct. 23

1203 A641 4c black, brown & yellow .25 .25
a. Yellow inverted, on cover, see note —

No. 1203a can only be collected on a cover postmarked before Nov. 16, 1962 (the date the Hammarskjold Special Printing, No. 1204, was issued), or tied on dated piece (unique used pair). Covers are known machine postmarked Cuyahoga Falls, Ohio, Nov. 14, 1962, and notarized in the lower left corner by George W. Schwartz, Notary Public. Other covers are reported postmarked Oct. 26, 1962, Brooklyn, NY, Vanderveer Station. Unaddressed, uncacheted first day covers also exist. Other covers may exist. All covers must be accompanied by certificates from recognized expertizing committees. Value of first-day cover, $3,000.

An unused pane of 50 was signed in the selvage by ten well-known philatelists attesting to its genuineness. This pane was donated to the American Philatelic Society in 1987.

An unknown number of "first day covers" exist bearing Artmaster cachets. These were contrived using examples of No. 1204.

Hammarskjold Special Printing

1962, Nov. 16

1204 A641 4c black, brown & yel (yellow inverted) .25 .25

No. 1204 was issued following discovery of No. 1203 with yellow background inverted.

CHRISTMAS ISSUE

Wreath and Candles — A642

1962, Nov. 1

1205 A642 4c green & red .25 .25

HIGHER EDUCATION ISSUE

Higher education's role in American cultural and industrial development and the centenary celebrations of the signing of the law creating land-grant colleges and universities.

Map of U.S. and Lamp A643

1962, Nov. 14

1206 A643 4c blue green & black .25 .25

WINSLOW HOMER ISSUE

Homer (1836-1910), painter, showing his oil, "Breezing Up," which hangs in the National Gallery, Washington, D.C.

"Breezing Up" — A644

1962, Dec. 15

1207 A644 4c multicolored .25 .25
a. Horiz. pair, imperf. btwn. and at right *7,000.*

FLAG ISSUE

Flag over White House — A645

1963-66

1208 A645 5c blue & red .25 .25
a. Tagged ('68) .25 .25
b. Horiz. pair, imperf. between, tagged *2,250.*

Beware of pairs with faint blind perfs between offered as No. 1208b.

REGULAR ISSUE

Andrew Jackson A646

George Washington A650

John J. Pershing A651

ROTARY PRESS PRINTING

1961-66 ***Perf. 11x10½***

1209 A646 1c green ('63) .25 .25
a. Tagged ('66) .25 .25
1213 A650 5c dk gray blue .25 .25
a. Booklet pane of 5 + label 3.00 *2.00*
b. Tagged ('63) .50 .25
c. As "a," tagged, ('63) 2.25 *1.50*
d. Horiz. pair, imperf. between, in #1213a with foldover or miscut *1,500.*
1214 A651 8c brown ('61) .25 .25

See Luminescence note after No. 1053.

Three different messages are found on the label in No. 1213a, and two messages on that of No. 1213c.

No. 1213d resulted from a paper foldover after perforating and before cutting into panes.

Unused catalogue numbers were left vacant for additional denominations.

COIL STAMPS
(Rotary Press)

1962-66 ***Perf. 10 Vertically***

1225 A646 1c green ('63) .40 .25
a. Tagged ('66) .40 .25
1229 A650 5c dk blue gray 1.50 .25
a. Tagged ('63) 2.50 .25
b. Imperf., pair *325.00*

CAROLINA CHARTER ISSUE

Tercentenary of the Carolina Charter granting to 8 Englishmen lands extending coast-to-coast roughly along the present border of Virginia to the north and Florida to the south. Original charter on display at Raleigh.

First Page of Carolina Charter A662

GIORI PRESS PRINTING

1963, Apr. 6 ***Perf. 11***

1230 A662 5c dark carmine & brown .25 .25

FOOD FOR PEACE-FREEDOM FROM HUNGER ISSUE

American "Food for Peace" program and the "Freedom from Hunger" campaign of the FAO.

Wheat — A663

1963, June 4

1231 A663 5c green, buff & red .25 .25

WEST VIRGINIA STATEHOOD, 100th ANNIV.

Map of West Virginia & State Capitol A664

1963, June 20

1232 A664 5c green, red & black .25 .25

EMANCIPATION PROCLAMATION ISSUE

Centenary of Lincoln's Emancipation Proclamation freeing about 3,000,000 slaves in 10 southern states.

Severed Chain A665

1963, Aug. 16

1233 A665 5c dark blue, black & red .25 .25

ALLIANCE FOR PROGRESS ISSUE

2nd anniv. of the Alliance for Progress, which aims to stimulate economic growth and raise living standards in Latin America.

Alliance Emblem A666

1963, Aug. 17

1234 A666 5c ultramarine & green .25 .25

CORDELL HULL ISSUE

Hull (1871-1955), Secretary of State (1933-44).

Cordell Hull (1871-1955), Sec. of State (1933-44) — A667

ROTARY PRESS PRINTING

1963, Oct. 5 ***Perf. 10½x11***

1235 A667 5c blue green .25 .25

ELEANOR ROOSEVELT ISSUE

Mrs. Franklin D. Roosevelt (1884-1962).

Mrs. Franklin D. Roosevelt (1884-1962) A668

1963, Oct. 11 ***Perf. 11x10½***

1236 A668 5c bright purple .25 .25

SCIENCE ISSUE

Honoring the sciences and in connection with the centenary of the Natl. Academy of Science.

"The Universe" A669

GIORI PRESS PRINTING

1963, Oct. 14 ***Perf. 11***

1237 A669 5c Prussian blue & black .25 .25

CITY MAIL DELIVERY ISSUE

Centenary of free city mail delivery.

Letter Carrier, 1863 — A670

1963, Oct. 26 **Tagged**

1238 A670 5c gray, dark blue & red .25 .25

RED CROSS CENTENARY ISSUE

A671

1963, Oct. 29

1239 A671 5c bluish black & red .25 .25

CHRISTMAS ISSUE

Natl. Christmas Tree & White House — A672

1963, Nov. 1

1240 A672 5c dk bl, bluish blk & red .25 .25
a. Tagged .65 .50
b. Horiz. pair, imperf between *7,500.*
c. Red missing (PS) —

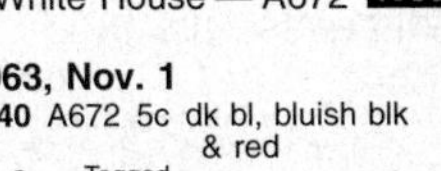

Columbia Jays — A673

Sam Houston — A674

JOHN JAMES AUDUBON ISSUE

Audubon (1785-1851), ornithologist and artist. The birds pictured are actually Collie's magpie jays. See No. C71.

1963, Dec. 7
1241 A673 5c dk blue & multi .25 .25

SAM HOUSTON ISSUE

Houston (1793-1863), soldier, president of Texas, US senator.

ROTARY PRESS PRINTING

1964, Jan. 10 ***Perf. 10½x11***
1242 A674 5c black .25 .25

CHARLES M. RUSSELL ISSUE

Russell (1864-1926), painter. The design is from a painting, Thomas Gilcrease Institute of American History and Art, Tulsa, Okla.

"Jerked Down" A675

GIORI PRESS PRINTING

1964, Mar. 19 ***Perf. 11***
1243 A675 5c multicolored .25 .25

NEW YORK WORLD'S FAIR ISSUE

New York World's Fair, 1964-65.

Mall with Unisphere & "Rocket Thrower," by Donald De Lue — A676

ROTARY PRESS PRINTING

1964, Apr. 22 ***Perf. 11x10½***
1244 A676 5c blue green .25 .25
a. All color omitted —

On No. 1244a, a clear albino impression of the design is present.

JOHN MUIR ISSUE

Muir (1838-1914), naturalist and conservationist.

John Muir (1838-1914), naturalist and conservationist and Redwood Forest — A677

GIORI PRESS PRINTING

1964, Apr. 29 ***Perf. 11***
1245 A677 5c brown, green, yellow green & olive .25 .25

KENNEDY MEMORIAL ISSUE

President John Fitzgerald Kennedy, (1917-1963).

Pres. John F. Kennedy (1917-63) and Eternal Flame A678

ROTARY PRESS PRINTING

1964, May 29 ***Perf. 11x10½***
1246 A678 5c blue gray .25 .25

NEW JERSEY TERCENTENARY ISSUE

300th anniv. of English colonization of New Jersey. The design is from a mural by Howard Pyle in the Essex County Courthouse, Newark, N.J.

Philip Carteret Landing at Elizabethtown & Map of New Jersey — A679

1964, June 15 ***Perf. 10½x11***
1247 A679 5c brt. ultramarine .25 .25

NEVADA STATEHOOD, 100th ANNIV.

Virginia City and Map of Nevada A680

GIORI PRESS PRINTING

1964, July 22 ***Perf. 11***
1248 A680 5c red, yellow & blue .25 .25

Flag A681

William Shakespeare A682

REGISTER AND VOTE ISSUE

Campaign to draw more voters to the polls.

1964, Aug. 1
1249 A681 5c dark blue & red .25 .25

SHAKESPEARE ISSUE

William Shakespeare (1564-1616).

ROTARY PRESS PRINTING

1964, Aug. 14 ***Perf. 10½x11***
1250 A682 5c black brown, *tan* .25 .25

DOCTORS MAYO ISSUE

Dr. William James Mayo (1861-1939) and his brother, Dr. Charles Horace Mayo (1865-1939), surgeons who founded the Mayo Foundation for Medical Education and Research in affiliation with the Univ. of Minnesota at Rochester. Heads on stamp are from a sculpture by James Earle Fraser.

Drs. William and Charles Mayo — A683

1964, Sept. 11
1251 A683 5c green .25 .25

AMERICAN MUSIC ISSUE

50th anniv. of the founding of the American Society of Composers, Authors and Publishers (ASCAP).

Lute, Horn, Laurel, Oak and Music Score A684

GIORI PRESS PRINTING

1964, Oct. 15 ***Perf. 11***
Gray Paper with Blue Threads
1252 A684 5c red, black & blue .25 .25
a. Blue omitted *750.00*
b. Blue missing (PS) —

Beware of examples offered as No. 1252a which have traces of blue.

HOMEMAKERS ISSUE

Honoring American women as homemakers and for the 50th anniv. of the passage of the Smith-Lever Act. By providing economic experts under an extension service of the U.S. Dept. of Agriculture, this legislation helped to improve homelife.

Farm Scene Sampler A685

Engraved (Giori Press); Background Lithographed

1964, Oct. 26
1253 A685 5c multicolored .25 .25

CHRISTMAS ISSUE

Holly A686

Mistletoe A687

Poinsettia A688

Sprig of Conifer A689

GIORI PRESS PRINTING

1964, Nov. 9
1254 A686 5c green, car & black .25 .25
a. Tagged .75 .50
b. Printed on gummed side *1,850.*
1255 A687 5c car, green & black .25 .25
a. Tagged .75 .50
1256 A688 5c car, green & black .25 .25
a. Tagged .75 .50
1257 A689 5c black, green & car .25 .25
a. Tagged .75 .50
b. Block of 4, #1254-1257 1.00 1.00
c. Block of 4, tagged 3.00 2.25

Tagged stamps issued Nov. 10.
No. 1254b resulted from a paper foldover before printing and perforating.

VERRAZANO-NARROWS BRIDGE ISSUE

Opening of the Verrazano-Narrows Bridge connecting Staten Island and Brooklyn.

Verrazano-Narrows Bridge and Map of NY Bay — A690

ROTARY PRESS PRINTING

1964, Nov. 21 ***Perf. 10½x11***
1258 A690 5c blue green .25 .25

FINE ARTS ISSUE

Abstract Design by Stuart Davis A691

GIORI PRESS PRINTING

1964, Dec. 2 ***Perf. 11***
1259 A691 5c ultra., black & dull red .25 .25

AMATEUR RADIO ISSUE

Issued to honor the radio amateurs on the 50th anniversary of the American Radio Relay League.

Radio Waves and Dial — A692

ROTARY PRESS PRINTING

1964, Dec. 15 ***Perf. 10½x11***
1260 A692 5c red lilac .25 .25

BATTLE OF NEW ORLEANS ISSUE

Battle of New Orleans, Chalmette Plantation, Jan. 8-18, 1815, established 150 years of peace and friendship between the US and Great Britain.

General Andrew Jackson and Sesquicentennial Medal — A693

GIORI PRESS PRINTING

1965, Jan. 8 ***Perf. 11***
1261 A693 5c deep carmine, violet blue & gray .25 .25

Discus Thrower A694

Microscope and Stethoscope A695

PHYSICAL FITNESS-SOKOL ISSUE

Publicizing the importance of physical fitness and for the centenary of the founding of the Sokol (athletic) organization in America.

1965, Feb. 15
1262 A694 5c maroon & black .25 .25

CRUSADE AGAINST CANCER ISSUE

Issued to publicize the "Crusade Against Cancer" and to stress the importance of early diagnosis.

1965, Apr. 1
1263 A695 5c black, purple & red orange .25 .25

CHURCHILL MEMORIAL ISSUE

Sir Winston Spencer Churchill (1874-1965), British statesman and World War II leader.

Winston Churchill — A696

ROTARY PRESS PRINTING

1965, May 13 ***Perf. 10½x11***

1264 A696 5c black .25 .25

MAGNA CARTA ISSUE

750th anniversary of the Magna Carta, the basis of English and American common law.

Procession of Barons and King John's Crown A697

GIORI PRESS PRINTING

1965, June 15 ***Perf. 11***

1265 A697 5c black, yellow ocher & red lilac .25 .25

INTERNATIONAL COOPERATION YEAR

ICY, 1965, and 20th anniv. of the UN.

ICY Emblem A698

1965, June 26

1266 A698 5c dull blue & black .25 .25

SALVATION ARMY ISSUE

Centenary of the founding of the Salvation Army by William Booth in London.

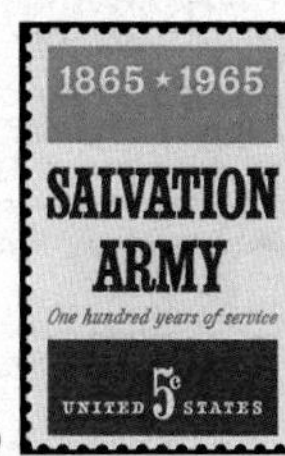

A699

1965, July 2

1267 A699 5c red, black & dark blue .25 .25

A700

A701

DANTE ISSUE

Dante Alighieri (1265-1321), Italian poet.

ROTARY PRESS PRINTING

1965, July 17 ***Perf. 10½x11***

1268 A700 5c maroon, *tan* .25 .25

HERBERT HOOVER ISSUE

President Herbert Clark Hoover, (1874-1964).

1965, Aug. 10

1269 A701 5c rose red .25 .25

ROBERT FULTON ISSUE

Fulton (1765-1815), inventor of the 1st commercial steamship.

Robert Fulton & Clermont A702

GIORI PRESS PRINTING

1965, Aug. 19 ***Perf. 11***

1270 A702 5c black & blue .25 .25

FLORIDA SETTLEMENT ISSUE

400th anniv. of the settlement of Florida, and the 1st permanent European settlement in the continental US, St. Augustine, Fla.

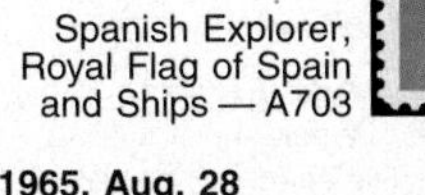

Spanish Explorer, Royal Flag of Spain and Ships — A703

1965, Aug. 28

1271 A703 5c red, yel & blk .25 .25

a. Yellow omitted *200.00*

See Spain No. 1312.

TRAFFIC SAFETY ISSUE

Issued to publicize traffic safety and the prevention of traffic accidents.

Traffic Signal A704

1965, Sept. 3

1272 A704 5c emer, red & blk .25 .25

JOHN SINGLETON COPLEY ISSUE

Copley (1738-1815), painter. The portrait of the artist's daughter is from the oil painting "The Copley Family," which hangs in the National Gallery of Art, Washington, D.C.

Elizabeth Clarke Copley — A705

1965, Sept. 17

1273 A705 5c blk, brn & olive .25 .25

INTERNATIONAL TELECOMMUNICATION UNION, 100th ANNIV.

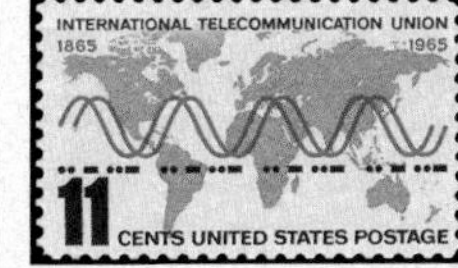

Gall Projection World Map & Radio Sine Wave A706

1965, Oct. 6

1274 A706 11c blk, car & bister .35 .25

ADLAI STEVENSON ISSUE

Adlai Ewing Stevenson (1900-65), governor of Illinois, US ambassador to the UN.

Adlai E. Stevenson — A707

LITHOGRAPHED, ENGRAVED (Giori)

1965, Oct. 23

1275 A707 5c pale bl, blk, car & vio bl .25 .25

CHRISTMAS ISSUE

Angel with Trumpet — A708

GIORI PRESS PRINTING

1965, Nov. 2

1276 A708 5c carmine, dark olive green & bister .25 .25

a. Tagged .75 .25

PROMINENT AMERICANS ISSUE

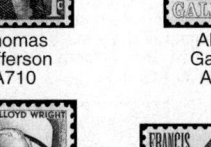

Thomas Jefferson A710

Albert Gallatin A711

Frank Lloyd Wright & Guggenheim Museum A712

Francis Parkman A713

Lincoln A714

Washington A715

Washington (Redrawn) A715a

Franklin D. Roosevelt A716

Albert Einstein A717

Andrew Jackson — A718

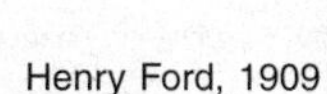

Henry Ford, 1909 Model T — A718a

John F. Kennedy A719

Oliver Wendell Holmes A720

Type 3 — A720a

George Catlett Marshall A721

Frederick Douglass A722

John Dewey — A723

Thomas Paine — A724

Lucy Stone A725

Eugene O'Neill A726

John Bassett Moore — A727

Types of 15c:

I. Necktie barely touches coat at bottom; crosshatching of tie strong and complete. Flag of "5" is true horizontal. Crosshatching of "15" is colorless when visible.

II. Necktie does not touch coat at bottom; LL to UR crosshatching lines strong, UL to LR lines very faint. Flag of "5" slants down slightly at right. Crosshatching of "15" is colored and visible when magnified.

III. Used only for No. 1288B; smaller in overall size and "15¢" is ¾mm closer to head.

ROTARY PRESS PRINTING

1965-78 ***Perf. 11x10½, 10½x11***

1278 A710 1c green, tagged .25 .25

a. Booklet pane of 8 1.00 .75

b. Bklt. pane of 4+2 labels .80 .60

c. Untagged (Bureau precanceled) 6.25 1.25

1279 A711 1¼c light green .25 .25

1280 A712 2c dk blue gray, tagged .25 .25

a. Bklt. pane of 5 + label 1.25 .80

b. Untagged (Bureau precanceled) 1.35 .40

c. Bklt. pane of 6 1.00 .75

1281 A713 3c violet, tagged .25 .25

a. Untagged (Bureau precanceled) 3.00 .75

1282 A714 4c black .25 .25

a. Tagged .25 .25

1283 A715 5c blue .25 .25

a. Tagged .25 .25

1283B A715a 5c blue, tagged .25 .25
d. Untagged (Bureau precanceled) 12.50 1.00

No. 1283B is redrawn; highlights, shadows softened.

1284 A716 6c gray brown .25 .25
a. Tagged .25 .25
b. Booklet pane of 8 1.50 1.00
c. Bklt. pane of 5+ label 1.50 1.00
d. Horiz. pair, imperf. between *2,350.*
1285 A717 8c violet .25 .25
a. Tagged .25 .25
1286 A718 10c lilac, tagged .25 .25
b. Untagged (Bureau precanceled) 55.00 1.75
1286A 718a 12c black, tagged .25 .25
c. Untagged (Bureau precanceled) 4.75 1.00
1287 A719 13c brown, tagged .30 .25
a. Untagged (Bureau precanceled) 6.00 1.00
1288 A720 15c mag, type I, tagged .30 .25
a. Untagged (Bureau precanceled) .75 .75
d. Type II .55 .25

Imperforates exist from printer's waste.
Values for No. 1288a are for the bars-only precancel. Also exists with city precancels, and worth more thus.

Perf. 10 on 2 or 3 Sides

1288B A720a 15c magenta, type III .35 .25
c. Booklet pane of 8 2.80 1.75
e. As "c," vert. imperf. between *1,750.*

No. 1288B issued in booklets only. All stamps have one or two straight edges. Plates made from redrawn die.

Perf. 11x10½, 10½x11

1289 A721 20c deep olive .40 .25
a. Tagged .40 .25
b. black olive .50 .25
c. As "a," double impression —
1290 A722 25c rose lake .55 .25
a. Tagged .45 .25
b. 25c magenta *25.00* —

Shades of No. 1290 rose lake exist that tend toward magenta, but are not. Competent identification is important for No. 1290b.

1291 A723 30c red lilac .65 .25
a. Tagged .50 .25
1292 A724 40c blue black .80 .25
a. Tagged .75 .25
1293 A725 50c rose magenta 1.00 .25
a. Tagged .80 .25
1294 A726 $1 dull purple 2.25 .25
a. Tagged 1.75 .25
b. $1 black violet 100.00 —
1295 A727 $5 gray black 10.00 2.25
a. Tagged 8.75 2.00
Nos. 1278-1295 (21) 19.35 7.25

Issued (without tagging) — 1965: 4c, 11/19.
1966: 5c, 2/22; 6c, 1/29; 8c, 3/14; $5, 12/3.
1967: 1¼c, 1/30; 20c, 10/24; 25c, 2/14; $1, 10/16.
1968: 30c, 10/21; 40c, 1/29; 50c, 8/13.
Dates for tagged: 1965: 4c, 12/1.
1966: 2c, 6/8; 5c, 2/23; 6c, 12/29; 8c, 7/6.
1967: 3c, 9/16; #1283B, 11/17; #1284b, 12/28; 10c, 3/15; 13c, 5/29.
1968: 1c, #1284c, 1/12; #1280a, 1/8; 12c, 7/30; 15c, 3/8.
1973: 20c, 25c, 30c, 40c, 50c, $1, $5, 4/3.
1978: No. 1288B, 6/14.

COIL STAMPS

Perf. 10 Horizontally

1966-81 **Tagged**
1297 A713 3c violet .25 .25
a. Imperf., pair 22.50
b. Untagged (Bureau precanceled) .40 .25
c. As "b," imperf. pair 6.00 —
1298 A716 6c gray brown .25 .25
a. Imperf., pair *1,750.*

Franklin D. Roosevelt — A727a

Perf. 10 Vertically

1299 A710 1c green .25 .25
a. Untagged (Bureau precanceled) 8.00 1.75
b. Imperf., pair *22.50* —
1303 A714 4c black .25 .25
a. Untagged (Bureau precanceled) 8.75 .75
b. Imperf., pair *650.00*
1304 A715 5c blue .25 .25
a. Untagged (Bureau precanceled) 6.50 .65
b. Imperf., pair *115.00*
e. As "a," imperf., pair *250.00*
f. Tagging omitted (not Bureau precanceled) — —

No. 1304b is valued in the grade of fine.
No. 1304e is precanceled Mount Pleasant, Iowa. Also exists from Chicago, Illinois; value $1,500 for pair.

1304C A715a 5c blue .25 .25
d. Imperf., pair *375.00*
1305 A727a 6c gray brown .25 .25
a. Imperf., pair 55.00
b. Untagged (Bureau precanceled) 20.00 1.00
1305E A720 15c magenta, type I .25 .25
f. Untagged (Bureau precanceled) 32.50 —
g. Imperf., pair, type I 20.00
h. Pair, imperf. between 125.00
i. Type II 1.50 .25
j. Imperf., pair, type II *55.00*
1305C A726 $1 dull purple 3.25 .40
d. Imperf., pair *1,500.*
Nos. 1297-1305C (9) 5.25 2.40

Issued: 1c, 1/12/68; 3c, 11/4/75; 4c, 5/28/66; #1304, 9/8/66; 6c, #1298, 12/28/67; #1305, 2/28/68;
$1, 1/12/73; 15c, 6/14/78.

MIGRATORY BIRD TREATY ISSUE

Migratory Birds over Canada-U.S. Border — A728

GIORI PRESS PRINTING

1966, Mar. 16 ***Perf. 11***
1306 A728 5c black, crimson & dark blue .25 .25

HUMANE TREATMENT OF ANIMALS ISSUE

Issued to promote humane treatment of all animals and for the centenary of the American Society for the Prevention of Cruelty to Animals.

Mongrel A729

LITHOGRAPHED, ENGRAVED (Giori)

1966, Apr. 9
1307 A729 5c orange brown & black .25 .25

Sesquicentennial Seal — A730

Clown — A731

INDIANA STATEHOOD, 150th ANNIV.

GIORI PRESS PRINTING

1966, Apr. 16
1308 A730 5c ocher, brown & violet blue .25 .25

AMERICAN CIRCUS ISSUE

Issued to honor the American Circus on the centenary of the birth of John Ringling.

1966, May 2
1309 A731 5c multicolored .25 .25

SIXTH INTERNATIONAL PHILATELIC EXHIBITION ISSUES

Sixth International Philatelic Exhibition (SIPEX), Washington, D.C., May 21-30.

Stamped Cover A732

LITHOGRAPHED, ENGRAVED (Giori)

1966
1310 A732 5c multicolored .25 .25

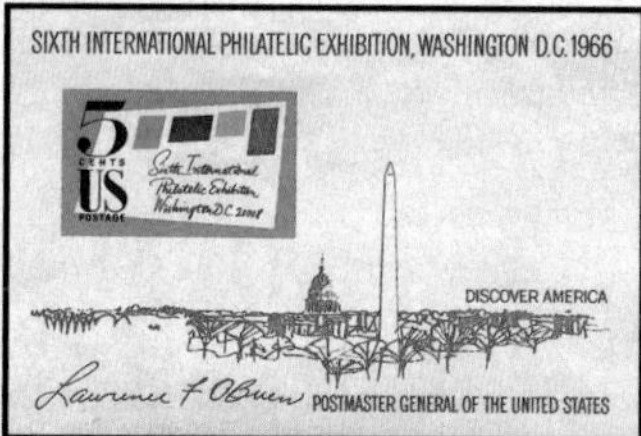

A733

SOUVENIR SHEET

Imperf

1311 A733 5c multicolored .25 .25

No. 1311 measures 108x74mm.

"Freedom" Checking "Tyranny" A734

Polish Eagle and Cross A735

BILL OF RIGHTS, 175th ANNIV.

GIORI PRESS PRINTING

1966, July 1 ***Perf. 11***
1312 A734 5c carmine, dark & light blue .25 .25

POLISH MILLENNIUM ISSUE

Adoption of Christianity in Poland, 1000th anniv.

ROTARY PRESS PRINTING

1966, July 30 ***Perf. 10½x11***
1313 A735 5c red .25 .25

Tagging Extended

During 1966, experimental use of tagged stamps was extended to the Cincinnati Postal Region covering offices in Indiana, Kentucky and Ohio. To supply these offices about 12 percent of the following nine issues (Nos. 1314-1322) were tagged.

NATIONAL PARK SERVICE ISSUE

50th anniv. of the Natl. Park Service of the Interior Dept. The design "Parkscape U.S.A." identifies Natl. Park Service facilities.

National Park Service Emblem A736

LITHOGRAPHED, ENGRAVED (Giori)

1966, Aug. 25 ***Perf. 11***
1314 A736 5c yellow, black & green .25 .25
a. Tagged .35 .35

MARINE CORPS RESERVE ISSUE

US Marine Corps Reserve founding, 50th anniv.

A737

1966, Aug. 29
1315 A737 5c black, bister, red & ultra .25 .25
a. Tagged .40 .25
b. Black & bister (engraved) missing (EP) *16,000.*

GENERAL FEDERATION OF WOMEN'S CLUBS ISSUE

75 years of service by the General Federation of Women's Clubs.

Women of 1890 and 1966 A738

GIORI PRESS PRINTING

1966, Sept. 12
1316 A738 5c black, pink & blue .25 .25
a. Tagged .40 .25

AMERICAN FOLKLORE ISSUE

Johnny Appleseed

Issued to honor Johnny Appleseed (John Chapman 1774-1845), who wandered over 100,000 square miles planting apple trees, and who gave away and sold seedlings to Midwest pioneers.

Johnny Appleseed — A739

1966, Sept. 24
1317 A739 5c green, red & black .25 .25
a. Tagged .40 .25

BEAUTIFICATION OF AMERICA ISSUE

Issued to publicize President Johnson's "Plant for a more beautiful America" campaign.

Jefferson Memorial A740

1966, Oct. 5
1318 A740 5c emerald, pink & black .25 .25
a. Tagged .40 .25

Compare with No. 4716c.

Central U.S. Map With Great River Road — A741

Statue of Liberty & "Old Glory" — A742

GREAT RIVER ROAD ISSUE

Issued to publicize the 5,600-mile Great River Road connecting New Orleans with Kenora, Ontario, and following the Mississippi most of the way.

LITHOGRAPHED, ENGRAVED (Giori)

1966, Oct. 21

1319 A741 5c vermilion, yellow, blue & green .25 .25
a. Tagged .45 .25

SAVINGS BOND-SERVICEMEN ISSUE

25th anniv. of US Savings Bonds, and honoring American servicemen.

1966, Oct. 26

1320 A742 5c red, dk bl, lt bl & blk .25 .25
a. Tagged .40 .25
b. Red, dark blue & black missing (EP) *4,000.*
c. Dark blue (engr.) missing (EP) *5,000.*

CHRISTMAS ISSUE

Madonna and Child — A743

Modeled after "Madonna and Child with Angels," by the Flemish artist Hans Memling (c.1430-1494), Mellon Collection, National Gallery of Art, Washington, D.C.

1966, Nov. 1

1321 A743 5c multicolored .25 .25
a. Tagged .40 .25

MARY CASSATT ISSUE

Cassatt (1844-1926), painter. The painting "The Boating Party" is in the Natl. Gallery of Art, Washington, D.C.

"The Boating Party" A744

GIORI PRESS PRINTING

1966, Nov. 17

1322 A744 5c multicolored .25 .25
a. Tagged .40 .25

Cassatt (1844-1926), painter. The original painting is in the Natl. Gallery of Art, Washington, DC.

NATIONAL GRANGE ISSUE

Centenary of the founding of the National Grange, American farmers' organization.

Grange Poster, 1870 — A745

1967, Apr. 17

1323 A745 5c org, yel, brn, grn & blk .25 .25

Phosphor Tagging

From No. 1323 onward, all postage issues are tagged, unless otherwise noted.

Tagging Omitted

Inadvertent omissions of tagging occurred on Nos. 1238, 1278, 1281, 1298 and 1305. In addition many tagged issues from 1967 on exist with tagging unintentionally omitted. These errors are listed in the *Scott Specialized Catalogue of United States Stamps and Covers.*

CANADA CENTENARY ISSUE

Centenary of Canada's emergence as a nation.

Canadian Landscape A746

1967, May 25

1324 A746 5c lt bl, dp grn, ultra, olive & blk .25 .25

ERIE CANAL ISSUE

150th anniversary of the Erie Canal ground-breaking ceremony at Rome, N.Y. The canal links Lake Erie and New York City.

Stern of Early Canal Boat A747

LITHOGRAPHED, ENGRAVED (Giori)

1967, July 4

1325 A747 5c ultra., greenish blue, black & crimson .25 .25

"SEARCH FOR PEACE" — LIONS ISSUE

Issued to publicize the search for peace. "Search for Peace" was the theme of an essay contest for young men and women sponsored by Lions International on its 50th anniversary.

Peace Dove A748

GIORI PRESS PRINTING

1967, July 5

Gray Paper with Blue Threads

1326 A748 5c blue, red & black .25 .25

HENRY DAVID THOREAU ISSUE

Henry David Thoreau (1817-1862), Writer — A749

1967, July 12

1327 A749 5c carmine, black & blue green .25 .25

NEBRASKA STATEHOOD, 100th ANNIV.

Hereford Steer and Corn A750

LITHOGRAPHED, ENGRAVED (Giori)

1967, July 29

1328 A750 5c dark red brown, lemon & yellow .25 .25

VOICE OF AMERICA ISSUE

25th anniv. of the radio branch of the United States Information Agency (USIA).

Radio Transmission Tower and Waves — A751

1967, Aug. 1

1329 A751 5c red, blue, black & carmine .25 .25

AMERICAN FOLKLORE ISSUE

Davy Crockett (1786-1836), frontiersman, hunter, and congressman from Tennessee who died at the Alamo.

Davy Crockett & Scrub Pines A752

1967, Aug. 17

1330 A752 5c green, black, & yellow .25 .25
a. Vertical pair, imperf. between *7,000.*
b. Green (engr.) missing (FO) —
c. Black & green (engr.) missing (FO) —

A foldover on a pane of No. 1330 resulted in one example each of Nos. 1330b-1330c. Part of the colors appear on the back of the selvage and one freak stamp. An engraved black-and-green-only impression appears on the gummed side of one almost-complete "stamp."

ACCOMPLISHMENTS IN SPACE ISSUE

US accomplishments in space. Printed with continuous design in horizontal rows of 5. In the left panes the astronaut stamp is 1st, 3rd and 5th, the spaceship 2nd and 4th. This arrangement is reversed in the right panes.

Space-Walking Astronaut — A753

Gemini 4 Capsule and Earth A754

1967, Sept. 29

1331 A753 5c multicolored .55 .25
1332 A754 5c multicolored .55 .25
b. Pair, #1331-1332 1.10 *1.25*

View of Model City — A755

Finnish Coat of Arms — A756

URBAN PLANNING ISSUE

Publicizing the importance of Urban Planning in connection with the Intl. Conf. of the American Institute of Planners, Washington, D.C., Oct. 1-6.

1967, Oct. 2

1333 A755 5c dark blue, light blue & black .25 .25

FINNISH INDEPENDENCE, 50th ANNIV.

ENGRAVED (Giori)

1967, Oct. 6

1334 A756 5c blue .25 .25

THOMAS EAKINS ISSUE

Eakins (1844-1916), painter and sculptor. The painting is in the Natl. Gallery of Art, Washington, D.C.

"The Biglin Brothers Racing" (Sculling on Schuylkill River, Philadelphia) — A757

Printed by Photogravure & Color Co., Moonachie, N.J.

PHOTOGRAVURE

1967, Nov. 2 *Perf. 12*

1335 A757 5c gold & multicolored .25 .25

CHRISTMAS ISSUE

Madonna and Child, by Hans Memling — A758

LITHOGRAPHED, ENGRAVED (Giori)

1967, Nov. 6 *Perf. 11*

1336 A758 5c multicolored .25 .25

See note on painting above No. 1321.

MISSISSIPPI STATEHOOD, 150th ANNIV.

Magnolia A759

GIORI PRESS PRINTING

1967, Dec. 11

1337 A759 5c brt grnsh bl, grn & red brn .25 .25

FLAG ISSUE

Flag and White House — A760

1968, Jan. 24

Size: 19x22mm

1338 A760 6c dk bl, red & grn .25 .25
- *k.* Vert. pair, imperf. btwn. 300.00 150.00
- *s.* Red missing (FO) —
- *u.* Vert. pair, imperf horiz. 325.00
- *v.* All color omitted —

No. 1338s is unique.

Beware of regumming on No. 1338u. Most examples have had the gum washed off to make it difficult or impossible to detect blind perfs. Check carefully for blind perfs. Value is for pair with original gum.

On No. 1338v, an albino impression of the engraved plate is present.

COIL STAMP

MULTICOLOR HUCK PRESS

1969, May 30 ***Perf. 10 Vertically***

Size: 18¼x21mm

1338A A760 6c dk bl, red & grn .25 .25
- *b.* Imperf., pair 350.00

MULTICOLOR HUCK PRESS

1970-71 ***Perf. 11x10½***

Size: 18¼x21mm

1338D A760 6c dk bl, red & grn .25 .25
- *e.* Horiz. pair, imperf. between 115.00

1338F A760 8c dk bl, red & slate grn ('71) .25 .25
- *i.* Imperf., vert. pair 35.00
- *j.* Horiz. pair, imperf. between 45.00
- *p.* Slate green omitted 300.00
- *t.* Horiz. pair, imperf. vertically —

Issued: #1338D, 8/7/70

COIL STAMP

MULTICOLOR HUCK PRESS

1971, May 10 ***Perf. 10 Vertically***

Size: 18¼x21mm

1338G A760 8c dk bl, red & slate grn .30 .25
- *h.* Imperf., pair 45.00

Farm House & Fields of Ripening Grain — A761

Map of North & South America — A762

ILLINOIS STATEHOOD, 150th ANNIV.

LITHOGRAPHED, ENGRAVED (Giori)

1968, Feb. 12 ***Perf. 11***

1339 A761 6c dk blue, blue, red & ocher .25 .25

HEMISFAIR '68 ISSUE

HemisFair '68 exhibition, San Antonio, Texas, Apr. 6-Oct. 6, for the 250th anniv. of San Antonio.

1968, Mar. 30

1340 A762 6c blue, rose red & white .25 .25
- *a.* White omitted 925.00

AIRLIFT ISSUE

Eagle Holding Pennant A763

1968, Apr. 4 **Untagged**

1341 A763 $1 sepia, dk. blue, ocher & brown red 2.00 1.25

Issued to pay for airlift of parcels from and to U.S. ports to servicemen overseas and in Alaska, Hawaii and P.R. Valid for all regular postage.

On Apr. 26, 1969, the POD ruled that henceforth No. 1341 "may be used toward paying the postage or fees for special services on airmail articles."

"SUPPORT OUR YOUTH" — ELKS ISSUE

Support Our Youth program, and honoring the Benevolent and Protective Order of Elks, which extended its youth service program in observance of its centennial year.

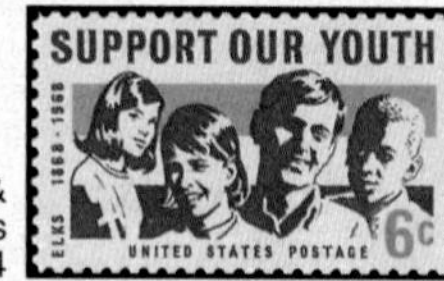

Girls & Boys A764

1968, May 1 **Tagged**

1342 A764 6c ultramarine & orange red .25 .25

Policeman and Small Boy — A765

Eagle Weather Vane — A766

LAW AND ORDER ISSUE

Publicizing the policeman as protector and friend and to encourage respect for law and order.

GIORI PRESS PRINTING

1968, May 17

1343 A765 6c chalky blue, black & red .25 .25

REGISTER AND VOTE ISSUE

Campaign to draw more voters to the polls. The weather vane is from an old house in the Russian Hill section of San Francisco, Cal.

LITHOGRAPHED, ENGRAVED (Giori)

1968, June 27

1344 A766 6c black, yellow & orange .25 .25

HISTORIC FLAG SERIES

Flags carried by American colonists and by citizens of the new United States. Printed se-tenant in vertical columns of 10. The flag sequence on the 2 upper panes is as listed. On the 2 lower panes the sequence is reversed with the Navy Jack in the 1st row and the Fort Moultrie flag in the 10th.

Ft. Moultrie, 1776 A767

Ft. McHenry, 1795-1818 A768

Washington's Cruisers, 1775 — A769

Bennington, 1777 A770

Rhode Island, 1775 A771

First Stars and Stripes, 1777 A772

Bunker Hill, 1775 A773

Grand Union, 1776 A774

Philadelphia Light Horse, 1775 — A775

First Navy Jack, 1775 A776

ENGR. (Giori) (#1345-1348, 1350);
ENGR. & LITHO. (#1349, 1351-1354)

1968, July 4

1345 A767 6c dark blue .40 .25
1346 A768 6c dark blue & red .40 .25
1347 A769 6c dark blue & olive green .30 .25
1348 A770 6c dark blue & red .30 .25
1349 A771 6c dark blue, yellow & red .30 .25
1350 A772 6c dark blue & red .30 .25
1351 A773 6c dark blue, olive green & red .30 .25
1352 A774 6c dark blue & red .30 .25
1353 A775 6c dark blue, yellow & red .30 .25
1354 A776 6c dark blue, red & yellow .30 .25
- *a.* Strip of ten, #1345-1354 3.25 3.25
- *b.* #1345b-1354b, any single, tagging omitted 65.00
- *c.* As "a," imperf 4,500.

WALT DISNEY ISSUE

Walt Disney (1901-1966), cartoonist, film producer and creator of Mickey Mouse.

Disney and Children of the World — A777

Printed by Achrovure Division of Union-Camp Corp., Englewood, N.J.

PHOTOGRAVURE

1968, Sept. 11 ***Perf. 12***

1355 A777 6c multicolored .40 .25
- *a.* Ocher omitted ("Walt Disney," "6c," etc.) 400.00 —
- *b.* Vert. pair, imperf. horiz. 575.00
- *c.* Imperf., pair 425.00
- *d.* Black omitted 1,850.
- *e.* Horiz. pair, imperf. between 3,500.
- *f.* Blue omitted 1,850.

FATHER MARQUETTE ISSUE

Father Jacques Marquette (1637-1675), French Jesuit missionary, who together with Louis Jolliet explored the Mississippi River and its tributaries.

Father Marquette and Louis Jolliet Exploring the Mississippi A778

LITHOGRAPHED, ENGRAVED (Giori)

1968, Sept. 20 ***Perf. 11***

1356 A778 6c black, apple green & orange brown .25 .25

AMERICAN FOLKLORE ISSUE

Daniel Boone (1734-1820), frontiersman and trapper.

Pennsylvania Rifle, Powder Horn, Tomahawk Pipe & Knife — A779

LITHOGRAPHED, ENGRAVED (Giori)

1968, Sept. 26

1357 A779 6c yel, dp yel, mar & blk .25 .25

ARKANSAS RIVER NAVIGATION ISSUE

Opening of the Arkansas River to commercial navigation.

Ship's Wheel, Power Transmission Tower & Barge — A780

1968, Oct. 1

1358 A780 6c bright blue, dark blue & black .25 .25

LEIF ERIKSON ISSUE

Leif Erikson, 11th century Norse explorer, called the 1st European to set foot on the American continent, at a place he called Vinland. The statue by the American sculptor A. Stirling Calder is in Reykjavik, Iceland.

Leif Erikson, by Stirling Calder — A781

1968, Oct. 9

1359 A781 6c light gray brown & black brown .25 .25

The luminescent element is in the light gray brown ink of the background. The engraved parts were printed on a rotary currency press.

CHEROKEE STRIP ISSUE

75th anniversary of the opening of the Cherokee Strip to settlers, Sept. 16, 1893.

Homesteaders Racing to Cherokee Strip — A782

ROTARY PRESS PRINTING

1968, Oct. 15 ***Perf. 11x10½***
1360 A782 6c brown .25 .25

JOHN TRUMBULL ISSUE

Trumbull (1756-1843), painter. The stamp shows Lt. Thomas Grosvenor and his attendant Peter Salem. The painting hangs at Yale University.

Detail from "The Battle of Bunker's Hill" — A783

LITHOGRAPHED, ENGRAVED (Giori)

1968, Oct. 18 ***Perf. 11***
1361 A783 6c multicolored .25 .25
b. Black (engr.) missing (FO) *11,000.* —

WATERFOWL CONSERVATION ISSUE

Wood Ducks A784

1968, Oct. 24
1362 A784 6c blk & multi .25 .25
a. Vertical pair, imperf. between *225.00* —
b. Red & dark blue omitted *425.00*
c. Red omitted *1,500.*

Dangerous fakes exist of Nos. 1362b and 1362c. Authentication by experts is required.

Gabriel, from van Eyck's Annunciation A785

Chief Joseph, by Cyrenius Hall A786

CHRISTMAS ISSUE

"The Annunciation" by the 15th century Flemish painter Jan van Eyck is in the National Gallery of Art, Washington, D.C.

ENGRAVED (Multicolor Huck press)

1968, Nov. 1
1363 A785 6c multicolored .25 .25
a. Untagged .25 .25
b. Imperf., pair, tagged *150.00*
c. Light yellow omitted *50.00* —
d. Imperf., pair, untagged *225.00*

AMERICAN INDIAN ISSUE

Honoring the American Indian and to celebrate the opening of the Natl. Portrait Gallery, Washington, D.C. Chief Joseph (Indian name, Thunder Traveling over the Mountains), a leader of the Nez Percé, was born in eastern Oregon about 1840 and died at the Colesville Reservation in Washington State in 1904.

LITHOGRAPHED, ENGRAVED (Giori)

1968, Nov. 4
1364 A786 6c black & multi .25 .25

BEAUTIFICATION OF AMERICA ISSUE

Publicizing the Natural Beauty Campaign for more beautiful cities, parks, highways and streets. In the left panes Nos. 1365 and 1367 appear in 1st, 3rd and 5th place, Nos. 1366 and 1368 in 2nd and 4th place. This arrangement is reversed in the right panes.

Capitol, Azaleas and Tulips A787

Washington Monument, Potomac River and Daffodils A788

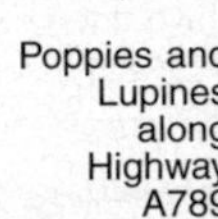

Poppies and Lupines along Highway A789

Blooming Crab Apples along Street A790

1969, Jan. 16 **Tagged**
1365 A787 6c multicolored .25 .25
1366 A788 6c multicolored .25 .25
1367 A789 6c multicolored .25 .25
1368 A790 6c multicolored .25 .25
a. Block of 4, #1365-1368 1.00 *1.25*

Compare with Nos. 4716a, 4716b, 4716d, 4716e.

Eagle from Great Seal of U.S. — A791

July Fourth, by Grandma Moses — A792

AMERICAN LEGION, 50th ANNIV.

1969, Mar. 15
1369 A791 6c red, blue & black .25 .25

AMERICAN FOLKLORE ISSUE

Grandma Moses (Anna Mary Robertson Moses, 1860-1961), primitive painter of American life.

1969, May 1
1370 A792 6c multicolored .25 .25
a. Horizontal pair, imperf. between *125.00* —
b. Engraved black ("6c U.S. Postage") & Prus. blue ("Grandma Moses") omitted *500.00*

Beware of pairs with blind perfs. being offered as No. 1370a.

No. 1370b often comes with mottled or disturbed gum. Such stamps sell for about two-thirds as much as examples with perfect gum.

APOLLO 8 ISSUE

Apollo 8 mission, which 1st put men into orbit around the moon, Dec. 21-27, 1968. The astronauts were: Col. Frank Borman, Capt. James Lovell and Maj. William Anders.

Moon Surface and Earth — A793

LITHOGRAPHED, ENGRAVED (Giori)

1969, May 5
1371 A793 6c black, blue & ocher .25 .25

Imperfs. exist from printer's waste.

W.C. HANDY ISSUE

Handy (1873-1958), jazz musician and composer.

W. C. Handy (1873-1958), Jazz Musician and Composer — A794

LITHOGRAPHED, ENGRAVED (Giori)

1969, May 17
1372 A794 6c violet, deep lilac & blue .25 .25

CALIFORNIA SETTLEMENT, 200th ANNIV.

Carmel Mission Belfry — A795

1969, July 16
1373 A795 6c orange, red, black & light blue .25 .25
b. Red (engr.) missing (CM) *400.00*

JOHN WESLEY POWELL ISSUE

Powell (1834-1902), geologist who explored the Green and Colorado Rivers 1869-75, and ethnologist.

Powell Exploring Colorado River A796

1969, Aug. 1
1374 A796 6c black, ocher & light blue .25 .25

ALABAMA STATEHOOD, 150th ANNIV.

Camellia & Yellow-shafted Flicker — A797

1969, Aug. 2
1375 A797 6c mag, rose red, yel, dk, grn & brn .25 .25

BOTANICAL CONGRESS ISSUE

11th Intl. Botanical Cong., Seattle, Wash., Aug. 24-Sept. 2. In left panes Nos. 1376 and 1378 appear in 1st, 3rd and 5th place; Nos. 1377 and 1379 in 2nd and 4th place. This arrangement is reversed in right panes.

Douglas Fir (Northwest) A798

Lady's-slipper (Northeast) — A799

Ocotillo (Southwest) — A800

Franklinia (Southeast) A801

1969, Aug. 23
1376 A798 6c multicolored .35 .25
1377 A799 6c multicolored .35 .25
1378 A800 6c multicolored .35 .25
1379 A801 6c multicolored .35 .25
a. Block of 4, #1376-1379 1.40 *1.75*

DARTMOUTH COLLEGE CASE ISSUE

150th anniv. of the Dartmouth College Case, which Daniel Webster argued before the Supreme Court, reasserting the sanctity of contracts.

Daniel Webster & Dartmouth Hall — A802

ROTARY PRESS PRINTING

1969, Sept. 22 ***Perf. 10½x11***
1380 A802 6c green .25 .25

PROFESSIONAL BASEBALL, 100th ANNIV.

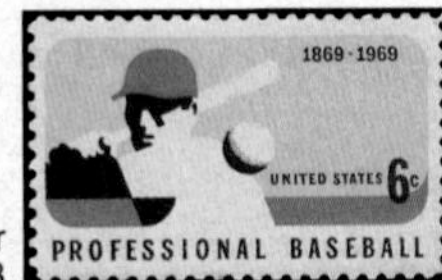

Batter A803

LITHOGRAPHED, ENGRAVED (Giori)

1969, Sept. 24 ***Perf. 11***
1381 A803 6c yellow, red, black & green .50 .25
a. Black omitted ("1869-1969, United States, 6c, Professional Baseball") *700.00*
c. Double impression of black (engr.) *5,750.*

INTERCOLLEGIATE FOOTBALL, 100th ANNIV.

Football Player & Coach A804

1969, Sept. 26

1382 A804 6c red & green .25 .25
b. Vert. pair, imperf horiz. *5,750.*

The engraved parts were printed on a rotary currency press.

No. 1382b is unique.

DWIGHT D. EISENHOWER ISSUE

Dwight D. Eisenhower A805

Designed by Robert J. Jones; photograph by Bernie Noble.

GIORI PRESS PRINTING

1969, Oct. 14

1383 A805 6c blue, black & red .25 .25
b. Blue ("U.S. 6c Postage") missing (PS) —

CHRISTMAS ISSUE

The painting, painted about 1870 by an unknown primitive artist, is the property of the N.Y. State Historical Association, Cooperstown, N.Y.

Winter Sunday in Norway, Maine A806

ENGRAVED (Multicolor Huck)

1969, Nov. 3 ***Perf. 11x10½***

1384 A806 6c dark green & multicolored .25 .25
Precancel .60 .25
b. Imperf., pair *600.00*
c. Light green omitted 25.00
d. Light green, red & yellow omitted *650.00* —
e. Yellow omitted *1,750.*
g. Red & yellow omitted *2,500.*
h. Light green and yellow omitted *500.00*
i. Light green and red omitted —
j. Vert. pair, top stamp Baltimore precancel, bottom stamp precancel missing (FO) —
k. Baltimore precancel printed on gum side *150.00*
l. Baltimore precancel, vert. pair, top stamp missing precancel, bottom stamp precancel printed inverted on reverse (FO) *500.00*
m. Inverted Baltimore precancel *600.00*
n. Baltimore precancel printed inverted on reverse (FO) *150.00*
p. Double impression of New Haven precancel —
q. Inverted Memphis precancel —

The precancel value applies to the least expensive of experimental precancels printed locally in four cities, on tagged stamps, with the names between lines 4½mm apart: in black or green, "ATLANTA, GA" and in green only "BALTIMORE, MD," "MEMPHIS, TN" and "NEW HAVEN, CT." They were sold freely to the public and could be used on any class of mail at all post offices during the experimental program and thereafter.

Most examples of No. 1384c show orange where the offset green was. Value is for this variety. Examples without orange sell for more.

On No. 1384i, almost all of the yellow is also omitted. Do not confuse with No. 1384d.

Cured Child — A807

HOPE FOR CRIPPLED ISSUE

Issued to encourage the rehabilitation of crippled children and adults and to honor the National Society for Crippled Children and Adults (Easter Seal Society) on its 50th anniversary.

LITHOGRAPHED, ENGRAVED (Giori)

1969, Nov. 20 ***Perf. 11***

1385 A807 6c multicolored .25 .25

WILLIAM M. HARNETT ISSUE

"Old Models" — A808

Harnett (1848-1892), painter. The painting hangs in the Museum of Fine Arts, Boston.

1969, Dec. 3

1386 A808 6c multicolored .25 .25
a. Red (engr.) missing (CM) —

NATURAL HISTORY ISSUE

Centenary of the American Museum of Natural History, New York City. Nos. 1387-1388 alternate in 1st row, Nos. 1389-1390 in 2nd row. This arrangement is repeated throughout the pane.

American Bald Eagle — A809

African Elephant Herd — A810

Tlingit Chief in Haida Ceremonial Canoe — A811

Brontosaurus, Stegosaurus & Allosaurus — A812

1970, May 6

1387 A809 6c multicolored .25 .25
1388 A810 6c multicolored .25 .25
1389 A811 6c multicolored .25 .25
1390 A812 6c multicolored .25 .25
a. Block of 4, #1387-1390 1.00 *1.00*

MAINE STATEHOOD, 150th ANNIV.

The painting hangs in the Metropolitan Museum of Art, New York City.

Lighthouse at Two Lights, Maine A813

1970, July 9 **Tagged** ***Perf. 11***

1391 A813 6c black & multi .25 .25

WILDLIFE CONSERVATION ISSUE

American Buffalo A814

ROTARY PRESS PRINTING

1970, July 20 ***Perf. 11x10½***

1392 A814 6c black, *light brown* .25 .25

REGULAR ISSUE
Dwight David Eisenhower

Dot between "R" and "U" A815

No dot between "R" and "U" — A815a

Benjamin Franklin A816

USPS Emblem A817

Fiorello H. LaGuardia A817a

Ernie Pyle Journalist USA 16c

Ernest Taylor Pyle — A818

Dr. Elizabeth Blackwell A818a

Amadeo P. Giannini A818b

ROTARY PRESS PRINTING

1970-74

1393 A815 6c dk blue gray .25 .25
a. Booklet pane of 8 2.00 2.00
b. Booklet pane of 5 + label 1.50 1.50
c. Untagged (Bureau precanceled) 12.75 3.00

Perf. 10½x11

1393D A816 7c bright blue ('73) .25 .25
e. Untagged (Bureau precanceled) 4.25 1.00

GIORI PRESS PRINTING

Perf. 11

1394 A815a 8c blk, red & bl gray ('71) .25 .25
b. Red missing (PS) *150.00*
c. Red missing (FO) *1,250.*
d. Red and blue missing (PS) —
e. Red and blue missing (FO) *1,000.*
f. All colors and tagging missing (FO) *1,000.*
g. Printed on gum side, tagged *1,000.*

No. 1394f must be collected se-tenant with No. 1394c, 1394e, or with a partially printed No. 1394.

ROTARY PRESS PRINTING

Perf. 11x10½ on 2 or 3 Sides

1395 A815 8c deep claret ('71) .25 .25
a. Booklet pane of 8 2.00 2.00
b. Booklet pane of 6 1.50 1.50
c. Booklet pane of 4 +2 ('72) 1.65 1.10
d. Booklet pane of 7 + label ('72) 1.90 1.90
e. Vert. pair, imperf. between, in #1395a or 1395d with foldover *600.00*

No. 1395 was issued only in booklets.

At least 4 pairs of No. 1395e are recorded from 3 panes (one No. 1395a and two 1395d) with different foldover patterns. A pane of No. 1395d also is known with a foldover resulting in a vertical pair of stamp and label, imperf between.

PHOTOGRAVURE (Andreotti)

Plates of 400 subjects in four panes of 100.

Perf. 11x10½

1396 A817 8c multi ('71) .25 .25

ROTARY PRESS PRINTING

1397 A817a 14c gray brown ('72) .25 .25
a. Untagged (Bureau precanceled) *125.00* 17.50
1398 A818 16c brown ('72) .35 .25
a. Untagged (Bureau precanceled) 22.50 5.00
1399 A818a 18c violet ('74) .35 .25
1400 A818b 21c green ('73) .40 .25
Nos. 1393-1400 (9) 2.60 2.25

Issued: 6c, 8/6/70; 7c, 10/20/72; #1394-1395, 5/10/71; #1396, 7/1/71; 14c, 4/24/72; 16c, 5/7/71; 18c, 1/23/74; 21c, 6/27/73.

COIL STAMPS
ROTARY PRESS PRINTING

1970-71 ***Perf. 10 Vert.***

1401 A815 6c dk blue gray .25 .25
a. Untagged (Bureau precanceled) 19.50 3.00
b. Imperf., pair *2,500.*
1402 A815 8c dp claret ('71) .25 .25
a. Imperf., pair 37.50
b. Untagged (Bureau precanceled) 6.75 .75
c. Pair, imperf. between *6,250.*

No. 1401b often found with small faults and/or without gum. Such examples sell for considerably less.

Issue dates: 6c, Aug. 6; 8c, May 10, 1971.

EDGAR LEE MASTERS ISSUE

A819

LITHOGRAPHED, ENGRAVED (Giori)

1970, Aug. 22 ***Perf. 11***

1405 A819 6c black & olive bister .25 .25

WOMAN SUFFRAGE ISSUE

50th anniversary of the 19th Amendment, which gave the vote to women.

Suffragettes, 1920 & Woman Voter, 1970 — A820

GIORI PRESS PRINTING

1970, Aug. 26

1406 A820 6c blue .25 .25

SOUTH CAROLINA ISSUE

300th anniv. of the founding of Charles Town (Charleston), the 1st permanent settlement of South Carolina. Against a background of pine wood the line drawings of the design represent the economic and historic development of South Carolina: the spire of St. Philip's Church, Capitol, state flag, a ship, 17th century man and woman, a Fort Sumter cannon, barrels, cotton, tobacco and yellow jasmine.

Symbols of South Carolina A821

LITHOGRAPHED, ENGRAVED (Giori)

1970, Sept. 12

1407 A821 6c bister, black & red .25 .25

STONE MOUNTAIN MEMORIAL ISSUE

Dedication of the Stone Mountain Confederate Memorial, Georgia, May 9, 1970.

A822

GIORI PRESS PRINTING

1970, Sept. 19

1408 A822 6c gray .25 .25

FORT SNELLING ISSUE

150th anniv. of Fort Snelling, Minnesota, an important outpost for the opening of the Northwest.

Fort Snelling, Keelboat & Tepees A823

LITHOGRAPHED, ENGRAVED (Giori)

1970, Oct. 17

1409 A823 6c yellow & multi .25 .25

ANTI-POLLUTION ISSUE

Issued to focus attention on the problems of pollution.

In left panes Nos. 1410 and 1412 appear in 1st, 3rd and 5th place; Nos. 1411 and 1413 in 2nd and 4th place. This arrangement is reversed in right panes.

Globe and Wheat A824

Globe and City A825

Globe and Bluegill A826

Globe and Seagull A827

PHOTOGRAVURE

1970, Oct. 28 *Perf. 11x10½*

1410 A824 6c multicolored .25 .25
1411 A825 6c multicolored .25 .25
1412 A826 6c multicolored .25 .25
1413 A827 6c multicolored .25 .25
a. Block of 4, #1410-1413 1.10 *1.25*

CHRISTMAS ISSUE

In left panes Nos. 1415 and 1417 appear in 1st, 3rd and 5th place; Nos. 1416 and 1418 in 2nd and 4th place. This arrangement is reversed in right panes.

Nativity — A828

Tin and Cast-iron Locomotive A829

Toy Horse on Wheels A830

Mechanical Tricycle A831

Doll Carriage A832

1970, Nov. 5 *Perf. 10½x11*

1414 A828 6c multicolored .25 .25
a. Precanceled .25 .25
b. Black omitted *400.00*
c. As "a," blue omitted *1,250.*
d. Type II .25 .25
e. Type II, precanceled .25 .25

No. 1414 has a slightly blurry impression, snowflaking in the sky and no gum breaker ridges. No. 1414d has shiny surfaced paper, sharper impression, no snowflaking and vertical and horizontal gum breaker ridges.

No. 1414a has a slightly blurry impression, snowflaking in the sky, no gum breaker ridges and the precancel is grayish black. No. 1414e has sharper impression, no snowflaking, gum breaker ridges and the precancel is intense black.

Perf. 11x10½

1415 A829 6c multicolored .30 .25
a. Precanceled .75 .25
b. Black omitted *2,250.*
1416 A830 6c multicolored .30 .25
a. Precanceled .75 .25
b. Black omitted *2,250.*
c. Imperf., pair (#1416, 1418) *2,500.*
1417 A831 6c multicolored .30 .25
a. Precanceled .75 .25
b. Black omitted *2,250.*
1418 A832 6c multicolored .30 .25
a. Precanceled .75 .25
b. Block of 4, #1415-1418 1.25 *1.40*
c. As "b," precanceled 3.25 *3.50*
d. Black omitted *2,250.*
e. As "b," black omitted *10,000.*
f. As "b," black omitted on #1417 & 1418 *4,500.*
g. P# block of 8, black omitted on #1415 & 1416 *4,500.*
Nos. 1415-1418 (4) 1.20 1.00

Nos. 1415-1418 and 1415a-1418a are known both without gum breaker ridges (common) and with gum breaker ridges (scarce).

The precanceled stamps, Nos. 1414a-1418a, were furnished to 68 cities. The plates include two straight (No. 1414a) or two wavy (Nos. 1415a-1418a) black lines that make up the precancellation. Unused values are for stamps with gum and used values are for stamps with an additional cancellation or without gum.

UNITED NATIONS, 25th ANNIV.

"UN" & UN Emblem A833

LITHOGRAPHED, ENGRAVED (Giori)

1970, Nov. 20 *Perf. 11*

1419 A833 6c blk, verm & ultra .25 .25

LANDING OF THE PILGRIMS ISSUE

350th anniv. of the landing of the Mayflower.

Mayflower & Pilgrims — A834

1970, Nov. 21

1420 A834 6c blk, org, yel, magenta, bl & brn .25 .25
a. Orange & yellow omitted *575.00*

DISABLED AMERICAN VETERANS AND SERVICEMEN ISSUE

No. 1421 for the 50th anniv. of the Disabled Veterans of America Organization; No. 1422 honors the contribution of servicemen, particularly those who were prisoners of war, missing or killed in action. Nos. 1421-1422 are printed se-tenant in horizontal rows of 10.

A835

A836

1970, Nov. 24

1421 A835 6c dark blue, red & multicolored .25 .25

ENGRAVED

1422 A836 6c dark blue, black & red .25 .25
a. Pair, #1421-1422 .50 .50

Ewe and Lamb A837

Douglas MacArthur A838

AMERICAN WOOL INDUSTRY ISSUE

450th anniv. of the introduction of sheep to the North American continent and the beginning of the American wool industry.

Plates of 200 subjects in four panes of 50.

1971, Jan. 19

1423 A837 6c multicolored .25 .25
b. Teal blue ("United States") missing (CM) *300.00*

GEN. DOUGLAS MacARTHUR ISSUE

MacArthur (1880-1964), Chief of Staff, Supreme Commander for the Allied Powers in the Pacific Area during World War II and Supreme Commander in Japan after the war.

GIORI PRESS PRINTING

1971, Jan. 26

1424 A838 6c black, red & dark blue .25 .25
a. Red missing (PS) —
c. Blue missing (PS) —

BLOOD DONOR ISSUE

Salute to blood donors and spur to increased participation in the blood donor program.

Giving Blood Saves Lives A839

LITHOGRAPHED, ENGRAVED (Giori)

1971, Mar. 12

1425 A839 6c bl, scarlet & ind .25 .25

MISSOURI STATEHOOD, 150th ANNIV.

The stamp design shows a Pawnee facing a hunter-trapper and a group of settlers. It is from a mural by Thomas Hart Benton in the Harry S Truman Library, Independence, Mo.

"Independence and the Opening of the West" — A840

PHOTOGRAVURE (Andreotti)

1971, May 8 *Perf. 11x10½*

1426 A840 8c multicolored .25 .25

See note on Andreotti printings and their color control markings in Information for Collectors under Printing, Photogravure.

WILDLIFE CONSERVATION ISSUE

Nos. 1427-1428 alternate in first row, Nos. 1429-1430 in second row. This arrangement repeated throughout pane.

Trout A841

Alligator — A842

Polar Bear, Cubs A843

California Condor — A844

LITHOGRAPHED, ENGRAVED (Giori)

1971, June 12 ***Perf. 11***

1427 A841 8c multicolored .25 .25
- *a.* Red omitted 1,250.
- *b.* Green (engr.) omitted —

1428 A842 8c multicolored .25 .25
1429 A843 8c multicolored .25 .25
1430 A844 8c multicolored .25 .25
- *a.* Block of 4, #1427-1430 1.00 1.00
- *b.* As "a," light green & dark green omitted from #1427-1428 3,750.
- *c.* As "a," red omitted from #1427, 1429-1430 3,000.

ANTARCTIC TREATY ISSUE

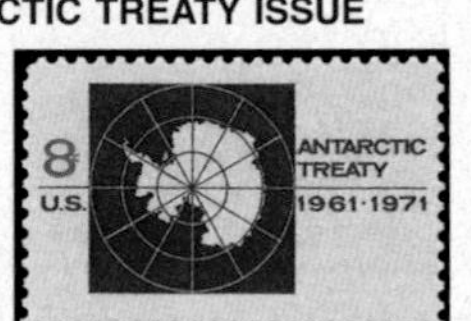

Map of Antarctica A845

Adapted from emblem on official documents of Consultative Meetings.

GIORI PRESS PRINTING

1971, June 23

1431 A845 8c red & dark blue .25 .25
- *b.* Both colors missing (EP) 500.00

No. 1431b should be collected se-tenant with a normal stamp and/or a partially printed stamp.

AMERICAN REVOLUTION BICENTENNIAL

Bicentennial Commission Emblem — A846

LITHOGRAPHED, ENGRAVED (Giori)

1971, July 4

1432 A846 8c gray, red, blue & black .25 .25
- *a.* Gray & black missing (EP) 450.00
- *b.* Gray ("U.S. Postage 8c") missing (EP) 700.00

JOHN SLOAN ISSUE

John Sloan (1871-1951), painter. The painting hangs in the Phillips Gallery, Washington, D.C.

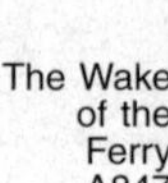

The Wake of the Ferry A847

1971, Aug. 2

1433 A847 8c multicolored .25 .25
- *b.* Red engr. ("John Sloan" and "8") missing (CM) 950.00

SPACE ACHIEVEMENT DECADE ISSUE

Decade of space achievements and the Apollo 15 moon exploration mission, July 26-Aug. 7. In the left panes the earth and sun stamp is 1st, 3rd and 5th, the rover 2nd and 4th. This arrangement is reversed in the right panes.

Earth, Sun, Landing Craft on Moon A848

Lunar Rover A849

1971, Aug. 2

1434 A848 8c blk, bl, gray, yel & red .25 .25
1435 A849 8c blk, bl, gray, yel & red .25 .25
- *b.* Pair, #1434-1435 .50 .50
- *d.* As "b," blue & red (litho.) omitted 900.00

Emily Elizabeth Dickinson A850

Sentry Box, Morro Castle, San Juan A851

EMILY DICKINSON ISSUE

1971, Aug. 28

1436 A850 8c **multi**, *greenish* .25 .25
- *a.* Black & olive (engr.) omitted 500.00
- *b.* Pale rose missing (EP) 5,500.
- *c.* Red omitted —

SAN JUAN ISSUE

450th anniversary of San Juan, Puerto Rico.

1971, Sept. 12

1437 A851 8c pale brn, blk, yel, red brn & dk brn .25 .25
- *b.* Dark brown (engr.) omitted —

VALUES FOR HINGED STAMPS AFTER NO. 771

This catalogue does not value unused stamps after No. 771 in hinged condition. Hinged unused stamps from No. 772 to the present are worth considerably less than the values given for unused stamps, which are for never-hinged examples.

Young Woman Drug Addict — A852

PREVENT DRUG ABUSE ISSUE

Drug Abuse Prevention Week, Oct. 3-9.

PHOTOGRAVURE (Andreotti)

1971, Oct. 4 ***Perf. 10½x11***

1438 A852 8c blue, deep blue & black .25 .25

CARE ISSUE

25th anniversary of CARE, a US-Canadian Cooperative for American Relief Everywhere.

1971, Oct. 27

1439 A853 8c blue, blk, vio & red lilac .25 .25
- *a.* Black omitted 1,600.

HISTORIC PRESERVATION ISSUE

Nos. 1440-1441 alternate in 1st row, Nos. 1442-1443 in 2nd row. This arrangement is repeated throughout the pane.

Decatur House, Washington, DC — A854

Whaling Ship Charles W. Morgan, Mystic, Conn. — A855

Cable Car, San Francisco — A856

San Xavier del Bac Mission, Tucson, Ariz. — A857

LITHOGRAPHED, ENGRAVED (Giori)

1971, Oct. 29 **Tagged** ***Perf. 11***

1440 A854 8c blk brn & ocher, *buff* .25 .25
1441 A855 8c blk brn & ocher, *buff* .25 .25
1442 A856 8c blk brn & ocher, *buff* .25 .25
1443 A857 8c blk brn & ocher, *buff* .25 .25
- *a.* Block of 4, #1440-1443 1.00 *1.00*
- *b.* As "a," black brown omitted 900.00
- *c.* As "a," ocher omitted 2,500.

CHRISTMAS ISSUE

Hands Reaching for CARE — A853

Adoration of the Shepherds, by Giorgione A858

Partridge in a Pear Tree, by Jamie Wyeth A859

No. 1444 after a painting by Giorgione in the National Gallery of Art, Washington D.C.

PHOTOGRAVURE (Andreotti)

1971, Nov. 10 ***Perf. 10½x11***

1444 A858 8c gold & multi .25 .25
- *a.* Gold omitted 350.00

1445 A859 8c dark green, red & multicolored .25 .25

Sidney Lanier (1842-1881) A860

Peace Corps Poster, by David Battle A861

SIDNEY LANIER ISSUE

Lanier (1842-81), poet, musician, lawyer, educator.

GIORI PRESS PRINTING

1972, Feb. 3 ***Perf. 11***

1446 A860 8c black, brown & light blue .25 .25

PEACE CORPS ISSUE

PHOTOGRAVURE (Andreotti)

1972, Feb. 11 ***Perf. 10½x11***

1447 A861 8c dark blue, light blue & red .25 .25

NATIONAL PARKS CENTENNIAL ISSUE

Centenary of Yellowstone National Park, the 1st National Park, and of the entire National Park System. See No. C84.

Hulk of Ship A862

Cape Hatteras Lighthouse A863

Laughing Gulls on Driftwood A864

Laughing Gulls and Dune A865

Wolf Trap Farm, Vienna, Va. — A866

Old Faithful, Yellowstone A867

Mt. McKinley, Alaska A868

LITHOGRAPHED, ENGRAVED (Giori)

1972 ***Perf. 11***

Plates of 400 subjects in 4 panes of 100 each

1448 A862 2c black & multi .25 .25
1449 A863 2c black & multi .25 .25
1450 A864 2c black & multi .25 .25
1451 A865 2c black & multi .25 .25
a. Block of 4, #1448-1451 .50 .50
b. As "a," black (litho.) omitted *1,250.*
1452 A866 6c black & multi .25 .25
1453 A867 8c blk, bl, brn & multi .25 .25
1454 A868 15c black & multi .30 .25
b. Yellow omitted *3,500.*

FAMILY PLANNING ISSUE

Family — A869

1972, Mar. 18

1455 A869 8c blk & multi .25 .25
a. Yellow omitted *375.00*
c. Dark brown missing (FO) *9,000.*

AMERICAN BICENTENNIAL ISSUE
Colonial American Craftsmen

In left panes Nos. 1456 and 1458 appear in 1st, 3rd and 5th place; Nos. 1457 and 1459 in 2nd and 4th place. This arrangement is reversed in right panes.

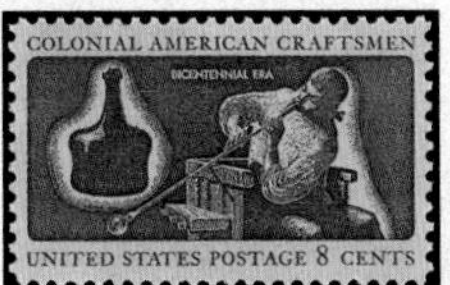

Glassmaker A870

Silversmith A871

Wigmaker A872

Hatter A873

ENGRAVED

1972, July 4 ***Perf. 11x10½***

1456 A870 8c deep brown .25 .25
1457 A871 8c deep brown .25 .25
1458 A872 8c deep brown .25 .25
1459 A873 8c deep brown .25 .25
a. Block of 4, #1456-1459 1.00 1.00

OLYMPIC GAMES ISSUE

11th Winter Olympic Games, Sapporo, Japan, Feb. 3-13 and 20th Summer Olympic Games, Munich, Germany, Aug. 26-Sept. 11. See No. C85.

Bicycling and Olympic Rings A874

Bobsledding A875

Running A876

PHOTOGRAVURE (Andreotti)

1972, Aug. 17 ***Perf. 11x10½***

1460 A874 6c blk, bl, red, emer & yel .25 .25
1461 A875 8c blk, bl, red, emer & yel .25 .25
1462 A876 15c blk, bl, red, emer & yel .30 .25
Nos. 1460-1462 (3) .80 .75

PARENT TEACHER ASSN., 75th ANNIV.

Blackboard A877

1972, Sept. 15

1463 A877 8c yellow & black .25 .25

WILDLIFE CONSERVATION ISSUE

Nos. 1464-1465 alternate in 1st row, Nos. 1468-1469 in 2nd row. This arrangement repeated throughout pane.

Fur Seals A878

Cardinal — A879

Brown Pelican — A880

Bighorn Sheep — A881

LITHOGRAPHED, ENGRAVED (Giori)

1972, Sept. 20 ***Perf. 11***

1464 A878 8c multicolored .25 .25
1465 A879 8c multicolored .25 .25
1466 A880 8c multicolored .25 .25
1467 A881 8c multicolored .25 .25
a. Block of 4, #1464-1467 1.00 *1.00*
b. As "a," brown omitted *3,250.*
c. As "a," green & blue omitted *3,250.*
d. As "a," red & brown omitted *3,500.*

MAIL ORDER BUSINESS ISSUE

Centenary of mail order business, originated by Aaron Montgomery Ward, Chicago. Design based on Headsville, W.Va., post office in Smithsonian Institution, Washington, D.C.

Rural Post Office Store A882

PHOTOGRAVURE (Andreotti)

1972, Sept, 27 ***Perf. 11x10½***

1468 A882 8c multicolored .25 .25

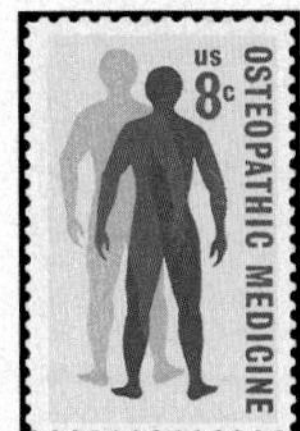

Man's Quest for Health A883

Tom Sawyer, by Norman Rockwell A884

OSTEOPATHIC MEDICINE ISSUE

75th anniv. of the American Osteopathic Assoc., founded by Dr. Andrew T. Still (1828-1917), who developed the principles of osteopathy in 1874.

1972, Oct. 9 ***Perf. 10½x11***

1469 A883 8c multicolored .25 .25

AMERICAN FOLKLORE ISSUE
Tom Sawyer

LITHOGRAPHED, ENGRAVED (Giori)

1972, Oct. 13 ***Perf. 11***

1470 A884 8c blk, red, yel, tan, bl & rose red .25 .25
a. Horiz. pair, imperf. between *7,250.*
b. Red & black (engr.) omitted *850.00*
c. Yellow & tan (litho.) omitted *1,100.*
e. Red (engr. 8c) missing (CM) *750.*

CHRISTMAS ISSUE

Angel from "Mary, Queen of Heaven" — A885

Santa Claus — A886

No. 1471, detail from a painting by the Master of the St. Lucy Legend in the National Gallery of Art, Washington, D.C.

PHOTOGRAVURE (Andreotti)

1972, Nov. 9 ***Perf. 10½x11***

1471 A885 8c multicolored .25 .25
a. Pink omitted *100.00*
b. Black omitted *2,750.*
1472 A886 8c multicolored .25 .25

PHARMACY ISSUE

Honoring American druggists in connection with the 120th anniversary of the American Pharmaceutical Association.

Mortar & Pestle, Bowl of Hygeia, 19th Century Medicine Bottles A887

LITHOGRAPHED, ENGRAVED (Giori)

1972, Nov. 10 ***Perf. 11***

1473 A887 8c black & multicolored .25 .25
a. Blue & orange omitted *600.00*
b. Blue omitted *1,250.*
c. Orange omitted *1,250.*
e. Vertical pair, imperf horiz. *1,850.*

STAMP COLLECTING ISSUE

Issued to publicize stamp collecting.

U.S. No. 1 Under Magnifying Glass A888

1972, Nov. 17

1474 A888 8c multicolored .25 .25
a. Black (litho.) omitted *425.00*

LOVE ISSUE

"Love," by Robert Indiana A889

PHOTOGRAVURE (Andreotti)

1973, Jan. 26 ***Perf. 11x10½***

1475 A889 8c red, emerald & violet blue .25 .25

AMERICAN BICENTENNIAL ISSUE
Communications in Colonial Times

Printer and Patriots Examining Pamphlet A890

Posting a Broadside A891

Postrider A892

Drummer A893

GIORI PRESS PRINTING

1973 ***Perf. 11***

1476 A890 8c ultra, greenish blk & red .25 .25
1477 A891 8c blk, vermilion & ultra .25 .25

LITHOGRAPHED, ENGRAVED (Giori)

1478 A892 8c bl, blk, red & grn .25 .25
a. Red missing (CM) —
1479 A893 8c bl, blk, yel & red .25 .25
Nos. 1476-1479 (4) 1.00 1.00

AMERICAN BICENTENNIAL ISSUE
Boston Tea Party

In left panes Nos. 1480 and 1482 appear in 1st, 3rd and 5th place, Nos. 1481 and 1483 appear in 2nd and 4th place. This arrangement is reversed in right panes.

British Merchantman — A894

British Three-master — A895

Boats and Ship's Hull A896

Boat and Dock A897

1973, July 4

1480	A894 8c black & multi		.25	.25
1481	A895 8c black & multi		.25	.25
1482	A896 8c black & multi		.25	.25
1483	A897 8c black & multi		.25	.25
a.	Block of 4, #1480-1483		1.00	1.00
b.	As "a," black (engraved) omitted		*950.00*	
c.	As "a," black (litho.) omitted		*800.00*	

AMERICAN ARTS ISSUE

George Gershwin (1898-1937), composer (No. 1484); Robinson Jeffers (1887-1962), poet (No. 1485); Henry Ossawa Tanner (1859-1937), black painter (No. 1486); Willa Cather (1873-1947), novelist (No. 1487).

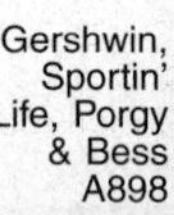

Gershwin, Sportin' Life, Porgy & Bess A898

Robinson Jeffers, Man & Children of Carmel with Burro A899

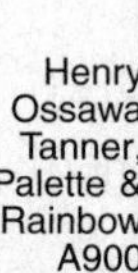

Henry Ossawa Tanner, Palette & Rainbow A900

Willa Cather, Pioneer Family & Covered Wagon A901

PHOTOGRAVURE (Andreotti)

1973

1484	A898 8c dp grn & multi		.25	.25
a.	Vertical pair, imperf. horiz.		*150.00*	
1485	A899 8c Prus bl & multi		.25	.25
a.	Vertical pair, imperf. horiz.		*175.00*	
1486	A900 8c yel brn & multi		.25	.25
1487	A901 8c dp brn & multi		.25	.25
a.	Vertical pair, imperf. horiz.		*175.00*	
	Nos. 1484-1487 (4)		1.00	1.00

Honoring: No. 1484, George Gershwin (1898-1937), composer. No. 1485, Robinson Jeffers (1887-1962), poet. No. 1486, Henry Ossawa Tanner (1859-1937), black painter (portrait by Thomas Eakins). No. 1487, Willa Sibert Cather (1873-1947), novelist.

Issued: No. 1484, Feb. 28; No. 1485, Aug. 13; No. 1486, Sept. 10; No. 1487, Sept. 20.

COPERNICUS ISSUE

Nicolaus Copernicus (1473-1543), Polish Astronomer — A902

LITHOGRAPHED, ENGRAVED (Giori)

1973, Apr. 23

1488	A902 8c black & orange		.25	.25
a.	Orange omitted		*650.00*	
b.	Black (engraved) omitted		*800.00*	

The orange can be chemically removed. Expertization of No. 1488a is required.

POSTAL SERVICE EMPLOYEES ISSUE

A tribute to US Postal Service employees. Nos. 1489-1498 are printed se-tenant in horizontal rows of 10. Emerald inscription on back, printed beneath gum in water-soluble ink, includes Postal Service emblem, "People Serving You" and a statement, differing for each of the 10 stamps, about some aspect of postal service.

Each stamp in top or bottom row has a tab with blue inscription enumerating various jobs in postal service.

Stamp Counter A903

Mail Collection A904

Letter Facing on Conveyor Belt — A905

Parcel Post Sorting — A906

Mail Canceling A907

Manual Letter Routing A908

Electronic Letter Routing — A909

Loading Mail on Truck — A910

Mailman A911

Rural Mail Delivery A912

PHOTOGRAVURE (Andreotti)

1973, Apr. 30 *Perf. 10½x11*

1489	A903 8c multicolored		.25	.25
1490	A904 8c multicolored		.25	.25
1491	A905 8c multicolored		.25	.25
1492	A906 8c multicolored		.25	.25
1493	A907 8c multicolored		.25	.25
1494	A908 8c multicolored		.25	.25
1495	A909 8c multicolored		.25	.25
1496	A910 8c multicolored		.25	.25
1497	A911 8c multicolored		.25	.25
1498	A912 8c multicolored		.25	.25
a.	Strip of 10, #1489-1498		2.50	2.50

HARRY S. TRUMAN ISSUE

Harry S Truman, 33rd President (1884-1972) A913

GIORI PRESS PRINTING

1973, May 8 *Perf. 11*

1499	A913 8c carmine rose, black & blue		.25	.25

ELECTRONICS PROGRESS ISSUE

See No. C86.

Marconi's Spark Coil and Gap A914

Transistors and Printed Circuit Board A915

Microphone, Speaker, Vacuum Tube, TV Camera Tube A916

LITHOGRAPHED, ENGRAVED (Giori)

1973, July 10

1500	A914 6c lilac & multi		.25	.25
1501	A915 8c tan & multi		.25	.25
a.	Black (inscriptions & "U.S. 8c") omitted		*300.00*	
b.	Tan (background) & lilac omitted		*700.00*	

Many examples of No. 1501b are hinged. Value about one-half never hinged value.

1502	A916 15c gray green & multicolored		.30	.25
a.	Black (inscriptions & "U.S. 15c") omitted		*900.00*	
	Nos. 1500-1502 (3)		.80	.75

See No. C86.

LYNDON B. JOHNSON ISSUE

Lyndon B. Johnson (1908-1973), 36th President A917

PHOTOGRAVURE (Andreotti)

1973, Aug. 27

1503	A917 8c black & multi		.25	.25
a.	Horiz. pair, imperf. vert.		*175.00*	

RURAL AMERICA ISSUE

Centenary of the introduction of Aberdeen Angus cattle into the US (#1504); of the Chautauqua Institution (#1505); and of the introduction of hard winter wheat into Kansas by Mennonite immigrants (#1506).

Angus and Longhorn Cattle A918

Chautauqua Tent and Buggies — A919

Wheat Fields and Train A920

No. 1504 after painting by F.C. "Frank" Murphy.

LITHOGRAPHED, ENGRAVED (Giori)

1973-74

1504	A918 8c multi		.25	.25
a.	Green & red brown omitted		*675.00*	
b.	Vert. pair, imperf. between			*5,000.*
1505	A919 10c multi		.25	.25
a.	Black (litho.) omitted			*1,750.*
1506	A920 10c multi		.25	.25
a.	Black and blue (engr.) omitted		*600.00*	
	Nos. 1504-1506 (3)		.75	.75

CHRISTMAS ISSUE

Small Cowper Madonna, by Raphael A921

Christmas Tree in Needlepoint A922

No. 1507 after painting in the National Gallery of Art, Washington, D.C.

PHOTOGRAVURE (Andreotti)

1973, Nov. 7 ***Perf. 10½x11***

1507 A921 8c multicolored .25 .25
1508 A922 8c multicolored .25 .25
a. Vertical pair, imperf. between *200.00*

50-Star & 13-Star Flags A923

Jefferson Memorial & Signature A924

Mail Transport A925

Liberty Bell A926

MULTICOLOR HUCK PRESS

1973-74 ***Perf. 11x10½***

1509 A923 10c red & blue .25 .25
a. Horizontal pair, imperf. between *40.00* —
b. Blue omitted *150.00* —
c. Imperf., vert. pair *600.00*
d. Horiz. pair, imperf. vert. *900.00*
f. Vert. pair, imperf between —

No. 1509 exists imperf and with red omitted from printer's waste.

ROTARY PRESS PRINTING

1510 A924 10c blue .25 .25
a. Untagged (Bureau precanceled) 4.00 1.00
b. Booklet pane of 5 + label 1.65 1.25
c. Booklet pane of 8 2.00 2.00
d. Booklet pane of 6 ('74) 5.25 1.75
e. Vert. pair, imperf. horiz. *325.00*
f. Vert. pair, imperf. btwn., in #1510c with miscut or with foldover *475.00*
i. As "b," double booklet pane of 10 plus stamps with 2 horiz. pairs imperf. btwn. plus stamp and label imperf. btwn. (FO) *1,750.*

No. 1510f resulted from a paper foldover after perforating and before cutting into booklet panes.

PHOTOGRAVURE (Andreotti)

1511 A925 10c multi .25 .25
a. Yellow omitted *45.00*

Beware of stamps with yellow chemically removed offered as No. 1511a.

COIL STAMPS
ROTARY PRESS PRINTING

1973-74 ***Perf. 10 Vert.***

1518 A926 6.3c brick red .25 .25
a. Untagged (Bureau precanceled) .35 .25
b. Imperf., pair *130.00*
c. As "a," imperf., pair *75.00*

No. 1518c is precanceled Washington, DC. Columbus, Ohio and Garden City, N.Y. Values for Columbus pair $425, for Garden City pair $850.

MULTICOLOR HUCK PRESS

1519 A923 10c red & blue .25 .25
a. Imperf., pair 35.00

ROTARY PRESS PRINTING

1520 A924 10c blue .25 .25
a. Untagged (Bureau precanceled) 5.50 1.25
b. Imperf., pair 30.00

VETERANS OF FOREIGN WARS ISSUE

75th anniversary of Veterans of Spanish-American and Other Foreign Wars.

V.F.W. Emblem A928

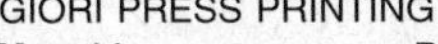
GIORI PRESS PRINTING

1974, Mar. 11 ***Perf. 11***

1525 A928 10c red & dark blue .25 .25
b. Blue missing (PS) —

ROBERT FROST ISSUE

Robert Frost (1874-1963), Poet — A929

1974, Mar. 26 ***Perf. 10½x11***

1526 A929 10c black .25 .25

EXPO '74 WORLD'S FAIR ISSUE

EXPO '74 World's Fair "Preserve the Environment," Spokane, Wash., May 4-Nov. 4.

"Cosmic Jumper" A930

PHOTOGRAVURE (Andreotti)

1974, Apr. 18 ***Perf. 11***

1527 A930 10c multicolored .25 .25

HORSE RACING ISSUE

Kentucky Derby, Churchill Downs, centenary.

Horses Rounding Turn A931

1974, May 4 ***Perf. 11x10½***

1528 A931 10c yellow & multicolored .25 .25
a. Blue ("Horse Racing") omitted *700.00*
b. Red ("U.S. postage 10 cents") omitted *1,750.*

Beware of stamps offered as No. 1528b that have traces of red.

SKYLAB ISSUE

First anniversary of the launching of Skylab I, honoring all who participated in the Skylab project.

Skylab A932

LITHOGRAPHED, ENGRAVED (Giori)

1974, May 14 ***Perf. 11***

1529 A932 10c multicolored .25 .25
a. Vert. pair, imperf. between —
c. Vert. pair, imperf. horiz. —

UNIVERSAL POSTAL UNION ISSUE

UPU cent. In the 1st row Nos. 1530-1537 are in sequence as listed. In the 2nd row Nos. 1534-1537 are followed by Nos. 1530-1533. Every row of 8 and every horizontal block of 8 contains all 8 designs. The letter writing designs are from famous works of art; some are details. The quotation on every second stamp, "Letters mingle souls," is from a letter by poet John Donne.

Michelangelo, from School of Athens — A933

Five Feminine Virtues — A934

Old Time Letter Rack — A935

Mlle. La Vergne — A936

Lady Writing Letter — A937

Inkwell and Quill — A938

Mrs. John Douglas — A939

Don Antonio Noreiga — A940

PHOTOGRAVURE (Andreotti)

1974, June 6

1530 A933 10c multicolored .25 .25
1531 A934 10c multicolored .25 .25
1532 A935 10c multicolored .25 .25
1533 A936 10c multicolored .25 .25
1534 A937 10c multicolored .25 .25
1535 A938 10c multicolored .25 .25
1536 A939 10c multicolored .25 .25
1537 A940 10c multicolored .25 .25
a. Block or strip of 8 (#1530-1537) 2.00 2.00
b. As "a," (block), imperf. vert. *2,500.*

MINERAL HERITAGE ISSUE

The sequence of stamps in 1st horizontal row is Nos. 1538-1541, 1538-1539. In 2nd row Nos. 1540-1541 are followed by Nos. 1538-1541.

Petrified Wood A941

Tourmaline — A942

Amethyst — A943

Rhodochrosite — A944

1974, June 13

1538 A941 10c blue & multi .25 .25
a. Light blue & yellow (litho.) omitted —
1539 A942 10c blue & multi .25 .25
a. Light blue (litho.) omitted —
b. Black & purple (engr.) omitted —
1540 A943 10c blue & multi .25 .25
a. Light blue & yellow (litho.) omitted —
1541 A944 10c blue & multi .25 .25
a. Block or strip of 4, #1538-1541 1.00 1.00
b. As "a," light blue & yellow (litho.) omitted *1,250.* —
c. Light blue (litho.) omitted —
d. Black & red (engr.) omitted —
e. Block of 4, two right stamps being Nos. 1539b and 1541d *7,000.*

No. 1541e is usually collected as a transition block of six or larger.

KENTUCKY SETTLEMENT, 200th ANNIV.

Fort Harrod, first settlement in Kentucky.

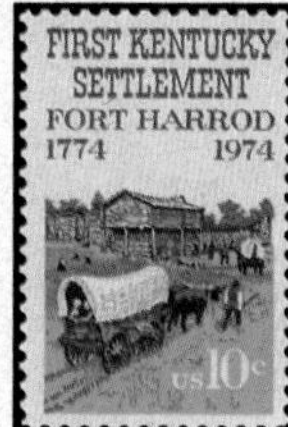

Fort Harrod — A945

1974, June 15

1542 A945 10c green & multi .25 .25
a. Dull black (litho.) omitted *525.00*
b. Green (engr. & litho.), black (engr. & litho.) & blue missing (EP) *2,500.*
c. Green (engr.) missing (EP) *3,000.*
d. Green (engr.) & black (litho.) missing (EP) —
f. Blue (litho.) omitted —

No. 1542f was caused by an occurrence that seems to be unique for U.S. total color omitted/missing errors. According to the BEP, oil on the printing blanket made a small area unreceptive to the blue ink. No blue at all was printed on one unique error stamp.

AMERICAN REVOLUTION BICENTENNIAL ISSUE

First Continental Congress

Nos. 1543-1544 alternate in 1st row, Nos. 1545-1546 in 2nd row. This arrangement is repeated throughout the pane.

Carpenters' Hall A946

A947

A948

Independence Hall — A949

1974, July 4

1543 A946 10c dark blue & red .25 .25
1544 A947 10c gray, dark blue & red .25 .25
1545 A948 10c gray, dark blue & red .25 .25
1546 A949 10c red & dark blue .25 .25
a. Block of 4, #1543-1546 1.00 1.00

ENERGY CONSERVATION ISSUE

Publicizing the importance of conserving all forms of energy.

A950

LITHOGRAPHED, ENGRAVED (Giori)

1974, Sept. 23

1547 A950 10c multicolored .25 .25
a. Blue & orange omitted *675.00*
b. Orange & green omitted *375.00*
c. Green omitted *550.00*

AMERICAN FOLKLORE ISSUE

Legend of Sleepy Hollow

The Headless Horseman in pursuit of Ichabod Crane from "Legend of Sleepy Hollow," by Washington Irving.

Legend of Sleepy Hollow A951

1974, Oct. 10

1548 A951 10c dk bl, blk, org & yel .25 .25

RETARDED CHILDREN ISSUE

Retarded Children Can Be Helped, theme of annual convention of the National Association of Retarded Citizens.

Retarded Child — A952

GIORI PRESS PRINTING

1974, Oct. 12

1549 A952 10c brown red & dark brown .25 .25

CHRISTMAS ISSUE

Angel, from Perussis Altarpiece, 1480 — A953

"The Road-Winter," by Currier & Ives — A954

Dove Weather Vane — A955

No. 1550, detail from the Perusus altarpiece painted by anonymous French artist, 1480, in Metropolitan Museum of Art, New York City. Currier and Ives print from drawing by Otto Knirsch

PHOTOGRAVURE (Andreotti)

1974, Oct. 23 ***Perf. 10½x11***

1550 A953 10c multicolored .25 .25

Perf. 11x10½

1551 A954 10c multicolored .25 .25
a. Buff omitted 12.50

No. 1551a is difficult to identify. Competent expertization is necessary.

Die Cut, Paper Backing Rouletted

1974, Nov. 15 **Untagged**

Self-adhesive; Inscribed "Precanceled"

1552 A955 10c multicolored .25 .25
Nos. 1550-1552 (3) .75 .75

Unused value of No. 1552 is for stamp on rouletted paper backing as issued. Used value is for stamp on piece, with or without postmark. **Most examples are becoming discolored from the adhesive. The Catalogue value is for discolored examples.**

Die cutting includes crossed slashes through dove, applied to prevent removal and re-use of the stamp. The stamp will separate into layers if soaked.

AMERICAN ARTS ISSUE

Benjamin West (1738-1820), painter (No. 1553); Paul Laurence Dunbar (1872-1906), poet (No. 1554); David (Lewelyn) Wark Griffith (1875-1948), motion picture producer (No. 1555).

Benjamin West — A956

Paul Laurence Dunbar — A957

D. W. Griffith & Projector A958

PHOTOGRAVURE (Andreotti)

1975 ***Perf. 10½x11***

1553 A956 10c multicolored .25 .25

Perf. 11

1554 A957 10c multicolored .25 .25
a. Imperf., pair *1,000.*

LITHOGRAPHED, ENGRAVED (Giori)

Perf. 11

1555 A958 10c brown & multicolored .25 .25
a. Brown (engr.) omitted *450.00*
Nos. 1553-1555 (3) .75 .75

SPACE ISSUES

US space accomplishments with unmanned craft. Pioneer 10 passed within 81,000 miles of Jupiter, Dec. 10, 1973. Mariner 10 explored Venus and Mercury in 1974 and Mercury again in 1975.

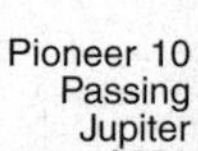

Pioneer 10 Passing Jupiter A959

Mariner 10, Venus & Mercury A960

LITHOGRAPHED, ENGRAVED (Giori)

1975 ***Perf. 11***

1556 A959 10c lt yel, dk yel, red, bl & 2 dk blues .25 .25
a. Red & dark yellow omitted *900.00*
b. Dark blues (engr.) omitted *525.00*
d. Dark yellow omitted —

Imperfs. exist from printer's waste.

1557 A960 10c blk, red, ultra & bister .25 .25
a. Red omitted *300.00* —
b. Ultramarine & bister omitted *1,250.*
d. Red missing (PS) *525.00*

COLLECTIVE BARGAINING ISSUE

Collective Bargaining law, enacted 1935, in Wagner Act.

"Labor and Management" — A961

PHOTOGRAVURE (Andreotti)

1975, Mar. 13

1558 A961 10c multicolored .25 .25

Imperforates exist from printer's waste.

AMERICAN BICENTENNIAL ISSUE

Contributors to the Cause

Sybil Ludington, age 16, rallied militia, Apr. 26, 1777; Salem Poor, black freeman, fought in Battle of Bunker Hill; Haym Salomon, Jewish immigrant, raised money to finance Revolutionary War; Peter Francisco, Portuguese-French immigrant, joined Continental Army at 15. Emerald inscription on back, printed beneath gum in water-soluble ink, gives thumbnail sketch of portrayed contributor.

Sybil Ludington A962

Salem Poor A963

Haym Salomon A964

Peter Francisco A965

1975, Mar. 25 ***Perf. 11x10½***

1559 A962 8c multicolored .25 .25
a. Back inscriptions omitted *150.00*
1560 A963 10c multicolored .25 .25
a. Back inscription omitted *150.00*

1561 A964 10c multicolored .25 .25
a. Back inscription omitted *150.00*
1562 A965 18c multicolored .35 .25
Nos. 1559-1562 (4) 1.10 1.00

Dangerous fakes exist of No. 1561 with red apparently omitted. Professional authentication is mandatory in order to establish such a stamp as a genuine error.

Lexington-Concord Battle, 200th Anniv.

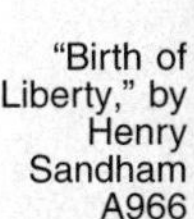

"Birth of Liberty," by Henry Sandham A966

1975, Apr. 19 ***Perf. 11***
1563 A966 10c multicolored .25 .25
a. Vert. pair, imperf. horiz. *300.00*

Bunker Hill Battle, 200th Anniv.

Battle of Bunker Hill, by John Trumbull — A967

1975, June 17
1564 A967 10c multicolored .25 .25

Military Uniforms

Bicentenary of US Military Services. Nos. 1565-1566 alternate in one row, Nos. 1567-1568 in next row.

Soldier with Flintlock Musket, Uniform Button — A968

Sailor with Grappling Hook, First Navy Jack, 1775 — A969

Marine with Musket, Full-rigged Ship — A970

Militiaman with Musket, Powder Horn — A971

1975, July 4
1565 A968 10c multicolored .25 .25
1566 A969 10c multicolored .25 .25
1567 A970 10c multicolored .25 .25
1568 A971 10c multicolored .25 .25
a. Block of 4, #1565-1568 1.00 1.00

APOLLO SOYUZ SPACE ISSUE

Apollo Soyuz space test project, Russo-American cooperation, launched July 15; link-up, July 17. Nos. In the 1st row, No. 1569 is in 1st and 3rd space, No. 1570 is 2nd space; in the 2nd row No. 1570 is in 1st and 3rd space, No. 1569 in 2nd space, etc.

Participating US and USSR crews: Thomas P. Stafford, Donald K. Slayton, Vance D. Brand, Aleksei A. Leonov, Valery N. Kubasov.

Apollo & Soyuz After Docking, Earth — A972

Spacecraft Before Docking, Earth & Project Emblem — A973

1975, July 15
1569 A972 10c multicolored .25 .25
1570 A973 10c multicolored .25 .25
a. Pair, #1569-1570 .50 .50
c. As "a," vert. pair, imperf. horiz. *1,400.*
d. As "a," yellow omitted *900.00*

Nos. 1569-1570 totally imperforate are printer's waste.

See Russia Nos. 4339-4340.

INTERNATIONAL WOMEN'S YEAR ISSUE

International Women's Year 1975.

Worldwide Equality for Women A974

1975, Aug. 26 ***Perf. 11x10½***
1571 A974 10c blue, orange & dark blue .25 .25

US POSTAL SERVICE BICENTENNIAL ISSUE

Nos. 1572-1573 alternate in 1st row, Nos. 1574-1575 in 2nd row. This arrangement is repeated throughout the pane.

Stagecoach and Trailer Truck A975

Old and New Locomotives — A976

Early Mail Plane and Jet — A977

Satellite for Transmission of Mailgrams — A978

1975, Sept. 3
1572 A975 10c multicolored .25 .25
1573 A976 10c multicolored .25 .25
1574 A977 10c multicolored .25 .25
1575 A978 10c multicolored .25 .25
a. Block of 4, #1572-1575 1.00 1.00
b. As "a," red "10c" omitted —

WORLD PEACE THROUGH LAW ISSUE

A prelude to 7th World Law Conference of the World Peace Through Law Center at Washington, D.C., Oct. 12-17.

Law Book, Olive Branch and Globe A979

GIORI PRESS PRINTING

1975, Sept. 29 ***Perf. 11***
1576 A979 10c green, Prussian blue & rose brown .25 .25
b. Horiz. pair, imperf vert. *7,500.*
c. All colors omitted —

No. 1576c is collected in a horiz. strip as two errors se-tenant with a partially printed stamp.

BANKING AND COMMERCE ISSUE

Banking and commerce in the U.S., and for the Centennial Convention of the American Bankers Association.

Engine Turning, Indian Head Penny & Morgan Silver Dollar A980

Seated Liberty Quarter, $20 Gold (Double Eagle), Engine Turning A981

LITHOGRAPHED, ENGRAVED (Giori)

1975, Oct. 6
1577 A980 10c multicolored .25 .25
1578 A981 10c multicolored .25 .25
a. Pair, #1577-1578 .50 .50
b. As "a," brown & blue (litho) omitted *1,750.*
c. As "a," brown, blue & yellow (litho) omitted *2,000.*

CHRISTMAS ISSUE

Madonna, by Domenico Ghirlandaio A982

Christmas Card, by Louis Prang, 1878 A983

PHOTOGRAVURE (Andreotti)

1975, Oct. 14
1579 A982 (10c) multicolored .25 .25
a. Imperf., pair *75.00*

Perf. 11.2

1580 A983 (10c) multicolored .25 .25
a. Imperf., pair *75.00*
c. Perf. 10.9 .25 .25

Perf. 10.5x11.3

1580B A983 (10c) multicolored .65 .25

AMERICANA ISSUE

Inkwell and Quill A984

Speaker's Stand A985

Early Ballot Box A987

Books, Bookmark, Eyeglasses A988

Dome of Capitol A994

Contemplation of Justice A995

Early American Printing Press — A996

Torch — A997

Liberty Bell A998

Eagle and Shield A999

Fort McHenry Flag A1001

Head, Statue of Liberty A1002

Old North Church, Boston A1003

Fort Nisqually A1004

Sandy Hook Lighthouse, NJ — A1005

Morris Township School No. 2, Devils Lake, ND — A1006

Iron "Betty" Lamp, 17th-18th Cent. A1007

Rush Lamp and Candle Holder A1008

Kerosene Table Lamp A1009

Railroad Conductor's Lantern, c. 1850 A1010

ROTARY PRESS PRINTING

1975-81 ***Perf. 11x10½***

Size: 18½x22½mm

1581 A984 1c dk bl, *grnish* .25 .25
a. Untagged (Bureau precanceled) 4.50 1.50
c. White paper, dull gum — —
1582 A985 2c red brn, *grnsh* .25 .25
a. Untagged (Bureau precanceled) 4.50 1.50
b. Cream paper ('81) .25 .25
1584 A987 3c olive, *grnsh* .25 .25
a. Untagged (Bureau precanceled) .75 .50

Values for No. 1584a are for the lines-only precancel. Also known with city precancels, and valued at $100 thus.

1585 A988 4c rose mag, *cream* .25 .25
a. Untagged (Bureau precanceled) 1.00 .75

The pair with horiz. gutter between also is misperfed through the stamps horizontally.
Values for No. 1585a are for the lines-only precancel. Also known with city precancels, and worth more thus.

Size: 17½x20½mm

Perf. 11x10½ on 3 Sides

1590 A994 9c slate green .45 *20.00*
From bklt. pane #1623a.

Perf. 10x9¾ on 3 Sides

1590A A994 9c slate green 14.00 *50.00*
From bklt. pane #1623Bc.

Nos. 1590 and 1590A used are valued with contemporaneous cancels only.

Size: 18½x22½mm

Perf. 11x10½

1591 A994 9c sl grn, *gray* .25 .25
a. Untagged (Bureau precanceled) 1.75 1.00

Values for No. 1591a are for the lines-only precancel. Also known with city precancels, and valued at $32.50 thus.

1592 A995 10c violet, *gray* .25 .25
a. Untagged (Bureau precanceled, Chicago) 9.50 5.00
1593 A996 11c orange, *gray* .25 .25
1594 A997 12c red brown, *beige* .25 .25

Perf. 11x10½ on 2 or 3 Sides

1595 A998 13c brown .30 .25
a. Booklet pane of 6 2.25 1.50
b. Booklet pane of 7 + label 2.25 1.50
c. Booklet pane of 8 2.25 1.50
d. Booklet pane of 5 + label, *Apr. 2, 1976* 1.75 1.25
e. Vert. pair, imperf. btwn., in #1595c with foldover *1,250.*
g. Horiz. pair, imperf. btwn., in #1595d with foldover —

Nos. 1595e and 1595g resulted from paper foldovers after perforating and before cutting into panes. Beware of printer's waste consisting of complete panes with perfs around all outside edges.

PHOTOGRAVURE (Andreotti)

Perf. 11.2

1596 A999 13c multicolored .25 .25
a. Imperf., pair *40.00* —
b. Yellow omitted *100.00*

ENGRAVED (Combination Press)

1597 A1001 15c gray, dk bl & red .30 .25
b. Gray omitted *325.00*
c. Vert. pair, imperf btwn and with natural straight edge at bottom *350.00*
e. Imperf., vert. pair *15.00*

ENGRAVED

Perf. 11x10½ on 2 or 3 Sides

1598 A1001 15c gray, dk bl & red .40 .25
a. Booklet pane of 8 4.25 1.50
1599 A1002 16c blue .35 .25
1603 A1003 24c red, *blue* .50 .25
1604 A1004 28c brown, *blue* .55 .25
1605 A1005 29c blue, *blue* .60 .25
1606 A1006 30c green, *blue* .55 .25

LITHOGRAPHED AND ENGRAVED

Perf. 11

1608 A1007 50c tan, blk & org .85 .25
a. Black omitted *225.00*
b. Vert. pair, imperf. horiz. *1,250.*

Beware of examples offered as No. 1608b that have blind perfs.

1610 A1008 $1 tan, brn, org & yel 2.00 .25
a. Brown (engraved) omitted *175.00*
b. Tan, orange & yellow omitted *200.00*
c. Brown (engraved) inverted *17,500.*
1611 A1009 $2 tan, dk grn, org & yel 3.75 .75
1612 A1010 $5 tan, red brn, yel & org 8.50 1.75
Nos. 1581-1612 (23) 35.35 77.25

Nos. 1590, 1590A, 1595, 1598, 1623 and 1623b were issued only in booklets. All stamps have one or two straight edges.
Years of issue: #1591, 1595-1596, 11c, 24c, 1975. #1590, 1c-4c, 10c, 1977. #1597-1598, 16c, 28c, 29c, $2, 1978. 30c-$1, $5, 1979. 12c, 1981.

Guitar A1011

Saxhorns A1012

Drum A1013

Piano A1014

Designers: 3.1c, George Mercer. 7.7c, Susan Robb. 7.9c, Bernard Glassman. 10c, Walter Brooks. 15c, V. Jack Ruther.

COIL STAMPS

ENGRAVED

1975-79 ***Perf. 10 Vertically***

1613 A1011 3.1c brown ('79) .25 .25
a. Untagged (Bureau precanceled, lines only) .35 .35
b. Imperf., pair *1,000.*
1614 A1012 7.7c brown ('76) .25 .25
a. Untagged (Bureau precanceled) .40 .30
b. As "a," imperf., pair *1,250.*

No. 1614b is precanceled Washington, DC. Also exists with Marion, OH precancel; value $1,950 for pair.

1615 A1013 7.9c carmine ('76) .25 .25
a. Untagged (Bureau precanceled) .40 .40
b. Imperf., pair *475.00*
1615C A1014 8.4c dak blue ('78) .25 .25
d. Untagged (Bureau precanceled) .50 .40
e. As "d," pair, imperf. between 45.00
f. As "d," imperf. pair, shiny gum 15.00

No. 1615Ce is precanceled with lines only. No. 1615Cf is precanceled with lines only (value shown) and also exists in pairs precanceled Newark, N.J. ($25)., Brownstown, Ind. ($900), Oklahoma City, Okla. ($1,500.) and Washington, DC ($1,250).

1616 A994 9c slate green ('75) .25 .25
a. Imperf., pair *125.00*
b. Untagged (Bureau precanceled) 1.15 .75
c. As "b," imperf., pair *600.00*

No. 1616c is precanceled Pleasantville, NY.

1617 A995 10c violet ('77) .25 .25
a. Untagged (Bureau precanceled) 42.50 1.35
b. Imperf., pair 60.00
c. As "a," imperf pair *3,500.*
1618 A998 13c brown ('75) .25 .25
a. Untagged (Bureau precanceled) 5.75 .75
b. Imperf., pair 22.50
g. Pair, imperf. between *600.00*
h. As "a," imperf., pair —

Values for No. 1618a with shiny gum are for the lines-only precancel. Also known with city precancels, and worth more thus.

1618C A1001 15c gray, dk bl & red ('78) .75 .25
d. Imperf., pair 22.50
e. Pair, imperf. between *100.00*
f. Gray omitted 30.00
1619 A1002 16c ultra ('78) .35 .25
a. Huck Press Printing .50 .25
Nos. 1613-1619 (9) 2.85 2.25

No. 1619a (the B press printing) has a white background without bluish tinge, is a fraction of a millimeter smaller than No. 1619 (the Cottrell press printing) and has no joint lines.
See Nos. 1811, 1813, 1816.

13-Star Flag, Independence Hall — A1015

Flag over Capitol — A1016

1975-81 ***Perf. 11x10¾***

1622 A1015 13c dk bl, red & brn red .25 .25
a. Horiz. pair, imperf. between 40.00
b. Vertical pair, imperf. *325.00*
e. Horiz. pair, imperf. vert. —

No. 1622 was printed on the Multicolored Huck Press. Plate markings are at top or bottom of pane.

Perf. 11¼

1622C A1015 13c dk bl, red & brn red ('81) 1.00 .25
d. Vertical pair, imperf 100.00

No. 1622C was printed on the Combination Press. Plate markings are at sides of pane.

BOOKLET STAMPS

Perf. 11x10½ on 2 or 3 Sides

1977, Mar. 11

1623 A1016 13c blue & red .25 .25
a. Booklet pane, 1 #1590 + 7 #1623 2.25 2.00
d. Pair, #1590 & #1623 .70 *1.00*

Perf. 10x9¾ on 2 or 3 Sides

1623B A1016 13c blue & red .80 .80
c. Booklet pane, 1 #1590A + 7 #1623B 20.00 —
e. Pair, #1590A & #1623B 15.00 15.00

COIL STAMP

1975, Nov. 15 ***Perf. 10 Vertically***

1625 A1015 13c dk blue, red & brown red .35 .25
a. Imperf., pair 20.00

AMERICAN BICENTENNIAL ISSUE

The Spirit of '76

Designed after painting by Archibald M. Willard in Abbot Hall, Marblehead, Massachusetts. Nos. 1629-1631 printed in continuous design.
Left panes contain 3 No. 1631a and one No. 1629; right panes contain one No. 1631 and 3 No. 1631a.

Drummer Boy A1019

Old Drummer A1020

Fifer — A1021

PHOTOGRAVURE (Andreotti)

1976, Jan. 1 ***Perf. 11***

1629 A1019 13c blue violet & multi .25 .25
a. Imperf., vert. pair —
1630 A1020 13c blue violet & multi .25 .25
1631 A1021 13c blue violet & multi .25 .25
a. Strip of 3, #1629-1631 .75 .75
b. As "a," imperf. *650.00*
c. Imperf., vert. pair, #1631 *600.00*

INTERPHIL ISSUE

Interphil 76 International Philatelic Exhibition, Philadelphia, Pa., May 29-June 6.

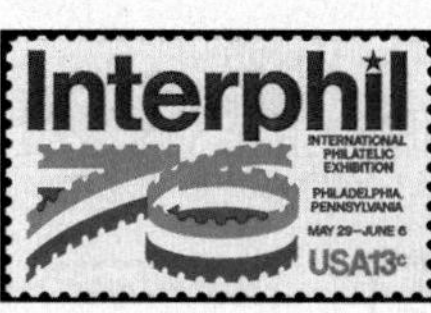

"Interphil 76" A1022

LITHOGRAPHED, ENGRAVED (Giori)

1976, Jan. 17

1632 A1022 13c dark blue & red (engr.), ultra. & red (litho.) .25 .25
a. Dark blue & red (engr.) missing (CM) —
c. Red (engr.) missing (CM) —

State Flags A1023

Photo.

1976, Feb. 23

1633 A1023 13c Delaware .30 .25
1634 A1024 13c Pennsylvania .30 .25
1635 A1025 13c New Jersey .30 .25
1636 A1026 13c Georgia .30 .25
1637 A1027 13c Connecticut .30 .25
1638 A1028 13c Massachusetts .30 .25
1639 A1029 13c Maryland .30 .25
1640 A1030 13c South Carolina .30 .25
1641 A1031 13c New Hampshire .30 .25
1642 A1032 13c Virginia .30 .25
1643 A1033 13c New York .30 .25
1644 A1034 13c North Carolina .30 .25
1645 A1035 13c Rhode Island .30 .25
1646 A1036 13c Vermont .30 .25
1647 A1037 13c Kentucky .30 .25
1648 A1038 13c Tennessee .30 .25
1649 A1039 13c Ohio .30 .25
1650 A1040 13c Louisiana .30 .25
1651 A1041 13c Indiana .30 .25
1652 A1042 13c Mississippi .30 .25
1653 A1043 13c Illinois .30 .25
1654 A1044 13c Alabama .30 .25
1655 A1045 13c Maine .30 .25
1656 A1046 13c Missouri .30 .25
1657 A1047 13c Arkansas .30 .25
1658 A1048 13c Michigan .30 .25
1659 A1049 13c Florida .30 .25
1660 A1050 13c Texas .30 .25
1661 A1051 13c Iowa .30 .25
1662 A1052 13c Wisconsin .30 .25
1663 A1053 13c California .30 .25

No.	Type	Description	Unused	Used
1664	A1054	13c Minnesota	.30	.25
1665	A1055	13c Oregon	.30	.25
1666	A1056	13c Kansas	.30	.25
1667	A1057	13c West Virginia	.30	.25
1668	A1058	13c Nevada	.30	.25
1669	A1059	13c Nebraska	.30	.25
1670	A1060	13c Colorado	.30	.25
1671	A1061	13c North Dakota	.30	.25
1672	A1062	13c South Dakota	.30	.25
1673	A1063	13c Montana	.30	.25
1674	A1064	13c Washington	.30	.25
1675	A1065	13c Idaho	.30	.25
1676	A1066	13c Wyoming	.30	.25
1677	A1067	13c Utah	.30	.25
1678	A1068	13c Oklahoma	.30	.25
1679	A1069	13c New Mexico	.30	.25
1680	A1070	13c Arizona	.30	.25
1681	A1071	13c Alaska	.30	.25
1682	A1072	13c Hawaii	.30	.25
a.		Pane of 50	17.50	15.00

TELEPHONE CENTENNIAL ISSUE

Centenary of first telephone call by Alexander Graham Bell, March 10, 1876.

Bell's Telephone Patent Application
A1073

ENGRAVED (Giori)

1976, Mar. 10

No.	Type	Description	Unused	Used
1683	A1073	13c black, purple & red, *tan*	.25	.25
a.		Black & purple missing (EP)	*450.00*	
b.		Red missing (EP)	—	
c.		All colors missing (EP)	—	

On No. 1683a, the errors have only tiny traces of red present, so are best collected as a horiz. strip of 5 with 2 or 3 error stamps. No. 1683c also must be collected as a transitional strip.

COMMERCIAL AVIATION ISSUE

50th anniversary of first contract air-mail flights: Dearborn, Mich. to Cleveland, Ohio, Feb. 15, 1926; and Pasco, Wash. to Elko, Nev., Apr. 6, 1926.

A1074

PHOTOGRAVURE (Andreotti)

1976, Mar. 19 Tagged *Perf. 11*

No.	Type	Description	Unused	Used
1684	A1074	13c blue & multicolored	.25	.25

CHEMISTRY ISSUE

Honoring American chemists, in conjunction with the centenary of the American Chemical Society.

A1075

PHOTOGRAVURE (Andreotti)

1976, Apr. 6

No.	Type	Description	Unused	Used
1685	A1075	13c multicolored	.25	.25

AMERICAN BICENTENNIAL ISSUES
SOUVENIR SHEETS

Designs, from Left to Right, No. 1686: a, Two British officers. b, Gen. Benjamin Lincoln. c, George Washington. d, John Trumbull, Col. Cobb, von Steuben, Lafayette, Thomas Nelson. e, Alexander Hamilton, John Laurens, Walter Stewart (all vert.).

No. 1687: a, John Adams, Roger Sherman, Robert R. Livingston. b, Jefferson, Franklin. c, Thomas Nelson, Jr., Francis Lewis, John Witherspoon, Samuel Huntington. d, John Hancock, Charles Thomson. e, George Read, John Dickinson, Edward Rutledge (a, d, vert., b, c, e, horiz.).

No. 1688: a, Boatsman. b, Washington. c, Flag bearer. d, Men in boat. e, Men on shore (a, d, horiz., b, c, e, vert.).

No. 1689: a, Two officers. b, Washington. c, Officer, black horse. d, Officer, white horse. e, Three soldiers (a, c, e, horiz., b, d, vert.).

LITHOGRAPHED

1976, May 29

No.	Type	Description	Unused	Used
1686	A1076	Pane of 5	3.25	2.25
a.-e.		13c multicolored	.45	.40
f.		"USA/13c" omitted on "b," "c" & "d," imperf, tagging omitted	—	*1,750.*
g.		"USA/13c" omitted on "a" & "e"	*500.00*	—
h.		Imperf., tagging omitted		*2,500.*
i.		"USA/13c" omitted on "b," "c" & "d"	*500.00*	
j.		"USA/13c" double on "b"	—	
k.		"USA/13c" omitted on "c" & "d"	*750.00*	
l.		"USA/13c" omitted on "e"	*475.00*	
m.		"USA/13c" omitted, imperf., tagging omitted		—
n.		As "g," imperf., tagging omitted		—
o.		"USA/13c" missing on "a" (PS)	*450.00*	
q.		"USA/13c" omitted on "a"	*1,100.*	
r.		Imperf., tagged		—
s.		"USA/13c" missing on "b" and "d" (PS)	—	
1687	A1077	Pane of 5	4.25	3.25
a.-e.		18c multicolored	.55	.55
f.		Design & marginal inscriptions omitted	*2,750.*	
g.		"USA/18c" omitted on "a" & "c"	*600.00*	—
h.		"USA/18c" omitted on "b," "d" & "e"	*400.00*	
i.		"USA/18c" omitted on "d"	*425.00*	*475.00*
j.		Black omitted in design	*1,500.*	
k.		"USA/18c" omitted, imperf., tagging omitted	*1,500.*	
m.		"USA/18c" omitted on "b" & "e"	*500.00*	
n.		"USA/18c" omitted on "b" & "d"	*1,000.*	
p.		Imperf. (tagged)	*1,000.*	
q.		"USA/18c" missing on "c" (CM)	—	
r.		Yellow omitted	*5,000.*	
s.		"USA/18c" missing on "a," "c" and "d" (PS)	—	
t.		"USA/18c" missing on "a" and "d" (PS)	*250.00*	
1688	A1078	Pane of 5	5.25	4.25
a.-e.		24c multicolored	.70	.70
f.		"USA/24c" omitted, imperf., tagging omitted	*950.00*	
g.		"USA/24c" omitted on "d" & "e"	*450.00*	*450.00*
h.		Design & marginal inscriptions omitted	*2,500.*	
i.		"USA/24c" omitted on "a," "b" & "c"	*450.00*	*400.00*
j.		Imperf., tagging omitted	*1,250.*	
k.		"USA/24c" of "d" & "e" inverted	*40,000.*	
l.		As "i," imperf, tagging omitted	*3,250.*	—
n.		As No. 1688, perfs inverted and reversed	—	
p.		"USA 24c" missing on "d" and "e" (CM)	—	
q.		"USA 24c" omitted on "b" and "c"	—	
1689	A1079	Pane of 5	6.25	5.25
a.-e.		31c multicolored	.85	.85
f.		"USA/31c" omitted, imperf.	*1,200.*	
g.		"USA/31c" omitted on "a" & "c"	*375.00*	
h.		"USA/31c" omitted on "b," "d" & "e"	*500.00*	—
i.		"USA/31c" omitted on "e"	*375.00*	
j.		Black omitted in design	*1,450.*	
k.		Imperf., tagging omitted		*2,150.*
l.		"USA/31c" omitted on "b" & "d"	*300.00*	
m.		"USA/31c" omitted on "a," "c" & "e"	*750.00*	
n.		As "m," imperf., tagging omitted	—	
p.		As "h," imperf., tagging omitted		*1,250.*
q.		As "g," imperf., tagging omitted	*2,500.*	
r.		"USA/31c" omitted on "d" & "e"	*600.00*	
s.		As "f," tagging omitted	*2,000.*	
t.		"USA/31c" omitted on "d"	*500.00*	
v.		As No. 1689, perfs and tagging inverted	*10,000.*	

A1076

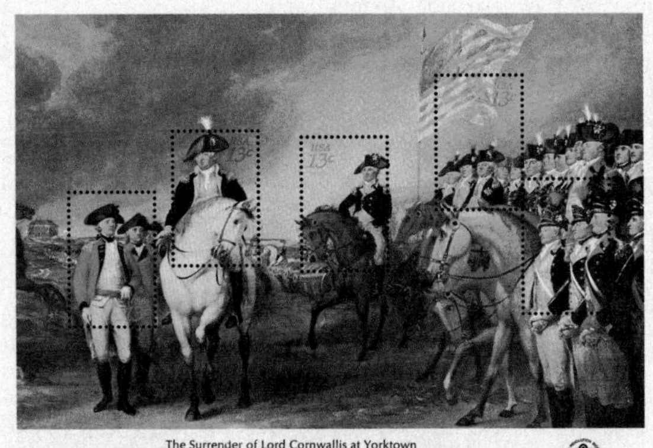

The Surrender of Lord Cornwallis at Yorktown
From a Painting by John Trumbull

A1077

The Declaration of Independence, 4 July 1776 at Philadelphia
From a Painting by John Trumbull

Washington Crossing the Delaware
From a Painting by Emanuel Leutze / Eastman Johnson

A1078

Washington Reviewing His Ragged Army at Valley Forge
From a Painting by William T. Trego

A1079

w.		"USA/31c" missing on "a," "b," "c" and "d" (PS)	—	
x.		"USA 31c" missing on "e" (CM)	—	
		Nos. 1686-1689 (4)	19.00	

Issued in connection with Interphil 76 International Philatelic Exhibition, Philadelphia, Pa., May 29-June 6. Size of panes: 203x152mm.

Benjamin Franklin

American Bicentennial: Benjamin Franklin (1706-1790), deputy postmaster general for the colonies (1753-1774) and statesman. Design based on marble bust by anonymous Italian sculptor after terra cotta bust by Jean Jacques Caffieri, 1777. Map published by R. Sayer and J. Bennett in London.

Franklin & Map of North America, 1776 A1080

LITHOGRAPHED, ENGRAVED (Giori)

1976, June 1

1690	A1080	13c multicolored	.25	.25
a.		Light blue omitted	*150.00*	

See Canada No. 691.

American Bicentennial Issue

A1081

A1082

A1083

A1084

Declaration of Independence, by John Trumbull

PHOTOGRAVURE (Andreotti)

1976, July 4

1691	A1081	13c multicolored	.30	.25
1692	A1082	13c multicolored	.30	.25
1693	A1083	13c multicolored	.30	.25
1694	A1084	13c multicolored	.30	.25
a.		Strip of 4, #1691-1694	1.20	1.10

OLYMPIC GAMES ISSUE

12th Winter Olympic Games, Innsbruck, Austria, Feb. 4-15, and 21st Summer Olympic Games, Montreal, Canada, July 17-Aug. 1. Nos. 1695-1696 alternate in one row, Nos. 1697-1698 in other row.

Diving — A1085

Skiing — A1086

Running A1087

Skating A1088

1976, July 16

1695	A1085	13c multicolored	.30	.25
1696	A1086	13c multicolored	.30	.25
1697	A1087	13c multicolored	.30	.25
1698	A1088	13c multicolored	.30	.25
a.		Block of 4, #1695-1698	1.20	1.20
b.		As "a," imperf.	*400.00*	

CLARA MAASS ISSUE

Clara Louise Maass (1876-1901), volunteer in fight against yellow fever, birth centenary.

Clara Maass, Newark German Hospital Pin — A1089

1976, Aug. 18

1699	A1089	13c multicolored	.25	.25
a.		Horiz. pair, imperf. vert.	*350.00*	

ADOLPH S. OCHS ISSUE

Adolph S. Ochs, Publisher of the NY Times, 1896-1935 A1090

GIORI PRESS PRINTING

1976, Sept. 18

1700	A1090	13c black & gray	.25	.25

CHRISTMAS ISSUE

Nativity, by John Singleton Copley A1091

Winter Pastime, by Nathaniel Currier A1092

PHOTOGRAVURE (Andreotti)

1976, Oct. 27

1701	A1091	13c multicolored	.25	.25
a.		Imperf., pair	*85.00*	
1702	A1092	13c multi, overall tagging	.25	.25
a.		Imperf., pair	*90.00*	

COMBINATION PRESS

1703	A1092	13c multicolored	.25	.25
a.		Imperf., pair	*75.00*	
b.		Vert. pair, imperf. between	*275.00*	
d.		Red omitted	*500.00*	
e.		Yellow omitted	—	

No. 1702 has overall tagging. Lettering at base is black and usually ½mm below design. As a rule, no "snowflaking" in sky or pond. Pane of 50 has margins on 4 sides with slogans. Plate Nos. 37465-37478.

No. 1703 has block tagging the size of printed area. Lettering at base is gray black and usually ¾mm below design. "Snowflaking" generally in sky and pond. Plate Nos. 37617-37621 or 37634-37638.

Examples of No. 1703 are known with various amounts of red or yellow missing. Nos. 1703d-1703e are stamps with the colors totally omitted. Expertization is recommended.

AMERICAN BICENTENNIAL ISSUE
Washington at Princeton

Washington's Victory over Lord Cornwallis at Princeton, N.J., bicentenary.

Washington, Nassau Hall, Hessians, 13-Star Flag — A1093

1977, Jan. 3

1704	A1093	13c multicolored	.25	.25
a.		Horiz. pair, imperf. vert.	*425.00*	
b.		Black (inscriptions) missing (PS)	—	

SOUND RECORDING ISSUE

Centenary of the invention of the phonograph by Thomas Alva Edison and development of sophisticated recording industry.

Tin Foil Phonograph A1094

LITHOGRAPHED, ENGRAVED (Giori)

1977, Mar. 23

1705	A1094	13c black & multi	.25	.25

AMERICAN FOLK ART SERIES
Pueblo Pottery

Pueblo art, 1880-1920, from Museums in New Mexico, Arizona and Colorado.

Zia — A1095

San Ildefonso A1096

Hopi — A1097

Acoma — A1098

PHOTOGRAVURE (Andreotti)

1977, Apr. 13

1706	A1095	13c multicolored	.25	.25
1707	A1096	13c multicolored	.25	.25
1708	A1097	13c multicolored	.25	.25
1709	A1098	13c multicolored	.25	.25
a.		Block or strip of 4, #1706-1709	1.00	1.00
b.		As "a," imperf. vert.	*1,500.*	

LINDBERGH FLIGHT ISSUE

Charles A. Lindbergh's solo transatlantic flight from New York to Paris, 50th anniversary.

Spirit of St. Louis A1099

1977, May 20

1710	A1099	13c multicolored	.25	.25
a.		Imperf., pair	*700.00*	

COLORADO STATEHOOD ISSUE

Issued to honor Colorado as the "Centennial State." It achieved statehood in 1876.

Columbine & Rocky Mountains — A1100

1977, May 21

1711	A1100	13c multicolored	.25	.25
a.		Horiz. pair, imperf. between and with natural straight edge at right	—	
b.		Horiz. pair, imperf. vertically	*600.00*	
c.		Perf. 11.2	.70	.25

BUTTERFLY ISSUE

Nos. 1712-1713 alternate in 1st row, Nos. 1714-1715 in 2nd row. This arrangement is repeated throughout the pane. Butterflies represent different geographic US areas.

Swallowtail A1101

Checkerspot — A1102

Dogface A1103

Orange Tip A1104

1977, June 6 Tagged Perf. 11

1712	A1101 13c tan & multi	.25	.25
1713	A1102 13c tan & multi	.25	.25
1714	A1103 13c tan & multi	.25	.25
1715	A1104 13c tan & multi	.25	.25
a.	Block of 4, #1712-1715	1.00	1.00
b.	As "a," imperf. horiz.	*9,500.*	

AMERICAN BICENTENNIAL ISSUES
Marquis de Lafayette

200th anniversary of Lafayette's Landing on the coast of South Carolina, north of Charleston.

Marquis de Lafayette A1105

GIORI PRESS PRINTING

1977, June 13

1716	A1105 13c blue, black & red	.25	.25
a.	Red missing (PS)	*250.00*	

Skilled Hands for Independence

Nos. 1717-1718 alternate in 1st row, Nos. 1719-1720 in 2nd row. This arrangement is repeated throughout the pane.

Seamstress A1106

Blacksmith A1107

Wheelwright A1108

Leatherworker — A1109

1977, July 4

1717	A1106 13c multicolored	.25	.25
1718	A1107 13c multicolored	.25	.25
1719	A1108 13c multicolored	.25	.25
1720	A1109 13c multicolored	.25	.25
a.	Block of 4, #1717-1720	1.00	1.00

PEACE BRIDGE ISSUE

50th anniversary of the Peace Bridge, connecting Buffalo (Fort Porter), N.Y. and Fort Erie, Ontario.

Peace Bridge & Dove A1110

ENGRAVED

1977, Aug. 4 Perf. 11x10½

1721	A1110 13c blue	.25	.25

AMERICAN BICENTENNIAL ISSUE
Battle of Oriskany

200th anniv. of the Battle of Oriskany, American Militia led by Brig. Gen. Nicholas Herkimer (1728-77).

Herkimer at Oriskany, by Yohn A1111

PHOTOGRAVURE (Andreotti)

1977, Aug. 6 Perf. 11

1722	A1111 13c multicolored	.25	.25

ENERGY ISSUE

Conservation and development of nation's energy resources. Nos. 1723-1724 se-tenant vertically.

Energy Conservation — A1112

Energy Development — A1113

1977, Oct. 20

1723	A1112 13c multicolored	.25	.25
1724	A1113 13c multicolored	.25	.25
a.	Pair, #1723-1724	.50	.50

ALTA CALIFORNIA ISSUE

Founding of El Pueblo de San José de Guadalupe, first civil settlement in Alta California, 200th anniversary.

Farm Houses A1114

LITHOGRAPHED, ENGRAVED (Giori)

1977, Sept. 9 Tagged Perf. 11

1725	A1114 13c black & multi	.25	.25

AMERICAN BICENTENNIAL ISSUE
Articles of Confederation

200th anniversary of drafting the Articles of Confederation, York Town, Pa.

Members of Continental Congress in Conference A1115

ENGRAVED (Giori)

1977, Sept. 30

1726	A1115 13c red & brn, *cream*	.25	.25
b.	Red omitted	*600.00*	
c.	Red & brown omitted	*400.00*	

No. 1726b also has most of the brown omitted. No. 1726c must be collected as a transition multiple, certainly with No. 1726b and preferably also with No. 1726.

TALKING PICTURES, 50th ANNIV.

Movie Projector and Phonograph A1116

LITHOGRAPHED, ENGRAVED (Giori)

1977, Oct. 6

1727	A1116 13c multicolored	.25	.25

AMERICAN BICENTENNIAL ISSUE
Surrender at Saratoga

200th anniversary of Gen. John Burgoyne's surrender at Saratoga.

Surrender of Burgoyne, by John Trumbull A1117

PHOTOGRAVURE (Andreotti)

1977, Oct. 7

1728	A1117 13c multicolored	.25	.25

CHRISTMAS ISSUE

Washington at Valley Forge A1118

Rural Mailbox A1119

PHOTOGRAVURE (Combination Press)

1977, Oct. 21

1729	A1118 13c multicolored	.25	.25
a.	Imperf., pair	*60.00*	

See Combination Press note after No. 1703.

PHOTOGRAVURE (Andreotti)

1730	A1119 13c multicolored	.25	.25
a.	Imperf., pair	*175.00*	

CARL SANDBURG ISSUE

Carl Sandburg (1878-1967), poet, biographer and collector of American folk songs, birth centenary.

Carl Sandburg, by William A. Smith, 1952 — A1120

GIORI PRESS PRINTING

1978, Jan. 6

1731	A1120 13c black & brown	.25	.25
a.	Brown omitted	*2,000.*	
c.	All colors omitted		—

No. 1731c is tagged and has a faint black tagging ghost. Authentication is advised.

CAPTAIN COOK ISSUE

Capt. James Cook, 200th anniversary of his arrival in Hawaii, at Waimea, Kauai, Jan. 20, 1778, and of his anchorage in Cook Inlet, near Anchorage, Alaska, June 1, 1778. Nos. 1732-1733 printed in panes of 50, containing 25 each of Nos. 1732-1733 including 5 No. 1733b.

Capt. Cook, by Nathaniel Dance, 1776 — A1121

"Resolution" and "Discovery," by John Webber — A1122

1978, Jan. 20

1732	A1121 13c dark blue	.25	.25
1733	A1122 13c green	.25	.25
a.	Vert. pair, imperf. horiz.	—	
b.	Pair, #1732-1733	.50	.50
c.	As "b," imperf. between	*4,250.*	

Indian Head Penny, 1877 A1123

Eagle A1124

Roses — A1126

ENGRAVED (Giori)

1978

1734	A1123 13c brown & blue green, *bister, Jan. 11, 1978*	.25	.25
a.	Horiz. pair, imperf. vert.	*175.00*	

PHOTOGRAVURE (Andreotti)

1735	A1124 (15c) orange, *May 22, 1978*	.30	.25
a.	Imperf., pair	*70.00*	
b.	Vert. pair, imperf. horiz.	*525.00*	
c.	Perf. 11.2	.35	.25

BOOKLET STAMPS
ENGRAVED

Perf. 11x10½ on 2 or 3 Sides

1736	A1124 (15c) orange	.30	.25
a.	Booklet pane of 8, *May 22, 1978*	2.50	1.50
c.	Vert. pair, imperf. btwn., in #1736a with foldover	*1,000.*	

Perf. 10 on 2 or 3 Sides

1737	A1126 15c multi	.30	.25
a.	Booklet pane of 8, *July 11, 1978*	2.50	2.00
b.	Imperf, pair	*450.00*	
c.	As "a," imperf	*2,000.*	

Robertson Windmill, Williamsburg A1127

Old Windmill, Portsmouth A1128

Cape Cod Windmill, Eastham A1129

Dutch Mill, Batavia A1130

Southwestern Windmill — A1131

BOOKLET STAMPS
ENGRAVED
Perf. 11 on 2 or 3 Sides

1980, Feb. 7

1738	A1127	15c sepia, *yellow*	.30	.25
1739	A1128	15c sepia, *yellow*	.30	.25
1740	A1129	15c sepia, *yellow*	.30	.25
1741	A1130	15c sepia, *yellow*	.30	.25
1742	A1131	15c sepia, *yellow*	.30	.25
a.		Booklet pane of 10, 2 each #1738-1742	3.50	3.00
b.		Strip of 5, #1738-1742	1.50	1.40

COIL STAMP

1978, May 22 ***Perf. 10 Vert.***

1743	A1124	(15c) orange	.30	.25
a.		Imperf., pair	65.00	

No. 1743a is valued in the grade of fine.

BLACK HERITAGE SERIES

Harriet Tubman (1820-1913), born a slave, helped more than 300 slaves escape to freedom.

Harriet Tubman (1820-1913), Cart Carrying Slaves — A1133

PHOTOGRAVURE (Andreotti)

1978, Feb. 1 ***Perf. 10½x11***

1744	A1133	13c multicolored	.25	.25

AMERICAN FOLK ART SERIES
Quilts
Basket Design

A1134

A1135

A1136

A1137

1978, Mar. 8 ***Perf. 11***

1745	A1134	13c multicolored	.25	.25
1746	A1135	13c multicolored	.25	.25
1747	A1136	13c multicolored	.25	.25
1748	A1137	13c multicolored	.25	.25
a.		Block of 4, #1745-1748	1.00	1.00

AMERICAN DANCE ISSUE

Ballet A1138

Theater A1139

Folk Dance A1140

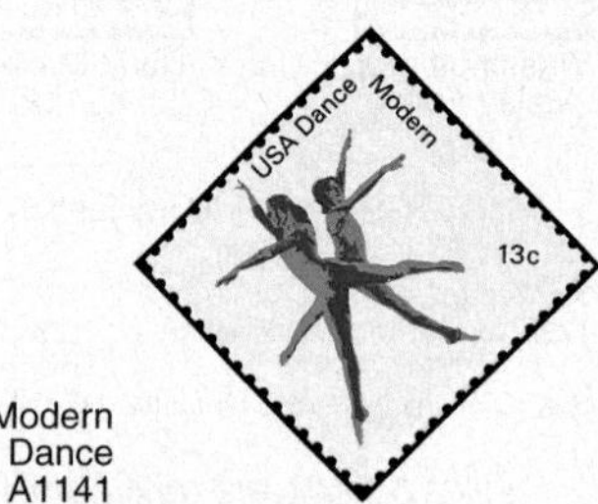

Modern Dance A1141

1978, Apr. 26

1749	A1138	13c multicolored	.25	.25
1750	A1139	13c multicolored	.25	.25
1751	A1140	13c multicolored	.25	.25
1752	A1141	13c multicolored	.25	.25
a.		Block of 4, #1749-1752	1.00	1.00

AMERICAN BICENTENNIAL ISSUE

French Alliance, signed in Paris, Feb. 6, 1778 and ratified by Continental Congress, May 4, 1778.

Louis XVI and Franklin, Porcelain Sculpture by C. G. Sauvage A1142

GIORI PRESS PRINTING

1978, May 4

1753	A1142	13c blue, black & red	.25	.25
a.		Red missing (PS)	—	

EARLY CANCER DETECTION ISSUE

George Papanicolaou, M.D. (1883-1962), cytologist and developer of Pap Test, early cancer detection in women.

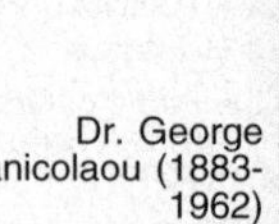
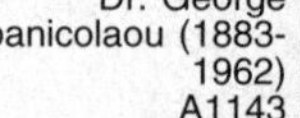

Dr. George Papanicolaou (1883-1962) A1143

ENGRAVED

1978, May 18 ***Perf. 10½x11***

1754	A1143	13c brown	.25	.25

PERFORMING ARTS SERIES

Jimmie Rodgers (1897-1933), the "Singing Brakeman, Father of Country Music" (No. 1755); George M. Cohan (1878-1942), actor and playwright (No. 1756).

Jimmie Rodgers and Locomotive A1144

George M. Cohan, "Yankee Doodle Dandy" and Stars A1145

PHOTOGRAVURE (Andreotti)

1978 ***Perf. 11***

1755	A1144	13c multicolored	.25	.25
1756	A1145	15c multicolored	.30	.25

CAPEX ISSUE

CAPEX '78, Canadian International Philatelic Exhibition, Toronto, Ont., June 9-18.

Wildlife from Canadian-U.S. Border — A1146

LITHOGRAPHED, ENGRAVED (Giori)

1978, June 10

1757	A1146	Block of 8, multicolored	2.00	2.00
a.		13c Cardinal	.25	.25
b.		13c Mallard	.25	.25
c.		13c Canada goose	.25	.25
d.		13c Blue jay	.25	.25
e.		13c Moose	.25	.25
f.		13c Chipmunk	.25	.25
g.		13c Red fox	.25	.25
h.		13c Raccoon	.25	.25
i.		As No. 1757, yellow, green, red, brown, blue, black (litho) omitted	*7,000.*	
j.		Strip of 4 (a-d), imperf. vert.	*5,000.*	
k.		Strip of 4 (e-h), imperf. vert.	*2,750.*	
l.		As No. 1757, "d" and "h" with black (engr.) omitted	—	
m.		As No. 1757, "b" with blue missing (PS)	—	
o.		Strip of 4 (e-h), all colors except black missing on "e," "f" and "g," all colors except black and brown missing on "h"	*1,250.*	

No. 1757k is worth more when contained in the block of 8. Value is for strip only.

PHOTOGRAPHY ISSUE

Photography's contribution to communications and understanding.

Photographic Equipment A1147

PHOTOGRAVURE (Andreotti)

1978, June 26

1758	A1147	15c multicolored	.30	.25

VIKING MISSIONS TO MARS ISSUE

Second anniv. of landing of Viking 1 on Mars.

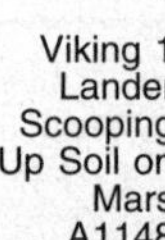

Viking 1 Lander Scooping Up Soil on Mars A1148

LITHOGRAPHED, ENGRAVED (Giori)

1978, July 20

1759	A1148	15c multicolored	.30	.25

WILDLIFE CONSERVATION

Nos. 1760-1761 alternate in one horizontal row. Nos. 1762-1763 in the next.

Great Gray Owl — A1149

Saw-whet Owl — A1150

Barred Owl — A1151

Great Horned Owl — A1152

1978, Aug. 26

1760	A1149	15c multicolored	.30	.25
1761	A1150	15c multicolored	.30	.25
1762	A1151	15c multicolored	.30	.25
1763	A1152	15c multicolored	.30	.25
a.		Block of 4, #1760-1763	1.25	1.25

AMERICAN TREES ISSUE

Giant Sequoia A1153

White Pine A1154

White Oak A1155

Gray Birch A1156

PHOTOGRAVURE (Andreotti)

1978, Oct. 9

1764 A1153 15c multicolored .30 .25
1765 A1154 15c multicolored .30 .25
1766 A1155 15c multicolored .30 .25
1767 A1156 15c multicolored .30 .25
a. Block of 4, #1764-1767 1.25 1.25
b. As "a," imperf. horiz. *17,500.*

No. 1767b is unique.

CHRISTMAS ISSUE

Madonna and Child with Cherubim, by Andrea della Robbia A1157

Child on Hobby-horse and Christmas Trees A1158

No. 1768, after terra cotta sculpture in National Gallery, Washington, D.C.

1978, Oct. 18 ***Perf. 11***

1768 A1157 15c blue & multicolored .30 .25
a. Imperf., pair *70.00*

Value for No. 1768a is for an uncreased pair.

1769 A1158 15c red & multicolored .30 .25
a. Imperf., pair *75.00*
b. Vert. pair, imperf. horiz. *1,000.*

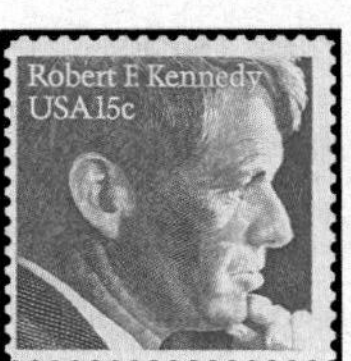

Robert F. Kennedy (1925-68), U.S. Attorney General A1159

Dr. Martin Luther King, Jr. (1929-68), and Civil Rights Marchers A1160

ROBERT F. KENNEDY ISSUE

ENGRAVED

1979, Jan. 12

1770 A1159 15c blue .35 .25

BLACK HERITAGE SERIES

Dr. Martin Luther King, Jr. (1929-1968), Civil Rights leader.

PHOTOGRAVURE (Andreotti)

1979, Jan. 13

1771 A1160 15c multicolored .40 .25
a. Imperf., pair *1,000.*

INTERNATIONAL YEAR OF THE CHILD ISSUE

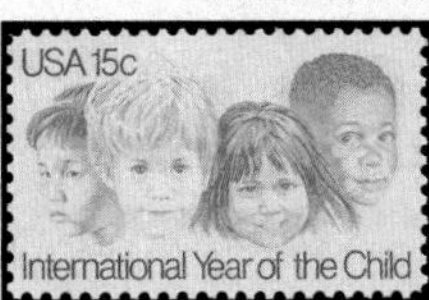

Children A1161

ENGRAVED

1979, Feb. 15

1772 A1161 15c orange red .30 .25

John Steinbeck A1162

Albert Einstein A1163

LITERARY ARTS SERIES

1979, Feb. 27 ***Perf. 10½x11***

1773 A1162 15c dark blue .30 .25

ALBERT EINSTEIN ISSUE

1979, Mar. 4

1774 A1163 15c chocolate .35 .25

AMERICAN FOLK ART SERIES
Pennsylvania Toleware, c. 1800

Coffeepot A1164

Tea Caddy — A1165

Sugar Bowl — A1166

Coffeepot A1167

PHOTOGRAVURE (Andreotti)

1979, Apr. 19 ***Perf. 11***

1775 A1164 15c multicolored .30 .25
1776 A1165 15c multicolored .30 .25
1777 A1166 15c multicolored .30 .25
1778 A1167 15c multicolored .30 .25
a. Block of 4, #1775-1778 1.25 1.25
b. As "a," imperf. horiz. *2,500.*

AMERICAN ARCHITECTURE SERIES

Virginia Rotunda, by Thomas Jefferson A1168

Baltimore Cathedral, by Benjamin Latrobe — A1169

Boston State House, by Charles Bulfinch A1170

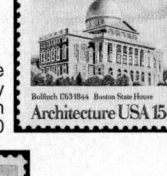

Philadelphia Exchange, by William Strickland A1171

ENGRAVED (Giori)

1979, June 4

1779 A1168 15c blk & brick red .30 .25
1780 A1169 15c blk & brick red .30 .25
1781 A1170 15c blk & brick red .30 .25
1782 A1171 15c blk & brick red .30 .25
a. Block of 4, #1779-1782 1.25 1.25

ENDANGERED FLORA ISSUE

Persistent Trillium A1172

Hawaiian Wild Broadbean A1173

Contra Costa Wallflower A1174

Antioch Dunes Evening Primrose A1175

PHOTOGRAVURE (Andreotti)

1979, June 7

1783 A1172 15c multicolored .30 .25
1784 A1173 15c multicolored .30 .25
1785 A1174 15c multicolored .30 .25
1786 A1175 15c multicolored .30 .25
a. Block of 4, #1783-1786 1.25 1.25
b. As "a," imperf. *200.00*

SEEING EYE DOGS ISSUE

1st guide dog program in the US, 50th anniv.

German Shepherd Leading Man — A1176

PHOTOGRAVURE (Combination Press)

1979, June 15

1787 A1176 15c multicolored .30 .25
a. Imperf., pair *325.00*

Child Holding Winner's Medal — A1177

John Paul Jones, by Charles Willson Peale — A1178

SPECIAL OLYMPICS ISSUE

Special Olympics for special children, Brockport, N.Y., Aug. 8-13.

PHOTOGRAVURE (Andreotti)

1979, Aug. 9

1788 A1177 15c multicolored .30 .25

JOHN PAUL JONES ISSUE

John Paul Jones (1747-1792), Naval Commander, American Revolution.

PHOTOGRAVURE (Champlain)

1979, Sept. 23 ***Perf. 11x12***

1789 A1178 15c multi .30 .25
c. Vert. pair, imperf. horiz. *125.00*

Imperforates on gummed stamp paper, including gutter pairs and blocks, are proofs from the ABNCo. archives. See No. 1789P in Proofs section of the Scott United States Specialized Catalogue.

Perf. 11

1789A A1178 15c multi .55 .25
d. Vertical pair, imperf. horiz. *115.00*

Perf. 12

1789B A1178 15c multi *3,250. 3,500.*

OLYMPIC GAMES ISSUE

22nd Summer Olympic Games, Moscow, July 19-Aug. 3, 1980. Nos. 1791-1792 alternate in one horizontal row, Nos. 1793-1794 in next.

Javelin — A1179

Running A1180

Swimming A1181

Rowing A1182

Equestrian A1183

PHOTOGRAVURE

1979, Sept. 5 ***Perf. 11***

1790 A1179 10c multicolored .25 .25

1979, Sept. 28

1791 A1180 15c multicolored .30 .25
1792 A1181 15c multicolored .30 .25
1793 A1182 15c multicolored .30 .25
1794 A1183 15c multicolored .30 .25
a. Block of 4, #1791-1794 1.25 1.25
b. As "a," imperf. *1,100.*

OLYMPIC GAMES ISSUE

13th Winter Olympic Games, Lake Placid, N.Y., Feb. 12-24. Nos. 1795-1796 alternate in one horizontal row, Nos. 1797-1798 in next.

Speed Skating A1184

Downhill Skiing A1185

Ski Jump A1186

Ice Hockey A1187

1980, Feb. 1 ***Perf. 11¼x10½***

1795 A1184 15c multicolored .35 .25
1796 A1185 15c multicolored .35 .25
1797 A1186 15c multicolored .35 .25
1798 A1187 15c multicolored .35 .25
b. Block of 4, #1795-1798 1.50 1.40

Perf. 11

1795A A1184 15c multicolored 1.10 .60
1796A A1185 15c multicolored 1.10 .60
1797A A1186 15c multicolored 1.10 .60
1798A A1187 15c multicolored 1.10 .60
c. Block of 4, #1795A-1798A 4.50 3.50

CHRISTMAS ISSUE

Virgin and Child, by Gerard David A1188

Santa Claus, Christmas Tree Ornament A1189

No. 1799 is designed after a painting in National Gallery of Art, Washington, D.C.

PHOTOGRAVURE (Andreotti)

1979, Oct. 18 ***Perf. 11***

1799 A1188 15c multicolored .30 .25
a. Imperf., pair *70.00*
b. Vert. pair, imperf. horiz. *500.00*
c. Vert. pair, imperf. between *950.00*

Perf. 11x10½

1800 A1189 15c multicolored .30 .25
a. Green & yellow omitted *450.00*
b. Green, yellow & tan omitted *400.00*
c. Vert. se-tenant pair, #1800a & 1800b *850.00*

Nos. 1800a and 1800b always have the remaining colors misaligned.

Nos. 1800a, 1800b and 1800c are valued in the grade of fine.

VALUES FOR HINGED STAMPS AFTER NO. 771

This catalogue does not value unused stamps after No. 771 in hinged condition. Hinged unused stamps from No. 772 to the present are worth considerably less than the values given for unused stamps, which are for never-hinged examples.

PERFORMING ARTS SERIES

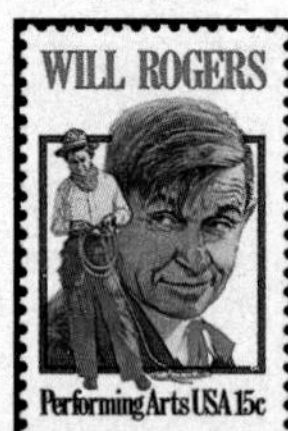

Will Rogers (1879-1935), Actor and Humorist — A1190

1979, Nov. 4 Tagged ***Perf. 11***

1801 A1190 15c multicolored .30 .25
a. Imperf., pair *125.00*

VIETNAM VETERANS ISSUE

A tribute to veterans of the Vietnam War.

Ribbon for Viet Nam Service Medal A1191

1979, Nov. 11

1802 A1191 15c multicolored .30 .25

W.C. Fields (1880-1946), Actor and Comedian A1192

Benjamin Banneker (1731-1806), Astronomer and Mathematician, Transverse A1193

PERFORMING ARTS SERIES

PHOTOGRAVURE

1980, Jan. 29

1803 A1192 15c multicolored .30 .25
a. Imperf., pair —

BLACK HERITAGE SERIES

1980, Feb. 15

1804 A1193 15c multicolored .30 .25
a. Horiz. pair, imperf. vert. *350.00*

Imperfs, including gutter pairs and blocks, exist from printer's waste. These have been fraudulently perforated to simulate No. 1804a. Genuine examples of No. 1804a do not have colors misregistered.

NATIONAL LETTER WRITING WEEK ISSUE

National Letter Writing Week, Feb. 24-Mar. 1. Nos. 1805-1810 are printed vertically se-tenant.

Letters Preserve Memories A1194

P.S. Write Soon A1195

Letters Lift Spirits A1196

Letters Shape Opinions A1197

1980, Feb. 25

1805 A1194 15c multicolored .30 .25
1806 A1195 15c purple & multi .30 .25
1807 A1196 15c multicolored .30 .25
1808 A1195 15c green & multi .30 .25
1809 A1197 15c multicolored .30 .25
1810 A1195 15c red & multi .30 .25
a. Vertical strip of 6, #1805-1810 1.85 *2.00*
Nos. 1805-1810 (6) 1.80 1.50

AMERICANA TYPE

Weaver Violins — A1199

COIL STAMPS

1980-81 Engr. ***Perf. 10 Vertically***

1811 A984 1c dark blue, *greenish* .25 .25
a. Imperf., pair *90.00*
1813 A1199 3.5c purple, *yellow* .25 .25
a. Untagged (Bureau precanceled, lines only) .25 .25
b. Imperf., pair *125.00*
1816 A997 12c red brown, *beige ('81)* .25 .25
a. Untagged (Bureau precanceled), red brown, *beige* 1.25 1.25
b. Imperf., pair 135.00
c. As "a," brownish red, *reddish beige* 1.25 1.25
Nos. 1811-1816 (3) .75 .75

A1207

PHOTOGRAVURE

1981, Mar. 15 Tagged ***Perf. 11x10½***

1818 A1207 (18c) violet .35 .25

BOOKLET STAMP

ENGRAVED

Perf. 10 on 2 or 3 Sides

1819 A1207 (18c) violet .40 .25
a. Booklet pane of 8 3.75 2.25

COIL STAMP

Perf. 10 Vert.

1820 A1207 (18c) violet .40 .25
a. Imperf., pair *80.00*

Frances Perkins A1208

Dolley Madison A1209

FRANCES PERKINS ISSUE

Frances Perkins (1882-1965), Secretary of Labor, 1933-1945 (first woman cabinet member).

ENGRAVED

1980, Apr. 10 ***Perf. 10½x11***

1821 A1208 15c Prussian blue .30 .25

DOLLEY MADISON ISSUE

Dolley Madison (1768-1849), First Lady, 1809-1817.

1980, May 20 ***Perf. 11***

1822 A1209 15c red brown & sepia .30 .25
a. Red brown missing (PS) *575.00*

Emily Bissell A1210

Helen Keller and Anne Sullivan A1211

EMILY BISSELL ISSUE

Emily Bissell (1861-1948), social worker; introduced Christmas seals in United States.

1980, May 31

1823 A1210 15c black & red .35 .25
a. Vert. pair, imperf. horiz. *250.00*
b. All colors missing (EP) —
c. Red missing (FO) —

HELEN KELLER ISSUE

Helen Keller (1880-1968), blind and deaf writer and lecturer taught by Anne Sullivan (1867-1936).

LITHOGRAPHED AND ENGRAVED

1980, June 27

1824 A1211 15c multicolored .30 .25

Veterans Administration Emblem A1212

Gen. Bernardo de Galvez A1213

VETERANS ADMINISTRATION, 50th ANNIV.

PHOTOGRAVURE

Plates of 200 subjects in four panes of 50.

1980, July 21

1825 A1212 15c carmine & violet blue .30 .25
a. Horiz. pair, imperf. vert. *375.00*

BERNARDO DE GALVEZ ISSUE

Gen. Bernardo de Galvez (1746-1786), helped defeat British in Battle of Mobile, 1780.

LITHOGRAPHED & ENGRAVED

1980, July 23

1826 A1213 15c multicolored .30 .25
- *a.* Red, brown & blue (engr.) omitted 500.00
- *b.* Blue, brown, red (engr.) & yellow (litho.) omitted 950.00

CORAL REEFS ISSUE

Brain Coral, Beaugregory Fish A1214

Elkhorn Coral, Porkfish A1215

Chalice Coral, Moorish Idol Fish — A1216

Finger Coral, Sabertooth Blenny Fish — A1217

PHOTOGRAVURE

1980, Aug. 26

1827 A1214 15c multi .30 .25
1828 A1215 15c multi .30 .25
1829 A1216 15c multi .30 .25
1830 A1217 15c multi .30 .25
- *a.* Block of 4, #1827-1830 1.25 1.10
- *b.* As "a," imperf. 400.00
- *c.* As "a," vert. imperf. between 1,750.
- *d.* As "a," imperf. vert. 2,750.

American Bald Eagle A1218

Edith Wharton A1219

ORGANIZED LABOR ISSUE

1980, Sept. 1

1831 A1218 15c multi .30 .25
- *a.* Imperf., pair 275.00

LITERARY ARTS SERIES

Edith Wharton (1862-1937), novelist.

ENGRAVED

1980, Sept. 5 ***Perf. 10½x11***

1832 A1219 15c purple .30 .25

EDUCATION ISSUE

"Homage to the Square: Glow," by Josef Albers — A1220

PHOTOGRAVURE

1980, Sept. 12 ***Perf. 11***

1833 A1220 15c multi .30 .25
- *a.* Horiz. pair, imperf. vert. 150.00

AMERICAN FOLK ART SERIES

Pacific Northwest Indian Masks

Heiltsuk, Bella Bella Tribe — A1221

Chilkat Tlingit Tribe — A1222

Tlingit Tribe — A1223

Bella Coola Tribe — A1224

1980, Sept. 25

1834 A1221 15c multi .35 .25
1835 A1222 15c multi .35 .25
1836 A1223 15c multi .35 .25
1837 A1224 15c multi .35 .25
- *a.* Block of 4, #1834-1837 1.50 1.25

AMERICAN ARCHITECTURE SERIES

Smithsonian Institution, by James Renwick A1225

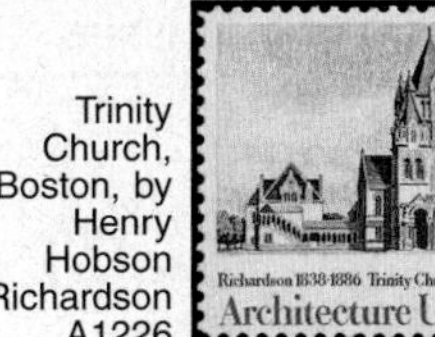

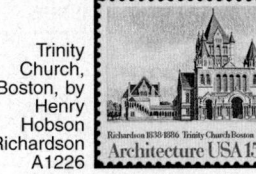

Trinity Church, Boston, by Henry Hobson Richardson A1226

Pennsylvania Academy of Fine Arts, by Frank Furness — A1227

Lyndhurst, Tarrytown, NY, by Alexander Jackson Davis A1228

ENGRAVED (Giori)

1980, Oct. 9

1838 A1225 15c black & red .30 .25
- *a.* Red missing (PS) —

1839 A1226 15c black & red .30 .25
1840 A1227 15c black & red .30 .25
1841 A1228 15c black & red .30 .25
- *a.* Block of 4, #1838-1841 1.25 1.25
- *b.* As "a," red missing on Nos. 1838, 1839 (PS) 400.00

CHRISTMAS ISSUE

Madonna and Child A1229

Wreath, Toys on Windowsill A1230

Design of No. 1842 after Epiphany Window, Washington Cathedral.

PHOTOGRAVURE

1980, Oct. 31

1842 A1229 15c multi .30 .25
- *a.* Imperf., pair 45.00

PHOTOGRAVURE (Combination Press)

1843 A1230 15c multi .30 .25
- *a.* Imperf., pair 50.00
- *b.* Buff omitted 22.50
- *c.* Vert. pair, imperf. horiz. —
- *d.* Horiz. pair, imperf. between 3,250.

No. 1843b is difficult to identify and should have a competent certificate.

GREAT AMERICANS ISSUE

A1231

A1232

A1233

A1234

A1235

A1236

A1237

A1238

A1239

A1240

A1241

A1242

A1243

A1244

A1245

A1246

A1247

A1248

A1249

A1250

A1251

A1252

A1253

A1254

A1255

A1256

ENGRAVED

Perf. 11x10½, 11 (1c, 6c-11c, 14c, No. 1862, 22c, 30c, 39c, 40c, 50c)

1980-85

1844 A1231 1c black ('83) .25 .25
- *a.* Imperf., pair 300.00
- *b.* Vert. pair, imperf. btwn. and with natural straight edge at bottom 1,400.
- *e.* Vert. pair, imperf. horiz. —

1845 A1232 2c brn blk ('82) .25 .25
1846 A1233 3c ol grn ('83) .25 .25
1847 A1234 4c violet ('83) .25 .25
1848 A1235 5c henna brn ('83) .30 .25
1849 A1236 6c org verm ('85) .25 .25
- *a.* Vert. pair, imperf. between and with natural straight edge at bottom 1,500.

1850 A1237 7c brt car ('85) .25 .25
1851 A1238 8c ol blk ('85) .25 .25
1852 A1239 9c dk grn ('86) .25 .25
1853 A1240 10c Prussian bl ('84) .25 .25
- *b.* Vert. pair, imperf. between 600.00
- *c.* Horiz. pair, imperf. between 1,750.
- *d.* Vert. pair, imperf horiz. —

Almost all examples of No. 1853b also have a natural straight edge at bottom. At least one pair has perfs at bottom and partial perfs at top.

Completely imperforate tagged or untagged stamps are from printer's waste. Known unused and used.

1854 A1241 11c dk blue ('85) .40 .25
1855 A1242 13c lt maroon ('82) .40 .25

1856 A1243 14c slate grn ('85) .30 .25
b. Vert. pair, imperf. horiz. *100.00*
c. Horiz. pair, imperf. between 8.00
d. Vert. pair, imperf. between *1,500.*
e. All color omitted —

No. 1856e comes from a partially printed pane and should be collected as a vertical strip of 10, one stamp normal, one stamp transitional and 8 stamps with color omitted.

1857 A1244 17c green ('81) .35 .25
1858 A1245 18c dk blue ('81) .35 .25
1859 A1246 19c brown .45 .25
1860 A1247 20c claret ('82) .40 .25
1861 A1248 20c green ('83) .50 .25
1862 A1249 20c black ('84) .40 .25
1863 A1250 22c dk chalky bl ('85) .75 .25
d. Vert. pair, imperf. horiz. *1,400.*
e. Vert. pair, imperf. between —
f. Horiz. pair, imperf. between *1,400.*
1864 A1251 30c ol gray ('84) .60 .25
b. Perf. 11.2, overall tagging 3.75 .25
1865 A1252 35c gray ('81) .75 .25
1866 A1253 37c blue ('82) .80 .25
1867 A1254 39c rose lilac ('85) 1.00 .25
a. Vert. pair, imperf. horiz. *400.00*
b. Vert. pair, imperf. between *1,500.*
1868 A1255 40c dk green ('84) 1.00 .25
1869 A1256 50c brown ('85) .95 .25
Nos. 1844-1869 (26) 11.95 6.50

A1261

A1262

EVERETT DIRKSEN (1896-1969)

Senate minority leader, 1960-1969.

ENGRAVED

1981, Jan. 4 *Perf. 11*
1874 A1261 15c gray .30 .25
a. All color omitted *500.00*

No. 1874a comes from a partially printed pane and may be collected as a vertical strip of 3 or 5 (1 or 3 stamps normal, one stamp transitional and one stamp with color omitted) or as a pair with one partially printed stamp.

BLACK HERITAGE SERIES

Whitney Moore Young, Jr. (1921-1971), civil rights leader.

PHOTOGRAVURE

1981, Jan. 30
1875 A1262 15c multi .35 .25

FLOWER ISSUE

A1263

A1264

A1265

A1266

1981, Apr. 23
1876 A1263 18c multicolored .35 .25
1877 A1264 18c multicolored .35 .25
1878 A1265 18c multicolored .35 .25
1879 A1266 18c multicolored .35 .25
a. Block of 4, #1876-1879 1.40 1.25

AMERICAN WILDLIFE

A1267

A1268

A1269

A1270

A1271

A1272

A1273 A1274

A1275

A1276

ENGRAVED

1981, May 14 **Dark brown**
1880 A1267 18c Bighorn .70 .25
1881 A1268 18c Puma .70 .25
1882 A1269 18c Harbor seal .70 .25
1883 A1270 18c American Buffalo .70 .25
1884 A1271 18c Brown bear .70 .25
1885 A1272 18c Polar bear .70 .25
1886 A1273 18c Elk (wapiti) .70 .25
1887 A1274 18c Moose .70 .25
1888 A1275 18c White-tailed deer .70 .25
1889 A1276 18c Pronghorn .70 .25
a. Booklet pane of 10, #1880-1889 7.00 6.00
Nos. 1880-1889 (10) 7.00 2.50

Nos. 1880-1889 issued in booklet only. All stamps have one or two straight edges.
Imperfs are from printer's waste.

FLAG AND ANTHEM ISSUE

A1277

A1278

A1279

A1280

ENGRAVED

1981, Apr. 24 *Perf. 11*
1890 A1277 18c multicolored .35 .25
a. Imperf., pair 70.00
b. Vert. pair, imperf. horiz. *550.00*
c. Vert. pair, imperf. between *550.00*

Coil Stamp

Perf. 10 Vert.

1891 A1278 18c multicolored .35 .25
a. Imperf., pair 17.50 —
b. Pair, imperf. between *1,750.*

Beware of pairs offered as No. 1891b that have faint blind perfs.
Vertical pairs and blocks exist from printer's waste.

Booklet Stamps

Perf. 11x10½ on 3 Sides

1892 A1279 6c dark blue & red .50 .25

Perf. 11x10½ on 2 or 3 Sides

1893 A1280 18c multicolored .30 .25
a. Booklet pane of 8 (2 #1892, 6 #1893) 3.00 2.50
b. As "a," vert. imperf. between 60.00
c. Se-tenant pair, #1892 & #1893 .90 1.00

Bureau Precanceled Coils
Starting with No. 1895b, Bureau precanceled coil stamps are valued unused as well as used. The coils issued with dull gum may be difficult to distinguish.
When used normally these stamps do not receive any postal markings so that used stamps with an additional postal cancellation of any kind are worth considerably less than the values shown here.

FLAG OVER SUPREME COURT ISSUE

A1281

1981, Dec. 17 *Perf. 11*
1894 A1281 20c blk, dk bl & red .40 .25
a. Vert. pair, imperf. 30.00
b. Vert. pair, imperf. horiz. *350.00*
c. Dark blue omitted *60.00*
d. Black omitted *225.00*

Coil Stamp

Perf. 10 Vert.

1895 A1281 20c blk, dk bl & red .40 .25
b. Untagged (Bureau precanceled, lines only) .50 .50
d. Imperf., pair 8.00 —
e. Pair, imperf. between *725.00*
f. Black omitted *45.00*
g. Dark blue omitted *1,200.*

The variety "black field of stars instead of blue" was caused by an inking roller smear.

BOOKLET STAMP

Perf. 11x10½ on 2 or 3 Sides

1896 A1281 20c blk, dk bl & red .40 .25
a. Booklet pane of 6 3.00 2.25
b. Booklet pane of 10, *June 1, 1982* 5.25 3.25

TRANSPORTATION ISSUE

A1283

A1284

COIL STAMPS
ENGRAVED

1981-84 *Perf. 10 Vert.*
1897 A1283 1c violet ('83) .25 .25
b. Imperf., pair *325.00*

The variety "black field of stars instead of blue" was caused by an inking roller smear.
See No. 2225.

1897A A1284 2c black ('82) .25 .25
c. Imperf., pair 45.00

See No. 2226.

A1284a

A1285

1898 A1284a 3c dk grn ('83) .25 .25
1898A A1285 4c reddish brn ('82) .25 .25
b. Untagged (Bureau precanceled, Nonprofit Org.) .25 .25
c. As "b," imperf., pair *450.00*
d. As No. 1898A, imperf. pair *450.00* —

See No. 2228.

A1286

A1287

1899 A1286 5c gray grn ('83) .25 .25
a. Imperf., pair *2,250.*
1900 A1287 5.2c car ('83) .25 .25
a. Untagged (Bureau precanceled, lines only) .25 .25

A1288

A1289

1901 A1288 5.9c blue ('82) .25 .25
a. Untagged (Bureau precanceled, lines only) .25 .25
b. As "a," imperf., pair *140.00*
1902 A1289 7.4c brown ('84) .25 .25
a. Untagged (Bureau precanceled, Blk. Rt. CAR-RT SORT) .25 .25

A1290

A1291

1903 A1290 9.3c car rose .30 .25
a. Untagged (Bureau precanceled, lines only) .25 .25
b. As "a," imperf., pair 90.00
1904 A1291 10.9c pur ('82) .30 .25
a. Untagged (Bureau precanceled, lines only) .30 .25
b. As "a," imperf., pair 125.00

A1292

A1293

1905 A1292 11c red ('84) .30 .25
a. Untagged *Sept. 1991* .25 .25

Untagged stamps from plate 1 come only Bureau precanceled with lines. Untagged stamps from plate 2 come only without precancel lines.

1906 A1293 17c ultra .35 .25
a. Untagged (Bureau precanceled, Presorted First Class) .35 .35
b. Imperf., pair 130.00
c. As "a," imperf., pair *400.00*

A1294

A1295

1907 A1294 18c dk brn .35 .25
a. Imperf., pair 95.00

1908 A1295 20c vermilion .35 .25
a. Imperf., pair 75.00
Nos. 1897-1908 (14) 3.95 3.50

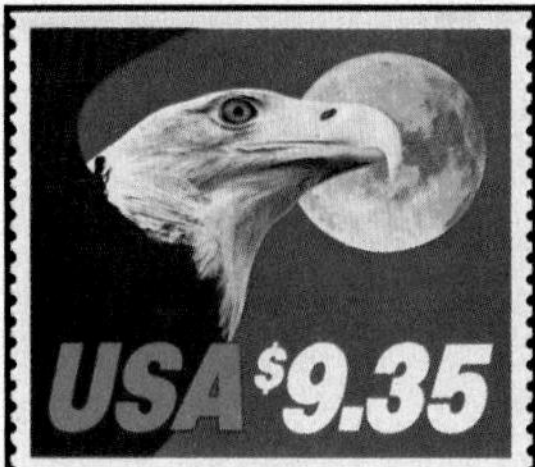

A1296

Booklet Stamp
PHOTOGRAVURE
Perf. 10 Vert. on 1 or 2 Sides

1983, Aug. 12 **Untagged**
1909 A1296 $9.35 multicolored 19.00 15.00
a. Booklet pane of 3 57.50 —

A1297

A1298

AMERICAN RED CROSS CENTENNIAL

Plates of 200 subjects in four panes of 50.

1981, May 1 ***Perf. 10½x11***
1910 A1297 18c multicolored .35 .25

SAVINGS & LOAN SESQUICENTENNIAL

1981, May 8 ***Perf. 11***
1911 A1298 18c multicolored .35 .25

SPACE ACHIEVEMENT ISSUE

A1299

A1302

A1300

A1301

A1303

A1306

A1304

A1305

Designs: A1299, Moon walk. A1300-A1301, A1304-A1305, Columbia space shuttle. A1302, Skylab. A1303, Pioneer 11. A1306, Telescope.

1981, May 21
1912 A1299 18c multicolored .40 .25
1913 A1300 18c multicolored .40 .25
1914 A1301 18c multicolored .40 .25
1915 A1302 18c multicolored .40 .25
1916 A1303 18c multicolored .40 .25
1917 A1304 18c multicolored .40 .25
1918 A1305 18c multicolored .40 .25
1919 A1306 18c multicolored .40 .25
a. Block of 8, #1912-1919 3.25 3.00
b. As "a," imperf. 5,000.
c. As "a," imperf. vert. —
e. As "a," top 4 stamps part perf, bottom 4 stamps imperf —

No. 1919c has blind horiz. perfs.

PROFESSIONAL MANAGEMENT EDUCATION CENTENARY

Joseph Wharton
A1307

1981, June 18
1920 A1307 18c blue & black .35 .25

PRESERVATION OF WILDLIFE HABITATS

A1308

A1309

A1310

A1311

1981, June 26
1921 A1308 18c multicolored .35 .25
1922 A1309 18c multicolored .35 .25
1923 A1310 18c multicolored .35 .25
1924 A1311 18c multicolored .35 .25
a. Block of 4, #1921-1924 1.50 1.25

INTERNATIONAL YEAR OF THE DISABLED

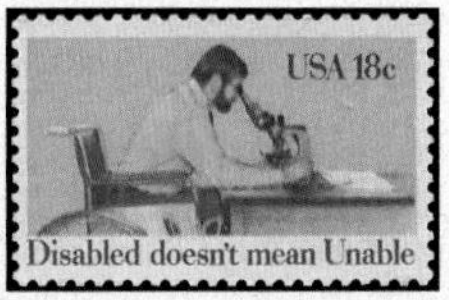

Man Looking through Microscope
A1312

1981, June 29
1925 A1312 18c multicolored .35 .25
a. Vert. pair, imperf. horiz. 2,000.

EDNA ST. VINCENT MILLAY ISSUE

A1313

LITHOGRAPHED AND ENGRAVED

1981, July 10
1926 A1313 18c multicolored .35 .25
a. Black (engr., inscriptions) omitted 200.00 —

ALCOHOLISM

A1314

ENGRAVED

1981, Aug. 19
1927 A1314 18c blue & black .45 .25
a. Imperf., pair 300.00
b. Vert. pair, imperf. horiz. 2,250.

AMERICAN ARCHITECTURE SERIES

New York University Library by Sanford White
A1315

Biltmore House by Richard Morris Hunt
A1316

Palace of the Arts by Bernard Maybeck
A1317

National Farmer's Bank by Louis Sullivan
A1318

1981, Aug. 28
1928 A1315 18c black & red .40 .25
1929 A1316 18c black & red .40 .25
1930 A1317 18c black & red .40 .25
1931 A1318 18c black & red .40 .25
a. Block of 4, #1928-1931 1.65 1.65

SPORTS PERSONALITIES

Mildred Didrikson Zaharias
A1319

Robert Tyre Jones
A1320

1981, Sept. 22 ***Perf. 10½x11***
1932 A1319 18c purple .40 .25
1933 A1320 18c green .60 .25

FREDERIC REMINGTON

Coming Through the Rye
A1321

LITHOGRAPHED AND ENGRAVED

1981, Oct. 9 ***Perf. 11***
1934 A1321 18c gray, olive green & brown .35 .25
a. Vert. pair, imperf. between 175.00
b. Brown omitted 225.00

JAMES HOBAN

Irish-American Architect of White House — A1322

PHOTOGRAVURE

1981, Oct. 13
1935 A1322 18c multicolored .35 .25
1936 A1322 20c multicolored .35 .25

See Ireland No. 504.

AMERICAN BICENTENNIAL

Battle of Yorktown
A1323

Battle of Virginia Capes
A1324

LITHOGRAPHED AND ENGRAVED

1981, Oct. 16
1937 A1323 18c multicolored .35 .25
1938 A1324 18c multicolored .35 .25
a. Pair, #1937-1938 .90 .75
b. As "a," black (engr., inscriptions) omitted 300.00
d. As "a," black (litho.) omitted —

CHRISTMAS

Madonna and Child, Botticelli — A1325

Felt Bear on Sled
A1326

PHOTOGRAVURE

1981, Oct. 28

1939	A1325 (20c) multicolored		.40	.25
a.	Imperf., pair		*90.00*	
b.	Vert. pair, imperf. horiz.		*850.00*	
1940	A1326 (20c) multicolored		.40	.25
a.	Imperf., pair		*175.00*	
b.	Vert. pair, imperf. horiz.		*2,500.*	

JOHN HANSON

First President of Continental Congress — A1327

1981, Nov. 5

1941	A1327 20c multicolored	.40	.25

DESERT PLANTS

Barrel Cactus — A1328

Agave — A1329

Beavertail Cactus — A1330

Saguaro — A1331

LITHOGRAPHED AND ENGRAVED

1981 Dec. 11

1942	A1328 20c multicolored	.35	.25
1943	A1329 20c multicolored	.35	.25
1944	A1330 20c multicolored	.35	.25
1945	A1331 20c multicolored	.35	.25
a.	Block of 4, #1942-1945	1.50	1.25
b.	As "a," deep brown (litho.) omitted	*3,750.*	
c.	No. 1945 imperf., vert. pair	*3,000.*	
d.	As "a," dark green & dark blue (engr.) missing (EP)	—	
e.	As "a," dark green (engr.) missing on left stamp (EP)	—	

A1332

A1333

PHOTOGRAVURE

1981, Oct. 11 ***Perf. 11x10½***

1946	A1332 (20c) brown	.40	.25
b.	All color omitted	*450.00*	

No. 1946b comes from a partially printed pane with most stamps normal. It must be collected as a vertical pair or strip with normal or partially printed stamps attached.

ENGRAVED

COIL STAMP

Perf. 10 Vert.

1947	A1332 (20c) brown	.60	.25
a.	Imperf. pair	*750.00*	

BOOKLET STAMPS

Perf. 11 on 2 or 3 Sides

1948	A1333 (20c) brown	.40	.25
a.	Booklet pane of 10	4.50	3.25

A1334

BOOKLET STAMP
ENGRAVED

Perf. 11 on 2 or 3 Sides

1982, Jan. 8

1949	A1334 20c dark blue	.55	.25
a.	Booklet pane of 10	5.50	2.50
b.	As "a," imperf. vert.	*90.00*	
c.	Type II	1.40	.25
d.	Type II, booklet pane of 10	14.00	—

No. 1949 is 18¾mm wide and has overall tagging. No. 1949c is 18½mm wide and has block tagging.

See No. 1880.

FRANKLIN DELANO ROOSEVELT

A1335

1982, Jan. 30 ***Perf. 11***

1950	A1335 20c blue	.40	.25

LOVE ISSUE

A1336

PHOTOGRAVURE

1982, Feb. 1 ***Perf. 11¼***

1951	A1336 20c multicolored	.40	.25
b.	Imperf., pair	*200.00*	
c.	Blue omitted	*200.00*	
d.	Yellow omitted	*650.00*	
e.	Purple omitted	—	

No. 1951c is valued in the grade of fine.

Perf. 11¼x10½

1951A	A1336 20c multicolored	.75	.25

GEORGE WASHINGTON

A1337

1982, Feb. 22 ***Perf. 11***

1952	A1337 20c multicolored	.40	.25

A1338

STATE BIRDS AND FLOWERS ISSUE

1982, Apr. 14 ***Perf. 10½x11¼***

1953	A1338	20c Alabama	.55	.30
1954	A1339	20c Alaska	.55	.30
1955	A1340	20c Arizona	.55	.30
1956	A1341	20c Arkansas	.55	.30
1957	A1342	20c California	.55	.30
1958	A1343	20c Colorado	.55	.30
1959	A1344	20c Connecticut	.55	.30
1960	A1345	20c Delaware	.55	.30
1961	A1346	20c Florida	.55	.30
1962	A1347	20c Georgia	.55	.30
1963	A1348	20c Hawaii	.55	.30
1964	A1349	20c Idaho	.55	.30
1965	A1350	20c Illinois	.55	.30
1966	A1351	20c Indiana	.55	.30
1967	A1352	20c Iowa	.55	.30
1968	A1353	20c Kansas	.55	.30
1969	A1354	20c Kentucky	.55	.30
1970	A1355	20c Louisiana	.55	.30
1971	A1356	20c Maine	.55	.30
1972	A1357	20c Maryland	.55	.30
1973	A1358	20c Massachusetts	.55	.30
1974	A1359	20c Michigan	.55	.30
1975	A1360	20c Minnesota	.55	.30
1976	A1361	20c Mississippi	.55	.30
1977	A1362	20c Missouri	.55	.30
1978	A1363	20c Montana	.55	.30
1979	A1364	20c Nebraska	.55	.30
1980	A1365	20c Nevada	.55	.30
1981	A1366	20c New Hampshire	.55	.30
b.		Black missing (EP)	*5,000.*	
1982	A1367	20c New Jersey	.55	.30
1983	A1368	20c New Mexico	.55	.30
1984	A1369	20c New York	.55	.30
1985	A1370	20c North Carolina	.55	.30
1986	A1371	20c North Dakota	.55	.30
1987	A1372	20c Ohio	.55	.30
1988	A1373	20c Oklahoma	.55	.30
1989	A1374	20c Oregon	.55	.30
1990	A1375	20c Pennsylvania	.55	.30
1991	A1376	20c Rhode Island	.55	.30
b.		Black missing (EP)	*5,000.*	
1992	A1377	20c South Carolina	.55	.30
1993	A1378	20c South Dakota	.55	.30
1994	A1379	20c Tennessee	.55	.30
1995	A1380	20c Texas	.55	.30
1996	A1381	20c Utah	.55	.30
1997	A1382	20c Vermont	.55	.30
1998	A1383	20c Virginia	.55	.30
1999	A1384	20c Washington	.55	.30
2000	A1385	20c West Virginia	.55	.30
2001	A1386	20c Wisconsin	.55	.30
b.		Black missing (EP)	*5,000.*	
2002	A1387	20c Wyoming	.55	.30
b.		A1338-A1387 Pane of 50, Nos. 1953-2002	27.50	20.00
d.		Pane of 50, imperf.	*27,500.*	

Perf. 11¼x11

1953A	A1338	20c Alabama	.65	.30
1954A	A1339	20c Alaska	.65	.30
1955A	A1340	20c Arizona	.65	.30
1956A	A1341	20c Arkansas	.65	.30
1957A	A1342	20c California	.65	.30
1958A	A1343	20c Colorado	.65	.30
1959A	A1344	20c Connecticut	.65	.30
1960A	A1345	20c Delaware	.65	.30
1961A	A1346	20c Florida	.65	.30
1962A	A1347	20c Georgia	.65	.30
1963A	A1348	20c Hawaii	.65	.30
1964A	A1349	20c Idaho	.65	.30
1965A	A1350	20c Illinois	.65	.30
1966A	A1351	20c Indiana	.65	.30
1967A	A1352	20c Iowa	.65	.30
1968A	A1353	20c Kansas	.65	.30
1969A	A1354	20c Kentucky	.65	.30
1970A	A1355	20c Louisiana	.65	.30
1971A	A1356	20c Maine	.65	.30
1972A	A1357	20c Maryland	.65	.30
1973A	A1358	20c Massachusetts	.65	.30
1974A	A1359	20c Michigan	.65	.30
1975A	A1360	20c Minnesota	.65	.30
1976A	A1361	20c Mississippi	.65	.30
1977A	A1362	20c Missouri	.65	.30
1978A	A1363	20c Montana	.65	.30
1979A	A1364	20c Nebraska	.65	.30
1980A	A1365	20c Nevada	.65	.30
1981A	A1366	20c New Hampshire	.65	.30
1982A	A1367	20c New Jersey	.65	.30
1983A	A1368	20c New Mexico	.65	.30
1984A	A1369	20c New York	.65	.30
1985A	A1370	20c North Carolina	.65	.30
1986A	A1371	20c North Dakota	.65	.30
1987A	A1372	20c Ohio	.65	.30
1988A	A1373	20c Oklahoma	.65	.30
1989A	A1374	20c Oregon	.65	.30
1990A	A1375	20c Pennsylvania	.65	.30
1991A	A1376	20c Rhode Island	.65	.30
1992A	A1377	20c South Carolina	.65	.30
1993A	A1378	20c South Dakota	.65	.30
1994A	A1379	20c Tennessee	.65	.30
1995A	A1380	20c Texas	.65	.30
1996A	A1381	20c Utah	.65	.30
1997A	A1382	20c Vermont	.65	.30
1998A	A1383	20c Virginia	.65	.30
1999A	A1384	20c Washington	.65	.30
2000A	A1385	20c West Virginia	.65	.30
2001A	A1386	20c Wisconsin	.65	.30
2002A	A1387	20c Wyoming	.65	.30
c.		A1338-A1387 Pane of 50, Nos. 1953A-2002A	32.50	22.50

US-NETHERLANDS

200th Anniv. of Diplomatic Recognition by the Netherlands
A1388

1982, Apr. 20 ***Perf. 11***

2003	A1388 20c multicolored	.40	.25
a.	Imperf., pair	*225.00*	

See Netherlands Nos. 640-641.

LIBRARY OF CONGRESS

A1389

ENGRAVED

1982, Apr. 21

2004	A1389 20c red & black	.40	.25
a.	All color missing	—	

No. 2004a must be collected as a right margin horiz. strip of 3, 4 or 5 with one No. 2004a, one transitional stamp and one or more normal stamps.

CONSUMER EDUCATION

A1390

Coil Stamp

1982, Apr. 27 ***Perf. 10 Vert.***

2005	A1390 20c sky blue	.55	.25
a.	Imperf., pair	75.00	

KNOXVILLE WORLD'S FAIR

A1391

A1392

A1393

A1394

PHOTOGRAVURE

1982, Apr. 29 *Perf. 11*

2006 A1391 20c multicolored .45 .25

2007 A1392 20c multicolored .45 .25

2008 A1393 20c multicolored .45 .25

2009 A1394 20c multicolored .45 .25

a. Block of 4, #2006-2009 1.80 1.50

HORATIO ALGER

Frontispiece from "Ragged Dick" — A1395

ENGRAVED

1982, Apr. 30

2010 A1395 20c red & black, *tan* .40 .25

a. Red and black omitted —

The Philatelic Foundation has issued a certificate for a pane of 50 with red and black colors omitted. Recognition of this error is by the paper and by a tiny residue of red ink from the tagging roller. The engraved plates did not strike the paper.

AGING TOGETHER

A1396

ENGRAVED

1982, May 21

2011 A1396 20c brown .40 .25

A1397

A1398

PERFORMING ARTS SERIES

PHOTOGRAVURE

1982, June 8

2012 A1397 20c multicolored .40 .25

a. Black missing (EP) —

John (1882-1942), Ethel (1879-1959), and Lionel (1878-1954) Barrymore, actors.

DR. MARY WALKER

1982, June 10

2013 A1398 20c multicolored .40 .25

Dr. Mary Walker (1832-1919), 1865 recipient of Medal of Honor.

INTERNATIONAL PEACE GARDEN

A1399

LITHOGRAPHED AND ENGRAVED

1982, June 30

2014 A1399 20c multicolored .50 .25

a. Black (engr.) omitted 200.00

A1400

A1401

AMERICA'S LIBRARIES

ENGRAVED

1982, July 13

2015 A1400 20c red & black .40 .25

a. Vert. pair, imperf. horiz. 200.00

c. All colors missing (EP) 175.00

On No. 2015c, an albino impression of the design is present.

BLACK HERITAGE SERIES

Jackie Robinson (1919-72), baseball player.

PHOTOGRAVURE

1982, Aug. 2 *Perf. 10½x11*

2016 A1401 20c multicolored 1.10 .25

TOURO SYNAGOGUE

A1402

PHOTOGRAVURE AND ENGRAVED

1982, Aug. 22 *Perf. 11*

2017 A1402 20c multicolored .45 .25

a. Imperf., pair 1,750.

WOLF TRAP FARM PARK

A1403

PHOTOGRAVURE

1982, Sept. 1

2018 A1403 20c multicolored .40 .25

AMERICAN ARCHITECTURE SERIES

Fallingwater, Mill Run, Pa., by Frank Lloyd Wright — A1404

Illinois Institute of Technology by Ludwig Mies van der Rohe A1405

Gropius House, Lincoln, Mass., by Walter Gropius A1406

Dulles Airport, by Eero Saarinen A1407

ENGRAVED

1982, Sept. 30

2019 A1404 20c black & brown .45 .25

b. Red missing (PS) —

2020 A1405 20c black & brown .45 .25

a. Red missing (PS) —

2021 A1406 20c black & brown .45 .25

2022 A1407 20c black & brown .45 .25

a. Block of 4, #2019-2022 2.00 1.75

FRANCIS OF ASSISI

A1408

PHOTOGRAVURE

1982, Oct. 7

2023 A1408 20c multicolored .40 .25

PONCE DE LEON

A1409

PHOTOGRAVURE (Combination press)

1982, Oct. 12

2024 A1409 20c multicolored .50 .25

a. Imperf., pair 575.00

b. Vert. pair, imperf. between and at top —

CHRISTMAS ISSUES

A1410

A1411

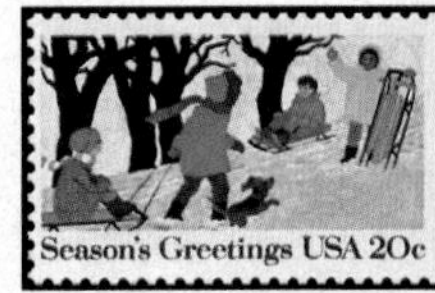

A1412

A1413

A1414

A1415

PHOTOGRAVURE

1982, Nov. 3

2025 A1410 13c multicolored .25 .25

a. Imperf., pair 300.00

PHOTOGRAVURE (Combination Press)

1982, Oct. 28

2026 A1411 20c multicolored .40 .25

a. Imperf. pair 115.00

b. Horiz. pair, imperf. vert. —

c. Vert. pair, imperf. horiz. —

PHOTOGRAVURE

2027 A1412 20c multicolored .60 .25

2028 A1413 20c multicolored .60 .25

2029 A1414 20c multicolored .60 .25

2030 A1415 20c multicolored .60 .25

a. Block of 4, #2027-2030 2.40 1.50

b. As "a," imperf. 1,250.

c. As "a," imperf. horiz. 700.00

Nos. 2025-2030 (6) 3.05 1.50

SCIENCE & INDUSTRY

A1416

LITHOGRAPHED AND ENGRAVED

1983, Jan. 19

2031 A1416 20c multicolored .40 .25

a. Black (engr.) omitted 1,000.

BALLOONS

A1417

A1420

A1418

A1419

PHOTOGRAVURE

1983, Mar. 31 **Tagged** *Perf. 11*

2032 A1417 20c multicolored .50 .25

2033 A1418 20c multicolored .50 .25

2034 A1419 20c multicolored .50 .25

2035 A1420 20c multicolored .50 .25

a. Block of 4, #2032-2035 2.00 1.50

b. As "a," imperf. 3,000.

c. As "a," right stamp perf., otherwise imperf. 3,000.

US-SWEDEN

A1421

ENGRAVED

1983, Mar. 24

2036 A1421 20c blue, blk & red brn .40 .25

See Sweden No. 1453.

CCC, 50th ANNIV.

A1422

PHOTOGRAVURE

1983, Apr. 5

2037 A1422 20c multicolored .40 .25
a. Imperf., pair *2,500.*
b. Vert. pair, imperf. horiz. —

JOSEPH PRIESTLEY

A1423

1983, Apr. 13

2038 A1423 20c multicolored .40 .25

VOLUNTEERISM

A1424

ENGRAVED (Combination Press)

1983, Apr. 20

2039 A1424 20c red & black .40 .25
a. Imperf., pair *225.00*

US-GERMANY

Concord, 1683
A1425

ENGRAVED

1983, Apr. 29

2040 A1425 20c brown .40 .25

See Germany No. 1397.

BROOKLYN BRIDGE

A1426

1983, May 17

2041 A1426 20c blue .40 .25
b. All color missing (EP) *75.00*

On No. 2041b, an albino impression of part of the design is evident.

TVA

A1427

PHOTOGRAVURE AND ENGRAVED (Combination Press)

1983, May 18

2042 A1427 20c multicolored .40 .25

A1428

PHOTOGRAVURE (Combination Press)

1983, May 14

2043 A1428 20c multicolored .40 .25

BLACK HERITAGE SERIES

A1429

PHOTOGRAVURE

1983, June 9

2044 A1429 20c multicolored .50 .25
a. Imperf., pair *300.00*

MEDAL OF HONOR

A1430

LITHOGRAPHED AND ENGRAVED

1983, June 7

2045 A1430 20c multicolored .55 .25
a. Red omitted *175.00*

A1431

A1432

GEORGE HERMAN RUTH (1895-1948)

ENGRAVED

1983, July 6 *Perf. 10½x11*

2046 A1431 20c blue 1.40 .25

LITERARY ARTS SERIES

Nathaniel Hawthorne (1804-1864), novelist.

PHOTOGRAVURE

1983, July 8 *Perf. 11*

2047 A1432 20c multicolored .45 .25

1984 SUMMER OLYMPICS

Discus
A1433

High Jump
A1434

Archery
A1435

Boxing
A1436

1983, July 28

2048 A1433 13c multicolored .35 .25
2049 A1434 13c multicolored .35 .25
2050 A1435 13c multicolored .35 .25
2051 A1436 13c multicolored .35 .25
a. Block of 4, #2048-2051 1.50 1.25

SIGNING OF TREATY OF PARIS

John Adams, Franklin, John Jay, David Hartley
A1437

1983, Sept. 2

2052 A1437 20c multicolored .40 .25

CIVIL SERVICE

A1438

PHOTOGRAVURE AND ENGRAVED

1983, Sept. 9

2053 A1438 20c buff, blue & red .40 .25

METROPOLITAN OPERA

A1439

LITHOGRAPHED AND ENGRAVED

1983, Sept. 14

2054 A1439 20c yellow & maroon .40 .25

AMERICAN INVENTORS

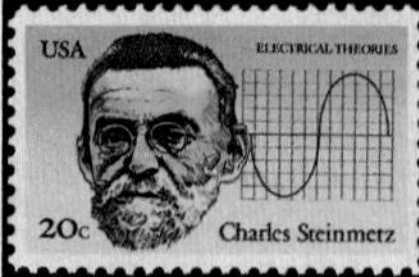

A1440

A1441

A1442

A1443

LITHOGRAPHED AND ENGRAVED

1983, Sept. 21

2055 A1440 20c multicolored .50 .25
2056 A1441 20c multicolored .50 .25
2057 A1442 20c multicolored .50 .25
2058 A1443 20c multicolored .50 .25
a. Block of 4, #2055-2058 2.00 1.50
b. As "a," black omitted *300.00*

STREETCARS

A1444

A1445

A1446

A1447

PHOTOGRAVURE AND ENGRAVED

1983, Oct. 8

2059 A1444 20c multicolored .50 .25
2060 A1445 20c multicolored .50 .25
a. Horiz. pair, black (engr.) missing on Nos. 2059, 2060 (EP) —
2061 A1446 20c multicolored .50 .25
a. Vert. pair, black (engr.) missing on Nos. 2059, 2061 (EP) —
2062 A1447 20c multicolored .50 .25
a. Block of 4, #2059-2062 2.00 1.50
b. As "a," black (engr.) omitted *275.00*
c. As "a," black (engr.) omitted on #2059, 2061 —

CHRISTMAS

A1448

A1449

PHOTOGRAVURE

1983, Oct. 28

2063 A1448 20c multicolored .40 .25
2064 A1449 20c multicolored .40 .25
a. Imperf., pair *100.00*

Martin Luther (1483-1546), German Religious Leader
A1450

Caribou and Alaska Pipeline
A1451

MARTIN LUTHER (1483-1546)

1983, Nov. 11

2065 A1450 20c multicolored .40 .25

ALASKA STATEHOOD, 25th ANNIV.

1984, Jan. 3

2066 A1451 20c multicolored .40 .25
a. Vert. pair, imperf. horiz. —

14th WINTER OLYMPIC GAMES

Ice Dancing
A1452

Downhill Skiing
A1453

Cross-country Skiing
A1454

Hockey
A1455

1984, Jan. 6 *Perf. 10½x11*

2067 A1452 20c multicolored .55 .25
2068 A1453 20c multicolored .55 .25
2069 A1454 20c multicolored .55 .25
2070 A1455 20c multicolored .55 .25
a. Block of 4, #2067-2070 2.20 1.75

A1456

LOVE LOVE LOVE LOVE LOVE USA 20c
A1457

FEDERAL DEPOSIT INSURANCE CORPORATION, 50TH ANNIV.

1984, Jan. 12 *Perf. 11*

2071 A1456 20c multicolored .40 .25

LOVE

PHOTOGRAVURE AND ENGRAVED
(Combination Press)

1984, Jan. 31 *Perf. 11x10½*

2072 A1457 20c multicolored .40 .25
a. Horiz. pair, imperf. vert. *125.00*

A1458

A1459

BLACK HERITAGE SERIES

Carter G. Woodson (1875-1950), Historian.

PHOTOGRAVURE

1984, Feb. 1 *Perf. 11*

2073 A1458 20c multicolored .40 .25
a. Horiz. pair, imperf. vert. *800.00*

SOIL & WATER CONSERVATION

1984, Feb. 6

2074 A1459 20c multicolored .40 .25

50TH ANNIV. OF CREDIT UNION ACT

Dollar Sign, Coin — A1460

1984, Feb. 10

2075 A1460 20c multicolored .40 .25

ORCHIDS

A1461

A1462

A1463

A1464

1984, Mar. 5

2076 A1461 20c multicolored .50 .25
2077 A1462 20c multicolored .50 .25
2078 A1463 20c multicolored .50 .25
2079 A1464 20c multicolored .50 .25
a. Block of 4, #2076-2079 2.00 1.50

HAWAII STATEHOOD, 25th ANNIV.

Eastern Polynesian Canoe, Golden Plover, Mauna Loa Volcano
A1465

1984, Mar. 12

2080 A1465 20c multicolored .40 .25

50TH ANNIV., NATIONAL ARCHIVES

Abraham Lincoln, George Washington
A1466

1984, Apr. 16

2081 A1466 20c multicolored .40 .25

LOS ANGELES SUMMER OLYMPICS

Diving — A1467

Long Jump — A1468

Wrestling
A1469

Kayak
A1470

1984, May 4

2082 A1467 20c multicolored .55 .25
2083 A1468 20c multicolored .55 .25
2084 A1469 20c multicolored .55 .25
2085 A1470 20c multicolored .55 .25
a. Block of 4, #2082-2085 2.40 1.90
b. As "a," imperf between vertically *9,500.*

LOUISIANA WORLD EXPOSITION

River Wildlife
A1471

1984, May 11

2086 A1471 20c multicolored .50 .25

HEALTH RESEARCH

Lab Equipment
A1472

1984, May 17

2087 A1472 20c multicolored .40 .25

A1473

A1474

PERFORMING ARTS

PHOTOGRAVURE AND ENGRAVED
(Combination Press)

1984, May 23

2088 A1473 20c multicolored .50 .25
b. Horiz. pair, imperf between —

JIM THORPE

ENGRAVED

1984, May 24

2089 A1474 20c dark brown .60 .25
a. All color omitted —

On No. 2089a, an albino impression of the design is evident.

PERFORMING ARTS

Tenor John McCormack (1884-1945)
A1475

PHOTOGRAVURE

1984, June 6

2090 A1475 20c multicolored .40 .25

See Ireland No. 594.

ST. LAWRENCE SEAWAY, 25th ANNIV.

Aerial View of Seaway, Freighters
A1476

1984, June 26

2091 A1476 20c multicolored .40 .25

WATERFOWL PRESERVATION ACT, 50th ANNIV.

"Mallards Dropping In," by Jay N. Darling
A1477

ENGRAVED

1984, July 2 *Perf. 11*

2092 A1477 20c blue .50 .25
a. Horiz. pair, imperf. vert. *275.00*

The Elizabeth
A1478

Herman Melville (1819-1891), Author
A1479

ROANOKE VOYAGES

PHOTOGRAVURE

1984, July 13

2093 A1478 20c multicolored .40 .25

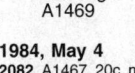

LITERARY ARTS SERIES

ENGRAVED

1984, Aug. 1

2094 A1479 20c sage green .40 .25

Junior Achievement Founder A1480

Smokey Bear A1481

HORACE MOSES (1862-1947), FOUNDER OF JUNIOR ACHIEVEMENT

ENGRAVED (Combination Press)

1984, Aug. 6

2095 A1480 20c orange & dark brown .45 .25

SMOKEY BEAR

LITHOGRAPHED AND ENGRAVED

1984, Aug. 13

2096 A1481 20c multicolored .40 .25
- *a.* Horiz. pair, imperf. btwn. *200.00*
- *b.* Vert. pair, imperf. btwn. *150.00*
- *c.* Block of 4, imperf. btwn. vert. and horiz. *2,750.*
- *d.* Horiz. pair, imperf. vert. *850.00*

ROBERTO CLEMENTE (1934-1972)

Clemente, Puerto Rican Flag — A1482

PHOTOGRAVURE

1984, Aug. 17

2097 A1482 20c multicolored 1.40 .25
- *a.* Horiz. pair, imperf. vert. *1,250.*

DOGS

Beagle, Boston Terrier A1483

Chesapeake Bay Retriever, Cocker Spaniel A1484

Alaskan Malamute, Collie A1485

Black & Tan Coonhound, American Foxhound A1486

1984, Sept. 7

2098 A1483 20c multicolored .50 .25
2099 A1484 20c multicolored .50 .25
2100 A1485 20c multicolored .50 .25
2101 A1486 20c multicolored .50 .25
- *a.* Block of 4, #2098-2101 2.00 1.90
- *b.* As "a," imperf horiz. —

CRIME PREVENTION

McGruff, The Crime Dog — A1487

1984, Sept. 26

2102 A1487 20c multicolored .40 .25

HISPANIC AMERICANS

A1488

1984, Oct. 31

2103 A1488 20c multicolored .40 .25
- *a.* Vert. pair, imperf. horiz. *1,500.*

FAMILY UNITY

A1489

PHOTOGRAVURE AND ENGRAVED (Combination Press)

1984, Oct. 1

2104 A1489 20c multicolored .40 .25
- *a.* Horiz. pair, imperf. vert. *325.00*
- *c.* Vert. pair, imperf. btwn. and at bottom —
- *d.* Horiz. pair, imperf. between —

A1490

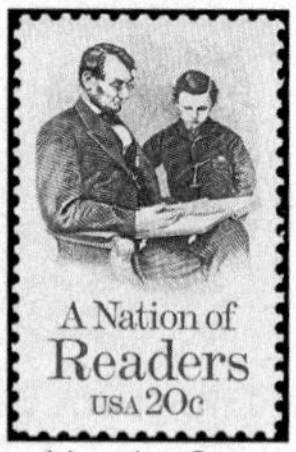

Lincoln, Son Tad — A1491

ELEANOR ROOSEVELT (1884-1962)

ENGRAVED

1984, Oct. 11

2105 A1490 20c deep blue .40 .25

NATION OF READERS

1984, Oct. 16

2106 A1491 20c brown & maroon .40 .25

CHRISTMAS

Madonna and Child by Fra Filippo Lippi — A1492

Santa Claus — A1493

PHOTOGRAVURE

1984, Oct. 30

2107 A1492 20c multicolored .40 .25
- *a.* Imperf., pair —

2108 A1493 20c multicolored .40 .25
- *a.* Horiz. pair, imperf. vert. *750.00*

No. 2108a is valued in the grade of fine.

VIETNAM VETERANS MEMORIAL

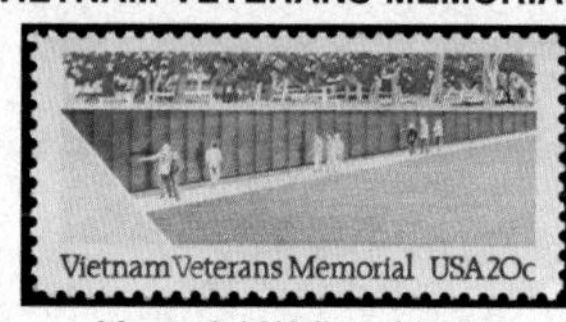

Memorial Wall — A1494

ENGRAVED

1984, Nov. 10

2109 A1494 20c multicolored .50 .25

PERFORMING ARTS

Composer Jerome Kern (1885-1945) A1495

PHOTOGRAVURE

1985, Jan. 23

2110 A1495 22c multicolored .45 .25

A1496

A1497

PHOTOGRAVURE

1985, Feb. 1 ***Perf. 11***

2111 A1496 (22c) green .60 .25
- *a.* Vert. pair, imperf. 35.00
- *b.* Vert. pair, imperf. horiz. *850.00*

COIL STAMP

Perf. 10 Vert.

2112 A1496 (22c) green .60 .25
- *a.* Imperf., pair *45.00*

BOOKLET STAMP

ENGRAVED

Perf. 11 on 2 or 3 Sides

2113 A1497 (22c) green .80 .25
- *a.* Booklet pane of 10 8.50 3.00
- *b.* As "a," Horiz. imperf. btwn. —

A1498

Flag over Capitol Dome A1499

ENGRAVED

1985, Mar. 29 ***Perf. 11***

2114 A1498 22c blue, red & black .45 .25
- *a.* All color missing (EP) —

No. 2114a should be collected se-tenant with a normal or a partially printed stamp.

COIL STAMP

Perf. 10 Vert.

2115 A1498 22c blue, red & black .45 .25
- *c.* Inscribed "T" at bottom ('87) .55 .40
- *f.* Imperf., pair 10.00

The variety "black field of stars instead of blue" was caused by an inking roller smear.

BOOKLET STAMP

Perf. 10 Horiz.

2116 A1499 22c blue, red & black .50 .25
- *a.* Booklet pane of 5 2.50 1.25

BOOKLET STAMPS

Frilled Dogwinkle A1500

Reticulated Helmet A1501

New England Neptune A1502

Calico Scallop A1503

Lightning Whelk — A1504

ENGRAVED

Perf. 10 on 2 or 3 Sides

1985, Apr. 4

2117 A1500 22c black & brown .45 .25
2118 A1501 22c black & multi .45 .25
2119 A1502 22c black & brown .45 .25
2120 A1503 22c black & violet .45 .25
2121 A1504 22c black & multi .45 .25
- *a.* Booklet pane of 10, 2 ea #2117-2121 4.50 3.00
- *b.* As "a," violet omitted on both Nos. 2120 *425.00*
- *c.* As "a," vert. imperf. between *375.00*
- *d.* As "a," imperf. —
- *e.* Strip of 5, Nos. 2117-2121 2.00 —

Eagle and Half Moon — A1505

TYPE I: washed out, dull appearance most evident in the black of the body of the eagle, and the red in the background between the eagle's shoulder and the moon. "$10.75" appears splotchy or grainy (P# 11111).

TYPE II: brighter, more intense colors most evident in the black on the eagle's body, and red in the background. "$10.75" appears smoother, brighter, and less grainy (P# 22222).

PHOTOGRAVURE

Perf. 10 Vert. on 1 or 2 Sides

1985, Apr. 29 **Untagged**

2122 A1505 $10.75 multi, type I 19.00 7.50
a. Booklet pane of 3 60.00 —
b. Type II, *June 19, 1989* 21.00 10.00
c. As "b," booklet pane of 3 65.00 —

TRANSPORTATION ISSUE

A1506

Buckboard 1880s USA 4.9

A1507

A1508

Tricycle 1880s 6 USA

A1509

A1510

Ambulance 1860s 8.3 USA

A1511

A1512

Oil Wagon 1890s 10.1 USA

A1513

A1514

Stanley Steamer 1909 USA 12

A1515

A1516

Iceboat 1880s USA 14

A1517

A1518

A1519

COIL STAMPS
ENGRAVED

1985-89 **Tagged** ***Perf. 10 Vert.***

2123 A1506 3.4c dk bluish green .25 .25
a. Untagged (Bureau precancel, Nonprofit Org. CAR-RT SORT) .25 .25
2124 A1507 4.9c brn blk .25 .25
a. Untagged (Bureau precancel, Nonprofit Org.) .25 .25
2125 A1508 5.5c dp mag ('86) .25 .25
a. Untagged (Bureau precancel, Nonprofit Org. CAR-RT SORT) .25 .25
2126 A1509 6c red brn .35 .25
a. Untagged (Bureau precancel, Nonprofit Org.) .25 .25
b. As "a," imperf., pair 175.00
2127 A1510 7.1c lake ('87) .25 .25
a. Untagged (Bureau precancel) .25 .25
c. As "a," black (precancel) omitted —

On. No. 2127c, an albino impression of the precancel is present.

2128 A1511 8.3c green .25 .25
a. Untagged (Bureau precancel, Blk. Rt. CAR-RT SORT) .25 .25

On No. 2231 "Ambulance 1860s" is 18mm long; on No. 2128, 18 ⅓mm long.

2129 A1512 8.5c dk Prus grn ('87) .25 .25
a. Untagged (Bureau precancel, Nonprofit Org.) .25 .25
2130 A1513 10.1c slate blue .55 .25
a. Untagged (Bureau precancel "Bulk Rate Carrier Route Sort" in red) ('88) .25 .25
b. As "a," red precancel, imperf, pair 15.00
As "a," black precancel, imperf, pair 70.00
2131 A1514 11c dk green .25 .25
2132 A1515 12c dk bl, I .35 .25
a. Untagged, type I (Bureau precancel, PRESORTED FIRST-CLASS), *Apr. 2* .25 .25
b. Untagged, type II (Bureau precancel, PRESORTED FIRST-CLASS) ('87) .40 .30

Type II has "Stanley Steamer 1909" ⅛mm shorter (17⅔mm) than No. 2132 (18mm).

2133 A1516 12.5c ol grn .35 .25
a. Untagged (Bureau precancel, Bulk Rate) .25 .25
b. As "a," imperf., pair 45.00
2134 A1517 14c sky bl, I .30 .25
a. Imperf., pair 80.00
b. Type II ('86) .30 .25
c. Tagging omitted, type I 35.00 —

Type II design is ¼mm narrower (17 ¼mm) than the original stamp (17 ½mm) and has block tagging. No. 2134 has overall tagging.

2135 A1518 17c brt bl ('86) .55 .25
a. Imperf., pair 325.00
2136 A1519 25c org brn ('86) .50 .25
a. Imperf., pair 11.00
b. Pair, imperf. between 525.00
Nos. 2123-2136 (14) 4.70 3.50

See Nos. 1897-1908, 2225-2231, 2252-2266, 2451-2468.

BLACK HERITAGE SERIES

Mary McLeod Bethune (1875-1955), Educator — A1520

PHOTOGRAVURE

1985, Mar. 5 ***Perf. 11***

2137 A1520 22c multicolored .60 .25

AMERICAN FOLK ART SERIES
Duck Decoys

Broadbill A1521

Mallard A1522

Canvasback A1523

Redhead A1524

1985, Mar. 22

2138 A1521 22c multicolored 1.00 .25
2139 A1522 22c multicolored 1.00 .25
2140 A1523 22c multicolored 1.00 .25
2141 A1524 22c multicolored 1.00 .25
a. Block of 4, #2138-2141 4.00 2.75

WINTER SPECIAL OLYMPICS

Ice Skater, Emblem, Skier A1525

1985, Mar. 25

2142 A1525 22c multicolored .50 .25
a. Vert. pair, imperf. horiz. 325.00

LOVE

A1526

1985, Apr. 17

2143 A1526 22c multicolored .45 .25
a. Imperf., pair 900.00

RURAL ELECTRIFICATION ADMINISTRATION

Electrified Farm A1527

PHOTOGRAVURE & ENGRAVED
(Combination Press)

1985, May 11

2144 A1527 22c multicolored .60 .25
a. Vert. pair, imperf between —

AMERIPEX '86

U.S. No. 134 — A1528

LITHOGRAPHED & ENGRAVED

1985, May 25

2145 A1528 22c multicolored .45 .25
a. Red, black & blue (engr.) omitted 150.00
b. Red & black omitted —
c. Red omitted 2,000.
d. Black missing (PS) —

ABIGAIL ADAMS (1744-1818)

Abigail Adams (1744-1818) A1529

PHOTOGRAVURE

1985, June 14

2146 A1529 22c multicolored .45 .25
a. Imperf., pair 200.00

FREDERIC AUGUSTE BARTHOLDI (1834-1904)

Frederic Auguste Bartholdi (1834-1904), Statue of Liberty — A1530

LITHOGRAPHED & ENGRAVED

1985, July 18

2147 A1530 22c multicolored .45 .25

Examples of No. 2147 exist with most, but not all, of the engraved black omitted.

George Washington, Washington Monument A1532

Envelopes A1533

COIL STAMPS
PHOTOGRAVURE

1985 ***Perf. 10 Vertically***

2149 A1532 18c multicolored .40 .25
a. Untagged (Bureau precancel) .35 .35
b. Imperf., pair 750.00
c. As "a," imperf., pair 575.00
2150 A1533 21.1c multicolored .40 .25
a. Untagged (Bureau Precancel) .40 .40

Precancellations on Nos. 2149a ("PRESORTED FIRST-CLASS") and 2150a ("ZIP+4") do not have lines.

KOREAN WAR VETERANS

American Troops in Korea A1535

ENGRAVED

1985, July 26 ***Perf. 11***

2152 A1535 22c gray green & rose red .45 .25

SOCIAL SECURITY ACT, 50th ANNIV.

Men, Women, Children, Corinthian Columns A1536

PHOTOGRAVURE

1985, Aug. 14

2153 A1536 22c deep & light blue .45 .25

WORLD WAR I VETERANS

The Battle of Marne, France, by Harvey Dunn A1537

ENGRAVED

1985, Aug. 26

2154 A1537 22c gray green & rose red .45 .25
a. Red missing (PS) 275.00

HORSES

Quarter Horse A1538

Morgan A1539

Saddlebred
A1540

Appaloosa
A1541

PHOTOGRAVURE

1985, Sept. 25

2155 A1538 22c multicolored 1.25 .25
2156 A1539 22c multicolored 1.25 .25
2157 A1540 22c multicolored 1.25 .25
2158 A1541 22c multicolored 1.25 .25
a. Block of 4, #2155-2158 5.00 4.00

PUBLIC EDUCATION IN AMERICA

Quill Pen, Apple, Spectacles, Penmanship Quiz — A1542

1985, Oct. 1

2159 A1542 22c multicolored .45 .25

INTERNATIONAL YOUTH YEAR

YMCA Youth Camping, Cent.
A1543

Boy Scouts, 75th Anniv.
A1544

Big Brothers/Big Sisters Fed., 40th Anniv. — A1545

Camp Fire, Inc., 75th Anniv.
A1546

1985, Oct. 7

2160 A1543 22c multicolored .70 .25
2161 A1544 22c multicolored .70 .25
2162 A1545 22c multicolored .70 .25
2163 A1546 22c multicolored .70 .25
a. Block of 4, #2160-2163 3.00 2.25

HELP END HUNGER

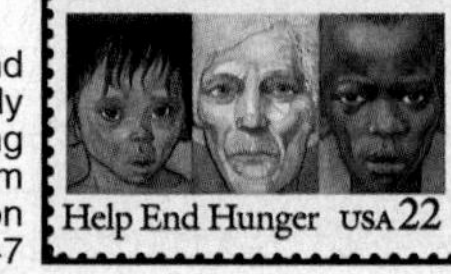
Youths and the Elderly Suffering from Malnutrition
A1547

PHOTOGRAVURE

1985, Oct. 15

2164 A1547 22c multicolored .45 .25

CHRISTMAS

Genoa Madonna, Enameled Terra-Cotta by Luca Della Robbia (1400-1482)
A1548

Poinsettia Plants
A1549

1985, Oct. 30

2165 A1548 22c multicolored .45 .25
a. Imperf., pair *55.00*
2166 A1549 22c multicolored .45 .25
a. Imperf., pair *85.00*

ARKANSAS STATEHOOD, 150th ANNIV.

Old State House, Little Rock
A1550

1986, Jan. 3

2167 A1550 22c multicolored .75 .25
a. Vert. pair, imperf. horiz. —

GREAT AMERICANS ISSUE

A1551

A1552

ENGRAVED

Perf. 11, 11½x11 (#2185), 11.2x11.1 (#2179)

1986-94

2168 A1551 1c brnsh ver .25 .25
b. 1c red brown .30 .30
2169 A1552 2c brt bl ('87) .25 .25
a. Untagged .25 .25

A1553

A1554

2170 A1553 3c bright blue .25 .25
a. Untagged ('94) .25 .25
2171 A1554 4c blue violet .25 .25
a. 4c grayish violet, untagged .25 .25
b. 4c deep grayish blue, untagged .25 .25
d. All color missing (EP) —

No. 2171d has an albino impression, and it also may be collected with a fully or partially printed stamp.

A1555

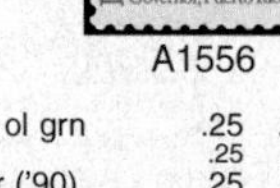
A1556

2172 A1555 5c dk ol grn .25 .25
b. 5c lt ol grn .25 .25
2173 A1556 5c car ('90) .25 .25
a. Untagged .25 .25

A1557

A1558

2175 A1557 10c lake ('87) .25 .25
e. 10c carmine .50 .25
f. All color omitted *200.00*

No. 2175f may be collected se-tenant with a partially printed stamp or longer vertical strip. Stamps not se-tenant with a partially printed stamp are identified by a light setoff on the gum side.

2176 A1558 14c crimson ('87) .30 .25

A1559

A1560

2177 A1559 15c claret ('88) .35 .25
d. All color omitted —

No. 2177d resulted from partially printed panes. It must be collected se-tenant with a partially printed stamp or in a longer horizontal strip showing error stamps plus partially/completely printed stamps.

2178 A1560 17c dull bl grn .35 .25

A1561

A1562

2179 A1561 20c red brn ('94) .40 .25
a. 20c orange brown .45 .25
b. 20c bright red brown 1.00 .25
2180 A1562 21c bl vio ('88) .45 .25

A1563

A1564

2181 A1563 23c pur ('88) .45 .25
2182 A1564 25c blue ('88) .50 .25
a. Booklet pane of 10, *May 3, 1988* 5.00 3.75
d. Horiz. pair, imperf between *750.00*
e. As "a," all color omitted on right stamps *1,250.*
f. As No. 2182 (sheet stamp), vert. pair, bottom stamp all color omitted —

No. 2182f may be collected se-tenant with a partially printed stamp or longer vertical strip.
See Nos. 2197, 2197a.

A1565

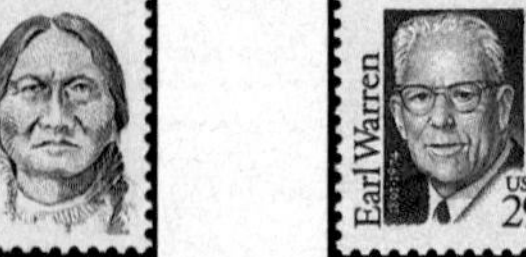
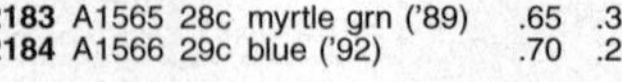
A1566

2183 A1565 28c myrtle grn ('89) .65 .35
2184 A1566 29c blue ('92) .70 .25

A1567

A1568

2185 A1567 29c indigo ('93) .65 .25
2186 A1568 35c black ('91) .75 .25

A1569

A1570

2187 A1569 40c dk bl ('90) .85 .25
2188 A1570 45c brt bl ('88) 1.00 .25
a. 45c blue ('90) 2.50 .25

Almost all examples of No. 2188a are in the grade of fine or fine-very fine. Values are for stamps in the grade of fine-very fine.

A1571

A1572

2189 A1571 52c pur ('91) 1.10 .25
2190 A1572 56c scarlet 1.20 .25

A1573

A1574

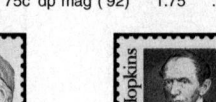

2191 A1573 65c dk bl ('88) 1.30 .25
2192 A1574 75c dp mag ('92) 1.75 .25

A1575

A1576

2193 A1575 $1 dk Prus grn 3.00 .50
a. All color omitted

No. 2193a must be collected se-tenant vertically with partially printed stamps.

2194 A1576 $1 intense dp bl ('89) 2.25 .50
b. $1 dp bl ('90) 2.50 .50
d. $1 dk bl ('92) 2.50 .50
e. $1 blue ('93) 2.75 .60

The intense deep blue of No. 2194 is much deeper than the deep blue and dark blue of the other $1 varieties.

A1577

A1578

2195 A1577 $2 brt violet 4.50 .50
2196 A1578 $5 copper red ('87) 9.00 1.00
Nos. 2168-2196 (28) 33.25 8.60

Booklet Stamp

Perf. 10 on 2 or 3 Sides

2197 A1564 25c blue ('88) .55 .25
a. Booklet pane of 6 3.30 2.50

Issued: No. 2182, 1/11; No. 2172, 2/27; $2, 3/19; 17c, 6/18; 1c, 6/30; 4c, 7/14; 56c, 9/3; 3c, 9/15; No. 2193, 9/23; 14c, 2/12/87; 2c, 2/28/87; 10c, 8/15/87; $5, 8/25/87; Nos. 2182a, 2197, 5/3/88; 15c, 6/6/88; 45c, 6/17/88; 21c, 10/21/88; 23c, 11/4/88; 65c, 11/5/88; No. 2194, 6/7/89; 28c, 9/14/89; No. 2173, 2/18/90; 40c, 9/6/90; Nos. 2188a, 2194b, 1990; 35c, 4/3/91; 52c, 6/3/91; No. 2173a, 1991; 75c, 2/16/92; No. 2184, 3/9/92; No. 2194d, 1992; No. 2185, 4/13/93; Nos. 2171b, 2194e, 1993; 20c, 10/24/94; Nos. 2170a, 2175e, 1994.

UNITED STATES - SWEDEN STAMP COLLECTING

Handstamped Cover, No. 213, Philatelic Memorabilia — A1581

Boy Examining Stamp Collection A1582

No. 836 Under Magnifying Glass, Sweden Nos. 268, 271 — A1583

1986 Presidents Miniature Sheet on First Day Cover A1584

BOOKLET STAMPS
LITHOGRAPHED & ENGRAVED

Perf. 10 Vert. on 1 or 2 Sides

1986, Jan. 23

2198 A1581 22c multicolored .45 .25
2199 A1582 22c multicolored .45 .25
2200 A1583 22c multicolored .45 .25
2201 A1584 22c multicolored .45 .25
a. Bklt. pane of 4, #2198-2201 2.00 1.75
b. As "a," black omitted on Nos. 2198, 2201 42.50 —
c. As "a," blue (litho.) omitted on Nos. 2198-2200 *1,750.*
d. As "a," buff (litho.) omitted —

See Sweden Nos. 1585-1588.

LOVE ISSUE

A1585

PHOTOGRAVURE

1986, Jan. 30 ***Perf. 11***

2202 A1585 22c multicolored .55 .25

Sojourner Truth (c. 1797-1883), Abolitionist A1586

Texas State Flag and Silver Spur A1587

BLACK HERITAGE SERIES

PHOTOGRAVURE

1986, Feb. 4

2203 A1586 22c multicolored .55 .25

REPUBLIC OF TEXAS, 150th ANNIV.

1986, Mar. 2

2204 A1587 22c dk bl, dk red & grayish blk .55 .25
a. Horiz. pair, imperf. vert. *700.00*
b. Dark red omitted *2,250.*
c. Dark blue omitted *6,000.*

FISH

Muskellunge — A1588

Atlantic Cod A1589

Largemouth Bass — A1590

Bluefin Tuna A1591

Catfish A1592

BOOKLET STAMPS
PHOTOGRAVURE

Perf. 10 Horiz. on 1 or 2 Sides

1986, Mar. 21

2205 A1588 22c multicolored 1.00 .25
2206 A1589 22c multicolored 1.00 .25
2207 A1590 22c multicolored 1.00 .25
2208 A1591 22c multicolored 1.00 .25
2209 A1592 22c multicolored 1.00 .25
a. Bklt. pane of 5, #2205-2209 6.00 2.75

The magenta used to print this issue is extremely fugitive. Dangerous fakes purported to be magenta omitted exist. No genuine examples are known. Panes apparently lacking red must be certified, and examples presently with certificates should be recertified.

PUBLIC HOSPITALS

A1593

1986, Apr. 11 ***Perf. 11***

2210 A1593 22c multicolored .45 .25
a. Vert. pair, imperf. horiz. *250.00*
b. Horiz. pair, imperf. vert. *950.00*

PERFORMING ARTS

Edward Kennedy "Duke" Ellington (1899-1974), Jazz Composer — A1594

1986, Apr. 29

2211 A1594 22c multicolored .45 .25
a. Vert. pair, imperf. horiz. *600.00*

AMERIPEX '86 ISSUE

Miniature Sheets

35 Presidents — A1599a

No. 2216: a, George Washington. b, John Adams. c, Thomas Jefferson. d, James Madison. e, James Monroe. f, John Quincy Adams. g, Andrew Jackson. h, Martin Van Buren. i, William H. Harrison.

No. 2217: a, John Tyler. b, James Knox Polk. c, Zachary Taylor. d, Millard Fillmore. e, Franklin Pierce. f, James Buchanan. g, Abraham Lincoln. h, Andrew Johnson. i, Ulysses S. Grant.

No. 2218: a, Rutherford B. Hayes. b, James A. Garfield. c, Chester A. Arthur. d, Grover Cleveland. e, Benjamin Harrison. f, William McKinley. g, Theodore Roosevelt. h, William H. Taft. i, Woodrow Wilson.

No. 2219: a, Warren G. Harding. b, Calvin Coolidge. c, Herbert Hoover. d, Franklin Delano Roosevelt. e, White House. f, Harry S. Truman. g, Dwight D. Eisenhower. h, John F. Kennedy. i, Lyndon B. Johnson.

LITHOGRAPHED & ENGRAVED

1986, May 22

2216 A1599a Pane of 9 7.50 4.00
a.-i. 22c, any single .75 .40
j. Blue (engr.) omitted *2,000.*
k. Black inscription omitted *1,750.*
l. Imperf. *10,500.*
m. As "k," double impression of red —
n. Blue omitted on a-c, e-f, h-i —
2217 A1599b Pane of 9 7.50 4.00
a-i. 22c, any single .75 .40
j. Black inscription omitted *2,000.*
2218 A1599c Pane of 9 7.50 4.00
a.-i. 22c, any single .75 .40
j. Brown (engr.) omitted —
k. Black inscription omitted *2,000.*
2219 A1599d Pane of 9 7.50 4.00
a.-i. 22c, any single .75 .40
j. Blackish blue (engr.) inscription omitted on a-b, d-e, g-h *2,000.*
l. Blackish blue (engr.) omitted on all stamps —
Nos. 2216-2219 (4) 30.00 16.00

Issued in conjunction with AMERIPEX '86 Intl. Philatelic Exhibition, Chicago, IL May 22-June 1.

ARCTIC EXPLORERS

Elisha Kent Kane A1600

Adolphus W. Greely A1601

Vilhjalmur Stefansson A1602

Robert E. Peary and Matthew Alexander Henson A1603

PHOTOGRAVURE

1986, May 28

2220 A1600 22c multicolored .65 .25
2221 A1601 22c multicolored .65 .25
2222 A1602 22c multicolored .65 .25
2223 A1603 22c multicolored .65 .25
a. Block of 4, #2220-2223 2.75 2.25
b. As "a," black omitted *6,000.*
c. As "a," Nos. 2220, 2221 black omitted —
d. As "a," Nos. 2222, 2223 black omitted —

STATUE OF LIBERTY, 100th ANNIVERSARY

Statue of Liberty, Cent. — A1604

ENGRAVED

1986, July 4

2224 A1604 22c scar & dk bl .45 .25
a. Scarlet omitted —

On No. 2224a, virtually all of the dark blue also is omitted, so the error stamp should be collected as part of a transition strip.

See France No. 2014.

TRANSPORTATION ISSUE

Types of 1982-85 and

A1604a

A1604b

COIL STAMPS
ENGRAVED

1986-90 ***Perf. 10 Vert.***

2225 A1604a 1c violet .25 .25
b. Untagged .25 .25
c. Imperf., pair *1,750.*
2226 A1604b 2c black .25 .25
a. Untagged .25 .25

REDUCED SIZE

2228 A1285 4c reddish brown .25 .25
b. Imperf., pair 175.00

Untagged

2231 A1511 8.3c green (Bureau precancel) .65 .25
Nos. 2225-2231 (4) 1.40 1.00

Issued: 1c, 11/26; 2c, 3/6/87. Earliest known usage of 4c, 8/15/86; 8.3c, 8/29.

On No. 2228 "Stagecoach 1890s" is 17¾mm long, on No. 1898A, 19½mm long. On No. 2231 "Ambulance 1860s" is 18mm long, on No. 2128, 18½mm long.

No. 2226 inscribed "2 USA"; No. 1897A inscribed "USA 2c".

AMERICAN FOLK ART SERIES
Navajo Art

A1605

A1606

A1607

A1608

LITHOGRAPHED & ENGRAVED

1986, Sept. 4 ***Perf. 11***

2235 A1605 22c multicolored .80 .25
2236 A1606 22c multicolored .80 .25
2237 A1607 22c multicolored .80 .25
2238 A1608 22c multicolored .80 .25
a. Block of 4, #2235-2238 3.25 2.25
b. As "a," black (engr.) omitted *300.00*

LITERARY ARTS SERIES

T. S. Eliot (1888-1965), Poet — A1609

ENGRAVED

1986, Sept. 26

2239 A1609 22c copper red .55 .25

AMERICAN FOLK ART SERIES
Woodcarved Figurines

Highlander Figure A1610

Ship Figurehead A1611

Nautical Figure — A1612

Cigar Store Figure — A1613

PHOTOGRAVURE

1986, Oct. 1

2240 A1610 22c multicolored .50 .25
2241 A1611 22c multicolored .50 .25
2242 A1612 22c multicolored .50 .25
2243 A1613 22c multicolored .50 .25
a. Block of 4, #2240-2243 2.00 1.50
b. As "a," imperf. vert. *750.00*

CHRISTMAS

Madonna, by Perugino (c. 1450-1523) A1614

Village Scene A1615

1986, Oct. 24

2244 A1614 22c multicolored .45 .25
a. Imperf., pair *475.00*
2245 A1615 22c multicolored .45 .25

MICHIGAN STATEHOOD, 150th ANNIV.

White Pine — A1616

1987, Jan. 26

2246 A1616 22c multicolored .55 .25

PAN AMERICAN GAMES

Runner in Full Stride A1617

1987, Jan. 29

2247 A1617 22c multicolored .45 .25
a. Silver omitted *850.00*

No. 2247a is valued in the grade of fine.

LOVE ISSUE

A1618

PHOTOGRAVURE

1987, Jan. 30 ***Perf. 11½x11***

2248 A1618 22c multicolored .45 .25

BLACK HERITAGE SERIES

Jean Baptiste Pointe du Sable (c. 1750-1818), Pioneer Trader, Founder of Chicago — A1619

1987, Feb. 20 ***Perf. 11***

2249 A1619 22c multicolored .50 .25

Enrico Caruso (1873-1921), Opera Tenor A1620

Fourteen Achievement Badges A1621

PERFORMING ARTS SERIES

PHOTOGRAVURE

1987, Feb. 27

2250 A1620 22c multicolored .45 .25
a. Black omitted *3,000.*

GIRL SCOUTS, 75TH ANNIVERSARY

LITHOGRAPHED & ENGRAVED

1987, Mar. 12

2251 A1621 22c multicolored .45 .25
a. All litho. colors omitted *2,000.*
b. Red & black (engr.) omitted *1,750.*

All known examples of No. 2251a have been expertized and certificate must accompany purchase. The unique pane of No. 2251b has been expertized and a certificate exists for the pane of 50.

TRANSPORTATION ISSUE

A1622

A1623

A1624

A1625

A1626

A1627

A1628

A1629

A1630

A1631

A1632

A1633

A1634

A1635

A1636

COIL STAMPS
ENGRAVED

1987-88 ***Perf. 10 Vert.***

2252 A1622 3c claret ('88) .25 .25
a. Untagged .25 .25
b. As "a," imperf. pair *1,350.*
2253 A1623 5c black .25 .25
2254 A1624 5.3c black (Bureau precancel in red), untagged ('88) .25 .25
2255 A1625 7.6c brown (Bureau precancel in red), untagged ('88) .25 .25
2256 A1626 8.4c dp clar (Bureau precancel in red), untagged ('88) .25 .25
a. Imperf., pair *400.00*
2257 A1627 10c blue .40 .25
e. Imperf. pair *1,500.*
2258 A1628 13c black (Bureau precancel in red), untagged ('88) .65 .25
2259 A1629 13.2c slate grn (Bureau precancel in red), untagged ('88) .25 .25
a. Imperf., pair 80.00
2260 A1630 15c violet ('88) .30 .25
c. Imperf., pair *500.00*
2261 A1631 16.7c rose (Bureau precancel in black), untagged ('88) .30 .30
a. Imperf., pair *125.00*

All known examples of No. 2261a are miscut top to bottom.

2262 A1632 17.5c dk vio .75 .25
a. Untagged (Bureau precancel in red) .65 .30
b. Imperf., pair *1,600.*
2263 A1633 20c blue vio ('88) .35 .25
a. Imperf., pair 50.00
2264 A1634 20.5c rose (Bureau precancel in black), untagged ('88) .75 .40
2265 A1635 21c olive grn (Bureau precancel in red), untagged ('88) .50 .40
a. Imperf., pair 42.50
2266 A1636 24.1c deep ultra (Bureau precancel in red), untagged ('88) .80 .45
Nos. 2252-2266 (15) 6.30 4.30

5.3c, 7.6c, 8.4c, 13.2c, 16.7c, 20.5c, 21c and 24.1c only available precanceled.

See Nos. 1897-1908, 2123-2136, 2225-2231, 2451-2468.

SPECIAL OCCASIONS

A1637

A1638

A1639

A1640

A1641

A1642

A1643

A1644

BOOKLET STAMPS
PHOTOGRAVURE
Perf. 10 on 1, 2 or 3 Sides

1987, Apr. 20

2267 A1637 22c multicolored .65 .25
2268 A1638 22c multicolored .80 .25
2269 A1639 22c multicolored .80 .25
2270 A1640 22c multicolored .80 .25
2271 A1641 22c multicolored .80 .25
2272 A1642 22c multicolored .65 .25
2273 A1643 22c multicolored 1.40 .25
2274 A1644 22c multicolored .80 .25
a. Bklt. pane of 10 (#2268-2271, 2273-2274, 2 each #2267, 2272) 10.00 5.00
Nos. 2267-2274 (8) 6.70 2.00

UNITED WAY, 100th ANNIV.

Six Profiles
A1645

LITHOGRAPHED & ENGRAVED

1987, Apr. 28 ***Perf. 11***

2275 A1645 22c multicolored .45 .25

A1646

A1647

A1648

A1649

Pheasant
A1649a

Grosbeak
A1649b

Owl —
A1649c

Honeybee
A1649d

Photo., Engr. (No. 2280). Litho. & Engr. (No. 2281)

1987-88 ***Perf. 11***

2276 A1646 22c multi .45 .25
a. Booklet pane of 20, *Nov. 30* 9.00 —
b. As "a," vert. pair, imperf. btwn. *1,250.*
c. As "a," miscut and inserted upside down into booklet cover, imperf between stamps and right selvage —
d. Yellow omitted —

All documented examples of No. 2276d show significant misregistration of the red ink.

2277 A1647 (25c) multi ('88) .50 .25
2278 A1648 25c multi ('88) .50 .25
Nos. 2276-2278 (3) 1.45 .75

COIL STAMPS
Perf. 10 Vert.

2279 A1647 (25c) multi ('88) .50 .25
a. Imperf., pair 55.00 —
2280 A1649 25c multi ('88) .50 .25
c. Imperf. pair 10.00
e. Black trees *90.00* —
f. Pair, imperf. between *400.00*
2281 A1649d 25c multi ('88) .50 .25
a. As No. 2281, imperf. pair 45.00
b. Black (engr.) omitted 45.00 —
c. Black (litho.) omitted *325.00*
d. Pair, imperf. between *600.00*
e. Yellow (litho.) omitted *800.00*
Nos. 2279-2281 (3) 1.50 .75

Beware of stamps with traces of the litho. black that are offered as No. 2281c.

Vertical pairs or blocks of No. 2281 and imperfs. with the engr. black missing are from printer's waste.

BOOKLET STAMPS

PHOTOGRAVURE
Perf. 10 on 2 or 3 Sides

2282 A1647 (25c) multi ('88) .50 .25
a. Booklet pane of 10 6.50 3.50

Perf. 11 on 2 or 3 Sides

2283 A1649a 25c multi ('88) .50 .25
a. Booklet pane of 10 6.00 3.50
b. 25c multicolored, red removed from sky 4.50 .25
c. As "b," bklt. pane of 10 45.00 —
d. Vert. pair, imperf. btwn. *275.00*

Imperf. panes exist from printers waste, and a large number exist. No. 2283d resulted from a foldover. Non-foldover pairs and multiples are printer's waste.

Perf. 10 on 2 or 3 Sides

2284 A1649b 25c multi ('88) .50 .25
2285 A1649c 25c multi ('88) .50 .25
b. Bklt. pane of 10, 5 each #2284-2285 5.00 3.50
d. Pair, Nos. 2284-2285 1.10 .50
2285A A1648 25c multi ('88) .50 .25
c. Booklet pane of 6 3.00 2.00
Nos. 2282-2285A (5) 2.50 1.25

Issued: #2276, 5/9; #2277, 2279, 2282, 3/22; #2278, 5/6; #2280, 5/20; #2281, 9/2; #2283, 4/29; #2284-2285, 5/28; #2285A, 7/5.

NORTH AMERICAN WILDLIFE

North American Wildlife — A1650

PHOTOGRAVURE

1987, June 13 ***Perf. 11***

2286 A1650 22c Barn swallow 1.00 .50
2287 A1651 22c Monarch butterfly 1.00 .50
2288 A1652 22c Bighorn sheep 1.00 .50
2289 A1653 22c Broad-tailed hummingbird 1.00 .50
2290 A1654 22c Cottontail 1.00 .50
2291 A1655 22c Osprey 1.00 .50
2292 A1656 22c Mountain lion 1.00 .50
2293 A1657 22c Luna moth 1.00 .50
2294 A1658 22c Mule deer 1.00 .50
2295 A1659 22c Gray squirrel 1.00 .50
2296 A1660 22c Armadillo 1.00 .50
2297 A1661 22c Eastern chipmunk 1.00 .50
2298 A1662 22c Moose 1.00 .50
2299 A1663 22c Black bear 1.00 .50
2300 A1664 22c Tiger swallowtail 1.00 .50
2301 A1665 22c Bobwhite 1.00 .50
2302 A1666 22c Ringtail 1.00 .50
2303 A1667 22c Red-winged blackbird 1.00 .50
2304 A1668 22c American lobster 1.00 .50
2305 A1669 22c Black-tailed jack rabbit 1.00 .50
2306 A1670 22c Scarlet tanager 1.00 .50
2307 A1671 22c Woodchuck 1.00 .50
2308 A1672 22c Roseate spoonbill 1.00 .50
2309 A1673 22c Bald eagle 1.00 .50
2310 A1674 22c Alaskan brown bear 1.00 .50
2311 A1675 22c Iiwi 1.00 .50
2312 A1676 22c Badger 1.00 .50
2313 A1677 22c Pronghorn 1.00 .50
2314 A1678 22c River otter 1.00 .50
2315 A1679 22c Ladybug 1.00 .50
2316 A1680 22c Beaver 1.00 .50
2317 A1681 22c White-tailed deer 1.00 .50
2318 A1682 22c Blue jay 1.00 .50
2319 A1683 22c Pika 1.00 .50
2320 A1684 22c American buffalo 1.00 .50
2321 A1685 22c Snowy egret 1.00 .50
2322 A1686 22c Gray wolf 1.00 .50
2323 A1687 22c Mountain goat 1.00 .50
2324 A1688 22c Deer mouse 1.00 .50
2325 A1689 22c Black-tailed prairie dog 1.00 .50
2326 A1690 22c Box turtle 1.00 .50
2327 A1691 22c Wolverine 1.00 .50
2328 A1692 22c American elk 1.00 .50
2329 A1693 22c California sea lion 1.00 .50
2330 A1694 22c Mockingbird 1.00 .50
2331 A1695 22c Raccoon 1.00 .50
2332 A1696 22c Bobcat 1.00 .50
2333 A1697 22c Black-footed ferret 1.00 .50
2334 A1698 22c Canada goose 1.00 .50
2335 A1699 22c Red fox 1.00 .50
a. A1650-A1699 Pane of 50, #2286-2335 50.00 35.00
2286b-2335b Any single, red omitted *2,500.*

RATIFICATION OF THE CONSTITUTION BICENTENNIAL

A1700

A1701

A1702

A1703

A1704

A1705

A1706

A1707

A1708

A1709

A1710

A1711

A1712

LITHOGRAPHED & ENGRAVED, PHOTOGRAVURE (#2337-2339, 2343-2344, 2347), ENGRAVED (#2341).

1987-90

2336 A1700 22c multi .60 .25
2337 A1701 22c multi .60 .25
2338 A1702 22c multi .60 .25
a. Black (engr.) omitted *4,500.*
2339 A1703 22c multi .60 .25
2340 A1704 22c multi .60 .25
2341 A1705 22c dk bl & dk red .60 .25
2342 A1706 22c multi .60 .25
2343 A1707 25c multi .60 .25
a. Strip of 3, vert. imperf btwn. *12,500.*
b. Red missing (PS) —
2344 A1708 25c multi .60 .25
2345 A1709 25c multi .60 .25
2346 A1710 25c multi .60 .25

2347 A1711 25c multi .60 .25
2348 A1712 25c multi .60 .25
Nos. 2336-2348 (13) 7.80 3.25

No. 2343b resulted either from a shifting of all colors or from a shift of both the perforations and the cutting of the pane.

Issued: No. 2336, 7/4; No. 2337, 8/26; No. 2338, 9/11; No. 2339, 1/6/88; No. 2340, 1/9/88; No. 2341, 2/6/88; No. 2342, 2/15/88; No. 2343, 5/23/88; No. 2344, 6/21/88; No. 2345, 6/25/88; No. 2346, 7/26/88; No. 2347, 8/22/89; No. 2348, 5/29/90.

Arabesque, Dar Batha Palace, Fez
A1713

William Cuthbert Faulkner (1897-1962), Novelist
A1714

US-MOROCCO DIPLOMATIC RELATIONS, 200th ANNIV.

LITHOGRAPHED & ENGRAVED

1987, July 17

2349 A1713 22c scar & blk .50 .25
a. Black (engr.) omitted *200.00*

See Morocco No. 642.

LITERARY ARTS SERIES

ENGRAVED

1987, Aug. 3

2350 A1714 22c bright green .55 .25

Used untagged imperfs exist from printer's waste.

AMERICAN FOLK ART SERIES

Lacemaking

A1715

A1716

A1717

A1718

LITHOGRAPHED & ENGRAVED

1987, Aug. 14

2351 A1715 22c ultra & white .45 .25
2352 A1716 22c ultra & white .45 .25
2353 A1717 22c ultra & white .45 .25
2354 A1718 22c ultra & white .45 .25
a. Block of 4, #2351-2354 1.90 1.90
b. As "a," white omitted *400.00*
c. Any single stamp, white omitted *90.00*

DRAFTING OF THE CONSTITUTION BICENTENNIAL

Excerpts from the Preamble

A1719

A1720

A1721

A1722

A1723

BOOKLET STAMPS

PHOTOGRAVURE

Perf. 10 Horiz. on 1 or 2 Sides

1987, Aug. 28

2355 A1719 22c multicolored .90 .25
a. Grayish green (background) omitted —
2356 A1720 22c multicolored .90 .25
a. Grayish green (background) omitted —
2357 A1721 22c multicolored .90 .25
a. Grayish green (background) omitted —
2358 A1722 22c multicolored .90 .25
a. Grayish green (background) omitted —
2359 A1723 22c multicolored .90 .25
a. Bklt. pane of 5, #2355-2359 4.50 2.25
b. Grayish green (background) omitted —

A1724

A1725

SIGNING OF THE CONSTITUTION

LITHOGRAPHED & ENGRAVED

1987, Sept. 17 ***Perf. 11***

2360 A1724 22c multicolored .55 .25

CERTIFIED PUBLIC ACCOUNTING

1987, Sept. 21

2361 A1725 22c multicolored 1.00 .25
a. Black (engr.) omitted *625.00*

LOCOMOTIVES

Stourbridge Lion, 1829 — A1726

Best Friend of Charleston, 1830 — A1727

John Bull, 1831
A1728

Brother Jonathan, 1832 — A1729

Gowan & Marx, 1839
A1730

BOOKLET STAMPS

Perf. 10 Horiz. on 1 or 2 Sides

1987, Oct. 1

2362 A1726 22c multi .55 .25
2363 A1727 22c multi .55 .25
2364 A1728 22c multi .55 .25
2365 A1729 22c multi .55 .25
a. Red omitted *900.00* *200.00*
2366 A1730 22c multi .55 .25
a. Bklt. pane of 5, #2362-2366 2.75 2.50
b. As No. 2366, black (engr.) omitted (single) —
c. As No. 2366, blue omitted (single) —

CHRISTMAS

Moroni Madonna
A1731

Christmas Ornaments
A1732

PHOTOGRAVURE

1987, Oct. 23 ***Perf. 11***

2367 A1731 22c multicolored .45 .25
2368 A1732 22c multicolored .45 .25

1988 WINTER OLYMPICS, CALGARY

Skiing — A1733

1988, Jan. 10

2369 A1733 22c multicolored .50 .25

AUSTRALIA BICENTENNIAL

Caricature of Australian Koala & American Bald Eagle — A1734

1988, Jan. 26

2370 A1734 22c multicolored .45 .25

See Australia No. 1052.

BLACK HERITAGE SERIES

James Weldon Johnson, Author, Lyricist — A1735

1988, Feb. 2

2371 A1735 22c multicolored .50 .25

CATS

Siamese, Exotic Shorthair
A1736

Abyssinian, Himalayan
A1737

Maine Coon, Burmese
A1738

American Shorthair, Persian
A1739

1988, Feb. 5

2372 A1736 22c multicolored .70 .25
2373 A1737 22c multicolored .70 .25
2374 A1738 22c multicolored .70 .25
2375 A1739 22c multicolored .70 .25
a. Block of 4, #2372-2375 2.80 1.90

AMERICAN SPORTS

Knute Rockne (1883-1931), Notre Dame football coach.

Francis Ouimet (1893-1967), 1st amateur golfer to win the US Open championship.

A1740

A1741

LITHOGRAPHED & ENGRAVED

1988, Mar. 9

2376 A1740 22c multicolored .50 .25

PHOTOGRAVURE

1988, June 13

2377 A1741 25c multicolored .60 .25

LOVE ISSUE

Rose A1742

Roses A1743

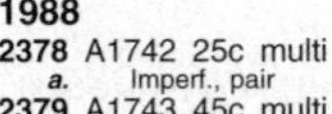

1988

2378 A1742 25c multi .50 .25
  a. Imperf., pair *1,750.*
2379 A1743 45c multi .85 .25

1988 SUMMER OLYMPICS, SEOUL

Gymnastic Rings A1744

1988, Aug. 19

2380 A1744 25c multicolored .50 .25

CLASSIC AUTOMOBILES

1928 Locomobile — A1745

1929 Pierce-Arrow A1746

1931 Cord A1747

1932 Packard A1748

1935 Duesenberg — A1749

LITHOGRAPHED & ENGRAVED
BOOKLET STAMPS
Perf. 10 Horiz. on 1 or 2 Sides

1988, Aug. 25

2381 A1745 25c multicolored .80 .25
2382 A1746 25c multicolored .80 .25
2383 A1747 25c multicolored .80 .25
2384 A1748 25c multicolored .80 .25
2385 A1749 25c multicolored .80 .25
  a. Bklt. pane of 5, #2381-2385 5.00 3.50

ANTARCTIC EXPLORERS

Nathaniel Palmer (1799-1877) — A1750

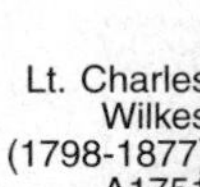

Lt. Charles Wilkes (1798-1877) A1751

Richard E. Byrd (1888-1957) — A1752

Lincoln Ellsworth (1880-1951) A1753

PHOTOGRAVURE

1988, Sept. 14 *Perf. 11*

2386 A1750 25c multicolored .65 .25
2387 A1751 25c multicolored .65 .25
2388 A1752 25c multicolored .65 .25
2389 A1753 25c multicolored .65 .25
  a. Block of 4, #2386-2389 2.75 2.00
  b. As "a," black omitted *1,000.*
  c. As "a," imperf. horiz. *1,500.*

AMERICAN FOLK ART SERIES

Carousel Animals

Deer — A1754

Horse — A1755

Camel — A1756

Goat — A1757

LITHOGRAPHED & ENGRAVED

1988, Oct. 1

2390 A1754 25c multicolored .75 .25
2391 A1755 25c multicolored .75 .25
2392 A1756 25c multicolored .75 .25
2393 A1757 25c multicolored .75 .25
  a. Block of 4, #2390-2393 3.00 2.00
  b. As "a," red omitted —

EXPRESS MAIL RATE

Eagle in Flight — A1758

1988, Oct. 4

2394 A1758 $8.75 multicolored 13.50 8.00

SPECIAL OCCASIONS

Happy Birthday — A1759

Best Wishes — A1760

Thinking of You — A1761

Love You — A1762

BOOKLET STAMPS
PHOTOGRAVURE
Perf. 11 on 2 or 3 Sides

1988, Oct. 22

2395 A1759 25c multicolored .50 .25
2396 A1760 25c multicolored .50 .25
  a. Bklt. pane of 6, 3 #2395 + 3 #2396 with gutter between 3.50 3.25
2397 A1761 25c multicolored .50 .25
2398 A1762 25c multicolored .50 .25
  a. Bklt. pane of 6, 3 #2397 + 3 #2398 with gutter between 3.50 3.25
  b. As "a," imperf. horiz. *2,000.*
  c. As "a," imperf. —
  Nos. 2395-2398 (4) 2.00 1.00

CHRISTMAS

Madonna and Child, by Botticelli A1763

One-horse Open Sleigh & Village Scene A1764

LITHOGRAPHED & ENGRAVED (No. 2399), PHOTOGRAVURE (No. 2400)

1988, Oct. 20 *Perf. 11½*

2399 A1763 25c multicolored .50 .25
  a. Gold omitted 25.00
2400 A1764 25c multicolored .50 .25

MONTANA STATEHOOD, 100th ANNIV.

C.M. Russell and Friends, by Charles M. Russell (1865-1926) A1765

LITHOGRAPHED & ENGRAVED

1989, Jan. 15 *Perf. 11*

2401 A1765 25c multicolored .55 .25

Imperfs without gum exist from printer's waste.

BLACK HERITAGE SERIES

Asa Philip Randolph (1889-1979), Labor & Civil Rights Leader — A1766

PHOTOGRAVURE

1989, Feb. 3

2402 A1766 25c multicolored .50 .25

NORTH DAKOTA STATEHOOD, 100th ANNIV.

Grain Elevator A1767

1989, Feb. 21

2403 A1767 25c multicolored .50 .25

WASHINGTON STATEHOOD, 100th ANNIV.

Mt. Rainier — A1768

1989, Feb. 22

2404 A1768 25c multicolored .50 .25

STEAMBOATS

Experiment, 1788-1790 — A1769

Phoenix, 1809 — A1770

New Orleans, 1812 — A1771

Washington, 1816 — A1772

Walk in the Water, 1818 — A1773

LITHOGRAPHED & ENGRAVED
BOOKLET STAMPS
Perf. 10 Horiz. on 1 or 2 Sides

1989, Mar. 3

2405 A1769 25c multicolored .50 .25
2406 A1770 25c multicolored .50 .25
2407 A1771 25c multicolored .50 .25
2408 A1772 25c multicolored .50 .25
2409 A1773 25c multicolored .50 .25
  a. Booklet pane of 5, #2405-2409 2.50 1.75

No. 122
A1774

Arturo Toscanini (1867-1957), Conductor
A1775

WORLD STAMP EXPO '89

Nov. 17-Dec. 3. Washington, D.C.

1989, Mar. 16 *Perf. 11*

2410 A1774 25c grayish brn, blk & car rose .50 .25

PERFORMING ARTS

PHOTOGRAVURE

1989, Mar. 25

2411 A1775 25c multicolored .50 .25

CONSTITUTION BICENTENNIAL SERIES

House of Representatives
A1776

Senate
A1777

Executive Branch
A1778

Supreme Court
A1779

LITHOGRAPHED & ENGRAVED

1989-90

2412 A1776 25c multi .50 .25
2413 A1777 25c multi .50 .25
2414 A1778 25c multi .50 .25
2415 A1779 25c multi .50 .25
Nos. 2412-2415 (4) 2.00 1.00

Issued: No. 2412, 4/4; No. 2413, 4/6; No. 2414, 4/16; No. 2415, 2/2/90.

SOUTH DAKOTA STATEHOOD, 100th ANNIV.

Pasque Flowers, Pioneer Woman and Sod House on Grasslands
A1780

PHOTOGRAVURE

1989, May 3

2416 A1780 25c multicolored .60 .25

Imperfs exist from printer's waste.

AMERICAN SPORTS

Lou Gehrig (1903-1941), New York Yankee Baseball Player — A1781

1989, June 10

2417 A1781 25c multicolored .60 .25

LITERARY ARTS SERIES

Ernest Hemingway (1899-1961), Nobel Prize-winner for Literature, 1954 — A1782

1989, July 17

2418 A1782 25c multicolored .50 .25
a. Vert. pair, imperf horiz. *1,000.*

Imperforates on gummed stamp paper, including gutter pairs and blocks, are proofs from the ABNCo. archives. See No. 2418P in Proofs section of the Scott U.S. Specialized Catalogue.

MOON LANDING, 20TH ANNIVERSARY

Raising the Flag on Lunar Surface, July 20, 1969
A1783

LITHOGRAPHED & ENGRAVED

1989, July 20 *Perf. 11x11½*

2419 A1783 $2.40 multi 4.75 2.00
a. Black (engr.) omitted *1,750.*
b. Imperf., pair *475.00*
c. Black (litho.) omitted *2,000.*

LETTER CARRIERS

Letter Carriers
A1784

PHOTOGRAVURE

2420 A1784 25c multicolored .50 .25

CONSTITUTION BICENTENNIAL

Bill of Rights — A1785

LITHOGRAPHED & ENGRAVED

1989, Sept. 25

2421 A1785 25c multicolored .50 .25
a. Black (engr.) omitted *225.00*

PREHISTORIC ANIMALS

Tyrannosaurus Rex — A1786

Pteranodon
A1787

Stegosaurus — A1788

Brontosaurus — A1789

1989, Oct. 1

2422 A1786 25c multicolored .70 .25
a. Black (engr.) omitted 80.00 —
2423 A1787 25c multicolored .70 .25
a. Black (engr.) omitted 80.00
2424 A1788 25c multicolored .70 .25
a. Black (engr.) omitted 80.00
2425 A1789 25c multicolored .70 .25
a. Black (engr.) omitted 80.00
b. Block of 4, #2422-2425 2.80 2.00
c. As "b," black (engr.) omitted *325.00*

The correct scientific name for Brontosaurus is Apatosaurus.

No. 2425c is valued in the grade of fine. Very fine blocks exist and sell for approximately $600.

PRE-COLUMBIAN AMERICA ISSUE

Southwest Carved Figure, A. D. 1150-1350 — A1790

PHOTOGRAVURE

1989, Oct. 12

2426 A1790 25c multicolored .60 .25

See No. C121.

CHRISTMAS

Madonna and Child, by Caracci
A1791

Sleigh Full of Presents
A1792

LITHOGRAPHED & ENGRAVED, PHOTOGRAVURE (#2428-2429)

1989, Oct. 19 *Perf. 11½*

2427 A1791 25c multicolored .50 .25
a. Booklet pane of 10 5.00 3.50
b. Red (litho.) omitted *575.00*
c. As "a," imperf. —

Perf. 11

2428 A1792 25c multicolored .50 .25
a. Vert. pair, imperf. horiz. *600.00*

BOOKLET STAMP

Perf. 11½ on 2 or 3 Sides

2429 A1792 25c multicolored .50 .25
a. Booklet pane of 10 5.00 3.50
c. As "a," horiz. imperf. between *2,250.*
d. As "a," red omitted *3,250.*
e. Imperf., pair —

Marked differences exist between Nos. 2428 and 2429: No. 2429 was printed in four colors, No. 2428 in five colors. The runners on the sleigh in No. 2429 are twice as thick as those on No. 2428. On No. 2429 the package at the upper left in the sleigh has a red bow, whereas the same package in No. 2428 has a red and black bow; and the ribbon on the upper right package in No. 2429 is green, whereas the same ribbon in No. 2428 is black.

Eagle and Shield — A1793

PHOTOGRAVURE
BOOKLET STAMP

1989, Nov. 10 *Die Cut*

Self-Adhesive

2431 A1793 25c multicolored .50 .25
a. Booklet pane of 18 11.00
b. Vert. pair, die cutting omitted between *325.00*
c. Die cutting omitted, pair *200.00*

Panes sold for $5.

Also available in strips of 18 with stamps spaced for use in affixing machines to service first day covers. Sold for $5.

No. 2431c will include part of the margins around the stamps.

Sold only in 15 test cities (Atlanta, Chicago, Cleveland, Columbus, OH, Dallas, Denver, Houston, Indianapolis, Kansas City, MO, Los Angeles, Miami, Milwaukee, Minneapolis, Phoenix, St. Louis) and through the philatelic agency.

WORLD STAMP EXPO '89

World Stamp Expo, Washington, DC, Nov. 17-Dec. 3 — A1794

LITHOGRAPHED & ENGRAVED

1989, Nov. 17 *Imperf.*

2433 A1794 Pane of 4 14.00 14.00
a. 90c like No. 122 3.50 3.00
b. 90c like 132TC4j 3.50 3.00
c. 90c like 132TC4i 3.50 3.00
d. 90c like 132TC4d 3.50 3.00

20th UPU CONGRESS
Traditional Mail Delivery

Stagecoach, c. 1850 — A1795

Paddlewheel Steamer A1796

Biplane — A1797

Depot-hack Type Automobile A1798

1989, Nov. 19 *Perf. 11*

2434 A1795 25c multicolored	.50	.25
2435 A1796 25c multicolored	.50	.25
2436 A1797 25c multicolored	.50	.25
2437 A1798 25c multicolored	.50	.25
a. Block of 4, #2434-2437	2.00	1.75
b. As "a," dark blue (engr.) omitted	*275.00*	

No. 2437b is valued in the grade of fine. Very fine blocks exist and sell for approximately $450.

Souvenir Sheet

1989, Nov. 28 *Imperf.*

2438 Sheet of 4	5.00	3.75
a. A1795 25c multicolored	1.25	.80
b. A1796 25c multicolored	1.25	.80
c. A1797 25c multicolored	1.25	.80
d. A1798 25c multicolored	1.25	.80
e. Dark blue & gray (engr.) omitted	*5,000.*	

20th Universal Postal Union Congress.

VALUES FOR HINGED STAMPS AFTER NO. 771

This catalogue does not value unused stamps after No. 771 in hinged condition. Hinged unused stamps from No. 772 to the present are worth considerably less than the values given for unused stamps, which are for never-hinged examples.

IDAHO STATEHOOD, 100th ANNIV.

Mountain Bluebird, Sawtooth Mountains — A1799

PHOTOGRAVURE

1990, Jan. 6 *Perf. 11*

2439 A1799 25c multicolored .55 .25

LOVE

A1800

PHOTOGRAVURE

1990, Jan. 18 *Perf. 12½x13*

2440 A1800 25c multi	.50	.25
a. Imperf., pair	*550.00*	

BOOKLET STAMP

Perf. 11½ on 2 or 3 Sides

2441 A1800 25c multi	.50	.25
a. Booklet pane of 10	5.00	3.50
b. Bright pink omitted	*85.00*	
c. As "a," bright pink omitted	*950.00*	

No. 2441b may be obtained from booklet panes containing both normal and color-omitted stamps.

BLACK HERITAGE SERIES

Ida B. Wells (1862-1931), Journalist — A1801

1990, Feb. 1 *Perf. 11*

2442 A1801 25c multicolored .75 .25

Beach Umbrella — A1802

BOOKLET STAMP

Perf. 11 on 2 or 3 Sides

1990, Feb. 3

2443 A1802 15c multicolored	.30	.25
a. Booklet pane of 10	3.00	2.50
b. Blue omitted	*115.00*	
c. As "a," blue omitted	*1,150.*	

WYOMING STATEHOOD, 100th ANNIV.

High Mountain Meadows, by Conrad Schwiering A1803

LITHOGRAPHED & ENGRAVED

1990, Feb. 23 *Perf. 11*

2444 A1803 25c multicolored	.80	.25
a. Black (engr.) omitted	*1,000.*	—

CLASSIC FILMS

Judy Garland and Toto (The Wizard of Oz) — A1804

Clark Gable & Vivien Leigh (Gone With the Wind) — A1805

Gary Cooper (Beau Geste) — A1806

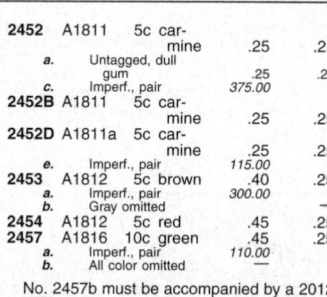

John Wayne (Stagecoach) A1807

PHOTOGRAVURE

1990, Mar. 23

2445 A1804 25c multicolored	1.50	.25
2446 A1805 25c multicolored	1.50	.25
2447 A1806 25c multicolored	1.50	.25
2448 A1807 25c multicolored	1.50	.25
a. Block of 4, #2445-2448	6.00	3.50

LITERARY ARTS SERIES

Marianne Craig Moore (1887-1972), Poet — A1808

1990, Apr. 18

2449 A1808 25c multicolored	.60	.25
a. All colors missing (EP)	—	

No. 2449a must be collected se-tenant with a partially printed stamp or in longer horizontal strips with a partially printed stamp and normal stamps.

TRANSPORTATION ISSUE

A1810

A1811

A1811a

A1812

A1816

A1822

A1823

A1825

A1827

COIL STAMPS
ENGRAVED, PHOTOGRAVURE
(#2452B, 2452D, 2454, 2458)

1990-95 *Perf. 9.8 Vert.*

Untagged (Nos. 2452B, 2452D, 2453, 2454, 2457-2458)

Bureau Precancel in Gray (#2453-2458)

2451 A1810 4c claret	.25	.25
a. Imperf., pair	*500.00*	
b. Untagged	.25	.25
2452 A1811 5c carmine	.25	.25
a. Untagged, dull gum	.25	.25
c. Imperf., pair	*375.00*	
2452B A1811 5c carmine	.25	.25
2452D A1811a 5c carmine	.25	.25
e. Imperf., pair	*115.00*	
2453 A1812 5c brown	.40	.25
a. Imperf., pair	*300.00*	
b. Gray omitted		—
2454 A1812 5c red	.45	.25
2457 A1816 10c green	.45	.25
a. Imperf., pair	*110.00*	
b. All color omitted	—	

No. 2457b must be accompanied by a 2012 certificate of authentication confirming that stamps are from the discovery coil roll that also contained normal and partially printed stamps.

2458 A1816 10c green	.55	.25
2463 A1822 20c green	.40	.25
a. Imperf., pair	*75.00*	
2464 A1823 23c dark blue	.45	.25
b. Imperf., pair	*100.00*	
2466 A1825 32c blue	.80	.25
a. Imperf., pair, shiny gum	*375.00*	
b. bright blue	3.00	2.25

Some specialists refer to No. 2466b as "Bronx blue," and it is considered to be an error of color.

2468 A1827 $1 bl & scar	2.25	.50
a. Imperf., pair	*2,000.*	*1,250.*
Nos. 2451-2468 (12)	6.75	3.25

Some mint pairs of No. 2468 appear to be imperf. but have faint blind perforations on the gum. Beware of examples with the gum removed.

Issued: $1, 4/20; No. 2452, 8/31; 4c, 1/25/91; 23c, 4/12/91; Nos. 2453, 2457, 5/25/91; No. 2454, 10/22/91; No. 2452B, 12/8/92; No. 2458, 5/25/94; Nos. 2452D, 3/20/95; 32c, 6/2/95; 20c, 6/9/95.

LIGHTHOUSES

Admiralty Head, WA — A1829

Cape Hatteras, NC — A1830

West Quoddy Head, ME — A1831

American Shoals, FL — A1832

Sandy Hook, NJ — A1833

BOOKLET STAMPS

LITHOGRAPHED & ENGRAVED

Perf. 10 Vert. on 1 or 2 Sides

1990, Apr. 26

2470 A1829 25c multicolored	1.75	.25
2471 A1830 25c multicolored	1.75	.25
2472 A1831 25c multicolored	1.75	.25
2473 A1832 25c multicolored	1.75	.25

2474 A1833 25c multicolored 1.75 .25
a. Bklt. pane of 5, #2470-2474 8.75 2.00
b. As "a," white ("USA 25") omitted 80.00 —

Perforations on Lighthouse booklet panes separate very easily. Careful handling is required.

FLAG

A1834

PHOTOGRAVURE

1990, May 18 Untagged *Die Cut*

Self-adhesive

Printed on Plastic

2475 A1834 25c dk red & dk bl .55 .25
a. Pane of 12 6.60

Sold only in panes of 12; peelable plastic backing inscribed in light ultramarine. Available for a test period of six months at 22 First National Bank automatic teller machines in Seattle.

FLORA AND FAUNA

A1840

American Kestrel A1841

Eastern Bluebird A1842

Fawn A1843

Cardinal A1844

Bobcat A1846

Pumpkinseed Sunfish — A1845

LITHOGRAPHED

Perf. 11, 11.2 (#2477)

1990-95 Untagged (1c, 3c)

2476 A1840 1c multi .25 .25
a. Quadruple impression of black inscriptions and denomination 850.00

Other colors on Nos. 2476a, 2476b and 2476c are misregistered and the stamps are poorly centered.

b. Quintuple impression of black inscriptions and denomination 1,500.
2477 A1841 1c multi .25 .25
2478 A1842 3c multi .25 .25
a. Vert. pair, imperf horiz. —
b. Double impression of all colors except yellow 200.00
c. Double impression of blue, triple impression of black —

Imperforates on gummed stamp paper, plus imperforate and perforated gutter pairs and blocks (including imperforate and perforated gutter pairs and blocks of No. 2476 se-tenant with No. 2478), are proofs from the ABNCo. archives. See Nos. 2476P and 2478P in Proofs section of the Scott U.S. Specialized Catalogue.

See Nos. 3031, 3031A, 3044. Compare design A1842 with design A2336.

PHOTOGRAVURE

2479 A1843 19c multi .35 .25
b. Red omitted *500.00*
c. Imperf, pair *900.00*

On No. 2479b other colors are shifted.

2480 A1844 30c multicolored, *June 22, 1991* .60 .25

LITHOGRAPHED & ENGRAVED

2481 A1845 45c multi .90 .25
a. Black (engr.) omitted *325.00* —

2482 A1846 $2 multi 3.50 1.25
a. Black (engr.) omitted *200.00*
Nos. 2476-2482 (7) 6.10 2.75

Issued: $2, 6/1; 19c, 3/11/91; No. 2476, 3c, 30c, 6/22/91; 45c, 12/2/92; No. 2477, 5/10/95.

Blue Jay — A1847

Wood Duck — A1848

African Violets A1849

Peach A1850

Pear A1851

Red Squirrel A1852

Rose A1853

Pine Cone A1854

PHOTOGRAVURE
BOOKLET STAMPS

Perf. 10.9x9.8 on 2 or 3 Sides

1991-95

2483 A1847 20c multi .50 .25
a. Booklet pane of 10 5.25 2.50
b. As "a," imperf —

Perf. 10 on 2 or 3 sides

2484 A1848 29c blk & multi .60 .25
a. Booklet pane of 10 6.00 3.75
b. Vert. pair, imperf. horiz. *175.00*
c. As "b," bklt. pane of 10 *850.00*
f. Vert. pair, imperf between and with natural straight edge at top or bottom *170.00*
g. As "f," bklt. pane of 10 *850.00*

Perf. 11 on 2 or 3 Sides

2485 A1848 29c red & multi .60 .25
a. Booklet pane of 10 6.00 4.00
b. Vert. pair, imperf. between *2,750.*
c. Imperf, pair *1,750.*

Perf. 10x11 on 2 or 3 Sides

2486 A1849 29c multi .60 .25
a. Booklet pane of 10 6.00 4.00

Perf. 11x10 on 2 or 3 Sides

2487 A1850 32c multi .65 .25
2488 A1851 32c multi .65 .25
a. Booklet pane, 5 each #2487-2488 6.50 4.25
b. Pair, #2487-2488 1.30 .30

Issued: Nos. 2484-2485, 4/12; No. 2486, 10/8/93; 20c, 6/15/95; 32c, 7/8/95.

PHOTOGRAVURE, ENGRAVED (#2491)

1993-95 *Die Cut*

Self-Adhesive

Booklet Stamps

2489 A1852 29c multi .65 .25
a. Booklet pane of 18 12.00
b. As "a," die cutting omitted —
2490 A1853 29c red, green & black .65 .25
a. Booklet pane of 18 12.00
2491 A1854 29c multi .60 .25
a. Booklet pane of 18 11.00
b. Horiz. pair, die cutting omitted between *175.00 125.00*
c. Coil with plate # B1 — 6.00

Stamps without plate number from coil strips are indistinguishable from booklet stamps once they are removed from the backing paper.

Serpentine Die Cut 11.3x11.7 on 2, 3 or 4 Sides

2492 A1853 32c pink, green & black .65 .25
a. Booklet pane of 20 + label 13.00
b. Booklet pane of 15 + label 9.75
c. Horiz. pair, die cutting omitted between —
d. As "a," 2 stamps and parts of 7 others printed on backing liner —
e. Booklet pane of 14 20.00
f. Booklet pane of 16 20.00
g. Coil with plate # S111 — 5.50
h. Vert. pair, die cutting omitted between (from No. 2492b) —
i. As "a," 6 pairs plus stamp and label die cutting omitted vert. btwn. (due to miscutting) —
j. As "f," with 2 vert. pairs at bottom die cutting omitted horiz., in full bklt. #BK178D —

Serpentine Die Cut 8.8 on 2, 3 or 4 Sides

2493 A1850 32c multi .65 .25
2494 A1851 32c multi .65 .25
a. Booklet pane, 10 each #2493-2494 + label 13.00
b. Pair, #2493-2494 1.30
c. As "b," die cutting omitted —

COIL STAMPS

Serpentine Die Cut 8.8 Vert.

2495 A1850 32c multi 2.00 .25
2495A A1851 32c multi 2.00 .25
b. Pair, #2495-2495A 4.00

Issued: No. 2489, 6/25; No. 2490, 8/19; No. 2491, 11/5; No. 2492, 6/2/95; Nos. 2493-2495A, 7/8/95.

See Nos. 3048-3049, 3053-3054.

Values for used self-adhesive stamps are for examples either on piece or off piece.

OLYMPIANS

Jesse Owens, 1936 A1855

Ray Ewry, 1900-08 A1856

Hazel Wightman, 1924 A1857

Eddie Eagan, 1920, 1932 A1858

Helene Madison, 1932 A1859

PHOTOGRAVURE

1990, July 6 *Perf. 11*

2496 A1855 25c multicolored .60 .25
2497 A1856 25c multicolored .60 .25
2498 A1857 25c multicolored .60 .25
2499 A1858 25c multicolored .60 .25
2500 A1859 25c multicolored .60 .25
a. Strip of 5, #2496-2500 3.25 2.50
b. As "a," blue omitted —

Imperforates on gummed stamp paper, including gutter pairs, strips and blocks, are proofs from the ABNCo. archives. See No. 2500aP in Proofs section of the Scott U.S. Specialized Catalogue.

INDIAN HEADDRESSES

Assiniboin A1860

Cheyenne A1861

Comanche A1862

Flathead A1863

Shoshone A1864

LITHOGRAPHED & ENGRAVED
BOOKLET STAMPS

Perf. 11 on 2 or 3 Sides

1990, Aug. 17

2501 A1860 25c multicolored 1.60 .25
2502 A1861 25c multicolored 1.60 .25
2503 A1862 25c multicolored 1.60 .25
a. Black (engr.) omitted —
2504 A1863 25c multicolored 1.60 .25
a. Black (engr.) omitted —
2505 A1864 25c multicolored 1.60 .25
a. Bklt. pane of 10, 2 each #2501-2505 16.00 7.50
b. As "a," black (engr.) omitted *2,750.*
c. Strip of 5, #2501-2505 8.00 2.50
d. As "a," horiz. imperf. between *2,400.*

The one example of No. 2505d that has been reported is actually split at the booklet fold and is a block of 4 and a block of 6.

MICRONESIA & MARSHALL ISLANDS

Canoe & Federated States of Micronesia Flag A1865

Stick Chart, Canoe & Republic of the Marshall Islands Flag A1866

1990, Sept. 28 *Perf. 11*

2506 A1865 25c multicolored .50 .25
2507 A1866 25c multicolored .50 .25
a. Pair, #2506-2507 1.00 .75
b. As "a," black (engr.) omitted *2,000.*

See Micronesia Nos. 124-126, Marshall Islands No. 381.

SEA CREATURES

Killer Whales A1867

Northern Sea Lions A1868

Sea Otter A1869

Common Dolphin A1870

1990, Oct. 3

2508 A1867 25c multicolored .55 .25
2509 A1868 25c multicolored .55 .25
2510 A1869 25c multicolored .55 .25
2511 A1870 25c multicolored .55 .25
a. Block of 4, #2508-2511 2.25 1.90
b. As "a," black (engr.) omitted *275.00*

See Russia Nos. 5933-5936.

PRE-COLUMBIAN AMERICA ISSUE

Grand Canyon A1871

PHOTOGRAVURE

1990, Oct. 12

2512 A1871 25c multicolored .55 .25

See No. C127.

DWIGHT D. EISENHOWER, BIRTH CENTENARY

A1872

1990, Oct. 13 **Tagged** *Perf. 11*

2513 A1872 25c multicolored .90 .25

Imperforates on gummed stamp paper are proofs from the ABNCo. archives. See No. 2513P in Proofs section of the Scott U.S. Specialized Catalogue.

CHRISTMAS

Madonna and Child by Antonello da Messina A1873

Christmas Tree A1874

LITHOGRAPHED & ENGRAVED

1990, Oct. 18 *Perf. 11½*

2514 A1873 25c multi .50 .25
b. Booklet pane of 10 5.00 3.25

PHOTOGRAVURE

Perf. 11

2515 A1874 25c multicolored .50 .25
a. Vert. pair, imperf. horiz. *625.00*
b. All colors missing (EP) —

No. 2515b must be collected se-tenant with normal and/or partially printed stamp(s).

BOOKLET STAMP

Perf. 11½x11 on 2 or 3 Sides

2516 A1874 25c multicolored .50 .25
a. Booklet pane of 10 5.00 3.25

Marked differences exist between Nos. 2515 and 2516. The background red on No. 2515 is even while that on No. 2516 is splotchy. The bands across the tree and "Greetings" are blue green on No. 2515 and yellow green on No. 2516.

A1875

This U.S. stamp, along with 25¢ of additional U.S. postage, is equivalent to the 'F' stamp rate

A1876

1991, Jan. 22 *Perf. 13*

2517 A1875 (29c) yel, blk, red & yel grn .60 .25
a. Imperf., pair *1,000.*
b. Horiz. pair, imperf. vert. *950.00*

See note after No. 2518.

Gutter pairs and blocks, and cross gutter blocks, all perforated, are proofs from the ABNCo. archives. See No. 2517P in Proofs section of the Scott U.S. Specialized Catalogue.

No. 2517a is usually collected as a vertical pair, though No. 2517 can be distinguished from the other "F" stamp issues.

COIL STAMP

Perf. 10 Vert.

2518 A1875 (29c) yel, blk, dull red & dk yel grn .60 .25
a. Imperf., pair 27.50

"For U.S. addresses only" is 17½mm long on No. 2517, 16½mm long on No. 2518. Design of No. 2517 measures 21½x17½mm, No. 2518, 21x18mm.

BOOKLET STAMPS

Perf. 11 on 2 or 3 Sides

2519 A1875 (29c) yel, blk, dull red & dk grn .60 .25
a. Booklet pane of 10 6.50 4.50

2520 A1875 (29c) pale yel, blk, red & brt grn 1.75 .25
a. Booklet pane of 10 18.00 4.50
b. As "a," imperf. horiz. —
c. Horiz. pair, imperf btwn., in error booklet pane of 12 stamps *450.00*
d. Imperf. vert., pair —

No. 2519 has bullseye perforations that measure approximately 11.2. No. 2520 has less pronounced black lines in the leaf, which is a much brighter green than on No. 2519.

No. 2520c is from a paper foldover before perforating.

LITHOGRAPHED

1991, Jan. 22 **Untagged** *Perf. 11*

2521 A1876 (4c) bister & carmine .25 .25
a. Vert. pair, imperf. horiz. 85.00
b. Imperf., pair 60.00

FLAG

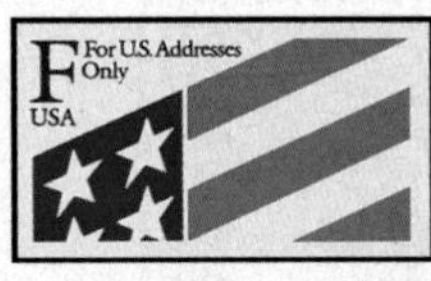

A1877

PHOTOGRAVURE

1991, Jan. 22 **Untagged** *Die Cut*

Self-Adhesive

Printed on Plastic

2522 A1877 (29c) blk, blue & dk red .60 .25
a. Pane of 12 7.25

Sold only in panes of 12; peelable plastic backing inscribed in light ultramarine. Available during a test period at First National Bank automatic teller machines in Seattle.

Flag Over Mt. Rushmore — A1878

COIL STAMPS

ENGRAVED

1991, Mar. 29 **Tagged** *Perf. 10 Vert.*

2523 A1878 29c bl, red & claret .75 .25
b. Imperf., pair 20.00
c. blue, red & brown 3.00 —

Specialists often call No. 2523c the "Toledo brown" variety.

PHOTOGRAVURE

1991, July 4

2523A A1878 29c blue, red & brown .75 .25

On No. 2523A, USA and 29 are not outlined in white and are farther from the bottom of the design.

Flower — A1879

PHOTOGRAVURE

1991-92 *Perf. 11*

2524 A1879 29c dull yel, blk, red & yel grn .60 .25

See note after No. 2527.

Perf. 13x12¾

2524A A1879 29c dull yel, blk, red & yel grn 1.00 .25

COIL STAMPS

Rouletted 10 Vert.

2525 A1879 29c pale yel, blk, red & yel grn .60 .25

Perf. 10 Vert.

2526 A1879 29c pale yel, blk, red & yel grn .80 .25

BOOKLET STAMP

Perf. 11 on 2 or 3 Sides

2527 A1879 29c pale yel, blk, red & bright grn .60 .25
a. Booklet pane of 10 6.00 3.50
b. Horiz. pair, imperf. between —
c. Horiz. pair, imperf. vert. *150.00*
d. As "a," imperf. horiz. *675.00*
e. As "a," imperf. vert. *500.00*

Flower on Nos. 2524-2524A has grainy appearance, inscriptions look rougher.

Issued: Nos. 2524, 2524A, 2527, 4/5; No. 2525, 8/16; No. 2526, 3/3/92.

Flag, Olympic Rings — A1880

BOOKLET STAMP

Perf. 11 on 2 or 3 Sides

1991, Apr. 21

2528 A1880 29c multicolored .60 .25
a. Booklet pane of 10 6.00 3.50
b. As "a," imperf. horiz. *2,750.*
c. Vert. pair, imperf. between, perfed at top and bottom *225.00*
d. Vert. strip of 3, top or bottom pair imperf. between —
e. Vert. pair, imperf. horiz. *650.00*
f. As "d," two pairs in #2528a with foldover —

No. 2528c comes from misperfed booklet panes. No. 2528d resulted from paper foldovers after normal perforating and before cutting into panes. Two No. 2528d are known. No. 2528e is valued in the grade of fine.

Fishing Boat A1881

Balloon A1882

COIL STAMPS

1991, Aug. 8 *Perf. 9.8 Vert.*

2529 A1881 19c multicolored, type I .40 .25
a. Type II ('93) .40 .25
b. As "a," untagged ('93) 1.00 .40

Design on Type II stamps is created by a finer dot pattern. Vertical sides of "1" are smooth on Type II and jagged on Type I stamps.

Imperforates are from printer's waste.

1994, June 25

2529C A1881 19c multicolored .50 .25

No. 2529C has one loop of rope tying boat to piling.

BOOKLET STAMP

Perf. 10 on 2 or 3 Sides

1991, May 17

2530 A1882 19c multicolored .40 .25
a. Booklet pane of 10 4.00 2.75

Flags on Parade — A1883

1991, May 30 *Perf. 11*

2531 A1883 29c multi .60 .25

Liberty Torch — A1884

1991, June 25 ***Die Cut***

Self-Adhesive

2531A A1884 29c black, gold & green .60 .25
b. Booklet pane of 18 11.00
c. Die cutting omitted, pair *1,400.*

Sold only in panes of 18; peelable paper backing inscribed in light blue. Available for consumer testing at First National Bank automatic teller machines in Seattle, WA.

SWITZERLAND

Switzerland, 700th Anniv. — A1887

1991, Feb. 22 ***Perf. 11***

2532 A1887 50c multicolored 1.00 .25
a. Vert. pair, imperf. horiz. *1,500.*

See Switzerland No. 888.
Imperfs exist from printer's waste.

A1888

A1889

VERMONT STATEHOOD, 200th ANNIV.

1991, Mar. 1

2533 A1888 29c multicolored .90 .25

SAVINGS BONDS, 50TH ANNIVERSARY

1991, Apr. 30 ***Perf. 11***

2534 A1889 29c multicolored .60 .25

LOVE

A1890

A1891

1991, May 9 ***Perf. 12½x13***

2535 A1890 29c multi .60 .25
b. Imperf., pair *1,650.*

Perf. 11

2535A A1890 29c multi .85 .25

BOOKLET STAMP (#2536)

Perf. 11.1x11.3 on 2 or 3 Sides

2536 A1890 29c multi .60 .25
a. Booklet pane of 10 6.00 3.50

"29" is closer to edge of design on No. 2536 than on No. 2535.

Perf. 11

2537 A1891 52c multi .90 .25

LITERARY ARTS SERIES

William Saroyan A1892

1991, May 22 ***Perf. 11***

2538 A1892 29c multicolored .60 .25
a. All colors missing (EP) —
b. All colors except black missing (EP) —

No. 2538a must be collected se-tenant with a partially printed stamp. On No. 2538b, only part of the black is present.
See Russia No. 6002.

Eagle, Olympic Rings — A1893

A1894

A1895

A1896

Futuristic Space Shuttle A1897

Space Shuttle Challenger A1898

Space Shuttle Endeavour — A1898a

1991, Sept. 29

2539 A1893 $1 gold & multi 2.00 .50
a. Black omitted —

LITHOGRAPHED & ENGRAVED

1991, July 7

2540 A1894 $2.90 multicolored 6.00 1.50
a. Vert. pair, imperf horiz. *900.00*
b. Black (engr.) omitted —

Imperforates on gummed stamp paper, including gutter pairs and blocks, are proofs from the ABNCo. archives. From the same source also come imperforate progressive proofs. See No. 2540P in Proofs section of the Scott U.S. Specialized Catalogue.

1991, June 16 **Untagged**

2541 A1895 $9.95 multicolored 20.00 6.00
a. Imperf., pair —

No. 2541 exists imperf plus black (engr.) omitted from printer's waste.

1991, Aug. 31 **Untagged**

2542 A1896 $14 multicolored 25.00 15.00
a. Red (engr. inscriptions) omitted *750.00*

No. 2542 exists imperf plus red omitted from printer's waste.

PHOTOGRAVURE

1993, June 3 ***Perf. 11x10½***

2543 A1897 $2.90 multicolored 6.00 1.75

Faked examples of No. 2543, unused and used, exist with red omitted due to bleaching.

1995, June 22 ***Perf. 11.2***

2544 A1898 $3 multicolored, dated "1995" 5.75 1.75
b. Dated "1996" 5.75 1.75
c. As "b," horiz. pair, imperf between —
d. As "b," imperf pair *1,000.*

1995, Aug. 4 ***Perf. 11***

2544A A1898a $10.75 multi 20.00 9.00

FISHING FLIES

Royal Wulff A1899

Jock Scott A1900

Apte Tarpon Fly A1901

Lefty's Deceiver A1902

Muddler Minnow A1903

PHOTOGRAVURE
BOOKLET STAMPS

Perf. 11 Horiz. on 1 or 2 Sides

1991, May 31

2545 A1899 29c multicolored 1.50 .25
a. Black omitted —
b. Horiz. pair, imperf. btwn., in #2549b with foldover *2,400.*
2546 A1900 29c multicolored 1.50 .25
a. Black omitted —
2547 A1901 29c multicolored 1.50 .25
a. Black omitted —
2548 A1902 29c multicolored 1.50 .25
2549 A1903 29c multicolored 2.00 .25
a. Bklt. pane of 5, #2545-2549 8.00 3.50

Horiz. pairs, imperf vert., exist from printer's waste.

No. 2545b is unique and resulted from a foldover after perfing but before cutting. Both stamps are creased.

Cole Porter (1891-1964), Composer A1904

S. W. Asia Service Medal A1905

PERFORMING ARTS

1991, June 8 ***Perf. 11***

2550 A1904 29c multicolored .60 .25
a. Vert. pair, imperf. horiz. *400.00*

OPERATIONS DESERT SHIELD & DESERT STORM

1991, July 2

2551 A1905 29c multicolored .60 .25
a. Vert. pair, imperf. horiz. *850.00*

No. 2551 is 21mm wide.

BOOKLET STAMP

Perf. 11 Vert. on 1 or 2 Sides

2552 A1905 29c multicolored .60 .25
a. Booklet pane of 5 3.00 2.25

No. 2552 is 20½mm wide. Inscriptions are shorter than on No. 2551.
No. 2552 Vert. pairs, imperf horiz., are from printer's waste.

1992 SUMMER OLYMPICS, BARCELONA

Pole Vault A1907

Discus A1908

Women's Sprints A1909

Javelin A1910

Women's Hurdles A1911

1991, July 12 ***Perf. 11***

2553 A1907 29c multicolored .60 .25
2554 A1908 29c multicolored .60 .25
2555 A1909 29c multicolored .60 .25
2556 A1910 29c multicolored .60 .25
2557 A1911 29c multicolored .60 .25
a. Strip of 5, #2553-2557 3.00 2.25

NUMISMATICS

1858 Flying Eagle Cent, 1907 Standing Liberty Double Eagle, Series 1875 $1 Note, Series 1902 $10 National Currency Note — A1912

LITHOGRAPHED & ENGRAVED

1991, Aug. 13

2558 A1912 29c multicolored .60 .25

WORLD WAR II

A1913

Designs and events of 1941: a, Military vehicles (Burma Road, 717-mile lifeline to China). b, Recruits (America's first peacetime draft). c, Shipments for allies (U.S. supports allies with Lend-Lease Act). d, Franklin D. Roosevelt, Winston Churchill (Atlantic Charter sets war aims of allies). e, Tank (America becomes the "arsenal of democracy.") f, Sinking of Destoyer Reuben James, Oct. 31. g, Gas mask, helmet (Civil defense mobilizes Americans at home). h, Liberty Ship, sea gull (First Liberty ship delivered December 30). i, Sinking ships (Japanese bomb Pearl Harbor, December 7). j, Congress in session (U.S. declares war on Japan, December 8). Central label is the size of 15 stamps and shows world map, extent of axis control.

LITHOGRAPHED & ENGRAVED

1991, Sept. 3

2559 A1913 Block of 10 7.50 5.00
a.-j. 29c any single .75 .45
k. Black (engr.) omitted *12,500.*

No. 2559 has selvage at left and right and either top or bottom.

BASKETBALL, 100TH ANNIVERSARY

Basketball, Hoop, Players' Arms — A1914

PHOTOGRAVURE

1991, Aug. 28

2560 A1914 29c multicolored .60 .25

DISTRICT OF COLUMBIA BICENTENNIAL

Capitol Building from Pennsylvania Avenue, Circa 1903 — A1915

LITHOGRAPHED & ENGRAVED

1991, Sept. 7

2561 A1915 29c multicolored .60 .25
a. Black (engr.) omitted *110.00*

COMEDIANS

Stan Laurel and Oliver Hardy A1916

Edgar Bergen and Charlie McCarthy A1917

Jack Benny A1918

Fanny Brice A1919

Bud Abbott and Lou Costello A1920

BOOKLET STAMPS

Perf. 11 on 2 or 3 Sides

1991, Aug. 29

2562 A1916 29c multicolored 1.00 .25
2563 A1917 29c multicolored 1.00 .25
2564 A1918 29c multicolored 1.00 .25
2565 A1919 29c multicolored 1.00 .25
2566 A1920 29c multicolored 1.00 .25
a. Strip of 5, #2562-2566 5.00 2.50
b. Bklt. pane of 10, 2 each #2562-2566 10.00 5.00
c. As "b," scar & brt violet (engr.) omitted *450.00*

BLACK HERITAGE SERIES

Jan E. Matzeliger (1852-1889), Inventor — A1921

PHOTOGRAVURE

1991, Sept. 15 ***Perf. 11***

2567 A1921 29c multicolored .60 .25
a. Horiz. pair, imperf. vert. *650.00*
b. Vert. pair, imperf. horiz. *650.00*
c. Imperf., pair *350.00*

SPACE EXPLORATION

Mercury, Mariner 10 A1922

Venus, Mariner 2 A1923

Earth, Landsat A1924

Moon, Lunar Orbiter A1925

Mars, Viking Orbiter A1926

Jupiter, Pioneer 11 A1927

Saturn, Voyager 2 A1928

Uranus, Voyager 2 A1929

Neptune, Voyager 2 A1930

Pluto A1931

PHOTOGRAVURE
BOOKLET STAMPS

Perf. 11 on 2 or 3 Sides

1991, Oct. 1

2568 A1922 29c multicolored 1.00 .25
2569 A1923 29c multicolored 1.00 .25
2570 A1924 29c multicolored 1.00 .25
2571 A1925 29c multicolored 1.00 .25
2572 A1926 29c multicolored 1.00 .25
2573 A1927 29c multicolored 1.00 .25
2574 A1928 29c multicolored 1.00 .25
2575 A1929 29c multicolored 1.00 .25
2576 A1930 29c multicolored 1.00 .25
2577 A1931 29c multicolored 1.00 .25
a. Bklt. pane of 10, #2568-2577 10.00 4.50

CHRISTMAS

Madonna and Child by Antoniazzo Romano A1933

Santa Claus in Chimney A1934

Santa Checking List — A1935

Santa with Present — A1936

Santa at Fireplace A1937

Santa and Sleigh — A1938

LITHOGRAPHED & ENGRAVED

1991, Oct. 17 ***Perf. 11***

2578 A1933 (29c) multi .60 .25
a. Booklet pane of 10 6.00 3.25
b. Red & black (engr.) omitted *3,250.*

PHOTOGRAVURE

2579 A1934 (29c) multi .60 .25
a. Horiz. pair, imperf. vert. 175.00
b. Vert. pair, imperf. horiz. *350.00*

BOOKLET STAMPS

Size: 25x18½mm

Perf. 11 on 2 or 3 Sides

2580 A1934 (29c) Type I 2.25 .25
2581 A1934 (29c) Type II 2.75 .25
a. Pair, #2580-2581 5.00 .55
b. Bklt. pane, 2 each, #2580, 2581 11.00 1.25
2582 A1935 (29c) multi .60 .25
a. Bklt. pane of 4 2.40 1.25
2583 A1936 (29c) multi .60 .25
a. Bklt. pane of 4 2.40 1.25
2584 A1937 (29c) multi .60 .25
a. Bklt. pane of 4 2.40 1.25
2585 A1938 (29c) multi .60 .25
a. Bklt. pane of 4 2.40 1.25
Nos. 2578-2585 (8) 8.60 2.00

The far left brick from the top row of the chimney is missing from Type II, No. 2581.

Imperfs of Nos. 2581, 2583-2585 are printer's waste.

A1939

A1942

A1944

ENGRAVED

1994-95 ***Perf. 11.2***

2587 A1939 32c red brown .65 .25

Perf. 11.5

2590 A1942 $1 blue 1.90 .50
2592 A1944 $5 slate green 8.00 2.50

Issued: $2, 5/5; $5, 8/19; 32c, 11/2/95.

Flag — A1946

Eagle and Shield — A1947

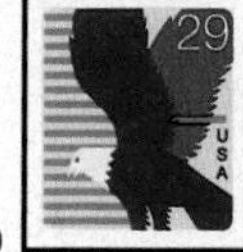

A1950

Statue of Liberty — A1951

BOOKLET STAMPS
PHOTOGRAVURE
Perf. 10 on 2 or 3 Sides

1992, Sept. 8

2593 A1946 29c black & multi .60 .25
a. Booklet pane of 10 6.00 4.25
d. Imperf, pair —

Perf. 11x10 on 2 or 3 Sides

2593B A1946 29c blk & multi 1.70 .50
c. Bklt. pane of 10, shiny gum 20.00 7.50

Perf. 11x10 on 2 or 3 Sides

1993, Apr. 8 (?)

2594 A1946 29c red & multi .65 .25
a. Booklet pane of 10 6.50 4.25

Denomination is red on #2594 and black on #2593 and 2593B.

LITHOGRAPHED & ENGRAVED (#2595), PHOTOGRAVURE

1992, Sept. 25 *Die Cut*

Self-Adhesive

2595 A1947 29c brown & multicolored .60 .25
a. Bklt. pane of 17 + label 13.00
b. Die cutting omitted, pair *125.00*
c. Brown omitted *300.00*
d. As "a," die cutting omitted *900.00*
2596 A1947 29c green & multicolored .60 .25
a. Bklt. pane of 17 + label 12.00
2597 A1947 29c red & multicolored .60 .25
a. Bklt. pane of 17 + label 10.50

Plate No. and inscription reads down on No. 2595a and up on Nos. 2596a-2597a. Design is sharper and more finely detailed on Nos. 2595, 2597.

Nos. 2595a-2597a sold for $5 each.

Nos. 2595-2597 also available in strips with stamps spaced for use in affixing machines to service first day covers.

1994 *Die Cut*

Self-Adhesive

2598 A1950 29c red, cream & blue .60 .25
a. Booklet pane of 18 11.00
b. Coil with P#111 — 5.00
c. Die cutting omitted, pair *1,000.*
2599 A1951 29c multi .60 .25
a. Booklet pane of 18 11.00
b. Coil with P#D1111 — 5.00

Except for Nos. 2598b and 2599b with plate numbers, coil stamps of Nos. 2595-2599 are indistinguishable from booklet stamps once they are removed from the backing paper.

See Nos. 3122-3122E.

Issued: No. 2598, 2/4; No. 2599, 6/24.

Scott values for used self-adhesive stamps are for examples either on piece or off piece.

A1956

A1957

A1959

A1960

Flag Over White House — A1961

COIL STAMPS

1991-93 **Untagged** *Perf. 10 Vert.*

2602 A1956 (10c) multi .30 .25
a. Imperf., pair —
2603 A1957 (10c) org yel & multi .30 .25
a. Imperf., pair 20.00
2604 A1957 (10c) gold & multi .25 .25
2605 A1959 23c multi .45 .40
a. Imperf, pair —

Vertical pairs uncut between on gummed stamp paper are proofs from the ABNCo. archives. See No. 2605P in Proofs section of the Scott U.S. Specialized Catalogue.

2606 A1960 23c multi .45 .40

"First-Class" is 9½mm long and "23" is 6mm long on No. 2606.

2607 A1960 23c multi .45 .40
c. Imperf., pair 65.00

"First-Class" is 9mm long and "23" is 6½mm long on No. 2607.

2608 A1960 23c vio bl, red & blk .80 .40

"First-Class" is 8½mm long and "23" is 6½mm long on No. 2608.

Nos. 2602-2608 are considered precancels by the USPS.

ENGRAVED
Tagged

2609 A1961 29c blue & red .60 .25
a. Imperf., pair 15.00
b. Pair, imperf. between 75.00
c. Indigo blue & red *22.50* —
Nos. 2602-2609 (8) 3.60 2.60

Beware of pairs with blind perfs sometimes offered as No. 2609b.

Issued: No. 2605, 9/27; No. 2602, 12/31; 29c, 4/23/92; No. 2606, 7/21/92; No. 2607, 10/9/92; Nos. 2603-2604, 5/29/93; No. 2608, 5/14/93.

See Nos. 2907, 3270-3271.

WINTER OLYMPICS

Hockey A1963

Figure Skating A1964

Speed Skating A1965

Skiing A1966

Bobsledding — A1967

PHOTOGRAVURE

1992, Jan. 11 *Perf. 11*

2611 A1963 29c multicolored .60 .25
2612 A1964 29c multicolored .60 .25
2613 A1965 29c multicolored .60 .25
2614 A1966 29c multicolored .60 .25
2615 A1967 29c multicolored .60 .25
a. Strip of 5, #2611-2615 3.00 2.50

Portion of Vignette of No. 129 — A1968

W.E.B. Du Bois (1868-1963), Civil Rights Leader — A1969

WORLD COLUMBIAN STAMP EXPO
LITHOGRAPHED & ENGRAVED

1992, Jan. 24

2616 A1968 29c multicolored .60 .25

BLACK HERITAGE SERIES

1992, Jan. 31

2617 A1969 29c multicolored .60 .25

A1970

A1971

LOVE
PHOTOGRAVURE

1992, Feb. 6

2618 A1970 29c multicolored .60 .25
a. Horiz. pair, imperf. vert. *300.00*
b. As "a," green omitted on right stamp *2,000.*

OLYMPIC BASEBALL

1992, Apr. 3 **Tagged** *Perf. 11*

2619 A1971 29c multicolored .60 .25

VOYAGES OF COLUMBUS

Seeking Queen Isabella's Support A1972

Crossing the Atlantic A1973

Approaching Land — A1974

Coming Ashore A1975

LITHOGRAPHED & ENGRAVED

1992, Apr. 24

2620 A1972 29c multicolored .65 .25
2621 A1973 29c multicolored .65 .25
2622 A1974 29c multicolored .65 .25
2623 A1975 29c multicolored .65 .25
a. Block of 4, #2620-2623 2.60 2.00

See Italy Nos. 1877-1880.

Souvenir Sheets

A1976

A1977

A1978

A1979

A1980

A1981

1992, May 22 ***Perf. 10½***

Tagged (15c-$5), Untagged

No.	Type	Description	Unused	Used
2624	A1976	Pane of 3	2.25	1.50
a.	A71	1c deep blue	.25	.25
b.	A74	4c ultramarine	.25	.25
c.	A82	$1 salmon	1.75	1.00
2625	A1977	Pane of 3	7.50	5.00
a.	A72	2c brown violet	.25	.25
b.	A73	3c green	.25	.25
c.	A85	$4 crimson lake	7.00	4.00
2626	A1978	Pane of 3	1.75	1.25
a.	A75	5c chocolate	.25	.25
b.	A80	30c orange brown	.60	.30
c.	A81	50c slate blue	.90	.50
2627	A1979	Pane of 3	6.00	3.75
a.	A76	6c purple	.25	.25
b.	A77	8c magenta	.25	.25
c.	A84	$3 yellow green	5.50	3.00
2628	A1980	Pane of 3	4.25	3.00
a.	A78	10c black brown	.25	.25
b.	A79	15c dark green	.30	.25
c.	A83	$2 brown red	3.50	2.00
2629	A1981	$5 Pane of 1	8.75	6.00
a.	A86	$5 black, single stamp	8.50	5.00
		Nos. 2624-2629 (6)	30.50	20.50

See Italy Nos. 1883-1888, Portugal Nos. 1918-1923 and Spain Nos. 2677-2682.

Imperforate souvenir sheets on gummed stamp paper, singly or in pairs and blocks, are proofs from the ABNCo. archives. Additionally, one imperforate essay, with the background of No. 2622 combined with the stamps of No. 2620, is recorded. See Nos. 2624P-2629P in Proofs section of the Scott U.S. Specialized Catalogue.

NEW YORK STOCK EXCHANGE BICENTENNIAL

A1982

1992, May 17 ***Perf. 11***

No.	Type	Description	Unused	Used
2630	A1982	29c green, red & black	.60	.25
a.		Black missing (EP)	*4,000.*	
b.		Black missing (CM)	*4,000.*	
c.		Center (black engr.) inverted	*18,500.*	
d.		Se-tenant pair, #2630b and #2630c	*24,000.*	

No. 2630a resulted from extraneous paper that blocked the black from appearing on the stamp paper. It is from a unique pane that contained four color-missing errors plus a fifth stamp missing half the black center.

No. 2630a must be collected se-tenant with a normal stamp or with a stamp with half of black engraving missing, or se-tenant with a normal stamp and an additional 2630a.

No. 2630b may be collected alone or se-tenant with No. 2630c.

Two panes, each containing 28 No. 2630c and 12 No. 2630b, have been documented.

SPACE ACCOMPLISHMENTS

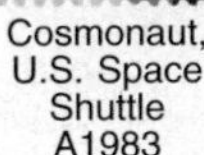

Cosmonaut, U.S. Space Shuttle A1983

Astronaut, Russian Space Station A1984

Sputnik, Vostok, Apollo Command & Lunar Modules A1985

Soyuz, Mercury and Gemini Spacecraft A1986

"Toaster Cord" Plate Flaw

PHOTOGRAVURE

1992, May 29

No.	Type	Description	Unused	Used
2631	A1983	29c multicolored	.60	.25
2632	A1984	29c multicolored	.60	.25
2633	A1985	29c multicolored	.60	.25
2634	A1986	29c multicolored	.60	.25
a.		Block of 4, #2631-2634	2.40	2.00
b.		As "a," yellow omitted	—	

The yellow color in Nos. 2631-2634 is easily removed by exposure to sunlight. Expertization of No. 2634b is essential.

See Russia Nos. 6080-6083.

ALASKA HIGHWAY, 50th ANNIVERSARY

A1987

LITHOGRAPHED & ENGRAVED

1992, May 30

No.	Type	Description	Unused	Used
2635	A1987	29c multicolored	.60	.25
a.		Black (engr.) omitted	*650.00*	—

Almost half the recorded No. 2635a errors are poorly centered. These sell for approximately $400.

KENTUCKY STATEHOOD BICENTENNIAL

A1988

PHOTOGRAVURE

1992, June 1

No.	Type	Description	Unused	Used
2636	A1988	29c multicolored	.60	.25
a.		Dark blue missing (EP)	—	
b.		Dark blue and red missing (EP)	—	
c.		All colors missing (EP)	—	

Nos. 2636a-2636c must be collected se-tenant with normal stamps.

SUMMER OLYMPICS

Soccer A1989

Gymnastics A1990

Volleyball A1991

Boxing A1992

Swimming A1993

1992, June 11

No.	Type	Description	Unused	Used
2637	A1989	29c multicolored	.60	.25
2638	A1990	29c multicolored	.60	.25
2639	A1991	29c multicolored	.60	.25
2640	A1992	29c multicolored	.60	.25
2641	A1993	29c multicolored	.60	.25
a.		Strip of 5, #2637-2641	3.00	2.50

HUMMINGBIRDS

Ruby-throated A1994

Broad-billed A1995

Costa's A1996

Rufous A1997

Calliope — A1998

BOOKLET STAMPS

Perf. 11 Vert. on 1 or 2 Sides

1992, June 15

No.	Type	Description	Unused	Used
2642	A1994	29c multicolored	.60	.25
2643	A1995	29c multicolored	.60	.25
2644	A1996	29c multicolored	.60	.25
2645	A1997	29c multicolored	.60	.25
2646	A1998	29c multicolored	.60	.25
a.		Bklt. pane of 5, #2642-2646	3.00	2.50

Imperforate singles, booklet panes and pane multiples or varieties on gummed stamp paper are proofs from the ABNCo. archives. From the same source also come imperforate progressive proofs. See No. 2646aP in Proofs section of the Scott U.S. Specialized Catalogue.

WILDFLOWERS

A1999

LITHOGRAPHED

1992, July 24 ***Perf. 11***

No.	Type	Description	Unused	Used
2647	A1999	29c Indian paintbrush	.80	.60
2648	A2000	29c Fragrant water lily	.80	.60
2649	A2001	29c Meadow beauty	.80	.60
2650	A2002	29c Jack-in-the-pulpit	.80	.60
2651	A2003	29c California poppy	.80	.60
2652	A2004	29c Large-flowered trillium	.80	.60
2653	A2005	29c Tickseed	.80	.60
2654	A2006	29c Shooting star	.80	.60
2655	A2007	29c Stream violet	.80	.60
2656	A2008	29c Bluets	.80	.60
2657	A2009	29c Herb Robert	.80	.60
2658	A2010	29c Marsh marigold	.80	.60
2659	A2011	29c Sweet white violet	.80	.60
2660	A2012	29c Claret cup cactus	.80	.60
2661	A2013	29c White mountain avens	.80	.60
2662	A2014	29c Sessile bellwort	.80	.60
2663	A2015	29c Blue flag	.80	.60
2664	A2016	29c Harlequin lupine	.80	.60
2665	A2017	29c Twinflower	.80	.60
2666	A2018	29c Common sunflower	.80	.60
2667	A2019	29c Sego lily	.80	.60
2668	A2020	29c Virginia bluebells	.80	.60
2669	A2021	29c Ohi'a lehua	.80	.60
2670	A2022	29c Rosebud orchid	.80	.60
2671	A2023	29c Showy evening primrose	.80	.60
2672	A2024	29c Fringed gentian	.80	.60
2673	A2025	29c Yellow lady's slipper	.80	.60
2674	A2026	29c Passionflower	.80	.60
2675	A2027	29c Bunchberry	.80	.60
2676	A2028	29c Pasqueflower	.80	.60
2677	A2029	29c Round-lobed hepatica	.80	.60
2678	A2030	29c Wild columbine	.80	.60
2679	A2031	29c Fireweed	.80	.60
2680	A2032	29c Indian pond lily	.80	.60
2681	A2033	29c Turk's cap lily	.80	.60
2682	A2034	29c Dutchman's breeches	.80	.60
2683	A2035	29c Trumpet honeysuckle	.80	.60
2684	A2036	29c Jacob's ladder	.80	.60
2685	A2037	29c Plains prickly pear	.80	.60
2686	A2038	29c Moss campion	.80	.60
2687	A2039	29c Bearberry	.80	.60
2688	A2040	29c Mexican hat	.80	.60
2689	A2041	29c Harebell	.80	.60
2690	A2042	29c Desert five spot	.80	.60
2691	A2043	29c Smooth Solomon's seal	.80	.60
2692	A2044	29c Red maids	.80	.60
2693	A2045	29c Yellow skunk cabbage	.80	.60
2694	A2046	29c Rue anemone	.80	.60
2695	A2047	29c Standing cypress	.80	.60
2696	A2048	29c Wild flax	.80	.60
a.		A1999-A2048 Pane of 50, #2647-2696	40.00	—

WORLD WAR II

A2049

No. 2697 — Events of 1942: a, B-25's take off to raid Tokyo, Apr. 18. b, Ration coupons (Food and other commodities rationed). c, Divebomber and deck crewman (US wins Battle of the Coral Sea, May). d, Prisoners of war (Corregidor falls to Japanese, May 6). e, Dutch Harbor buildings on fire (Japan invades Aleutian Islands, June). f, Headphones, coded message (Allies decipher secret enemy codes). g, Yorktown lost, U.S. wins at Midway. h, Woman with drill (Millions of women join war effort). i, Marines land on Guadalcanal, Aug. 7. j, Tank in desert (Allies land in North Africa, Nov.).

Central label is the size of 15 stamps and shows world map, extent of axis control.

LITHOGRAPHED & ENGRAVED

1992, Aug. 17

2697	A2049	Block of 10	7.50	5.00
a.-j.		29c any single	.75	.30
k.		Red (litho.) omitted	*5,000.*	

No. 2697 has selvage at left and right and either top or bottom.

A2050

A2051

LITERARY ARTS SERIES

PHOTOGRAVURE

1992, Aug. 22

2698 A2050 29c multicolored .60 .25

Dorothy Parker (1893-1967), author.

THEODORE VON KARMAN

1992, Aug. 31

2699 A2051 29c multicolored .60 .25

Von Karman (1881-1963), rocket scientist.

MINERALS

Azurite — A2052

Copper — A2053

Variscite A2054

Wulfenite A2055

LITHOGRAPHED & ENGRAVED

1992, Sept. 17

2700	A2052	29c multicolored	.60	.25
2701	A2053	29c multicolored	.60	.25
2702	A2054	29c multicolored	.60	.25
2703	A2055	29c multicolored	.60	.25
a.		Block or strip of 4, #2700-2703	2.40	2.00
b.		As "a," silver (litho.) omitted	*7,750.*	
c.		As "a," red (litho.) omitted	—	
d.		As "a," silver omitted on two stamps	—	

Specialists have questioned the existence of No. 2703c as a genuine error. The editors would like to see authenticated evidence of its existence.

JUAN RODRIGUEZ CABRILLO

Cabrillo, Ship, Map of San Diego Bay Area — A2056

1992, Sept. 28

2704	A2056	29c multicolored	.60	.25
a.		Black (engr.) omitted	*2,250.*	

WILD ANIMALS

Giraffe A2057

Giant Panda A2058

Flamingo A2059

King Penguins A2060

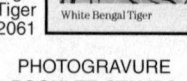

White Bengal Tiger A2061

PHOTOGRAVURE
BOOKLET STAMPS

Perf. 11 Horiz. on 1 or 2 Sides

1992, Oct. 1

2705	A2057	29c multicolored	.65	.25
2706	A2058	29c multicolored	.65	.25
2707	A2059	29c multicolored	.65	.25
2708	A2060	29c multicolored	.65	.25
2709	A2061	29c multicolored	.65	.25
a.		Booklet pane of 5, #2705-2709	3.25	2.25
b.		As "a," imperf.	*2,000.*	

CHRISTMAS

Madonna and Child, by Giovanni Bellini — A2062

A2063

A2064

A2065

A2066

LITHOGRAPHED & ENGRAVED

1992 ***Perf. 11½x11***

2710	A2062	29c multicolored	.60	.25
a.		Booklet pane of 10	6.00	3.50

LITHOGRAPHED

2711	A2063	29c multicolored	.75	.25
2712	A2064	29c multicolored	.75	.25
2713	A2065	29c multicolored	.75	.25
2714	A2066	29c multicolored	.75	.25
a.		Block of 4, #2711-2714	3.00	1.10

Booklet Stamps

PHOTOGRAVURE

Perf. 11 on 2 or 3 Sides

2715	A2063	29c multicolored	.85	.25
2716	A2064	29c multicolored	.85	.25
2717	A2065	29c multicolored	.85	.25
2718	A2066	29c multicolored	.85	.25
a.		Booklet pane of 4, #2715-2718	3.50	1.25

Imperforates and part-perforates on gummed stamp paper are proofs from the ABNCo. archives. From the same source come imperforates with Toys only and imperforates without denominations. See No. 2718aP in Proofs section of the Scott U.S. Specialized Catalogue.

Self-Adhesive

Die Cut

2719	A2065	29c multicolored	.65	.25
a.		Booklet pane of 18	12.00	

"Greetings" is 27mm long on Nos. 2711-2714, 25mm long on Nos. 2715-2718 and 21½mm long on No. 2719. Nos. 2715-2719 differ in color from Nos. 2711-2714.

Issued: #2710-2718, 10/22; #2719, 10/28.

CHINESE NEW YEAR

Year of the Rooster A2067

LITHOGRAPHED & ENGRAVED

1992, Dec. 30 ***Perf. 11***

2720 A2067 29c multicolored .60 .25

See No. 3895j.

AMERICAN MUSIC SERIES

Elvis Presley A2068

Oklahoma! A2069

Hank Williams A2070

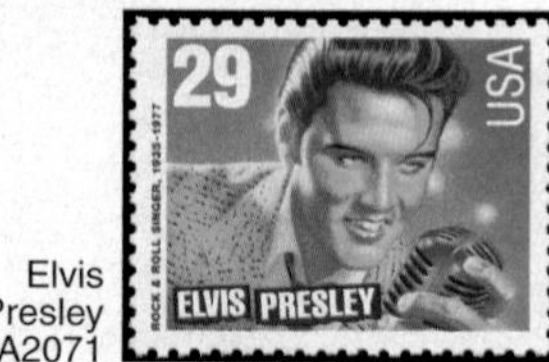

Elvis Presley A2071

Bill Haley A2072

Clyde McPhatter A2073

Ritchie Valens A2074

Otis Redding A2075

Buddy Holly A2076

Dinah Washington A2077

PHOTOGRAVURE

1993 ***Perf. 11***

2721	A2068	29c multicolored	.60	.25
a.		Imperf, pair	—	

Perf. 10

2722	A2069	29c multicolored	.60	.25
2723	A2070	29c multicolored	.75	.25

Perf. 11.2x11.5

2723A A2070 29c multicolored 18.00 10.00

1993, June 16 ***Perf. 10***

2724	A2071	29c multicolored	.70	.25
2725	A2072	29c multicolored	.70	.25
2726	A2073	29c multicolored	.70	.25
2727	A2074	29c multicolored	.70	.25
2728	A2075	29c multicolored	.70	.25
2729	A2076	29c multicolored	.70	.25
2730	A2077	29c multicolored	.70	.25
a.		Vert. strip of 7, #2724-2730	5.50	3.00

Booklet Stamps

Perf. 11 Horiz. on 1 or 2 Sides

2731	A2071	29c multicolored	.60	.25
2732	A2072	29c multicolored	.60	.25
2733	A2073	29c multicolored	.60	.25
2734	A2074	29c multicolored	.60	.25
2735	A2075	29c multicolored	.60	.25
2736	A2076	29c multicolored	.60	.25
2737	A2077	29c multicolored	.60	.25
a.		Booklet pane, 2 #2731, 1 each #2732-2737	5.00	2.25
b.		Booklet pane, #2731, 2735-2737 + tab	2.40	1.50

Nos. 2731-2737 have smaller design sizes, brighter colors and shorter inscriptions than Nos. 2724-2730, as well as framelines around the designs and other subtle design differences.

No. 2737b without tab is indistinguishable from broken No. 2737a.

Imperforates of both No. 2737a and 2737b on gummed stamp paper are proofs from the ABNCo. archives. Perforated booklet pane multiples and varieties also exist from the same source. See Nos. 2737aP-2737bP in Proofs section of the Scott U.S. Specialized Catalogue.

See Nos. 2769, 2771, 2775 and designs A2112-A2117.

SPACE FANTASY

A2086

A2087

A2088

A2089

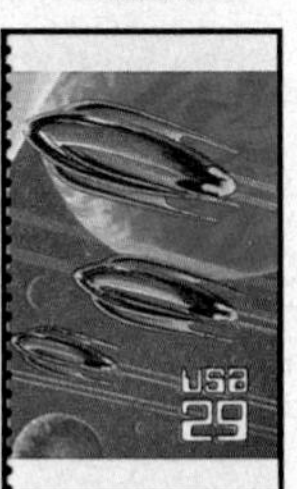

A2090

BOOKLET STAMPS

1993, Jan. 25 ***Perf. 11 Vert.***

2741	A2086	29c multicolored	.60	.25
2742	A2087	29c multicolored	.60	.25
2743	A2088	29c multicolored	.60	.25
2744	A2089	29c multicolored	.60	.25
2745	A2090	29c multicolored	.60	.25
a.		Booklet pane of 5, #2741-2745	3.00	2.25

BLACK HERITAGE SERIES

Percy Lavon Julian (1899-1975), Chemist — A2091

LITHOGRAPHED & ENGRAVED

1993, Jan. 29 ***Perf. 11***

2746	A2091	29c multicolored	.60	.25

OREGON TRAIL

A2092

1993, Feb. 12

2747	A2092	29c multicolored	.60	.25
b.		Blue omitted	—	

WORLD UNIVERSITY GAMES

A2093

PHOTOGRAVURE

1993, Feb. 25

2748	A2093	29c multicolored	.60	.25

GRACE KELLY (1929-1982)

Actress, Princess of Monaco — A2094

ENGRAVED

1993, Mar. 24

2749	A2094	29c blue	.60	.25

See Monaco No. 1851.

CIRCUS

Clown — A2095

Ringmaster A2096

Trapeze Artist — A2097

Elephant A2098

LITHOGRAPHED

1993, Apr. 6

2750	A2095	29c multicolored	.60	.25
2751	A2096	29c multicolored	.60	.25
2752	A2097	29c multicolored	.60	.25
2753	A2098	29c multicolored	.60	.25
a.		Block of 4, #2750-2753	2.40	1.75

CHEROKEE STRIP LAND RUN, CENTENNIAL

A2099

LITHOGRAPHED & ENGRAVED

1993, Apr. 17

2754	A2099	29c multicolored	.60	.25

Imperforates on gummed stamp paper, including gutter pairs and blocks, are proofs from the ABNCo. archives. From the same source also come perforated gutter pairs and blocks, plus imperforates missing the red text and black denomination and "USA." An approved die proof also is recorded. See No. 2754P in Proofs section of the Scott U.S. Specialized Catalogue.

DEAN ACHESON (1893-1971)

Secretary of State — A2100

ENGRAVED

1993, Apr. 21

2755	A2100	29c greenish gray	.60	.25

SPORTING HORSES

Steeplechase — A2101

Thoroughbred Racing — A2102

Harness Racing A2103

Polo A2104

LITHOGRAPHED & ENGRAVED

1993, May 1 ***Perf. 11x11½***

2756	A2101	29c multicolored	.60	.25
2757	A2102	29c multicolored	.60	.25
2758	A2103	29c multicolored	.60	.25
2759	A2104	29c multicolored	.60	.25
a.		Block of 4, #2756-2759	2.40	2.00
b.		As "a," black (engr.) omitted	*525.00*	

GARDEN FLOWERS

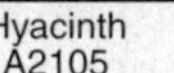

Hyacinth A2105

Daffodil A2106

Tulip — A2107

Iris — A2108

Lilac — A2109

LITHOGRAPHED & ENGRAVED
BOOKLET STAMPS

1993, May 15 ***Perf. 11 Vert.***

2760	A2105	29c multicolored	.75	.25
2761	A2106	29c multicolored	.75	.25
2762	A2107	29c multicolored	.75	.25
2763	A2108	29c multicolored	.75	.25
2764	A2109	29c multicolored	.75	.25
a.		Booklet pane of 5, #2760-2764	3.75	2.25
b.		As "a," black (engr.) omitted	*140.00*	
c.		As "a," imperf.	*850.00*	

WORLD WAR II

A2110

Designs and events of 1943: a, Destroyers (Allied forces battle German U-boats). b, Military medics treat the wounded. c, Amphibious landing craft on beach (Sicily attacked by Allied forces, July). d, B-24s hit Ploesti refineries, August. e, V-mail delivers letters from home. f, PT boat (Italy invaded by Allies, Sept.). g, Nos. WS7, WS8, savings bonds, (Bonds and stamps help war effort). h, "Willie and Joe" keep spirits high. i, Banner in window (Gold Stars mark World War II losses). j, Marines assault Tarawa, Nov.

Central label is the size of 15 stamps and shows world map with extent of Axis control and Allied operations.

1993, May 31 *Perf. 11*

2765 A2110 Block of 10 7.50 5.00
a.-j. 29c any single .75 .40

No. 2765 has selvage at left and right and either top or bottom.

JOE LOUIS (1914-1981)

A2111

LITHOGRAPHED & ENGRAVED

1993, June 22

2766 A2111 29c multicolored .60 .25

AMERICAN MUSIC SERIES

Oklahoma! Type and

Show Boat
A2112

Porgy & Bess
A2113

My Fair Lady
A2114

BOOKLET STAMPS
PHOTOGRAVURE

Perf. 11 Horiz. on 1 or 2 Sides

1993, July 14

2767 A2112 29c multicolored .60 .25
2768 A2113 29c multicolored .60 .25
2769 A2069 29c multicolored .60 .25
2770 A2114 29c multicolored .60 .25
a. Booklet pane of 4, #2767-2770 2.75 2.25

No. 2769 has smaller design size, brighter colors and shorter inscription than No. 2722, as well as a frameline around the design and other subtle design differences.

Imperforate booklet panes, singly or in multiples, on gummed stamp paper are proofs from the ABNCo. archives. From the same source come imperforate progressive proofs, plus imperforate proofs/essays showing slightly altered designs. See No. 2770aP in Proofs section of the Scott U.S. Specialized Catalogue.

AMERICAN MUSIC SERIES

Hank Williams Type and

Patsy Cline
A2115

The Carter Family
A2116

Bob Wills
A2117

PHOTOGRAVURE

1993, Sept. 25 *Perf. 10*

2771 A2070 29c multicolored .75 .25
2772 A2115 29c multicolored .75 .25
2773 A2116 29c multicolored .75 .25
2774 A2117 29c multicolored .75 .25
a. Block or horiz. strip of 4, #2771-2774 3.00 1.75

Booklet Stamps

Perf. 11 Horiz. on one or two sides

With Black Frameline

2775 A2070 29c multicolored .60 .25
2776 A2116 29c multicolored .60 .25
2777 A2115 29c multicolored .60 .25
2778 A2117 29c multicolored .60 .25
a. Booklet pane of 4, #2775-2778 2.50 2.00

Inscription at left measures 27½mm on No. 2723, 27mm on No. 2771 and 22mm on No. 2775. No. 2723 shows only two tuning keys on guitar, while No. 2771 shows those two and parts of two others.

Imperforate booklet panes on gummed stamp paper, singly or in multiples, are proofs from the ABNCo. archives. From the same source come panes perfed horiz. but uncut vertically, plus imperforate progressive proofs and other die proof varieties. See No. 2778aP in Proofs section in the Scott U.S. Specialized Catalogue.

NATIONAL POSTAL MUSEUM

Independence Hall, Benjamin Franklin, Printing Press, Colonial Post Rider — A2118

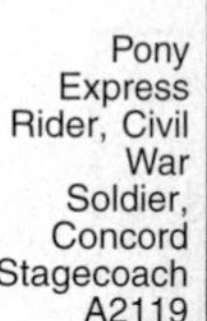

Pony Express Rider, Civil War Soldier, Concord Stagecoach
A2119

JN-4H Biplane, Charles Lindbergh, Railway Mail Car, 1931 Model A Ford Mail Truck
A2120

California Gold Rush Miner's Letter, Nos. 39, 295, C3a, C13, Barcode & Circular Date Stamp
A2121

LITHOGRAPHED AND ENGRAVED

1993, July 30 **Tagged** *Perf. 11*

2779 A2118 29c multicolored .60 .25
2780 A2119 29c multicolored .60 .25
2781 A2120 29c multicolored .60 .25
2782 A2121 29c multicolored .60 .25
a. Block or strip of 4, #2779-2782 2.40 2.00
b. As "a," engr. maroon (USA/29) and black ("My dear...") omitted —
c. As "a," imperf *2,750.*

AMERICAN SIGN LANGUAGE

A2122

A2123

PHOTOGRAVURE

1993, Sept. 20 *Perf. 11½*

2783 A2122 29c multicolored .60 .25
2784 A2123 29c multicolored .60 .25
a. Pair, #2783-2784 1.20 .75

CLASSIC BOOKS

A2124

A2125

A2126

A2127

Designs: No. 2785, Rebecca of Sunnybrook Farm, by Kate Douglas Wiggin. No. 2786, Little House on the Prairie, by Laura Ingalls Wilder. No. 2787, The Adventures of Huckleberry Finn, by Mark Twain. No. 2788, Little Women, by Louisa May Alcott.

LITHOGRAPHED & ENGRAVED

1993, Oct. 23 *Perf. 11*

2785 A2124 29c multicolored .60 .25
2786 A2125 29c multicolored .60 .25
2787 A2126 29c multicolored .60 .25
2788 A2127 29c multicolored .60 .25
a. Block or horiz. strip of 4, #2785-2788 2.40 2.00

Imperforates on gummed stamp paper, including gutter pairs and blocks, are proofs from the ABNCo. archives. See No. 2788aP in Proofs section of the Scott U.S. Specialized Catalogue.

CHRISTMAS

Madonna and Child in a Landscape, by Giovanni Battista Cima — A2128

Jack-in-the-Box
A2129

Red-Nosed Reindeer
A2130

Snowman
A2131

Toy Soldier Blowing Horn
A2132

1993, Oct. 21

2789 A2128 29c multicolored .60 .25

Booklet Stamp

Size: 18x25mm

Perf. 11½x11 on 2 or 3 Sides

2790 A2128 29c multicolored .60 .25
a. Booklet pane of 4 2.40 1.75
b. Imperf., pair —
c. As "a," imperf —

Nos. 2789-2790 have numerous design differences.

1993

PHOTOGRAVURE

Perf. 11½

2791 A2129 29c multicolored .60 .25
2792 A2130 29c multicolored .60 .25
2793 A2131 29c multicolored .60 .25
2794 A2132 29c multicolored .60 .25
a. Block or strip of 4, #2791-2794 2.40 2.00

Booklet Stamps

Size: 18x21mm

Perf. 11x10 on 2 or 3 Sides

2795 A2132 29c multicolored .85 .25
2796 A2131 29c multicolored .85 .25
2797 A2130 29c multicolored .85 .25
2798 A2129 29c multicolored .85 .25
a. Booklet pane, 3 each #2795-2796, 2 each #2797-2798 8.50 4.00
b. Booklet pane, 3 each #2797-2798, 2 each #2795-2796 8.50 4.00
c. Block of 4, #2795-2798 3.40 1.75

Self-Adhesive

Size: 19½x26½mm

Die Cut

2799 A2131 29c multicolored .65 .25
- *a.* Coil with plate # V1111111 — 6.00

2800 A2132 29c multicolored .65 .25
2801 A2129 29c multicolored .65 .25
2802 A2130 29c multicolored .65 .25
- *a.* Booklet pane, 3 each #2799-2802 8.00
- *b.* Block of 4, #2799-2802 2.60

Except for No. 2799a with plate number, coil stamps are indistinguishable from booklet stamps once they are removed from the backing paper.

Size: 17x20mm

2803 A2131 29c multicolored .60 .25
- *a.* Booklet pane of 18 11.00

Snowman on Nos. 2793, 2799 has three buttons and seven snowflakes beneath nose (placement differs on both stamps). No. 2796 has two buttons and five snowflakes beneath nose. No. 2803 has two orange buttons and four snowflakes beneath nose.

Issued: #2791-2798, 10/21; #2799-2803, 10/28.

MARIANA ISLANDS

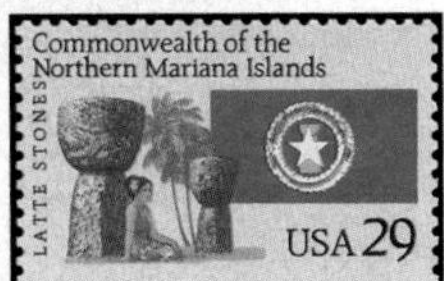

A2133

LITHOGRAPHED AND ENGRAVED

1993, Nov. 4 ***Perf. 11***

2804 A2133 29c multicolored .60 .25

COLUMBUS' LANDING IN PUERTO RICO, 500th ANNIVERSARY

A2134

PHOTOGRAVURE

1993, Nov. 19 ***Perf. 11.2***

2805 A2134 29c multicolored .60 .25

AIDS AWARENESS

A2135

1993, Dec. 1

2806 A2135 29c black & red .60 .25
- *a.* Perf. 11 vert. on 1 or 2 sides, from bklt. pane .70 .25
- *b.* As "a," booklet pane of 5 3.50 2.00

WINTER OLYMPICS

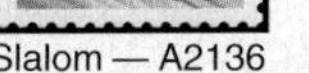

Slalom — A2136

Luge — A2137

Ice Dancing A2138

Cross-Country Skiing A2139

Ice Hockey — A2140

LITHOGRAPHED

1994, Jan. 6

2807 A2136 29c multicolored .60 .25
2808 A2137 29c multicolored .60 .25
2809 A2138 29c multicolored .60 .25
2810 A2139 29c multicolored .60 .25
2811 A2140 29c multicolored .60 .25
- *a.* Strip of 5, #2807-2811 3.00 2.50

EDWARD R. MURROW, JOURNALIST (1908-65)

A2141

ENGRAVED

1994, Jan. 21

2812 A2141 29c brown .60 .25

LOVE

A2142

A2143

A2144

Booklet Stamps

LITHOGRAPHED & ENGRAVED

1994 ***Die Cut***

Self-adhesive

2813 A2142 29c multicolored .60 .25
- *a.* Booklet pane of 18 11.00
- *b.* Coil with plate # B1 — 3.75

Except for No. 2813b with plate number, coil stamps are indistinguishable from booklet stamps once they are removed from the backing paper.

PHOTOGRAVURE

Perf. 10.9x11.1 on 2 or 3 sides

2814 A2143 29c multicolored .60 .25
- *a.* Booklet pane of 10 6.00 3.50
- *b.* Imperf, pair —
- *d.* As "a," imperf. —

Horiz. pairs, imperf between, are printer's waste.

No. 2814 was issued in booklets only.

LITHOGRAPHED & ENGRAVED

Perf. 11.1

2814C A2143 29c multicolored .70 .25

Size of No. 2814C is 20x28mm. No. 2814 is 18x24½mm.

PHOTOGRAVURE & ENGRAVED

Perf. 11.2

2815 A2144 52c multicolored 1.00 .25

Issued: No. 2813, Jan. 27; Nos. 2814-2815, Feb. 14; No. 2814C, June 11.

BLACK HERITAGE SERIES

Dr. Allison Davis (1902-83), Social Anthropologist, Educator — A2145

ENGRAVED

1994, Feb. 1 ***Perf. 11.2***

2816 A2145 29c red brown & brown .60 .25

CHINESE NEW YEAR

Year of the Dog A2146

PHOTOGRAVURE

1994, Feb. 5

2817 A2146 29c multicolored .80 .25

See No. 3895k.

BUFFALO SOLDIERS

A2147

LITHOGRAPHED & ENGRAVED

1994, Apr. 22 ***Perf. 11.5x11.2***

2818 A2147 29c multicolored .60 .25
- *a.* Double impression (second impression light) of red brown (engr. inscriptions) —

SILENT SCREEN STARS

Rudolph Valentino (1895-1926) A2148

Clara Bow (1905-65) A2149

Charlie Chaplin (1889-1977) A2150

Lon Chaney (1883-1930) A2151

John Gilbert (1895-1936) A2152

Zasu Pitts (1898-1963) A2153

Harold Lloyd (1894-1971) A2154

Keystone Cops A2155

Theda Bara (1885-1955) A2156

Buster Keaton (1895-1966) A2157

1994, Apr. 27 ***Perf. 11.2***

2819 A2148 29c red, blk & brt vio 1.10 .30
2820 A2149 29c red, blk & brt vio 1.10 .30
2821 A2150 29c red, blk & brt vio 1.10 .30
2822 A2151 29c red, blk & brt vio 1.10 .30
2823 A2152 29c red, blk & brt vio 1.10 .30
2824 A2153 29c red, blk & brt vio 1.10 .30
2825 A2154 29c red, blk & brt vio 1.10 .30
2826 A2155 29c red, blk & brt vio 1.10 .30
2827 A2156 29c red, blk & brt vio 1.10 .30
2828 A2157 29c red, blk & brt vio 1.10 .30
- *a.* Block of 10, #2819-2828 11.00 5.00
- *b.* As "a," black (litho.) omitted —
- *c.* As "a," blk, red & brt vio (litho.) omitted —

GARDEN FLOWERS

Lily — A2158

Zinnia — A2159

Gladiola A2160

Marigold A2161

Rose — A2162

1994, Apr. 28 ***Perf. 10.9 Vert.***

Booklet Stamps

2829	A2158 29c multicolored		.65	.25
2830	A2159 29c multicolored		.65	.25
2831	A2160 29c multicolored		.65	.25
2832	A2161 29c multicolored		.65	.25
2833	A2162 29c multicolored		.65	.25
a.	Booklet pane of 5, #2829-2833		3.25	2.25
b.	As "a," imperf		*650.00*	
c.	As "a," black (engr.) omitted		*150.00*	

1994 WORLD CUP SOCCER CHAMPIONSHIPS

A2163

A2163a

A2164

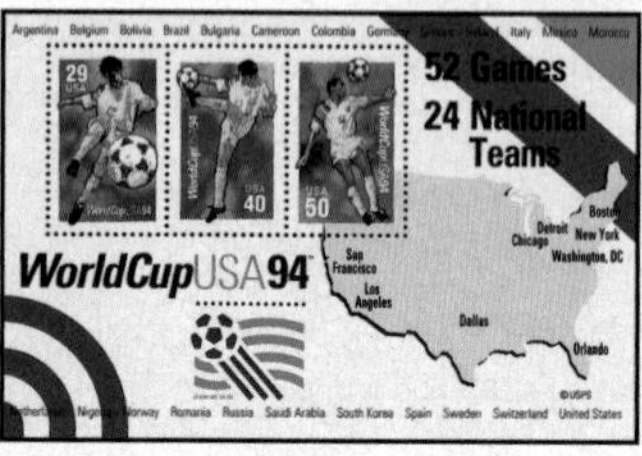

A2165

Design: 40c, Soccer player, diff.

PHOTOGRAVURE

1994, May 26 ***Perf. 11.1***

2834	A2163 29c multicolored	.60	.25
2835	A2163a 40c multicolored	.80	.25
2836	A2164 50c multicolored	1.00	.25
	Nos. 2834-2836 (3)	2.40	.75

Souvenir Sheet of 3

2837	A2165 #a.-#c.	4.50	3.00

No. 2837c has a portion of the yellow map in the LR corner.

WORLD WAR II

A2166

Designs and events of 1944: a, Allied forces retake New Guinea. b, P-51s escort B-17s on bombing raids. c, Troops running from landing craft (Allies in Normandy, D-Day, June 6). d, Airborne units spearhead attacks. e, Officer at periscope (Submarines shorten war in Pacific). f, Parade (Allies free Rome, June 4; Paris, Aug. 25). g, Soldier firing flamethrower (US troops clear Saipan bunkers). h, Red Ball Express speeds vital supplies. i, Battleship firing main battery (Battle for Leyte Gulf, Oct. 23-26). j, Soldiers in snow (Bastogne and Battle of the Bulge, Dec.).

Central label is size of 15 stamps and shows world map with extent of Axis control and Allied operations.

Illustration reduced.

LITHOGRAPHED & ENGRAVED

1994, June 6 ***Perf. 10.9***

2838	A2166 Block of 10	17.00	10.00
a.-j.	29c any single	1.70	.50

No. 2838 has selvage at left and right and either top or bottom.

NORMAN ROCKWELL

A2167

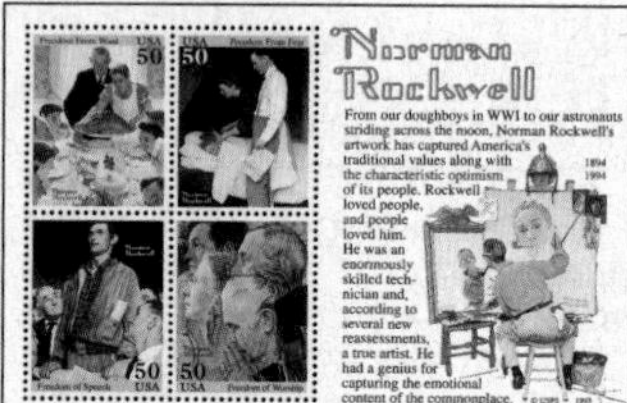

A2168

1994, July 1 ***Perf. 10.9x11.1***

2839	A2167 29c multicolored	.60	.25

Souvenir Sheet

LITHOGRAPHED

2840	A2168 Sheet of 4	4.50	2.75
a.	50c Freedom From Want	1.10	.65
b.	50c Freedom From Fear	1.10	.65
c.	50c Freedom of Speech	1.10	.65
d.	50c Freedom of Worship	1.10	.65

Moon Landing, 25th Anniv.

A2169

A2170

Miniature Sheet

1994, July 20 ***Perf. 11.2x11.1***

2841	A2169 29c Sheet of 12	10.50	—
a.	Single stamp	.85	.60

LITHOGRAPHED & ENGRAVED

Perf. 10.7x11.1

2842	A2170 $9.95 multicolored	20.00	16.00

LOCOMOTIVES

Hudson's General A2171

McQueen's Jupiter A2172

Eddy's No. 242 A2173

Ely's No. 10 A2174

Buchanan's No. 999 A2175

PHOTOGRAVURE

1994, July 28 ***Perf. 11 Horiz.***

Booklet Stamps

2843	A2171 29c multicolored	.70	.25
2844	A2172 29c multicolored	.70	.25
2845	A2173 29c multicolored	.70	.25
2846	A2174 29c multicolored	.70	.25
2847	A2175 29c multicolored	.70	.25
a.	Booklet pane of 5, #2843-2847	3.50	2.00
b.	As "a," imperf.	*2,500.*	

GEORGE MEANY, LABOR LEADER (1894-1980)

A2176

ENGRAVED

1994, Aug. 16 ***Perf. 11.1x11***

2848	A2176 29c blue	.60	.25

AMERICAN MUSIC SERIES

Popular Singers

Al Jolson (1886-1950) A2177

Bing Crosby (1904-77) A2178

Ethel Waters (1896-1977) A2179

Nat "King" Cole (1919-65) A2180

Ethel Merman (1908-84) A2181

Jazz Singers

Bessie Smith (1894-1937) A2182

Muddy Waters (1915-83) A2183

Billie Holiday (1915-59) A2184

Robert Johnson (1911-38) A2185

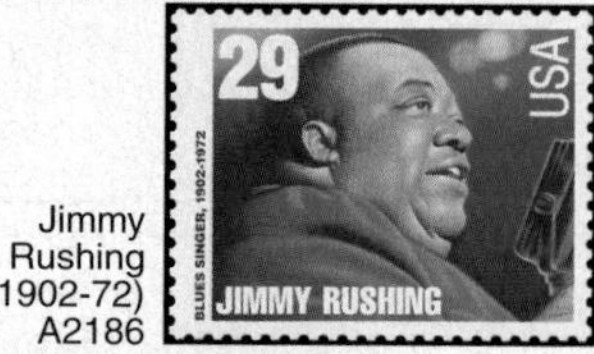

Jimmy Rushing (1902-72) A2186

"Ma" Rainey (1886-1939) A2187

Mildred Bailey (1907-51) A2188

Howlin' Wolf (1910-76) A2189

PHOTOGRAVURE

1994, Sept. 1 ***Perf. 10.1x10.2***

2849 A2177 29c multicolored .85 .25
2850 A2178 29c multicolored .85 .25
2851 A2179 29c multicolored .85 .25
2852 A2180 29c multicolored .85 .25
2853 A2181 29c multicolored .85 .25
a. Vert. strip of 5, #2849-2853 4.25 2.00
b. Pane of 20, imperf *4,600.*

1994, Sept. 17 ***Perf. 11x10.8***

LITHOGRAPHED

2854 A2182 29c multicolored 1.50 .25
2855 A2183 29c multicolored 1.50 .25
2856 A2184 29c multicolored 1.50 .25
2857 A2185 29c multicolored 1.50 .25
2858 A2186 29c multicolored 1.50 .25
2859 A2187 29c multicolored 1.50 .25
2860 A2188 29c multicolored 1.50 .25
2861 A2189 29c multicolored 1.50 .25
a. Block of 10, #2854-2861 +2 additional stamps 15.00 4.50

LITERARY ARTS SERIES

James Thurber (1894-1961) A2190

LITHOGRAPHED & ENGRAVED

1994, Sept. 10 ***Perf. 11***

2862 A2190 29c multicolored .60 .25

WONDERS OF THE SEA

Diver, Motorboat A2191

Diver, Ship A2192

Diver, Ship's Wheel A2193

Diver, Coral A2194

LITHOGRAPHED

1994, Oct. 3 ***Perf. 11x10.9***

2863 A2191 29c multicolored .75 .25
2864 A2192 29c multicolored .75 .25
2865 A2193 29c multicolored .75 .25
2866 A2194 29c multicolored .75 .25
a. Block of 4, #2863-2866 3.00 1.50
b. As "a," imperf *500.00*

CRANES

Black-Necked A2195

Whooping A2196

LITHOGRAPHED & ENGRAVED

1994, Oct. 9 ***Perf. 10.8x11***

2867 A2195 29c multicolored .70 .25
2868 A2196 29c multicolored .70 .25
a. Pair, #2867-2868 1.40 .75
b. As "a," black & magenta (engr.) omitted *1,500.*
c. As "a," double impression of engr. black (Birds' names and "USA") & magenta ("29") *4,750.*
d. As "a," double impression of engr. black ("USA") & magenta ("29") —

LEGENDS OF THE WEST

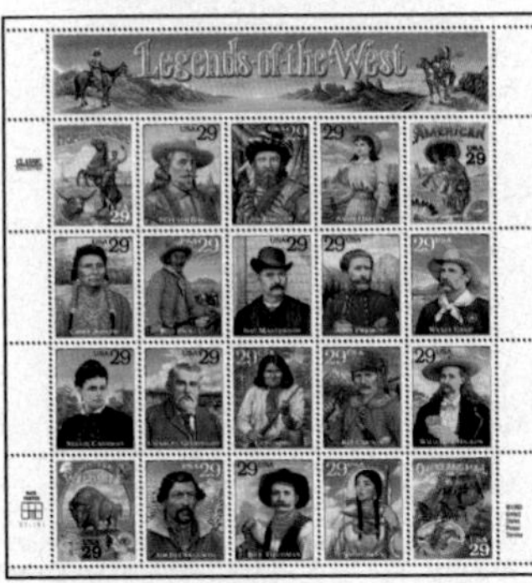

A2197

g. Bill Pickett (1870-1932) (Revised)

Designs: a, Home on the Range. b, Buffalo Bill Cody (1846-1917). c, Jim Bridger (1804-81). d, Annie Oakley (1860-1926). e, Native American Culture. f, Chief Joseph (c. 1840-1904). h, Bat Masterson (1853-1921). i, John C. Fremont (1813-90). j, Wyatt Earp (1848-1929). k, Nellie Cashman (c. 1849-1925).

l, Charles Goodnight (1826-1929). m, Geronimo (1823-1909). n, Kit Carson (1809-68). o, Wild Bill Hickok (1837-76). p, Western Wildlife. q, Jim Beckwourth (c. 1798-1866). r, Bill Tilghman (1854-1924). s, Sacagawea (c. 1787-1812). t, Overland Mail.

PHOTOGRAVURE

1994, Oct. 18 ***Perf. 10.1x10***

2869 A2197 Pane of 20 15.00 10.00
a.-t. 29c any single .75 .50
u. As No. 2869, a.-e. imperf. f.-j. part perf. —

LEGENDS OF THE WEST (Recalled)

g. Bill Pickett (Recalled)

Nos. 2870b-2870d, 2870f-2870o, 2870q-2870s have a frameline around the vignette that is half the width of the frameline on similar stamps in No. 2869. Other design differences may exist.

1994

2870 A2197 29c Pane of 20 230.00 —

150,000 panes of No. 2870 were made available through a drawing. Panes were delivered in an envelope. Value is for pane without envelope. Panes with envelopes sell for somewhat more.

CHRISTMAS

Madonna and Child, by Elisabetta Sirani A2200

Stocking A2201

Santa Claus A2202

Cardinal in Snow A2203

LITHOGRAPHED & ENGRAVED

1994, Oct. 20 ***Perf. 11¼***

2871 A2200 29c multi .60 .25

BOOKLET STAMP

Perf. 9¾x11

2871A A2200 29c multi .60 .25
b. Booklet pane of 10 6.25 3.50
c. Imperf, pair *425.00*

LITHOGRAPHED

Perf. 11¼

2872 A2201 29c multi .60 .25
a. Booklet pane of 20 12.50 6.00
b. Imperf., pair —
c. Vert. pair, imperf. horiz. —
d. Quadruple impression of black, triple impression of blue, double impressions of red and yellow, green normal —
e. Vert. pair, imperf. between —
f. As "a," imperf. —

PHOTOGRAVURE

BOOKLET STAMPS

Self-Adhesive

Die Cut

2873 A2202 29c multi .70 .25
a. Booklet pane of 12 8.50
b. Coil with plate # V1111 — 6.00

Except for No. 2873b with plate number, coil stamps are indistinguishable from booklet stamps once they are removed from the backing paper.

2874 A2203 29c multi .60 .25
a. Booklet pane of 18 11.00

BUREAU OF ENGRAVING & PRINTING

Souvenir Sheet

A2204

LITHOGRAPHED & ENGRAVED

1994, Nov. 3 ***Perf. 11***

2875 A2204 $2 Pane of 4 16.00 13.50
a. Single stamp 4.00 2.00

CHINESE NEW YEAR

Year of the Boar A2205

PHOTOGRAVURE

1994, Dec. 30 ***Perf. 11.2x11.1***

2876 A2205 29c multicolored .70 .25

See No. 3895l.

A2206

A2207

Old Glory
USA G
For U.S. addresses only

A2208

USA G
For U.S. addresses only

A2208a

A2209

LITHOGRAPHED

Perf. 11x10.8

1994, Dec. 13 **Untagged**

2877 A2206 (3c) tan, brt bl & red .25 .25
a. Imperf., pair *115.00*
b. Double impression of red *175.00*

No. 2877 imperf and with blue omitted is known from printer's waste.

Perf. 10.8x10.9

Untagged

2878 A2206 (3c) tan, dk bl & red .25 .25

Inscriptions on #2877 are in a thin typeface. Those on #2878 are in heavy, bold type.

PHOTOGRAVURE

Perf. 11.2x11.1

2879 A2207 (20c) black "G," yel & multi .40 .25
a. Imperf., pair —

Perf. 11x10.9

2880 A2207 (20c) red "G," yel & multi .75 .25

Perf. 11.2x11.1

2881 A2208 (32c) black "G" & multi 1.25 .25
a. Booklet pane of 10 12.50 5.00

Perf. 11x10.9

2882 A2208a (32c) red "G" & multi .60 .25

Distance on #2882 from bottom of red G to top of flag immediately above is 13¾mm. Illustration A2208a shows #2885 superimposed over #2882.

BOOKLET STAMPS

Perf. 10x9.9 on 2 or 3 Sides

2883 A2208 (32c) black "G" & multi .65 .25
a. Booklet pane of 10 6.50 3.75

Perf. 10.9 on 2 or 3 Sides

2884 A2208 (32c) blue "G" & multi .65 .25
a. Booklet pane of 10 6.50 3.75
b. As "a," imperf *1,700.*

Perf. 11x10.9 on 2 or 3 Sides

2885 A2208a (32c) red "G" & multi .90 .25
a. Booklet pane of 10 9.00 4.50
b. Horiz. pair, imperf vert. *750.00*
c. Horiz. pair, imperf between —
d. Horiz. pair, imperf. btwn., in #2885a with foldover —

Distance on #2885 from bottom of red G to top of flag immediately above is 13½mm. See note below #2882.

No. 2885c resulted from a paper foldover after perforating and before cutting into panes.

A2208b A2208c

Die Cut
Self-Adhesive

2886 A2208b (32c) gray, bl, lt bl, red & blk .75 .25
a. Booklet pane of 18 14.00
b. Coil with plate # V11111 — 10.00

No. 2886 is printed on prephosphored paper that is opaque, thicker and brighter than that of No. 2887 and has only a small number of blue shading dots in the white stripes immediately below the flag's blue field.

Except for No. 2886b with plate number, coil stamps are indistinguishable from booklet stamps once they are removed from the backing paper.

2887 A2208c (32c) black, blue & red .75 .25
a. Booklet pane of 18 13.50

No. 2887 has noticeable blue shading in the white stripes immediately below the blue field and has overall tagging. The paper is translucent, thinner and duller than No. 2886.

COIL STAMPS

Perf. 9.8 Vert.

2888 A2209 (25c) black "G" .90 .50
2889 A2208 (32c) black "G" 1.50 .25
a. Imperf., pair *250.00*
2890 A2208 (32c) blue "G" .65 .25
2891 A2208 (32c) red "G" .85 .25

Rouletted 9.8 Vert.

2892 A2208 (32c) red "G" .75 .25

A2210

Flag Over Porch — A2212

COIL STAMP

1995 **Untagged** ***Perf. 9.8 Vert.***

2893 A2210 (5c) green & multi .50 .25

1995, May 19 ***Perf. 10.4***

2897 A2212 32c multicolored .75 .25
a. Imperf., vert. pair 55.00

See Nos. 2913-2916, 2920-2921, 3133.

Butte A2217 Mountain A2218

Auto — A2220 Auto Tail Fin — A2223

Juke Box A2225 Flag Over Field A2230

COIL STAMPS

Self-Adhesive (#2902B, 2904A-2904B, 2906-2907, 2910, 2912A, 2912B, 2915-2915D, 2919-2921)

1995-97 ***Perf. 9.8 Vert.***

Untagged (Nos. 2902-2912B)

2902 A2217 (5c) yel, red & bl .25 .25
a. Imperf., pair 450.00

Serpentine Die Cut 11.5 Vert.

Untagged

2902B A2217 (5c) yel, red & bl ('96) .35 .25

Perf. 9.8 Vert.

Untagged

2903 A2218 (5c) purple & multi ('96) .25 .25

Letters of inscription "USA NONPROFIT ORG." outlined in purple on #2903.

Untagged

2904 A2218 (5c) blue & multi ('96) .25 .25
c. Imperf., pair 350.00

Letters of inscription have no outline on #2904.

Serpentine Die Cut 11.2 Vert.

Untagged

2904A A2218 (5c) purple & multi ('96) .40 .25

Serpentine Die Cut 9.8 Vert.

Untagged

2904B A2218 (5c) purple & multi ('97) .25 .25

Letters of inscription outlined in purple on #2904B, not outlined on No. 2904A.

Perf. 9.8 Vert.

Untagged

2905 A2220 (10c) blk, red brn & brn, small "1995" date .25 .25
a. Medium "1995" date .25 .25
b. Large "1995" date ('96) .50 .25
c. As "b," brown omitted, P#S33 single 400.00

Date on 2905 is approximately 1.9mm long, on No. 2905a 2mm long, and on No. 2905b 2.1mm long.

Serpentine Die Cut 11.5 Vert.

Untagged

2906 A2220 (10c) blk, brn & red brn ('96) .50 .25

Untagged

2907 A1957 (10c) gold & multi ('96) .75 .25

Perf. 9.8 Vert.

Untagged

2908 A2223 (15c) dk org yel & multi .30 .30

No. 2908 has dark, bold colors, heavy shading lines and heavily shaded chrome.

Untagged

2909 A2223 (15c) buff & multi .30 .30

No. 2909 has shinier chrome, more subdued colors and finer details than No. 2908.

Serpentine Die Cut 11.5 Vert.

Untagged

2910 A2223 (15c) buff & multi ('96) .30 .30

Perf. 9.8 Vert.

Untagged

2911 A2225 (25c) dk red, dk yel grn & multi .50 .50
a. Imperf, pair *400.00*

No. 2911 has dark, saturated colors and dark blue lines in the music selection board.

Untagged

2912 A2225 (25c) brt org red, brt yel grn & multi .75 .50

No. 2912 has bright colors, less shading and light blue lines in the music selection board.

Serpentine Die Cut 11.5 Vert.

Untagged

2912A A2225 (25c) brt org red, brt yel grn & multi ('96) .50 .50

Serpentine Die Cut 9.8 Vert.

Untagged

2912B A2225 (25c) dk red, dk yel grn & multi ('97) .75 .50

See No. 3132.

Perf. 9.8 Vert.

2913 A2212 32c bl, tan, brn, red & lt bl .65 .25
a. Imperf., pair 30.00

No. 2913 has pronounced light blue shading in the flag and red "1995" at left bottom. See No. 3133.

2914 A2212 32c bl, yel brn, red & gray .80 .25

No. 2914 has pale gray shading in the flag and blue "1995" at left bottom.

Serpentine Die Cut 8.7 Vert.

2915 A2212 32c multi 1.25 .30

Serpentine Die Cut 9.8 Vert.

2915A A2212 32c dk bl, tan, brn, red & lt bl ('96) .65 .25
h. Die cutting omitted, pair 32.50
i. Tan omitted —
j. Double die cutting 30.00

No. 2915A has red "1996" at left bottom.

Sky on No. 3133 shows color gradation at LR not on No. 2915A.

On No. 2915Ai all other colors except brown are severely shifted.

On No. 2915Aj, the second die cutting is a different gauge than the normal 9.8.

Serpentine Die Cut 11.5 Vert.

2915B A2212 32c dk bl, tan, brn, red & lt bl ('96) 1.00 *.90*

Serpentine Die Cut 10.9 Vert.

2915C A2212 32c dk bl, tan, brn, red & lt bl 2.50 .40

Serpentine Die Cut 9.8 Vert.

2915D A2212 32c dk bl, tan, brn, red & lt bl ('97) 2.00 *.90*

Stamps on multiples of No. 2915A touch, and are on a peelable backing the same size as the stamps, while those of No. 2915D are separated on the peelable backing, which is larger than the stamps.

No. 2915D has red "1997" at left bottom; No. 2915A has red "1996" at left bottom.

Sky on No. 3133 shows color gradation at LR not on No. 2915D, and it has blue "1996" at left bottom.

BOOKLET STAMPS

Perf. 10.8x9.8 on 2 or 3 Adjacent Sides

2916 A2212 32c bl, tan, brn, red & lt bl .65 .25
a. Booklet pane of 10 6.50 3.25
b. As "a," imperf. —

Die Cut

2919 A2230 32c multi .65 .25
a. Booklet pane of 18 12.00
b. Vert. pair, die cutting omitted btwn. —

Serpentine Die Cut 8.7 on 2, 3 or 4 Adjacent Sides

2920 A2212 32c multi, dated blue "1995" .65 .25
a. Booklet pane of 20+label 13.00
b. Small date 6.00 .35
c. As "b," booklet pane of 20+label 100.00
f. As No. 2920, pane of 15+label 10.00
g. As "a," partial pane of 10, 3 stamps and parts of 7 stamps printed on backing liner —
h. As No. 2920, booklet pane of 15 *47.50*
i. As No. 2920, die cutting omitted, pair —
j. Dark blue omitted (from No. 2920a) *1,750.*
k. Vert. pair, die cutting missing btwn., in No. 2920a with shift in die cutting —

Date on No. 2920 is nearly twice as large as date on No. 2920b. No. 2920f comes in various configurations.

No. 2920h is a pane of 16 with one stamp removed. The missing stamp is the lower right stamp in the pane or (more rarely) the upper left stamp. No. 2920h cannot be made from No. 2920f, a pane of 15 + label. The label is located in the sixth or seventh row of the pane and is die cut. If the label is removed, an impression of the die cutting appears on the backing paper.

Serpentine Die Cut 11.3 on 3 sides

2920D A2212 32c multi, dated blue "1996" ('96) .80 .25
e. Booklet pane of 10 8.00

Serpentine Die Cut 9.8 on 2 or 3 Adjacent Sides

2921 A2212 32c dk bl, tan, brn, red & lt bl, dated red "1996" ('96) .90 .25
a. Booklet pane of 10, dated red "1996" 9.00
b. As No. 2921, dated red "1997," *Jan. 24, 1997* 1.20 .25
c. As "a," dated red "1997" 12.00
d. Booklet pane of 5 + label, dated red "1997," *Jan. 24, 1997* 8.00
e. As "a," die cutting omitted 200.00

Issued: #2902, 2905, 3/10/95; #2908-2909, 2911-2912, 2919, 3/17/95; #2915, 2920, 4/18/95; #2897, 2913-2914, 2916, 5/19/95; #2920d, 1/20/96; #2904B, 2912B, 2915D, 2921b-2921d, 1/24/97; #2903-2904, 3/16/96; #2915A, 5/21/97; #2907, 2921, 5/21/96; #2902B, 2904A, 2906, 2910, 2912A, 2915B, 6/15/96; #2915C, 5/21/96.

See Nos. 3132-3133.

Scott values for used self-adhesive stamps are for examples either on piece or off piece.

GREAT AMERICANS ISSUE

A2248

A2249

A2250

A2251

A2253

A2255

A2256

A2257

A2258

ENGRAVED

1995-99

Self-Adhesive (#2941-2942)

Perf. 11.2, Serpentine Die Cut 11.7x11.5 (#2941-2942)

2933 A2248 32c brown .75 .25
2934 A2249 32c green ('96) .75 .25
2935 A2250 32c lake ('98) .65 .35
2936 A2251 32c blue ('98) .65 .35
a. 32c light blue .65 .35
2938 A2253 46c carmine .90 .30
2940 A2255 55c green 1.15 .25
a. Imperf, pair —
2941 A2256 55c black ('99) 1.10 .25
2942 A2257 77c blue ('98) 1.50 .40
2943 A2258 78c bright violet 1.60 .25
a. 78c dull violet 1.60 .25
b. 78c pale violet 1.75 .30
Nos. 2933-2943 (9) 9.05 2.65

The pale violet ink on No. 2943b luminesces bright pink under long-wave ultraviolet light.

LOVE

A2263

Cherub from Sistine Madonna, by Raphael — A2264

LITHOGRAPHED & ENGRAVED

1995, Feb. 1 ***Perf. 11.2***

2948 A2263 (32c) multi .65 .25

Self-Adhesive

Die Cut

2949 A2264 (32c) multi .65 .25
a. Booklet pane of 20 + label 13.00
b. Red (engr.) omitted *250.00*
c. As "a," red (engr.) omitted *4,000.*
d. Red (engr.) missing (CM) —

No. 2949d must be collected se-tenant with a normal stamp.

See Nos. 2957-2960, 3030.

FLORIDA STATEHOOD

A2265

LITHOGRAPHED

1995, Mar. 3 ***Perf. 11.1***

2950 A2265 32c multicolored .65 .25

EARTH DAY

Earth Clean-Up A2266

Solar Energy A2267

Tree Planting A2268

Beach Clean-Up A2269

1995, Apr. 20 ***Perf. 11.1x11***

2951 A2266 32c multicolored .65 .25
2952 A2267 32c multicolored .65 .25
2953 A2268 32c multicolored .65 .25
2954 A2269 32c multicolored .65 .25
a. Block of 4, #2951-2954 2.60 1.75

Richard M. Nixon, 37th President (1913-94) A2270

Bessie Coleman, Aviator A2271

RICHARD M. NIXON

LITHOGRAPHED & ENGRAVED

1995, Apr. 26 ***Perf. 11.2***

2955 A2270 32c multicolored .65 .25
a. Red (engr.) missing (CM) *750.00*

No. 2955 is known with red (engr. "Richard Nixon") inverted, and with red engr. omitted but only half the Nixon portrait present, both from printer's waste. No. 2955a shows a complete Nixon portrait.

BLACK HERITAGE SERIES

ENGRAVED

1995, Apr. 27

2956 A2271 32c red & black .85 .25

LOVE

A2272

A2273

A2274

LITHOGRAPHED & ENGRAVED

1995, May 12

2957 A2272 32c multicolored .65 .25

Compare with No. 3030.

2958 A2273 55c multicolored 1.10 .25

BOOKLET STAMPS

Perf. 9.8x10.8

2959 A2272 32c multicolored .65 .25
a. Booklet pane of 10 6.50 3.25
b. Imperf, pair *100.00*
c. As "a," imperf. *500.00*

Self-Adhesive

Die Cut

2960 A2274 55c multicolored 1.10 .25
a. Booklet pane of 20 + label 22.50

RECREATIONAL SPORTS

Volleyball A2275

Softball A2276

Bowling A2277

Tennis A2278

Golf A2279

LITHOGRAPHED

1995, May 20

2961 A2275 32c multicolored .65 .25
2962 A2276 32c multicolored .65 .25
2963 A2277 32c multicolored .65 .25
2964 A2278 32c multicolored .65 .25
2965 A2279 32c multicolored .65 .25
a. Vert. strip of 5, #2961-2965 3.25 2.00
b. As "a," imperf *2,000.*
c. As "a," yellow omitted *1,750.*
d. As "a," yellow, blue & magenta omitted *1,750.*

PRISONERS OF WAR & MISSING IN ACTION

A2280

1995, May 29

2966 A2280 32c multicolored .65 .25

LEGENDS OF HOLLYWOOD

Marilyn Monroe (1926-62) — A2281

PHOTOGRAVURE

1995, June 1 ***Perf. 11.1***

2967 A2281 32c multicolored .80 .25
a. Imperf., pair *300.00*

Perforations in corner of each stamp are star-shaped.

TEXAS STATEHOOD

A2282

LITHOGRAPHED

1995, June 16 ***Perf. 11.2***

2968 A2282 32c multicolored .75 .25

GREAT LAKES LIGHTHOUSES

Split Rock, Lake Superior A2283

St. Joseph, Lake Michigan A2284

Spectacle Reef, Lake Huron — A2285

Marblehead, Lake Erie — A2286

Thirty Mile Point, Lake Ontario — A2287

PHOTOGRAVURE

BOOKLET STAMPS

1995, June 17 ***Perf. 11.2 Vert.***

2969 A2283 32c multicolored 1.20 .30
2970 A2284 32c multicolored 1.20 .30
2971 A2285 32c multicolored 1.20 .30
2972 A2286 32c multicolored 1.20 .30
2973 A2287 32c multicolored 1.20 .30
a. Booklet pane of 5, #2969-2973 6.00 3.00
b. As "a," two vert. pairs imperf. horiz. of #2972 and 2973, in pane of 7+ stamps in cplt. bklt. #BK230 (due to foldover) —

U.N., 50th ANNIV.

A2288

ENGRAVED

1995, June 26 *Perf. 11.2*
2974 A2288 32c blue .65 .25

CIVIL WAR

A2289

Designs: a, Monitor and Virginia. b, Robert E. Lee. c, Clara Barton. d, Ulysses S. Grant. e, Battle of Shiloh. f, Jefferson Davis. g, David Farragut. h, Frederick Douglass. i, Raphael Semmes. j, Abraham Lincoln. k, Harriet Tubman. l, Stand Watie. m, Joseph E. Johnston. n, Winfield Hancock. o, Mary Chesnut. p, Battle of Chancellorsville. q, William T. Sherman. r, Phoebe Pember. s, "Stonewall" Jackson. t, Battle of Gettysburg.

PHOTOGRAVURE

1995, June 29 *Perf. 10.1*
2975 A2289 Pane of 20 32.50 17.50
a.-t. 32c any single 1.50 .60
u. As No. 2975, a.-e. imperf, f.-j. part perf, others perf *1,000.*
v. As No. 2975, k.-t. imperf, f.-j. part perf, others perf *1,750.*
w. As No. 2975, imperf *1,150.*
x. Block of 9 (f.-h., k.-m., p.-r.) k.-l. & p.-q. imperf. vert. —
y. As No. 2975, a.-b. perf, c., f.-h. part perf, others imperf *850.00*
z. As No. 2975, o. and t. imperf, j., n. & s. part perf, others perf —

AMERICAN FOLK ART SERIES
Carousel Horses

A2290

A2291

A2292

A2293

LITHOGRAPHED

1995, July 21 *Perf. 11*
2976 A2290 32c multicolored .65 .25
2977 A2291 32c multicolored .65 .25
2978 A2292 32c multicolored .65 .25
2979 A2293 32c multicolored .65 .25
a. Block of 4, #2976-2979 2.60 2.00

WOMAN SUFFRAGE

A2294

LITHOGRAPHED & ENGRAVED

1995, Aug. 26 *Perf. 11.1x11*
2980 A2294 32c multicolored .65 .25
a. Black (engr.) omitted *350.00*
b. Imperf., pair *1,000.*
c. Vert. pair, imperf between and at bottom *650.00*

No. 2980a is valued in the grade of fine. Very fine examples exist and sell for much more.

WORLD WAR II

A2295

Designs and events of 1945: a, Marines raise flag on Iwo Jima. b, Fierce fighting frees Manila by March 3, 1945. c, Soldiers advancing (Okinawa, the last big battle). d, Destroyed bridge (US and Soviets link up at Elbe River). e, Allies liberate Holocaust survivors. f, Germany surrenders at Reims. g, Refugees (By 1945, World War II has uprooted millions). h, Truman announces Japan's surrender. i, Sailor kissing nurse (News of victory hits home). j, Hometowns honor their returning veterans.

Central label is size of 15 stamps and shows world map with extent of Axis control and Allied operations.

1995, Sept. 2 *Perf. 11.1*
2981 A2295 Block of 10 15.00 7.50
a.-j. 32c any single 1.50 .50

No. 2981 has selvage at left and right and either top or bottom.

AMERICAN MUSIC SERIES

Louis Armstrong A2296

Coleman Hawkins A2297

James P. Johnson A2298

Jelly Roll Morton A2299

Charlie Parker A2300

Eubie Blake A2301

Charles Mingus A2302

Thelonious Monk A2303

John Coltrane A2304

Erroll Garner A2305

LITHOGRAPHED

Plates of 120 in six panes of 20

1995 *Perf. 11.1x11*
2982 A2296 32c white denomination .90 .25
a. Imperf, pair —
2983 A2297 32c multicolored 2.25 .30
2984 A2296 32c black denomination 2.25 .30
2985 A2298 32c multicolored 2.25 .30
2986 A2299 32c multicolored 2.25 .30
2987 A2300 32c multicolored 2.25 .30
2988 A2301 32c multicolored 2.25 .30
2989 A2302 32c multicolored 2.25 .30
2990 A2303 32c multicolored 2.25 .30
2991 A2304 32c multicolored 2.25 .30
2992 A2305 32c multicolored 2.25 .30
a. Vert. block of 10, #2983-2992 23.00 7.50
b. Pane of 20, dark blue (inscriptions) omitted —
c. Imperf pair of Nos. 2991-2992 —

GARDEN FLOWERS

A2306

A2307

A2308

A2309

A2310

LITHOGRAPHED & ENGRAVED
BOOKLET STAMPS

1995, Sept. 19 *Perf. 10.9 Vert.*
2993 A2306 32c multicolored .65 .25
2994 A2307 32c multicolored .65 .25
2995 A2308 32c multicolored .65 .25
2996 A2309 32c multicolored .65 .25
2997 A2310 32c multicolored .65 .25
a. Booklet pane of 5, #2993-2997 3.25 2.25
b. As "a," imperf *2,250.*

EDDIE RICKENBACKER (1890-1973), AVIATOR

A2311

PHOTOGRAVURE

1995, Sept. 25 *Perf. 11¼*
2998 A2311 60c multicolored, small "1995" year date 1.40 .50
a. Large "1995" date, *Oct., 1999* 2.00 .50

Date on No. 2998 is 1mm long, on No. 2998a 1½mm long.

REPUBLIC OF PALAU

A2312

LITHOGRAPHED

1995, Sept. 29 *Perf. 11.1*
2999 A2312 32c multicolored .65 .25

See Palau Nos. 377-378.

COMIC STRIPS

A2313

Designs: a, The Yellow Kid. b, Katzenjammer Kids. c, Little Nemo in Slumberland. d, Bringing Up Father. e, Krazy Kat. f, Rube Goldberg's Inventions. g, Toonerville Folks. h, Gasoline Alley. i, Barney Google. j, Little Orphan Annie. k, Popeye. l, Blondie. m, Dick Tracy. n, Alley Oop. o, Nancy. p, Flash Gordon. q, Li'l Abner. r, Terry and the Pirates. s, Prince Valiant. t, Brenda Starr, Reporter.

PHOTOGRAVURE

1995, Oct. 1 ***Perf. 10.1***

3000	A2313	Pane of 20	13.00	10.00
a.-t.		32c any single	.65	.50
u.		As No. 3000, a.-h. imperf., i.-l. part perf	—	
v.		As No. 3000, m.-t. imperf., i.-l. part perf	*2,750.*	
w.		As No. 3000, a.-l. imperf.,m.-t. imperf vert.	—	
x.		As No. 3000, imperf	—	

U.S. NAVAL ACADEMY, 150th ANNIVERSARY

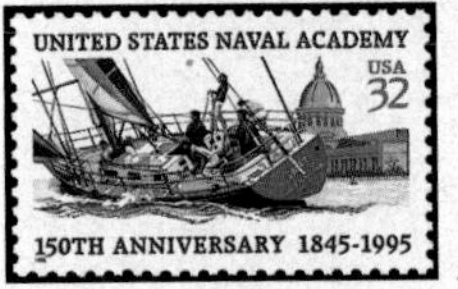

A2314

LITHOGRAPHED

1995, Oct. 10 ***Perf. 10.9***

3001	A2314	32c multicolored	.65	.25

LITERARY ARTS SERIES

Tennessee Williams (1911-83) A2315

1995, Oct. 13 ***Perf. 11.1***

3002	A2315	32c multicolored	.65	.25

CHRISTMAS

Madonna and Child A2316

Santa Claus Entering Chimney A2317

Child Holding Jumping Jack — A2318

Child Holding Tree — A2319

Santa Claus Working on Sled A2320

Midnight Angel A2321

Children Sledding — A2322

LITHOGRAPHED & ENGRAVED

1995 ***Perf. 11.2***

3003	A2316	32c multicolored	.65	.25
c.		Black (engr., denomination) omitted	*175.00*	

BOOKLET STAMP

Perf. 9.8x10.9

3003A	A2316	32c multicolored	.65	.25
b.		Booklet pane of 10	6.50	4.00

LITHOGRAPHED

Perf. 11.25

3004	A2317	32c multicolored	.70	.25
3005	A2318	32c multicolored	.70	.25
3006	A2319	32c multicolored	.70	.25
3007	A2320	32c multicolored	.70	.25
a.		Block or strip of 4, #3004-3007	2.80	1.25
b.		Booklet pane of 10, 3 each #3004-3005, 2 each #3006-3007	8.00	4.00
c.		Booklet pane of 10, 2 each #3004-3005, 3 each #3006-3007	8.00	4.00
d.		As "a," imperf	*375.00*	
e.		As "b," miscut and inserted upside down into booklet cover, with full bottom selvage	—	

PHOTOGRAVURE

Self-Adhesive Stamps

Serpentine Die Cut 11.25 on 2, 3 or 4 sides

3008	A2320	32c multicolored	.95	.25
3009	A2318	32c multicolored	.95	.25
3010	A2317	32c multicolored	.95	.25
3011	A2319	32c multicolored	.95	.25
a.		Booklet pane of 20, 5 each #3008-3011 + label	19.00	

LITHOGRAPHED

Serpentine Die Cut 11.3x11.6 on 2, 3 or 4 sides

3012	A2321	32c multicolored	.65	.25
a.		Booklet pane of 20 + label	13.00	
b.		Vert. pair, die cutting omitted between	—	
c.		Booklet pane of 15 + label, *1996*	13.00	
d.		Booklet pane of 15	*30.00*	

No. 3012a comes either with no die cutting in the label (1995 printing) or with the die cutting from the 1996 printing.

No. 3012d is a pane of 16 with one stamp removed. The missing stamp can be from either row 1, 2, 3, 7 or 8 of the pane. No. 3012d cannot be made from No. 3012c, a pane of 15 + label. The label is die cut. If the label is removed, an impression of the die cutting appears on the backing paper.

PHOTOGRAVURE

Die Cut

3013	A2322	32c multicolored	.65	.25
a.		Booklet pane of 18	12.00	

Self-Adhesive Coil Stamps

Serpentine Die Cut 11.2 Vert.

3014	A2320	32c multicolored	3.00	.30
3015	A2318	32c multicolored	3.00	.30
3016	A2317	32c multicolored	3.00	.30
3017	A2319	32c multicolored	3.00	.30
a.		Strip of 4, #3014-3017	12.00	

LITHOGRAPHED

Serpentine Die Cut 11.6 Vert.

3018	A2321	32c multicolored	1.10	.30

Nos. 3005-3006 have "USA" printed in green. It is red on the self-adhesive stamps.

Issued: #3003-3003A, 3012-3013, 3018, 10/19; #3004-3011, 3014-3017, 9/30.

ANTIQUE AUTOMOBILES

1893 Duryea A2323

1894 Haynes A2324

1898 Columbia A2325

1899 Winton A2326

1901 White A2327

PHOTOGRAVURE

1995, Nov. 3 ***Perf. 10.1x11.1***

3019	A2323	32c multicolored	.90	.25
3020	A2324	32c multicolored	.90	.25
3021	A2325	32c multicolored	.90	.25
3022	A2326	32c multicolored	.90	.25
3023	A2327	32c multicolored	.90	.25
a.		Vert. or horiz. strip of 5, #3019-3023	4.50	2.00

Vert. and horiz. strips are all in different order.

UTAH STATEHOOD CENTENARY

Delicate Arch, Arches Natl. Park — A2328

LITHOGRAPHED

1996, Jan. 4 ***Perf. 11.1***

3024	A2328	32c multicolored	.75	.25

GARDEN FLOWERS

Crocus A2329

Winter Aconite A2330

Pansy A2331

Snowdrop A2332

Anemone — A2333

LITHOGRAPHED & ENGRAVED

BOOKLET STAMPS

1996, Jan. 19 ***Perf. 10.9 Vert.***

3025	A2329	32c multi	.75	.25
3026	A2330	32c multi	.75	.25
3027	A2331	32c multi	.75	.25
3028	A2332	32c multi	.75	.25
3029	A2333	32c multi	.75	.25
a.		Booklet pane of 5, #3025-3029	3.75	2.50
b.		As "a," imperf.	—	

LOVE

Cherub from Sistine Madonna, by Raphael — A2334

BOOKLET STAMP

Serpentine Die Cut 11.3x11.7

1996, Jan. 20

Self-Adhesive

3030	A2334	32c multicolored	.65	.25
a.		Booklet pane of 20 + label	13.00	
b.		Booklet pane of 15 + label	10.00	
c.		Red (engr. "Love") omitted	*150.00*	
d.		Red (engr. "Love") missing (CM)	—	
e.		Double impression of red (engr. "Love")	*450.00*	
f.		Die cutting omitted, pair	*225.00*	
g.		As "a," stamps 1-5 double impression of red (engr. "LOVE")	*1,000.*	
h.		As "a," red (engr. "LOVE") omitted	*1,250.*	
i.		As "a," die cutting omitted	—	
j		As "e," two examples in booklet pane of 20 (No. 3030a)	*1,000.*	

No. 3030d must be collected se-tenant with a stamp bearing the red engraving.

FLORA AND FAUNA SERIES

Kestrel, Blue Jay and Rose Types of 1993-95 and

Red-headed Woodpecker A2335

Eastern Bluebird A2336

Red Fox A2339

Ring-necked Pheasant A2350

Coral Pink Rose — A2351

Serpentine Die Cut 10½

1996-2002 Untagged

Self-Adhesive (#3031, 3031A)

3031 A1841 1c multicolored .25 .25
c. Die cutting omitted, pair —

Serpentine Die Cut 11¼

Untagged

3031A A1841 1c multicolored .25 .25
b. Die cutting omitted, pair —

No. 3031A has blue inscription and year.

Perf. 11

Untagged

3032 A2335 2c multicolored .25 .25
3033 A2336 3c multicolored .25 .25

Serpentine Die Cut 11½x11¼

Self-Adhesive

3036 A2339 $1 multicolored 3.75 .50
a. Serpentine die cut 11¾x11 ('02) 4.00 .50

Beginning with Nos. 3036 and 3036a, hidden 3-D images can be seen on some stamps when they are viewed with a special "Stamp Decoder" lens sold by the USPS. See the *Scott Specialized Catalogue of U.S. Stamps and Covers* for descriptions of these images. Stamps with 3-D images are 3036-3036a, 3167, 3168-3172, 3178, 3206, 3230-3234, 3238-3242, 3261-3262, 3321-3324, 3472-3473, 3647-3648, 3651, 3771, 3787-3791, 3808-3811, 3838 and 3862.

COIL STAMPS

Untagged

Perf. 9¾ Vert.

3044 A1841 1c multicolored, small date .25 .25
a. Large date .25 .25

Date on No. 3044 is 1mm long, on No. 3044a 1.5mm long.

Untagged

3045 A2335 2c multicolored .25 .25

Issued: #3032, 2/2/96; #3033, 4/3/96; #3044, 1/20/96; #3036, 8/14/98; #3045, 6/22/99; #3031, 11/19/99; #3031A, 10/00.

BOOKLET STAMPS

PHOTOGRAVURE

Self-Adhesive

3048 A1847 20c multi .40 .25
a. Booklet pane of 10 4.00
b. Booklet pane of 4 35.00
c. Booklet pane of 6 50.00

Nos. 3048b-3048c are from the vending machine booklet No. BK237 that has a glue strip at the top edge of the top pane, the peelable strip removed and the rouletting line 2mm lower than on No. 3048a on some booklets, when the panes are compared with bottoms aligned. Vending booklets with plate #S2222 always have gauge 8½ rouletting on booklet covers. Convertible booklets (No. 3048a) with plate #S2222 always have gauge 12½ rouletting on booklet covers. Vending booklets with plate #S1111 can have either 8½ or 12½ gauge rouletting on booklet cover, and it may be impossible to tell a vending booklet with 12½ gauge rouletting and plate #S1111 from a convertible booklet with peelable strip removed.

Serpentine Die Cut 11.3x11.7 on 2, 3 or 4 Sides

3049 A1853 32c yel, org, grn & blk .65 .25
a. Booklet pane of 20 + label 13.00
b. Booklet pane of 4 2.60
c. Booklet pane of 5 + label 3.50
d. Booklet pane of 6 4.00

Serpentine Die Cut 11.2 on 3 Sides

3050 A2350 20c multi .65 .25
a. Booklet pane of 10, all stamps upright 6.50
b. Serpentine die cut 11 3.25 .25
c. As "b," booklet pane of 10, all stamps upright 35.00

Serpentine Die Cut 10½x11 on 3 Sides

3051 A2350 20c multi .75 .25

Serpentine Die Cut 10.6x10.4 on 3 Sides

3051A A2350 20c multicolored 7.00 .50
b. Booklet pane of 5, 4 #3051, 1 #3051A turned sideways at top 10.00
c. Booklet pane of 5, 4 #3051, 1 #3051A turned sideways at bottom 10.00

No. 3051 represents the eight upright stamps on the booklet panes Nos. 3051Ab and 3051Ac. The two stamps turned sideways on those panes are No. 3051A.

Serpentine Die Cut 11½x11¼ on 2, 3 or 4 Sides

3052 A2351 33c multi .90 .25
a. Booklet pane of 4 3.60
b. Booklet pane of 5 + label 4.50
c. Booklet pane of 6 5.50
d. Booklet pane of 20 + label 17.50
j. Die cutting omitted, pair —
k. As "d," die cutting omitted —

Serpentine Die Cut 10¾x10½ on 2 or 3 sides

3052E A2351 33c multi .80 .25
f. Booklet pane of 20 16.00
g. Black ("33 USA," etc.) omitted 350.00
h. As "f," all 12 stamps on one side with black omitted —
i. Horiz. pair, die cutting missing between (PS) —
j. As "f," vert. die cutting missing between (PS) —

No. 3052Ef is a double-sided booklet pane with 12 stamps on one side and 8 stamps plus label on the other side.

COIL STAMPS

Serpentine Die Cut 11½ Vert.

3053 A1847 20c multi .50 .25

Yellow Rose, Ring-necked Pheasant Types of 1996-98

COIL STAMPS

LITHOGRAPHED

Self-Adhesive

3054 A1853 32c yel, mag, blk & grn .65 .25
a. Die cutting omitted, pair 75.00
b. Black, yellow & green omitted —
c. Black, yellow & green omitted, die cutting omitted, pair —
d. Black omitted —
e. Black omitted, die cutting omitted, pair —
f. All colors omitted, die cutting omitted —
g. Pair, die cutting omitted, containing one stamp each of "c" and "e" —

Nos. 3054b and 3054d also are miscut and with shifted die cuttings.

No. 3054f must be collected se-tenant with a partially printed stamp(s).

3055 A2350 20c multi .40 .25
a. Die cutting omitted, pair 125.00

No. 3055a exists miscut. It is more common in this form and is valued thus.

Issued: #3048, 3053, 8/2/96; #3049, 10/24/96; #3054, 8/1/97; #3050, 3055, 7/31/98; #3051, 7/99; #3052, 8/13/99; #3052E, 4/7/00.

BLACK HERITAGE SERIES

Ernest E. Just (1883-1941), Marine Biologist — A2358

LITHOGRAPHED

1996, Feb. 1 ***Perf. 11.1***

3058 A2358 32c gray & black .65 .25

SMITHSONIAN INSTITUTION, 150TH ANNIVERSARY

A2359

1996, Feb. 7

3059 A2359 32c multicolored .65 .25

CHINESE NEW YEAR

Year of the Rat — A2360

PHOTOGRAVURE

1996, Feb. 8

3060 A2360 32c multicolored .90 .25
a. Imperf., pair 675.00

See No. 3895a.

PIONEERS OF COMMUNICATION

Eadweard Muybridge A2361

Ottmar Mergenthaler — A2362

Frederic E. Ives A2363

William Dickson A2364

LITHOGRAPHED

1996, Feb. 22 ***Perf. 11.1x11***

3061 A2361 32c multicolored .65 .25
3062 A2362 32c multicolored .65 .25
3063 A2363 32c multicolored .65 .25
3064 A2364 32c multicolored .65 .25
a. Block or strip of 4, #3061-3064 2.60 2.00

Muybridge (1830-1904), Photographer; Mergenthaler (1854-99), Inventor of Linotype; Ives (1856-1937), Developer of Halftone Process; Dickson (1860-1935), Co-developer of Kinetoscope.

FULBRIGHT SCHOLARSHIPS, 50th ANNIVERSARY

A2365

LITHOGRAPHED & ENGRAVED

1996, Feb. 28 ***Perf. 11.1***

3065 A2365 32c multicolored .75 .25

JACQUELINE COCHRAN (1910-80), PILOT

A2366

1996, Mar. 9

3066 A2366 50c multicolored 1.00 .40
a. Black (engr.) omitted 45.00

MARATHON

A2367

LITHOGRAPHED

1996, Apr. 11

3067 A2367 32c multicolored .65 .25

1996 SUMMER OLYMPIC GAMES

A2368

Designs: a, Decathlon (javelin). b, Men's canoeing. c, Women's running. d, Women's diving. e, Men's cycling. f, Freestyle wrestling. g, Women's gymnastics. h, Women's sailboarding. i, Men's shot put. j, Women's soccer. k, Beach volleyball. l, Men's rowing. m, Men's sprints. n, Women's swimming. o, Women's softball. p, Men's hurdles. q, Men's swimming. r, Men's gymnastics (pommel horse). s, Equestrian. t, Men's basketball.

PHOTOGRAVURE

1996, May 2 ***Perf. 10.1***

3068 A2368 Pane of 20 14.00 10.00
a.-t. 32c any single .70 .50
u. As No. 3068, imperf 800.00
v. As No. 3068, back inscriptions omitted on a., f., k. & p., incorrect back inscriptions on others —
w. As No. 3068, e. imperf, d., i.-j. part perf, all others perf —

GEORGIA O'KEEFFE (1887-1986)

A2369

PHOTOGRAVURE

1996, May 23 ***Perf. 11.6x11.4***

3069 A2369 32c multicolored .85 .25
a. Imperf., pair 125.00

TENNESSEE STATEHOOD BICENTENNIAL

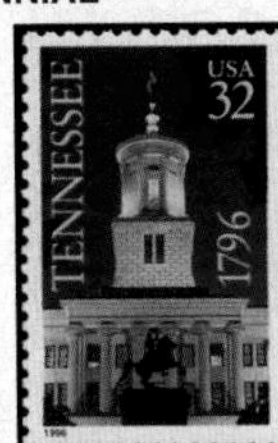

A2370

1996, May 31 ***Perf. 11.1***

3070 A2370 32c multicolored .75 .25

Booklet Stamp

Self-Adhesive

Serpentine Die Cut 9.9x10.8

3071 A2370 32c multicolored .75 .30
a. Booklet pane of 20, #S11111 15.00
b. Horiz. pair, die cutting omitted btwn. — —
c. Die cutting omitted, pair —
d. Horiz. pair, die cutting omitted vert. — —

AMERICAN INDIAN DANCES

A2371

A2372

A2373

A2374

A2375

LITHOGRAPHED

1996, June 7 ***Perf. 11.1***

3072 A2371 32c Fancy 1.20 .25
3073 A2372 32c Butterfly 1.20 .25
3074 A2373 32c Traditional 1.20 .25
3075 A2374 32c Raven 1.20 .25
3076 A2375 32c Hoop 1.20 .25
a. Strip of 5, #3072-3076 6.00 2.50

PREHISTORIC ANIMALS

A2376

A2377

A2378

A2379

1996, June 8 ***Perf. 11.1x11***

3077 A2376 32c Eohippus .65 .25
3078 A2377 32c Woolly Mammoth .65 .25
3079 A2378 32c Mastodon .65 .25
3080 A2379 32c Saber-tooth Cat .65 .25
a. Block or strip of 4, #3077-3080 2.60 2.00

A2380

A2381

BREAST CANCER AWARENESS

1996, June 15 ***Perf. 11.1***

3081 A2380 32c multicolored .65 .25

LEGENDS OF HOLLYWOOD

James Dean (1931-55)

PHOTOGRAVURE

1996, June 24

3082 A2381 32c multicolored .65 .25
a. Imperf., pair *100.00*
b. As "a," red (USA 32c) missing (CM) and tan (JAMES DEAN) omitted —
c. As "a," tan (JAMES DEAN) omitted —
d. As "a," top stamp red missing (CM) and tan (JAMES DEAN) omitted, bottom stamp tan omitted —
e. As No. 3082 pane of 20, right two columns perf, left three columns imperf *1,750.*

Perforations in corner of each stamp are star-shaped. No. 3082 was also available on the first day of issue in at least 127 Warner Bros. Studio stores.

Nos. 3082b-3082d come from the same error pane. The top row is No. 3082b; rows 2-4 are No. 3082c. No. 3082d is a vertical pair with one stamp from No. 3082b at top and one stamp from No. 3082c at bottom.

FOLK HEROES

A2382

A2383

A2384

A2385

LITHOGRAPHED

1996, July 11 ***Perf. 11.1x11***

3083 A2382 32c multicolored .65 .25
3084 A2383 32c multicolored .65 .25
3085 A2384 32c multicolored .65 .25
3086 A2385 32c multicolored .65 .25
a. Block or strip of 4, #3083-3086 2.60 2.00

Myron's Discobolus
A2386

Young Corn, by Grant Wood
A2387

CENTENNIAL OLYMPIC GAMES

ENGRAVED

1996, July 19 Tagged ***Perf. 11.1***

3087 A2386 32c brown .75 .25

Sheet margin of the pane of 20 is lithographed.

IOWA STATEHOOD, 150TH ANNIVERSARY

LITHOGRAPHED

1996, Aug. 1

3088 A2387 32c multicolored .80 .25

BOOKLET STAMP

Self-Adhesive

Serpentine Die Cut 11.6x11.4

3089 A2387 32c multicolored .70 .30
a. Booklet pane of 20 14.00

RURAL FREE DELIVERY, CENT.

A2388

LITHOGRAPHED & ENGRAVED

1996, Aug. 7 ***Perf. 11.2x11***

3090 A2388 32c multicolored .80 .25

RIVERBOATS

Robt. E. Lee
A2389

Sylvan Dell
A2390

Far West
A2391

Rebecca Everingham
A2392

Bailey Gatzert
A2393

PHOTOGRAVURE

Serpentine Die Cut 11x11.1

1996, Aug. 22

Self-Adhesive

3091 A2389 32c multicolored .65 .40
3092 A2390 32c multicolored .65 .40
3093 A2391 32c multicolored .65 .40
3094 A2392 32c multicolored .65 .40
3095 A2393 32c multicolored .65 .40
a. Vert. strip of 5, #3091-3095 3.25
b. Strip of 5, #3091-3095, with special die cutting, die cut 11 ¼ *65.00 50.00*

The serpentine die cutting runs through the peelable backing to which Nos. 3091-3095 are affixed. No. 3095a exists with stamps in different sequences.

On the long side of each stamp in No. 3095b, the die cutting is missing 3 "perforations" between the stamps, one near each end and one in the middle. This allows a complete strip to be removed from the backing paper for use on a first day cover.

AMERICAN MUSIC SERIES

Big Band Leaders

Count Basie
A2394

Tommy & Jimmy Dorsey
A2395

Glenn Miller
A2396

Benny Goodman
A2397

Songwriters

Harold Arlen
A2398

Johnny Mercer
A2399

Dorothy Fields
A2400

Hoagy Carmichael A2401

LITHOGRAPHED

1996, Sept. 11 *Perf. 11.1x11*

3096	A2394 32c multicolored		.75	.25
3097	A2395 32c multicolored		.75	.25
3098	A2396 32c multicolored		.75	.25
3099	A2397 32c multicolored		.75	.25
a.	Block or strip of 4, #3096-3099		3.00	2.00
3100	A2398 32c multicolored		.75	.25
3101	A2399 32c multicolored		.75	.25
3102	A2400 32c multicolored		.75	.25
3103	A2401 32c multicolored		.75	.25
a.	Block or strip of 4, #3100-3103		3.00	2.00

LITERARY ARTS SERIES

F. Scott Fitzgerald (1896-1940) A2402

PHOTOGRAVURE

1996, Sept. 27 *Perf. 11.1*

3104 A2402 23c multicolored .55 .25

ENDANGERED SPECIES

A2403

Designs: a, Black-footed ferret. b, Thick-billed parrot. c, Hawaiian monk seal. d, American crocodile. e, Ocelot. f, Schaus swallowtail butterfly. g, Wyoming toad. h, Brown pelican. i, California condor. j, Gila trout. k, San Francisco garter snake. l, Woodland caribou. m, Florida panther. n, Piping plover. o, Florida manatee.

LITHOGRAPHED

1996, Oct. 2 *Perf. 11.1x11*

3105 A2403 Pane of 15 12.00 8.00
a.-o. 32c any single .80 .50

See Mexico No. 1995.

COMPUTER TECHNOLOGY

A2404

LITHOGRAPHED & ENGRAVED

1996, Oct. 8 *Perf. 10.9x11.1*

3106 A2404 32c multicolored .65 .25

CHRISTMAS

Madonna and Child from Adoration of the Shepherds, by Paolo de Matteis — A2405

Family at Fireplace A2406

Decorating Tree A2407

Dreaming of Santa Claus A2408

Holiday Shopping A2409

Skaters — A2410

LITHOGRAPHED & ENGRAVED

1996 *Perf. 11.1x11.2*

3107 A2405 32c multicolored .65 .25
a. Black (engr.) omitted *600.00*

LITHOGRAPHED

Perf. 11.3

3108	A2406 32c multicolored	.65	.25
3109	A2407 32c multicolored	.65	.25
3110	A2408 32c multicolored	.65	.25
3111	A2409 32c multicolored	.65	.25
a.	Block or strip of 4, #3108-3111	2.60	1.75
b.	Strip of 4, #3110-3111, 3108-3109, with #3109 imperf., #3108 imperf. at right	—	
c.	Strip of 4, #3108-3111, with #3111 imperf, #3110 imperf at right	—	

BOOKLET STAMPS

Self-Adhesive

LITHOGRAPHED & ENGRAVED

Serpentine Die Cut 10 on 2, 3 or 4 Sides

3112	A2405 32c multicolored	.75	.25
a.	Booklet pane of 20 + label	15.00	
b.	Die cutting omitted, pair	50.00	
c.	As "a," die cutting omitted	—	

LITHOGRAPHED

Serpentine Die Cut 11.8x11.5 on 2, 3 or 4 Sides

3113	A2406 32c multicolored	.75	.25
3114	A2407 32c multicolored	.75	.25
3115	A2408 32c multicolored	.75	.25
3116	A2409 32c multicolored	.75	.25
a.	Booklet pane of 20, 5 ea #3113-3116	15.00	
b.	Strip of 4, #3113-3116, die cutting omitted	*500.00*	
c.	Block of 6, die cutting omitted	*700.00*	
d.	As "a," die cutting omitted	*1,750.*	

PHOTOGRAVURE

Die Cut

3117 A2410 32c multicolored .65 .25
a. Booklet pane of 18 12.00

Issued: #3108-3111, 3113-3117, 10/8; #3107, 3112, 11/1.

HANUKKAH

A2411

Serpentine Die Cut 11.1

1996, Oct. 22

Self-Adhesive

3118 A2411 32c multicolored .65 .25

See Nos. 3352, 3547, 3672, Israel No. 1289. For booklet see No. BK258.

CYCLING

Souvenir Sheet

A2412

1996, Nov. 1 *Perf. 11x11.1*

3119	A2412 Sheet of 2	2.75	2.00
a.	50c orange & multi	1.30	1.00
b.	50c blue green & multi	1.30	1.00

No. 3119 exists overprinted in gold and in silver for the Tour of China '96. This overprint is a private production. Value, set of 2 sheets $17.50.

CHINESE NEW YEAR

Year of the Ox A2413

1997, Jan. 5 *Perf. 11.2*

3120 A2413 32c multicolored .80 .25

See No. 3895b.

BLACK HERITAGE SERIES

Brig. Gen. Benjamin O. Davis, Sr. (1880-1970) A2414

LITHOGRAPHED

Serpentine Die Cut 11.4

1997, Jan. 28

Self-Adhesive

3121 A2414 32c multicolored .70 .25

Statue of Liberty Type of 1994

PHOTOGRAVURE

Serpentine Die Cut 11 on 2, 3 or 4 Sides

1997, Feb. 1

Self-Adhesive

3122	A1951 32c red, lt bl, dk bl & yel	.70	.25
a.	Booklet pane of 20 + label	14.00	
b.	Booklet pane of 4	2.80	
c.	Booklet pane of 5 + label	3.75	
d.	Booklet pane of 6	4.25	
h.	As "a," die cutting omitted	—	

Serpentine Die Cut 11.5x11.8 on 2, 3 or 4 Sides

1997

Self-Adhesive

3122E	A1951 32c red, lt bl, dk bl & yel	1.50	.25
f.	Booklet pane of 20 + label	40.00	
g.	Booklet pane of 6	9.00	

LOVE

A2415

Swans — A2416

LITHOGRAPHED

Serpentine Die Cut 11.8x11.6 on 2, 3 or 4 Sides

1997, Feb. 4

Self-Adhesive

3123	A2415 32c multicolored	.65	.25
a.	Booklet pane of 20 + label	13.00	
b.	Die cutting omitted, pair	*115.00*	
c.	As "a," die cutting omitted	*1,150.*	
d.	As "a," black omitted	—	

Serpentine Die Cut 11.6x11.8 on 2, 3 or 4 Sides

3124	A2416 55c multicolored	1.10	.25
a.	Booklet pane of 20 + label	22.00	

HELPING CHILDREN LEARN

A2417

PHOTOGRAVURE

Serpentine Die Cut 11.6x11.7

1997, Feb. 18

Self-Adhesive

3125 A2417 32c multicolored .65 .25

MERIAN BOTANICAL PRINTS

Citron, Moth, Larvae, Pupa, Beetle A2418

Flowering Pineapple, Cockroaches A2419

No. 3128 (r), No. 3129 (l), No. 3128a below

Serpentine Die Cut 10.9x10.2 on 2, 3 or 4 Sides

1997, Mar. 3

Self-Adhesive

3126	A2418 32c multicolored	.65	.25
3127	A2419 32c multicolored	.65	.25
a.	Booklet pane, 10 ea #3126-3127 + label	13.00	
b.	Pair, #3126-3127	1.30	
c.	Vert. pair, die cutting omitted between	*425.00*	

Size: 18.5x24mm

Serpentine Die Cut 11.2x10.8 on 2 or 3 Sides

3128	A2418 32c multicolored	1.00	.25
a.	See footnote	2.50	.25
b.	Booklet pane, 2 ea #3128-3129, 1 #3128a	6.50	

3129 A2419 32c multicolored 1.00 .25
a. See footnote 4.50 .35
b. Booklet pane, 2 ea #3128-3129, 1 #3129a 8.50
c. Pair, #3128-3129 2.00

Nos. 3128a-3129a are placed sideways on the pane and are serpentine die cut 11.2 on top and bottom, 10.8 on left side. One of the two No. 3128a per pane has a straight edge at left. The right side is 11.2 broken by a sloping die cut where the stamp meets the vertical die cutting of the two stamps above it. See illustration above.

PACIFIC 97

Sailing Ship — A2420

Stagecoach — A2421

ENGRAVED

1997, Mar. 13 Tagged ***Perf. 11.2***

3130 A2420 32c blue .65 .30
3131 A2421 32c red .65 .30
a. Pair, #3130-3131 1.30 .75

Juke Box and Flag Over Porch Types of 1995

PHOTOGRAVURE

COIL STAMPS

1997, Mar. 14 Untagged ***Imperf.***

Self-Adhesive

3132 A2225 (25c) brt org red, brt yel grn & multi 1.50 .50

Tagged

Serpentine Die Cut 9.9 Vert.

3133 A2212 32c dk bl, tan, brn, red & lt bl 1.75 .25

Nos. 3132-3133 were issued without backing paper. No. 3132 has simulated perforations ending in black bars at the top and bottom edges of the stamp. Sky on No. 3133 shows color gradation at LR not on Nos. 2915A or 2915D, and it has blue "1996" at left bottom.

LITERARY ARTS SERIES

Thornton Wilder (1897-1975) A2422

LITHOGRAPHED

1997, Apr. 17 ***Perf. 11.1***

3134 A2422 32c multicolored .65 .25

RAOUL WALLENBERG (1912-47)

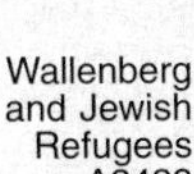

Wallenberg and Jewish Refugees A2423

1997, Apr. 24

3135 A2423 32c multicolored .65 .25

DINOSAURS

A2424

Designs: a, Ceratosaurus. b, Camptosaurus. c, Camarasaurus. d, Brachiosaurus. e, Goniopholis. f, Stegosaurus. g, Allosaurus. h, Opisthias. i, Edmontonia. j, Einiosaurus. k, Daspletosaurus. l, Palaeosaniwa. m, Corythosaurus. n, Ornithomimus. o, Parasaurolophus.

1997, May 1 ***Perf. 11x11.1***

3136 A2424 Sheet of 15 10.00 8.00
a.-o. 32c any single .65 .50
p. As No. 3136, bottom 7 stamps imperf. *3,750.*
q. As No. 3136, top 8 stamps imperf *3,750.*
r. As No. 3136, all colors and tagging missing (EP) —

No. 3136r resulted from double sheeting in the sheet-fed press. It is properly gummed and perforated.

BUGS BUNNY

A2425

PHOTOGRAVURE

1997, May 22 ***Serpentine Die Cut 11***

Self-Adhesive

3137 Pane of 10 6.75
a. A2425 32c single .65 .25
b. Pane of 9 #3137a 6.00
c. Pane of 1 #3137a .65

Die cutting on #3137 does not extend through the backing paper.

3138 Pane of 10 160.00
a. A2425 32c single 3.50
b. Pane of 9 #3138a 32.50
c. Pane of 1, no die cutting 120.00

Die cutting on #3138b extends through the backing paper.

An untagged promotional piece similar to No. 3137c exists on the same backing paper as the pane, with the same design image, but without Bugs' signature and the single stamp. Replacing the stamp is an enlarged "32 / USA" in the same style as used on the stamp. This promotional piece was not valid for postage.

PACIFIC 97

Franklin A2426

Washington A2427

LITHOGRAPHED & ENGRAVED

1997 ***Perf. 10.5x10.4***

3139 Pane of 12 12.00 9.00
a. A2426 50c single 1.00 .50
3140 Pane of 12 14.50 11.00
a. A2427 60c single 1.20 .60

Selvage on Nos. 3139-3140 is lithographed. Issued: No. 3139, 5/29; No. 3140, 5/30.

MARSHALL PLAN, 50TH ANNIV.

Gen. George C. Marshall, Map of Europe — A2428

1997, June 4 ***Perf. 11.1***

3141 A2428 32c multicolored .65 .25

CLASSIC AMERICAN AIRCRAFT

A2429

Designs: a, Mustang. b, Model B. c, Cub. d, Vega. e, Alpha. f, B-10. g, Corsair. h, Stratojet. i, GeeBee. j, Staggerwing. k, Flying Fortress. l, Stearman. m, Constellation. n, Lightning. o, Peashooter. p, Tri-Motor. q, DC-3. r, 314 Clipper. s, Jenny. t, Wildcat.

PHOTOGRAVURE

1997, July 19 ***Perf. 10.1***

3142 A2429 Pane of 20 13.00 10.00
a.-t. 32c any single .65 .50

FOOTBALL COACHES

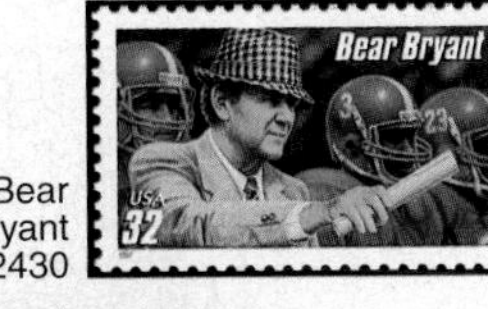

Bear Bryant A2430

Pop Warner A2431

Vince Lombardi A2432

George Halas A2433

LITHOGRAPHED

1997 ***Perf. 11.2***

3143 A2430 32c multicolored .65 .25
3144 A2431 32c multicolored .65 .25
3145 A2432 32c multicolored .65 .25
3146 A2433 32c multicolored .65 .25
a. Block or strip of 4, #3143-3146 2.60 1.50

With Red Bar Above Coach's Name

Perf. 11

3147 A2432 32c multicolored .65 .45
3148 A2430 32c multicolored .65 .45
3149 A2431 32c multicolored .65 .45
3150 A2433 32c multicolored .65 .45

Issued: #3143-3146, 7/25; #3147, 8/5; #3148, 8/7; #3149, 8/8; #3150, 8/16.

AMERICAN DOLLS

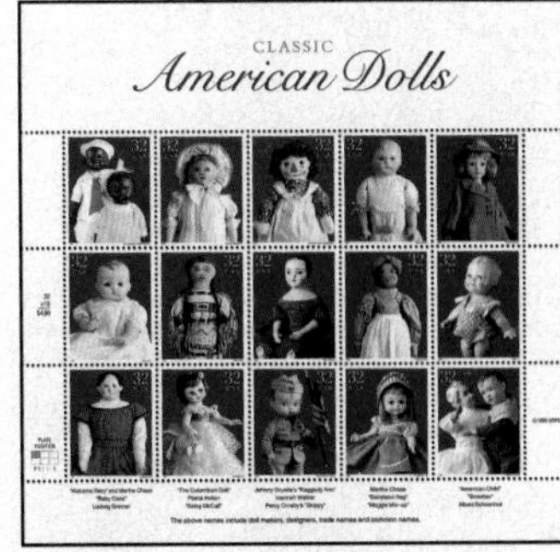

A2434

Designs: a, "Alabama Baby," and doll by Martha Chase. b, "Columbian Doll." c, Johnny Gruelle's "Raggedy Ann." d, Doll by Martha Chase. e, "American Child." f, "Baby Coos." g, Plains Indian. h, Doll by Izannah Walker. i, "Babyland Rag." j, "Scootles." k, Doll by Ludwig Greiner. l, "Betsy McCall." m, Percy Crosby's "Skippy." n, "Maggie Mix-up." o, Dolls by Albert Schoenhut.

1997, July 28 ***Perf. 10.9x11.1***

3151 A2434 Pane of 15 13.50 —
a.-o. 32c any single .90 .60

A2435

A2436

LEGENDS OF HOLLYWOOD

Humphrey Bogart (1899-1957).

PHOTOGRAVURE

1997, July 31 ***Perf. 11.1***

3152 A2435 32c multicolored .85 .25

Perforations in corner of each stamp are star-shaped.

"THE STARS AND STRIPES FOREVER!"

1997, Aug. 21

3153 A2436 32c multicolored .65 .25

AMERICAN MUSIC SERIES

Opera Singers

Lily Pons A2437

Richard Tucker A2438

Lawrence Tibbett A2439

Rosa Ponselle A2440

Classical Composers & Conductors

Leopold Stokowski A2441

Arthur Fiedler A2442

George Szell A2443

Eugene Ormandy A2444

Samuel Barber A2445

Ferde Grofé A2446

Charles Ives A2447

Louis Moreau Gottschalk A2448

LITHOGRAPHED

1997 *Perf. 11*

3154 A2437 32c multicolored .75 .25
3155 A2438 32c multicolored .75 .25
3156 A2439 32c multicolored .75 .25
3157 A2440 32c multicolored .75 .25
a. Block or strip of 4, #3154-3157 3.00 2.00
3158 A2441 32c multicolored 1.50 .25
3159 A2442 32c multicolored 1.50 .25
3160 A2443 32c multicolored 1.50 .25
3161 A2444 32c multicolored 1.50 .25
3162 A2445 32c multicolored 1.50 .25
3163 A2446 32c multicolored 1.50 .25
3164 A2447 32c multicolored 1.50 .25
3165 A2448 32c multicolored 1.50 .25
a. Block of 8, #3158-3165 12.00 4.00

Issued: #3154-3157, 9/10; #3158-3165, 9/12.

PADRE FÉLIX VARELA (1788-1853)

A2449

1997, Sept. 15 *Perf. 11.2*

3166 A2449 32c purple .65 .25

DEPARTMENT OF THE AIR FORCE, 50TH ANNIV.

Thunderbirds Aerial Demonstration Squadron — A2450

1997, Sept. 18 *Perf. 11.2x11.1*

3167 A2450 32c multicolored .65 .25

CLASSIC MOVIE MONSTERS

A2451

A2452

A2453

A2454

A2455

PHOTOGRAVURE

1997, Sept. 30 *Perf. 10.2*

3168 A2451 32c multicolored .75 .25
3169 A2452 32c multicolored .75 .25
3170 A2453 32c multicolored .75 .25
3171 A2454 32c multicolored .75 .25
3172 A2455 32c multicolored .75 .25
a. Strip of 5, #3168-3172 3.75 2.25

FIRST SUPERSONIC FLIGHT, 50TH ANNIV.

A2456

LITHOGRAPHED

Serpentine Die Cut 11.4

1997, Oct. 14

Self-Adhesive

3173 A2456 32c multicolored .65 .25

WOMEN IN MILITARY SERVICE

A2457

1997, Oct. 18 *Perf. 11.1*

3174 A2457 32c multicolored .65 .25

KWANZAA

A2458

PHOTOGRAVURE

1997, Oct. 22 *Serpentine Die Cut 11*

Self-Adhesive

3175 A2458 32c multicolored .65 .25

See Nos. 3368, 3548, 3673.

CHRISTMAS

Madonna and Child A2459

Holly A2460

LITHOGRAPHED

Serpentine Die Cut 9.9 on 2, 3 or 4 Sides

1997

Booklet Stamps

Self-Adhesive

3176 A2459 32c multicolored .65 .25
a. Booklet pane of 20 + label 13.00

Serpentine Die Cut 11.2x11.6 on 2, 3 or 4 Sides

3177 A2460 32c multicolored .65 .25
a. Booklet pane of 20 + label 13.00
b. Booklet pane of 4 2.60
c. Booklet pane of 5 + label 3.25
d. Booklet pane of 6 3.90

Madonna and Child, by Sano di Pietro.
Issued: No. 3176, 10/27; No. 3177, 10/30.

MARS PATHFINDER

Souvenir Sheet

Mars Rover Sojourner — A2461

PHOTOGRAVURE

1997, Dec. 10 Tagged *Perf. 11x11.1*

3178 A2461 $3 multicolored 6.00 4.00
a. $3, single stamp 5.50 3.00
b. Single souvenir sheet from sheet of 18 7.00 —

The perforations at the bottom of the stamp contain the letters "USA." Vertical rouletting extends from the vertical perforations of the stamp to the bottom of the souvenir sheet.

Sheet of 18 has vertical perforations separating the three columns of souvenir sheets. These were cut away when No. 3178 was produced. Thus, the souvenir sheet from the sheet of 18 is wider and has vertical perforations on one or two sides.

CHINESE NEW YEAR

Year of the Tiger — A2462

1998, Jan. 5 *Perf. 11.2*

3179 A2462 32c multicolored .80 .25

See No. 3895c.

A2463

A2464

ALPINE SKIING

LITHOGRAPHED

1998, Jan. 22 *Perf. 11.2*

3180 A2463 32c multicolored .75 .25

BLACK HERITAGE SERIES

Serpentine Die Cut 11.6x11.3

1998, Jan. 28

Self-Adhesive

3181 A2464 32c sepia & black .70 .25

CELEBRATE THE CENTURY

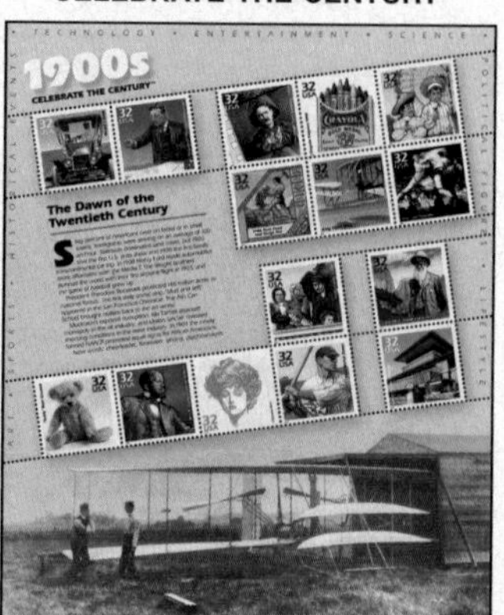

1900s — A2465

No. 3182: a, Model T Ford. b, Theodore Roosevelt. c, Motion picture "The Great Train Robbery," 1903. d, Crayola Crayons introduced, 1903. e, St. Louis World's Fair, 1904. f, Design used on Hunt's Remedy stamp

(#RS56), Pure Food & Drug Act, 1906. g, Wright Brothers first flight, Kitty Hawk, 1903. h, Boxing match shown in painting "Stag at Sharkey's," by George Bellows of the Ash Can School. i, Immigrants arrive. j, John Muir, preservationist. k, "Teddy" Bear created. l, W.E.B. Du Bois, social activist. m, Gibson Girl. n, First baseball World Series, 1903. o, Robie House, Chicago, designed by Frank Lloyd Wright.

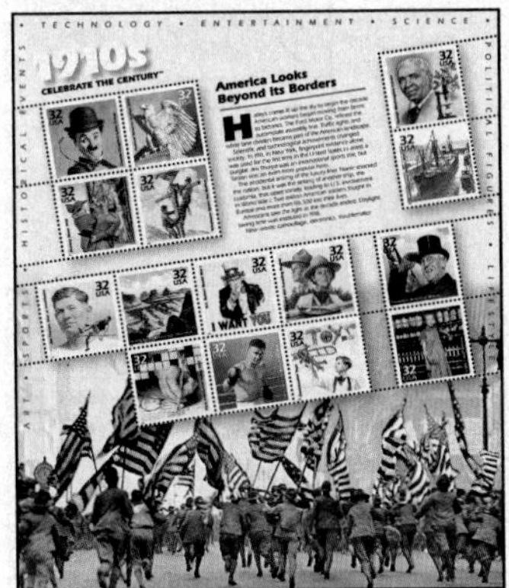

1910s — A2466

No. 3183: a, Charlie Chaplin as the Little Tramp. b, Federal Reserve System created, 1913. c, George Washington Carver. d, Avant-garde art introduced at Armory Show, 1913. e, First transcontinental telephone line, 1914. f, Panama Canal opens, 1914. g, Jim Thorpe wins decathlon at Stockholm Olympics, 1912. h, Grand Canyon National Park, 1919. i, U.S. enters World War I. j, Boy Scouts started in 1910, Girl Scouts formed in 1912. k, Woodrow Wilson. l, First crossword puzzle published, 1913. m, Jack Dempsey wins heavyweight title, 1919. n, Construction toys. o, Child labor reform.

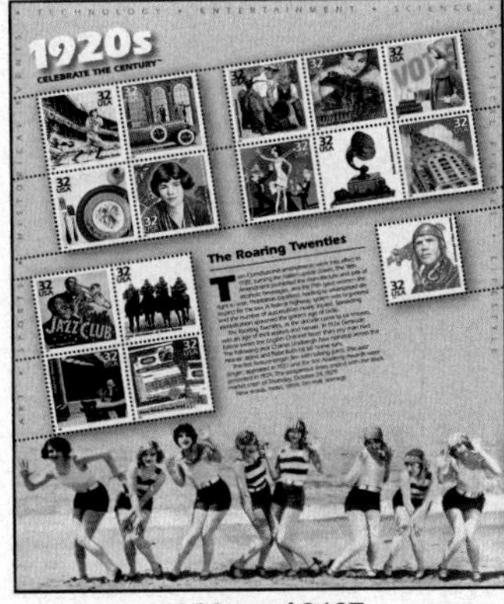

1920s — A2467

No. 3184: a, Babe Ruth. b, The Gatsby style. c, Prohibition enforced. d, Electric toy trains. e, 19th Amendment (woman voting). f, Emily Post's Etiquette. g, Margaret Mead, anthropologist. h, Flappers do the Charleston. i, Radio entertains America. j, Art Deco style (Chrysler Building). k, Jazz flourishes. l, Four Horsemen of Notre Dame. m, Lindbergh flies the Atlantic. n, American realism (Automat, by Edward Hopper). o, Stock Market crash, 1929.

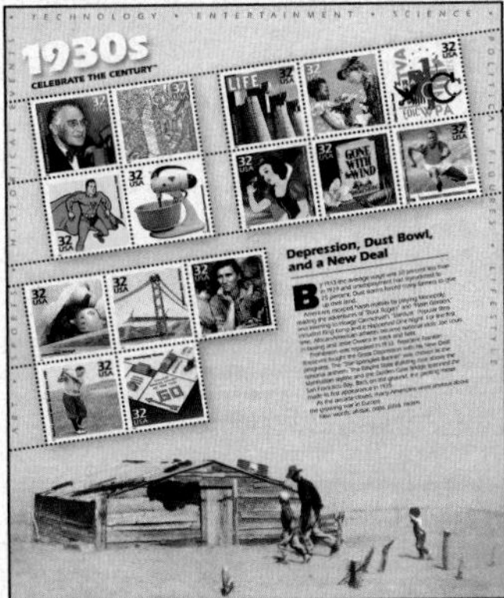

1930s — A2468

No. 3185: a, Franklin D. Roosevelt. b, The Empire State Building. c, 1st Issue of Life Magazine, 1936. d, Eleanor Roosevelt. e, FDR's New Deal. f, Superman arrives, 1938. g, Household conveniences. h, "Snow White and the Seven Dwarfs," 1937. i, "Gone with the Wind," 1936. j, Jesse Owens. k, Streamline design. l, Golden Gate Bridge. m, America survives the Depression. n, Bobby Jones wins golf Grand Slam, 1938. o, The Monopoly Game.

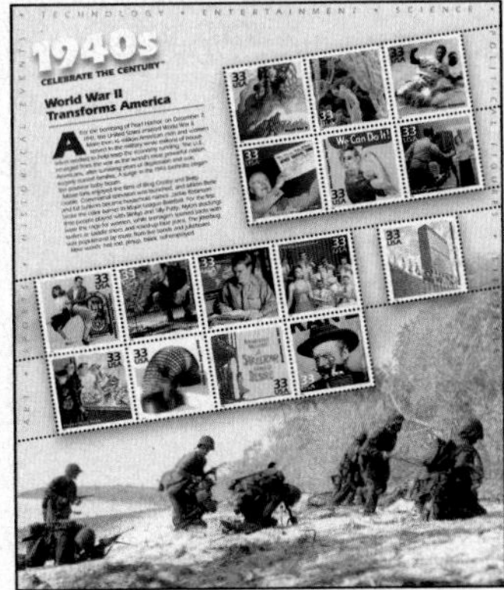

1940s — A2469

No. 3186: a, World War II. b, Antibiotics save lives. c, Jackie Robinson. d, Harry S Truman. e, Women support war effort. f, TV entertains America. g, Jitterbug sweeps nation. h, Jackson Pollock, Abstract Expressionism. i, GI Bill, 1944. j, Big Band Sound. k, Intl. style of architecture (UN Headquarters). l, Postwar baby boom. m, Slinky, 1945. n, "A Streecar Named Desire," 1947. o, Orson Welles' "Citizen Kane."

1950s — A2470

No. 3187: a, Polio vaccine developed. b, Teen fashions. c, The "Shot Heard 'Round the World." d, US launches satellites. e, Korean War. f, Desegregating public schools. g, Tail fins, chrome. h, Dr. Seuss' "The Cat in the Hat." i, Drive-in movies. j, World Series rivals. k, Rocky Marciano, undefeated boxer. l, "I Love Lucy." m, Rock 'n Roll. n, Stock car racing. o, Movies go 3-D.

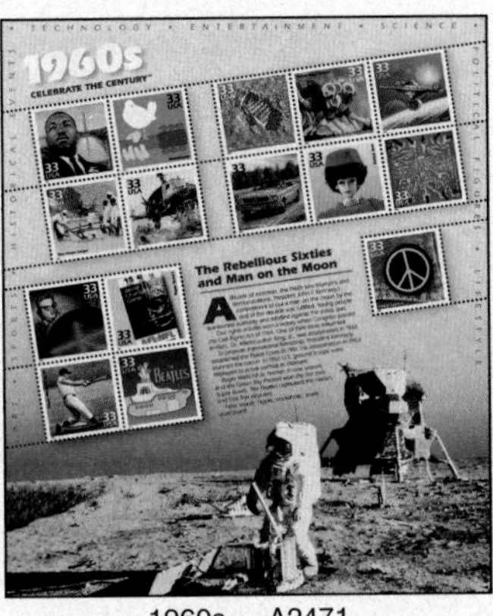

1960s — A2471

No. 3188: a, Martin Luther King, Jr., "I Have a Dream." b, Woodstock. c, Man walks on the moon. d, Green Bay Packers. e, Star Trek. f, The Peace Corps. g, Viet Nam War. h, Ford Mustang. i, Barbie Doll. j, Integrated circuit. k, Lasers. l, Super Bowl I. m, Peace symbol. n, Roger Maris, 61 in '61. o, The Beatles "Yellow Submarine."

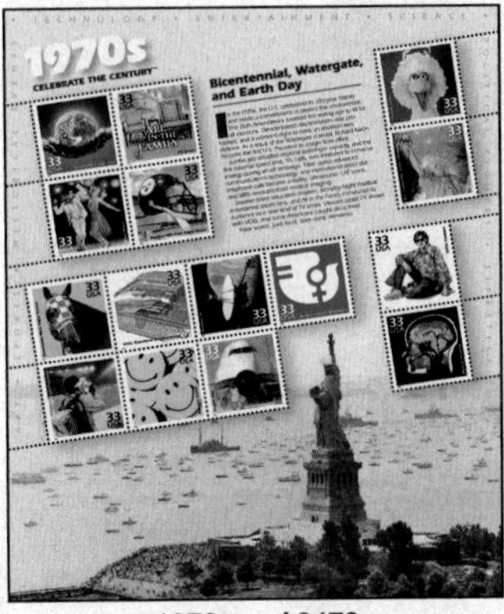

1970s — A2472

No. 3189: a, Earth Day celebrated. b, "All in the Family" television series. c, "Sesame Street" television series character, Big Bird. d, Disco music. e, Pittsburgh Steelers win four Super Bowls. f, US Celebrates 200th birthday. g, Secretariat wins Triple Crown. h, VCRs transform entertainment. i, Pioneer 10. j, Women's rights movement. k, 1970s fashions. l, "Monday Night Football." m, Smiley face buttons. n, Jumbo jets. o, Medical imaging.

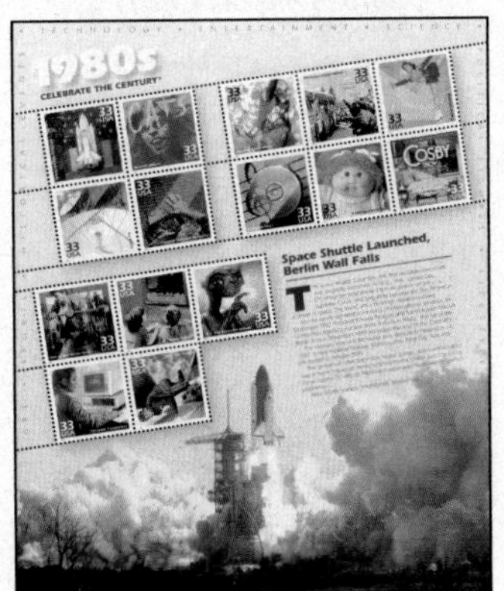

1980s — A2473

No. 3190: a, Space shuttle program. b, "Cats" Broadway show. c, San Francisco 49ers. d, Hostages in Iran come home. e, Figure skating. f, Cable TV. g, Vietnam Veterans Memorial. h, Compact discs. i, Cabbage Patch Kids. j, "The Cosby Show" television series. k, Fall of the Berlin Wall. l, Video games. m, "E. T. The Extra-Terrestrial" movie. n, Personal computers. o, Hip-hop culture.

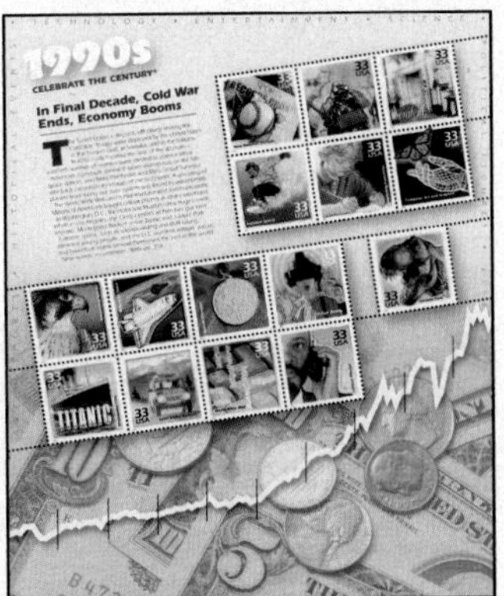

1990s — A2474

No. 3191: a, New baseball records. b, Gulf War. c, "Seinfeld" television series. d, Extreme sports. e, Improving education. f, Computer art and graphics. g, Recovering species. h, Return to space. i, Special Olympics. j, Virtual reality. k, Movie "Jurassic Park." l, Movie "Titanic." m, Sport utility vehicles. n, World Wide Web. o, Cellular phones.

LITHOGRAPHED, ENGRAVED
(#3182m, 3183f, 3184m, 3185b, 3186k, 3187a, 3188c, 3189h)

1998-2000			***Perf. 11½***	
3182	A2465	Pane of 15	10.00	8.50
a.-o.		32c any single	.75	.65
p.		Engr. red (No. 3182m, Gibson girl) omitted, in pane of 15	*3,000.*	
3183	A2466	Pane of 15	10.00	8.50
a.-o.		32c any single	.75	.65
p.		Nos. 3183g, 3183 l-3183o imperf, in pane of 15	*7,000.*	
3184	A2467	Pane of 15	12.50	8.50
a.-o.		32c any single	.80	.65
3185	A2468	Pane of 15	12.50	8.50
a.-o.		32c any single	.80	.65
3186	A2469	Pane of 15	13.00	8.50
a.-o.		33c any single	.85	.65
3187	A2470	Pane of 15	13.00	8.50
a.-o.		33c any single	.85	.65
3188	A2471	Pane of 15	13.00	8.50
a.-o.		33c any single	.85	.65
3189	A2472	Pane of 15	13.00	8.50
a.-o.		33c any single	.85	.65
3190	A2473	Pane of 15	13.00	8.50
a.-o.		33c any single	.85	.65
3191	A2474	Pane of 15	13.00	8.50
a.-o.		33c any single	.85	.65
		Nos. 3182-3191 (10)	123.00	85.00

Issued: #3182-3183, 2/3; #3184, 5/28; #3185, 9/10; #3186, 2/18/99; #3187, 5/26/99; #3188, 9/17/99; #3189, 11/18/99; #3190, 1/12/00; #3191, 5/2/00.

"REMEMBER THE MAINE"

A2475

LITHOGRAPHED & ENGRAVED

1998, Feb. 15			***Perf. 11.2x11***	
3192	A2475	32c red & black	.70	.25

FLOWERING TREES

Southern Magnolia A2476

Blue Paloverde A2477

Yellow Poplar — A2478

Prairie Crab Apple — A2479

Pacific Dogwood
A2480

LITHOGRAPHED

1998, Mar. 19 ***Die Cut Perf 11.3***

Self-Adhesive

3193 A2476 32c multicolored .65 .40
3194 A2477 32c multicolored .65 .40
3195 A2478 32c multicolored .65 .40
3196 A2479 32c multicolored .65 .40
3197 A2480 32c multicolored .65 .40
a. Strip of 5, #3193-3197 3.25
b. As "a," die cutting omitted —

ALEXANDER CALDER (1898-1976), SCULPTOR

Black Cascade, 13 Verticals, 1959 — A2481

Untitled, 1965 — A2482

Rearing Stallion, 1928 — A2483

Portrait of a Young Man, c. 1945 — A2484

Un Effet du Japonais, 1945 — A2485

PHOTOGRAVURE

1998, Mar. 25 ***Perf. 10.2***

3198 A2481 32c multicolored .65 .25
3199 A2482 32c multicolored .65 .25
3200 A2483 32c multicolored .65 .25
3201 A2484 32c multicolored .65 .25
3202 A2485 32c multicolored .65 .25
a. Strip of 5, #3198-3202 3.25 2.25

A2486

CINCO DE MAYO

Serpentine Die Cut 11.7x10.9

1998, Apr. 16

Self-Adhesive

3203 A2486 32c multicolored .65 .25

See Mexico #2066. For 33c version, see #3309.

A2487

A2488

SYLVESTER & TWEETY

Serpentine Die Cut 11.1

1998, Apr. 27

Self-Adhesive

3204 Pane of 10 6.75
a. A2487 32c single .65 .25
b. Pane of 9 #3204a 6.00
c. Pane of 1 #3204a .65

Die cutting on #3204b does not extend through the backing paper.

3205 Pane of 10 15.00
a. A2487 32c single 1.00
b. Pane of 9 #3205a *9.00*
c. Pane of 1, no die cutting *4.00*

Die cutting on #3205a extends through the backing paper.

WISCONSIN STATEHOOD

Serpentine Die Cut 10.8x10.9

1998, May 29

Self-Adhesive

3206 A2488 32c multicolored .65 .30

Wetlands
A2489

Diner
A2490

COIL STAMPS

1998 **Untagged** ***Perf. 10 Vert.***

3207 A2489 (5c) multicolored .25 .25

Serpentine Die Cut 9.8 Vert.

Self-adhesive

Untagged

3207A A2489 (5c) multicolored, small date .25 .25
b. Large date .30 .25

Date on No. 3207A is approximately 1.4mm long, on No. 3207Ab approx. 1.6mm long.

Perf. 10 Vert.

Untagged

3208 A2490 (25c) multicolored .50 .50

Serpentine Die Cut 9.8 Vert.

Self-Adhesive

Untagged

3208A A2490 (25c) multicolored .50 .50

Issued: #3207-3208, 6/5; #3208A, 9/30; #3207A, 12/14.

1898 TRANS-MISSISSIPPI STAMPS, CENT.

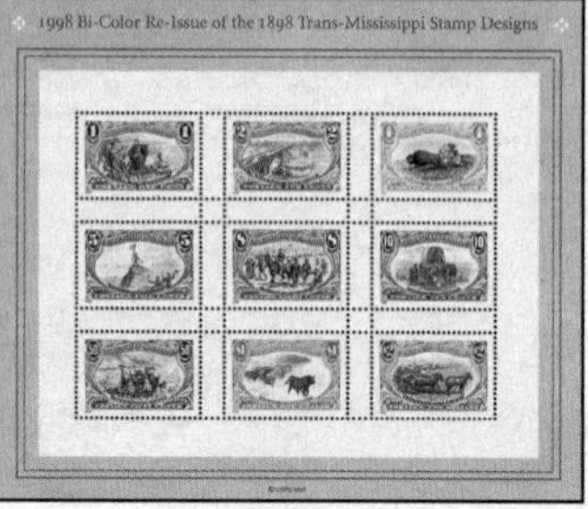

A2491

LITHOGRAPHED & ENGRAVED

1998, June 18 ***Perf. 12x12.4***

3209 A2491 Pane of 9 9.50 7.00
a. A100 1c green & black .25 .25
b. A108 2c red brown & black .25 .25
c. A102 4c orange & black .25 .25
d. A103 5c blue & black .25 .25
e. A104 8c dark lilac & black .25 .25
f. A105 10c purple & black .25 .25
g. A106 50c green & black 1.25 .60
h. A107 $1 red & black 2.50 1.25
i. A101 $2 red brown & black 4.25 2.50

Vignettes on Nos. 3209b and 3209i are reversed in comparison to the original issue.

3210 A107 $1 Pane of 9 #3209h 22.50 —

BERLIN AIRLIFT, 50th ANNIV.

A2492

PHOTOGRAVURE

1998, June 26 ***Perf. 11.2***

3211 A2492 32c multicolored .65 .25

AMERICAN MUSIC SERIES
Folk Singers

Huddie "Leadbelly" Ledbetter
A2493

Woody Guthrie
A2494

Sonny Terry
A2495

Josh White
A2496

1998, June 26 ***Perf. 10.1x10.2***

3212 A2493 32c multicolored .90 .25
3213 A2494 32c multicolored .90 .25
3214 A2495 32c multicolored .90 .25
3215 A2496 32c multicolored .90 .25
a. Block or strip of 4, #3212-3215 3.60 2.00

AMERICAN MUSIC SERIES
Gospel Singers

Mahalia Jackson
A2497

Roberta Martin
A2498

Clara Ward
A2499

Sister Rosetta Tharpe
A2500

1998, July 15 ***Perf. 10.1x10.3***

3216 A2497 32c multicolored 1.00 .25
3217 A2498 32c multicolored 1.00 .25
3218 A2499 32c multicolored 1.00 .25
3219 A2500 32c multicolored 1.00 .25
a. Block or strip of 4, #3216-3219 4.00 2.00

SPANISH SETTLEMENT OF THE SOUTHWEST

La Mision de San Miguel de San Gabriel, Española, NM — A2501

LITHOGRAPHED

1998, July 11 ***Perf. 11.2***

3220 A2501 32c multicolored .65 .25

LITERARY ARTS SERIES

Stephen Vincent Benét — A2502

1998, July 22 ***Perf. 11.2***

3221 A2502 32c multicolored .65 .25

TROPICAL BIRDS

Antillean Euphonia — A2503

Green-throated Carib — A2504

Crested Honeycreeper — A2505

Cardinal Honeyeater A2506

1998, July 29

3222 A2503 32c multicolored .65 .25
3223 A2504 32c multicolored .65 .25
3224 A2505 32c multicolored .65 .25
3225 A2506 32c multicolored .65 .25
a. Block or strip of 4, #3222-3225 2.60 2.00

LEGENDS OF HOLLYWOOD

A2507

PHOTOGRAVURE

1998, Aug. 3 ***Perf. 11.1***

3226 A2507 32c multicolored .75 .25

Perforations in corner of each stamp are star-shaped.

ORGAN & TISSUE DONATION

A2508

Serpentine Die Cut 11.7

1998, Aug. 5

Self-Adhesive

3227 A2508 32c multicolored .65 .25

MODERN BICYCLE

A2509

COIL STAMP

Serpentine Die Cut 9.8 Vert.

1998, Aug. 14 **Untagged**

Self-Adhesive (#3228)

3228 A2509 (10c) multicolored, small "1998" year date .25 .25
a. Large date .25 .25

Date on No. 3228a is approximately 1 ½mm; on No. 3228 approximately 1mm.

Untagged

Perf. 9.9 Vert.

3229 A2509 (10c) multicolored .25 .25

Date on No. 3229 is approximately 2mm wide.

BRIGHT EYES

Dog A2510

Fish A2511

Cat A2512

Parakeet A2513

Hamster A2514

Serpentine Die Cut 9.9

1998, Aug. 20

Self-Adhesive

3230 A2510 32c multicolored .75 .40
3231 A2511 32c multicolored .75 .40
3232 A2512 32c multicolored .75 .40
3233 A2513 32c multicolored .75 .40
3234 A2514 32c multicolored .75 .40
a. Strip of 5, #3230-3234 3.75

KLONDIKE GOLD RUSH, CENTENNIAL

A2515

LITHOGRAPHED

1998, Aug. 21 ***Perf. 11.1***

3235 A2515 32c multicolored .65 .25

AMERICAN ART

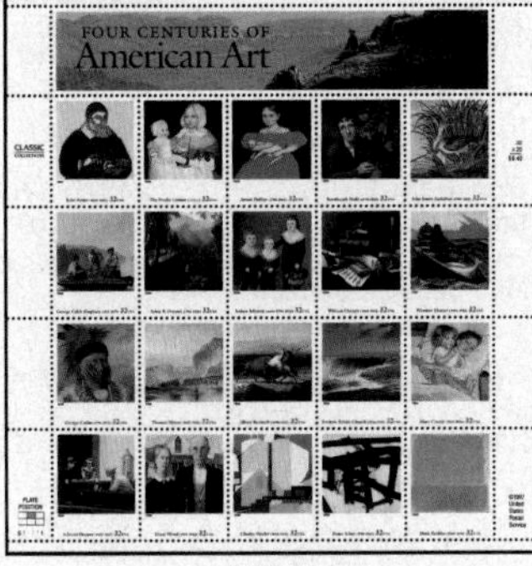

A2516

Paintings: a, "Portrait of Richard Mather," by John Foster. b, "Mrs. Elizabeth Freake and Baby Mary," by The Freake Limner. c, "Girl in Red Dress with Cat and Dog," by Ammi Phillips. d, "Rubens Peale with a Geranium," by Rembrandt Peale. e, "Long-billed Curlew, Numenius Longrostris," by John James Audubon. f, "Boatmen on the Missouri," by George Caleb Bingham. g, "Kindred Sprits," by Asher B. Durand. h, "The Westwood Children," by Joshua Johnson. i, "Music and Literature," by William Harnett. j, "The Fog Warning," by Winslow Homer. k, "The White Cloud, Head Chief of the Iowas," by George Catlin. l, "Cliffs of Green River," by Thomas Moran. m, "The Last of the Buffalo," by Alfred Bierstadt. n, "Niagara," by Frederic Edwin Church. o, "Breakfast in Bed," by Mary Cassatt. p, "Nighthawks," by Edward Hopper. q, "American Gothic," by Grant Wood. r, "Two Against the White," by Charles Sheeler. s, "Mahoning," by Franz Kline. t, "No. 12," by Mark Rothko.

PHOTOGRAVURE

1998, Aug. 27 ***Perf. 10.2***

3236 A2516 Pane of 20 18.00 10.00
a.-t. 32c any single .90 .60

AMERICAN BALLET

A2517

LITHOGRAPHED

1998, Sept. 16 ***Perf. 10.9x11.1***

3237 A2517 32c multicolored .65 .25

SPACE DISCOVERY

A2518

A2519

A2520

A2521

A2522

PHOTOGRAVURE

1998, Oct. 1 ***Perf. 11.1***

3238 A2518 32c multicolored .65 .25
3239 A2519 32c multicolored .65 .25
3240 A2520 32c multicolored .65 .25
3241 A2521 32c multicolored .65 .25
3242 A2522 32c multicolored .65 .25
a. Strip of 5, #3238-3242 3.25 2.25

GIVING AND SHARING

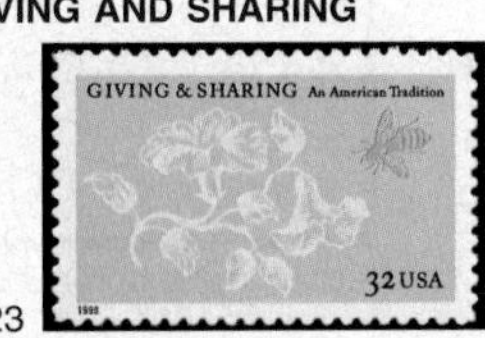

A2523

Serpentine Die Cut 11.1

1998, Oct. 7

Self-Adhesive

3243 A2523 32c multicolored .65 .25

CHRISTMAS

Madonna and Child — A2524

Evergreen A2525

Victorian A2526

Chili Pepper A2527

Tropical A2528

LITHOGRAPHED

Serpentine Die Cut 10.1x9.9 on 2, 3 or 4 Sides

1998, Oct. 15

Self-Adhesive

Booklet Stamps

3244 A2524 32c multicolored .65 .25
a. Booklet pane of 20 + label 13.00
b. Die cutting omitted, pair —

Size: 22x25mm

Serpentine Die Cut 11.3x11.7 on 2 or 3 Sides

3245 A2525 32c multicolored 5.00 .25
3246 A2526 32c multicolored 5.00 .25
3247 A2527 32c multicolored 5.00 .25
3248 A2528 32c multicolored 5.00 .25
a. Booklet pane of 4, #3245-3248 20.00
b. Booklet pane of 5, #3245-3246, 3248, 2 #3247 + label 25.00
c. Booklet pane of 6, #3247-3248, 2 each #3245-3246 30.00
d. As "a," die cutting omitted —
e. As "b," die cutting omitted —
f. As "c," die cutting omitted —

Size: 23x30mm

Serpentine Die Cut 11.4x11.5 on 2, 3, or 4 Sides

3249 A2525 32c multicolored 2.00 .25
a. Serp. die cut 11.7x11.6 on 2, 3, or 4 sides 2.50 .25
3250 A2526 32c multicolored 2.00 .25
a. Serp. die cut 11.7x11.6 on 3 or 4 sides 2.50 .25
3251 A2527 32c multicolored 2.00 .25
a. Serp. die cut 11.7x11.6 on 3 or 4 sides 2.50 .25
3252 A2528 32c multicolored + label 2.00 .25
a. Serp. die cut 11.7x11.6 on 2, 3, or 4 sides 2.50 .25
b. Block or strip of 4, #3249-3252 8.00
c. Booklet pane of 20, 5 each #3249-3252 + label 40.00
d. Block or strip of 4, #3249a-3252a 10.00
e. Booklet pane of 20, 5 each #3249a-3252a + label 50.00
f. Block or strip of 4, #3249-3252, red ("Greetings 32 USA" and "1998") omitted on #3249, 3252 *625.00*
g. Block or strip of 4, #3249-3252, red ("Greetings 32 USA" and "1998") omitted on #3249, 3252; green (same) omitted on #3250, 3251 —
h. As "b," die cutting omitted —
i. As "c," die cutting omitted *4,500.*

Madonna and Child, Florence, 15th Cent.

Dedicated printing plates were used to print the red and green denominations, salutations and dates. Red and green appearing in the wreaths come from other plates and, therefore, are not part of the color omissions.

Weather Vane — A2529

Uncle Sam — A2530

Uncle Sam's Hat — A2531

Space Shuttle Landing — A2532

Piggyback Space Shuttle — A2533

1998 Untagged *Perf. 11.2*

3257 A2532 (1c) multi .25 .25
a. Black omitted 125.00

Untagged

3258 A2529 (1c) multi .25 .25

No. 3257 is 18mm high, has thin letters, white USA, and black 1998. No. 3258 is 17mm high, has thick letters, pale blue USA and blue 1998.

PHOTOGRAVURE

Serpentine Die Cut 10.8

Self-Adhesive (#3259, 3261-3263, 3265-3269)

3259 A2530 22c multi .45 .25
a. Die cut 10.8x10.5 2.50 .25
b. Vert. pair, No. 3259 + 3259a 3.50

See No. 3353.

Perf. 11.2

3260 A2531 (33c) multi .65 .25

LITHOGRAPHED

Serpentine Die Cut 11.5

3261 A2532 $3.20 multi 6.00 1.50
3262 A2533 $11.75 multi 22.50 10.00

Hidden 3-D images (ENTERPRISE/COLUMBIA /CHALLENGER/ATLANTIS/ENDEAVOR/DISCOVERY) can be seen on Nos. 3261 and 3262 when viewed with a special "Stamp Decoder" lens sold by the USPS.

COIL STAMPS

PHOTOGRAVURE

Serpentine Die Cut 9.9 Vert.

3263 A2530 22c multi .45 .25
a. Die cutting omitted, pair —

See No. 3353.

Perf. 9.8 Vert.

3264 A2531 (33c) multi .65 .25
a. Imperf, pair —

Serpentine Die Cut 9.9 Vert.

3265 A2531 (33c) multi .80 .25
a. Die cutting omitted, pair 65.00 —
b. Red omitted *525.00*
c. Black omitted *1,750.*
d. Black omitted, die cutting omitted, pair *675.00*
e. Red omitted, die cutting omitted, pair *500.00*
f. Blue omitted —

Unused examples of No. 3265 are on backing paper the same size as the stamps. Corners of the stamp are 90 degree angles.

On No. 3265b, the blue and gray colors are shifted down and to the right.

On No. 3265f, the red is misregistered to right by 10½ stamps and gray by 3mm.

Serpentine Die Cut 9.9 Vert.

3266 A2531 (33c) multi 1.75 .25

Unused examples of No. 3266 are on backing paper larger than the stamps, and the stamps are spaced approximately 2mm. apart. Corners of stamps are rounded.

BOOKLET STAMPS

Serpentine Die Cut 9.9 on 2 or 3 Sides

3267 A2531 (33c) multi .75 .25
a. Booklet pane of 10 7.50

Serpentine Die Cut 11¼ on 3 Sides (#3268, 3268a)

or 11 on 2, 3 or 4 sides (#3268b, 3268c)

3268 A2531 (33c) multi .75 .25
a. Booklet pane of 10 7.50
b. Serpentine die cut 11 .75 .25
c. As "b," booklet pane of 20 + label 15.00

Die Cut 8 on 2, 3 or 4 Sides

3269 A2531 (33c) multi .65 .25
a. Booklet pane of 18 12.00

Issued: No. 3262, 11/19; others, 11/9.

Unused and used examples of an "H" nondenominated stamp inscribed "Postcard Rate" exist in the marketplace. There is no evidence that these stamps were ever officially issued. Values: unused $3,000; used $2,250.

A2534

PHOTOGRAVURE

COIL STAMPS

Perf. 9.8 Vert.

1998, Dec. 14 Untagged

3270 A2534 (10c) multicolored, small date .25 .25
a. Large date .45 .25

Self-Adhesive

Untagged

Serpentine Die Cut 9.9 Vert.

3271 A2534 (10c) multicolored, small date .25 .25
a. Large date 1.00 .25

Dates on Nos. 3270a and 3271a are approximately 1¾mm; on Nos. 3270-3271 approximately 1¼mm.

Compare to Nos. 2602-2604, 2907.

Scott values for used self-adhesive stamps are for examples either on piece or off piece.

CHINESE NEW YEAR

Year of the Rabbit — A2535

1999, Jan. 5 *Perf. 11.2*

3272 A2535 33c multicolored .80 .25

See No. 3895d.

BLACK HERITAGE SERIES

Malcolm X — A2536

LITHOGRAPHED

Serpentine Die Cut 11.4

1999, Jan. 20

Self-Adhesive

3273 A2536 33c multicolored .85 .25

LOVE

A2537

A2538

PHOTOGRAVURE

1999, Jan. 28 *Die Cut*

Booklet Stamp

Self-Adhesive

3274 A2537 33c multicolored .65 .25
a. Booklet pane of 20 13.00
b. Die cutting omitted, pair *115.00*
c. As "a," die cutting omitted *1,150.*
3275 A2538 55c multicolored 1.10 .25

HOSPICE CARE

A2539

LITHOGRAPHED

Serpentine Die Cut 11.4

1999, Feb. 9

3276 A2539 33c multicolored .65 .25

Flag & City A2540

Flag & Chalkboard A2541

PHOTOGRAVURE

1999, Feb. 25 *Perf. 11.2*

Self-Adhesive (#3278, 3278F, 3279, 3281-3282)

3277 A2540 33c multi .70 .25

No. 3277 has red date.

Serpentine Die Cut 11 on 2, 3 or 4 Sides

3278 A2540 33c multi .65 .25
a. Booklet pane of 4 2.60
b. Booklet pane of 5 + label 3.25
c. Booklet pane of 6 3.90
d. Booklet pane of 10 14.00
e. Booklet pane of 20 + label 17.00
h. As "e," die cutting omitted —
i. Serpentine die cut 11¼ 1.50 .25
j. As "i," booklet pane of 10 15.00

No. 3278 has black date.

BOOKLET STAMPS

Serpentine Die Cut 11½x11¾ on 2, 3 or 4 Sides

3278F A2540 33c multi 1.40 .25
g. Booklet pane of 20 + label 28.00

No. 3278F has black date.

Serpentine Die Cut 9.8 on 2 or 3 Sides

3279 A2540 33c multi .85 .25
a. Booklet pane of 10 8.50

No. 3279 has red date.

COIL STAMPS

Perf. 9.9 Vert.

3280 A2540 33c multi, small "1999" year date .65 .25
a. Large date 1.50 .25
b. As No. 3280, imperf pair — *150.00*

Serpentine Die Cut 9.8 Vert.

Two types of No. 3281: Type I, Long vertical feature at left and right of tallest building consists of 3 separate lines; Type II, Same features consist of solid color.

3281 A2540 33c multi, type I, large "1999" year date .65 .25
a. As No. 3281, die cutting omitted, pair 30.00
b. Light blue and yellow omitted *275.00*
c. Small date, type II .65 .25
d. Small date, type I 5.00 .30
e. As "c," die cutting omitted, pair —

Corners are square on #3281. Unused examples are on backing paper the same size as the stamps, and the stamps are adjoining.

Date on Nos. 3280a and 3281 is approximately 1¾mm; on Nos. 3280, 3281c and 3281d approximately 1¼mm.

3282 A2540 33c multi .65 .25

Corners are rounded on #3282. Unused examples are on backing paper larger than the stamps, and the stamps are spaced approximately 2mm. apart.

PHOTOGRAVURE

Serpentine Die Cut 7.9 on 2, 3 or 4 Sides

1999, Mar. 13

Self-Adhesive

BOOKLET STAMP

3283 A2541 33c multicolored .65 .25
a. Booklet pane of 18 12.00

IRISH IMMIGRATION

A2542

LITHOGRAPHED

1999, Feb. 26 *Perf. 11.2*

3286 A2542 33c multicolored .65 .25

See Ireland No. 1168.

PERFORMING ARTS SERIES

Alfred Lunt (1892-1977), Lynn Fontanne (1887-1983), Actors

A2543

1999, Mar. 2

3287 A2543 33c multicolored .65 .25

ARCTIC ANIMALS

A2544

A2545

A2546

A2547

A2548

1999, Mar. 12 ***Perf. 11***

3288 A2544 33c Arctic Hare .85 .25
3289 A2545 33c Arctic Fox .85 .25
3290 A2546 33c Snowy Owl .85 .25
3291 A2547 33c Polar Bear .85 .25
3292 A2548 33c Gray Wolf .85 .25
a. Strip of 5, #3288-3292 4.25 —

SONORAN DESERT

A2549

Designs: a, Cactus wren, brittlebush, teddy bear cholla. b, Desert tortoise. c, White-winged dove, prickly pear. d, Gambel quail. e, Saguaro cactus. f, Desert mule deer. g, Desert cottontail, hedgehog cactus. h, Gila monster. i, Western diamondback rattlesnake, cactus mouse. j, Gila woodpecker.

Serpentine Die Cut Perf 11.2

1999, Apr. 6

Self-Adhesive

3293 A2549 Pane of 10 8.00
a.-j. 33c any single .80 .50

BERRIES

Blueberries
A2550

Raspberries
A2551

Strawberries
A2552

Blackberries
A2553

PHOTOGRAVURE

Serpentine Die Cut 11¼x11½ on 2, 3 or 4 Sides (Nos. 3294-3297), or 2 or 3 sides (Nos. 3294a-3297a)

1999, Apr. 10

Self-Adhesive

3294 A2550 33c multicolored .85 .25
a. Dated "2000" 1.25 .25
3295 A2551 33c multicolored .85 .25
a. Dated "2000" 1.25 .25
3296 A2552 33c multicolored .85 .25
a. Dated "2000" 1.25 .25
3297 A2553 33c multicolored .85 .25
a. Dated "2000" 1.25 .25
b. Booklet pane of 20, 5 each #3294-3297 + label 17.50
c. Block of 4, #3294-3297 3.50
d. Booklet pane of 20, 5 #3297e + label 25.00
e. Block of 4, #3294a-3297a 5.00

No. 3297d is a double-sided booklet pane, with 12 stamps on one side and eight stamps plus label on the other side.

Serpentine Die Cut 9½x10 on 2 or 3 Sides

3298 A2550 33c multicolored 1.00 .25
3299 A2552 33c multicolored 1.00 .25
3300 A2551 33c multicolored 1.00 .25
3301 A2553 33c multicolored 1.00 .25
a. Booklet pane of 4, #3298-3301 4.00
b. Booklet pane of 5, #3298, 3299, 3301, 2 #3300 + label 5.00
c. Booklet pane of 6, #3300, 3301, 2 #3298, 3299 6.00
d. Block of 4, #3298-3301 4.00

COIL STAMPS

Serpentine Die Cut 8.5 Vert.

3302 A2550 33c multicolored 1.75 .25
3303 A2551 33c multicolored 1.75 .25
3304 A2553 33c multicolored 1.75 .25
3305 A2552 33c multicolored 1.75 .25
a. Strip of 4, #3302-3305 7.00

A2554

A2555

DAFFY DUCK

PHOTOGRAVURE

Serpentine Die Cut 11.1

1999, Apr. 16

Self-Adhesive

3306 Pane of 10 6.75
a. A2554 33c single .65 .25
b. Pane of 9 #3306a 6.00
c. Pane of 1 #3306a .65

Die cutting on #3306b does not extend through the backing paper.

3307 Pane of 10 15.00
a. A2554 33c single 1.25
b. Pane of 9 #3307a 12.00
c. Pane of 1, no die cutting 2.75
d. As "a," vert. pair, die cutting omitted btwn. pos. 6 and 9 (unique) *4,250.*

Die cutting on #3307b extends through the backing paper.

LITERARY ARTS SERIES

Ayn Rand (1905-82).

LITHOGRAPHED

1999, Apr. 22 ***Perf. 11.2***

3308 A2555 33c multicolored .65 .25

Cinco De Mayo Type of 1998

Serpentine Die Cut 11.6x11.3

1999, Apr. 27

Self-Adhesive

3309 A2486 33c multicolored .70 .25

TROPICAL FLOWERS

Bird of Paradise
A2556

Royal Poinciana
A2557

Gloriosa Lily
A2558

Chinese Hibiscus
A2559

PHOTOGRAVURE

BOOKLET STAMPS

Serpentine Die Cut 10.9 on 2 or 1 Sides

1999, May 1

Self-Adhesive

3310 A2556 33c multicolored .65 .30
3311 A2557 33c multicolored .65 .30
3312 A2558 33c multicolored .65 .30
3313 A2559 33c multicolored .65 .30
a. Block of 4, #3310-3313 2.60
b. Booklet pane, 5 each #3313a 13.00

No. 3313b is a double-sided booklet pane with 12 stamps on one side and 8 stamps plus label on the other side.

A2560

A2561

JOHN (1699-1777) & WILLIAM (1739-1823) BARTRAM, BOTANISTS

LITHOGRAPHED

Serpentine Die Cut 11½

1999, May 18

Self-Adhesive

3314 A2560 33c Franklinia alatamaha, by William Bartram .65 .25

PROSTATE CANCER AWARENESS

PHOTOGRAVURE

1999, May 28 ***Serpentine Die Cut 11***

Self-Adhesive

3315 A2561 33c multicolored .65 .25

CALIFORNIA GOLD RUSH, 150TH ANNIV.

A2562

LITHOGRAPHED

1999, June 18 ***Perf. 11¼***

3316 A2562 33c multicolored .65 .25

AQUARIUM FISH

Reef Fish

A2563

A2564

A2565

A2566

Designs: No. 3317, Yellow fish, red fish, cleaner shrimp. No. 3318, Fish, thermometer. No. 3319, Red fish, blue & yellow fish. No. 3320, Fish, heater/aerator.

Serpentine Die Cut 11½

1999, June 24

Self-Adhesive

3317 A2563 33c multicolored .65 .30
3318 A2564 33c multicolored .65 .30
3319 A2565 33c multicolored .65 .30
3320 A2566 33c multicolored .65 .30
b. Strip of 4, #3317-3320 2.60

EXTREME SPORTS

A2567

A2568

A2569

A2570

PHOTOGRAVURE

Serpentine Die Cut 11

1999, June 25

Self-Adhesive

3321 A2567 33c multicolored .75 .30
3322 A2568 33c multicolored .75 .30
3323 A2569 33c multicolored .75 .30
3324 A2570 33c multicolored .75 .30
a. Block or strip of 4, #3321-3324 3.00

AMERICAN GLASS

Free-Blown Glass — A2571

Mold-Blown Glass — A2572

Pressed Glass — A2573

Art Glass — A2574

LITHOGRAPHED

1999, June 29 ***Perf. 11***

3325 A2571 33c multicolored 1.90 .25
3326 A2572 33c multicolored 1.90 .25
3327 A2573 33c multicolored 1.90 .25
3328 A2574 33c multicolored 1.90 .25
a. Strip or block of 4, #3325-3328 7.75 3.00

A2575

A2576

LEGENDS OF HOLLYWOOD

James Cagney (1899-1986)

PHOTOGRAVURE

1999, July 22 ***Perf. 11***

3329 A2575 33c multicolored .80 .25

Perforations in corner of each stamp are star-shaped.

GEN. WILLIAM "BILLY" L. MITCHELL (1879-1936), AVIATION PIONEER

Serpentine Die Cut 9¾x10

1999, July 30

Self-Adhesive

3330 A2576 55c multicolored 1.10 .30

HONORING THOSE WHO SERVED

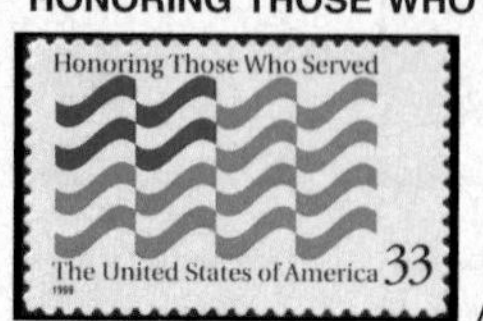

A2577

Serpentine Die Cut 11

1999, Aug. 16

Self-Adhesive

3331 A2577 33c black, blue & red .65 .25

UNIVERSAL POSTAL UNION

A2578

LITHOGRAPHED

1999, Aug. 25 ***Perf. 11***

3332 A2578 45c multicolored 1.00 .45

FAMOUS TRAINS

Daylight A2579

Congressional — A2580

20th Century Limited A2581

Hiawatha A2582

Super Chief A2583

1999, Aug. 26

3333 A2579 33c multicolored .75 .25
3334 A2580 33c multicolored .75 .25
3335 A2581 33c multicolored .75 .25
3336 A2582 33c multicolored .75 .25
3337 A2583 33c multicolored .75 .25
a. Strip of 5, #3333-3337 3.75 —

Stamps in No. 3337a are arranged in four different orders.

FREDERICK LAW OLMSTED (1822-1903), LANDSCAPE ARCHITECT

A2584

1999, Sept. 12

3338 A2584 33c multicolored .65 .25

AMERICAN MUSIC SERIES
Hollywood Composers

Max Steiner (1888-1971) — A2585

Dimitri Tiomkin (1894-1975) — A2586

Bernard Herrmann (1911-75) A2587

Franz Waxman (1906-67) A2588

Alfred Newman (1907-70) A2589

Erich Wolfgang Korngold (1897-1957) — A2590

1999, Sept. 16 ***Perf. 11***

3339 A2585 33c multicolored 1.40 .25
3340 A2586 33c multicolored 1.40 .25
3341 A2587 33c multicolored 1.40 .25
3342 A2588 33c multicolored 1.40 .25
3343 A2589 33c multicolored 1.40 .25
3344 A2590 33c multicolored 1.40 .25
a. Block of 6, #3339-3344 8.50 4.50

AMERICAN MUSIC SERIES
Broadway Songwriters

Ira (1896-1983) & George (1898-1937) Gershwin — A2591

Alan Jay Lerner (1918-86) & Frederick Loewe (1901-88) A2592

Lorenz Hart (1895-1943) — A2593

Richard Rodgers (1902-79) & Oscar Hammerstein II (1895-1960) — A2594

Meredith Willson (1902-84) A2595

Frank Loesser (1910-69) A2596

1999, Sept. 21

3345 A2591 33c multicolored 1.25 .25
3346 A2592 33c multicolored 1.25 .25
3347 A2593 33c multicolored 1.25 .25
3348 A2594 33c multicolored 1.25 .25
3349 A2595 33c multicolored 1.25 .25
3350 A2596 33c multicolored 1.25 .25
a. Block of 6, #3345-3350 7.50 4.50

INSECTS & SPIDERS

A2597

Designs: a, Black widow. b, Elderberry longhorn. c, Lady beetle. d, Yellow garden spider. e, Dogbane beetle. f, Flower fly. g, Assassin bug. h, Ebony jewelwing. i, Velvet ant. j, Monarch caterpillar. k, Monarch butterfly. l, Eastern Hercules beetle. m, Bombardier beetle. n, Dung beetle. o, Spotted water beetle. p, True katydid. q, Spinybacked spider. r, Periodical cicada. s, Scorpionfly. t, Jumping spider.

1999, Oct. 1 ***Perf. 11***

3351 A2597 Pane of 20 14.00 10.00
a.-t. 33c any single .70 .50

Hanukkah Type of 1996

PHOTOGRAVURE

1999, Oct. 8 ***Serpentine Die Cut 11***

Self-Adhesive

3352 A2411 33c multicolored .65 .25

Uncle Sam Type of 1998

COIL STAMP

1999, Oct. 8 ***Perf. 9¾ Vert.***

3353 A2530 22c multicolored .45 .25

NATO, 50TH ANNIV.

A2598

LITHOGRAPHED

1999, Oct. 13 ***Perf. 11¼***

3354 A2598 33c multicolored .65 .25

CHRISTMAS

Madonna and Child, by Bartolomeo Vivarini A2599

Deer A2600

Serpentine Die Cut 11¼ on 2 or 3 sides

1999, Oct. 20

Booklet Stamp

Self-Adhesive

3355 A2599 33c multicolored 1.00 .25
a. Booklet pane of 20 20.00

Serpentine Die Cut 11¼

3356 A2600 33c gold & red 2.25 .25
3357 A2600 33c gold & blue 2.25 .25
3358 A2600 33c gold & purple 2.25 .25
3359 A2600 33c gold & green 2.25 .25
a. Block or strip of 4, #3356-3359 9.00

Booklet Stamps

Serpentine Die Cut 11¼ on 2, 3 or 4 sides

3360 A2600 33c gold & red 1.40 .25
3361 A2600 33c gold & blue 1.40 .25
3362 A2600 33c gold & purple 1.40 .25
3363 A2600 33c gold & green 1.40 .25
a. Booklet pane of 20, 5 each #3360-3363 28.00
b. Block of 4, #3360-3363 5.60
c. As "b," die cutting omitted *250.00*
d. As "a," die cutting omitted *1,250.*

Size: 21x19mm

Serpentine Die Cut 11½x11¼ on 2 or 3 sides

3364 A2600 33c gold & red 2.00 .25
3365 A2600 33c gold & blue 2.00 .25
3366 A2600 33c gold & purple 2.00 .25
3367 A2600 33c gold & green 2.00 .25
a. Booklet pane of 4, #3364-3367 8.00
b. Booklet pane of 5, #3364, 3366, 3367, 2 #3365 + label 10.00
c. Booklet pane of 6, #3365, 3367, 2 each #3364 & 3366 12.00
d. Block of 4, #3364-3367 8.00

The frame on Nos. 3356-3359 is narrow and the space between it and the hoof is a hairline. The frame on Nos. 3360-3363 is much thicker, and the space between it and the hoof is wider.

Kwanzaa Type of 1997

PHOTOGRAVURE

1999, Oct. 29 ***Serpentine Die Cut 11***

Self-Adhesive

3368 A2458 33c multicolored .65 .25

YEAR 2000

Baby New Year — A2601

LITHOGRAPHED

Serpentine Die Cut 11¼

1999, Dec. 27

Self-Adhesive

3369 A2601 33c multicolored .65 .25

CHINESE NEW YEAR

Year of the Dragon — A2602

2000, Jan. 6 ***Perf. 11¼***

3370 A2602 33c multicolored .80 .25

See No. 3895e.

BLACK HERITAGE SERIES

Patricia Roberts Harris — A2603

Serpentine Die Cut 11½x11¼

2000, Jan. 27

Self-Adhesive

3371 A2603 33c indigo .65 .25

SUBMARINES

S Class A2604

Los Angeles Class A2605

Ohio Class A2606

USS Holland A2607

Gato Class — A2608

2000, Mar. 27 ***Perf. 11***

3372 A2605 33c multicolored, with microprinted "USPS" at base of sail .75 .25

BOOKLET STAMPS

3373 A2604 22c multicolored 1.25 .75
3374 A2605 33c multicolored, no microprinting 1.75 1.00
3375 A2606 55c multicolored 2.75 1.25
3376 A2607 60c multicolored 3.00 1.50
3377 A2608 $3.20 multicolored 16.00 5.00
a. Booklet pane of 5, #3373-3377 22.50 —

No. 3377a was issued with two types of text in the selvage.

PACIFIC COAST RAIN FOREST

A2609

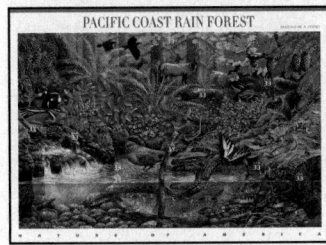

Designs: a, Harlequin duck. b, Dwarf oregongrape, snail-eating ground beetle. c, American dipper, horiz. d, Cutthroat trout, horiz. e, Roosevelt elk. f, Winter wren. g, Pacific giant salamander, Rough-skinned newt. h, Western tiger swallowtail, horiz. i, Douglas squirrel, foliose lichen. j, Foliose lichen, banana slug.

Serpentine Die Cut 11¼x11½, 11½ (horiz. stamps)

2000, Mar. 29

Self-Adhesive

3378 A2609 Pane of 10 10.00
a.-j. 33c any single 1.00 .50

LOUISE NEVELSON (1899-1988), SCULPTOR

Silent Music I — A2610

Royal Tide I — A2611

Black Chord — A2612

Nightsphere-Light — A2613

Dawn's Wedding Chapel I — A2614

2000, Apr. 6 ***Perf. 11x11¼***

3379 A2610 33c multicolored .65 .25
3380 A2611 33c multicolored .65 .25
3381 A2612 33c multicolored .65 .25
3382 A2613 33c multicolored .65 .25
3383 A2614 33c multicolored .65 .25
a. Strip of 5, #3379-3383 3.25 —

HUBBLE SPACE TELESCOPE IMAGES

Eagle Nebula — A2615

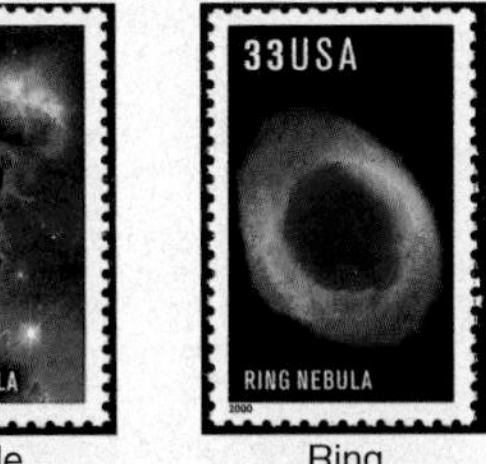
Ring Nebula — A2616

Lagoon Nebula — A2617

Egg Nebula — A2618

Galaxy NGC 1316 — A2619

PHOTOGRAVURE

2000, Apr. 10 ***Perf. 11***

3384 A2615 33c multicolored .65 .25
3385 A2616 33c multicolored .65 .25
3386 A2617 33c multicolored .65 .25
3387 A2618 33c multicolored .65 .25
3388 A2619 33c multicolored .65 .25
a. Strip of 5, #3384-3388 3.25 2.00
b. As "a," imperf *1,150.*

AMERICAN SAMOA

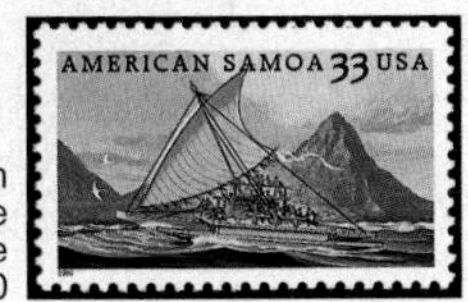
Samoan Double Canoe A2620

LITHOGRAPHED

2000, Apr. 17

3389 A2620 33c multicolored .85 .25

LIBRARY OF CONGRESS

A2621

2000, Apr. 24

3390 A2621 33c multicolored .65 .25

ROAD RUNNER & WILE E. COYOTE

A2622

Serpentine Die Cut 11

2000, Apr. 26

Self-Adhesive

3391 Pane of 10 10.00
- *a.* A2622 33c single .85 .25
- *b.* Pane of 9 #3391a 8.00
- *c.* Pane of 1 #3391a 1.50
- *d.* All die cutting omitted, pane of 10 *2,400.*

Die cutting on #3391b does not extend through the backing paper.

3392 Pane of 10 *40.00*
- *a.* A2622 33c single *2.75*
- *b.* Pane of 9 #3392a *30.00*
- *c.* Pane of 1, imperf. *5.00*

Die cutting on #3392a extends through the backing paper. Used examples of No. 3392a are identical to those of No. 3391a.

Nos. 3391b-3391c and 3392b-3392c are separated by a vertical line of microperforations.

DISTINGUISHED SOLDIERS

A2623

A2624

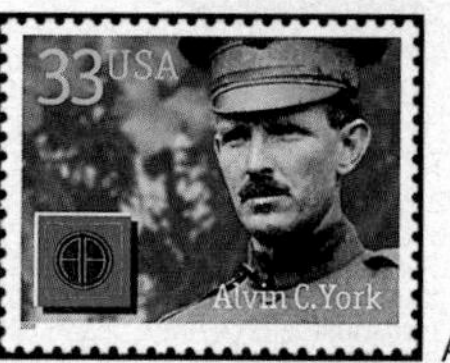

A2625

A2626

Designs: No. 3393, Maj. Gen. John L. Hines. No. 3394, Gen. Omar N. Bradley. No. 3395, Sgt. Alvin C. York. No. 3396, Second Lt. Audie L. Murphy.

2000, May 3 ***Perf. 11***

3393 A2623 33c multicolored .70 .25
3394 A2624 33c multicolored .70 .25
3395 A2625 33c multicolored .70 .25
3396 A2626 33c multicolored .70 .25
- *a.* Block or strip of 4, #3393-3396 2.80 1.50

SUMMER SPORTS

Runners A2627

2000, May 5

3397 A2627 33c multicolored .65 .25

ADOPTION

Stick Figures — A2628

Serpentine Die Cut 11½

2000, May 10

Self-Adhesive

3398 A2628 33c multicolored .75 .25
- *a.* Die cutting omitted, pair —

See note after No. 1549.

YOUTH TEAM SPORTS

A2629

A2630

A2631

A2632

2000, May 27 ***Perf. 11***

3399 A2629 33c Basketball .70 .25
3400 A2630 33c Football .70 .25
3401 A2631 33c Soccer .70 .25
3402 A2632 33c Baseball .70 .25
- *a.* Block or strip of 4, #3399-3402 2.80 1.75

THE STARS AND STRIPES

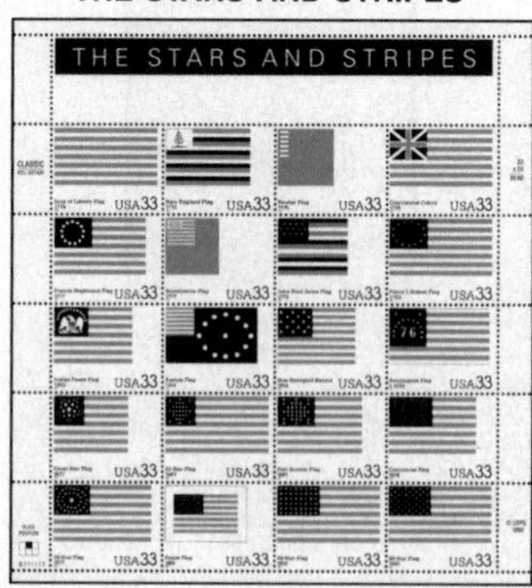

A2633

Designs: a, Sons of Liberty Flag, 1775. b, New England Flag, 1775. c, Forster Flag, 1775. d, Continental Colors, 1776. e, Francis Hopkinson Flag, 1777. f, Brandywine Flag, 1777. g, John Paul Jones Flag, 1779. h, Pierre L'Enfant Flag, 1783. i, Indian Peace Flag, 1803. j, Easton Flag, 1814. k, Star-Spangled Banner, 1814. l, Bennington Flag, c. 1820. m, Great Star Flag, 1837. n, 29-Star Flag, 1847. o, Fort Sumter Flag, 1861. p, Centennial Flag, 1876. q, 38-Star Flag, 1877. r, Peace Flag, 1891. s, 48-Star Flag, 1912. t, 50-Star Flag, 1960.

2000, June 14 ***Perf. 10½x11***

3403 A2633 Pane of 20 15.00 11.00
- *a.-t.* 33c any single .75 .50

BERRIES

Blueberries A2634

Strawberries A2635

Blackberries A2636

Raspberries A2637

See designs A2550-A2553.

PHOTOGRAVURE

COIL STAMPS

Serpentine Die Cut 8½ Horiz.

2000, June 16 **Tagged**

Self-Adhesive

3404 A2634 33c multicolored 3.50 .25
3405 A2635 33c multicolored 3.50 .25
3406 A2636 33c multicolored 3.50 .25
3407 A2637 33c multicolored 3.50 .25
- *a.* Strip of 4, #3404-3407 15.00

Nos. 3404-3407 are linerless coils issued without backing paper. The adhesive is strong and can remove the ink from stamps in the roll.

LEGENDS OF BASEBALL

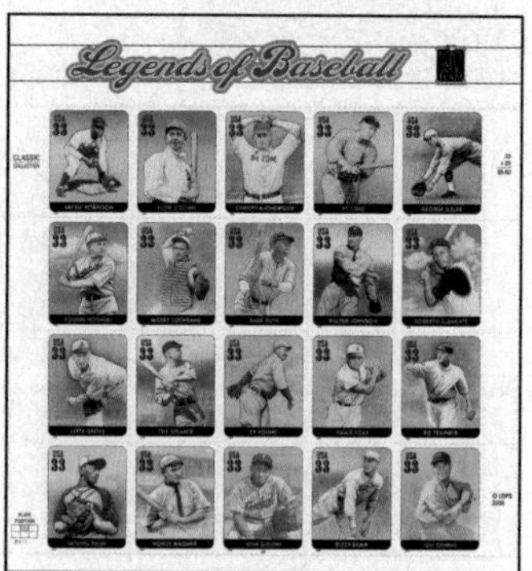

A2638

Designs: a, Jackie Robinson. b, Eddie Collins. c, Christy Mathewson. d, Ty Cobb. e, George Sisler. f, Rogers Hornsby. g, Mickey Cochrane. h, Babe Ruth. i, Walter Johnson. j, Roberto Clemente. k, Lefty Grove. l, Tris Speaker. m, Cy Young. n, Jimmie Foxx. o, Pie Traynor. p, Satchel Paige. q, Honus Wagner. r, Josh Gibson. s, Dizzy Dean. t, Lou Gehrig.

LITHOGRAPHED

Serpentine Die Cut 11¼

2000, July 6

Self-Adhesive

3408 A2638 Pane of 20 15.00
- *a.-t.* 33c any single .75 .50

SPACE

Souvenir Sheets

A2639

A2640

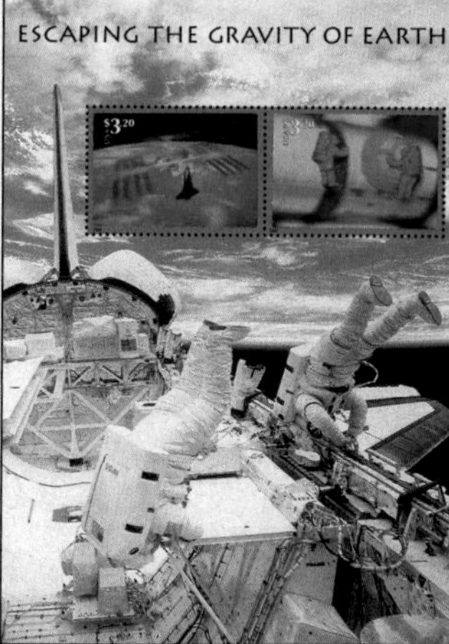

A2641

A2642

A2643

Designs: No. 3409: a, Hubble Space Telescope. b, Radio interferometer very large array, New Mexico. c, Optical and infrared telescopes, Keck Observatory, Hawaii. d, Optical telescopes, Cerro Tololo Observatory, Chile. e, Optical telescope, Mount Wilson Observatory, California. f, Radio telescope, Arecibo Observatory, Puerto Rico.

No. 3410: a, Sun and corona. b, Cross-section of sun. c, Sun and earth. d, Sun and solar flare. e, Sun and clouds.

No. 3411: a, Space Shuttle and Space Station. b, Astronauts working in space.

PHOTOGRAVURE

2000 ***Perf. 10½x11***

3409 A2639 Sheet of 6 15.00 7.00
a.-f. 60c any single 2.25 1.00

Perf. 10¾

3410 A2640 Sheet of 5 + label 17.50 10.00
a.-e. $1 any single 3.00 1.75
f. As No. 3410, imperf *3,250.*
g As No. 3410, with hologram from No. 3411b applied —

Untagged

Photogravure with Hologram Affixed

Perf. 10½, 10¾ (#3412)

3411 A2641 Sheet of 2 22.50 10.00
a.-b. $3.20 any single 10.00 4.00
c. Hologram omitted on right stamp —
3412 A2642 multicolored 40.00 17.50
a. $11.75 single 35.00 15.00
b. Hologram omitted —
c. Hologram omitted on No. 3412 in uncut sheet of 5 panes —
3413 A2643 multicolored 40.00 17.50
a. $11.75 single 35.00 15.00
b. Double hologram *4,250.*
c. Double hologram on No. 3413 in uncut sheet of 5 panes —
d. Hologram omitted on No. 3413 in uncut sheet of 5 panes —
Nos. 3409-3413 (5) 135.00 62.00

Issued: No. 3409, 7/10; No. 3410, 7/11; No. 3411, 7/9; No. 3412, 7/7; No. 3413, 7/8.

The holograms on Nos. 3411-3413 scratch easily. Values are for examples with minimal scratches. Examples without scratches are worth more.

Warning: Soaking in water may affect holographic images.

STAMPIN' THE FUTURE CHILDREN'S STAMP DESIGN CONTEST WINNERS

by Zachary Canter A2644

by Sarah Lipsey A2645

by Morgan Hill A2646

by Ashley Young A2647

LITHOGRAPHED

Serpentine Die Cut 11¼

2000, July 13

Self-Adhesive

3414 A2644 33c multicolored .65 .30
3415 A2645 33c multicolored .65 .30
3416 A2646 33c multicolored .65 .30
3417 A2647 33c multicolored .65 .30
a. Horiz. strip of 4, #3414-3417 2.60

DISTINGUISHED AMERICANS

Gen. Joseph W. Stilwell A2650

Wilma Rudolph (1940-94), Athlete A2652

Sen. Claude Pepper A2656

Sen. Margaret Chase Smith (1897-1995) A2657

James A. Michener (1907-97), Author — A2657a

Dr. Jonas Salk (1914-95), Polio Vaccine Pioneer A2658

Harriet Beecher Stowe (1811-96), Author A2660

Sen. Hattie Caraway (1878-1950) — A2661

Edward Trudeau (1848-1915), Phthisiologist — A2661a

Mary Lasker (1900-94), Philanthropist — A2661b

Edna Ferber (1887-1968), Writer A2662

Edna Ferber (With Curving Shoulder) A2663

Dr. Albert Sabin (1906-93), Polio Vaccine Pioneer — A2664

LITHOGRAPHED & ENGRAVED, LITHOGRAPHED (#3436)

Perf. 11 (#3420, 3426), Serpentine Die Cut 11¼x10¾ (#3422, 3430, 3432B), 11¼x11 (#3427A, 3428, 3432A, 3435), 11 (#3427, 3431), 11½x11 (#3432), 11x11¾ (#3433), 11¼ (#3434)

2000-09

Self-Adhesive (All Except #3420, 3426)

3420 A2650 10c red & black .25 .25
a. Imperf, pair *325.00*
3422 A2652 23c red & black .45 .25
a. Imperf, pair —
3426 A2656 33c red & black .65 .25
3427 A2657 58c red & black 1.25 .25
b. Black (engr.) omitted *475.00*
3427A A2657a 59c multi 1.30 .25
3428 A2658 63c red & black 1.25 .25
a. Black (litho.) omitted —
3430 A2660 75c red & black 1.50 .25
3431 A2661 76c red & black 1.50 .25
3432 A2661 76c red & black *4.00* *2.00*
3432A A2661a 76c multi 1.50 .25
3432B A2661b 78c multi 1.60 .25
3433 A2662 83c red & black 1.70 .30
3434 A2663 83c red & black 1.60 .30
3435 A2664 87c red & black 1.75 .30

BOOKLET STAMP

Serpentine Die Cut 11¼x10¾ on 3 Sides

Self-Adhesive

3436 A2652 23c red & black .45 .25
a. Booklet pane of 4 1.80
b. Booklet pane of 6 2.70
c. As "a" & "b" in cplt booklet of 10 (No. BK279A), die cutting omitted and peel strip intact, P#P44 —
d. Booklet pane of 10 4.50
e. As "d," die cutting omitted —

The backing on No. 3436b has a different product number (672900) than that found on the lower portion of No. 3436d (673000).

Issued: 10c, 8/24; 33c, 9/7; No. 3432, 2/21/01; No. 3433, 7/29/02; No. 3434, Aug. 2003; 23c, 7/14/04; 63c, 87c, 3/2/06; 58c, 75c, 6/13/07; 59c, No. 3432A, 5/12/08; No. 3432B, 5/15/09.

CALIFORNIA STATEHOOD, 150TH ANNIV.

Big Sur and Iceplant — A2668

PHOTOGRAVURE

2000, Sept. 8 ***Serpentine Die Cut 11***

Self-Adhesive

3438 A2668 33c multicolored .75 .25

DEEP SEA CREATURES

Fanfin Anglerfish A2669

Sea Cucumber A2670

Fangtooth A2671

Amphipod A2672

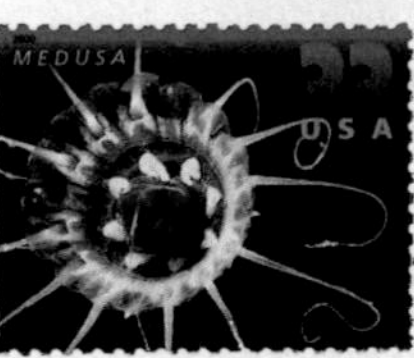

Medusa A2673

2000, Oct. 2 Tagged ***Perf. 10x10¼***

3439 A2669 33c multicolored .75 .25
3440 A2670 33c multicolored .75 .25
3441 A2671 33c multicolored .75 .25
3442 A2672 33c multicolored .75 .25
3443 A2673 33c multicolored .75 .25
a. Vert. strip of 5, #3439-3443 3.75 2.00

LITERARY ARTS SERIES

Thomas Wolfe (1900-38), Novelist — A2674

LITHOGRAPHED

2000, Oct. 3 ***Perf. 11***

3444 A2674 33c multicolored .65 .25

WHITE HOUSE, 200TH ANNIV.

A2675

Serpentine Die Cut 11¼

2000, Oct. 18

Self-Adhesive

3445 A2675 33c multicolored 1.00 .25

LEGENDS OF HOLLYWOOD

Edward G. Robinson (1893-1973), Actor — A2676

PHOTOGRAVURE

2000, Oct. 24 ***Perf. 11***

3446 A2676 33c multicolored 1.75 .25

Perforations in corner of each stamp are star-shaped.

New York Public Library Lion — A2677

PHOTOGRAVURE
COIL STAMP

Serpentine Die Cut 11½ Vert.

2000, Nov. 9 Untagged

Self-Adhesive

3447 A2677 (10c) multicolored, "2000" year date .25 .25
a. "2003" year date .25 .25

See No. 3769.

Flag Over Farm — A2678

LITHOGRAPHED (#3448-3449), PHOTOGRAVURE (#3450)

2000, Dec. 15 ***Perf. 11¼***

3448 A2678 (34c) multicolored 1.00 .25

Self-Adhesive

Serpentine Die Cut 11¼

3449 A2678 (34c) multicolored 1.00 .25

Booklet Stamp

Self-Adhesive

Serpentine Die Cut 8 on 2, 3 or 4 Sides

3450 A2678 (34c) multicolored .85 .25
a. Booklet pane of 18 16.00
b. Die cutting omitted, pair —

A2679

Statue of Liberty — A2680

PHOTOGRAVURE

Serpentine Die Cut 11 on 2, 3 or 4 Sides

2000, Dec. 15

Self-Adhesive (#3451, 3453)

Booklet Stamp

3451 A2679 (34c) multicolored .70 .25
a. Booklet pane of 20 14.00
b. Booklet pane of 4 3.00
c. Booklet pane of 6 5.75
d. As "a," die cutting omitted —

Coil Stamps

Perf. 9¾ Vert.

3452 A2680 (34c) multicolored .70 .25

Serpentine Die Cut 10 Vert.

3453 A2680 (34c) multicolored, small date .70 .25
a. Die cutting omitted, pair *300.00*
b. Large date .75 .25

The date on No. 3453 is 1.4mm long, on No. 3453b 1.55mm long and darker in color.

A2681

A2682

A2683

Flowers — A2684

PHOTOGRAVURE

Serpentine Die Cut 10½x10¾ on 2 or 3 Sides

2000, Dec. 15

Booklet Stamps

Self-Adhesive

3454 A2681 (34c) purple & multi 1.00 .25
3455 A2682 (34c) tan & multi 1.00 .25
3456 A2683 (34c) green & multi 1.00 .25
3457 A2684 (34c) red & multi 1.00 .25
a. Block of 4, #3454-3457 4.00
b. Booklet pane of 4, #3454-3457 4.00
c. Booklet pane of 6, #3456, 3457, 2 each #3454-3455 6.00
d. Booklet pane of 6, #3454, 3455, 2 each #3456-3457 6.00
e. Booklet pane of 20, 5 each #3454-3457 + label 20.00

No. 3457e is a double-sided booklet pane, with 12 stamps on one side and eight stamps plus label on the other side.

Serpentine Die Cut 11½x11¾ on 2 or 3 Sides

3458 A2681 (34c) purple & multi 3.50 .25
3459 A2682 (34c) tan & multi 3.50 .25
3460 A2683 (34c) green & multi 3.50 .25
3461 A2684 (34c) red & multi 3.50 .25
a. Block of 4, #3458-3461 14.00
b. Booklet pane of 20, 2 each #3461a, 3 each #3457a 45.00
c. Booklet pane of 20, 2 each #3457a, 3 each #3461a 60.00

Nos. 3461b and 3461c are double-sided booklet panes, with 12 stamps on one side and eight stamps plus label on the other side.

Coil Stamps

Serpentine Die Cut 8½ Vert.

3462 A2683 (34c) green & multi 4.50 .25
3463 A2684 (34c) red & multi 4.50 .25
3464 A2682 (34c) tan & multi 4.50 .25
3465 A2681 (34c) purple & multi 4.50 .25
a. Strip of 4, #3462-3465 18.00

Lettering on No. 3462 has black outline not found on No. 3456. Zeroes of "2000" are rounder on Nos. 3454-3457 than on Nos. 3462-3465.

Statue of Liberty A2685

George Washington A2686

American Buffalo A2687

Flag Over Farm A2688

Statue of Liberty — A2689

A2690

A2691

A2692

Flowers A2693

Apple A2694

Orange A2695

Eagle A2696

Capitol Dome — A2697

Washington Monument A2698

Serpentine Die Cut 9¾ Vert.

2001, Jan. 7

Coil Stamp

Self-Adhesive

3466 A2685 34c multi .70 .25

Self-Adhesive (#3468-3468A, 3470-3473)

2001 ***Perf. 11¼x11***

3467 A2687 21c multi .50 .25

Serpentine Die Cut 11

3468 A2687 21c multi .50 .25

Litho.

Serpentine Die Cut 11¼x11¾

3468A A2686 23c green .50 .25

Photo.

Perf. 11¼

3469 A2688 34c multi .75 .25

Serpentine Die Cut 11¼

3470 A2688 34c multi 1.00 .25

Serpentine Die Cut 10¾

3471 A2696 55c multi 1.10 .25
3471A A2696 57c multi 1.10 .25

Serpentine Die Cut 11¼x11½

Litho.

3472 A2697 $3.50 multi 7.00 2.00
a. Die cutting omitted, pair —
3473 A2698 $12.25 multi 22.50 10.00

COIL STAMPS

Self-Adhesive (#3475-3475A, 3477-3481)

Photo.

Serpentine Die Cut 8½ Vert.

3475 A2687 21c multi .50 .25
3475A A2686 23c green .75 .25

Compare No. 3475A ("2001" date at lower left) with No. 3617 ("2002" date at lower left).

Perf. 9¾ Vert.

3476 A2685 34c multi .70 .25

Serpentine Die Cut 9¾ Vert.

3477 A2685 34c multi .80 .25
a. Die cutting omitted, pair *75.00*

No. 3477 has right angle corners and backing paper as high as the stamp. No. 3466 has rounded corners and is on backing paper larger than the stamp.

Serpentine Die Cut 8½ Vert.

3478 A2690 34c green & multi .90 .25
3479 A2691 34c red & multi .90 .25
3480 A2692 34c tan & multi .90 .25
3481 A2693 34c purple & multi .90 .25
a. Strip of 4, #3478-3481 3.60

BOOKLET STAMPS

Litho.

Self-Adhesive

Serpentine Die Cut 11¼x11 on 3 Sides

3482 A2686 20c dk car .55 .25
a. Booklet pane of 10 5.50
b. Booklet pane of 4 2.20
c. Booklet pane of 6 3.30

Serpentine Die Cut 10½x11 on 3 Sides

3483 A2686 20c dk car 5.00 1.25
a. Booklet pane of 4, 2 #3482 at L, 2 #3483 at R 14.00
b. Booklet pane of 6, 3 #3482 at L, 3 #3483 at R 20.00
c. Booklet pane of 10, 5 #3482 at L, 5 #3483 at R 28.00
d. Booklet pane of 4, 2 #3483 at L, 2 #3482 at R 14.00
e. Booklet pane of 6, 3 #3483 at L, 3 #3482 at R 20.00
f. Booklet pane of 10, 5 #3483 at L, 5 #3482 at R 28.00
g. Pair, #3482 at L, #3483 at R 5.75
h. Pair, #3483 at L, #3482 at R 5.75

Serpentine Die Cut 11¼ on 3 Sides

3484 A2687 21c multi .60 .25
b. Booklet pane of 4 2.40
c. Booklet pane of 6 3.60
d. Booklet pane of 10 6.00

Serpentine Die Cut 10½x11¼

3484A A2687 21c multi 5.00 1.50
e. Booklet pane of 4, 2 #3484 at L, 2 #3484A at R 14.00
f. Booklet pane of 6, 3 #3484 at L, 3 #3484A at R 20.00
g. Booklet pane of 10, 5 #3484 at L, 5 #3484A at R 28.00
h. Booklet pane of 4, 2 #3484A at L, 2 #3484 at R 14.00
i. Booklet pane of 6, 3 #3484A at L, 3 #3484 at R 20.00
j. Booklet pane of 10, 5 #3484A at L, 5 #3484 at R 28.00
k. Pair, #3484 at L, #3484A at R 5.75
l. Pair, #3484A at L, #3484 at R 5.75

Photo.

Serpentine Die Cut 11 on 2, 3 or 4 Sides

3485 A2689 34c multi .70 .25
a. Booklet pane of 10 7.00
b. Booklet pane of 20 14.00
c. Booklet pane of 4 3.00
d. Booklet pane of 6 4.50
e. Die cutting omitted, pair (from No. 3485b) —
f. As "e," booklet pane of 20 —

Serpentine Die Cut 10½x10¾ on 2 or 3 Sides

3487 A2693 34c purple & multi .85 .25
3488 A2692 34c tan & multi .85 .25
3489 A2690 34c green & multi .85 .25
3490 A2691 34c red & multi .85 .25
a. Block of 4, #3487-3490 3.50
b. Booklet pane of 4, #3487-3490 3.50
c. Booklet pane of 6, #3489-3490, 2 each #3487-3488 5.00
d. Booklet pane of 6, #3487-3488, 2 each #3489-3490 5.00
e. Booklet pane of 20, 5 each #3490a + label 17.50

No. 3490e is a double-sided booklet pane, with 12 stamps on one side and eight stamps plus label on the other side.

Litho.

Serpentine Die Cut 11¼ on 2, 3 or 4 Sides

3491 A2694 34c multi .70 .25
3492 A2695 34c multi .70 .25
a. Pair, #3491-3492 1.40
b. Booklet pane, 10 each #3491-3492 14.00
c. As "a," black ("34 USA") omitted —
d. As "a," die cutting omitted —
e. As "b," die cutting omitted —
f. As "b," right four stamps yellow omitted *3,500.*

Serpentine Die Cut 11½x10¾ on 2 or 3 Sides

3493 A2694 34c multi 1.25 .25
3494 A2695 34c multi 1.25 .25
a. Pair, #3493-3494 2.50
b. Booklet pane, 2 each #3493-3494 5.00

c. Booklet pane, 3 each #3493-3494, #3493 at UL 7.50
d. Booklet pane, 3 each #3493-3494, #3494 at UL 7.50

Serpentine Die Cut 8 on 2, 3, or 4 Sides

3495 A2688 34c multi 1.25 .25
a. Booklet pane of 18 22.50

Issued: Nos. 3472-3473, 1/29; Nos. 3469, 3476-3481, 3485, 3487-3490, 2/7; Nos. 3468, 3471, 3475, 3482, 3483, 2/22; Nos. 3470, 3491-3492, 3/6; Nos. 3493-3494, May; Nos. 3467, 3468A, 3471A, 3475A, 3483, 3484A, 9/20; No. 3495, 12/17.
See Nos. 3616-3619.

LOVE

Rose, Apr. 20, 1763 Love Letter by John Adams A2699

Rose, Apr. 20, 1763 Love Letter by John Adams A2700

Rose, Aug. 11, 1763 Love Letter by Abigail Smith (Abigail Adams in 1764) — A2701

LITHOGRAPHED

Serpentine Die Cut 11¼ on 2, 3 or 4 Sides

2001

Self-Adhesive

Booklet Stamps (Nos. 3496-3498)

3496 A2699 (34c) multi .90 .25
a. Booklet pane of 20 18.00
b. Vert. pair, die cutting omitted between —

Serpentine Die Cut 11¼ on 2, 3 or 4 Sides

3497 A2700 34c multi .90 .25
a. Booklet pane of 20 18.00
b. Vertical pair, die cutting omitted between —

Size: 18x21mm

Serpentine Die Cut 11½x10¾ on 2 or 3 Sides

3498 A2700 34c multi 1.00 .25
a. Booklet pane of 4 4.00
b. Booklet pane of 6 6.00

Serpentine Die Cut 11¼

3499 A2701 55c multi 1.10 .25

Issued: No. 3496, 1/19; others, 2/14.
See No. 3551.

CHINESE NEW YEAR

Year of the Snake A2702

2001, Jan. 20 ***Perf. 11¼***

3500 A2702 34c multicolored .75 .25

See No. 3895f.

BLACK HERITAGE SERIES

Roy Wilkins (1901-81), Civil Rights Leader — A2703

Serpentine Die Cut 11½x11¼

2001, Jan. 24

Self-Adhesive

3501 A2703 34c blue .70 .25

AMERICAN ILLUSTRATORS

A2704

No. 3502: a, Marine Corps poster "First in the Fight, Always Faithful," by James Montgomery Flagg. b, "Interlude (The Lute Players)," by Maxfield Parrish. c, Advertisement for Arrow Collars and Shirts, by J. C. Leyendecker. d, Advertisement for Carrier Corp. Refrigeration, by Robert Fawcett. e, Advertisement for Luxite Hosiery, by Coles Phillips. f, Illustration for correspondence school lesson, by Al Parker. g, "Br'er Rabbit," by A. B. Frost. h, "An Attack on a Galleon," by Howard Pyle. i, Kewpie and Kewpie Doodle Dog, by Rose O'Neill. j, Illustration for cover of True Magazine, by Dean Cornwell. k, "Galahad's Departure," by Edwin Austin Abbey. l, "The First Lesson," by Jessie Willcox Smith. m, Illustration for cover of McCall's Magazine, by Neysa McMein. n, "Back Home For Keeps," by Jon Whitcomb. o, "Something for Supper," by Harvey Dunn. p, "A Dash for the Timber," by Frederic Remington. q, Illustration for "Moby Dick," by Rockwell Kent. r, "Captain Bill Bones," by N. C. Wyeth. s, Illustration for cover of The Saturday Evening Post, by Norman Rockwell. t, "The Girl He Left Behind," by John Held, Jr.

PHOTOGRAVURE

Serpentine Die Cut 11¼

2001, Feb. 1

Self-Adhesive

3502 A2704 Pane of 20 19.00
a.-t. 34c any single .90 .60

DIABETES AWARENESS

A2705

LITHOGRAPHED

Serpentine Die Cut 11¼x11½

2001, Mar. 16

Self-Adhesive

3503 A2705 34c multicolored .65 .25

NOBEL PRIZE CENTENARY

Alfred Nobel and Obverse of Medals A2706

LITHOGRAPHED & ENGRAVED

2001, Mar. 22 ***Perf. 11***

3504 A2706 34c multicolored .70 .25
a. Imperf, pair —

See Sweden No. 2415.

PAN-AMERICAN EXPOSITION INVERT STAMPS, CENT.

A2707

No. 3505: Reproductions (dated 2001) of: a, #294a. b, #295a. c, #296a. d, Commemorative "cinderella" stamp depicting a buffalo.

LITHOGRAPHED (#3505d), ENGRAVED (others)

Perf. 12 (#3505d), 12½x12 (others)

2001, Mar. 29

Tagged (#3505d), Untagged (others)

3505 A2707 Pane of 7, #3505a-3505c, 4 #3505d 10.00 7.00
a. A109 1c green & black .75 .25
b. A110 2c carmine & black .75 .25
c. A111 4c deep red brown & black .75 .25
d. 80c red & blue 1.90 .35

GREAT PLAINS PRAIRIE

A2708

No. 3506 — Wildlife and flowers: a, Pronghorns, Canada geese. b, Burrowing owls, American buffalos. c, American buffalo, Black-tailed prairie dogs, wild alfalfa, horiz. d, Black-tailed prairie dog, American buffalos,. e, Painted lady butterfly, American buffalo, prairie coneflowers, prairie wild roses, horiz. f, Western meadowlark, camel cricket, prairie coneflowers, prairie wild roses. g, Badger, harvester ants. h, Eastern short-horned lizard, plains pocket gopher. i, Plains spadefoot, dung beetle, prairie wild roses, horiz. j, Two-striped grasshopper, Ord's kangaroo rat.

LITHOGRAPHED

Serpentine Die Cut 10

2001, Apr. 19

Self-Adhesive

3506 A2708 Pane of 10 10.00
a.-j. 34c Any single 1.00 .50

PEANUTS COMIC STRIP

Snoopy A2709

Serpentine Die Cut 11¼x11½

2001, May 17

Self-Adhesive

3507 A2709 34c multicolored .80 .25

HONORING VETERANS

A2710

2001, May 23

Self-Adhesive

3508 A2710 34c multicolored .80 .25

FRIDA KAHLO (1907-54), PAINTER

Self-portrait A2711

2001, June 21 ***Perf. 11¼***

3509 A2711 34c multicolored .70 .25

LEGENDARY PLAYING FIELDS

Ebbets Field A2712

Tiger Stadium A2713

Crosley Field A2714

Yankee Stadium A2715

Polo Grounds A2716

Forbes Field A2717

Fenway Park A2718

Comiskey Park A2719

Shibe Park A2720

Wrigley Field A2721

PHOTOGRAVURE

Serpentine Die Cut 11¼x11½

2001, June 27 **Self-Adhesive**

3510	A2712 34c multicolored	.90	.60
3511	A2713 34c multicolored	.90	.60
3512	A2714 34c multicolored	.90	.60
3513	A2715 34c multicolored	.90	.60
3514	A2716 34c multicolored	.90	.60
3515	A2717 34c multicolored	.90	.60
3516	A2718 34c multicolored	.90	.60
3517	A2719 34c multicolored	.90	.60
3518	A2720 34c multicolored	.90	.60
3519	A2721 34c multicolored	.90	.60
a.	Block of 10, #3510-3519	9.00	

ATLAS STATUE, NEW YORK CITY

A2722

COIL STAMP

Serpentine Die Cut 8½ Vert.

2001, June 29 **Untagged**

Self-Adhesive

3520 A2722 (10c) multicolored .25 .25

See No. 3770.

No. 3520 is known with extremely faint tagging, most likely from contamination in the paper-making process.

LEONARD BERNSTEIN (1918-90), CONDUCTOR

A2723

LITHOGRAPHED

2001, July 10 ***Perf. 11¼***

3521 A2723 34c multicolored .70 .25

WOODY WAGON

A2724

PHOTOGRAVURE

COIL STAMP

Serpentine Die Cut 11½ Vert.

2001, Aug. 3 **Untagged**

Self-Adhesive

3522 A2724 (15c) multicolored .30 .25

LEGENDS OF HOLLYWOOD

Lucille Ball (1911-89) — A2725

LITHOGRAPHED

2001, Aug. 6 ***Serpentine Die Cut 11***

Self-Adhesive

3523 A2725 34c multicolored 1.00 .25

a. Die cutting omitted, pair *875.00*

AMERICAN TREASURES SERIES

Amish Quilts

Diamond in the Square, c. 1920 — A2726

Lone Star, c. 1920 — A2727

Sunshine and Shadow, c. 1910 — A2728

Double Ninepatch Variation A2729

Serpentine Die Cut 11¼x11½

2001, Aug. 9

Self-Adhesive

3524	A2726 34c multicolored	.70	.30
3525	A2727 34c multicolored	.70	.30
3526	A2728 34c multicolored	.70	.30
3527	A2729 34c multicolored	.70	.30
a.	Block or strip of 4, #3524-3527	2.80	

CARNIVOROUS PLANTS

Venus Flytrap A2730

Yellow Trumpet A2731

Cobra Lily — A2732

English Sundew — A2733

PHOTOGRAVURE

Serpentine Die Cut 11½

2001, Aug. 23

Self-Adhesive

3528	A2730 34c multicolored	.70	.25
3529	A2731 34c multicolored	.70	.25
3530	A2732 34c multicolored	.70	.25
3531	A2733 34c multicolored	.70	.25
a.	Block or strip of 4, #3528-3531	2.80	

EID

"Eid Mubarak" — A2734

Serpentine Die Cut 11¼

2001, Sept. 1

Self-Adhesive

3532 A2734 34c multicolored .70 .25

See Nos. 3674, 4117, 4202, 4351, 4416.

ENRICO FERMI (1901-54), PHYSICIST

A2735

LITHOGRAPHED

2001, Sept. 29 ***Perf. 11***

3533 A2735 34c multicolored .70 .25

THAT'S ALL FOLKS!

Porky Pig at Mailbox — A2736

PHOTOGRAVURE

2001, Oct. 1 ***Serpentine Die Cut 11***

Self-Adhesive

3534	Pane of 10	7.00	
a.	A2736 34c single	.70	.25
b.	Pane of 9 #3534a	6.25	
c.	Pane of 1 #3534a	.70	

Die cutting on No. 3534b does not extend through the backing paper.

3535	Pane of 10	60.00	
a.	A2736 34c single	3.00	
b.	Pane of 9 #3535a	27.50	
c.	Pane of 1, no die cutting	30.00	

Die cutting on No. 3535a extends through backing paper.

Nos. 3534b-3534c and 3535b-3535c are separated by a vertical line of microperforations.

CHRISTMAS

Virgin and Child, by Lorenzo Costa — A2737

A2738 A2739

A2740 A2741

19th Century Chromolithographs of Santa Claus

Serpentine Die Cut 11½ on 2, 3 or 4 Sides

2001, Oct. 10

Self-Adhesive

Booklet Stamps (#3536, 3537a-3540a, 3537b, 3538b, 3539b, 3540e, 3541-3544)

3536	A2737 34c multicolored	.75	.25
a.	Booklet pane of 20	15.00	

Serpentine Die Cut 10¾x11

Black Inscriptions

3537	A2738 34c multicolored, large date	.70	.25
a.	Small date (from booklet pane)	.90	.25
b.	Large date (from booklet pane)	2.00	.25
3538	A2739 34c multicolored, large date	.70	.25
a.	Small date (from booklet pane)	.90	.25
b.	Large date (from booklet pane)	2.00	.25
3539	A2740 34c multicolored, large date	.70	.25
a.	Small date (from booklet pane)	.90	.25
b.	Large date (from booklet pane)	2.00	.25
3540	A2741 34c multicolored, large date	.70	.25
a.	Small date (from booklet pane)	.90	.25
b.	Block of 4, #3537-3540	2.80	
c.	Block of 4, small date, #3537a-3540a	3.60	
d.	Booklet pane of 20, 5 #3540c + label	18.00	
e.	Large date (from booklet pane)	2.00	.25
f.	Block of 4, large date, #3537b-3539b, 3540e	8.00	
g.	Booklet pane of 20, 5 #3540f + label	40.00	

Nos. 3540d and 3540g are double-sided booklet panes, with 12 stamps on one side and eight stamps plus label on the other side.

Numerals "3" and "4" are distinctly separate on Nos. 3537-3540, and touching or separated by a slight hairline on the booklet pane stamps.

Designs of booklet stamps Nos. 3537a-3539a and 3537b-3539b are slightly taller than Nos. 3537-3539. Nos. 3540a and 3540e measure the same as No. 3540.

Serpentine Die Cut 11 on 2 or 3 Sides

Size: 21x18½mm

Green and Red Inscriptions

3541	A2738 34c multicolored	1.10	.25
3542	A2739 34c multicolored	1.10	.25
3543	A2740 34c multicolored	1.10	.25
3544	A2741 34c multicolored	1.10	.25
a.	Block of 4, #3541-3544	4.40	
b.	Booklet pane of 4, #3541-3544	4.40	
c.	Booklet pane of 6, #3543-3544, 2 #3541-3542	6.60	
d.	Booklet pane of 6, #3541-3542, 2 #3543-3544	6.60	
	Nos. 3536-3544 (9)	7.95	2.25

JAMES MADISON (1751-1836)

Madison and His Home, Montpelier A2742

LITHOGRAPHED & ENGRAVED

2001, Oct. 18 ***Perf. 11x11¼***

3545 A2742 34c green & black .70 .25

THANKSGIVING

Cornucopia
A2743

LITHOGRAPHED
Serpentine Die Cut 11¼

2001, Oct. 19

Self-Adhesive

3546 A2743 34c multicolored .70 .25

Hanukkah Type of 1996
PHOTOGRAVURE

2001, Oct. 21 ***Serpentine Die Cut 11***

Self-Adhesive

3547 A2411 34c multicolored .70 .25

Kwanzaa Type of 1997

2001, Oct. 21

Self-Adhesive

3548 A2458 34c multicolored .70 .25

UNITED WE STAND

A2744

LITHOGRAPHED
BOOKLET STAMPS
Serpentine Die Cut 11¼ on 2, 3, or 4 Sides

2001, Oct. 24

Self-Adhesive

3549 A2744 34c multicolored .75 .25
a. Booklet pane of 20 15.00

PHOTOGRAVURE
Serpentine Die Cut 10½x10¾ on 2 or 3 Sides

2002, Jan.

Self-Adhesive

3549B A2744 34c multicolored 1.00 .25
c. Booklet pane of 4 4.00
d. Booklet pane of 6 6.00
e. Booklet pane of 20 20.00

No. 3549Be is a double-sided booklet pane, with 12 stamps on one side and eight stamps plus label on the other side.

"First day covers" of No. 3549B are dated Oct. 24, 2001.

COIL STAMPS

Serpentine Die Cut 9¾ Vert.

2001, Oct. 24

Self-Adhesive

3550 A2744 34c multicolored 1.25 .25
3550A A2744 34c multicolored 1.25 .25

No. 3550 has right angle corners and backing paper as high as the stamp. No. 3550A has rounded corners, the backing paper larger than the stamp, and the stamps are spaced approximately 2mm apart.

Love Letters Type of 2001
LITHOGRAPHED
Serpentine Die Cut 11¼

2001, Nov. 19

Self-Adhesive

3551 A2701 57c multicolored 1.10 .25

WINTER OLYMPICS

Ski Jumping
A2745

Snowboarding — A2746

Ice Hockey
A2747

Figure Skating
A2748

PHOTOGRAVURE
Serpentine Die Cut 11½x10¾

2002, Jan. 8

Self-Adhesive

3552 A2745 34c multicolored .70 .30
3553 A2746 34c multicolored .70 .30
3554 A2747 34c multicolored .70 .30
3555 A2748 34c multicolored .70 .30
a. Block or strip of 4, #3552-3555 2.80
b. Die cutting inverted, pane of 20 —
c. Die cutting omitted, block of 4 *825.00*

MENTORING A CHILD

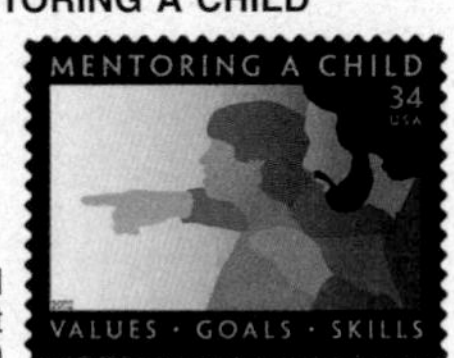

Child and Adult
A2749

Serpentine Die Cut 11x10¾

2002, Jan. 10

Self-Adhesive

3556 A2749 34c multicolored .70 .25

BLACK HERITAGE SERIES

Langston Hughes (1902-67), Writer — A2750

LITHOGRAPHED
Serpentine Die Cut 10¼x10½

2002, Feb. 1

Self-Adhesive

3557 A2750 34c multicolored .70 .25
a. Die cutting omitted, pair *850.00*

Beware of pairs/panes with extremely faint die cutting offered as imperf errors.

HAPPY BIRTHDAY

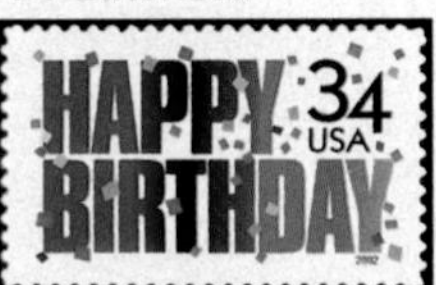

A2751

PHOTOGRAVURE

2002, Feb. 8 ***Serpentine Die Cut 11***

Self-Adhesive

3558 A2751 34c multicolored .75 .25

See Nos. 3695, 4079.

CHINESE NEW YEAR

Year of the Horse
A2752

LITHOGRAPHED
Serpentine Die Cut 10½x10¼

2002, Feb. 11

Self-Adhesive

3559 A2752 34c multicolored .75 .25
a. Horiz. pair, vert. die cutting omitted —

See No. 3895g.

U.S. MILITARY ACADEMY, BICENT.

Military Academy Coat of Arms — A2753

PHOTOGRAVURE
Serpentine Die Cut 10½x11

2002, Mar. 16

Self-Adhesive

3560 A2753 34c multicolored .75 .25

GREETINGS FROM AMERICA

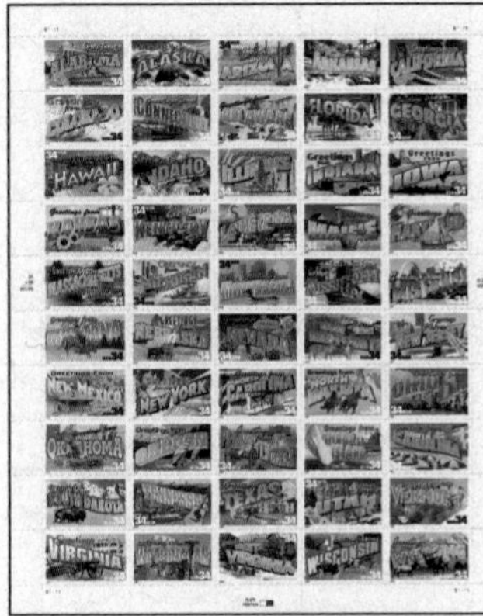

A2754-A2803

Serpentine Die Cut 10¾

2002, Apr. 4

Self-Adhesive

No.	Design	Value	Description	Unused	Used
3561	A2754	34c	Alabama	.70	.60
3562	A2755	34c	Alaska	.70	.60
3563	A2756	34c	Arizona	.70	.60
3564	A2757	34c	Arkansas	.70	.60
3565	A2758	34c	California	.70	.60
3566	A2759	34c	Colorado	.70	.60
3567	A2760	34c	Connecticut	.70	.60
3568	A2761	34c	Delaware	.70	.60
3569	A2762	34c	Florida	.70	.60
3570	A2763	34c	Georgia	.70	.60
3571	A2764	34c	Hawaii	.70	.60
3572	A2765	34c	Idaho	.70	.60
3573	A2766	34c	Illinois	.70	.60
3574	A2767	34c	Indiana	.70	.60
3575	A2768	34c	Iowa	.70	.60
3576	A2769	34c	Kansas	.70	.60
3577	A2770	34c	Kentucky	.70	.60
3578	A2771	34c	Louisiana	.70	.60
3579	A2772	34c	Maine	.70	.60
3580	A2773	34c	Maryland	.70	.60
3581	A2774	34c	Massachusetts	.70	.60
3582	A2775	34c	Michigan	.70	.60
3583	A2776	34c	Minnesota	.70	.60
3584	A2777	34c	Mississippi	.70	.60
3585	A2778	34c	Missouri	.70	.60
3586	A2779	34c	Montana	.70	.60
3587	A2780	34c	Nebraska	.70	.60
3588	A2781	34c	Nevada	.70	.60
3589	A2782	34c	New Hampshire	.70	.60
3590	A2783	34c	New Jersey	.70	.60
3591	A2784	34c	New Mexico	.70	.60
3592	A2785	34c	New York	.70	.60
3593	A2786	34c	North Carolina	.70	.60
3594	A2787	34c	North Dakota	.70	.60
3595	A2788	34c	Ohio	.70	.60
3596	A2789	34c	Oklahoma	.70	.60
3597	A2790	34c	Oregon	.70	.60
3598	A2791	34c	Pennsylvania	.70	.60
3599	A2792	34c	Rhode Island	.70	.60
3600	A2793	34c	South Carolina	.70	.60
3601	A2794	34c	South Dakota	.70	.60
3602	A2795	34c	Tennessee	.70	.60
3603	A2796	34c	Texas	.70	.60
3604	A2797	34c	Utah	.70	.60
3605	A2798	34c	Vermont	.70	.60
3606	A2799	34c	Virginia	.70	.60
3607	A2800	34c	Washington	.70	.60
3608	A2801	34c	West Virginia	.70	.60
3609	A2802	34c	Wisconsin	.70	.60
3610	A2803	34c	Wyoming	.70	.60
a.			Pane of 50, #3561-3610	35.00	

See Nos. 3696-3745.

LONGLEAF PINE FOREST

A2804

No. 3611 — Wildlife and flowers: a, Bachman's sparrow. b, Northern bobwhite, yellow pitcher plants. c, Fox squirrel, red-bellied woodpecker. d, Brown-headed nuthatch. e, Broadhead skink, yellow pitcher plants, pipeworts. f, Eastern towhee, yellow pitcher plants, Savannah meadow beauties, toothache grass. g, Gray fox, gopher tortoise, horiz. h, Blind click beetle, sweetbay, pine woods treefrog. i, Rosebud orchid, pipeworts, southern toad, yellow pitcher plants. j, Grass-pink orchid, yellow-sided skimmer, pipeworts, yellow pitcher plants, horiz.

Serpentine Die Cut 10½x10¾, 10¾x10½

2002, Apr. 26

Self-Adhesive

3611 A2804 Pane of 10 19.00
a.-j. 34c Any single 1.90 .50
k. As No. 3611, die cutting omitted *2,500.*

AMERICAN DESIGN SERIES

Toleware Coffeepot — A2805

PHOTOGRAVURE
COIL STAMP
Perf. 9¾ Vert.

2002, May 31 **Untagged**

3612 A2805 5c multicolored .25 .25
a. Imperf, pair —

No. 3612a is valued with disturbed gum. It is also known without gum and is valued only slightly less thus.

See Nos. 3756-3756A.

Star — A2806

LITHOGRAPHED, PHOTOGRAVURE
(No. 3614, 3615)
Serpentine Die Cut 11

2002, June 7 **Untagged**

Self-Adhesive (#3613-3614)

Year at Lower Left

3613 A2806 3c red, blue & black .25 .25
a. Die cutting omitted, pair —

Serpentine Die Cut 10

Year at Lower Right

Untagged

3614 A2806 3c red, blue & black .25 .25

Coil Stamp
Perf. 9¾ Vert.

Year at Lower Left

Untagged

3615 A2806 3c red, blue & black .25 .25

Washington Type of 2001
LITHOGRAPHED, PHOTOGRAVURE
(#3617)

2002, June 7 ***Perf. 11¼***

3616 A2686 23c green .50 .25

Self-Adhesive

Coil Stamp

Serpentine Die Cut 8½ Vert.

3617 A2686 23c gray green .45 .25
a. Die cutting omitted, pair —

Compare No. 3617 ("2002" date at lower left) with No. 3475A ("2001" date at lower left).

Booklet Stamps

Serpentine Die Cut 11¼x11 on 3 Sides

3618 A2686 23c green .50 .25
a. Booklet pane of 4 2.00
b. Booklet pane of 6 3.00
c. Booklet pane of 10 5.00

Serpentine Die Cut 10½x11 on 3 Sides

3619 A2686 23c green 4.50 1.75
a. Booklet pane of 4, 2 #3619 at L, 2 #3618 at R 10.00
b. Booklet pane of 6, 3 #3619 at L, 3 #3618 at R 15.00
c. Booklet pane of 4, 2 #3618 at L, 2 #3619 at R 10.00
d. Booklet pane of 6, 3 #3618 at L, 3 #3619 at R 15.00
e. Booklet pane of 10, 5 #3619 at L, 5#3618 at R 27.50
f. Booklet pane of 10, 5 #3618 at L, 5 #3619 at R 27.50
g. Pair, #3619 at L, #3618 at R 5.00
h. Pair, #3618 at L, #3619 at R 5.00
i. Nos. 3619c and 3619d, in bklt. of 10 (#BK289A), imperf. vert. btwn. on both panes —

Flag — A2807

LITHOGRAPHED, PHOTOGRAVURE (#3622, 3624, 3625)

2002, June 7 ***Perf. 11¼x11***

3620 A2807 (37c) multicolored .85 .25

Self-Adhesive

Serpentine Die Cut 11¼x11

3621 A2807 (37c) multicolored 1.00 .25

Coil Stamp

Serpentine Die Cut 10 Vert.

3622 A2807 (37c) multicolored .75 .25
a. Die cutting omitted, pair —

Booklet Stamps

Serpentine Die Cut 11¼ on 2, 3 or 4 Sides

3623 A2807 (37c) multicolored .75 .25
a. Booklet pane of 20 15.00

Serpentine Die Cut 10½x10¾ on 2 or 3 Sides

3624 A2807 (37c) multicolored .75 .25
a. Booklet pane of 4 3.00
b. Booklet pane of 6 4.50
c. Booklet pane of 20 15.00

Serpentine Die Cut 8 on 2, 3 or 4 Sides

3625 A2807 (37c) multicolored .75 .25
a. Booklet pane of 18 13.50

Toy Mail Wagon A2808

Toy Locomotive A2809

Toy Taxicab A2810

Toy Fire Pumper A2811

PHOTOGRAVURE

Serpentine Die Cut 11 on 2, 3 or 4 Sides

2002, June 7

Booklet Stamps

Self-Adhesive

3626 A2808 (37c) multicolored .75 .25
3627 A2809 (37c) multicolored .75 .25
3628 A2810 (37c) multicolored .75 .25
3629 A2811 (37c) multicolored .75 .25
a. Block of 4, #3626-3629 3.00
b. Booklet pane of 4, #3626-3629 3.00
c. Booklet pane of 6, #3627, 3629, 2 each #3626, 3628 4.50
d. Booklet pane of 6, #3626, 3628, 2 each #3627, 3629 4.50
e. Booklet pane of 20, 5 each #3626-3629 15.00

Flag — A2812

LITHOGRAPHED, PHOTOGRAVURE (#3631-3633, 3634, 3636, 3636D)

2002-05 ***Perf. 11¼***

3629F A2812 37c multi .90 .25
g. Imperf, pair *250.00*

No. 3629F has microprinted "USA" in top red stripe of flag.

Serpentine Die Cut 11¼x11

Self-Adhesive (#3630, 3632-3637)

3630 A2812 37c multi .90 .25

No. 3630 has microprinted "USA" in top red stripe of flag.

COIL STAMPS

Perf. 9¾ Vert.

3631 A2812 37c multi .75 .25

Serpentine Die Cut 9¾ Vert.

3632 A2812 37c multi .75 .25
b. Die cutting omitted, pair 50.00 50.00

Serpentine Die Cut 10¼ Vert.

3632A A2812 37c multi .75 .25
f. Die cutting omitted, pair —

No. 3632A lacks points of stars at margin at left top, and was printed in "logs" of adjacent coil rolls that are connected at the top or bottom, wherein each roll could be separated from an adjacent roll as needed.

No. 3632 has "2002" date at left bottom. No. 3632A has "2003" date at left bottom.

Serpentine Die Cut 11¾ Vert.

3632C A2812 37c multi .75 .25

No. 3632C is the only 37c Flag coil stamp with a "2004" date at left bottom.

Serpentine Die Cut 8½ Vert.

3633 A2812 37c multi .75 .25
3633A A2812 37c multi 2.25 .25

No. 3633A has right angle corners and backing paper as high as the stamp, and is dated "2003." No. 3633 is dated "2002," has rounded corners, the backing paper larger than the stamp, and the stamps are spaced approximately 2mm apart.

Serpentine Die Cut 9½ Vert.

3633B A2812 37c multi 5.50 .25

No. 3633B has microprinted "USA" in top red stripe of flag, and has "2005" date at bottom left.

Booklet Stamps

Serpentine Die Cut 11.1 on 3 Sides (#3634)

3634 A2812 37c multi, large "2002" year date .75 .25
a. Booklet pane of 10 7.50
b. Small "2003" date, die cut 11 .75 .25
c. Booklet pane, 4 #3634b 3.00
d. Booklet pane, 6 #3634b 4.50
e. As #3634, die cut 11.3 .85 .25
f. As "e," booklet pane of 10 8.50

Serpentine Die Cut 11.3 on 2, 3 or 4 Sides

3635 A2812 37c multi .75 .25
a. Booklet pane of 20 15.00
b. Black omitted *3,000.*

No. 3635 has "USPS" microprinted in the top red flag stripe and has a small "2002" year date.

Serpentine Die Cut 10½x10¾ on 2 or 3 Sides

3636 A2812 37c multi .75 .25
a. Booklet pane of 4 3.00
b. Booklet pane of 6 4.50
c. Booklet pane of 20 15.00
f. As "c," 11 stamps and part of 12th stamp on reverse printed on backing liner, the 8 stamps on front side die cutting omitted —

No. 3636c is a double-sided booklet pane, with 12 stamps on one side and eight stamps plus label on the other side.

Serpentine Die Cut 11¼x11 on 2 or 3 Sides

3636D A2812 37c multi 1.25 .25
e. Booklet pane of 20 25.00

No. 3636D lacks points of stars at margin at UL. No. 3636D is the only 37c Flag booklet stamp with a "2004" date at left bottom. No. 3636De is a double-sided booklet pane with 12 stamps on one side and eight stamps plus label on the other side.

Serpentine Die Cut 8 on 2, 3 or 4 Sides

3637 A2812 37c multi .75 .25
a. Booklet pane of 18 13.50

Issued: Nos. 3630-3632, 3633, 3634, 3635-3636, 6/7; No. 3637, 2/4/03; No. 3633A, Apr. 2003; No. 3632A, 8/7/03; No. 3634b, 10/23/03; No. 3629F, 11/24/03; No. 3636D, July 2004; No. 3632C, 2004; No. 3633B, 6/7/05.

Toy Locomotive A2813

Toy Mail Wagon A2814

Toy Fire Pumper A2815

Toy Taxicab A2816

PHOTOGRAVURE

Serpentine Die Cut 8½ Horiz.

2002-03

Self-Adhesive

Coil Stamps

3638 A2813 37c multi 1.00 .25
3639 A2814 37c multi 1.00 .25
3640 A2815 37c multi 1.00 .25
3641 A2816 37c multi 1.00 .25
a. Strip of 4, #3638-3641 4.00

Serpentine Die Cut 11 on 2, 3 or 4 Sides

Booklet Stamps

3642 A2814 37c multi, "2002" year date .75 .25
a. Serpentine die cut 11x11¼ on 2 or 3 sides, dated "2003" .75 .25
3643 A2813 37c multi, "2002" year date .75 .25
a. Serpentine die cut 11x11¼ on 2 or 3 sides, dated "2003" .75 .25
3644 A2816 37c multi, "2002" year date .75 .25
a. Serpentine die cut 11x11¼ on 2 or 3 sides, dated "2003" .75 .25
3645 A2815 37c multi, "2002" year date .75 .25
a. Block of 4, #3642-3645 3.00
b. Booklet pane of 4, #3642-3645 3.00
c. Booklet pane of 6, #3643, 3645, 2 each #3642, 3644 4.50
d. Booklet pane of 6, #3642, 3644, 2 each #3643, 3645 4.50
e. Booklet pane of 20, 5 each #3642-3645 15.00
f. Serpentine die cut 11x11¼ on 2 or 3 sides, dated "2003" .75 .25
g. Block of 4, #3642a, 3643a, 3644a, 3645f 3.00
h. Booklet pane of 20, 5 #3645g 15.00

No. 3645h is a double-sided booklet with 12 stamps on one side and 8 stamps plus label (booklet cover) on the other side. Nos. 3642a, 3643a, 3644a and 3645f have slightly narrower designs than Nos. 3642-3645.

Issued: Nos. 3638-3645, 7/26; Nos. 3642a, 3643a, 3644a, 3645f, 9/3/03.

Coverlet Eagle — A2817

LITHOGRAPHED

Serpentine Die Cut 11x11¼

2002, July 12

Self-Adhesive

3646 A2817 60c multicolored 1.25 .25

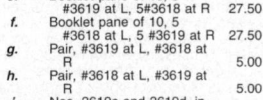

Jefferson Memorial A2818

Capitol Dome — A2819

Serpentine Die Cut 11¼ (#3647, 3648), 11x10¾ (#3647A)

2002-03 **Tagged**

Self-Adhesive

3647 A2818 $3.85 multi 7.50 2.00
3647A A2818 $3.85 multi 8.50 2.00
3648 A2819 $13.65 multi 27.50 10.00

No. 3647A is dated 2003.

MASTERS OF AMERICAN PHOTOGRAPHY

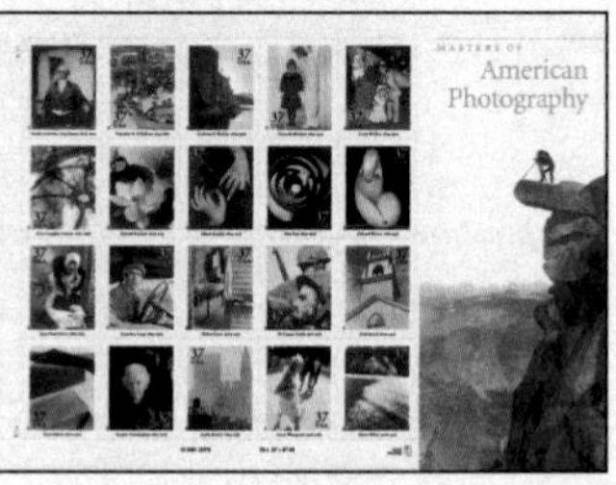

A2820

No. 3649: a, Portrait of Daniel Webster, by Albert Sands Southworth and Josiah Johnson Hawes. b, Gen. Ulysses S. Grant and Officers, by Timothy H. O'Sullivan. c, "Cape Horn, Columbia River," by Carleton E. Watkins. d, "Blessed Art Thou Among Women," by Gertrude Käsebier. e, "Looking for Lost Luggage, Ellis Island," by Lewis W. Hine. f, "The Octopus," by Alvin Langdon Coburn. g, "Lotus, Mount Kisco, New York," by Edward Steichen. h, "Hands and Thimble," by Alfred Stieglitz. i, "Rayograph," by Man Ray. j, "Two Shells," by Edward Weston. k, "My Corsage," by James VanDerZee. l, "Ditched, Stalled, and Stranded, San Joaquin Valley, California," by Dorothea Lange. m, "Washroom and Dining Area of Floyd Burroughs' Home, Hale County, Alabama," by Walker Evans. n, "Frontline Soldier with Canteen, Saipan," by W. Eugene Smith. o, "Steeple," by Paul Strand. p, "Sand Dunes, Sunrise," by Ansel Adams. q, "Age and Its Symbols," by Imogen Cunningham. r, New York cityscape, by André Kertész. s, Photograph of pedestrians, by Garry Winogrand. t, "Bristol, Vermont," by Minor White.

PHOTOGRAVURE

Serpentine Die Cut 10½x10¾

2002, June 13

Self-Adhesive

3649 A2820 Pane of 20 15.00
a.-t. 37c Any single .75 .50
u. As No. 3649, die cutting omitted —

AMERICAN TREASURES SERIES

Scarlet and Louisiana Tanagers, by John James Audubon — A2821

Serpentine Die Cut 10¾

2002, June 27

Self-Adhesive

3650 A2821 37c multicolored 1.00 .25

HARRY HOUDINI (1874-1926), MAGICIAN

A2822

LITHOGRAPHED

Serpentine Die Cut 11¼

2002, July 3

Self-Adhesive

3651	A2822 37c multicolored		.75	.25

ANDY WARHOL (1928-87), ARTIST

Self-Portrait A2823

PHOTOGRAVURE

Serpentine Die Cut 10½x10¾

2002, Aug. 9

Self-Adhesive

3652	A2823 37c multicolored		.75	.25

TEDDY BEARS, CENTENNIAL

Bruin Bear, c. 1907 — A2824

"Stick" Bear, 1920s — A2825

Gund Bear, c. 1948 — A2826

Ideal Bear, c. 1905 — A2827

Serpentine Die Cut 10½

2002, Aug. 15

Self-Adhesive

3653 A2824 37c multicolored		1.00	.30
3654 A2825 37c multicolored		1.00	.30
3655 A2826 37c multicolored		1.00	.30
3656 A2827 37c multicolored		1.00	.30
a. Block or vert. strip of 4, #3653-3656		4.00	

LOVE

A2828 A2829

LITHOGRAPHED (#3657), PHOTOGRAVURE

Serpentine Die Cut 11 on 2, 3 or 4 Sides

2002, Aug. 16

Booklet Stamp (#3657)

Self-Adhesive

3657 A2828 37c multicolored		.75	.25
a. Booklet pane of 20		15.00	
b. As "a," silver ("Love 37 USA") missing on top five stamps (CM)		*750.00*	

Serpentine Die Cut 11

3658 A2829 60c multicolored		1.25	.25

Beware of examples of No. 3658 with gold ink fraudulently removed.

LITERARY ARTS

Ogden Nash (1902-71), Poet A2830

PHOTOGRAVURE

Serpentine Die Cut 11

2002, Aug. 19

Self-Adhesive

3659 A2830 37c multicolored		.75	.25

DUKE KAHANAMOKU (1890-1968), "FATHER OF SURFING" AND OLYMPIC SWIMMER

Kahanamoku and Surfers at Waikiki Beach — A2831

PHOTOGRAVURE

Serpentine Die Cut 11½x11¾

2002, Aug. 24

Self-Adhesive

3660 A2831 37c multicolored		.75	.25

AMERICAN BATS

Red Bat A2832

Leaf-nosed Bat A2833

Pallid Bat A2834

Spotted Bat A2835

Serpentine Die Cut 10¾

2002, Sept. 13

Self-Adhesive

3661 A2832 37c multicolored		.75	.30
3662 A2833 37c multicolored		.75	.30
3663 A2834 37c multicolored		.75	.30
3664 A2835 37c multicolored		.75	.30
a. Block or horiz. strip of 4, #3661-3664		3.00	

WOMEN IN JOURNALISM

Nellie Bly (1864-1922) — A2836

Ida M. Tarbell (1857-1944) — A2837

Ethel L. Payne (1911-91) A2838

Marguerite Higgins (1920-66) A2839

Serpentine Die Cut 11x10½

2002, Sept. 14

Self-Adhesive

3665 A2836 37c multicolored		1.00	.30
3666 A2837 37c multicolored		1.00	.30
3667 A2838 37c multicolored		1.00	.30
3668 A2839 37c multicolored		1.00	.30
a. Block or horiz. strip of 4, #3665-3668		4.00	

IRVING BERLIN (1888-1989), COMPOSER

Berlin and Score of "God Bless America" — A2840

Serpentine Die Cut 11

2002, Sept. 15

Self-Adhesive

3669 A2840 37c multicolored		.75	.25

NEUTER AND SPAY

Kitten A2841

Puppy A2842

Serpentine Die Cut 10¾x10½

2002, Sept. 20

Self-Adhesive

3670 A2841 37c multicolored		1.00	.25
3671 A2842 37c multicolored		1.00	.25
a. Horiz. or vert. pair, #3670-3671		2.00	

Hanukkah Type of 1996

2002, Oct. 10 ***Serpentine Die Cut 11***

Self-Adhesive

3672 A2411 37c multicolored		.75	.25

Kwanzaa Type of 1997

2002, Oct. 10 ***Serpentine Die Cut 11***

Self-Adhesive

3673 A2458 37c multicolored		.75	.25

Eid Type of 2001

2002, Oct. 10 ***Serpentine Die Cut 11***

Self-Adhesive

3674 A2734 37c multicolored		.75	.25

CHRISTMAS

Madonna and Child, by Jan Gossaert — A2843

LITHOGRAPHED

Serpentine Die Cut 11x11¼ on 2, 3 or 4 Sides

2002, Oct. 10

Self-Adhesive

Booklet Stamp

Design size: 19x27mm

3675 A2843 37c multicolored		.75	.25
a. Booklet pane of 20		15.00	

Compare to No. 3820, which measures 19½x28mm

CHRISTMAS

Snowman with Red and Green Plaid Scarf — A2844

Snowman with Blue Plaid Scarf — A2845

Snowman with Pipe — A2846

Snowman with Top Hat — A2847

Snowman with Blue Plaid Scarf — A2848

Snowman with Pipe — A2849

Snowman with Top Hat — A2850

Snowman with Red and Green Plaid Scarf — A2851

PHOTOGRAVURE

Serpentine Die Cut 11

2002, Oct. 28 **Tagged**

Self-Adhesive

3676 A2844 37c multicolored .90 .25
3677 A2845 37c multicolored .90 .25
3678 A2846 37c multicolored .90 .25
3679 A2847 37c multicolored .90 .25
a. Block or vert. strip of 4, #3676-3679 3.75

COIL STAMPS

Serpentine Die Cut 8½ Vert.

3680 A2848 37c multicolored 3.25 .25
3681 A2849 37c multicolored 3.25 .25
3682 A2850 37c multicolored 3.25 .25
3683 A2851 37c multicolored 3.25 .25
a. Strip of 4, #3680-3683 13.00

BOOKLET STAMPS

Serpentine Die Cut 10¾x11 on 2 or 3 Sides

3684 A2844 37c multicolored 1.25 .25
3685 A2845 37c multicolored 1.25 .25
3686 A2846 37c multicolored 1.25 .25
3687 A2847 37c multicolored 1.25 .25
a. Block of 4, #3684-3687 5.00
b. Booklet pane of 20, 5 #3687a + label 25.00

No. 3687b is a double-sided booklet pane with 12 stamps on one side and eight stamps plus label on the other side.

Colors of Nos. 3684-3687 are deeper and designs are slightly smaller than those found on Nos. 3676-3679.

Serpentine Die Cut 11 on 2 or 3 Sides

3688 A2851 37c multicolored 1.25 .25
3689 A2848 37c multicolored 1.25 .25
3690 A2849 37c multicolored 1.25 .25
3691 A2850 37c multicolored 1.25 .25
a. Block of 4, #3688-3691 5.00
b. Booklet pane of 4, #3688-3691 5.00
c. Booklet pane of 6, #3690-3691, 2 each #3688-3689 7.50
d. Booklet pane of 6, #3688-3689, 2 each #3690-3691 7.50
Nos. 3676-3691 (16) 26.60 4.00

LEGENDS OF HOLLYWOOD

Cary Grant (1904-86), Actor — A2852

Serpentine Die Cut 10¾

2002, Oct. 15

Self-Adhesive

3692 A2852 37c multicolored 1.25 .25

Sea Coast — A2853

PHOTOGRAVURE
COIL STAMP

Serpentine Die Cut 8½ Vert.

2002, Oct. 21

Self-Adhesive

3693 A2853 (5c) multicolored .25 .25

See Nos. 3775, 3785, 3864, 3874, 3875.

HAWAIIAN MISSIONARY STAMPS

A2854

No. 3694: a, 2c stamp of 1851 (Hawaii Scott 1). b, 5c stamp of 1851 (Hawaii Scott 2) c, 13c stamp of 1851 (Hawaii Scott 3). d, 13c stamp of 1852 (Hawaii Scott 4).

LITHOGRAPHED

2002, Oct. 24 **Tagged** ***Perf. 11***

3694 A2854 Pane of 4 5.00 2.50
a.-d. 37c Any single 1.25 .50

Happy Birthday Type of 2002

PHOTOGRAVURE

2002, Oct. 25 ***Serpentine Die Cut 11***

Self-Adhesive

3695 A2751 37c multicolored .75 .25

Greetings From America Type of 2002

Serpentine Die Cut 10¾

2002, Oct. 25

Self-Adhesive

No.	Type	Value	Design	Unused	Used
3696	A2754	37c	Alabama	.75	.60
3697	A2755	37c	Alaska	.75	.60
3698	A2756	37c	Arizona	.75	.60
3699	A2757	37c	Arkansas	.75	.60
3700	A2758	37c	California	.75	.60
3701	A2759	37c	Colorado	.75	.60
3702	A2760	37c	Connecticut	.75	.60
3703	A2761	37c	Delaware	.75	.60
3704	A2762	37c	Florida	.75	.60
3705	A2763	37c	Georgia	.75	.60
3706	A2764	37c	Hawaii	.75	.60
3707	A2765	37c	Idaho	.75	.60
3708	A2766	37c	Illinois	.75	.60
3709	A2767	37c	Indiana	.75	.60
3710	A2768	37c	Iowa	.75	.60
3711	A2769	37c	Kansas	.75	.60
3712	A2770	37c	Kentucky	.75	.60
3713	A2771	37c	Louisiana	.75	.60
3714	A2772	37c	Maine	.75	.60
3715	A2773	37c	Maryland	.75	.60
3716	A2774	37c	Massachusetts	.75	.60
3717	A2775	37c	Michigan	.75	.60
3718	A2776	37c	Minnesota	.75	.60
3719	A2777	37c	Mississippi	.75	.60
3720	A2778	37c	Missouri	.75	.60
3721	A2779	37c	Montana	.75	.60
3722	A2780	37c	Nebraska	.75	.60
3723	A2781	37c	Nevada	.75	.60
3724	A2782	37c	New Hampshire	.75	.60
3725	A2783	37c	New Jersey	.75	.60
3726	A2784	37c	New Mexico	.75	.60
3727	A2785	37c	New York	.75	.60
3728	A2786	37c	North Carolina	.75	.60
3729	A2787	37c	North Dakota	.75	.60
3730	A2788	37c	Ohio	.75	.60
3731	A2789	37c	Oklahoma	.75	.60
3732	A2790	37c	Oregon	.75	.60
3733	A2791	37c	Pennsylvania	.75	.60
3734	A2792	37c	Rhode Island	.75	.60
3735	A2793	37c	South Carolina	.75	.60
3736	A2794	37c	South Dakota	.75	.60
3737	A2795	37c	Tennessee	.75	.60
3738	A2796	37c	Texas	.75	.60
3739	A2797	37c	Utah	.75	.60
3740	A2798	37c	Vermont	.75	.60
3741	A2799	37c	Virginia	.75	.60
3742	A2800	37c	Washington	.75	.60
3743	A2801	37c	West Virginia	.75	.60
3744	A2802	37c	Wisconsin	.75	.60
3745	A2803	37c	Wyoming	.75	.60
a.			Pane of 50, #3696-3745	37.50	

BLACK HERITAGE SERIES

Thurgood Marshall (1908-93), Supreme Court Justice — A2855

LITHOGRAPHED

Serpentine Die Cut 11½

2003, Jan. 7

Self-Adhesive

3746 A2855 37c black & gray .75 .25

CHINESE NEW YEAR

Year of the Ram A2856

Serpentine Die Cut 11½

2003, Jan. 15

Self-Adhesive

3747 A2856 37c multicolored .75 .25

See No. 3895h.

LITERARY ARTS

Zora Neale Hurston (1891-1960), Writer — A2857

PHOTOGRAVURE

Serpentine Die Cut 10¾

2003, Jan. 24

Self-Adhesive

3748 A2857 37c multicolored .85 .25

AMERICAN DESIGN SERIES

Toleware Coffeepot Type of 2002 and

Navajo Necklace A2858

Chippendale Chair A2859

American Clock A2860

Tiffany Lamp A2866

Silver Coffeepot — A2868

LITHOGRAPHED, PHOTOGRAVURE (#3750, 3751, 3756, 3758, 3758A, 3758B, 3759, 3761, 3761A, 3762)

Self-Adhesive (#3749-3757)

2003-11 ***Serpentine Die Cut 11¼x11***

Untagged (#3749-3756A, 3758-3762, 3763a)

3749 A2866 1c multi .25 .25
3749A A2866 1c multi .25 .25

No. 3749A has "USPS" microprinted on a white field high on the lamp stand, just below the shade and is dated "2008." No. 3749 has "USPS" microprinted lower on the lamp stand and not on a white field and is dated "2007."

Serpentine Die Cut 11

3750 A2858 2c multi .25 .25

A reprinting of No. 3750 shows the borders in a much brighter deep turquoise blue shade.

Serpentine Die Cut 11¼x11½

3751 A2858 2c multi .30 .25

Serpentine Die Cut 11¼x11

With "USPS" Microprinting

3752 A2858 2c multi .25 .25

Serpentine Die Cut 11¼x10¾

3753 A2858 2c multi .25 .25

Serpentine Die Cut 11¼x11

3754 A2868 3c multi .25 .25

Microprinted "USPS" on No. 3752 is found on top silver appendage next to and below the middle turquoise stone on the right side of the necklace. Microprinting on No. 3753 is found on the top silver appendage next to and below the lower turquoise stone on the left side of the necklace. Nos. 3751 and 3752 are dated "2006." No. 3753 is dated "2007."

Serpentine Die Cut 10¾x10¼

3755 A2859 4c multi .25 .25

Serpentine Die Cut 11¼x11¾

3756 A2805 5c multi .25 .25

Serpentine Die Cut 11¼x10¾

3756A A2805 5c multi .25 .25

No. 3756A has microprinting on the lower part of the coffeepot handle and is dated "2007." No. 3756 has no microprinting and is dated "2004." Existence of No. 3756A was reported in Aug. 2008.

No. 3756A is known printed with non-reactive cream-colored background ink and also with luminescent cream-colored ink that glows orange under both shortwave and longwave ultraviolet light.

3757 A2860 10c multi .25 .25
a. Die cutting omitted, pair —

COIL STAMPS

Perf. 9¾ Vert.

3758 A2866 1c multi .25 .25
3758A A2866 1c multi .25 .25
3758B A2858 2c multi .25 .25

No. 3758A has microprinted "USPS" on lamp stand just below the lampshade and is dated "2008." No. 3758 lacks microprinting and is dated "2003."

3759 A2868 3c multi .25 .25
3761 A2859 4c multi, dated "2007" at LL .25 .25
3761A A2859 4c multi, dated "2013" at UL .25 .25

No. 3761 is dated "2007" at lower left. On plate number singles, the plate number is at the lower right on No. 3761 and centered at bottom on No. 3761A.

3762 A2860 10c multi .25 .25
3763 A2860 10c multi .25 .25

Nos. 3763 and 3763a are dated "2008," have a microprinted "USPS" as the middle "I" in "VIII," and have network of beige dots on clock face. No. 3762 is dated "2006," lacks microprinting, and has network of gray dots on clock face.

Issued: No. 3757, 1/24; No. 3758, 3/1; No. 3755, 3/5/04; No. 3756, 6/25/04; No. 3750, 8/20/04; No. 3759, 9/16/05; Nos. 3751-3752, 12/8/05; No. 3762, 8/4/06; Nos. 3749, 3754, 3/16/07; No. 3753, 5/12/07; No. 3761, 7/19/07; No. 3749A, 3/7/08; No. 3758A, 6/7/08; No. 3758B, 2/12/11; No. 3763, 7/15/08; No. 3756A, Aug. 2008.

This is an ongoing set. Numbers may change.

See No. 3612.

AMERICAN CULTURE SERIES

Wisdom, Rockefeller Center, New York City — A2875

LITHOGRAPHED

Serpentine Die Cut 11¼x11

2003, Feb. 28

Self-Adhesive

3766 A2875 $1 multicolored 2.00 .40
a. Dated "2008" 2.00 .40

New York Public Library Lion Type of 2000

PHOTOGRAVURE

COIL STAMP

Perf. 9¾ Vert.

2003, Feb. 4 **Untagged**

3769 A2677 (10c) multicolored .25 .25

Atlas Statue Type of 2001

PHOTOGRAVURE

Serpentine Die Cut 11 Vert.

2003, Oct. **Untagged**

Coil Stamp

Self-Adhesive

3770 A2722 (10c) multicolored .25 .25

No. 3770 is dated 2003.

SPECIAL OLYMPICS

Athlete with Medal — A2879

Serpentine Die Cut 11

2003, Feb. 13

Self-Adhesive

3771 A2879 80c multicolored 1.60 .35

AMERICAN FILMMAKING: BEHIND THE SCENES

A2880

No. 3772: a, Screenwriting (segment of script from *Gone With the Wind*). b, Directing (John Cassavetes). c, Costume design (Edith Head). d, Music (Max Steiner working on score). e, Makeup (Jack Pierce working on Boris Karloff's makeup for *Frankenstein*). f, Art direction (Perry Ferguson working on sketch for *Citizen Kane*). g, Cinematography (Paul Hill, assistant cameraman for *Nagana*). h, Film editing (J. Watson Webb editing *The Razor's Edge*). i, Special effects (Mark Siegel working on model for *E.T. The Extra-Terrestrial*). j, Sound (Gary Summers works on control panel).

Serpentine Die Cut 11 Horiz.

2003, Feb. 25

Self-Adhesive

3772 A2880 Pane of 10 12.00

a.-j. 37c Any single 1.20 .50

OHIO STATEHOOD BICENTENNIAL

Aerial View of Farm Near Marietta — A2881

LITHOGRAPHED

Serpentine Die Cut 11¾x11½

2003, Mar. 1

Self-Adhesive

3773 A2881 37c multicolored .75 .25

PELICAN ISLAND NATIONAL WILDLIFE REFUGE, CENT.

Brown Pelican — A2882

Serpentine Die Cut 12x11½

2003, Mar. 14

Self-Adhesive

3774 A2882 37c multicolored .75 .25

Sea Coast Type of 2002

PHOTOGRAVURE

COIL STAMP

Perf. 9¾ Vert.

2003, Mar. 19 **Untagged**

3775 A2853 (5c) multicolored .25 .25

See No. 3864. No. 3775 has "2003" year date in blue, dots that run together in surf area, and a distinct small orange cloud. No. 3864 has "2004" year date in black, rows of distinctly separated dots in surf area, and the small orange cloud is indistinct.

OLD GLORY

Uncle Sam on Bicycle with Liberty Flag, 20th Cent. — A2883

1888 Presidential Campaign Badge — A2884

1893 Silk Bookmark A2885

Modern Hand Fan A2886

Carving of Woman with Flag and Sword, 19th Cent. — A2887

LITHOGRAPHED

BOOKLET STAMPS

Serpentine Die Cut 10x9¾

2003, Apr. 3

Self-Adhesive

3776 A2883 37c multicolored .75 .50

3777 A2884 37c multicolored .75 .50

3778 A2885 37c multicolored .75 .50

3779 A2886 37c multicolored .75 .50

3780 A2887 37c multicolored .75 .50

a. Horiz. strip of 5, #3776-3780 3.75

b. Booklet pane, 2 #3780a 7.50

No. 3780b was issued with two types of backing.

CESAR E. CHAVEZ (1927-93), LABOR ORGANIZER

A2888

Serpentine Die Cut 11¾x11½

2003, Apr. 23

Self-Adhesive

3781 A2888 37c multicolored .75 .25

LOUISIANA PURCHASE, BICENTENNIAL

English Translation of Treaty, Map of U.S., Treaty Signers — A2889

PHOTOGRAVURE

Serpentine Die Cut 10¾

2003, Apr. 30

Self-Adhesive

3782 A2889 37c multicolored .95 .40

FIRST FLIGHT OF WRIGHT BROTHERS, CENT.

Orville Wright Piloting 1903 Wright Flyer A2890

2003, May 22 ***Serpentine Die Cut 11***

Self-Adhesive

3783 Pane of 10 9.00

a. A2890 37c single .90 .40

b. Pane of 9 #3783a 8.00

c. Pane of 1 #3783a .90

PURPLE HEART

A2891

LITHOGRAPHED

2003 ***Serpentine Die Cut 11¼x10¾***

Self-Adhesive

3784 A2891 37c multi .75 .25

b. Printed on back of backing paper —

d. Die cutting omitted, pair —

Serpentine Die Cut 10¾x10¼

3784A A2891 37c multi .75 .25

e. Die cutting omitted, pair 150.00

f. Die cutting omitted, pane of 20 *1,600.*

See Nos. 4032, 4164, 4263-4264, 4390.

Sea Coast Type of 2002

COIL STAMP

PHOTOGRAVURE

Serpentine Die Cut 9½x10

2003, June **Untagged**

Self-Adhesive

3785 A2853 (5c) multicolored .25 .25

a. Serp. die cut 9¼x10 .25 .25

On No. 3785, the stamps are spaced on backing paper that is taller than the stamps.

One printing of No. 3785 has more of a scarlet shade in the sky than do other examples of Nos. 3785 and 3785a. Nos. 3785 and 3785a have black "2003" year date.

LEGENDS OF HOLLYWOOD

Audrey Hepburn (1929-93), Actress — A2892

Serpentine Die Cut 10¾

2003, June 11

Self-Adhesive

3786 A2892 37c multicolored 1.25 1.00

SOUTHEASTERN LIGHTHOUSES

Old Cape Henry, Virginia A2893

Cape Lookout, North Carolina A2894

Morris Island, South Carolina A2895

Tybee Island, Georgia A2896

Hillsboro Inlet, Florida — A2897

Serpentine Die Cut 10¾

2003, June 13

Self-Adhesive

3787 A2893 37c multicolored 1.10 .30

3788 A2894 37c multicolored 1.10 .30

a. Bottom of "USA" even with top of upper half-diamond of lighthouse (pos. 2) 4.00 2.50

3789 A2895 37c multicolored 1.10 .30

3790 A2896 37c multicolored 1.10 .30

3791 A2897 37c multicolored 1.10 .30

a. Strip of 5, #3787-3791 5.50

b. Strip of 5, #3787, 3788a, 3789-3791 9.50

Eagle in Gold on Colored Background A2898

Colored Eagle on Gold Background A2899

COIL STAMPS

Dated "2003"

Serpentine Die Cut 11¾ Vert.

2003, June 26 **Untagged**

Self-Adhesive

3792 A2898 (25c) gray & gold .50 .25

3793 A2899 (25c) gold & red .50 .25

3794 A2898 (25c) dull blue & gold .50 .25

3795 A2899 (25c) gold & Prussian blue .50 .25

3796 A2898 (25c) green & gold .50 .25
3797 A2899 (25c) gold & gray .50 .25
3798 A2898 (25c) Prussian blue & gold .50 .25
3799 A2899 (25c) gold & dull blue .50 .25
3800 A2898 (25c) red & gold .50 .25
3801 A2899 (25c) gold & green .50 .25
b. Strip of 10, #3792-3801 5.00

Dated "2005"

Serpentine Die Cut 11½ Vert.

2005, Aug. 5 Untagged

3792d A2898 (25c) gray & gold .50 .25
3793d A2899 (25c) gold & red .50 .25
3794d A2898 (25c) dull blue & gold .50 .25
3795d A2899 (25c) gold & Prussian blue .50 .25
3796d A2898 (25c) green & gold .50 .25
3797d A2899 (25c) gold & gray .50 .25
3798d A2898 (25c) Prussian blue & gold .50 .25
3799d A2899 (25c) gold & dull blue .50 .25
3800d A2898 (25c) red & gold .50 .25
3801d A2899 (25c) gold & green .50 .25
e. Strip of 10, #3792d-3801d 5.00

See Nos. 3844-3853.

ARCTIC TUNDRA

A2900

No. 3802 — Wildlife and vegetation: a, Gyrfalcon. b, Gray wolf, vert. c, Common raven, vert. d, Musk oxen and caribou, vert. e, Grizzly bears, caribou. f, Caribou, willow ptarmigans. g, Arctic ground squirrel, vert. h, Willow ptarmigan, bearberry. i, Arctic grayling. j, Singing vole, thin-legged wolf spider, lingonberry, Labrador tea.

LITHOGRAPHED

Serpentine Die Cut 10¾x10½, 10½x10¾

2003, July 2

Self-Adhesive

3802 A2900 Pane of 10 8.50
a.-j. 37c Any single .85 .50

KOREAN WAR VETERANS MEMORIAL

Memorial in Snow A2901

Serpentine Die Cut 11½x11¾

2003, July 27

Self-Adhesive

3803 A2901 37c multicolored .75 .25

MARY CASSATT PAINTINGS

Young Mother, 1888 — A2902

Children Playing on the Beach, 1884 — A2903

On a Balcony, 1878-79 A2904

Child in a Straw Hat, c. 1886 A2905

PHOTOGRAVURE

Serpentine Die Cut 10¾ on 2 or 3 Sides

2003, Aug. 7

Self-Adhesive

Booklet Stamps

3804 A2902 37c multicolored .75 .30
3805 A2903 37c multicolored .75 .30
3806 A2904 37c multicolored .75 .30
3807 A2905 37c multicolored .75 .30
a. Block of 4, #3804-3807 3.00
b. Booklet pane of 20, 5 #3807a 15.00

No. 3807b is a double-sided booklet with 12 stamps on one side and 8 stamps plus label (booklet cover) on the other side.

EARLY FOOTBALL HEROES

Bronko Nagurski (1908-90) A2906

Ernie Nevers (1903-76) A2907

Walter Camp (1859-1925) A2908

Red Grange (1903-91) A2909

Serpentine Die Cut 11½x11¾

2003, Aug. 8

Self-Adhesive

3808 A2906 37c multicolored .75 .30
3809 A2907 37c multicolored .75 .30
3810 A2908 37c multicolored .75 .30
3811 A2909 37c multicolored .75 .30
a. Block of 4, #3808-3811 3.00

ROY ACUFF

Acuff (1903-92), Country Music Artist, and Fiddle — A2910

Serpentine Die Cut 11

2003, Sept. 13

Self-Adhesive

3812 A2910 37c multicolored .75 .25

DISTRICT OF COLUMBIA

Map, National Mall, Row Houses and Cherry Blossoms — A2911

2003, Sept. 23

Self-Adhesive

3813 A2911 37c multicolored .80 .25

REPTILES AND AMPHIBIANS

Scarlet Kingsnake A2912

Blue-Spotted Salamander — A2913

Reticulate Collared Lizard A2914

Ornate Chorus Frog A2915

Ornate Box Turtle A2916

2003, Oct. 7

Self-Adhesive

3814 A2912 37c multicolored .80 .40
3815 A2913 37c multicolored .80 .40
3816 A2914 37c multicolored .80 .40
3817 A2915 37c multicolored .80 .40
3818 A2916 37c multicolored .80 .40
a. Vert. strip of 5, #3814-3818 4.00

Washington Type of 2002

PHOTOGRAVURE

2003, Oct. ***Serpentine Die Cut 11***

Self-Adhesive

3819 A2686 23c gray green 1.00 .25

Christmas Type of 2002

LITHOGRAPHED

Serpentine Die Cut 11¼ on 2 or 3 Sides

2003, Oct. 23

Self-Adhesive

Booklet Stamp

Size: 19½x28mm

3820 A2843 37c multicolored .75 .25
a. Booklet pane of 20 15.00
b. Die cutting omitted, pair —

No. 3820a is a double-sided booklet with 12 stamps on one side and 8 stamps plus label (booklet cover) on the other side.

Compare to No. 3675, which measures 19x27mm.

CHRISTMAS

Reindeer with Pan Pipes A2917

Santa Claus with Drum A2918

Santa Claus with Trumpet A2919

Reindeer with Horn A2920

Reindeer with Pan Pipes A2921

Santa Claus with Drum A2922

Santa Claus with Trumpet A2923

Reindeer with Horn A2924

PHOTOGRAVURE

Serpentine Die Cut 11¾x11

2003, Oct. 23

Self-Adhesive

3821 A2917 37c multicolored 1.00 .25
3822 A2918 37c multicolored 1.00 .25
3823 A2919 37c multicolored 1.00 .25
3824 A2920 37c multicolored 1.00 .25
a. Block of 4, #3821-3824 4.00
b. Booklet pane of 20, 5 each #3821-3824 20.00

No. 3824b is a double-sided booklet with 12 stamps on one side and 8 stamps plus label (booklet cover) on the other side.

BOOKLET STAMPS

Serpentine Die Cut 10½x10¾ on 2 or 3 Sides

3825 A2921 37c multicolored 1.10 .25
3826 A2922 37c multicolored 1.10 .25
3827 A2923 37c multicolored 1.10 .25
3828 A2924 37c multicolored 1.10 .25
a. Block of 4, #3825-3828 4.40
b. Booklet pane of 4, #3825-3828 4.40

c. Booklet pane of 6, #3827-3828, 2 each #3825-3826 6.60
d. Booklet pane of 6, #3825-3826, 2 each #3827-3828 6.60

Snowy Egret — A2925

COIL STAMPS
PHOTOGRAVURE
Serpentine Die Cut 8½ Vert.
2003-04 Tagged
Self-Adhesive

3829 A2925 37c multi .75 .25
b. Black omitted — —

LITHOGRAPHED
Serpentine Die Cut 9½ Vert.

3829A A2925 37c multi .85 .25

Serpentine Die Cut 11½x11 on 2, 3 or 4 Sides
Booklet Stamps
PHOTOGRAVURE

3830 A2925 37c multi .75 .25
a. Booklet pane of 20 15.00
b. As "a," die cutting omitted —

With "USPS" Microprinted on Bird's Breast
Litho.

3830D A2925 37c multi *5.50* .25
e. Booklet pane of 20 *110.00*
f. Die cutting omitted, pair *150.00*
g. As "e," die cutting omitted *1,200.*

Issued: No. 3829, 10/24; No. 3830, 1/30/04; No. 3829A, Mar. 2004; No. 3830D, 2004.

PACIFIC CORAL REEF

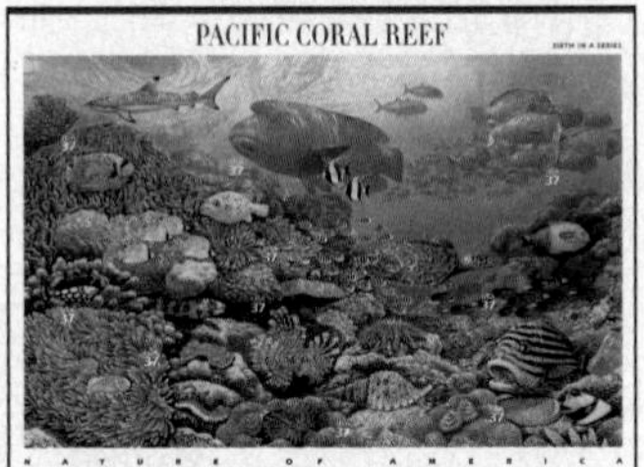

A2926

No. 3831 — Marine life: a, Emperor angelfish, blue coral, mound coral, vert. b, Humphead wrasse, Moorish idol. c, Bumphead parrotfish, vert. d, Black-spotted puffer, threadfin butterflyfish, staghorn coral. e, Hawksbill turtle, palette surgeonfish. f, Pink anemonefish, magnificent sea anemone, vert. g, Snowflake moray eel, Spanish dancer. h, Lionfish, vert. i, Triton's trumpet. j, Oriental sweetlips, bluestreak cleaner wrasse, mushroom coral, vert.

PHOTOGRAVURE
Serpentine Die Cut 10¾
2004, Jan. 2
Self-Adhesive

3831 A2926 Pane of 10 9.00
a.-j. 37c Any single .90 .40

CHINESE NEW YEAR

Year of the Monkey A2927

Serpentine Die Cut 10¾
2004, Jan. 13
Self-Adhesive

3832 A2927 37c multicolored .75 .25

See No. 3895i.

LOVE

Candy Hearts — A2928

BOOKLET STAMP
Serpentine Die Cut 10¾ on 2, 3 or 4 Sides
2004, Jan. 14
Self-Adhesive

3833 A2928 37c multicolored .75 .25
a. Booklet pane of 20 15.00

BLACK HERITAGE SERIES

Paul Robeson (1898-1976), Actor, Singer, Athlete and Activist — A2929

PHOTOGRAVURE
Serpentine Die Cut 10¾
2004, Jan. 20
Self-Adhesive

3834 A2929 37c multicolored .75 .25

THEODOR SEUSS GEISEL (DR. SEUSS)

Dr. Seuss (1904-91), Children's Book Writer, and Book Characters A2930

PHOTOGRAVURE
Serpentine Die Cut 10¾x10½
2004, Mar. 2
Self-Adhesive

3835 A2930 37c multicolored .85 .25
a. Die cutting omitted, pair *2,250.*

FLOWERS

White Lilacs and Pink Roses A2931

Five Varieties of Pink Roses A2932

LITHOGRAPHED (#3836), PHOTOGRAVURE
BOOKLET STAMP (#3836)
Serpentine Die Cut 10¾ on 2, 3 or 4 Sides
2004, Mar. 4
Self-Adhesive

3836 A2931 37c multicolored .75 .25
a. Booklet pane of 20 15.00

Serpentine Die Cut 11½x11

3837 A2932 60c multicolored 1.40 .25

UNITED STATES AIR FORCE ACADEMY, 50TH ANNIV.

Cadet Chapel A2933

PHOTOGRAVURE
Serpentine Die Cut 10¾
2004, Apr. 1
Self-Adhesive

3838 A2933 37c multicolored .75 .25

HENRY MANCINI

Henry Mancini (1924-94), Composer, and Pink Panther A2934

2004, Apr. 13
Self-Adhesive

3839 A2934 37c multicolored .75 .25

AMERICAN CHOREOGRAPHERS

Martha Graham (1893-1991) — A2935

Alvin Ailey (1931-89), and Dancers A2936

Agnes de Mille (1909-93), and Dancers A2937

George Balanchine (1904-83), and Dancers A2938

LITHOGRAPHED
2004, May 4
Self-Adhesive

3840 A2935 37c multicolored .75 .30
3841 A2936 37c multicolored .75 .30
3842 A2937 37c multicolored .75 .30
3843 A2938 37c multicolored .75 .30
a. Horiz. strip of 4, #3840-3843 3.00
b. Strip of 4, die cutting omitted *275.00*
c. Pane of 20 misprinted and miscut to show 5 #3843 and half of 5 #3842 at left, lower center plate position diagram at center, and 10 blank stamps at right. —

Eagle Types of 2003
PHOTOGRAVURE
COIL STAMPS
Perf. 9¾ Vert.
2004, May 12 Untagged

3844 A2898 (25c) gray & gold .50 .25
3845 A2899 (25c) gold & green .50 .25
3846 A2898 (25c) red & gold .50 .25
3847 A2899 (25c) gold & dull blue .50 .25
3848 A2898 (25c) Prussian blue & gold .50 .25
3849 A2899 (25c) gold & gray .50 .50
3850 A2898 (25c) green & gold .50 .25
3851 A2899 (25c) gold & Prussian blue .50 .25
3852 A2898 (25c) dull blue & gold .50 .25
3853 A2899 (25c) gold & red .50 .25
a. Strip of 10, #3844-3853 5.00 —

LEWIS & CLARK EXPEDITION, BICENTENNIAL

Meriwether Lewis (1774-1809) and William Clark (1770-1838) On Hill — A2939

Lewis — A2940

Clark — A2941

LITHOGRAPHED & ENGRAVED
Serpentine Die Cut 10¾
2004, May 14
Self-Adhesive

3854 A2939 37c green & multi 1.10 .25

Booklet Stamps
Serpentine Die Cut 10½x10¾

3855 A2940 37c blue & multi .90 .45
3856 A2941 37c red & multi .90 .45
a. Horiz. or vert. pair, #3855-3856 1.80
b. Booklet pane, 5 each #3855-3856 9.00

Nos. 3855-3856 were issued in booklets containing two No. 3856b, each with a different backing. The booklets sold for $8.95.

ISAMU NOGUCHI (1904-88), SCULPTOR

Akari 25N — A2942

Margaret La Farge Osborn A2943

Black Sun — A2944

Mother and Child — A2945

Figure (Detail) — A2946

LITHOGRAPHED

Serpentine Die Cut 10½x10¾

2004, May 18

Self-Adhesive

3857	A2942 37c black		.90	.40
3858	A2943 37c black		.90	.40
3859	A2944 37c black		.90	.40
3860	A2945 37c black		.90	.40
3861	A2946 37c black		.90	.40
a.	Horiz. strip of 5, #3857-3861		4.50	

NATIONAL WORLD WAR II MEMORIAL

A2947

Serpentine Die Cut 10¾

2004, May 29

Self-Adhesive

3862 A2947 37c multicolored .75 .25

Scott values for used self-adhesive stamps are for examples either on piece or off piece.

OLYMPIC GAMES, ATHENS, GREECE

Stylized Runner A2948

2004, June 9

Self-Adhesive

3863 A2948 37c multicolored .75 .25

Sea Coast Type of 2002

PHOTOGRAVURE

COIL STAMP

Perf. 9¾ Vert.

2004, June 11 **Untagged**

3864 A2853 (5c) multicolored .25 .25

No. 3864 has "2004" year date in black, rows of distinctly separated dots in surf area, and the small orange cloud is indistinct. No. 3775 has "2003" year date in blue, dots that run together in surf area, and a distinct small orange cloud.

THE ART OF DISNEY: FRIENDSHIP

Goofy, Mickey Mouse, Donald Duck — A2949

Bambi, Thumper A2950

Mufasa, Simba — A2951

Jiminy Cricket, Pinocchio A2952

LITHOGRAPHED

Serpentine Die Cut 10½x10¾

2004, June 23

Self-Adhesive

3865	A2949 37c multicolored	1.00	.30
3866	A2950 37c multicolored	1.00	.30
3867	A2951 37c multicolored	1.00	.30
3868	A2952 37c multicolored	1.00	.30
a.	Block or vert. strip of 4, #3865-3868	4.00	

U.S.S. CONSTELLATION

A2953

ENGRAVED

Serpentine Die Cut 10½

2004, June 30

Self-Adhesive

3869 A2953 37c brown .75 .25

R. BUCKMINSTER FULLER (1895-1983), ENGINEER

Time Magazine Cover Depicting Fuller, by Boris Artzybasheff A2954

LITHOGRAPHED

Serpentine Die Cut 10½x10¾

2004, July 12

Self-Adhesive

3870 A2954 37c multicolored .75 .25

LITERARY ARTS

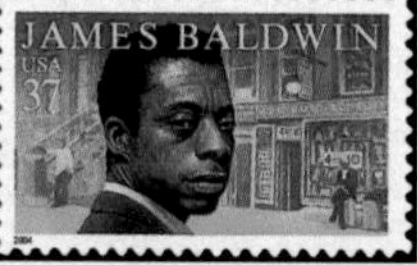
James Baldwin (1924-87), Writer A2955

Serpentine Die Cut 10¾

2004, July 23

Self-Adhesive

3871	A2955 37c multicolored	.75	.25
a.	Die cutting omitted, pair	*750.00*	

AMERICAN TREASURES SERIES

Giant Magnolias on a Blue Velvet Cloth, by Martin Johnson Heade A2956

PHOTOGRAVURE

BOOKLET STAMP

Serpentine Die Cut 10¾ on 2 or 3 Sides

2004, Aug. 12

Self-Adhesive

3872	A2956 37c multicolored	.70	.25
a.	Booklet pane of 20	15.00	
b.	Die cutting omitted, pair, in #3872a with foldover	—	

No. 3872a is a double-sided booklet pane with 12 stamps on one side and eight stamps plus label on the other side.

ART OF THE AMERICAN INDIAN

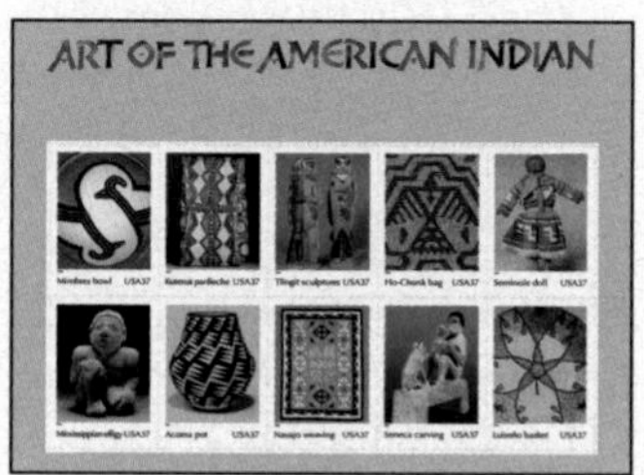

A2957

No. 3878: a, Mimbres bowl. b, Kutenai parfleche. c, Tlingit sculptures. d, Ho-Chunk bag. e, Seminole doll. f, Mississippian effigy. g, Acoma pot. h, Navajo weaving. i, Seneca carving. j, Luiseño basket.

Serpentine Die Cut 10¾x11

2004, Aug. 21

Self-Adhesive

3873	A2957 Pane of 10	25.00	
a.-j.	37c Any single	2.50	.40

Sea Coast Type of 2002

PHOTOGRAVURE

COIL STAMPS

Serpentine Die Cut 10 Vert.

2004-05 **Untagged**

Self-Adhesive

3874	A2853 (5c) multicolored, large "2003" year date	.25	.25
a.	Small "2003" year date ('05)	.25	.25

Serpentine Die Cut 11½ Vert.

Untagged

3875 A2853 (5c) multicolored, "2004" year date .25 .25

On Nos. 3874, 3874a and 3875, the stamps are spaced on backing paper that is taller than the stamps.

LEGENDS OF HOLLYWOOD

John Wayne (1907-79), Actor — A2958

Serpentine Die Cut 10¾

2004, Sept. 9

Self-Adhesive

3876 A2958 37c multicolored .85 .25

SICKLE CELL DISEASE AWARENESS

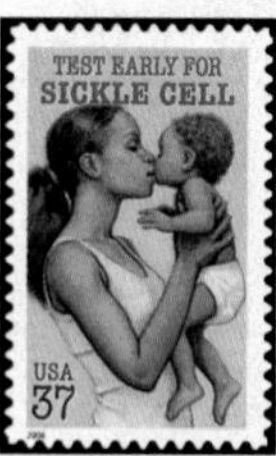

Mother and Child — A2959

Serpentine Die Cut 11

2004, Sept. 29

Self-Adhesive

3877 A2959 37c multicolored .75 .25

CLOUDSCAPES

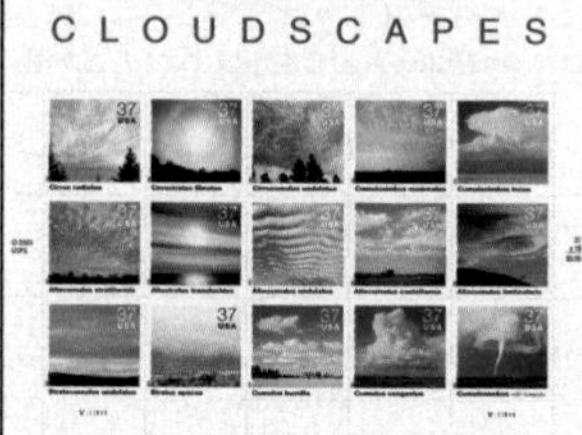

A2960

No. 3878 — Clouds: a, Cirrus radiatus. b, Cirrostratus fibratus. c, Cirrocumulus undulatus. d, Cumulonimbus mammatus. e, Cumulonimbus incus. f, Altocumulus stratiformis. g, Altostratus translucidus. h, Altocumulus undulatus. i, Altocumulus castellanus. j, Altocumulus lenticularis. k, Stratocumulus undulatus. l, Stratus opacus. m, Cumulus humilis. n, Cumulus congestus. o, Cumulonimbus with tornado.

2004, Oct. 4

Self-Adhesive

3878	A2960 Pane of 15	15.00	
a.-o.	37c Any single	1.00	.50

CHRISTMAS

Madonna and Child, by Lorenzo Monaco — A2961

LITHOGRAPHED

BOOKLET STAMP

Serpentine Die Cut 10¾x11 on 2 or 3 Sides

2004, Oct. 14

Self-Adhesive

3879	A2961 37c multicolored	.75	.25
a.	Booklet pane of 20	15.00	
b.	As "a," die cutting omitted	—	

No. 3879a is a double-sided booklet pane with 12 stamps on one side and eight stamps plus label that serves as a booklet cover on the other side.

HANUKKAH

Dreidel — A2962

Serpentine Die Cut 10¾

2004, Oct. 15

Self-Adhesive

3880	A2962 37c multicolored	.75	.25
a.	Die cuts applied to wrong sides of stamp (hyphen-hole die cuts and wavy line on face, die cut 10¾ on reverse)	—	—

See Nos. 4118, 4219, 4372.

KWANZAA

People in Robes — A2963

Serpentine Die Cut 10¾

2004, Oct. 16

Self-Adhesive

3881 A2963 37c multicolored .75 .25

See Nos. 4119, 4220, 4373.

LITERARY ARTS

Moss Hart (1904-61), Playwright A2964

PHOTOGRAVURE

2004, Oct. 25 ***Serpentine Die Cut 11***

Self-Adhesive

3882 A2964 37c multicolored .75 .25

CHRISTMAS

Purple Santa Ornament A2965

Green Santa Ornament A2966

Blue Santa Ornament A2967

Red Santa Ornament A2968

Purple Santa Ornament A2969

Green Santa Ornament A2970

Blue Santa Ornament A2971

Red Santa Ornament A2972

Serpentine Die Cut 11½x11

2004, Nov. 16

Self-Adhesive

3883 A2965 37c purple & multi 1.00 .25
3884 A2966 37c green & multi 1.00 .25
3885 A2967 37c blue & multi 1.00 .25
3886 A2968 37c red & multi 1.00 .25
a. Block or strip of 4, #3883-3886 4.00
b. Booklet pane of 20, 5 #3886a blocks 20.00

Booklet Stamps

Serpentine Die Cut 10¼x10¾ on 2 or 3 Sides

3887 A2969 37c purple & multi 1.00 .25
3888 A2970 37c green & multi 1.00 .25
3889 A2971 37c blue & multi 1.00 .25
3890 A2972 37c red & multi 1.00 .25
a. Block of 4, #3887-3890 4.00
b. Booklet pane of 4, #3887-3890 4.00
c. Booklet pane of 6, #3889-3890, 2 each #3887-3888 6.00
d. Booklet pane of 6, #3887-3888, 2 each #3889-3890 6.00

Serpentine Die Cut 8 on 2, 3 or 4 Sides

3891 A2970 37c green & multi 1.35 .25
3892 A2969 37c purple & multi 1.35 .25
3893 A2972 37c red & multi 1.35 .25
3894 A2971 37c blue & multi 1.35 .25
a. Block of 4, #3891-3894 5.40
b. Booklet pane of 18, 6 each #3891, 3893, 3 each #3892, 3894 24.50
Nos. 3883-3894 (12) 13.40 3.00

No. 3886b is a double-sided booklet with 12 stamps on one side and 8 stamps plus label that serves as a booklet cover on the other side.

The design of No. 3894b shows ornaments in a wooden box. The pattern of the wooden box dividers creates three types of each design. Rows 1 and 4 are Type 1, with a top horizontal strip of frame extending from edge to edge while the bottom strip of frame stops at the design's width. Rows 2 and 5 are Type 2, with both top and bottom strips of frame stopping at the design's width. Rows 3 and 6 are Type 3, with the top strip of frame stopping at design's width while the bottom strip of frame extends from edge to edge. Each variety is equally common.

Chinese New Year Types of 1992-2004

Serpentine Die Cut 10¾

2005, Jan. 6

Self-Adhesive

3895 Double sided pane of 24, 2 each #a-l 18.00
a. A2360 37c Rat .75 .40
b. A2413 37c Ox .75 .40
c. A2462 37c Tiger .75 .40
d. A2535 37c Rabbit .75 .40
e. A2602 37c Dragon .75 .40
f. A2702 37c Snake .75 .40
g. A2752 37c Horse .75 .40
h. A2856 37c Ram .75 .40
i. A2927 37c Monkey .75 .40
j. A2067 37c Rooster .75 .40
k. A2146 37c Dog .75 .40
l. A2205 37c Boar .75 .40
m. As No. 3895, die cutting missing on "a," "b," and "c" on reverse side (PS) *1,250.*

No. 3895h has "2005" year date and is photogravure while No. 3747 has "2003" year date and is lithographed.

Stamps are on the right side of the front and on the left side of the reverse.

BLACK HERITAGE SERIES

Marian Anderson (1897-1993), Singer — A2973

2005, Jan. 27

Self-Adhesive

3896 A2973 37c multicolored .85 .25

RONALD REAGAN

Ronald Reagan (1911-2004), 40th President — A2974

2005, Feb. 9

Self-Adhesive

3897 A2974 37c multicolored .75 .25

See No. 4078.

LOVE

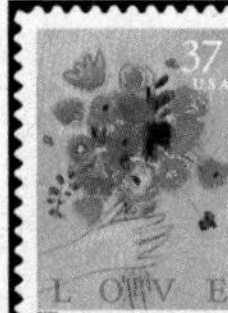

Hand and Flower Bouquet — A2975

BOOKLET STAMP

Serpentine Die Cut 10¾x11 on 2, 3 or 4 Sides

2005, Feb. 18

Self-Adhesive

3898 A2975 37c multicolored .75 .25
a. Booklet pane of 20 15.00

NORTHEAST DECIDUOUS FOREST

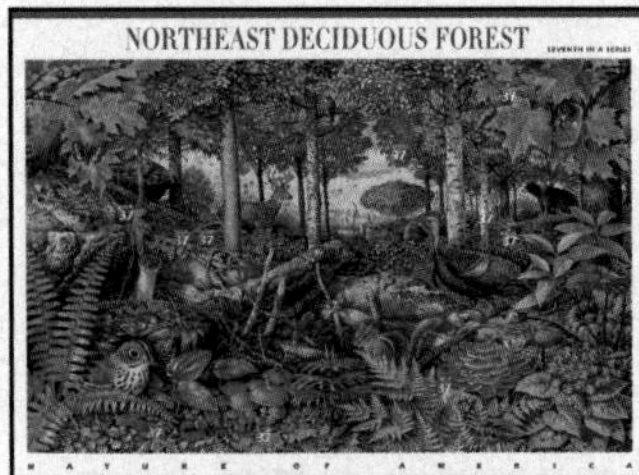

A2976

No. 3899 — Wildlife: a, Eastern buckmoth, vert. b, Red-shouldered hawk. c, Eastern red bat. d, White-tailed deer. e, Black bear. f, Long-tailed weasel, vert. g, Wild turkey, vert. h, Ovenbird, vert. i, Red eft. j, Eastern chipmunk.

Serpentine Die Cut 10¾

2005, Mar. 3

Self-Adhesive

3899 A2976 Pane of 10 8.50
a.-j. 37c Any single .85 .40

SPRING FLOWERS

Hyacinth A2977

Daffodil A2978

Tulip — A2979

Iris — A2980

LITHOGRAPHED BOOKLET STAMPS

Serpentine Die Cut 10¾ on 2 or 3 Sides

2005, Mar. 15

Self-Adhesive

3900 A2977 37c multicolored .85 .30
3901 A2978 37c multicolored .85 .30
3902 A2979 37c multicolored .85 .30
3903 A2980 37c multicolored .85 .30
a. Block of 4, #3900-3903 3.40
b. Booklet pane of 20, 5 each #3900-3903 17.00
c. As "b," die cutting omitted on side with 8 stamps —

No. 3903b is a double-sided booklet with 12 stamps on one side and 8 stamps plus label (booklet cover) on the other side.

LITERARY ARTS

Robert Penn Warren (1905-89), Writer A2981

PHOTOGRAVURE

Serpentine Die Cut 10¾

2005, Apr. 22

Self-Adhesive

3904 A2981 37c multicolored .75 .25

EDGAR Y. "YIP" HARBURG

Harburg (1896-1981), Lyricist — A2982

LITHOGRAPHED

2005, Apr. 28

Self-Adhesive

3905 A2982 37c multicolored .75 .25

AMERICAN SCIENTISTS

Barbara McClintock (1902-92), Geneticist A2983

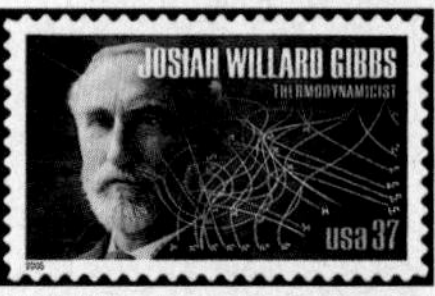

Josiah Willard Gibbs (1839-1903), Thermodynamicist — A2984

John von Neumann (1903-57), Mathematician — A2985

Richard Feynman (1918-88), Physicist A2986

2005, May 4

Self-Adhesive

3906 A2983 37c multicolored 1.00 .30
3907 A2984 37c multicolored 1.00 .30
3908 A2985 37c multicolored 1.00 .30
a. Vert. pair, die cutting omitted, #3906 & 3908 —
3909 A2986 37c multicolored 1.00 .30
a. Block or horiz. strip of 4, #3906-3909 4.00
b. All colors omitted, tagging omitted, pane of 20 —
c. As "a," printing on back of stamps omitted —
d. Vert. pair, die cutting omitted, #3907 & 3909 —

On No. 3909b, the printing on the back of the pane and all die cutting is normal.

MODERN AMERICAN ARCHITECTURE

A2987

No. 3910 — Buildings: a, Guggenheim Museum, New York. b, Chrysler Building, New York. c, Vanna Venturi House, Philadelphia. d, TWA Terminal, New York. e, Walt Disney Concert Hall, Los Angeles. f, 860-880 Lake Shore

Drive, Chicago. g, National Gallery of Art, Washington, DC. h, Glass House, New Canaan, CT. i, Yale Art and Architecture Building, New Haven, CT. j, High Museum of Art, Atlanta. k, Exeter Academy Library, Exeter, NH. l, Hancock Center, Chicago.

Serpentine Die Cut 10¾x11

2005, May 19

Self-Adhesive

3910 A2987 Pane of 12 11.00
a.-l. 37c Any single .90 .50
m. As No. 3910, orange yellow omitted *350.00* —

LEGENDS OF HOLLYWOOD

Henry Fonda (1905-82), Actor — A2988

Sheets of 180 in nine panes of 20

Serpentine Die Cut 11x10¾

2005, May 20

Self-Adhesive

3911 A2988 37c multicolored .90 .25

THE ART OF DISNEY: CELEBRATION

Pluto, Mickey Mouse — A2989

Mad Hatter, Alice — A2990

Flounder, Ariel — A2991

Snow White, Dopey — A2992

Serpentine Die Cut 10½x10¾

2005, June 30

Self-Adhesive

3912 A2989 37c multicolored .85 .30
3913 A2990 37c multicolored .85 .30
3914 A2991 37c multicolored .85 .30
3915 A2992 37c multicolored .85 .30
a. Block or vert. strip of 4, #3912-3915 3.40
b. Die cutting omitted, pane of 20 — *1,400.*
c. Printed on backing paper, pane of 20 —

On the unique used pane of No. 3915b, the outer selvage was removed by cutting.

ADVANCES IN AVIATION

Boeing 247 A2993

Consolidated PBY Catalina — A2994

Grumman F6F Hellcat A2995

Republic P-47 Thunderbolt A2996

Engineering and Research Corporation Ercoupe 415 A2997

Lockheed P-80 Shooting Star A2998

Consolidated B-24 Liberator — A2999

Boeing B-29 Superfortress — A3000

Beechcraft 35 Bonanza A3001

Northrop YB-49 Flying Wing A3002

Serpentine Die Cut 10¾x10½

2005, July 29

Self-Adhesive

3916 A2993 37c multicolored .80 .40
3917 A2994 37c multicolored .80 .40
3918 A2995 37c multicolored .80 .40
3919 A2996 37c multicolored .80 .40
3920 A2997 37c multicolored .80 .40
3921 A2998 37c multicolored .80 .40
3922 A2999 37c multicolored .80 .40
3923 A3000 37c multicolored .80 .40
3924 A3001 37c multicolored .80 .40
3925 A3002 37c multicolored .80 .40
a. Block of 10, #3916-3925 8.00

RIO GRANDE BLANKETS

A3003

A3004

A3005

A3006

LITHOGRAPHED BOOKLET STAMPS

Serpentine Die Cut 10¾ on 2 or 3 Sides

2005, July 30

Self-Adhesive

3926 A3003 37c multicolored .75 .30
3927 A3004 37c multicolored .75 .30
3928 A3005 37c multicolored .75 .30
3929 A3006 37c multicolored .75 .30
a. Block of 4, #3926-3929 3.00
b. Booklet pane, 5 each #3926-3929 15.00

No. 3929b is a double-sided booklet with 12 stamps on one side and 8 stamps plus label (booklet cover) on the other side.

PRESIDENTIAL LIBRARIES ACT, 50th ANNIV.

Presidential Seal — A3007

Serpentine Die Cut 10¾

2005, Aug. 4

Self-Adhesive

3930 A3007 37c multicolored .80 .25

SPORTY CARS OF THE 1950S

1953 Studebaker Starliner A3008

1954 Kaiser Darren A3009

1953 Chevrolet Corvette A3010

1952 Nash Healey A3011

1955 Ford Thunderbird — A3012

BOOKLET STAMPS

Serpentine Die Cut 10¾ on 2 or 3 Sides

2005, Aug. 20 **Tagged**

Self-Adhesive

3931 A3008 37c multicolored .90 .40
3932 A3009 37c multicolored .90 .40
3933 A3010 37c multicolored .90 .40
3934 A3011 37c multicolored .90 .40
3935 A3012 37c multicolored .90 .40
a. Vert. strip of 5, #3931-3935 4.50
b. Booklet pane, 4 each #3931-3935 18.00

Stamps in No. 3935a are not adjacent, as rows of selvage are between stamps one and two, and between stamps three and four.

No. 3935b is a double-sided booklet pane with 12 stamps on one side (2 each #3931, 3933, 3935, and 3 each #3932, 3934) and eight stamps (1 each #3932, 3934, and 2 each #3931, 3933, 3935) plus label on the other side.

ARTHUR ASHE

Arthur Ashe (1943-93), Tennis Player — A3013

Serpentine Die Cut 10¾

2005, Aug. 27

Self-Adhesive

3936 A3013 37c multicolored .75 .25

TO FORM A MORE PERFECT UNION

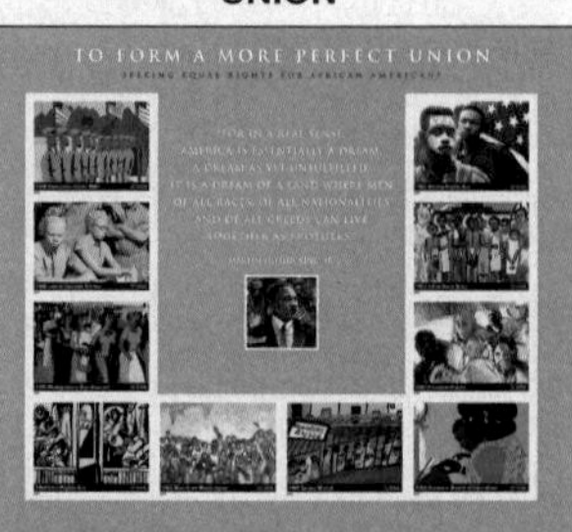

A3014

No. 3937 — Inscriptions and artwork: a, 1948 Executive Order 9981 (Training for War, by William H. Johnson). b, 1965 Voting Rights Act (Youths on the Selma March, 1965, photograph by Bruce Davidson). c, 1960 Lunch Counter Sit-ins (National Civil Rights Museum exhibits, by StudioEIS). d, 1957 Little Rock Nine (America Cares, by George Hunt). e,

1955 Montgomery Bus Boycott (Walking, by Charles Alston). f, 1961 Freedom Riders (Freedom Riders, by May Stevens). g, 1964 Civil Rights Act (Dixie Café, by Jacob Lawrence). h, 1963 March on Washington (March on Washington, by Alma Thomas). i, 1965 Selma March (Selma March, by Bernice Sims). j, 1954 Brown v. Board of Education (The Lamp, by Romare Bearden).

Serpentine Die Cut 10¾x10½

2005, Aug. 30

Self-Adhesive

3937 A3014 Pane of 10 9.00
a.-j. 37c Any single .90 .40

CHILD HEALTH

Child and Doctor — A3015

PHOTOGRAVURE

Serpentine Die Cut 10½x11

2005, Sept. 7

Self-Adhesive

3938 A3015 37c multicolored .75 .25

LET'S DANCE

Merengue A3016

Salsa — A3017

Cha Cha Cha — A3018

Mambo A3019

Serpentine Die Cut 10¾

2005, Sept. 17

Self-Adhesive

3939 A3016 37c multicolored 1.00 .30
3940 A3017 37c multicolored 1.00 .30
3941 A3018 37c multicolored 1.00 .30
3942 A3019 37c multicolored 1.00 .30
a. Vert. strip of 4, #3939-3942 4.00

Stamps in the vertical strip are not adjacent as rows of selvage are between the stamps. The backing paper of stamps from the 2nd and 4th columns have Spanish inscriptions, while the other columns have English inscriptions.

GRETA GARBO

Garbo (1905-90), Actress A3020

ENGRAVED

2005, Sept. 23

Self-Adhesive

3943 A3020 37c black .75 .25

See Sweden No. 2517.

JIM HENSON AND THE MUPPETS

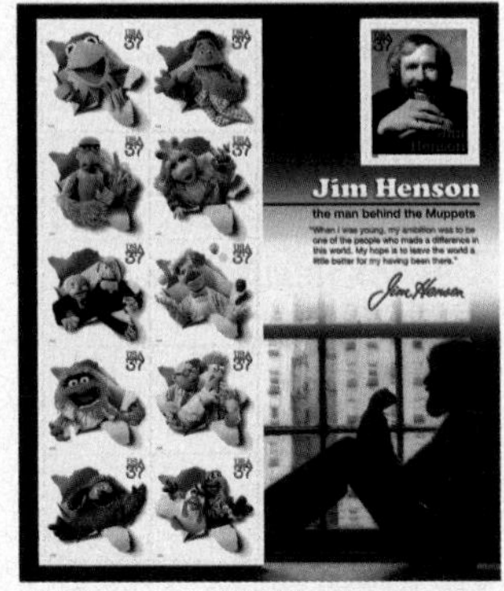

A3021

No. 3944: a, Kermit the Frog. b, Fozzie Bear. c, Sam the Eagle and flag. d, Miss Piggy. e, Statler and Waldorf. f, The Swedish Chef and fruit. g, Animal. h, Dr. Bunsen Honeydew and Beaker. i, Rowlf the Dog. j, The Great Gonzo and Camilla the Chicken. k, Jim Henson.

Nos. 3944a-3944j are 30x30mm; No. 3944k, 28x37mm.

PHOTOGRAVURE

Serpentine Die Cut 10½, 10½x10¾ (#3944k)

2005, Sept. 28

Self-Adhesive

3944 A3021 Pane of 11 9.00
a.-k. 37c Any single .80 .50

CONSTELLATIONS

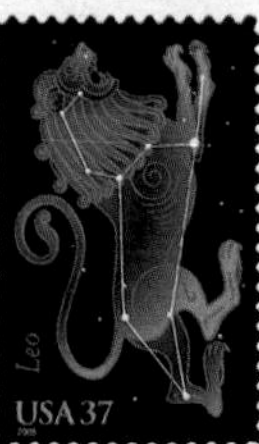

Leo — A3022

Orion — A3023

Lyra A3024

Pegasus A3025

LITHOGRAPHED

Serpentine Die Cut 10¾

2005, Oct. 3

Self-Adhesive

3945 A3022 37c multicolored .85 .30
3946 A3023 37c multicolored .85 .30
3947 A3024 37c multicolored .85 .30
3948 A3025 37c multicolored .85 .30
a. Block or vert. strip of 4, #3945-3948 3.40
b. As "a," die cutting omitted 750.00

CHRISTMAS COOKIES

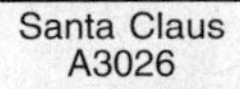

Santa Claus A3026

Snowmen A3027

Angel — A3028

Elves — A3029

Santa Claus A3030

Snowmen A3031

Angel A3032

Elves A3033

LITHOGRAPHED, PHOTOGRAVURE (#3953-3960)

Serpentine Die Cut 10¾x11

2005, Oct. 20

Self-Adhesive

Design Size: 19x26mm

3949 A3026 37c multicolored .85 .25
3950 A3027 37c multicolored .85 .25
3951 A3028 37c multicolored .85 .25
3952 A3029 37c multicolored .85 .25
a. Block or vert. strip of 4, #3949-3952 3.50

Booklet Stamps

Serpentine Die Cut 10¾x11 on 2 or 3 Sides

Design Size: 19½x27mm

3953 A3026 37c multicolored 1.00 .25
3954 A3027 37c multicolored 1.00 .25
3955 A3028 37c multicolored 1.00 .25
3956 A3029 37c multicolored 1.00 .25
a. Block of 4, #3953-3956 4.00
b. Booklet pane of 20, 5 #3956a 20.00

Serpentine Die Cut 10½x10¾

3957 A3030 37c multicolored 1.25 .25
3958 A3031 37c multicolored 1.25 .25
3959 A3032 37c multicolored 1.25 .25
3960 A3033 37c multicolored 1.25 .25
a. Block of 4, #3957-3960 5.00
b. Booklet pane of 4, #3957-3960 5.00
c. Booklet pane of 6, #3959-3960, 2 each #3957-3958 7.50
d. Booklet pane of 6, #3957-3958, 2 each #3959-3960 7.50

No. 3956b is a double-sided booklet pane with 12 stamps on one side and eight stamps plus label that serves as a booklet cover on the other side. Nos. 3949-3952 have a small "2005" year date, while Nos. 3953-3956 have a large year date. Other design differences caused by different cropping of the images can be found, with Nos. 3953-3956 showing slightly more design features on one or more sides.

DISTINGUISHED MARINES

Lt. Gen. John A. Lejeune (1867-1942), 2nd Infantry Division Insignia — A3034

Lt. Gen. Lewis B. Puller (1898-1971), 1st Marine Division Insignia — A3035

Sgt. John Basilone (1916-45), 5th Marine Division Insignia A3036

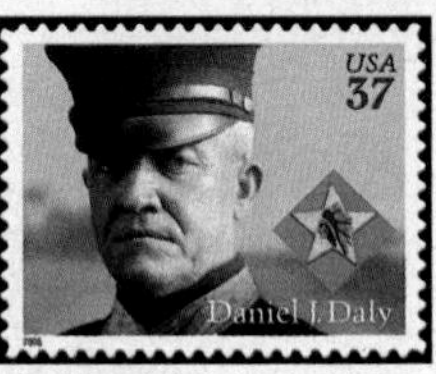

Sgt. Major Daniel J. Daly (1873-1937), 73rd Machine Gun Company, 6th Marine Regiment Insignia — A3037

LITHOGRAPHED

Serpentine Die Cut 11x10½

2005, Nov. 10

Self-Adhesive

3961 A3034 37c multicolored 1.00 .30
3962 A3035 37c multicolored 1.00 .30
3963 A3036 37c multicolored 1.00 .30
3964 A3037 37c multicolored 1.00 .30
a. Block or horiz. strip of 4, #3961-3964 4.00

Flag and Statue of Liberty — A3038

LITHOGRAPHED (#3965, 3966, 3970, 3974), PHOTOGRAVURE

2005, Dec. 8 ***Perf. 11¼***

3965 A3038 (39c) multicolored .80 .25

Self-Adhesive (#3966, 3968-3975)

Serpentine Die Cut 11¼x10¾

3966 A3038 (39c) multicolored .80 .25
a. Booklet pane of 20 16.00
b. As "a," die cutting omitted —

COIL STAMPS

Perf. 9¾ Vert.

3967 A3038 (39c) multicolored .80 .25

Serpentine Die Cut 8½ Vert.

3968 A3038 (39c) multicolored .80 .25

Serpentine Die Cut 10¼ Vert.

3969 A3038 (39c) multicolored 1.20 .25

Serpentine Die Cut 9½ Vert.

3970 A3038 (39c) multicolored 2.00 .25

BOOKLET STAMPS

Serpentine Die Cut 11¼x10¾ on 2 or 3 Sides

3972 A3038 (39c) multicolored .80 .25
a. Booklet pane of 20 16.00

Serpentine Die Cut 10½x10¾ on 2 or 3 Sides

3973 A3038 (39c) multicolored .80 .25
a. Booklet pane of 20 16.00

On both Nos. 3972 and 3973, the sky immediately above the date is bright blue and extends from the left side to beyond the "6" in the date, the left arm of the star at the upper left barely touches the frame line and is without the "USPS" microprinting. They are distinguishable by the die cutting. Nos. 3872a and 3973a are double-sided booklet panes with 12 stamps on one side and eight stamps plus label that serves as a booklet cover on the other side.

No. 3973 was not available until January 2006.

Serpentine Die Cut 11¼x10¾ on 2 or 3 Sides

3974 A3038 (39c) multicolored .80 .25
a. Booklet pane of 4 3.20
b. Booklet pane of 6 4.80

Serpentine Die Cut 8 on 2, 3 or 4 Sides

3975 A3038 (39c) multicolored .80 .25
a. Booklet pane of 18 14.50
Nos. 3965-3975 (10) 9.60 2.50

Nos. 3965-3975 are dated "2006."

On No. 3966, the sky immediately above the date is bright blue and extends from the left side to beyond the "6" in the date, the left arm of the star at upper left is clear of the top frame, and "USPS" is microprinted on the top red flag stripe.

On No. 3974, the sky immediately above the date is dark blue and extends from the left side to the second "0" in the date, the left arm of the star at upper left touches the top frame, and lacks the microprinting found on No. 3966.

Nos. 3965 and 3970 also have "USPS" microprinted on the top red flag stripe.

Nos. 3966a and 3972a are double-sided booklet panes with 12 stamps on one side and eight stamps plus label that serves as a booklet cover on the other side. On No. 3966a, the stamps on one side are upside-down with relation to the stamps on the other side. On No. 3972a the stamps are all aligned the same on both sides.

LOVE

Birds — A3039

PHOTOGRAVURE

Serpentine Die Cut 11 on 2, 3, or 4 Sides

2006, Jan. 3

BOOKLET STAMP

Self-Adhesive

3976 A3039 (39c) multicolored 1.00 .25
a. Booklet pane of 20 20.00

Flag and Statue of Liberty — A3040

LITHOGRAPHED (#3978, 3981), PHOTOGRAVURE (#3979-3980, 3983, 3985)

2006 *Serpentine Die Cut 11¼x10¾*

Self-Adhesive (#3978, 3980-3985)

3978 A3040 39c multi .85 .25
a. Booklet pane of 10 8.50
b. Booklet pane of 20 17.00
c. As "b," die cutting omitted on side with 8 stamps —
d. Die cutting omitted, pair —

No. 3978 has "USPS" microprinted on top red flag stripe.

No. 3978b is a double-sided booklet with 12 stamps on one side and 8 stamps plus label (booklet cover) on the other side.

COIL STAMPS

Perf. 9¾ Vert.

3979 A3040 39c multi 1.00 .25

Serpentine Die Cut 11 Vert.

3980 A3040 39c multi .80 .25

No. 3980 has rounded corners and lacks microprinting. Unused examples are on backing paper taller than the stamp, and the stamps are spaced approximately 3mm apart.

Serpentine Die Cut 9½ Vert.

3981 A3040 39c multi 1.00 .25
a. Die cutting omitted, pair —

No. 3981 has "USPS" microprinted on top red flag stripe.

Serpentine Die Cut 10¼ Vert.

3982 A3040 39c multi 1.00 .25
a. Vert. pair, unslit between *500.00*

Serpentine Die Cut 8½ Vert.

3983 A3040 39c multi .80 .25

BOOKLET STAMP

Serpentine Die Cut 11¼x10¾ on 2 or 3 Sides

3985 A3040 39c multi .80 .25
a. Booklet pane of 20 16.00
b. Serpentine die cut 11.1 on 2 or 3 sides .80 .25
c. Booklet pane of 4 #3985b 3.20
d. Booklet pane of 6 #3985b 4.80

Nos. 3983 and 3985 lack the microprinting found on Nos. 3978 and 3981. No. 3982 was not made available until June, despite the official first day of issue. No. 3983 was not made available until July and No. 3985 was not made available until August, despite the official first day of issue. No. 3985a is a double-sided booklet with 12 stamps on one side and 8 stamps plus label (booklet cover) on the other side.

Issued: No. 3980, 1/9; No. 3979, 3/8; Nos. 3978, 3981, 3982, 3985, 4/8.

CHILDREN'S BOOK ANIMALS

The Very Hungry Caterpillar, from *The Very Hungry Caterpillar,* by Eric Carle A3041

Wilbur, from *Charlotte's Web,* by E. B. White A3042

Fox in Socks, from *Fox in Socks,* by Dr. Seuss A3043

Maisy, from *Maisy's ABC,* by Lucy Cousins A3044

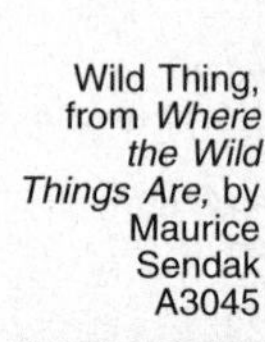

Wild Thing, from *Where the Wild Things Are,* by Maurice Sendak A3045

Curious George, from *Curious George,* by Margaret and H. A. Rey — A3046

Olivia, from *Olivia,* by Ian Falconer A3047

Frederick, from *Frederick,* by Leo Lionni A3048

PHOTOGRAVURE

Serpentine Die Cut 10¾

2006, Jan. 10

Self-Adhesive

3987 A3041 39c multicolored .80 .40
3988 A3042 39c multicolored .80 .40
3989 A3043 39c multicolored .80 .40
3990 A3044 39c multicolored .80 .40
3991 A3045 39c multicolored .80 .40
3992 A3046 39c multicolored .80 .40
3993 A3047 39c multicolored .80 .40
3994 A3048 39c multicolored .80 .40
a. Block of 8, #3987-3994 6.50

See Great Britain Nos. 2340-2341.

2006 WINTER OLYMPICS, TURIN, ITALY

Skier A3049

LITHOGRAPHED

2006, Jan. 11

Self-Adhesive

3995 A3049 39c multicolored .80 .25

BLACK HERITAGE SERIES

Hattie McDaniel (1895-1952), Actress — A3050

2006, Jan. 25

Self-Adhesive

3996 A3050 39c multicolored .80 .25

Chinese New Year Types of 1992-2004

2006, Jan. 29

Self-Adhesive

3997 Pane of 12 12.00
a. A2360 39c Rat 1.00 .50
b. A2413 39c Ox 1.00 .50
c. A2462 39c Tiger 1.00 .50
d. A2535 39c Rabbit 1.00 .50
e. A2602 39c Dragon 1.00 .50
f. A2702 39c Snake 1.00 .50
g. A2752 39c Horse 1.00 .50
h. A2856 39c Ram 1.00 .50
i. A2927 39c Monkey 1.00 .50
j. A2067 39c Rooster 1.00 .50
k. A2146 39c Dog 1.00 .50
l. A2205 39c Boar 1.00 .50

WEDDING DOVES

Dove Facing Left — A3051

Dove Facing Right — A3052

BOOKLET STAMPS

Serpentine Die Cut 10¾x11 on 2, 3 or 4 Sides

2006, Mar. 1

Self-Adhesive

3998 A3051 39c pale lilac .80 .25
a. Booklet pane of 20 16.00
b. As "a," die cutting omitted —

Serpentine Die Cut 10¾x11

3999 A3052 63c pale yellow green 1.40 .50
a. Booklet pane, 20 each #3998-3999 45.00
b. Horiz. pair, #3998-3999 with vertical gutter between 2.25 1.50

Common Buckeye Butterfly — A3053

LITHOGRAPHED (#4000), PHOTOGRAVURE (#4001-4002)

2006, Mar. 8 ***Perf. 11¼***

4000 A3053 24c multicolored .50 .25

Self-Adhesive

Serpentine Die Cut 11

4001 A3053 24c multicolored .55 .25
a. Serpentine die cut 10¾x11¼ on 3 sides (from booklet panes) .50 .25
b. Booklet pane of 10 #4001a 5.00
c. Booklet pane of 4 #4001a 2.00
d. Booklet pane of 6 #4001a 3.00

No. 4001b is a convertible booklet that was sold flat. It has a self-adhesive panel that covers the rouletting on the inside of the booklet cover. Nos. 4001c and 4001d are component panes of a vending machine booklet, which was sold pre-folded and sealed, and which does not have the self-adhesive panel covering the rouletting on the inside of the booklet cover.

COIL STAMP

Serpentine Die Cut 8½ Horiz.

4002 A3053 24c multicolored .50 .25

CROPS OF THE AMERICAS

Chili Peppers A3054

Beans A3055

Sunflower and Seeds A3056

Squashes A3057

Corn — A3058

PHOTOGRAVURE (#4003-4012), LITHOGRAPHED (#4013-4017)

Serpentine Die Cut 10¼ Horiz.

2006, Mar. 16

Self-Adhesive

Coil Stamps

4003 A3054 39c multicolored 1.25 .35
4004 A3055 39c multicolored 1.25 .35
4005 A3056 39c multicolored 1.25 .35
4006 A3057 39c multicolored 1.25 .35
4007 A3058 39c multicolored 1.25 .35
a. Strip of 5, #4003-4007 6.25

Booklet Stamps

Serpentine Die Cut 10¾x10½ on 2 or 3 Sides

4008 A3058 39c multicolored 1.00 .35
4009 A3057 39c multicolored 1.00 .35
4010 A3056 39c multicolored 1.00 .35
4011 A3055 39c multicolored 1.00 .35
4012 A3054 39c multicolored 1.00 .35
a. Horiz. strip of 5, #4008-4012 5.00
b. Booklet pane, 4 each #4008-4012 20.00

Serpentine Die Cut 10¾x11¼ on 2 or 3 Sides

4013 A3054 39c multicolored 1.00 .35
4014 A3058 39c multicolored 1.00 .35
4015 A3057 39c multicolored 1.00 .35
4016 A3056 39c multicolored 1.00 .35
a. Booklet pane of 4, #4013-4016 4.00
4017 A3055 39c multicolored 1.00 .35
a. Horiz. strip of 5, #4013-4017 5.00
b. Booklet pane of 4, #4013-4015, 4017 4.00
c. Booklet pane of 6, #4013-4016, 2 #4017 6.00
d. Booklet pane of 6, #4013-4015, 4017, 2 #4016 6.00

Stamps in Nos. 4012a and 4017a are not adjacent, as one or two rows of selvage is between stamps (or a blank space where selvage was removed by the manufacturer).

No. 4012b is a double-sided booklet with 12 stamps on one side and 8 stamps plus label (booklet cover) on the other side.

"USA" is at right of "39" on No. 4004, at left of "39" on Nos. 4011, 4017. Top of "USA" is aligned with top of "39" on No. 4013, with bottom of "39" on Nos. 4003, 4012.

X-PLANES

A3059

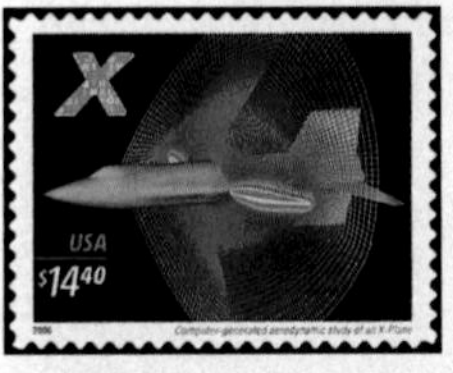

A3060

LITHOGRAPHED WITH HOLOGRAM AFFIXED

Serpentine Die Cut 10¾x10½

2006, Mar. 17 **Self-Adhesive**

4018	A3059	$4.05 multi	8.00	5.00
a.		Silver foil ("X") omitted	—	
4019	A3060	$14.40 multi	27.50	15.00

Beware of Nos. 4018 and 4019 with "X" hologram chemically removed. Certification is strongly recommended.

SUGAR RAY ROBINSON (1921-89), BOXER

A3061

PHOTOGRAVURE

2006, Apr. 7 *Serpentine Die Cut 11*

Self-Adhesive

4020	A3061	39c red & blue	.80	.25

BENJAMIN FRANKLIN (1706-90)

Statesman A3062

Scientist A3063

Printer A3064

Postmaster A3065

2006, Apr. 7 **Self-Adhesive**

4021	A3062	39c multicolored	1.25	.30
4022	A3063	39c multicolored	1.25	.30
4023	A3064	39c multicolored	1.25	.30
4024	A3065	39c multicolored	1.25	.30
a.		Block or horiz. strip of 4	5.00	

THE ART OF DISNEY: ROMANCE

Mickey and Minnie Mouse — A3066

Cinderella and Prince Charming A3067

Beauty and the Beast — A3068

Lady and Tramp — A3069

LITHOGRAPHED

Serpentine Die Cut 10½x10¾

2006, Apr. 21

Self-Adhesive

4025	A3066	39c multicolored	.80	.30
4026	A3067	39c multicolored	.80	.30
4027	A3068	39c multicolored	.80	.30
4028	A3069	39c multicolored	.80	.30
a.		Block or vert. strip of 4, #4025-4028	3.20	

LOVE

Birds — A3070

PHOTOGRAVURE

Serpentine Die Cut 11 on 2, 3 or 4 Sides

2006, May 1

Self-Adhesive

Booklet Stamp

4029	A3070	39c multicolored	.95	.25
a.		Booklet pane of 20	19.00	

LITERARY ARTS

Katherine Anne Porter (1890-1980), Author — A3071

LITHOGRAPHED

Serpentine Die Cut 10¾

2006, May 15

Self-Adhesive

4030	A3071	39c multicolored	.80	.25

AMBER ALERT

Mother and Child A3072

PHOTOGRAVURE

Serpentine Die Cut 10¾

2006, May 25

Self-Adhesive

4031	A3072	39c multicolored	.80	.25

Purple Heart Type of 2003

LITHOGRAPHED

Serpentine Die Cut 11¼x11

2006, May 26

Self-Adhesive

4032	A2891	39c multicolored	.80	.25

WONDERS OF AMERICA

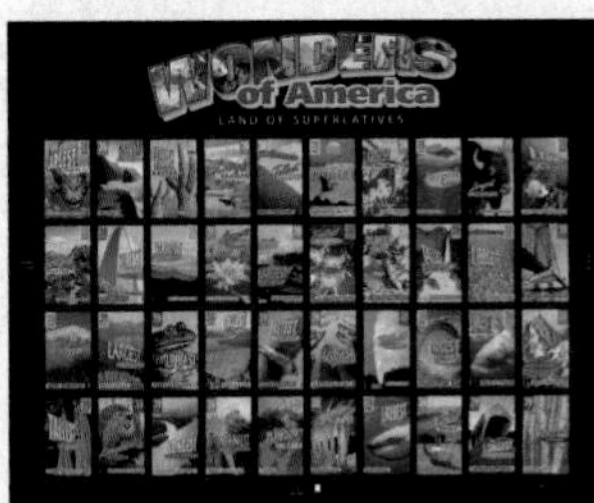

A3073-3112

Designs: No. 4033, American alligator, largest reptile. No. 4034, Moloka'i, highest sea cliffs. No. 4035, Saguaro, tallest cactus. No. 4036, Bering Glacier, largest glacier. No. 4037, Great Sand Dunes, tallest dunes. No. 4038, Chesapeake Bay, largest estuary. No. 4039, Cliff Palace, largest cliff dwelling. No. 4040, Crater Lake, deepest lake. No. 4041, American bison, largest land mammal. No. 4042, Off the Florida Keys, longest reef. No. 4043, Pacific Crest Trail, longest hiking trail. No. 4044, Gateway Arch, tallest man-made monument. No. 4045, Appalachians, oldest mountains. No. 4046, American lotus, largest flower. No. 4047, Lake Superior, largest lake. No. 4048, Pronghorn, fastest land animal. No. 4049, Bristlecone pines, oldest trees. No. 4050, Yosemite Falls, tallest waterfall. No. 4051, Great Basin, largest desert. No. 4052, Verrazano-Narrows Bridge, longest span. No. 4053, Mount Washington, windiest place. No. 4054, Grand Canyon, largest canyon. No. 4055, American bullfrog, largest frog. No. 4056, Oroville Dam, tallest dam. No. 4057, Peregrine falcon, fastest bird. No. 4058, Mississippi River Delta, largest delta. No. 4059, Steamboat, tallest geyser. No. 4060, Rainbow Bridge, largest natural bridge. No. 4061, White sturgeon, largest freshwater fish. No. 4062, Rocky Mountains, longest mountain chain. No. 4063, Coast redwoods, tallest trees. No. 4064, American beaver, largest rodent. No. 4065, Mississippi-Missouri, longest river system. No. 4066, Mount Wai'ale'ale, rainiest spot. No. 4067, Kilauea, most active volcano. No. 4068, Mammoth Cave, longest cave. No. 4069, Blue whale, loudest animal. No. 4070, Death Valley, hottest spot. No. 4071, Cornish-Windsor Bridge, longest covered bridge. No. 4072, Quaking aspen, largest plant.

PHOTOGRAVURE

Serpentine Die Cut 10¾

2006, May 27

Self-Adhesive

4033	A3073	39c multicolored	.80	.60
4034	A3074	39c multicolored	.80	.60
4035	A3075	39c multicolored	.80	.60
4036	A3076	39c multicolored	.80	.60
4037	A3077	39c multicolored	.80	.60
4038	A3078	39c multicolored	.80	.60
4039	A3079	39c multicolored	.80	.60
4040	A3080	39c multicolored	.80	.60
4041	A3081	39c multicolored	.80	.60
4042	A3082	39c multicolored	.80	.60
4043	A3083	39c multicolored	.80	.60
4044	A3084	39c multicolored	.80	.60
4045	A3085	39c multicolored	.80	.60
4046	A3086	39c multicolored	.80	.60
4047	A3087	39c multicolored	.80	.60
4048	A3088	39c multicolored	.80	.60
4049	A3089	39c multicolored	.80	.60
4050	A3090	39c multicolored	.80	.60
4051	A3091	39c multicolored	.80	.60
4052	A3092	39c multicolored	.80	.60
4053	A3093	39c multicolored	.80	.60
4054	A3094	39c multicolored	.80	.60
4055	A3095	39c multicolored	.80	.60
4056	A3096	39c multicolored	.80	.60
4057	A3097	39c multicolored	.80	.60
4058	A3098	39c multicolored	.80	.60
4059	A3099	39c multicolored	.80	.60
4060	A3100	39c multicolored	.80	.60
4061	A3101	39c multicolored	.80	.60
4062	A3102	39c multicolored	.80	.60
4063	A3103	39c multicolored	.80	.60
4064	A3104	39c multicolored	.80	.60
4065	A3105	39c multicolored	.80	.60
4066	A3106	39c multicolored	.80	.60
4067	A3107	39c multicolored	.80	.60
4068	A3108	39c multicolored	.80	.60
4069	A3109	39c multicolored	.80	.60
4070	A3110	39c multicolored	.80	.60
4071	A3111	39c multicolored	.80	.60
4072	A3112	39c multicolored	.80	.60
a.		Pane of 40, #4033-4072	32.00	

EXPLORATION OF EAST COAST BY SAMUEL DE CHAMPLAIN, 400TH ANNIV.

Ship and Map — A3113

A3114

LITHOGRAPHED & ENGRAVED

Serpentine Die Cut 10¾

2006, May 28

Self-Adhesive (#4073)

4073	A3113	39c multicolored	.85	.25

Souvenir Sheet

Perf. 11

4074	A3114	Pane of 4, 2 each #4074a, Canada #2156a	8.50	3.00
a.		A3113 39c multicolored	2.00	.25

Washington 2006 World Philatelic Exhibition (#4074). Canada No. 2156, which was sold only by Canada Post, has a bar code in the lower left margin of the pane. No. 4074, which was sold only by the United States Postal Service for $1.75, lacks this bar code.

WASHINGTON 2006 WORLD PHILATELIC EXHIBITION

Souvenir Sheet

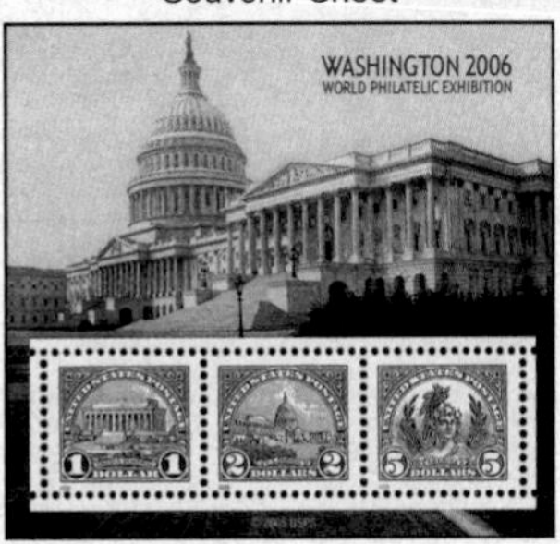

A3115

LITHOGRAPHED (MARGIN) & ENGRAVED

2006, May 29 ***Perf. 10¾x10½***

4075	A3115	Pane of 3	16.00	6.00
a.		A174 $1 violet brown	2.00	.50
b.		A175 $2 deep blue	4.00	1.00
c.		A176 $5 carmine & blue	10.00	2.50

DISTINGUISHED AMERICAN DIPLOMATS

Souvenir Sheet

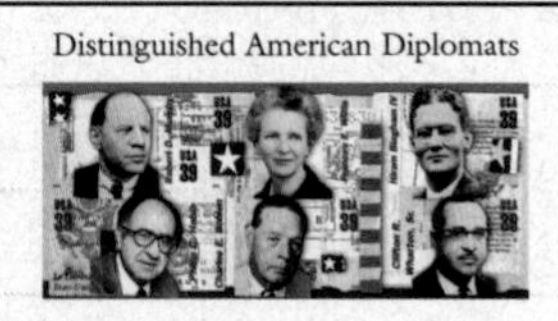

A3116

No. 4076: a, Robert D. Murphy (1894-1978). b, Frances E. Willis (1899-1983). c, Hiram Bingham IV (1903-88). d, Philip C. Habib (1920-92). e, Charles E. Bohlen (1904-74). f, Clifton R. Wharton, Sr. (1899-1990).

PHOTOGRAVURE

Serpentine Die Cut 10¾

2006, May 29

Self-Adhesive

4076	A3116 Pane of 6	6.00	
a.-f.	39c any single	1.00	.40

LEGENDS OF HOLLYWOOD

Judy Garland (1922-69), Actress — A3117

LITHOGRAPHED

2006, June 10

Self-Adhesive

4077 A3117 39c multicolored	1.00	.25
a. Pair, die cutting omitted	—	

Ronald Reagan Type of 2005

PHOTOGRAVURE

2006, June 14

Self-Adhesive

4078 A2974 39c multicolored	.90	.25

Happy Birthday Type of 2002

Serpentine Die Cut 11

2006, June 23

Self-Adhesive

4079 A2751 39c multicolored	.80	.25

BASEBALL SLUGGERS

Roy Campanella (1921-93) A3118

Hank Greenberg (1911-86) A3119

Mel Ott (1909-58) A3120

Mickey Mantle (1931-95) A3121

Serpentine Die Cut 10¾

2006, July 15

Self-Adhesive

4080 A3118 39c multicolored	.80	.30
4081 A3119 39c multicolored	.80	.30
4082 A3120 39c multicolored	.80	.30
4083 A3121 39c multicolored	.80	.30
a. Block or vert. strip of 4, #4080-4083	3.20	

DC COMICS SUPERHEROES

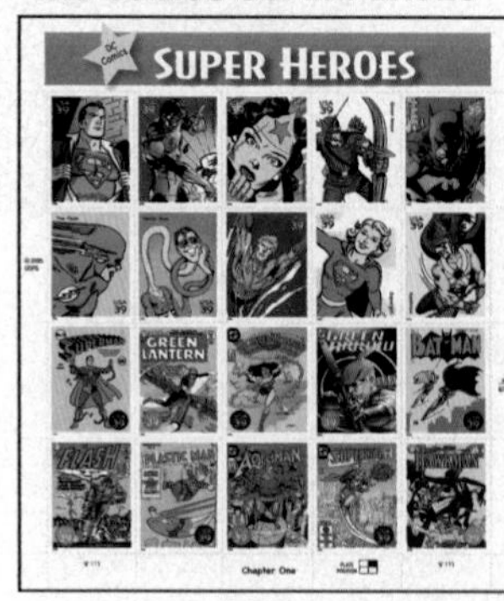

A3122

No. 4084: a, Superman. b, Green Lantern. c, Wonder Woman. d, Green Arrow. e, Batman. f, The Flash. g, Plastic Man. h, Aquaman. i, Supergirl. j, Hawkman. k, Cover of *Superman #11*. l, Cover of *Green Lantern #4*. m, Cover of *Wonder Woman #22 (Second Series)*. n, Cover of *Green Arrow #15*. o, Cover of *Batman #1*. p, Cover of *The Flash #111*. q, Cover of *Plastic Man #4*. r, Cover of *Aquaman #5 (of 5)*. s, Cover of *The Daring New Adventures of Supergirl #1*. t, Cover of *The Brave and the Bold Presents Hawkman #36*.

Serpentine Die Cut 10½x10¾

2006, July 20

Self-Adhesive

4084 A3122 Pane of 20	16.00	
a.-t. 39c Any single	.80	.50
u. As No. 4084, all inscriptions omitted on reverse	—	

MOTORCYCLES

1940 Indian Four A3123

1918 Cleveland A3124

Generic "Chopper," c. 1970 A3125

1965 Harley-Davidson Electra-Glide — A3126

Serpentine Die Cut 10¾x10½

2006, Aug. 7

Self-Adhesive

4085 A3123 39c multicolored	1.00	.30
4086 A3124 39c multicolored	1.00	.30
4087 A3125 39c multicolored	1.00	.30
4088 A3126 39c multicolored	1.00	.30
a. Block or horiz. strip of 4, #4085-4088	4.00	

AMERICAN TREASURES SERIES

Quilts of Gee's Bend, Alabama

Housetop Variation, by Mary Lee Bendolph A3127

Pig in a Pen Medallion, by Minnie Sue Coleman A3128

Nine Patch, by Ruth P. Mosely A3129

Housetop Four Block Half Log Cabin Variation, by Lottie Mooney A3130

Roman Stripes Variation, by Loretta Pettway A3131

Chinese Coins Variation, by Arlonzia Pettway A3132

Blocks and Strips, by Annie Mae Young A3133

Medallion, by Loretta Pettway A3134

Bars and String-pieced Columns, by Jessie T. Pettway A3135

Medallion With Checkerboard Center, by Patty Ann Williams A3136

BOOKLET STAMPS

Serpentine Die Cut 10¾ on 2 or 3 Sides

2006, Aug. 24

Self-Adhesive

4089 A3127 39c multicolored	1.10	.40
4090 A3128 39c multicolored	1.10	.40
4091 A3129 39c multicolored	1.10	.40
4092 A3130 39c multicolored	1.10	.40
4093 A3131 39c multicolored	1.10	.40
4094 A3132 39c multicolored	1.10	.40
4095 A3133 39c multicolored	1.10	.40
4096 A3134 39c multicolored	1.10	.40
4097 A3135 39c multicolored	1.10	.40
4098 A3136 39c multicolored	1.10	.40
a. Block of 10, #4089-4098	11.00	
b. Booklet pane of 20, 2 each #4089-4098	22.50	

No. 4098b is a double-sided booklet pane with 12 stamps on one side (1 each #4090-4093, 4095-4098, and 2 each #4089, 4094) and eight stamps (1 each #4090-4093, 4095-4098) plus label (booklet cover) on the other side.

SOUTHERN FLORIDA WETLAND

A3137

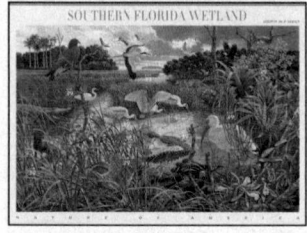

No. 4099 — Wildlife: a, Snail kite. b, Wood storks. c, Florida panther. d, Bald eagle, horiz. e, American crocodile, horiz. f, Roseate spoonbills, horiz. g, Everglades mink. h, Cape Sable seaside sparrow, horiz. i, American alligator, horiz. j, White ibis.

Serpentine Die Cut 10¾

2006, Oct. 4

Self-Adhesive

4099 A3137 Pane of 10	9.00	
a.-j. 39c any single	.90	.40

CHRISTMAS

Madonna and Child with Bird, by Ignacio Chacón A3138

Snowflake A3139

Snowflake A3140

Snowflake A3141

Snowflake — A3142

LITHOGRAPHED, PHOTOGRAVURE (#4113-4116)

Serpentine Die Cut 10¾x11 on 2 or 3 Sides

2006

Self-Adhesive

Booklet Stamps (#4100, 4105-4116)

4100 A3138 39c multi	.80	.25
a. Booklet pane of 20	16.00	

Base of Denomination Higher Than Year Date

Serpentine Die Cut 11¼x11

4101 A3139 39c multi	.90	.25
4102 A3140 39c multi	.90	.25
4103 A3141 39c multi	.90	.25
4104 A3142 39c multi	.90	.25
a. Block or vert. strip of 4, #4101-4104	3.60	

Base of Denominations Even With Year Date

Serpentine Die Cut 11¼x11½ on 2 or 3 Sides

4105 A3139 39c multi	.80	.25
a. Red missing (PS)	—	
4106 A3140 39c multi	.80	.25
a. Red missing (PS)	—	

4107 A3141 39c multi .80 .25

4108 A3142 39c multi .80 .25
- *a.* Block of 4, #4105-4108 3.20
- *b.* Booklet pane of 20, 5 #4108a 16.00
- *c.* As "a," red ("USA") and green ("39") omitted —

Serpentine Die Cut 11¼x10¾ on 2 or 3 Sides

4109 A3139 39c multi 1.00 .25

4110 A3140 39c multi 1.00 .25

4111 A3141 39c multi 1.00 .25

4112 A3142 39c multi 1.00 .25
- *a.* Block of 4, #4109-4112 4.00
- *b.* Booklet pane of 4, #4109-4112 4.00
- *c.* Booklet pane of 6, #4111-4112, 2 each #4109-4110 6.00
- *d.* Booklet pane of 6, #4109-4110, 2 each #4111-4112 6.00

Serpentine Die Cut 8 on 2, 3 or 4 Sides

4113 A3139 39c multi 1.20 .25
- *a.* Red and green missing (PS) —

4114 A3141 39c multi 1.20 .25

4115 A3140 39c multi 1.20 .25

4116 A3142 39c multi 1.20 .25
- *a.* Block of 4, #4113-4116 4.80
- *b.* Booklet pane of 18, 4 each #4114, 4116, 5 each #4113, 4115 22.00

Nos. 4100-4116 (17) 16.40 4.25

No. 4108b is a double-sided booklet pane with 12 stamps on one side and eight stamps plus label that serves as a booklet cover on the other side. Snowflakes on Nos. 4101-4104 are slightly smaller than those on Nos. 4105-4116.

Issued: No. 4100, 10/17, Nos. 4101-4116, 10/5.

Eid Type of 2001

PHOTOGRAVURE

2006, Oct. 6 *Serpentine Die Cut 11*

Self-Adhesive

4117 A2734 39c multicolored .80 .25

Hanukkah Type of 2004

LITHOGRAPHED

Serpentine Die Cut 10¾x11

2006, Oct. 6

Self-Adhesive

4118 A2962 39c multicolored .80 .25
- *a.* Die cutting omitted, pane of 20 —

Kwanzaa Type of 2004

Serpentine Die Cut 11x10¾

2006, Oct. 6

Self-Adhesive

4119 A2963 39c multicolored .80 .25

BLACK HERITAGE SERIES

Ella Fitzgerald (1917-96), Singer — A3143

Serpentine Die Cut 11

2007, Jan. 10

Self-Adhesive

4120 A3143 39c multicolored .80 .25

OKLAHOMA STATEHOOD, 100TH ANNIV.

Cimarron River A3144

2007, Jan. 11

Self-Adhesive

4121 A3144 39c multicolored .80 .25

LOVE

Hershey's Kiss — A3145

PHOTOGRAVURE

Serpentine Die Cut 10¾x11 on 2, 3 or 4 Sides

2007, Jan. 13

BOOKLET STAMP

Self-Adhesive

4122 A3145 39c multicolored .80 .25
- *a.* Booklet pane of 20 16.00

INTERNATIONAL POLAR YEAR

Souvenir Sheet

A3146

No. 4123: a, Aurora borealis. b, Aurora australis.

LITHOGRAPHED

Serpentine Die Cut 10¾

2007, Feb. 21

Self-Adhesive

4123 A3146 Pane of 2 4.00
- *a.-b.* 84c Either single 2.00 .50

LITERARY ARTS

Henry Wadsworth Longfellow (1807-82), Poet A3147

2007, Mar. 15

Self-Adhesive

4124 A3147 39c multicolored .80 .25

"FOREVER" STAMP

Liberty Bell — A3148

Large Microprinting (#4125, 4128)

Small Microprinting (#4126)

Medium Microprinting (#4127)

PHOTOGRAVURE, LITHOGRAPHED (#4126, 4127)

Serpentine Die Cut 11¼x10¾ on 2 or 3 Sides

2007-09

Booklet Stamps

Self-Adhesive

Large Microprinting, Bell 16mm Wide

4125 A3148 (41c) multicolored, dated "2007," Apr. 12 .90 .25
- *a.* Booklet pane of 20 18.00
- *b.* (42c) Dated "2008" .90 .25
- *c.* Booklet pane of 20 #4125b 18.00
- *d.* As "c," copper ("FOREVER") omitted —
- *e.* As "c," copper ("FOREVER") omitted on side with 12 stamps, copper splatters on side with 8 stamps —
- *f.* (44c) Dated "2009" (*'09*) .90 .25
- *g.* Booklet pane of 20 #4125f 18.00
- *h.* As No. 4125, copper ("FOREVER") omitted, on cover —
- *i.* As No. 4125, die cutting missing, horiz. pair (PS) —

Small Microprinting, Bell 16mm Wide

4126 A3148 (41c) multicolored, dated "2007" .90 .25
- *a.* Booklet pane of 20 18.00
- *b.* (42c) Dated "2008" (*'08*) .90 .25
- *c.* Booklet pane of 20 #4126b 18.00
- *d.* (44c) Dated "2009" in copper (*'09*) .90 .25
- *e.* Booklet pane of 20 #4126d 18.00
- *f.* As "b," copper ("FOREVER") omitted 1,400.

Medium Microprinting, Bell 15mm Wide

4127 A3148 (41c) multicolored, dated "2007" (*'07*) .90 .25
- *a.* Booklet pane of 20 18.00
- *b.* Booklet pane of 4 3.60
- *c.* Booklet pane of 6 5.50
- *d.* (42c) Dated "2008" (*'08*) .90 .25
- *e.* As "d," booklet pane of 20 18.00
- *f.* (42c) Dated "2008," date in smaller type (*'08*) .90 .25
- *g.* As "f," booklet pane of 4 3.60
- *h.* As "f," booklet pane of 6 5.50
- *i.* (44c) Dated "2009" in copper (*'09*) .90 .25
- *j.* As "i," booklet pane of 20 18.00
- *k.* As "i," die cutting omitted, pair —
- *l.* As No. 4127, copper ("FOREVER") and "USA FIRST-CLASS" missing (PS) —
- *m.* As "e," die cutting omitted 500.00

Large Microprinting, Bell 16mm Wide

Serpentine Die Cut 8 on 2, 3 or 4 Sides

4128 A3148 (41c) multicolored, dated "2007" .90 .25
- *a.* Booklet pane of 18 16.50
- *b.* (42c) Dated "2009" (*'09*) .90 .25
- *c.* As "b," booklet pane of 18 16.50

Nos. 4125-4128 (4) 3.60 1.00

Nos. 4125-4128 were sold for 41c on the day of issue and will be valid for the one ounce first class postage rate after any new rates go into effect. As of May 12, 2008, any "Forever" stamp (Nos. 4125-4128 and 4127d) in stock was sold for 42c. As of May 15, 2009, all "Forever" stamps in stock were sold for 44c, etc.

Nos. 4125a, 4125c, 4126a, 4126c, 4127a, 4127e and 4127j are double-sided booklet panes, with 12 stamps on one side and eight stamps plus a label that serves as a booklet cover on the other side.

Nos. 4127b and 4127c exist with rouletting on backing paper of either gauge 9½ or 13.

See No. 4437.

Flag — A3149

LITHOGRAPHED, PHOTOGRAVURE (#4134, 4135)

2007, Apr. 12 *Perf. 11¼*

4129 A3149 (41c) multicolored .90 .40

Self-Adhesive (#4130, 4132-4135)

Serpentine Die Cut 11¼x10¾

4130 A3149 (41c) multicolored .90 .25

COIL STAMPS

Perf. 9¾ Vert.

4131 A3149 (41c) multicolored .90 .40

With Perpendicular Corners

Serpentine Die Cut 9½ Vert.

4132 A3149 (41c) multicolored .90 .25

Serpentine Die Cut 11 Vert.

4133 A3149 (41c) multicolored .90 .25
- *a.* Die cutting omitted, pair 1,250.

Serpentine Die Cut 8½ Vert.

4134 A3149 (41c) multicolored .90 .25

With Rounded Corners

Serpentine Die Cut 11 Vert.

4135 A3149 (41c) multicolored .90 .75

Nos. 4129-4135 (7) 6.30 2.55

Nos. 4132-4134 are on backing paper as high as the stamp. No. 4135 is on backing paper that is larger than the stamp.

SETTLEMENT OF JAMESTOWN, 400TH ANNIV.

Ships Susan Constant, Godspeed and Discovery — A3150

LITHOGRAPHED

Serpentine Die Cut 10½x10½x10¾

2007, May 11

Self-Adhesive

4136 A3150 41c multicolored 1.10 .25

WILDLIFE

Bighorn Sheep A3151

Florida Panther A3152

LITHOGRAPHED, PHOTOGRAVURE (#4138, 4142)

2007 *Perf. 11¼x11*

4137 A3152 26c multi .60 .25

Self-Adhesive

Serpentine Die Cut 11

4138 A3151 17c multi .35 .25

Serpentine Die Cut 11¼x11

4139 A3152 26c multi .55 .25

Coil Stamps

Serpentine Die Cut 11 Vert.

4140 A3151 17c multi .35 .25

4141 A3152 26c multi .75 .25
- *a.* Die cutting omitted, pair —

Booklet Stamp

Serpentine Die Cut 11¼x11 on 3 Sides

4142 A3152 26c multi .55 .25
- *a.* Booklet pane of 10 5.50

Nos. 4137 and 4139 have microprinted "USPS" to the left and above the lower left whisker. No. 4140 has microprinted "USPS" on right horn. No. 4141 has microprinted "USPS" along the right edge of the stamp just above the panther. Nos. 4138 and 4142 lack microprinting.

Issued: Nos. 4137, 4139, 4141, 4142, 5/12; No. 4138, 5/14; No. 4140, 5/21.

PREMIERE OF MOVIE "STAR WARS," 30TH ANNIVERSARY

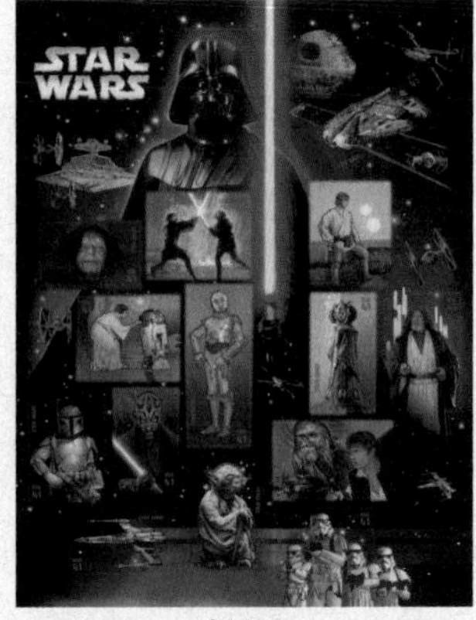

A3153

No. 4143: a, Darth Vader (40x53mm). b, Millennium Falcon (47x25mm). c, Emperor Palpatine (41x26mm). d, Anakin Skywalker and Obi-Wan Kenobi (41x33mm). e, Luke Skywalker (31x41mm). f, Princess Leia and R2-D2 (41x33mm). g, C-3PO (21x65mm). h, Queen Padmé Amidala (26x48mm). i, Obi-Wan Kenobi (31x48mm). j, Boba Fett (32x40mm). k, Darth Maul (26x41mm). l, Chewbacca and Han Solo (48x31mm). m, X-wing Starfighter (41x26mm). n, Yoda (31x48mm). o, Stormtroopers (41x31mm).

LITHOGRAPHED

2007, May 25 ***Serpentine Die Cut 11***

Self-Adhesive

4143 A3153 Pane of 15 13.00
a.-o. 41c Any single .85 .50

PRESIDENTIAL AIRCRAFT

Air Force One A3154

Marine One A3155

LITHOGRAPHED & ENGRAVED (#4144), LITHOGRAPHED (#4145)

Serpentine Die Cut 10¾

2007, June 13

Self-Adhesive

4144 A3154 $4.60 multi 9.25 5.00
a. Black (engr.) omitted *275.00*
4145 A3155 $16.25 multi 27.50 16.00

PACIFIC LIGHTHOUSES

Diamond Head Lighthouse, Hawaii — A3156

Five Finger Lighthouse, Alaska — A3157

Grays Harbor Lighthouse, Washington A3158

Umpqua River Lighthouse, Oregon A3159

St. George Reef Lighthouse, California — A3160

PHOTOGRAVURE

Serpentine Die Cut 11

2007, June 21

Self-Adhesive

4146 A3156 41c multicolored 1.20 .40
4147 A3157 41c multicolored 1.20 .40
4148 A3158 41c multicolored 1.20 .40
4149 A3159 41c multicolored 1.20 .40
4150 A3160 41c multicolored 1.20 .40
a. Horiz. strip of 5, #4146-4150 6.00

WEDDING HEARTS

Heart With Lilac Background A3161

Heart With Pink Background A3162

LITHOGRAPHED (#4151), PHOTOGRAVURE (#4152) BOOKLET STAMP (#4151)

Serpentine Die Cut 10¾ on 2, 3 or 4 Sides

2007, June 27

Self-Adhesive

4151 A3161 41c multicolored 1.00 .25
a. Booklet pane of 20 20.00

Serpentine Die Cut 10¾x11

4152 A3162 58c multicolored 1.25 .25

POLLINATION

Purple Nightshade, Morrison's Bumblebee A3163

Hummingbird Trumpet, Calliope Hummingbird — A3164

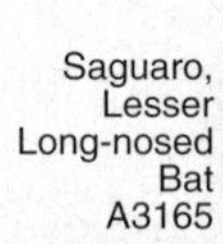

Saguaro, Lesser Long-nosed Bat A3165

Prairie Ironweed, Southern Dogface Butterfly A3166

No. 4153: Type I, Tip of bird wing is directly under center of "U" in "USA," straight edge at left. Type II, Tip of bird wing is directly under the right line of the "U" in "USA," straight edge at right.

No. 4154: Type I, Tip of bird wing is even with the top of denomination, straight edge at right. Type II, Tip of bird wing is well above denomination, straight edge at left.

No. 4155: Type I, Top of "USA" is even with the lower portion of the nearest unopened green saguaro flower bud, straight edge at left. Type II, Top of "USA" is even with the point where the flower and unopened green saguaro bud meet, straight edge at right.

No. 4156: Type I, Bottom of denomination is even with top point of the white triangle found between the bottom of the purple flower and the green leaf below it, straight edge at right. Type II, Bottom of denomination is even with the lower point of the white triangle found between the bottom of the purple flower and the green leaf below it, straight edge at left.

LITHOGRAPHED

Serpentine Die Cut 11 on 2, 3 or 4 Sides

2007, June 29 **Tagged**

Self-Adhesive

Booklet Stamps

4153 A3163 41c multicolored, Type I .85 .30
a. Type II .85 .30
4154 A3164 41c multicolored, Type I .85 .30
a. Type II .85 .30
4155 A3165 41c multicolored, Type I .85 .30
a. Type II .85 .30
4156 A3166 41c multicolored, Type I .85 .30
a. Type II .85 .30
b. Block of 4, #4153-4156 3.40
c. Block of 4, #4153a-4156a 3.40
d. Booklet pane of 20, 3 each #4153-4156, 2 each #4153a-4156a 17.00

No. 4156d is a double-sided booklet with 12 stamps (2 each #4153-4156, 1 each #4153a-4156a) on one side and 8 stamps plus label (booklet cover) on the other side.

Patriotic Banner — A3167

PHOTOGRAVURE (#4157), LITHOGRAPHED (#4158)

Serpentine Die Cut 11 Vert.

2007, July 4 **Untagged**

Coil Stamps

Self-Adhesive

4157 A3167 (10c) red, gold & blue .25 .25

Serpentine Die Cut 11¾ Vert.

4158 A3167 (10c) red, gold & blue .25 .25

See No. 4385.

MARVEL COMICS SUPERHEROES

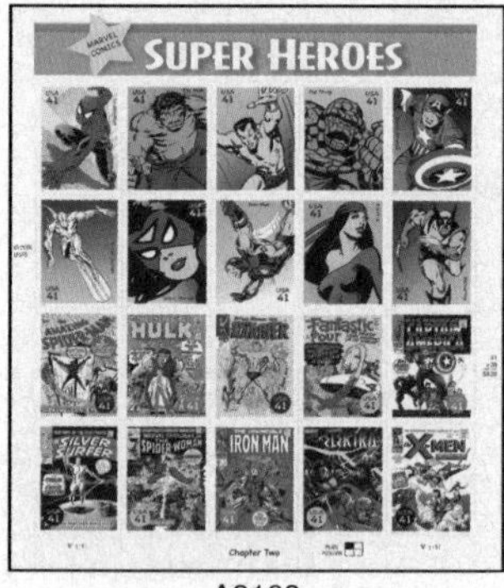

A3168

No. 4159: a, Spider-man. b, The Hulk. c, Sub-Mariner. d, The Thing. e, Captain America. f, Silver Surfer. g, Spider-Woman. h, Iron Man. i, Elektra. j, Wolverine. k, Cover of *The Amazing Spider-Man #1*. l, Cover of *The Incredible Hulk #1*. m, Cover of *Sub-Mariner #1*. n, Cover of *The Fantastic Four #3*. o, Cover of *Captain America #100*. p, Cover of *The Silver Surfer #1*. q, Cover of *Marvel Spotlight on The Spider-Woman #32*. r, Cover of *Iron Man #1*. s, Cover of *Daredevil #176 Featuring Elektra*. t, Cover of *The X-Men #1*.

PHOTOGRAVURE

Serpentine Die Cut 10½x10¾

2007, July 26

Self-Adhesive

4159 A3168 Pane of 20 17.00
a.-t. 41c Any single .85 .50

VINTAGE MAHOGANY SPEEDBOATS

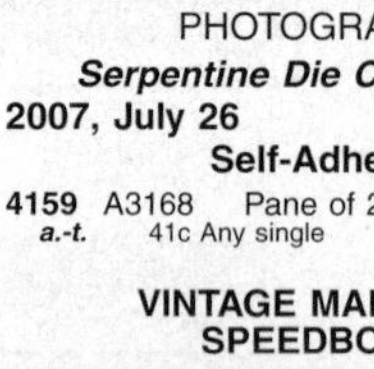

1915 Hutchinson A3169

1954 Chris-Craft A3170

1939 Hacker-Craft A3171

1931 Gar Wood — A3172

LITHOGRAPHED

Serpentine Die Cut 10½

2007, Aug. 4

Self-Adhesive

4160 A3169 41c multicolored .85 .30
4161 A3170 41c multicolored .85 .30
4162 A3171 41c multicolored .85 .30
4163 A3172 41c multicolored .85 .30
a. Horiz. strip of 4, #4160-4163 3.40

Purple Heart Type of 2003

LITHOGRAPHED

Serpentine Die Cut 11¼x10¾

2007, Aug. 7

Self-Adhesive

4164 A2891 41c multicolored .85 .25

AMERICAN TREASURES SERIES

Magnolia and Irises, Stained Glass by Louis Comfort Tiffany — A3173

BOOKLET STAMP

Serpentine Die Cut 10¾ on 2 or 3 Sides

2007, Aug. 9

Self-Adhesive

4165 A3173 41c multicolored .85 .25
a. Booklet pane of 20 17.00

No. 4165a is a double-sided booklet pane with 12 stamps on one side and eight stamps plus label (booklet cover) on the other side.

FLOWERS

Iris — A3174

Dahlia — A3175

Magnolia A3176

Red Gerbera Daisy A3177

Coneflower A3178

Tulip A3179

Water Lily — A3180

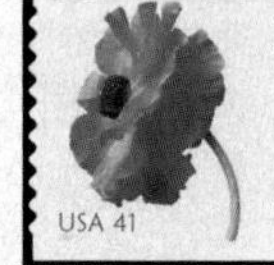
Poppy — A3181

Chrysanthemum A3182

Orange Gerbera Daisy A3183

LITHOGRAPHED, PHOTOGRAVURE (#4176-4185)

Serpentine Die Cut 9½ Vert.

2007, Aug. 10

COIL STAMPS

Self-Adhesive

4166 A3174 41c multicolored 1.75 .35
4167 A3175 41c multicolored 1.75 .35
4168 A3176 41c multicolored 1.75 .35
4169 A3177 41c multicolored 1.75 .35
4170 A3178 41c multicolored 1.75 .35
4171 A3179 41c multicolored 1.75 .35
4172 A3180 41c multicolored 1.75 .35
4173 A3181 41c multicolored 1.75 .35
4174 A3182 41c multicolored 1.75 .35
4175 A3183 41c multicolored 1.75 .35
a. Strip of 10, #4166-4175 17.50

BOOKLET STAMPS

Serpentine Die Cut 11¼x11½ on 2 or 3 Sides

4176 A3182 41c multicolored 1.50 .35
4177 A3183 41c multicolored 1.50 .35
4178 A3174 41c multicolored 1.50 .35
4179 A3175 41c multicolored 1.50 .35
4180 A3176 41c multicolored 1.50 .35
4181 A3177 41c multicolored 1.50 .35
4182 A3180 41c multicolored 1.50 .35
4183 A3181 41c multicolored 1.50 .35
4184 A3178 41c multicolored 1.50 .35
4185 A3179 41c multicolored 1.50 .35
a. Booklet pane of 20, 2 each #4176-4185 30.00
b. As "a," die cutting missing on Nos. 4178 & 4183 on side with 8 stamps (PS) —

No. 4185a is a double-sided booklet pane with 12 stamps on one side (2 each #4176-4177, 1 each #4178-4185) and eight stamps (#4178-4185) plus label (booklet cover) on the other side.

Flag — A3184

LITHOGRAPHED, PHOTOGRAVURE (#4188, 4189)

Serpentine Die Cut 9½ Vert.

2007, Aug. 15

COIL STAMPS

Self-Adhesive

With "USPS" Microprinted on Right Side of Flagpole

With Perpendicular Corners

4186 A3184 41c multicolored .85 .25

With "USPS" Microprinted on Left Side of Flagpole

Serpentine Die Cut 11 Vert.

4187 A3184 41c multicolored .85 .25

Without "USPS" Microprinting on Flagpole

Serpentine Die Cut 8½ Vert.

4188 A3184 41c multicolored .85 .25

Serpentine Die Cut 11 Vert.

With Rounded Corners

4189 A3184 41c multicolored .85 .25

No. 4188 is on backing paper as high as the stamp. No. 4189 is on backing paper that is larger than the stamp.

BOOKLET STAMPS

Serpentine Die Cut 11¼x10¾ on 3 Sides

With "USPS" Microprinted on Right Side of Flagpole

4190 A3184 41c multicolored .85 .25
a. Booklet pane of 10 8.50

With "USPS" Microprinted on Left Side of Flagpole

Serpentine Die Cut 11¼x10¾ on 2 or 3 Sides

4191 A3184 41c multicolored .85 .25
a. Booklet pane of 20 17.00

The microprinting on Nos. 4190 and 4191 is under the ball of the flagpole. The flagpole is light gray on No. 4190 and dark gray on No. 4191. No. 4191a is a double-sided booklet with 12 stamps on one side of the peelable backing and 8 stamps plus label (booklet cover) on the other side.

THE ART OF DISNEY: MAGIC

Mickey Mouse A3185

Peter Pan and Tinker Bell — A3186

Dumbo and Timothy Mouse A3187

Aladdin and Genie — A3188

PHOTOGRAVURE

Serpentine Die Cut 10½x10¾

2007, Aug. 16

Self-Adhesive

4192 A3185 41c multicolored .85 .30
4193 A3186 41c multicolored .85 .30
4194 A3187 41c multicolored .85 .30
4195 A3188 41c multicolored .85 .30
a. Block of 4, #4192-4195 3.40

CELEBRATE

A3189

LITHOGRAPHED

Serpentine Die Cut 10¾

2007, Aug. 17

Self-Adhesive

4196 A3189 41c multicolored .85 .25

See Nos. 4335, 4407.

LEGENDS OF HOLLYWOOD

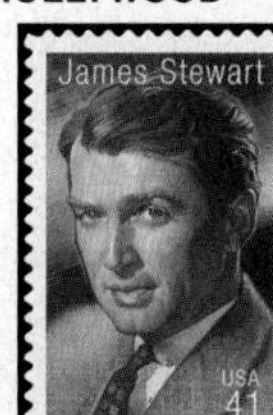
James Stewart (1908-97), Actor — A3190

2007, Aug. 17

Self-Adhesive

4197 A3190 41c multicolored .90 .25

ALPINE TUNDRA

A3191

No. 4198 — Wildlife: a, Elk. b, Golden eagle, horiz. c, Yellow-bellied marmot. d, American pika. e, Bighorn sheep. f, Magdalena alpine butterfly. g, White-tailed ptarmigan. h, Rocky Mountain parnassian butterfly. i, Melissa arctic butterfly, horiz. j, Brown-capped rosy-finch, horiz.

PHOTOGRAVURE

2007, Aug. 28

Self-Adhesive

4198 A3191 Pane of 10 8.50
a.-j. 41c any single .85 .40

GERALD R. FORD

Gerald R. Ford (1913-2006), 38th President — A3192

LITHOGRAPHED

Serpentine Die Cut 11

2007, Aug. 31

Self-Adhesive

4199 A3192 41c multicolored .85 .25

JURY DUTY

Twelve Jurors — A3193

Serpentine Die Cut 10½

2007, Sept. 12

Self-Adhesive

4200 A3193 41c multicolored .85 .25

MENDEZ v. WESTMINSTER, 60th ANNIV.

A3194

LITHOGRAPHED

Serpentine Die Cut 11

2007, Sept. 14

Self-Adhesive

4201 A3194 41c multicolored .85 .25

Eid Type of 2001

PHOTOGRAVURE

Serpentine Die Cut 11

2007, Sept. 28

Self-Adhesive

4202 A2734 41c multicolored .90 .25

AURORAS

Aurora Borealis A3195

Aurora Australis A3196

LITHOGRAPHED

Serpentine Die Cut 10¾

2007, Oct. 1

Self-Adhesive

4203 A3195 41c multicolored 1.25 .25
4204 A3196 41c multicolored 1.25 .25
a. Horiz. or vert. pair, #4203-4204 2.50

YODA

A3197

Serpentine Die Cut 10½x10¾

2007, Oct. 25

Self-Adhesive

4205 A3197 41c multicolored .85 .25

CHRISTMAS

Madonna of the Carnation, by Bernardino Luini A3198

Knit Reindeer A3199

Knit Christmas Tree A3200

Knit Snowman A3201

Knit Bear A3202

Knit Reindeer A3203

Knit Christmas Tree A3204

Knit Snowman A3205

Knit Bear — A3206

LITHOGRAPHED, PHOTOGRAVURE (#4215-4218)

Serpentine Die Cut 10¾x11 on 2 or 3 Sides

2007, Oct. 25

Self-Adhesive

Booklet Stamps (#4206, 4210b, 4211-4218)

4206 A3198 41c multicolored .85 .25
a. Booklet pane of 20 17.00

No. 4206a is a double-sided booklet pane with 12 stamps on one side and eight stamps plus label that serves as a booklet cover on the other side.

Serpentine Die Cut 10¾ on 2, 3 or 4 Sides

4207 A3199 41c multicolored .85 .25
4208 A3200 41c multicolored .85 .25
4209 A3201 41c multicolored .85 .25
4210 A3202 41c multicolored, overall tagging .85 .25
b. Block or vert. strip of 4, #4207-4210 3.40
d. Booklet pane of 20 17.00

No. 4210d is a double-sided booklet pane with 12 stamps on one side and eight stamps plus label that serves as a booklet cover on the other side.

Serpentine Die Cut 11¼x11 on 2 or 3 Sides

4211 A3203 41c multicolored .85 .25
4212 A3204 41c multicolored .85 .25
4213 A3205 41c multicolored .85 .25
4214 A3206 41c multicolored .85 .25
a. Block of 4, #4211-4214 3.40
b. Booklet pane of 4, #4211-4214 3.40
c. Booklet pane of 6, #4213-4214, 2 each #4211-4212 5.10
d. Booklet pane of 6, #4211-4212, 2 each #4213-4214 5.10

Serpentine Die Cut 8 on 2, 3 or 4 Sides

4215 A3203 41c multicolored 1.00 .25
4216 A3204 41c multicolored 1.00 .25
4217 A3205 41c multicolored 1.00 .25
4218 A3206 41c multicolored 1.00 .25
a. Block of 4, #4215-4218 4.00
b. Booklet pane of 18, 4 each #4215, 4218, 5 each #4216, 4217 18.00
Nos. 4206-4218 (13) 11.65 3.25

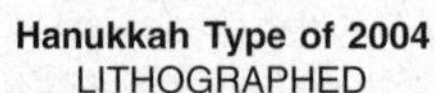

Hanukkah Type of 2004

LITHOGRAPHED

Serpentine Die Cut 10¾x11

2007, Oct. 26

Self-Adhesive

4219 A2962 41c multicolored .85 .25

Kwanzaa Type of 2004

LITHOGRAPHED

Serpentine Die Cut 11x10¾

2007, Oct. 26

Self-Adhesive

4220 A2963 41c multicolored .85 .25

CHINESE NEW YEAR

Year of the Rat A3207

PHOTOGRAVURE

Serpentine Die Cut 10¾

2008, Jan. 9

Self-Adhesive

4221 A3207 41c multicolored .85 .25

BLACK HERITAGE SERIES

Charles W. Chesnutt (1858-1932), Writer — A3208

Serpentine Die Cut 11

2008, Jan. 31 **Self-Adhesive**

4222 A3208 41c multicolored .85 .25

LITERARY ARTS SERIES

Marjorie Kinnan Rawlings (1896-1953), Writer — A3209

Self-Adhesive

4223 A3209 41c multicolored .85 .25

AMERICAN SCIENTISTS

Gerty Cori (1896-1957), Biochemist — A3210

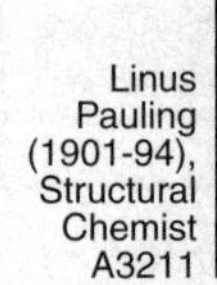

Linus Pauling (1901-94), Structural Chemist A3211

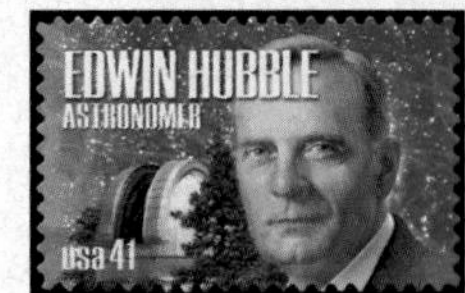

Edwin Hubble (1889-1953), Astronomer — A3212

John Bardeen (1908-91), Theoretical Physicist A3213

2008, Mar. 6

Self-Adhesive

4224 A3210 41c multicolored 1.00 .30
4225 A3211 41c multicolored 1.00 .30
4226 A3212 41c multicolored 1.00 .30
4227 A3213 41c multicolored 1.00 .30
a. Horiz. strip of 4, #4224-4227 4.00

Flag at Dusk — A3214

Flag at Night — A3215

Flag at Dawn A3216

Flag at Midday A3217

PHOTOGRAVURE (#4228-4231, 4240-4247), LITHOGRAPHED (#4232-4239)

2008, Apr. 18 ***Perf. 9¾ Vert.***

COIL STAMPS

4228 A3214 42c multicolored 1.50 .40
4229 A3215 42c multicolored 1.50 .40
4230 A3216 42c multicolored 1.50 .40
4231 A3217 42c multicolored 1.50 .40
a. Horiz. strip of 4, #4228-4231 6.00 1.60

Self-Adhesive

With Perpendicular Corners

Serpentine Die Cut 9½ Vert.

4232 A3214 42c multicolored 1.50 .25
4233 A3215 42c multicolored 1.50 .25
4234 A3216 42c multicolored 1.50 .25
4235 A3217 42c multicolored 1.50 .25
a. Horiz. strip of 4, #4232-4235 6.00

Serpentine Die Cut 11 Vert.

4236 A3214 42c multicolored 1.50 .25
4237 A3215 42c multicolored 1.50 .25
4238 A3216 42c multicolored 1.50 .25
4239 A3217 42c multicolored 1.50 .25
a. Horiz. strip of 4, #4236-4239 6.00

Serpentine Die Cut 8½ Vert.

4240 A3214 42c multicolored 1.50 .25
4241 A3215 42c multicolored 1.50 .25
4242 A3216 42c multicolored 1.50 .25
4243 A3217 42c multicolored 1.50 .25
a. Horiz. strip of 4, #4240-4243 6.00

Serpentine Die Cut 11 Vert.

With Rounded Corners

4244 A3214 42c multicolored 1.00 .30
4245 A3215 42c multicolored 1.00 .30
4246 A3216 42c multicolored 1.00 .30
4247 A3217 42c multicolored 1.00 .30
a. Horiz. strip of 4, #4244-4247 5.00
Nos. 4228-4247 (20) 28.00 5.80

Nos. 4232-4243 are on backing paper as high as the stamp. Nos. 4244-4247 are on backing paper that is larger than the stamp. Nos. 4232-4235 have "USPS" microprinted on the right side of a white flag stripe. Nos. 4236-4239 have "USPS" micorprinted on red flag stripes. On Nos. 4244-4247, the paper, vignette size and "2008" year date are slightly larger than those features on Nos. 4236-4239.

AMERICAN JOURNALISTS

Martha Gellhorn (1908-98) A3218

John Hersey (1914-93) A3219

George Polk (1913-48) A3220

Ruben Salazar (1928-70) A3221

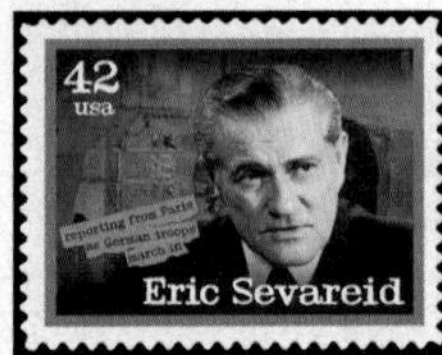

Eric Sevareid (1912-92) A3222

LITHOGRAPHED

Serpentine Die Cut 10¾x10½

2008, Apr. 22

Self-Adhesive

4248 A3218 42c multicolored 1.25 .40
4249 A3219 42c multicolored 1.25 .40
4250 A3220 42c multicolored 1.25 .40
4251 A3221 42c multicolored 1.25 .40
4252 A3222 42c multicolored 1.25 .40
a. Vert. strip of 5, #4248-4252 6.25

TROPICAL FRUIT

Pomegranate A3223

Star Fruit A3224

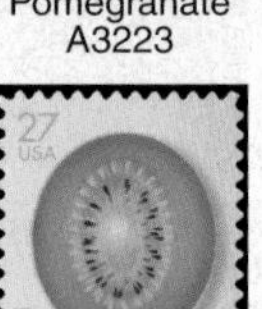

Kiwi A3225

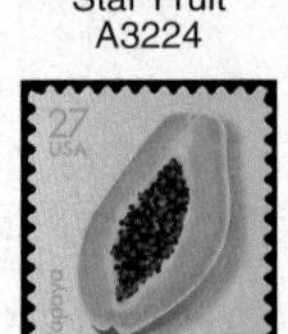

Papaya A3226

Guava — A3227

LITHOGRAPHED (#4253-4257), PHOTOGRAVURE (#4258-4262)

Serpentine Die Cut 11¼x10¾

2008, Apr. 25

Self-Adhesive

4253 A3223 27c multicolored .90 .25
4254 A3224 27c multicolored .90 .25
4255 A3225 27c multicolored .90 .25
4256 A3226 27c multicolored .90 .25
4257 A3227 27c multicolored .90 .25
a. Horiz. strip of 5, #4253-4257 4.50

COIL STAMPS

Serpentine Die Cut 8½ Vert.

4258 A3226 27c multicolored 1.25 .25
4259 A3227 27c multicolored 1.25 .25
4260 A3223 27c multicolored 1.25 .25
4261 A3224 27c multicolored 1.25 .25

4262 A3225 27c multicolored 1.25 .25
a. Strip of 5, #4258-4262 6.25
b. As No. 4262, light green ("27 USA," "Kiwi" and year date) omitted —
Nos. 4253-4262 (10) 10.75 2.50

Purple Heart Type of 2003
LITHOGRAPHED

2008, Apr. 30 ***Perf. 11¼***
4263 A2891 42c multicolored .90 .25

Self-Adhesive
Serpentine Die Cut 11¼x10¾
4264 A2891 42c multicolored .85 .25

FRANK SINATRA

Frank Sinatra (1915-98), Singer and Actor — A3228

Serpentine Die Cut 10¾
2008, May 13
Self-Adhesive
4265 A3228 42c multicolored .85 .25

MINNESOTA STATEHOOD, 150th ANNIV.

Bridge Over Mississippi River Near Winona — A3229

Serpentine Die Cut 10¾
2008, May 17
Self-Adhesive
4266 A3229 42c multicolored .85 .25

WILDLIFE

Dragonfly — A3230

LITHOGRAPHED
Serpentine Die Cut 11¼x11
2008, May 19
Self-Adhesive
4267 A3230 62c multicolored 1.25 .25

AMERICAN LANDMARKS

Mount Rushmore A3231

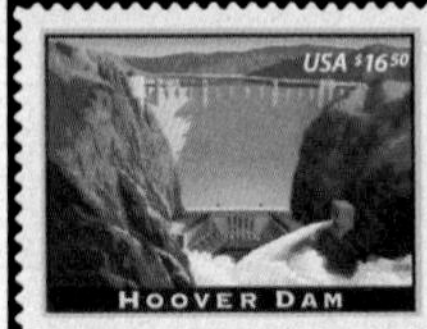

Hoover Dam A3232

2008 ***Serpentine Die Cut 10¾x10½***
Self-Adhesive
4268 A3231 $4.80 multicolored 9.75 5.00
4269 A3232 $16.50 multicolored 30.00 17.00

Issued: $4.80, 6/6; $16.50, 6/20.

LOVE

Man Carrying Heart — A3233

PHOTOGRAVURE
Serpentine Die Cut 10¾ on 2, 3, or 4 Sides
2008, June 10
Booklet Stamp
Self-Adhesive
4270 A3233 42c multicolored .85 .25
a. Booklet pane of 20 17.00

WEDDING HEARTS

Heart With Light Green Background A3234

Heart With Buff Background A3235

LITHOGRAPHED (#4271), PHOTOGRAVURE (#4272) BOOKLET STAMP (#4271)
Serpentine Die Cut 10¾ on 2, 3 or 4 Sides
2008, June 10
Self-Adhesive
4271 A3234 42c multicolored .90 .25
a. Booklet pane of 20 18.00

Serpentine Die Cut 10¾
4272 A3235 59c multicolored 1.25 .25

FLAGS OF OUR NATION

American Flag and Clouds — A3236

Alabama Flag and Shrimp Boat — A3237

Alaska Flag and Humpback Whale — A3238

American Samoa Flag and Island Peaks and Trees — A3239

Arizona Flag and Saguaro Cacti A3240

Arkansas Flag and Wood Duck — A3241

California Flag and Coast — A3242

Colorado Flag and Mountain — A3243

Connecticut Flag, Sailboats and Buoy — A3244

Delaware Flag and Beach — A3245

PHOTOGRAVURE
Serpentine Die Cut 11 Vert.
2008, June 14
Self-Adhesive
Coil Stamps
4273 A3236 42c multicolored .85 .30
4274 A3237 42c multicolored .85 .30
4275 A3238 42c multicolored .85 .30
4276 A3239 42c multicolored .85 .30
4277 A3240 42c multicolored .85 .30
a. Strip of 5, #4273-4277 4.25
4278 A3241 42c multicolored .85 .30
4279 A3242 42c multicolored .85 .30
4280 A3243 42c multicolored .85 .30
4281 A3244 42c multicolored .85 .30
4282 A3245 42c multicolored .85 .30
a. Strip of 5, #4278-4282 4.25
b. P # set of 10, #4277a + 4282a 8.50

No. 4273 always has a plate number. No. 4282b may be collected as one continuous strip, but the item will not fit in any standard album.

District of Columbia Flag and Cherry Tree — A3246

Florida Flag and Anhinga A3247

Georgia Flag, Fence and Lamppost — A3248

Guam Flag, Fish and Tropicbird — A3249

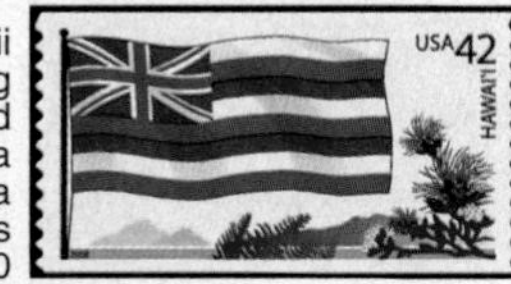

Hawaii Flag and Ohia Lehua Flowers A3250

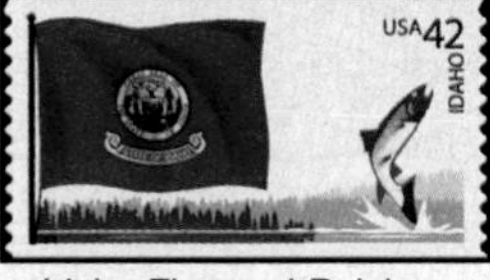

Idaho Flag and Rainbow Trout — A3251

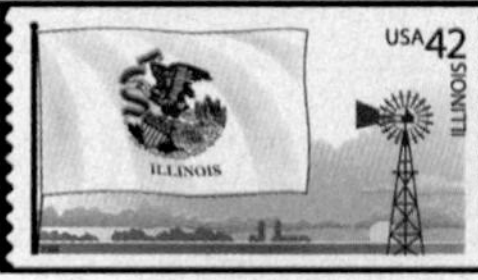

Illinois Flag and Windmill A3252

Indiana Flag and Tractor A3253

Iowa Flag, Farm Field and Cornstalks — A3254

Kansas Flag and Farm Buildings — A3255

2008, Sept. 2
Self-Adhesive
Coil Stamps
4283 A3246 42c multicolored .85 .30
4284 A3247 42c multicolored .85 .30
4285 A3248 42c multicolored .85 .30
4286 A3249 42c multicolored .85 .30
4287 A3250 42c multicolored .85 .30
a. Strip of 5, #4283-4287 4.25
4288 A3251 42c multicolored .85 .30
4289 A3252 42c multicolored .85 .30
4290 A3253 42c multicolored .85 .30
4291 A3254 42c multicolored .85 .30
4292 A3255 42c multicolored .85 .30
a. Strip of 5, #4288-4292 4.25
b. P # set of 10, #4287a + 4192a 8.50

No. 4283 always has a plate number. No. 4292b may be collected as one continuous strip, but the item will not fit in any standard album.

Kentucky Flag, Fence and Horses — A3256

Louisiana Flag and Brown Pelicans — A3257

Maine Flag and Moose A3258

Maryland Flag and Red-winged Blackbird — A3259

Massachusetts Flag, Sea Birds and Sailboats — A3260

Michigan Flag and Great Lakes Ships — A3261

Minnesota Flag, Swans and Grain Elevator — A3262

Mississippi Flag and Black Bears — A3263

Missouri Flag and Paddle Wheeler A3264

American Flag and Wheat — A3265

2009, Aug. 6

Self-Adhesive

Coil Stamps

4293	A3256	44c	multicolored	.90	.30
4294	A3257	44c	multicolored	.90	.30
4295	A3258	44c	multicolored	.90	.30
4296	A3259	44c	multicolored	.90	.30
4297	A3260	44c	multicolored	.90	.30
a.	Strip of 5, #4293-4297			4.50	
4298	A3261	44c	multicolored	.90	.30
4299	A3262	44c	multicolored	.90	.30
4300	A3263	44c	multicolored	.90	.30
4301	A3264	44c	multicolored	.90	.30
4302	A3265	44c	multicolored	.90	.30
a.	Strip of 5, #4298-4302			4.50	
b.	P # set of 10, #4297a + 4302a			9.00	

No. 4293 always has a plate number. No. 4302b may be collected as one continuous strip, but the item will not fit in any standard album.

American Flag and Mountains — A3266

Montana Flag and Mountain Lion — A3267

Nebraska Flag and Central-pivot Irrigation System — A3268

Nevada Flag, Mountains and Ocotillos — A3269

New Hampshire Flag and Loon — A3270

New Jersey Flag and Sand Castle A3271

New Mexico Flag, Mountains and Hot Air Balloons — A3272

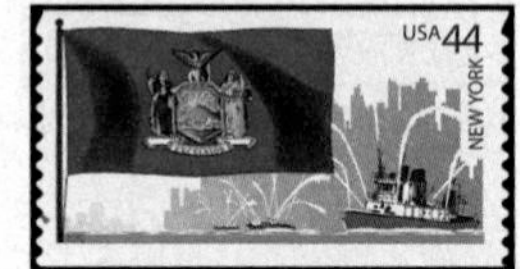

New York Flag, Fireboats and City Skyline — A3273

North Carolina Flag, Great Blue Heron and Cape Hatteras Lighthouse — A3274

North Dakota Flag and Elk A3275

2010, Apr. 16

Self-Adhesive

Coil Stamps

4303	A3266	44c	multicolored	.90	.30
4304	A3267	44c	multicolored	.90	.30
4305	A3268	44c	multicolored	.90	.30
4306	A3269	44c	multicolored	.90	.30
4307	A3270	44c	multicolored	.90	.30
a.	Strip of 5, #4303-4307			4.50	
4308	A3271	44c	multicolored	.90	.30
4309	A3272	44c	multicolored	.90	.30
4310	A3273	44c	multicolored	.90	.30
4311	A3274	44c	multicolored	.90	.30
4312	A3275	44c	multicolored	.90	.30
a.	Strip of 5, #4308-4312			4.50	
b.	P # set of 10, #4307a + 4312a			9.00	

No. 4303 always has a plate number. No. 4312b may be collected as one continuous strip, but the item will not fit in any standard album.

Northern Marianas Flag, Beach and Palm Trees — A3276

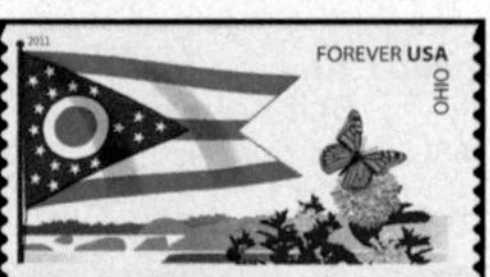

Ohio Flag, Butterfly, Milkweed Flowers and River — A3277

Oklahoma Flag and Oil Pumps — A3278

Oregon Flag, Mount Hood and Camas Lilies A3279

Pennsylvania Flag and White-tailed Deer — A3280

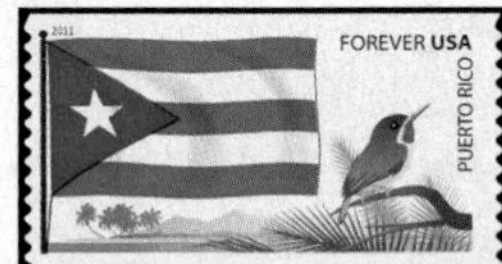

Puerto Rico Flag and Puerto Rican Tody Bird A3281

Rhode Island Flag and Sailboat A3282

South Carolina Flag, Marsh and Gazebo A3283

South Dakota Flag and Bison A3284

Tennessee Flag and Scarlet Tanagers — A3285

PHOTOGRAVURE

Serpentine Die Cut 11 Vert.

2011, Aug. 11

Self-Adhesive

Coil Stamps

4313	A3276	(44c)	multicolored	.95	.30
4314	A3277	(44c)	multicolored	.95	.30
4315	A3278	(44c)	multicolored	.95	.30
4316	A3279	(44c)	multicolored	.95	.30
4317	A3280	(44c)	multicolored	.95	.30
a.	Strip of 5, #4313-4317			4.75	
4318	A3281	(44c)	multicolored	.95	.30
4319	A3282	(44c)	multicolored	.95	.30
4320	A3283	(44c)	multicolored	.95	.30
4321	A3284	(44c)	multicolored	.95	.30
4322	A3285	(44c)	multicolored	.95	.30
a.	Strip of 5, #4318-4322			4.75	
b.	P# set of 10, #4317a + 4322a			9.50	

Alternating examples of the five examples of No. 4313 in the roll have a plate number. No. 4322b may be collected as one continuous strip, but the item will not fit in any standard album.

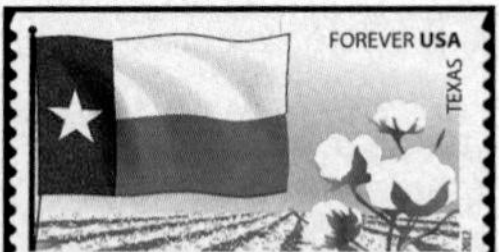

Texas Flag, Cotton Plant and Field A3286

Utah Flag, Cactus and Rock Arch A3287

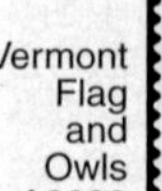

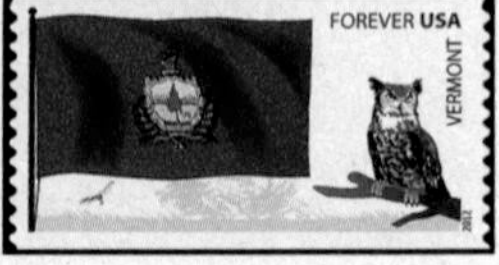

Vermont Flag and Owls A3288

Virgin Islands Flag, Sailfish and Boat A3289

Virginia Flag and Replicas of Ships that Carried Settlers to Jamestown — A3290

Washington Flag and Evergreen Forest — A3291

West Virginia Flag and Wild Turkeys A3292

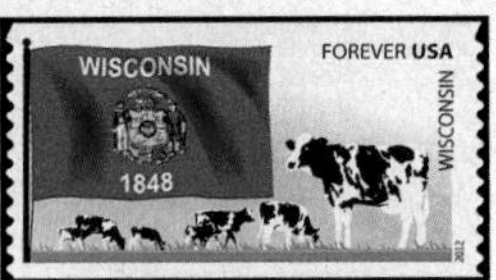

Wisconsin Flag and Dairy Cows — A3293

Wyoming Flag and Bighorn Sheep — A3294

American Flag and Fruited Plain — A3295

PHOTOGRAVURE

Serpentine Die Cut 11 Vert.

2012, Aug. 16

Self-Adhesive

Coil Stamps

4323	A3286	(45c)	multicolored	.95	.30
4324	A3287	(45c)	multicolored	.95	.30
4325	A3288	(45c)	multicolored	.95	.30
4326	A3289	(45c)	multicolored	.95	.30
4327	A3290	(45c)	multicolored	.95	.30
a.	Strip of 5, #4323-4327			4.75	
4328	A3291	(45c)	multicolored	.95	.30
4329	A3292	(45c)	multicolored	.95	.30
4330	A3293	(45c)	multicolored	.95	.30
4331	A3294	(45c)	multicolored	.95	.30
4332	A3295	(45c)	multicolored	.95	.30
a.	Strip of 5, #4328-4332			4.75	
b.	P# set of 10, #4327a + 4332a			9.50	

Alternating examples of the five examples of No. 4323 in the roll have a plate number. No. 4332b may be collected as one continuous strip, but the item will not fit in any standard album.

CHARLES (1907-78) AND RAY (1912-88) EAMES, DESIGNERS

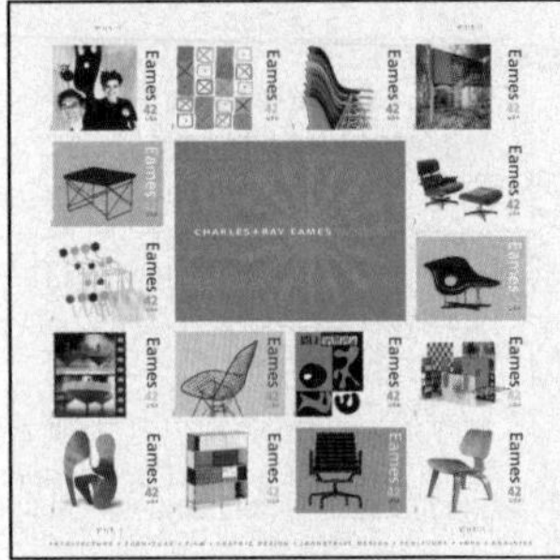
A3296

No. 4333: a, Christmas card depicting Charles and Ray Eames. b, "Crosspatch" fabric design. c, Stacking chairs. d, Case Study House #8, Pacific Palisades, CA. e, Wire-base table. f, Lounge chair and ottoman. g, Hang-it-all. h, La Chaise. i, Scene from film, "Tops." j, Wire mesh chair. k, Cover of May 1943 edition of *California Arts & Architecture* Magazine. l, House of Cards. m, Molded plywood sculpture. n, Eames Storage Unit. o, Aluminum group chair. p, Molded plywood chair.

PHOTOGRAVURE

Serpentine Die Cut 10¾x10½

2008, June 17

Self-Adhesive

4333	A3296	Pane of 16 + label	18.00	
a.-p.	42c Any single		1.10	.50

SUMMER OLYMPIC GAMES, BEIJING, CHINA

Gymnast A3297

LITHOGRAPHED

Serpentine Die Cut 10¾

2008, June 19

Self-Adhesive

4334	A3297	42c	multicolored	.85	.25

Celebrate Type of 2007

Serpentine Die Cut 10¾

2008, July 10

Self-Adhesive

4335	A3189	42c	multicolored	.85	.25

VINTAGE BLACK CINEMA

Poster for "Black and Tan" — A3298

Poster for "The Sport of the Gods" — A3299

Poster for "Prinsesse Tam-Tam" A3300

Poster for "Caldonia" A3301

Poster for "Hallelujah" — A3302

Serpentine Die Cut 10¾

2008, July 16 **Tagged**

Self-Adhesive

4336	A3298	42c	multicolored	.85	.40
4337	A3299	42c	multicolored	.85	.40
4338	A3300	42c	multicolored	.85	.40
4339	A3301	42c	multicolored	.85	.40
4340	A3302	42c	multicolored	.85	.40
a.	Horiz. strip of 5, #4336-4340			4.25	

"TAKE ME OUT TO THE BALLGAME," CENT.

Baseball Players and First Six Notes of Song — A3303

PHOTOGRAVURE

Serpentine Die Cut 11

2008, July 16

Self-Adhesive

4341	A3303	42c	multicolored	.85	.25

THE ART OF DISNEY: IMAGINATION

Pongo and Pup — A3304

Steamboat Willie — A3305

Princess Aurora, Flora, Fauna and Merryweather A3306

Mowgli and Baloo — A3307

Serpentine Die Cut 10½x10¾

2008, Aug. 7

Self-Adhesive

4342	A3304	42c	multicolored	.85	.30
4343	A3305	42c	multicolored	.85	.30
4344	A3306	42c	multicolored	.85	.30
4345	A3307	42c	multicolored	.85	.30
a.	Block of 4, #4342-4345			3.40	

AMERICAN TREASURES SERIES

Valley of the Yosemite, by Albert Bierstadt A3308

LITHOGRAPHED

BOOKLET STAMP

Serpentine Die Cut 11 on 2 or 3 Sides

2008, Aug. 14

Self-Adhesive

4346	A3308	42c	multicolored	.85	.25
a.	Booklet pane of 20			17.00	

No. 4346a is a double-sided booklet pane with 12 stamps on one side and eight stamps plus label (booklet cover) on the other side.

Sunflower — A3309

BOOKLET STAMP

Serpentine Die Cut 11¼x10¾ on 2 or 3 Sides

2008, Aug. 15

Self-Adhesive

4347	A3309	42c	multicolored	.85	.25
a.	Booklet pane of 20			17.00	

No. 4347a is a double-sided booklet pane with 12 stamps on one side and eight stamps plus label (booklet cover) on the other side.

Sea Coast Type of 2002

LITHOGRAPHED

COIL STAMP

Perf. 9¾ Vert.

2008, Sept. 5 **Untagged**

4348	A2853	(5c)	multicolored	.25	.25

No. 4348 has "2008" year date in black, and microprinted "USPS" at the end of the purple rock to the right of the crashing wave.

LATIN JAZZ

Musicians A3310

PHOTOGRAVURE

Serpentine Die Cut 11x10¾

2008, Sept. 8

Self-Adhesive

4349	A3310	42c	multicolored	.85	.25

LEGENDS OF HOLLYWOOD

Bette Davis (1908-89), Actress — A3311

LITHOGRAPHED

Serpentine Die Cut 10¾

2008, Sept. 18

Self-Adhesive

4350 A3311 42c multicolored 1.00 .25

Eid Type of 2001

PHOTOGRAVURE

Serpentine Die Cut 11

2008, Sept. 23

Self-Adhesive

4351 A2734 42c multicolored .85 .25

GREAT LAKES DUNES

A3312

No. 4352 — Wildlife: a, Vesper sparrow. b, Red fox, vert. c, Piping plover. d, Eastern hog-nose snake. e, Common mergansers. f, Spotted sandpiper, vert. g, Tiger beetle, vert. h, White-footed mouse, vert. i, Piping plover nestlings. j, Red admiral butterfly, vert.

Serpentine Die Cut 10¾

2008, Oct. 2

Self-Adhesive

4352 A3312 Pane of 10 8.50
a.-j. 42c Any single .85 .40

AUTOMOBILES OF THE 1950s

1959 Cadillac Eldorado A3313

1957 Studebaker Golden Hawk A3314

1957 Pontiac Safari A3315

1957 Lincoln Premiere A3316

1957 Chrysler 300C A3317

LITHOGRAPHED

2008, Oct. 3

Self-Adhesive

4353 A3313 42c multicolored .85 .40
4354 A3314 42c multicolored .85 .40
4355 A3315 42c multicolored .85 .40
4356 A3316 42c multicolored .85 .40
4357 A3317 42c multicolored .85 .40
a. Vert. strip of 5, #4353-4357 4.25

ALZHEIMER'S DISEASE AWARENESS

A3318

PHOTOGRAVURE

Serpentine Die Cut 10¾

2008, Oct. 17

Self-Adhesive

4358 A3318 42c multicolored .85 .25

CHRISTMAS

Virgin and Child with the Young John the Baptist, by Sandro Botticelli A3319

Drummer Nutcracker A3320

Santa Claus Nutcracker A3321

King Nutcracker A3322

Soldier Nutcracker A3323

Drummer Nutcracker A3324

Santa Claus Nutcracker A3325

King Nutcracker A3326

Soldier Nutcracker — A3327

LITHOGRAPHED, PHOTOGRAVURE (#4368-4371)

Serpentine Die Cut 10¾x11 on 2 or 3 Sides

2008, Oct. 23

Self-Adhesive

Booklet Stamps

4359 A3319 42c multicolored .85 .25
a. Booklet pane of 20 17.00
b. Die cutting omitted, pair —
4360 A3320 42c multicolored 1.00 .25
4361 A3321 42c multicolored 1.00 .25
4362 A3322 42c multicolored 1.00 .25
4363 A3323 42c multicolored 1.00 .25
a. Block of 4, #4360-4363 4.00
b. Booklet pane of 20, 5 each #4360-4363 20.00

No. 4359a is a double-sided booklet pane with 12 stamps on one side and eight stamps plus label that serves as a booklet cover on the other side. No. 4363b is a double-sided booklet pane with 12 stamps on one side (3 each of Nos. 4360-4363) and eight stamps (2 each of Nos. 4360-4363) plus label that serves as a booklet cover on the other side.

Serpentine Die Cut 11¼x11 on 2 or 3 Sides

4364 A3324 42c multicolored 1.00 .25
4365 A3325 42c multicolored 1.00 .25
4366 A3326 42c multicolored 1.00 .25
4367 A3327 42c multicolored 1.00 .25
a. Block of 4, #4364-4367 4.00
b. Booklet pane of 4, #4364-4367 4.00
c. Booklet pane of 6, #4366-4367, 2 each #4364-4365 6.00
d. Booklet pane of 6, #4364-4365, 2 each #4366-4367 6.00

Serpentine Die Cut 8 on 2, 3 or 4 Sides

4368 A3324 42c multicolored 1.00 .25
4369 A3325 42c multicolored 1.00 .25
4370 A3326 42c multicolored 1.00 .25
4371 A3327 42c multicolored 1.00 .25
a. Block of 4, #4368-4371 4.00
b. Booklet pane of 18, 5 each #4368-4369, 4 each #4370-4371 18.00
Nos. 4359-4371 (13) 12.85 3.25

Hanukkah Type of 2004

LITHOGRAPHED

Serpentine Die Cut 10¾x11

2008, Oct. 24

Self-Adhesive

4372 A2962 42c multicolored .85 .25

Kwanzaa Type of 2004

Serpentine Die Cut 11x10¾

2008, Oct. 24

Self-Adhesive

4373 A2963 42c multicolored .85 .25

ALASKA STATEHOOD, 50TH ANNIV.

Dogsledder Near Rainy Pass A3328

Serpentine Die Cut 10¾

2009, Jan. 3

Self-Adhesive

4374 A3328 42c multicolored .85 .25

CHINESE NEW YEAR

Year of the Ox A3329

2009, Jan. 8

Self-Adhesive

4375 A3329 42c multicolored .85 .25

OREGON STATEHOOD, 150TH ANNIV.

Pacific Coast of Oregon A3330

2009, Jan. 14

Self-Adhesive

4376 A3330 42c multicolored .85 .25

EDGAR ALLAN POE

Edgar Allan Poe (1809-49), Writer — A3331

PHOTOGRAVURE

2009, Jan. 16

Self-Adhesive

4377 A3331 42c multicolored .90 .25

AMERICAN LANDMARKS

Redwood Forest A3332

Old Faithful A3333

LITHOGRAPHED

Serpentine Die Cut 10¾x10½

2009, Jan. 16

Self-Adhesive

4378 A3332 $4.95 multi 10.00 5.00
4379 A3333 $17.50 multi 32.50 20.00

ABRAHAM LINCOLN (1809-65), 16TH PRESIDENT

Lincoln as Rail-splitter A3334

Lincoln as Lawyer A3335

Lincoln as Politician A3336

Lincoln as President A3337

Serpentine Die Cut 10¾

2009, Feb. 9

Self-Adhesive

4380 A3334 42c multicolored 1.50 .30
4381 A3335 42c multicolored 1.50 .30
4382 A3336 42c multicolored 1.50 .30
4383 A3337 42c multicolored 1.50 .30
a. Horiz. strip of 4, #4380-4383 6.00

CIVIL RIGHTS PIONEERS

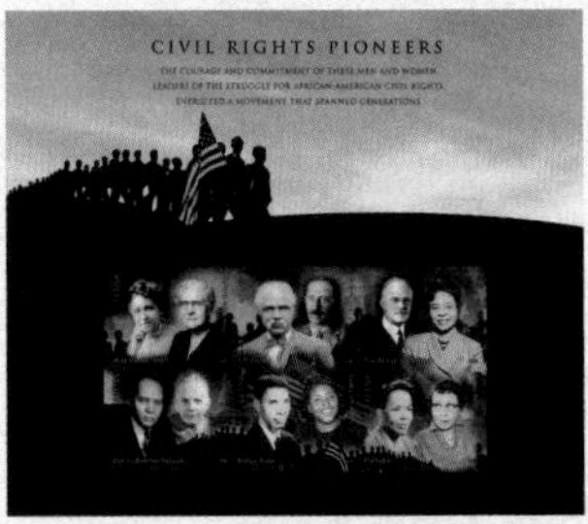

A3338

No. 4384: a, Mary Church Terrell (1863-1954), writer, Mary White Ovington (1865-1951), journalist. b, J. R. Clifford (1848-1933), attorney, Joel Elias Spingarn (1875-1939), educator. c, Oswald Garrison Villard (1872-1949), co-founder of National Association for the Advancement of Colored People (NAACP), Daisy Gatson Bates (1914-99), mentor of black Little Rock Central High School students. d, Charles Hamilton Houston (1895-1950), lawyer, Walter White (1893-1955), chief secretary of NAACP. e, Medgar Evers (1925-63), assassinated Mississippi NAACP field secretary, Fannie Lou Hamer (1917-77), voting rights activist. f, Ella Baker (1903-86), activist, Ruby Hurley (1909-80), NAACP Southeast Regional Director.

PHOTOGRAVURE

2009, Feb. 21

Self-Adhesive

4384 A3338 Pane of 6 5.10
a.-f. 42c Any single .85 .40

Patriotic Banner Type of 2007

LITHOGRAPHED

COIL STAMP

Perf. 9¾ Vert.

2009, Feb. 24 **Untagged**

4385 A3167 (10c) multicolored .25 .25

LITERARY ARTS

Richard Wright (1908-60), Author A3339

Serpentine Die Cut 10¾

2009, Apr. 9

Self-Adhesive

4386 A3339 61c multicolored 1.25 .25

WILDLIFE

Polar Bear A3340

Dolphin A3341

LITHOGRAPHED (#4387), PHOTOGRAVURE

2009 ***Serpentine Die Cut 11¼x11***

Self-Adhesive

4387 A3340 28c multi .60 .25

Serpentine Die Cut 11

4388 A3341 64c multi 1.40 .25

COIL STAMP

Serpentine Die Cut 8½ Vert.

4389 A3340 28c multi .60 .25

Issued: Nos. 4387, 4389, 4/16; No. 4388, 6/12.

Purple Heart Type of 2003

LITHOGRAPHED

Serpentine Die Cut 11¼x10¾

2009, Apr. 28

Self-Adhesive

4390 A2891 44c multicolored .90 .25

Flag — A3342

LITHOGRAPHED, PHOTOGRAVURE (#4394, 4395, 4396)

2009 ***Perf. 9¾ Vert.***

COIL STAMPS

4391 A3342 44c multi .90 .90

Self-Adhesive

Serpentine Die Cut 11 Vert.

With Pointed Corners

4392 A3342 44c multi 1.50 .25
a. Die cutting omitted, pair —

Serpentine Die Cut 9½ Vert.

4393 A3342 44c multi 1.50 .25

Serpentine Die Cut 8½ Vert.

4394 A3342 44c multi 1.50 .25

Serpentine Die Cut 11 Vert.

With Rounded Corners

4395 A3342 44c multi .90 .25

BOOKLET STAMP

Serpentine Die Cut 11¼x10¾ on 3 Sides

4396 A3342 44c multi .90 .25
a. Booklet pane of 10 9.00

Nos. 4392-4394 are on backing paper as high as the stamp. No. 4395 is on backing paper that is taller than the stamp. No. 4393 has microprinted "USPS" on white stripe below the blue field.

Issued: Nos. 4391, 4395, 5/1; Nos. 4392-4394, 5/8, No. 4396, 6/5.

WEDDINGS

Wedding Rings — A3343

Wedding Cake — A3344

LITHOGRAPHED, PHOTOGRAVURE (#4398)

Serpentine Die Cut 10¾

2009, May 1

Self-Adhesive

4397 A3343 44c multicolored .90 .25
4398 A3344 61c multicolored 1.25 .25

See Nos. 4521, 4602.

THE SIMPSONS TELEVISION SHOW, 20TH ANNIV.

Homer Simpson A3345

Marge Simpson A3346

Bart Simpson A3347

Lisa Simpson A3348

Maggie Simpson — A3349

LITHOGRAPHED BOOKLET STAMPS

Serpentine Die Cut 10¾ on 2, 3 or 4 Sides

2009, May 7

Self-Adhesive

4399 A3345 44c multicolored .90 .40
4400 A3346 44c multicolored .90 .40
4401 A3347 44c multicolored .90 .40
4402 A3348 44c multicolored .90 .40
4403 A3349 44c multicolored .90 .40
a. Horiz. strip of 5, #4399-4403 4.50
b. Booklet pane of 20, 4 each #4399-4403 18.00

LOVE

King of Hearts A3350

Queen of Hearts A3351

PHOTOGRAVURE BOOKLET STAMPS

Serpentine Die Cut 10¾ on 2, 3 or 4 Sides

2009, May 8

Self-Adhesive

4404 A3350 44c multicolored 1.00 .25
4405 A3351 44c multicolored 1.00 .25
a. Horiz. or vert. pair, #4404-4405 2.00
b. Booklet pane of 20, 10 each #4404-4405 20.00

BOB HOPE

Bob Hope (1903-2003), Actor, Comedian — A3352

LITHOGRAPHED

Serpentine Die Cut 10¾

2009, May 29

Self-Adhesive

4406 A3352 44c multicolored .90 .25

Celebrate Type of 2007

2009, June 10

Self-Adhesive

4407 A3189 44c multicolored .90 .25
a. Die cutting omitted, pair *275.00*

BLACK HERITAGE

Anna Julia Cooper (c. 1858-1964), Educator — A3353

2009, June 11

Self-Adhesive

4408 A3353 44c multicolored .90 .25

GULF COAST LIGHTHOUSES

Matagorda Island Lighthouse, Texas A3354

Sabine Pass Lighthouse, Louisiana A3355

Biloxi Lighthouse, Mississippi A3356

Sand Island Lighthouse, Alabama A3357

Fort Jefferson Lighthouse, Florida — A3358

Serpentine Die Cut 11x10¾

2009, July 23

Self-Adhesive

4409 A3354 44c multicolored .90 .40
4410 A3355 44c multicolored .90 .40
4411 A3356 44c multicolored .90 .40
4412 A3357 44c multicolored .90 .40
4413 A3358 44c multicolored .90 .40
a. Horiz. strip of 5, #4409-4413 4.50

EARLY TV MEMORIES

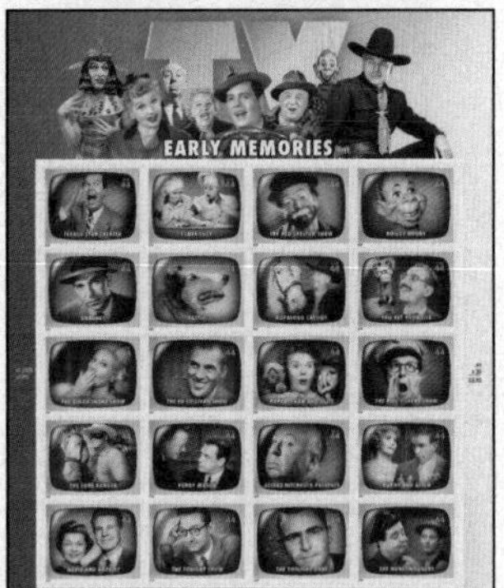

A3359

No. 4414: a, Milton Berle in "Texaco Star Theater." b, Lucille Ball and Vivian Vance in "I Love Lucy." c, Red Skelton in "The Red Skelton Show." d, Marionette Howdy Doody in "Howdy Doody." e, Jack Webb in "Dragnet." f, Lassie in "Lassie." g, William Boyd and horse, Topper, in "Hopalong Cassidy." h, Groucho Marx in "You Bet Your Life." i, Dinah Shore in "The Dinah Shore Show." j, Ed Sullivan in "The Ed Sullivan Show." k, Fran Allison and puppets, Kukla and Ollie in "Kukla, Fran and Ollie." l, Phil Silvers in "The Phil Silvers Show." m, Clayton Moore and horse, Silver, in "The Lone Ranger." n, Raymond Burr and William Talman in "Perry Mason." o, Alfred Hitchcock in "Alfred Hitchcock Presents." p, George Burns and Gracie Allen in "Burns and Allen." q, Ozzie and Harriet Nelson in "Ozzie and Harriet." r, Steve Allen in "The Tonight Show." s, Rod Serling in "The Twilight Zone." t, Jackie Gleason and Art Carney in "The Honeymooners."

Serpentine Die Cut 10¾x10½

2009, Aug. 11

Self-Adhesive

4414 A3359 Pane of 20 20.00
a.-t. 44c Any single 1.00 .50

HAWAII STATEHOOD, 50TH ANNIV.

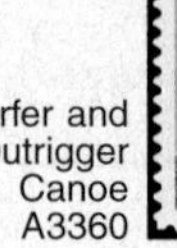

Surfer and Outrigger Canoe
A3360

PHOTOGRAVURE

Serpentine Die Cut 11

2009, Aug. 21

Self-Adhesive

4415 A3360 44c multicolored 1.25 .25

Eid Type of 2001

2009, Sept. 3

Self-Adhesive

4416 A2734 44c multicolored .90 .25

THANKSGIVING DAY PARADE

Crowd, Street Sign, Bear Balloon
A3361

Drum Major, Musicians
A3362

Musicians, Balloon, Horse
A3363

Cowboy, Turkey Balloon, Crowd, Television Cameraman — A3364

Serpentine Die Cut 11x10¾

2009, Sept. 9

Self-Adhesive

4417 A3361 44c multicolored .90 .30
4418 A3362 44c multicolored .90 .30
4419 A3363 44c multicolored .90 .30
4420 A3364 44c multicolored .90 .30
a. Horiz. strip of 4, #4417-4420 3.60

LEGENDS OF HOLLYWOOD

Gary Cooper (1901-61), Actor — A3365

Serpentine Die Cut 11

2009, Sept. 10

Self-Adhesive

4421 A3365 44c multicolored 1.00 .25

SUPREME COURT JUSTICES

Souvenir Sheet

A3366

No. 4422: a, Felix Frankfurter (1882-1965). b, William J. Brennan, Jr. (1906-97). c, Louis D. Brandeis (1856-1941). d, Joseph Story (1779-1845).

LITHOGRAPHED

Serpentine Die Cut 11x10½

2009, Sept. 22

Self-Adhesive

4422 A3366 Pane of 4 3.60
a.-d. 44c Any single .90 .30

KELP FOREST

A3367

Wildlife: a, Brown pelican. b, Western gull, southern sea otters, red sea urchin. c, Harbor seal. d, Lion's mane nudibranch, vert. e, Yellowtail rockfish, white-spotted rose anemone. f, Vermilion rockfish. g, Copper rockfish. h, Pacific rock crab, jeweled top snail. i, Northern kelp crab, vert. j, Treefish, Monterey turban snail, brooding sea anemones.

PHOTOGRAVURE

Serpentine Die Cut 10¾

2009, Oct. 1

Self-Adhesive

4423 A3367 Pane of 10 9.00
a.-j. 44c Any single .90 .40

CHRISTMAS

Madonna and Sleeping Child, by Sassoferrato (Giovanni Battista Salvi)
A3368

Reindeer
A3369

Snowman
A3370

Gingerbread Man
A3371

Toy Soldier
A3372

Reindeer
A3373

Snowman
A3374

Gingerbread Man
A3375

Toy Soldier — A3376

LITHOGRAPHED, PHOTOGRAVURE (#4429-4432)

Serpentine Die Cut 10¾x11 on 2 or 3 Sides

2009

Self-Adhesive

Booklet Stamps

4424 A3368 44c multicolored .90 .25
a. Booklet pane of 20 18.00
4425 A3369 44c multicolored .90 .25
4426 A3370 44c multicolored .90 .25
4427 A3371 44c multicolored .90 .25
4428 A3372 44c multicolored .90 .25
a. Block of 4, #4425-4428 3.60
b. Booklet pane of 20, 5 each #4425-4428 18.00
c. As "b," die cutting omitted on side with 12 stamps —
d. As "b," die cutting omitted on side with 8 stamps —
e. As "a," die cutting omitted *325.00*

Serpentine Die Cut 8 on 2, 3 or 4 Sides

4429 A3373 44c multicolored 1.00 .25
4430 A3374 44c multicolored 1.00 .25
4431 A3375 44c multicolored 1.00 .25
4432 A3376 44c multicolored 1.00 .25
a. Block of 4, #4429-4432 4.00
b. Booklet pane of 18, 5 each #4429, 4431, 4 each #4430, 4432 18.00
Nos. 4424-4432 (9) 8.50 2.25

No. 4424a is a double-sided booklet pane with 12 stamps on one side and eight stamps plus label that serves as a booklet cover on the other side. No. 4428b is a double-sided booklet pane with 12 stamps on one side (3 each of Nos. 4425-4428) and eight stamps (2 each of Nos. 4425-4428) plus label that serves as a booklet cover on the other side.

HANUKKAH

Menorah — A3377

LITHOGRAPHED

Serpentine Die Cut 10¾x11

2009, Oct. 9

Self-Adhesive

4433 A3377 44c multicolored .90 .25

KWANZAA

Family — A3378

2009, Oct. 9

Self-Adhesive

4434 A3378 44c multicolored .90 .25

CHINESE NEW YEAR

Year of the Tiger
A3379

Designed by Ethel Kessler. Printed by Avery Dennison.

PHOTOGRAVURE

Serpentine Die Cut 11

2010, Jan. 14 **Tagged**

Self-Adhesive

4435 A3379 44c multicolored 1.10 .25

2010 WINTER OLYMPICS, VANCOUVER

Snowboarder
A3380

Designed by Howard E. Paine. Printed by Avery Dennison.

PHOTOGRAVURE

Serpentine Die Cut 11

2010, Jan. 22 **Tagged**

Self-Adhesive

4436 A3380 44c multicolored .90 .25
P# block of 4, 6# + V 4.00
Pane of 20 20.00

"Forever" Liberty Bell Type of 2007

Printed by Ashton-Potter (USA) Ltd.

Serpentine Die Cut 11¼x10¾ on 2, 3 or 4 Sides

2010, Feb. 3 **Litho.**

Booklet Stamp

Self-Adhesive

Medium Microprinting, Bell 16mm Wide

Dated "2009" in Copper

4437 A3148 (44c) multicolored .95 .25
a. Booklet pane of 18 17.00

On No. 4437, the "2009" date is smaller than that on No. 4127i, which has a 15mm wide bell. The bell on No. 4437 is also 17mm tall while No. 4127i is 16mm tall. The microprinted "Forever" is on a dotted background on No. 4437 and on a white background on No. 4127i.

See also No. 4128c.

AMERICAN LANDMARKS

Mackinac Bridge, Michigan
A3381

Bixby Creek Bridge, California
A3382

PHOTOGRAVURE

Serpentine Die Cut 10¾x10½

2010, Feb. 3 **Tagged**

Self-Adhesive

4438 A3381 $4.90 multi 10.00 5.00
P# block of 4, 4# +V 40.00
Pane of 20 200.00
4439 A3382 $18.30 multi 35.00 18.00
P# block of 4, 4# +V 140.00
Pane of 20 700.00

DISTINGUISHED SAILORS

Admiral William S. Sims (1858-1936), Emblem of USS W.S. Sims — A3383

Admiral Arleigh A. Burke (1901-96), Emblem of USS Arleigh Burke A3384

Lieutenant Commander John McCloy (1876-1945), Emblem of USS McCloy — A3385

Petty Officer 3rd Class Doris Miller (1919-43), Emblem of USS Miller A3386

PHOTOGRAVURE

Serpentine Die Cut 10¾x10½

2010, Feb. 4 Tagged

Self-Adhesive

4440	A3383 44c multicolored	.90	.30
4441	A3384 44c multicolored	.90	.30
4442	A3385 44c multicolored	.90	.30
4443	A3386 44c multicolored	.90	.30
a.	Block or horiz. strip of 4, #4440-4443	3.60	
	P# block of 4, 6# + V	4.00	
	P# block of 8, 2 sets of 6# + V + top label	7.20	
	Pane of 20	19.50	

ABSTRACT EXPRESSIONISTS

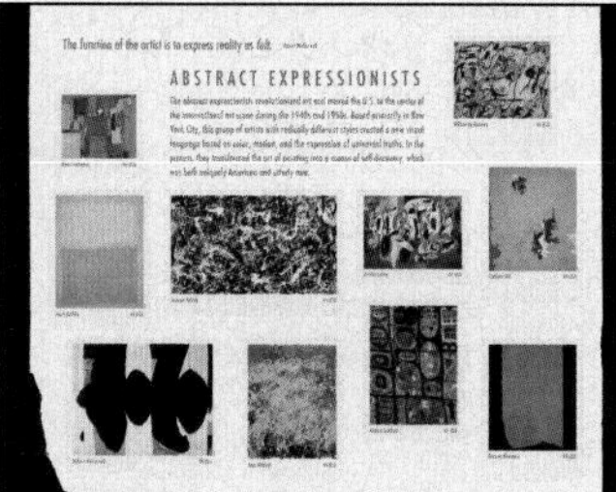

A3387

No. 4444: a, The Golden Wall, by Hans Hofmann (30x30mm). b, Asheville, by Willem de Kooning (38x38mm). c, Orange and Yellow, by Mark Rothko (35x49mm). d, Convergence, by Jackson Pollock (63x43mm). e, The Liver Is the Cock's Comb, by Arshile Gorky (39x32mm). f, 1948-C, by Clyfford Still (35x49mm). g, Elegy to the Spanish Republic No. 34, by Robert Motherwell (54x49mm). h, La Grande Vallée 0, by Joan Mitchell (35x49mm). i, Romanesque Façade, by Adolph Gottlieb (35x49mm). j, Achilles, by Barnett Newman (35x49mm).

LITHOGRAPHED

Serpentine Die Cut 10¾x11, 10¾ (#4444a, 4444b, 4444e), 11x10¾ (#4444d)

2010, Mar. 11 Tagged

Self-Adhesive

4444	A3387 Pane of 10	10.00	
a.-j.	44c Any single	1.00	.40

BILL MAULDIN (1921-2003), CARTOONIST

A3388

LITHOGRAPHED

Serpentine Die Cut 10¾

2010, Mar. 31 Tagged

Self-Adhesive

4445	A3388 44c multicolored	.90	.25
	P# block of 4, 4# + P	3.60	
	Pane of 20	18.00	

COWBOYS OF THE SILVER SCREEN

Roy Rogers (1911-98) A3389

Tom Mix (1880-1940) A3390

William S. Hart (1864-1946) A3391

Gene Autry (1907-98) A3392

LITHOGRAPHED

Serpentine Die Cut 10½x10¾

2010, Apr. 17

Self-Adhesive

4446	A3389 44c multicolored	1.25	.30
4447	A3390 44c multicolored	1.25	.30
4448	A3391 44c multicolored	1.25	.30
4449	A3392 44c multicolored	1.25	.30
a.	Block of 4, #4446-4449	5.00	

LOVE

Pansies in a Basket — A3393

PHOTOGRAVURE

Serpentine Die Cut 10¾

2010, Apr. 22

Self-Adhesive

4450	A3393 44c multicolored	.90	.25

ANIMAL RESCUE

Wire-haired Jack Russell Terrier — A3394

Maltese — A3395

Calico — A3396

Yellow Labrador Retriever A3397

Golden Retriever A3398

Gray, White and Tan Cat — A3399

Black, White and Tan Cat — A3400

Australian Shepherd A3401

Boston Terrier — A3402

Orange Tabby — A3403

LITHOGRAPHED

Serpentine Die Cut 10¾

2010, Apr. 30

Self-Adhesive

4451	A3394 44c multicolored	1.25	.40
4452	A3395 44c multicolored	1.25	.40
4453	A3396 44c multicolored	1.25	.40
4454	A3397 44c multicolored	1.25	.40
4455	A3398 44c multicolored	1.25	.40
4456	A3399 44c multicolored	1.25	.40
4457	A3400 44c multicolored	1.25	.40
4458	A3401 44c multicolored	1.25	.40
4459	A3402 44c multicolored	1.25	.40
4460	A3403 44c multicolored	1.25	.40
a.	Block of 10, #4451-4460	12.50	

LEGENDS OF HOLLYWOOD

Katharine Hepburn (1907-2003), Actress — A3404

PHOTOGRAVURE

Serpentine Die Cut 10¾

2010, May 12

Self-Adhesive

4461	A3404 44c black	1.00	.25

MONARCH BUTTERFLY

A3405

PHOTOGRAVURE

Serpentine Die Cut 10½

2010, May 17

Self-Adhesive

4462	A3405 64c multicolored	1.30	.25

KATE SMITH

Kate Smith (1907-86), Singer — A3406

PHOTOGRAVURE

2010, May 27 ***Serpentine Die Cut 11***

Self-Adhesive

4463	A3406 44c multicolored	.90	.25

BLACK HERITAGE

Oscar Micheaux (1884-1951), Film Director — A3407

Serpentine Die Cut 11

2010, June 22

Self-Adhesive

4464	A3407 44c multicolored	.90	.25

NEGRO LEAGUES BASEBALL

Play at the Plate A3408

Andrew "Rube" Foster (1879-1930), Founder of Negro National League — A3409

PHOTOGRAVURE

Serpentine Die Cut 11

2010, July 15

Self-Adhesive

4465 A3408 44c multicolored .90 .30
4466 A3409 44c multicolored .90 .30
a. Horiz. pair, #4465-4466 1.80

SUNDAY FUNNIES

Beetle Bailey — A3410

Calvin and Hobbes A3411

Archie — A3412

Garfield A3413

Dennis the Menace A3414

LITHOGRAPHED

Serpentine Die Cut 10½x10¾

2010, July 16

Self-Adhesive

4467 A3410 44c multicolored .90 .30
4468 A3411 44c multicolored .90 .30
4469 A3412 44c multicolored .90 .30
4470 A3413 44c multicolored .90 .30
4471 A3414 44c multicolored .90 .30
a. Horiz. strip of 5, #4467-4471 4.50

BOY SCOUTS OF AMERICA, CENTENNIAL

Boy Scouts — A3415

PHOTOGRAVURE

Serpentine Die Cut 11

2010, July 27

Self-Adhesive

4472 A3415 44c multicolored .90 .25

Boys in a Pasture, by Winslow Homer (1836-1910) — A3416

Serpentine Die Cut 10¾

2010, Aug. 12

Self-Adhesive

4473 A3416 44c multicolored .90 .25

HAWAIIAN RAIN FOREST

A3417

No. 4474: a, Hawaii 'amakihi, Hawaii 'elepaio, ohi'a lehua. b, 'Akepa, 'ope'ape'a, vert. c, 'I'iwi, haha. d, 'Oma'o, kanawao, 'ohelo kau la'au, vert. e, 'Oha, vert. f, Pulelehua butterfly, kolea lau nui, 'ilihia. g, Koele Mountain damselfly, 'akala, vert. h, 'Apapane, Hawaiian mint, vert. i, Jewel orchid, vert. j, Happyface spider, 'ala'ala wai nui, vert.

LITHOGRAPHED

Serpentine Die Cut 10¾

2010, Sept. 1

Self-Adhesive

4474 A3417 Pane of 10 9.00
a.-j. 44c Any single .90 .40

MOTHER TERESA

Mother Teresa (1910-97), Humanitarian, 1979 Nobel Peace Laureate — A3418

PHOTOGRAVURE

2010, Sept. 5 ***Serpentine Die Cut 11***

Self-Adhesive

4475 A3418 44c multicolored .90 .25

LITERARY ARTS

Julia de Burgos (1914-53), Poet A3419

PHOTOGRAVURE

Serpentine Die Cut 11

2010, Sept. 14

Self-Adhesive

4476 A3419 44c multicolored .90 .25

CHRISTMAS

Angel with Lute, Detail of Fresco by Melozzo da Forli — A3420

Ponderosa Pine — A3421

Eastern Red Cedar A3422

Balsam Fir A3423

Blue Spruce A3424

Ponderosa Pine A3425

Eastern Red Cedar A3426

Balsam Fir A3427

Blue Spruce — A3428

Designed by Terrence W. McCaffrey (#4477), Howard E. Paine

Printed by Avery Dennison (#4477), Banknote Corporation of America for Sennett Security Products (#4478-4481), Ashton-Potter (USA) Ltd. (#4482-4485).

PHOTOGRAVURE (#4477), LITHOGRAPHED

Serpentine Die Cut 10¾

2010, Oct. 21 **Tagged**

Self-Adhesive

4477 A3420 44c multicolored .90 .25
P# block of 4, 5#+V 3.60
Pane of 20 18.00

Booklet Stamps

Serpentine Die Cut 11 on 2 or 3 Sides

4478 A3421 (44c) multicolored .95 .25
4479 A3422 (44c) multicolored .95 .25
4480 A3423 (44c) multicolored .95 .25
4481 A3424 (44c) multicolored .95 .25
a. Block of 4, #4478-4481 3.80
b. Booklet pane of 20, 5 each #4478-4481 19.00
c. As "a," die cutting omitted — —
d. As "b," die cutting omitted on side with 12 stamps —
e. As "b," die cutting omitted on side with 8 stamps *800.00*
f. As "b," die cutting omitted on side with 12 stamps, die cutting omitted on bottom 4 stamps on side with 8 stamps —

Serpentine Die Cut 11¼x10¾ on 2, 3 or 4 Sides

4482 A3425 (44c) multicolored .95 .25
4483 A3426 (44c) multicolored .95 .25
4484 A3427 (44c) multicolored .95 .25
4485 A3428 (44c) multicolored .95 .25
a. Block of 4, #4482-4485 3.80
b. Booklet pane of 18, 5 each #4482, 4484, 4 each #4483, 4485 17.00
Nos. 4477-4485 (9) 8.50 2.25

No. 4481b is a double-sided booklet pane with 12 stamps on one side (3 each of Nos. 4478-4481) and eight stamps (2 each of Nos. 4478-4481) plus label that serves as a booklet cover on the other side.

Statue of Liberty A3429

Flag A3430

LITHOGRAPHED (#4486-4489), PHOTOGRAVURE

Serpentine Die Cut 9½ Vert.

2010, Dec. 1

COIL STAMPS

Self-Adhesive

4486 A3429 (44c) multicolored .95 .25
4487 A3430 (44c) multicolored .95 .25
a. Pair, #4486-4487 1.90

Serpentine Die Cut 11 Vert.

4488 A3429 (44c) multicolored .95 .25
a. Vert. pair, horiz. unslit btwn. —
4489 A3430 (44c) multicolored .95 .25
a. Pair, #4488-4489 1.90
b. Block of 4 (one pair each from two different coil rolls), horiz. unslit btwn. —

Serpentine Die Cut 8½ Vert.

4490 A3429 (44c) multicolored .95 .25
4491 A3430 (44c) multicolored .95 .25
a. Pair, #4490-4491 1.90
Nos. 4486-4491 (6) 5.70 1.50

Microprinting reads "4evR" on Nos. 4486-4487, "4evr" on Nos. 4488-4489, and "4EVR" on Nos. 4490-4491. The microprinting is found above the Statue of Liberty's hair, and at the bottom of the lowest red stripe of the flag.

CHINESE NEW YEAR

Year of the Rabbit A3431

PHOTOGRAVURE

Serpentine Die Cut 11

2011, Jan. 22

Self-Adhesive

4492 A3431 (44c) multicolored .95 .25

KANSAS STATEHOOD, 150TH ANNIV.

Windmill and Wind Turbines A3432

LITHOGRAPHED

Serpentine Die Cut 11

2011, Jan. 27

Self-Adhesive

4493 A3432 (44c) multicolored .95 .25

PRES. RONALD REAGAN (1911-2004)

Pres. Ronald Reagan — A3433

PHOTOGRAVURE
Serpentine Die Cut 10½
2011, Feb. 10
Self-Adhesive

4494 A3433 (44c) multicolored .95 .25

Art Deco Bird — A3434

LITHOGRAPHED
Serpentine Die Cut 10 Vert.
2011, Feb. 11 Untagged
COIL STAMP
Self-Adhesive

4495 A3434 (5c) multicolored .25 .25

Quill and Inkwell — A3435

LITHOGRAPHED
Serpentine Die Cut 11¾ Vert.
2011, Feb. 14
COIL STAMP
Self-Adhesive

4496 A3435 44c multicolored .95 .25

LATIN MUSIC LEGENDS

Tito Puente (1923-2000) A3436

Carmen Miranda (1909-55) A3437

Selena (1971-95) A3438

Carlos Gardel (1890-1935) A3439

Celia Cruz (1925-2003) A3440

PHOTOGRAVURE
Serpentine Die Cut 10¾
2011, Mar. 16
Self-Adhesive

4497 A3436 (44c) multicolored .95 .40
4498 A3437 (44c) multicolored .95 .40
4499 A3438 (44c) multicolored .95 .40
4500 A3439 (44c) multicolored .95 .40
4501 A3440 (44c) multicolored .95 .40
a. Horiz. strip of 5, #4497-4501 4.75

CELEBRATE

A3441

PHOTOGRAVURE
Serpentine Die Cut 11x11½
2011, Mar. 25
Self-Adhesive

4502 A3441 (44c) multicolored .95 .25

JAZZ

Musicians A3442

PHOTOGRAVURE
Serpentine Die Cut 10¾
2011, Mar. 26
Self-Adhesive

4503 A3442 (44c) multicolored .95 .25

See note after No. 1549.

Statue of Liberty and Flag Types of 2010 and

George Washington A3443

Oregano A3444

Flax A3445

Foxglove A3446

Lavender A3447

Sage A3448

Oveta Culp Hobby (1905-95), First Health, Education and Welfare Department Secretary A3449

New River Gorge Bridge, West Virginia — A3450

LITHOGRAPHED (#4504, 4511, 4512, 4518-4519), PHOTOGRAVURE (#4505-4510, 4513-4517)

2011 ***Serpentine Die Cut 11¼x10¾***
Self-Adhesive

4504 A3443 20c multicolored .40 .25

Serpentine Die Cut 11

4505 A3444 29c multicolored .60 .25
4506 A3445 29c multicolored .60 .25
4507 A3446 29c multicolored .60 .25
4508 A3447 29c multicolored .60 .25
4509 A3448 29c multicolored .60 .25
a. Horiz. strip of 5, #4505-4509 3.00
4510 A3449 84c multicolored 1.75 .35

Serpentine Die Cut 10¾x10½

4511 A3450 $4.95 multicolored 10.00 5.00
Nos. 4504-4511 (7) 13.40 6.50

Coil Stamps
Serpentine Die Cut 9½ Vert.

4512 A3443 20c multicolored .40 .25

Serpentine Die Cut 8½ Vert.

4513 A3446 29c multicolored .80 .25
4514 A3447 29c multicolored .80 .25
4515 A3448 29c multicolored .80 .25
4516 A3444 29c multicolored .80 .25
4517 A3445 29c multicolored .80 .25
a. Horiz. strip of 5, #4513-4517 4.00
Nos. 4512-4517 (6) 4.40 1.50

Booklet Stamps
Thin Paper
Serpentine Die Cut 11¼x10¾ on 2, 3, or 4 Sides

4518 A3429 (44c) multicolored .95 .25
4519 A3430 (44c) multicolored .95 .25
a. Pair, #4518-4519 1.90
b. Booklet pane of 18, 9 each #4518-4519 17.00

Issued: Nos. 4504, 4511, 4512, 4/11; Nos. 4505-4509, 4513-4517, 4/7; No. 4510, 4/15; Nos. 4518-4519. 4/8.

Wedding Cake Type of 2009 With "USA" in Serifed Type and

Wedding Roses — A3450a

LITHOGRAPHED (#4520), PHOTOGRAVURE (#4521)

2011 ***Serpentine Die Cut 11***
Self-Adhesive

4520 A3450a (44c) multicolored .95 .25
a. Die cutting omitted, pair —
4521 A3344 64c multicolored 1.30 .25

Issued: No. 4520, 4/21; No. 4521, 4/11.

CIVIL WAR SESQUICENTENNIAL

Battle of Fort Sumter — A3451

First Battle of Bull Run — A3452

LITHOGRAPHED
Serpentine Die Cut 11
2011, Apr. 12
Self-Adhesive

4522 A3451 (44c) multicolored .95 .25
4523 A3452 (44c) multicolored .95 .25
a. Pair, #4522-4523 1.90

GO GREEN

A3453

No. 4524 — Messages: a, Buy local produce, reuse bags. b, Fix water leaks. c, Share rides. d, Turn off lights not in use. e, Choose to walk. f, Go Green, reduce our environmental footprint step by step. g, Compost. h, Let nature do the work. i, Recycle more. j, Ride a bike. k, Plant trees. l, Insulate the home. m, Use public transportation. n, Use efficient light bulbs. o, Adjust the thermostat. p, Maintain tire pressure.

PHOTOGRAVURE
Serpentine Die Cut 10¾
2011, Apr. 14
Self-Adhesive

4524 A3453 Pane of 16 15.25
a.-p. (44c) Any single .95 .50

HELEN HAYES

Helen Hayes (1900-93), Actress — A3454

Serpentine Die Cut 11
2011, Apr. 25 Tagged
Self-Adhesive

4525 A3454 (44c) multicolored .95 .25

LEGENDS OF HOLLYWOOD

Gregory Peck (1916-2003), Actor — A3455

Serpentine Die Cut 10¾
2011, Apr. 28
Self-Adhesive

4526 A3455 (44c) black .95 .25

SPACE FIRSTS

Alan B. Shepard, Jr. (1923-98), First American in Space A3456

Messenger, First Spacecraft to Orbit Mercury — A3457

LITHOGRAPHED

2011, May 4 ***Serpentine Die Cut 11***

Self-Adhesive

4527 A3456 (44c) multicolored .95 .25
4528 A3457 (44c) multicolored .95 .25
a. Horiz. pair, #4527-4528 1.90

Purple Heart and Ribbon — A3458

Serpentine Die Cut 11¼x10¾

2011, May 5

Self-Adhesive

4529 A3458 (44c) multicolored .95 .25

INDIANAPOLIS 500, CENT.

Ray Harroun Driving Marmon Wasp A3459

Designed by Phil Jordan. Printed by Banknote Corporation of America for Sennett Security Products.

LITHOGRAPHED

Serpentine Die Cut 10¾

2011, May 20

Self-Adhesive

4530 A3459 (44c) multicolored .95 .25
P# block of 4, 6#+S 3.80
Pane of 20 19.00

GARDEN OF LOVE

Pink Flower A3460

Red Flower A3461

Blue Flowers A3462

Butterfly A3463

Green Vine Leaves A3464

Blue Flower A3465

Doves A3466

Orange Red Flowers A3467

Strawberry A3468

Yellow Orange Flowers A3469

Designed by Derry Noyes. Printed by Avery Dennison.

PHOTOGRAVURE

Serpentine Die Cut 10¾

2011, May 23

Self-Adhesive

4531 A3460 (44c) multicolored .95 .40
4532 A3461 (44c) multicolored .95 .40
4533 A3462 (44c) multicolored .95 .40
4534 A3463 (44c) multicolored .95 .40
4535 A3464 (44c) multicolored .95 .40
4536 A3465 (44c) multicolored .95 .40
4537 A3466 (44c) multicolored .95 .40
4538 A3467 (44c) multicolored .95 .40
4539 A3468 (44c) multicolored .95 .40
4540 A3469 (44c) multicolored .95 .40
a. Block of 10, #4531-4540 9.50
Nos. 4531-4540 (10) 9.50 4.00

The two blocks of 10 on the pane are separated by a gutter.

AMERICAN SCIENTISTS

Melvin Calvin (1911-97), Chemist A3470

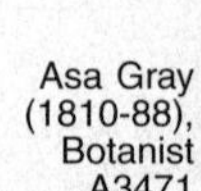

Asa Gray (1810-88), Botanist A3471

Maria Goeppert Mayer (1906-72), Physicist A3472

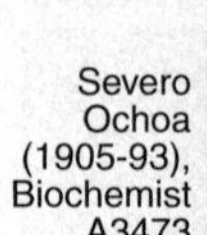

Severo Ochoa (1905-93), Biochemist A3473

LITHOGRAPHED

Serpentine Die Cut 11

2011, June 16

Self-Adhesive

4541 A3470 (44c) multicolored .95 .30
4542 A3471 (44c) multicolored .95 .30
4543 A3472 (44c) multicolored .95 .30
4544 A3473 (44c) multicolored .95 .30
a. Horiz. strip of 4, #4541-4544 3.80
b. Horiz. strip of 4, die cutting missing on backing paper (from misaligned die-cutting mat) —

LITERARY ARTS

Mark Twain (Samuel L. Clemens) (1835-1910), Writer — A3474

PHOTOGRAVURE

Serpentine Die Cut 11

2011, June 25

Self-Adhesive

4545 A3474 (44c) multicolored .95 .25

PIONEERS OF AMERICAN INDUSTRIAL DESIGN

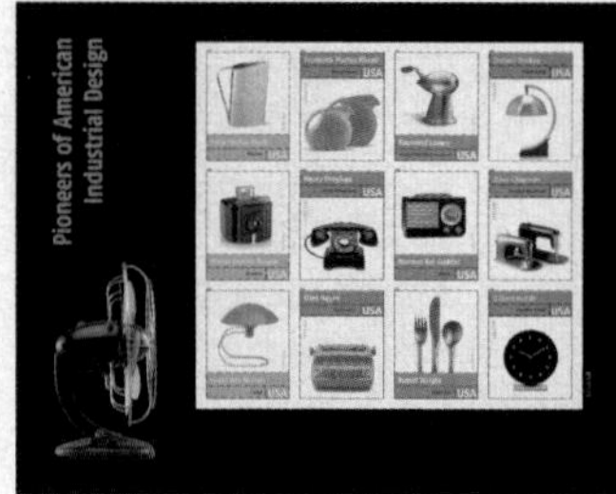

A3475

No. 4546: a, "Normandie" pitcher, designed by Peter Müller-Munk (1904-67). b, Fiesta dinnerware, designed by Frederick Hurten Rhead (1880-1942). c, Streamlined pencil sharpener, designed by Raymond Loewy (1893-1986). d, Table lamp, designed by Donald Deskey (1894-1989). e, Kodak "Baby Brownie" camera, designed by Walter Dorwin Teague (1883-1960). f, Model 302 Bell telephone, designed by Henry Dreyfuss (1904-72). g, Emerson "Patriot" radio, designed by Norman Bel Geddes (1893-1958). h, Streamlined sewing machines, designed by Dave Chapman (1909-78). i, "Anywhere" lamp, designed by Greta von Nessen (1900-74). j, IBM "Selectric" typewriter, designed by Eliot Noyes (1910-77). k, "Highlight/Pinch" flatware, designed by Russel Wright (1904-76). l, Herman Miller electric clock, designed by Gilbert Rohde (1894-1944).

PHOTOGRAVURE

Serpentine Die Cut 10¾

2011, June 29

Self-Adhesive

4546 A3475 Pane of 12 11.50
a.-l. (44c) Any single .95 .50

OWNEY, THE POSTAL DOG

Owney, His Medals and Tags A3476

PHOTOGRAVURE

Serpentine Die Cut 11

2011, July 27

Self-Adhesive

4547 A3476 (44c) multicolored 1.00 .25

U.S. MERCHANT MARINE

Clipper Ship A3477

Auxiliary Steamship A3478

Liberty Ship A3479

Container Ship A3480

PHOTOGRAVURE

Serpentine Die Cut 11

2011, July 28

Self-Adhesive

4548 A3477 (44c) multicolored .95 .30
4549 A3478 (44c) multicolored .95 .30
4550 A3479 (44c) multicolored .95 .30
4551 A3480 (44c) multicolored .95 .30
a. Block or horiz. strip of 4, #4548-4551 3.80

EID

"Eid Mubarak" — A3481

PHOTOGRAVURE

Serpentine Die Cut 11¼

2011, Aug. 12

Self-Adhesive

4552 A3481 (44c) mar, gray & gold .90 .25

CHARACTERS FROM DISNEY-PIXAR FILMS

Send a Hello

Lightning McQueen and Mater from *Cars* — A3482

Remy the Rat and Linguini from *Ratatouille* A3483

Buzz Lightyear and Aliens from *Toy Story* — A3484

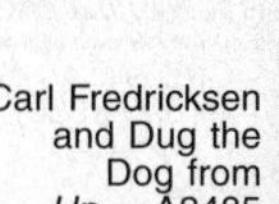

Carl Fredricksen and Dug the Dog from *Up* — A3485

WALL-E from *WALL-E* A3486

PHOTOGRAVURE

Serpentine Die Cut 10½

2011, Aug. 19

Self-Adhesive

4553 A3482 (44c) multicolored .95 .40
4554 A3483 (44c) multicolored .95 .40
4555 A3484 (44c) multicolored .95 .40
4556 A3485 (44c) multicolored .95 .40
4557 A3486 (44c) multicolored .95 .40
a. Horiz. strip of 5, #4553-4557 4.75

Adjacent horizontal or vertical stamps will have selvage between the stamps.

AMERICAN TREASURES SERIES

The Long Leg, by Edward Hopper (1882-1967) — A3487

PHOTOGRAVURE

Serpentine Die Cut 11

2011, Aug. 24

Self-Adhesive

4558 A3487 (44c) multicolored .95 .25

Statue of Liberty and Flag Types of 2010

LITHOGRAPHED (#4559-4562), PHOTOGRAVURE

Serpentine Die Cut 11¼x11 on 2 or 3 Sides

2011, Sept. 14

BOOKLET STAMPS

Self-Adhesive

4559 A3429 (44c) multicolored .95 .25
4560 A3430 (44c) multicolored .95 .25
a. Pair, #4559-4560 1.90
b. Booklet pane of 20, 10 each #4559-4560 19.00
4561 A3429 (44c) multicolored .95 .25
4562 A3430 (44c) multicolored .95 .25
a. Pair, #4561-4562 1.90
b. Booklet pane of 20, 10 each #4561-4562 19.00

Serpentine Die Cut 11¼x11½ on 2 or 3 Sides

4563 A3429 (44c) multicolored .95 .25
4564 A3430 (44c) multicolored .95 .25
a. Pair, #4563-4564 1.90
b. Booklet pane of 20, 10 each #4563-4564 19.00
Nos. 4559-4564 (6) 5.40 1.20

Microprinting reads "4evR" on Nos. 4559-4560, "4evr" on Nos. 4561-4562, and "4EVR" on Nos. 4563-4564. The microprinting is found above the Statue of Liberty's hair, and at the bottom of the lowest red stripe of the flag. Nos. 4560b, 4562b and 4564b are double-sided booklet panes with 12 stamps one one side (6 each of types A3429-A3430) and 8 stamps (4 each of types A3429-A3430) on the other side. The paper used on Nos. 4561-4562 is thicker than that used on Nos. 4518-4519.

BLACK HERITAGE

Barbara Jordan (1936-96), Congresswoman A3488

LITHOGRAPHED

Serpentine Die Cut 10¾

2011, Sept. 16

Self-Adhesive

4565 A3488 (44c) multicolored .95 .25

ART OF ROMARE BEARDEN (1911-88)

Conjunction A3489

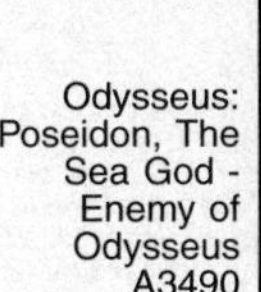

Odysseus: Poseidon, The Sea God - Enemy of Odysseus A3490

Prevalence of Ritual: Conjur Woman A3491

Falling Star — A3492

PHOTOGRAVURE

Serpentine Die Cut 10¾

2011, Sept. 28

Self-Adhesive

4566 A3489 (44c) multicolored .95 .30
4567 A3490 (44c) multicolored .95 .30
4568 A3491 (44c) multicolored .95 .30
4569 A3492 (44c) multicolored .95 .30
a. Horiz. strip of 4, #4566-4569 3.80

CHRISTMAS

Madonna of the Candelabra, by Raphael — A3493

A3494 A3495

A3496 A3497

A3498 A3499

Ornaments
A3500 A3501

LITHOGRAPHED

Serpentine Die Cut 10¾x 11 on 2 or 3 Sides

2011, Oct. 13

Booklet Stamps

Self-Adhesive

4570 A3493 (44c) multicolored .95 .25
a. Booklet pane of 20 19.00

With "USPS" Microprinted on Collar of Ornament

4571 A3494 (44c) multicolored .95 .25
4572 A3495 (44c) multicolored .95 .25
4573 A3496 (44c) multicolored .95 .25
4574 A3497 (44c) multicolored .95 .25
a. Block of 4, #4571-4574 3.80
b. Booklet pane of 20, 5 each #4571-4574 19.00

Microprinted "USPS" in Places Other Than Collar of Ornament

4575 A3494 (44c) multicolored .95 .25
4576 A3495 (44c) multicolored .95 .25
4577 A3496 (44c) multicolored .95 .25
4578 A3497 (44c) multicolored .95 .25
a. Block of 4, #4575-4578 3.80
b. Booklet pane of 20, 5 each #4575-4578 19.00

Serpentine Die Cut 11¼x11 on 2, 3 or 4 Sides

4579 A3498 (44c) multicolored .95 .25
4580 A3499 (44c) multicolored .95 .25
4581 A3500 (44c) multicolored .95 .25
4582 A3501 (44c) multicolored .95 .25
a. Block of 4, #4579-4582 3.80
b. Booklet pane of 18, 5 each #4579, 4582, 4 each #4580-4581 17.00
Nos. 4570-4582 (13) 11.70 2.60

The microprinted "USPS" is to the left of the third stripe on Nos. 4575 and 4579, on the left side of the bottom ribbon of the ribbon cluster above the ornament collar on Nos. 4576 and 4578, below the bottom stripe near the bottom tip on No. 4577, on the vertical ribbon on No. 4580, on a curved ribbon above the collar on No. 4581, and on the left side of the ornament, below the collar, on No. 4582.

No. 4570a is a double-sided booklet with 12 stamps on one side and eight stamps plus a label that serves as a booklet cover on the other side. Nos. 4574b and 4578b are double sided booklets with 12 stamps (3 each of types A3494-A3497) on one side and eight stamps (2 each of types A3494-A3497) plus a label that serves as a booklet cover on the other side.

HANUKKAH

A3502

Serpentine Die Cut 11x10¾

2011, Oct. 14

Self-Adhesive

4583 A3502 (44c) multicolored .95 .25

KWANZAA

Family — A3503

Serpentine Die Cut 10¾x11

2011, Oct. 14

Self-Adhesive

4584 A3503 (44c) multicolored .95 .25

Eagle — A3504

PHOTOGRAVURE

Serpentine Die Cut 11 Vert.

2012, Jan. 3

Coil Stamps

Self-Adhesive

Color Behind "USA"

4585 A3504 (25c) green .50 .25
4586 A3504 (25c) blue green .50 .25
4587 A3504 (25c) blue .50 .25
4588 A3504 (25c) red violet .50 .25
4589 A3504 (25c) brown orange .50 .25
4590 A3504 (25c) yellow orange .50 .25
a. Strip of 6, #4585-4590 3.00

NEW MEXICO STATEHOOD CENTENNIAL

Sanctuary II, Painting by Doug West A3505

PHOTOGRAVURE

2012, Jan. 6 ***Serpentine Die Cut 11***

Self-Adhesive

4591 A3505 (44c) multicolored .95 .25

ALOHA SHIRTS

Surfers and Palm Trees A3506

Surfers A3507

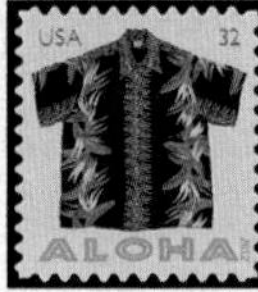

Bird of Paradise Flowers A3508

Kilauea Volcano A3509

Fossil Fish, Shells and Starfish — A3510

PHOTOGRAVURE, LITHOGRAPHED (#4597-4601)

Serpentine Die Cut 11

2012, Jan. 19

Self-Adhesive

4592 A3506 32c multicolored .65 .30
4593 A3507 32c multicolored .65 .30
4594 A3508 32c multicolored .65 .30
4595 A3509 32c multicolored .65 .30
4596 A3510 32c multicolored .65 .30
a. Horiz. strip of 5, #4592-4596 3.25

Coil Stamps

Serpentine Die Cut 11 Vert.

4597 A3510 32c multicolored .65 .30
4598 A3506 32c multicolored .65 .30
4599 A3507 32c multicolored .65 .30
4600 A3508 32c multicolored .65 .30
4601 A3509 32c multicolored .65 .30
a. Strip of 5, #4597-4601 3.25
b. As "a," die cutting omitted —
Nos. 4592-4601 (10) 6.50 2.50

On Nos. 4592-4596, the top of the shirt collars are all higher than the cross line of the "A" in "USA," and on Nos. 4597-4601, they are even with or slightly below the cross line.

Wedding Cake Type of 2009

LITHOGRAPHED

Serpentine Die Cut 10¾

2012, Jan. 20

Self-Adhesive

4602 A3344 65c multicolored 1.30 .25

BALTIMORE CHECKERSPOT BUTTERFLY

A3511

PHOTOGRAVURE

Serpentine Die Cut 10¾

2012, Jan. 20

Self-Adhesive

4603 A3511 65c multicolored 1.30 .25

DOGS AT WORK

Seeing Eye Dog — A3512

Therapy Dog — A3513

Military Dog — A3514

Rescue Dog — A3515

PHOTOGRAVURE

Serpentine Die Cut 10¾

2012, Jan. 20

Self-Adhesive

4604 A3512 65c multicolored 1.30 .30
4605 A3513 65c multicolored 1.30 .30
4606 A3514 65c multicolored 1.30 .30
4607 A3515 65c multicolored 1.30 .30
a. Block or vert. strip of 4, #4604-4607 5.20

BIRDS OF PREY

Northern Goshawk A3516

Peregrine Falcon A3517

Golden Eagle A3518

Osprey A3519

Northern Harrier — A3520

LITHOGRAPHED

Serpentine Die Cut 11¼x10¾

2012, Jan. 20

Self-Adhesive

4608 A3516 85c multicolored 1.75 .35
4609 A3517 85c multicolored 1.75 .35
4610 A3518 85c multicolored 1.75 .35
4611 A3519 85c multicolored 1.75 .35
4612 A3520 85c multicolored 1.75 .35
a. Horiz. strip of 5, #4608-4612 8.75

WEATHER VANES

Rooster With Perch — A3521

Cow — A3522

Eagle — A3523

Rooster Without Perch — A3524

Centaur — A3525

LITHOGRAPHED

Serpentine Die Cut 11¾ Vert.

2012, Jan. 20

Coil Stamps
Self-Adhesive

4613 A3521 45c multicolored .90 .30
4614 A3522 45c multicolored .90 .30
4615 A3523 45c multicolored .90 .30
4616 A3524 45c multicolored .90 .30
4617 A3525 45c multicolored .90 .30
a. Strip of 5, #4613-4617 4.50

BONSAI

Sierra Juniper — A3526

Black Pine — A3527

Banyan — A3528

Trident Maple — A3529

Azalea — A3530

LITHOGRAPHED

Serpentine Die Cut 11x10¾ on 2 or 3 Sides

2012, Jan. 23

Booklet Stamps
Self-Adhesive

4618 A3526 (45c) multicolored .95 .40
4619 A3527 (45c) multicolored .95 .40
4620 A3528 (45c) multicolored .95 .40
4621 A3529 (45c) multicolored .95 .40
4622 A3530 (45c) multicolored .95 .40
a. Vert. strip of 5, #4618-4622 4.75
b. Booklet pane of 20, 4 each #4618-4622 19.00

Stamps in No. 4622a are not adjacent, as rows of selvage are between stamps two and three, and between stamps four and five.

No. 4622b is a double-sided booklet with 12 stamps on one side (3 each #4618, 4621, 2 each #4619, 4620, 4622) and eight stamps (#4618, 4621, 2 each #4619, 4620, 4622) plus label that serves as a booklet cover on the other side.

CHINESE NEW YEAR

Year of the Dragon A3531

PHOTOGRAVURE

Serpentine Die Cut 11x10¾

2012, Jan. 23

Self-Adhesive

4623 A3531 (45c) multicolored .95 .25

BLACK HERITAGE

John H. Johnson (1918-2005), Magazine Publisher — A3532

LITHOGRAPHED

Serpentine Die Cut 10¾

2012, Jan. 31

Self-Adhesive

4624 A3532 (45c) multicolored .95 .25

HEART HEALTH

Tree, Man, Sun and Apple — A3533

PHOTOGRAVURE

2012, Feb. 9 ***Serpentine Die Cut 11***

Self-Adhesive

4625 A3533 (45c) multicolored .95 .25

LOVE

Ribbons A3534

LITHOGRAPHED

Serpentine Die Cut 10¾

2012, Feb. 14

Self-Adhesive

4626 A3534 (45c) red .95 .25
a. Die cutting omitted, pair —

Postal Service officials declared on Feb. 2 that No. 4626 could be sold in post offices as of that date to make the stamp available to customers before St. Valentine's Day, but the first day ceremony for the stamp was held Feb. 14 in Colorado Springs, CO. Official first day covers have that date and city.

ARIZONA STATEHOOD CENTENNIAL

Cathedral Rock A3535

PHOTOGRAVURE

Serpentine Die Cut 11

2012, Feb. 14

Self-Adhesive

4627 A3535 (45c) multicolored .95 .25

DANNY THOMAS

Thomas (1912-91), Comedian, and St. Jude's Children's Research Hospital, Memphis A3536

LITHOGRAPHED

Serpentine Die Cut 10¾x10½

2012, Feb. 16

Self-Adhesive

4628 A3536 (45c) multicolored .95 .25

Flag and "Equality" A3537

Flag and "Justice" A3538

Flag and "Freedom" A3539

Flag and "Liberty" A3540

PHOTOGRAVURE (#4629-4632), LITHOGRAPHED (#4633-4648)

Serpentine Die Cut 8½ Vert.

2012, Feb. 22

Coil Stamps
Self-Adhesive

4629 A3537 (45c) multicolored .95 .25
4630 A3538 (45c) multicolored .95 .25
4631 A3539 (45c) multicolored .95 .25
4632 A3540 (45c) multicolored .95 .25
a. Strip of 4, #4629-4632 3.80

Serpentine Die Cut 9½ Vert.

4633 A3537 (45c) multicolored .95 .25
4634 A3538 (45c) multicolored .95 .25
4635 A3539 (45c) multicolored .95 .25
4636 A3540 (45c) multicolored .95 .25
b. Strip of 4, #4633-4636 3.80

Serpentine Die Cut 11 Vert.

4637 A3537 (45c) multicolored .95 .25
4638 A3538 (45c) multicolored .95 .25
4639 A3539 (45c) multicolored .95 .25
4640 A3540 (45c) multicolored .95 .25
a. Strip of 4, #4637-4640 3.80
b. As "a," die cutting omitted —
Nos. 4629-4640 (12) 10.80 3.00

Booklet Stamps
Colored Dots in Stars
18½mm From Lower Left to Lower Right Corners of Flag

Serpentine Die Cut 11¼x10¾ on 2 or 3 Sides

4641 A3539 (45c) multicolored .95 .25
4642 A3540 (45c) multicolored .95 .25
4643 A3537 (45c) multicolored .95 .25
4644 A3538 (45c) multicolored .95 .25
b. Block of 4, #4641-4644 3.80
c. Booklet pane of 20, 5 each #4641-4644 19.00

Dark Dots Only in Stars
19mm from Lower Left to Lower Right Corners of Flag

4645 A3539 (45c) multicolored .95 .25
4646 A3540 (45c) multicolored .95 .25
4647 A3537 (45c) multicolored .95 .25
4648 A3538 (45c) multicolored .95 .25
a. Block of 4, #4645-4648 3.80
b. Booklet pane of 20, 5 each #4645-4648 19.00
Nos. 4641-4648 (8) 7.60 2.00

On Nos. 4641-4644, the blue canton of the flag is made up of blue and red inks. The paper is tagged over each block of 4, with no tagging on the paper between the blocks. The tagging is a dull yellow green under ultraviolet light. The words are slightly longer than those on Nos. 4645-4648.

On Nos. 4645-4648, the blue canton is made up of blue and dull blue inks. The paper is prephosphored with the tagging appearing bright yellow green under ultraviolet light. The words are slightly shorter than those on Nos. 4641-4644.

No. 4644b is a double-sided booklet with 12 stamps on one side (3 each #4641-4644) and eight stamps (2 each #4641-4644) plus label that serves as a booklet cover on the other side.

No. 4648b is a double-sided booklet with 12 stamps on one side (3 each #4645-4648) and eight stamps (2 each #4645-4648) plus label that serves as a booklet cover on the other side.

See Nos. 4673-4676.

AMERICAN LANDMARKS ISSUE

Sunshine Skyway Bridge, Florida A3541

Carmel Mission, Carmel, CA A3542

LITHOGRAPHED

Serpentine Die Cut 10¾x10½

2012, Feb. 28

Self-Adhesive

4649	A3541	$5.15 multi	10.50	5.75
4650	A3542	$18.95 multi	37.50	19.00

CHERRY BLOSSOM CENTENNIAL

Cherry Blossoms and Washington Monument — A3543

Cherry Blossoms and Jefferson Memorial A3544

LITHOGRAPHED

Serpentine Die Cut 10¾

2012, Mar. 24 **Tagged**

Self-Adhesive

4651	A3543 (45c) multicolored		.95	.25
4652	A3544 (45c) multicolored		.95	.25
a.	Horiz. pair, #4651-4652		1.90	

See Japan No. 3413.

AMERICAN TREASURES SERIES

Flowers, by William H. Johnson (1901-70) — A3545

PHOTOGRAVURE

Sheets of 200 in 10 panes of 20

Serpentine Die Cut 10¾

2012, Apr. 11 **Tagged**

Self-Adhesive

4653	A3545 (45c) multicolored	1.00	.35

TWENTIETH CENTURY POETS

Joseph Brodsky (1940-96) A3546

Gwendolyn Brooks (1917-2000) A3547

William Carlos Williams (1883-1963) A3548

Robert Hayden (1913-80) A3549

Sylvia Plath (1932-63) A3550

Elizabeth Bishop (1911-79) A3551

Wallace Stevens (1879-1955) A3552

Denise Levertov (1923-97) A3553

E. E. Cummings (1894-1962) A3554

Theodore Roethke (1908-63) A3555

LITHOGRAPHED

Sheets of 160 in eight panes of 20

Serpentine Die Cut 10¾x11

2012, Apr. 21 **Tagged**

Self-Adhesive

4654	A3546 (45c) multicolored	.95	.40
4655	A3547 (45c) multicolored	.95	.40
4656	A3548 (45c) multicolored	.95	.40
4657	A3549 (45c) multicolored	.95	.40
4658	A3550 (45c) multicolored	.95	.40
4659	A3551 (45c) multicolored	.95	.40
4660	A3552 (45c) multicolored	.95	.40
4661	A3553 (45c) multicolored	.95	.40
4662	A3554 (45c) multicolored	.95	.40
4663	A3555 (45c) multicolored	.95	.40
a.	Block of 10, #4654-4663	9.50	
	Nos. 4654-4663 (10)	9.50	4.00

CIVIL WAR SESQUICENTENNIAL

Battle of New Orleans — A3556

Battle of Antietam — A3557

LITHOGRAPHED

Double-sided sheets of 72 in six panes of 12 (60 on one side, 12 on other side)

Serpentine Die Cut 11

2012, Apr. 24 **Tagged**

Self-Adhesive

4664	A3556 (45c) multicolored	.95	.25
4665	A3557 (45c) multicolored	.95	.25
a.	Pair, #4664-4665	1.90	

DISTINGUISHED AMERICANS

José Ferrer (1912-92), Actor — A3558

LITHOGRAPHED

Sheets of 160 in eight panes of 20

Serpentine Die Cut 10¾x11

2012, Apr. 26 **Tagged**

Self-Adhesive

4666	A3558 (45c) multicolored	.95	.25

LOUISIANA STATEHOOD BICENTENNIAL

Sunset Over Flat Lake — A3559

PHOTOGRAVURE

Sheets of 160 in eight panes of 20

Serpentine Die Cut 11

2012, Apr. 30 **Tagged**

Self-Adhesive

4667	A3559 (45c) multicolored	.95	.25

GREAT FILM DIRECTORS

John Ford (1894-1973), Scene From *The Searchers,* Starring John Wayne — A3560

Frank Capra (1897-1991), Scene From *It Happened One Night,* Starring Clark Gable and Claudette Colbert — A3561

Billy Wilder (1906-2002), Scene From *Some Like It Hot,* Starring Marilyn Monroe — A3562

John Huston (1906-87), Scene From *The Maltese Falcon,* Starring Humphrey Bogart A3563

PHOTOGRAVURE

Serpentine Die Cut 10¾

2012, May 23

Self-Adhesive

4668	A3560 (45c) multicolored	.95	.30
4669	A3561 (45c) multicolored	.95	.30
4670	A3562 (45c) multicolored	.95	.30
4671	A3563 (45c) multicolored	.95	.30
a.	Block or horiz. strip of 4, #4668-4671	3.80	

WILDLIFE

Bobcat — A3564

LITHOGRAPHED

Serpentine Die Cut 10 Vert.

2012, June 1

Coil Stamp

Self-Adhesive

4672	A3564 1c multicolored	.25	.25

Flags Type of 2012

PHOTOGRAVURE

Serpentine Die Cut 11¼x10¾ on 3 Sides

2012, June 1 **Tagged**

Booklet Stamps

Self-Adhesive

Colored Dots in Stars

19¼mm From Lower Left to Lower Right Corners of Flag

4673	A3539 (45c) multicolored	.95	.25
4674	A3540 (45c) multicolored	.95	.25
4675	A3537 (45c) multicolored	.95	.25
4676	A3538 (45c) multicolored	.95	.25
a.	Block of 4, #4673-4676	3.80	
b.	Booklet pane of 10, 3 each #4673-4674, 2 each #4675-4676	9.50	

Nos. 4673 and No. 4675 have straight edge on left side only. Nos. 4674 and 4676 have straight edge on right side only. Nos. 4641-4648 each have a straight edge at top or bottom. The letters in the "USPS" microprinting on Nos. 4673-4676, found at the right side of the bottom white flag stripe, are printed in a distinct curve, with the tops of the middle letters, "SP," being below the tops of the outside letters, "U" and "S," and the letters can be difficult to distinguish against the shading on the stripe. The letters in the microprinting on Nos. 4641-4648, found in the same place on the stamp, are printed in a straight line, and are printed boldly, making them easily distinguishable from the shading. The lettering on Nos. 4673-4767 has a fuzzier, less distinct appearance under magnification than the lettering on Nos. 4641-4648, which is most evident in the year "2012."

CHARACTERS FROM DISNEY-PIXAR FILMS

Mail a Smile

Flik and Dot From *A Bug's Life* — A3565

Bob Parr and Dashiell Parr From *The Incredibles* A3566

Nemo and Squirt From *Finding Nemo* — A3567

Jessie, Woody and Bullseye From *Toy Story 2* — A3568

Boo, Mike Wazowski and James P. "Sulley" Sullivan From *Monsters, Inc.* — A3569

PHOTOGRAVURE

Serpentine Die Cut 10½

2012, June 1

Self-Adhesive

4677 A3565 (45c) multicolored .95 .40
4678 A3566 (45c) multicolored .95 .40
4679 A3567 (45c) multicolored .95 .40
4680 A3568 (45c) multicolored .95 .40
4681 A3569 (45c) multicolored .95 .40
a. Horiz. strip of 5, #4677-4681 4.75

Adjacent horizontal or vertical stamps will have selvage between the stamps.

Aloha Shirts Type of 2012

LITHOGRAPHED

Serpentine Die Cut 11¼x10¾ on 3 Sides

2012, June 2

Booklet Stamps
Self-Adhesive

4682 A3506 32c multicolored .65 .30
4683 A3508 32c multicolored .65 .30
4684 A3510 32c multicolored .65 .30
4685 A3507 32c multicolored .65 .30
4686 A3509 32c multicolored .65 .30
a. Vert. strip of 5, #4682-4686 3.25
b. Booklet pane of 10, 2 each #4682-4686 6.50

BICYCLING

Child on Bicycle with Training Wheels A3570

Commuter on Bicycle with Panniers A3571

Road Racer A3572

BMX Rider A3573

LITHOGRAPHED

Serpentine Die Cut 10¾

2012, June 7

Self-Adhesive

4687 A3570 (45c) multicolored .95 .30
4688 A3571 (45c) multicolored .95 .30
4689 A3572 (45c) multicolored .95 .30
4690 A3573 (45c) multicolored .95 .30
a. Horiz. strip of 4, #4687-4690 3.80

GIRL SCOUTS OF AMERICA, CENT.

Girl Scouts — A3574

LITHOGRAPHED

Serpentine Die Cut 10¾

2012, June 9

Self-Adhesive

4691 A3574 (45c) multicolored .95 .25
a. Die cutting omitted, pair —

MUSICIANS

Edith Piaf (1915-63), Singer — A3575

Miles Davis (1926-91), Jazz Trumpet Player — A3576

PHOTOGRAVURE

Serpentine Die Cut 10¾x11

2012, June 12 **Self-Adhesive**

4692 A3575 (45c) multicolored .95 .25
4693 A3576 (45c) multicolored .95 .25
a. Horiz. pair, #4692-4693 1.90

See France Nos. 4256-4257.

Imperforate Uncut Press Sheets
Beginning with Nos. 4694-4697, the United States Postal Service made available for sale imperforate uncut press sheets of selected commemorative and definitive issues. These sheets, along with their corresponding multiples, are described and valued in footnotes following each issue in the *Scott Specialized Catalogue of United States Stamps and Covers*. **For descriptions and illustrations of typical press-sheet multiples, see the note after No. 2868 in the Scott U.S. Specialized catalogue.**

MAJOR LEAGUE BASEBALL ALL-STARS

Ted Williams (1918-2002) — A3577

Larry Doby (1923-2003) — A3578

Willie Stargell (1940-2001) — A3579

Joe DiMaggio (1914-99) A3580

PHOTOGRAVURE

Serpentine Die Cut 10¾x11

2012, July 20

Self-Adhesive

4694 A3577 (45c) multicolored .95 .30
4695 A3578 (45c) multicolored .95 .30
4696 A3579 (45c) multicolored .95 .30
4697 A3580 (45c) multicolored .95 .30
a. Horiz. strip or block of 4, #4694-4697 3.80

Panes containing 20 of the same stamp were issued on July 21 in Boston, MA (for No. 4694), Cleveland, OH (for No. 4695), Pittsburgh, PA (for No. 4696) and New York, NY (for No. 4697).

INNOVATIVE CHOREOGRAPHERS

Isadora Duncan (1877-1927) A3581

José Limón (1908-72) A3582

Katherine Dunham (1909-2006) A3583

Bob Fosse (1927-87) A3584

LITHOGRAPHED

Serpentine Die Cut 10¾x11

2012, July 28

Self-Adhesive

4698 A3581 (45c) multicolored .95 .30
4699 A3582 (45c) multicolored .95 .30
4700 A3583 (45c) multicolored .95 .30
4701 A3584 (45c) multicolored .95 .30
a. Vert. strip of 4, #4698-4701 3.80

EDGAR RICE BURROUGHS

Edgar Rice Burroughs (1875-1950), Writer, and Tarzan — A3585

LITHOGRAPHED

Serpentine Die Cut 10¾

2012, Aug. 17

Self-Adhesive

4702 A3585 (45c) multicolored .95 .25

WAR OF 1812 BICENTENNIAL

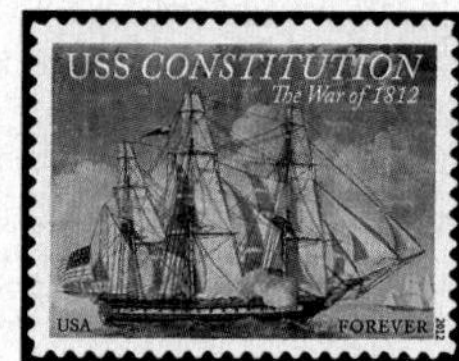

Painting of U.S.S. Constitution, by Michele Felice Corné — A3586

PHOTOGRAVURE

Serpentine Die Cut 10¾x10½

2012, Aug. 18

Self-Adhesive

4703 A3586 (45c) multicolored 1.10 .25

Purple Heart and Ribbon — A3587

Designed by Jennifer Arnold. Printed by Avery Dennison.

PHOTOGRAVURE

Sheets of 420 in 21 panes of 20

2012, Sept. 4 ***Serpentine Die Cut 11***

Self-Adhesive

4704 A3587 (45c) multicolored .95 .25

Compare with Type A3458.

LITERARY ARTS

O. Henry (William S. Porter) (1862-1910), New York City Buildings and Elevated Trains — A3588

PHOTOGRAVURE

Serpentine Die Cut 11

2012, Sept. 11

Self-Adhesive

4705 A3588 (45c) multicolored .95 .25

Flags Type of 2012
Booklet Stamps Self-Adhesive
Colored Dots in Stars 18½mm From Lower Left to Lower Right Corners of Flag Thin Paper

LITHOGRAPHED

Serpentine Die Cut 11¼x10¾ on 2, 3 or 4 Sides

2012, Sept. 22

4706 A3539 (45c) multicolored .95 .25
4707 A3540 (45c) multicolored .95 .25
4708 A3537 (45c) multicolored .95 .25
4709 A3538 (45c) multicolored .95 .25
a. Block of 4, #4706-4709 3.80
b. Booklet pane of 18, 5 each #4706-4707, 4 each #4708-4709 17.00
Nos. 4706-4709 (4) 3.80 1.00

The overall-tagged paper used for Nos. 4706-4709 is glossier than that used on Nos. 4641-4644. The blue canton of the flag on Nos. 4706-4709 is made up of blue and red inks, similar to Nos. 4641-4644.

EARTHSCAPES

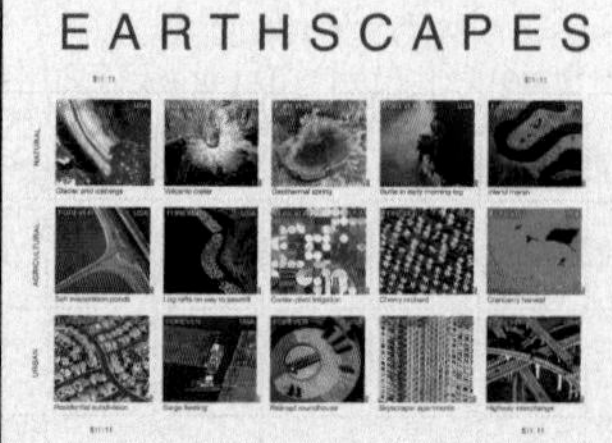

A3589

No. 4710: a, Glacier and icebergs. b, Volcanic crater. c, Geothermal spring. d, Butte in early morning fog. e, Inland marsh. f, Salt evaporation ponds. g, Log rafts on way to sawmill. h, Center-pivot irrigation. i, Cherry orchard. j, Cranberry harvest. k, Residential subdivision. l, Barge fleeting. m, Railroad roundhouse. n, Skyscraper apartments. o, Highway interchange.

LITHOGRAPHED

Serpentine Die Cut 10¾

2012, Oct. 1

Self-Adhesive

4710	A3589	Pane of 15	16.50	
a.-o.		(45c) Any single	1.10	.50

CHRISTMAS

Holy Family and Donkey A3590

Reindeer in Flight, Moon A3591

Santa Claus and Sleigh — A3592

Reindeer Over Roof — A3593

Snow-covered Buildings A3594

LITHOGRAPHED

Serpentine Die Cut 11 on 2 or 3 Sides

2012

Booklet Stamps

Self-Adhesive

4711	A3590 (45c) multi		.95	.25
a.	Booklet pane of 20		19.00	

Serpentine Die Cut 11x10¾ on 2 or 3 sides

4712	A3591 (45c) multi		.95	.25
4713	A3592 (45c) multi		.95	.25
4714	A3593 (45c) multi		.95	.25
4715	A3594 (45c) multi		.95	.25
a.	Block of 4, #4712-4715		3.80	
b.	Booklet pane of 20, 5 each #4712-4715		19.00	
	Nos. 4711-4715 (5)		4.50	1.25

Issued: No. 4711, Oct. 10, Nos. 4712-4715, Oct. 13.

No. 4711a is a double-sided booklet with 12 stamps on one side and eight stamps plus a label that serves as a booklet cover on the other side. No. 4715b is a double-sided booklet with 12 stamps on one side (3 each of Nos. 4712-4715) and eight stamps (2 each of Nos. 4712-4715) plus a label that serves as a booklet cover on the other side.

See No. 4813.

LADY BIRD JOHNSON

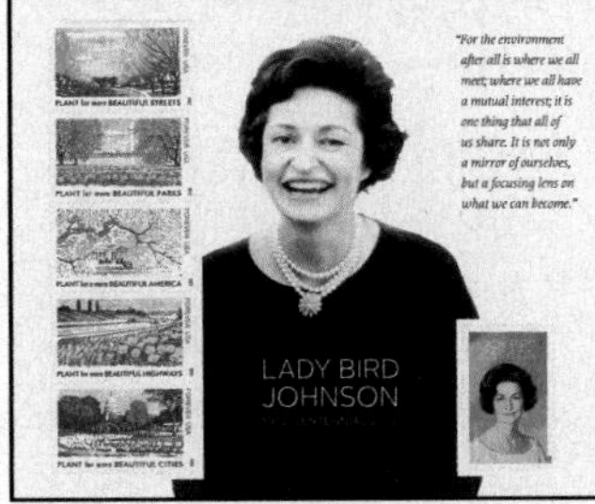

A3595

No. 4716: a, Blooming crab apples lining avenue (Plant for more Beautiful Streets). b, Washington Monument, Potomac River and daffodils (Plant for more Beautiful Parks). c, Jefferson Memorial, Tidal Basin and cherry blossoms (Plant for a more Beautiful America). d, Poppies and lupines along highway (Plant for more Beautiful Highways). e, Capitol, azaleas and tulips (Plant for more Beautiful Cities). f, Lady Bird Johnson (1912-2007), First Lady, vert.

LITHOGRAPHED

Serpentine Die Cut 10¾

2012, Nov. 30

Self-Adhesive

4716	A3595	Pane of 6	5.75	
a.-f.		(45c) Any single	.95	.40

WAVES OF COLOR

A3596

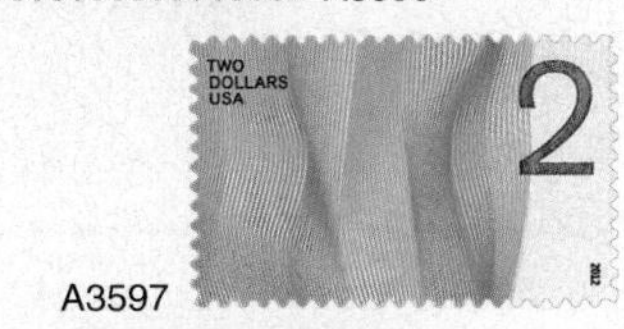

A3597

A3598

TEN DOLLARS USA

A3599

LITHOGRAPHED & ENGRAVED

Serpentine Die Cut 11, 10¾ (#4719)

2012, Dec. 1

Self-Adhesive

4717	A3596 $1 multi	2.00	.50
4718	A3597 $2 multi	3.75	1.25
4719	A3598 $5 multi	8.75	2.50
4720	A3599 $10 multi	17.50	9.00
	Nos. 4717-4720 (4)	32.00	13.25

Adjacent horizontal or vertical stamps have selvage between the stamps. Plate blocks have sheet margins on the top or bottom and both sides.

EMANCIPATION PROCLAMATION, 150th ANNIV.

A3600

PHOTOGRAVURE

2013, Jan. 1 ***Serpentine Die Cut 11***

Self-Adhesive

4721	A3600 (45c) multicolored	.95	.25

KALEIDOSCOPE FLOWERS

A3601

USA 46

A3602

USA 46

A3603

USA 46

A3604

LITHOGRAPHED

Serpentine Die Cut 11 Vert.

2013, Jan. 14

Coil Stamps

Self-Adhesive

Color of Large Outer Leaves

4722	A3601 46c yellow orange	.95	.25
4723	A3602 46c yellow green	.95	.25
4724	A3603 46c red violet	.95	.25
4725	A3604 46c red	.95	.25
a.	Strip of 4, #4722-4725	3.80	
	Nos. 4722-4725 (4)	3.80	1.00

CHINESE NEW YEAR

Year of the Snake A3605

PHOTOGRAVURE

Serpentine Die Cut 11

2013, Jan. 16

Self-Adhesive

4726	A3605 (45c) multicolored	.95	.25

APPLES

Northern Spy Apple A3606

Golden Delicious Apple A3607

Granny Smith Apple A3608

Baldwin Apple A3609

LITHOGRAPHED

Serpentine Die Cut 11¼x10¾

2013, Jan. 17

Self-Adhesive

4727	A3606 33c multicolored	.70	.25
4728	A3607 33c multicolored	.70	.25
4729	A3608 33c multicolored	.70	.25
4730	A3609 33c multicolored	.70	.25
a.	Block of 4, #4727-4730	2.80	

Coil Stamps

Serpentine Die Cut 11 Vert.

4731	A3609 33c multicolored	.70	.25
4732	A3606 33c multicolored	.70	.25
4733	A3607 33c multicolored	.70	.25
4734	A3608 33c multicolored	.70	.25
a.	Strip of 4, #4731-4734	2.80	
	Nos. 4727-4734 (8)	5.60	2.00

Wedding Cake Type of 2009

LITHOGRAPHED

Serpentine Die Cut 10¾

2013, Jan. 18

Self-Adhesive

4735	A3344 66c multicolored	1.40	.25

SPICEBUSH SWALLOWTAIL BUTTERFLY

A3610

PHOTOGRAVURE

Serpentine Die Cut 10¾

2013, Jan. 23

Self-Adhesive

4736	A3610 66c multicolored	1.40	.25

TUFTED PUFFINS

A3611

LITHOGRAPHED

Serpentine Die Cut 11¼x10¾

2013, Jan. 23

Solid Color in "Tufted Puffins" and "86"

"2013" in Orange Red

Self-Adhesive

4737	A3611 86c multicolored	1.75	.35

AMERICAN LANDMARKS ISSUE

Arlington Green Bridge, Vermont A3612

Grand Central Terminal, New York City A3613

PHOTOGRAVURE

2013 ***Serpentine Die Cut 10¾x10½***

Self-Adhesive

4738	A3612 $5.60 multi	11.00	6.25
4739	A3613 $19.95 multi	40.00	21.00
	Pane of 10	400.00	

Earth
A3614

PHOTOGRAVURE

2013, Jan. 28 ***Serpentine Die Cut***

Self-Adhesive

4740	A3614 ($1.10) multi		2.25	.50

Unused values are for stamps with surrounding selvage. Adjacent stamps are separated by rouletting.

LOVE

Envelope With Wax Seal — A3615

PHOTOGRAVURE

Serpentine Die Cut 10¾

2013, Jan. 30

Self-Adhesive

4741	A3615 (46c) multicolored		.95	.25

ROSA PARKS

Parks (1913-2005), Civil Rights Pioneer — A3616

PHOTOGRAVURE

Serpentine Die Cut 10¾

2013, Feb. 4

Self-Adhesive

4742	A3616 (46c) multicolored		.95	.25

MUSCLE CARS

1969 Dodge Charger Daytona
A3617

1966 Pontiac GTO
A3618

1967 Ford Mustang Shelby GT 500
A3619

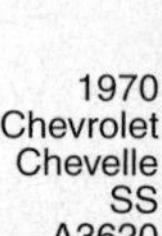

1970 Chevrolet Chevelle SS
A3620

1970 Plymouth Hemi Barracuda
A3621

Designed by Carl T. Herrman. Printed by Avery Dennison.

PHOTOGRAVURE

Sheets of 200 in 10 panes of 20

Serpentine Die Cut 10¾

2013, Feb. 22 **Tagged**

Self-Adhesive

4743	A3617 (46c) multicolored		.95	.30
4744	A3618 (46c) multicolored		.95	.30
4745	A3619 (46c) multicolored		.95	.30
4746	A3620 (46c) multicolored		.95	.30
4747	A3621 (46c) multicolored		.95	.30
a.	Vert. strip of 5, #4743-4747		4.75	
	Vert. P# block of 10, 5# + V		9.50	
	Horiz. P# block of 8, 2 sets of 5# + V		7.60	
	Pane of 20		19.00	
	Nos. 4743-4747 (5)		4.75	1.50

MODERN ART IN AMERICA

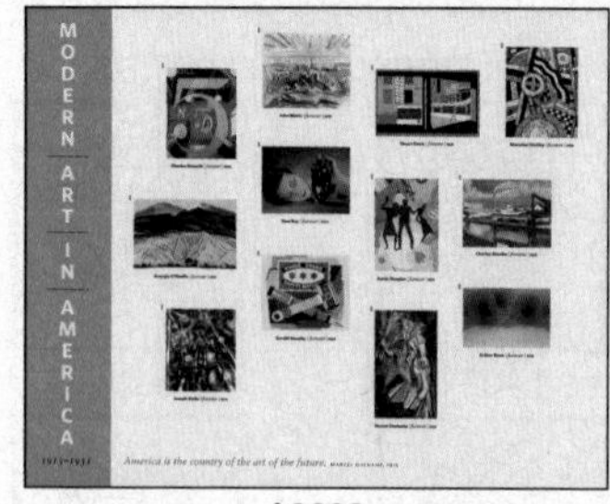

A3622

No. 4748: a, I Saw the Figure 5 in Gold, by Charles Demuth (37x51mm). b, Sunset, Maine Coast, by John Marin (43x43mm). c, House and Street, by Stuart Davis (51x41mm). d, Painting, Number 5, by Marsden Hartley (37x51mm). e, Black Mesa Landscape, New Mexico/Out Back of Marie's II, by Georgia O'Keeffe (51x41mm). f, Noire et Blanche, by Man Ray (43x41mm). g, The Prodigal Son, by Aaron Douglas (34x51mm). h, American Landscape, by Charles Sheeler (43x41mm). i, Brooklyn Bridge, by Joseph Stella (38x47mm). j, Razor, by Gerald Murphy (43x43mm). k, Nude Descending a Staircase, No. 2, by Marcel Duchamp (34x58mm). l, Fog Horns, by Arthur Dove (43x37mm).

PHOTOGRAVURE

Serpentine Die Cut 10½

2013, Mar. 7

Self-Adhesive

4748	A3622 Pane of 12		11.50	
a.-l.	(46c) Any single		.95	.50

Armory Show, cent.

Patriotic Star — A3623

LITHOGRAPHED

Serpentine Die Cut 10¾ Vert.

2013, Mar. 19

Coil Stamp

Self-Adhesive

4749	A3623 46c multicolored		.95	.25

LA FLORIDA

A3624 A3625

A3626 A3627

PHOTOGRAVURE

Serpentine Die Cut 10½x10¾

2013, Apr. 3

Self-Adhesive

4750	A3624 (46c) multicolored		.95	.25
4751	A3625 (46c) multicolored		.95	.25
4752	A3626 (46c) multicolored		.95	.25
4753	A3627 (46c) multicolored		.95	.25
a.	Block of 4, #4750-4753		3.80	
	Nos. 4750-4753 (4)		3.80	1.00

Naming of Florida, 500th anniv.

VINTAGE SEED PACKETS

Phlox
A3628

Calendula
A3629

Digitalis
A3630

Linum
A3631

Alyssum
A3632

Zinnias
A3633

Pinks
A3634

Cosmos
A3635

Aster
A3636

Primrose
A3637

PHOTOGRAVURE

Serpentine Die Cut 10¾ on 2 or 3 Sides

2013, Apr. 5

Booklet Stamps

Self-Adhesive

4754	A3628 (46c) multicolored		.95	.25
4755	A3629 (46c) multicolored		.95	.25
4756	A3630 (46c) multicolored		.95	.25
4757	A3631 (46c) multicolored		.95	.25
4758	A3632 (46c) multicolored		.95	.25
4759	A3633 (46c) multicolored		.95	.25
4760	A3634 (46c) multicolored		.95	.25
4761	A3635 (46c) multicolored		.95	.25
4762	A3636 (46c) multicolored		.95	.25
4763	A3637 (46c) multicolored		.95	.25
a.	Block of 10, #4754-4763		9.50	
b.	Booklet pane of 20, 2 each #4754-4763		19.00	
	Nos. 4754-4763 (10)		9.50	2.50

No. 4763b is a double-sided booklet pane with 12 stamps on one side (2 each #4754, 4759, 1 each #4755-4758, 4760-4763), and eight stamps (1 each #4755-4758, 4760-4763) plus label (booklet cover) on the other side.

WEDDING FLOWERS

Flowers — A3638

Flowers and "Yes I Do"
A3639

PHOTOGRAVURE

Serpentine Die Cut 10¾

2013, Apr. 11

Self-Adhesive

4764	A3638 (46c) multicolored		.95	.25
4765	A3639 66c multicolored		1.40	.30

Flag in Autumn
A3640

Flag in Winter
A3641

Flag in Spring
A3642

Flag in Summer
A3643

PHOTOGRAVURE (#4766-4769),
LITHOGRAPHED (#4770-4785)

2013 ***Serpentine Die Cut 8½ Vert.***

Coil Stamps

Self-Adhesive

4766	A3640 (46c) multicolored		.95	.25
4767	A3641 (46c) multicolored		.95	.25
4768	A3642 (46c) multicolored		.95	.25
4769	A3643 (46c) multicolored		.95	.25
a.	Strip of 4, #4766-4769		3.80	

Serpentine Die Cut 9½ Vert.

4770	A3640 (46c) multicolored		.95	.25
4771	A3641 (46c) multicolored		.95	.25
4772	A3642 (46c) multicolored		.95	.25
4773	A3643 (46c) multicolored		.95	.25
a.	Strip of 4, #4770-4773		3.80	

Serpentine Die Cut 11 Vert.

4774	A3641 (46c) multicolored		.95	.25
4775	A3642 (46c) multicolored		.95	.25
4776	A3643 (46c) multicolored		.95	.25
4777	A3640 (46c) multicolored		.95	.25
a.	Strip of 4, #4774-4777		3.80	
	Nos. 4766-4777 (12)		11.40	3.00

Booklet Stamps
With Microprinted "USPS" at Lower Left Corner of Flag
Serpentine Die Cut 11¼x10¾ on 2 or 3 Sides

4778 A3642 (46c) multicolored .95 .25
4779 A3643 (46c) multicolored .95 .25
4780 A3640 (46c) multicolored .95 .25
4781 A3641 (46c) multicolored .95 .25
a. Block of 4, #4778-4781 3.80
b. Booklet pane of 20, 5 each #4778-4781 19.00

With Microprinted "USPS" Near Top of Pole or at Lower Left Corner Near Rope (#4783)
Pre-phosphored Paper

4782 A3642 (46c) multicolored .95 .25
4783 A3643 (46c) multicolored .95 .25
4784 A3640 (46c) multicolored .95 .25
4785 A3641 (46c) multicolored .95 .25
b. Block of 4, #4782-4785 3.80
c. Booklet pane of 20, 5 each #4782-4785 19.00
e. Booklet pane of 10, 3 each #4784a, 4785a, 2 each #4782a, 4783a 9.50
Nos. 4778-4785 (8) 7.60 2.00

Issued: Nos. 4766-4777, 5/3; Nos. 4778-4785, 5/17. No. 4781b is a double-sided booklet with 12 stamps on one side (3 each #4778-4781) and eight stamps (2 each #4778-4781) plus label that serves as a booklet cover on the other side.

No. 4785c is a double-sided booklet with 12 stamps on one side (3 each #4782-4785) and eight stamps (2 each #4782-4785) plus label that serves as a booklet cover on the other side.

A microprinted "USPS" is found on tree trunk to the left of the "F" in "Forever" on No. 4766, on tree trunk near lower left corner of flag on No. 4767, on white flag stripe at lower right on No. 4768, and on the top of the flagpole below the ball on No. 4769. Nos. 4770-4773 are microprinted "USPS" in the same places as on Nos. 4778-4781. Nos. 4774-4777 are microprinted "USPS" in the same places as on Nos. 4782-4785.

No. 4785e comprises stamps printed on paper with overall tagging. For detailed listings, see the *Scott Specialized Catalogue of United States Stamps and Covers.*

See Nos. 4796-4799.

MUSIC ICONS

Lydia Mendoza (1916-2007), Tejano Music Recording Artist — A3644

PHOTOGRAVURE
Serpentine Die Cut 10¾
2013, May 15
Self-Adhesive

4786 A3644 (46c) multicolored .95 .25

Adjacent horizontal or vertical stamps have selvage between the stamps.

CIVIL WAR SESQUICENTENNIAL

Battle of Vicksburg — A3645

Battle of Gettysburg — A3646

LITHOGRAPHED
2013, May 23 ***Serpentine Die Cut 11***
Self-Adhesive

4787 A3645 (46c) multicolored .95 .25
4788 A3646 (46c) multicolored .95 .25
a. Pair, #4787-4788 1.90

MUSIC ICONS

Johnny Cash (1932-2003), Country Music Recording Artist — A3647

PHOTOGRAVURE
Serpentine Die Cut 10¾
2013, June 5
Self-Adhesive

4789 A3647 (46c) multicolored .95 .25

WEST VIRGINIA STATEHOOD, 150th ANNIV.

Hills in Monongahela National Forest — A3648

PHOTOGRAVURE
Serpentine Die Cut 11
2013, June 20
Self-Adhesive

4790 A3648 (46c) multicolored .95 .25

NEW ENGLAND COASTAL LIGHTHOUSES

Portland Head Lighthouse, Maine A3649

Portsmouth Harbor Lighthouse, New Hampshire A3650

Boston Harbor Lighthouse, Massachusetts A3651

Point Judith Lighthouse, Rhode Island A3652

New London Harbor Lighthouse, Connecticut A3653

LITHOGRAPHED
Serpentine Die Cut 11x10¾
2013, July 13
Self-Adhesive

4791 A3649 (46c) multicolored .95 .40
4792 A3650 (46c) multicolored .95 .40
4793 A3651 (46c) multicolored .95 .40
4794 A3652 (46c) multicolored .95 .40
4795 A3653 (46c) multicolored .95 .40
a. Horiz. strip of 5, #4791-4795 4.75
Nos. 4791-4795 (5) 4.75 1.25

Flag Types of 2013
PHOTOGRAVURE
Serpentine Die Cut 11¼x11½ on 2 or 3 Sides
2013, Aug. 8
Booklet Stamps
Self-Adhesive

4796 A3642 (46c) multicolored .95 .25
4797 A3643 (46c) multicolored .95 .25
4798 A3640 (46c) multicolored .95 .25
4799 A3641 (46c) multicolored .95 .25
a. Block of 4, #4796-4799 3.80
b. Booklet pane of 20, 5 each #4796-4799 19.00
Nos. 4796-4799 (4) 3.80 1.00

No. 4799b is a double-sided booklet with 12 stamps on one side (3 each #4796-4799) and eight stamps (2 each #4796-4799) plus label that serves as a booklet cover on the other side. Nos. 4796-4799 are microprinted "USPS" in the same places as Nos. 4766-4769.

EID

"Eid Mubarak" — A3654

LITHOGRAPHED
2013, Aug. 8 ***Serpentine Die Cut 11***
Self-Adhesive

4800 A3654 (46c) dk grn, gray & gold .95 .25

BUILDING A NATION

Airplane Mechanic, Photograph by Lewis Hine — A3655

Derrick Man on Empire State Building, Photograph by Lewis Hine — A3656

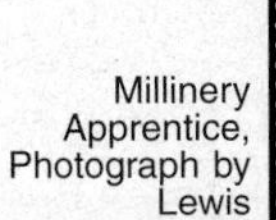

Millinery Apprentice, Photograph by Lewis Hine — A3657

Man on Hoisting Ball on Empire State Building, Photograph by Lewis Hine — A3658

Linotype Operator, Photograph by Lewis Hine — A3659

Welder on Empire State Building, Photograph by Lewis Hine — A3660

Coal Miner, by Anonymous Photographer A3661

Riveters on Empire State Building, Photograph by Lewis Hine — A3662

Powerhouse Mechanic, Photograph by Lewis Hine — A3663

Railroad Track Walker, Photograph by Lewis Hine — A3664

Textile Worker, Photograph by Lewis Hine — A3665

Man Guiding Beam on Empire State Building, Photograph by Lewis Hine — A3666

PHOTOGRAVURE

Serpentine Die Cut 10½x10¾

2013, Aug. 8

Self-Adhesive

4801 Pane of 12 11.50
a. A3655 (46c) black & gray .95 .50
b. A3656 (46c) black & gray .95 .50
c. A3657 (46c) black & gray .95 .50
d. A3658 (46c) black & gray .95 .50
e. A3659 (46c) black & gray .95 .50
f. A3660 (46c) black & gray .95 .50
g. A3661 (46c) black & gray .95 .50
h. A3662 (46c) black & gray .95 .50
i. A3663 (46c) black & gray .95 .50
j. A3664 (46c) black & gray .95 .50
k. A3665 (46c) black & gray .95 .50
l. A3666 (46c) black & gray .95 .50

No. 4801 was printed with five different sheet margins depicting coal miner from No. 4801g, man on hoisting ball on Empire State Building, man measuring bearings in large gearwheel, man on cable at Empire State Building, and woman welder. Value is for sheet with any margin.

Bobcat Type of 2012

LITHOGRAPHED

2013, Aug. 9 ***Perf. 9¾ Vert.***

Coil Stamp

4802 A3564 1c multicolored .25 .25

BLACK HERITAGE

Althea Gibson (1927-2003), Tennis Player — A3667

PHOTOGRAVURE

Serpentine Die Cut 11

2013, Aug. 23

Self-Adhesive

4803 A3667 (46c) multicolored .95 .25

MARCH ON WASHINGTON, 50th ANNIV.

Marchers and Washington Monument — A3668

PHOTOGRAVURE

Serpentine Die Cut 10¾

2013, Aug. 23

Self-Adhesive

4804 A3668 (46c) multicolored .95 .25

WAR OF 1812 BICENTENNIAL

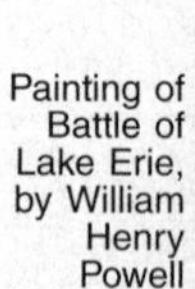

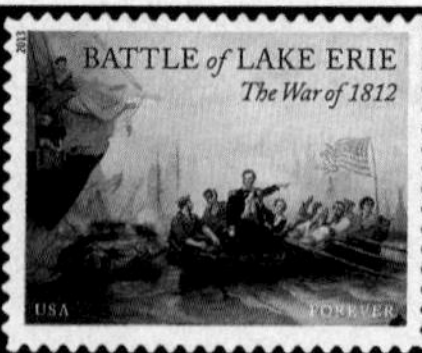

Painting of Battle of Lake Erie, by William Henry Powell A3669

LITHOGRAPHED

Serpentine Die Cut 10¾

2013, Sept. 10

Self-Adhesive

4805 A3669 (46c) multicolored .95 .25

INVERTED JENNY

Miniature Sheet

A3670

LITHOGRAPHED & ENGRAVED

Serpentine Die Cut 10½x11¼

2013, Sept. 22

Self-Adhesive

4806 A3670 multicolored 24.00
a. $2 Single stamp 4.00 1.25

No. 4806, along with a piece of white cardboard backing, was placed in a sealed envelope. The envelope, along with a piece of gray cardboard backing, was inside a sealed plastic outerwrap. One hundred panes were produced that contain the airplane right-side up. These panes were included in the same envelope and outerwrap and were distributed randomly. No returns or refunds were offered for any opened packages. Values for No. 4806 are for panes removed from the envelope.

A book containing an unused and a first-day canceled example of No. 4806, along with items that are termed "proofs" and "die wipes," sold for $200.

MUSIC ICONS

Ray Charles (1930-2004), Recording Artist — A3671

LITHOGRAPHED

Serpentine Die Cut 10½

2013, Sept. 23

Self-Adhesive

4807 A3671 (46c) multicolored .95 .25

Adjacent horizontal or vertical stamps have selvage between the stamps.

SNOWFLAKES

A3672  A3673

A3674  A3675

A3676

PHOTOGRAVURE

Serpentine Die Cut 11 Vert.

2013, Oct. 1

Coil Stamps

Self-Adhesive

4808 A3672 (10c) lt bl & multi .25 .25
4809 A3673 (10c) pale bl & multi .25 .25
4810 A3674 (10c) lt bl & multi .25 .25
4811 A3675 (10c) pale bl & multi .25 .25
4812 A3676 (10c) lil & multi .25 .25
a. Strip of 5, #4808-4812 1.25
Nos. 4808-4812 (5) 1.25 1.25

Holy Family and Donkey Type of 2012 Dated "2013" and

Wreath A3677

Virgin and Child, by Jan Gossaert A3678

Poinsettia A3679

Gingerbread House With Red Door — A3680

Gingerbread House With Blue Door — A3681

Gingerbread House With Green Door — A3682

Gingerbread House With Orange Door — A3683

Poinsettia — A3684

LITHOGRAPHED, PHOTOGRAVURE (#4821)

2013 ***Serpentine Die Cut 11***

Self-Adhesive

4813 A3590 (46c) multicolored .95 .25

Serpentine Die Cut

4814 A3677 ($1.10) multicolored 2.25 .50

Booklet Stamps

Serpentine Die Cut 11 on 2 or 3 Sides

4815 A3678 (46c) multicolored .95 .25
a. Booklet pane of 20 19.00
4816 A3679 (46c) multicolored .95 .25
a. Booklet pane of 20 19.00
4817 A3680 (46c) multicolored .95 .25
4818 A3681 (46c) multicolored .95 .25
4819 A3682 (46c) multicolored .95 .25
4820 A3683 (46c) multicolored .95 .25
a. Block of 4, #4817-4820 3.80
b. Booklet pane of 20, 5 each #4817-4820 19.00

Serpentine Die Cut 8 on 2, 3 or 4 Sides

4821 A3684 (46c) multicolored .95 .25
a. Booklet pane of 18 17.50
Nos. 4815-4821 (7) 6.65 1.75

Issued: Nos. 4813, 4815, 10/11; No. 4814, 10/24; Nos. 4816, 4821, 10/10; Nos. 4817-4820, 11/6.

MEDALS OF HONOR

Navy Medal of Honor — A3685

Army Medal of Honor — A3686

LITHOGRAPHED

Serpentine Die Cut 11

2013, Nov. 11

Self-Adhesive

4822 A3685 (46c) multicolored .95 .25
4823 A3686 (46c) multicolored .95 .25
a. Pair, #4822-4823 1.90

HANUKKAH

Menorah A3687

LITHOGRAPHED

Sheets of 160 in eight panes of 20

Serpentine Die Cut 11

2013, Nov. 19

Self-Adhesive

4824 A3687 (46c) multicolored .95 .25

Postal Service officials declared on Nov. 8 that No. 4824 could be sold in post offices on Nov. 9, but the first day ceremony was held on Nov. 19 in New York, NY. Official first day covers have that date and city.

SCENES FROM HARRY POTTER MOVIES

Harry Potter — A3688

Harry Potter and Ron Weasley A3689

Harry Potter, Ron Weasley, Hermione Granger A3690

Hermione Granger — A3691

Harry Potter and Fawkes the Phoenix A3692

Hedwig the Owl — A3693

Dobby the House Elf — A3694

Harry Potter and Buckbeak the Hippogriff A3695

Headmaster Albus Dumbledore A3696

Professor Severus Snape A3697

Rubeus Hagrid A3698

Professor Minerva McGonagall A3699

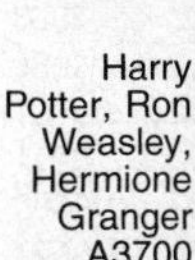

Harry Potter, Ron Weasley, Hermione Granger A3700

Luna Lovegood A3701

Fred and George Weasley A3702

Ginny Weasley A3703

Draco Malfoy — A3704

Harry Potter A3705

Lord Voldemort A3706

Bellatrix Lestrange — A3707

LITHOGRAPHED

Serpentine Die Cut 11

2013, Nov. 19

Booklet Stamps
Self-Adhesive

4825	A3688 (46c) multicolored	.95	.25
4826	A3689 (46c) multicolored	.95	.25
4827	A3690 (46c) multicolored	.95	.25
4828	A3691 (46c) multicolored	.95	.25
a.	Booklet pane of 4, #4825-4828, + central label	3.80	
4829	A3692 (46c) multicolored	.95	.25
4830	A3693 (46c) multicolored	.95	.25
4831	A3694 (46c) multicolored	.95	.25
4832	A3695 (46c) multicolored	.95	.25
a.	Booklet pane of 4, #4829-4832, + central label	3.80	
4833	A3696 (46c) multicolored	.95	.25
4834	A3697 (46c) multicolored	.95	.25
4835	A3698 (46c) multicolored	.95	.25
4836	A3699 (46c) multicolored	.95	.25
a.	Booklet pane of 4, #4833-4836, + central label	3.80	
4837	A3700 (46c) multicolored	.95	.25
4838	A3701 (46c) multicolored	.95	.25
4839	A3702 (46c) multicolored	.95	.25
4840	A3703 (46c) multicolored	.95	.25
a.	Booklet pane of 4, #4837-4840, + central label	3.80	
4841	A3704 (46c) multicolored	.95	.25
4842	A3705 (46c) multicolored	.95	.25
4843	A3706 (46c) multicolored	.95	.25
4844	A3707 (46c) multicolored	.95	.25
a.	Booklet pane of 4, #4841-4844, + central label	3.80	
	Nos. 4825-4844 (20)	19.00	5.00

KWANZAA

People, Candles and Book — A3708

LITHOGRAPHED

Serpentine Die Cut 11

2013, Nov. 26

Self-Adhesive

4845	A3708 (46c) multicolored	.95	.25

SUBJECT INDEX OF REGULAR, COMMEMORATIVE & AIR POST ISSUES

UNITED STATES

SEMI-POSTAL STAMPS

BREAST CANCER RESEARCH

SP1

PHOTOGRAVURE

Serpentine Die Cut 11

1998, July 29

Self-Adhesive

B1 SP1 (32c+8c) multicolored .95 .25

HEROES OF 2001

Firemen Atop World Trade Center Rubble — SP2

LITHOGRAPHED

Serpentine Die Cut 11¼

2002, June 7

Self-Adhesive

B2 SP2 (34c+11c) multicolored .95 .35

STOP FAMILY VIOLENCE

SP3

PHOTOGRAVURE

2003, Oct. 8 ***Serpentine Die Cut 11***

Self-Adhesive

B3 SP3 (37c+8c) multicolored .95 .45

SAVE VANISHING SPECIES

Amur Tiger Cub — SP4

PHOTOGRAVURE

Serpentine Die Cut 10¾

2011, Sept. 20

Self-Adhesive

B4 SP4 (44c+11c) multicolored 1.10 .55

The 11c surtax was for the Multinational Species Conservation Funds of the U.S. Fish and Wildlife Service.

AIR POST STAMPS

Curtiss Jenny — AP1

FLAT PLATE PRINTINGS

1918 Unwmk. Engr. *Perf. 11*

C1 AP1 6c orange 60. 30.
Never hinged 120.
C2 AP1 16c green 65. 35.
Never hinged 130.
C3 AP1 24c car rose & blue 70. 35.
Never hinged 140.
a. Center inverted *400,000.*
Never hinged *850,000.*
Nos. C1-C3 (3) 195.00 100.00
Nos. C1-C3, never hinged 390.00

Wooden Propeller and Radiator — AP2

Emblem of Air Service — AP3

De Havilland Biplane — AP4

1923

C4 AP2 8c dark green 20.00 15.00
Never hinged 40.00
C5 AP3 16c dark blue 65.00 30.00
Never hinged 130.00
C6 AP4 24c carmine 70.00 30.00
Never hinged 140.00
Nos. C4-C6 (3) 155.00 75.00
Nos. C4-C6, never hinged 310.00

Map of U.S. and Two Mail Planes — AP5

1926-27

C7 AP5 10c dark blue 2.50 .35
Never hinged 4.50
C8 AP5 15c olive brown 2.75 2.50
Never hinged 5.25
C9 AP5 20c yellow green 7.00 2.00
Never hinged 13.50
Nos. C7-C9 (3) 12.25 4.85
Nos. C7-C9, never hinged 23.25

Lindbergh's Airplane "Spirit of St. Louis" — AP6

1927, June 18

C10 AP6 10c dark blue 7.00 2.50
Never hinged 13.00
a. Booklet pane of 3 75.00 *65.00*
Never hinged 120.00
b. Double impression *16,500.*

Singles from No. C10a are imperf. at sides or imperf. at sides and bottom.

Only one example is recorded of No. C10b.

Beacon on Rocky Mountains AP7

1928, July 25

C11 AP7 5c carmine and blue 5.00 .75
Never hinged 9.50
a. Vert. pair, imperf. between *7,000.*

No. C11a is unique. It is torn and valued thus.

Winged Globe — AP8

1930, Feb. 10

Stamp design: 46½x19mm

C12 AP8 5c violet 9.50 .50
Never hinged 18.00
a. Horiz. pair, imperf. between *4,500.*

See Nos. C16-C17, C19.

GRAF ZEPPELIN ISSUE

Zeppelin over Atlantic Ocean — AP9

Zeppelin between Continents — AP10

Zeppelin Passing Globe — AP11

1930, Apr. 19

C13 AP9 65c green 180. 165.
Never hinged 275.
C14 AP10 $1.30 brown 400. 375.
Never hinged 650.
C15 AP11 $2.60 blue 575. 600.
Never hinged 975.
Nos. C13-C15 (3) 1,155. 1,140.
Nos. C13-C15, never hinged 1,900.

ROTARY PRESS PRINTING

1931-32 ***Perf. 10½x11***

Stamp design: 47½x19mm

C16 AP8 5c violet 5.00 .60
Never hinged 8.75

C17 AP8 8c olive bister ('32) 2.25 .40
Never hinged 4.00

CENTURY OF PROGRESS ISSUE

Airship "Graf Zeppelin" — AP12

FLAT PLATE PRINTING

1933, Oct. 2 ***Perf. 11***

C18 AP12 50c green 47.50 47.50
Never hinged 82.50

Catalogue values for unused stamps in this section, from this point to the end, are for Never Hinged items.

Type of 1930 Issue

ROTARY PRESS PRINTING

1934, June 30 ***Perf. 10½x11***

C19 AP8 6c dull orange 3.50 .25

TRANSPACIFIC ISSUES

The "China Clipper" over the Pacific AP13

FLAT PLATE PRINTING

1935, Nov. 22 ***Perf. 11***

C20 AP13 25c blue 1.40 1.00

The "China Clipper" over the Pacific AP14

1937, Feb. 15

C21 AP14 20c green 11.00 1.75
C22 AP14 50c carmine 11.00 5.00

Eagle Holding Shield, Olive Branch and Arrows AP15

1938, May 14

C23 AP15 6c dark blue & carmine .70 .25
a. Vert. pair, imperf. horiz. *300.00* —
b. Horiz. pair, imperf. vert. *12,500.*
c. 6¢ ultra & car 150.00 *1,500.*
On cover *1,750.*

TRANSATLANTIC ISSUE

Winged Globe — AP16

1939, May 16

C24 AP16 30c dull blue 12.00 1.50

Twin-Motored Transport Plane — AP17

ROTARY PRESS PRINTING

1941-44 *Perf. 11x10½*

C25 AP17 6c carmine .25 .25
a. Booklet pane of 3 4.00 1.50
b. Horiz. pair, imperf. between *2,000.*

Singles from No. C25a are imperf. at sides or at sides and bottom.

Value of No. C25b is for pair without blue crayon P. O. rejection mark on front. Very fine pairs with crayon mark sell for about $1,500.

C26 AP17 8c olive green .25 .25
a. All color omitted —

No. C26a has an albino impression and exists as a pair of stamps within a double-paper spliced strip of six stamps.

C27 AP17 10c violet 1.25 .25
C28 AP17 15c brown carmine 2.25 .35
C29 AP17 20c bright green 2.25 .30
C30 AP17 30c blue 2.25 .35
C31 AP17 50c orange 11.00 3.25
Nos. C25-C31 (7) 19.50 5.00

DC-4 Skymaster AP18

1946, Sept. 25 *Perf. 11x10½*

C32 AP18 5c carmine .25 .25

DC-4 Skymaster — AP19

1947, Mar. 26 *Perf. 10½x11*

C33 AP19 5c carmine .25 .25

Pan American Union Building, Washington, DC — AP20

Statue of Liberty & New York Skyline AP21

Plane over San Francisco-Oakland Bay Bridge — AP22

1947 *Perf. 11x10½*

C34 AP20 10c black .25 .25
a. Dry printing .40 .25
C35 AP21 15c bright blue green .35 .25
a. Horiz. pair, imperf. between *2,000.*
b. Dry printing .55 .25
C36 AP22 25c blue .90 .25
a. Dry printing 1.20 .25
Nos. C34-C36 (3) 1.50 .75

See note on wet and dry printings following No. 1029.

No. C35a is valued in the grade of fine.

Type of 1947

ROTARY PRESS COIL STAMP

1948, Jan. 15 *Perf. 10 Horizontally*

C37 AP19 5c carmine 1.00 .80

NEW YORK CITY ISSUE

Map of Five Boroughs, Circular Band & Planes — AP23

50th anniv. of the consolidation of the five boroughs of New York City.

ROTARY PRESS PRINTING

1948, July 31 *Perf. 11x10½*

C38 AP23 5c bright carmine .25 .25

Type of 1947

1949 *Perf. 10½x11*

C39 AP19 6c carmine .25 .25
a. Booklet pane of 6 12.00 5.00
b. Dry printing .50 .25
c. As "a," dry printing 25.00 —

See note on wet and dry printings following No. 1029.

ALEXANDRIA BICENTENNIAL ISSUE

Home of John Carlyle, Alexandria Seal & Gadsby's Tavern AP24

200th anniv. of the founding of Alexandria, Va.

1949, May 11 *Perf. 11x10½*

C40 AP24 6c carmine .25 .25

Type of 1947

ROTARY PRESS COIL STAMP

1949, Aug. 25 *Perf. 10 Horizontally*

C41 AP19 6c carmine 3.00 .25

UNIVERSAL POSTAL UNION ISSUE

Post Office Department Building AP25

Globe & Doves Carrying Messages AP26

Boeing Stratocruiser & Globe — AP27

ROTARY PRESS PRINTING

1949 *Perf. 11x10½*

C42 AP25 10c violet .25 .25
C43 AP26 15c ultramarine .30 .25
C44 AP27 25c rose carmine .60 .40
Nos. C42-C44 (3) 1.15 .90

WRIGHT BROTHERS ISSUE

Wilbur & Orville Wright and their Plane AP28

1949, Dec. 17

C45 AP28 6c magenta .25 .25

Diamond Head, Honolulu, Hawaii AP29

1952, Mar. 26

C46 AP29 80c bright red violet 4.75 1.25

POWERED FLIGHT, 50th ANNIV.

First Plane and Modern Plane AP30

1953, May 29

C47 AP30 6c carmine .25 .25

Eagle in Flight — AP31

Issued primarily for use on domestic post cards.

1954, Sept. 3

C48 AP31 4c bright blue .25 .25

AIR FORCE, 50th ANNIV.

B-52 Stratofortress and F-104 Starfighters — AP32

1957, Aug. 1

C49 AP32 6c blue .25 .25

Type of 1954

1958, July 31

C50 AP31 5c red .25 .25

Silhouette of Jet Airliner — AP33

1958, July 31 *Perf. 10½x11*

C51 AP33 7c blue .25 .25
a. Booklet pane of 6 8.00 6.00
b. Vert. pair, imperf. between (from booklet pane) —

No. C51b resulted from a paper foldover after perforating and before cutting into panes. Two pairs are known.

ROTARY PRESS COIL STAMP

Perf. 10 Horizontally

C52 AP33 7c blue 2.00 .25

ALASKA STATEHOOD ISSUE

Big Dipper, North Star & Map of Alaska AP34

ROTARY PRESS PRINTING

1959, Jan. 3 *Perf. 11x10½*

C53 AP34 7c dark blue .25 .25

BALLOON JUPITER ISSUE

Balloon & Crowd — AP35

Centenary of the carrying of mail by the balloon Jupiter from Lafayette to Crawfordsville, Ind.

GIORI PRESS PRINTING

1959, Aug. 17 *Perf. 11*

C54 AP35 7c dark blue & red .30 .25

HAWAII STATEHOOD ISSUE

Alii Warrior, Map of Hawaii & Star of Statehood AP36

ROTARY PRESS PRINTING

1959, Aug. 21 *Perf. 11x10½*

C55 AP36 7c rose red .25 .25

PAN AMERICAN GAMES ISSUE

Runner Holding Torch — AP37

3rd Pan American Games, Chicago, Aug. 27-Sept. 7, 1959.

GIORI PRESS PRINTING

1959, Aug. 27 *Perf. 11*

C56 AP37 10c red, white & blue .25 .25

Liberty Bell AP38

Statue of Liberty AP39

Abraham Lincoln AP40

1959-66

C57 AP38 10c black & green ('60) 1.00 .70
C58 AP39 15c black & orange .35 .25
C59 AP40 25c black & maroon ('60) .50 .25
a. Tagged ('66) .60 .30
Nos. C57-C59 (3) 1.85 1.20

Airmail stamps starting with No. C69 are tagged unless otherwise noted.

Type of 1958
ROTARY PRESS PRINTING

1960, Aug. 12 ***Perf. 10½x11***

C60 AP33 7c carmine .25 .25
a. Booklet pane of 6 8.50 7.00
b. Vert. pair, imperf between (from booklet pane) *5,500.*

No. C60b resulted from a paper foldover after perforating and before cutting into panes. Two pairs are known.

Type of 1958
ROTARY PRESS COIL STAMP

1960, Oct. 22 ***Perf. 10 Horizontally***

C61 AP33 7c carmine 4.00 .25

Type of 1959-60 and

Statue of Liberty AP41

GIORI PRESS PRINTING

1961-67 ***Perf. 11***

C62 AP38 13c black & red .40 .25
a. Tagged ('67) .75 .50
C63 AP41 15c black & orange .30 .25
a. Tagged ('67) .35 .25
b. As "a," horiz. pair, imperf. vert. *15,000.*
c. As "a," horiz. pair, imperf between and at left *2,750.*
d. All color omitted *100.00*

On No. C63d, there is a clear albino plate impression.

Jet Airliner Over Capitol — AP42

ROTARY PRESS PRINTING

1962, Dec. 5 ***Perf. 10½x11***

C64 AP42 8c carmine .25 .25
a. Tagged ('63) .25 .25
b. Booklet pane of 5 + label 6.00 3.00
c. As "b," tagged ('64) 1.75 .75

Nos. C64a and C64c were made by overprinting Nos. C64 and C64b with phosphorescent ink. No. C64a was first issued at Dayton, O., for experiments in high speed mail sorting. The tagging is visible in ultraviolet light.

COIL STAMP; ROTARY PRESS
Perf. 10 Horizontally

C65 AP42 8c carmine .40 .25
a. Tagged ('64) .35 .25

MONTGOMERY BLAIR ISSUE

Montgomery Blair — AP43

Montgomery Blair (1813-83), Postmaster General (1861-64), who called the 1st Intl. Postal Conf., Paris, 1863, forerunner of the UPU.

GIORI PRESS PRINTING

1963, May 3 ***Perf. 11***

C66 AP43 15c dull red, dark brown & blue .55 .50

Bald Eagle — AP44

Issued primarily for use on domestic post cards.

ROTARY PRESS PRINTING

1963, July 12 ***Perf. 11x10½***

C67 AP44 6c red .25 .25
a. Tagged ('67) 4.00 3.00

AMELIA EARHART ISSUE

Amelia Earhart & Lockheed Electra — AP45

GIORI PRESS PRINTING

1963, July 24 ***Perf. 11***

C68 AP45 8c carmine & maroon .25 .25

ROBERT H. GODDARD ISSUE

Robert H. Goddard, Atlas Rocket & Launching Tower, Cape Kennedy AP46

1964, Oct. 5

C69 AP46 8c blue, red & bister .35 .25

Luminescence

Air Post stamps issued after mid-1964 are tagged.

ALASKA PURCHASE ISSUE

Tlingit Totem, Southern Alaska — AP47

1967, Mar. 30

C70 AP47 8c brown .25 .25

"Columbia Jays," by Audubon AP48

50-Star Runway AP49

1967, Apr. 26

C71 AP48 20c multicolored .75 .25

See note over No. 1241.

ROTARY PRESS PRINTING

1968, Jan. 5 ***Perf. 11x10½***

C72 AP49 10c carmine .25 .25
b. Booklet pane of 8 2.25 2.00
c. Booklet pane of 5 + label 3.75 1.25
d. Vert. pair, imperf. btwn., in #C72b with foldover *5,000.*

No. C72d resulted from a paper foldover after perforating and before cutting into panes. Two pairs are recorded from different panes.

ROTARY PRESS COIL STAMP
Perf. 10 Vertically

C73 AP49 10c carmine .30 .25
a. Imperf., pair *475.00*

The $1 Airlift stamp is listed as No. 1341.

50th ANNIVERSARY OF AIR MAIL ISSUE

Curtiss Jenny AP50

50th anniv. of regularly scheduled air mail service.

LITHOGRAPHED, ENGRAVED (GIORI)

1968, May 15 ***Perf. 11***

C74 AP50 10c blue, black & red .25 .25

USA and Jet — AP51

1968, Nov. 22

C75 AP51 20c red, blue & black .35 .25

See No. C81.

MOON LANDING ISSUE

First Man on the Moon AP52

1969, Sept. 9

C76 AP52 10c multicolored .25 .25
a. Rose red (litho.) omitted *500.00* —

On No. C76a, the lithographed rose red is missing from the entire vignette-the dots on top of the yellow areas as well as the flag shoulder patch.

Silhouette of Delta Wing Plane AP53

Silhouette of Jet Airliner AP54

Winged Airmail Envelope — AP55

Statue of Liberty AP56

ROTARY PRESS PRINTING

1971-73 ***Perf. 10½x11***

C77 AP53 9c red .25 .25

No. C77 issued primarily for use on domestic post cards.

Perf. 11x10½

C78 AP54 11c carmine .25 .25
a. Booklet pane of 4 + 2 labels 1.25 1.00
b. Untagged (Bureau precanceled) .85 .85
C79 AP55 13c carmine ('73) .25 .25
a. Booklet pane of 5 + label ('73) 1.50 1.00
b. Untagged (Bureau precanceled) .85 .85
c. Green instead of red tagging (single from booklet pane) —

No. C78b Bureau precanceled "WASHINGTON D.C." (or "DC" - more valuable thus), No. C79b "WASHINGTON DC" only; both for use of Congressmen, but available to any permit holder.

GIORI PRESS PRINTING
Perf. 11

C80 AP56 17c bluish black, red, & dark green .35 .25

"USA" & Jet Type of 1968
LITHOGRAPHED, ENGRAVED (GIORI)

C81 AP51 21c red, blue & black .40 .25
b. Black (engr.) missing (FO) *2,750.*

The two recorded examples of No. C81b are in a single full pane. Catalogue value is for both errors.

COIL STAMPS
ROTARY PRESS PRINTING

1971-73 ***Perf. 10 Vertically***

C82 AP54 11c carmine .25 .25
a. Imperf., pair *250.00*
C83 AP55 13c carmine ('73) .30 .25
a. Imperf., pair 65.00

NATIONAL PARKS CENTENNIAL ISSUE
City of Refuge, Hawaii

Kii Statue & Temple, City of Refuge, Hawaii — AP57

LITHOGRAPHED, ENGRAVED (GIORI)

1972, May 3 ***Perf. 11***

C84 AP57 11c orange & multicolored .25 .25
a. Blue & green (litho.) omitted *750.00*

OLYMPIC GAMES ISSUE

Skiing & Olympic Rings AP58

11th Winter Olympic Games, Sapporo, Japan, Feb. 3-13, and 20th Summer Olympic Games, Munich, Germany, Aug. 26-Sept. 11.

PHOTOGRAVURE (Andreotti)

1972, Aug. 17 ***Perf. 11x10½***

C85 AP58 11c black, blue, red, emerald & yellow .25 .25

ELECTRONICS PROGRESS ISSUE

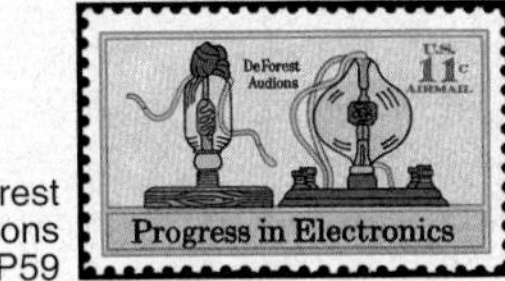

De Forest Audions AP59

LITHOGRAPHED, ENGRAVED (GIORI)

1973, July 10 ***Perf. 11***

C86 AP59 11c multicolored .30 .25
a. Vermilion & olive (litho.) omitted *825.00*
c. Olive omitted *1,150.*

Statue of Liberty AP60

Mt. Rushmore National Memorial AP61

GIORI PRESS PRINTING

1974

C87 AP60 18c carmine, black & ultramarine .35 .30
C88 AP61 26c ultramarine, black & carmine .60 .25

Plane & Globes AP62

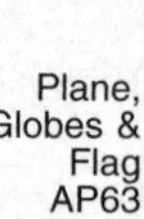

Plane, Globes & Flag AP63

1976, Jan. 2

C89 AP62 25c red, blue & black .50 .25
C90 AP63 31c red, blue & black .60 .25
b. All colors omitted —

On No. C90b, there is a colorless embossed image and a tagging ghost plane visible under UV light.

WRIGHT BROTHERS ISSUE

Orville and Wilbur Wright, Flyer A AP64

Wright Brothers, Flyer A and Shed AP65

LITHOGRAPHED, ENGRAVED (GIORI)

1978, Sept. 23

C91 AP64 31c ultra & multi .65 .30
C92 AP65 31c ultra & multi .65 .30
a. Vert. pair, #C91-C92 1.30 1.20
b. As "a," ultra. & black (engr.) omitted *600.00*
c. As "a," black (engr.) omitted *2,500.*
d. As "a," black, yellow, magenta, blue & brown (litho.) omitted *2,250.*

OCTAVE CHANUTE ISSUE

Chanute & Biplane Hangglider AP66

Biplane Hanggliders & Chanute AP67

1979, Mar. 29

C93 AP66 21c blue & multi .70 .35
C94 AP67 21c blue & multi .70 .35
a. Vert. pair, #C93-C94 1.40 1.20
b. As "a," ultra & black (engr.) omitted *4,500.*

WILEY POST ISSUE

Wiley Post & "Winnie Mae" AP68

NR-105 W, Post in Pressurized Suit, Portrait AP69

1979, Nov. 20

C95 AP68 25c blue &multi .95 .45
C96 AP69 25c blue & multi .95 .45
a. Vert. pair, #C95-C96 1.90 1.50

OLYMPIC GAMES ISSUE

High Jump AP70

PHOTOGRAVURE

1979, Nov. 1

C97 AP70 31c multicolored .70 .30

PHILIP MAZZEI (1730-1816)

Philip Mazzei (1730-1816), Italian-born Political Writer — AP71

1980, Oct. 13

C98 AP71 40c multicolored .80 .25
b. Imperf., pair *3,000.*

1982 ***Perf. 10½x11¼***

C98A AP71 40c multicolored 7.00 1.50
c. Horiz. pair, imperf. vert. *4,250.*

BLANCHE STUART SCOTT

Blanche Stuart Scott (1886-1970) AP72

1980, Dec. 30 ***Perf. 11***

C99 AP72 28c multicolored .60 .25
a. Imperf., pair *2,150.*

GLENN CURTISS

Glenn Curtiss (1878-1930) — AP73

1980, Dec. 30

C100 AP73 35c multicolored .65 .25
a. Light blue (background) omitted *2,000.*

SUMMER OLYMPICS 1984

Women's Gymnastics AP74

Hurdles AP75

Women's Basketball AP76

Soccer AP77

Shot Put — AP78

Men's Gymnastics AP79

Women's Swimming AP80

Weight Lifting AP81

Women's Fencing AP82

Cycling AP83

Women's Volleyball AP84

Pole Vaulting AP85

1983, June 17

C101 AP74 28c multicolored 1.00 .30
C102 AP75 28c multicolored 1.00 .30
C103 AP76 28c multicolored 1.00 .30
C104 AP77 28c multicolored 1.00 .30
a. Block of 4, #C101-C104 4.25 2.50
b. As "a," imperf. vert. *7,500.*

1983, Apr. 8 ***Perf. 11.2 Bullseye***

C105 AP78 40c multicolored .90 .40
C106 AP79 40c multicolored .90 .40
C107 AP80 40c multicolored .90 .40
C108 AP81 40c multicolored .90 .40
b. Block of 4, #C105-C108 4.25 3.00
d. Block of 4, imperf. *900.00*

1983, Nov. 4 ***Perf. 11***

C109 AP82 35c multicolored .90 .55
C110 AP83 35c multicolored .90 .55
C111 AP84 35c multicolored .90 .55
C112 AP85 35c multicolored .90 .55
a. Block of 4, #C109-C112 4.00 3.25

AVIATION PIONEERS

Alfred V. Verville AP86

Lawrence & Elmer Sperry AP87

1985, Feb. 13 **Tagged** ***Perf. 11***

C113 AP86 33c multicolored .65 .25
a. Imperf., pair *675.00*
C114 AP87 39c multicolored .80 .25
a. Imperf., pair *1,250.*

TRANSPACIFIC AIRMAIL

50th Anniversary

Transpacific Airmail AP88

1985, Feb. 15

C115 AP88 44c multicolored .85 .25
a. Imperf., pair *675.00*

FR. JUNIPERO SERRA (1713-1784)

California Missionary

Outline Map of Southern California, Portrait, San Gabriel Mission AP89

1985, Aug. 22

C116 AP89 44c multicolored 1.00 .35
a. Imperf., pair *1,000.*

SETTLING OF NEW SWEDEN, 350th ANNIV.

Settling of New Sweden, 350th Anniv. AP90

LITHOGRAPHED AND ENGRAVED

1988, Mar. 29

C117 AP90 44c multicolored 1.00 .25

See Sweden No. 1672 and Finland No. 768.

SAMUEL P. LANGLEY (1834-1906)

Langley and Unmanned Aerodrome No. 5 AP91

1988, May 14
C118 AP91 45c multicolored 1.00 .25

IGOR SIKORSKY (1889-1972)

Sikorsky and VS300 Helicopter, 1939 AP92

PHOTOGRAVURE AND ENGRAVED

1988, June 23
C119 AP92 36c multicolored .70 .25
a. Red, dk blue & black (engraved) omitted *2,500.*

Beware of examples with traces of engraved red offered as "red omitted" varieties.

FRENCH REVOLUTION BICENTENNIAL

Liberty, Equality and Fraternity — AP93

LITHOGRAPHED AND ENGRAVED

1989, July 14 ***Perf. 11½x11***
C120 AP93 45c multicolored .95 .25

See France Nos. 2143-2145a.

PRE-COLUMBIAN AMERICA ISSUE

UPAE Emblem & *Key Marco Cat* — AP94

PHOTOGRAVURE

1989, Oct. 12 ***Perf. 11***
C121 AP94 45c multicolored .90 .25

20th UPU CONGRESS
Futuristic Mail Delivery

Spacecraft AP95

Air-suspended Hover Car — AP96

Moon Rover — AP97

Space Shuttle — AP98

LITHOGRAPHED & ENGRAVED

1989, Nov. 27
C122 AP95 45c multicolored 1.00 .50
C123 AP96 45c multicolored 1.00 .50
C124 AP97 45c multicolored 1.00 .50
C125 AP98 45c multicolored 1.00 .50
a. Block of 4, #C122-C125 4.00 3.00
b. As "a," light blue (engr.) omitted *575.00*

Souvenir Sheet
LITHOGRAPHED & ENGRAVED

1989, Nov. 24 ***Imperf.***
C126 Sheet of 4 5.00 4.00
a. AP95 45c multicolored 1.25 .50
b. AP96 45c multicolored 1.25 .50
c. AP97 45c multicolored 1.25 .50
d. AP98 45c multicolored 1.25 .50

PRE-COLUMBIAN AMERICA ISSUE

Tropical Coast AP99

PHOTOGRAVURE

1990, Oct. 12 ***Perf. 11***
C127 AP99 45c multicolored .90 .25

HARRIET QUIMBY, 1ST AMERICAN WOMAN PILOT

Harriet Quimby, Bleriot Aircraft AP100

1991, Apr. 27
C128 AP100 50c multicolored 1.00 .25
a. Vert. pair, imperf. horiz. *1,000.*
b. Perf. 11.2, prephosphored uncoated paper ('93) 1.20 .25

WILLIAM T. PIPER, AIRCRAFT MANUFACTURER

William T. Piper, Piper Cub AP101

1991, May 17
C129 AP101 40c multicolored .80 .25

Blue sky is plainly visible all the way across stamp above Piper's head.
See No. C132.

ANTARCTIC TREATY, 30TH ANNIVERSARY

Antarctic Treaty, 30th Anniv. AP102

1991, June 21
C130 AP102 50c multicolored 1.00 .35

PRE-COLUMBIAN AMERICA ISSUE

First Americans Crossed Over From Asia AP103

1991, Oct. 12
C131 AP103 50c multicolored 1.00 .35

Piper Type of 1991

1993 ***Perf. 11.2***
C132 AP101 40c multicolored 3.50 .65

Piper's hair touches top edge of design. No selvage inscriptions.
Bullseye perf.

"All LC (Letters and Cards) mail receives First-Class Mail service in the United States, is dispatched by the fastest transportation available, and travels by airmail or priority service in the destination country. All LC mail should be marked 'AIRMAIL' or 'PAR AVION.'" (U.S. Postal Service, Pub. 51).

No. C133 listed below was issued to meet the LC rate to Canada and Mexico and is inscribed with the silhouette of a jet plane next to the denomination indicating the need for airmail service. This is unlike No. 2998, which met the LC rate to other countries, but contained no indication that it was intended for that use.

Future issues that meet a specific international airmail rate and contain the airplane silhouette will be treated by Scott as Air Post stamps. Stamps similar to No. 2998 will be listed in the Postage section.

SCENIC AMERICAN LANDSCAPES

Niagara Falls AP104

1999, May 12 ***Serpentine Die Cut 11***
Self-Adhesive
C133 AP104 48c multicolored .95 .25

Rio Grande AP105

1999, July 30
Self-Adhesive
C134 AP105 40c multicolored .80 .60

Grand Canyon AP106

LITHOGRAPHED
Serpentine Die Cut 11¼x11½

2000, Jan. 20
Self-Adhesive
C135 AP106 60c multi 1.25 .25
a. Die cutting omitted, pair *1,500.*
b. Vert. pair, die cutting omitted horiz. —
c. Horiz. pair, die cutting omitted between —
d. Horiz. pair, die cutting omitted vert. —

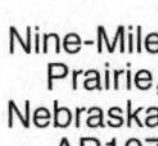

Nine-Mile Prairie, Nebraska AP107

LITHOGRAPHED

2001, Mar. 6
Self-Adhesive
C136 AP107 70c multi 1.40 .30

Mt. McKinley AP108

PHOTOGRAVURE
Serpentine Die Cut 11

2001, Apr. 17
Self-Adhesive
C137 AP108 80c multi 1.60 .35

Acadia National Park AP109

LITHOGRAPHED
Serpentine Die Cut 11.25x11.5

2001-05
Self-Adhesive
C138 AP109 60c multi 1.25 .25
a. Serpentine die cut 11½x11¾ 1.25 .25
b. As "a," with "2005" year date 1.25 .25
c. As "b," printed on back of backing paper —

Bryce Canyon National Park AP110

Great Smoky Mountains National Park AP111

LITHOGRAPHED
Serpentine Die Cut 10¾

2006, Feb. 24
Self-Adhesive
C139 AP110 63c multicolored 1.25 .25
a. Die cutting omitted, pair *450.00*
C140 AP111 75c multicolored 1.50 .35
a. Die cutting omitted, pair —

Yosemite National Park AP112

PHOTOGRAVURE
Serpentine Die Cut 11

C141 AP112 84c multicolored 1.75 .35
Nos. C139-C141 (3) 4.50 .95

Okefenokee Swamp, Georgia and Florida AP113

Hagatña Bay, Guam
AP114

LITHOGRAPHED (#C142), PHOTOGRAVURE (#C143)

Serpentine Die Cut 10¾

2007, June 1

Self-Adhesive

C142 AP113 69c multicolored 1.40 .30

Serpentine Die Cut 11

C143 AP114 90c multicolored 1.80 .40

13-Mile Woods, New Hampshire
AP115

Trunk Bay, St. John, Virgin Islands
AP116

LITHOGRAPHED (#C144), PHOTOGRAVURE (#C145)

Serpentine Die Cut 10¾

2008, May 16

Self-Adhesive

C144 AP115 72c multicolored 1.50 .30

Serpentine Die Cut 11

C145 AP116 94c multicolored 1.90 .45

AP117

AP118

LITHOGRAPHED, PHOTOGRAVURE (#C147)

Serpentine Die Cut 10¾

2009, June 28

Self-Adhesive

C146 AP117 79c multicolored ⓢ 1.60 .35

Serpentine Die Cut 11

C147 AP118 98c multicolored ⓢ 2.00 .45

See note after No. 1549.

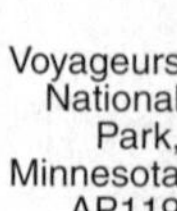

Voyageurs National Park, Minnesota
AP119

LITHOGRAPHED

Serpentine Die Cut 10¾

2011, Apr. 11

Self-Adhesive

C148 AP119 80c multicolored ⓢ 1.60 .25

See note after No. 1549.

Glacier National Park, Montana — AP120

Amish Horse and Buggy on Road, Lancaster County, Pennsylvania — AP121

LITHOGRAPHED

2012 ***Serpentine Die Cut 10¾***

Self-Adhesive

C149 AP120 85c multicolored 1.75 .35
C150 AP121 $1.05 multicolored 2.10 .45
a. Die cutting omitted on front, pair *1,100.*
b. Silver (airplane silhouette) missing (PS) —

Issued: 85c, 1/19; $1.05, 1/20.

AIR POST SPECIAL DELIVERY STAMPS

To provide for the payment of both the postage and the special delivery fee in one stamp.

Great Seal of United States
APSD1

1934, Aug. 30 **Unwmk.** ***Perf. 11***

CE1 APSD1 16c dark blue .70 .80
Never hinged .90

For imperforate variety see No. 771.

Type of 1934

1936, Feb. 10

CE2 APSD1 16c red & blue .45 .35
Never hinged .60
a. Horiz. pair, imperf. vert. *4,250.*
Never hinged *5,250.*

SPECIAL DELIVERY STAMPS

When affixed to any letter or article of mailable matter, secured immediate delivery, between 7 A. M. and midnight, at any post office.

Messenger Running — SD1

Flat Plate Printing

1885 **Unwmk.** ***Perf. 12***

E1 SD1 10c blue 550.00 80.00
Never hinged 1,250.

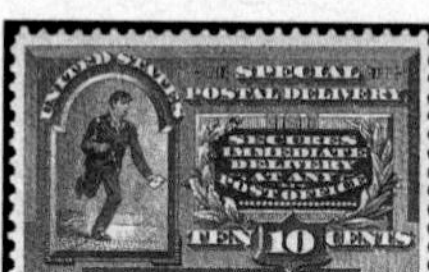

Messenger Running
SD2

1888, Sept. 6

E2 SD2 10c blue 500.00 45.00
Never hinged 1,150.

COLUMBIAN EXPOSITION ISSUE

Though not issued expressly for the Exposition, No. E3 is considered to be part of that issue.

1893, Jan. 24

E3 SD2 10c orange 300.00 50.00
Never hinged 675.00

Messenger Running
SD3

1894, Oct. 10

Line under "TEN CENTS"

E4 SD3 10c blue 900.00 100.00
Never hinged 2,250.

No. E5a

1895, Aug. 16 **Wmk. 191**

E5 SD3 10c blue 210.00 12.50
Never hinged 500.00
a. Dots in curved frame above messenger (Pl. 882) 350.00 45.00
Never hinged 700.00
b. Printed on both sides —

Messenger on Bicycle
SD4

1902, Dec. 9

E6 SD4 10c ultramarine 230.00 10.00
Never hinged 525.00
a. 10c blue 300.00 12.50
Never hinged 800.00

Helmet of Mercury and Olive Branch — SD5

1908, Dec. 12

E7 SD5 10c green 70.00 50.00
Never hinged 150.00

1911, Jan. **Wmk. 190** ***Perf. 12***

E8 SD4 10c ultramarine 110.00 10.00
Never hinged 240.00
b. 10c violet blue 140.00 14.00
Never hinged 300.00

1914, Sept. ***Perf. 10***

E9 SD4 10c ultramarine 190.00 12.00
Never hinged 425.00
a. 10c blue 250.00 15.00
Never hinged 550.00

1916, Oct. 19 **Unwmk.** ***Perf. 10***

E10 SD4 10c pale ultramarine 320.00 50.00
Never hinged 700.00
a. 10c blue 375.00 50.00
Never hinged 800.00

1917, May 2 ***Perf. 11***

E11 SD4 10c ultramarine 20.00 .75
Never hinged 45.00
b. 10c gray violet 30.00 3.00
Never hinged 65.00
c. 10c blue 90.00 5.00
Never hinged 190.00
d. Perf. 10 at left —

Postman and Motorcycle
SD6

Post Office Truck
SD7

1922, July 12

E12 SD6 10c gray violet 45.00 3.00
Never hinged 95.00
a. 10c deep ultramarine 55.00 3.50
Never hinged 130.00

1925

E13 SD6 15c deep orange 40.00 3.75
Never hinged 75.00
E14 SD7 20c black 2.00 1.00
Never hinged 4.00
Nos. E12-E14 (3) 87.00 7.75

Motorcycle Type of 1922

ROTARY PRESS PRINTING

1927-31 ***Perf. 11x10½***

E15 SD6 10c gray violet .65 .25
Never hinged 1.20
On cover .50
a. 10c red lilac .80 .25
Never hinged 1.40
b. 10c gray lilac .90 .25
Never hinged 1.55
c. Horizontal pair, imperf. between *300.00*
Never hinged *500.00*
E16 SD6 15c orange ('31) .60 .25
Never hinged .90

Catalogue values for unused stamps in this section, from this point to the end, are for Never Hinged items.

1944-51

E17 SD6 13c blue .60 .25
E18 SD6 17c orange yellow 3.50 2.50
E19 SD7 20c black ('51) 1.20 .25

Special Delivery Letter, Hand to Hand
SD8

1954, Oct. 13 ***Perf. 11x10½***

E20 SD8 20c deep blue .40 .25

1957, Sept. 3

E21 SD8 30c lake .50 .25

Arrows
SD9

GIORI PRESS PRINTING

1969, Nov. 21 ***Perf. 11***

E22 SD9 45c carmine & violet blue 1.20 .25

1971, May 10

E23 SD9 60c violet blue & carmine 1.25 .25

REGISTRATION STAMP

Issued for the prepayment of registry fees; not usable for postage.

Eagle — RS1

1911, Dec. 1 **Wmk. 190** ***Perf. 12***

F1 RS1 10c ultramarine 80.00 15.00
Never hinged 175.00

CERTIFIED MAIL STAMP

For use on first-class mail for which no indemnity value is claimed, but for which proof of mailing and proof of delivery are available at less cost than registered mail.

Catalogue value for the unused stamp in this section is for a Never Hinged item.

Letter Carrier — CM1

ROTARY PRESS PRINTING

1955, June 6 Unwmk. ***Perf. 10½x11***

FA1 CM1 15c red .75 .75

POSTAGE DUE STAMPS

For affixing, by a postal clerk to any piece of mailable matter, to denote the amount to be collected from the addressee because of insufficient prepayment of postage.

D1

Printed by the American Bank Note Co.

Plates of 200 subjects in two panes of 100 each.

1879 Unwmk. Engr. ***Perf. 12***

J1 D1 1c brown 90.00 14.00
Never hinged 260.00
J2 D1 2c brown 400.00 25.00
Never hinged 1,050.
J3 D1 3c brown 100.00 6.00
Never hinged 280.00
J4 D1 5c brown 775.00 70.00
Never hinged 1,900.
J5 D1 10c brown 900.00 70.00
Never hinged *2,500.*
a. Imperf., pair *2,500.*
J6 D1 30c brown 350.00 65.00
Never hinged 800.00
J7 D1 50c brown 600.00 90.00
Never hinged 1,600.
Nos. J1-J7 (7) 3,215. 340.00

Special Printing

J8 D1 1c deep brown *22,500.*
Never hinged —
J9 D1 2c deep brown *19,000.*
J10 D1 3c deep brown *25,000.*
J11 D1 5c deep brown *15,000.*
J12 D1 10c deep brown *8,500.*
J13 D1 30c deep brown *9,750.*
J14 D1 50c deep brown *8,750.*

1884

J15 D1 1c red brown 70.00 7.00
Never hinged 190.00
J16 D1 2c red brown 80.00 6.00
Never hinged 225.00
J17 D1 3c red brown 1,050. 350.00
Never hinged 2,500.
J18 D1 5c red brown 600.00 50.00
Never hinged 1,450.
J19 D1 10c red brown 600.00 35.00
Never hinged 1,450.
J20 D1 30c red brown 200.00 70.00
Never hinged 500.00
J21 D1 50c red brown 1,750. 250.00
Never hinged 3,750.
Nos. J15-J21 (7) 4,350. 768.00

1891

J22 D1 1c bright claret 30.00 2.00
Never hinged 85.00
J23 D1 2c bright claret 32.50 2.00
Never hinged 90.00
J24 D1 3c bright claret 67.50 16.00
Never hinged 180.00
J25 D1 5c bright claret 100.00 16.00
Never hinged 290.00
J26 D1 10c bright claret 165.00 30.00
Never hinged 500.00
J27 D1 30c bright claret 575.00 225.00
Never hinged 1,700.
J28 D1 50c bright claret 600.00 225.00
Never hinged 1,750.
Nos. J22-J28 (7) 1,570. 516.00

See Die and Plate Proofs in the Scott U.S. Specialized catalog for imperfs. on stamp paper.

D2

Printed by the Bureau of Engraving and Printing.

1894

J29 D2 1c vermilion 2,250. 725.
Never hinged *5,750.*
J30 D2 2c vermilion 775. 350.
Never hinged 1,900.

1894-95

J31 D2 1c deep claret 72.50 12.00
Never hinged 260.00
b. Vertical pair, imperf. horiz. —
J32 D2 2c deep claret 62.50 10.00
Never hinged 240.00
J33 D2 3c deep claret ('95) 200.00 50.00
Never hinged 575.00
J34 D2 5c deep claret ('95) 300.00 55.00
Never hinged 850.00
J35 D2 10c deep claret 350.00 40.00
Never hinged 1,000.
J36 D2 30c deep claret ('95) 550.00 250.00
Never hinged 1,250.
a. 30c carmine 675.00 275.00
Never hinged 1,600.
b. 30c pale rose 450.00 200.00
Never hinged 1,100.
J37 D2 50c deep claret ('95) 1,800. 800.00
Never hinged 4,250.
a. 50c pale rose 1,600. 725.00
Never hinged 3,750.
Nos. J31-J37 (7) 3,335. 1,217.

Shades are numerous in the 1894 and later issues.

See Die and Plate Proofs in the Scott U.S. Specialized catalog for imperfs. on stamp paper.

1895-97 Wmk. 191

J38 D2 1c deep claret 13.50 1.00
Never hinged 40.00
J39 D2 2c deep claret 13.50 1.00
Never hinged 40.00
J40 D2 3c deep claret 100.00 5.00
Never hinged 260.00
J41 D2 5c deep claret 110.00 5.00
Never hinged 280.00
J42 D2 10c deep claret 110.00 7.50
Never hinged 280.00
J43 D2 30c deep claret ('97) 600.00 75.00
Never hinged 1,500.
J44 D2 50c deep claret ('96) 375.00 60.00
Never hinged 1,000.
Nos. J38-J44 (7) 1,322. 154.50

1910-12 Wmk. 190

J45 D2 1c deep claret 40.00 5.00
Never hinged 115.00
a. 1c rose carmine 35.00 5.00
Never hinged 105.00
J46 D2 2c deep claret 40.00 2.00
Never hinged 115.00
a. 2c rose carmine 35.00 2.00
Never hinged 105.00
J47 D2 3c deep claret 625.00 60.00
Never hinged 1,600.
J48 D2 5c deep claret 120.00 12.00
Never hinged 275.00
a. 5c rose carmine 120.00 12.00
Never hinged 275.00
J49 D2 10c deep claret 125.00 20.00
Never hinged 280.00
a. 10c rose carmine 125.00 20.00
Never hinged 280.00
J50 D2 50c deep claret ('12) 1,100. 175.00
Never hinged 2,900.
a. 50c rose carmine 1,150. 190.00
Never hinged *3,000.*
Nos. J45-J50 (6) 2,050. 274.00

1914 ***Perf. 10***

J52 D2 1c carmine lake 80.00 15.00
Never hinged 220.00
a. 1c dull rose 85.00 15.00
Never hinged 230.00
J53 D2 2c carmine lake 62.50 1.00
Never hinged 170.00
a. 2c dull rose 67.50 2.00
Never hinged 180.00
b. 2c vermilion 67.50 2.00
Never hinged 180.00
J54 D2 3c carmine lake 1,050. 75.00
Never hinged 3,000.
a. 3c dull rose 1,000. 75.00
Never hinged 2,900.
J55 D2 5c carmine lake 50.00 6.00
Never hinged 140.00
a. 5c dull rose 45.00 4.00
Never hinged 130.00
J56 D2 10c carmine lake 75.00 4.00
Never hinged 200.00
a. 10c dull rose 80.00 5.00
Never hinged 210.00
J57 D2 30c carmine lake 225.00 55.00
Never hinged 525.00
J58 D2 50c carmine lake *11,500.* 1,600.
Never hinged *21,000.*
Nos. J52-J58 (7) 13,042. 1,756.

No. J58 unused is valued in the grade of fine to very fine.

1916 Unwmk. ***Perf. 10***

J59 D2 1c rose 4,000. 750.00
Never hinged 9,000.
J60 D2 2c rose 275.00 85.00
Never hinged 750.00

1917 ***Perf. 11***

J61 D2 1c carmine rose 2.75 .25
Never hinged 9.00
a. 1c rose red 2.75 .25
Never hinged 9.00
b. 1c deep claret 2.75 .25
Never hinged 9.00
J62 D2 2c carmine rose 2.75 .25
Never hinged 9.00
a. 2c rose red 2.75 .25
Never hinged 9.00
b. 2c deep claret 2.75 .25
Never hinged 9.00
J63 D2 3c carmine rose 13.50 .80
Never hinged 35.00
a. 3c rose red 13.50 .80
Never hinged 35.00
b. 3c deep claret 13.50 .80
Never hinged 35.00
J64 D2 5c carmine 11.00 .80
Never hinged 32.50
a. 5c rose red 11.00 .80
Never hinged 32.50
b. 5c deep claret 11.00 .80
Never hinged 32.50
J65 D2 10c carmine rose 22.50 1.00
Never hinged 65.00
a. 10c rose red 22.50 1.00
Never hinged 65.00
b. 10c deep claret 22.50 1.00
Never hinged 65.00
J66 D2 30c carmine rose 80.00 2.00
Never hinged 220.00
a. 30c deep claret 80.00 2.00
Never hinged 220.00
b. As "a," perf 10 at top, precanceled *21,000.*

No. J66b is valued with small faults and fine centering, as the two recorded examples are in this condition and grade.

J67 D2 50c carmine rose 140.00 1.00
Never hinged 325.00
a. 50c rose red 140.00 1.00
Never hinged 325.00
b. 50c deep claret 140.00 1.00
Never hinged 325.00
Nos. J61-J67 (7) 272.50 6.10

1925

J68 D2 ½c dull red 1.00 .25
Never hinged 1.75

D3

D4

1930 ***Perf. 11***

J69 D3 ½c carmine 4.25 1.90
Never hinged 9.50
J70 D3 1c carmine 2.75 .35
Never hinged 6.25
J71 D3 2c carmine 3.75 .35
Never hinged 8.50
J72 D3 3c carmine 20.00 2.75
Never hinged 47.50
J73 D3 5c carmine 18.00 5.00
Never hinged 42.50
J74 D3 10c carmine 42.50 2.00
Never hinged 95.00
J75 D3 30c carmine 125.00 4.00
Never hinged 275.00
J76 D3 50c carmine 175.00 2.00
Never hinged 375.00
J77 D4 $1 carmine 32.50 .35
Never hinged 65.00
a. $1 scarlet 27.50 .35
Never hinged 55.00
J78 D4 $5 scarlet 37.50 .35
Never hinged 85.00
b. carmine 37.50 .35
Never hinged 70.00
Nos. J69-J78 (10) 461.25 19.05

Type of 1930-31 Issue

Rotary Press Printing

1931 ***Perf. 11x10½***

J79 D3 ½c dull carmine .90 .25
Never hinged 1.30
a. ½c scarlet .90 .25
Never hinged 1.30
J80 D3 1c scarlet .25 .25
Never hinged .30
b. dull carmine .25 .25
Never hinged .30
J81 D3 2c scarlet .25 .25
Never hinged .30
b. dull carmine .25 .25
Never hinged .30
J82 D3 3c scarlet .30 .25
Never hinged .45
b. dull carmine .25 .25
Never hinged .40
J83 D3 5c scarlet .50 .25
Never hinged .75
b. dull carmine .40 .25
Never hinged .60
J84 D3 10c scarlet 1.25 .25
Never hinged 1.90
b. 10c dull carmine 1.10 .25
Never hinged 1.80
J85 D3 30c dull carmine 7.50 .25
Never hinged 11.50
a. 30c scarlet 7.50 .25
Never hinged 11.50
J86 D3 50c dull carmine 9.00 .25
Never hinged 15.00
a. 50c scarlet 9.00 .25
Never hinged 15.00

Design measures 22½x19mm

1956 ***Perf. 10½x11***

J87 D4 $1 scarlet 30.00 .25
Never hinged 52.50
Nos. J79-J87 (9) 49.95 2.25

For listings of other color shades and printing varieties see the *Scott Specialized Catalogue of United States Stamps and Covers.*

Catalogue values for unused stamps in this section, from this point to the end, are for Never Hinged items.

D5

Rotary Press Printing

Denominations added in black by rubber plates in an operation similar to precanceling.

Perf. 11x10½

1959, June 19 Unwmk.

Denomination in Black

J88 D5 ½c carmine rose 1.50 1.10
J89 D5 1c carmine rose .25 .25
a. Denomination omitted 200.00
b. Pair, one without "1 CENT" *400.00*
J90 D5 2c carmine rose .25 .25
J91 D5 3c carmine rose .25 .25
a. Pair, one without "3 CENTS" *600.00*
J92 D5 4c carmine rose .25 .25
J93 D5 5c carmine rose .25 .25
a. Pair, one without "5 CENTS" *1,100.*
J94 D5 6c carmine rose .25 .25
a. Pair, one without "6 CENTS" *800.00*
J95 D5 7c carmine rose .25 .25
J96 D5 8c carmine rose .25 .25
a. Pair, one without "8 CENTS" *750.00*
J97 D5 10c carmine rose .25 .25
J98 D5 30c carmine rose .70 .25
J99 D5 50c carmine rose 1.10 .25

Straight Numeral Outlined in Black

J100 D5 $1 carmine rose 2.00 .25
J101 D5 $5 carmine rose 9.00 .25
Nos. J88-J101 (14) 16.55 4.35

All single stamps with denomination omitted are catalogued as No. J89a.

1978-85

Denomination in Black

J102 D5 11c carmine rose .25 .25
J103 D5 13c carmine rose .25 .25
J104 D5 17c carmine rose ('85) .40 .35

UNITED STATES OFFICES IN CHINA

Issued for sale by the postal agency at Shanghai, at their surcharged value in local currency. Valid to the amount of their original values for the prepayment of postage on mail dispatched from the U.S. postal agency at Shanghai to addresses in the U.S.

Nos. 498-499, 502-504, 506-510, 512, 514-518 Surcharged

1919 Unwmk. *Perf. 11*
K1 A140 2c on 1c green 25.00 *70.00*
Never hinged 70.00
K2 A140 4c on 2c rose, type I 25.00 *70.00*
Never hinged 70.00
K3 A140 6c on 3c vio, type II 60.00 *140.00*
Never hinged 150.00
K4 A140 8c on 4c brown 60.00 *140.00*
Never hinged 150.00
K5 A140 10c on 5c blue 65.00 *140.00*
Never hinged 170.00
K6 A140 12c on 6c red org 85.00 *210.00*
Never hinged 220.00
K7 A140 14c on 7c black 87.50 *210.00*
Never hinged 225.00
K8 A148 16c on 8c ol bis 70.00 *160.00*
Never hinged 180.00
a. 16c on 8c ol grn 60.00 *140.00*
Never hinged 160.00
K9 A148 18c on 9c sal red 65.00 *175.00*
Never hinged 170.00
K10 A148 20c on 10c org yel 60.00 *140.00*
Never hinged 160.00
K11 A148 24c on 12c brn car 80.00 *160.00*
Never hinged 200.00
a. 24c on 12c cl brn 110.00 *225.00*
Never hinged 275.00
K12 A148 30c on 15c gray 87.50 *230.00*
Never hinged 210.00
K13 A148 40c on 20c deep ultra 130.00 *325.00*
Never hinged 300.00
K14 A148 60c on 30c org red 120.00 *275.00*
Never hinged 280.00
K15 A148 $1 on 50c lt vio 575.00 *1,000.*
Never hinged 1,300.
K16 A148 $2 on $1 vio brn 450.00 *750.00*
Never hinged 1,000.
a. Double surcharge *10,500.* *12,500.*
Never hinged *17,500.*
Nos. K1-K16 (16) 2,045. *4,195.*

Fake surcharges exist, but most are rather crudely made.

Nos. 498 and 528B Surcharged

1922, July 3
K17 A140 2c on 1c green 110.00 *225.00*
Never hinged 250.00
K18 A140 4c on 2c car, type VII 100.00 *200.00*
Never hinged 230.00
a. "SHANGHAI" omitted *7,500.*
b. "CHINA" only *15,000.*

OFFICIAL STAMPS

The franking privilege having been abolished, as of July 1, 1873, these stamps were provided for each of the departments of Government for the prepayment of postage on official matter.

Penalty franks were first authorized in 1877, and their expanded use after 1879 reduced the need for official stamps, the use of which was finally abolished on July 5, 1884.

Designs, except Post Office, resemble those illustrated but are not identical. Each bears the name of Department. Portraits are as follows: 1c, Franklin; 2c, Jackson; 3c, Washington; 6c, Lincoln; 7c, Stanton; 10c, Jefferson; 12c, Clay; 15c, Webster; 24c, Scott; 30c, Hamilton; 90c, Perry.

Special printings overprinted "SPECIMEN" follow No. O120.

Printed by the Continental Bank Note Co.
Thin Hard Paper

O1

Franklin—O2

AGRICULTURE

1873 Engr. Unwmk. *Perf. 12*
O1 O1 1c yellow 280.00 *200.00*
Never hinged 600.00
No gum 160.00
O2 O1 2c yellow 240.00 100.00
Never hinged 500.00
No gum 100.00
O3 O1 3c yellow 220.00 17.50
Never hinged 460.00
No gum 80.00
O4 O1 6c yellow 260.00 60.00
Never hinged 550.00
No gum 95.00
O5 O1 10c yellow 525.00 200.00
Never hinged 1,150.
No gum 220.00
O6 O1 12c yellow 450.00 260.00
Never hinged 950.00
No gum 250.00
O7 O1 15c yellow 425.00 230.00
Never hinged 950.00
No gum 225.00
O8 O1 24c yellow 425.00 250.00
Never hinged 950.00
No gum 225.00
O9 O1 30c yellow 550.00 280.00
Never hinged 1,200.
No gum 275.00
Nos. O1-O9 (9) 3,375. 1,597.

EXECUTIVE

1873
O10 O2 1c carmine 850.00 475.00
Never hinged 2,250.
No gum 450.00
O11 O2 2c carmine 550.00 240.00
Never hinged 1,250.
No gum 240.00
O12 O2 3c carmine 700.00 210.00
Never hinged 1,600.
No gum 270.00
a. 3c violet rose 1,000. 250.00
Never hinged 2,250.
No gum 375.00
On cover —
O13 O2 6c carmine 900.00 550.00
Never hinged —
No gum 325.00
O14 O2 10c carmine 1,200. 650.00
Never hinged —
No gum 600.00
Nos. O10-O14 (5) 4,200. 2,125.

O3

O4

INTERIOR

1873
O15 O3 1c vermilion 75.00 10.00
Never hinged 170.00
No gum 30.00
O16 O3 2c vermilion 70.00 12.00
Never hinged 160.00
No gum 30.00
O17 O3 3c vermilion 80.00 6.00
Never hinged 175.00
No gum 35.00
O18 O3 6c vermilion 70.00 10.00
Never hinged 160.00
No gum 27.50
O19 O3 10c vermilion 70.00 20.00
Never hinged 160.00
No gum 27.50
O20 O3 12c vermilion 90.00 12.00
Never hinged 200.00
No gum 35.00
O21 O3 15c vermilion 200.00 25.00
Never hinged 450.00
No gum 80.00
O22 O3 24c vermilion 180.00 20.00
Never hinged 400.00
No gum 60.00
a. Double impression —
O23 O3 30c vermilion 290.00 20.00
Never hinged 625.00
No gum 110.00
O24 O3 90c vermilion 325.00 50.00
Never hinged 700.00
No gum 120.00
Nos. O15-O24 (10) 1,450. 185.00

JUSTICE

1873
O25 O4 1c purple 250.00 100.00
Never hinged 550.00
No gum 100.00
O26 O4 2c purple 310.00 110.00
Never hinged 700.00
No gum 120.00
O27 O4 3c purple 320.00 35.00
Never hinged 725.00
No gum 110.00
O28 O4 6c purple 310.00 45.00
Never hinged 700.00
No gum 110.00
O29 O4 10c purple 310.00 100.00
Never hinged 700.00
No gum 120.00
O30 O4 12c purple 260.00 75.00
Never hinged 575.00
No gum 95.00
O31 O4 15c purple 475.00 200.00
Never hinged 1,050.
No gum 210.00
O32 O4 24c purple 1,250. 425.00
Never hinged —
No gum 550.00
O33 O4 30c purple 1,300. 350.00
Never hinged —
No gum 550.00
O34 O4 90c purple 1,900. 900.00
Never hinged —
No gum 800.00
Nos. O25-O34 (10) 6,685. 2,340.

O5

O6

NAVY

1873
O35 O5 1c ultramarine 160.00 50.00
Never hinged 350.00
No gum 65.00
a. 1c dull blue 160.00 50.00
Never hinged 350.00
No gum 65.00
O36 O5 2c ultramarine 160.00 25.00
Never hinged 350.00
No gum 65.00
a. 2c dull blue 160.00 25.00
Never hinged 350.00
No gum 65.00
O37 O5 3c ultramarine 170.00 15.00
Never hinged 375.00
No gum 60.00
a. 3c dull blue 170.00 15.00
Never hinged 375.00
No gum 60.00
O38 O5 6c ultramarine 150.00 25.00
Never hinged 325.00
No gum 55.00
a. 6c dull blue 150.00 25.00
Never hinged 325.00
No gum 55.00
O39 O5 7c ultramarine 650.00 230.00
Never hinged —
No gum 250.00
a. 7c dull blue 650.00 230.00
Never hinged —
No gum 250.00
O40 O5 10c ultramarine 210.00 45.00
Never hinged 475.00
No gum 75.00
a. 10c dull blue 210.00 45.00
Never hinged 475.00
No gum 75.00
O41 O5 12c ultramarine 220.00 45.00
Never hinged 500.00
No gum 80.00
O42 O5 15c ultramarine 375.00 75.00
Never hinged —
No gum 135.00
O43 O5 24c ultramarine 400.00 85.00
Never hinged —
No gum 160.00
a. 24c dull blue 375.00 80.00
Never hinged —
No gum 150.00
O44 O5 30c ultramarine 325.00 50.00
Never hinged —
No gum 125.00
O45 O5 90c ultramarine 1,050. 375.00
Never hinged —
No gum 450.00
a. Double impression *20,000.*
Nos. O35-O45 (11) 3,870. 1,020.

POST OFFICE

Stamps of the Post Office Department are often on paper with a gray surface. This is essentially a wiping problem, caused by an over-milled carbon black pigment that released acid and etched the plates. There is no premium for stamps on paper with a gray surface.

1873
O47 O6 1c black 25.00 12.00
Never hinged 60.00
No gum 12.00
O48 O6 2c black 30.00 10.00
Never hinged 75.00
No gum 13.00
a. Double impression 700.00 400.00
O49 O6 3c black 10.00 2.00
Never hinged 25.00
No gum 3.00
a. Printed on both sides *7,500.*
O50 O6 6c black 30.00 8.00
Never hinged 75.00
No gum 12.00
a. Diagonal half used as 3c on cover *5,000.*
b. Double impression *3,000.*
O51 O6 10c black 140.00 55.00
Never hinged 325.00
No gum 60.00
O52 O6 12c black 120.00 12.00
Never hinged 275.00
No gum 40.00
O53 O6 15c black 140.00 20.00
Never hinged 325.00
No gum 50.00
O54 O6 24c black 200.00 25.00
Never hinged 450.00
No gum 70.00
O55 O6 30c black 200.00 25.00
Never hinged 450.00
No gum 70.00
O56 O6 90c black 220.00 25.00
Never hinged 500.00
No gum 80.00
Nos. O47-O56 (10) 1,115. 194.00

STATE

Franklin — O7

Seward — O8

1873
O57 O7 1c dark green 260.00 75.00
Never hinged 575.00
No gum 110.00
O58 O7 2c dark green 310.00 100.00
Never hinged —
No gum 120.00
O59 O7 3c dark green 220.00 25.00
Never hinged 500.00
No gum 85.00
O60 O7 6c dark green 220.00 30.00
Never hinged 500.00
No gum 85.00
O61 O7 7c dark green 290.00 65.00
Never hinged 650.00
No gum 95.00
O62 O7 10c dark green 230.00 55.00
Never hinged 525.00
No gum 100.00
O63 O7 12c dark green 310.00 125.00
Never hinged 700.00
No gum 140.00
O64 O7 15c dark green 320.00 90.00
Never hinged 725.00
No gum 130.00
O65 O7 24c dark green 525.00 230.00
Never hinged —
No gum 275.00
O66 O7 30c dark green 500.00 180.00
Never hinged —
No gum 240.00
O67 O7 90c dark green 1,050. 325.00
Never hinged —
No gum 525.00
O68 O8 $2 green & black 1,800. 3,000.
Never hinged 3,750.
No gum 850.00
O69 O8 $5 green & black 8,000. *13,000.*
Never hinged —
No gum 3,750.
O70 O8 $10 green & black 5,000. *7,500.*
Never hinged 11,500.
No gum 2,750.
O71 O8 $20 green & black 5,500. 5,500.
Never hinged 12,500.
No gum 2,500.

No. O71 used is valued with a blue or red handstamp favor cancel. Nos. O68-O71 with pen cancels sell for approximately 25-40% of the values shown.

TREASURY

O9

1873
O72 O9 1c brown 120.00 10.00
Never hinged 250.00
No gum 45.00
O73 O9 2c brown 125.00 8.00
Never hinged 275.00
No gum 45.00
O74 O9 3c brown 110.00 2.00
Never hinged 230.00
No gum 40.00
a. Double impression *5,000.*
O75 O9 6c brown 120.00 4.00
Never hinged 250.00
No gum 45.00
O76 O9 7c brown 250.00 35.00
Never hinged 550.00
No gum 95.00
O77 O9 10c brown 240.00 12.00
Never hinged 525.00
No gum 90.00
O78 O9 12c brown 300.00 10.00
Never hinged 650.00
No gum 100.00
O79 O9 15c brown 300.00 12.00
Never hinged 650.00
No gum 100.00
O80 O9 24c brown 675.00 100.00
Never hinged —
No gum 270.00
O81 O9 30c brown 400.00 12.00
Never hinged —
No gum 140.00
O82 O9 90c brown 400.00 15.00
Never hinged —
No gum 140.00
Nos. O72-O82 (11) 3,040. 220.00

WAR

O10

1873
O83 O10 1c rose 240.00 15.00
Never hinged 525.00
No gum 90.00
O84 O10 2c rose 240.00 15.00
Never hinged 525.00
No gum 90.00
O85 O10 3c rose 240.00 5.00
Never hinged 525.00
No gum 90.00
O86 O10 6c rose 625.00 10.00
Never hinged 1,350.
No gum 250.00
O87 O10 7c rose 160.00 90.00
Never hinged 360.00
No gum 80.00
O88 O10 10c rose 140.00 25.00
Never hinged 300.00
No gum 45.00
O89 O10 12c rose 275.00 12.00
Never hinged 600.00
No gum 110.00
O90 O10 15c rose 85.00 15.00
Never hinged 190.00
No gum 30.00
O91 O10 24c rose 85.00 12.00
Never hinged 190.00
No gum 30.00
O92 O10 30c rose 130.00 12.00
Never hinged 275.00
No gum 45.00
O93 O10 90c rose 225.00 60.00
Never hinged 500.00
No gum 80.00
Nos. O83-O93 (11) 2,445. 271.00

Printed by the American Bank Note Co.

1879 **Soft Porous Paper**

AGRICULTURE

O94 O1 1c yel, no gum 6,000.
O95 O1 3c yellow 550.00 150.00
Never hinged 1,250.
No gum 240.00

INTERIOR

O96 O3 1c vermilion 300.00 *275.00*
Never hinged 550.00
No gum 160.00
O97 O3 2c vermilion 10.00 3.00
Never hinged 17.50
No gum 3.00
O98 O3 3c vermilion 10.00 3.00
Never hinged 22.50
No gum 3.00
O99 O3 6c vermilion 10.00 *12.50*
Never hinged 17.50
No gum 3.00
O100 O3 10c vermilion 110.00 75.00
Never hinged 250.00
No gum 60.00
O101 O3 12c vermilion 230.00 115.00
Never hinged 525.00
No gum 130.00
O102 O3 15c pale vermilion 400.00 260.00
Never hinged 900.00
No gum 200.00
O103 O3 24c pale vermilion 4,500. —
Never hinged 10,000.
No gum 2,100.
Nos. O96-O103 (8) 5,570. 743.50

JUSTICE

O106 O4 3c bluish pur 190.00 125.00
Never hinged 425.00
No gum 80.00
O107 O4 6c bluish pur 475.00 300.00
Never hinged 1,050.
No gum 210.00

POST OFFICE

O108 O6 3c black 30.00 10.00
Never hinged 70.00
No gum 10.00

TREASURY

O109 O9 3c brown 80.00 10.00
Never hinged 175.00
No gum 35.00
O110 O9 6c brown 200.00 50.00
Never hinged 450.00
No gum 65.00
O111 O9 10c brown 260.00 80.00
Never hinged 575.00
No gum 90.00
O112 O9 30c brown 2,400. 425.00
Never hinged —
No gum 875.00
O113 O9 90c brown 5,500. 750.00
Never hinged —
No gum 2,000.
Nos. O109-O113 (5) 8,440. 1,315.

WAR

O114 O10 1c rose red 6.00 4.00
Never hinged 11.00
No gum 2.50
O115 O10 2c rose red 12.00 4.00
Never hinged 22.50
No gum 4.00
O116 O10 3c rose red 12.00 2.00
Never hinged 22.50
No gum 4.00
a. Imperf., pair *5,000.*
b. Double impression *7,500.*
O117 O10 6c rose red 11.00 3.00
Never hinged 20.00
No gum 4.00
O118 O10 10c rose red 65.00 50.00
Never hinged 120.00
No gum 26.00
O119 O10 12c rose red 60.00 14.00
Never hinged 110.00
No gum 20.00
O120 O10 30c rose red 225.00 100.00
Never hinged 450.00
No gum 90.00
Nos. O114-O120 (7) 391.00 177.00

SPECIAL PRINTINGS

Special printings of Official stamps were made in 1875 at the time the other Reprints, Re-issues and Special Printings were printed. They are ungummed.

Although perforated, these stamps were sometimes (but not always) cut apart with scissors. As a result the perforations may be mutilated and the design damaged.

All values exist imperforate.

Printed by the Continental Bank Note Co.

Overprinted in Block Letters

1875 ***Perf. 12***

Thin, hard white paper
Type D

AGRICULTURE

Carmine Overprint

O1S D 1c yellow 32.50
a. "Sepcimen" error *2,500.*
b. Horiz. ribbed paper 37.50
c. As "b," small dotted "i" in "Specimen" 500.00
O2S D 2c yellow 55.00
a. "Sepcimen" error *3,000.*
O3S D 3c yellow 400.00
a. "Sepcimen" error *12,500.*
O4S D 6c yellow 400.00
a. "Sepcimen" error *20,000.*
O5S D 10c yellow 400.00
a. "Sepcimen" error *17,500.*
O6S D 12c yellow 400.00
a. "Sepcimen" error *12,500.*
O7S D 15c yellow 400.00
a. "Sepcimen" error *12,500.*
O8S D 24c yellow 400.00
a. "Sepcimen" error *12,500.*
O9S D 30c yellow 400.00
a. "Sepcimen" error *13,500.*
Nos. O1S-O9S (9) 2,887.

EXECUTIVE

Blue Overprint

O10S D 1c carmine 32.50
a. Horiz. ribbed paper 40.00
b. As "a," small dotted "i" in "Specimen" 500.00
O11S D 2c carmine 55.00
O12S D 3c carmine 67.50
O13S D 6c carmine 67.50
O14S D 10c carmine 67.50
Nos. O10S-O14S (5) 290.00

INTERIOR

Blue Overprint

O15S D 1c vermilion 60.00
O16S D 2c vermilion 140.00
a. "Sepcimen" error *12,500.*
O17S D 3c vermilion *2,500.*
O18S D 6c vermilion *2,500.*
O19S D 10c vermilion *2,500.*
O20S D 12c vermilion *2,500.*
O21S D 15c vermilion *2,500.*
O22S D 24c vermilion *2,500.*
O23S D 30c vermilion *2,500.*
O24S D 90c vermilion *2,500.*
Nos. O15S-O24S (10) *20,200.*

JUSTICE

Blue Overprint

O25S D 1c purple 32.50
a. "Sepcimen" error *1,900.*
b. Horiz. ribbed paper 35.00
c. As "b," small dotted "i" in "Specimen" 500.00
O26S D 2c purple 55.00
a. "Sepcimen" error *2,500.*
O27S D 3c purple 1,250.
a. "Sepcimen" error *11,000.*
O28S D 6c purple 1,250.
O29S D 10c purple 1,250.
O30S D 12c purple 1,250.
a. "Sepcimen" error *17,500.*
O31S D 15c purple 1,250.
a. "Sepcimen" error *17,500.*
O32S D 24c purple 1,250.
a. "Sepcimen" error *20,000.*
O33S D 30c purple 1,250.
a. "Sepcimen" error *15,000.*
O34S D 90c purple 1,250.
Nos. O25S-O34S (10) 10,087.

NAVY

Carmine Overprint

O35S D 1c ultramarine 35.00
a. "Sepcimen" error *2,500.*
b. Double "Specimen" overprint *1,900.*
O36S D 2c ultramarine 75.00
a. "Sepcimen" error *3,250.*
O37S D 3c ultramarine 1,400.
O38S D 6c ultramarine 1,400.
O39S D 7c ultramarine 550.00
a. "Sepcimen" error *10,000.*
O40S D 10c ultramarine 1,400.
a. "Sepcimen" error *17,500.*
O41S D 12c ultramarine 1,400.
a. "Sepcimen" error *17,500.*
O42S D 15c ultramarine 1,400.
a. "Sepcimen" error *15,000.*
O43S D 24c ultramarine 1,400.
a. "Sepcimen" error *15,000.*
O44S D 30c ultramarine 1,400.
a. "Sepcimen" error *17,500.*
O45S D 90c ultramarine 1,400.
Nos. O35S-O45S (11) 11,860.

POST OFFICE

Carmine Overprint

O47S D 1c black 45.00
a. "Sepcimen" error *2,750.*
b. Inverted overprint *2,750.*
O48S D 2c black 325.00
a. "Sepcimen" error *9,000.*
O49S D 3c black 1,600.
a. "Sepcimen" error —
O50S D 6c black 1,600.
O51S D 10c black 1,100.
a. "Sepcimen" error *15,000.*
O52S D 12c black 1,600.
O53S D 15c black 1,600.
a. "Sepcimen" error *20,000.*
O54S D 24c black 1,600.
a. "Sepcimen" error *20,000.*
O55S D 30c black 1,600.
O56S D 90c black 1,600.
a. "Sepcimen" error *20,000.*
Nos. O47S-O56S (10) 12,670.

STATE

Carmine Overprint

O57S D 1c bluish green 32.50
a. "Sepcimen" error *1,900.*
b. Horiz. ribbed paper 35.00
c. As "b," small dotted "i" in "Specimen" 550.00
d. Double "Specimen" overprint *3,850.*
O58S D 2c bluish green 90.00
a. "Sepcimen" error *2,500.*
O59S D 3c bluish green 140.00
a. "Sepcimen" error *6,000.*
O60S D 6c bluish green 350.00
a. "Sepcimen" error *11,000.*
O61S D 7c bluish green 140.00
a. "Sepcimen" error *8,250.*
O62S D 10c bluish green 550.00
a. "Sepcimen" error *17,500.*
O63S D 12c bluish green 550.00
a. "Sepcimen" error *17,500.*
O64S D 15c bluish green 600.00
O65S D 24c bluish green 600.00
a. "Sepcimen" error *17,500.*
O66S D 30c bluish green 600.00
a. "Sepcimen" error *17,500.*
O67S D 90c bluish green 600.00
a. "Sepcimen" error *15,000.*
O68S D $2 green & blk *25,000.*
O69S D $5 green & blk *30,000.*
O70S D $10 green & blk *60,000.*
O71S D $20 green & blk *100,000.*
Nos. O57S-O67S (11) 4,252.

TREASURY

Blue Overprint

O72S D 1c dark brown 80.00
O73S D 2c dark brown 450.00
O74S D 3c dark brown 1,600.
O75S D 6c dark brown 1,600.
O76S D 7c dark brown 950.00
O77S D 10c dark brown 1,600.
O78S D 12c dark brown 1,600.
O79S D 15c dark brown 1,600.
O80S D 24c dark brown 1,600.
O81S D 30c dark brown 1,600.
O82S D 90c dark brown 1,650.
Nos. O72S-O82S (11) 14,330.

WAR

Blue Overprint

O83S D 1c deep rose 35.00
a. "Sepcimen" error *2,750.*
O84S D 2c deep rose 125.00
a. "Sepcimen" error *3,250.*
O85S D 3c deep rose 1,300.
a. "Sepcimen" error *25,000.*
O86S D 6c deep rose 1,300.
a. "Sepcimen" error *27,500.*
O87S D 7c deep rose 425.00
a. "Sepcimen" error *17,500.*
O88S D 10c deep rose 1,400.
a. "Sepcimen" error *30,000.*
O89S D 12c deep rose 1,400.
a. "Sepcimen" error *30,000.*
O90S D 15c deep rose 1,400.
a. "Sepcimen" error *30,000.*
O91S D 24c deep rose 1,400.
a. "Sepcimen" error *30,000.*
O92S D 30c deep rose 1,400.
a. "Sepcimen" error *30,000.*
O93S D 90c deep rose 1,400.
a. "Sepcimen" error *30,000.*
Nos. O83S-O93S (11) 11,585.

Printed by the American Bank Note Co.

SOFT POROUS PAPER

EXECUTIVE

1881

Blue Overprint

O10xS D 1c violet rose 95.00

NAVY

Carmine Overprint

O35xS D 1c gray blue 100.00
a. Double overprint 1,200.

STATE

O57xS D 1c yellow green 180.00

OFFICIAL POSTAL SAVINGS MAIL

These stamps were used to prepay postage on official correspondence of the Postal Savings Division of the POD. Discontinued Sept. 23, 1914.

O11

Printed by the Bureau of Engraving & Printing

1910-11 **Engr.** **Wmk. 191**
O121 O11 2c black 17.50 2.00
Never hinged 40.00
O122 O11 50c dark green 160.00 60.00
Never hinged 375.00
O123 O11 $1 ultramarine 200.00 15.00
Never hinged 450.00

Wmk. 190

O124 O11 1c dark violet 10.00 2.00
Never hinged 22.50
O125 O11 2c black 55.00 7.00
Never hinged 135.00
O126 O11 10c carmine 20.00 2.00
Never hinged 50.00
Nos. O121-O126 (6) 462.50 88.00

Catalogue values for unused stamps in this section, from this point to the end, are for Never Hinged items.

Catalogue values for used stamps are for regularly used examples, not for examples removed from first day covers.

From No. O127 onward, all official stamps are tagged unless noted.

OFFICIAL MAIL

O12

Engraved
Unwmk.

1983, Jan. 12-1985 ***Perf. 11***
O127 O12 1c red, blue & black .25 .25
O128 O12 4c red, blue & black .25 .25
O129 O12 13c red, blue & black .50 *15.00*
O129A O12 14c red, blue & black .45 .50
O130 O12 17c red, blue & black .55 .40
O132 O12 $1 red, blue & black 2.25 1.00
O133 O12 $5 red, blue & black 9.50 *20.00*
Nos. O127-O133 (7) 13.75 37.40

No. O129A does not have a "c" after the "14."

COIL STAMPS

Perf. 10 Vert.

O135 O12 20c red, blue & black 1.75 2.00
a. Imperf., pair *1,000.*

O136 O12 22c red, blue & blk ('85) 1.00 *2.00*
a. Tagging omitted —

Inscribed: Postal Card Rate D

1985, Feb. 4 ***Perf. 11***
O138 O12 (14c) red, blue & black 7.50 *15.00*

Frame line completely around blue design — O13

Inscribed: No. O139, Domestic Letter Rate D; No. O140, Domestic Mail E.

COIL STAMPS

Litho., Engr. (#O139)

1985-88 ***Perf. 10 Vert.***
O138A O13 15c red, blue & blk .50 .50
O138B O13 20c red, blue & blk .50 .30
O139 O12 (22c) red, blue & blk 5.25 *20.00*
O140 O13 (25c) red, blue & blk .75 *2.00*
O141 O13 25c red, blue & blk .65 .50
a. Imperf., pair *1,000.* —
Nos. O138A-O141 (5) 7.65 *23.30*

Issue dates: 1985; E, Mar. 22, 1988; 15c, June 11; 20c, May 19; 25c, June 11.
See Nos. O143, O145-O151, O153-O156.

1989, July 5 **Litho.** ***Perf. 11***
O143 O13 1c red, blue & black .25 .25

On No. O143, the denomination is shown as "1". See No. O154.

Type of 1985 and

O14

COIL STAMPS

1991 **Litho.** ***Perf. 10 Vert.***
O144 O14 (29c) red, blue & blk .80 .50
O145 O13 29c red, blue & blk .70 .30

1991-93 **Litho.** ***Perf. 11***
O146 O13 4c red, blue & blk .25 .30
O146A O13 10c red, blue & blk .30 .30
O147 O13 19c red, blue & blk .40 .50
O148 O13 23c red, blue & blk .50 .30

Perf. 11¼
O151 O13 $1 red, blue & blk 5.00 .75
Nos. O146-O151 (5) 6.45 2.15

Nos. O146A, O151 have a line of microscopic printing below eagle.
See No. O156 for 23c with microscopic text below eagle.
Imperfs of No. O148 are printer's waste.
Issued: No. O146, 4/6; Nos. O147-O148, 5/24; 10c, 10/19/93; No. O151, 9/1993.

COIL STAMPS

Inscribed: No. O152, For U.S. addresses only G.

Perf. 9.8 Vert.
O152 O14 (32c) red, blue & blk .65 .50
O153 O13 32c red, blue & blk 1.50 .50

Nos. O146A, O151, O153 have a line of microscopic text below the eagle.

1995, May 9 **Untagged** ***Perf. 11.2***
O154 O13 1c red, blue & black .25 .50

Denomination on No. O154 has a cent sign. See No. O143.

O155 O13 20c red, blue & black .55 .50
O156 O13 23c red, blue & black .60 .50

COIL STAMP

1999, Oct. 8 ***Perf. 9¾ Vert.***
O157 O13 33c red, blue & black 2.25 —

Type of 1985
COIL STAMP

2001, Feb. 27 ***Perf. 9¾ Vert.***
O158 O13 34c red, blue & black 2.25 .50

Nos. O154-O158 have a line of microscopic text below the eagle.

Type of 1985
COIL STAMP

2002, Aug. 2 **Photo.** ***Perf. 10 Vert.***
O159 O13 37c red, blue & black .75 .50

Type of 1985
COIL STAMP

2006, Mar. 8 ***Perf. 10 Vert.***
O160 O13 39c red, blue & black .80 *.80*

Type of 1988
LITHOGRAPHED

2006, Sept. 29 ***Perf. 11¼***
O161 O13 $1 red, blue & black 3.50 *1.25*

No. O161 has a solid blue background. No. O151 has a background of crosshatched lines.

Type of 1985
COIL STAMP

2007, June 25 ***Perf. 9¾***
O162 O13 41c red, blue & black 1.00 *1.00*

Nos. O159-O162 have solid blue backgrounds. Nos. O138A-O158 have a background of crosshatched lines.

Type of 1985
Serpentine Die Cut 11½x10¾
2009, Feb. 24 **Untagged**
Self-Adhesive
O163 O13 1c red, blue & black .25 *.40*

NEWSPAPER STAMPS

For the prepayment of postage on bulk shipments of newspapers and periodicals. From 1875 on, the stamps were affixed to pages of receipt books, sometimes canceled and retained by the post office. Discontinued on July 1, 1898.

Virtually all used stamps of Nos. PR1-PR4 are canceled by blue brush strokes. All are rare. Most used stamps of Nos. PR9-PR32, PR57-PR79 and PR81-PR89 are pen canceled (or uncanceled), with some of Nos. PR9-PR32 also known canceled by a thick blue brush stroke.

Handstamp cancellations on any of these issues are rare and sell for much more than catalogue values which are for pen-canceled examples.

Used values for Nos. PR90-PR125 are for stamps with handstamp cancellations.

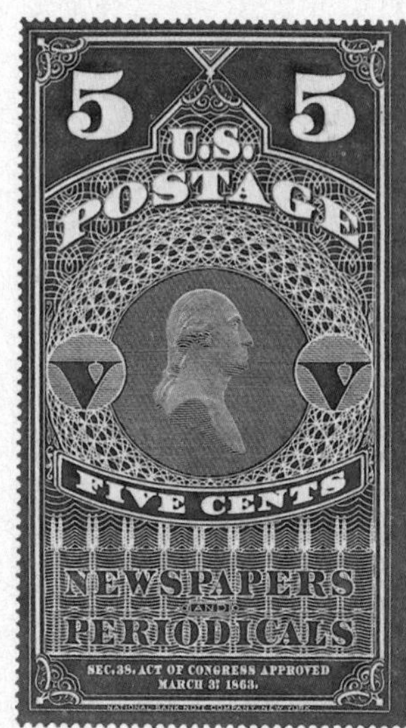

Washington — N1

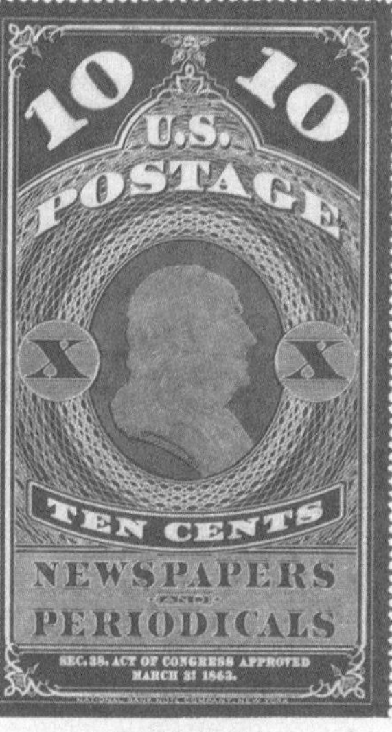

Franklin — N2

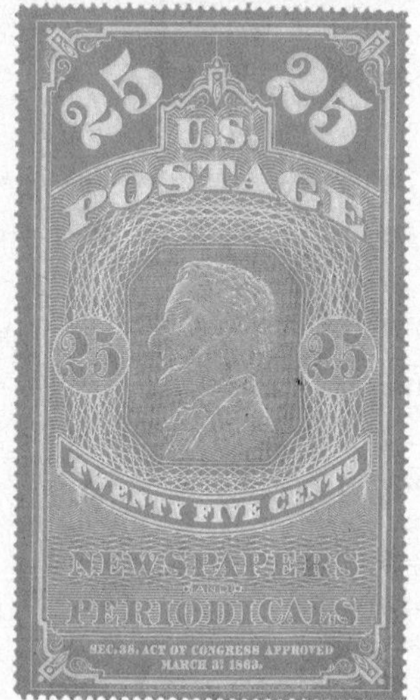

Lincoln — N3

Values for Nos. PR1-PR8 are for examples with perforations on all four sides. Examples with natural straight edges sell for somewhat less. Some panes were fully perforated, while others have natural straight edges either at top or bottom affecting five stamps in the pane of ten.

Printed by the National Bank Note Co.
Typographed and Embossed
1865 **Unwmk.** ***Perf. 12***
Thin hard paper, without gum
Size of design: 51x95mm
Colored Border

PR1 N1 5c dark blue 750.00 *2,000.*
a. 5c light blue 1,000. —
PR2 N2 10c blue green 300.00 *1,800.*
a. 10c green 300.00 *1,800.*
b. Pelure paper 400.00 *1,800.*
PR3 N3 25c orange red 400.00 *2,500.*
a. 25c carmine red 425.00 *2,500.*
b. Pelure paper 450.00

Nos. PR1-PR3 used are valued with faults.

White Border
Yellowish paper

PR4 N1 5c light blue 550.00 *2,400.*
a. 5c dark blue 550.00 —
b. Pelure paper 600.00 —
Nos. PR1-PR4 (4) 2,000.

REPRINTS of 1865 ISSUE
Printed by the Continental Bank Note Co. using the original National Bank Note Co. plates

1875
Hard white paper, without gum
5c White Border, 10c and 25c Colored Border

PR5 N1 5c dull blue 225.00
a. Printed on both sides *5,750.*
PR6 N2 10c dark bluish green 250.00
a. Printed on both sides *4,250.*
PR7 N3 25c dark carmine 300.00
Nos. PR5-PR7 (3) 775.00

The 5c has white border, 10c and 25c have colored borders.
Many fakes exist of Nos. PR1-PR7, some of high quality. Certification is highly recommended.
The Continental Bank Note Co. made another special printing from new plates, which did not have the colored border. These exist imperforate and perforated, but they were not regularly issued. Value, imperf. set $3,750.

Printed by the American Bank Note Co.
Soft porous paper, without gum
White Border

1881
PR8 N1 5c dark blue 700.00

Statue of Freedom — N4

"Justice" — N5

Ceres — N6

"Victory" — N7

Clio — N8

Minerva — N9

Vesta — N10

"Peace" N11

"Commerce" N12

Hebe — N13

Indian Maiden — N14

Values for used examples of Nos. PR9-PR113 are for fine-very fine examples for denominations to $3, and fine for denominations of $5 or higher. Used examples of some Scott numbers might not exist without faults.

Printed by the Continental Bank Note Co.
Size of design: 24x35mm

1875, Jan. 1 **Engr.**

Thin hard paper

PR9	N4	2c black	300.00	40.00
		No gum	120.00	
PR10	N4	3c black	300.00	45.00
		No gum	120.00	
PR11	N4	4c black	300.00	40.00
		No gum	120.00	
PR12	N4	6c black	300.00	45.00
		No gum	120.00	
PR13	N4	8c black	350.00	65.00
		No gum	135.00	
PR14	N4	9c black	500.00	125.00
		No gum	185.00	
PR15	N4	10c black	375.00	60.00
		No gum	135.00	
PR16	N5	12c rose	800.00	100.00
		No gum	325.00	
PR17	N5	24c rose	850.00	125.00
		No gum	350.00	
PR18	N5	36c rose	850.00	150.00
		No gum	350.00	
PR19	N5	48c rose	1,250.	400.00
		No gum	450.00	
PR20	N5	60c rose	1,250.	115.00
		No gum	450.00	
PR21	N5	72c rose	1,500.	375.00
		No gum	550.00	
PR22	N5	84c rose	1,850.	375.00
		No gum	650.00	
PR23	N5	96c rose	1,350.	250.00
		No gum	525.00	
PR24	N6	$1.92 dk brn	1,650.	250.00
		No gum	650.00	
PR25	N7	$3 ver	1,800.	450.00
		No gum	700.00	
PR26	N8	$6 ultra	3,600.	550.00
		No gum	1,400.	
PR27	N9	$9 yel org	4,000.	*1,000.*
		No gum	1,600.	
PR28	N10	$12 bl grn	4,500.	*1,100.*
		No gum	1,750.	
PR29	N11	$24 dk gray vio	4,750.	*1,200.*
		No gum	1,850.	
PR30	N12	$36 brn rose	5,000.	*1,400.*
		No gum	2,000.	
PR31	N13	$48 red brn	7,000.	*1,600.*
		No gum	2,600.	
PR32	N14	$60 violet	6,500.	*1,750.*
		No gum	2,400.	

SPECIAL PRINTING of 1875 ISSUE
Printed by the Continental Bank Note Co.
Hard white paper, without gum

1875

PR33	N4	2c gray black	650.00
a.		Horiz. ribbed paper	500.00
PR34	N4	3c gray black	650.00
a.		Horiz. ribbed paper	500.00
PR35	N4	4c gray black	700.00
a.		Horiz. ribbed paper	1,000.
PR36	N4	6c gray black	900.00
PR37	N4	8c gray black	975.00
PR38	N4	9c gray black	1,050.
PR39	N4	10c gray black	1,400.
PR40	N5	12c pale rose	1,500.
PR41	N5	24c pale rose	2,100.
PR42	N5	36c pale rose	2,800.
PR43	N5	48c pale rose	4,000.
PR44	N5	60c pale rose	4,000.
PR45	N5	72c pale rose	4,500.
PR46	N5	84c pale rose	5,500.
PR47	N5	96c pale rose	*8,500.*
PR48	N6	$1.92 dk brn	*22,500.*
PR49	N7	$3 vermilion	*45,000.*
PR50	N8	$6 ultra	*80,000.*
PR51	N9	$9 yellow org	*250,000.*
PR52	N10	$12 blue green	*125,000.*
PR53	N11	$24 dk gray vio	—
PR54	N12	$36 brn rose	*250,000.*
PR55	N13	$48 red brown	—
PR56	N14	$60 violet	—

Although four examples of No. PR51 were sold, only one is currently documented.

No. PR54 is valued in the grade of fine. Although two stamps were sold, only one is currently documented.

All values of this issue, Nos. PR33 to PR56, exist imperforate but were not regularly issued thus. Value, set $60,000.

Printed by the American Bank Note Co.
Soft porous paper

1879

PR57	N4	2c black	75.00	15.00
		No gum	30.00	
PR58	N4	3c black	85.00	20.00
		No gum	35.00	
PR59	N4	4c black	85.00	20.00
		No gum	35.00	
a.		Double paper	—	
PR60	N4	6c black	125.00	35.00
		No gum	50.00	
PR61	N4	8c black	135.00	35.00
		No gum	55.00	
PR62	N4	10c black	135.00	35.00
		No gum	55.00	
PR63	N5	12c red	500.00	125.00
		No gum	210.00	
PR64	N5	24c red	500.00	125.00
		No gum	210.00	
PR65	N5	36c red	1,000.	325.00
		No gum	475.00	
PR66	N5	48c red	1,000.	300.00
		No gum	450.00	
PR67	N5	60c red	1,000.	275.00
		No gum	450.00	
a.		Imperf., pair	*4,000.*	
PR68	N5	72c red	1,250.	425.00
		No gum	575.00	
PR69	N5	84c red	1,250.	350.00
		No gum	575.00	
PR70	N5	96c red	1,200.	275.00
		No gum	525.00	
PR71	N6	$1.92 pale brn	550.00	175.00
		No gum	225.00	
PR72	N7	$3 red ver	625.00	200.00
		No gum	250.00	
PR73	N8	$6 blue	1,050.	300.00
		No gum	400.00	
PR74	N9	$9 orange	800.00	225.00
		No gum	325.00	
PR75	N10	$12 yel grn	850.00	250.00
		No gum	325.00	
PR76	N11	$24 dk vio	800.00	300.00
		No gum	300.00	
PR77	N12	$36 Indian red	850.00	350.00
		No gum	350.00	
PR78	N13	$48 yel brn	900.00	450.00
		No gum	350.00	
PR79	N14	$60 purple	850.00	400.00
		No gum	350.00	
		Nos. PR57-PR70 (14)	8,340.	2,360.

See the Scott U.S. Specialized Catalogue Die and Plate Proof section for imperforates.

SPECIAL PRINTING of 1879 ISSUE
Printed by the American Bank Note Co.
Without gum

1883

PR80	N4	2c intense black	1,700.

REGULAR ISSUE
With gum

1885, July 1

PR81	N4	1c black	95.00	12.50
		No gum	42.50	
PR82	N5	12c carmine	200.00	30.00
		No gum	85.00	
PR83	N5	24c carmine	200.00	32.50
		No gum	85.00	
PR84	N5	36c carmine	300.00	57.50
		No gum	125.00	
PR85	N5	48c carmine	425.00	75.00
		No gum	180.00	
PR86	N5	60c carmine	550.00	100.00
		No gum	240.00	
PR87	N5	72c carmine	550.00	110.00
		No gum	240.00	
PR88	N5	84c carmine	850.00	250.00
		No gum	325.00	
PR89	N5	96c carmine	750.00	190.00
		No gum	300.00	
		Nos. PR81-PR89 (9)	3,920.	857.50

See the Scott U.S. Specialized Catalogue Die and Plate Proof section for imperforates.

Printed by the Bureau of Engraving and Printing

1894

Soft wove paper, with pale, whitish gum

PR90	N4	1c intense black	425.00	*4,500.*
		Never hinged	1,000.	
		No gum	175.00	
PR91	N4	2c intense black	500.00	
		Never hinged	1,200.	
		No gum	210.00	
PR92	N4	4c intense black	550.00	*13,500.*
		Never hinged	1,400.	
		No gum	225.00	
PR93	N4	6c intense black	4,500.	
		Never hinged	*11,500.*	
		No gum	1,900.	
PR94	N4	10c intense black	1,200.	
		No gum	525.00	
PR95	N5	12c pink	2,600.	*4,500.*
		No gum	1,100.	
PR96	N5	24c pink	3,750.	*4,750.*
		No gum	1,850.	
PR97	N5	36c pink	*50,000.*	
PR98	N5	60c pink	*55,000.*	*16,000.*
PR99	N5	96c pink	*52,500.*	
PR100	N7	$3 scarlet	*60,000.*	
PR101	N8	$6 pale blue	*60,000.*	—
		No gum	*30,000.*	

Nos. PR90, PR95-PR98 used are valued with fine centering and small faults.

No. PR97 unused is valued in the grade of very good to fine. No. PR98 unused is valued in the grade of fine. Nos. PR99-PR100 unused are valued in the grade of fine-very fine.

Statue of Freedom N15

"Justice" N16

"Victory" — N17

Clio — N18

Vesta — N19

"Peace" — N20

"Commerce" N21

Indian Maiden N22

1895, Feb. 1

Size of designs: 1c-50c, 21x34mm
$2-$100, 24x35mm

PR102	N15	1c black	230.00	*125.00*
		Never hinged	500.00	
		No gum	90.00	
PR103	N15	2c black	230.00	*125.00*
		Never hinged	500.00	
		No gum	90.00	
PR104	N15	5c black	300.00	*175.00*
		Never hinged	650.00	
		No gum	125.00	
PR105	N15	10c black	550.00	*400.00*
		Never hinged	1,150.	
		No gum	225.00	
PR106	N16	25c car	750.00	*500.00*
		Never hinged	1,650.	
		No gum	300.00	
PR107	N16	50c car	*2,750.*	*800.00*
		Never hinged	*6,250.*	
		No gum	*875.00*	
PR108	N17	$2 scarlet	1,500.	*1,100.*
		Never hinged	3,250.	
		No gum	575.00	
PR109	N18	$5 ultra	2,100.	*1,750.*
		Never hinged	4,500.	
		No gum	800.00	
PR110	N19	$10 green	2,500.	*2,000.*
		Never hinged	5,250.	
		No gum	900.00	
PR111	N20	$20 slate	3,250.	*2,500.*
		Never hinged	6,750.	
		No gum	1,200.	
PR112	N21	$50 dull rose	2,900.	*750.00*
		Never hinged	6,250.	
		No gum	1,100.	
PR113	N22	$100 purple	3,500.	*7,000.*
		Never hinged	7,250.	
		No gum	1,400.	
		Nos. PR102-PR113 (12)	20,560.	17,225.

1895-97 **Wmk. 191**

PR114	N15	1c black	8.00	*25.00*
		Never hinged	20.00	
		No gum	2.75	
PR115	N15	2c black	8.00	*25.00*
		Never hinged	20.00	
		No gum	2.75	
PR116	N15	5c black	13.00	*40.00*
		Never hinged	27.50	
		No gum	4.25	
PR117	N15	10c black	13.00	*25.00*
		Never hinged	27.50	
		No gum	4.25	
PR118	N16	25c carmine	20.00	*65.00*
		Never hinged	45.00	
		No gum	7.00	
PR119	N16	50c carmine	25.00	*75.00*
		Never hinged	55.00	
		No gum	8.50	
PR120	N17	$2 scarlet	30.00	*110.00*
		Never hinged	75.00	
		No gum	10.00	
PR121	N18	$5 dark bl	40.00	*175.00*
		Never hinged	100.00	
		No gum	13.50	
a.		$5 light blue	200.00	*500.00*
		Never hinged	500.00	
		No gum	67.50	
PR122	N19	$10 green	42.50	*160.00*
		Never hinged	105.00	
		No gum	14.00	
PR123	N20	$20 slate	45.00	*180.00*
		Never hinged	110.00	
		No gum	15.00	
PR124	N21	$50 dull rose	75.00	*225.00*
		Never hinged	170.00	
		No gum	27.50	
PR125	N22	$100 purple	65.00	*240.00*
		Never hinged	150.00	
		No gum	22.50	
		Nos. PR114-PR125 (12)	384.50	*1,345.*
		Nos. PR114-PR125, never hinged	905.00	

In 1899 the Government sold 26,989 sets of these stamps, but, as the stock of high values was not sufficient to make up the required number, an additional printing was made of the $5, $10, $20, $50 and $100. These are virtually indistinguishable from earlier printings.

For overprints, see Nos. R159-R160.

PARCEL POST STAMPS

Issued for the prepayment of postage on parcel post packages only.

Post Office Clerk — PP1

City Carrier PP2

Railway Postal Clerk — PP3

Rural Carrier PP4

Mail Train — PP5

Steamship and Mail Tender PP6

Automobile Service PP7

Airplane Carrying Mail — PP8

Manufacturing — PP9

Dairying PP10

Harvesting PP11

Fruit Growing PP12

1913 Wmk. 190 Engr. *Perf. 12*

Q1	PP1	1c carmine rose	4.50	1.75
		Never hinged	11.00	
Q2	PP2	2c carmine rose	5.25	1.40
		Never hinged	12.50	
a.		2c lake	*1,750.*	
b.		2c carmine lake	*350.00*	

No. Q2a is valued in the grade of fine to very fine.

Q3	PP3	3c carmine	9.50	6.50
		Never hinged	26.00	
Q4	PP4	4c carmine rose	30.00	3.50
		Never hinged	85.00	
Q5	PP5	5c carmine rose	25.00	2.50
		Never hinged	67.50	
Q6	PP6	10c carmine rose	42.50	3.50
		Never hinged	95.00	
Q7	PP7	15c carmine rose	62.50	15.00
		Never hinged	175.00	
Q8	PP8	20c carmine rose	120.00	30.00
		Never hinged	280.00	
Q9	PP9	25c carmine rose	57.50	8.50
		Never hinged	160.00	
Q10	PP10	50c carmine rose	250.00	50.00
		Never hinged	625.00	
Q11	PP11	75c carmine rose	85.00	40.00
		Never hinged	200.00	
Q12	PP12	$1 carmine rose	300.00	45.00
		Never hinged	700.00	
		Nos. Q1-Q12 (12)	991.75	207.65
		Nos. Q1-Q12, never hinged	2,468.	

PARCEL POST POSTAGE DUE STAMPS

For affixing by a postal clerk to any parcel post package, to denote the amount to be collected from the addressee because of insufficient prepayment of postage.

PPD1

1913 Wmk. 190 Engr. *Perf. 12*

JQ1	PPD1	1c dark green	8.50	4.25
		Never hinged	21.00	
JQ2	PPD1	2c dark green	65.00	18.00
		Never hinged	160.00	
JQ3	PPD1	5c dark green	10.50	5.00
		Never hinged	25.00	
JQ4	PPD1	10c dark green	120.00	45.00
		Never hinged	300.00	
JQ5	PPD1	25c dark green	75.00	4.75
		Never hinged	190.00	
		Nos. JQ1-JQ5 (5)	279.00	77.00
		Nos. JQ1-JQ5, never hinged	696.00	

SPECIAL HANDLING STAMPS

For use on fourth-class mail to secure the same expeditious handling accorded to first-class mail matter.

PP13

1925-28 Engr. Unwmk. *Perf. 11*

QE1	PP13	10c yel grn ('28)	2.00	1.00
		Never hinged	4.25	
QE2	PP13	15c yel grn ('28)	2.25	.90
		Never hinged	4.75	
QE3	PP13	20c yel grn ('28)	3.75	1.50
		Never hinged	7.75	
QE4	PP13	25c dp grn ('25)	20.00	3.75
		Never hinged	37.50	
a.		yel grn ('28)	16.50	*22.50*
		Never hinged	32.50	
		Nos. QE1-QE4 (4)	28.00	7.15
		Nos. QE1-QE4, never hinged	54.25	

COMPUTER VENDED POSTAGE

CVP1

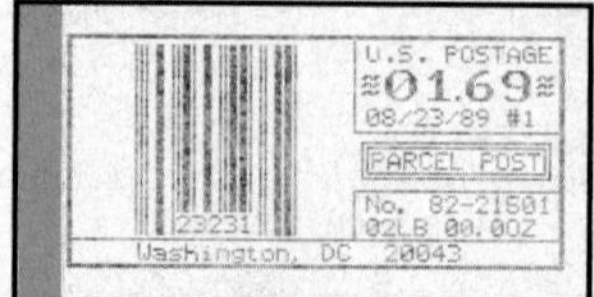

CVP2

1989, Aug. 23 Tagged *Guillotined*
Self-Adhesive

Washington, DC, Machine 82
Date Other Than First Day

CVP1	CVP1	25c First Class	6.00	—
a.		First day dated, serial Nos. 12501-15500	5.00	—
b.		First day dated, serial Nos. 00001-12500	5.00	—
c.		First day dated, over No. 27500	—	—
CVP2	CVP1	$1 Third Class	—	—
a.		First day dated, serial Nos. 24501-27500	—	—
b.		First day dated, over No. 27500	—	—
CVP3	CVP2	$1.69 Parcel Post	—	—
a.		First day dated, serial Nos. 21501-24500	—	—
b.		First day dated, over No. 27500	—	—
CVP4	CVP1	$2.40 Priority Mail	—	—
a.		First day dated, serial Nos. 18501-21500	—	—
b.		Priority Mail , with bar code (CVP2)	*100.00*	
c.		First day dated, over No. 27500	—	—
CVP5	CVP1	$8.75 Express Mail	—	—
a.		First day dated, serial Nos. 15501-18500	—	—
b.		First day dated, over No. 27500	—	—

Washington, DC, Machine 83
Date Other Than First Day

CVP6	CVP1	25c First Class	6.00	—
a.		First day dated, serial Nos. 12501-15500	5.00	—
b.		First day dated, serial Nos. 00001-12500	5.00	—
c.		First day dated, over No. 27500	—	—
CVP7	CVP1	$1 Third Class	—	—
a.		First day dated, serial Nos. 24501-27500	—	—
b.		First day dated, over No. 27500	—	—
CVP8	CVP2	$1.69 Parcel Post	—	—
a.		First day dated, serial Nos. 21501-24500	—	—
b.		First day dated, over No. 27500	—	—
CVP9	CVP1	$2.40 Priority Mail	—	—
a.		First day dated, serial Nos. 18501-21500	—	—
b.		First day dated, over No. 27500	—	—
c.		Priority Mail , with bar code (CVP2)	*100.00*	

Error date 11/18/90 exists.

CVP10	CVP1	$8.75 Express Mail	—	—
a.		First day dated, serial Nos. 15501-18500	—	—
b.		First day dated, over No. 27500	—	—

1989, Sept. 1

Kensington, MD, Machine 82
Date Other Than First Day

CVP11	CVP1	25c First Class	6.00	—
a.		First day dated, serial Nos. 12501-15500	5.00	—
b.		First day dated, serial Nos. 00001-12500	5.00	—
c.		First day dated, over No. 27500	—	—
CVP12	CVP1	$1 Third Class	—	—
a.		First day dated, serial Nos. 24501-27500	—	—
b.		First day dated, over No. 27500	—	—
CVP13	CVP2	$1.69 Parcel Post	—	—
a.		First day dated, serial Nos. 21501-24500	—	—
b.		First day dated, over No. 27500	—	—
CVP14	CVP1	$2.40 Priority Mail	—	—
a.		First day dated, serial Nos. 18501-21500	—	—
b.		First day dated, over No. 27500	—	—
c.		Priority Mail , with bar code (CVP2)	*100.00*	
CVP15	CVP1	$8.75 Express Mail	—	—
a.		First day dated, serial Nos. 15501-18500	—	—
b.		First day dated, over No. 27500	—	—

Kensington, MD, Machine 83
Date Other Than First Day

CVP16	CVP1	25c First Class	6.00	—
a.		First day dated, serial Nos. 12501-15500	5.00	—
b.		First day dated, serial Nos. 00001-12500	5.00	—
c.		First day dated, over No. 27500	—	—
CVP17	CVP1	$1 Third Class	—	—
a.		First day dated, serial Nos. 24501-27500	—	—
b.		First day dated, over No. 27500	—	—
CVP18	CVP2	$1.69 Parcel Post	—	—
a.		First day dated, serial Nos. 21501-24500	—	—
b.		First day dated, over No. 27500	—	—
CVP19	CVP1	$2.40 Priority Mail	—	—
a.		First day dated, serial Nos. 18501-21500	—	—
b.		First day dated, over No. 27500	—	—
c.		Priority Mail , with bar code (CVP2)	100.00	
CVP20	CVP1	$8.75 Express Mail	—	—
a.		First day dated, serial Nos. 15501-18500	—	—
b.		First day dated, over No. 27500	—	—

1989, Nov.

Washington, DC, Machine 11

CVP21	CVP1	25c First Class	*150.00*	
a.		First Class, with bar code (CVP2)		—

Stamps in CVP1 design with $1.10 denominations exist (certified first class).

CVP22	CVP1	$1 Third Class	*500.00*	
CVP23	CVP2	$1.69 Parcel Post	*500.00*	
CVP24	CVP1	$2.40 Priority Mail	*500.00*	
a.		Priority Mail , with bar code (CVP2)		—
CVP25	CVP1	$8.75 Express Mail	*500.00*	

Washington, DC, Machine 12

CVP26	CVP1	25c First Class	*150.00*	

A $1.10 certified First Class stamp, dated Nov. 20, exists on cover.

CVP27	CVP1	$1 Third Class		—

A $1.40 Third Class stamp of type CVP2, dated Dec. 1 is known on a Dec. 2 cover.

CVP28	CVP2	$1.69 Parcel Post		—
CVP29	CVP1	$2.40 Priority Mail		—
a.		Priority Mail , with bar code (CVP2)		—
CVP30	CVP1	$8.75 Express Mail		—

An $8.50 Express Mail stamp, dated Dec. 2, exists on cover.

CVP3 — Type I CVP3 — Type II

1992, Aug. 20 Engr. *Perf. 10 Horiz.*
Coil Stamp

CVP31	CVP3	29c red & blue, type I	.75	.25
c.		32c Type II ('94)	1.00	.40

No. CVP31 was available in all denominations from 1c to $99.99.

The listing is for the first class rate. Other denominations, se-tenant combinations, or "errors" are not listed.

Type II denomination has large sans-serif numerals preceded by an asterisk measuring 2mm across. No. CVP31 has small numerals with serifs preceded by an asterisk 1½mm across.

CVP4

1994, Feb. 19 Photo. *Perf. 9.9 Vert.*

CVP32	CVP4	29c dark red & dark blue	.70	.35

No. CVP32 was available in all denominations from 19c to $99.99.

The listing is for the first class rate at time of issue. Other denominations, se-tenant combinations, or "errors" will not be listed.

1996, Jan. 26

CVP33	CVP4	32c bright red & blue, "1996" below design	.70	.25

Letters in "USA" on No. CVP33 are thicker than on No. CVP32. Numerous other design differences exist in the moire pattern and in the bunting. No. CVP33 has "1996" in the lower left corner; No. CVP32 has no date.

For No. CVP33, the 32c value has been listed because it was the first class rate in effect at the time the stamp was issued.

CVP5

1999 Tagged *Die Cut*
Self-Adhesive

CVP34	CVP5	33c black	*50.00*	—
a.		"Priority Mail" under encryption at LL	—	—
b.		"Express Mail" under encryption at LL	—	—

No. CVP34 was available from 15 NCR Automated Postal Center machines located in central Florida. Machines could produce values in any denomination required. The backing paper is taller and wider than the stamp.

Sales of No. CVP34 were discontinued in 2000 or 2001.

CVP6

1999, May 7 Tagged *Die Cut*

Self-Adhesive

Size: 77½x39mm

Microprinting Above Red Orange Line

CVP35	CVP6 33c black & red orange, control numbers only at LL, round corners		20.00	—
a.	"Priority Mail" at LL, square corners		150.00	—
b.	"Priority Mail AS" and text string at LL, square corners		150.00	—

No Microprinting Above Red Orange Line

CVP36	CVP6 33c black & red orange, control numbers only at LL, round corners	10.00	—
a.	"Priority Mail" at LL, square corners	125.00	—
b.	"Priority Mail AS" and text string at LL, square corners	125.00	—

Size: 73½x42mm

CVP37	CVP6 33c black & pink, control numbers only at LL	3.75	—
a.	"Priority Mail" at LL	5.00	—
b.	"Priority Mail AS" and text string at LL	5.00	—

Nos. CVP35-CVP37 were available from 18 IBM Neopost machines located in central Florida. The backing paper is taller than the stamp. Any denomination could be printed up to $99.99.

Simplypostage.com — CVP8

2001

Self-Adhesive

Serpentine Die Cut 8 at Right

Eagle and Stars Background

CVP39	CVP8 34c black, blue & orange, *2001*	—	—
CVP40	CVP8 34c black, blue & orange, with control number at UL, *2001*	—	—

Flag Background

CVP41	CVP8 34c black, blue & orange, with control number at UL, *2001*	—	—
CVP42	CVP8 34c black, blue & orange, with control number at LL, *2001*	—	20.00

Neopostage.com — CVP9

Serpentine Die Cut 8¾ at Right

2002, June

Self-Adhesive

CVP43	CVP9	21c black, blue & orange	—	
a.	Booklet pane of 10		—	
CVP44	CVP9	23c black, blue & orange	—	—
a.	Booklet pane of 10		90.00	
CVP45	CVP9	34c black, blue & orange	—	—
a.	Booklet pane of 10		—	
CVP46	CVP9	37c black, blue & orange	—	—
a.	Booklet pane of 10		60.00	
CVP47	CVP9	50c black, blue & orange	—	—
a.	Booklet pane of 10		180.00	
CVP47B	CVP9	57c black, blue & orange	—	
a.	Booklet pane of 10		—	
CVP48	CVP9	60c black, blue & orange	—	—
a.	Booklet pane of 10		160.00	
CVP49	CVP9	70c black, blue & orange	—	—
a.	Booklet pane of 10		180.00	
CVP50	CVP9	80c black, blue & orange	—	—
a.	Booklet pane of 10		180.00	
CVP51	CVP9	$3.50 black, blue & orange	—	—
a.	Booklet pane of 1		—	
b.	Booklet pane of 2		—	
c.	Booklet pane of 5		—	
d.	Booklet pane of 10		—	
CVP52	CVP9	$3.85 black, blue & orange	—	
a.	Booklet pane of 1		—	
b.	Booklet pane of 2		—	
c.	Booklet pane of 5		—	
d.	Booklet pane of 10		—	
CVP52E	CVP9	$12.45 black, blue & orange	—	
a.	Booklet pane of 1		—	
CVP53	CVP9	$13.65 black, blue & orange	—	—
a.	Booklet pane of 1		—	
b.	Booklet pane of 2		—	
c.	Booklet pane of 5		—	
d.	Booklet pane of 10		—	

Nos. CVP43-CVP53 were printed only with the stated values.

Denominations of 34c, 57c, $3.50 and perhaps others exist with a ICNOVA kiosk location designation. These were produced during pre-issue testing at a location not publicly accessible and are not considered to be valid postage. Stamps from the ICNOVA location have much smaller 2-D bar code squares. The denominations listed above come from other publicly accessible kiosk locations from June 20, 2002, forward. Official sales of these stamps began on June 20, 2002, or later for some denominations.

The 21c, 34c, 57c, $3.50 and $12.45 denominations were only sold from June 21 to June 29, 2002. They are all scarce, and some are rare. The 37c, $3.85 and $13.65 denominations were not sold until June 30, 2002, when the rate change took effect.

While the name on Nos. CVP39-CVP42 reads simplypostage.com and the name on Nos. CVP43-CVP53 reads neopostage.com, both were products of Neopost.

Issued: Nos. CVP43-CVP49, CVP51-CVP53, 6/2002; No. CVP50, 7/2002.

Earliest documented use: Nos. CVP43, CVP47, CVP51-CVP52, not known used; Nos. CVP44, CVP46, CVP48-CVP49, CVP53, 6/30; No. CVP45, 6/21; No. CVP50, 7/3.

CVP10

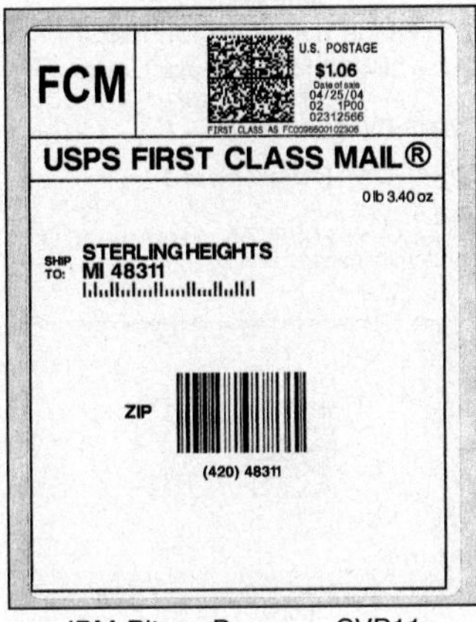

IBM Pitney Bowes — CVP11

2004, Apr. 14 *Die Cut*

Self-Adhesive

CVP54	CVP10 37c black & pink	5.75	—
a.	"First Class Mail" under encryption at LL	2.50	—
b.	"Priority Mail" under encryption at LL	2.50	—
c.	"Parcel Post" under encryption at LL	2.50	—
d.	"International" under encryption at LL	2.50	—
CVP55	CVP11 37c black, "US Postage" under encryption at LL	2.50	—
a.	"First Class Mail" under encryption at LL	—	—
b.	"Priority Mail" under encryption at LL	—	—
c.	"Parcel Post" under encryption at LL	—	—
d.	"International" under encryption at LL	—	—

Nos. CVP54-CVP55 could be printed in any denomination up to $99.99. Catalogue values for Nos. CVP54-CVP54d and CVP55 are for stamps with low denominations. Stamps with denominations appropriate to the service described are valued correspondingly higher.

CVP12

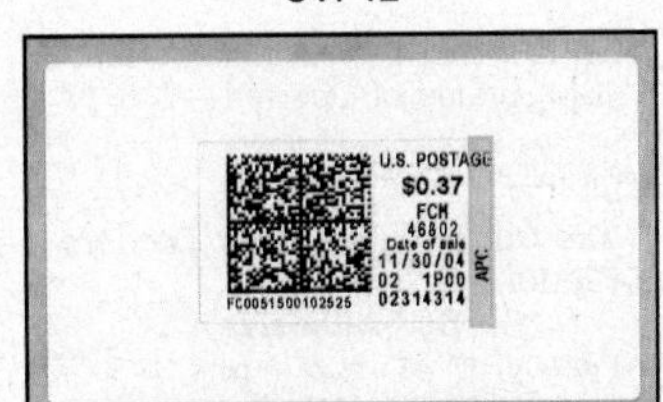

IBM Pitney Bowes — CVP13

2004, Nov. 19 *Die Cut*

Self-Adhesive

Serial Number Under Encryption APC

CVP56	CVP12	37c black	2.50	.25
CVP57	CVP13	37c black & pink	1.00	.25

Nos. CVP56-CVP57 could be printed in any denomination. No. CVP56 could be printed with three different rate inscriptions under the denomination. No. CVP57 could be printed with 18 different rate inscriptions and/or service indicators under the denomination, and with at least 27 different rate inscriptions and or/service indicators under the denomination on stamps with a four-digit code after the zip code.

Blank Under Denomination

"IM" and Numbers Under Encryption

CVP58	CVP13	60c black & pink	3.00	.50
CVP59	CVP13	80c black & pink	3.75	.50

"PM" and Numbers Under Encryption

CVP60	CVP13	$3.85 black & pink	15.00	.50

"EM" and Numbers Under Encryption

CVP61	CVP13	$13.65 black & pink	42.50	1.00

"IB" and Numbers Under Encryption

CVP62	CVP13	$1 black & pink	4.00	.25

Nos. CVP58-CVP61 could only be printed in denominations listed. No. CVP62 could be printed in any denomination above 99c. As of May 12, 2008, it was possible to create stamps with "IB" and numbers under encryption in any denomination. The computer software was later changed to once again only permit stamps of certain denominations to be created with "IB" and numbers under the encryption.

IBM Pitney Bowes Type of 2004

2006 *Die Cut*

Self-Adhesive

Blank Under Denomination

"IM" and Numbers Under Encryption

CVP63	CVP13	48c black & pink	1.50	.40
CVP64	CVP13	63c black & pink	1.75	.50
CVP65	CVP13	84c black & pink	2.25	.50

"PM" and Numbers Under Encryption

CVP66	CVP13	$4.05 black & pink	11.00	.50
CVP66A	CVP13	$8.10 black & pink	30.00	1.00

"EM" and Numbers Under Encryption

CVP67	CVP13	$14.40 black & pink	32.50	1.00

Nos. CVP63-CVP67 could only be printed in denominations listed.

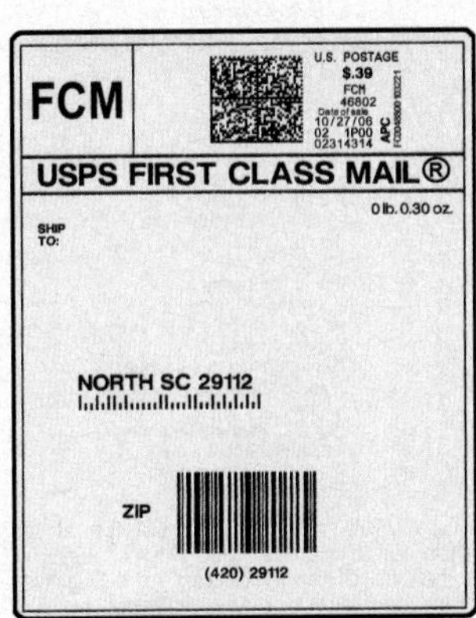

IBM Pitney Bowes — CVP14

2006 ***Die Cut***

Self-Adhesive
No Inscription Under Encryption
Serial Number to Right of "APC"
"Ship To:" Above Destination City

CVP69 CVP14 39c black 2.25 .25

Nos. CVP69 could be printed in any denomination, with 14 different rate inscriptions and/or service indicators under the denomination on stamps having "Ship To:" at the left and no code below the weight, and at least 29 different rate inscriptions and/or service indicators under the denomination on stamps having a four-digit code at the right that is even with the words "Ship To:" and below the weight.

IBM Pitney Bowes Type of 2004

2006(?)-07 ***Die Cut***

Self-Adhesive
Blank Under Denomination
"IB" and Numbers Under Encryption

CVP70 CVP13 39c black & pink 1.00 .50
CVP71 CVP13 41c black & pink 1.75 .50
CVP72 CVP13 69c black & pink 2.50 .70

"IM" and Numbers Under Encryption

CVP73 CVP13 61c black & pink 2.25 .50
CVP74 CVP13 90c black & pink 3.50 .95

Nos. CVP70-CVP74 could only be printed in the denominations listed.

Nos. CVP71-CVP74 issued May, 2007. No. CVP70 was issued before the May rate change. As of May 12, 2008, it was possible to create stamps with "IB" and numbers under encryption in any denomination. The computer software was later changed to once again only permit stamps of certain denominations to be created with "IB" and numbers under the encryption. No. CVP70 was available for sale from Nov. 2006 to May 13, 2007. Nos. CVP71-CVP72 were available for sale from May 14, 2007 to May 11, 2008.

Pitney Bowes — CVP15

2006, Dec. ***Die Cut***

Self-Adhesive

CVP75 CVP15 41c black & pink 1.50 —
a. "Mailed From Zip Code ..." on bottom line .20 —
b. "Postcard" on bottom line .55 —
c. "First Class Mail Intl" on bottom line 1.25 —
d. "Parcel Post" on bottom line 7.50 —
e. "Priority" on bottom line 9.25 —
f. "Express Mail" on bottom line 33.00 —
g. Numeric code and date sold on bottom line, eagle at left, encryption at right — —
h. As "g," "Postcard" on bottom line — —
i. As "g," "First Class Mail" on bottom line — —
j. As "g," "First Class Mail Intl" on bottom line — —
k. As "g," "Priority Envelope" on bottom line — —
l. As "g," "Priority Mail" on bottom line — —
m. As "g," "Priority Tube" on bottom line — —
n. As "g," "Priority Box" on bottom line — —
o. As "g," "Priority - Irregular Shape" on bottom line — —
p. As "g," "Parcel Post" on bottom line — —
q. As "g," "Express Mail" on bottom line — —

No. CVP75 was put into service at large companies and universities in Dec. 2006, with the majority of the machines not being available to the general public. Information about this stamp was not made available until 2007. Other rates and inscriptions might be available.

Nos. CVP75a could be printed in any denomination. Nos. CVP75b-CVP75f could be printed only in pre-programmed denominations based on the current rates for the service, or in any denominations at or above the minimum rates for the service. Values are for stamps with low denominations. A stamp with "First Class" on the bottom line has been reported but has not been seen by the editors. Inscriptions generated by the software may vary from machine to machine depending on when the software was installed.

Issued: No. CVP75g, 10/18/11. No. CVP75g was made available at Mail & Go postal stations in Super Target stores in the Dallas, TX area, and presumably could be printed in any denomination.

IBM Pitney Bowes Type of 2004

2008, May ***Die Cut***

Self-Adhesive
Blank Under Denomination
"IM" and Numbers Under Encryption

CVP76 CVP13 94c black & pink 3.00 .60
CVP77 CVP13 $1.20 black & pink 3.75 1.25

Nos. CVP76-CVP77 could only be printed in the denominations listed.

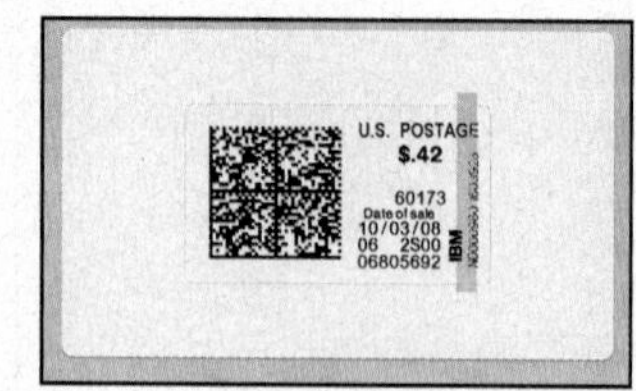

IBM — CVP16

Die Cut With Rounded Corners

2008, June 4

Self-Adhesive

CVP78 CVP16 42c black & pink 4.25 —

Die Cut With Perpendicular Corners

CVP79 CVP16 42c black & pink 4.25 —
a. Pane of 6 —
b. Pane of 7 —
c. Pane of 8 —
d. Pane of 9 —
e. Pane of 10 —

Nos. CVP78-CVP79 were made available during a pilot study to evaluate a new IBM kiosk at Schaumburg, IL. No. CVP78 could be printed in any denomination from 1c to $25. Because each kiosk transaction was limited to $100, No. CVP79e could only be bought with stamps denominated from 1c to $10. Individual panes with 6, 7, 8, 9 or 10 stamps could be purchased as long as the total face value of the pane did not exceed $100. Stamps denominated from $10.01 to $16.66 could only be purchased in panes containing fewer than 10 stamps. Stamps denominated from $16.67 to $25 could only be purchased as a single stamp.

No. CVP79e exists with the vertical pink tagging strip along the left side of the stamps.

IBM Pitney Bowes Type of 2004

2009 ***Die Cut***

Self-Adhesive
Blank Under Denomination
"IM" and Numbers Under Encryption

CVP80 CVP13 98c black & pink 2.00 .60
CVP81 CVP13 $1.24 black & pink 2.50 1.25

Nos. CVP80-CVP81 could only be printed in denominations listed.

IBM (Statue of Liberty) — CVP17

Illustration reduced.

Die Cut With Rounded Corners

2009, June 5

Self-Adhesive

CVP82 CVP17 44c black & pink 7.50 —

Die Cut With Perpendicular Corners

CVP83 CVP17 44c black & pink 7.50 —
a. Pane of 6 (1c to $16.66) —
b. Pane of 7 (1c to $14.28) —
c. Pane of 8 (1c to $12.50) —
d. Pane of 9 (1c to $11.11) —
e. Pane of 10 (1c to $10) —

No. CVP82 could be printed in any denomination from 1c to $25. Nos. CVP82-CVP83 were made available during a pilot study to evaluate a new IBM kiosk at Schaumburg, IL. The machine study at Schaumburg was scheduled to end on July 31, 2009. No. CVP82 was created for purchases of one to five individual stamps or any extra stamps beyond multiples of 10 ending in numerals 1 to 5. Nos. CVP83a-CVP83e were created when stamps purchased ended in numerals 6 to 0.

Flag
CVP18

Serpentine Die Cut 13¼x12½

2011, Oct. 18

Self-Adhesive

CVP84 CVP18 44c multicolored, date sold only on bottom line — —
a. Date sold and "Postcard" on bottom line — —
b. Date sold and "First-Class" on bottom line — —

No. CVP84 was issued in panes of 10. It was made available at Mail & Go postal stations in Super Target stores in the Dallas, TX area. Panes could be printed in any denomination from 29c to $9.99. Serpentine die cut 9 examples of No. CVP84 with dates earlier than Oct. 18 were produced at Pitney Bowes facilities. This serpentine die cut 9 sticker stock is not known to have been sent out for use in machines that were available for sale by the general public. No. CVP84 was made available in 2013 with dozens of images other than the flag shown. These optional images are for various holidays and events, as well as social causes, such as support for breast cancer, education and recycling. One image, for bridal showers, has been made available in two different types.

APC
CVP19

Die Cut With Rounded Corners

2012, Apr. 12

Self-Adhesive

CVP85 CVP19 45c black & pink — —
a. Die cut with perpendicular corners, colored bar at left, "Fold Here" at center, 100x38mm — —

No. CVP85 has "APC" reading upwards at right. No. CVP78 has "IBM" reading upwards at right. No. CVP85 was available during a nationwide test of machines, and could be printed in any denomination from 1c to $99.99. Only one to six examples of No. CVP85 could be purchased and printed at one time.

No. CVP85a was produced on label stock normally used for No. CVP87 when machines ran out of label stock to produce orders for No. CVP85.

APC Variable Vignette Stamp — CVP20

Die Cut With Rounded Corners

2012, Apr. 12

Self-Adhesive

CVP86 CVP20 (45c) black & pink — —
a. Die cut with perpendicular corners, colored bar at left, "Fold Here" at center, 100x38mm — —

No. CVP86 was available during a nationwide test of machines, and could be printed only as "Forever" stamps. The vignette portion of the stamp at left could be chosen from a gallery of six images (Mr. Zip, Heart, Flowers, Flag, Eagle, and Balloons and "Celebrate!", which is depicted). Values are for any vignette, or for any other vignette that may be programmed into the machine at a later date. Each vignette design could be purchased in a quantities ranging from 1 stamp to 100 stamps, but because a $1 minimum purchase was required, at least three examples of the first stamp chosen had to be purchased. A maximum of ten stamps could be printed on a sheet. Sales of stamps that are not in multiples of 10 were printed in strips, smaller-sized sheets containing an even number of stamps, or in sheets having one label inscribed "This Block Is Not Valid Postage" when the sheet contained an odd number of stamps.

No. CVP86a was produced on label stock normally used for No. CVP87 when machines ran out of label stock to produce orders for No. CVP86.

Examples of No. CVP86 without a printed image at left are the result of machines having their image-printing capability shut off so preprinted label stock for producing No. CVP88 could be substituted for the blank label stock used for Nos. CVP85 and CVP86. See footnote under No. CVP88 for information about examples of No. CVP86 with date of purchase inscriptions to right of "Forever."

APC — CVP21

Die Cut With Perpendicular Corners

2012, Apr. 12

Self-Adhesive

CVP87 CVP21 45c black & pink — —

No. CVP87 was available during a nationwide test of machines, and could be printed in any denomination from 1c to $99.99. Stamps can be inscribed with a variety of different service inscriptions.

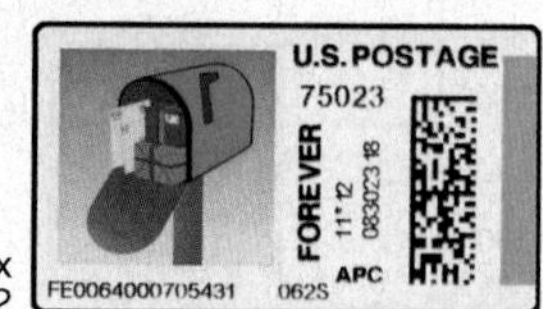

Mailbox
CVP22

Die Cut With Rounded Corners

2012

Self-Adhesive

CVP88 CVP22 (45c) multicolored — —

The mailbox vignette is preprinted on No. CVP88. This preprinted stock was placed in machines in November 2012 and is supposed to be removed from machines on December 31, 2012. The earliest known date of sale is Nov. 10, 2012.

Examples of No. CVP88 with the mailbox design covered by images used for Nos. CVP85 and CVP86 were the result of machines having their blank label stock replaced with the pre-printed label stock while the machine's image-printing capability was not shut off to accommodate the preprinted stock.

On No. CVP88, the number of the month and last two digits of the year in which the stamp was purchased, separated by an asterisk, appear to the right of "Forever." Some examples of No. CVP86 might have the date included if the programming for this was done and the blank label stock was still in the machine.

Labels inscribed "This Block Is Not Valid For Postage" differ from similar labels created with No. CVP86. Various sizes of "Void" overprints on these labels exist.

Reindeer — CVP23

Die Cut With Rounded Corners

2013

Self-Adhesive

CVP89	CVP23 (46c) multicolored	—	—

The reindeer vignette is preprinted on No. CVP89. This preprinted stock was placed in machines in November 2013 and was supposed to be removed from machines sometime after Dec. 25, 2013.

PERSONAL COMPUTER POSTAGE

Personal computer postage, approved by the US Postal Service, was created by subscribing to Stamps.com, an Internet website. Customers ordered self-adhesive labels showing vignettes, but lacking any franking value. The franking value indicia of the stamps could be printed at the customer's convenience at any computer with an Internet connection, using the customer's access codes. Any postage printed would be charged against the customer's account.

Neopost

CVPA1

2000 ***Serpentine Die Cut 8***

Self-Adhesive

1CVP1	CVPA1 33c black, yellow & pink	—	—

Stamps.com

Flag and Star — CVPA1a

Serpentine Die Cut 5¾ at Left

2002, July

"Stamps.com" in Lower Case Letters

Identification Code Below Zip Code

No Mail Class Inscribed

1CVP2	CVPA1a 37c black, blue & orange	7.00	3.00

Identification Code Above Zip Code

Inscribed "US Postage" only

1CVP2A	CVPA1a 37c black, blue & orange	4.00	3.00
a.	"First Class" below "US Postage"	2.75	2.00
b.	"Priority" below "US Postage"	8.25	2.50
c.	"Express" below "US Postage"	25.00	5.00
d.	"Media Mail" below "US Postage"	7.75	2.50
e.	"Parcel Post" below "US Postage"	7.75	2.50
f.	"Bound Printed Matter" below "US Postage"	7.75	2.50
g.	"BPM" below "US Postage"	7.75	2.50

See Nos. 1CVP9, 1CVP21.

No. 1CVP2 apparently could be printed in denominations up to and including 37c. The 37c denomination comes with "FIRST-CLASS" between the Zip code and the identification code.

Later versions of the Stamps.com software allow any denomination to be printed, as well as additional or different mail-class inscriptions, on any basic stamp except for No. 1CVP2.

Values for Nos. 1CVP2A and 1CVP3-1CVP42 are for items appropriate to the service described. Stamps with denominations far lower than those appropriate to the service are valued correspondingly lower.

The software changes allow Nos. 1CVP2A and 1CVP3-1CVP37 to be printed with the mail-class inscriptions described for Nos. 1CVP38f-1CVP38p.

Later software changes allow Nos. 1CVP2A, 1CVP3-1CVP42 and 1CVP51-1CVP58 to be printed with mail-class inscriptions "Library Mail," "Intl. First Class," "Intl Priority," "Intl Express," and "M-Bag" with any denomination.

Love — CVPA2

2002 ***Serpentine Die Cut 5¾ at Left***

1CVP3	CVPA2 37c black, blue & orange	4.00	4.00
a.	"First Class" below "US Postage"	2.75	2.00
b.	"Priority" below "US Postage"	8.25	2.50
c.	"Express" below "US Postage"	25.00	5.00
d.	"Media Mail" below "US Postage"	7.75	2.50
e.	"Parcel Post" below "US Postage"	7.75	2.50
f.	"Bound Printed Matter" below "US Postage"	7.75	2.50
g.	"BPM" below "US Postage"	7.75	2.50

Statue of Liberty and Flag — CVPA3

Liberty Bell and Flag — CVPA4

Eagle and Flag — CVPA5

George Washington and Flag — CVPA6

Capitol Building and Flag — CVPA7

Serpentine Die Cut 5¾ at Left

2003, June

1CVP4	CVPA3 37c black, blue & orange	3.50	2.00
a.	"First Class" below "US Postage"	3.25	2.00
b.	"Priority" below "US Postage"	8.00	1.00
c.	"Express" below "US Postage"	25.00	3.00
d.	"Media Mail" below "US Postage"	7.50	1.00
e.	"Parcel Post" below "US Postage"	7.50	1.00
f.	"Bound Printed Matter" below "US Postage"	7.50	1.00
g.	"BPM" below "US Postage"	7.50	1.00
1CVP5	CVPA4 37c black, blue & orange	3.50	2.00
a.	"First Class" below "US Postage"	3.25	2.00
b.	"Priority" below "US Postage"	8.00	1.00
c.	"Express" below "US Postage"	25.00	3.00
d.	"Media Mail" below "US Postage"	7.50	1.00
e.	"Parcel Post" below "US Postage"	7.50	1.00
f.	"Bound Printed Matter" below "US Postage"	7.50	1.00
g.	"BPM" below "US Postage"	7.50	1.00
1CVP6	CVPA5 37c black, blue & orange	3.50	2.00
a.	"First Class" below "US Postage"	3.25	2.00
b.	"Priority" below "US Postage"	8.00	1.00
c.	"Express" below "US Postage"	25.00	3.00
d.	"Media Mail" below "US Postage"	7.50	1.00
e.	"Parcel Post" below "US Postage"	7.50	1.00
f.	"Bound Printed Matter" below "US Postage"	7.50	1.00
g.	"BPM" below "US Postage"	7.50	1.00
1CVP7	CVPA6 37c black, blue & orange	3.50	2.00
a.	"First Class" below "US Postage"	3.25	.25
b.	"Priority" below "US Postage"	8.00	1.00
c.	"Express" below "US Postage"	25.00	3.00
d.	"Media Mail" below "US Postage"	7.50	1.00
e.	"Parcel Post" below "US Postage"	7.50	1.00
f.	"Bound Printed Matter" below "US Postage"	7.50	1.00
g.	"BPM" below "US Postage"	7.50	1.00
1CVP8	CVPA7 37c black, blue & orange	3.50	2.00
a.	"First Class" below "US Postage"	3.25	.25
b.	"Priority" below "US Postage"	8.00	1.00
c.	"Express" below "US Postage"	25.00	3.00
d.	"Media Mail" below "US Postage"	7.50	1.00
e.	"Parcel Post" below "US Postage"	7.50	1.00
f.	"Bound Printed Matter" below "US Postage"	7.50	1.00
g.	"BPM" below "US Postage"	7.50	1.00
h.	Strip of 5, #1CVP4-1CVP8	17.50	

Flag and Star Type of 2002 Redrawn With "Stamps.com" in Upper Case Letters

Serpentine Die Cut 5¾ at Left

2003, June

Identification Code Above Zip Code

1CVP9	CVPA1a 37c black, blue & orange, "US Postage" only	3.00	1.50
a.	"First Class" below "US Postage"	2.00	.25
b.	"Priority" below "US Postage"	8.00	1.00
c.	"Express" below "US Postage"	25.00	3.00
d.	"Media Mail" below "US Postage"	7.50	1.00
e.	"Parcel Post" below "US Postage"	7.50	1.00
f.	"Bound Printed Matter" below "US Postage"	7.50	1.00
g.	"BPM" below "US Postage"	7.50	1.00

Snowman CVPA8

Snowflakes CVPA9

Holly CVPA10

Dove CVPA11

Gingerbread Man and Candy CVPA12

Serpentine Die Cut 4½ at Left

2003, Dec.

1CVP10	CVPA8 37c black, blue & orange	3.00	1.50
a.	"First Class" below "US Postage"	2.00	1.00
b.	"Priority" below "US Postage"	8.00	1.00
c.	"Express" below "US Postage"	25.00	3.00
d.	"Media Mail" below "US Postage"	7.50	1.00

e. "Parcel Post" below "US Postage" 7.50 1.00
f. "Bound Printed Matter" below "US Postage" 7.50 1.00
g. "BPM" below "US Postage" 7.50 1.00

1CVP11 CVPA9 37c black, blue & orange 3.00 1.50
a. "First Class" below "US Postage" 2.00 1.00
b. "Priority" below "US Postage" 8.00 1.00
c. "Express" below "US Postage" 25.00 3.00
d. "Media Mail" below "US Postage" 7.50 1.00
e. "Parcel Post" below "US Postage" 7.50 1.00
f. "Bound Printed Matter" below "US Postage" 7.50 1.00
g. "BPM" below "US Postage" 7.50 1.00

1CVP12 CVPA10 37c black, blue & orange 3.00 1.50
a. "First Class" below "US Postage" 2.00 1.00
b. "Priority" below "US Postage" 8.00 1.00
c. "Express" below "US Postage" 25.00 3.00
d. "Media Mail" below "US Postage" 7.50 1.00
e. "Parcel Post" below "US Postage" 7.50 1.00
f. "Bound Printed Matter" below "US Postage" 7.50 1.00
g. "BPM" below "US Postage" 7.50 1.00

1CVP13 CVPA11 37c black, blue & orange 3.00 1.50
a. "First Class" below "US Postage" 2.00 1.00
b. "Priority" below "US Postage" 8.00 1.00
c. "Express" below "US Postage" 25.00 3.00
d. "Media Mail" below "US Postage" 7.50 1.00
e. "Parcel Post" below "US Postage" 7.50 1.00
f. "Bound Printed Matter" below "US Postage" 7.50 1.00
g. "BPM" below "US Postage" 7.50 1.00

1CVP14 CVPA12 37c black, blue & orange 3.00 1.50
a. "First Class" below "US Postage" 2.00 1.00
b. "Priority" below "US Postage" 8.00 1.00
c. "Express" below "US Postage" 25.00 3.00
d. "Media Mail" below "US Postage" 7.50 1.00
e. "Parcel Post" below "US Postage" 7.50 1.00
f. "Bound Printed Matter" below "US Postage" 7.50 1.00
g. "BPM" below "US Postage" 7.50 1.00
h. Strip of 5, #1CVP10-1CVP14 12.50

Mailbox
CVPA13

Serpentine Die Cut 6½ at Left

2004, Mar.

1CVP15 CVPA13 37c black, blue & orange 25.00 15.00
a. "First Class" below "US Postage" 25.00 15.00
b. "Priority" below "US Postage" — —
c. "Express" below "US Postage" — —
d. "Media Mail" below "US Postage" — —
e. "Parcel Post" below "US Postage" — —
f. "Bound Printed Matter" below "US Postage" — —
g. "BPM" below "US Postage" — —

Blank sheets of No. 1CVP15 were sent free of charge to those who responded to special Stamps.com promotions which offered a fixed amount of free postage as an enticement to new subscribers. The franking portion of the stamps could only be applied after subscribing.

George Washington
CVPA14

Thomas Jefferson
CVPA15

Abraham Lincoln
CVPA16

Theodore Roosevelt
CVPA17

John F. Kennedy
CVPA18

Serpentine Die Cut 6½ at Left

2004, Apr.

1CVP16 CVPA14 37c black, blue & orange 2.00 1.00
a. "First Class" below "US Postage" 1.10 .75
b. "Priority" below "US Postage" 5.00 2.50
c. "Express" below "US Postage" 20.00 5.00
d. "Media Mail" below "US Postage" 5.00 2.50
e. "Parcel Post" below "US Postage" 5.00 2.50
f. "Bound Printed Matter" below "US Postage" 5.00 2.50
g. "BPM" below "US Postage" 5.00 2.50

1CVP17 CVPA15 37c black, blue & orange 2.00 1.00
a. "First Class" below "US Postage" 1.10 .75
b. "Priority" below "US Postage" 5.00 2.50
c. "Express" below "US Postage" 20.00 5.00
d. "Media Mail" below "US Postage" 5.00 2.50
e. "Parcel Post" below "US Postage" 5.00 2.50
f. "Bound Printed Matter" below "US Postage" 5.00 2.50
g. "BPM" below "US Postage" 5.00 2.50

1CVP18 CVPA16 37c black, blue & orange 2.00 1.00
a. "First Class" below "US Postage" 1.10 .75
b. "Priority" below "US Postage" 5.00 2.50
c. "Express" below "US Postage" 20.00 5.00
d. "Media Mail" below "US Postage" 5.00 2.50
e. "Parcel Post" below "US Postage" 5.00 2.50
f. "Bound Printed Matter" below "US Postage" 5.00 2.50
g. "BPM" below "US Postage" 5.00 2.50

1CVP19 CVPA17 37c black, blue & orange 2.00 1.00
a. "First Class" below "US Postage" 1.10 .75
b. "Priority" below "US Postage" 5.00 2.50
c. "Express" below "US Postage" 20.00 5.00
d. "Media Mail" below "US Postage" 5.00 2.50
e. "Parcel Post" below "US Postage" 5.00 2.50
f. "Bound Printed Matter" below "US Postage" 5.00 2.50
g. "BPM" below "US Postage" 5.00 2.50

1CVP20 CVPA18 37c black, blue & orange 2.00 1.00
a. "First Class" below "US Postage" 1.10 .75
b. "Priority" below "US Postage" 5.00 2.50
c. "Express" below "US Postage" 20.00 5.00
d. "Media Mail" below "US Postage" 5.00 2.50
e. "Parcel Post" below "US Postage" 5.00 2.50
f. "Bound Printed Matter" below "US Postage" 5.00 2.50
g. "BPM" below "US Postage" 5.00 2.50
h. Horiz. strip of 5, #1CVP16-1CVP20 10.00

Flag and Star Type of 2002 Redrawn With Orange Stars and Text at Left

Serpentine Die Cut 6½ at Left

2004, Apr.

"Stamps.com" in Upper Case Letters

Identification Code Above Zip Code

1CVP21 CVPA1a 37c black, blue & orange 2.00 1.00
a. "First Class" below "US Postage" 1.35 .75
b. "Priority" below "US Postage" 6.00 2.50
c. "Express" below "US Postage" 22.50 5.00
d. "Media Mail" below "US Postage" 6.00 2.50
e. "Parcel Post" below "US Postage" 6.00 2.50
f. "Bound Printed Matter" below "US Postage" 6.00 2.50
g. "BPM" below "US Postage" 6.00 2.50

Bicycling
CVPA19

Running
CVPA20

Swimming
CVPA21

Boxing
CVPA22

Equestrian
CVPA23

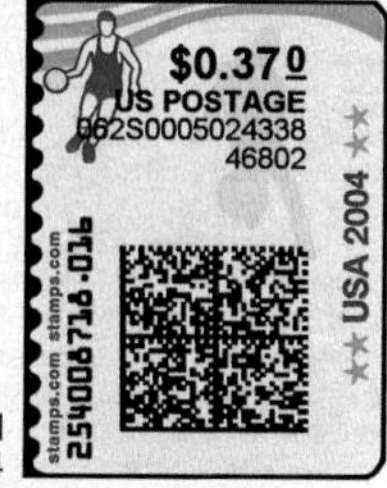

Basketball
CVPA24

Judo
CVPA25

Soccer
CVPA26

Gymnastics
CVPA27

Tennis
CVPA28

Serpentine Die Cut 6½ at Left

2004, Apr.

1CVP22 CVPA19 37c black, blue & orange 3.00 2.00
- *a.* "First Class" below "US Postage" 2.50 1.50
- *b.* "Priority" below "US Postage" 8.00 1.00
- *c.* "Express" below "US Postage" 25.00 3.00
- *d.* "Media Mail" below "US Postage" 7.50 1.00
- *e.* "Parcel Post" below "US Postage" 7.50 1.00
- *f.* "Bound Printed Matter" below "US Postage" 7.50 1.00
- *g.* "BPM" below "US Postage" 7.50 1.00

1CVP23 CVPA20 37c black, blue & orange 3.00 2.00
- *a.* "First Class" below "US Postage" 2.50 1.50
- *b.* "Priority" below "US Postage" 8.00 1.00
- *c.* "Express" below "US Postage" 25.00 3.00
- *d.* "Media Mail" below "US Postage" 7.50 1.00
- *e.* "Parcel Post" below "US Postage" 7.50 1.00
- *f.* "Bound Printed Matter" below "US Postage" 7.50 1.00
- *g.* "BPM" below "US Postage" 7.50 1.00

1CVP24 CVPA21 37c black, blue & orange 3.00 2.00
- *a.* "First Class" below "US Postage" 2.50 1.50
- *b.* "Priority" below "US Postage" 8.00 1.00
- *c.* "Express" below "US Postage" 25.00 3.00
- *d.* "Media Mail" below "US Postage" 7.50 1.00
- *e.* "Parcel Post" below "US Postage" 7.50 1.00
- *f.* "Bound Printed Matter" below "US Postage" 7.50 1.00
- *g.* "BPM" below "US Postage" 7.50 1.00

1CVP25 CVPA22 37c black, blue & orange 3.00 2.00
- *a.* "First Class" below "US Postage" 2.50 1.50
- *b.* "Priority" below "US Postage" 8.00 1.00
- *c.* "Express" below "US Postage" 25.00 3.00
- *d.* "Media Mail" below "US Postage" 7.50 1.00
- *e.* "Parcel Post" below "US Postage" 7.50 1.00
- *f.* "Bound Printed Matter" below "US Postage" 7.50 1.00
- *g.* "BPM" below "US Postage" 7.50 1.00

1CVP26 CVPA23 37c black, blue & orange 3.00 2.00
- *a.* "First Class" below "US Postage" 2.50 1.50
- *b.* "Priority" below "US Postage" 8.00 1.00
- *c.* "Express" below "US Postage" 25.00 3.00
- *d.* "Media Mail" below "US Postage" 7.50 1.00
- *e.* "Parcel Post" below "US Postage" 7.50 1.00
- *f.* "Bound Printed Matter" below "US Postage" 7.50 1.00
- *g.* "BPM" below "US Postage" 7.50 1.00
- *h.* Horiz. strip of 5, #1CVP22-1CVP26 15.00

1CVP27 CVPA24 37c black, blue & orange 3.00 2.00
- *a.* "First Class" below "US Postage" 2.50 1.50
- *b.* "Priority" below "US Postage" 8.00 1.00
- *c.* "Express" below "US Postage" 25.00 3.00
- *d.* "Media Mail" below "US Postage" 7.50 1.00
- *e.* "Parcel Post" below "US Postage" 7.50 1.00
- *f.* "Bound Printed Matter" below "US Postage" 7.50 1.00
- *g.* "BPM" below "US Postage" 7.50 1.00

1CVP28 CVPA25 37c black, blue & orange 3.00 2.00
- *a.* "First Class" below "US Postage" 2.50 1.50
- *b.* "Priority" below "US Postage" 8.00 1.00
- *c.* "Express" below "US Postage" 25.00 3.00
- *d.* "Media Mail" below "US Postage" 7.50 1.00
- *e.* "Parcel Post" below "US Postage" 7.50 1.00
- *f.* "Bound Printed Matter" below "US Postage" 7.50 1.00
- *g.* "BPM" below "US Postage" 7.50 1.00

1CVP29 CVPA26 37c black, blue & orange 3.00 2.00
- *a.* "First Class" below "US Postage" 2.50 1.50
- *b.* "Priority" below "US Postage" 8.00 1.00
- *c.* "Express" below "US Postage" 25.00 3.00
- *d.* "Media Mail" below "US Postage" 7.50 1.00
- *e.* "Parcel Post" below "US Postage" 7.50 1.00
- *f.* "Bound Printed Matter" below "US Postage" 7.50 1.00
- *g.* "BPM" below "US Postage" 7.50 1.00

1CVP30 CVPA27 37c black, blue & orange 3.00 2.00
- *a.* "First Class" below "US Postage" 2.50 1.50
- *b.* "Priority" below "US Postage" 8.00 1.00
- *c.* "Express" below "US Postage" 25.00 3.00
- *d.* "Media Mail" below "US Postage" 7.50 1.00
- *e.* "Parcel Post" below "US Postage" 7.50 1.00
- *f.* "Bound Printed Matter" below "US Postage" 7.50 1.00
- *g.* "BPM" below "US Postage" 7.50 1.00

1CVP31 CVPA28 37c black, blue & orange 3.00 2.00
- *a.* "First Class" below "US Postage" 2.50 1.50
- *b.* "Priority" below "US Postage" 8.00 1.00
- *c.* "Express" below "US Postage" 25.00 3.00
- *d.* "Media Mail" below "US Postage" 7.50 1.00
- *e.* "Parcel Post" below "US Postage" 7.50 1.00
- *f.* "Bound Printed Matter" below "US Postage" 7.50 1.00
- *g.* "BPM" below "US Postage" 7.50 1.00
- *h.* Horiz. strip of 5, #1CVP27-1CVP31 15.00

The item pictured above was produced by Stamps.com for a special promotional mailing of its own and was not made available unused to customers.

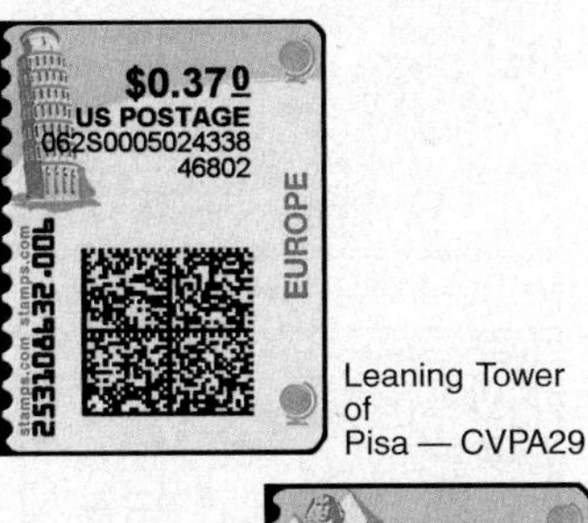

Leaning Tower of Pisa — CVPA29

Sphinx and Pyramids CVPA30

Sydney Opera House CVPA31

Mayan Pyramid CVPA32

Asian Temple CVPA33

Serpentine Die Cut 6½ at Left

2004, July

1CVP32 CVPA29 37c black, blue & orange 3.00 2.00
- *a.* "First Class" below "US Postage" 2.30 1.50
- *b.* "Priority" below "US Postage" 8.00 1.00
- *c.* "Express" below "US Postage" 25.00 3.00
- *d.* "Media Mail" below "US Postage" 7.50 1.00
- *e.* "Parcel Post" below "US Postage" 7.50 1.00
- *f.* "Bound Printed Matter" below "US Postage" 7.50 1.00
- *g.* "BPM" below "US Postage" 7.50 1.00

1CVP33 CVPA30 37c black, blue & orange 3.00 2.00
- *a.* "First Class" below "US Postage" 2.30 1.50
- *b.* "Priority" below "US Postage" 8.00 1.00
- *c.* "Express" below "US Postage" 25.00 3.00
- *d.* "Media Mail" below "US Postage" 7.50 1.00
- *e.* "Parcel Post" below "US Postage" 7.50 1.00
- *f.* "Bound Printed Matter" below "US Postage" 7.50 1.00
- *g.* "BPM" below "US Postage" 7.50 1.00

1CVP34 CVPA31 37c black, blue & orange 3.00 2.00
- *a.* "First Class" below "US Postage" 2.30 1.50
- *b.* "Priority" below "US Postage" 8.00 1.00
- *c.* "Express" below "US Postage" 25.00 3.00
- *d.* "Media Mail" below "US Postage" 7.50 1.00
- *e.* "Parcel Post" below "US Postage" 7.50 1.00
- *f.* "Bound Printed Matter" below "US Postage" 7.50 1.00
- *g.* "BPM" below "US Postage" 7.50 1.00

1CVP35 CVPA32 37c black, blue & orange 3.00 2.00
- *a.* "First Class" below "US Postage" 2.30 1.50
- *b.* "Priority" below "US Postage" 8.00 1.00
- *c.* "Express" below "US Postage" 25.00 3.00
- *d.* "Media Mail" below "US Postage" 7.50 1.00
- *e.* "Parcel Post" below "US Postage" 7.50 1.00
- *f.* "Bound Printed Matter" below "US Postage" 7.50 1.00
- *g.* "BPM" below "US Postage" 7.50 1.00

1CVP36 CVPA33 37c black, blue & orange 3.00 2.00
- *a.* "First Class" below "US Postage" 2.30 1.50
- *b.* "Priority" below "US Postage" 8.00 1.00
- *c.* "Express" below "US Postage" 25.00 3.00
- *d.* "Media Mail" below "US Postage" 7.50 1.00
- *e.* "Parcel Post" below "US Postage" 7.50 1.00
- *f.* "Bound Printed Matter" below "US Postage" 7.50 1.00
- *g.* "BPM" below "US Postage" 7.50 1.00
- *h.* Strip of 5, #1CVP32-1CVP36 15.00

Computer and Letters CVPA34

Serpentine Die Cut 6½ at Left

2005, Mar.

1CVP37 CVPA34 37c black, blue & orange 25.00 15.00
- *a.* "First Class" below "US Postage" 25.00 15.00
- *b.* "Priority" below "US Postage" — —
- *c.* "Express" below "US Postage" — —
- *d.* "Media Mail" below "US Postage" — —
- *e.* "Parcel Post" below "US Postage" — —
- *f.* "Bound Printed Matter" below "US Postage" — —
- *g.* "BPM" below "US Postage" — —

Blank sheets of No. 1CVP37 were sent free of charge to those who responded to special Stamps.com promotions which offered a fixed amount of free postage as an enticement to new subscribers. The franking portion of the stamps could only be applied after subscribing.

Logo CVPA35

2005, Aug. ***Die Cut Perf. 6½ at Left***

1CVP38 CVPA35 37c black, blue & orange 1.00 .30
- *a.* "Priority" below "US Postage" 8.00 1.00
- *b.* "Express" below "US Postage" 25.00 3.00
- *c.* "Media Mail" below "US Postage" 7.50 1.00
- *d.* "Parcel Post" below "US Postage" 7.50 1.00
- *e.* "BPM" below "US Postage" 7.50 1.00
- *f.* "Aerogramme" below "US Postage" 1.40 1.00
- *g.* "Intl Air Letter" below "US Postage" 1.25 1.00
- *h.* "Intl Eco Letter" (Economy Letter Mail) below "US Postage" 5.50 1.00
- *i.* "GXG" (Global Express Guaranteed) below "US Postage" 50.00 6.00
- *j.* "EMS" (Global Express Mail) below "US Postage" 32.50 4.00
- *k.* "GPM" (Global Priority Mail) below "US Postage" 8.00 1.00
- *l.* "Intl Air Parcel" (Air Parcel Post) below "US Postage" 26.00 3.00
- *m.* "Intl Eco Parcel" (Economy Parcel Post) below "US Postage" 32.50 4.00
- *n.* "M-Bag (Air)" below "US Postage" 35.00 5.00
- *o.* "M-Bag (Economy)" below "US Postage" 18.00 3.00
- *p.* "Mat for Blind" below "US Postage" 1.25 —

Values for lettered varieties on Nos. 1CVP38 are based on the prices set as the minimum values for each service classification in the software available at the time the stamps were issued. In mid-December 2005, the software was changed to allow for a 1c minimum value for any of these lettered varieties.

In 2006, No. 1CVP38 was made available on a coil roll. Value, $1.40.

Snowman — CVPA36

Candy Cane — CVPA37

Dove — CVPA38

Stylized Christmas Tree and Window — CVPA39

2005, Nov. ***Die Cut Perf. 6 at Right***

1CVP39 CVPA36 37c multi 1.60 .25
- *a.* "Priority" below "US Postage" 8.00 1.00
- *b.* "Express" below "US Postage" 25.00 3.00
- *c.* "Media Mail" below "US Postage" 7.50 1.00
- *d.* "Parcel Post" below "US Postage" 7.50 1.00
- *e.* "BPM" below "US Postage" 7.50 1.00
- *f.* "Aerogramme" below "US Postage" 1.40 1.00
- *g.* "Intl Air Letter" below "US Postage" 1.25 1.00
- *h.* "Intl Eco Letter" (Economy Letter Mail) below "US Postage" 5.50 1.00
- *i.* "GXG" (Global Express Guaranteed) below "US Postage" 50.00 6.00
- *j.* "EMS" (Global Express Mail) below "US Postage" 32.50 4.00
- *k.* "GPM" (Global Priority Mail) below "US Postage" 8.00 1.00
- *l.* "Intl Air Parcel" (Air Parcel Post) below "US Postage" 26.00 3.00
- *m.* "Intl Eco Parcel" (Economy Parcel Post) below "US Postage" 32.50 4.00
- *n.* "M-Bag (Air)" below "US Postage" 35.00 5.00
- *o.* "M-Bag (Economy)" below "US Postage" 18.00 3.00
- *p.* "Mat for Blind" below "US Postage" .25 —

1CVP40 CVPA37 37c multi 1.60 .25
- *a.* "Priority" below "US Postage" 8.00 1.00
- *b.* "Express" below "US Postage" 25.00 3.00
- *c.* "Media Mail" below "US Postage" 7.50 1.00
- *d.* "Parcel Post" below "US Postage" 7.50 1.00
- *e.* "BPM" below "US Postage" 7.50 1.00
- *f.* "Aerogramme" below "US Postage" 1.40 1.00
- *g.* "Intl Air Letter" below "US Postage" 1.25 1.00
- *h.* "Intl Eco Letter" (Economy Letter Mail) below "US Postage" 5.50 1.00
- *i.* "GXG" (Global Express Guaranteed) below "US Postage" 50.00 6.00
- *j.* "EMS" (Global Express Mail) below "US Postage" 32.50 4.00
- *k.* "GPM" (Global Priority Mail) below "US Postage" 8.00 1.00
- *l.* "Intl Air Parcel" (Air Parcel Post) below "US Postage" 26.00 3.00
- *m.* "Intl Eco Parcel" (Economy Parcel Post) below "US Postage" 32.50 4.00
- *n.* "M-Bag (Air)" below "US Postage" 35.00 5.00
- *o.* "M-Bag (Economy)" below "US Postage" 18.00 3.00
- *p.* "Mat for Blind" below "US Postage" .25 —

1CVP41 CVPA38 37c multi 1.60 .25
- *a.* "Priority" below "US Postage" 8.00 1.00
- *b.* "Express" below "US Postage" 25.00 3.00
- *c.* "Media Mail" below "US Postage" 7.50 1.00
- *d.* "Parcel Post" below "US Postage" 7.50 1.00
- *e.* "BPM" below "US Postage" 7.50 1.00
- *f.* "Aerogramme" below "US Postage" 1.40 1.00
- *g.* "Intl Air Letter" below "US Postage" 1.25 1.00
- *h.* "Intl Eco Letter" (Economy Letter Mail) below "US Postage" 5.50 1.00
- *i.* "GXG" (Global Express Guaranteed) below "US Postage" 50.00 6.00
- *j.* "EMS" (Global Express Mail) below "US Postage" 32.50 4.00
- *k.* "GPM" (Global Priority Mail) below "US Postage" 8.00 1.00
- *l.* "Intl Air Parcel" (Air Parcel Post) below "US Postage" 26.00 3.00
- *m.* "Intl Eco Parcel" (Economy Parcel Post) below "US Postage" 32.50 4.00
- *n.* "M-Bag (Air)" below "US Postage" 35.00 5.00
- *o.* "M-Bag (Economy)" below "US Postage" 18.00 3.00
- *p.* "Mat for Blind" below "US Postage" .25 —

1CVP42 CVPA39 37c multi 1.60 .25
- *a.* "Priority" below "US Postage" 8.00 1.00
- *b.* "Express" below "US Postage" 25.00 3.00
- *c.* "Media Mail" below "US Postage" 7.50 1.00
- *d.* "Parcel Post" below "US Postage" 7.50 1.00
- *e.* "BPM" below "US Postage" 7.50 1.00
- *f.* "Aerogramme" below "US Postage" 1.40 1.00
- *g.* "Intl Air Letter" below "US Postage" 1.25 1.00
- *h.* "Intl Eco Letter" (Economy Letter Mail) below "US Postage" 5.50 1.00
- *i.* "GXG" (Global Express Guaranteed) below "US Postage" 50.00 6.00
- *j.* "EMS" (Global Express Mail) below "US Postage" 32.50 4.00
- *k.* "GPM" (Global Priority Mail) below "US Postage" 8.00 1.00
- *l.* "Intl Air Parcel" (Air Parcel Post) below "US Postage" 26.00 3.00
- *m.* "Intl Eco Parcel" (Economy Parcel Post) below "US Postage" 32.50 4.00
- *n.* "M-Bag (Air)" below "US Postage" 35.00 5.00
- *o.* "M-Bag (Economy)" below "US Postage" 18.00 3.00
- *p.* "Mat for Blind" below "US Postage" .25 —
- *q.* Vert. strip, 2 each #1CVP39-1CVP42 6.00

Values for lettered varieties on Nos. 1CVP39-1CVP42 are based on the prices set as the minimum values for each service classification in the software available at the time the stamps were issued. In mid-December 2005, the software was changed to allow for a 1c minimum value for any of these lettered varieties.

Endicia.com

CVPA40

CVPA41

2005-06 ***Serpentine Die Cut 10¼***

1CVP43 CVPA40 24c black & bright rose 10.00 4.00
- *a.* 39c "First Class" under "US Postage" 2.00 .50
- *b.* 63c "Intl. Mail" under "US Postage" 3.25 2.50
- *c.* $4.05 "Priority Mail" under "US Postage" 12.00 2.50

Coil Stamps

Serpentine Die Cut 10½x10¼ on 2 Sides

1CVP44 CVPA41 24c black & pink 11.00 4.00
- *a.* 39c "First Class" under "US Postage" 2.25 .50
- *b.* 63c "Intl. Mail" under "US Postage" 3.50 2.50
- *c.* $4.05 "Priority Mail" under "US Postage" 12.50 2.50

Issued: Nos. 1CVP43, Nov. 2005; Nos. 1CVP44, Jan. 2006.

Originally, face values of 2c, 52c, 63c, 87c, $1.11, $1.35, $1.59, $1.83, $2.07, $2.31, $2.55, $2.79, $3.03, and $3.27 could also be printed on stamps with the "First class" inscription. Additionally, an 84c face value could be printed on stamps with the "Intl. Mail" inscription, and a $8.10 face value could be printed on stamps with the "Priority Mail" inscription. Values for Nos. 1CVP43-1CVP44 are for stamps with the listed face values and mail-class inscription. Values for stamps with lower or higher face values are correspondingly lower or higher.

In 2007, software changes permitted Nos. 1CVP43 and 1CVP44 to be printed with mail class inscriptions "Media Mail," "BPM," "Parcel Post," "Library Mail," and "Express Mail," as well as any face value for any mail-class inscription.

Nos. 1CVP43 and 1CVP44 printed after the software changes are inscribed "First Class" under "US Postage" and sell for considerably less than the values shown. Stamps printed before the software changes are inscribed "Postcard" under "US Postage," as shown in the illustrations.

Stamps.com

Flag and Mount Rushmore — CVPA42

Flag and Eagle — CVPA43

Flag and Statue of Liberty — CVPA44

Flag and Liberty Bell — CVPA45

2006, Mar. ***Die Cut Perf. 6 at Right***

1CVP51 CVPA42 39c multi .80 .25
1CVP52 CVPA43 39c multi .80 .25
1CVP53 CVPA44 39c multi .80 .25
1CVP54 CVPA45 39c multi .80 .25
- *a.* Vert. strip of 8, 2 each #1CVP51-1CVP54 8.00

Other service inscriptions with any possible face value can be printed on Nos. 1CVP51-1CVP54.

Stamps.com

Leaning Tower of Pisa — CVPA46

Taj Mahal — CVPA47

Eiffel Tower — CVPA48

Parthenon — CVPA49

2006 ***Die Cut Perf 6 at Right***

1CVP55 CVPA46 39c multi .80 .25
1CVP56 CVPA47 39c multi .80 .25
1CVP57 CVPA48 39c multi .80 .25
1CVP58 CVPA49 39c multi .80 .25
- *a.* Vert. strip, 2 each #1CVP55-1CVP58 8.00

With the introduction of the new software in December 2005, any stamp could have any denomination 1c and above, and any service classification.

Pitney Bowes Stamp Expressions

CVPA50

2006 ***Die Cut Perf. 6 Horiz.***

Inscribed "pitneybowes.com/se" at Right

1CVP59 CVPA50 39c black + label 1.35 .80

The stamp and label are separated by vertical roulettes. Users could create their own label images on the Pitney Bowes Stamp Expressions website (which required approval of the image from Pitney Bowes before it could be used), or download various pre-approved label images from the website into their personal computers. Stamps could be printed without label images. Stamps were printed on rolls of tagged thermal paper from a device that could be operated without a direct connection to the personal computer. See No. 1CVT1.

Stamps.com

CVPA51

Personalizable Images — CVPA52

2006, Sept. ***Die Cut Perf. 6 at Right***

1CVP60 CVPA51 39c multi 1.50 .95
  a. Numerals in denomination 2½mm high, thicker text 1.50 .95

Perf. Die Cut Perf. 6 at Top

1CVP61 CVPA52 39c multi 1.50 .95
  a. Numerals in denomination 2½mm high, thicker text 1.50 .95

Users could requisition sheets of Nos. 1CVP60 and 1CVP61 with images of their choice from Stamps.com at $4.99 per sheet of 24. Priority and Express service classifications could also be printed on Nos. 1CVP60-1CVP61 with any denomination. Stamps exist with slightly larger die cutting (60x30mm and 30x60mm) in both squared and rounded corners. The denomination type shown on Nos. 1CVP60-1CVP61 can be placed on label types CVPA36-CVPA39, CVPA42-CVPA49, CVPA53-CVPA60 and any later stamps.com labels of this size.

Numerals in denomination are 3mm tall on Nos. 1CVP60-1CVP61. Serial numbers on Nos. 1CPVP60-1CVP61 lack periods and have small bank-check style numerals.

Autumn Leaves — CVPA53

Pumpkins — CVPA54

Basket of Apples, Sheaf of Wheat, Falling Leaves and Pumpkins — CVPA55

Leaves and Carved Pumpkin — CVPA56

2006 ***Die Cut Perf. 6 at Right***

1CVP62 CVPA53 39c multi 1.25 .25
1CVP63 CVPA54 39c multi 1.25 .25
1CVP64 CVPA55 39c multi 1.25 .25
1CVP65 CVPA56 39c multi 1.25 .25
  a. Vert. strip, 2 each #1CVP62-1CVP65 10.00

See note after No. 1CVP58.

"Season's Greetings" — CVPA57

Christmas Trees — CVPA58

Snowman — CVPA59

Dove — CVPA60

2006 ***Die Cut Perf. 6 at Right***

1CVP66 CVPA57 39c multi 1.25 .25
1CVP67 CVPA58 39c multi 1.25 .25
1CVP68 CVPA59 39c multi 1.25 .25
1CVP69 CVPA60 39c multi 1.25 .25
  a. Vert. strip, 2 each #1CVP66-1CVP69 10.00

See note after No. 1CVP58.

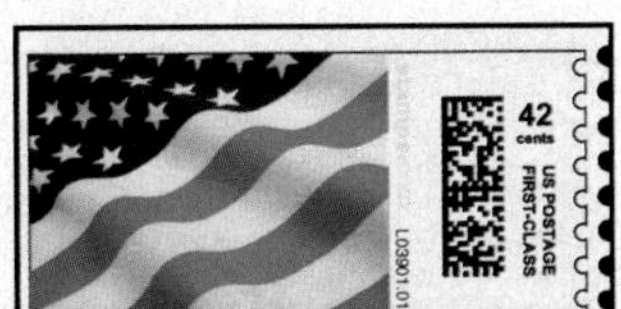

Flag — CVPA61

Statue of Liberty and Flag — CVPA62

Bald Eagle and Flag — CVPA63

Flag Painted on Building — CVPA64

2008 ***Die Cut Perf. 5½ at Right***

Serial Number With Period, Large Letters and Numerals

1CVP70 CVPA61 42c multi 1.25 .25
1CVP71 CVPA62 42c multi 1.25 .25
1CVP72 CVPA63 42c multi 1.25 .25
1CVP73 CVPA64 42c multi 1.25 .25

On Nos. 1CVP70-1CVP105, and perhaps on other stamps, placement of the stamp serial number and the stamps.com logo might differ on various printings of the label stock. Descriptive text outside the frame might also vary or not be present on these various printings.

Autumn — CVPA65

Designs: No. 1CVP74, Oak leaves. No. 1CVP75, Pumpkin patch. No. 1CVP76, Autumn reflection. No. 1CVP77, Pumpkins and gourds.

2008

Serial Number With Period, Large Letters and Numerals

1CVP74 CVPA65 42c multi 1.25 .25
1CVP75 CVPA65 42c multi 1.25 .25
1CVP76 CVPA65 42c multi 1.25 .25
1CVP77 CVPA65 42c multi 1.25 .25

Flowers — CVPA66

Designs: No. 1CVP78, Sunflowers. No. 1CVP79, Daisies. No. 1CVP80, Sunflower sky. No. 1CVP81, Treasure flowers.

2008

Serial Number With Period, Large Letters and Numerals

1CVP78 CVPA66 42c multi 1.25 .25
1CVP79 CVPA66 42c multi 1.25 .25
1CVP80 CVPA66 42c multi 1.25 .25
1CVP81 CVPA66 42c multi 1.25 .25

Endangered Animals — CVPA67

Designs: No. 1CVP82, Bengal tiger. No. 1CVP83, Hawksbill turtle. No. 1CVP84, Panda. No. 1CVP85, African rhino.

2008

Serial Number With Period, Large Letters and Numerals

1CVP82 CVPA67 42c multi 1.25 .25
1CVP83 CVPA67 42c multi 1.25 .25
1CVP84 CVPA67 42c multi 1.25 .25
1CVP85 CVPA67 42c multi 1.25 .25

Parks — CVPA68

Designs: No. 1CVP86, Grand Canyon National Park, Arizona. No. 1CVP87, Yosemite National Park, California. No. 1CVP88, Niagara Falls. No. 1CVP89, Arches National Park, Utah.

2008

Serial Number With Period, Large Letters and Numerals

1CVP86 CVPA68 42c multi 1.25 .25
1CVP87 CVPA68 42c multi 1.25 .25
1CVP88 CVPA68 42c multi 1.25 .25
1CVP89 CVPA68 42c multi 1.25 .25

City Skylines — CVPA69

Designs: No. 1CVP90, New York City. No. 1CVP91, St. Louis. No. 1CVP92, Chicago. No. 1CVP93, San Francisco.

2008

Serial Number With Period, Large Letters and Numerals

1CVP90 CVPA69 42c multi 1.25 .25
1CVP91 CVPA69 42c multi 1.25 .25
1CVP92 CVPA69 42c multi 1.25 .25
1CVP93 CVPA69 42c multi 1.25 .25

Presidential Memorials — CVPA70

Designs: No. 1CVP94, Washington Monument. No. 1CVP95, Lincoln Memorial. No. 1CVP96, Jefferson Memorial. No. 1CVP97, Mount Rushmore.

2008

Serial Number With Period, Large Letters and Numerals

1CVP94 CVPA70 42c multi 1.25 .25
1CVP95 CVPA70 42c multi 1.25 .25
1CVP96 CVPA70 42c multi 1.25 .25
1CVP97 CVPA70 42c multi 1.25 .25

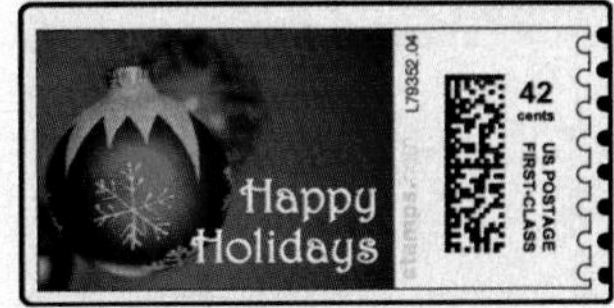

Christmas — CVPA71

Designs: No. 1CVP98, Ornament, "Happy Holidays." No. 1CVP99, Gingerbread men, "Season's Greetings." No. 1CVP100, Snowflake, "Happy Holidays." No. 1CVP101, Christmas tree, "Season's Greetings."

2008

Serial Number With Period, Large Letters and Numerals

Without Year or Text at Left

1CVP98 CVPA71 42c multi 1.25 .25
1CVP99 CVPA71 42c multi 1.25 .25
1CVP100 CVPA71 42c multi 1.25 .25
1CVP101 CVPA71 42c multi 1.25 .25

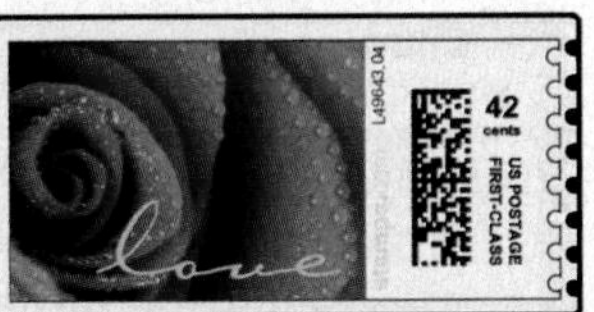

Love — CVPA72

"Love" and: No. 1CVP102, Rose. No. 1CVP103, Small hearts. No. 1CVP104, Large heart. No. 1CVP105, Hearts on curtain.

2009

Serial Number With Period, Large Letters and Numerals

Without Year or Text at Left

1CVP102 CVPA72 42c multi 1.25 .25
1CVP103 CVPA72 42c multi 1.25 .25
1CVP104 CVPA72 42c multi 1.25 .25
1CVP105 CVPA72 42c multi 1.25 .25

Wavy Lines
CVPA73

2009 ***Die Cut Perf 6½ at Right***

1CVP106 CVPA73 44c multi 1.25 .25

Endicia .com

Globe
CVPA74

2009 ***Serpentine Die Cut 10¼x10½***

1CVP107 CVPA74 44c orange & black 1.25 .25

Software allowed for six other inscriptions below "US Postage" (Priority Mail, Media Mail, Parcel Post, Library Mail, Express Mail and Intl Mail) and any face value for any mail-class inscription.

Stamps.com

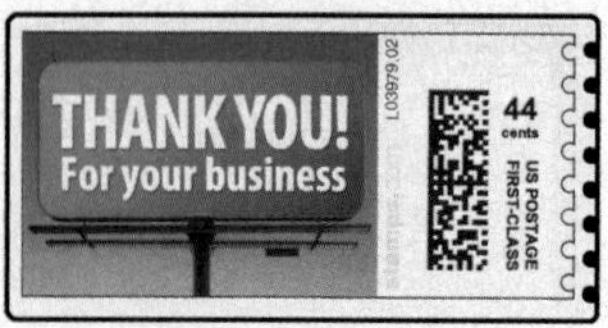

Thank You For Your Business — CVPA75

Text: No. 1CVP108, On billboard. No. 1CVP109, And building. No. 1CVP110, On red background. No. 1CVP111, And two people shaking hands.

2009 ***Die Cut Perf. 5½ at Right***

Serial Number With Period, Large Letters and Numerals

Without Year or Text at Left

1CVP108 CVPA75 44c multi 1.25 .25
1CVP109 CVPA75 44c multi 1.25 .25
1CVP110 CVPA75 44c multi 1.25 .25
1CVP111 CVPA75 44c multi 1.25 .25

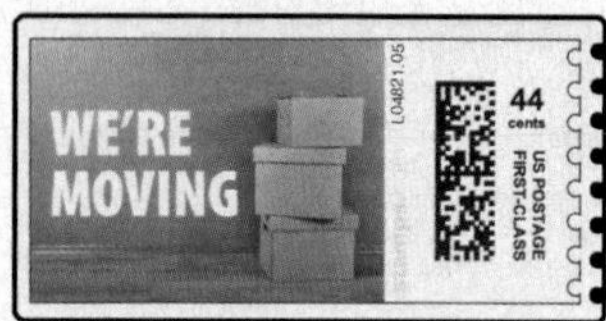

We're Moving — CVPA76

Text: No. 1CVP112, Stack of three boxes, green background. No. 1CVP113, Eleven boxes, orange background. No. 1CVP114, Four boxes, green background. No. 1CVP115, Four boxes, red background.

2009

Serial Number With Period, Large Letters and Numerals

Without Year or Text at Left

1CVP112 CVPA76 44c multi 1.25 .25
1CVP113 CVPA76 44c multi 1.25 .25
1CVP114 CVPA76 44c multi 1.25 .25
1CVP115 CVPA76 44c multi 1.25 .25

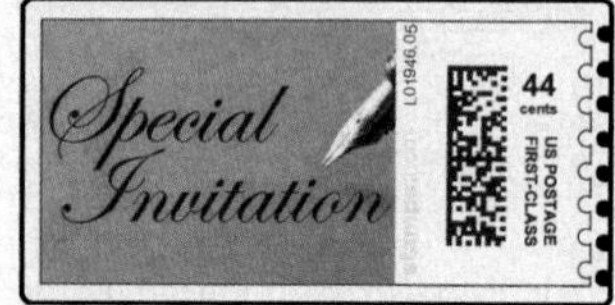

Special Invitation — CVPA77

Text: No. 1CVP116, And pen nib. No. 1CVP117, And circled "15" on calendar. No. 1CVP118, On card on envelope. No. 1CVP119, On wax seal.

2009

Serial Number With Period, Large Letters and Numerals

Without Year or Text at Left

1CVP116 CVPA77 44c multi 1.25 .25
1CVP117 CVPA77 44c multi 1.25 .25
1CVP118 CVPA77 44c multi 1.25 .25
1CVP119 CVPA77 44c multi 1.25 .25

US Flag — CVPA78

Flag: No. 1CVP120, On flagpole. No. 1CVP121, Behind Statue of Liberty. No. 1CVP122, Behind bald eagle. No. 1CVP123, On United States map.

2009

Serial Number With Period, Large Letters and Numerals

Without Year or Text at Left

1CVP120 CVPA78 44c multi 1.25 .25
1CVP121 CVPA78 44c multi 1.25 .25
1CVP122 CVPA78 44c multi 1.25 .25
1CVP123 CVPA78 44c multi 1.25 .25

Patriotic Symbols — CVPA79

Designs: No. 1CVP124, Statue of Liberty. No. 1CVP125, Flag. No. 1CVP126, Bald eagle.

2010 ***Die Cut Perf. 5½ Vert.***

1CVP124 CVPA79 44c multi 1.25 .25
1CVP125 CVPA79 44c multi 1.25 .25
1CVP126 CVPA79 44c multi 1.25 .25

Jewish Symbols — CVPA80

Designs: No. 1CVP127, Menorah. No. 1CVP125, Dreidel. No. 1CVP126, Star of David.

2010 ***Die Cut Perf. 5½ Vert.***

1CVP127 CVPA80 44c multi 1.25 .25
1CVP128 CVPA80 44c multi 1.25 .25
1CVP129 CVPA80 44c multi 1.25 .25

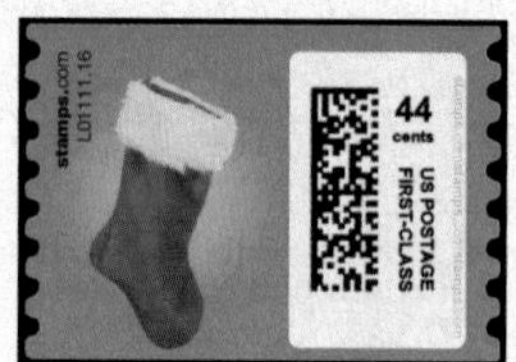

Christmas — CVPA81

Designs: No. 1CVP130, Christmas stocking. No. 1CVP131, Christmas tree. No. 1CVP132, Santa Claus.

2010 ***Die Cut Perf. 5½ Vert.***

1CVP130 CVPA81 44c multi 1.25 .25
1CVP131 CVPA81 44c multi 1.25 .25
1CVP132 CVPA81 44c multi 1.25 .25

Valentine's Day — CVPA82

Designs: No. 1CVP133, Hearts. No. 1CVP134, Rose. No. 1CVP135, Candy hearts.

2011 ***Die Cut Perf. 5½ Vert.***

1CVP133 CVPA82 44c multi 1.25 .25
1CVP134 CVPA82 44c multi 1.25 .25
1CVP135 CVPA82 44c multi 1.25 .25

Christian Symbols — CVPA83

Designs: No. 1CVP136, Cross. No. 1CVP137, Fish. No. 1CVP138, Rosary beads.

2011 ***Die Cut Perf. 5½ Vert.***

1CVP136 CVPA83 44c multi 1.25 .25
1CVP137 CVPA83 44c multi 1.25 .25
1CVP138 CVPA83 44c multi 1.25 .25

NON-PERSONALIZABLE POSTAGE

Stamps.com

These stamps, approved by the USPS, were non-personalizable stamps that could be purchased directly from private manufacturers, which shipped them to the customer. Other non-personalizable stamps have been created by a variety of companies, all sold at excessive amounts over face value as "collectibles". Such items are not listed here. Most items created that sold for excessive amounts over face value have vignettes that are licensed images, usually depicting sport team emblems or other sports-related themes, or celebrities.

Personalized postage stamps, first available in 2004, created by a variety of different companies, and heretofore listed with Scott numbers having a "2CVP" prefix, are no longer listed. Personalized stamps, though valid for postage, are not sold at any U.S. Postal Service post office. They are available only by on-line ordering through the company's website. Stamps are only available from the companies in full panes of 20. Each pane is sold at a significant premium above the stated face value to cover the costs of personalization, shipping and handling.

In recent years, there has been a steadily increasing number of private companies, either directly licensed by the USPS or created as spinoff companies of these licensees, creating distinctly different personalized stamps. None of the companies has issued fewer than seven stamps for each rate change, with one issuing as many as 42 different stamps. Because mailing rates set by the USPS are expected to change yearly, the collective output of distinctly different, rate-based stamps from these various companies likely will increase. There are no restrictions in place to prevent more firms from bringing personalized stamps to the marketplace, or to keep stamp producers from offering even more customer options. Some personalized stamps do not differ in any appreciable manner from some of the non-personalizable stamps sold as collectibles and not listed here.

CVPC1

CVPC2

2007, May ***Die Cut***

Self-Adhesive

3CVP1 CVPC1 2c black & gray .25 .25
a. Inscribed "US Postag" — —

Die Cut Perf. 5¼ at Right

3CVP2 CVPC2 2c multicolored .25 .25
a. Tagged *1.40 1.40*

2008 ***Die Cut***

3CVP3 CVPC1 1c black & gray .25 .25

No. 3CVP1 was printed in sheets of 40 stamps. Stamps with serial numbers ending in "06" are No. 3CVP1a. Sheets were sold for face value plus a shipping charge and were obtainable through the stamps.com website.

No. 3CVP2 was printed in sheets of 20. Full sheets were given free of charge to first-time stamps.com customers, but the full sheets were available for sale to other customers at face value plus a shipping charge through the stamps.com website.

CARRIERS' STAMPS

GENERAL ISSUE CARRIER STAMPS

Issued by the U.S. Government to facilitate payment of fees for delivering and collecting letters.

Franklin
OC1

Eagle
OC2

1851 **Engr.** **Unwmk.** ***Imperf.***

LO1 OC1 (1c) dull blue, *rose* 7,000. *8,000.*

LO2 OC2 1c blue (shades) 50.00 *80.00*

1875

Franklin Reprints

Imperf

LO3 OC1 (1c) blue, *rose* 50.

Perf. 12

LO4 OC1 (1c) blue *16,000.*

No. LO4 is valued in the grade of average to fine.

Eagle Reprints

Imperf.

LO5 OC2 1c blue 25.

Perf. 12

LO6 OC2 1c blue 175.

Reprints of the Franklin Carrier are printed in dark blue, instead of the dull blue or deep blue of the originals. Two reprintings of 10,000 each were made in 1875 on the same rose paper as the originals. A third reprinting of 5,000 in 1881 is on soft wove paper.

The first two reprintings of 10,000 each of the Eagle carrier are on hard white paper, ungummed and sometimes perforated. A third reprinting of 10,000 stamps in 1881 is on soft wove paper. Originals are on yellowish paper with brown gum.

No. LO6 is valued with the perfs cutting slightly into the design.

CITY CARRIER DEPARTMENT STAMPS

Issued by officials or employees of the U.S. Government for the purpose of securing or indicating payment of carriers' fees.

All are imperforate.

Baltimore, Md.

C1

1850-55 **Typo.**

Settings of 10 (2x5) varieties

1LB1 C1 1c red, *bluish* 180. 160.
1LB2 C1 1c blue, *bluish* 200. 150.
a. Bluish laid paper — —
1LB3 C1 1c blue 160. 100.
a. Laid paper 200. 150.
b. Block of 14 containing three tete-beche gutter pairs (unique) *4,000.*
1LB4 C1 1c green — 1,000.
1LB5 C1 1c red 2,250. 1,750.

C2

1856 **Typo.**

1LB6 C2 1c blue (shades) 130. 90.
1LB7 C2 1c red (shades) 130. 90.

C3

Plate of 10 (2x5); 10 Varieties

The sheet consisted of at least four panes of 10 placed horizontally, the two center panes tete beche. This makes possible five horizontal tete beche gutter pairs.

1857

1LB8 C3 1c black (shades) 65. 50.
a. "SENT" 100. 75.
b. Short rays 100. 75.
1LB9 C3 1c red 100. 90.
a. "SENT" 140. 110.
b. Short rays 140. 110.
c. As "b," double impression *800.*

Boston, Mass.

C6

Several Varieties

1849-50 **Pelure Paper** **Typeset**

3LB1 C6 1c blue 375. 180.
a. Wrong ornament at left *400.*

C7

1851

Wove Paper Colored Through

3LB2 C7 1c blue (shades), *slate* 190. 100.

Charleston, S. C.

Honour's City Express

C8

1849 **Typo.**

Wove Paper Colored Through

4LB1 C8 2c blk, *brn rose* *10,000.*
Cut to shape *4,000.* *4,000.*
4LB2 C8 2c blk, *yel,* cut to shape —

No. 4LB1 unused is a unique uncanceled stamp on piece. The used cut-to-shape stamp is also unique. In addition two covers exist bearing No. 4LB1.

No. 4LB2 unused (uncanceled) off cover is unique; three known on cover.

See the Scott U.S. Specialized Catalogue.

4LB2A C8 2c blk, *bl gray,* on cover, cut to shape —

No. 4LB2A is unique.

C10

1854 **Wove Paper** **Typeset**

4LB3 C10 2c black *1,500.*

C11

Several Varieties

1849-50

Wove Paper Colored Through

4LB5 C11 2c black, *bluish,* pelure *750.* *500.*
a. "Ceuts" *5,750.*
4LB7 C11 2c black, *yellow* *750.* *1,000.*
a. "Cnnts," ms. tied on cover *14,500.*

No. 4LB5a is unique. It is without gum and is valued thus. No. 4LB7a also is unique.

C13

C14

C15

Several varieties of each type

1851-58 **Typeset**

Wove Paper Colored Through

4LB8 C13 2c black, *bluish* 350. 175.
a. Period after "PAID" 500. 250.
b. "Cens" 700. *900.*
c. "Conours" and "Bents" —

The No. 4LB8 with No. 2 combination cover is unique. It is a cover front only and is valued thus.

4LB9 C13 2c black, *bluish,* pelure *850.* *950.*
4LB10 C13 2c black, *pink,* pelure, on cover *7,000.*
4LB11 C14 (2c) black, *bluish* — *375.*
4LB12 C14 (2c) black, *bluish,* pelure — —
4LB13 C15 (2c) black, *bluish* ('58) 750. 400.
a. Comma after "PAID" *1,100.*
b. No period after "Post" *1,400.*

Kingman's City Post

C16

C17

Several varieties of each

1851(?)-58(?) **Typeset**

Wove Paper Colored Through

4LB14 C16 2c black, *bluish* *1,400.* *900.*
a. "Kingman's" erased *5,000.*
4LB15 C17 2c black, *bluish* *800.* *800.*
a. "Kingman's" erased, on cover with 3c #11, tied by pen cancel (unique) *4,500.*

Martin's City Post

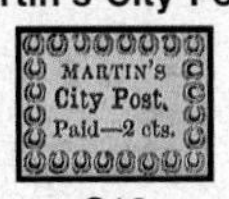

C18

Several varieties

1858 **Typeset**

Wove Paper Colored Through

4LB16 C18 2c black, *bluish* *8,000.*

Beckman's City Post

Same as C19, but inscribed "Beckmann's City Post."

1860

4LB17 C19 2c black, on cover —

No. 4LB17 is unique.

Steinmeyer's City Post

C19

C20

Several varieties of Type C19

Type C20 printed from plate of 10 (2x5) varieties

1859 **Typeset**

Wove Paper Colored Through

4LB18 C19 2c black, *bluish* *21,000.*
4LB19 C20 2c black, *bluish* *4,500.* —
4LB20 C20 2c black, *pink* *200.* —
4LB21 C20 2c black, *yellow* 200.

Cincinnati, Ohio

Williams' City Post

C20a

1854 **Wove Paper** **Litho.**

9LB1 C20a 2c brown — *4,000.*

Cleveland, Ohio

Bishop's City Post

C20b

C20c

1854 **Wove Paper** **Litho.**

10LB1 C20b blue *5,000.* *4,000.*

Vertically Laid Paper

10LB2 C20c 2c black, *bluish* *4,000.* *6,000.*

No. 10LB2 unused is unique. It is cut in at bottom and without gum, and is valued thus.

Louisville, Ky.

Wharton's U.S.P.O. Despatch

C21

1857 **Lithographed**

5LB1 C21 (2c) bluish green (shades) 125.

Brown & McGill's U. S. P. O. Despatch

C22

1858, Nov.-1860 **Lithographed**

5LB2 C22 (2c) blue (shades) 250. *750.*

1858, Feb.-Aug.

5LB3 C22 (2c) black *4,500.* *15,000.*
On cover, not tied, with 3c #26 *17,500.*

The value for No. 5LB3 used refers to the finer of the two known used (canceled) examples; it is extremely fine and on a piece with a 3c #26.

New York, N. Y.

United States City Despatch Post

C23

Wove Paper Colored Through

1842 **Engr.**

6LB1 C23 3c black, *grayish* *2,000.*

Used examples are Carriers' stamps only when canceled with the regular government cancellation "U.S." in octagonal frame (see illustration), "U.S.CITY DESPATCH POST," or New York circular postmark.

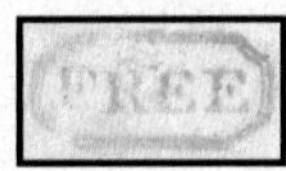

When canceled "FREE" in frame they were used as local stamps. See No. 40L1 in the Scott Specialized Catalogue of United States Stamps.

C24

Wove Paper (unsurfaced) Colored Through

1842-45

6LB2 C24 3c black, *rosy buff* *5,000.*
6LB3 C24 3c black, *light blue* *1,500.* 750.
6LB4 C24 3c black, *green* *11,500.*

Some authorities consider No. 6LB2 to be an essay, and No. 6LB4 a color changeling. No. 6LB2 unused is valued without gum.

Glazed Paper, Surface Colored

6LB5 C24 3c black, *blue green* (shades) 200. 175.
a. Double impression *1,500.*
b. 3c black, *blue* 650. *300.*
c. As "b," double impression *850.*
d. 3c black, *green* 1,000. *750.*
black, *apple green* *2,000.*
e. As "d," double impression —
6LB6 C24 3c black, *pink,* on cover front *14,500.*

No. 6LB6 is unique.

No. 6LB5 Surcharged in Red — C25

1846

6LB7 C25 2c on 3c black, *bluish grn,* on cover *14,000.*
On cover, not tied, with certificate *70,000.*

The City Despatch 2c red is listed in the Scott U.S. Specialized Catalogue as a Local stamp.

U.S. MAIL

C27

1849 **Typo.**

Wove Paper, Colored Through

6LB9	C27	1c black, *rose*	100.	100.

1849-50

Glazed Surface Paper

6LB10	C27	1c black, *yellow*	100.	100.
6LB11	C27	1c black, *buff*	100.	100.
a.		Pair, one stamp sideways	*2,850.*	

Philadelphia, Pa.

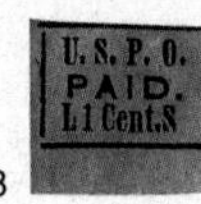

C28

Several Varieties

Thick Wove Paper Colored Through

1849-50 **Typeset**

7LB1	C28	1c black, *rose* (with "L P")	450.	
7LB2	C28	1c black, *rose* (with "S")	*3,000.*	
7LB3	C28	1c black, *rose* (with "H")	275.	
7LB4	C28	1c black, *rose* (with "L S")	400.	*500.*
7LB5	C28	1c black, *rose* (with "J J")		*7,500.*

The unique used No. 7LB5 is an uncanceled stamp on a cover front.

C29

Several Varieties

7LB6	C29	1c black, *rose*	300.	250.
7LB7	C29	1c black, *blue*, glazed	*1,000.*	
7LB8	C29	1c blk, *ver*, glazed	*700.*	
7LB9	C29	1c blk, *yel*, glazed	*2,750.*	*2,250.*

Cancellations on Nos. 7LB1-7LB9: Normally these stamps were left uncanceled on the letter, but occasionally were accidentally tied by the Philadelphia town postmark which was normally struck in blue ink.

A 1c black on buff (unglazed) of type C29 is believed to be a color changeling.

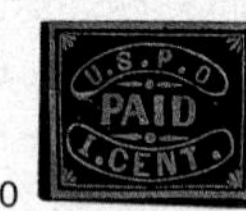

C30

1850-52 **Litho.**

7LB11	C30	1c gold, *black*, glazed	175.	110.
7LB12	C30	1c blue	400.	275.
7LB13	C30	1c black	*750.*	*550.*

25 varieties of C30.

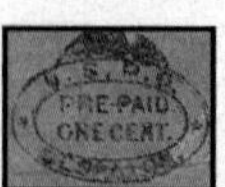

C31

Handstamped

7LB14	C31	1c blue, *buff*	3,250.	

1855(?)

7LB16	C31	1c black		*5,000.*

C32

1856(?) **Handstamped**

7LB18	C32	1c black	*1,250.*	*2,000.*

P. O. PAID 1 Cent. P. O. PAID 1 Cent.

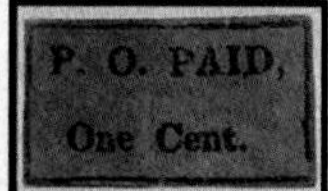

Labels of these designs are believed by most specialists not to be carrier stamps. Those seen are uncanceled, either off cover or affixed to stampless covers of the early 1850s. Some students believe they should be given carrier status.

St. Louis, Mo.

C36

C37

Illustrations enlarged to show details of the two types (note upper corners especially). Sizes of actual designs are 17 1/2x22mm.

1849 **White Wove Paper** **Litho.**

Two Types

8LB1	C36	2c black	*7,000.*	*3,000.*
8LB2	C37	2c black	*6,000.*	—

Cancellation on Nos. 8LB1-8LB2: Black town.

C38

1857 **Litho.**

8LB3	C38	2c blue		*22,500.*

The used example off cover is unique. Five covers are recorded.

Cancellations on No. 8LB3: Black boxed "1ct," "Paid" in arc, black pen.

STAMPED ENVELOPES & WRAPPERS

VALUES

Unless otherwise noted, values are for cut squares in a grade of very fine.

Very fine cut squares will have the design well centered within moderately large margins. Precanceled cut squares must include the entire precancellation.

Values for unused entires are for those without printed or manuscript address. Values for letter sheets are for folded entires. Unfolded examples sell for more. A "full corner" includes back and side flaps and commands a premium.

Entire envelopes and wrappers are listed in the Scott U.S. Specialized Catalogue.

Wrappers are listed with envelopes of corresponding designs, and indicated by prefix letter "W" instead of "U."

An ALBINO impression is where two or more envelope blanks are fed into the printing press. The one adjacent to the printing die receives the color and the embossing, while the others are embossed only. Albinos are printing errors and are sometimes worth more than normal, inked impressions. Because of the nature of the printing process, many albinos were produced, and most collectors will not pay much, or any, premium for most of them. Albinos of earlier issues, canceled while current, are scarce.

The papers of these issues vary greatly in texture, and in color from yellowish to bluish white and from amber to dark buff.

"+" Some authorities claim that Nos. U37, U48, U49, U110, U124, U125, U130, U133A, U137A, U137B, U137C, W138, U145, U162, U178A, U185, U220, U285, U286, U298, U299, UO3, UO32, UO38, UO45 and UO45A (each with "+" before number) were not regularly issued and are not known to have been used.

U1

"THREE" in short label with curved ends; 13mm wide at top. Twelve varieties.

Washington — U2

"THREE" in short label with straight ends; 15½mm wide at top. Three varieties.

U3

"THREE" in short label with octagonal ends. Two varieties.

U4

"THREE" in wide label with straight ends; 20mm wide at top.

U5

"THREE" in medium wide label with curved ends; 14½mm wide at top. Ten varieties. A sub-variety shows curved lines at either end of label omitted; both T's have longer cross stroke; R is smaller (20 varieties).

U6

Four varieties.

U7

"TEN" in short label; 15½mm wide at top.

U8

"TEN" in wide label; 20mm wide at top.

1853-55

On Diagonally Laid Paper (Early printings of No. U1 on Horizontally Laid Paper)

U1	U1	3c red	350.00	35.00
U2	U1	3c red, *buff*	90.00	30.00
U3	U2	3c red	950.00	50.00
U4	U2	3c red, *buff*	425.00	45.00
U5	U3	3c red ('54)	5,750.	500.00
U6	U3	3c red, *buff* ('54)	4,250.	100.00
U7	U4	3c red	5,000.	150.00
U8	U4	3c red, *buff*	*8,250.*	175.00
U9	U5	3c red ('54)	40.00	4.00
U10	U5	3c red, *buff* ('54)	20.00	4.00
U11	U6	6c red	300.00	90.00
U12	U6	6c red, *buff*	145.00	90.00
U13	U6	6c green	260.00	150.00
U14	U6	6c green, *buff*	200.00	125.00
U15	U7	10c green ('55)	425.00	100.00
U16	U7	10c green, *buff* ('55)	175.00	90.00
a.		10c pale green, *buff*	135.00	70.00
U17	U8	10c green ('55)	375.00	140.00
a.		10c pale green	275.00	125.00
U18	U8	10c green, *buff* ('55)	375.00	100.00
a.		10c pale green, *buff*	350.00	100.00

Nos. U9, U10, U11, U12, U13, U14, U17, and U18 have been reprinted on white and buff papers, wove or vertically laid, and are not known entire. The originals are on diagonally laid paper. Value, set of 8 reprints on laid, $225. Reprints on wove sell for more.

The first printings of Nos. U1, U2, U3, U4 and U7 have G.F. Nesbitt crests printed on the envelope flaps. These sell for a premium. Such examples of Nos. U1-U4 with 1853 year-dated cancels sell for a very large premium.

No. U1 with watermark having a space between lines and on horizontally laid paper sells for a substantial premium.

U9

Period after "POSTAGE." (Eleven varieties.)

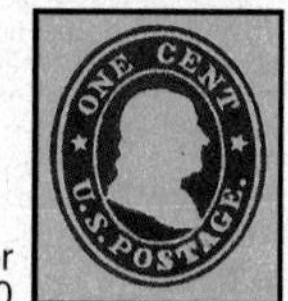

Franklin, Period after "POSTAGE." — U10

Bust touches inner frame-line at front and back.

No period after "POSTAGE" — U11

No period after "POSTAGE." (Two varieties.)

Washington — U12

Nine varieties of type U12.

Envelopes are on diagonally laid paper.

Wrappers on vertically or horizontally laid paper, or on unwatermarked wove paper (Nos. U21A, W22, W25)

1860-61

W18B	U9	1c blue ('61)	*5,500.*	
U19	U9	1c blue, *buff*	35.00	12.50
W20	U9	1c bl, *buff* ('61)	65.00	50.00
W21	U9	1c bl, *man* ('61)	55.00	45.00
U21A	U9	1c bl, *org*		*350.00*
W22	U9	1c bl, *org* ('61)	*3,500.*	
U23	U10	1c bl, *org*	625.00	350.00
U24	U11	1c bl, *amb*	350.00	110.00
W25	U11	1c bl, *man* ('61)	*7,000.*	*1,750.*
U26	U12	3c red	27.50	17.50
U27	U12	3c red, *buff*	22.50	12.50

U28	U12+U9	3c +1c red & bl	250.00	225.00
U29	U12+U9	3c +1c red & bl, *buff*	250.00	250.00
U30	U12	6c red	2,500.	1,500.
U31	U12	6c red, *buff*	3,500.	1,450.
U32	U12	10c green	1,250.	450.00
U33	U12	10c green, *buff*	1,450.	400.00

Nos. U26, U27, U30 to U33 have been reprinted on the same vertically laid paper as the reprints of the 1853-55 issue, and are not known entire. Value, Nos. U26-U27, $75 each; Nos. U30-U33, $75 each.

U13

U14

U15

Washington — U16

Envelopes are on diagonally laid paper.

U36 and U45 come on vertically or horizontally laid paper.

1861

U34	U13	3c pink	27.50	5.00
U35	U13	3c pink, *buff*	32.50	6.00
U36	U13	3c pink, *blue* (Letter Sheet)	70.00	70.00
+U37	U13	3c pink, *orange*	*4,250.*	
U38	U14	6c pink	100.00	80.00
U39	U14	6c pink, *buff*	60.00	60.00
U40	U15	10c yellow green	40.00	30.00
a.		10c blue green	40.00	30.00
U41	U15	10c yel grn, *buff*	40.00	30.00
a.		10c blue green, *buff*	40.00	30.00
U42	U16	12c red & brn, *buff*	180.00	180.00
a.		12c lake & brown, *buff*	*1,250.*	
U43	U16	20c red & bl, *buff*	250.00	225.00
U44	U16	24c red & grn, *buff*	210.00	210.00
a.		24c lake & green, *salmon*	260.00	225.00
U45	U16	40c blk & red, *buff*	300.00	400.00

Nos. U38 and U39 have been reprinted on the same papers as the reprints of the 1853-55 issue, and are not known entire. Value, set of 2 reprints, $60.

Jackson — U17

"U.S. POSTAGE" above. Downstroke and tail of "2" unite near the point (seven varieties).

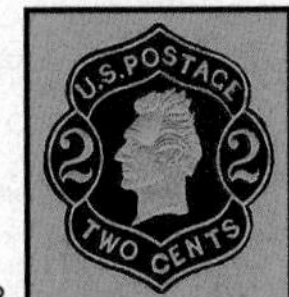
Jackson — U18

"U.S. POSTAGE" above. The downstroke and tail of the "2" touch but do not merge.

Jackson — U19

"U.S. POST" above. Stamp 24-25mm wide (Sixteen varieties).

Jackson — U20

"U.S. POST" above. Stamp 25½-26¼mm wide. (Twenty-five varieties.)
Envelopes are on diagonally laid paper. Wrappers on vertically or horizontally laid paper.

Envelopes are on diagonally laid paper.
Wrappers on vertically or horizontally laid paper.

1863-64

U46	U17	2c black, *buff*	50.00	24.00
W47	U17	2c black, *dark manila*	90.00	65.00
+U48	U18	2c black, *buff*	*2,250.*	
+U49	U18	2c black, *orange*	1,900.	
U50	U19	2c black, *buff* ('64)	17.50	11.00
W51	U19	2c black, *buff* ('64)	450.00	275.00
U52	U19	2c black, *orange* ('64)	20.00	11.00
W53	U19	2c black, *dark manila* ('64)	47.50	40.00
U54	U20	2c black, *buff* ('64)	17.50	9.50
W55	U20	2c black, *buff* ('64)	95.00	65.00
U56	U20	2c black, *orange* ('64)	22.50	10.00
W57	U20	2c black, *light manila* ('64)	22.50	14.00

Washington — U21

79 varieties for Nos. U58-U61; 2 varieties for Nos. U63-U65.

Washington U22

1864-65

U58	U21	3c pink	10.00	1.60
U59	U21	3c pink, *buff*	10.00	1.25
U60	U21	3c brown ('65)	65.00	40.00
U61	U21	3c brown, *buff* ('65)	50.00	30.00
U62	U21	6c pink	90.00	29.00
U63	U21	6c pink, *buff*	45.00	27.50
U64	U21	6c purple ('65)	55.00	26.00
U65	U21	6c purple, *buff* ('65)	45.00	20.00
U66	U22	9c lemon, *buff* ('65)	375.00	250.00
U67	U22	9c orange, *buff* ('65)	125.00	90.00
a.		9c orange yellow, *buff*	125.00	90.00
U68	U22	12c brown, *buff* ('65)	275.00	275.00
U69	U22	12c red brown, *buff* ('65)	125.00	55.00
U70	U22	18c red, *buff* ('65)	80.00	95.00
U71	U22	24c blue, *buff* ('65)	80.00	95.00
U72	U22	30c green, *buff* ('65)	100.00	80.00
a.		30c yellow green, *buff*	95.00	80.00
U73	U22	40c rose, *buff* ('65)	100.00	*250.00*

Printed by George H. Reay, Brooklyn, N. Y.

The engravings in this issue are finely executed.

Franklin — U23

Bust points to the end of the "N" of "ONE."

Jackson — U24

Bust narrow at back. Small, thick figures of value.

Washington — U25

Queue projects below bust.

Lincoln — U26

Neck very long at the back.

Stanton — U27

Bust pointed at the back; figures "7" are normal.

Jefferson — U28

Queue forms straight line with the bust.

Clay — U29

Ear partly concealed by hair, mouth large, chin prominent.

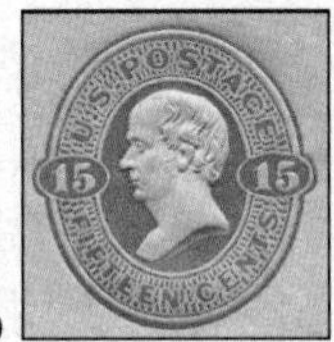
Webster — U30

Has side whiskers.

Scott — U31

Straggling locks of hair at top of head; ornaments around the inner oval end in squares.

Hamilton — U32

Back of bust very narrow, chin almost straight; labels containing figures of value are exactly parallel.

Perry — U33

Front of bust very narrow and pointed; inner lines of shields project very slightly beyond the oval.

1870-71

No.	Design	Denom.	Description	Unused	Used
U74	U23	1c	blue	37.50	30.00
a.		1c	ultramarine	65.00	35.00
U75	U23	1c	blue, *amber*	30.00	27.50
a.		1c	ultramarine, *amber*	62.50	30.00
U76	U23	1c	blue, *orange*	17.00	15.00
W77	U23	1c	blue, *manila*	37.50	35.00
U78	U24	2c	brown	35.00	16.00
U79	U24	2c	brown, *amber*	17.50	10.00
U80	U24	2c	brown, *orange*	10.00	6.50
W81	U24	2c	brown, *manila*	25.00	20.00
U82	U25	3c	green	7.00	1.00
a.		3c	brown (error), entire	*8,500.*	
U83	U25	3c	green, *amber*	6.00	2.00
U84	U25	3c	green, *cream*	8.00	4.50
U85	U26	6c	dark red	25.00	16.00
a.		6c	vermilion	25.00	16.00
U86	U26	6c	dark red, *amber*	37.50	20.00
a.		6c	vermilion, *amber*	37.50	20.00
U87	U26	6c	dark red, *cream*	37.50	25.00
a.		6c	vermilion, *cream*	32.50	20.00
U88	U27	7c	vermilion, *amber* ('71)	55.00	175.00
U89	U28	10c	olive black	800.00	900.00
U90	U28	10c	olive black, *amber*	800.00	800.00
U91	U28	10c	brown	82.50	70.00
U92	U28	10c	brown, *amber*	85.00	52.50
a.		10c	dark brown, *amber*	85.00	75.00
U93	U29	12c	plum	100.00	82.50
U94	U29	12c	plum, *amber*	110.00	100.00
U95	U29	12c	plum, *cream*	225.00	200.00
U96	U30	15c	red orange	75.00	75.00
a.		15c	orange	75.00	
U97	U30	15c	red orange, *amber*	160.00	275.00
a.		15c	orange, *amber*	170.00	
U98	U30	15c	red orange, *cream*	325.00	375.00
a.		15c	orange, *cream*	325.00	
U99	U31	24c	purple	125.00	125.00
U100	U31	24c	purple, *amber*	200.00	300.00
U101	U31	24c	purple, *cream*	275.00	450.00
U102	U32	30c	black	65.00	120.00
U103	U32	30c	black, *amber*	250.00	450.00
U104	U32	30c	black, *cream*	190.00	450.00
U105	U33	90c	carmine	140.00	300.00
U106	U33	90c	carmine, *amber*	350.00	900.00
U107	U33	90c	carmine, *cream*	175.00	*2,250.*

Printed by Plimpton Manufacturing Co.

The profiles in this issue are inferior to the fine engraving of the Reay issue.

U34

Bust forms an angle at the back near the frame. Lettering poorly executed. Distinct circle in "O" of "Postage."

U35

Lower part of bust points to the end of the "E" in "ONE." Head inclined downward.

U36

Bust narrow at back. Thin numerals. Head of "P" narrow. Bust broad at front, ending in sharp corners.

U37

Bust broad. Figures of value in long ovals.

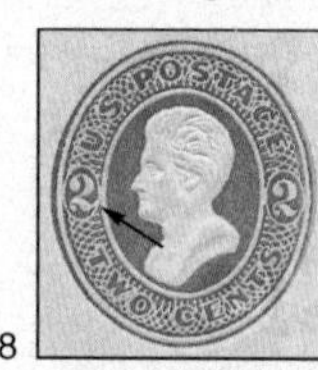

U38

Similar to U37 but the figure "2" at the left touches the oval.

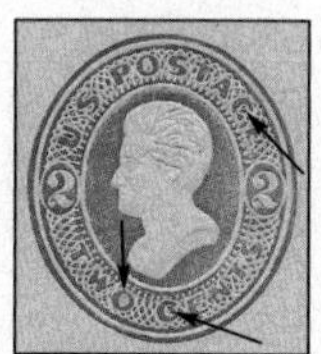

U39

Similar to U37 but the "O" of "TWO" has the center netted instead of plain and the "G" of "POSTAGE" and the "C" of "CENTS" have diagonal crossline.

U40

Bust broad: numerals in ovals short and thick.

U41

Similar to U40 but the ovals containing the numerals are much heavier. A diagonal line runs from the upper part of the "U" to the white frame-line.

U42

Similar to U40 but the middle stroke of "N" in "CENTS" is as thin as the vertical strokes.

U43

Bottom of bust cut almost semi-circularly.

U44

Thin lettering, long thin figures of value.

U45

Thick lettering, well-formed figures of value, queue does not project below bust.

U46

Top of head egg-shaped; knot of queue well marked and projects triangularly.

Taylor — U47

Die 1

Die 2

Die 1: Figures of value with thick, curved tops.

Die 2: Figures of value with long, thin tops.

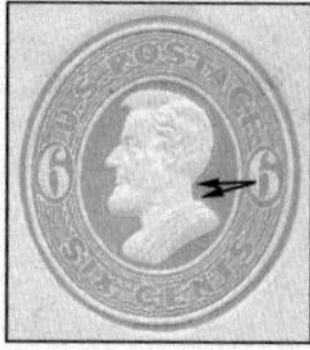

U48

Neck short at back.

U49

Figures of value turned up at the ends.

U50

Very large head.

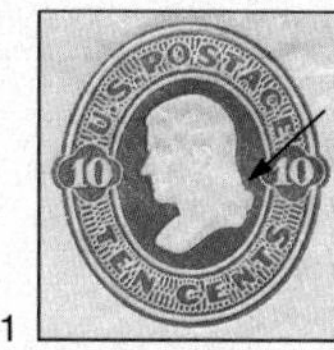

U51

Knot of queue stands out prominently.

U52

Ear prominent, chin receding.

U53

No side whiskers, forelock projects above head.

U54

Hair does not project; ornaments around the inner oval end in points.

U55

Back of bust rather broad, chin slopes considerably; labels containing figures of value are not exactly parallel.

U56

Front of bust sloping; inner lines of shields project considerably into the inner oval.

1874-86

Design U34

No.	Denom.	Description	Unused	Used
U108	1c	dark blue	175.00	70.00
a.	1c	light blue	175.00	70.00
U109	1c	dk bl, *amb*	150.00	75.00
+U110	1c	dk blue, *cr*	1,100.	
U111	1c	dk blue,*org*	15.00	17.50
a.		dk blue, *org*	12.50	12.50
W112	1c	dk blue, *man*	62.50	40.00

Design U35

No.	Denom.	Description	Unused	Used
U113	1c	light blue	2.25	1.00
a.	1c	dark blue	8.00	7.00

U114	1c lt blue, *amb*	3.25	3.25
a.	dk blue, *amb*	17.50	10.00
U115	1c blue, *cr*	4.75	4.25
a.	dk blue, *cr*	17.50	8.50
U116	1c lt blue, *org*	.75	.40
a.	dk blue, *org*	4.00	2.50
I117	1c lt bl, *bl* ('80)	7.50	5.00
U118	1c lt bl, *fawn* ('79)	7.50	5.00
U119	1c lt bl, *man* ('86)	8.00	3.25
W120	1c lt bl, *man*	1.25	1.10
a.	dk bl, *man*	8.00	7.00
U121	1c lt bl, *amb man*	17.50	10.00

Design U36

U122	2c brown	140.00	65.00
U123	2c brown, *amb*	67.50	40.00
+U124	2c brn, *crm*	*1,100.*	
+U125	2c brn, *org*	*18,000.*	
W126	2c brn, *man*	140.00	85.00
W127	2c ver, *man*	2,750.	500.00

Design U37

U128	2c brown	60.00	35.00
U129	2c brn, *amb*	80.00	45.00
+U130	2c brn, *cr*	*40,000.*	
W131	2c brn, *man*	17.50	15.00

Design U38

U132	2c brown	70.00	27.50
U133	2c brn, *amb*	325.00	70.00
+U133A	2c brn, *cr*	*70,000.*	

Design U39

U134	2c brown	1,100.	160.00
U135	2c brn, *amb*	425.00	150.00
U136	2c brn, *org*	50.00	27.50
W137	2c brn, *man*	75.00	40.00
+U137A	2c ver	*32,500.*	
+U137B	2c ver, *amb*	*30,000.*	
+U137C	2c ver, *org*	*70,000.*	
+W138	2c ver, *man*	*25,000.*	

Design U40

U139	2c brn ('75)	57.50	37.50
U140	2c brn,*amb* ('75)	85.00	62.50
+U140A	2c reddish brn, *org* ('75)	*17,500.*	
W141	2c brn, *man* ('75)	32.50	25.00
U142	2c ver ('75)	8.00	5.00
a.	2c pink	8.00	5.00
U143	2c ver, *amb* ('75)	9.00	5.00
U144	2c ver, *cr* ('75)	17.50	7.00
+U145	2c ver, *org* ('75)	*35,000.*	
U146	2c ver, *bl* ('80)	110.00	40.00
U147	2c ver, *fawn* ('75)	8.00	5.00
W148	2c ver, *man* ('75)	4.00	3.50

Design U41

U149	2c ver ('78)	45.00	25.00
a.	2c pink	52.50	27.00
U150	2c ver, *amb* ('78)	35.00	15.00
U151	2c ver, *bl* ('80)	10.00	8.00
a.	2c pink, *blue*	11.00	8.00
U152	2c ver, *fawn* ('78)	10.00	4.00

Design U42

U153	2c ver ('76)	75.00	30.00
U154	2c ver, *amb* ('76)	300.00	90.00
W155	2c ver, *man* ('76)	20.00	10.00

Design U43

U156	2c ver ('81)	1,250.	175.00
U157	2c ver, *amb* ('81)	*47,500.*	*27,500.*
W158	2c ver, *man* ('81)	90.00	55.00

Design U44

U159	3c green	35.00	10.00
U160	3c grn, *amb*	35.00	10.00
U161	3c grn, *cr*	35.00	12.00
+U162	3c grn, *bl*	*75,000.*	

Design U45

U163	3c green	1.40	.30
U164	3c grn, *amb*	1.50	.70
U165	3c grn, *cr*	8.50	6.50
U166	3c grn, *bl*	7.50	6.00
U167	3c grn, *fawn* ('75)	4.75	3.50

Design U46

U168	3c grn ('81)	1,250.	80.00
U169	3c grn, *amb*	550.00	140.00
U170	3c grn, *bl* ('81)	*11,500.*	*2,750.*
U171	3c grn, *fawn* ('81)	*40,000.*	*2,750.*

Design U47

U172	5c bl, die I ('75)	12.50	10.00
U173	5c bl, die I, *amb* ('75)	12.50	11.00
U174	5c bl, die I, *cr* ('75)	95.00	45.00
U175	5c bl, die I, *bl* ('75)	30.00	17.50
U176	5c bl, die I, *fawn* ('75)	160.00	65.00
U177	5c bl, die 2 ('75)	11.00	9.00
U178	5c bl, die 2, *amb* ('75)	9.00	8.00
+U178A	5c bl, die 2, *cr* ('76)	*11,000.*	
U179	5c bl, die 2, *bl* ('75)	25.00	12.50
U180	5c bl, die 2, *fawn* ('75)	125.00	50.00

Design U48

U181	6c red	8.00	6.50
a.	6c vermilion	8.00	6.50
U182	6c red, *amber*	12.50	6.50
a.	6c ver, *amb*	12.50	6.50
U183	6c red, *cream*	50.00	17.50
a.	6c ver, *cr*	45.00	15.00
U184	6c red, *fawn* ('75)	17.50	12.50

Design U49

+U185	7c vermilion	*1,200.*	
U186	7c ver, *amb*	125.00	75.00

Design U50

U187	10c brown	40.00	20.00
U188	10c brn, *amb*	75.00	35.00

Design U51

U189	10c choc ('75)	6.00	4.00
a.	10c bister brown	7.00	5.00
b.	10c yellow ocher	*4,250.*	
U190	10c choc, *amb* ('75)	7.00	6.00
a.	10c bis brn, *amb*	7.00	6.00
b.	10c yel ocher, *amb*	*3,250.*	
U191	10c brn, *oriental buff* ('86)	12.50	8.75
U192	10c brn, *bl* ('86)	12.50	8.00
a.	10c gray blk, *bl*	12.50	7.50
b.	10c red brn, *bl*	12.50	7.50
U193	10c brn, *man* ('86)	12.50	10.00
a.	10c red brn, *man*	12.50	10.00
U194	10c brn, *amb man* ('86)	17.50	9.00
a.	10c red brn, *amb man*	17.50	9.00

Design U52

U195	12c plum	300.00	100.00
U196	12c plum, *amb*	200.00	160.00
U197	12c plum, *cr*	180.00	130.00

Design U53

U198	15c orange	50.00	35.00
U199	15c org, *amb*	140.00	130.00
U200	15c org, *cr*	500.00	300.00

Design U54

U201	24c purple	175.00	150.00
U202	24c pur, *amb*	180.00	100.00
U203	24c pur, *cr*	170.00	100.00

Design U55

U204	30c black	60.00	25.00
U205	30c blk, *amb*	70.00	60.00
U206	30c blk, *cr* ('75)	325.00	325.00
U207	30c blk, *oriental buff* ('81)	100.00	80.00
U208	30c blk, *bl* ('81)	100.00	80.00
U209	30c blk, *man* ('81)	90.00	70.00
U210	30c blk, *amb man* ('86)	180.00	100.00

Design U56

U211	90c carmine ('75)	95.00	75.00
U212	90c car, *amb* ('75)	175.00	250.00
U213	90c car, *cr* ('75)	1,250.	
U214	90c car, *oriental buff* ('86)	140.00	250.00
U215	90c car, *bl* ('86)	175.00	250.00
U216	90c car, *man* ('86)	140.00	225.00
U217	90c car, *amb man* ('86)	160.00	*200.00*

Note: No. U206 has watermark #2; No. U207 watermark #6 or #7. No U213 has watermark #2; No. U214 watermark #7. These envelopes cannot be positively identified except by the watermark.

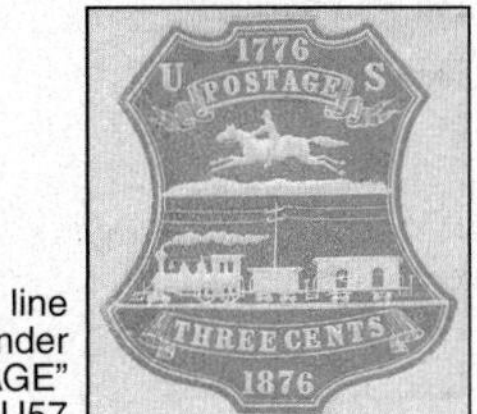

Single line under "POSTAGE" U57

Double line under "POSTAGE" U58

1876

U218	U57	3c red	35.00	25.00
U219	U57	3c green	35.00	17.50
+U220	U58	3c red	*27,500.*	
U221	U58	3c green	35.00	25.00

Cent. of the U.S., and the World's Fair at Philadelphia.

Used examples of Nos. U218-U221 with exposition cancels and/or typed addresses sell for a premium.

See No. U582.

Garfield — U59

1882-86

U222	U59	5c brown	5.00	3.00
U223	U59	5c brn, *amb*	5.25	3.50
+U224	U59	5c brn, *oriental buff* ('86)	140.00	
+U225	U59	5c brn, *bl*	75.00	
U226	U59	5c brn, *fawn*	325.00	

Washington — U60

1883, October

U227	U60	2c red	5.50	2.25
a.		2c brown (error), entire	*9,500.*	
U228	U60	2c red, *amb*	6.50	2.75
U229	U60	2c red, *blue*	8.00	5.00
U230	U60	2c red, *fawn*	9.00	5.25

Wavy lines fine and clear — U61

1883, November

Four Wavy Lines in Oval

U231	U61	2c red	5.00	2.50
U232	U61	2c red, *amb*	6.00	3.75
U233	U61	2c red, *blue*	10.00	7.50
U234	U61	2c red, *fawn*	7.50	4.75
W235	U61	2c red, *man*	20.00	6.25

Wavy lines thick and blurred — U62

Retouched die.

1884, June

U236	U62	2c red	15.00	4.00
U237	U62	2c red, *amber*	20.00	10.00
U238	U62	2c red, *blue*	29.00	12.00
U239	U62	2c red, *fawn*	20.00	11.00

See Nos. U260-W269.

3½ links over left "2" — U63

U240	U63	2c red	90.00	45.00
U241	U63	2c red, *amb*	675.00	300.00
U242	U63	2c red, *fawn*		*30,000.*

2 links below right "2" — U64

U243	U64	2c red	130.00	75.00
U244	U64	2c red, *amb*	325.00	100.00
U245	U64	2c red, *blue*	375.00	210.00
U246	U64	2c red, *fawn*	375.00	200.00

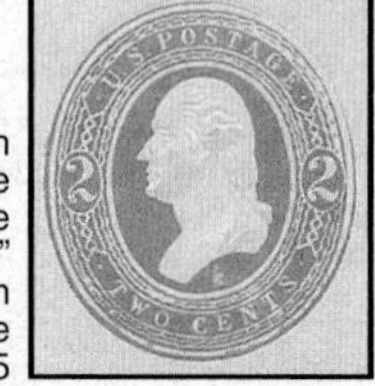

Round "O" in "TWO." White lines above "WO" of "TWO" joined to form thick white dash. — U65

U247	U65	2c red	3,000.	400.00
U248	U65	2c red, *amb*	4,500.	750.00
U249	U65	2c red, *fawn*	1,100.	500.00

See Nos. U270-U276.

Jackson — U66

Die 1

Die 2

Die 1: Numeral at left is 2¾mm wide. Die 2: Numeral at left is 3¼mm wide.

1883-86

U250	U66	4c green, die 1	4.00	3.50
U251	U66	4c grn, die 1, *amb*	5.00	3.50
U252	U66	4c grn, die 1, *oriental buff* ('86)	13.00	9.00
U253	U66	4c green, die 1, *blue* ('86)	13.00	6.50
U254	U66	4c grn, die 1, *man* ('86)	16.00	7.50
U255	U66	4c grn, die 1, *amb man* ('86)	22.50	10.00
U256	U66	4c green, die 2	10.00	5.00
U257	U66	4c grn, die 2, *amb*	12.50	7.00
U258	U66	4c grn, die 2, *man* ('86)	12.50	7.50
U259	U66	4c grn, die 2, *amb man* ('86)	12.50	7.50

1884, May

U260	U61	2c brown	17.50	5.75
U261	U61	2c brown, *amber*	17.50	6.50
U262	U61	2c brown, *blue*	20.00	10.00
U263	U61	2c brown, *fawn*	17.50	9.25
W264	U61	2c brown, *manila*	18.00	11.50

1884, June

Retouched Die

U265	U62	2c brown	18.00	6.50
U266	U62	2c brn, *amb*	60.00	40.00
U267	U62	2c brown, *blue*	22.50	9.00
U268	U62	2c brown, *fawn*	17.00	11.00
W269	U62	2c brn, *man*	27.50	15.00

2 Links Below Right "2"

U270	U64	2c brown	130.00	50.00
U271	U64	2c brn, *amb*	425.00	125.00
U272	U64	2c brown, *fawn*		*2,000.*

Round "O" in "Two"

U273 U65 2c brown 250.00 100.00
U274 U65 2c brn, *amb* 250.00 100.00
U275 U65 2c brown, *blue* *12,500.*
U276 U65 2c brown, *fawn* 800.00 750.00

U67

Extremity of bust below the queue forms a point.

Washington — U68

Extremity of bust is rounded.

Similar to U61
Two wavy lines in oval

1884-86

U277 U67 2c brown .50 .25
a. 2c brown lake, die 1 22.50 21.00
U278 U67 2c brn, *amb* .65 .50
a. 2c brown lake, *amber* 35.00 25.00
U279 U67 2c brn, *oriental buff* ('86) 7.00 2.10
U280 U67 2c brown, *blue* 3.00 2.10
U281 U67 2c brown, *fawn* 3.75 2.40
U282 U67 2c brn, *man* ('86) 13.00 4.00
W283 U67 2c brn, *man* 8.00 5.00
U284 U67 2c brn, *amb man* ('86) 9.00 5.75
+U285 U67 2c red 700.00
+U286 U67 2c red, *blue* 275.00
W287 U67 2c red, *manila* 150.00
U288 U68 2c brown 275.00 50.00
U289 U68 2c brn, *amb* 20.00 13.00
U290 U68 2c brown, *blue* 1,400. 325.00
U291 U68 2c brown, *fawn* 35.00 25.00
W292 U68 2c brn, *man* 35.00 19.00

Grant — US1

1886

Letter Sheet, 160x271mm
Creamy White Paper

U293 US1 2c green, entire 30.00 20.00

See the Scott U.S. Specialized Catalogue for perforation and inscription varieties.

Franklin — U69

Washington U70

Bust points between third and fourth notches of inner oval "G" of "POSTAGE" has no bar.

U71

Bust points between second and third notches of inner oval; "G" of "POSTAGE" has a bar; ear is indicated by one heavy line; one vertical line at corner of mouth.

U72

Frame same as U71; upper part of head more rounded; ear indicated by two curved lines with two locks of hair in front; two vertical lines at corner of mouth.

Jackson — U73

Grant — U74

There is a space between the beard and the collar of the coat. A button is on the collar.

U75

The collar touches the beard and there is no button.

1887-94

Design U69

U294 1c blue .55 .25
U295 1c dk bl ('94) 7.00 2.50
U296 1c bl, *amb* 3.25 1.25
U297 1c dk bl, *amb* ('94) 47.50 22.50
+U298 1c bl, *oriental buff* *12,500.*
+U299 1c bl, *bl* *15,000.*
U300 1c bl, *man* .65 .35
W301 1c bl, *man* .45 .30
U302 1c dk bl, *man* ('94) 27.50 12.50
W303 1c DK bl, *man* ('94) 16.00 10.00
U304 1c bl, *amb man* 12.50 5.00

Design U70

U305 2c green 15.00 10.00
U306 2c grn, *amb* 40.00 17.50
U307 2c grn, *oriental buff* 100.00 40.00
U308 2c grn, *bl* 3,500.
U309 2c grn, *man* *12,500.* 1,000.
U310 2c grn, *amb man* *27,500.* *2,500.*

Design U71

U311 2c green .30 .25
a. 2c dark green ('94) .45 .30
U312 2c grn, *amb* .40 .25
a. Double impression —
b. 2c dk grn, *amb* ('94) .55 .35
U313 2c grn, *oriental buff* .55 .25
a. 2c dk grn, *oriental buff* ('94) 2.00 1.00
b. Double impression 150.00
U314 2c grn, *bl* .60 .30
a. 2c dk grn, *bl* ('94) .80 .40
U315 2c grn, *man* 2.00 .50
a. 2c dk grn, *man* ('94) 2.75 .75
W316 2c grn, *man* 3.50 2.50
U317 2c grn, *amb man* 2.50 1.90
a. 2c dk grn, *amb man* ('94) 3.50 3.00

Design U72

U318 2c green 125.00 12.50
U319 2c grn, *amb* 175.00 27.50
U320 2c grn, *oriental buff* 140.00 40.00
U321 2c grn, *bl* 175.00 70.00
U322 2c grn, *man* 240.00 70.00
U323 2c grn, *amb man* 400.00 100.00

Design U73

U324 4c carmine 3.25 2.00
a. 4c lake 3.50 2.00
b. 4c scarlet ('94) 3.50 2.00
U325 4c car, *amb* 3.50 3.50
a. 4c lake, *amber* 3.50 3.50
b. 4c scarlet, *amber* ('94) 4.00 3.75
U326 4c car, *oriental buff* 7.50 3.50
a. 4c lake, *oriental buff* 7.50 3.50
U327 4c car, *bl* 6.00 4.00
a. 4c lake, *blue* 6.50 4.00
U328 4c car, *man* 9.00 7.00
a. 4c lake, *manila* 9.00 6.00
b. 4c pink, *manila* 15.00 10.00
U329 4c car, *amb man* 7.00 3.25
a. 4c lake, *amb man* 7.00 3.25
b. 4c pink, *amb man* 15.00 10.00

Design U74

U330 5c blue 3.75 4.00
U331 5c bl, *amb* 5.00 2.50
a. Double impression, entire —
U332 5c bl, *oriental buff* 5.50 4.00
U333 5c blue, *blue* 9.00 6.00

Design U75

U334 5c blue ('94) 25.00 12.50
U335 5c bl, *amb* ('94) 12.50 7.50

Design U55

U336 30c red brn 50.00 45.00
a. 30c yellow brown 50.00 45.00
b. 30c chocolate 50.00 45.00
U337 30c red brn, *amb* 50.00 45.00
a. 30c yel brn, *amb* 50.00 45.00
b. 30c choc, *amb* 50.00 45.00
U338 30c red brn, *oriental buff* 50.00 45.00
a. 30c yel brn, *oriental buff* 50.00 45.00
U339 30c red brn, *bl* 50.00 45.00
a. 30c yel brn, *bl* 50.00 45.00
U340 30c red brn, *man* 50.00 45.00
a. 30c brown, *manila* 50.00 45.00
U341 30c red brn, *amb man* 50.00 45.00
a. 30c yel brn, *amb man* 50.00 45.00

Design U56

U342 90c purple 67.50 85.00
U343 90c pur, *amb* 82.50 85.00
U344 90c pur, *oriental buff* 82.50 85.00
U345 90c pur, *bl* 82.50 85.00
U346 90c pur, *man* 85.00 85.00
U347 90c pur, *amb man* 85.00 85.00

Columbus and Liberty — U76

1893

U348 U76 1c deep blue 2.25 1.25
U349 U76 2c violet 1.75 .50
a. 2c dark slate (error) *2,500.*
U350 U76 5c chocolate 7.50 7.00
a. 5c slate brown (error) *850.00* *950.00*
U351 U76 10c slate brown 30.00 27.50
Nos. U348-U351 (4) 41.50 36.25

Franklin U77

Washington U78

Bust points to first notch of inner oval and is only slightly concave below.

U79

Bust points to middle of second notch of inner oval and is quite hollow below. Queue has ribbon around it.

U80

Same as die 2, but hair flowing. No ribbon on queue.

Lincoln — U81

Bust pointed but not draped.

U82

Bust broad and draped.

U83

Head larger, inner oval has no notches.

Grant — U84

Similar to design of 1887-95 but smaller.

1899

U352 U77 1c green 2.00 .25
U353 U77 1c green, *amber* 5.50 1.50
U354 U77 1c green, *oriental buff* 10.00 2.75
U355 U77 1c green, *blue* 12.50 7.50
U356 U77 1c green, *manila* 2.50 .95
W357 U77 1c green, *manila* 2.75 1.10
U358 U78 2c carmine 3.00 1.75
U359 U78 2c car, *amb* 20.00 12.50
U360 U78 2c carmine, *oriental buff* 20.00 11.00
U361 U78 2c carmine, *blue* 60.00 35.00
U362 U79 2c carmine .35 .25
a. 2c dark lake 30.00 30.00
U363 U79 2c car, *amb* 1.75 .25
U364 U79 2c carmine, *oriental buff* 1.20 .25
U365 U79 2c carmine, *blue* 1.50 .55
W366 U79 2c car, *man* 9.00 3.25
U367 U80 2c carmine 6.00 2.75
U368 U80 2c car, *amb* 10.00 6.50
U369 U80 2c carmine, *oriental buff* 22.50 12.50
U370 U80 2c carmine, *blue* 12.50 10.00
U371 U81 4c brown 15.00 12.50
U372 U81 4c brown, *amber* 15.00 12.50
U373 U82 4c brown *7,500.* 1,100.
U374 U83 4c brown 12.50 8.00
U375 U83 4c brown, *amber* 60.00 25.00
W376 U83 4c brown, *manila* 20.00 12.50
U377 U84 5c blue 11.00 9.00
U378 U84 5c blue, *amber* 12.50 10.00

Franklin — U85

Washington — U86

"D" of "UNITED" contains vertical line at right that parallels the left vertical line. One short and two long vertical lines at the right of "CENTS."

Grant — U87

Lincoln — U88

1903

U379	U85	1c green	.75	.25
U380	U85	1c green, *amber*	14.00	2.00
U381	U85	1c green, *oriental buff*	17.50	2.50
U382	U85	1c green, *blue*	22.50	2.50
U383	U85	1c green, *manila*	4.00	.90
W384	U85	1c green, *manila*	2.50	.40
U385	U86	2c carmine	.40	.25
a.		2c pink	2.00	1.50
b.		2c red	2.00	1.50
U386	U86	2c carmine, *amber*	2.00	.50
a.		2c pink, *amber*	5.50	3.00
b.		2c red, *amber*	14.00	7.00
U387	U86	2c carmine, *oriental buff*	2.00	.30
a.		2c pink, *oriental buff*	3.50	2.00
b.		2c red, *oriental buff*	4.00	2.25
U388	U86	2c carmine, *blue*	1.75	.50
a.		2c pink, *blue*	22.50	14.00
b.		2c red, *blue*	22.50	14.00
W389	U86	2c carmine, *manila*	19.00	9.00
U390	U87	4c choc	20.00	11.00
U391	U87	4c choc, *amber*	22.50	11.00
W392	U87	4c choc, *manila*	25.00	12.50
U393	U88	5c blue	19.00	11.00
U394	U88	5c blue, *amber*	19.00	11.00

U89

Re-cut die — "D" of "UNITED" is well rounded at right. The three lines at the right of "CENTS" and at the left of "TWO" are usually all short; the lettering is heavier and the ends of the ribbons slightly changed.

1904

Re-cut Die

U395	U89	2c carmine	.75	.25
a.		2c pink	5.50	2.50
U396	U89	2c carmine, *amber*	8.00	1.00
a.		2c pink, *amber*	9.00	3.00
U397	U89	2c carmine, *oriental buff*	5.50	1.10
a.		2c pink, *oriental buff*	7.00	2.75
U398	U89	2c carmine, *blue*	4.00	.90
a.		2c pink, *blue*	5.50	2.50
W399	U89	2c carmine, *manila*	14.00	8.00
a.		2c pink, *manila*	27.50	17.50
b.		Double impression, entire	*375.00*	

Franklin — U90

Die 1

Die 2

Die 3

Die 4

Die 1 — Wide "D" in "UNITED."
Die 2 — Narrow "D" in "UNITED."
Die 3 — Wide "S-S" in "STATES" (1910).
Die 4 — Sharp angle at back of bust, "N" and "E" of "ONE" are parallel (1912).

1907-16 **Die 1**

U400	U90	1c green	.35	.25
a.		Die 2	.85	.25
b.		Die 3	.85	.35
c.		Die 4	.90	.30
U401	U90	1c green, *amber*	2.00	.40
a.		Die 2	2.50	.70
b.		Die 3	3.25	.75
c.		Die 4	2.00	.65
U402	U90	1c green, *oriental buff*	10.00	1.00
a.		Die 2	13.00	1.50
b.		Die 3	15.00	1.50
c.		Die 4	10.00	1.50
U403	U90	1c green, *blue*	10.00	1.50
a.		Die 2	13.00	3.00
b.		Die 3	12.50	3.00
c.		Die 4	9.50	1.25
U404	U90	1c green, *manila*	3.00	1.90
a.		Die 3	4.50	3.00
W405	U90	1c green, *manila*	1.00	.25
a.		Die 2	65.00	25.00
b.		Die 3	12.00	4.00
c.		Die 4	90.00	—

Washington — U91 — brown red

Die 1, Washington — U91 — carmine

Die 2

Die 3

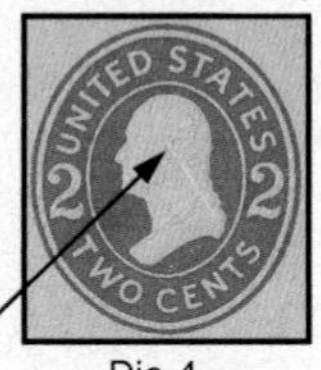
Die 4

Die 5

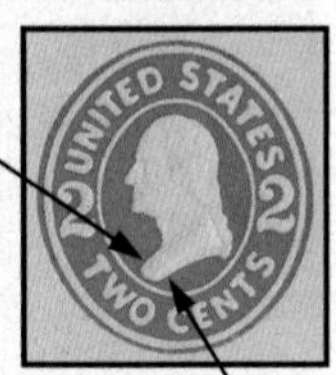
Die 6

Die 7

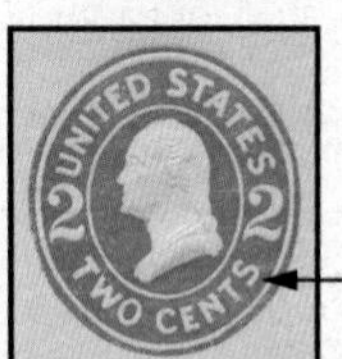
Die 8

Die 1 — Oval "O" in "TWO" and "C" in "CENTS." Front of bust broad.

Die 2 — Similar to 1 but hair re-cut in two distinct locks at top of head.

Die 3 — Round "O" in "TWO" and "C" in "CENTS," coarse lettering.

Die 4 — Similar to 3 but lettering fine and clear, hair lines clearly embossed. Inner oval thin and clear.

Die 5 — All "S's" wide (1910).

Die 6 — Similar to 1 but front of bust narrow (1913).

Die 7 — Similar to 6 but upper corner of front of bust cut away (1916).

Die 8 — Similar to 7 but lower stroke of "S" in "CENTS" is a straight line. Hair as in Die 2 (1916).

Die 1

U406	U91	2c brown red	.90	.25
a.		Die 2	42.50	7.00
b.		Die 3	.80	.25
U407	U91	2c brown red, *amber*	6.50	2.00
a.		Die 2	375.00	65.00
b.		Die 3	4.50	1.25
U408	U91	2c brown red, *oriental buff*	8.75	1.50
a.		Die 2	325.00	125.00
b.		Die 3	7.50	2.50
U409	U91	2c brn red, *blue*	5.75	2.00
a.		Die 2	400.00	200.00
b.		Die 3	5.75	1.75
W410	U91	2c brn red, *man*	40.00	35.00
U411	U91	2c carmine	.35	.25
a.		Die 2	.90	.25
b.		Die 3	.80	.35
c.		Die 4	.65	.25
d.		Die 5	.65	.30
e.		Die 6	.60	.25
f.		Die 7	40.00	25.00
g.		Die 8	40.00	25.00
h.		#U411 with added impression of #U400, entire	475.00	
i.		#U411 with added impression of #U416a, entire	475.00	
k.		As No. U411, double impression, entire	175.00	
U412	U91	2c carmine, *amb*	.30	.25
a.		Die 2	2.10	.25
b.		Die 3	2.25	.45
c.		Die 4	.55	.25
d.		Die 5	.90	.35
e.		Die 6	.70	.35
f.		Die 7	37.50	25.00
U413	U91	2c car, *oriental buff*	.55	.25
a.		Die 2	2.25	.45
b.		Die 3	9.00	3.00
c.		Die 4	.55	.25
d.		Die 5	3.50	1.25
e.		Die 6	.70	.35
f.		Die 7	105.00	45.00
g.		Die 8	27.50	17.50
U414	U91	2c carmine, *blue*	.60	.25
a.		Die 2	2.25	.35
b.		Die 3	2.75	.60
c.		Die 4	.70	.25
d.		Die 5	2.25	.30
e.		Die 6	.65	.30
f.		Die 7	42.50	25.00
g.		Die 8	42.50	25.00
W415	U91	2c car, *manila*	5.00	2.00
a.		Die 2	5.50	1.25
b.		Die 5	5.50	2.50
c.		Die 7	130.00	97.50

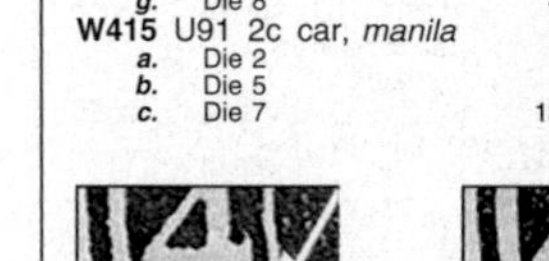

U90 4c Die 1 U90 4c Die 2

Die 1 — "F" close to (1mm) left "4."
Die 2 — "F" far from (1¾mm) left "4."

U416	U90	4c black, die 2	7.50	3.00
a.		Die 1	7.50	3.00
U417	U90	4c black, *amb*, die 2	7.50	2.50
a.		Die 1	7.50	2.50

Die 1 — Tall "F" in "FIVE"

Die 2 — Short "F" in "FIVE"

U418	U91	5c blue, die 2	7.00	2.25
a.		Die 1	7.00	2.25
b.		5c blue, *buff*, die 2 (error)	*3,500.*	
c.		5c blue, *blue*, die 2 (error)	*3,250.*	
d.		As "c," die 1 (error), entire	*6,250.*	
U419	U91	5c blue, *amber*, die 2	17.50	12.00
a.		Die 1	17.50	12.00

Franklin — U92

Die 1

Die 2

Die 3 Die 4 Die 5

(The 1c and 4c dies are the same except for figures of value.)

Die 1 — UNITED nearer inner circle than outer circle.

Die 2 — Large U; large NT closely spaced.

Die 3 — Knob of hair at back of neck. Large NT widely spaced.

Die 4 — UNITED nearer outer circle than inner circle.

Die 5 — Narrow oval C, (also O and G).

1915-32 **Die 1**

U420	U92	1c green ('17)	.25	.25
a.		Die 2	110.00	55.00
b.		Die 3	.35	.25
c.		Die 4	.55	.40
d.		Die 5	.45	.35
U421	U92	1c grn, *amber* ('17)	.55	.30
a.		Die 2	425.00	175.00
b.		Die 3	1.40	.65
c.		Die 4	1.90	.85
d.		Die 5	1.10	.55
U422	U92	1c grn, *oriental buff* ('17)	2.40	.90
a.		Die 4	5.50	1.25
U423	U92	1c grn, *bl* ('17)	.50	.35
a.		Die 3	.80	.45
b.		Die 4	1.40	.65
c.		Die 5	.85	.35
U424	U92	1c grn, *manila* (unglazed) ('16)	6.50	4.00
W425	U92	1c grn, *manila* (unglazed) ('16)	.30	.25
a.		Die 3	190.00	125.00

U426 U92 1c grn, *brown* (glazed) ('20) 47.50 16.00

W427 U92 1c grn, *brown* (glazed) ('20) 70.00 35.00
- *a.* Printed on unglazed side *400.00*
  - Entire *750.00*
- *b.* Unglazed on both sides *150.00*

U428 U92 1c grn, *brown* (unglazed) ('20) 15.00 7.50

W428A U92 1c grn, *brown* (unglazed) ('20) *3,000.*

Washington — U93

Die 1

Die 2

Die 3

Die 4

Die 5

Die 6

Die 7

Die 8

Die 9

(The 1½c, 2c, 3c, 5c, and 6c dies are the same except for figures of value.)

Die 1 — Letters broad. Numerals vertical. Large head (9¼mm). from tip of nose to back of neck. E closer to inner circle than N of cents.

Die 2 — Similar to 1; but U far from left circle.

Die 3 — Similar to 2; but all inner circles very thin (Rejected die).

Die 4 — Large head as in Die 1. C of CENTS close to circle. Baseline of right numeral "2" slants downward to right. Left numeral "2" is larger.

Die 5 — Small head (8¾mm) from tip of nose to back of neck. T and S of CENTS close at bottom.

Die 6 — Similar to 5; but T and S of CENTS far apart at bottom. Left numeral slopes to right.

Die 7 — Large head. Both numerals slope to right. Clean cut lettering. All letters T have short top strokes.

Die 8 — Similar to 7; but all letters T have long top strokes.

Die 9 — Narrow oval C (also O and G).

1915-32 — Die 1

U429 U93 2c carmine .25 .25
- *a.* Die 2 16.00 7.00
- *b.* Die 3 47.50 50.00
- *c.* Die 4 30.00 15.00
- *d.* Die 5 .55 .35
- *e.* Die 6 .65 .30
- *f.* Die 7 .70 .25
- *g.* Die 8 .50 .25
- *h.* Die 9 .50 .25
- *i.* 2c green (error), die 1, entire *12,500.*
- *j.* #U429 with added impression of #U420 600.00
- *k.* #U429 with added impression of #U416a, entire *3,500.*
- *l.* #U429 with added impression of #U400, entire 950.00
- *m.* #U429, double impression, entire 1,750.
- *n.* As "f," double impression, entire *750.00*
- *o.* As "e," triple impression —
- *p.* As "m," second impression on side flap, entire *250.00*

U430 U93 2c car, *amber* ('16) .30 .25
- *a.* Die 2 21.00 12.50
- *b.* Die 4 52.50 25.00
- *c.* Die 5 1.60 .35
- *d.* Die 6 1.25 .40
- *e.* Die 7 .75 .35
- *f.* Die 8 .70 .30
- *g.* Die 9 .65 .25
- *h.* As No. U430, with added impression of 4c black (#U416a), entire *650.00*
- *i.* As "g," with added impression of 2c car. die 1 on side flap, entire —

U431 U93 2c car, *oriental buff* ('16) 2.25 .65
- *a.* Die 2 200.00 75.00
- *b.* Die 4 77.50 60.00
- *c.* Die 5 3.50 2.00
- *d.* Die 6 3.50 2.00
- *e.* Die 7 3.50 2.00

U432 U93 2c car, *blue* ('16) .30 .25
- *b.* Die 2 42.50 25.00
- *c.* Die 3 165.00 90.00
- *d.* Die 4 67.50 50.00
- *e.* Die 5 1.10 .30
- *f.* Die 6 1.10 .40
- *g.* Die 7 .85 .35
- *h.* Die 8 .65 .25
- *i.* Die 9 1.00 .30
- *j.* 2c purple (error), die 9 —

U432A U93 2c car, *manila*, die 7, entire *50,000.*

W433 U93 2c car, *manila*, ('16) .25 .25

W434 U93 2c car, *brn* (glazed) ('20) 75.00 45.00

W435 U93 2c car, *brn* (unglazed) ('20) 100.00 60.00

U436 U93 3c purple ('32) .30 .25
- *a.* 3c dark violet, die 1 ('17) .60 .25
- *b.* 3c dark violet, die 5 ('17) 1.75 .75
- *c.* 3c dark violet, die 6 ('17) 2.10 1.40
- *d.* 3c dark violet, die 7 ('17) 1.50 .95
- *e.* 3c purple, die 7 ('32) .70 .30
- *f.* 3c purple, die 9 ('32) .45 .25
- *g.* 3c carmine (error), die 1 37.50 35.00
- *h.* 3c carmine (error), die 5 32.50 —
- *i.* #U436 with added impression of #U420, entire 900.00
- *j.* #U436 with added impression of #U429, entire 900.00 950.00
- *k.* As "f," double impression, preprinted, entire *600.00*

U437 U93 3c purple, *amb* ('32) .35 .25
- *a.* 3c dk vio, die 1 ('17) 5.50 1.25
- *b.* 3c dk vio, die 5 ('17) 8.50 2.50
- *c.* 3c dk vio, die 6 ('17) 8.50 2.50
- *d.* 3c dk vio, die 7 ('17) 8.50 2.25
- *e.* 3c pur, die 7 ('32) .75 .25
- *f.* 3c pur, die 9 ('32) .55 .25
- *g.* 3c carmine (error), die 5 450.00 400.00
- *h.* 3c black (error), die 1 200.00 —

U438 U93 3c dk vio, *oriental buff* ('17) 25.00 5.50
- *a.* Die 5 25.00 5.50
- *b.* Die 6 32.50 8.00
- *c.* Die 7 32.50 10.00

U439 U93 3c purple, *bl* ('32) .35 .25
- *a.* 3c dark violet, die 1 ('17) 7.50 2.00
- *b.* 3c dark violet, die 5 ('17) 8.50 6.00
- *c.* 3c dark violet, die 6 ('17) 8.50 6.00
- *d.* 3c dark violet, die 7 ('17) 11.00 6.00
- *e.* 3c purple, die 7 ('32) .75 .25
- *f.* 3c purple, die 9 ('32) .60 .25
- *g.* 3c carmine (error), die 5 275.00 300.00

U440 U92 4c black ('18) 1.75 .60
- *a.* With added impression of 2c carmine (#U429), die 1, entire 450.00

U441 U92 4c black, *amb* ('18) 3.00 .85
- *a.* 4c black, *amb*, with added impression of 2c car (#U429), die 1 175.00

U442 U92 4c blk, *bl* ('21) 3.25 .85

U443 U93 5c blue ('18) 3.25 2.75

U444 U93 5c blue, *amber* ('18) 4.00 1.60

U445 U93 5c bl, *blue* ('21) 3.75 3.25

For 1½c and 6c see Nos. U481-W485, U529-U531.

Double or triple surcharge listings of 1920-25 are for examples with surcharge directly or partly upon the stamp.

Surcharged on 1874-1920 Envelopes indicated by Numbers in Parentheses

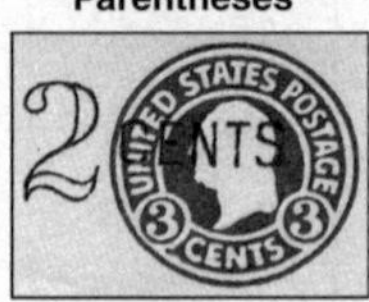

Type 1

1920-21

Surcharged in Black

U446 U93 2c on 3c dark vio (U436a, die 1) 15.00 10.00
- *a.* On No. U436b (die 5) 15.00 10.00
- *b.* As "a," double surcharge 140.00

Surcharged

Type 2

Rose Surcharge

U447 U93 2c on 3c dark vio (U436a, die 1) 9.00 7.50
- *b.* On No. U436c (die 6) 13.00 8.50

Black Surcharge

U447A U92 2c on 1c green (U420, die 1) Entire *3,500.*

U447C U93 2c on 2c carmine (U429, die 1) —

U447D U93 2c on 2c car, *amb* (U430, die 1) 15,000.

U448 U93 2c on 3c dark vio (U436a, die 1) 2.75 2.00
- *a.* On No. U436b (die 5) 2.75 2.00
- *b.* On No. U436c (die 6) 3.50 2.00
- *c.* On No. U436d (die 7) 2.75 2.00

U449 U93 2c on 3c dk vio, *amb* (U437a, die 1) 7.50 6.00
- *a.* On No. U437b (die 5) 13.00 7.50
- *b.* On No. U437c (die 6) 9.50 6.00
- *c.* On No. U437d (die 7) 8.50 6.50

U450 U93 2c on 3c dk vio, *oriental buff* (U438, die 1) 17.50 15.00
- *a.* On No. U438a (die 5) 17.50 15.00
- *b.* On No. U438b (die 6) 17.50 15.00
- *c.* On No. U438c (die 7) 130.00 90.00

U451 U93 2c on 3c dk vio, *blue* (U439a, die 1) 15.00 10.50
- *b.* On No. U439b (die 5) 15.00 10.50
- *c.* On No. U439c (die 6) 15.00 10.50
- *d.* On No. U439d (die 7) 27.50 22.50

Surcharged

Type 3

Bars 2mm apart, 25 to 26mm in length

U451A U90 2c on 1c green (U400, die 1) *25,000.*

U452 U92 2c on 1c green (U420, die 1) 2,500.
- *a.* On No. U420b (die 3) 3,000.
- *b.* As No. U452, double surcharge 3,750.

U453 U91 2c on 2c car (U411b, die 3) 4,500.
- *a.* On No. U411 (die 1) 4,500.

U453B U91 2c on 2c car, *bl* (U414e, die 6) 2,000. 750.00

U453C U91 2c on 2c car, *oriental buff* (U413e, die 6) 1,600. *750.00*
- *d.* On No. U413 (die 1) 1,600.

U454 U93 2c on 2c car (U429e, die 6) 150.00
- *a.* On No. U429 (die 1) 325.00
- *b.* On No. U429d (die 5) 500.00
- *c.* On No. U429f (die 7) 150.00

U455 U93 2c on 2c car, *amb* (U430, die 1) 1,600.
- *a.* On No. U430d (die 6) 1,750.
- *b.* On No. U430e (die 7) 1,750.

U456 U93 2c on 2c car, *oriental buff* (U431a, die 2) 250.00
- *a.* On No. U431c (die 5) 250.00
- *b.* On No. U431e (die 7) 800.00
- *c.* As No. U456, double surcharge 700.00

U457 U93 2c on 2c car, *bl* (U432f, die 6) 375.00
a. On No. U432e (die 5) 325.00
b. On No. U432g (die 7) 800.00
U458 U93 2c on 3c dark vio (U436a, die 1) .50 .35
a. On No. U436b (die 5) .50 .40
b. On No. U436c (die 6) .50 .35
c. On No. U436d (die 7) .50 .35
d. As #U458, double surcharge 25.00 7.50
e. As #U458, triple surcharge 100.00
f. As #U458, dbl. surch., 1 in magenta 100.00
g. As #U458, dbl. surch., types 2 & 3 140.00
h. As "a," double surcharge 27.50 15.00
i. As "a," triple surcharge 110.00
j. As "a," double surch., both magenta 110.00
k. As "b," double surcharge 25.00 8.00
l. As "c," double surcharge 25.00 8.00
m. As "c," triple surcharge 110.00
n. Double impression of indicia, single surcharge, entire 450.00
U459 U93 2c on 3c dk vio, *amb* (U437c, die 6) 3.00 1.00
a. On No. U437a (die 1) 4.00 1.00
b. On No. U437b (die 5) 4.00 1.00
c. On No. U437d (die 7) 3.00 1.00
d. As #U459, double surcharge 35.00
e. As "a," double surcharge 35.00
f. As "b," double surcharge 35.00
g. As "b," double surcharge, types 2 & 3 125.00
h. As "c," double surcharge 35.00
U460 U93 2c on 3c dk vio, *oriental buff* (U438a, die 5) 3.50 2.00
a. On No. U438 (die 1) 3.50 2.00
b. On No. U438b (die 6) 4.00 2.00
c. As #U460, double surcharge 20.00
d. As "a," double surcharge 20.00
e. As "b," double surcharge 20.00
f. As "b," triple surcharge 150.00
U461 U93 2c on 3c dk vio, *bl* (U439a, die 1) 6.00 1.00
a. On No. U439b (die 5) 6.00 1.00
b. On No. U439c (die 6) 6.00 2.50
c. On No. U439d (die 7) 12.50 7.50
d. As #U461, double surcharge 20.00
e. As "a," double surcharge 20.00
f. As "b," double surcharge 20.00
g. As "c," double surcharge 20.00
U462 U87 2c on 4c choc (U390) 525.00 260.00
U463 U87 2c on 4c choc, *amb* (U391) 850.00 350.00
U463A U90 2c on 4c black (U416, die 2) 900.00 400.00
U464 U93 2c on 5c blue (U443) 1,000.

Surcharged

Type 4

Bars 1 mm apart, 21 to 23 mm in length

U465 U92 2c on 1c green (U420, die 1) 1,100.
a. On No. U420b (die 3) 1,400.
U466 U91 2c on 2c car (U411e, die 6), entire
Entire 22,500.
U466A U93 2c on 2c carmine (U429, die 1) 800.00
c. On No. U429d (die 5) 900.00
d. On No. U429e (die 6) 900.00
e. On No. U429f (die 7) 900.00
U466B U93 2c on 2c car, *amb* (U430) *14,000.*
U466C U93 2c on 2c car, *oriental buff* (U431), entire *20,000.*
U466D U25 2c on 3c green, die 2 (U82) *7,500.*

U467 U45 2c on 3c green, die 2 (U163) 350.00
U468 U93 2c on 3c dark vio (U436a, die 1) .70 .45
a. On No. U436b (die 5) .70 .50
b. On No. U436c (die 6) .70 .50
c. On No. U436d (die 7) .70 .50
d. As #U468, double surcharge 20.00
e. As #U468, triple surcharge 100.00
f. As #U468, dbl. surch., types 2 & 4 125.00
g. As "a," double surcharge 20.00
h. As "b," double surcharge 20.00
i. As "c," double surcharge 20.00
j. As "c," triple surcharge 100.00
k. As "c," inverted surcharge 75.00
l. 2c on 3c carmine (error), (U436h) 650.00
m. As #U468, triple surcharge, one inverted, entire *700.00*
U469 U93 2c on 3c dk vio, *amb* (U437a, die 1) 3.75 2.25
a. On No. U437b (die 5) 3.75 2.25
b. On No. U437c (die 6) 3.75 2.25
c. On No. U437d (die 7) 3.75 2.25
d. As #U469, double surcharge 30.00
e. As "a," double surcharge 30.00
f. As "a," double surcharge, types 2 & 4 100.00
g. As "b," double surcharge 30.00
h. As "c," double surcharge 30.00
U470 U93 2c on 3c dk vio, *oriental buff* (U438, die 1) 6.00 2.50
a. On No. U438a (die 5) 6.00 2.50
b. On No. U438b (die 6) 6.00 2.50
c. On No. U438c (die 7) 42.50 32.50
d. As #U470, double surcharge 25.00
e. As #U470, double surch., types 2 & 4 90.00
f. As "a," double surcharge 25.00
g. As "b," double surcharge 25.00
U471 U93 2c on 3c dk vio, *bl* (U439a, die 1) 6.75 1.75
a. On No. U439b (die 5) 7.50 1.75
b. On No. U439c (die 6) 7.50 1.75
c. On No. U439d (die 7) 12.00 10.00
d. As #U471, double surcharge 30.00
e. As #U471, double surch., types 2 & 4 175.00
f. As "a," double surcharge 30.00
g. As "b," double surcharge 30.00
U471A U83 2c on 4c brown, (U374), entire 625.00
U472 U87 2c on 4c choc (U390) 15.00 12.00
a. Double surcharge 150.00
U473 U87 2c on 4c choc, *amb* (U391) 17.00 10.00

Surcharged

Double Surcharge, Type 4 and 1c as above

U474 U93 2c on 1c on 3c dark violet (U436a, die 1) 250. *500.*
a. On No. U436b (die 5) 250.
b. On No. U436d (die 7) 900.
U475 U93 2c on 1c on 3c dk vio, *amb* (U437a, die 1) 225.

Surcharged

Type 5

U476 U93 2c on 3c dk vio, *amb* (U437a, die 1) 275.
a. On No. U437c (die 6) 800.
b. As #U476, double surcharge —

Surcharged

Type 6

U477 U93 2c on 3c dark vio (U436a, die 1) 130.
a. On No. U436b (die 5) 250.
b. On No. U436c (die 6) 250.
c. On No. U436d (die 7) 250.
U478 U93 2c on 3c dk vio, *amb* (U437a, die 1) 290.

Handstamped Surcharge in Black or Violet — Type 7

U479 U93 2c on 3c dark violet (Bk) (U436a, die 1) 250. —
a. On No. U436b (die 5) 650.
b. On No. U436d (die 7) 450.
U480 U93 2c on 3c dark violet (V) (U436d, die 7) *5,000.*
a. Double overprint —

Expertization by competent authorities is required for Nos. U476-U480.

1925-34

Type of 1916-32 Issue

Die 1

U481 U93 1½c brown .25 .25
a. Die 8 .70 .25
b. 1½c purple, die 1 (error) ('34) 70.00
U482 U93 1½c brown, *amber* .90 .40
a. Die 8 1.75 .75
U483 U93 1½c brown, *bl* 1.60 .95
a. Die 8 2.40 1.25
U484 U93 1½c brown, *manila* 6.50 3.00
W485 U93 1½c brown, *manila* .85 .25
a. With added impression of #W433 120.00 —

Surcharged Type 8

1925

U486 U71 1½c on 2c grn (U311) 600.
U487 U71 1½c on 2c green, *amb* (U312) 1,000.
U488 U77 1½c on 1c green (U352) 450.
U489 U77 1½c on 1c grn, *amb* (U353) 110. 60.
U490 U90 1½c on 1c green (U400, die 1) 6.25 3.50
a. On No. U400a (die 2) 17.00 9.00
b. On No. U400b (die 3) 40.00 17.50
c. On No. U400c (die 4) 9.00 2.50

U491 U90 1½c on 1c grn, *amb* (U401c, die 4) 8.00 3.00
a. On No. U401 (die 1) 12.50 3.50
b. On No. U401a (die 2) 120.00 70.00
c. On No. U401b (die 3) 60.00 50.00
U492 U90 1½c on 1c grn, *oriental buff* (U402a, die 2) 500.00 150.00
a. On No. U402c (die 4) 750.00 250.00
U493 U90 1½c on 1c grn, *bl* (U403c, die 4) 110.00 65.00
a. On No. U403a (die 2) 110.00 67.50
U494 U90 1½c on 1c grn, *man* (U404, die 1) 300.00 100.00
a. On No. U404a (die 3) 1,250.
U495 U92 1½c on 1c green (U420, die 1) .80 .25
a. On No. U420a (die 2) 85.00 52.50
b. On No. U420b (die 3) 2.10 .70
c. On No. U420c (die 4) 2.10 .85
d. As #U495, double surcharge 10.00 3.00
e. As "b," double surcharge 10.00 3.00
f. As "c," double surcharge 10.00 3.00
U496 U92 1½c on 1c grn, *amb* (U421, die 1) 18.00 12.50
a. On No. U421b (die 3) 725.00
b. On No. U421c (die 4) 18.00 12.50
U497 U92 1½c on 1c grn, *oriental buff* (U422, die 1) 3.75 1.90
a. On No. U422b (die 4) 67.50
U498 U92 1½c on 1c grn, *bl* (U423c, die 4) 1.40 .75
a. On No. U423 (die 1) 2.40 1.50
b. On No. U423b (die 3) 1.75 1.50
U499 U92 1½c on 1c grn, *man* (U424) 12.50 6.00
U500 U92 1½c on 1c grn, *brn* (unglazed) (U428) 75.00 30.00
U501 U92 1½c on 1c grn, *brn* (glazed) (U426) 75.00 30.00
U502 U93 1½c on 2c car (U429, die 1) 225.00 —
a. On No. U429d (die 5) 275.00
b. On No. U429f (die 7) 275.00
c. On No. U429e (die 6) 350.00
d. On No. U429g (die 8) 475.00
U503 U93 1½c on 2c car, *oriental buff* (U431c, die 5) 225.00 —
a. Double surcharge —
b. Double surcharge, one inverted *700.00*
U504 U93 1½c on 2c car, *bl* (U432, die 1) 400.00 —
a. On No. U432g (die 7) 400.00
b. As "a," double surcharge, entire —
c. On No. U432f (die b), entire *450.00*
U505 U93 1½c on 1½c brn (U481, die 1) 325.00
a. On No. U481a (die 8) 325.00
b. As No. U505, double surcharge, entire *2,000.*
U506 U93 1½c on 1½c brn, *bl* (U483a, die 8) 225.00
a. On No. U483 (die 1) 325.00

The paper of No. U500 is not glazed and appears to be the same as that used for the wrappers of 1920.

Surcharged Type 9

Black Surcharge

U507 U69 1½c on 1c blue (U294) 2,000.
U507A U69 1½c on 1c blue, *amb* (U296) —

U507B	U69	1½c on 1c blue, *manila* (U300)	5,000.	
U508	U77	1½c on 1c grn, *amb* (U353)	65.00	
U508A	U85	1½c on 1c grn (U379)	3,750.	
U509	U85	1½c on 1c grn, *amb* (U380)	15.00	10.00
a.		Double surcharge	75.00	
U509B	U85	1½c on 1c green, *oriental buff* (U381)	45.00	40.00
U510	U90	1½c on 1c green (U400, die 1)	2.75	1.25
b.		On No. U400a (die 2)	9.00	4.00
c.		On No. U400b (die 3)	37.50	8.00
d.		On No. U400c (die 4)	3.50	1.25
e.		As No. U510, double surcharge	25.00	
U511	U90	1½c on 1c grn, *amb* (U401, die 1)	210.00	100.00
U512	U90	1½c on 1c grn, *oriental buff* (U402, die 1)	8.00	4.00
a.		On No. U402c (die 4)	21.00	14.00
U513	U90	1½c on 1c grn, *bl* (U403, die 1)	6.00	4.00
a.		On No. U403c (die 4)	6.00	4.00
U514	U90	1½c on 1c grn, *man* (U404, die 1)	35.00	9.00
a.		On No. U404a (die 3)	77.50	40.00
U515	U92	1½c on 1c green (U420, die 1)	.40	.25
a.		On No. U420a (die 2)	20.00	15.00
b.		On No. U420b (die 3)	.40	.25
c.		On No. U420c (die 4)	.40	.25
d.		As #U515, double surcharge	10.00	
e.		As #U515, inverted surcharge	20.00	
f.		As #U515, triple surcharge	20.00	
g.		As #U515, dbl. surch., one invtd., entire	—	
h.		As "b," double surcharge	10.00	
i.		As "b," inverted surcharge	20.00	
j.		As "b," triple surcharge	30.00	
k.		As "c," double surcharge	10.00	
l.		As "c," inverted surcharge	20.00	
U516	U92	1½c on 1c grn, *amb* (U421c, die 4)	55.00	27.50
a.		On No. U421 (die 1)	60.00	32.50
U517	U92	1½c on 1c grn, *oriental buff* (U422, die 1)	6.25	1.25
a.		On No. U422a (die 4)	7.25	1.50
U518	U92	1½c on 1c grn, *bl* (U423b, die 4)	5.00	1.50
a.		On No. U423 (die 1)	8.25	4.50
b.		On No. U423a (die 3)	27.50	7.50
c.		As "a," double surcharge	30.00	
U519	U92	1½c on 1c grn, *man* (U424, die 1)	30.00	12.00
a.		Double surcharge	100.00	
U520	U93	1½c on 2c car (U429, die 1)	325.00	—
a.		On No. U429d (die 5)	300.00	
b.		On No. U429e (die 6)	300.00	
c.		On No. U429f (die 7)	350.00	
U520D	U93	1½c on 2c car, *amber* (U430c, die 5), entire		—
U520E	U92	1½c on 4c black (U440, die 1), entire		—

Magenta Surcharge

U521	U92	1½c on 1c grn (U420b, die 3)	4.25	3.50
a.		Double surcharge	75.00	

Sesquicentennial Exposition Issue

150th anniversary of the Declaration of Independence.

Liberty Bell — U94

Die 1. The center bar of "E" of "postage" is shorter than top bar.

Die 2. The center bar of "E" of "postage" is of same length as top bar.

1926, July 27

U522	U94	2c carmine, die 1	1.00	.50
a.		Die 2	6.50	3.75

Washington Bicentennial Issue

200th anniversary of the birth of George Washington.

Mount Vernon — U95

2c Die 1 — "S" of "Postage" normal.
2c Die 2 — "S" of "Postage" raised.

1932

U523	U95	1c olive green	1.00	.80
U524	U95	1½c chocolate	2.00	1.50
U525	U95	2c car, die 1	.40	.25
a.		2c carmine, die 2	70.00	20.00
b.		2c carmine, *blue,* die 1 (error) entire	*30,000.*	
U526	U95	3c violet	1.75	.35
U527	U95	4c black	17.50	17.50
U528	U95	5c dark blue	3.50	3.50
		Nos. U523-U528 (6)	26.15	23.90

1932, Aug. 18

U529	U93	6c orange, die 7	6.00	4.00
U530	U93	6c orange, *amber,* die 7	12.00	10.00
U531	U93	6c orange, *blue,* die 7	12.00	10.00

Franklin — U96

Die 1

Die 2

Die 3

Die 1 — Short (3½mm) and thick "I" in thick circle.

Die 2 — Tall (4½mm) and thin "1" in thin circle; upper and lower bars of E in ONE long and 1mm from circle.

Die 3 — As in Die 2, but E normal and 1½mm from circle.

1950

U532	U96	1c green, die 1	5.00	1.75
a.		Die 2	6.50	3.00
b.		Die 3	6.50	3.00
		Precanceled, die 3		1.25

Washington — U97

Die 1

Die 2

Die 3

Die 4

Die 1 — Thick "2" in thick circle; toe of "2" is acute angle.

Die 2 — Thin "2" in thin circle; toe of "2" is almost right angle; line through left stand of "N" in UNITED and stand of "E" in POSTAGE goes considerably below tip of chin; "N" of UNITED is tall; "O" of TWO is high.

Die 3 — Figure "2" as in Die 2. Short UN in UNITED thin crossbar in A of STATES.

Die 4 — Tall UN in UNITED; thick crossbar in A of STATES; otherwise like Die 3.

U533	U97	2c carmine, die 3	.70	.25
a.		Die 1	.80	.30
b.		Die 2	1.40	.85
c.		Die 4	1.30	.60

Die 1

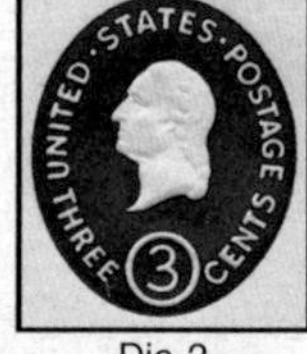
Die 2

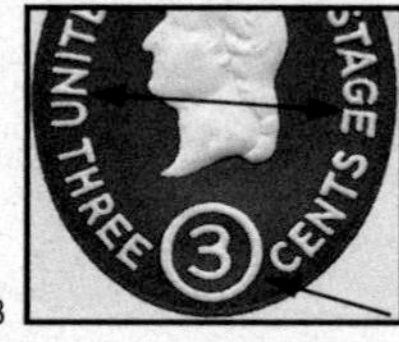
Die 3

Die 4

Die 5

Die 1 — Thick and tall (4½mm) "3" in thick circle; long top bars and short stems in T's of STATES.

Die 2 — Thin and tall (4½mm) "3" in medium circle; short top bars and long stems in T's of STATES.

Die 3 — Thin and short (4mm) "3" in thin circle; lettering wider than Dies 1 and 2; line from left stand of N to stand of E is distinctly below tip of chin.

Die 4 — Figure and letters as in Die 3. Line hits tip of chin; short N in UNITED and thin crossbar in A of STATES.

Die 5 — Figure, letter and chin line as in Die 4; but tall N in UNITED and thick crossbar in A of STATES.

U534	U97	3c dark violet, die 4	.35	.25
a.		Die 1	1.90	.70
b.		Die 2	.75	.50
c.		Die 3	.55	.25
d.		Die 5	.75	.45
e.		As "c," double impression	*300.00*	

Washington — U98

1952

U535	U98	1½c brown	4.50	3.50
		Precanceled		1.25

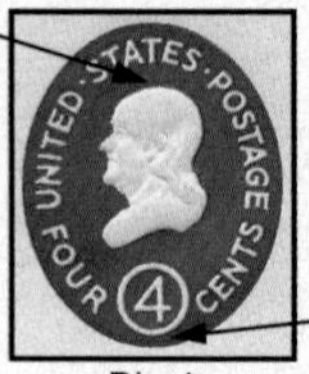
Die 1

Die 2

Die 3

Die 1 — Head high in oval (2mm below T of STATES). Circle near (1mm) bottom of colored oval.

Die 2 — Head low in oval (3mm). Circle 1½mm from edge of oval. Right leg of A in POSTAGE shorter than left. Short leg on P.

Die 3 — Head centered in oval (2½mm). Circle as in Die 2. Legs of A of POSTAGE about equal. Long leg on P.

1958

U536	U96	4c red violet, die 1	.75	.25
a.		Die 2	.90	.25
b.		Die 3	.90	.25

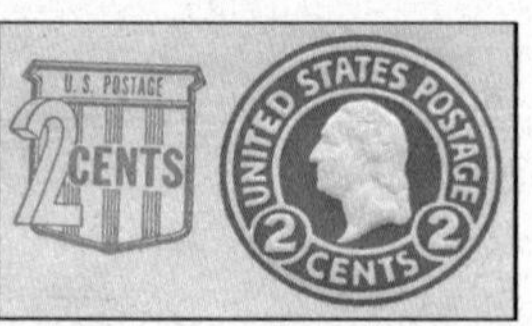

Nos. U429, U429f, U429h, U533, U533a-U533c Surcharged in Red — b

1958

U537	U93	2c + 2c carmine, die 1	3.25	1.50
a.		Die 7	10.00	7.00
b.		Die 9	4.75	5.00
U538	U97	2c + 2c carmine, die 1	.70	.80
a.		Die 2	.90	1.00
b.		Die 3	.70	.70
c.		Die 4	.70	1.00

Nos. U436a, U436e-U436f, U534a-U534d Surcharged in Green — a

U539	U93	3c + 1c purple, die 1	12.50	9.00
a.		Die 7	11.00	7.50
b.		Die 9	20.00	15.00
U540	U97	3c + 1c dark violet, die 3	.40	1.00
a.		Die 2, entire	*3,500.*	—
b.		Die 4	.65	1.00
c.		Die 5	.70	1.00

Benjamin Franklin — U99

George Washington U100

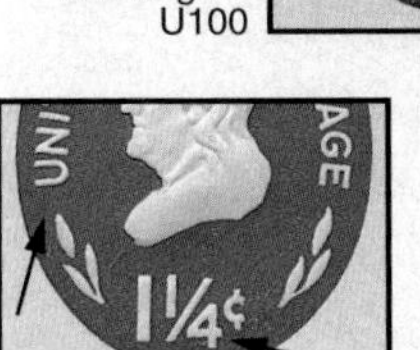

Die 1

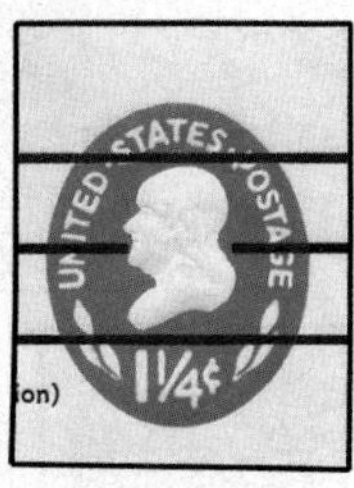

Die 2

Dies of 1¼c

Die 1 — The "4" is 3mm high. Upper leaf in left cluster is 2mm from "U."

Die 2 — The "4" is 3½mm high. Leaf clusters are larger. Upper leaf at left is 1mm from "U."

1960

U541 U99 1¼c turquoise, die 1 .65 .50
Die 1, precanceled .25
a. Die 2, precanceled 1.25
U542 U100 2½c dull blue .80 .50
Precanceled .25

Precanceled cut squares

Precanceled envelopes do not normally receive another cancellation. Since the lack of a cancellation makes it impossible to distinguish between cut squares from used and unused envelopes, they are valued here as used only.

Pony Express Centennial Issue

Pony Express Rider — U101

Envelope White Outside, Blue Inside.

1960

U543 U101 4c brown .55 .30

Abraham Lincoln — U102

Die 1

Die 2

Die 3

Die 1 — Center bar of E of POSTAGE is above the middle. Center bar of E of STATES slants slightly upward. Nose sharper, more pointed. No offset ink specks inside envelope on back of die impression.

Die 2 — Center bar of E of POSTAGE in middle. P of POSTAGE has short stem. Ink specks on back of die impression.

Die 3 — FI of FIVE closer than Die 1 or 2. Second T of STATES seems taller than ES. Ink specks on back of die impression.

1962

U544 U102 5c dark blue, die 2 .80 .25
a. Die 1 .80 .25
b. Die 3 .85 .35
c. Die 2 with albino impression of 4c (#U536) 60.00 —
d. Die 3 with albino impression of 4c (#U536), entire *140.00* —
e. Die 3 on complete impression of 4c (#U536), cut square *125.00*

No. U536 Surcharged in Green at left of Stamp

Two types of surcharge:

Type I — "U.S. POSTAGE" 18½mm high. Serifs on cross of T both diagonal. Two lines of shading in C of CENT.

Type II — "U.S. POSTAGE" 17½mm high. Right serif on cross of T is vertical. Three shading lines in C.

1962

U545 U96 4c + 1c red vio, die 1, type I 1.25 1.10
a. Type II 1.25 1.10

New York World's Fair Issue

Issued to publicize the New York World's Fair, 1964-65.

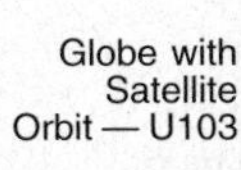
Globe with Satellite Orbit — U103

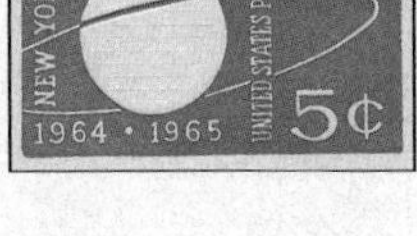

1964

U546 U103 5c maroon .55 .40

Liberty Bell — U104

Old Ironsides U105

Eagle — U106

Head of Statue of Liberty — U107

1965-69

U547 U104 1¼c brown .50
U548 U104 1⁴⁄₁₀c brown ('68) .50
U548A U104 1⁶⁄₁₀c orange ('69) .50
b. 1⁶⁄₁₀c brown (error), entire *5,000.*
U549 U105 4c bright blue .90 .25
U550 U106 5c bright purple .75 .25
a. Bar tagged ('67) 3.00 1.00

Tagged

U551 U107 6c lt green ('68) .70 .25
a. 6c dark gray green, entire 200.00 —

Nos. U549-U550 Surcharged Types "b" and "a" in Red or Green at Left of Stamp

1968, Feb. 5

U552 U105 4c + 2c bright blue (R) 3.25 2.00
U553 U106 5c + 1c bright purple (G) 3.00 2.75
a. Tagged 3.00 2.75
b. With 2c surcharge type "b" (error) 400.00

Tagged

Envelopes from No. U554 onward are tagged, except for bulk-rate and non-profit envelopes, which are untagged. The tagging element is in the ink through No. 608 unless otherwise noted. From No. 611 on, envelopes have bar or block tagging unless otherwise noted.

Herman Melville Issue

Issued to honor Herman Melville (1819-1891), writer, and the whaling industry.

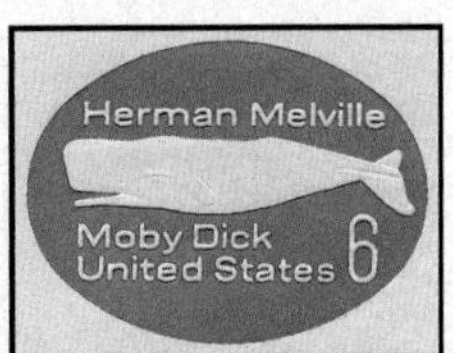

Moby Dick U108

1970, Mar. 7

U554 U108 6c blue .50 .25

Youth Conference Issue

Issued to publicize the White House Conference on Youth, Estes Park, Colo., Apr. 18-22.

Youth Conference Emblem — U109

1971, Feb. 24

U555 U109 6c light blue .70 1.00

Liberty Bell Type of 1965 and U110

Eagle — U110

1971

U556 U104 1⁷⁄₁₀c deep lilac, untagged .35
U557 U110 8c ultramarine .40 .25

Nos. U551 and U555 Surcharged in Green at Left of Stamp

1971, May 16

U561 U107 6c + (2c) light green .90 1.25
a. Inverted surcharge, entire *225.00*
U562 U109 6c + (2c) light blue 2.00 2.50
a. Inverted surcharge printed on reverse, entire —

Bowling Issue

Issued as a salute to bowling and in connection with the 7th World Tournament of the International Bowling Federation, Milwaukee, Wis.

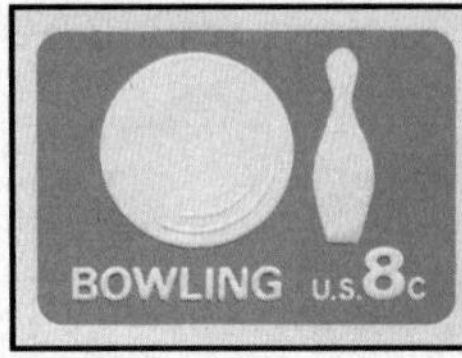

Bowling Ball and Pin U111

1971, Aug. 21

U563 U111 8c rose red .60 .25

Aging Conference Issue

White House Conference on Aging, Washington, D.C., Nov. 28-Dec. 2, 1971.

Conference Symbol U112

1971, Nov. 15

U564 U112 8c light blue .50 .25

International Transportation Exhibition Issue

U.S. International Transportation Exhibition, Dulles International Airport, Washington, D.C., May 27-June 4.

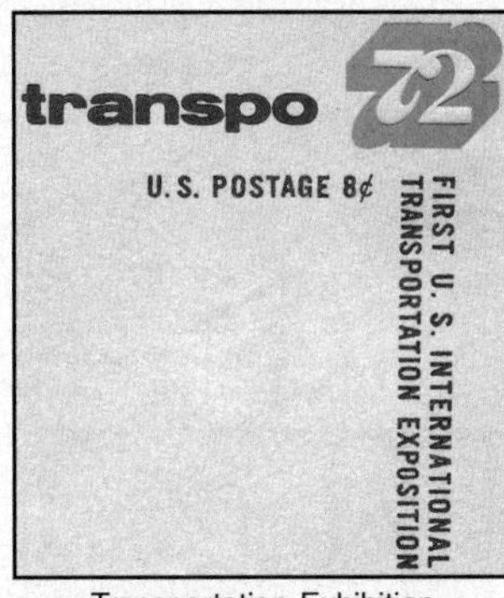

Transportation Exhibition Emblem — U113

1972, May 2

U565 U113 8c ultramarine & rose red .50 .25

No. U557 Surcharged Type "b" (like Nos. U537-U538) in Ultramarine at Left of Stamp

1973, Dec. 1

U566 U110 8c + 2c brt. ultramarine .40 1.25

Liberty Bell — U114

1973, Dec. 5
U567 U114 10c emerald .40 .25

"Volunteer Yourself" U115

1974, Aug. 23
Untagged
U568 U115 1⁸⁄₁₀c blue green .25

Tennis Centenary Issue

Centenary of tennis in the United States.

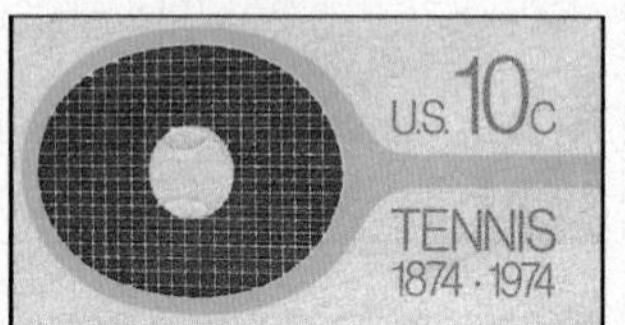

Tennis Racquet — U116

1974, Aug. 31 **Block Tagged**
U569 U116 10c yellow, brt. blue & light green .55 .25

Bicentennial Era Issue

The Seafaring Tradition — Compass Rose — U118

The American Homemaker — Quilt Pattern — U119

The American Farmer — Sheaf of Wheat — U120

The American Doctor — U121

The American Craftsman — Tools, c. 1750 — U122

Designs (in brown on left side of envelope): 10c, Norwegian sloop Restaurationen. No. U572, Spinning wheel. No. U573, Plow. No. U574, Colonial era medical instruments and bottle. No. U575, Shaker rocking chair.

1975-76 **Embossed**
Light Brown Diagonally Laid Paper

U571 U118 10c brown & blue .30 .25
a. Brown ("10c/USA," etc.) omitted, entire 110.00
U572 U119 13c brown & blue green .35 .25
a. Brown ("13c/USA," etc.) omitted, entire 110.00
U573 U120 13c brown & bright green .35 .25
a. Brown ("13c/USA," etc.) omitted, entire 110.00
U574 U121 13c brown & orange .35 .25
a. Brown ("13c/USA," etc.) omitted, entire 110.00
U575 U122 13c brown & carmine .35 .25
a. Brown ("13c/USA," etc.) omitted, entire 110.00
Nos. U571-U575 (5) 1.70 1.25

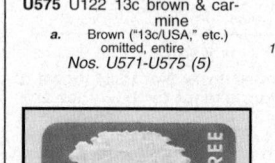

Liberty Tree, Boston, 1646 U123

1975, Nov. 8 **Embossed**
U576 U123 13c orange brown .30 .25

Star and Pinweel U124

U125

U126

Eagle — U127

"Uncle Sam" — U128

1976-78 **Embossed**
U577 U124 2c red, untagged .25
U578 U125 2.1c green, untagged .25
U579 U126 2.7c green, untagged .25
U580 U127 (15c) orange .40 .25
U581 U128 15c red, ink tagged .40 .25
a. Bar tagged 7.00 7.00

For No. U581 with surcharge, see No. U586b.

Bicentennial Issue

Centennial Envelope, 1876 — U129

1976, Oct. 15 **Embossed**
U582 U129 13c emerald .35 .25

Golf Issue

Golf Club in Motion and Golf Ball — U130

Photogravure and Embossed
1977, Apr. 7
U583 U130 13c black, blue & yellow green .65 .25
a. Black omitted, entire 500.00
b. Black & blue omitted, entire 500.00
c. Black, blue & yellow green omitted, entire 500.00

On No. U583c, the embossing is present.

Energy Issue

Conservation and development of national resources.

Energy Conservation U131

Energy Development U132

1977, Oct. 20 **Embossed**
Bar Tagged
U584 U131 13c black, red & yellow .45 .25
a. Red, yellow & tagging omitted, entire 190.00
b. Yellow & tagging omitted, entire 150.00
c. Black omitted, entire 135.00
d. Black & red omitted, entire 260.00
U585 U132 13c black, red & yellow .45 .25

Olive Branch and Star — U133

1978, July 28 **Embossed**
Black Surcharge
U586 U133 15c on 16c blue .40 .25
a. Surcharge omitted, entire 250.00 1,000.
b. Surcharge on No. U581, entire 150.00 260.00
c. As "a," with surcharge printed on envelope flap 175.00 —
d. Surcharge inverted (in lower left corner), entire 300.00 —

Auto Racing Issue

Indianapolis 500 Racing Car — U134

1978, Sept. 2 **Embossed**
U587 U134 15c red, blue & black .45 .25
a. Black omitted, entire 100.00
b. Black & blue omitted, entire 170.00
c. Red & tagging omitted, entire 100.00
d. Red, blue & tagging omitted, entire 170.00

No. U576 Surcharged Like No. U586

1978, Nov. 28 **Embossed**
U588 U123 15c on 13c orange brown .40 .25
a. Surcharge inverted (in lower left corner), entire —

U135

Weaver Violins — U136

U137

Eagle — U138

Star — U139

Eagle — U140

Embossed
1979, May 18 **Untagged**
U589 U135 3.1c ultramarine .35

1980, June 23 **Untagged**
U590 U136 3.5c purple .35
a. 3.5c violet, tagged (in ink), error of color and tagging using ink intended for No. U592, entire *300.00* *500.00*

1982, Feb. 17 **Untagged**
U591 U137 5.9c brown .35

1981, Mar. 15
U592 U138 (18c) violet .45 .25

1981, Apr. 2
U593 U139 18c dark blue .45 .25

1981, Oct. 11
U594 U140 (20c) brown .45 .25

Veterinary Medicine Issue

Seal of Veterinarians — U141

Design at left side of envelope shows 5 animals and bird in brown, "Veterinary Medicine" in gray.

1979, July 24
U595 U141 15c brown & gray .50 .25
a. Gray omitted, entire *425.00*
b. Brown omitted, entire *500.00*
c. Gray & brown omitted, entire *325.00*

On No. 595c, the embossing of the seal is present.

Olympic Games Issue

22nd Olympic Games, Moscow, July 19-Aug. 3, 1980.

U142

Design (multicolored on left side of envelope) shows two soccer players with ball.

1979, Dec. 10
U596 U142 15c red, green & black .60 .25
a. Red & green omitted, tagging omitted, entire *190.00*
b. Black omitted, tagging omitted, entire *190.00*
c. Black & green omitted, entire *190.00*
d. Red omitted, tagging omitted, entire *325.00*
e. All colors omitted *250.00*

No. U596c exists with a portion of the green present in the Olympics 1980 design at the lower left corner of the envelope.

On No. U596e, the blind embossing of "USA 15c" remains.

Highwheeler Bicycle — U143

Design (blue on left side of envelope) shows racing bicycle.

1980, May 16
U597 U143 15c blue & rose claret .40 .25
a. Blue ("15c USA") omitted, entire 100.00
b. As "a," tagging omitted *100.00*

Racing Yacht — U144

1980, Sept. 15
U598 U144 15c blue & red .40 .25

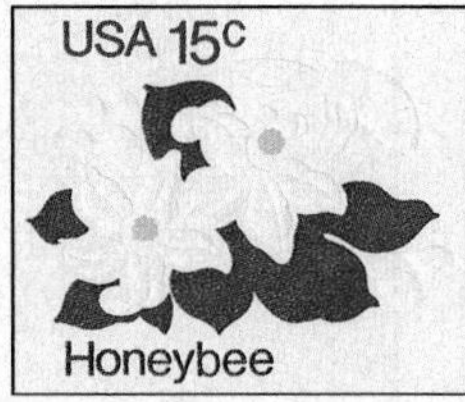

Italian Honeybee and Orange Blossoms U145

Bee and petals colorless embossed.

Photogravure and Embossed

1980, Oct. 10
U599 U145 15c brown, green & yellow .35 .25
a. Brown ("USA 15c") omitted, entire *100.00*
b. Green omitted, entire *100.00*

No. U599b also has almost all of the brown color missing.

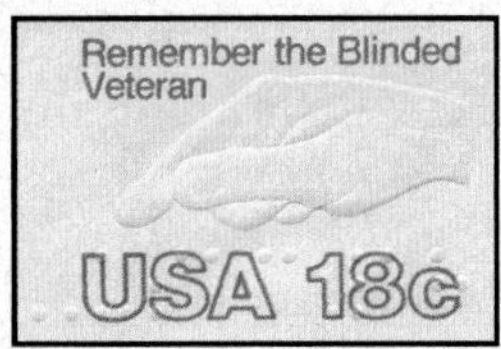

U146

Hand and braille colorless embossed.

1981, Aug. 13 **Embossed**
U600 U146 18c blue & red .45 .25
a. Blue omitted, entire *300.00*
b. Red omitted, entire *210.00*

Capitol Dome U147

1981, Nov. 13
U601 U147 20c deep magenta, ink tagged .45 .25
a. Bar tagged 4.50 1.50

U148

1982, June 15
U602 U148 20c dark blue, black & magenta .45 .25
a. Dark blue omitted, entire *175.00*
b. Dark blue & magenta omitted, entire *175.00*
c. All colors omitted, entire *175.00*

On No. 602c, the colorless embossed impression of the Great Seal is present.

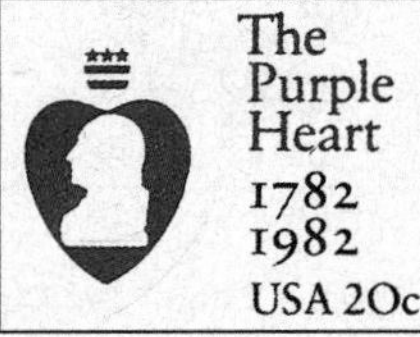

U149

1982, Aug. 6
U603 U149 20c purple & black .75 .25
a. Black omitted, entire *80.00*
b. Purple omitted, entire *200.00*

U150

1983, Mar. 21 **Untagged**
U604 U150 5.2c orange .90

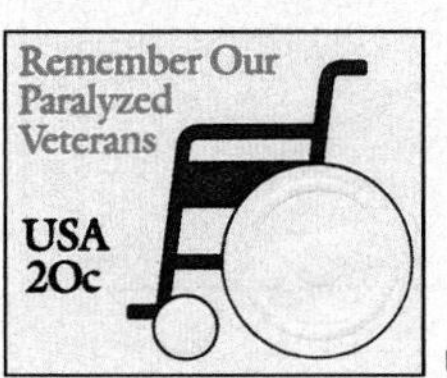

U151

1983, Aug. 3
U605 U151 20c red, blue & black .45 .25
a. Red omitted, entire *260.00*
b. Blue omitted, entire *260.00*
c. Red & black omitted, entire *125.00*
d. Blue & black omitted, entire *125.00*
e. Black omitted, entire *260.00*

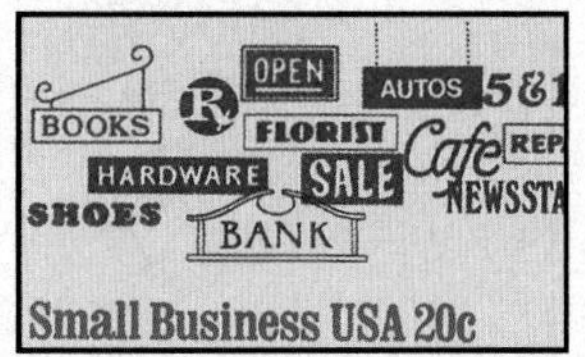

U152

Design shows storefronts at lower left. Stamp and design continue on back of envelope.

1984, May 7 **Photo.**
U606 U152 20c multi .50 .25

U153

1985, Feb. 1 **Embossed**
U607 U153 (22c) deep green .55 .30

American Buffalo U154

1985, Feb. 25
U608 U154 22c violet brown, ink tagged .55 .25
a. Untagged, 3 blue precancel lines, unwmk'd ('86) .25
b. Bar tagged 2.00 1.00

Frigate U.S.S. Constitution, "Old Ironsides" U155

1985, May 3 **Untagged**
U609 U155 6c green blue .35

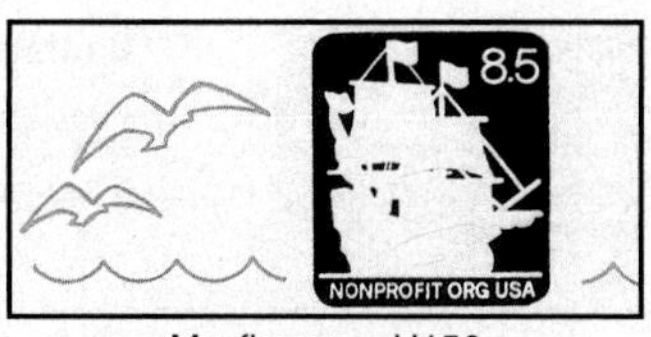

Mayflower — U156

1986, Dec. 4 **Untagged**
Precanceled
U610 U156 8.5c black & gray .65

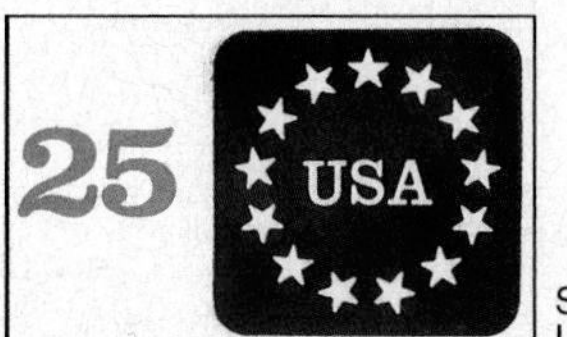

Stars U157

1988, Mar. 26 **Typo. & Embossed**
U611 U157 25c dark red & deep blue .60 .25
a. Dark red omitted, tagging omitted 50.00 —
c. Dark red omitted, tagging not omitted *60.00*

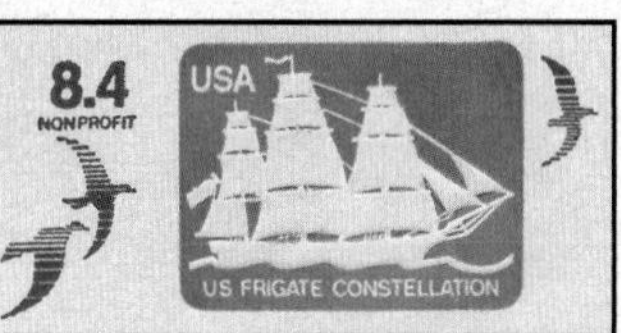

Sea Gulls, Frigate USS Constellation — U158

1988, Apr. 12 **Untagged**
Precanceled
U612 U158 8.4c black & bright blue .65
a. Black omitted, entire *500.00*

Snowflake — U159

"Holiday Greetings!" inscribed in lower left.

1988, Sept. 8 **Typo.**
U613 U159 25c dark red & green 1.25 *20.00*

Stars and "*Philatelic Mail*" Continuous in Dark Red Below Vignette — U160

"Philatelic Mail" and asterisks in dark red below vignette; continuous across envelope face and partly on reverse.

1989, Mar. 10
U614 U160 25c dark red & deep blue .50 .25
b. Red omitted, entire 125.00

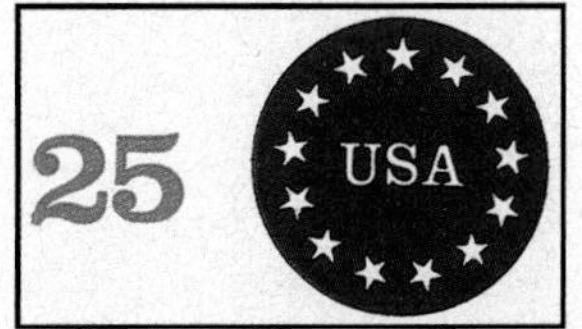

"USA" and Stars — U161

1989, July 10 **Unwmk.**

U615 U161 25c dark red & deep blue .50 .25
a. Dark red omitted, entire *425.00*

Lined with a blue design to provide security for enclosures.

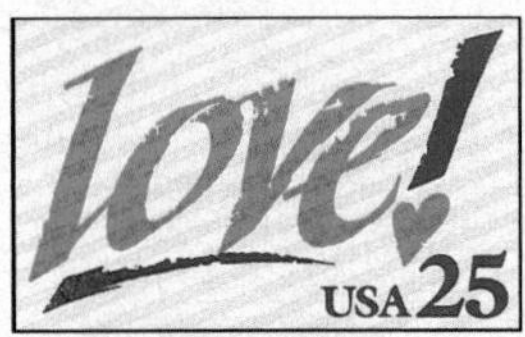

Love — U162

Litho. & Typo.

1989, Sept. 22 **Unwmk.**

U616 U162 25c dark red & bright blue .50 .75
a. Dark red and bright blue omitted, entire 150.00
b. Bright blue omitted, entire 150.00

No. U616 has light blue lines printed diagonally over the entire surface of the envelope.

Shuttle Docking at Space Station — U163

1989, Dec. 3 **Typo.** **Unwmk.**
Die Cut

U617 U163 25c ultramarine .90 .60
a. Ultramarine omitted, entire *400.00*

A hologram, visible through the die cut window to the right of "USA 25," is affixed to the inside of the envelope.

See Nos. U625, U639.

Vince Lombardi Trophy, Football Players — U164

1990, Sept. 9 **Unwmk.** ***Die Cut***

U618 U164 25c vermilion .90 .60

A hologram, visible through the die cut window to the right of "USA 25," is affixed to the inside of the envelope.

Star — U165

Typo. & Embossed

1991, Jan. 24 **Wmk.**

U619 U165 29c ultramarine & rose .60 .30
a. Ultramarine omitted, entire *375.00*
b. Rose omitted, tagged, entire *300.00*
c. Rose omitted, tagging omitted, entire —
d. Tagging omitted, entire —

See No. U623.

Birds — U166

Stamp and design continue on back of envelope.

1991, May 3 **Typo.** **Wmk.**
Untagged, Precanceled

U620 U166 11.1c blue & red — .90
a. Blue omitted, entire

Love — U167

1991, May 9 **Litho.** **Unwmk.**

U621 U167 29c light blue, purple & bright rose .60 .60
a. Bright rose omitted, entire *400.00*
b. Purple omitted, entire *400.00*

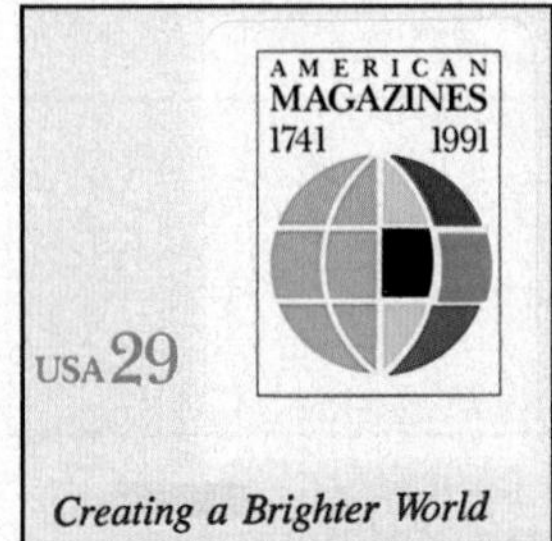

Magazine Industry, 250th Anniv. — U168

Photo. & Typo.

1991, Oct. 7 **Unwmk.**

U622 U168 29c multicolored .70 1.00

The photogravure vignette, visible through the die cut window to the right of "USA 29", is affixed to the inside of the envelope.

Star U169

Stamp and design continue on back of envelope.

1991, July 20 **Typo.** **Unwmk.**

U623 U169 29c ultra & rose .60 .30
a. Ultra omitted, entire *500.00*
b. Rose omitted, entire *200.00*

Lined with a blue design to provide security for enclosures.

Country Geese U170

1991, Nov. 8 **Litho. & Typo.** **Wmk.**

U624 U170 29c blue gray & yellow .60 .60

Space Shuttle Type of 1989
Unwmk.

1992, Jan. 21 **Typo.** ***Die Cut***

U625 U163 29c yellow green .80 .50

A hologram, visible through the die cut window to the right of "USA 29," is affixed to the inside of the envelope.

U171

Typo. & Litho.

1992, Apr. 10 ***Die Cut***

U626 U171 29c multicolored .60 1.00

The lithographed vignette, visible through the die cut window to the right of "USA 29," is affixed to the inside of the envelope.

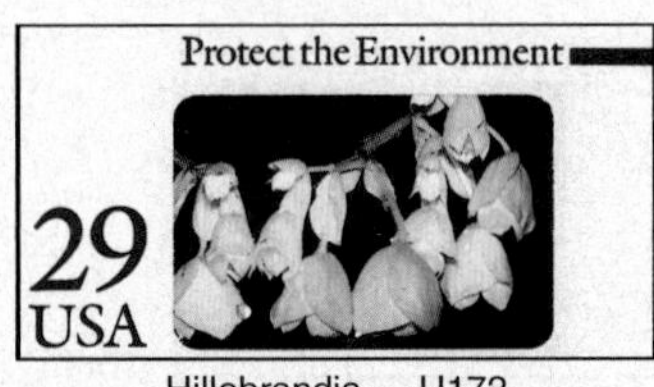

Hillebrandia — U172

1992, Apr. 22

U627 U172 29c multicolored .65 1.00

The lithographed vignette, visible through the die cut window to the right of "29 USA," is affixed to the inside of the envelope.

U173

Typo. & Embossed

1992, May 19 **Precanceled**
Untagged

U628 U173 19.8c red & blue .40

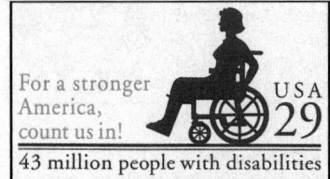

For a stronger America, count us in!
USA
29
43 million people with disabilities

U174

1992, July 22 **Typo.**

U629 U174 29c red & blue .60 .30

U175

1993, Oct. 2 **Typo. & Litho.** ***Die Cut***

U630 U175 29c multicolored 1.10 1.10

The lithographed vignette, visible through the die cut window to the right of "USA 29," is affixed to the inside of the envelope.

U176

Typo. & Embossed

1994, Sept. 17

U631 U176 29c brown & black .70 1.25
a. Black ("29/USA") omitted, entire *325.00*

Liberty Bell — U177

1995, Jan. 3 **Typo. & Embossed**

U632 U177 32c greenish blue & blue .65 .30
a. Greenish blue omitted *100.00*
b. Blue ("USA 32") omitted 90.00

See No. U638.

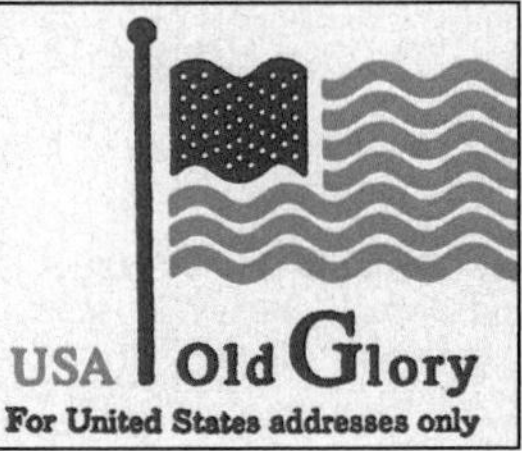

U178

Design sizes: 49x38mm (#U633), 53x44mm (U634). Stamp and design continue on back of envelope.

1995 **Typo.**

U633 U178 (32c) blue & red 1.25 2.00
U634 U178 (32c) blue & red 1.25 2.00
a. Red & tagging omitted, entire *325.00*
b. Blue omitted, entire *325.00*

Originally, Nos. U633-U634 were only available through the Philatelic Fullfillment Center after their announcement 1/12/95.

U179

Stamp and design continue on back of envelope.

1995, Mar. 10
Precanceled, Untagged

U635 U179 (5c) green & red brown .40

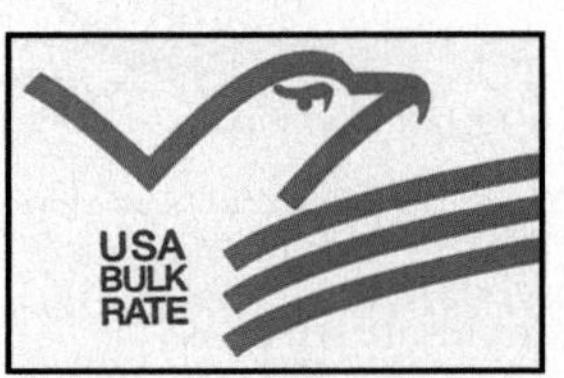

Graphic Eagle — U180

1995, Mar. 10
Precanceled, Untagged

U636 U180 (10c) dark carmine & blue 1.50

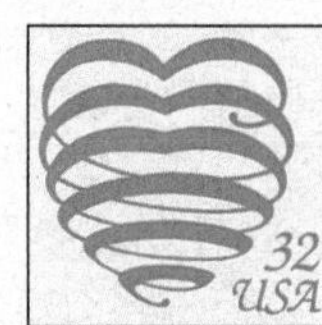

Spiral Heart — U181

1995, May 12
U637 U181 32c red, *light blue* .65 .30
a. Red omitted, entire *200.00*

Liberty Bell Type of 1995

1995, May 16
U638 U177 32c greenish blue & blue .70 .30
a. Greenish blue omitted, entire *175.00*

Space Shuttle Type of 1989

1995, Sept. 22 ***Die Cut***
U639 U163 32c carmine rose .75 .35

A hologram, visible through the die cut window to the right of "USA 32," is affixed to the inside of the envelope.

U182

Typo. & Litho.

1996, Apr. 20 ***Die Cut***
U640 U182 32c multicolored .70 .30

The lithographed vignette, visible through the die cut window to the right of "USA 32c," is affixed to the inside of the envelope.

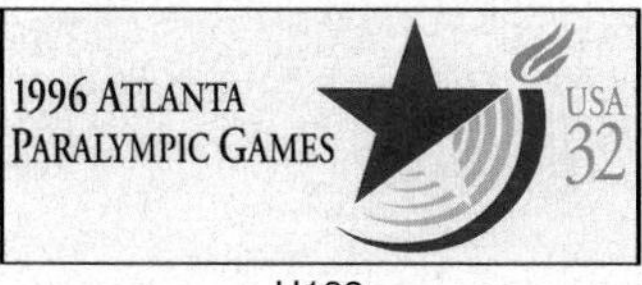

U183

1996, May 2
U641 U183 32c multicolored .70 .30
a. Blue & red omitted, entire *260.00*
b. Blue & gold omitted, entire *550.00*
c. Red omitted, entire *260.00*
d. Black & red omitted, entire *450.00*
e. Blue omitted, entire *300.00*

U184

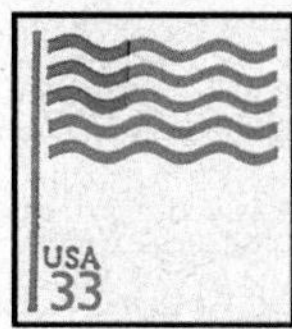

U184a

1999, Jan. 11 **Typo. & Embossed**
U642 U184 33c yellow, blue & red, tagging bar to left of design 1.00 .30
a. Tagging bar to right of design 7.50 3.00
b. As "a," blue omitted, entire *200.00*
c. As "a," yellow omitted, entire *175.00*
d. As "a," yellow and blue omitted, entire *175.00*
e. As "a," blue and red omitted, entire *175.00*
f. As "a," all colors omitted, entire *175.00*
g. As No. U642, red omitted, entire —
h. As No. U642, yellow and red omitted, entire —
i. As No. U642, blue and red omitted, entire —

On No. U642f, the distinctive tagging bar is present. Expertization is required.

1999, Jan. 11 **Typo.**
U643 U184a 33c blue & red 1.00 .30
a. Tagging bar to right of design 10.00 5.00

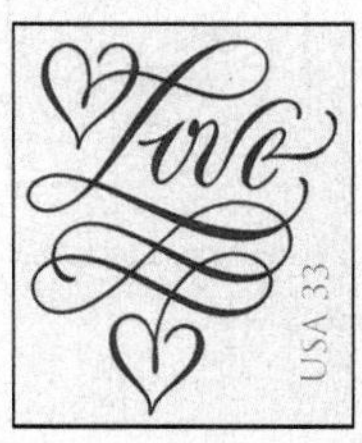

U185

1999, Jan. 28 **Litho.**
U644 U185 33c violet .65 .30
a. Tagging bar to right of design .65 .30

Lincoln — U186

1999, June 5 **Typo. & Litho.**
U645 U186 33c blue & black .65 .30

Eagle U187

2001, Jan. 7 **Typo.**
U646 U187 34c blue gray & gray .70 .30
a. Blue gray omitted 175.00

Many color shades known.

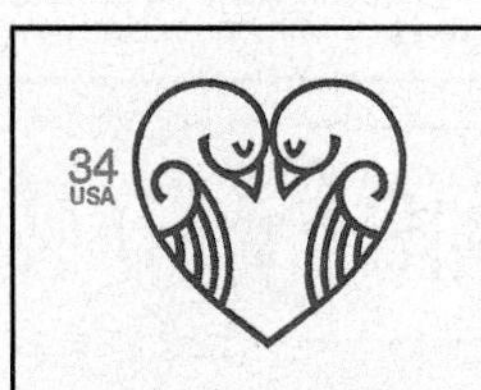

Lovebirds — U188

2001, Feb. 14 **Litho.**
U647 U188 34c rose & dull violet .70 .30

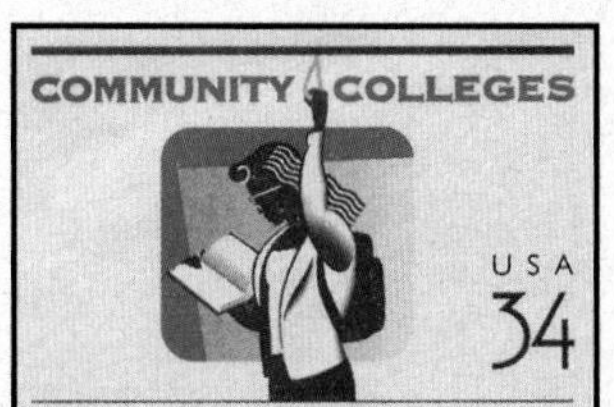

Community Colleges, Cent. — U189

2001, Feb. 20 **Typo.**
U648 U189 34c dark blue & orange brown .70 .30

Ribbon Star — U190

2002, June 7
U649 U190 37c red, blue & gray .75 .35
a. Gray omitted, entire —
b. Blue and gray omitted, entire —

All No. U649 were printed on recycled paper. It was also produced using a different blue-gray recycled paper starting in 2002.

Type of 1995 Inscribed "USA / Presorted / Standard"

2002, Aug. 8 **Untagged**

Precanceled

U650 U180 (10c) dark carmine & blue .25

Nurturing Love — U191

2003, Jan. 25
U651 U191 37c olive green & yellow orange .80 .35

Jefferson Memorial Type

2003, Dec. 29
U652 A2818 $3.85 multicolored 11.00 6.25

On No. U652, the stamp indicia is printed on the flap of the envelope.

Disney Type of 2004 Letter Sheet

2004, June 23 **Litho.**
U653 A2949 37c multicolored 2.50 2.25
U654 A2950 37c multicolored 2.50 2.25
U655 A2951 37c multicolored 2.50 2.25
a. All color missing on reverse, entire —
U656 A2952 37c multicolored 2.50 2.25
a. Booklet of 12 letter sheets, 3 each #U653-U656 30.00

No. U656a sold for $14.95.

White Lilacs and Pink Roses Type of 2004 Letter Sheet

2005, Mar. 3
U657 A2931 37c multicolored 2.50 2.50

No. U657 was sold in pads of 12 for $14.95.

Computer-generated Study of an X-Plane — U192

2006, Jan. 5 **Typo.**
U658 U192 $4.05 multicolored 8.25 7.50

Benjamin Franklin — U193

2006, Jan. 9
U659 U193 39c blue green & black .80 .40
a. All color omitted, entire —

On No. 659a, the tagging bar and the blue green printing on the reverse are present.

Air Force One U194

2007, May 6
U660 U194 $4.60 multicolored 9.25 7.00

Marine One U195

2007, May 6
U661 U195 $16.25 multicolored 33.00 17.00

Horses — U196

2007, May 12
U662 U196 41c reddish brown & black .85 .40

Elk U197

2008, May 2
U663 U197 42c green & black, tagging bar 20mm tall .85 .40
a. Tagging bar 26mm tall .85 .40
b. As No. U663, litho., tagging bar 19mm tall .85 .40
c. Black omitted, entire 85.00
d. Black over entire stamp area 100.00

No. U663 was printed by National Envelope for Ashton-Potter (USA) Ltd. No. U663a was printed by Westvaco.

No. U663b was printed by Ashton-Potter (USA) Ltd. The lithographed impressions of No. U663b are slightly sharper (some tree branches are slightly thinner and more distinct) than the typographed impressions on Nos. U663 and U663a, but because of the nature of the design are nonetheless difficult to distinguish without measuring the tagging bar.

Mount Rushmore — U198

2008, May 12
U664 U198 $4.80 multicolored 9.75 7.00

Sunflower Type of 2008 Letter Sheet

2008, Aug. 15 **Litho.**
U665 A3309 42c multicolored 3.00 3.00

No. U665 was sold in packs of 10 for $14.95.

Redwood Forest Type of 2009

2009, Jan. 16 Typo.
U666 A3332 $4.95 multicolored 10.00 7.50

U199

2009-11 Litho.
U667 U199 (44c) multicolored .90 .90
a. As #U667, typographed .90 .45
b. As #U667, dated "2011," "FOREVER" multicolored (with color dots) .90 .90
c. As #U667b, "FOREVER" in brown (solid color) .90 .90

Issued: No. U667, 5/11; No. U667a, 8/16; Nos. U667b, U667c, 1/3/11.

No. U667 had a franking value of 44c on the day of issue and will be valid for the one ounce first class postage rate after any new rates go into effect.

The typographed version (No. U667a) can be distinguished from No. U667 by the position of the recycle logo on the back. On the litho. version it is to the right of the recycle text; on the typo. version it is to the left of the text.

U200

2009, May 11
U668 U200 44c multicolored .90 .45
a. As #U668, typographed .90 .45
b. As No. U668, triple impression of black, entire —

On No. U668a, the screened blue dots cover the entire area between the "S" and the "C" on No. U668, but appear more random on No. U668a. The pattern of blue dots running towards the shoulder under the head and neck of the horse is long and distinct on No. U668, but barely noticeable, with only a few dots showing, on No. U668a.

See second paragraph of No. U667 footnote, which also applies to Nos. U668 and U668a.

Gulf Coast Lighthouses Type of 2009

2009, July 23 Litho.
U669 A3354 44c multicolored 3.25 3.00
U670 A3355 44c multicolored 3.25 3.00
U671 A3356 44c multicolored 3.25 3.00
U672 A3357 44c multicolored 3.25 3.00
U673 A3358 44c multicolored 3.25 3.00
Nos. U669-U673 (5) 16.25 15.00

Pack of ten, containing two of each letter sheet, sold for $15.95.

Mackinac Bridge U201

Designed by Carl T. Herrman.

2010, Jan. 4 Typo. Unwmk.
U674 U201 $4.90 multicolored 10.00 7.50

No. U674 was sold only in packs of 5.

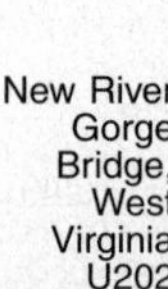

New River Gorge Bridge, West Virginia U202

Designed by Carl T. Herrman.

2011, Jan. 3 Typo. Unwmk.
U675 U202 $4.95 multicolored 10.00 7.50

No. U675 was sold only in packs of 5.

Sunshine Skyway Bridge, Florida U203

Designed by Carl T. Hermann.

2012, Jan. 3 Typo. Unwmk.
U676 U203 $5.15 multicolored 10.50 7.50
Entire 10.50 7.50
Entire, first day cancel, Liberty, MO 10.50

No. U676 was sold only in packs of 5.

Purple Martin — U204

Designed by William J. Gicker.

2012, Jan. 23 Litho. Unwmk.

Design Size: 48x33mm

U677 U204 (45c) multicolored .95 .50
Entire 1.10 .55
Entire, first day cancel, Mulberry, FL 2.40

Design Size: 50x35mm

U678 U204 (45c) multicolored .95 .50
Entire 1.10 .55
Entire, first day cancel, Mulberry, FL 2.40

No. U677 was from No. 6¾ size envelopes only. No. U678 was from No. 9 and No. 10 size envelopes.

No. U678 was reprinted in June 2012 without the 'Cradle to Cradle' recycling logo on the back.

Arlington Green Bridge Type of 2013

2013, Jan. 25 Typo. Unwmk.
U679 A3612 $5.60 multicolored 11.00 8.00

No. U679 was sold only in packs of 5.

Bank Swallows U205

Designed by William J. Gicker.

2013, Mar. 1 Litho. Unwmk.

Design Size: 38x35mm

U680 U205 (46c) multicolored .95 .50

Design Size: 41x38mm

U681 U205 (46c) multicolored .95 .50

No. U680 is from No. 6¾ size envelopes only. No. U681 is from No. 9 and No. 10 size envelopes.

Eagle, Shield and Flags U206

Designed by Richard Sheaff.

2013, Aug. 9 Litho. Unwmk.
U682 U206 (46c) multicolored .95 .50

AIR POST STAMPED ENVELOPES & AIR LETTER SHEETS

UC1

5c — Vertical rudder is not semi-circular but slopes down to the left. The tail of the plane projects into the G of POSTAGE.

UC2

Die 2 (5c and 8c): Vertical rudder is semi-circular. The tail of the plane touches but does not project into the G of POSTAGE.

Die 2 (6c) — Same as UC2 except three types of numeral.

2a — The numeral "6" is 6½mm wide.
2b — The numeral "6" is 6mm wide.
2c — The numeral "6" is 5½mm wide.

Die 3 (6c): Vertical rudder leans forward. S closer to O than to T of POSTAGE. E of POSTAGE has short center bar. Border types b and d, also without border.

1929-44
UC1 UC1 5c blue 3.25 2.00
a. Orange and blue border, type b 375.00 *450.00*
UC2 UC2 5c blue, die 2 11.00 5.00
UC3 UC2 6c orange, die 2a ('34) 1.25 .40
a. With added impression of 3c purple (#U436a), entire without border *4,000.*
UC4 UC2 6c orange, die 2b ('42) 3.00 2.00
UC5 UC2 6c orange, die 2c ('44) .70 .30
UC6 UC2 6c orange, die 3 ('42) 1.00 .35
a. 6c orange, *blue,* die 3 (error) Entire, without border *15,000.* *10,000.*
UC7 UC2 8c olive green, die 2 ('32) 12.50 3.50

Surcharged in black on envelopes indicated by number in parenthesis

1945
UC8 U93 6c on 2c carmine (U429, die 1) 1.25 .65
a. On U429f, die 7 2.25 1.50
b. On U429g, die 8 1.90 1.10
c. On U429h, die 9 11.00 7.50
d. 6c on 1c green (error) (U420) *1,750.*
e. 6c on 3c dk violet (error) (U436a) *2,000.*
f. 6c on 3c dk violet (error), *amber* (U437a) *3,000.*
g. 6c on 3c violet (error) (U526) *3,000.*
UC9 U95 6c on 2c carmine (U525) 55.00 35.00

Surcharged in Black

Surcharged on 6c orange air post envelopes without borders.

1946
UC10 UC2 5c on 6c orange, die 2a 2.75 1.50
a. Double surcharge 75.00
UC11 UC2 5c on 6c orange, die 2b 10.00 5.50
UC12 UC2 5c on 6c orange, die 2c .75 .50
a. Double surcharge 75.00 *300.00*
UC13 UC2 5c on 6c orange, die 3 .70 .60
a. Double surcharge 75.00 50.00
c. Double surcharge, one on reverse —
UC13B U93 5c on 6c (UC8a), entire —

The 6c borderless envelopes and the revalued envelopes were issued primarily for use to and from members of the armed forces. The 5c rate came into effect Oct. 1, 1946.

DC-4 Skymaster UC3

Die 1 — The end of the wing at the right is a smooth curve. The juncture of the front end of the plane and the engine forms an acute angle. The first T of STATES and the E's of UNITED STATES lean to the left.

Die 2 — The end of the wing at the right is a straight line. The juncture of the front end of the plane and the engine is wide open. The first T of STATES and the E's of UNITED STATES lean to the right.

1946
UC14 UC3 5c carmine, die 1 .75 .25
UC15 UC3 5c carmine, die 2 .75 .25

See Nos. UC18, UC26.

DC-4 Skymaster — UC4

1947-55 Typo.

Letter Sheets for Foreign Postage

UC16 UC4 10c brt red, *pale bl,* entire 8.50 7.00
e. Blue omitted, entire 425.00
f. Overlay omitted front & back, entire *100.00*
g. Overlay omitted from front only, entire *500.00*
a. "Air Letter" on face, 4-line inscription on back ('51), entire 17.50 10.00
b. As "a," 10c chocolate, *pale bl,* entire 450.00
c. "Air Letter" and "Aerogramme" on face, 4-line inscription on back ('53), entire 45.00 12.50
d. As "c," 3-line inscription on back ('55), entire 9.00 8.00

Postage Stamp Centenary Issue

Centenary of the first postage stamps issued by the United States Government.

Washington & Franklin, Early and Modern Mail-carrying Vehicles — UC5

Two dies: Rotary, design measures 22¼mm high; and flat bed press, design 21¾mm high.

Embossed, Rotary Press Printing

1947, May 21

For Domestic Postage

UC17 UC5 5c carmine (rotary) .50 .30
a. Flat plate printing .50 .30

Type of 1946

Type I: 6's lean to right.
Type II: 6's upright.

1950, Sept. 22
UC18 UC3 6c carmine, type I .75 .25
a. Type II .90 .25

Several other types differ slightly from the two listed.

Nos. UC14, UC15, UC18 Surcharged in Red

1951
UC19 UC3 6c on 5c carmine, die 1 .85 1.50
a. Surcharge inverted at lower left, entire —
UC20 UC3 6c on 5c carmine, die 2 .85 1.50
a. 6c on 6c carmine (error) entire *1,500.*
b. Double surcharge *975.00* —

To qualify as No. UC20b, both surcharges must be to the left of the indicia.

Nos. UC14, UC15 and UC17 Surcharged in Red at Left of Stamp

1952
UC21 UC3 6c on 5c carmine, die 1 27.50 20.00
a. Double surcharge, entire *600.00*
UC22 UC3 6c on 5c carmine, die 2 3.75 2.50
a. Double surcharge 250.00
b. Triple surcharge, entire 275.00

To qualify as Nos. UC22a or UC22b, all surcharges must be to the left of the indicia.

Same Surcharge in Red on No. UC17

UC23 UC5 6c on 5c carmine *1,000.*

The 6c on 4c black (No. U440) is believed to be a favor printing.

Fifth International Philatelic Exhibition Issue

FIPEX, the Fifth International Philatelic Exhibition, New York, N.Y., Apr. 28-May 6, 1956.

Eagle in Flight — UC6

1956, May 2
UC25 UC6 6c red .75 .50

Two types exist, differing slightly in the clouds at top.

Skymaster Type of 1946

1958, July 31
UC26 UC3 7c blue .65 .50

Nos. UC3-UC5, UC18 and UC25 Surcharged in Green

1958
UC27 UC2 6c + 1c orange, die 2a 325.00 *300.00*
UC28 UC2 6c + 1c orange, die 2b 80.00 80.00
UC29 UC2 6c + 1c orange, die 2c 40.00 55.00
UC30 UC3 6c + 1c carmine, type I 1.00 .50
a. Type II 1.00 .50
UC31 UC6 6c + 1c red 1.00 .50

Jet Airliner UC7

Letter Sheet for Foreign Postage

Type I: Back inscription in 3 lines.
Type II: Back inscription in 2 lines.

Typographed, Without Embossing

1958-59
UC32 UC7 10c blue & red, *blue,* II ('59), entire 6.00 5.00
a. Type I ('58), entire 10.00 5.00
b. Red omitted, II, entire *850.00*
c. Blue omitted, II, entire *850.00*
d. Red omitted, I, entire *1,000.*

Silhouette of Jet Airliner — UC8

1958, Nov. 21 **Embossed**
UC33 UC8 7c blue .60 .25

1960, Aug. 18
UC34 UC8 7c carmine .60 .25

Jet Plane and Globe UC9

Letter Sheet for Foreign Postage

Typographed, Without Embossing

1961, June 16
UC35 UC9 11c red & blue, *blue,* entire 3.00 3.50
a. Red omitted, entire *900.00*
b. Blue omitted, entire *1,000.*

UC10

1962, Nov. 17 **Embossed**
UC36 UC10 8c red .55 .25

UC11

1965-67
UC37 UC11 8c red .45 .25
a. Tagged 4.50 .30

No. UC37a has a 8x24mm panel at left of stamp that glows orange red under ultraviolet light.

Pres. John F. Kennedy and Jet Plane UC12

Letter Sheets for Foreign Postage

Typographed, Without Embossing

1965, May 29
UC38 UC12 11c red & dark blue, *blue,* entire 3.75 4.00

1967, May 29
UC39 UC12 13c red & dark blue, *blue,* entire 3.25 4.00
a. Red omitted, entire *600.00*
b. Dark blue omitted, entire *500.00*

UC13

1968, Jan. 8 **Tagged** **Embossed**
UC40 UC13 10c red .50 .25

1968, Feb. 5
UC41 UC11 8c + 2c red .65 .25

Tagging

Envelopes and Letter Sheets from No. UC42 onward are tagged unless otherwise noted.

Human Rights Year Issue

Issued for International Human Rights Year, and to commemorate the 20th anniversary of the United Nations' Declaration of Human Rights.

Globes and Flock of Birds — UC14

Letter Sheet for Foreign Postage

1968, Dec. 3 **Photo.**
UC42 UC14 13c gray, brown, orange & black, *blue,* entire 8.00 7.50
a. Orange omitted, entire *1,000.*
b. Brown omitted, entire *375.00*
c. Black omitted, entire *800.00*
d. Gray and black omitted, entire —

No. UC42 has a luminescent panel ⅜x1 inch on the right globe. The panel glows orange red under ultraviolet light.

UC15

1971, May 6 **Embossed (Plane)**
UC43 UC15 11c red & blue .50 *1.75*

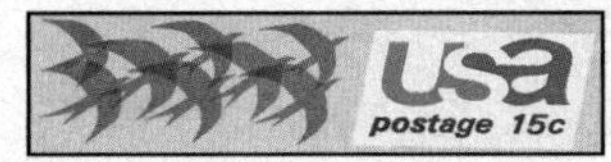

Birds in Flight and "usa" — UC16

Letter Sheet for Foreign Postage

1971 **Photo.**
UC44 UC16 15c gray, red, white & blue, *blue,* entire 1.50 *7.50*
a. "AEROGRAMME" added to inscription, entire 1.50 *7.50*
b. As #UC44, red omitted, entire *300.00*
c. As "a," red omitted, entire —

Folding instructions (2 steps) in capitals on No. C44; (4 steps) in upper and lower case on No. UC44a.

On Nos. UC44-UC44a the white rhomboid background of "USA postage 15c" is luminescent. No. UC44 is inscribed: "VIA AIR MAIL-PAR AVION". "postage 15c" is in gray. See No. UC46.

No. UC40 Surcharged in Green

1971, June 28 **Embossed**
UC45 UC13 10c + (1c) red 1.50 .75

HOT AIR BALLOONING CHAMPIONSHIPS ISSUE

Hot Air Ballooning World Championships, Albuquerque, N.M., Feb. 10-17, 1973.

"usa" Type of 1971

Design: Three balloons and cloud at left in address section; no birds beside stamp. Inscribed "INTERNATIONAL HOT AIR BALLOONING." "postage 15c" in blue.

Letter Sheet for Foreign Postage

1973, Feb. 10
UC46 UC16 15c red, white & blue, *blue,* entire 1.00 *7.50*

Folding instructions as on No. UC44a. See notes after No. UC44.

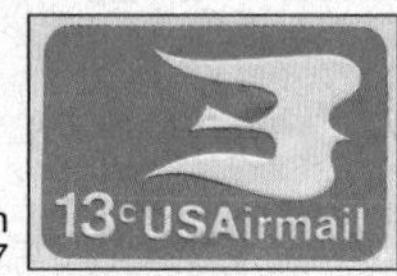

Bird in Flight — UC17

1973, Dec. 1 **Luminescent Ink**
UC47 UC17 13c rose red .30 .25

Beginning with No. UC48, all listings are letter sheets for foreign postage.

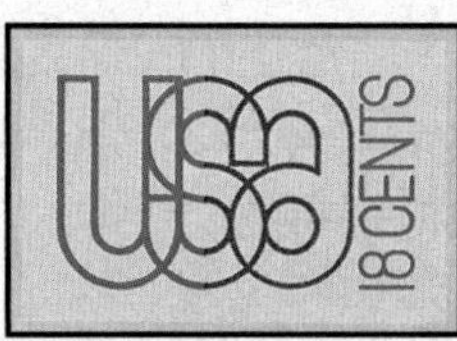

UC18

1974, Jan. 4 **Photo.**
UC48 UC18 18c red & blue, *blue,* entire 1.00 *6.00*
a. Red omitted, entire *200.00*

25TH ANNIVERSARY OF NATO ISSUE

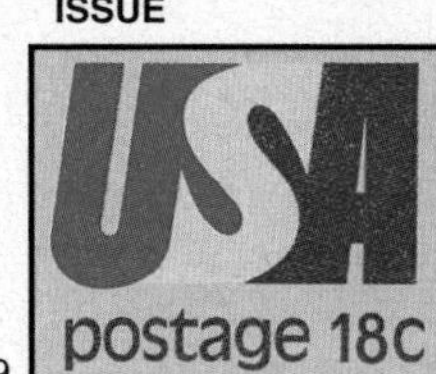

UC19

Design: "NATO" and NATO emblem at left in address section.

1974, Apr. 4
UC49 UC19 18c red & blue, *blue,* entire 1.00 *6.00*
Die cutting reversed, entire *100.00*

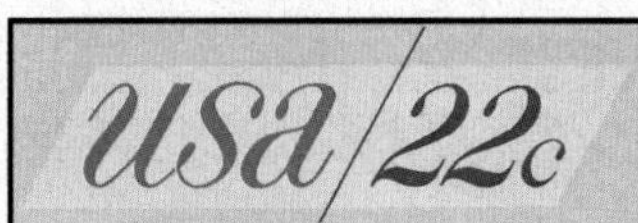

UC20

1976, Jan. 16
UC50 UC20 22c red & blue, *blue,* entire 1.00 *6.00*
a. Red color missing due to foldover and die cutting —

UC21

1978, Nov. 3

UC51 UC21 22c blue, *blue,* entire 1.00 *3.00*

22nd OLYMPIC GAMES, MOSCOW, JULY 19-AUG. 3, 1980.

UC22

Design (multicolored in bottom left corner) shows discus thrower.

1979, Dec. 5

UC52 UC22 22c red, black & green, *bluish,* entire 1.50 *6.00*

UC23

Design (brown on No. UC53, green and brown on No. UC54): lower left, Statue of Liberty. Inscribed "Tour the United States." Folding area shows tourist attractions.

1980, Dec. 29

UC53 UC23 30c blue, red & brown, *blue,* entire .85 *6.00*
- *a.* Red omitted, entire 70.00

1981, Sept. 21

UC54 UC23 30c yellow, magenta, blue & black, *blue,* entire .65 *6.00*

UC24

Design: "Made in USA . . . world's best buys!" on flap, ship, tractor in lower left. Reverse folding area shows chemicals, jet silhouette, wheat, typewriter and computer tape disks.

1982, Sept. 16

UC55 UC24 30c multi, *blue,* entire .80 *6.00*

WORLD COMMUNICATIONS YEAR

World Map Showing Locations of Satellite Tracking Stations — UC25

Design: Reverse folding area shows satellite, tracking station.

1983, Jan. 7

UC56 UC25 30c multi, *blue,* entire .90 *8.00*

1984 OLYMPICS

UC26

Indicia in black, multicolor design of woman equestrian at lower left with montage of competitive events on reverse folding area.

1983, Oct. 14

UC57 UC26 30c black & multi, *light blue,* entire .85 *8.00*

WEATHER SATELLITES, 25TH ANNIV.

UC27

Design: Landsat orbiting the earth at lower left with three Landsat photographs on reverse folding area. Inscribed: "Landsat views the Earth."

1985, Feb. 14

UC58 UC27 36c multi, *blue,* entire 1.25 *12.50*

NATIONAL TOURISM WEEK

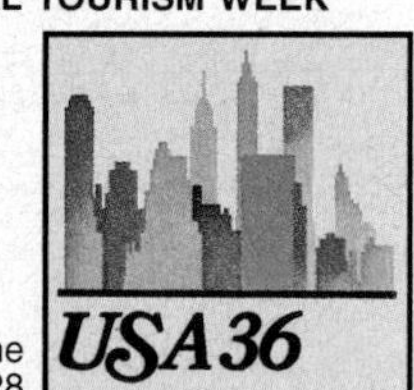

Urban Skyline UC28

Design: Inscribed "Celebrate America" at lower left and "Travel. . . the perfect freedom" on folding area. Skier, Indian chief, cowboy, jazz trumpeter and pilgrims on reverse folding area.

1985, May 21

UC59 UC28 36c multi, *blue,* entire 1.25 *12.50*
- *a.* Black omitted, entire *600.00* —

MARK TWAIN AND HALLEY'S COMET

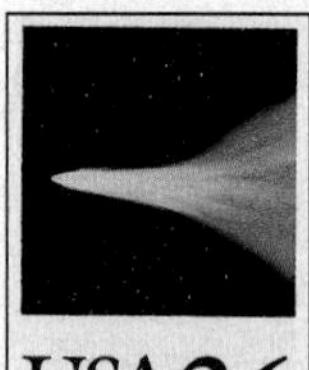

Comet Tail Viewed from Space — UC29

Design: Portrait of Twain at lower left and inscribed "I came in with Halley's Comet in 1835. It is coming again next year, and I expect to go out with it. It will be the greatest disappointment of my life if I don't go out with Halley's Comet." "1835 . Mark Twain . 1910 . Halley's Comet . 1985" and Twain, Huckleberry Finn, steamboat and comet on reverse folding areas.

1985, Dec. 4

UC60 UC29 36c multi, entire 2.00 *12.50*

UC30

1988, May 9 **Litho.**

UC61 UC30 39c multi, entire 1.25 *12.50*
- *a.* Tagging bar to left of design ('89) 1.25 *1.50*

On No. UC61, the tagging bar is between "USA" and "39."

MONTGOMERY BLAIR, POSTMASTER GENERAL 1861-64

Montgomery Blair and Pres. Lincoln — UC31

Design: Mail bags and "Free city delivery," "Railway mail service" and "Money order system" at lower left. Globe, locomotive, bust of Blair, UPU emblem and "The Paris conference of 1863, initiated by Postmaster General Blair, led, in 1874, to the founding of the Universal Postal Union" contained on reverse folding area.

1989, Nov. 20

UC62 UC31 39c multicolored, entire 1.40 *16.00*
- *a.* Double impression —
- *b.* Triple impression —
- *c.* Quadruple impression —

UC32

1991, May 17

UC63 UC32 45c gray, red & blue, *blue,* entire 1.40 *10.00*
- *a.* White paper, entire 1.00 *10.00*

Thaddeus Lowe (1832-1913), Balloonist — UC33

1995, Sept. 23

UC64 UC33 50c multicolored, *blue,* entire 1.50 *10.00*

Voyageurs Natl. Park, Minnesota UC34

1999, May 15

UC65 UC34 60c multicolored, *blue,* entire 1.75 *12.50*

No. UC65 used is often found with additional postage affixed.

OFFICIAL STAMPED ENVELOPES

By the Act of Congress, January 31, 1873, the franking privilege of officials was abolished as of July 1, 1873 and the Postmaster General was authorized to prepare official envelopes. At the same time official stamps were prepared for all Departments. Department envelopes became obsolete July 5, 1884. After that, government offices began to use franked envelopes of varied design. These indicate no denomination and lie beyond the scope of this Catalogue.

Post Office Department

"2" 9mm high — UO1

"3" 9mm high — UO2

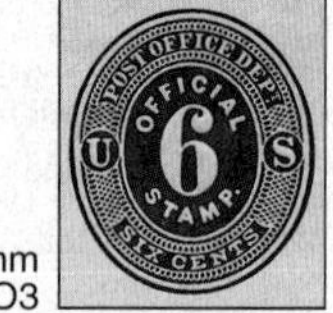

"6" 9 ½mm high — UO3

1873

UO1 UO1 2c black, *lemon* 25.00 10.00

UO2 UO2 3c black, *lemon* 20.00 6.50

+UO3 UO2 3c black *30,000.*

UO4 UO3 6c black, *lemon* 27.50 17.50

"2" 9 ¼mm high — UO4

"3" 9 ¼mm high — UO5

"6" 10 ½mm high — UO6

1874-79

UO5 UO4 2c black, *lemon* 11.00 4.25

UO6 UO4 2c black 140.00 37.50

UO7 UO5 3c black, *lemon* 2.75 .85

UO8 UO5 3c black 2,750. 1,200.

UO9 UO5 3c black, *amber* 150.00 40.00

UO10 UO5 3c black, *blue* *42,500.*

UO11	UO5	3c blue, *blue* ('75)	*42,500.*	
UO12	UO6	6c black, *lemon*	16.00	6.50
UO13	UO6	6c black	2,500.	2,100.

Fakes exist of Nos. UO3, UO8 and UO13.

Postal Service

UO7

1877

UO14	UO7	black	6.00	4.50
UO15	UO7	black, *amber*	250.00	50.00
UO16	UO7	blue, *amber*	225.00	40.00
UO17	UO7	blue, *blue*	9.00	6.75

War Department

Franklin — UO8

Bust points to the end of "N" of "ONE".

Jackson — UO9

Bust narrow at the back.

Washington — UO10

Queue projects below the bust.

Lincoln — UO11

Neck very long at the back.

Jefferson — UO12

Queue forms straight line with bust.

Clay — UO13

Ear partly concealed by hair, mouth large, chin prominent.

Webster — UO14

Has side whiskers.

Scott UO15

Hamilton UO16

Back of bust very narrow; chin almost straight; the labels containing the letters "U S" are exactly parallel.

Reay Issue

1873

UO18	UO8	1c dk red	575.00	300.00
WO18A	UO8	1c dk red, *man,* entire		—
UO19	UO9	2c dk red	2,000.	400.00
UO20	UO10	3c dk red	70.00	42.50
UO21	UO10	3c dk red, *amb*	*40,000.*	
UO22	UO10	3c dk red, *cr*	900.00	300.00
UO23	UO11	6c dk red	325.00	100.00
UO24	UO11	6c dk red, *cr*	6,000.	425.00
UO25	UO12	10c dk red	*17,500.*	2,250.
UO26	UO13	12c dk red	180.00	60.00
UO27	UO14	15c dk red	160.00	55.00
UO28	UO15	24c dk red	175.00	50.00
UO29	UO16	30c dk red	500.00	150.00
UO30	UO8	1c ver	200.00	
WO31	UO8	1c ver, *man*	20.00	14.00
+UO32	UO9	2c ver	425.00	
WO33	UO9	2c ver, *man*	280.00	
UO34	UO10	3c ver	90.00	40.00
UO35	UO10	3c ver, *amb*	110.00	
UO36	UO10	3c ver, *cr*	15.00	12.50
UO37	UO11	6c ver	100.00	
+UO38	UO11	6c ver, *cr*	500.00	
UO39	UO12	10c ver	350.00	
UO40	UO13	12c ver	150.00	
UO41	UO14	15c ver	275.00	
UO42	UO15	24c ver	350.00	
UO43	UO16	30c ver	375.00	

UO17

Bottom serif on "S" is thick and short; bust at bottom below hair forms a sharp point.

UO18

Bottom serif on "S" is thick and short; front part of bust is rounded.

UO19

Bottom serif on "S" is short; queue does not project below bust.

UO20

Neck very short at the back.

UO21

Knot of queue stands out prominently.

UO22

Ear prominent, chin receding.

UO23

Has no side whiskers; forelock projects above head.

UO24

Back of bust rather broad; chin slopes considerably; the label containing letters "U S" are not exactly parallel.

Plimpton Issue

1875

UO44	UO17	1c red	175.00	85.00
+UO45	UO17	1c red, *amb*	900.00	
+UO45A	UO17	1c red, *org*	*37,500.*	
WO46	UO17	1c red, *man*	4.50	2.75
UO47	UO18	2c red	125.00	—
UO48	UO18	2c red, *amber*	37.50	17.50
UO49	UO18	2c red, *orange*	60.00	17.50
WO50	UO18	2c red, *manila*	120.00	50.00
UO51	UO19	3c red	17.50	10.00
UO52	UO19	3c red, *amber*	20.00	10.00
UO53	UO19	3c red, *cream*	7.00	3.75
UO54	UO19	3c red, *blue*	4.00	2.75
UO55	UO19	3c red, *fawn*	6.50	2.75
UO56	UO20	6c red	65.00	30.00
UO57	UO20	6c red, *amber*	90.00	40.00
UO58	UO20	6c red, *cream*	200.00	85.00
UO59	UO21	10c red	180.00	80.00
UO60	UO21	10c red, *amber*	950.00	
UO61	UO22	12c red	55.00	40.00
UO62	UO22	12c red, *amber*	675.00	
UO63	UO22	12c red, *cream*	600.00	
UO64	UO23	15c red	250.00	140.00
UO65	UO23	15c red, *amber*	825.00	
UO66	UO23	15c red, *cream*	600.00	
UO67	UO24	30c red	175.00	140.00
UO68	UO24	30c red, *amber*	850.00	
UO69	UO24	30c red, *cream*	800.00	

POSTAL SAVINGS ENVELOPES

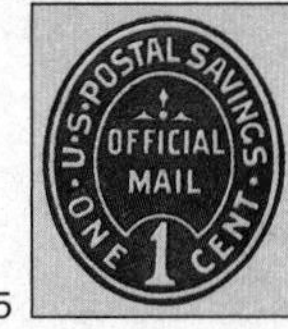

UO25

1911

UO70	UO25	1c green	85.00	25.00
UO71	UO25	1c green, *oriental buff*	225.00	85.00
UO72	UO25	2c carmine	13.00	4.00
a.		2c carmine, *manila* (error)	*1,750.*	*1,000.*

Used Values

Catalogue values for regularly used entires. Those with first-day cancels generally sell for much less.

Tagged

Envelopes from No. UO73 onward are tagged unless otherwise noted.

OFFICIAL MAIL

UO26

1983, Jan. 12 **Typo. & Embossed**

UO73	UO26	20c blue, entire	1.10	*30.00*

UO27

1985, Feb. 26 **Typo. & Embossed**

UO74	UO27	22c blue, entire	.90	*30.00*

UO28

1987, Mar. 2 **Typo.**

UO75	UO28	22c blue, entire	1.50	*35.00*

Used exclusively to mail U.S. Savings Bonds.

UO29

1988, Mar. 22

UO76	UO29	(25c) black & blue, entire	1.50	*35.00*

Used exclusively to mail U.S. Savings Bonds.

UO30

UO31

1988, Apr. 11 Typo. & Embossed

UO77 UO30 25c black & blue, entire .85 *25.00*
a. Denomination & lettering as on No. UO78, entire *5.00 20.00*

Used exclusively to mail U.S. Savings Bonds.

Typo.

UO78 UO31 25c black & blue, entire 1.10 *35.00*
a. Denomination & lettering as on No. UO77, entire 1.00 *35.00*

Used to mail U.S. Savings Bonds. Also used by the Department of Agriculture.

Used Values

Postally used examples of Nos. UO79-UO94 seldom appear in the marketplace and thus cannot be valued with as much certainty as the editors would like. They must show evidence of postal usage. Clear cancels are valued even higher. The editors would like to have records of sales of examples of these used envelopes. If a value exists, it is based on a known transaction(s) or consultation with experts.

1990, Mar. 17

Stars and "E Pluribus Unum" illegible. "Official" is 13mm, "USA" is 16mm long.

UO79 UO31 45c black & blue, entire 1.25 *200.00*
UO80 UO31 65c black & blue, entire 1.75 *200.00*

Used exclusively to mail U.S. passports.

UO32

Stars and "E Pluribus Unum" clear and sharply printed. "Official" is 14½mm, "USA" is 17mm long.

1990, Aug. 10 Litho.

UO81 UO32 45c black & blue, entire 1.25 —
UO82 UO32 65c black & blue, entire 1.75 —

Used exclusively to mail U.S. passports.

UO33

1991, Jan. 22 Typo. Wmk.

UO83 UO33 (29c) black & blue, entire 1.10 *35.00*

Used exclusively to mail U.S. Savings Bonds.

UO34

Litho. & Embossed

1991, Apr. 6 Wmk.

UO84 UO34 29c black & blue, entire .80 *20.00*

UO35

1991, Apr. 17 Wmk.

UO85 UO35 29c black & blue, entire .80 *20.00*

Used exclusively to mail U.S. Savings Bonds.

Consular Service, Bicent. UO36

1992, July 10 Litho. Unwmk.

UO86 UO36 52c blue & red, entire 6.00 *150.00*
a. 52c blue & red, *blue-white*, entire 1.50 *150.00*
UO87 UO36 75c blue & red, entire 11.00 *150.00*
a. 75c blue & red, *blue-white*, entire 2.50 *150.00*

Used exclusively to mail U.S. passports. Available only in 4⅜ inch x 8⅞ inch size with self-adhesive flap.

UO37

1995-99 Typo. & Embossed

UO88 UO37 32c blue & red, entire 1.00 *20.00*
UO89 UO37 33c blue & red, entire 1.00 *20.00*

Type of 1995

2001, Feb. 27

UO90 UO37 34c blue & red, entire 1.00 *20.00*

Type of 1995

2002, Aug. 2

UO91 UO37 37c blue & red, type I, entire 1.00 *15.00*
a. Type II, entire 1.00 *35.00*

Type I has 29x28mm blue panel, top of "USA" even with the bottom of the eagle's neck and is made with "100% recycled paper" as noted on reverse. Type II has a 27½x27½mm blue panel, top of "USA" even with the highest arrow, and has no mention of "100% recycled paper" on reverse.

Type of 1995

2006, Jan. 9

UO92 UO37 39c blue & red, entire 2.00 *25.00*

Type of 1995

2007, May 12

UO93 UO37 41c blue & red, entire 2.00 *25.00*

Type of 1995

2008, June 20 Typo.

UO94 UO37 42c blue & red, entire 2.00 *15.00*

REVENUE STAMPS

Nos. R1-R102 were used to pay taxes on documents and proprietary articles including playing cards. Until Dec. 25, 1862, the law stated that a revenue stamp could be used only for payment of the tax upon the particular instrument or article specified on its face. After that date stamps, except the Proprietary, could be used indiscriminately.

Values quoted are for pen-canceled stamps. Stamps with handstamped cancellations sell at higher prices. Stamps canceled with cuts, punches or holes sell for less. See the Scott U.S. Specialized Catalogue.

General Issue

First Issue

Head of Washington in Oval. Various Frames as Illustrated.

Nos. R1b to R42b, part perforate, occur perforated sometimes at sides only and sometimes at top and bottom only. The higher values, part perforate, are perforated at sides only. Imperforate and part perforate revenues often bring much more in pairs or blocks than as single stamps. Part perforate revenues with an asterisk (*) after the value exist imperforate horizontally or vertically.

The experimental silk paper is a variety of the old paper and has only a very few minute fragments of fiber.

Some of the stamps were in use eight years and were printed several times. Many color variations occurred, particularly when unstable pigments were used and the color was intended to be purple or violet, such as the 4c Proprietary, 30c and $2.50 stamps. Before 1868 dull colors predominate on these and the early red stamps. In later printings of the 4c Proprietary, 30c and $2.50 stamps, red predominates in the mixture, and on the dollar values the red is brighter. The early $1.90 stamp is dull purple, imperf. or perforated. In a later printing, perforated only, the purple is darker.

R1

R2

Old Paper

1862-71 Engr. *Perf. 12*

R1 R1 1c Express, red
a. Imperf. 75.00
b. Part perf. 55.00*
c. Perf. 1.50
d. Silk paper 150.00
e. As No. R1c, vertical pair, imperf. between *200.00*

R2 R1 1c Playing Cards, red
a. Imperf. 3,000.
b. Part perf. 2,000.
c. Perf. 210.00

R3 R1 1c Proprietary, red
a. Imperf. 1,250.
b. Part perf. 275.00*
c. Perf. .50
d. Silk paper 57.50

R4 R1 1c Telegraph, red
a. Imperf. 750.00
c. Perf. 20.00

R5 R2 2c Bank Check, blue
a. Imperf. 1.50
b. Part perf. 5.50*
c. Perf. .50
e. As No. R5c, Double impression 800.00
f. As No. R5c, pair imperf between 400.00

R6 R2 2c Bank Check, orange
b. Part perf. 60.00*
c. Perf. .45
d. Silk paper 275.00
e. As No. R6c, orange, *green* 700.00
f. As No. R6c, vert. half used as 1c on document —

R7 R2 2c Certificate, blue
a. Imperf. 17.50
c. Perf. 32.50

R8 R2 2c Certificate, orange
c. Perf. 45.00

R9 R2 2c Express, blue
a. Imperf. 15.00
b. Part perf. 35.00*
c. Perf. .40

R10 R2 2c Express, orange
b. Part perf. *800.00*
c. Perf. 14.00
d. Silk paper 160.00

R11 R2 2c Playing Cards, blue
a. Imperf. *1,500.*
b. Part perf. 325.00
c. Perf. 4.50

R12 R2 2c Playing Cards, org
c. Perf. 55.00

R13 R2 2c Proprietary, blue
a. Imperf. 1,200.
b. Part perf. 350.
c. Perf. .40
d. Silk paper 175.00
e. ultramarine 300.00

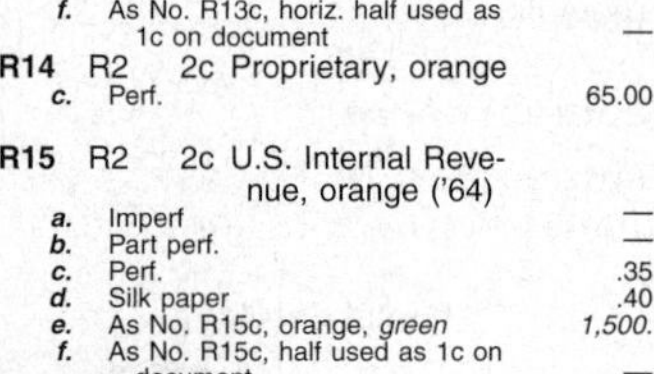

f. As No. R13c, horiz. half used as 1c on document —

R14 R2 2c Proprietary, orange
c. Perf. 65.00

R15 R2 2c U.S. Internal Revenue, orange ('64)
a. Imperf —
b. Part perf. —
c. Perf. .35
d. Silk paper .40
e. As No. R15c, orange, *green* *1,500.*
f. As No. R15c, half used as 1c on document —

R3

R16 R3 3c Foreign Exchange, green
b. Part perf. 950.00
c. Perf. 5.00
d. Silk paper 175.00

R17 R3 3c Playing Cards, green ('63)
a. Imperf. *40,000.*
c. Perf. 175.00

R18 R3 3c Proprietary, green
b. Part perf. 1,000.
c. Perf. 9.00
d. Silk paper 125.00
e. As No. R18c, double impression *1,000.*
f. As No. R18c, printed on both sides *3,500.*

R19 R3 3c Telegraph, green
a. Imperf. 100.00
b. Part perf. 30.00
c. Perf. 3.00

R20 R3 4c Inland Exchange, brown ('63)
c. Perf. 2.25
d. Silk paper 175.00

R21 R3 4c Playing Cards, slate ('63)
c. Perf. 800.00

R22 R3 4c Proprietary, purple
a. Imperf. —
b. Part perf. 650.00
c. Perf. 8.50
d. Silk paper 250.00

There are shade and color variations of Nos. R21-R22.

R23 R3 5c Agreement, red
c. Perf. .50
d. Silk paper 4.50
e. As No. R23c, diag. half used as 2c on document *2,500.*

R24 R3 5c Certificate, red
a. Imperf. 4.00
b. Part perf. 15.00
c. Perf. .50
d. Silk paper 1.10
e. As No. R24c, half used as 2c on document —
f. As No. R24d, impression of No. R3 on back *2,750.*

R25 R3 5c Express, red
a. Imperf. 8.00
b. Part perf. 8.00*
c. Perf. .40

R26 R3 5c Foreign Exchange, red
b. Part perf. —
c. Perf. .50
d. Silk paper 500.00

R27 R3 5c Inland Exchange, red
a. Imperf. 10.00
b. Part perf. 6.75
c. Perf. .60
d. Silk paper 17.50
e. As No. R27c, double impression —

R28 R3 5c Playing Cards, red ('63)
c. Perf. 40.00
e. Double impression *1,200.*

R29 R3 5c Proprietary, red ('64)
c. Perf. 30.00
d. Silk paper 300.00

R30 R3 6c Inland Exchange, orange ('63)
c. Perf. 2.25
d. Silk paper 160.00

R31 R3 6c Proprietary, orange ('71)
c. Perf. *2,000.*

Nearly all examples of No. R31 are faulty or repaired and poorly centered. The catalogue value is for a fine centered stamp with minor faults which do not detract from its appearance.

R32 R3 10c Bill of Lading, blue
a. Imperf. 55.00
b. Part perf. 500.00
c. Perf. 1.75
e. As No. R32c, half used as 5c on document *300.00*

R33 R3 10c Certificate, blue
a. Imperf. 350.00
b. Part perf. 950.00*
c. Perf. .35
d. Silk paper 6.00
e. As No. R33c, half used as 5c on document *300.00*

R34 R3 10c Contract, blue
b. Part perf. 575.00
be. As No. R34b, ultramarine 750.00
c. Perf. .50
ce. As No. R34c, ultramarine 1.00

d. Silk paper 4.25
f. As No. R34c, vertical half used as 5c on document *300.00*

R35 R3 10c Foreign Exchange, blue
c. Perf. 14.00
d. Silk paper —
e. As No. R35c, ultramarine 20.00

R36 R3 10c Inland Exchange, blue
a. Imperf. 500.00
b. Part perf. 4.50*
c. Perf. .30
d. Silk paper 100.00
e. As No. R36c, half used as 5c on document *300.00*

R37 R3 10c Power of Attorney, blue
a. Imperf. 1,100.
b. Part perf. 30.00
c. Perf. 1.00
e. As No. R37c, half used as 5c on document *300.00*

R38 R3 10c Proprietary, blue ('64)
c. Perf. 19.00

R39 R3 15c Foreign Exchange, brown ('63)
c. Perf. 17.00
e. Double impression *1,000.*

R40 R3 15c Inland Exchange, brown
a. Imperf. 45.00
b. Part perf. 14.00
c. Perf. 2.00
e. As No. R40b, double impression *1,900.*
f. As No. R40c, double impression *550.00*

R41 R3 20c Foreign Exchange, red
a. Imperf. 95.00
c. Perf. 80.00
d. Silk paper 350.00

R42 R3 20c Inland Exchange, red
a. Imperf. 17.00
b. Part perf. 22.50
c. Perf. .45
d. Silk paper —
e. As No. R42c, half used as 5c on document *300.00*

R4 R5

R43 R4 25c Bond, red
a. Imperf. 300.00
b. Part perf. 6.75
c. Perf. 3.75

R44 R4 25c Certificate, red
a. Imperf. 11.00
b. Part perf. 6.75*
c. Perf. .50
d. Silk paper 2.75
e. As No. R44c, printed on both sides *3,500.*
f. As No. R44c, impression of No. R48 on back *6,500.*

R45 R4 25c Entry of Goods, red
a. Imperf. 22.50
b. Part perf. 300.00*
c. Perf. 1.50
d. Silk paper 90.00

R46 R4 25c Insurance, red
a. Imperf. 12.50
b. Part perf. 19.00
c. Perf. .30
d. Silk paper 7.00
e. As No. R46c, double impression *500.00*

R47 R4 25c Life Insurance, red
a. Imperf. 50.00
b. Part perf. 950.00
c. Perf. 11.00

R48 R4 25c Power of Attorney, red
a. Imperf. 10.00
b. Part perf. 45.00
c. Perf. 1.00

R49 R4 25c Protest, red
a. Imperf. 35.00
b. Part perf. 1,000.
c. Perf. 10.00

R50 R4 25c Warehouse Receipt, red
a. Imperf. 55.00
b. Part perf. 1,100.
c. Perf. 45.00

R51 R4 30c Foreign Exchange, lilac
a. Imperf. 200.00
b. Part perf. *5,000.*
c. Perf. 60.00
d. Silk paper *600.00*

R52 R4 30c Inland Exchange, lilac
a. Imperf. 72.50
b. Part perf. 90.00
c. Perf. 8.50
d. Silk paper —

R53 R4 40c Inland Exchange, brown
a. Imperf. 2,000.
b. Part perf. 9.00
c. Perf. 8.00
d. Silk paper 575.00
f. As No. R53c, double impression —

R54 R5 50c Conveyance, blue
a. Imperf. 20.00
b. Part perf. 3.50
c. Perf. .35
ce. As No. R54c, ultramarine .50
d. Silk paper, blue 3.00
de. As No. R54d, ultramarine —

R55 R5 50c Entry of Goods, blue
b. Part perf. 17.50
c. Perf. .60
d. Silk paper 110.00

R56 R5 50c Foreign Exchange, blue
a. Imperf. 75.00
b. Part perf. 125.00
c. Perf. 7.50
e. As No. R56c, double impression *500.00*
f. As No. R56c, half used as 25c on document *300.00*

R57 R5 50c Lease, blue
a. Imperf. 35.00
b. Part perf. 250.00
c. Perf. 10.00

R58 R5 50c Life Insurance, blue
a. Imperf. 45.00
b. Part perf. 200.00
c. Perf. 1.75
e. As No. R58c, double impression *800.00*

R59 R5 50c Mortgage, blue
a. Imperf. 22.50
b. Part perf. 5.00
c. Perf. .70
d. Silk paper —
e. As No. R59a, double impression —
f. As No. R59c, double impression —

R60 R5 50c Original Process, blue
a. Imperf. 5.50
b. Part perf. *650.00*
c. Perf. 1.00
d. Silk paper 7.50
e. As No. R60c, half used as 25c on document —

R61 R5 50c Passage Ticket, blue
a. Imperf. 140.00
b. Part perf. 500.00
c. Perf. 2.25

R62 R5 50c Probate of Will, blue
a. Imperf. 55.00
b. Part perf. 250.00
c. Perf. 22.50

R63 R5 50c Surety Bond, blue
a. Imperf. 400.00
b. Part perf. 2.75
c. Perf. .30
e. As No. R63c, ultramarine .75

R64 R5 60c Inland Exchange, orange
a. Imperf. 110.00
b. Part perf. 82.50
c. Perf. 9.00
d. Silk paper 85.00

R65 R5 70c Foreign Exchange, green
a. Imperf. 725.00
b. Part perf. 200.00
c. Perf. 14.00
d. Silk paper 110.00

R6

R7

R66 R6 $1 Conveyance, red
a. Imperf. 27.50
b. Part perf. *3,000.*
c. Perf. 27.50
d. Silk paper 175.00

R67 R6 $1 Entry of Goods, red
a. Imperf. 50.00
c. Perf. 2.75
d. Silk paper 150.00

R68 R6 $1 Foreign Exchange, red
a. Imperf. 90.00
c. Perf. .75
d. Silk paper 125.00
e. As No. R68d, diagonal half used as 50c on document *300.00*

R69 R6 $1 Inland Exchange, red
a. Imperf. 17.00
b. Part perf. *3,000.**
c. Perf. .70
d. Silk paper 6.00

R70 R6 $1 Lease, red
a. Imperf. 50.00
c. Perf. 4.50
e. As No. R70c, half used as 50c on document —

R71 R6 $1 Life Insurance, red
a. Imperf. 300.00
c. Perf. 10.00
d. Silk paper *500.00*
e. As No. R71c, half used as 50c on document —

R72 R6 $1 Manifest, red
a. Imperf. 47.50
c. Perf. 40.00

R73 R6 $1 Mortgage, red
a. Imperf. 27.50
c. Perf. 300.00

R74 R6 $1 Passage Ticket, red
a. Imperf. 350.00
c. Perf. 350.00

R75 R6 $1 Power of Attorney, red
a. Imperf. 100.00
c. Perf. 2.75
e. As No. R75c, horiz. half used as 50c on document —

R76 R6 $1 Probate of Will, red
a. Imperf. 100.00
c. Perf. 55.00

R77 R7 $1.30 Foreign Exchange, orange ('63)
a. Imperf. *9,000.*
c. Perf. 85.00

R78 R7 $1.50 Inland Exchange, blue
a. Imperf. 32.50
c. Perf. 7.00

R79 R7 $1.60 Foreign Exchange, green ('63)
a. Imperf. 1,300.
c. Perf. 180.00

R80 R7 $1.90 Foreign Exchange, purple ('63)
a. Imperf. *12,500.*
c. Perf. 200.00
d. Silk paper 300.00

R8

R81 R8 $2 Conveyance, red
a. Imperf. 225.00
b. Part perf. 2,750.
c. Perf. 4.00
d. Silk paper 40.00
e. As No. R81c, half used as $1 on document *600.00*

R82 R8 $2 Mortgage, red
a. Imperf. 150.00
c. Perf. 7.00
d. Silk paper 60.00
e. As No. R82c, half used as $1 on document —

R83 R8 $2 Probate of Will, red ('63)
a. Imperf. *7,750.*
c. Perf. 90.00
e. As No. R83c, horiz. half used as $1 on document *750.00*

R84 R8 $2.50 Inland Exchange, purple ('63)
a. Imperf. *10,000.*
c. Perf. 22.50
d. Silk paper 30.00
e. As No. R84c, double impression *1,400.*

There are many shade and color variations of Nos. R84c and R84d.

R85 R8 $3 Charter Party, green
a. Imperf. 200.00
c. Perf. 11.00
d. Silk paper 150.00
e. As No. R85c, printed on both sides *7,000.*
f. As No. R85c, half used as $1.50 on document —
g. As No. R85c, impression of No. RS208 on back *17,000.*

R86 R8 $3 Manifest, green
a. Imperf. 200.00
c. Perf. 55.00

R87 R8 $3.50 Inland Exchange, blue ('63)
a. Imperf. *9,000.*
c. Perf. 70.00
e. As No. R87c, printed on both sides *4,000.*

The $3.50 has stars in upper corners.

R9

R10

R88 R9 $5 Charter Party, red
a. Imperf. 300.00
c. Perf. 10.00
d. Silk paper 100.00

R89 R9 $5 Conveyance, red
a. Imperf. 50.00
c. Perf. 11.00
d. Silk paper 140.00

R90 R9 $5 Manifest, red
a. Imperf. 250.00
c. Perf. 120.00

R91 R9 $5 Mortgage, red
a. Imperf. 200.00
c. Perf. 25.00

R92 R9 $5 Probate of Will, red
a. Imperf. 800.00
c. Perf. 27.50

R93 R9 $10 Charter Party, green
a. Imperf. 900.00
c. Perf. 37.50

R94 R9 $10 Conveyance, green
a. Imperf. 175.00
c. Perf. 77.50

R95 R9 $10 Mortgage, green
a. Imperf. 900.00
c. Perf. 40.00

R96 R9 $10 Probate of Will, green
a. Imperf. 3,500.
c. Perf. 45.00

R97 R10 $15 Mortgage, blue
a. Imperf. 3,500.
c. Perf. 300.00
e. As No. R97c, ultramarine 325.00
f. As No. R97c, milky blue 350.00

R98 R10 $20 Conveyance, orange
a. Imperf. 175.00
c. Perf. 125.00
d. Silk paper 175.00

R99 R10 $20 Probate of Will, orange
a. Imperf. 2,750.
c. Perf. 2,500.

R100 R10 $25 Mortgage, red ('63)
a. Imperf. 2,200.
c. Perf. 250.00
d. Silk paper 275.00
e. As No. R100c, horiz. pair, imperf. between *2,250.*

R101 R10 $50 U.S. Internal Revenue, green ('63)
a. Imperf. 325.00
c. Perf. 210.00

R11

R102 R11 $200 U.S. Int. Rev., green & red ('64)
a. Imperf. 2,750.
c. Perf. 1,000.

DOCUMENTARY STAMPS
Second Issue

After release of the First Issue revenue stamps, the Bureau of Internal Revenue received many reports of fraudulent cleaning and re-use. The Bureau ordered a Second Issue with new designs and colors, using a patented "chameleon" paper which is usually violet or pinkish, with silk fibers.

While designs are different from those of the first issue, stamp sizes and make up of the plates are the same as for corresponding denominations.

R12

R12a

George Washington

Various Frames and Numeral Arrangements

1871 ***Perf. 12***

R103 R12 1c blue & black 90.00
Cut cancel 35.00
a. Inverted center *1,600.*
R104 R12 2c blue & black 2.75
Cut cancel .30
a. Inverted center *5,000.*
R105 R12a 3c blue & black 50.00
Cut cancel 20.00
R106 R12a 4c blue & black 125.00
Cut cancel 45.00
a. Horiz. half used as 2c on document *500.00*
b. Vert. half used as 2c on document *1,000.*
R107 R12a 5c blue & black 2.00
Cut cancel .50
a. Inverted center *3,500.*
R108 R12a 6c blue & black 250.00
Cut cancel 80.00
R109 R12a 10c blue & black 1.50
Cut cancel .30
a. Inverted center *2,000.*
b. Double impression of center —
c. Half used as 5c on document *300.00*

No. R109a is valued in the grade of fine.

R110 R12a 15c blue & black 85.00
Cut cancel 30.00
R111 R12a 20c blue & black 8.00
Cut cancel 3.00
a. Inverted center *7,000.*

No. R111a is valued in the grade of fine and with small faults, as almost all examples have faults.

R13

R13a

R112 R13 25c blue & black 1.50
Cut cancel .30
a. Inverted center *11,000.*
b. Sewing machine perf. 125.00
Cut cancel 70.00
c. Perf. 8 475.00
R113 R13 30c blue & black 160.00
Cut cancel 60.00
R114 R13 40c blue & black 130.00
Cut cancel 40.00
R115 R13a 50c blue & black 1.40
Cut cancel .35
a. Sewing machine perf. 450.00
b. Inverted center 1,250.
Punch cancel 350.00
R116 R13a 60c blue & black 225.00
Cut cancel 70.00
R117 R13a 70c blue & black 85.00
Cut cancel 27.50
a. Inverted center *4,000.*
Cut cancel *1,250.*

R13b

R118 R13b $1 blue & black 10.00
Cut cancel 2.25
a. Inverted center *5,000.*
Punch cancel *900.00*
R119 R13b $1.30 blue & black 600.00
Cut cancel 160.00
R120 R13b $1.50 blue & black 22.50
Cut cancel 9.00
a. Sewing machine perf. *2,500.*
R121 R13b $1.60 blue & black 750.00
Cut cancel 350.00
R122 R13b $1.90 blue & black 500.00
Cut cancel 150.00

R13c

R123 R13c $2 blue & black 22.50
Cut cancel 10.00
R124 R13c $2.50 blue & black 50.00
Cut cancel 25.00
R125 R13c $3 blue & black 65.00
Cut cancel 30.00
R126 R13c $3.50 blue & black 425.00
Cut cancel 130.00

R13d

R127 R13d $5 blue & black 32.50
Cut cancel 11.00
a. Inverted center *3,000.*
Punch cancel *1,100.*
R128 R13d $10 blue & black 230.00
Cut cancel 80.00

R13e

R129 R13e $20 blue & black 1,000.
Cut cancel 350.00
R130 R13e $25 blue & black 1,150.
Cut cancel 390.00
R131 R13e $50 blue & black 1,200.
Cut cancel 400.00

R13f

R132 R13f $200 red, blue & black *8,500.*
Cut cancel *3,500.*

Printed in sheets of one.

R13g

R133 R13g $500 red orange, green & black *17,500.*

Printed in sheets of one.

Value for No. R133 is for a very fine appearing example with a light circular cut cancel or with minor flaws.

Inverted Centers: Fraudulently produced inverted centers exist, some excellently made.

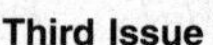

Confusion resulting from the fact that all 1c through $50 denominations of the Second Issue were uniform in color, caused the ordering of a new printing with values in distinctive colors.

Plates used were those of the preceding issue.

Third Issue

Various Frames and Numeral Arrangements.

Violet "Chameleon" Paper with Silk Fibers.

1871-72 ***Perf. 12***

R134 R12 1c claret & black ('72) 55.00
Cut cancel 25.00
R135 R12 2c orange & black .40
Cut cancel .25
a. 2c vermilion & black (error) *800.00*
b. Inverted center 650.00
c. Imperf., pair —
d. As No. R135, double impression of frame *1,500.*
e. As No. R135, frame printed on both sides *1,600.*
f. As No. R135, double impression of center *150.00*
R136 R12a 4c brown & black ('72) 95.00
Cut cancel 35.00
R137 R12a 5c orange & black .35
Cut cancel .25
a. Inverted center *4,500.*

No. R137a is valued in the grade of fine.

R138 R12a 6c orange & black ('72) 110.00
Cut cancel 35.00

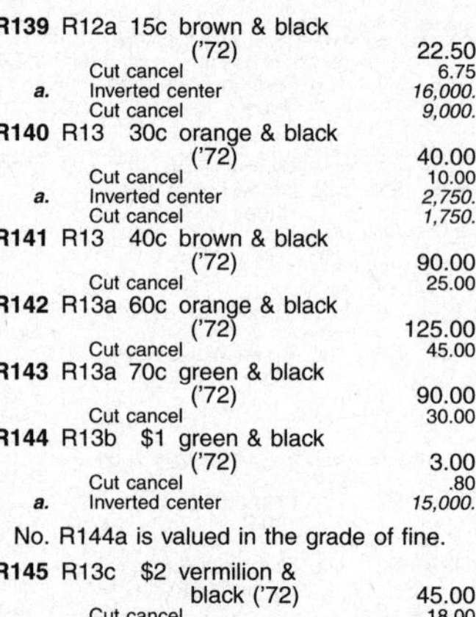

R139 R12a 15c brown & black ('72) 22.50
Cut cancel 6.75
a. Inverted center *16,000.*
Cut cancel *9,000.*
R140 R13 30c orange & black ('72) 40.00
Cut cancel 10.00
a. Inverted center *2,750.*
Cut cancel *1,750.*
R141 R13 40c brown & black ('72) 90.00
Cut cancel 25.00
R142 R13a 60c orange & black ('72) 125.00
Cut cancel 45.00
R143 R13a 70c green & black ('72) 90.00
Cut cancel 30.00
R144 R13b $1 green & black ('72) 3.00
Cut cancel .80
a. Inverted center *15,000.*

No. R144a is valued in the grade of fine.

R145 R13c $2 vermilion & black ('72) 45.00
Cut cancel 18.00
R146 R13c $2.50 claret & black ('72) 90.00
Cut cancel 27.50
a. Inverted center *22,500.*
R147 R13c $3 green & black ('72) 85.00
Cut cancel 27.50
R148 R13d $5 vermilion & black ('72) 42.50
Cut cancel 15.00
R149 R13d $10 green & black ('72) 400.00
Cut cancel 85.00
R150 R13e $20 orange & black ('72) 800.00
Cut cancel 325.00
a. $20 vermilion & black (error) 1,200.

See note on Inverted Centers after No. R133.

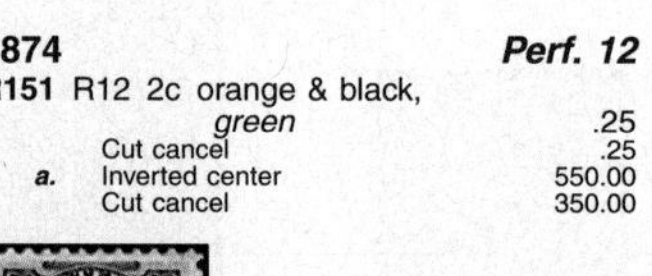

1874 ***Perf. 12***

R151 R12 2c orange & black, *green* .25
Cut cancel .25
a. Inverted center 550.00
Cut cancel 350.00

Liberty — R14

1875-78 ***Perf. 12***

R152 R14 2c bl, *blue*
a. silk paper .45
b. Wmk. 191R ('78) .35
c. Wmk. 191R, rouletted 6 32.50
d. As "a," vert. pair, imperf. horiz. 525.00
e. As "b," imperf., pair *350.00*
f. As "b," vert. pair, imperf. horiz. 350.00

The watermarked paper came into use in 1878. The rouletted stamps probably were introduced in 1881.

Nos. 279, 267a, 267, 279Bg, 279B, 272-274 Overprinted in Red or Blue

a

b

1898 **Wmk. 191** ***Perf. 12***

For Nos. R153-R160, values in the first column are for unused examples, values in the second column are for used.

R153 A87 (a) 1c green (R) 5.00 2.75
R154 A87 (b) 1c green (R) .35 .35
a. Overprint inverted 35.00 22.50
b. Overprint on back instead of face, inverted *4,000.*
c. Pair, one without overprint *10,000.*
R155 A88 (b) 2c pink, III (Bl) .30 .25
b. 2c **carmine**, type III (Bl) .35 .25
c. As No. R155, overprint inverted 6.50 4.50
d. Vertical pair, one without overprint *1,750.*
e. Horiz. pair, one without overprint —
f. As No. R155, overprint on back instead of face, inverted 350.00
i. Double ovt., one split *750.00*

R155A A88 (b) 2c pink, IV (Bl) .25 .25
g. 2c **carmine,** type IV (Bl) .25 .25
h. As No. R155A, overprint inverted 2.75 2.00

Handstamped Type "b" in Magenta

R156 A93 8c violet brown *5,500.*
R157 A94 10c dark green *4,250.*
R158 A95 15c dark blue *6,500.*

Nos. R156-R158 were emergency provisionals, privately prepared, not officially issued.

Privately Prepared Provisionals

No. 285 Overprinted in Red

1898 Wmk. 191 *Perf. 12*
R158A A100 1c dark yellow green *12,500. 12,500.*

Same Overprinted "I.R./P.I.D. & Son" in Red

R158B A100 1c dark yellow green *30,000. 30,000.*

No. R158B is valued with small faults as each of the four recorded examples have faults.

Nos. R158A-R158B were overprinted with federal government permission by the Purvis Printing Co. upon order of Capt. L. H. Chapman of the Chapman Steamboat Line. Both the Chapman Line and P. I. Daprix & Son operated freight-carrying steamboats on the Erie Canal. The Chapman Line touched at Syracuse, Utica, Little Falls and Fort Plain; the Daprix boat ran between Utica and Rome. Overprintings of 250 of each stamp were made.

Dr. Kilmer & Co. provisional overprints and St. Louis provisional proprietary stamps are listed under "Private Die Medicine Stamps" in the Scott U.S. Specialized Catalogue.

Newspaper Stamp No. PR121 Surcharged Vertically in Red

1898 *Perf. 12*
R159 N18 $5 dark blue, surcharge reading down 550.00 325.00
R160 N18 $5 dark blue, surcharge reading up 150.00 140.00

Battleship — R15

Inscribed: "Series of 1898" and "Documentary."

There are 2 styles of rouletting for the 1898 proprietary and documentary stamps, an ordinary roulette 5½ and one where small rectangles of the paper are cut out, called hyphen hole perf. 7.

1898 Wmk. 191R *Rouletted 5½*
R161 R15 ½c orange 4.00 *17.50*
R162 R15 ½c dark gray .30 .25
a. Vert. pair, imperf. horiz. 100.00
R163 R15 1c pale blue .25 .25
a. Vert. pair, imperf. horiz. 8.00
b. Imperf., pair *500.00*
c. Diagonal half used as ½c, on piece 800.00
R164 R15 2c car rose .30 .30
a. Vert. pair, imperf. horiz. 100.00
b. Imperf., pair 300.00
c. Horiz. pair, imperf. vert. 325.00
R165 R15 3c dark blue 3.50 .35
R166 R15 4c pale rose 2.50 .35
a. Vert. pair, imperf. horiz. 175.00
R167 R15 5c lilac .65 .35
a. Pair, imperf. horiz. or vert. 275.00 175.00
b. Horiz. pair, imperf. btwn. *650.00*
R168 R15 10c dark brown 2.00 .25
a. Vert. pair, imperf. horiz. 40.00 35.00
b. Horiz. pair, imperf. vert. —
R169 R15 25c pur brown 5.00 .50
R170 R15 40c blue lilac 125.00 1.50
Cut cancellation .35
R171 R15 50c slate violet 30.00 .25
a. Imperf., pair *325.00*
b. Horiz. pair, imperf. btwn. *375.00*
R172 R15 80c bister 110.00 .50
Cut cancellation .25

No. R167b may not be genuine.

Hyphen Hole Perf. 7

R163p 1c .30 .25
R164p 2c .35 .25
R165p 3c 35.00 1.40
R166p 4c 13.00 1.60
R167p 5c 13.00 .35
R168p 10c 7.50 .25
R169p 25c 15.00 .50
R170p 40c 175.00 30.00
Cut cancellation 12.50
R171p 50c 60.00 1.00
b. Horiz. pair, imperf. btwn. — *250.00*
R172p 80c 210.00 50.00
Cut cancellation 20.00

Commerce — R16

1898 *Rouletted 5½*
R173 R16 $1 dark green 25.00 .25
a. Vert. pair, imperf. horiz. 800.00
b. Horiz. pair, imperf. vert. — 325.00
p. Hyphen hole perf. 7 37.50 2.00
Cut cancel .75
R174 R16 $3 dark brown 45.00 1.25
Cut cancellation .30
a. Horiz. pair, imperf. vert. 500.00
p. Hyphen hole perf. 7 80.00 3.50
Cut cancellation .40
R175 R16 $5 orange red 75.00 2.00
Cut cancellation .30
R176 R16 $10 black 160.00 3.50
Cut cancellation .65
a. Horiz. pair, imperf. vert. —
R177 R16 $30 red 500.00 160.00
Cut cancellation 47.50
R178 R16 $50 gray brown 275.00 7.00
Cut cancellation 2.50

See Nos. R182-R183.

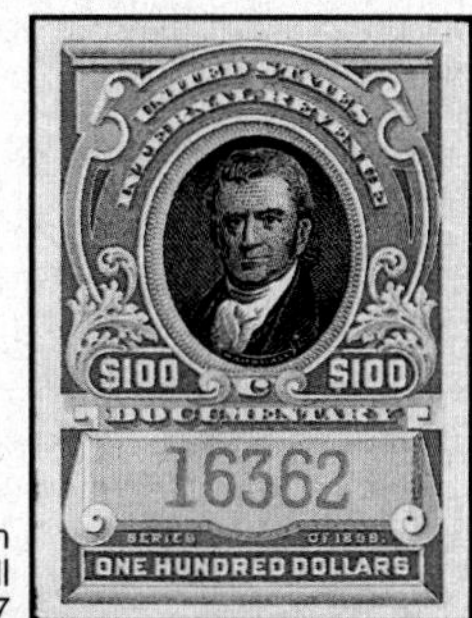

John Marshall R17

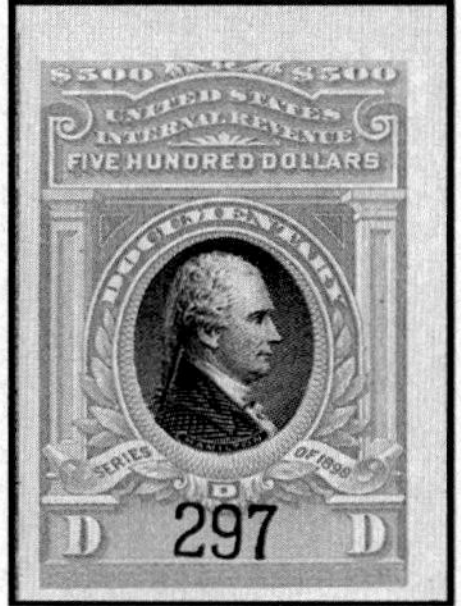

Alexander Hamilton R18

James Madison R19

1899 *Imperf.*

Without Gum

R179 R17 $100 yel brn & blk 300.00 40.00
Cut cancel 22.50
R180 R18 $500 car lake & blk 2,100. 800.00
Cut cancel 350.00
R181 R19 $1000 grn & blk 1,500. 400.00
Cut cancel 160.00

1900 *Hyphen-hole perf. 7*

Allegorical Figure of Commerce

R182 R16 $1 carmine 45.00 .55
Cut cancel .30
R183 R16 $3 lake (fugitive ink) 300.00 60.00
Cut cancel 10.00

Warning: The ink on No. R183 will run in water.

a

Surcharged type "a"

1900
R184 R16 $1 gray 35.00 .40
Cut cancel .30
a. Horiz. pair, imperf vert —
b. Surcharge omitted 140.00
As "b," cut cancel 82.50
R185 R16 $2 gray 35.00 .40
Cut cancel .25
R186 R16 $3 gray 175.00 15.00
Cut cancel 6.00
R187 R16 $5 gray 85.00 11.00
Cut cancel 1.60
R188 R16 $10 gray 225.00 25.00
Cut cancel 4.50
R189 R16 $50 gray 2,000. 575.00
Cut cancel 140.00

b

Surcharged type "b"

Warning: If Nos. R190-R194 are soaked, the center part of the surcharged numeral may wash off. Before the surcharging, a square of soluble varnish was applied to the middle of some stamps.

1902
R190 R16 $1 green 50.00 3.50
Cut cancel .30
a. Inverted surcharge *190.00*
R191 R16 $2 green 50.00 2.50
Cut cancel .45
a. Surcharged as No. R185 150.00 90.00
b. Surcharged as No. R185, in violet *2,000.* —
c. As "a," double surcharge *150.00*
d. As "a," triple surcharge *850.00*
e. Pair, Nos. R191c and R191d *1,650.*
R192 R16 $5 green 240.00 42.50
Cut cancel 5.00
a. Surcharge omitted 300.00
b. Pair, one without surcharge *500.00*
R193 R16 $10 green 525.00 225.00
Cut cancel 80.00
R194 R16 $50 green 2,750. 1,250.
Cut cancel 325.00

R20

Inscribed "Series of 1914"

Offset Printing

1914 Wmk. 190 *Perf. 10*
R195 R20 ½c rose 14.00 5.00
R196 R20 1c rose 2.75 .30
R197 R20 2c rose 4.00 .30
R198 R20 3c rose 100.00 40.00
R199 R20 4c rose 30.00 2.50
R200 R20 5c rose 10.00 .40
R201 R20 10c rose 8.00 .25
R202 R20 25c rose 50.00 .60
R203 R20 40c rose 32.50 3.00
R204 R20 50c rose 13.00 .35
R205 R20 80c rose 210.00 17.00
Nos. R195-R205 (11) 474.25 69.70

Wmk. 191R

R206 R20 ½c rose 1.60 .50
R207 R20 1c rose .25 .25
R208 R20 2c rose .30 .25
R209 R20 3c rose 1.50 .25
R210 R20 4c rose 4.50 .50
R211 R20 5c rose 2.00 .35
R212 R20 10c rose .80 .25
R213 R20 25c rose 8.00 1.50
R214 R20 40c rose 125.00 15.00
Cut cancel .50
R215 R20 50c rose 27.50 .40
Cut cancel .25
R216 R20 80c rose 200.00 35.00
Cut cancel 1.25
Nos. R206-R216 (11) 371.45 54.25

Liberty — R21

Inscribed "Series 1914"

Engr.

R217 R21 $1 green 75.00 .55
Cut cancel .25
a. $1 yellow green 50.00 .25
R218 R21 $2 carmine 125.00 1.00
Cut cancel .25
R219 R21 $3 purple 150.00 5.00
Cut cancel .80
R220 R21 $5 blue 105.00 4.50
Cut cancel .65
R221 R21 $10 yellow orange 325.00 7.50
Cut cancel 1.10
R222 R21 $30 vermilion 775.00 21.00
Cut cancel 2.25
R223 R21 $50 violet 2,000. 1,200.
Cut cancel 450.00

See Nos. R240-R245, R257-R259, R276-R281.

Portrait Types of 1899 Inscribed "Series of 1915" (#R224), or "Series of 1914"

1914-15 Without Gum *Perf. 12*
R224 R19 $60 brown *(Lincoln)* 250.00 150.00
Cut cancel 70.00
R225 R17 $100 green *(Washington)* 77.50 45.00
Cut cancel 16.00
R226 R18 $500 blue *(Hamilton)* — 700.00
Cut cancel 275.00
R227 R19 $1000 orange *(Madison)* — 800.00
Cut cancel 300.00

The stamps of types R17, R18 and R19 in this and subsequent issues were issued in vertical strips of 4 which are imperforate at the top, bottom and right side; therefore, single stamps are always imperforate on one or two sides.

R22

Offset Printing

1917 Wmk. 191R *Perf. 11*

R228 R22 1c carmine rose .35 .25
R229 R22 2c carmine rose .25 .25
R230 R22 3c carmine rose 1.75 .40
R231 R22 4c carmine rose .75 .25
R232 R22 5c carmine rose .30 .25
R233 R22 8c carmine rose 3.00 .35
R234 R22 10c carmine rose .40 .25
R235 R22 20c carmine rose .75 .25
R236 R22 25c carmine rose 1.75 .25
R237 R22 40c carmine rose 2.25 .50
R238 R22 50c carmine rose 2.50 .25
R239 R22 80c carmine rose 9.00 .35
Nos. R228-R239 (12) 23.05 3.60

Liberty Type of 1914 without "Series 1914"

1917-33 **Engr.**

R240 R21 $1 yellow green 10.00 .30
a. $1 green 7.25 .25
R241 R21 $2 rose 17.50 .25
R242 R21 $3 violet 60.00 1.50
Cut cancel .30
R243 R21 $4 yellow brown ('33) 40.00 2.00
Cut cancel .30
R244 R21 $5 dark blue 27.50 .35
Cut cancel .25
R245 R21 $10 orange 60.00 1.40
Cut cancel .30

Portrait Types of 1899 without "Series of" and Date

Portraits: $30, Grant. $60, Lincoln. $100, Washington. $500, Hamilton. $1,000, Madison.

1917 Without Gum *Perf. 12*

R246 R17 $30 dp org, green numerals 55.00 13.00
Cut cancel 2.25
a. As "b," imperf. pair 750.00
b. Numerals in blue 125.00 3.50
Cut cancel 1.50
R247 R19 $60 brown 65.00 8.00
Cut cancel .85
R248 R17 $100 green 45.00 2.00
Cut cancel .50
R249 R18 $500 blue, red numerals 375.00 50.00
Cut cancel 15.00
a. Numerals in orange 425.00 65.00
R250 R19 $1000 orange 175.00 20.00
Cut cancel 7.50
a. Imperf., pair 2,000.

See note after No. R227.

1928-29 Offset Printing *Perf. 10*

R251 R22 1c carmine rose 2.10 1.60
R252 R22 2c carmine rose .60 .30
R253 R22 4c carmine rose 7.00 4.00
R254 R22 5c carmine rose 1.75 .55
R255 R22 10c carmine rose 2.75 1.25
R256 R22 20c carmine rose 6.00 4.50

Engr.

R257 R21 $1 green 200.00 45.00
Cut cancel 5.00
R258 R21 $2 rose 90.00 5.00
R259 R21 $10 orange 325.00 75.00
Cut cancel 30.00

1929 Offset Printing *Perf. 11x10*

R260 R22 2c carmine rose ('30) 3.00 2.75
R261 R22 5c carmine rose ('30) 2.00 1.90
R262 R22 10c carmine rose 9.25 6.75
R263 R22 20c carmine rose 15.00 8.25

Used values for Nos. R264-R734 are for stamps which are neither cut nor perforated with initials. Examples with cut cancellations or perforated initials are valued in the Scott U. S. Specialized Catalogue.

Types of 1917-33 Overprinted in Black

SERIES 1940

Offset Printing

1940 Wmk. 191R *Perf. 11*

R264 R22 1c rose pink 3.75 2.40
R265 R22 2c rose pink 5.00 2.25
R266 R22 3c rose pink 11.00 5.00
R267 R22 4c rose pink 5.00 .80
R268 R22 5c rose pink 5.00 1.25
R269 R22 8c rose pink 22.50 17.00
R270 R22 10c rose pink 2.50 .65
R271 R22 20c rose pink 3.25 .80
R272 R22 25c rose pink 8.00 1.50
R273 R22 40c rose pink 6.75 .90
R274 R22 50c rose pink 11.00 .55
R275 R22 80c rose pink 14.00 1.75

Engr.

R276 R21 $1 green 75.00 1.25
R277 R21 $2 rose 75.00 2.00
R278 R21 $3 violet 100.00 37.50
R279 R21 $4 yellow brown 190.00 35.00
R280 R21 $5 dark blue 85.00 20.00
R281 R21 $10 orange 240.00 50.00

Types of 1917 Handstamped "Series 1940" like R264-R281 in Blue (Nos. R282-R283), Green (Nos. R283-R284, R286) or Violet (No. R285)

1940 Wmk. 191R *Perf. 12*

Without Gum

R282 R17 $30 vermilion 1,100.
a. With black 2-line handstamp in larger type 22,500.
R283 R19 $60 brown 2,400.
a. As #R282a, cut cancel 12,500.
R284 R17 $100 green 3,000.
R285 R18 $500 blue 3,000.
a. As #R282a 3,250. 4,250.
b. Blue handstamp; double transfer —
R286 R19 $1000 orange 900.
a. Double overprint, cut cancel —

Alexander Hamilton R23

Levi Woodbury R24

Overprinted in Black SERIES 1940

Various Portraits: 2c, Oliver Wolcott, Jr. 3c, Samuel Dexter. 4c, Albert Gallatin. 5c. G. W. Campbell. 8c, Alexander Dallas. 10c, William H. Crawford. 20c, Richard Rush. 25c, S. D. Ingham. 40c. Louis McLane. 50c, William J. Duane. 80c, Roger B. Taney. $2, Thomas Ewing. $3, Walter Forward. $4, J. C. Spencer. $5, G. M. Bibb. $10, R. J. Walker. $20, William M. Meredith.

1940 Engr. Wmk. 191R *Perf. 11*

R288 R23 1c carmine 5.75 4.50
a. Imperf, pair, without gum 250.00
R289 R23 2c carmine 8.50 4.00
a. Imperf, pair, without gum 250.00
R290 R23 3c carmine 30.00 12.00
a. Imperf, pair, without gum 250.00
R291 R23 4c carmine 62.50 27.50
a. Imperf, pair, without gum 250.00
R292 R23 5c carmine 4.75 .80
a. Imperf, pair, without gum 250.00
R293 R23 8c carmine 85.00 60.00
a. Imperf, pair, without gum 250.00
R294 R23 10c carmine 4.25 .60
a. Imperf, pair, without gum 250.00
R295 R23 20c carmine 5.50 4.25
a. Imperf, pair, without gum 250.00
R296 R23 25c carmine 5.00 .75
a. Imperf, pair, without gum 250.00
R297 R23 40c carmine 75.00 30.00
a. Imperf, pair, without gum 250.00
R298 R23 50c carmine 8.00 .60
a. Imperf, pair, without gum 250.00
R299 R23 80c carmine 175.00 100.00
a. Imperf, pair, without gum 475.00
R300 R24 $1 carmine 42.50 .60
a. Imperf, pair, without gum 250.00
R301 R24 $2 carmine 80.00 .90
R302 R24 $3 carmine 190.00 95.00
a. Imperf, pair, without gum 1,400.
R303 R24 $4 carmine 125.00 50.00
R304 R24 $5 carmine 70.00 3.00
R305 R24 $10 carmine 125.00 10.00
R305A R24 $20 carmine 3,000. 1,100.
b. Imperf, pair, without gum 700.00

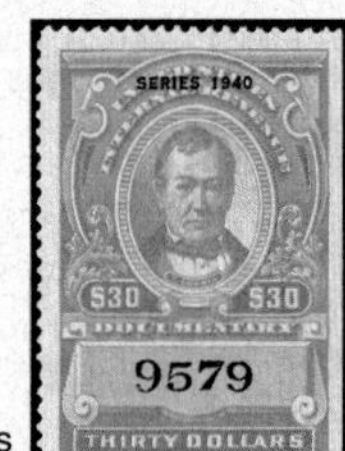
Thomas Corwin — R25

Various Frames and Portraits: $50, James Guthrie. $60, Howell Cobb. $100, P. F. Thomas. $500, J. A. Dix, $1,000, S. P. Chase.

Perf. 12

Without Gum

R306 R25 $30 carmine 200.00 75.00
R306A R25 $50 carmine — 10,000.
R307 R25 $60 carmine 375.00 80.00
a. Vert. pair, imperf. btwn. 2,750. 1,450.
R308 R25 $100 carmine 275.00 100.00
R309 R25 $500 carmine — 5,500.
R310 R25 $1000 carmine — 550.00

The $30 to $1,000 denominations in this and following similar issues, and the $2,500, $5,000 and $10,000 stamps of 1952-58 have straight edges on one or two sides. They were issued without gum through No. R723.

Nos. R288-R310 Overprinted

SERIES 1941

1941 Wmk. 191R *Perf. 11*

R311 R23 1c carmine 5.00 2.75
R312 R23 2c carmine 5.25 1.10
R313 R23 3c carmine 10.00 4.25
R314 R23 4c carmine 7.50 1.75
R315 R23 5c carmine 1.50 .40
R316 R23 8c carmine 21.00 8.50
R317 R23 10c carmine 2.00 .35
R318 R23 20c carmine 4.75 .65
R319 R23 25c carmine 2.40 .65
R320 R23 40c carmine 16.00 3.25
R321 R23 50c carmine 3.50 .30
R322 R23 80c carmine 65.00 12.00
R323 R24 $1 carmine 15.00 .30
R324 R24 $2 carmine 20.00 .50
R325 R24 $3 carmine 32.50 3.50
R326 R24 $4 carmine 47.50 27.50
R327 R24 $5 carmine 60.00 1.10
R328 R24 $10 carmine 100.00 6.00
R329 R24 $20 carmine 850.00 400.00

Perf. 12

Without Gum

R330 R25 $30 carmine 200.00 55.00
R331 R25 $50 carmine 1,100. 900.00
R332 R25 $60 carmine 225.00 87.50
R333 R25 $100 carmine 110.00 37.50
R334 R25 $500 carmine — 375.00
R335 R25 $1000 carmine — 225.00

Nos. R288-R310 Overprinted

SERIES 1942

1942 Wmk. 191R *Perf. 11*

R336 R23 1c carmine .65 .60
R337 R23 2c carmine .60 .60
R338 R23 3c carmine .90 .80
R339 R23 4c carmine 1.75 1.10
R340 R23 5c carmine .60 .35
R341 R23 8c carmine 9.50 4.75
R342 R23 10c carmine 1.75 .35
R343 R23 20c carmine 1.75 .60
R344 R23 25c carmine 3.00 .55
R345 R23 40c carmine 6.50 1.75
R346 R23 50c carmine 4.00 .35
R347 R23 80c carmine 27.50 13.00
R348 R24 $1 carmine 12.50 .25
R349 R24 $2 carmine 15.00 .30
R350 R24 $3 carmine 27.50 3.25
R351 R24 $4 carmine 35.00 7.50
R352 R24 $5 carmine 37.50 1.50
R353 R24 $10 carmine 85.00 3.75
R354 R24 $20 carmine 200.00 45.00
a. Imperf., perf. initials —

Perf. 12

Without Gum

R355 R25 $30 carmine 100.00 42.50
R356 R25 $50 carmine 1,900. 1,500.
R357 R25 $60 carmine 2,500. 2,000.
R358 R25 $100 carmine 275.00 175.00
R359 R25 $500 carmine *1,600.* 275.00
R360 R25 $1000 carmine — 150.00

Nos. R288-R310 Overprinted in Black

SERIES 1943

1943 Wmk. 191R *Perf. 11*

R361 R23 1c carmine .80 .65
R362 R23 2c carmine .65 .55
R363 R23 3c carmine 3.75 3.50
R364 R23 4c carmine 1.60 1.50
R365 R23 5c carmine .70 .45
R366 R23 8c carmine 6.00 4.00
R367 R23 10c carmine .85 .30
R368 R23 20c carmine 2.50 .80
R369 R23 25c carmine 2.75 .50
R370 R23 40c carmine 7.50 4.00
R371 R23 50c carmine 2.00 .30
R372 R23 80c carmine 27.50 8.00
R373 R24 $1 carmine 9.00 .35
R374 R24 $2 carmine 18.00 .35
R375 R24 $3 carmine 30.00 3.00
R376 R24 $4 carmine 55.00 10.00
R377 R24 $5 carmine 52.50 .75
R378 R24 $10 carmine 85.00 5.00
R379 R24 $20 carmine 210.00 60.00

Perf. 12

Without Gum

R380 R25 $30 carmine 125.00 25.00
R381 R25 $50 carmine 200.00 75.00
R382 R25 $60 carmine 325.00 125.00
R383 R25 $100 carmine 35.00 22.50
R384 R25 $500 carmine *375.00* 325.00
R385 R25 $1000 carmine *350.00* 200.00

Nos. R288-R310 Overprinted

Series 1944

1944 Wmk. 191R *Perf. 11*

R386 R23 1c carmine .50 .45
R387 R23 2c carmine .65 .55
R388 R23 3c carmine .65 .40
R389 R23 4c carmine .75 .65
R390 R23 5c carmine .40 .25
R391 R23 8c carmine 2.25 1.75
R392 R23 10c carmine .50 .25
R393 R23 20c carmine 1.10 .35
R394 R23 25c carmine 2.00 .30
R395 R23 40c carmine 3.75 .80
R396 R23 50c carmine 4.00 .35
R397 R23 80c carmine 21.00 5.50
R398 R24 $1 carmine 10.00 .30
R399 R24 $2 carmine 15.00 .45
R400 R24 $3 carmine 25.00 2.40
R401 R24 $4 carmine 32.50 11.50
R402 R24 $5 carmine 32.50 .50
R403 R24 $10 carmine 65.00 1.60
R404 R24 $20 carmine 200.00 19.00

Perf. 12

Without Gum

R405 R25 $30 carmine 95.00 35.00
R406 R25 $50 carmine 42.50 22.50
R407 R25 $60 carmine 275.00 75.00
R408 R25 $100 carmine 52.50 12.50
R409 R25 $500 carmine — *3,250.*
R410 R25 $1000 carmine *4,000.* 500.00

Nos. R288-R310 Overprinted

Series 1945

1945 Wmk. 191R *Perf. 11*

R411 R23 1c carmine .40 .30
R412 R23 2c carmine .40 .30
R413 R23 3c carmine .75 .50
R414 R23 4c carmine .45 .35
R415 R23 5c carmine .45 .30
R416 R23 8c carmine 6.25 2.75
R417 R23 10c carmine 1.25 .25
R418 R23 20c carmine 8.00 1.50
R419 R23 25c carmine 1.75 .30
R420 R23 40c carmine 9.00 1.25
R421 R23 50c carmine 4.00 .25
R422 R23 80c carmine 26.00 14.00
R423 R24 $1 carmine 13.50 .30
R424 R24 $2 carmine 13.50 .40
R425 R24 $3 carmine 27.50 3.00
R426 R24 $4 carmine 35.00 4.25
R427 R24 $5 carmine 35.00 .50
R428 R24 $10 carmine 65.00 2.50
R429 R24 $20 carmine 140.00 16.00

Perf. 12

Without Gum

R430 R25 $30 carmine 175.00 40.00
R431 R25 $50 carmine 200.00 45.00
R432 R25 $60 carmine 375.00 80.00

R433	R25	$100	carmine	40.00	20.00
R434	R25	$500	carmine	500.00	325.00
R435	R25	$1000	carmine	375.00	125.00

Nos. R288-R310 Overprinted

Series 1946

1946		**Wmk. 191R**			***Perf. 11***
R436	R23	1c	carmine	.30	.30
R437	R23	2c	carmine	.45	.35
R438	R23	3c	carmine	.55	.40
R439	R23	4c	carmine	.80	.65
R440	R23	5c	carmine	.45	.30
R441	R23	8c	carmine	2.50	2.00
R442	R23	10c	carmine	1.10	.30
R443	R23	20c	carmine	1.75	.50
R444	R23	25c	carmine	6.00	.35
R445	R23	40c	carmine	4.50	.85
R446	R23	50c	carmine	6.00	.30
R447	R23	80c	carmine	17.50	5.00
R448	R24	$1	carmine	16.00	.30
R449	R24	$2	carmine	19.00	.30
R450	R24	$3	carmine	27.50	5.00
R451	R24	$4	carmine	60.00	20.00
R452	R24	$5	carmine	40.00	.50
R453	R24	$10	carmine	72.50	1.75
R454	R24	$20	carmine	140.00	16.00

Perf. 12
Without Gum

R455	R25	$30	carmine	60.00	17.50
R456	R25	$50	carmine	50.00	12.50
R457	R25	$60	carmine	95.00	22.50
R458	R25	$100	carmine	70.00	12.50
R459	R25	$500	carmine	*625.00*	150.00
R460	R25	$1000	carmine	*375.00*	160.00

Nos. R288-R310 Overprinted

Series 1947

1947		**Wmk. 191R**			***Perf. 11***
R461	R23	1c	carmine	.85	.55
R462	R23	2c	carmine	.75	.55
R463	R23	3c	carmine	.85	.55
R464	R23	4c	carmine	.90	.75
R465	R23	5c	carmine	.55	.40
R466	R23	8c	carmine	1.75	.80
R467	R23	10c	carmine	1.40	.30
R468	R23	20c	carmine	2.25	.55
R469	R23	25c	carmine	3.00	.70
R470	R23	40c	carmine	5.50	1.10
R471	R23	50c	carmine	3.75	.40
R472	R23	80c	carmine	12.00	8.00
R473	R24	$1	carmine	8.25	.35
R474	R24	$2	carmine	14.00	.65
R475	R24	$3	carmine	17.50	6.00
R476	R24	$4	carmine	19.00	5.00
R477	R24	$5	carmine	27.50	.60
R478	R24	$10	carmine	67.50	3.00
R479	R24	$20	carmine	110.00	14.00

Perf. 12
Without Gum

R480	R25	$30	carmine	150.00	27.50
R481	R25	$50	carmine	72.50	17.50
R482	R25	$60	carmine	175.00	60.00
R483	R25	$100	carmine	65.00	15.00
R484	R25	$500	carmine	*500.00*	250.00
R485	R25	$1000	carmine	*275.00*	100.00

Nos. R288-R310 Overprinted

Series 1948

1948		**Wmk. 191R**			***Perf. 11***
R486	R23	1c	carmine	.35	.30
R487	R23	2c	carmine	.50	.45
R488	R23	3c	carmine	.60	.40
R489	R23	4c	carmine	.55	.40
R490	R23	5c	carmine	.50	.25
R491	R23	8c	carmine	1.00	.50
R492	R23	10c	carmine	1.00	.25
R493	R23	20c	carmine	2.50	.40
R494	R23	25c	carmine	2.25	.30
R495	R23	40c	carmine	7.00	1.75
R496	R23	50c	carmine	2.50	.30
R497	R23	80c	carmine	12.00	8.00
R498	R24	$1	carmine	10.50	.30
R499	R24	$2	carmine	18.00	.40
R500	R24	$3	carmine	24.00	3.50
R501	R24	$4	carmine	35.00	4.00
R502	R24	$5	carmine	30.00	.50
R503	R24	$10	carmine	70.00	1.50
a.	Pair, one dated "1946"				—
R504	R24	$20	carmine	400.00	18.00

Perf. 12
Without Gum

R505	R25	$30	carmine	125.00	35.00
R506	R25	$50	carmine	150.00	27.50
a.	Vert. pair, imperf. btwn.			*2,500.*	
R507	R25	$60	carmine	250.00	75.00
a.	Vert. pair, imperf. btwn.			*2,500.*	
R508	R25	$100	carmine	100.00	20.00
a.	Vert. pair, imperf. btwn.			*2,000.*	
R509	R25	$500	carmine	1,000.	200.00
R510	R25	$1000	carmine	300.00	125.00

Nos. R288-R310 Overprinted

Series 1949

1949		**Wmk. 191R**			***Perf. 11***
R511	R23	1c	carmine	.40	.35
R512	R23	2c	carmine	.75	.45
R513	R23	3c	carmine	.60	.50
R514	R23	4c	carmine	.80	.60
R515	R23	5c	carmine	.55	.30
R516	R23	8c	carmine	1.00	.70
R517	R23	10c	carmine	.60	.35
R518	R23	20c	carmine	1.75	.75
R519	R23	25c	carmine	2.25	.85
R520	R23	40c	carmine	6.50	2.75
R521	R23	50c	carmine	5.00	.40
R522	R23	80c	carmine	15.00	7.50
R523	R24	$1	carmine	13.50	.85
R524	R24	$2	carmine	17.00	2.50
R525	R24	$3	carmine	27.50	8.00
R526	R24	$4	carmine	30.00	8.00
R527	R24	$5	carmine	32.50	4.25
R528	R24	$10	carmine	72.50	5.25
R529	R24	$20	carmine	150.00	15.00

Perf. 12
Without Gum

R530	R25	$30	carmine	125.00	35.00
R531	R25	$50	carmine	160.00	60.00
R532	R25	$60	carmine	250.00	70.00
R533	R25	$100	carmine	80.00	21.00
R534	R25	$500	carmine	*500.00*	250.00
R535	R25	$1000	carmine	*375.00*	160.00

Nos. R288-R310 Overprinted

Series 1950

1950		**Wmk. 191R**			***Perf. 11***
R536	R23	1c	carmine	.40	.25
R537	R23	2c	carmine	.40	.35
R538	R23	3c	carmine	.50	.40
R539	R23	4c	carmine	.70	.50
R540	R23	5c	carmine	.45	.35
R541	R23	8c	carmine	1.75	.80
R542	R23	10c	carmine	.80	.30
R543	R23	20c	carmine	1.40	.45
R544	R23	25c	carmine	2.00	.45
R545	R23	40c	carmine	6.00	2.10
R546	R23	50c	carmine	8.00	.35
R547	R23	80c	carmine	15.00	8.50
R548	R24	$1	carmine	15.00	.40
R549	R24	$2	carmine	17.50	2.75
R550	R24	$3	carmine	20.00	6.00
R551	R24	$4	carmine	27.50	7.50
R552	R24	$5	carmine	35.00	1.00
R553	R24	$10	carmine	70.00	10.00
R554	R24	$20	carmine	150.00	15.00

Perf. 12
Without Gum

R555	R25	$30	carmine	125.00	70.00
R556	R25	$50	carmine	100.00	22.50
a.	Vert. pair, imperf. horiz.				—
R557	R25	$60	carmine	210.00	75.00
R558	R25	$100	carmine	85.00	22.50
R559	R25	$500	carmine	*300.00*	125.00
R560	R25	$1000	carmine	*300.00*	95.00

Nos. R288-R310 Overprinted

Series 1951

1951		**Wmk. 191R**			***Perf. 11***
R561	R23	1c	carmine	.30	.25
R562	R23	2c	carmine	.30	.35
R563	R23	3c	carmine	.30	.35
R564	R23	4c	carmine	.30	.35
R565	R23	5c	carmine	.30	.35
R566	R23	8c	carmine	1.25	.45
R567	R23	10c	carmine	.30	.35
R568	R23	20c	carmine	.30	.55
R569	R23	25c	carmine	.30	.50
R570	R23	40c	carmine	3.75	1.60
R571	R23	50c	carmine	3.00	.60
R572	R23	80c	carmine	10.00	3.25
R573	R24	$1	carmine	16.00	.30
R574	R24	$2	carmine	21.00	.55
R575	R24	$3	carmine	16.00	4.00
R576	R24	$4	carmine	20.00	12.50
R577	R24	$5	carmine	10.00	.70
R578	R24	$10	carmine	18.00	2.50
R579	R24	$20	carmine	55.00	16.00

Perf. 12
Without Gum

R580	R25	$30	carmine	125.00	25.00
a.	Imperf., pair			*2,500.*	*775.00*
R581	R25	$50	carmine	200.00	45.00
R582	R25	$60	carmine	225.00	75.00
R583	R25	$100	carmine	70.00	25.00
R584	R25	$500	carmine	*400.00*	175.00
R585	R25	$1000	carmine	*375.00*	150.00

No. R583 is known imperf horizontally. It exists as a reconstructed used vertical strip of 4 that was separated into single stamps.

Documentary Stamps and Types of 1940 Overprinted in Black

Series 1952

Designs: 55c, $1.10, $1.65, $2.20, $2.75, $3.30, L. J. Gage; $2500, William Windom; $5000, C. J. Folger; $10,000, W. Q. Gresham.

1952		**Wmk. 191R**			***Perf. 11***
R586	R23	1c	carmine	.35	.30
R587	R23	2c	carmine	.50	.35
R588	R23	3c	carmine	.40	.35
R589	R23	4c	carmine	.45	.30
R590	R23	5c	carmine	.35	.30
R591	R23	8c	carmine	.90	.60
R592	R23	10c	carmine	.50	.30
R593	R23	20c	carmine	1.25	.40
R594	R23	25c	carmine	2.50	.45
R595	R23	40c	carmine	6.00	1.75
R596	R23	50c	carmine	3.50	.30
R597	R23	55c	carmine	.60	15.00
R598	R23	80c	carmine	19.00	4.00
R599	R24	$1	carmine	7.00	1.50
R600	R24	$1.10	carmine	25.00	30.00
R601	R24	$1.65	carmine	175.00	62.50
R602	R24	$2	carmine	17.00	.90
R603	R24	$2.20	carmine	160.00	70.00
R604	R24	$2.75	carmine	190.00	70.00
R605	R24	$3	carmine	32.50	6.00
a.	Horiz. pair, imperf. btwn.			*1,300.*	
R606	R24	$3.30	carmine	225.00	90.00
R607	R24	$4	carmine	37.50	6.00
R608	R24	$5	carmine	32.50	1.25
R609	R24	$10	carmine	60.00	1.25
R610	R24	$20	carmine	92.50	16.00

Perf. 12
Without Gum

R611	R25	$30	carmine	70.00	27.50
R612	R25	$50	carmine	75.00	35.00
R613	R25	$60	carmine	475.00	70.00
R614	R25	$100	carmine	75.00	10.00
R615	R25	$500	carmine	*750.00*	150.00
R616	R25	$1000	carmine	*250.00*	75.00
R617	R25	$2500	carmine	*375.00*	275.00
R618	R25	$5000	carmine	—	*5,500.*
R619	R25	$10,000	carmine	—	*1,400.*

Documentary Stamps and Types of 1940 Overprinted in Black

Series 1953

1953		**Wmk. 191R**			***Perf. 11***
R620	R23	1c	carmine	.40	.35
R621	R23	2c	carmine	.40	.30
R622	R23	3c	carmine	.45	.35
R623	R23	4c	carmine	.60	.45
R624	R23	5c	carmine	.50	.30
a.	Vert. pair, imperf. horiz.			*650.00*	
R625	R23	8c	carmine	1.10	.85
R626	R23	10c	carmine	.65	.35
R627	R23	20c	carmine	1.50	.50
R628	R23	25c	carmine	1.75	.65
R629	R23	40c	carmine	2.50	.90
R630	R23	50c	carmine	3.00	.35
R631	R23	55c	carmine	7.00	2.00
a.	Horiz. pair, imperf. vert.			*375.00*	
R632	R23	80c	carmine	10.00	2.10
R633	R24	$1	carmine	5.25	.35
R634	R24	$1.10	carmine	12.00	2.50
a.	Horiz. pair, imperf. vert.			*700.00*	
b.	Imperf. pair			*600.00*	
R635	R24	$1.65	carmine	12.00	4.50
R636	R24	$2	carmine	9.00	.75
R637	R24	$2.20	carmine	20.00	6.00
R638	R24	$2.75	carmine	1.75	7.00
R639	R24	$3	carmine	17.00	4.00
R640	R24	$3.30	carmine	50.00	17.50
R641	R24	$4	carmine	40.00	15.00
R642	R24	$5	carmine	27.50	1.25
R643	R24	$10	carmine	60.00	2.25
R644	R24	$20	carmine	140.00	22.50

Perf. 12
Without Gum

R645	R25	$30	carmine	100.00	20.00
R646	R25	$50	carmine	160.00	42.50
R647	R25	$60	carmine	700.00	425.00
R648	R25	$100	carmine	55.00	15.00
R649	R25	$500	carmine	*2,000.*	175.00
R650	R25	$1000	carmine	550.00	80.00
R651	R25	$2500	carmine	2,000.	1,750.
R652	R25	$5000	carmine	—	*6,000.*
R653	R25	$10,000	carmine	—	*3,250.*

Types of 1940
Without Overprint

1954		**Wmk. 191R**			***Perf. 11***
R654	R23	1c	carmine	.25	.25
a.	Horiz. pair, imperf. vert.				*1,500.*
R655	R23	2c	carmine	.25	.30
R656	R23	3c	carmine	.25	.30
R657	R23	4c	carmine	.25	.30
R658	R23	5c	carmine	.25	.25
a.	Vert. pair, imperf. horiz.			—	
R659	R23	8c	carmine	.25	.25
R660	R23	10c	carmine	.25	.25
R661	R23	20c	carmine	.30	.40
R662	R23	25c	carmine	.35	.45
R663	R23	40c	carmine	.75	.60
R664	R23	50c	carmine	1.00	.25
a.	Horiz. pair, imperf. vert.			600.00	
R665	R23	55c	carmine	.90	1.25
R666	R23	80c	carmine	1.50	1.90
R667	R24	$1	carmine	.90	.35
R668	R24	$1.10	carmine	2.00	2.50
R669	R24	$1.65	carmine	25.00	7.50
R670	R24	$2	carmine	1.00	.45
R671	R24	$2.20	carmine	2.25	3.75
R672	R24	$2.75	carmine	25.00	55.00
R673	R24	$3	carmine	2.00	2.00
R674	R24	$3.30	carmine	3.50	5.00
R675	R24	$4	carmine	2.75	4.00
R676	R24	$5	carmine	3.25	.50
R677	R24	$10	carmine	5.00	1.50
R678	R24	$20	carmine	10.00	6.50

Documentary Stamps & Type of 1940 Ovptd. in Black

1954		**Wmk. 191R**			***Perf. 12***
		Without Gum			
R679	R25	$30	carmine	55.00	17.50
a.	Booklet pane of 4			*225.00*	
R680	R25	$50	carmine	55.00	29.00
a.	Booklet pane of 4			*225.00*	
R681	R25	$60	carmine	55.00	30.00
a.	Booklet pane of 4			*225.00*	
R682	R25	$100	carmine	55.00	7.50
a.	Booklet pane of 4			*225.00*	
R683	R25	$500	carmine	*150.00*	87.50
a.	Booklet pane of 4			*600.00*	
R684	R25	$1000	carmine	300.00	90.00
a.	Booklet pane of 4			*1,200.*	
R685	R25	$2500	carmine	*350.00*	350.00
a.	Booklet pane of 4			*1,400.*	
R686	R25	$5000	carmine	*1,750.*	1,250.
a.	Booklet pane of 4			*7,000.*	
R687	R25	$10,000	carmine	*1,750.*	*2,250.*
a.	Booklet pane of 4			*7,000.*	

Documentary Stamps and Type of 1940 Overprinted in Black

Series 1955

1955		**Wmk. 191R**			***Perf. 12***
		Without Gum			
R688	R25	$30	carmine	90.00	17.50
R689	R25	$50	carmine	100.00	30.00
R690	R25	$60	carmine	160.00	45.00
R691	R25	$100	carmine	125.00	20.00
R692	R25	$500	carmine	750.00	200.00
R693	R25	$1000	carmine	*275.00*	80.00
R694	R25	$2500	carmine	*500.00*	275.00
R695	R25	$5000	carmine	*2,500.*	*2,000.*
R696	R25	$10,000	carmine	—	1,250.

Documentary Stamps and Type of 1940 Overprinted in Black "Series 1956"

1956		**Wmk. 191R**			***Perf. 12***
		Without Gum			
R697	R25	$30	carmine	140.00	20.00
R698	R25	$50	carmine	200.00	27.50
R699	R25	$60	carmine	190.00	60.00
R700	R25	$100	carmine	110.00	15.00
R701	R25	$500	carmine	*650.00*	150.00
R702	R25	$1000	carmine	600.00	100.00
R703	R25	$2500	carmine	—	800.00
R704	R25	$5000	carmine	—	2,250.
R705	R25	$10,000	carmine	—	800.00

Documentary Stamps and Type of 1940 Overprinted in Black "Series 1957"

1957 Wmk. 191R ***Perf. 12***

Without Gum

R706 R25 $30 carmine 225.00 60.00
R707 R25 $50 carmine 125.00 47.50
R708 R25 $60 carmine *1,000.* 350.00
R709 R25 $100 carmine 110.00 20.00
R710 R25 $500 carmine 450.00 200.00
R711 R25 $1000 carmine *300.00* 100.00
R712 R25 $2500 carmine — 1,200.
R713 R25 $5000 carmine *4,000.* 1,800.
R714 R25 $10,000 carmine — 600.00

Documentary Stamps and Type of 1940 Overprinted in Black "Series 1958"

1958 Wmk. 191R ***Perf. 12***

Without Gum

R715 R25 $30 carmine 110.00 27.50
R716 R25 $50 carmine 150.00 35.00
R717 R25 $60 carmine 160.00 42.50
R718 R25 $100 carmine 80.00 15.00
R719 R25 $500 carmine 350.00 125.00
R720 R25 $1000 carmine *425.00* 90.00
R721 R25 $2500 carmine — 1,500.
R722 R25 $5000 carmine — *4,250.*
R723 R25 $10,000 carmine — 2,250.

Documentary Stamps and Type of 1940 Without Overprint

1958 Wmk. 191R ***Perf. 12***

With Gum

R724 R25 $30 carmine 11.00 7.00
a. Booklet pane of 4 *57.50*
b. Vert. pair, imperf. horiz. *2,250.*
R725 R25 $50 carmine 12.00 7.00
a. Booklet pane of 4 *60.00*
b. Vert. pair, imperf. horiz. *3,500.*
R726 R25 $60 carmine 17.50 21.00
a. Booklet pane of 4 *90.00*
R727 R25 $100 carmine 13.00 4.75
a. Booklet pane of 4 *65.00*
R728 R25 $500 carmine 17.50 26.00
a. Booklet pane of 4 *90.00*
R729 R25 $1000 carmine 16.00 21.00
a. Booklet pane of 4 *80.00*
b. Vert. pair, imperf. horiz. *1,750.*
R730 R25 $2500 carmine *175.00* 175.00
a. Booklet pane of 4 *800.00*
R731 R25 $5000 carmine 275.00 175.00
a. Booklet pane of 4 *1,200.*
R732 R25 $10,000 carmine *275.00* 140.00
a. Booklet pane of 4 *1,200.*

Internal Revenue Building, Washington, DC — R26

Centenary of the Internal Revenue Service.

Giori Press Printing

1962, July 2 Unwmk. ***Perf. 11***

R733 R26 10c violet blue & bright green 1.00 .40
Never hinged 1.25

1963

"Established 1862" Removed

R734 R26 10c violet blue & bright green 3.00 .70
Never hinged 5.00

Documentary revenue stamps were no longer required after Dec. 31, 1967.

PROPRIETARY STAMPS

Stamps for use on proprietary articles were included in the first general issue of 1862-71. They are Nos. R3, R13-R14, R18, R22, R29, R31, R38.

Washington — RB1

RB1a

Various Frame Designs

1871-74 Engr. ***Perf. 12***

RB1 RB1 1c grn & blk
a. Violet paper ('71) 8.00
b. Green paper ('74) 14.00
c. As "a," Imperf. 80.00
d. As "a." Inverted center *5,250.*
RB2 RB1 2c grn & blk
a. Violet paper ('71) 8.75
b. Green paper ('74) 30.00
c. As "a," Invtd. center *45,000.*
d. As "b," Invtd. center *8,000.*
e. As "b," vert. half used as 1c on document —

Only two examples recorded of the inverted center on violet paper, No. RB2e. Value is for example with very good to fine centering and very small faults.

RB2d is valued with fine centering and small faults.

RB3 RB1a 3c grn & blk
a. Violet paper ('71) 32.50
b. Green paper ('74) 67.50
c. As "a," sewing machine perf. 650.00
d. As "a," inverted center *14,000.*

No. RB3d is valued with small faults as 7 of the 8 recorded examples have faults.

RB4 RB1a 4c grn & blk
a. Violet paper ('71) 16.00
b. Green paper ('74) 25.00
c. As "a." inverted center *15,000.*
d. As "b," vert. half used as 2c on document —

No. RB4c is valued with small faults as 6 of the 7 recorded examples have faults.

RB5 RB1a 5c grn & blk
a. Violet paper ('71) 175.00
b. Green paper ('74) 250.00
c. As "a," inverted center *130,000.*

No. RB5c is unique. Value represents price realized in 2000 auction sale.

RB6 RB1a 6c grn & blk
a. Violet paper ('71) 57.50
b. Green paper ('74) 140.00
RB7 RB1a 10c grn & blk ('73)
a. Violet paper ('71) 300.00
b. Green paper ('74) 65.00

RB1b

RB8 RB1b 50c grn & blk ('73)
a. Violet paper ('71) 1,000.
b. Green paper ('74) 850.00
RB9 RB1b $1 grn & blk ('73)
a. Violet paper ('71) *3,500.*
b. Green paper ('74) *12,500.*

RB1c

RB10 RB1c $5 grn & blk ('73)
a. Violet paper ('71) *11,000.*
b. Green paper ('74) *85,000.*

No. RB10b is valued with small faults.

Washington — RB2

RB2a

Various Frame Designs
Green Paper

1875-81 ***Perf.***

Unmwkd. (Silk Paper), Wmk. 191R

RB11 RB2 1c green
a. Silk paper 2.25
b. Wmk 191R .50
c. Rouletted 6 160.00
d. As No. RB11b, vert. pair, imperf btwn. *300.00*
RB12 RB2 2c brown
a. Silk paper 3.25
b. Wmk 191R 2.00
c. Rouletted 6 175.00
RB13 RB2a 3c orange
a. Silk paper 14.00
b. Wmk 191R 4.00
c. Rouletted 6 140.00
d. As No. RB13c, horiz. pair, imperf. between —
e. As No. RB13c, vert. pair, imperf. between *1,900.*
RB14 RB2a 4c red brown
a. Silk paper 10.00
b. Wmk 191R 9.00
c. Rouletted 6 *21,000.*
RB15 RB2a 4c red
b. Wmk 191R 6.00
c. Rouletted 6 400.00
RB16 RB2a 5c black
a. Silk paper 175.00
b. Wmk 191R 125.00
c. Rouletted 6 *1,850.*
RB17 RB2a 6c violet blue
a. Silk paper 35.00
b. Wmk 191R 25.00
c. Rouletted 6 *900.00*
RB18 RB2a 6c violet
b. Wmk 191R 35.00
c. Rouletted 6 *1,500.*
RB19 RB2a 10c blue ('81)
b. Wmk 191R 400.00

Many fraudulent roulettes exist.

Battleship — RB3

Inscribed "Series of 1898." and "Proprietary."

See note on rouletting preceding No. R161.

Rouletted 5½

1898 Wmk. 191R Engr.

RB20 RB3 ⅛c yellow green .25 .25
a. Vert. pair, imperf. horiz. —
b. Vert. pair, imperf. btwn. *800.00*
RB21 RB3 ¼c brown .25 .25
a. ¼c red brown .25 .25
b. ¼c yellow brown .25 .25
c. ¼c orange brown .25 .25
d. ¼c bister .25 .25
e. Vert. pair, imperf. horiz. — —
f. Printed on both sides —
RB22 RB3 ⅜c deep orange .30 .30
a. Horiz. pair, imperf. vert. 12.50
b. Vert. pair, imperf. horiz. —
RB23 RB3 ⅝c deep ultra .25 .25
a. Vert. pair, imperf. horiz. 85.00 —
b. Horiz. pair, imperf. btwn. *350.00* *200.00*
RB24 RB3 1c dark green 2.25 .50
a. Vert. pair, imperf. horiz. *325.00*
RB25 RB3 1¼c violet .35 .25
a. 1¼c brown violet .25 .25
b. Vert. pair, imperf. btwn. —
RB26 RB3 1⅞c dull blue 15.00 2.00
RB27 RB3 2c violet brown 1.40 .35
a. Horiz. pair, imperf. vert. 60.00
RB28 RB3 2½c lake 5.00 .35
a. Vert. pair, imperf. horiz. 225.00
RB29 RB3 3¾c olive gray 42.50 15.00
RB30 RB3 4c purple 16.00 1.50
RB31 RB3 5c brown orange 15.00 1.50
a. Vert. pair, imperf. horiz. — *400.00*
b. Horiz. pair, imperf. vert. — *425.00*
Nos. RB20-RB31 (12) 98.55 22.50

Hyphen Hole Perf. 7

RB20p ⅛c .30 .25
RB21p ¼c .25 .25
b. ¼c yellow brown .25 .25
c. ¼c orange brown .25 .25
d. ¼c bister .25 .25
RB22p ⅜c .50 .35
RB23p ⅝c .30 .25
RB24p 1c 30.00 15.00
RB25p 1¼c .30 .30
a. 1¼c brown violet .25 .25
RB26p 1⅞c 35.00 9.00
RB27p 2c 7.25 1.00
RB28p 2½c 6.00 .40
RB29p 3¾c 90.00 27.50
RB30p 4c 62.50 22.50
RB31p 5c 75.00 25.00

See note before No. R161.

RB4

Inscribed "Series of 1914"

Offset Printing

1914 Wmk. 190 ***Perf. 10***

RB32 RB4 ⅛c black .25 .35
RB33 RB4 ¼c black 4.00 1.50
RB34 RB4 ⅜c black .35 .35
RB35 RB4 ⅝c black 7.75 3.00
RB36 RB4 1¼c black 5.00 1.75
RB37 RB4 1⅞c black 67.50 22.50
RB38 RB4 2½c black 16.00 3.50
RB39 RB4 3⅛c black 200.00 67.50
RB40 RB4 3¾c black 65.00 27.50
RB41 RB4 4c black 90.00 45.00
RB42 RB4 4⅜c black *3,000.* —
RB43 RB4 5c black 175.00 110.00
Nos. RB32-RB41,RB43 (11) 630.85 282.95

Wmk. 191R

RB44 RB4 ⅛c black .35 .30
RB45 RB4 ¼c black .25 .25
RB46 RB4 ⅜c black .75 .45
RB47 RB4 ½c black 4.25 3.75
RB48 RB4 ⅝c black .30 .25
RB49 RB4 1c black 5.50 5.50
RB50 RB4 1¼c black .65 .40
RB51 RB4 1½c black 4.25 3.00
RB52 RB4 1⅞c black 1.35 .90
RB53 RB4 2c black 7.50 6.00
RB54 RB4 2½c black 2.00 1.40
RB55 RB4 3c black 6.00 4.00
RB56 RB4 3⅛c black 8.00 5.00
RB57 RB4 3¾c black 17.50 11.00
RB58 RB4 4c black .50 .30
RB59 RB4 4⅜c black 20.00 11.00
RB60 RB4 5c black 4.50 3.75
RB61 RB4 6c black 80.00 52.50
RB62 RB4 8c black 25.00 16.00
RB63 RB4 10c black 18.00 11.00
RB64 RB4 20c black 35.00 24.00
Nos. RB44-RB64 (21) 241.65 160.75

RB5

1919 Offset Printing *Perf. 11*

RB65 RB5 1c dark blue .25 .25
RB66 RB5 2c dark blue .35 .25
RB67 RB5 3c dark blue 1.50 .75
RB68 RB5 4c dark blue 2.25 .75
RB69 RB5 5c dark blue 3.00 1.25
RB70 RB5 8c dark blue 22.50 16.00
RB71 RB5 10c dark blue 11.00 4.25
RB72 RB5 20c dark blue 17.50 6.00
RB73 RB5 40c dark blue 65.00 20.00
Nos. RB65-RB73 (9) 123.35 49.50

FUTURE DELIVERY STAMPS

Issued to facilitate the collection of a tax upon each sale, agreement of sale or agreement to sell any products or merchandise at any exchange or board of trade, or other similar place for future delivery.

Documentary Stamps of 1917 Overprinted in Black or Red

Documentary Stamps Nos. R228-R250 Overprinted in Black or Red

Offset Printing

1918-34 Wmk. 191R *Perf. 11*

Overprint Horizontal (Lines 8mm apart)

Left Value — Unused
Right Value — Used

RC1 R22 2c carmine rose 8.75 .25
RC2 R22 3c carmine rose ('34) 47.50 37.50
Cut cancel 20.00
RC3 R22 4c carmine rose 15.00 .25
b. Double impression of stamp 10.00
RC3A R22 5c carmine rose ('33) 90.00 7.50
RC4 R22 10c carmine rose 24.00 .35
a. Double overprint — 5.25
b. "FUTURE" omitted — *325.00*
c. "DELIVERY FUTURE" 37.50
RC5 R22 20c carmine rose 35.00 .25
a. Double overprint 21.00
RC6 R22 25c carmine rose 75.00 .60
Cut cancel .30
RC7 R22 40c carmine rose 85.00 1.25
Cut cancel .35
RC8 R22 50c carmine rose 22.50 .35
a. "DELIVERY" omitted — *110.00*
RC9 R22 80c carmine rose 175.00 15.00
Cut cancel 4.00
a. Double overprint 37.50

Engr.

Overprint Vertical, Reading Up (Lines 2mm apart)

RC10 R21 $1 green (R) 65.00 .35
Cut cancel .25
a. Overprint reading down *300.00*
b. Black overprint —
Cut cancel 125.00
RC11 R21 $2 rose 75.00 .45
Cut cancel .25
RC12 R21 $3 violet (R) 225.00 3.50
Cut cancel .30
a. Overprint reading down — 52.50
RC13 R21 $5 dark blue (R) 125.00 .60
Cut cancel .25
RC14 R21 $10 orange 150.00 1.35
Cut cancel .30
a. "DELIVERY FUTURE" *110.00*
RC15 R21 $20 olive bister 400.00 9.00
Cut cancel .80

Overprint Horizontal (Lines 11⅔mm apart)

Perf. 12

Without Gum

RC16 R17 $30 vermilion, green numerals 125.00 5.50
Cut cancel 1.75
a. Numerals in blue 110.00 4.75
Cut cancel 2.00
b. Imperf., blue numerals *110.00*
RC17 R19 $50 olive green *(Cleveland)* 100.00 3.00
Cut cancel .90
a. $50 olive bister 100.00 2.75
Cut cancel .25
RC18 R19 $60 brown 140.00 9.00
Cut cancel 1.20
a. Vert. pair, imperf. horiz. *550.00*
RC19 R17 $100 yellow green ('34) 225.00 37.50
Cut cancel 9.00
RC20 R18 $500 blue, red numerals (R) 275.00 25.00
Cut cancel 9.00
a. Numerals in orange — 60.00
Cut cancel 12.50
RC21 R19 $1000 orange 200.00 7.50
Cut cancel 2.00
a. Vert. pair, imperf. horiz. *1,350.*

See note after No. R227.

1923-24 Offset Printing *Perf. 11*

Overprint Horizontal (Lines 2mm apart)

RC22 R22 1c carmine rose 1.25 .25
RC23 R22 80c carmine rose 175.00 3.50
Cut cancel .70

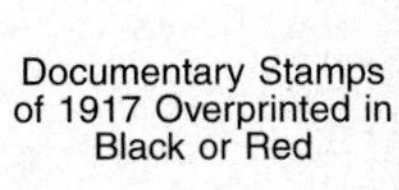

Documentary Stamps of 1917 Overprinted in Black or Red

1925-34 Engr.

RC25 R21 $1 green (R) 85.00 2.00
Cut cancel .45
RC26 R21 $10 orange (Bk) ('34) 225.00 29.00
Cut cancel 18.00

Overprint Type I

1928-29 Offset Printing *Perf. 10*

RC27 R22 10c carmine rose *5,000.*
RC28 R22 20c carmine rose *5,000.*

Some specialists have questioned the status of No. RC28, believing known examples to be either fraudulently reperforated examples of No. RC5, or examples of No. R256 with fake overprints applied. The editors would like to see authenticated evidence of the existence of No. RC28.

STOCK TRANSFER STAMPS

Issued to facilitate the collection of a tax on all sales or agreements to sell, or memoranda of sales or delivery of, or transfers of legal title to shares or certificates of stock.

Documentary Stamps Nos. R228-R259 Overprinted in Black or Red

Offset Printing

1918-22 Wmk. 191R *Perf. 11*

Overprint Horizontal (Lines 8mm apart)

RD1 R22 1c carmine rose 1.00 .25
a. Double overprint — —
RD2 R22 2c carmine rose .25 .25
a. Double overprint — 15.00
Double overprint, cut cancel 7.50
RD3 R22 4c carmine rose .25 .25
a. Double overprint — 4.25
Double overprint, cut cancel 2.10
b. "STOCK" omitted 10.50
d. Ovpt. lines 10mm apart —
RD4 R22 5c carmine rose .30 .25
RD5 R22 10c carmine rose .30 .25
a. Double overprint — 5.25
Double overprint, cut cancel 2.75
b. "STOCK" omitted —
RD6 R22 20c carmine rose .55 .25
a. Double overprint 6.25
b. "STOCK" double —
RD7 R22 25c carmine rose 2.25 .30
Cut cancel .25
RD8 R22 40c carmine rose ('22) 2.25 .25
RD9 R22 50c carmine rose .80 .25
a. Double overprint —
RD10 R22 80c carmine rose 9.00 .45
Cut cancel .25

Engr.

Overprint Vertical, Reading Up (Lines 2mm apart)

RD11 R21 $1 green (R) 190.00 35.00
Cut cancel 9.50
a. Overprint reading down 225.00 35.00
Overprint reading down, cut cancel 10.00
RD12 R21 $1 green (Bk) 3.00 .30
a. Pair, one without overprint — *160.00*
b. Overprinted on back instead of face, inverted — *110.00*
c. Overprint reading down — 7.50
d. $1 yellow green 3.00 .25
RD13 R21 $2 rose 3.00 .25
a. Overprint reading down 11.50
Overprint reading down, cut cancel 1.50
b. Vert. pair, imperf. horiz. *500.00*
RD14 R21 $3 violet (R) 27.50 6.00
Cut cancel .30
RD15 R21 $4 yellow brown 12.00 .30
Cut cancel .25
RD16 R21 $5 dark blue (R) 8.00 .30
Cut cancel .25
a. Overprint reading down 42.50 1.35
Overprint reading down, cut cancel .25
RD17 R21 $10 orange 30.00 .45
Cut cancel .25
RD18 R21 $20 olive bister ('21) 130.00 18.00
Cut cancel 4.50
a. Overprint reading down —

Overprint Horizontal (Lines 11½mm apart)

1918 Without Gum *Perf. 12*

RD19 R17 $30 ver, grn numerals 42.50 6.50
Cut cancel 2.25
a. Numerals in blue 175.00 75.00
RD20 R19 $50 ol grn, *Cleveland* 140.00 62.50
Cut cancel 26.00
RD21 R19 $60 brown 275.00 25.00
Cut cancel 10.50
RD22 R17 $100 green 45.00 7.50
Cut cancel 3.00
RD23 R18 $500 blue (R) 425.00 150.00
Cut cancel 75.00
a. Numerals in orange 150.00
RD24 R19 $1,000 orange 275.00 95.00
Cut cancel 32.50

See note after No. R227.

1928 Offset Printing *Perf. 10*

Overprint Horizontal (Lines 8mm apart)

RD25 R22 2c carmine rose 5.50 .30
RD26 R22 4c carmine rose 5.50 .30
RD27 R22 10c carmine rose 5.50 .30
a. Inverted overprint *1,400.*
b. Ovpt. lines 9½mm apart —
RD28 R22 20c carmine rose 6.50 .35
RD29 R22 50c carmine rose 10.00 .50

Engr.

Overprint Vertical, Reading Up (Lines 2mm apart)

RD30 R21 $1 green 50.00 .35
a. $1 yellow green 50.00 .50
RD31 R21 $2 carmine rose 45.00 .35
a. Pair, one without overprint *225.00* *190.00*
RD32 R21 $10 orange 45.00 .50

Overprinted Horiz. in Black

1920 Offset Printing *Perf. 11*

RD33 R22 2c carmine rose 12.50 1.00
RD34 R22 10c carmine rose 3.00 .35
b. Inverted overprint *1,500.* *1,250.*
RD35 R22 20c carmine rose 5.75 .25
a. Horiz. pair, one without overprint 175.00
d. Inverted overprint (perf. initials) —
RD36 R22 50c carmine rose 5.00 .30

Engr.

RD37 R21 $1 green 70.00 13.50
RD38 R21 $2 rose 80.00 13.50

Offset Printing

Perf. 10

RD39 R22 2c carmine rose 13.00 1.10
RD40 R22 10c carmine rose 5.25 .55
RD41 R22 20c carmine rose 6.00 .25

Used values for Nos. RD42-RD372 are for stamps which are neither cut nor perforated with initials. Stamps with cut cancellations or perforated initials are valued in the Scott U.S. Specialized Catalogue.

Documentary Stamps of 1917-33 Overprinted in Black

1940 *Perf. 11*

RD42 R22 1c rose pink 4.50 .65
a. "Series 1940" inverted *600.00* *450.00*

No. RD42a always comes with a natural straight edge at left.

RD43 R22 2c rose pink 4.75 .65
RD45 R22 4c rose pink 5.50 .35
RD46 R22 5c rose pink 6.00 .25
RD48 R22 10c rose pink 11.00 .35
RD49 R22 20c rose pink 12.50 .35
RD50 R22 25c rose pink 12.50 1.10
RD51 R22 40c rose pink 9.25 1.00
RD52 R22 50c rose pink 10.50 .35
RD53 R22 80c rose pink 250.00 100.00

Engr.

RD54 R21 $1 green 42.50 .60
RD55 R21 $2 rose 47.50 1.00
RD56 R21 $3 violet 300.00 18.00
RD57 R21 $4 yellow brown 110.00 1.60
RD58 R21 $5 dark blue 85.00 2.00
RD59 R21 $10 orange 250.00 10.00
RD60 R21 $20 olive bister 500.00 150.00

Nos. RD19-RD24 Handstamped in Blue "Series 1940"

1940 *Perf. 12*

Without Gum

RD61 R17 $30 vermilion *1,250.* 1,250.
RD62 R19 $50 olive green *2,250.* *2,250.*
a. Double ovpt., perf. initial *1,000.*
RD63 R19 $60 brown *3,000.* *3,000.*
RD64 R17 $100 green *2,000.* 900.
RD65 R18 $500 blue 3,250.
RD66 R19 $1,000 orange

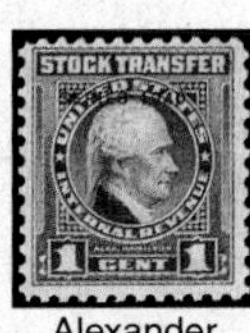

Alexander Hamilton
ST1

Levi Woodbury
ST2

Overprinted in Black **SERIES 1940**

Same Portraits as Nos. R288-R310.

1940 Engr. *Perf. 11*

RD67 ST1 1c bright green 14.00 3.25
a. Imperf, pair, without gum *250.00*
RD68 ST1 2c bright green 9.00 1.75
RD70 ST1 4c bright green 16.00 4.50
RD71 ST1 5c bright green 10.00 1.75
a. Imperf, pair, without gum *250.00*
b. Without overprint, cut cancel *400.00*
RD73 ST1 10c bright green 14.00 2.10
RD74 ST1 20c bright green 16.00 2.40
RD75 ST1 25c bright green 55.00 10.50
RD76 ST1 40c bright green 110.00 45.00
RD77 ST1 50c bright green 14.00 2.10
RD78 ST1 80c bright green 160.00 65.00
RD79 ST2 $1 bright green 60.00 4.25
a. Without overprint, perf. initial *400.00*
RD80 ST2 $2 bright green 65.00 12.00
RD81 ST2 $3 bright green 90.00 15.00

No.	Type	Value	Color	Unused	Used
RD82	ST2	$4	bright green	500.00	275.00
RD83	ST2	$5	bright green	90.00	16.00
RD84	ST2	$10	bright green	225.00	60.00
RD85	ST2	$20	bright green	1,250.	125.00

Nos. RD67-RD85 exist imperforate, without overprint. Value, set of pairs, $1,100.

Thomas Corwin — ST3

Overprinted "SERIES 1940"

Various frames and portraits as Nos. R306-R310.

Perf. 12
Without Gum

No.	Type	Value	Color	Unused	Used
RD86	ST3	$30	bright green	*1,750.*	175.00
RD87	ST3	$50	bright green	800.00	500.00
RD88	ST3	$60	bright green	*3,000.*	1,750.
RD89	ST3	$100	bright green	*600.00*	375.00
RD90	ST3	$500	bright green	—	*2,750.*
RD91	ST3	$1,000	bright green	—	*3,750.*

Nos. RD86-RD91 exist as unfinished imperforates with complete receipt tabs, without overprints or serial numbers. Known in singles, pairs (Nos. RD86-RD88 and Nos. RD90-RD91, value $300 per pair; No. RD89, value $150 per pair), panes of four with plate number, uncut sheets of four panes (with two plate numbers), cross gutter blocks of eight, and blocks of four with vertical gutter between and plate number.

Nos. RD67-RD91 Overprinted Instead: **SERIES 1941**

1941 ***Perf. 11***

No.	Type	Value	Color	Unused	Used
RD92	ST1	1c	bright green	.80	.55
RD93	ST1	2c	bright green	.60	.30
RD95	ST1	4c	bright green	.65	.25
RD96	ST1	5c	bright green	.60	.25
RD98	ST1	10c	bright green	1.10	.25
RD99	ST1	20c	bright green	2.40	.30
RD100	ST1	25c	bright green	2.40	.45
RD101	ST1	40c	bright green	3.75	.75
RD102	ST1	50c	bright green	5.00	.35
RD103	ST1	80c	bright green	30.00	10.00
RD104	ST2	$1	bright green	21.00	.25
RD105	ST2	$2	bright green	22.50	.30
RD106	ST2	$3	bright green	32.50	1.50
RD107	ST2	$4	bright green	57.50	8.50
RD108	ST2	$5	bright green	57.50	.65
RD109	ST2	$10	bright green	125.00	5.50
RD110	ST2	$20	bright green	350.00	90.00

Perf. 12
Without Gum

No.	Type	Value	Color	Unused	Used
RD111	ST3	$30	bright green	1,250.	325.00
RD112	ST3	$50	bright green	1,000.	650.00
RD113	ST3	$60	bright green	*1,350.*	350.00
RD114	ST3	$100	bright green	300.00	190.00
RD115	ST3	$500	bright green	2,750.	*2,250.*
RD116	ST3	$1,000	bright green	—	*2,250.*

Nos. RD67-RD91 overprinted instead: **SERIES 1942**

1942 ***Perf. 11***

No.	Type	Value	Color	Unused	Used
RD117	ST1	1c	bright green	.75	.30
RD118	ST1	2c	bright green	.65	.35
RD119	ST1	4c	bright green	3.50	1.10
RD120	ST1	5c	bright green	.70	.25
a.			Overprint inverted		*750.00*
RD121	ST1	10c	bright green	2.25	.25
RD122	ST1	20c	bright green	2.75	.25
RD123	ST1	25c	bright green	2.50	.25
RD124	ST1	40c	bright green	5.75	.40
RD125	ST1	50c	bright green	6.50	.25
RD126	ST1	80c	bright green	27.50	6.00
RD127	ST2	$1	bright green	24.00	.40
RD128	ST2	$2	bright green	37.50	.40
RD129	ST2	$3	bright green	42.50	1.10
RD130	ST2	$4	bright green	57.50	24.00
RD131	ST2	$5	bright green	50.00	.40
a.			Double overprint, perf. initial		*1,250.*
RD132	ST2	$10	bright green	110.00	9.50
RD133	ST2	$20	bright green	250.00	55.00

Perf. 12
Without Gum

No.	Type	Value	Color	Unused	Used
RD134	ST3	$30	bright green	425.00	100.00
RD135	ST3	$50	bright green	425.00	175.00
RD136	ST3	$60	bright green	500.00	240.00
RD137	ST3	$100	bright green	*625.00*	100.00
RD138	ST3	$500	bright green	—	*15,000.*
RD139	ST3	$1,000	bright green	—	700.00

Nos. RD67-RD91 overprinted instead **SERIES 1943**

1943 ***Perf. 11***

No.	Type	Value	Color	Unused	Used
RD140	ST1	1c	bright green	.55	.30
RD141	ST1	2c	bright green	.60	.40
RD142	ST1	4c	bright green	2.10	.25
RD143	ST1	5c	bright green	.60	.25
RD144	ST1	10c	bright green	1.50	.25
RD145	ST1	20c	bright green	2.25	.25
RD146	ST1	25c	bright green	6.75	.35
RD147	ST1	40c	bright green	6.25	.30
RD148	ST1	50c	bright green	5.75	.30
RD149	ST1	80c	bright green	30.00	7.50
RD150	ST2	$1	bright green	22.50	.25
RD151	ST2	$2	bright green	25.00	.50
RD152	ST2	$3	bright green	30.00	2.50
RD153	ST2	$4	bright green	75.00	27.50
RD154	ST2	$5	bright green	80.00	.60
RD155	ST2	$10	bright green	125.00	7.50
RD156	ST2	$20	bright green	325.00	75.00

Perf. 12
Without Gum

No.	Type	Value	Color	Unused	Used
RD157	ST3	$30	bright green	500.00	300.00
RD158	ST3	$50	bright green	2,250.	210.00
RD159	ST3	$60	bright green	—	1,900.
RD160	ST3	$100	bright green	225.00	80.00
RD161	ST3	$500	bright green	—	2,250.
RD162	ST3	$1,000	bright green	1,000.	650.00

Stock Transfer Stamps and Type of 1940 Overprinted in Black

Series 1944

1944 ***Perf. 11***

No.	Type	Value	Color	Unused	Used
RD163	ST1	1c	bright green	.90	.75
RD164	ST1	2c	bright green	.70	.25
RD165	ST1	4c	bright green	.70	.35
RD166	ST1	5c	bright green	.65	.25
RD167	ST1	10c	bright green	1.00	.30
RD168	ST1	20c	bright green	2.25	.25
RD169	ST1	25c	bright green	3.25	.90
RD170	ST1	40c	bright green	15.00	8.00
RD171	ST1	50c	bright green	5.50	.30
RD172	ST1	80c	bright green	14.50	6.25
RD173	ST2	$1	bright green	14.50	.50
RD174	ST2	$2	bright green	50.00	.75
RD175	ST2	$3	bright green	47.50	2.00
RD176	ST2	$4	bright green	80.00	15.00
RD177	ST2	$5	bright green	55.00	3.50
RD178	ST2	$10	bright green	125.00	7.25
RD179	ST2	$20	bright green	275.00	20.00

Perf. 12
Without Gum

Designs: $2,500, William Windom. $5,000, C. J. Folger. $10,000, W. Q. Gresham.

No.	Type	Value	Color	Unused	Used
RD180	ST3	$30	bright green	350.00	110.00
RD181	ST3	$50	bright green	275.00	125.00
RD182	ST3	$60	bright green	*1,500.*	325.00
RD183	ST3	$100	bright green	375.00	100.00
RD184	ST3	$500	bright green	*2,250.*	*1,750.*
RD185	ST3	$1,000	bright green	*2,750.*	1,900.
RD185A	ST3	$2,500	bright green		—
RD185B	ST3	$5,000	bright green		*75,000.*
RD185C	ST3	$10,000	bright green, cut cancel		*27,500.*

Stock Transfer Stamps and Type of 1940 Overprinted in Black

Series 1945

1945 ***Perf. 11***

No.	Type	Value	Color	Unused	Used
RD186	ST1	1c	bright green	.45	.25
RD187	ST1	2c	bright green	.45	.35
RD188	ST1	4c	bright green	.50	.35
RD189	ST1	5c	bright green	.45	.25
RD190	ST1	10c	bright green	1.25	.35
RD191	ST1	20c	bright green	2.25	.45
RD192	ST1	25c	bright green	3.50	.40
RD193	ST1	40c	bright green	5.00	.25
RD194	ST1	50c	bright green	10.00	.45
RD195	ST1	80c	bright green	15.00	4.75
RD196	ST2	$1	bright green	17.50	.30
RD197	ST2	$2	bright green	32.50	.90
RD198	ST2	$3	bright green	55.00	1.75
RD199	ST2	$4	bright green	55.00	4.25
RD200	ST2	$5	bright green	35.00	1.00
RD201	ST2	$10	bright green	85.00	12.00
RD202	ST2	$20	bright green	210.00	20.00

Perf. 12
Without Gum

No.	Type	Value	Color	Unused	Used
RD203	ST3	$30	bright green	225.00	90.00
RD204	ST3	$50	bright green	125.00	60.00
RD205	ST3	$60	bright green	1,200.	325.00
RD206	ST3	$100	bright green	150.00	65.00
RD207	ST3	$500	bright green	—	1,400.
RD208	ST3	$1,000	bright green	*3,250.*	1,400.
RD208A	ST3	$2,500	bright green, perf. initial		*20,000.*
RD208B	ST3	$5,000	bright green		*22,250.*
RD208C	ST3	$10,000	bright green, cut cancel		*22,500.*

Stock Transfer Stamps and Type of 1940 Overprinted in Black

Series 1946

1946 ***Perf. 11***

No.	Type	Value	Color	Unused	Used
RD209	ST1	1c	bright green	.50	.35
a.			Pair, one dated "1945"	*550.00*	
RD210	ST1	2c	bright green	.50	.25
RD211	ST1	4c	bright green	.50	.25
RD212	ST1	5c	bright green	.55	.25
RD213	ST1	10c	bright green	1.25	.25
RD214	ST1	20c	bright green	2.50	.30
RD215	ST1	25c	bright green	3.00	.40
RD216	ST1	40c	bright green	6.50	1.25
RD217	ST1	50c	bright green	6.75	.25
RD218	ST1	80c	bright green	20.00	9.50
RD219	ST2	$1	bright green	14.50	.90
RD220	ST2	$2	bright green	16.00	1.00
RD221	ST2	$3	bright green	30.00	2.25
RD222	ST2	$4	bright green	30.00	9.00
RD223	ST2	$5	bright green	50.00	2.25
RD224	ST2	$10	bright green	87.50	4.25
RD225	ST2	$20	bright green	325.00	62.50

Perf. 12
Without Gum

No.	Type	Value	Color	Unused	Used
RD226	ST3	$30	bright green	250.00	62.50
RD227	ST3	$50	bright green	190.00	75.00
RD228	ST3	$60	bright green	375.00	225.00
RD229	ST3	$100	bright green	225.00	90.00
RD230	ST3	$500	bright green	*700.00*	300.00
RD231	ST3	$1,000	bright green	425.00	250.00
RD232	ST3	$2,500	bright green		*27,500.*
RD233	ST3	$5,000	bright green, cut cancel		*20,000.*
RD234	ST3	$10,000	bright green, cut cancel		*16,500.*

Stock Transfer Stamps and Type of 1940 Overprinted in Black

Series 1947

1947 ***Perf. 11***

No.	Type	Value	Color	Unused	Used
RD235	ST1	1c	bright green	2.75	.90
RD236	ST1	2c	bright green	2.75	.90
RD237	ST1	4c	bright green	2.00	.70
RD238	ST1	5c	bright green	2.00	.60
RD239	ST1	10c	bright green	2.00	.90
RD240	ST1	20c	bright green	3.75	.90
RD241	ST1	25c	bright green	5.00	.90
RD242	ST1	40c	bright green	4.50	1.40
RD243	ST1	50c	bright green	5.00	.35
RD244	ST1	80c	bright green	27.50	14.00
RD245	ST2	$1	bright green	20.00	1.00
RD246	ST2	$2	bright green	32.50	1.25
RD247	ST2	$3	bright green	45.00	2.50
RD248	ST2	$4	bright green	62.50	9.50
RD249	ST2	$5	bright green	45.00	3.25
RD250	ST2	$10	bright green	200.00	11.00
RD251	ST2	$20	bright green	160.00	42.50

Perf. 12
Without Gum

No.	Type	Value	Color	Unused	Used
RD252	ST3	$30	bright green	600.00	75.00
RD253	ST3	$50	bright green	500.00	225.00

RD254 ST3 $60 bright green 1,150. 225.00
RD255 ST3 $100 bright green 175.00 62.50
RD256 ST3 $500 bright green 850.00 650.00
RD257 ST3 $1,000 bright green 650.00 175.00
RD258 ST3 $2,500 bright green —
RD259 ST3 $5,000 bright green 700.00
RD260 ST3 $10,000 bright green —
a. Vert. pair, imperf. horiz., cut cancel —

Stock Transfer Stamps and Type of 1940 Overprinted in Black

Series 1948

1948		*Perf. 11*	
RD261 ST1	1c bright green	.45	.35
RD262 ST1	2c bright green	.45	.35
RD263 ST1	4c bright green	.80	.45
RD264 ST1	5c bright green	.45	.25
RD265 ST1	10c bright green	.55	.35
RD266 ST1	20c bright green	1.60	.40
RD267 ST1	25c bright green	1.90	.55
RD268 ST1	40c bright green	3.50	1.00
RD269 ST1	50c bright green	5.75	.45
RD270 ST1	80c bright green	27.50	9.50
RD271 ST2	$1 bright green	14.00	.50
RD272 ST2	$2 bright green	27.50	1.00
RD273 ST2	$3 bright green	55.00	10.00
RD274 ST2	$4 bright green	60.00	20.00
RD275 ST2	$5 bright green	70.00	5.00
RD276 ST2	$10 bright green	80.00	7.25
RD277 ST2	$20 bright green	160.00	25.00

Perf. 12

Without Gum

RD278 ST3 $30 bright green 225.00 90.00
RD279 ST3 $50 bright green 175.00 85.00
RD280 ST3 $60 bright green 350.00 225.00
RD281 ST3 $100 bright green 140.00 30.00
RD282 ST3 $500 bright green 600.00 325.00
RD283 ST3 $1,000 bright green 425.00 250.00
RD284 ST3 $2,500 bright green 850.00 500.00
RD285 ST3 $5,000 bright green 650.00 425.00
RD286 ST3 $10,000 bright green —

Stock Transfer Stamps and Type of 1940 Overprinted in Black

Series 1949

1949		*Perf. 11*	
RD287 ST1	1c bright green	2.25	.70
RD288 ST1	2c bright green	2.25	.75
RD289 ST1	4c bright green	2.50	.75
RD290 ST1	5c bright green	3.00	.75
RD291 ST1	10c bright green	6.00	1.00
RD292 ST1	20c bright green	10.00	1.00
RD293 ST1	25c bright green	11.00	1.25
RD294 ST1	40c bright green	25.00	3.25
RD295 ST1	50c bright green	30.00	.45
RD296 ST1	80c bright green	37.50	10.00
RD297 ST2	$1 bright green	27.50	1.00
RD298 ST2	$2 bright green	50.00	1.75
RD299 ST2	$3 bright green	85.00	10.00
RD300 ST2	$4 bright green	90.00	20.00
RD301 ST2	$5 bright green	72.50	3.00
RD302 ST2	$10 bright green	125.00	12.50
RD303 ST2	$20 bright green	250.00	22.50

Perf. 12

Without Gum

RD304 ST3 $30 bright green 325.00 125.00
RD305 ST3 $50 bright green 375.00 250.00
RD306 ST3 $60 bright green 550.00 400.00
RD307 ST3 $100 bright green 225.00 80.00
RD308 ST3 $500 bright green *900.00* 375.00
RD309 ST3 $1,000 bright green *450.00* 125.00
RD310 ST3 $2,500 bright green —
RD311 ST3 $5,000 bright green —
RD312 ST3 $10,000 bright green — 475.00
a. Pair, one without ovpt., cut cancel *8,000.*

No. RD312a is unique.

Stock Transfer Stamps and Type of 1940 Overprinted in Black

Series 1950

1950		*Perf. 11*	
RD313 ST1	1c bright green	.80	.40
RD314 ST1	2c bright green	.70	.35
RD315 ST1	4c bright green	.65	.40
RD316 ST1	5c bright green	.75	.25
RD317 ST1	10c bright green	3.25	.30
RD318 ST1	20c bright green	5.00	.80
RD319 ST1	25c bright green	8.00	1.00
RD320 ST1	40c bright green	12.00	1.50
RD321 ST1	50c bright green	15.00	.50
RD322 ST1	80c bright green	22.50	7.25
RD323 ST2	$1 bright green	22.50	.55
RD324 ST2	$2 bright green	35.00	1.25
RD325 ST2	$3 bright green	60.00	8.50
RD326 ST2	$4 bright green	75.00	20.00
RD327 ST2	$5 bright green	60.00	3.25
RD328 ST2	$10 bright green	190.00	12.50
RD329 ST2	$20 bright green	225.00	50.00

Perf. 12

Without Gum

RD330 ST3 $30 bright green 275.00 175.00
a. Booklet pane of 4 *3,300.*
RD331 ST3 $50 bright green 350.00 200.00
a. Booklet pane of 4 *3,300.*
RD332 ST3 $60 bright green 325.00 200.00
a. Booklet pane of 4 *4,750.*
RD333 ST3 $100 bright green 125.00 55.00
a. Vert. pair, imperf. btwn. 2,000. *1,750.*
RD334 ST3 $500 bright green 650.00 300.00
RD335 ST3 $1,000 bright green 225.00 85.00
RD336 ST3 $2,500 bright green — *2,000.*
a. Booklet pane of 4 *10,000.*
RD337 ST3 $5,000 bright green — 1,100.
a. Booklet pane of 4 *10,000.*
RD338 ST3 $10,000 bright green — 1,500.
a. Booklet pane of 4 *10,000.*

Stock Transfer Stamps and Type of 1940 Overprinted in Black

Series 1951

1951		*Perf. 11*	
RD339 ST1	1c bright green	3.00	.75
RD340 ST1	2c bright green	2.50	.50
RD341 ST1	4c bright green	3.00	.75
RD342 ST1	5c bright green	2.25	.55
RD343 ST1	10c bright green	3.00	.35
RD344 ST1	20c bright green	7.50	1.25
RD345 ST1	25c bright green	10.00	1.50
RD346 ST1	40c bright green	45.00	12.50
RD347 ST1	50c bright green	17.00	1.50
RD348 ST1	80c bright green	35.00	14.00
RD349 ST2	$1 bright green	32.50	1.25
RD350 ST2	$2 bright green	45.00	1.75
RD351 ST2	$3 bright green	60.00	14.00
RD352 ST2	$4 bright green	300.00	25.00
RD353 ST2	$5 bright green	75.00	4.00
RD354 ST2	$10 bright green	150.00	11.00
RD355 ST2	$20 bright green	250.00	30.00

Perf. 12

Without Gum

RD356 ST3 $30 bright green 325.00 150.00
RD357 ST3 $50 bright green 325.00 125.00
RD358 ST3 $60 bright green — *1,600.*
RD359 ST3 $100 bright green 210.00 100.00
RD360 ST3 $500 bright green 750.00 450.00
RD361 ST3 $1,000 bright green 225.00 140.00
RD362 ST3 $2,500 bright green — *5,000.*
RD363 ST3 $5,000 bright green — *2,000.*
RD364 ST3 $10,000 bright green *2,000.* 250.00

Stock Transfer Stamps and Type of 1940 Overprinted in Black

Series 1952

1952 *Perf. 11*
RD365 ST1 1c bright green 42.50 27.50
RD366 ST1 10c bright green 45.00 27.50
RD367 ST1 20c bright green 450.00 —
RD368 ST1 25c bright green 600.00 —
RD369 ST1 40c bright green 140.00 55.00
RD370 ST2 $4 bright green *1,750.* 800.00
RD371 ST2 $10 bright green *4,250.* —
RD372 ST2 $20 bright green *7,000.* —

Stock Transfer Stamps were discontinued in 1952.

HUNTING PERMIT STAMPS

Catalogue values for all unused stamps in this section are for stamps with never-hinged original gum. Minor natural gum skips and bends are normal on Nos. RW1-RW20. No-gum stamps are without signature or other cancel.

Department of Agriculture
Various Designs Inscribed
"U. S. Department of Agriculture"

Mallards Alighting — HP1

Engraved: Flat Plate Printing

1934 **Unwmk.** *Perf. 11*

Inscribed "Void after June 30, 1935"
RW1 HP1 $1 blue 750. 150.
Hinged 375.
No gum 175.
a. Imperf., vertical pair —
b. Vert. pair, imperf. horiz. —

Used value is for stamp with handstamp or manuscript cancel.

It is almost certain that No. RW1a is No. RW1b with vertical perfs trimmed off. No horizontal pairs of No. RW1a are known. All recorded pairs are vertical, with narrow side margins. Both varieties probably are printer's waste since examples exist with gum on front or without gum.

1935
Inscribed "Void after June 30, 1936"
RW2 HP2 $1 rose lake 725. 160.00
Hinged 360.
No gum 200.

1936
Inscribed "Void after June 30, 1937"
RW3 HP3 $1 brown black 350. 90.00
Hinged 175.
No gum 100.

1937
Inscribed "Void after June 30, 1938"
RW4 HP4 $1 light green 325. 70.00
Hinged 150.
No gum 90.

1938
Inscribed "Void after June 30, 1939"
RW5 HP5 $1 light violet 425. 75.00
Hinged 200.
No gum 90.

Department of the Interior
Various Designs Inscribed
"U. S. Department of the Interior"

Green-Winged Teal — HP6

1939
Inscribed "Void after June 30, 1940"
RW6 HP6 $1 chocolate 250. 45.00
Hinged 110.
No gum 50.

1940
Inscribed "Void after June 30, 1941"
RW7 HP7 $1 sepia 225. 45.00
Hinged 110.
No gum 50.

1941
Inscribed "Void after June 30, 1942"
RW8 HP8 $1 brown carmine 225. 45.00
Hinged 110.
No gum 50.

1942
Inscribed "Void after June 30, 1943"
RW9 HP9 $1 violet brown 225. 45.00
Hinged 110.
No gum 50.

1943
Inscribed "Void After June 30, 1944"
RW10 HP10 $1 deep rose 120.00 35.00
Hinged 65.00
No gum 40.00

1944
Inscribed "Void after June 30, 1945"
RW11 HP11 $1 red orange 130.00 50.00
Hinged 60.00
No gum 40.00

1945
Inscribed "Void after June 30, 1946"
RW12 HP12 $1 black 95.00 25.00
Hinged 45.00
No gum 30.00

1946
Inscribed "Void after June 30, 1947"
RW13 HP13 $1 red brown 50.00 15.00
No gum 18.00
a. $1 bright rose pink *35,000.*

1947
Inscribed "Void after June 30, 1948"
RW14 HP14 $1 black 55.00 15.00
No gum 18.00

1948
Inscribed "Void after June 30, 1949"
RW15 HP15 $1 bright blue 55.00 15.00
No gum 18.00

Goldeneye Ducks — HP16

1949
Inscribed "Void after June 30, 1950"
RW16 HP16 $2 bright green 70.00 15.00
No gum 22.50

1950
Inscribed "Void after June 30, 1951"
RW17 HP17 $2 violet 90.00 15.00
No gum 22.50

1951
Inscribed "Void After June 30, 1952"
RW18 HP18 $2 gray black 90.00 15.00
No gum 22.50

1952
Inscribed "Void after June 30, 1953"
RW19 HP19 $2 dp ultra 90.00 15.00
No gum 22.50

1953
Inscribed "Void after June 30, 1954"
RW20 HP20 $2 dp rose brn 90.00 15.00
No gum 22.50

No. RW21 and following issues are printed on dry, pregummed paper and the back inscription is printed on top of the gum, except for the self-adhesive stamp issues starting in 1998.

1954
Inscribed "Void after June 30, 1955"

RW21 HP21 $2 black 85.00 12.00
No gum 20.00

1955
Inscribed "Void after June 30, 1956"

RW22 HP22 $2 dark blue 85.00 12.00
No gum 20.00
a. Back inscription inverted *5,500.* *4,500.*

1956
Inscribed "Void after June 30, 1957"

RW23 HP23 $2 black 85.00 12.00
No gum 20.00

1957
Inscribed "Void after June 30, 1958"

RW24 HP24 $2 emerald 85.00 12.00
No gum 20.00
a. Back inscription inverted *5,000.*

1958
Inscribed "Void after June 30, 1959"

RW25 HP25 $2 black 85.00 12.00
No gum 20.00
a. Back inscription inverted —

Labrador Retriever Carrying Mallard Drake — HP26

Giori Press Printing

1959
Inscribed "Void after June 30, 1960"

RW26 HP26 $3 multi 120.00 15.00
No gum 40.00
a. Back inscription inverted *27,500.* —

Redhead Ducks — HP27

1960
Inscribed "Void after June 30, 1961"

RW27 HP27 $3 multi 90.00 12.00
No gum 35.00

1961
Inscribed "Void after June 30, 1962"

RW28 HP28 $3 multicolored 95.00 12.00
No gum 45.00

Pintail Drakes — HP29

1962
Inscribed "Void after June 30, 1963"

RW29 HP29 $3 multicolored 100.00 12.00
No gum 45.00
a. Back inscription omitted —

1963
Inscribed "Void after June 30, 1964"

RW30 HP30 $3 multicolored 100.00 12.00
No gum 45.00

1964
Inscribed "Void after June 30, 1965"

RW31 HP31 $3 multicolored 100.00 12.00
No gum 45.00

1965
Inscribed "Void after June 30, 1966"

RW32 HP32 $3 multicolored 100.00 12.00
No gum 50.00

Whistling Swans — HP33

1966
Inscribed "Void after June 30, 1967"

RW33 HP33 $3 multi 100.00 12.00
No gum 50.00

1967
Inscribed "Void after June 30, 1968"

RW34 HP34 $3 multicolored 110.00 12.00
No gum 55.00

1968
Inscribed "Void after June 30, 1969"

RW35 HP35 $3 multicolored 65.00 11.00
No gum 25.00
a. Back inscription omitted —

White-winged Scoters — HP36

1969
Inscribed "Void after June 30, 1970"

RW36 HP36 $3 multi 65.00 8.00
No gum 25.00

1970 **Engraved & Lithographed**
Inscribed "Void after June 30, 1971"

RW37 HP37 $3 multi 65.00 8.00
No gum 25.00

1971
Inscribed "Void after June 30, 1972"

RW38 HP38 $3 multi 40.00 8.00
No gum 20.00

1972
Inscribed "Void after June 30, 1973"

RW39 HP39 $5 multi 27.50 7.00
No gum 10.00

1973
Inscribed "Void after June 30, 1974"

RW40 HP40 $5 multi 20.00 7.00
No gum 10.00

1974
Inscribed "Void after June 30, 1975"

RW41 HP41 $5 multi 20.00 6.00
No gum 9.00
a. Back inscription missing, but printed vertically on face of stamp and selvage, from foldover *4,750.*

1975
Inscribed "Void after June 30, 1976"

RW42 HP42 $5 multi 16.00 6.00
No gum 9.00

1976 **Engr.**
Inscribed "Void after June 30, 1977"

RW43 HP43 $5 grn & blk 16.00 6.00
No gum 9.00

1977 **Litho. & Engr.**
Inscribed "Void after June 30, 1978"

RW44 HP44 $5 multi 16.00 6.00
No gum 9.00

Hooded Merganser — HP45

1978
Inscribed "Void after June 30, 1979"

RW45 HP45 $5 multicolored 16.00 6.00
No gum 8.00

1979
Inscribed "Void after June 30, 1980"

RW46 HP46 $7.50 multi 16.00 7.00
No gum 9.00

1980
Inscribed "Void after June 30, 1981"

RW47 HP47 $7.50 multi 16.00 7.00
No gum 9.00

1981
Inscribed "Void after June 30, 1982"

RW48 HP48 $7.50 multi 18.00 7.00
No gum 9.00

1982
Inscribed "Void after June 30, 1983"

RW49 HP49 $7.50 multi 16.00 7.00
No gum 9.00
a. Orange and violet omitted *10,000.*

A certificate from a recognized expertization committee is required for No. RW49a.

1983
Inscribed "Void after June 30, 1984"

RW50 HP50 $7.50 multi 16.00 7.00
No gum 9.00

1984
Inscribed "Void after June 30, 1985"

RW51 HP51 $7.50 multi 16.00 7.00
No gum 9.00

See Special Printings section that follows.

1985
Inscribed "Void after June 30, 1986"

RW52 HP52 $7.50 multi 16.00 8.00
No gum 9.00
a. Light blue (litho.) omitted *20,000.*

The omitted color on No. RW52a coincides with a double paper splice affecting the top row of five stamps from the sheet and top ⅓ of stamps in the second row. There is also a color changeling of the brownish red ducks and their reflections in the water to yellow and yellow orange, respectively, on the error stamps. This error currently exists as three vertical strips of 6 (top stamp the error) and a plate number block of 12 (2x6, top two stamps the error).

1986
Inscribed "Void after June 30, 1987"

RW53 HP53 $7.50 multi 16.00 7.00
No gum 9.00
a. Black omitted *2,000.*

1987 ***Perf. 11½x11***
Inscribed "Void after June 30, 1988"

RW54 HP54 $10 multi 16.00 10.00
No gum 9.00

1988
Inscribed "Void after June 30, 1989"

RW55 HP55 $10 multicolored 16.00 10.00
No gum 10.00

1989
Inscribed "Void after June 30, 1990"

RW56 HP56 $12.50 multi 20.00 10.00
No gum 11.00

1990
Inscribed "Void after June 30, 1991"

RW57 HP57 $12.50 multi 20.00 10.00
No gum 12.00
a. Back inscription omitted *300.00*
b. Black inscription printed on the stamp paper rather than the gum —
No gum —

The back inscription is normally on top of the gum so beware of examples with gum removed offered as No. RW57a. Full original gum must be intact on No. RW57a. Used examples of No. RW57a cannot exist.

All known examples of No. RW57b are used or have no gum. Expertization is recommended.

King Eiders — HP58

1991
Inscribed "Void after June 30, 1992"

RW58 HP58 $15 multi 27.50 12.00
No gum 15.00
a. Black (engr.) omitted *20,000.*

1992
Inscribed "Void after June 30, 1993"

RW59 HP59 $15 multi 27.50 12.00
No gum 15.00

1993
Inscribed "Void after June 30, 1994"

RW60 HP60 $15 multi 27.50 12.00
No gum 15.00
a. Black (engr.) omitted *2,250.*

1994 ***Perf. 11¼x11***
Inscribed "Void after June 30, 1995"

RW61 HP61 $15 multi 27.50 12.00
No gum 15.00

1995
Inscribed "Void after June 30, 1996"

RW62 HP62 $15 multi 32.50 12.00
No gum 15.00

1996
Inscribed "Void after June 30, 1997"

RW63 HP63 $15 multi 32.50 12.00
No gum 12.50

1997

Inscribed "Void after June 30, 1998"

RW64 HP64 $15 multi 27.50 12.00
No gum 15.00

1998 ***Perf. 11¼***

Inscribed "Void after June 30, 1999"

RW65 HP65 $15 multi 45.00 22.50
No gum 22.50

Self-Adhesive

Die Cut Perf. 10

RW65A HP65 $15 *Barrow's Goldeneye* 35.00 15.00
No gum 15.00

Nos. RW65 and later issues were sold in panes of 30 (RW65 and RW66) or 20 (RW67 and later issues), with four plate numbers per pane. The self-adhesives starting with No. RW65A were sold in panes of 1. The self-adhesives are valued unused as complete panes and used as single stamps.

1999 ***Perf. 11¼***

Inscribed "Void after June 30, 2000"

RW66 HP66 $15 multi 42.50 20.00
No gum 25.00

Self-Adhesive

Die Cut Perf. 10

RW66A HP66 $15 multi 25.00 12.00
No gum 15.00

2000 ***Perf. 11¼***

Inscribed "Void after June 30, 2001"

RW67 HP67 $15 multi 30.00 15.00
No gum 17.50

Self-Adhesive

Die Cut Perf. 10

RW67A HP67 $15 multi 25.00 14.00
No gum 17.50

2001 ***Perf. 11¼***

Inscribed "Void after June 30, 2002"

RW68 HP68 $15 multi 30.00 16.00
No gum 17.50

Self-Adhesive

Die Cut Perf. 10

RW68A HP68 $15 multi 25.00 10.00
No gum 15.00

Printed by Banknote Corporation of America.

2002 ***Perf. 11¼***

Inscribed "Void after June 30, 2003"

RW69 HP69 $15 multi 30.00 16.00
No gum 17.50

Self-Adhesive

Serpentine Die Cut 11x10¾

RW69A HP69 $15 multi 25.00 10.00
No gum 15.00

Printed by Ashton-Potter (USA) Ltd.

2003 ***Perf. 11***

Inscribed "Void after June 30, 2004"

RW70 HP70 $15 multi 25.00 16.00
No gum 17.50
b. Imperf, pair *7,000.*
c. Back inscription omitted *4,500.*

Self-Adhesive

Serpentine Die Cut 11x10¾

RW70A HP70 $15 multi 25.00 10.00
No gum 15.00

Printed by Banknote Corporation of America for Sennett Security Products.

2004 ***Perf. 11***

Inscribed "Void after June 30, 2005"

RW71 HP71 $15 multicolored 25.00 11.00
No gum 16.00

Self-Adhesive

Serpentine Die Cut 11x10¾

RW71A HP71 $15 multicolored 25.00 10.00
No gum 15.00

Printed by Banknote Corporation of America for Sennett Security Products.

Two types of RW72: I, No framelines at top, right or bottom (from left two panes of the press sheet); II, Gray framelines at top, right and bottom (from right two panes of the press sheet).

2005 **Litho. & Engr.** ***Perf. 11***

Inscribed "Void after June 30, 2006"

RW72 HP72 $15 multi, type I 22.50 11.00
No gum 16.00
b. Souvenir sheet of 1 1,900.
c. Type II 22.50 11.00
No gum 16.00

There are two types of RW72: type I has no frame lines; type II has gray frame lines at top, right and bottom edges of design. No. RW72c, the type II stamp, is any stamp from the right two panes of the sheet of four panes. No. RW72, the Type I stamp, is any stamp from the left two panes.

Self-Adhesive

Litho. & Debossed

Serpentine Die Cut 11x10¾

RW72A HP72 $15 multi 22.50 11.00
No gum 15.00

No. RW72b sold for $20. 1,000 No. RW72b were issued. Approximately 750 were signed by the artist in black, value $2,000 as shown. Approximately 150 were signed in blue ink, value $2,500. Approximately 100 were signed in gold ink, value $3,000. Most examples of No. RW72b are in the grade of F-VF. Catalogue values are for Very Fine examples.

The Duck Stamp Office never announced the existence of No. RW72b to the public through a press release or a website announcement during the time the sheet was on sale, apparently because it was not clear beforehand that the souvenir sheet could be produced successfully and on time. No. RW72b sold out before a public announcement of the item's existence could be made.

Ross's Goose — HP73

Printed by Banknote Corporation of America for Sennett Security Products

2006 **Litho. & Engr.** ***Perf. 11***

Inscribed "Void after June 30, 2007"

RW73 HP73 $15 multi 22.50 11.00
No gum 15.00
b. Souvenir sheet of 1 175.00 —
c. As "b," without artist's signature (error) *2,500.*

Self-Adhesive

Serpentine Die Cut 11x10¾

RW73A HP73 $15 multi 22.50 11.00
No gum 15.00

No. RW73b sold for $25. All examples of No. RW73b have a black signature of the artist on a designated line in the sheet margin. Ten thousand were issued.

The sheet margin has a line designated for the signature of the engraver, Piotr Naszarkowski, but no sheets were sold with his signature. Naszarkowski signed approximately 2,500 sheets during three days at the Washington 2006 World Philatelic Exhibition, and he signed another 2,500 or more after the conclusion of the exhibition. Value $250.

Ring-necked Ducks — HP74

Designed by Richard C. Clifton. Printed by Banknote Corporation of America for Sennett Security Products.

2007 **Litho.** ***Perf. 11***

Inscribed "Void after June 30, 2008"

RW74 HP74 $15 multi 25.00 11.00
No gum 15.00
b. Souvenir sheet of 1 140.00
c. As "b", without artist's signature (error) *2,750.*

Self-Adhesive

Serpentine Die Cut 11x10¾

RW74A HP74 $15 multi 22.50 11.00
No gum 15.00

No. RW74b sold for $25 plus a shipping fee. The artist signed No. RW74b on a designated line in the sheet margin. Ten thousand were issued. There is no back inscription on No. RW74b.

Northern Pintails — HP75

Designed by Joe Hautman. Printed by Ashton-Potter (USA) Ltd.

2008 **Litho.** ***Perf. 13¼***

Inscribed "Void after June 30, 2009"

RW75 HP75 $15 multi 25.00 11.00
No gum 15.00
b. Souvenir sheet of 1 70.00 —
c. As "b," without artist's signature (error) *500.00*

Self-Adhesive

Serpentine Die Cut 10¾

RW75A HP75 $15 multi 22.50 11.00
No gum 20.00

A sheet commemorating the 75th anniversary of Hunting Permit stamps containing one example of No. RW75 and a label with the vignette of No. RW1 sold for $50. Value, $90.

No. RW75b sold for $30 plus a shipping fee. The artist signed No. RW75b on a designated line in the sheet margin. Ten thousand were prepared. There is no back inscription on No. RW75b.

Designed by Joshua Spies. Printed by Ashton-Potter (USA) Ltd.

2009 **Litho.** ***Perf. 13¼***

Inscribed "Void after June 30, 2010"

RW76 HP76 $15 multi 25.00 11.00
No gum 15.00
b. Souvenir sheet of 1 55.00
c. As "b," without artist's signature (error) *400.00*

No. RW76b sold for $30 plus a shipping fee. The artist signed No. RW76b on a designated line in the sheet margin. Ten thousand were prepared.

Self-Adhesive

Serpentine Die Cut 11x10¾

RW76A HP76 $15 multi 22.50 11.00
No gum 20.00

2010 **Litho.** ***Perf. 11¼x11***

Inscribed "Void after June 30, 2011"

RW77 HP77 $15 multi 25.00 11.00
No gum 15.00
b. Souvenir sheet of 1, perf. 13¼ 55.00
c. As "b," without artist's signature (error) *175.00*

Self-Adhesive

Serpentine Die Cut 11x10¾

RW77A HP77 $15 multi 22.50 11.00
No gum 20.00

No. RW77b was sold for $30 plus a shipping fee. The artist signed No. RW77b on a designated line in the sheet margin. Ten thousand were prepared. There is no back inscription on No. RW77b.

White-fronted Geese — HP78

Designed by James Hautman. Printed by Ashton-Potter (USA) Ltd..

2011 **Litho.** ***Perf. 13¼***

Inscribed "Void after June 30, 2012"

RW78 HP78 $15 multi 25.00 11.00
No gum 15.00
b. Souvenir sheet of 1 50.00
c. As "b," without artist's signature (error) *175.00*

Self-Adhesive

Serpentine Die Cut 11x10¾

RW78A HP78 $15 multi 22.50 11.00
No gum 20.00

No. RW78b was sold for $25 plus a shipping fee. The artist signed No. RW78b on a designated line in the sheet margin. Ten thousand were prepared.

Wood Duck — HP79

Designed by Joseph Hautman. Printed by Ashton-Potter (USA) Ltd.

2012 **Litho.** ***Perf. 13¼***

Inscribed "Void after June 30, 2013"

RW79 HP79 $15 multi 25.00 11.00
No gum 15.00
b. Souvenir sheet of 1 50.00
c. As "b," without artist's signature (error) *1,750.*

Self-Adhesive

Serpentine Die Cut 11x10¾

RW79A HP79 $15 multi 22.50 11.00
No gum 20.00

No. RW79b was sold for $25 plus a shipping fee. The artist signed No. RW79b on a designated line in the sheet margin. One No. RW79b was signed in red ink as a "surprise" for a random buyer. This was not authorized.

Common Goldeneye — HP80

Designed by Robert Steiner. Printed by Ashton-Potter (USA) Ltd.

2013 Litho. *Perf. 13¼*
Inscribed "Void after June 30, 2014"

RW80	HP80 $15 multi	25.00	11.00
	No gum	15.00	
	P# block of 4	100.00	
b.	Souvenir sheet of 1	50.00	

Self-Adhesive
Serpentine Die Cut 11x10¾

RW80A	HP80 $15 multi	22.50	11.00
	No gum	20.00	

No. RW80b was sold for $25 plus a shipping fee. The artist signed No. RW80b on a designated line in the sheet margin.

CONFEDERATE STATES OF AMERICA

3¢ 1861 POSTMASTERS' PROVISIONALS

With the secession of South Carolina from the Union on Dec. 20, 1860, a new era began in U.S. history as well as its postal history. Other Southern states quickly followed South Carolina's lead, which in turn led to the formation of the provisional government of the Confederate States of America on Feb. 4, 1861.

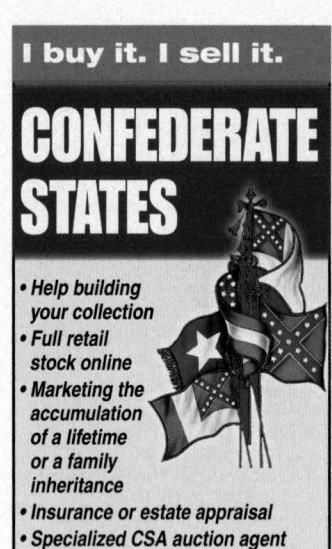

President Jefferson Davis' cabinet was completed Mar. 6, 1861, with the acceptance of the position of Postmaster General by John H. Reagan of Texas. The provisional government had already passed regulations that required payment for postage in cash and that effectively carried over the U.S. 3c rate until the new Confederate Post Office Department took over control of the system.

Soon after entering on his duties, Reagan directed the postmasters in the Confederate States and in the newly seceded states to "continue the performance of their duties as such, and render all accounts and pay all moneys (sic) to the order of the Government of the U.S. as they have heretofore done, until the Government of the Confederate States shall be prepared to assume control of its postal affairs."

As coinage was becoming scarce, postal patrons began having problems buying individual stamps or paying for letters individually, especially as stamp stocks started to run short in certain areas. Even though the U.S. Post Office Department was technically in control of the postal system and southern postmasters were operating under Federal authority, the U.S.P.O. was hesitant in re-supplying seceded states with additional stamps and stamped envelopes.

The U.S. government had made the issuance of postmasters' provisionals illegal many years before, but the southern postmasters had to do what they felt was necessary to allow patrons to pay for postage and make the system work. Therefore, a few postmasters took it upon themselves to issue provisional stamps in the 3c rate then in effect.

Interestingly, these were stamps and envelopes that the U.S. government did not recognize as legal, but they did do postal duty unchallenged in the Confederate States. Yet the proceeds were to be remitted to the U.S. government in Washington! Six authenticated postmasters' provisionals in the 3c rate have been recorded.

On May 13, 1861, Postmaster General Reagan issued his proclamation "assuming control and direction of postal service within the limits of the Confederate States of America on and after the first day of June," with new postage rates and regulations.

The Federal government suspended operations in the Confederate States (except for western Virginia and the seceding state of Tennessee) by a proclamation issued by Postmaster General Montgomery Blair on May 27, 1861, effective from May 31, 1861, and June 10 for western and middle Tennessee.

As Tennessee did not join the Confederacy until July 2, 1861, the unissued 3c Nashville provisional was produced in a state that was in the process of seceding, while the other provisionals were used in the Confederacy before the June 1 assumption of control of postal service by the Confederate States of America.

Illustrations are reduced in size.

XU numbers are envelope entires.

HILLSBORO, N.C.

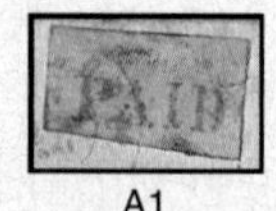

A1

Handstamped Adhesive

1AX1	A1 3c bluish black, on cover	—

No. 1AX1 is unique. This is the same handstamp as used for No. 39X1. 3c usage is determined from the May 27, 1861 circular date stamp.

JACKSON, MISS.

E1

Handstamped Envelope

2AXU1	E1 3c black	*3,500.*

See Nos. 43XU1-43XU4.

MADISON COURT HOUSE, FLA.

A1

"CNETS"

Typeset Adhesive

3AX1	A1 3c gold	—	*20,000.*
a.	"CNETS"		*25,000.*

No. 3AX1a is unique.

See No. 137XU1.

NASHVILLE, TENN.

A1

Typeset Adhesive (5 varieties)

4AX1	A1 3c carmine	350.

No. 4AX1 was prepared by Postmaster McNish with the U.S. rate, but the stamp was never issued.

See Nos. 61X2-61XU2.

SELMA, ALA.

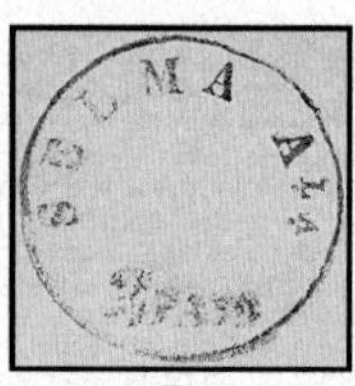

E1

Handstamped Envelope

5AXU1	E1 3c black	*2,500.*

See Nos. 77XU1-77XU3.

TUSCUMBIA, ALA.

E1

Handstamped Envelope, impression at upper right

6AXU1	E1 3c dull red, *buff*	*17,500.*

Dangerous forgeries exist of No. 6AXU1.
See Nos. 84XU1-84XU3.

POSTMASTERS' PROVISIONAL ISSUES

These stamps and envelopes were issued by individual postmasters generally between June 1, 1861, when the use of U.S. stamps stopped in the Confederacy, and Oct. 16, 1861, when the 1st Confederate Government stamps were issued.

They were occasionally issued at later periods, especially in Texas, when regular issues of Government stamps were unavailable.

Canceling stamps of the post offices were often used to produce envelopes, some of which were supplied in advance by private citizens.

These envelopes and other stationery therefore may be found in a wide variety of papers, colors, sizes & shapes, including patriotic and semi-official types.

It is often difficult to determine whether the impression made by the canceling stamp indicates provisional usage or merely postage paid at the time the letter was deposited in the post office. Occasionally the same mark was used for both purposes.

The *press-printed* provisional envelopes are in a different category. They were produced in quantity, using envelopes procured in advance by the postmaster, such as those of Charleston, Lynchburg, Memphis, etc.

The press-printed envelopes are listed and valued on all known papers.

The handstamped provisional envelopes are listed and valued according to type and variety of handstamp, but not according to paper. Many exist on such a variety of papers that they defy accurate, complete listing.

The value of a handstamped provisional envelope is determined *primarily* by the clarity of the markings and its overall condition and attractiveness, rather than type of paper.

All handstamped provisional envelopes, when used, should also show the postmark of the town of issue.

Most handstamps are impressed at top right, although they exist from some towns in other positions.

Illustrations in this section are reduced in size.

XU numbers are envelope entires.

ABERDEEN, MISS.

E1

Handstamped Envelopes

1XU1	E1 5c black	*7,000.*
a.	10c (ms.) on 5c black	*12,500.*

No. 1XU1a is unique.

ABINGDON, VA.

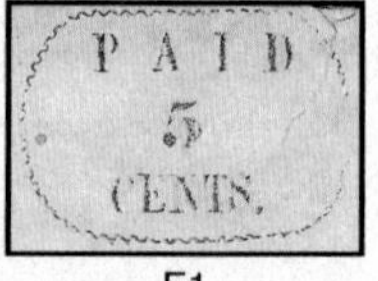

E1

Handstamped Envelopes

2XU1	E1 2c black		*12,500.*
a.	5c (ms.) on 2c black		*15,000.*
2XU2	E1 5c black		1,750.
2XU3	E1 10c black	*2,200.*	3,500.

No. 2XU1 is unique. No. 2XU3 unused and used are each unique.

ALBANY, GA.

E1

E2

E3

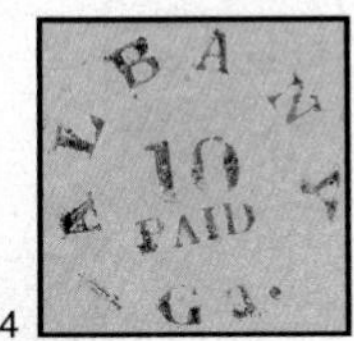
E4

Handstamped Envelopes

3XU1	E1	5c greenish blue	900.
3XU2	E2	10c greenish blue	*1,750.*
a.		10c on 5c greenish blue	*3,500.*
3XU5	E3	5c greenish blue	—
3XU6	E4	10c greenish blue	*3,500.*

Only one example each recorded of Nos. 3XU2, 3XU2a and 3XU6. No. 3XU2 is a cover front only and is valued as such. No. 3XU2a is the unique Confederate example of one provisional marking revaluing another.

The existence of No. 3XU5 is in question. The editors would like to see an authenticated example of this marking.

ANDERSON COURT HOUSE, S.C.

E1

E2

Handstamped Envelopes

4XU1	E1	5c black	1,000.	2,250.
4XU2	E2	10c (ms.) black		*3,000.*
4XU3	E1	(2c) black, denomination omitted (circular rate)		*2,250.*

ATHENS, GA

A1 — Type I

A1 — Type II

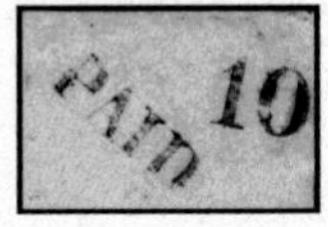
E1

Typographed Adhesives (from woodcuts of two types)

Pairs, both horizontal and vertical, always show one of each type.

5X1	A1	5c purple (shades)	1,000.	1,750.
a.		Tete beche pair (vertical)		*7,500.*
5X2	A1	5c red	5,750.	5,500.

The colorless ornaments in the four corners of No. 5X2 were recut making them wider than those in No. 5X1.

Dangerous fakes exist of Nos. 5X1 and 5X2. Certificates of authenticity from recognized committees are strongly recommended.

Handstamped Envelopes

5XU1	E1	10c black, on patriotic cover	*2,500.*

The markings on No. 5XU1 are the same as those used on stampless envelopes. On the unique listed example of No. 5XU1, there is a handwritten note on the inside of the flap: 'Andrew had these envelopes stamped & I am obliged to use them or loose the postage.' Two or more similar covers from the same correspondence are known, but without the note under the flap. While these also may be provisional use, it cannot be proven, and these covers are considered handstamp paid covers.

ATLANTA, GA.

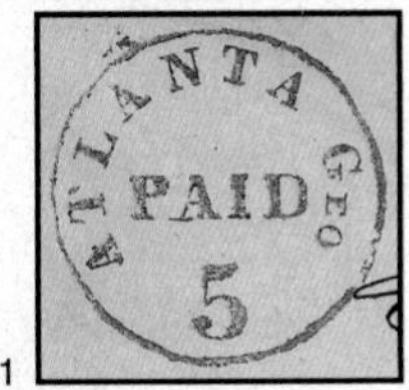
E1

E2

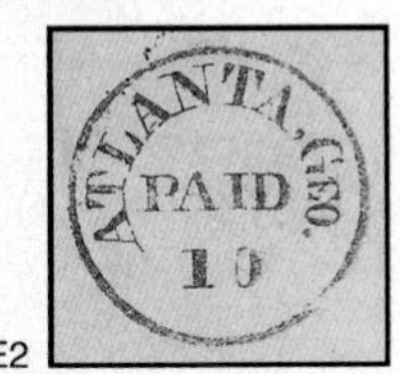
E2

Handstamped Envelopes

6XU1	E1	5c red		*5,000.*
6XU2	E1	5c black	175.	1,000.
a.		10c on 5c black		*2,500.*

No. 6UX3 was probably used for drop letters and circulars.

6XU4	E3	2c black	*3,000.*
6XU5	E3	5c black	1,500.
a.		10c on 5c black	*2,500.*
6XU6	E3	10c black	950.

Only one example recorded of No. 6XU1.

E3

Handstamped Envelopes

6XU8	E3	5c black	3,500.
6XU9	E3	10c black ("10" upright)	3,250.

Only one example recorded of No. 6XU8.

AUSTIN, MISS.

E1

Press-printed Envelope (typeset)

8XU1	E1	5c red, *amber*	*75,000.*

One example recorded.

AUSTIN, TEX.

E1a

Handstamped Adhesive

9X1	E1a	10c black	—

Handstamped Envelope

9XU1	E1a	10c black	1,750.

AUTAUGAVILLE, ALA.

E1

E2

Handstamped Envelopes

10XU1	E1	5c black	*20,000.*
10XU2	E2	5c black	*20,000.*

No. 10XU2 is unique.

BALCONY FALLS, VA.

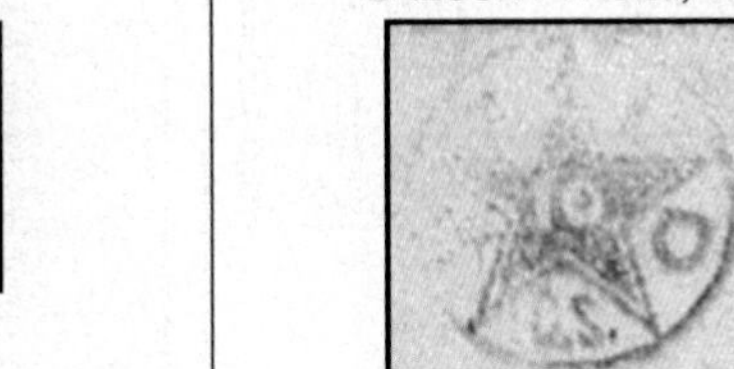
E1

Handstamped Envelope

122XU1	E1	10c blue	*2,000.*

The use of No. 122XU1 as a provisional marking is in question. The editors would like to see authenticated evidence of its use as a provisional.

BARNWELL COURT HOUSE, S. C.

E1

Handstamped Envelope

123XU1	E1	5c black	*3,000.*

These are two separate handstamps.

All recorded uses are on addressed covers without postmarks.

BATON ROUGE, LA.

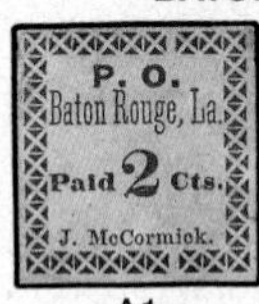

A1

A2

Typeset Adhesives

Ten varieties of each

11X1	A1	2c green	*8,250.*	*5,000.*
a.		"McCcrmick"	*40,000.*	*40,000.*
11X2	A2	5c **green & carmine**	1,500.	1,400.
a.		"McCcrmick"	*10,000.*	*3,500.*

Only one example each is recorded of No. 11X1a unused, used and on cover.

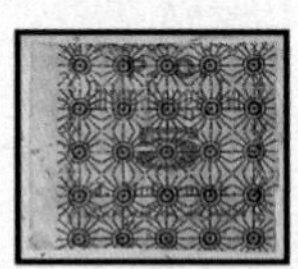

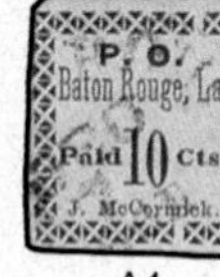

A3 A4

Ten varieties of each

11X3 A3 5c green & carmine *10,000.* *2,750.*
a. "McCcrmick" *6,000.*
11X4 A4 10c blue *50,000.*

BEAUMONT, TEX.

A1 A2

Typeset Adhesives

Several varieties of each

12X1 A1 10c black, *yellow* *12,500.*
12X2 A1 10c black, *pink* *12,500.*

No. 12X1 is smaller than No. 12X2.

12X3 A2 10c black, *yellow,* on cover *90,000.*

One example recorded of No. 12X3.

BLUFFTON, S. C.

E1

Handstamped Envelope

124XU1 E1 5c black *8,000.*

Only one example recorded of No. 124XU1.

BRIDGEVILLE, ALA.

A1

Handstamped Adhesive in black within red pen-ruled squares

13X1 A1 5c black & red, pair on cover *20,000.*

CAMDEN, S. C.

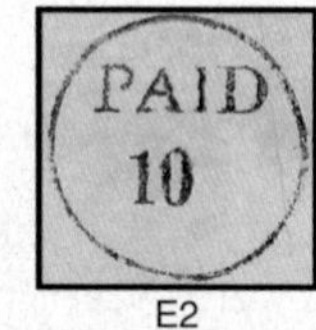

E1 E2

Handstamped Envelopes

125XU1 E1 5c black *2,500.*
125XU2 E2 10c black *750.*

No. 125XU2 unused was privately carried and is addressed but has no postal markings. No. 125XU2 is indistinguishable from a handstamp paid cover when used.

CANTON, MISS.

E1

"P" in star is initial of Postmaster William Priestly.

Handstamped Envelopes

14XU1 E1 5c black 4,000.
a. 10c (ms.) on 5c black 5,000.

CAROLINA CITY, N. C.

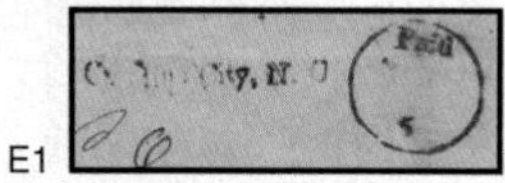

E1

Handstamped Envelope

118XU1 E1 5c black *5,000.*

CARTERSVILLE, GA.

E1

Handstamped Envelope

126XU1 E1 (5c) red *1,500.*

CHAPEL HILL, N. C.

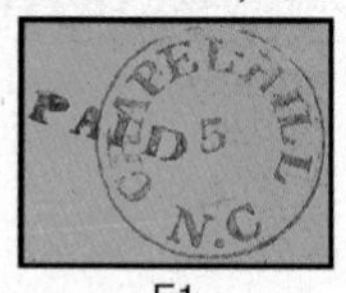

E1

Handstamped Envelope

15XU1 E1 5c black 3,750.

CHARLESTON, S. C.

A1 E1

E2

Lithographed Adhesive

16X1 A1 5c blue 1,200. 850.

Values are for stamps showing parts of the outer frame lines on at least 3 sides.

Press-printed Envelopes (typographed from woodcut)

16XU1 E1 5c blue 1,250. *3,500.*
16XU2 E1 5c blue, *amber* 1,250. *3,500.*
16XU3 E1 5c blue, *orange* 1,250. *3,500.*
16XU4 E1 5c blue, *buff* 1,250. *3,500.*
16XU5 E1 5c blue, *blue* 1,250. *3,500.*
16XU6 E2 10c blue, *orange* *80,000.*

The No. 16XU6 used entire is unique; value based on 1997 auction sale.

Beware of fakes of the E1 design.

Handstamped Cut Square

16XU7 E2 10c black *3,000.*

There is only one example of No. 16XU7. It is a cutout, not an entire. It may not have been mailed from Charleston, and it may not have paid postage.

CHARLOTTE, N. C.

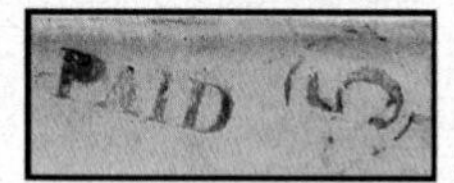

E1

146XU1 E1 5c blue, "5" in circle and straight line "PAID" *3,500.*

CHARLOTTESVILLE, VA.

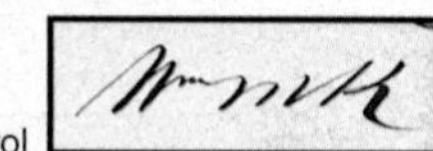

Control

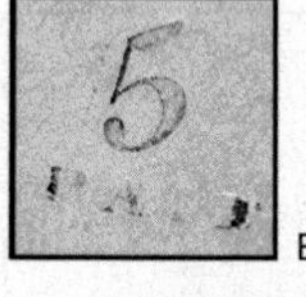

E1

Handstamped Envelopes, Manuscript Initials

127XU1 E1 5c blue —
127XU2 E1 10c blue —

CHATTANOOGA, TENN.

E1

E2

Handstamped Envelopes

17XU2 E1 5c black 2,500.
17XU3 E2 5c on 2c black *5,000.*

No. 17XU3 is unique.

CHRISTIANSBURG, VA.

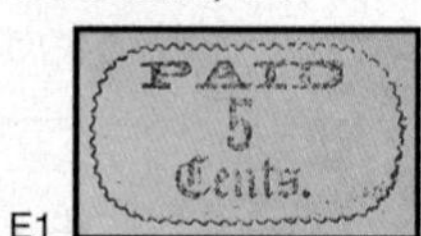

E1

Handstamped Envelopes

Impressed at top right

99XU1 E1 5c black *2,250.*
99XU2 E1 5c blue *2,000.*
99XU4 E1 5c green on U.S. envelope No. U27 *4,500.*
99XU5 E1 10c blue *3,500.*

The absence of 5c and 10c handstamped paid markings from this town suggests that Nos. 99XU1-99XU5 were used as both provisional and handstamped paid markings.

COLAPARCHEE, GA.

E1

Control

Handstamped Envelope

119XU1 E1 5c black *3,500.*

There are only two recorded examples of No. 119XU1, and both are used from Savannah with a general issue stamp.

COLUMBIA, S. C.

E1

E2

Handstamped Envelopes

18XU1 E1 5c blue 550. 900.
a. 10c on 5c blue *3,500.*
18XU2 E1 5c black 600. 1,250.

Three types of "PAID," one in circle

18XU4 E2 5c blue, seal on front *7,500.*
a. Seal on back *1,250.*
18XU5 E2 10c blue, seal on back *6,000.*

Three types of "PAID" for Nos. 18XU4-18XU5, one in circle.

Circular Seal similar to E2, 27mm diameter

18XU6 E2 5c blue (seal on back) *4,000.*

COLUMBIA, TENN.

E1

Handstamped Envelope

113XU1 E1 5c red *7,500.*

One example recorded.

COLUMBUS, GA.

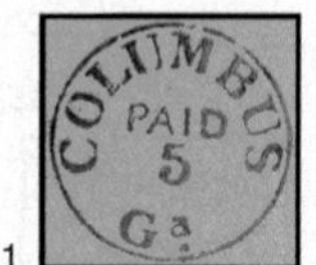

E1

Handstamped Envelopes

19XU1 E1 5c blue *1,200.*
19XU2 E1 10c red *3,250.*

COURTLAND, ALA.

E1

Handstamped Envelopes (from woodcut)

103XU1 E1 5c red *10,000.*

CUTHBERT, GA

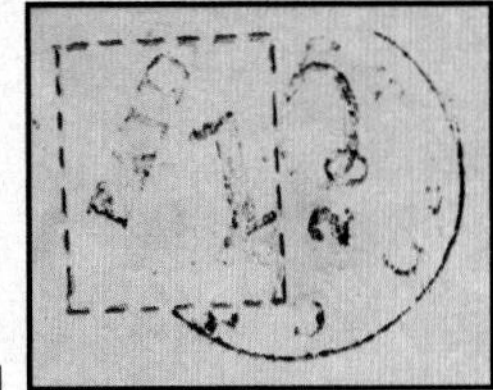
E1

Handstamped Envelope

95XU1 E1 10c black *750.*

The unique example of No. 95XU1 was used by having a C.S.A. 10c #12c placed over it.

DALTON, GA

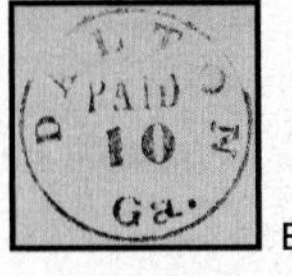
E1

Handstamped Envelopes

20XU1 E1 5c black *750.*
- ***a.*** Denomination omitted (5c rate) *875.*
- ***b.*** 10c (ms.) on 5c black 1,500.
- ***c.*** 20c (ms.) on 5c black —

20XU2 E1 10c black 1,250.

DANVILLE, VA.

A1

Design measures 60x37mm — E1

E2

E3

E4

Typeset Adhesive
Wove Paper

21X1 A1 5c red *6,500.*

Two varieties known.

Laid Paper

21X2 A1 5c red *10,000.*

No. 21X2 is unique.

Press-printed Envelopes (typographed)

Two types: "SOUTHERN" in straight or curved line

Impressed (usually) at top left

21XU1 E1 5c black *9,000.*
21XU2 E1 5c black, *amber* —
21XU3 E1 5c black, *dark buff* *9,000.*

The existence of No. 21XU2 is in question. The editors would like to see authenticated evidence of its existence.

Unissued 10c envelopes (type E1, in red) are known. All recorded examples are envelopes that show evidence of added stamps being torn off.

Dangerous forgeries exist of No. 21XU1.

Handstamped Envelopes

21XU3A E4 5c black (ms "WBP" initials) *1,000.*
21XU4 E2 10c black *2,500.*
21XU6 E3 10c black *2,750.*
21XU7 E4 10c black (ms "WBP" initials) —

Types E2 and E3 both exist on one cover.

DEMOPOLIS, ALA.

E1

Handstamped Envelopes, Signature in ms.

22XU1 E1 5c black ("Jno. Y. Hall") *3,500.*
22XU2 E1 5c black ("J. Y. Hall") *3,500.*
22XU3 E1 5c (ms.) black ("J. Y. Hall") *4,000.*

EATONTON, GA.

E1

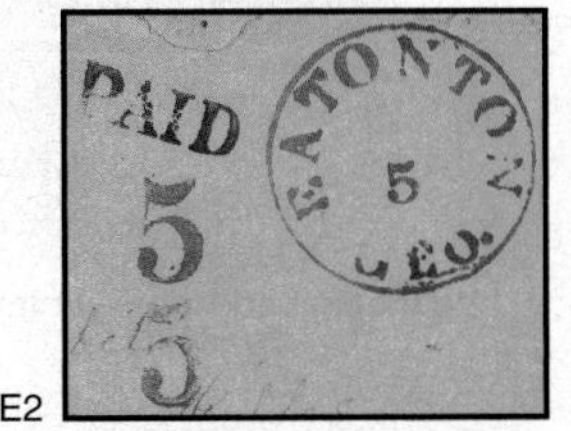
E2

Handstamped Envelopes

23XU1 E1 5c black *3,000.*
23XU2 E2 5c + 5c black *5,000.*

EMORY, VA.

A1

Handstamped Adhesives ("PAID" and "5" in circle on selvage of U.S. 1c 1857 issue)
Perf. 15 on three sides

24X1 A1 5c blue, on cover, tied *27,500.*

Also known with "5" above "PAID."

E1

E2

Handstamped Envelopes

24XU1 E1 5c blue *2,000.*
24XU2 E2 10c blue *10,000.*

Only one example recorded of No. 24XU2.

FINCASTLE, VA.

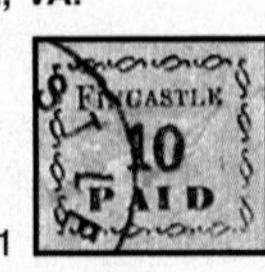
E1

Press-printed Envelope (typeset)

Impressed at top right

104XU1 E1 10c black *20,000.*

One example recorded of No. 104XU1.

FORSYTH, GA.

E1 E2

Handstamped Envelope

120XU1 E1 10c black *2,000.*
120XU2 E2 10c black *1,250.*

Only one example each recorded of Nos. 120XU1 and 120XU2.

FORT VALLEY, GA.

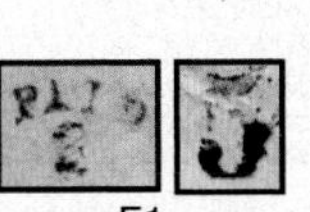
E1

E2

Handstamped Envelope

148XU1 E1 5c on 3c black —

Black circle control on front of envelope. Unique.

FRANKLIN, N. C.

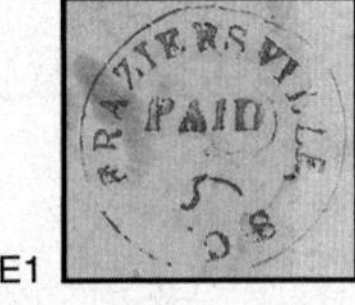
E1

Press-printed Envelope (typeset) (No. 25XU1)
Impressed at top right

25XU1 E1 5c blue, *buff* *30,000.*
25XU2 5c black, large "5" woodcut in 31mm circular town mark *2,500.*

The one known No. 25XU1 envelope shows black circular Franklin postmark with manuscript date.

FRAZIERSVILLE, S. C.

E1

Handstamped Envelope, "5" manuscript

128XU1 E1 5c black *5,000.*

Only one example recorded of No. 128XU1.

FREDERICKSBURG, VA.

A1

Sheets of 20, two panes of 10 varieties each

Typeset Adhesives
Thin bluish paper

26X1 A1 5c blue, *bluish* 900. 1,250.
26X2 A1 10c red (shades), *bluish* 2,250.

GAINESVILLE, ALA.

E1

E2

E2

Handstamped Envelopes

27XU1 E1 5c black *4,500.*
27XU2 E2 5c black *5,000.*
27XU3 E3 10c ("01") black *6,000.*

GALVESTON, TEX.

E1

Handstamped Envelopes

98XU1 E1 5c black 500. *1,500.*
98XU2 E1 10c black *2,000.*

E2

E3

Handstamped Envelopes

98XU3 E2 10c black 550. *2,500.*
98XU4 E2 20c black *3,500.*
98XU5 E3 5c black *4,500.*

GASTON, N. C.

E1

Handstamped Envelope

129XU1 E1 5c black *6,000.*

Only one example recorded of No. 129XU1.

GEORGETOWN, S. C.

E1

Control

E2

Handstamped Envelopes

28XU1 E1 5c black 1,200.
28XU2 E2 5c black, separate "5" and straightline "PAID" handstamps, control on reverse — 2,000.

GOLIAD, TEX.

A1

A2

Typeset Adhesives

29X1 A1 5c black 12,000.
29X2 A1 5c black, *gray* 11,500.
29X3 A1 5c black, *rose* 12,000.
29X4 A1 10c black — 12,000.
29X5 A1 10c black, *rose* 12,000.

Type A1 stamps are signed "Clarke-P.M." vertically in black or red.

29X6 A2 5c black, *gray* 10,000.
a. "GOILAD" 12,000.
29X7 A2 10c black, *buff* 12,000.
a. "GOILAD" 15,000.
29X8 A2 5c black, *dark blue,* on cover 12,000.
29X9 A2 10c black, *dark blue* 20,000.

GONZALES, TEX.

Colman & Law were booksellers when John B. Law (of the firm) was appointed Postmaster. The firm used a small lithographed label on drugs and on the front or inside of books they sold.

A1

Lithographed Adhesives on colored glazed paper

30X1 A1 (5c) gold, *dark blue,* pair on cover, *1861* 15,000.
30X2 A1 (10c) gold, *garnet,* on cover, *1864* 25,000.
30X3 A1 (10c) gold, *black,* on cover, *1865* —

No. 30X1 must bear double-circle town cancel as validating control. The control was applied to the labels in the sheet before their sale as stamps. When used, the stamps bear an additional Gonzales double-circle postmark.

GREENSBORO, ALA.

E1

E2

Handstamped Envelopes

31XU1 E1 5c black 3,000.
31XU2 E1 10c black 2,750.
31XU3 E2 10c black 6,000.

GREENSBORO, N. C.

E1

Handstamped Envelope

32XU1 E1 10c red 1,250.

GREENVILLE, ALA.

A1

A2

Typeset Adhesives
On pinkish surface-colored glazed paper.

33X1 A1 5c blue & red *25,000.*
33X2 A2 10c red & blue —

Two used examples each are known of Nos. 33X1-33X2, and all are on covers. Covers bear a postmark but it was not used to cancel the stamps.

The former No. 33X1a has been identified as a counterfeit.

GREENVILLE, TENN.

E1

144XU1 E1 5c black *5,000.*

Only one example of No. 144XU1 is recorded.

GREENVILLE COURT HOUSE, S. C.

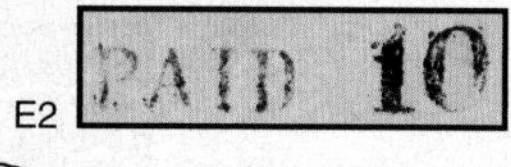

E1

E2

Control

Handstamped Envelopes (Several types)

34XU1 E1 5c black *2,000.*
34XU2 E2 10c black *2,000.*
a. 20c (ms.) on 10c black *3,000.*

Envelopes must bear one of three different postmark controls on the back.

GREENWOOD DEPOT, VA.

A1

"PAID" Handstamped Adhesive ("PAID" with value and signature in ms.)
Laid Paper

35X1 A1 10c black, *gray blue,* on cover 22,500.

GRIFFIN, GA.

E1

Handstamped Envelopes

102XU1 E1 5c black 2,250.
102XU2 E1 10c black *5,000.*

No. 102XU2 is on a large piece of an envelope with July 25 postmark at left. It is unique.

GROVE HILL, ALA.

A1

Handstamped Adhesive (from woodcut)

36X1 A1 5c black —

Two examples are recorded. One is on cover tied by the postmark. The other is canceled by magenta pen on a cover front.

HALLETTSVILLE, TEX.

A1

Handstamped Adhesive
Ruled Letter Paper

37X1 A1 10c black, *gray blue,* on cover *15,000.*

One example known.

HAMBURGH, S. C.

E1

Handstamped Envelope

112XU1 E1 5c black *9,000.*

HARRISBURGH (Harrisburg), TEX.

E1

E2

Handstamped Envelope

130XU1 E1 5c black —
130XU2 E2 10c black —

HELENA, TEX.

A1

Typeset Adhesives
Several varieties

38X1 A1 5c black, *buff* *12,500. 10,000.*
38X2 A1 10c black, *gray* *10,000.*

On 10c "Helena" is in upper and lower case italics.

Used examples are valued with small faults or repairs, as all recorded have faults.

HILLSBORO, N. C.

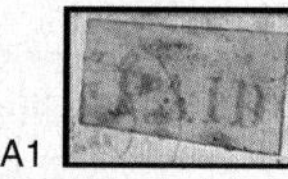

A1

Handstamped Adhesive

39X1 A1 5c black, on cover *15,000.*

See 3c 1861 Postmaster's Provisional No. 1AX1.

Ms./Handstamped Envelope

39XU1 E1 10c "paid 10" in manuscript with undated blue town cancel as control on face —

HOLLANDALE, TEX.

E1

Handstamped Envelope

132XU1 E1 5c black —

HOUSTON, TEX.

E1

Handstamped Envelopes

40XU1 E1 5c red — 750.
a. 10c (ms.) on 5c red *3,000.*
40XU2 E1 10c red — *1,500.*
40XU3 E1 10c black *2,250.*
40XU4 E1 5c +10c red *2,500.*
40XU5 E1 10c +10c red *2,500.*

Nos. 40XU2-40XU5 show "TEX" instead of "TXS."

HUNTSVILLE, TEX.

PAID
5

E1 Control

Handstamped Envelope

92XU1 E1 5c black *5,000.*

No. 92XU1 exists with "5" outside or within control circle.

INDEPENDENCE, TEX.

A1

A2

Handstamped Adhesives

41X1 A1 10c black, *buff,* on cover, uncanceled, cut to shape *20,000.*

41X2 A1 10c black, *dull rose,* on cover —

With small "10" and "Pd" in manuscript

41X3 A2 10c black, *buff,* on cover, uncanceled, cut to shape *32,500.*

No. 41X1 is unique.

All known examples of Nos. 41X1-41X3 are uncanceled on covers with black "INDEPENDANCE TEX." (sic) postmark.

The existence of No. 41X2 has been questioned by specialists. The editors would like to see authenticated evidence of the existence of this item.

ISABELLA, GA.

E1

Handstamped Envelope, Manuscript "5"

133XU1 E1 5c black *5,000.*

Only one example recorded of No. 133XU1.

IUKA, MISS.

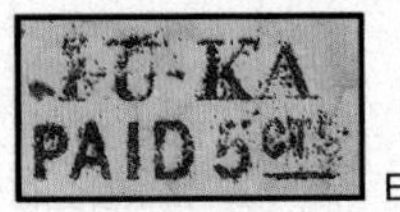

E1

Handstamped Envelope

42XU1 E1 5c black *1,750.*

JACKSON, MISS.

E1

Handstamped Envelopes

Two types of numeral

43XU1 E1 5c black 750.
a. 10c on 5c black *2,750.*
43XU2 E1 10c black *2,000.*
a. 5c on 10c black *3,750.*
43XU4 E1 10c on 5c blue *2,750.*

The 5c also exists on a lettersheet.

See 3c 1861 Postmaster's Provisional No. 2AXU1.

JACKSONVILLE, ALA.

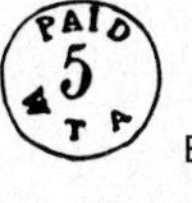

E1

Handstamped Envelope

110XU1 E1 5c black — *3,000.*

JACKSONVILLE, FLA.

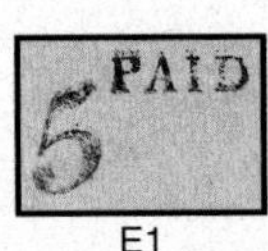

E1 Control

Handstamped Envelope

134XU1 E1 5c black —

Undated double circle postmark control on reverse.

JETERSVILLE, VA.

A1 

Handstamped Adhesive ("5" with ms. "AHA." initials) Laid Paper

44X1 A1 5c black, vertical pair on cover, uncanceled *16,000.*

JONESBORO, TENN.

E1

Handstamped Envelopes

45XU1 E1 5c black *7,000.*
45XU2 E1 5c dark blue *7,000.*

KINGSTON, GA.

E1

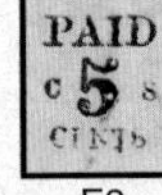

E2

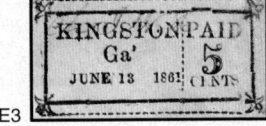

E3

E4

Typeset Envelopes (design types E1-E2, E4 are handstamps; typeset design E3 probably impressed by hand but possibly press printed)

46XU1 E1 5c black 3,000.
46XU2 E2 5c black 3,250.
46XU4 E3 5c black *12,500.*
46XU5 E4 5c black *2,000.*

There is only one recorded example of No. 46XU4.

KNOXVILLE, TENN.

A1

Typographed Adhesives (stereotype from woodcut) Grayish Laid Paper

47X1 A1 5c brick red *1,750.* 1,400.
47X2 A1 5c carmine *2,750.* *2,250.*
47X3 A1 10c green, on cover *57,750.*

The #47X3 cover is unique. Value is based on 1997 auction sale.

E1 E2

Press-printed Envelopes (typographed)

47XU1 E1 5c blue *2,500.*
47XU2 E1 5c blue, *orange* *3,500.*
47XU3 E1 10c red (cut to shape) *7,500.*
47XU4 E1 10c red, *orange* (cut to shape) *7,500.*

Only one example each recorded of Nos. 47XU3 and 47XU4.

Dangerous fakes exist of Nos. 47XU1 and 47XU2.

Handstamped Envelopes

47XU5 E2 5c black *1,500.*
a. 10c on 5c black *3,500.*

Type E2 exists with "5" above or below "PAID."

LA GRANGE, TEX.

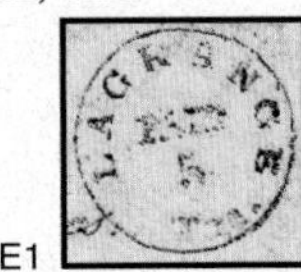

E1

Handstamped Envelopes

48XU1 E1 5c black — 2,250.
48XU2 E1 10c black 3,000.

LAKE CITY, FLA.

E1 Control

Handstamped Envelope

96XU1 E1 10c black *3,500.*

Envelopes have black circle control mark, or printed name of E. R. Ives, postmaster, on face or back.

LAURENS COURT HOUSE, S. C.

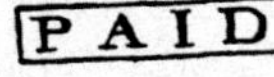

E1

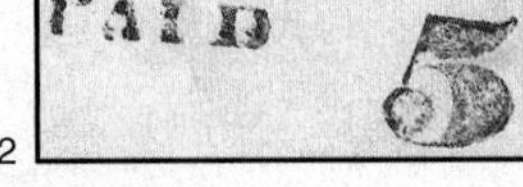

E2

Control

Handstamped Envelopes

116XU1 E1 5c black *2,250.*
116XU2 E2 5c black *2,250.*

Envelopes have a 25mm undated control mark on reverse.

LENOIR, N. C.

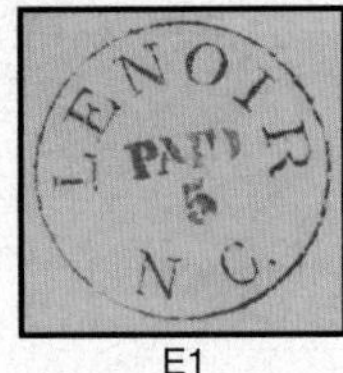

A1 E1

Handstamped Adhesive (from woodcut) White wove paper with cross-ruled orange lines

49X1 A1 5c blue & orange *7,250.* *6,750.*

Handstamped Envelopes

49XU1 A1 5c blue *4,000.*
49XU2 A1 10c (5c+5c) blue *25,000.*
49XU3 E1 5c blue *4,500.*
49XU4 E1 5c black *4,500.*

No. 49XU2 is unique.

LEXINGTON, MISS.

E1

Handstamped Envelopes

50XU1 E1 5c black *5,000.*
50XU2 E1 10c black *6,000.*

Only one example is recorded of No. 50XU2.

LEXINGTON, VA.

E1

Handstamped Envelopes

135XU1 E1 5c blue *500.*
135XU2 E1 10c blue *750.*

Nos. 135XU1-135XU2 by themselves are indistinguishable from stampless covers when used.

LIBERTY, VA. (and Salem, Va.)

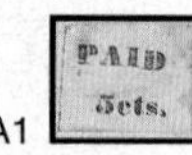

A1

Typeset Adhesive (probably impressed by hand)

Laid Paper

74X1 A1 5c black, on cover, uncanceled *35,000.*

Two known on covers with Liberty, Va. postmark; one cover known with the nearby Salem, Va. office postmark.

LIMESTONE SPRINGS, S. C.

A1

Handstamped Adhesive

121X1 A1 5c black, *light blue*, on cover *10,000.*
121X2 A1 5c black, *white*, two on cover *32,500.*

Stamps are cut round or rectangular. Covers are not postmarked. The No. 121X2 cover bears the only two recorded examples of this stamp.

LIVINGSTON, ALA.

A1

Lithographed Adhesive

51X1 A1 5c blue *15,000.*

LYNCHBURG, VA.

A1

E1

Typographed Adhesive (stereotype from woodcut)

52X1 A1 5c blue (shades) *1,800.* *1,500.*

Press-printed Envelopes (typographed)

Impressed at top right or left

52XU1 E1 5c black *700.00* *4,000.*
52XU2 E1 5c black, *amber* *4,000.*
52XU3 E1 5c black, *buff* *4,000.*
52XU4 E1 5c black, *brown* *4,000.*

MACON, GA.

A1

A2

FIVE CENTS.
A3

TWO CENTS
A4

Typeset Adhesives

Several varieties of type A1, 10 of A2, 5 of A3

Wove Paper

53X1 A1 5c black, *light blue green* (shades) 1,250. 1,000.

Warning: Dangerous forgeries exist of the normal variety and the Comma after "OFFICE" variety. Certificates of authenticity from recognized committees are strongly recommended.

53X3 A2 5c black, *yellow* 2,500. 1,250.
53X4 A3 5c black, *yellow* (shades) 3,000. 1,750.
a. Vertical tête bêche pair —
53X5 A4 2c black, *gray green* —

Laid Paper

53X6 A2 5c black, *yellow* *6,000.* *6,000.*
53X7 A3 5c black, *yellow* *6,000.*
53X8 A1 5c black, *light blue green* 1,750. *2,250.*

No. 53X4a is unique.

E1

Handstamped Envelope

Two types: "PAID" over "5," "5" over "PAID"

53XU1 E1 5c black 250. 650.

Values are for "PAID" over "5" variety. "5" over "PAID" is much scarcer.

MADISON, GA.

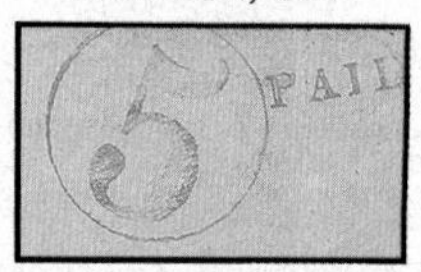

E1

Handstamped Envelope

136XU1 E1 5c red *600.*

No. 136XU1 is indistinguishable from a handstamp paid cover when used.

MADISON COURT HOUSE, FLA.

E1

Typeset Envelope

137XU1 E1 5c black, *yellow* *25,000.*

No. 137XU1 is unique.

See 3c 1861 Postmaster's Provisional No. 3AX1.

MARIETTA, GA.

E1

Control

PAID

E2 5

Handstamped Envelopes

54XU1 E1 5c black 500.
a. 10c on 5c black *1,750.*

With Double Circle Control

54XU3 E1 10c black
54XU4 E2 5c black *2,000.*

The existence of No. 54XU3 has been questioned by specialists. The editors would like to see authenticated evidence that verifies this listing.

MARION, VA.

A1

Adhesives with Typeset frame and Handstamped numeral in center

55X1 A1 5c black *7,500.*
55X2 A1 10c black *16,500.* *10,000.*
55X3 A1 5c black, *bluish*, laid paper — —

The 2c, 3c, 15c and 20c are believed to be bogus items printed later using the original typeset frame.

MARS BLUFF, S. C.

E1

145XU1 E1 5c black —

The No. 145XU1 marking is a provisional only when unused, used from another town or used under a general issue.

MEMPHIS, TENN.

A1

56X1a
Partial Print

A2

Typographed Adhesives (stereotyped from woodcut)

56X1 A1 2c blue (shades) 100. *1,250.*
a. Partial print 250. —
56X2 A2 5c red (shades) 150. *250.*
a. Tête bêche pair 1,500.
b. Pair, one sideways 2,500.
c. Pelure paper — —

Press-printed Envelopes (typographed)

56XU1 A2 5c red (shades) *3,000.*
56XU2 A2 5c red, *amber* *3,000.*
56XU3 A2 5c red, *orange* *3,000.*
56XU4 A2 5c red, *cream* *5,750.*

Only one example of No. 56XU4 is recorded. It is on a cover on which a C.S.A. No. 11 is affixed over the provisional to pay the postage.

MICANOPY, FLA.

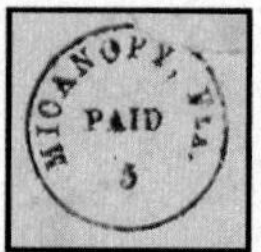

E1

Handstamped Envelope

105XU1 E1 5c black *11,500.*

One example recorded.

MILLEDGEVILLE, GA.

E1

E2

E3

Handstamped Envelopes

Two types of No. 57XU5: Type I, tall, thin "1" and "0" of "10"; Type II, short, fat "1" and "0" of "10."

57XU1 E1 5c black 500.
a. Wide spacing between "I" and "D" of "PAID" 600.
b. 10c on 5c black 1,000.
57XU2 E1 5c blue 800.
57XU4 E2 10c black 375. 1,200.
a. Wide spacing between "I" and "D" of "PAID" 1,200.
57XU5 E3 10c black, type I 125. 800.
a. Type II 1,500.

On No. 57XU4, the "PAID/10" virtually always falls outside the Milledgeville control marking (as in illustration E1).

The existence of No. 57XU2 as a provisional has been questioned by specialists. The editors would like to see authenticated evidence of provisional use of this marking.

MILTON, N. C.

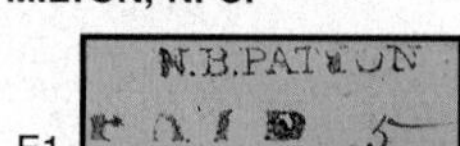

E1

Handstamped Envelope, "5" Manuscript

138XU1 E1 5c black *3,000.*

MOBILE, ALA.

A1

Lithographed Adhesives

58X1 A1 2c black 2,250. 1,200.
58X2 A1 5c blue 350. 450.

MONTGOMERY, ALA.

E1

E1a

Handstamped Envelopes

59XU1 E1 5c red *1,100.*
a. 10c on 5c red *2,750.*

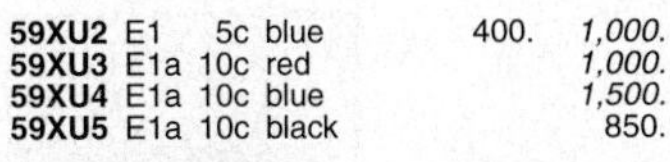

59XU2 E1 5c blue 400. *1,000.*
59XU3 E1a 10c red *1,000.*
59XU4 E1a 10c blue *1,500.*
59XU5 E1a 10c black 850.

E2

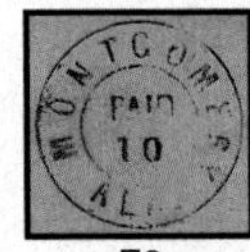
E3

59XU7 E2 2c red *2,500.*
59XU7A E2 2c blue *3,500.*
59XU8 E2 5c black *2,250.*
59XU9 E3 10c black *3,250.*
59XU10 E3 10c red *1,750.*

The existence of No. 59XU10 is in question. The editors would like to see an authenticated example of this marking.

MT. LEBANON, LA.

A1

Woodcut Adhesive (mirror image of design)

60X1 A1 5c red brown, on cover *255,000.*

One example known. Value represents sale price at 2009 auction.

NASHVILLE, TENN.

A2

E1

Typographed Adhesives (stereotyped from woodcut)

Gray Blue Ribbed Paper

61X2 A2 5c carmine (shades) 1,000. 600.
a. Vertical tête bêche pair *4,000.*
61X3 A2 5c brick red (shades) 1,000. 1,000.
61X4 A2 5c gray (shades) 1,250. 1,500.
61X5 A2 5c violet brown (shades) 1,250. 750.
a. Vertical tete beche pair 5,000. *7,500.*
61X6 A2 10c green — *7,500.*

Handstamped Envelopes

61XU1 E1 5c blue 900.
61XU2 E1 5c +10c blue *2,750.*

See 3c Postmaster's Provisional No. 4AX1.

NEW ORLEANS, LA.

A1

A2

Typographed Adhesives (stereotyped from woodcut)

62X1 A1 2c blue 225. *550.*
a. Printed on both sides, on cover *10,500.*
62X2 A1 2c red (shades) 190. *1,000.*
62X3 A2 5c brown, *white* 300. 200.
a. Printed on both sides *3,750.*
b. 5c ocher 700. 625.
62X4 A2 5c red brn, *bluish* 325. 200.
a. Printed on both sides *3,250.*

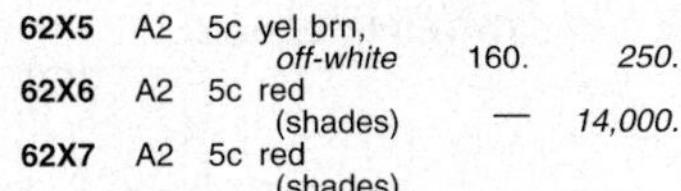

62X5 A2 5c yel brn, *off-white* 160. *250.*
62X6 A2 5c red (shades) — *14,000.*
62X7 A2 5c red (shades), *bluish* *15,000.*

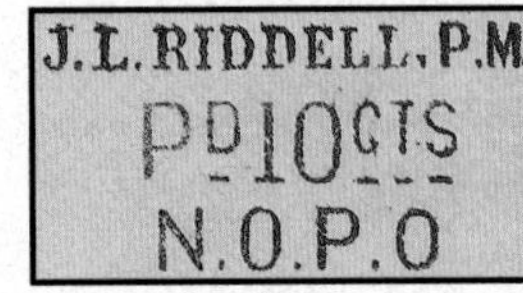

E1

Handstamped Envelopes

62XU1 E1 5c black 4,500.
62XU2 E1 10c black *11,500.*

"J. L. RIDDELL, P. M." omitted

62XU3 E1 2c black *9,500.*

Some authorities question the use of No. 62XU3 as a provisional.

NEW SMYRNA, FLA.

A1

Handstamped Adhesive

On white paper with blue ruled lines

63X1 A1 10c ("O1") on 5c black *50,000.*

One example known. It is uncanceled on a postmarked patriotic cover.

NORFOLK, VA.

E1

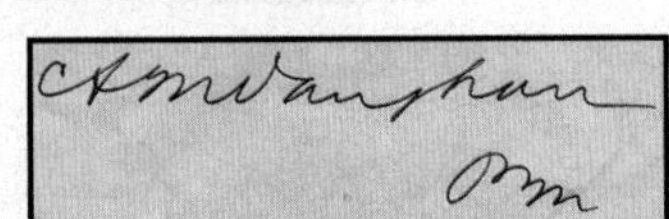
Manuscript Signature

Handstamped Envelopes

Ms Signature on Front or Back

139XU1 E1 5c blue — *1,500.*
139XU2 E1 10c blue *1,750.*

OAKWAY, S. C.

A1

Handstamped Adhesive (from woodcut)

115X1 A1 5c black, on cover *60,000.*

Two used examples of No. 115X1 are recorded, both on cover. Value represents 2012 auction realization for the cover on which the stamp is tied by manuscript "Paid."

PENSACOLA, FLA.

E1

Handstamped Envelopes

106XU1 E1 5c black *3,750.*
a. 10c (ms.) on 5c black *4,250.*

PETERSBURG, VA.

A1

Typeset Adhesive

Ten varieties

65X1 A1 5c red (shades) *2,250.* 750.

PITTSYLVANIA COURT HOUSE, VA.

A1

Typeset Adhesives

66X1 A1 5c dull red, wove paper *7,500.* *6,500.*
66X2 A1 5c dull red, laid paper *5,500.*

PLAINS OF DURA, GA.

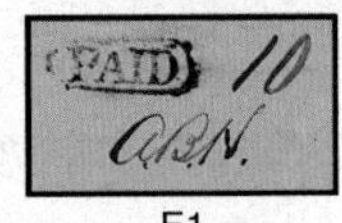

E1

Handstamped Envelopes, Ms. Initials

140XU1 E1 5c black —
140XU2 E1 10c black *5,000.*

No. 140XU2 is unique.

PLEASANT SHADE, VA.

A1

Typeset Adhesive

Five varieties

67X1 A1 5c blue *5,000.* *20,000.*

PLUM CREEK, TEX.

E1

Manuscript Adhesive

141X1 E1 10c black, *blue,* on cover —

The stamps have ruled lines with the value "10" in manuscript. Size and shape vary.

PORT GIBSON, MISS.

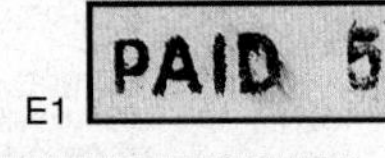

E1

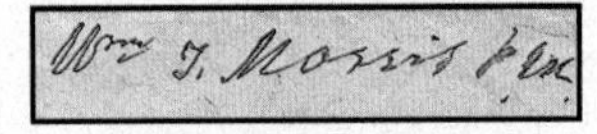
Manuscript Signature

Handstamped Envelope, Ms Signature

142XU1 E1 5c black —

PORT LAVACA, TEX.

A1

Typeset Adhesive

107X1 A1 10c black, on cover *25,000.*

One example known. It is uncanceled on a postmarked cover.

RALEIGH, N. C.

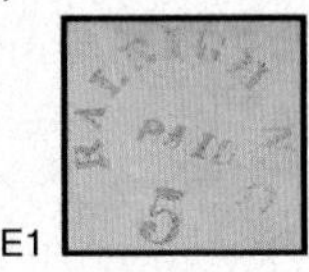
E1

Handstamped Envelopes

68XU1 E1 5c red 600.
68XU2 E1 5c blue *3,000.*

RHEATOWN, TENN.

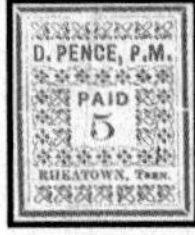
A1

Typeset Adhesive

Three varieties

69X1 A1 5c red *6,000.* *7,500.*

RICHMOND, TEX.

E1

Handstamped Envelopes or Letter Sheets

70XU1 E1 5c red 2,500.
a. 10c on 5c red *5,000.*
70XU2 E1 10c red 2,000.
a. 15c (ms.) on 10c red *5,000.*

RINGGOLD, GA.

E1

Handstamped Envelope

71XU1 E1 5c blue black *9,000.*

RUTHERFORDTON, N. C.

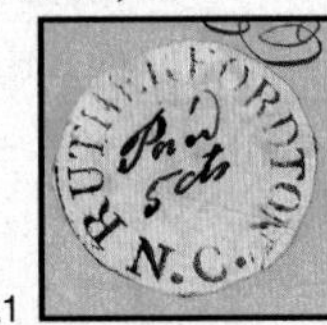
A1

Handstamped Adhesive, Ms. "Paid 5cts"

72X1 A1 5c black, cut round, on cover (uncanceled) *35,000.*

No. 72X1 is unique.

SALEM, N. C.

"Paid 5" in Ms. — E1

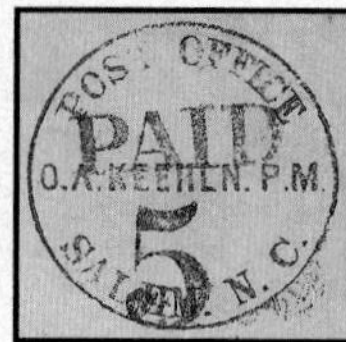

"Paid 5" Handstamped — E2

Handstamped Envelopes

73XU1	E1	5c black	1,750.
73XU2	E1	10c black	*2,250.*
73XU3	E2	5c black	*2,250.*
a.		10c on 5c black	*2,800.*

Reprints exist on various papers. They either lack the "Paid" and value or have them counterfeited.

Salem, Va.
See No. 74X1 under Liberty, Va.

SALISBURY, N. C.

E1

Press-printed Envelope (typeset)
Impressed at top left

75XU1	E1	5c black, *greenish*	*5,000.*

One example known. Part of envelope is torn away, leaving part of design missing.

SAN ANTONIO, TEX.

E1

E2

Control

Handstamped Envelopes

76XU1	E1	10c black	500.	*2,000.*
76XU1A	E2	5c black		*1,500.*
76XU2	E2	10c black		*2,500.*

Black circle control mark is on front or back.

SAVANNAH, GA.

E1

Control

PAID 10

E2

Handstamped Envelopes

101XU1	E1	5c black	400.
a.		10c on 5c black	1,500.
101XU2	E2	5c black	600.
a.		20c on 5c black	*2,000.*
101XU3	E1	10c black	750.
101XU4	E2	10c black	750.

Envelopes must have octagonal control mark. One example is known of No.101XU2a.

SELMA, ALA.

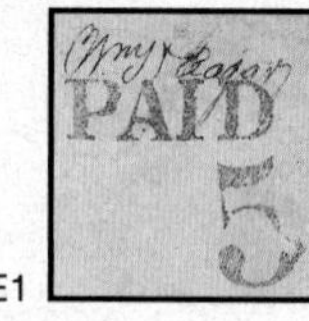

E1

Handstamped Envelopes; Signature in Ms.

77XU1	E1	5c black	*1,250.*
a.		10c on 5c black	*3,000.*
77XU2	E1	10c black	*2,500.*

Signature is that of Postmaster William H. Eagar.
See 3c 1861 Postmaster's Provisional No. 5AX1.

SPARTA, GA.

E1

Handstamped Envelopes

93XU1	E1	5c red	—	2,250.
93XU2	E1	10c red		*5,000.*

Only one example recorded of No. 93XU2.

SPARTANBURG, S. C.

A1

A2

Handstamped Adhesives
(on ruled or plain wove paper)

78X1	A1	5c black, cut to shape	
a.		"Paid" instead of denomination, revalued to 5c with "PAID" and "5" in small circle handstamps	—
78X2	A2	5c black, *bluish*	*4,000.*
78X3	A2	5c black, *brown*	*4,000.*

Most examples of Nos. 78X1-78X3 are cut round. Cut square examples in sound condition are worth much more.

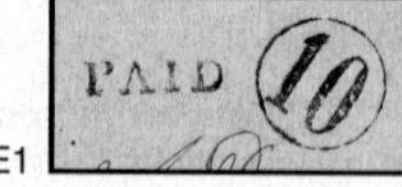

E1

Control

Handstamped Envelopes

78XU1	E1	10c black (control on reverse)	*5,000.*

STATESVILLE, N. C.

E1

Handstamped Envelopes

79XU1	E1	5c black	*900.*
a.		10c on 5c black	*2,500.*

Unused examples of No. 79XU1 are reprints.

SUMTER, S. C.

E1

Handstamped Envelopes

80XU1	E1	5c black	500.	
a.		10c on 5c black		*900.*
80XU2	E1	10c black	600.	
a.		2c (ms.) on 10c black		*1,100.*

Used examples of Nos. 80XU1-80XU2 are indistinguishable from handstamped "Paid" covers.

TALBOTTON, GA.

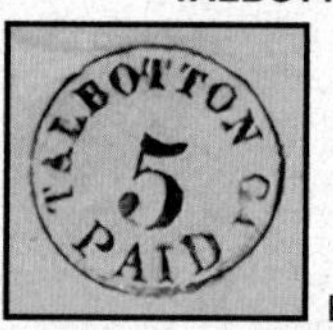

E1

Handstamped Envelopes

94XU1	E1	5c black	1,000.
a.		10c on 5c black	*2,000.*
94XU2	E1	10c black	1,000.

TALLADEGA, ALA.

E1

Handstamped Envelopes

143XU1	E1	5c black	*1,500.*	—
143XU2	E1	10c black	*1,500.*	—

These same markings were used on handstamped "Paid" covers.

TELLICO PLAINS, TENN.

A1

Typeset Adhesives
Laid Paper

81X1	A1	5c red	2,500.	—
81X2	A1	10c red	4,000.	

THOMASVILLE, GA.

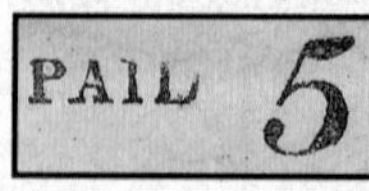

E1

Control

Handstamped Envelopes

82XU1	E1	5c black	750.

On No. 82XU1, the control is on the reverse of the cover. The dated control is known with four different dates, including June 18, June 21 and August 23. The patriotic cover use is unique.

E2

82XU2	E2	5c black	900.

TULLAHOMA, TENN.

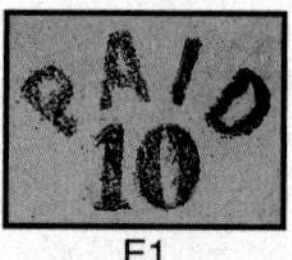

E1

Control

Handstamped Envelope

111XU1	E1	10c black	*4,250.*

TUSCALOOSA, ALA.

PAID
5

E1

Handstamped Envelopes

83XU1	E1	5c black	250.
83XU2	E1	10c black	250.

Used examples of Nos. 83XU1-83XU2 are indistinguishable from handstamped "Paid" covers.

TUSCUMBIA, ALA.

E1

Handstamped Envelopes

84XU1	E1	5c black	4,000.
84XU2	E1	5c red	*5,000.*
84XU3	E1	10c black	*5,250.*

See 3c 1861 Postmaster's Provisional No. 6AXU1.

UNIONTOWN, ALA.

A1

Typeset Adhesives
(settings of 4 (2x2), 4 varieties of each value)
Laid Paper

86X1	A1	2c dark blue, *gray blue, on cover*	—

86X2 A1 2c dark blue, sheet of 4 *40,000.*
86X3 A1 5c green, *gray blue* *4,000.* *3,250.*
86X4 A1 5c green *4,000.* *3,250.*
86X5 A1 10c red, *gray blue* —

Two examples known of No. 86X1, both on cover (drop letters), one uncanceled and one pen canceled.

The only recorded examples of No. 86X2 are in a unique sheet of 4.

The item listed as No. 86X5 used is an uncanceled stamp on a large piece with part of addressee's name in manuscript.

UNIONVILLE, S. C.

A1

Handstamped Adhesive
"PAID" and "5" applied separately

Paper with Blue Ruled Lines

87X1 A1 5c black, *grayish* —

VALDOSTA, GA.

E1

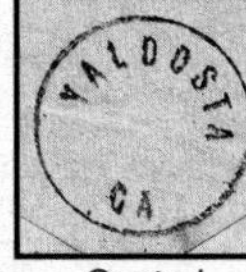

Control

Handstamped Envelopes

100XU1 E1 10c black *9,000.*
100XU2 E1 5c +5c black —

The black circle control must appear on front of the No. 100XU2 envelope and on the back of the No. 100XU1 envelope.

There is one recorded cover each of Nos. 100XU1-100XU2.

VICTORIA, TEX.

A1

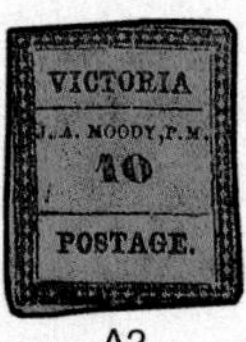

A2

Typeset Adhesives

Surface colored paper

88X1 A1 5c red brown, *green* *20,000.*
88X2 A1 10c red brown, *green* *22,500.*
88X3 A2 10c red brown, *green, pelure paper* *27,500.* *30,000.*

WALTERBOROUGH, S. C.

E1

Handstamped Envelopes

108XU1 E1 10c black, *buff* —
108XU2 E1 10c carmine *4,250.*

The existence of No. 108XU1 is in question. The editors would like to see authenticated evidence of its existence.

WARRENTON, GA.

E1

Handstamped Envelopes

89XU1 E1 5c black 1,250.
a. 10c (ms.) on 5c black 1,000.

Fakes of the Warrenton provisional marking based on the illustration shown are known on addressed but postally unused covers.

WASHINGTON, GA.

E1

Handstamped Envelope

117XU1 E1 10c black *2,000.*

Envelopes must have black circle postmark control on the back. Examples with the undated control on the front are not considered provisional unless a dated postmark is also present.

WEATHERFORD, TEX.

E1

Handstamped Envelopes (woodcut with "PAID" inserted in type)

109XU1 E1 5c black *2,000.*
109XU2 E1 5c +5c black *11,000.*

One example is known of No. 109XU2.

WILKESBORO, N. C.

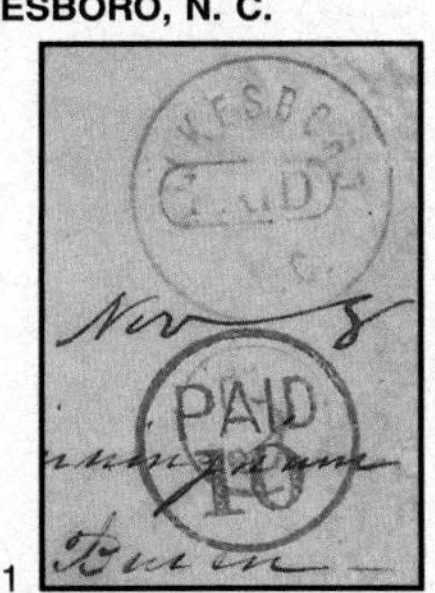

E1

Handstamped Envelope

147XU1 E1 5c black, revalued to 10c —

No. 147XU1 is unique.

WINNSBOROUGH, S. C.

Control

E1

Handstamped Envelopes

97XU1 E1 5c black *2,000.*
97XU2 E1 10c black *3,500.*

Envelopes must have black circle control on front or back.

WYTHEVILLE, VA.

E1

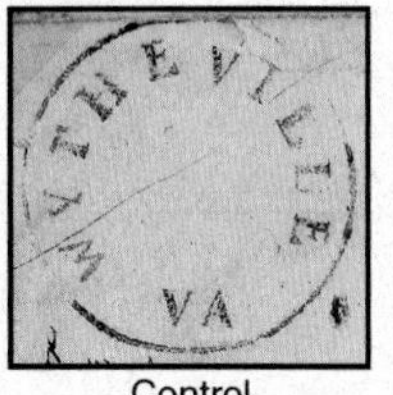

Control

Handstamped Envelope

114XU1 E1 5c black 900.

For later additions, listed out of numerical sequence, see:
#*74X1*, Liberty, Va.
#*92XU1*, Huntsville, Tex.
#*93XU1*, Sparta, Ga.
#*94XU1*, Talbotton, Ga.
#*95XU1*, Cuthbert, GA
#*96XU1*, Lake City, Fla.
#*97XU1*, Winnsborough, S.C.
#*98XU1*, Galveston, Tex.
#*99XU1*, Christiansburg, Va.
#*100XU1*, Valdosta, Ga.
#*101XU1*, Savannah, Ga.
#*102XU1*, Griffin, Ga.
#*103XU1*, Courtland, Ala.
#*104XU1*, Fincastle, Va.
#*105XU1*, Micanopy, Fla.
#*106XU1*, Pensacola, Fla.
#*107X1*, Port Lavaca, Tex.
#*108XU1*, Walterborough, S.C.
#*109XU1*, Weatherford, Tex.
#*110XU1*, Jacksonville, Ala.
#*111XU1*, Tullahoma, Tenn.
#*112XU1*, Hamburgh, S.C.
#*113XU1*, Columbia, Tenn.
#*114XU1*, Wytheville, Va.
#*115X1*, Oakway, S.C.
#*116XU1*, Laurens Court House, S.C.
#*117XU1*, Washington, Ga.
#*118XU1*, Carolina City, N.C.
#*119XU1*, Colaparchee, Ga.
#*120XU1*, Forsyth, Ga.
#*121XU1*, Limestone Springs, S.C.
#*122XU1*, Balcony Falls, Va.
#*123XU1*, Barnwell Court House, S.C.
#*124XU1*, Bluffton, S.C.
#*125XU1*, Camden, S.C.
#*126XU1*, Cartersville, Ga.
#*127XU1*, Charlottesville, Va.
#*128XU1*, Fraziersville, S.C.
#*129XU1*, Gaston, N.C.
#*130XU1*, Harrisburgh, Tex.
#*132XU1*, Hollandale, Tex.
#*133XU1*, Isabella, Ga.
#*134XU1*, Jacksonville, Fla.
#*135XU1*, Lexington, Va.
#*136XU1*, Madison, Ga.
#*137XU1*, Madison Court House, Fla.
#*138XU1*, Milton, N.C.
#*139XU1*, Norfolk, Va.
#*140XU1*, Plains of Dura, Ga.
#*141X1*, Plum Creek, Tex.
#*142XU1*, Port Gibson, Miss.
#*143XU1*, Talladega, Ala.
#*144XU1*, Greenville, Tenn.
#*145XU1*, Mars Bluff, S.C.
#*146XU1*, Charlotte, N.C.
#*147XU1*, Wilkesboro, N.C.
#*148XU1*, Fort Valley, Ga.

GENERAL ISSUES

Jefferson Davis — A1

1861 **Unwmk.** **Litho.** ***Imperf.***

1 A1 5c green (shades) 275. 175.
No gum 160.
a. 5c light green 275. 175.
No gum 160.
b. 5c dark green 375. 250.
No gum 225.
c. 5c olive green 400. 250.
No gum 240.

Thomas Jefferson — A2

1861-62

2 A2 10c blue 300. 200.
No gum 175.
a. 10c light blue 300. 200.
No gum 175.
b. 10c dark blue 700. 300.
No gum 400.
c. 10c indigo *5,000.* *3,500.*
No gum *2,500.*
d. Printed on both sides *1,750.*
e. light milky blue 1,100. 325.
No gum 650.

Specialists have questioned the existence of No. 2bd, the Hoyer & Ludwig printed on both sides. The editors would like to see authenticated evidence of its existence.

The earliest printings of No. 2 were made by Hoyer & Ludwig, the later ones by J. T. Paterson & Co.

Stamps of the later printings usually have a small colored dash below the lowest point of the upper left spandrel.

See Nos. 4-5.

Andrew Jackson — A3

1862

3 A3 2c green 950. 750.
No gum 550.
a. 2c bright yellow green *2,000.* —
No gum *1,300.*

4 A1 5c blue 225. 125.
No gum 130.
a. 5c dark blue 275. 175.
No gum 150.
b. 5c light milky blue 300. 200.
No gum 170.

5 A2 10c rose (shades) 1,750. 500.
No gum 1,000.
a. 10c carmine *3,500.* *1,900.*
No gum *2,100.*

Jefferson Davis — A4

Typo.

6 A4 5c light blue 16. 28.
No gum 7.

7 A4 5c blue (De La Rue thin paper) 20. 22.
No gum 10.
a. 5c deep blue 25. 30.
No gum 12.
b. Printed on both sides *2,500.* *1,400.*

No. 6 has fine, clear impression. No. 7 has coarser impression and the color is duller and often blurred.

Both 2c and 10c stamps, types A4 and A10, were privately printed in various colors.

Andrew Jackson — A5

1863 **Engr.**

8 A5 2c brown red 75. *350.*
No gum 40.
a. 2c pale red 90. *450.*
No gum 45.

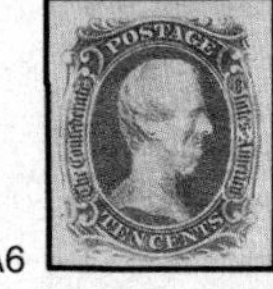

A6

Thick or Thin Paper

9 A6 10c blue 900. 550.
No gum 575.
a. 10c milky blue (first printing) 950. 600.
No gum 575.
b. 10c gray blue 1,000. 650.
No gum 625.

Jefferson Davis — A6a

10 A6a 10c blue (with frame line) 5,000. 1,900.
No gum 3,500.
a. 10c milky blue 5,000. 1,900.
No gum 3,500.
b. 10c greenish blue 5,500. 1,900.
No gum 4,000.
c. 10c dark blue 5,500. 1,900.
No gum 4,000.

Values of Nos. 10, 10a, 10b and 10c are for examples showing parts of lines on at least three sides. Used stamps showing 4 complete lines sell for approximately 3 to 4 times the values given. Unused stamps showing 4 complete lines are exceedingly rare (only two recorded), and the one sound example is valued at $25,000.

A7

There are many slight differences between A7 and A8, the most noticeable being the additional line outside the ornaments at the four corners of A8.

1863-64

11 A7 10c blue 16. *20.*
No gum 7.
a. 10c milky blue 50. 60.
No gum 27.
b. 10c dark blue 25. 30.
No gum 12.
c. 10c greenish blue 30. 20.
No gum 17.
d. 10c green 75. *80.*
No gum 45.
e. Officially perforated 12½ (A. & D.) 350. 275.

A8

12 A8 10c blue 20. 25.
No gum 10.
a. 10c milky blue 50. 60.
No gum 25.
b. 10c light blue 19. 22.
No gum 9.
c. 10c greenish blue 40. *55.*
No gum 20.
d. 10c dark blue 22. 25.
No gum 11.
e. 10c green 125. 140.
No gum 75.
f. Officially perforated 12½ (A. & D.) 375. 300.

The paper of Nos. 11 and 12 varies from thin hard to thick soft. The so-called laid paper is probably due to thick streaky gum.

George Washington — A9

1863

13 A9 20c green 45. *400.*
No gum 27.
a. 20c yellow green 70. *450.*
No gum 45.
b. 20c dark green 65. *500.*
No gum 40.
c. 20c bluish green 100. —
No gum 65.
d. Diagonal half used as 10c on cover *2,000.*
e. Horizontal half used as 10c on cover *3,500.*

John C. Calhoun — A10

1862 **Typo.**

14 A10 1c orange 100.
No gum 60.
a. 1c deep orange 130.
No gum 75.

No. 14 was never put in use.

CANAL ZONE

kə-'nal 'zōn

LOCATION — A strip of land 10 miles wide, extending through the Republic of Panama, between the Atlantic and Pacific Oceans.
GOVT. — From 1904-79 a U.S. Government Reservation; from 1979-99 under joint control of the Republic of Panama and the U.S.
AREA — 552.8 sq. mi.
POP. — 41,800 (est. 1976)

The Canal Zone, site of the Panama Canal, was leased in perpetuity to the U.S. for a cash payment of $10,000,000 and a yearly rental. Treaties between the two countries provided for joint jurisdiction by the U.S. and Panama, 1979-1999, with Panama handling postal service. At the end of 1999, the canal, in its entirety, reverted to Panama.

100 Centavos = 1 Peso
100 Centesimos = 1 Balboa
100 Cents = 1 Dollar

Catalogue values for unused stamps in this country are for Never Hinged items, beginning with Scott 118 in the regular postage section and Scott C6 in the air post section.

Watermarks

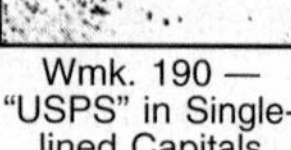

Wmk. 190 — "USPS" in Single-lined Capitals

Wmk. 191 — Double-lined "USPS" in Capitals

Map of Panama — A1

Violet to Violet-Blue Handstamp on Panama Nos. 72, 72a-72c, 78, 79.

On the 2c "PANAMA" is normally 13mm long. On the 5c and 10c it measures about 15mm.

On the 2c, "PANAMA" reads up on the upper half of the sheet and down on the lower half. On the 5c and 10c, "PANAMA" reads up at left and down at right on each stamp.

On the 2c only, varieties exist with inverted "V" for "A," accent on "A," inverted "N," etc., in "PANAMA."

Unwmk.

1904, June 24 **Engr.** ***Perf. 12***

1 A1 2c rose, both "PANAMA" reading up or down 650. 400.
a. "CANAL ZONE" inverted *1,000.* 850.
b. "CANAL ZONE" double *3,250.* 2,000.
c. "CANAL ZONE" double, both inverted *20,000.*
d. "PANAMA" reading down and up 750. 650.
e. As "d," "CANAL ZONE" invtd. *9,000.* *9,000.*
f. Vert. pair, "PANAMA" reading up on top 2c, down on other *2,100.* *2,100.*
g. As "f," "CANAL ZONE" inverted *20,000.*
2 A1 5c blue 300. 190.
a. "CANAL ZONE" inverted 775. 600.
b. "CANAL ZONE" double 2,250. 1,500.
c. Pair, one without "CANAL ZONE" overprint *5,000.* *5,000.*
d. "CANAL ZONE" overprint diagonal, reading down to right 800. 700.
3 A1 10c yellow 400. 230.
a. "CANAL ZONE" inverted 775. 600.
b. "CANAL ZONE" double *14,000.*
c. Pair, one without "CANAL ZONE" overprint *6,000.* *5,000.*
Nos. 1-3 (3) 1,350. 820.00

Cancellations consist of town and/or bars in magenta or black, or a mixture of both colors.
Nos. 1-3 were withdrawn July 17, 1904.
Forgeries of the "Canal Zone" overprint and cancellations are numerous.

United States Nos. 300, 319, 304, 306 and 307 Overprinted in Black

1904, July 18 **Wmk. 191**

4 A115 1c blue green 40.00 22.50
5 A129 2c carmine 35.00 25.00
a. 2c scarlet 35.00 30.00
6 A119 5c blue 100.00 65.00
7 A121 8c violet black 160.00 85.00
8 A122 10c pale red brown 140.00 90.00
Nos. 4-8 (5) 475.00 287.50

Beware of fake overprints.

A2

A3

CANAL ZONE
Regular Type

CANAL ZONE
Antique Type

1904-06 **Unwmk.**

Black Overprint on Stamps of Panama

9 A2 1c green 2.75 2.00
a. "CANAL" in antique type 100.00 100.00
b. "ZONE" in antique type 70.00 70.00
c. Inverted overprint *7,500.* *6,000.*
d. Double overprint *2,750.* *2,000.*
10 A2 2c rose 4.50 3.00
a. Inverted overprint 225.00 275.00
b. "L" of "CANAL" sideways 2,500. 2,500.

"PANAMA" (15mm long) reading up at left, down at right

Overprint "CANAL ZONE" in Black, "PANAMA" and Bar in Red

11 A3 2c rose 7.00 5.00
a. "ZONE" in antique type 200.00 200.00
b. "PANAMA" overprint inverted, bar at bottom 600.00 *675.00*
12 A3 5c blue 8.00 3.50
a. "CANAL" in antique type 75.00 65.00
b. "ZONE" in antique type 75.00 65.00
c. "CANAL ZONE" double 800.00 800.00
d. "PANAMA" double 1,100. 1,000.
e. "PANAMA" inverted, bar at bottom 1,000. 2,000.
13 A3 10c yellow 20.00 12.50
a. "CANAL" in antique type 200.00 200.00
b. "ZONE" in antique type 175.00 160.00
c. "PANAMA" ovpt. double 650.00 650.00
d. "PANAMA" overprint in red brown 27.50 27.50
Nos. 11-13 (3) 35.00 21.00

With Added Surcharge in Red

a

14 A3 8c on 50c bister brown 30.00 22.50
a. "ZONE" in antique type 1,150. 1,150.
b. "CANAL ZONE" inverted 450.00 425.00
c. "PANAMA" overprint in rose brown 40.00 40.00
d. As "c," "CANAL" in antique type *1,750.* *850.00*
e. As "c," "ZONE" in antique type *1,750.*
f. As "c," "8 cts" double *1,100.*
g. As "c," "8" omitted *4,500.*
h. As "c," "cts 8" —

Nos. 11-14 are overprinted or surcharged on Panama Nos. 77, 77e, 78, 78c, 78d, 78f, 78g, 78h, 79 79c, 79e, 79g and 81 respectively.

On No. 14 with original gum, the gum is almost always disturbed. Unused stamps are valued thus.

Panama No. 74a, 74b Overprinted "CANAL ZONE" in Regular Type in Black and Surcharged Type "a" in Red Both "PANAMA" (13mm long) Reading Up

15 A3(a) 8c on 50c bister brown 2,250. *4,750.*
a. "PANAMA" reading down and up *7,000.* —

On No. 15 with original gum, the gum is almost always disturbed. Unused stamps are valued thus.

Map of Panama — A4

Panama Nos. 19 and 21 Surcharged in Black

a
PANAMA CANAL ZONE 1 ct. PANAMA

b
PANAMA CANAL ZONE 1 ct. PANAMA

c
PANAMA CANAL ZONE 1 ct. PANAMA

d
PANAMA CANAL ZONE 2 cts. PANAMA

e
PANAMA CANAL ZONE 2 cts. PANAMA

f
PANAMA CANAL ZONE 2 cts. PANAMA

1906

There were three printings of each denomination, differing principally in the relative position of the various parts of the surcharges. Varieties occur with inverted "V" for the final "A" in "PANAMA," "CA" spaced, "ZO" spaced, "2c" spaced, accents in various positions, and with bars shifted so that two bars appear on top or bottom of the stamp (either with or without the corresponding bar on top or bottom) and sometimes with only one bar at top or bottom.

16 A4	1c on 20c violet, type a	2.00	1.60
a.	Type b	2.00	1.60
b.	Type c	2.00	1.60
c.	As No. 16, double surcharge		*2,000.*
17 A4	2c on 1p lake, type d	2.75	2.75
a.	Type e	2.75	2.75
b.	Type f	20.00	20.00

Panama Nos. 74, 74a and 74b Overprinted "CANAL ZONE" in Regular Type in Black and Surcharged in Red

b

c

1905-06

Both "PANAMA" Reading Up

18 A3(b)	8c on 50c bister brown	50.00	50.00
a.	"ZONE" in antique type	200.00	180.00
b.	"PANAMA" reading down and up	175.00	160.00
19 A3(c)	8c on 50c bister brown	55.00	40.00
a.	"CANAL" in antique type	210.00	180.00
b.	"ZONE" in antique type	210.00	180.00
c.	"8 cts" double	*1,100.*	*1,100.*
d.	"PANAMA" reading down and up	110.00	90.00

On Nos. 18-19 with original gum, the gum is usually disturbed. Unused stamps are valued thus.

Panama No. 81 Overprinted "CANAL ZONE" in Regular Type in Black and Surcharged in Red Type "c" plus Period

"PANAMA" reading up and down

20 A3(c)	8c on 50c bister brown	37.50	37.50
a.	"CANAL" antique type	200.00	180.00
b.	"ZONE" in antique type	200.00	180.00
c.	"8 cts" omitted	800.00	800.00
d.	"cts 8"	*1,500.*	
e.	"cts 8" double		—

Nos. 14 and 18-20 exist without CANAL ZONE overprint but were not regularly issued and are considered printer's waste. Forgeries of the overprint varieties of Nos. 9-15 and 18-20 are known.

On No. 20 with original gum, the gum is usually disturbed. Unused stamps are valued thus.

Francisco Hernandez de Cordoba — A5

Vasco Nunez de Balboa — A6

Fernández de Córdoba A7

Justo Arosemena A8

Manuel J. Hurtado — A9

Jose de Obaldia — A10

Stamps of Panama Overprinted in Black

1906-07 *Perf. 12*

Overprint Reading Up

21 A5	2c red & black	30.00	30.00
a.	"CANAL" only	*4,000.*	

Overprint Reading Down

22 A6	1c green & black	2.00	1.00
a.	Horiz. pair, imperf. btwn.	1,100.	1,100.
b.	Vert. pair, imperf. btwn.	*2,000.*	*2,000.*
c.	Vert. pair, imperf. horiz.	*2,250.*	*1,750.*
d.	Inverted overprint reading up	550.00	550.00
e.	Double overprint	275.00	275.00
f.	Double overprint, one inverted	1,750.	1,600.
g.	Invtd. center, ovpt. reading up	*3,750.*	*4,750.*
h.	Horiz. pair, imperf vert.	*5,000.*	
23 A7	2c red & black	3.00	1.10
a.	Horizontal pair, imperf. between	2,250.	2,000.
b.	Vertical pair, one without overprint	2,500.	2,500.
c.	Double overprint	700.00	700.00
d.	Double overprint, one diagonal	800.00	800.00
e.	Double overprint, one diagonal, in pair with normal	2,500.	
f.	2c carmine red & black	5.00	2.75
g.	As "f," inverted center and overprint reading up		*14,000.*
h.	As "d," one "ZONE CANAL"	*4,000.*	
i.	"CANAL" double	*5,000.*	
24 A8	5c ultramarine & black	5.75	2.25
c.	Double overprint	500.00	400.00
d.	"CANAL" only	*5,500.*	
e.	"ZONE CANAL"	*5,000.*	
25 A9	8c purple & black	20.00	8.00
a.	Horizontal pair, imperf. between and at left margin	*1,750.*	*4,000.*
26 A10	10c violet & black	20.00	7.50
a.	Dbl. ovpt., one reading up	*5,000.*	
b.	Overprint reading up	*5,500.*	
	Nos. 22-26 (5)	50.75	19.85

Nos. 22-25 occur with "CA" of "CANAL" spaced ½mm further apart on position No. 50 of the setting.

The used pair of No. 25a is unique.

Cordoba A11

Arosemena A12

Hurtado — A13

Jose de Obaldia — A14

1909

Overprint Reading Down

27 A11	2c vermilion & black	12.50	5.00
a.	Horizontal pair, one without overprint	*2,600.*	
b.	Vert. pair, one without ovpt.	*3,500.*	
28 A12	5c deep blue & black	40.00	12.50
29 A13	8c violet & black	40.00	14.00
30 A14	10c violet & black	37.50	14.00
a.	Horizontal pair, one with "ZONE" omitted	*3,000.*	
b.	Vertical pair, one without overprint	*4,000.*	
	Nos. 27-30 (4)	130.00	45.50

Nos. 27-30 occur with "CA" spaced (position 50).

Do not confuse No. 27 with Nos. 39d or 53a.

On No. 30a, the stamp with "ZONE" omitted is also missing most of "CANAL."

For designs A11-A14 with overprints reading up, see Nos. 32-35, 39-41, 47-48, 53-54, 56-57.

Black Overprint Reading Up

Vasco Nunez de Balboa — A15

Type I

Type I Overprint: "C" with serifs both top and bottom. "L," "Z" and "E" with slanting serifs.

Compare Type I overprint with Types II to V illustrated before Nos. 38, 46, 52 and 55.

1909-10

31 A15	1c dark green & black	4.25	1.25
a.	Inverted center and overprint reading down		*22,500.*
c.	Bklt. pane of 6, handmade, perf. margins	*500.00*	
32 A11	2c vermilion & black	4.50	1.25
a.	Vert. pair, imperf. horiz.	1,000.	1,000.
c.	Bklt. pane of 6, handmade, perf. margins	*800.00*	
d.	Double overprint (I)		*6,000.*
33 A12	5c deep blue & black	17.00	3.50
a.	Double overprint	375.00	375.00
34 A13	8c violet & black	12.00	6.00
a.	Vertical pair, one without overprint	*1,750.*	
35 A14	10c violet & black	47.50	20.00
	Nos. 31-35 (5)	85.25	32.00

No. 32d is unique and has small faults.

See Nos. 38, 46, 52, 55.

A16

A17

Black Surcharge

1911, Jan. 14

36 A16	10c on 13c gray	6.00	2.25
a.	"10 cts" inverted	350.00	300.00
b.	"10 cts" omitted	350.00	

Many used stamps offered as No. 36b are merely No. 36 from which the surcharge has been chemically removed.

1914, Jan. 6

37 A17	10c gray	50.00	12.50

Black Overprint Reading Up

Type II: "C" with serif at top only. "L" and "E" with vertical serifs. "O" tilts to left

1912-16

38 A15	1c green & black	11.00	3.00
a.	Vertical pair, one without overprint	1,750.	1,750.
b.	Booklet pane of 6, imperf. margins	575.00	
c.	Booklet pane of 6, handmade, perf. margins	*1,000.*	
39 A11	2c vermilion & black	8.00	1.10
a.	Horiz. pair, right stamp without overprint	*1,250.*	
b.	Horiz. pair, left stamp without overprint	*1,750.*	
c.	Booklet pane of 6, imperf. margins	550.00	
d.	Overprint reading down	200.00	
e.	As "d," inverted center	650.00	*750.00*
f.	As "e," booklet pane of 6, handmade, perf. margins	*8,000.*	
g.	As "c," handmade, perf. margins	900.00	800.00
h.	As No. 39, "CANAL" only		1,100.
40 A12	5c deep blue & black	20.00	2.50
a.	With Cordoba portrait of 2c		*12,500.*
41 A14	10c violet & black	57.50	8.00
	Nos. 38-41 (4)	96.50	14.60

Map of Panama Canal A18

Balboa Takes Possession of the Pacific Ocean A19

Gatun Locks — A20

Culebra Cut — A21

1915, Mar. 1

Blue Overprint, Type II

42 A18	1c dark green & black	8.75	6.50
43 A19	2c carmine & black	12.00	4.25
44 A20	5c blue & black	11.00	5.75
45 A21	10c orange & black	20.00	11.00
	Nos. 42-45 (4)	51.75	27.50

Black Overprint Reading Up

Type III Overprint: Similar to Type I but letters appear thinner, particularly the lower bar of "L," "Z" and "E." Impressions are often light, rough and irregular, and not centered.

1915-20

46 A15	1c green & black	175.00	125.00
a.	Overprint reading down	375.00	
b.	Double overprint	225.00	
c.	"ZONE" double	*6,500.*	
d.	Double overprint, one reads "ZONE CANAL"	2,000.	
47 A11	2c orange vermilion & black	2,750.	60.00
48 A12	5c deep blue & black	450.00	130.00
	Nos. 46-48 (3)	3,375.	315.00

Spacing between words of overprint on Nos. 46-48 is 9¼mm; spacing varieties are not known. This should not be confused with a fairly common 9¼mm spacing of the 2c value of type I, nor with an uncommon 9¼mm spacing variety of the 5c of type I.

S.S. "Panama" in Culebra Cut — A22

S.S. "Panama" in Culebra Cut — A23

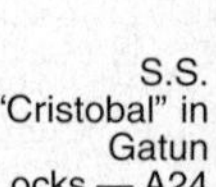

S.S. "Cristobal" in Gatun Locks — A24

1917, Jan. 23

Blue Overprint, Type II

49 A22 12c purple & black 17.50 5.25
50 A23 15c bright blue & black 50.00 17.50
51 A24 24c yellow brown & black 37.50 14.00
Nos. 49-51 (3) 105.00 36.75

Black Overprint Reading Up

Type IV: "C" thick at bottom, "E" with center bar same length as top and bottom bars

1918-20

52 A15 1c green & black 32.50 11.00
a. Overprint reading down 175.00 —
b. Booklet pane of 6 600.00
c. Booklet pane of 6, left vertical row of 3 without overprint 7,500.
d. Booklet pane of 6, right vertical row of 3 with double overprint 7,500.
e. Horiz. bklt. pair, left stamp without overprint 3,000.
f. Horiz. bklt. pair, right stamp with double overprint 3,000.
g. Double overprint, booklet single 3,000.
53 A11 2c vermilion & black 110.00 6.50
a. Overprint reading down 150.00 150.00
b. Horiz. pair, right stamp without ovpt. (from misregistered overprints) 2,000.
c. Booklet pane of 6 1,050.
d. Booklet pane of 6, left vertical row of 3 without overprint 15,000.
e. Horiz. bklt. pair, left stamp without overprint 3,000.
f. Horiz. sheet pair, one without overprint (from foldover) 1,750.
54 A12 5c deep blue & black 150.00 35.00
Nos. 52-54 (3) 292.50 52.50

No. 53e used is unique and is on cover.

Black Overprint Reading Up

Type V: Smaller block type 1¾mm high. "A" with flat top

1920-21

55 A15 1c light green & black 22.50 3.50
a. Overprint reading down 300.00 225.00
b. Horiz. pair, right stamp without ovpt. 1,750.
c. Horiz. pair, left stamp without ovpt. 1,000.
d. "ZONE" only 4,000. —
e. Booklet pane of 6 2,250.
f. As No. 55, "CANAL" double 2,000.
56 A11 2c orange vermilion & black 8.50 1.75
a. Double overprint 600.00
b. Double overprint, one reading down 650.00
c. Horiz. pair, right stamp without overprint 1,500.
d. Horiz. pair, left stamp without overprint 1,000.
e. Vertical pair, one without overprint 1,500.
f. "ZONE" double 1,000.
g. Booklet pane of 6 850.00
h. As No. 56, "CANAL" double 800.
57 A12 5c deep blue & black 300.00 47.50
a. Horiz. pair, right stamp without overprint 2,250.
b. Horiz. pair, left stamp without overprint 2,250.
Nos. 55-57 (3) 331.00 52.75

Drydock at Balboa A25

Ship in Pedro Miguel Locks — A26

1920, Sept.

Black Overprint Type V

58 A25 50c orange & black 260.00 160.00
59 A26 1b dark violet & black 175.00 50.00

Jose Vallarino — A27

The "Land Gate" — A28

Bolivar's Tribute — A29

Municipal Building in 1821 and 1921 — A30

Statue of Balboa — A31

Tomas Herrera — A32

Jose de Fabrega — A33

Type V overprint in black, reading up, on all values except the 5c which is overprinted with larger type in red

1921, Nov. 13

60 A27 1c green 4.00 1.50
a. "CANAL" double 2,250.
b. Booklet pane of 6 900.00
61 A28 2c carmine 2.75 1.00
a. Overprint reading down 200.00 225.00
b. Double overprint 900.00
c. Vertical pair, one without overprint 3,500.
d. "CANAL" double 1,900.
f. Booklet pane of 6 2,000.
62 A29 5c blue (R) 10.00 3.50
a. Overprint reading down (R) 60.00
63 A30 10c violet 18.00 7.50
a. Overprint, reading down 90.00
64 A31 15c light blue 50.00 17.50
65 A32 24c black brown 70.00 22.50
66 A33 50c black 150.00 85.00
Nos. 60-66 (7) 304.75 138.50

Experts question the status of the 5c with a small type V overprint in red or black.

Type III overprint in black, reading up

1924, Jan. 28

67 A27 1c green 500. 200.
a. "ZONE CANAL" reading down 800.
b. "ZONE" only, reading down 1,900.
c. Se-tenant pair, #67a and 67b 2,750.

Coat of Arms — A34

1924, Feb.

68 A34 1c dark green 10.00 4.50
69 A34 2c carmine 7.00 2.75

The 5c to lb values were prepared but never issued. See listing in the Scott U.S. specialized catalogue.

United States Nos. 551-554, 557, 562, 564-566, 569, 570 and 571 Overprinted in Red (No. 70) or Black (all others)

Type A: Letters "A" with Flat Tops

1924-25 Unwmk. *Perf. 11*

70 A154 ½c olive brown .25 .70
Never hinged .45
71 A155 1c deep green 1.25 1.00
Never hinged 2.30
a. Inverted overprint 500.00 500.00
b. "ZONE" inverted 350.00 325.00
c. "CANAL" only 1,250.
d. "ZONE CANAL" 500.00
e. Booklet pane of 6 80.00
72 A156 1½c yellow brown 2.00 1.70
Never hinged 3.25
73 A157 2c carmine 7.00 1.70
Never hinged 11.00
a. Booklet pane of 6 175.00
74 A160 5c dark blue 17.50 7.50
Never hinged 27.50
75 A165 10c orange 42.50 20.00
Never hinged 70.00
76 A167 12c brown violet 32.50 32.50
Never hinged 62.50
a. "ZONE" inverted 3,750. 2,250.
77 A168 14c dark blue 27.50 22.50
Never hinged 42.50
78 A169 15c gray 47.50 37.50
Never hinged 75.00
79 A172 30c olive brown 32.50 20.00
Never hinged 52.50
80 A173 50c lilac 75.00 45.00
Never hinged 150.00
81 A174 $1 violet brown 225.00 95.00
Never hinged 375.00
Nos. 70-81 (12) 510.50 285.10

Normal spacing between words of the overprint is 9¼mm. Minor spacing variations are known.

All examples of Nos. 71b and 76a have a natural straight edge at right.

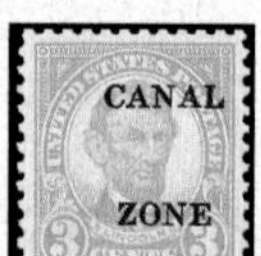
Type B: Letters "A" with Sharp Pointed Tops

1925-28

84 A157 2c carmine 27.50 8.00
Never hinged 45.00
a. "CANAL" only 2,250.
b. "ZONE CANAL" 500.00
c. Horizontal pair, one without overprint 3,500.
d. Booklet pane of 6 175.00
e. Vertical pair, "a" and "b" se-tenant 3,500.
85 A158 3c violet 3.75 3.00
Never hinged 6.00
a. "ZONE ZONE" 550.00 550.00
86 A160 5c dark blue 3.50 2.75
Never hinged 6.00
a. "ZONE ZONE" (LR18) 1,000.
b. "CANAL" inverted (LR7) 950.00
c. Inverted overprint 500.00
d. Horizontal pair, one without overprint 3,250.
e. Overprinted "ZONE CANAL" 350.00
f. "ZONE" only 2,000.
g. Vertical pair, one without overprint, other overprint inverted 2,500.
h. "CANAL" only 2,250.
87 A165 10c orange 35.00 12.00
Never hinged 52.50
a. "ZONE ZONE" (LR18) 3,000.
88 A167 12c brown violet 20.00 12.50
Never hinged 34.00
a. "ZONE ZONE" (LR18) 5,000.
89 A168 14c dark blue 27.50 16.00
Never hinged 42.50
90 A169 15c gray 7.50 4.50
Never hinged 11.50
a. "ZONE ZONE" (LR18) 5,500.
91 A187 17c black 4.50 3.00
Never hinged 7.50
a. "ZONE" only 1,000.
b. "CANAL" only 2,000.
c. "ZONE CANAL" 275.00
92 A170 20c carmine rose 7.25 3.25
Never hinged 11.00
a. "CANAL" inverted (UR48) 6,500.
b. "ZONE" inverted (LL76) 4,750.
c. "ZONE CANAL" (LL91) 4,750.
93 A172 30c olive brown 5.75 3.75
Never hinged 9.00
94 A173 50c lilac 225.00 165.00
Never hinged 375.00
95 A174 $1 violet brown 120.00 55.00
Never hinged 265.00
Nos. 84-95 (12) 487.25 288.75

1926

96 A188 2c carmine rose 4.50 3.75
Never hinged 6.75

On this stamp there is a space of 5mm instead of 9mm between the two words of the overprint.

Overprint Type B in Black on U.S. Nos. 583, 584, 591

1926-27 *Perf. 10*

97 A157 2c carmine 47.50 11.00
Never hinged 80.00
a. Pair, one without overprint 2,750.
b. Booklet pane of 6 500.00
c. "CANAL" only 2,000.
d. "ZONE" only 2,750.
98 A158 3c violet 7.50 4.25
Never hinged 11.00
99 A165 10c orange 18.00 7.50
Never hinged 27.50
Nos. 97-99 (3) 73.00 22.75

No. 97d is valued in the grade of fine. Very fine examples are not known.

Overprint Type B in Black on U.S. Nos. 632, 634 (Type I), 635, 637, 642

1927-31 *Perf. 11x10½*

100 A155 1c green 1.60 1.40
Never hinged 2.40
a. Vertical pair, one without overprint 3,750.
101 A157 2c carmine 1.75 1.00
Never hinged 2.50
a. Booklet pane of 6 200.00
102 A158 3c violet 4.50 2.75
Never hinged 6.75
a. Booklet pane of 6, hand-made, perf. margins 6,500.
103 A160 5c dark blue 25.00 10.00
Never hinged 45.00
104 A165 10c orange 17.50 10.00
Never hinged 26.00
Nos. 100-104 (5) 50.35 25.15

Wet and Dry Printings

Canal Zone stamps printed by both the "wet" and "dry" process are Nos. 105, 108-109, 111-114, 117, 138-140, C21-C24, C26, J25, J27. Starting with Nos. 147 and C27, the Bureau of Engraving and Printing used the "dry" method exclusively. Late dry printings of Nos. 105, 108, 112-114, 117, 138 and 152 also exist with dull gum.

See note on Wet and Dry Printings following U.S. No. 1029.

Maj. Gen. William Crawford Gorgas A35

Maj. Gen. George Washington Goethals A36

Gaillard Cut — A37

Maj. Gen. Harry Foote Hodges A38

Lt. Col. David DuB. Gaillard A39

Maj. Gen. William L. Sibert — A40

Jackson Smith — A41

Rear Adm. Harry H. Rousseau A42

Col. Sydney B. Williamson A43

J.C.S. Blackburn — A44

1928-40 *Perf. 11*

105	A35	1c green	.25	.25
		Never hinged	.25	
106	A36	2c carmine	.25	.25
		Never hinged	.30	
	a.	Booklet pane of 6	15.00	*20.00*
		Never hinged	22.50	
107	A37	5c blue	1.00	.40
		Never hinged	1.30	
108	A38	10c orange	.25	.25
		Never hinged	.25	
109	A39	12c brown violet	.75	.60
		Never hinged	1.00	
110	A40	14c blue	.85	.85
		Never hinged	1.20	
111	A41	15c gray black	.40	.35
		Never hinged	.55	
112	A42	20c dark brown	.60	.25
		Never hinged	.80	
113	A43	30c black	.80	.70
		Never hinged	1.10	
114	A44	50c rose lilac	1.50	.65
		Never hinged	2.00	
		Nos. 105-114 (10)	6.65	4.55

For surcharges and overprints, see Nos. J21-J24, O1-O8.
Coils are listed as Nos. 160-161.

United States Nos. 720 and 695 Overprinted type B

1933, Jan. 14 *Perf. 11x10½*

115	A226	3c deep violet	2.75	.25
		Never hinged	4.00	
	b.	"CANAL" only	*2,600.*	
	c.	Booklet pane of 6, handmade, perf. margins	80.00	—
116	A168	14c dark blue	4.50	3.50
		Never hinged	7.00	
	a.	"ZONE CANAL"	*1,500.*	

Gen. George Washington Goethals — A45

20th anniversary of the opening of the Panama Canal.

1934 *Perf. 11*

117	A45	3c red violet	.25	.25
		Never hinged	.30	
	a.	Booklet pane of 6	*12.50*	*32.50*
	b.	As "a," handmade, perf. margins	160.00	—

Coil is listed as No. 153.

Catalogue values for unused stamps in this section, from this point to the end, are for Never Hinged items.

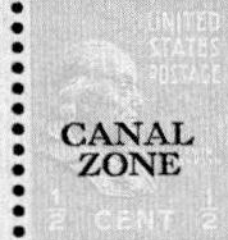

United States Nos. 803 and 805 Overprinted in Black

1939, Sept. 1 *Perf. 11x10½*

118	A275	½c red orange	.25	.25
119	A277	1½c bister brown	.25	.25

Panama Canal Anniversary Issue

Balboa-Before — A46

Balboa-After — A47

Gaillard Cut-Before A48

Gaillard Cut-After A49

Bas Obispo-Before — A50

Bas Obispo-After A51

Gatun Locks-Before — A52

Gatun Locks-After A53

Canal Channel-Before A54

Canal Channel-After — A55

Gamboa-Before A56

Gamboa-After — A57

Pedro Miguel Locks-Before — A58

Pedro Miguel Locks-After A59

Gatun Spillway-Before A60

Gatun Spillway-After — A61

25th anniversary of the opening of the Panama Canal.

1939, Aug. 15

120	A46	1c yellow green	.60	.30
121	A47	2c rose carmine	.70	.35
122	A48	3c purple	.70	.25
123	A49	5c dark blue	2.00	1.25
124	A50	6c red orange	4.50	3.00
125	A51	7c black	5.00	3.00
126	A52	8c green	7.00	3.50
127	A53	10c ultramarine	5.50	5.00
128	A54	11c blue green	11.00	8.00
129	A55	12c brown carmine	11.00	7.50
130	A56	14c dark violet	11.00	7.00
131	A57	15c olive green	14.00	5.75
132	A58	18c rose pink	16.00	8.50
133	A59	20c brown	17.50	7.50
134	A60	25c orange	27.50	17.50
135	A61	50c violet brown	30.00	6.00
		Nos. 120-135 (16)	164.00	84.40

Maj. Gen. George W. Davis A62

Gov. Charles E. Magoon A63

Theodore Roosevelt A64

John F. Stevens A65

John F. Wallace — A66

1946-49

Size: 19x22mm

136	A62	½c bright red	.40	.25
137	A63	1½c chocolate	.40	.25
138	A64	2c light rose carmine	.25	.25
139	A65	5c dark blue	.35	.25
140	A66	25c green	.85	.55
		Nos. 136-140 (5)	2.25	1.55

See Nos. 155, 162, 164. For overprint, see No. O9.

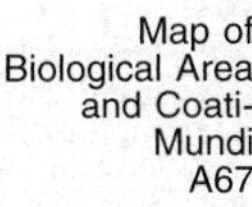

Map of Biological Area and Coati-Mundi A67

25th anniversary of the establishment of the Canal Zone Biological Area on Barro Colorado Island.

1948, Apr. 17

141	A67	10c black	1.75	1.00

"Forty-niners" Arriving at Chagres A68

Journey by "Bungo" to Las Cruces A69

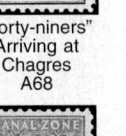

Las Cruces Trail to Panama A70

Departure for San Francisco A71

Centenary of the California Gold Rush.

1949, June 1

142	A68	3c blue	.65	.25
143	A69	6c violet	.65	.30
144	A70	12c bright blue green	1.75	.90
145	A71	18c deep red lilac	2.00	1.50
		Nos. 142-145 (4)	5.05	2.95

Workers in Culebra Cut — A72

Early Railroad Scene — A73

Contribution of West Indian laborers in the construction of the Panama Canal.

1951, Aug. 15

146	A72	10c carmine	3.50	1.50

Centenary of the completion of the Panama Railroad and the first transcontinental railroad trip in the Americas.

1955, Jan. 28

147	A73	3c violet	1.00	.60

Gorgas Hospital and Ancon Hill — A74

75th anniversary of Gorgas Hospital.

1957, Nov. 17
148 A74 3c black .45 .35

S.S. Ancon A75

1958, Aug. 30
149 A75 4c greenish blue .40 .30

Roosevelt Medal and Map — A76

Centenary of the birth of Theodore Roosevelt (1858-1919).

1958, Nov. 15
150 A76 4c brown .60 .30

Boy Scout Badge — A77

Administration Building — A78

50th anniversary of the Boy Scouts of America.

1960, Feb. 8 Giori Press Printing
151 A77 4c dark blue, red & bister .55 .40

1960, Nov. 1
152 A78 4c rose lilac .25 .25

Types of 1934, 1960 and 1946 Coil Stamps

1960-62 Unwmk. ***Perf. 10 Vertically***
153 A45 3c deep violet .25 .25

Perf. 10 Horizontally
154 A78 4c dull rose lilac .25 .25

Perf. 10 Vertically
155 A65 5c deep blue .25 .25
Nos. 153-155 (3) .75 .75

Girl Scout Badge and Camp at Gatun Lake A79

50th anniversary of the Girl Scouts.

Giori Press Printing

1962, Mar. 12 ***Perf. 11***
156 A79 4c blue, dark green & bister .40 .30

Thatcher Ferry Bridge and Map of Western Hemisphere A80

Opening of the Thatcher Ferry Bridge, spanning the Panama Canal.

Giori Press Printing

1962, Oct. 12
157 A80 4c black & silver .35 .25
a. Silver (bridge) omitted *(50)* 8,000.
Hinged 6,000.

Goethals Memorial, Balboa A81

Fort San Lorenzo A82

1968-71 Giori Press Printing
158 A81 6c green & ultra. .30 .30
159 A82 8c slate green, blue, dark brown & ocher .35 .25

Types of 1928, 1932 and 1948 Coil Stamps

1975, Feb. 14 ***Perf. 10 Vertically***
160 A35 1c green .25 .25
161 A38 10c orange .70 .40
162 A66 25c yellow green 2.75 2.75
Nos. 160-162 (3) 3.70 3.40

Dredge Cascadas A83

Giori Press Printing

1976, Feb. 23
163 A83 13c multicolored .35 .25
a. Booklet pane of 4 3.00 —

No. 163a exists with and without staple holes in selvage tab.

Stevens Type of 1946

1977 ***Perf. 11x10½***

Size: 19x22½mm

164 A65 5c deep blue .60 .85
a. Tagged, dull gum 12.00 15.00

No. 164 exists with both shiny gum and dull gum. Stamps with dull gum exist with and without tagging.

No. 164a exists even though there was no equipment in the Canal Zone to detect tagging.

Towing Locomotive, Ship in Lock — A84

1978, Oct. 25 ***Perf. 11***
165 A84 15c dp grn & bl grn .35 .25

AIR POST STAMPS

Nos. 105-106 Surcharged in Dark Blue

Type I - Flag of "Five" pointing up

Type II - Flag of "5" curved

1929-31 Engr. Unwmk. ***Perf. 11***
C1 A35 15c on 1c green, type I 7.50 5.00
C2 A35 15c on 1c yellow green, type II 65.00 47.50
C3 A36 25c on 2c carmine 3.50 2.00
Nos. C1-C3 (3) 76.00 54.50

Nos. 114 and 106 Surcharged

AIR MAIL
≡10c

1929, Dec. 31
C4 A44 10c on 50c lilac 8.00 5.75
C5 A36 20c on 2c carmine 4.50 1.25
a. Dropped "2" in surcharge 85.00 60.00

Catalogue values for unused stamps in this section, from this point to the end, are for Never Hinged items.

Gaillard Cut — AP1

1931-49
C6 AP1 4c red violet .75 .65
C7 AP1 5c yellow green .60 .30
C8 AP1 6c yellow brown .75 .35
C9 AP1 10c orange 1.00 .35
C10 AP1 15c blue 1.25 .30
C11 AP1 20c red violet 2.00 .25
C12 AP1 30c rose lake 6.50 1.50
C13 AP1 40c yellow 3.50 1.10
C14 AP1 $1 black 9.00 1.60
Nos. C6-C14 (9) 25.35 6.40

For overprints, see Nos. CO1-CO14.

Douglas Plane over Sosa Hill — AP2

Planes and Map of Central America AP3

Pan American Clipper and Scene near Fort Amador AP4

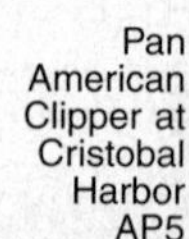

Pan American Clipper at Cristobal Harbor AP5

Pan American Clipper over Gaillard Cut — AP6

Pan American Clipper Landing AP7

10th anniversary of Air Mail service and the 25th anniversary of the opening of the Panama Canal.

1939, July 15
C15 AP2 5c greenish black 4.00 2.25
C16 AP3 10c dull violet 3.50 3.00
C17 AP4 15c light brown 5.00 1.00
C18 AP5 25c blue 17.50 8.00
C19 AP6 30c rose carmine 17.50 6.00
C20 AP7 $1 green 45.00 27.50
Nos. C15-C20 (6) 92.50 47.75

Globe and Wing — AP8

1951, July 16
C21 AP8 4c lt red violet .75 .35
C22 AP8 6c lt brown .50 .25
C23 AP8 10c lt red orange .90 .35
C24 AP8 21c lt blue 8.00 4.00
C25 AP8 31c cerise 9.50 3.75
a. Horiz. pair, imperf. vert. 1,250. —
C26 AP8 80c lt gray black 6.00 1.50
Nos. C21-C26 (6) 25.65 10.20

Flat Plate Printing

1958, Aug. 16 Unwmk. ***Perf. 11***
C27 AP8 5c yellow green 1.00 .60
C28 AP8 7c olive 1.00 .45
C29 AP8 15c brown violet 4.50 2.75
C30 AP8 25c orange yellow 12.50 2.75
C31 AP8 35c dark blue 9.00 2.75
Nos. C27-C31 (5) 28.00 9.30
Nos. C21-C31 (11) 53.65 19.50

See No. C34.

Emblem of U.S. Army Caribbean School AP9

US Army Caribbean School for Latin America at Fort Gulick.

1961, Nov. 21
C32 AP9 15c red & blue 1.60 .75

Malaria Eradication Emblem and Mosquito AP10

World Health Organization drive to eradicate malaria.

1962, Sept. 24
C33 AP10 7c yellow & black .50 .40

Globe-Wing Type of 1951

1963, Jan. 7 ***Perf. 10½x11***
C34 AP8 8c carmine .75 .30

Alliance Emblem AP11

2nd anniv. of the Alliance for Progress, which aims to stimulate economic growth and raise living standards in Latin America.

1963, Aug. 17 ***Perf. 11***
C35 AP11 15c gray, grn & dk ultra 1.50 .85

Jet over Canal Zone Views AP12

50th anniversary of the opening of the Panama Canal.

Designs: 6c, Cristobal. 8c, Gatun Locks. 15c, Madden Dam. 20c, Gaillard Cut. 30c, Miraflores Locks. 80c, Balboa.

1964, Aug. 15

C36	AP12	6c green & black	.60	.35
C37	AP12	8c rose red & black	.60	.35
C38	AP12	15c blue & black	1.25	.75
C39	AP12	20c rose lilac & black	1.60	1.00
C40	AP12	30c reddish brown & black	2.75	2.25
C41	AP12	80c olive bister & black	4.75	3.00
		Nos. C36-C41 (6)	11.55	7.70

Seal and Jet Plane
AP13

1965, July 15

C42	AP13	6c green & black	.50	.30
C43	AP13	8c rose red & black	.45	.25
C44	AP13	15c blue & black	.75	.25
C45	AP13	20c lilac & black	.80	.30
C46	AP13	30c redsh brn & blk	1.10	.30
C47	AP13	80c bister & black	2.50	.75
		Nos. C42-C47 (6)	6.10	2.15

1968-76

C48	AP13	10c dull orange & black	.35	.25
a.		Booklet pane of 4	4.25	—
C49	AP13	11c olive & black	.35	.25
a.		Booklet pane of 4	3.50	—
C50	AP13	13c emerald & black	.85	.25
a.		Booklet pane of 4	6.00	—
C51	AP13	22c vio & blk	1.10	*2.00*
C52	AP13	25c pale yellow green & black	.80	.70
C53	AP13	35c salmon & black	1.25	*2.00*
		Nos. C48-C53 (6)	4.70	*5.45*

AIR POST OFFICIAL STAMPS

Beginning in March 1915, stamps for use on official mail were identified by a large "P" perforated through each stamp. These were replaced by overprinted issues in 1941. The use of official stamps was discontinued December 31, 1951. During their currency, they were not for sale in mint condition and were sold to the public only when canceled with a parcel post rotary canceler reading "Balboa Heights, Canal Zone" between two wavy lines.

After having been withdrawn from use, mint stamps (except Nos. CO8-CO12 and O3, O8) were made available to the public at face value for three months beginning Jan. 2, 1952. **Values for used examples of Nos. CO1-CO7, CO14, O1-O2, O4-O9, are for canceled-to-order stamps with original gum, postally used stamps being worth more.**

Nos. C7, C9-C14 Overprinted in Black

Two types of overprint

Type I — "PANAMA CANAL" 19-20mm long

1941-42 — Unwmk. — *Perf. 11*

CO1	AP1	5c yellow green	6.50	1.50
CO2	AP1	10c orange	8.50	1.75
CO3	AP1	15c blue	11.00	1.75
CO4	AP1	20c red violet	13.00	4.00
CO5	AP1	30c rose lake	17.50	5.00
CO6	AP1	40c yellow	17.50	7.50
CO7	AP1	$1 black	20.00	10.00
		Nos. CO1-CO7 (7)	94.00	31.50

Overprint varieties occur on Nos. CO1-CO7 and CO14: "O" of "OFFICIAL" over "N" of "PANAMA" (entire third row). "O" of "OFFICIAL" broken at top (position 31). "O" of "OFFICIAL" over second "A" of "PANAMA" (position 45). First "F" of "OFFICIAL" over second "A" of "PANAMA" (position 50).

1941, Sept. 22

Type II — "PANAMA CANAL" 17mm long

CO8	AP1	5c yellow green	—	160.00
CO9	AP1	10c orange	—	275.00
CO10	AP1	20c red violet	—	175.00
CO11	AP1	30c rose lake	*1,000.*	65.00
CO12	AP1	40c yellow	—	180.00
		Nos. CO8-CO12 (5)		855.00

1947, Nov.

Type I — "PANAMA CANAL" 19-20mm long

CO14	AP1	6c yellow brown	13.00	5.50
a.		Inverted overprint *(50)*		*2,500.*

POSTAGE DUE STAMPS

Prior to 1914, many of the postal issues were handstamped "Postage Due" and used as postage due stamps.

Postage Due Stamps of the U.S. Nos. J45a, J46a and J49a Overprinted in Black

1914, Mar. — Wmk. 190 — *Perf. 12*

J1	D2	1c rose carmine	85.00	15.00
J2	D2	2c rose carmine	250.00	42.50
J3	D2	10c rose carmine	1,000.	40.00
		Nos. J1-J3 (3)	1,335.	97.50

Castle Gate (See footnote) — D1

Statue of Columbus
D2

Pedro J. Sosa
D3

1915, Mar. — Unwmk.

Blue Overprint, Type II, on Postage Due Stamps of Panama

J4	D1	1c olive brown	12.50	5.00
J5	D2	2c olive brown	225.00	17.50
J6	D3	10c olive brown	50.00	10.00
		Nos. J4-J6 (3)	287.50	32.50

Type D1 was intended to show a gate of San Lorenzo Castle, Chagres, and is so labeled. By error the stamp actually shows the main gate of San Geronimo Castle, Portobelo.

Surcharged in Red

1915, Nov.

J7	D1	1c on 1c olive brown	110.00	15.00
J8	D2	2c on 2c olive brown	25.00	7.50
J9	D3	10c on 10c olive brown	22.50	5.00
		Nos. J7-J9 (3)	157.50	27.50

Columbus Statue — D4

Capitol, Panama City — D5

1919, Dec.

Surcharged in Carmine by Panama Canal Press, Mount Hope, C. Z.

"Canal Zone" Type III

J10	D4	2c on 2c olive brown	30.00	12.50
J11	D5	4c on 4c olive brown	35.00	15.00
a.		"ZONE" omitted	*9,250.*	
b.		"4" omitted	*8,500.*	

Blue Overprint, Type V, on Postage Due Stamp of Panama

1922

J11C	D1	1c dark olive brown	—	10.00
d.		"CANAL ZONE" reading down	200.00	

U.S. Postage Due Stamps Nos. J61, J26b and J65b Overprinted in Black.

Type A

Letters "A" with Flat Tops

1924, July 1 — *Perf. 11*

J12	D2	1c carmine rose	110.00	27.50
J13	D2	2c deep claret	55.00	15.00
J14	D2	10c deep claret	250.00	50.00
		Nos. J12-J14 (3)	415.00	92.50

U.S. Postage Stamps Nos. 552, 554 and 562 Overprinted Type A and additional Overprint in Red or Blue

1925, Feb.

J15	A155	1c deep green (R)	90.00	15.00
J16	A157	2c carmine (Bl)	22.50	7.00
J17	A165	10c orange (R)	55.00	11.00
a.		"POSTAGE DUE" double	800.00	
b.		"E" of "POSTAGE" omitted	750.00	
c.		As "b," "POSTAGE DUE" double	*3,250.*	
		Nos. J15-J17 (3)	167.50	33.00

Overprinted Type B

Letters "A" with Sharp Pointed Tops On U.S. Postage Due Stamps Nos. J61, J62, J65, J65a

1925, June 24

J18	D2	1c carmine rose	8.00	3.00
a.		"ZONE ZONE" (LR18)	1,500.	
J19	D2	2c carmine rose	15.00	3.00
a.		"ZONE ZONE" (LR18)	1,500.	
J20	D2	10c carmine rose	150.00	20.00
a.		Vert. pair, one without ovpt.	*3,000.*	
b.		10c rose red	*250.00*	150.00
c.		As "b," double overprint	*450.00*	—
		Nos. J18-J20 (3)	173.00	26.00

Regular Issue of 1928-29 Surcharged

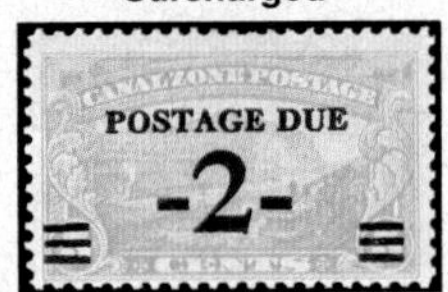

1929-30

J21	A37	1c on 5c blue	3.75	1.75
		Never hinged	7.50	
a.		"POSTAGE DUE" missing	*5,500.*	
J22	A37	2c on 5c blue	6.50	2.50
		Never hinged	13.00	
J23	A37	5c on 5c blue	6.50	2.75
		Never hinged	13.00	
J24	A37	10c on 5c blue	6.50	2.75
		Never hinged	13.00	
		Nos. J21-J24 (4)	23.25	9.75

On No. J23 the three short horizontal bars in the lower corners of the surcharge are omitted.

Canal Zone Seal — D6

1932-41

J25	D6	1c claret	.25	.25
		Never hinged	.30	
J26	D6	2c claret	.25	.25
		Never hinged	.30	
J27	D6	5c claret	.35	.25
		Never hinged	.50	
J28	D6	10c claret	1.75	1.50
		Never hinged	2.25	
J29	D6	15c claret	1.25	1.00
		Never hinged	1.60	
		Nos. J25-J29 (5)	3.85	3.25

OFFICIAL STAMPS

See note at beginning of Air Post Official Stamps

Regular Issues of 1928-34 Overprinted in Black

Type 1

Type 2

Type 1 — "PANAMA" 10mm long
Type 1a — "PANAMA" 9mm long

Unwmk.

1941, Mar. 31 — Engr. — *Perf. 11*

O1	A35	1c yellow green, type 1	2.00	.40
O2	A45	3c deep violet, type 1	3.75	.75
O3	A37	5c blue, type 2	*1,000.*	25.00
O4	A38	10c orange, type 1	7.50	1.90
O5	A41	15c gray black, type 1	15.00	2.25
O6	A42	20c olive brown, type 1	17.50	2.75
O7	A44	50c lilac, type 1	42.50	5.50
O8	A44	50c rose lilac, type 1a		600.00

No. 139 with Same Overprint in Black

1947, Feb.

O9	A65	5c deep blue, type 1	12.50	3.75

CUBA

'kyü-bə

LOCATION — The largest island of the West Indies; south of Florida.
GOVT. — socialist; under US military governor 1899-1902 and US provisional governor 1906-1909.
AREA — 44,206 sq. mi.
POP. — 9,710,000 (1981)
CAPITAL — Havana

Formerly a Spanish possession, Cuba's attempts to gain freedom led to US intervention in 1898. Under Treaty of Paris of that year, Spain relinquished the island to US trust. In 1902, a republic was established and Cuban Congress took over government from US military authorities.

100 Cents = 1 Dollar

Watermark

Wmk. 191 — Double-lined "USPS" in Capitals

Values for Nos. 176-220 are for stamps in the grade of fine and in sound condition where such exist. Values for Nos. 221-J4 are for very fine examples.

King Alfonso XIII — N2

Issued under Administration of the United States

Puerto Principe Issue

Issues of Cuba of 1898 and 1896 Surcharged

a

b

Black Surcharge on Nos. 156-158, 160

1898-99

Types a, c, d, e, f, g and h are 17½mm high, the others are 19½mm high.

176 A19 (a) 1c on 1m org brn 50.00 30.00
177 A19 (b) 1c on 1m org brn 45.00 35.00
a. Broken figure "1" 75.00 65.00
b. Inverted surcharge 200.00
d. As "a," inverted *250.00*

c

d

178 A19 (c) 2c on 2m org brn 24.00 20.00
a. Inverted surcharge 250.00 50.00
179 A19 (d) 2c on 2m org brn 40.00 35.00
a. Inverted surcharge 350.00 100.00

k

l

179B A19 (k) 3c on 1m org brn 300. 175.
c. Double surcharge 1,500. 750.

An unused example is known with "cents" omitted.

179D A19 (l) 3c on 1m org brn *1,500.* *750.*
e. Double surcharge — —

e

f

179F A19 (e) 3c on 2m org brn *1,500.*

Value is for examples with minor faults.

179G A19 (f) 3c on 2m org brn — *2,000.*

Value is for examples with minor faults.

180 A19 (e) 3c on 3m org brn 30. *30.*
a. Inverted surcharge 110.
181 A19 (f) 3c on 3m org brn 75. 75.
a. Inverted surcharge *200.*

g

h

i

j

182 A19 (g) 5c on 1m org brn 700. 200.
a. Inverted surcharge *500.*
183 A19 (h) 5c on 1m org brn *1,300.* *500.*
a. Inverted surcharge *700.*
184 A19 (g) 5c on 2m org brn 750. 275.
185 A19 (h) 5c on 2m org brn 1,500. 500.
186 A19 (g) 5c on 3m org brn 650. 175.
a. Inverted surcharge 1,200. 700.
187 A19 (h) 5c on 3m org brn 400.
a. Inverted surcharge 1,000.
188 A19 (g) 5c on 5m org brn 80. 60.
a. Inverted surcharge 400. 200.
b. Double surcharge — —
189 A19 (h) 5c on 5m org brn 350. 250.
a. Inverted surcharge 425.
b. Double surcharge — —

The 2nd printing of Nos. 188-189 has shiny ink. Values are for the 1st printing.

189C A19 (i) 5c on 5m org brn *7,500.*

Black Surcharge on No. P25

190 N2 (g) 5c on ½m bl grn 250. 75.
a. Inverted surcharge 500. 150.
b. Pair, one without surcharge 500.

Value for 190b is for pair with unsurcharged stamp at right. Also exists with unsurcharged stamp at left.

191 N2 (h) 5c on ½m bl grn 300. 90.
a. Inverted surcharge 200.
192 N2 (i) 5c on ½m bl grn 550. 200.
a. Dbl. surch., one diagonal *11,500.*
193 N2 (j) 5c on ½m bl grn 800. 300.

Red Surcharge on No. 161

196 A19 (k) 3c on 1c blk vio 65. 35.
a. Inverted surcharge 325.
197 A19 (l) 3c on 1c blk vio 125. 55.
a. Inverted surcharge 400.
198 A19 (i) 5c on 1c blk vio 25. 30.
a. Inverted surcharge 125.
b. Surcharge vert. reading up *3,500.*
c. Double surcharge *400.* *600.*
d. Double invtd. surch. —

Value for No. 198b is for surcharge reading up. One example is known with surcharge reading down.

199 A19 (j) 5c on 1c blk vio 55. 55.
a. Inverted surcharge 250.
b. Vertical surcharge *2,000.*
c. Double surcharge 1,000. 700.

m

200 A19 (m) 10c on 1c blk vio 20. *50.*
a. Broken figure "1" 40. *100.*

Black Surcharge on Nos. P26-P30

201 N2 (k) 3c on 1m bl grn 350. 350.
a. Inverted surcharge 450.
b. "EENTS" 550. 450.
c. As "b", inverted 850.
202 N2 (l) 3c on 1m bl grn 550. 400.
a. Inverted surcharge 850.
203 N2 (k) 3c on 2m bl grn 850. 400.
a. "EENTS" 1,250. 500.
b. Inverted surcharge 1,150.
c. As "a," inverted 950.
204 N2 (l) 3c on 2m bl grn 1,250. 600.
a. Inverted surcharge 750.
205 N2 (k) 3c on 3m bl grn 900. 400.
a. Inverted surcharge 750.
b. "EENTS" 1,250. 450.
c. As "b," inverted 700.
206 N2 (l) 3c on 3m bl grn 1,200. 550.
a. Inverted surcharge 700.
211 N2 (i) 5c on 1m bl grn 1,800.
a. "EENTS" — 2,500.
212 N2 (j) 5c on 1m bl grn 2,250.
213 N2 (i) 5c on 2m bl grn 1,800.
a. "EENTS" — 1,900.
214 N2 (j) 5c on 2m bl grn 1,750.
215 N2 (i) 5c on 3m bl grn 550.
a. "EENTS" 1,000.
216 N2 (j) 5c on 3m bl grn — 1,000.
217 N2 (i) 5c on 4m bl grn *2,500.* 900.
a. "EENTS" *3,000.* 1,500.
b. Inverted surcharge *2,000.*
c. As "a," inverted 2,000.
218 N2 (j) 5c on 4m bl grn *1,500.*
a. Inverted surcharge *2,000.*
219 N2 (i) 5c on 8m bl grn *2,500.* 1,250.
a. Inverted surcharge 1,500.
b. "EENTS" — 1,800.
c. As "b," inverted 2,500.
220 N2 (j) 5c on 8m bl grn 2,000.
a. Inverted surcharge 2,500.

Beware of forgeries of the Puerto Principe issue. Obtaining expert opinions is recommended.

United States Stamps Nos. 279, 267, 267b, 279Bf, 279Bh, 268, 281, 282C and 283 Surcharged in Black

CUBA 1 c. de PESO.

1899 **Wmk. 191** ***Perf. 12***

221 A87 1c on 1c yel grn 5.00 .40
Never hinged 12.50
222 A88 2c on 2c reddish car, III 10.00 .75
Never hinged 25.00
b. 2c on 2c vermilion, type III 10.00 .75
222A A88 2c on 2c reddish car, IV 6.00 .40
Never hinged 15.00
c. 2c on 2c vermilion, IV 6.00 .40
d. As No. 222A, inverted surcharge *5,500.* *4,500.*
223 A88 2½c on 2c reddish car, III 5.00 .80
Never hinged 12.50
b. 2½c on 2c vermilion, III 5.00 .80
223A A88 2½c on 2c reddish car, IV 3.50 .50
Never hinged 8.75
c. 2½c on 2c vermilion, IV 3.50 .50
224 A89 3c on 3c purple 12.00 1.75
Never hinged 30.00
a. Period between "B" and "A" 40.00 35.00
225 A91 5c on 5c blue 12.50 2.00
Never hinged 30.00
226 A94 10c on 10c brn, I 24.00 6.50
Never hinged 70.00
b. "CUBA" omitted *7,000.* *4,000.*
226A A94 10c on 10c brn, II *6,000.*
Nos. 221-226 (8) 78.00 13.10

The 2½c was sold and used as a 2c stamp.
Excellent counterfeits of this and the preceding issue exist, especially inverted and double surcharges.

Issues of the Republic under US Military Rule

Statue of Columbus A20

Royal Palms A21

"Cuba" — A22

Ocean Liner — A23

Cane Field — A24

1899 **Wmk. US-C (191C)** ***Perf. 12***

227 A20 1c yellow green 3.50 .25
Never hinged 8.75
228 A21 2c carmine 3.50 .25
Never hinged 8.75
a. scarlet 3.50 .25
b. Booklet pane of 6 *5,500.*
229 A22 3c purple 3.50 .30
Never hinged 8.75
230 A23 5c blue 4.50 .30
Never hinged 11.00
231 A24 10c brown 11.00 .80
Never hinged 27.50
Nos. 227-231 (5) 26.00 1.90

No. 228b was issued by the Republic.
See Nos. 233-237 in Scott Standard Catalogue Vol 2. For surcharge see No. 232.

SPECIAL DELIVERY STAMPS

Issued under Administration of the United States

US No. E5 Surcharged in Red

1899 **Wmk. 191** ***Perf. 12***

E1 SD3 10c blue 130. 100.
Never hinged 300.
a. No period after "CUBA" 575. 400.

Issue of the Republic under US Military Rule

Special Delivery Messenger SD2

Printed by the US Bureau of Engraving and Printing

1899 Wmk. US-C (191C)

Inscribed: "Immediata"

E2 SD2 10c orange 52.50 15.00
Never hinged 120.00

POSTAGE DUE STAMPS

Issued under Administration of the United States

Postage Due Stamps of the United States Nos. J38, J39, J41 and J42 Surcharged in Black Like Nos. 221-226A

D2

1899 Wmk. 191 *Perf. 12*

J1 D2 1c dp claret 45.00 5.25
Never hinged 110.00
J2 D2 2c dp claret 45.00 5.25
Never hinged 110.00
a. Inverted surcharge *4,000.*
J3 D2 5c dp claret 45.00 5.25
Never hinged 110.00
J4 D2 10c dp claret 24.00 2.50
Never hinged 60.00
Nos. J1-J4 (4) 159.00 18.25

DANISH WEST INDIES

'dā-nish 'west 'in-dēs

LOCATION — Group of islands in the West Indies, lying east of Puerto Rico
GOVT. — Danish colony
AREA — 132 sq. mi.
POP. — 27,086 (1911)
CAPITAL — Charlotte Amalie

The US bought these islands in 1917 and they became the US Virgin Islands, using US stamps and currency.

100 Cents = 1 Dollar
100 Bit = 1 Franc (1905)

Wmk. 111 — Small Crown

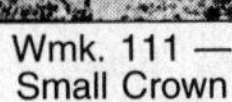

Wmk. 112 — Crown

Wmk. 113 — Crown

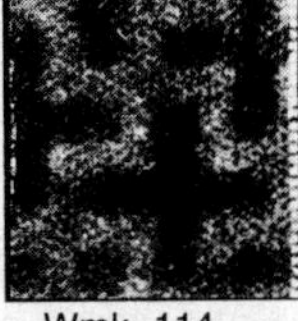

Wmk. 114 — Multiple Crosses

Coat of Arms — A1

Yellowish Paper
Yellow Wavy-line Burelage, UL to LR

1856 Typo. Wmk. 111 *Imperf.*

1 A1 3c dark carmine, brown gum 200. *275.*
a. 3c dark carmine, yellow gum 225. *275.*
b. 3c carmine, white gum *4,250.* —

The brown and yellow gums were applied locally.

Reprint: 1981, carmine, back-printed across two stamps ("Reprint by Dansk Post og Telegrafmuseum 1978"), value, pair, $10.

White Paper
Yellow Wavy-line Burelage UR to LL

1866

2 A1 3c rose 40. *75.*

No. 2 reprints, unwatermarked: 1930, carmine, value $100. 1942, rose carmine, back-printed across each row ("Nytryk 1942 G. A. Hagemann Danmark og Dansk Vestindiens Frimaerker Bind 2"), value $50.

1872 *Perf. 12½*

3 A1 3c rose 100. *275.*

Without Burelage

1873

4 A1 4c dull blue 250. *475.*
a. Imperf., pair 775.
b. Horiz. pair, imperf. vert. 575.

The 1930 reprint of No. 4 is ultramarine, unwatermarked and imperf., value $100.

The 1942 4c reprint is blue, unwatermarked, imperf. and has printing on back (see note below No. 2), value $60.

A2

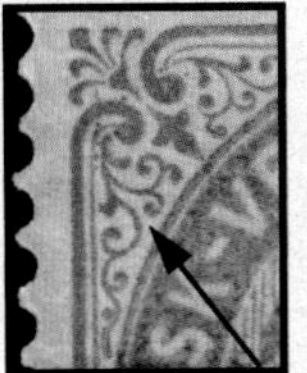

Normal Frame

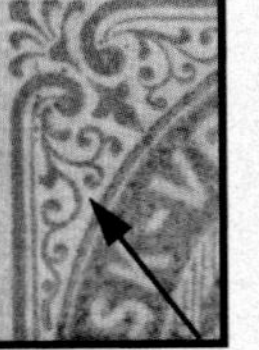

Inverted Frame

The arabesques in the corners have a main stem and a branch. When the frame is in normal position, in the upper left corner the branch leaves the main stem half way between two little leaflets. In the lower right corner the branch starts at the foot of the second leaflet. When the frame is inverted the corner designs are, of course, transposed.

White Wove Paper
Varying from Thin to Thick

1874-79 Wmk. 112 *Perf. 14x13½*

Values for inverted frames, covers and blocks are for the cheapest variety.

5 A2 1c green & brown red 22.50 *30.00*
a. 1c green & rose lilac, thin paper 80.00 *125.00*
b. 1c green & red violet, medium paper 45.00 *65.00*
c. 1c green & claret, thick paper 20.00 *30.00*
e. As "c," inverted frame 25.00 *32.50*
f. As "a," inverted frame *475.00*

No. 5 exists with "b" surcharge, "10 CENTS 1895." See note below No. 15.

6 A2 3c blue & carmine 27.50 20.00
a. 3c light blue & rose carmine, thin paper 65.00 50.00
b. 3c deep blue & dark carmine, medium paper 40.00 17.00
c. 3c greenish blue & lake, thick paper 32.50 17.00
d. Imperf., pair 375.00 —
e. Inverted frame, thick paper 30.00 20.00
f. As "a," inverted frame *350.00*
7 A2 4c brown & dull blue 16.00 *19.00*
b. 4c brown & ultramarine, thin paper 225.00 *225.00*
c. Diagonal half used as 2c on cover 140.00
d. As "b," inverted frame *900.00 1,400.*
8 A2 5c grn & gray ('76) 30.00 25.00
a. 5c yellow green & dark gray, thin paper 55.00 37.50
b. Inverted frame, thick paper 30.00 25.00

9 A2 7c lilac & orange 35.00 *95.00*
a. 7c lilac & yellow 90.00 *100.00*
b. Inverted frame 65.00 *150.00*
10 A2 10c blue & brn ('76) 30.00 30.00
a. 10c dark blue & black brown, thin paper 70.00 45.00
b. Period between "t" & "s" of "cents" 35.00 30.00
c. Inverted frame 27.50 *32.50*
11 A2 12c red lil & yel grn ('77) 42.50 *175.00*
a. 12c lilac & deep green 160.00 *200.00*
12 A2 14c lilac & green 650.00 *1,250.*
a. Inverted frame *2,500. 3,500.*
13 A2 50c vio, thin paper ('79) 190.00 *300.00*
a. 50c gray violet, thick paper 250.00 *375.00*
Nos. 5-13 (9) 1,043. 1,944.

The central element in the fan-shaped scrollwork at the outside of the lower left corner of Nos. 5a and 7b looks like an elongated diamond.

See Nos. 16-20. For surcharges see Nos. 14-15, 23-28, 40.

Nos. 9 and 13 Surcharged in Black

a

b

1887

14 A2 (a) 1c on 7c lilac & orange 100.00 *200.00*
a. 1c on 7c lilac & yellow 120.00 *225.00*
b. Double surcharge 250.00 *500.00*
c. Inverted frame 110.00 *350.00*

1895

15 A2 (b) 10c on 50c violet, thin paper 42.50 *67.50*

The "b" surcharge also exists on No. 5, with "10" found in two sizes. These are essays.

Type of 1874-79

1896-1901 *Perf. 13*

16 A2 1c green & red violet, inverted frame ('98) 15.00 *22.50*
a. Normal frame 300.00 *450.00*
17 A2 3c blue & lake, inverted frame ('98) 12.00 *17.50*
a. Normal frame 250.00 *425.00*
18 A2 4c bister & dull blue ('01) 17.50 15.00
a. Diagonal half used as 2c on cover 100.00
b. Inverted frame 60.00 *85.00*
c. As "b," diagonal half used as 2c on cover 350.00
19 A2 5c green & gray, inverted frame 35.00 35.00
a. Normal frame 800.00 *1,200.*
20 A2 10c blue & brown ('01) 80.00 *150.00*
a. Inverted frame 1,000. *2,000.*
b. Period between "t" and "s" of "cents" 170.00 160.00
Nos. 16-20 (5) 159.50 *240.00*

Arms — A5

1900

21 A5 1c light green 3.00 3.00
22 A5 5c light blue 17.50 *25.00*

See Nos. 29-30. For surcharges see Nos. 41-42.

Nos. 6, 17, 20 Surcharged

c

Surcharge "c" in Black

1902 *Perf. 14x13½*

23 A2 2c on 3c blue & carmine, inverted frame 700.00 *900.00*
a. "2" in date with straight tail 750.00 *950.00*
b. Normal frame —

Perf. 13

24 A2 2c on 3c blue & lake, inverted frame 10.00 *27.50*
a. "2" in date with straight tail 12.00 *32.50*
b. Dated "1901" 750.00 750.00
c. Normal frame 175.00 *300.00*
d. Dark green surcharge 2,750.
e. As "d" & "a" — —
f. As "d" & "c" —

Only one example of No. 24f can exist.

25 A2 8c on 10c blue & brown 25.00 *42.50*
a. "2" with straight tail 30.00 *45.00*
b. On No. 20b 32.50 *45.00*
c. Inverted frame 250.00 *425.00*

d

Surcharge "d" in Black

1902 *Perf. 13*

27 A2 2c on 3c blue & lake, inverted frame 12.00 *32.50*
a. Normal frame 240.00 *425.00*
28 A2 8c on 10c blue & brown 12.00 14.00
a. On No. 20b 18.50 *25.00*
b. Inverted frame 225.00 *400.00*
Nos. 23-28 (5) 759.00 1,016.

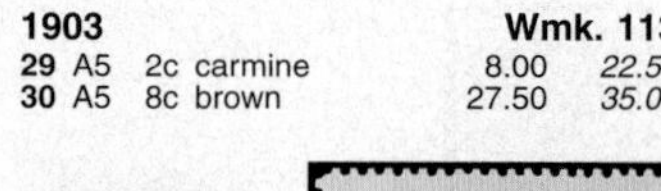

1903 **Wmk. 113**

29 A5 2c carmine 8.00 *22.50*
30 A5 8c brown 27.50 *35.00*

King Christian IX — A8

St. Thomas Harbor — A9

1905 **Typo.** ***Perf. 13***

31 A8 5b green 3.75 3.25
32 A8 10b red 3.75 3.25
33 A8 20b green & blue 8.75 8.25
34 A8 25b ultramarine 8.75 *10.50*
35 A8 40b red & gray 8.25 8.25
36 A8 50b yellow & gray 10.00 12.00

Perf. 12

Wmk. Two Crowns (113)

Frame Typographed, Center Engraved

37 A9 1fr green & blue 17.50 *45.00*
38 A9 2fr orange red & brown 30.00 *60.00*
39 A9 5fr yellow & brown 77.50 *275.00*
Nos. 31-39 (9) 168.25 *425.50*

Favor cancels exist on Nos. 37-39. Value 25% less.

Nos. 18, 22 and 30 Surcharged in Black

1905 **Wmk. 112**

40 A2 5b on 4c bister & dull blue 16.00 *50.00*
a. Inverted frame 45.00 *90.00*
41 A5 5b on 5c light blue 12.50 *47.50*

Wmk. 113

42 A5 5b on 8c brown 14.00 *50.00*
Nos. 40-42 (3) 42.50 147.50

Favor cancels exist on Nos. 40-42. Value 25% less.

Frederik VIII — A10

Frame Typographed, Center Engraved

1908

43 A10 5b green 1.90 1.90
44 A10 10b red 1.90 1.90
45 A10 15b violet & brown 3.75 *4.50*
46 A10 20b green & blue 30.00 27.50
47 A10 25b blue & dark blue 1.90 *2.50*
48 A10 30b claret & slate 50.00 *52.50*
49 A10 40b vermilion & gray 5.75 *9.50*
50 A10 50b yellow & brown 5.75 *14.00*
Nos. 43-50 (8) 100.95 114.30

Christian X — A11

1915 **Wmk. 114** ***Perf. 14x14½***

51 A11 5b yellow green 4.00 *5.50*
52 A11 10b red 4.00 *55.00*
53 A11 15b lilac & red brown 4.00 *55.00*
54 A11 20b green & blue 4.00 *55.00*
55 A11 25b blue & dark blue 4.00 *17.50*
56 A11 30b claret & black 4.00 *100.00*
57 A11 40b orange & black 4.00 *100.00*
58 A11 50b yellow & brown 3.75 *100.00*
Nos. 51-58 (8) 31.75 *488.00*

Forged and favor cancellations exist.

POSTAGE DUE STAMPS

Royal Cipher, "Christian 9 Rex" D1

1902 **Litho.** **Unwmk.** ***Perf. 11½***

J1 D1 1c dark blue 5.00 *17.50*
J2 D1 4c dark blue 12.50 *22.50*
J3 D1 6c dark blue 22.50 *60.00*
J4 D1 10c dark blue 20.00 *65.00*
Nos. J1-J4 (4) 60.00 *165.00*

There are five types of each value. On the 4c they may be distinguished by differences in the figure "4"; on the other values differences are minute.

Used values of Nos. J1-J8 are for canceled stamps. Uncanceled stamps without gum have probably been used. Value 60% of unused.

Excellent counterfeits of Nos. J1-J4 exist.

Numeral of value — D2

1905-13 ***Perf. 13***

J5 D2 5b red & gray 4.50 *6.75*
J6 D2 20b red & gray 7.50 *14.00*
J7 D2 30b red & gray 6.75 *14.00*
J8 D2 50b red & gray 6.00 *35.00*
a. Perf. 14x14½ ('13) 37.50 *140.00*
b. Perf. 11½ 325.00
Nos. J5-J8 (4) 24.75 *69.75*

All values of this issue are known imperforate, but were not regularly issued.

Used values of Nos. J5-J8 are for canceled stamps. Uncanceled examples without gum have probably been used. Value 60% of unused.

Counterfeits of Nos. J5-J8 exist.

Danish West Indies stamps were replaced by those of the U.S. in 1917, after the U.S. bought the islands.

GUAM

'gwäm

LOCATION — One of the Mariana Islands in the Pacific Ocean, about 1450 miles east of the Philippines
GOVT. — United States Possession
AREA — 206 sq. mi.
POP. — 9,000 (est. 1899)
CAPITAL — Agaña

Formerly a Spanish possession, Guam was ceded to the United States in 1898 following the Spanish-American War. Stamps overprinted "Guam" were superseded by the regular postage stamps of the United States in 1901.

100 Cents = 1 Dollar

United States Nos. 279, 279B, 279Bc, 268, 280a, 281, 282, 272, 282C, 283, 284, 275, 275a, 276 and 276A Overprinted

1899 **Wmk. 191** ***Perf. 12***

Black Overprint

1 A87 1c deep green 20.00 *25.00*
Never hinged 40.00

A bogus inverted overprint exists.

2 A88 2c red, type IV 17.50 *25.00*
Never hinged 35.00
a. rose carmine, type IV 30.00 30.00
Never hinged 60.00
3 A89 3c purple 140.00 *175.00*
Never hinged 275.00
4 A90 4c lilac brown 125.00 *175.00*
Never hinged 250.00
5 A91 5c blue 32.50 *45.00*
Never hinged 65.00
6 A92 6c lake 125.00 *190.00*
Never hinged 250.00
7 A93 8c violet brown 125.00 *160.00*
Never hinged 275.00
8 A94 10c brown, type I 45.00 *55.00*
Never hinged 90.00
9 A94 10c brown, type II *3,250.* —
Never hinged *6,500.*
10 A95 15c olive green 150.00 140.00
Never hinged 300.00
11 A96 50c orange 350.00 *400.00*
Never hinged 700.00
a. 50c red orange 550.00 —
Never hinged 1,100.

Red Overprint

12 A97 $1 black, type I 350.00 *400.00*
Never hinged 700.00
13 A97 $1 black, type II *4,250.*
Never hinged —
Nos. 1-8,10-12 (11) 1,480. *1,790.*

Counterfeits of the overprint exist.
No. 13 exists only in the special printing.

SPECIAL DELIVERY STAMP

United States No. E5 Overprinted in Red

1899 **Wmk. 191** ***Perf. 12***

E1 SD3 10c blue 150.00 *200.00*
Never hinged 275.00
a. Dots in curved frame above messenger (Plate 882) 200.00
Never hinged 400.00

Counterfeits of the overprint exist.

The special stamps for Guam were replaced by the regular issues of the United States.

Guam Guard Mail stamps of 1930 are listed in the Scott U.S. specialized catalogue.

HAWAII

hə-'wä-yē

LOCATION — Group of 20 islands in the Pacific Ocean, about 2,000 miles southwest of San Francisco.
GOVT. — Former Kingdom and Republic
AREA — 6,435 sq. mi.
POP. — 150,000 (est. 1899)
CAPITAL — Honolulu

Until 1893 an independent kingdom, from 1893 to 1898 a republic, the Hawaiian Islands were annexed to the US in 1898. The Territory of Hawaii achieved statehood in 1959.

100 Cents = 1 Dollar

Values for Nos. 1-4 are for examples with minor damage that has been skillfully repaired.

Values of Hawaii stamps vary considerably according to condition. For Nos. 1-4, values are for examples with minor damage that has been skillfully repaired.

A1

A2

A3

1851-52 Unwmk. Typeset *Imperf.*
Pelure Paper

1 A1 2c blue *660,000. 250,000.*
2 A1 5c blue *55,000. 35,000.*
3 A2 13c blue *37,000. 28,000.*
4 A3 13c blue *52,500. 35,000.*

Nos. 1-4 are known as the "Missionaries."
Two varieties of each. Nos. 1-4, off cover, are almost invariably damaged.
No. 1 unused is unique.

Values for Nos. 5-82 are for very fine examples. Extremely fine to superb stamps sell at much higher prices, and inferior or poor stamps sell at reduced prices, depending on the condition of the individual example.

King Kamehameha III

A4

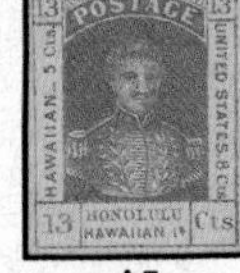

A5

Printed in Sheets of 20 (4x5)

1853 Engr.
Thick White Wove Paper

5 A4 5c blue 1,900. 1,900.
   a. Line through "Honolulu" (Pos. 2) *3,000. 3,000.*
6 A5 13c dark red 850. *1,700.*

See Nos. 8-11.

A6

1857

7 A6 5c on 13c dark red *7,000. 10,000.*

1857 Thin White Wove Paper

8 A4 5c blue 700. *750.*
   a. Line through "Honolulu" (Pos. 2) *1,350. 1,350.*
   b. Double impression *3,500. 4,750.*

1861 Thin Bluish Wove Paper

9 A4 5c blue 375. 375.
   a. Line through "Honolulu" (Pos. 2) *950. 1,000.*

1868

RE-ISSUE

Ordinary White Wove Paper

10 A4 5c blue 27.50
   a. Line through "Honolulu" (Pos. 2) 75.
11 A5 13c dull rose 325.

Remainders of Nos. 10 and 11 were overprinted "SPECIMEN." See Nos. 10S-11Sb in the Scott U.S. Specialized Catalogue.

Nos. 10 and 11 were never placed in use but stamps (both with and without overprint) were sold at face value at the Honolulu post office.

REPRINTS (Official Imitations)

Original

Reprint

Original

Reprint

5c — *Originals have two small dots near the left side of the square in the upper right corner. These dots are missing in the reprints.*

13c — *The bottom of the 3 of 13 in the upper left corner is flattened in the originals and rounded in the reprints. The "t" of "Cts" on the left side is as tall as the "C" in the reprints, but shorter in the originals.*

1889

10R A4 5c blue 65.
11R A5 13c orange red 300.

On August 19, 1892, the remaining supply of reprints was overprinted in black "REPRINT." The reprints (both with and without overprint) were sold at face value. See the Scott U.S. Specialized Catalogue.

Values for the Numeral stamps, Nos. 12-26, are for four-margin examples. Unused values are for stamps without gum.

A7

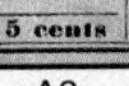
A8

A9

1859-62 Typeset

12 A7 1c light blue, *bluish white* *17,500. 15,000.*
   a. "1 Ce" omitted *22,500.*
   b. "nt" omitted — —

No. 12a is unique.

13 A7 2c light blue, *bluish white* *6,250. 5,000.*
   a. 2c dark blue, *grayish white* *6,750. 5,000.*
   b. Comma after "Cents" — *6,750.*
   c. No period after "LETA" — —
14 A7 2c black, *greenish blue* ('62) *8,000. 6,000.*
   a. "2-Cents." —

1859-63

15 A7 1c black, *grayish* ('63) 650. *2,750.*
   a. Tête bêche pair *9,000.*
   b. "NTER" —
   c. Period omitted after "Postage" 850.
16 A7 2c black, *grayish* 1,000. 850.
   a. "2" at top of rectangle *3,750. 3,750.*
   b. Printed on both sides — *21,000.*
   c. "NTER" *3,250. 6,500.*
   d. 2c black, *grayish white* 1,000. 850.
   e. Period omitted after "Cents" —
   f. Overlapping impressions — —
   g. "TAGE" —
17 A7 2c dark blue, *bluish* ('63) *12,000. 8,750.*
   a. "ISL" — —
18 A7 2c black, *blue gray* ('63) *3,500. 6,000.*

1864-65

19 A7 1c black 550. *10,000.*
20 A7 2c black 775. *1,500.*
21 A8 5c blue, *blue* ('65) 900. 700.
   a. Tête bêche pair *10,500.*
   b. 5c bluish black, *grayish white* *14,000. 3,750.*

No. 21b unused is unique. No. 21b used is also unique but defective.

22 A9 5c blue, *blue* ('65) 575. *900.*
   a. Tête bêche pair *20,000.*
   b. 5c blue, *grayish white* —
   c. Overlapping impressions —

1864 Laid Paper

23 A7 1c black 300. *2,500.*
   a. "HA" instead of "HAWAIIAN" *3,500.*
   b. Tête bêche pair *6,250.*
   c. Tête bêche pair, Nos. 23, 23a *18,000.*
24 A7 2c black 325. *1,050.*
   a. "NTER" *3,500.*
   b. "S" of "POSTAGE" omitted *1,500.*
   c. Tête bêche pair *7,000.*

A10

1865 Wove Paper

25 A10 1c dark blue 350.
   a. Double impression —
   b. With inverted impression of No. 21 on face *18,500.*
26 A10 2c dark blue 350.

Nos. 12 to 26 were typeset and were printed in settings of ten, each stamp differing from the others.

King Kamehameha IV
A11

1861-63 Litho.

Horizontally Laid Paper

27 A11 2c pale rose 350. 350.
   a. 2c carmine rose ('63) 3,000. 2,850.

Vertically Laid Paper

28 A11 2c pale rose 325. 325.
   a. 2c carmine rose ('63) 350. *400.*

RE-ISSUE

1869 Engr. Thin Wove Paper

29 A11 2c red 45.00 —

No. 29 was not issued for postal purposes although canceled examples are known. It was sold only at the Honolulu post office, at first without overprint and later with overprint "CANCELLED." See No. 29S in the Scott U.S. Specialized Catalogue.

See Nos. 50-51 and note following No. 51.

Princess Victoria Kamamalu — A12

King Kamehameha IV — A13

A14

King Kamehameha V — A15

Mataio Kekuanaoa — A16

1864-86 Engr. *Perf. 12*
Wove Paper

30 A12 1c purple ('86) 11.00 8.00
   Never hinged 27.50
   a. 1c mauve ('71) 60.00 20.00
   Never hinged 100.00
   b. 1c violet ('78) 20.00 10.00
   Never hinged 50.00
31 A13 2c rose vermilion 65.00 10.00
   Never hinged 160.00
   a. 2c vermilion ('86) 50.00 20.00
   Never hinged 120.00
   b. Half used as 1c on cover with #32 *8,500.*
32 A14 5c blue ('66) 175.00 30.00
   Never hinged 400.00
33 A15 6c yellow green ('71) 45.00 10.00
   Never hinged 110.00
   a. 6c bluish green ('78) 35.00 10.00
   Never hinged 85.00
   b. As "a," horiz. pair, imperf. *2,250.*
34 A16 18c dull rose ('71) 95.00 37.50
   Never hinged 225.00
   Nos. 30-34 (5) 391.00 95.50
   Set, never hinged 922.50

No. 32 has traces of rectangular frame lines surrounding the design. Nos. 39 and 52C have no such frame lines.

For overprints see Nos. 53, 58-60, 65, 66C, 71.

King David Kalakaua
A17

Prince William Pitt Leleiohoku
A18

1875

35 A17 2c brown 9.00 3.00
   Never hinged 22.00
36 A18 12c black 65.00 27.50
   Never hinged 165.00

See Nos. 38, 43, 46. For overprints see Nos. 56, 62-63, 66, 69.

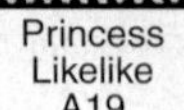
Princess Likelike A19

King David Kalakaua A20

Queen Kapiolani — A21

Statue of King Kamehameha I — A22

King William Lunalilo — A23

Queen Emma Kaleleonalani — A24

1882

37 A19 1c blue 11.00 6.00
Never hinged 29.00
38 A17 2c lilac rose 125.00 45.00
Never hinged 275.00
39 A14 5c ultramarine 15.00 3.00
Never hinged 37.50
a. Vert. pair, imperf. horiz. *5,000. 6,000.*
40 A20 10c black 47.50 22.50
Never hinged 120.00
41 A21 15c red brown 65.00 25.00
Never hinged 160.00
Nos. 37-41 (5) 263.50 101.50
Set, never hinged 621.50

1883-86

42 A19 1c green 3.00 2.00
Never hinged 8.00
43 A17 2c rose ('86) 5.00 1.00
Never hinged 12.00
a. 2c dull red 62.50 21.00
Never hinged 140.00
44 A20 10c red brown ('84) 37.50 10.00
Never hinged 95.00
45 A20 10c vermilion 42.50 12.50
Never hinged 105.00
46 A18 12c red lilac 85.00 35.00
Never hinged 225.00
47 A22 25c dark violet 150.00 60.00
Never hinged 350.00
48 A23 50c red 190.00 85.00
Never hinged 425.00
49 A24 $1 rose red 275.00 250.00
Never hinged 625.00 *8,000.*
Maltese cross cancellation 100.00
Nos. 42-49 (8) 788.00 455.50
Set, never hinged 1,845.

Other fiscal cancellations exist on No. 49.

Nos. 48-49 are valued used with postal cancels. Canceled-to-order cancels exist and are worth less.

REPRODUCTION and REPRINT

Yellowish Wove Paper

1886-89 Engr. *Imperf.*

50 A11 2c orange vermilion 160.00
Never hinged 275.00
51 A11 2c carmine ('89) 30.00
Never hinged 50.00

In 1885, the Postmaster General wished to have on sale complete sets of Hawaii's portrait stamps, but was unable to find either the stone from which Nos. 27 and 28 were printed, or the plate from which No. 29 was printed. He therefore sent an example of No. 29 to the American Bank Note Company, with an order to engrave a new plate like it and print 10,000 stamps therefrom, of which 5000 were overprinted "SPECIMEN" in blue.

The original No. 29 was printed in sheets of fifteen (5x3), but the plate of these "Official Imitations" was made up of fifty stamps (10x5). Later, in 1887, the original die for No. 29 was discovered, and, after retouching, a new plate was made and 37,500 stamps were printed (No. 51). These, like the originals, were printed in sheets of fifteen. They were delivered during 1889 and 1890. In 1892, all remaining unsold in the Post Office were overprinted "Reprint".

No. 29 is red in color, and printed on very thin white wove paper. No. 50 is orange vermilion in color, on medium, white to buff paper. In No. 50 the vertical line on the left side of the portrait touches the horizontal line over the label "Elua Keneta", while in the other two varieties, Nos. 29 and 51, it does not touch the horizontal line by half a millimeter. In No. 51 there are three parallel lines on the left side of the King's nose, while in No. 29 and No. 50 there are no such lines. No. 51 is carmine in color and printed on thick, yellowish to buff, wove paper.

It is claimed that both Nos. 50 and 51 were available for postage, although not made to fill a postal requirement. They exist with favor cancellation. No. 51 also is known postally used. See Nos. 50S-51S in the Scott U.S. specialized catalogue.

Queen Liliuokalani — A25

1890-91 *Perf. 12*

52 A25 2c dull violet ('91) 15.00 1.50
Never hinged 25.00
a. Vert. pair, imperf. horiz. *3,750.*
52C A14 5c deep indigo 120.00 150.00
Never hinged 275.00

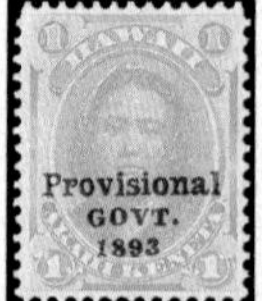

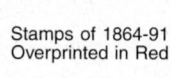

Stamps of 1864-91 Overprinted in Red

Three categories of double overprints:
I. Both overprints heavy.
II. One overprint heavy, one of moderate strength.
III. One overprint heavy, one of light or weak strength.

1893

Overprinted in Red

53 A12 1c purple 9.00 13.00
Never hinged 21.00
a. "189" instead of "1893" 600.00 —
b. No period after "GOVT" *265.00 250.00*
f. Double overprint (III) *600.00*
54 A19 1c blue 9.00 *15.00*
Never hinged 21.00
b. No period after "GOVT" *140.00 140.00*
e. Double overprint (II) *1,500.*
f. Double overprint (III) *400.00*
55 A19 1c green 2.00 *3.00*
Never hinged 4.50
d. Double overprint (I) *650.00 650.00*
f. Double overprint (III) *225.00 250.00*
g. Pair, one without ovpt. *10,000.*
56 A17 2c brown 12.00 *20.00*
Never hinged 28.50
b. No period after "GOVT" *300.00* —
57 A25 2c dull violet 1.50 1.10
Never hinged 3.00
a. "18 3" instead of "1893" *850.00 950.00*
d. Double overprint (I) *1,300. 700.00*
f. Double overprint (III) *190.00 190.00*
g. Inverted overprint *4,000. 4,750.*
58 A14 5c deep indigo 13.00 *25.00*
Never hinged 32.00
b. No period after "GOVT" *250.00 250.00*
f. Double overprint (III) *1,250. 675.00*
59 A14 5c ultramarine 7.00 3.00
Never hinged 15.00
d. Double overprint (I) *6,500.*
e. Double overprint (II) *4,000. 4,000.*
f. Double overprint (III) *600.00*
g. Inverted overprint *1,500. 1,500.*
60 A15 6c green 17.50 *25.00*
Never hinged 40.00
e. Double overprint (II) *1,100.*
61 A20 10c black 13.00 *20.00*
Never hinged 30.00
e. Double overprint (II) *1,000. 750.00*
f. Double overprint (III) *225.00*
61B A20 10c red brown *17,500. 29,000.*
62 A18 12c black 12.00 *20.00*
Never hinged 30.00
d. Double overprint (I) *2,000.*
e. Double overprint (II) *1,750.*
63 A18 12c red lilac 165.00 *250.00*
Never hinged 400.00
64 A22 25c dark violet 32.00 *40.00*
Never hinged 72.00
b. No period after "GOVT" *350.00 350.00*
f. Double overprint (III) *1,100.*
Nos. 53-61,62-64 (12) 293.00 *435.10*
Nos. 53-61, 62-64 never hinged 697.00

Virtually all known examples of No. 61B are cut in at the top.

Overprinted in Black

65 A13 2c vermilion 80.00 *85.00*
Never hinged 200.00
b. No period after "GOVT" *275.00 275.00*
66 A17 2c rose 1.75 *2.25*
Never hinged 3.00
b. No period after "GOVT" 65.00 65.00
d. Double overprint (I) *4,000.*
e. Double overprint (II) *2,750.*
f. Double overprint (III) *300.00*
66C A15 6c green *17,500. 29,000.*
67 A20 10c vermilion 20.00 *30.00*
Never hinged 50.00
f. Double overprint (III) *1,250.*
68 A20 10c red brown 10.00 *13.00*
Never hinged 25.00
f. Double overprint (III) *4,000.*
69 A18 12c red lilac 325.00 *500.00*
Never hinged 575.00
70 A21 15c red brown 25.00 *35.00*
Never hinged 55.00
e. Double overprint (II) *2,000.*
71 A16 18c dull rose 35.00 *35.00*
Never hinged 75.00
a. "18 3" instead of "1893" *525.00 525.00*
b. No period after "GOVT" *325.00 300.00*
d. Double overprint (I) *650.00*
f. Double overprint (III) *275.00* —
g. Pair, one without ovpt. *3,500.*
h. As "b," double overprint (II) *1,750.*
72 A23 50c red 80.00 *110.00*
Never hinged 175.00
b. No period after "GOVT" *475.00 475.00*
Never hinged 725.00
f. Double overprint (III) *1,000.*
73 A24 $1 rose red 150.00 *175.00*
Never hinged 325.00
b. No period after "GOVT" *475.00* 450.00
Nos. 65-66,67-73 (9) 726.75 *985.25*
Nos. 65-66, 67-73 never hinged 1,483.

Coat of Arms — A26

View of Honolulu — A27

Statue of Kamehameha I — A28

Stars and Palms — A29

S. S. "Arawa" — A30

Pres. Sanford Ballard Dole — A31

"CENTS" Added — A32

1894

74 A26 1c yellow 2.00 1.50
Never hinged 5.00
75 A27 2c brown 2.00 .60
Never hinged 5.00
76 A28 5c rose lake 5.00 2.00
Never hinged 13.00
77 A29 10c yellow green 8.00 5.00
Never hinged 22.50
78 A30 12c blue 17.50 *20.00*
Never hinged 42.50
79 A31 25c deep blue 22.50 16.00
Never hinged 55.00
Nos. 74-79 (6) 57.00 *45.10*
Set, never hinged 144.00

Numerous double transfers exist on Nos. 75 and 81.

1899

80 A26 1c dark green 2.00 1.50
Never hinged 5.00
81 A27 2c rose 1.50 1.00
Never hinged 4.00
a. 2c salmon 1.50 1.50
Never hinged 4.00
b. Vert. pair, imperf. horiz. *4,250.*
82 A32 5c blue 8.00 3.50
Never hinged 20.00
Nos. 80-82 (3) 11.50 6.00
Set, never hinged 29.00

OFFICIAL STAMPS

Lorrin Andrews Thurston — O1

1896 Engr. Unwmk. *Perf. 12*

O1 O1 2c green 45.00 20.00
Never hinged 110.00
O2 O1 5c black brown 45.00 20.00
Never hinged 110.00
O3 O1 6c deep ultramarine 45.00 20.00
Never hinged 110.00
O4 O1 10c bright rose 45.00 20.00
Never hinged 110.00
O5 O1 12c orange 55.00 22.50
Never hinged 135.00
O6 O1 25c gray violet 65.00 22.50
Never hinged 160.00
Nos. O1-O6 (6) 300.00 125.00
Set, never hinged 735.00

Used values for Nos. O1-O6 are for stamps canceled-to-order "FOREIGN OFFICE/HONOLULU H.I." in double circle without date. Values of postally used stamps: Nos. O1-O2, O4, $40 each; No. O3, $110; No. O5, $140; No. O6, $175.

The stamps of Hawaii were replaced by those of the United States.

PHILIPPINES

ˌfi-lə-ˈpēnz

LOCATION — Group of 7,100 islands and islets in the Malay Archipelago, north of Borneo, in the North Pacific Ocean
GOVT. — US Admin., 1898-1946
AREA — 115,748 sq. mi.
POP. — 16,971,100 (est. 1941)
CAPITAL — Quezon City

The islands were ceded to the US by Spain in 1898. On Nov. 15, 1935, they were given their independence, subject to a transition period which ended July 4, 1946. On that date the Commonwealth became the "Republic of the Philippines."

100 Cents = 1 Dollar (1899)
100 CENTAVOS = 1 PESO (1906)

Wmk. 191PI — Double-lined PIPS

Wmk. 190PI — Single-lined PIPS

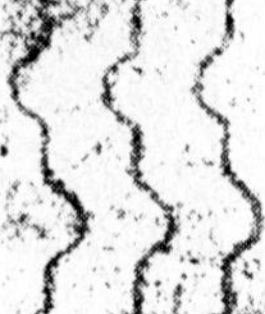
Wmk. 257 — Curved Wavy Lines

Issued under U.S. Administration

Regular Issues of the United States Overprinted in Black

1899-1901 Unwmk. *Perf. 12*

On U.S. Stamp No. 260

212 A96 50c orange 300. 225.
Never hinged 775.

On U.S. Stamps Nos. 279, 279B, 279Bd, 279Be, 279Bf, 279Bc, 268, 281, 282C, 283, 284, 275, 275a

Wmk. Double-lined USPS (191)

213 A87 1c yellow green 4.00 .60
Never hinged 10.00
a. Inverted overprint *77,500.*
214 A88 2c red, type IV 1.75 .60
Never hinged 4.25
a. 2c orange red, type IV, ('01) 1.75 .60
Never hinged 4.25
b. Bklt. pane of 6, red, type IV ('00) 250.00 *300.00*
Never hinged 600.00
c. 2c reddish carmine, type IV 2.50 1.00
Never hinged 6.00
d. 2c rose carmine, type IV 3.00 1.10
Never hinged 7.25
215 A89 3c purple 9.00 1.25
Never hinged 21.50
216 A91 5c blue 9.00 1.00
Never hinged 21.50
a. Inverted overprint *6,500.*

No. 216a is valued in the grade of fine.

217 A94 10c brown, type I 35.00 4.00
Never hinged 80.00
217A A94 10c orange brown, type II 125.00 27.50
Never hinged 325.00
218 A95 15c olive green 40.00 8.00
Never hinged 95.00
219 A96 50c orange 125.00 37.50
Never hinged 300.00
a. 50c red orange 250.00 55.00
Never hinged 600.00
Nos. 213-219 (8) 348.75 80.45

Regular Issue

1901, Aug. 30

Same Overprint in Black On U.S. Stamps Nos. 280b, 282 and 272

220 A90 4c orange brown 35.00 5.00
Never hinged 80.00
221 A92 6c lake 40.00 7.00
Never hinged 95.00
222 A93 8c violet brown 40.00 7.50
Never hinged 95.00
Nos. 220-222 (3) 115.00 19.50

Same Overprint in Red On U.S. Stamps Nos. 276, 276A, 277a and 278

223 A97 $1 black, type I 300.00 200.00
Never hinged 1,000.
223A A97 $1 black, type II 2,000. 750.00
Never hinged 5,000.
224 A98 $2 dark blue 350.00 325.00
Never hinged 1,150.
225 A99 $5 dark green 650.00 *875.00*
Never hinged 1,600.

Regular Issue

1903-04

Same Overprint in Black On U.S. Stamps Nos. 300 to 310 and shades

226 A115 1c blue green 7.00 .40
Never hinged 15.50
227 A116 2c carmine 9.00 1.10
Never hinged 20.00
228 A117 3c bright violet 67.50 12.50
Never hinged 150.00
229 A118 4c brown 80.00 22.50
Never hinged 175.00
a. 4c orange brown 80.00 20.00
Never hinged 175.00
230 A119 5c blue 17.50 1.00
Never hinged 40.00
231 A120 6c brownish lake 85.00 22.50
Never hinged 190.00
232 A121 8c violet black 50.00 15.00
Never hinged 125.00
233 A122 10c pale red brown 35.00 2.25
Never hinged 80.00
a. 10c red brown 35.00 3.00
Never hinged 80.00
b. Pair, one without overprint *1,500.*
234 A123 13c purple black 35.00 17.50
Never hinged 80.00
a. 13c brown violet 35.00 17.50
Never hinged 80.00
235 A124 15c olive green 60.00 15.00
Never hinged 135.00
236 A125 50c orange 125.00 35.00
Never hinged 275.00
Nos. 226-236 (11) 571.00 144.75
Set, never hinged 1,285.

Same Overprint in Red On U.S. Stamps Nos. 311, 312 and 313

237 A126 $1 black 300.00 200.00
Never hinged 800.00
238 A127 $2 dark blue 650.00 *800.00*
Never hinged 1,500.
239 A128 $5 dark green 900.00 *3,750.*
Never hinged 1,800.

Same Overprint in Black On U.S. Stamp Nos. 319 and 319c

240 A129 2c carmine 8.00 2.25
Never hinged 17.50
a. Booklet pane of 6 *2,000.*
b. 2c scarlet 8.00 2.75
Never hinged 19.00
c. As "b," booklet pane of 6 —

José Rizal — A40

Designs: 4c, McKinley. 6c, Ferdinand Magellan. 8c, Miguel Lopez de Legaspi. 10c, Gen. Henry W. Lawton. 12c, Lincoln. 16c, Adm. William T. Sampson. 20c, Washington. 26c, Francisco Carriedo. 30c, Franklin. 1p-10p, Arms of City of Manila.

Wmk. Double-lined PIPS (191)

1906, Sept. 8 *Perf. 12*

241 A40 2c deep green .40 .25
Never hinged 1.00
a. 2c yellow green ('10) .60 .25
Never hinged 1.50
b. Booklet pane of 6 750.00 *800.00*
Never hinged *1,500.*
242 A40 4c carmine .50 .25
Never hinged 1.25
a. 4c carmine lake ('10) 1.00 .25
Never hinged 2.50
b. Booklet pane of 6 *650.00* *700.00*
Never hinged *1,250.*
243 A40 6c violet 2.50 .25
Never hinged 6.25
244 A40 8c brown 4.50 .90
Never hinged 11.00
245 A40 10c blue 3.50 .30
Never hinged 8.75
a. 10c dark blue 3.50 .30
Never hinged 8.75
246 A40 12c brown lake 9.00 2.50
Never hinged 22.50
247 A40 16c violet black 6.00 .35
Never hinged 15.00
248 A40 20c orange brown 7.00 .35
Never hinged 17.50
249 A40 26c violet brown 11.00 3.00
Never hinged 27.50
250 A40 30c olive green 6.50 1.75
Never hinged 16.00
251 A40 1p orange 50.00 7.50
Never hinged 120.00
252 A40 2p black 50.00 1.75
Never hinged 130.00
253 A40 4p dark blue 160.00 20.00
Never hinged 375.00
254 A40 10p dark green 225.00 80.00
Never hinged 575.00
Nos. 241-254 (14) 535.90 119.15
Set, never hinged 1,316.

1909-13 Change of Colors

255 A40 12c red orange 11.00 3.00
Never hinged 27.50
256 A40 16c olive green 6.00 .75
Never hinged 15.00
257 A40 20c yellow 9.00 1.25
Never hinged 22.50
258 A40 26c blue green 3.50 1.25
Never hinged 8.75
259 A40 30c ultramarine 13.00 3.50
Never hinged 32.50
260 A40 1p pale violet 45.00 5.00
Never hinged 110.00
260A A40 2p violet brown ('13) 100.00 12.00
Never hinged 250.00
Nos. 255-260A (7) 187.50 26.75
Set, never hinged 466.25

Wmk. Single-lined PIPS (190)

1911

261 A40 2c green .75 .25
Never hinged 1.80
a. Booklet pane of 6 *800.00* *900.00*
Never hinged *1,400.*
262 A40 4c carmine lake 3.00 .25
Never hinged 6.75
a. 4c carmine — —
b. Booklet pane of 6 *600.00* *700.00*
Never hinged *1,100.*
263 A40 6c deep violet 3.00 .25
Never hinged 6.75
264 A40 8c brown 9.50 .50
Never hinged 21.50
265 A40 10c blue 4.00 .25
Never hinged 9.00
266 A40 12c orange 4.00 .45
Never hinged 9.00
267 A40 16c olive green 4.50 .40
Never hinged 10.00
a. 16c pale olive green 4.50 .50
Never hinged 10.00
268 A40 20c yellow 3.50 .25
Never hinged 7.75
a. 20c orange 4.00 .30
Never hinged 9.00
269 A40 26c blue green 6.00 .30
Never hinged 13.50
270 A40 30c ultramarine 6.00 .50
Never hinged 13.50
271 A40 1p pale violet 27.50 .60
Never hinged 62.50
272 A40 2p violet brown 45.00 1.00
Never hinged 100.00
273 A40 4p deep blue 600.00 110.00
Never hinged 1,200.
274 A40 10p deep green 200.00 30.00
Never hinged 400.00
Nos. 261-274 (14) 916.75 145.00
Set, never hinged 1,862.

1914

275 A40 30c gray 12.00 .50
Never hinged 27.50

1914 *Perf. 10*

276 A40 2c green 3.00 .25
Never hinged 7.00
a. Booklet pane of 6 *750.00* *800.00*
Never hinged *1,250.*
277 A40 4c carmine 4.00 .30
Never hinged 9.00
a. Booklet pane of 6 *750.00*
Never hinged *1,300.*
278 A40 6c light violet 45.00 9.50
Never hinged 100.00
a. 6c deep violet 50.00 6.25
Never hinged 110.00
279 A40 8c brown 55.00 10.50
Never hinged 125.00
280 A40 10c dark blue 30.00 .25
Never hinged 67.50
281 A40 16c olive green 100.00 5.00
Never hinged 225.00
282 A40 20c orange 40.00 1.00
Never hinged 85.00
283 A40 30c gray 60.00 4.50
Never hinged 130.00
284 A40 1p pale violet 150.00 3.75
Never hinged 350.00
Nos. 276-284 (9) 487.00 35.05
Set, never hinged 1,020.

1918 *Perf. 11*

285 A40 2c green 21.00 4.25
Never hinged 40.00
a. Booklet pane of 6 *750.00* *800.00*
Never hinged *1,300.*
286 A40 4c carmine 26.00 6.00
Never hinged 55.00
a. Booklet pane of 6 *1,350.* *2,000.*
287 A40 6c deep violet 40.00 6.00
Never hinged 90.00
287A A40 8c light brown 220.00 25.00
Never hinged 400.00
288 A40 10c dark blue 60.00 3.00
Never hinged 140.00
289 A40 16c olive green 110.00 10.00
Never hinged 250.00
289A A40 20c orange 175.00 12.00
Never hinged 400.00
289C A40 30c gray 95.00 18.00
Never hinged 215.00
289D A40 1p pale violet 100.00 25.00
Never hinged 225.00
Nos. 285-289D (9) 847.00 109.25
Set, never hinged 1,815.

1917 Unwmk. *Perf. 11*

290 A40 2c yellow green .25 .25
Never hinged .55
a. 2c dark green .30 .25
Never hinged .65
b. Vert. pair, imperf. horiz. *2,000.*
c. Horiz. pair, imperf. between *1,500.* —
d. Vertical pair, imperf. btwn. *1,750.* *1,000.*
e. Booklet pane of 6 27.50 *30.00*
Never hinged 60.00
291 A40 4c carmine .30 .25
Never hinged .65
a. 4c light rose .30 .25
Never hinged .65
b. Booklet pane of 6 20.00 *22.50*
Never hinged 35.00
292 A40 6c deep violet .35 .25
Never hinged .70
a. 6c lilac .40 .25
Never hinged .80
b. 6c red violet .40 .25
Never hinged .70
c. Booklet pane of 6 *550.00* *800.00*
Never hinged *900.00*
293 A40 8c yellow brown .30 .25
Never hinged .50
a. 8c orange brown .30 .25
Never hinged .50
294 A40 10c deep blue .30 .25
Never hinged .65
295 A40 12c red orange .35 .25
Never hinged .75
296 A40 16c light olive green 65.00 .25
Never hinged 130.00
a. 16c olive bister 65.00 .50
Never hinged 130.00
297 A40 20c orange yellow .35 .25
Never hinged .75
298 A40 26c green .50 .45
Never hinged 1.10
a. 26c blue green .60 .25
Never hinged 1.35
299 A40 30c gray .55 .25
Never hinged 1.35
300 A40 1p pale violet 40.00 1.00
Never hinged 90.00
a. 1p red lilac 40.00 1.00
Never hinged 90.00
b. 1p pale rose lilac 40.00 1.10
Never hinged 90.00
301 A40 2p violet brown 35.00 1.00
Never hinged 77.50
302 A40 4p blue 32.50 .50
Never hinged 72.50
a. 4p dark blue 35.00 .55
Never hinged 77.50
Nos. 290-302 (13) 175.75 5.20
Set, never hinged 377.00

1923-26

Design: 16c, Adm. George Dewey.

303 A40 16c olive bister 1.00 .25
Never hinged 2.25
a. 16c olive green 1.25 .25
Never hinged 2.75
304 A40 10p deep green ('26) 50.00 20.00
Never hinged 110.00

Legislative Palace A42

1926, Dec. 20 *Perf. 12*

319 A42 2c green & black .50 .25
Never hinged 1.25
a. Horiz. pair, imperf. between *300.00*
b. Vert. pair, imperf. between *575.00*
320 A42 4c carmine & black .55 .40
Never hinged 1.20
a. Horiz. pair, imperf. between *325.00*
b. Vert. pair, imperf. between *600.00*
321 A42 16c olive green & black 1.00 .65
Never hinged 2.25
a. Horiz. pair, imperf. between *350.00*
b. Vert. pair, imperf. between *625.00*
c. Double impression of center *675.00*
322 A42 18c light brown & black 1.10 .50
Never hinged 2.50
a. Double impression of center *1,250.*
b. Vertical pair, imperf. between *675.00*
323 A42 20c orange & black 2.00 1.00
Never hinged 4.50
a. 20c orange & brown *600.00* —
b. As No. 323, imperf., pair *575.00* *575.00*
c. As "a," imperf., pair *1,750.*
d. Vert. pair, imperf. between *700.00*
324 A42 24c gray & black 1.00 .55
Never hinged 2.25
a. Vert. pair, imperf. between *700.00*
325 A42 1p rose lilac & black 47.50 50.00
Never hinged 70.00
a. Vert. pair, imperf. between *700.00*
Nos. 319-325 (7) 53.65 53.35
Set, never hinged 83.95

Opening of the Legislative Palace.
No. 322a is valued in the grade of fine.
For overprints, see Nos. O1-O4.

Rizal Type of 1906

Coil Stamp

1928 *Perf. 11 Vertically*

326 A40 2c green 7.50 *12.50*
Never hinged 18.75

Types of 1906-1923

1925-31 *Imperf.*

340 A40 2c yel green ('31) .50 .50
Never hinged .90
a. 2c green ('25) .80 .75
Never hinged 1.80
341 A40 4c car rose ('31) .50 *1.00*
Never hinged 1.00
a. 4c carmine ('25) 1.20 1.00
Never hinged 2.75
342 A40 6c violet ('31) 3.00 3.75
Never hinged 5.00
a. 6c deep violet ('25) 12.00 8.00
Never hinged 26.00
343 A40 8c brown ('31) 2.00 *5.00*
Never hinged 4.00
a. 8c yellow brown ('25) 13.00 8.00
Never hinged 26.00
344 A40 10c blue ('31) 5.00 *7.50*
Never hinged 12.00
a. 10c deep blue ('25) 45.00 20.00
Never hinged 100.00
345 A40 12c dp orange ('31) 8.00 10.00
Never hinged 15.00
a. 12c red orange ('25) 60.00 35.00
Never hinged 135.00
346 A40 16c olive green 6.00 7.50
Never hinged 11.00
a. 16c bister green ('25) 42.50 18.00
Never hinged 100.00
347 A40 20c dp yel orange ('31) 5.00 *7.50*
Never hinged 11.00
a. 20c yellow orange ('25) 45.00 20.00
Never hinged 100.00
348 A40 26c green ('31) 6.00 *9.00*
Never hinged 11.00
a. 26c blue green ('25) 45.00 25.00
Never hinged 110.00
349 A40 30c light gray ('31) 8.00 10.00
Never hinged 16.00
a. 30c gray ('25) 45.00 25.00
Never hinged 110.00
350 A40 1p light violet ('31) 10.00 *15.00*
Never hinged 20.00
a. 1p violet ('25) 200.00 100.00
Never hinged 425.00
351 A40 2p brn vio ('31) 30.00 *45.00*
Never hinged 80.00
a. 2p violet brown ('25) 400.00 400.00
Never hinged 675.00
352 A40 4p blue ('31) 80.00 90.00
Never hinged 150.00
a. 4p deep blue ('25) 2,200. 1,000.
Never hinged 3,500.

353 A40 10p green ('31) 175.00 *225.00*
Never hinged 300.00
a. 10p deep green ('25) 3,000. *3,250.*
Never hinged 5,000.
Nos. 340-353 (14) 339.00 436.75
Set, never hinged 636.90
Nos. 340a-353a (14) 6,109. 4,910.

Nos. 340a-353a were the original post office issue. These were reprinted twice in 1931 for sale to collectors (Nos. 340-353).

Mount Mayon, Luzon A43

Post Office, Manila A44

Pier No. 7, Manila Bay — A45

(See footnote) — A46

Rice Planting A47

Rice Terraces A48

Baguio Zigzag A49

1932, May 3 ***Perf. 11***

354 A43 2c yellow green .75 .30
Never hinged 1.25
355 A44 4c rose carmine .75 .30
Never hinged 1.25
356 A45 12c orange 1.00 .75
Never hinged 1.25
357 A46 18c red orange 50.00 15.00
Never hinged 80.00
358 A47 20c yellow 1.10 .75
Never hinged 1.75
359 A48 24c deep violet 1.75 1.00
Never hinged 3.00
360 A49 32c olive brown 1.75 1.00
Never hinged 3.00 6.50
Nos. 354-360 (7) 57.10 19.10
Set, never hinged 91.50

The 18c vignette was intended to show Pagsanjan Falls in Laguna, central Luzon, and is so labeled. Through error the stamp pictures Vernal Falls in Yosemite National Park, California.

For overprints see #C29-C35, C47-C51, C63.

Nos. 302, 302a Surcharged in Orange or Red

1932

368 A40 1p on 4p blue (O) 7.50 1.00
Never hinged 12.00
a. 1p on 4p dark blue (O) 7.50 1.00
Never hinged 12.00
369 A40 2p on 4p dark blue (R) 10.00 1.50
Never hinged 17.00
a. 2p on 4p blue (R) 10.00 1.00
Never hinged 17.00

Far Eastern Championship

Issued in commemoration of the Tenth Far Eastern Championship Games.

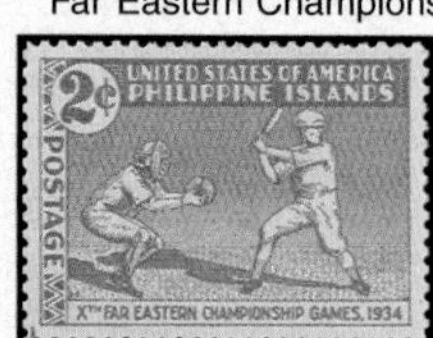

Baseball Players A50

Tennis Player — A51

Basketball Players — A52

1934, Apr. 14 ***Perf. 11½***

380 A50 2c yellow brown 1.50 .80
Never hinged 2.25
381 A51 6c ultramarine .25 .25
Never hinged .30
a. Vertical pair, imperf. between *1,100.*
382 A52 16c violet brown .50 .50
Never hinged .75
a. Vert. pair, imperf. horiz. *1,500.*
Nos. 380-382 (3) 2.25 1.55
Set, never hinged 3.30

José Rizal — A53

Woman and Carabao A54

La Filipina — A55

Pearl Fishing A56

Fort Santiago A57

Salt Spring — A58

Magellan's Landing, 1521 — A59

"Juan de la Cruz" — A60

Rice Terraces A61

"Blood Compact," 1565 — A62

Barasoain Church, Malolos A63

Battle of Manila Bay, 1898 A64

Montalban Gorge A65

George Washington A66

1935, Feb. 15 ***Perf. 11***

383 A53 2c rose .25 .25
Never hinged .25
384 A54 4c yellow green .25 .25
Never hinged .25
385 A55 6c dark brown .25 .25
Never hinged .35
386 A56 8c violet .25 .25
Never hinged .35
387 A57 10c rose carmine .30 .25
Never hinged .45
388 A58 12c black .35 .25
Never hinged .50
389 A59 16c dark blue .35 .25
Never hinged .55
390 A60 20c light olive green .35 .25
Never hinged .45
391 A61 26c indigo .40 .40
Never hinged .60
392 A62 30c orange red .40 .40
Never hinged .60
393 A63 1p red orange & black 2.00 1.25
Never hinged 3.00
394 A64 2p bister brown & black 12.00 2.00
Never hinged 16.00
395 A65 4p blue & black 12.00 4.00
Never hinged 16.00
396 A66 5p green & black 25.00 5.00
Never hinged 50.00
Nos. 383-396 (14) 54.15 15.05
Set, never hinged 74.45

For overprints & surcharges see Nos. 411-424, 433-446, 449, 463-466, 468, 472-474, 478-484, 485-494, C52-C53, O15-O36, O38, O40-O43, N2-N9, N28, NO2-NO6.

Issues of the Commonwealth

Issued to commemorate the inauguration of the Philippine Commonwealth, Nov. 15, 1935.

The Temples of Human Progress — A67

1935, Nov. 15

397 A67 2c carmine rose .25 .25
Never hinged .30
398 A67 6c deep violet .25 .25
Never hinged .30
399 A67 16c blue .25 .25
Never hinged .35
400 A67 36c yellow green .40 .30
Never hinged .60
401 A67 50c brown .60 .55
Never hinged .90
Nos. 397-401 (5) 1.75 1.60
Set, never hinged 2.45

Jose Rizal Issue

75th anniversary of the birth of Jose Rizal (1861-1896), national hero of the Filipinos.

Jose Rizal — A68

1936, June 19 ***Perf. 12***

402 A68 2c yellow brown .25 .25
Never hinged .25
403 A68 6c slate blue .25 .25
Never hinged .25
a. Imperf. vertically, pair *1,000.*
Never hinged *1,500.*
404 A68 36c red brown .50 *.70*
Never hinged .75
Nos. 402-404 (3) 1.00 1.20
Set, never hinged 1.25

Commonwealth Anniversary Issue

Issued in commemoration of the first anniversary of the Commonwealth.

President Manuel L. Quezon — A69

1936, Nov. 15 ***Perf. 11***

408 A69 2c orange brown .25 .25
Never hinged .30
409 A69 6c yellow green .25 .25
Never hinged .30
410 A69 12c ultramarine .25 .25
Never hinged .30
Nos. 408-410 (3) .75 .75
Set, never hinged .90

Stamps of 1935 Overprinted in Black

a

b 

1936-37

411 A53(a) 2c rose .25 .25
Never hinged .25
a. Bklt. pane of 6 ('37) 2.50 2.00
Never hinged 4.00
b. Hyphen omitted 125.00 100.00
412 A54(b) 4c yel grn ('37) .50 *4.00*
Never hinged .75
413 A55(a) 6c dark brown .25 .25
Never hinged .25
414 A56(b) 8c violet ('37) .25 .25
Never hinged .35
415 A57(b) 10c rose carmine .25 .25
Never hinged .25
a. "COMMONWEALT" 20.00 —
Never hinged 30.00
416 A58(b) 12c black ('37) .25 .25
Never hinged .30
417 A59(b) 16c dark blue .30 .25
Never hinged .45
418 A60(a) 20c lt ol grn ('37) 1.00 .40
Never hinged 1.60
419 A61(b) 26c indigo ('37) .90 .35
Never hinged 1.50
420 A62(b) 30c orange red .50 .25
Never hinged .80
421 A63(b) 1p red org & blk 1.00 .25
Never hinged 1.60
422 A64(b) 2p bis brn & blk ('37) 15.00 4.00
Never hinged 25.00
423 A65(b) 4p bl & blk ('37) 50.00 8.00
Never hinged 80.00
424 A66(b) 5p grn & blk ('37) 15.00 *30.00*
Never hinged 25.00
Nos. 411-424 (14) 85.45 48.75
Set, never hinged 110.75

Eucharistic Congress Issue

Issued to commemorate the 33rd International Eucharistic Congress held at Manila, Feb. 3-7, 1937.

Map of Philippines — A70

1937, Feb. 3

425 A70 2c yellow green .25 .25
Never hinged .25
426 A70 6c light brown .25 .25
Never hinged .25
427 A70 12c sapphire .25 .25
Never hinged .25
428 A70 20c deep orange .30 .25
Never hinged .50
429 A70 36c deep violet .55 .40
Never hinged .80
430 A70 50c carmine .70 .35
Never hinged 1.10
Nos. 425-430 (6) 2.30 1.75
Set, never hinged 3.15

Arms of Manila — A71

1937, Aug. 27

431 A71 10p gray 6.00 2.00
Never hinged 8.50
432 A71 20p henna brown 5.00 1.40
Never hinged 8.00

Stamps of 1935 Overprinted in Black

a 

b 

1938-40

433 A53(a) 2c rose ('39) .25 .25
Never hinged .25
a. Booklet pane of 6 3.50 3.50
Never hinged 5.50
b. As "a," lower left-hand stamp overprinted "WEALTH COMMON-" *3,000.*
Never hinged *5,000.*
c. Hyphen omitted 100.00 50.00
434 A54(b) 4c yel grn ('40) 3.00 *30.00*
Never hinged 4.75
435 A55(a) 6c dk brn ('39) .25 .25
Never hinged .40
a. 6c golden brown .25 .25
Never hinged .40
436 A56(b) 8c violet ('39) .25 .25
Never hinged .25
a. "COMMONWEALT" (LR 31) 90.00
Never hinged 140.00
437 A57(b) 10c rose car ('39) .25 .25
Never hinged .25
a. "COMMONWEALT" (LR 31) 65.00 —
Never hinged 100.00
438 A58(b) 12c black ('40) .25 .25
Never hinged .25
439 A59(b) 16c dark blue .25 .25
Never hinged .25
440 A60(a) 20c lt ol grn ('39) .25 .25
Never hinged .25
441 A61(b) 26c indigo ('40) 1.00 1.00
Never hinged 1.50
442 A62(b) 30c org red ('39) 3.00 .70
Never hinged 5.00
443 A63(b) 1p red org & blk .60 .25
Never hinged 1.00
444 A64(b) 2p bis brn & blk ('39) 10.00 1.00
Never hinged 15.00
445 A65(b) 4p bl & blk ('40) 175.00 250.00
Never hinged 350.00
446 A66(b) 5p grn & blk ('40) 20.00 6.00
Never hinged 35.00
Nos. 433-446 (14) 214.35 *290.70*
Set, never hinged 414.15

Overprint "b" measures 18½x1¾mm.

No. 433b occurs in booklet pane, No. 433a, position 5; all examples are straight-edged, left and bottom.

First Foreign Trade Week Issue
Nos. 384, 298a and 432 Surcharged in Red, Violet or Black

a 

b

c

1939, July 5

449 A54(a) 2c on 4c yellow green (R) .25 .25
Never hinged .35
450 A40(b) 6c on 26c blue green (V) .25 .50
Never hinged .35
a. 6c on 26c green 3.00 1.00
Never hinged 5.00
451 A71(c) 50c on 20p henna brown (Bk) 1.25 1.00
Never hinged 2.00 5.00
Nos. 449-451 (3) 1.75 1.75
Set, never hinged 2.70

Commonwealth 4th Anniversary Issue (#452-460)

Triumphal Arch — A72

1939, Nov. 15

452 A72 2c yellow green .25 .25
Never hinged .25
453 A72 6c carmine .25 .25
Never hinged .25
454 A72 12c bright blue .25 .25
Never hinged .25
Nos. 452-454 (3) .75 .75
Set, never hinged .75

For overprints see Nos. 469, 476.

Malacañan Palace A73

1939, Nov. 15

455 A73 2c green .25 .25
Never hinged .25
456 A73 6c orange .25 .25
Never hinged .25
457 A73 12c carmine .25 .25
Never hinged .25
Nos. 455-457 (3) .75 .75
Set, never hinged .75

For overprint, see No. 470.

Pres. Quezon Taking Oath of Office — A74

1940, Feb. 8

458 A74 2c dark orange .25 .25
Never hinged .25
459 A74 6c dark green .25 .25
Never hinged .25
460 A74 12c purple .25 .25
Never hinged .30
Nos. 458-460 (3) .75 .75
Set, never hinged .80

For overprints, see Nos. 471, 477.

José Rizal — A75

ROTARY PRESS PRINTING

1941, Apr. 14 ***Perf. 11x10½***

Size: 19x22½mm

461 A75 2c apple green .25 *.50*
Never hinged .25

FLAT PLATE PRINTING

1941, Nov. 14 ***Perf. 11***

Size: 18¾x22¼mm

462 A75 2c pale apple green 1.00 —
Never hinged 1.25
a. Booklet pane of 6 6.00 —
Never hinged 7.50

No. 461 was issued only in sheets. No. 462 was issued only in booklet panes on Nov. 14, 1941, just before the war, and only a few used stamps and covers exist. All examples have one or two straight edges. Mint booklets reappeared after the war. In August 1942, the booklet pane was reprinted in a darker shade (apple green). However, the apple green panes were available only to U.S. collectors during the war years, so no war-period used stamps from the Philippines exist. Value of apple green booklet pane, never hinged, $6.

For type A75 overprinted, see Nos. 464, O37, O39, N1 and NO1.

Philippine Stamps of 1935-41, Handstamped in Violet

1944 ***Perf. 11, 11x10½***

463 A53 2c rose (On 411) *325.00 160.00*
a. Booklet pane of 6 *(28)* *12,500.*
463B A53 2c rose (On 433) *2,000. 1,750.*
464 A75 2c apple grn (On 461) 10.00 10.00
Never hinged 17.50
a. Pair, one without ovpt. — —
465 A54 4c yel grn (On 384) 42.50 *42.50*
Never hinged 70.00
466 A55 6c dk brn (On 385) *3,500. 2,000.*
467 A69 6c yel grn (On 409) 225.00 *150.00*
Never hinged *400.00*
468 A55 6c dk brn (On 413) *4,750. 825.00*
469 A72 6c car (On 453) *350.00 125.00*
470 A73 6c org (On 456) *1,750. 725.00*
471 A74 6c dk grn (On 459) *275.00 225.00*
472 A56 8c vio (On 436) 17.50 *24.00*
Never hinged 30.00
473 A57 10c car rose (On 415) *300.00 150.00*
474 A57 10c car rose (On 437) *275.00 200.00*
Never hinged *475.00*
475 A69 12c ultra (On 410) *1,100. 400.00*
476 A72 12c brt bl (On 454) *7,000. 2,500.*
477 A74 12c pur (On 460) *375.00 275.00*
478 A59 16c dk bl (On 389) *3,000.* —
479 A59 16c dk bl (On 417) *1,500. 1,000.*
480 A59 16c dk bl (On 439) *500.00 200.00*
481 A60 20c lt ol grn (On 440) 110.00 35.00
Never hinged 185.00
482 A62 30c org red (On 420) *450.00 1,500.*
483 A62 30c org red (On 442) *750.00 375.00*
484 A63 1p red org & blk (On 443) *6,250. 4,500.*

Nos. 463-484 are valued in the grade of fine to very fine.

No. 463 comes only from the booklet pane. All examples have one or two straight edges.

Types of 1935-37 Overprinted

a 

b

Nos. 431-432 Overprinted in Black — c

1945 ***Perf. 11***

485 A53(a) 2c rose .25 .25
Never hinged .25
486 A54(b) 4c yellow green .25 .25
Never hinged .25
487 A55(a) 6c golden brown .25 .25
Never hinged .25
488 A56(b) 8c violet .25 .25
Never hinged .25
489 A57(b) 10c rose carmine .25 .25
Never hinged .25
490 A58(b) 12c black .25 .25
Never hinged .25
491 A59(b) 16c dark blue .25 .25
Never hinged .30
492 A60(a) 20c lt olive green .30 .25
Never hinged .40
493 A62(b) 30c orange red .50 .35
Never hinged .75
494 A63(b) 1p red orange & black 1.10 .25
Never hinged 1.60
495 A71(c) 10p gray 55.00 13.50
Never hinged 90.00
496 A71(c) 20p henna brown 50.00 15.00
Never hinged 75.00
Nos. 485-496 (12) 108.65 31.10
Set, never hinged 169.55

José Rizal — A76

1946, May 28 ***Perf. 11x10½***

497 A76 2c sepia .25 .25
Never hinged .25

For overprints see Nos. 503, O44.

Later issues, released by the Philippine Republic on July 4, 1946, and thereafter, are listed in Scott's Standard Postage Stamp Catalogue, Vol. 5.

AIR POST STAMPS

Madrid-Manila Flight Issue

Issued to commemorate the flight of Spanish aviators Gallarza and Loriga from Madrid to Manila.

Regular Issue of 1917-26 Overprinted in Red or Violet

Designs: Nos. C7-C8, Adm. William T. Sampson. No. C9, Adm. George Dewey.

1926, May 13 Unwmk. *Perf. 11*

C1 A40 2c green (R) 20.00 17.50
Never hinged 45.00
C2 A40 4c carmine (V) 30.00 20.00
Never hinged 55.00
a. Inverted overprint *4,000.* —
C3 A40 6c lilac (R) 75.00 75.00
Never hinged 125.00
C4 A40 8c orange brown (V) 75.00 60.00
Never hinged 125.00
C5 A40 10c deep blue (R) 75.00 60.00
Never hinged 140.00
C6 A40 12c red orange (V) 80.00 65.00
Never hinged 150.00
C7 A40 16c light olive green (V) *3,250. 3,250.*
C8 A40 16c olive bister (R) *5,000. 5,000.*
C9 A40 16c olive green (V) 100.00 70.00
Never hinged 160.00
C10 A40 20c org ye (V) 100.00 80.00
Never hinged 160.00
C11 A40 26c blue green (V) 100.00 80.00
Never hinged 160.00
C12 A40 30c gray (V) 100.00 80.00
Never hinged 160.00
C13 A40 2p vio brn (R) 600.00 600.00
Never hinged 1,100.
C14 A40 4p dark blue (R) 750.00 750.00
Never hinged 1,300.
C15 A40 10p deep green (V) 1,350. 1,350.

Same Overprint on No. 269

Wmk. Single-lined PIPS (190)

Perf. 12

C16 A40 26c blue green (V) *6,250.*

Same Overprint on No. 284

Perf. 10

C17 A40 1p pale violet (V) 300.00 225.00
Never hinged 450.00

Flight of Spanish aviators Gallarza and Loriga from Madrid to Manila.

London-Orient Flight Issue

Issued Nov. 9, 1928, to celebrate the arrival of a British squadron of hydroplanes.

Regular Issue of 1917-25 Overprinted in Red

1928, Nov. 9 *Perf. 11*

C18 A40 2c green 1.00 1.00
Never hinged 2.00
C19 A40 4c carmine 1.25 1.50
Never hinged 2.00
C20 A40 6c violet 5.00 3.00
Never hinged 10.00
C21 A40 8c orange brown 5.00 3.00
Never hinged 10.00
C22 A40 10c deep blue 5.00 3.00
Never hinged 10.00
C23 A40 12c red orange 8.00 4.00
Never hinged 12.00
C24 A40 16c olive green (No. 303a) 8.00 4.00
Never hinged 12.00
C25 A40 20c orange yellow 8.00 4.00
Never hinged 12.00
C26 A40 26c blue green 20.00 8.00
Never hinged 35.00
C27 A40 30c gray 20.00 8.00
Never hinged 35.00

Same Overprint on No. 271

Wmk. Single-lined PIPS (190)

Perf. 12

C28 A40 1p pale violet 55.00 30.00
Never hinged 90.00
Nos. C18-C28 (11) 136.25 69.50
Set, never hinged 230.00

Von Gronau Issue

Commemorating the visit of Capt. Wolfgang von Gronau's airplane on its round-the-world flight.

Nos. 354-360 Overprinted

1932, Sept. 27 Unwmk. *Perf. 11*

C29 A43 2c yellow green .90 .60
Never hinged 1.40
C30 A44 4c rose carmine .90 .40
Never hinged 1.40
C31 A45 12c orange 1.25 .65
Never hinged 2.00
C32 A46 18c red orange 5.00 5.00
Never hinged 8.00
C33 A47 20c yellow 4.00 4.00
Never hinged 6.50
C34 A48 24c deep violet 4.00 4.00
Never hinged 6.50
C35 A49 32c olive brown 3.50 3.00
Never hinged 5.75
Nos. C29-C35 (7) 19.55 17.65
Set, never hinged 31.55

Rein Issue

Commemorating the flight from Madrid to Manila of the Spanish aviator Fernando Rein y Loring.

Regular Issue of 1917-25 Overprinted

1933, Apr. 11

C36 A40 2c green .75 .45
Never hinged 1.10
C37 A40 4c carmine .90 .45
Never hinged 1.40
C38 A40 6c deep violet 1.10 .80
Never hinged 1.75
C39 A40 8c orange brown 3.75 2.00
Never hinged 5.75
C40 A40 10c dark blue 3.75 2.25
Never hinged 5.75
C41 A40 12c orange 3.75 2.00
Never hinged 5.75
C42 A40 16c olive green 3.50 2.00
Never hinged 5.25
C43 A40 20c yellow 3.75 2.00
Never hinged 5.75
C44 A40 26c green 3.75 2.75
Never hinged 5.75
a. 26c blue green 4.00 2.00
Never hinged 6.00
C45 A40 30c gray 4.00 3.00
Never hinged 6.00
Nos. C36-C45 (10) 29.00 17.70
Set, never hinged 44.25

No. 290a Overprinted

1933, May 26

C46 A40 2c green .65 .40
Never hinged 1.00

Regular Issue of 1932 Overprinted

C47 A44 4c rose carmine .30 .25
Never hinged .45
C48 A45 12c orange .60 .25
Never hinged .90
C49 A47 20c yellow .60 .25
Never hinged .90
C50 A48 24c deep violet .65 .25
Never hinged 1.00
C51 A49 32c olive brown .85 .35
Never hinged 1.40
Nos. C46-C51 (6) 3.65 1.75
Set, never hinged 5.65

Transpacific Issue

Issued to commemorate the China Clipper flight from Manila to San Francisco, Dec. 2-5, 1935.

Nos. 387, 392 Overprinted in Gold

1935, Dec. 2

C52 A57 10c rose carmine .40 .25
Never hinged .60
C53 A62 30c orange red .60 .35
Never hinged .90

Manila-Madrid Flight Issue

Issued to commemorate the Manila-Madrid flight by aviators Antonio Arnaiz and Juan Calvo.

Regular Issue of 1917-25 Surcharged in Various Colors

1936, Sept. 6

C54 A40 2c on 4c carmine (Bl) .25 .25
Never hinged .25
C55 A40 6c on 12c red orange (V) .25 .25
Never hinged .30
C56 A40 16c on 26c blue green (Bk) .25 .25
Never hinged .40
a. 16c on 26c green 2.00 .70
Never hinged 3.00
Nos. C54-C56 (3) .75 .75
Set, never hinged .95

Air Mail Exhibition Issue

Issued to commemorate the first Air Mail Exhibition, held Feb. 17-19, 1939.

Regular Issue of 1917-37 Surcharged in Black or Red

1939, Feb. 17

C57 A40 8c on 26c blue green (Bk) 2.00 2.00
Never hinged 4.00
a. 8c on 26c green (Bk) 10.00 4.00
Never hinged 16.00
C58 A71 1p on 10p gray (R) 8.00 4.00
Never hinged 12.00

Moro Vinta and Clipper AP1

1941, June 30

C59 AP1 8c carmine 2.00 .60
Never hinged 2.75
C60 AP1 20c ultramarine 3.00 .50
Never hinged 4.00
C61 AP1 60c blue green 3.00 1.00
Never hinged 4.00
C62 AP1 1p sepia .70 .50
Never hinged 1.00
Nos. C59-C62 (4) 8.70 2.60
Set, never hinged 11.75

For overprint see No. NO7. For surcharges see Nos. N10-N11, N35-N36.

No. C47 Hstmpd. in Violet

1944, Dec. 3

C63 A44 4c rose carmine *3,750. 2,750.*

SPECIAL DELIVERY STAMPS

United States No. E5 Overprinted in Red

Wmk. Double-lined USPS (191)

1901, Oct. 15 *Perf. 12*

E1 SD3 10c dark blue 100. 80.
Never hinged 185.
a. Dots in curved frame above messenger (Pl. 882) *175. 160.*

Special Delivery Messenger SD2

1906, Sept. 8

E2 SD2 20c deep ultra 45.00 8.00
Never hinged 90.00
b. 20c pale ultramarine 35.00 8.00
Never hinged 70.00

See Nos. E3-E6. For overprints see Nos. E7-E10, EO1.

SPECIAL PRINTING

U.S. No. E6 Overprinted in Red

Wmk. Double-lined USPS (191)

1907

E2A SD4 10c ultramarine *2,750.*

Wmk. Single-lined PIPS (190)

1911, Apr.

E3 SD2 20c deep ultra 22.00 1.75
Never hinged 42.00

1916 *Perf. 10*

E4 SD2 20c deep ultra 175.00 90.00
Never hinged 275.00

1919 Unwmk. *Perf. 11*

E5 SD2 20c ultramarine .60 .25
Never hinged .90
a. 20c pale blue .75 .25
Never hinged 1.00
b. 20c dull violet .60 .25
Never hinged .90

Type of 1906 Issue

1925-31 *Imperf.*

E6 SD2 20c dull violet ('31) 30.00 *75.00*
Never hinged 45.00
a. 20c violet blue ('25) 50.00 —
Never hinged 80.00

Type of 1919 Overprinted in Black

1939, Apr. 27 *Perf. 11*

E7 SD2 20c blue violet .25 .25
Never hinged .40

Nos. E5b and E7, Hstmpd. in Violet

1944

E8 SD2 20c dull violet (On E5b) *1,400. 550.00*
E9 SD2 20c blue violet (On E7) *550.00 250.00*

Type SD2 Overprinted

1945, May 1

E10 SD2 20c blue violet .70 .55
Never hinged 1.10
a. "IC" close together 3.25 2.75
Never hinged 4.75

SPECIAL DELIVERY OFFICIAL STAMP

Type of 1906 Issue Overprinted

1931 Unwmk. *Perf. 11*

EO1 SD2 20c dull violet 3.00 *75.00*
Never hinged 4.50
a. No period after "B" 50.00 *250.00*
Never hinged 75.00
b. Double overprint —

It is strongly recommended that expert opinion be acquired for No. EO1 used.

POSTAGE DUE STAMPS

U.S. Nos. J38-J44 Overprinted in Black

Wmk. Double-lined USPS (191)

1899, Aug. 16 *Perf. 12*

J1 D2 1c deep claret 7.50 2.50
Never hinged 15.00
J2 D2 2c deep claret 7.50 2.50
Never hinged 15.00
J3 D2 5c deep claret 15.00 2.50
Never hinged 30.00
J4 D2 10c deep claret 19.00 5.50
Never hinged 37.50
J5 D2 50c deep claret 200.00 100.00
Never hinged 335.00

No. J1 was used to pay regular postage Sept. 5-19, 1902.

1901, Aug. 31

J6 D2 3c deep claret 17.50 7.00
Never hinged 35.00
J7 D2 30c deep claret 250.00 110.00
Never hinged 415.00
Nos. J1-J7 (7) 516.50 230.00
Set, never hinged 882.50

Post Office Clerk — D3

1928, Aug. 21 Unwmk. *Perf. 11*

J8 D3 4c brown red .25 .25
Never hinged .25
J9 D3 6c brown red .30 .75
Never hinged .45
J10 D3 8c brown red .25 .75
Never hinged .35
J11 D3 10c brown red .30 .75
Never hinged .45
J12 D3 12c brown red .25 .75
Never hinged .35
J13 D3 16c brown red .30 .75
Never hinged .45
J14 D3 20c brown red .30 .75
Never hinged .45
Nos. J8-J14 (7) 1.95 4.75
Set, never hinged 2.75

No. J8 Surcharged in Blue

1937, July 29 Unwmk. *Perf. 11*

J15 D3 3c on 4c brown red .25 .25
Never hinged .35

See note after No. NJ1.

Nos. J8 to J14 Handstamped in Violet

1944, Dec. 3

J16 D3 4c brown red *150.00* —
J17 D3 6c brown red *90.00* —
J18 D3 8c brown red *95.00* —
J19 D3 10c brown red *90.00* —
J20 D3 12c brown red *90.00* —
J21 D3 16c brown red *95.00* —
a. Pair, one without ovpt. —
J22 D3 20c brown red *95.00* —
Nos. J16-J22 (7) *705.00*

OFFICIAL STAMPS

Official Handstamped Overprints

"Officers purchasing stamps for government business may, if they so desire, surcharge them with the letters O.B. either in writing with black ink or by rubber stamps but in such a manner as not to obliterate the stamp that postmasters will be unable to determine whether the stamps have been previously used." C.M. Cotterman, Director of Posts, December 26, 1905.

Beginning January 1, 1906, all branches of the Insular Government used postage stamps to prepay postage instead of franking them as before. Some officials used manuscript, some utilized the typewriting machines but by far the larger number provided themselves with rubber stamps. The majority of these read "O.B." but other forms were: "OFFICIAL BUSINESS" or "OFFICIAL MAIL" in two lines, with variations on many of these.

These "O.B." overprints are known on U.S. 1899-1901 stamps; on 1903-06 stamps in red and blue; on 1906 stamps in red, blue, black, yellow and green.

"O.B." overprints were also made on the centavo and peso stamps of the Philippines, per order of May 25, 1907.

Beginning in 1926 the Bureau of Posts issued press-printed official stamps, but many government offices continued to handstamp ordinary postage stamps "O.B." The press-printed "O.B." overprints are listed below.

During the Japanese occupation period 1942-45, the same system of handstamped official overprints prevailed, but the handstamp usually consisted of "K.P.", initials of the Tagalog words, "Kagamitang Pampamahalaan" (Official Business), and the two Japanese characters used in the printed overprint on Nos. NO1 to NO4.

Regular Issue of 1926 Ovptd. in Red

1926, Dec. 20 Unwmk. *Perf. 12*

O1 A42 2c green & black 3.00 1.00
Never hinged 4.50
O2 A42 4c car & blk 3.00 1.25
Never hinged 4.50
a. Vertical pair, imperf. between 750.00
O3 A42 18c lt brn & blk 8.00 4.00
Never hinged 12.00
O4 A42 20c org & blk 7.75 1.75
Never hinged 11.50
Nos. O1-O4 (4) 21.75 8.00
Set, never hinged 32.50

Opening of the Legislative Palace.

Regular Issue of 1917-26 Overprinted

1931 *Perf. 11*

O5 A40 2c green .40 .25
Never hinged .65
a. No period after "B" 17.50 17.50
Never hinged 27.50
b. No period after "O" 40.00 30.00
O6 A40 4c carmine .45 .25
Never hinged .70
a. No period after "B" 40.00 20.00
Never hinged 60.00
O7 A40 6c deep violet .75 .25
Never hinged 1.25
O8 A40 8c yellow brown .75 .25
Never hinged 1.25
O9 A40 10c deep blue 1.20 .25
Never hinged 1.90
O10 A40 12c red orange 2.00 .25
Never hinged 3.00
a. No period after "B" 80.00 80.00
Never hinged 120.00
O11 A40 16c light olive green 1.00 .25
Never hinged 1.50
a. 16c olive bister 2.00 .25
Never hinged 3.00
O12 A40 20c orange yellow 1.25 .25
Never hinged 1.90
a. No period after "B" 80.00 80.00
Never hinged 120.00
O13 A40 26c green 2.00 1.00
Never hinged 3.25
a. 26c blue green 2.50 1.50
Never hinged 4.00
O14 A40 30c gray 2.00 .25
Never hinged 3.25
Nos. O5-O14 (10) 11.80 3.25
Set, never hinged 18.65

Overprinted on Nos. 383-392

1935

O15 A53 2c rose .25 .25
Never hinged .30
a. No period after "B" 15.00 10.00
Never hinged 22.50
b. No period after "O" — —
O16 A54 4c yellow green .25 .25
Never hinged .30
a. No period after "B" 15.00 *40.00*
Never hinged 22.50
O17 A55 6c dark brown .25 .25
Never hinged .40
a. No period after "B" 35.00 35.00
Never hinged 52.50
O18 A56 8c violet .30 .25
Never hinged .45
O19 A57 10c rose carmine .30 .25
Never hinged .45
O20 A58 12c black .75 .25
Never hinged 1.10
O21 A59 16c dark blue .55 .25
Never hinged .85
O22 A60 20c light olive green .60 .25
Never hinged .90
O23 A61 26c indigo .90 .25
Never hinged 1.50
O24 A62 30c orange red .80 .25
Never hinged 1.20
Nos. O15-O24 (10) 4.95 2.50
Set, never hinged 7.40

Nos. 411 and 418 with Additional Overprint in Black

1937-38

O25 A53 2c rose .25 .25
Never hinged .30
a. No period after "B" 25.00 25.00
Never hinged 45.00
b. Period after "B" raised (UL 4) 150.00
O26 A60 20c lt ol grn ('38) .70 .50
Never hinged 1.10

Regular Issue of 1935 Overprinted In Black

a

b

1938-40

O27 A53(a) 2c rose .25 .25
Never hinged .30
a. Hyphen omitted 10.00 10.00
Never hinged 15.00
b. No period after "B" 20.00 *30.00*
Never hinged 30.00
O28 A54(b) 4c yellow green .75 1.00
Never hinged 1.10
O29 A55(a) 6c dark brown .30 .25
Never hinged .45
O30 A56(b) 8c violet .75 .85
Never hinged 1.10
O31 A57(b) 10c rose carmine .25 .25
Never hinged .30
a. No period after "O" 50.00 40.00
Never hinged 75.00
O32 A58(b) 12c black .30 .25
Never hinged .45
O33 A59(b) 16c dark blue .30 .25
Never hinged .45
O34 A60(a) 20c light olive green ('40) .55 .85
Never hinged .85
O35 A61(b) 26c indigo 1.50 *2.00*
Never hinged 2.25
O36 A62(b) 30c orange red .75 .85
Never hinged 1.10
Nos. O27-O36 (10) 5.70 6.80
Set, never hinged 8.25

No. 461 Overprinted in Black — c

1941, Apr. 14 *Perf. 11x10½*

O37 A75(c) 2c apple green .25 *.40*
Never hinged .30

Official Stamps Handstamped in Violet

1944 *Perf. 11, 11x10½*

O38 A53 2c rose (On O27) *375.00 150.00*
Block of 4 *2,000.*
O39 A75 2c apple grn (On O37) 10.00 10.00
Never hinged 15.00
O40 A54 4c yel grn (On O16) *42.50 30.00*
Never hinged 75.00
O40A A55 6c dk brn (On O29) *8,000.* —
O41 A57 10c rose car (On O31) *500.00*
a. No period after "O" *4,000.*
O42 A60 20c lt ol grn (On O22) *8,000.*
O43 A60 20c lt ol grn (On O26) *1,750.*

No. 497 Overprinted Type "c" in Black

1946, June 19 *Perf. 11x10½*

O44 A76 2c sepia .25 .25
Never hinged .25
a. Vertical pair, bottom stamp without ovpt. —

OCCUPATION STAMPS

Issued Under Japanese Occupation

Nos. 461, 438 and 439 Overprinted with Bars in Black

1942-43 Unwmk. *Perf. 11x10½, 11*

N1 A75 2c apple green .25 *1.00*
Never hinged .30
a. Pair, one without overprint —
N2 A58 12c black ('43) .25 *2.00*
Never hinged .40
N3 A59 16c dark blue 5.00 3.75
Never hinged 7.50
Nos. N1-N3 (3) 5.50 6.75
Set, never hinged 8.20

Nos. 435a, 435, 442, 443, and 423 Surcharged in Black

a

b

c

d

1942-43 *Perf. 11*

N4 A55(a) 5(c) on 6c golden brown .25 *.75*
Never hinged .35
a. Top bar shorter and thinner .25 *1.00*
Never hinged .35
b. 5(c) on 6c dark brown .25 *.85*
Never hinged .35
c. As "b," top bar shorter and thinner .25 *1.00*
Never hinged .35
d. Double surcharge, on cover —
N5 A62(b) 16(c) on 30c org red ('43) .25 *.60*
Never hinged .45
N6 A63(c) 50c on 1p red org & blk ('43) .75 *1.25*
Never hinged 1.10
a. Double surcharge *300.00*
N7 A65(d) 1p on 4p bl & blk ('43) 100.00 *200.00*
Never hinged 155.00
Nos. N4-N7 (4) 101.25 202.60
Set, never hinged 156.90

On Nos. N4 and N4b, the top bar measures 1½x22½mm. On Nos. N4a and N4c, the top bar measures 1x21mm and the "5" is smaller and thinner.

The used value for No. N7 is for postal cancellation. Used stamps exist with first day cancellations. They are worth somewhat less.

No. 384 Surcharged in Black

1942, May 18

N8 A54 2(c) on 4c yellow green 6.00 6.00
Never hinged 8.75

Issued to commemorate Japan's capture of Bataan and Corregidor. The American-Filipino forces finally surrendered May 7, 1942. No. N8 exists with "R" for "B" in BATAAN.

No. 384 Surcharged in Black

1942, Dec. 8

N9 A54 5(c) on 4c yellow green .50 *1.00*
Never hinged .75

1st anniversary of the "Greater East Asia War."

Nos. C59 and C62 Surcharged in Black

1943, Jan. 23

N10 AP1 2(c) on 8c carmine .25 *1.00*
Never hinged .35
N11 AP1 5c on 1p sepia .50 *1.50*
Never hinged .75

1st anniv. of the Philippine Executive Commission.

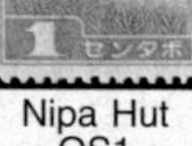

Nipa Hut
OS1

Rice Planting
OS2

Mt. Mayon and Mt. Fuji — OS3

Moro Vinta — OS4

The "c" currency is indicated by four Japanese characters, "p" currency by two.

Engraved; Typographed (2c, 6c, 25c)

1943-44 **Wmk. 257** *Perf. 13*

N12 OS1 1c dp orange .25 .40
Never hinged .30
N13 OS2 2c brt green .25 .40
Never hinged .30
N14 OS1 4c slate green .25 .40
Never hinged .30
N15 OS3 5c orange brown .25 .40
Never hinged .30
N16 OS2 6c red .25 .60
Never hinged .30
N17 OS3 10c blue green .25 .40
Never hinged .30
N18 OS4 12c steel blue 1.00 1.50
Never hinged 1.50
N19 OS4 16c dk brown .25 .40
Never hinged .30
N20 OS1 20c rose violet 1.25 1.75
Never hinged 1.90
N21 OS3 21c violet .25 .40
Never hinged .35
N22 OS2 25c pale brown .25 .40
Never hinged .35
N23 OS3 1p dp carmine .75 1.25
Never hinged 1.15
N24 OS4 2p dull violet 6.50 6.50
Never hinged 10.00
N25 OS4 5p dark olive 16.00 18.00
Never hinged 25.00
Nos. N12-N25 (14) 27.75 32.80
Set, never hinged 42.00

Issued: Nos. N13, N15, 4/1; Nos. N12, N14, N23, 6/7; Nos. N16-N19, 7/14; Nos. N20-N22, 8/16; No. N24, 9/16; No. N25, 4/1/44.

For surcharges see Nos. NB5-NB7.

OS5

1943, May 7 **Photo.** **Unwmk.**

N26 OS5 2c carmine red .25 *.75*
Never hinged .30
N27 OS5 5c bright green .25 *1.00*
Never hinged .35

1st anniversary of the fall of Bataan and Corregidor.

No. 440 Surcharged in Black

1943, June 20 **Engr.** *Perf. 11*

N28 A60 12(c) on 20c light olive green .25 *.75*
Never hinged .35
a. Double surcharge —

350th anniversary of the printing press in the Philippines. "Limbagan" is Tagalog for "printing press."

Rizal Monument, Filipina and Philippine Flag — OS6

1943, Oct. 14 **Photo.** *Perf. 12*

N29 OS6 5c light blue .25 *.90*
Never hinged .30
a. Imperf. .25 .90
N30 OS6 12c orange .25 *.90*
Never hinged .30
a. Imperf. .25 *.90*
N31 OS6 17c rose pink .25 *.90*
Never hinged .30
a. Imperf. .25 *.90*
Nos. N29-N31 (3) .75 *2.70*
Set, never hinged .90

"Independence of the Philippines." Japan granted "independence" Oct. 14, 1943, when the puppet republic was founded.

The imperforate stamps were issued without gum.

José Rizal — OS7

Rev. José Burgos — OS8

Apolinario Mabini — OS9

1944, Feb. 17 **Litho.**

N32 OS7 5c blue .25 *1.00*
Never hinged .30
a. Imperf. .25 *2.00*
Never hinged .35
N33 OS8 12c carmine .25 *1.00*
Never hinged .30
a. Imperf. .25 *2.00*
Never hinged .35
N34 OS9 17c deep orange .25 *1.00*
Never hinged .30
a. Imperf. .25 *2.00*
Never hinged .35
Nos. N32-N34 (3) .75 *3.00*
Set, never hinged .90

See No. NB8.

Nos. C60 and C61 Surcharged in Black

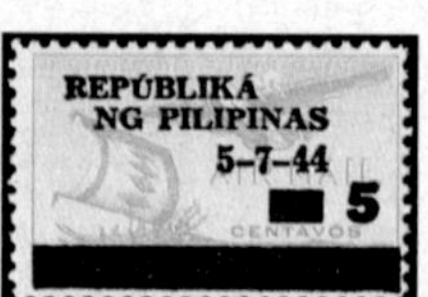

1944, May 7 *Perf. 11*

N35 AP1 5(c) on 20c ultramarine .50 1.00
Never hinged .75
N36 AP1 12(c) on 60c blue green 1.75 1.75
Never hinged 2.50

2nd anniversary of the fall of Bataan and Corregidor.

OS10

1945, Jan. 12 **Litho.** *Imperf.*
Without Gum

N37 OS10 5c dull violet brown .25 *.50*
Never hinged .30
N38 OS10 7c blue green .25 *.50*
Never hinged .30
N39 OS10 20c chalky blue .25 *.50*
Never hinged .30
Nos. N37-N39 (3) *.75* 1.50
Set, never hinged .90

Issued belatedly on Jan. 12, 1945, to commemorate the first anniversary of the puppet Philippine Republic, Oct. 14, 1944. "S" stands for "sentimos."

OCCUPATION SEMI-POSTAL STAMPS

Woman, Farming and Cannery — OSP1

Unwmk.

1942, Nov. 12 **Litho.** *Perf. 12*

NB1 OSP1 2c + 1c pale violet .25 *.60*
Never hinged .30
NB2 OSP1 5c + 1c bright green .25 *1.00*
Never hinged .30
NB3 OSP1 16c + 2c orange 30.00 *32.50*
Never hinged 42.00
Nos. NB1-NB3 (3) 30.50 34.10
Set, never hinged 42.60

Issued to promote the campaign to produce and conserve food. The surtax aided the Red Cross.

Souvenir Sheet

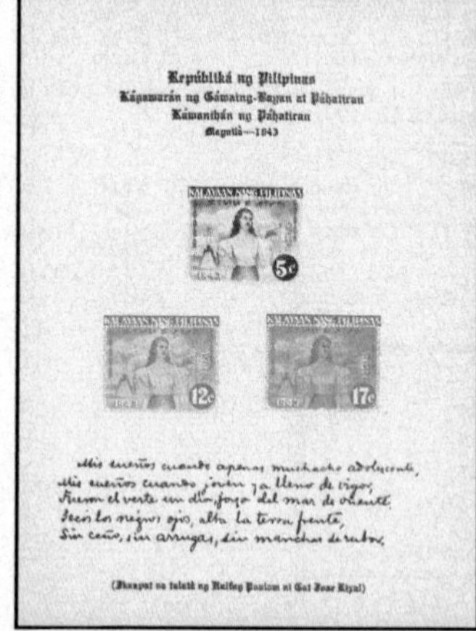

OSP2

1943, Oct. 14 **Without Gum** *Imperf.*

NB4 OSP2 Sheet of 3 75.00 *17.50*

"Independence of the Philippines."

No. NB4 contains one each of Nos. N29a-N31a. Marginal inscription is from Rizal's "Last Farewell." Sold for 2.50p.

The value of No. NB4 used is for a sheet from a first day cover. Commercially used sheets are extremely scarce and worth much more.

Nos. N18, N20 and N21 Surcharged in Black

1943, Dec. 8 Wmk. 257 *Perf. 13*

NB5 OS4 12c + 21c steel blue .25 *1.50*
Never hinged .30
NB6 OS1 20c + 36c rose violet .25 *1.50*
Never hinged .30
NB7 OS3 21c + 40c violet .25 *2.00*
Never hinged .30
Nos. NB5-NB7 (3) .75 *5.00*
Set, never hinged .90

The surtax was for the benefit of victims of a Luzon flood. "Baha" is Tagalog for "flood."

Souvenir Sheet

OSP3

Unwmk.
1944, Feb. 9 Litho. *Imperf.*
Without Gum

NB8 OSP3 Sheet of 3 6.50 3.50

#NB8 contains 1 each of #N32a-N34a.

Sheet sold for 1p, surtax going to a fund for the care of heroes' monuments.

The value for No. NB8 used is for a stamp from a first day cover. Commercially used examples are worth much more.

OCCUPATION POSTAGE DUE STAMP

No. J15 Overprinted with Bar in Blue

1942, Oct. 14 Unwmk. *Perf. 11*

NJ1 D3 3c on 4c brown red 25.00 *35.00*
Never hinged 37.50

On examples of No. J15, two lines were drawn in India ink with a ruling pen across "United States of America" by employees of the Short Paid Section of the Manila Post Office to make a provisional 3c postage due stamp which was used from Sept. 1, 1942 (when the letter rate was raised from 2c to 5c) until Oct. 14 when No. NJ1 went on sale. Value on cover, $175.

OCCUPATION OFFICIAL STAMPS

Nos. 461, 413, 435, 435a and 442 Ovptd. or Srchd. in Black with Bars and

1943-44 Unwmk. *Perf. 11x10½, 11*

NO1 A75 2c apple green .25 *.75*
Never hinged .30
a. Double overprint *400.00*
Never hinged *600.00*
NO2 A55 5(c) on 6c dk brn (On No. 413) ('44) 40.00 *45.00*
Never hinged 55.00
NO3 A55 5(c) on 6c golden brn (On No. 435a) .25 *.90*
Never hinged .35
a. Narrower spacing between bars .25 *.90*
Never hinged .35
b. 5(c) on 6c dark brown (On No. 435) .25 *.90*
Never hinged .35
c. As "b," narrower spacing between bars .25 *.90*
Never hinged .35
d. Double overprint —
NO4 A62 16(c) on 30c org red .30 *1.25*
Never hinged .45
a. Wider spacing between bars .30 *1.25*
Never hinged .45
Nos. NO1-NO4 (4) 40.80 47.90
Set, never hinged 56.10

On Nos. NO3 and NO3b the bar deleting "United States of America" is 9¾ to 10mm above the bar deleting "Common." On Nos. NO3a and NO3c, the spacing is 8 to 8½mm.

On No. NO4, the center bar is 19mm long, 3½mm below the top bar and 6mm above the Japanese characters. On No. NO4a, the center bar is 20½mm long, 9mm below the top bar and 1mm above the Japanese characters.

"K.P." stands for Kagamitang Pampamahalaan, "Official Business" in Tagalog.

Nos. 435 & 435a Surcharged in Black

1944, Aug. 28 *Perf. 11*

NO5 A55 (5c) on 6c golden brown .30 *.40*
Never hinged .45
a. 5(c) on 6c dark brown .30 *.40*
Never hinged .45

Nos. O34 and C62 Overprinted in Black

a

b

NO6 A60(a) 20c light olive green .40 *.50*
Never hinged .60
NO7 AP1(b) 1p sepia .90 *1.00*
Never hinged 1.45
Nos. NO5-NO7 (3) 1.60 1.90
Set, never hinged 2.05

PUERTO RICO

ˌpwer-tə-ˈrē-ˌₒkō

(Porto Rico)

LOCATION — Large island in the West Indies, east of Hispaniola
GOVT. — Former Spanish possession
AREA — 3,435 sq. mi.
POP. — 953,243 (1899)
CAPITAL — San Juan

The island was ceded to the US by the Treaty of 1898.

Spanish issues of 1855-73 used in both Puerto Rico and Cuba are listed as Cuba Nos. 1-4, 9-14, 18-21, 32-34, 35A-37, 39-41, 43-45, 47-49, 51-53, 55-57.

Spanish issues of 1873-1898 for Puerto Rico only are listed in Vol. 4 of this Catalogue.

100 Cents = 1 Dollar (1898)

Issued under U.S. Administration
PROVISIONAL ISSUES

Ponce Issue

A11

Handstamped
1898 Unwmk. *Imperf.*

200 A11 5c violet, *yellowish* *7,500.* —

The only way No. 200 is known used is handstamped on envelopes. Unused stamps always have a violet control mark. Used envelopes do not have the control mark. The same handstamp used to prepare No. 200 also is known handstamped on an unused envelope, also without the control mark. Research into whether the envelopes represent prepaid postmaster provisional usage is ongoing.

Uses on 2c U.S. stamps on cover were strictly as a cancellation, not as provisional postage.

Dangerous forgeries exist.

Coamo Issue

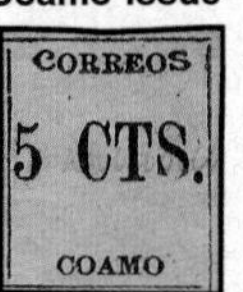

A12

Typeset, setting of 10
1898, Aug.

201 A12 5c black 650. *1,050.*

See the Scott U.S. Specialized Catalogue for more detailed listings.

The stamps bear the control mark "F. Santiago" in violet. About 500 were issued.

Dangerous forgeries exist.

Regular Issue

United States Nos. 279, 279Bf, 281, 272 and 282C Overprinted in Black at 36 degree angle

1899 Wmk. 191 *Perf. 12*

210 A87 1c yellow green 6.00 1.40
a. Overprint at 25 degree angle 8.00 2.25
211 A88 2c redsh car, type IV 5.00 1.25
a. Overprint at 25 degree angle, *Mar. 15* 6.50 2.25
212 A91 5c blue 12.50 2.50
213 A93 8c violet brown 40.00 17.50
a. Overprint at 25 degree angle 45.00 19.00
c. "PORTO RIC" 150.00 110.00
214 A94 10c brown, type I 24.00 6.00
Nos. 210-214 (5) 87.50 28.65

Misspellings of the overprint on Nos. 210-214 (PORTÖ RICU, PORTU RICO, FORTO RICO) are actually broken letters.

United States Nos. 279 and 279B Overprinted Diagonally in Black

1900

215 A87 1c yellow green 7.50 1.40
216 A88 2c red, type IV 5.50 2.00
b. Inverted overprint *12,500.*

POSTAGE DUE STAMPS

United States Nos. J38, J39 and J42 Overprinted in Black at 36 degree angle

1899 Wmk. 191 *Perf. 12*

J1 D2 1c deep claret 22.50 5.50
a. Overprint at 25 degree angle 22.50 7.50
J2 D2 2c deep claret 20.00 6.00
a. Overprint at 25 degree angle 20.00 7.00
J3 D2 10c deep claret 180.00 55.00
a. Overprint at 25 degree angle 160.00 75.00
Nos. J1-J3 (3) 222.50 66.50

Stamps of Puerto Rico were replaced by those of the United States.

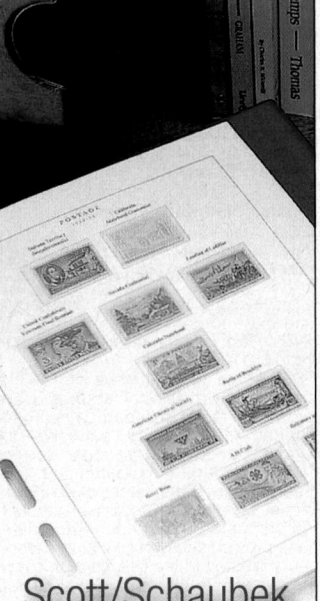

RYUKYU ISLANDS

rē-'yü-ˌ,kyü 'ī-ləndz

LOCATION — Chain of 63 islands between Japan and Formosa, separating the East China Sea from the Pacific Ocean.
GOVT. — Semi-autonomous under United States administration.
AREA — 848 sq. mi.
POP. — 945,465 (1970)
CAPITAL — Naha, Okinawa

The Ryukyus were part of Japan until American forces occupied them in 1945. The islands reverted to Japan May 15, 1972.

Before the general issue of 1948, a number of provisional stamps were used. These included a mimeographed-handstamped adhesive for Kume Island, and various current stamps of Japan handstamped with chops by the postmasters of Okinawa, Amami, Miyako and Yaeyama. Although authorized by American authorities, these provisionals were local in nature, so are omitted in the listings that follow. They are listed in the *Scott United States Specialized Catalogue.*

100 Sen = 1 Yen
100 Cents = 1 Dollar (1958).

Catalogue values for unused stamps in this country are for Never Hinged items.

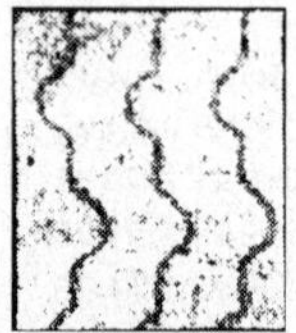
Wmk. 257

Cycad — A1

Lily — A2

Sailing Ship — A3

Farmer — A4

1948-49 Typo. Wmk. 257 *Perf. 13*
Second Printing, July 18, 1949

1	A1 5s magenta	2.25	2.25
2	A2 10s yellow green	5.50	5.50
3	A1 20s yellow green	3.25	3.25
4	A3 30s vermilion	1.40	1.40
5	A2 40s magenta	1.40	1.40
6	A3 50s ultramarine	5.50	*4.00*
7	A4 1y ultramarine	5.50	5.50
	Nos. 1-7 (7)	24.80	23.30

First Printing, July 1, 1948

1a	A1 5s magenta	3.00	*3.50*
2a	A2 10s yellow green	2.00	*2.00*
3a	A1 20s yellow green	2.00	*2.00*
4a	A3 30s vermilion	4.00	*3.50*
5a	A2 40s magenta	60.00	60.00
6a	A3 50s ultramarine	4.00	4.00
7a	A4 1y ultramarine	475.00	350.00
	Nos. 1a-7a (7)	550.00	425.00

First printing: thick yellow gum, dull colors, rough perforations, grayish paper. Second printing: white gum, sharp colors, cleancut perforations, white paper.

Tile Rooftop and Shishi — A5

Ryukyu University — A6

Designs: 50s, Tile rooftop & Shishi. 1y, Ryukyu girl. 2y, Shuri Castle. 3y, Guardian dragon. 4y, Two women. 5y, Sea shells.

Perf. 13x13½
1950, Jan. 21 Photo. Unwmk.
Off-white Paper

8	A5 50s dark carmine rose	.25	.25
a.	White paper, third printing, *Sept. 6, 1958*	.50	.50
b.	"White Sky" variety (pos. 76)	3.50	3.50
9	A5 1y deep blue	3.50	3.00
10	A5 2y rose violet	10.00	6.00
11	A5 3y carmine rose	25.00	11.00
12	A5 4y greenish gray	12.50	11.00
13	A5 5y blue green	6.75	6.00
	Nos. 8-13 (6)	58.00	37.25

No. 8a has colorless gum and an 8-character imprint in the sheet margin. The original 1950 first two printings on off-white paper have yellowish gum and a 5-character imprint.

For No. 8b, a defect in pos. 76 of the plates used for the first two printings resulted in the sky above the tile roof being predominantly white. A new master negative and plate was made for the third printing, so pos. 76 for this printing does not have the "white sky" variety.

For surcharges see Nos. 16-17.

1951, Feb. 12 *Perf. 13½x13*

14	A6 3y red brown	50.00	25.00

Opening of Ryukyu University, Feb. 12.

Pine Tree — A7

1951, Feb. 19 *Perf. 13*

15	A7 3y dark green	40.00	20.00

Reforestation Week, Feb. 18-24.

No. 8 surcharged in Black

Type I

Type II

Type III

There are three types of 10y surcharge:

Type I: narrow-spaced rules, "10" normal spacing, "Kai Tei" characters in 9-point type. First printing, Jan. 1, 1952.

Type II: wide-spaced rules, "10" normal spacing, "Kai Tei" characters in 9-point type. Second printing, June 5, 1952.

Type III: rules and "10" both wide-spaced, "Kai Tei" characters in 8-point type. Third printing, Dec. 8, 1952.

Both eight and nine point type were used in overprinting Nos. 16-17. In the varieties listed below, the first number indicates the size of the "Kai" character, and the second number is the size of the "Tei" character.

1952 *Perf. 13½x13*

16	A5 10y on 50s dark carmine rose (II)	10.00	10.00
c.	8/8 point Kai Tei	10.00	10.00
d.	9/8 point Kai Tei	80.00	80.00
e.	Surcharge transposed	900.00	—
f.	Legend of surcharge only (no obliteration bars)	1,200.	
g.	Wrong font for "0" (pos. 59)	150.00	150.00
h.	Wrong font for "Yen" symbol (pos. 69)	150.00	150.00
i.	Surcharge on "white sky" variety (No. 8b) (pos. 76)	150.00	150.00

On No. 16e, the entire obliteration-bars portion of the surcharge normally under the 10 Yen must be visible at the top of the stamp. Ten examples of No. 16e exist (pos. 91-100) with the full obliteration bars also in the bottom selvage.

Forgeries to defraud the Postal Agency of revenue are known, used only, at the Gusikawa Post Office. Two types. Value, $500 each.

16A	A5 10y on 50s dark carmine rose (I)	35.00	35.00
a.	8/8 point Kai Tei	35.00	35.00
b.	Bottom two bars inverted (pos. 17)	150.00	150.00
c.	Wrong font for "0" (pos. 73)	250.00	250.00
d.	Surcharge on "white sky" variety (No. 8b) (pos. 76)	250.00	250.00
e.	Wide spaced obliterating bars (pos. 72)	150.00	150.00
f.	Wide spaced bottom obliterating bars (pos. 86, 95)	80.00	80.00
16B	A5 10y on 50s dark carmine rose (III)	45.00	35.00
a.	Wrong font for "Yen" symbol (pos. 25, 35, 85)	200.00	200.00
b.	Wrong font for "Tei" (pos. 26)	350.00	350.00
c.	Asterisk missing (pos. 54)	—	—
d.	"Kai Tei" 1.25mm above asterisk (pos. 54)	350.00	350.00
e.	"Kai" omitted (pos. 71)	—	
f.	Narrow spaced "10" (pos. 96)	350.00	350.00
g.	Surcharge on "white sky" variety (No. 8b)	350.00	350.00
h.	Extra wide spaced "10" (pos. 60)	200.00	200.00
i.	Asterisk within 2.0mm of "Kai Tei" (pos. 87)	200.00	200.00

The Kai Tei of the third printing measures the same as the 8-point type in the earlier printings but has differing characteristics. The Top curved line of the Kai is shorter and the lower curved line is also much shorter.

No. 10 surcharged 100y in black

17	A5 100y on 2y rose violet, Kai Tei characters in 9/9-point type, June 16, 1952	2,250.	1,600.
a.	8/8 point Kai Tei	2,250.	1,600.
b.	9/8 point Kai Tei	3,500.	3,500.
c.	Center "0" in wrong font, stamp with 9/9 Kai Tei (pos. 42)	5,000.	5,000.
d.	Center "0" in wrong font, stamp with 8/8 Kai Tei (pos. 67, 86)	3,500.	3,500.
e.	Center "0" in wrong font, stamp with 9/8 Kai Tei (pos. 53)	5,000.	5,000.
f.	Wrong font for last "0" (pos. 59)	5,000.	5,000.
g.	Wrong font for "yen" symbol (pos. 69)	5,000.	5,000.

Varieties of shifted and damaged surcharge characters exist, most notably a damaged ("clipped") Kai.

See note after 16B to differentiate between 8-point and 9-point charaters.

Surcharge forgeries are known. Authentication by competant experts is recommended.

Dove, Bean Sprout and Map — A8

Madanbashi Bridge — A9

1952, Apr. 1 *Perf. 13½x13*

18	A8 3y deep plum	90.00	40.00

Establishment of the Government of the Ryukyu Islands (GRI), April 1, 1952.

1952-53

Designs: 2y, Main Hall, Shuri Castle. 3y, Shurei Gate. 6y, Stone Gate, Soenji Temple, Naha. 10y, Benzaiten-do Temple. 30y, Sonohan Utaki (altar) at Shuri Castle. 50y, Tamaudun (royal mausoleum), Shuri. 100y, Stone Bridge, Hosho Pond, Enkaku Temple.

19	A9 1y red	.30	.30
20	A9 2y green	.40	.40
21	A9 3y aquamarine	.50	.50
22	A9 6y blue	2.00	2.00
23	A9 10y crimson rose	2.50	1.00
24	A9 30y olive green	10.00	7.50
a.	30y light olive green, *1958*	50.00	
25	A9 50y rose violet	14.00	9.00
26	A9 100y claret	17.50	5.00
	Nos. 19-26 (8)	47.20	25.70

Issued: 1y, 2y and 3y, 11/20/52. Others,1/20/53.

Reception at Shuri Castle — A10

Perry and American Fleet A11

1953, May 26 *Perf. 13½x13, 13x13½*

27	A10 3y deep magenta	12.00	6.50
28	A11 6y dull blue	1.25	1.50

Centenary of the arrival of Commodore Matthew Calbraith Perry at Naha, Okinawa.

Chofu Ota and Pencil-shaped Matrix — A12

Shigo Toma and Pen — A13

1953, Oct. 1 *Perf. 13½x13*

29	A12 4y yellow brown	11.00	5.00

Third Newspaper Week.

1954, Oct. 1

30	A13 4y blue	10.00	7.50

Fourth Newspaper Week.

Ryukyu Pottery — A14

Noguni Shrine and Sweet Potato Plant — A15

Designs: 15y, Lacquerware. 20y, Textile design.

1954-55 Photo. *Perf. 13*

31	A14 4y brown	1.00	.60
32	A14 15y vermilion	4.00	4.00
33	A14 20y yellow orange	2.50	2.50
	Nos. 31-33 (3)	7.50	7.10

For surcharges see Nos. C19, C21, C23.

1955, Nov. 26

34	A15 4y blue	11.50	7.00

350th anniv. of the introduction of the sweet potato to the Ryukyu Islands.

Stylized Trees — A16

Willow Dance — A17

1956, Feb. 18 **Unwmk.**
35 A16 4y bluish green 10.00 6.00

Arbor Week, Feb. 18-24.

1956, May 1 ***Perf. 13***

8y, Straw hat dance. 14y, Dancer in warrior costume with fan.

36 A17 5y rose lilac 1.00 .60
37 A17 8y violet blue 2.00 2.00
38 A17 14y reddish brown 3.00 3.00
Nos. 36-38 (3) 6.00 5.60

For surcharges see Nos. C20, C22.

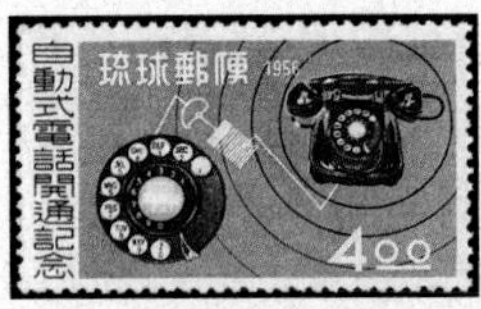

Telephone — A18

1956, June 8
39 A18 4y violet blue 12.50 8.00

Establishment of dial telephone system.

Garland of Pine, Bamboo and Plum — A19

Map of Okinawa and Pencil Rocket — A20

1956, Dec. 1 ***Perf. 13½x13***
40 A19 2y multicolored 1.80 2.00

New Year, 1957.

1957, Oct. 1 **Photo.** ***Perf. 13½x13***
41 A20 4y deep violet blue 1.00 1.00

7th annual Newspaper Week, Oct. 1-7.

Phoenix — A21

1957, Dec. 1 **Unwmk.** ***Perf. 13***
42 A21 2y multicolored .25 .25

New Year, 1958.

Ryukyu Stamps — A22

1958, July 1 ***Perf. 13½***
43 A22 4y multicolored .80 .80

10th anniv. of 1st Ryukyu stamps.

Yen Symbol and Dollar Sign — A23

Perf. 10.3, 10.8, 11.1 & Compound

1958, Sept. 16 **Typo.**

Without Gum

44 A23 ½c orange .90 .90
a. Imperf., pair *1,750.*
b. Horiz. pair, imperf. between 150.00
c. Vert. pair, imperf. between 200.00
d. Vert. strip of 4, imperf. between 800.00
45 A23 1c yellow green 1.40 1.40
a. Horiz. pair, imperf. between 200.00
b. Vert. pair, imperf. between 150.00
c. Vert. strip of 3, imperf. between 700.00
d. Vert. strip of 4, imperf. between 800.00
e. Block of 4, imperf. btwn. vert. & horiz. *10,000.*
46 A23 2c dark blue 2.25 2.25
a. Horiz. pair, imperf. between 200.00
b. Vert. pair, imperf. between *2,000.*
c. Horiz. strip of 3, imperf. between 450.00
d. Horiz. strip of 4, imperf. between 800.00
47 A23 3c deep carmine 1.75 1.50
a. Horiz. pair, imperf. between 200.00
b. Vert. pair, imperf. between 150.00
c. Vert. strip of 3, imperf. between 450.00
d. Vert. strip of 4, imperf. between 800.00
e. Block of 4, imperf. btwn. vert. & horiz. *10,000.*
48 A23 4c bright green 2.25 2.25
a. Horiz. pair, imperf. between *450.00*
b. Vert. pair, imperf. between 200.00
49 A23 5c orange 4.25 3.75
a. Horiz. pair, imperf. between 225.00
b. Vert. pair, imperf. between *850.00*
50 A23 10c aquamarine 5.75 4.75
a. Horiz. pair, imperf. between 300.00
b. Vert. pair, imperf. between 200.00
c. Vert. strip of 3, imperf. between 800.00
51 A23 25c bright violet blue 8.00 6.00
a. Gummed paper, perf. 10.3 ('61) 15.00 15.00
b. Horiz. pair, imperf. between *2,000.*
c. Vert. pair, imperf. between *5,000.*
d. Vert. strip of 3, imperf. between 900.00
52 A23 50c gray 17.50 10.00
a. Gummed paper, perf. 10.3 ('61) 15.00 15.00
b. Horiz. pair, imperf. between *1,750.*
53 A23 $1 rose lilac 12.50 5.50
a. Horiz. pair, imperf. between 500.00
b. Vert. pair, imperf. between *2,500.*
Nos. 44-53 (10) 56.55 38.30

Printed locally. Perforation, paper and shade varieties exist. Nos. 51a and 52a are on off-white paper and perf 10.3.

Gate of Courtesy — A24

1958, Oct. 15 **Photo.** ***Perf. 13½***
54 A24 3c multicolored 1.25 1.25

Restoration of Shureimon, Gate of Courtesy, on road leading to Shuri City.

Imitations of this stamp were distributed in 1972 to discourage speculation in Ryukyuan stamps. The imitations were printed without gum and have a lengthy message in light blue printed on the back. A second type exists, with printed black perforations and three Japanese characters on the back ("Mozo Hin" — imitation) in black. Value, sheet of 10 $15.

Lion Dance A25

Trees and Mountains A26

1958, Dec. 10 **Unwmk.** ***Perf. 13½***
55 A25 1½c multicolored .30 .30

New Year, 1959.

1959, Apr. 30 **Litho.** ***Perf. 13½x13***
56 A26 3c blue, yellow green, green & red .70 .60

"Make the Ryukyus Green" movement.

Yonaguni Moth A27

1959, July 23 **Photo.** ***Perf. 13***
57 A27 3c multicolored 1.20 1.00

Meeting of the Japanese Biological Education Society in Okinawa.

Hibiscus A28

Toy (Yakaji) A29

Designs: 3c, Fish (Moorish idol). 8c, Sea shell (Phalium bandatum). 13c, Butterfly (Kallinia Inachus Eucerca), denomination at left, butterfly going up. 17c, Jellyfish (Dactylometra pacifera Goette).

Inscribed 琉球郵便

1959, Aug. 10 ***Perf. 13x13½***
58 A28 ½c multicolored .30 .25
59 A28 3c multicolored .75 .40
60 A28 8c light ultramarine, black & ocher 10.00 5.50
61 A28 13c light blue, gray & orange 1.75 1.75
62 A28 17c violet blue, red & yellow 20.00 9.00
Nos. 58-62 (5) 32.80 16.90

Four-character inscription measures 10x2mm on ½c; 12x3mm on 3c, 8c; 8½x2mm on 13c, 17c. See Nos. 76-80.

1959, Dec. 1 **Litho.**
63 A29 1½c gold & multicolored .55 .45

New Year, 1960.

University Badge A30

1960, May 22 **Photo.** ***Perf. 13***
64 A30 3c multicolored .95 .75

10th anniv. opening of Ryukyu University.

Dancer — A31

Designs: Various Ryukyu Dances.

1960, Nov. 1 **Photo.** ***Perf. 13***

Dark Gray Background

65 A31 1c yellow, red & violet 2.00 .80
66 A31 2½c crimson, blue & yellow 3.00 1.00
67 A31 5c dark blue, yellow & red 1.00 .50
68 A31 10c dark blue, yellow & red 1.00 .70
Nos. 65-68 (4) 7.00 3.00

See Nos. 81-87, 220.

Torch and Nago Bay A32

Runners at Starting Line A33

1960, Nov. 8
72 A32 3c light blue, green & red 5.00 3.00
73 A33 8c orange & slate green 1.00 .75

8th Kyushu Inter-Prefectural Athletic Meet, Nago, Northern Okinawa, Nov. 6-7.

Little Egret and Rising Sun A34

1960, Dec. 1 **Unwmk.** ***Perf. 13***
74 A34 3c reddish brown 5.00 3.50

National census.

Okinawa Bull Fight — A35

1960, Dec. 10 ***Perf. 13½***
75 A35 1½c bister, dark blue & red brown 1.50 1.50

New Year, 1961.

Type of 1959 With Japanese Inscription Redrawn

A28a

1960-61 **Photo.** ***Perf. 13x13½***
76 A28a ½c multicolored, *Oct. 1961* .60 .45
77 A28a 3c multicolored, *Aug. 23, 1961* 1.00 .35
78 A28a 8c light ultramarine, black & ocher, *July 1, 1960* 1.25 .80
79 A28a 13c blue, brown & red, *July 1, 1960* 1.50 .90

80 A28a 17c violet blue, red & yellow, *July 1, 1960* 12.50 6.00
Nos. 76-80 (5) 16.85 8.50

Size of Japanese inscription on Nos. 78-80 is 10½x1½mm. On No. 79 the denomination is at right, butterfly going down.

Dancer Type of 1960 with "RYUKYUS" Added in English

1961-64 ***Perf. 13***

81 A31 1c multicolored .25 .25
82 A31 2½c multicolored .25 .25
83 A31 5c multicolored .25 .25
84 A31 10c multicolored .45 .40
84A A31 20c multicolored 3.25 1.40
85 A31 25c multicolored 1.00 .90
86 A31 50c multicolored 2.50 1.40
87 A31 $1 multicolored 6.00 .25
Nos. 81-87 (8) 13.95 5.10

Issued: Nos. 86-87, 9/1/61; No. 81, 12/5/61; No. 85, 2/1/62; Nos. 82-84, 6/20/62; No. 84A, 1/20/64.

Pine Tree — A36

1961, May 1 **Photo.** ***Perf. 13***
88 A36 3c yellow green & red 1.80 1.25

"Make the Ryukyus Green" movement.

Naha, Steamer and Sailboat A37

1961, May 20
89 A37 3c aquamarine 2.25 1.50

40th anniv. of Naha.

White Silver Temple — A38

Unwmk.

1961, Oct. 1 **Typo.** ***Perf. 11***
90 A38 3c red brown 2.50 2.00
a. Horiz. pair, imperf. between *1,000.*
b. Vert. pair, imperf. between *700.00*

Merger of townships Takamine, Kanegushiku and Miwa with Itoman.

A 3-cent stamp to commemorate the merger of two cities, Shimoji-cho and Hirara-shi of Miyako Island, was scheduled to be issued on Oct. 30, 1961. However, the merger was called off and the stamp never issued. It features a white chaplet on Kiyako linen on a blue background.

Books and Bird — A39

1961, Nov. 12 **Litho.** ***Perf. 13***
91 A39 3c multicolored 1.10 .90

Book Week.

Rising Sun and Eagles — A40

1961, Dec. 10 **Photo.** ***Perf. 13½***
92 A40 1½c gold, vermilion & black 2.00 2.00

New Year, 1962.

Symbolic Steps, Trees and Government Building — A41

Design: 3c, Government Building.

1962, Apr. 1 **Unwmk.** ***Perf. 13½***
93 A41 1½c multicolored .60 .60
94 A41 3c bright green, red & gray .80 .80

10th anniv. of the Government of the Ryukyu Islands (GRI).

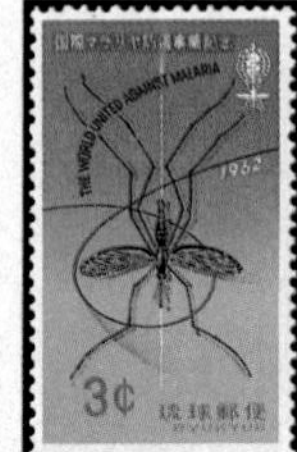

Anopheles Hyrcanus Sinensis — A42

Design: 8c, Malaria eradication emblem and Shurei gate.

1962, Apr. 7 ***Perf. 13½x13***
95 A42 3c multicolored .60 .60
96 A42 8c multicolored .90 .75

World Health Organization drive to eradicate malaria.

Dolls and Toys — A43

1962, May 5 **Litho.** ***Perf. 13½***
97 A43 3c red, black, blue & buff 1.10 1.00

Children's Day, 1962.

Linden or Sea Hibiscus — A44

Flowers: 3c, Indian coral tree. 8c, Iju (Schima liukiuensis Nakal). 13c, Touch-me-not (garden balsam). 17c, Shell flower (Alpinia speciosa).

1962, June 1 **Photo.**
98 A44 ½c multicolored .35 .25
99 A44 3c multicolored .30 .25
100 A44 8c multicolored .55 .45
101 A44 13c multicolored .75 .60
102 A44 17c multicolored 1.25 .80
Nos. 98-102 (5) 3.20 2.35

See Nos. 107 and 114 for 1½c and 15c flower stamps. For surcharge see No. 190.

Earthenware A45

1962, July 5 ***Perf. 13½x13***
103 A45 3c multicolored 3.50 2.50

Philatelic Week.

Japanese Fencing (Kendo) A46

1962, July 25 ***Perf. 13***
104 A46 3c multicolored 3.50 2.50

All-Japan Kendo Meeting in Okinawa, July 25, 1962.

Rabbit Playing near Water, Bingata Cloth Design — A47

1962, Dec. 10 ***Perf. 13x13½***
105 A47 1½c gold & multicolored 1.00 .80

New Year, 1963.

Young Man and Woman, Stone Relief — A48

1963, Jan. 15 **Photo.** ***Perf. 13½***
106 A48 3c gold, black & blue .90 .80

Gooseneck Cactus — A49

Trees and Wooded Hills — A50

1963, Apr. 5 ***Perf. 13x13½***
107 A49 1½c dark blue green, yellow & pink .30 .25

1963, Mar. 25 ***Perf. 13½x13***
108 A50 3c ultramarine, green & red brown 1.00 .80

"Make the Ryukyus Green" movement.

Map of Okinawa — A51

1963, Apr. 30 **Unwmk.** ***Perf. 13½***
109 A51 3c multicolored 1.25 1.00

Opening of the Round Road on Okinawa.

Hawks over Islands — A52

1963, May 10 **Photo.**
110 A52 3c multicolored 1.10 .95

Bird Day, May 10.

Shioya Bridge — A53

1963, June 5
111 A53 3c multicolored 1.10 .95

Opening of Shioya Bridge over Shioya Bay.

Tsuikin-wan Lacquerware Bowl — A54

1963, July 1 **Unwmk.** ***Perf. 13½***
112 A54 3c multicolored 2.75 2.50

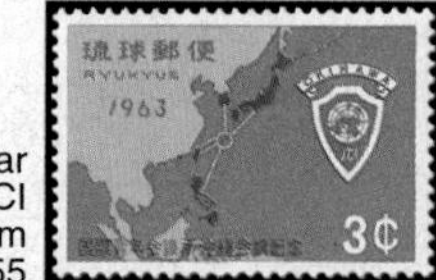

Map of Far East and JCI Emblem A55

1963, Sept. 16 **Photo.** ***Perf. 13½***
113 A55 3c multicolored .70 .70

Meeting of the International Junior Chamber of Commerce (JCI), Naha, Okinawa, Sept. 16-19.

Mamaomoto — A56

1963, Oct. 15 ***Perf. 13x13½***
114 A56 15c multicolored 1.25 .80

Site of Nakagusuku Castle — A57

1963, Nov. 1 ***Perf. 13½x13***
115 A57 3c multicolored .60 .60

Protection of national cultural treasures.

Flame — A58

Dragon — A59

1963, Dec. 10 ***Perf. 13½***

116 A58 3c red, dark blue & yellow .65 .60

15th anniv. of the Universal Declaration of Human Rights.

1963, Dec. 10 **Photo.**

117 A59 1½c multicolored .55 .50

New Year, 1964.

Carnation A60

Pineapples and Sugar Cane A61

1964, May 10 ***Perf. 13½***

118 A60 3c blue, yellow, black & carmine .40 .35

Mothers Day.

1964, June 1

119 A61 3c multicolored .40 .35

Agricultural census.

Minsah Obi (Sash Woven of Kapok) — A62

1964, July 1 **Unwmk.** ***Perf. 13½***

120 A62 3c deep blue, rose pink & ocher .50 .50

a. 3c deep blue, deep carmine & ocher .65 .65

Philatelic Week.

Girl Scout and Emblem A63

1964, Aug. 31 **Photo.**

121 A63 3c multicolored .40 .35

10th anniv. of Ryukyuan Girl Scouts.

Shuri Relay Station — A64

Parabolic Antenna and Map — A65

1964, Sept. 1 **Unwmk.** ***Perf. 13½***

Black Overprint

122 A64 3c deep green .65 .65

a. Figure "1" inverted 30.00 30.00

b. Overprint inverted *1,500.*

c. Overprint missing *3,500.*

d. Overprint inverted and figure "1" inverted *5,000.*

123 A65 8c ultramarine 1.25 1.25

a. Overprint missing *3,500.*

Opening of the Ryukyu Islands-Japan microwave system carrying telephone and telegraph messages. The overprints indicate the system was not actually opened until 1964.

Many of the stamps with overprint errors listed above are damaged. The values listed here are for stamps in very fine condition.

Gate of Courtesy, Olympic Torch and Emblem — A66

1964, Sept. 7 **Photo.** ***Perf. 13½x13***

124 A66 3c ultramarine, yellow & red .30 .25

Relaying the Olympic torch on Okinawa en route to Tokyo.

"Naihanchi," Karate Stance — A67

"Makiwara," Strengthening Hands and Feet — A68

"Kumite," Simulated Combat — A69

1964-65 **Photo.** ***Perf. 13½***

125 A67 3c dull claret, yel & blk .50 .45

126 A68 3c yel & multi .40 .40

127 A69 3c gray, red & blk .40 .40

Nos. 125-127 (3) 1.30 1.25

Karate, Ryukyuan self-defense sport. Issued: No. 125, 10/5/64; No. 126, 2/5/65; No. 127, 6/5/65.

Miyara Dunchi — A70

Snake and Iris (Bingata) — A71

1964, Nov. 1 ***Perf. 13½***

128 A70 3c multicolored .30 .25

Protection of national cultural treasures. Miyara Dunchi was built as a residence by Miyara-pechin Toen in 1819.

1964, Dec. 10 **Photo.**

129 A71 1½c multicolored .30 .25

New Year, 1965.

Boy Scouts — A72

1965, Feb. 6 ***Perf. 13½***

130 A72 3c light blue & multi .45 .40

10th anniv. of Ryukyuan Boy Scouts.

Main Stadium, Onoyama A73

1965, July 1 ***Perf. 13x13½***

131 A73 3c multicolored .25 .25

Inauguration of the main stadium of the Onoyama athletic facilities.

Samisen of King Shoko — A74

1965, July 1 **Photo.** ***Perf. 13½***

132 A74 3c buff & multicolored .45 .40

Philatelic Week.

Kin Power Plant — A75

ICY Emblem, Ryukyu Map — A76

1965, July 1

133 A75 3c green & multi .25 .25

Completion of Kin power plant.

1965, Aug. 24 **Photo.** ***Perf. 13½***

134 A76 3c multicolored .25 .25

20th anniv. of the UN and International Cooperation Year, 1964-65.

Naha City Hall — A77

1965, Sept. 18 **Unwmk.** ***Perf. 13½***

135 A77 3c blue & multicolored .25 .25

Completion of Naha City Hall.

Chinese Box Turtle — A78

Turtles: No. 137, Hawksbill turtle (denomination at top, country name at bottom). No. 138, Asian terrapin (denomination and country name on top).

1965-66 **Photo.** ***Perf. 13½***

136 A78 3c golden brown & multi .30 .30

137 A78 3c black, yel & brown .30 .30

138 A78 3c gray & multicolored .30 .30

Nos. 136-138 (3) .90 .90

Issued: No. 136, 10/20/65; No. 137, 1/20/66; No. 138, 4/20/66.

Horse (Bingata) — A79

1965, Dec. 10 **Photo.** ***Perf. 13½***

139 A79 1½c multicolored .25 .25

a. Gold omitted *2,000.* *2,000.*

New Year, 1966.

There are 92 unused and 2 used examples of No. 139a known.

Noguchi's Okinawa Woodpecker A80

Sika Deer — A81

Design: No. 142, Dugong.

1966 **Photo.** ***Perf. 13½***

140 A80 3c blue green & multi .25 .25

141 A81 3c bl, red, blk, brn & grn .25 .25

142 A81 3c bl, yel grn, blk & red .25 .25

Nos. 140-142 (3) .75 .75

Nature Conservation. Issued No. 140, 2/15; No. 141, 3/15; No. 142, 4/20.

Ryukyu Bungalow Swallow — A82

1966, May 10 **Photo.** ***Perf. 13½***

143 A82 3c sky blue, black & brown .25 .25

4th Bird Week, May 10-16.

Lilies and Ruins A83

1966, June 23 ***Perf. 13x13½***

144 A83 3c multicolored .25 .25

Memorial Day, end of the Battle of Okinawa, June 23, 1945.

University of the Ryukyus A84

1966, July 1

145 A84 3c multicolored .25 .25

Transfer of the University of the Ryukyus from U.S. authority to the Ryukyu Government.

Lacquerware, 18th Century — A85

Tile-Roofed House and UNESCO Emblem — A86

1966, Aug. 1 ***Perf. 13½***

146 A85 3c gray & multicolored .25 .25

Philatelic Week.

1966, Sept. 20 Photo. ***Perf. 13½***

147 A86 3c multicolored .25 .25

20th anniv. of UNESCO.

Government Museum and Dragon Statue — A87

1966, Oct. 6

148 A87 3c multicolored .25 .25

Completion of the GRI (Government of the Ryukyu Islands) Museum, Shuri.

Tomb of Nakasone-Tuimya Genga, Ruler of Miyako — A88

1966, Nov. 1 Photo. ***Perf. 13½***

149 A88 3c multicolored .25 .25

Protection of national cultural treasures.

Ram in Iris Wreath (Bingata) — A89

1966, Dec. 10 Photo. ***Perf. 13½***

150 A89 1½c dark blue & multicolored .25 .25

New Year, 1967.

Clown Fish — A90

Fish: No. 152, Young boxfish (white numeral at lower left). No. 153, Forceps fish (pale buff numeral at lower right). No. 154, Spotted triggerfish (orange numeral). No. 155, Saddleback butterflyfish (carmine numeral, lower left).

1966-67

151 A90 3c orange red & multi .25 .25
152 A90 3c org yel & multi .25 .25
153 A90 3c multicolored .40 .25
154 A90 3c multicolored .35 .25
155 A90 3c multicolored .30 .25
Nos. 151-155 (5) 1.55 1.25

Issued No. 151, 12/20/66; No. 152, 1/10/67; No. 153, 4/10/67; No. 154, 5/25/67; No. 155, 6/10/67.

A 3-cent stamp to commemorate Japanese-American-Ryukyuan Joint Arbor Day was scheduled for release on March 16, 1967. However, it was not released. The stamp in light blue and white features American and Japanese flags joined by a shield containing a tree.

Tsuboya Urn — A91

Episcopal Miter — A92

1967, Apr. 20

156 A91 3c yellow & multicolored .25 .25

Philatelic Week.

1967-68 Photo. ***Perf. 13½***

Seashells: No. 158, Venus comb murex. No. 159, Chiragra spider. No. 160, Green truban. No. 161, Euprotomus bulla.

157 A92 3c light green & multi .25 .25
158 A92 3c grnsh bl & multi .25 .25
159 A92 3c emerald & multi .25 .25
160 A92 3c light blue & multi .30 .25
161 A92 3c bright blue & multi .60 .50
Nos. 157-161 (5) 1.65 1.50

Issued: No. 157, 6/20/67; No. 159, 1/18/68; No. 160, 2/20/68; No. 161, 6/5/68; No. 158, 8/30/68.

Red-tiled Roofs and ITY Emblem A93

1967, Sept. 11 Photo. ***Perf. 13½***

162 A93 3c multicolored .25 .25

International Tourist Year.

Mobile TB Clinic — A94

1967, Oct. 13 Photo. ***Perf. 13½***

163 A94 3c lilac & multicolored .25 .25

15th anniv. of the Anti-Tuberculosis Society.

Hojo Bridge, Enkaku Temple, 1498 — A95

1967, Nov. 1

164 A95 3c blue green & multi .25 .25

Protection of national cultural treasures.

Monkey (Bingata) — A96

TV Tower and Map — A97

1967, Dec. 11 Photo. ***Perf. 13½***

165 A96 1½c silver & multi .25 .25

New Year, 1968.

1967, Dec. 22

166 A97 3c multicolored .25 .25

Opening of Miyako and Yaeyama television stations.

Dr. Kijin Nakachi and Helper — A98

Pill Box (Inro) — A99

1968, Mar. 15 Photo. ***Perf. 13½***

167 A98 3c multicolored .30 .25

120th anniv. of the first vaccination in the Ryukyu Islands, by Dr. Kijin Nakachi.

1968, Apr. 18

168 A99 3c gray & multicolored .45 .45

Philatelic Week.

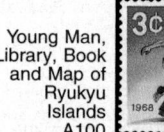

Young Man, Library, Book and Map of Ryukyu Islands A100

1968, May 13

169 A100 3c multicolored .30 .25

10th International Library Week.

Mailmen's Uniforms and Stamp of 1948 A101

1968, July 1 Photo. ***Perf. 13x13½***

170 A101 3c multicolored .30 .25

First Ryukyuan postage stamps, 20th anniv.

Main Gate, Enkaku Temple A102

Photo. & Engr.

1968, July 15 ***Perf. 13½***

171 A102 3c multicolored .30 .25

Restoration of the main gate Enkaku Temple, built 1492-1495, destroyed during World War II.

Old Man's Dance — A103

Mictyris Longicarpus A104

1968, Sept. 15 Photo. ***Perf. 13½***

172 A103 3c gold & multicolored .30 .25

Old People's Day.

1968-69 Photo. ***Perf. 13½***

Crabs: No. 174, Uca dubia stimpson. No. 175, Baptozius vinosus. No. 176, Cardisoma carnifex. No. 177, Ocypode ceratophthalma pallas.

173 A104 3c blue, ocher & black .30 .25
174 A104 3c lt bl grn & multi .35 .30
175 A104 3c light green & multi .35 .30
176 A104 3c light ultra & multi .45 .40
177 A104 3c light ultra & multi .45 .40
Nos. 173-177 (5) 1.90 1.65

Issued: No. 173, 10/10/68; No. 174, 2/5/69; No. 175, 3/5/69; No. 176, 5/15/69; No. 177, 6/2/69.

Saraswati Pavilion A105

1968, Nov. 1 Photo. ***Perf. 13½***

178 A105 3c multicolored .30 .25

Restoration of the Sarawati Pavilion (in front of Enkaku Temple), destroyed during World War II.

Tennis Player A106

Cock and Iris (Bingata) A107

1968, Nov. 23 Photo. ***Perf. 13½***

179 A106 3c green & multi .40 .35

35th All-Japan East-West Men's Soft-ball Tennis Tournament, Naha City, Nov. 23-24.

1968, Dec. 10

180 A107 1½c orange & multi .25 .25

New Year, 1969.

Boxer — A108

Ink Slab Screen — A109

1969, Jan. 3

181 A108 3c gray & multi .40 .30

20th All-Japan Amateur Boxing Championships held at the University of the Ryukyus, Jan. 3-5.

1969, Apr. 17 Photo. *Perf. 13½*

182 A109 3c salmon, indigo & red .40 .35

Philatelic Week.

Box Antennas and Map of Radio Link A110

Gate of Courtesy and Emblems A111

1969, July 1 Photo. *Perf. 13½*

183 A110 3c multicolored .30 .25

Opening of the UHF (radio) circuit system between Okinawa and the outlying Miyako-Yaeyama Islands.

1969, Aug. 1 Photo. *Perf. 13½*

184 A111 3c Prussian blue, gold & vermilion .30 .25

22nd All-Japan Formative Education Study Conf., Naha, Aug. 1-3.

Tug of War Festival A112

Hari Boat Race A113

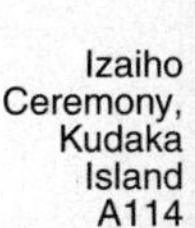

Izaiho Ceremony, Kudaka Island A114

Mortardrum Dance — A115

Sea God Dance A116

1969-70 Photo. *Perf. 13*

185 A112 3c multicolored .30 .25
186 A113 3c multicolored .35 .30
187 A114 3c multicolored .35 .30
188 A115 3c multicolored .50 .45
189 A116 3c multicolored .50 .45
Nos. 185-189 (5) 2.00 1.75

Folklore. Issued, No. 185, 8/1/69; No. 186, 9/5/69; No. 187, 10/3/69; No. 188, 1/20/70; No. 189, 2/27/70.

No. 99 Surcharged

1969, Oct. 15 Photo. *Perf. 13½*

190 A44 ½c on 3c multicolored 1.00 1.00
a. "1/2c" only surcharge 950.00

No. 190a are right margin stamps from a pane with a leftward misregistration of the surcharging plate.

Nakamura-ke Farm House, Built 1713-51 A117

1969, Nov. 1 Photo. *Perf. 13½*

191 A117 3c multicolored .25 .25

Protection of national cultural treasures.

Statue of Kyuzo Toyama, Maps of Hawaiian and Ryukyu Islands A118

1969, Dec. 5 Photo. *Perf. 13½*

192 A118 3c light ultra & multi .50 .50
a. Without overprint *3,000.*
b. Wide-spaced bars *700.00 500.00*

70th anniv. of Ryukyu-Hawaii emigration led by Kyuzo Toyama.
The overprint "1969" at lower left and bars across "1970" at upper right was applied before No. 192 was issued.

Dog and Flowers (Bingata) — A119

Sake Flask Made from Coconut A120

1969, Dec. 10

193 A119 1½c pink & multi .25 .25

New Year, 1970.

1970, Apr. 15 Photo. *Perf. 13½*

194 A120 3c multicolored .25 .25

Philatelic Week, 1970.

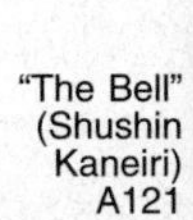

"The Bell" (Shushin Kaneiri) A121

Child and Kidnapper (Chu-nusudu) A122

Robe of Feathers (Mekarushi) A123

Vengeance of Two Young Sons (Nidotichiuchi) A124

The Virgin and the Dragon (Kokonomaki) A125

1970 Photo. *Perf. 13½*

195 A121 3c dull blue & multi .60 .40
a. Souvenir sheet of 4 5.00 5.00
196 A122 3c light blue & multi .60 .40
a. Souvenir sheet of 4 5.00 5.00
197 A123 3c bluish grn & multi .60 .40
a. Souvenir sheet of 4 5.00 5.00
198 A124 3c dull bl grn & multi .60 .40
a. Souvenir sheet of 4 5.00 5.00
199 A125 3c multicolored .60 .40
a. Souvenir sheet of 4 5.00 5.00
Nos. 195-199 (5) 3.00 2.00
Nos. 195a-199a (5) 25.00 25.00

Classic Opera. Issued No. 195, 4/28; No. 196, 5/29; No. 197, 6/30; No. 198, 7/30; No. 199, 8/25.

Underwater Observatory and Tropical Fish — A126

1970, May 22

200 A126 3c blue green & multi .30 .25

Completion of the underwater observatory of Busena-Misaki, Nago.

Noboru Jahana (1865-1908), Politician A127

Map of Okinawa and People A128

Portraits: No. 202, Saion Gushichan Bunjaku (1682-1761), statesman. No. 203, Choho Giwan (1823-1876), regent and poet.

1970-71 Engr. *Perf. 13½*

201 A127 3c rose claret .50 .45
202 A127 3c dull blue green .75 .65
203 A127 3c black .50 .45
Nos. 201-203 (3) 1.75 1.55

Issued: No. 201, 9/25.70; No. 202, 12/22/70; No. 203, 1/22/71.

1970, Oct. 1 Photo.

204 A128 3c red & multicolored .25 .25

Oct. 1, 1970 census.

Great Cycad of Une — A129

1970, Nov. 2 Photo. *Perf. 13½*

205 A129 3c gold & multicolored .25 .25

Protection of national treasures.

Japanese Flag, Diet and Map of Ryukyus A130

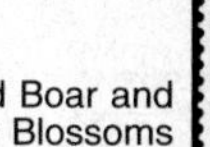

Wild Boar and Cherry Blossoms (Bingata) — A131

1970, Nov. 15 Photo. *Perf. 13½*

206 A130 3c ultra & multi .80 .75

Citizen's participation in national administration to Japanese law of Apr. 24, 1970.

1970, Dec. 10

207 A131 1½c multicolored .25 .25

New Year, 1971.

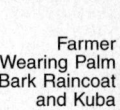

Low Hand Loom (Jibata) A132

Farmer Wearing Palm Bark Raincoat and Kuba Leaf Hat — A133

Fisherman's Wooden Box and Scoop A134

Designs: No. 209, Woman running a filature (reel). No. 211, Woman hulling rice with cylindrical "Shiri-ushi."

1971 Photo. *Perf. 13½*

208 A132 3c light blue & multi .30 .25
209 A132 3c pale grn & multi .30 .25
210 A133 3c light blue & multi .35 .30
211 A132 3c yellow & multi .40 .35
212 A134 3c gray & multi .35 .30
Nos. 208-212 (5) 1.70 1.45

Issued: No. 208, 2/16; No. 209, 3/16; No. 210, 4/30; No. 211, 5/20; No. 212, 6/15.

Water Carrier (Taku) — A135

1971, Apr. 15 Photo. *Perf. 13½*

213 A135 3c blue grn & multi .35 .30

Philatelic Week, 1971.

Old and New Naha, and City Emblem A136

1971, May 20 *Perf. 13*

214 A136 3c ultra & multi .25 .25

50th anniv. of Naha as a municipality.

Caesalpinia Pulcherrima — A137

Design: 2c, Madder (Sandanka).

1971 Photo. *Perf. 13*

215	A137	2c gray & multi	.25	.25
216	A137	3c gray & multi	.25	.25

Issued No. 216, 5/10; No. 215, 9/30.

View from Mabuni Hill — A138

Mt. Arashi from Haneji Sea — A139

Yabuchi Island from Yakena Port — A140

1971-72

217	A138	3c green & multi	.25	.25
218	A139	3c blue & multi	.25	.25
219	A140	4c multicolored	.25	.25
		Nos. 217-219 (3)	.75	.75

Government parks. Issued: No. 217, 7/30/71; No. 218, 8/31/71; No. 219, 1/20/72.

For the 4-cent unissued "stamp" picturing Iriomote Park, originally planned for issue in 1971 but never released, see the note after No. RQ8 in the Scott U.S. Specialized catalogue.

Dancer — A141

Deva King, Torinji Temple — A142

1971, Nov. 1 Photo. *Perf. 13*

220	A141	4c Prussian blue & multicolored	.25	.25

1971, Dec. 1

221	A142	4c dp blue & multi	.25	.25

Protection of national cultural treasures.

Rat and Chrysanthemums A143

Student Nurse A144

1971, Dec. 10

222	A143	2c brown orange & multi	.25	.25

New Year, 1972.

1971, Dec. 24

223	A144	4c lilac & multi	.25	.25

Nurses' training, 25th anniversary.

Birds on Seashore A145

Sun over Islands A147

Coral Reef — A146

1972 Photo. *Perf. 13*

224	A145	5c brt blue & multi	.40	.35
225	A146	5c gray & multi	.40	.35
226	A147	5c ocher & multi	.40	.35
		Nos. 224-226 (3)	1.20	1.05

Issued: No. 226, 3/21; No. 225, 3/30; No. 224, 4/14.

Dove, US and Japanese Flags — A148

1972, Apr. 17 Photo. *Perf. 13*

227	A148	5c bright blue & multi	.80	.80

Antique Sake Pot (Yushibin) — A149

1972, Apr. 20

228	A149	5c ultra & multi	.60	.60

Ryukyu stamps were replaced by those of Japan after May 15, 1972.

AIR POST STAMPS

Catalogue values for all unused stamps in this section are for Never Hinged items.

Dove and Map of Ryukyus — AP1

Perf. 13x13½

1950, Feb. 15 Photo. Unwmk.

C1	AP1	8y bright blue	130.00	40.00
C2	AP1	12y green	25.00	17.50
C3	AP1	16y rose carmine	12.50	10.00
		Nos. C1-C3 (3)	167.50	67.50

Heavenly Maiden AP2

1951-54

C4	AP2	13y blue	2.00	2.00
C5	AP2	18y green	3.00	3.00
C6	AP2	30y cerise	4.50	1.50
C7	AP2	40y red violet	6.50	6.50
C8	AP2	50y yellow orange	7.50	7.50
		Nos. C4-C8 (5)	23.50	20.50

Issued: Nos. C4-C6, 10/1/51; Nos. C7-C8, 8/16/54.

Heavenly Maiden Playing Flute — AP3

1957, Aug. 1 Engr. *Perf. 13½*

C9	AP3	15y blue green	7.50	4.00
C10	AP3	20y rose carmine	10.00	7.00
C11	AP3	35y yellow green	11.00	8.00
a.		35y light yellow green, 1958	*125.00*	
C12	AP3	45y reddish brown	15.00	10.00
C13	AP3	60y gray	17.50	12.00
		Nos. C9-C13 (5)	61.00	41.00

On one printing of No. C10, position 49 shows an added spur on the right side of the second character from the left. Value unused, $175.

Same Surcharged in Brown Red or Light Ultramarine

1959, Dec. 20

C14	AP3	9c on 15y blue green (BrR)	2.50	2.00
a.		Inverted surcharge	*950.00*	
b.		Pair, one without surcharge	—	
C15	AP3	14c on 20y rose carmine (L.U.)	3.25	4.00
C16	AP3	19c on 35y light yellow green (BrR)	7.00	6.00
C17	AP3	27c on 45y reddish brown (L.U.)	15.00	6.00
C18	AP3	35c on 60y gray (BrR)	12.50	9.00
		Nos. C14-C18 (5)	40.25	27.00

No. C15 is found with the variety described below No. C13. Value unused, $125.

Nos. 31-33, 36 and 38 Surcharged in Black, Brown, Red, Blue or Green

1960, Aug. 3 Photo. *Perf. 13*

C19	A14	9c on 4y brown	2.50	1.00
a.		Surcharge inverted and transposed	*15,000.*	*15,000.*
b.		Inverted surcharge (legend only)	*12,000.*	
c.		Surcharge transposed	*1,200.*	
d.		Legend of surcharge only	*3,500.*	
e.		Vert. pair, one without surcharge	*6,000.*	

Nos. C19c and C19d are from a single sheet of 100 with surcharge shifted downward. Ten examples of No. C19c exist with "9c" also in bottom selvage. No. C19d is from the top row of the sheet.

No. C19e is unique, pos. 100, caused by paper foldover.

C20	A17	14c on 5y rose lilac (Br)	3.00	3.00
C21	A14	19c on 15y vermilion (R)	2.50	3.00
C22	A17	27c on 14y reddish brown (Bl)	7.00	2.50
C23	A14	35c on 20y yellow orange (G)	5.00	5.00
		Nos. C19-C23 (5)	20.00	14.50

Wind God — AP4

Designs: 9c, Heavenly Maiden (as on AP2). 14c, Heavenly Maiden (as on AP3). 27c, Wind God at right. 35c, Heavenly Maiden over treetops.

1961, Sept. 21 Unwmk. *Perf. 13½*

C24	AP4	9c multicolored	.30	.25
C25	AP4	14c multicolored	.65	.80
C26	AP4	19c multicolored	.75	.90
C27	AP4	27c multicolored	3.25	.60
C28	AP4	35c multicolored	2.25	1.25
		Nos. C24-C28 (5)	7.20	3.80

Jet over Gate of Courtesy AP5

Jet Plane AP6

1963, Aug. 28 *Perf. 13x13½*

C29	AP5	5½c multicolored	.25	.25
C30	AP6	7c multicolored	.30	.30

SPECIAL DELIVERY STAMP

Catalogue value for the unused stamp in this section is for a Never Hinged item.

Sea Horse and Map of Ryukyus — SD1

Perf. 13x13½

1950, Feb. 15 Unwmk. Photo.

E1	SD1	5y bright blue	25.00	17.50

UNITED NATIONS, OFFICES IN NEW YORK

yu-ˌnī-təd ˈnā-shənz

United Nations stamps are used on UN official mail sent from UN Headquarters in New York City, the UN European Office in Geneva, Switzerland, or from the Donaupark Vienna International Center or Atomic Energy Agency in Vienna, Austria to points throughout the world. They may be used on private correspondence sent through the UN post offices and are valid only at the individual UN post offices.

The UN stamps issued for use in Geneva and Vienna are listed in separate sections. Geneva issues were denominated in centimes and francs and Vienna issues in schillings (now cents and euros) and are valid only in Geneva or Vienna. The UN stamps issued for use in New York, denominated in cents and dollars, are valid only in New York.

Letters bearing Nos. 170-174 provide an exception as they were carried by the Canadian postal system.

See Switzerland Nos. 7O1-7O39 in Volume 6 of the Scott *Standard Postage Stamp Catalogue* for stamps issued by the Swiss Government for official use of the UN European Office and other UN affiliated organizations. See France official stamp listings for stamps issued by the French Government for official use of UNESCO.

Catalogue values for all unused stamps in this section are for Never Hinged items.

Stamps are inscribed in English, French, or Spanish or are multilingual.

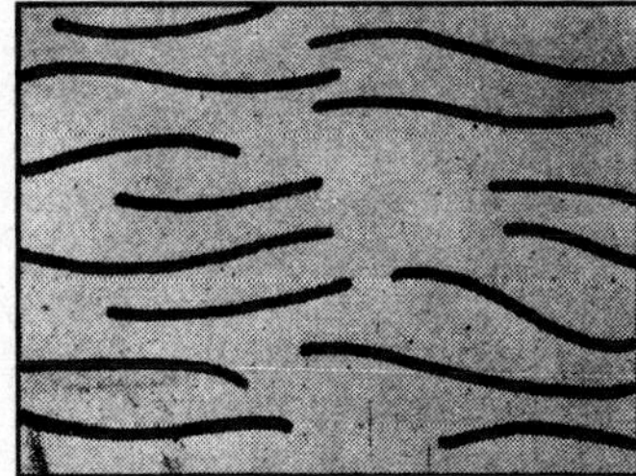

Wmk. 309 — Wavy Lines

Peoples of the World — A1

UN Headquarters Building — A2

"Peace, Justice, Security" — A3

UN Flag — A4

UN Children's Fund — A5

World Unity — A6

Perf. 13x12½, 12½x13

1951 Engr. and Photo. Unwmk.

1	A1	1c magenta	.25	.25
2	A2	1½c blue green	.25	.25
3	A3	2c purple	.25	.25
4	A4	3c magenta & blue	.25	.25
5	A5	5c blue	.25	.25
6	A1	10c chocolate	.25	.25
7	A4	15c violet & blue	.35	.25
8	A6	20c dark brown	.40	.30
9	A4	25c olive gray & blue	.50	.30
10	A2	50c indigo	4.75	2.00
11	A3	$1 red	2.25	1.10
		Nos. 1-11 (11)	9.75	5.45

Veteran's War Memorial Building, San Francisco A7

7th anniversary of the signing of the United Nations Charter.

1952, Oct. 24 *Perf. 12*

12	A7	5c blue	.65	.35

Globe and Encircled Flame A8

4th anniversary of the adoption of the Universal Declaration of Human Rights.

1952, Dec. 10 *Perf. 13½x14*

13	A8	3c deep green	.45	.35
14	A8	5c blue	.55	.40

Refugee Family — A9

Issued to publicize "Protection for Refugees."

1953, Apr. 24 *Perf. 12½x13*

15	A9	3c dark red brown & rose brown	.25	.25
16	A9	5c indigo & blue	.45	.40

Envelope, UN Emblem and Map — A10

Issued to honor the UPU.

1953, June 12 *Perf. 13*

17	A10	3c black brown	.40	.40
18	A10	5c dark blue	1.25	1.00

Gearwheels and UN Emblem — A11

UN activities in the field of technical assistance.

1953, Oct. 24 *Perf. 13x12½*

19	A11	3c dark gray	.25	.25
20	A11	5c dark green	.40	.45

Hands Reaching Toward Flame — A12

Human Rights Day.

1953, Dec. 10 *Perf. 12½x13*

21	A12	3c bright blue	.30	.30
22	A12	5c rose red	1.00	1.00

Ear of Wheat — A13

UN Emblem and Anvil — A14

Issued to honor the FAO.

1954, Feb. 11 *Perf. 12½x13*

23	A13	3c dark green & yellow	.30	.25
24	A13	8c indigo & yellow	.75	.50

1954, May 10 *Perf. 12½x13*

Issued to honor the ILO.

25	A14	3c brown	.25	.25
26	A14	8c magenta	1.00	.85

UN European Office, Geneva A15

Issued on the occasion of UN Day.

1954, Oct. 25 *Perf. 14*

27	A15	3c dark blue violet	1.25	1.00
28	A15	8c red	.35	.30

Mother and Child — A16

Human Rights Day.

1954, Dec. 10 *Perf. 14*

29	A16	3c red orange	10.00	4.00
30	A16	8c olive green	2.00	.35

Symbol of Flight
A17

International Civil Aviation Organization.

1955, Feb. 9 *Perf. 13½x14*
31 A17 3c blue 1.00 .75
32 A17 8c rose carmine .60 .50

UNESCO Emblem
A18

Issued to honor the UN Educational, Scientific and Cultural Organization.

1955, May 11 *Perf. 13½x14*
33 A18 3c lilac rose .35 .30
34 A18 8c light blue .30 .30

UN Charter
A19

10th anniversary of the United Nations.

1955, Oct. 24 *Perf. 13½x14*
35 A19 3c deep plum .90 .55
36 A19 4c dull green .50 .35
37 A19 8c bluish black .35 .25
Nos. 35-37 (3) 1.75 1.15

Souvenir Sheet

1955, Oct. 24 **Wmk. 309** *Imperf.*
38 A19 Sheet of 3 90.00 40.00
a. 3c deep plum 12.50 5.00
b. 4c dull green 12.50 5.00
c. 8c bluish black 12.50 5.00
d. As No. 38, corrected plates (see footnote) 100.00 50.00

Two printings were made of the sheet: No. 38 (200,000) and No. 38d (50,000). No. 38 may be distinguished by the broken lines in the background shading on the 8c. It leaves a small white spot below the left leg of the "n" of "Unies." On No. 38d, the broken line was retouched, eliminating the white spot. The 4c was also retouched.

Hand Holding Torch — A20

Issued in honor of Human Rights Day.

1955, Dec. 9 **Unwmk.** *Perf. 14x13½*
39 A20 3c ultramarine .30 .30
40 A20 8c green .40 .30

Symbols of Telecommunication — A21

Honoring the International Telecommunication Union.

1956, Feb. 17 *Perf. 14*
41 A21 3c turquoise blue .25 .25
42 A21 8c deep carmine .30 .30

Globe & Caduceus — A22

Issued in honor of the World Health Organization.

1956, Apr. 6 *Perf. 14*
43 A22 3c bright greenish blue .25 .25
44 A22 8c golden brown .25 .25

General Assembly
A23

Issued to commemorate UN Day.

1956, Oct. 24 *Perf. 14*
45 A23 3c dark blue .25 .25
46 A23 8c gray olive .25 .25

Flame and Globe
A24

Issued to publicize Human Rights Day.

1956, Dec. 10 *Perf. 14*
47 A24 3c plum .25 .25
48 A24 8c dark blue .25 .25

Weather Balloon — A25

Issued to honor the World Meterological Organization.

1957, Jan. 28 *Perf. 14*
49 A25 3c violet blue .25 .25
50 A25 8c dark carmine rose .25 .25

Badge of UN Emergency Force — A26

Issued in honor of the UN Emergency Force.

1957, Apr. 8 *Perf. 14x12½*
51 A26 3c light blue .25 .25
52 A26 8c rose carmine .25 .25

Nos. 51-52 Re-engraved

1957, Apr.-May *Perf. 14x12½*
53 A26 3c blue .25 .25
54 A26 8c rose carmine .35 .25

On Nos. 53-54 the background within and around the circles is shaded lightly, giving a halo effect. The lettering is more distinct with a line around each letter.

UN Emblem and Globe — A27

Issued to honor the Security Council.

1957, Oct. 24 *Perf. 12½x13*
55 A27 3c orange brown .25 .25
56 A27 8c dark blue green .25 .25

Flaming Torch — A28

Issued in honor of Human Rights Day.

1957, Dec. 10 *Perf. 14*
57 A28 3c red brown .25 .25
58 A28 8c black .25 .25

Atom & UN Emblem — A29

Issued in honor of the International Atomic Energy Agency.

1958, Feb. 10 *Perf. 12*
59 A29 3c olive .25 .25
60 A29 8c blue .25 .25

Central Hall, Westminster
A30

UN Seal
A31

Central Hall, Westminster, London, was the site of the first session of the United Nations General Assembly, 1946.

1958, Apr. 14 *Perf. 12*
61 A30 3c violet blue .25 .25
62 A30 8c rose claret .25 .25

1958, Oct. 24 *Perf. 13½x14*
63 A31 4c red orange .25 .25

1958, June 2 *Perf. 13x14*
64 A31 8c bright blue .25 .25

Issue dates: 4c, Oct. 24; 8c, June 2.

Gearwheels — A32

Issued to honor the Economic and Social Council.

1958, Oct. 24 **Unwmk.** *Perf. 12*
65 A32 4c dark blue green .25 .25
66 A32 8c vermilion .25 .25

Hands Upholding Globe — A33

Human Rights Day and to commemorate the 10th anniversary of the signing of the Universal Declaration of Human Rights.

1958, Dec. 10 **Unwmk.** *Perf. 12*
67 A33 4c yellow green .25 .25
68 A33 8c red brown .25 .25

New York City Building, Flushing Meadows
A34

Site of many General Assembly meetings, 1946-50.

1959, Mar. 30 **Unwmk.** *Perf. 12*
69 A34 4c light lilac rose .25 .25
70 A34 8c aquamarine .25 .25

UN Emblems and Symbols of Agriculture, Industry and Trade — A35

Figure Adapted from Rodin's "Age of Bronze" — A36

Issued to honor the Economic Commission for Europe.

1959, May 18 **Unwmk.** *Perf. 12*
71 A35 4c blue .25 .25
72 A35 8c red orange .25 .25

1959, Oct. 23 **Unwmk.** *Perf. 12*

Issued to honor the Trusteeship Council.

73 A36 4c bright red .25 .25
74 A36 8c dark olive green .25 .25

World Refugee Year Emblem — A37

World Refugee Year, July 1, 1959-June 30, 1960.

1959, Dec. 10 **Unwmk.** *Perf. 12*
75 A37 4c olive & red .25 .25
76 A37 8c olive & bright greenish blue .25 .25

Chaillot Palace, Paris — A38

Chaillot Palace in Paris was the site of General Assembly meetings in 1948 and 1951.

1960, Feb. 29 **Unwmk.** *Perf. 14*
77 A38 4c rose lilac & blue .25 .25
78 A38 8c dull green & brown .25 .25

Map of Far East and Steel Beam A39

Honoring the Economic Commission for Asia and the Far East (ECAFE).

Perf. 13x13½

1960, Apr. 11 Photo. Unwmk.

79 A39 4c deep claret, blue green & dull yellow .25 .25
80 A39 8c olive green, blue & rose .25 .25

Tree, FAO and UN Emblems — A40

Fifth World Forestry Congress, Seattle, Washington, Aug. 29-Sept. 10.

Perf. 13½

1960, Aug. 29 Photo. Unwmk.

81 A40 4c dark blue, green & orange .25 .25
82 A40 8c yellow green, black & orange .25 .25

UN Headquarters and Preamble to UN Charter — A41

Issued to commemorate the 15th anniversary of the United Nations.

1960, Oct. 24 Unwmk. *Perf. 11*

83 A41 4c blue .25 .25
84 A41 8c gray .25 .25

Souvenir Sheet

Imperf

85 Sheet of 2 1.25 1.25
a. A41 4c blue .55 .55
b. A41 8c gray .55 .55

Block and Tackle — A42

Scales of Justice — A43

Honoring the International Bank for Reconstruction and Development.

Perf. 13½x13

1960, Dec. 9 Photo. Unwmk.

86 A42 4c multicolored .25 .25
87 A42 8c multicolored .25 .25

Perf. 13½x13

1961, Feb. 13 Photo. Unwmk.

Issued to honor the International Court of Justice.

88 A43 4c yellow, orange brown & black .25 .25
89 A43 8c yellow, green & black .25 .25

Seal of International Monetary Fund — A44

Issued to honor the International Monetary Fund.

Perf. 13x13½

1961, Apr. 17 Photo. Unwmk.

90 A44 4c bright bluish green .25 .25
91 A44 7c terra cotta & yellow .25 .25

Abstract Group of Flags — A45

Perf. 11½

1961, June 5 Photo. Unwmk.

92 A45 30c multicolored .45 .30

See UN Offices in Geneva No. 10.

Cogwheel and Map of Latin America — A46

Issued to honor the Economic Commission for Latin America.

Perf. 13½

1961, Sept. 18 Photo. Unwmk.

93 A46 4c blue, red & citron .25 .25
94 A46 11c green, lilac & orange vermilion .25 .25

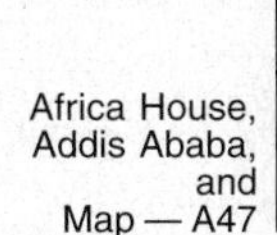

Africa House, Addis Ababa, and Map — A47

Issued to honor the Economic Commission for Africa.

Perf. 11½

1961, Oct. 24 Photo. Unwmk.

95 A47 4c ultramarine, orange, yellow & brown .25 .25
96 A47 11c emerald, orange, yellow & brown .25 .25

Mother Bird Feeding Young and UNICEF Seal — A48

15th anniversary of the United Nations Children's Fund.

Perf. 11½

1961, Dec. 4 Photo. Unwmk.

97 A48 3c brown, gold, orange & yellow .25 .25
98 A48 4c brown, gold, blue & emerald .25 .25
99 A48 13c deep green, gold, purple & pink .25 .25
Nos. 97-99 (3) .75 .75

Family and Symbolic Buildings A49

UN program for housing and urban development,

Perf. 14½x14

1962, Feb. 28 Photo. Unwmk.

Central design multicolored

100 A49 4c bright blue .25 .25
a. Black omitted 200.00
b. Yellow omitted —
c. Brown omitted —
101 A49 7c orange brown .25 .25
a. Red omitted —
b. Black omitted —
c. Gold omitted —

"The World Against Malaria" — A50

Issued in honor of the WHO and to call attention to the international campaign to eradicate malaria from the world.

Perf. 14x14½

1962, Mar. 30 Photo. Unwmk.

Word frame in gray

102 A50 4c orange, yellow, brown, green & black .25 .25
103 A50 11c green, yellow, brown & indigo .25 .25

"Peace" — A51

UN Flag — A52

Hands Combining "UN" and Globe — A53

UN Emblem over Globe A54

Photo.; Engr. (5c)

Perf. 14x14½

1962, May 25 Unwmk.

104 A51 1c vermilion, blue, black & gray .25 .25
105 A52 3c light green, Prussian blue, yellow & gray .25 .25

Perf. 12

106 A53 5c dark carmine rose .25 .25

Perf. 12½

107 A54 11c dark & light blue & gold .25 .25
Nos. 104-107 (4) 1.00 1.00

See #167 and UN Offices in Geneva #2, 6. Compare A51 with A76.

Flag at Half-mast and UN Headquarters A55

World Map Showing Congo A56

Issued on the 1st anniversary of the death of Dag Hammarskjold, Secretary General of the United Nations 1953-61, in memory of those who died in the service of the United Nations.

Perf. 11½

1962, Sept. 17 Photo. Unwmk.

108 A55 5c black, light blue & blue .25 .25
109 A55 15c black, gray olive & blue .25 .25

Perf. 11½

1962, Oct. 24 Photo. Unwmk.

Issued to commemorate the United Nations Operation in the Congo.

110 A56 4c olive, orange, black & yellow .25 .25
111 A56 11c blue green, orange, black & yellow .25 .25

Globe in Universe and Palm Frond — A57

Issued to honor the Committee on Peaceful Uses of Outer Space.

Perf. 14x13½

1962, Dec. 3 Engr. Unwmk.

112 A57 4c violet blue .25 .25
113 A57 11c rose claret .25 .25

Development Decade Emblem — A58

UN Development Decade and UN Conference on the Application of Science and Technology for the Benefit of the Less Developed Areas, Geneva, Feb. 4-20.

Perf. 11½

1963, Feb. 4 Photo. Unwmk.

114 A58 5c pale green, maroon, dark blue & Prussian blue .25 .25
115 A58 11c yellow, maroon, dark blue & Prussian blue .25 .25

Stalks of Wheat — A59

Issued for the "Freedom from Hunger" campaign of the Food and Agriculture Organization.

Perf. 11½

1963, Mar. 22 Photo. Unwmk.

116 A59 5c vermilion, green & yellow .25 .25
117 A59 11c vermilion, deep claret & yellow .25 .25

Bridge over Map of New Guinea — A60

1st anniversary of the United Nations Temporary Executive Authority (UNTEA) in West New Guinea (West Irian).

Perf. 11½

1963, Oct. 1 Photo. Unwmk.

118 A60 25c blue, green & gray .50 .40

General Assembly Building, New York — A61

Since October 1955 all sessions of the General Assembly have been held in the General Assembly Hall, UN Headquarters, NY.

Unwmk.

1963, Nov. 4 Photo. *Perf. 13*

119 A61 5c violet blue, blue, yellow green & red .25 .25
120 A61 11c green, yellow green, blue, yellow & red .25 .25

Flame — A62

15th anniversary of the signing of the Universal Declaration of Human Rights.

Unwmk.

1963, Dec. 10 Photo. *Perf. 13*

121 A62 5c green, gold, red & yellow .25 .25
122 A62 11c carmine, gold, blue & yellow .25 .25

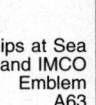

Ships at Sea and IMCO Emblem A63

Issued to honor the Intergovernmental Maritime Consultative Organization.

Perf. 11½

1964, Jan. 13 Photo. Unwmk.

123 A63 5c blue, olive, ocher & yellow .25 .25
124 A63 11c dark blue, dark green, emerald & yellow .25 .25

Map of the World — A64

UN Emblem — A65

Three Men United Before Globe — A66

Stylized Globe and Weather Vane — A67

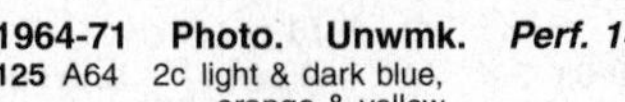

1964-71 Photo. Unwmk. *Perf. 14*

125 A64 2c light & dark blue, orange & yellow green .25 .25
a. Perf. 13x13½ .25 .25

Perf. 11½

126 A65 7c dark blue, orange brown & black .25 .25
127 A66 10c blue green, olive green & black .25 .25
128 A67 50c multicolored .55 .45
Nos. 125-128 (4) 1.30 1.20

Issued: 2c, 7c, May 29; 50c, Mar. 6.
See UN Offices in Geneva Nos. 3, 12.

Arrows Showing Global Flow of Trade A68

Issued to commemorate the UN Conference on Trade and Development, Geneva, Mar. 23-June 15.

Unwmk.

1964, June 15 Photo. *Perf. 13*

129 A68 5c black, red & yellow .25 .25
130 A68 11c black, olive & yellow .25 .25

Poppy Capsule and Hands A69

Honoring international efforts and achievements in the control of narcotics.

Unwmk.

1964, Sept. 21 Engr. *Perf. 12*

131 A69 5c rose red & black .25 .25
132 A69 11c emerald & black .25 .25

Padlocked Atomic Blast — A70

Signing of the nuclear test ban treaty pledging an end to nuclear explosions in the atmosphere, outer space and under water.

Litho. and Engr.

Perf. 11x11½

1964, Oct. 23 Unwmk.

133 A70 5c dark red & dark brown .25 .25

"Education for Progress" A71

Issued to publicize the UNESCO world campaign for universal literacy and for free compulsory primary education.

Perf. 12½

1964, Dec. 7 Photo. Unwmk.

134 A71 4c orange, red, bister, green & blue .25 .25
135 A71 5c bister, red, dark & light blue .25 .25
136 A71 11c green, light blue, black & rose .25 .25
Nos. 134-136 (3) .75 .75

Progress Chart, Key & Globe — A72

Issued to publicize the Special Fund program to speed economic growth and social advancement in low-income countries.

Perf. 13½x13

1965, Jan. 25 Photo. Unwmk.

137 A72 5c dull blue, dark blue, yellow & red .25 .25
138 A72 11c yellow green, dark blue, yellow & red .25 .25
a. Black omitted (UN emblem on key) —

Leaves & View of Cyprus — A73

Issued to honor the United Nations Peacekeeping Force on Cyprus.

Perf. 11½

1965, Mar. 4 Photo. Unwmk.

139 A73 5c orange, olive & black .25 .25
140 A73 11c yellow green, blue green & black .25 .25

"From Semaphore to Satellite" A74

Centenary of the International Telecommunication Union.

Perf. 11½

1965, May 17 Photo. Unwmk.

141 A74 5c aquamarine, orange, blue & purple .25 .25
142 A74 11c light violet, red orange, bister & bright green .25 .25

ICY Emblem — A75

20th anniversary of the United Nations and International Cooperation Year.

Perf. 14x13½

1965, June 26 Engr. Unwmk.

143 A75 5c dark blue .25 .25
144 A75 15c lilac rose .25 .25

Souvenir Sheet

145 A75 Sheet of two .35 .35

"Peace" — A76

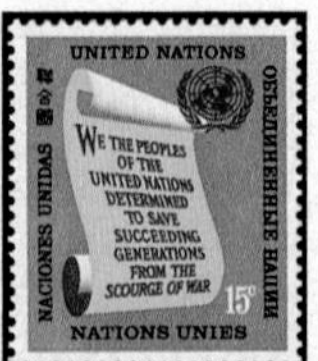

Opening Words, UN Charter — A77

UN Headquarters, Emblem — A78

UN Emblem — A79

UN Emblem A80

Perf. 13½x13

1965-66 Photo. Unwmk.

146 A76 1c vermilion, blue, black & gray .25 .25

Perf. 14

147 A77 15c olive bister, dull yellow, black & deep claret .25 .25

Perf. 12

148 A78 20c dark blue, blue, red & yellow .25 .25
a. Yellow omitted —

Litho. and Embossed

Perf. 14

149 A79 25c light & dark blue .30 .25
a. 25c light & dark blue, new dk blue plate/cylinder (see footnote) .30 .25
b. As "a," tagged 10.00 10.00

Photo.

Perf. 11½

150 A80 $1 aquamarine & sapphire 1.60 1.60
Nos. 146-150 (5) 2.65 2.60

Issued: 1c, No. 149, 9/20/65; No. 149a, 11/5/65; 15c, 20c, 10/25/65; $1, 3/25/66.

On No. 149, the dark blue "halo" of the U.N. emblem is large, overlapping the "25c." On No. 149a, a new dark blue plate/cylinder was used, making the "halo" of the U.N. emblem smaller.

See UN Offices in Geneva Nos. 5, 9, 11.

Fields & People — A81

Issued to emphasize the importance of the world's population growth and its problems and to call attention to population trends and development.

Unwmk.

1965, Nov. 29 Photo. *Perf. 12*

151 A81 4c multicolored .25 .25
152 A81 5c multicolored .25 .25
153 A81 11c multicolored .25 .25
Nos. 151-153 (3) .75 .75

Globe & Flags of UN Members — A82

Issued to honor the World Federation of United Nations Associations.

Perf. 11½

1966, Jan. 31 Photo. Unwmk.

154 A82 5c multicolored .25 .25
155 A82 15c multicolored .25 .25

WHO Headquarters, Geneva — A83

Issued to commemorate the opening of the World Health Organization Headquarters, Geneva.

1966, May 26 Photo. *Perf. 12½x12*

Granite Paper

156 A83 5c lt & dk blue, orange, green & bister .25 .25
157 A83 11c orange, lt & dark blue, green & bister .25 .25

Coffee — A84

Issued to commemorate the International Coffee Agreement of 1962.

1966, Sept. 19 Photo. ***Perf. 13½x13***

158 A84 5c orange, lt blue, green, red & dk brown .25 .25
159 A84 11c lt blue, yellow, green, red & dk brown .25 .25

UN Observer — A85

Issued to honor the Peace Keeping United Nation Observers.
Printed by Courvoisier, S.A. Panes of 50. Designed by Ole S. Hamann.

1966, Oct. 24 Photo. ***Perf. 11½***
Granite Paper

160 A85 15c steel blue, orange, black & green .25 .25

Children of Various Races — A86

20th anniversary of the United Nations Children's Fund (UNICEF).

1966, Nov. 28 Litho. ***Perf. 13x13½***

161 A86 4c pink & multi .25 .25
162 A86 5c pale green & multi .25 .25
a. Yellow omitted — —
163 A86 11c light ultramarine & multi .25 .25
b. Dark blue omitted —
Nos. 161-163 (3) .75 .75

Hand Rolling up Sleeve & Chart Showing Progress A87

United Nations Development Program.

1967, Jan. 23 Photo. ***Perf. 12½***

164 A87 5c green, yellow, purple & orange .25 .25
165 A87 11c blue, chocolate, light green & orange .25 .25

Type of 1962 and

UN Headquarters, New York & World Map — A88

1967 Photo. ***Perf. 11½***

166 A88 1½c ultramarine, black, orange & ocher .25 .25

Size: 33x23mm

167 A53 5c red brown, brown & orange yellow .25 .25

Issue dates: 1½c, Mar. 17; 5c, Jan. 23.
See UN Offices in Geneva No. 1.

Fireworks — A89

Issued to honor all nations which gained independence since 1945.

1967, Mar. 17 Photo. ***Perf. 14x14½***

168 A89 5c dark blue & multi .25 .25
169 A89 11c brown lake & multi .25 .25

"Peace" — A90

UN Pavilion, EXPO '67 — A91

EXPO '67, International Exhibition, Montreal, Apr. 28-Oct. 27, 1967.

Engr. & Litho.

1967, Apr. 28 ***Perf. 11***

170 A90 4c red & red brown .25 .25
171 A90 5c blue & red brown .25 .25

Litho.

172 A91 8c multicolored .25 .25

Engr. and Litho.

173 A90 10c green & red brown .25 .25
174 A90 15c dark brown & red brown .25 .25
Nos. 170-174 (5) 1.25 1.25

Luggage Tags and UN Emblem A92

Issued to publicize International Tourist Year, 1967.

1967, June 19 Litho. ***Perf. 14***

175 A92 5c reddish brown & multi .25 .25
176 A92 15c ultramarine & multi .25 .25

Quotation from Isaiah 2:4 — A93

Issued to publicize the UN General Assembly's resolutions on general and complete disarmament and for suspension of nuclear and thermonuclear tests.

1967, Oct. 24 Photo. ***Perf. 14***

177 A93 6c ultramarine, yellow, gray & brown .25 .25
178 A93 13c magenta, yellow, gray & brown .25 .25

Art at UN Issue
Miniature Sheet

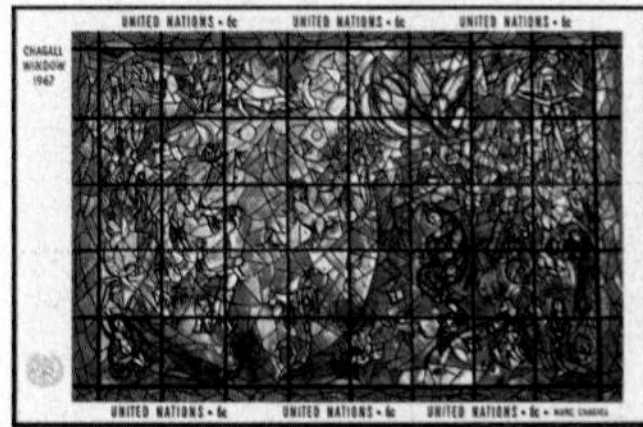
Memorial Window — A94

"The Kiss of Peace" — A95

1967, Nov. 17 Litho. ***Rouletted 9***

179 A94 6c Sheet of 6, #a.-f. .40 .40

Perf. 13x13½

180 A95 6c multicolored .25 .25

No. 179 contains six 6c stamps, each rouletted on 3 sides, imperf. on fourth side. Size: 124x80mm. On Nos. 179a-179c, "United Nations 6c" appears at top; on Nos. 179d-179f, at bottom. No. 179f includes name "Marc Chagall."

Globe and Major UN Organs A96

Issued to honor the United Nations Secretariat.

1968, Jan. 16 Photo. ***Perf. 11½***

181 A96 6c multicolored .25 .25
182 A96 13c multicolored .25 .25

Art at UN Issue

Statue by Henrik Starcke — A97

1968, Mar. 1 Photo. ***Perf. 11½***

183 A97 6c blue & multi .25 .25
184 A97 75c rose lake & multi 1.10 .90

The 6c is part of the "Art at the UN" series. The 75c belongs to the regular definitive series. The teakwood Starcke statue, which stands in the Trusteeship Council Chamber, represents mankind's search for freedom and happiness.
See UN Offices in Geneva No. 13.

Factories and Chart — A98

Issued to publicize the UN Industrial Development Organization.

1968, Apr. 18 Litho. ***Perf. 12***

185 A98 6c greenish blue, lt greenish blue, black & dull claret .25 .25
186 A98 13c dull red brown, light red brown, black & ultra .25 .25

UN Headquarters A99

1968, May 31 Litho. ***Perf. 12x13½***

187 A99 6c green, blue, black & gray .25 .25

Radarscope and Globes A100

Issued to publicize World Weather Watch, a new weather system directed by the World Meteorological Organization.

1968, Sept. 19 Photo. ***Perf. 13x13½***

188 A100 6c green, black, ocher, red & blue .25 .25
189 A100 20c lilac, black, ocher, red & blue .30 .25

Human Rights Flame — A101

Issued for International Human Rights Year, 1968.

Photo.; Foil Embossed

1968, Nov. 22 ***Perf. 12½***

190 A101 6c bright blue, deep ultra & gold .25 .25
191 A101 13c rose red, dark red & gold .25 .25

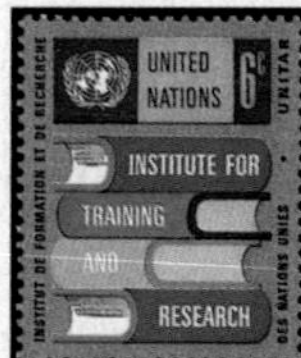

Books and UN Emblem — A102

United Nations Institute for Training and Research (UNITAR).

1969, Feb. 10 Litho. ***Perf. 13½***

192 A102 6c yellow green & multi .25 .25
193 A102 13c bluish lilac & multi .25 .25

UN Building, Santiago, Chile A103

The UN Building in Santiago, Chile, is the seat of the UN Economic Commission for Latin America and of the Latin American Institute for Economic and Social Planning.

1969, Mar. 14 Litho. ***Perf. 14***

194 A103 6c light blue, violet blue & light green .25 .25
195 A103 15c pink, cream & red brown .25 .25

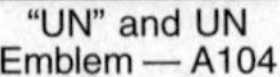

"UN" and UN Emblem — A104

UN Emblem and Scales of Justice — A105

1969, Mar. 14 Photo. *Perf. 13½*

196 A104 13c bright blue, black & gold .25 .25

See UN Offices in Geneva No. 7.

1969, Apr. 21 Photo. *Perf. 11½*

20th anniversary session of the UN International Law Commission.

Granite Paper

197 A105 6c bright green, ultra & gold .25 .25

198 A105 13c crimson, lilac & gold .25 .25

Allegory of Labor, Emblems of UN and ILO A106

Issued to publicize "Labor and Development" and to commemorate the 50th anniversary of the International Labor Organization.

1969, June 5 Photo. *Perf. 13*

199 A106 6c blue, deep blue, yellow & gold .25 .25

200 A106 20c orange vermilion, magenta, yellow & gold .25 .25

Art at UN Issue

Ostrich, Tunisian Mosaic, 3rd Century — A107

Design: 13c, Pheasant; French inscription.

1969, Nov. 21 Photo. *Perf. 14*

201 A107 6c blue & multi .25 .25

202 A107 13c red & multi .25 .25

Art at UN Issue

Peace Bell, Gift of Japanese A108

The Peace Bell was a gift of the people of Japan in 1954, cast from donated coins and metals. It is housed in a Japanese cypress structure at UN Headquarters, New York.

1970, Mar. 13 Photo. *Perf. 13½x13*

203 A108 6c violet blue & multi .25 .25

204 A108 25c claret & multi .30 .25

Mekong River, Power Lines and Map of Delta — A109

Issued to publicize the Lower Mekong Basin Development project under UN auspices.

1970, Mar. 13 *Perf. 14*

205 A109 6c dark blue & multi .25 .25

206 A109 13c deep plum & multi .25 .25

"Fight Cancer" A110

Issued to publicize the fight against cancer in connection with the 10th International Cancer Congress of the International Union Against Cancer, Houston, Texas, May 22-29.

1970, May 22 Litho. *Perf. 14*

207 A110 6c blue & black .25 .25

208 A110 13c olive & black .25 .25

UN Emblem and Olive Branch A111

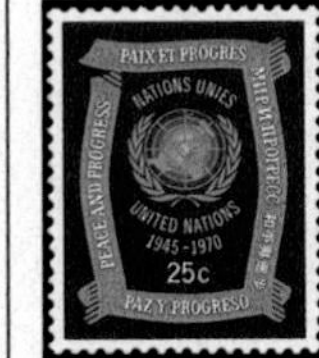

UN Emblem — A112

25th anniv. of the UN. First day covers were postmarked at UN Headquarters, NY, and at San Francisco.

1970, June 26 Photo. *Perf. 11½*

209 A111 6c red, gold, dark & light blue .25 .25

210 A111 13c dark blue, gold, green & red .25 .25

Perf. 12½

211 A112 25c dark blue, gold & light blue .35 .25

Nos. 209-211 (3) .85 .75

Souvenir Sheet

Imperf

212 Sheet of 3 .85 .85

a. A111 6c red, gold & multicolored .25 .25

b. A111 13c violet blue, gold & multi .25 .25

c. A112 25c violet blue, gold & light blue .35 .35

Scales, Olive Branch, Progress Symbol A113

Sea Bed, Fish, Underwater Research A114

Issued to publicize "Peace, Justice and Progress" in connection with the 25th anniversary of the United Nations.

1970, Nov. 20 Photo. *Perf. 13½*

213 A113 6c gold & multi .25 .25

214 A113 13c silver & multi .25 .25

Photo. & Engr.

1971, Jan. 25 *Perf. 13*

Issued to publicize peaceful uses of the sea bed.

215 A114 6c blue & multi .25 .25

See UN Offices in Geneva No. 15.

Refugees, Sculpture by Kaare K. Nygaard A115

International support for refugees.

1971, Mar. 2 Litho. *Perf. 13x12½*

216 A115 6c brown, ocher & black .25 .25

217 A115 13c ultramarine, greenish blue & black .25 .25

See UN Offices in Geneva No. 16.

Wheat and Globe — A116

Publicizing the UN World Food Program.

1971, Apr. 13 Photo. *Perf. 14*

218 A116 13c red & multicolored .25 .25

See UN Offices in Geneva No. 17.

UPU Headquarters, Bern — A117

Opening of new Universal Postal Union Headquarters, Bern.

1971, May 28 Photo. *Perf. 11½*

219 A117 20c brown orange & multi .30 .25

See UN Offices in Geneva No. 18.

"Eliminate Racial Discrimination" A118

A119

International Year Against Racial Discrimination.

1971, Sept. 21 Photo. *Perf. 13½*

220 A118 8c yellow green & multi .25 .25

221 A119 13c blue & multi .25 .25

See UN Offices in Geneva Nos. 19-20.

UN Headquarters, New York — A120

UN Emblem and Symbolic Flags A121

1971, Oct. 22 Photo. *Perf. 13½*

222 A120 8c violet blue & multi .25 .25

Perf. 13

223 A121 60c ultra & multi .80 .80

Maia by Pablo Picasso — A122

To publicize the UN International School.

1971, Nov. 19 Photo. *Perf. 11½*

224 A122 8c olive & multi .25 .25

225 A122 21c ultra & multi .25 .25

Letter Changing Hands A123

1972, Jan. 5 Litho. *Perf. 14*

226 A123 95c carmine & multi 1.30 1.10

"No More Nuclear Weapons" A124

To promote non-proliferation of nuclear weapons.

1972, Feb. 14 Photo. *Perf. 13½x14*

227 A124 8c dull rose, black, blue & gray .25 .25

See UN Offices in Geneva No. 23.

Proportions of Man (c. 1509), by Leonardo da Vinci A125

"Human Environment" A126

World Health Day, Apr. 7.

Litho. & Engr.

1972, Apr. 7 *Perf. 13x13½*

228 A125 15c black & multi .25 .25

See UN Offices in Geneva No. 24.

Litho. & Embossed

1972, June 5 *Perf. 12½x14*

UN Conf. on Human Environment, Stockholm, June 5-16, 1972.

229 A126 8c red, buff, green & blue .25 .25

230 A126 15c blue green, buff, green & blue .25 .25

See UN Offices in Geneva Nos. 25-26.

"Europe" and UN Emblem — A127

The Five Continents, by José Maria Sert — A128

Economic Commission for Europe, 25th anniversary.

1972, Sept. 11 Litho. *Perf. 13x13½*

231 A127 21c yellow brown & multi .30 .30

See UN Offices in Geneva No. 27.

Art at UN Issue

1972, Nov. 17 Photo. *Perf. 12x12½*

232 A128 8c gold, brown & golden brown .25 .25
233 A128 15c gold, blue green & brown .25 .25

See UN Offices in Geneva Nos. 28-29.

Olive Branch and Broken Sword A129

Disarmament Decade, 1970-79.

1973, Mar. 9 Litho. *Perf. 13½x13*

234 A129 8c blue & multi .25 .25
235 A129 15c lilac rose & multi .25 .25

See UN Offices in Geneva Nos. 30-31.

Poppy Capsule and Skull — A130

Fight against drug abuse.

1973, Apr. 13 Photo. *Perf. 13½*

236 A130 8c deep orange & multi .25 .25
237 A130 15c pink & multi .25 .25

See UN Offices in Geneva No. 32.

Honeycomb A131

5th anniversary of the United Nations Volunteer Program.

1973, May 25 Photo. *Perf. 14*

238 A131 8c olive bister & multi .25 .25
239 A131 21c gray blue & multi .30 .30

See UN Offices in Geneva No. 33.

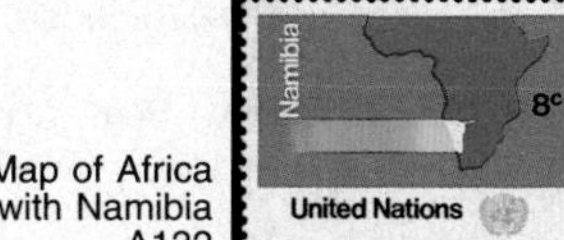

Map of Africa with Namibia A132

To publicize Namibia (South-West Africa) for which the UN General Assembly ended the mandate of South Africa and established the UN Council for Namibia to administer the territory until independence.

1973, Oct. 1 Photo. *Perf. 14*

240 A132 8c emerald & multi .25 .25
241 A132 15c bright rose & multi .25 .25

See UN Offices in Geneva No. 34.

UN Emblem, Human Rights Flame A133

25th anniversary of the adoption and proclamation of the Universal Declaration of Human Rights.

1973, Nov. 16 Photo. *Perf. 13½*

242 A133 8c deep carmine & multi .25 .25
243 A133 21c blue green & multi .25 .25

See UN Offices in Geneva Nos. 35-36.

ILO Headquarters, Geneva A134

New Headquarters of International Labor Organization.

1974, Jan. 11 Photo. *Perf. 14*

244 A134 10c ultra & multi .25 .25
245 A134 21c blue green & multi .30 .25

See UN Offices in Geneva Nos. 37-38.

Post Horn Encircling Globe A135

Centenary of Universal Postal Union.

1974, Mar. 22 Litho. *Perf. 12½*

246 A135 10c gold & multi .25 .25

See UN Offices in Geneva Nos. 39-40.

Art at UN Issue

Peace Mural, by Candido Portinari A136

The mural, a gift of Brazil, is in the Delegates' Lobby, General Assembly Building.

1974, May 6 Photo. *Perf. 14*

247 A136 10c gold & multi .25 .25
248 A136 18c ultra & multi .35 .30

See UN Offices in Geneva Nos. 41-42.

Dove & UN Emblem A137

UN Headquarters A138

Globe, UN Emblem, Flags A139

1974, June 10 Photo. *Perf. 14*

249 A137 2c dark & light blue .25 .25
250 A138 10c multicolored .25 .25
251 A139 18c multicolored .25 .25
Nos. 249-251 (3) .75 .75

Children of the World — A140

Law of the Sea — A141

World Population Year.

1974, Oct. 18 Photo. *Perf. 14*

252 A140 10c light blue & multi .25 .25
253 A140 18c lilac & multi .35 .25

See UN Offices in Geneva Nos. 43-44.

1974, Nov. 22 Photo. *Perf. 14*

Declaration of UN General Assembly that the sea bed is common heritage of mankind, reserved for peaceful purposes.

254 A141 10c green & multi .25 .25
255 A141 26c orange red & multi .35 .30

See UN Offices in Geneva No. 45.

Satellite and Globe — A142

Peaceful uses (meteorology, industry, fishing, communications) of outer space.

1975, Mar. 14 Litho. *Perf. 13*

256 A142 10c multicolored .25 .25
257 A142 26c multicolored .35 .30

See UN Offices in Geneva Nos. 46-47.

Equality Between Men and Women — A143

International Women's Year.

1975, May 9 Litho. *Perf. 15*

258 A143 10c multicolored .25 .25
259 A143 18c multicolored .35 .30

See UN Offices in Geneva Nos. 48-49.

UN Flag and "XXX" — A144

30th anniversary of the United Nations.

1975, June 26 Litho. *Perf. 13*

260 A144 10c olive bister & multi .25 .25
261 A144 26c purple & multi .40 .35

Souvenir Sheet

Imperf

262 Sheet of 2 .60 .50
a. A144 10c olive bister & multicolored .25 .25
b. A144 26c purple & multicolored .35 .25

See Offices in Geneva Nos. 50-52.

Hand Reaching up over Map of Africa & Namibia — A145

"Namibia-United Nations direct responsibility." See note after No. 241.

1975, Sept. 22 Photo. *Perf. 13½*

263 A145 10c multicolored .25 .25
264 A145 18c multicolored .30 .30

See UN Offices in Geneva Nos. 53-54.

Wild Rose Growing from Barbed Wire — A146

United Nations Peace-keeping Operations.

1975, Nov. 21 Engr. *Perf. 12½*

265 A146 13c ultramarine .25 .25
266 A146 26c rose carmine .40 .40

See UN Offices in Geneva Nos. 55-56.

Symbolic Flags Forming Dove — A147

UN Emblem — A149

People of All Races A148

UN Flag A150

Dove and Rainbow A151

1976 Litho. *Perf. 13x13½, 13½x13*

267 A147 3c multicolored .25 .25
268 A148 4c multicolored .25 .25

Photo.

Perf. 14

269 A149 9c multicolored .25 .25

Litho.

Perf. 13x13½

270 A150 30c blue, emerald & black .35 .35
271 A151 50c yellow green & multi .65 .65
Nos. 267-271 (5) 1.75 1.75

Issue dates: 3c, 4c, 30c, 50c, Jan. 6; 9c, Nov. 19.

See UN Offices in Vienna No. 8.

Interlocking Bands — A152

World Federation of United Nations Associations.

1976, Mar. 12 Photo. *Perf. 14*
272 A152 13c blue, green & black .25 .25
273 A152 26c green & multi .35 .30
See UN Offices in Geneva No. 57.

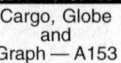

Cargo, Globe and Graph — A153

Houses Around Globe — A154

UN Conference on Trade and Development (UNCTAD), Nairobi, Kenya, May 1976.

1976, Apr. 23 Photo. *Perf. 11½*
274 A153 13c deep magenta & multi .25 .25
275 A153 31c dull blue & multi .40 .30
See UN Offices in Geneva No. 58.

1976, May 28 Photo. *Perf. 14*

Habitat, UN Conference on Human Settlements, Vancouver, Canada, May 31-June 11.

276 A154 13c red brown & multi .25 .25
277 A154 25c green & multi .40 .30
See UN Offices in Geneva Nos. 59-60.

Magnifying Glass, Sheet of Stamps, UN Emblem A155

United Nations Postal Administration, 25th anniversary.

1976, Oct. 8 Photo. *Perf. 11½*
278 A155 13c blue & multi .25 .25
279 A155 31c green & multi 1.40 1.40
See UN Offices in Geneva Nos. 61-62.

Grain — A156

World Food Council.

1976, Nov. 19 Litho. *Perf. 14½*
280 A156 13c multicolored .25 .25
See UN Offices in Geneva No. 63.

WIPO Headquarters, Geneva — A157

World Intellectual Property Organization (WIPO).

1977, Mar. 11 Photo. *Perf. 14*
281 A157 13c citron & multi .25 .25
282 A157 31c bright green & multi .45 .35
See UN Offices in Geneva No. 64.

Drops of Water Falling into Funnel — A158

UN Water Conference, Mar del Plata, Argentina, Mar. 14-25.

1977, Apr. 22 Photo. *Perf. 13½x13*
283 A158 13c yellow & multi .25 .25
284 A158 25c salmon & multi .40 .35
See UN Offices in Geneva Nos. 65-66.

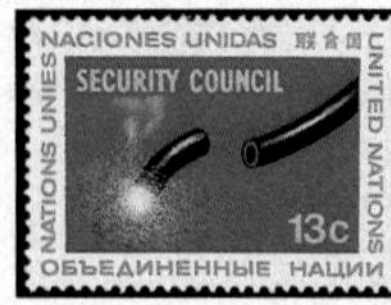

Burning Fuse Severed A159

UN Security Council.

1977, May 27 Photo. *Perf. 14*
285 A159 13c purple & multi .25 .25
286 A159 31c dark blue & multi .45 .30
See UN Offices in Geneva Nos. 67-68.

"Combat Racism" A160

Fight against racial discrimination.

1977, Sept. 19 Litho. *Perf. 13½x13*
287 A160 13c black & yellow .25 .25
288 A160 25c black & vermilion .40 .30
See UN Offices in Geneva Nos. 60-70.

Atom, Grain, Fruit and Factory — A161

Peaceful uses of atomic energy.

1977, Nov. 18 Photo. *Perf. 14*
289 A161 13c yellow bister & multi .25 .25
290 A161 18c dull green & multi .30 .25
See UN Offices in Geneva Nos. 71-72.

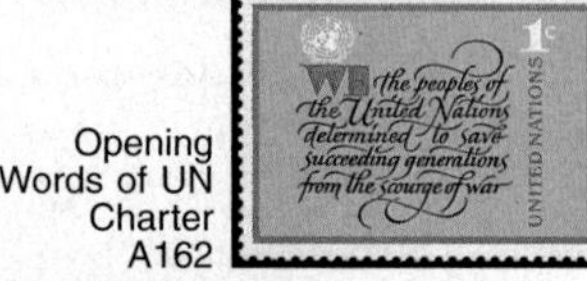

Opening Words of UN Charter A162

"Live Together in Peace" A163

People of the World — A164

1978, Jan. 27 Litho. *Perf. 14½*
291 A162 1c gold, brown & red .25 .25
292 A163 25c multicolored .35 .30
293 A164 $1 multicolored 1.25 1.25
Nos. 291-293 (3) 1.85 1.80
See UN Offices in Geneva No. 73.

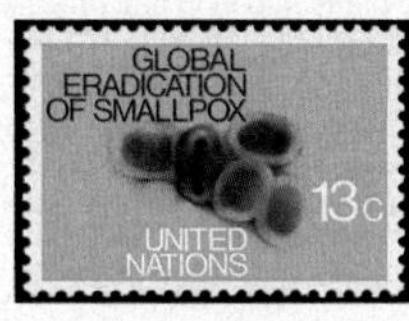

Smallpox Virus — A165

Global eradication of smallpox.

1978, Mar. 31 Photo. *Perf. 12x11½*
294 A165 13c rose & black .25 .25
295 A165 31c blue & black .40 .40
See UN Offices in Geneva Nos. 74-75.

Open Handcuff A166

Multicolored Bands and Clouds A167

Liberation, justice and cooperation for Namibia.

1978, May 5 Photo. *Perf. 12*
296 A166 13c multicolored .25 .25
297 A166 18c multicolored .30 .25
See UN Offices in Geneva No. 76.

1978, June 12 Photo. *Perf. 14*

International Civil Aviation Organization for "Safety in the Air."

298 A167 13c multicolored .25 .25
299 A167 25c multicolored .35 .30
See UN Offices in Geneva Nos. 77-78.

General Assembly A168

1978, Sept. 15 Photo. *Perf. 13½*
300 A168 13c multicolored .25 .25
301 A168 18c multicolored .35 .30
See UN Offices in Geneva Nos. 79-80.

Hemispheres as Cogwheels A169

Technical Cooperation Among Developing Countries Conference, Buenos Aires, Argentina, Sept. 1978.

1978, Nov. 17 Photo. *Perf. 14*
302 A169 13c multicolored .25 .25
303 A169 31c multicolored .50 .40
See UN Offices in Geneva No. 81.

Hand Holding Olive Branch — A170

Tree of Various Races — A171

Globe, Dove with Olive Branch — A172

Birds and Globe — A173

1979, Jan. 19 Photo. *Perf. 14*
304 A170 5c multicolored .25 .25
305 A171 14c multicolored .25 .25
306 A172 15c multicolored .25 .25
307 A173 20c multicolored .30 .25
Nos. 304-307 (4) 1.05 1.00

UNDRO Against Fire and Water — A174

Office of the UN Disaster Relief Coordinator (UNDRO).

1979, Mar. 9 Photo. *Perf. 14*
308 A174 15c multicolored .25 .25
309 A174 20c multicolored .35 .30
See UN Offices in Geneva Nos. 82-83.

Child and ICY Emblem A175

International Year of the Child.

1979, May 4 Photo. *Perf. 14*
310 A175 15c multicolored .25 .25
311 A175 31c multicolored .35 .35
See UN Offices in Geneva Nos. 84-85.

Map of Namibia, Olive Branch — A176

Scales and Sword of Justice — A177

For a free and independent Namibia.

1979, Oct. 5 Litho. *Perf. 13½*
312 A176 15c multicolored .25 .25
313 A176 31c multicolored .30 .35
See UN Offices in Geneva No. 86.

1979, Nov. 9 Litho. *Perf. 13x13½*

International Court of Justice, The Hague, Netherlands.

314 A177 15c multicolored .25 .25
315 A177 20c multicolored .30 .35
See UN Offices in Geneva Nos. 87-88.

Graph of Economic Trends — A178

Key — A179

New International Economic Order.

1980, Jan. 11 Litho. ***Perf. 15x14½***

316 A178 15c multicolored .25 .25
317 A179 31c multicolored .45 .35

See UN Offices in Geneva No. 89; Vienna No. 7.

Women's Year Emblems A180

United Nations Decade for Women.

1980, Mar. 7 Litho. ***Perf. 14½x15***

318 A180 15c multicolored .25 .25
319 A180 20c multicolored .30 .25

See UN Offices in Geneva Nos. 90-91; Vienna Nos. 9-10.

UN Emblem and "UN" on Helmet A181

Arrows and UN Emblem A182

United Nations Peace-keeping Operations.

1980, May 16 Litho. ***Perf. 14x13***

320 A181 15c blue & black .25 .25
321 A182 31c multicolored .40 .40

See UN Offices in Geneva No. 92; Vienna No. 11.

"35" and Flags — A183

Globe and Laurel — A184

35th Anniversary of the United Nations.

1980, June 26 Litho. ***Perf. 13x13½***

322 A183 15c multicolored .25 .25
323 A184 31c multicolored .40 .35

Souvenir Sheet

Imperf

324 Sheet of 2 .65 .65
a. A183 15c multicolored .25 .25
b. A184 31c multicolored .40 .40

See UN Offices in Geneva Nos. 93-95; Vienna Nos. 12-14.

Flag of Turkey A185

1980, Sept. 26 Litho. ***Perf. 12***

Granite Paper

325 A185 15c shown .25 .25
326 A185 15c Luxembourg .25 .25
327 A185 15c Fiji .25 .25
328 A185 15c Viet Nam .25 .25
a. Se-tenant block of 4, #325-328 1.10 1.10
329 A185 15c Guinea .25 .25
330 A185 15c Surinam .25 .25
331 A185 15c Bangladesh .25 .25
332 A185 15c Mali .25 .25
a. Se-tenant block of 4, #329-332 1.10 1.10
333 A185 15c Yugoslavia .25 .25
334 A185 15c France .25 .25
335 A185 15c Venezuela .25 .25
336 A185 15c El Salvador .25 .25
a. Se-tenant block of 4, #333-336 1.10 1.10
337 A185 15c Madagascar .25 .25
338 A185 15c Cameroon .25 .25
339 A185 15c Rwanda .25 .25
340 A185 15c Hungary .25 .25
a. Se-tenant block of 4, #337-340 1.10 1.10
Nos. 325-340 (16) 4.00 4.00

Issued in 4 panes of 16. Each pane contains 4 blocks of 4 (Nos. 325-328, 329-332, 333-336, 337-340). A se-tenant block of 4 designs centers each pane.

See Nos. 350-365, 374-389, 399-414, 425-440, 450-465, 477-492, 499-514, 528-543, 554-569, 690-697, 719-726, 744-751, 795-802, 921-924.

Symbolic Flowers A186

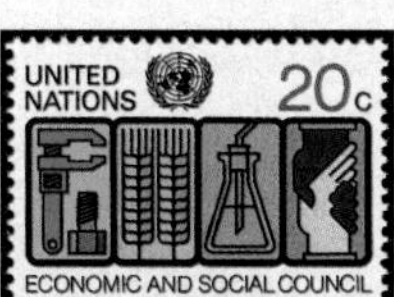

Symbols of Progress A187

1980, Nov. 21 Litho. ***Perf. 13½x13***

341 A186 15c multicolored .25 .25
342 A187 20c multicolored .40 .35

See UN Offices in Geneva, Nos. 96-97; Vienna Nos. 15-16.

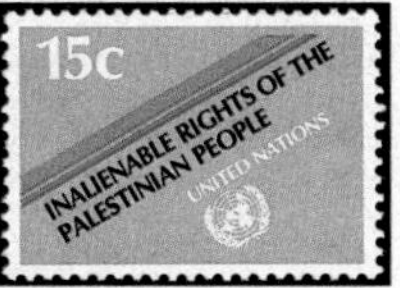

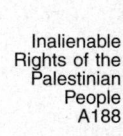

Inalienable Rights of the Palestinian People A188

1981, Jan. 30 Photo. ***Perf. 12x11½***

343 A188 15c multicolored .30 .25

See UN Offices in Geneva No. 98; Vienna No. 17.

Interlocking Puzzle Pieces — A189

Stylized Person — A190

International Year of the Disabled.

1981, Mar. 6 Photo. ***Perf. 14***

344 A189 20c multicolored .25 .25
345 A190 35c black & orange .40 .45

See UN Offices in Geneva Nos. 99-100; Vienna Nos. 18-19.

Art at UN Issue

Divislava and Sebastocrator Kaloyan, Bulgarian Mural, 1259, Boyana Church, Sofia — A191

1981, Apr. 15 Photo. ***Perf. 11½***

Granite Paper

346 A191 20c multicolored .25 .25
347 A191 31c multicolored .40 .45

See UN Offices in Geneva No. 101; Vienna No. 20.

Solar Energy A192

Conference Emblem A193

Conference on New and Renewable Sources of Energy, Nairobi, Aug. 10-21.

1981, May 29 Litho. ***Perf. 13***

348 A192 20c multicolored .25 .25
349 A193 40c multicolored .50 .50

See UN Offices in Geneva No. 102; Vienna No. 21.

Flag Type of 1980

1981, Sept. 25 Litho.

Granite Paper

350 A185 20c Djibouti .25 .25
351 A185 20c Sri Lanka .25 .25
352 A185 20c Bolivia .25 .25
353 A185 20c Equatorial Guinea .25 .25
a. Se-tenant block of 4, #350-353 1.60 1.60
354 A185 20c Malta .25 .25
355 A185 20c Czechoslovakia .25 .25
356 A185 20c Thailand .25 .25
357 A185 20c Trinidad & Tobago .25 .25
a. Se-tenant block of 4, #354-357 1.60 1.60
358 A185 20c Ukrainian SSR .25 .25
359 A185 20c Kuwait .25 .25
360 A185 20c Sudan .25 .25
361 A185 20c Egypt .25 .25
a. Se-tenant block of 4, #358-361 1.60 1.60
362 A185 20c US .40 .25
363 A185 20c Singapore .25 .25
364 A185 20c Panama .25 .25
365 A185 20c Costa Rica .25 .25
a. Se-tenant block of 4, #362-365 1.60 1.60
Nos. 350-365 (16) 4.15 4.00

See note after No. 340.

Seedling and Tree Cross Section A194

"10" and Symbols of Progress A195

United Nations Volunteers Program, 10th anniv.

1981, Nov. 13 Litho.

366 A194 18c multicolored .25 .25
367 A195 28c multicolored .55 .55

See UN Offices in Geneva Nos. 103-104; Vienna Nos. 22-23.

Respect for Human Rights — A196

Independence of Colonial Countries and People — A197

Second Disarmament Decade — A198

1982, Jan. 22 ***Perf. 11½x12***

368 A196 17c multicolored .25 .25
369 A197 28c multicolored .45 .40
370 A198 40c multicolored .75 .70
Nos. 368-370 (3) 1.45 1.35

A199

A200

10th Anniversary of United Nations Environment Program.

1982, Mar. 19 Litho. ***Perf. 13½x13***

371 A199 20c multicolored .25 .25
372 A200 40c multicolored .65 .65

See UN Offices in Geneva Nos. 107-108; Vienna Nos. 25-26.

UN Emblem and Olive Branch in Outer Space A201

Exploration and Peaceful Uses of Outer Space.

1982, June 11 Litho. ***Perf. 13x13½***

373 A201 20c multicolored .45 .45

See UN Offices in Geneva Nos. 109-110; Vienna No. 27.

Flag Type of 1980

1982, Sept. 24 Litho. ***Perf. 12***

Granite Paper

374 A185 20c Austria .25 .25
375 A185 20c Malaysia .25 .25
376 A185 20c Seychelles .25 .25
377 A185 20c Ireland .25 .25
a. Se-tenant block of 4, #374-377 1.60 1.60
378 A185 20c Mozambique .25 .25
379 A185 20c Albania .25 .25
380 A185 20c Dominica .25 .25
381 A185 20c Solomon Islnads .25 .25
a. Se-tenant block of 4, #378-381 1.60 1.60
382 A185 20c Philippines .25 .25
383 A185 20c Swaziland .25 .25
384 A185 20c Nicaragua .25 .25
385 A185 20c Burma .25 .25
a. Se-tenant block of 4, #382-385 1.60 1.60
386 A185 20c Cape Verde .25 .25
387 A185 20c Guyana .25 .25
388 A185 20c Belgium .25 .25
389 A185 20c Nigeria .25 .25
a. Se-tenant block of 4, #386-389 1.60 1.60
Nos. 374-389 (16) 4.00 4.00

See note after No. 340.

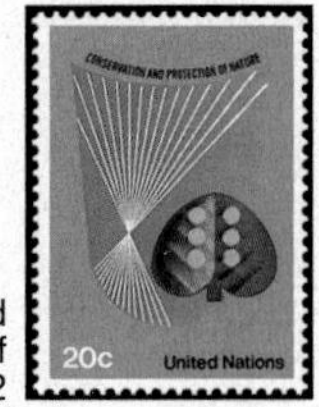

Conservation and Protection of Nature — A202

1982, Nov. 19 **Photo.** ***Perf. 14***

390 A202 20c Leaf .30 .30
391 A202 28c Butterfly .55 .50

See UN Offices in Geneva Nos. 111-112; Vienna Nos. 28-29.

A203

World Communications Year — A204

World Communications Year.

1983, Jan. 28 **Litho.** ***Perf. 13***

392 A203 20c multicolored .25 .25
393 A204 40c multicolored .65 .65

See UN Offices in Geneva No. 113; Vienna No. 30.

A205

Safety at Sea — A206

Safety at Sea.

1983, Mar. 18 **Litho.** ***Perf. 14½***

394 A205 20c multicolored .25 .25
395 A206 37c multicolored .60 .55

See UN Offices in Geneva Nos. 114-115; Vienna Nos. 31-32.

World Food Program A207

1983, Apr. 22 **Engr.** ***Perf. 13½***

396 A207 20c rose lake .35 .35

See UN Offices in Geneva No. 116; Vienna Nos. 33-34.

A208

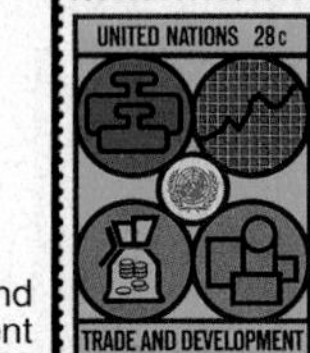

Trade and Development A209

UN Conference on Trade and Development.

1983, June 6 **Litho.** ***Perf. 14***

397 A208 20c multicolored .25 .35
398 A209 28c multicolored .70 .65

See UN Offices in Geneva Nos. 117-118; Vienna Nos. 35-36.

Flag Type of 1980

1983, Sept. 23 **Photo.** ***Perf. 12***

Granite Paper

399 A185 20c Great Britain .25 .25
400 A185 20c Barbados .25 .25
401 A185 20c Nepal .25 .25
402 A185 20c Israel .25 .25
a. Se-tenant block of 4, #399-402 1.90 1.90
403 A185 20c Malawi .25 .25
404 A185 20c Byelorussian SSR .25 .25
405 A185 20c Jamaica .25 .25
406 A185 20c Kenya .25 .25
a. Se-tenant block of 4, #403-406 1.90 1.90
407 A185 20c People's Republic of China .25 .25
408 A185 20c Peru .25 .25
409 A185 20c Bulgaria .25 .25
410 A185 20c Canada .25 .25
a. Se-tenant block of 4, #407-410 1.90 1.90
411 A185 20c Somalia .25 .25
412 A185 20c Senegal .25 .25
413 A185 20c Brazil .25 .25
414 A185 20c Sweden .25 .25
a. Se-tenant block of 4, #411-414 1.90 1.90
Nos. 399-414 (16) 4.00 4.00

See note after No. 340.

A210

35th Anniv. of the Universal Declaration of Human Rights — A211

35th Anniversary of the Universal Declaration of Human Rights.

Photo. & Engr.

1983, Dec. 9 ***Perf. 13½***

415 A210 20c multicolored .30 .25
416 A211 40c multicolored .70 .65

See UN Offices in Geneva Nos. 119-120; Vienna Nos. 37-38.

Intl. Population Conference A212

1984, Feb. 3 **Litho.** ***Perf. 14***

417 A212 20c multicolored .25 .25
418 A212 40c multicolored .65 .65

See UN Offices in Geneva No. 121; Vienna No. 39.

Tractor Plowing A213

Rice Paddy A214

World Food Day, Oct. 16.

1984, Mar. 15 **Litho.** ***Perf. 14½***

419 A213 20c multicolored .30 .30
420 A214 40c multicolored .60 .60

See UN Offices in Geneva Nos. 122-123; Vienna Nos. 40-41.

Grand Canyon A215

Ancient City of Polonnaruwa, Sri Lanka A216

World Heritage.

1984, Apr. 18 **Litho.** ***Perf. 14***

421 A215 20c multicolored .25 .25
422 A216 50c multicolored .75 .75

See Nos. 601-602, UN Offices in Geneva Nos. 124-125, 211-212; Vienna Nos. 42-43, 125-126.

A217

A218

Future for Refugees.

1984, May 29 **Photo.** ***Perf. 11½***

423 A217 20c multicolored .30 .30
424 A218 50c multicolored .90 .90

See UN Offices in Geneva Nos. 126-127; Vienna Nos. 44-45.

Flag Type of 1980

1984, Sept. 21 **Photo.** ***Perf. 12***

Granite Paper

425 A185 20c Burundi .35 .35
426 A185 20c Pakistan .35 .35
427 A185 20c Benin .35 .35
428 A185 20c Italy .35 .35
a. Se-tenant block of 4, #425-428 2.75 2.75
429 A185 20c Tanzania .35 .35
430 A185 20c United Arab Emirates .35 .35
431 A185 20c Ecuador .35 .35
432 A185 20c Bahamas .35 .35
a. Se-tenant block of 4, #429-432 2.75 2.75
433 A185 20c Poland .35 .35
434 A185 20c Papua New Guinea .35 .35
435 A185 20c Uruguay .35 .35
436 A185 20c Chile .35 .35
a. Se-tenant block of 4, #433-436 2.75 2.75
437 A185 20c Paraguay .35 .35
438 A185 20c Bhutan .35 .35
439 A185 20c Central African Republic .35 .35
440 A185 20c Australia .35 .35
a. Se-tenant block of 4, #437-440 2.75 2.75
Nos. 425-440 (16) 5.60 5.60

See note after No. 340.

Intl. Youth Year — A219

ILO Turin Center — A220

1984, Nov. 15 **Litho.** ***Perf. 13½***

441 A219 20c multicolored .35 .35
442 A219 35c multicolored .85 .85

See UN Offices in Geneva No. 128; Vienna Nos. 46-47.

1985, Feb. 1 **Engr.** ***Perf. 13½***

443 A220 23c blue .45 .45

See UN Offices in Geneva Nos. 129-130; Vienna No. 48.

UN University A221

1985, Mar. 15 **Photo.** ***Perf. 13½***

444 A221 50c Farmer plowing, discussion group .95 .95

See UN Offices in Geneva Nos. 131-132; Vienna No. 49.

Peoples of the World — A222

Painting UN Emblem A223

1985, May 10 **Litho.** ***Perf. 14***

445 A222 22c multicolored .30 .30
446 A223 $3 multicolored 3.75 1.50

See UN Offices in Geneva Nos. 133-134; Vienna Nos. 50-51.

The Corner A224

Alvaro Raking Hay A225

UN 40th anniversary. Oil paintings (details) by American artist Andrew Wyeth (b. 1917).

Perf. 12 x 11½

1985, June 26 **Photo.**

447 A224 22c multicolored .35 .35
448 A225 45c multicolored 1.00 1.00

Souvenir Sheet

Imperf

449 Sheet of 2 1.30 1.30
a. A224 22c multicolored .50 .50
b. A225 45c multicolored .80 .80

See UN Offices in Geneva Nos. 135-137; Vienna Nos. 52-54.

Flag Type of 1980

1985, Sept. 20 Photo. *Perf. 12*

Granite Paper

450 A185 22c Grenada .45 .45
451 A185 22c Federal Republic of Germany .45 .45
452 A185 22c Saudi Arabia .45 .45
453 A185 22c Mexico .45 .45
a. Se-tenant block of 4, #450-453 3.25 3.25
454 A185 22c Uganda .45 .45
455 A185 22c St. Thomas & Prince .45 .45
456 A185 22c USSR .45 .45
457 A185 22c India .45 .45
a. Se-tenant block of 4, #454-457 3.25 3.25
458 A185 22c Liberia .45 .45
459 A185 22c Mauritius .45 .45
460 A185 22c Chad .45 .45
461 A185 22c Dominican Republic .45 .45
a. Se-tenant block of 4, #458-461 3.25 3.25
462 A185 22c Sultanate of Oman .45 .45
463 A185 22c Ghana .45 .45
464 A185 22c Sierra Leone .45 .45
465 A185 22c Finland .45 .45
a. Se-tenant block of 4, #462-465 3.25 3.25
Nos. 450-465 (16) 7.20 7.20

See note after 340.

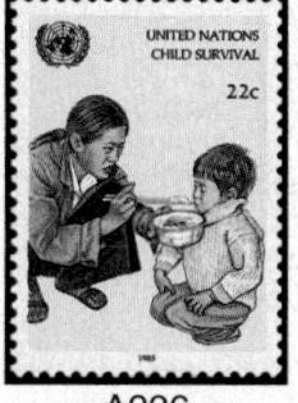

A226

A227

UNICEF Child Survival Campaign.

Photo. & Engr.

1985, Nov. 22 *Perf. 13½*

466 A226 22c Asian Toddler .30 .30
467 A226 33c Breastfeeding .65 .65

See UN Offices in Geneva Nos. 138-139; Vienna Nos. 55-56.

1986, Jan. 31 Photo. *Perf. 11½x12*

Africa in Crisis, campaign against hunger.

468 A227 22c multicolored .40 .40

See UN Offices in Geneva No. 140; Vienna No. 57.

Water Resources A228

1986, Mar. 14 Photo. *Perf. 13½*

469 A228 22c Dam .80 .80
470 A228 22c Irrigation .80 .80
471 A228 22c Hygiene .80 .80
472 A228 22c Well .80 .80
a. Block of 4, #469-472 4.00 4.00

UN Development Program. No. 472a has continuous design. See UN Offices in Geneva Nos. 141-144; Vienna Nos. 58-61.

Human Rights Stamp of 1954 — A229

Stamp collecting: 44c, Engraver.

1986, May 22 Engr. *Perf. 12½*

473 A229 22c dark violet & bright blue .25 .25
474 A229 44c brown & emerald green .75 .75

See UN Offices in Geneva Nos. 146-147; Vienna Nos. 62-63.

Birds Nest in Tree — A230

Peace in Seven Languages A231

Photo. & Embossed

1986, June 20 *Perf. 13½*

475 A230 22c multicolored .50 .50
476 A231 33c multicolored 1.25 1.25

International Peace Year.
See UN Offices in Geneva Nos. 148-149; Vienna Nos. 64-65.

Flag Type of 1980

1986, Sept. 19 Photo. *Perf. 12*

Granite Paper

477 A185 22c New Zealand .50 .50
478 A185 22c Lao PDR .50 .50
479 A185 22c Burkina Faso .50 .50
480 A185 22c Gambia .50 .50
a. Se-tenant block of 4, #477-480 3.25 3.25
481 A185 22c Maldives .50 .50
482 A185 22c Ethiopia .50 .50
483 A185 22c Jordan .50 .50
484 A185 22c Zambia .50 .50
a. Se-tenant block of 4, #481-484 3.25 3.25
485 A185 22c Iceland .50 .50
486 A185 22c Antigua & Barbuda .50 .50
487 A185 22c Angola .50 .50
488 A185 22c Botswana .50 .50
a. Se-tenant block of 4, #485-488 3.25 3.25
489 A185 22c Romania .50 .50
490 A185 22c Togo .50 .50
491 A185 22c Mauritania .50 .50
492 A185 22c Colombia .50 .50
a. Se-tenant block of 4, #489-492 3.25 3.25
Nos. 477-492 (16) 8.00 8.00

See note after No. 340.

World Federation of UN Associations, 40th Anniv. — A232

22c, Mother Earth, by Edna Hibel, U.S. 33c, Watercolor by Salvador Dali (b. 1904), Spain. 39c, New Dawn, by Dong Kingman, U.S. 44c, Watercolor by Chaim Gross, U.S.

1986, Nov. 14 Litho. *Perf. 13x13½*

Souvenir Sheet

493 Sheet of 4 3.00 3.00
a. A232 22c multicolored .40 .40
b. A232 33c multicolored .50 .40
c. A232 39c multicolored .75 .50
d. A232 44c multicolored 1.10 .75

See UN Offices in Geneva No. 150; Vienna No. 66.

Trygve Halvdan Lie (1896-1968), 1st Secretary-General A233

Photo. & Engr.

1987, Jan. 30 *Perf. 13½*

494 A233 22c multicolored .75 .75

See Offices in Geneva No. 151; Vienna No. 67.

Intl. Year of Shelter for the Homeless A234

22c, Surveying and blueprinting. 44c, Cutting lumber.

Perf. 13½x12½

1987, Mar. 13 Litho.

495 A234 22c multicolored .35 .35
496 A234 44c multicolored .90 .90

See Offices in Geneva Nos. 154-155; Vienna Nos. 68-69.

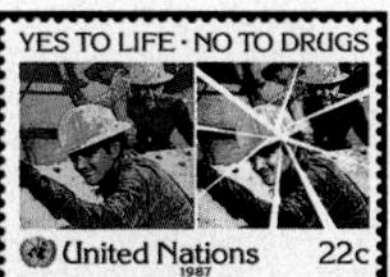

Fight Drug Abuse A235

22c, Construction. 33c, Education.

1987, June 12 Litho. *Perf. 14½x15*

497 A235 22c multicolored .45 .45
498 A235 33c multicolored .90 .90

See Offices in Geneva Nos. 156-157; Vienna Nos. 70-71.

Flag Type of 1980

1987, Sept. 18 Photo. *Perf. 12*

Granite Paper

499 A185 22c Comoros .50 .50
500 A185 22c Yemen PDR .50 .50
501 A185 22c Mongolia .50 .50
502 A185 22c Vanuatu .50 .50
a. Se-tenant block of 4, #499-502 3.25 3.25
503 A185 22c Japan .50 .50
504 A185 22c Gabon .50 .50
505 A185 22c Zimbabwe .50 .50
506 A185 22c Iraq .50 .50
a. Se-tenant block of 4, #503-506 3.25 3.25
507 A185 22c Argentina .50 .50
508 A185 22c Congo .50 .50
509 A185 22c Niger .50 .50
510 A185 22c St. Lucia .50 .50
a. Se-tenant block of 4, #507-510 3.25 3.25
511 A185 22c Bahrain .50 .50
512 A185 22c Haiti .50 .50
513 A185 22c Afghanistan .50 .50
514 A185 22c Greece .50 .50
a. Se-tenant block of 4, #511-514 3.25 3.25
Nos. 499-514 (16) 8.00 8.00

See note after No. 340.

UN Day — A236

Multinational people in various occupations.

1987, Oct. 23 Litho. *Perf. 14½x15*

515 A236 22c multicolored .35 .35
516 A236 39c multicolored .55 .55

See Offices in Geneva Nos. 158-159; Vienna Nos. 74-75.

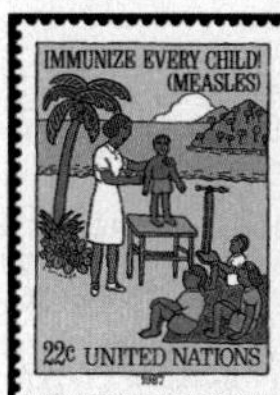

Immunize Every Child — A237

22c, Measles. 44c, Tetanus.

1987, Nov. 20 Litho. *Perf. 15x14½*

517 A237 22c multicolored .75 .75
518 A237 44c multicolored 1.50 1.50

See Offices in Geneva Nos. 160-161; Vienna Nos. 76-77.

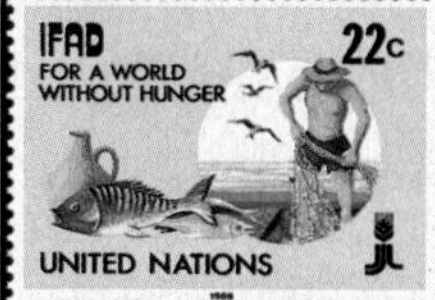

Intl. Fund for Agricultural Development (IFAD) — A238

22c, Fishing. 33c, Farming.

1988, Jan. 29 Litho. *Perf. 13½*

519 A238 22c multicolored .35 .35
520 A238 33c multicolored .75 .75

See Offices in Geneva Nos. 162-163; Vienna Nos. 78-79.

A239

1988, Jan. 29 Photo. *Perf. 13½x14*

521 A239 3c multicolored .25 .25

Survival of the Forests A240

Tropical rain forest: 25c, Treetops. 44c, Ground vegetation and tree trunks. Printed se-tenant in a continuous design.

1988, Mar. 18 Litho. *Perf. 14x15*

522 A240 25c multicolored .75 .75
523 A240 44c multicolored 1.00 1.00
a. Pair, #522-523 3.00 3.00

See Offices in Geneva Nos. 165-166; Vienna Nos. 80-81.

Intl. Volunteer Day — A241

25c, Edurahon. 50c, Vocational training, horiz.

Perf. 13x14, 14x13

1988, May 6 Litho.

524 A241 25c multicolored .45 .45
525 A241 50c multicolored .95 .95

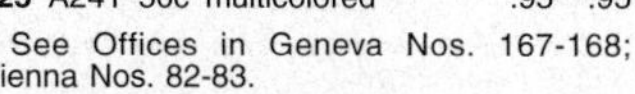

See Offices in Geneva Nos. 167-168; Vienna Nos. 82-83.

Health in Sports A242

25c, Cycling, vert. 35c, Marathon.

Perf. 13½x13, 13x13½

1988, June 17 Litho.

526 A242 25c multicolored .45 .45
527 A242 38c multicolored 1.00 1.00

See Offices in Geneva Nos. 169-170; Vienna Nos. 84-85.

Flag Type of 1980

1988, Sept. 15 Photo. *Perf. 12*

Granite Paper

528 A185 25c Spain .50 .50
529 A185 25c St. Vincent & Grenadines .50 .50
530 A185 25c Ivory Coast .50 .50
531 A185 25c Lebanon .50 .50
a. Se-tenant block of 4, #528-531 3.25 3.25
532 A185 25c Yemen (Arab Republic) .50 .50
533 A185 25c Cuba .50 .50
534 A185 25c Denmark .50 .50
535 A185 25c Libya .50 .50
a. Se-tenant block of 4, #532-535 3.25 3.25
536 A185 25c Qatar .50 .50
537 A185 25c Zaire .50 .50
538 A185 25c Norway .50 .50
539 A185 25c German Democratic Republic .50 .50
a. Se-tenant block of 4, #536-539 3.25 3.25
540 A185 25c Iran .50 .50
541 A185 25c Tunisia .50 .50
542 A185 25c Samoa .50 .50
543 A185 25c Belize .50 .50
a. Se-tenant block of 4, #540-543 3.25 3.25
Nos. 528-543 (16) 8.00 8.00

See note after No. 340.

A243

Photo. & Engr.

1988, Dec. 9 *Perf. 11x11½*

544 A243 25c multicolored .45 .45

Souvenir Sheet

545 A243 $1 multicolored 1.25 1.25

Universal Declaration of Human Rights, 40th anniv.

See Offices in Geneva Nos. 171-172; Vienna Nos. 86-87.

A244

UN Peace-Keeping Force, 1988 Nobel Peace Prize Winner — A245

1989, Jan. 27 Litho. *Perf. 13x14*

546 A244 25c Energy and nature .60 .60
547 A244 45c Agriculture 1.10 1.10

World Bank. See Offices in Geneva Nos. 173-174; Vienna Nos. 88-89.

1989, Mar. 17 Litho. *Perf. 14x13½*

UN Peace-Keeping Force, awarded 1988 Nobel Peace Prize.

548 A245 25c multicolored .45 .45

See Offices in Geneva No. 175; Vienna No. 90.

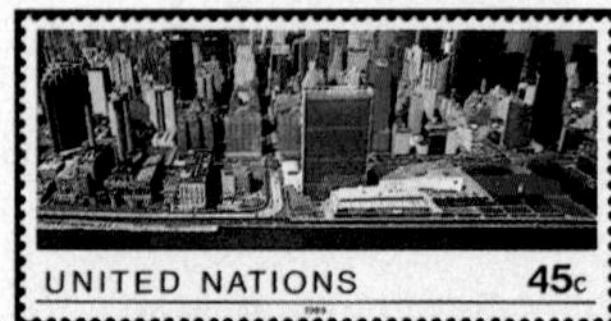

Aerial Photograph of New York Headquarters — A246

1989, Mar. 17 Litho. *Perf. 14½x14*

549 A246 45c multicolored .65 .65

World Weather Watch, 25th Anniv. (in 1988) — A247

Satellite photographs: 25c, Storm system off the U.S. east coast. 36c, Typhoon Abby in the north-west Pacific.

1989, Apr. 21 Litho. *Perf. 13x14*

550 A247 25c multicolored .50 .50
551 A247 36c multicolored 1.10 1.10

See Offices in Geneva Nos. 176-177; Vienna Nos. 91-92.

A248 A249

Photo. & Engr., Photo. (90c)

1989, Aug. 23 *Perf. 14*

552 A248 25c multicolored 1.25 1.25
553 A249 90c multicolored 2.75 2.75

See Offices in Geneva Nos. 178-179; Vienna Nos. 93-94.

Flag Type of 1980

1989, Sept. 22 Photo. *Perf. 12*

Granite Paper

554 A185 25c Indonesia .60 .60
555 A185 25c Lesotho .60 .60
556 A185 25c Guatemala .60 .60
557 A185 25c Netherlands .60 .60
a. Se-tenant block of 4, #554-557 4.00 4.00
558 A185 25c South Africa .60 .60
559 A185 25c Portugal .60 .60
560 A185 25c Morocco .60 .60
561 A185 25c Syrian Arab Republic .60 .60
a. Se-tenant block of 4, #558-561 4.00 4.00
562 A185 25c Honduras .60 .60
563 A185 25c Kampuchea .60 .60
564 A185 25c Guinea-Bissau .60 .60
565 A185 25c Cyprus .60 .60
a. Se-tenant block of 4, #562-565 4.00 4.00
566 A185 25c Algeria .60 .60
567 A185 25c Brunei .60 .60
568 A185 25c St. Kitts and Nevis .60 .60
569 A185 25c United Nations .60 .60
a. Se-tenant block of 4, #566-569 4.00 4.00
Nos. 554-569 (16) 9.60 9.60

See note after No. 340.

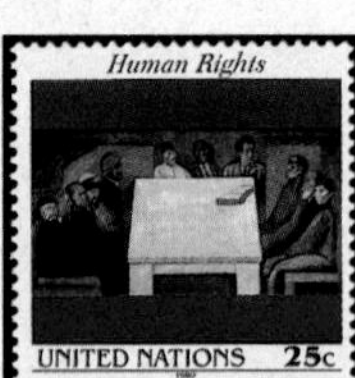

Declaration of Human Rights, 40th Anniv. (in 1988) — A250

Paintings: 25c, The Table of Universal Brotherhood, by Jose Clemente Orozco. 45c, Study for Composition II, by Vassily Kandinsky.

1989, Nov. 17 Litho. *Perf. 13½*

570 A250 25c multicolored .35 .35
571 A250 45c multicolored .80 .80

Panes of 12+12 se-tenant labels containing Articles 1 (25c) or 2 (45c) inscribed in English, French or German.

See Nos. 582-583, 599-600, 616-617, 627-628; Offices in Geneva Nos. 180-181, 193-194, 209-210, 224-225, 234-235; Vienna Nos. 95-96, 108-109, 123-124, 139-140, 150-151.

Intl. Trade Center A251

1990, Feb. 2 Litho. *Perf. 14½x15*

572 A251 25c multicolored 1.00 1.00

See Offices in Geneva No. 182; Vienna No. 97.

Fight AIDS Worldwide A252

40c, Shadow over crowd.

Perf. 13½x12½

1990, Mar. 16 Litho.

573 A252 25c multicolored .35 .35
574 A252 40c multicolored 1.15 1.15

See Offices in Geneva Nos. 184-185, Vienna Nos. 99-100.

Medicinal Plants — A253

1990, May 4 Photo. *Perf. 11½*

Granite Paper

575 A253 25c Catharanthus roseus .45 .45
576 A253 90c Panax quinquefolium 1.40 1.40

See Offices in Geneva Nos. 186-187, Vienna Nos. 101-102.

United Nations, 45th Anniv. A254

45c, "45," emblem.

1990, June 26 Litho. *Perf. 14½x13*

577 A254 25c multicolored .50 .50
578 A254 45c multicolored 1.90 1.90

Souvenir Sheet

579 Sheet of 2, #577-578 3.50 3.50

See Offices in Geneva Nos. 188-190; Vienna Nos. 103-105.

Crime Prevention — A255

1990, Sept. 13 Photo. *Perf. 14*

580 A255 25c Crimes of youth .65 .65
581 A255 36c Organized crime 1.25 1.25

See Offices in Geneva Nos. 191-192; Vienna Nos. 106-107.

Human Rights Type of 1989

25c, Fragment from the sarcophagus of Plotinus, c. 270 A.D. 45c, Combined Chambers of the High Court of Appeal by Charles Paul Renouard.

1990, Nov. 16 Litho. *Perf. 13½*

582 A250 25c black, gray & tan .35 .35
583 A250 45c black & brown .65 .65

See Offices in Geneva Nos. 193-194; Vienna Nos. 108-109.

Economic Commission for Europe A256

1991, Mar. 15 Litho. *Perf. 14*

584 A256 30c Two storks 1.10 1.10
585 A256 30c Woodpecker, ibex 1.10 1.10
586 A256 30c Capercaille, plover 1.10 1.10
587 A256 30c Falcon, marmot 1.10 1.10
a. Block of 4, #584-587 4.50 4.50

See Offices in Geneva Nos. 195-198; Vienna Nos. 110-113.

Namibian Independence A257

1991, May 10 Litho. *Perf. 14*

588 A257 30c Dunes, Namib Desert .50 .50
589 A257 50c Savanna 1.10 1.00

See Offices in Geneva Nos. 199-200; Vienna Nos. 114-115.

A258

The Golden Rule by Norman Rockwell — A259

UN Headquarters, New York — A260

1991 Litho. *Perf. 13½*

590 A258 30c multi .60 .60

Photo.

Perf. 12x11½

591 A259 50c multi 1.00 1.00

Engr.

592 A260 $2 dark blue 2.75 2.75

Rights of the Child — A261

1991, June 14 Litho. *Perf. 14½*

593 A261 30c Children, globe 1.00 1.00
594 A261 70c House, rainbow 2.00 2.00

See Offices in Geneva Nos. 203-204; Vienna Nos. 117-118.

Banning of Chemical Weapons A262

90c, Hand holding back chemical drums.

1991, Sept. 11 Litho. *Perf. 13½*
595 A262 30c multicolored .75 .75
596 A262 90c multicolored 2.25 2.25

See Offices in Geneva Nos. 205-206; Vienna Nos. 119-120.

UN Postal Administration, 40th Anniv. — A263

1991, Oct. 24 Litho. *Perf. 14x15*
597 A263 30c No. 1 .65 .65
598 A263 40c No. 3 .85 .85

See Offices in Geneva Nos. 207-208; Vienna Nos. 121-122.

Human Rights Type of 1989

30c, The Last of England, by Ford Madox Brown. 40c, The Emigration to the East, by Tito Salas.

1991, Nov. 20 Litho. *Perf. 13½*
599 A250 30c multicolored .40 .40
600 A250 50c multicolored .80 1.00

See Offices in Geneva Nos. 209-210; Vienna Nos. 123-124.

World Heritage Type of 1984

30c, Uluru Natl. Park, Australia. 50c, The Great Wall of China.

1992, Jan. 24 Litho. *Perf. 13*
Size: 35x28mm
601 A215 30c multicolored .55 .55
602 A215 50c multicolored .90 .90

See Offices in Geneva Nos. 211-212; Vienna Nos. 125-126.

Clean Oceans — A264

1992, Mar. 13 Litho. *Perf. 14*
603 A264 29c Ocean surface .50 .50
604 A264 29c Ocean bottom .50 .50
a. Pair, #603-604 1.10 1.10

See Offices in Geneva Nos. 214-215, Vienna Nos. 127-128.

Earth Summit — A265

No. 605, Globe at LR. No. 606, Globe at LL. No. 607, Globe at UR. No. 608, Globe at UL.

1992, May 22 Photo. *Perf. 11½*
605 A265 29c multicolored .65 .65
606 A265 29c multicolored .65 .65
607 A265 29c multicolored .65 .65
608 A265 29c multicolored .65 .65
a. Block of 4, #605-608 4.00 3.50

See Offices in Geneva Nos. 216-219, Vienna Nos. 129-132.

Mission to Planet Earth — A266

No. 609, Satellites over city, sailboats, fishing boat. No. 610, Satellite over coast, passenger liner, dolphins, whale, volcano.

1992, Sept. 4 Photo. *Rouletted 8*
Granite Paper
609 A266 29c multicolored 1.25 1.25
610 A266 29c multicolored 1.25 1.25
a. Pair, #609-610 2.50 2.50

See Offices in Geneva Nos. 220-221, Vienna Nos. 133-134.

Science and Technology for Development — A267

50c, Animal, man drinking.

1992, Oct. 2 Litho. *Perf. 14*
611 A267 29c multicolored .40 .40
612 A267 50c multicolored .70 .70

UN University Building, Tokyo A268

UN Headquarters A269

40c, UN University Building, Tokyo, diff.

Perf. 14, 13½x13 (29c)
1992, Oct. 2 Litho.
613 A268 4c multicolored .25 .25
614 A269 29c multicolored .50 .50
615 A268 40c multicolored .65 .65
Nos. 613-615 (3) 1.40 1.40

Human Rights Type of 1989

29c, Lady Writing a Letter with her Maid, by Vermeer. 50c, The Meeting, by Ester Almqvist.

1992, Nov. 20 Litho. *Perf. 13½*
616 A250 29c multicolored .40 .40
617 A250 50c multicolored .60 .60

See Offices in Geneva Nos. 224-225; Vienna Nos. 139-140.

Aging With Dignity — A270

29c, Elderly couple, family. 52c, Old man, physician, woman holding fruit basket.

1993, Feb. 5 Litho. *Perf. 13*
618 A270 29c multicolored .45 .45
619 A270 52c multicolored 1.00 1.00

See Offices in Geneva Nos. 226-227; Vienna Nos. 141-142.

Endangered Species A271

No. 620, Hairy-nosed wombat. No. 621, Whooping crane. No. 622, Giant clam. No. 623, Giant sable antelope.

1993, Mar. 2 Litho. *Perf. 13x12½*
620 A271 29c multicolored .45 .45
621 A271 29c multicolored .45 .45
622 A271 29c multicolored .45 .45
623 A271 29c multicolored .45 .45
a. Block of 4, #620-623 2.00 2.00

See Nos. 639-642, 657-660, 674-677, 700-703, 730-733, 757-760, 773-776; Offices in Geneva Nos. 228-231, 246-249, 264-267, 280-283, 298-301, 318-321, 336-339, 352-355; Vienna Nos. 143-146, 162-165, 180-183, 196-199, 214-217, 235-238, 253-256, 269-272.

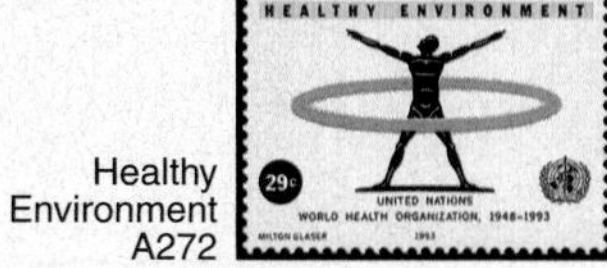
Healthy Environment A272

29c, Personal. 50c, Family.

1993, May 7 Litho. *Perf. 15x14½*
624 A272 29c Man .50 .50
625 A272 50c Family .90 .90

See Offices in Geneva Nos. 232-233; Vienna Nos. 147-148.

A273

1993, May 7 Litho. *Perf. 15x14*
626 A273 5c multicolored .25 .25

Human Rights Type of 1989

29c, Shocking Corn, by Thomas Hart Benton. 35c, The Library, by Jacob Lawrence.

1993, June 11 Litho. *Perf. 13½*
627 A250 29c multicolored .40 .40
628 A250 35c multicolored .45 .45

See Offices in Geneva Nos. 234-235; Vienna Nos. 150-151.

Intl. Peace Day — A274

Denomination at: #629, UL. #630, UR. #631, LL. #632, LR.

Rouletted 12½
1993, Sept. 21 Litho. & Engr.
629 A274 29c blue & multi 1.00 1.00
630 A274 29c blue & multi 1.00 1.00
631 A274 29c blue & multi 1.00 1.00
632 A274 29c blue & multi 1.00 1.00
a. Block of 4, #629-632 6.00 6.00

See Offices in Geneva Nos. 236-239; Vienna Nos. 152-155.

Environment-Climate — A275

#633, Chameleon. #634, Palm trees, top of funnel cloud. #635, Bottom of funnel cloud, deer, antelope. #636, Bird of paradise.

1993, Oct. 29 Litho. *Perf. 14½*
633 A275 29c multicolored .75 .75
634 A275 29c multicolored .75 .75
635 A275 29c multicolored .75 .75
636 A275 29c multicolored .75 .75
a. Strip of 4, #633-636 4.00 4.00

See Offices in Geneva Nos. 240-243; Vienna Nos. 156-159.

Intl. Year of the Family — A276

29c, Mother holding child, two children, woman. 45c, People tending crops.

1994, Feb. 4 Litho. *Perf. 13.1*
637 A276 29c green & multi .70 .70
638 A276 45c blue & multi .90 .90

See Offices in Geneva Nos. 244-245; Vienna Nos. 160-161.

Endangered Species Type of 1993

No. 639, Chimpanzee. No. 640, St. Lucia Amazon. No. 641, American crocodile. No. 642, Dama gazelle.

1994, Mar. 18 Litho. *Perf. 12.7*
639 A271 29c multicolored .45 .45
640 A271 29c multicolored .45 .45
641 A271 29c multicolored .45 .45
642 A271 29c multicolored .45 .45
a. Block of 4, #639-642 2.00 2.00

See Offices in Geneva Nos. 246-249; Vienna Nos. 162-165.

Protection for Refugees — A277

1994, Apr. 29 Litho. *Perf. 14.3x14.8*
643 A277 50c multicolored .90 .90

See Offices in Geneva No. 250; Vienna No. 166.

Dove of Peace — A278

Sleeping Child, by Stanislaw Wyspianski A279

Mourning Owl, by Vanessa Isitt A280

1994, Apr. 29 Litho. *Perf. 12.9*
644 A278 10c multicolored .25 .25
645 A279 19c multicolored .30 .30

Engr.
Perf. 13.1
646 A280 $1 red brown 1.50 1.50
Nos. 644-646 (3) 2.05 2.05

Intl. Decade for Natural Disaster Reduction A281

Earth seen from space, outline map of: #647, North America. #648, Eurasia. #649, South America, #650, Australia and South Asia.

1994, May 27 Litho. *Perf. 13.9x14.2*
647 A281 29c multicolored 1.75 1.75
648 A281 29c multicolored 1.75 1.75
649 A281 29c multicolored 1.75 1.75
650 A281 29c multicolored 1.75 1.75
a. Block of 4, #647-650 7.50 7.50

See Offices in Geneva Nos. 251-254; Vienna Nos. 170-173.

Population and Development — A282

29c, Children playing. 52c, Family with house, car, other possessions.

1994, Sept. 1 Litho. *Perf. 13.2x13.6*
651 A282 29c multicolored .40 .40
652 A282 52c multicolored .80 .80

See Offices in Geneva Nos. 258-259; Vienna Nos. 174-175.

UNCTAD, 30th Anniv. A283

1994, Oct. 28
653 A283 29c multicolored .40 .40
654 A283 50c multi, diff. .80 .80

See Offices in Geneva Nos. 260-261; Vienna Nos. 176-177.

UN, 50th Anniv. — A284

Litho. & Engr.
1995, Jan. 1 *Perf. 13.4*
655 A284 32c multicolored .90 .90

See Offices in Geneva No. 262; Vienna No. 178.

Social Summit, Copenhagen A285

656 A285 50c multicolored 1.00 1.00

See Offices in Geneva No. 263; Vienna No. 179.

Endangered Species Type of 1993

No. 657, Giant armadillo. No. 658, American bald eagle. No. 659, Fijian/Tongan banded iguana. No. 660, Giant panda.

1995, Mar. 24 Litho. *Perf. 13x12½*
657 A271 32c multicolored .40 .40
658 A271 32c multicolored .40 .40
659 A271 32c multicolored .40 .40
660 A271 32c multicolored .40 .40
a. Block of 4, 657-660 2.25 2.25

See Offices in Geneva Nos. 264-267; Vienna Nos. 180-183.

Intl. Youth Year, 10th Anniv. — A286

32c, Seated child. 55c, Children cycling.

1995, May 26 Litho. *Perf. 14.4x14.7*
661 A286 32c multicolored .55 .55
662 A286 55c multicolored .95 .95

See Offices in Geneva Nos. 268-269; Vienna Nos. 184-185.

UN, 50th Anniv. — A287

32c, Hand with pen signing UN Charter, flags. 50c, Veterans' War Memorial, Opera House, San Francisco.

Perf. 13.3x13.6
1995, June 26 Engr.
663 A287 32c black .55 .55
664 A287 50c maroon 1.00 1.00

Souvenir Sheet
Litho. & Engr.
Imperf

665 Sheet of 2, #663-664 2.75 2.75
a. A287 32c black 1.00 1.00
b. A287 50c maroon 1.25 1.25

No. 665 exists with gold China 1996 overprint. Value $20.

See Offices in Geneva Nos. 270-272; Vienna Nos. 186-188.

4th World Conference on Women, Beijing A288

32c, Mother and child. 40c, Seated woman, cranes flying above.

1995, Sept. 5 Photo. *Perf. 12*
666 A288 32c multicolored .50 .50

Size: 28x50mm

667 A288 40c multicolored .85 .85

See Offices in Geneva Nos. 273-274; Vienna Nos. 189-190.

UN Headquarters — A289

1995, Sept. 5 Litho. *Perf. 15*
668 A289 20c multicolored .35 .35

Miniature Sheet

United Nations, 50th Anniv. — A290

1995, Oct. 24 Litho. *Perf. 14*
669 Sheet of 12 12.00 12.00
a.-l. A290 32c any single .80 .80
670 Souvenir booklet 14.00
a. A290 32c Booklet pane of 3, vert. strip of 3 from UL of sheet 3.50 3.50
b. A290 32c Booklet pane of 3, vert. strip of 3 from UR of sheet 3.50 3.50
c. A290 32c Booklet pane of 3, vert. strip of 3 from LL of sheet 3.50 3.50
d. A290 32c Booklet pane of 3, vert. strip of 3 from LR of sheet 3.50 3.50

See Offices in Geneva Nos. 275-276; Vienna Nos. 191-192.

WFUNA, 50th Anniv. — A291

1996, Feb. 2 Litho. *Perf. 13x13½*
671 A291 32c multicolored .50 .50

See Offices in Geneva No. 277; Vienna No. 193.

Mural, by Fernand Leger — A292

1996, Feb. 2 Litho. *Perf. 14½x15*
672 A292 32c multicolored .45 .45
673 A292 60c multi, diff. .95 .95

Endangered Species Type of 1993

Printed by Johann Enschede and Sons, the Netherlands. Designed by Diane Bruyninckx, Belgium.

No. 674, Masdevallia veitchiana. No. 675, Saguaro cactus. No. 676, West Australian pitcher plant. No. 677, Encephalartos horridus.

1996, Mar. 14 Litho. *Perf. 12½*
674 A271 32c multicolored .45 .45
675 A271 32c multicolored .45 .45
676 A271 32c multicolored .45 .45
677 A271 32c multicolored .45 .45
a. Block of 4, #674-677 2.25 2.25

See Offices in Geneva Nos. 280-283; Vienna Nos. 196-199.

City Summit (Habitat II) — A293

No. 678, Deer. No. 679, Man, child, dog sitting on hill, overlooking town. No. 680, People walking in park, city skyline. No. 681, Tropical park, Polynesian woman, boy. No. 682, Polynesian village, orchids, bird.

1996, June 3 Litho. *Perf. 14x13½*
678 A293 32c multicolored .80 .80
679 A293 32c multicolored .80 .80
680 A293 32c multicolored .80 .80
681 A293 32c multicolored .80 .80
682 A293 32c multicolored .80 .80
a. Strip of 5, #678-682 7.00 7.00

See Offices in Geneva Nos. 284-288; Vienna Nos. 200-204.

Sport and the Environment A294

32c, Men's basketball. 50c, Women's volleyball, horiz.

Perf. 14x14½, 14½x14
1996, July 19 Litho.
683 A294 32c multicolored .65 .65
684 A294 50c multicolored 1.40 1.40

Souvenir Sheet

685 A294 Sheet of 2, #683-684 2.50 2.50

See Offices in Geneva Nos. 289-291; Vienna Nos. 205-207.

1996 Summer Olympic Games, Atlanta, GA.

Plea for Peace — A295

32c, Doves. 60c, Stylized dove.

1996, Sept. 17 Litho. *Perf. 14½x15*
686 A295 32c multicolored .50 .50
687 A295 60c multicolored .90 .90

See Offices in Geneva Nos. 292-293; Vienna Nos. 208-209.

UNICEF, 50th Anniv. — A296

Fairy Tales: 32c, Yeh-Shen, China. 60c, The Ugly Duckling, by Hans Christian Andersen.

1996, Nov. 20 Litho. *Perf. 14½x15*
688 A296 32c multicolored .45 .45
689 A296 60c multicolored 1.10 1.10

See Offices in Geneva Nos. 294-295; Vienna Nos. 210-211.

Flag Type of 1980

1997, Feb. 12 Photo. *Perf. 12*
Granite Paper
690 A185 32c Tadjikistan 1.00 1.00
691 A185 32c Georgia 1.00 1.00
692 A185 32c Armenia 1.00 1.00
693 A185 32c Namibia 1.00 1.00
a. Block of 4, #690-693 13.00 13.00
694 A185 32c Liechtenstein 1.00 1.00
695 A185 32c Republic of Korea 1.00 1.00
696 A185 32c Kazakhstan 1.00 1.00
697 A185 32c Latvia 1.00 1.00
a. Block of 4, #694-697 13.00 13.00

See note after No. 340.

Cherry Blossoms, UN Headquarters A297

Peace Rose — A298

1997, Feb. 12 Litho. *Perf. 14½*
698 A297 8c multicolored .25 .25
699 A298 55c multicolored .90 .90

Endangered Species Type of 1993

No. 700, African elephant. No. 701, Major Mitchell's cockatoo. No. 702, Black-footed ferret. No. 703, Cougar.

1997, Mar. 13 Litho. *Perf. 12½*

700 A271 32c multicolored .40 .40
701 A271 32c multicolored .40 .40
702 A271 32c multicolored .40 .40
703 A271 32c multicolored .40 .40
a. Block of 4, #700-703 2.25 2.25

See Offices in Geneva Nos. 298-301; Vienna Nos. 214-217.

Earth Summit, 5th Anniv. A299

No. 704, Sailboat. No. 705, Three sailboats. No. 706, Two people watching sailboat, sun. No. 707, Person, sailboat.

$1, Combined design similar to Nos. 704-707.

1997, May 30 Photo. *Perf. 11.5*

Granite Paper

704 A299 32c multicolored .90 .90
705 A299 32c multicolored .90 .90
706 A299 32c multicolored .90 .90
707 A299 32c multicolored .90 .90
a. Block of 4, #704-707 5.00 5.00

Souvenir Sheet

708 A299 $1 multicolored 2.75 2.75
a. Ovptd. in sheet margin *17.50 17.50*

See Offices in Geneva Nos. 302-306; Vienna Nos. 218-222.

No. 708 contains one 60x43mm stamp. Overprint in sheet margin of No. 708a reads "PACIFIC 97 / World Philatelic Exhibition / San Francisco, California / 29 May - 8 June 1997".

Transportation A300

Ships: No. 709, Clipper ship. No. 710, Paddle steamer. No. 711, Ocean liner. No. 712, Hovercraft. No. 713, Hydrofoil.

1997, Aug. 29 Litho. *Perf. 14x14½*

709 A300 32c multicolored .60 .60
710 A300 32c multicolored .60 .60
711 A300 32c multicolored .60 .60
712 A300 32c multicolored .60 .60
713 A300 32c multicolored .60 .60
a. Strip of 5, #709-713 4.00 4.00

See Offices in Geneva Nos. 307-311; Vienna Nos. 223-227.

No. 713a has continuous design.

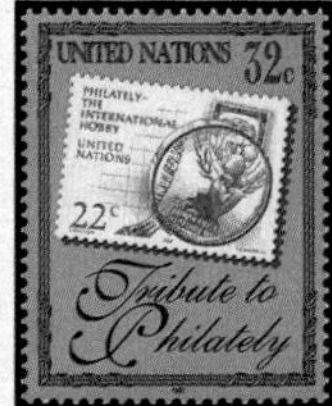

Philately — A301

32c, No. 473. 50c, No. 474.

1997, Oct. 14 Litho. *Perf. 13½x14*

714 A301 32c multicolored .60 .60
715 A301 50c multicolored 1.50 1.50

See Offices in Geneva Nos. 312-313; Vienna Nos. 228-229.

World Heritage Convention, 25th Anniv. — A302

Terracotta warriors of Xian: 32c, Single warrior. 60c, Massed warriors. No. 718a, like #716. No. 718b, like #717. No. 718c, like Geneva #314. No. 718d, like Geneva #315. No. 718e, like Vienna #230. No. 718f, like Vienna #231.

1997, Nov. 19 Litho. *Perf. 13½*

716 A302 32c multicolored .75 .75
717 A302 60c multicolored 1.25 1.25
718 Souvenir booklet 10.00
a.-f. A302 8c any single .50 .50
g. Booklet pane of 4 #718a 2.00 2.00
h. Booklet pane of 4 #718b 2.00 2.00
i. Booklet pane of 4 #718c 2.00 2.00
j. Booklet pane of 4 #718d 2.00 2.00
k. Booklet pane of 4 #718e 2.00 2.00
l. Booklet pane of 4 #718f 2.00 2.00

See Offices in Geneva Nos. 314-316; Vienna Nos. 230-232.

Flag Type of 1980

1998, Feb. 13 Photo. *Perf. 12*

Granite Paper

719 A185 32c Micronesia .80 .80
720 A185 32c Slovakia .80 .80
721 A185 32c Democratic People's Republic of Korea .80 .80
722 A185 32c Azerbaijan .80 .80
a. Block of 4, #719-722 12.50 12.50
723 A185 32c Uzbekistan .80 .80
724 A185 32c Monaco .80 .80
725 A185 32c Czech Republic .80 .80
726 A185 32c Estonia .80 .80
a. Block of 4, #723-726 12.50 12.50
Nos. 719-726 (8) 6.40 6.40

A303

A304

A305

Perf. 14½x15, 15x14½

1998, Feb. 13 Litho.

727 A303 1c multicolored .25 .25
728 A304 2c multicolored .25 .25
729 A305 21c multicolored .40 .40
Nos. 727-729 (3) .90 .90

Endangered Species Type of 1993

No. 730, Lesser galago. No. 731, Hawaiian goose. No. 732, Golden birdwing. No. 733, Sun bear.

1998, Mar. 13 Litho. *Perf. 12½*

730 A271 32c multicolored .45 .45
731 A271 32c multicolored .45 .45
732 A271 32c multicolored .45 .45
733 A271 32c multicolored .45 .45
a. Block of 4, #730-733 2.25 2.25

See Offices in Geneva Nos. 318-321; Vienna Nos. 235-238.

Intl. Year of the Ocean — A306

1998, May 20 Litho. *Perf. 13x13½*

734 A306 Sheet of 12 12.50 12.50
a.-l. 32c any single 1.00 1.00

See Offices in Geneva No. 322; Vienna No. 239.

Rain Forests A307

1998, June 19 Litho. *Perf. 13x13½*

735 A307 32c Jaguar .50 .50

Souvenir Sheet

736 A307 $2 like #735 3.00 3.00

See Offices in Geneva Nos. 323-324; Vienna Nos. 240-241.

U.N. Peacekeeping Forces, 50th Anniv. — A308

33c, Commander with binoculars. 40c, Two soldiers on vehicle.

1998, Sept. 15 Photo. *Perf. 12*

737 A308 33c multicolored .50 .50
738 A308 40c multicolored .75 .75

See Offices in Geneva Nos. 325-326; Vienna Nos. 242-243.

Universal Declaration of Human Rights, 50th Anniv. — A309

Stylized people: 32c, Carrying flag. 55c, Carrying pens.

Litho. & Photo.

1998, Oct. 27 *Perf. 13*

739 A309 32c multicolored .45 .45
740 A309 55c multicolored .90 .90

See Offices in Geneva Nos. 327-328; Vienna Nos. 244-245.

Schönbrun Palace, Vienna — A310

33c, #743f, The Gloriette. 60c, #743b, Wall painting on fabric (detail), by Johann Wenzl Bergl, vert. No. 743a, Blue porcelain vase, vert. No. 743c, Porcelain stove, vert. No. 743d, Palace. No. 743e, Great Palm House (conservatory).

1998, Dec. 4 Litho. *Perf. 14*

741 A310 33c multicolored .55 .55
742 A310 60c multicolored 1.25 1.00

Souvenir Booklet

743 Booklet 24.00
a.-c. A310 11c any single .50 .50
d.-f. A310 15c any single 1.60 1.60
g. Booklet pane of 4 #743d 6.50 6.50
h. Booklet pane of 3 #743a 1.50 1.50
i. Booklet pane of 3 #743b 1.50 1.50
j. Booklet pane of 3 #743c 1.50 1.50
k. Booklet pane of 4 #743e 6.50 6.50
l. Booklet pane of 4 #743f 6.50 6.50

See Offices in Geneva Nos. 329-331; Vienna Nos. 246-248.

Flag Type of 1980

1999, Feb. 5 Photo. *Perf. 12*

744 A185 33c Lithuania .85 .85
745 A185 33c San Marino .85 .85
746 A185 33c Turkmenistan .85 .85
747 A185 33c Marshall Islands .85 .85
a. Block of 4, #744-747 13.00 13.00
748 A185 33c Moldova .85 .85
749 A185 33c Kyrgyzstan .85 .85
750 A185 33c Bosnia & Herzegovina .85 .85
751 A185 33c Eritrea .85 .85
a. Block of 4, #748-751 13.00 13.00
Nos. 744-751 (8) 6.80 6.80

See note after No. 340.

Flags and Globe — A311

Roses — A312

1999, Feb. 5 Litho. *Perf. 14x13½*

752 A311 33c multicolored .50 .50

Photo.

Granite Paper

Perf. 11½x12

753 A312 $5 multicolored 8.00 8.00

World Heritage Sites, Australia A313

33c, #756f, Willandra Lakes region. 60c, #756b, Wet tropics of Queensland. No. 756a, Tasmanian wilderness. No. 756c, Great Barrier Reef. No. 756d, Uluru-Kata Tjuta Natl. Park. No. 756e, Kakadu Natl. Park.

1999, Mar. 19 Litho. *Perf. 13*

754 A313 33c multicolored .60 .60
755 A313 60c multicolored 1.25 1.25

Souvenir Booklet

756 Booklet 16.00
a.-c. A313 5c any single .30 .30
d.-f. A313 15c any single 1.00 1.00
g. Booklet pane of 4, #756a 1.20 1.20
h. Booklet pane of 4, #756d 4.00 4.00
i. Booklet pane of 4, #756b 1.20 1.20
j. Booklet pane of 4, #756e 4.00 4.00
k. Booklet pane of 4, #756c 1.20 1.20
l. Booklet pane of 4, #756f 4.00 4.00

See Offices in Geneva Nos. 333-335; Vienna Nos. 250-252.

Endangered Species Type of 1993

No. 757, Tiger. No. 758, Secretary bird. No. 759, Green tree python. No. 760, Long-tailed chinchilla.

1999, Apr. 22 Litho. *Perf. 12½*

757 A271 33c multicolored .60 .60
758 A271 33c multicolored .60 .60
759 A271 33c multicolored .60 .60
760 A271 33c multicolored .60 .60
a. Block of 4, #757-760 2.40 2.40

See Offices in Geneva Nos. 336-339; Vienna Nos. 253-256.

UNISPACE III, Vienna — A314

No. 761, Probe on planet's surface. No. 762, Planetary rover. No. 763, Composite of #761-762.

1999, July 7 Photo. *Rouletted 8*

761 A314 33c multicolored .50 .50
762 A314 33c multicolored .50 .50
a. Pair, #761-762 1.75 1.75

Souvenir Sheet

Perf. 14½

763 A314 $2 multicolored 4.00 4.00
a. Ovptd. in sheet margin 18.00 8.00

No. 763a was issued 7/7/00 and is overprinted in violet blue "WORLD STAMP EXPO 2000 / ANAHEIM, CALIFORNIA / U.S.A./ 7-16 JULY 2000."

See Offices in Geneva Nos. 340-342; Vienna Nos. 257-259.

UPU, 125th Anniv. — A315

Various people, 19th century methods of mail transportation, denomination at: No. 764, UL. No. 765, UR. No. 766, LL. No. 767, LR.

1999, Aug. 23 Photo. *Perf. 11¾*

764 A315 33c multicolored .45 .45
765 A315 33c multicolored .45 .45
766 A315 33c multicolored .45 .45
767 A315 33c multicolored .45 .45
a. Block of 4, #764-767 2.50 2.50

See Offices in Geneva Nos. 343-346; Vienna Nos. 260-263.

In Memoriam A316

Designs: 33c, $1, UN Headquarters. Size of $1 stamp: 34x63mm.

1999, Sept. 21 Litho. *Perf. 14½x14*

768 A316 33c multicolored .80 .80

Souvenir Sheet

Perf. 14

769 A316 $1 multicolored 2.00 2.00

Education, Keystone to the 21st Century — A317

Perf. 13½x13¾

1999, Nov. 18 Litho.

770 A317 33c Two readers .50 .50
771 A317 60c Heart 1.00 1.00

See Offices in Geneva Nos. 349-350, Vienna Nos. 266-267.

International Year of Thanksgiving A318

2000, Jan. 1 Litho. *Perf. 13¼x13½*

772 A318 33c multicolored .75 .75

On No. 772 parts of the design were applied by a thermographic process producing a shiny, raised effect. See Offices in Geneva No. 351, Vienna No. 268.

Endangered Species Type of 1993

No. 773, Brown bear. No. 774, Black-bellied bustard. No. 775, Chinese crocodile lizard. No. 776, Pygmy chimpanzee.

2000, Apr. 6 Litho. *Perf. 12¾x12½*

773 A271 33c multicolored .50 .50
774 A271 33c multicolored .50 .50
775 A271 33c multicolored .50 .50
776 A271 33c multicolored .50 .50
a. Block of 4, #773-776 2.50 2.50

See Offices in Geneva Nos. 352-355; Vienna Nos. 269-272.

Our World 2000 A319

Winning artwork in Millennium painting competition: 33c, Crawling Toward the Millennium, by Sam Yeates, US. 60c, Crossing, by Masakazu Takahata, Japan, vert.

Perf. 13x13½, 13½x13

2000, May 30 Litho.

777 A319 33c multicolored .60 .60
778 A319 60c multicolored 1.00 1.00

See Offices in Geneva No. 356-357, Vienna No. 273-274.

UN, 55th Anniv. — A320

33c, Workmen removing decorative discs in General Assembly Hall, 1956. 55c, UN Building in 1951.

2000, July 7 Litho. *Perf. 13¼x13*

779 A320 33c multicolored .55 .55
780 A320 55c multicolored .95 .95

Souvenir Sheet

781 A320 Sheet of 2, #779-780 3.00 3.00

See Offices in Geneva No. 358-360, Vienna No. 275-277.

International Flag of Peace — A321

2000, Sept. 15 Litho. *Perf. 14½x14*

782 A321 33c multicolored .65 .65

The UN in the 21st Century — A322

No. 783: a, Farmers, animals in rice paddy. b, Vehicle chassis being lifted. c, People voting. d, Baby receiving inoculation. e, Woman, man at pump. f, Mason, construction workers.

2000, Sept. 15 Litho. *Perf. 14*

783 A322 Sheet of 6 9.00 9.00
a.-f. 33c any single 1.25 1.25

See Offices in Geneva No. 361; Vienna No. 278.

World Heritage Sites, Spain — A323

Nos. 784, 786a, Alhambra, Generalife and Albayzin, Granada. Nos. 785, 786d, Amphitheater of Mérida. #786b, Walled Town of Cuenca. #786c, Aqueduct of Segovia. #786e, Toledo. #786f, Güell Park, Barcelona.

2000, Oct. 6 Litho. *Perf. 14¾x14½*

784 A323 33c multicolored .55 .55
785 A323 60c multicolored 1.10 1.10

Souvenir Booklet

786 Booklet 15.00
a.-c. A323 5c any single .45 .45
d.-f. A323 15c any single .80 .80
g. Booklet pane of 4, #786a 1.80 1.80
h. Booklet pane of 4, #786d 3.20 3.20
i. Booklet pane of 4, #786b 1.80 1.80
j. Booklet pane of 4, #786e 3.20 3.20
k. Booklet pane of 4, #786c 1.80 1.80
l. Booklet pane of 4, #786f 3.20 3.20

See Offices in Geneva Nos. 362-364, Vienna Nos. 279-281.

Respect for Refugees A324

2000, Nov. 9 Litho. *Perf. 13¼x12¾*

787 A324 33c multicolored .75 .75

Souvenir Sheet

788 A324 $1 multicolored 2.00 2.00

See Offices in Geneva Nos. 365-366, Vienna Nos. 282-283.

Endangered Species Type of 1993

No. 789, Common spotted cuscus. No. 790, Resplendent quetzal. No. 791, Gila monster. No. 792, Guereza.

2001, Feb. 1 Litho. *Perf. 12¾x12½*

789 A271 34c multicolored .60 .60
790 A271 34c multicolored .60 .60
791 A271 34c multicolored .60 .60
792 A271 34c multicolored .60 .60
a. Block of 4, #789-792 2.40 2.40

See Offices in Geneva Nos. 367-370; Vienna Nos. 284-287.

Intl. Volunteers Year — A325

Paintings by: 34c, Jose Zaragoza, Brazil. 80c, John Terry, Australia.

2001, Mar. 29 Litho. *Perf. 13¼*

793 A325 34c multicolored .65 .65
794 A325 80c multicolored 1.60 1.60

See Offices in Geneva Nos. 371-372; Vienna Nos. 288-289.

Flag Type of 1980

2001, May 25 Photo. *Perf. 12*

Granite Paper

795 A185 34c Slovenia 1.25 1.25
796 A185 34c Palau 1.25 1.25
797 A185 34c Tonga 1.25 1.25
798 A185 34c Croatia 1.25 1.25
a. Block of 4, #795-798 15.00 15.00
799 A185 34c Former Yugoslav Republic of Macedonia 1.25 1.25
800 A185 34c Kiribati 1.25 1.25
801 A185 34c Andorra 1.25 1.25
802 A185 34c Nauru 1.25 1.25
a. Block of 4, #799-802 15.00 15.00
Nos. 795-802 (8) 10.00 10.00

Sunflower — A326

Rose — A327

2001, May 25 Litho. *Perf. 13¼x13¾*

803 A326 7c multicolored .25 .25
804 A327 34c multicolored .60 .60

World Heritage Sites, Japan — A328

34c, #807a, Kyoto. 70c, #807d, Shirakawa-Go and Gokayama. #807b, Nara. #807c, Himeji-Jo. #807e, Itsukushima Shinto Shrine. #807f, Nikko.

2001, Aug. 1 Litho. *Perf. 12¾x13¼*

805 A328 34c multicolored .60 .60
806 A328 70c multicolored 1.25 1.25

Souvenir Booklet

807 Booklet 16.00
a.-c. A328 5c any single .50 .50
d.-f. A328 20c any single .80 .80
g. Booklet pane of 4, #807a 2.00 2.00
h. Booklet pane of 4, #807d 3.20 3.20
i. Booklet pane of 4, #807b 2.00 2.00
j. Booklet pane of 4, #807e 3.20 3.20
k. Booklet pane of 4, #807c 2.00 2.00
l. Booklet pane of 4, #807f 3.20 3.20

See Offices in Geneva Nos. 373-375, Vienna Nos. 290-292.

Dag Hammarskjöld (1905-61), UN Secretary General — A329

2001, Sept. 18 Engr. *Perf. 11x11¼*

808 A329 80c blue 1.50 1.50

See Offices in Geneva No. 376, Vienna No. 293.

A330

UN Postal Administration, 50th Anniv. — A331

2001, Oct. 18 Litho. *Perf. 13½*

809 A330 34c Stamps, streamers .55 .55
810 A330 80c Stamps, gifts 1.50 1.50

Souvenir Sheet

811 A331 Sheet of 2 #811a 8.00 8.00
a. $1 blue & light blue, 38mm diameter 4.00 4.00

See Offices in Geneva Nos. 377-379, Vienna Nos. 294-296.

Climate Change — A332

No. 812, Canada geese, greenhouses, butterfly, thistle. No. 813, Canada geese, iceberg, penguins, tomato plant. No. 814, Palm tree, solar collector. No. 815, Hand planting ginkgo cutting.

2001, Nov. 16 Litho. *Perf. 13¼*

812 A332 34c multicolored 1.00 1.00
813 A332 34c multicolored 1.00 1.00
814 A332 34c multicolored 1.00 1.00
815 A332 34c multicolored 1.00 1.00
a. Horiz. strip, #812-815 4.00 4.00

See Offices in Geneva Nos. 380-383, Vienna Nos. 297-300.

Awarding of Nobel Peace Prize to Secretary General Kofi Annan and UN — A333

2001, Dec. 10 Litho. *Perf. 13¼*

816 A333 34c multicolored .70 .70

See Offices in Geneva Nos. 384, Vienna Nos. 301.

Children and Stamps A334

2002, Mar. 1 Litho. *Perf. 13¾*

817 A334 80c multicolored 1.40 1.40

Endangered Species Type of 1993

No. 818, Hoffmann's two-toed sloth. No. 819, Bighorn sheep. No. 820, Cheetah. No. 821, San Esteban Island chuckwalla.

2002, Apr. 4 Litho. *Perf. 12¾x12½*

818 A271 34c multicolored .80 .80
819 A271 34c multicolored .80 .80
820 A271 34c multicolored .80 .80
821 A271 34c multicolored .80 .80
a. Block of 4, #818-821 3.25 3.25

See Offices in Geneva Nos. 386-389; Vienna 308-311.

Independence of East Timor — A335

34c, Wooden ritual mask. 57c, Decorative door panel.

2002, May 20 Litho. *Perf. 14x14½*

822 A335 34c multicolored .70 .70
823 A335 57c multicolored 1.20 1.20

See Offices in Geneva Nos. 390-391; Vienna Nos. 312-313.

Intl. Year of Mountains A336

No. 824, Khan Tengri, Kyrgyzstan. No. 825, Mt. Kilimanjaro, Tanzania. No. 826, Mt. Foraker, US. No. 827, Paine Grande, Chile.

2002, May 24 Litho. *Perf. 13x13¼*

824 A336 34c multicolored 1.00 1.00
825 A336 34c multicolored 1.00 1.00
826 A336 80c multicolored 2.00 2.00
827 A336 80c multicolored 2.00 2.00
a. Vert. strip or block of four, #824-827 10.00 10.00

See Offices in Geneva Nos. 392-395; Vienna Nos. 314-317.

World Summit on Sustainable Development, Johannesburg — A337

No. 828, Sun, Earth, planets, stars. No. 829, Three women. No. 830, Sailboat. No. 831, Three faceless people.

2002, June 27 Litho. *Perf. 14½x14*

828 A337 37c multicolored 1.00 1.00
829 A337 37c multicolored 1.00 1.00
830 A337 60c multicolored 2.00 2.00
831 A337 60c multicolored 2.00 2.00
a. Vert. strip or block of four, #828-831 9.00 9.00

See Offices in Geneva Nos. 396-399; Vienna Nos. 318-321.

World Heritage Sites, Italy — A338

37c, #834d, Florence. 70c, #834a, Amalfi Coast. #834b, Aeolian Islands. #834c, Rome. #834e, Pisa. #834f, Pompeii.

Perf. 13½x13¼

2002, Aug. 30 Litho.

832 A338 37c multicolored .70 .70
833 A338 70c multicolored 1.40 1.40

Souvenir Booklet

834 Booklet 22.50
a.-c. A338 5c any single .60 .60
d.-f. A338 15c any single 1.25 1.25
g. Booklet pane of 4, #834d 4.50 4.50
h. Booklet pane of 4, #834a 2.40 2.40
i. Booklet pane of 4, #834e 4.50 4.50
j. Booklet pane of 4, #834b 2.40 2.40
k. Booklet pane of 4, #834f 4.50 4.50
l. Booklet pane of 4, #834c 2.40 2.40

See Offices in Geneva Nos. 400-402, Vienna Nos. 322-324.
See Italy Nos. 2506-2507.

AIDS Awareness A339

2002, Oct. 24 Litho. *Perf. 13½*

835 A339 70c multicolored 1.50 1.50

See No. B1, Offices in Geneva Nos. 403, B1, Vienna Nos. 325, B1.

Indigenous Art — A340

No. 836: a, Detail of Paracas textile, Peru. b, Sinu culture anthropo-zoomorphic pendant, Colombia. c, Hicholi Indian embroidery, Mexico. d, Rigpaktsa back ornament, Brazil. e, Wool crafts, Chile. f, Huari feathered woven hat, Bolivia.

2003, Jan. 31 Litho. *Perf. 14¼*

836 A340 Sheet of 6 10.00 10.00
a.-f. 37c Any single 1.60 1.60

See Offies in Geneva No. 405; Vienna No. 326.

Clasped Hands — A341

UN Emblem A342

UN Headquarters A343

2003, Mar. 28 Litho. *Perf. 14¼*

837 A341 23c multicolored .40 .40

Litho. with Foil Application

838 A342 37c gold & multicolored .60 .60

Litho. with Hologram

839 A343 70c multicolored 1.40 1.40

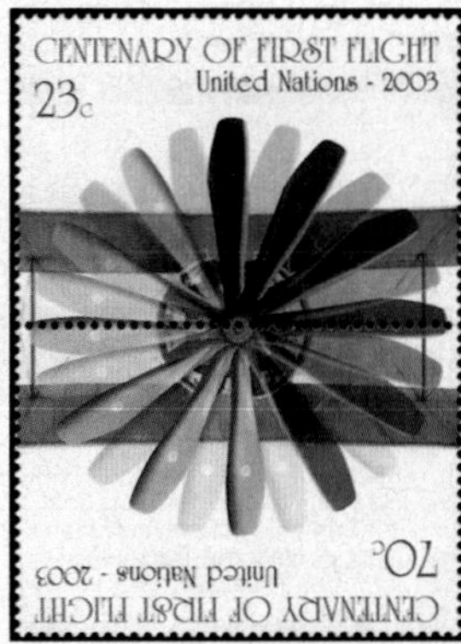

Powered Flight, Cent. — A344

Perf. 13½x13¾

2003, Mar. 28 Litho.

840 23c multicolored 1.25 1.25
841 70c multicolored 2.75 2.75
a. A344 Tete beche pair, #840-841 4.00 4.00

Endangered Species Type of 1993

No. 842, Great hornbill. No. 843, Scarlet ibis. No. 844, Knob-billed goose. No. 845, White-faced whistling duck.

2003, Apr. 3 Litho. *Perf. 12¾x12½*

842 A271 37c multicolored .80 .80
843 A271 37c multicolored .80 .80
844 A271 37c multicolored .80 .80
845 A271 37c multicolored .80 .80
a. Block of 4, #842-845 3.25 3.25

See Offices in Geneva Nos. 407-410; Vienna 329-332.

Intl. Year of Freshwater A345

Perf. 14¼x14½

2003, June 20 Litho.

846 A345 23c Wildlife, garbage 1.50 1.50
847 A345 37c Trees, canoe 2.00 2.00
a. Horiz. pair, #846-847 7.50 7.50

See Offices in Geneva, Nos. 411-412; Vienna Nos. 333-334.

Ralph Bunche (1903-71), Diplomat — A346

Litho. With Foil Application

2003, Aug. 7 ***Perf. 13½x14***

848 A346 37c blue & multicolored .80 .80

See Offices in Geneva No. 413; Vienna No. 336.

In Memoriam of Victims of Aug. 19 Bombing of UN Complex in Baghdad, Iraq — A347

2003, Oct. 24 Litho. ***Perf. 13¼x13***

849 A347 60c multicolored 1.25 1.25

See Offices in Geneva No. 414, Vienna No. 337.

World Heritage Sites, United States A348

37c, #852a, Yosemite National Park. 60c, #852d, Hawaii Volcanoes National Park. #852b, Great Smoky Mountains National Park. #852c, Olympic National Park. #852e, Everglades National Park. #852f, Yellowstone National Park.

2003, Oct. 24 Litho. ***Perf. 14½x14¼***

850 A348 37c multicolored .90 .90
851 A348 60c multicolored 1.50 1.50

Souvenir Booklet

852 Booklet 12.00
a.-c. A348 10c any single .30 .30
d.-f. A348 20c any single .60 .60
g. Booklet pane of 4 #852a 1.20 1.20
h. Booklet pane of 4 #852d 2.40 2.40
i. Booklet pane of 4 #852b 1.20 1.20
j. Booklet pane of 4 #852e 2.40 2.40
k. Booklet pane of 4 #852c 1.20 1.20
l. Booklet pane of 4 #852f 2.40 2.40

See Offices in Geneva Nos. 415-417, Vienna Nos. 338-340.

UN Security Council — A349

UN Emblem — A350

UN General Assembly — A351

Flags — A352

UN Headquarters — A353

2003, Nov. 26 Litho. ***Perf. 13¼***

853 A349 37c multicolored + label 10.00 10.00
854 A350 37c multicolored + label 10.00 10.00
855 A351 37c multicolored + label 10.00 10.00
856 A352 37c multicolored + label 10.00 10.00
857 A353 37c multicolored + label 10.00 10.00
a. Vert. strip of 5, #853-857, + 5 labels 50.00 50.00

The full sheet sold for $14.95 with or without personalized labels. The personalization of labels was available only at UN Headquarters, and not through mail order.

One thousand full sheets with sheet margins inscribed "Hong Kong Stamp Expo" were sold only at that venue. Value $150. Also exists with sheet margins inscribed "Essen." Value $140.

A sheet containing two strips of five stamps similar to Nos. 853-857 but dated "2005" and ten labels sold for $4.95. These sheets were only available canceled. Value $110. An imperforate error of this sheet is known.

Endangered Species Type of 1993

No. 858, American black bear. No. 859, Musk deer. No. 860, Golden snub-nosed monkey. No. 861, Wild yak.

2004, Jan. 29 Litho. ***Perf. 12¾x12½***

858 A271 37c multicolored 1.10 1.10
859 A271 37c multicolored 1.10 1.10
860 A271 37c multicolored 1.10 1.10
861 A271 37c multicolored 1.10 1.10
a. Block of 4, #858-861 4.50 4.50

See Offices in Geneva Nos. 418-421; Vienna Nos. 342-345.

Indigenous Art Type of 2003

No. 862: a, Viking wood carving depicting Saga of Sigurd Favnesbane, Norway. b, Stele, Italy. c, Detail of matador's suit, Spain. d, Amphora, Greece. e, Bronze figurine of bull, Czech Republic. f, Detail of lacquer box illustration depicting scene from "On the Seashore," by Alexander Pushkin, Russia.

2004, Mar. 4 Litho. ***Perf. 13¼***

862 A340 Sheet of 6 9.00 9.00
a.-f. 37c Any single 1.25 1.25

See Offices in Geneva No. 422; Vienna No. 346.

Road Safety A354

Road map art with: 37c, Automobile with road signs, city skyline. 70c, Automobile, hand, vert.

Perf. 13x13¼, 13¼x13

2004, Apr. 7 Litho.

863 A354 37c multicolored .85 .85
864 A354 70c multicolored 1.40 1.40

See Offices in Geneva Nos. 423-424, Vienna Nos. 347-348.

Japanese Peace Bell, 50th Anniv. — A355

Litho. & Engr.

2004, June 3 ***Perf. 13¼x13***

865 A355 80c multicolored 1.50 1.50

See Offices in Geneva No. 425; Vienna No. 349.

World Heritage Sites, Greece — A356

No. 866, Acropolis, Athens. Nos. 867, 868e, Delos. No. 868a, Delphi. No. 868b, Pythagoreion and Heraion of Samos. No. 868c, Olympia. No. 868d, Mycenae and Tiryns.

2004, Aug. 12 Litho. ***Perf. 14x13¼***

866 A356 37c multicolored .70 .70
a. Booklet pane of 4 3.00 —
867 A356 60c multicolored 1.10 1.10

Souvenir Booklet

868 Booklet, #866a, 868f-868j 15.00
a.-d. A356 23c any single .55 .55
e. A356 37c multi .90 .90
f. Booklet pane of 4 #868a 2.20 2.20
g. Booklet pane of 4 #868b 2.20 2.20
h. Booklet pane of 4 #868c 2.20 2.20
i. Booklet pane of 4 #868d 2.20 2.20
j. Booklet pane of 4 #868e 3.60 3.60

See Offices in Geneva Nos. 426-428, Vienna Nos. 350-352. No. 868 sold for $7.20.

My Dream for Peace — A357

Winning designs of Lions Club International children's global peace poster contest by: 37c, Sittichok Pariyaket, Thailand. 80c, Bayan Fais Abu Bial, Israel.

2004, Sept. 21 Litho. ***Perf. 14***

869 A357 37c multicolored .60 .60
870 A357 80c multicolored 1.40 1.40

See Offices in Geneva Nos. 429-430, Vienna Nos. 353-354.

A358

Human Rights — A359

2004, Oct. 14 Litho. ***Perf. 11¼***

871 A358 37c multicolored .75 .75
872 A359 70c multicolored 1.40 1.40

See Offices in Geneva Nos. 431-432, Vienna Nos. 355-356.

Disarmament A360

2004, Oct. 15 Litho. ***Perf. 13¾***

873 A360 37c multicolored .80 .80

United Nations, 60th Anniv. — A361

Litho. & Engr.

2005, Feb. 4 ***Perf. 11x11¼***

874 A361 80c multicolored 1.50 1.50

Souvenir Sheet

Litho.

Imperf

875 A361 $1 multicolored 16.00 16.00

See Offices in Geneva Nos. 434-435; Vienna Nos. 357-358.

Endangered Species Type of 1993

Designs: No. 876, Blue orchid. No. 877, Swan orchid. No. 878, Christmas orchid. No. 879, Aerangis modesta.

2005, Mar. 3 Litho. ***Perf. 12¾x12½***

876 A271 37c multicolored 1.10 1.10
877 A271 37c multicolored 1.10 1.10
878 A271 37c multicolored 1.10 1.10
879 A271 37c multicolored 1.10 1.10
a. Block of 4, #876-879 4.50 4.50

See Offices in Geneva Nos. 436-439; Vienna Nos. 360-363.

Non-Violence, Sculpture by Carl Fredrik Reuterswärd, New York — A362

Armillary Sphere, Sculpture by Paul Manship, Geneva — A363

Terra Cotta Warriors, Vienna — A364

Single Form, Sculpture by Barbara Hepworth, New York — A365

Sphere Within a Sphere, Sculpture by Arnaldo Pomodoro, New York — A366

2005, Mar. 3 Litho. *Perf. 13¼*

880 A362 80c multicolored + label *25.00 25.00*
881 A363 80c multicolored + label *25.00 25.00*
882 A364 80c multicolored + label *25.00 25.00*
883 A365 80c multicolored + label *25.00 25.00*
884 A366 80c multicolored + label *25.00 25.00*
a. Vert. strip of 5, #880-884, + 5 labels *125.00 125.00*
b. Sheet of 10, both #884 37c (error) *3,250.*
c. Vert. strip of 5, #884 37c (error) *1,450.*

The full sheet sold for $14.95 with or without personalized labels. The personalization of labels was available only at UN Headquarters, and not through mail order.

The full sheet exists with sheet margins and labels commemorating the Riccione 2005 Philatelic Exhibition. This sheet went on sale 8/20/05 and was also sold for $14.95. Value $140.

Nature's Wisdom — A367

37c, Ice climber, Norway. 80c, Egret, Japan.

2005, Apr. 21 Litho. *Perf. 13½x13¼*

885 A367 37c multicolored .65 .65
886 A367 80c multicolored 1.50 1.50

See Offices in Geneva Nos. 440-441, Vienna Nos. 364-365.

Intl. Year of Sport A368

2005, June 3 Litho. *Perf. 13x13¼*

887 A368 37c Sailing .65 .65
888 A368 70c Running 1.25 1.25

See Offices in Geneva Nos. 442-443; Vienna Nos. 366-367.

World Heritage Sites, Egypt — A369

Nos. 889, 891a, Memphis and its Necropolis. Nos. 890, 891d, Ancient Thebes. No. 891b, Philae. No. 891c, Abu Mena. No. 891e, Islamic Cairo. No. 891f, St. Catherine area.

2005, Aug. 4 Litho. *Perf. 14x13¼*

889 A369 37c multicolored .60 .60
890 A369 80c multicolored 1.40 1.40

Souvenir Booklet

891 Booklet, #891g-891l 15.00
a.-c. A369 23c any single .50 .50
d.-f. A369 37c any single .75 .75
g. Booklet pane of 4 #891a 2.00 2.00
h. Booklet pane of 4 #891b 2.00 2.00
i. Booklet pane of 4 #891c 2.00 2.00
j. Booklet pane of 4 #891d 3.00 3.00
k. Booklet pane of 4 #891e 3.00 3.00
l. Booklet pane of 4 #891f 3.00 3.00

See Offices in Geneva Nos. 444-446, Vienna Nos. 368-370.

My Dream for Peace Type of 2004

Winning designs of Lions Club International children's global peace poster contest by: 37c, Vittoria Sansebastiano, Italy. 80c, Jordan Harris, US.

2005, Sept. 21 Litho. *Perf. 14*

892 A357 37c multicolored .60 .60
893 A357 80c multicolored 1.40 1.40

See Offices in Geneva Nos. 447-448, Vienna Nos. 371-372.

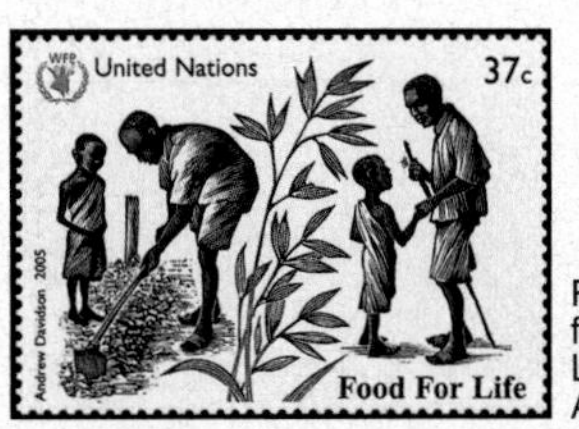

Food for Life A370

37c, Oats, children and adults. 80c, Wheat, mothers breastfeeding babies.

2005, Oct. 20 Litho. *Perf. 13¾*

894 A370 37c multicolored .60 .60
895 A370 80c multicolored 1.40 1.40

See Offices in Geneva Nos. 449-450; Vienna Nos. 373-374.

Stylized Flags in Heart and Hands A371

2006, Feb. 3 Litho. *Perf. 13x13¼*

896 A371 25c multicolored .75 .75

Indigenous Art Type of 2003

No. 897 — Musical instruments: a, Drum, Ivory Coast. b, Drum, Tunisia. c, Stringed instruments, Morocco. d, Drums, Sudan. e, Instruments, Cameroun. f, Harp, Congo.

2006, Feb. 3 Litho. *Perf. 13¼*

897 A340 Sheet of 6 10.00 10.00
a.-f. 37c Any single 1.50 1.50

See Offices in Geneva No. 452; Vienna No. 375.

UN Symbols Type of 2003

2006, Mar. 6 Litho. *Perf. 13¼*

898 A349 39c multicolored + label 3.50 3.50
899 A350 39c multicolored + label 3.50 3.50
900 A351 39c multicolored + label 3.50 3.50
901 A352 39c multicolored + label 3.50 3.50
902 A353 39c multicolored + label 3.50 3.50
a. Vert. strip of 5, #898-902, + 5 labels 17.50 17.50

The full sheet sold for $14.95 with or without personalized labels. The personalization of labels was available only at UN Headquarters, and not through mail order.

Sculpture Type of 2005

2006, Mar. 6 Litho. *Perf. 13¼*

903 A362 84c multicolored + label 7.00 7.00
a. Perf. 14½x14 + label 15.00 15.00
904 A363 84c multicolored + label 7.00 7.00
a. Perf. 14½x14 + label 15.00 15.00
905 A364 84c multicolored + label 7.00 7.00
a. Perf. 14½x14 + label 15.00 15.00
906 A365 84c multicolored + label 7.00 7.00
a. Perf. 14½x14 + label 15.00 15.00
907 A366 84c multicolored + label 7.00 7.00
a. Perf. 14½x14 + label 15.00 15.00
b. Vert. strip of 5, #903-907, + 5 labels *35.00 35.00*
c. Vert. strip of 5, #903a-907a, + 5 labels *75.00 75.00*

The full sheet sold for $14.95 with or without personalized labels. The personalization of labels was available only at UN Headquarters, and not through mail order.

Nos. 903a-907a issued 9/21/06. Nos. 903a-907a were from sheet for 2006 Berlin Stamp Show. The year "2006" is slightly smaller on Nos. 903a-907a than on Nos. 903-907.

Full sheets with different margins were sold at the Washington 2006 World Philatelic Exhibition, where the labels could be personalized. These are worth slightly more than the generic No. 907b sheet.

Endangered Species Type of 1993

No. 908, Golden mantella. No. 909, Panther chameleon. No. 910, Peruvian rainbow boa. No. 911, Dyeing poison frog.

Perf. 12¾x12½

2006, Mar. 16 Litho.

908 A271 39c multicolored .90 .90
909 A271 39c multicolored .90 .90
910 A271 39c multicolored .90 .90
911 A271 39c multicolored .90 .90
a. Block of 4, #908-911 3.60 3.60

See Offices in Geneva Nos. 453-456; Vienna Nos. 376-379.

Dove Between War and Peace — A372

2006, Apr. 10 Litho. *Perf. 13¼*

912 A372 75c multicolored + label 5.00 5.00

The full sheet sold for $14.95 with or without personalized labels. The personalization of labels was available only at UN Headquarters, and not through mail order.

Intl. Day of Families A373

39c, Family harvesting grapes. 84c, Children playing with toy sailboats.

2006, May 27 Litho. *Perf. 14x13½*

913 A373 39c multicolored .70 .70
914 A373 84c multicolored 1.50 1.50

See Offices in Geneva Nos. 457-458; Vienna Nos. 380-381.

World Heritage Sites, France — A374

Eiffel Tower and: Nos. 915, 917a, Banks of the Seine. Nos. 916, 917d, Roman Aqueduct. No. 917b, Provins. No. 917c, Carcasonne. No. 917e, Mont Saint-Michel. No. 917f, Chateau de Chambord.

Litho. & Embossed with Foil Application

2006, June 17 *Perf. 13½x13¼*

915 A374 39c multicolored .75 .75
916 A374 84c multicolored 1.75 1.75

Souvenir Booklet

917 Booklet, #917g-917l 16.00
a.-c. A374 24c any single .50 .50
d.-f. A374 39c any single .80 .80
g. Booklet pane of 4 #917a 2.00 2.00
h. Booklet pane of 4 #917b 2.00 2.00
i. Booklet pane of 4 #917c 2.00 2.00
j. Booklet pane of 4 #917d 3.25 3.25
k. Booklet pane of 4 #917e 3.25 3.25
l. Booklet pane of 4 #917f 3.25 3.25

See Offices in Geneva Nos. 459-461, Vienna Nos. 382-384.

My Dream for Peace Type of 2004

Winning designs of Lions Club International children's global peace poster contest by: 39c, Cheuk Tat Li, Hong Kong. 84c, Kosshapan Paitoon, Thailand.

2006, Sept. 21 Litho. *Perf. 13½x13*

918 A357 39c multicolored .80 .80
919 A357 84c multicolored 1.75 1.75

See Offices in Geneva Nos. 462-463; Vienna Nos. 385-386.

Flags and Coins — A375

No. 920 — Flag of: a, People's Republic of China, 1 yuan coin. b, Australia, 1 dollar coin. c, Ghana, 50 cedi coin. d, Israel, 10 agorot coin. e, Russia, 1 ruble coin. f, Mexico, 10 peso coin. g, Japan, 10 yen coin. h, Cambodia, 200 riel coin.

2006, Oct. 5 Litho. *Perf. 13¼x13*

920 Sheet of 8 10.00 10.00
a.-h. A375 39c Any single 1.25 1.25

A column of rouletting in the middle of the sheet separates it into two parts. See Nos. 930, 953, 998, 1022, 1039, 1078; Offices in Geneva Nos. 464, 469, 484, 512, 532, 546, 576; Vienna Nos. 387, 392, 421, 459, 483, 507, 539.

Flag Type of 1980

2007, Feb. 2 Litho. *Perf. 14*

921 A185 39c Tuvalu 1.00 1.00
922 A185 39c Switzerland 1.00 1.00
923 A185 39c Timor-Leste 1.00 1.00

924 A185 39c Montenegro 1.00 1.00
a. Block of 4, #921-924 12.00 12.00
Nos. 921-924 (4) 4.00 4.00

Endangered Species Type of 1993

No. 925, Drill. No. 926, Common squirrel monkey. No. 927, Ring-tailed lemur. No. 928, Collared mangabey.

Perf. 12¾x12½

2007, Mar. 15 Litho.
925 A271 39c multicolored .85 .85
926 A271 39c multicolored .85 .85
927 A271 39c multicolored .85 *.85*
928 A271 39c multicolored .85 .85
a. Block of 4, #925-928 3.50 3.50

See Offices in Geneva Nos. 465-468; Vienna Nos. 388-391.

UN Emblem — A376

2007, Feb. 5 Litho. ***Perf. 14½x14***
929 A376 84c dark blue + label *17.50 17.50*

The full sheet sold for $14.95. The sheet has two each of five different labels that could not be personalized. The sheet was distributed to members of the Japanese mission on Sept. 21, 2006, but it was not sold to the public until 2007. The sheet's availability to the public was not announced through press releases or on the UNPA website prior to the day of issue or afterward. It was sent to standing order customers in May 2007.
Compare with Type A377.

Flags and Coins Type of 2006

No. 930 — Flag of: a, Brazil, 50 centavo coin. b, Thailand, 1 baht coin. c, Viet Nam, 5,000 dong coin. d, Ecuador, 10 centavo coin. e, India, 5 rupee coin. f, South Africa, 5 cent coin. g, Barbados, 25 cent coin. h, Republic of Korea, 500 won coin.

2007, May 3 Litho. ***Perf. 13¼x13***
930 Sheet of 8 8.00 8.00
a.-h. A375 39c Any single 1.00 1.00

A column of rouletting in the middle of the sheet separates it into two parts. See Offices in Geneva No. 469; Vienna No. 392.

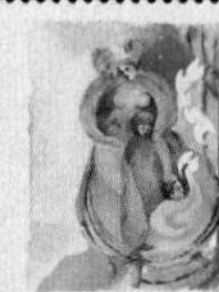

UN Emblem — A377

2007, June 1 Litho. ***Perf. 13¼***
931 A377 84c blue + label *5.50 5.50*

The full sheet sold for $14.95. The sheet has two each of five different labels that could not be personalized.
Compare with Type A376.

Peaceful Visions — A378

39c, "Nest." 84c, "Sisters Weave the Olive Branch."

2007, June 1 Litho. ***Perf. 13x12½***
932 A378 39c multicolored .90 .90
933 A378 84c multicolored 1.80 1.80

See Offices in Geneva Nos. 470-471; Vienna Nos. 398-399.

UN Symbols Type of 2003

2007, May 14 Litho. ***Perf. 13¼***
934 A349 41c multicolored + label 2.50 2.50
935 A350 41c multicolored + label 2.50 2.50
936 A351 41c multicolored + label 2.50 2.50
937 A352 41c multicolored + label 2.50 2.50
938 A353 41c multicolored + label 2.50 2.50
a. Vert. strip of 5, #934-938, + 5 labels 15.00 15.00

The full sheet sold for $14.95 with or without personalized labels. The personalization of labels was available only at UN Headquarters, and not through mail order.

UN Flag — A379

2007, May 14 Litho. ***Perf. 13¼***
939 A379 90c blue + label *9.00 9.00*

The full sheet sold for $14.95. The sheet has two each of five different labels that could not be personalized.
A second printing of No. 939 has the "U" and "N" more closely spaced, and it has different labels and different pane borders. Value about the same.

Helmet of UN Peacekeeper A380

2007, Aug. 9 Litho. ***Perf. 12½x13¼***
940 A380 90c multicolored 1.90 1.90

World Heritage Sites, South America — A381

No. 941, Galapagos Islands, Ecuador. Nos. 942, 943a, Rapa Nui, Chile. No. 943b, Cueva de las Manos, Argentina. No. 943c, Machu Picchu, Peru. No. 943d, Tiwanaku, Bolivia. No. 943e, Iguaçu National Park, Brazil.

2007, Aug. 9 Litho. ***Perf. 13¼x13***
941 A381 41c multicolored .85 .85
a. Booklet pane of 4 3.40 —
942 A381 90c multicolored 1.90 1.90

Souvenir Booklet

943 Booklet, #941a, 943f-943j 17.00
a.-c. A381 26c Any single .60 .60
d.-e. A381 41c Either single 1.00 1.00
f. Booklet pane of 4 #943a 2.40 2.40
g. Booklet pane of 4 #943b 2.40 2.40
h. Booklet pane of 4 #943c 2.40 2.40
i. Booklet pane of 4 #943d 4.00 4.00
j. Booklet pane of 4 #943e 4.00 4.00

See Offices in Geneva Nos. 472-474, Vienna Nos. 400-402. No. 943 sold for $8.50.

Humanitarian Mail — A382

2007, Sept. 6 Litho. ***Perf. 12½x13¼***
944 A382 90c multicolored 1.90 1.90

See Offices in Geneva No. 475, Vienna No. 403, Switzerland No. 9O21.

Space for Humanity A383

41c, Space Shuttle. 90c, Astronauts spacewalking.
$1, International Space Station.

2007, Oct. 25 Litho. ***Perf. 13½x14***
945 A383 41c multicolored .85 .85
946 A383 90c multicolored 1.90 1.90

Souvenir Sheet

947 A383 $1 multicolored 2.50 2.50
a. With World Space Week emblem in margin 3.00 3.00

See Offices in Geneva Nos. 476-478, Vienna Nos. 409-411.

Intl. Holocaust Remembrance Day — A384

2008, Jan. 27 Litho. ***Perf. 13***
948 A384 41c multicolored .85 .85

See Offices in Geneva No. 479, Vienna No. 412, Israel No. 1715.

Endangered Species Type of 1993

No. 949, South African fur seal. No. 950, Orange cup coral. No. 951, Longsnout seahorse. No. 952, Gray whale.

2008, Mar. 6 Litho. ***Perf. 12¾x12½***
949 A271 41c multicolored 1.00 1.00
950 A271 41c multicolored 1.00 1.00
941 A271 41c multicolored 1.00 1.00
952 A271 41c multicolored 1.00 1.00
a. Block of 4, #949-952 4.00 4.00

See Offices in Geneva Nos. 480-483; Vienna Nos. 417-420.

Flags and Coins Type of 2006

No. 953 — Flag of: a, United Kingdom, 2 pound coin. b, Singapore, 5 dollar coin. c, Colombia, 500 peso coin. d, Sri Lanka, 10 rupee coin. e, Philippines, 1 peso coin. f, Indonesia, 500 rupiah coin. g, United Arab Emirates, 1 dirham coin. h, Libya, 50 dinar coin.

2008, May 8 Litho. ***Perf. 13¼x13***
953 Sheet of 8 7.00 7.00
a.-h. A375 41c Any single .85 .85

A column of rouletting in the middle of the sheet separates it into two parts. See Offices in Geneva No. 484; Vienna No. 421.

Sculpture and Flags — A385

UN Flag — A386

UN General Assembly — A387

Flags — A388

UN Headquarters — A389

2008, May 12 Litho. ***Perf. 13¼***
954 A385 42c multicolored + label *2.00 2.00*
955 A386 42c multicolored + label *2.00 2.00*
956 A387 42c multicolored + label *2.00 2.00*
957 A388 42c multicolored + label *2.00 2.00*
958 A389 42c multicolored + label *2.00 2.00*
a. Vert. strip of 5, #954-958, + 5 labels *12.00 12.00*

The full sheet sold for $14.95 with or without personalized labels. The personalization of labels was available only at UN Headquarters, and not through mail order.

UN Emblem — A390

2008, May 12 Litho. ***Perf. 13¼***
959 A390 94c blue + label *3.50 3.50*

The full sheet sold for $14.95 with or without labels that could be personalized. There are five non-personalized labels. The personalization of labels was available only at UN Headquarters, and not through mail order.

Wheelchair Accessibility Symbol — A391

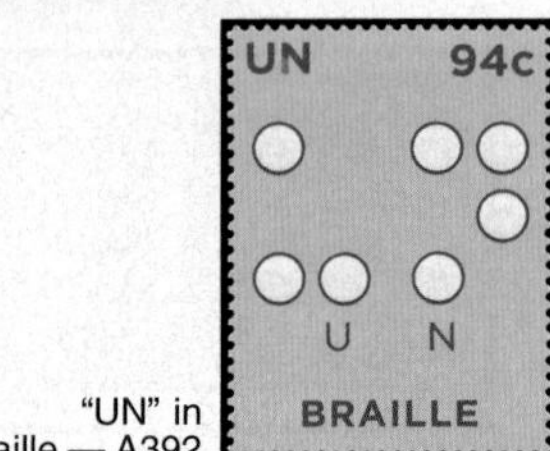

"UN" in Braille — A392

Litho. & Embossed

2008, June 6 *Perf. 14x13¼*

960 A391 42c blue & yellow .85 .85
961 A392 94c yellow & blue 1.90 1.90

Convention on the Rights of Persons with Disabilities. See Offices in Geneva Nos. 485-486, Vienna Nos. 427-428.

Sport for Peace — A393

42c, $1.25, Sprinter. 94c, Hurdler.

2008, Aug. 8 Litho. *Perf. 14½*

962 A393 42c multicolored .85 .85
963 A393 94c multicolored 1.90 1.90

Souvenir Sheet

Perf. 12¾x13¼

964 A393 $1.25 multicolored 6.00 6.00

2008 Summer Olympics, Beijing. See Offices in Geneva Nos. 487-489, Vienna Nos. 429-431.

Sport for Peace — A394

2008, Aug. 8 Litho. *Perf. 13¼*

965 A394 94c multicolored + label *3.75 3.75*

2008 Summer Olympics, Beijing. The full pane sold for $14.95 with or without personalized labels. There are two non-personalized labels. The personalization of labels was available only at UN Headquarters, and not through mail order.

"We Can End Poverty" — A395

Winning designs in children's art contest by: 42c, Grace Tsang, Hong Kong. 94c, Bryan Jevoncia, Indonesia, vert.

Perf. 12¾x12½

2008, Sept. 18 Litho.

966 A395 42c multicolored .85 .85

Perf. 12½x12¾

967 A395 94c multicolored 1.90 1.90

See Offices in Geneva Nos. 490-491, Vienna Nos. 432-433.

Climate Change Types of Geneva and Vienna and

A396

Climate Change — A397

No. 968 — Parched ground and snail shell with quarter of Earth in: a, LR. b, LL. c, UR. d, UL.

No. 969 — Coral reef with quarter of Earth in: a, LR. b, LL. c, UR. d, UL.

No. 970: a, Like #969a. b, Like #969b. c, Like #969c. d, Like #969d. e, Like Geneva #493a. f, Like Geneva #493b. g, Like Geneva #493c. h, Like Geneva #493d. i, Like Vienna #434a. j, Like Vienna #434b. k, Like Vienna #434c. l, Like Vienna #434d. m, Like Geneva #492a. n, Like Geneva #492b. o, Like Geneva #492c. p, Like Geneva #492d. q, Like Vienna #435a. r, Like Vienna #435b. s, Like Vienna #435c. t, Like Vienna #435d.

All stamps have blue panels inscribed "Climate Change."

2008, Oct. 23 Litho. *Perf. 13¼x13*

968 Sheet of 4 4.75 4.75
a.-d. A396 42c Any single 1.10 1.10
e. Booklet pane of 4, #968a-968d 6.00 6.00
969 Sheet of 4 10.00 10.00
a.-d. A397 94c Any single 2.50 2.50

Souvenir Booklet

970 Booklet, #968e, 970u-970y 20.00
a.-d. A397 27c Any single .75 .75
e.-h. G77 27c Any single .75 .75
i.-l. V72 27c Any single .75 .75
m.-p. G76 42c Any single 1.00 1.00
q.-t. V73 42c Any single 1.00 1.00
u. Booklet pane of 4, #970a-970d 3.00 3.00
v. Booklet pane of 4, #970e-970h 3.00 3.00
w. Booklet pane of 4, #970i-970l 3.00 3.00
x. Booklet pane of 4, #970m-970p 4.00 4.00
y. Booklet pane of 4, #970q-970t 4.00 4.00

No. 970 sold for $9. See Offices in Geneva Nos. 492-494, Vienna Nos. 434-436.

A398

Designs: 1c, Cielo rosado. 9c, Rosa de sangre. 10c, Espíritu de mujer.

2009, Feb. 6 Litho. *Perf. 13¼*

971 A398 1c multicolored .25 .25
972 A398 9c multicolored .25 .25
973 A398 10c multicolored .25 .25
Nos. 971-973 (3) .75 .75

A399

Litho. With Foil Application

2009, Feb. 6 *Perf. 14x13½*

974 A399 94c purple & multicolored 2.00 2.00

See Offices in Geneva No. 495, Vienna No. 437.

Endangered Species Type of 1993

No. 975, Emperor dragonfly. No. 976, Southern wood ant. No. 977, Rosalia longicorn. No. 978, Apollo butterfly.

2009, Apr. 16 Litho. *Perf. 12¾x12½*

975 A271 42c multicolored 1.00 1.00
976 A271 42c multicolored 1.00 1.00
977 A271 42c multicolored 1.00 1.00
978 A271 42c multicolored 1.00 1.00
a. Block of 4, #975-978 4.00 4.00
b. Pane of 16, imperf. —

See Offices in Geneva Nos. 496-499; Vienna Nos. 438-441.

A400

Nos. 979, 981a, Town Hall and Roland on the Marketplace, Bremen. Nos. 980, 981d, Aachen Cathedral. No. 981b, Wartburg Castle. No. 981c, Palaces and Parks of Potsdam and Berlin. No. 981e, Luther Memorials in Eisleben and Wittenberg. No. 981f, Monastic Island of Reichenau.

2009, May 7 Litho. *Perf. 14x13½*

979 A400 44c multicolored .90 .90
980 A400 98c multicolored 2.00 2.00

Souvenir Booklet

981 Booklet, #981g-981l 17.50
a.-c. A400 27c any single .55 .55
d.-f. A400 42c any single .85 .85
g. Booklet pane of 4 #981a 2.25 2.25
h. Booklet pane of 4 #981b 2.25 2.25
i. Booklet pane of 4 #981c 2.25 2.25
j. Booklet pane of 4 #981d 3.50 3.50
k. Booklet pane of 4 #981e 3.50 3.50
l. Booklet pane of 4 #981f 3.50 3.50

See Offices in Geneva Nos. 500-502, Vienna Nos. 442-444.

UN Flag — A401

Let Us Beat Swords Into Plowshares, Sculpture by Evgeny Vuchetich — A402

Single Form, Sculpture by Barbara Hepworth — A403

Window Cleaner — A404

UN Headquarters — A405

2009, June 5 *Perf. 13¼*

982 A401 44c multicolored + label 2.00 2.00
a. Perf. 11¼x11 + label 8.00 8.00
b. Perf. 14¼x14½ + label 1.80 1.80
983 A402 44c multicolored + label 2.00 2.00
a. Perf. 11¼x11 + label 8.00 8.00
b. Perf. 14¼x14½ + label 1.80 1.80
984 A403 44c multicolored + label 2.00 2.00
a. Perf. 11¼x11 + label 8.00 8.00
b. Perf. 14¼x14½ + label 1.80 1.80
985 A404 44c multicolored + label 2.00 2.00
a. Perf. 11¼x11 + label 8.00 8.00
b. Perf. 14¼x14½ + label 1.80 1.80
986 A405 44c multicolored + label 2.00 2.00
a. Perf. 11¼x11 + label 8.00 8.00
b. Perf. 14¼x14½ + label 1.80 1.80
c. Vert. strip of 5, #982-986, + 5 labels 10.00 10.00
d. Vert. strip of 5, #982a-986a, + 5 labels 40.00 40.00
e. Vert. strip of 5, #982b-986b, + 5 labels 9.00 7.50

The full sheets sold for $14.95 with or without personalized labels. The personalization of labels was available only at UN Headquarters, and not through mail order. The sheet of No. 986d has "ver. 2" in the lower right selvage. The sheet of No. 986e has "Ver. 3" in the lower right selvage.

Flags and UN Headquarters — A406

Single Form, Sculpture by Barbara Hepworth — A407

UN Flag — A408

Sphere Within a Sphere, Sculpture by Arnaldo Pomodoro — A409

UN Headquarters and Chrysler Building — A410

2009, June 5

987 A406 98c multicolored + label 3.50 3.50
a. Perf. 11¼x11 + label 8.00 8.00
b. Perf. 14¼x14½ + label 3.50 3.50
988 A407 98c multicolored + label 3.50 3.50
a. Perf. 11¼x11 + label 8.00 8.00
b. Perf. 14¼x14½ + label 3.50 3.50
989 A408 98c multicolored + label 3.50 3.50
a. Perf. 11¼x11 + label 8.00 8.00
b. Perf. 14¼x14½ + label 3.50 3.50
990 A409 98c multicolored + label 3.50 3.50
a. Perf. 11¼x11 + label 8.00 8.00
b. Perf. 14¼x14½ + label 3.50 3.50

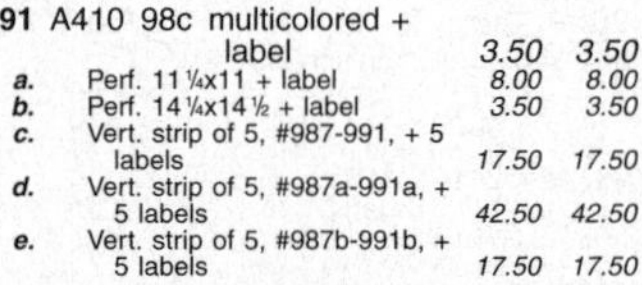

991 A410 98c multicolored + label 3.50 3.50
- *a.* Perf. 11¼x11 + label 8.00 8.00
- *b.* Perf. 14¼x14½ + label 3.50 3.50
- *c.* Vert. strip of 5, #987-991, + 5 labels 17.50 17.50
- *d.* Vert. strip of 5, #987a-991a, + 5 labels 42.50 42.50
- *e.* Vert. strip of 5, #987b-991b, + 5 labels 17.50 17.50

The full sheets sold for $14.95 with or without personalized labels. The personalization of labels was available only at UN Headquarters, and not through mail order. The sheet of No. 991d has "ver. 2" in the lower right selvage. The sheet of No. 991e has "VER. 3" in the lower right selvage.

Economic and Social Council — A411

Designs: 44c, Water and sanitation. 98c, Traditional medicines.

2009, Aug. 6 ***Perf. 12¾x12½***

992 A411 44c multicolored .90 .90
993 A411 98c multicolored 2.00 2.00

See Offices in Geneva Nos. 503-504, Vienna Nos. 450-451.

UN Emblem — A412

2009, Sept. 22 ***Perf. 13¼***

994 A412 98c multicolored + label 5.00 5.00
- *a.* Perf. 11¼x11 + label 5.00 5.00

The full sheets sold for $14.95 with or without personalized labels. There are five different non-personalized labels. The personalization of labels was available only at UN Headquarters, and not through mail order. The sheet of No. 994a has "ver. 2" in the lower right selvage.

Miniature Sheet

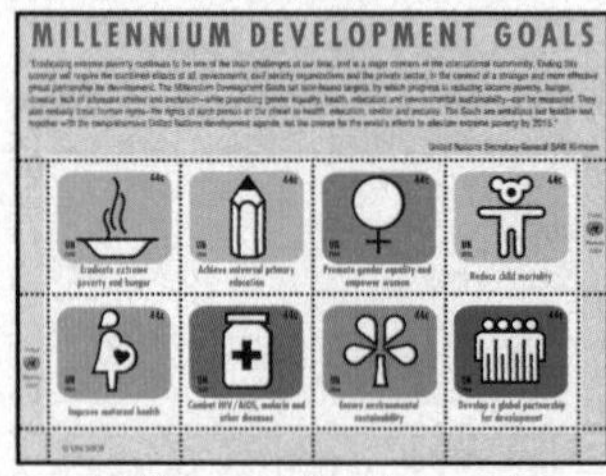

Millennium Development Goals — A413

No. 995: a, Bowl of hot food. b, Pencil. c, Female symbol. d, Teddy bear. e, Pregnant woman, heart. f, Medicine bottle. g, Stylized tree. h, Conjoined people.

2009, Sept. 25

995 A413 Sheet of 8 7.25 7.25
- *a.-h.* 44c Any single .90 .90

See Offies in Geneva No. 505; Vienna No. 457.

Mohandas K. Gandhi — A414

2009, Oct. 2

996 A414 $1 multicolored 2.00 2.00

Miniature Sheet

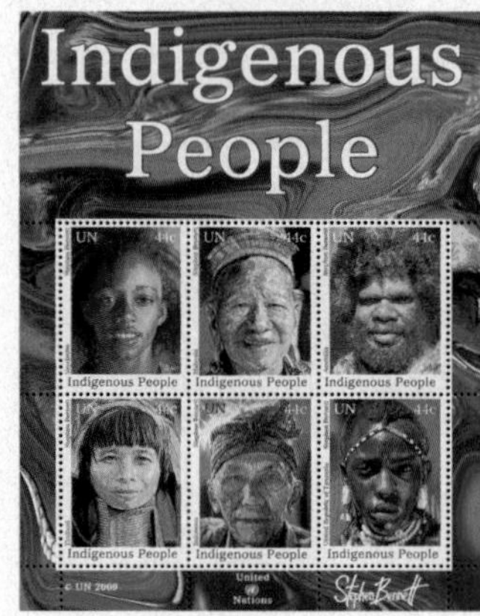

Indigenous People — A415

No. 997 — Portraits of person from: a, Seychelles. b, Malaysia. c, Australia. d, Thailand. e, Indonesia. f, Tanzania.

2009, Oct. 8 ***Perf. 12½***

997 A415 Sheet of 6 5.50 5.50
- *a.-f.* 44c Any single .90 .90

See Offices in Geneva No. 511, Vienna No. 458.

Flags and Coins Type of 2006

No. 998 — Flag of: a, Bahamas, 10 cent coin. b, Jamaica, 20 dollar coin. c, Honduras, 50 centavo coin. d, Kuwait, 100 fils coin. e, Panama, 1 cuarto de Balboa coin. f, Guatemala, 50 centavo coin. g, St. Lucia, 1 cent coin. h, Yemen, 20 rial coin.

2010, Feb. 5 Litho. ***Perf. 13¼x13***

998 Sheet of 8 8.00 8.00
- *a.-h.* A375 44c Any single 1.00 1.00
- First day cover 9.00

A column of rouletting in the middle of the sheet separates it into two parts. See Offices in Geneva No. 512; Vienna No. 459.

Endangered Species Type of 1993

No. 999, Monkey puzzle tree. No. 1000, Quiver tree. No. 1001, Bristlecone pine tree. No. 1002, Scarlet ball cactus.

2010, Apr. 15 Litho. ***Perf. 12¾x12½***

999 A271 44c multicolored 1.25 1.25
1000 A271 44c multicolored 1.25 1.25
1001 A271 44c multicolored 1.25 1.25
1002 A271 44c multicolored 1.25 1.25
- *a.* Block of 4, #999-1002 5.00 5.00

See Offices in Geneva Nos. 513-516; Vienna Nos. 465-468.

The stamp pictured above was printed in limited quantities and sold for far more than face value. The label attached to the stamp could not be personalized. Value for stamp and label, $3. A similar stamp dated "2011" with a different label attached exists.

One Planet, One Ocean Types of Geneva and Vienna and

A416

One Planet, One Ocean — A417

No. 1003: a, Turtle at top, eel at left, fish at LR. b, Fish at LL, turtle's flipper at bottom. c, Fish at left, yellow sponge at LR, Lobster at right. d, Lobster at left, turtle at right.

No. 1004: a, Octopus at left, fish at LR. b, Fish at left and right, turtle's head at bottom. c, Lobster at left. fish at LL and LR. d, Fish at LL and LR, turtle's body at UR.

No. 1005: a, Like #1003a. b, Like #1003b, c, Like #1003c, d, Like #1003d. e, Like Vienna #471a. f, Like Vienna #471b. g, Like Vienna #471c, h, Like Vienna #471d. i, Like Geneva #519a. j, Like Geneva #519b, k, Like Geneva #519c. l, Like Geneva #519d. m, Like #1004a. n, Like #1004b. o, Like #1004c, p, Like #1004d. q, Like Vienna #472a. r, Like Vienna #472b. s, Like Vienna #472c. t, Like Vienna #472d. u, Like Geneva #520a. v, Like Geneva #520b. w, Like Geneva #520c. x, Like Geneva #520d.

2010, May 6 Litho. ***Perf. 14x13¼***

1003 A416 Sheet of 4 3.60 3.60
- *a.-d.* 44c Any single .90 .90

1004 A417 Sheet of 4 8.00 8.00
- *a.-d.* 98c Any single 2.00 2.00

Souvenir Booklet

Perf. 13¼x13

1005 Booklet, #1005y-1005z, 1005aa-1005ad 18.00
- *a.-d.* A416 28c any single .60 .60
- *e.-h.* V91 28c any single .60 .60
- *i.-l.* G85 28c any single .60 .60
- *m.-p.* A417 44c any single .90 .90
- *q.-t.* V92 44c any single .90 .90
- *u.-x.* G86 44c any single .90 .90
- *y.* Booklet pane of 4 #1005a-1005d 2.40 2.40
- *z.* Booklet pane of 4 #1005e-1005h 2.40 2.40
- *aa.* Booklet pane of 4 #1005i-1005l 2.40 2.40
- *ab.* Booklet pane of 4 #1005m-1005p 3.60 3.60
- *ac.* Booklet pane of 4 #1005q-1005t 3.60 3.60
- *ad.* Booklet pane of 4 #1005u-1005x 3.60 3.60

Intl. Oceanographic Commission, 50th anniv. See Offices in Geneva Nos. 519-521, Vienna Nos. 471-473.

People of Different Cultures — A418

People of Different Cultures as New York Buildings A419

2010, June 4 Litho. ***Perf. 13***

1006 A418 3c multicolored .25 .25
1007 A419 4c multicolored .25 .25

UN Headquarters and New York Skyline — A420

Shanghai Skyline — A421

2010, June 4 Litho. ***Perf. 13¼***

1008 A420 98c multicolored 3.00 3.00
1009 A421 98c multicolored 3.00 3.00
- *a.* Horiz. pair, #1008-1009 6.00 6.00

Expo 2010, Shanghai. Nos. 1008 -1009 were sold only in full panes for $14.95.

United Nations, 65th Anniv. — A422

Litho. With Foil Application

2010, June 28 ***Perf. 13¼***

1010 A422 98c light blue & gold 2.00 2.00

Souvenir Sheet

1011 Sheet of 2 #1011a 4.00 4.00
- *a.* A422 98c dark blue & gold 2.00 2.00

See Offices in Geneva No. 522, Vienna No. 474.

A423

A424

A425

A426

United Nations Sea Transport — A427

2010, Sept. 2 Litho. *Perf. 13¼x13*

1012 A423 44c multicolored .90 .90
1013 A424 44c multicolored .90 .90
1014 A425 44c multicolored .90 .90
1015 A426 44c multicolored .90 .90
1016 A427 44c multicolored .90 .90
a. Horiz. strip of 5, #1012-1016 4.50 4.50

See Offices in Geneva Nos. 523-527, Vienna Nos. 475-479.

Intl. Year of Biodiversity A428

Drawings from Art Forms from Nature, by Ernst Heinrich: 15c, Hummingbird. $1.50, Liverwort.

2010, Oct. 18 Litho. *Perf. 13*

1017 A428 15c multicolored .30 .30
1018 A428 $1.50 multicolored 3.00 3.00

See Offices in Geneva Nos. 517-518; Vienna Nos. 469-470.

Miniature Sheet

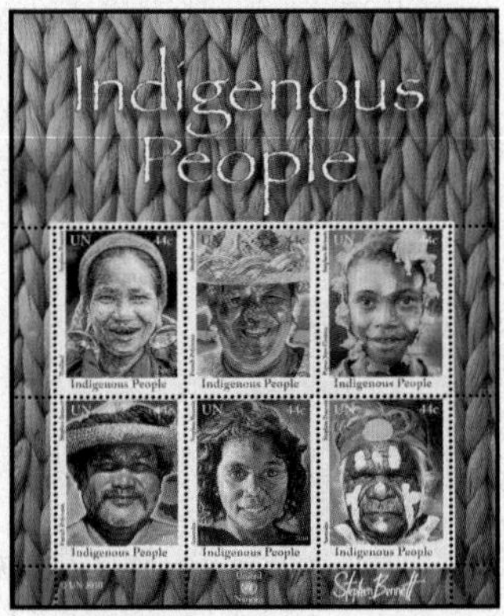

Indigenous People — A429

No. 1019 — Portraits of person from: a, Thailand. b, French Polynesia (woman, denomination in black). c, Papua New Guinea. d, French Polynesia (man, denomination in white). e, Australia (child). f, Australia (old man with headband).

2010, Oct. 21 Litho. *Perf. 13*

1019 A429 Sheet of 6 6.00 6.00
a.-f. 44c Any single 1.00 1.00

See Offices in Geneva No. 529; Vienna No. 480.

United Nations Headquarters, New York — A430

United Nations Headquarters: 11c, Aerial view. $5, Ground-level view.

2011, Feb. 4 Litho. *Perf. 13*

1020 A430 11c multicolored .25 .25
1021 A430 $5 multicolored 10.00 10.00

See Offices in Geneva Nos. 530-531; Vienna Nos. 481-482.

Flags and Coins Type of 2006

No. 1022 — Flag of: a, Mauritius, 1 rupee coin. b, Guyana, 10 dollar coin. c, Timor, 5 cent coin. d, Iceland, 100 krónur coin. e, Chile, 1 peso coin. f, Norway, 20 kroner coin. g, Fiji, 50 cent coin. h, Comoro Islands, 100 franc coin.

2011, Mar. 3 Litho. *Perf. 13¼x13*

1022 Sheet of 8 8.75 8.75
a.-h. A375 44c Any single 1.10 1.10

A column of rouletting in the middle of the sheet separates it into two parts. See Offices in Geneva No. 532; Vienna No. 483.

UN Emblem — A431

2011, Apr. 7 Litho. *Perf. 14¾*

1023 A431 98c blue + label *3.00 3.00*

Printed in sheets of 10 + 10 different labels which are not personalizable. The full sheet sold for $14.95

Human Space Flight, 50th Anniv. — A432

No. 1023: Various parts of outer space scene.

No. 1024: a, Cosmonaut and rocket. b, Astronaut on ladder of Lunar Module.

2011, Apr. 12 Litho. *Perf. 13x13¼*

1024 A432 Sheet of 16 14.50 14.50
a.-p. 44c any single .90 .90

Souvenir Sheet

1025 A432 Sheet of 2 3.00 3.00
a. 44c multi .90 .90
b. 98c multi 2.00 2.00

See Offices in Geneva Nos. 533-534; Vienna Nos. 484-485. No. 1024 contains two 40x48mm stamps that were printed as part of a larger sheet of six stamps, Vienna No. 485c, which was broken up into its component two-stamp souvenir sheets, and also sold as one unit.

UNESCO World Heritage Sites in Nordic Countries — A433

Designs: 44c, Surtsey Volcanic Island, Iceland. 98c, Drottningholm Castle, Sweden.

2011, May 5 Litho. *Perf. 14x13½*

1026 A433 44c multicolored .90 .90
1027 A433 98c multicolored 2.00 2.00

See Offices in Geneva Nos. 535-536; Vienna Nos. 496-497.

AIDS Ribbon — A434

2011, June 3 Litho. *Die Cut*

Self-Adhesive

1028 A434 44c red & blue 1.00 1.00

See Offices in Geneva No. 537; Vienna No. 498.

Economic and Social Council (ECOSOC) — A435

2011, July 1 Litho. *Perf. 14¼*

1029 A435 44c multicolored .90 .90
1030 A435 98c multicolored 2.00 2.00

See Offices in Geneva Nos. 538-539; Vienna Nos. 499-500.

Endangered Species Type of 1993

Designs: No. 1031, Bali starling. No. 1032, California condor. No. 1033, Japanese crane. No. 1034, Black-fronted piping-guan.

2011, Sept. 7 *Perf. 12¾x12½*

1031 A271 44c multicolored 1.00 1.00
1032 A271 44c multicolored 1.00 1.00
1033 A271 44c multicolored 1.00 1.00
1034 A271 44c multicolored 1.00 1.00
a. Block of 4, #1031-1034 4.00 4.00

See Offices in Geneva Nos. 540-543; Vienna Nos. 501-504.

Intl. Year of Forests — A436

Designs: 44c, Tree with wildlife, man with mask. 98c, Tree roots.

Litho. With Foil Application

2011, Oct. 13 *Perf. 12½*

1035 44c multicolored 1.00 1.00
1036 98c multicolored 2.00 2.00
a. A436 Vert. pair, #1035-1036 3.00 3.00

See Offices in Geneva Nos. 544-545; Vienna Nos. 505-506.

UN Emblem — A437

2012, Jan. 23 Litho. *Perf. 14¾*

1037 A437 $1.05 blue + label *3.00 3.00*
Sheet of 10 + 10 labels *30.00* —

The full sheet sold for $14.95. The generic label exists as shown, and with dragon in yellow against red background. Labels could be personalized. The personalization of labels was available only at UN Headquarters, and not through mail order.

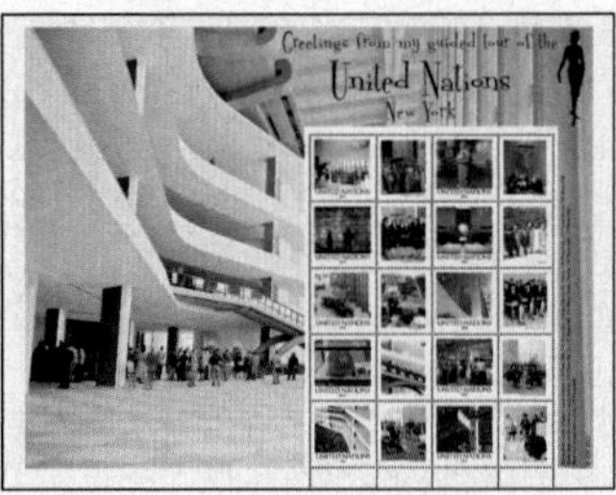

A438

No. 1038: a, Desk in lobby. b, Sculpture of Jesus holding lamb. c, Stained-glass window. d, Meeting room. e, Guided tour. f, Flags in front of United Nations buildings. g, United Nations Peacekeepers helmet in showcase. h, Gift shop. i, View of curved floors above lobby. j, Street signs.

2012, Jan. 23 Litho. *Perf. 14¾*

1038 A438 Sheet of 10 *30.00 30.00*
a.-j. $1.05 Any single + label *3.00 3.00*

The full sheet sold for $14.95. The generic labels are shown. Labels could be personalized. The personalization of labels was available only at UN Headquarters, and not through mail order.

Flags and Coins Type of 2006

No. 1039 — Flag of: a, Nepal, 1 rupee coin. b, Bahrain, 100 fils coin. c, Paraguay, 1000 guarani coin. d, Ethiopia, 25 cent coin. e, Peru, 1 sol coin. f, Solomon Islands, 20 cent coin. g, Dominican Republic, 1 peso coin. h, Canada, 1 dollar coin.

2012, Feb. 3 Litho. *Perf. 13¼x13*

1039 Sheet of 8 7.25 7.25
a.-h. A375 45c Any single .90 .90

A column of rouletting in the middle of the sheet separates it into two parts. See Offices in Geneva No. 546; Vienna No. 507.

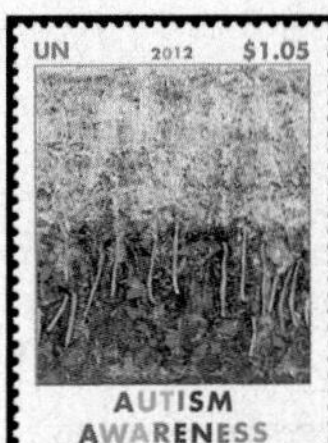

A439

Autism Awareness A440

Drawings by autistic people: No. 1040, An Abstract Garden II, by Trent Altman, U.S. No. 1041, Crazy Love, by Hannah Kandel, U.S.

2012, Apr. 2 Litho. *Perf. 14x13½*

1040 A439 $1.05 multicolored 2.10 2.10
1041 A440 $1.05 multicolored 2.10 2.10
a. Pair, #1040-1041 4.20 4.20

See Offices in Geneva Nos. 547-548; Vienna Nos. 508-509.

Endangered Species Type of 1993

Designs: No. 1042, Giant panda. No. 1043, Short-horned chameleon. No. 1044, Oncilla. No. 1045, Cotton-headed tamarin.

2012, Apr. 19 Litho. *Perf. 12¾x12½*

1042 A271 45c multicolored .90 .90
1043 A271 45c multicolored .90 .90
1044 A271 45c multicolored .90 .90
1045 A271 45c multicolored .90 .90
a. Block of 4, #1042-1045 3.60 3.60

See Offices in Geneva Nos. 549-552; Vienna Nos. 511-514.

Tinker Bell — A441

Tinker Bell — A442

2012, June 1 Litho. *Perf. 14¾*

1046 A441 $1.05 multicolored + label *3.00 3.00*
1047 A442 $1.05 multicolored + label *3.00 3.00*
a. Vert. pair, #1046-1047, + 2 labels *6.00 6.00*
Sheet of 10, 5 each #1046-1047, + 10 labels *30.00 30.00*

The full sheet sold for $14.95. The generic labels are shown. Labels could be personalized. The personalization of labels was available only at UN Headquarters, and not through mail order.

Rio + 20 Conference on Sustainable Development, Rio de Janeiro A443

2012, June 1 Litho. *Perf. 13x13¼*

1048 A443 $1.05 multicolored 2.10 2.10

See Offices in Geneva No. 553; Vienna No. 515.

Sport for Peace — A444

2012 Paralympics events: 45c, Goalball. $1.05, Sitting volleyball.

Litho. With Foil Application

2012, Aug. 17 *Perf. 14½*

1049 A444 45c multicolored .90 .90
1050 A444 $1.05 multicolored 2.10 2.10
a. Souvenir sheet of 1 2.10 2.10

See Offices in Geneva Nos. 554-555; Vienna Nos. 516-517.

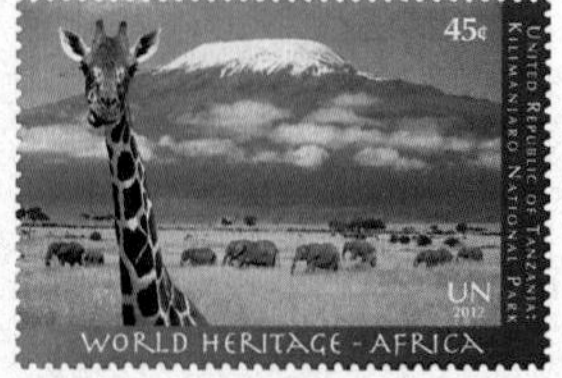

UNESCO World Heritage Sites in Africa — A445

Designs: 45c, Kilamanjaro National Park, Tanzania. $1.05, Old Towns of Djenné, Mali.

2012, Sept. 5 Litho. *Perf. 13¼*

1051 A445 45c multicolored .90 .90
1052 A445 $1.05 multicolored 2.10 2.10

See Offices in Geneva Nos. 556-557; Vienna Nos. 518-519.

Miniature Sheet

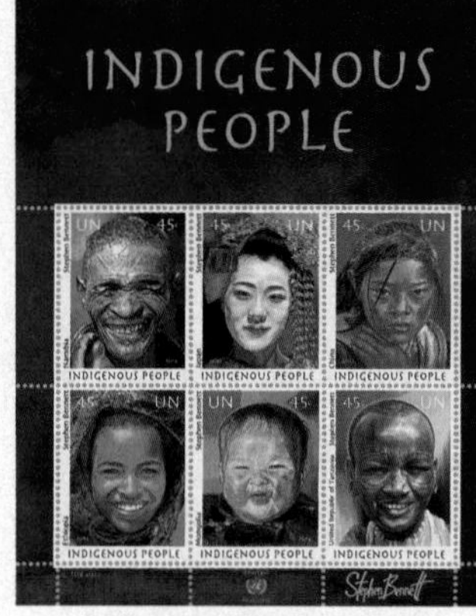

Indigenous People — A446

No. 1053 — Portrait of person from: a, Namibia. b, Japan. c, China. d, Ethiopia. e, Mongolia. f, Tanzania.

2012, Oct. 11 Litho. *Perf. 13¼x13*

1053 A446 Sheet of 6 5.50 5.50
a.-f. 45c Any single .90 .90

See Offices in Geneva No. 558; Vienna No. 520.

UN Emblem — A447

2013, Jan. 28 Litho. *Perf. 14¾*

1054 A447 $1.10 multicolored + label *3.00 3.00*
Sheet of 10 + 10 labels *30.00* —

The full sheet sold for $14.95. The generic label exists as shown, and with snake against red background. Labels could be personalized. The personalization of labels was available only at UN Headquarters, and not through mail order.

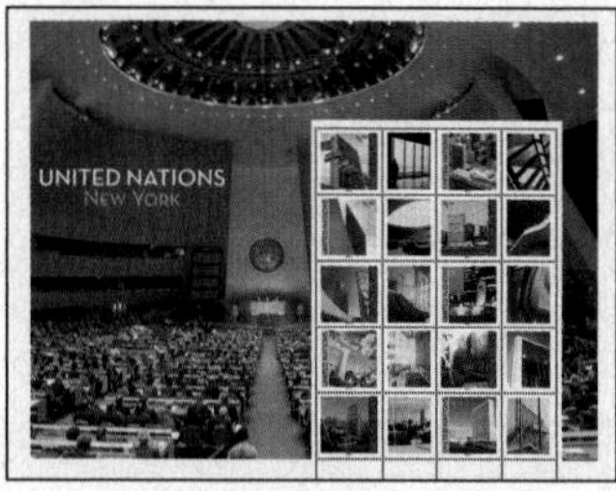

A448

No. 1055: a, Flags in front of Secretariat Building, brown panel at right. b, Aerial view of headquarters and East River, yellow orange panel at left. c, Secretariat Building and wall of General Assembly building, yellow orange panel at left. d, Headquarters and East River, brown panel at right. e, General Asembly and Secretariat Buildings, flags at right, brown panel at right. f, Sculpture and fountain at night, yellow orange panel at left. g, Secretariat Building and cherry blossoms, yellow orange panel at left. h, Secretariat Building, trees without leaves, flags at left, brown panel at right. i, Aerial view of headquarters at night, brown panel at right. j, Headquarters, yellow panel at left.

2013, Jan. 28 Litho. *Perf. 14¾*

1055 A448 Sheet of 10 *30.00 30.00*
a.-j. $1.10 Any single + label *3.00 3.00*

The full sheet sold for $14.95. The generic labels are shown. Labels could be personalized. The personalization of labels was available only at UN Headquarters, and not through mail order.

World Radio Day — A449

Designs: 46c, Radio antenna. $1.10, Audrey Hepburn at microphone.

2013, Feb. 13 Litho. *Perf. 13¼x13*

1056 A449 46c multicolored .95 .95
1057 A449 $1.10 multicolored 2.25 2.25

See Offices in Geneva Nos. 559-560; Vienna Nos. 521-522.

Circle of People A450

United Nations Headquarters A451

2013, Mar. 5 Litho. *Perf. 14x13½*

1058 A450 $1.10 multicolored 2.25 2.25

Perf. 13½x14

1059 A451 $3 multicolored 6.00 6.00

See Offices in Geneva Nos. 561-562; Vienna Nos. 523-524.

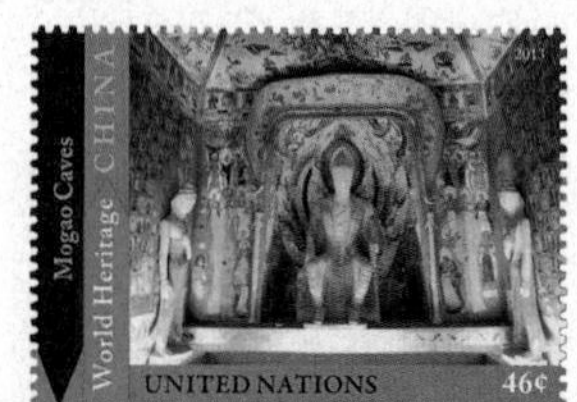

World Heritage Sites, China — A452

Designs: Nos. 1060, 1062a, Mogao Caves. Nos. 1061, 1062d, Imperial Palace, Beijing. No. 1062b, Potala Palace, Lhasa. No. 1062c, Great Wall of China. No. 1062e, Mount Huangshan. No. 1062f, Mausoleum of the First Qing Emperor.

2013, Apr. 11 Litho. *Perf. 14x13½*

1060 A452 46c multicolored .95 .95
1061 A452 $1.10 multicolored 2.25 2.25

Souvenir Booklet

1062 Booklet, #1062g-1062l 20.00
a.-c. A452 33c any single .70 .70
d.-f. A452 46c any single .95 .95
g. Booklet pane of 4 #1062a 2.80 —
h. Booklet pane of 4 #1062b 2.80 —
i. Booklet pane of 4 #1062c 2.80 —
j. Booklet pane of 4 #1062d 3.80 —
k. Booklet pane of 4 #1062e 3.80 —
l. Booklet pane of 4 #1062f 3.80 —

See Offices in Geneva Nos. 563-565, Vienna Nos. 525-527.

Flag Type of 1980

2013, May 2 Litho. *Perf. 13*

1063 A185 $1.10 Myanmar 2.25 2.25
1064 A185 $1.10 Russian Federation 2.25 2.25
1065 A185 $1.10 South Sudan 2.25 2.25
1066 A185 $1.10 Cape Verde 2.25 2.25
a. Block of 4, #1063-1066 9.00 9.00
Nos. 1063-1066 (4) 9.00 9.00

World Oceans Day — A453

No. 1067 — Fish from *One Fish, Two Fish, Red Fish, Blue Fish,* by Dr. Seuss: a, Green fish, red fish, sign. b, Red fish facing right. c, Green fish facing left, sign. d, Yellow fish, sign. e, Blue fish. f, Red fish facing left, sign. g, Red fish facing right, water droplets, tail of yellow and red fish, sign. h, Yellow and red fish, green fish, side of blue fish. i, Head of blue fish, sign post. j, Sign and wave. k, Sign, red fish, side and tail of blue fish, wave. l, Side of blue fish, green fish, wave.

2013, May 31 Litho. *Perf. 13*

1067 A453 Sheet of 12 11.50 11.50
a.-l. 46c any single .95 .95

See Offices in Geneva No. 566; Vienna No. 528.

Nebulae — A454

Designs: No. 1068, V838 Mon. No. 1069, WR 25, Tr16-244.
46c, 30 Doradus.

2013, Aug. 9 Litho. *Perf. 13¼*

1068 A454 $1.10 multicolored 2.25 2.25
1069 A454 $1.10 multicolored 2.25 2.25
a. Pair, #1068-1069 4.50 4.50

Souvenir Sheet

1070 A454 46c multicolored .95 .95

No. 1070 contains one 44x44mm stamp. See Offices in Geneva Nos. 567-569; Vienna Nos. 529-531.

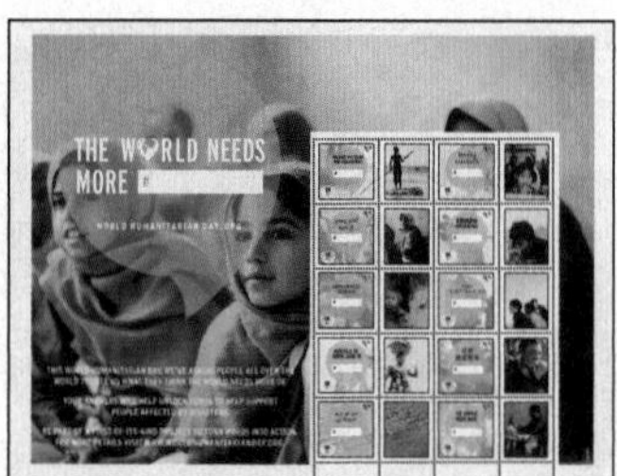

World Humanitarian Day — A455

No. 1071 — "The World Needs More" in speech balloon in: a, Somali (Uduunku. . .). b, Thai. c, Arabic (people in background). d, Portuguese (O Mundo. . .). e, Russian. f, Korean. g, Swahili (Mahitaji. . .). h, Chinese. i, Urdu (aerial view of village in background). j, English.

2013, Aug. 19 Litho. *Perf. 14¾*

1071 A455 Sheet of 10 *30.00 30.00*
a.-j. $1.10 Any single + label *3.00 3.00*

The full sheet sold for $14.95. The generic labels are shown. Labels could be personalized. The personalization of labels was available only at UN Headquarters, and not through mail order.

Works of Disabled Artists — A456

Designs: 46c, Self-portrait II by Chuck Close, U.S. $1.10, Tears and Laughter, by Josephine King, United Kingdom.

2013, Sept. 20 Litho. *Perf. 13¼x13*

1072	A456	46c multicolored	.95	.95
1073	A456	$1.10 multicolored	2.25	2.25

See Offices in Geneva Nos. 570-571; Vienna Nos. 532-533.

Endangered Species Type of 1993

Designs: No. 1074, Asian tapir. No. 1075, Mongoose lemur. No. 1076, Flat-headed cat. No. 1077, Aye-aye.

2013, Oct. 10 Litho. *Perf. 12¾x12½*

1074	A271	$1.10 multicolored	2.25	2.25
1075	A271	$1.10 multicolored	2.25	2.25
1076	A271	$1.10 multicolored	2.25	2.25
1077	A271	$1.10 multicolored	2.25	2.25
a.		Block of 4, #1074-1077	9.00	9.00

See Offices in Geneva Nos. 572-575; Vienna Nos. 534-537.

Flags and Coins Type of 2006

No. 1078 — Flag of: a, Montenegro, 20 cent coin. b, Grenada, 5 cent coin. c, United States, 25 cent coin. d, Gabon, 100 franc coin. e, Palau, 1 cent coin. f, Niger, 100 franc coin. g, Saint Kitts and Nevis, 5 cent coin. h, Venezuela, 1 bolivar coin.

2013, Nov. 6 Litho. *Perf. 13¼x13*

1078		Sheet of 8	7.75	7.75
a.-h.	A375	46c Any single	.95	.95

A column of rouletting in the middle of the sheet separates it into two parts. See Offices in Geneva No. 576; Vienna No. 539.

SEMI-POSTAL STAMPS

Souvenir Sheet

AIDS Awareness — SP1

2002, Oct. 24 Litho. *Perf. 14½*

B1	SP1	37c + 6c multicolored	3.50	3.50

See Offices in Geneva No. B1, Vienna No. B1.

AIR POST STAMPS

Plane and Gull — AP1

Swallows and UN Emblem AP2

1951, Dec. 14 Unwmk. *Perf. 14*

C1	AP1	6c henna brown	.25	.25
C2	AP1	10c bright blue green	.30	.30
C3	AP2	15c deep ultramarine	.40	.40
a.		15c Prussian blue	65.00	
C4	AP2	25c gray black	.85	.85
		Nos. C1-C4 (4)	1.80	1.80

Airplane Wing and Globe — AP3

1957, May 27 *Perf. 12½x14*

C5	AP3	4c maroon	.25	.25

Type of 1957 and

UN Flag and Plane AP4

Perf. 12½x13½

1959, Feb. 9 Unwmk.

C6	AP3	5c rose red	.25	.25
		Perf. 13½x14		
C7	AP4	7c ultramarine	.25	.25

Outer Space — AP5

UN Emblem — AP6

Bird of Laurel Leaves — AP7

Perf. 11½

1963, June 17 Photo. Unwmk.

C8	AP5	6c black, blue & yellow green	.25	.25
C9	AP6	8c yellow, olive green & red	.25	.25
		Perf. 12½x12		
C10	AP7	13c ultra, aquamarine, gray & carmine	.25	.25

"Flight Across Globe" — AP8

Jet Plane and Envelope AP9

Perf. 11½x12, 12x11½

1964, May 1 Photo. Unwmk.

C11	AP8	15c violet, buff, gray & pale green	.30	.30
a.		Gray omitted	—	
C12	AP9	25c yellow, orange, gray, blue & red	.50	.50
		Nos. C8-C12 (5)	1.55	1.55

See UN Offices in Geneva No. 8.

Jet Plane and UN Emblem AP10

1968, Apr. 18 Litho. *Perf. 13*

C13	AP10	20c multicolored	.35	.35

Wings, Envelopes and UN Emblem AP11

1969, Apr. 21 Litho. *Perf. 13*

C14	AP11	10c orange vermilion, orange, yellow & black	.25	.25

UN Emblem and Stylized Wing — AP12

Birds in Flight — AP13

Clouds AP14

"UN" and Plane — AP15

Litho. & Engr.

1972, May 1 *Perf. 13x13½*

C15	AP12	9c light blue, dark red & violet blue	.25	.25
		Photo.		
		Perf. 14x13½		
C16	AP13	11c blue & multicolored	.25	.25
		Perf. 13½x14		
C17	AP14	17c yellow, red & orange	.25	.25
		Perf. 13		
C18	AP15	21c silver & multi	.25	.25
		Nos. C15-C18 (4)	1.00	1.00

Globe and Jet — AP16

Pathways Radiating from UN Emblem AP17

Bird in Flight, UN Headquarters AP18

Perf. 13, 12½x13 (18c)

1974, Sept. 16 Litho.

C19	AP16	13c multicolored	.25	.25
C20	AP17	18c gray olive & multicolored	.25	.25
C21	AP18	26c blue & multi	.35	.35
		Nos. C19-C21 (3)	.85	.85

Winged Airmail Letter — AP19

Symbolic Globe and Plane — AP20

1977, June 27 Photo. *Perf. 14*

C22	AP19	25c greenish blue & multi	.35	.35
C23	AP20	31c magenta	.45	.45

OFFICES IN GENEVA, SWITZERLAND

For use only on mail posted at the Palais des Nations (UN European Office), Geneva. Inscribed in French unless otherwise stated.

100 Centimes = 1 Franc

Catalogue values for all unused stamps in this country are for Never Hinged items.

Types of United Nations Issues 1961-69 and

UN European Office, Geneva — G1

Designs: 5c, UN Headquarters, New York, and world map. 10c, UN flag. 20c, Three men united before globe. 50c, Opening words of UN Charter. 60c, UN emblem over globe. 70c, "un" and UN emblem. 75c, "Flight Across Globe." 80c, UN Headquarters and emblem. 90c, Abstract group of flags. 1fr, UN emblem. 2fr, Stylized globe and weather vane. 3fr, Statue by Henrik Starcke. 10fr, "Peace, Justice, Security."

The 20c, 80c and 90c are inscribed in French. The 75c and 10fr carry French inscription at top, English at bottom.

1969-70 Photo. Unwmk.
Perf. 13 (5c, 70c, 90c); 12½x12 (10c);

1 A88 5c purple & multi .25 .25
a. Green omitted —
2 A52 10c salmon & multi .25 .25

Perf. 11½ (20c-60c, 3fr)

3 A66 20c black & multi .25 .25
4 G1 30c dark blue & multi .25 .25
5 A77 50c ultra & multi .30 .30
6 A54 60c dark brown, salmon & gold .35 .35
7 A104 70c red, black & gold .40 .40

Perf. 11½x12 (75c)

8 AP8 75c carmine rose & multi .45 .45

Perf. 13½x14 (80c)

9 A78 80c blue green, red & yellow .45 .45
10 A45 90c blue & multi .50 .50

Litho. & Embossed
Perf. 14 (1fr)

11 A79 1fr light & dark green .50 .50

Photo.
Perf. 12x11½ (2fr)

12 A67 2fr blue & multi 1.00 1.00
13 A97 3fr olive & multi 1.25 1.25

Engr.
Perf. 12 (10fr)

14 A3 10fr dark blue 4.50 4.50
Nos. 1-14 (14) 10.70 10.70

Sea Bed Type of UN
Photo. & Engr.
1971, Jan. 25 ***Perf. 13***
15 A114 30c green & multi .25 .25

Refugee Type of UN
1971, Mar. 12 Litho. ***Perf. 13x12½***
16 A115 50c deep carmine, deep orange & black .25 .25

World Food Program Type of UN
1971, Apr. 13 Photo. ***Perf. 14***
17 A116 50c dark violet & multi .25 .25

UPU Headquarters Type of UN
1971, May 28 Photo. ***Perf. 11½***
18 A117 75c green & multi .35 .35

Eliminate Racial Discrimination Types of UN
1971, Sept. 21 Photo. ***Perf. 13½***
19 A118 30c blue & multi .25 .25
20 A119 50c yellow green & multi .25 .25

Picasso Type of UN
1971, Nov. 19 Photo. ***Perf. 11½***
21 A122 1.10fr multicolored .75 .75

Palais des Nations, Geneva G2

1972, Jan. 5 Photo. ***Perf. 11½***
22 G2 40c olive, blue, salmon & dark green .25 .25

Nuclear Weapons Type of UN
1972, Feb. 14 Photo. ***Perf. 13½x14***
23 A124 40c yellow, green, black, rose & gray .25 .25

World Health Day Type of UN
Litho. & Engr.
1972, Apr. 7 ***Perf. 13x13½***
24 A125 80c black & multi .45 .45

Human Environment Type of UN
Lithographed & Embossed
1972, June 5 ***Perf. 12½x14***
25 A126 40c olive, lemon, green & blue .25 .25
26 A126 80c ultra, pink, green & blue .45 .45

Economic Commission for Europe Type of UN
1972, Sept. 11 Litho. ***Perf. 13x13½***
27 A127 1.10fr red & multi 1.00 1.00

Art at UN (Sert) Type of UN
1972, Nov. 17 Photo. ***Perf. 12x12½***
28 A128 40c gold, red & brown .30 .30
29 A128 80c gold, brown & olive .60 .60

Disarmament Decade Type of UN
1973, Mar. 9 Litho. ***Perf. 13½x13***
30 A129 60c violet & multi .40 .40
31 A129 1.10fr olive & multi .85 .85

Drug Abuse Type of UN
1973, Apr. 13 Photo. ***Perf. 13½***
32 A130 60c blue & multi .45 .45

Volunteers Type of UN
1973, May 25 Photo. ***Perf. 14***
33 A131 80c gray green & multi .35 .35

Namibia Type of UN
1973, Oct. 1 Photo. ***Perf. 13½***
34 A132 60c red & multi .35 .35

Human Rights Type of UN
1973, Nov. 16 Photo. ***Perf. 13½***
35 A133 40c ultramarine & multi .30 .30
36 A133 80c olive & multi .50 .50

ILO Headquarters Type of UN
1974, Jan. 11 Photo. ***Perf. 14***
37 A134 60c violet & multi .45 .45
38 A134 80c brown & multi .65 .65

Centenary of UPU Type of UN
1974, Mar. 22 Litho. ***Perf. 12½***
39 A135 30c gold & multi .25 .25
40 A135 60c gold & multi .60 .60

Art at UN (Portinari) Type of UN
1974, May 6 Photo. ***Perf. 14***
41 A136 60c dark red & multi .40 .40
42 A136 1fr green & multi .70 .70

World Population Year Type of UN
1974, Oct. 18 Photo. ***Perf. 14***
43 A140 60c bright green & multi .50 .50
44 A140 80c brown & multi .70 .70

Law of the Sea Type of UN
1974, Nov. 22 Photo. ***Perf. 14***
45 A141 1.30fr blue & multicolored 1.00 1.00

Outer Space Type of UN
1975, Mar. 14 Litho. ***Perf. 13***
46 A142 60c multicolored .50 .50
47 A142 90c multicolored .75 .75

International Women's Year Type of UN
1975, May 9 Litho. ***Perf. 15***
48 A143 60c multicolored .40 .40
49 A143 90c multicolored .70 .70

30th Anniversary Type of UN
1975, June 26 Litho. ***Perf. 13***
50 A144 60c green & multi .40 .40
51 A144 90c violet & multi .70 .70

Souvenir Sheet
Imperf

52 Sheet of 2 1.00 1.00
a. A144 60c green & multicolored .30 .30
b. A144 90c violet & multicolored .60 .60

Namibia Type of UN
1975, Sept. 22 Photo. ***Perf. 13½***
53 A145 50c multicolored .30 .30
54 A145 1.30fr multicolored .85 .85

Peace-keeping Operations Type of UN
1975, Nov. 21 Engr. ***Perf. 12½***
55 A146 60c greenish blue .35 .35
56 A146 70c bright violet .65 .65

WFUNA Type of UN
1976, Mar. 12 Photo. ***Perf. 14***
57 A152 90c multicolored .90 .90

UNCTAD Type of UN
1976, Apr. 23 Photo. ***Perf. 11½***
58 A153 1.10fr sepia & multi .90 .90

Habitat Type of UN
1976, May 28 Photo. ***Perf. 14***
59 A154 40c dull blue & multi .25 .25
60 A154 1.50fr violet & multi .75 .75

UN Emblem, Post Horn and Rainbow G3

UN Postal Administration, 25th anniversary.

1976, Oct. 8 Photo. ***Perf. 11½***
61 G3 80c tan & multicolored .50 .50
62 A3 1.10fr light green & multi 1.60 1.60

World Food Council Type of UN
1976, Nov. 19 Litho. ***Perf. 14½***
63 A156 70c multicolored .50 .50

WIPO Type of UN
1977, Mar. 11 Photo. ***Perf. 14***
64 A157 80c red & multi .60 .60

Drop of Water and Globe — G4

UN Water Conference, Mar del Plata, Argentina, Mar. 14-25.

1977, Apr. 22 Photo. ***Perf. 13½x13***
65 G4 80c ultra & multi .50 .50
66 G4 1.10fr dark carmine & multi .80 .80

Hands Protecting UN Emblem — G5

UN Security Council.

1977, May 27 Photo. ***Perf. 11***
67 G5 80c blue & multi .50 .50
68 G5 1.10fr emerald & multi .80 .80

Colors of Five Races Spun into One Firm Rope — G6

Fight against racial discrimination.

1977, Sept. 19 Litho. ***Perf. 13½x13***
69 G6 40c multicolored .25 .25
70 G6 1.10fr multicolored .65 .65

Atomic Energy Turning Partly into Olive Branch — G7

Peaceful uses of atomic energy.

1977, Nov. 18 Photo. ***Perf. 14***
71 G7 80c dark carmine & multi .55 .55
72 G7 1.10fr Prussian blue & multi .75 .75

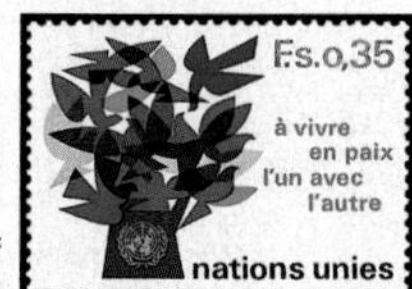

"Tree" of Doves — G8

1978, Jan. 27 Litho. ***Perf. 14½***
73 G8 35c multicolored .25 .25

Globes with Smallpox Distribution G9

Global eradication of smallpox.

1978, Mar. 31 Photo. ***Perf. 12x11½***
74 G9 80c yellow & multi .60 .60
75 G9 1.10fr light green & multi .90 .90

Namibia Type of UN
1978, May 5 Photo. ***Perf. 12***
76 A166 80c multicolored .85 .85

Jets and Flight Patterns — G10

International Civil Aviation Organization for "Safety in the Air."

1978, June 12 Photo. ***Perf. 14***
77 G10 70c multicolored .40 .40
78 G10 80c multicolored .70 .70

General Assembly, Flags and Globe — G11

1978, Sept. 15 Photo. ***Perf. 13½***
79 G11 70c multicolored .45 .45
80 G11 1.10fr multicolored .85 .85

Technical Cooperation Type of UN

1978, Nov. 17 Photo. *Perf. 14*

81 A169 80c multicolored .70 .70

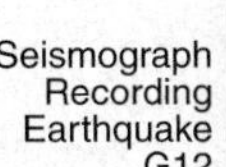

Seismograph Recording Earthquake G12

Office of the UN Disaster Relief Coordinator (UNDRO).

1979, Mar. 9 Photo. *Perf. 14*

82 G12 80c multicolored .50 .50
83 G12 1.50fr multicolored .80 .80

Children and Rainbow G13

International Year of the Child.

1979, May 4 Photo. *Perf. 14*

84 G13 80c multicolored .35 .35
85 G13 1.10fr multicolored .65 .65

Namibia Type of UN

1979, Oct. 5 Litho. *Perf. 13½*

86 A176 1.10fr multicolored .60 .60

International Court of Justice, Scales — G14

International Court of Justice, The Hague, Netherlands.

1979, Nov. 9 Litho. *Perf. 13x13½*

87 G14 80c multicolored .40 .40
88 G14 1.10fr multicolored .60 .60

New Economic Order Type of UN

1980, Jan. 11 Litho. *Perf. 15x14½*

89 A179 80c multicolored .85 .85

Women's Year Emblem G15

United Nations Decade for Women.

1980, Mar. 7 Litho. *Perf. 14½x15*

90 G15 40c multicolored .30 .30
91 G15 70c multicolored .70 .70

Peace-keeping Operations Type of UN

1980, May 16 Litho. *Perf. 14x13*

92 A181 1.10fr blue & green .85 .85

Dove and "35" — G16

35th Anniversary of the United Nations.

1980, June 26 Litho. *Perf. 13x13½*

93 G16 40c blue green & black .35 .30
94 A183 70c multicolored .65 .65

Souvenir Sheet

Imperf

95 Sheet of 2 1.10 1.10
a. G16 40c blue green & black .30 .30
b. A183 70c multicolored .80 .80

ECOSOC Type of UN and

Family Climbing Line Graph — G17

1980, Nov. 21 Litho. *Perf. 13½x13*

96 A186 40c multicolored .30 .30
97 G17 70c multicolored .60 .60

Palestinian Rights

1981, Jan. 30 Photo. *Perf. 12x11½*

98 A188 80c multicolored .55 .55

International Year of the Disabled.

1981, Mar. 6 Photo. *Perf. 14*

99 A190 40c black & blue .25 .25
100 V4 1.50fr black & red 1.00 1.00

Art Type of UN

1981, Apr. 15 Photo. *Perf. 11½*

Granite Paper

101 A191 80c multicolored .80 .80

Energy Type of 1981

1981, May 29 Litho. *Perf. 13*

102 A192 1.10fr multicolored .75 .75

Volunteers Program Type and

Volunteers Program Type and Symbols of Science, Agriculture and Industry G18

1981, Nov. 13 Litho.

103 A194 40c multicolored .45 .45
104 G18 70c multicolored .90 .90

Fight Against Apartheid — G19

Flower of Flags — G20

1982, Jan. 22 *Perf. 11½x12*

105 G19 30c multicolored .25 .25
106 G20 1fr multicolored .80 .80

Human Environment Type of UN and:

Human Environment — G21

10th Anniversary of United Nations Environment Program.

1982, Mar. 19 Litho. *Perf. 13½x13*

107 G21 40c multicolored .30 .30
108 A199 1.20fr multicolored 1.10 1.25

Outer Space Type of UN and

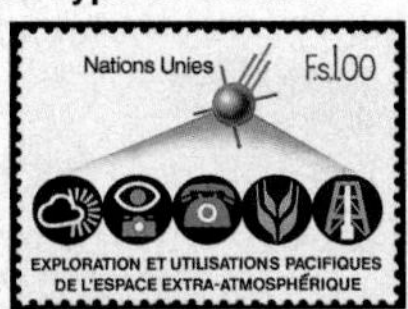

Satellite Applications of Space Technology G22

Exploration and Peaceful Uses of Outer Space.

1982, June 11 Litho. *Perf. 13x13½*

109 A201 80c multicolored .60 .60
110 G22 1fr multicolored .80 .80

Conservation & Protection of Nature

1982, Nov. 19 Photo. *Perf. 14*

111 A202 40c Bird .45 .45
112 A202 1.50fr Reptile 1.10 1.10

World Communications Year

1983, Jan. 28 Litho. *Perf. 13*

113 A204 1.20fr multicolored 1.25 1.25

Safety at Sea Type of UN and

Life Preserver and Radar — G23

1983, Mar. 18 Litho. *Perf. 14½*

114 A205 40c multicolored .40 .40
115 G23 80c multicolored .80 .80

World Food Program

1983, Apr. 22 Engr. *Perf. 13½*

116 A207 1.50fr blue 1.25 1.25

Trade Type of UN and

G24

1983, June 6 Litho. *Perf. 14*

117 A208 80c multicolored .50 .50
118 G24 1.10fr multicolored .90 .90

G25

35th Anniv. of the Universal Declaration of Human Rights — G26

Photo. & Engr.

1983, Dec. 9 *Perf. 13½*

119 G25 40c multicolored .45 .45
120 G26 1.20fr multicolored .95 .95

International Conference on Population Type

1984, Feb. 3 Litho. *Perf. 14*

121 A212 1.20fr multicolored .90 .90

Fishing G27

Women Farm Workers, Africa G28

World Food Day, Oct. 16

1984, Mar. 15 Litho. *Perf. 14½*

122 G27 50c multicolored .30 .30
123 G28 80c multicolored .60 .60

Valletta, Malta — G29

Los Glaciares Natl. Park, Argentina G30

World Heritage

1984, Apr. 18 Litho. *Perf. 14*

124 G29 50c multicolored .60 .60
125 G30 70c multicolored .85 .85

G31

G32

Future for Refugees

1984, May 29 Photo. *Perf. 11½*

126 G31 35c multicolored .30 .30
127 G32 1.50fr multicolored 1.10 1.10

International Youth Year — G33

1984, Nov. 15 Litho. *Perf. 13½*

128 G33 1.20fr multicolored 1.25 1.25

ILO Type of UN and

Turin Center — G34

1985, Feb. 1 Engr. *Perf. 13½*

129 A220 80c dull red .70 .70
130 G34 1.20fr U Thant Pavilion 1.10 1.10

UN University Type

1985, Mar. 15 Photo. *Perf. 13½*

131 A221 50c Pastoral scene, advanced communications .60 .60
132 A221 80c like No. 131 1.00 1.00

Postman G35

Doves — G36

1985, May 10 Litho. *Perf. 14*

133 G35 20c multicolored .25 .25
134 G36 1.20fr multicolored 1.25 1.25

40th Anniversary Type

Perf. 12 x 11½

1985, June 26 **Photo.**

135 A224 50c multicolored .60 .60
136 A225 70c multicolored .90 .90

Souvenir Sheet

Imperf

137 Sheet of 2 2.25 2.25
a. A224 50c multicolored .85 .85
b. A225 70c multicolored 1.10 1.10

UNICEF Child Survival Campaign Type

Photo. & Engr.

1985, Nov. 22 ***Perf. 13½***

138 A226 50c Three girls .40 .40
139 A226 1.20fr Infant drinking 1.10 1.10

Africa in Crisis Type

1986, Jan. 31 Photo. ***Perf. 11½x12***

140 A227 1.40fr Mother, hungry children 1.25 1.25

UN Development Program Type

Forestry.

1986, Mar. 14 Photo. ***Perf. 13½***

141 A228 35c Erosion control 1.75 1.75
142 A228 35c Logging 1.75 1.75
143 A228 35c Lumber transport 1.75 1.75
144 A228 35c Nursery 1.75 1.75
a. Block of 4, #141-144 7.50 7.50

Doves and Sun — G37

1986, Mar. 14 Litho. ***Perf. 15x14½***

145 G37 5c multicolored .25 .25

Stamp Collecting Type

Designs: 50c, UN Human Rights stamp. 80c, UN stamps.

1986, May 22 Engr. ***Perf. 12½***

146 A229 50c dark green & henna brown .60 .60
147 A229 80c dark green & yellow orange .90 .90

Flags and Globe as Dove — G38

Peace in French — G39

International Peace Year.

Photo. & Embossed

1986, June 20 ***Perf. 13½***

148 G38 45c multicolored .60 .60
149 G39 1.40fr multicolored 1.25 1.25

WFUNA Anniversary Type

Souvenir Sheet

Designs: 35c, Abstract by Benigno Gomez, Honduras. 45c, Abstract by Alexander Calder (1898-1976), US. 50c, Abstract by Joan Miro (b. 1893), Spain. 70c, Sextet with Dove, by Ole Hamann, Denmark.

1986, Nov. 14 Litho. ***Perf. 13x13½***

150 Sheet of 4 3.75 3.75
a. A232 35c multicolored .50 .50
b. A232 45c multicolored .70 .70
c. A232 50c multicolored .90 .90
d. A232 70c multicolored 1.25 1.25

No. 150 has inscribed margin picturing UN and WFUNA emblems.

Trygve Lie Type

Photo. & Engr.

1987, Jan. 30 ***Perf. 13½***

151 A233 1.40fr multicolored 1.10 1.10

Sheaf of Colored Bands, by Georges Mathieu — G40

Armillary Sphere, Palais des Nations — G41

Photo., Photo. & Engr. (#153)

1987, Jan. 30 ***Perf. 11½x12, 13½***

152 G40 90c multicolored .65 .65
153 G41 1.40fr multicolored 1.25 1.25

Shelter for the Homeless Type

Designs: 50c, Cement-making and brick-making. 90c, Interior construction and decorating.

Perf. 13½x12½

1987, Mar. 13 **Litho.**

154 A234 50c multicolored .50 .50
155 A234 90c multicolored 1.00 1.00

Fight Drug Abuse Type

Designs: 80c, Mother and child. 1.20fr, Workers in rice paddy.

1987, June 12 Litho. ***Perf. 14½x15***

156 A235 80c multicolored .50 .50
157 A235 1.20fr multicolored 1.00 1.00

UN Day Type

Designs: Multinational people in various occupations.

1987, Oct. 23 Litho. ***Perf. 14½x15***

158 A236 35c multicolored .55 .55
159 A236 50c multicolored .80 .80

Immunize Every Child Type

Designs: 90c, Whooping cough. 1.70fr, Tuberculosis.

1987, Nov. 20 Litho. ***Perf. 15x14½***

160 A237 90c multicolored 1.50 1.50
161 A237 1.70fr multicolored 2.75 2.75

IFAD Type

Designs: 35c, Flocks, dairy products. 1.40fr, Fruit.

1988, Jan. 29 Litho. ***Perf. 13½***

162 A238 35c multicolored .35 .35
163 A238 1.40fr multicolored 1.40 1.40

G42

1988, Jan. 29 Photo. ***Perf. 14***

164 G42 50c multicolored .80 .80

Survival of the Forests Type

Pine forest: 50c, Treetops, mountains. 1.10fr, Lake, tree trunks. Printed se-tenant in a continuous design.

1988, Mar. 18 Litho. ***Perf. 14x15***

165 A240 50c multicolored 1.25 1.25
166 A240 1.10fr multicolored 3.50 3.50
a. Pair, #165-166 5.50 5.50

Intl. Volunteer Day Type

Designs: 80c, Agriculture, vert. 90c, Veterinary medicine.

Perf. 13x14, 14x13

1988, May 6 **Litho.**

167 A241 80c multicolored .80 .80
168 A241 90c multicolored 1.00 1.00

Health in Sports Type

Paintings by LeRoy Neiman, American sports artist: 50c, Soccer, vert. 1.40fr, Swimming.

Perf. 13½x13, 13x13½

1988, June 17 **Litho.**

169 A242 50c multicolored .40 .40
170 A242 1.40fr multicolored 1.40 1.40

Universal Declaration of Human Rights 40th Anniv. Type

Photo. & Engr.

1988, Dec. 9 ***Perf. 12***

171 A243 90c multicolored .70 .70

Souvenir Sheet

172 A243 2fr multicolored 2.75 2.75

World Bank Type

1989, Jan. 27 Litho. ***Perf. 13x14***

173 A244 80c Telecommunications 1.00 1.00
174 A244 1.40fr Industry 2.00 2.00

Peace-Keeping Force Type

1989, Mar. 17 ***Perf. 14x13½***

175 A245 90c multicolored 1.25 1.25

World Weather Watch Type

Satellite photographs: 90c, Europe under the influence of Arctic air. 1.10fr, Surface temperatures of sea, ice and land surrounding the Kattegat between Denmark and Sweden.

1989, Apr. 21 Litho. ***Perf. 13x14***

176 A247 90c multicolored 1.25 1.25
177 A247 1.10fr multicolored 2.00 2.00

G43 G44

Photo., Photo. & Engr. (2fr)

1989, Aug. 23 ***Perf. 14***

178 G43 50c multicolored 1.00 1.00
179 G44 2fr multicolored 3.50 3.50

Offices in Vienna, 10th anniv.

Human Rights Type of 1989

Artwork: 35c, Young Mother Sewing, by Mary Cassatt. 80c, The Unknown Slave, sculpture by Albert Mangones.

1989, Nov. 17 Litho. ***Perf. 13½***

180 A250 35c multicolored .35 .35
181 A250 80c multicolored 1.00 1.00

Printed in panes of 12+12 se-tenant labels containing Articles 3 (35c) or 4 (80c) inscribed in English, French or German.

See Nos. 193-194, 209-210,34-235.

Intl. Trade Center Type

1990, Feb. 2 Litho. ***Perf. 14½x15***

182 A251 1.50fr multicolored 2.25 2.25

G45

1990, Feb. 2 Photo. ***Perf. 14x13½***

183 G45 5fr multicolored 4.75 4.75

G46

Fight AIDS Worldwide — G46a

Fight AIDS Type

Designs: 50c, "SIDA." 80c, Proportional drawing of man like the illustration by Leonardo da Vinci.

Perf. 13½x12½

1990, Mar. 16 **Litho.**

184 G46 50c multicolored 1.00 1.00
185 G46a 80c multicolored 1.75 1.75

Medicinal Plants Type

1990, May 4 Photo. ***Perf. 11½***

Granite Paper

186 A253 90c Plumeria rubra 1.00 1.00
187 A253 1.40fr Cinchona officinalis 2.00 2.00

UN 45th Anniv. Type

"45," emblem and: 90c, Symbols of clean environment, transportation and industry. 1.10fr, Dove in silhouette.

1990, June 26 Litho. ***Perf. 14½x13***

188 A254 90c multicolored 1.10 1.10
189 A254 1.10fr multicolored 2.25 2.25

Souvenir Sheet

190 Sheet of 2, #188-189 6.00 6.00

Crime Prevention Type

1990, Sept. 13 Photo. ***Perf. 14***

191 A255 50c Official corruption 1.25 1.25
192 A255 2fr Environmental crime 3.00 3.00

Human Rights Type of 1989

Artwork: 35c, The Prison Courtyard by Vincent Van Gogh. 90c, Katho's Son Redeems the Evil Doer From Execution by Albrecht Durer.

1990, Nov. 16 Litho. ***Perf. 13½***

193 A250 35c multicolored .45 .45
194 A250 90c black & brown 1.25 1.25

Economic Commission for Europe Type

1991, Mar. 15 Litho. ***Perf. 14***

195 A256 90c Owl, gull 1.25 1.25
196 A256 90c Bittern, otter 1.25 1.25
197 A256 90c Swan, lizard 1.25 1.25
198 A256 90c Great crested grebe 1.25 1.25
a. Block of 4, #195-198 5.00 5.00

Namibian Independence Type

1991, May 10 Litho. ***Perf. 14***

199 A257 70c Mountains 1.00 1.00
200 A257 90c Baobab tree 2.00 2.00

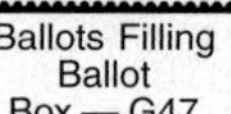

Ballots Filling Ballot Box — G47

UN Emblem — G48

1991, May 10 Litho. ***Perf. 15x14½***

201 G47 80c multicolored .75 .75
202 G48 1.50fr multicolored 2.00 2.00

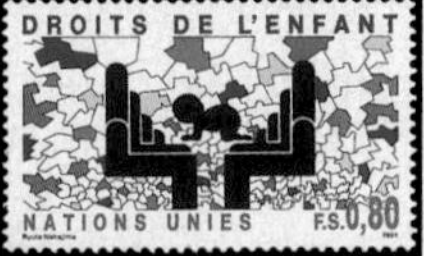

G49

Rights of the Child G50

1991, June 14 Litho. ***Perf. 14½***

203 G49 80c Hands holding infant 1.00 1.00
204 G50 1.10fr Children, flowers 2.00 2.00

G51

Banning of Chemical Weapons
G52

1991, Sept. 11 Litho. *Perf. 13½*
205 G51 80c multicolored 2.00 2.00
206 G52 1.40fr multicolored 3.00 3.00

UN Postal Administration, 40th Anniv. Type

1991, Oct. 24 *Perf. 14x15*
207 A263 50c UN NY No. 7 .80 .80
208 A263 1.60fr UN NY No. 10 2.20 2.20

Human Rights Type of 1989

Artwork: 50c, Early Morning in Rio...1925, by Paul Klee. 90c, Marriage of Giovanni (?) Arnolfini and Giovanna Cenami (?), by Jan Van Eyck.

1991, Nov. 20 Litho. *Perf. 13½*
209 A250 50c multicolored .75 .75
210 A250 90c multicolored 1.25 1.25

Panes of 12+12 se-tenant labels containing Articles 15 (50c) or 16 (90c) inscribed in French, German or English.

World Heritage Type of 1984

Designs: 50c, Sagarmatha Natl. Park, Nepal. 1.10fr, Stonehenge, United Kingdom.

1992, Jan. 24 Litho. *Perf. 13*
Size: 35x28mm
211 G29 50c multicolored .80 .80
212 G29 1.10fr multicolored 1.90 1.90

G53

1992, Jan. 24 Litho. *Perf. 15x14½*
213 G53 3fr multicolored 3.00 3.00

Clean Oceans Type

1992, Mar. 13 Litho. *Perf. 14*
214 A264 80c Ocean surface, diff. .90 .90
215 A264 80c Ocean bottom, diff. .90 .90
a. Pair, #214-215 1.80 *2.00*

Earth Summit Type

Designs: No. 216, Rainbow. No. 217, Two clouds shaped as faces. No. 218, Two sailboats. No. 219, Woman with parasol, boat, flowers.

1992, May 22 Photo. *Perf. 11½*
216 A265 75c multicolored 1.50 1.50
217 A265 75c multicolored 1.50 1.50
218 A265 75c multicolored 1.50 1.50
219 A265 75c multicolored 1.50 1.50
a. Block of 4, #216-219 6.00 6.00

Mission to Planet Earth Type

Designs: No. 220, Space station. No. 221, Probes near Jupiter.

1992, Sept. 4 Photo. *Rouletted 8*
Granite Paper
220 A266 1.10fr multicolored 2.00 2.00
221 A266 1.10fr multicolored 2.00 2.00
a. Pair, #220-221 4.00 4.00

Science and Technology Type of 1992

Designs: 90c, Doctor, nurse. 1.60fr, Graduate seated before computer.

1992, Oct. 2 Litho. *Perf. 14*
222 A267 90c multicolored 1.25 1.25
223 A267 1.60fr multicolored 3.00 3.00

Human Rights Type of 1989

Artwork: 50c, The Oath of the Tennis Court, by Jacques Louis David. 90c, Rocking Chair I, by Henry Moore.

1992, Nov. 20 Litho. *Perf. 13½*
224 A250 50c multicolored .75 .75
225 A250 90c multicolored 1.25 1.25

Panes of 12+12 se-tenant labels containing Articles 21 (50c) and 22 (90c) inscribed in French, German or English.

Aging With Dignity Type

Designs: 50c, Older man coaching soccer. 1.60fr, Older man working at computer terminal.

1993, Feb. 5 Litho. *Perf. 13*
226 A270 50c multicolored .50 .50
227 A270 1.60fr multicolored 1.50 1.50

Endangered Species Type

Designs: No. 228, Pongidae (gorilla). No. 229, Falco peregrinus (peregrine falcon). No. 230, Trichechus inunguis (Amazonian manatee). No. 231, Panthera uncia (snow leopard).

1993, Mar. 2 Litho. *Perf. 13x12½*
228 A271 80c multicolored 1.10 1.10
229 A271 80c multicolored 1.10 1.10
230 A271 80c multicolored 1.10 1.10
231 A271 80c multicolored 1.10 1.10
a. Block of 4, #228-231 4.50 4.50

Healthy Environment Type

1993, May 7 Litho. *Perf. 15x14½*
232 A272 60c Neighborhood .75 .75
233 A272 1fr Urban skyscrapers 1.75 1.75

Human Rights Type of 1989

Artwork: 50c, Three Musicians, by Pablo Picasso. 90c, Voice of Space, by Rene Magritte.

1993, June 11 Litho. *Perf. 13½*
234 A250 50c multicolored .75 .75
235 A250 90c multicolored 1.75 1.75

Printed in panes of 12 + 12 se-tenant labels containing Article 27 (50c) and 28 (90c) inscribed in French, German or English.

Intl. Peace Day Type

Denomination at: No. 236, UL. No. 237, UR. No. 238, LL. No. 239, LR.

Rouletted 12½
1993, Sept. 21 Litho. & Engr.
236 A274 60c purple & multi 2.00 2.00
237 A274 60c purple & multi 2.00 2.00
238 A274 60c purple & multi 2.00 2.00
239 A274 60c purple & multi 2.00 2.00
a. Block of 4, #236-239 8.00 8.00

Environment-Climate Type

1993, Oct. 29 Litho. *Perf. 14½*
240 A275 1.10fr Polar bears 2.00 2.00
241 A275 1.10fr Whale sounding 2.00 2.00
242 A275 1.10fr Elephant seal 2.00 2.00
243 A275 1.10fr Penguins 2.00 2.00
a. Strip of 4, #240-243 8.00 8.00

Intl. Year of the Family Type of 1993

Designs: 80c, Parents teaching child to walk. 1fr, Two women and child picking plants.

1994, Feb. 4 Litho. *Perf. 13.1*
244 A276 80c rose violet & multi 1.00 1.00
245 A276 1fr brown & multi 1.40 1.40

Endangered Species Type of 1993

Designs: No. 246, Mexican prairie dog. No. 247, Jabiru. No. 248, Blue whale. No. 249, Golden lion tamarin.

1994, Mar. 18 Litho. *Perf. 12.7*
246 A271 80c multicolored 1.10 1.10
247 A271 80c multicolored 1.10 1.10
248 A271 80c multicolored 1.10 1.10
249 A271 80c multicolored 1.10 1.10
a. Block of 4, #246-249 4.50 4.50

Protection for Refugees Type of 1994

Design: 1.20fr, Hand lifting figure over chasm.

1994, Apr. 29 Litho. *Perf. 14.3x14.8*
250 A277 1.20fr multicolored 2.25 2.25

Intl. Decade for Natural Disaster Reduction Type of 1994

Earth seen from space, outline map of: No. 251, North America. No. 252, Eurasia. No. 253, South America. No. 254, Australia and South Pacific region.

1994, May 27 Litho. *Perf. 13.9x14.2*
251 A281 60c multicolored 1.75 1.75
252 A281 60c multicolored 1.75 1.75
253 A281 60c multicolored 1.75 1.75
254 A281 60c multicolored 1.75 1.75
a. Block of 4, #251-254 7.00 7.00

Palais des Nations, Geneva
G54

Creation of the World, by Oili Maki — G55

1994, Sept. 1 Litho. *Perf. 14.3x14.6*
255 G54 60c multicolored .75 .75
256 G55 80c multicolored 1.00 1.00
257 G54 1.80fr multi, diff. 2.25 2.25
Nos. 255-257 (3) 4.00 4.00

Population and Development Type of 1994

Designs: 60c, People shopping at open-air market. 80c, People on vacation crossing bridge.

1994, Sept. 1 Litho. *Perf. 13.2x13.6*
258 A282 60c multicolored 1.00 1.00
259 A282 80c multicolored 1.25 1.25

UNCTAD Type of 1994

1994, Oct. 28
260 A283 80c multi, diff. 1.10 1.10
261 A283 1fr multi, diff. 1.50 1.50
a. Grayish green omitted —

UN 50th Anniv. Type of 1995

Litho. & Engr.
1995, Jan. 1 *Perf. 13.4*
262 A284 80c multicolored 1.10 1.10

Social Summit Type of 1995

Photo. & Engr.
1995, Feb. 3 *Perf. 13.6x13.9*
263 A285 1fr multi, diff. 1.25 1.25

Endangered Species Type of 1993

Designs: No. 264, Crowned lemur, Lemur coronatus. No. 265, Giant Scops owl, Otus gurneyi. No. 266, Zetek's frog, Atelopus varius zeteki. No. 267, Wood bison, Bison bison athabascae.

1995, Mar. 24 Litho. *Perf. 13x12½*
264 A271 80c multicolored 1.10 1.10
265 A271 80c multicolored 1.10 1.10
266 A271 80c multicolored 1.10 1.10
267 A271 80c multicolored 1.10 1.10
a. Block of 4, 264-267 4.50 4.50

Intl. Youth Year Type of 1995

Designs: 80c, Farmer on tractor, fields at harvest time. 1fr, Couple standing by fields at night.

1995, May 26 Litho. *Perf. 14.4x14.7*
268 A286 80c multicolored 1.25 1.25
269 A286 1fr multicolored 2.00 2.00

UN, 50th Anniv. Type of 1995

Designs: 60c, Like No. 663. 1.80fr, Like No. 664.

Perf. 13.3x13.6
1995, June 26 Engr.
270 A287 60c maroon .80 .80
271 A287 1.80fr green 3.00 3.00

Souvenir Sheet
Litho. & Engr.
Imperf
272 Sheet of 2, #270-271 3.75 3.75
a. A287 60c maroon .75 .75
b. A287 1.80fr green 3.00 3.00

Conference on Women Type of 1995

Designs: 60c, Black woman, cranes flying above. 1fr, Women, dove.

1995, Sept. 5 Photo. *Perf. 12*
273 A288 60c multicolored 1.00 1.00
Size: 28x50mm
274 A288 1fr multicolored 2.00 2.00

UN People, 50th Anniv. Type of 1995

1995, Oct. 24 Litho. *Perf. 14*
275 Sheet of 12 14.00 14.00
a.-l. A290 30c each 1.10 1.10
276 Souvenir booklet 14.00
a. A290 30c Booklet pane of 3, vert. strip of 3 from UL of sheet 3.50 3.50
b. A290 30c Booklet pane of 3, vert. strip of 3 from UR of sheet 3.50 3.50
c. A290 30c Booklet pane of 3, vert. strip of 3 from LL of sheet 3.50 3.50
d. A290 30c Booklet pane of 3, vert. strip of 3 from LR of sheet 3.50 3.50

WFUNA, 50th Anniv. Type

Design: 80c, Fishing boat, fish in net.

1996, Feb. 2 Litho. *Perf. 13x13½*
277 A291 80c multicolored 1.25 1.25

The Galloping Horse Treading on a Flying Swallow, Chinese Bronzework, Eastern Han Dynasty (25-220 A.D.) — G56

Palais des Nations, Geneva
G57

1996, Feb. 2 Litho. *Perf. 14½x15*
278 G56 40c multicolored .50 .50
279 G57 70c multicolored .90 .90

Endangered Species Type of 1993

Designs: No. 280, Paphiopedilum delenatii. No. 281, Pachypodium baronii. No. 282, Sternbergia lutea. No. 283, Darlingtonia californica.

1996, Mar. 14 Litho. *Perf. 12½*
280 A271 80c multicolored 1.00 1.00
281 A271 80c multicolored 1.00 1.00
282 A271 80c multicolored 1.00 1.00
283 A271 80c multicolored 1.00 1.00
a. Block of 4, #280-283 4.00 4.00

City Summit Type of 1996

Designs: No. 284, Asian family. No. 285, Oriental garden. No. 286, Fruit, vegetable vendor, mosque. No. 287, Boys playing ball. No. 288, Couple reading newspaper.

1996, June 3 Litho. *Perf. 14x13½*
284 A293 70c multicolored 1.50 1.50
285 A293 70c multicolored 1.50 1.50
286 A293 70c multicolored 1.50 1.50
287 A293 70c multicolored 1.50 1.50
288 A293 70c multicolored 1.50 1.50
a. Strip of 5, #284-288 7.50 7.50

Sport and the Environment Type

Designs: 70c, Cycling, vert. 1.10fr, Sprinters.

Perf. 14x14½, 14½x14
1996, July 19 Litho.
289 A294 70c multicolored 1.00 1.00
290 A294 1.10fr multicolored 1.50 1.50

Souvenir Sheet
291 A294 Sheet of 2, #289-290 3.00 3.00

Plea for Peace Type

Designs: 90c, Tree filled with birds, vert. 1.10fr, Bouquet of flowers in rocket tail vase, vert.

1996, Sept. 17 Litho. *Perf. 15x14½*
292 A295 90c multicolored 1.25 1.25
293 A295 1.10fr multicolored 1.50 1.50

UNICEF Type

Fairy Tales: 70c, The Sun and the Moon, South America. 1.80fr, Ananse, Africa.

1996, Nov. 20 Litho. *Perf. 14½x15*

294 A296 70c multicolored .80 .80
295 A296 1.80fr multicolored 2.00 2.00

UN Flag — G58

Palais des Nations Under Construction, by Massimo Campigli G59

1997, Feb. 12 Litho. *Perf. 14½*

296 G58 10c multicolored .25 .25
297 G59 1.10fr multicolored 1.25 1.25

Endangered Species Type of 1993

Designs: No. 298, Ursus maritimus (polar bear). No. 299, Goura cristata (blue-crowned pigeon). No. 300, Amblyrhynchus cristatus (marine iguana). No. 301, Lama guanicoe (guanaco).

1997, Mar. 13 Litho. *Perf. 12½*

298 A271 80c multicolored .90 .90
299 A271 80c multicolored .90 .90
300 A271 80c multicolored .90 .90
301 A271 80c multicolored .90 .90
a. Block of 4, #298-301 3.60 3.60

Earth Summit Anniv. Type

Designs: No. 302, Person flying over mountain. No. 303, Mountain, person's face. No. 304, Person standing on mountain, sailboats. No. 305, Person, mountain, trees.

1.10fr, Combined design similar to Nos. 302-305.

1997, May 30 Photo. *Perf. 11½*
Granite Paper

302 A299 45c multicolored 1.00 1.00
303 A299 45c multicolored 1.00 1.00
304 A299 45c multicolored 1.00 1.00
305 A299 45c multicolored 1.00 1.00
a. Block of 4, #302-305 4.00 4.00

Souvenir Sheet

306 A299 1.10fr multicolored 3.50 3.50

Transportation Type of 1997

Air transportation: No. 307, Zeppelin, Fokker tri-motor. No. 308, Boeing 314 Clipper, Lockheed Constellation. No. 309, DeHavilland Comet. No. 310, Boeing 747, Illyushin jet. No. 311, Concorde.

1997, Aug. 29 Litho. *Perf. 14x14½*

307 A300 70c multicolored 1.00 1.00
308 A300 70c multicolored 1.00 1.00
309 A300 70c multicolored 1.00 1.00
310 A300 70c multicolored 1.00 1.00
311 A300 70c multicolored 1.00 1.00
a. Strip of 5, #307-311 5.00 5.00

Philately Type

Designs: 70c, No. 146. 1.10fr, No. 147.

1997, Oct. 14 Litho. *Perf. 13½x14*

312 A301 70c multicolored .80 .80
313 A301 1.10fr multicolored 1.50 1.50

World Heritage Convention Type

Terracotta warriors of Xian: 45c, Single warrior. 70c, Massed warriors. No. 316a, like NY No. 716. No. 316b, like NY No. 717. No. 316c, like Geneva No. 314. No. 316d, like Geneva No. 315. No. 316e, like Vienna No. 230. No. 316f, like Vienna No. 231.

1997, Nov. 19 Litho. *Perf. 13½*

314 A302 45c multicolored 1.25 1.25
315 A302 70c multicolored 2.25 2.25
316 Souvenir booklet 11.00
a.-f. A302 10c any single .45 .45
g. Booklet pane of 4 #316a 1.80 1.80
h. Booklet pane of 4 #316b 1.80 1.80
i. Booklet pane of 4 #316c 1.80 1.80
j. Booklet pane of 4 #316d 1.80 1.80
k. Booklet pane of 4 #316e 1.80 1.80
l. Booklet pane of 4 #316f 1.80 1.80

Palais des Nations, Geneva G60

1998, Feb. 13 Litho. *Perf. 14½x15*

317 G60 2fr multicolored 1.50 1.50

Endangered Species Type of 1993

Designs: No. 318, Macaca thibetana (short-tailed Tibetan macaque). No. 319, Phoenicopterus ruber (Caribbean flamingo). No. 320, Ornithoptera alexandrae (Queen Alexandra's birdwing). No. 321, Dama mesopotamica (Persian fallow deer).

1998, Mar. 13 Litho. *Perf. 12½*

318 A271 80c multicolored 1.00 1.00
319 A271 80c multicolored 1.00 1.00
320 A271 80c multicolored 1.00 1.00
321 A271 80c multicolored 1.00 1.00
a. Block of 4, #318-321 4.00 4.00

Intl. Year of the Ocean — G61

1998, May 20 Litho. *Perf. 13x13½*

322 G61 Pane of 12 11.00 11.00
a.-l. 45c any single .90 .90

Rain Forests Type

1998, June 19 *Perf. 13x13½*

323 A307 70c Orangutans .90 .90

Souvenir Sheet

324 A307 3fr like #323 4.00 *7.00*

Peacekeeping Type

Designs: 70c, Soldier with two children. 90c, Two soldiers, children.

1998, Sept. 15 Photo. *Perf. 12*

325 A308 70c multicolored .85 .85
326 A308 90c multicolored 1.40 1.40

Declaration of Human Rights Type of 1998

Designs: 90c, Stylized birds. 1.80fr, Stylized birds flying from hand.

Litho. & Photo.

1998, Oct. 27 *Perf. 13*

327 A309 90c multicolored .95 .95
328 A309 1.80fr multicolored 2.00 2.00

Schönbrunn Palace Type

Designs: 70c, No. 331b, Great Palm House. 1.10fr, No. 331d, Blue porcelain vase, vert. No. 331a, Palace. No. 331c, The Gloriette (archway). No. 331e, Wall painting on fabric (detail), by Johann Wenzl Bergl, vert. No. 331f, Porcelain stove, vert.

1998, Dec. 4 Litho. *Perf. 14*

329 A310 70c multicolored .90 .90
330 A310 1.10fr multicolored 1.20 1.20

Souvenir Booklet

331 Booklet 18.00
a.-c. A310 10c any single .50 .50
d.-f. A310 30c any single 1.50 1.50
g. Booklet pane of 4 #331a 2.00 2.00
h. Booklet pane of 3 #331d 4.50 4.50
i. Booklet pane of 3 #331e 4.50 4.50
k. Booklet pane of 4 #331b 2.00 2.00
l. Booklet pane of 4 #331c 2.00 2.00

Palais Wilson, Geneva G62

1999, Feb. 5 Photo. *Perf. 11½*
Granite Paper

332 G62 1.70fr brown red 1.75 1.75

World Heritage, Australia Type

Designs: 90c, No. 335e, Kakadu Natl. Park. 1.10fr, No. 335c, Great Barrier Reef. No. 335a, Tasmanian Wilderness. No. 335b, Wet tropics of Queensland. No. 335d, Uluru-Kata Tjuta Natl. Park. No. 335f, Willandra Lakes region.

1999, Mar. 19 Litho. *Perf. 13*

333 A313 90c multicolored 1.25 1.25
334 A313 1.10fr multicolored 1.50 1.50

Souvenir Booklet

335 Booklet 12.00
a.-c. A313 10c any single .30 .30
d.-f. A313 20c any single .70 .70
g. Booklet pane of 4, #335a 1.20 1.20
h. Booklet pane of 4, #335d 2.80 2.80
i. Booklet pane of 4, #335b 1.20 1.20
j. Booklet pane of 4, #335e 2.80 2.80
k. Booklet pane of 4, #335c 1.20 1.20
l. Booklet pane of 4, #335f 2.80 2.80

Endangered Species Type of 1993

Designs: No. 336, Equus hemionus (Asiatic wild ass). No. 337, Anodorhynchus hyacinthinus (hyacinth macaw). No. 338, Epicrates subflavus (Jamaican boa). No. 339, Dendrolagus bennettianus (Bennetts' tree kangaroo).

1999, Apr. 22 Litho. *Perf. 12½*

336 A271 90c multicolored 1.00 1.00
337 A271 90c multicolored 1.00 1.00
338 A271 90c multicolored 1.00 1.00
339 A271 90c multicolored 1.00 1.00
a. Block of 4, #336-339 4.00 4.00

UNISPACE III Type

Designs: No. 340, Farm, satellite dish. No. 341, City, satellite in orbit. No. 342, Composite of Nos. 340-341.

1999, July 7 Photo. *Rouletted 8*

340 A314 45c multicolored .90 .90
341 A314 45c multicolored .90 .90
a. Pair, #340-341 2.00 2.00

Souvenir Sheet
Perf. 14½

342 A314 2fr multicolored 4.50 4.50
a. Ovptd. in sheet margin 9.50 9.50

UPU Type

Various people, early 20th century methods of mail transportation, denomination at: No. 343, UL. No. 344, UR. No. 345, LL. No. 346, LR.

1999, Aug. 23 Photo. *Perf. 11¾*

343 A315 70c multicolored .90 .90
344 A315 70c multicolored .90 .90
345 A315 70c multicolored .90 .90
346 A315 70c multicolored .90 .90
a. Block of 4, #343-346 3.60 3.60

In Memoriam Type

Designs: 1.10fr, 2fr, Armillary sphere, Palais de Nations. Size of 2fr stamp: 34x63mm.

1999, Sept. 21 Litho. *Perf. 14½x14*

347 A316 1.10fr multicolored 1.25 1.25

Souvenir Sheet
Perf. 14

348 A316 2fr multicolored 3.00 3.00

Education Type

Perf. 13½x13¾

1999, Nov. 18 Litho.

349 A317 90c Rainbow over globe .75 .75
350 A317 1.80fr Fish, tree, globe, book 1.75 1.75

Intl. Year Of Thanksgiving Type

2000, Jan 1 Litho. *Perf. 13¼x13½*

351 A318 90c multicolored 1.00 1.00

On No. 351 portions of the design were applied by a thermographic process producing a shiny, raised effect.

Endangered Species Type of 1993

Designs: No. 352, Hippopotamus amphibius (hippopotamus). No. 353, Coscoroba coscoroba (Coscoroba swan). No. 354, Varanus prasinus (emerald monitor). No. 355, Enhydra lutris (sea otter).

2000, Apr. 6 Litho. *Perf. 12¾x12½*

352 A271 90c multicolored 1.25 1.25
353 A271 90c multicolored 1.25 1.25
354 A271 90c multicolored 1.25 1.25
355 A271 90c multicolored 1.25 1.25
a. Block of 4, #352-355 5.00 5.00

Our World 2000 Type

Winning artwork in Millennium painting competition: 90c, The Embrace, by Rita Adaimy, Lebanon. 1.10fr, Living Single, by Richard Kimanthi, Kenya, vert.

Perf. 13x13½, 13½x13

2000, May 30 Litho.

356 A319 90c multicolored 1.00 1.00
357 A319 1.10fr multicolored 1.25 1.25

55th Anniversary Type

Designs: 90c, Trygve Lie, Harry S Truman, workers at cornerstone dedication ceremony, 1949. 1.40fr, Window cleaner on Secretariat Building, General Assembly Hall under construction, 1951.

2000, July 7 Litho. *Perf. 13¼x13*

358 A320 90c multicolored 1.00 1.00
359 A320 1.40fr multicolored 1.50 1.50

Souvenir Sheet

360 A320 Sheet of 2, #358-359 3.50 3.50

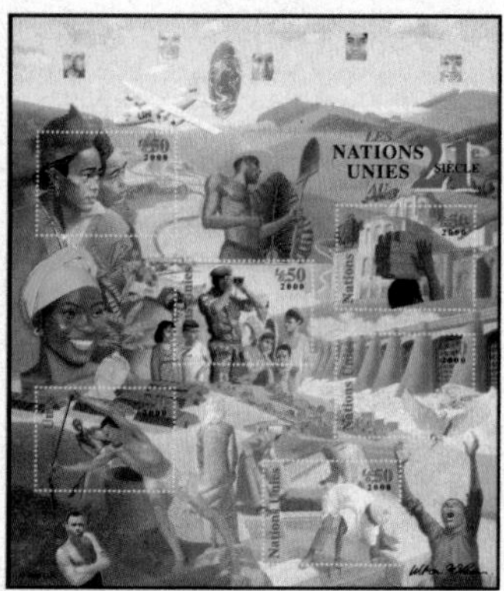

The UN in the 21st Century — G63

No. 361: a, Two people, terraced rice paddy. b, Man carrying bricks on head. c, UN Peacekeeper with binoculars. d, Dam, doves. e, Men with shovels. f, People working on irrigation system.

2000, Sept. 15 Litho. *Perf. 14*

361 G63 Pane of 6 9.00 9.00
a.-f. 50c any single 1.50 1.50

World Heritage, Spain Type

Designs: Nos. 362, 364b, Walled Town of Cuenca. Nos. 363, 364e, Toledo. No. 364a, Alhambra, Generalife and Albayzin, Granada. No. 364c, Aqueduct of Segovia. No. 364d, Amphitheater of Mérida. No. 364f, Güell Park, Barcelona.

2000, Oct. 6 Litho. *Perf. 14¾x14½*

362 A323 1fr multicolored 1.40 1.40
363 A323 1.20fr multicolored 1.60 1.60

Souvenir Booklet

364 Booklet 11.00
a.-c. A323 10c any single .30 .30
d.-f. A323 20c any single .60 .60
g. Booklet pane of 4, #364a 1.20 1.20
h. Booklet pane of 4, #364d 2.40 2.40
i. Booklet pane of 4, #364b 1.20 1.20
j. Booklet pane of 4, #364e 2.40 2.40
k. Booklet pane of 4, #364c 1.20 1.20
l. Booklet pane of 4, #364f 2.40 2.40

Respect for Refugees Type

Designs: 80c, 1.80fr, Refugee with cane, four other refugees.

2000, Nov. 9 Litho. *Perf. 13¼x12¾*

365 A324 80c multicolored 1.25 1.25

Souvenir Sheet

366 A324 1.80fr multicolored 2.50 2.50

Endangered Species Type of 1993

Designs: No. 367, Felis lynx canadensis (North American lynx). No. 368, Pavo muticus (green peafowl). No. 369, Geochelone elephantopus (Galapagos giant tortoise). No. 370, Lepilemur spp. (sportive lemur).

2001, Feb. 1 Litho. *Perf. 12¾x12½*

367 A271 90c multicolored 1.25 1.25
368 A271 90c multicolored 1.25 1.25
369 A271 90c multicolored 1.25 1.25
370 A271 90c multicolored 1.25 1.25
a. Block of 4, #367-370 5.00 5.00

Intl. Volunteers Year — G64

Paintings by: 90c, Ernest Pignon-Ernest, France. 1.30fr, Paul Siché, France.

2001, Mar. 29 Litho. *Perf. 13¼*

371 G64 90c multicolored 1.10 1.10
372 G64 1.30fr multicolored 1.60 1.60

World Heritage, Japan Type

Designs: 1.10fr, No. 375b, Nara. 1.30fr, No. 375e, Itsukushima Shinto Shrine. No. 375a, Kyoto. No. 375c, Himeji-Jo. No. 375d, Shirakawa-Go and Gokayama. No. 375f, Nikko.

2001, Aug. 1 Litho. *Perf. 12¾x13¼*

373 A328 1.10fr multicolored 1.30 1.30
374 A328 1.30fr multicolored 1.50 1.50

Souvenir Booklet

375 Booklet 15.00
a.-c. A328 10c any single .50 .50
d.-f. A328 30c any single .75 .75
g. Booklet pane of 4, #375a 2.00 2.00
h. Booklet pane of 4, #375d 3.00 3.00
i. Booklet pane of 4, #375b 2.00 2.00
j. Booklet pane of 4, #375e 3.00 3.00
k. Booklet pane of 4, #375c 2.00 2.00
l. Booklet pane of 4, #375f 3.00 3.00

Dag Hammarskjöld Type

2001, Sept. 18 Engr. *Perf. 11x11¼*

376 A329 2fr carmine lake 2.50 2.50

UN Postal Administration, 50th Anniv. Types

2001, Oct. 18 Litho. *Perf. 13½*

377 A330 90c Stamps, globe 1.00 1.00
378 A330 1.30fr Stamps, horns 1.75 1.75

Souvenir Sheet

379 A331 Sheet of 2 12.50 12.50
a. 1.30fr red & light blue, 38mm diameter 5.00 5.00
b. 1.80fr red & light blue, 38mm diameter 7.50 7.50

Climate Change Type

Designs: No. 380, Lizard, flowers, shoreline. No. 381, Windmills, construction workers. No. 382, Non-polluting factory. No. 383, Solar oven, city, village, picnickers.

2001, Nov. 16 Litho. *Perf. 13¼*

380 A332 90c multicolored 1.10 1.10
381 A332 90c multicolored 1.10 1.10
382 A332 90c multicolored 1.10 1.10
383 A332 90c multicolored 1.10 1.10
a. Horiz. strip, #380-383 4.50 4.50

Nobel Peace Prize Type

2001, Dec. 10 Litho. *Perf. 13¼*

384 A333 90c multicolored 1.10 1.10

Palais des Nations — G65

2002, Mar. 1 Litho. *Perf. 13¾*

385 G65 1.30fr multicolored 1.40 1.40

Endangered Species Type of 1993

Designs: No. 386, Cacajao calvus (white uakari). No. 387, Mellivora capensis (honey badger). No. 388, Otocolobus manul (manul). No. 389, Varanus exantematicus (Bosc's monitor).

2002, Apr. 4 Litho. *Perf. 12¾x12½*

386 A271 90c multicolored 1.50 1.50
387 A271 90c multicolored 1.50 1.50
388 A271 90c multicolored 1.50 1.50
389 A271 90c multicolored 1.50 1.50
a. Block of 4, #386-389 6.00 6.00

Independence of East Timor Type

Designs: 90c, Wooden statue of male figure. 1.30fr, Carved wooden container.

2002, May 20 Litho. *Perf. 14x14½*

390 A335 90c multicolored 1.25 1.25
391 A335 1.30fr multicolored 1.75 1.75

Intl. Year of Mountains Type

Designs: No. 392, Weisshorn, Switzerland. No. 393, Mt. Fuji, Japan. No. 394, Vinson Massif, Antarctica. No. 395, Mt. Kamet, India.

2002, May 24 Litho. *Perf. 13x13¼*

392 A336 70c multicolored 1.00 1.00
393 A336 70c multicolored 1.00 1.00
394 A336 1.20fr multicolored 1.75 1.75
395 A336 1.20fr multicolored 1.75 1.75
a. Vert. strip or block of four, #392-395 8.00 8.00

World Summit on Sustainable Development (Peter Max) Type

Designs: No. 396, Sun, birds, flowers, heart. No. 397, Three faceless people, diff. No. 398, Three women, diff. No. 399, Sailboat, mountain.

2002, June 27 Litho. *Perf. 14½x14*

396 A337 90c multicolored 1.40 1.40
397 A337 90c multicolored 1.40 1.40
398 A337 1.80fr multicolored 2.75 2.75
399 A337 1.80fr multicolored 2.75 2.75
a. Vert. strip or block of four, #396-399 12.00 12.00

World Heritage, Italy Type

Designs: 90c, No. 402e, Pisa. 1.30fr, No. 402b, Aeolian Islands. No. 402a, Amalfi Coast. No. 402c, Rome. No. 402d, Florence. No. 402f, Pompeii.

Perf. 13½x13¼

2002, Aug. 30 Litho.

400 A338 90c multicolored 1.25 1.25
401 A338 1.30fr multicolored 2.00 2.00

Souvenir Booklet

402 Booklet 33.00 33.00
a.-c. A338 10c any single .75 .75
d.-f. A338 20c any single 2.00 2.00
g. Booklet pane of 4, #402d 8.00 8.00
h. Booklet pane of 4, #402a 3.00 3.00
i. Booklet pane of 4, #402e 8.00 8.00
j. Booklet pane of 4, #402b 3.00 3.00
k. Booklet pane of 4, #402f 8.00 8.00
l. Booklet pane of 4, #402c 3.00 3.00

AIDS Awareness Type

2002, Oct. 24 Litho. *Perf. 13½*

403 A339 1.30fr multicolored 2.00 2.00

Entry of Switzerland into United Nations G66

2002, Oct. 24 Litho. *Perf. 14½x14¾*

404 G66 3fr multicolored 3.50 3.50

Indigenous Art — G67

No. 405: a, Detail of Inca poncho, Peru. b, Bahia culture seated figure, Brazil. c, Blanket, Ecuador. d, Mayan stone sculpture, Belize. e, Embroidered fabric, Guatemala. f, Colima terra-cotta dog sculpture, Mexico.

2003, Jan. 31 Litho. *Perf. 14¼*

405 G67 Pane of 6 10.00 10.00
a.-f. 90c Any single 1.50 1.50

New Inter-Parliamentary Union Headquarters, Geneva — G68

2003, Feb. 20 Litho. *Perf. 14½x14*

406 G68 90c multicolored 1.75 1.75

Endangered Species Type of 1993

Designs: No. 407, Branta ruficollis (red-breasted goose). No. 408, Geronticus calvus (bald ibis). No. 409, Dendrocygna bicolor (fulvous whistling duck). No. 410, Ramphastos vitellinus (channel-billed toucan).

2003, Apr. 3 Litho. *Perf. 12¾x12½*

407 A271 90c multicolored 1.25 1.25
408 A271 90c multicolored 1.25 1.25
409 A271 90c multicolored 1.25 1.25
410 A271 90c multicolored 1.25 1.25
a. Block of 4, #407-410 5.00 5.00

International Year of Freshwater Type of 2003

Perf. 14¼x14½

2003, June 20 Litho.

411 A345 70c Waterfall 1.00 1.00
412 A345 1.30fr People, mountain 2.00 2.00
a. Horiz. pair, #411-412 4.00 4.00

Ralph Bunche Type

Litho. With Foil Application

2003, Aug. 7 *Perf. 13½x14*

413 A346 1.80fr brown red & multicolored 2.75 2.75

In Memoriam Type of 2003

2003, Oct. 24 Litho. *Perf. 13¼x13*

414 A347 85c multicolored 1.50 1.50

World Heritage Sites, United States Type

Designs: 90c, No. 417b, Great Smoky Mountains National Park. 1.30fr, No. 417f, Yellowstone National Park. No. 417a, Yosemite National Park. No. 417c, Olympic National Park. No. 417d, Hawaii Volcanoes National Park. No. 417e, Everglades National Park.

2003, Oct. 24 Litho. *Perf. 14½x14¼*

415 A348 90c multicolored 1.50 1.50
416 A348 1.30fr multicolored 2.25 2.25

Souvenir Booklet

417 Booklet 10.00
a.-c. A348 10c any single .25 .25
d.-f. A348 30c any single .55 .55
g. Booklet pane of 4 #417a 1.00 1.00
h. Booklet pane of 4 #417d 2.25 2.25
i. Booklet pane of 4 #417b 1.00 1.00
j. Booklet pane of 4 #417e 2.25 2.25
k. Booklet pane of 4 #417c 1.00 1.00
l. Booklet pane of 4 #417f 2.25 2.25

Endangered Species Type of 1993

Designs: No. 418, Ursus thibetanus (Asiatic black bear). No. 419, Hippocamelus antisensis (Northern Andean deer). No. 420, Macaca silenus (Lion-tailed macaque). No. 421, Bos gaurus (Gaur).

2004, Jan. 29 Litho. *Perf. 12¾x12½*

418 A271 1fr multicolored 1.60 1.60
419 A271 1fr multicolored 1.60 1.60
420 A271 1fr multicolored 1.60 1.60
421 A271 1fr multicolored 1.60 1.60
a. Block of 4, #418-421 6.50 6.50

Indigenous Art Type of 2003

No. 422: a, Decoration for cows, Switzerland. b, Stone Age terra cotta sculpture of seated woman, Romania. c, Butter stamps, France. d, Detail of herald's tabard, United Kingdom. e, Woodcut print of medieval Cologne, Germany. f, Mesolithic era terra cotta sculpture of mother and child, Serbia and Montenegro.

2004, Mar. 4 Litho. *Perf. 13¼*

422 G67 Sheet of 6 10.00 10.00
a.-f. 1fr Any single 1.50 1.50

Road Safety Type

Road map art with: 85c, Man on hand. 1fr, Person, seat belt, vert.

Perf. 13x13¼, 13¼x13

2004, Apr. 7 Litho.

423 A354 85c multicolored 1.40 1.40
424 A354 1fr multicolored 1.75 1.75

See France No. 3011.

Japanese Peace Bell, 50th Anniv. Type

Litho. & Engr.

2004, June 3 *Perf. 13¼x13*

425 A355 1.30fr multicolored 2.00 2.00

World Heritage Sites, Greece Type

Designs: 1fr, No. 428b, Delphi. 1.30fr, No. 428e, Pythagoreion and Heraion of Samos. No. 428a, Acropolis, Athens. No. 428c, Olympia. No. 428d, Delos. No. 428f, Mycenae and Tiryns.

2004, Aug. 12 Litho. *Perf. 14x13¼*

426 A356 1fr multicolored 1.50 1.50
427 A356 1.30fr multicolored 2.00 2.00

Souvenir Booklet

428 Booklet 13.50
a.-c. A356 20c any single .30 .30
d.-f. A356 50c any single .80 .80
g. Booklet pane of 4 #428a 1.25 1.25
h. Booklet pane of 4 #428b 1.25 1.25
i. Booklet pane of 4 #428c 1.25 1.25
j. Booklet pane of 4 #428d 3.25 3.25
k. Booklet pane of 4 #428e 3.25 3.25
l. Booklet pane of 4 #428f 3.25 3.25

My Dream for Peace Type

Winning designs of Lions Club International children's global peace poster contest by: 85c, Anggun Sita Rustinya, Indonesia. 1.20fr, Amanda Nunez, Belize.

2004, Sept. 21 Litho. *Perf. 14*

429 A357 85c multicolored 1.40 1.40
430 A357 1.20fr multicolored 2.00 2.00

G69

Human Rights — G70

2004, Oct. 14 Litho. *Perf. 11¼*

431 G69 85c multicolored 1.25 1.25
432 G70 1.30fr multicolored 2.25 2.25

Sports G71

2004, Nov. 23 Litho. *Perf. 13x13½*

433 G71 180c multicolored 3.25 3.25

See Switzerland No. 1196.

United Nations, 60th Anniv. Type of 2005

Litho. & Engr.

2005, Feb. 4 *Perf. 11x11¼*

434 A361 1.30fr multicolored 2.50 2.50

Souvenir Sheet

Litho.

Imperf

435 A361 3fr multicolored 7.50 7.50

Endangered Species Type of 1993

Designs: No. 436, Laelia milleri. No. 437, Psygmorchis pusilla. No. 438, Dendrobium cruentum. No. 439, Orchis purpurea.

2005, Mar. 3 Litho. *Perf. 12¾x12½*

436 A271 1fr multicolored 2.00 2.00
437 A271 1fr multicolored 2.00 2.00
438 A271 1fr multicolored 2.00 2.00
439 A271 1fr multicolored 2.00 2.00
a. Block of 4, #436-439 8.00 8.00

Nature's Wisdom — G72

Designs: 1fr, Children collecting water, India. 80c, Ruby brittle star, Bahamas.

2005, Apr. 21 Litho. *Perf. 13½x13¼*
440 G72 1fr multicolored 1.75 1.75
441 G72 1.30fr multicolored 2.00 2.00

Intl. Year of Sport Type

2005, June 3 Litho. *Perf. 13x13¼*
442 A368 1fr Wheelchair racing 1.75 1.75
443 A368 1.30fr Cycling 2.25 2.25

World Heritage Sites, Egypt Type

Designs: Nos. 444, 446b, Philae. Nos. 445, 446e, Islamic Cairo. No. 446a, Memphis and its Necropolis. No. 446c, Abu Mena. No. 446d, Ancient Thebes. No. 446f, St. Catherine area.

2005, Aug. 4 Litho. *Perf. 14x13¼*
444 A369 1fr multicolored 2.00 2.00
445 A369 1.30fr multicolored 2.50 2.50

Souvenir Booklet

446 Booklet, #446g-446l 16.50
a.-c. A369 20c any single .40 .40
d.-f. A369 50c any single .90 .90
g. Booklet pane of 4 #446a 1.60 1.60
h. Booklet pane of 4 #446b 1.60 1.60
i. Booklet pane of 4 #446c 1.60 1.60
j. Booklet pane of 4 #446d 3.75 3.75
k. Booklet pane of 4 #446e 3.75 3.75
l. Booklet pane of 4 #446f 3.75 3.75

My Dream for Peace Type

Winning designs of Lions Club International children's global peace poster contest by: 1fr, Marisa Harun, Indonesia. 1.30fr, Carlos Javier Parramón Teixidó, Spain.

2005, Sept. 21 Litho. *Perf. 14*
447 A357 1fr multicolored 1.75 1.75
448 A357 1.30fr multicolored 2.00 2.00

Food for Life Type

Designs: 1fr, Rye, airplane dropping parcels, camel caravan. 1.30fr, Sorghum, people carrying grain sacks, trucks.

2005, Oct. 20 Litho. *Perf. 13¾*
449 A370 1fr multicolored 1.90 1.90
450 A370 1.30fr multicolored 2.40 2.40

Armillary Sphere, Palais des Nations — G73

Litho. with Hologram

2006, Feb. 3 *Perf. 13¼x13½*
451 G73 1.30fr multicolored 2.25 2.25

Indigenous Art Type of 2003

No. 452 — Musical instruments: a, Bell, Benin. b, Drum, Swaziland. c, Sanza, Congo. d, Stringed instruments, Cape Verde. e, Caixixi, Ghana. f, Bells, Central Africa.

2006, Feb. 3 Litho. *Perf. 13¼*
452 G67 Pane of 6 12.00 12.00
a.-f. 1.20fr Any single 2.00 2.00

Endangered Species Type of 1993

Designs: No. 453, Dyscophus antongilii. No. 454, Chamaeleo dilepsis. No. 455, Corallus caninus. No. 456, Phyllobates vittatus.

Perf. 12¾x12½

2006, Mar. 16 Litho.
453 A271 1fr multicolored 1.75 1.75
454 A271 1fr multicolored 1.75 1.75
455 A271 1fr multicolored 1.75 1.75
456 A271 1fr multicolored 1.75 1.75
a. Block of 4, #453-456 7.00 7.00

Intl. Day of Families Type

Designs: 1fr, Family reading together. 1.30fr, Family on motorcycle.

2006, May 27 Litho. *Perf. 14x13½*
457 A373 1fr multicolored 1.25 1.25
458 A373 1.30fr multicolored 1.75 1.75

World Heritage Sites, France Type

Eiffel Tower and: Nos. 459, 461b, Provins. Nos. 460, 461e, Mont Saint-Michel. No. 461a, Banks of the Seine. No. 461c, Carcassonne. No. 461d, Roman Aqueduct. No. 446f, Chateau de Chambord.

Litho. & Embossed with Foil Application

2006, June 17 *Perf. 13½x13¼*
459 A374 1fr multicolored 1.75 1.75
460 A374 1.30fr multicolored 2.25 2.25

Souvenir Booklet

461 Booklet, #461g-461l 15.00
a.-c. A374 20c any single .35 .35
d.-f. A374 50c any single .85 .85
g. Booklet pane of 4 #461a 1.40 1.40
h. Booklet pane of 4 #461b 1.40 1.40
i. Booklet pane of 4 #461c 1.40 1.40
j. Booklet pane of 4 #461d 3.50 3.50
k. Booklet pane of 4 #461e 3.50 3.50
l. Booklet pane of 4 #461f 3.50 3.50

See France Nos. 3219-3220.

My Dream for Peace Type of 2004

Winning designs of Lions Club International children's global peace poster contest by: 85c, Ariam Boaglio, Italy. 1.20fr, Sierra Spicer, US.

2006, Sept. 21 Litho. *Perf. 13½x13*
462 A357 85c multicolored 1.60 1.60
463 A357 1.20fr multicolored 2.25 2.25

Flags and Coins Type

No. 464 — Flag of: a, Uganda, 500 shilling coin. b, Luxembourg, 1 euro coin. c, Cape Verde, 20 escudo coin. d, Belgium, 1 euro coin. e, Italy, 1 euro coin. f, New Zealand, 1 dollar coin. g, Switzerland, 2 franc coin. h, Lebanon, 500 pound coin.

2006, Oct. 5 Litho. *Perf. 13¼x13*
464 Pane of 8 15.00 15.00
a.-h. A375 85c Any single 1.50 1.50

A column of rouletting in the middle of the pane separates it into two parts.

Endangered Species Type of 1993

Designs: No. 465, Theropithecus gelada. No. 466, Cercopithecus neglectus. No. 467, Varecia variegata. No. 468, Hylobates moloch.

Perf. 12¾x12½

2007, Mar. 15 Litho.
465 A271 1fr multicolored 1.75 1.75
466 A271 1fr multicolored 1.75 1.75
467 A271 1fr multicolored 1.75 1.75
468 A271 1fr multicolored 1.75 1.75
a. Block of 4, #465-468 7.00 7.00

Flags and Coins Type of 2006

No. 469 — Flag of: a, Burkina Faso, 500 franc coin. b, France, 50 cent coin. c, Moldova, 50 bani coin. d, Papua New Guinea, 1 kina coin. e, Bolivia, 1 boliviano coin. f, Myanmar, 100 kyat coin. g, Mali, 500 franc coin. h, Tunisia, 5 dinar coin.

2007, May 3 Litho. *Perf. 13¼x13*
469 Sheet of 8 12.50 12.50
a.-h. A375 85c Any single 1.50 1.50

A column of rouletting in the middle of the sheet separates it into two parts.

Peaceful Visions Type of 2007

Designs: 1.20fr, "Harvest for All." 1.80fr, "This Dream Has Wings."

2007, June 1 Litho. *Perf. 13x12½*
470 A378 1.20fr multicolored 2.25 2.25
471 A378 1.80fr multicolored 3.25 3.25

World Heritage Sites, South America Type

Designs: Nos. 472, 474a, Tiwanaku, Bolivia. Nos. 473, 474f, Machu Picchu, Peru. No. 474b, Iguaçu National Park, Brazil. No. 474c, Galapagos Islands, Ecuador. No. 474d, Rapa Nui, Chile. No. 474e, Cueva de las Manos, Argentina.

2007, Aug. 9 Litho. *Perf. 13¼x13*
472 A381 1fr multicolored 1.90 1.90
473 A381 1.80fr multicolored 3.25 3.25

Souvenir Booklet

474 Booklet, #474g-474l 16.00
a.-c. A381 20c Any single .40 .40
d.-f. A381 50c Any single .90 .90
g. Booklet pane of 4 #474a 1.60 1.60
h. Booklet pane of 4 #474b 1.60 1.60
i. Booklet pane of 4 #474c 1.60 1.60
j. Booklet pane of 4 #474d 3.60 3.60
k. Booklet pane of 4 #474e 3.60 3.60
l. Booklet pane of 4 #474f 3.60 3.60

Humanitarian Mail Type

2007, Sept. 6 Litho. *Perf. 12½x13¼*
475 A382 1.80fr multicolored 3.25 3.25

Space for Humanity Type

Designs: 1fr, Astronaut spacewalking. 1.80fr, International Space Station, space probe, Jupiter.
3fr, Astronauts spacewalking.

2007, Oct. 25 Litho. *Perf. 13½x14*
476 A383 1fr multicolored 1.90 1.90
477 A383 1.80fr multicolored 3.25 3.25

Souvenir Sheet

478 A383 3fr multicolored 7.50 7.50

Intl. Holocaust Remembrance Day Type

2008, Jan. 27 Litho. *Perf. 13*
479 A384 85c multicolored 3.00 3.00

Endangered Species Type of 1993

Designs: No. 480, Odobenus rosmarus. No. 481, Platygyra daedalea. No. 482, Hippocampus bargibanti. No. 483, Delphinapterus leucas.

2008, Mar. 6 Litho. *Perf. 12¾x12½*
480 A271 1fr multicolored 2.00 2.00
481 A271 1fr multicolored 2.00 2.00
482 A271 1fr multicolored 2.00 2.00
483 A271 1fr multicolored 2.00 2.00
a. Block of 4, #480-483 8.00 8.00

Flags and Coins Type of 2006

No. 484 — Flag of: a, Madagascar, 1 ariary coin. b, Rwanda, 50 franc coin. c, Benin, 10 franc coin. d, Iran, 500 rial coin. e, Namibia, 5 dollar coin. f, Maldives, 1 rufiyaa coin. g, Albania, 10 lek coin. h, Turkey, 1 lira coin.

2008, May 8 Litho. *Perf. 13¼x13*
484 Sheet of 8 15.00 15.00
a.-h. A375 85c Any single 1.75 1.75

A column of rouletting in the middle of the sheet separates it into two parts.

Handshake G74

Sign Language — G75

Litho. & Embossed

2008, June 6 *Perf. 14x13¼*
485 G74 1fr orange & red 2.25 2.25
486 G75 1.80fr red & orange 4.00 4.00

Convention on the Rights of Persons with Disabilities.

Sport for Peace Type of 2008

Designs: 1fr, 3fr, Gymnast. 1.80fr, Tennis player.

2008, Aug. 8 Litho. *Perf. 14½*
487 A393 1fr multicolored 2.25 2.25
488 A393 1.80fr multicolored 4.00 4.00

Souvenir Sheet

Perf. 12¾x13¼
489 A393 3fr multicolored 9.00 9.00

2008 Summer Olympics, Beijing.

"We Can End Poverty" Type of 2008

Winning designs in children's art contest by: 1fr, Ranajoy Banerjee, India, vert. 1.80fr, Elizabeth Elaine Chun Nig Au, Hong Kong, vert.

Perf. 12½x12¾

2008, Sept. 18 Litho.
490 A395 1fr multicolored 2.25 2.25
491 A395 1.80fr multicolored 3.75 3.75

Climate Change Types of New York and Vienna and

G76

Climate Change — G77

No. 492 — Polar bear with quarter of Earth in: a, LR. b, LL. c, UR. d, UL.
No. 493 — Ship and sea ice with quarter of Earth in: a, LR. b, LL. c, UR. d, UL.
No. 494: a, Like New York #969a. b, Like New York #969b. c, Like New York #969c. d, Like New York #969d. e, Like Geneva #493a. f, Like Geneva #493b. g, Like Geneva #493c. h, Like Geneva #493d. i, Like Vienna #434a. j, Like Vienna #434b. k, Like Vienna #434c. l, Like Vienna #434d. m, Like New York #968a. n, Like New York #968b, o, Like New York #968c, p, Like New York #968d. q, Like Geneva #492a. r, Like Geneva #492b. s, Like Geneva #492c. t, Like Geneva #492d. u, Like Vienna #435a. v, Like Vienna #435b. w, Like Vienna #435c. x, Like Vienna #435d.
All stamps have red panels inscribed "Changement de climat."

2008, Oct. 23 Litho. *Perf. 13¼x13*
492 Sheet of 4 10.50 10.50
a.-d. G76 1.20fr Any single 2.60 2.60
493 Sheet of 4 15.50 15.50
a.-d. G77 1.80fr Any single 3.75 3.75

Souvenir Booklet

494 Booklet, #494y-494ad 25.00
a.-d. A397 35c Any single .75 .75
e.-h. G77 35c Any single .75 .75
i.-l. V72 35c Any single .75 .75
m.-p. A396 50c Any single 1.00 1.00
q.-t. G76 50c Any single 1.00 1.00
u.-x. V73 50c Any single 1.00 1.00
y. Booklet pane of 4, #494a-494d 3.00 3.00
z. Booklet pane of 4, #494e-494h 3.00 3.00
aa. Booklet pane of 4, #494i-494l 3.00 3.00
ab. Booklet pane of 4, #494m-494p 4.25 4.25
ac. Booklet pane of 4, #494q-494t 4.25 4.25
ad. Booklet pane of 4, #494u-494x 4.25 4.25

U Thant Type of 2009

Litho. With Foil Application

2009, Feb. 6 *Perf. 14x13½*
495 A399 1.30fr red & multi 3.25 3.25

Endangered Species Type of 1993

No. 496, Maculinea arion. No. 497, Dolomedes plantarius. No. 498, Cerambyx cerdo. No. 499, Coenagrion mercuriale.

2009, Apr. 16 Litho. *Perf. 12¾x12½*
496 A271 1fr multicolored 1.90 1.90
497 A271 1fr multicolored 1.90 1.90
498 A271 1fr multicolored 1.90 1.90
499 A271 1fr multicolored 1.90 1.90
a. Block of 4, #496-499 7.75 7.75

World Heritage Sites, Germany Type of 2009

Designs: Nos. 500, 502b, Wartburg Castle. Nos. 501, 502f, Monastic Island of Reichenau. No. 502a, Town Hall and Roland on the Marketplace, Bremen. No. 502c, Palaces and Parks of Potsdam and Berlin. No. 502d, Aachen Cathedral. No. 502e, Luther Memorials in Eisleben and Wittenberg.

2009, May 7 Litho. *Perf. 14x13½*
500 A400 1fr multicolored 2.25 2.25
501 A400 1.30fr multicolored 2.75 2.75

Souvenir Booklet

502 Booklet, #502g-502l 18.00
a.-c. A400 30c any single .55 .55
d.-f. A400 50c any single .90 .90

g. Booklet pane of 4 #502a 2.25 2.25
h. Booklet pane of 4 #502b 2.25 2.25
i. Booklet pane of 4 #502c 2.25 2.25
j. Booklet pane of 4 #502d 3.75 3.75
k. Booklet pane of 4 #502e 3.75 3.75
l. Booklet pane of 4 #502f 3.75 3.75

Economic and Social Council (ECOSOC) Type of 2009

Designs: 85c, Improving maternal health. 1.80fr, Access to essential medicines.

2009, Aug. 6 ***Perf. 12¾x12½***
503 A411 85c multicolored 2.00 2.00
504 A411 1.80fr multicolored 4.00 4.00

Millennium Development Goals Type of 2009

Miniature Sheet

No. 505: a, Bowl of hot food. b, Pencil. c, Female symbol. d, Teddy bear. e, Pregnant woman, heart. f, Medicine bottle. g, Stylized tree. h, Conjoined people.

2009, Sept. 25 ***Perf. 13¼***
505 A413 Sheet of 8 18.00 18.00
a.-h. 1.10fr Any single 2.25 2.25

Palais des Nations — G78

Palais des Nations — G79

Flags of United Nations and Switzerland — G80

Meeting Room — G81

Armillary Sphere — G82

2009, Oct. 2 ***Perf. 13¼***
506 G78 1fr multi + label *6.00 6.00*
a. Perf. 11¼x11 + label *5.00 5.00*
507 G79 1fr multi + label *6.00 6.00*
a. Perf. 11¼x11 + label *5.00 5.00*
508 G80 1fr multi + label *6.00 6.00*
a. Perf. 11¼x11 + label *5.00 5.00*
509 G81 1fr multi + label *6.00 6.00*
a. Perf. 11¼x11 + label *5.00 5.00*
510 G82 1fr multi + label *6.00 6.00*
a. Perf. 11¼x11 + label *5.00 5.00*
b. Vert. strip of 5, #506-510, + 5 labels *30.00 30.00*
c. Vert. strip of 5, #506a-510a, + 5 labels *25.00 25.00*

United Nations Postal Administration in Geneva, 40th anniv. The full sheets sold for €19.90 or $14.95. Labels could not be personalized. The sheet of No. 510c has "VER. 2" in the lower right selvage.

Miniature Sheet

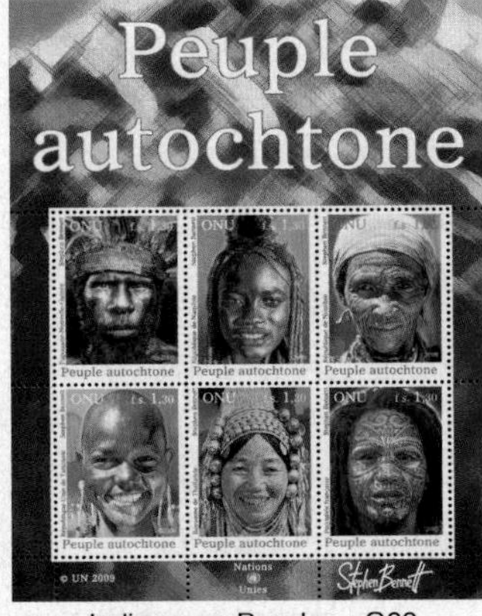

Indigenous People — G83

No. 511 — Portraits of person from: a, Papua New Guinea. b, Namibia (young woman). c, Namibia (old man). d, Tanzania. e, Thailand. f, French Polynesia.

2009, Oct. 8 ***Perf. 12½***
511 G83 Sheet of 6 16.00 16.00
a.-f. 1.30fr Any single 2.60 2.60

Flags and Coins Type of 2006

No. 512 — Flag of: a, Equatorial Guinea, 100 franc coin. b, Laos, 20 kip coin. c, Seychelles, 5 rupee coin. d, Mauritania, 1 ougiya coin. e, Argentina, 1 peso coin. f, Morocco, 1 dirham coin. g, Sudan, 20 piaster coin. h, Brunei, 50 cent coin.

2010, Feb. 5 Litho. ***Perf. 13¼x13***
512 Sheet of 8 15.00 15.00
a.-h. A375 85c Any single 1.75 1.75

A column of rouletting in the middle of the sheet separates it into two parts.

Endangered Species Type of 1993

No. 513, Fouquieria columnaris. No. 514, Aloe arborescens. No. 515, Galanthus krasnovii. No. 516, Dracaena draco.

2010, Apr. 15 Litho. ***Perf. 12¾x12½***
513 A271 1fr multicolored 2.25 2.25
514 A271 1fr multicolored 2.25 2.25
515 A271 1fr multicolored 2.25 2.25
516 A271 1fr multicolored 2.25 2.25
a. Block of 4, #513-516 9.00 9.00

Intl. Year of Biodiversity G84

Drawings from Art Forms from Nature, by Ernst Heinrich: 1.60fr, Arachnid. 1.90fr, Starfish.

2010, Apr. 15 Litho. ***Perf. 13***
517 G84 1.60fr multicolored 3.75 3.75
518 G84 1.90fr multicolored 4.25 4.25

One Planet, One Ocean Types of New York and Vienna and

G85

G86

No. 519: a, Turtles at left and top, fish at bottom. b, Hammerhead shark. c, Fish at left and center, corals. d, Fish at left, coral.

No. 520: a, Dolphins. b, Shark, head of fish at right, small fish in background. c, Ray and fish. d, Fish at bottom, coral and sponges.

No. 521: a, Like New York #1003a. b, Like New York #1003b, c, Like New York #1003c, d, Like New York #1003d. e, Like Vienna #471a. f, Like Vienna #471b. g, Like Vienna #471c, h, Like Vienna #471d. i, Like #519a. j, Like #519b, k, Like #519c. l, Like #519d. m, Like New York #1004a. n, Like New York #1004b. o, Like New York #1004c, p, Like New York #1004d. q, Like Vienna #472a. r, Like Vienna #472b. s, Like Vienna #472c. t, Like Vienna #472d. u, Like #520a. v, Like #520b. w, Like #520c. x, Like #520d.

2010, May 6 Litho. ***Perf. 14x13¼***
519 G85 Sheet of 4 8.00 8.00
a.-d. 85c Any single 2.00 2.00
520 G86 Sheet of 4 10.00 10.00
a.-d. 1fr Any single 2.50 2.50

Souvenir Booklet

Perf. 13¼x13

521 Booklet, #521y-521z, 521aa-521ad 22.00
a.-d. A416 30c any single .70 .70
e.-h. V91 30c any single .70 .70
i.-l. G85 30c any single .70 .70
m.-p. A417 50c any single 1.10 1.10
q.-t. V92 50c any single 1.10 1.10
u.-x. G86 50c any single 1.10 1.10
y. Booklet pane of 4 #521a-521d 2.80 2.80
z. Booklet pane of 4 #521e-521h 2.80 2.80
aa. Booklet pane of 4 #521i-521l 2.80 2.80
ab. Booklet pane of 4 #521m-521p 4.40 4.40
ac. Booklet pane of 4 #521q-521t 4.40 4.40
ad. Booklet pane of 4 #521u-521x 4.40 4.40

Intl. Oceanographic Commission, 50th anniv.

United Nations, 65th Anniv. Type of 2010

Litho. With Foil Application

2010, June 28 ***Perf. 13¼***
522 A422 1.90fr red & gold 4.00 4.00
a. Souvenir sheet of 2 *(40,500)+* 8.00 8.00

G87

G88

G89

G90

United Nations Land Transport — G91

2010, Sept. 2 Litho. ***Perf. 13¼x13***
523 G87 1fr multicolored 1.80 1.80
524 G88 1fr multicolored 1.80 1.80
525 G89 1fr multicolored 1.80 1.80
526 G90 1fr multicolored 1.80 1.80
527 G91 1fr multicolored 1.80 1.80

Miniature Sheet

Campaign Against Child Labor — G92

No. 528: a, Child, buildings, road, burning can. b, Child with full basket on back, children playing in background. c, Child working, children on school bus. d, Child with mining helmet, three other children. e, Child near tubs, children working, child being beaten. f, Child with hoe. g, Marionette, traffic light. h, Child carrying basket on head. i, Children on rock field near hills. j, Child holding bags in road.

2010, Sept. 2 Litho. ***Perf. 14¾***
528 G92 Sheet of 10 + 10 labels 32.50 32.50
a.-j. 1.90fr Any single + label 3.25 3.25

No. 528 sold for $14.95, 15fr and €11.46, each of which was far lower than the level at which 19fr, the total face value of the stamps on the sheet, was worth on the day of issue. Labels could not be personalized.

Miniature Sheet

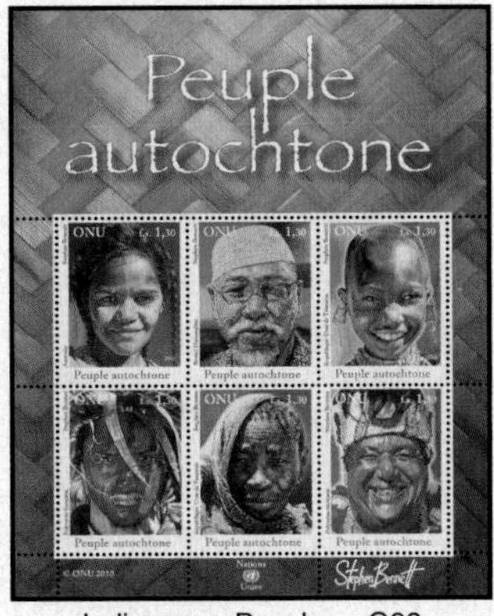

Indigenous People — G93

No. 529 — Portraits of person from: a, Australia. b, Brunei. c, Tanzania (girl with bald head). d, French Polynesia (man with headdress of leaves). e, Tanzania (man with headdress). f, French Polynesia (man with white headdress).

2010, Oct. 21 Litho. ***Perf. 13***
529 G93 Pane of 6 16.50 16.50
a.-f. 1.30fr Any single 2.75 2.75

United Nations Headquarters, Geneva — G94

United Nations Headquarters, Geneva: 10c, Aerial view. 50c, Ground-level view.

2011, Feb. 4 Litho. *Perf. 13*

530 G94 10c multicolored .35 .35
531 G94 50c multicolored 1.25 1.25

Flags and Coins Type of 2006

No. 532 — Flag of: a, Mongolia, 500 tugrik coin. b, Senegal, 500 franc coin. c, Egypt, 100 piaster coin. d, Congo, 100 franc coin. e, Nicaragua, 1 Córdoba coin. f, Central African Republic, 100 franc coin. g, Algeria, 5 dinar coin. h, Ukraine, 5 hryvnia coin.

2011, Mar. 3 Litho. *Perf. 13¼x13*

532 Sheet of 8 15.00 15.00
a.-h. A375 85c Any single 1.75 1.75

A column of rouletting in the middle of the sheet separates it into two parts.

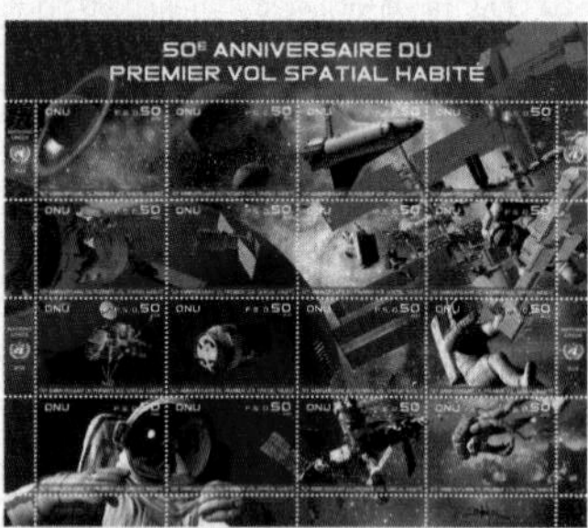

Human Space Flight, 50th Anniv. — G95

No. 533: Various parts of outer space scene.

No. 534, vert.: a, International Space Station. b, International Space Station, diff.

2011, Apr. 12 Litho. *Perf. 13x13¼*

533 G95 Sheet of 16 18.00 18.00
a.-p. 50c any single 1.10 1.10

Souvenir Sheet

534 G95 Sheet of 2 7.50 7.50
a. 85c multi 3.25 3.25
b. 1fr multi 4.25 4.25

No. 534 contains two 40x48mm stamps that were printed as part of a larger sheet of six stamps, Vienna No. 485c, which was broken up into its component two-stamp souvenir sheets, and also sold as one unit.

UNESCO World Heritage Sites in Nordic Countries Type of 2011

Designs: 85c, Kronborg Castle, Denmark. 1fr, Suomenlinna Fortress, Finland.

2011, May 5 Litho. *Perf. 14x13½*

535 A433 85c multicolored 1.90 1.90
536 A433 1fr multicolored 2.25 2.25

AIDS Ribbon Type of 2011

2011, June 3 Litho. *Die Cut*

Self-Adhesive

537 A434 1.30fr red & orange 4.00 4.00

ECOSOC Type of 2011

2011, July 1 Litho. *Perf. 14¼*

538 A435 1fr multicolored 3.00 3.00
539 A435 1.30fr multicolored 4.00 4.00

Endangered Species Type of 1993

Designs: No. 540, Strigops habroptilus (Kakapo). No. 541, Lophophorus impejanus (Himalayan monal). No. 542, Ciconia nigra (Black stork). No. 543, Pithecophaga jeffreyi (Philippine eagle).

2011, Sept. 7 Litho. *Perf. 12¾x12½*

540 A271 1fr multicolored 2.60 2.60
541 A271 1fr multicolored 2.60 2.60
542 A271 1fr multicolored 2.60 2.60
543 A271 1fr multicolored 2.60 2.60
a. Block of 4, #540-543 10.40 10.40

Intl. Year of Forests Type of 2011

Designs: 85c, Birds and butterflies, tree tops. 1.40fr, Fish and coral.

Litho. With Foil Application

2011, Oct. 13 *Perf. 12½*

544 85c multicolored 2.25 2.25
545 1.40fr multicolored 3.75 3.75
a. A436 Vert. pair, #544-545 6.00 6.00

Flags and Coins Type of 2006

No. 546 — Flag of: a, Saudi Arabia, 100 halala coin. b, Georgia, 2 lari coin. c, Democratic People's Republic of Korea, 50 won coin. d, Lesotho, 50 lisente coin. e, Serbia, 5 dinar coin. f, Djibouti, 20 franc coin. g, Belize, 1 dollar coin. h, Liechtenstein, 20 centime coin.

2012, Feb. 3 Litho. *Perf. 13¼x13*

546 Sheet of 8 16.50 16.50
a.-h. A375 85c Any single 2.00 2.00

A column of rouletting in the middle of the sheet separates it into two parts.

G96

Autism Awareness G97

Drawings by autistic people: No. 547, Victory, by J.A Tan, Canada. No. 548, Untitled drawing, by Michael Augello, U.S.

2012, Apr. 2 Litho. *Perf. 14x13½*

547 G96 1.40fr multicolored 3.50 3.50
548 G97 1.40fr multicolored 3.50 3.50
a. Pair, #547-548 7.00 7.00

Endangered Species Type of 1993

Designs: No. 549, Panthera tigris altaica. No. 550, Psitacella picta. No. 551, Iguana iguana. No. 552, Propithecus tattersalli.

2012, Apr. 19 Litho. *Perf. 12¾x12½*

549 A271 1fr multicolored 2.40 2.40
550 A271 1fr multicolored 2.40 2.40
551 A271 1fr multicolored 2.40 2.40
552 A271 1fr multicolored 2.40 2.40
a. Block of 4, #549-552 9.75 9.75

Rio + 20 Type of 2012

2012, June 1 Litho. *Perf. 13x13¼*

553 A443 1.40fr multicolored 4.00 4.00

Sport for Peace Type of 2012

2012 Paralympics events: 1fr, Track. 1.40fr, Archery.

Litho. With Foil Application

2012, Aug. 17 *Perf. 14½*

554 A444 1fr multicolored 2.40 2.40
555 A444 1.40fr multicolored 3.50 3.50
a. Souvenir sheet of 1 3.50 3.50

UNESCO World Heritage Sites in Africa Type of 2012

Designs: 85c, Virunga National Park, Congo Democratic Republic. 1fr, Amphitheater of El Jem, Tunisia.

2012, Sept. 5 Litho. *Perf. 13¼*

556 A445 85c multicolored 2.00 2.00
557 A445 1fr multicolored 2.40 2.40

Miniature Sheet

Indigenous People — G98

No. 558 — Portrait of person from: a, China. b, Tibet, China. c, Mongolia. d, Mexico. e, Papua New Guinea. f, Haiti.

2012, Oct. 11 Litho. *Perf. 13¼x13*

558 G98 Sheet of 6 13.50 13.50
a.-f. 85c Any single 2.25 2.25

World Radio Day Type of 2013

Designs: 1.40fr, Reporter with microphone and tape recorder. 1.90fr, Engineers in studio.

2013, Feb. 13 Litho. *Perf. 13¼x13*

559 A448 1.40fr multicolored 3.50 3.50
560 A448 1.90fr multicolored 4.50 4.50

Person on Leaf G99

Dove and People — G100

2013, Mar. 5 Litho. *Perf. 14x13½*

561 G99 1fr multicolored 2.40 2.40

Perf. 13½x14

562 G100 1.40fr multicolored 3.50 3.50

World Heritage Sites, China, Type of 2013

Designs: Nos. 563, 565b, Potala Palace, Lhasa. Nos. 564, 565e, Mount Huangshan. No. 565a, Mogao Caves. No. 565c, Great Wall of China. No. 565d, Imperial Palace, Beijing. No. 565f, Mausoleum of the First Qing Emperor.

2013, Apr. 11 Litho. *Perf. 14x13½*

563 A452 1.40fr multicolored 3.50 3.50
564 A452 1.90fr multicolored 4.50 4.50

Souvenir Booklet

565 Booklet, #565g-565l 24.00
a.-c. A452 30c any single .75 .75
d.-f. A452 50c any single 1.25 1.25
g. Booklet pane of 4 #565a 3.00 —
h. Booklet pane of 4 #565b 3.00 —
i. Booklet pane of 4 #565c 3.00 —
j. Booklet pane of 4 #565d 5.00 —
k. Booklet pane of 4 #565e 5.00 —
l. Booklet pane of 4 #565f 5.00 —

World Oceans Day — G101

No. 566 — Fish from *One Fish, Two Fish, Red Fish, Blue Fish,* by Dr. Seuss: a, Three red fish facing right. b, Green fish, tail of yellow fish. c, Three red fish facing right, part of tail of red fish. d, Two entire green fish facing left, tail of bottom fish ends above "n" in "océan." e, Red fish with eye open facing left. f, Tail of red fish, yellow and red fish facing left. g, Red fish facing right, water droplets. h, Yellow and red fish facing right. i, Two green fish facing left, tail of bottom fish ends to right of "océan." j, Red fish and wave. k, Two green fish, red fish, wave. l, Yellow fish in car, wave.

2013, May 31 Litho. *Perf. 13*

566 G101 Sheet of 12 24.50 24.50
a.-l. 85c any single 2.00 2.00

Nebulae Type of 2013

Designs: No. 567, NGC 2346. No. 568, Sh 2-106.

1fr, Messier 16.

2013, Aug. 9 Litho. *Perf. 13¼*

567 A454 1.40fr multicolored 3.50 3.50
568 A454 1.40fr multicolored 3.50 3.50
a. Pair, #567-568 7.00 7.00

Souvenir Sheet

569 A454 1fr multicolored 2.40 2.40

No. 569 contains one 44x44mm stamp.

Works of Disabled Artists Type of 2013

Designs: 1.40fr, See the Girl with the Red Dress On, by Sargy Mann, United Kingdom. 1.90fr, Performers in China Disabled People's Performing Art Troupe, People's Republic of China.

2013, Sept. 20 Litho. *Perf. 13¼x13*

570 A456 1.40fr multicolored 3.50 3.50
571 A456 1.90fr multicolored 4.50 4.50

Endangered Species Type of 1993

Designs: No. 572, Smutsia temminckii. No. 573, Perodicticus potto. No. 574, Tarsius syrichta. No. 575, Pteropus livingstonii.

2013, Oct. 10 Litho. *Perf. 12¾x12½*

572 A271 1.40fr multicolored 3.25 3.25
573 A271 1.40fr multicolored 3.25 3.25
574 A271 1.40fr multicolored 3.25 3.25
575 A271 1.40fr multicolored 3.25 3.25
a. Block of 4, #572-575 13.00 13.00

Flags and Coins Type of 2006

No. 576 — Flag of: a, Ivory Coast, 100 franc coin. b, Marshall Islands, 10 cent coin. c, Andorra, 20 cent coin. d, Guinea-Bissau, 100 franc coin. e, Kenya, 20 shilling coin. f, Antigua and Barbuda, 5 cent coin. g, Tajikistan, 50 diram coin. h, Micronesia, 5 cent coin.

2013, Nov. 6 Litho. *Perf. 13¼x13*

576 Sheet of 8 26.00 26.00
a.-h. A375 1.40fr Any single 3.25 3.25

A column of rouletting in the middle of the sheet separates it into two parts.

SEMI-POSTAL STAMPS

AIDS Awareness Semi-postal Type

Souvenir Sheet

2002, Oct. 24 Litho. *Perf. 14½*

B1 SP1 90c + 30c multicolored 4.00 4.00

V31

1993, May 7 Photo. *Perf. 11½*
Granite Paper

149 V31 13s multicolored 2.00 2.25

Human Rights Type of 1989

Artwork: 5s, Lower Austrian Peasants' Wedding, by Ferdinand G. Waldmuller. 6s, Outback, by Sally Morgan.

1993, June 11 Litho. *Perf. 13½*

150 A250 5s multicolored .80 .90
151 A250 6s multicolored 1.00 1.10

Intl. Peace Day Type

Denomination at: No. 152, UL. No. 153, UR. No. 154, LL. No. 155, LR.

Rouletted 12½
1993, Sept. 21 Litho. & Engr.

152 A274 5.50s green & multi 1.80 2.00
153 A274 5.50s green & multi 1.80 2.00
154 A274 5.50s green & multi 1.80 2.00
155 A274 5.50s green & multi 1.80 2.00
a. Block of 4, #152-155 7.25 8.25

Environment-Climate Type

Designs: No. 156, Monkeys. No. 157, Bluebird, industrial pollution, volcano. No. 158, Volcano, nuclear power plant, tree stumps. No. 159, Cactus, tree stumps, owl.

1993, Oct. 29 Litho. *Perf. 14½*

156 A275 7s multicolored 2.00 2.25
157 A275 7s multicolored 2.00 2.25
158 A275 7s multicolored 2.00 2.25
159 A275 7s multicolored 2.00 2.25
a. Strip of 4, #156-159 8.00 9.00

Intl. Year of the Family Type of 1993

Designs: 5.50s, Adults, children holding hands. 8s, Two adults, child planting crops.

1994, Feb. 4 Litho. *Perf. 13.1*

160 A276 5.50s blue green & multi 1.00 1.10
161 A276 8s red & multi 1.25 1.40

Endangered Species Type of 1993

Designs: No. 162, Ocelot. No. 163, White-breasted silver-eye. No. 164, Mediterranean monk seal. No. 165, Asian elephant.

1994, Mar. 18 Litho. *Perf. 12.7*

162 A271 7s multicolored 1.00 1.10
163 A271 7s multicolored 1.00 1.10
164 A271 7s multicolored 1.00 1.10
165 A271 7s multicolored 1.00 1.10
a. Block of 4, #162-165 4.00 4.40

Protection for Refugees Type

Design: 12s, Protective hands surround group of refugees.

1994, Apr. 29 Litho. *Perf. 14.3x14.8*

166 A277 12s multicolored 1.50 1.75

V32

V33

V34

1994, Apr. 29 Litho. *Perf. 12.9*

167 V32 50g multicolored .25 .30
168 V33 4s multicolored .40 .45
169 V34 30s multicolored 4.00 4.50
Nos. 167-169 (3) 4.65 5.25

Intl. Decade for Natural Disaster Reduction Type

Earth seen from space, outline map of: No. 170, North America. No. 171, Eurasia. No. 172, South America. No. 173, Australia and South Asia.

1994, May 27 Litho. *Perf. 13.9x14.2*

170 A281 6s multicolored 1.75 1.90
171 A281 6s multicolored 1.75 1.90
172 A281 6s multicolored 1.75 1.90
173 A281 6s multicolored 1.75 1.90
a. Block of 4, #170-173 7.00 7.75

Population and Development Type

Designs: 5.50s, Women teaching, running machine tool, coming home to family. 7s, Family on tropical island.

1994, Sept. 1 Litho. *Perf. 13.2x13.6*

174 A282 5.50s multicolored .90 1.00
175 A282 7s multicolored 1.50 1.75

UNCTAD Type

1994, Oct. 28

176 A283 6s multi, diff. .90 1.00
177 A283 7s multi, diff. 1.50 1.75

UN 50th Anniv. Type

Litho. & Engr.
1995, Jan. 1 *Perf. 13.4*

178 A284 7s multicolored 1.25 1.40

Social Summit Type

Photo. & Engr.
1995, Feb. 3 *Perf. 13.6x13.9*

179 A285 14s multi, diff. 2.00 2.25

Endangered Species Type of 1993

Designs: No. 180, Black rhinoceros, Diceros bicornis. No. 181, Golden conure, Aratinga guarouba. No. 182, Douc langur, Pygathrix nemaeus. No. 183, Arabian oryx, Oryx leucoryx.

1995, Mar. 24 Litho. *Perf. 13x12½*

180 A271 7s multicolored 1.00 1.10
181 A271 7s multicolored 1.00 1.10
182 A271 7s multicolored 1.00 1.10
183 A271 7s multicolored 1.00 1.10
a. Block of 4, 180-183 4.00 4.50

Intl. Youth Year Type

Designs: 6s, Village in winter. 7s, Teepees.

1995, May 26 Litho. *Perf. 14.4x14.7*

184 A286 6s multicolored .80 .90
185 A286 7s multicolored 1.00 1.10

UN, 50th Anniv. Type

Designs: 7s, Like No. 663. 10s, Like No. 664.

Perf. 13.3x13.6
1995, June 26 Engr.

186 A287 7s green 1.00 1.10
187 A287 10s black 1.50 1.70

Souvenir Sheet
Litho. & Engr.
Imperf

188 Sheet of 2, #186-187 2.50 2.80
a. A287 7s green 1.00 1.10
b. A287 10s black 1.50 1.70

Conference on Women Type

Designs: 5.50s, Women amid tropical plants. 6s, Woman reading, swans on lake.

1995, Sept. 5 Photo. *Perf. 12*

189 A288 5.50s multicolored .80 .90

Size: 28x50mm

190 A288 6s multicolored 1.20 1.30

UN People, 50th Anniv. Type

1995, Oct. 24 Litho. *Perf. 14*

191 Sheet of 12 12.00 13.00
a.-l. A290 3s any single 1.00 1.10
192 Souvenir booklet 14.00
a. A290 3s Booklet pane of 3, vert. strip of 3 from UL of sheet 3.50 4.00
b. A290 3s Booklet pane of 3, vert. strip of 3 from UR of sheet 3.50 4.00
c. A290 3s Booklet pane of 3, vert. strip of 3 from LL of sheet 3.50 4.00
d. A290 3s Booklet pane of 3, vert. strip of 3 from LR of sheet 3.50 4.00

WFUNA, 50th Anniv. Type

Design: 7s, Harlequin holding dove.

1996, Feb. 2 Litho. *Perf. 13x13½*

193 A291 7s multicolored 1.00 1.10

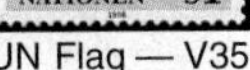

UN Flag — V35

Abstract, by Karl Korab — V36

1996, Feb. 2 Litho. *Perf. 15x14½*

194 V35 1s multicolored .25 .30
195 V36 10s multicolored 1.60 1.75

Endangered Species Type of 1993

Designs: No. 196, Cypripedium calceolus. No. 197, Aztekium ritteri. No. 198, Euphorbia cremersii. No. 199, Dracula bella.

1996, Mar. 14 Litho. *Perf. 12½*

196 A271 7s multicolored .75 .85
197 A271 7s multicolored .75 .85
198 A271 7s multicolored .75 .85
199 A271 7s multicolored .75 .85
a. Block of 4, #196-199 3.00 3.40

City Summit Type

Designs: No. 200, Arab family selling fruits, vegetables. No. 201, Women beside stream, camels. No. 202, Woman carrying bundle on head, city skyline. No. 203, Woman threshing grain, yoke of oxen in field. No. 204, Native village, elephant.

1996, June 3 Litho. *Perf. 14x13½*

200 A293 6s multicolored 1.50 1.75
201 A293 6s multicolored 1.50 1.75
202 A293 6s multicolored 1.50 1.75
203 A293 6s multicolored 1.50 1.75
204 A293 6s multicolored 1.50 1.75
a. Strip of 5, #200-204 7.50 9.00

Sport and the Environment Type

6s, Men's parallel bars (gymnastics), vert. 7s, Hurdles.

Perf. 14x14½, 14½x14
1996, July 19 Litho.

205 A294 6s multicolored .80 .90
206 A294 7s multicolored .90 1.00

Souvenir Sheet

207 A294 Sheet of 2, #205-206 1.75 1.90

Plea for Peace Type

Designs: 7s, Dove and butterflies. 10s, Stylized dove, diff.

1996, Sept. 17 Litho. *Perf. 14½x15*

208 A295 7s multicolored .80 .90
209 A295 10s multicolored 1.20 1.40

UNICEF Type

Fairy Tales: 5.50s, Hansel and Gretel, by the Brothers Grimm. 8s, How Maui Stole Fire from the Gods, South Pacific.

1996, Nov. 20 Litho. *Perf. 14½x15*

210 A296 5.50s multicolored .90 1.00
211 A296 8s multicolored 1.40 1.60

V37

Phoenixes Flying Down (Detail), by Sagenji Yoshida — V38

1997, Feb. 12 Litho. *Perf. 14½*

212 V37 5s multicolored .80 .90
213 V38 6s multicolored .90 1.00

Endangered Species Type of 1993

Designs: No. 214, Macaca sylvanus (Barbary macaque). No. 215, Anthropoides paradisea (blue crane). No. 216, Equus przewalskii (Przewalski horse). No. 217, Myrmecophaga tridactyla (giant anteater).

1997, Mar. 13 Litho. *Perf. 12½*

214 A271 7s multicolored .75 .85
215 A271 7s multicolored .75 .85
216 A271 7s multicolored .75 .85
217 A271 7s multicolored .75 .85
a. Block of 4, #214-217 3.00 3.40

Earth Summit Anniv. Type

Designs: No. 218, Person running. No. 219, Hills, stream, trees. No. 220, Tree with orange leaves. No. 221, Tree with pink leaves.

11s, Combined design similar to Nos. 218-221.

1997, May 30 Photo. *Perf. 11.5*
Granite Paper

218 A299 3.50s multicolored 1.50 1.75
219 A299 3.50s multicolored 1.50 1.75
220 A299 3.50s multicolored 1.50 1.75
221 A299 3.50s multicolored 1.50 1.75
a. Block of 4, #218-221 6.00 7.00

Souvenir Sheet

222 A299 11s multicolored 2.00 2.25

Transportation Type

Ground transportation: No. 223, 1829 Rocket, 1901 Darraque. No. 224, Steam engine from Vladikawska Railway, trolley. No. 225, Double-decker bus. No. 226, 1950s diesel locomotive, semi-trailer. No. 227, High-speed train, electric car.

1997, Aug. 29 Litho. *Perf. 14x14½*

223 A300 7s multicolored 1.25 1.40
224 A300 7s multicolored 1.25 1.40
225 A300 7s multicolored 1.25 1.40
226 A300 7s multicolored 1.25 1.40
227 A300 7s multicolored 1.25 1.40
a. Strip of 5, #223-227 6.25 7.00

No. 227a has continuous design.

Philately Type

Designs: 6.50s, No. 62. 7s, No. 63.

1997, Oct. 14 Litho. *Perf. 13½x14*

228 A301 6.50s multicolored .80 .90
229 A301 7s multicolored .90 1.00

World Heritage Convention Type

Terracotta warriors of Xian: 3s, Single warrior. 6s, Massed warriors. No. 232a, like No. 716. No. 232b, like No. 717. No. 232c, like Geneva No. 314. No. 232d, like Geneva No. 315. No. 232e, like Vienna No. 230. No. 232f, like Vienna No. 231.

1997, Nov. 19 Litho. *Perf. 13½*

230 A302 3s multicolored 1.00 1.10
231 A302 6s multicolored 2.00 2.25
232 Souvenir booklet 12.00
a.-f. A302 1s any single .50 .55
g. Booklet pane of 4 #232a 2.00 2.25
h. Booklet pane of 4 #232b 2.00 2.25
i. Booklet pane of 4 #232c 2.00 2.25
j. Booklet pane of 4 #232d 2.00 2.25
k. Booklet pane of 4 #232e 2.00 2.25
l. Booklet pane of 4 #232f 2.00 2.25

Japanese Peace Bell, Vienna — V39

Vienna Subway, Vienna Intl. Center — V40

1998, Feb. 13 Litho. *Perf. 15x14½*

233 V39 6.50s multicolored .80 .90
234 V40 9s multicolored 1.00 1.10

Endangered Species Type of 1993

Designs: No. 235, Chelonia mydas (green turtle). No. 236, Speotyto cunicularia (burrowing owl). No. 237, Trogonoptera brookiana (Rajah Brooke's birdwing). No. 238, Ailurus fulgens (lesser panda).

1998, Mar. 13 Litho. *Perf. 12½*

235 A271 7s multicolored .75 .85
236 A271 7s multicolored .75 .85
237 A271 7s multicolored .75 .85
238 A271 7s multicolored .75 .85
a. Block of 4, #235-238 3.00 3.40

Intl. Year of the Ocean — V41

1998, May 20 Litho. *Perf. 13x13½*
239 V41 Sheet of 12 11.00 12.00
a.-l. 3.50s any single .90 1.00

Rain Forests Type

1998, June 19 *Perf. 13x13½*
240 A307 6.50s Ocelot .90 1.00

Souvenir Sheet
241 A307 22s like #240 3.00 3.25

Peacekeeping Type of 1998

Designs: 4s, Soldier passing out relief supplies. 7.50s, UN supervised voting.

1998, Sept. 15 Photo. *Perf. 12*
242 A308 4s multicolored .50 .60
243 A308 7.50s multicolored 1.00 1.10

Declaration of Human Rights Type

Designs: 4.50s, Stylized person. 7s, Gears.

Litho. & Photo.
1998, Oct. 27 *Perf. 13*
244 A309 4.50s multicolored .80 .90
245 A309 7s multicolored 1.25 1.40

Schönbrunn Palace Type

Designs: 3.50s, No. 248d, Palace. 7s, No. 248c, Porcelain stove, vert. No. 248a, Blue porcelain vase, vert. No. 248b, Wall painting on fabric (detail), by Johann Wenzl Bergl, vert. No. 248e, Great Palm House (conservatory). No. 248f, The Gloriette (archway).

1998, Dec. 4 Litho. *Perf. 14*
246 A310 3.50s multicolored .60 .70
247 A310 7s multicolored 1.10 1.25

Souvenir Booklet
248 Booklet 20.00
a.-c. A310 1s any single .60 .70
d.-f. A310 2s any single 1.20 1.30
g. Booklet pane of 4 #248d 4.80 5.25
h. Booklet pane of 3 #248a 1.80 2.00
i. Booklet pane of 3 #248b 1.80 2.00
j. Booklet pane of 3 #248c 1.80 2.00
k. Booklet pane of 4 #248e 4.80 5.25
l. Booklet pane of 4 #248f 4.80 5.25

Volcanic Landscape — V42

1999, Feb. 5 Litho. *Perf. 13x13½*
249 V42 8s multicolored 1.25 1.40

World Heritage, Australia Type

Designs: 4.50s, No. 252d, Uluru-Kata Tjuta Natl. Park. 6.50s, No. 252a, Tasmanian Wilderness. No. 252b, Wet tropics of Queensland. No. 252c, Great Barrier Reef. No. 252e, Kakadu Natl. Park. No. 252f, Willandra Lakes region.

1999, Mar. 19 Litho. *Perf. 13*
250 A313 4.50s multicolored .75 .85
251 A313 6.50s multicolored 1.10 1.25

Souvenir Booklet
252 Booklet 9.00
a.-c. A313 1s any single .25 .30
d.-f. A313 2s any single .45 .50
g. Booklet pane of 4, #252a 1.00 1.10
h. Booklet pane of 4, #252d 1.80 2.00
i. Booklet pane of 4, #252b 1.00 1.10
j. Booklet pane of 4, #252e 1.80 2.00
k. Booklet pane of 4, #252c 1.00 1.10
l. Booklet pane of 4, #252f 1.80 2.00

Endangered Species Type of 1993

Designs: No. 253, Pongo pygmaeus (orangutan). No. 254, Pelecanus crispus (Dalmatian pelican). No. 255, Eunectes notaeus (yellow anaconda). No. 256, Caracal.

1999, Apr. 22 Litho. *Perf. 12½*
253 A271 7s multicolored .75 .85
254 A271 7s multicolored .75 .85
255 A271 7s multicolored .75 .85
256 A271 7s multicolored .75 .85
a. Block of 4, #253-256 3.00 3.40

UNISPACE III Type

Designs: No. 257, Satellite over ships. No. 258, Satellite up close. No. 259, Composite of Nos. 257-258.

1999, July 7 Photo. *Rouletted 8*
257 A314 3.50s multicolored .75 .85
258 A314 3.50s multicolored .75 .85
a. Pair, #257-258 1.60 1.70

Souvenir Sheet
Perf. 14½
259 A314 13s multicolored 4.50 5.00

UPU Type

Various people, late 20th century methods of mail transportation, denomination at: No. 260, UL. No. 261, UR. No. 262, LL. No. 263, LR.

1999, Aug. 23 Photo. *Perf. 11¾*
260 A315 6.50s multicolored 1.00 1.10
261 A315 6.50s multicolored 1.00 1.10
262 A315 6.50s multicolored 1.00 1.10
263 A315 6.50s multicolored 1.00 1.10
a. Block of 4, #260-263 4.00 4.50

In Memoriam Type

Designs: 6.50s, 14s, Donaupark. Size of 14s stamp: 34x63mm.

1999, Sept. 21 Litho. *Perf. 14½x14*
264 A316 6.50s multicolored .90 1.00

Souvenir Sheet
Perf. 14
265 A316 14s multicolored 3.00 3.25

Education Type

Perf. 13½x13¾
1999, Nov. 18 Litho.
266 A317 7s Boy, girl, book .75 .85
267 A317 13s Group reading 1.75 1.90

Intl. Year of Thanksgiving Type

2000, Jan. 1 Litho. *Perf. 13¼x13½*
268 A318 7s multicolored 1.00 1.10

On No. 268 parts of the design were applied by a thermographic process producing a shiny, raised effect.

Endangered Species Type of 1993

Designs: No. 269, Panthera pardus (leopard). No. 270, Platalea leucorodia (white spoonbill). No. 271, Hippocamelus bisulcus (huemal). No. 272, Orcinus orca (killer whale).

2000, Apr. 6 Litho. *Perf. 12¾x12½*
269 A271 7s multicolored 1.10 1.25
270 A271 7s multicolored 1.10 1.25
271 A271 7s multicolored 1.10 1.25
272 A271 7s multicolored 1.10 1.25
a. Block of 4, #269-272 4.50 5.00

Our World 2000 Type

Winning artwork in Millennium painting competition: 7s, Tomorrow's Dream, by Voltaire Perez, Philippines. 8s, Remembrance, by Dimitris Nalbandis, Greece, vert.

Perf. 13x13½, 13½x13
2000, May 30 Litho.
273 A319 7s multicolored .60 .70
274 A319 8s multicolored .75 .85

55th Anniversary Type

Designs: 7s, Secretariat Building, unfinished dome of General Assembly Hall, 1951. 9s, Trygve Lie and Headquraters Advisory Committee at topping-out ceremony, 1949.

2000, July 7 Litho. *Perf. 13¼x13*
275 A320 7s multicolored .90 1.00
276 A320 9s multicolored 1.25 1.40

Souvenir Sheet
277 A320 Sheet of 2, #275-276 2.75 3.25

The UN in the 21st Century — V43

No. 278: a, Farm machinery. b, UN Peacekeepers and children. c, Oriental farm workers. d, Peacekeepers searching for mines. e, Medical research. f, Handicapped people.

2000, Sept. 15 Litho. *Perf. 14*
278 V43 Sheet of 6 7.50 8.50
a.-f. 3.50s any single 1.25 1.40

World Heritage, Spain Type

Designs: Nos. 279, 281c, Aqueduct of Segovia. Nos. 280, 281f, Güell Park, Barcelona. No. 281a, Alhambra, Generalife and Albayzin, Granada. No. 281b, Walled Town of Cuenca. No. 281d, Amphitheater of Mérida. No. 281e, Toledo.

2000, Oct. 6 Litho. *Perf. 14¾x14½*
279 A323 4.50s multicolored .80 .90
280 A323 6.50s multicolored 1.20 1.40

Souvenir Booklet
281 Booklet 9.00
a.-c. A323 1s any single .25 .30
d.-f. A323 2s any single .50 .55
g. Booklet pane of 4, #281a 1.00 1.10
h. Booklet pane of 4, #281d 2.00 2.25
i. Booklet pane of 4, #281b 1.00 1.10
j. Booklet pane of 4, #281e 2.00 2.25
k. Booklet pane of 4, #281c 1.00 1.10
l. Booklet pane of 4, #281f 2.00 2.25

Respect for Refugees Type

Designs: 7s, 25s, Refugee with hat, three other refugees.

2000, Nov. 9 Litho. *Perf. 13¼x12¾*
282 A324 7s multicolored 1.10 1.25

Souvenir Sheet
283 A324 25s multicolored 3.75 4.25

Endangered Species Type of 1993

Designs: No. 284, Tremarctos ornatus (spectacled bear). No. 285, Anas laysanensis (Laysan duck). No. 286, Proteles cristatus (aardwolf). No. 287, Trachypithecus cristatus (silvered leaf monkey).

2001, Feb. 1 Litho. *Perf. 12¾x12½*
284 A271 7s multicolored 1.10 1.25
285 A271 7s multicolored 1.10 1.25
286 A271 7s multicolored 1.10 1.25
287 A271 7s multicolored 1.10 1.25
a. Block of 4, #284-287 4.50 5.00

Intl. Volunteers Year — V44

Paintings by: 10s, Nguyen Thanh Chuong, Viet Nam. 12s, Ikko Tanaka, Japan.

2001, Mar. 29 Litho. *Perf. 13¼*
288 V44 10s multicolored 1.40 1.60
289 V44 12s multicolored 1.75 1.90

World Heritage, Japan Type

Designs: 7s, No. 290c, Himeji-Jo. 15s, No. 291f, Nikko. No. 292a, Kyoto. No. 292b, Nara. No. 292d, Shirakawa-Go and Gokayama. No. 292e, Itsukushima Shinto Shrine.

2001, Aug. 1 Litho. *Perf. 12¾x13¼*
290 A328 7s multicolored 1.00 1.10
291 A328 15s multicolored 2.10 2.25

Souvenir Booklet
292 Booklet 11.50
a.-c. A328 1s any single .30 .35
d.-f. A328 2s any single .60 .70
g. Booklet pane of 4, #292a 1.20 1.40
h. Booklet pane of 4, #292d 2.40 2.75
i. Booklet pane of 4, #292b 1.20 1.40
j. Booklet pane of 4, #292e 2.40 2.75
k. Booklet pane of 4, #292c 1.20 1.40
l. Booklet pane of 4, #292f 2.40 2.75

Dag Hammarskjöld Type

2001, Sept. 18 Engr. *Perf. 11x11¼*
293 A329 7s green 1.00 1.10

UN Postal Administration, 50th Anniv. Types

2001, Oct. 18 Litho. *Perf. 13½*
294 A330 7s Stamps, balloons 1.00 1.10
295 A330 8s Stamps, cake 1.10 1.25

Souvenir Sheet
296 A331 Sheet of 2 7.50 8.00
a. 7s green & light blue, 38mm diameter 2.50 2.75
b. 21s green & light blue, 38mm diameter 5.00 5.50

Climate Change Type

Designs: No. 297, Solar panels, automobile at pump. No. 298, Blimp, bicyclists, horse and rider. No. 299, Balloon, sailboat, lighthouse, train. No. 300, Bird, train, traffic signs.

2001, Nov. 16 Litho. *Perf. 13¼*
297 A332 7s multicolored 1.00 1.10
298 A332 7s multicolored 1.00 1.10
299 A332 7s multicolored 1.00 1.10
300 A332 7s multicolored 1.00 1.10
a. Horiz. strip, #297-300 5.00 5.50

Nobel Peace Prize Type

2001, Dec. 10 Litho. *Perf. 13¼*
301 A333 7s multicolored 1.00 .55

100 Cents = 1 Euro (€)

Austrian Tourist Attractions V45

Designs: 7c, Semmering Railway. 51c, Pferdschwemme, Salzburg. 58c, Aggstein an der Donau Ruins. 73c, Hallstatt. 87c, Melk Abbey. €2.03, Kapitelschwemme, Salzburg.

2002, Mar. 1 Litho. *Perf. 14½x14*
302 V45 7c multicolored .25 .30
303 V45 51c multicolored .90 1.25
304 V45 58c multicolored 1.00 1.10
305 V45 73c multicolored 1.25 1.40
306 V45 87c multicolored 1.75 2.00
307 V45 €2.03 multicolored 3.50 3.75
Nos. 302-307 (6) 8.65 9.80

Endangered Species Type of 1993

Designs: No. 308, Hylobates syndactylus (siamang). No. 309, Spheniscus demersus (jackass penguin). No. 310, Prionodon linsang (banded linsang). No. 311, Bufo retiformis (Sonoran green toad).

2002, Apr. 4 Litho. *Perf. 12¾x12½*
308 A271 51c multicolored 1.25 1.25
309 A271 51c multicolored 1.25 1.25
310 A271 51c multicolored 1.25 1.25
311 A271 51c multicolored 1.25 1.25
a. Block of 4, #308-311 5.00 5.00

Independence of East Timor Type

Designs: 51c, Deer horn container with carved wooden stopper. €1.09, Carved wooden tai weaving loom.

2002, May 20 Litho. *Perf. 14x14½*
312 A335 51c multicolored 1.00 1.00
313 A335 €1.09 multicolored 2.25 2.25

Intl. Year of Mountains Type

Designs: No. 314, Mt. Cook, New Zealand. No. 315, Mt. Robson, Canada. No. 316, Mt. Rakaposhi, Pakistan. No. 317, Mt. Everest (Sagarmatha), Nepal.

2002, May 24 Litho. *Perf. 13x13¼*
314 A336 22c multicolored .40 .40
315 A336 22c multicolored .40 .40
316 A336 51c multicolored 1.00 1.00
317 A336 51c multicolored 1.00 1.00
a. Vert. strip or block of four, #314-317 6.50 6.50

World Summit on Sustainable Development (Peter Max) Type

Designs: No. 318, Rainbow. No. 319, Three women, diff. No. 320, Three faceless people. No. 321, Birds, wave.

2002, June 27 Litho. ***Perf. 14½x14***
318 A337 51c multicolored 1.00 1.00
319 A337 51c multicolored 1.00 1.00
320 A337 58c multicolored 1.25 1.25
321 A337 58c multicolored 1.25 1.25
a. Vert. strip or block of four, #318-321 8.50 8.50

World Heritage, Italy Type

Designs: 51c, No. 324f, Pompeii. 58c, No. 324c, Rome. No. 324a, Amalfi Coast. No. 324b, Aeolian Islands. No. 324d, Florence. No. 324e, Pisa.

Perf. 13½x13¼

2002, Aug. 30 Litho.
322 A338 51c multicolored 1.10 1.10
323 A338 58c multicolored 1.25 1.25

Souvenir Booklet

324 Booklet 15.00
a.-c. A338 7c any single .40 .40
d.-f. A338 15c any single .85 .85
g. Booklet pane of 4, #324d 3.40 3.40
h. Booklet pane of 4, #324a 1.60 1.60
i. Booklet pane of 4, #324e 3.40 3.40
j. Booklet pane of 4, #324b 1.60 1.60
k. Booklet pane of 4, #324f 3.40 3.40
l. Booklet pane of 4, #324c 1.60 1.60

AIDS Awareness Type

2002, Oct. 24 Litho. ***Perf. 13½***
325 A339 €1.53 multicolored 2.50 2.75

Indigenous Art — V46

No. 326: a, Mola, Panama. b, Mochican llama-shaped spouted vessel, Peru. c, Tarabuco woven cloth, Bolivia. d, Masks, Cuba. e, Aztec priest's feather headdress, Mexico. f, Bird-shaped staff head, Colombia.

2003, Jan. 31 Litho. ***Perf. 14¼***
326 V46 Sheet of 6 8.00 8.00
a.-f. 51c Any single 1.30 1.30

Austrian Tourist Attractions Type of 2002

Designs: 25c, Kunsthistorisches Museum, Vienna. €1, Belvedere Palace, Vienna.

2003, Mar. 28 Litho. ***Perf. 14½x14***
327 V45 25c multicolored .55 .55
328 V45 €1 multicolored 2.25 2.25

Endangered Species Type of 1993

Designs: No. 329, Anas formosa (Baikal teal). No. 330, Bostrychia hagedash (Hadada ibis). No. 331, Ramphastos toco (toco toucan). No. 332, Alopochen aegyptiacus (Egyptian goose).

2003, Apr. 3 Litho. ***Perf. 12¾x12½***
329 A271 51c multicolored 1.25 1.25
330 A271 51c multicolored 1.25 1.25
331 A271 51c multicolored 1.25 1.25
332 A271 51c multicolored 1.25 1.25
a. Block of 4, #329-332 5.00 5.00

International Year of Freshwater Type of 2003

Perf. 14¼x14½

2003, June 20 Litho.
333 A345 55c Bridge, bird 3.00 3.00
334 A345 75c Horse, empty river 5.00 5.00
a. Horiz. pair, #333-334 8.00 8.00

Austrian Tourist Attractions Type of 2002

Design: 4c, Schloss Eggenberg, Graz.

2003, Aug. 7 Litho. ***Perf. 14x13¼***
335 V45 4c multicolored .45 .45

Ralph Bunche Type

Litho. With Foil Application

2003, Aug. 7 ***Perf. 13½x14***
336 A346 €2.10 olive green & multicolored 3.50 3.50

In Memoriam Type of 2003

2003, Oct. 24 Litho. ***Perf. 13¼x13***
337 A347 €2.10 multicolored 5.00 5.00

World Heritage Sites, United States Type

Designs: 55c, No. 340c, Olympic National Park. 75c, No. 340e, Everglades National Park. No. 340a, Yosemite National Park. No. 340b, Great Smoky Mountains National Park. No. 340d, Hawaii Volcanoes National Park. No. 340f, Yellowstone National Park.

2003, Oct. 24 Litho. ***Perf. 14½x14¼***
338 A348 55c multicolored 1.50 .75
339 A348 75c multicolored 2.00 1.00

Souvenir Booklet

340 Booklet 12.00
a.-c. A348 15c any single .45 .45
d.-f. A348 20c any single .55 .55
g. Booklet pane of 4 #340a 1.80 1.80
h. Booklet pane of 4 #340d 2.20 2.20
i. Booklet pane of 4 #340b 1.80 1.80
j. Booklet pane of 4 #340e 2.20 2.20
k. Booklet pane of 4 #340c 1.80 1.80
l. Booklet pane of 4 #340f 2.20 2.20

Austrian Tourist Attractions Type of 2002

Design: 55c, Schloss Schönbrunn, Vienna.

2004, Jan. 29 Litho. ***Perf. 13x13¼***
341 V45 55c multicolored 1.50 1.50

Endangered Species Type of 1993

Designs: No. 342, Melursus ursinus (Sloth bear). No. 343, Cervus eldi (Eld's deer). No. 344, Cercocebus torquatus (Cherry-crowned mangabey). No. 345, Bubalus arnee (Wild water buffalo).

2004, Jan. 29 Litho. ***Perf. 12¾x12½***
342 A271 55c multicolored 1.50 1.50
343 A271 55c multicolored 1.50 1.50
344 A271 55c multicolored 1.50 1.50
345 A271 55c multicolored 1.50 1.50
a. Block of 4, #342-345 6.00 6.00

Indigenous Art Type of 2003

No. 346: a, Illuminated illustration from the Book of Kells, Ireland. b, Easter eggs, Ukraine. c, Venus of Willendorf, Paleolithic age limestone statue, Austria. d, Flatatunga panel, Iceland. e, Neolithic era idol, Hungary. f, Illuminated illustration from medical treatise, Portugal.

2004, Mar. 4 Litho. ***Perf. 13¼***
346 V46 Sheet of 6 10.50 10.50
a.-f. 55c Any single 1.75 1.75

Road Safety Type

Road map art with: 55c, Automobile, alcohol bottles. 75c, Road, clouds in traffic light colors, vert.

Perf. 13x13¼, 13¼x13

2004, Apr. 7 Litho.
347 A354 55c multicolored 1.25 1.25
348 A354 75c multicolored 1.75 1.75

Japanese Peace Bell, 50th Anniv. Type

Litho. & Engr.

2004, June 3 ***Perf. 13¼x13***
349 A355 €2.10 multicolored 4.50 4.50

World Heritage Sites, Greece Type

Designs: 55c, No. 352f, Mycenae and Tiryns. 75c, No. 352e, Olympia. No. 352a, Acropolis, Athens. No. 352b, Delos. No. 352c, Delphi. No. 352d, Pythagoreion and Heraion of Samos.

2004, Aug. 12 Litho. ***Perf. 14x13¼***
350 A356 55c multicolored 1.75 1.75
351 A356 75c multicolored 2.25 2.25

Souvenir Booklet

352 Booklet 16.00
a.-d. A356 25c any single .60 .60
e.-f. A356 30c either single .70 .70
g. Booklet pane of 4 #352a 2.40 2.40
h. Booklet pane of 4 #352b 2.40 2.40
i. Booklet pane of 4 #352c 2.40 2.40
j. Booklet pane of 4 #352d 2.40 2.40
k. Booklet pane of 4 #352e 2.80 2.80
l. Booklet pane of 4 #352f 2.80 2.80

My Dream for Peace Type

Winning designs of Lions Club International children's global peace poster contest by: 55c, Henry Ulfe Renteria, Peru. €1, Michelle Fortaliza, Philippines.

2004, Sept. 21 Litho. ***Perf. 14***
353 A357 55c multicolored 1.40 1.40
354 A357 €1 multicolored 2.50 2.50

V47

Human Rights — V48

2004, Oct. 14 Litho. ***Perf. 11¼***
355 V47 55c multicolored 1.00 1.00
356 V48 €1.25 multicolored 3.00 3.00

United Nations, 60th Anniv. Type of 2005

Litho. & Engr.

2005, Feb. 4 ***Perf. 11x11¼***
357 A361 55c multicolored 2.50 2.50

Souvenir Sheet

Litho.

Imperf

358 A361 €2.10 multicolored 6.50 6.50

International Center, Vienna — V49

Litho. with Hologram

2005, Feb. 4 ***Perf. 13½x13¼***
359 V49 75c multicolored 2.25 2.25

Endangered Species Type of 1993

Designs: No. 360, Ansellia africana. No. 361, Phragmipedium kovachii. No. 362, Cymbidium ensifolium. No. 363, Renanthera imschootiana.

2005, Mar. 3 Litho. ***Perf. 12¾x12½***
360 A271 55c multicolored 1.40 1.40
361 A271 55c multicolored 1.40 1.40
362 A271 55c multicolored 1.40 1.40
363 A271 55c multicolored 1.40 1.40
a. Block of 4, #360-363 6.00 6.00

Nature's Wisdom — V50

Designs: 55c, Desert landscape, China. 80c, Cheetah family, Africa.

2005, Apr. 21 Litho. ***Perf. 13½x13¼***
364 V50 55c multicolored 1.60 1.60
365 V50 75c multicolored 2.25 2.25

Intl. Year of Sport Type

2005, June 3 Litho. ***Perf. 13x13¼***
366 A368 55c Equestrian 1.60 1.60
367 A368 €1.10 Soccer 3.25 3.25

World Heritage Sites, Egypt Type

Designs: Nos. 368, 370c, Abu Mena. Nos. 369, 370f, St. Catherine area. No. 370a, Memphis and its Necropolis. No. 370b, Philae. No. 370d, Ancient Thebes. No. 370e, Islamic Cairo.

2005, Aug. 4 Litho. ***Perf. 14x13¼***
368 A369 55c multicolored 1.60 1.60
369 A369 75c multicolored 2.25 2.25

Souvenir Booklet

370 Booklet, #370g-370l 19.50
a.-c. A369 25c any single .75 .75
d.-f. A369 30c any single .85 .85
g. Booklet pane of 4 #370a 3.00 3.00
h. Booklet pane of 4 #370b 3.00 3.00
i. Booklet pane of 4 #370c 3.00 3.00
j. Booklet pane of 4 #370d 3.50 3.50
k. Booklet pane of 4 #370e 3.50 3.50
l. Booklet pane of 4 #370f 3.50 3.50

No. 370 sold for €6.80.

My Dream for Peace Type

Winning designs of Lions Club International children's global peace poster contest by: 55c, Lee Min Gi, Republic of Korea. €1, Natalie Chan, US.

2004, Sept. 21 Litho. ***Perf. 14***
371 A357 55c multicolored 1.60 1.60
372 A357 €1 multicolored 2.75 2.75

Food for Life Type

Designs: 55c, Corn, people with food bowls, teacher and students. €1.25, Rice, helicopter dropping food, elephant caravan.

2005, Oct. 20 Litho. ***Perf. 13¾***
373 A370 55c multicolored 1.60 1.60
374 A370 €1.25 multicolored 3.50 3.50

Indigenous Art Type of 2003

No. 375 — Musical instruments: a, Drum, Guinea. b, Whistle, Congo. c, Horn, Botswana. d, Drums, Burundi. e, Harp, Gabon. f, Bell, Nigeria.

2006, Feb. 3 Litho. ***Perf. 13¼***
375 V46 Sheet of 6 10.00 10.00
a.-f. 55c Any single 1.60 1.60

Endangered Species Type of 1993

Designs: No. 376, Dendrobates pumilio. No. 377, Furcifer lateralis. No. 378, Corallus hortulanus. No. 379, Dendrobates leucomelas.

Perf. 12¾x12½

2006, Mar. 16 Litho.
376 A271 55c multicolored 1.50 1.50
377 A271 55c multicolored 1.50 1.50
378 A271 55c multicolored 1.50 1.50
379 A271 55c multicolored 1.50 1.50
a. Block of 4, #376-379 6.00 6.00

Intl. Day of Families Type

Designs: 55c, Family at water pump. €1.25, Family preparing food.

2006, May 27 Litho. ***Perf. 14x13½***
380 A373 55c multicolored 1.25 1.25
381 A373 €1.25 multicolored 2.50 2.50

World Heritage Sites, France Type

Eiffel Tower and: Nos. 382, 384c, Carcasonne. Nos. 383, 384f, Chateau de Chambord. No. 384a, Banks of the Seine. No. 384b, Provins. No. 384d, Roman Aqueduct. No. 384e, Mont Saint-Michel.

Litho. & Embossed with Foil Application

2006, June 17 ***Perf. 13½x13¼***
382 A374 55c multicolored 1.50 1.50
383 A374 75c multicolored 2.00 2.00

Souvenir Booklet

384 Booklet, #384g-384l 18.00
a.-c. A374 25c any single .65 .65
d.-f. A374 30c any single .80 .80
g. Booklet pane of 4 #384a 2.60 2.60
h. Booklet pane of 4 #384b 2.60 2.60
i. Booklet pane of 4 #384c 2.60 2.60
j. Booklet pane of 4 #384d 3.25 3.25
k. Booklet pane of 4 #384e 3.25 3.25
l. Booklet pane of 4 #384f 3.25 3.25

No. 384 sold for €6.80.

My Dream for Peace Type of 2004

Winning designs of Lions Club International children's global peace poster contest by: 55c, Klara Thein, Germany. €1, Laurensia Levina, Indonesia.

2006, Sept. 21 Litho. *Perf. 13½x13*
385 A357 55c multicolored 1.60 1.60
386 A357 €1 multicolored 3.00 3.00

Flags and Coins Type

No. 387 — Flag of: a, Gambia, 1 dalasi coin. b, Pakistan, 1 rupee coin. c, Afghanistan, 2 afghani coin. d, Austria, 1 euro coin. e, Germany, 50 cent coin. f, Haiti, 50 centimes coin. g, Denmark, 20 krone coin. h, Netherlands, 1 euro coin.

2006, Oct. 5 Litho. *Perf. 13¼x13*
387 Sheet of 8 14.00 14.00
a.-h. A375 55c Any single 1.75 1.75

A column of rouletting in the middle of the sheet separates it into two parts.

Endangered Species Type of 1993

Designs: No. 388, Chlorocebus aethiops. No. 389, Nasalis larvatus. No. 390, Papio hamadryas. No. 391, Erythrocebus patas.

Perf. 12¾x12½
2007, Mar. 15 Litho.
388 A271 55c multicolored 1.60 1.60
389 A271 55c multicolored 1.60 1.60
390 A271 55c multicolored 1.60 1.60
391 A271 55c multicolored 1.60 1.60
a. Block of 4, #388-391 6.40 6.40

Flags and Coins Type of 2006

No. 392 — Flag of: a, Trinidad and Tobago, 50 cent coin. b, Sierra Leone, 10 cent coin. c, Hungary, 100 forint coin. d, San Marino, 2 euro coin. e, Croatia, 1 kuna coin. f, Spain, 1 euro coin. g, Kazakhstan, 100 tenge coin. h, Ireland, 5 cent coin.

2007, May 3 Litho. *Perf. 13¼x13*
392 Sheet of 8 13.00 13.00
a.-h. A375 55c Any single 1.60 1.60

A column of rouletting in the middle of the sheet separates it into two parts.

Five 55c stamps depicting views of the Vienna International Center and the United Nations flag were released May 3, 2007. The editors have reason to believe that these stamps were not sold at the UN Post Office in Vienna. Value, strip of 5 with labels $40, sheet of 10 $80.

Peaceful Visions Type of 2007

Designs: 55c, "The Sowers." €1.25, "We All Thrive Under the Same Sky."

2007, June 1 Litho. *Perf. 13x12½*
398 A378 55c multicolored 1.60 1.60
399 A378 €1.25 multicolored 3.75 3.75

World Heritage Sites, South America Type

Designs: Nos. 400, 402e, Iguaçu National Park, Brazil. Nos. 401, 402b, Cueva de las Manos, Argentina. No. 402a, Rapa Nui, Chile. No. 402c, Machu Picchu, Peru. No. 402d, Tiwanaku, Bolivia. No. 474f, Galapagos Islands, Ecuador.

2007, Aug. 9 Litho. *Perf. 13¼x13*
400 A381 55c multicolored 2.00 2.00
401 A381 75c multicolored 2.75 2.75

Souvenir Booklet

402 Booklet, #402g-402l 20.00
a.-c. A381 25c Any single .75 .75
d.-f. A381 30c Any single .90 .90
g. Booklet pane of 4 #402a 3.00 3.00
h. Booklet pane of 4 #402b 3.00 3.00
i. Booklet pane of 4 #402c 3.00 3.00
j. Booklet pane of 4 #402d 3.60 3.60
k. Booklet pane of 4 #402e 3.60 3.60
l. Booklet pane of 4 #402f 3.60 3.60

Humanitarian Mail Type

2007, Sept. 6 Litho. *Perf. 12½x13¼*
403 A382 75c multicolored 2.25 2.25

Five 65c stamps depicting the International Space Station, astronauts and planets were released Oct. 1, 2007. The editors have reason to believe that these stamps were not sold at the UN Post Office in Vienna. Value, strip of 5 with labels $45, sheet of 10 $90.

Space for Humanity Type

Designs: 65c, Space stations. €1.15, Space Station.
€2.10, Space probe, Jupiter.

2007, Oct. 25 Litho. *Perf. 13½x14*
409 A383 65c multicolored 2.00 2.00
410 A383 €1.15 multicolored 3.50 3.50

Souvenir Sheet

411 A383 €2.10 multicolored 8.00 8.00

Intl. Holocaust Remembrance Day Type

2008, Jan. 27 Litho. *Perf. 13*
412 A384 65c multicolored 3.00 3.00

Johann Strauss Memorial, Vienna — V61

Pallas Athene Fountain, Vienna V62

Pegasus Fountain, Salzburg V63

Statue, Belvedere Palace Gardens, Vienna V64

2008, Jan. 28 Litho. *Perf. 13½x14*
413 V61 10c black .35 .35

Perf. 14x13½
414 V62 15c black .50 .50
415 V63 65c black 2.25 2.25
416 V64 €1.40 black 4.75 4.75
Nos. 413-416 (4) 7.85 7.85

Endangered Species Type of 1993

Designs: No. 4170, Mirounga angustirostris. No. 418, Millepora alcicornis. No. 419, Hippocampus histrix. No. 420, Physeter catodon.

2008, Mar. 6 Litho. *Perf. 12¾x12½*
417 A271 65c multicolored 2.50 2.50
418 A271 65c multicolored 2.50 2.50
419 A271 65c multicolored 2.50 2.50
420 A271 65c multicolored 2.50 2.50
a. Block of 4, #417-420 10.00 10.00

Flags and Coins Type of 2006

No. 421 — Flag of: a, Poland, 5 zloty coin. b, Latvia, 1 lat coin. c, Portugal, 1 euro coin. d, Armenia, 500 dram coin. e, Sweden, 1 krona coin. f, Cyprus, 1 euro coin. g, Slovakia, 1 koruna coin. h, Qatar, 50 dirham coin.

2008, May 8 Litho. *Perf. 13¼x13*
421 Sheet of 8 18.00 18.00
a.-h. A375 65c Any single 2.25 2.25

A column of rouletting in the middle of the sheet separates it into two parts.

Five 65c stamps depicting the Vienna International Center and its artwork were released May 12, 2008. The editors have reason to believe that these stamps were not sold at the UN Post Office in Vienna. Value, strip of 5 with labels $30, sheet of 10 $60.

Graduate — V70

Stylized Person, Heart, Brain, Hands — V71

Litho. & Embossed

2008, June 6 *Perf. 14x13¼*
427 V70 55c green & violet 2.00 2.00
428 V71 €1.40 violet & green 5.00 5.00

Convention on the Rights of Persons with Disabilities.

Sport for Peace Type of 2008

Designs: 65c, Man on rings. €1.30, €2.10, Swimmer.

2008, Aug. 8 Litho. *Perf. 14½*
429 A393 65c multicolored 2.25 2.25
430 A393 €1.30 multicolored 4.50 4.50

Souvenir Sheet

Perf. 12¾x13¼
431 A393 €2.10 multicolored 9.00 9.00
a. Overprinted in sheet margin 10.00 10.00

2008 Summer Olympics, Beijing. No. 431a is overprinted in black "Peking 2008" and medals with UN emblem.

"We Can End Poverty" Type of 2008

Winning designs in children's art contest: 65c, By Mariam Marukian, Armenia. 75c, By Rufaro Duri, Zimbabwe, vert.

Perf. 12¾x12½
2008, Sept. 18 Litho.
432 A395 65c multicolored 2.25 2.25

Perf. 12½x12¾
433 A395 75c multicolored 2.60 2.60

Five €1.40 stamps depicting views of the Vienna International Center and its artwork were released Sept. 18, 2008. The editors have reason to believe that these stamps were not sold at the UN Post Office in Vienna. Value, strip of 5 with labels $40, sheet of 10 $80.

Climate Change Types of New York and Geneva and

V72

Climate Change — V73

No. 434 — Smokestacks with quarter of Earth in: a, LR. b, LL. c, UR. d, UL.
No. 435 — Cut trees with quarter of Earth in: a, LR. b, LL. c, UR. d, UL.
No. 436: a, Like New York #969a. b, Like New York #969b. c, Like New York #969c. d, Like New York #969d. e, Like Geneva #493a. f, Like Geneva #493b. g, Like Geneva #493c. h, Like Geneva #493d. i, Like Vienna #434a. j, Like Vienna #434b. k, Like Vienna #434c. l, Like Vienna #434d. m, Like New York #968a. n, Like New York #968b, o, Like New York #968c, p, Like New York #968d. q, Like Geneva #492a. r, Like Geneva #492b. s, Like Geneva #492c. t, Like Geneva #492d. u, Like Vienna #435a. v, Like Vienna #435b. w, Like Vienna #435c. x, Like Vienna #435d.
All stamps have green panels inscribed "Klimawandel."

2008, Oct. 23 Litho. *Perf. 13¼x13*
434 Sheet of 4 9.00 9.00
a.-d. V72 65c Any single 2.25 2.25
435 Sheet of 4 16.00 16.00
a.-d. V73 €1.15 Any single 4.00 4.00

Souvenir Booklet

436 Booklet, #436y-436ad 27.00
a.-d. A397 30c Any single 1.00 1.00
e.-h. G77 30c Any single 1.00 1.00
i.-l. V72 30c Any single 1.00 1.00
m.-p. A396 35c Any single 1.10 1.10
q.-t. G76 35c Any single 1.10 1.10
u.-x. V73 35c Any single 1.10 1.10
y. Booklet pane of 4, #436a-436d 4.25 4.25
z. Booklet pane of 4, #436e-436h 4.25 4.25
aa. Booklet pane of 4, #436i-436l 4.25 4.25
ab. Booklet pane of 4, #436m-436p 4.75 4.75
ac. Booklet pane of 4, #436q-436t 4.75 4.75
ad. Booklet pane of 4, #436u-436x 4.75 4.75

U Thant Type of 2009

Litho. With Foil Application

2009, Feb. 6 *Perf. 14x13½*
437 A399 €1.15 green & multi 4.50 4.50

Endangered Species Type of 1993

Designs: No. 438, Trogonoptera brookiana. No. 439, Pandinus imperator. No. 440, Carabus intricatus. No. 441, Brachypelma smithi.

2009, Apr. 16 Litho. *Perf. 12¾x12½*
438 A271 65c multicolored 2.00 2.00
439 A271 65c multicolored 2.00 2.00
440 A271 65c multicolored 2.00 2.00
441 A271 65c multicolored 2.00 2.00
a. Block of 4, #438-441 8.00 8.00

World Heritage Sites, Germany Type of 2009

Designs: Nos. 442, 444c, Palaces and Parks of Potsdam and Berlin. Nos. 443, 444e, Luther Memorials in Eisleben and Wittenberg. No. 444a, Town Hall and Roland on the Marketplace, Bremen. No. 444b, Wartburg Castle. No. 444d, Aachen Cathedral. No. 444f, Monastic Island of Reichenau.

2009, May 7 Litho. *Perf. 14x13½*
442 A400 65c multicolored 1.90 1.90
443 A400 €1.40 multicolored 4.00 4.00

Souvenir Booklet

444 Booklet, #444g-444l 22.50
a.-c. A400 30c any single .85 .85
d.-f. A400 35c any single 1.00 1.00
g. Booklet pane of 4 #444a 3.50 3.50
h. Booklet pane of 4 #444b 3.50 3.50
i. Booklet pane of 4 #444c 3.50 3.50
j. Booklet pane of 4 #444d 4.00 4.00
k. Booklet pane of 4 #444e 4.00 4.00
l. Booklet pane of 4 #444f 4.00 4.00

Memorial Plaza, Vienna International Center — V74

The First Swallows, Sculpture by Juozas Mikenas — V75

Conference Building, Vienna International Center — V76

Butterfly Tree, by Rudolf Hausner — V77

Flags in Memorial Plaza — V78

2009, May 7 ***Perf. 13¼***

445	V74 65c multicolored + label	5.00	5.00
a.	Perf. 11¼x11	10.00	10.00
446	V75 65c multicolored + label	5.00	5.00
a.	Perf. 11¼x11	10.00	10.00
447	V76 65c multicolored + label	5.00	5.00
a.	Perf. 11¼x11	10.00	10.00
448	V77 65c multicolored + label	5.00	5.00
a.	Perf. 11¼x11	10.00	10.00
449	V78 65c multicolored + label	5.00	5.00
a.	Perf. 11¼x11	10.00	10.00
b.	Vert. strip of 5, #445-449, + 5 labels	25.00	25.00
c.	Vert. strip of 5, #445a-449a, + 5 labels	50.00	50.00

The sheet of No. 449c has "ver. 2" in the lower right selvage.

Economic and Social Council (ECOSOC) Type of 2009

Designs: 55c, Combat HIV/AIDS, malaria and other diseases. 65c, Reduce child mortality.

2009, Aug. 6 Litho. ***Perf. 12¾x12½***

450	A411 55c multicolored	2.25	2.25
451	A411 65c multicolored	3.50	3.50

V79

V80

V81

V82

Vienna International Center, 30th Anniv. — V83

2009, Aug. 24 ***Perf. 13¼***

452	V79 €1.40 multicolored + label	6.00	6.00
a.	Perf. 11¼x11	20.00	20.00
453	V80 €1.40 multicolored + label	6.00	6.00
a.	Perf. 11¼x11	20.00	20.00
454	V81 €1.40 multicolored + label	6.00	6.00
a.	Perf. 11¼x11	20.00	20.00
455	V82 €1.40 multicolored + label	6.00	6.00
a.	Perf. 11¼x11	20.00	20.00
456	V83 €1.40 multicolored + label	6.00	6.00
a.	Perf. 11¼x11	20.00	20.00
b.	Vert. strip of 5, #452-456, + 5 labels	30.00	30.00
c.	Vert. strip of 5, #452a-456a, + 5 labels	100.00	100.00

The sheet of No. 456c has "ver. 2" in the lower right selvage.

Millennium Development Goals Type of 2009

Miniature Sheet

No. 457: a, Bowl of hot food. b, Pencil. c, Female symbol. d, Teddy bear. e, Pregnant woman, heart. f, Medicine bottle. g, Stylized tree. h, Conjoined people.

2009, Sept. 25

457	A413	Sheet of 8	16.00	16.00
a.-h.		65c Any single	2.00	2.00

Miniature Sheet

Indigenous People — V84

No. 458 — Portraits of person from: a, Tanzania. b, Australia. c, Namibia (small child). d, Indonesia. e, Namibia (young girl). f, Untied Arab Emirates.

2009, Oct. 8 ***Perf. 12½***

458	V84	Sheet of 6	12.00	12.00
a.-f.		65c Any single	2.00	2.00

Flags and Coins Type of 2006

No. 459 — Flag of: a, Romania, 1 ban coin. b, Slovenia, 5 cent coin. c, Azerbaijan, 10 giapik coin. d, Bangladesh, 5 taka coin. e, Belarus, 1 ruble coin. f, Malta, 1 euro coin. g, Swaziland, 1 lilangeni coin. h, Jordan, 10 piaster coin.

2010, Feb. 5 Litho. ***Perf. 13¼x13***

459	Sheet of 8	17.50	17.50
a.-h.	A375 65c Any single	2.10	2.10

A column of rouletting in the middle of the sheet separates it into two parts.

People Pulling Rope — V85

Person With Hands Over Eyes — V86

Woman Touching Her Shoulder — V87

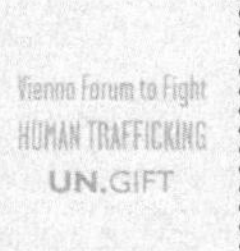

Man With Wheelbarrow — V88

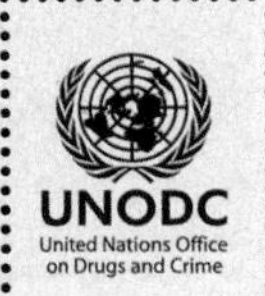

Blue Heart — V89

Designed by Rorie Katz, US.

2010, Feb. 5 Litho. ***Perf. 11¼x11***

460	V85 65c multicolored + label	4.50	4.50
461	V86 65c multicolored + label	4.50	4.50
462	V87 65c multicolored + label	4.50	4.50
463	V88 65c multicolored + label	4.50	4.50
464	V89 65c multicolored + label	4.50	4.50
a.	Vert. strip of 5, #460-464, + 5 labels	22.50	22.50

The full sheet sold for $14.95 or €19.90. The labels could not be personalized.

Endangered Species Type of 1993

Designs: No. 465, Mammillaria zeilmanniana. No. 466, Hoodia gordonii. No. 467, Welwitschia mirabilis. No. 468, Euphorbia milii.

2010, Apr. 15 Litho. ***Perf. 12¾x12½***

465	A271 65c multicolored	2.25	2.25
466	A271 65c multicolored	2.25	2.25
467	A271 65c multicolored	2.25	2.25
468	A271 65c multicolored	2.25	2.25
a.	Block of 4, #465-468	9.00	9.00

Intl. Year of Biodiversity V90

Drawings from Art Forms from Nature, by Ernst Heinrich: 5c, Colonial algae. 20c, Boxfish.

2010, Apr. 15 Litho. ***Perf. 13***

469	V90 5c multicolored	.25	.25
470	V90 20c multicolored	.70	.70

One Planet, One Ocean Types of New York and Geneva and

V91

V92

No. 471: a, Dolphin at left, fish at right. b, Fish at top, shark in center. c, Dolphin at left, fish at right and bottom. d, Fish at left, top and right.

No. 472: a, Dolphins. b, Shark and fish at center, ray at bottom. c, Fish at left, turtle at bottom. d, Fish and coral.

No. 473: a, Like New York #1003a. b, Like New York #1003b, c, Like New York #1003c, d, Like New York #1003d. e, Like #471a. f, Like #471b. g, Like #471c, h, Like #471d. i, Like Geneva #519a. j, Like Geneva #519b, k, Like Geneva #519c. l, Like Geneva #519d. m, Like New York #1004a. n, Like New York #1004b. o, Like New York #1004c, p, Like New York #1004d. q, Like #472a. r, Like #472b. s, Like #472c. t, Like #472d. u, Like Geneva #520a. v, Like Geneva #520b. w, Like Geneva #520c. x, Like Geneva #520d.

2010, May 6 Litho. ***Perf. 14x13¼***

471	V91	Sheet of 4	7.75	7.75
a.-d.		55c Any single	1.90	1.90
472	V92	Sheet of 4	9.00	9.00
a.-d.		65c Any single	2.25	2.25

Souvenir Booklet

Perf. 13¼x13

473	Booklet, #473y-473z, 473aa-473ad	27.00	
a.-d.	A416 30c any single	1.00	1.00
e.-h.	V91 30c any single	1.00	1.00
i.-l.	G85 30c any single	1.00	1.00
m.-p.	A417 35c any single	1.25	1.25
q.-t.	V92 35c any single	1.25	1.25
u.-x.	G86 35c any single	1.25	1.25
y.	Booklet pane of 4 #473a-473d	4.00	4.00
z.	Booklet pane of 4 #473e-473h	4.00	4.00
aa.	Booklet pane of 4 #473i-473l	4.00	4.00
ab.	Booklet pane of 4 #473m-473p	5.00	5.00
ac.	Booklet pane of 4 #473q-473t	5.00	5.00
ad.	Booklet pane of 4 #473u-473x	5.00	5.00

Intl. Oceanographic Commission, 50th anniv.

United Nations, 65th Anniv. Type of 2010

Litho. With Foil Application

2010, June 28 ***Perf. 13¼***

474	A422 75c green & gold	3.00	3.00
a.	Souvenir sheet of 2	6.00	6.00

V93

V94

V95

V96

V97

2010, Sept. 2 Litho. *Perf. 13¼x13*

475	V93	65c multicolored	1.90	1.90
476	V94	65c multicolored	1.90	1.90
477	V95	65c multicolored	1.90	1.90
478	V96	65c multicolored	1.90	1.90
479	V97	65c multicolored	1.90	1.90
a.		Horiz. strip of 5, #475-479	9.50	9.50

Miniature Sheet

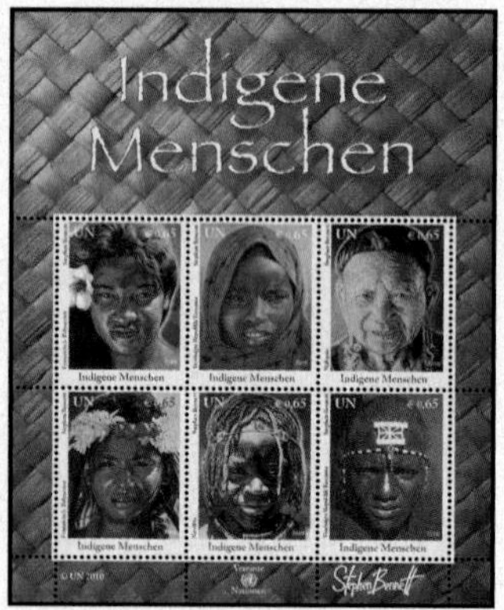

Indigenous People — V98

No. 480 — Portraits of person from: a, French Polynesia (denomination in white). b, Tanzania (child with cloth head covering). c, Malaysia. d, French Polynesia (denomination in white and green). e, Namibia. f, Tanzania (man with band around forehead).

2010, Oct. 21 Litho. *Perf. 13*

480	V98	Pane of 6	11.50	11.50
a.-f.		65c Any single	1.90	1.90

United Nations Headquarters, Vienna — V99

United Nations Headquarters, Geneva: €1.25, Aerial view. €2.85, Ground-level view.

2011, Feb. 4 Litho. *Perf. 13*

481	V99	€1.25 multicolored	3.75	3.75
482	V99	€2.85 multicolored	8.25	8.25

Flags and Coins Type of 2006

No. 483 — Flag of: a, Lithuania, 2 lita coin. b, Greece, 1 euro coin. c, Kyrgyzstan, 50 tyiyn coin. d, Oman, 100 baisa coin. e, Estonia, 2 euro coin. f, Czech Republic, 5 koruna coin. g, Uzbekistan, 100 som coin. h, Monaco, 1 euro coin.

2011, Mar. 3 Litho. *Perf. 13¼x13*

483		Sheet of 8	15.00	15.00
a.-h.	A375	65c Any single	1.75	1.75

A column of rouletting in the middle of the sheet separates it into two parts.

Human Space Flight, 50th Anniv. — V100

No. 484: Various parts of outer space scene.

No. 485, vert.: a, Space Shuttle. b, Space Station.

2011, Apr. 12 Litho. *Perf. 13x13¼*

484	V100	Sheet of 16	16.50	16.50
a.-p.		35c any single	1.00	1.00

Souvenir Sheet

485	V100	Sheet of 2	5.00	5.00
a.		55c multi	2.25	2.25
b.		65c multi	2.75	2.75
c.		Souvenir sheet of 6, New York #1024a-1024b, Geneva #534a-b, Vienna #485a-485b	11.00	11.00

No. 485 contains two 40x48mm stamps that were printed as part of a larger sheet of six stamps, No. 485c, which was broken up into its component two-stamp souvenir sheets, and also sold as one unit.

Vienna International Center and Flagpoles — V101

Fish-eye View of Vienna International Center and Flagpole — V102

Vienna International Center and Train — V103

Aerial View of Vienna International Center — V104

Vienna International Center and Water — V105

Detail From La Pioggia, Stadt Unter de Regen, by Friedensreich Hundertwasser — V106

Hand in Hand, by Hans Dietrich — V107

The Scholars Pavilion — V108

Detail From Grupo Expectante, by Alfredo Sosabravo — V109

Yes to Life, No to Drugs, by Sami Burhan — V110

2011, May 1 Litho. *Perf. 14¾*

486	V101	62c multi + label	*2.50*	*2.50*
487	V102	62c multi + label	*2.50*	*2.50*
488	V103	62c multi + label	*2.50*	*2.50*
489	V104	62c multi + label	*2.50*	*2.50*
490	V105	62c multi + label	*2.50*	*2.50*
a.		Vert. strip of 5, #486-490, + 5 labels	*15.00*	*15.00*
491	V106	70c multi + label	*3.00*	*3.00*
492	V107	70c multi + label	*3.00*	*3.00*
493	V108	70c multi + label	*3.00*	*3.00*
494	V109	70c multi + label	*3.00*	*3.00*
495	V110	70c multi + label	*3.00*	*3.00*
a.		Vert. strip of 5, #491-495, + 5 labels	*17.50*	*17.50*
		Nos. 486-495 (10)	*25.50*	*25.50*

The full sheet of Nos. 486-490 sold for $21.45 or €12.40. The full sheet of Nos. 491-495 sold for $14.26 or €9.90. The labels could be personalized.

UNESCO World Heritage Sites in Nordic Countries Type of 2011

Designs: 62c, Urnes Stave Church, Norway. 1fr, Struve Geodetic Arc, Norway, Finland and Sweden.

2011, May 5 Litho. *Perf. 14x13½*

496	A433	62c multicolored	1.90	1.90
497	A433	70c multicolored	2.10	2.10

AIDS Ribbon Type of 2011

2011, June 3 Litho. *Die Cut*

Self-Adhesive

498	A434	70c red & green	2.40	2.40

ECOSOC Type of 2011

2011, July 1 Litho. *Perf. 14¼*

499	A435	62c multicolored	3.00	3.00
500	A435	70c multicolored	4.00	4.00

Endangered Species Type of 1993

Designs: No. 501, Cyanoramphus novaezelandiae (Red-fronted parakeet). No. 502, Haliaeetus albicilla (White-tailed eagle). No. 503, Probosciger aterrimus (Black palm cockatoo). No. 504, Caloenas nicobarica (Nicobar pigeon).

2011, Sept. 7 Litho. *Perf. 12¾x12½*

501	A271	70c multicolored	2.50	2.50
502	A271	70c multicolored	2.50	2.50
503	A271	70c multicolored	2.50	2.50
504	A271	70c multicolored	2.50	2.50
a.		Block of 4, #501-504	10.00	10.00

Intl. Year of Forests Type of 2011

Designs: 62c, Tree top, crosses, circles and ovals. 70c, Stylized people and trees.

Litho. With Foil Application

2011, Oct. 13 *Perf. 12½*

505		62c multicolored	2.00	2.00
506		70c multicolored	2.25	2.25
a.	A436	Vert. pair, #505-506	4.25	4.25

Flags and Coins Type of 2006

No. 507 — Flag of: a, Cameroun, 100 franc coin. b, Samoa, 2 tala coin. c, Surinam, 5 cent coin. d, Macedonia, 50 denar coin. e, Bulgaria, 50 stotinka coin. f, Tanzania, 100 shilling coin. g, Finland, 1 euro coin. h, Cuba, 1 peso coin.

2012, Feb. 3 Litho. *Perf. 13¼x13*

507		Sheet of 8	16.50	16.50
a.-h.	A375	70c Any single	2.00	2.00

A column of rouletting in the middle of the sheet separates it into two parts.

V111

Autism Awareness V112

Drawings by autistic people: No. 508, The Path, by Ryan Smoluk, Canada. No. 509, Untitled drawing, by Colm Isherwood, Ireland.

2012, Apr. 2 Litho. *Perf. 14x13½*

508	V111	70c multicolored	2.25	2.25
509	V112	70c multicolored	2.25	2.25
a.		Pair, #508-509	4.50	4.50

UN Emblem — V113

2012, Apr. 12 Litho. *Perf. 14½*

510	V113	70c black + label	*3.50*	*3.50*
		Sheet of 10 + 10 labels	*35.00*	*35.00*

The full sheet sold for $14.52 or €9.90. The labels could be personalized.

Endangered Species Type of 1993

Designs: No. 511, Panthera uncia. No. 512, Polyplectron schleiermacheri. No. 513, Tyto novaehollandiae. No. 514, Ambystoma mexicanum.

2012, Apr. 19 Litho. ***Perf. 12¾x12½***
511 A271 70c multicolored 2.25 2.25
512 A271 70c multicolored 2.25 2.25
513 A271 70c multicolored 2.25 2.25
514 A271 70c multicolored 2.25 2.25
a. Block of 4, #511-514 9.00 9.00

Rio + 20 Type of 2012

2012, June 1 Litho. ***Perf. 13x13¼***
515 A443 70c multicolored 2.10 2.10

Sport for Peace Type of 2012

Litho. With Foil Application

2012, Aug. 17 ***Perf. 14½***
516 A444 62c multicolored 1.90 1.90
517 A444 70c multicolored 2.10 2.10
a. Souvenir sheet of 1 2.10 2.10

UNESCO World Heritage Sites in Africa Type of 2012

Designs: 62c, Kenya Lake System, Kenya. 70c, Medina of Marrakesh, Morocco.

2012, Sept. 5 Litho. ***Perf. 13¼***
518 A445 62c multicolored 1.75 1.75
519 A445 70c multicolored 2.00 2.00

Miniature Sheet

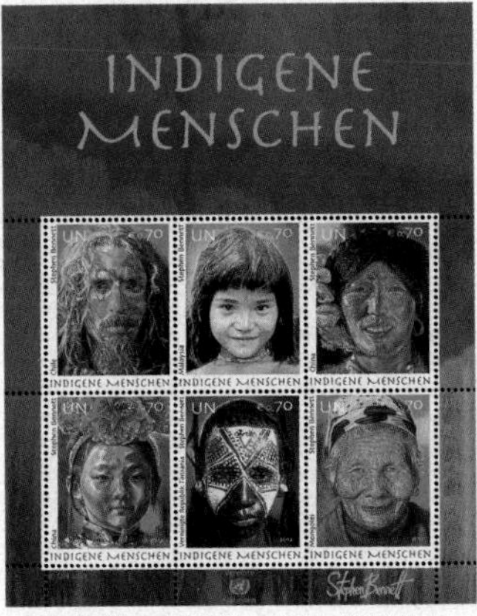

Indigenous People — V114

No. 520 — Portrait of person from: a, Chile. b, Malaysia. c, China (woman with black hair). d, China (woman with flower in hair). e, Tanzania. f, Mongolia.

2012, Oct. 11 Litho. ***Perf. 13¼x13***
520 V114 Sheet of 6 11.50 11.50
a.-f. 70c Any single 1.90 1.90

World Radio Day Type of 2013

Designs: 70c, Microphone and scripts. €1.70, Boy with radio.

2013, Feb. 13 Litho. ***Perf. 13¼x13***
521 A448 70c multicolored 2.00 2.00
522 A448 €1.70 multicolored 5.00 5.00

People in Handprint V115

People in Heart — V116

2013, Mar. 5 Litho. ***Perf. 14x13½***
523 V115 62c multicolored 1.90 1.90

Perf. 13½x14

524 V116 €2.20 multicolored 6.50 6.50

World Heritage Sites, China, Type of 2013

Designs: Nos. 525, 527c, Great Wall of China. Nos. 526, 527f, Mausoleum of the First Qing Emperor. No. 527a, Mogao Caves. No. 527b, Potala Palace, Lhasa. No. 527d, Imperial Palace, Beijing. No. 527e, Mount Huangshan.

2013, Apr. 11 Litho. ***Perf. 14x13½***
525 A452 70c multicolored 2.00 2.00
526 A452 €1.70 multicolored 5.00 5.00

Souvenir Booklet

527 Booklet, #527g-527l 25.00
a.-c. A452 30c any single .85 .85
d.-f. A452 40c any single 1.10 1.10
g. Booklet pane of 4 #527a 3.50 —
h. Booklet pane of 4 #527b 3.50 —
i. Booklet pane of 4 #527c 3.50 —
j. Booklet pane of 4 #527d 4.75 —
k. Booklet pane of 4 #527e 4.75 —
l. Booklet pane of 4 #527f 4.75 —

World Oceans Day — V117

No. 528 — Fish from *One Fish, Two Fish, Red Fish, Blue Fish*, by Dr. Seuss: a, Green fish facing left, wave. b, Red fish facing right. c, Three green fish on plate. d, Red fish, back half of red fish, wave. e, Red fish facing left, front half of red fish facing right. f, Two red fish facing left. g, Two green fish facing right, wave. h, Red fish facing right, head of blue fish wearing hat. i, Yellow fish with green star, wave. j, Yellow fish, back of blue fish, wave. k, Two red fish, body of blue fish. l, Tail of yellow fish, two green fish facing left, wave.

2013, May 31 Litho. ***Perf. 13***
528 V117 Sheet of 12 24.00 24.00
a.-l. 70c any single 2.00 2.00

Nebulae Type of 2013

Designs: No. 567, NGC 2346. No. 568, Sh 2-106.
1fr, Messier 16.

2013, Aug. 9 Litho. ***Perf. 13¼***
529 A454 €1.70 multicolored 5.00 5.00
530 A454 €1.70 multicolored 5.00 5.00
a. Pair, #529-530 10.00 10.00

Souvenir Sheet

531 A454 62c multicolored 1.90 1.90

No. 531 contains one 44x44mm stamp.

Works of Disabled Artists Type of 2013

Designs: 70c, Electro Man, by Pete Eckert, U.S. €1.70, Dive Bomb, by Matt Sesow, U.S.

2013, Sept. 20 Litho. ***Perf. 13¼x13***
532 A456 70c multicolored 2.00 2.00
533 A456 €1.70 multicolored 5.00 5.00

Endangered Species Type of 1993

Designs: No. 534, Hemigalus derbyanus. No. 535, Bubo ascalaphus. No. 536, Nycticebus coucang. No. 537, Zaglossus spp.

2013, Oct. 10 Litho. ***Perf. 12¾x12½***
534 A271 70c multicolored 2.00 2.00
535 A271 70c multicolored 2.00 2.00
536 A271 70c multicolored 2.00 2.00
537 A271 70c multicolored 2.00 2.00
a. Block of 4, #534-537 8.00 8.00

UN Emblem — V118

2013, Oct. 24 Litho. ***Perf. 14½***
538 V118 70c gray blue & blue + label *3.00 3.00*

The full sheet sold for $14.20 or €9.90. The labels could be personalized.

Flags and Coins Type of 2006

No. 539 — Flag of: a, Malaysia, 50 sen coin. b, Nigeria, 1 naira coin. c, Zambia, 20 ngwee coin. d, Togo, 100 franc coin. e, Dominica, 5 cent coin. f, Chad, 100 franc coin. g, St. Vincent and the Grenadines, 5 cent coin. h, Syria, 25 pound coin.

2013, Nov. 6 Litho. ***Perf. 13¼x13***
539 Sheet of 8 16.00 16.00
a.-h. A375 70c Any single 2.00 2.00

A column of rouletting in the middle of the sheet separates it into two parts.

SEMI-POSTAL STAMPS

AIDS Awareness Semi-postal Type

Souvenir Sheet

2002, Oct. 24 Litho. ***Perf. 14½***
B1 SP1 51c + 25c multicolored 3.50 3.50

U.N. TEMPORARY EXECUTIVE AUTHORITY, WEST NEW GUINEA

Temporary Executive Authority

LOCATION — Western half of New Guinea, southwest Pacific Ocean
GOVT. — Province of Indonesia
AREA — In 1958, the size was 151,789 sq. mi.
POP. — estimated at 730,000 in 1958
CAPITAL — Hollandia

The former Netherlands New Guinea became a territory under the administration of the United Nations Temporary Executive Authority on Oct. 1, 1962.

The territory came under Indonesian administration on May 1, 1963. For stamps issued by Indonesia see West Irian in Volume 3.

100 Cents = 1 Gulden

100 Cents = 1 Gulden

Catalogue values for all unused stamps in this country are for Never Hinged items.

First Printing (Hollandia)

Netherlands New Guinea Stamps of 1950-60 Overprinted

Overprint size: 17x3½mm. Top of "N" is slightly lower than the "U," and the base of the "T" is straight, or nearly so.

Photo.; Litho. (#4, 6, 8)

Perf. 12½x12, 12½x13½

1962 **Unwmk.**
1 A4 1c vermilion & yellow .25 .25
2 A1 2c deep orange .25 .25
3 A4 5c chocolate & yellow .25 .25
4 A5 7c org red, bl & brn vio .25 *.35*
5 A4 10c aqua & red brown .25 *.35*
6 A5 12c green, bl & brn vio .25 *.35*
7 A4 15c deep yel & red brn .50 .50
8 A5 17c brown violet & blue .60 *.75*
9 A4 20c lt bl grn & red brn .60 *.75*
10 A6 25c red .35 *.55*
11 A6 30c deep blue .80 .80
12 A6 40c deep orange .80 .80
13 A6 45c dark olive 1.40 *1.60*
14 A6 55c slate blue *20.00* 1.75
15 A6 80c dull gray violet 5.75 5.75
16 A6 85c dark violet brown 3.00 3.00
17 A6 1g plum 9.75 3.00

Engr.

18 A3 2g reddish brown 12.00 25.00
19 A3 5g green 9.00 7.00
Nos. 1-19 (19) 66.05 53.05

Overprinted locally and sold in West New Guinea. Stamps of the second printing were used to complete sets sold to collectors.

Second Printing (Haarlen, Netherlands)

Overprint size: 17x3½mm. Top of the "N" is slightly higher than the "U," and the base of the "T" is concave.

Photo.; Litho. (#4a, 6a, 8a)

Perf. 12½x12, 12½x13½

1962 **Unwmk.**
1a A4 1c vermilion & yellow .25 .25
2a A1 2c deep orange .25 .25
3a A4 5c chocolate & yellow .25 .25
4a A5 7c org red, bl & brn vio .25 .25
5a A4 10c aqua & red brown .25 .25
6a A5 12c green, bl & brn vio .25 .25
7a A4 15c deep yel & red brn .55 .25
8a A5 17c brown violet & blue .70 .40
9a A4 20c lt blue grn & red brn .70 .40
10a A6 25c red .40 .35
11a A6 30c deep blue 1.00 .40
12a A6 40c deep orange 1.00 .40
13a A6 45c dark olive 1.90 .85
14a A6 55c slate blue 6.00 1.10
15a A6 80c dull gray violet 8.00 *10.00*
16a A6 85c dark violet brown 4.00 *5.00*
17a A6 1g plum 4.50 2.25

Engr.

18a A3 2g reddish brown 15.00 *20.00*
19a A3 5g green 7.50 6.00
Nos. 1a-19a (19) 52.75 48.90

Third Printing

Overprint 14mm long.

Photo.; Litho. (#4b, 6b, 8b)

Perf. 12½x12

1963, Mar. Photo. Unwmk.
1b A4 1c vermilion & yellow *6.00 3.00*
3b A4 5c chocolate & yellow *7.00 4.00*
4b A5 7c org red, bl & brn vio *25.00 25.00*
5b A4 10c aqua & red brown *7.00 4.00*
6b A5 12c green, bl & brn vio *37.50 37.50*
7b A4 15c deep yel & red brn *120.00 130.00*
8b A5 17c brown violet & blue *15:00 15.00*
9b A4 20c lt blue grn & red brn *8.00 5.00*
Nos. 1b-9b (8) 225.50 223.50

The third printing was applied in West New Guinea and it is doubtful whether it was regularly issued. Used values are for canceled to order stamps.

Fourth Printing

Overprint 19mm long.

Photogravure

1963, Mar. Unwmk. ***Perf. 12½x12***
1c A4 1c vermilion & yellow *45.00 45.00*
5c A4 10c aqua & red brown *130.00 130.00*

The fourth printing was applied in West New Guinea and it is doubtful whether it was regularly issued. Used values are for canceled to order stamps.

U.N. TRANSITIONAL AUTHORITY IN EAST TIMOR

A30

2000, Apr. 29 Litho. ***Perf. 12x11¾***

350	A30	Dom. red & multi	*40.00*	*50.00*
351	A30	Int. blue & multi	*60.00*	*75.00*

No. 350 sold for 10c and No. 351 sold for 50c on day of issue.

U.N. INTERIM ADMINISTRATION, KOSOVO

These stamps were issued by the United Nations Interim Administration Mission in Kosovo and the Post & Telecommunications of Kosovo. Service was local for the first two months, with international use to start in mid-May.

100 pfennigs = 1 mark
100 cents = €1 (2002)

Catalogue values for all unused stamps in this country are for Never Hinged items.

Peace in Kosovo — A1

Designs: 20pf, Mosaic depicting Orpheus, c. 5th-6th cent., Podujeve. 30pf, Dardinian idol, Museum of Kosovo. 50pf, Silver coin of Damastion from 4th cent. B.C. 1m, Statue of Mother Teresa, Prizren. 2m, Map of Kosovo.

Perf. 13½x13, 13½x13¼ (30pf)

2000, Mar. 14 Litho. Unwmk.

1	A1	20pf multicolored	1.00	.75
2	A1	30pf multicolored	1.25	1.00
3	A1	50pf multicolored	1.60	1.40
4	A1	1m multicolored	2.75	2.00
5	A1	2m multicolored	5.50	4.00
		Nos. 1-5 (5)	12.10	9.15

Beginning with No. 6, Kosovan stamps were not available to collectors through the United Nations Postal Administration.

Peace in Kosovo — A2

Designs: 20pf, Bird. 30pf, Street musician. 50pf, Butterfly and pear. 1m, Children and stars. 2m, Globe and handprints.

2001, Nov. 12 Litho. ***Perf. 14***

6	A2	20pf multicolored	1.50	1.00
7	A2	30pf multicolored	1.75	1.25
8	A2	50pf multicolored	3.25	2.25
9	A2	1m multicolored	7.00	5.00
10	A2	2m multicolored	13.50	10.00
		Nos. 6-10 (5)	27.00	19.50

Peace in Kosovo Type of 2001 With Denominations in Euros Only

2002, May 2 Litho. ***Perf. 14***

11	A2	10c Like #6	1.50	1.00
12	A2	15c Like #7	1.75	1.25
13	A2	26c Like #8	3.25	2.25
14	A2	51c Like #9	7.50	6.00
15	A2	€1.02 Like #10	15.00	12.50
		Nos. 11-15 (5)	29.00	23.00

Christmas — A3

Designs: 50c, Candles and garland. €1, Stylized men.

2003, Dec. 20 Litho. ***Perf. 14***

16	A3	50c multicolored	*14.00*	*12.50*
17	A3	€1 multicolored	*27.50*	*20.00*

Return of Refugees — A4

Five Years of Peace — A5

2004, June 29 Litho. ***Perf. 13¼x13***

18	A4	€1 multicolored	*15.00*	*15.00*
19	A5	€2 multicolored	*30.00*	*30.00*

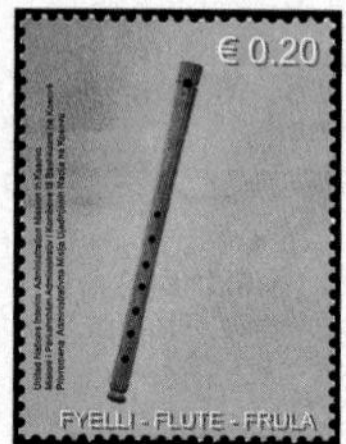

Musical Instruments — A6

2004, Aug. 31 Litho. ***Perf. 13¼x13***

20	A6	20c Flute	*12.50*	*12.50*
21	A6	30c Ocarina	*22.50*	*22.50*

Aprons A7

Vests — A8

Designs: 20c, Apron from Prizren. 30c, Apron from Rugova. 50c, Three vests. €1, Two vests.

2004, Oct. 28 Litho. ***Perf. 13x13¼***

22	A7	20c multicolored	*8.00*	*8.00*
23	A7	30c multicolored	*11.00*	*11.00*
24	A8	50c multicolored	*18.50*	*18.50*
25	A8	€1 multicolored	*37.50*	*37.50*
		Nos. 22-25 (4)	*75.00*	*75.00*

Mirusha Waterfall A9

2004, Nov. 26 Litho. ***Perf. 13x13¼***

26	A9	€2 multicolored	*15.00*	*15.00*

House A10

2004, Dec. 14 Litho. ***Perf. 13x13¼***

27	A10	50c multicolored	*7.50*	*7.50*

Flowers — A11

2005, June 29 Litho. ***Perf. 13½***

28	A11	15c Peony	*3.00*	*3.00*
29	A11	20c Poppies	*4.00*	*4.00*
30	A11	30c Gentian	*7.00*	*7.00*
		Nos. 28-30 (3)	*14.00*	*14.00*

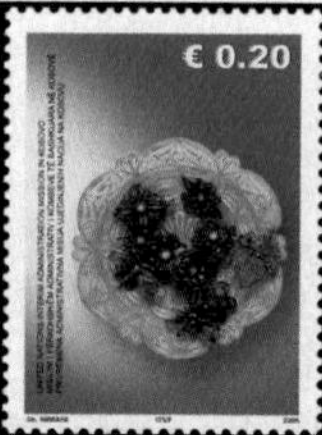

A12

Handicrafts A13

2005, July 20 ***Perf. 13¼x13***

31	A12	20c shown	*2.50*	*2.50*
32	A12	30c Cradle	*4.00*	*4.00*
33	A13	50c shown	*6.00*	*6.00*
34	A12	€1 Necklace	*7.50*	*7.50*
		Nos. 31-34 (4)	*20.00*	*20.00*

Village A14

Town A15

City — A16

2005, Sept. 15 ***Perf. 13x13½***

35	A14	20c multicolored	*3.00*	*3.00*
36	A15	50c multicolored	*6.00*	*6.00*
37	A16	€1 multicolored	*10.00*	*10.00*
		Nos. 35-37 (3)	*19.00*	*19.00*

Archaeological Artifacts — A17

2005, Nov. 2 ***Perf. 13½x13***

38	A17	20c shown	*2.00*	*2.00*
39	A17	30c Statue	*3.50*	*3.50*
40	A17	50c Sculpture	*5.00*	*5.00*
41	A17	€1 Helmet	*10.00*	*10.00*
		Nos. 38-41 (4)	*20.50*	*20.50*

Minerals A18

2005, Dec. 10 ***Perf. 13x13½***

42	A18	€2 multicolored	*15.00*	*15.00*

A19 Europa — A20

2006, July 20 ***Perf. 13¼x13***

43	A19	50c multicolored	*2.00*	*2.00*
44	A20	€1 multicolored	*4.00*	*4.00*

Fauna A21

2006, May 23 Litho. ***Perf. 13***

45	A21	15c Wolf	*1.00*	*1.00*
46	A21	20c Cow	*1.25*	*1.25*
47	A21	30c Pigeon	*1.50*	*1.50*
48	A21	50c Swan	*1.75*	*1.75*
49	A21	€1 Dog	*3.25*	*3.25*
	a.	Souvenir sheet, #45-49, + label	*10.00*	*10.00*
		Nos. 45-49 (5)	*8.75*	*8.75*

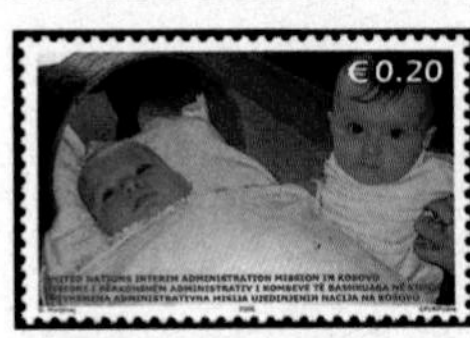

Children A22

Designs: 20c, Children in cradle. 30c, Children reading. 50c, Girls dancing. €1, Child in water.

2006, June 30 Litho. *Perf. 13*
50 A22 20c multicolored *1.00 1.00*
51 A22 30c multicolored *1.25 1.25*
52 A22 50c multicolored *1.75 1.75*
53 A22 €1 multicolored *4.00 4.00*
a. Souvenir sheet, #50-53 *9.00 9.00*
Nos. 50-53 (4) 8.00 8.00

A23

A24

A25

Tourist Attractions — A26

2006, Sept. 1 Litho. *Perf. 13*
54 A23 20c multicolored *1.00 1.00*
55 A24 30c multicolored *1.25 1.25*
56 A25 50c multicolored *1.75 1.75*
57 A26 €1 multicolored *3.75 3.75*
a. Souvenir sheet, #54-57 *11.00 11.00*
Nos. 54-57 (4) 7.75 7.75

Intl. Peace Day — A27

2006, Sept. 21 Litho. *Perf. 13*
58 A27 €2 multicolored *12.50 12.50*

Ancient Coins — A28

Various coins.

2006, Nov. 1 Litho. *Perf. 13*
59 A28 20c multicolored *1.00 1.00*
60 A28 30c multicolored *1.50 1.50*
61 A28 50c multicolored *2.25 2.25*
62 A28 €1 multicolored *4.00 4.00*
a. Souvenir sheet, #59-62 *10.00 10.00*
Nos. 59-62 (4) 8.75 8.75

Sculpture — A29

2006, Dec. 1 Litho. *Perf. 13*
63 A29 €2 multicolored *8.75 8.75*
a. Miniature sheet, #45-57, 59-63, + 2 labels *75.00 75.00*

Convention on the Rights of Persons With Disabilities — A30

Emblems of handicaps and: 20c, Children and butterfly. 50c, Handicapped women. 70c, Map of Kosovo. €1, Stylized flower.

2007, Apr. 23 Litho. *Perf. 14x14¼*
64 A30 20c multicolored *1.25 1.25*
65 A30 50c multicolored *2.50 2.50*
66 A30 70c multicolored *3.50 3.50*
67 A30 €1 multicolored *4.50 4.50*
a. Souvenir sheet, #64-67 *12.50 12.50*
Nos. 64-67 (4) 11.75 11.75

Scouting, Cent. — A31

Europa — A32

2007, May 12 Litho. *Perf. 13¼*
68 A31 70c multicolored *4.50 4.50*
69 A32 €1 multicolored *7.00 7.00*
a. Souvenir sheet, #68-69 *100.00 100.00*

A33

A34

A35

International Children's Day — A36

2007, June 1 Litho. *Perf. 13¼*
70 A33 20c multicolored *1.25 1.25*
71 A34 30c multicolored *1.50 1.50*
72 A35 70c multicolored *3.00 3.00*
73 A36 €1 multicolored *5.00 5.00*
Nos. 70-73 (4) 10.75 10.75

Native Costumes — A37

Designs: 20c, Serbian woman. 30c, Prizren Region woman. 50c, Sword dancer. 70c, Drenica Region woman. €1, Shepherd, Rugova.

2007, July 6 Litho. *Perf. 13½x13¼*
74 A37 20c multicolored *1.25 1.25*
75 A37 30c multicolored *1.75 1.75*
76 A37 50c multicolored *2.00 2.00*
77 A37 70c multicolored *3.25 3.25*
78 A37 €1 multicolored *4.25 4.25*
a. Souvenir sheet, #74-78, + label *25.00 25.00*
Nos. 74-78 (5) 12.50 12.50

Masks — A38

Various masks.

Perf. 13½x13¼
2007, Sept. 11 Litho.
79 A38 15c multicolored *.75 .75*
80 A38 30c multicolored *1.00 1.00*
81 A38 50c multicolored *1.75 1.75*
82 A38 €1 multicolored *3.50 3.50*
Nos. 79-82 (4) 7.00 7.00

Sports — A39

Designs: 20c, Soccer ball, basketball, two people standing, person in wheelchair. 50c, Wrestlers. €1, Symbols of 24 sports.

2007, Oct. 2 Litho. *Perf. 13¼x13½*
83 A39 20c multicolored *1.00 1.00*
84 A39 50c multicolored *2.25 2.25*
85 A39 €1 multicolored *4.50 4.50*
Nos. 83-85 (3) 7.75 7.75

Architecture A40

Designs: 30c, Stone bridge, Vushtrri. 50c, Hamam, Prizren. 70c, Tower. €1, Tower, diff.

2007, Nov. 6 Litho. *Perf. 13¼*
86 A40 30c multicolored *2.00 2.00*
87 A40 50c multicolored *3.50 3.50*
88 A40 70c multicolored *4.00 4.00*
89 A40 €1 multicolored *5.00 5.00*
Nos. 86-89 (4) 14.50 14.50

Locomotives A41

Designs: €1, Diesel locomotive. €2, Steam locomotive

2007, Dec. 7 Litho. *Perf. 13¼*
90 A41 €1 multicolored *7.50 7.50*
91 A41 €2 multicolored *15.00 15.00*

Skanderbeg (1405-68), Albanian National Hero — A42

2008, Jan. 17 Litho. *Perf. 13¼*
92 A42 €2 multicolored *8.75 8.75*

Kosovo declared its independence from Serbia on Feb. 17, 2008, ending the United Nations Interim Administration.

ABU DHABI

,ä-bü-'thä-bē

LOCATION — Arabia, on Persian Gulf
GOVT. — Sheikdom under British protection
POP. — 25,000 (estimated)
CAPITAL — Abu Dhabi

Abu Dhabi is one of six Persian Gulf sheikdoms to join the United Arab Emirates, which proclaimed its independence Dec. 2, 1971. See United Arab Emirates.

100 Naye Paise = 1 Rupee
1000 Fils = 1 Dinar (1966)

Catalogue values for all unused stamps in this country are for Never Hinged items.

Sheik Shakbut bin Sultan — A1

Palace — A2

Designs: 40np, 50np, 75np, Gazelle. 5r, 10r, Oil rig and camels.

Perf. 14½

1964, Mar. 30 Photo. Unwmk.

1 A1 5np brt yellow green 2.00 *3.25*
2 A1 15np brown 2.50 2.00
3 A1 20np brt ultra 3.00 1.75
a. Perf 13x13½ 500.00
4 A1 30np red orange 3.25 1.25
5 A1 40np brt violet 5.50 1.00
6 A1 50np brown olive 5.00 2.25
7 A1 75np gray 7.00 4.00

Engr. *Perf. 13x13½*

8 A2 1r light green 6.50 2.50
9 A2 2r black 11.00 5.00
10 A2 5r carmine rose 24.00 17.50
11 A2 10r dark blue 32.50 22.50
Nos. 1-11 (11) 102.25 63.00

For surcharges see Nos. 15-25.

Falcon Perched on Wrist — A3

40np, Falcon facing left. 2r, Falcon facing right.

1965, Mar. 30 Photo. *Perf. 14½*

12 A3 20np chlky blue & brn 17.50 3.50
13 A3 40np ultra & brown 21.00 5.50
14 A3 2r brt blue grn & gray brn 32.50 20.00
Nos. 12-14 (3) 71.00 29.00

Nos. 1-11 Surcharged

a

b

c

1966, Oct. 1 Photo. *Perf. 14½*

15 A1 (a) 5f on 5np 11.00 6.00
16 A1 (a) 15f on 15np 13.00 8.00
17 A1 (a) 20f on 20np, perf 13x13½ (#3a) 15.00 10.00
a. Perf 14½ (#3) 250.00
18 A1 (a) 30f on 30np 15.00 *17.50*
19 A1 (b) 40f on 40np 14.00 2.00
20 A1 (b) 50f on 50np 40.00 *40.00*
21 A1 (b) 75f on 75np 40.00 *40.00*

Engr.
Perf. 13x13½

22 A2 (c) 100f on 1r 19.00 5.25
23 A2 (c) 200f on 2r 24.00 16.00
24 A2 (c) 500f on 5r 45.00 *50.00*
25 A2 (c) 1d on 10r 70.00 *80.00*
Nos. 15-25 (11) 306.00 *274.75*

Overprint on No. 25 has "1 Dinar" on 1 line and 3 bars through old denomination.

Sheik Zaid bin Sultan al Nahayan
A4 A6

Dorcas Gazelle — A5

Designs: 5f, 15f, 20f, 35f, Crossed flags of Abu Dhabi. 200f, Falcon. 500f, 1d, Palace.

Engr.; Flags Litho.

1967, Apr. 1 *Perf. 13x13½*

26 A4 5f dull grn & red .35 .25
27 A4 15f dk brown & red .50 .25
28 A4 20f dk blue & red .85 .25
29 A4 35f purple & red 1.00 .30

Engr.

30 A4 40f green 1.40 .30
31 A4 50f brown 1.75 .40
32 A4 60f blue 1.90 .45
33 A4 100f car rose 3.00 .65

Litho.

34 A5 125f green & brn ol 7.50 2.00
35 A5 200f sky blue & brn 30.00 6.50
36 A5 500f org & brt pur 27.50 9.00
37 A5 1d green & vio bl 55.00 19.00
Nos. 26-37 (12) 130.75 39.35

For surcharge, see No. 55A.

1967, Aug. 6 Photo. *Perf. 14½x14*

38 A6 40f Prussian green 4.50 2.50
39 A6 50f brown 5.50 2.00
40 A6 60f blue 18.00 4.00
41 A6 100f carmine rose 27.50 10.00
Nos. 38-41 (4) 55.50 18.50

Human Rights Flame and Sheik Zaid — A6a

Perf. 14½x14

1968, Apr. 1 Photo. Unwmk.

Emblem in Red and Green

42 A6a 35f peacock bl & gold 2.25 .90
43 A6a 60f dk blue & gold 3.50 1.25
44 A6a 150f dk brown & gold 9.00 3.00
Nos. 42-44 (3) 14.75 5.15

International Human Rights Year.

Sheik Zaid and Coat of Arms A7

Perf. 14x14½

1968, Aug. 6 Photo. Unwmk.

45 A7 5f multicolored 4.25 .60
46 A7 10f multicolored 4.25 .85
47 A7 100f multicolored 11.50 3.25
48 A7 125f multicolored 17.50 4.75
Nos. 45-48 (4) 37.50 9.45

Accession of Sheik Zaid, 2nd anniversary.

Abu Dhabi Airport — A8

5f, Buildings under construction and earth-moving equipment. 35f, New bridge and falcon. Each stamp shows different portrait of Sheik Zaid.

Perf. 12, 12½x13 (10f)

1969, Mar. 28 Litho.

Size: 5f, 35f, 59x34mm

49 A8 5f multicolored 2.75 .55
50 A8 10f multicolored 7.75 1.00
51 A8 35f multicolored 30.00 8.00
Nos. 49-51 (3) 40.50 9.55

Issued to publicize progress made in Abu Dhabi during preceding 2 years.

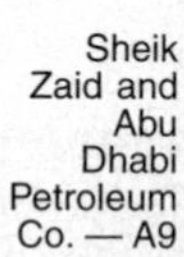

Sheik Zaid and Abu Dhabi Petroleum Co. — A9

Designs: 60f, Abu Dhabi Marine Areas drilling platform and helicopter. 125f, Zakum Field separator at night. 200f, Tank farm.

1969, Aug. 6 Litho. *Perf. 14x13½*

52 A9 35f olive grn & multi 1.75 .85
53 A9 60f yel brown & multi 8.25 2.25
54 A9 125f multicolored 11.00 3.25
55 A9 200f red brown & multi 13.00 4.75
Nos. 52-55 (4) 34.00 11.10

Accession of Sheik Zaid, 3rd anniversary.

No. 27 Surcharged "25" in Arabic

1969, Dec. 13

55A A4 25f on 15f dk brown & red 225.00 125.00

Because of local demand for 25f stamps for mailing Christmas greeting card abroad, the Director of Posts ordered that 20,000 examples of No. 27 be surcharged "25" in Arabic for emergency use. This surcharge was applied locally, using a hand numbering machine. All stamps were sold at post office counters between Dec. 13 and Dec. 24, and the majority were used on mail during this period.

Sheik Zaid — A10

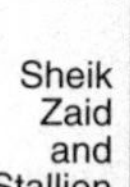

Sheik Zaid and Stallion A11

5f, 25f, 60f, 90f, Oval frame around portrait. 150f, Gazelle and Sheik. 500f, Fort Jahili and Sheik. 1d, Grand Mosque and Sheik.

1970-71 Litho. *Perf. 14*

56 A10 5f lt green & multi .90 .25
57 A10 10f bister & multi 1.10 .25
58 A10 25f lilac & multi 1.75 .25
59 A10 35f violet & multi 2.00 .25
60 A10 50f sepia & multi 2.75 .40
61 A10 60f violet & multi 3.25 .50
62 A10 70f rose red & multi 5.50 .65
63 A10 90f car rose & multi 7.00 1.00
64 A11 125f multi ('71) 10.00 2.00
65 A11 150f multi ('71) 13.50 2.50
66 A11 500f multi ('71) 42.50 11.00
67 A11 1d multi ('71) 77.50 22.50
Nos. 56-67 (12) 167.75 41.55

For surcharge see No. 80.

Sheik Zaid and Mt. Fuji — A12

1970, Aug. Litho. *Perf. 13½x13*

68 A12 25f multicolored 4.75 1.25
69 A12 35f multicolored 6.25 2.00
70 A12 60f multicolored 11.50 3.50
Nos. 68-70 (3) 22.50 6.75

Issued to publicize EXPO '70 International Exhibition, Osaka, Japan, Mar. 15-Sept. 13.

Abu Dhabi Airport A13

Designs: 60f, Airport entrance. 150f, Aerial view of Abu Dhabi Town, vert.

Perf. 14x13½, 13½x14

1970, Sept. 22 Litho.

71 A13 25f multicolored 4.75 .85
72 A13 60f multicolored 9.25 2.00
73 A13 150f multicolored 21.00 5.25
Nos. 71-73 (3) 35.00 8.10

Accession of Sheik Zaid, 4th anniversary.

Gamal Abdel Nasser — A14

1971, May 3 Litho. *Perf. 14*

74 A14 25f deep rose & blk 9.00 3.50
75 A14 35f rose violet & blk 12.00 5.25

In memory of Gamal Abdel Nasser (1918-1970), President of UAR.

Scout Cars A15

Designs: 60f, Patrol boat. 125f, Armored car in desert. 150f, Meteor jet fighters.

1971, Aug. 6 Litho. *Perf. 13*

No.	Type	Description	Unused	Used
76	A15	35f multicolored	6.50	1.50
77	A15	60f multicolored	8.50	2.25
78	A15	125f multicolored	19.00	3.50
79	A15	150f multicolored	23.00	6.50
		Nos. 76-79 (4)	57.00	13.75

Accession of Sheik Zaid, 5th anniversary.

No. 60 Surcharged in Green

1971, Dec. 8 *Perf. 14*

No.	Type	Description	Unused	Used
80	A10	5f on 50f multi	*110.00*	*110.00*

Dome of the Rock, Jerusalem — A16

Different views of Dome of the Rock.

1972, June 3 *Perf. 13*

No.	Type	Description	Unused	Used
81	A16	35f lt violet & multi	30.00	5.75
82	A16	60f lt violet & multi	55.00	9.50
83	A16	125f lilac & multi	100.00	20.00
		Nos. 81-83 (3)	185.00	35.25

Nos. 80-83 were issued after Abu Dhabi joined the United Arab Emirates Dec. 2, 1971. Stamps of UAE replaced those of Abu Dhabi. UAE Nos. 1-12 were used only in Abu Dhabi except the 10f and 25f which were issued later in Dubai and Sharjah.

ADEN

'ä-dən

LOCATION — Southern Arabia
GOVT. — British colony and protectorate
AREA — 112,075 sq. mi.
POP. — 220,000 (est. 1964)
CAPITAL — Aden

Aden used India stamps before 1937.

In January, 1963, the colony of Aden (the port) and the sheikdoms and emirates of the Western Aden Protectorate formed the Federation of South Arabia. This did not include the Eastern Aden Protectorate with Kathiri and Qu'aiti States. Stamps of Aden, except those of Kathiri and Qu'aiti States, were replaced Apr. 1, 1965, by those of the Federation of South Arabia. See South Arabia and People's Democratic Republic of Yemen, Vol. 6.

12 Pies = 1 Anna
16 Annas = 1 Rupee
100 Cents = 1 Shilling (1951)

Catalogue values for unused stamps in this country are for Never Hinged items.

ISSUES UNDER BRITISH ADMINISTRATION

Dhow — A1

Perf. 13x11½

1937, Apr. 1 Engr. Wmk. 4

No.	Type	Description	Unused	Used
1	A1	½a lt green	4.50	2.50
2	A1	9p dark green	4.25	3.50
3	A1	1a black brown	4.25	2.00
4	A1	2a red	4.75	3.00
5	A1	2½a blue	6.75	2.00
6	A1	3a carmine rose	11.00	9.00
7	A1	3½a gray blue	8.50	5.75
8	A1	8a rose lilac	30.00	10.00
9	A1	1r brown	60.00	12.00
10	A1	2r orange yellow	110.00	40.00
11	A1	5r rose violet	240.00	*150.00*
12	A1	10r olive green	625.00	*550.00*
		Nos. 1-12 (12)	1,109.	*789.75*
		Set, hinged	800.00	

Common Design Types pictured following the introduction.

Coronation Issue

Common Design Type

1937, May 12 *Perf. 13½x14*

No.	Type	Description	Unused	Used
13	CD302	1a black brown	.80	1.25
14	CD302	2½a blue	.95	*1.60*
15	CD302	3½a gray blue	1.25	*3.25*
		Nos. 13-15 (3)	3.00	*6.10*
		Set, hinged	2.00	

Aidrus Mosque — A2

¾a, 5r, Camel Corpsman. 1a, 2r, Aden Harbor. 1½a, 1r, Adenese dhow. 2½a, 8a, Mukalla. 3a, 14a, 10r, Capture of Aden, 1839.

1939-48 Engr. Wmk. 4 *Perf. 12½*

No.	Type	Description	Unused	Used
16	A2	½a green (7/42)	1.75	.60
17	A2	¾a red brn	3.00	1.40
18	A2	1a brt lt blue	.75	.50
19	A2	1½a red	2.75	*.65*
20	A2	2a dark brown	1.25	.40
21	A2	2½a brt ultra	2.00	.45
22	A2	3a rose car & dk brn	1.90	.25
23	A2	8a orange	2.25	.40
23A	A2	14a lt bl & brn blk ('45)	4.25	1.25
24	A2	1r bright green	5.25	2.75
25	A2	2r dp mag & bl blk ('44)	11.00	3.00
26	A2	5r dp ol & lake brn (1/44)	30.00	15.00
27a	A2	10r dk pur & lake brn	45.00	17.50
		Nos. 16-27a (13)	96.25	41.45
		Set, hinged	70.00	

For shades, see the *Scott Classic Specialized Catalogue.*

Peace Issue

Common Design Type

Perf. 13½x14

1946, Oct. 15 Engr. Wmk. 4

No.	Type	Description	Unused	Used
28	CD303	1½a carmine	.25	*1.50*
29	CD303	2½a deep blue	.45	.80

Return to peace at end of World War II.

Silver Wedding Issue

Common Design Types

1949, Jan. 17 Photo. *Perf. 14x14½*

No.	Type	Description	Unused	Used
30	CD304	1½a scarlet	.40	*2.50*

Engraved; Name Typographed

Perf. 11½x11

No.	Type	Description	Unused	Used
31	CD305	10r purple	37.50	*45.00*

25th anniv. of the marriage of King George VI and Queen Elizabeth.

UPU Issue

Common Design Types

Srchd. in Annas & Rupees

Engr.; Name typo. on Nos. 33-34

1949, Oct. 10 *Perf. 13½, 11x11½*

No.	Type	Description	Unused	Used
32	CD306	2½a on 20c dp ultra	.70	*1.60*
33	CD307	3a on 30c dp car	2.25	1.60
34	CD308	8a on 50c org	1.75	*1.75*
35	CD309	1r on 1sh blue	1.90	*4.00*
		Nos. 32-35 (4)	6.60	*8.95*

75th anniv. of the formation of the UPU.

Nos. 18 and 20-27 Surcharged in Black or Carmine

1951, Oct. 1 Wmk. 4 *Perf. 12½*

No.	Type	Description	Unused	Used
36	A2	5c on 1a #18a	.35	*.50*
37	A2	10c on 2a #20a	.35	*.55*
38	A2	15c on 2½a	.45	*1.50*
a.		Double surcharge	*1,600.*	
		Hinged	*950.00*	
39	A2	20c on 3a	.50	.50
40	A2	30c on 8a #23b (C)	.55	*.70*
41	A2	50c on 8a #23b	.75	.50
42	A2	70c on 14a (#23A)	2.50	1.75
43	A2	1sh on 1r #24a	3.00	.40
44	A2	2sh on 2r #25	14.00	3.50
45	A2	5sh on 5r #26	27.50	14.00
46	A2	10sh on 10r #27	37.50	15.50
		Nos. 36-46 (11)	87.45	39.40

Surcharge on No. 40 includes 2 bars.

Coronation Issue

Common Design Type

1953, June 2 Engr. *Perf. 13½x13*

No.	Type	Description	Unused	Used
47	CD312	15c dark grn & black	1.25	1.25

Minaret — A10

Camel Transport — A11

15c, Crater. 25c, Mosque. 35c, Dhow. 50c, Map. 70c, Salt works. 1sh, Dhow building. 1sh, 25c, Colony Badge. 2sh, Aden Protectorate levy. 5sh, Crater Pass. 10sh, Tribesman. 20sh, Aden in 1572.

Perf. 12, 12x13½ ('56)

1953-59 Engr. Wmk. 4

Size: 29x23, 23x29mm

No.	Type	Description	Unused	Used
48	A10	5c grn, perf 12x13½ ('56)	.25	.25
a.		Perf. 12 ('55)	2.00	*3.50*
b.		5c bluish grn, perf 12x13½ ('56)	.25	*.55*
49	A11	10c orange	.45	.25
a.		10c vermilion ('55)	.25	*.35*
50	A11	15c blue green	1.25	.60
a.		15c grayish grn ('59)	8.00	6.00
51	A11	25c carmine	.85	.55
a.		25c deep rose red ('56)	4.50	1.50
52	A10	35c ultra, perf. 12	2.50	1.50
a.		35c dp bl, perf 12x13½ ('58)	7.00	4.50
b.		35c vio bl, perf 12x13½ ('59)	13.50	4.00
53	A10	50c blue, perf 12	.30	.25
a.		As "b," perf 12x13½ ('56)	1.00	.25
b.		50c deep bl, perf 12 ('55)	2.75	1.50
54	A10	70c gray, perf 12	.30	.25
a.		As "b," perf 12x13½ ('56)	1.75	.25
b.		70c grayish blk, perf 12 ('54)	1.25	.35
55	A11	1sh pur & sepia	.40	.25
55A	A11	1sh vio & black ('55)	1.75	.25
56	A10	1sh25c blk & lt blue ('56)	10.00	.65
57	A10	2sh car rose & sep	1.75	.65
57A	A10	2sh car & black ('56)	13.00	.60
58	A10	5sh blue & sepia	1.75	1.00
58A	A10	5sh dk blue & blk ('56)	14.00	1.75
59	A10	10sh olive & sepia	1.90	*8.00*
60	A10	10sh ol gray & blk ('54)	17.50	2.00

Size: 36½x27mm

Perf. 13½x13

No.	Type	Description	Unused	Used
61	A11	20sh rose vio & dk brn	7.00	*11.00*
61A	A11	20sh lt vio & blk ('57)	62.50	20.00
		Nos. 48-61A (18)	137.45	49.80

No. 60 has heavier shading on tribesman's lower garment than No. 59.

See Nos. 66-75. For overprints see Nos. 63-64.

Type of 1953

Inscribed: "Royal Visit 1954"

1954, Apr. 27 *Perf. 12*

No.	Type	Description	Unused	Used
62	A11	1sh purple & sepia	.65	*.60*

Nos. 50 & 56 Overprinted in Red

No. 63

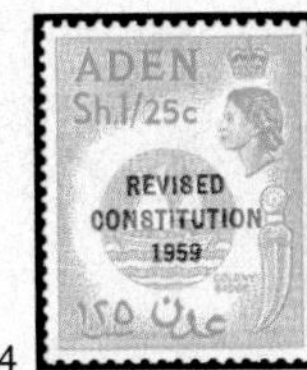

No. 64

1959, Jan. 26 *Perf. 12, 12x13½*

No.	Type	Description	Unused	Used
63	A11	15c dark blue green	.50	*1.75*
64	A10	1sh25c blk & light blue	1.50	1.00

Introduction of a revised constitution.

Freedom from Hunger Issue

Common Design Type

Perf. 14x14½

1963, June 4 Photo. Wmk. 314

No.	Type	Description	Unused	Used
65	CD314	1sh25c green	1.75	*1.75*

Types of 1953-57

Perf. 12x13½, 12 (#67-69, 73)

1964-65 Engr. Wmk. 314

No.	Type	Description	Unused	Used
66	A10	5c green ('65)	3.75	*10.00*
67	A11	10c orange	1.25	1.25
68	A11	15c Prus green	.85	*5.00*
69	A11	25c carmine	2.75	.45
70	A10	35c dk blue	8.00	6.00
71	A10	50c dull blue	.60	.50
72	A10	70c gray	1.75	*3.25*
73	A11	1sh vio & black	13.00	3.00
74	A10	1sh25c blk & lt blue	18.50	2.50
75	A10	2sh car & blk ('65)	6.50	*32.50*
		Nos. 66-75 (10)	56.95	*64.45*

KATHIRI STATE OF SEIYUN

LOCATION — In Eastern Aden Protectorate
GOVT. — Sultanate
CAPITAL — Seiyun

The stamps of the Kathiri State of Seiyun were valid for use throughout Aden. Used stamps generally bear Aden GPO or Aden Camp cancels. Examples with cancels from offices in the Eastern Protectorate command a premium.

Sultan Ja'far bin Mansur al Kathiri — A1

Seiyun — A2

Minaret at Tarim — A3

Designs: 2½a, Mosque at Seiyun. 3a, Palace at Tarim. 8a, Mosque at Seiyun, horiz. 1r, South Gate, Tarim. 2r, Kathiri House. 5r, Mosque at Tarim.

1942 Engr. Wmk. 4 *Perf. 13¾x14*
1 A1 ½a dark green .25 *1.75*
2 A1 ¾a copper brown .45 *4.00*
3 A1 1a deep blue .80 *2.00*

Perf. 13x11½, 11½x13
4 A2 1½a dark car rose .80 *2.50*
5 A3 2a sepia brown .50 *2.50*
6 A3 2½a deep blue 1.50 2.25
7 A2 3a dk car rose & dull brn 2.00 *4.00*
8 A2 8a orange red 2.50 1.00
9 A3 1r green 6.00 4.50
10 A2 2r rose vio & dk blue 12.00 *22.50*
11 A3 5r gray green & fawn 32.50 30.00
Nos. 1-11 (11) 59.30 *77.00*

For surcharges see Nos. 20-27.

Nos. 4, 6 Ovptd. in Black or Red

a

b

Perf. 13x11½, 11½x13
1946, Oct. 15 Wmk. 4
12 A2 (a) 1½a dark car rose .25 .65
13 A3 (b) 2½a deep blue (R) .25 .25
a. Inverted overprint 1,100.
Hinged 700.
b. Double overprint 1,500.
Hinged 1,000.

Victory of the Allied Nations in WWII.
All examples of No. 13b have the 2nd overprint almost directly over the 1st.

Silver Wedding Issue
Common Design Types

1949, Jan. 17 Photo. *Perf. 14x14½*
14 CD304 1½a scarlet .50 *3.00*

Engraved; Name Typo.
Perf. 11½x11
15 CD305 5r green 21.00 *13.00*

25th anniv. of the marriage of King George VI and Queen Elizabeth.

UPU Issue
Common Design Types

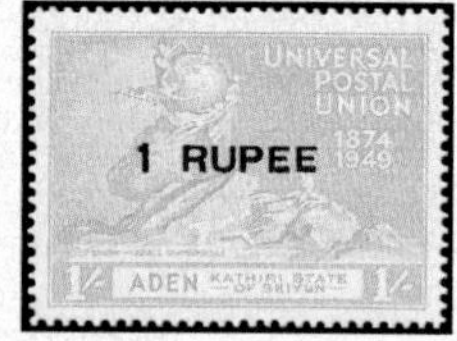

Srchd. in Annas and Rupees

Engr.; Name Typo. on Nos. 17-18
1949, Oct. 10 *Perf. 13½, 11x11½*
16 CD306 2½a on 20c dp ultra .25 *.80*
17 CD307 3a on 30c dp car 1.25 *2.00*
18 CD308 8a on 50c orange .40 *2.75*
19 CD309 1r on 1sh blue .50 *1.25*
Nos. 16-19 (4) 2.40 *6.80*

75th anniv. of the formation of the UPU.

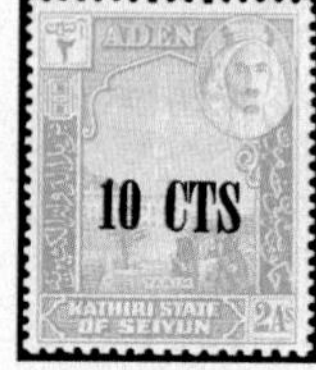

Nos. 3 and 5-11 Srchd. in Carmine or Black

Perf. 14, 13x11½, 11½x13
1951, Oct. 1 Engr. Wmk. 4
20 A1 5c on 1a (C) .25 *1.75*
21 A3 10c on 2a #5a .30 *1.25*
22 A3 15c on 2½a .30 *2.25*
23 A2 20c on 3a #7 .25 *2.75*
24 A2 50c on 8a .30 *1.25*
25 A3 1sh on 1r 1.25 *3.00*
26 A2 2sh on 2r #10 11.00 *37.50*
27 A3 5sh on 5r 32.50 *50.00*
Nos. 20-27 (8) 46.15 99.75

Coronation Issue
Common Design Type

1953, June 2 *Perf. 13½x13*
28 CD312 15c dk green & blk .40 *1.50*

Sultan Hussein A10

Seiyun Scene A11

25c, Minaret at Tarim, vert. 35c, Mosque at Seiyun, vert. 50c, Palace at Tarim. 1sh, Mosque at Seiyun. 2sh, South Gate, Tarim, vert.. 5sh, Kathiri house. 10sh, Mosque entrance, Tarim, vert.

1954, Jan. 15 Engr. *Perf. 12½*
29 A10 5c dark brown .25 .25
30 A10 10c deep blue .25 .25

Perf. 13x11½, 11½x13
31 A11 15c dk blue green .25 .25
32 A11 25c dk car rose .25 .25
33 A11 35c deep blue .25 .25
34 A11 50c dk car rose & dk brn .25 .25
35 A11 1sh deep orange .25 .25
36 A11 2sh gray green 4.25 2.25
37 A11 5sh vio & dk blue 9.50 8.50
38 A11 10sh vio & yel brn 10.00 *8.50*
Nos. 29-38 (10) 25.50 *21.00*

Perf. 11½x13, 13x11½
1964, July 1 Wmk. 314

Designs: 70c, Qarn Adh Dhabi. 1sh25c, Seiyun, horiz. 1sh50c, View of Gheil Omer, horiz.

39 A11 70c black 3.00 2.00
40 A11 1sh25c bright green 3.00 *8.50*
41 A11 1sh50c purple 3.00 *9.00*
Nos. 39-41 (3) 9.00 *19.50*

QUAITI STATE OF SHIHR AND MUKALLA

LOCATION — In Eastern Aden Protectorate
GOVT. — Sultanate
CAPITAL — Mukalla

The stamps of the Quaiti State of Shihr and Mukalla were valid for use throughout Aden. Used stamps generally bear Aden GPO or Aden Camp cancels. Examples with cancels from offices in the Eastern Protectorate command a premium.

Sultan Sir Saleh bin Ghalib al Qu'aiti — A1

Mukalla Harbor — A2

Buildings at Shibam — A3

Designs: 2a, Gateway of Shihr. 3a, Outpost of Mukalla. 8a, View of 'Einat. 1r, Governor's Castle, Du'an. 2r, Mosque in Hureidha. 5r, Meshhed.

1942 Engr. Wmk. 4 *Perf. 13¾x14*
1 A1 ½a blue green 1.50 .50
2 A1 ¾a copper brown 2.50 .40
3 A1 1a deep blue 1.00 1.00

Perf. 13x11½, 11½x13
4 A2 1½a dk car rose 2.00 .50
5 A2 2a black brown 2.00 *2.00*
6 A3 2½a deep blue .50 .30
7 A2 3a dk car rose & dl brn 1.25 1.00
8 A3 8a orange red 1.25 .40
9 A2 1r green 7.50 4.25
a. Missing "A" in "CA" of watermark 1,200. *1,100.*
10 A3 2r rose vio & dk blue 16.00 12.00
11 A3 5r gray green & fawn 32.50 17.00
Nos. 1-11 (11) 68.00 39.35

For surcharges see Nos. 20-27.

Nos. 4, 6 Ovptd. in Black or Carmine like Kathiri Nos. 12-13

1946, Oct. 15 *Perf. 11½x13, 13x11½*
12 A2 (b) 1½a dk car rose .25 *.80*
13 A3 (a) 2½a deep blue (C) .25 .25

Victory of the Allied Nations in WWII.

Silver Wedding Issue
Common Design Types

1949, Jan. 17 Photo. *Perf. 14x14½*
14 CD304 1½a scarlet 1.00 *4.50*

Engraved; Name Typo.
Perf. 11½x11
15 CD305 5r green 21.00 14.00

25th anniv. of the marriage of King George VI and Queen Elizabeth.

UPU Issue
Common Design Types
Surcharged with New Values in Annas and Rupees

Engr.; Name Typo. on Nos. 17 and 18
1949, Oct. 10 *Perf. 13½, 11x11½*
16 CD306 2½a on 20c dp ultra .25 .25
17 CD307 3a on 30c dp car 1.50 1.25
18 CD308 8a on 50c org .35 *1.25*
19 CD309 1r on 1sh blue .45 .50
a. Surcharge omitted *4,000.*
Hinged *3,250.*
Nos. 16-19 (4) 2.55 3.25

Nos. 3, 5-11 & Types Srchd. in Carmine or Black

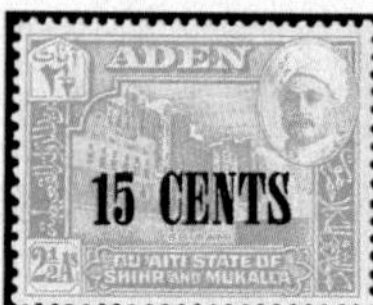

Perf. 14, 13x11½, 11½x13
1951, Oct. 1 Engr. Wmk. 4
20 A1 5c on 1a (C) .25 .25
21 A2 10c on 2a .25 .25
22 A3 15c on 2½a .25 .25
23 A2 20c on 3a #7 .35 *.90*
24 A3 50c on 8a org red .60 *2.50*
25 A2 1sh on 1r 2.25 .60
26 A3 2sh on 2r 8.50 *25.00*
27 A3 5sh on 5r 17.50 *32.50*
Nos. 20-27 (8) 29.95 *62.25*

Coronation Issue
Common Design Type

1953, June 2 Engr. *Perf. 13½x13*
28 CD312 15c dk blue & black 1.10 .60

Qu'aiti State in Hadhramaut

Metal Work — A10

Fisheries A11

Designs: 10c, Mat making. 15c, Weaving. 25c, Pottery. 35c, Building. 50c, Date cultivation. 90c, Agriculture. 1sh25c, 10sh, Lime burning. 2sh, Dhow building. 5sh, Agriculture.

Perf. 11½x13, 13½x14
1955, Sept. 1 Engr. Wmk. 4
29 A10 5c greenish blue .85 .25
30 A10 10c black .90 .25
31 A10 15c dk green .70 .35
32 A10 25c carmine .50 .25
33 A10 35c ultra .90 .25
34 A10 50c red orange .70 .30
35 A10 90c brown .70 .25
36 A11 1sh purple & blk .75 .25
37 A11 1sh25c red org & blk .80 .65
38 A11 2sh dk blue & blk 4.00 .75
39 A11 5sh green & blk 5.00 2.00
40 A11 10sh car & black 11.00 8.00
Nos. 29-40 (12) 26.80 13.55

Types of 1955 with Portrait of Sultan Awadh Bin Saleh El-Qu'aiti

Design: 70c, Agriculture. Others as before.

1963, Oct. 20 Wmk. 314
41 A10 5c greenish blue .25 *1.50*
42 A10 10c black .25 *1.25*
43 A10 15c dark green .25 *1.50*
44 A10 25c carmine .25 *.75*
45 A10 35c ultra .25 *1.75*
46 A10 50c red orange .25 *1.00*
47 A10 70c brown .30 .75
48 A11 1sh purple & blk .35 .35
49 A11 1sh25c red org & blk .75 *4.75*
50 A11 2sh dk blue & blk 3.25 2.00
51 A11 5sh green & blk 14.00 *30.00*
52 A11 10sh car & black 27.50 *30.00*
Nos. 41-52 (12) 47.65 *75.60*

AFARS & ISSAS

French Territory of the

'ä-ˌfär z̦ and ē-'sä z̦

LOCATION — East Africa
GOVT. — French Overseas Territory
AREA — 8,880 sq. mi.
POP. — 150,000 (est. 1974)
CAPITAL — Djibouti (Jibuti)

The French overseas territory of Somali Coast was renamed the French Territory of the Afars and Issas in 1967. It became the Djibouti Republic on June 27, 1977.

100 Centimes = 1 Franc

Catalogue values for all unused stamps in this country are for Never Hinged items.

Imperforates

Most stamps of Afars and Issas exist imperforate in issued and trial colors, and also in small presentation sheets in issued colors.

Grayheaded Kingfisher — A48

1967 Unwmk. Engr. *Perf. 13*

310 A48 10fr Halcyon leucocephala 4.25 3.25
311 A48 15fr Haematopus ostralegus 5.50 4.00
312 A48 50fr Tringa nebularia 12.50 8.00
313 A48 55fr Coracias abyssinicus 17.50 13.00
314 A48 60fr Xerus rutilus, vert. 24.00 17.00
Nos. 310-314 (5) 63.75 45.25
Nos. 310-314,C50 (6) 91.25 62.75

Issued: 10fr, 55fr, Aug. 21; 15fr, 50fr, 60fr, Sept. 25. See No. C50.

Soccer A49

1967, Dec. 18 Engr. *Perf. 13*

315 A49 25fr shown 3.25 2.75
316 A49 30fr Basketball 3.75 3.50

Common Design Types
Pictured in section at front of book.

WHO Anniversary Issue

Common Design Type

1968, May 4 Engr. *Perf. 13*

317 CD126 15fr multicolored 3.25 2.25

20th anniv. of WHO.

Damerdjog Fortress A50

Administration Buildings: 25fr, Ali Adde. 30fr, Dorra. 40fr, Assamo.

1968, May 17 Engr. *Perf. 13*

318 A50 20fr slate, brn & emer 1.40 1.40
319 A50 25fr brt grn, bl & brn 1.60 1.60
320 A50 30fr brn ol, brn org & sl 2.00 1.90
321 A50 40fr brn ol, sl & brt grn 3.50 2.75
Nos. 318-321 (4) 8.50 7.65

Human Rights Year Issue

Common Design Type

1968, Aug. 10 Engr. *Perf. 13*

322 CD127 10fr purple, ver & org 2.50 1.75
323 CD127 70fr green, pur & org 4.50 2.50

International Human Rights Year.

Radio-television Station, Djibouti — A52

High Commission Palace, Djibouti — A53

Designs: 2fr, Justice Building. 5fr, Chamber of Deputies. 8fr, Great Mosque. 15fr, Monument of Free French Forces, vert. 40fr, Djibouti Post Office. 70fr, Residence of Gov. Léonce Lagarde at Obock. No. 332, Djibouti Harbormaster's Building. No. 333, Control tower, Djibouti Airport.

1968-70 Engr. *Perf. 13*

324 A52 1fr multicolored .65 .65
325 A52 2fr multicolored .90 .75
326 A52 5fr multicolored 1.25 1.00
327 A52 8fr multicolored 1.50 1.25
328 A52 15fr multicolored 5.75 3.75
329 A52 40fr multicolored 3.75 2.75
330 A53 60fr multicolored 3.25 2.25
331 A53 70fr multicolored 4.75 3.00
332 A53 85fr multicolored 6.25 3.75
333 A52 85fr multicolored 7.50 4.50
Nos. 324-333 (10) 35.55 23.65

Issued: No. 330, 1968; Nos. 324-328, 331-332, 1969; Nos. 329, 333, 1970.
See Nos. C54-C55.

Locust A54

Designs: 50fr, Pest control by helicopter. 55fr, Pest control by plane.

1969, Oct. 6 Engr. *Perf. 13*

334 A54 15fr brn, grn & slate 5.25 2.25
335 A54 50fr dk grn, bl & ol brn 3.00 2.25
336 A54 55fr red brn, bl & brn 3.75 2.50
Nos. 334-336 (3) 12.00 7.00

Campaign against locusts.

ILO Issue

Common Design Type

1969, Nov. 24 Engr. *Perf. 13*

337 CD131 30fr org, gray & lil 3.00 2.25

Afar Dagger in Ornamental Scabbard A56

1970, Apr. 3 Engr. *Perf. 13*

338 A56 10fr multicolored 1.50 1.00
339 A56 15fr multicolored 1.75 1.10
340 A56 20fr multicolored 2.00 1.25
341 A56 25fr multicolored 2.50 1.40
Nos. 338-341 (4) 7.75 4.75

See No. 364.

UPU Headquarters Issue

Common Design Type

1970, May 20 Engr. *Perf. 13*

342 CD133 25fr brn, brt grn & choc 3.25 1.75

Trapshooting — A57

Motorboats A58

Designs: 50fr, Steeplechase. 55fr, Sailboat, vert. 60fr, Equestrians.

1970 Engr. *Perf. 13*

343 A57 30fr dp brn, yel grn & brt bl 3.25 1.75
344 A58 48fr blue & multi 6.50 2.75
345 A58 50fr cop red, bl & pur 6.50 2.75
346 A58 55fr red brn, bl & ol 6.50 2.75
347 A58 60fr ol, blk & red brn 7.00 3.75
Nos. 343-347 (5) 29.75 13.75

Issued: 30fr, 6/5; 48fr, 10/9; 50fr, 60fr, 11/6.

Automatic Ferry, Tadjourah A59

1970, Nov. 25

348 A59 48fr blue, brn & grn 4.75 2.75

Volcanic Geode A60

Diabase and Chrysolite A61

10fr, Doleritic basalt. 15fr, Olivine basalt.

1971 Photo. *Perf. 13*

349 A61 10fr black & multi 3.25 1.25
350 A61 15fr black & multi 4.25 1.75
351 A60 25fr black, crim & brn 8.50 3.75
352 A61 40fr black & multi 11.50 5.75
Nos. 349-352 (4) 27.50 12.50

Issued: 10fr, 11/22; 15fr, 10/8; 25fr, 4/26; 40fr, 1/25.

A62

4fr, Manta birostris. 5fr, Coryphaena hippurus. 9fr, Pristis pectinatus.

1971, July 1 Photo. *Perf. 12x12½*

353 A62 4fr mulitcolored 2.75 1.25
354 A62 5fr multicolored 3.50 2.00
355 A62 9fr multicolored 4.75 2.40
Nos. 353-355 (3) 11.00 5.65

See No. C60.

De Gaulle Issue

Common Design Type

Designs: 60fr, Gen. Charles de Gaulle, 1940. 85fr, Pres. de Gaulle, 1970.

1971, Nov. 9 Engr. *Perf. 13*

356 CD134 60fr dk vio bl & blk 7.50 4.25
357 CD134 85fr dk vio bl & blk 8.50 5.25

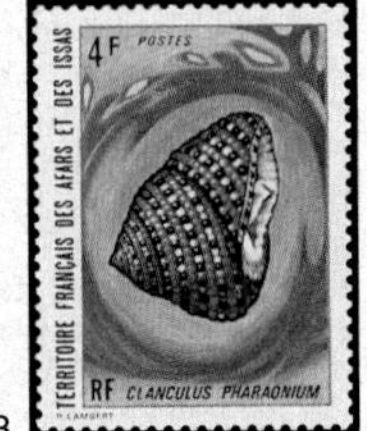

A63

Shells: 4fr, Strawberry Top. 9fr, Cypraea pantherina. 20fr, Bull-mouth helmet. 50fr, Ethiopian volute.

1972, Mar. 8 Photo. *Perf. 12½x13*

358 A63 4fr olive & multi 2.50 1.50
359 A63 9fr dk blue & multi 3.00 1.75
360 A63 20fr dp green & multi 5.00 2.75
361 A63 50fr dp claret & multi 9.00 4.50
Nos. 358-361 (4) 19.50 10.50

Shepherd — A64

Design: 10fr, Dromedary breeding.

1973, Apr. 11 Photo. *Perf. 13*

362 A64 9fr blue & multi 2.00 1.00
363 A64 10fr blue & multi 2.25 1.00

Afar Dagger — A65

1974, Jan. 29 Engr. *Perf. 13*

364 A65 30fr slate grn & dk brn 1.90 1.00

For surcharge see No. 379.

Flamingos, Lake Abbe — A66

Flamingos and different views of Lake Abbe.

1974, Feb. 22 Photo. *Perf. 13*

370 A66 5fr multicolored 3.50 1.10
371 A66 15fr multicolored 3.00 1.25
372 A66 50fr multicolored 5.00 2.00
Nos. 370-372 (3) 11.50 4.35

Soccer Ball — A67

1974, May 24 Engr. *Perf. 13*

373 A67 25fr black & emerald 3.50 1.75

World Cup Soccer Championship, Munich, June 13-July 7.

Letters Around UPU Emblem — A68

1974, Oct. 9 Engr. *Perf. 13*
374 A68 20fr multicolored 1.75 .80
375 A68 100fr multicolored 4.50 2.75

Centenary of Universal Postal Union.

Oleo Chrysophylla A69

Designs: 15fr, Ficus species. 20fr, Solanum adoense.

1974, Nov. 22 Photo.
376 A69 10fr shown 2.25 1.00
377 A69 15fr multicolored 2.75 1.50
378 A69 20fr multicolored 3.75 2.00
Nos. 376-378 (3) 8.75 4.50

Day Primary Forest.

No. 364 Surcharged in Red

1975, Jan. 1 Engr. *Perf. 13*
379 A65 40fr on 30fr multi 2.75 1.50

Treasury — A70

Design: 25fr, Government buildings.

1975, Jan. 7 Engr. *Perf. 13*
380 A70 8fr blue, gray & red .80 .50
381 A70 25fr red, blue & indigo 1.75 1.00

Darioconus Textile — A71

Sea Shells: No. 383, Murex palmarosa. 10fr, Conus sumatrensis. 15fr, Cypraea pulchra. No. 386, 45fr, Murex scolopax. No. 387, Cypraea exhusta. 40fr, Ranella spinosa. 55fr, Cypraea erythraensis. 60fr, Conus taeniatus.

1975-76 Engr. *Perf. 13*
382 A71 5fr blue grn & brn 1.50 1.00
383 A71 5fr blue & multi ('76) 1.50 1.10
384 A71 10fr lilac, blk & brn 3.00 1.25
385 A71 15fr blue, ind & brn 4.25 1.50
386 A71 20fr purple & lt brn 6.50 3.50
387 A71 20fr brt grn & multi ('76) 3.00 1.50
388 A71 40fr green & brown 5.00 2.75
389 A71 45fr green, bl & bister 5.75 2.75
390 A71 55fr turq & multi ('76) 4.50 3.00
391 A71 60fr buff & sepia ('76) 8.00 3.50
Nos. 382-391 (10) 43.00 21.85

Hypolimnas Misippus A72

Butterflies: 40fr, Papilio nireus. 50fr, Acraea anemosa. 65fr, Holocerina smilax menieri. 70fr, Papilio demodocus. No. 397, Papilio dardanus. No. 398, Balachowsky gonimbrasca. 150fr, Vanessa cardui.

1975-76 Photo. *Perf. 13*
392 A72 25fr emerald & multi 5.00 2.50
393 A72 40fr yellow & multi 5.25 2.75
394 A72 50fr ultra & multi ('76) 6.50 3.50
395 A72 65fr ol & multi ('76) 6.25 3.50
396 A72 70fr violet & multi 8.00 4.50
397 A72 100fr blue & multi 9.50 5.25
398 A72 100fr Prus bl & multi ('76) 8.50 5.00
399 A72 150fr grn & multi ('76) 10.00 5.75
Nos. 392-399 (8) 59.00 32.75

A73

No. 400, Hyaena hyaena. No. 401, Cercopithecus aethiops. No. 402, Equus asinus somalicus. No. 403, Dorcatragus megalotis. No. 404, Ichneumia albicauda. No. 405, Hystrix galeata. No. 406, Ictonyx striatus. No. 407, Orycteropus afer.

Perf. 13x12½, 12½x13
1975-76 Photo.
400 A73 10fr multicolored 1.75 1.25
401 A73 15fr multicolored 3.00 1.75
402 A73 15fr multicolored 2.75 1.50
403 A73 30fr multicolored 3.75 2.50
404 A73 50fr multicolored 4.75 2.50
405 A73 60fr multicolored 6.50 3.25
406 A73 70fr multicolored 8.75 4.00
407 A73 200fr multicolored 12.00 7.00
Nos. 400-407 (8) 43.25 23.75

Nos. 401-402, 405 are vert.
Issued: 50fr, 60fr, 70fr, 2/21; No. 401, 200fr, 10/24; 10fr, No. 402, 30fr, 2/4/76.

A74

No. 413, Vidua macroura. No. 414, Psittacula krameri. No. 415, Cinnyris venustus. No. 416, Ardea goliath. No. 417, Scopus umbretta. No. 418, Oena capensis. No. 419, Platalea alba.

1975-76 Photo. *Perf. 12½x13*
413 A74 20fr multicolored 3.50 1.75
414 A74 25fr multicolored 3.25 1.25
415 A74 50fr multicolored 6.25 3.00
416 A74 60fr multicolored 7.50 3.75
417 A74 100fr multicolored 14.00 6.00
418 A74 100fr multicolored 8.25 3.75
419 A74 300fr multicolored 16.00 8.50
Nos. 413-419 (7) 58.75 28.00

Issued: 300fr, 6/15/76; 25fr, No. 418, 10/13/76; others 11/21 and 12/19/75.

A75

1975, Dec. 19 Engr. *Perf. 13*
421 A75 20fr Palms 3.00 1.00

Satellite and Alexander Graham Bell — A76

1976, Mar. 10 Engr. *Perf. 13*
422 A76 200fr dp bl, org & sl grn 6.00 4.00

Centenary of the first telephone call by Alexander Graham Bell, Mar. 10, 1876.

Basketball A77

1976, July 7 Litho. *Perf. 12½*
423 A77 10fr shown 1.50 .70
424 A77 15fr Bicycling 1.50 .80
425 A77 40fr Soccer 2.25 1.25
426 A77 60fr Running 3.00 2.00
Nos. 423-426 (4) 8.25 4.75

21st Olympic Games, Montreal, Canada, July 17-Aug. 1.

Pterois Radiata — A78

1976, Aug. 10 Photo. *Perf. 13x13½*
428 A78 45fr blue & multi 4.00 2.50

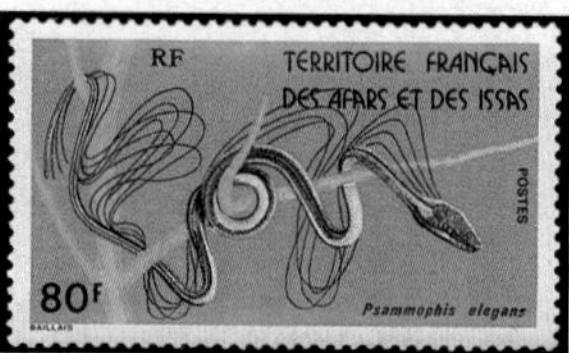

Psammophis Elegans — A79

Design: 70fr, Naja nigricollis, vert.

Perf. 13x13½, 13½x13
1976, Sept. 27 Photo.
430 A79 70fr ocher & multi 6.00 3.00
431 A79 80fr emerald & multi 8.25 4.00

Motorcyclist A80

1977, Jan. 27 Litho. *Perf. 12x12½*
432 A80 200fr multicolored 9.00 5.75

Moto-Cross motorcycle race.

Conus Betulinus — A81

Sea Shells: 5fr, Cyprea tigris. 70fr, Conus striatus. 85fr, Cyprea mauritiana.

1977 Engr. *Perf. 13*
433 A81 5fr multicolored 3.25 1.75
434 A81 30fr multicolored 4.50 1.75
435 A81 70fr multicolored 11.00 4.50
436 A81 85fr multicolored 11.00 4.50
Nos. 433-436 (4) 29.75 12.50

Gaterin Gaterinus A82

1977, Apr. 15 Photo. *Perf. 13x12½*
437 A82 15fr shown 2.00 1.25
438 A82 65fr Barracudas 5.00 2.25

AIR POST STAMPS

AP16

200fr, Aquila rapax belisarius.

Unwmk.
1967, Aug. 21 Engr. *Perf. 13*
C50 AP16 200fr multicolored 27.50 17.50

AP17

48fr, Parachutists. 85fr, Water skier & skin diver.

1968 Engr. *Perf. 13*

C51 AP17 48fr multicolored 7.50 2.50
C52 AP17 85fr multicolored 7.50 6.00

Issue dates: 48fr, Jan. 5; 85fr, Mar. 15.

Aerial Map of the Territory — AP18

1968, Nov. 15 Engr. *Perf. 13*

C53 AP18 500fr bl, dk brn & ocher 30.00 11.00

Buildings Type of Regular Issue

100fr, Cathedral. 200fr, Sayed Hassan Mosque.

1969 Engr. *Perf. 13*

C54 A53 100fr multi, vert. 6.50 3.00
C55 A53 200fr multi, vert. 9.50 6.00

Issue dates: 100fr, Apr. 4; 200fr, May 8.

Concorde Issue

Common Design Type

1969, Apr. 17

C56 CD129 100fr org red & ol 30.00 18.00

Arta Ionospheric Station — AP19

1970, May 8 Engr. *Perf. 13*

C57 AP19 70fr multicolored 5.00 3.25

Japanese Sword Guard, Fish Design — AP20

200fr, Japanese sword guard, horse design.

Gold embossed

1970, Oct. 26 *Perf. 12½*

C58 AP20 100fr multicolored 13.00 8.50
C59 AP20 200fr multicolored 16.00 12.00

EXPO '70 International Exposition, Osaka, Japan, Mar. 15-Sept. 13.

Scarus vetula — AP21

1971, July 1 Photo. *Perf. 12½*

C60 AP21 30fr black & multi 7.00 4.50

Djibouti Harbor — AP22

1972, Feb. 3

C61 AP22 100fr blue & multi 6.50 3.50

New Djibouti harbor.

AP23

30fr, Pterocles lichtensteini. 49fr, Uppupa epops. 66fr, Capella media. 500fr, Francolinus ochropectus.

1972 Photo. *Perf. 12½x13*

C62 AP23 30fr multi 5.00 3.00
C63 AP23 49fr multi 7.25 4.25
C64 AP23 66fr multi 12.00 6.50
C65 AP23 500fr multi 40.00 18.00
Nos. C62-C65 (4) 64.25 31.75

Issue dates: No. C65, Nov. 3; others Apr. 21.

AP24

Olympic Rings and: 5fr, Running. 10fr, Basketball. 55fr, Swimming, horiz. 60fr, Olympic torch and Greek frieze, horiz.

1972, June 8 Engr. *Perf. 13*

C66 AP24 5fr multicolored 1.25 .90
C67 AP24 10fr multicolored 1.50 .90
C68 AP24 55fr multicolored 3.00 1.75
C69 AP24 60fr multicolored 3.75 2.00
Nos. C66-C69 (4) 9.50 5.55

20th Olympic Games, Munich, 8/26-9/11.

Louis Pasteur — AP25

100fr, Albert Calmette and C. Guérin.

1972, Oct. 5 Engr. *Perf. 13*

C70 AP25 20fr multicolored 3.00 1.25
C71 AP25 100fr multicolored 5.75 4.25

Pasteur, Calmette, Guerin, chemists and bacteriologists, benefactors of mankind.

Map and Views of Territory — AP26

200fr, Woman and Mosque of Djibouti, vert.

1973, Jan. 15 Photo. *Perf. 13*

C72 AP26 30fr brown & multi 7.75 4.75
C73 AP26 200fr multicolored 14.50 9.50

Visit of Pres. Georges Pompidou of France, Jan. 15-17.

AP27

30fr, Oryx beisa. 50fr, Madoqua saltiana. 66fr, Felis caracal.

1973, Feb. 26 Photo. *Perf. 13x12½*

C74 AP27 30fr multicolored 3.75 2.00
C75 AP27 50fr multicolored 5.25 3.50
C76 AP27 66fr multicolored 7.00 3.75
Nos. C74-C76 (3) 16.00 9.25

See Nos. C94-C96.

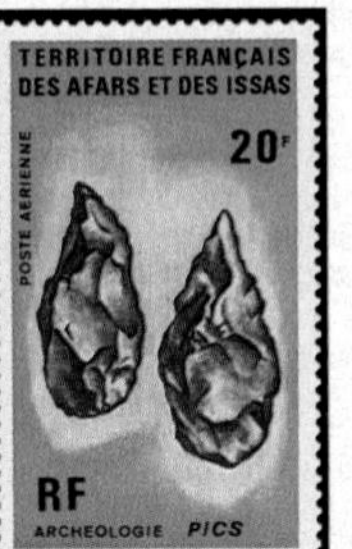

Celts — AP28

Various pre-historic flint tools. 40fr, 60fr, horiz.

1973 *Perf. 13*

C77 AP28 20fr yel grn, blk & brn 5.50 3.00
C78 AP28 40fr yellow & multi 5.50 3.75
C79 AP28 49fr lilac & multi 10.00 5.00
C80 AP28 60fr blue & multi 8.00 5.50
Nos. C77-C80 (4) 29.00 17.25

Issued: 20fr, 49fr, 3/16; 40fr, 60fr, 9/7.

AP29

40fr, Octopus macropus. 60fr, Halicore dugong.

1973, Mar. 16

C81 AP29 40fr multicolored 5.00 2.25
C82 AP29 60fr multicolored 9.75 4.75

AP30

Copernicus: 8fr, Nicolaus Copernicus, Polish astronomer. 9fr, William C. Roentgen, physicist, X-ray discoverer. No. C85, Edward Jenner, physician, discoverer of vaccination. No. C86, Marie Curie, discoverer of radium and polonium. 49fr, Robert Koch, physician and bacteriologist. 50fr, Clement Ader (1841-1925), French aviation pioneer. 55fr, Guglielmo Marconi, Italian electrical engineer, inventor. 85fr, Moliere, French playwright. 100fr, Henri Farman (1874-1937), French aviation pioneer. 150fr, Andre-Marie Ampere (1775-1836), French physicist. 250fr, Michelangelo Buonarroti (1475-1564), Italian sculptor, painter and architect.

1973-75 Engr. *Perf. 13*

C83 AP30 8fr multicolored 1.50 1.00
C84 AP30 9fr multicolored 2.25 1.50
C85 AP30 10fr multicolored 2.25 1.50
C86 AP30 10fr multicolored 2.00 1.50
C87 AP30 49fr multicolored 4.25 3.00
C88 AP30 50fr multicolored 4.25 3.00
C89 AP30 55fr multicolored 3.00 2.25
C90 AP30 85fr multicolored 7.25 3.00
C91 AP30 100fr multicolored 6.50 3.75
C92 AP30 150fr multicolored 6.50 3.75
C93 AP30 250fr multicolored 11.00 7.00
Nos. C83-C93 (11) 50.75 31.25

Issued: 8fr, 85fr, 5/9/73; 9fr, No. C85, 49fr, 10/12/73; 100fr, 1/29/74; 55fr, 3/22/74; No. C86, 8/23/74; 150fr, 7/24/75; 250fr, 6/26/75; 50fr, 9/25/75.

AP31

20fr, Papio anubis. 50fr, Genetta tigrina, horiz. 66fr, Lapus habessinicus.

Perf. 12½x13, 13x12½

1973, Dec. 12 Photo.

C94 AP31 20fr multicolored 3.25 1.50
C95 AP31 50fr multicolored 5.00 2.25
C96 AP31 66fr multicolored 7.00 2.75
Nos. C94-C96 (3) 15.25 6.50

Spearfishing — AP32

1974, Apr. 14 Engr. *Perf. 13*

C97 AP32 200fr multicolored 13.50 8.00

No. C97 was prepared for release in Nov. 1972, for the 3rd Underwater Spearfishing Contest in the Red Sea. Dates were obliterated with a rectangle and the stamp was not issued without this obliteration. Value $400.

Rock Carvings, Balho — AP33

1974, Apr. 26

C98	AP33	200fr carmine & slate	16.00	8.25

Lake Assal — AP34

Designs (Lake Assal): 50fr, Rock formations on shore. 85fr, Crystallized wood.

1974, Oct. 25 Photo. *Perf. 13*

C99	AP34	49fr multicolored	3.00	2.00
C100	AP34	50fr multicolored	3.25	2.25
C101	AP34	85fr multicolored	6.50	4.25
		Nos. C99-C101 (3)	12.75	8.50

Columba Guinea — AP35

1975, May 23 Photo. *Perf. 13*

C102	AP35	500fr multicolored	30.00	14.00

Djibouti Airport — AP36

1977, Mar. 1 Litho. *Perf. 12*

C103	AP36	500fr multicolored	17.00	11.00

Opening of new Djibouti Airport.

Thomas A. Edison and Phonograph — AP37

Design: 75fr, Alexander Volta, electric train, lines and light bulb.

1977, May 5 Engr. *Perf. 13*

C104	AP37	55fr multicolored	5.50	3.00
C105	AP37	75fr multicolored	8.50	5.00

Famous inventors: Thomas Alva Edison and Alexander Volta (1745-1827).

POSTAGE DUE STAMPS

Nomad's Milk Jug — D3

Perf. 14x13

1969, Dec. 15 Engr. Unwmk.

J49	D3	1fr red brn, red lil & sl	.70	*1.00*
J50	D3	2fr red brn, emer & sl	.80	*1.00*
J51	D3	5fr red brn, bl & slate	1.25	*1.50*
J52	D3	10fr red brn, brn & slate	2.00	*2.25*
		Nos. J49-J52 (4)	4.75	*5.75*

AFGHANISTAN

af-ˈga-nə-ˌstan

LOCATION — Central Asia, bounded by Iran, Turkmenistan, Uzbekistan, Tajikistan, Pakistan, and China
GOVT. — Republic
AREA — 251,773 sq. mi.
POP. — 23,500,000 (1995 est.)
CAPITAL — Kabul

Afghanistan changed from a constitutional monarchy to a republic in July 1973.

12 Shahi = 6 Sanar = 3 Abasi =
2 Krans = 1 Rupee Kabuli
60 Paisas = 1 Rupee (1921)
100 Pouls = 1 Rupee Afghani (1927)

Catalogue values for unused stamps in this country are for Never Hinged items, beginning with Scott 364 in the regular postage section, Scott B1 in the semi-postal section, Scott C7 in the airpost section, Scott O8 in officials section, and Scott RA6 in the postal tax section.

CHARACTERS OF VALUE.

Shahi. 1871-78 A7 1876 A8

Sanar. 1871-78 Abasi. 1871 6 Shahi. 1872

1 Rupee. 1874 ½ Rupee. 1876(A8) 1876 (A7)

1 Rupee. 1872 Rupee. 1874 1876 (A8) 1877-78

From 1871 to 1892 and 1898, the Moslem year date appears on the stamp. Numerals as follows:

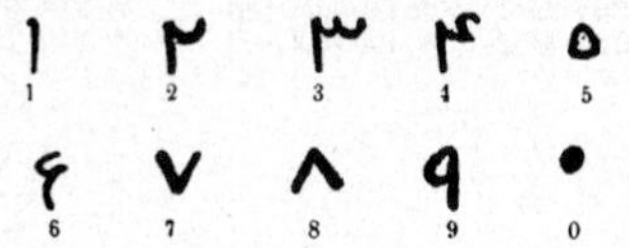

Until 1891, cancellation consisted of cutting or tearing a piece from the stamps. Such examples should not be considered as damaged.

Values are for cut square examples of good color. Cut to shape or faded examples sell for much less, particularly Nos. 2-10.

Nos. 2-108 are on laid paper of varying thickness except where wove is noted.

Until 1907, all stamps were issued ungummed.

The tiger's head on types A2 to A11 symbolizes the name of the contemporary amir, Sher (Tiger) Ali.

Kingdom of Kabul

Tiger's Head, Type I — A2

Tiger's Head, Type II — A2a

Both circles dotted. Type I: has well-defined inner and outer circles with evenly spaced dots.

Type II: has no well-defined inner and outer circles, and the dots are randomly spaced.

1871 Unwmk. Litho. *Imperf.*
Dated "1288"

2	A2	1sh black	550.00	25.00
2A	A2a	1sh black	525.00	35.00
3	A2	1sa black	650.00	32.50
3A	A2a	1sa black	210.00	55.00
4	A2	1ab black	250.00	50.00
4A	A2a	1ab black	100.00	32.50
		Nos. 2-4 (3)	1,450.	107.50

Thirty varieties of the shahi, 10 of the sanar and 5 of the abasi.

Similar designs without the tiger's head in the center are revenues.

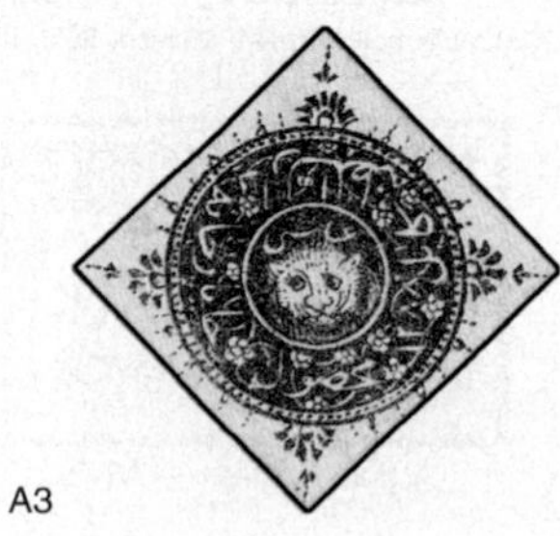

A3

Outer circle dotted

Dated "1288"

5	A3	1sh black	525.00	35.00
6	A3	1sa black	300.00	50.00
7	A3	1ab black	110.00	32.50
		Nos. 5-7 (3)	935.00	117.50

Five varieties of each.

A4

Toned Wove Paper

1872 Dated "1289"

8	A4	6sh violet	*1,250.*	*800.*
9	A4	1rup violet	*1,750.*	*1,250.*

Two varieties of each. Date varies in location. Printed in sheets of 4 (2x2) containing two of each denomination.

Most used examples are smeared with a greasy ink cancel.

A4a

White Laid Paper

1873 Dated "1290"

10	A4a	1sh black	25.00	12.00
a.		Corner ornament missing	*550.00*	*500.00*
b.		Corner ornament retouched	*75.00*	*40.00*

15 varieties. Nos. 10a, 10b are the sixth stamp on the sheet.

A5

1873

11	A5	1sh black	22.50	11.00
11A	A5	1sh violet	*500.00*	

Sixty varieties of each.

1874 Dated "1291"

12	A5	1ab black	90.00	55.00
13	A5	½rup black	37.50	20.00
14	A5	1rup black	40.00	24.00
		Nos. 12-14 (3)	167.50	99.00

Five varieties of each.

Nos. 12-14 were printed on the same sheet. Se-tenant varieties exist.

A6

A7

1875 Dated "1292"

15	A6	1sa black	*375.00*	*350.00*
a.		Wide outer circle	*1,200.*	*750.00*
16	A6	1ab black	425.00	400.00
17	A6	1sa brown violet	75.00	30.00
a.		Wide outer circle	300.00	*185.00*
18	A6	1ab brown violet	115.00	67.50

Ten varieties of the sanar, five of the abasi.

Nos. 15-16 and 17-18 were printed in the same sheets. Se-tenant pairs exist.

1876 **Dated "1293"**

No.	Type	Denom.	Color	Unused	Used
19	A7	1sh	black	325.00	175.00
20	A7	1sa	black	375.00	200.00
21	A7	1ab	black	750.00	425.00
22	A7	½rup	black	450.00	275.00
23	A7	1rup	black	875.00	275.00
24	A7	1sh	violet	450.00	275.00
25	A7	1sa	violet	425.00	275.00
26	A7	1ab	violet	525.00	275.00
27	A7	½rup	violet	225.00	60.00
28	A7	1rup	violet	225.00	75.00

12 varieties of the shahi and 3 each of the other values.

A8

1876 **Dated "1293"**

No.	Type	Denom.	Color	Unused	Used
29	A8	1sh	gray	16.00	6.00
30	A8	1sa	gray	16.00	8.00
31	A8	1ab	gray	42.50	20.00
32	A8	½rup	gray	50.00	25.00
33	A8	1rup	gray	37.50	17.50
34	A8	1sh	olive blk	140.00	80.00
35	A8	1sa	olive blk	190.00	100.00
36	A8	1ab	olive blk	400.00	250.00
37	A8	½rup	olive blk	275.00	275.00
38	A8	1rup	olive blk	375.00	400.00
39	A8	1sh	green	30.00	8.00
40	A8	1sa	green	40.00	24.00
41	A8	1ab	green	80.00	60.00
42	A8	½rup	green	125.00	80.00
43	A8	1rup	green	110.00	125.00
44	A8	1sh	ocher	32.50	15.00
45	A8	1sa	ocher	40.00	24.00
46	A8	1ab	ocher	80.00	50.00
47	A8	½rup	ocher	90.00	65.00
48	A8	1rup	ocher	140.00	125.00
49	A8	1sh	violet	37.50	15.00
50	A8	1sa	violet	37.50	15.00
51	A8	1ab	violet	50.00	15.00
52	A8	½rup	violet	70.00	27.50
53	A8	1rup	violet	100.00	40.00

24 varieties of the shahi, 4 of which show denomination written:

12 varieties of the sanar, 6 of the abasi and 3 each of the ½ rupee and rupee.

A9

1877 **Dated "1294"**

No.	Type	Denom.	Color	Unused	Used
54	A9	1sh	gray	10.00	15.00
55	A9	1sa	gray	6.00	6.00
56	A9	1ab	gray	11.00	9.00
57	A9	½rup	gray	14.50	20.00
58	A9	1rup	gray	14.50	20.00
59	A9	1sh	black	18.00	27.50
60	A9	1sa	black	25.00	10.00
61	A9	1ab	black	42.50	15.00
62	A9	½rup	black	45.00	30.00
63	A9	1rup	black	45.00	30.00
64	A9	1sh	green	32.50	32.50
a.			Wove paper	35.00	
65	A9	1sa	green	12.00	12.00
a.			Wove paper	16.00	15.00
66	A9	1ab	green	16.00	16.00
a.			Wove paper	30.00	
67	A9	½rup	green	27.50	30.00
a.			Wove paper	32.50	42.50
68	A9	1rup	green	27.50	30.00
a.			Wove paper	32.50	42.50
69	A9	1sh	ocher	11.00	5.25
70	A9	1sa	ocher	8.00	7.25
71	A9	1ab	ocher	32.50	24.50
72	A9	½rup	ocher	40.00	35.00
73	A9	1rup	ocher	45.00	35.00
74	A9	1sh	violet	11.00	5.00
75	A9	1sa	violet	11.00	5.00
76	A9	1ab	violet	19.00	12.00
77	A9	½rup	violet	27.50	30.00
78	A9	1rup	violet	27.50	30.00

25 varieties of the shahi, 8 of the sanar, 3 of the abasi and 2 each of the ½ rupee and rupee.

Some examples of Nos. 54-78 show a "94" year date. These are valued less.

A10

A11

1878 **Dated "1295"**

No.	Type	Denom.	Color	Unused	Used
79	A10	1sh	gray	5.00	10.00
80	A10	1sa	gray	7.00	10.00
81	A10	1ab	gray	7.00	10.00
82	A10	½rup	gray	12.00	15.00
83	A10	1rup	gray	12.00	15.00
84	A10	1sh	black	9.50	
85	A10	1sa	black	9.50	
86	A10	1ab	black	32.50	
87	A10	½rup	black	35.00	
88	A10	1rup	black	35.00	
89	A10	1sh	green	32.50	55.00
90	A10	1sa	green	8.00	9.00
91	A10	1ab	green	35.00	30.00
92	A10	½rup	green	32.50	30.00
93	A10	1rup	green	60.00	40.00
94	A10	1sh	ocher	24.00	8.00
95	A10	1sa	ocher	12.00	15.00
96	A10	1ab	ocher	45.00	35.00
97	A10	½rup	ocher	65.00	45.00
98	A10	1rup	ocher	27.50	30.00
99	A10	1sh	violet	8.00	15.00
100	A10	1sa	violet	30.00	25.00
101	A10	1ab	violet	16.00	15.00
102	A10	½rup	violet	55.00	35.00
103	A10	1rup	violet	45.00	30.00
104	A11	1sh	gray	5.50	5.00
105	A11	1sh	black	90.00	50.00
106	A11	1sh	green	8.00	4.00
107	A11	1sh	ocher	8.00	7.25
108	A11	1sh	violet	6.50	5.00

40 varieties of the shahi, 30 of the sanar, 6 of the abasi and 2 each of the ½ rupee and 1 rupee.

Some examples of Nos. 79-108 show a "95" year date. These are valued less.

The 1876, 1877 and 1878 issues were printed in separate colors for each main post office on the Peshawar-Kabul-Khulm (Tashkurghan) postal route. Some specialists consider the black printings to be proofs or trial colors.

There are many shades of these colors.

1ab, Type I (26mm) — A12

1ab, Type II (28mm) — A13

A14

A15

Dated "1298", numerals scattered through design

Handstamped, in watercolor

1881-90

Thin White Laid Batonne Paper

No.	Type	Denom.	Color	Unused	Used
109	A12	1ab	violet	4.00	2.00
109A	A13	1ab	violet	8.00	3.00
110	A12	1ab	black brn	5.00	2.00
111	A12	1ab	rose	12.00	3.00
b.			Se-tenant with No. 111A	16.00	
111A	A13	1ab	rose	6.00	2.00
112	A14	2ab	violet	8.00	2.00
113	A14	2ab	black brn	10.00	6.00
114	A14	2ab	rose	20.00	10.00
115	A15	1rup	violet	10.00	2.00
116	A15	1rup	black brn	12.00	8.00
117	A15	1rup	rose	11.00	6.00

Thin White Wove Batonne Paper

No.	Type	Denom.	Color	Unused	Used
118	A12	1ab	violet	12.00	5.00
119	A12	1ab	vermilion	30.00	9.00
120	A12	1ab	rose	30.00	25.00
121	A14	2ab	violet	30.00	25.00
122	A14	2ab	vermilion	30.00	16.00
122A	A14	2ab	black brn		
123	A15	1rup	violet	15.00	8.00
124	A15	1rup	vermilion	14.00	7.50
125	A15	1rup	black brn	19.00	8.00

Thin White Laid Batonne Paper

No.	Type	Denom.	Color	Unused	Used
126	A12	1ab	brown org	20.00	8.00
126A	A13	1ab	brn org (II)	20.00	8.00
127	A12	1ab	carmine lake	20.00	8.00
a.			Laid paper	20.00	8.00
128	A14	2ab	brown org	20.00	8.00
129	A14	2ab	carmine lake	20.00	8.00
130	A15	1rup	brown org	35.00	15.00
131	A15	1rup	car lake	35.00	15.00

Yellowish Laid Batonne Paper

No.	Type	Denom.	Color	Unused	Used
132	A12	1ab	purple	10.00	10.00
133	A12	1ab	red	10.00	5.00

1884 **Colored Wove Paper**

No.	Type	Denom.	Color	Unused	Used
133A	A13	1ab	purple, *yel* (II)	17.50	17.50
134	A12	1ab	purple, *grn*	20.00	
135	A12	1ab	purple, *blue*	32.50	21.00
136	A12	1ab	red, *grn*	37.50	
137	A12	1ab	red, *yel*	30.00	
139	A12	1ab	red, *rose*	50.00	
140	A14	2ab	red, *yel*	30.00	
142	A14	2ab	red, *rose*	30.00	
143	A15	1rup	red, *yel*	55.00	20.00
145	A15	1rup	red, *rose*	65.00	25.00

Thin Colored Ribbed Paper

No.	Type	Denom.	Color	Unused	Used
146	A14	2ab	red, *yellow*	40.00	
147	A15	1rup	red, *yellow*	80.00	
148	A12	1ab	lake, *lilac*	40.00	
149	A14	2ab	lake, *lilac*	40.00	
150	A15	1rup	lake, *lilac*	40.00	
151	A12	1ab	lake, *green*	40.00	
152	A14	2ab	lake, *green*	40.00	
153	A15	1rup	lake, *green*	40.00	

1886-88 **Colored Wove Paper**

No.	Type	Denom.	Color	Unused	Used
155	A12	1ab	black, *magenta*	60.00	
156	A12	1ab	claret brn, *org*	50.00	
156A	A12	1ab	red, *org*	40.00	
156B	A14	2ab	red, *org*	40.00	
156C	A15	1rup	red, *org*	40.00	

Laid Batonné Paper

No.	Type	Denom.	Color	Unused	Used
157	A12	1ab	black, *lavender*	40.00	
158	A12	1ab	cl brn, *grn*	40.00	
159	A12	1ab	black, *pink*	60.00	
160	A14	2ab	black, *pink*	100.00	
161	A15	1rup	black, *pink*	70.00	

Laid Paper

No.	Type	Denom.	Color	Unused	Used
162	A12	1ab	black, *pink*	80.00	
163	A14	2ab	black, *pink*	80.00	
164	A15	1rup	black, *pink*	80.00	
165	A12	1ab	brown, *yel*	80.00	
166	A14	2ab	brown, *yel*	80.00	
167	A15	1rup	brown, *yel*	80.00	
168	A12	1ab	blue, *grn*	80.00	
169	A14	2ab	blue, *grn*	80.00	
170	A15	1rup	blue, *grn*	80.00	

1891 **Colored Wove Paper**

No.	Type	Denom.	Color	Unused	Used
175	A12	1ab	green, *rose*	100.00	
176	A15	1rup	pur, *grn batonne*	100.00	

Nos. 109-176 fall into three categories:

1. Those regularly issued and in normal postal use from 1881 on, handstamped on thin white laid or wove paper in strip sheets containing 12 or more impressions of the same denomination arranged in two irregular rows, with the impressions often touching or overlappng.

2. The 1884 postal issues provisionally printed on smooth or ribbed colored wove paper as needed to supplement low stocks of the normal white paper stamps.

3. The "special" printings made in a range of colors on several types of laid or wove colored papers, most of which were never used for normal printings. These were produced periodically from 1886 to 1891 to meet philatelic demands. Although nominally valid for postage, most of the special printings were exported directly to fill dealers' orders, and few were ever postally used. Many of the sheets contained all three denominations with impressions separated by ruled lines. Sometimes different colors were used, so se-tenant multiples of denomination or color exist. Many combinations of stamp and paper colors exist besides those listed.

Various shades of each color exist.

Type A12 is known dated "1297."

Counterfeits, lithographed or typographed, are plentiful.

Kingdom of Afghanistan

A16

A17

A18

Dated "1309"

1891 **Pelure Paper** **Litho.**

No.	Type	Denom.	Color	Unused	Used
177	A16	1ab	slate blue	2.00	2.00
a.			Tete beche pair	19.00	
178	A17	2ab	slate blue	12.00	12.00
179	A18	1rup	slate blue	27.50	27.50
			Nos. 177-179 (3)	41.50	41.50

Revenue stamps of similar design exist in various colors.

Nos. 177-179 were printed in panes on the same sheet, so se-tenant gutter pairs exist. Examples in black or red are proofs.

A Mosque Gate and Crossed Cannons (National Seal) — A19

Dated "1310" in Upper Right Corner

1892 **Flimsy Wove Paper**

No.	Type	Denom.	Color	Unused	Used
180	A19	1ab	black, *green*	3.50	3.00
181	A19	1ab	black, *orange*	4.50	4.50
182	A19	1ab	black, *yellow*	3.50	3.00
183	A19	1ab	black, *pink*	4.00	3.25
184	A19	1ab	black, *lil rose*	4.00	4.00
185	A19	1ab	black, *blue*	6.00	5.50
186	A19	1ab	black, *salmon*	4.50	3.75
187	A19	1ab	black, *magenta*	4.00	4.00
188	A19	1ab	black, *violet*	4.00	4.00
188A	A19	1ab	black, *scarlet*	4.00	3.00

Many shades exist.

A20

A21

Undated

1894 **Flimsy Wove Paper**

No.	Type	Denom.	Color	Unused	Used
189	A20	2ab	black, *green*	12.00	8.00
190	A21	1rup	black, *green*	14.50	13.00

24 varieties of the 2 abasi and 12 varieties of the rupee.

Nos. 189-190 and F3 were printed se-tenant in the same sheet. Pairs exist.

A21a

Dated "1316"

1898 Flimsy Wove Paper

191 A21a 2ab black, *pink* 3.00
192 A21a 2ab black, *magenta* 3.00
193 A21a 2ab black, *yellow* 1.40
193A A21a 2ab black, *salmon* 3.50
194 A21a 2ab black, *green* 1.75
195 A21a 2ab black, *purple* 2.40
195A A21a 2ab black, *blue* 22.50
Nos. 191-195A (7) 37.55

Nos. 191-195A were not regularly issued. Genuinely used examples are scarce. No. 195A was found in remainder stocks and probably was never released.

A22

A23

A24

1907 Engr. *Imperf.*

Medium Wove Paper

196 A22 1ab blue green 50.00 30.00
a. 1ab emerald 75.00 20.00
b. Double impression *500.00*
c. Printed on both sides 450.00
197 A22 1ab brt blue 35.00 35.00
198 A23 2ab deep blue 45.00 25.00
a. Double impression *550.00*
199 A24 1rup green 100.00 50.00
a. 1rup blue green 100.00 75.00

Zigzag Roulette 10

200 A22 1ab green *2,750.* 350.00
a. Double impression *1,500.*
b. Printed on both sides *1,750.*
c. Double impression and printed on both sides *2,500.*
d. 1ab blue green *2,750.* 350.00
201 A23 2ab blue *2,500.* —

1908 *Serrate Roulette 13*

201A A22 1ab green — —
b. 1ab emerald green, on cover *1,250.*
201B A23 2ab blue *3,500.*

Nos. 201A and 201Ab are only known used on cover.
No. 201B is known only unused.

Perf. 12 on 2, 3 or 4 Sides

202 A22 1ab green — 65.00
203 A23 2ab deep blue 35.00 20.00
a. Horiz. pair, imperf between 450.00
204 A24 1rup blue green 125.00 65.00
Nos. 202-204 (3) 160.00 150.00

Twelve varieties of the 1 abasi, 6 of the 2 abasi, 4 of the 1 rupee.
Nos. 196-204 were issued in small sheets containing 3 or 4 panes. Gutter pairs, normal and tete beche, exist.
Two plates were used for the 1 abasi: plate I, inner vert. lines extend into lower left panel; plate II, inner vert. lines do not extend into lower left panel.

A25

A26

A27

1909-19 Typo. *Perf. 12*

205 A25 1ab ultra 7.00 2.00
a. Imperf., pair 48.00
206 A25 1ab red ('16) 1.60 1.25
a. Imperf. 30.00
207 A25 1ab rose ('18) 1.60 1.00
208 A26 2ab green 2.75 2.25
a. Imperf., pair 48.00
b. Horiz. pair, imperf. btwn.
208C A26 2ab yellow ('16) 3.25 2.75
209 A26 2ab bis ('18-'19) 3.25 *3.25*
210 A27 1rup lilac brn 6.75 6.50
a. 1rup red brown 7.50 7.50
211 A27 1rup ol bis ('16) 9.75 8.00
Nos. 205-211 (8) 35.95 27.00

A28

1913

212 A28 2pa drab brown 20.00 6.00
a. 2pa red brown 20.00 6.00

No. 212 is inscribed "Tiket waraq dak" (Postal card stamps). It was usable only on postcards and not accepted for postage on letters.
Nos. 196-212 sometimes show letters of a papermaker's watermark, "Howard & Jones, London."

Royal Star — A29

1920, Aug. 24 *Perf. 12*

Size: 39x46mm

214 A29 10pa rose 175.00 100.00
215 A29 20pa red brown 275.00 175.00
216 A29 30pa green 375.00 250.00
Nos. 214-216 (3) 825.00 525.00

2nd Independence Day. Issued to commemorate the first anniversary of the signing of the armistice that ended the war of independence (Third Afghan War).
Issued in sheets of two.
No. 214 exists in two sizes: 38.5mmx45mm, position 1 in sheet; 38.5mmx46mm, position 2.

1921, Mar. Size: 22½x28¼mm

217 A29 10pa rose 2.50 1.25
a. Perf. 11 ('27) 22.50 13.00
218 A29 20pa red brown 4.50 2.50
219 A29 30pa yel green 6.50 3.00
a. Tete beche pair 55.00 32.50
b. 30pa green 6.50 3.50
c. As "b," Tete beche pair 55.00 32.50
Nos. 217-219 (3) 13.50 6.75

3rd Independence Day.
Two types of the 10pa, three of the 20pa.

Hstmpd. in black on Nos. 217-219

1923, Feb. 26

219D A29a 10pa rose — 100.00
219E A29a 20pa red brown — 100.00
219F A29a 30pa yel green 350.00 —

5th Independence Day.
Two types of handstamp exist.
Forgeries exist.
See No. Q13B-Q13E.

These handstamps were used by Afghan post offices on incoming foreign mail from 1921 until Afghanistan joined the Universal Postal Union April 1, 1928. Afghan stamps were applied to foreign mail arriving in the country and were canceled with these postage-due handstamps to indicate that postage was to be collected from the addressee. The handstamps were applied primarily to Nos. 217-219, 227-235, 236, and 237-246. Values are the same as for stamps with postal cancellations. A third type of handstamp exists with no distinctive outer border.

A30

1924, Feb. 26 *Perf. 12*

220 A30 10pa chocolate 45.00 30.00
a. Tete beche pair 150.00 100.00

6th Independence Day.
Printed in sheets of four consisting of two tete beche pairs, and in sheets of two. Two types exist.

Some authorities believe that Nos. Q15-Q16 were issued as regular postage stamps.

Crest of King Amanullah
A32

Size: 29x37mm

1925, Feb. 26 *Perf. 12*

222 A32 10pa light brown 70.00 45.00

7th Independence Day.
Printed in sheets of 8 (two panes of 4).

Wove Paper

1926, Feb. 28 Size: 26x33mm

224 A32 10pa dark blue 8.00 8.00
a. Imperf., pair 32.50
b. Horiz. pair, imperf. btwn. 75.00
c. Vert. pair, imperf. btwn.
d. Laid paper 40.00 13.00

7th anniv. of Independence. Printed in sheets of 4, and in sheets of 8 (two panes of 4). Tete beche gutter pairs exist.

Tughra and Crest of Amanullah
A33

1927, Feb.

225 A33 10pa magenta 14.00 12.00
a. Vertical pair, imperf. between 75.00

Dotted Background

226 A33 10pa magenta 20.00 13.00
a. Horiz. pair, imperf. between 75.00

The surface of No. 226 is covered by a net of fine dots.
8th anniv. of Independence. Printed in sheets of 8 (two panes of 4).
Tete-beche gutter pairs exist. Value, pair $85.

National Seal — A34

A35

A35a

A36

1927, Oct. *Imperf.*

227 A34 15p pink 1.40 1.40
228 A35 30p Prus green 2.75 1.25
229 A36 60p light blue 3.75 3.25
a. Tete beche pair 10.00
Nos. 227-229 (3) 7.90 5.90

1927-30 *Perf. 11, 12*

230 A34 15p pink 1.75 1.40
231 A34 15p ultra ('29) 1.75 1.40
232 A35 30p Prus green 3.25 1.40
233 A35a 30p dp green ('30) 1.75 1.25
234 A36 60p bright blue 3.50 2.00
a. Tete beche pair 17.50 17.50
235 A36 60p black ('29) 4.00 2.25
Nos. 230-235 (6) 16.00 9.70

Nos. 230, 232 and 234 are usually imperforate on one or two sides.
No. 233 has been redrawn. A narrow border of pearls has been added and "30," in European and Arabic numerals, inserted in the upper spandrels.

Tughra and Crest of Amanullah — A37

1928, Feb. 27

236 A37 15p pink 5.00 5.00
a. Tete beche pair 12.00 10.00
b. Horiz. pair, imperf. vert. 22.50 19.00
c. As "a," imperf. vert., block of 4 65.00

9th anniv. of Independence. This stamp is always imperforate on one or two sides.

A 15p blue of somewhat similar design was prepared for the 10th anniv., but was not issued due to Amanullah's dethronement. Value, $15.

A38

A39

A40

A41

A42

1928-30 ***Perf. 11, 12***

237 A38 2p dull blue 5.25 4.50
a. Vertical pair, imperf. between 20.00
238 A38 2p lt rose ('30) .45 .55
239 A39 10p gray green 1.25 .40
a. Tete beche pair 14.00 6.50
b. Vert. pair, imperf. horiz. 11.00 11.00
c. Vertical pair, imperf. between
240 A39 10p choc ('30) 2.00 1.25
a. 10p brown purple ('29) 8.50 4.00
241 A40 25p car rose 1.50 .40
242 A40 25p Prus green ('29) 2.75 1.25
243 A41 40p ultra 2.00 .75
a. Tete beche pair 15.00 *16.00*
244 A41 40p rose ('29) 2.25 1.25
a. Tete beche pair 14.50
b. Vert. pair, imperf. horiz. 11.00
245 A42 50p red 2.50 1.00
246 A42 50p dk blue ('29) 3.25 1.50
Nos. 237-246 (10) 23.20 12.85

The sheets of these stamps are often imperforate at the outer margins.

Nos. 237-238 are newspaper stamps.

This handstamp was used for ten months by the Revolutionary Gov't in Kabul as a control mark on outgoing mail. It occasionally fell on the stamps but there is no evidence that it was officially used as an overprint. Unused examples were privately made.

Independence Monument A46

Laid Paper
Without Gum

Wmk. Large Seal in the Sheet

1931, Aug. **Litho.** ***Perf. 12***

262 A46 20p red 2.50 1.25

13th Independence Day.

National Assembly Chamber A47

A48

A50

National Assembly Building A49

National Assembly Chamber A51

National Assembly Building A52

Wove Paper

1932 **Unwmk.** **Typo.** ***Perf. 12***

263 A47 40p olive 1.00 .40
264 A48 60p violet 1.25 .80
265 A49 80p dark red 1.75 1.25
266 A50 1af black 13.50 7.50
267 A51 2af ultra 6.00 4.00
268 A52 3af gray green 6.50 3.50
Nos. 263-268 (6) 30.00 17.45

Formation of the Natl. Council. Imperforate or perforated examples on ungummed chalky paper are proofs.

See Nos. 304-305.

Mosque at Balkh — A53

Kabul Fortress A54

Parliament House, Darul Funun — A55

Parliament House, Darul Funun — A56

Arch of Qalai Bist — A57

Memorial Pillar of Knowledge and Ignorance A58

Independence Monument A59

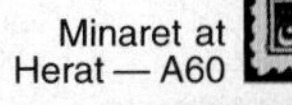

Minaret at Herat — A60

Arch of Paghman A61

Ruins at Balkh — A62

Minarets of Herat — A63

Great Buddha at Bamian — A64

1932 **Typo.** ***Perf. 12***

269 A53 10p brown .65 .25
270 A54 15p dk brown .50 .30
271 A55 20p red .75 .25
272 A56 25p dk green 1.10 .25
273 A57 30p red 1.10 .25
274 A58 40p orange 1.40 .50
275 A59 50p blue 1.90 1.40
a. Tete beche pair 12.00
276 A60 60p blue 1.75 .90
277 A61 80p violet 3.25 2.00
278 A62 1af dark blue 5.75 .80
279 A63 2af dk red violet 6.25 2.25
280 A64 3af claret 7.75 3.00
Nos. 269-280 (12) 32.15 12.15

Counterfeits of types A53-A65 exist.

See Nos. 290-295, 298-299, 302-303.

Entwined 2's — A65

Two types:

Type I — Numerals shaded. Size about 21x29mm.

Type II — Numerals unshaded. Size about 21¾x30mm.

1931-38 ***Perf. 12, 11x12***

281 A65 2p red brn (I) .40 .50
282 A65 2p olive blk (I) ('34) .30 .80
283 A65 2p grnsh gray (I) ('34) .40 .75
283A A65 2p black (II) ('36) .25 .75
284 A65 2p salmon (II) ('38) .50 .75
284A A65 2p rose (I) ('38) .50 .90
b. Imperf., pair 10.00

Imperf

285 A65 2p black (II) ('37) .75 .75
286 A65 2p salmon (II) ('38) .75 .75
Nos. 281-286 (8) 3.85 5.95

The newspaper rate was 2 pouls.

A66

1932, Aug. ***Perf. 12***

287 A66 1af Independence Monument 5.50 3.25

14th Independence Day.

A67

1929 Liberation Monument, Kabul.

1932, Oct. **Typo.**

288 A67 80p red brown 2.00 1.50

Arch of Paghman — A68

1933, Aug.

289 A68 50p light ultra 3.00 1.50

15th Independence Day.
No. 289 exists imperf. Value, $5.

Types of 1932 and

Royal Palace, Kabul A69

Darrah- Shikari Pass, Hindu Kush — A70

1934-38	**Typo.**	***Perf. 12***		
290	A53	10p deep violet	.30	.25
291	A54	15p turq green	.50	.25
292	A55	20p magenta	.50	.25
293	A56	25p deep rose	.60	.25
294	A57	30p orange	.65	.30
295	A58	40p blue black	.75	.30
296	A69	45p dark blue	2.75	1.50
297	A69	45p red ('38)	.50	.25
298	A59	50p orange	.80	.25
299	A60	60p purple	1.00	.45
300	A70	75p red	4.00	2.00
301	A70	75p dk blue ('38)	1.00	.65
302	A61	80p brown vio	1.60	.80
303	A62	1af red violet	3.25	1.60
304	A51	2af gray black	5.25	2.40
305	A52	3af ultra	6.00	3.00
		Nos. 290-305 (16)	29.45	14.50

Nos. 290, 292, 300, 304, 305 exist imperf.

Independence Monument — A71

1934, Aug. Litho. Without Gum

306 A71 50p pale green 3.25 2.75
a. Tete beche pair 11.50 11.50

16th year of Independence. Each sheet of 40 (4x10) included 4 tete beche pairs as lower half of sheet was inverted.

Independence Monument — A74

1935, Aug. 15 Laid Paper

309 A74 50p dark blue 3.50 2.40

17th year of Independence.

Fireworks Display A75

Wove Paper

1936, Aug. 15 ***Perf. 12***

310 A75 50p red violet 3.25 2.50

18th year of Independence.

Independence Monument and Nadir Shah — A76

1937

311 A76 50p vio & bis brn 2.75 2.10
a. Imperf., pair 9.50 9.50

19th year of Independence.

Mohammed Nadir Shah
A77 A78

1938 Without Gum ***Perf. 11x12***

315 A77 50p brt blue & sepia 2.75 2.40
a. Imperf. pair 24.00 19.00

20th year of Independence.

1939 ***Perf. 11, 12x11***

317 A78 50p deep salmon 2.40 1.50

21st year of Independence.

National Arms A79

Parliament House, Darul Funun — A80

Royal Palace, Kabul A81

Independence Monument — A82

Independence Monument and Nadir Shah — A83

Mohammed Zahir Shah — A84

Mohammed Zahir Shah A85

Perf. 11, 11x12, 12x11, 12

1939-61			**Typo.**	
318	A79	2p intense blk	.30	*.70*
318A	A79	2p brt pink ('61)	.30	*.70*
		Size: 36.5x24mm		
319	A80	10p brt purple	.30	.25
		Size: 31.5x21mm		
320	A80	15p brt green	.35	.25
		Size: 34x22.5mm		
321	A80	20p red lilac	.50	.25
322	A81	25p rose red	.60	.30
322A	A81	25p green ('41)	.35	.25
323	A81	30p orange	.50	.25
a.		Vert. pair, imperf between		—
324	A81	40p dk gray	1.00	.50
325	A82	45p brt carmine	1.00	.40
326	A82	50p dp orange	.80	.25
327	A82	60p violet	1.00	.25
328	A83	75p ultra	3.00	.80
328A	A83	75p red vio ('41)	2.25	1.60
328C	A83	75p brt red ('44)	4.00	3.00
328D	A83	75p chnt brn ('49)	4.00	3.00
329	A83	80p chocolate	2.00	1.00
a.		80p dull red violet (error)		
330	A84	1af brt red violet	2.25	.80
330A	A85	1af brt red vio ('44)	2.25	.90
331	A85	2af copper red	3.00	.80
a.		2af deep rose red	4.25	1.75
332	A84	3af deep blue	5.00	2.40
		Nos. 318-332 (21)	34.75	18.65

Many shades exist in this issue.
On No. 332, the King faces slightly left.
No. 318A issued with and without gum.
See Nos. 795A-795B. For similar design see No. 907A.

Mohammed Nadir Shah — A86

1940, Aug. 23 ***Perf. 11***

333 A86 50p gray green 2.00 1.50

22nd year of Independence.

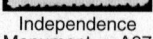

Independence Monument — A87

Arch of Paghman — A88

1941, Aug. 23 ***Perf. 12***

334 A87 15p gray green 12.00 5.75
335 A88 50p red brown 2.50 2.10

23rd year of Independence.

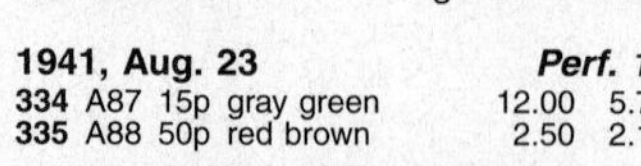

Sugar Factory, Baghlan A89

1942, Apr. ***Perf. 12***

336 A89 1.25af blue (shades) 2.00 1.50
a. 1.25af ultra 2.50 1.75

In 1949, a 1.50af brown, type A89, was sold for 3af by the Philatelic Office, Kabul. It was not valid for postage. Value $6.

Independence Monument — A90

Mohammed Nadir Shah and Arch of Paghman A91

1942, Aug. 23 ***Perf. 12***

337 A90 35p bright green 3.75 3.50
338 A91 125p chalky blue 3.00 2.00

24th year of Independence.

Independence Monument and Nadir Shah — A92

Mohammed Nadir Shah — A93

Perf. 11x12, 12x11

1943, Aug. 25 Typo. Unwmk.

339 A92 35p carmine 17.50 15.00
340 A93 1.25af dark blue 3.50 2.50

25th year of Independence.

Tomb of Gohar Shad, Herat — A94

Ruins of Qalai Bist — A95

1944, May 1 ***Perf. 12, 11x12***

341 A94 35p orange 1.50 1.00
342 A95 70p violet 2.00 1.00
a. 70p rose lilac 2.00 1.00

A96

A97

1944, Aug. *Perf. 12*
343 A96 35p crimson 1.25 .65
344 A97 1.25af ultra 2.25 1.75

26th year of Independence.

Catalogue values for unused stamps in this section, from this point to the end of the section, are for Never Hinged items.

A98

A99

1945, July
345 A98 35p deep red lilac 2.50 .80
346 A99 1.25af blue 4.00 2.00

27th year of Independence.

Mohammed Zahir Shah — A100

Independence Monument A101 | Mohammed Nadir Shah A102

1946, July
347 A100 15p emerald 1.25 .50
348 A101 20p dp red lilac 2.00 .75
349 A102 125p blue 3.75 1.75
Nos. 347-349 (3) 7.00 3.00

28th year of Independence.

Zahir Shah and Ruins of Qalai Bist — A103

A104

Begging Child A106

A105

1947, Aug.
350 A103 15p yellow green .80 .55
351 A104 35p plum 1.00 .65
352 A105 125p deep blue 2.75 1.60
Nos. 350-352 (3) 4.55 2.80

29th year of Independence.

A107

1948, May Unwmk. Typo. *Perf. 12*
353 A106 35p yel green 4.75 4.00
354 A107 125p gray blue 4.75 4.00

Children's Day, May 29, 1948, and valid only on that day. Proceeds were used for Child Welfare.

A108 A109

A110

1948, Aug.
355 A108 15p green .65 .30
356 A109 20p magenta .80 .30
357 A110 125p dark blue 1.60 .80
Nos. 355-357 (3) 3.05 1.40

30th year of Independence.

United Nations Emblem — A111

1948, Oct. 24
358 A111 125p dk violet blue 9.50 8.00

UN, 3rd anniv. Valid one day only. Sheets of 9.

Maiwand Victory Column, Kandahar — A112

Zahir Shah and Ruins of Qalai Bist A113

Independence Monument and Nadir Shah — A114

1949, Aug. 24 Typo. *Perf. 12*
359 A112 25p green 1.25 .50
360 A113 35p magenta 1.50 .65
361 A114 1.25af blue 2.50 1.25
Nos. 359-361 (3) 5.25 2.40

31st year of Independence.

Nadir Shah — A117

1950, Aug.
364 A117 35p red brown .75 .30
365 A117 125p blue 2.00 .50

32nd year of Independence.

Medical School and Nadir Shah A119

Size: 38x25mm

1950, Dec. 22 Typo. *Perf. 12*
367 A119 35p emerald 1.25 .65

Size: 46x30mm

368 A119 1.25af deep blue 4.00 2.00
a. 1.25af black (error) — —

19th anniv. of the founding of Afghanistan's Faculty of Medicine. On sale and valid for use on Dec. 22-28, 1950.

See Nos. RA9-RA10.

Minaret, Herat A120

Zahir Shah A121

Mosque of Khodja Abu Parsar, Balkh — A122

A123

A124

20p, Buddha at Bamian. 40p, Ruined arch. 45p, Maiwand Victory monument. 50p, View of Kandahar. 60p, Ancient tower. 70p, Afghanistan flag. 80p, 1af, Profile of Zahir Shah in uniform.

Imprint: "Waterlow & Sons Limited, London"

Photogravure, Engraved, Engraved and Lithographed
Perf. 12, 12½, 13x12½, 13½

1951, Mar. 21 Unwmk.
369 A120 10p yellow & brn .30 .25
370 A120 15p blue & brn .55 .25
371 A120 20p black 10.00 5.50
372 A121 25p green .50 .25
373 A122 30p cerise .65 .25
374 A121 35p violet .70 .25
375 A122 40p chestnut brn .70 .25
376 A120 45p deep blue .70 .25
377 A122 50p olive black 2.00 .25
378 A120 60p black 1.60 .30
379 A122 70p dk grn, blk, red & grn .90 .25
380 A123 75p cerise 1.25 .50
381 A123 80p carmine & blk 2.10 .90
382 A123 1af dp grn & vio 1.60 .65
383 A124 1.25af rose lil & blk 1.90 1.00
384 A124 2af ultra 2.75 .80
385 A124 3af ultra & blk 6.00 1.25
Nos. 369-385 (17) 34.20 13.15

Nos. 372, 374 and 381 to 385 are engraved, No. 379 is engraved and lithographed.

Imperfs. exist of the photogravure stamps.

See Nos. 445-451, 453, 552A-552D. For surcharges see Nos. B1-B2.

Arch of Paghman A125

Nadir Shah and Independence Monument — A126

Overprint in Violet

Perf. 13½x13, 13

1951, Aug. 25 Engr.
386 A125 35p dk green & blk 1.10 .65
387 A126 1.25af deep blue 3.00 1.40

Overprint reads "Sol 33 Istiqlal" or "33rd Year of Independence." Overprint measures about 11mm wide.

See Nos. 398-399B, 441-442.

Proposed Flag of Pashtunistan — A127

Design: 125p, Flag and Pashtunistan warrior.

1951, Sept. 2 Litho. *Perf. 11½*

388 A127 35p dull chocolate 1.50 .75
389 A127 125p blue 3.00 2.00

Issued to publicize "Free Pashtunistan" Day. Exist Imperf.

Imperforates

From 1951 to 1958, quantities of nearly all locally-printed stamps were left imperforate and sold by the government at double face. From 1959 until March, 1964, many of the imperforates were sold for more than face value.

Avicenna — A128

1951, Nov. 4 Typo. *Perf. 11½*

390 A128 35p deep claret 7.50 1.50
391 A128 125p blue 3.00 *4.00*

20th anniv. of the founding of the national Graduate School of Medicine.
Exist imperf. Value $27.50.

A129

Dove and UN Symbols A130

1951, Oct. 24

392 A129 35p magenta .90 .40
393 A130 125p blue 2.25 1.75

7th anniv. of the UN. Exist imperf.

Amir Sher Ali Khan and Tiger Head Stamp A131

Nos. 395, 397, Zahir Shah and stamp.

1951, Dec. 23 Litho.

394 A131 35p chocolate .85 .40
395 A131 35p rose lilac .85 .40
396 A131 125p ultra 1.25 .80
a. Cliche of 35p in plate of 125p 110.00 100.00
397 A131 125p aqua 1.25 .80
Nos. 394-397 (4) 4.20 2.40

76th anniv. of the UPU. Exist imperf. Values, set: unused $9; used $17.50.

Stamps of 1951 Without Overprint

Perf. 13½x13, 13

1952, Aug. 24 Engr.

398 A125 35p dk green & blk 1.50 .55
399 A126 1.25af deep blue 3.25 1.25

For overprints see Nos. 399A-399B, 441-442.

Same Overprinted in Violet

399A A125 35p dk grn & blk 4.00 2.25
399B A126 1.25af deep blue 4.00 2.25

Nos. 398-399B issued for 34th Independence Day.

Globe — A132

Perf. 11½

1952, Oct. 25 Unwmk. Litho.

400 A132 35p rose .80 .65
401 A132 125p aqua 1.60 1.10

Issued to honor the United Nations. Exist Imperf. Values, set: unused $6; used $7.25.

Symbol of Medicine A134

1952, Nov. *Perf. 11½*

403 A134 35p chocolate .70 .50
404 A134 125p violet blue 2.00 1.40

21st anniv. of the natl. Graduate School of Medicine.
No. 404 is inscribed in French with white letters on a colored background.
Exist Imperf. Values, set: unused $3.50; used $4.50.

Tribal Warrior, Natl. Flag — A135

1952, Sept. 1 *Perf. 11*

405 A135 35p red .80 .80
406 A135 125p dark blue 1.25 1.25

No. 406 is inscribed in French "Pashtunistan Day, 1952."
Exist imperf. Values, set, unused or used, $2.75.

Flags of Afghanistan & Pashtunistan A139

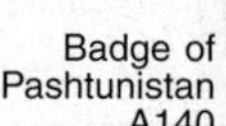

Badge of Pashtunistan A140

Perf. 10½x11, 11

1953, Sept. 1 Unwmk.

411 A139 35p vermilion .50 .25
412 A140 125p blue 1.00 .60

Issued to publicize "Free Pashtunistan" Day."
Exist imperf. Values, set: unused, $3.50; used, $4.

Nadir Shah and Flag Bearer A141

A142

1953, Aug. 24 *Perf. 11*

413 A141 35p green .40 .25
414 A142 125p violet .80 .55

35th anniv. of Independence.
Exist imperf. Values, set: unused, $3.50; used, $4.

United Nations Emblem — A143

1953, Oct. 24

415 A143 35p lilac 1.00 .80
416 A143 125p violet blue 2.00 1.50

United Nations Day, 1953.
Exist imperf. Values, set, unused or used, $9.

A144

Nadir Shah — A145

1953, Nov. 29

417 A144 35p orange 1.50 1.50
418 A145 125p chalky blue 3.00 3.00

22nd anniv. of the founding of the Natl. Graduate School of Medicine.
Exist imperf. Values, set: unused, $9; used, $12.50.

35p. Original — Right character in second line of Persian inscription

Redrawn — Persian character

Original

Redrawn

1953

419 A144 35p deep orange 9.50 9.50
420 A145 125p chalky blue 9.50 9.50

Exist imperf.

Nadir Shah and Symbols of Independence — A146

1954, Aug. Typo. *Perf. 11*

421 A146 35p carmine rose .70 .40
422 A146 125p violet blue 2.00 .80

36th year of Independence.
Exist imperf. Values, set: unused, $6; used, $7.

Raising Flag of Pashtunistan A147

1954, Sept. *Perf. 11½*

423 A147 35p chocolate .70 .40
424 A147 125p blue 2.00 .80

Issued to publicize "Free Pashtunistan" Day.
Exist imperf. Values, set: unused, $4.75; used, $6.50.

UN Flag and Map — A148

1954, Oct. 24 *Perf. 11*

425 A148 35p carmine rose 1.25 1.25
426 A148 125p dk violet blue 3.25 2.25

9th anniv. of the United Nations.
Exist imperf. Values, set: unused, $9; used, $10.

UN Symbols
A149

Design: 125p, UN emblem & flags.

1955, June 26 Litho. *Perf. 11*

Size: 26½x36mm

427 A149 35p dark green 1.10 .55

Size: 28½x36mm

428 A149 125p aqua 2.00 1.00

10th anniv. of the UN charter.
Exist imperf. Values, set: unused, $12; used, $12.50.

Nadir Shah (center) and Brothers
A150

1929 Civil War Scene and Zahir Shah — A151

1955, Aug. Unwmk. *Perf. 11*

429 A150 35p brt pink .65 .40
430 A150 35p violet blue .65 .40
431 A151 125p rose lilac 1.40 .90
432 A151 125p light violet 1.40 .90
Nos. 429-432 (4) 4.10 2.60

37th anniv. of Independence.
Exist imperf. Values, set: unused, $12; used, $13.50.

Tribal Elders' Council and Pashtun Flag — A152

1955, Sept. 5

433 A152 35p orange brown .60 .25
434 A152 125p yellow green 2.00 .55

Issued for "Free Pashtunistan" Day.
Exist imperf. Values, set: unused, $7; used, $9.

UN Flag — A153

1955, Oct. 24 Unwmk. *Perf. 11*

435 A153 35p orange brown 1.10 .60
436 A153 125p brt ultra 2.00 1.10

10th anniv. of the United Nations.
Exist imperf. Value for set: unused, $15; used, $17.50.

A154

1956, Aug. Litho.

437 A154 35p lt green .55 .30
438 A154 140p lt violet blue 2.25 .90

38th year of Independence.
Exist imperf. Value for set: unused, $3; used, $4.

Jesh'n Exhibition Hall
A155

1956, Aug. 25

439 A155 50p chocolate .90 .40
440 A155 50p lt violet blue .90 .40

International Exposition at Kabul.
Of the 50p face value, only 35p paid postage. The remaining 15p went to the Exposition.
Exist imperf. Value for set: unused, $7; used, $8.

Nos. 398-399 Handstamped in Violet

a

b

1957, Aug. Engr. *Perf. 13½x13, 13*

441 A125 (a) 35p dk green & blk .65 .30
442 A126 (b) 1.25af deep blue 1.00 .70

Arabic overprint measures 19mm.
39th year of independence.

Pashtunistan Flag — A156

1957, Sept. 1 Litho. *Perf. 11*

443 A156 50p pale lilac rose 1.00 .55
444 A156 155p light violet 1.50 1.00

Issued for "Free Pashtunistan" Day. French inscription on No. 444. 15p of each stamp went to the Pashtunistan Fund.
Exist imperf. Values, set: unused, $4; used, $4.50.

Types of 1951 and

Game of Buzkashi
A157

Perf. 12, 12½, 12½x13, 13, 13x12, 13x12½, 13½x14

Photo., Engr., Engr.& Litho.

1957, Nov. 23 Unwmk.

Imprint: "Waterlow & Sons Limited, London"

445 A122 30p brown .40 .25
446 A122 40p rose red .55 .25
447 A122 50p yellow .65 .25
448 A120 60p ultra .80 .25
449 A123 75p brt violet 1.00 .25
450 A123 80p violet & brn 1.10 .25
451 A123 1af carmine & ultra 1.75 .25
452 A157 140p olive & dp claret 2.75 .65
453 A124 3af orange & blk 2.75 .90
Nos. 445-453 (9) 11.75 3.30

No. 452 lacks imprint.

Nadir Shah and Flag-bearer
A158

1958, Aug. 25 *Perf. 13½x14*

454 A158 35p dp yellow green .50 .25
455 A158 140p brown 1.25 1.00

40th year of Independence.

Exposition Buildings
A159

1958, Aug. 23 Litho. *Perf. 11*

456 A159 35p brt blue green .50 .25
457 A159 140p vermilion 1.25 1.00

International Exposition at Kabul.
Exist imperf. Value set, unused or used, $4.

Pres. Celal Bayar of Turkey — A160

1958, Sept. 13 Unwmk.

458 A160 50p lt blue .30 .25
459 A160 100p brown .65 .30

Visit of President Celal Bayar of Turkey.
Values, set: unused, $2.25; used, $3.25.

Flags of UN and Afghanistan
A161

1958, Oct. 24 Photo. *Perf. 14x13½*

Flags in Original Colors

460 A161 50p dark gray .65 .65
461 A161 100p green 1.40 1.10

United Nations Day, Oct. 24.
Exist imperf. Value set, unused or used, $4.50.

Atomic Energy Encircling the Hemispheres — A162

1958, Oct. 20 *Perf. 13½x14*

462 A162 50p blue .75 .50
463 A162 100p dp red lilac 1.10 .65

Issued to promote Atoms for Peace.
Exist imperf. Value set, unused or used, $3.50.

UNESCO Building, Paris
A163

1958, Nov. 3

464 A163 50p dp yellow grn .80 .65
465 A163 100p brown olive .80 .80

UNESCO Headquarters in Paris opening, Nov. 3.
Exist imperf. Value set, unused or used, $6.

Globe and Torch
A164

Perf. 13½x14

1958, Dec. 10 Unwmk.

466 A164 50p lilac rose .50 .50
467 A164 100p maroon 1.00 *1.10*

10th anniv. of the signing of the Universal Declaration of Human Rights.
Exist imperf. Value set, unused or used, $4.50.

Nadir Shah and Flags
A165

1959, Aug. Litho. *Perf. 11 Rough*

468 A165 35p light vermilion .55 .50
469 A165 165p light violet 1.50 .65

41st year of Independence.
Exist imperf. Value set, unused or used, $2.50.

Uprooted Oak Emblem — A166

1960, Apr. 7 *Perf. 11*

470 A166 50p deep orange .35 .25
471 A166 165p blue .45 .25

World Refugee Year, 7/1/59-6/30/60.
Two imperf. souvenir sheets exist. Both contain a 50p and a 165p, type A166, with marginal inscriptions and WRY emblem in maroon. On one sheet the stamps are in the colors of Nos. 470-471 (size 108x81mm). Value $6. On the other, the 50p is blue and the 165p is deep orange (size 107x80mm). Value $7.
For surcharges see Nos. B35-B36.
Exist imperf. Value set, unused or used, $4.50.

Buzkashi
A167

1960, May 4 *Perf. 11, Imperf.*

472 A167 25p rose red .75 .25
473 A167 50p bluish green 1.75 .90
a. Cliche of 25p in plate of 50p 27.50 27.50

Exist imperf. Value set, unused or used, $2.75.
See Nos. 549-550A.

Independence Monument A168

1960, Aug. ***Perf. 11, 12***
474 A168 50p light blue .45 .25
475 A168 175p bright pink 1.25 .40

42nd Independence Day.
Exist imperf. Value set, unused or used, $1.75.

Globe and Flags A169

1960, Oct. 24 Litho. ***Perf. 11, 12***
476 A169 50p rose lilac .25 .25
477 A169 175p ultra 1.00 .65

UN Day.
Exist imperf. Value set, unused or used, $2.50.
An imperf. souvenir sheet contains one each of Nos. 476-477 with marginal inscriptions ("La Journée des Nations Unies 1960" in French and Persian) and UN emblem in light blue. Size: 127x85½mm. Value $6.
This sheet was surcharged "+20ps" in 1962. Value $5.50.

Teacher Pointing to Globe A170

1960, Oct. 23 ***Perf. 11***
478 A170 50p brt pink .40 .30
479 A170 100p brt green 1.00 .50

Issued to publicize Teacher's Day.
Exist imperf. Value set, unused or used, $2.50.

Mohammed Zahir Shah — A171

1960, Oct. 15
480 A171 50p red brown .65 .25
481 A171 150p dk car rose 1.60 .55

Honoring the King on his 46th birthday.
Exist imperf. Value set, unused or used, $2.50.

Buzkashi A172

1960, Nov. 9 ***Perf. 11***
482 A172 175p lt red brown 2.40 .50

Exists imperf. Value, unused or used, $3.
See Nos. 551-552.

No. 482 Overprinted in Bright Green

1960, Dec. 24
483 A172 175p red brown 2.00 2.00
a. Souv. sheet of 1, imperf. 6.00 *8.00*

17th Olympic Games, Rome, 8/25-9/11.
Value, unused or used, $4.50.

Mir Wais — A173

1961, Jan. 5 Unwmk. ***Perf. 10½***
484 A173 50p brt rose lilac .70 .40
485 A173 175p ultra 1.25 .50
a. Souv. sheet, #484-485, imperf. 3.75 3.75

Mir Wais (1665-1708), national leader.
Exist imperf. Value set, unused or used, $2.75.

No Postal Need

existed for the 1p-15p denominations issued with sets of 1961-63 (between Nos. 486 and 649, B37 and B65).
The lowest denomination actually used for non-philatelic postage in that period was 25p (except for the 2p newspaper rate for which separate stamps were provided).

Horse, Sheep and Camel A174

Designs: No. 487, 175p, Rock partridge. 10p, 100p, Afghan hound. 15p, 150p, Grain & grasshopper, vert.

1961, Mar. 29 Photo. ***Perf. 13½x14***
486 A174 2p maroon & buff .25 .25
487 A174 2p ultra & org .25 .25
488 A174 5p brown & yel .25 .25
489 A174 10p black & salmon .25 .25
490 A174 15p blue grn & yel .25 .25
491 A174 25p black & pink .25 .25
492 A174 50p black & citron .30 .30
493 A174 100p black & pink .45 .40
494 A174 150p green & yel .65 .65
495 A174 175p ultra & pink .80 .65
Nos. 486-495 (10) 3.70 3.50

Two souvenir sheets, perf. and imperf., contain 2 stamps, 1 each of No. 492-493. Value $3 each.

Afghan Fencing A175

Designs: No. 497, 5p, 25p, 50p, Wrestlers. 10p, 100p, Man with Indian clubs. 15p, 150p, Afghan fencing. 175p, Children skating.

1961, July 6 ***Perf. 13½x14***
496 A175 2p green & rose lil .25 .25
497 A175 2p brown & citron .25 .25
498 A175 5p gray & rose .25 .25
499 A175 10p blue & bister .25 .25
500 A175 15p sl bl & dl lil .25 .25
501 A175 25p black & dl bl .25 .25
502 A175 50p sl grn & bis brn .25 .25
503 A175 100p brown & bl grn .55 .55
504 A175 150p brown & org yel .90 .90
505 A175 175p black & blue .95 .95
Nos. 496-505 (10) 4.15 4.15

Issued for Children's Day.
A souvenir sheet exists, perf. and imperf., containing one each of Nos. 502-503. Value $5 each.
For surcharges see Nos. B37-B41.

Bande Amir Lakes A176

1961, Aug. 7 Photo. ***Perf. 13½x14***
506 A176 3af brt blue .50 .25
507 A176 10af rose claret 1.40 1.25

Nadir Shah — A177

1961, Aug. 23 ***Perf. 14x13½***
508 A177 50p rose red & blk .55 .50
509 A177 175p brt grn & org brn .95 .70

43rd Independence Day.
Exist imperf. Value set, unused or used, $2.50.
Two souvenir sheets, perf. and imperf., contain one each of Nos. 508-509. Value, each $3.00.

Girl Scout — A178

Perf. 14x13½

1961, July 23 **Unwmk.**
510 A178 50p dp car & dk gray .40 .25
511 A178 175p dp grn & rose brn 1.00 .50

Issued for Women's Day.
Exist imperf. Value set, unused or used, $4.50.
Two souvenir sheets exist, perf. and imperf., containing one each of Nos. 510-511. Value $4.50 each.

Exhibition Hall, Kabul A179

1961, Aug. 23 ***Perf. 13½x14***
512 A179 50p yel brn & yel grn .25 .25
513 A179 175p blue & brn .70 .50

International Exhibition at Kabul.

Pathan with Pashtunistan Flag — A180

1961, Aug. 31 Photo. ***Perf. 14x13½***
514 A180 50p blk, lil & red .30 .25
515 A180 175p brn, grnsh bl & red .65 .55

Issued for "Free Pashtunistan Day."
Exist imperf. Value set, unused or used, $1.60.
Souvenir sheets exist perf. and imperf. containing one each of Nos. 514-515. Value $2.25 each.

Assembly Building A181

1961, Sept. 10 ***Perf. 12***
516 A181 50p dk gray & brt grn .25 .25
517 A181 175p ultra & brn .65 .50

Anniv. of the founding of the Natl. Assembly.
Exist imperf. Value set, unused or used, $1.25.
Souvenir sheets exist, perf. and imperf., containing one each of Nos. 516-517. Value $1.50 each.

Exterminating Anopheles Mosquito — A182

1961, Oct. 5 ***Perf. 13½x14***
518 A182 50p blk & brn lil .75 .30
519 A182 175p maroon & brt grn 2.00 .90

Anti-Malaria campaign.
Exist imperf. Value set, unused or used, $4.
Souvenir sheets exist, perf. and imperf., containing one each of Nos. 518-519. Value $4.50 each.

Zahir Shah — A183

1961, Oct. 15 ***Perf. 13½***
520 A183 50p lilac & blue .30 .25
521 A183 175p emerald & red brn .90 .50

Issued to honor King Mohammed Zahir Shah on his 47th birthday.
See Nos. 609-612.

Pomegranates — A184

Fruit: No. 523, 5p, 25p, 50p, Grapes. 10p, 150p, Apples. 15p, 175p, Pomegranates. 100p, Melons.

1961, Oct. 16 ***Perf. 13½x14***

Fruit in Natural Colors

522 A184 2p black .25 .25
523 A184 2p green .25 .25
524 A184 5p lilac rose .25 .25
525 A184 10p lilac .25 .25
526 A184 15p dk blue .25 .25
527 A184 25p dull red .25 .25
528 A184 50p purple .25 .25
529 A184 100p brt blue .55 .55
530 A184 150p brown .90 .90
531 A184 175p olive gray .95 .95
Nos. 522-531 (10) 4.15 4.15

For Afghan Red Crescent Society.

Souvenir sheets exist, perf. and imperf., containing one each of Nos. 528-529. Value $2.25 each.

For surcharges see Nos. B42-B46.

UN Headquarters, NY — A185

1961, Oct. 24 ***Perf. 13½x14***

Vertical Borders in Emerald, Red and Black

532 A185 1p rose lilac .25 .25
533 A185 2p slate .25 .25
534 A185 3p brown .25 .25
535 A185 4p ultra .25 .25
536 A185 50p rose red .25 .25
537 A185 75p gray .25 .25
538 A185 175p brt green .55 .55
Nos. 532-538 (7) 2.05 2.05

16th anniv. of the UN.

Nos. 536-538 exist imperf. Values, unused or used: 50p, 40c; 75p, 65c; 175p, $1.40.

Souvenir sheets exist, perf. and imperf., containing one each of Nos. 536-538. Value $2.50 each.

Children Giving Flowers to Teacher — A186

Designs: No. 540, 5p, 25p, 50p, Tulips. 10p, 100p, Narcissus. 15p, 150p, Children giving flowers to teacher. 175p, Teacher with children in front of school.

1961, Oct. 26 **Photo.** ***Perf. 12***

539 A186 2p multicolored .25 .25
540 A186 2p multicolored .25 .25
541 A186 5p multicolored .25 .25
542 A186 10p multicolored .25 .25
543 A186 15p multicolored .25 .25
544 A186 25p multicolored .25 .25
545 A186 50p multicolored .25 .25
546 A186 100p multicolored .50 .50
547 A186 150p multicolored .80 .80
548 A186 175p multicolored .90 .90
Nos. 539-548 (10) 3.95 3.95

Issued for Teacher's Day.

Souvenir sheets exist, perf. and imperf. containing one each of Nos. 545-546. Value, 2 sheets, $4.50.

For surcharges see Nos. B47-B51.

Buzkashi Types of 1960

1961-72 **Litho.** ***Perf. 10½, 11***

549 A167 25p violet 1.40 .25
b. 25p brt vio, typo. ('72) .25 .25
549A A167 25p citron ('63) 2.50 .25
550 A167 50p blue 2.00 .25
550A A167 50p yel org ('69) .50 .30
551 A172 100p citron .80 .25
551A A172 150p orange ('64) .65 .30
552 A172 2af lt green 1.50 1.00
Nos. 549-552 (7) 9.35 2.60

Zahir Shah Types of 1951

Imprint: "Thomas De La Rue & Co. Ltd."

Photo., Engr., Engr. & Litho.

1962 ***Perf. 13x12, 13***

552A A123 75p brt purple 2.75 .25
552B A123 1af car & ultra 3.50 .30
552C A124 2af blue 7.25 .80
552D A124 3af orange & blk 10.00 1.00
Nos. 552A-552D (4) 23.50 2.35

People Raising UNESCO Symbol — A187

1962, July 2 **Photo.** ***Perf. 14x13½***

553 A187 2p rose lil & brn .25 .25
554 A187 2p ol bis & brn .25 .25
555 A187 5p dp org & dk grn .25 .25
556 A187 10p gray & mag .25 .25
557 A187 15p blue & brn .25 .25
558 A187 25p org yel & pur .25 .25
559 A187 50p lt grn & pur .25 .25
560 A187 75p brt cit & brn .25 .25
561 A187 100p dp org & brn .30 .30
Nos. 553-561 (9) 2.30 2.30

15th anniv. of UNESCO. Souvenir sheets exist, perf. and imperf. One contains Nos. 558-559; the other contains Nos. 560-561. Value, $3.25 each perforated, $2.40 each imperf.

For surcharges see Nos. B52-B60.

Ahmad Shah — A188

1962, Feb. 24 **Photo.** ***Perf. 13½***

562 A188 50p red brn & gray .25 .25
563 A188 75p green & salmon .30 .25
564 A188 100p claret & bister .40 .30
Nos. 562-564 (3) .95 .80

Ahmad Shah (1724-73), founded the Afghan kingdom in 1747 and ruled until 1773.

Afghan Hound — A189

Designs: 5p, 75p, Afghan cock. 10p, 100p, Kondjid plant. 15p, 125p, Astrakhan skins.

1962, Apr. 21 ***Perf. 14x13½***

565 A189 2p rose & brn .25 .25
566 A189 2p lt green & brn .25 .25
567 A189 5p dp rose & claret .25 .25
568 A189 10p lt grn & sl grn .25 .25
569 A189 15p blue grn & blk .25 .25
570 A189 25p blue & brn .25 .25
571 A189 50p gray & brn .30 .25
572 A189 75p rose lil & lil .50 .30
573 A189 100p gray & dl grn .55 .40
574 A189 125p rose brn & blk .65 .50
Nos. 565-574 (10) 3.50 2.95

Agriculture Day. Perf. and imperf. souvenir sheets exist. Set of 4 sheets, value $11.00.

Athletes with Flag and Nadir Shah — A190

1962, Aug. 23 ***Perf. 12***

575 A190 25p multicolored .25 .25
576 A190 50p multicolored .25 .25
577 A190 150p multicolored .40 .30
Nos. 575-577 (3) .90 .80

44th Independence Day.

Woman in National Costume — A191

1962, Aug. 30 ***Perf. 11½x12***

578 A191 25p lilac & brn .25 .25
579 A191 50p green & brn .25 .25
Nos. 578-579,C15-C16 (4) 2.10 2.10

Issued for Women's Day. A souvenir sheet exists containing one each of Nos. 578-579, C15-C16. Value $4.50.

Man and Woman with Flag — A192

Malaria Eradication Emblem and Swamp — A193

1962, Aug. 31 **Photo.**

580 A192 25p black, pale bl & red .25 .25
581 A192 50p black, grn & red .25 .25
582 A192 150p black, pink & red .55 .40
Nos. 580-582 (3) 1.05 .90

Issued for "Free Pashtunistan Day."

1962, Sept. 5 ***Perf. 14x13½***

583 A193 2p dk grn & ol gray .25 .25
584 A193 2p dk green & sal .25 .25
585 A193 5p red brn & ol .25 .25
586 A193 10p red brn & brt grn .25 .25
587 A193 15p red brn & gray .25 .25
588 A193 25p brt bl & bluish grn .25 .25
589 A193 50p brt bl & rose lil .25 .25
590 A193 75p black & blue .25 .25
591 A193 100p black & brt pink .30 .25
592 A193 150p black & bis brn .50 .40
593 A193 175p black & orange .55 .50
Nos. 583-593 (11) 3.35 3.15

WHO drive to eradicate malaria. Perf. and imperf. souvenir sheets exist. Set of 4 sheets, value $14.

For surcharges see Nos. B61-B71.

National Assembly Building — A194

Perf. 10½, 11 (100p)

1962, Sept. 10 **Unwmk.** **Litho.**

594 A194 25p lt green .25 .25
595 A194 50p blue .45 .45
596 A194 75p rose .60 .60
597 A194 100p violet .75 .75
598 A194 125p ultra 1.00 1.00
Nos. 594-598 (5) 3.05 3.05

Establishment of the National Assembly.

Horse Racing — A195

Designs: 2p, Horse racing. 3p, Wrestling. 4p, Weight lifting. 5p, Soccer.

1962, Sept. 22 **Photo.** ***Perf. 12***

Black Inscriptions

599 A195 1p lt ol & red brn .25 .25
600 A195 2p lt grn & red brn .25 .25
601 A195 3p yellow & dk pur .25 .25
602 A195 4p pale bl & grn .25 .25
603 A195 5p bluish grn & dk brn .25 .25
Nos. 599-603,C17-C22 (11) 5.30 5.30

4th Asian Games, Djakarta, Indonesia.

Exist imperf. Value, set of 11, unused or used, $17.50.

Two souvenir sheets exist. A perforated one contains a 125p blue, dark blue and brown stamp in horse racing design. An imperf. one contains a 2af buff, purple and black stamp in soccer design. Value, $3.50 each.

Runners A196

1p, 2p, Diver, vert. 4p, Peaches. 5p, Iris, vert.

Perf. 11½x12, 12x11½

1962, Oct. 2 **Unwmk.**

604 A196 1p rose lil & brn .25 .25
605 A196 2p blue & brn .25 .25
606 A196 3p brt blue & lil .25 .25
607 A196 4p ol gray & multi .25 .25
608 A196 5p gray & multi .25 .25
Nos. 604-608,C23-C25 (8) 4.90 4.90

Issued for Children's Day.

Exist imperf. Value, set of 8, unused or used, $27.50.

Zahir Shah Type of 1961, Dated "1962"

1962, Oct. 15 ***Perf. 13½***

Various Frames

609 A183 25p lilac rose & brn .25 .25
610 A183 50p orange brn & grn .30 .25
611 A183 75p blue & lake .40 .25
612 A183 100p green & red brn .55 .25
Nos. 609-612 (4) 1.50 1.00

Issued to honor King Mohammed Zahir Shah on his 48th birthday.

Grapes A197

1962, Oct. 16 ***Perf. 12***

613 A197 1p shown .25 .25
614 A197 2p Grapes .25 .25
615 A197 3p Pears .25 .25
616 A197 4p Wistaria .25 .25
617 A197 5p Blossoms .25 .25
Nos. 613-617,C26-C28 (8) 2.50 2.50

For the Afghan Red Crescent Society.

Exist imperf. Value, set of 8, unused or used, $20.

UN Headquarters, NY and Flags of UN and Afghanistan — A198

1962, Oct. 24 **Unwmk.**

618 A198 1p multicolored .25 .25
619 A198 2p multicolored .25 .25
620 A198 3p multicolored .25 .25
621 A198 4p multicolored .25 .25
622 A198 5p multicolored .25 .25
Nos. 618-622,C29-C31 (8) 2.70 2.70

UN Day.

Exist imperf. Value, set of 8, unused or used, $9.50.

Souvenir sheets exist. One contains a single 4af ultramarine stamp, perforated; the other, a 4af ocher stamp, imperf. Value, 2 sheets, $9.25.

Boy Scout — A199

1962, Oct. 18 **Photo.** ***Perf. 12***

623 A199 1p yel, dk grn & sal .25 .25
624 A199 2p dl yel, slate & sal .25 .25
625 A199 3p rose, blk & sal .25 .25
626 A199 4p multicolored .25 .25
Nos. 623-626,C32-C35 (8) 3.90 3.90

Issued to honor the Boy Scouts.

Exist imperf. Value, set of 8, unused or used, $27.50.

Pole Vault — A200

3p, High jump. 4p, 5p, Different blossoms.

1962, Oct. 25 **Unwmk.** ***Perf. 12***

627 A200 1p lilac & dk grn .25 .25
628 A200 2p yellow grn & brn .25 .25
629 A200 3p bister & vio .25 .25
630 A200 4p sal pink, grn & ultra .25 .25
631 A200 5p yellow, grn & bl .25 .25
Nos. 627-631,C36-C37 (7) 2.85 2.85

Issued for Teacher's Day.

Exist imperf. Value, set of 7, unused or used, $12.

Rockets A201

1962, Nov. 29

632 A201 50p pale lil & dk bl .70 .70
633 A201 100p lt blue & red brn 1.50 1.50

UN World Meteorological Day.

Exist imperf. Value, set, unused or used, $27.50.

A souvenir sheet contains one 5af pink and green stamp. Value $6.

Ansari Mausoleum, Herat — A202

Perf. 13½

1963, Jan. 3 **Unwmk.** **Photo.**

634 A202 50p purple & grn .25 .25
635 A202 75p gray & magenta .25 .25
636 A202 100p orange brn & brn .40 .40
Nos. 634-636 (3) .90 .90

Khwaja Abdullah Ansari, Sufi, religious leader and poet, on the 900th anniv. of his death.

Sheep A203

Silkworm, Cocoons, Moth and Mulberry Branch A204

1963, Mar. 1 ***Perf. 12***

637 A203 1p grnsh blue & blk .25 .25
638 A203 2p yellow grn & blk .25 .25
639 A203 3p lilac rose & blk .25 .25
640 A204 4p gray, grn & brn .25 .25
641 A204 5p red lil, grn & brn .25 .25
Nos. 637-641,C42-C44 (8) 3.25 3.25

Issued for the Day of Agriculture.

Exist imperf. Value, set of 8, unused or used, $12.

Rice — A205

Designs: 3p, Corn. 300p, Wheat emblem.

1963, Mar. 27 **Unwmk.** ***Perf. 14***

642 A205 2p gray, claret & grn .25 .25
643 A205 3p green, yel & ocher .25 .25
644 A205 300p dk blue & yel .75 .75
Nos. 642-644,C45 (4) 2.65 2.65

FAO "Freedom from Hunger" campaign.

Meteorological Measuring Instrument — A206

Designs: 3p, 10p, Weather station. 4p, 5p, Rockets in space.

1963, May 23 **Photo.** ***Perf. 13½x14***

645 A206 1p dp magenta & brn .25 .25
646 A206 2p brt blue & brn .25 .25
647 A206 3p red & brown .25 .25
648 A206 4p orange & lilac .25 .25
649 A206 5p green & dl vio .25 *.25*

Imperf

650 A206 10p red brn & grn .45 .40
Nos. 645-650,C46-C50 (11) 12.30 12.25

3rd UN World Meteorological Day, Mar. 23.

Independence Monument A207

1963, Aug. 23 **Litho.** ***Perf. 10½***

651 A207 25p lt green .25 .25
652 A207 50p orange .40 .25
653 A207 150p rose carmine .65 .30
Nos. 651-653 (3) 1.30 .80

45th Independence Day.

Pathans in Forest A208

1963, Aug. 31 **Unwmk.** ***Perf. 10½***

654 A208 25p pale violet .25 .25
655 A208 50p sky blue .30 .25
655A A208 150p dull red brn .80 .40
Nos. 654-655A (3) 1.35 .90

Issued for "Free Pashtunistan Day."

4th Asian Games, Djakarta — A208a

2p, 250p, 300p, Wrestling. 3p, 10p, Tennis. 4p, 500p, Javelin. 5p, 9af, Shot put.

1963, Sept. 3 **Litho.** ***Perf. 12***

656 A208a 2p rose vio & brn .25 .25
656A A208a 3p olive grn & brn .25 .25
656B A208a 4p blue & brn .25 .25
656C A208a 5p yel grn & brn .25 .25
656D A208a 10p lt bl grn & brn .25 .25
656E A208a 300p yellow & vio .50 .50
656F A208a 500p lt yel bis & brn .90 .90
656G A208a 9af pale grn & vio 1.50 1.50
Nos. 656-656G (8) 4.15 4.15

Souvenir Sheets

656H A208a 250p lilac & vio 2.00 2.00
656I A208a 300p blue & blk 2.00 2.00

Nos. 656E-656F are airmail. Nos. 656-656I exist imperf. Values, unused or used: set, $12; souvenir sheets, each $11.

National Assembly Building — A209

1963, Sept. 10 ***Perf. 11***

657 A209 25p gray .25 .25
658 A209 50p dull red .25 .25
659 A209 75p brown .25 .25
660 A209 100p olive .25 .25
661 A209 125p lilac .40 .25
Nos. 657-661 (5) 1.40 1.25

Issued to honor the National Assembly.

Balkh Gate A210

1963, Oct. 8

662 A210 3af choc (screened margins) 1.00 .30
a. White margins 2.50 .55

In the original printing a halftone screen extended across the plate, covering the space between the stamps. A retouch removed the screen between the stamps (No. 662a).

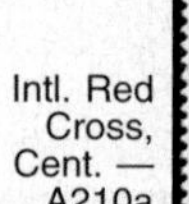

Intl. Red Cross, Cent. — A210a

4p, 5p, 200p, 3af, Nurse holding patient, vert. 10p, 4af, 6af, Crown Prince Ahmed Shah.

1963, Oct. 9 ***Perf. 13½***

662B A210a 2p olive, blk & red .25 .25
662C A210a 3p blue, blk & red .25 .25
662D A210a 4p lt grn, blk & red .25 .25
662E A210a 5p lt vio, blk & red .25 .25
662F A210a 10p gray grn, red & blk .25 .25
662G A210a 100p dull bl grn, red & blk .25 .25
662H A210a 200p lt brn, blk & red .25 .25
662I A210a 4af brt bl grn, red & blk .25 .25
m. Souvenir sheet of 1 1.75 1.60
662J A210a 6af lt brn, red & blk .25 .25
Nos. 662B-662J (9) 2.25 2.25

Souvenir Sheet

662K A210a 3af dl blue, blk & red 1.75

Nos. 662G-662K are airmail.

Nos. 662B-662K exist imperf. Values, unused or used: set, $12; souvenir sheets, each $11.

Zahir Shah — A211

1963, Oct. 15 ***Perf. 10½***

663 A211 25p green .25 .25
663A A211 50p gray .25 .25
663B A211 75p carmine rose .30 .25
663C A211 100p dull redsh brn .50 .25
Nos. 663-663C (4) 1.30 1.00

King Mohammed Zahir Shah, 49th birthday.

Kemal Ataturk — A212

1963, Oct. 10 ***Perf. 10½***

664 A212 1af blue .25 .25
665 A212 3af rose lilac .65 .50

25th anniv. of the death of Kemal Ataturk, president of Turkey.

Protection of Nubian Monuments A213

Designs: 5af, 7.50af, 10af, Ruins, vert.

Perf. 12, Imperf. (150p, 250p, 10af)

1963, Nov. 16 **Photo.**

666 A213 100p lil rose & blk .25 .25
666A A213 150p rose lil & blk .25 *.30*
666B A213 200p brown & blk .40 .40
666C A213 250p ultra & blk .50 .50
666D A213 500p green & blk 1.00 1.00
666E A213 5af greenish blue & gray bl 1.00 1.00
666F A213 7.50af red brn & gray bl 1.75 1.75
666G A213 10af ver & gray bl 1.90 1.90
Nos. 666-666G (8) 7.05 7.10

Nos. 666E-666G are airmail. No. 666D exists imperf. Value, unused or used, 95¢.

Women's Day — A213a

1964, Jan. 5 ***Perf. 14x13½***

667 A213a 2p multicolored .25 .25
667A A213a 3p multicolored .25 .25
667B A213a 4p multicolored .25 .25
667C A213a 5p multicolored .25 .25
667D A213a 10p multicolored .25 .25
Nos. 667-667D (5) 1.25 1.25

Exist imperf. Value set, unused or used, $2.40.

A213b

Boy and Girl Scouts — A213c

Nos. 668F-668G, 668K-668M, Girl with flag.

1964, Jan. 5 *Perf. 13½x14, 14x13½*

668 A213b 2p multi .25 .25
668A A213b 3p multi .25 .25
668B A213b 4p multi .25 .25
668C A213b 5p multi .25 .25
668D A213b 10p multi .25 .25
668E A213c 2af multi .25 .25
668F A213c 2af multi .25 .25
668G A213c 2.50af multi .25 .25
668H A213c 3af multi .30 .30
668I A213c 4af multi .40 .40
668J A213c 5af multi .50 .50
668K A213c 12af multi 1.25 1.25
Nos. 668-668K (12) 4.45 4.45

Souvenir Sheets

668L A213c 5af multi 1.25 1.25
668M A213c 6af multi 1.25 2.00
668N A213c 6af multi 2.50 2.50
668O A213c 10af multi 2.50 2.50

Nos. 668E-668O are airmail.

Nos 668-668K, 668N-668O exist imperf. Values, unused or used: set, $15; souvenir sheets, each $7.

Children — A213d

2p, Playing ball. 4p, Swinging, jumping rope, vert. 5p, Skiing, vert.

1964, Jan. 22 *Perf. 12*

669 A213d 2p multi .25 .25
669A A213d 3p like #669 .25 .25
669B A213d 4p multi .25 .25
669C A213d 5p multi .25 .25
669D A213d 10p like #669 .25 .25
669E A213d 200p like #669C .75 .75
669F A213d 300p like #669B 1.10 1.10
Nos. 669-669F (7) 3.10 3.10

Nos. 669E-669F are airmail.

Nos. 669-669F exist imperf. Value set, unused or used, $27.50.

Red Crescent Society — A213e

Designs: 100p, 200p, Pierre and Marie Curie, physicists. 2.50af, 7.50af Nurse examining child. 3.50af, 5af, Nurse and patients.

Perf. 14, Imperf. (#670A, 670C-670D)

1964, Feb. 8

670 A213e 100p multi .50 .50
670A A213e 100p multi .50 .50
670B A213e 200p multi .80 .80
670C A213e 2.50af multi 1.25 1.25
670D A213e 3.50af multi 1.90 1.90
670E A213e 5af multi 2.10 2.10
670F A213e 7.50af multi 3.00 3.00
Nos. 670-670F (7) 10.05 10.05

Nos. 670A and 670E-F are airmail.

Teachers' Day — A213f

Flowers: 2p, 3p, 3af, 4af, Tulips. 4p, 5p, 3.50af, 6af, Flax. 10p, 1.50af, 2af, Iris.

Perf. 12, Imperf. (1.50af, 2af)

1964, Mar. 3

671 A213f 2p multicolored .25 .25
671A A213f 3p multicolored .25 .25
671B A213f 4p multicolored .25 .25
671C A213f 5p multicolored .25 .25
671D A213f 10p multicolored .25 .25
671E A213f 1.50af multicolored 2.25 2.25
671F A213f 2af multicolored 3.00 3.00
671G A213f 3af multicolored .90 .90
671H A213f 3.50af multicolored 1.10 1.10
Nos. 671-671H (9) 8.50 8.50

Souvenir Sheets

671I A213f 4af multi 2.40 2.40
671J A213f 6af multi, imperf 5.00 5.00

Nos. 671E-671J are airmail. Nos. 671-671D exist imperf. Value, each 20¢.

A213g

UN Day: 5p, 10p, 2af, 3af, 4af, Doctor and nurse, vert.

1964, Mar. 9 *Perf. 14*

672 A213g 2p multicolored .25 .25
672A A213g 3p multicolored .25 .25
672B A213g 4p multicolored .25 .25
672C A213g 5p multicolored .25 .25
672D A213g 10p multicolored .25 .25
672E A213g 100p multicolored .65 .65
672F A213g 2af multicolored 1.20 1.20
672G A213g 3af multicolored 1.75 1.75
Nos. 672-672G (8) 4.85 4.85

Souvenir Sheets

672H A213g 4af multi, imperf. 14.50 14.50
672I A213g 5af multi 3.25 3.25

Nos. 672E-672G are airmail.

Nos. 672-672G exist imperf. Value set, unused or used, $20.

For surcharges see Nos. B71A-B71J.

UNICEF — A213h

Design: 5af, 7.50af, 10af, Children eating.

Perf. 14x13½, Imperf. (150p, 250p, 10af)

1964, Mar. 15

673 A213h 100p multi .30 .30
673A A213h 150p multi 1.75 1.75
673B A213h 200p multi .65 .65
673C A213h 250p multi 3.00 3.00
673D A213h 5af multi 1.50 1.50
673E A213h 7.50af multi 2.40 2.40
673F A213h 10af multi 12.50 12.50
Nos. 673-673F (7) 22.10 22.10

Nos. 673D-673F are airmail.

Eradication of Malaria — A213i

4p, 5p, 5af, 10af Spraying mosquitoes.

1964, Mar. 15 *Perf. 13½*

674 A213i 2p lt red brn & yel grn .25 .25
674A A213i 3p olive grn & buff .25 .25
674B A213i 4p dk vio & bl grn .25 .25
674C A213i 5p brn & grn .25 .25
674D A213i 2af Prus bl & ver .65 .30
h. Souvenir sheet of 1 4.75 4.75
674E A213i 5af dk grn & lt red brn, imperf. 5.25 5.25
i. Souv. sheet of 1, imperf. 14.50 14.50
674F A213i 10af red brn & grnsh bl 2.75 1.75
Nos. 674-674F (7) 9.65 8.30

No. 674B Surcharged in Black

674G A213i 10p on 4p Prus bl & rose .90 .25

No. 674G not issued without surcharge. Nos. 674D-674F are airmail.

Nos. 674-674C, 674G exist imperf. Values, each $2.75.

"Tiger's Head" of 1878 — A214

1964, Mar. 22 **Photo.** *Perf. 12*

675 A214 1.25af gold, grn & blk .25 .25
676 A214 5af gold, rose car & blk .55 .35

Issued to honor philately.

Unisphere and Flags A215

1964, May 3 *Perf. 13½x14*

677 A215 6af crimson, gray & grn .25 .25

New York World's Fair, 1964-65.

Hand Holding Torch — A216

1964, May 12 **Photo.** *Perf. 14x13½*

678 A216 3.75af multicolored .25 .25

1st UN Seminar on Human Rights in Kabul, May 1964. The denomination in Persian at right erroneously reads "3.25" but the stamp was sold and used as 3.75af.

Kandahar Airport A217

1964, Apr. **Litho.** *Perf. 10½, 11*

679 A217 7.75af dk red brown .65 .40
680 A217 9.25af lt green .90 .80
681 A217 10.50af lt green 1.10 .95
682 A217 13.75af carmine rose 1.40 1.00
Nos. 679-682 (4) 4.05 3.15

Inauguration of Kandahar Airport.

Snow Leopard A218

50p, Ibex, vert. 75p, Head of argali. 5af, Yak.

1964, June 25 **Photo.** *Perf. 12*

683 A218 25p yellow & blue 1.75 .25
684 A218 50p dl red & grn 2.00 .25
685 A218 75p Prus bl & lil 2.40 .25
686 A218 5af brt grn & dk brn 2.50 .90
Nos. 683-686 (4) 8.65 1.65

View of Herat A219

Flag and Map of Afghanistan A220

Tourist publicity: 75p, Tomb of Queen Gowhar Shad, vert.

1964, July 12 *Perf. 13½x14, 14x13½*

687 A219 25p sepia & bl .25 .25
688 A219 75p dp blue & buff .30 .25
689 A220 3af red, blk & grn .55 .25
Nos. 687-689 (3) 1.10 .75

Wrestling A221

25p, Hurdling, vert. 1af, Diving, vert. 5af, Soccer.

1964, July 26 *Perf. 12*

690 A221 25p ol bis, blk & car .25 .25
691 A221 1af bl grn, blk & car .25 .25
692 A221 3.75af yel grn, blk & car .40 .25
693 A221 5af brn, blk & car .50 .30
a. Souv. sheet, #690-693, imperf. 1.25 1.25
Nos. 690-693 (4) 1.40 1.05

18th Olympic Games, Tokyo, Oct. 10-25, 1964. No. 693a sold for 15af. The additional 5af went to the Afghanistan Olympic Committee.

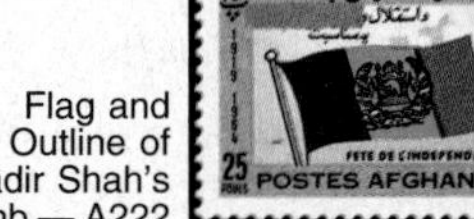

Flag and Outline of Nadir Shah's Tomb — A222

1964, Aug. 24 **Photo.**

695 A222 25p multicolored .25 .25
696 A222 75p multicolored .30 .25

Independence Day. The stamps were printed with an erroneous inscription in upper left corner: "33rd year of independence." This was locally obliterated with a typographed gold bar. Value, each $4.

Pashtunistan Flag — A223

1964, Sept. 1 **Unwmk.**
697 A223 100p gold, blk, red, bl & grn .55 .25

Issued for "Free Pashtunistan Day."

Zahir Shah — A225

1964, Oct. 17 ***Perf. 14x13½***
699 A225 1.25af gold & yel grn .25 .25
700 A225 3.75af gold & rose .40 .40
701 A225 50af gold & gray 3.50 2.25
Nos. 699-701 (3) 4.15 2.90

King Mohammed Zahir Shah, 50th birthday.

Coat of Arms of Afghanistan and UN Emblem A226

1964, Oct. 24 ***Perf. 13½x14***
702 A226 5af gold, blk & dl bl .25 .25

Issued for United Nations Day.

Emblem of Afghanistan Women's Association A227

1964, Nov. 9 **Photo.** **Unwmk.**
703 A227 25p pink, dk bl & emer .55 .30
704 A227 75p aqua, dk bl & emer .90 .40
705 A227 1af sil, dk bl & emer 1.25 .55
Nos. 703-705 (3) 2.70 1.25

Issued for Women's Day.

Poet Mowlana Nooruddin Abdul Rahman Jami (1414-1492) A228

Perf. 11 Rough

1964, Nov. 23 **Litho.**
706 A228 1.50af blk, emer & yel .95 .95

No. 706 also exists clean-cut perf 10½.

Woodpecker A229

Birds: 3.75af, Black-throated jay, vert. 5af, Impeyan pheasant, vert.

Perf. 13½x14, 14x13½

1965, Apr. 20 **Photo.** **Unwmk.**
707 A229 1.25af multi 3.00 .40
708 A229 3.75af multi 5.25 .90
709 A229 5af multi 6.00 2.00
Nos. 707-709 (3) 14.25 3.30

ITU Emblem, Old and New Communication Equipment — A230

1965, May 17 ***Perf. 13½x14***
710 A230 5af lt bl, blk & red .50 .35

Cent. of the ITU.

"Red City," Bamian — A231

Designs: 3.75af, Ruins of ancient Bamian city. 5af, Bande Amir, mountain lakes.

1965, May 30 ***Perf. 13x13½***
711 A231 1.25af pink & multi .40 .25
712 A231 3.75af lt blue & multi .65 .25
713 A231 5af yellow & multi .95 .25
Nos. 711-713 (3) 2.00 .75

Issued for tourist publicity.

ICY Emblem A232

1965, June 25 ***Perf. 13½x13***
714 A232 5af multicolored .50 .30

International Cooperation Year, 1965.

ARIANA Air Lines Emblem and DC-3 A233

5af, DC-6 at right. 10af, DC-3 on top.

Perf. 13½x14

1965, July 15 **Photo.** **Unwmk.**
715 A233 1.25af brt bl, gray & blk .30 .25
716 A233 5af red lil, blk & bl .90 .25
717 A233 10af bis, blk, bl gray & grn 1.60 .55
a. Souv. sheet, #715-717, imperf 3.00 3.00
Nos. 715-717 (3) 2.80 1.05

10th anniv. of Afghan Air Lines, ARIANA.

Nadir Shah — A234

1965, Aug. 23 ***Perf. 14x13½***
718 A234 1af dl grn, blk & red brn .40 .25

For the 47th Independence Day.

Flag of Pashtunistan — A235

Perf. 13½x14

1965, Aug. 31 **Photo.** **Unwmk.**
719 A235 1af multicolored .40 .25

Issued for "Free Pashtunistan Day."

Zahir Shah Signing Constitution — A236

1965, Sept. 11 ***Perf. 13x13½***
720 A236 1.50af brt grn & blk .40 .25

Promulgation of the new Constitution.

Zahir Shah and Oak Leaves — A237

1965, Oct. 14 ***Perf. 14x13½***
721 A237 1.25af blk, ultra & salmon .25 .25
722 A237 6af blk, lt bl & rose lil .40 .35

King Mohammed Zahir Shah, 51st birthday.

Flags of UN and Afghanistan A238

1965, Oct. 24 ***Perf. 13½x14***
723 A238 5af multicolored .25 .25

Issued for United Nations Day.

Dappled Ground Gecko A239

Designs: 4af, Caucasian agamid (lizard). 8af, Horsfield's tortoise.

Perf. 13½x14

1966, May 10 **Photo.** **Unwmk.**
724 A239 3af tan & multi 1.00 .25
725 A239 4af brt grn & multi 1.25 .30
726 A239 8af violet & multi 2.25 .65
Nos. 724-726 (3) 4.50 1.20

Soccer Player and Globe — A240

1966, July 31 **Litho.** ***Perf. 14x13½***
727 A240 2af rose red & blk .70 .25
728 A240 6af violet bl & blk 1.25 .30
729 A240 12af bister brn & blk 2.50 .70
Nos. 727-729 (3) 4.45 1.25

World Cup Soccer Championship, Wembley, England, July 11-30.

Cotton Flower and Boll — A241

5af, Silkworm. 7af, Farmer plowing with oxen.

1966, July 31 ***Perf. 13½x14***
730 A241 1af multicolored .90 .25
731 A241 5af multicolored 1.75 .30
732 A241 7af multicolored 2.50 .50
Nos. 730-732 (3) 5.15 1.05

Issued for the Day of Agriculture.

Independence Monument — A242

1966, Aug. 23 **Photo.** ***Perf. 13½x14***
733 A242 1af multicolored .30 .25
734 A242 3af multicolored .90 .30

Issued to commemorate Independence Day.

Flag of Pashtunistan — A243

Perf. 11 Rough

1966, Aug. 31 **Litho.**
735 A243 1af bright blue .55 .25

"Free Pashtunistan Day."

Bagh-i-Bala Park Casino A244

Tourist publicity: 2af, Map of Afghanistan. 8af, Tomb of Abd-er-Rahman. The casino on 4af is the former summer palace of Abd-er-Rahman near Kabul.

1966, Oct. 3 **Photo.** ***Perf. 13½x14***
736 A244 2af red & multi .40 .25
737 A244 4af multicolored .80 .35
738 A244 8af multicolored 1.20 .80
a. Souvenir sheet of 3, #736-738, imperf. 3.50 3.50
Nos. 736-738 (3) 2.40 1.40

Zahir Shah — A245

1966, Oct. 14 ***Perf. 14x13½***

739	A245	1af dk slate grn	.25	.25
740	A245	5af red brown	.55	.30

King Mohammed Zahir Shah, 52nd birthday. See Nos. 760-761.

UNESCO Emblem — A246

1967, Mar. 6 **Litho.** ***Perf. 12***

741	A246	2af multicolored	.30	.25
742	A246	6af multicolored	.50	.25
743	A246	12af multicolored	1.10	.25
		Nos. 741-743 (3)	1.90	.75

20th anniv. of UNESCO.

Zahir Shah and UN Emblem A247

1967 **Photo.**

744	A247	5af multicolored	.40	.25
745	A247	10af multicolored	.80	.30

UN Intl. Org. for Refugees, 20th anniv.

New Power Station A248

5af, Carpet, vert. 8af, Cement factory.

1967, Jan. 7 **Photo.** ***Perf. 13½x14***

746	A248	2af red lil & ol grn	.30	.25
747	A248	5af multicolored	.30	.25
748	A248	8af blk, dk bl & tan	.60	.30
		Nos. 746-748 (3)	1.20	.80

Issued to publicize industrial development.

International Tourist Year Emblem A249

Designs: 6af, International Tourist Year emblem and map of Afghanistan.

1967, May 11 **Photo.** ***Perf. 12***

749	A249	2af yel, blk & lt bl	.40	.25
750	A249	6af bis brn, blk & lt bl	.65	.25
a.		Souv. sheet, #749-750, imperf	2.00	1.25

Intl. Tourist Year, 1967. No. 750a sold for 10af.

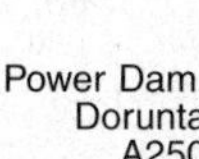

Power Dam, Doruntа A250

6af, Sirobi Dam, vert. 8af, Reservoir at Jalalabad.

1967, July 2 **Photo.** ***Perf. 12***

751	A250	1af dk green & lil	.40	.25
752	A250	6af red brn & grnsh bl	.80	.25
753	A250	8af plum & dk bl	1.20	.40
		Nos. 751-753 (3)	2.40	.90

Progress in agriculture through electricity.

Macaque — A251

Designs: 6af, Striped hyena, horiz. 12af, Persian gazelles, horiz.

1967, July 28 **Photo.** ***Perf. 12***

754	A251	2af dull yel & indigo	.75	.25
755	A251	6af lt green & sepia	1.50	.30
756	A251	12af lt bl & red brn	2.25	.80
		Nos. 754-756 (3)	4.50	1.35

Pashtun Dancers A252

1967, Sept. 1 **Photo.** ***Perf. 12***

757	A252	2af magenta & violet	.70	.25

Issued for "Free Pashtunistan Day."

Retreat of British at Maiwand A253

1967, Aug. 24

758	A253	1af dk brn & org ver	.40	.25
759	A253	2af dk brn & brt pink	.80	.25

Issued to commemorate Independence Day.

King Type of 1966

1967, Oct. 15 **Photo.** ***Perf. 14x13½***

760	A245	2af brown red	.25	.25
761	A245	8af dark blue	.65	.30

Issued to honor King Mohammed Zahir Shah on his 53rd birthday.

Fireworks and UN Emblem — A254

1967, Oct. 24 **Litho.** ***Perf. 12***

762	A254	10af violet bl & multi	.70	.40

Issued for United Nations Day.

Greco-Roman Wrestlers A255

Design: 6af, Free style wrestlers.

1967, Nov. 20 **Photo.**

763	A255	4af ol grn & rose lil	.50	.25
764	A255	6af dp carmine & brn	.95	.25
a.		Souv. sheet, #763-764, imperf	2.10	2.10

1968 Olympic Games.

Said Jamalluddin Afghan — A256

1967, Nov. 27

765	A256	1af magenta	.25	.25
766	A256	5af brown	.40	.25

Said Jamalluddin Afghan, politician (1839-97).

Bronze Vase, 11th-12th Centuries — A257

Design: 7af, Bronze vase, Ghasnavide era, 11th-12th centuries.

1967, Dec. 23 **Photo.** ***Perf. 12***

767	A257	3af lt green & brn	.65	.25
768	A257	7af yel & slate grn	1.20	.30
a.		Souv. sheet, #767-768, imperf	3.00	3.00

WHO Emblem A258

1968, Apr. 7 **Photo.** ***Perf. 12***

769	A258	2af citron & brt bl	.25	.25
770	A258	7af rose & brt bl	.50	.30

20th anniv. of the WHO.

Karakul A259

1968, May 20 **Photo.** ***Perf. 12***

771	A259	1af yellow & blk	.30	.25
772	A259	6af lt blue & blk	1.00	.30
773	A259	12af ultra & dk brn	1.75	.50
		Nos. 771-773 (3)	3.05	1.05

Issued for the Day of Agriculture.

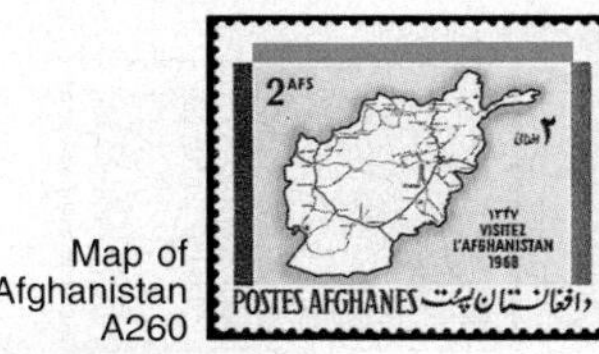

Map of Afghanistan A260

Victory Tower, Ghazni — A261

Design: 16af, Mausoleum, Ghazni.

1968, June 3 ***Perf. 13½x14, 12***

774	A260	2af red, blk, lt bl & grn	.40	.25
775	A261	3af yel, dk brn & lt bl	.50	.25
776	A261	16af pink & multi	1.60	.55
		Nos. 774-776 (3)	2.50	1.05

Issued for tourist publicity.

Cinereous Vulture — A262

6af, Eagle owl. 7af, Greater flamingoes.

1968, July 3 ***Perf. 12***

777	A262	1af sky blue & multi	1.75	.65
778	A262	6af yellow & multi	4.00	2.00
779	A262	7af multicolored	6.00	2.25
		Nos. 777-779 (3)	11.75	4.90

Game of "Pegsticking" A263

2af, Olympic flame & rings, vert. 12af, Buzkashi.

1968, July 20 **Photo.** ***Perf. 12***

780	A263	2af multicolored	.50	.25
781	A263	8af orange & multi	.85	.40
782	A263	12af multicolored	1.25	.65
		Nos. 780-782 (3)	2.60	1.30

19th Olympic Games, Mexico City, 10/12-27.

Flower-decked Armored Car — A264

1968, Aug. 23

783	A264	6af multicolored	.75	.25

Issued to commemorate Independence Day.

Flag of Pashtunistan A265

1968 Aug. 31 **Photo.** ***Perf. 12***

784	A265	3af multicolored	.30	.25

Issued for "Free Pashtunistan Day."

Zahir Shah — A266

1968, Oct. 14 **Photo.** ***Perf. 12***

785	A266	2af ultra	.25	.25
786	A266	8af brown	.55	.30

King Mohammed Zahir Shah, 54th birthday.

Human Rights Flame — A267

1968, Oct. 24

787	A267	1af multicolored	.30	.25
788	A267	2af violet, bis & blk	.30	.25
789	A267	6af vio blk, bis & vio	.60	.25
		Nos. 787-789 (3)	1.20	.75

Souvenir Sheet
Imperf

790 A267 10af plum, bis & red org 1.75 1.75

International Human Rights Year.

Maolana Djalalodine Balkhi — A268

1968, Nov. 26 Photo. *Perf. 12*

791 A268 4af dk green & mag .30 .25

Balkhi (1207-73), historian.

Kushan Mural — A269

Design: 3af, Jug shaped like female torso.

1969, Jan. 2 *Perf. 12*

792 A269 1af dk grn, mar & yel .55 .25
793 A269 3af violet, gray & mar 1.20 .25
a. Souv. sheet, #792-793, imperf 2.40 1.75

Archaeological finds at Bagram, 1st cent. B.C. to 2nd cent. A.D.

ILO Emblem A270

1969, Mar. 23 Photo. *Perf. 12*

794 A270 5af lt yel, lemon & blk .30 .25
795 A270 8af lt bl, grnsh bl & blk .55 .30

50th anniv. of the ILO.

Arms Type of 1939

1969, May (?) Typo.

795A A79 100p dark green .40 .25
795B A79 150p deep brown .55 .25

Nos. 795A-795B were normally used as newspaper stamps.

Badakhshan Scene A271

Tourist Publicity: 2af, Map of Afghanistan. 7af, Three men on mules ascending the Pamir Mountains.

1969, July 6 Photo. *Perf. 13½x14*

796 A271 2af ocher & multi .70 .25
797 A271 4af multicolored .90 .30
798 A271 7af multicolored 1.40 .65
a. Souv. sheet, #796-798, imperf 3.00 2.40
Nos. 796-798 (3) 3.00 1.20

No. 798a sold for 15af.

Bust, from Hadda Treasure, 3rd-5th Centuries — A272

Designs: 5af, Vase and jug. 10af, Statue of crowned woman. 5af and 10af from Bagram treasure, 1st-2nd centuries.

1969, Aug. 3 Photo. *Perf. 14x13½*

799 A272 1af olive grn & gold .40 .25
800 A272 5af purple & gold .70 .25
801 A272 10af dp blue & gold 1.10 .30
Nos. 799-801 (3) 2.20 .80

Zahir Shah and Queen Humeira — A273

1969, Aug. 23 *Perf. 12*

802 A273 5af gold, dk bl & red brn .40 .25
803 A273 10af gold, dp lil & bl grn .70 .40

Issued to commemorate Independence Day.

Map of Pashtunistan and Rising Sun — A274

1969, Aug. 31 Typo. *Perf. 10½*

804 A274 2af lt blue & red .40 .25

Issued for "Free Pashtunistan Day."

Zahir Shah — A275

1969, Oct. 14 Photo. *Perf. 12*

Portrait in Natural Colors

805 A275 2af dk brown & gold .25 .25
806 A275 6af brown & gold .55 .25

King Mohammed Zahir Shah, 55th birthday.

UN Emblem and Flag of Afghanistan — A276

1969, Oct. 24 Litho. *Perf. 13½*

807 A276 5af blue & multi .30 .25

Issued for United Nations Day.

ITU Emblem — A277

1969, Nov. 12

808 A277 6af ultra & multi .30 .25
809 A277 12af rose & multi .70 .40

Issued for World Telecommunications Day.

Crested Porcupine A278

1af, Long-tailed porcupine. 8af, Red deer.

1969, Dec. 7 Photo. *Perf. 12*

810 A278 1af yellow & multi .50 .30
811 A278 3af blue & multi 1.10 .50
812 A278 8af pink & multi 2.00 1.00
Nos. 810-812 (3) 3.60 1.80

Man's First Footprints on Moon, and Earth — A279

1969, Dec. 28 *Perf. 13½x14*

813 A279 1af yel grn & multi .25 .25
814 A279 3af yellow & multi .30 .25
815 A279 6af blue & multi .50 .25
816 A279 10af rose & multi .70 .40
Nos. 813-816 (4) 1.75 1.15

Moon landing. See note after Algeria No. 427.

Anti-cancer Symbol — A280

1970, Apr. 7 Photo. *Perf. 14*

817 A280 2af dk grn & rose car .25 .25
818 A280 6af dk bl & rose claret .50 .25

Issued to publicize the fight against cancer.

Mirza Abdul Quader Bedel — A281

1970, May 6 *Perf. 14x13½*

819 A281 5af multicolored .40 .25

Mirza Abdul Quader Bedel (1643-1720), poet.

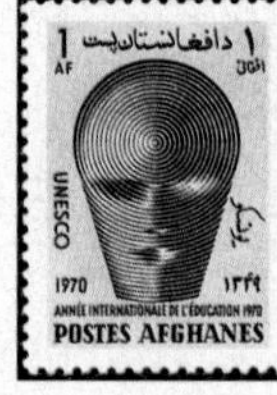

Education Year Emblem — A282

1970, June 7 Photo. *Perf. 12*

820 A282 1af black .25 .25
821 A282 6af deep rose .40 .25
822 A282 12af green .90 .40
Nos. 820-822 (3) 1.55 .90

International Education Year 1970.

Mother and Child — A283

1970, June 15 *Perf. 13½*

823 A283 6af yellow & multi .30 .25

Issued for Mother's Day.

UN Emblem, Scales of Justice, Spacecraft A284

1970, June 26

824 A284 4af yel, dk bl & dp bl .25 .25
825 A284 6af pink, dk bl & brt bl .40 .25

25th anniversary of United Nations.

Mosque of the Amir of the two Swords, Kabul A285

2af, Map of Afghanistan. 7af, Arch of Paghman.

1970, July 6 *Perf. 12*

Size: 30½x30½mm

826 A285 2af lt bl, blk & citron .30 .25

Size: 36x26mm

827 A285 3af pink & multi .50 .25
828 A285 7af yellow & multi .95 .25
Nos. 826-828 (3) 1.75 .75

Issued for tourist publicity.

Zahir Shah Reviewing Troops — A286

1970, Aug. 23 Photo. *Perf. 13½*

829 A286 8af multicolored .40 .25

Issued to commemorate Independence Day.

Pathans — A287

1970, Aug. 31 Typo. *Perf. 10½*

830 A287 2af ultra & red .40 .25

Issued for "Free Pashtunistan Day."

Quail — A288

4af, Golden eagle. 6af, Ringnecked pheasant.

1970, Sept. Photo. *Perf. 12*

831 A288 2af multicolored 2.10 .65
832 A288 4af multicolored 4.00 .95
833 A288 6af multicolored 5.25 1.60
Nos. 831-833 (3) 11.35 3.20

Zahir Shah — A289

1970, Oct. 14 Photo. *Perf. 14x13½*

834 A289 3af green & vio .25 .25
835 A289 7af dk bl & vio brn .70 .30

King Mohammed Zahir Shah, 56th birthday.

Red Crescents A290

1970, Oct. 16 Typo. *Perf. 10½*

836 A290 2af black, gold & red .30 .25

Issued for the Red Crescent Society.

UN Emblem and Charter A291

1970, Oct. 24 Photo. *Perf. 14*

837 A291 1af gold & multi .25 .25
838 A291 5af gold & multi .30 .25

United Nations Day.

Tiger Heads of 1871 — A292

1970, Nov. 10 *Perf. 12*

839 A292 1af sal, lt grnsh bl & blk .30 .25
840 A292 4af lt ultra, yel & blk .55 .25
841 A292 12af lilac, lt bl & blk .95 .40
Nos. 839-841 (3) 1.80 .90

Cent. of the 1st Afghan postage stamps. The postal service was established in 1870, but the 1st stamps were issued in May, 1871.

Globe and Waves A293

1971, May 17 Photo. *Perf. 13½*

842 A293 12af green, blk & bl .65 .40

3rd World Telecommunications Day.

Callimorpha Principalis A294

Designs: 3af, Epizygaenella species. 5af, Parnassius autocrator.

1971, May 30 *Perf. 13½x14*

843 A294 1af vermilion & multi 1.25 .55
844 A294 3af yellow & multi 2.50 1.10
845 A294 5af ultra & multi 3.50 1.75
Nos. 843-845 (3) 7.25 3.40

"UNESCO" and Half of Ancient Kushan Statue — A295

1971, June 26 Photo. *Perf. 13½*

846 A295 6af ocher & vio .50 .25
847 A295 10af lt blue & mar .80 .35

UNESCO-sponsored Intl. Kushani Seminar.

Tughra and Independence Monument — A296

1971, Aug. 23

848 A296 7af rose red & multi .55 .25
849 A296 9af red orange & multi .90 .35

Independence Day.

Pashtunistan Square, Kabul — A297

1971, Aug. 31 Typo. *Perf. 10½*

850 A297 5af deep rose lilac .50 .25

"Free Pashtunistan Day."

Zahir Shah — A298

1971, Oct. 14 Photo. *Perf. 12½x12*

851 A298 9af lt green & multi .55 .30
852 A298 17af yellow & multi 1.10 .65

King Mohammed Zahir Shah, 57th birthday.

A299

Design: Map of Afghanistan, red crescent, various activities.

1971, Oct. 16 *Perf. 14x13½*

853 A299 8af lt bl, red, grn & blk .50 .30

For Afghan Red Crescent Society.

Equality Year Emblem A300

1971, Oct. 24 *Perf. 12*

854 A300 24af brt blue 1.50 .80

International Year Against Racial Discrimination and United Nations Day.

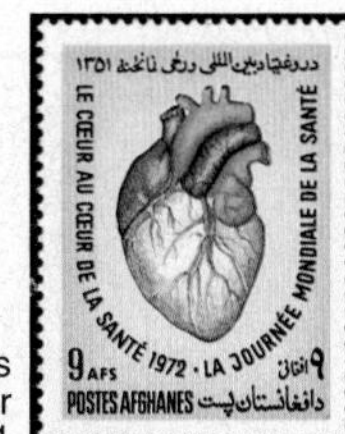

"Your Heart is your Health" — A301

1972, Apr. 7 Photo. *Perf. 14*

855 A301 9af pale yellow & multi .90 .30
856 A301 12af gray & multi 1.75 .40

World Health Day.

Tulip — A302

Designs: 10af, Rock partridge, horiz. 12af, Lynx, horiz. 18af, Allium stipitatum (flower).

1972, June 5 Photo. *Perf. 14*

857 A302 7af green & multi 1.25 .70
858 A302 10af blue & multi 7.00 1.60
859 A302 12af lt green & multi 2.40 1.25
860 A302 18af blue grn & multi 2.40 1.40
Nos. 857-860 (4) 13.05 4.95

Buddhist Shrine, Hadda A302a

Designs: 7af, Greco-Bactrian animal seal, 250 B.C. 9af, Greco-Oriental temple, Ai-Khanoum, 3rd-2nd centuries B.C.

1972, July 16 Photo. *Perf. 12*

861 A302a 3af brown & dl bl .65 .25
862 A302a 7af rose claret & dl grn .95 .30
863 A302a 9af green & lilac 1.40 .40
Nos. 861-863 (3) 3.00 .95

Tourist publicity.

King and Queen Reviewing Parade — A303

1972, Aug. 23 Photo. *Perf. 13½*

864 A303 25af gold & multi 4.50 1.25

Independence Day.

Used as a provisional in 1978 with king and queen portion removed.

Wrestling A304

10af, 19af, 21af, Wrestling, different hold.

1972, Aug. 26

865 A304 4af ol bis & multi .30 .25
866 A304 8af lt blue & multi .55 .25
867 A304 10af yel grn & multi .70 .30
868 A304 19af multicolored 1.50 .50
869 A304 21af lilac & multi 1.60 .55
a. Souv. sheet, #865-869, imperf 3.25 3.25
Nos. 865-869 (5) 4.65 1.85

20th Olympic Games, Munich, Aug. 26-Sept. 11. No. 869a sold for 60af.

Pathan and View of Tribal Territory — A305

1972, Aug. 31 *Perf. 12½x12*

870 A305 5af ultra & multi .55 .25

Pashtunistan day.

Zahir Shah — A306

1972, Oct. 14 Photo. *Perf. 14x13½*

871 A306 7af gold, blk & Prus bl .70 .25
872 A306 14af gold, blk & lt brn 1.10 .40

58th birthday of King Mohammed Zahir Shah.

City Destroyed by Earthquake, Refugees — A307

1972, Oct. 16 ***Perf. 13½***

873 A307 7af lt bl, red & blk .65 .25

For Afghan Red Crescent Society.

UN Emblem A308

1972, Oct. 24

874 A308 12af lt ultra & blk .70 .30

UN Economic Commission for Asia and the Far East (ECAFE), 25th anniv.

Ceramics A309

Designs: 9af, Leather coat, vert. 12af, Metal ware, vert. 16af, Inlaid artifacts.

1972, Dec. 10 **Photo.** ***Perf. 12***

875 A309 7af gold & multi .50 .25
876 A309 9af gold & multi .75 .35
877 A309 12af gold & multi .90 .40
878 A309 16af gold & multi 1.50 .50
a. Souv. sheet, #875-878, imperf 4.00 4.00
Nos. 875-878 (4) 3.65 1.50

Handicraft industries. No. 878a sold for 45af.

WMO and National Emblems — A310

1973, Apr. 3 **Photo.** ***Perf. 14***

879 A310 7af lt lil & dk grn .55 .25
880 A310 14af lt bl & dp claret 1.40 .40

Cent. of intl. meteorological cooperation.

Abu Rayhan al-Biruni — A311

1973, June 16 **Photo.** ***Perf. 13½***

881 A311 10af multicolored .65 .40

Millennium of birth (973-1048), philosopher and mathematician.

Family — A312

1973, June 30 **Photo.** ***Perf. 13½***

882 A312 9af orange & red lil .75 .25

Intl. Family Planning Fed., 21st anniv.

Republic

Impeyan Pheasant A313

Birds: 9af, Great crested grebe. 12af, Himalayan snow cock.

1973, July 29 **Photo.** ***Perf. 12x12½***

883 A313 8af yellow & multi 3.00 2.00
884 A313 9af blue & multi 3.75 2.40
885 A313 12af multicolored 4.50 3.25
Nos. 883-885 (3) 11.25 7.65

Stylized Buzkashi Horseman A314

1973, Aug. ***Perf. 13½***

886 A314 8af black .55 .30

Tourist publicity.

Fireworks A315

1973, Aug. 23 **Photo.** ***Perf. 12***

887 A315 12af multicolored .65 .40

55th Independence Day.

Lake Abassine, Pashtunistan Flag — A316

1973, Aug. 31 ***Perf. 14x13½***

888 A316 9af multicolored .65 .35

Pashtunistan Day.

Red Crescent A317

1973, Oct. 16 ***Perf. 13½***

889 A317 10af red, blk & gold .95 .30

Red Crescent Society.

Kemal Ataturk A318

1973, Oct. 28 **Litho.** ***Perf. 10½***

890 A318 1af blue .25 .25
891 A318 7af reddish brown 1.25 .25

50th anniversary of the Turkish Republic.

Human Rights Flame, Arms of Afghanistan A319

1973, Dec. 10 **Photo.** ***Perf. 12***

892 A319 12af sil, blk & lt bl .55 .40

25th anniversary of the Universal Declaration of Human Rights.

Asiatic Black Bears A320

1974, Mar. 26 **Litho.** ***Perf. 12***

893 A320 5af shown .65 .25
894 A320 7af Afghan hound 1.00 .40
895 A320 10af Persian goat 1.40 .50
896 A320 12af Leopard 1.75 .55
a. Souv. sheet, #893-896, imperf 10.00 10.00
Nos. 893-896 (4) 4.80 1.70

Worker and Farmer A321

1974, May 1 **Photo.** ***Perf. 13½x12½***

897 A321 9af rose red & multi .70 .30

International Labor Day, May 1.

Independence Monument and Arch — A322

1974, May 27 **Photo.** ***Perf. 12***

898 A322 4af blue & multi .40 .25
899 A322 11af gold & multi .55 .25

56th Independence Day.

Arms of Afghanistan and Symbol of Cooperation — A323

Pres. Mohammad Daoud Khan — A324

5af, Flag of Republic of Afghanistan. 15af, Soldiers, coat of arms of the Republic.

Sizes: 4af, 15af, 36x22mm; 5af, 7af, 36x26, 26x36mm

1974, July 25 ***Perf. 13½x12½, 14***

900 A323 4af multicolored .40 .25
901 A323 5af multicolored .55 .25
902 A324 7af green, brn & blk .65 .25
a. Souv. sheet, #901-902, imperf 1.75 1.75
903 A323 15af multicolored 1.25 .30
a. Souv. sheet, #900, 903, imperf 2.00 2.00
Nos. 900-903 (4) 2.85 1.05

1st anniv. of the Republic of Afghanistan.

Lesser Spotted Eagle A325

Birds: 6af, White-fronted goose, ruddy shelduck and gray-lag goose. 11af, European coots and European crane.

1974, Aug. 6 **Photo.** ***Perf. 13½x13***

904 A325 1af car rose & multi 2.00 .50
905 A325 6af blue & multi 4.50 .80
906 A325 11af yellow & multi 7.00 1.40
a. Strip of 3, #904-906 14.00 14.00

Flags of Pashtunistan and Afghanistan — A326

1974, Aug. 31 **Photo.** ***Perf. 14***

907 A326 5af multicolored .30 .25

Pashtunistan Day.

Natl. Arms A326a

1974, Aug. **Typo.** ***Rough Perf. 11***

907A A326a 100p green .80 .25

Coat of Arms A327

1974, Oct. 9

908 A327 7af gold, grn & blk .30 .25

Centenary of Universal Postal Union.

"un" and UN Emblem A328

1974, Oct. 24 Photo. *Perf. 14*

909 A328 5af lt ultra & dk bl .40 .25

United Nations Day.

Minaret of Jam — A329

Buddha, Hadda — A330

14af, Lady riding griffin, 2nd century, Bagram.

1975, May 5 Photo. *Perf. 13½*

910	A329	7af multicolored	.30	.25
911	A330	14af multicolored	.65	.40
912	A330	15af multicolored	.80	.40
a.		Souv. sheet, #910-912, imperf.	3.50	3.50
		Nos. 910-912 (3)	1.75	1.05

South Asia Tourism Year 1975.

New Flag of Afghanistan A331

1975, May 27 Photo. *Perf. 12*

913 A331 16af multicolored .80 .25

57th Independence Day.

Celebrating Crowd — A332

1975, July 17 Photo. *Perf. 13½*

914	A332	9af blue & multi	.50	.25
915	A332	12af carmine & multi	.65	.30

Second anniversary of the Republic.

Women's Year Emblems A333

1975, Aug. 24 Photo. *Perf. 12*

916 A333 9af car, lt bl & blk .50 .25

International Women's Year 1975.

Pashtunistan Flag, Sun Rising Over Mountains A334

Mohammed Akbar Khan A335

1975, Aug. 31 *Perf. 13½*

917 A334 10af multicolored .40 .25

Pashtunistan Day.

1976, Feb. 4 Photo. *Perf. 14*

918 A335 15af lt brown & multi .55 .40

Mohammed Akbar Khan (1816-1846), warrior son of Amir Dost Mohammed Khan.

A336

Pres. Mohammad Daoud Khan — A337

1974-78 Photo. *Perf. 14*

919	A336	10af multi	.65	.25
920	A336	16af multi ('78)	2.40	.90
921	A336	19af multi	.90	.50
922	A336	21af multi	1.40	.55
923	A336	22af multi ('78)	3.50	1.90
924	A336	30af multi ('78)	4.75	2.75
925	A337	50af multi ('75)	2.75	1.40
926	A337	100af multi ('75)	5.50	2.40
		Nos. 919-926 (8)	21.85	10.65

Arms of Republic, Independence Monument — A338

1976, June 1 Photo. *Perf. 14*

927 A338 22af blue & multi .70 .50

58th Independence Day.

Flag Raising — A339

1976, July 17 Photo. *Perf. 14*

928 A339 30af multicolored .80 .55

Republic Day.

Mountain Peaks and Flag of Pashtunistan A340

1976, Aug. 31 Photo. *Perf. 14*

929 A340 16af multicolored .65 .50

Pashtunistan Day.

Coat of Arms A340a

1976, Sept. Litho. *Perf. 11 Rough*

930	A340a	25p salmon	.50	.30
931	A340a	50p lt green	.55	.25
932	A340a	1af ultra	.55	.25
		Nos. 930-932 (3)	1.60	.80

Flag and Views on Open Book A341

1977, May 27 Photo. *Perf. 14*

937 A341 20af green & multi .70 .60

59th Independence Day.

Pres. Daoud and National Assembly — A342

President Taking Oath of Office A343

Designs: 10af, Inaugural address. 18af, Promulgation of Constitution.

1977, June 22

938	A342	7af multicolored	.80	.55
939	A343	8af multicolored	.90	.70
940	A343	10af multicolored	1.10	.90
941	A342	18af multicolored	1.90	1.50
a.		Souvenir sheet of 4	3.50	3.50
		Nos. 938-941 (4)	4.70	3.65

Election of 1st Pres. and promulgation of Constitution. No. 941a contains 4 imperf. stamps similar to Nos. 938-941.

Jamalluddin Medal A344

1977, July 6 Photo. *Perf. 14*

942 A344 12af blue, blk & gold .40 .30

Sajo Jamalluddin Afghani, reformer, 80th death anniversary.

Afghanistan Flag over Crowd — A345

1977, July 17

943 A345 22af multicolored .70 .55

Dancers, Fountain, Pashtunistan Flag — A346

1977, Aug. 31

944 A346 30af multicolored 1.10 .90

Pashtunistan Day.

Arms and Carrier Pigeon — A346a

1977, Oct. 30 Litho. *Perf. 11*

944A A346a 1af black & blue .40 .25

Members of Parliament Congratulating Pres. Daoud — A347

1978, Feb. 5 Litho. *Perf. 14*

945 A347 20af multicolored 2.00 1.10

Election of first president, first anniversary.

Map of Afghanistan, UPU Emblem — A348

1978, Apr. 1 Photo. *Perf. 14*

946 A348 10af green, blk & gold .40 .25

Afghanistan's UPU membership, 50th anniv.

Wall Telephone and Satellite Station A349

1978, Apr. 12

947 A349 8af multicolored .40 .25

Afghanistan's ITU membership, 50th anniv.

Democratic Republic

Arrows Pointing to Crescent, Cross and Lion — A350

1978, July 6 Litho. *Perf. 11 Rough*

948 A350 3af black 1.25 .65

50th anniv. of Afghani Red Crescent Soc.

Khalq Party Emblem — A350a

1978, Aug. Litho. *Perf. 11*

948A A350a 1af rose red & gold 1.50 .65

948B A350a 4af rose red & gold 2.10 .90

Qalai Bist Arch A351

Hazara Women — A351a

1978, Aug. 19 *Perf. 14*

949 A351 16af Bamian Buddha 1.25 .50

949A A351 22af shown 1.50 .65

949B A351a 30af shown 2.10 1.10

Nos. 949-949B (3) 4.85 2.25

Men with Pashtunistan Flag — A352

1978, Aug. 31 *Perf. 11 Rough*

950 A352 7af ultra & red .50 .25

Pashtunistan Day.

Coat of Arms and Emblems A353

1978, Sept. 8 *Perf. 11*

951 A353 20af rose red .90 .40

World Literacy Day.

A354

Perf. 11½ Rough

1978, Oct. 25 Litho.

952 A354 18af light green .95 .40

Hero of Afghanistan.

Khalq Party Flag A355

1978, Oct. 19 Photo. *Perf. 11½*

953 A355 8af black, red & gold .65 .25

954 A355 9af black, red & gold .95 .25

"The mail serving the people."

Nour Mohammad Taraki — A356

1979, Jan. 1 Litho. *Perf. 12*

955 A356 12af multicolored .70 .25

Nour Mohammad Taraki, founder of People's Democratic Party of Afghanistan, installation as president.

Woman Breaking Chain — A357

1979, Mar. 8 Litho. *Perf. 11*

956 A357 14af red & ultra 1.25 .50

Women's Day. Inscribed "POSSTES."

Map of Afghanistan, Census Emblem — A358

1979, Mar. 25 Litho. *Perf. 12*

957 A358 3af multicolored .90 .70

First comprehensive population census.

Farmers A359

1979, Mar. 21

958 A359 1af multicolored .65 .30

Agricultural advances.

Pres. Taraki Reading First Issue of Khalq — A360

1979, Apr. 11 *Perf. 12½x12*

959 A360 2af multicolored .65 .25

Khalq, newspaper of People's Democratic Republic of Afghanistan.

Pres. Noor Mohammad Taraki A361

Plaza with Tank Monument and Fountain — A362

House where Revolution Started — A363

Designs: 50p, Taraki, tank. 12af, House where 1st Khalq Party Congress was held.

Perf. 12, 12½x12 (A362)

1979, Apr. 27 Litho.

959A A363 50p multicolored .65 .25

960 A361 4af multicolored .40 .25

961 A362 5af multicolored .55 .25

962 A363 6af multicolored .70 .25

963 A363 12af multicolored .80 .25

Nos. 959A-963 (5) 3.10 1.25

1st anniversary of revolution.

Carpenter and Blacksmith A364

1979, May 1 *Perf. 12*

964 A364 10af multicolored 1.10 .25

Int'l Labor Day.

Children, Flag and Map of Afghanistan — A366

1979, June 1 Litho. *Perf. 12½x12*

966 A366 16af multicolored 2.00 .90

International Year of the Child.

Doves Circling Asia in Globe A366a

1979 Litho. *Perf. 11x10½*

966A A366a 2af red & blue 1.25 .25

Armed Afghans, Kabul Memorial and Arch — A367

1979, Aug. 19 Litho. *Perf. 12*

967 A367 30af multicolored 1.50 .90

60th independence day.

Pashtunistan Citizens, Flag — A368

1979, Aug. 31

968 A368 9af multicolored .70 .25

Pashtunistan Day.

UPU Day A369

1979, Oct. 9 Litho. *Perf. 12*

969 A369 15af multicolored .65 .25

Tombstone — A369a

1979, Oct. 25 Litho. ***Perf. 12½x12***
969A A369a 22af multicolored 2.40 1.25

International Women's Day — A370

1980, Mar. 8 Litho. ***Perf. 12***
970 A370 8af multicolored 1.50 .50

Farmers' Day — A371

1980, Mar. 21 Litho. ***Perf. 11½x12***
971 A371 2af multicolored 2.25 .70

Non-smoker and Smoker A372

1980, Apr. 7 ***Perf. 11½***
972 A372 5af multicolored 1.75 .70

Anti-smoking campaign; World Health Day.

Lenin, 110th Birth Anniversary A373

1980, Apr. 22 ***Perf. 12x12½***
973 A373 12af multicolored 2.50 .85

People and Fist on Map of Afghanistan — A374

1980, Apr. 27 Litho. ***Perf. 12½x12***
974 A374 1af multicolored .70 .25

Saur Revolution, 2nd anniversary.

International Workers' Solidarity Day — A375

1980, May 1
975 A375 9af multicolored .50 .25

Wrestling, Moscow '80 Emblem A376

1980, July 19 ***Perf. 12x12½, 12½x12***

976 A376	3af Soccer, vert.	.60	.25
977 A376	6af shown	.70	.25
978 A376	9af Buzkashi	.80	.25
979 A376	10af Pegsticking	.95	.25
	Nos. 976-979 (4)	3.05	1.00

22nd Summer Olympic Games, Moscow, July 19-Aug. 3.

61st Anniversary of Independence — A377

1980, Aug. 19 Litho. ***Perf. 12½x12***
980 A377 3af multicolored .85 .25

Pashtunistan Day — A378

1980, Aug. 30
981 A378 25af multicolored 1.00 .45

Intl. UPU Day A379

1980, Oct. 9 Litho. ***Perf. 12½x12***
982 A379 20af multicolored 1.00 .45

The resistance group headed by Amin Wardak released some stamps in 1980. Some of these are inscribed "WARDAK AFGHANISTAN," others "Solidarite Internationale Avec la Resistance Afghane." The status of these labels is questionable.

International Women's Day — A381

1981, Mar. 9 Litho. ***Perf. 12½x12***
984 A381 15af multicolored 1.25 .35

Farmers' Day — A382

1981, Mar. 20 Litho. ***Perf. 12½x12***
985 A382 1af multicolored 1.00 .25

Bighorn Mountain Sheep (Protected Species) A383

1981, Apr. 4 ***Perf. 12x12½***
986 A383 12af multicolored 2.40 .70

Saur Revolution, 3rd Anniversary A384

1981, Apr. 27 ***Perf. 11***
987 A384 50p brown .70 .25

Intl. Workers' Solidarity Day — A385

1981, May 1 ***Perf. 12½x12***
988 A385 10af multicolored .95 .35

13th World Telecommunications Day — A387

1981, May 17 Litho. ***Perf. 12½x12***
990 A387 9af multicolored .70 .25

Intl. Children's Day — A388

1981, June 1 ***Perf. 12x12½***
991 A388 15af multicolored .95 .45

People's Independence Monument 62nd Anniv. of Independence — A389

1981, Aug. 19
992 A389 4af multicolored 1.10 .30

Pashtunistan Day — A390

1981, Aug. 31 Litho. ***Perf. 12***
992A A390 2af multicolored .70 .25

Intl. Tourism Day — A391

1981, Sept. 27 ***Perf. 12½x12***
993 A391 5af multicolored .70 .25

World Food Day — A392

1981, Oct. 16
995 A392 7af multicolored .85 .25

Asia-Africa Solidarity Meeting — A393

1981, Nov. 18 Litho. ***Perf. 11***
996 A393 8af blue .80 .25

Struggle Against Apartheid — A394

1981, Dec. 1 ***Perf. 12½x12***
997 A394 4af multicolored 1.00 .25

1300th Anniv. of Bulgaria A395

1981, Dec. 9 ***Perf. 12x12½***
998 A395 20af multicolored 1.75 .50

Buzkashi Game — A395a

1980 Photo. *Perf. 14*
998A A395a 50af multicolored 2.25 1.25
998B A395a 100af multicolored 4.50 1.75

Intl. Women's Day A396

1982, Mar. 8 Litho. *Perf. 12*
999 A396 6af multicolored .60 .25

Farmers' Day — A397

1982, Mar. 21
1000 A397 4af multicolored .70 .25

Judas Trees — A398

Designs: Various local plants.

1982, Apr. 9 Litho. *Perf. 12*
1001 A398 3af shown .40 .25
1002 A398 4af Rose of Sharon .70 .25
1003 A398 16af Rhubarb plant 1.60 .35
Nos. 1001-1003 (3) 2.70 .85

Saur Revolution, 4th Anniv. — A399

1982, Apr. 27
1004 A399 1af multicolored 1.50 .25

George Dimitrov (1882-1947), First Prime Minister of Bulgaria — A400

1982, Apr. 30
1005 A400 30af multicolored 2.40 .85

Intl. Workers' Solidarity Day A401

1982, May 1
1006 A401 10af multicolored .85 .25

Storks — A402

1982, May 31
1007 A402 6af shown 1.75 .50
1008 A402 11af Nightingales 2.75 .60

Hedgehogs A403

1982, July 6 Litho. *Perf. 12*
1009 A403 3af shown .85 .25
1010 A403 14af Cobra 2.00 .25

See Nos. 1020-1022.

63rd Anniv. of Independence — A404

1982, Aug. 19
1011 A404 20af multicolored 1.25 .50

Pashtunistan Day — A405

1982, Aug. 31
1012 A405 32af multicolored 2.50 .75

World Tourism Day A406

1982, Sept. 27 Litho. *Perf. 12*
1013 A406 9af multicolored .85 .35

UPU Day A407

1982, Oct. 9
1014 A407 4af multicolored .95 .25

World Food Day A408

1982, Oct. 16
1015 A408 9af multicolored 1.50 .35

37th Anniv. of UN — A409

1982, Oct. 24
1016 A409 15af multicolored 1.00 .45

ITU Plenipotentiaries Conference, Nairobi, Sept. — A410

1982, Oct. 26
1017 A410 8af multicolored .80 .25

TB Bacillus Centenary — A411

1982, Nov. 24 Litho. *Perf. 12*
1018 A411 7af multicolored .50 .25

Human Rights Declaration, 34th Anniv. — A412

1982, Dec. 10
1019 A412 5af multicolored .45 .25

Animal Type of 1982

1982, Dec. 16
1020 A403 2af Lions .45 .25
1021 A403 7af Donkeys .95 .35
1022 A403 12af Marmots, vert. 2.00 .50
Nos. 1020-1022 (3) 3.40 1.10

Intl. Women's Day — A413

1983, Mar. 8
1023 A413 3af multicolored .25 .25

Mir Alicher Nawai Research Decade — A414

1983, Mar. 19
1024 A414 22af multicolored .95 .35

Farmers' Day A415

1983, Mar. 21 Litho. *Perf. 12*
1025 A415 10af multicolored .85 .25

5th Anniv. of Saur Revolution A416

1983, Apr. 27 Litho. *Perf. 12*
1026 A416 15af multicolored .70 .35

Intl. Workers' Solidarity Day — A417

1983, May 1
1027 A417 2af multicolored .70 .25

World Communications Year — A418

1983, May 17
1028 A418 4af Modes of communication .45 .25
1029 A418 11af Building .75 .25

Intl. Children's Day — A419

1983, June 1 Litho. *Perf. 12*
1030 A419 25af multicolored .80 .35

2nd Anniv. of National Front — A420

1983, June 15
1031 A420 1af multicolored .35 .25

Local Butterflies A421

Various butterflies. 9af, 13af vert.

1983, July 6

1032 A421 9af multicolored 1.10 .80
1033 A421 13af multicolored 2.50 1.40
1034 A421 21af multicolored 3.25 1.75
Nos. 1032-1034 (3) 6.85 3.95

Struggle Against Apartheid — A422

1983, Aug. 1 Litho. *Perf. 12*

1035 A422 10af multicolored .55 .25

64th Anniv of Independence — A423

1983, Aug. 19

1036 A423 6af multicolored .45 .25

Parliament House — A423a

1983, Sept. Litho. *Perf. 12*

1036A A423a 50af shown 1.75 .35
1036B A423a 100af Afghan Woman, Camel 4.25 .45

A424

World Tourism Day — A425

1983, Sept. 27 Litho. *Perf. 12*

1037 A424 5af shown .45 .25
1038 A425 7af shown .60 .25
1039 A424 12af Golden statues .95 .25
1040 A425 16af Stone carving 1.25 .25
Nos. 1037-1040 (4) 3.25 1.00

World Communications Year — A426

1983, Oct. 9 Litho. *Perf. 12*

1041 A426 14af Dish antenna, dove .90 .25
1042 A426 15af Building, flag .90 .25

World Food Day — A427

1983, Oct. 16 Litho. *Perf. 12*

1043 A427 14af multicolored .90 .25

Sports A428

1983, Nov. 1 Litho. *Perf. 12*

1044 A428 1af Soccer .25 .25
1045 A428 18af Boxing 1.00 .35
1046 A428 21af Wrestling 1.25 .35
Nos. 1044-1046 (3) 2.50 .95

Pashtunistan Day — A428a

1983, Nov. Litho. *Perf. 12*

1046A A428a 3af Pathans Waving Flag .45 .25

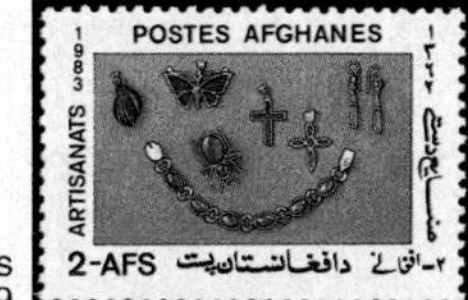

Handicrafts A429

1983, Nov. 22

1047 A429 2af Jewelry .25 .25
1048 A429 8af Stone ashtrays, dishes .35 .25
1049 A429 19af Furniture .60 .25
1050 A429 30af Leather goods 1.50 .40
Nos. 1047-1050 (4) 2.70 1.15

UN Declaration of Human Rights, 35th Anniv. A430

1983, Dec. 10 Litho. *Perf. 12*

1051 A430 20af multicolored .95 .25

Kabul Polytechnical Institute, 20th Anniv. — A431

1983, Dec. 28 *Perf. 12½x12*

1052 A431 30af multicolored 1.25 .35

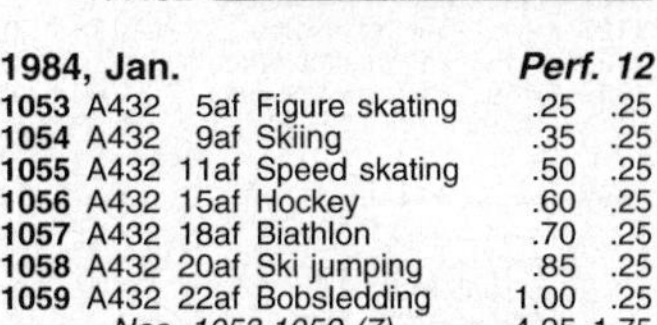

1984 Winter Olympics A432

1984, Jan. *Perf. 12*

1053 A432 5af Figure skating .25 .25
1054 A432 9af Skiing .35 .25
1055 A432 11af Speed skating .50 .25
1056 A432 15af Hockey .60 .25
1057 A432 18af Biathlon .70 .25
1058 A432 20af Ski jumping .85 .25
1059 A432 22af Bobsledding 1.00 .25
Nos. 1053-1059 (7) 4.25 1.75

Intl. Women's Day — A433

1984, Mar. 8

1060 A433 4af multicolored .50 .25

Farmers' Day A434

Various agricultural scenes.

1984, Mar. 21 Litho. *Perf. 12*

1061 A434 2af multicolored .25 .25
1062 A434 4af multicolored .25 .25
1063 A434 7af multicolored .25 .25
1064 A434 9af multicolored .25 .25
1065 A434 15af multicolored .45 .25
1066 A434 18af multicolored .50 .25
1067 A434 20af multicolored .70 .25
Nos. 1061-1067 (7) 2.65 1.75

World Aviation Day A435

1984, Apr. 12

1068 A435 5af Luna 1 .35 .25
1069 A435 8af Luna 2 .45 .25
1070 A435 11af Luna 3 .55 .25
1071 A435 17af Apollo 11 .70 .25
1072 A435 22af Soyuz 6 .90 .35
1073 A435 28af Soyuz 7 .90 .35
1074 A435 34af Soyuz 6, 7, 8 1.10 .45
Nos. 1068-1074 (7) 4.95 2.15

Souvenir Sheet

Perf. 12x12½

1075 A435 25af S. Koroliov 1.50 .90

No. 1075 contains one 30x41mm stamp.

Saur Revolution, 6th Anniv. A436

1984, Apr. 27 *Perf. 12*

1076 A436 3af multicolored .45 .25

65th Anniv. of Independence — A437

1984, Aug. 19 Litho. *Perf. 12*

1077 A437 6af multicolored .65 .25

Pashto's and Balutchi's Day A438

1984, Aug. 31

1078 A438 3af Symbolic sun, tribal terr. .45 .25

Wildlife A439

1af, Cape hunting dog, vert. 2af, Argali sheep, vert. 6af, Przewalski's horse. 8af, Wild boar, vert. 17af, Snow leopard. 19af, Tiger. 22af, Indian elephant, vert.

Perf. 12½x12, 12x12½

1984, May 5 Litho.

1079 A439 1af multicolored .25 .25
1080 A439 2af multicolored .25 .25
1081 A439 6af multicolored .60 .25
1082 A439 8af multicolored .90 .25
1083 A439 17af multicolored 1.75 .25
1084 A439 19af multicolored 3.00 .25
1085 A439 22af multicolored 3.25 .35
Nos. 1079-1085 (7) 10.00 1.85

19th UPU Congress, Hamburg A440

25af, German postman, 17th cent. 35af, Postrider, 16th cent. 40af, Carrier pigeon, letter.

50af, Hamburg No. 3 in black.

1984, June 18 *Perf. 12x12½*

1086 A440 25af multicolored .95 .30
1087 A440 35af multicolored 1.50 .45
1088 A440 40af multicolored 1.90 .55
Nos. 1086-1088 (3) 4.35 1.30

Souvenir Sheet

1089 A440 50af multicolored 2.50 1.50

No. 1089 contains one 30x40mm stamp.

Natl. Aviation, 40th Anniv. A441

Soviet civil aircraft.

1984, June 29

1090 A441 1af Antonov AN-2 .25 .25
1091 A441 4af Ilyushin IL-12 .25 .25
1092 A441 9af Tupolev TU-104 .60 .25
1093 A441 10af Ilyushin IL-18 .90 .25
1094 A441 13af Tupolev TU-134 1.10 .25
1095 A441 17af Ilyushin IL-62 1.50 .30
1096 A441 21af Ilyushin IL-28 1.75 .40
Nos. 1090-1096 (7) 6.35 1.95

Ettore Bugatti (1881-1947), Type 43, Italy — A442

Classic automobiles and their designers: 5af, Henry Ford, 1903 Model A, US. 8af, Rene Panhard (1841-1908), 1899 Landau, France. 11af, Gottlieb Daimler (1834-1900), 1935 Daimler-Benz, Germany. 12af, Carl Benz (1844-1929), 1893 Victoris, Germany. 15af, Armand Peugeot (1848-1915), 1892 Vis-a-Vis, France. 22af, Louis Chevrolet (1879-1941), 1925 Sedan, US.

1984, June 30

1097 A442 2af multicolored .25 .25
1098 A442 5af multicolored .35 .25
1099 A442 8af multicolored .60 .25
1100 A442 11af multicolored .75 .25
1101 A442 12af multicolored 1.00 .25
1102 A442 15af multicolored 1.10 .25
1103 A442 22af multicolored 1.50 .35
Nos. 1097-1103 (7) 5.55 1.85

Qalai Bist Arch A443

World Tourism Day: 2af, Ornamental buckled harness. 5af, Victory Monument and Memorial Arch, Kabul. 9af, Standing sculpture of Afghani ruler and attendants. 15af, Buffalo riders in snow. 19af, Camel driver, tent, camel in caparison. 21af, Horsemen playing buzkashi.

1984, Sept. 27

1104 A443 1af multicolored .25 .25
1105 A443 2af multicolored .25 .25
1106 A443 5af multicolored .25 .25
1107 A443 9af multicolored .25 .25
1108 A443 15af multicolored .45 .25
1109 A443 19af multicolored .90 .25
1110 A443 21af multicolored 1.00 .25
Nos. 1104-1110 (7) 3.35 1.75

UN World Food Day — A444

Fruit-bearing trees.

1984, Oct. 16

1111 A444 2af multicolored .25 .25
1112 A444 4af multicolored .25 .25
1113 A444 6af multicolored .35 .25
1114 A444 9af multicolored .50 .25
1115 A444 13af multicolored .60 .25
1116 A444 15af multicolored .75 .25
1117 A444 26af multicolored 1.25 .25
Nos. 1111-1117 (7) 3.95 1.75

People's Democratic Party, 20th Anniv. A445

1985, Jan. 1

1118 A445 25af multicolored 1.25 .45

Farmer's Day A446

1af, Oxen. 3af, Mare, foal. 7af, Brown horse. 8af, White horse, vert. 15af, Sheep, sheepskins. 16af, Shepherd, cattle, sheep. 25af, Family, camels.

1985, Mar. 2

1119 A446 1af multicolored .35 .25
1120 A446 3af multicolored .35 .25
1121 A446 7af multicolored .35 .25
1122 A446 8af multicolored .60 .25
1123 A446 15af multicolored .95 .25
1124 A446 16af multicolored 1.10 .35
1125 A446 25af multicolored 1.60 .45
Nos. 1119-1125 (7) 5.30 2.05

Geologist's Day — A447

1985, Apr. 5

1126 A447 4af multicolored .35 .25

Lenin and Peasant Petitioners A448

Lenin and: 10af, Lenin and Peasant Petitioners. 15af, Revolutionaries, 1917, Leningrad. 25af, Lenin leading Revolutionary Guards, 1917. 50af, Portrait.

1985, Apr. 21 ***Perf. 12x12½***

1127 A448 10af multicolored .70 .25
1128 A448 15af multicolored .85 .25
1129 A448 25af multicolored 1.50 .40
Nos. 1127-1129 (3) 3.05 .90

Souvenir Sheet

1130 A448 50af multicolored 2.50 1.50

Saur Revolution, 7th Anniv. — A449

1985, Apr. 27

1131 A449 21af multicolored 1.00 .30

Berlin-Treptow Soviet War Memorial, Red Army at Siege of Berlin, 1945 — A450

9af, Victorious Motherland monument, fireworks over Kremlin. 10af, Caecilienhof, site of Potsdam Treaty signing, Great Britain, USSR & US flags.

1985, May 9 ***Perf. 12½x12***

1132 A450 6af multicolored .60 .25
1133 A450 9af multicolored .85 .25
1134 A450 10af multicolored 1.10 .25
Nos. 1132-1134 (3) 2.55 .75

End of World War II, defeat of Nazi Germany, 40th anniv.

INTELSAT, 20th Anniv. A451

Designs: 6af, INTELSAT I satellite orbiting Earth. 9af, INTELSAT VI. 10af, Delta D rocket launch, Cape Canaveral, vert.

Perf. 12x12½, 12½x12

1985, Apr. 6 **Litho.**

1135 A451 6af multicolored .50 .25
1136 A451 9af multicolored .70 .25
1137 A451 10af multicolored .95 .25
Nos. 1135-1137 (3) 2.15 .75

12th World Youth Festival, Moscow — A452

7af, Olympic stadium, Moscow. 12af, Festival emblem. 13af, Kremlin. 18af, Folk doll, emblem.

1985, May 5

1138 A452 7af multicolored .25 .25
1139 A452 12af multicolored .45 .25
1140 A452 13af multicolored .55 .35
1141 A452 18af multicolored .70 .60
Nos. 1138-1141 (4) 1.95 1.45

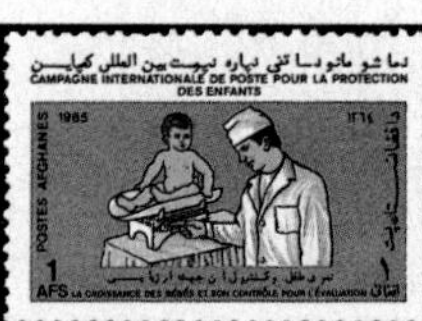

Intl. Child Survival Campaign A453

1985, June 1

1142 A453 1af Weighing child .25 .25
1143 A453 2af Immunization .25 .25
1144 A453 4af Breastfeeding .35 .25
1145 A453 5af Mother, child .40 .25
Nos. 1142-1145 (4) 1.25 1.00

Flowers A454

1985, July 5

1146 A454 2af Oenothera affinis .25 .25
1147 A454 4af Erythrina crista-galli .35 .25
1148 A454 8af Tillandsia aeranthos .60 .25
1149 A454 13af Vinca major .95 .25
1150 A454 18af Mirabilis jalapa 1.40 .35
1151 A454 25af Cypella herbertii 1.90 .45
1152 A454 30af Clytostoma callistegioides 2.50 .60
Nos. 1146-1152 (7) 7.95 2.40

Souvenir Sheet

Perf. 12½x11½

1153 A454 75af Sesbania punicea, horiz. 6.00 3.50

ARGENTINA '85.

Independence, 66th Anniv. — A455

1985, Aug. 19 ***Perf. 12x12½***

1154 A455 33af Mosque 1.50 .45

Pashto's and Balutchi's Day A456

1985, Aug. 30

1155 A456 25af multicolored 1.50 .25

UN Decade for Women A457

1985, Sept. 22

1156 A457 10af Emblems .70 .25

World Tourism Day, 10th Anniv. — A457a

1af, Guldara Stupa. 2af, Mirwais Tomb, vert. 10af, Statue of Bamyan, vert. 13af, No Gumbad Mosque, vert. 14af, Pule Kheshti Mosque. 15af, Bost Citadel. 20af, Ghazni Minaret, vert.

1985, Sept. 27 **Litho.** ***Perf. 12***

1156A A457a 1af multi .25 .25
1156B A457a 2af multi .25 .25
1156C A457a 10af multi .60 .25
1156D A457a 13af multi .85 .25
1156E A457a 14af multi .95 .25
1156F A457a 15af multi 1.00 .25
1156G A457a 20af multi 1.40 .25
Nos. 1156A-1156G (7) 5.30 1.75

Sports — A457b

Perf. 12x12½, 12½x12

1985, Oct. 3 **Litho.**

1156H A457b 1af Boxing .25 .25
1156I A457b 2af Volleyball .25 .25
1156J A457b 3af Soccer, vert. .50 .25
1156K A457b 12af Buzkashi .75 .25
1156L A457b 14af Weight lifting .95 .25
1156M A457b 18af Wrestling 1.00 .25
1156N A457b 25af Peg sticking 1.25 .35
Nos. 1156H-1156N (7) 4.95 1.85

World Food Day — A457c

1985, Oct. 16

1156O A457c 25af multicolored .95 .30

UN 40th Anniv. — A458

1985, Oct. 24 ***Perf. 12½x12***
1157 A458 22af multicolored 1.10 .30

Birds — A459

1985, Oct. 25 ***Perf. 12½x12, 12x12½***
1158 A459 2af Jay .25 .25
1159 A459 4af Plover, hummingbird 1.00 .50
1160 A459 8af Pheasant 1.10 .50
1161 A459 13af Hoopoe 1.75 .95
1162 A459 18af Falcon 2.00 1.00
1163 A459 25af Partridge 3.00 1.60
1164 A459 30af Pelicans, horiz. 4.00 1.90
Nos. 1158-1164 (7) 13.10 6.70

Souvenir Sheet
Perf. 12x12½
1165 A459 75af Parakeets 7.50 5.00

Mushrooms A460

3af, Tricholomopsis rutilans. 4af, Boletus miniatoporus. 7af, Amanita rubescens. 11af, Boletus scaber. 12af, Coprinus atramentarius. 18af, Hypholoma. 20af, Boletus aurantiacus.

1985, June 10 Litho. ***Perf. 12½x12***
1165A A460 3af multicolored .25 .25
1166 A460 4af multicolored .45 .25
1167 A460 7af multicolored .70 .35
1168 A460 11af multicolored .95 .60
1169 A460 12af multicolored 1.25 .60
1170 A460 18af multicolored 1.75 .75
1171 A460 20af multicolored 2.00 .75
Nos. 1165A-1171 (7) 7.35 3.55

World Wildlife Fund — A461

1985, Nov. 25
1172 A461 2af Leopard, cubs *1.00* *.25*
1173 A461 9af Adult's head *2.25* *.50*
1174 A461 11af Adult *3.00* *1.00*
1175 A461 15af Cub *4.50* *1.50*
Nos. 1172-1175 (4) *10.75* *3.25*

Motorcycle, Cent. — A462

Designs: Different makes and landmarks.

1985, Dec. 16
1176 A462 2af multicolored .25 .25
1177 A462 4af multicolored .35 .25
1178 A462 8af multicolored .60 .25
1179 A462 13af multicolored .95 .25
1180 A462 18af multicolored 1.10 .25
1181 A462 25af multicolored 1.60 .35
1182 A462 30af multicolored 2.50 .40
Nos. 1176-1182 (7) 7.35 2.00

Souvenir Sheet
Perf. 11½x12½
1183 A462 75af multicolored 5.00 2.50

People's Democratic Party, 21st Anniv. — A463

1986, Jan. 1 ***Perf. 12½x12***
1184 A463 2af multicolored .35 .25

27th Soviet Communist Party Congress — A464

1986, Mar. 31
1185 A464 25af Lenin .85 .40

First Man in Space, 25th Anniv. — A465

Designs: 3af, Spacecraft. 7af, Soviet space achievement medal, vert. 9af, Rocket lift-off, vert. 11af, Yuri Gagarin, military decorations, vert. 13af, Gagarin, cosmonaut. 15af, Gagarin, politician. 17af, Gagarin wearing flight suit, vert.

Perf. 12½x12, 12x12½
1986, Apr. 12 **Litho.**
1186 A465 3af multicolored .25 .25
1187 A465 7af multicolored .25 .25
1188 A465 9af multicolored .40 .25
1189 A465 11af multicolored .50 .25
1190 A465 13af multicolored .60 .25
1191 A465 15af multicolored .65 .25
1192 A465 17af multicolored .75 .25
Nos. 1186-1192 (7) 3.40 1.75

Loya Jirgah (Grand Assembly) of the People's Democratic Republic, 1st Anniv. A465a

1986, Apr. 23 Litho. ***Perf. 12x12½***
1192A A465a 3af multicolored .40 .25

Intl. Day of Labor Solidarity — A465b

1986, May 1 ***Perf. 12½x12***
1192B A465b 5af multicolored .50 .25

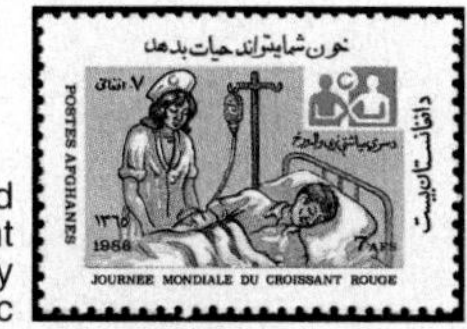

Intl. Red Crescent Day A465c

1986, May 8 ***Perf. 12x12½***
1192C A465c 7af multicolored .50 .25

Intl. Children's Day A466

1af, Mother, children, vert. 3af, Mother, child, vert. 9af, Children, map.

1986, June 1 ***Perf. 12***
1193 A466 1af multicolored .25 .25
1194 A466 3af multicolored .25 .25
1195 A466 9af multicolored .40 .25
Nos. 1193-1195 (3) .90 .75

World Youth Day A466a

1986, July 31 ***Perf. 12x12½***
1195A A466a 15af multicolored .70 .45

Pashtos' and Baluchis' Day A467

1986, Aug. 31 ***Perf. 12x12½***
1196 A467 4af multicolored .25 .25

Intl. Peace Year — A468

1986, Sept. 30 Photo. ***Perf. 12½x12***
1197 A468 12af black & Prus blue .60 .25

A469

1986 World Cup Soccer Championships, Mexico — A470

Various soccer plays.

1986, Apr. 15 Litho. ***Perf. 12***
1198 A469 3af multi, vert. .25 .25
1199 A469 4af multicolored .35 .25
1200 A469 7af multicolored .40 .25
1201 A469 11af multi, vert. .70 .25
1202 A469 12af multicolored .85 .25
1203 A469 18af multi, vert. 1.25 .25
1204 A469 20af multi, vert. 1.50 .25
Nos. 1198-1204 (7) 5.30 1.75

Souvenir Sheet
Perf. 12½x12
1205 A470 75af multicolored 4.75 3.00

A471

1986, Apr. 21 ***Perf. 12½x12***
1206 A471 16af Lenin .75 .45

A472

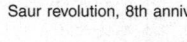

1986, Apr. 27 Litho. ***Perf. 12½x12***
1207 A472 8af multicolored .60 .25

Saur revolution, 8th anniv.

Natl. Independence, 67th Anniv. — A473

1986, Aug. 19 Litho. ***Perf. 12½x12***
1208 A473 10af multicolored .50 .25

Literacy Day A474

1986, Sept. 18 ***Perf. 12x12½***
1209 A474 2af multicolored .25 .25

Dogs — A475

1986, May 19 Litho. *Perf. 12x12½*

1210 A475 5af St. Bernard .25 .25
1211 A475 7af Collie .40 .25
1212 A475 8af Pointer .50 .25
1213 A475 9af Golden retriever .60 .25
1214 A475 11af German shepherd .70 .25
1215 A475 15af Bulldog .95 .25
1216 A475 20af Afghan hound 1.25 .30
Nos. 1210-1216 (7) 4.65 1.80

Lizards — A476

1986, July 7 *Perf. 12x12½, 12½x12*

1217 A476 3af Cobra .25 .25
1218 A476 4af shown .25 .25
1219 A476 5af Praying mantis .35 .25
1220 A476 8af Beetle .50 .25
1221 A476 9af Tarantula .60 .30
1222 A476 10af Python .70 .35
1223 A476 11af Scorpions .85 .35
Nos. 1217-1223 (7) 3.50 2.00

Nos. 1217, 1219, 1221-1223 horiz.

STOCKHOLMIA '86 — A477

Ships.

1986, Aug. 28 *Perf. 12½x12*

1224 A477 4af multicolored .40 .25
1225 A477 5af multicolored .60 .25
1226 A477 6af multicolored .70 .25
1227 A477 7af multicolored .85 .25
1228 A477 8af multicolored 1.00 .25
1229 A477 9af multicolored 1.10 .25
1230 A477 11af multicolored 1.40 .25
Nos. 1224-1230 (7) 6.05 1.75

Souvenir Sheet

1231 A477 50af Galley 4.25 2.00

A479

1986, Sept. 14 *Perf. 12*

1232 A479 3af lt blue, blk & olive gray .40 .25

Reunion of Afghan tribes under the Supreme Girgah.

A480

1986, Oct. 25 *Perf. 12½x12*

1233 A480 3af black & brt ver .40 .25

Natl. youth solidarity.

Locomotives — A481

1986, June 21 *Perf. 12½x12*

1234 A481 4af multicolored .25 .25
1235 A481 5af multicolored .35 .25
1236 A481 6af multicolored .45 .25
1237 A481 7af multicolored .50 .25
1238 A481 8af multicolored .65 .25
1239 A481 9af multicolored .85 .25
1240 A481 11af multicolored 1.25 .25
Nos. 1234-1240 (7) 4.30 1.75

Fish A482

Various fish.

1986, May 25

1241 A482 5af multicolored .25 .25
1242 A482 7af multicolored .40 .25
1243 A482 8af multicolored .50 .25
1244 A482 9af multicolored .60 .25
1245 A482 11af multicolored .85 .25
1246 A482 15af multicolored 1.10 .35
1247 A482 20af multicolored 1.50 .35
Nos. 1241-1247 (7) 5.20 1.95

Saur Revolution, 9th Anniv. A483

1987, Apr. 27 *Perf. 12*

1248 A483 3af multicolored .25 .25

Natl. Reconciliation — A484

1987, May 27 *Perf. 12x12½*

1249 A484 3af multicolored .25 .25

A485

A486

UN Child Survival Campaign — A487

1987, June 1 *Perf. 12*

1250 A485 1af multicolored .25 .25
1251 A486 5af multicolored .25 .25
1252 A487 9af multicolored .35 .25
Nos. 1250-1252 (3) .85 .75

Conference of Clergymen and Ulema, 1st Anniv. A488

1987, June 30

1253 A488 5af multicolored .35 .25

Butterflies — A489

1987, July 3

1254 A489 7af multicolored .60 .35
1255 A489 9af multi, diff. .75 .35
1256 A489 10af multi, diff. 1.00 .50
1257 A489 12af multi, diff. 1.50 .50
1258 A489 15af multi, diff. 1.60 .70
1259 A489 22af multi, diff. 2.25 .95
1260 A489 25af multi, diff. 2.50 .95
Nos. 1254-1260 (7) 10.20 4.30

10af, 15af and 22af horiz.

A490

1987, Aug. 11

1261 A490 1af multicolored .25 .25

1st election of local representatives for State Power and Administration.

Natl. Independence, 68th Anniv. — A490a

1987, Aug. 19

1261A A490a 3af multicolored .25 .25

1st Artificial Satellite (Sputnik), 30th Anniv. — A491

1987, Oct. 4 Litho. *Perf. 12½x12*

1262 A491 10af Sputnik .40 .25
1263 A491 15af Rocket launch .60 .25
1264 A491 25af Soyuz .85 .25
Nos. 1262-1264 (3) 1.85 .75

World Post Day A492

1987, Oct. 9 *Perf. 12x12½*

1265 A492 22af multicolored 1.10 .60

Intl. Communications and Transport Day — A493

1987, Oct. 24 *Perf. 12½x12*

1266 A493 42af multicolored 4.75 1.00

October Revolution in Russia, 70th Anniv. — A494

1987, Nov. 7

1267 A494 25af Lenin 1.25 .70

Mice — A495

Various mice. Nos. 1269-1272 horiz.

1987, Dec. 6 *Perf. 12½x12, 12x12½*

1268 A495 2af multicolored .40 .25
1269 A495 4af multi, diff. .50 .25
1270 A495 8af multi, diff. .60 .25
1271 A495 16af multi, diff. 1.00 .25
1272 A495 20af multi, diff. 1.25 .25
Nos. 1268-1272 (5) 3.75 1.25

Medicinal Plants — A496

1987, Nov. 11 Litho. *Perf. 12*

1273 A496 3af Castor bean .25 .25
1274 A496 6af Licorice .45 .25
1275 A496 9af Chamomile .75 .25
1276 A496 14af Datura 1.00 .25
1277 A496 18af Dandelion 1.25 .30
Nos. 1273-1277 (5) 3.70 1.30

Pashto's and Baluchis' Day — A497

1987, Aug. 30

1278 A497 4af multicolored .25 .25

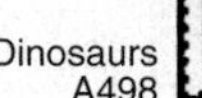

Dinosaurs A498

Perf. 12½x12, 12x12½

1988, June 6 **Litho.**

1279 A498 3af Mesosaurus .25 .25
1280 A498 5af Styracosaurus .25 .25
1281 A498 10af Uinatherium .50 .25
1282 A498 15af Protoceratops .75 .25
1283 A498 20af Stegosaurus 1.00 .30
1284 A498 25af Ceratosaurus 1.40 .35
1285 A498 30af Dinornis maximus 1.90 .60
Nos. 1279-1285 (7) 6.05 2.25

Nos. 1280-1283 horiz.

Pashtos' and Baluchis' Day — A499

1988, Aug. 30 *Perf. 12½x12*

1286 A499 23af multicolored .95 .60

Afghan-Soviet Joint Space Flight — A500

1988, Aug. 30

1287 A500 32af multicolored 1.25 .50

Valentina Tereshkova, 1st Woman in Space, 25th Anniv. — A501

1988, Oct. 16 *Perf. 12x12½, 12½x12*

1288 A501 10af Portrait, rocket, horiz. .85 .35
1289 A501 15af Lift-off, dove .85 .30
1290 A501 25af Spacecraft, Earth, horiz. 1.00 .45
Nos. 1288-1290 (3) 2.70 1.10

Traditional Crafts — A502

Perf. 12x12½, 12½x12

1988, Nov. 9 **Litho.**

1291 A502 2af Pitcher, bowls .25 .25
1292 A502 4af Vases .25 .25
1293 A502 5af Dress .25 .25
1294 A502 9af Mats, napkins .35 .25
1295 A502 15af Pocketbooks .60 .25
1296 A502 23af Jewelry .95 .25
1297 A502 50af Furniture 1.90 .25
Nos. 1291-1297 (7) 4.55 1.75

Nos. 1291-1292, 1294-1297 horiz.

Precious and Semiprecious Gems — A503

1988, Dec. 5 *Perf. 12½x12*

1298 A503 13af Emeralds 1.00 .25
1299 A503 37af Lapiz lazuli 2.25 .60
1300 A503 40af Rubies 2.50 .75
Nos. 1298-1300 (3) 5.75 1.60

1988 Winter Olympics, Calgary — A504

1988, Dec. 25

1301 A504 2af Women's figure skating .25 .25
1301A A504 5af Skiing .25 .25
1301B A504 9af Bobsledding .50 .25
1301C A504 22af Biathlon 1.00 .35
1301D A504 37af Speed skating 2.25 .65

Size: 80x60mm

1302 A504 75af Ice hockey 4.50 3.50
Nos. 1301-1302 (6) 8.75 5.25

A510

A511

A512

A513

A513a

Flowers — A514

Various flowering plants.

Perf. 12x12½, 12½x12

1988, Jan. 27 **Litho.**

1303 A510 3af multicolored .25 .25
1304 A511 5af multicolored .35 .25
1305 A511 7af multi, vert. .50 .25
1306 A512 9af multicolored .70 .25
1307 A513 12af multicolored 1.25 .35
1308 A513a 15af multicolored 1.60 .35
1309 A514 24af multicolored 2.25 .35
Nos. 1303-1309 (7) 6.90 2.05

Traditional Musical Instruments A515

String and percussion instruments.

1988, Jan. 15 **Litho.** *Perf. 12*

1310 A515 1af shown .25 .25
1311 A515 3af drums .25 .25
1312 A515 5af multi, diff. .30 .25
1313 A515 15af multi, diff. .70 .25
1314 A515 18af multi, diff. 1.00 .30
1315 A515 25af multi, diff. 1.40 .30
1316 A515 33af multi, diff. 1.90 .30
Nos. 1310-1316 (7) 5.80 1.90

Admission of Afghanistan to the ITU and UPU, 60th Anniv. — A516

1988, Apr. 13 **Litho.** *Perf. 12*

1317 A516 20af multicolored .85 .50

Saur Revolution, 10th Anniv. A517

1988, Apr. 23

1318 A517 10af multicolored .50 .35

Fruit A518

1988, July 18 **Litho.** *Perf. 12*

1319 A518 2af Baskets, compote .25 .25
1320 A518 4af Four baskets .35 .25
1321 A518 7af Basket .45 .25
1322 A518 8af Grapes, vert. .50 .25
1323 A518 16af Market .85 .35
1324 A518 22af Market, diff. 1.25 .35
1325 A518 25af Vendor, vert. 1.90 .35
Nos. 1319-1325 (7) 5.55 2.05

Jawaharlal Nehru (1889-1964), 1st Prime Minister of Independent India — A519

1988, Nov. 14

1326 A519 40af multicolored 2.25 .85

Natl. Independence, 69th Anniv. — A520

1988, Aug. 1

1327 A520 24af multicolored 1.25 .70

Intl. Red Cross and Red Crescent Organizations, 125th Annivs. — A521

1988, Sept. 26

1328 A521 10af multicolored .85 .50

Natl. Reconciliation Institute, 2nd Anniv. — A522

1989, Jan. 4

1329 A522 4af multicolored .25 .25

Chess A523

Boards, early matches and hand-made chessmen.

1989, Feb. 2 Litho. *Perf. 12x12½*

1330 A523 2af Bishop .25 .25
1331 A523 3af Queen .35 .25
1332 A523 4af King (bust) .45 .25
1333 A523 7af King, diff. .70 .25
1334 A523 16af Knight 1.10 .25
1335 A523 24af Pawn 1.60 .35
1336 A523 45af Bishop, diff. 2.75 .45
Nos. 1330-1336 (7) 7.20 2.05

Paintings by Picasso — A524

Designs: 4af, *The Old Jew.* 6af, *The Two Mountebanks.* 8af, *Portrait of Ambrouse Vollar.* 22af, *Woman of Majorca.* 35af, *Acrobat on the Ball.* 75af, *Usine a Horta de Ebro.*

1989, Feb. 13 Litho. *Perf. 12½x12*

1341 A524 4af multicolored .35 .25
1342 A524 6af multicolored .45 .25
1343 A524 8af multicolored .55 .25
1344 A524 22af multicolored 1.25 .25
1345 A524 35af multicolored 2.50 .25

Size: 71x90mm

Imperf

1346 A524 75af multicolored 4.75 1.25
Nos. 1341-1346 (6) 9.85 2.50

Fauna — A525

3af, Allactaga euphratica. 4af, Equus hemionus. 14af, Felis lynx. 35af, Gypaetus barbatus. 44af, Capra falconeri.
100af, Naja oxiana.

1989, Feb. 20 Litho. *Perf. 12½x12*

1347 A525 3af multicolored .35 .25
1348 A525 4af multicolored .35 .25
1349 A525 14af multicolored 1.00 .35
1350 A525 35af multicolored 3.75 1.60
1351 A525 44af multicolored 2.50 1.25

Size: 71x91mm

Imperf

1352 A525 100af multicolored 7.75 3.00
Nos. 1347-1352 (6) 15.70 6.70

Intl. Women's Day — A526

1989, Mar. 8 *Perf. 12½x12*

1353 A526 8af multicolored .45 .25

Restoration and Development of San'a, Yemen — A527

1988, Dec. 27 Litho. *Perf. 12*

1354 A527 32af multicolored 1.60 1.10

Agriculture Day A528

1989, Mar. 21

1355 A528 1af Cattle .25 .25
1356 A528 2af Old and new plows .25 .25
1357 A528 3af Field workers .25 .25
Nos. 1355-1357 (3) .75 .75

World Meteorology Day — A529

1989, Mar. 23

1358 A529 27af shown 1.25 .25
1359 A529 32af Emblems 1.75 .25
1360 A529 40af Weather station, balloon, vert. 2.25 .25
Nos. 1358-1360 (3) 5.25 .75

Saur Revolution, 11th Anniv. A530

1989, Apr. 27

1361 A530 20af multicolored 1.10 .25

Classic Automobiles — A531

5af, 1910 Duchs, Germany. 10af, 1911 Ford, US. 20af, 1911 Renault, France. 25af, 1911, Russo-Balte, Russia. 30af, 1926 Fiat, Italy.

1989, Dec. 30 Litho. *Perf. 12½x12*

1362 A531 5af multi .45 .25
1363 A531 10af multi .75 .25
1364 A531 20af multi 1.40 .25
1365 A531 25af multi 1.60 .35
1366 A531 30af multi 1.90 .35
Nos. 1362-1366 (5) 6.10 1.45

Asia-Pacific Telecommunity, 10th Anniv. — A532

1989, Aug. 3 *Perf. 12*

1367 A532 3af shown .25 .25
1368 A532 27af Emblem, satellite dish 1.10 .25

Teacher's Day A533

1989, May 30 Litho. *Perf. 12*

1369 A533 42af multicolored 2.25 .35

French Revolution, Bicent. — A534

1989, July Litho. *Perf. 12*

1370 A534 25af multicolored 1.60 .95

Natl. Independence, 70th Anniv. — A535

1989, Aug. 18 Litho. *Perf. 12*

1371 A535 25af multicolored 1.25 .35

A536

1989, Aug. 30

1372 A536 3af multicolored .25 .25

Pashtos' and Baluchis' Day.

Birds — A537

3af, Platalea leucorodia. 5af, Porphyrio porhyrio. 10af, Botaurus stellaris, horiz. 15af, Pelecanus onocrotalus. 20af, Netta rufina. 25af, Cygnus olor. 30af, Phalacrocorax carbo, horiz.

1989, Dec. 5 Litho. *Perf. 12*

1373 A537 3af multicolored .25 .25
1374 A537 5af multicolored .50 .25
1375 A537 10af multicolored .95 .45
1376 A537 15af multicolored 1.25 .55
1377 A537 20af multicolored 1.60 .60
1378 A537 25af multicolored 2.25 .70
1379 A537 30af multicolored 2.50 .95
Nos. 1373-1379 (7) 9.30 3.75

Tourism — A538

1989, Dec.

1380 A538 1af Mosque 1.60 —
1381 A538 2af Minaret 3.25 —
1382 A538 3af Buzkashi, horiz. 4.75 —
1383 A538 4af Jet over Hendo Kush, horiz. 6.50 —
Nos. 1380-1383 (4) 16.10

Mavlavi Allahdad Balkhi, President of Post of the Afghanistan Postal Administration, has declared that "the stamps which have been printed after year 1989 are false stamps."

The following stamps have been condemned as unauthorized by the Afghan Ministry of Communications:

Dated 1996: *Mushrooms,* 6 stamps + souvenir sheet. *Bears,* 5 stamps + souvenir sheet. *1998 Word Soccer Cup Championships,* 6 stamps + souvenir sheet. *Silkworms,* 6 stamps + souvenir sheet. *Domestic Cats,* 6 stamps + souvenir sheet. *Horses,* 5 stamps + souvenir sheet. *Islamic Revolution,* 6 stamps. *Independence Anniv./Honoring Prophet Mohammed,* 2 stamps.

Dated 1997: *Tulips,* 6 stamps + souvenir sheet. *Llamas & Camels,* 6 stamps + souvenir sheet. *Domestic Cats,* 6 stamps + souvenir sheet. *Wildflowers,* 6 stamps + souvenir sheet. *Early Sailing Ships* (triangles), 6 stamps + souvenir sheet. *1998 Word Soccer Cup Championships,* 6 stamps + souvenir sheet. *Mushrooms,* 6 stamps + souvenir sheet.

Dated 1998: *Mushrooms,* 6 stamps + souvenir sheet. *Butterflies,* 6 stamps + souvenir sheet. *Princess Diana,* 9 stamps in a miniature sheet. *WWF (Wild Sheep),* strip of 4 stamps. *Wildlife,* 12 stamps. *Dogs,* 6 stamps + souvenir sheet. *Locomotives,* 6 stamps + souvenir sheet. *Prehistoric Animals,* 6 stamps + souvenir sheet. *Antique Cars,* 6 stamps + souvenir sheet. *Fish,* 6 stamps + souvenir sheet. *Birds,* 6 stamps + souvenir sheet.

Dated 1999: *Chess,* 6 stamps + souvenir sheet. *Mushrooms,* 6 stamps + souvenir sheet. *Locomotives,* 6 stamps + souvenir sheet. *Dogs,* 6 stamps + souvenir sheet. *Minerals,* 6 stamps + souvenir sheet. *Snails,* 6 stamps + souvenir sheet. *Vintage Race Cars,* 6 stamps + souvenir sheet. *China '99,* 12 stamps in a miniature sheet. *Cacti,* 6 stamps + souvenir sheet. *Horses,* 6 stamps + souvenir sheet. *Ferrari Automobiles,* 6 stamps + souvenir sheet. *Orchids,* 6 stamps + souvenir sheet. *Parrots,* 6 stamps + souvenir sheet. *Sailing Ships,* 6 stamps + souvenir sheet.

Dated 2000: *Cats,* 6 stamps + souvenir sheet. *WIPA 2000 (Birds),* 6 stamps + souvenir sheet.

Dated 2001: *Mushrooms,* 6 stamps + souvenir sheet. *Locomotives,* 6 stamps + souvenir sheet.

In addition to these sets, a number of bogus illegal issues have appeared. These issues include:

Beetles: miniature sheet of 9 different stamps.

Birds: 2 miniature sheets of 9 different stamps each.

Boats: 3 miniature sheets of 9 different stamps each.

Cars (Vintage): 3 miniature sheets of 9 different stamps each.

Cats: 3 miniature sheets of 9 different stamps each.

Chess: 3 miniature sheets of 9 different stamps each.

Dinosaurs: 3 miniature sheets of 9 different stamps each.

Dogs: 3 miniature sheets of 9 different stamps each.

Eagles & Owls: miniature sheet of 9 different stamps.

Eagles: miniature sheet of 9 different stamps.

Elvis Presley: 3 miniature sheets of 9 different stamps each.

Fauna of Afghanistan: miniature sheet of 9 different stamps.

Fish: miniature sheet of 9 different stamps.

Great People of the 20th Century: miniature sheet of 9 different stamps.

Horses: 2 miniature sheets of 9 different stamps each.

Korea/Japan World Soccer Cup: 2 souvenir sheets.

Locomotives: 2 souvenir sheets inscribed "Trains."

Locomotives: miniature sheet of 9 different stamps, inscribed "English Trains."

Marilyn Monroe: 3 miniature sheets of 9 different stamps each.

Marilyn Monroe: Block of 4 different stamps.

Mother Teresa & Pope John Paul II: 3 miniature sheets of 6 different stamps each + 3 souvenir sheets.

Osama Ben Laden Wanted Poster: 1 stamp in miniature sheet of 9.

Owls: 3 miniature sheets of 9 different stamps each + 2 souvenir sheets.

Paintings (Classic Posters): miniature sheet of 9 different stamps.

Paintings (Impressionists): 3 miniature sheets of 6 different stamps each + 3 souvenir sheets.

Plants: miniature sheet of 9 different stamps + souvenir sheet depicting orchid.

Princess Diana: miniature sheet of 9 different stamps.

Sports: 4 miniature sheets of 9 different stamps each, inscribed "Formula 2000."

Transitional Islamic State

Ahmed Shah Masood (1953?-2001), Military Leader — A539

2002 Litho. ***Perf. 13½x13***
1384 A539 14,000af multi 5.00 —

National Understanding — A540

2002, July 18 Litho. ***Perf. 13x13½***
1385 A540 11,000af multi 3.00 3.00

Destruction of Bamyan Buddha Statue by Taliban Government A541

2002, July 18 ***Perf. 13½x13***
1386 A541 25,000af multi 5.00 5.00

Universal Declaration of Human Rights, 55th Anniv. — A542

2002, Dec. 10 Litho. ***Perf. 13x12¾***
1387 A542 4af multi 3.50 3.50

Farmer's Day A543

Designs: 3af, Tractor. 6af, Oxen pulling plow.

2003, Mar. 21 Litho. ***Perf. 12¾x13***
1388 A543 3af shown 5.00 —
1389 A453 6af multi 10.00 —

Miniature Sheet

Orchids — A544

No. 1390: a, 9af, Calanthe veitchii. b, 13af, Eulanthe sanderiana. c, 17af, Ordontioda vuylstekeae. d, 20af, Dendrobium infundibulum. e, 30af, Miltonsiopsis roezlii. f, 40af, Cattleya labiata. g, 100af, Vanda coerulea.

2003, Apr. 17 Litho. ***Perf. 13x12¾***
1390 A544 Sheet of 7, #a-g, + 2 labels 22.50 22.50

Birthday of Mohammed — A545

2003, May 14 Litho. ***Perf. 12¾x13***
1391 A545 10af multi 6.00 6.00

World Tuberculosis Day — A546

Designs: 1af, Boy and girl holding sign. 4af, Caricatures of doctors and patients, horiz. 9af, Caricatures of patients, horiz.

Perf. 13x12¾, 12¾x13
2003, May 18 Litho.
1392-1394 A546 Set of 3 6.00 6.00

Loya Jurga A547

2003, June 16 Litho. ***Perf. 12¾x13***
1395 A547 20af multi 4.00 4.00

Day Against Narcotics — A548

Designs: 1af, Map of Afghanistan, poppy. 2af, Poppy capsule, skulls, vert. 5af, Farmer and tractor in poppy field.
10af, Poppy capsule, skulls.

Perf. 12¾x13, 13x12¾
2003, June 25 Litho.
1396-1398 A548 Set of 3 3.50 3.50

Souvenir Sheet

1398A A548 10af multi 2.75 2.75

Dogs — A549

Designs: 10af, Rottweiler. 20af, Cocker spaniel. 30af, Doberman pinscher. 40af, Afghan hound. 50af, Giant schnauzer. 60af, Boxer.
150af, Afghan hound, diff.

2003, July 4 Litho. ***Perf. 13x12¾***
1399-1404 A549 Set of 6 20.00 20.00

Souvenir Sheet

1405 A549 150af multi 14.50 14.50

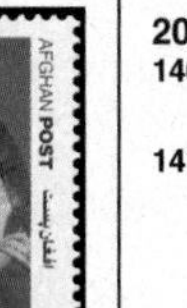

Lighthouses A550

Designs: 10af, Bird Island, South Africa. 20af, Cordouan, France. 30af, Mahota Pagoda, China. 50af, Bay Canh, Viet Nam. 60af, Cap Roman Rock, South Africa. 100af, Mikomoto Shima, Japan.
150af, Bell Rock, Great Britain.

2003, Aug. 5
1406-1411 A550 Set of 6 22.50 22.50

Souvenir Sheet

1412 A550 150af multi 14.50 14.50

Independence, 84th Anniv. — A551

2003, Aug. 19 Litho. ***Perf. 12¾x13***
1413 A551 15af multi 3.50 3.50

Intl. Literacy Day A552

2003, Sept. 8 Litho. ***Perf. 12¾x13***
1414 A552 2af multi 1.00 1.00

Miniature Sheet

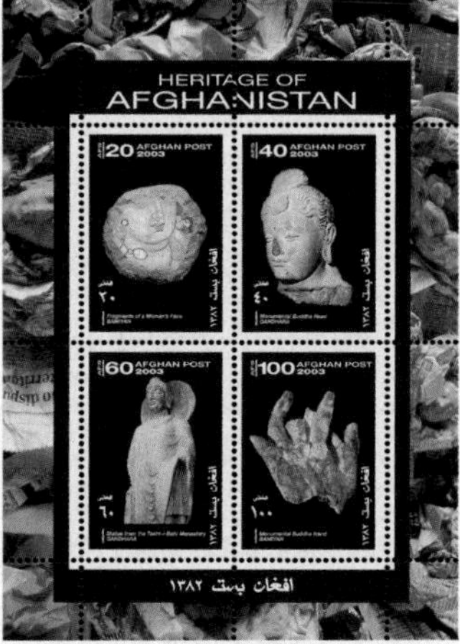

Heritage of Afghanistan — A553

No. 1415: a, 20af, Fragments of rock drawing depicting a woman, Bamiyan. b, 40af, Head of Buddha, Gandhara. c, 60af, Statue from Takht-i-Bahi Monastery, Gandhara. d, 100af, Hand of Buddha, Bamiyan.

2003, Oct. 10 Litho. ***Perf. 13x12¾***
1415 A553 Sheet of 4, #a-d 22.50 22.50

Revelation of the Koran to Mohammed — A554

2003, Nov. 23 Litho. ***Perf. 12¾x13***
1416 A554 9af multi 6.50 6.50

A555

Afghanistan Tourism Day—A555a

Designs: 8af, 25af, Fort. 12af, Bust, jar, historical artifacts.

2003, Dec. 16 Litho. ***Perf. 12¾x13***

1417 A555 4af shown .75 .75
1418 A555a 8af ol grn & multi 1.00 1.00
1418A A555 12afmulti 1.25 1.25
Nos. 1417-1418A (3) 3.00 3.00

Souvenir Sheet

1418B A555a 25aflil & multi 3.00 3.00

Animals A556

Designs: 6af, Leopard. 11af, Jackal. 15af, Wild goat.
40af, Leopard facing left.

2003 Litho. ***Perf. 12¾***

1419-1421 A556 Set of 3 5.00 5.00

Souvenir Sheet

1422 A556 40af multi 8.25 8.25

World Post Day A557

2003, Oct. 9 Litho. ***Perf. 12¾x13***

1423 A557 8af multi 2.50 2.50

Int'l. Women's Day — A558

2004 Litho. ***Perf. 12¾x13***

1424 A558 6af multi 1.50 1.50

World Tuberculosis Day — A559

Designs: 1af, Woman, hands holding medicine and bloody tissue. 4af, Woman wearing mask, child. 9af, Eight men. 12af, Man, map of Afghanistan, vert. 15af, Doctor touching patient, people in white in background, vert.

Perf. 12¾x13, 13x12¾

2004, Mar. 23 Litho.

1425 A559 1af multi .35 .35
1426 A559 4af multi .75 .75
1427 A559 9af multi 1.50 1.50
1428 A559 12af multi 2.00 2.00
1429 A559 15af multi 2.50 2.50
Nos. 1425-1429 (5) 7.10 7.10

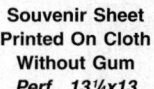

Pres. Hamid Karzai — A560

Karzai and Map of Afghanistan A561

2004, Oct. 7 ***Perf. 13x12¾***

1430 A560 12af multi 3.00 3.00
1431 A561 12af multi 5.00 5.00

Oath of Pres. Karzai.

First Direct Presidential Election — A562

Denominations: 15af, 25af.

2004, Oct. 9 Litho. ***Perf. 12¾x13***

1432-1433 A562 Set of 2 7.00 7.00

Two types of Arabic inscriptions exist on each stamp. Values the same.

Afghanistan postal officials declared a set of eight stamps depicting soccer players and a set of eight stamps depicting FIFA Presidents as "not authorized."

The editors are seeking more information about the status of a set of four Worldwide Fund for Nature stamps depicting the Himalayan musk deer.

Souvenir Sheet

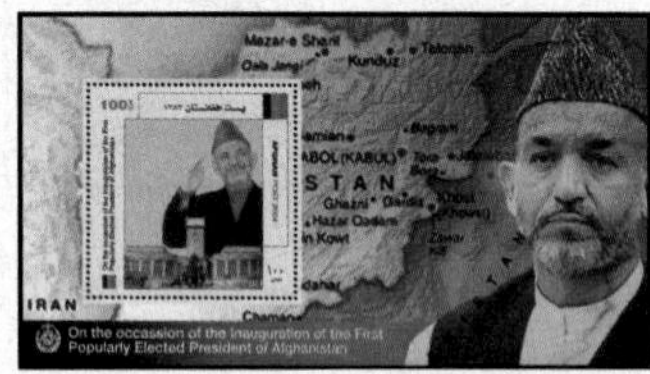

Inauguration of Pres. Karzai — A563

2004, Dec. 7 Litho. ***Perf. 13½***

1434 A563 100af multi 18.00 18.00

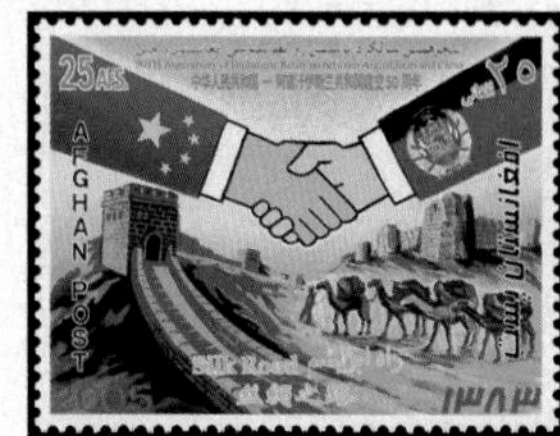

Diplomatic Relations Between Afghanistan and People's Republic of China, 50th Anniv. — A564

2005, Jan. 20 Litho. ***Perf. 12***

1435 A564 25af multi 3.00 3.00

Souvenir Sheet
Printed On Cloth
Without Gum
Perf. 13¼x13

1436 A564 150af multi 24.00 24.00

No. 1436 contains one 60x40mm stamp.

Mine Clearance Campaign A565

Designs: 1af, Mine danger warning sign. 2af, Mine clearer with dog, vert. 3af. Mine clearer with metal detector, vert.

2006, Apr. 4 ***Perf. 13¼x13, 13x13¼***

1437-1439 A565 Set of 3 2.00 2.00

Independence, 87th Anniv. — A566

2006, Aug. 19 ***Perf. 13x13¼***

1440 A566 45af multi 8.00 8.00

World Literacy Day — A567

2006, Sept. 8

1441 A567 12af multi 2.00 2.00

World Post Day A568

Color of "2006": No. 1442, 15af, Light green. No. 1443, 15af, Black.

2006, Sept. 9 ***Perf. 13¼x13***

1442-1443 A568 Set of 2 4.50 4.50

The length of the Arabic inscription on the top of the stamp is longer on No. 1442 than on No. 1443.

World Tourism Day A569

Designs: 15af, Lamp, pitchers, bowl, building. 30af, Pitchers, cup, mountain.

2006, Sept. 27 Litho. ***Perf. 13¼x13***

1444 A569 15af multi 2.50 2.50
1445 A569 30af multi 4.50 4.50

Campaign for Elimination of Violence Against Women — A570

Designs: 12af, Woman behind barbed wire, chain, hands unlocking lock. 14af, Woman, roots. 19af, Eyes of woman, needle and thread closing eye hole of burqa, horiz.

Perf. 13x13¼, 13¼x13

2006, Nov. 25 Litho.

1446-1448 A570 Set of 3 6.75 6.75

Mevlana Jalal ad-Din ar-Rumi (1207-73), Islamic Philosopher A571

Designs: 65af, Birthplace at Balkh. 85af, Mevlana and whirling dervishes, vert.
150af, Mevlana, whirling dervishes, birthplace at Balkh, horiz.

Perf. 13¼x13, 13x13¼

2006, Nov. 26

1449-1450 A571 Set of 2 15.00 15.00

Size: 106x78mm
Imperf

1451 A571 150af multi 30.00 30.00

No. 1451 contains two perforated labels lacking country name or value. See Iran No. 2911, Syria No. 1574, Turkey No. 2971.

Successful Completion of Bonn Process A572

2007, Apr. 19 ***Perf. 13¼x13***

1452 A572 25af multi 4.00 4.00

Dated 2006.

Mevlana Jalal ad-Din ar-Rumi (1207-73), Islamic Philosopher A573

2007, May 24

1453 A573 40af multi 6.00 6.00

Milli Attan Dance A574

2007, Aug. 19

1454 A574 38af multi 6.00 6.00

Natl. Day of Fine Arts — A575

Singers: 20af, Ustad Awal Mir. 22af, Mirmun Parwin.

2007, Sept. 25 ***Perf. 13x13¼***
1455-1456 A575 Set of 2 *7.50 7.50*

Third Meeting of Economic Cooperation Organization Postal Authorities, Tehran — A576

2007, Dec. 22 ***Perf. 13¼x13***
1457 A576 8af multi *2.00 2.00*

National Unity — A577

Emperors: 25af, Ahmad Shah Baba (c. 1723-73). 30af, Mirwais Nika. 34af, Sultan Mahmood Ghaznawi (979-1030).

2007, Dec. 22 ***Perf. 13x13¼***
1458-1460 A577 Set of 3 *12.00 12.00*

Red Crescent Society — A578

2009, Jan. 21 Litho. ***Perf. 13x13¼***
1461 A578 17af multi *2.40 2.40*

Rudaki (c. 859-c.940), Poet — A579

2009, Jan. 21
1462 A579 55af multi *6.50 6.50*

SEMI-POSTAL STAMPS

Catalogue values for unused stamps in this section are for Never Hinged items.

No. 373 Surcharged in Violet

1952, July 12 Unwmk. ***Perf. 12½***
B1 A122 40p + 30p cerise 5.25 3.00
B2 A122 125p + 30p cerise 7.75 3.50

1000th anniv. of the birth of Avicenna.

Children at Play — SP1

1955, July 3 Typo. ***Perf. 11***
B3 SP1 35p + 15p dk green 1.25 .70
B4 SP1 125p + 25p purple 2.50 1.25

The surtax was for child welfare.
Exist imperf. Values, set: unused $6.50; used $7.

Amir Sher Ali Khan, Tiger Head Stamp and Zahir Shah — SP2

1955, July 2 Litho.
B5 SP2 35p + 15p carmine 1.00 .55
B6 SP2 125p + 25p pale vio bl 1.90 1.00

85th anniv. of the Afghan post.
Exist imperf. Values, set: unused $5; used $6.

Children at Play — SP3

1956, June 20 Typo.
B7 SP3 35p + 15p brt vio bl .90 .40
B8 SP3 140p + 15p dk org brn 2.25 .85

Issued for Children's Day. The surtax was for child welfare. No. B8 inscribed in French.
Exist imperf. Values, set: unused $8; used $8.75.

Pashtunistan Monument, Kabul — SP4

1956, Sept. 1 Litho.
B9 SP4 35p + 15p dp violet .40 .25
B10 SP4 140p + 15p dk brown 1.10 .75

"Free Pashtunistan" Day. The surtax aided the "Free Pashtunistan" movement.
No. B9 measures 30½x19½mm; No. B10, 29x19mm. On sale and valid for use only on Sept. 1-2.
Exist imperf. Values, set: unused $6; used $7.50.

Globe and Sun — SP5

1956, Oct. 24 ***Perf. 11***
B11 SP5 35p + 15p ultra 1.25 1.10
B12 SP5 140p + 15p red brown 2.10 1.75

Afghanistan's UN admission, 10th anniv.
Exist imperf. Values, set: unused $14; used $17.50.

Children on Seesaw SP6

1957, June 20 Unwmk.
B13 SP6 35p + 15p brt rose .85 .55
B14 SP6 140p + 15p ultra 1.60 1.40

Children's Day. Surtax for child welfare.
Exist imperf. Values, set: unused $3.25; used $4.

UN Headquarters and Emblems SP7

1957, Oct. 24 ***Perf. 11 Rough***
B15 SP7 35p + 15p red brown .60 .40
B16 SP7 140p + 15p lt ultra 1.10 1.10

United Nations Day.
Exist imperf. Values, set: unused $6; used $7.50.

Swimming Pool and Children SP8

1958, June 22 ***Perf. 11***
B17 SP8 35p + 15p rose .65 .40
B18 SP8 140p + 15p dl red brn .80 .65

Children's Day. Surtax for child welfare.
Exist imperf. Values, set: unused $5; used $6.

Pashtunistan Flag — SP9

1958, Aug. 31
B19 SP9 35p + 15p lt blue .40 .25
B20 SP9 140p + 15p red brown 1.00 .65

Issued for "Free Pashtunistan Day."
Exist imperf. Values, set: unused $4; used $5.

Children Playing Tug of War — SP10

1959, June 23 Litho. ***Perf. 11***
B21 SP10 35p + 15p brown vio .60 .35
B22 SP10 165p + 15p brt pink 1.25 .50

Children's Day. Surtax for child welfare.
Exist imperf. Value set, unused or used, $5.

Pathans in Tribal Dance SP11

Perf. 11 Rough

1959, Sept. Unwmk.
B23 SP11 35p + 15p green .60 .35
B24 SP11 165p + 15p orange 1.25 .75

Issued for "Free Pashtunistan Day."
Exist imperf. Value set, unused or used, $2.50.

Afghan Cavalryman with UN Flag — SP12

1959, Oct. 24 ***Perf. 11 Rough***
B25 SP12 35p + 15p orange .35 .25
B26 SP12 165p + 15p lt bl grn .75 .45

Issued for United Nations Day.
Exist imperf. Value set, unused or used, $2.50.

Children SP13

1960, Oct. 23 Litho.
B27 SP13 75p + 25p lt ultra .90 .35
B28 SP13 175p + 25p lt green 1.75 .50

Children's Day. Surtax for child welfare.
Exist imperf. Value set, unused or used, $2.75.

Man with Spray Gun SP14

1960, Sept. 6 ***Perf. 11 Rough***
B29 SP14 50p + 50p orange 1.40 1.25
B30 SP14 175p + 50p red brown 3.50 2.75

11th anniversary of the WHO malaria control program in Afghanistan.
Exist imperf. Value set, unused or used, $7.50.

SP15

1960, Sept. 1 Unwmk.
B31 SP15 50p + 50p rose .60 .30
B32 SP15 175p + 50p dk blue 1.40 1.10

Issued for "Free Pashtunistan Day."
Exist imperf. Value set, unused or used, $3.25.

Ambulance — SP16

1960, Oct. 16 ***Perf. 11***
Crescent in Red
B33 SP16 50p + 50p violet .65 .50
B34 SP16 175p + 50p blue 1.75 1.00

Issued for the Red Crescent Society.
Exist imperf. Value set, unused or used, $3.25.

Nos. 470-471 Surcharged in Blue or Orange

1960, Dec. 31 Litho. *Perf. 11*

B35 A166 50p + 25p dp org (Bl) 1.75 1.75
B36 A166 165p + 25p blue (O) 1.75 1.75

Exist imperf. Value set, unused or used, $11.

The souvenir sheets described after No. 471 were surcharged in carmine "+25 Ps" on each stamp. Values: normal colors, unused $6, used $6.50; reversed colors, unused $7.50, used $9.50.

See general note after No. 485.

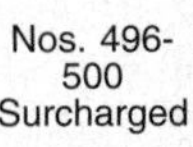
Nos. 496-500 Surcharged

Perf. 13½x14

1961, July 6 Unwmk. Photo.

B37 A175 2p + 25p green & rose lil .50 .50
B38 A175 2p + 25p brown & cit .50 .50
B39 A175 5p + 25p gray & rose .50 .50
B40 A175 10p + 25p blue & bis .50 .50
B41 A175 15p + 25p sl bl & dl lil .50 .50
Nos. B37-B41 (5) 2.50 2.50

UNICEF. The same surcharge was applied to an imperf. souvenir sheet like that noted after No. 505. Value $5.

Nos. 522-526 Surcharged "+25PS" and Crescent in Red

1961, Oct. 16 *Perf. 13½x14*

B42 A184 2p + 25p black .50 .50
B43 A184 2p + 25p green .50 .50
B44 A184 5p + 25p lilac rose .50 .50
B45 A184 10p + 25p lilac .50 .50
B46 A184 15p + 25p dk blue .50 .50
Nos. B42-B46 (5) 2.50 2.50

Issued for the Red Crescent Society.

Nos. 539-543 Surcharged in Red: "UNESCO + 25PS"

1962 *Perf. 12*

B47 A186 2p + 25p multi .40 .40
B48 A186 2p + 25p multi .40 .40
B49 A186 5p + 25p multi .40 .40
B50 A186 10p + 25p multi .40 .40
B51 A186 15p + 25p multi .40 .40
Nos. B47-B51 (5) 2.00 2.00

UNESCO. The same surcharge was applied to the souvenir sheets mentioned after No. 548. Value, 2 sheets, $10.

Nos. 553-561 Surcharged: "Dag Hammarskjöld +20PS"

1962, Sept. 17 *Perf. 14x13½*

B52 A187 2p + 20p .25 .25
B53 A187 2p + 20p .25 .25
B54 A187 5p + 20p .25 .25
B55 A187 10p + 20p .25 .25
B56 A187 15p + 20p .25 .25
B57 A187 25p + 20p .25 .25
B58 A187 50p + 20p .30 .30
B59 A187 75p + 20p .50 .50
B60 A187 100p + 20p .80 .80
Nos. B52-B60 (9) 3.10 3.10

In memory of Dag Hammarskjold, Sec. Gen. of the UN, 1953-61. Perf. and imperf. souvenir sheets exist. Value, 2 sheets, $6.50.

Nos. 583-593 Surcharged "+15PS"

1963, Mar. 15 *Perf. 14x13½*

B61 A193 2p + 15p 1.00 1.00
B62 A193 2p + 15p 1.00 1.00
B63 A193 5p + 15p 1.00 1.00
B64 A193 10p + 15p 1.00 1.00
B65 A193 15p + 15p 1.00 1.00
B66 A193 25p + 15p 1.00 1.00
B67 A193 50p + 15p 1.00 1.00
B68 A193 75p + 15p 1.00 1.00
B69 A193 100p + 15p 1.00 1.00
B70 A193 150p + 15p 1.00 1.00
B71 A193 175p + 15p 1.00 1.00
Nos. B61-B71 (11) 11.00 11.00

WHO drive to eradicate malaria.

Nos. 672-672G, 672I Surcharged in Various Positions

1964, Mar. 9

B71A A213g 2p + 50p .25 .25
B71B A213g 3p + 50p .25 .25
B71C A213g 4p + 50p .25 .25
B71D A213g 5p + 50p .25 .25
B71E A213g 10p + 50p .25 .25
B71F A213g 100p + 50p .70 .70
B71G A213g 2af + 50p 1.50 1.50
B71H A213g 3af + 50p 2.10 2.10
Nos. B71A-B71H (8) 5.55 5.55

Souvenir Sheet

B71J A213g 5af + 50p 4.50 4.50

Nos. B71E-B71G are airmail semi-postals.

Blood Transfusion Kit — SP17

1964, Oct. 18 Litho. *Perf. 10½*

B72 SP17 1af + 50p black & rose .40 .30

Issued for the Red Crescent Society and Red Crescent Week, Oct. 18-24.

First Aid Station SP18

1965, Oct. 16 Photo. *Perf. 13½x14*

B73 SP18 1.50af + 50p multi .35 .25

Issued for the Red Crescent Society.

Children Playing SP19

1966, Nov. 28 Photo. *Perf. 13½x14*

B74 SP19 1af + 1af yel grn & cl .30 .25
B75 SP19 3af + 2af yel & brn .65 .25
B76 SP19 7af + 3af rose lil & grn .95 .50
Nos. B74-B76 (3) 1.90 1.00

Children's Day.

Nadir Shah Presenting Society Charter SP20

1967, Feb. 15 Photo. *Perf. 13x14*

B77 SP20 2af + 1af red & dk grn .35 .25
B78 SP20 5af + 1af lil rose & brn .75 .35

Issued for the Red Crescent Society.

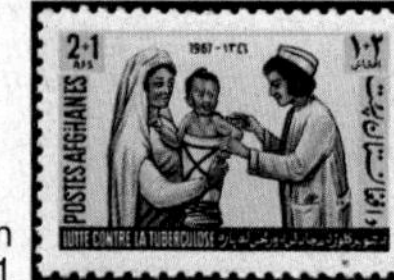

Vaccination SP21

1967, June 6 Photo. *Perf. 12*

B79 SP21 2af + 1af yellow & blk .25 .25
B80 SP21 5af + 2af pink & brn .65 .35

The surtax was for anti-tuberculosis work.

Red Crescent — SP22

1967, Oct. 18 Photo. *Perf. 12*

Crescent in Red

B81 SP22 3af + 1af gray ol & blk .25 .25
B82 SP22 5af + 1af dl bl & blk .40 .25

Issued for the Red Crescent Society.

Queen Humeira — SP23

1968, June 14 Photo. *Perf. 12*

B83 SP23 2af + 2af red brown .35 .25
B84 SP23 7af + 2af dull green .90 .60

Issued for Mother's Day.

Red Crescent — SP24

1968, Oct. 16 Photo. *Perf. 12*

B85 SP24 4af + 1af yel, blk & red .60 .25

Issued for the Red Crescent Society.

Red Cross, Crescent, Lion and Sun Emblems — SP25

1969, May 5 Litho. *Perf. 14x13½*

B86 SP25 3af + 1af multicolored .65 .35
B87 SP25 5af + 1af multicolored .80 .35

League of Red Cross Societies, 50th anniv.

Mother and Child — SP26

1969, June 14 Photo. *Perf. 12*

B88 SP26 1af + 1af yel org & brn .30 .25
B89 SP26 4af + 1af rose lil & pur .50 .35
a. Souvenir sheet of 2 2.50 2.50

Mother's Day. No. B89a contains 2 imperf. stamps similar to Nos. B88-B89. Sold for 10af.

Red Crescent — SP27

1969, Oct. 16 Photo. *Perf. 12*

B90 SP27 6af + 1af multi .80 .30

Issued for the Red Crescent Society.

UN and FAO Emblems, Farmer — SP28

1973, May 24 Photo. *Perf. 13½*

B91 SP28 14af + 7af grnsh bl & lil 1.40 .90

World Food Program, 10th anniversary.

Dome of the Rock, Jerusalem SP29

1977, Sept. 11 Photo. *Perf. 14*

B92 SP29 12af + 3af multi 2.10 .60

Surtax for Palestinian families and soldiers.

15 Cent. (lunar) of Islamic Pilgrimage (Hegira) — SP30

1981, Jan. 17 Litho. *Perf. 12½x12*

B93 SP30 13af + 2af multi 1.75 .30

Red Crescent Aid Programs SP31

1981, May 8 *Perf. 12x12½*

B94 SP31 1af + 4af multi .65 .80

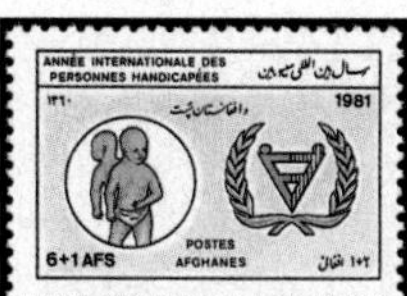
Intl. Year of the Disabled SP32

1981, Oct. 12 *Perf. 12x12½*
B95 SP32 6af + 1af multi .90 .50

AIR POST STAMPS

Plane over Kabul AP1

Perf. 12, 12x11, 11

1939, Oct. 1 Typo. Unwmk.
C1 AP1 5af orange 6.00 4.50
a. Imperf., pair ('47) 29.00 29.00
b. Horiz. pair, imperf. vert. 32.50 32.50
C2 AP1 10af blue 6.50 4.50
a. 10af lt bl 8.00 6.00
b. Imperf., pair ('47) 29.00
c. Horiz. pair, imperf. vert. 32.50
C3 AP1 20af emerald 12.00 7.50
a. Imperf., pair ('47) 29.00
b. Horiz. pair, imperf. vert. 32.50
c. Vert. pair, imperf. horiz. 35.00
Nos. C1-C3 (3) 24.50 16.50

These stamps come with clean-cut or rough perforations. Counterfeits exist.

Catalogue values for unused stamps in this section, from this point to the end of the section, are for Never Hinged items.

1948, June 14 *Perf. 12x11½*
C4 AP1 5af emerald 24.00 24.00
C5 AP1 10af red orange 24.00 24.00
C6 AP1 20af blue 24.00 24.00
Nos. C4-C6 (3) 72.00 72.00

Imperforates exist.

Plane over Palace Grounds, Kabul AP2

Imprint: "Waterlow & Sons, Limited, London"

1951-54 Engr. *Perf. 13½*
C7 AP2 5af henna brn 3.50 .70
C8 AP2 5af dp grn ('54) 2.00 .45
C9 AP2 10af gray 9.75 2.50
C10 AP2 20af dark blue 11.50 3.25

1957
C11 AP2 5af ultra 2.10 .60
C12 AP2 10af dark vio 3.25 1.10
Nos. C7-C12 (6) 32.10 8.60

See No. C38.

Ariana Plane over Hindu Kush AP3

Perf. 11, Imperf.

1960-63 Litho. Unwmk.
C13 AP3 75p light vio .65 .25
C14 AP3 125p blue .80 .40

Perf. 10½, 11

C14A AP3 5af citron ('63) 1.50 1.00
Nos. C13-C14A (3) 2.95 1.65

Imperf examples of Nos. C13-C14 are valued at approx. 50 percent more than the values shown.

Girl Scout — AP4

1962, Aug. 30 Photo. *Perf. 11½x12*
C15 AP4 100p ocher & brn .60 .60
C16 AP4 175p brt yel grn & brn 1.00 1.00

Women's Day. See Nos. 578-579 and note on souvenir sheet.

Sports Type of Regular Issue, 1962

25p, 50p, Horse racing. 75p, 100p, Wrestling. 150p, Weight lifting. 175p, Soccer.

1962, Sept. 25 Unwmk. *Perf. 12*
Black Inscriptions
C17 A195 25p rose & red brn .25 .25
C18 A195 50p gray & red brn .30 .30
C19 A195 75p pale vio & dk grn .55 .55
C20 A195 100p gray ol & dk pur .70 .70
C21 A195 150p rose lil & grn 1.00 1.00
C22 A195 175p sal & brn 1.25 1.25
Nos. C17-C22 (6) 4.00 4.00

Children's Day Type of Regular Issue

Perf. 11½x12, 12x11½

1962, Oct. 14 Unwmk.
C23 A196 75p Runners .65 .65
C24 A196 150p Peaches 1.25 1.25
C25 A196 200p Iris, vert. 1.75 1.75
Nos. C23-C25 (3) 3.65 3.65

A souvenir sheet contains one each of Nos. C23-C25. Value $4.00.

Red Crescent Type of Regular Issue

1962, Oct. 16 *Perf. 12*
Fruit and Flowers in Natural Colors; Carmine Crescent
C26 A197 25p Grapes .25 .25
C27 A197 50p Pears .30 .30
C28 A197 100p Wistaria .70 .70
Nos. C26-C28 (3) 1.20 1.20

Two souvenir sheets exist. One contains a 150p gray brown stamp in blossom design, the other a 200p gray stamp in wistaria design, imperf. Value, each $5.00.

UN Type of Regular Issue

1962, Oct. 24 Photo.
Flags in Original Colors, Black Inscriptions
C29 A198 75p blue .30 .30
C30 A198 100p lt brn .50 .50
C31 A198 125p brt grn .65 .65
Nos. C29-C31 (3) 1.45 1.45

Boy Scout Type of Regular Issue

1962, Oct. 25 Unwmk. *Perf. 12*
C32 A199 25p gray, blk, dl grn & sal .30 .30
C33 A199 50p grn, brn & sal .60 .60
C34 A199 75p bl grn, red brn & sal .90 .90
C35 A199 100p bl, slate & sal 1.10 1.10
Nos. C32-C35 (4) 2.90 2.90

Teacher's Day Type of Regular Issue

1962, Oct. 25
C36 A200 100p Pole vault .65 .65
C37 A200 150p High jump .95 .95

A souvenir sheet contains one 250p pink and slate green stamp in design of 150p. Values: perf $3; imperf $24.

Type of 1951-54
Imprint: "Thomas De La Rue & Co. Ltd."

1962 Engr. *Perf. 13½*
C38 AP2 5af ultra 13.50 1.00

Agriculture Types of Regular Issue
Unwmk.

1963, Mar. 1 Photo. *Perf. 12*
C42 A204 100p dk car, grn & brn .40 .40
C43 A203 150p ocher & blk .65 .65
C44 A204 200p ultra, grn & brn .95 .95
Nos. C42-C44 (3) 2.00 2.00

Hands Holding Wheat Emblem AP5

1963, Mar. 27 Photo. *Perf. 14*
C45 AP5 500p lil, lt brn & brn 1.40 1.40

FAO "Freedom from Hunger" campaign.
Two souvenir sheets exist. One contains a 1000p blue green, light brown and brown, type AP5, imperf. The other contains a 200p brown and green and 300p ultramarine, yellow and ocher in rice and corn designs, type A205. Values $6.50 and $4.50.

Meteorological Day Type of Regular Issue

Designs: 100p, 500p, Meteorological measuring instrument. 200p, 400p, Weather station. 300p, Rockets in space.

1963, May 23 *Imperf.*
C46 A206 100p brn & bl 3.25 3.25

Perf. 13½x14

C47 A206 200p brt grn & lil 1.00 1.00
C48 A206 300p dk bl & rose 1.50 1.50
C49 A206 400p bl & dl red brn 2.10 2.10
C50 A206 500p car rose & gray grn 2.75 2.75
Nos. C47-C50 (4) 7.35 7.35

Nos. C47 and C50 printed se-tenant.
Nos. C47 and C50 exist imperf. Values, unused or used: 200p, $6.75; 500p, $17.50.
Two souvenir sheets exist. One contains a 125p red and brown stamp in rocket design. The other contains a 100p blue and dull red brown in "rockets in space" design. Values $5 and $13.

Kabul International Airport — AP8

Perf. 12x11½

1964, Apr. Unwmk. Photo.
C57 AP8 10af red lil & grn .80 .25
C58 AP8 20af dk grn & red lil 1.00 .40
a. Perf. 12 ('68) 5.00 3.00
C59 AP8 50af dk bl & grnsh bl 2.75 1.25
a. Perf. 12 ('68) 8.00 5.00
Nos. C57-C59 (3) 4.55 1.90

Inauguration of Kabul Airport Terminal.
Nos. C58a-C59a are 36mm wide. Nos. C58-C59 are 35½mm wide.

Zahir Shah and Kabul Airport — AP9

100af, Zahir Shah and Ariana Plane.

1971 Photo. *Perf. 12½x13½*
C60 AP9 50af multi 4.50 4.50
C61 AP9 100af blk, red & grn 5.75 3.50

Remainders of No. C60 were used, summer in 1978, with king's portrait torn or cut off.

REGISTRATION STAMPS

R1

Dated "1309"
Pelure Paper

1891 Unwmk. Litho. *Imperf.*
F1 R1 1r slate blue 2.40
a. Tete beche pair 13.50

Genuinely used examples of No. F1 are rare. Counterfeit cancellations exist.

R2

Dated "1311"

1893 Thin Wove Paper
F2 R2 1r black, *green* 2.00

Genuinely used examples of No. F2 are rare. Counterfeit cancellations exist.

R3

1894 Undated
F3 R3 2ab black, *green* 9.50 *11.00*

12 varieties. See note below Nos. 189-190.

R4

1898-1900 Undated
F4 R4 2ab black, *deep rose* 4.50 4.50
F5 R4 2ab black, *lilac rose* 6.50 5.00
F6 R4 2ab black, *magenta* 8.00 5.00
F7 R4 2ab black, *salmon* 4.50 3.50
F8 R4 2ab black, *orange* 4.50 4.50
F9 R4 2ab black, *yellow* 4.50 3.50
F10 R4 2ab black, *green* 4.50 3.50
Nos. F4-F10 (7) 37.00 30.50

Many shades of paper.
Nos. F4-F10 come in two sizes, measured between outer frame lines: 52x36mm, 1st printing; 46x33mm, 2nd printing. The outer frame line (not pictured) is 3-6mm from inner frame line.
Used on P.O. receipts.

OFFICIAL STAMPS

(Used only on interior mail.)

Coat of Arms O1

1909 Unwmk. Typo. *Perf. 12*
Wove Paper
O1 O1 red 1.25 1.25
a. Carmine ('19?) 2.50 6.50

Later printings of No. O1 in scarlet, vermilion, claret, etc., on various types of paper, were issued until 1927.

Coat of Arms — O2

1939-68? **Typo.** ***Perf. 11, 12***

O3 O2 15p emerald 1.10 .80
O4 O2 30p ocher ('40) 1.50 1.50
O5 O2 45p dark carmine 1.25 1.25
O6 O2 50p brt car ('68) .70 .70
a. 50p carmine rose ('55) 1.25 .70
O7 O2 1af brt red violet 2.00 1.75
Nos. O3-O7 (5) 6.55 6.00

Size of 50p, 24x31mm, others 22½x28mm.

Catalogue values for unused stamps in this section, from this point to the end of the section, are for Never Hinged items.

1964-65 **Litho.** ***Perf. 11***

O8 O2 50p rose .90 .90
a. 50p salmon ('65) 2.00 2.00

Stamps of this type are revenues.

PARCEL POST STAMPS

Coat of Arms — PP1

PP2

PP3

PP4

1909 **Unwmk.** **Typo.** ***Perf. 12***

Q1 PP1 3sh bister 1.25 *2.25*
a. Imperf., pair —
Q2 PP2 1kr olive gray 3.50 *3.50*
a. Imperf., pair —
Q3 PP3 1r orange 3.25 3.25
Q4 PP3 1r olive green 24.00 4.50
Q5 PP4 2r red 4.00 4.00
Nos. Q1-Q5 (5) 36.00 17.50

1916-18

Q6 PP1 3sh green 1.75 *3.50*
Q7 PP2 1kr pale red 3.00 1.50
a. 1kr rose red ('18) 4.00 4.00
Q8 PP3 1r brown org 3.50 1.75
a. 1r deep brown ('18) 12.00 3.00
Q9 PP4 2r blue 6.25 *6.50*
Nos. Q6-Q9 (4) 14.50 *13.25*

Nos. Q1-Q9 sometimes show letters of the papermaker's watermark "HOWARD & JONES LONDON."

Ungummed stamps are remainders. They sell for one-third the price of mint stamps.

Old Habibia College, Near Kabul — PP5

1921 **Wove Paper**

Q10 PP5 10pa chocolate 5.00 5.75
a. Tete beche pair 22.50 22.50
Q11 PP5 15pa light brn 7.00 7.50
a. Tete beche pair 27.50 27.50
Q12 PP5 30pa red violet 12.50 7.50
a. Tete beche pair 40.00 40.00
b. Laid paper *15.00* *15.00*
Q13 PP5 1r brt blue 14.00 14.00
a. Tete beche pair 65.00 65.00
Nos. Q10-Q13 (4) 38.50 34.75

Stamps of this issue are usually perforated on one or two sides only.

The laid paper of No. Q12b has a papermaker's watermark in the sheet.

Handstamped in black on Nos. Q10-Q13

PP5a

1923, Feb. 26

Q13B PP5a 10pa chocolate — —
Q13C PP5a 15pa light brn — —
Q13D PP5a 30pa red violet — —
Q13E PP5a 1r brt blue — —

5th Independence Day.
Two types of handstamp exist.
Forgeries exist.

PP6

1924-26 **Wove Paper**

Q15 PP6 5kr ultra ('26) 50.00 50.00
Q16 PP6 5r lilac 20.00 25.00

A 15r rose exists, but is not known to have been placed in use. Value, unused $350.

PP7

PP8

1928-29 ***Perf. 11, 11xImperf.***

Q17 PP7 2r yellow orange 8.00 7.00
Q18 PP7 2r green ('29) 7.50 7.50
Q19 PP8 3r deep green 10.50 10.50
Q20 PP8 3r brown ('29) 9.50 10.50
Nos. Q17-Q20 (4) 35.50 35.50

POSTAL TAX STAMPS

Aliabad Hospital near Kabul PT1

Pierre and Marie Curie PT2

Perf. 12x11½, 12

1938, Dec. 22 **Typo.** **Unwmk.**

RA1 PT1 10p peacock grn 3.25 *5.00*
RA2 PT2 15p dull blue 3.25 *5.00*

Obligatory on all mail Dec. 22-28, 1938. The money was used for the Aliabad Hospital. See note with CD80.

Catalogue values for unused stamps in this section, from this point to the end of the section, are for Never Hinged items.

PT3

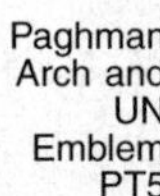

Begging Child — PT4

1949, May 28 **Typo.** ***Perf. 12***

RA3 PT3 35p red orange 3.25 2.10
RA4 PT4 125p ultra 4.00 2.10

United Nations Children's Day, May 28. Obligatory on all foreign mail on that date. Proceeds were used for child welfare.

Paghman Arch and UN Emblem PT5

1949, Oct. 24

RA5 PT5 125p dk blue green 15.00 9.00

4th anniv. of the UN. Valid one day only. Issued in sheets of 9 (3x3).

Zahir Shah and Map of Afghanistan — PT6

1950, Mar. 30 **Typo.**

RA6 PT6 125p blue green 4.50 1.50

Return of Zahir Shah from a trip to Europe for his health. Valid for two weeks. The tax was used for public health purposes.

Hazara Youth — PT7

1950, May 28 **Typo.** ***Perf. 11½***

RA7 PT7 125p dk blue green 4.50 2.50

Tax for Child Welfare. Obligatory and valid only on May 28, 1950, on foreign mail.

Ruins of Qalai Bist and Globe — PT8

1950, Oct. 24

RA8 PT8 1.25af ultramarine 9.00 5.25

5th anniv. of the UN. Proceeds went to Afghanistan's UN Projects Committee.

Zahir Shah and Medical Center PT9

1950, Dec. 22 Typo. *Perf. 11½*

Size: 38x25mm

RA9 PT9 35p carmine 1.25 .60

Size: 46x30mm

RA10 PT9 1.25af black 7.50 2.50

The tax was for the national Graduate School of Medicine.

Koochi Girl with Lamb PT10

Kohistani Boy and Sheep — PT11

1951, May 28

RA11 PT10 35p emerald 1.50 .90
RA12 PT11 1.25af ultramarine 1.50 .90

The tax was for Child Welfare.

Distributing Gifts to Children — PT12

Qandahari Boys Dancing the "Attan" PT13

1952, May 28 Litho.

RA13 PT12 35p chocolate .80 .65
RA14 PT13 125p violet 1.60 .95

The tax was for Child Welfare.
Exist imperf. Values, set: unused $6; used $9.50.

Soldier Receiving First Aid — PT14

1952, Oct. 19

RA15 PT14 10p light green .80 .65

Exist imperf. Value: unused $2.50; used $4.

Stretcher-bearers and Wounded — PT15

Soldier Assisting Wounded — PT16

1953, Oct.

RA16 PT15 10p yel grn & org red .80 .80
RA17 PT16 10p vio brn & org red .80 .80

Exist imperf. Values, set: unused $4; used $5.

Prince Mohammed Nadir — PT17

1953, May 28

RA18 PT17 35p orange yellow .50 .25
RA19 PT17 125p chalky blue .90 .55

No. RA19 is inscribed in French "Children's Day." The tax was for child welfare.
Exist imperf. Values, set: unused $4; used $5.

Map and Young Musicians PT18

1954, May 28 Unwmk. *Perf. 11*

RA20 PT18 35p purple .65 .40
RA21 PT18 125p ultra 1.90 1.25

No. RA21 is inscribed in French. The tax was for child welfare.
Exist imperf. Values, set: unused $4.50; used $6.50.

PT19

1954, Oct. 17 *Perf. 11½*

RA22 PT19 20p blue & red .75 .35

Exists imperf. Values: unused $2; used $2.50.

Red Crescent PT20

1955, Oct. 18 *Perf. 11*

RA23 PT20 20p dull grn & car .70 .35

Exists imperf. Values: unused $1.50; used $2.

Zahir Shah and Red Crescent PT21

1956, Oct. 18

RA24 PT21 20p lt grn & rose car .40 .25

Exists imperf. Value, unused or used, $1.25.

Red Crescent Headquarters, Kabul — PT22

1957, Oct. 17

RA25 PT22 20p lt ultra & car .90 .60

Exists imperf. Values: unused $2; used $2.50.

Map and Crescent PT23

1958, Oct. Unwmk. *Perf. 11*

RA26 PT23 25p yel grn & red .40 .30

Exists imperf. Values: unused 50¢; used 80¢.

PT24

1959, Oct. 17 Litho. *Perf. 11*

RA27 PT24 25p lt violet & red .40 .25

The tax on Nos. RA15-RA17, RA22-RA27 was for the Red Crescent Society. Use of these stamps was required for one week.
Exists imperf. Values: unused 50¢; used 80¢.

AGÜERA, LA

ä-gwā'rä

LOCATION — An administrative district in southern Rio de Oro on the northwest coast of Africa.
GOVT. — Spanish possession
AREA — Because of indefinite political boundaries, figures for area and population are not available.

100 Centimos = 1 Peseta

Type of 1920 Issue of Rio de Oro Overprinted

1920, June Typo. Unwmk. *Perf. 13*

1	A8	1c blue green	2.60	2.60
2	A8	2c olive brown	2.60	2.60
3	A8	5c deep green	2.60	2.60
4	A8	10c light red	2.60	2.60
5	A8	15c yellow	2.60	2.60
6	A8	20c lilac	2.60	2.60
7	A8	25c deep blue	2.60	2.60
8	A8	30c dark brown	2.60	2.60
9	A8	40c pink	2.60	2.60
10	A8	50c bright blue	8.50	8.50
11	A8	1p red brown	15.50	15.50
12	A8	4p dark violet	50.00	50.00
13	A8	10p orange	95.00	95.00
		Nos. 1-13 (13)	192.40	192.40
		Set, never hinged	400.00	

Very fine examples of Nos. 1-13 will be somewhat off center. Well-centered examples are uncommon and will sell for more.

King Alfonso XIII — A2

1922, June

14	A2	1c turquoise bl (I)	1.25	1.10
15	A2	2c dark green	1.40	1.10
16	A2	5c blue green	1.40	1.10
17	A2	10c red	1.40	1.10
18	A2	15c red brown	1.40	1.10
19	A2	20c yellow	1.40	1.10
20	A2	25c deep blue	1.40	1.10
21	A2	30c dark brown	1.40	1.10
22	A2	40c rose red	1.60	1.40
23	A2	50c red violet	5.50	4.50
24	A2	1p rose	11.00	9.25
25	A2	4p violet	30.00	24.00
26	A2	10p orange	45.00	37.50
		Nos. 14-26 (13)	104.15	85.45
		Set, never hinged	200.00	

For later issues, see Spanish Sahara.

AITUTAKI

ˌit-ə-'täk-ē

LOCATION — One of the larger Cook Islands, in the South Pacific Ocean northeast of New Zealand
GOVT. — A dependency of New Zealand
AREA — 7 sq. mi.
POP. — 2,335 (1981)

The Cook Islands were attached to New Zealand in 1901. Stamps of Cook Islands were used in 1892-1903 and 1932-72.

Aitutaki acquired its own postal service in August 1972, though remaining part of Cook Islands.

12 Pence = 1 Shilling
100 Cents = 1 Dollar (1972)

Catalogue values for unused stamps in this country are for Never Hinged items, beginning with Scott 37.

Watermark

Wmk. 61- Single-lined NZ and Star Close Together

Stamps of New Zealand Surcharged in Red or Blue

a

b

c

d

e

f

1903 Engr. Wmk. 61 *Perf. 14*

1	A18(a)	½p green (R)	5.00	*7.25*
2	A35(b)	1p rose (Bl)	5.25	*6.25*

Perf. 11

3	A22(c)	2½p blue (R)	17.00	13.00
4	A23(d)	3p yellow brn (Bl)	20.00	*16.50*
5	A26(e)	6p red (Bl)	32.50	27.50
6	A29(f)	1sh scarlet (Bl)	60.00	*95.00*
a.		1sh orange red (Bl)	77.50	*105.00*

1911, Sept. Typo. *Perf. 14x15*

7	A41(a)	½p yellow grn (R)	1.10	*6.50*

Engr.
Perf. 14

9	A22(c)	2½p deep blue (R)	8.75	*20.00*

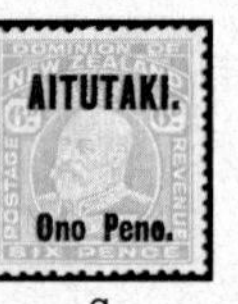

g

h

1913-16 Typo.

10	A42(b)	1p rose (Bl)	3.25	*14.00*

Engr.

12	A41(g)	6p car rose (Bl) ('16)	50.00	*140.00*
13	A41(h)	1sh ver (Bl) ('14)	60.00	*160.00*

1916-17 *Perf. 14x13½, 14x14½*

17	A45(g)	6p car rose (Bl)	9.00	*29.00*
18	A45(h)	1sh ver (Bl) ('17)	14.00	*100.00*
		Nos. 1-18 (13)	285.85	*635.00*

New Zealand Stamps of 1909-19 Overprinted in Red or Dark Blue

1917-20 Typo. *Perf. 14x15*

19	A43	½p yellow grn ('20)	1.10	*6.50*
20	A42	1p car (Bl) ('20)	4.75	*32.50*
21	A47	1½p gray black	4.25	*32.50*
22	A47	1½p brown org ('19)	.90	*7.75*
23	A43	3p choc (Bl) ('19)	3.75	*19.00*

Perf. 14x13½, 14x14½
Engr.

24	A44	2½p dull blue ('18)	1.90	*17.50*
25	A45	3p vio brn (Bl) ('18)	1.75	*29.00*
26	A45	6p car rose (Bl)	5.25	*22.50*
27	A45	1sh vermilion (Bl)	13.00	*35.00*
		Nos. 19-27 (9)	36.65	202.25

Landing of Capt. Cook A15

Avarua Waterfront A16

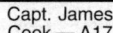

Capt. James Cook — A17

Palm — A18

Houses at Arorangi — A19

Avarua Harbor — A20

1920 Engr. Unwmk. *Perf. 14*

28	A15	½p green & black	4.00	27.50
29	A16	1p carmine & black	4.00	19.00
30	A17	1½p brown & blk	6.50	*13.00*
31	A18	3p dp blue & blk	2.75	*15.00*
32	A19	6p slate & red brn	6.25	15.00
33	A20	1sh claret & blk	10.50	*22.50*
		Nos. 28-33 (6)	34.00	*112.00*

Inverted centers, double frames, etc. are from printers waste.

Rarotongan Chief (Te Po) — A21

1924-27 Wmk. 61 *Perf. 14*

34	A15	½p green & blk ('27)	2.25	*20.00*
35	A16	1p carmine & blk	6.50	*8.25*
36	A21	2½p blue & blk ('27)	8.25	*77.50*
		Nos. 34-36 (3)	17.00	*105.75*

Catalogue values for unused stamps in this section, from this point to the end of the section, are for Never Hinged items.

Cook Islands Nos. 199-200, 202, 205-206, 210, 212-213, 215-217 Ovptd.

1972 Photo. Unwmk. *Perf. 14x13½*

37	A34	½c gold & multi	.55	*1.00*
38	A34	1c gold & multi	1.25	*1.75*
39	A34	2½c gold & multi	3.00	*9.00*
40	A34	4c gold & multi	1.25	*1.25*
41	A34	5c gold & multi	3.50	*10.00*
42	A34	10c gold & multi	3.50	*7.00*
43	A34	20c gold & multi	4.00	*1.50*
44	A34	25c gold & multi	1.25	*1.50*
45	A34	50c gold & multi	3.00	*4.00*
46	A35	$1 gold & multi	5.50	*7.00*
47	A35	$2 gold & multi	.90	*1.10*
		Nos. 37-47 (11)	27.70	*45.10*

Overprint horizontal on Nos. 46-47. On $2, overprint is in capitals of different font; size: 21x3mm.

Issued: Nos. 37-46, Aug. 9; No. 47, Nov. 24.

Same Overprint Horizontal in Silver On Cook Islands Nos. 330-332

1972, Oct. 27 *Perf. 13½*

48	A53	1c gold & multi	.25	.25
49	A53	5c gold & multi	.25	.25
50	A53	10c gold & multi	.40	.40
		Nos. 48-50 (3)	.90	.90

Fluorescence

Starting in 1972, stamps carry a "fluorescent security underprinting" in a multiple pattern of New Zealand's coat of arms with "Aitutaki" above, "Cook Islands" below and two stars at each side.

Silver Wedding Type of Cook Islands

1972, Nov. 20 Photo. *Perf. 13½*

Size: 29x40mm

51	A54	5c silver & multi	3.50	3.00

Size: 66x40mm

52	A54	15c silver & multi	1.50	1.25

25th anniversary of the marriage of Queen Elizabeth II and Prince Philip. Nos. 51-52 printed in sheets of 5 stamps and one label.

Flower Issue of Cook Islands Overprinted

1972, Dec. 11 Photo. *Perf. 14x13½*

53	A34	½c on #199	.25	.25
54	A34	1c on #200	.25	.25
55	A34	2½c on #202	.30	.25
56	A34	4c on #205	.35	.25
57	A34	5c on #206	.35	.25
58	A34	10c on #210	.45	.35
59	A34	20c on #212	1.40	.55
60	A34	25c on #213	.65	*.75*
61	A34	50c on #215	1.00	*1.00*
62	A35	$1 on #216	1.40	*2.00*
		Nos. 53-62 (10)	6.40	*5.90*

See Nos. 73-76.

The Passion of Christ, by Mathias Grunewald — A22

Paintings: No. 63b, St. Veronica, by Rogier van der Weyden. No. 63c, Crucifixion, by Raphael. No. 63d, Resurrection, by della Francesca. No. 64a, Last Supper, by Master of Amiens. No. 64b, Condemnation of Christ, by Hans Holbein, the Elder. No. 64c, Crucifixion, by Rubens. No. 64d, Resurrection, by El Greco. No. 65a, Passion of Christ, by El Greco. No. 65b, St. Veronica, by Jakob Cornelisz. No. 65c, Crucifixion, by Rubens. No. 65d, Resurrection, by Dierik Bouts.

Perf. 13½

1973, Apr. 6 Photo. Unwmk.

No.	Description	Unused	Used
63	Block of 4	1.00	.35
a.-d.	A22 1c any single	.25	.25
64	Block of 4	1.25	1.00
a.-d.	A22 5c any single	.30	.25
65	Block of 4	2.50	2.00
a.-d.	A22 10c any single	.60	.40
	Nos. 63-65 (3)	4.75	3.35

Easter. Printed in blocks of 4 in sheets of 40. Design descriptions in top and bottom margins.

Coin Type of Cook Islands

Queen Elizabeth II Coins: 1c, Taro leaf. 2c, Pineapples. 5c, Hibiscus. 10c, Oranges. 20c, Fairy terns. 50c, Bonito. $1, Tangaroa, Polynesian god of creation, vert.

1973, May 14 *Perf. 13x13½*

Size: 37x24mm

No.	Description	Unused	Used
66	A55 1c dp car & multi	.25	.25
67	A55 2c blue & multi	.25	.25
68	A55 5c green & multi	.25	.25
	Size: 46x30mm		
69	A55 10c vio blue & multi	.25	.25
70	A55 20c green & multi	.30	.30
71	A55 50c dp car & multi	.75	.50
	Size: 32x54½mm		
72	A55 $1 blue, blk & sil	1.00	.60
	Nos. 66-72 (7)	3.05	2.40

Cook Islands coinage commemorating silver wedding anniv. of Queen Elizabeth II.

Printed in sheets of 20 stamps and label showing Westminster Abbey.

Cook Islands Nos. 208, 210, 212 and 215 Overprinted Like Nos. 53-62 and: "TENTH ANNIVERSARY/ CESSATION/ OF/ NUCLEAR TESTING/ TREATY"

1973, July Photo. *Perf. 14x13½*

No.	Description	Unused	Used
73	A34 8c gold & multi	.25	.25
74	A34 10c gold & multi	.25	.25
75	A34 20c gold & multi	.45	.45
76	A34 50c gold & multi	1.00	1.00
	Nos. 73-76 (4)	1.95	1.95

Nuclear Test Ban Treaty, 10th anniv., protest against French nuclear testing on Mururoa Atoll.

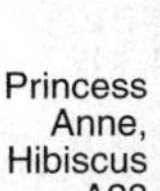

Princess Anne, Hibiscus A23

Design: 30c, Mark Phillips and hibiscus.

1973, Nov. 14 Photo. *Perf. 13½x14*

No.	Description	Unused	Used
77	A23 25c gold & multi	.25	.25
78	A23 30c gold & multi	.35	.35
a.	Souvenir sheet of 2, #77-78	.70	.70

Wedding of Princess Anne and Capt. Mark Phillips.

Virgin and Child, by Il Perugino — A24

Paintings of the Virgin and Child by various masters — No. 79: a, Van Dyck. b, Bartolommeo Montagna. c, Carlo Crivelli. d, Il Perugino. No. 80: a, Cima da Conegliano. b, Memling. c, Veronese. d, Veronese. No. 81: a, Raphael. b, Lorenzo Lotto. c, Del Colle. d, Memling.

1973, Dec. Photo. *Perf. 13*

No.	Description	Unused	Used
79	A24 1c Block of 4, #a.-d.	.50	.50
80	A24 5c Block of 4, #a.-d.	1.00	1.00
81	A24 10c Block of 4, #a.-d.	2.00	2.00
	Nos. 79-81 (3)	3.50	3.50

Christmas. Printed in blocks of 4 in sheets of 48. Design descriptions in margins.

Murex Ramosus A25

Terebra Maculata — A26

Pacific Shells: 1c, Nautilus macromphalus. 2c, Harpa major. 3c, Phalium strigatum. 4c, Cypraea talpa. 5c, Mitra stictica. 8c, Charonia tritonis. 10c, Murex triremis. 20c, Oliva sericea. 25c, Tritonalia rubeta. 60c, Strombus latissimus. $1, Biplex perca. $5, Cypraea hesitata.

1974-75 Photo. *Perf. 13*

No.	Description	Unused	Used
82	A25 ½c silver & multi	1.00	.90
83	A25 1c silver & multi	1.00	.90
84	A25 2c silver & multi	1.00	.90
85	A25 3c silver & multi	1.00	.90
86	A25 4c silver & multi	1.00	.90
87	A25 5c silver & multi	1.00	.90
88	A25 8c silver & multi	1.00	.90
89	A25 10c silver & multi	1.00	.85
90	A25 20c silver & multi	1.50	.85
91	A25 25c silver & multi	1.50	.85
92	A25 60c silver & multi	4.00	1.25
93	A25 $1 silver & multi	3.00	1.50
	Perf. 14		
94	A26 $2 silver & multi	6.00	6.00
95	A26 $5 silver & multi	30.00	13.50
	Nos. 82-95 (14)	54.00	31.10

Issued: Nos. 82-93, 1/31/74; $2, 1/20/75; $5, 2/28/75.

For overprints see Nos. O1-O16.

William Bligh and "Bounty" A27

No. 96, shown. No. 97, "Bounty" at sea. No. 98, Bligh and "Bounty" off Aitutaki. No. 99, Chart of Aitutaki, 1856. No. 100, James Cook and "Resolution". No. 101, Maps of Aitutaki and Pacific Ocean.

Size: 38x22mm

1974, Apr. 11 Photo. *Perf. 13*

No.	Description	Unused	Used
96	A27 1c multicolored	.55	.55
97	A27 1c multicolored	.55	.55
a.	Pair, #96-97	1.10	1.10
98	A27 5c multicolored	1.10	1.10
99	A27 5c multicolored	1.10	1.10
a.	Pair, #98-99	2.20	2.20
100	A27 8c multicolored	1.50	1.50
101	A27 8c multicolored	1.50	1.50
a.	Pair, #100-101	3.00	3.00
	Nos. 96-101,C1-C6 (12)	12.60	12.30

Capt. William Bligh (1754-1817), European discoverer of Aitutaki, Apr. 11, 1789.

Aitutaki Nos. 1 & 2 Map and UPU Emblem A28

Design: 50c, Aitutaki Nos. 4 and 28, map of Aitutaki and UPU emblem.

1974, July 15 Photo. *Perf. 13½*

No.	Description	Unused	Used
102	A28 25c blue & multi	.75	.75
103	A28 50c blue & multi	1.25	1.25
a.	Souvenir sheet of 2, #102-103	2.50	2.50

UPU, cent. Printed in sheets of 5 plus label showing UPU emblem.

A29

Designs: Paintings of the Virgin and Child by: 1c, Van der Goes. 5c, Giovanni Bellini. 8c, Gerard David. 10c, Antonello da Messina. 25c, Joos van Cleve. 30c, Maitre de St. Catherine.

1974, Oct. 11 Photo. *Perf. 13½*

No.	Description	Unused	Used
104	A29 1c multicolored	.35	.25
105	A29 5c multicolored	.35	.25
106	A29 8c multicolored	.35	.25
107	A29 10c multicolored	.35	.25
108	A29 25c multicolored	.65	.50
109	A29 30c multicolored	.85	.65
a.	Souvenir sheet of 6, #104-109	2.25	2.25
	Nos. 104-109 (6)	2.90	2.15

Christmas. Nos. 104-109 printed in sheets of 15 stamps and corner label. See Nos. B1-B6.

A30

Designs: Churchill portraits — 10c, Dublin, Age 5. 25c, As young man. 30c, Inspecting troops, WWII. 50c, Painting. $1, Giving V sign.

1974, Nov. 29 Photo. *Perf. 14*

No.	Description	Unused	Used
110	A30 10c multicolored	.25	.25
111	A30 25c multicolored	.30	.25
112	A30 30c multicolored	.35	.25
113	A30 50c multicolored	.70	.40
114	A30 $1 multicolored	1.25	.85
a.	Souvenir sheet of 5, #110-114 + label, perf. 13½	4.50	4.50
	Nos. 110-114 (5)	2.85	2.00

Sir Winston Churchill (1874-1965). Nos. 110-114 printed in sheets of 5 stamps and corner label.

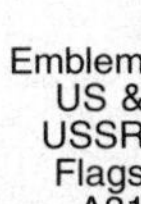

Emblem US & USSR Flags A31

50c, Icarus and Apollo Soyuz spacecraft.

1975, July 24 Photo. *Perf. 13x14½*

No.	Description	Unused	Used
115	A31 25c multicolored	.30	.30
116	A31 50c multicolored	1.00	1.00
a.	Souvenir sheet of 2	1.60	1.60

Apollo Soyuz space test project (Russo-American cooperation), launching July 15; link-up July 17. Nos. 115 and 116 each printed in sheets of 5 stamps and one label showing area of Apollo splash-downs. No. 116a contains one each of Nos. 115-116 with gold and black border and inscription.

Madonna and Child, by Pietro Lorenzetti — A32

Paintings: 7c, Adoration of the Kings, by Rogier van der Weyden. 15c, Madonna and Child, by Bartolommeo Montagna. 20c, Adoration of the Shepherds.

1975, Nov. 24 Photo. *Perf. 14x13½*

No.	Description	Unused	Used
117	A32 Strip of 3	.40	.40
a.	6c St. Francis	.25	.25
b.	6c Madonna and Child	.25	.25
c.	6c St. John the Evangelist	.25	.25
118	A32 Strip of 3	.40	.40
a.	7c One King	.25	.25
b.	7c Madonna and Child	.25	.25
c.	7c Two Kings	.25	.25
119	A32 Strip of 3	.90	.90
a.	15c St. Joseph	.30	.25
b.	15c Madonna and Child	.30	.25
c.	15c St. John the Baptist	.30	.25
120	A32 Strip of 3	1.10	1.10
a.	20c One Shepherd	.35	.35
b.	20c Madonna and Child	.35	.35
c.	20c Two Shepherds	.35	.35
d.	Souv. sheet of 12, #117-120, perf. 13½	3.50	3.50
	Nos. 117-120 (4)	2.80	2.80

Christmas. Nos. 117-120 printed in sheets of 30 (10 strips of 3).

For surcharges see Nos. B7-B10.

Descent from the Cross, detail — A33

Designs (Painting, Flemish School, 16th Century): 30c, Virgin Mary, disciple and body of Jesus. 35c, Mary Magdalene and disciple.

1976, Apr. 5 Photo. *Perf. 13½*

No.	Description	Unused	Used
121	A33 15c gold & multi	.25	.25
122	A33 30c gold & multi	.30	.30
123	A33 35c gold & multi	.75	.75
a.	Souvenir sheet of 3	1.50	1.50
	Nos. 121-123 (3)	1.30	1.30

Easter. No. 123a contains 3 stamps similar to Nos. 121-123, perf. 13, in continuous design without gold frames and white margins.

Declaration of Independence — A34

Paintings by John Trumbull: 35c, Surrender of Cornwallis at Yorktown. 50c, Washington's Farewell Address. a, "1976 BICENTENARY." b, "UNITED STATES." c, "INDEPENDENCE 1776."

1976, June 1 Photo. *Perf. 13½*

No.	Description	Unused	Used
124	A34 Strip of 3	1.50	1.50
a.-c.	30c any single	.45	.45
125	A34 Strip of 3	2.00	2.00
a.-c.	35c any single	.65	.65
126	A34 Strip of 3	2.50	2.50
a.-c.	50c any single	.80	.80
d.	Souvenir sheet of 9 (3x3)	6.00	6.00
	Nos. 124-126 (3)	6.00	6.00

American Bicentennial. Nos. 124-126 printed in sheets of 5 strips of 3 and 3-part corner label showing portrait of John Trumbull, commemorative inscription and portraits of Washington (30c), John Adams (35c) and Jefferson (50c). No. 126d contains 3 strips similar to Nos. 124-126.

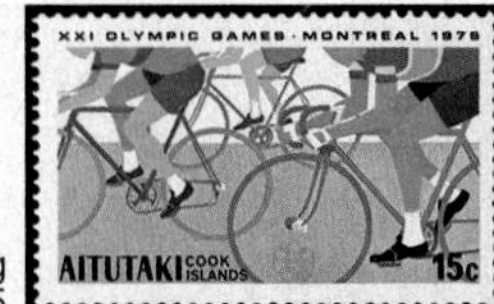

Bicycling
A35

Montreal Olympic Games Emblem and: 35c, Sailing. 60c, Field hockey. 70c, Running.

1976, July 15 Photo. *Perf. 13x14*

127 A35 15c multicolored .30 .25
128 A35 35c multicolored .60 .50
129 A35 60c multicolored .95 .80
130 A35 70c multicolored 1.25 .90
a. Souvenir sheet of 4 3.50 3.50
Nos. 127-130 (4) 3.10 2.45

21st Olympic Games, Montreal, Canada, July 17-Aug. 1. Nos. 127-130 printed in sheets of 5 stamps and label showing coat of Arms and Montreal Olympic Games emblem. No. 130a contains 4 stamps similar to Nos. 127-130 with gold margin around each stamp.

Nos. 127-130a Overprinted

1976, July 30

131 A35 15c multicolored .25 .25
132 A35 35c multicolored .60 .60
133 A35 60c multicolored .85 .85
134 A35 70c multicolored 1.10 1.10
a. Souvenir sheet of 4 3.00 3.00
Nos. 131-134 (4) 2.80 2.80

Visit of Queen Elizabeth II to Montreal and official opening of the Games. Each stamp of No. 134a has diagonal overprint. Sheet margin has additional overprint: "ROYAL VISIT OF H.M. QUEEN ELIZABETH II/OFFICIALLY OPENED 17 JULY 1976."

Annunciation — A36

Designs: Nos. 137-138, Angel appearing to the shepherds. Nos. 139-140, Nativity. Nos. 141-142, Three Kings.

1976, Oct. 18 *Perf. 13½x13*

135 6c dk green & gold .25 .25
136 6c dk green & gold .25 .25
a. A36 Pair, #135-136 .25 .25
137 7c dk brown & gold .25 .25
138 7c dk brown & gold .25 .25
a. A36 Pair, #137-138 .25 .25
139 15c dk blue & gold .25 .25
140 15c dk blue & gold .25 .25
a. A36 Pair, #139-140 .30 .30
141 20c purple & gold .25 .25
142 20c purple & gold .25 .25
a. A36 Pair, #141-142 .50 .50
b. Souvenir sheet of 8 2.00 2.00
Nos. 135-142 (8) 2.00 2.00

Christmas. No. 142b contains 8 stamps similar to Nos. 135-142 with white margin around each pair of stamps.
For overprints see Nos. B11-B18.

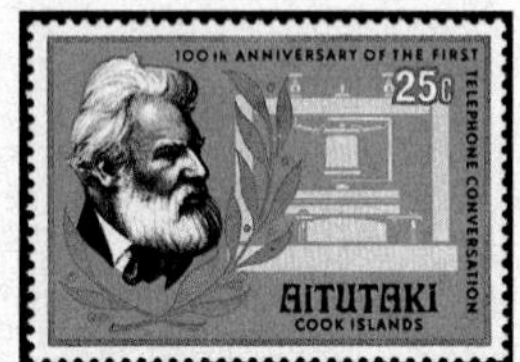

A. G. Bell and 1876 Telephone — A38

Design: 70c, Satellite and radar.

1977, Mar. 3 Photo. *Perf. 13½x13*

143 A38 25c rose & multi .25 .25
144 A38 70c violet & multi .65 .65
a. Souvenir sheet of 2 1.75 1.75

Centenary of first telephone call by Alexander Graham Bell, Mar. 10, 1876. No. 144a contains a 25c in colors of 70c and 70c in colors of 25c.

Calvary (detail), by Rubens
A39

Paintings by Rubens: 20c, Lamentation. 35c, Descent from the Cross.

1977, Mar. 31 Photo. *Perf. 13½x14*

145 A39 15c gold & multi .55 .55
146 A39 20c gold & multi .70 .70
147 A39 35c gold & multi 1.00 1.00
a. Souv. sheet, #145-147, perf. 13 2.50 2.50
Nos. 145-147 (3) 2.25 2.25

Easter, and 400th birth anniv. of Peter Paul Rubens (1577-1640), Flemish painter.

Capt. Bligh, "Bounty" and George III — A40

Designs: 35c, Rev. John Williams, George IV, First Christian Church. 50c, British flag, map of Aitutaki, Queen Victoria. $1, Elizabeth II and family on balcony after coronation.

1977, Apr. 21 *Perf. 13½*

148 A40 25c gold & multi .25 .25
149 A40 35c gold & multi .30 .30
150 A40 50c gold & multi .50 .50
151 A40 $1 gold & multi 1.75 1.75
a. Souvenir sheet of 4, #148-151 2.50 2.50
Nos. 148-151 (4) 2.80 2.80

Reign of Queen Elizabeth II, 25th anniv.
For overprint & surcharge see Nos. O11, O15.

Annunciation — A41

Designs: No. 154, Virgin, Child and ox. No. 155, Joseph and donkey (Nativity). No. 156, Three Kings. No. 157, Virgin and Child. No. 158, Joseph. No. 159, Virgin, Child and donkey (Flight into Egypt).

1977, Oct. 14 Photo. *Perf. 13½x14*

152 6c multicolored .25 .25
153 6c multicolored .25 .25
a. A41 Pair, #152-153 .25 .25
154 7c multicolored .25 .25
155 7c multicolored .25 .25
a. A41 Pair, #154-155 .25 .25
156 15c multicolored .25 .25
157 15c multicolored .25 .25
a. A41 Pair, #156-157 .40 .40
158 20c multicolored .25 .25
159 20c multicolored .25 .25
a. A41 Pair, #158-159 .50 .50
b. Souvenir sheet of 8, #152-159 2.00 2.00
Nos. 152-159 (8) 2.00 2.00

Christmas.
For surcharges see Nos. B19-B26a.

Hawaiian Wood Figurine — A43

Designs: 50c, Talbot hunting dog, figurehead of "Resolution", horiz. $1, Temple figure.

1978, Jan. 19 Litho. *Perf. 13½*

160 A43 35c multicolored .60 .60
161 A43 50c multicolored .85 .85
162 A43 $1 multicolored 1.40 1.40
a. Souvenir sheet of 3, #160-162 3.00 3.00
Nos. 160-162 (3) 2.85 2.85

Bicentenary of Capt. Cook's arrival in Hawaii. Nos. 160-162 issued in sheets of 6.

Jesus Carrying Cross, by Simone di Martini
A44

Paintings: 20c, Avignon Pietà, 15th Century. 35c, Christ at Emmaus, by Rembrandt.

1978, Mar. 17 Photo. *Perf. 13½x14*

163 A44 15c gold & multi .25 .25
164 A44 20c gold & multi .30 .30
165 A44 35c gold & multi .40 .40
a. Souvenir sheet of 3 1.10 1.10
Nos. 163-165 (3) .95 .95

Easter. No. 165a contains one each of Nos. 163-165, perf. 13½, and label showing Louvre, Paris. See Nos. B27-B29.

Souvenir Sheet

25th Anniv. of Coronation of Queen Elizabeth II. — A45

1978, June 15 Photo. *Perf. 13½x13*

166 Sheet of 6 2.75 2.75
a. A45 $1 Yale of Beaufort .40 .40
b. A45 $1 Elizabeth II .40 .40
c. A45 $1 Ancestral statue .40 .40
d. Souvenir sheet of 6 2.50 2.50

No. 166d contains 2 strips of Nos. 166a-166c separated by horizontal slate green gutter showing Royal family on balcony, silver marginal inscription.

Virgin and Child, by Dürer — A46

Designs: Various paintings of the Virgin and Child by Albrecht Dürer.

1978, Dec. 4 Photo. *Perf. 14½x13*

167 A46 15c multicolored .40 .25
168 A46 17c multicolored .50 .30
169 A46 30c multicolored .75 .50
170 A46 35c multicolored .75 .60
Nos. 167-170 (4) 2.40 1.65

Christmas; 450th death anniv. of Albrecht Dürer (1471-1528), German painter. Nos. 167-170 issued in sheets of 5 stamps and corner label. See No. B30.

Capt. Cook, by Nathaniel Dance — A47

Design: 75c, "Resolution" and "Adventure," by William Hodges.

1979, July 20 Photo. *Perf. 14x13½*

171 A47 50c multicolored 1.75 1.25
172 A47 75c multicolored 2.25 1.75
a. Souvenir sheet of 2, #171-172 3.25 3.25

Capt. James Cook (1728-1779), explorer, death bicentenary.

Boy Holding Hibiscus, IYC Emblem — A48

IYC Emblem and: 35c, Boy playing guitar. 65c, Boys in outrigger canoe.

1979, Oct. 1 Photo. *Perf. 14x13½*

173 A48 30c multicolored .25 .25
174 A48 35c multicolored .40 .40
175 A48 65c multicolored .55 .55
Nos. 173-175 (3) 1.20 1.20

See No. B31.

Aitutaki No. 102, Hill, Penny Black
A49

Designs: Nos. 176, 178-179, 181, paintings of letter writers, Flemish School, 17th century.

1979, Nov. 14 Photo. *Perf. 13*

176 A49 50c Gabriel Metsu .55 .55
177 A49 50c shown .55 .55
178 A49 50c Jan Vermeer .55 .55
a. Strip of 3, #176-178 1.75 1.75
179 A49 65c Gerard Terborch .70 .70
180 A49 65c No. 103 (like No. 177) .70 .70
181 A49 65c Jan Vermeer .70 .70
a. Strip of 3, #179-181 2.25 2.25
Nos. 176-181 (6) 3.75 3.75

Souvenir Sheet

182 Sheet of 6 3.00 3.00
a. A49 30c like No. 176 .50 .50
b. A49 30c like No. 177 .50 .50
c. A49 30c like No. 178 .50 .50
d. A49 30c like No. 179 .50 .50
e. A49 30c like No. 180 .50 .50
f. A49 30c like No. 181 .50 .50

Sir Rowland Hill (1795-1879), originator of penny postage. Nos. 176-178 and 179-181 printed in sheets of 9.

Descent from the Cross, Detail — A50

Easter: 30c, 35c, Descent from the Cross, by Quentin Metsys (details).

1980, Apr. 3 Photo. *Perf. 13x13½*

183 A50 20c multicolored .55 .45
184 A50 30c multicolored .65 .60
185 A50 35c multicolored .80 .70
Nos. 183-185 (3) 2.00 1.75

See No. B32.

Albert Einstein — A51

No. 187, Formula, atom structure. No. 188, Portrait, diff. No. 189, Atomic blast. No. 190, Portrait, diff. No. 191, Atomic blast, trees.

1980, July 21 Photo. *Perf. 14*

186 A51 12c shown .80 .80
187 A51 12c multicolored .80 .80
a. Pair, #186-187 1.75 1.75
188 A51 15c multicolored .85 .85
189 A51 15c multicolored .85 .85
a. Pair, #188-189 1.75 1.75
190 A51 20c multicolored 1.00 1.00
191 A51 20c multicolored 1.00 1.00
a. Pair, #190-191 2.10 2.10
b. Souv. sheet of 6, #186-191, perf. 13 5.50 5.50
Nos. 186-191 (6) 5.30 5.30

Albert Einstein (1879-1955), theoretical physicist.

A52

No. 192, Ancestral Figure, Aitutaki. No. 193, God image staff, Rarotonga. No. 194, Trade adze, Mangaia. No. 195, Tangaroa carving, Rarotonga. No. 196, Wooden image, Aitutaki. No. 197, Hand club, Rarotonga. No. 198, Carved mace, Mangaia. No. 199, Fisherman's god, Rarotonga. No. 200, Ti'i image, Aitutaki. No. 201, Fisherman's god, diff. No. 202, Carved mace, Cook Islands. No. 203, Tangaroa, diff. No. 204, Chief's headdress, Aitutaki. No. 205, Carved mace, diff. No. 206, God image staff, diff.

1980, Sept. 26 Photo. *Perf. 14*

192 A52 6c multicolored .25 .25
193 A52 6c multicolored .25 .25
194 A52 6c multicolored .25 .25
195 A52 6c multicolored .25 .25
a. Block of 4, #192-195 .65 .65
196 A52 12c multicolored .25 .25
197 A52 12c multicolored .25 .25
198 A52 12c multicolored .25 .25
199 A52 12c multicolored .25 .25
a. Block of 4, #196-199 1.00 1.00
200 A52 15c multicolored .25 .25
201 A52 15c multicolored .25 .25
202 A52 15c multicolored .25 .25
203 A52 15c multicolored .25 .25
a. Block of 4, #200-203 1.10 1.10
204 A52 20c multicolored .40 .40
205 A52 20c multicolored .40 .40
206 A52 20c multicolored .40 .40
207 A52 20c like #195 .40 .40
a. Block of 4, #204-207 1.60 1.60
b. Souvenir sheet of 16, #192-207 4.25

Third South Pacific Arts Festival, Port Moresby, Papua New Guinea.

A53

Virgin and Child, Sculptures.

1980, Nov. 21 Photo. *Perf. 13x13½*

208 A53 15c 13th cent. .25 .25
209 A53 20c 14th cent. .25 .25
210 A53 25c 15th cent. .30 .30
211 A53 35c 15th cent., diff. .55 .55
Nos. 208-211 (4) 1.35 1.35

Christmas. See No. B33.

Mourning Virgin, by Pedro Roldan — A54

Easter (Roldan Sculptures): 40c, Christ. 50c, Mourning St. John.

1981, Mar. 31 Photo. *Perf. 14*

212 A54 30c green & gold .35 .35
213 A54 40c brt purple & gold .45 .45
214 A54 50c dk blue & gold .50 .50
Nos. 212-214 (3) 1.30 1.30

See No. B34.

Sturnus Vulgaris — A55

1981-82 *Perf. 14x13½, 13½x14*

215 A55 1c shown .45 .25
216 A55 1c Poephila gouldiae .45 .25
a. Pair, #215-216 1.00 .30
217 A55 2c Petroica multicolor .50 .25
218 A55 2c Pachycephala pectoralis .50 .25
a. Pair, #217-218 1.10 .30
219 A55 3c Falco peregrinus .60 .25
220 A55 3c Rhipidura rufifrons .60 .25
a. Pair, #219-220 1.25 .30
221 A55 4c Tyto alba .70 .25
222 A55 4c Padda oryzivora .70 .25
a. Pair, #221-222 1.50 .35
223 A55 5c Artamus leucorhynchus .75 .25
224 A55 5c Vini peruviana .75 .25
a. Pair, #223-224 1.60 .40
225 A55 6c Columba livia .80 .25
226 A55 6c Porphyrio porphyria .80 .25
a. Pair, #225-226 1.75 .40
227 A55 10c Geopelia striata .90 .30
228 A55 10c Lonchura castaneothorax .90 .30
a. Pair, #227-228 2.00 .75
229 A55 12c Acridotheres tristis 1.00 .40
230 A55 12c Egretta sacra 1.00 .40
a. Pair, #229-230 2.10 .85
231 A55 15c Diomeda melanophris 1.25 .50
232 A55 15c Numenius phaeopus 1.25 .50
a. Pair, #231-232 2.75 1.10
233 A55 20c Gygis alba 1.50 .60
234 A55 20c Pluvialis dominica 1.50 .60
a. Pair, #233-234 3.50 1.25
235 A55 25c Sula leucogaster 1.75 .70
236 A55 25c Anas superciliosa 1.75 .70
a. Pair, #235-236 4.00 1.50
237 A55 30c Anas acuta 2.00 .80
238 A55 30c Fregata minor 2.00 .80
a. Pair, #237-238 4.25 1.75
239 A55 35c Stercorarius pomarinus 2.10 .90
240 A55 35c Conopoderas caffra 2.10 .90
a. Pair, #239-240 4.50 2.00
241 A55 40c Lalage maculosa 2.25 1.00
242 A55 40c Gallirallus philippensis 2.25 1.00
a. Pair, #241-242 5.00 2.25
243 A55 50c Vini stepheni 2.50 1.50
244 A55 50c Diomedea epomophora 2.50 1.50
a. Pair, #243-244 5.50 3.25
245 A55 70c Ptilinopus victor 5.75 2.40
246 A55 70c Erythrura cyaneovirens 5.75 2.40
e. Pair, #245-246 12.00 4.80

Photo. *Perf. 13½*

Size: 35x47mm

246A A55 $1 Myiagra azureocapilla 6.00 4.00
246B A55 $2 Myiagra vanikorensis 6.50 *8.00*
246C A55 $4 Amandava amandava 10.00 *14.00*
246D A55 $5 Halcyon recurvirostris 12.00 *16.00*
Nos. 215-246D (36) 84.10 63.20

Issued: Nos. 215-230, 4/6; Nos. 231-238, 5/8; Nos. 239-246, 1/14/82; Nos. 246A-246B, 2/15/82.

Nos. 231-246 horiz.

For surcharges and overprint see Nos. 293-306, 452-454, O40-O41.

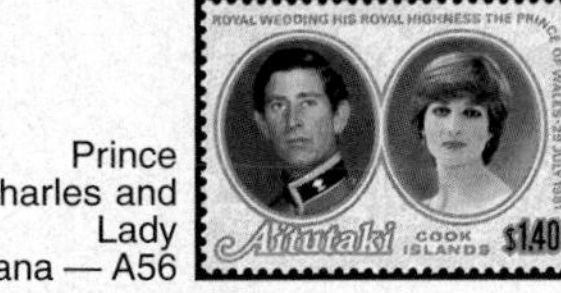

Prince Charles and Lady Diana — A56

Perf. 13x13½, 13½x13

1981, June 10 Photo.

247 A56 60c Charles, vert. .50 .50
248 A56 80c Lady Diana, vert. .60 .60
Complete booklet, one sheet of 4 each #247-248 6.00
249 A56 $1.40 Shown .85 .85
Nos. 247-249 (3) 1.95 1.95

Royal Wedding. Issued in sheets of 4.

For overprints and surcharges see Nos. 265-267, 307, 309, 355, 405-407, B35-B37.

1982 World Cup Soccer — A57

Designs: Various soccer players.

1981, Nov. 30 Photo. *Perf. 14*

250 A57 12c Pair, #250a-250b 1.40 1.25
251 A57 15c Pair, #251a-251b 1.50 1.40
252 A57 20c Pair, #252a-252b 1.75 1.40
253 A57 25c Pair, #253a-253b 2.00 1.50
Nos. 250-253 (4) 6.65 5.55

See No. B38.

Christmas A58

Rembrandt Etchings: 15c, Holy Family, 1632, vert. 30c, Virgin with Child, 1634, vert. 40c, Adoration of the Shepherds, 1654. 50c, Holy Family with Cat, 1644.

1981, Dec. 10 *Perf. 14*

254 A58 15c gold & dk brown .60 .60
255 A58 30c gold & dk brown .85 .85
256 A58 40c gold & dk brown 1.00 1.00
257 A58 50c gold & dk brown 1.25 1.25
Nos. 254-257 (4) 3.70 3.70

Souvenir Sheets

258 A58 80c + 5c like #254 1.00 .90
259 A58 80c + 5c like #255 1.00 .90
260 A58 80c + 5c like #256 1.00 .90
261 A58 80c + 5c like #257 1.00 .90

Nos. 258-261 have multicolored margins showing entire etching. Surtax on Nos. 258-261 was for local charities.

21st Birthday of Princess Diana — A59

1982, June 24 Photo. *Perf. 14*

262 A59 70c shown 2.00 .90
263 A59 $1 Wedding portrait 2.00 1.00
264 A59 $2 Diana, diff. 3.50 1.75
a. Souvenir sheet of 3, #262-264 7.00 7.00
Nos. 262-264 (3) 7.50 3.65

See Nos. 268-270a. For surcharges see Nos. 308, 310.

Nos. 247-249 Overprinted

a

b

1982, July 13 *Perf. 13x13½, 13½x13*

265 A56 60c Pair, #a.-b. 1.50 1.25
266 A56 80c Pair, #a.-b. 2.25 2.00
267 A56 $1.40 Pair, #a.-b. 3.75 3.25
Nos. 265-267 (3) 7.50 6.50

Nos. 265-267 were overprinted with alternating inscriptions within the sheet.

Nos. 262-264a Inscribed: "Royal Birth 21 June 1982 Prince William Of Wales"

1982, Aug. 5 *Perf. 14*

268 A59 70c multicolored .80 .80
269 A59 $1 multicolored 1.75 1.75
270 A59 $2 multicolored 2.75 2.75
a. Souvenir sheet of 3 6.00 6.00
Nos. 268-270 (3) 5.30 5.30

Christmas — A60

Madonna and Child Sculptures, 12th-15th Cent.

1982, Dec. 10 Photo. *Perf. 13*

271 A60 18c multicolored .75 .75
272 A60 36c multicolored .90 .90
273 A60 48c multicolored 1.00 1.00
274 A60 60c multicolored 1.40 1.40
Nos. 271-274 (4) 4.05 4.05

Souvenir Sheet

275 Sheet of 4 5.00 5.00
a. A60 18c + 2c like 18c .80 .80
b. A60 36c + 2c like 36c .90 .90
c. A60 48c + 2c like 48c 1.10 1.10
d. A60 60c + 2c like 60c 1.60 1.60

Surtax was for children's charities.

Commonwealth Day — A61

1983, Mar. 14 Photo. ***Perf. 13x13½***

276 A61 48c Bananas 1.10 1.10
277 A61 48c Ti'i statuette 1.10 1.10
278 A61 48c Boys canoeing 1.10 1.10
279 A61 48c Capt. Bligh, Bounty 1.10 1.10
a. Block of 4, #276-279 5.25 5.25

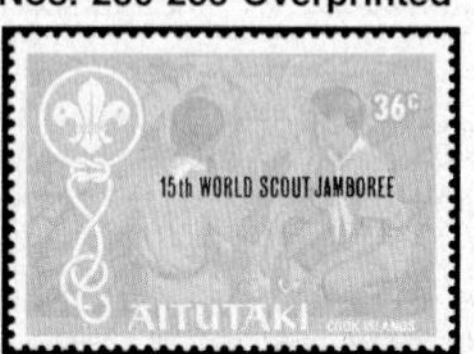

Scouting Year A62

1983, Apr. 18 Photo. ***Perf. 14***

280 A62 36c Campfire .60 .60
281 A62 48c Salute .70 .70
282 A62 60c Hiking .75 .75
Nos. 280-282 (3) 2.05 2.05

Souvenir Sheet

Perf. 13½

283 Sheet of 3 2.75 2.75
a. A62 36c + 3c like #280 .70 .70
b. A62 48c + 3c like #281 .80 .80
c. A62 60c + 3c like #282 1.10 1.10

Surtax was for benefit of Scouting.

Nos. 280-283 Overprinted

1983, July 11 Photo. ***Perf. 14***

284 A62 36c multicolored 1.00 1.00
285 A62 48c multicolored 1.25 1.25
286 A62 60c multicolored 1.50 1.50
Nos. 284-286 (3) 3.75 3.75

Souvenir Sheet

287 Sheet of 3 3.50 3.50
a. A62 36c + 3c like #284 .75 .75
b. A62 48c + 3c like #285 .90 .90
c. A62 60c + 3c like #286 1.25 1.25

A63

Manned Flight Bicentenary: Modern sport balloons.

1983, July 22 Photo. ***Perf. 14x13***

288 A63 18c multicolored .75 .75
289 A63 36c multicolored 1.00 1.00
290 A63 48c multicolored 1.25 1.25
291 A63 60c multicolored 1.50 1.50
Nos. 288-291 (4) 4.50 4.50

Souvenir Sheet

292 A63 $2.50 multicolored 3.25 3.25

Nos. 293-306, 308, 310-311 Surcharged in Black

Nos. 307, 309 Surcharged in Black and Gold

1983, Sept. 22

293 A55 18c on 20c, #233 3.00 1.10
294 A55 18c on 20c, #234 3.00 1.10
a. Pair, #293-294 6.25 2.20
295 A55 36c on 25c, #235 3.50 1.50
296 A55 36c on 25c, #236 3.50 1.50
a. Pair, #295-296 7.50 3.00
297 A55 36c on 30c, #237 3.50 1.50
298 A55 36c on 30c, #238 3.50 1.50
a. Pair, #297-298 7.50 3.00
299 A55 36c on 35c, #239 3.75 1.50
300 A55 36c on 35c, #240 3.75 1.50
a. Pair, #299-300 7.75 3.00
301 A55 48c on 40c, #241 5.00 1.50
302 A55 48c on 40c, #242 5.00 1.50
a. Pair, #301-302 10.50 3.00
303 A55 48c on 50c, #243 5.00 1.50
304 A55 48c on 50c, #244 5.00 1.50
a. Pair, #303-304 10.50 3.00
305 A55 72c on 70c, #245 8.50 3.00
306 A55 72c on 70c, #246 8.50 3.00
a. Pair, #305-306 17.50 6.00
307 A56 96c on 80c, #248 3.25 2.50
308 A59 96c on $1, #263 3.00 2.25
309 A56 $1.20 on $1.40, #249 3.25 2.50
310 A59 $1.20 on $2, #264 3.00 2.25

Size: 35x47mm

311 A55 $5.60 on $5, #246D 22.50 11.00
Nos. 293-311 (19) 99.50 43.70

Nos. 307-308, 310-311 vert.

A64

60, Global coverage. 96c, Communications satellite.

1983, Sept. 29 Photo. ***Perf. 14***

312 A64 48c shown .90 .65
313 A64 60c multicolored 1.40 .75
314 A64 96c multicolored 1.75 1.50
a. Souvenir sheet of 3, #312-314 3.50 3.50
Nos. 312-314 (3) 4.05 2.90

World Communications Year.

Christmas A65

Raphael Paintings — 36c, Madonna of the Chair. 48c, Alba Madonna. 60c, Connestabile Madonna.

1983, Nov. 21 Photo. ***Perf. 13½x14***

315 A65 36c multicolored .90 .50
316 A65 48c multicolored 1.25 1.00
317 A65 60c multicolored 1.75 1.25
Nos. 315-317 (3) 3.90 2.75

Souvenir Sheet

318 Sheet of 3 3.50 3.50
a. A65 36c + 3c like #315 1.00 1.00
b. A65 48c + 3c like #316 1.10 1.10
c. A65 60c + 3c like #317 1.25 1.25

1983, Dec. 15 ***Imperf.***

Size: 46x46mm

319 A65 85c + 5c like #315 1.75 1.75
320 A65 85c + 5c like #316 1.75 1.75
321 A65 85c + 5c like #317 1.75 1.75
Nos. 319-321 (3) 5.25 5.25

Surtax was for children's charities.

Local Birds — A66

1984 Photo. ***Perf. 14***

322 A66 2c as No. 216 2.00 .80
323 A66 3c as No. 215 2.00 .80
324 A66 5c as No. 217 2.00 .95
325 A66 10c as No. 218 2.75 .95
326 A66 12c as No. 220 2.75 .95
327 A66 18c as No. 219 2.75 1.25
328 A66 24c as No. 221 2.75 1.25
329 A66 30c as No. 222 2.75 1.25
330 A66 36c as No. 223 2.75 1.25
331 A66 48c as No. 224 2.75 1.25
332 A66 50c as No. 225 3.00 1.90
333 A66 60c as No. 226 3.00 1.90
334 A66 72c as No. 227 3.50 1.90
335 A66 96c as No. 228 3.50 1.90
336 A66 $1.20 as No. 229 3.50 2.75
337 A66 $2.10 as No. 230 4.00 3.75
338 A66 $3 as No. 246A 5.75 5.00
339 A66 $4.20 as No. 246B 4.50 *6.50*
340 A66 $5.60 as No. 246C 5.75 *8.25*
341 A66 $9.60 as No. 246D 8.75 *11.50*
Nos. 322-341 (20) 70.50 56.05

For overprints and surcharges see Nos. O17-O39.

1984 Summer Olympics — A67

1984, July 24 Photo. ***Perf. 13x13½***

342 A67 36c Javelin .55 .55
343 A67 48c Shot put .65 .65
344 A67 60c Hurdles .75 .75
345 A67 $2 Handball 2.75 2.75
Nos. 342-345 (4) 4.70 4.70

Souvenir Sheet

346 Sheet of 4 4.00 4.00
a. A67 36c + 5c like #342 .50 .50
b. A67 48c + 5c like #343 .65 .65
c. A67 60c + 5c like #344 .75 .75
d. A67 $2 + 5c like #345 1.75 1.75

Surtax was for benefit of local sports.

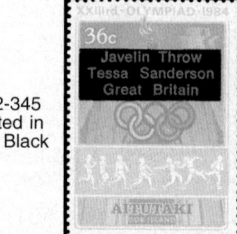

Nos. 342-345 Overprinted in Gold and Black

1984, Aug. 21 Photo. ***Perf. 13x13½***

347 A67 36c multicolored .50 .50
348 A67 48c multicolored .60 .60
349 A67 60c multicolored .70 .70
350 A67 $2 multicolored 2.25 2.25
Nos. 347-350 (4) 4.05 4.05

Ausipex '84 — A68

60c, William Bligh, map. 96c, Bounty, map. $1.40, Stamps, map.

1984, Sept. 14 Photo. ***Perf. 14***

351 A68 60c multicolored 4.50 4.50
352 A68 96c multicolored 4.50 4.50
353 A68 $1.40 multicolored 4.50 4.50
Nos. 351-353 (3) 13.50 13.50

Souvenir Sheet

354 Sheet of 3 8.50 8.50
a. A68 60c + 5c like #351 1.75 1.75
b. A68 96c + 5c like #352 2.50 2.50
c. A68 $1.40 + 5c like #353 3.75 3.75

For overprint see No. 399.

No. 247 Surcharged

1984, Oct. 10 Photo. ***Perf. 13x13½***

355 A56 $3 multicolored 3.25 3.25

Issued in sheets of 4.

A69

1984, Nov. 16 Photo. ***Perf. 13***

356 A69 36c Annunciation .55 .55
357 A69 48c Nativity .65 .65
358 A69 60c Epiphany .75 .75
359 A69 96c Flight into Egypt 1.00 1.00
Nos. 356-359 (4) 2.95 2.95

Souvenir Sheets

Size: 45x53mm

Imperf

360 A69 90c + 7c like #356 1.25 1.25
361 A69 90c + 7c like #357 1.25 1.25
362 A69 90c + 7c like #358 1.25 1.25
363 A69 90c + 7c like #359 1.25 1.25

Christmas.

A70

1984, Dec. 10 Photo. ***Perf. 13½x14***

364 A70 48c Diana, Henry 2.75 2.75
365 A70 60c William, Henry 2.75 2.75
366 A70 $2.10 Family 3.50 3.50
Nos. 364-366 (3) 9.00 9.00

Souvenir Sheet

367 Sheet of 3 8.00 8.00
a. A70 96c + 7c like #364 2.50 2.50
b. A70 96c + 7c like #365 2.50 2.50
c. A70 96c + 7c like #366 2.50 2.50

Christmas, Birth of Prince Henry, Sept. 15.

Surtax was for benefit of local children's charities.

Audubon Birth Bicentenary A71

Illustrations of bird species by John J. Audubon — 55c, Gray kingbird. 65c, Bohemian waxwing. 75c, Summer tanager. 95c, Cardinal. $1.15, White-winged crossbill.

1985, Mar. 22 Litho. ***Perf. 13***

368 A71 55c multicolored 1.25 1.25
369 A71 65c multicolored 1.50 1.50
370 A71 75c multicolored 1.75 1.75
371 A71 95c multicolored 2.00 2.00
372 A71 $1.15 multicolored 3.00 3.00
Nos. 368-372 (5) 9.50 9.50

Queen Mother, 85th Birthday A72

Photographs: 55c, Lady Elizabeth Bowes-Lyon, age 7. 65c, Engaged to the Duke of York, 75c, Duchess of York with daughter, Elizabeth. $1.30, Holding the infant Prince Charles. $3, Portrait taken on 63rd birthday.

1985-86 ***Perf. 13½x13***

373 A72 55c multicolored .75 .75
374 A72 65c multicolored .85 .85
375 A72 75c multicolored 1.00 1.00
376 A72 $1.30 multicolored 1.50 1.50
a. Souvenir sheet of 4, #373-376 9.00 7.50
Nos. 373-376 (4) 4.10 4.10

Souvenir Sheet

377 A72 $3 multicolored 5.00 5.00

Nos. 373-376 printed in sheets of 4.
Issued: No. 376a, 8/4/86; others, 6/14/85.
For overprint see No. 446.

Intl. Youth Year A73

Designs: 75c, The Calmady Children, by Thomas Lawrence (1769-1830). 90c, Madame Charpentier's Children, by Renoir (1841-1919). $1.40, Young Girls at Piano, by Renoir.

1985, Sept. 16 **Photo.** ***Perf. 13***

378 A73 75c multicolored 3.00 3.00
379 A73 90c multicolored 3.00 3.00
380 A73 $1.40 multicolored 4.00 4.00
Nos. 378-380 (3) 10.00 10.00

Souvenir Sheet

381 Sheet of 3 8.00 8.00
a. A73 75c + 10c like #378 2.00 2.00
b. A73 90c + 10c like #379 2.25 2.25
c. A73 $1.40 + 10c like #380 3.00 3.00

Surcharged for children's activities.

Adoration of the Magi, by Giotto di Bondone (1276-1337) — A74

1985, Nov. 15 **Photo.** ***Perf. 13½x13***

382 A74 95c multicolored 2.00 2.00
383 A74 95c multicolored 2.00 2.00
a. Pair, #382-383 4.50 4.50
384 A74 $1.15 multicolored 2.00 2.00
385 A74 $1.15 multicolored 2.00 2.00
a. Pair, #384-385 4.50 4.50
Nos. 382-385 (4) 8.00 8.00

Souvenir Sheet

Imperf

386 A74 $6.40 multicolored 16.50 16.50

Christmas, return of Halley's Comet, 1985-86.

Halley's Comet A75

Designs: 90c, Halley's Comet, A.D. 684, wood engraving, Nuremberg Chronicles. $1.25, Sighting of 1066, Bayeux Tapestry, detail, c. 1092, France. $1.75, The Comet Inflicting Untold Disasters, 1456, Lucerne Chronicles, by Diebolt Schilling. $4.20, Melancolia I, engraving by Durer.

1986, Feb. 25 **Photo.** ***Perf. 13½x13***

387 A75 90c multicolored 1.25 1.25
388 A75 $1.25 multicolored 1.75 1.75
389 A75 $1.75 multicolored 2.75 2.75
Nos. 387-389 (3) 5.75 5.75

Souvenir Sheets

390 Sheet of 3 + label 7.50 7.50
a. A75 95c, like #387 2.25 2.25
b. A75 95c, like #388 2.25 2.25
c. A75 95c, like #389 2.25 2.25

Imperf

391 A75 $4.20 multicolored 7.00 7.00

Elizabeth II, 60th Birthday — A76

1986, Apr. 21 ***Perf. 14***

392 A76 95c Coronation portrait 1.25 1.25

Souvenir Sheet

Perf. 13½

393 A76 $4.20 Portrait, diff. 6.50 6.50

No. 392 printed in sheets of 5 with label picturing U.K. flag and Queen's flag for New Zealand.

Statue of Liberty, Cent. A77

1986, June 27 **Photo.** ***Perf. 14***

394 A77 $1 Liberty head 1.75 1.75
395 A77 $2.75 Statue 3.50 3.50

Souvenir Sheet

Perf. 13½

396 Sheet of 2 3.50 3.50
a. A77 $1.25 like $1 1.60 1.60
b. A77 $1.25 like $2.75 1.60 1.60

For surcharges see Nos B45, B49.

Wedding of Prince Andrew and Sarah Ferguson — A78

1986, July 23 ***Perf. 14***

397 A78 $2 multicolored 3.00 3.00

Souvenir Sheet

Perf. 13½

398 A78 $5 multicolored 7.00 7.00

No. 397 printed in sheets of 5 plus label picturing Westminster Abbey.
For surcharge see No. B48.

No. 354 Overprinted

1986, Aug. 4 **Photo.** ***Perf. 14***

399 Sheet of 3 14.50 14.50
a. A68 60c + 5c like #351 3.50 3.50
b. A68 96c + 5c like #352 4.00 4.00
c. A68 $1.40 + 5c like #353 6.50 6.50

STAMPEX '86, Adelaide, Aug. 4-10.

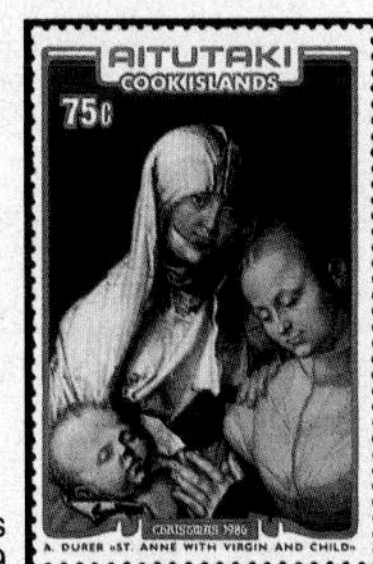

Christmas A79

Paintings by Albrecht Durer: 75c, No. 404a, St. Anne with Virgin and Child. $1.35, No. 404b, Virgin and Child. $1.95, No. 404c, Adoration of the Magi. $2.75, No. 404d, Rosary Festivity.

1986, Nov. 21 **Litho.** ***Perf. 13½***

400 A79 75c multicolored 1.50 1.50
401 A79 $1.35 multicolored 2.50 2.50
402 A79 $1.95 multicolored 3.50 3.50
403 A79 $2.75 multicolored 5.00 5.00
Nos. 400-403 (4) 12.50 12.50

Souvenir Sheet

404 Sheet of 4 17.00 17.00
a.-d. A79 $1.65 any single 4.00 4.00

For surcharges see Nos. B39-B44, B46-B47, B50-B54.

Nos. 247-249 Srchd. in Gold and Black

1987, Nov. 20 **Photo.** ***Perf. 13x12½***

405 A56 $2.50 on 60c No. 247 2.75 2.75
406 A56 $2.50 on 80c No. 248 2.75 2.75
407 A56 $2.50 on $1.40 No. 249 2.75 2.75
Nos. 405-407 (3) 8.25 8.25

Issued in sheets of 4 with margin inscriptions overprinted with gold bar and "40th Anniversary of the Royal Wedding / 1947-1987" in black; "OVERPRINTED BY NEW ZEALAND GOVERNMENT PRINTER, / WELLINGTON, NOVEMBER 1987" at left.

A80

The Virgin with Garland, by Rubens — A81

Painting details.

1987, Dec. 10 **Photo.** ***Perf. 13x13½***

408 A80 70c UL 2.25 2.25
409 A80 85c UR 2.75 2.75
410 A80 $1.50 LL 3.25 3.25
411 A80 $1.85 LR 4.00 4.00
Nos. 408-411 (4) 12.25 12.25

Souvenir Sheets

412 Sheet of 4 14.50 14.50
a. A80 95c like No. 408 3.50 3.50
b. A80 95c like No. 409 3.50 3.50
c. A80 95c like No. 410 3.50 3.50
d. A80 95c like No. 411 3.50 3.50

Perf. 13

413 A81 $6 multicolored 16.00 16.00

Christmas.

1988 Summer Olympics, Seoul — A82

Flags of Korea, Aitutaki, ancient and modern events, and Seoul Games emblem or $50 silver coin issued to commemorate the participation of Aitutaki athletes in the Olympics for the first time: 70c, No. 418a, Obverse of silver coin, chariot race, running. 85c, Emblem, running, soccer. 95c, Emblem, boxing, handball. $1.40, No. 418b, Reverse of coin, spearmen, women's tennis.

1988, Aug. 22 **Photo.** ***Perf. 14½x15***

414 A82 70c multicolored 2.50 2.50
415 A82 85c multicolored 2.75 2.75
416 A82 95c multicolored 2.75 2.75
417 A82 $1.40 multicolored 3.50 3.50
Nos. 414-417 (4) 11.50 11.50

Souvenir Sheet

418 Sheet of 2 9.00 9.00
a.-b. A82 $2 any single 4.25 4.25

Nos. 414-417 Ovptd. with Names of 1988 Olympic Gold Medalists

a

b

c

d

1988, Oct. 10 Litho. *Perf. 14½x15*

419	A82 (a)	70c on No. 414	2.00	2.00
420	A82 (b)	85c on No. 415	2.00	2.00
421	A82 (c)	95c on No. 416	2.00	2.00
422	A82 (d)	$1.40 on No. 417	4.25	4.25
		Nos. 419-422 (4)	10.25	10.25

Griffith is spelled incorrectly on No. 419.

Christmas A83

Paintings by Rembrandt: 55c, Adoration of the Shepherds (detail), National Gallery, London. 70c, Holy Family, Alte Pinakothek, Munich. 85c, Presentation in the Temple, Kunsthalle, Hamburg. 95c, The Holy Family, Louvre, Paris. $1.15, Presentation in the Temple, diff., Mauritshuis, The Hague. $4.50, Adoration of the Shepherds (entire painting).

1988, Nov. 2 Photo. *Perf. 13½*

423	A83	55c multicolored	2.00	2.00
424	A83	70c multicolored	2.25	2.25
425	A83	85c multicolored	2.50	2.50
426	A83	95c multicolored	2.75	2.75
427	A83	$1.15 multicolored	3.25	3.25
		Nos. 423-427 (5)	12.75	12.75

Souvenir Sheet

Perf. 14

428	A83	$4.50 multicolored	9.50	9.50

No. 428 contains one 52x34mm stamp.

A84

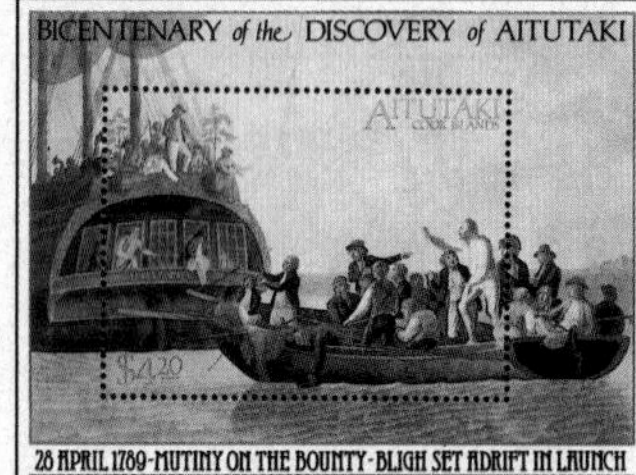

Mutiny on the *Bounty,* 200th Anniv. — A85

55c, Ship, Capt. Bligh. 65c, Breadfruit. 75c, Bligh, chart. 95c, Bounty off Aitutaki. $1.65, Christian, Bligh.
$4.20, Castaways.

1989, July 3 Photo. *Perf. 13½*

429	A84	55c multicolored	2.25	2.25
430	A84	65c multicolored	2.75	2.75
431	A84	75c multicolored	3.00	3.00
432	A84	95c multicolored	3.50	3.50
433	A84	$1.65 multicolored	4.25	4.25
		Nos. 429-433 (5)	15.75	15.75

Souvenir Sheet

434	A85	$4.20 multicolored	13.50	13.50

Discovery of Aitutaki by William Bligh, bicent.

1st Moon Landing, 20th Anniv. — A86

Apollo 11 mission emblem, American flag, eagle, "The Eagle has landed" and: 75c, Astronaut standing on the lunar surface. $1.15, Conducting an experiment in front of the lunar module. $1.80, Carrying equipment. $6.40, Raising the flag.

1989, July 28 Photo. *Perf. 13½x13*

435	A86	75c multicolored	3.00	3.00
436	A86	$1.15 multicolored	3.50	3.50
437	A86	$1.80 multicolored	4.50	4.50
		Nos. 435-437 (3)	11.00	11.00

Souvenir Sheet

Perf. 13½

438	A86	$6.40 multicolored	11.50	11.50

No. 438 contains one 42x31mm stamp.

Christmas — A87

Details from *Virgin in Glory,* by Titian: 70c, Virgin. 85c, Christ child. 95c, Angel. $1.25, Cherubs. $6, Entire painting.

1989, Nov. 20 Photo. *Perf. 13½x13*

439	A87	70c multicolored	2.50	2.50
440	A87	85c multicolored	3.00	3.00
441	A87	95c multicolored	3.50	3.50
442	A87	$1.25 multicolored	4.25	4.25
		Nos. 439-442 (4)	13.25	13.25

Souvenir Sheet

Perf. 13½

443	A87	$6 multicolored	13.00	13.00

No. 443 contains one 45x60mm stamp.

World Environmental Protection — A88

Designs: a, Human comet, World Philatelic Programs emblem. b, Comet tail and "Protect The Endangered Earth!" $3, Human comet, emblem and inscription.

1990, Feb. 16 Photo. *Perf. 13½x13*

444	A88	Pair	7.25	7.25
a.-b.		$1.75 any single	3.25	3.25

Souvenir Sheet

445	A88	$3 multicolored	8.00	8.00

No. 376a Overprinted

Designs: 55c, Lady Elizabeth Bowes-Lyon, 1907. 65c, Lady Elizabeth engaged to Duke of York. 75c, As Duchess of York with daughter Elizabeth. $1.30, As Queen Mother with grandson.

1990, July 16 Litho. *Perf. 13½x13*

446		Sheet of 4	16.00	16.00
a.		A72 55c multicolored	2.50	2.50
b.		A72 65c multicolored	3.25	3.25
c.		A72 75c multicolored	4.00	4.00
d.		A72 $1.30 multicolored	6.25	6.25

Christmas — A89

Paintings: 70c, Madonna of the Basket by Correggio. 85c, Virgin and Child by Morando. 95c, Adoration of the Child by Tiepolo. $1.75, Mystic Marriage of St. Catherine by Memling. $6, Donne Triptych by Memling.

1990, Nov. 28 Litho. *Perf. 14*

447	A89	70c multicolored	1.90	1.90
448	A89	85c multicolored	2.10	2.10
449	A89	95c multicolored	2.50	2.50
450	A89	$1.75 multicolored	3.50	3.50
		Nos. 447-450 (4)	10.00	10.00

Souvenir Sheet

451	A89	$6 multicolored	15.00	15.00

Nos. 246A-246B Overprinted

1990, Dec. 5 Photo. *Perf. 13½*

452	A55	$1 multicolored	6.50	6.50
453	A55	$2 multicolored	7.50	7.50

Birdpex '90, 20 Intl. Ornithological Congress, New Zealand.

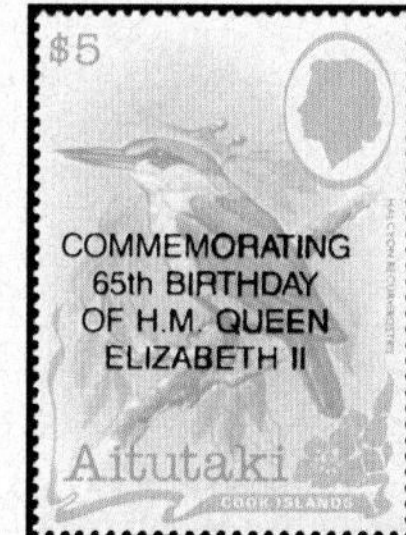

No. 246D Overprinted

1991, Apr. 22 Photo. *Perf. 13*

454	A55	$5 multicolored	13.00	13.00

Christmas — A90

Paintings: 80c, The Holy Family, by Mengs. 90c, Virgin and Child, by Fra Filippo Lippi. $1.05, Virgin and Child, by Durer. $1.75, Adoration of the Shepherds, by De La Tour. $6, The Holy Family, by Michelangelo.

1991, Nov. 13 Litho. *Perf. 14*

455	A90	80c multicolored	1.90	1.90
456	A90	90c multicolored	2.10	2.10
457	A90	$1.05 multicolored	2.50	2.50
458	A90	$1.75 multicolored	3.50	3.50
		Nos. 455-458 (4)	10.00	10.00

Souvenir Sheet

459	A90	$6 multicolored	16.00	16.00

1992 Summer Olympics, Barcelona — A91

1992, July 29 Litho. *Perf. 14*

460	A91	95c Hurdles	2.75	2.75
461	A91	$1.25 Weight lifting	3.00	3.00
462	A91	$1.50 Judo	3.50	3.50
463	A91	$1.95 Soccer	3.75	3.75
		Nos. 460-463 (4)	13.00	13.00

6th Festival of Pacific Arts, Rarotonga — A92

Canoes: 30c, Vaka Motu. 50c, Hamatafua. 95c, Alia Kalia Ndrua. $1.75, Hokule'a Hawaiian. $1.95, Tuamotu Pahi.

1992, Oct. 16 Litho. *Perf. 14x15*

464	A92	30c multicolored	.90	.90
465	A92	50c multicolored	1.10	1.10
466	A92	95c multicolored	2.25	2.25
467	A92	$1.75 multicolored	3.25	2.75
468	A92	$1.95 multicolored	4.00	4.00
		Nos. 464-468 (5)	11.50	11.00

For overprints see Nos. 524-528.

Nos. 464-468 Overprinted

1992, Oct. 16

469	A92	30c on #464	1.25	1.25
470	A92	50c on #465	2.00	2.00
471	A92	95c on #466	3.25	3.25
472	A92	$1.75 on #467	4.50	4.50
473	A92	$1.95 on #468	5.50	5.50
		Nos. 469-473 (5)	16.50	16.50

Christmas
A93

Designs: Different details from Virgin's Nativity, by Guido Reni.

1992, Nov. 19 Litho. *Perf. 13½*

474 A93 80c multicolored 2.25 2.25
475 A93 90c multicolored 2.25 2.25
476 A93 $1.05 multicolored 2.40 2.40
477 A93 $1.75 multicolored 3.75 3.75
Nos. 474-477 (4) 10.65 10.65

Souvenir Sheet

478 A93 $6 like #476 10.00 10.00

No. 478 contains one 39x50mm stamp.

Discovery of America, 500th Anniv. — A94

Designs: $1.25, Columbus being blessed as he departs from Spain. $1.75, Map of Columbus' four voyages. $1.95, Columbus landing in New World.

1992, Dec. 11 *Perf. 14x15*

479 A94 $1.25 multicolored 3.50 3.50
480 A94 $1.75 multicolored 4.25 4.25
481 A94 $1.95 multicolored 4.75 4.75
Nos. 479-481 (3) 12.50 12.50

Coronation of Queen Elizabeth II, 40th Anniv. — A95

Designs: a, Victoria, Edward VII. b, George V, George VI. c, Elizabeth II.

1993, June 4 Litho. *Perf. 14*

482 A95 $1.75 Strip of 3, #a.-c. 12.50 12.50

Christmas — A96

Religious sculpture: 80c, Madonna and Child, by Nino Pisano. 90c, Virgin on Rosebush, by Luca Della Robbia. $1.15, Virgin with Child and St. John, by Juan Francisco Rustici. $1.95, Virgin with Child, by Michelangelo. $3, Madonna and Child, by Jacopo Della Quercia.

1993, Oct. 29 Litho. *Perf. 14*

483 A96 80c multicolored 1.25 1.25
484 A96 90c multicolored 1.60 1.60
485 A96 $1.15 multicolored 2.00 2.00
486 A96 $1.95 multicolored 3.25 3.25

Size: 32x47mm

Perf. 13½

487 A96 $3 multicolored 5.50 5.50
Nos. 483-487 (5) 13.60 13.60

1994 Winter Olympics, Lillehammer — A97

Designs: a, Ice hockey. b, Ski jumping. c, Cross-country skiing.

1994, Feb. 11 Litho. *Perf. 14*

488 A97 $1.15 Strip of 3, #a.-c. 13.50 13.50

Flowers — A98

Hibiscus
A98a

1994-97 Litho. *Perf. 13½*

489 A98 5c Prostrate morning glory .25 .25
490 A98 10c White frangipani .25 .25
491 A98 15c Red hibiscus .35 .25
492 A98 20c Yellow allamanda .45 .25
493 A98 25c Royal poinciana .50 .25
494 A98 30c White gardenia .75 .40
495 A98 50c Pink frangipani 1.10 .85
496 A98 80c Morning glory 1.40 1.25
497 A98 85c Yellow mallow 1.60 1.40
498 A98 90c Red coral tree 1.60 1.40
499 A98 $1 Cup of gold 2.00 1.50
500 A98 $2 Red cordia 2.75 2.75
501 A98a $3 multicolored 4.50 4.50
502 A98a $5 multicolored 6.50 6.50
503 A98a $8 multicolored 10.00 10.00
Nos. 489-503 (15) 34.00 31.80

Issued: 5c-90c, 2/17; $1, $2, 4/29; $3, $5, 11/18; $8, 11/21/97.

First Manned Moon Landing, 25th Anniv. A99

Designs: No. 506, Astronauts Collins, Armstrong, Aldrin. No. 507, Splash down in South Pacific.

1994, July 20 Litho. *Perf. 14*

506 A99 $2 multicolored 8.25 8.25
507 A99 $2 multicolored 8.25 8.25

Christmas — A100

Paintings: No. 508a, The Madonna of the Basket, by Corregio. b, Virgin & Child with Saints, by Hans Memling. c, The Virgin & Child with Flowers, by Dolci. d, Virgin & Child with Angels, by Bergognone.

No. 509a, The Adoration of the Kings, by Dosso. b, The Virgin & Child, by Bellini. c, The Virgin & Child, by Schiavone. d, Adoration of the Kings, by Dolci.

1994, Nov. 30 Litho. *Perf. 14*

508 A100 85c Block of 4, #a.-d. 6.25 6.25
509 A100 90c Block of 4, #a.-d. 6.75 6.75

End of World War II, 50th Anniv. — A101

Designs: a, Battle of Britain, 1940. b, Battle of Midway, June 1942.

1995, Sept. 4 Litho. *Perf. 13½x13*

510 A101 $4 Pair, #a.-b. 27.50 27.50

No. 510 issued in sheets of 4 stamps.

Queen Mother, 95th Birthday A102

1995, Sept. 14 Litho. *Perf. 13x13½*

511 A102 $4 multicolored 12.50 12.50

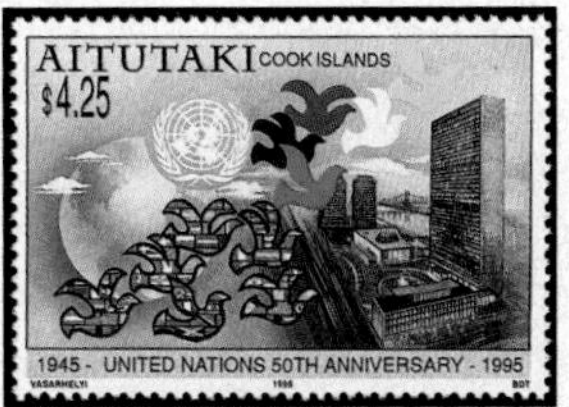

UN, 50th Anniv. — A103

1995, Oct. 18 Litho. *Perf. 13½*

512 A103 $4.25 multicolored 10.00 10.00

Year of the Sea Turtle A104

1995, Dec. 1 Litho. *Perf. 14x13½*

513 A104 95c Green 3.50 3.50
514 A104 $1.15 Leatherback 3.75 3.75
515 A104 $1.50 Olive Ridley 4.00 4.00
516 A104 $1.75 Loggerhead 4.50 4.50
Nos. 513-516 (4) 15.75 15.75

Queen Elizabeth II, 70th Birthday A105

1996, June 24 Litho. *Perf. 14*

517 A105 $4.50 multicolored 9.50 9.50

No. 517 was issued in sheets of 4.

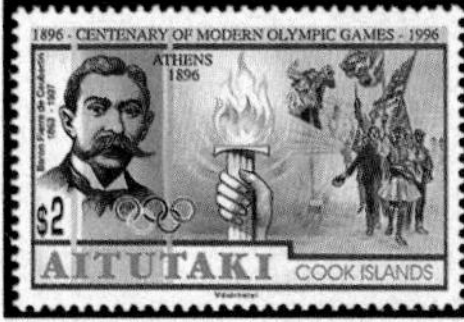

Modern Olympic Games, Cent. A106

Designs: No. 518, Pierre de Coubertin, Olympic torch, parading athletes, 1896. No. 519, Modern sprinters, US flag, Atlanta, 1996.

1996, July 11 Litho. *Perf. 14*

518 A106 $2 multicolored 6.00 6.00
519 A106 $2 multicolored 6.00 6.00
a. Pair, #518-519 12.00 12.00

Queen Elizabeth II and Prince Philip, 50th Wedding Anniv. A107

Designs: $2.50, Queen Elizabeth II, Prince Philip, Queen Mother, and King George VI. $6, like No. 520, close-up.

1997, Nov. 20 Litho. *Perf. 14*

520 A107 $2.50 multicolored 4.50 4.50

Souvenir Sheet

521 A107 $6 multicolored 10.00 10.00

No. 520 was issued in sheets of 4.

Diana, Princess of Wales (1961-97) — A108

1998, Apr. 15 Litho. *Perf. 14*

522 A108 $1 multicolored 1.25 1.25

Souvenir Sheet

523 A108 $4 like #522 6.00 6.00

No. 522 was issued in sheets of 5 + label. No. 523 is a continuous design.

For surcharge see No. B55.

Nos. 464-468 Overprinted

1999, Dec. 31 Litho. *Perf. 14x15*
524 A92 30c on #464 .40 .40
525 A92 50c on #465 .65 .65
526 A92 95c on #466 1.10 1.10
527 A92 $1.75 on #467 2.25 2.25
528 A92 $1.95 on #468 2.50 2.50
Nos. 524-528 (5) 6.90 6.90

Queen Mother, 100th Birthday — A109

No. 529: a, Wearing crown, blue-toned photograph. b, Wearing crown, color photograph. c, Wearing hat. d, With King George VI.

2000, Oct. 20 Litho. *Perf. 14*
529 A109 $3 Sheet of 4, #a-d 12.00 12.00

Souvenir Sheet

530 A109 $7.50 With flowers 8.00 8.00

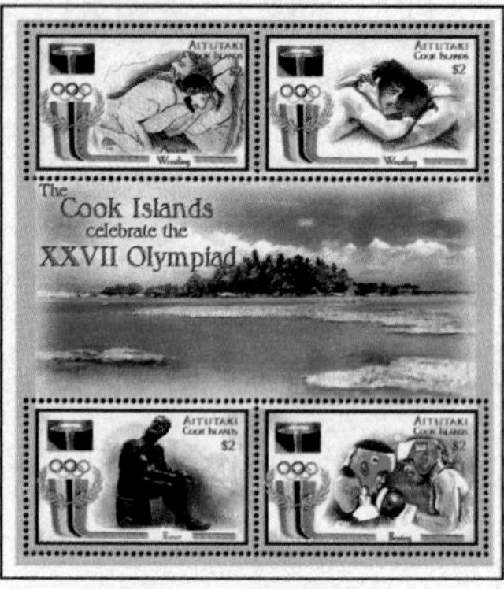

2000 Summer Olympics, Sydney — A110

No. 531: a, Ancient wrestling. b, Wrestling. c, Ancient boxer. d, Boxing.

2000, Dec. 14 Litho. *Perf. 14*
531 A110 $2 Sheet of 4, #a-d 8.75 8.75

Souvenir Sheet

532 A110 $2.75 Torch relay 3.50 3.50

Worldwide Fund for Nature (WWF) A111

Various views of two blue lorikeets: 80c, 90c, $1.15, $1.95.

2002, Sept. 3 Litho. *Perf. 14*
533-536 A111 Set of 4 6.50 6.50

United We Stand — A112

2003, Sept. 30 Litho. *Perf. 14*
537 A112 $1.15 multi 2.10 2.10

Printed in sheets of 4.

Pope John Paul II (1920-2005) A113

2005, Nov. 11 Litho. *Perf. 14*
538 A113 $1.95 multi 3.75 3.75

Printed in sheets of 5 + label.

Worldwide Fund for Nature (WWF) — A114

Blue moon butterfly: 80c, Caterpillar and chrysalis. 90c, Female. $1.15, Male. $1.95. Male, diff.

2008, Nov. 18 Litho. *Perf. 13½*
539-542 A114 Set of 4 6.00 6.00

Nos. 539-542 were each printed in sheets of 4.

Worldwide Fund for Nature (WWF) — A115

Designs: 80c, Tomato grouper. 90c, Peacock grouper. $1.10, Pair of Tomato groupers. $1.20, Head of Peacock grouper.

2010, Dec. 9 *Perf. 14*
543-546 A115 Set of 4 5.00 5.00

Tourism A116

Designs: 10c, Airplane, island. 20c, Bent palm tree, sun on horizon. 30c, Beach. 40c, Ship, islands. 50c, Road in forest. 60c, Islands and beach (at right) under dark skies. 70c, People fishing. 80c, Bent palm tree. 90c, Huts. $1, Islands and beach (at left). $1.10, Fence near beach. $1.20, Sun at horizon. $1.50, Moon above island. $2, Mountain on island. $3, Building and courtyard.

2010, Dec. 10
547 A116 10c multi .25 .25
548 A116 20c multi .30 .30
549 A116 30c multi .45 .45
550 A116 40c multi .60 .60
551 A116 50c multi .75 .75
552 A116 60c multi .90 .90
553 A116 70c multi 1.10 1.10
554 A116 80c multi 1.25 1.25
555 A116 90c multi 1.40 1.40
556 A116 $1 multi 1.50 1.50
557 A116 $1.10 multi 1.60 1.60
558 A116 $1.20 multi 1.75 1.75
559 A116 $1.50 multi 2.00 2.00
560 A116 $2 multi 2.75 2.75
561 A116 $3 multi 4.25 4.25
a. Sheet of 15, #547-561 21.00 21.00
Nos. 547-561 (15) 20.85 20.85

A117

Engagement of Prince William and Catherine Middleton — A118

Designs: Nos. 562, 565a, 567, 50c, Middleton. Nos. 563, 565b, 568, $5, Prince playing polo.

No. 564: a, Prince in military uniform. b, Prince playing polo. c, Middleton, fence. d, Prince, man and woman in background. e, Middleton, woman in background. f, Couple, Prince at left. g, Middleton with black hat. h, Prince. i, Couple, Middleton at left. j, Hands of couple, engagement ring.

$8.10, Couple, Prince in uniform at left.

2011, Jan. 14 *Perf. 14*
562 A117 50c multi .75 .75
563 A117 $5 multi 7.75 7.75

Miniature Sheets

564 A118 $1 Sheet of 10, #a-j 15.50 15.50

Perf. 13¾x13½

565 A117 Sheet of 2, #a-b 8.50 8.50

Souvenir Sheets

Perf. 14¼

566 A117 $8.10 multi 12.50 12.50
567 A117 $11 multi 17.00 17.00
568 A117 $11 multi 17.00 17.00
Nos. 566-568 (3) 46.50 46.50

No. 565 contains two 28x44mm stamps. Nos. 566-568 each contain one 38x50mm stamp.

Peonies A119

2011, Apr. 8 Litho. *Perf. 13¼*
569 A119 90c multi 1.40 1.40

Souvenir Sheet

Perf. 14¾x14

570 A119 $6.60 Peonies in vase, horiz. 10.50 10.50

No. 569 was printed in sheets of 6. No. 570 contains one 48x42mm stamp.

Souvenir Sheet

Wedding of Prince William and Catherine Middleton — A120

No. 571 — Bride and groom: a, $1.10, Walking down aisle. b, $1.20, Kneeling.

2011, July 15 *Perf. 15x14¼*
571 A120 Sheet of 2, #a-b 4.00 4.00

Aitutaki Marine Research Center — A121

Designs: 10c, Suspended cages underwater. 20c, Station manager Richard Story. 80c, Tridacna maxima. 90c, Tridacna maxima, diff. $1.10, Tridacna derasa. $1.20, Tridacna derasa, diff.

No. 578, vert.: a, $2, Researcher underwater. b, $3, Researcher lifting cage on boat.

2011, July 25 *Perf. 14¼x14*
572-577 A121 Set of 6 7.25 7.25

Souvenir Sheet

Perf. 13¾

578 A121 Sheet of 2, #a-b 8.50 8.50

Nos. 572-577 each were printed in sheets of 4. No. 578 contains two 30x38mm stamps.

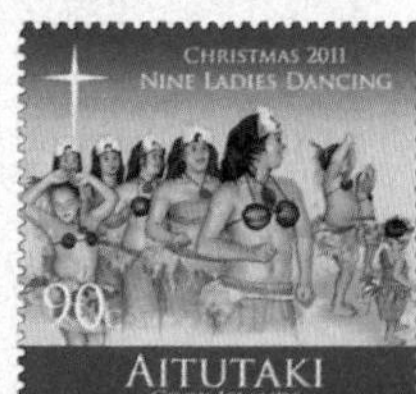

Christmas A122

No. 579 — Items from Christmas song "The Twelve Days of Christmas": a, Nine ladies dancing. b, Ten lords a leaping. c, Eleven pipers piping. d, Twelve drummers drumming.

2011, Dec. 24 Litho. *Perf. 13¼*
579 Horiz. strip of 4 8.25 8.25
a. A122 90c multi 1.50 1.50
b. A122 $1 multi 1.60 1.60
c. A122 $1.20 multi 1.90 1.90
d. A122 $2 multi 3.25 3.25
e. Souvenir sheet of 4, #579a-579d 8.25 8.25

No. 579 was printed in sheets containing three strips.

Beatification of Pope John Paul II — A123

No. 580: a, $1.10, Pope Benedict XVI. b, $5.10, Pope John Paul II.

2012, Jan. 10 *Perf. 13¾*
580 A123 Horiz. pair, #a-b 10.50 10.50

No. 580 was printed in sheets containing two pairs.

Cetaceans — A124

Designs: Nos. 581, 593a, 20c, Humpback whale. Nos. 582, 593b, 30c, Humpback whale tail. Nos. 583, 593c, 50c, Humpback whale, diff. Nos. 584, 593d, 80c, Striped dolphins. Nos. 585, 593e, 90c, Striped dolphins, diff. Nos. 586, 593f, $1, Striped dolphins, diff. Nos. 587, 593g, $1.10, Striped dolphin. Nos. 588, 593h, $1.20, Striped dolphins, diff. Nos. 589, 593i, $5, Striped dolphins, diff. Nos. 590, 593j, $6, Humpback whale tail, diff. Nos. 591, 593k, $7.50, Humpback whale, diff. Nos. 592, 593l, $10, Humpback whale, diff.

2012, June 22 *Perf. 14*

Stamps Without Dark Blue Frame Near Denomination

581-592 A124 Set of 12 55.00 55.00

Stamps With Dark Blue Frame All Around

593 A124 Sheet of 12, #a-l 55.00 55.00

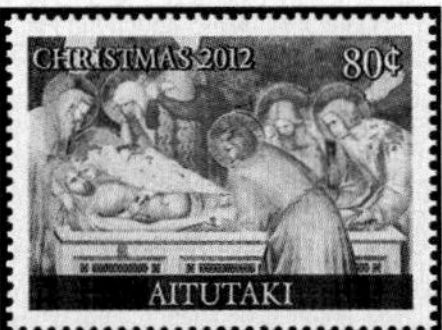

Entombment of Christ, by Pietro Lorenzetti — A125

The Last Supper, by Lorenzetti A126

Madonna with St. Francis and St. John the Evangelist, by Lorenzetti A127

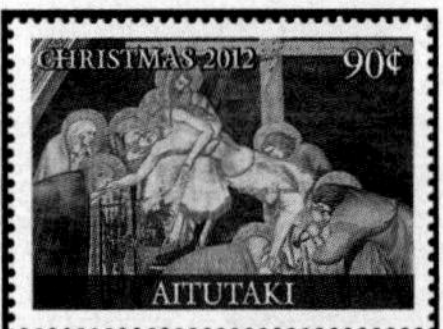

Deposition of Christ from the Cross, by Lorenzetti A128

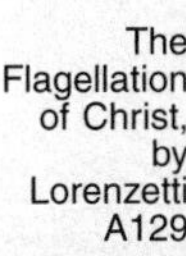

The Flagellation of Christ, by Lorenzetti A129

Entry of Christ Into Jerusalem, by Lorenzetti A130

Perf. 14¾x14¼

2012, Nov. 16 **Litho.**

Stamps With White Frames

594 Horiz. pair 2.80 2.80
a. A125 80c multi 1.40 1.40
b. A126 80c multi 1.40 1.40
595 Horiz. pair 3.00 3.00
a. A127 90c multi 1.50 1.50
b. A128 90c multi 1.50 1.50
596 Horiz. pair 10.00 10.00
a. A129 $3 multi 5.00 5.00
b. A130 $3 multi 5.00 5.00
Nos. 594-596 (3) 15.80 15.80

Miniature Sheet

Stamps Without White Frame

597 Sheet of 6 16.00 16.00
a. A125 80c multi 1.40 1.40
b. A126 80c multi 1.40 1.40
c. A127 90c multi 1.50 1.50
d. A128 90c multi 1.50 1.50
e. A129 $3 multi 5.00 5.00
f. A130 $3 multi 5.00 5.00

Christmas.

Personalizable Stamp — A131

2012, Dec. 21 **Litho.** *Perf. 14x14¾*
598 A131 $4 multi 6.75 6.75

Miniature Sheet

New Year 2013 (Year of the Snake) — A132

No. 599 — Snake with background color of: a, Green. b, Yellow, c, Pink. d, Violet.

2013, Feb. 21 **Litho.** *Perf. 14¾x14*
599 A132 $1.20 Sheet of 4, #a-d 8.00 8.00

Cetaceans — A133

Various boats and: Nos. 600, 612a, 10c, Humpback whale. Nos. 601, 612b, 40c, Humpback whale, diff. Nos. 602, 612c, 60c, Humpback whale, diff. Nos. 603, 612d, 70c, Striped dolphin. Nos. 604, 612e, $1.50, Striped dolphin, diff. Nos. 605, 612f, $1.80, Striped dolphin, diff. Nos. 606, 612g, $2, Striped dolphin, diff. Nos. 607, 612h, $2.25, Striped dolphin, diff. Nos. 608, 612i, $2.50, Striped dolphin, diff. Nos. 609, 612j, Humpback whale, diff. Nos. 610, 612k, $4, Humpback whale, diff. Nos. 611, 612l, $20, Humpback whale, diff.

2013, June 5 **Litho.** *Perf. 14*

Stamps With White Frames

600-611 A133 Set of 12 62.50 62.50

Miniature Sheet

Stamps Without White Frames

612 A133 Sheet of 12, #a-l 62.50 62.50

Souvenir Sheet

Birth of Prince George of Cambridge — A134

No. 613: a, $1.30, Duchess of Cambridge. b, $1.50, Duchess of Cambridge reviewing Scouts, Duchess and Duke of Cambridge kissing. c, $1.70, Duchess of Cambridge, diff.

2013, Aug. 1 **Litho.** *Perf. 13½*
613 A134 Sheet of 3, #a-c 7.25 7.25

Souvenir Sheet

China International Collection Expo — A135

No. 614: a, $1.50, Painting by Paul Gauguin. b, $1.70, Beijing Exhibition Center.

2013, Sept. 26 **Litho.** *Perf. 12*
614 A135 Sheet of 2, #a-b 5.50 5.50

Pres. John F. Kennedy (1917-63) A136

Designs: $2.50, Kennedy and quotation. $2.90, Kennedy.

2013, Nov. 8 **Litho.** *Perf. 14¼*
615-616 A136 Set of 2 9.00 9.00

Christmas — A137

Religious paintings by: $1, William Brassey Hole. $1.30, Bernardino Luini.

No. 619 — Religious paintings by: a, $2, Gentile da Fabriano. b, $2.40, Marten de Vos. c, $2.60, Pietro Perugino.

2013, Nov. 18 **Litho.** *Perf. 13¼*
617-618 A137 Set of 2 4.00 4.00

Souvenir Sheet

619 A137 Sheet of 3, #a-c 11.50 11.50

SEMI-POSTAL STAMPS

Christmas Type of 1974

Designs: 1c+1c, like No. 104. 5c+1c, like No. 105. 8c+1c, like No. 106. 10c+1c, like No. 107. 25c+1c, like No. 108. 30c+1c, like No. 109.

1974, Dec. 2 **Photo.** *Perf. 13½*
B1 A29 1c + 1c multicolored .25 .25
B2 A29 5c + 1c multicolored .25 .25
B3 A29 8c + 1c multicolored .25 .25
B4 A29 10c + 1c multicolored .25 .25
B5 A29 25c + 1c multicolored .30 .30
B6 A29 30c + 1c multicolored .30 .30
Nos. B1-B6 (6) 1.60 1.60

Surtax was for child welfare.

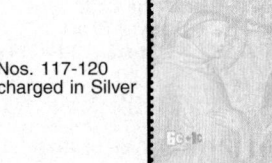

Nos. 117-120 Surcharged in Silver

1975, Dec. 19 **Photo.** *Perf. 14x13½*
B7 A32 Strip of 3 .45 .45
a.-c. 6c+1c any single .25 .25
B8 A32 Strip of 3 .50 .50
a.-c. 7c+1c any single .25 .25
B9 A32 Strip of 3 1.00 1.00
a.-c. 15c+1c any single .30 .30
B10 A32 Strip of 3 1.50 1.50
a.-c. 20c+1c any single .45 .45
Nos. B7-B10 (4) 3.45 3.45

Christmas. The surtax was for children's activities during holiday season.

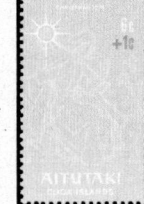

Nos. 135-142a Surcharged in Silver

1976, Nov. 19 **Photo.** *Perf. 13½x13*
B11 6c + 1c multicolored .25 .25
B12 6c + 1c multicolored .25 .25
a. A36 Pair, #B11-B12 .25 .25
B13 7c + 1c multicolored .25 .25
B14 7c + 1c multicolored .25 .25
a. A36 Pair, #B13-B14 .25 .25
B15 15c + 1c multicolored .25 .25
B16 15c + 1c multicolored .25 .25
a. A36 Pair, #B15-B16 .45 .45
B17 20c + 1c multicolored .30 .30
B18 20c + 1c multicolored .50 .50
a. A36 Pair, #B17-B18 1.00 1.00
b. Souvenir sheet of 8 2.00 2.00

Surtax was for child welfare. Stamps of No. B18b each surcharged 2c.

Nos. 152-159a Surcharged in Black

1977, Nov. 15 *Perf. 13½x14*
B19 6c + 1c multicolored .25 .25
B20 6c + 1c multicolored .25 .25
a. A41 Pair, #B19-B20 .25 .25
B21 7c + 1c multicolored .25 .25
B22 7c + 1c multicolored .25 .25
a. A41 Pair, #B21-B22 .25 .25
B23 15c + 1c multicolored .25 .25
B24 15c + 1c multicolored .25 .25
a. A41 Pair, #B23-B24 .50 .50

B25 20c + 1c multicolored .30 .30
B26 20c + 1c multicolored .30 .30
a. A41 Pair, #B25-B26 .65 .65
b. Souvenir sheet of 8 2.50 2.50
Nos. B19-B26 (8) 2.10 2.10

Surtax was for child welfare. Stamps of No. B26b each surcharged 2c.

Easter Type of 1978
Souvenir Sheets

Paintings: No. B27, like No. 163. No. B28, like No. 164. No. B29, like No. 165.

1978, Mar. 17 Photo. *Perf. 14*
B27 A44 50c + 5c multicolored .65 .65
B28 A44 50c + 5c multicolored .65 .65
B29 A44 50c + 5c multicolored .65 .65

Nos. B27-B29 contain one stamp 33x25mm.

Christmas Type of 1978
Souvenir Sheet

1978, Dec. 4 Photo. *Perf. 14½x13*
B30 Sheet of 4 2.60 2.60
a. A46 15c + 2c like #167 .35 .35
b. A46 17c + 2c like #168 .40 .40
c. A46 30c + 2c like #169 .60 .60
d. A46 35c + 2c like #170 .75 .75

Year of the Child Type
Souvenir Sheet

1979, Oct. 1 Photo. *Perf. 14x13½*
B31 Sheet of 3 1.25 1.25
a. A48 30c + 3c like #173 .30 .30
b. A48 35c + 3c like #174 .35 .35
c. A48 65c + 3c like #175 .45 .45

Easter Type of 1980
Souvenir Sheet

No. B32 shows entire painting in continuous design. Nos. B32a-B32c similar to Nos. 183-185. Size of Nos. B32a-B32c: 25x50mm.

1980, Apr. 3 Photo. *Perf. 13x13½*
B32 Sheet of 3 1.90 1.90
a. A50 20c + 2c multicolored .45 .45
b. A50 30c + 2c multicolored .60 .60
c. A50 35c + 2c multicolored .75 .75

Christmas Type of 1980
Souvenir Sheet

1980, Nov. 21 Photo. *Perf. 13x13½*
B33 Sheet of 4 1.50 1.50
a. A53 15c + 2c like #208 .25 .25
b. A53 20c + 2c like #209 .30 .30
c. A53 25c + 2c like #210 .35 .35
d. A53 35c + 2c like #211 .45 .45

Easter Type of 1981
Souvenir Sheet

1981, Mar. 31 Photo. *Perf. 13½*
B34 Sheet of 3 1.65 1.65
a. A54 30c + 2c like #212 .35 .35
b. A54 40c + 2c like #213 .50 .50
c. A54 50c + 2c like #214 .65 .65

Nos. 247-249 Surcharged

1981, Nov. 23 Photo. *Perf. 13x13½*
B35 A56 60 + 5c multi .65 .65
B36 A56 80 + 5c multi .70 .70
B37 A56 $1.40 + 5c multi .90 .90
Nos. B35-B37 (3) 2.25 2.25

Intl. Year of the Disabled. Surtax was for the handicapped.

Soccer Type of 1981
Souvenir Sheet

1981, Nov. 30 *Perf. 14*
B38 A57 Sheet of 8, multi 6.00 6.00

No. B38 contains stamps with 2c surtax similar to Nos. 250-253. Surtax was for local sports.

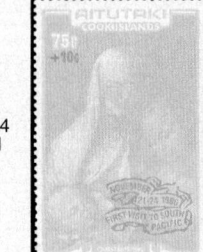

Nos. 400-404 Surcharged

1986, Nov. 25 Litho. *Perf. 13½*
B39 A79 75c + 10c multi 3.75 3.25
B40 A79 $1.35 + 10c multi 4.25 3.75
B41 A79 $1.95 + 10c multi 6.00 5.00
B42 A79 $2.75 + 10c multi 7.00 7.50
Nos. B39-B42 (4) 21.00 19.50

Souvenir Sheet

B43 Sheet of 4 22.50 22.50
a.-d. A79 $1.65 +10c on #404a-404d, each 6.00 6.00

State visit of Pope John Paul II.
For surcharges see Nos. B51-B54.

Nos. 394-395, 397 and 400-403 Surcharged in Silver or Black

1987, Apr. 29 Litho. *Perf. 13½, 14*
B44 A79 75c + 50c #400 3.50 2.50
B45 A77 $1 + 50c #394 (B) 4.25 3.50
B46 A79 $1.35 + 50c #401 5.75 5.00
B47 A79 $1.95 + 50c #402 6.25 5.00
B48 A78 $2 + 50c #397 6.50 5.00
B49 A77 $2.75 + 50c #395 (B) 8.00 6.25
B50 A79 $2.75 + 50c #403 8.50 7.25
Nos. B44-B50 (7) 42.75 34.50

Nos. B39-B42 Surcharged in Silver

1987, Apr. 29 Litho. *Perf. 13½*
B51 A79 75c + 50c No. B39 4.00 4.00
B52 A79 $1.35 + 50c No. B40 4.50 4.50
B53 A79 $1.95 + 50c No. B41 4.75 4.75
B54 A79 $2.75 + 50c No. B42 6.00 6.00
Nos. B51-B54 (4) 19.25 19.25

No. 523 Surcharged in Silver

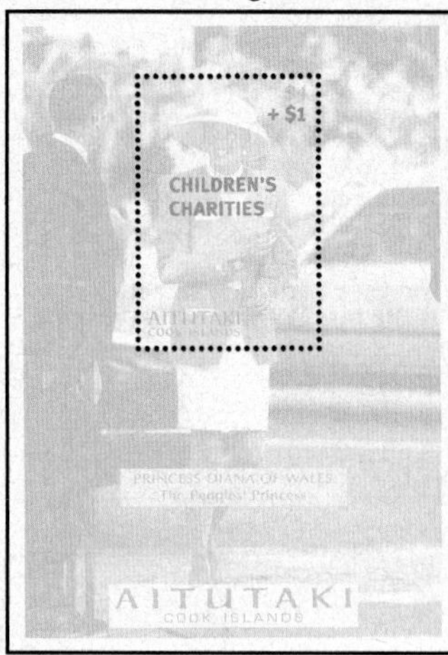

Souvenir Sheet

1998, Nov. 19 Litho. *Perf. 14*
B55 A108 $4 + $1 multicolored 6.25 6.25

AIR POST STAMPS

Capt. Bligh Type of 1974

1974, Sept. 9 Litho. *Perf. 13*
Size: 46x26mm
C1 A27 10c Bligh and "Bounty" .75 .60
C2 A27 10c "Bounty" at sea .75 .60
a. Pair, #C1-C2 1.75 1.60
C3 A27 25c Bligh and "Bounty" .90 .90
C4 A27 25c Chart, 1856 .90 .90
a. Pair, #C3-C4 2.00 2.00
C5 A27 30c Cook and "Resolution" 1.50 1.50
C6 A27 30c Maps 1.50 1.50
a. Pair, #C5-C6 3.25 3.25
Nos. C1-C6 (6) 6.30 6.00

See note after No. 101.

OFFICIAL STAMPS

Nos. 83-90, 92-95, 150-151 Ovptd. or Srchd. in Black, Silver or Gold

1978-79 Photo. *Perf. 13x13½*
O1 A25 1c multi 1.10 .25
O2 A25 2c multi 1.75 .25
O3 A25 3c multi 1.75 .25
O4 A25 4c multi (G) 1.75 .25
O5 A25 5c multi 1.75 .25
O6 A25 8c multi 1.75 .25
O7 A25 10c multi 2.00 .25
O8 A25 15c on 60c multi 3.50 .25
O9 A25 18c on 60c multi 3.50 .25
O10 A25 20c multi (G) 3.50 .25
O11 A40 50c multi 1.50 .70
O12 A25 60c multi 12.00 .80
O13 A25 $1 multi 12.00 1.00
O14 A26 $2 multi 11.00 .80
O15 A40 $4 on $1 multi (S) 2.50 .80
O16 A26 $5 multi 13.00 1.50
Nos. O1-O16 (16) 74.35 8.10

Overprint on 4c, 20c, $1 diagonal.
Issued: Nos. O14-O16, 2/20/79; others, 11/3/78.

Stamps of 1983-84 Ovptd. or Surcharged in Green

or Gold (#O29-O32)

1985, Aug. 9 *Perf. 14, 13x13½*
O17 A66 2c No. 322 2.10 2.10
O18 A66 5c No. 324 2.50 2.50
O19 A66 10c No. 325 3.00 3.00
O20 A66 12c No. 326 3.25 3.00
O21 A66 18c No. 327 4.00 3.50
O22 A66 20c on 24c No. 328 4.50 3.75
O23 A66 30c No. 329 3.50 2.50
O24 A66 40c on 36c No. 330 3.50 2.50
O25 A66 50c No. 332 3.50 2.50
O26 A66 55c on 48c No. 331 3.50 2.50
O27 A66 60c No. 333 4.00 2.75
O28 A66 65c on 72c No. 334 4.00 2.75
O29 A61 75c on 48c No. 276 2.50 2.10
O30 A61 75c on 48c No. 277 2.50 2.10
O31 A61 75c on 48c No. 278 2.50 2.10
O32 A61 75c on 48c No. 279 2.50 2.10
a. Block of 4, Nos. O29-O32 11.00 11.00
O33 A66 80c on 96c No. 335 4.00 3.75
Nos. O17-O33 (17) 55.35 45.50

Nos. 336-341 Overprinted Like Nos. O17-O21, O23, O25, O27 in Metallic Green

1986, Oct. 1 *Perf. 14*
O34 A66 $3 multi 8.50 6.50
O35 A66 $4.20 multi 11.00 8.50
O36 A66 $5.60 multi 12.00 10.00
O37 A66 $9.60 multi 15.00 12.00

1988-91 *Perf. 14*
O38 A66 $1.20 multi 5.00 2.50
O39 A66 $2.10 multi 7.50 4.00

Nos. 246C-246D Surcharged in Metallic Blue

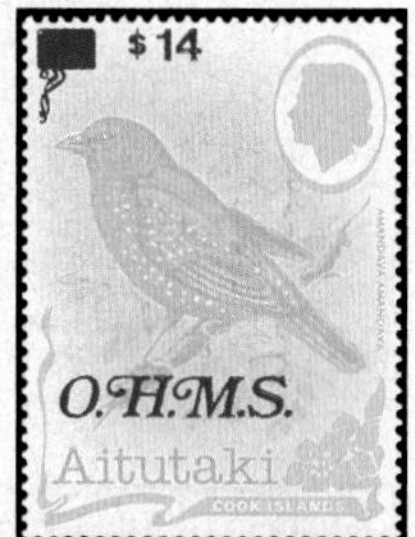

O40 A55 $14 on $4 (B) 17.50 14.00
O41 A55 $18 on $5 (B) 22.50 19.00
Nos. O34-O41 (8) 99.00 76.50

Issue dates: July 2, 1991; others, June 15.

AJMAN

äj-'man

LOCATION — Oman Peninsula, Arabia, on Persian Gulf
GOVT. — Sheikdom under British Protection
AREA — 100 sq. mi.
POP. — 4,400
CAPITAL — Ajman

Ajman is one of six Persian Gulf sheikdoms to join the United Arab Emirates, which proclaimed its independence Dec. 2, 1971. See United Arab Emirates.

100 Naye Paise = 1 Rupee

Catalogue values for all unused stamps in this country are for Never Hinged items.

Sheik Rashid bin Humaid al Naimi & Arab Stallion A1

Designs: 2np, 50np, Regal angelfish. 3np, 70np, Camel. 4np, 1r, Angelfish. 5np, 1.50r, Green turtle. 10np, 2r, Jewelfish. 15np, 3r, White storks. 20np, 5r, White-eyed gulls. 30np, 10r, Lanner falcon. 40np as 1np.

Photo. & Litho.

1964 Unwmk. *Perf. 14*

Size: 35x22mm

No.	Type	Description	Unused	Used
1	A1	1np gold & multi	.25	.25
2	A1	2np gold & multi	.25	.25
3	A1	3np gold & multi	.25	.25
4	A1	4np gold & multi	.25	.25
5	A1	5np gold & multi	.25	.25
6	A1	10np gold & multi	.25	.25
7	A1	15np gold & multi	.25	.25
8	A1	20np gold & multi	.25	.25
9	A1	30np gold & multi	.25	.25

Size: 42x27mm

No.	Type	Description	Unused	Used
10	A1	40np gold & multi	.25	.25
11	A1	50np gold & multi	.25	.25
12	A1	70np gold & multi	.25	.25
13	A1	1r gold & multi	.40	.25
14	A1	1.50r gold & multi	.50	.35
15	A1	2r gold & multi	.85	.50

Size: 53x33½mm

No.	Type	Description	Unused	Used
16	A1	3r gold & multi	1.25	.90
17	A1	5r gold & multi	3.25	2.00
18	A1	10r gold & multi	5.00	3.50
		Nos. 1-18 (18)	14.25	10.50

Issued: Nos. 1-9, 6/20; Nos. 10-15, 9/7; Nos. 16-18, 11/4. Exist imperf. Value, set $22.

Pres. and Mrs. John F. Kennedy with Caroline — A2

Pres. Kennedy: 10np, As a boy in football uniform. 15np, Diving. 50np, As navy lieutenant, receiving Navy and Marine Corps Medal from Capt. Frederic L. Conklin. 1r, Sailing with Jacqueline Kennedy. 2r, With Eleanor Roosevelt. 5r, With Lyndon B. Johnson and Hubert H. Humphrey. 10r, Portrait.

1964, Dec. 15 Photo. *Perf. 13½x14*

No.	Type	Description	Unused	Used
19	A2	10np grn & red lil	.25	.25
20	A2	15np Prus bl & vio	.25	.25
21	A2	50np org brn & dk bl	.25	.25
22	A2	1r brn & Prus grn	.50	.30
23	A2	2r red lil & dp ol	.75	.40
24	A2	3r grn & red brn	1.25	.50
25	A2	5r vio & brn	2.25	1.50
26	A2	10r dk bl & red brn	4.75	2.25
		Nos. 19-26 (8)	10.25	5.70

John F. Kennedy (1917-63). Exist imperf. Value, set $14. A souvenir sheet contains one each of Nos. 23-26. Value, perf or imperf, $14.

Runners at Start — A3

10np, 1.50r, Boxing. 25np, 2r, Judo. 50np, 5r, Gymnast on vaulting horse. 1r, 3r, Sailing yacht.

1965, Jan. 12 Photo. *Perf. 13½x14*

No.	Type	Description	Unused	Used
27	A3	5np red brn, brt pink & Prus grn	.25	.25
28	A3	10np dk ol grn, bl gray & red brn	.25	.25
29	A3	15np dk vio, grn & sep	.25	.25
30	A3	25np bl sal pink & blk	.25	.25
31	A3	50np mar, bl & ind	.25	.25
32	A3	1r dk grn, lil & ultra	.40	.25
33	A3	1.50r lil, grn & brn	.60	.40
34	A3	2r red org, bis & dk bl	1.00	.70
35	A3	3r dk brn, grnsh bl & lil	1.75	.95
36	A3	5r grn, yel & red brn	2.50	1.60
		Nos. 27-36 (10)	7.50	5.15

18th Olympic Games, Tokyo, Oct. 10-25, 1964. Exist imperf. Value, set $7.50. A souvenir sheet contains four stamps similar to Nos. 33-36 in changed colors. Values: perf $5; imperf $9.

Stanley Gibbons Catalogue, 1865, U.S. No. 1X2 — A4

Designs: 10np, Austria, Scarlet Mercury 1856. 15np, British Guiana 1c, 1856. 25np, Canada 12p, 1851. 50np, Hawaii 2c, 1851. 1r, Mauritius 2p, 1847. 3r, Switzerland, Geneva 10c, 1843. 5r, Tuscany 31, 1860. 5np, 15np, 50np and 3r show first edition of Stanley Gibbons Catalogue; 10np, 25np, 1r and 5r show 1965 Elizabethan Catalogue.

1965, May 6 Unwmk. *Perf. 13*

No.	Type	Description	Unused	Used
37	A4	5np multi	.25	.25
38	A4	10np multi	.25	.25
39	A4	15np multi	.25	.25
40	A4	25np multi	.25	.25
41	A4	50np multi	.25	.25
42	A4	1r multi	.45	.25
43	A4	3r multi	1.25	.50
a.		Souv. sheet of 4, #38-39, 42-43	3.75	
44	A4	5r multi	2.25	.95
a.		Souv. sheet of 4, #37, 40-41, 44	3.25	
		Nos. 37-44 (8)	5.20	2.95

Gibbons Catalogue Cent. Exhib., London, Feb. 17-20. Nos. 43a and 44a for 125th anniv. of 1st postage stamp. Exist imperf. Value, set $6.50. Sheets exist imperf. Value for both sheets, $7.

Stamps of Ajman were replaced in 1972 by those of United Arab Emirates.

AIR POST STAMPS

Type of Regular Issue, 1964

Designs: 15np, Arab stallion. 25np, Regal angelfish. 35np, Camel. 50np, Angelfish. 75np, Green turtle. 1r, Jewelfish. 2r, White storks. 3r, White-eyed gulls. 5r, Lanner falcon.

Photo. & Litho.

1965 Unwmk. *Perf. 14*

Size: 42x25½mm

No.	Type	Description	Unused	Used
C1	A1	15np silver & multi	.25	.25
C2	A1	25np silver & multi	.25	.25
C3	A1	35np silver & multi	.25	.25
C4	Al	50np silver & multi	.30	.25
C5	A1	75np silver & multi	.55	.25
C6	A1	1r silver & multi	.40	.25

Size: 53x33½mm

No.	Type	Description	Unused	Used
C7	A1	2r silver & multi	1.00	.50
C8	A1	3r silver & multi	2.50	.75
C9	A1	5r silver & multi	3.75	1.00
		Nos. C1-C9 (9)	9.25	3.75

Issued: Nos. C1-C6, 11/15; Nos. C7-C9, 12/18. Exist imperf. Value, set $10.

AIR POST OFFICIAL STAMPS

Type of Regular Issue, 1964

Designs: 75np, Jewelfish. 2r, White storks. 3r, White-eyed gulls. 5r, Lanner falcon.

Photo. & Litho.

1965, Dec. 18 Unwmk. *Perf. 14*

Size: 42x25½mm

No.	Type	Description	Unused	Used
CO1	A1	75np gold & multi	.60	.25

Size: 53x33½mm

No.	Type	Description	Unused	Used
CO2	A1	2r gold & multi	2.00	.40
CO3	A1	3r gold & multi	2.50	.90
CO4	A1	5r gold & multi	4.25	1.25
		Nos. CO1-CO4 (4)	9.35	2.80

OFFICIAL STAMPS

Type of Regular Issue, 1964

25np, Arab stallion. 40np, Regal angelfish. 50np, Camel. 75np, Angelfish. 1r, Green turtle.

Photo. & Litho.

1965, Dec. 1 Unwmk. *Perf. 14*

Size: 42x25½mm

No.	Type	Description	Unused	Used
O1	A1	25np gold & multi	.25	.25
O2	A1	40np gold & multi	.35	.25
O3	A1	50np gold & multi	.45	.30
O4	A1	75np gold & multi	.55	.35
O5	A1	1r gold & multi	.80	.40
		Nos. O1-O5 (5)	2.40	1.55

ALAOUITES

'al-au-ˌwïtz

LOCATION — A division of Syria, in Western Asia
GOVT. — Under French Mandate
AREA — 2,500 sq. mi.
POP. — 278,000 (approx. 1930)
CAPITAL — Latakia

This territory became an independent state in 1924, although still administered under the French Mandate. In 1930, it was renamed Latakia, and Syrian stamps overprinted "Lattaquie" superseded the stamps of Alaouites. For these and subsequent issues, see Latakia and Syria.

100 Centimes = 1 Piaster

Issued under French Mandate

Stamps of France Surcharged

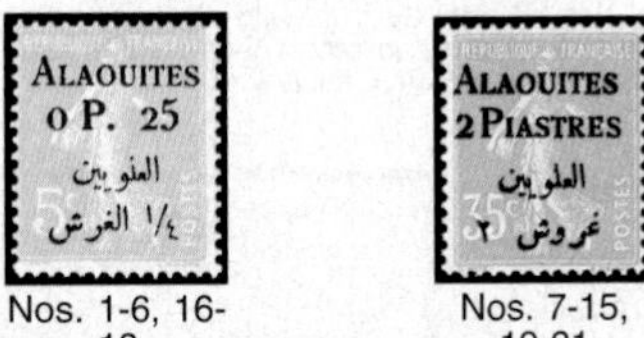

Nos. 1-6, 16-18 — Nos. 7-15, 19-21

1925 Unwmk. *Perf. 14x13½*

No.	Type	Description	Unused	Used
1	A16	10c on 2c vio brn	3.50	3.50
2	A22	25c on 5c orange	3.50	3.50
3	A20	75c on 15c gray grn	6.50	6.50
4	A22	1p on 20c red brn	3.50	3.50
5	A22	1.25p on 25c blue	4.00	4.00
6	A22	1.50p on 30c red	12.50	12.50
7	A22	2p on 35c violet	4.00	*4.00*
8	A18	2p on 40c red & pale bl	4.75	4.75
9	A18	2p on 45c grn & bl	17.00	17.00
10	A18	3p on 60c vio & ultra	7.50	7.50
11	A20	3p on 60c lt vio	12.00	12.00
b.		Double surcharge	160.00	160.00
12b	A20	4p on 85c vermilion	3.00	*3.00*
c.		As "b," inverted surcharge	50.00	50.00
13	A18	5p on 1fr cl & ol grn	7.50	7.50
14	A18	10p on 2fr org & pale bl	11.00	11.00
15	A18	25p on 5fr bl & buff	14.00	14.00
		Nos. 1-15 (15)	113.75	99.00

Two types of surcharge exist on the 4p and on the 5p-25p. For detailed listings, see the *Scott Classic Specialized Catalogue of Stamps and Covers 1840-1940.*

For overprints, see Nos. C1-C4.

Same Surcharges on Pasteur Stamps of France

No.	Type	Description	Unused	Used
16	A23	50c on 10c green	3.00	3.00
17	A23	75c on 15c green	3.75	3.75
18	A23	1.50p on 30c red	3.00	3.00
19	A23	2p on 45c red	3.75	3.75
20	A23	2.50p on 50c blue	5.25	5.25
21	A23	4p on 75c blue	9.00	9.00
		Nos. 16-21 (6)	27.75	*27.75*

Two types of overprints exist on No. 21. For detailed listings, see *Scott Classic Specialized Catalogue of Stamps and Covers 1840-1940.*

Inverted Surcharges

No.	Type	Description	Value
1a	A16	10c on 2c vio brn	32.50
2a	A22	25c on 5c orange	32.50
3a	A20	75c on 15c gray grn	40.00
4a	A22	1p on 20c red brn	32.50
5a	A22	1.25p on 25c blue	32.50
6a	A22	1.50p on 30c red	47.50
7a	A22	2p on 35c violet	47.50
8a	A18	2p on 40c red & pale bl	47.50
9a	A18	2p on 45c grn & bl	47.50
10a	A18	3p on 60c vio & ultra	45.00
11a	A20	3p on 60c lt vio	47.50
12a	A20	4p on 85c vermilion	37.50
13a	A18	5p on 1fr cl & ol grn	37.50
14a	A18	10p on 2fr org & pale bl	37.50
15a	A18	25p on 5fr bl & buff	37.50
16a	A23	50c on 10c green	30.00
17a	A23	75c on 15c green	37.50
18a	A23	1.50p on 30c red	45.00
19a	A23	2p on 45c red	35.00
20a	A23	2.50p on 50c blue	30.00
21a	A23	4p on 75c blue	35.00

Stamps of Syria, 1925, Overprinted in Red, Black or Blue

On A3, A5

On A4

1925, Mar. 1 *Perf. 12½, 13½*

No.	Type	Description	Unused	Used
25	A3	10c dk violet (R)	1.50	*2.25*
a.		Double overprint	40.00	40.00
b.		Inverted overprint	32.50	
c.		Black overprint	35.00	35.00
e.		"ALAOUITE," instead of "ALAOUITES"	27.50	*27.50*
26	A4	25c olive black (R)	2.25	*3.00*
a.		Inverted overprint	37.50	
b.		Blue overprint	47.50	47.50
27	A4	50c yellow green	1.75	1.75
a.		Inverted overprint	37.50	37.50
b.		Blue overprint	45.00	45.00
c.		Red overprint	45.00	45.00
e.		Double overprint	45.00	45.00
28	A4	75c brown orange	2.00	*2.25*
a.		Inverted overprint	40.00	*60.00*
b.		Double overprint	42.50	*65.00*
29	A5	1p magenta	2.75	2.75
a.		Inverted overprint	37.50	*47.50*
30	A4	1.25p deep green	3.25	*3.50*
a.		Red overprint	45.00	45.00
b.		Double overprint		70.00
31	A4	1.50p rose red (Bl)	2.75	*3.00*
a.		Inverted overprint	40.00	40.00
b.		Black overprint	37.50	37.50
c.		As "b", inverted	70.00	
32	A4	2p dk brown (R)	2.75	*3.50*
a.		Blue overprint	60.00	60.00
b.		Inverted overprint	35.00	35.00

33 A4 2.50p pck blue (R) 4.00 *4.50*
a. Black overprint 60.00 60.00
34 A4 3p orange brown 2.50 *2.75*
a. Inverted overprint 35.00 35.00
b. Blue overprint 65.00 65.00
c. Double overprint 75.00
35 A4 5p violet 3.50 *4.00*
a. Red overprint 65.00 65.00
b. Inverted overprint 37.50
36 A4 10p violet brown 5.00 *6.00*
37 A4 25p ultra (R) 8.00 *10.00*
Nos. 25-37 (13) 42.00 *49.25*

For overprints see Nos. C5-C19.

Stamps of Syria, 1925, Surcharged in Black or Red

Nos. 38-42

Nos. 43-45

1926

38 A4 3.50p on 75c brn org 2.50 *2.75*
a. Surcharged on face and back 19.00 19.00
39 A4 4p on 25c ol blk 2.50 *2.50*
40 A4 6p on 2.50p pck bl (R) 3.00 *3.25*
41 A4 12p on 1.25p dp grn 3.25 *3.50*
a. Inverted surcharge 32.50 32.50
42 A4 20p on 1.25p dp grn 5.25 5.25
43 A4 4.50p on 75c brn org 5.25 3.25
a. Inverted surcharge 50.00 50.00
b. Double surcharge 45.00 45.00
44 A4 7.50p on 2.50p pck bl 4.75 3.25
45 A4 15p on 25p ultra 8.75 5.50
Nos. 38-45 (8) 35.25 *29.25*

Two types of overprints exist on No. 39. For detailed listings, see *Scott Classic Specialized Catalogue of Stamps and Covers 1840-1940.*
For overprint, see No. C21.

Syria No. 199 Ovptd. in Red like No. 25

1928

46 A3 5c on 10c dk violet 2.00 1.75
a. Double surcharge 35.00

Syria Nos. 178 and 174 Surcharged like Nos. 43-45 in Red

47 A4 2p on 1.25p dp green 16.00 8.00
a. Double surcharge 50.00
b. Inverted surcharge 47.50 47.50
48 A4 4p on 25c olive black 11.00 6.50
a. Double surcharge 40.00 40.00
b. Inverted surcharge 40.00 40.00

For overprint see No. C20.

49 A4 4p on 25c olive black 82.50 50.00
a. Double impression 135.00
Nos. 46-49 (4) 111.50 66.25

AIR POST STAMPS

Nos. 8, 10, 13 & 14 with Additional Ovpt. in Black

1925, Jan. 1 Unwmk. ***Perf. 14x13½***

C1b A18 2p on 40c 14.00 14.00
C2 A18 3p on 60c 20.00 *17.50*
a. Inverted overprint 110.00 110.00
C3 A18 5p on 1fr 15.00 12.00
a. Inverted overprint 32.50 *32.50*
C4 A18 10p on 2fr 19.00 15.00
a. Inverted overprint 32.50 *32.50*
Nos. C1-C4 (4) 66.00 *56.50*

Two types of overprints exist on Nos. C1-C4. For detailed listings, see *Scott Classic Specialized Catalogue of Stamps and Covers 1840-1940.*

Nos. 32, 34, 35 & 36 With Additional Ovpt. in Green

1925, Mar. 1 ***Perf. 13½***

C5 A4 2p dark brown 6.00 5.00
a. Inverted overprint 55.00 55.00
b. Red overprint 100.00
C6 A4 3p orange brown 6.00 5.00
a. Inverted overprint 55.00 55.00
b. Red overprint 100.00
C7 A4 5p violet 6.00 5.00
a. Inverted overprint 55.00 55.00
b. Red overprint 100.00
C8 A4 10p violet brown 6.00 5.00
a. Inverted overprint 55.00 55.00
b. Red overprint 100.00
Nos. C5-C8 (4) 24.00 20.00

Nos. 32, 34, 35 & 36 With Additional Ovpt. in Red

1926, May 1

C9 A4 2p dark brown 6.50 6.50
a. Red overprint double 160.00 160.00
b. Black overprint double 160.00 160.00
c. Black overprint inverted 70.00 70.00
C10 A4 3p orange brown 6.50 6.50
a. Black overprint inverted 70.00 70.00
C11 A4 5p violet 7.50 7.50
a. Black overprint inverted 70.00 70.00
C12 A4 10p violet brown 7.50 7.50
a. Black overprint inverted 70.00 70.00
Nos. C9-C12 (4) 28.00 28.00

No. C9 has the original overprint in black. Double or inverted overprints, original or plane, are known on most of Nos. C9-C12. Value, each $75.
The red plane overprint was also applied to Nos. C5-C8. These are believed to have been essays, and were not regularly issued. Value, each $100.

Nos. 27c, 37 and Syria No. 177 With Addtl. Ovpt. of Airplane in Red or Black

1929, June-July

C17 A4 50c yel grn (R) 5.00 5.00
a. Plane overprint double 225.00
b. Plane ovpt. on face and back 50.00
c. Pair with plane overprint Tête-bêche 275.00
d. Double overprint 190.00 190.00
e. Overprint inverted 100.00
f. Plane only inverted 225.00
C18 A5 1p magenta (Bk) 9.00 9.00
a. Red overprint 45.00
C19 A4 25p ultra (R) 52.50 40.00
a. Plane overprint inverted 100.00 100.00
b. Surcharge double 125.00 125.00
Nos. C17-C19 (3) 66.50 54.00

Nos. 28 and 30 exist with additional overprint of airplane in red. These stamps were never issued. Value, each $100.

Nos. 47 and 45 With Additional Ovpt. of Airplane in Red

1929-30

C20 A4 2p on 1.25p ('30) 7.25 7.25
a. Surcharge inverted 50.00 50.00
b. Double surcharge 60.00 60.00
c. Triple surcharge 125.00
C21 A4 15p on 25p (Bk + R) 55.00 47.50
a. Plane overprint inverted 190.00 190.00

POSTAGE DUE STAMPS

Postage Due Stamps of France, 1893-1920, Surcharged Like No. 1 (Nos. J1-J2) or No. 7 (Nos. J3-J5)

1925 Unwmk. ***Perf. 14x13½***

J1 D2 50c on 10c choc 8.50 8.50
J2 D2 1p on 20c ol grn 8.50 8.50
J3 D2 2p on 30c red 8.50 8.50
J4 D2 3p on 50c vio brn 8.50 8.50
J5 D2 5p on 1fr red brn, *straw* 8.50 8.50
Nos. J1-J5 (5) 42.50 *42.50*

Two types of overprints exist on No. J5. For detailed listings, see *Scott Classic Specialized Catalogue of Stamps and Covers 1840-1940.*

Postage Due Stamps of Syria, 1925, Overprinted Like No. 26 (Type D5) or No. 25 (Type D6) in Black, Blue or Red

1925 ***Perf. 13½***

J6 D5 50c brown, *yel* 5.00 *5.00*
a. Blue overprint 40.00
b. Red overprint 60.00
c. Overprint inverted 30.00 30.00
J7 D6 1p vio, *rose* (Bl) 4.50 *4.50*
a. Black overprint 125.00 100.00
b. Double overprint (Bk + Bl) 150.00 125.00
c. Overprint inverted 40.00 40.00
J8 D5 2p blk, *blue* (R) 6.00 6.00
a. Blue overprint 40.00
J9 D5 3p blk, *red org* 8.00 8.00
a. Overprint inverted 30.00
J10 D5 5p blk, *bl grn* (R) 10.00 10.00
a. Overprint inverted 30.00 30.00
b. Black overprint 45.00
Nos. J6-J10 (5) 33.50 33.50

The stamps of Alaouites were superseded in 1930 by those of Latakia.

ALBANIA

al-'bā-nē-ə

LOCATION — Southeastern Europe
GOVT. — Republic
AREA — 11,101 sq. mi.
POP. — 3,364,571 (1999 est.)
CAPITAL — Tirana

After the outbreak of World War I, the country fell into a state of anarchy when the Prince and all members of the International Commission left Albania. Subsequently General Ferrero in command of Italian troops declared Albania an independent country. A constitution was adopted and a republican form of government was instituted which continued until 1928 when, by constitutional amendment, Albania was declared to be a monarchy. The President of the republic, Ahmed Zogu, became king of the new state. Many unlisted varieties or surcharges and lithographed labels are said to have done postal duty in Albania and Epirus during this unsettled period.

On April 7, 1939, Italy invaded Albania. King Zog fled but did not abdicate. The King of Italy acquired the crown.

Germany occupied Albania from September, 1943, until late 1944 when it became an independent state. The People's Republic began in January, 1946.

40 Paras = 1 Piaster = 1 Grossion
100 Centimes = 1 Franc (1917)
100 Qintar = 1 Franc
100 Qintar (Qindarka) = 1 Lek (1947)

Catalogue values for unused stamps in this country are for Never Hinged items, beginning with Scott 458 in the regular postage section, Scott B34 in the semi-postal section, and Scott C67 in the airpost section.

Watermarks

Wmk. 125 — Lozenges

Wmk. 220 — Double Headed Eagle

Issues of 1908 Turkey Stamps Handstamped

Perf. 12, 13½ and Compound

1913, June Unwmk.

1 A19 2½pi violet brown 750.00 650.00

With Additional Overprint in Carmine

2 A19 10pa blue green 675.00 650.00

Handstamped on Issue of 1909

4 A21 5pa ocher 450.00 450.00
5 A21 10pa blue green 350.00 225.00
6 A21 20pa car rose 350.00 250.00
7 A21 1pi ultra 325.00 250.00
8 A21 2pi blue black 500.00 450.00
10 A21 5pi dark violet 1,400. 1,500.
11 A21 10pi dull red *5,000.* *4,750.*

For surcharge see No. 19.
Additional values of 25pi dark green and 50pi red brown were overprinted and sold only to dealers. Values, 25pi $8,000, 50pi $16,000.

With Additional Overprint in Blue or Carmine

13A A21 10pa blue green 900.00 850.00
14 A21 20pa car rose (Bl) 800.00 850.00
15 A21 1pi brt blue (C) 1,900. 1,750.

Handstamped on Newspaper Stamp of 1911

17 A21 2pa olive green 425.00 425.00

Handstamped on Postage Due Stamp of 1908

18 A19 1pi black, *dp rose* 3,000. 2,500.

No. 18 was used for regular postage.

No. 6 Surcharged With New Value

19 A21 10pa on 20pa car rose 1,250. 1,250.

The overprint on #1-19 was handstamped and is found inverted, double, etc.
Nos. 6, 7 and 8 exist with the handstamp in red, blue or violet, but these varieties are not known to have been regularly issued.
A 2pa on 5pa newspaper stamp and a 2pi Postage due stamp exist with the handstamp, but these are not known to have been regularly issued. Values, $1,800 and $725, respectively.
Excellent counterfeits exist of Nos. 1 to 19.

A1

Handstamped on White Laid Paper Without Eagle and Value Issued Without Gum

1913, July *Imperf.*
20 A1 (1pi) black 325.00 *525.00*
Cut to shape 190.00 *275.00*
a. Sewing machine perf. 575.00 *725.00*

Value Typewritten in Violet Issued Without Gum

1913, Aug. **With Eagle**
21 A1 10pa violet 16.00 16.00
a. Double impression — —
22 A1 20pa red & black 22.00 18.00
a. "2p para" — —
23 A1 1gr black 22.00 22.00
24 A1 2gr blue & violet 27.00 21.00
25 A1 5gr violet & blue 32.50 27.00
26 A1 10gr blue 32.50 27.00
Nos. 21-26 (6) 152.00 131.00

Nos. 21-26 exist with the eagle inverted or omitted and with numerous errors in the figures of value and the spelling of the word "grosh."

A2

Skanderbeg (George Castriota) — A3

Handstamped on White Laid Paper Eagle and Value in Black Issued Without Gum

1913, Nov. *Perf. 11½*
27 A2 10pa green 5.50 4.25
b. Eagle and value in green 2,350. 2,300.
c. 10pa red (error) 32.50 32.50
d. 10pa violet (error) 32.50 32.50
29 A2 20pa red 8.25 6.25
b. 20pa green (error) 42.50 32.50
30 A2 30pa violet 8.25 6.25
a. 30pa ultramarine (error) 32.50 32.50
b. 30pa red (error) 32.50 32.50
31 A2 1gr ultramarine 11.00 9.50
a. 1gr green (error) 32.50 32.50
b. 1gr black (error) 32.50 32.50
c. 1gr violet (error) 32.50 32.50
33 A2 2gr black 16.00 10.50
a. 2gr violet (error) 40.00 40.00
b. 2gr blue (error) 40.00 40.00
Nos. 27-33 (5) 49.00 36.75

The stamps of this issue are known with eagle or value inverted or omitted.
1st anniv. of Albanian independence.
Counterfeits exist.

1913, Dec. **Typo.** *Perf. 14*
35 A3 2q orange brn & buff 5.50 2.50
36 A3 5q green & blue grn 5.50 2.50
37 A3 10q rose red 5.50 2.50
38 A3 25q dark blue 5.50 2.50
39 A3 50q violet & red 13.00 5.25
40 A3 1fr deep brown 30.00 16.00
Nos. 35-40 (6) 65.00 *31.25*

For overprints and surcharges see Nos. 41-52, 105, J1-J9.

Nos. 35-40 Handstamped in Black or Violet

1914, Mar. 7
41 A3 2q orange brn & buff 75.00 *85.00*
42 A3 5q grn & bl grn (V) 75.00 *85.00*
43 A3 10q rose red 75.00 *85.00*
44 A3 25q dark blue (V) 75.00 *85.00*
45 A3 50q violet & red 75.00 *85.00*
46 A3 1fr deep brown 75.00 *85.00*
Nos. 41-46 (6) 450.00 510.00

Issued to celebrate the arrival of Prince Wilhelm zu Wied on Mar. 7, 1914.

Nos. 35-40 Surcharged in Black

a

b

1914, Apr. 2
47 A3 (a) 5pa on 2q 3.25 3.25
48 A3 (a) 10pa on 5q 3.25 3.25
49 A3 (a) 20pa on 10q 5.50 4.25
50 A3 (b) 1gr on 25q 5.50 4.25
51 A3 (b) 2gr on 50q 5.50 5.25
52 A3 (b) 5gr on 1fr 22.00 16.00
Nos. 47-52 (6) 45.00 36.25

For overprints see Nos. 105, J6-J9.

Inverted Surcharge

47a A3 (a) 5pa on 2q 24.00 24.00
48a A3 (a) 10pa on 5q 22.50 22.50
49a A3 (a) 20pa on 10q 24.00 24.00
50a A3 (b) 1gr on 25q 24.00 24.00
51a A3 (b) 2gr on 50q 28.00 28.00
52b A3 (b) 5gr on 1fr 90.00 90.00
Nos. 47a-52b (6) 212.50 212.50

Korce (Korytsa) Issues

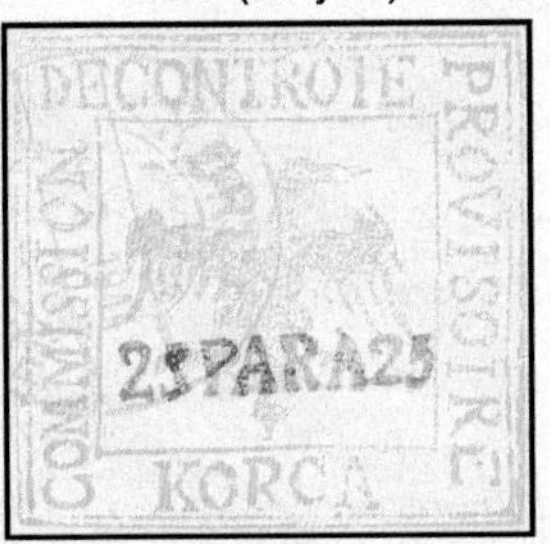

A4

1914 **Handstamped** *Imperf.*
52A A4 10pa violet & red 200.00 200.00
c. 10pa black & red 325.00 325.00
53 A4 25pa violet & red 200.00 200.00
a. 25pa black & red 425.00 425.00

Nos. 52A-53a were handstamped directly on the cover, so the paper varies. They were also produced in sheets; these are rarely found. Nos. 52A-53a were issued by Albanian military authorities.
Counterfeits exists of Nos. 52A and 53.

A5

1917 **Typo. & Litho.** *Perf. 11½*
54 A5 1c dk brown & grn 17.50 12.00
55 A5 2c red & green 17.50 12.00
56 A5 3c gray grn & grn 17.50 12.00
57 A5 5c green & black 16.00 8.00
58 A5 10c rose red & black 16.00 8.00
59 A5 25c blue & black 16.00 8.00
60 A5 50c violet & black 16.00 10.00
61 A5 1fr brown & black 16.00 10.00
Nos. 54-61 (8) 132.50 80.00

A6

1917-18
62 A6 1c dk brown & grn 2.75 2.40
63 A6 2c red brown & grn 2.75 2.40
a. "CTM" for "CTS" 72.50 120.00
64 A6 3c black & green 2.75 2.40
a. "CTM" for "CTS" 80.00 135.00
65 A6 5c green & black 4.00 4.00
66 A6 10c dull red & black 4.00 4.00
67 A6 50c violet & black 7.25 6.50
68 A6 1fr red brn & black 20.00 17.50
Nos. 62-68 (7) 43.50 39.20

Counterfeits abound of Nos. 54-68, 80-81.

No. 65 Surcharged in Red

1918
80 A6 25c on 5c green & blk 275.00 *325.00*

A7

1918
81 A7 25c blue & black 72.50 95.00

General Issue

A8

A9

Handstamped in Rose or Blue XVI MCMXIX

1919 *Perf. 12½*
84 A8 (2)q on 2h brown 15.00 15.00
85 A8 5q on 16h green 15.00 15.00
86 A8 10q on 8h rose (Bl) 15.00 15.00
87 A8 25q on 64h blue 15.00 15.00
88 A9 25q on 64h blue *375.00 375.00*
89 A8 50q on 32h violet 15.00 15.00
90 A8 1fr on 1.28k org, *bl* 15.00 15.00
Nos. 84-90 (7) *465.00 465.00*

See Nos. J10-J13. Compare with types A10-A14. For overprints see Nos 91-104.

Handstamped in Rose or Blue

1919, Jan. 16
91 A8 (2)q on 2h brown 16.00 16.00
92 A8 5q on 16h green 12.00 12.00
93 A8 10q on 8h rose (Bl) 12.00 12.00
94 A8 25q on 64h blue 160.00 160.00
95 A9 25q on 64h blue 52.50 60.00
96 A8 50q on 32h violet 16.00 16.00
97 A8 1fr on 1.28k org, *bl* 16.00 16.00
Nos. 91-97 (7) 284.50 292.00

Handstamped in Violet

1919
98 A8 (2)q on 2h brown 20.00 20.00
99 A8 5q on 16h green 20.00 20.00
100 A8 10q on 8h rose 20.00 20.00
101 A8 25q on 64h blue 20.00 20.00
102 A9 25q on 64h blue 160.00 160.00
103 A8 50q on 32h violet 20.00 20.00
104 A8 1fr on 1.28k org, *bl* 20.00 20.00
Nos. 98-104 (7) 280.00 280.00

No. 50 Overprinted in Violet

1919 *Perf. 14*
105 A3 1gr on 25q blue 32.50 25.00

A10

A11

1919, June 5 *Perf. 11½, 12½*
106 A10 10q on 2h brown 8.00 6.00
107 A11 15q on 8h rose 8.00 6.00
108 A11 20q on 16h green 8.00 6.00
109 A10 25q on 64h blue 8.00 6.00
110 A11 50q on 32h violet 8.00 6.00
111 A11 1fr on 96h orange 8.00 6.00
112 A10 2fr on 1.60k vio, *buff* 29.00 24.00
Nos. 106-112 (7) 77.00 60.00

Nos. 106-108, 110 exist with inverted surcharge.

A12

A13

Surcharged in Black or Violet

1919
113 A12 10q on 8h car 8.00 6.00
114 A12 15q on 8h car (V) 8.00 6.00
115 A13 20q on 16h green 8.00 6.00
116 A13 25q on 32h violet 8.00 6.00
117 A13 50q on 64h blue 22.50 16.00
118 A13 1fr on 96h orange 9.75 8.00
119 A12 2fr on 1.60k vio, *buff* 16.00 12.00
Nos. 113-119 (7) 80.25 60.00

A14

Overprinted in Blue or Black Without New Value

1920 *Perf. 12½*
120 A14 1q gray (Bl) 100.00 95.00
121 A14 10q rose (Bk) 14.00 *32.50*
a. Double overprint 150.00 *150.00*
122 A14 20q brown (Bl) 45.00 47.50
123 A14 25q blue (Bk) 525.00 *600.00*
124 A14 50q brown vio (Bk) 60.00 *80.00*
Nos. 120-124 (5) 744.00 855.00

Counterfeit overprints exist of Nos. 120-128.

Surcharged in Black with New Value
125 A14 2q on 10q rose (R) 16.00 *24.00*
126 A14 5q on 10q rose (G) 16.00 *20.00*
127 A14 25q on 10q rose (Bl) 16.00 *24.00*
128 A14 50q on 10q rose (Br) 16.00 *32.50*
Nos. 125-128 (4) 64.00 100.50

Stamps of type A14 (Portrait of the Prince zu Wied) were not placed in use without overprint or surcharge.

A15

Post Horn Overprinted in Black

1920 ***Perf. 14x13***

129 A15 2q orange 12.00 9.75
130 A15 5q deep green 20.00 17.50
131 A15 10q red 35.00 35.00
132 A15 25q light blue 65.00 35.00
133 A15 50q gray green 14.50 12.00
134 A15 1fr claret 14.50 12.00
Nos. 129-134 (6) 161.00 121.25

Type A15 was never placed in use without post horn or "Besa" overprint.

Stamps of Type A15 (No Post Horn) Overprinted

1921

135 A15 2q orange 8.00 8.00
136 A15 5q deep green 8.00 8.00
137 A15 10q red 16.00 14.00
138 A15 25q light blue 29.00 24.00
139 A15 50q gray green 16.00 14.00
140 A15 1fr claret 16.00 14.00
Nos. 135-140 (6) 93.00 82.00

For surcharge & overprints see Nos. 154, 156-157.

Stamps of these types, and with "TAKSE" overprint, were unauthorized and never placed in use. They are common.

Gjirokaster
A18

Korcha
A19

Designs: 5q, Kanina. 10q, Berati. 25q, Bridge at Vezirit. 50q, Rozafat. 2fr, Dursit.

1923 **Typo.** ***Perf. 12½, 11½***

147 A18 2q orange 1.25 2.10
148 A18 5q yellow green 1.10 1.60
149 A18 10q carmine 1.10 1.60
150 A18 25q dark blue 1.10 1.60
151 A18 50q dark green 1.10 1.60
152 A19 1fr dark violet 1.10 1.60
153 A19 2fr olive green 6.50 8.25
Nos. 147-153 (7) 13.25 18.35

For overprints & surcharges see Nos. 158-185, B1-B8.

No. 135 Surcharged

1922 ***Perf. 14x13***

154 A15 1q on 2q orange 3.25 8.00

Stamps of Type A15 (No Post Horn) Overprinted

1922

156 A15 5q deep green 5.00 8.00
157 A15 10q red 5.00 8.00

Nos. 147-151 Ovptd. in Black and Violet

1924, Jan. ***Perf. 12½***

158 A18 2q red orange 10.00 20.00
159 A18 5q yellow green 10.00 20.00
160 A18 10q carmine 7.50 14.50
161 A18 25q dark blue 7.50 14.50
162 A18 50q dark green 11.50 20.00
Nos. 158-162 (5) 46.50 89.00

The words "Mbledhje Kushtetuese" are in taller letters on the 25q than on the other values. Opening of the Constituent Assembly.

Counterfeits of Nos. 158 and 161 are plentiful.

No. 147 Surcharged

1924

163 A18 1q on 2q red orange 3.00 8.00

Nos. 163, 147-152 Overprinted

1924

164 A18 1q on 2q orange 2.75 7.25
165 A18 2q orange 2.75 7.25
166 A18 5q yellow green 2.75 7.25
167 A18 10q carmine 2.75 7.25
168 A18 25q dark blue 2.75 7.25
169 A18 50q dark green 6.25 14.00
170 A19 1fr dark violet 6.25 17.50
Nos. 164-170 (7) 26.25 67.75

Issued to celebrate the return of the Government to the Capital after a revolution.

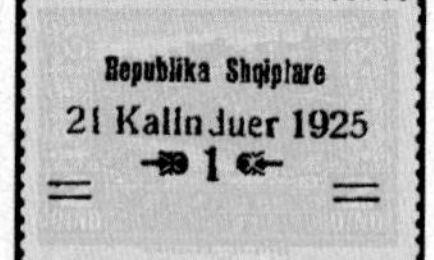

Nos. 163, 147-152 Overprinted

1925

171 A18 1q on 2q orange 3.25 8.00
172 A18 2q orange 3.25 8.00
173 A18 5q yellow green 3.25 8.00
174 A18 10q carmine 3.25 8.00
175 A18 25q dark blue 3.25 8.00
176 A18 50q dark green 3.25 12.00
177 A19 1fr dark violet 6.25 16.00
Nos. 171-177 (7) 25.75 68.00

Proclamation of the Republic, Jan. 21, 1925. The date "1921" instead of "1925" occurs once in each sheet of 50.

Counterfeits exist.

Nos. 163, 147-153 Overprinted

1925

178 A18 1q on 2q orange 1.10 1.60
a. Inverted overprint 12.50 12.50
179 A18 2q orange 1.10 1.60
180 A18 5q yellow green 1.10 1.60
a. Inverted overprint 12.50 12.50
181 A18 10q carmine 1.10 1.60
182 A18 25q dark blue 1.10 1.60
183 A18 50q dark green 1.10 1.60
184 A19 1fr dark violet 5.00 4.00
185 A19 2fr olive green 7.50 4.00
Nos. 178-185 (8) 19.10 17.60

Counterfeits exist.

President Ahmed Zogu
A25 A26

1925 ***Perf. 13½, 13½x13***

186 A25 1q orange .25 .25
187 A25 2q red brown .25 2.00
188 A25 5q green .25 .25
189 A25 10q rose red .25 .25
190 A25 15q gray brown .75 2.00
191 A25 25q dark blue .25 .25
192 A25 50q blue green .85 1.50
193 A26 1fr red & ultra 1.75 2.00
194 A26 2fr green & orange 1.90 2.00
195 A26 3fr brown & violet 4.00 5.00
196 A26 5fr violet & black 4.50 6.75
Nos. 186-196 (11) 15.00 22.25

No. 193 in ultramarine and brown, and No. 194 in green and brown were not regularly issued. Value, set $15.

For overprints & surcharges see Nos. 197-209, 238-248.

Nos. 186-196 Overprinted in Various Colors

1927

197 A25 1q orange (V) .60 1.00
198 A25 2q red brn (G) .25 .30
199 A25 5q green (R) 1.25 .50
200 A25 10q rose red (Bl) .25 .30
201 A25 15q gray brn (G) 7.00 14.00
202 A25 25q dk blue (R) .50 .40
203 A25 50q blue grn (Bl) .50 .40
204 A26 1fr red & ultra (Bk) 1.40 .55
205 A26 2fr green & org (Bk) 1.50 .80
206 A26 3fr brown & vio (Bk) 2.40 1.60
207 A26 5fr violet & blk (Bk) 3.50 2.75
Nos. 197-207 (11) 19.15 22.60

No. 200 exists perf. 11.

For surcharges see Nos. 208-209, 238-240.

Nos. 200, 202 Surcharged in Black or Red

1928

208 A25 1q on 10q rose red .50 .55
a. Inverted surcharge 4.00 4.00
209 A25 5q on 25q dk blue (R) .50 .55
a. Inverted surcharge 4.00 4.00

A27

King Zog I — A28

Black Overprint

1928 ***Perf. 14x13½***

210 A27 1q orange brown 5.00 9.50
211 A27 2q slate 5.00 9.50
212 A27 5q blue green 5.00 12.00
213 A27 10q rose red 4.00 12.00
214 A27 15q bister 15.00 47.50
215 A27 25q deep blue 6.00 12.00
216 A27 50q lilac rose 10.00 15.00

Red Overprint

Perf. 13½x14

217 A28 1fr blue & slate 10.00 12.00
Nos. 210-217 (8) 60.00 129.50

Compare with types A29-A32.

A29

A30

Black or Red Overprint

1928 ***Perf. 14x13½***

218 A29 1q orange brown 12.50 25.00
219 A29 2q slate (R) 12.50 25.00
220 A29 5q blue green 10.00 20.00
221 A29 10q rose red 10.00 16.00
222 A29 15q bister 15.00 27.50
223 A29 25q deep blue (R) 10.00 16.00
224 A29 50q lilac rose 10.00 16.00

Perf. 13½x14

225 A30 1fr blue & slate (R) 12.50 20.00
226 A30 2fr green & slate (R) 12.50 20.00
Nos. 218-226 (9) 105.00 185.50

Proclamation of Ahmed Zogu as King of Albania.

A31

A32

Black Overprint

1928 ***Perf. 14x13½***

227 A31 1q orange brown .40 1.25
228 A31 2q slate .40 1.25
229 A31 5q blue green 2.75 3.50
230 A31 10q rose red .40 1.25
231 A31 15q bister 15.00 24.00
232 A31 25q deep blue .40 1.25
233 A31 50q lilac rose .75 2.00

Perf. 13½x14

234 A32 1fr blue & slate 1.50 2.50
235 A32 2fr green & slate 1.50 4.00
236 A32 3fr dk red & ol bis 7.50 12.00
237 A32 5fr dull vio & gray 7.50 16.00
Nos. 227-237 (11) 38.10 69.00

The overprint reads "Kingdom of Albania."

Nos. 203, 202, 200 Surcharged in Black

1929 ***Perf. 13½x13, 11½***

238 A25 1q on 50q blue green .40 .55
239 A25 5q on 25q dark blue .40 .55
240 A25 15q on 10q rose red .60 1.00
Nos. 238-240 (3) 1.40 2.10

Nos. 186-189, 191-194 Overprinted in Black or Red

1929 ***Perf. 11½, 13½***

241 A25 1q orange 7.50 20.00
242 A25 2q red brown 7.50 20.00
243 A25 5q green 7.50 20.00
244 A25 10q rose red 7.50 20.00
245 A25 25q dark blue 7.50 20.00

No.	Type	Description	Unused	Used
246	A25	50q blue green (R)	10.00	*24.00*
247	A26	1fr red & ultra	14.00	*35.00*
248	A26	2fr green & orange	14.00	*35.00*
		Nos. 241-248 (8)	75.50	194.00

34th birthday of King Zog. The overprint reads "Long live the King."

Lake Butrinto — A33

King Zog I — A34

Zog Bridge — A35

Ruin at Zog Manor — A36

Perf. 14, 14½

1930, Sept. 1 Photo. Wmk. 220

No.	Type	Description	Unused	Used
250	A33	1q slate	.25	.25
251	A33	2q orange red	.25	.25
252	A34	5q yellow green	.25	.25
253	A34	10q carmine	.25	.25
254	A34	15q dark brown	.25	.25
255	A34	25q dark ultra	.25	.25
256	A33	50q slate green	.70	.55
257	A35	1fr violet	1.10	1.00
258	A35	2fr indigo	1.50	1.10
259	A36	3fr gray green	3.50	2.25
260	A36	5fr orange brown	4.50	3.50
		Nos. 250-260 (11)	12.80	9.90

2nd anniversary of accession of King Zog I.

For overprints see Nos. 261-270, 299-309, J39. For surcharges see Nos. 354-360.

Nos. 250-259 Overprinted in Black

1934, Dec. 24

No.	Type	Description	Unused	Used
261	A33	1q slate	8.50	*12.00*
262	A33	2q orange red	8.50	*12.00*
263	A34	5q yellow green	8.50	9.50
264	A34	10q carmine	9.25	*12.00*
265	A34	15q dark brown	9.25	*12.00*
266	A34	25q dark ultra	9.25	*12.00*
267	A33	50q slate green	10.00	*16.00*
268	A35	1fr violet	11.00	*20.00*
269	A35	2fr indigo	12.00	*25.00*
270	A36	3fr gray green	15.00	*35.00*
		Nos. 261-270 (10)	101.25	165.50

Tenth anniversary of the Constitution.

Allegory of Death of Skanderbeg A37

Albanian Eagle in Turkish Shackles A38

5q, 25q, 40q, 2fr, Eagle with wings spread.

1937 Unwmk. *Perf. 14*

No.	Type	Description	Unused	Used
271	A37	1q brown violet	.25	.25
272	A38	2q brown	.50	.35
273	A38	5q lt green	.50	.50
274	A37	10q olive brown	.50	*.80*
275	A38	15q rose red	.80	*1.00*
276	A38	25q blue	1.50	*2.00*
277	A37	50q deep green	3.75	3.25
278	A38	1fr violet	9.00	6.00
279	A38	2fr orange brown	12.00	9.00
		Nos. 271-279 (9)	28.80	23.15

Souvenir Sheet

No.	Type	Description	Unused	Used
280		Sheet of 3	17.50	*150.00*
a.	A37	20q red violet	3.50	*6.25*
b.	A38	30q olive brown	3.50	*6.25*
c.	A38	40q red	3.50	*6.25*

25th anniv. of independence from Turkey, proclaimed Nov. 26, 1912.

Queen Geraldine and King Zog — A40

1938 *Perf. 14*

No.	Type	Description	Unused	Used
281	A40	1q slate violet	.30	.40
282	A40	2q red brown	.30	.40
283	A40	5q green	.30	.40
284	A40	10q olive brown	1.10	.80
285	A40	15q rose red	1.10	.80
286	A40	25q blue	2.75	2.00
287	A40	50q Prus green	5.75	4.00
288	A40	1fr purple	11.50	8.00
		Nos. 281-288 (8)	23.10	16.80

Souvenir Sheet

No.	Type	Description	Unused	Used
289		Sheet of 4	35.00	*175.00*
a.	A40	20q dark red violet	7.75	*9.75*
b.	A40	30q brown olive	7.75	*9.75*

Wedding of King Zog and Countess Geraldine Apponyi, Apr. 27, 1938.

No. 289 contains 2 each of Nos. 289a, 289b.

Queen Geraldine — A42

National Emblems — A43

Designs: 10q, 25q, 30q, 1fr, King Zog.

1938

No.	Type	Description	Unused	Used
290	A42	1q dp red violet	.25	*.55*
291	A43	2q red orange	.25	*.55*
292	A42	5q deep green	.50	.50
293	A42	10q red brown	.50	*1.00*
294	A42	15q deep rose	1.00	*1.25*
295	A42	25q deep blue	1.40	1.40
296	A43	50q gray black	8.50	6.00
297	A42	1fr slate green	12.50	9.00
		Nos. 290-297 (8)	24.90	20.25

Souvenir Sheet

No.	Type	Description	Unused	Used
298		Sheet of 3	22.50	*100.00*
b.	A43	20q Prussian green	7.00	*12.00*
c.	A42	30q deep violet	7.00	*12.00*

10th anniv. of royal rule. They were on sale for 3 days (Aug. 30-31, Sept. 1) only, during which their use was required on all mail.

No. 298 contains Nos. 294, 298b, 298c.

Issued under Italian Dominion

Nos. 250-260 Overprinted in Black

1939 Wmk. 220 *Perf. 14*

No.	Type	Description	Unused	Used
299	A33	1q slate	1.25	*1.25*
300	A33	2q orange red	1.25	*1.25*
301	A34	5q yellow green	1.25	*1.25*
302	A34	10q carmine	1.25	*1.25*
303	A34	15q dark brown	2.00	*3.75*
304	A34	25q dark ultra	2.00	*3.75*
305	A33	50q slate green	2.50	*5.00*
306	A35	1fr violet	2.50	*5.00*
307	A35	2fr indigo	3.25	*9.50*
308	A36	3fr gray green	7.75	*22.50*
309	A36	5fr orange brown	10.00	*25.00*
		Nos. 299-309 (11)	35.00	79.50

Resolution adopted by the Natl. Assembly, Apr. 12, 1939, offering the Albanian Crown to Italy.

A46

A47

Native Costumes — A48

King Victor Emmanuel III A49 A50

Native Costume — A51

Monastery A52

Designs: 2fr, Bridge at Vezirit. 3fr, Ancient Columns. 5fr, Amphitheater.

1939 Unwmk. Photo. *Perf. 14*

No.	Type	Description	Unused	Used
310	A46	1q blue gray	1.25	.50
311	A47	2q olive green	1.25	.50
312	A48	3q golden brown	1.25	.50
313	A49	5q green	1.25	.25
314	A50	10q brown	1.25	.25
315	A50	15q crimson	1.25	.25
316	A50	25q sapphire	2.00	.80
317	A50	30q brt violet	2.50	1.40
318	A51	50q dull purple	3.25	3.25
319	A49	65q red brown	5.00	11.50
320	A52	1fr myrtle green	7.50	9.50
321	A52	2fr brown lake	11.50	19.00
322	A52	3fr brown black	19.00	35.00
323	A52	5fr gray violet	25.00	*50.00*
		Nos. 310-323 (14)	83.25	132.70

For overprints and surcharges see Nos. 331-353.

King Victor Emmanuel III — A56

1942 Photo.

No.	Type	Description	Unused	Used
324	A56	5q green	1.25	*2.00*
325	A56	10q brown	1.25	*2.00*
326	A56	15q rose red	1.25	*2.00*
327	A56	25q blue	1.25	*2.00*
328	A56	65q red brown	3.50	*4.00*
329	A56	1fr myrtle green	3.50	*4.00*
330	A56	2fr gray violet	3.50	*4.00*
		Nos. 324-330 (7)	15.50	20.00

Conquest of Albania by Italy, 3rd anniv.

No. 311 Surcharged in Black

No.	Type	Description	Unused	Used
331	A47	1q on 2q olive green	1.60	*4.00*

Issued under German Administration

Stamps of 1939 Overprinted in Carmine or Brown

1943

No.	Type	Description	Unused	Used
332	A47	2q olive green	1.00	*4.00*
333	A48	3q golden brown	1.00	*4.00*
334	A49	5q green	1.00	*4.00*
335	A50	10q brown	1.00	*4.00*
336	A50	15q crimson (Br)	1.00	*4.00*
337	A50	25q sapphire	1.00	*4.00*
338	A50	30q brt violet	1.00	*4.00*
339	A49	65q red brown	1.50	*8.00*
340	A52	1fr myrtle green	6.25	*24.00*
341	A52	2fr brown lake	7.75	*80.00*
342	A52	3fr brown black	60.00	*200.00*

Surcharged with New Values

No.	Type	Description	Unused	Used
343	A48	1q on 3q gldn brn	1.00	*8.00*
344	A49	50q on 65q red brn	1.50	*12.00*
		Nos. 332-344 (13)	85.00	*360.00*

Proclamation of Albanian independence.

The overprint "14 Shtator 1943" on Nos. 324 to 328 is private and fraudulent.

Independent State

Nos. 312 to 317 and 319 to 321 Surcharged with New Value and Bars in Black or Carmine, and:

1945

No.	Type	Description	Unused	Used
345	A48	30q on 3q gldn brn	3.75	*12.00*
346	A49	40q on 5q green	3.75	*12.00*
347	A50	50q on 10q brown	3.75	*12.00*
348	A50	60q on 15q crimson	3.75	*12.00*
349	A50	80q on 25q saph (C)	3.75	*12.00*
350	A50	1fr on 30q brt violet	3.75	*12.00*
351	A49	2fr on 65q red brn	3.75	*12.00*
352	A52	3fr on 1fr myr green	3.75	*12.00*
353	A52	5fr on 2fr brown lake	3.75	*12.00*
		Nos. 345-353 (9)	33.75	*108.00*

"DEMOKRATIKE" is not abbreviated on Nos. 352 and 353.

Nos. 250, 251, 256 and 258 Surcharged in Black or Carmine, and

1945 Wmk. 220

No.	Type	Description	Unused	Used
354	A33	30q on 1q slate	2.75	*6.00*
355	A33	60q on 1q slate	2.75	*6.00*
356	A33	80q on 1q slate	2.75	*6.00*
357	A33	1fr on 1q slate	6.00	*12.00*
358	A33	2fr on 2q org red	7.00	*13.50*
359	A33	3fr on 50q sl grn	15.00	*25.00*
360	A35	5fr on 2fr indigo	20.00	*40.00*
		Nos. 354-360 (7)	56.25	*108.50*

Albanian Natl. Army of Liberation, 2nd anniv.

The surcharge on No. 360 is condensed to fit the size of the stamp.

Country House, Labinot — A57

40q, 60q, Bridge at Berat. 1fr, 3fr, Permet.

Perf. 11½

1945, Nov. 28 Unwmk. Typo.

No.	Type	Description	Unused	Used
361	A57	20q bluish green	.40	*1.40*
362	A57	30q deep orange	.60	*2.00*
363	A57	40q brown	.60	*2.00*
364	A57	60q red violet	.90	*2.75*
365	A57	1fr rose red	2.25	*6.00*
366	A57	3fr dark blue	16.00	*24.00*
		Nos. 361-366 (6)	20.75	*38.15*

Counterfeits: lithographed; genuine: typographed.

For overprints and surcharges see Nos. 367-378, 418-423, B28-B33.

Nos. 361 to 366 Overprinted in Black

1946

No.	Type	Description	Unused	Used
367	A57	20q bluish green	.85	*1.60*
368	A57	30q deep orange	1.10	*2.00*
369	A57	40q brown	1.40	*2.50*
370	A57	60q red violet	2.50	*4.00*
371	A57	1fr rose red	9.00	*14.50*
372	A57	3fr dark blue	14.00	*25.00*
		Nos. 367-372 (6)	28.85	*49.60*

Convocation of the Constitutional Assembly, Jan. 10, 1946.

People's Republic

#361-366 Overprinted in Black

1946 *Perf. 11*

No.	Type	Value	Color	Unused	Used
373	A57	20q	bluish green	1.00	*1.25*
374	A57	30q	deep orange	1.25	*1.75*
375	A57	40q	brown	1.75	*4.00*
376	A57	60q	red violet	3.50	*7.00*
377	A57	1fr	rose red	10.00	*16.00*
378	A57	3fr	dark blue	15.00	*24.50*
			Nos. 373-378 (6)	32.50	*54.50*

Proclamation of the Albanian People's Republic.
Some values exist perf 11½.
For surcharges see Nos. 418-423.

Globe, Dove and Olive Branch — A60

Perf. 11½, Imperf.

1946, Mar. 8 **Typo.**

Denomination in Black

No.	Type	Value	Color	Unused	Used
379	A60	20q	lilac & dull red	.25	*1.25*
380	A60	40q	dp lilac & dull red	.45	*1.75*
381	A60	50q	violet & dull red	.90	*2.50*
382	A60	1fr	lt blue & red	1.75	*5.00*
383	A60	2fr	dk blue & red	2.25	*8.00*
			Nos. 379-383 (5)	5.60	*18.50*

International Women's Congress.
Counterfeits exist.

Athletes with Shot and Indian Club A61

Perf. 11½

1946, Oct. 6 **Litho.** **Unwmk.**

No.	Type	Value	Color	Unused	Used
384	A61	1q	grnsh black	7.50	*10.00*
385	A61	2q	green	7.50	*10.00*
386	A61	5q	brown	7.50	*10.00*
387	A61	10q	crimson	7.50	*10.00*
388	A61	20q	ultra	7.50	*10.00*
389	A61	40q	rose violet	7.50	*10.00*
390	A61	1fr	deep orange	17.50	*27.50*
			Nos. 384-390 (7)	62.50	*87.50*

Balkan Games, Tirana, Oct. 6-13.

Qemal Stafa — A62

1947, May 5 *Perf. 12½x11½*

No.	Type	Value	Color	Unused	Used
391	A62	20q	brn & yel brn	7.00	*12.00*
392	A62	28q	dk blue & blue	7.00	*12.00*
393	A62	40q	brn blk & gray brn	7.00	*12.00*
a.			Souvenir sheet, #391-393	80.00	*100.00*
			Nos. 391-393 (3)	21.00	*36.00*

5th anniv. of the death of Qemal Stafa.

Young Railway Laborers A64

1947, May 16 *Perf. 11½*

No.	Type	Value	Color	Unused	Used
395	A64	1q	brn blk & gray brn	2.75	1.40
396	A64	4q	dk green & green	2.75	1.40
397	A64	10q	blk brn & bis brn	2.75	1.60
398	A64	15q	dk red & red	2.75	1.60
399	A64	20q	indigo & bl gray	6.00	3.00
400	A64	28q	dk blue & blue	8.00	2.50
401	A64	40q	brn vio & rose vio	17.50	14.50

Perf. 13x12½

No.	Type	Value	Color	Unused	Used
402	A64	68q	dk brn & org brn	21.50	*25.00*
			Nos. 395-402 (8)	64.00	51.00

Issued to publicize the construction of the Durres Elbasan Railway by Albanian youths.
The 4q, 20q, 28q and 40q exist perf 13x12½.

Citizens Led by Hasim Zeneli A65

Enver Hoxha and Vasil Shanto — A66

Inauguration of Vithkuq Brigade — A67

Vojo Kushi — A68

1947, July 10 **Litho.**

No.	Type	Value	Color	Unused	Used
403	A65	16q	brn org & red brn	5.00	*8.00*
404	A66	20q	org brn & dk brn	5.00	*8.00*
405	A67	28q	blue & dk blue	5.00	*8.00*
406	A68	40q	lilac & dk brn	5.00	*8.00*
			Nos. 403-406 (4)	20.00	*32.00*

4th anniv. of the formation of Albania's army, July 10, 1943.

Conference Building Ruins, Peza — A69

1947, Sept. 16

No.	Type	Value	Color	Unused	Used
407	A69	2 l	red violet	3.75	*6.00*
408	A69	2.50 l	deep blue	3.75	*6.00*

Peza Conf., Sept. 16, 1942, 5th anniv.

Disabled Soldiers — A70

1947, Nov. 17 *Perf. 12½x11½*

No.	Type	Value	Color	Unused	Used
408A	A70	1 l	red	10.00	*12.00*

Disabled War Veterans Cong., 11/14-20/47.

A71

A73

2 l, Banquet. 2.50 l, Peasants rejoicing.

Perf. 11½x12½, 12½x11½

1947, Nov. 17 **Unwmk.**

No.	Type	Value	Color	Unused	Used
409	A71	1.50 l	dull violet	5.50	*8.00*
410	A71	2 l	brown	5.50	*8.00*
411	A71	2.50 l	blue	5.50	*8.00*
412	A73	3 l	rose red	5.50	*8.00*
			Nos. 409-412 (4)	22.00	*32.00*

Agrarian reform law of 11/17/46, 1st anniv.

Burning Farm Buildings A74

Designs: 2.50 l, Trench scene. 5 l, Firing line. 8 l, Winter advance. 12 l, Infantry column.

1947, Nov. 29 *Perf. 11½x12½*

No.	Type	Value	Color	Unused	Used
413	A74	1.50 l	red	2.75	*4.00*
414	A74	2.50 l	rose brown	2.75	*4.00*
415	A74	5 l	blue	5.75	6.50
416	A74	8 l	purple	8.50	*10.00*
417	A74	12 l	brown	14.00	*16.00*
			Nos. 413-417 (5)	33.75	*40.50*

3rd anniv. of Albania's liberation.

Nos. 373 to 378 Surcharged with New Value and Bars in Black

1948, Feb. 22 *Perf. 11*

No.	Type	Value	Color	Unused	Used
418	A57	50q	on 30q dp org	.40	*.55*
419	A57	1 l	on 20q bluish grn	1.00	1.00
420	A57	2.50 l	on 60q red vio	1.60	*2.75*
421	A57	3 l	on 1fr rose red	2.00	*3.50*
422	A57	5 l	on 3fr dk bl	4.50	*6.00*
423	A57	12 l	on 40q brown	12.00	*16.00*
			Nos. 418-423 (6)	21.50	*29.80*

The two bars consist of four type squares each set close together.
Some values exist perf 11½.

Map, Train and Construction Workers — A75

1948, June 1 **Litho.** *Perf. 11½*

No.	Type	Value	Color	Unused	Used
424	A75	50q	dk car rose	1.60	1.25
425	A75	1 l	lt green & blk	1.60	1.40
426	A75	1.50 l	deep rose	3.00	2.00
427	A75	2.50 l	org brn & dk brn	4.25	2.50
428	A75	5 l	dull blue	7.00	4.50
429	A75	8 l	sal & dk brn	12.00	8.00
430	A75	12 l	red vio & dk vio	14.50	10.00
431	A75	20 l	olive gray	27.50	20.00
			Nos. 424-431 (8)	71.45	49.65

Issued to publicize the construction of the Durres-Tirana Railway.

Marching Soldiers A76

Design: 8 l, Battle scene.

1948, July 10

No.	Type	Value	Color	Unused	Used
432	A76	2.50 l	yellow brown	4.00	4.00
433	A76	5 l	dark blue	5.75	5.75
434	A76	8 l	violet gray	9.25	8.00
			Nos. 432-434 (3)	19.00	17.75

5th anniv. of the formation of Albania's army.

Bricklayer, Flag, Globe and "Industry" — A77

Map and Soldier — A78

1949, May 1 **Photo.** *Perf. 12½x12*

No.	Type	Value	Color	Unused	Used
435	A77	2.50 l	olive brown	.90	*2.00*
436	A77	5 l	blue	1.90	*3.25*
437	A77	8 l	violet brown	3.25	*5.25*
			Nos. 435-437 (3)	6.05	*10.50*

Issued to publicize Labor Day, May 1, 1949.

1949, July 10 **Unwmk.**

No.	Type	Value	Color	Unused	Used
438	A78	2.50 l	brown	.90	*2.00*
439	A78	5 l	light ultra	1.90	*3.00*
440	A78	8 l	brown orange	3.25	*5.25*
			Nos. 438-440 (3)	6.05	10.25

6th anniv. of the formation of Albania's army.

Enver Hoxha — A79

Albanian Citizen and Spasski Tower, Kremlin — A80

1949, Oct. 16 **Engr.** *Perf. 12½*

No.	Type	Value	Color	Unused	Used
441	A79	50q	purple	.25	.25
442	A79	1 l	dull green	.25	.25
443	A79	1.50 l	car lake	.25	.25
444	A79	2.50 l	brown	.65	.25
445	A79	5 l	violet blue	1.25	.80
446	A79	8 l	sepia	2.50	2.40
447	A79	12 l	rose lilac	6.50	4.25
448	A79	20 l	gray blue	8.50	5.25
			Nos. 441-448 (8)	20.15	13.70

1949, Sept. 10 **Photo.** *Perf. 12½x12*

No.	Type	Value	Color	Unused	Used
449	A80	2.50 l	orange brown	.75	*1.50*
450	A80	5 l	deep ultra	1.75	*3.50*

Albanian-Soviet friendship.

Albanian Soldier and Flag — A81

Battle Scene — A82

1949, Nov. 29 Unwmk. *Perf. 12*

451 A81 2.50 l brown .75 *1.25*
452 A82 3 l dark red .75 *2.25*
453 A81 5 l violet 1.50 *3.00*
454 A82 8 l black 3.00 *5.50*
Nos. 451-454 (4) 6.00 *12.00*

Fifth anniversary of Albania's liberation.

Joseph V. Stalin — A83

1949, Dec. 21

455 A83 2.50 l dark brown .60 *1.60*
456 A83 5 l violet blue 1.60 *2.75*
457 A83 8 l rose brown 4.25 *6.75*
Nos. 455-457 (3) 6.45 *11.10*

70th anniv. of the birth of Joseph V. Stalin.

Canceled to Order

Beginning in 1950, Albania sold some issues in sheets canceled to order. Values in second column, when much less than unused, are for "CTO" examples. Postally used stamps are valued at slightly less than, or the same as, unused.

Catalogue values for unused stamps in this section, from this point to the end of the section, are for Never Hinged items.

Symbols of UPU and Postal Transport A84

1950, July 1 Photo. *Perf. 12x12½*

458 A84 5 l blue 3.00 1.40
459 A84 8 l rose brown 5.50 1.90
460 A84 12 l sepia 11.00 2.40
Nos. 458-460 (3) 19.50 5.70

75th anniv. (in 1949) of the UPU.

Sami Frasheri — A85

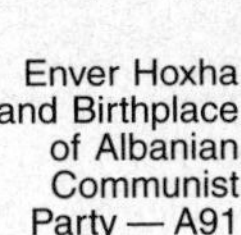

Arms and Albanian Flags — A86

Authors: 2.50 l, Andon Zako. 3 l, Naim Frasheri. 5 l, Kostandin Kristoforidhi.

1950, Nov. 5 *Perf. 14*

461 A85 2 l dark green 1.60 .40
462 A85 2.50 l red brown 2.25 .45
463 A85 3 l brown carmine 4.25 .65
464 A85 5 l deep blue 5.50 .80
Nos. 461-464 (4) 13.60 2.30

"Jubilee of the Writers of the Renaissance."

1951, Jan. 11 Engr. *Perf. 14x13½*

465 A86 2.50 l brown carmine 2.25 .30
466 A86 5 l deep blue 4.25 .65
467 A86 8 l sepia 7.00 1.25
Nos. 465-467 (3) 13.50 2.20

5th anniv. of the formation of the Albanian People's Republic.

Skanderbeg — A87

1951, Mar. 1

468 A87 2.50 l brown 2.25 .30
469 A87 5 l violet 4.25 .55
470 A87 8 l olive bister 7.00 1.10
Nos. 468-470 (3) 13.50 1.95

483rd anniv. of the death of George Castriota (Skanderbeg).

Enver Hoxha and Congress of Permet — A88

1951, May 24 Photo. *Perf. 12*

471 A88 2.50 l dark brown 1.10 .25
472 A88 3 l rose brown 1.25 .35
473 A88 5 l violet blue 2.75 .55
474 A88 8 l rose lilac 5.00 .85
Nos. 471-474 (4) 10.10 2.00

Congress of Permet, 7th anniversary.

Child and Globe — A89

Weighing Baby — A90

1951, July 16

475 A89 2 l green 2.75 .80
476 A90 2.50 l brown 3.75 .95
477 A90 3 l red 4.25 1.25
478 A89 5 l blue 6.25 1.40
Nos. 475-478 (4) 17.00 4.40

Intl. Children's Day, June 1, 1951.

Enver Hoxha and Birthplace of Albanian Communist Party — A91

1951, Nov. 8 Photo. *Perf. 14*

479 A91 2.50 l olive brown .75 .25
480 A91 3 l rose brown .75 .40
481 A91 5 l dark slate blue 1.75 .65
482 A91 8 l black 3.25 .90
Nos. 479-482 (4) 6.50 2.20

Albanian Communist Party, 10th anniv.

Battle Scene A92

Designs: 5 l, Schoolgirl, "Agriculture and Industry." 8 l, Four portraits.

1951, Nov. 28 *Perf. 12x12½*

483 A92 2.50 l brown 1.10 .25
484 A92 5 l blue 2.25 .50
485 A92 8 l brown carmine 5.00 .85
Nos. 483-485 (3) 8.35 1.60

Albanian Communist Youth Org., 10th anniv.

Albanian Heroes (Haxhija, Lezha, Giylbegaj, Mazi and Deda) — A93

Designs: Nos. 486-489 each show 5 "Heroes of the People"; No. 490 shows 2 (Stafa and Shanto).

1950, Dec. 25 Unwmk. *Perf. 14*

486 A93 2 l dark green 1.40 .25
487 A93 2.50 l purple 1.60 .25
488 A93 3 l scarlet 3.25 .35
489 A93 5 l brt blue 5.50 .45
490 A93 8 l olive brown 11.00 1.25
Nos. 486-490 (5) 22.75 2.55

6th anniv. of Albania's liberation.

Tobacco Factory, Shkoder A94

Composite, Lenin Hydroelectric Plant — A95

Designs: 1 l, Canal. 2.50 l, Textile factory. 3 l, "8 November" Cannery. 5 l, Motion Picture Studio, Tirana. 8 l, Stalin Textile Mill, Tirana. 20 l, Central Hydroelectric Dam.

1953, Aug. 1 *Perf. 12x12½, 12½x12*

491 A94 50q red brown .80 .25
492 A94 1 l dull green 1.10 .25
493 A94 2.50 l brown 1.50 .25
494 A94 3 l rose brown 1.90 .25
495 A94 5 l blue 3.25 .25
496 A94 8 l brown olive 3.75 .25
497 A95 12 l deep plum 5.75 .40
498 A94 20 l slate blue 11.00 .60
Nos. 491-498 (8) 29.05 2.50

Liberation Scene — A96

1954, Nov. 29 *Perf. 12x12½*

499 A96 50q brown violet .45 .25
500 A96 1 l olive green .70 .25
501 A96 2.50 l yellow brown 1.25 .25
502 A96 3 l carmine rose 2.25 .25
503 A96 5 l gray blue 3.50 .25
504 A96 8 l rose brown 6.50 .65
Nos. 499-504 (6) 14.65 1.90

10th anniversary of Albania's liberation.

School — A97

Pandeli Sotiri, Petro Nini Luarasi, Nuci Naci — A98

1956, Feb. 23 Unwmk.

505 A97 2 l rose violet .55 .25
506 A98 2.50 l lt green .90 .25
507 A98 5 l ultra 2.00 .40
508 A97 10 l brt grnsh blue 6.50 .75
Nos. 505-508 (4) 9.95 1.65

Opening of the 1st Albanian school, 70th anniv.

Flags — A99

Designs: 5 l, Labor Party headquarters, Tirana. 8 l, Marx and Lenin.

1957, June 1 Engr. *Perf. 11½x11*

509 A99 2.50 l brown 1.00 .25
510 A99 5 l lt violet blue 2.10 .25
511 A99 8 l rose lilac 3.25 1.00
Nos. 509-511 (3) 6.35 1.50

Albania's Labor Party, 15th anniv.

Congress Emblem A100

1957, Oct. 4 Unwmk. *Perf. 11½*

512 A100 2.50 l gray brown 1.25 .25
513 A100 3 l rose red 1.25 .25
514 A100 5 l dark blue 1.25 .25
515 A100 8 l green 3.25 .65
Nos. 512-515 (4) 7.00 1.40

4th Intl. Trade Union Cong., Leipzig, 10/4-15.

Lenin and Cruiser "Aurora" A101

1957, Nov. 7 Litho. *Perf. 10½*

516 A101 2.50 l violet brown .85 .25
517 A101 5 l violet blue 2.40 .25
518 A101 8 l gray 2.40 .35
Nos. 516-518 (3) 5.65 .85

40th anniv. of the Russian Revolution.

Albanian Fighter Holding Flag — A102

1957, Nov. 28 *Perf. 10½*

519 A102 1.50 l magenta 1.00 .25
520 A102 2.50 l brown 1.75 .25
521 A102 5 l blue 2.25 .35
522 A102 8 l green 5.00 .65
Nos. 519-522 (4) 10.00 1.50

Proclamation of independence, 45th anniv.

Naum Veqilharxhi — A103

1958, Feb. 1 **Unwmk.**

523 A103 2.50 l dark brown .80 .25
524 A103 5 l violet blue 1.60 .25
525 A103 8 l rose lilac 3.25 .60
Nos. 523-525 (3) 5.65 1.10

160th anniv. of the birth of Naum Veqilharxhi, patriot and writer.

Luigj Gurakuqi (1879-1925), Writer & Politician — A104

1958, Apr. 15 **Photo.** ***Perf. 10½***

526 A104 1.50 l dark green .65 .25
527 A104 2.50 l brown .65 .25
528 A104 5 l blue .65 .25
529 A104 8 l sepia 3.25 .50
Nos. 526-529 (4) 5.20 1.25

Transfer of the ashes of Luigj Gurakuqi.

Soldiers A105

2.50 l, 11 l, Airman, sailor, soldier and tank.

1958, July 10 **Litho.**

530 A105 1.50 l blue green .45 .25
531 A105 2.50 l dark red brown .65 .25
532 A105 8 l rose red 1.60 .30
533 A105 11 l bright blue 2.50 .50
Nos. 530-533 (4) 5.20 1.30

15th anniversary of Albanian army.

Cerciz Topulli and Mihal Grameno A106

Buildings and Tree A107

1958, July 1

534 A106 2.50 l dk olive bister .70 .25
535 A107 3 l green .70 .25
536 A106 5 l blue 1.60 .25
537 A107 8 l red brown 2.75 .40
Nos. 534-537 (4) 5.75 1.15

50th anniversary, Battle of Mashkullore.

Ancient Amphitheater and Goddess of Butrinto A108

1959, Jan. 25 **Litho.** ***Perf. 10½***

538 A108 2.50 l redsh brown 1.10 .25
539 A108 6.50 l lt blue green 3.00 .30
540 A108 11 l dark blue 5.00 .75
Nos. 538-540 (3) 9.10 1.30

Cultural Monuments Week.

Frederic Joliot-Curie and World Peace Congress Emblem — A109

1959, July 1 **Unwmk.**

541 A109 1.50 l carmine rose 2.75 .25
542 A109 2.50 l rose violet 5.50 .30
543 A109 11 l blue 13.50 1.50
Nos. 541-543 (3) 21.75 2.05

10th anniv. of the World Peace Movement.

Basketball — A110

Sports: 2.50 l, Soccer, 5 l, Runner. 11 l, Man and woman runners with torch and flags.

1959, Nov. 20 ***Perf. 10½***

544 A110 1.50 l bright violet 1.10 .25
545 A110 2.50 l emerald 1.10 .25
546 A110 5 l carmine rose 2.40 .25
547 A110 11 l ultra 6.50 1.75
Nos. 544-547 (4) 11.10 2.50

1st Albanian Spartacist Games.

Fighter and Flags — A111

Designs: 2.50 l, Miner with drill standing guard. 3 l, Farm woman with sheaf of grain. 6.50 l, Man and woman in laboratory.

1959, Nov. 29

548 A111 1.50 l brt carmine 1.50 .25
549 A111 2.50 l red brown 2.00 .25
550 A111 3 l brt blue green 2.75 .30
551 A111 6.50 l bright red 6.00 .50
a. Souvenir sheet 12.25 12.25
Nos. 548-551 (4) 12.25 1.30

15th anniversary of Albania's liberation.

No. 551a contains one each of Nos. 548-551, imperf. and all in bright carmine. Inscribed ribbon frame of sheet and frame lines for each stamp are blue green.

Mother and Child, UN Emblem A112

1959, Dec. 5 **Unwmk.**

552 A112 5 l lt grnsh blue 8.00 1.00
a. Miniature sheet 9.50 9.50

10th anniv. (in 1958) of the signing of the Universal Declaration of Human Rights.

No. 552a contains one imperf. stamp similar to No. 552; ornamental border.

Woman with Olive Branch — A113

1960, Mar. 8 **Litho.** ***Perf. 10½***

553 A113 2.50 l chocolate 1.25 .25
554 A113 11 l rose carmine 4.75 .50

50th anniv. of Intl. Women's Day, Mar. 8.

Alexander Moissi — A114

1960, Apr. 20

555 A114 3 l deep brown .70 .25
556 A114 11 l Prus green 3.00 .35

80th anniversary of the birth of Alexander Moissi (Moisiu) (1880-1935), German actor.

Lenin — A115

1960, Apr. 22

557 A115 4 l Prus blue 2.50 .25
558 A115 11 l lake 7.50 .40

90th anniversary of birth of Lenin.

School Building — A116

1960, May 30 **Litho.** ***Perf. 10½***

559 A116 5 l green 2.75 .35
560 A116 6.50 l plum 2.75 .35

1st Albanian secondary school, 50th anniv.

Soldier on Guard Duty — A117

1960, May 12 **Unwmk.** ***Perf. 10½***

561 A117 1.50 l carmine rose .55 .25
562 A117 11 l Prus blue 3.25 .40

15th anniversary of the Frontier Guards.

Liberation Monument, Tirana, Family and Policeman — A118

1960, May 14

563 A118 1.50 l green .55 .25
564 A118 8.50 l brown 3.25 .40

15th anniversary of the People's Police.

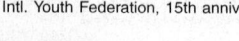

Congress Site — A119

1960, Mar. 25

565 A119 2.50 l sepia .55 .25
566 A119 7.50 l dull blue 1.65 .25

40th anniversary, Congress of Louchnia.

Pashko Vasa — A120

Designs: 1.50 l, Jani Vreto. 6.50 l, Sami Frasheri. 11 l, Page of statutes of association.

1960, May 5

567 A120 1 l gray olive .65 .25
568 A120 1.50 l brown 1.00 .25
569 A120 6.50 l blue 2.10 .25
570 A120 11 l rose red 5.75 .35
Nos. 567-570 (4) 9.50 1.10

80th anniv. (in 1959) of the Association of Albanian Authors.

Albanian Fighter and Cannon — A121

1960, Aug. 2 **Litho.** ***Perf. 10½***

571 A121 1.50 l olive brown .75 .25
572 A121 2.50 l maroon 1.40 .35
573 A121 5 l dark blue 3.00 .45
Nos. 571-573 (3) 5.15 1.05

Battle of Viona (against Italian troops), 40th anniv.

TU-104 Plane, Clock Tower, Tirana, and Kremlin, Moscow A122

1960, Aug. 18

574 A122 1 l redsh brown 1.25 .25
575 A122 7.50 l brt grnsh blue 4.00 .35
576 A122 11.50 l gray 6.75 .60
Nos. 574-576 (3) 12.00 1.20

TU-104 flights, Moscow-Tirana, 2nd anniv.

Rising Sun and Federation Emblem — A123

1960, Nov. 10 **Unwmk.** ***Perf. 10½***

577 A123 1.50 l ultra .60 .25
578 A123 8.50 l red 2.25 .35

Intl. Youth Federation, 15th anniv.

Ali Kelmendi — A124

1960, Dec. 5 **Litho.** ***Perf. 10½***

579 A124 1.50 l pale gray grn .55 .25
580 A124 11 l dull rose lake 2.25 .30

Ali Kelmendi, communist leader, 60th birthday.

Flags of Russia and Albania and Clasped Hands — A125

1961, Jan. 10 Unwmk. *Perf. 10½*

581 A125 2 l violet .55 .25
582 A125 8 l dull red brown 2.40 .35

15th anniv. of the Albanian-Soviet Friendship Society.

Marx and Lenin — A126

1961, Feb. 13 Litho.

583 A126 2 l rose red .55 .25
584 A126 8 l violet blue 2.40 .25

Fourth Communist Party Congress.

Man from Shkoder — A127

Costumes: 1.50 l, Woman from Shkoder. 6.50 l, Man from Lume. 11 l, Woman from Mirdite.

1961, Apr. 28 *Perf. 10½*

585 A127 1 l slate 1.25 .25
586 A127 1.50 l dull claret 1.25 .25
587 A127 6.50 l ultra 5.00 .55
588 A127 11 l red 7.50 1.40
Nos. 585-588 (4) 15.00 2.45

Otter — A128

Designs: 6.50 l, Badger. 11 l, Brown bear.

1961, June 25 Unwmk. *Perf. 10½*

589 A128 2.50 l grayish blue 4.00 .25
590 A128 6.50 l blue green 8.00 .50
591 A128 11 l dark red brown 17.50 .85
Nos. 589-591 (3) 29.50 1.60

Dalmatian Pelicans — A129

1961, Sept. 30 *Perf. 14*

592 A129 1.50 l shown 4.75 .25
593 A129 7.50 l Gray herons 7.00 .60
594 A129 11 l Little egret 8.75 .75
Nos. 592-594 (3) 20.50 1.60

Cyclamen — A130

1961, Oct. 27 Litho.

595 A130 1.50 l shown 2.25 .25
596 A130 8 l Forsythia 6.00 .50
597 A130 11 l Lily 7.50 .60
Nos. 595-597 (3) 15.75 1.35

Milosh G. Nikolla — A131

1961, Oct. 30 *Perf. 14*

598 A131 50q violet brown .65 .25
599 A131 8.50 l Prus green 2.25 .35

50th anniv. of the birth of Milosh Gjergi Nikolla, poet.

Flag with Marx and Lenin — A132

1961, Nov. 8

600 A132 2.50 l vermilion .65 .25
601 A132 7.50 l dull red brown 2.25 .35

20th anniv. of the founding of Albania's Communist Party.

Worker, Farm Woman and Emblem — A133

1961, Nov. 23 Unwmk. *Perf. 14*

602 A133 2.50 l violet blue .65 .25
603 A133 7.50 l rose claret 2.25 .30

20th anniv. of the Albanian Workers' Party.

Yuri Gagarin and Vostok 1 — A134

1962, Feb. 15 Unwmk. *Perf. 14*

604 A134 50q blue 1.50 *1.75*
605 A134 4 l red lilac 4.25 *4.75*
606 A134 11 l dk slate grn 11.00 *11.50*
Nos. 604-606 (3) 16.75 *18.00*

1st manned space flight, made by Yuri A. Gagarin, Soviet astronaut, Apr. 12, 1961.

Nos. 604-606 were overprinted with an overall yellow tint and with "POSTA AJRORE" (Air Mail) in maroon or black in 1962. Value: set, maroon ovpt., $90 mint, $130 used; set, black ovpt., $300 mint, $400 used.

Petro Nini Luarasi — A135

1962, Feb. 28 Litho.

607 A135 50q Prus blue .50 .25
608 A135 8.50 l olive gray 4.25 .25

50th anniv. (in 1961) of the death of Petro Nini Luarasi, Albanian patriot.

Malaria Eradication Emblem — A136

1962, Apr. 30 Unwmk. *Perf. 14*

609 A136 1.50 l brt green .55 .25
610 A136 2.50 l brown red .55 .25
611 A136 10 l red lilac 1.10 .25
612 A136 11 l blue 1.40 .35
Nos. 609-612 (4) 3.60 1.10

WHO drive to eradicate malaria.

Souvenir sheets, perf. and imperf., contain one each of Nos. 609-612. Value $30 each. Nos. 609-612 imperf., value, set $25.

Camomile — A137

Medicinal plants.

1962, May 10

613 A137 50q shown .55 .30
614 A137 8 l Linden 2.00 .60
615 A137 11.50 l Garden sage 3.25 .90
Nos. 613-615 (3) 5.80 1.80

Value, imperf. set $30 mint, $40 used.

Woman Diver — A138

2.50 l, Pole vault. 3 l, Mt. Fuji & torch, horiz. 9 l, Woman javelin thrower. 10 l, Shot putting.

1962, May 31 *Perf. 14*

616 A138 50q brt grnsh bl & blk .25 .25
617 A138 2.50 l gldn brn & sepia .40 .25
618 A138 3 l blue & gray .55 .25
619 A138 9 l rose car & dk brn 2.25 .25
620 A138 10 l olive & blk 2.40 .30
Nos. 616-620 (5) 5.85 1.30

1964 Olympic Games, Tokyo. Value, imperf set, $50 mint, $70 used. A 15 l (like 3 l) exists in souv. sheet, perf. and imperf. Value, each $35 mint, $50 used.

Globe and Orbits — A139

Dog Laika and Sputnik 2 — A140

Designs: 1.50 l, Rocket to the sun. 20 l, Lunik 3 photographing far side of the moon.

1962, June Unwmk. *Perf. 14*

621 A139 50q violet & org .60 .25
622 A140 1 l blue grn & brn 1.10 .30
623 A140 1.50 l yellow & ver 1.60 .40
624 A139 20 l magenta & bl 11.00 5.50
Nos. 621-624 (4) 14.30 6.45

Russian space explorations.

Nos. 621-624 exist imperf in changed colors. Value, mint $65, used $75.

Two miniature sheets exist, containing one 14-lek picturing Sputnik 1. The perforated 14-lek is yellow and brown; the imperf. red and brown. Value, each mint $65, used $75.

Soccer Game, Map of South America — A141

2.50 l, 15 l, Soccer game and globe as ball.

1962, July Litho.

625 A141 1 l org & dk pur .55 .25
626 A141 2.50 l emer & bluish grn 1.40 .25
627 A141 6.50 l lt brn & pink 1.40 .25
628 A141 15 l bluish grn & mar 3.00 .40
Nos. 625-628 (4) 6.35 1.15

World Soccer Championships, Chile, 5/30-6/17.

Exist imperforate in changed colors. Value, mint $40, used $75.

Two miniature sheets exist, each containing a single 20-lek in design similar to A141. The perf. sheet is brown and green; the imperf., brown and orange. Value, mint $40, used $75.

Map of Europe and Albania — A142

Designs: 1 l, 2.50 l, Map of Adriatic Sea and Albania and Roman statue.

1962, Aug.

630 A142 50q multicolored .45 *1.00*
631 A142 1 l ultra & red .95 *2.75*
632 A142 2.50 l blue & red 7.25 *8.50*
633 A142 11 l multicolored 10.00 *17.50*
Nos. 630-633 (4) 18.65 *29.75*

Tourist propaganda. Imperforates in changed colors exist. Value, mint $35, used $70.

Miniature sheets containing a 7 l and 8 l stamp, perf. and imperf., exist. Value, mint $40, used $75.

Woman of Dardhe — A143

Regional Costumes: 1 l, Man from Devoll. 2.50 l, Woman from Lunxheri. 14 l, Man from Gjirokaster.

1962, Sept.

635 A143 50q car, bl & pur .45 .25
636 A143 1 l red brn & ocher .55 .25
637 A143 2.50 l vio, yel grn & blk 1.60 .60
638 A143 14 l red brn & pale grn 6.75 1.60
Nos. 635-638 (4) 9.35 2.70

Exist imperf. Value, set, mint $40, used $60.

Chamois — A144

Animals: 1 l, Lynx, horiz. 1.50 l, Wild boar, horiz. 15 l, 20 l, Roe deer.

1963, Oct. 24 Unwmk. *Perf. 14*

639 A144 50q sl grn & dk pur .55 .25
640 A144 1 l orange & blk 2.25 .25
641 A144 1.50 l red brn & blk 2.75 .25
642 A144 15 l yel ol & red brn 22.00 1.00
Nos. 639-642 (4) 27.55 1.75

Miniature Sheet

643 A144 20 l yel ol & red brn 135.00 145.00

Imperfs. in changed colors, value Nos. 639-642 $75, No. 643 $125.

Ismail Qemali — A145

Designs: 1 l, Albania eagle. 16 l, Eagle over fortress formed by "RPSH."

1962, Dec. 28 Litho.

644 A145 1 l red & red brn .75 .25
645 A145 3 l org brn & blk 3.75 .25
646 A145 16 l dk car rose & blk 6.75 .50
Nos. 644-646 (3) 11.25 1.00

50th anniv. of independence. Imperfs. in changed colors, value, set $40 mint, $60 used.

Monument of October Revolution — A146

1963, Jan. 5 Unwmk. *Perf. 14*

647 A146 5 l shown 1.25 .25
648 A146 10 l Lenin statue 3.00 .35

October Revolution (Russia, 1917), 45th anniv.

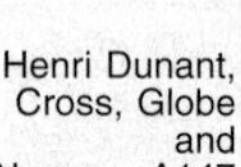

Henri Dunant, Cross, Globe and Nurse — A147

1963, Jan 25 Unwmk. *Perf. 14*

649 A147 1.50 l rose lake, red & blk .70 .25
650 A147 2.50 l lt bl, red & blk 1.10 .25
651 A147 6 l emerald, red & blk 2.25 .25
652 A147 10 l dull yel, red & blk 3.75 .60
Nos. 649-652 (4) 7.80 1.35

Cent. of the Geneva Conf., which led to the establishment of the Intl. Red Cross in 1864.
Imperfs. in changed colors, value, set $60.

Stalin and Battle of Stalingrad A148

1963, Feb. 2

653 A148 8 l dk green & slate 11.00 1.00

Battle of Stalingrad, 20th anniv. See No. C67.

Andrian G. Nikolayev — A149

Designs: 7.50 l, Vostoks 3 and 4 and globe, horiz. 20 l, Pavel R. Popovich. 25 l, Nikolayev, Popovich and globe with trajectories.

1963, Feb. 28 Litho.

654 A149 2.50 l vio bl & sepia .60 .40
655 A149 7.50 l lt blue & blk 1.60 .80
656 A149 20 l violet & sepia 4.25 2.25
Nos. 654-656 (3) 6.45 3.45

Miniature Sheet

657 A149 25 l vio bl & sepia 45.00 45.00

1st group space flight of Vostoks 3 and 4, Aug. 11-15, 1962. Imperfs in changed colors, value: Nos. 654-656 $45 mint or used; No. 657 perf, $45 mint or used; No. 657 imperf, $50 mint or used.

"Albania" Decorating Police Officer — A150

1963, Mar. 20 Unwmk. *Perf. 14*

658 A150 2.50 l crim, mag & blk 1.10 .25
659 A150 7.50 l org ver, dk red & blk 3.75 .25

20th anniversary of the security police.

Polyphylla Fullo — A151

Beetles: 1.50 l, Lucanus cervus. 8 l, Procerus gigas. 10 l, Cicindela albanica.

1963, Mar. 20

660 A151 50q ol grn & brn 1.25 .25
661 A151 1.50 l blue & brn 2.00 .25
662 A151 8 l dl rose & blk vio 7.50 1.25
663 A151 10 l brt citron & blk 9.75 1.40
Nos. 660-663 (4) 20.50 3.15

1913 Stamp and Postmark A152

10 l, Stamps of 1913, 1937 and 1962.

1963, May 5

664 A152 5 l yel, buff, bl & blk 2.25 .25
665 A152 10 l car rose, grn & blk 3.75 .45

50th anniversary of Albanian stamps.

Boxer — A153

Designs: 3 l, Basketball baskets. 5 l, Volleyball. 6 l, Bicyclists. 9 l, Gymnast. 15 l, Hands holding torch, and map of Japan.

1963, May 25 *Perf. 13½*

666 A153 2 l yel, blk & red brn .70 *1.00*
667 A153 3 l ocher, brn & bl .90 *2.00*
668 A153 5 l gray bl, red brn & brn 1.40 *2.75*
669 A153 6 l gray, dk gray & grn 1.90 *5.00*
670 A153 9 l rose, red brn & bl 3.75 *7.50*
Nos. 666-670 (5) 8.65 *18.25*

Miniature Sheet

671 A153 15 l lt bl, car, blk & brn 20.00 20.00

1964 Olympic Games in Tokyo. Value, imperfs. Nos. 666-670 $20, No. 671 $20.

Crested Grebe — A154

Birds: 3 l, Golden eagle. 6.50 l, Gray partridges. 11 l, Capercaillie.

1963, Apr. 20 Litho. *Perf. 14*

672 A154 50q multicolored 1.50 .25
673 A154 3 l multicolored 3.00 .50
674 A154 6.50 l multicolored 7.50 1.25
675 A154 11 l multicolored 10.00 2.00
Nos. 672-675 (4) 22.00 4.00

Soldier and Building A155

2.50 l, Soldier with pack, ship, plane. 5 l, Soldier in battle. 6 l, Soldier, bulldozer.

1963, July 10 Unwmk. *Perf. 12*

676 A155 1.50 l brick red, yel & blk .55 .25
677 A155 2.50 l bl, ocher & brn 1.10 .25
678 A155 5 l bluish grn, gray & blk 1.60 .25
679 A155 6 l red brn, buff & bl 2.25 .25
Nos. 676-679 (4) 5.50 1.00

Albanian army, 20th anniversary.

Maj. Yuri A. Gagarin A156

Designs: 5 l, Maj. Gherman Titov. 7 l, Maj. Andrian G. Nikolayev. 11 l, Lt. Col. Pavel R. Popovich. 14 l, Lt. Col. Valeri Bykovski. 20 l, Lt. Valentina Tereshkova.

1963, July 30

Portraits in Yellow and Black

680 A156 3 l brt purple 1.10 .25
681 A156 5 l dull blue 1.30 .25
682 A156 7 l gray 1.60 .25
683 A156 11 l deep claret 3.25 .35
684 A156 14 l blue green 5.00 .60
685 A156 20 l ultra 7.50 1.10
Nos. 680-685 (6) 19.75 2.80

Man's conquest of space. Value, imperf. set $55.

Volleyball A157

1963, Aug. 31 *Perf. 12x12½*

686 A157 2 l shown .55 .25
687 A157 3 l Weight lifting .85 .25
688 A157 5 l Soccer 1.10 .25
689 A157 7 l Boxing 1.60 .25
690 A157 8 l Rowing 3.75 .30
Nos. 686-690 (5) 7.85 1.30

European championships. Imperfs. in changed colors, value set $35.

Papilio Podalirius A158

1963, Sept. 29 Litho.

Various Butterflies and Moths in Natural Colors

691 A158 1 l red .65 *.25*
692 A158 2 l blue 1.10 *.25*
693 A158 4 l dull lilac 2.25 *.60*
694 A158 5 l pale green 3.25 *.60*
695 A158 8 l bister 5.50 *1.25*
696 A158 10 l light blue 7.00 *1.75*
Nos. 691-696 (6) 19.75 *4.70*

Oil Refinery, Cerrik — A159

2.50 l, Food processing plant, Tirana, horiz. 30 l, Fruit canning plant. 50 l, Tannery, horiz.

1963, Nov. 15 Unwmk. *Perf. 14*

697 A159 2.50 l rose red, *pnksh* 1.10 .25
698 A159 20 l slate grn, *grnsh* 4.25 .25
699 A159 30 l dull pur, *grysh* 9.75 .55
700 A159 50 l ocher, *yel* 11.00 .85
Nos. 697-700 (4) 26.10 1.90

Industrial development in Albania.
For surcharges see Nos. 841-846.

Flag and Shield — A160

1963, Nov. 24 *Perf. 12½x12*

701 A160 2 l grnsh bl, blk, ocher & red .75 .25
702 A160 8 l blue, blk, ocher & red 2.25 .50

1st Congress of Army Aid Assn.

Chinese, Caucasian and Negro Men — A161

1963, Dec. 10 *Perf. 12x11½*

703 A161 3 l bister & blk .65 .25
704 A161 5 l bister & ultra 1.25 .25
705 A161 7 l bister & vio 2.75 .30
Nos. 703-705 (3) 4.65 .80

15th anniv. of the Universal Declaration of Human Rights.

Slalom Ascent — A162

Designs: 50q, Bobsled, horiz. 6.50 l, Ice hockey, horiz. 12.50 l, Women's figure skating. No. 709A, Ski jumper.

1963, Dec. 25 ***Perf. 14***

No.	Type	Value	Description	Mint	Used
706	A162	50q	grnsh bl & blk	.55	.25
707	A162	2.50 l	red, gray & blk	1.00	.25
708	A162	6.50 l	yel, blk & gray	1.40	.25
709	A162	12.50 l	red, blk & yel grn	2.75	.55
			Nos. 706-709 (4)	5.70	1.30

Miniature Sheet

No.	Type	Value	Description	Mint	Used
709A	A162	12.50 l	multi	30.00	30.00

9th Winter Olympic Games, Innsbruck, Jan. 29-Feb. 9, 1964. Imperfs. in changed colors, value Nos. 706-709 $90, No. 709A $65.

Lenin — A163

1964, Jan. 21 ***Perf. 12½x12***

No.	Type	Value	Description	Mint	Used
710	A163	5 l	gray & bister	1.25	.25
711	A163	10 l	gray & ocher	2.25	.30

40th anniversary, death of Lenin.

Hurdling — A164

Designs: 3 l, Track, horiz. 6.50 l, Rifle shooting, horiz. 8 l, Basketball.

Perf. 12½x12, 12x12½

1964, Jan. 30 **Litho.**

No.	Type	Value	Description	Mint	Used
712	A164	2.50 l	pale vio & ultra	.55	.25
713	A164	3 l	lt grn & red brn	1.10	.35
714	A164	6.50 l	blue & claret	1.60	1.00
715	A164	8 l	lt blue & ocher	2.75	1.60
			Nos. 712-715 (4)	6.00	3.20

1st Games of the New Emerging Forces, GANEFO, Jakarta, Indonesia, Nov. 10-22, 1963.

Fish — A165

1964, Feb. 26 **Unwmk.** ***Perf. 14***

No.	Type	Value	Description	Mint	Used
716	A165	50q	Sturgeon	.55	.25
717	A165	1 l	Gilthead	1.10	.25
718	A165	1.50 l	Striped mullet	1.60	.25
719	A165	2.50 l	Carp	2.25	.25
720	A165	6.50 l	Mackerel	3.25	.40
721	A165	10 l	Lake Ohrid trout	5.50	.50
			Nos. 716-721 (6)	14.25	1.90

Wild Animals A166

1964, Mar. 28 ***Perf. 12½x12***

No.	Type	Value	Description	Mint	Used
722	A166	1 l	Red Squirrel	.55	.25
723	A166	1.50 l	Beech marten	.85	.25
724	A166	2 l	Red fox	1.10	.40
725	A166	2.50 l	Hedgehog	1.60	.40
726	A166	3 l	Hare	2.25	.60
727	A166	5 l	Jackal	2.75	.60
728	A166	7 l	Wildcat	4.25	.60
729	A166	8 l	Wolf	5.50	.95
			Nos. 722-729 (8)	18.85	4.05

Lighting Olympic Torch — A167

5 l, Torch, globes. 7 l, 15 l, Olympic flag, Mt. Fuji. 10 l, National Stadium, Tokyo.

1964, May 18 ***Perf. 12x12½***

No.	Type	Value	Description	Mint	Used
730	A167	3 l	lt yel grn, yel & buff	.55	*.70*
731	A167	5 l	red & vio blue	.75	*1.00*
732	A167	7 l	lt bl, ultra & yel	1.10	*1.50*
733	A167	10 l	orange, bl & vio	1.60	*2.50*
			Nos. 730-733 (4)	4.00	*5.70*

Miniature Sheet

No.	Type	Value	Description	Mint	Used
734	A167	15 l	lt bl, ultra & org	22.50	22.50

18th Olympic Games, Tokyo, Oct. 10-25, 1964. No. 734 contains one 49x62mm stamp. Imperfs. in changed colors, value Nos. 730-733 $20, No. 734 $22.50.

See No. 745.

Partisans — A168

5 l, Arms of Albania. 8 l, Enver Hoxha.

Perf. 12½x12

1964, May 24 **Litho.** **Unwmk.**

No.	Type	Value	Description	Mint	Used
735	A168	2 l	orange, red & blk	1.25	.25
736	A168	5 l	multicolored	3.00	.30
737	A168	8 l	red brn, blk & red	6.25	.90
			Nos. 735-737 (3)	10.50	1.45

20th anniv. of the Natl. Anti-Fascist Cong. of Liberation, Permet, May 24, 1944. The label attached to each stamp, without perforations between, carries a quotation from the 1944 Congress.

Albanian Flag and Revolutionists A169

Perf. 12½x12

1964, June 10 **Litho.** **Unwmk.**

No.	Type	Value	Description	Mint	Used
738	A169	2.50 l	red & gray	.50	.25
739	A169	7.50 l	lilac rose & gray	1.25	.25

Albanian revolution of 1924, 40th anniv.

Full Moon — A170

Designs: 5 l, New moon. 8 l, Half moon. 11 l, Waning moon. 15 l, Far side of moon.

1964, June 27 ***Perf. 12x12½***

No.	Type	Value	Description	Mint	Used
740	A170	1 l	purple & yel	.50	.25
741	A170	5 l	violet & yel	1.00	.25
742	A170	8 l	blue & yel	1.60	.30
743	A170	11 l	green & yel	4.50	.45
			Nos. 740-743 (4)	7.60	1.25

Miniature Sheet

Perf. 12 on 2 sides

No.	Type	Value	Description	Mint	Used
744	A170	15 l	ultra & yel	17.00	17.00

No. 744 contains one stamp, size: 35x36mm, perforated at top and bottom. Imperfs. in changed colors, value Nos. 740-743 $18, No. 744 $17.

No. 733 with Added Inscription: "Rimini 25-VI-64"

1964 ***Perf. 12x12½***

No.	Type	Value	Description	Mint	Used
745	A167	10 l	orange, bl & vio	8.00	8.00

"Toward Tokyo 1964" Phil. Exhib. at Rimini, Italy, June 25-July 6.

Wren — A171

Birds: 1 l, Penduline titmouse. 2.50 l, Green woodpecker. 3 l, Tree creeper.4 l, Nuthatch. 5 l, Great titmouse. 6 l, Goldfinch. 18 l, Oriole.

1964, July 31 ***Perf. 12x12½***

No.	Type	Value	Description	Mint	Used
746	A171	50q	multi	.50	.25
747	A171	1 l	orange & multi	1.00	.25
748	A171	2.50 l	multi	1.50	.40
749	A171	3 l	blue & multi	2.00	.40
750	A171	4 l	yellow & multi	2.50	.80
751	A171	5 l	blue & multi	3.00	.80
752	A171	6 l	lt vio & multi	3.50	1.25
753	A171	18 l	pink & multi	7.50	2.75
			Nos. 746-753 (8)	21.50	6.90

Running and Gymnastics A172

Sport: 2 l, Weight lifting, judo. 3 l, Equestrian, bicycling. 4 l, Soccer, water polo. 5 l, Wrestling, boxing. 6 l, Pentathlon, hockey. 7 l, Swimming, sailing. 8 l, Basketball, volleyball. 9 l, Rowing, canoeing. 10 l, Fencing, pistol shooting. 20 l, Three winners.

Perf. 12x12½

1964, Sept. 25 **Litho.** **Unwmk.**

No.	Type	Value	Description	Mint	Used
754	A172	1 l	lt bl, rose & emer	.25	.25
755	A172	2 l	bis brn, bluish grn & vio	.25	.25
756	A172	3 l	vio, red org & ol bis	.25	.25
757	A172	4 l	grnsh bl, ol & ultra	.50	.35
758	A172	5 l	grnsh bl, car & pale lil	.50	.35
759	A172	6 l	dk bl, org & lt bl	1.00	.75
760	A172	7 l	dk bl, lt ol & org	1.00	.75
761	A172	8 l	emer, gray & yel	1.00	.75
762	A172	9 l	bl, yel & lil rose	1.00	.75
763	A172	10 l	brt grn, org brn & yel grn	1.60	1.00
			Nos. 754-763 (10)	7.35	5.45

Miniature Sheet

Perf. 12

No.	Type	Value	Description	Mint	Used
764	A172	20 l	violet & lemon	25.00	30.00

18th Olympic Games, Tokyo, Oct. 10-25. No. 764 contains one stamp, size: 41x68mm. Imperfs in changed colors, value: Nos. 754-763, $20 mint, $30 used; No. 764, $25 mint, $30 used.

Arms of People's Republic of China — A173

Mao Tse-tung and Flag A174

1964, Oct. 1 ***Perf. 11½x12, 12x11½***

No.	Type	Value	Description	Mint	Used
765	A173	7 l	black, red & yellow	10.00	4.50
766	A174	8 l	black, red & yellow	10.00	6.00

People's Republic of China, 15th anniv.

Karl Marx A175

Designs: 5 l, St. Martin's Hall, London. 8 l, Friedrich Engels.

1964, Nov. 5 ***Perf. 12x11½***

No.	Type	Value	Description	Mint	Used
767	A175	2 l	red, lt vio & blk	1.10	.45
768	A175	5 l	gray blue	2.50	1.40
769	A175	8 l	ocher, blk & red	5.00	1.75
			Nos. 767-769 (3)	8.60	3.60

Centenary of First Socialist International.

Jeronim de Rada — A176

1964, Nov. 15 ***Perf. 12½x11½***

No.	Type	Value	Description	Mint	Used
770	A176	7 l	slate green	1.60	.35
771	A176	8 l	dull violet	2.75	.60

Birth of Jeronim de Rada, poet, 150th anniv.

Arms of Albania — A177

Factories A178

Designs: 3 l, Combine harvester. 4 l, Woman chemist. 10 l, Hands holding Communist Party book, hammer and sickle.

Perf. 11½x12, 12x11½

1964, Nov. 29

No.	Type	Value	Description	Mint	Used
772	A177	1 l	multicolored	.50	.40
773	A178	2 l	red, yel & vio bl	1.00	.80
774	A178	3 l	red, yel & brn	1.50	1.25

775 A178 4 l red, yel & gray grn 2.00 1.60
776 A177 10 l red, bl & blk 5.00 4.00
Nos. 772-776 (5) 10.00 8.05

20th anniversary of liberation.

Planet Mercury — A179

Planets: 2 l, Venus and rocket. 3 l, Earth, moon and rocket. 4 l, Mars and rocket. 5 l, Jupiter. 6 l, Saturn. 7 l, Uranus. 8 l, Neptune. 9 l, Pluto. 15 l, Solar system and rocket.

1964, Dec. 15 ***Perf. 12x12½***

777 A179 1 l yellow & pur .25 .25
778 A179 2 l multicolored .50 .25
779 A179 3 l multicolored .70 .40
780 A179 4 l multicolored .70 .40
781 A179 5 l yel, dk pur & brn 1.00 .60
782 A179 6 l lt grn, vio brn & yel 1.50 .60
783 A179 7 l yellow & grn 1.75 .90
784 A179 8 l yellow & vio 2.00 1.00
785 A179 9 l lt grn, yel & blk 2.25 1.25
Nos. 777-785 (9) 10.65 5.65

Miniature Sheet

Perf. 12 on 2 sides

786 A179 15 l car, bl, yel & grn 35.00 35.00

No. 786 contains one stamp, size: 62x51mm, perforated at top and bottom. Imperfs. in changed colors. Value Nos. 777-785, $35; No. 786, $32.50.

European Chestnut — A180

1965, Jan. 25 ***Perf. 11½x12***

787 A180 1 l shown .35 .25
788 A180 2 l Medlars .55 .25
789 A180 3 l Persimmon .75 .25
790 A180 4 l Pomegranate 1.10 .40
791 A180 5 l Quince 2.25 .50
792 A180 10 l Orange 4.25 1.00
Nos. 787-792 (6) 9.25 2.65

Symbols of Industry — A181

Designs: 5 l, Books, triangle and compass. 8 l, Beach, trees and hotel.

1965, Feb. 20

793 A181 2 l blk, car rose & pink *7.50* 7.00
794 A181 5 l yel, gray & blk *12.00* 10.50
795 A181 8 l blk, vio bl & lt bl *15.00* 13.00
Nos. 793-795 (3) *34.50* 30.50

Professional trade associations, 20th anniv.

Water Buffalo A182

Various designs: Water buffalo.

1965, Mar. ***Perf. 12x11½***

796 A182 1 l lt yel grn, yel & brn blk 1.00 .35
797 A182 2 l lt bl, dk gray & blk 2.10 .65
798 A182 3 l yellow, brn & grn 3.25 1.10
799 A182 7 l brt grn, yel & brn blk 7.25 1.50
800 A182 12 l pale lil, dk brn & ind 12.00 1.75
Nos. 796-800 (5) 25.60 5.35

Mountain View, Valbona — A183

1.50 l, Seashore. 3 l, Glacier and peak. 4 l, Gorge. 5 l, Mountain peaks. 9 l, Lake and hills.

1965, Mar. **Litho.** ***Perf. 12***

801 A183 1.50 l multi 1.60 .35
802 A183 2.50 l multi 3.50 .70
803 A183 3 l multi, vert. 3.75 .70
804 A183 4 l multi, vert. 5.00 1.25
805 A183 5 l multi 6.00 1.50
806 A183 9 l multi 16.00 3.00
Nos. 801-806 (6) 35.85 7.50

Frontier Guard — A184

1965, Apr. 25 **Unwmk.**

807 A184 2.50 l lt blue & multi 1.75 .25
808 A184 12.50 l lt ultra & multi 8.50 .90

20th anniversary of the Frontier Guards.

Small-bore Rifle Shooting, Prone — A185

Designs: 2 l, Rifle shooting, standing. 3 l, Target over map of Europe, showing Bucharest. 4 l, Pistol shooting. 15 l, Rifle shooting, kneeling.

1965, May 10

809 A185 1 l lil, car rose, blk & brn .45 .25
810 A185 2 l bl, blk, brn & vio bl .45 .25
811 A185 3 l pink & car rose 1.10 .25
812 A185 4 l bis, blk & vio brn 2.00 .25
813 A185 15 l brt grn, brn & vio brn 5.00 .50
Nos. 809-813 (5) 9.00 1.50

European Shooting Championships, Bucharest.

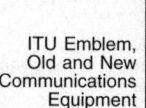

ITU Emblem, Old and New Communications Equipment A186

1965, May 17 ***Perf. 12½x12***

814 A186 2.50 l brt grn, blk & lil rose 1.10 .25
815 A186 12.50 l vio, blk & brt bl 6.50 .30

Centenary of the ITU.

Col. Pavel Belyayev — A187

Designs: 2 l, Voskhod II. 6.50 l, Lt. Col. Alexei Leonov. 20 l, Leonov floating in space.

1965, June 15 ***Perf. 12***

816 A187 1.50 l lt blue & brn .30 .25
817 A187 2 l dk bl, lt vio & lt ultra .35 .25
818 A187 6.50 l lilac & brn 1.10 .25
819 A187 20 l chlky bl, yel & blk 4.25 .40
Nos. 816-819 (4) 6.00 1.15

Miniature Sheet

Perf. 12 on 2 sides

820 A187 20 l brt bl, org & blk 20.00 20.00

Space flight of Voskhod II and 1st man walking in space, Lt. Col. Alexei Leonov. No. 820 contains one stamp, size: 51x59½mm, perforated at top and bottom. Imperf., brt grn background, value $20.

Marx and Lenin — A188

1965, June 21 ***Perf. 12***

821 A188 2.50 l dk brn, red & yel 1.10 .25
822 A188 7.50 l sl grn, org ver & buff 3.50 .25

6th Conf. of Postal Ministers of Communist Countries, Peking, June 21-July 15.

Mother and Child — A189

2 l, Pioneers. 3 l, Boy and girl at play, horiz. 4 l, Child on beach. 15 l, Girl with book.

Perf. 12½x12, 12x12½

1965, June 29 **Litho.** **Unwmk.**

823 A189 1 l brt bl, rose lil & blk .25 .25
824 A189 2 l salmon, vio & blk .60 .25
825 A189 3 l green, org & vio .80 .25
826 A189 4 l multicolored 1.10 .25
827 A189 15 l lil rose, brn & ocher 4.25 .50
Nos. 823-827 (5) 7.00 1.50

Issued for International Children's Day.

Statue of Magistrate — A190

Designs: 1 l, Amphora. 2 l, Illyrian armor. 3 l, Mosaic, horiz. 15 l, Torso, Apollo statue.

1965, July 20 ***Perf. 12***

828 A190 1 l lt ol, org & brn .25 .25
829 A190 2 l gray grn, grn & brn .55 .25
830 A190 3 l tan, brn, car & lil .75 .25
831 A190 4 l green, bis & brn 1.60 .25
832 A190 15 l gray & pale claret 4.00 .65
Nos. 828-832 (5) 7.15 1.65

Flowers — A191

1965, Aug. 11 ***Perf. 12½x12***

833 A191 1 l Fuchsia .25 .25
834 A191 2 l Cyclamen .75 .25
835 A191 3 l Tiger lily 1.30 .25
836 A191 3.50 l Iris 1.60 .25
837 A191 4 l Dahlia 1.75 .25
838 A191 4.50 l Hydrangea 2.25 .25
839 A191 5 l Rose 2.40 .30
840 A191 7 l Tulips 3.25 .35
Nos. 833-840 (8) 13.55 2.15

Nos. 698-700 Surcharged New Value and Two Bars

1965, Aug. 16 ***Perf. 14***

841 A159 5q on 30 l 1.00 1.00
842 A159 15q on 30 l 1.00 1.00
843 A159 25q on 50 l 1.60 1.60
844 A159 80q on 50 l 3.50 3.50
845 A159 1.10 l on 20 l 5.00 5.00
846 A159 2 l on 20 l 8.00 8.00
Nos. 841-846 (6) 20.10 20.10

White Stork — A192

Migratory Birds: 20q, Cuckoo. 30q, Hoopoe. 40q, European bee-eater. 50q, European nightjar. 1.50 l, Quail.

1965, Aug. 31 ***Perf. 12***

847 A192 10q yel, blk & gray .55 .40
848 A192 20q brt pink, blk & dk bl 1.10 .40
849 A192 30q violet, blk & bis 1.60 .60
850 A192 40q emer, blk yel & org 2.25 .80
851 A192 50q ultra, brn & red brn 2.75 .95
852 A192 1.50 l bis, red brn & dp org 8.25 2.75
Nos. 847-852 (6) 16.50 5.90

"Homecoming," by Bukurosh Sejdini — A193

1965, Sept. 26 **Litho.** ***Perf. 12x12½***

853 A193 25q olive black 3.25 .40
854 A193 65q blue black 8.25 1.60
855 A193 1.10 l black 11.00 3.25
Nos. 853-855 (3) 22.50 5.25

Second war veterans' meeting.

Hunting — A194

1965, Oct. 6 **Litho.** **Unwmk.**

856 A194 10q Capercaillie .50 .25
857 A194 20q Deer 1.00 .25
858 A194 30q Pheasant 1.50 .25
859 A194 40q Mallards 2.00 .25
860 A194 50q Boar 2.50 .25
861 A194 1 l Rabbit 5.00 .55
Nos. 856-861 (6) 12.50 1.80

Oleander — A195

Flowers: 20q, Forget-me-nots. 30q, Pink. 40q, White water lily. 50q, Bird's foot. 1 l, Corn poppy.

1965, Oct. 26 *Perf. 12½x12*

No.	Type	Denom.	Colors	Unused	Used
862	A195	10q	brt bl, grn & car rose	.25	.25
863	A195	20q	org red, bl, brn & grn	.55	.25
864	A195	30q	vio, car rose & grn	.75	.25
865	A195	40q	emerald, yel & blk	1.30	.30
866	A195	50q	org brn, yel & grn	1.60	.40
867	A195	1 l	yel grn, blk & rose red	4.25	1.60
			Nos. 862-867 (6)	8.70	3.05

Hotel Turizmi, Fier — A196

Buildings: 10q, Hotel, Peshkopi. 15q, Sanatorium, Tirana. 25q, Rest home, Pogradec. 65q, Partisan Sports Arena, Tirana. 80q, Rest home, Mali Dajt. 1.10 l, Culture House, Tirana. 1.60 l, Hotel Adriatik, Durres. 2 l, Migjeni Theater, Shkoder. 3 l, Alexander Moissi House of Culture, Durres.

1965, Oct. 27 *Perf. 12x12½*

No.	Type	Denom.	Colors	Unused	Used
868	A196	5q	blue & blk	.25	.25
869	A196	10q	ocher & blk	.25	.25
870	A196	15q	dull grn & blk	.25	.25
871	A196	25q	violet & blk	.75	.25
872	A196	65q	lt brn & blk	1.60	.50
873	A196	80q	yel grn & blk	2.25	.50
874	A196	1.10 l	lilac & blk	2.75	.50
875	A196	1.60 l	lt vio bl & blk	4.25	1.40
876	A196	2 l	dull rose & blk	5.25	1.40
877	A196	3 l	gray & blk	10.50	2.50
			Nos. 868-877 (10)	28.10	7.80

Freighter "Teuta" — A197

Ships: 20q, Raft. 30q, Sailing ship, 19th cent. 40q, Sailing ship, 18th cent. 50q, Freighter "Vlora." 1 l, Illyric galleys.

1965, Nov. 16

No.	Type	Denom.	Colors	Unused	Used
878	A197	10q	brt grn & dk grn	.35	.25
879	A197	20q	ol bis & dk grn	.45	.25
880	A197	30q	lt & dp ultra	.55	.25
881	A197	40q	vio & dp vio	.75	.25
882	A197	50q	pink & dk red	1.60	.25
883	A197	1 l	bister & brn	3.75	.45
			Nos. 878-883 (6)	7.45	1.70

Brown Bear — A198

Various Albanian bears. 50q, 55q, 60q, horiz.

1965, Dec. 7 *Perf. 11½x12*

No.	Type	Denom.	Colors	Unused	Used
884	A198	10q	bister & dk brn	.45	.25
885	A198	20q	pale brn & dk brn	.55	.25
886	A198	30q	bis, dk brn & car	1.10	.25
887	A198	35q	pale brn & dk brn	1.30	.25
888	A198	40q	bister & dk brn	1.60	.25
889	A198	50q	bister & dk brn	2.75	.25
890	A198	55q	bister & dk brn	3.25	.30
891	A198	60q	pale brn, dk brn & car	6.00	.50
			Nos. 884-891 (8)	17.00	2.30

Basketball and Players — A199

10q, Games' emblem (map of Albania and basket). 30q, 50q, Players with ball (diff. designs). 1.40 l, Basketball medal on ribbon.

1965, Dec. 15 **Litho.** *Perf. 12½x12*

No.	Type	Denom.	Colors	Unused	Used
892	A199	10q	blue, yel & car	.35	.25
893	A199	20q	rose lil, lt brn & blk	.45	.25
894	A199	30q	bis, lt brn, red & blk	.75	.25
895	A199	50q	lt grn, lt brn & blk	1.60	.25
896	A199	1.40 l	rose, blk, brn & yel	3.25	.50
			Nos. 892-896 (5)	6.40	1.50

7th Balkan Basketball Championships, Tirana, Dec. 15-19.

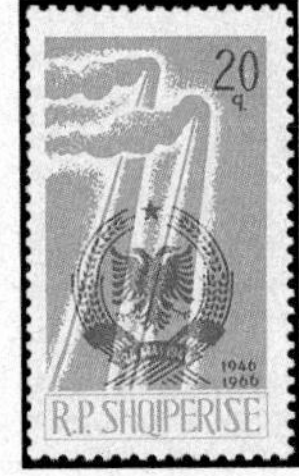

Arms of Republic and Smokestacks A200

Arms and: 10q, Book. 30q, Wheat. 60q, Book, hammer & sickle. 80q, Factories.

1966, Jan. 11 **Litho.** *Perf. 11½x12*
Coat of Arms in Gold

No.	Type	Denom.	Colors	Unused	Used
897	A200	10q	crimson & brn	.30	.25
898	A200	20q	blue & vio bl	.35	.25
899	A200	30q	org yel & brn	.75	.25
900	A200	60q	yel grn & brt grn	1.75	.25
901	A200	80q	crimson & brn	2.25	.25
			Nos. 897-901 (5)	5.40	1.25

Albanian People's Republic, 20th anniv.

Cow A201

1966, Feb. 25 *Perf. 12½x12, 12x12½*

No.	Type	Denom.	Design	Unused	Used
902	A201	10q	shown	.25	.25
903	A201	20q	Pig	.55	.25
904	A201	30q	Ewe & lamb	1.25	.30
905	A201	35q	Ram	1.60	.30
906	A201	40q	Dog	2.25	.30
907	A201	50q	Cat, vert.	2.75	.30
908	A201	55q	Horse, vert.	3.00	.40
909	A201	60q	Ass, vert.	5.50	.60
			Nos. 902-909 (8)	17.15	2.70

Soccer Player and Map of Uruguay — A202

5q, Globe in form of soccer ball. 15q, Player, map of Italy. 20q, Goalkeeper, map of France. 25q, Player, map of Brazil. 30q, Player, map of Switzerland. 35q, Player, map of Sweden. 40q, Player, map of Chile. 50q, Player, map of Great Britain. 70q, World Championship cup & ball.

1966, Mar. 20 **Litho.** *Perf. 12*

No.	Type	Denom.	Colors	Unused	Used
910	A202	5q	gray & dp org	.25	.25
911	A202	10q	lt brn, bl & vio	.25	.25
912	A202	15q	cit, dk bl & brt bl	.30	.25
913	A202	20q	org, vio bl & brt bl	.35	.25
914	A202	25q	salmon & sepia	.45	.25
915	A202	30q	lt yel grn & brn	.55	.25
916	A202	35q	lt ultra & emer	.85	.25
917	A202	40q	pink & brown	.90	.25
918	A202	50q	pale grn, mag & rose red	1.10	.25
919	A202	70q	gray, brn, yel & blk	1.60	.30
			Nos. 910-919 (10)	6.60	2.55

World Cup Soccer Championship, Wembley, England, July 11-30.

Andon Zako Cajupi — A203

1966, Mar. 27 **Unwmk.**

No.	Type	Denom.	Colors	Unused	Used
920	A203	40q	bluish blk	1.10	.25
921	A203	1.10 l	dark green	3.25	.40

Andon Zako Cajupi, poet, birth centenary.

Painted Lady — A204

Designs: 20q, Blue dragonfly. 30q, Cloudless sulphur butterfly. 35q, 40q, Splendid dragonfly. 50q, Machaon swallow-tail. 55q, Sulphur butterfly. 60q, Whitemarbled butterfly.

1966, Apr. 21 **Litho.** *Perf. 11½x12*

No.	Type	Denom.	Colors	Unused	Used
922	A204	10q	multicolored	.45	.25
923	A204	20q	yellow & multi	.55	.25
924	A204	30q	yellow & multi	.75	.25
925	A204	35q	sky blue & multi	1.10	.25
926	A204	40q	multicolored	1.60	.25
927	A204	50q	rose & multi	2.25	.25
928	A204	55q	multicolored	2.75	.25
929	A204	60q	multicolored	7.00	.35
			Nos. 922-929 (8)	16.45	2.10

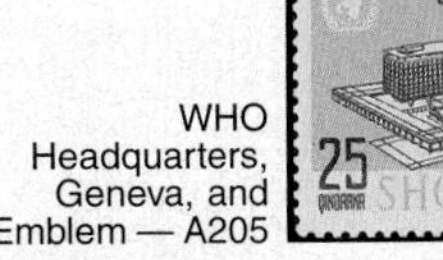

WHO Headquarters, Geneva, and Emblem — A205

Designs (WHO Emblem and): 35q, Ambulance and stretcher bearers, vert. 60q, Albanian mother and nurse weighing infant, vert. 80q, X-ray machine and hospital.

Perf. 12x12½, 12½x12
1966, May 3 **Litho.**

No.	Type	Denom.	Colors	Unused	Used
930	A205	25q	lt blue & blk	.50	.25
931	A205	35q	salmon & ultra	1.10	.25
932	A205	60q	lt grn, bl & red	1.50	.25
933	A205	80q	yel, bl, grn & lt brn	2.25	.25
			Nos. 930-933 (4)	5.35	1.00

Inauguration of the WHO Headquarters, Geneva.

Bird's Foot Starfish A206

Designs: 25q, Starfish. 35q, Brittle star. 45q, But-thorn starfish. 50q, Starfish. 60q, Sea cucumber. 70q, Sea urchin.

1966, May 10 *Perf. 12x12½*

No.	Type	Denom.	Colors	Unused	Used
934	A206	15q	multicolored	.45	.25
935	A206	25q	multicolored	.75	.30
936	A206	35q	multicolored	1.25	.40
937	A206	45q	multicolored	1.60	.45
938	A206	50q	multicolored	1.75	.55
939	A206	60q	multicolored	2.75	.75
940	A206	70q	multicolored	3.25	1.90
			Nos. 934-940 (7)	11.80	4.60

Luna 10 — A207

30q, 80q, Trajectory of Luna 10, earth & moon.

1966, June 10 *Perf. 12x12½*

No.	Type	Denom.	Colors	Unused	Used
941	A207	20q	blue, yel & blk	.55	.25
942	A207	30q	yel grn, blk & bl	1.10	.25
943	A207	70q	vio, yel & blk	2.25	.25
944	A207	80q	yel, vio, grn & blk	3.75	.50
			Nos. 941-944 (4)	7.65	1.25

Launching of the 1st artificial moon satellite, Luna 10, Apr. 3, 1966.

Jules Rimet Cup and Soccer A208

Designs: Various scenes of soccer play.

1966, July 12 **Litho.** *Perf. 12x12½*
Black Inscriptions

No.	Type	Denom.	Colors	Unused	Used
945	A208	10q	ocher & lilac	.40	.25
946	A208	20q	lt blue & cit	.50	.25
947	A208	30q	brick red & Prus bl	.75	.25
948	A208	35q	lt ultra & rose	1.00	.25
949	A208	40q	yel grn & lt red brn	1.00	.25
950	A208	50q	lt red brn & yel grn	1.25	.25
951	A208	55q	rose lil & yel grn	1.25	.25
952	A208	60q	dp rose & ocher	2.50	.25
			Nos. 945-952 (8)	8.65	2.00

World Cup Soccer Championship, Wembley, England, July 11-30.

Water Level Map of Albania — A209

30q, Water measure & fields. 70q, Turbine & pylon. 80q, Hydrological decade emblem.

1966, July *Perf. 12½x12*

No.	Type	Denom.	Colors	Unused	Used
953	A209	20q	brick red, blk & org	.55	.25
954	A209	30q	emer, blk & lt brn	.85	.25
955	A209	70q	brt violet & blk	1.60	.25
956	A209	80q	brt bl, org, yel & blk	2.75	.45
			Nos. 953-956 (4)	5.75	1.20

Hydrological Decade (UNESCO), 1965-74.

Greek Turtle — A210

Designs: 15q, Grass snake. 25q, European pond turtle. 30q, Wall lizard. 35q, Wall gecko. 45q, Emerald lizard. 50q, Slowworm. 90q, Horned viper (or sand viper).

1966, Aug. 10 Litho. *Perf. 12½x12*

No.	Type	Description	Unused	Used
957	A210	10q gray & multi	.35	.25
958	A210	15q yellow & multi	.50	.25
959	A210	25q ultra & multi	.55	.25
960	A210	30q multicolored	.65	.25
961	A210	35q multicolored	1.10	.25
962	A210	45q multicolored	1.25	.25
963	A210	50q orange & multi	1.40	.30
964	A210	90q lilac & multi	2.75	.55
		Nos. 957-964 (8)	8.55	2.35

Persian Cat A211

Cats: 10q, Siamese, vert. 15q, European tabby, vert. 25q, Black kitten. 60q, 65q, 80q, Various Persians.

Perf. 12x12½, 12½x12

1966, Sept. 20 Litho.

No.	Type	Description	Unused	Used
965	A211	10q multicolored	.45	.25
966	A211	15q blk, sepia & car	.55	.25
967	A211	25q blk, dk & lt brn	1.10	.25
968	A211	45q blk, org & yel	1.75	.25
969	A211	60q blk, brn & yel	2.75	.30
970	A211	65q multicolored	3.00	.40
971	A211	80q blk, gray & yel	3.75	.50
		Nos. 965-971 (7)	13.35	2.20

Pjeter Budi, Writer — A212

1966, Oct. 5 *Perf. 12x12½*

No.	Type	Description	Unused	Used
972	A212	25q buff & slate grn	1.10	.25
973	A212	1.75 l gray & dull claret	3.25	.45

UNESCO Emblem A213

Designs (UNESCO Emblem and): 15q, Open book, rose and school. 25q, Male folk dancers. 1.55 l, Jug, column and old building.

1966, Oct. 20 Litho. *Perf. 12*

No.	Type	Description	Unused	Used
974	A213	5q lt gray & multi	.35	.25
975	A213	15q dp blue & multi	.45	.25
976	A213	25q gray & multi	.75	.25
977	A213	1.55 l multi	3.25	.50
		Nos. 974-977 (4)	4.80	1.25

20th anniv. of UNESCO.

A214

Designs: 15q, Hand holding book with pictures of Marx, Engels, Lenin and Stalin. 25q, Map of Albania, hammer and sickle, symbols of agriculture and industry. 65q, Symbolic grain and factories. 95q, Fists holding rifle, spade, axe, sickle and book.

1966, Nov. 1 Litho. *Perf. 11½x12*

No.	Type	Description	Unused	Used
978	A214	15q vermilion & gold	.35	.25
979	A214	25q multicolored	.60	.25
980	A214	65q brn, brn org & gold	1.60	.25
981	A214	95q yellow & multi	2.25	.40
		Nos. 978-981 (4)	4.80	1.15

Albanian Communist Party, 5th Cong.

A215

Designs: 15q, Hammer and sickle, Party emblem in sunburst. 25q, Partisan and sunburst. 65q, Steel worker and blast furnace. 95q, Combine harvester, factories, and pylon.

1966, Nov. 8

No.	Type	Description	Unused	Used
982	A215	15q orange & multi	.55	.25
983	A215	25q red & multi	.75	.25
984	A215	65q multicolored	1.60	.25
985	A215	95q blue & multi	2.25	.40
		Nos. 982-985 (4)	5.15	1.15

25th anniv. of the founding of the Albanian Workers Party.

Russian Wolfhound — A216

Dogs: 15q, Sheep dog. 25q, English setter. 45q, English springer spaniel. 60q, Bulldog. 65q, Saint Bernard. 80q, Dachshund.

1966, Oct. 30 Litho. *Perf. 12½x12*

No.	Type	Description	Unused	Used
986	A216	10q green & multi	.55	.25
987	A216	15q multicolored	.75	.25
988	A216	25q lilac & multi	1.25	.25
989	A216	45q rose & multi	2.00	.35
990	A216	60q brown & multi	2.25	.40
991	A216	65q ultra & multi	3.00	.45
992	A216	80q blue grn & multi	4.25	.50
		Nos. 986-992 (7)	14.05	2.45

Ndre Mjeda — A217

1966 *Perf. 12½x12*

No.	Type	Description	Unused	Used
993	A217	25q brt bl & dk brn	.65	.25
994	A217	1.75 l brt grn & dk brn	3.75	.65

Birth Centenary of the priest Ndre Mjeda.

Proclamation A218

Designs: 10q, Banner, man and woman holding gun and axe, horiz. 1.85 l, man with axe and banner and partisan with gun.

1966, Dec. 25 *Perf. 11½x12, 12x11½*

No.	Type	Description	Unused	Used
995	A218	5q lt brn, red & blk	.35	.25
996	A218	10q red, blk, gray & bl	.55	.25
997	A218	1.85 l red, blk & salmon	3.50	.30
		Nos. 995-997 (3)	4.40	.80

Albanian Communist Party, 25th anniv.

Golden Eagle — A219

Birds of Prey: 15q, European sea eagle. 25q, Griffon vulture. 40q, Common sparrowhawk. 50q, Osprey. 70q, Egyptian vulture. 90q, Kestrel.

1966, Dec. 20 Litho. *Perf. 11½x12*

No.	Type	Description	Unused	Used
998	A219	10q gray & multi	.55	.25
999	A219	15q multicolored	.75	.25
1000	A219	25q citron & multi	1.10	.25
1001	A219	40q multicolored	1.30	.25
1002	A219	50q multicolored	1.75	.30
1003	A219	70q yellow & multi	2.75	.40
1004	A219	90q multicolored	3.75	.50
		Nos. 998-1004 (7)	11.95	2.20

Hake A220

Fish: 15q, Red mullet. 25q, Opah. 40q, Atlantic wolf fish. 65q, Lumpfish. 80q, Swordfish. 1.15 l, Shorthorn sculpin.

1967, Jan. 20 Photo. *Perf. 12x11½*

Fish in Natural Colors

No.	Type	Description	Unused	Used
1005	A220	10q blue	.45	.25
1006	A220	15q lt yellow grn	.55	.25
1007	A220	25q Prus blue	1.10	.25
1008	A220	40q emerald	1.30	.25
1009	A220	65q brt blue grn	1.60	.30
1010	A220	80q blue	2.75	.40
1011	A220	1.15 l brt green	3.25	.65
		Nos. 1005-1011 (7)	11.00	2.35

White Pelican A221

Designs: Various groups of pelicans.

1967, Feb. 22 Litho. *Perf. 12*

No.	Type	Description	Unused	Used
1012	A221	10q pink & multi	.30	.25
1013	A221	15q pink & multi	.55	.25
1014	A221	25q pink & multi	1.60	.25
1015	A221	50q pink & multi	3.25	.25
1016	A221	2 l pink & multi	8.25	.75
		Nos. 1012-1016 (5)	13.95	1.75

Camellia A222

Flowers: 10q, Chrysanthemum. 15q, Hollyhock. 25q, Flowering Maple. 35q, Peony. 65q, Gladiolus. 80q, Freesia. 1.15 l, Carnation.

Unwmk.

1967, Apr. 12 Litho. *Perf. 12*

Flowers in Natural Colors

No.	Type	Description	Unused	Used
1017	A222	5q pale brown	.25	.25
1018	A222	10q lt lilac	.25	.25
1019	A222	15q gray	.35	.25
1020	A222	25q ultra	1.10	.25
1021	A222	35q lt blue	1.30	.25
1022	A222	65q lt blue grn	2.20	.25
1023	A222	80q lt bluish gray	2.75	.30
1024	A222	1.15 l dull yellow	3.25	.45
		Nos. 1017-1024 (8)	11.45	2.25

Congress Emblem and Power Station — A223

1967, Apr. 24 Litho. *Perf. 12*

No.	Type	Description	Unused	Used
1025	A223	25q multi	1.10	.25
1026	A223	1.75 l multi	3.25	.55

Cong. of the Union of Professional Workers, Tirana, Apr. 24.

Rose — A224

Various Roses in Natural Colors.

1967, May 15 *Perf. 12x12½*

No.	Type	Description	Unused	Used
1027	A224	5q blue gray	.65	.25
1028	A224	10q brt blue	.65	.25
1029	A224	15q rose violet	.65	.25
1030	A224	25q lemon	.75	.25
1031	A224	35q brt grnsh blue	1.25	.25
1032	A224	65q gray	1.40	.25
1033	A224	80q brown	1.60	.30
1034	A224	1.65 l gray green	3.75	.50
		Nos. 1027-1034 (8)	10.70	2.30

Seashore, Bregdet Borsh — A225

Views: 15q, Buthrotum, vert. 25q, Shore, Fshati Piqeras. 45q, Shore, Bregdet. 50q, Shore, Bregdet Himare. 65q, Ship, Sarande (Santi Quaranta). 80q, Shore, Dhermi. 1 l, Sunset, Bregdet, vert.

Perf. 12x12½, 12½x12

1967, June 10

No.	Type	Description	Unused	Used
1035	A225	15q multicolored	.45	.25
1036	A225	20q multicolored	.55	.25
1037	A225	25q multicolored	1.10	.35
1038	A225	45q multicolored	1.30	.35
1039	A225	50q multicolored	1.50	.35
1040	A225	65q multicolored	2.20	.50
1041	A225	80q multicolored	2.40	.70
1042	A225	1 l multicolored	3.25	1.00
		Nos. 1035-1042 (8)	12.75	3.75

Fawn A226

Roe Deer: 20q, Stag, vert. 25q, Doe, vert. 30q, Young stag and doe. 35q, Doe and fawn. 40q, Young stag, vert. 65q, Stag and doe, vert. 70q, Running stag and does.

Perf. 12½x12, 12x12½

1967, July 20 Litho.

No.	Type	Description	Unused	Used
1043	A226	15q multicolored	.55	.25
1044	A226	20q multicolored	.55	.25
1045	A226	25q multicolored	1.10	.25
1046	A226	30q multicolored	1.10	.25

No.	Type	Description	Unused	Used
1047	A226	35q multicolored	1.60	.25
1048	A226	40q multicolored	1.60	.25
1049	A226	65q multicolored	3.25	.35
1050	A226	70q multicolored	4.25	.55
		Nos. 1043-1050 (8)	14.00	2.40

Man and Woman from Madhe A227

Regional Costumes: 20q, Woman from Zadrimes. 25q, Dancer and drummer, Kukesit. 45q, Woman spinner, Dardhes. 50q, Farm couple, Myseqese. 65q, Dancer with tambourine, Tirana. 80q, Man and woman, Dropullit. 1 l, Piper, Laberise.

1967, Aug. 25 ***Perf. 12***

No.	Type	Description	Unused	Used
1051	A227	15q tan & multi	.45	.25
1052	A227	20q lt yellow grn	.50	.25
1053	A227	25q multicolored	.55	.25
1054	A227	45q sky blue & multi	.95	.25
1055	A227	50q lemon & multi	1.00	.30
1056	A227	65q pink & multi	1.30	.40
1057	A227	80q multicolored	2.25	.45
1058	A227	1 l gray & multi	2.25	.60
		Nos. 1051-1058 (8)	9.25	2.75

Fighters and Newspaper — A228

75q, Printing plant, newspapers, microphone. 2 l, People holding newspaper.

1967, Aug. 25 ***Perf. 12½x12***

No.	Type	Description	Unused	Used
1059	A228	25q multicolored	.65	.25
1060	A228	75q pink & multi	1.75	.50
1061	A228	2 l multicolored	4.25	1.25
		Nos. 1059-1061 (3)	6.65	2.00

Issued for the Day of the Press.

Street Scene, by Kole Idromeno — A229

Hakmarrja Battalion, by Sali Shijaku — A230

Designs: 20q, David, fresco by Onufri, 16th century, vert. 45q, Woman's head, ancient mosaic, vert. 50q, Men on horseback from 16th century icon, vert. 65q, Farm Women, by Zef Shoshi. 80q, Street Scene, by Vangjush Mio. 1 l, Bride, by Kolé Idromeno, vert.

Perf. 12, 12x12½, (A230)

1967, Oct. 25 **Litho.**

No.	Type	Description	Unused	Used
1062	A229	15q multicolored	.55	.25
1063	A229	20q multicolored	.75	.25
1064	A230	25q multicolored	1.10	.25
1065	A229	45q multicolored	1.25	.25
1066	A229	50q multicolored	1.60	.25
1067	A230	65q multicolored	2.25	.25
1068	A230	80q multicolored	2.25	.30
1069	A230	1 l multicolored	4.50	.35
		Nos. 1062-1069 (8)	14.25	2.15

Lenin at Storming of Winter Palace — A231

Designs: 15q, Lenin and Stalin, horiz. 50q, Lenin and Stalin addressing meeting. 1.10 l, Storming of the Winter Palace, horiz.

1967, Nov. 7 ***Perf. 12***

No.	Type	Description	Unused	Used
1070	A231	15q red & multi	.35	.25
1071	A231	25q slate grn & blk	.75	.25
1072	A231	50q brn, blk & brn vio	1.10	.25
1073	A231	1.10 l lilac, gray & blk	2.40	.30
		Nos. 1070-1073 (4)	4.60	1.05

50th anniv. of the Russian October Revolution.

Rabbit — A232

Designs: Various hares and rabbits. The 15q, 25q, 35q, 40q and 1 l are horizontal.

1967, Sept. 30

No.	Type	Description	Unused	Used
1074	A232	15q orange & multi	.35	.25
1075	A232	20q brt yel & multi	.45	.25
1076	A232	25q lt brn & multi	.65	.25
1077	A232	35q multicolored	1.10	.25
1078	A232	40q yellow & multi	1.30	.25
1079	A232	50q pink & multi	2.25	.25
1080	A232	65q multicolored	2.50	.35
1081	A232	1 l lilac & multi	3.50	.55
		Nos. 1074-1081 (8)	12.10	2.40

University, Torch and Book — A233

1967, Sept. 15 **Litho.** ***Perf. 12***

No.	Type	Description	Unused	Used
1082	A233	25q multi	.55	.25
1083	A233	1.75 l multi	3.50	.35

10th anniv. of the founding of the State University, Tirana.

Coat of Arms and Soldiers A234

65q, Arms, Factory, grain, flag, gun, radio tower. 1.20 l, Arms, hand holding torch.

1967, Sept. 16 ***Perf. 12x11½***

No.	Type	Description	Unused	Used
1084	A234	15q multi	.35	.25
1085	A234	65q multi	1.10	.25
1086	A234	1.20 l multi	2.40	.25
		Nos. 1084-1086 (3)	3.85	.75

25th anniversary of the Democratic Front.

Turkey A235

Designs: 20q, Duck. 25q, Hen. 45q, Rooster. 50q, Guinea fowl. 65q, Goose, horiz. 80q, Mallard, horiz. 1 l, Chicks, horiz.

Perf. 12x12½, 12½x12

1967, Nov. 25 **Photo.**

No.	Type	Description	Unused	Used
1087	A235	15q gold & multi	.25	.25
1088	A235	20q gold & multi	.35	.25
1089	A235	25q gold & multi	.55	.25
1090	A235	45q gold & multi	1.10	.25
1091	A235	50q gold & multi	1.25	.25
1092	A235	65q gold & multi	1.60	.25
1093	A235	80q gold & multi	2.25	.35
1094	A235	1 l gold & multi	3.25	.45
		Nos. 1087-1094 (8)	10.60	2.30

Skanderbeg A236

Designs: 10q, Arms of Skanderbeg. 25q, Helmet and sword. 30q, Kruje Castle. 35q, Petreles Castle. 65q, Berati Castle. 80q, Skanderbeg addressing national chiefs. 90q, Battle of Albulenes.

1967, Dec. 10 **Litho.** ***Perf. 12x12½***

Medallion in Bister and Dark Brown

No.	Type	Description	Unused	Used
1095	A236	10q gold & violet	.25	.25
1096	A236	15q gold & rose car	.35	.25
1097	A236	25q gold & vio bl	.55	.25
1098	A236	30q gold & dk blue	.65	.25
1099	A236	35q gold & maroon	.75	.25
1100	A236	65q gold & green	1.10	.25
1101	A236	80q gold & gray brn	2.25	.30
1102	A236	90q gold & ultra	2.50	.35
		Nos. 1095-1102 (8)	8.40	2.15

500th anniv. of the death of Skanderbeg (George Castriota), national hero.

10th Winter Olympic Games, Grenoble, France, Feb. 6-18 — A237

Designs: 15q, 2 l, Winter Olympics emblem. 25q, Ice hockey. 30q, Women's figure skating. 50q, Slalom. 80q, Downhill skiing. 1 l, Ski jump.

1967-68

No.	Type	Description	Unused	Used
1103	A237	15q multicolored	.25	.25
1104	A237	25q multicolored	.25	.25
1105	A237	30q multicolored	.35	.25
1106	A237	50q multicolored	.55	.25
1107	A237	80q multicolored	1.10	.25
1108	A237	1 l multicolored	2.40	.25
		Nos. 1103-1108 (6)	4.90	1.50

Miniature Sheet

Imperf

No.	Type	Description	Unused	Used
1109	A237	2 l red, gray & brt bl ('68)	9.25	9.25

Nos. 1103-1108 issued Dec. 29, 1967.

Skanderbeg Monument, Kruje — A238

Designs: 10q, Skanderbeg monument, Tirana. 15q, Skanderbeg portrait, Uffizi Galleries, Florence. 25q, engraved portrait of Gen. Tanush Topia. 35q, Portrait of Gen. Gjergj Arianti, horiz. 65q, Portrait bust of Skanderbeg by O. Paskali. 80q, Title page of "The Life of Skanderbeg." 90q, Skanderbeg battling the Turks, painting by S. Rrota, horiz.

Perf. 12x12½, 12½x12

1968, Jan. 17 **Litho.**

No.	Type	Description	Unused	Used
1110	A238	10q multicolored	.45	.25
1111	A238	15q multicolored	.55	.25
1112	A238	25q blk, yel & lt bl	1.00	.25
1113	A238	30q multicolored	1.10	.25
1114	A238	35q lt vio, pink & blk	1.30	.25
1115	A238	65q multicolored	2.25	.30
1116	A238	80q pink, blk & yel	3.00	.50
1117	A238	90q beige & multi	3.50	.65
		Nos. 1110-1117 (8)	13.15	2.70

500th anniv. of the death of Skanderbeg (George Castriota), national hero.

Carnation A239

1968, Feb. 15 ***Perf. 12***

Various Carnations in Natural Colors

No.	Type	Description	Unused	Used
1118	A239	15q green	.25	.25
1119	A239	20q dk brown	.25	.25
1120	A239	25q brt blue	.35	.25
1121	A239	50q gray olice	1.10	.25
1122	A239	80q bluish gray	1.60	.25
1123	A239	1.10 l violet gray	2.25	.40
		Nos. 1118-1123 (6)	5.80	1.65

"Electrification" A240

65q, Farm tractor, horiz. 1.10 l, Cow & herd.

1968, Mar. 5 **Litho.** ***Perf. 12***

No.	Type	Description	Unused	Used
1124	A240	25q multi	.55	.25
1125	A240	65q multi	1.60	.30
1126	A240	1.10 l multi	2.25	.40
		Nos. 1124-1126 (3)	4.40	.95

Fifth Farm Cooperatives Congress.

Goat A241

Various goats. 15q, 20q, 25q are vertical.

1968, Mar. 25 ***Perf. 12x12½, 12½x12***

No.	Type	Description	Unused	Used
1127	A241	15q multi	.25	.25
1128	A241	20q multi	.35	.25
1129	A241	25q multi	.45	.25
1130	A241	30q multi	.55	.25

1131 A241 40q multi .65 .25
1132 A241 50q multi .75 .25
1133 A241 80q multi 1.60 .25
1134 A241 1.40 l multi 3.25 .40
Nos. 1127-1134 (8) 7.85 2.15

Zef N. Jubani — A242

1968, Mar. 30 *Perf. 12*
1135 A242 25q yellow & choc .55 .25
1136 A242 1.75 l lt violet & blk 2.75 .50

Sesquicentennial of the birth of Zef N. Jubani, writer and scholar.

Physician and Hospital — A243

Designs (World Health Organization Emblem and): 65q, Hospital and microscope, horiz. 1.10 l, Mother feeding child.

Perf. 12½x12, 12x12½
1968, Apr. 7 **Litho.**
1137 A243 25q green & claret .35 .25
1138 A243 65q black, yel & bl 1.30 .30
1139 A243 1.10 l black & dp org 1.60 .40
Nos. 1137-1139 (3) 3.25 .95

20th anniv. of WHO.

Scientist A244

Women: 15q, Militia member. 60q, Farm worker. 1 l, Factory worker.

1968, Apr. 14 *Perf. 12*
1140 A244 15q ver & dk red .45 .25
1141 A244 25q blue grn & grn .60 .25
1142 A244 60q dull yel & brn 1.60 .25
1143 A244 1 l lt vio & vio 2.75 .40
Nos. 1140-1143 (4) 5.40 1.15

Albanian Women's Organization, 25th anniv.

Karl Marx A245

Designs: 25q, Marx lecturing to students. 65q, "Das Kapital," "Communist Manifesto" and marching crowd. 95q, Full-face portrait.

1968, May 5 **Litho.** *Perf. 12*
1144 A245 15q gray, dk bl & bis 1.00 .25
1145 A245 25q brn vio, dk brn & dl yel 1.40 .25
1146 A245 65q gray, blk, brn & car 2.25 .25
1147 A245 95q gray, ocher & blk 3.75 .50
Nos. 1144-1147 (4) 8.40 1.25

Karl Marx, 150th birth anniversary.

Heliopsis A246

Flowers: 20q, Red flax. 25q, Orchid. 30q, Gloxinia. 40q, Turk's-cap lily. 80q, Amaryllis. 1.40 l, Red magnolia.

1968, May 10 *Perf. 12x12½*
1148 A246 15q gold & multi .30 .25
1149 A246 20q gold & multi .35 .25
1150 A246 25q gold & multi .45 .25
1151 A246 30q gold & multi .55 .25
1152 A246 40q gold & multi .55 .25
1153 A246 80q gold & multi 1.60 .40
1154 A246 1.40 l gold & multi 2.75 .60
Nos. 1148-1154 (7) 6.55 2.25

Proclamation of Prizren — A247

25q, Abdyl Frasheri. 40q, House in Prizren.

1968, June 10 **Litho.** *Perf. 12*
1155 A247 25q emerald & blk .55 .25
1156 A247 40q multicolored 1.10 .25
1157 A247 85q yellow & multi 1.60 .30
Nos. 1155-1157 (3) 3.25 .80

League of Prizren against the Turks, 90th anniv.

Shepherd, by A. Kushi — A248

Paintings from Tirana Art Gallery: 20q, View of Tirana, by V. Mio, horiz. 25q, Mountaineer, by G. Madhi. 40q, Refugees, by A. Buza. 80q, Guerrillas of Shahin Matrakut, by S. Xega. 1.50 l, Portrait of an Old Man, by S. Papadhimitri. 1.70 l, View of Scutari, by S. Rrota. 2.50 l, Woman in Scutari Costume, by Z. Colombi.

1968, June 20 *Perf. 12x12½*
1158 A248 15q gold & multi .25 .25
1159 A248 20q gold & multi .25 .25
1160 A248 25q gold & multi .30 .25
1161 A248 40q gold & multi .55 .25
1162 A248 80q gold & multi 1.10 .25
1163 A248 1.50 l gold & multi 2.75 .30
1164 A248 1.70 l gold & multi 3.25 .55
Nos. 1158-1164 (7) 8.45 2.10

Miniature Sheet

Perf. 12½xImperf.

1165 A248 2.50 l multi 4.00 4.00

No. 1165 contains one stamp, size: 50x71mm.

Soldier and Guns — A249

25q, Sailor, warships. 65q, Aviator, planes, vert. 95q, Militiamen, woman.

1968, July 10 **Litho.** *Perf. 12*
1166 A249 15q multicolored .55 .25
1167 A249 25q multicolored .65 .25
1168 A249 65q multicolored 2.25 .25
1169 A249 95q multicolored 3.75 .25
Nos. 1166-1169 (4) 7.20 1.00

25th anniversary of the People's Army.

Squid A250

Designs: 20q, Crayfish. 25q, Whelk. 50q, Crab. 70q, Spiny lobster. 80q, Shore crab. 90q, Norway lobster.

1968, Aug. 20
1170 A250 15q multicolored .55 .25
1171 A250 20q multicolored .55 .25
1172 A250 25q multicolored .55 .25
1173 A250 50q multicolored .75 .25
1174 A250 70q multicolored 1.25 .30
1175 A250 80q multicolored 2.25 .35
1176 A250 90q multicolored 2.50 .40
Nos. 1170-1176 (7) 8.40 2.05

Women's Relay Race — A251

Sport: 20q, Running. 25q, Women's discus. 30q, Equestrian. 40q, High jump. 50q, Women's hurdling. 80q, Soccer. 1.40 l, Woman diver. 2 l, Olympic stadium.

1968, Sept. 23 **Photo.** *Perf. 12*
1177 A251 15q multicolored .25 .25
1178 A251 20q multicolored .25 .25
1179 A251 25q multicolored .25 .25
1180 A251 30q multicolored .45 .25
1181 A251 40q multicolored .45 .25
1182 A251 50q multicolored .45 .25
1183 A251 80q multicolored 1.10 .25
1184 A251 1.40 l multicolored 2.25 .35
Nos. 1177-1184 (8) 5.45 2.10

Souvenir Sheet

Perf. 12½ Horizontally

1185 A251 2 l multicolored 4.00 4.00

19th Olympic Games, Mexico City, Oct. 12-27. No. 1185 contains one rectangular stamp, size: 64x54mm. Value of imperfs., Nos. 1177-1184 $12.50, No. 1185 $9.

Enver Hoxha — A252

1968, Oct. 16 **Litho.** *Perf. 12*
1186 A252 25q blue gray .45 .25
1187 A252 35q rose brown .65 .25
1188 A252 80q violet 1.40 .35
1189 A252 1.10 l brown 1.75 .50
Nos. 1186-1189 (4) 4.25 1.35

Souvenir Sheet

Imperf

1190 A252 1.50 l rose red, bl vio & gold *140.00 140.00*

60th birthday of Enver Hoxha, First Secretary of the Central Committee of the Communist Party of Albania.

Book and Pupils A253

1968, Nov. 14 **Photo.**
1191 A253 15q mar & slate grn .65 .25
1192 A253 85q gray olive & sepia 3.25 .25

60th anniv. of the Congress of Monastir, Nov. 14-22, 1908, which adopted a unified Albanian alphabet.

Waxwing — A254

Birds: 20q, Rose-colored starling. 25q, Kingfishers. 50q, Long-tailed tits. 80q, Wallcreeper. 1.10 l, Bearded tit.

1968, Nov. 15 **Litho.**

Birds in Natural Colors

1193 A254 15q lt blue & blk .35 .25
1194 A254 20q bister & blk .55 .25
1195 A254 25q pink & blk .75 .25
1196 A254 50q lt yel grn & blk 1.10 .25
1197 A254 80q bis brn & blk 2.25 .35
1198 A254 1.10 l pale grn & blk 3.25 .55
Nos. 1193-1198 (6) 8.25 1.90

Mao Tse-tung — A255

1968, Dec. 26 **Litho.** *Perf. 12½x12*
1199 A255 25q gold, red & blk 1.25 .40
1200 A255 1.75 l gold, red & blk 7.50 3.50

75th birthday of Mao Tse-tung.

Adem Reka and Crane — A256

Portraits: 10q, Pjeter Lleshi and power lines. 15q, Mohammed Shehu and Myrteza Kepi. 25q, Shkurte Vata and women railroad workers. 65q, Agron Elezi, frontier guard. 80q, Ismet Bruçaj and mountain road. 1.30 l, Fuat Cela, blind revolutionary.

1969, Feb. 10 **Litho.** *Perf. 12x12½*
1201 A256 5q multicolored .35 .25
1202 A256 10q multicolored .35 .25
1203 A256 15q multicolored .75 .25
1204 A256 25q multicolored 1.10 .25
1205 A256 65q multicolored 1.50 .25
1206 A256 80q multicolored 1.50 .25
1207 A256 1.30 l multicolored 2.25 .25
Nos. 1201-1207 (7) 7.80 1.75

Contemporary heroine and heroes.

Meteorological Instruments — A257

Designs: 25q, Water gauge. 1.60 l, Radar, balloon and isobars.

1969, Feb. 25 *Perf. 12*

1208 A257 15q multicolored .55 .25
1209 A257 25q ultra, org & blk .85 .25
1210 A257 1.60 l rose vio, yel & blk 4.25 .60
Nos. 1208-1210 (3) 5.65 1.10

20th anniv. of Albanian hydrometeorology.

Partisans, 1944, by F. Haxmiu — A258

Paintings: 5q, Student Revolutionists, by P. Mele, vert. 65q, Steel Mill, by C. Ceka. 80q, Reconstruction, by V. Kilica. 1.10 l, Harvest, by N. Jonuzi. 1.15 l, Terraced Landscape, by S. Kaceli. 2 l, Partisans' Meeting.

Perf. 12x12½, 12½x12

1969, Apr. 25 **Litho.**

Size: 31½x41½mm

1211 A258 5q buff & multi .25 .25

Size: 51½x30½mm

1212 A258 25q buff & multi .35 .25

Size: 40½x32mm

1213 A258 65q buff & multi .55 .25

Size: 51½x30½mm

1214 A258 80q buff & multi .70 .25
1215 A258 1.10 l buff & multi 1.25 .25
1216 A258 1.15 l buff & multi 1.75 .25
Nos. 1211-1216 (6) 4.85 1.50

Miniature Sheet

Imperf

Size: 111x90mm

1217 A258 2 l ocher & multi 2.75 2.00

Leonardo da Vinci, Self-portrait A259

Designs (after Leonardo da Vinci): 35q, Lilies. 40q, Design for a flying machine, horiz. 1 l, Portrait of Beatrice. No. 1222, Portrait of a Noblewoman. No. 1223, Mona Lisa.

Perf. 12x12½, 12½x12

1969, May 2 **Litho.**

1218 A259 25q gold & sepia .35 .25
1219 A259 35q gold & sepia .65 .25
1220 A259 40q gold & sepia .85 .25
1221 A259 1 l gold & multi 2.25 .25
1222 A259 2 l gold & sepia 4.25 .55
Nos. 1218-1222 (5) 8.35 1.55

Miniature Sheet

Imperf

1223 A259 2 l gold & multi 7.00 4.50

Leonardo da Vinci (1452-1519), painter, sculptor, architect and engineer.

First Congress Meeting Place A260

Designs: 1 l, Albanian coat of arms. 2.25 l, Two partisans with guns and flag.

1969, May 24 *Perf. 12*

1224 A260 25q lt grn, blk & red .55 .25
1225 A260 2.25 l multi 4.25 1.00

Souvenir Sheet

1226 A260 1 l gold, bl, blk & red 50.00 50.00

25th anniversary of the First Anti-Fascist Congress of Permet, May 24, 1944.

Albanian Violet — A261

Designs: Violets and Pansies.

1969, June 30 **Litho.** *Perf. 12x12½*

1227 A261 5q gold & multi .25 .25
1228 A261 10q gold & multi .25 .25
1229 A261 15q gold & multi .40 .25
1230 A261 20q gold & multi .50 .25
1231 A261 25q gold & multi .50 .25
1232 A261 80q gold & multi 1.60 .35
1233 A261 1.95 l gold & multi 2.75 .65
Nos. 1227-1233 (7) 6.25 2.25

Plum, Fruit and Blossoms A262

Designs: Blossoms and Fruits.

1969, Aug. 10 **Litho.** *Perf. 12*

1234 A262 10q shown .25 .25
1235 A262 15q Lemon .25 .25
1236 A262 25q Pomegranate .55 .25
1237 A262 50q Cherry 1.10 .25
1238 A262 80q Peach 1.75 .25
1239 A262 1.20 l Apple 2.75 .40
Nos. 1234-1239 (6) 6.65 1.65

Basketball A263

Designs: 10q, 80q, 2.20 l, Various views of basketball game. 25q, Hand aiming ball at basket and map of Europe, horiz.

1969, Sept. 15 **Litho.** *Perf. 12*

1240 A263 10q multi .45 .25
1241 A263 15q buff & multi .45 .25
1242 A263 25q blue & multi .55 .25
1243 A263 80q multi 1.60 .25
1244 A263 2.20 l multi 3.25 .50
Nos. 1240-1244 (5) 6.30 1.50

16th European Basketball Championships, Naples, Italy, Sept. 27-Oct. 5.

Runner A264

Designs: 5q, Games' emblem. 10q, Woman gymnast. 20q, Pistol shooting. 25q, Swimmer at start. 80q, Bicyclist. 95q, Soccer.

1969, Sept. 30

1245 A264 5q multicolored .25 .25
1246 A264 10q multicolored .25 .25
1247 A264 15q multicolored .50 .25
1248 A264 20q multicolored .50 .25
1249 A264 25q multicolored .55 .25
1250 A264 80q multicolored 1.60 .25
1251 A264 95q multicolored 2.25 .25
Nos. 1245-1251 (7) 5.90 1.75

Second National Spartakiad.

Electronic Technicians, Steel Ladle — A265

25q, Mao Tse-tung with microphones. 1.40 l, Children holding Mao's red book.

1969, Oct. 1 **Litho.** *Perf. 12*

1252 A265 25q multi, vert. 2.50 .60
1253 A265 85q multi 7.50 2.25
1254 A265 1.40 l multi, vert. 12.00 4.00
Nos. 1252-1254 (3) 22.00 6.85

People's Republic of China, 20th anniv.

Enver Hoxha A266

Designs: 80q, Pages from Berat resolution. 1.45 l, Partisans with flag.

1969, Oct. 20 **Litho.** *Perf. 12*

1255 A266 25q multicolored .35 .25
1256 A266 80q gray & multi .85 .25
1257 A266 1.45 l ocher & multi 2.25 .45
Nos. 1255-1257 (3) 3.45 .95

25th anniv. of the 2nd reunion of the Natl. Antifascist Liberation Council, Berat.

Soldiers — A267

Designs: 30q, Oil refinery. 35q, Combine harvester. 45q, Hydroelectric station and dam. 55q, Militia woman, man and soldier. 1.10 l, Dancers and musicians.

1969, Nov. 29

1258 A267 25q multi .45 .25
1259 A267 30q multi .55 .25
1260 A267 35q multi .75 .25
1261 A267 45q multi 1.25 .25
1262 A267 55q multi 1.75 .30
1263 A267 1.10 l multi 3.25 .45
Nos. 1258-1263 (6) 8.00 1.75

25th anniv. of the socialist republic.

Joseph V. Stalin, (1879-1953), Russian Political Leader — A268

1969, Dec. 21 **Litho.** *Perf. 12*

1264 A268 15q lilac .25 .25
1265 A268 25q slate blue .55 .25
1266 A268 1 l brown 1.90 .25
1267 A268 1.10 l violet blue 2.25 .25
Nos. 1264-1267 (4) 4.95 1.00

Head of Woman A269

Greco-Roman Mosaics: 25q, Geometrical floor design, horiz. 80q, Bird and tree, horiz. 1.10 l, Floor with birds and grapes, horiz. 1.20 l, Fragment with corn within oval design.

1969, Dec. 25 *Perf. 12½x12*

1268 A269 15q gold & multi .25 .25
1269 A269 25q gold & multi .35 .25
1270 A269 80q gold & multi 1.10 .25
1271 A269 1.10 l gold & multi 1.60 .25
1272 A269 1.20 l gold & multi 2.25 .35
Nos. 1268-1272 (5) 5.55 1.35

Cancellation of 1920 — A270

25q, Proclamation and congress site.

1970, Jan. 21 **Litho.** *Perf. 12*

1273 A270 25q red, gray & blk .55 .25
1274 A270 1.25 l dk grn, yel & blk 3.25 .25

Congress of Louchnia, 50th anniversary.

Worker, Student and Flag A271

1970, Feb. 11 *Perf. 12½x12*

1275 A271 25q red & multi .55 .25
1276 A271 1.75 l red & multi 3.25 .50

Vocational organizations in Albania, 25th anniv.

Turk's-cap Lily — A272

Lilies: 5q, Cernum, vert. 15q, Madonna, vert. 25q, Royal, vert. 1.10 l, Tiger. 1.15 l, Albanian.

Perf. 11½x12, 12x11½

1970, Mar. 10				**Litho.**	
1277	A272	5q	multi	.40	.25
1278	A272	15q	multi	.40	.25
1279	A272	25q	multi	.70	.25
1280	A272	80q	multi	2.00	.25
1281	A272	1.10 l	multi	2.50	.25
1282	A272	1.15 l	multi	3.25	.30
	Nos. 1277-1282 (6)			9.25	1.55

Lenin A273

Designs (Lenin): 5q, Portrait, vert. 25q, As volunteer construction worker. 95q, Addressing crowd. 1.10 l, Saluting, vert.

1970, Apr. 22		**Litho.**		***Perf. 12***	
1283	A273	5q	multi	.25	.25
1284	A273	15q	multi	.35	.25
1285	A273	25q	multi	.55	.25
1286	A273	95q	multi	1.10	.25
1287	A273	1.10 l	multi	2.00	.25
	Nos. 1283-1287 (5)			4.25	1.25

Centenary of birth of Lenin (1870-1924).

Frontier Guard A274

1970, Apr. 25					
1288	A274	25q	multi	.55	.25
1289	A274	1.25 l	multi	2.75	.50

25th anniversary of Frontier Guards.

Soccer Players — A275

Designs: 5q, Jules Rimet Cup and globes. 10q, Aztec Stadium, Mexico City. 25q, Defending goal. 65q, 80q, No. 1296, Two soccer players in various plays. No. 1297, Mexican horseman and volcano Popocatepetl.

1970, May 15	**Litho.**			***Perf. 12½x12***	
1290	A275	5q	multicolored	.25	.25
1291	A275	10q	multicolored	.25	.25
1292	A275	15q	multicolored	.25	.25
1293	A275	25q	lt green & multi	.25	.25
1294	A275	65q	pink & multi	.55	.25
1295	A275	80q	lt blue & multi	1.10	.40
1296	A275	2 l	yellow & multi	2.75	1.00
	Nos. 1290-1296 (7)			5.40	2.65

Souvenir Sheet

Perf 12 x Imperf

1297	A275	2 l	multicolored	4.00	3.00

World Soccer Championships for the Jules Rimet Cup, Mexico City, May 31-June 21, 1970. No. 1297 contains one large horizontal stamp. Nos. 1290-1297 exist imperf. Value: Nos. 1290-1296, mint or used, $12; No. 1297, mint $10, used $5.

UPU Headquarters and Monument, Bern — A276

1970, May 30	**Litho.**			***Perf. 12½x12***	
1298	A276	25q	ultra, gray & blk	.35	.25
1299	A276	1.10 l	org, buff & blk	1.60	.25
1300	A276	1.15 l	grn, gray & blk	1.75	.30
	Nos. 1298-1300 (3)			3.70	.80

Inauguration of the new UPU Headquarters in Bern.

Bird and Grapes Mosaic A277

Mosaics, 5th-6th centuries, excavated near Pogradec: 10q, Waterfowl and grapes. 20q, Bird and tree stump. 25q, Bird and leaves. 65q, Fish. 2.25 l, Peacock, vert.

1970, July 10		***Perf. 12½x12, 12x12½***			
1301	A277	5q	multi	.25	.25
1302	A277	10q	multi	.35	.25
1303	A277	20q	multi	.55	.25
1304	A277	25q	multi	.60	.25
1305	A277	65q	multi	1.10	.25
1306	A277	2.25 l	multi	3.75	.35
	Nos. 1301-1306 (6)			6.60	1.60

Fruit Harvest and Dancers A278

Designs: 25q, Contour-plowed fields and conference table. 80q, Cattle and newspapers. 1.30 l, Wheat harvest.

1970, Aug. 28	**Litho.**			***Perf. 12x11½***	
1307	A278	15q	brt violet & blk	.45	.25
1308	A278	25q	dp blue & blk	.55	.25
1309	A278	80q	dp brown & blk	1.60	.25
1310	A278	1.30 l	org brn & blk	2.25	.25
	Nos. 1307-1310 (4)			4.85	1.00

25th anniv. of the agrarian reform law.

Attacking Partisans — A279

Designs: 25q, Partisans with horses and flag. 1.60 l, Partisans.

1970, Sept. 3				***Perf. 12***	
1311	A279	15q	org brn & blk	.35	.25
1312	A279	25q	brn, yel & blk	.75	.25
1313	A279	1.60 l	dp grn & blk	2.50	.35
	Nos. 1311-1313 (3)			3.60	.85

50th anniversary of liberation of Vlona.

Miners, by Nexhmedin Zajmi — A280

Paintings from the National Gallery, Tirana: 5q, Bringing in the Harvest, by Isuf Sulovari, vert. 15q, The Activists, by Dhimitraq Trebicka, vert. 65q, Instruction of Partisans, by Hasan Nallbani. 95q, Architectural Planning, by Vilson Kilica. No. 1319, Woman Machinist, by Zef Shoshi, vert. No. 1320, Partisan Destroying Tank, by Sali Shijaku, vert.

Perf. 12½x12, 12x12½

1970, Sept. 25				**Litho.**	
1314	A280	5q	multicolored	.25	.25
1315	A280	15q	multicolored	.25	.25
1316	A280	25q	multicolored	.25	.25
1317	A280	65q	multicolored	.55	.25
1318	A280	95q	multicolored	1.10	.25
1319	A280	2 l	multicolored	3.25	.35
	Nos. 1314-1319 (6)			5.65	1.60

Miniature Sheet

Imperf

1320	A280	2 l	multicolored	3.75	2.50

Electrification Map of Albania — A281

Designs: 25q, Light bulb, hammer and sickle emblem, map of Albania and power graph. 80q, Linemen at work. 1.10 l, Use of electricity on the farm, in home and business.

1970, Oct. 25		**Litho.**		***Perf. 12***	
1321	A281	15q	multi	.35	.25
1322	A281	25q	multi	.55	.25
1323	A281	80q	multi	1.60	.25
1324	A281	1.10 l	multi	1.75	.25
	Nos. 1321-1324 (4)			4.25	1.00

Albanian village electrification completion.

Friedrich Engels A282

Designs: 1.10 l, Engels as young man. 1.15 l, Engels addressing crowd.

1970, Nov. 28	**Litho.**			***Perf. 12x12½***	
1325	A282	25q	bister & dk bl	.55	.25
1326	A282	1.10 l	bis & dp claret	1.60	.25
1327	A282	1.15 l	bis & dk ol grn	1.75	.30
	Nos. 1325-1327 (3)			3.90	.80

150th anniv. of the birth of Friedrich Engels (1820-95), German socialist, collaborator with Karl Marx.

Factories — A282a

Designs: 10q, Tractor factory, Tirana, horiz. 15q, Fertilizer factory, Fier. 20q, Superphosphate factory, Lac, horiz. 25q, Cement factory, Elbasan, horiz. 80q, Coking plant, Qyteti Stalin, horiz.

1970-71		**Litho.**		***Perf. 12***	
1327A	A282A	10q	multi	250.00	160.00
1327B	A282A	15q	multi	250.00	160.00
1327C	A282A	20q	multi	250.00	160.00
1327D	A282A	25q	multi	250.00	160.00
1327E	A282A	80q	multi	250.00	160.00
	Nos. 1327A-1327E (5)			1,250.	800.00

Issue dates: 15q, 12/4/70. 10q, 20q, 25q, 80q, 1/20/71.

Ludwig van Beethoven A283

Designs: 5q, Birthplace, Bonn. 25q, 65q, 1.10 l, various portraits. 1.80 l, Scene from Fidelio, horiz.

1970, Dec. 16		**Litho.**		***Perf. 12***	
1328	A283	5q	dp plum & gold	.25	.25
1329	A283	15q	brt rose lil & sil	.35	.25
1330	A283	25q	green & gold	.55	.25
1331	A283	65q	magenta & sil	1.40	.25
1332	A283	1.10 l	dk blue & gold	2.50	.30
1333	A283	1.80 l	black & sil	4.50	.50
	Nos. 1328-1333 (6)			9.55	1.80

Ludwig van Beethoven (1770-1827), composer.

Coat of Arms A284

Designs: 25q, Proclamation. 80q, Enver Hoxha reading proclamation. 1.30 l, Young people and proclamation.

1971, Jan. 11		**Litho.**		***Perf. 12***	
1334	A284	15q	lt bl, gold, blk & red	.35	.25
1335	A284	25q	rose lil, blk, gold & gray	.45	.25
1336	A284	80q	emerald, blk & gold	1.30	.25
1337	A284	1.30 l	yel org, blk & gold	1.75	.30
	Nos. 1334-1337 (4)			3.85	1.05

Declaration of the Republic, 25th anniv.

"Liberty" — A285

Designs: 50q, Women's brigade. 65q, Street battle, horiz. 1.10 l, Execution, horiz.

Perf. 12x11½, 11½x12

1971, Mar. 18				**Litho.**	
1338	A285	25q	dk bl & bl	.55	.25
1339	A285	50q	slate green	.75	.25
1340	A285	65q	dk brn & chest	1.10	.25
1341	A285	1.10 l	purple	2.25	.25
	Nos. 1338-1341 (4)			4.65	1.00

Centenary of the Paris Commune.

Black Men — A286

1.10 l, Men of 3 races. 1.15 l, Black protest.

1971, Mar. 21				***Perf. 12x12½***	
1342	A286	25q	blk & bis brn	.35	.25
1343	A286	1.10 l	blk & rose car	1.10	.25
1344	A286	1.15 l	blk & ver	1.30	.25
	Nos. 1342-1344 (3)			2.75	.75

Intl. year against racial discrimination.

Tulip — A287

Designs: Various tulips.

1971, Mar. 25

1345 A287 5q multi .25 .25
1346 A287 10q yellow & multi .25 .25
1347 A287 15q pink & multi .50 .25
1348 A287 20q lt blue & multi .50 .25
1349 A287 25q multi .50 .25
1350 A287 80q multi 1.60 .25
1351 A287 1 l multi 2.75 .25
1352 A287 1.45 l citron & multi 4.25 .30
Nos. 1345-1352 (8) 10.60 2.05

Horseman, by Dürer — A288

Art Works by Dürer: 15q, Three peasants. 25q, Dancing peasant couple. 45q, The bagpiper. 65q, View of Kalkrebut, horiz. 2.40 l, View of Trent, horiz. 2.50 l, Self-portrait.

Perf. 11½x12, 12x11½

1971, May 15 **Litho.**

1353 A288 10q blk & pale grn .25 .25
1354 A288 15q black & pale lil .60 .25
1355 A288 25q black & pale bl .60 .25
1356 A288 45q blk & pale rose 1.10 .25
1357 A288 65q black & multi 2.25 .25
1358 A288 2.40 l black & multi 5.25 .40
Nos. 1353-1358 (6) 10.05 1.65

Miniature Sheet

Imperf

1359 A288 2.50 l multi 5.50 3.75

Albrecht Dürer (1471-1528), German painter and engraver.

Satellite Orbiting Globe — A289

Designs: 1.20 l, Government Building, Tirana, and Red Star emblem. 2.20 l, like 60q. 2.50 l, Flag of People's Republic of China forming trajectory around globe.

1971, June 10 **Litho.** ***Perf. 12x12½***

1360 A289 60q purple & multi 1.10 .25
1361 A289 1.20 l ver & multi 2.25 .30
1362 A289 2.20 l green & multi 4.25 .50

Imperf

1363 A289 2.50 l vio blk & multi 6.50 3.75
Nos. 1360-1363 (4) 14.10 4.80

Space developments of People's Republic of China.

Mao Tse-tung A290

Designs: 1.05 l, House where Communist Party was founded, horiz. 1.20 l, Peking crowd with placards, horiz.

1971, July 1 ***Perf. 12x12½, 12½x12***

1364 A290 25q silver & multi .85 .25
1365 A290 1.05 l silver & multi 2.25 2.00
1366 A290 1.20 l silver & multi 3.25 2.25
Nos. 1364-1366 (3) 6.35 4.50

50th anniv. of Chinese Communist Party.

Crested Titmouse — A291

1971, Aug. 15 **Litho.** ***Perf. 12½x12***

1367 A291 5q shown .30 .25
1368 A291 10q European serin .45 .25
1369 A291 15q Linnet .65 .25
1370 A291 25q Firecrest 1.10 .25
1371 A291 45q Rock thrush 1.60 .25
1372 A291 60q Blue tit 2.40 .50
1373 A291 2.40 l Chaffinch 9.50 2.75
a. Block of 7, #1367-1373 + label 24.00 19.00
Nos. 1367-1373 (7) 16.00 4.50

Continuous design with bird's nest label at upper left.

Nos. 1367-1372 exist in blocks of 8, with two labels.

Olympic Rings and Running — A292

Designs (Olympic Rings and): 10q, Hurdles. 15q, Canoeing. 25q, Gymnastics. 80q, Fencing. 1.05 l, Soccer. 2 l, Runner at finish line. 3.60 l, Diving, women's.

1971, Sept. 15

1374 A292 5q green & multi .25 .25
1375 A292 10q multicolored .25 .25
1376 A292 15q blue & multi .25 .25
1377 A292 25q violet & multi .55 .25
1378 A292 80q lilac & multi 1.10 .25
1379 A292 1.05 l multicolored 1.30 .25
1380 A292 3.60 l multicolored 4.50 .50
Nos. 1374-1380 (7) 8.20 2.00

Souvenir Sheet

Imperf

1381 A292 2 l brt blue & multi 2.75 2.00

20th Olympic Games, Munich, Aug. 26-Sept. 10, 1972.

Workers with Flags A293

Designs: 1.05 l, Party Headquarters, Tirana, and Red Star. 1.20 l, Rifle, star, flag and "VI."

1971, Nov. 1 ***Perf. 12***

1382 A293 25q multi .55 .25
1383 A293 1.05 l multi 1.50 .25
1384 A293 1.20 l multi, vert. 2.10 .30
Nos. 1382-1384 (3) 4.15 .80

6th Congress of Workers' Party.

Factories and Workers A294

Designs: 80q, "XXX" and flag, vert. 1.55 l, Enver Hoxha and flags.

1971, Nov. 8

1385 A294 15q gold, sil, lil & yel .25 .25
1386 A294 80q gold, sil & red 1.40 .25
1387 A294 1.55 l gold, sil, red & brn 2.75 .30
Nos. 1385-1387 (3) 4.40 .80

30th anniversary of Workers' Party.

Construction Work, by M. Fushekati — A295

Contemporary Albanian Paintings: 5q, Young Man, by R. Kuci, vert. 25q, Partisan, by D. Jukniu, vert. 80q, Fliers, by S. Kristo. 1.20 l, Girl in Forest, by A. Sadikaj. 1.55 l, Warriors with Spears and Shields, by S. Kamberi. 2 l, Freedom Fighter, by I. Lulani.

Perf. 12x12½, 12½x12

1971, Nov. 20

1388 A295 5q gold & multi .25 .25
1389 A295 15q gold & multi .25 .25
1390 A295 25q gold & multi .25 .25
1391 A295 80q gold & multi 1.10 .25
1392 A295 1.20 l gold & multi 1.40 .25
1393 A295 1.55 l gold & multi 1.60 .30
Nos. 1388-1393 (6) 4.85 1.55

Miniature Sheet

Imperf

1394 A295 2 l gold & multi 4.00 3.00

Young Workers' Emblem — A296

1971, Nov. 23 ***Perf. 12x12½***

1395 A296 15q lt blue & multi .25 .25
1396 A296 1.35 l grnsh gray & multi 2.00 .30

Albanian Young Workers' Union, 30th anniv.

"Halili and Hajria" Ballet — A297

Scenes from "Halili and Hajria" Ballet: 10q, Brother and sister. 15q, Hajria before Sultan Suleiman. 50q, Hajria and husband. 80q, Execution of Halili. 1.40 l, Hajria killing her husband.

1971, Dec. 27 ***Perf. 12½x12***

1397 A297 5q silver & multi .25 .25
1398 A297 10q silver & multi .25 .25
1399 A297 15q silver & multi .25 .25
1400 A297 50q silver & multi 1.00 .50
1401 A297 80q silver & multi 1.75 1.00
1402 A297 1.40 l silver & multi 3.00 1.75
Nos. 1397-1402 (6) 6.50 4.00

Albanian ballet Halili and Hajria after drama by Kol Jakova.

Biathlon and Olympic Rings — A298

Designs (Olympic Rings and): 10q, Sledding. 15q, Ice hockey. 20q, Bobsledding. 50q, Speed skating. 1 l, Slalom. 2 l, Ski jump. 2.50 l, Figure skating, pairs.

1972, Feb. 10

1403 A298 5q lt olive & multi .25 .25
1404 A298 10q lt violet & multi .25 .25
1405 A298 15q multicolored .25 .25
1406 A298 20q pink & multi .25 .25
1407 A298 50q lt blue & multi .85 .25
1408 A298 1 l ocher & multi 1.30 .25
1409 A298 2 l lilac & multi 2.40 .40
Nos. 1403-1409 (7) 5.55 1.90

Souvenir Sheet

Imperf

1410 A298 2.50 l blue & multi 4.00 3.00

11th Winter Olympic Games, Sapporo, Japan, Feb. 3-13.

Wild Strawberries A299

Wild Fruits and Nuts: 10q, Blackberries. 15q, Hazelnuts. 20q, Walnuts. 25q, Strawberry-tree fruit. 30q, Dogwood berries. 2.40 l, Rowan berries.

1972, Mar. 20 **Litho.** ***Perf. 12***

1411 A299 5q lt grn & multi .25 .25
1412 A299 10q yellow & multi .25 .25
1413 A299 15q lt vio & multi .25 .25
1414 A299 20q pink & multi .45 .25
1415 A299 25q multi .55 .25
1416 A299 30q multi .80 .25
1417 A299 2.40 l multi 4.25 .50
Nos. 1411-1417 (7) 6.80 2.00

"Your Heart is your Health" A300

World Health Day: 1.20 l, Cardiac patient and electrocardiogram.

1972, Apr. 7 ***Perf. 12x12½***

1418 A300 1.10 l multicolored 1.75 .40
1419 A300 1.20 l rose & multi 2.00 .85

Worker and Student — A301

7th Trade Union Cong., May 8: 2.05 l, Assembly Hall, dancers and emblem.

1972, Apr. 24 **Litho.** ***Perf. 11½x12½***

1420 A301 25q multi .75 .25
1421 A301 2.05 l blue & multi 3.00 .40

Qemal Stafa A302

Designs: 15q, Memorial flame. 25q, Monument "Spirit of Defiance," vert.

1972, May 5 ***Perf. 12½x12, 12x12½***

No.	Type	Value	Color	Mint	Used
1422	A302	15q	gray & multi	.25	.25
1423	A302	25q	sal rose, blk & gray	.55	.25
1424	A302	1.90 l	dull yel & blk	2.25	.35
			Nos. 1422-1424 (3)	3.05	.85

30th anniversary of the murder of Qemal Stafa and of Martyrs' Day.

Camellia A303

Designs: Various camellias.

1972, May 10 ***Perf. 12x12½***

Flowers in Natural Colors

No.	Type	Value	Color	Mint	Used
1425	A303	5q	lt blue & blk	.25	.25
1426	A303	10q	citron & blk	.25	.25
1427	A303	15q	grnsh gray & blk	.25	.25
1428	A303	25q	pale sal & blk	.55	.25
1429	A303	45q	gray & blk	.75	.25
1430	A303	50q	sal pink & blk	1.30	.25
1431	A303	2.50 l	bluish gray & blk	5.00	.90
			Nos. 1425-1431 (7)	8.35	2.40

High Jump — A304

Designs (Olympic and Motion Emblems and): 10q, Running. 15q, Shot put. 20q, Bicycling. 25q, Pole vault. 50q, Hurdles, women's. 75q, Hockey. 2 l, Swimming. 2.50 l, Diving, women's.

1972, June 30 **Litho.** ***Perf. 12½x12***

No.	Type	Value	Color	Mint	Used
1432	A304	5q	multicolored	.25	.25
1433	A304	10q	lt brn & multi	.25	.25
1434	A304	15q	lt lil & multi	.25	.25
1435	A304	20q	multicolored	.35	.25
1436	A304	25q	lt vio & multi	.45	.25
1437	A304	50q	lt grn & multi	.55	.25
1438	A304	75q	multicolored	1.10	.25
1439	A304	2 l	multicolored	3.25	.35
			Nos. 1432-1439 (8)	6.45	2.10

Miniature Sheet

Imperf

No.	Type	Value	Color	Mint	Used
1440	A304	2.50 l	multi	4.00	3.00

20th Olympic Games, Munich, Aug. 26-Sept. 11. Nos. 1432-1439 each issued in sheets of 8 stamps and one label (3x3) showing Olympic rings in gold.

Autobus A305

25q, Electric train. 80q, Ocean liner Tirana. 1.05 l, Automobile. 1.20 l, Trailer truck.

1972, July 25 **Litho.** ***Perf. 12***

No.	Type	Value	Color	Mint	Used
1441	A305	15q	org brn & multi	.25	.25
1442	A305	25q	gray & multi	.55	.25
1443	A305	80q	dp grn & multi	.75	.25
1444	A305	1.05 l	multi	1.30	.25
1445	A305	1.20 l	multi	2.25	.25
			Nos. 1441-1445 (5)	5.10	1.25

Arm Wrestling A306

Folk Games: 10q, Piggyback ball game. 15q, Women's jumping. 25q, Rope game (srum). 90q, Leapfrog. 2 l, Women throwing pitchers.

1972, Aug. 18

No.	Type	Value	Color	Mint	Used
1446	A306	5q	multi	.25	.25
1447	A306	10q	lt bl & multi	.25	.25
1448	A306	15q	rose & multi	.25	.25
1449	A306	25q	lt bl & multi	.55	.25
1450	A306	90q	ocher & multi	1.75	.25
1451	A306	2 l	lt grn & multi	2.75	.30
			Nos. 1446-1451 (6)	5.80	1.55

1st National Festival of People's Games.

Mastheads — A307

30th Press Day: 25q, Printing press. 1.90 l, Workers reading paper.

1972, Aug. 25

No.	Type	Value	Color	Mint	Used
1452	A307	15q	lt bl & blk	.25	.25
1453	A307	25q	red, grn & blk	.35	.25
1454	A307	1.90 l	lt vio & blk	2.25	.40
			Nos. 1452-1454 (3)	2.85	.90

Map of Peza Area, Memorial Tablet A308

25q, Guerrillas with flag. 1.90 l, Peza Conference memorial.

1972, Sept. 16

No.	Type	Value	Color	Mint	Used
1455	A308	15q	shown	.35	.25
1456	A308	25q	multicolored	.55	.25
1457	A308	1.90 l	multicolored	3.00	.40
			Nos. 1455-1457 (3)	3.90	.90

30th anniversary, Conference of Peza.

Partisans, by Sotir Capo — A309

Paintings: 10q, Woman, by Ismail Lulani, vert. 15q, "Communists," by Lec Shkreli, vert. 20q, View of Nendorit, 1941, by Sali Shijaku, vert. 50q, Woman with Sheaf, by Zef Shoshi, vert. 1 l, Landscape with Children, by Dhimitraq Trebicka. 2 l, Women on Bicycles, by Vilson Kilica. 2.30 l, Folk Dance, by Abdurrahim Buza.

Perf. 12½x12, 12x12½

1972, Sept. 25 **Litho.**

No.	Type	Value	Color	Mint	Used
1458	A309	5q	gold & multi	.25	.25
1459	A309	10q	gold & multi	.25	.25
1460	A309	15q	gold & multi	.25	.25
1461	A309	20q	gold & multi	.35	.25
1462	A309	50q	gold & multi	.65	.25
1463	A309	1 l	gold & multi	1.30	.25
1464	A309	2 l	gold & multi	2.75	.40
			Nos. 1458-1464 (7)	5.80	1.90

Miniature Sheet

Imperf

No.	Type	Value	Color	Mint	Used
1465	A309	2.30 l	gold & multi	4.00	3.00

No. 1465 contains one 41x68mm stamp.

Congress Emblem — A310

Design: 2.05 l, Young worker with banner.

1972, Oct. 23 **Litho.** ***Perf. 12***

No.	Type	Value	Color	Mint	Used
1466	A310	25q	silver, red & gold	.75	.25
1467	A310	2.05 l	silver & multi	3.00	.50

Union of Working Youth, 6th Congress.

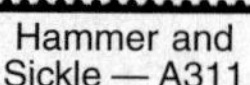

Hammer and Sickle — A311

Ismail Qemali — A312

Design: 1.20 l, Lenin as orator.

1972, Nov. 7 **Litho.** ***Perf. 11½x12***

No.	Type	Value	Color	Mint	Used
1468	A311	1.10 l	multi	1.40	.25
1469	A311	1.20 l	multi	3.00	.30

Russian October Revolution, 55th anniv.

Perf. 12x11½, 11½x12

1972, Nov. 29

Designs: 15q, Albanian fighters, horiz. 65q, Rally, horiz. 1.25 l, Coat of arms.

No.	Type	Value	Color	Mint	Used
1470	A312	15q	red, brt bl & blk	.25	.25
1471	A312	25q	yel, blk & red	.25	.25
1472	A312	65q	red, sal & blk	.85	.25
1473	A312	1.25 l	dl red & blk	2.75	.25
			Nos. 1470-1473 (4)	4.10	1.00

60th anniv. of independence.

Cock, Mosaic A313

Mosaics, 2nd-5th centuries, excavated near Buthrotium and Apollonia: 10q, Bird, vert. 15q, Partridges, vert. 25q, Warrior's legs. 45q, Nymph riding dolphin, vert. 50q, Fish, vert. 2.50 l, Warrior with helmet.

1972, Dec. 10 ***Perf. 12½x12, 12x12½***

No.	Type	Value	Color	Mint	Used
1474	A313	5q	silver & multi	.25	.25
1475	A313	10q	silver & multi	.25	.25
1476	A313	15q	silver & multi	.25	.25
1477	A313	25q	silver & multi	.45	.25
1478	A313	45q	silver & multi	.55	.25
1479	A313	50q	silver & multi	.75	.25
1480	A313	2.50 l	silver & multi	3.75	.80
			Nos. 1474-1480 (7)	6.25	2.30

Nicolaus Copernicus A314

Designs: 10q, 25q, 80q, 1.20 l, Various portraits of Copernicus. 1.60 l, Heliocentric solar system.

1973, Feb. 19 **Litho.** ***Perf. 12x12½***

No.	Type	Value	Color	Mint	Used
1481	A314	5q	lil rose & multi	.25	.25
1482	A314	10q	dull ol & multi	.25	.25
1483	A314	25q	multicolored	.25	.25
1484	A314	80q	lt violet & multi	.75	.25
1485	A314	1.20 l	blue & multi	2.25	.30
1486	A314	1.60 l	gray & multi	3.25	.40
			Nos. 1481-1486 (6)	7.00	1.70

500th anniversary of the birth of Nicolaus Copernicus (1473-1543), Polish astronomer.

Flowering Cactus — A315

Designs: Various flowering cacti.

1973, Mar. 25 **Litho.** ***Perf. 12***

No.	Type	Value	Color	Mint	Used
1487	A315	10q	multicolored	.25	.25
1488	A315	15q	multicolored	.25	.25
1489	A315	20q	beige & multi	.25	.25
1490	A315	25q	gray & multi	.55	.25
1491	A315	30q	beige & multi	4.25	1.50
1492	A315	65q	gray & multi	.85	.25
1493	A315	80q	multicolored	1.10	.25
1494	A315	2 l	multicolored	2.25	.60
a.			Block of 8, #1487-1494	18.00	10.00
			Nos. 1487-1494 (8)	9.75	3.60

A block containing Nos. 1487-1490, 1492-1494 and a label exists.

Guard and Factories — A316

1.80 l, Guard and guards with prisoner.

1973, Mar. 20 **Litho.** ***Perf. 12½x12***

No.	Type	Value	Color	Mint	Used
1495	A316	25q	ultra & blk	.55	.25
1496	A316	1.80 l	dk red & multi	3.00	.40

30th anniv. of the State Security Branch.

Common Tern — A317

Sea Birds: 15q, White-winged black terns, vert. 25q, Black-headed gull, vert. 45q, Great black-headed gull. 80q, Slender-billed gull, vert. 2.40 l, Sandwich terns.

1973, Apr. 30 ***Perf. 12½x12, 12x12½***

No.	Type	Value	Color	Mint	Used
1497	A317	5q	gold & multi	.25	.25
1498	A317	15q	gold & multi	.45	.25
1499	A317	25q	gold & multi	.55	.25
1500	A317	45q	gold & multi	1.10	.25

1501 A317 80q gold & multi 2.25 .25
1502 A317 2.40 l gold & multi 4.25 .55
Nos. 1497-1502 (6) 8.85 1.80

Letters, 1913 Cancellation and Post Horn — A318

Design: 1.80 l, Mailman, 1913 cancel.

1973, May, 5 Litho. ***Perf. 12x11½***
1503 A318 25q red & multi 1.10 .25
1504 A318 1.80 l red & multi 4.25 .55

60th anniversary of Albanian stamps.

Farmer, Worker, Soldier A319

Design: 25q, Woman and factory, vert.

1973, June 4 ***Perf. 12***
1505 A319 25q carmine rose .55 .25
1506 A319 1.80 l yel, dp org & blk 3.25 .50

7th Congress of Albanian Women's Union.

Creation of General Staff, by G. Madhi — A320

Designs: 40q, "August 1949," sculpture by Sh. Haderi, vert. 60q, "Generation after Generation," sculpture by H. Dule, vert. 80q, "Defend Revolutionary Victories," by M. Fushekati.

1973, July 10 Litho. ***Perf. 12½x12***
1507 A320 25q gold & multi *13.00 11.00*
1508 A320 40q gold & multi *13.00 11.00*
1509 A320 60q gold & multi *13.00 11.00*
1510 A320 80q gold & multi *13.00 11.00*
Nos. 1507-1510 (4) *52.00 44.00*

30th anniversary of the People's Army.

"Electrification," by S. Hysa — A321

Albanian Paintings: 10q, Woman Textile Worker, by N. Nallbani. 15q, Gymnasts, by M. Fushekati. 50q, Aviator, by F. Stamo. 80q, Fascist Prisoner, by A. Lakuriqi. 1.20 l, Workers with Banner, by P. Mele. 1.30 l, Farm Woman, by Zef Shoshi. 2.05 l, Battle of Tenda, by F. Haxhiu. 10q, 50q, 80q, 1.20 l, 1.30 l, vertical.

Perf. 12½x12, 12x12½

1973, Aug. 10
1511 A321 5q gold & multi .25 .25
1512 A321 10q gold & multi .25 .25
1513 A321 15q gold & multi .25 .25
1514 A321 50q gold & multi .65 .25
1515 A321 80q gold & multi .75 .25
1516 A321 1.20 l gold & multi 1.10 .25
1517 A321 1.30 l gold & multi 2.25 .25
Nos. 1511-1517 (7) 5.50 1.75

Souvenir Sheet

Imperf

1518 A321 2.05 l multi 4.00 3.00

Mary Magdalene, by Caravaggio A322

Paintings by Michelangelo da Caravaggio: 10q, The Lute Player, horiz. 15q, Self-portrait. 50q, Boy Carrying Fruit and Flowers. 80q, Still Life, horiz. 1.20 l, Narcissus. 1.30 l, Boy Peeling Apple. 2.05 l, Man with Feathered Hat.

Perf. 12x12½, 12½x12

1973, Sept. 28
1519 A322 5q gold & multi .25 .25
1520 A322 10q gold & multi .25 .25
1521 A322 15q gold, blk & gray .25 .25
1522 A322 50q gold & multi .65 .25
1523 A322 80q gold & multi .90 .25
1524 A322 1.20 l gold & multi 1.30 .30
1525 A322 1.30 l gold & multi 2.25 .30
Nos. 1519-1525 (7) 5.85 1.85

Souvenir Sheet

Imperf

1526 A322 2.05 l multi 6.00 5.25

Michelangelo da Caravaggio (Merisi; 1573?-1609), Italian painter. No. 1526 contains one stamp, size: 63x73mm.

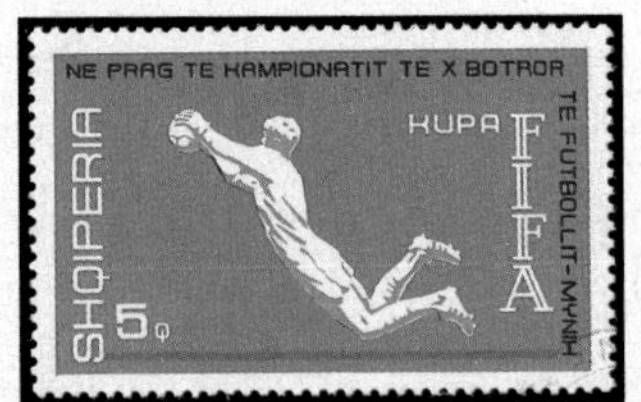

Soccer — A323

Designs: 5q-1.25 l, Various soccer scenes. 2.05 l, Ball in goal and list of cities where championships were held.

1973, Oct. 30 Litho. ***Perf. 12½x12***
1527 A323 5q multi .25 .25
1528 A323 10q multi .25 .25
1529 A323 15q multi .25 .25
1530 A323 20q multi .25 .25
1531 A323 25q multi .25 .25
1532 A323 90q multi 1.30 .25
1533 A323 1.20 l multi 1.50 .25
1534 A323 1.25 l multi 2.25 .25
Nos. 1527-1534 (8) 6.30 2.00

Minature Sheet

Imperf

1535 A323 2.05 l multi 4.50 3.25

World Soccer Cup, Munich 1974.

Weight Lifter — A324

Designs: Various stages of weight lifting. 1.20 l, 1.60 l, horiz.

1973, Oct. 30 Litho. ***Perf. 12***
1536 A324 5q multi .25 .25
1537 A324 10q multi .25 .25
1538 A324 25q multi .25 .25
1539 A324 90q multi .75 .25
1540 A324 1.20 l multi 1.10 .25
1541 A324 1.60 l multi 2.25 .25
Nos. 1536-1541 (6) 4.85 1.50

Weight Lifting Championships, Havana, Cuba.

Ballet — A325

Harvester Combine A326

Designs: 5q, Cement factory, Kavaje. 10q, Ali Kelmendi truck factory and tank cars, horiz. 25q, "Communication." 35q, Skiers and hotel, horiz. 60q, Resort, horiz. 80q, Mountain lake. 1 l, Mao Tse-tung textile mill. 1.20 l, Steel workers. 2.40 l, Welder and pipe. 3 l, Skanderbeg Monument, Tirana. 5 l, Roman arches, Durres.

Perf. 12½x12, 12x12½

1973-74 Litho.
1543 A325 5q gold & multi .25 .25
1544 A325 10q gold & multi .25 .25
1545 A325 15q gold & multi .55 .25
1545A A326 20q gold & multi .25 .25
1546 A326 25q gold & multi .75 .25
1547 A326 35q gold & multi .65 .25
1548 A326 60q gold & multi 1.10 .25
1549 A326 80q gold & multi 1.75 .25
1549A A326 1 l gold & multi .40 .25
1549B A326 1.20 l gold & multi 1.25 .25
1549C A326 2.40 l gold & multi 2.75 .35
1550 A326 3 l gold & multi 4.25 .35
1551 A326 5 l gold & multi 5.00 .60
Nos. 1543-1551 (13) 19.20 3.80

Issue dates: Nos. 1545-1546, 1549-1550, Dec. 5, 1973; others, 1974.

Mao Tse-tung — A327

80th birthday of Mao Tse-tung: 1.20 l, Mao Tse-tung addressing crowd.

1973, Dec. 26 ***Perf. 12***
1552 A327 85q multicolored *11.00* 1.25
1553 A327 1.20 l multicolored *17.00* 2.25

Old Man and Dog, by Gericault A328

Paintings by Jean Louis André Theodore Gericault: 10q, Horse's Head. 15q, Male Model. 25q, Head of Black Man. 1.20 l, Self-portrait. 2.05 l, Raft of the Medusa, horiz. 2.20 l, Battle of the Giants.

Perf. 12x12½, 12½x12

1974, Jan. 18 Litho.
1554 A328 10q gold & multi .25 .25
1555 A328 15q gold & multi .25 .25
1556 A328 20q gold & multi .25 .25
1557 A328 25q gold & blk .55 .25
1558 A328 1.20 l gold & multi 2.25 .25
1559 A328 2.20 l gold & multi 3.75 .40
Nos. 1554-1559 (6) 7.30 1.65

Souvenir Sheet

Imperf

1560 A328 2.05 l gold & multi 4.00 3.00

No. 1560 contains one 87x78mm stamp.

Lenin, by Pandi Mele — A329

Designs: 25q, Lenin with Sailors on Cruiser Aurora, by Dhimitraq Trebicka, horiz. 1.20 l, Lenin, by Vilson Kilica.

1974, Jan. 21 ***Perf. 12½x12, 12x12½***
1561 A329 25q gold & multi .90 .25
1562 A329 60q gold & multi 2.10 .25
1563 A329 1.20 l gold & multi 6.00 .55
Nos. 1561-1563 (3) 9.00 1.05

50th anniv. of the death of Lenin.

Swimming Duck, Mosaic — A330

Designs: Mosaics from the 5th-6th Centuries A.D., excavated near Buthrotium, Pogradec and Apollonia.

1974, Feb. 20 Litho. ***Perf. 12½x12***
1564 A330 5q shown .25 .25
1565 A330 10q Bird, flower .25 .25
1566 A330 15q Vase, grapes .25 .25
1567 A330 25q Duck .25 .25
1568 A330 40q Donkey, bird .45 .25
1569 A330 2.50 l Sea horse 2.75 .40
Nos. 1564-1569 (6) 4.20 1.65

Soccer — A331

Various scenes from soccer. 2.05 l, World Soccer Cup & names of participating countries.

1974, Apr. 25 Litho. ***Perf. 12½x12***
1570 A331 10q gold & multi .25 .25
1571 A331 15q gold & multi .25 .25
1572 A331 20q gold & multi .25 .25
1573 A331 25q gold & multi .35 .25
1574 A331 40q gold & multi .55 .25
1575 A331 80q gold & multi 1.10 .25
1576 A331 1 l gold & multi 1.30 .30
1577 A331 1.20 l gold & multi 1.75 .40
Nos. 1570-1577 (8) 5.80 2.20

Souvenir Sheet

Imperf

1578 A331 2.05 l gold & multi 4.50 3.00

World Cup Soccer Championship, Munich, June 13-July 7. No. 1578 contains one stamp (60x60mm) with simulated perforations. Nos. 1570-1577 exist imperf, No. 1578 with simulated perfs omitted. Values $10 and $25, respectively.

Arms of Albania, Soldier — A332

Design: 1.80 l, Soldier and front page of 1944 Congress Book.

1974, May 24 **Litho.** ***Perf. 12***
1579 A332 25q multicolored .55 .25
1580 A332 1.80 l multicolored 2.25 .30

30th anniversary of the First Anti-Fascist Liberation Congress of Permet.

Medicinal Plants A333

10q, Bittersweet. 15q, Arbutus. 20q, Lilies of the valley. 25q, Autumn crocus. 40q, Borage, horiz. 80q, Soapwort, horiz. 2.20 l, Gentian, horiz.

1974, May 5 ***Perf. 12x12½***
1581 A333 10q multicolored .25 .25
1582 A333 15q multicolored .25 .25
1583 A333 20q multicolored .25 .25
1584 A333 25q multicolored .55 .25
1585 A333 40q multicolored .80 .25
1586 A333 80q multicolored 1.30 .25
1587 A333 2.20 l multicolored 3.75 .45
Nos. 1581-1587 (7) 7.15 1.95

Revolutionaries with Albanian Flag — A334

1.80 l, Portraits of 5 revolutionaries, vert.

Perf. 12½x12, 12x12½
1974, June 10
1588 A334 25q red, blk & lil .55 .25
1589 A334 1.80 l yel, red & blk 2.25 .45

50th anniversary Albanian Bourgeois Democratic Revolution.

European Redwing — A335

Designs: Songbirds; Nos. 1597-1600 vert.

Perf. 12½x12, 12x12½
1974, July 15 **Litho.**
1594 A335 10q shown .25 .25
1595 A335 15q European robin .25 .25
1596 A335 20q Greenfinch .35 .25
1597 A335 25q Bullfinch .55 .25
1598 A335 40q Hawfinch .85 .25
1599 A335 80q Blackcap 2.25 .25
1600 A335 2.20 l Nightingale 4.25 .50
Nos. 1594-1600 (7) 8.75 2.00

Globe — A336

Cent. of UPU: 1.20 l, UPU emblem. 2.05 l, Jet over globe.

1974, Aug. 25 **Litho.** ***Perf. 12x12½***
1601 A336 85q grn & multi 1.75 .25
1602 A336 1.20 l vio & ol grn 2.75 .25

Miniature Sheet

Imperf

1603 A336 2.05 l blue & multi 25.00 25.00

Widows, by Sali Shijaku — A337

Albanian Paintings: 15q, Drillers, by Danish Jukniu, vert. 20q, Workers with Blueprints, by Clirim Ceka. 25q, Call to Action, by Spiro Kristo, vert. 40q, Winter Battle, by Sabaudin Xhaferi. 80q, Comrades, by Clirim Ceka, vert. 1 l, Aiding the Partisans, by Guri Madhi. 1.20 l, Teacher with Pupils, by Kleo Nini Brezat. 2.05 l, Comrades in Arms, by Guri Madhi.

Perf. 12½x12, 12x12½
1974, Sept. 25
1604 A337 10q silver & multi .25 .25
1605 A337 15q silver & multi .25 .25
1606 A337 20q silver & multi .25 .25
1607 A337 25q silver & multi .40 .25
1608 A337 40q silver & multi .55 .25
1609 A337 80q silver & multi 1.10 .25
1610 A337 1 l silver & multi 1.60 .25
1611 A337 1.20 l silver & multi 2.25 .25
Nos. 1604-1611 (8) 6.65 2.00

Miniature Sheet

Imperf

1612 A337 2.05 l silver & multi 4.00 3.00

Crowd on Tien An Men Square A338

Design: 1.20 l, Mao Tse-tung, vert.

1974, Oct. 1 ***Perf. 12***
1613 A338 85q gold & multi *6.00* 1.50
1614 A338 1.20 l gold & multi *9.50* 2.50

25th anniversary of the proclamation of the People's Republic of China.

Women's Volleyball A339

Spartakiad Medal and: 15q, Women hurdlers. 20q, Women gymnasts. 25q, Mass exercises in Stadium. 40q, Weight lifter. 80q, Wrestlers. 1 l, Military rifle drill. 1.20 l, Soccer.

1974, Oct. 9 ***Perf. 12x12½***
1615 A339 10q multi .25 .25
1616 A339 15q multi .25 .25
1617 A339 20q multi .25 .25
1618 A339 25q gray & multi .25 .25
1619 A339 40q multi .55 .25
1620 A339 80q multi .75 .25
1621 A339 1 l multi 1.10 .25
1622 A339 1.20 l tan & multi 1.75 .25
Nos. 1615-1622 (8) 5.15 2.00

National Spartakiad, Oct. 9-17.

View of Berat — A340

Designs: 80q, Enver Hoxha addressing Congress, bas-relief, horiz. 1 l, Hoxha and leaders leaving Congress Hall.

Perf. 12x12½, 12½x12
1974, Oct. 20 **Litho.**
1623 A340 25q rose car & blk .35 .25
1624 A340 80q yel, brn & blk 1.10 .25
1625 A340 1 l dp lilac & blk 2.25 .30
Nos. 1623-1625 (3) 3.70 .80

30th anniversary of 2nd Congress of Berat.

Anniversary Emblem, Factory Guards — A341

35q, Chemical industry. 50q, Agriculture. 80q, Arts. 1 l, Atomic diagram & computer. 1.20 l, Youth education. 2.05 l, Crowd & History Book.

1974, Nov. 29 **Litho.** ***Perf. 12½x12***
1626 A341 25q green & multi .25 .25
1627 A341 35q ultra & multi .25 .25
1628 A341 50q brown & multi .30 .25
1629 A341 80q multicolored .65 .25
1630 A341 1 l violet & multi .85 .25
1631 A341 1.20 l multicolored 1.60 .30
Nos. 1626-1631 (6) 3.90 1.55

Miniature Sheet

Imperf

1632 A341 2.05 l gold & multi 4.00 3.00

30th anniv. of liberation from Fascism.

Artemis, from Apolloni A342

1974, Dec. 25 **Photo.** ***Perf. 12x12½***
1633 A342 10q shown .25 .25
1634 A342 15q Zeus statue .25 .25
1635 A342 20q Poseidon statue .25 .25
1636 A342 25q Illyrian helmet .40 .25
1637 A342 40q Amphora .80 .25
1638 A342 80q Agrippa 1.25 .25
1639 A342 1 l Demosthenes 1.60 .30
1640 A342 1.20 l Head of Bilia 2.75 .35
Nos. 1633-1640 (8) 7.55 2.15

Miniature Sheet

Imperf

1641 A342 2.05 l Artemis & amphora 4.00 3.00

Archaeological discoveries in Albania.

Workers and Factories A343

25q, Handshake, tools and book, vert.

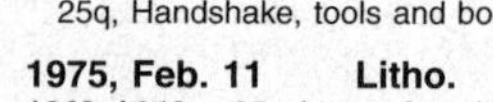

1975, Feb. 11 **Litho.** ***Perf. 12***
1642 A343 25q brown & multi .45 .25
1643 A343 1.80 l yellow & multi 1.75 .35

Albanian Trade Unions, 30th anniversary.

Chicory A344

1975, Feb. 15
1644 A344 5q shown .25 .25
1645 A344 10q Houseleek .25 .25
1646 A344 15q Columbine .25 .25
1647 A344 20q Anemone .25 .25
1648 A344 25q Hibiscus .25 .25
1649 A344 30q Gentian .25 .25
1650 A344 35q Hollyhock .55 .25
1651 A344 2.70 l Iris 2.50 .45
Nos. 1644-1651 (8) 4.55 2.20

Protected flowers.

Jesus, from Doni Madonna A345

Works by Michelangelo: 10q, Slave, sculpture. 15q, Head of Dawn, sculpture. 20q, Awakening Giant, sculpture. 25q, Cumaenian Sybil, Sistine Chapel. 30q, Lorenzo di Medici, sculpture. 1.20 l, David, sculpture. 2.05 l, Self-portrait. 3.90 l, Delphic Sybil, Sistine Chapel.

1975, Mar. 20 **Litho.** ***Perf. 12x12½***
1652 A345 5q gold & multi .25 .25
1653 A345 10q gold & multi .25 .25
1654 A345 15q gold & multi .25 .25
1655 A345 20q gold & multi .25 .25
1656 A345 25q gold & multi .25 .25
1657 A345 30q gold & multi .35 .25
1658 A345 1.20 l gold & multi 1.00 .25
1659 A345 3.90 l gold & multi 2.75 .50
Nos. 1652-1659 (8) 5.35 2.25

Miniature Sheet

Imperf

1660 A345 2.05 l gold & multi 4.50 3.25

Michelangelo Buonarroti (1475-1564), Italian sculptor, painter and architect.

Two-wheeled Cart — A346

Albanian Transportation of the Past: 5q, Horseback rider. 15q, Lake ferry. 20q, Coastal three-master. 25q, Phaeton. 3.35 l, Early automobile on bridge.

1975, Apr. 15 **Litho.** ***Perf. 12½x12***
1661 A346 5q bl grn & multi .25 .25
1662 A346 10q ol & multi .25 .25
1663 A346 15q lil & multi .25 .25
1664 A346 20q multi .25 .25
1665 A346 25q multi .25 .25
1666 A346 3.35 l ocher & multi 3.25 .50
Nos. 1661-1666 (6) 4.50 1.75

Guard at Frontier Stone — A347

Guardsman and Militia — A348

1975, Apr. 25 *Perf. 12*

1667 A347 25q multi .55 .25
1668 A348 1.80 l multi 2.10 .35

30th anniversary of Frontier Guards.

Posting Illegal Poster — A349

Designs: 60q, Partisans in battle. 1.20 l, Partisan killing German soldier, and Albanian coat of arms.

1975, May 9 *Perf. 12½x12*

1669 A349 25q multi .35 .25
1670 A349 60q multi .75 .25
1671 A349 1.20 l red & multi 1.60 .30
Nos. 1669-1671 (3) 2.70 .80

30th anniversary of victory over Fascism.

European Widgeons — A350

Waterfowl: 5q, Anas penelope. 10q, Netta rufina. 15q, Anser albifrons. 20q, Anas acuta. 25q, Mergus serrator. 30q, Pata somateria. 35q, Cignus cignus. 2.70 l, Spatula clypeata.

1975, June 15 **Litho.** *Perf. 12*

1672 A350 5q brt blue & multi .25 .25
1673 A350 10q yel grn & multi .25 .25
1674 A350 15q brt rose lil & multi .25 .25
1675 A350 20q bl grn & multi .25 .25
1676 A350 25q multicolored .35 .25
1677 A350 30q multicolored .60 .25
1678 A350 35q orange & multi .80 .25
1679 A350 2.70 l multi 4.75 .90
Nos. 1672-1679 (8) 7.50 2.65

Shyqyri Kanapari, by Musa Qarri — A351

Albanian Paintings: 10q, Woman Saving Children in Sea, by Agim Faja. 15q, "November 28, 1912" (revolution), by Petrit Ceno, horiz. 20q, "Workers Unite," by Sali Shijaku. 25q, The Partisan Shota Galica, by Ismail Lulani. 30q, Victorious Resistance Fighters, 1943, by Nestor Jonuzi. 80q, Partisan Couple in Front of Red Flag, by Vilson Halimi. 2.05 l, Dancing Procession, by Abdurahim Buza. 2.25 l, Republic Day Celebration, by Fatmir Haxhiu, horiz.

Perf. 12x12½, 12½x12

1975, July 15 **Litho.**

1680 A351 5q gold & multi .25 .25
1681 A351 10q gold & multi .25 .25
1682 A351 15q gold & multi .25 .25
1683 A351 20q gold & multi .25 .25
1684 A351 25q gold & multi .25 .25
1685 A351 30q gold & multi .25 .25
1686 A351 80q gold & multi .65 .25
1687 A351 2.25 l gold & multi 2.75 .45
Nos. 1680-1687 (8) 4.90 2.20

Miniature Sheet

Imperf

1688 A351 2.05 l gold & multi 3.75 2.75

Nos. 1680-1687 issued in sheets of 8 stamps and gold center label showing palette and easel.

Farmer Holding Reform Law — A352

Design: 2 l, Produce and farm machinery.

1975, Aug. 28 *Perf. 12*

1689 A352 15q multicolored .55 .25
1690 A352 2 l multicolored 2.50 .50

Agrarian reform, 30th anniversary.

Alcynonium Palmatum A353

Corals: 10q, Paramuricea chamaeleon. 20q, Coralium rubrum. 25q, Eunicella covalini. 3.70 l, Cladocora cespitosa.

1975, Sept. 25 **Litho.** *Perf. 12*

1691 A353 5q blue, ol & blk .25 .25
1692 A353 10q blue & multi .25 .25
1693 A353 20q blue & multi .25 .25
1694 A353 25q blue & blk .35 .25
1695 A353 3.70 l blue & blk 5.25 .80
Nos. 1691-1695 (5) 6.35 1.80

Bicycling A354

Designs (Montreal Olympic Games Emblem and): 10q, Canoeing. 15q, Fieldball. 20q, Basketball. 25q, Water polo. 30q, Hockey. 1.20 l, Pole vault. 2.05 l, Fencing. 2.15 l, Montreal Olympic Games emblem and various sports.

1975, Oct. 20 **Litho.** *Perf. 12½*

1696 A354 5q multi .25 .25
1697 A354 10q multi .25 .25
1698 A354 15q multi .25 .25
1699 A354 20q multi .40 .25
1700 A354 25q multi .45 .25
1701 A354 30q multi .55 .25
1702 A354 1.20 l multi 1.50 .30
1703 A354 2.05 l multi 2.75 .45
Nos. 1696-1703 (8) 6.40 2.25

Miniature Sheet

Imperf

1704 A354 2.15 l org & multi 6.50 5.25

21st Olympic Games, Montreal, July 18-Aug. 8, 1976. Nos. 1696-1703 exist imperf. Value $10.

Power Lines Leading to Village A355

Designs: 25q, Transformers and insulators. 80q, Dam and power station. 85q, Television set, power lines, grain and cogwheel.

1975, Oct. 25 *Perf. 12x12½*

1705 A355 15q ultra & yel .25 .25
1706 A355 25q brt vio & pink .30 .25
1707 A355 80q lt grn & gray .90 .25
1708 A355 85q ocher & brn 2.00 .45
Nos. 1705-1708 (4) 3.45 1.20

General electrification, 5th anniversary.

Child, Rabbit and Teddy Bear Planting Tree — A356

Fairy Tales: 10q, Mother fox. 15q, Ducks in school. 20q, Little pigs building house. 25q, Animals watching television. 30q, Rabbit and bear at work. 35q, Working and playing ants. 2.70 l, Wolf in sheep's clothes.

1975, Dec. 25 **Litho.** *Perf. 12½x12*

1709 A356 5q black & multi .25 .25
1710 A356 10q black & multi .25 .25
1711 A356 15q black & multi .25 .25
1712 A356 20q black & multi .30 .25
1713 A356 25q black & multi .40 .25
1714 A356 30q black & multi .50 .25
1715 A356 35q black & multi .55 .25
1716 A356 2.70 l black & multi 3.00 .75
Nos. 1709-1716 (8) 5.50 2.50

Arms, People, Factories A357

Design: 1.90 l, Arms, government building, celebrating crowd.

1976, Jan. 11 **Litho.** *Perf. 12*

1717 A357 25q gold & multi .55 .25
1718 A357 1.90 l gold & multi 3.00 .35

30th anniversary of proclamation of Albanian People's Republic.

Ice Hockey, Olympic Games' Emblem A358

Designs: 10q, Speed skating. 15q, Biathlon. 50q, Ski jump. 1.20 l, Slalom. 2.15 l, Figure skating, pairs. 2.30 l, One-man bobsled.

1976, Feb. 4

1719 A358 5q silver & multi .25 .25
1720 A358 10q silver & multi .25 .25
1721 A358 15q silver & multi .25 .25
1722 A358 50q silver & multi .35 .25
1723 A358 1.20 l silver & multi 1.10 .25
1724 A358 2.30 l silver & multi 2.00 .40
Nos. 1719-1724 (6) 4.20 1.65

Miniature Sheet

Perf. 12 on 2 sides x Imperf.

1725 A358 2.15 l silver & multi 3.25 2.00

12th Winter Olympic Games, Innsbruck, Austria, Feb. 4-15.

Meadow Saffron A359

Medicinal Plants: 10q, Deadly night-shade. 15q, Yellow gentian. 20q, Horse chestnut. 70q, Shield fern. 80q, Marshmallow. 2.30 l, Thorn apple.

1976, Apr. 10 **Litho.** *Perf. 12x12½*

1726 A359 5q black & multi .25 .25
1727 A359 10q black & multi .25 .25
1728 A359 15q black & multi .25 .25
1729 A359 20q black & multi .25 .25
1730 A359 70q black & multi .75 .25
1731 A359 80q black & multi 1.25 .25
1732 A359 2.30 l black & multi 2.75 .35
Nos. 1726-1732 (7) 5.75 1.85

Bowl and Spoon — A360

15q, Flask, vert. 20q, Carved handles, vert. 25q, Pistol and dagger. 80q, Wall hanging, vert. 1.20 l, Earrings and belt buckle. 1.40 l, Jugs, vert.

1976 Litho. ***Perf. 12½x12, 12x12½***

1733 A360 10q lilac & multi .25 .25
1734 A360 15q gray & multi .25 .25
1735 A360 20q multi .25 .25
1736 A360 25q car & multi .25 .25
1737 A360 80q yellow & multi .75 .25
1738 A360 1.20 l multi 1.10 .30
1739 A360 1.40 l tan & multi 2.00 .40
Nos. 1733-1739 (7) 4.85 1.95

Natl. Ethnographic Conf., Tirana, June 28.
For surcharge see No. 1873.

Founding of Cooperatives, by Zef Shoshi — A361

Paintings: 10q, Going to Work, by Agim Zajmi, vert. 25q, Crowd Listening to Loudspeaker, by Vilson Kilica. 40q, Woman Welder, by Sabaudin Xhaferi, vert. 50q, Factory, by Isuf Sulovari, vert. 1.20 l, 1942 Revolt, by Lec Shkreli, vert. 1.60 l, Coming Home from Work, by Agron Dine. 2.05 l, Honoring a Young Pioneer, by Andon Lakuriqi.

Perf. 12½x12, 12x12½

1976, Aug. 8 **Litho.**

1740 A361 5q gold & multi .25 .25
1741 A361 10q gold & multi .25 .25
1742 A361 25q gold & multi .25 .25
1743 A361 40q gold & multi .40 .25
1744 A361 50q gold & multi .70 .25
1745 A361 1.20 l gold & multi 1.10 .55
1746 A361 1.60 l gold & multi 1.60 .85
Nos. 1740-1746 (7) 4.55 2.65

Miniature Sheet

Perf. 12 on 2 sides x Imperf.

1747 A361 2.05 l gold & multi 3.00 2.00

Red Flag, Agricultural Symbols — A362

Design: 1.20 l, Red flag and raised pickax.

1976, Nov. 1

1748 A362 25q multi .55 .25
1749 A362 1.20 l multi 2.00 .50

7th Workers Party Congress.

Enver Hoxha, Partisans and Albanian Flag — A363

1.90 l, Demonstrators with Albanian flag.

1976, Oct. 28 ***Perf. 12x12½***

1750 A363 25q multi .50 .25
1751 A363 1.90 l multi 2.50 .65

Anti-Fascist demonstrations, 35th anniv.

Attacking Partisans, Meeting House A364

Designs (Red Flag and): 25q, Partisans, pickax and gun. 80q, Workers, soldiers, pickax and gun. 1.20 l, Agriculture and industry. 1.70 l, Dancers, symbols of science and art.

1976, Nov. 8 **Litho.** ***Perf. 12x12½***

1752 A364 15q gold & multi .25 .25
1753 A364 25q gold & multi .50 .25
1754 A364 80q gold & multi 1.10 .25
1755 A364 1.20 l gold & multi 1.50 .25
1756 A364 1.70 l gold & multi 2.10 .25
Nos. 1752-1756 (5) 5.45 1.25

35th anniv. of 1st Workers Party Congress.

Young Workers and Track A365

1.25 l, Young soldiers and Albanian flag.

1976, Nov. 23 ***Perf. 12***

1757 A365 80q yellow & multi 1.25 .35
1758 A365 1.25 l carmine & multi 2.25 .50

Union of Young Communists, 35th anniv.

"Cuca e Maleve" Ballet A366

Scenes from ballet "Mountain Girl."

1976, Dec. 14 ***Perf. 12***

1759 A366 10q gold & multi .25 *.50*
1760 A366 15q gold & multi .25 *.50*
1761 A366 20q gold & multi .35 *1.00*
1762 A366 25q gold & multi .55 *2.00*
1763 A366 80q gold & multi 1.25 *3.00*
1764 A366 1.20 l gold & multi 1.75 *4.00*
1765 A366 1.40 l gold & multi 2.25 *4.00*
Nos. 1759-1765 (7) 6.65 *15.00*

Miniature Sheet

Perf. 12 on 2 sides x Imperf.

1766 A366 2.05 l gold & multi 4.75 *5.25*

Bashtove Castle A367

Albanian Castles: 15q, Gjirokastres. 20q, Ali Pash Tepelene. 25q, Petrele. 80q, Berat. 1.20 l, Durres. 1.40 l, Kruje.

1976, Dec. 30 **Litho.** ***Perf. 12***

1767 A367 10q black & dull bl .25 .25
1768 A367 15q black & grn .25 .25
1769 A367 20q black & gray .25 .25
1770 A367 25q black & brn .35 .25
1771 A367 80q black & rose 1.00 .35
1772 A367 1.20 l black & vio 1.60 .50
1773 A367 1.40 l black & brn red 1.75 .55
Nos. 1767-1773 (7) 5.45 2.40

Skanderbeg's Shield and Spear — A368

Skanderbeg's Weapons: 80q, Helmet, sword and scabbard. 1 l, Halberd, quiver with arrows, crossbow and spear.

1977, Jan. 28 **Litho.** ***Perf. 12***

1774 A368 15q silver & multi 2.25 .60
1775 A368 80q silver & multi 7.00 3.50
1776 A368 1 l silver & multi 10.50 8.50
Nos. 1774-1776 (3) 19.75 12.60

Skanderbeg (1403-1468), national hero.

Ilia Qiqi, Messenger in Storm — A369

Modern Heroes: 10q, Ilia Dashi, sailor in battle. 25q, Fran Ndue Ivanaj, fisherman in storm. 80q, Zeliha Allmetaj, woman rescuing child. 1 l, Ylli Zaimi, rescuing goats from flood. 1.90 l, Isuf Plloci, fighting forest fire.

1977, Feb. 28 **Litho.** ***Perf. 12x12½***

1777 A369 5q brown & multi .25 .25
1778 A369 10q ultra & multi .25 .25
1779 A369 25q blue & multi .50 .25
1780 A369 80q ocher & multi 1.50 .35
1781 A369 1 l brown & multi 1.75 .45
1782 A369 1.90 l brown & multi 3.50 1.40
Nos. 1777-1782 (6) 7.75 2.95

Polyvinylchloride Plant, Vlore — A370

6th Five-year plan: 25q, Naphtha fractioning plant, Ballsh. 65q, Hydroelectric station and dam, Fjerzes. 1 l, Metallurgical plant and blast furance, Elbasan.

1977, Mar. 29 **Litho.** ***Perf. 12½x12***

1783 A370 15q silver & multi .35 .25
1784 A370 25q silver & multi .55 .25
1785 A370 65q silver & multi 1.50 .35
1786 A370 1 l silver & multi 2.40 .65
Nos. 1783-1786 (4) 4.80 1.50

Qerime Halil Galica — A371

Design: 1.25 l, Qerime Halil Galica "Shota" and father Azem Galica.

1977, Apr. 20 **Litho.** ***Perf. 12***

1787 A371 80q dark red 1.50 .30
1788 A371 1.25 l gray blue 2.10 .70

"Shota" Galica, communist fighter.

Victory Monument, Tirana — A372

Red Star and: 80q, Clenched fist, Albanian flag. 1.20 l, Bust of Qemal Stafa, poppies.

1977, May 5 **Litho.** ***Perf. 12***

1789 A372 25q multi .45 .25
1790 A372 80q multi 1.60 .45
1791 A372 1.20 l multi 3.00 .85
Nos. 1789-1791 (3) 5.05 1.55

35th anniversary of Martyrs' Day.

Physician Visiting Farm, Mobile Clinic — A373

10q, Cowherd, cattle ranch. 20q, Militia woman helping with harvest, rifle, combine. 80q, Modern village, highway, power lines. 2.95 l, Tractor, greenhouses.

1977, June 18

1792 A373 5q multi .25 .25
1793 A373 10q multi .25 .25
1794 A373 20q multi .25 .25
1795 A373 80q multi 1.60 .25
1796 A373 2.95 l multi 5.25 1.75
Nos. 1792-1796 (5) 7.60 2.75

"Socialist transformation of the villages."

Armed Workers, Flag and Factory — A374

1.80 l, Workers with proclamation and flags.

1977, June 20

1797 A374 25q multi .55 .25
1798 A374 1.80 l multi 3.25 .80

9th Labor Unions Congress.

Kerchief Dance — A375

Designs: Various folk dances.

1977, Aug. 20 **Litho.** ***Perf. 12***

1799 A375 5q multi .25 .25
1800 A375 10q multi .25 .25
1801 A375 15q multi .25 .25
1802 A375 25q multi .25 .25
1803 A375 80q multi .75 .25
1804 A375 1.20 l multi 1.10 .35
1805 A375 1.55 l multi 1.60 .45
Nos. 1799-1805 (7) 4.45 2.05

Miniature Sheet

Perf. 12 on 2 sides x Imperf.

1806 A375 2.05 l multi 4.00 3.25

See Nos. 1836-1840, 1884-1888.

Attack A376

Designs: 25q, Enver Hoxha addressing Army. 80q, Volunteers and riflemen. 1 l, Volunteers, hydrofoil patrolboat and MiG planes. 1.90 l, Volunteers and Albanian flag.

1977, July 10 **Litho.** ***Perf. 12***

1807 A376 15q gold & multi .40 .25
1808 A376 25q gold & multi .40 .25
1809 A376 80q gold & multi 1.50 .35
1810 A376 1 l gold & multi 2.50 .50
1811 A376 1.90 l gold & multi 3.75 .90
Nos. 1807-1811 (5) 8.55 2.25

"One People-One Army."

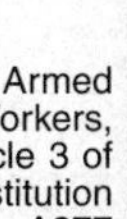

Armed Workers, Article 3 of Constitution A377

Design: 1.20 l, Symbols of farming and fertilizer industry, Article 25 of Constitution.

1977, Oct.

1812	A377	25q	red, gold & blk	.55	.25
1813	A377	1.20 l	red, gold & blk	2.50	.50

New Constitution.

Picnic — A378

Film Frames: 15q, Telephone lineman in winter. 25q, Two men and a woman. 80q, Workers. 1.20 l, Boys playing in street. 1.60 l, Harvest.

1977, Oct. 25 Litho. ***Perf. 12½x12***

1814	A378	10q	blue green	.50	.50
1815	A378	15q	multi	.50	.50
1816	A378	25q	black	.50	.50
1817	A378	80q	multi	1.75	1.75
1818	A378	1.20 l	deep claret	2.75	2.75
1819	A378	1.60 l	multi	3.00	3.00
	Nos. 1814-1819 (6)			9.00	9.00

Albanian films.

Farm Workers in Field, by V. Mio A379

Paintings by V. Mio: 10q, Landscape in Snow. 15q, Grazing Sheep under Walnut Tree in Spring. 25q, Street in Korce. 80q, Horseback Riders on Mountain Pass. 1 l, Boats on Shore. 1.75 l, Tractors Plowing Fields. 2.05 l, Self-portrait.

1977, Dec. 25 Litho. ***Perf. 12½x12***

1820	A379	5q	gold & multi	.25	.25
1821	A379	10q	gold & multi	.25	.25
1822	A379	15q	gold & multi	.25	.25
1823	A379	25q	gold & multi	.25	.25
1824	A379	80q	gold & multi	.65	.25
1825	A379	1 l	gold & multi	1.00	.25
1826	A379	1.75 l	gold & multi	1.75	.25
	Nos. 1820-1826 (7)			4.40	1.75

Miniature Sheet

Imperf.; Perf. 12 Horiz. between Vignette and Value Panel

1827	A379	2.05 l	gold & multi	4.00	3.25

Pan Flute — A380

Folk Musical Instruments: 25q, Single-string goat's-head fiddle. 80q, Woodwind. 1.20 l, Drum. 1.70 l, Bagpipe. Background shows various woven folk patterns.

1978, Jan. 20 ***Perf. 12x12½***

1828	A380	15q	multi	.55	.25
1829	A380	25q	multi	1.10	.25
1830	A380	80q	multi	3.00	1.00
1831	A380	1.20 l	multi	7.25	2.00
1832	A380	1.70 l	multi	12.00	3.50
	Nos. 1828-1832 (5)			23.90	7.00

Albanian Flag, Monument and People — A381

25q, Ismail Qemali, fighters, horiz. 1.65 l, People dancing around Albanian flag, horiz.

1978 ***Perf. 12½x12, 12x12½***

1833	A381	15q	multi	.30	.25
1834	A381	25q	multi	.60	.30
1835	A381	1.65 l	multi	3.00	1.10
	Nos. 1833-1835 (3)			3.90	1.65

65th anniversary of independence.

Folk Dancing Type of 1977

Designs: Various dances.

1978, Feb. 15 Litho. ***Perf. 12***

1836	A375	5q	multi	.25	.25
1837	A375	25q	multi	.35	.25
1838	A375	80q	multi	1.10	.40
1839	A375	1 l	multi	1.10	.40
1840	A375	2.30 l	multi	3.25	1.75
	Nos. 1836-1840 (5)			6.05	3.05

Nos. 1836-1840 have white background around dancers, Nos. 1799-1805 have pinkish shadows.

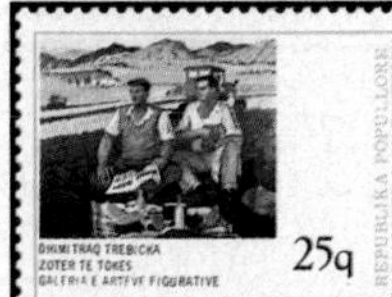

Tractor Drivers, by Dhimitraq Trebicka A382

Working Class Paintings: 80q, Steeplejack, by Spiro Kristo. 85q, "A Point in the Discussion," by Skender Milori. 90q, Oil rig crew, by Anesti Cini, vert. 1.60 l, Metal workers, by Ramadan Karanxha. 2.20 l, Political discussion, by Sotiraq Sholla.

1978, Mar. 25 Litho. ***Perf. 12***

1841	A382	25q	multi	.30	.25
1842	A382	80q	multi	.75	.60
1843	A382	85q	multi	.95	.60
1844	A382	90q	multi	.95	.60
1845	A382	1.60 l	multi	2.00	1.25
	Nos. 1841-1845 (5)			4.95	3.30

Miniature Sheet

Perf. 12 on 2 sides x Imperf.

1846	A382	2.20 l	multi	7.50	5.00

Woman with Rifle and Pickax A383

1.95 l, Farm & Militia women, industrial plant.

1978, June 1 Litho. ***Perf. 12***

1847	A383	25q	gold & red	.55	.25
1848	A383	1.95 l	gold & red	8.25	1.50

8th Congress of Women's Union.

Children and Flowers — A384

Designs: 10q, Children with rifle, ax, book and flags. 25q, Dancing children in folk costume. 1.80 l, Children in school.

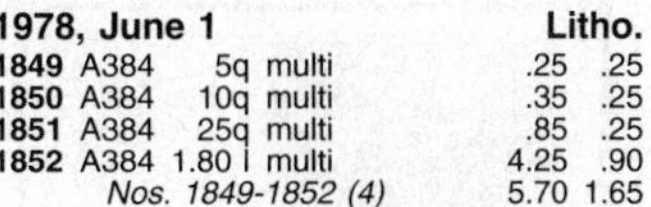

1978, June 1 **Litho.**

1849	A384	5q	multi	.25	.25
1850	A384	10q	multi	.35	.25
1851	A384	25q	multi	.85	.25
1852	A384	1.80 l	multi	4.25	.90
	Nos. 1849-1852 (4)			5.70	1.65

International Children's Day.

Spirit of Skanderbeg as Conqueror A385

10q, Battle at Mostar Bridge. 80q, Marchers, Albanian flag. 1.20 l, Riflemen in winter battle. 1.65 l, Abdyl Frasheri (1839-92). 2.20 l, Rifles, scroll, pen, League building. 2.60 l, League headquarters, Prizren.

1978, June 10 Litho. ***Perf. 12***

1853	A385	10q	multi	.25	.25
1854	A385	25q	multi	.35	.30
1855	A385	80q	multi	1.60	1.10
1856	A385	1.20 l	multi	2.50	1.50
1857	A385	1.65 l	multi	3.75	2.00
1858	A385	2.60 l	multi	6.00	4.75
	Nos. 1853-1858 (6)			14.45	9.90

Miniature Sheet

Perf. 12 on 2 sides x Imperf.

1859	A385	2.20 l	multi	6.00	4.25

Centenary of League of Prizren.

Guerrillas and Flag, 1943 — A386

Designs: 25q, Soldier, sailor, airman, militiaman, horiz. 1.90 l, Members of armed forces, civil guards, and Young Pioneers.

1978, July 10 ***Perf. 11½x12½***

1860	A386	5q	multi	1.00	.50
1861	A386	25q	multi	2.75	1.50
1862	A386	1.90 l	multi	9.00	7.50
	Nos. 1860-1862 (3)			12.75	9.50

35th anniversary of People's Army.

Woman with Machine Carbine — A387

25q, Man with target rifle, horiz. 95q, Man shooting with telescopic sights, horiz. 2.40 l, Woman target shooting with pistol.

Perf. 12½x12, 12x12½

1978, Sept. 20 **Litho.**

1863	A387	25q	black & yel	.30	.25
1864	A387	80q	orange & blk	.85	.55
1865	A387	95q	red & blk	1.40	.80
1866	A387	2.40 l	carmine & blk	3.75	2.40
	Nos. 1863-1866 (4)			6.30	4.00

32nd National Rifle-shooting Championships, Sept. 20.

Kerchief Dance — A388

15q, Musicians. 25q, Fiddler with single-stringed instrument. 80q, Dancers, men. 1.20 l, Saber dance. 1.90 l, Singers, women.

1978, Oct. 6 ***Perf. 12***

1867	A388	10q	multi	.25	.25
1868	A388	15q	multi	.25	.25
1869	A388	25q	multi	.25	.25
1870	A388	80q	multi	.60	.60
1871	A388	1.20 l	multi	1.40	.90
1872	A388	1.90 l	multi	2.75	2.00
	Nos. 1867-1872 (6)			5.50	4.25

National Folklore Festival.

See Nos. 2082-2085, 2289-2290.

No. 1736 Surcharged with New Value, 2 Bars and "RICCIONE 78"

1978 Litho. ***Perf. 12½x12***

1873	A360	3.30 l on 25q	multi	22.50	20.00

Riccione 78 Philatelic Exhibition.

Enver Hoxha A389

1978, Oct. 16 Litho. ***Perf. 12x12½***

1874	A389	80q	red & multi	.55	.50
1875	A389	1.20 l	red & multi	1.10	.50
1876	A389	2.40 l	red & multi	2.25	1.50
	Nos. 1874-1876 (3)			3.90	2.50

Miniature Sheet

Perf. 12½ on 2 sides x Imperf.

1877	A389	2.20 l	red & multi	4.50	3.00

70th birthday of Enver Hoxha, First Secretary of Central Committee of the Communist Party of Albania.

Woman and Wheat — A390

25q, Woman with egg crates. 80q, Shepherd, sheep. 2.60 l, Milkmaid, cows.

1978, Dec. 15 ***Perf. 12x12½***

1878	A390	15q	multicolored	.75	.75
1879	A390	25q	multicolored	1.00	.75
1880	A390	80q	multicolored	3.00	2.10
1881	A390	2.60 l	multicolored	11.00	8.00
	Nos. 1878-1881 (4)			15.75	11.60

Dora d'Istria — A391

Design: 1.10 l, Full portrait of Dora d'Istria, author; birth sesquicentennial.

1979, Jan. 22 Litho. ***Perf. 12***

1882	A391	80q	lt grn & blk	1.60	1.00
1883	A391	1.10 l	vio brn & blk	2.75	2.00

Folk Dancing Type of 1977

Designs: Various folk dances.

1979, Feb. 25

1884	A375	15q	multi	.45	.25
1885	A375	25q	multi	.45	.25
1886	A375	80q	multi	1.75	.90
1887	A375	1.20 l	multi	2.25	1.25
1888	A375	1.40 l	multi	2.75	1.75
	Nos. 1884-1888 (5)			7.65	4.40

Nos. 1884-1888 have white background. Denomination in UL on No. 1885, in UR on No. 1802; LL on No.1886, UL on No. 1803.

Tower House — A392

Traditional Houses: 15q, Stone gallery house, horiz. 80q, House with wooden galleries, horiz. 1.20 l, Galleried tower house. 1.40 l, 1.90 l, Tower houses, diff.

1979, Mar. 20

1889	A392	15q multi	.25	.25
1890	A392	25q multi	.35	.25
1891	A392	80q multi	1.10	.45
1892	A392	1.20 l multi	1.60	.75
1893	A392	1.40 l multi	2.25	1.25
		Nos. 1889-1893 (5)	5.55	2.95

Miniature Sheet

Perf. 12 on 2 sides x Imperf.

1894	A392	1.90 l multi	8.00	5.25

See Nos. 2015-2018.

Soldier, Factories, Wheat A393

1.65 l, Soldiers, workers and coat of arms.

1979, May 14 Litho. *Perf. 12*

1895	A393	25q multi	1.00	.60
1896	A393	1.65 l multi	5.00	2.00

Congress of Permet, 35th anniversary.

Albanian Flag A394

1979, June 4

1897	A394	25q multi	1.00	.60
1898	A394	1.65 l multi	5.00	2.75

5th Congress of Albanian Democratic Front.

Alexander Moissi, (1880-1935), Actor — A395

1979, Apr 2

1899	A395	80q multi	1.60	.65
1900	A395	1.10 l multi, diff.	2.25	1.40

Vasil Shanto, (1913-44) A396

Design: 25q, 90q, Qemal Stafa (1921-42).

1979, May 5

1901	A396	15q multi	.25	.25
1902	A396	25q multi	.55	.25
1903	A396	60q multi	2.25	.60
1904	A396	90q multi	3.25	.90
		Nos. 1901-1904 (4)	6.30	2.00

Shanto and Stafa, anti-Fascist fighters.
For similar design see A410.

Winter Campaign, by Arben Basha — A397

Paintings of Military Scenes by: 25q, Ismail Lulani. 80q, Myrteza Fushekati. 1.20 l, Muhamet Deliu. 1.40 l, Jorgji Gjikopulli. 1.90 l, Fatmir Haxhiu.

1979, July 15 Litho. *Perf. 12½x12*

1905	A397	15q multi	.25	.25
1906	A397	25q multi	.25	.25
1907	A397	80q multi	1.10	.30
1908	A397	1.20 l multi	1.75	.90
1909	A397	1.40 l multi	2.25	.90
		Nos. 1905-1909 (5)	5.60	2.60

Miniature Sheet

Perf. 12 on 2 sides x Imperf.

1910	A397	1.90 l multi	6.00	4.50

Athletes Surrounding Flag — A398

1979, Oct. 1 Litho. *Perf. 12*

1911	A398	15q shown	.25	.25
1912	A398	25q Shooting	.25	.25
1913	A398	80q Dancing	.90	.30
1914	A398	1.20 l Soccer	1.60	.45
1915	A398	1.40 l High jump	2.00	.60
		Nos. 1911-1915 (5)	5.00	1.85

Liberation Spartakiad, 35th anniversary.

Literary Society Headquarters A399

Albanian Literary Society Centenary: 25q, Seal and charter. 80q, Founder. 1.55 l, 1879 Headquarters.
1.90 l, Founders.

1979, Oct. 12

1916	A399	25q multi	.35	.25
1917	A399	80q multi	1.10	.35
1918	A399	1.20 l multi	1.60	.60
1919	A399	1.55 l multi	2.25	.75
		Nos. 1916-1919 (4)	5.30	1.95

Miniature Sheet

Perf. 12½ on 2 sides x Imperf.

1920	A399	1.90 l multi	3.75	3.25

Children Entering School, Books — A401

10q, Communications. 15q, Steel workers. 20q, Dancers, instruments. 25q, Newspapers, radio, television. 60q, Textile worker. 80q, Armed forces. 1.20 l, Industry. 1.60 l, Transportation. 2.40 l, Agriculture. 3 l, Medicine.

1979 Litho. *Perf. 12½x12*

1923	A401	5q shown	.25	.25
1924	A401	10q multi	.25	.25
1925	A401	15q multi	.25	.25
1926	A401	20q multi	.25	.25
1927	A401	25q multi	.25	.25
1928	A401	60q multi	1.00	.25
1929	A401	80q multi	1.40	.25
1930	A401	1.20 l multi	2.40	.25
1931	A401	1.60 l multi	3.25	.40
1932	A401	2.40 l multi	5.00	.45
1932A	A401	3 l multi	6.75	.60
		Nos. 1923-1932A (11)	21.05	3.45

Workers and Factory A402

Worker, Red Flag and: 80q, Hand holding sickle and rifle. 1.20 l, Red star and open book. 1.55 l, Open book and cogwheel.

1979, Nov. 29

1933	A402	25q multi	.35	.25
1934	A402	80q multi	1.10	.90
1935	A402	1.20 l multi	1.60	1.40
1936	A402	1.55 l multi	2.25	2.00
		Nos. 1933-1936 (4)	5.30	4.55

35th anniversary of independence.

Joseph Stalin — A403

Design: 1.10 l, Stalin on dais, horiz.

1979, Dec. 21 Litho. *Perf. 12*

1937	A403	80q red & dk bl	1.60	1.50
1938	A403	1.10 l red & dk bl	2.25	2.00

Joseph Stalin (1879-1953), birth centenary.

Fireplace and Pottery, Korcar A404

Home Furnishings: 80q, Cupboard bed, dagger, pistol, ammunition pouch, Shkodar. 1.20 l, Stool, pot, chair, Mirdit. 1.35 l, Chimney, dagger, jacket, Gjirokaster.

1980, Feb. 27 Litho. *Perf. 12*

1939	A404	25q multi	.40	.35
1940	A404	80q multi	.75	.65
1941	A404	1.20 l multi	1.75	1.50
1942	A404	1.35 l multi	2.25	2.00
		Nos. 1939-1942 (4)	5.15	4.50

See Nos. 1985-1988.

Pipe, Painted Flask A405

80q, Leather handbags. 1.20 l, Carved eagle, embroidered rug. 1.35 l, Lace.

1980, Mar. 4

1943	A405	25q shown	.40	.35
1944	A405	80q multi	.75	.65
1945	A405	1.20 l multi	1.75	1.50
1946	A405	1.35 l multi	2.25	2.00
		Nos. 1943-1946 (4)	5.15	4.50

Prof. Aleksander Xhuvanit Birth Centenary A406

1980, Mar. 14

1947	A406	80q multi	2.50	2.50
1948	A406	1 l multi	3.00	3.00

Revolutionaries on Horseback — A407

Insurrection at Kosove, 70th Anniversary: 1 l, Battle scene.

1980, Apr. 4

1949	A407	80q red & black	2.25	1.75
1950	A407	1 l red & black	3.25	2.75

Soldiers and Workers Laboring to Aid the Stricken Populations, by D. Jukniu and I. Lulani — A408

1980, Apr. 15 Litho. *Perf. 12½*

1951	A408	80q lt blue & multi	2.25	1.75
1952	A408	1 l lt blue grn & multi	3.25	2.75

Lenin, 110th Birth Anniversary A409

1980, Apr. 22

1953	A409	80q multi	2.25	1.75
1954	A409	1 l multi	3.25	2.75

Misto Mame and Ali Demi, War Martyrs A410

War Martyrs: 80q, Sadik Staveleci, Vojo Kusji, Hoxhi Martini. 1.20 l, Bule Naipi, Persefoni Kokedhima. 1.35 l, Ndoc Deda, Hydajet Lezha, Naim Gyylbegu, Ndoc Mazi, Ahmed Haxha.

Congress Statute, Coat of Arms — A400

1979, Oct. 20 Photo. *Perf. 12x12½*

1921	A400	25q multi	2.10	2.10
1922	A400	1.65 l multi	6.50	6.50

2nd Congress of Berat, 35th anniversary.

1980, May 5

1955 A410 25q multi .35 .30
1956 A410 80q multi 1.10 .90
1957 A410 1.20 l multi 1.75 1.50
1958 A410 1.35 l multi 2.25 2.00
Nos. 1955-1958 (4) 5.45 4.70

See Nos. 2012A-2012D, 2025-2028, 2064-2067, 2122-2125, 2171-2174, 2207-2209.

Scene from "Mirela" A411

1980, June 7

1959 A411 15q shown .25 .25
1960 A411 25q The Scribbler .25 .25
1961 A411 80q Circus Bears 1.25 1.00
1962 A411 2.40 l Waterdrops 4.25 3.00
Nos. 1959-1962 (4) 6.00 4.50

Carrying Iron Castings in the Enver Hoxha Tractor Combine, by S. Shijaku and M. Fushekati — A412

Paintings (Gallery of Figurative Paintings, Tirana): 80q, The Welder, by Harilla Dhima. 1.20 l, Steel Erectors, by Petro Kokushta. 1.35 l, Pandeli Lena, 1.80 l Communists, by Vilson Kilica.

1980, July 22

1963 A412 25q multi .35 .30
1964 A412 80q multi 1.10 .90
1965 A412 1.20 l multi 1.75 1.50
1966 A412 1.35 l multi 2.25 2.00
Nos. 1963-1966 (4) 5.45 4.70

Imperf

1967 A412 1.80 l multi 5.00 5.00

No. 1967 measures 66x82mm and has a row of perforations above and below the vignette.

Gate, Parchment Miniature, 11th Cent. — A413

Bas reliefs of the Middle Ages: 80q, Eagle, 13th cent. 1.20 l, Heraldic lion, 14th cent. 1.35 l, Pheasant, 14th cent.

1980, Sept. 27 Litho. *Perf. 12*

1968 A413 25q gold & blk .25 .25
1969 A413 80q gold & blk .65 .65
1970 A413 1.20 l gold & blk 1.60 1.60
1971 A413 1.35 l gold & blk 1.60 1.60
Nos. 1968-1971 (4) 4.10 4.10

Divjaka National Park A414

1980, Nov. 6 Photo.

1972 A414 80q shown 1.10 .90
1973 A414 1.20 l Lura 1.60 1.40
1974 A414 1.60 l Thethi 2.75 2.25
Nos. 1972-1974 (3) 5.45 4.55

Souvenir Sheet

Perf. 12½ Horiz.

1975 A414 1.80 l Llogara Park 5.50 5.50

Citizens, Flag and Arms of Albania A415

1 l, People's Party Headquarters, Tirana.

1981, Jan. 11 Litho. *Perf. 12*

1976 A415 80q multi 1.60 1.50
1977 A415 1 l multicolored 2.40 2.25

35th anniversary of the Republic.

Child's Bed A416

80q, Wooden bucket, brass bottle. 1.20 l, Shoes. 1.35 l, Jugs.

1981, Mar. 20 Litho. *Perf. 12*

1978 A416 25q multicolored .35 .35
1979 A416 80q multicolored .70 .70
1980 A416 1.20 l multicolored 1.10 1.10
1981 A416 1.35 l multicolored 1.60 1.60
Nos. 1978-1981 (4) 3.75 3.75

A417

1981, Apr. 20

1982 A417 80q Soldiers 1.25 1.10
1983 A417 1 l Sword combat 1.60 1.40

Souvenir Sheet

Perf. 12½ Vert.

1984 A417 1.80 l Soldier with pistol 5.00 5.00

Battle of Shtimje centenary.

Home Furnishings Type of 1980

25q, House interior, Labara. 80q, Labara, diff. 1.20 l, Mat. 1.35 l, Dibres.

1981, Feb. 25 Litho. *Perf. 12*

1985 A404 25q multicolored .30 .30
1986 A404 80q multicolored .65 .60
1987 A404 1.20 l multicolored 1.30 1.10
1988 A404 1.35 l multicolored 1.90 1.60
Nos. 1985-1988 (4) 4.15 3.60

A419

Designs: Children's circus.

1981, June *Perf. 12*

1989 A419 15q multi .35 .30
1990 A419 25q multi .35 .30
1991 A419 80q multi .70 .60
1992 A419 2.40 l multi 2.25 1.90
Nos. 1989-1992 (4) 3.65 3.10

Soccer Players A420

1982 World Cup Soccer Elimination Games: Various soccer players.

1981, Mar. 31 Litho. *Perf. 12*

1993 A420 25q multi 1.50 .90
1994 A420 80q multi 5.00 3.00
1995 A420 1.20 l multi 7.00 4.00
1996 A420 1.35 l multi 9.00 5.00
Nos. 1993-1996 (4) 22.50 12.90

Allies, by S. Hysa A421

Paintings: 80q, Warriors, by A. Buza. 1.20 l, Rallying to the Flag, Dec. 1911, by A. Zajmi, vert. 1.35 l, My Flag is My Heart, by L. Cefa, vert. 1.80 l, Circling the Flag in a Common Cause, by N. Vasia.

1981, July 10 *Perf. 12½x12*

1997 A421 25q multi .55 .55
1998 A421 80q multi .80 .80
1999 A421 1.20 l multi 1.10 1.10
2000 A421 1.35 l multi 1.50 1.50
Nos. 1997-2000 (4) 3.95 3.95

Souvenir Sheet

Perf. 12½ Horiz.

2001 A421 1.80 l multi 5.00 5.00

No. 2001 contains one 55x55mm stamp.

Rifleman A422

1981, Aug. 30 *Perf. 12*

2002 A422 25q shown .40 .35
2003 A422 80q Weight lifting .90 .75
2004 A422 1.20 l Volleyball 1.25 1.00
2005 A422 1.35 l Soccer 1.50 1.25
Nos. 2002-2005 (4) 4.05 3.35

Albanian Workers' Party, 8th Congress A423

1981, Nov. 1

2006 A423 80q Flag, star .75 .75
2007 A423 1 l Flag, hammer & sickle 1.25 1.25

Albanian Workers' Party, 40th Anniv. — A424

1981, Nov. 8

2008 A424 80q Symbols of industrialization .55 .50
2009 A424 2.80 l Fist, emblem 2.75 2.40

Souvenir Sheet

Perf. 12 Horiz.

2010 A424 1.80 l Enver Hoxha, Memoirs 5.50 5.50

Communist Youth Org., 40th Anniv. — A425

1981, Nov. 23

2011 A425 80q Star, ax, map 1.25 1.00
2012 A425 1 l Flags, star 2.75 2.00

War Martyrs Type of 1980

25q, Perlat Rexhepi (1919-42) and Branko Kadia (1921-42). 80q, Xheladin Beqiri (1908-44) and Hajdar Dushi (1916-44). 1.20 l, Koci Bako (1905-41), Vasil Laci (1923-41) and Mujo Ulqinaku (1898-1939). 1.35 l, Mine Peza (1875-1942) and Zoja Cure (1920-44).

1981, May 5 Litho. *Perf. 12*

2012A A410 25q silver & multi .60 .25
2012B A410 80q gold & multi 1.50 .75
2012C A410 1.20 l silver & multi 2.00 1.25
2012D A410 1.35 l gold & multi 2.75 1.40
Nos. 2012A-2012D (4) 6.85 3.65

Fan S. Noli, Writer, Birth Centenary A426

1982, Jan. 6 Litho. *Perf. 12*

2013 A426 80q lt ol grn & gold 1.50 .80
2014 A426 1.10 l lt red brn & gold 2.00 1.40

Traditional Houses Type of 1979

1982, Feb. *Perf. 12½x12*

2015 A392 25q Bulqize .30 .30
2016 A392 80q Lebush 1.50 1.10
2017 A392 1.20 l Bicaj 2.25 1.60
2018 A392 1.55 l Klos 3.25 2.25
Nos. 2015-2018 (4) 7.30 5.25

TB Bacillus Centenary A428

1982, Mar. 24 *Perf. 12*

2019 A428 80q Globe 6.00 2.50
2020 A428 1.10 l Koch 9.00 4.25

Albanian League House, Prizren, by K. Buza — A429

Kosova Landscapes: 25q, Castle at Prizrenit, by G. Madhi. 1.20 l, Mountain Gorge at Rogove, by K. Buza. 1.55 l, Street of the Hadhji at Zekes, by G. Madhi. 25q, 1.20 l, 1.55 l vert.

Perf. 12x12½, 12½x12

1982, Apr. 15 Litho.

2021 A429 25q multi .75 .40
2022 A429 80q multi 2.00 1.25
2023 A429 1.20 l multi 3.50 2.10
2024 A429 1.55 l multi 4.75 3.00
Nos. 2021-2024 (4) 11.00 6.75

War Martyrs Type of 1980

Designs: 25q, Hibe Palikuqi, Liri Gero. 80q, Mihal Duri, Kajo Karafili. 1.20 l, Fato Dudumi, Margarita Tutulani, Shejnaze Juka. 1.55 l, Memo Meto, Gjok Doci.

1982, May *Perf. 12*

2025	A410	25q multi	.75	.50
2026	A410	80q multi	1.25	1.00
2027	A410	1.20 l multi	2.00	1.60
2028	A410	1.55 l multi	2.75	2.25
		Nos. 2025-2028 (4)	6.75	5.35

Loading Freighter — A430

Children's Paintings.

1982, June 15 *Perf. 12½x12*

2029	A430	15q shown	.80	.45
2030	A430	80q Forest	1.60	1.25
2031	A430	1.20 l City	2.50	2.00
2032	A430	1.65 l Park	5.00	3.00
		Nos. 2029-2032 (4)	9.90	6.70

9th Congress of Trade Unions A431

1982, June 6 **Litho.** *Perf. 12*

2033	A431	80q Workers, factories	6.50	3.75
2034	A431	1.10 l Emblem, flag	8.50	5.00

Alpine Village Festival, by Danish Jukniu A432

Industrial Development Paintings: 80q, Hydroelectric Station Builders, by Ali Miruku. 1.20 l, Steel Workers, by Clirim Ceka. 1.55 l, Oil drillers, by Pandeli Lena. 1.90 l, Trapping the Furnace, by Jorgji Gjikopulli.

1982, July *Perf. 12½*

2035	A432	25q multi	.50	.25
2036	A432	80q multi	1.50	1.40
2037	A432	1.20 l multi	2.25	1.60
2038	A432	1.55 l multi	3.00	1.90
		Nos. 2035-2038 (4)	7.25	5.15

Souvenir Sheet

Perf. 12 Horiz.

2039	A432	1.90 l multi	7.50	4.00

No. 2039 contains one 54x48mm stamp.

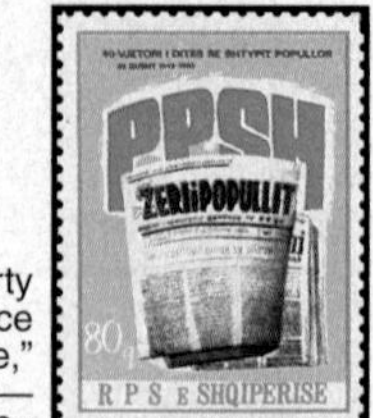

Communist Party Newspaper "Voice of the People," 40th Anniv. — A432a

80q, Newspapers. 1.10 l, Paper, press.

1982, Aug. 25 **Litho.** *Perf. 12*

2039A	A432a	80q multi	*120.00*	*100.00*
2039B	A432a	1.10 l multi	*120.00*	*100.00*

40th Anniv. of Democratic Front A433

80q, Glory to the Heroes of Peza Monument. 1.10 l, Marchers.

1982, Sept. 16 *Perf. 12*

2040	A433	80q multi	*12.00*	5.50
2041	A433	1.10 l multi	*17.50*	7.50

8th Youth Congress — A434

1982, Oct. 4

2042	A434	80q multi	*12.00*	5.50
2043	A434	1.10 l multi	*18.00*	7.50

Handmade Shoulder Bags — A435

25q, Rug, horiz. 1.20 l, Wooden pots, bowls, horiz. 1.55 l, Jug.

1982, Nov.

2044	A435	25q multi	.65	.35
2045	A435	80q multi	1.60	.90
2046	A435	1.20 l multi	2.25	1.25
2047	A435	1.55 l multi	3.50	2.00
		Nos. 2044-2047 (4)	8.00	4.50

70th Anniv. of Independence — A436

1982, Nov. 28

2048	A436	20q Ishamil Qemali	.60	.40
2049	A436	1.20 l Partisans	2.50	1.50
2050	A436	2.40 l Partisans, diff.	5.00	3.00
		Nos. 2048-2050 (3)	8.10	4.90

Souvenir Sheet

Perf. 12 Horiz.

2051	A436	1.90 l Independence Monument, Tirana	7.50	7.50

Dhermi Beach A437

1982, Dec. 20

2052	A437	25q shown	.40	.40
2053	A437	80q Sarande	1.10	1.10
2054	A437	1.20 l Ksamil	1.50	1.50
2055	A437	1.55 l Lukove	2.10	2.10
		Nos. 2052-2055 (4)	5.10	5.10

Handkerchief Dancers — A438

Folkdancers — 80q, With kerchief, drum. 1.20 l, With guitar, flute, tambourine. 1.55 l, Women.

1983, Feb. 20 **Litho.** *Perf. 12*

2056	A438	25q multi	.25	.25
2057	A438	80q multi	1.25	.55
2058	A438	1.20 l multi	2.00	.90
2059	A438	1.55 l multi	2.50	1.10
		Nos. 2056-2059 (4)	6.00	2.80

A439

1983, Mar. 14 **Litho.** *Perf. 12*

2060	A439	80q multi	2.25	1.75
2061	A439	1.10 l multi	2.75	2.10

Karl Marx (1818-83).

A440

80q, Electricity generation. 1.10 l, Gas & oil production.

1983, Apr. 20

2062	A440	80q multi	1.50	1.25
2063	A440	1.10 l multi	2.10	1.40

Energy development.

War Martyrs Type of 1980

Designs: 25q, Asim Zeneli (1916-43), Nazmi Rushiti (1919-42). 80q, Shyqyri Ishmi (1922-42), Shyqyri Alimerko (1923-43), Myzafer Asqeriu (1918-42). 1.20 l, Qybra Sokoli (1924-44), Qeriba Derri (1905-44), Ylbere Bilibashi (1928-44). 1.55 l, Themo Vasi (1915-43), Abaz Shehu (1905-42).

1983, May 5 **Litho.** *Perf. 12*

2064	A410	25q multi	.45	.30
2065	A410	80q multi	1.40	1.00
2066	A410	1.20 l multi	2.25	1.50
2067	A410	1.55 l multi	3.25	2.25
		Nos. 2064-2067 (4)	7.35	5.05

Women's Union, 9th Congress A441

1983, June 1 **Litho.** *Perf. 12x12½*

2068	A441	80q red & gold	2.25	1.25
2069	A441	1.10 l blue & gold	2.75	1.90

Bicycling A442

1983, June 20 *Perf. 12*

2070	A442	25q shown	.40	.25
2071	A442	80q Chess	1.25	.65
2072	A442	1.20 l Gymnastics	2.00	1.25
2073	A442	1.55 l Wrestling	2.50	1.50
		Nos. 2070-2073 (4)	6.15	3.65

40th Anniv. of People's Army — A443

1983, July 10

2074	A443	20q Armed services	.50	.25
2075	A443	1.20 l Soldier, gun barrels	2.25	1.25
2076	A443	2.40 l Factory guard, crowd	4.25	2.10
		Nos. 2074-2076 (3)	7.00	3.60

Sunny Day, by Myrteza Fushekati — A444

Paintings: 80q, Messenger of the Grasp, by Niko Progi. 1.20 l, 29 November 1944, by Harilla Dhimo. 1.55 l, Fireworks, by Pandi Mele. 1.90 l, Partisan Assault, by Sali Shijaku and M. Fushekati.

1983, Aug. 28 **Litho.** *Perf. 12½x12*

2077	A444	25q multi	.35	.35
2078	A444	80q multi	1.25	1.25
2079	A444	1.20 l multi	1.50	1.50
2080	A444	1.55 l multi	2.25	2.25
		Nos. 2077-2080 (4)	5.35	5.35

Souvenir Sheet

Perf. 12

2081	A444	1.90 l multi	14.00	10.00

Folklore Festival Type of 1978

Gjirokaster Folklore Festival: folkdances.

1983, Oct. 6 **Litho.** *Perf. 12*

2082	A388	25q Sword dance	.35	.25
2083	A388	80q Kerchief dance	2.25	1.40
2084	A388	1.20 l Shepherd flautists	2.75	1.90
2085	A388	1.55 l Garland dance	4.50	3.00
		Nos. 2082-2085 (4)	9.85	6.55

World Communications Year — A446

1983, Nov. 10

2086	A446	60q multi	.75	.60
2087	A446	1.20 l multi	2.25	1.25

75th Birthday of Enver Hoxha A447

1983, Oct. 16 **Litho.** *Perf. 12½*

2088	A447	80q multi	.90	.75
2089	A447	1.20 l multi	1.50	1.25
2090	A447	1.80 l multi	2.00	1.75
		Nos. 2088-2090 (3)	4.40	3.75

Souvenir Sheet

Perf. 12 Horiz.

2091	A447	1.90 l multi	4.25	4.25

The Right to a Joint Triumph, by J. Keraj A448

Era of Skanderbeg in Figurative Art: 80q, The Heroic Center of the Battle of Krujes, by N. Bakalli. 1.20 l, The Rights of the Enemy after our Triumph, by N. Progri. 1.55 l, The Discussion at Lezhes, by B. Ahmeti. 1.90 l, Victory over the Turks, by G. Madhi.

1983, Dec. 10 ***Perf. 12½x12***

2092 A448 25q multi .60 .50
2093 A448 80q multi 1.75 1.60
2094 A448 1.20 l multi 2.25 2.10
2095 A448 1.55 l multi 3.25 3.00
Nos. 2092-2095 (4) 7.85 7.20

Souvenir Sheet

Perf. 12 Horiz.

2096 A448 1.90 l multi 9.50 9.50

Greco-Roman Ruins of Illyria — A449

80q, Amphitheater, Buthroxtum. 1.20 l, Colonnade, Apollonium. 1.80 l, Vaulted gallery, amphitheater at Epidamnus.

1983, Dec. 28 ***Perf. 12***

2097 A449 80q multicolored 2.50 2.00
2098 A449 1.20 l multicolored 3.50 3.00
2099 A449 1.80 l multicolored 3.50 3.00
Nos. 2097-2099 (3) 9.50 8.00

Archeological Discoveries A450

Designs: Apollo, 3rd cent. 25q, Tombstone, Korce, 3rd cent. 80q, Apollo, diff. 1st cent. 1.10 l, Earthenware pot (child's head), Tren, 1st cent. 1.20 l, Man's head, Dyrrah, 2.20 l, Eros with Dolphin, statue Bronze Dyrrah, 3rd cent.

1984, Feb. 25 ***Perf. 12x12½***

2100 A450 15q multi .25 .25
2101 A450 25q multi .35 .35
2102 A450 80q multi 1.25 1.00
2103 A450 1.10 l multi 1.50 1.25
2104 A450 1.20 l multi 2.25 1.60
2105 A450 2.20 l multi 4.00 2.75
Nos. 2100-2105 (6) 9.60 7.20

Clock Towers — A451

1984, Mar. 30 **Litho.** ***Perf. 12***

2106 A451 15q Gjirokaster .30 .25
2107 A451 25q Kavaje .40 .25
2108 A451 80q Elbasan 1.25 .75
2109 A451 1.10 l Tirana 1.50 1.10
2110 A451 1.20 l Peqin 2.25 1.50
2111 A451 2.20 l Kruje 3.75 2.50
Nos. 2106-2111 (6) 9.45 6.35

40th Anniv. of Liberation A452

15q, Student & microscope. 25q, Guerrilla with flag. 80q, Children with flag. 1.10 l, Soldier. 1.20 l, Workers with flag. 2.20 l, Militia at dam.

1984, Apr. 20 **Litho.** ***Perf. 12***

2112 A452 15q multi .25 .25
2113 A452 25q multi .45 .35
2114 A452 80q multi 1.50 1.10
2115 A452 1.10 l multi 2.00 1.25
2116 A452 1.20 l multi 2.50 1.60
2117 A452 2.20 l multi 4.00 2.75
Nos. 2112-2117 (6) 10.70 7.30

Children — A453

1984, May **Litho.** ***Perf. 12***

2118 A453 15q Children reading .65 .45
2119 A453 25q Young pioneers 1.25 .90
2120 A453 60q Gardening 2.50 1.75
2121 A453 2.80 l Kite flying 6.50 4.00
Nos. 2118-2121 (4) 10.90 7.10

War Martyrs Type of 1980

Designs: 15q, Manush Almani, Mustafa Matohiti, Kastriot Muco. 25q, Zaho Koka, Reshit Collaku, Maliq Muco. 1.20 l, Lefter Talo, Tom Kola, Fuat Babani. 2.20 l, Myslysm Shyri, Dervish Hexali, Skender Caci.

1984, May 5 **Litho.** ***Perf. 12***

2122 A410 15q multi .75 .65
2123 A410 25q multi 1.75 1.10
2124 A410 1.20 l multi 3.00 2.00
2125 A410 2.20 l multi 6.25 3.75
Nos. 2122-2125 (4) 11.75 7.50

A454

1984, May 24 **Litho.** ***Perf. 12***

2126 A454 80q Enver Hoxha 4.00 2.75
2127 A454 1.10 l Resistance fighter 4.50 3.25

40th anniv. of Permet Congress.

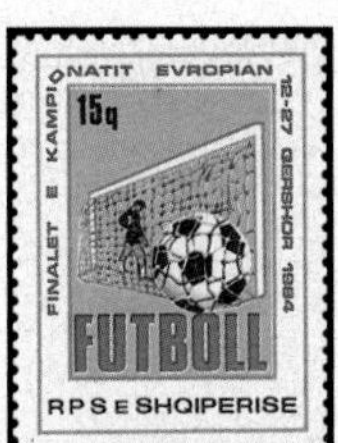
A455

1984, June 12 **Litho.** ***Perf. 12***

2128 A455 15q Goalkeeper 1.50 1.00
2129 A455 25q Referee 1.50 1.00
2130 A455 1.20 l Map of Europe 5.00 3.00
2131 A455 2.20 l Field diagram 5.75 3.50
Nos. 2128-2131 (4) 13.75 8.50

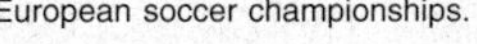
European soccer championships.

Freedom Came, by Myrteza Fushekati — A456

Paintings, Tirana Gallery of Figurative Art: 25q, Morning, by Zamir Mati, vert. 80q, My Darling, by Agim Zajmi, vert. 2.60 l, For the Partisans, by Arben Basha. 1.90 l, Eagle, by Zamir Mati, vert.

1984, June 12 ***Perf. 12½***

2132 A456 15q multi .60 .50
2133 A456 25q multi 1.25 1.00
2134 A456 80q multi 3.25 3.00
2135 A456 2.60 l multi 5.00 4.50
Nos. 2132-2135 (4) 10.10 9.00

Souvenir Sheet

Perf. 12 Horiz.

2136 A456 1.90 l multi 13.00 8.00

Flora — A457

15q, Moraceae L. 25q, Plantaginaceae L. 1.20 l, Hypericaceae L. 2.20 l, Leontopodium alpinum.

1984, Aug. 20 **Litho.** ***Perf. 12***

2137 A457 15q multicolored 3.25 .85
2138 A457 25q multicolored 4.25 1.25
2139 A457 1.20 l multicolored 13.00 4.75
2140 A457 2.20 l multicolored 24.00 9.00
Nos. 2137-2140 (4) 44.50 15.85

AUSIPEX '84, Melbourne, Sept. 21-30 — A458

Perf. 12 Horiz.

1984, Sept. 21 **Litho.**

2141 A458 1.90 l Sword dancers, emblem 6.00 6.00

A459

Forestry, logging, UNFAO emblem — 15q, Beech trees, transport. 25q, Pine forest, logging cable. 1.20 l, Firs, sawmill. 2.20 l, Forester clearing woods.

1984, Sept. 25 ***Perf. 12***

2142 A459 15q multi 1.50 .80
2143 A459 25q multi 2.00 1.50
2144 A459 1.20 l multi 6.50 4.50
2145 A459 2.20 l multi 10.00 5.50
Nos. 2142-2145 (4) 20.00 12.30

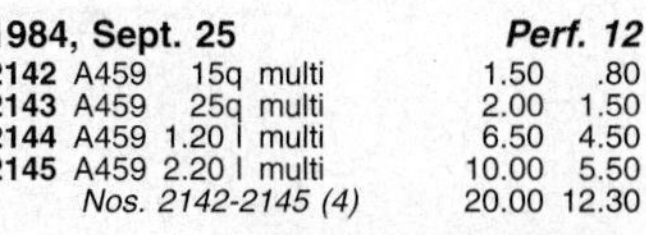

A460

1984, Oct. 13 ***Perf. 12½***

2146 A460 1.20 l View of Gjirokaster 3.25 2.50

EURPHILA '84, Rome.

5th National Spartakiad A461

1984, Oct. 19 ***Perf. 12***

2147 A461 15q Soccer .25 .25
2148 A461 25q Women's track & field .60 .55
2149 A461 80q Weight lifting 1.25 1.10
2150 A461 2.20 l Pistol shooting 3.25 3.25
Nos. 2147-2150 (4) 5.35 5.15

Souvenir Sheet

Perf. 12 Horiz.

2151 A461 1.90 l Opening ceremony, red flags 4.75 4.75

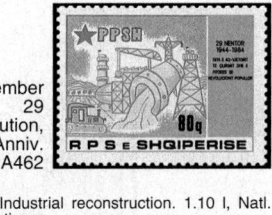

November 29 Revolution, 40th Anniv. A462

80q, Industrial reconstruction. 1.10 l, Natl. flag, partisans.
1.90 l, Gen. Enver Hoxha reading 1944 declaration.

1984, Nov. 29 ***Perf. 12***

2152 A462 80q multicolored 3.00 1.50
2153 A462 1.10 l multicolored 3.75 2.10

Souvenir Sheet

Perf. 12 Horiz.

2154 A462 1.90 l multicolored 4.50 4.50

Archaeological Discoveries from Illyria — A463

Designs: 15q, Iron Age water container. 80q, Terra-cotta woman's head, 6th-7th cent. B.C. 1.20 l, Aphrodite, bust, 3rd cent. B.C. 1.70 l, Nike, A.D. 1st-2nd cent. bronze statue.

1985, Feb. 25 ***Perf. 12x12½***

2155 A463 15q multi .70 .25
2156 A463 80q multi 2.25 1.10
2157 A463 1.20 l multi 3.00 1.50
2158 A463 1.70 l multi 4.75 2.25
Nos. 2155-2158 (4) 10.70 5.10

Hysni Kapo (1915-1980), Natl. Labor Party Leader — A464

1985, Mar. 4 *Perf. 12*

2159 A464 90q red & blk 2.25 2.25
2160 A464 1.10 l chlky bl & blk 2.75 2.75

OLYMPHILEX '85, Lausanne — A465

1985, Mar. 18

2161 A465 25q Women's track & field .30 .30
2162 A465 60q Weight lifting 1.00 1.00
2163 A465 1.20 l Soccer 1.75 1.75
2164 A465 1.50 l Women's pistol shooting 3.00 3.00
Nos. 2161-2164 (4) 6.05 6.05

Johann Sebastian Bach — A466

1985, Mar. 31

2165 A466 80q Portrait, manuscript 25.00 20.00
2166 A466 1.20 l Eisenach, birthplace 32.50 25.00

Gen. Enver Hoxha (1908-1985) A467

1985, Apr. 11 *Perf. 12½*

2167 A467 80q multicolored 2.75 1.90

Souvenir Sheet

Imperf

2168 A467 1.90 l multicolored 4.25 4.25

Natl. Frontier Guards, 40th Anniv. A468

1985, Apr. 25 *Perf. 12*

2169 A468 25q Guardsman, family 1.75 1.00
2170 A468 80q At frontier post 5.00 3.00

War Martyrs Type of 1980

25q, Mitro Xhani (1916-44), Nimete Progonati (1929-44), Kozma Nushi (1909-44). 40q, Ajet Xhindoli (1922-43), Mustafa Kacaci (1903-44), Estref Caka Osaja (1919-44). 60q, Celo Sinani (1929-44), Lt. Ambro Andoni (1920-44), Meleq Gosnishti (1913-44). 1.20 l, Thodhori Mastora (1920-44), Fejzi Micoli (1919-45), Hysen Cino (1920-44).

1985, May 5

2171 A410 25q multi .85 .75
2172 A410 40q multi 1.40 1.25
2173 A410 60q multi 2.25 2.00
2174 A410 1.20 l multi 3.75 3.25
Nos. 2171-2174 (4) 8.25 7.25

Victory over Fascism A469

25q, Rifle, red flag, inscribed May 9. 80q, Hand holding rifle, globe, broken swastika.

1985, May 9

2175 A469 25q multi *32.50 30.00*
2176 A469 80q multi *85.00 125.00*

End of World War II, 40th anniv.

Primary School, by Thoma Malo A470

Paintings, Tirana Gallery of Figurative Art: 80q, The Heroes, by Hysen Devolli, vert. 90q, In Our Days, by Angjelin Dodmasej, vert. 1.20 l, Going Off to Sow, by Ksenofon Dilo. 1.90 l, Foundry Workers, by Mikel Gurashi.

1985, June 25 *Perf. 12½*

2177 A470 25q multi .40 .30
2178 A470 80q multi 1.60 1.00
2179 A470 90q multi 2.00 1.40
2180 A470 1.20 l multi 2.50 1.75
Nos. 2177-2180 (4) 6.50 4.45

Souvenir Sheet

Perf. 12 Horiz.

2181 A470 1.90 l multi 6.50 5.00

Basketball Championships, Spain — A471

Various plays.

1985, July 20 Litho. *Perf. 12*

2182 A471 25q dull bl & blk .35 .25
2183 A471 80q dull grn & blk 1.40 .80
2184 A471 1.20 l dl vio & blk 2.10 1.40
2185 A471 1.60 l dl rose & blk 3.00 2.25
Nos. 2182-2185 (4) 6.85 4.70

Fruits — A472

1985, Aug. 20

2186 A472 25q Oranges .75 .75
2187 A472 80q Plums 3.25 3.00
2188 A472 1.20 l Apples 5.50 5.00
2189 A472 1.60 l Cherries 6.50 6.00
Nos. 2186-2189 (4) 16.00 14.75

Architecture A473

1985, Sept. 20

2190 A473 25q Kruja .50 .50
2191 A473 80q Gjirokastra 2.50 2.25
2192 A473 1.20 l Berati 3.25 3.00
2193 A473 1.60 l Shkodera 4.75 4.25
Nos. 2190-2193 (4) 11.00 10.00

Natl. Folk Theater Festival — A474

Various scenes from folk plays.

1985, Oct. 6

2194 A474 25q multi .55 .50
2195 A474 80q multi 1.60 1.50
2196 A474 1.20 l multi 2.25 2.10
2197 A474 1.60 l multi 2.75 2.50

Size: 56x82mm

Imperf

2198 A474 1.90 l multi 5.00 4.00
Nos. 2194-2198 (5) 12.15 10.60

Socialist People's Republic, 40th Anniv. — A475

1986, Jan. 11 Litho. *Perf. 12½*

2199 A475 25q Natl. crest, vert. 2.00 1.00
2200 A475 80q Proclamation, 1946 4.00 2.25

A476

Designs: 25q, Dam, River Drin, Melgun. 80q, Bust of Enver Hoxha, dam power house.

1986, Feb. 20 *Perf. 12*

2201 A476 25q multi *8.50* 3.50
2202 A476 80q multi *20.00* 13.00

Enver Hoxha hydro-electric power station, Koman.

A477

Flowers: 25q, Gymnospermium shqipetarum. 1.20 l, Leucojum valentinum.

1986, Mar. 20 Litho. *Perf. 12*

2203 A477 25q multi 2.75 2.25
2204 A477 1.20 l multi 10.00 9.00
a. Pair, #2203-2204 15.00 15.00

Nos. 2203-2204 exist imperf. Value, pair: mint $60, used $50.

A478

Famous Men — A479

Designs: 25q, Maxim Gorky, Russian author. 80q, Andre Marie Ampere, French physicist. 1.20 l, James Watt, English inventor of modern steam engine. 2.40 l, Franz Liszt, Hungarian composer.

1986, Apr. 20

2205 Strip of 4 *20.00* 11.50
a. A478 25q dull red brown .50 .30
b. A478 80q dull violet 2.00 2.00
c. A478 1.20 l blue green 3.50 3.00
d. A478 2.40 l dull lilac rose 7.00 5.50

Size: 88x72mm

Imperf

2206 A479 1.90 l multi *10.00* 9.00

No. 2206 has central area picturing Gorky, Ampere, Watt and Liszt, perf. 12½.

War Martyrs Type of 1980

25q, Ramiz Aranitasi (1923-43), Inajete Dumi (1924-44) and Laze Nuro Ferraj (1897-1944). 80q, Dine Kalenja (1919-44), Kozma Naska (1921-44), Met Hasa (1929-44) and Fahri Ramadani (1920-44). 1.20 l, Hiqmet Buzi (1927-44), Bajram Tusha (1922-42), Mumin Selami (1923-42) and Hajrfdin Bylyshi (1923-42).

1986, May 5 *Perf. 12*

2207 A410 25q multi 3.00 2.75
2208 A410 80q multi 7.25 6.75
2209 A410 1.20 l multi 12.00 10.50
Nos. 2207-2209 (3) 22.25 20.00

A480

1986 World Cup Soccer Championships, Mexico — A481

1986, May 31 Litho. *Perf. 12*

2210 A480 25q Globe, world cup .75 .45
2211 A480 1.20 l Player, soccer ball 4.00 2.25

Size: 97x64mm
Imperf

2212 A481 1.90 l multi 4.75 4.25
Nos. 2210-2212 (3) 9.50 6.95

No. 2212 has central label, perf. 12½.

Transportation Workers' Day, 40th Anniv. — A482

1986, Aug. 10 Litho. *Perf. 12*
2213 A482 1.20 l multi 18.00 9.75

Prominent Albanians A483

Designs: 30q, Naim Frasheri (1846-1900), poet. 60q, Ndre Mjeda (1866-1937), poet. 90q, Petro Nini Luarasi (1865-1911), poet, journalist. 1 l, Andon Zako Cajupi (1866-1930), poet. 1.20 l, Millosh Gjergj Nikolla Migjeni (1911-1938), novelist. 2.60 l, Urani Rumbo (1884-1936), educator.

1986, Sept. 20 Litho. *Perf. 12*
2214 A483 30q multi 1.00 .60
2215 A483 60q multi 2.00 1.10
2216 A483 90q multi 2.75 2.00
2217 A483 1 l multi 3.50 2.50
2218 A483 1.20 l multi 4.50 3.00
2219 A483 2.60 l multi 12.00 6.75
Nos. 2214-2219 (6) 25.75 15.95

Albanian Workers' Party, 9th Congress, Tirana A484

1986, Nov. 3 Litho. *Perf. 12*
2220 A484 30q multi *22.50* 17.00

No. 2220 exists with country name misspelled "SHQIPERSIE." Value, mint, $150.

A485

Albanian Workers' Party, 45th Anniv.: 30q, Handstamp, signature of Hoxha. 1.20 l, Marx, Engels, Lenin and Stalin, party building.

1986, Nov. 8
2221 A485 30q multi *6.00* 4.25
2222 A485 1.20 l multi *17.50* 13.00

A486

Statue of Mother Albania.

1986, Nov. 29 *Perf. 12x12½*
2223 A486 10q peacock blue .25 .25
2224 A486 20q henna brn .25 .25
2225 A486 30q vermilion .25 .25
2226 A486 50q dk olive bis .25 .25
2227 A486 60q lt olive grn .35 .25
2228 A486 80q rose .55 .40
2229 A486 90q ultra .75 .45
2230 A486 1.20 l green 1.10 .60
2231 A486 1.60 l red vio 1.60 .60
2232 A486 2.20 l myrtle grn 2.25 1.25
2233 A486 3 l brn org 2.75 1.75
2234 A486 6 l yel bister 5.50 3.25
Nos. 2223-2234 (12) 15.85 9.55

For surcharges see Nos. 2435-2439.

Artifacts A487

Designs: 30q, Head of Aesoulapius, 5th cent. B.C. Byllis, marble. 80q, Aphrodite, 3rd cent. B.C., Fier, terracotta. 1 l, Pan, 3rd-2nd cent, B.C., Byllis, bronze. 1.20 l, Jupiter, A.D. 2nd cent., Tirana, limestone.

1987, Feb. 20
2235 A487 30q multi 1.10 .75
2236 A487 80q multi 2.25 1.25
2237 A487 1 l multi 3.25 1.75
2238 A487 1.20 l multi 4.25 3.00
Nos. 2235-2238 (4) 10.85 6.75

A488

Gun, quill pen, book of the alphabet and: 30q, Monument, vert. 80q, School, Korca. 1.20 l, Students.

1987, Mar. 7 *Perf. 12*
2239 A488 30q multi .60 .50
2240 A488 80q multi 1.40 1.10
2241 A488 1.20 l multi 2.25 2.00
Nos. 2239-2241 (3) 4.25 3.60

First Albanian school, cent.

A489

Famous Men: 30q, Victor Hugo, French author. 80q, Galileo Galilei, Italian mathematician, philosopher. 90q, Charles Darwin, British biologist. 1.30 l, Miguel Cervantes, Spanish novelist.

1987, Apr. 20
2242 A489 30q multi .65 .45
2243 A489 80q multi 1.50 1.00
2244 A489 90q multi 2.25 1.60
2245 A489 1.30 l multi 3.00 2.25
Nos. 2242-2245 (4) 7.40 5.30

World Food Day — A490

30q, Forsythia europaea. 90q, Moltkia doerfleri. 2.10 l, Wulfenia baldacii.

1987, May 20
2246 A490 30q multicolored .90 .50
2247 A490 90q multicolored 2.00 1.25
2248 A490 2.10 l multicolored 4.00 2.75
Nos. 2246-2248 (3) 6.90 4.50

10th Trade Unions Cong. — A491

1987, June 25
2249 A491 1.20 l multi 6.00 6.00

Sowing, by Bujar Asllani — A492

Paintings in the Eponymous Museum, Tirana: 30q, The Sustenance of Industry, by Myrteza Fushekati, vert. 80q, The Gifted Partisan, by Skender Kokobobo, vert. 1.20 l, At the Forging Block, by Clirim Ceka.

Perf. 12x12½, 12½x12
1987, July 20 Litho.
2250 A492 30q multi .55 .40
2251 A492 80q multi 1.10 1.00
2252 A492 1 l shown 1.75 1.50
2253 A492 1.20 l multi 2.25 2.00
Nos. 2250-2253 (4) 5.65 4.90

A493

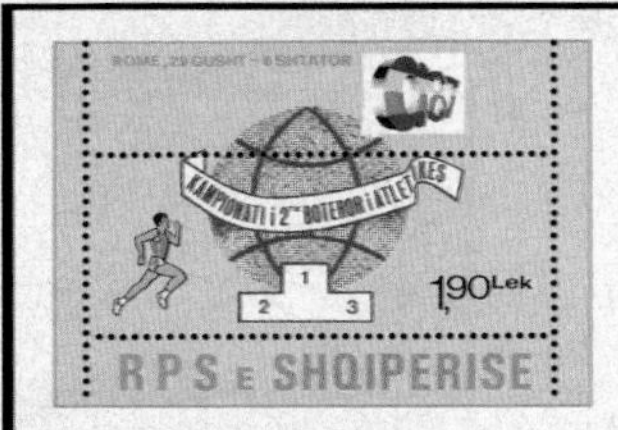

OLYMPHILEX '87, Rome, Aug. 29-Sept. 6 — A494

1987, Aug. 29 Litho. *Perf. 12½*
2254 A493 30q Hammer throw .60 .60
2255 A493 90q Running 1.50 1.50
2256 A493 1.10 l Shot put 1.50 1.50

Size: 85x60mm

2257 A494 1.90 l Runner, globe 4.25 4.25
Nos. 2254-2257 (4) 7.85 7.85

Famous Men A495

Designs: 30q, Themistokli Germenji (1871-1917), author, politician. 80q, Bajram Curri (1862-1925), founder of the Albanian League. 90q, Aleks Stavre Drenova (1872-1947), poet. 1.30 l, Gjerasim D. Qiriazi (1861-1894), teacher, journalist.

1987, Sept. 30 *Perf. 12*
2258 A495 30q multi .30 .30
2259 A495 80q multi 1.50 1.10
2260 A495 90q multi 1.75 1.25
2261 A495 1.30 l multi 2.75 2.25
Nos. 2258-2261 (4) 6.30 4.90

Albanian Labor Party Congress, Tirana A496

1987, Oct. 22 Litho. *Perf. 12*
2262 A496 1.20 l multi 8.00 6.00

Natl. Independence, 75th Anniv. — A497

1987, Nov. 27
2263 A497 1.20 l State flag 8.00 6.75

Postal Administration, 75th Anniv. — A498

1987, Dec. 5
2264 A498 90q P.O. emblem 9.50 6.25
2265 A498 1.20 l State seal 13.00 9.00

Art & Literature — A499

Portraits: 30q, Lord Byron (1788-1824), English Poet. 1.20 l, Eugene Delacroix (1798-1863), French painter.

1988, Mar. 10
2266 A499 30q org brn & blk *8.00* 4.25
2267 A499 1.20 l pale vio & blk *25.00* 16.00

WHO, 40th Anniv. — A500

1988, Apr. 7
2268 A500 90q multi *60.00* 45.00
2269 A500 1.20 l multi *90.00* 60.00

Flowers — A501

Designs: 30q, Sideritis raeseri. 90q, Lunaria telekiana. 2.10 l, Sanguisorba albanica.

1988, May 20 Booklet Stamps

2270 A501 30q multicolored 11.00 9.00
2271 A501 90q multicolored 22.50 15.00
2272 A501 2.10 l multicolored 32.50 19.00
a. Bklt. pane of 3, plus label 80.00 80.00
Nos. 2270-2272 (3) 66.00 43.00

10th Women's Federation Congress A502

1988, June 6

2273 A502 90q blk, red & dark org 25.00 22.00

European Soccer Championships — A503

Various athletes.
1.90 l, Goalie designs of Nos. 2274-2276.

1988, June 10

2274 A503 30q multicolored 2.75 2.50
2275 A503 80q multicolored 4.00 3.50
2276 A503 1.20 l multicolored 6.00 5.50

Size: 79x68mm

Imperf

2277 A503 1.90 l multicolored 16.00 15.00
Nos. 2274-2277 (4) 28.75 26.50

League of Prizren, 110th Anniv. — A504

1988, June 10 Litho. *Perf. 12*

2278 A504 30q Hands *45.00 45.00*
2279 A504 1.20q House *85.00 85.00*

People's Army, 45th Anniv. — A505

1988, July 10

2280 A505 60q shown *45.00 45.00*
2281 A505 90q Soldier statue *85.00 85.00*

Famous Albanians A506

Designs: 30q, Mihal Grameno (1871-1931), author. 90q, Bajo Topulli (1868-1930), freedom fighter. 1 l, Murat Toptani (1868-1917), poet. 1.20 l, Jul Variboba, poet.

1988, Aug. 15

2282 A506 30q multi *17.50 17.50*
2283 A506 90q multi *30.00 30.00*
2284 A506 1 l multi *40.00 40.00*
2284A A506 1.20 l multi *50.00 50.00*
Nos. 2282-2284A (4) *137.50 137.50*

Migjeni (1911-1938), Poet — A507

1988, Aug. 26 Litho. *Perf. 12*

2285 A507 90q silver & brown *25.00 25.00*

Ballads A508

1988, Sept. 5

2286 A508 30q Dede Skurra 12.50 8.00
2287 A508 90q Omeri Iri 30.00 21.00
2288 A508 1.20 l Gjergj Elez Alia 37.50 27.50
Nos. 2286-2288 (3) 80.00 56.50

Folklore Festival Type of 1978

30q, Kerchief Dance. 1.20 l, Dancers with raised arm.

1988, Oct. 6

2289 A388 30q multi *35.00 35.00*
2290 A388 1.20 l multi *125.00 110.00*

Enver Hoxha Museum A510

Perf. 12x12½, 12½x12

1988, Oct. 16 Litho.

2291 A510 90q Portrait, vert. 6.00 6.00
2292 A510 1.20 l shown 9.00 9.00

Hoxha (1908-85), Communist leader.

Monastir Congress, 80th Anniv. A511

1988, Nov. 14 Litho. *Perf. 12*

2293 A511 60q Scroll *30.00* 25.00
2294 A511 90q Book, building *55.00* 45.00

Locomotives, Map Showing Rail Network — A512

1989, Feb. 28 Litho. *Perf. 12½x12*

2295 A512 30q 1947 .40 .30
2296 A512 90q 1949 1.25 1.00
2297 A512 1.20 l 1978 1.50 1.25
2298 A512 1.80 l 1985 2.25 1.90
2299 A512 2.40 l 1988 5.00 4.50
Nos. 2295-2299 (5) 10.40 8.95

Archaeological Treasures — A513

30q, Illyrian grave. 90q, Warrior on horseback.

1989, Mar. 10 Litho. *Perf. 12*

2300 A513 30q blk & tan .35 .30
2301 A513 90q blk & dl grn 1.25 1.00
2302 A513 2.10 l shown 2.25 1.90
Nos. 2300-2302 (3) 3.85 3.20

Folklore A514

1989, Apr. 5 Litho. *Perf. 12x12½*

2303 A514 30q multicolored .55 .50
2304 A514 80q multi, diff. 1.10 1.00
2305 A514 1 l multi, diff. 1.25 1.00
2306 A514 1.20 l multi, diff. 1.75 1.50
Nos. 2303-2306 (4) 4.65 4.00

Flowers — A515

Designs: 30q, Aster albanicus. 90q, Orchis x paparisti. 2.10 l, Orchis albanica.

1989, May 10 *Perf. 12*

2307 A515 30q multicolored .35 .30
2308 A515 90q multicolored 1.30 1.10
2309 A515 2.10 l multicolored 2.25 1.75
Nos. 2307-2309 (3) 3.90 3.15

Famous People — A516

Designs: 30q, Johann Strauss the Younger (1825-1899), composer. 80q, Marie Curie (1867-1834), chemist. 1 l, Federico Garcia Lorca (1898-1936), poet. 1.20 l, Albert Einstein (1879-1955), physicist.

1989, June 3

2310 A516 30q gold & blk brn .55 .50
2311 A516 80q gold & blk brn 1.10 1.00
2312 A516 1 l gold & blk brn 1.60 1.50
2313 A516 1.20 l gold & blk brn 2.25 2.00
a. Block of 4, #2310-2313 8.00 8.00
Nos. 2310-2313 (4) 5.50 5.00

6th Congress of Albanian Democratic Front A517

1989, June 26

2314 A517 1.20 l multicolored 12.00 10.00

French Revolution, Bicent. — A518

90q, Storming of the Bastille. 1.20 l, Statue.

1989, July 7 Litho. *Perf. 12½*

2315 A518 90q multicolored 1.00 1.00
2316 A518 1.20 l shown 2.00 2.00

Illyrian Ship A519

1989, July 25 *Perf. 12*

2317 A519 30q shown .55 .45
2318 A519 80q Caravel 1.00 .90
2319 A519 90q 3-masted schooner 1.10 .90
2320 A519 1.30 l Modern cargo ship 1.60 1.40
Nos. 2317-2320 (4) 4.25 3.65

A520

Famous Men: 30q, Pjeter Bogdani (1625-1689), writer. 80q, Gavril Dara (1826-1889), poet. 90q, Thimi Mitko (1820-1890), writer. 1.30 l, Kole Idromeno (1860-1939), painter.

1989, Aug. 30 Litho. *Perf. 12*

2321 A520 30q multicolored .40 .25
2322 A520 80q multicolored 1.00 .90
2323 A520 90q multicolored 1.40 1.00
2324 A520 1.30 l multicolored 2.00 1.40
Nos. 2321-2324 (4) 4.80 3.55

A521

1989, Sept. 29

2325	A521	90q	shown	1.10	1.10
2326	A521	1.20 l	Workers	1.60	1.60

First Communist International, 125th anniv.

Spartakiad Games
A522

1989, Oct. 27 ***Perf. 12x12½***

2327	A522	30q	Gymnastics	.25	.25
2328	A522	80q	Soccer	.75	.75
2329	A522	1 l	Cycling	1.00	1.00
2330	A522	1.20 l	Running	1.10	1.10
			Nos. 2327-2330 (4)	3.10	3.10

Miniature Sheet

45th Anniv. of Liberation — A523

1989, Nov. 29 ***Perf. 12x12½***

2331	A523 Sheet of 4		6.00	6.00
a.	30q Revolutionary		.60	.50
b.	80q "45"		1.25	1.00
c.	1 l Coat of arms		1.25	1.00
d.	1.20 l Workers		1.75	1.50

Rupicapra Rupicapra
A524

1990, Mar. 15 ***Perf. 12***

2332	A524	10q	Two adults	.40	.40
2333	A524	30q	Adult, kid	1.00	1.00
2334	A524	80q	Adult	2.50	2.50
2335	A524	90q	Adult head	2.75	2.75
a.			Block of 4, #2332-2335	7.50	7.50

World Wildlife Fund.

Tribal Masks
A525

1990, Apr. 4 ***Perf. 12x12½***

2336	A525	30q	shown	.35	.35
2337	A525	90q	multi, diff.	.85	.85
2338	A525	1.20 l	multi, diff.	1.10	1.10
2339	A525	1.80 l	multi, diff.	1.60	1.60
			Nos. 2336-2339 (4)	3.90	3.90

Mushrooms
A526

30q, Amanita caesarea. 90q, Lepiota procera. 1.20 l, Boletus edulis. 1.80 l, Clathrus cancelatus.

1990, Apr. 28 **Litho.** ***Perf. 12***

2340	A526	30q	multicolored	.35	.35
2341	A526	90q	multicolored	1.25	1.25
2342	A526	1.20 l	multicolored	1.75	1.75
2343	A526	1.80 l	multicolored	2.75	2.75
			Nos. 2340-2343 (4)	6.10	6.10

First Postage Stamp, 150th Anniv.
A527

1990, May 6 ***Perf. 12***

2344	A527	90q	shown	1.00	.50
2345	A527	1.20 l	Post rider	1.25	.75
2346	A527	1.80 l	Carriage	1.75	1.40
a.			Bklt. pane of 3, #2344-2346 + label	4.25	
			Nos. 2344-2346 (3)	4.00	2.65

World Cup Soccer, Italy
A528

1990, June **Litho.** ***Perf. 12***

2347	A528	30q	multicolored	.30	.30
2348	A528	90q	multi, diff.	1.00	1.00
2349	A528	1.20 l	multi, diff.	1.75	1.75

Size: 80x63mm

Imperf

2350	A528	3.30 l	multi, diff.	5.00	5.00
			Nos. 2347-2350 (4)	8.05	8.05

Vincent Van Gogh, Death Cent.
A529

Self portraits and: 30q, Details from various paintings. 90q, Woman in field. 2.10 l, Asylum. 2.40 l, Self-portrait.

1990, July 27

2351	A529	30q	multicolored	.40	.40
2352	A529	90q	multicolored	1.10	1.10
2353	A529	2.10 l	multicolored	2.50	2.50

Size: 87x73mm

Imperf

2354	A529	2.40 l	multicolored	4.25	4.25
			Nos. 2351-2354 (4)	8.25	8.25

Albanian Folklore — A530

Scenes from medieval folktale of "Gjergj Elez Alia": 30q, Alia lying wounded. 90q, Alia being helped onto horse. 1.20 l, Alia fighting Bajloz. 1.80 l, Alia on horseback over severed head of Bajloz.

1990, Aug. 30 ***Perf. 12½x12***

2355	A530	30q	multicolored	.45	.45
2356	A530	90q	multicolored	.85	.85
2357	A530	1.20 l	multicolored	1.10	1.10
2358	A530	1.80 l	multicolored	1.75	1.75
			Nos. 2355-2358 (4)	4.15	4.15

Founding of Berat, 2400th Anniv. — A531

Designs: 30q, Xhamia E Plumbit. 90q, Kisha E Shen Triadhes. 1.20 l, Ura E Beratit. 1.80 l, Onufri-Piktor Mesjetar. 2.40 l, Nikolla-Piktor Mesjetar.

1990, Sept. 20 ***Perf. 12½***

2359	Block of 5 + 4 labels	7.00	7.00
a.	A531 30q multi	.25	.25
b.	A531 90q multi	.80	.80
c.	A531 1.20 l multi	1.00	1.00
d.	A531 1.80 l multi	1.75	1.75
e.	A531 2.40 l multi	1.90	1.90

No. 2359 was sold in souvenir folders for 9.90 l.

Illyrian Heroes — A532

1990, Oct. 20 ***Perf. 12***

2360	A532	30q	Pirroja	.25	.25
2361	A532	90q	Teuta	.75	.75
2362	A532	1.20 l	Bato	.85	.85
2363	A532	1.80 l	Bardhyli	1.25	1.25
			Nos. 2360-2363 (4)	3.10	3.10

Intl. Literacy Year
A533

1990, Oct. 30

2364	A533	90q	lt bl & multi	.80	.80
2365	A533	1.20 l	pink & multi	1.25	1.25

Albanian Horseman by Eugene Delacroix
A534

Designs: 1.20 l, Albanian Woman by Camille Corot. 1.80 l, Skanderbeg by unknown artist.

1990, Nov. 30 ***Perf. 12x12½***

2366	A534	30q	multicolored	.40	.40
2367	A534	1.20 l	multicolored	1.00	1.00
2368	A534	1.80 l	multicolored	1.60	1.60
			Nos. 2366-2368 (3)	3.00	3.00

A535

1991, Jan. 23 **Litho.** ***Perf. 12x12½***

2369	A535	90q	shown	.75	.75
2370	A535	1.20 l	Boletini standing	1.10	1.10

Isa Boletini (1864-1916), freedom fighter.

A536

1991, Jan. 30 **Litho.** ***Perf. 12***

Background Color

2371	A536	90q	pale yellow	.75	.75
2372	A536	1.20 l	pale gray	1.10	1.10

Arberi State, 800th anniv.

Pierre Auguste Renoir (1841-1919), Painter — A537

Paintings: 30q, Girl Reading, 1876, vert. 90q, The Swing, 1876, vert. 1.20 l, Boating Party, 1868-1869. 1.80 l, Flowers and grapes, 1878. 3 l, Self-portrait.

1991, Feb. 25 ***Perf. 12½x12***

2373	A537	30q	multicolored	.55	.55
2374	A537	90q	multicolored	.85	.85
2375	A537	1.20 l	multicolored	1.25	1.25
2376	A537	1.80 l	multicolored	2.25	2.25

Size: 95x75mm

Imperf

2377	A537	3 l	multicolored	4.25	4.25
			Nos. 2373-2377 (5)	9.15	9.15

Flowers — A538

30q, Cistus albanicus. 90q, Trifolium pilczii. 1.80 l, Lilium albanicum.

1991, Mar. 30 ***Perf. 12***

2378	A538	30q	multicolored	.30	.30
2379	A538	90q	multicolored	1.00	1.00
2380	A538	1.80 l	multicolored	1.60	1.60
			Nos. 2378-2380 (3)	2.90	2.90

Legend of Rozafa
A539

Various scenes from legend.

1991, Sept. 30 **Litho.** ***Perf. 12x12½***

2381	A539	30q	multicolored	.35	.35
2382	A539	90q	multicolored	.85	.85
2383	A539	1.20 l	multicolored	1.25	1.25
2384	A539	1.80 l	multicolored	1.75	1.75
			Nos. 2381-2384 (4)	4.20	4.20

For surcharges see Nos. 2586, 2604.

Wolfgang Amadeus Mozart, Death Bicent. — A540

1991, Oct. 5 **Litho.** ***Perf. 12***

2385 A540 90q Conducting 1.00 1.00
2386 A540 1.20 l Portrait 1.25 1.25
2387 A540 1.80 l Playing piano 2.10 2.10

Size: 89x70mm

Imperf

2388 A540 3 l Medal, score 5.50 5.50
Nos. 2385-2388 (4) 9.85 9.85

Airplanes — A541

Designs: 30q, Glider, Otto Lilienthal, 1896. 80q, Avion III, Clement Ader, 1897. 90q, Flyer, Wright Brothers, 1903. 1.20 l, Concorde. 1.80 l, Tupolev 114. 2.40 l, Dornier 31 E.

1992, Jan. 27 **Litho.** ***Perf. 12½x12***

2389 A541 30q multicolored .35 .35
2390 A541 80q multicolored .60 .60
2391 A541 90q multicolored .90 .90
2392 A541 1.20 l multicolored 1.25 1.25
2393 A541 1.80 l multicolored 1.25 1.25
2394 A541 2.40 l multicolored 2.25 2.25
Nos. 2389-2394 (6) 6.60 6.60

No. 2393 misidentifies a Tupolev 144.

Explorers — A542

1992, Jan. 10

2395 A542 30q Bering .35 .35
2396 A542 90q Columbus 1.10 1.10
2397 A542 1.80 l Magellan 2.25 2.25
Nos. 2395-2397 (3) 3.70 3.70

1992 Winter Olympics, Albertville A543

1992, Feb. 15 **Litho.** ***Perf. 12½***

2398 A543 30q Ski jumping .30 .30
2399 A543 90q Cross country skiing .75 .75
2400 A543 1.20 l Pairs figure skating 1.10 1.10
2401 A543 1.80 l Luge 1.60 1.60
Nos. 2398-2401 (4) 3.75 3.75

For surcharge see No. 2598.

Participation of Albania in Conference on Security and Cooperation in Europe, Berlin (1991) — A544

1992, Mar. 31 **Litho.** ***Perf. 12½x12***

2402 A544 90q shown 1.25 1.25
2403 A544 1.20 l Flags, map 1.50 1.50
a. Pair, #2402-2403 4.00 4.00

Dated 1991. Issued in sheets containing 2 No. 2403a, 3 each Nos. 2402-2403 + 2 labels. No. 2402 was also issued in sheets of 16.

Albanian Admission to CEPT — A545

1992, Apr. 25 **Litho.** ***Perf. 12½***

2404 A545 90q Envelopes, CEPT emblem 1.10 1.10
2405 A545 1.20 l blk, pur & red lil 1.40 1.40
a. Pair, #2404-2405 2.50 2.50

Issued in sheets containing 2 No. 2405a, 3 each Nos. 2404-2405 and 2 labels.

Martyrs' Day — A546

1992, May 5 ***Perf. 12x12½***

2406 A546 90q Freedom flame, vert. 1.00 1.00

Perf. 12½x12

2407 A546 4.10 l Flowers 4.50 4.50

European Soccer Championships, Sweden'92 — A547

Various stylized designs of soccer plays.

1992, June 10 **Litho.** ***Perf. 12***

2408 A547 30q green & lt grn .60 .60
2409 A547 90q blue & pink 1.25 1.25
2410 A547 10.80 l henna & tan 7.00 7.00

Size: 90x70mm

Imperf

2411 A547 5 l tan, lt green & pink 5.50 5.50
Nos. 2408-2411 (4) 14.35 14.35

1992 Summer Olympics, Barcelona A548

1992, June 14 **Litho.** ***Perf. 12***

2412 A548 30q Tennis .45 .45
2413 A548 90q Baseball 1.25 1.25
2414 A548 1.80 l Table tennis 2.25 2.25

Size: 90x70mm

Imperf

2415 A548 5 l Torch bearer 5.25 5.25
Nos. 2412-2415 (4) 9.20 9.20

United Europe A549

1992, July 10 **Litho.** ***Perf. 12***

2416 A549 1.20 l multicolored 1.50 1.25

Horses A550

1992, Aug. 10 **Litho.** ***Perf. 12***

2417 A550 30q Native .30 .30
2418 A550 90q Nonius .50 .50
2419 A550 1.20 l Arabian, vert. .70 .70
2420 A550 10.60 l Haflinger, vert. 7.00 7.00
Nos. 2417-2420 (4) 8.50 8.50

For surcharge, see No. 2781.

Discovery of America, 500th Anniv. A551

Map of North and South America and: 60q, Columbus, sailing ships. 3.20 l, Columbus meeting natives.

1992, Aug. 20

2421 A551 60q blk, bl & gray *.60 .60*
2422 A551 3.20 l blk, brn & gray *4.00 4.00*

Size: 90x70mm

Imperf

2423 A551 5 l Map, Columbus *70.00 70.00*

Mother Theresa, Infant — A552

1992, Oct. 4 **Litho.** ***Perf. 12x12½***

2424 A552 40q fawn .30 .30
2425 A552 60q brown .30 .30
2426 A552 1 l violet .30 .30
2427 A552 1.80 l gray .30 .30
2428 A552 2 l red .40 .40
2429 A552 2.40 l green .45 .45
2430 A552 3.20 l blue .60 .60
2431 A552 5.60 l rose violet .90 .90
2432 A552 7.20 l olive 1.25 1.25
2433 A552 10 l org brn 1.50 1.50
Nos. 2424-2433 (10) 6.30 6.30

See Nos. 2472-2476.
For surcharge, see No. 2786.

A553

1993, Apr. 25 **Litho.** ***Perf. 12***

2434 A553 16 l multicolored 3.50 3.50

Visit of Pope John Paul II.

Nos. 2223-2226, 2229 Surcharged

1993, May 2 **Litho.** ***Perf. 12x12½***

2435 A486 3 l on 10q .30 .30
2436 A486 6.50 l on 20q 1.00 1.00
2437 A486 13 l on 30q 2.25 2.25
2438 A486 20 l on 90q 3.50 3.50
2439 A486 30 l on 50q 5.25 5.25
Nos. 2435-2439 (5) 12.30 12.30

Lef Nosi (1873-1945), Minister of Posts A554

1993, May 5 **Litho.** ***Perf. 12***

2440 A554 6.50 l olive brn & bister 1.25 1.25

First Albanian postage stamps, 80th anniv.

Europa A555

Contemporary paintings by: 3 l, A. Zajmi, vert. 7 l, E. Hila. 20 l, B. Ahmeti-Peizazh.

1993, May 28 **Litho.** ***Perf. 12***

2441 A555 3 l multicolored 1.25 1.25
2442 A555 7 l multicolored 4.50 4.50

Size: 116x122mm

2443 A555 20 l multicolored 9.00 9.00
Nos. 2441-2443 (3) 14.75 14.75

1993 Mediterranean Games, France — A556

1993, June 20 **Litho.** ***Perf. 12***

2444 A556 3 l Running .30 .30
2445 A556 16 l Kayaking 2.25 2.25
2446 A556 21 l Cycling 3.00 3.00

Size: 111x78mm

Imperf

2447 A556 20 l Mediterranean map 4.25 4.25
Nos. 2444-2447 (4) 9.80 9.80

For surcharge, see No. 2789.

Frang Bardhi, Author, 350th Death Anniv. A557

1993, Aug. 20 Litho. *Perf. 12x12½*
2448 A557 6.50 l shown 1.25 1.25

Size: 89x101mm

Imperf

2449 A557 20 l Writing at desk 4.75 4.75

A558

1994, July 17 Litho. *Perf. 12*
2450 A558 42 l shown 1.40 1.40
2451 A558 68 l Mascot, ball, US map 2.40 2.40

1994 World Cup Soccer Championships, US.

A559

European Inventors, Discoveries: 50 l, Gjovalin Gjadri, engineer. 100 l, Karl von Ghega, Austrian engineer. 150 l, Sketch of road project.

1994, Dec. 31 Litho. *Perf. 14*
2452 A559 50 l multicolored 2.25 2.25
2453 A559 100 l multicolored 3.50 3.50

Size: 50x70mm

Imperf

2454 A559 150 l multicolored 5.75 5.75
Nos. 2452-2454 (3) 11.50 11.50

Europa (No. 2454).

Ali Pasa of Tepelene (Lion of Janina) (1744-1822) — A560

1995, Jan. 28 *Perf. 14*
2455 A560 60 l shown 2.10 2.10

Size: 70x50mm

Imperf

2456 A560 100 l Tepelene Palace 3.50 3.50

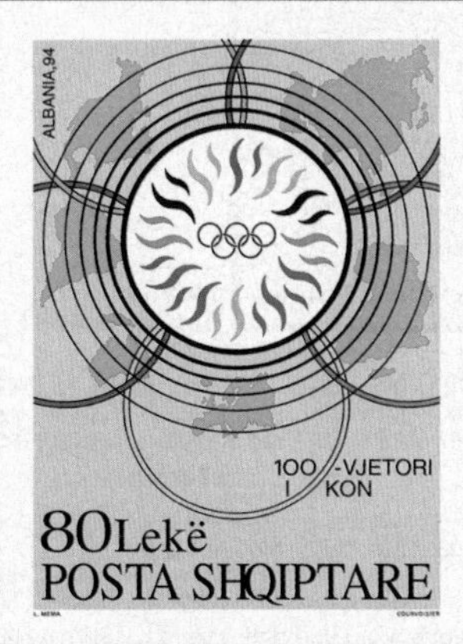

Intl. Olympic Committee, Cent. — A561

1995, Feb. 2 *Imperf.*
2457 A561 80 l multicolored 2.75 2.75

Karl Benz (1844-1929), Automobile Pioneer — A562

Designs: 5 l, Automobile company emblem, Benz. 10 l, Modern Mercedes Benz automobile. 60 l, First four-wheel Benz 1886 motor car. 125 l, Pre-war Mercedes touring car.

1995, Jan. 21 Litho. *Perf. 14*
2458 A562 5 l multicolored .30 .30
2459 A562 10 l multicolored .30 .30
2460 A562 60 l multicolored 1.75 1.75
2461 A562 125 l multicolored 4.00 4.00
Nos. 2458-2461 (4) 6.35 6.35

Liberation, 50th Anniv. (in 1994) A563

1995, Jan. 28 Litho. *Perf. 14*
2462 A563 50 l black, gray & red 1.90 1.90

Dated 1994.

Miniature Sheet

Albania '93 — A564

Composers: a, 3 l, Wagner. b, 6.50 l, Grieg. c, 11 l, Gounod. d, 20 l, Tchaikovsky.

1995, Jan. 26 *Perf. 12*
2463 A564 Sheet of 4, #a.-d. 2.50 2.50

Voskopoja Academy, 250th Anniv. — A565

Buildings of Voskopoja.

1995, Feb. 2
2464 A565 42 l multicolored 1.25 1.25
2465 A565 68 l multicolored 2.00 2.00
a. Pair, #2464-2465 3.50 3.50

Bleta Apricula — A566

1995, Aug. 20 Litho. *Perf. 12*
2466 A566 5 l On flower .30 .30
2467 A566 10 l Honeycomb, bee .40 .40
2468 A566 25 l Emerging from cell of honeycomb 1.40 1.40
Nos. 2466-2468 (3) 2.10 2.10

Peace & Freedom — A567

Stylized hands reaching for: 50 l, Olive branch. 100 l, Peace dove.
150 l, Stylized person.

1995, Aug. 10 *Perf. 13½x14*
2469 A567 50 l multicolored 2.25 2.25
2470 A567 100 l multicolored 4.50 4.50

Size: 80x60mm

Imperf

2471 A567 150 l multicolored 7.00 7.00
Nos. 2469-2471 (3) 13.75 13.75

Europa.
For surcharges, see Nos. B39-B40.

Mother Teresa Type of 1992

1994-95 Litho. *Perf. 12x12½*
2472 A552 5 l violet .30 .30
2473 A552 18 l orange 1.75 1.75
2474 A552 20 l rose lilac .70 .70
2475 A552 25 l green 2.50 2.50
2476 A552 60 l olive 2.50 2.50
Nos. 2472-2476 (5) 7.75 7.75

Issued: 20 l, 1994; 60 l, 1995; others, 7/94.

Arctic Explorers — A568

Designs: a, Fridtjof Nansen (1861-1930), Norway. b, James Cook (1728-79), England. c, Roald Amundsen (1872-1928), Norway. d, Robert F. Scott (1872-1928), Great Britain.

1995, Sept. 14 Litho. *Perf. 13½x14*
2477 A568 25 l Block of 4, #a.-d. 5.00 5.00

For surcharges, see No. 2790.

UN, 50th Anniv. A569

1995, Sept. 14 Litho. *Perf. 14x13½*
2478 A569 2 l shown .25 .25
2479 A569 100 l like #2478, flags streaming to right 3.00 3.00

For surcharge, see No. 2782.

Poets — A570

1995 *Perf. 13½x14*
2480 A570 25 l Paul Éluard 1.00 1.00
2481 A570 50 l Sergei Yesenin 1.75 1.75
a. Pair, #2480-2481 3.00 3.00

Entry into Council of Europe A571

Designs: 25 l, Doves flying from headquarters, Strasbourg. 85 l, Albanian eagle over map of Europe.

1995 *Perf. 14x13½*
2482 A571 25 l multicolored 1.10 1.10
2483 A571 85 l multicolored 3.50 3.50

For surcharge see No. 2583

Jan Kukuzeli, Composer A572

Stylized figure: 18 l, Writing. 20 l, Holding hand to head. 100 l, Holding up scroll of paper.

1995, Oct. 17 ***Perf. 13½x14***

2484 A572 18 l multicolored .75 .75
2485 A572 20 l multicolored .75 .75

Size: 74x74mm

2486 A572 100 l multicolored 3.50 3.50
Nos. 2484-2486 (3) 5.00 5.00

For surcharge, see No. 2787.

World Tourism Organization, 20th Anniv. — A573

Stylized designs: 18 l, Church, saint holding scroll. 20 l, City, older buildings. 42 l, City, modern buildings.

1995, Oct. 17

2487 A573 18 l multicolored .70 .70
2488 A573 20 l multicolored .80 .80
2489 A573 42 l multicolored 2.10 2.10
Nos. 2487-2489 (3) 3.60 3.60

For surcharge, see No. 2788.

Fables of Jean de la Fontaine (1621-95) A574

Designs: 2 l, Raptor, turtle, wolf, goose, mouse, lion, rats. 3 l, Crow, goose, dog, foxes. 25 l, Insect, doves, frogs. 60 l, Drawings of Da la Fontaine, animals, birds.

1995, Aug. 20 **Litho.** ***Perf. 14x13½***

2490 A574 2 l multicolored .25 .25
2491 A574 3 l multicolored .25 .25
2492 A574 25 l multicolored 1.00 1.00

Imperf

Size: 73x56mm

2493 A574 60 l multicolored 2.75 2.75
Nos. 2490-2493 (4) 4.25 4.25

For surcharges, see Nos. 2783, 2784, 2791.

Motion Pictures, Cent. — A576

1995, Nov. 17

2496 A576 10 l Louis Lumiere .35 .35
2497 A576 85 l Auguste Lumiere 3.00 3.00
a. Pair, #2496-2497 3.50 3.50

Elvis Presley (1935-77) A577

1995, Nov. 20 **Litho.** ***Perf. 14x13½***

2498 A577 3 l orange & multi .35 .35
2499 A577 60 l green & multi 2.50 2.50

For surcharge, see No. 2785.

A578

1995, Nov. 25 ***Perf. 13½x14***

2500 A578 10 l 1925 Bank notes .40 .40
2501 A578 25 l 1995 Bank notes 1.00 1.00

National Bank, 70th anniv.

A579

1995, Nov. 27 **Litho.** ***Perf. 13½x14***

2502 A579 5 l shown .25 .25
2503 A579 50 l Maiden planting tree 1.75 1.75

Democracy, 5th anniv.

A580

Designs: 25 l, Soccer ball, British flag, map of Europe, stadium. 100 l, Soccer ball, player.

1996, June 4 ***Perf. 14***

2504 A580 25 l multicolored 1.10 1.10
2505 A580 100 l multicolored 3.25 3.25

Euro '96, European Soccer Championships, Great Britain.

For surcharge, see No. 2792.

Mother Teresa — A581

1996, May 5 ***Perf. 13½x14***

2506 A581 25 l blue & multi 1.25 1.25
2507 A581 100 l red & multi 4.00 4.00

Size: 52x74mm

Imperf

2508 A581 150 l Mother Teresa, diff. 8.25 8.25
Nos. 2506-2508 (3) 13.50 13.50

Europa. For overprints see Nos. 2551, 2582.

GSM Cellular Telephone Transmission A582

Designs: 10 l, Satellite transmitting signals. 60 l, Uses for cellular telephone, vert.

Perf. 13x13½, 13½x13

1996, Aug. 1 **Litho.**

2509 A582 10 l multicolored .35 .35
2510 A582 60 l multicolored 2.00 2.00

1996 Summer Olympic Games, Atlanta — A583

Stylized designs.

1996, Aug. 3 **Litho.** ***Perf. 13x14***

2511 A583 5 l Runners .25 .25
2512 A583 25 l Throwers .90 .90
2513 A583 60 l Jumpers 2.10 2.10

Size: 52x37mm

Imperf

2514 A583 100 l Emblem, US flag 3.00 3.00
Nos. 2511-2514 (4) 6.25 6.25

Gottfried Wilhelm Leibniz (1646-1716), Mathematician — A584

85 l, René Descartes (1596-1650), mathematician.

1996, Sept. 20 **Litho.** ***Perf. 14***

2515 A584 10 l multicolored .60 .60
2516 A584 85 l multicolored 3.00 3.00

Paintings by Francisco Goya (1746-1828) A585

Designs: 10 l, The Naked Maja. 60 l, Dona Isabel Cobos de Porcel. 100 l, Self portrait.

1996, Sept. 25 ***Perf. 14x13½***

2517 A585 10 l multicolored .60 .60
2518 A585 60 l multicolored 2.25 2.25

Souvenir Sheet

2519 A585 100 l multicolored 3.25 3.25

Religious Engravings — A586

Designs: a, 5 l, Book cover showing crucifixion, angels. b, 25 l, Medallion of crucifixion. c, 85 l, Book cover depicting life of Christ.

1996, Nov. 5 ***Perf. 13x13½***

2520 A586 Block of 3, #a.-c. + label 4.00 4.00

UNICEF, 50th Anniv. — A587

Children's paintings: 5 l, Fairy princess. 10 l, Doll, sun. 25 l, Sea life. 50 l, House, people.

1996, Nov. 11 ***Perf. 13½***

2521 A587 5 l multicolored .30 .30
2522 A587 10 l multicolored .35 .35
2523 A587 25 l multicolored 1.25 1.25
2524 A587 50 l multicolored 1.75 1.75
Nos. 2521-2524 (4) 3.65 3.65

Gjergj Fishta (1871-1940), Writer, Priest — A588

1996, Dec. 20 ***Perf. 13½x14***

2525 A588 10 l shown .50 .50
2526 A588 60 l Battle scene, portrait 2.00 2.00

Omar Khayyam — A589

1997, Mar. 6 ***Perf. 14***

2527 A589 20 l shown .85 .85
2528 A589 50 l Portrait, diff. 1.75 1.75

A590

1997, Mar. 20 ***Perf. 14x14½***

2529 A590 20 l Portrait .90 .90
2530 A590 60 l Printing press 2.10 2.10
a. Pair, #2529-2530 3.00 3.00

Johannes Gutenberg (1397?-1468).

A591

The Azure Eye (Stories and Legends): 30 l, Dragon on rock looking at warrior, donkey. 100 l, Dragon drinking water from pond, warrior.

1997, May 5 **Litho.** ***Perf. 13x14***

2531 A591 30 l multicolored 1.25 1.25
2532 A591 100 l multicolored 3.75 3.75

Europa.

A592

1997, Apr. 10 ***Perf. 14***

2533 A592 10 l Pelicanus crispus .25 .25
2534 A592 80 l Pelicans, diff. 2.25 2.25
a. Pair, #2533-2534 2.50 2.50

No. 2534a is a continuous design.

A593

1997, June 25 **Litho.** ***Perf. 14***

2535 A593 10 l blk & dark brn .35 .35
2536 A593 25 l blk & blue blk 1.00 1.00

Souvenir Sheet

2537 A593 80 l gray brown 3.00 3.00

Faik Konica (1875-1942), writer and politician.
No. 2537 contains one 22x26mm stamp.

A594

1997 Mediterranean Games, Bari: 20 l, Man running. 30 l, Woman running, 3-man canoe. 100 l, Man breaking finish line, silhouettes of man and woman.

1997, June 13

2538 A594 20 l Man running .60 .60
2539 A594 30 l Woman running, canoe 1.25 1.25

Size: 52x74mm

Imperf

2540 A594 100 l multicolored 3.25 3.25

Skanderbeg — A595

1997, Aug. 25 **Litho.** ***Perf. 13***

2541 A595 5 l red brn & red .25 .25
2542 A595 10 l dp ol & ol .40 .40
2543 A595 20 l dp grn & grn .80 .80
2544 A595 25 l dp mag & red lil 1.00 1.00
2545 A595 30 l dk vio & vio 1.25 1.25
2546 A595 50 l black 2.00 2.00
2547 A595 60 l brn & lt brn 2.40 2.40
2548 A595 80 l dk brown & brn 3.25 3.25
2549 A595 100 l dk red brown & red brn 4.00 4.00
2550 A595 110 l dark blue 4.25 4.25
Nos. 2541-2550 (10) 19.60 19.60

No. 2507 Ovptd. in Silver "HOMAZH / 1910-1997"

1997 ***Perf. 13½x14***

2551 A581 100 l red & multi 4.50 4.50

Religious Manuscripts — A596

Albanian Codex: a, 10 l, 11th cent. b, 25 l, 6th cent. c, 60 l, 6th cent., diff.

1997, Nov. 15 **Litho.** ***Perf. 13x14***

2552 A596 Block of 3, #a.-c. + label 3.25 3.25

See No. 2575.

Post and Telecommunications Administration, 85th Anniv. — A597

1997, Dec. 4 ***Perf. 13½***

2553 A597 10 l multi .25 .25
2554 A597 30 l multi, diff. .90 .90

A598

1998, Mar. 25 **Litho.** ***Perf. 14***

2555 A598 30 l red brn & multi .85 .85
2556 A598 100 l tan & multi 2.40 2.40
a. Pair, #2555-2556 3.25 3.25

Nikete Dardani, musician.

A599

Legends of Pogradecit: a, 30 l, Old man seated at table. b, 50 l, Three Graces. c, 60 l, Two women, fountain. d, 80 l, Iceman.

1998, Apr. 15

2557 A599 Block of 4, #a.-d. 4.75 4.75

A600

1998, May 5 **Litho.** ***Perf. 13x14***

2558 A600 60 l shown 1.75 1.75
2559 A600 100 l multi, diff. 2.75 2.75

Size: 50x72mm

Imperf

2560 A600 150 l multi, diff. 4.50 4.50

Europa (folk festivals).

A601

Albanian League of Prizren, 120th anniv.: a, 30 l, Abdyl Frasheri. b, 50 l, Sulejman Vokshi. c, 60 l, Iljaz Pashe Dibra. d, 80 l, Ymer Prizreni.

1998, June 10 **Litho.** ***Perf. 13½x13***

2561 A601 Block of 4, #a.-d. 4.75 4.75

1998 World Cup Soccer Championships, France — A602

Stylized soccer players.

1998, June 10 ***Perf. 13½***

2562 A602 60 l multicolored 1.50 1.50
2563 A602 100 l multicolored 2.25 2.25

Size: 50x73mm

Imperf

2564 A602 120 l Mascot 3.50 3.50

European Youth Greco-Roman Wrestling Championships, Albania — A603

1998, July 5 ***Perf. 13½***

2565 A603 30 l shown .85 .85
2566 A603 60 l Wrestlers, diff. 1.40 1.40
a. Pair, #2565-2566 2.50 2.50

Eqerem Cabej (1908-1980), Albanian Etymologist — A604

1998, Aug. 7 ***Perf. 14***

2567 A604 60 l yel brn & multi 1.00 1.00
2568 A604 80 l brn red & multi 1.50 1.50
a. Pair, #2567-2568 2.75 2.75

Paul Gauguin (1848-1903) A605

Paintings (details): 60 l, The Vision after the Sermon. 80 l, Ea Haere la Oe.
120 l, Stylized design to resemble self-portrait.

1998, Sept. 10 ***Perf. 13½***

2569 A605 60 l multicolored 1.25 1.25
2570 A605 80 l multicolored 1.75 1.75
a. Pair, #2569-2570 3.25 3.25

Size: 50x73mm

Imperf

2571 A605 120 l multicolored 3.00 3.00

Epitaph of Gllavenica, 14th Cent. Depiction of Christ — A606

Designs: 30 l, Entire cloth showing artwork. 80 l, Closer view.
100 l, Upper portion of cloth, vert.

1998, Oct. 5 ***Perf. 14½x14***

2572 A606 30 l multicolored .75 .75
2573 A606 80 l multicolored 1.90 1.90

Souvenir Sheet

Perf. 13

2574 A606 100 l multicolored 2.75 2.75

No. 2574 contains one 25x29mm stamp.

Religious Manuscripts Type of 1997

Illustrations from Purple Codex, Gold Codex: a, 30 l, Manuscript, columns on sides, arched top. b, 50 l, Manuscript cover with embossed pictures of icons. c, 80 l, Manuscript picturing cathedral, birds.

1998, Oct. 15 ***Perf. 13x14***

2575 A596 Block of 3, #a.-c. + label 4.00 4.00

Mikel Koliqi (1902-97), First Albanian Cardinal — A607

1998, Nov. 28 *Perf. 14*

2576 A607 30 l shown .75 .75
2577 A607 100 l Portrait, facing 2.25 2.25
a. Pair, #2576-2577 3.25 3.25

Mother Teresa (1910-97) — A608

Perf. 14x13½, 13½x14

1998, Sept. 5 **Photo.**

2578 A608 60 l With child, horiz. 1.50 1.50
2579 A608 100 l shown 2.75 2.75

See Italy Nos. 2254-2255.

Diana, Princess of Wales (1961-97) — A609

1998, Aug. 31 **Litho.** *Perf. 13½*

2580 A609 60 l shown *4.50 4.50*
2581 A609 100 l With Mother Teresa *6.50 6.50*

No. 2508 Overprinted in Blue

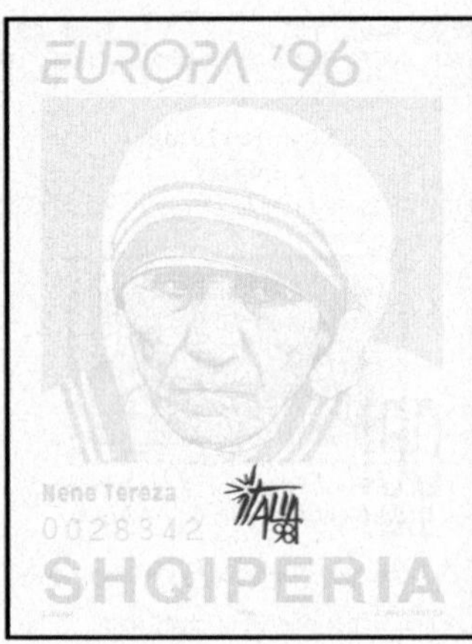

1998, Oct. 23 **Litho.** *Imperf.*

2582 A581 150 l multicolored 10.00 10.00

No. 2482 Surcharged

1999, Apr. 20 **Litho.** *Perf. 14x13½*

2583 A571 150 l on 25 l multi 5.00 5.00

Famous Americans — A610

a, Washington. b, Lincoln. c. Martin Luther King, Jr.

1999, Mar. 15 *Perf. 14*

2584 A610 150 l Block of 3, #a.-c. + label 12.00 12.00

Monachus Albiventer — A611

Seals: a, 110 l, One looking left, one looking right. b, 150 l, Both looking right. c, 110 l, Mirror image of No. 2585b. d, 150 l, Mirror image of No. 2585a.

1999, Apr. 10

2585 A611 Sheet of 4, #a.-d. 15.00 15.00

No. 2382 Surcharged

1999, Apr. 24 **Litho.** *Perf. 12x12¼*

2586 A539 150 l on 90 l multi 4.00 4.00

IBRA '99, Nuremburg.

A612

1999, Apr. 25 **Litho.** *Perf. 13½x13¾*

2587 A612 10 l blue & multi 1.00 1.00
2588 A612 100 l green & multi 5.00 5.00

Souvenir Sheet

Perf. 13

2589 A612 250 l green & multi 7.00 7.00

NATO, 50th anniv. No. 2589 contains one 30x50mm stamp.

A613

Cartoon mouse: a, 80 l, Writing. b, 110 l, Holding chin. c, 150 l, Wearing bow tie. d, 60 l, Pointing.

1999, Apr. 30 **Litho.** *Perf. 13x13¾*

2590 A613 Strip of 4, #a.-d. 11.00 11.00

Animated films.

Europa A614

1999, May 1 **Litho.** *Perf. 13¾x13*

2591 A614 90 l Thethi Park 3.00 3.00
2592 A614 310 l Lura Park 7.50 7.50

Imperf

Size: 80x60mm

2592A A614 350 l Kombetare Park 11.00 11.00
Nos. 2591-2592A (3) 21.50 21.50

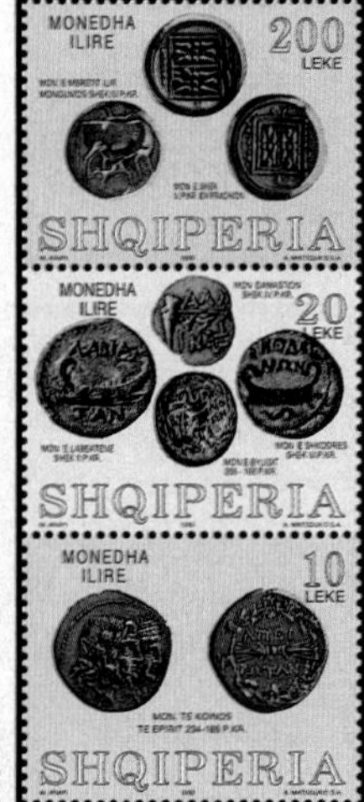
Illyrian Coins A615

Designs: a, 200 l, Kings of Illyria — Monumiou c. 300-280 BC cow suckling calf, square containing double stellate pattern, and Epidamos-Dyrrachium c. 623 BC, square with double stellate. b, 20 l, Damastion c. 395-380 BC siver drachm portable ingot, Byllis c. 238-168 BC AE13 serpent entwined around cornucopia, Skodra after 168 BC, AE17 war galley, and other war galley coin. c, 10l, Epirote Republic before 238 BC silver tetraobol with jugate busts of Zeus and Dione on obverse and thunderbolt within oak wreath reverse.

310 l, Kings of Illyria — Genthos c. 197-168 BC head wearing kausia.

1999, June 1 **Litho.** *Perf. 13¾x13¼*

2593 A615 Strip of 3, #a.-c. 8.00 8.00

Souvenir Sheet

Perf. 13

2594 A615 310 l multicolored 9.50 9.50

Charlie Chaplin — A616

Designs: 30 l, Holding cigarette. 50 l, Tipping hat. 250 l, Dancing.

1999, June 20 **Litho.** *Perf. 14x14¼*

2595 A616 30 l multicolored 1.10 1.10
2596 A616 50 l multicolored 2.00 2.00
2597 A616 250 l multicolored 8.25 8.25
a. Booklet pane, 2 each #2595-2597, perf. 14¼ vert. 23.00
Complete booklet 23.00
Nos. 2595-2597 (3) 11.35 11.35

In No. 2597a, the 30 l stamps are at the ends of the pane and the 250 l stamps are in the middle.

No. 2398 Surcharged

1999, July 2 **Litho.** *Perf. 12½*

2598 A543 150 l on 30q multi 4.25 4.25

PhilexFrance 99.

Holocaust — A617

1999, July 6 **Litho.** *Perf. 14x14¼*

2599 A617 30 l brown & multi 1.10 1.10
2600 A617 150 l gray & multi 5.25 5.25

First Manned Moon Landing, 30th Anniv. — A618

No. 2601: a, 30 l, Astronaut, earth. b, 150 l, Lunar Module. c, 300 l, Astronaut, flag.
280 l, Lift-off.

1999, July 25 **Litho.** *Perf. 13¼x14*

2601 A618 Strip of 3, #a.-c 17.00 17.00

Souvenir Sheet

Perf. 13

2602 A618 280 l multicolored 9.00 9.00

No. 2602 contains one 25x29mm stamp.

UPU, 125th Anniv. — A619

Background colors: a, 20 l, aquamarine and brown. b, 60 l, bister and dark blue.

1999, Aug. 1 **Litho.** *Perf. 14x14¼*

2603 A619 Pair, #a.-b. 2.50 2.50

No. 2383 Surcharged in Brown, Symbol in Red and Green

1999 **Method & Perf. as Before**

2604 A539 150 l on 1.20 l multi 4.25 4.25

China 1999 World Philatelic Exhibition.

A620

Background colors: a, 10 l, Yellow. b, 20 l, Orange. c, 200 l, Green.

1999, Sept. 2 Litho. ***Perf. 14x14¼***
2605 A620 Strip of 3, #a.-c. 7.00 7.00

First Natl. Track & Field Championships, 70th anniv.

A621

1999, Oct. 30 ***Perf. 14***
2606 A621 30 l Madonna and Child 1.50 1.50
2607 A621 300 l shown 7.50 7.50
a. Souv. sheet, 2 ea #2606-2607 18.00 18.00

Art by Onufri of Elbasan.

Famous Albanians — A622

Designs: a, 10 l, Bilal Golemi (1899-1955), veterinarian. b, 20 l, Azem Galica (1889-1924), freedom fighter. c, 50 l, Viktor Eftimiu (1889-1972), writer. d, 300 l, Lasgush Poradeci (1900-87), poet.

1999, Nov. 28 Litho. ***Perf. 14¼x14***
2608 A622 Block of 4, #a.-d. 11.00 11.00

Carnival Masks — A623

1999, Dec. 1 ***Perf. 13¾***
2609 A623 30 l shown 1.75 1.75
2610 A623 300 l Turkey head 7.75 7.75

Millennium A624

2000, Mar. 27 Litho. ***Perf. 13½x14***
2611 A624 40 l red & multi 1.25 1.25
2612 A624 90 l blue & multi 2.75 2.75

Native Costumes — A625

a, 5 l, Librazhdi. b, 10 l, Malesia e Madhe woman. c, 15 l, Malesia e Madhe man. d, 20 l, Tropoje. e, 30 l, Dumrea. f, 35 l, Tirana man. g, 40 l, Tirana woman. h, 45 l, Arbereshe. i, 50 l, Gjirokaster. j, 55 l, Lunxheri. k, 70 l, Cameria. l, 90 l, Laberia.

2000, Mar. 28 ***Perf. 13x13¾***
2613 Booklet pane of 12 18.00 18.00
Booklet, #2613 20.00

Gustave Mayer (1850-1900), Student of Albanian Culture — A626

Colors: a, 50 l, olive green. b, 130 l, carmine lake.

2000, Mar. 30 ***Perf. 13½x14***
2614 A626 Pair, #a-b 5.00 5.00

Cartoon Duck — A627

Duck with: a, 250 l, Top hat. b, 10 l, Ten-gallon hat. c, 30 l, Cap. d, 90 l, Bow.

2000, Apr. 6 Litho. ***Perf. 13x13¾***
2615 A627 Strip of 4, #a-d 10.00 10.00

Grand Prix Race Cars — A628

Various cars.

2000, Apr. 10 Litho. ***Perf. 14¼x14***
2616 Bklt. pane of 10 + 2 labels 12.50 12.50
a.-j. A628 30 l any single 1.25 1.25
Booklet, #2616 15.00

Holy Year 2000 A629

Designs: 15 l, Church with bell tower. 40 l, Church with conical roof. 90 l, Ruins. 250 l, Aerial view of ruins.

2000, Apr. 22 Litho. ***Perf. 13¾x14***
2617-2619 A629 Set of 3 5.50 5.50

Souvenir Sheet

Perf. 13¾

2620 A629 250 l multi 6.75 6.75

No. 2620 contains one 38x38mm stamp.

Europa, 2000

Common Design Type

2000, May 9 ***Perf. 13x13¾***
2621 CD17 130 l multi 3.50 3.50

Souvenir Sheet

Perf. 13

2622 CD17 300 l Detail of #2621 9.50 9.50

No. 2622 contains one 25x29mm stamp.

Miniature Sheet

Wild Animals — A630

No. 2623: a, 10 l, Canis lupus. b, 40 l, Ursus arctos. c, 90 l, Sus scrofa. d, 220 l, Vulpes vulpes.

2000, May 17 ***Perf. 14¼x13¾***
2623 A630 Sheet of 4, #a-d 11.00 11.00

Gustav Mahler (1860-1911), Composer A631

2000, May 30 ***Perf. 13½x14***
2624 A631 130 l multi 3.75 3.75

WIPA 2000 Stamp Exhibition, Vienna.

European Soccer Championships — A632

10 l, Goalie. 120 l, Player heading ball. 260 l, Player kicking ball.

2000, June 1 ***Perf. 13¾x13¼***
2625-2626 A632 Set of 2 3.75 3.75

Imperf

Size: 81x60mm

2627 A632 260 l multi 7.75 7.75

Paintings by Pablo Picasso — A633

Various unnamed paintings or self-portraits: 30 l, Brown panel. 40 l, Green panel. 130 l, Self-portrait, with Espana 2000 philatelic exhibition emblem, vert. 250 l, Blue panel.

2000 Litho. ***Perf. 13¾***
2628-2631 A633 Set of 4 11.00 11.00

Souvenir Sheet

Perf. 13

2632 A633 400 l Self-portrait 13.00 13.00

No. 2632 contains one 25x29mm stamp.
Issued: 130 l, 10/6; others 6/7.

2000 Summer Olympics, Sydney — A634

No. 2633: a, 10 l, Basketball. b, 40 l, Soccer. c, 90 l, Runner. d, 250 l, Cycling.

2000, July 1 ***Perf. 14x14¼***
2633 A634 Block of 4, #a-d 13.00 13.00

First Zeppelin Flight, Cent. — A635

No. 2634: a, 15 l, LZ-1 over Friedrichshafen. b, 30 l, Airship over Paris. c, 300 l, R34 over New York.

2000, July 2 ***Perf. 13¾x13***
2634 A635 Sheet of 3, #a-c 10.00 10.00

Souvenir Sheet

Perf. 13

2635 A635 300 l Ferdinand von Zeppelin 9.00 9.00

No. 2634 contains three 40x28mm stamps.

Flowers — A636

No. 2636: a, 50 l, Gentiana lutea. b, 70 l, Gentiana cruciata.

2000, Oct. 10 ***Perf. 13¼x14***
2636 A636 Pair, #a-b 3.50 3.50

Famous Albanians — A637

a, 30 l, Naim Frasheri, writer (1845-1900). b, 50 l, Bajram Curri, politician (1862-1925).

2000, Nov. 28 ***Perf. 14¼x13¾***
2637 A637 Pair, #a-b 2.50 2.50

UN High Commissioner on Refugees, 50th Anniv. — A638

50 l, Mother & child. 90 l, Mother & child, diff.

2000, Dec. 14 ***Perf. 13¾x14¼***
2638-2639 A638 Set of 2 4.25 4.25

Famous Albanians — A639

No. 2640: a, Ahmed Myftar Dede. b, Sali Njazi Dede.

2001, Feb. 22 Litho. ***Perf. 14¼x14***
2640 A639 90 l Horiz. pair, #a-b 4.50 4.50

Native Costumes — A640

No. 2641: a, Man from Tropoje. b, Woman from Lume. c, Woman from Mirdite. d, Man from Lume. e, Woman from Zadrime. f, Woman from Shpati. g, Man from Kruje. h, Woman from Macukulli. i, Woman from Dardhe. j, Man from Lushnje. k, Woman from Dropulli. l, Woman from Shmili.

2001, Mar. 15 ***Perf. 13x13¾***
2641 A640 20 l Sheet of 12, #a-l 6.00 6.00
Booklet, #2641 8.00

See Nos. 2669, 2701, 2760, 2770.

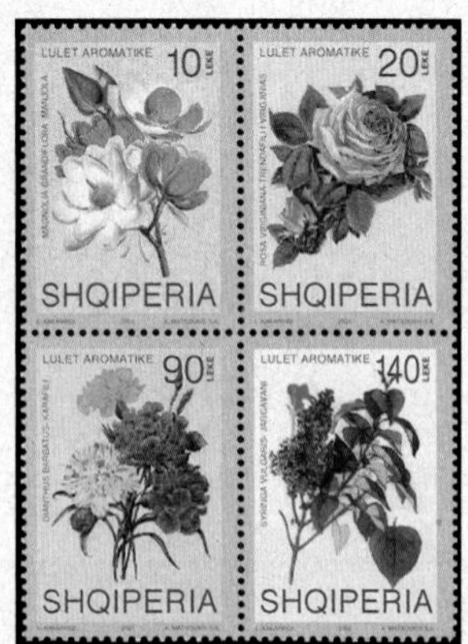

Flowers — A641

No. 2642: a, 10 l, Magnolia grandiflora. b, 20 l, Rosa virginiana. c, 90 l, Dianthus barbatus. d, 140 l, Syringa vulgaris.

2001, Mar. 30 ***Perf. 14x14¼***
2642 A641 Block of 4, #a-d 7.50 7.50

Cartoon Dog — A642

Denominations: a, 50 l. b, 90 l. c, 140 l, d, 20 l.

2001, Apr. 6 ***Perf. 13x13¾***
2643 A642 Strip of 4, #a-d 7.00 7.00

Opera Composers — A643

Designs: No. 2644, 90 l, Vincenzo Bellini (1801-35). No. 2645, 90 l, Giuseppe Verdi (1813-1901).
300 l, Bellini and Verdi.

2001, Apr. 20 ***Perf. 13¾x13***
2644-2645 A643 Set of 2 3.75 3.75

Souvenir Sheet
Perf. 13¾

2646 A643 300 l multi 6.00 6.00

Europa A644

Designs: 40 l, Waterfall, cliffs. 110 l, Waterfall, boulders. 200 l, Water, shoreline.
350 l, Ripples in water, vert.

2001, Apr. 29 ***Perf. 13¾x14***
2647-2649 A644 Set of 3 9.00 9.00

Souvenir Sheet
Perf. 12¾x13

2650 A644 350 l multi 11.00 11.00

No. 2650 contains one 25x29mm stamp.

Domestic Animals — A645

No. 2651: a, 10 l, Horse. b, 15 l, Donkey. c, 80 l, Cat. d, 90 l, Dog.
300 l, Cat.

2001, May 17 ***Perf. 14¼x14***
2651 A645 Sheet of 4, #a-d 4.50 4.50

Souvenir Sheet
Perf. 12¾x13

2652 A645 300 l shown 6.75 6.75

No. 2651 contains four 42x26mm stamps.

2001 Mediterranean Games, Tunis, Tunisia — A646

No. 2653: a, 10 l, Swimmer. b, 90 l, Runners. c, 140 l, Cyclists.
260 l, Discus thrower.

2001, June 1 ***Perf. 14¼x14***
2653 A646 Vert. strip of 3, #a-c 5.00 5.00

Souvenir Sheet
Perf. 13x12¾

2654 A646 260 l multi 5.25 5.25

No. 2654 contains one 29x25mm stamp.

History of Aviation — A647

No. 2655: a, Clement Ader's flight of Eole, Oct. 9, 1890. b, Louis Blériot's flight of Blériot IX over English Channel, July 25, 1909. c, Charles Lindbergh's solo transatlantic flight of Spirit of St. Louis, May, 1927. d, Flight over Tirana, May 30, 1925. e, Antonov AN-10, 1956. f, First Concorde flight, Feb. 9, 1969. g, First Boeing 747 flight, Jan. 22, 1970. h, First flight of Space Shuttle Columbia, Apr. 12, 1981.

2001, June 20 ***Perf. 13¾x13***
2655 A647 40 l Sheet of 8, #a-h 8.00 8.00

Bridges — A648

No. 2656: a, 10 l, Tabakeve. b, 20 l, Kamares. c, 40 l, Golikut. d, 90 l, Mesit.
250 l, Tabakeve.

2001, July 20 ***Perf. 13¾x13¼***
2656 A648 Sheet of 4, #a-d 3.25 3.25

Souvenir Sheet
Perf. 12¾x13

2657 A648 250 l shown 5.00 5.00

No. 2656 contains four 38x30mm stamps.

Coats of Arms — A649

Arms of: 20 l, Dimitri of Arber. 45 l, Balsha. 50 l, Muzaka. 90 l, George Castrioti (Skanderbeg).

2001, Sept. 12 ***Perf. 12¾x13***
2658 A649 20 l multi .50 .50
a. Booklet pane of 4 2.00
2659 A649 45 l multi 1.00 1.00
a. Booklet pane of 4 9.00
2660 A649 50 l multi 1.10 1.10
a. Booklet pane of 4 4.50
2661 A649 90 l multi 2.00 2.00
a. Booklet pane of 4 8.00
Booklet, #2658a-2661a 24.00
Nos. 2658-2661 (4) 4.60 4.60

See Nos. 2681-2684, 2709-2712, 2775.

Year of Dialogue Among Civilizations A650

Colors of denomination: 45 l, Green. 50 l, Black. 120 l, White.

2001, Oct. 6 ***Perf. 13½x14***
2662-2664 A650 Set of 3 5.50 5.50

Nobel Prizes, Cent. A651

Laureates: 10 l, Doctors Without Borders, Peace, 1999. 20 l , Wilhelm C. Roentgen, Physics, 1901. 90 l, Ferid Murad, Physiology or Medicine, 1988. 200 l, Mother Teresa, Peace, 1979.

2001, Dec. 1 ***Perf. 13¾x13¼***
2665-2668 A651 Set of 4 10.00 10.00

Costumes Type of 2001

No. 2669: a, Man from Gjakova. b, Woman from Prizren. c, Man from Shkoder. d, Woman from Shkoder. e, Man from Berat. f, Woman from Berat. g, Woman from Elbasan. h, Man from Elbasan. i, Woman from Vlore. j, Man from Vlore. k, Woman from Gjirokaster. l, Woman from Delvina.

2002, Mar. 20 Litho. ***Perf. 13x13¾***
2669 A640 30 l Sheet of 12, #a-l 8.75 8.75
Complete booklet, #2669 9.75

Cartoon Deer — A652

No. 2670: a, 50 l, Deer. b, 90 l, Deer and rabbit. c, 140 l, Deer, diff. d, 20 l, Deer and rabbit, diff.

2002, Apr. 8 ***Perf. 13x13¾***
2670 A652 Horiz. strip of 4, #a-d 7.25 7.25

Fireplaces — A653

Fireplace color: a, 30 l, Deep brown. b, 40 l, Henna brown. 50 l, Orange brown. 90 l, Chestnut.

2002, Apr. 15 Litho. *Perf. 14*
2671 A653 Sheet of 4, #a-d 4.75 4.75

Europa — A654

Designs: 40 l, High wire act. 90 l, Acrobats. 220 l, Contortionist.
350 l, Trained horse act.

2002, May 1 Litho. *Perf. 13x13¾*
2672-2674 A654 Set of 3 10.00 10.00

Souvenir Sheet
Perf. 13¾

2675 A654 350 l multi 10.00 10.00

No. 2675 contains one 37x37mm stamp.

2002 World Cup Soccer Championships, Japan and Korea — A655

Emblem, soccer ball and stylized players: 20 l, 30 l, 90 l, 120 l
360 l, Stylized player and emblem.

2002, May 6 Litho. *Perf. 13¾x13¼*
2676-2679 A655 Set of 4 6.00 6.00

Souvenir Sheet
Perf. 13

2680 A655 360 l multi 7.25 7.25

No. 2680 contains one 50x29mm stamp.

Arms Type of 2001

2002, May 12 *Perf. 13*

2681	A649 20 l Gropa	.50	.50
a.	Booklet pane of 4	2.00	—
2682	A649 45 l Skurra	1.10	1.10
a.	Booklet pane of 4	4.50	—
2683	A649 50 l Bua	1.25	1.25
a.	Booklet pane of 4	5.00	—
2684	A649 90 l Topia	2.50	2.50
a.	Booklet pane of 4	10.00	—
	Complete booklet, #2681a-2684a	22.50	
	Nos. 2681-2684 (4)	5.35	5.35

Cacti — A656

No. 2685: a, Opuntia catingola. b, Neoporteria pseudoreicheana. c, Lobivia shaferi. d, Hylocereus undatus. e, Borzicactus madisoniorum.

2002, May 17 *Perf. 14*
2685 A656 50 l Sheet of 5, #a-e 6.00 6.00

Blood Donation — A657

Letters "A," "B," and "O" with: No. 2686, 90 l, Stylized people. No. 2687, 90 l, Wings.

2002, June 16 *Perf. 13¾x14¼*
2686-2687 A657 Set of 2 4.75 4.75

Sportsmen A658

No. 2688: a, Naim Kryeziu, soccer player. b, Riza Lushta, soccer player. c, Ymer Pampuri, weight lifter.
300 l, Loro Borici, soccer player, vert.

2002, July 3 *Perf. 14¼x14*
2688 Horiz. strip of 3 3.50 3.50
a.-c. A658 50 l Any single 1.10 1.10

Size: 60x80mm
Imperf

2689 A658 300 l multi 7.00 7.00

Intl. Federation of Stamp Dealers Associations, 50th Anniv. A659

Designs: 50 l, Man, #2471. 100 l, Map of Albania, Europe, cube of blue spheres.

2002, Sept. 1 Litho. *Perf. 13¾x13¼*
2690-2691 A659 Set of 2 4.00 4.00

Anti-Terrorism — A660

Designs: 100 l, Statue of Liberty. 150 l, World Trade Center on fire.
350 l, Statue of Liberty and World Trade Center, vert.

2002, Sept. 11 *Perf. 13¾x13*
2692-2693 A660 Set of 2 8.00 8.00

Souvenir Sheet
Perf. 13

2694 A660 350 l multi 9.00 9.00

No. 2694 contains one 29x50mm stamp.

Mediterranean Sealife — A661

No. 2695: a, Caretta caretta. b, Delphinus delphis. c, Prionace glauca. d, Balaenoptera physalus. e, Torpedo torpedo. f, Octopus vulgaris.

Perf. 14¼x14¾
2002, Sept. 12 Litho.
2695 A661 50 l Sheet of 6, #a-f 12.00 12.00

Famous Albanians — A662

No. 2696: a, Tefta Tashko Koço (1910-47), singer. b, Naim Frasheri (1923-75), actor. c, Kristaq Antoniu (1909-79), singer. d, Panajot Kanaçi (1923-96), choreographer.

2002, Oct. 6 *Perf. 13¾*
2696 A662 50 l Block of 4, #a-d 5.00 5.00

Independence, 90th Anniv. — A663

Designs: 20 l, Flags of Albania and other nations. 90 l, People, Albanian flag.

2002, Nov. 28 Litho. *Perf. 13½x14*
2697-2698 A663 Set of 2 2.75 2.75

Post and Telecommunications Administration, 90th Anniv. — A664

Designs: 20 l, Satellite dish. 90 l, Telegraph, air mail envelope.

2002, Dec. 4
2699-2700 A664 Set of 2 2.75 2.75

Costumes Type of 2001

No. 2701: a, Woman from Kelmendi. b, Man from Zadrime. c, Woman from Zerqani. d, Man from Peshkopi. e, Man from Malesia e Tiranes. f, Woman from Malesia e Tiranes. g, Woman from Fushe Kruje. h, Man from Shpati. i, Woman from Myzeqe. j, Woman from Labinoti. k, Man from Korce. l, Woman from Laberi.

2003, Apr. 1 Litho. *Perf. 13¼*
2701 A640 30 l Sheet of 12, #a-l 12.00 12.00
Booklet, #2701 12.00

Characterizations of Popeye — A665

No. 2702: a, 80 l, Popeye and Olive Oyl. b, 150 l, Popeye smoking pipe. c, 40 l, Popeye and Brutus. d, 50 l, Popeye walking.

2003, Apr. 6
2702 A665 Strip of 4, #a-d 9.00 9.00

Castles — A666

No. 2703: a, 10 l, Porto Palermo. b, 20 l, Petrela. c, 50 l, Kruja. d, 120 l, Preza.

2003, Apr. 15 Litho. *Perf. 13¼*
2703 A666 Sheet of 4, #a-d 5.75 5.75

Europa — A667

Poster art: 150 l, Onufri. 200 l, Various posters.
350 l, Face from Onufri poster.

2003, Apr. 30 *Perf. 14*
2704-2705 A667 Set of 2 *10.00 10.00*

Souvenir Sheet

2706 A667 350 l multi *10.00 10.00*

First Albanian Stamps, 90th Anniv. A668

Designs: 50 l, Stamped envelopes, sheets of stamps. 1000 l, Seal of Post, Telegraph and Telephone Ministry.

2003, May 12 *Perf. 13¼*
2707-2708 A668 Set of 2 *30.00 30.00*

Arms Type of 2001

Family arms: 10 l, Arianiti. 20 l, Jonima. 70 l, Dukagjini. 120 l, Kopili.

2003, May 12

2709	A649 10 l multi	.35	.35
a.	Booklet pane of 4	1.50	—
2710	A649 20 l multi	.75	.75
a.	Booklet pane of 4	3.00	—
2711	A649 70 l multi	2.25	2.25
a.	Booklet pane of 4	9.00	—
2712	A649 120 l multi	4.00	4.00
a.	Booklet pane of 4	16.00	—
	Complete booklet, #2709a, 2710a, 27111a, 2712a	30.00	
	Nos. 2709-2712 (4)	7.35	7.35

Fruit — A669

No. 2713: a, 50 l, Punica gramatunil. b, 60 l, Citrus medica. c, 70 l, Cucumis melo. d, 80 l, Ficus.

Serpentine Die Cut 6¼

2003, May 17 **Self-Adhesive**

2713 A669 Sheet of 4, #a-d 7.25 7.25

Roman Emperors from Illyria and Coins Depicting Them — A670

No. 2714: a, Diocletian (c. 245-c. 313). b, Justinian I (483-565). c, Claudius II (214-70). d, Constantine I (the Great) (d. 337).

2003, June 20 **Litho.** ***Perf. 13¼***

2714 A670 70 l Block of 4, #a-d 8.50 8.50

Birds — A671

No. 2715: a, Ciconia ciconia. b, Aquilia chrysaetos. c, Bubo bubo. d, Tetrao urogallos.

2003, Aug. 20 ***Perf. 14½x14¼***

2715 A671 70 l Sheet of 4, #a-d 8.50 8.50

First International Soccer Match in Albania, 90th Anniv. — A672

No. 2716: a, Denomination at right. b, Denomination at left.

2003, Sept. 2

2716 A672 80 l Horiz. pair, #a-b 5.00 5.00

Paintings by Edouard Manet — A673

Designs: 40 l, Lunch in the Workshop (detail). 100 l, The Fifer.
250 l, Manet, horiz.

2003, Sept. 20 ***Perf. 14½x14¼***

2717-2718 A673 Set of 2 4.00 4.00

Souvenir Sheet

Perf. 14¼x14½

2719 A673 250 l multi 7.00 7.00

Sculptors — A674

No. 2720: a, Odhise Paskali. b, Janaq Paco. c, Llazar Nikolla. d, Murat Toptani.

2003, Oct. 6 ***Perf. 13¼***

2720 A674 50 l Block of 4, #a-d 5.75 5.75

Beatification of Mother Teresa — A675

Sculptures of Mother Teresa: 40 l, Profile. 250 l, Front view.
350 l, Mother Teresa praying.

2003, Oct. 19 ***Perf. 13¼***

2721-2722 A675 Set of 2 8.25 8.25

Souvenir Sheet

Perf.

2723 A675 350 l multi 10.00 10.00

No. 2723 contains one 40mm diameter stamp.

Natural Monuments — A676

Designs: 20 l, Divjaka Forest Park. 30 l, Fir trees, Hotova. 200 l, Fir tree, Drenova.

2003, Oct. 20 ***Perf. 13¼***

2724-2726 A676 Set of 3 7.00 7.00

Tour de France Bicycle Race, Cent. A677

Designs: 50 l, Cyclist, "100," map of France. 100 l, Cyclists, French flag.

2003, Nov. 1 ***Perf. 14¼x14½***

2727-2728 A677 Set of 2 4.25 4.25

Europa — A678

Various vacation spots with country name in: No. 2729, 200 l, White. No. 2730, 200 l, Light blue.
350 l, Orange.

2004, June 23 **Litho.** ***Perf. 13½***

2729-2730 A678 Set of 2 11.50 11.50
a. Booklet pane, 4 each #2729-2730, perf. 13½ on 3 sides 46.00 —
Complete booklet, #2730a 46.00

Souvenir Sheet

Perf. 14¼x13½

2731 A678 350 l multi 11.50 11.50

No. 2731 contains one 29x37mm stamp.
In No. 2730a, the two columns in the middle are tete-beche pairs of Nos. 2729-2730.

European Soccer Championships, Portugal — A679

Various players: 20 l, 40 l, 50 l, 200 l.
350 l, Player (37mm diameter stamp).

2004, June 24 ***Perf. 14***

2732-2735 A679 Set of 4 10.00 10.00

Souvenir Sheet

Perf.

2736 A679 350 l multi 11.50 11.50

2004 Summer Olympics, Athens — A680

Designs: 10 l, Statue of discus thrower. 200 l, Bust.
350 l, Torch bearer.

2004, Aug. 12 ***Perf. 13½***

2737-2738 A680 Set of 2 7.00 7.00

Souvenir Sheet

Perf. 13½x13¾

2739 A680 350 l multi 11.50 11.50

No. 2739 contains one 38x54mm stamp.

Prince Wilhelm zu Wied (1876-1945), Appointed Ruler of Albania A681

Designs: 40 l, With hat. 150 l, Without hat.

2004, Aug. 30 **Litho.** ***Perf. 13½***

2740-2741 A681 Set of 2 4.75 4.75

Characterizations of Bugs Bunny — A682

No. 2742 — Background color: a, 40 l, Orange. b, 50 l, Light blue. c, 80 l, Purple. d, 150 l, Green.

2004, Sept. 15

2742 A682 Horiz. strip of 4, #a-d 8.25 8.25

Icons Painted by Nikolla Onufri A683

Various saints: 10 l, 20 l, 1000 l.

2004, Oct. 3 ***Perf. 14***

2743-2745 A683 Set of 3 27.00 27.00

Souvenir Sheet

Perf. 13½x14¼

2746 A683 400 l Saint, diff. 9.75 9.75

Souvenir Sheet

Ladybugs — A684

No. 2747: a, With 12 spots, on flower. b, With 5 spots, on flower. c, With wings extended. d, On leaves.

2004, Oct. 10 ***Perf. 14***

2747 A684 80 l Sheet of 4, #a-d 8.25 8.25

Entertainment Personalities — A685

No. 2748: a, Ndrek Luca (1924-93), actor. b, Jorgjia Truja (1909-94), singer, film director. c, Maria Kraja (1911-99), opera singer. d, Zina Andri (1924-80), actress, theater director.

2004, Oct. 12 ***Perf. 13¾x13½***

2748 A685 50 l Block of 4, #a-d 7.00 7.00

Coats of Arms — A686

Designs: 20 l, Spani. 40 l, Gjuraj. 80 l, Zahariaj. 150 l, Dushmani.

2004, Oct. 25 ***Perf. 13¾x14***

2749 A686 20 l multi .50 .50
a. Booklet pane of 4 2.00 —
2750 A686 40 l multi 1.00 1.00
a. Booklet pane of 4 4.00 —

2751 A686 80 l multi 2.00 2.00
a. Booklet pane of 4 8.00 —
2752 A686 150 l multi 3.75 3.75
a. Booklet pane of 4 15.00 —
Complete booklet, #2749a-2752a 29.00
Nos. 2749-2752 (4) 7.25 7.25

Souvenir Sheet

Dahlias — A687

No. 2753: a, Pink flower with small petals, large bud in front. b, Bud in back. c, Small flower at right. d, Red flower with large petals, small bud in front.

2004, Nov. 1 ***Perf. 14***
2753 A687 80 l Sheet of 4, #a-d 8.25 8.25

Art in National Gallery — A688

No. 2745 — Art by: a, Unknown artist (Madonna and Child). b, Mihal Anagnosti. c, Onufer Qiprioti. d, Cetiret. e, Onuferi. f, Kel Kodheli. g, Vangjush Mio. h, Abdurahim Buza. i, Mustafa Arapi. j, Guri Madhi. k, Janaq Paço. l, Zef Kolombi. m, Hasan Reçi. n, Vladimir Jani. o, Halim Beqiri. p, Edison Gjergo. q, Naxhi Bakalli. r, Agron Bregu. s, Edi Hila. t, Artur Muharremi. u, Rembrandt. v, Gazmend Leka. w, Damien Hirst. x, Edvin Rama. y, Ibrahim Kodra.

2004, Nov. 20 ***Perf. 14***
2754 Sheet of 25 12.50 12.50
a.-y. A688 20 l Any single .50 .50

NATO in Kosovo, 5th Anniv. — A689

NATO emblem and: 100 l, Pennants and stars. 200 l, Doves, UN flag.
350 l, Buildings, Albanian flag.

2004, Nov. 28 ***Perf. 14¼x13½***
2755-2756 A689 Set of 2 9.25 9.25

Souvenir Sheet

2757 A689 350 l multi 11.00 11.00

Liberation From Nazi Occupation, 60th Anniv. — A690

Designs: 50 l, Two doves. 200 l, One dove.

2004, Nov. 29 ***Perf. 13¾x13½***
2758-2759 A690 Set of 2 7.75 7.75

Native Costumes Type of 2001

No. 2760: a, Woman from Gramshi (showing back). b, Woman from Gramshi (showing front). c, Woman from Korça with blue skirt. d, Man from Kolonja. e, Woman from Korça with red dress. f, Woman from Librazhdi. g, Woman from Permeti. h, Woman from Pogradeci. i, Man from Skrapari. j, Woman from Skrapari. k, Woman from Tepelena. l, Woman from Vlora.

2004, Dec. 4 ***Perf. 13½***
2760 A640 30 l Sheet of 12, #a-l 11.50 11.50
Complete booklet, #2760 11.50

Europa Stamps, 50th Anniv. (in 2006) — A691

Vignettes similar to: 200 l, #2558. 250 l, #2471, horiz.
500 l, #2675.

2005, Oct. 1 **Litho.** ***Perf. 13¾***
2761-2762 A691 Set of 2 14.50 14.50

Souvenir Sheet

2763 A691 500 l multi 16.00 16.00

No. 2763 contains one 38x38mm stamp.

A692

Europa — A693

2005, Oct. 5 ***Perf. 14x13¾***
2764 A692 200 l multi 7.00 7.00
a. Perf. 13¼x13¾ on 2 or 3 sides 7.00 7.00
2765 A693 200 l multi 7.00 7.00
a. Perf. 13¼x13¾ on 2 or 3 sides 7.00 7.00

Souvenir Sheet
Perf. 12¾x13

2766 A633 350 l Stuffed cabbage 12.00 12.00
a. Booklet pane, #2766, 3 each #2764a, 2765a 55.00 —
Complete booklet, #2766a 55.00

No. 2766 contains one 25x30mm stamp. Serial number is at top right of sheet margin on No. 2766, and on binding stub on No. 2766a. No. 2766a sold for 1650 l.

Admission to the United Nations, 50th Anniv. — A694

2005, Oct. 19 ***Perf. 12¾***
2767 A694 40 l multi 1.40 1.40

Cartoon Characters: — A695

No. 2768 — Tom & Jerry: a, 150 l, Tom. b, 40 l, Tom & Jerry. c, 50 l, Tom & Jerry, diff. d, 80 l, Jerry.

2005, Oct. 20 ***Perf. 14***
2768 A695 Horiz. strip of 4, #a-d 10.00 10.00

Paintings A696

Various unattributed paintings: a, Mountain, town and river. b, Castle and aqueduct. c, Crowd, minaret. d, Castle on mountain, people near river.

2005, Oct. 21
2769 Horiz. strip of 4 35.00 35.00
a. A696 10 l multi .35 .35
b. A696 20 l multi .65 .65
c. A696 30 l multi 1.00 1.00
d. A696 1000 l multi 32.50 32.50

Costumes Type of 2001

No. 2770: a, Man, Tirana. b, Woman, Bende Tirana. c, Woman, Zall Dajt. d, Man, Kavaje-Durres. e, Woman, Has. f, Man, Mat. g, Woman, Liqenas. h, Woman, Klenje. i, Woman, Maleshove. j, Woman, German. k, Woman, Kruje. l, Man, Reç.

2005, Oct. 24 ***Perf. 14x13¾***
2770 A640 30 l Sheet of 12, #a-l 11.50 11.50
Complete booklet, #2770 15.00

Complete booklet sold for 460 l.

2005 Mediterranean Games, Almería, Spain — A697

2005, Oct. 25 ***Perf. 14¼x13¾***
2771 Horiz. strip of 3 6.50 6.50
a. A697 20 l Runner in blocks .65 .65
b. A697 60 l Gymnastics 2.00 2.00
c. A697 120 l Relay race 3.75 3.75

Souvenir Sheet
Perf. 12¾x13

2772 A697 300 l Diver 9.50 9.50

No. 2772 contains one 50x30mm stamp.

Rotary International, Cent. — A698

Rotary International emblem and: 30 l, Map of North America. 150 l, Rays and "100 Vjet," vert.

2005, Nov. 11 ***Perf. 13¾***
2773-2774 A698 Set of 2 6.00 6.00

Arms Type of 2001

No. 2775 — Arms of: a, Bua Despots. b, Karl Topia. c, Dukagjini II. d, Engjej.

2005, Nov. 14 ***Perf. 12¾***
2775 Horiz. strip of 4 9.75 9.75
a. A649 10 l multi .35 .35
b. A649 30 l multi 1.00 1.00
c. A649 100 l multi 3.50 3.50
d. A649 150 l multi 5.00 5.00
e. Booklet pane, 4 #2775a 1.30 —
f. Booklet pane, 4 #2775b 4.25 —
g. Booklet pane, 4 #2775c 13.50 —
h. Booklet pane, 4 #2775d 20.00 —
Complete booklet, #2775e-2775h 40.00

Souvenir Sheet

Portulaca Flowers — A699

No. 2776: a, Yellow flowers. b, Three white flowers. c, Red and bright yellow flowers. d, Pink flower. e, Red flower.

2005, Nov. 17 ***Perf. 14***
2776 A699 70 l Sheet of 5, #a-e 11.50 11.50

Cycling in Albania, 80th Anniv. — A700

2005, Nov. 20 ***Perf. 13¼x13¾***
2777 Strip of 3 8.25 8.25
a. A700 50 l blue & multi 1.75 1.75
b. A700 60 l red & multi 2.10 2.10
c. A700 120 l bright red & multi 4.50 4.50

Souvenir Sheet

Skanderbeg (1405-68), National Hero — A701

No. 2778 — Various scenes of warriors in battle: a, 40 l (50x30mm). b, 50 l (50x30mm). c, 60 l (50x30mm). d, 70 l (50x30mm). e, 80 l (30mm diameter). f, 90 l (30mm diameter).

2005, Nov. 28 ***Perf. 13***
2778 A701 Sheet of 6, #a-f 14.00 14.00

End of World War II, 60th Anniv. — A702

No. 2779: a, 50 l, Doves, roses, army helmet. b, 200 l, Statues, flags, dove.

2005, Nov. 29 ***Perf. 14x13¾***
2779 A702 Horiz. pair, #a-b 9.00 9.00

Marubi Family Artists A703

No. 2780: a, Matia Kodheli-Marubi. b, Gege Marubi. c, Pjeter Marubi. d, Kel Marubi.

2005, Dec. 4
2780 Horiz. strip of 4 9.50 9.50
a. A703 10 l multi .35 .35
b. A703 20 l multi .65 .65
c. A703 70 l multi 2.25 2.25
d. A703 200 l multi 6.25 6.25

Nos. 2417, 2433, 2446, 2477, 2478, 2484, 2487, 2490-2492, 2498 and 2504 Surcharged

Methods and Perfs as Before

2006
2781 A550 on 30q #2417 *3.25* *3.25*
2782 A569 on 2 l #2478 *3.25* *3.25*
2783 A574 on 2 l #2490 *3.25* *3.25*

2784	A574	on 3 l #2491	*3.25*	*3.25*
2785	A577	on 3 l #2498	*3.25*	*3.25*
2786	A552	on 10 l #2433	*3.25*	*3.25*
2787	A572	on 18 l #2484	*3.25*	*3.25*
2788	A573	on 18 l #2487	*3.25*	*3.25*
2789	A556	on 21 l #2446	*3.25*	*3.25*
2790	A568	on 25 l #2477 (block of 4, #a-d)	*210.00*	*210.00*
2791	A574	on 25 l #2492	*3.25*	*3.25*
2792	A580	on 25 l #2504	*3.25*	*3.25*
		Nos. 2781-2789,2791-2792 (11)	35.75	35.75

Location of surcharge varies.

Visit of Pres. George W. Bush to Albania — A704

No. 2793 — Photograph of Bush in: a, 20 l, Blue. b, 40 l, Green. c, 80 l, Full color.
200 l, Statue of Liberty, flags of US and Albania, horiz.

Perf. 13¼x13½

2007, June 10 **Litho.**

2793 A704 Horiz. strip of 3, #a-c 3.50 3.50

Souvenir Sheet

Perf. 13½x13¼

2794 A704 200 l multi 5.25 5.25

Italian Delegation of Experts in Albania, 10th Anniv. — A705

Perf. 13¼x13½

2007, Sept. 15 **Litho.**

Granite Paper

2795 A705 40 l multi 1.75 1.75

Europa — A707

Men and women and: No. 2805, 200 l, Flag of European Union, map of Europe. No. 2806, 200 l, Flag and map of Albania.
350 l, Men, women, flags of Albania and European Union, horiz.

2007, Oct. 23 **Litho.** ***Perf. 13x13¼***

2805-2806 A707 Set of 2 12.00 12.00

Souvenir Sheet

Perf. 13¼x13

2807 A707 350 l multi 11.00 11.00

No. 2807 contains one 30x25mm stamp. Dated 2006.

Europa — A708

Designs: 100 l, Scouts, flags, mountain. 150 l, Scouts, flags, mountain, diff.
250 l, Knot, horiz.

2007, Oct. 24 ***Perf. 13¼x13***

2808-2809 A708 Set of 2 7.50 7.50

Souvenir Sheet

2810 A708 250 l multi 7.50 7.50

Scouting, cent. No. 2810 contains one 30x25mm stamp.

Pink Panther — A709

No. 2811 — Pink Panther: a, 150 l, Wearing uniform. b, 40 l, Wearing bowtie. c, 50 l, With inspector. d, 80 l, With elbow resting on orange panel.

2007, Oct. 25 ***Perf. 13***

2811 A709 Horiz. strip of 4, #a-d 11.00 11.00

Children's Art — A710

No. 2812 — Art by: a, 10 l, Arkida Lema. b, 40 l, Amarilda Prifti. c, 50 l, Iliaz Kasa. d, 80 l, Klaudia Mezini, horiz.

2007, Oct. 29 ***Perf. 13***

2812 A710 Horiz. strip of 4, #a-d 7.00 7.00

Frescoes — A712

Designs: 70 l, sower, by David Selenices. 110 l, Floral mural, Et'hem Bey Mosque, Tirana.

2007, Oct. 31 **Litho.** ***Perf. 13***

2814-2815 A712 Set of 2 4.75 4.75

Miniature Sheet

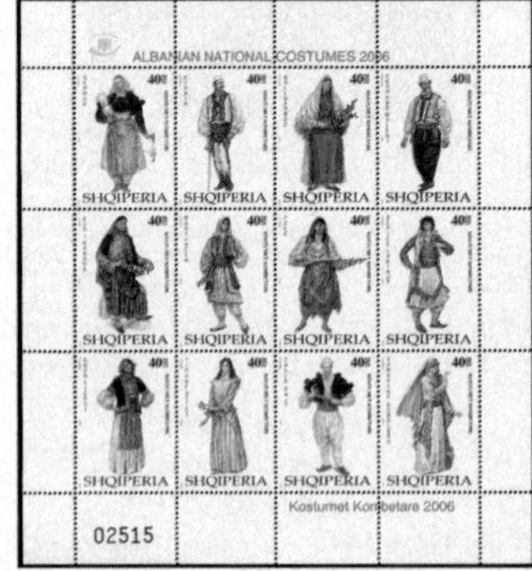

Native Costumes — A713

No. 2816: a, German woman. b, Kurbin man. c, Golloborde woman. d, Kerrabe Malesi man. e, Gur i Bardhe woman. f, Martanesh woman. g, Puke woman. h, Serice Labinot woman. i, Shen Gjergj woman. j, Tirane Qytet woman. k, Zalle Dajt man. l, Zaranike Godolesh woman.

2008, Nov. 1 **Litho.** ***Perf. 13***

2816 A713 40 l Sheet of 12, #a-l 17.00 17.00

Dated 2006. A sheet of 20 l stamps depicting native costumes with country name at left was issued on Nov. 2 in limited quantities to those with reservations to purchase the sheet, and later was sold at an inflated price.

Tourism A714

No. 2817: a, Thethi National Park (Parku Kombetar Thethit). b, Lures Lake (Liqenet e Lures). c, Kanina Castle (Kalaja e Kanines). d, Karavasta Lagoon (Laguna e Karavastase).

2007, Nov. 5

2817		Horiz. strip of 4	8.50	8.50
a.	A714	40 l green & multi	1.60	1.60
b.	A714	50 l red violet & multi	1.90	1.90
c.	A714	60 l red & multi	2.25	2.25
d.	A714	70 l blue violet & multi	2.75	2.75

Trees of Elbasan A715

Designs: 70 l, Tree and pond. 90 l, Hollowed-out tree.

2007, Nov. 8 ***Perf. 13x13¼***

2818-2819 A715 Set of 2 5.50 5.50

Dated 2006.

Pope Clement XI (1649-1721) A716

No. 2820: a, 30 l, Red background. b, 120 l, Blue background.

2007, Nov. 9 ***Perf. 13¼x13***

2820 A716 Vert. pair, #a-b 5.00 5.00

Dated 2006.

Léopold Sédar Senghor (1906-2001), First President of Senegal — A717

Color of photograph: 40 l, Sepia. 80 l, Black.

2007, Nov. 10

2821-2822 A717 Set of 2 6.00 6.00

Dated 2006.

Albania as Balkan Soccer Champions, 60th Anniv. (in 2006) — A718

Background colors: 10 l, Buff and red. 80 l, Light and dark blue.

2007, Nov. 11 ***Perf. 13x13¼***

2823-2824 A718 Set of 2 8.00 8.00

Dated 2006.

Miniature Sheet

Gjirokaster UNESCO World Heritage Site — A719

No. 2825: a, 10 l, Cannons. b, 20 l, Wall decoration. c, 30 l, Building. d, 60 l, Bridge. e, 80 l, Aerial view of town. f, 90 l, Castle atop cliff.

2007, Nov. 12 ***Perf. 13¼x13***

2825 A719 Sheet of 6, #a-f 12.00 12.00

Dated 2006.

Participation of Albanian Military in International Missions, 10th Anniv. (in 2006) — A720

Designs: 10 l, Soldier in gas mask. 100 l, Soldiers in raft.

2008, Nov. 13

2826-2827 A720 Set of 2 4.75 4.75

Dated 2006.

Mother Teresa (1910-97), 1978 Nobel Peace Laureate — A721

Background color: 60 l, Orange yellow. 130 l, Brown.

2007, Nov. 15 ***Perf. 13¼x13***

2828-2829 A721 Set of 2 8.00 8.00

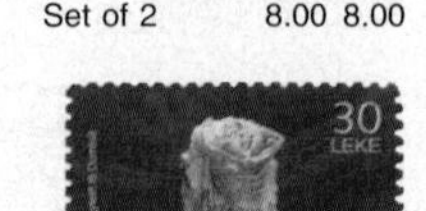

Statue of Gaia Found Near Durres — A722

No. 2831: a, 30 l, Small image of statue. b, 120 l, Large image of statue.

2007, Nov. 16 Litho. *Perf. 13¼x13*
2831 A722 Vert. pair, #a-b 10.00 10.00

A 200 l souvenir sheet issued with this set was sold in limited quantities to those with reservations to purchase the sheet, and later was sold at an inflated price. Value, $100.

Prehistoric Cave and Rock Drawings A723

Designs: 20 l, Rock drawings, Lepenice. 100 l, Rock drawing, Tren.
300 l, Cave drawing, Tren.

2007, Nov. 19 *Perf. 13¼x13*
2832-2833 A723 Set of 2 5.50 5.50

Souvenir Sheet
Perf. 13x13¼

2834 A723 300 l multi 12.50 12.50

Dated 2006.

Famous Men A724

No. 2835: a, Osman Kazazi (1917-99), resistance leader. b, Pjeter Arbnori (1935-2006), politician. c, Lasgush Poradeci (1899-1987), writer. d, Cesk Zadeja (1927-97), musician.

2007, Nov. 22 *Perf. 13¼x13*
2835 Horiz. strip of 4 8.00 8.00
a. A724 10 l multi .40 .40
b. A724 20 l multi .80 .80
c. A724 60 l multi 2.50 2.50
d. A724 100 l multi 4.25 4.25

Famous Men — A725

No. 2836: a, Abdurrahim Buza (1905-87), painter. b, Aleks Buda (1911-93), historian. c, Thimi Mitko (1820-90), writer. d, Martin Camaj (1925-94), writer.

2007, Nov. 22 *Perf. 13x13¼*
2836 Horiz. strip of 4 8.00 8.00
a.-d. A725 50 l Any single 2.00 2.00

Dated 2006.

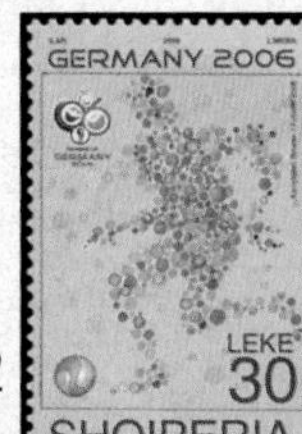

2006 World Cup Soccer Championships, Germany — A726

Stylized soccer players with background colors of: 30 l, Yellow. 60 l, Red. 120 l, Black.
350 l, Emblem of 2006 World Cup.

2007, Nov. 26
2837-2839 A726 Set of 3 10.00 10.00

Souvenir Sheet

2840 A726 350 l multi 15.00 15.00

Dated 2006.

Independence, 95th Anniv. — A727

Ismail Qemali (1844-1919), first Albanian Prime Minister and: 50 l, Heraldic eagle and years. 110 l, Text.

2007, Nov. 28 *Perf. 13x13¼*
2841-2842 A727 Set of 2 6.50 6.50

Vegetables A728

No. 2843: a, Garlic. b, Onions. c, Peppers. d, Tomatoes.

2007, Dec. 3 Litho. *Perf. 12¾*
2843 Horiz. strip of 4 + 3 labels 12.50 12.50
a.-d. A728 80 l Any single 3.00 3.00

Wulfenia Baldacci A729

2007, Dec. 4 Litho. *Perf. 13*
2844 Horiz. pair + central label 10.00 10.00
a. A729 70 l lilac & multi 3.75 3.75
b. A729 100 l buff & multi 5.25 5.25

Albanian Post and Telecommunications Department, 95th Anniv. — A730

Denomination in: 80 l, Red. 90 l, Black.

2007, Dec. 5 *Perf. 13¼x13*
2845-2846 A730 Set of 2 6.50 6.50

Miniature Sheet

Infrastructure Development — A731

No. 2847: a, 10 l, Trans-Balkan Road. b, 20 l, Port of Durres. c, 30 l, Road, Tirana. d, 40 l, Mother Teresa Terminal. e, 50 l, Road, Shkoder. f, 60 l, Tepelene-Gjirokaster Road. g, 70 l, Fier-Lushnje Road. h, 80 l, Kalimash-Morine Road.
150 l, Mother Teresa Air Terminal, Tirana.

2007, Dec. 7 *Perf. 13¼x12¾*
2847 A731 Sheet of 8, #a-h 14.00 14.00

Souvenir Sheet

2848 A731 150 l multi 4.75 4.75

Invitation to Join NATO — A732

No. 2849 — NATO emblem and: a, 40 l, Flags of member nations. b, 60 l, Heraldic eagles.

2008, Apr. 12 Litho. *Perf. 13x13¼*
2849 A732 Horiz. pair, #a-b 3.75 3.75

Children's Drawings — A733

No. 2850 — Dove and: a, 40 l, Black doves and flowers. b, 70 l, Boat on water.

2008, June 1 Litho. *Perf. 13x13¼*
2850 A733 Horiz. pair, #a-b 4.00 4.00

UEFA Euro 2008 Soccer Championships, Austria and Switzerland — A734

No. 2851: a, 50 l, Map of Switzerland. b, 250 l, Map of Austria
200 l, Mascots, vert.

2008, June 16 *Perf. 13x13¼*
2851 A734 Horiz. pair, #a-b 12.00 12.00

Souvenir Sheet
Perf. 13¼x13

2852 A734 200 l multi 7.50 7.50

Prizren League, 130th Anniv. — A735

No. 2853: a, 100 l, Handwritten document. b, 150 l, Building, Albanian flag.

2008, June 27 *Perf. 13¼x13*
Granite Paper
2853 A735 Vert. pair, #a-b 9.50 9.50

First Albanian Postage Stamps, 95th Anniv. — A736

2008, June 30 Litho.
2854 A736 40 l multi 2.00 2.00

Famous People of Albanian Heritage A737

No. 2855: a, John Belushi (1949-82), actor. b, Gjon Mili (1904-84), photographer. c, Mimar Sinan (1489-1588), architect. d, Ibrahim Kodra (1918-2006), artist.

2008, July 9 *Perf. 13x13¼*
2855 Horiz. strip of 4 7.50 7.50
a. A737 5 l multi .25 .25
b. A737 10 l multi .30 .30
c. A737 20 l multi .65 .65
d. A737 200 l multi 6.25 6.25

A738

Europa — A739

Hand holding quill pen and: 100 l, Map of Europe. 150 l, Map of Albania and Adriatic region.

2008, July 15 *Perf. 13¼x13*
Granite Paper (#2856-2857)
2856-2857 A738 Set of 2 9.50 9.50

Souvenir Sheet
Perf. 13x13¼

2858 A739 250 l multi 9.50 9.50

Poppies — A740

No. 2859: a, 50 l, Two poppies. b, 150 l, One poppy.

2008, July 30 ***Perf. 13¼x13***
Granite Paper

2859 A740 Vert. pair, #a-b 7.50 7.50

2008 Summer Olympics, Beijing — A741

No. 2860: a, Soccer. b, Water polo. c, Running. d, Cycling.

2008, Aug. 8 ***Perf. 13x13¼***

2860 Horiz. strip of 4 5.50 5.50
a. A741 20 l multi .80 .80
b. A741 30 l multi 1.10 1.10
c. A741 40 l multi 1.60 1.60
d. A741 50 l multi 2.00 2.00

Landscapes — A742

No. 2861: a, 60 l, Osumit Canyon. b, 250 l, Komanit Lake.

2008, Aug. 25 ***Perf. 13***

2861 A742 Horiz. pair, #a-b 12.00 12.00

King Zog (1895-1961) — A743

No. 2862 — Denomination color: a, 40 l, Black. b, 100 l, Red.

2008, Sept. 1 ***Perf. 13x13¼***

2862 A743 Horiz. pair, #a-b 5.50 5.50

Freedom Fighters — A744

No. 2863: a, 40 l, Azem Hajdari (1963-98), assassinated politician. b, 200 l, Adem Jashari (1955-98), Kosovar independence leader.

2008, Sept. 12

2863 A744 Horiz. pair, #a-b 9.00 9.00

Independence of Kosovo — A745

No. 2864: a, 20 l, Ymer Prizreni (1820-87), political leader. b, 30 l, Isa Boletini (1864-1916), military leader. c, 40 l, Ibrahim Rugova (1944-2006), President of Kosovo. d, 50 l, Azem Galica (1889-1924), military leader. e, 70 l, Adem Jashari (1955-98), independence leader.

2008, Sept. 20 ***Perf. 13¼x13***

2864 A745 Block of 5, #a-e, + 4 labels 7.50 7.50

Roman Emperors of Illyrian Origin — A746

No. 2865: a, 30 l, Decius (201-51). b, 200 l, Maximinus Thrax (173-238).

2008, Oct. 3 ***Perf. 13***

2865 A746 Vert. pair, #a-b 8.00 8.00

Harry Potter — A747

No. 2866 — Harry Potter and: a, 20 l, Professor Dumbledore. b, 30 l, House-elf Dobby. c, 50 l, Hermione Granger and friends. d, 100 l, Lord Voldemort.

2008, Oct. 15 ***Perf. 13x13¼***

2866 A747 Block of 4, #a-d 7.50 7.50

A booklet containing a pane of Nos. 2866a-2866d sold for 550 l.

Monastir Congress, Cent. — A748

No. 2867: a, 40 l, Building. b, 100 l, Pages with handwritten Albanian alphabet.

2008, Nov. 14 ***Perf. 13***

2867 A748 Horiz. pair, #a-b 5.25 5.25

Archaeology — A749

No. 2868: a, Ruins of synagogue, Sarande. b, Site at Orikumit. c, Site at Antigonese.

2008, Dec. 5 ***Perf. 13***

2868 Horiz. strip of 3 5.25 5.25
a. A749 10 l multi .35 .35
b. A749 50 l multi 1.90 1.90
c. A749 80 l multi 3.00 3.00

Universal Postal Union, 135th Anniv. — A750

No. 2869 — Emblems of Albania Post and UPU, world map and background color of: a, 100 l, Yellow bister. b, 200 l, Light blue, vert.

Perf. 13x13¼ (#2869a), 13¼x13 (#2869b)

2009, Oct. 9 **Litho.**

2869 A750 Pair, #a-b 10.50 10.50

Stan Laurel (1890-1965) and Oliver Hardy (1892-1957), Comedians A751

No. 2870 — Laurel and Hardy: a, 150 l, Holdings hats. b, 200 l, Wearing hats.

300 l, Laurel and Hardy wearing mortarboards, horiz.

2009, Oct. 16 **Litho.** ***Perf. 13¼x13***

2870 A751 Vert. pair, #a-b 12.00 12.00

Souvenir Sheet

Perf. 13x13¼

2871 A751 300 l multi 10.50 10.50

Weight Lifting — A752

No. 2872 — Various weight lifters and: a, 10 l, Oval with latitudinal and longitudinal lines. b, 60 l, Olympic rings. c, 120 l, Circles and stars. d, 150 l, Double-headed eagle of Albanian arms.

2009, Oct. 21 ***Perf. 13¼x13***

2872 A752 Block of 4, #a-d 12.00 12.00

European Court of Human Rights, 50th Anniv. A753

2009, Oct. 30 ***Perf. 13***

2873 A753 200 l multi 6.75 6.75

Council of Europe, 60th Anniv. A754

2009, Nov. 2

2874 A754 150 l multi 7.00 7.00

Albanian Painters — A755

No. 2875: a, 40 l, Abidin Dino (1913-93). b, 50 l, Lin Delija (1926-94). c, 60 l, Lika Janko (1928-2001). d, 150 l, Artur Tashko (1901-94).

2009, Nov. 11

2875 A755 Block of 4, #a-d 10.50 10.50

Traffic Safety — A756

No. 2876 — Traffic officer: a, 5 l, Holding matador's red cape. 1000 l, Stopping traffic.

2009, Nov. 16 ***Perf. 13¼x13***

2876 A756 Horiz. pair, #a-b *27.50 27.50*

Diplomatic Relations Between Albania and People's Republic of China, 60th Anniv. — A757

2009, Nov. 23 ***Perf. 13***
2877 A757 20 l multi .50 .50

Albanian Iso-polyphonic Singers, UNESCO Intangible Cultural Heritage — A758

No. 2878: a, 40 l, Singers. b, 250 l, Musicians.

2009, Nov. 25 ***Perf. 13¼x13***
2878 A758 Horiz. pair, #a-b 10.50 10.50

End of World War II, 65th Anniv. — A759

No. 2879 — Double-headed eagle and: a, 70 l, Soldier. b, 200 l, Bombers.

2009, Nov. 29 ***Perf. 13x13¼***
2879 A759 Horiz. pair, #a-b 8.75 8.75

Legend of Mujit and Halitit — A760

No. 2880: a, 30 l, Man being held against giant's breasts. b, 200 l, Man and woman on horse.

2009, Dec. 5
2880 A760 Horiz. pair, #a-b 8.00 8.00

Religious Art and Buildings — A761

No. 2881: a, Mosque, Berat. b, Church, Korçe. c, Church, Lezhe.

2009, Dec. 9 ***Perf. 13¼x13***

2881	Horiz. strip of 3	10.00	10.00
a.	A761 90 l multi	3.00	3.00
b.	A761 100 l multi	3.25	3.25
c.	A761 120 l multi	3.75	3.75

Europa A762

Designs: 200 l, Planets, dish antenna. 250 l, Spacecraft and exploration vehicle on Mars. 350 l, Satellite above planet.

2009, Dec. 11 ***Perf. 13x13¼***
2882 A762 200 l multi 6.75 6.75
2883 A762 250 l multi 8.25 8.25

Souvenir Sheet

Perf. 13¼x13

2884	A762 350 l multi	12.00	12.00
a.	Booklet pane, #2882-2884	27.00	—
	Complete booklet, #2884a	27.00	

Intl. Year of Astronomy. No. 2884 contains one 30x25mm stamp.

Archaeological Sites — A763

No. 2885: a, 30 l, Fort, Tirana. b, 250 l, Tomb, Kamenica.

2009, Dec. 16 ***Perf. 13***
2885 A763 Horiz. pair, #a-b 9.25 9.25

National Theater A764

No. 2886 — Scenes from plays: a, Shi ne Plazh. b, Pallati 176. c, Apologjia e Vertete e Sokratit.

2009, Dec. 21

2886	Horiz. strip of 3	10.00	10.00
a.	A764 20 l multi	.65	.65
b.	A764 80 l multi	2.60	2.60
c.	A764 200 l multi	6.75	6.75

Central State Archives, 60th Anniv. — A765

No. 2887: a, 40 l, Book, handwritten manuscript. b, 60 l, Scroll.

2009, Dec. 28
2887 A765 Horiz. pair, #a-b 3.50 3.50

Albanian-Italian Friendship — A766

2010, Apr. 12 **Litho.** ***Perf. 13***
2888 A766 40 l multi .80 .80

Mother Teresa (1910-97), Humanitarian A767

2010, Aug. 26
2889 A767 100 l multi 1.90 1.90

See Kosovo No. 154, Macedonia No. 529.

Visaless Entry Into Europe for Albanians A768

2010, Nov. 8 ***Perf. 13x13¼***
2890 A768 40 l multi .80 .80

National Library. 50th Anniv. — A769

No. 2891: a, 10 l, Man reading book. b, 1000 l, Man at computer.

2011, Feb. 18
2891 A769 Horiz. pair, #a-b 20.00 20.00

Dated 2010.

Student's Protest Movement, 20th Anniv. — A770

No. 2892: a, 40 l, Protestors, man at microphone. b, 60 l, Toppling of Enver Hoxha statue.
200 l, Students giving "V" for victory hand sign, vert.

2011, Feb. 20 ***Perf. 13***
2892 A770 Horiz. pair, #a-b 2.00 2.00

Souvenir Sheet

2893 A770 200 l multi 4.00 4.00

Dated 2010.

Europa — A771

No. 2894 — Characters from children's stories: a, 100 l, Sun, donkey and rooster. b, 150 l, Bird and cat in balloons, girl.
250 l, Girl, stack of books, horiz.

2011, Feb. 25 ***Perf. 13¼x13***
2894 A771 Vert. pair, #a-b 5.00 5.00

Souvenir Sheet

Perf. 13x13¼

2895 A771 250 l multi 5.00 5.00

Dated 2010.

Underwater Archaeology — A772

No. 2896: a, 50 l, Close-up of underwater artifact. b, 250 l, Items on seabed.

2011, Mar. 2 ***Perf. 13¼x13***
2896 A772 Horiz. pair, #a-b 6.00 6.00

Dated 2010.

2010 World Cup Soccer Championships, South Africa — A773

No. 2897 — Emblem, ball and players: a, 80 l. b, 120 l.
200 l, Two players.

2011, Mar. 10 ***Perf. 13¼x13***
2897 A773 Horiz. pair, #a-b 4.00 4.00

Souvenir Sheet

2898 A773 200 l multi 4.00 4.00

Dated 2010.

Albanian Peacekeeping Force — A774

No. 2899: a, 50 l, Helicopter, soldiers. b, 200 l, Soldier, tank.

2011, Mar. 21
2899 A774 Horiz. pair, #a-b 5.25 5.25

Dated 2010.

Lushnja Congress, 90th Anniv. — A775

No. 2900: a, 70 l, Document and seal. b, 150 l, Building.

2011, Mar. 23
2900 A775 Horiz. pair, #a-b 4.50 4.50

Dated 2010.

National Cultural Heritage Day — A776

No. 2901: a, House, Gjirokaster. b, Apron, Dumre. c, Fortress, Tirana. d, Lute, Shkoder.
200 l, Woman, Zadrime.

2011, Mar. 31 ***Perf. 13x13¼***

2901	Horiz. strip of 4	5.75	5.75
a.	A776 10 l multi	.25	.25
b.	A776 70 l multi	1.40	1.40
c.	A776 80 l multi	1.60	1.60
d.	A776 120 l multi	2.50	2.50

Souvenir Sheet

2902 A776 200 l multi 4.25 4.25

Dated 2010.

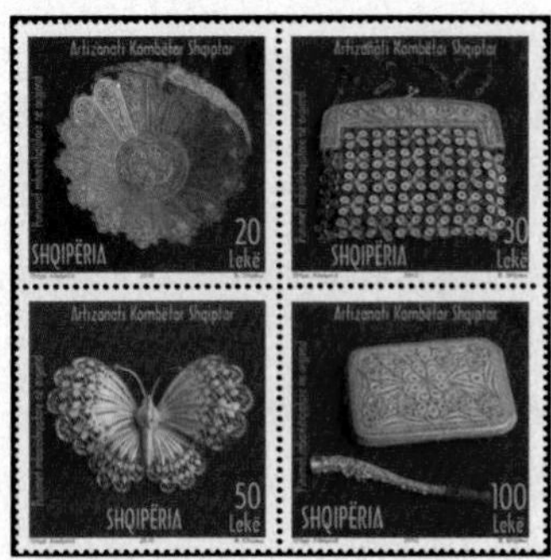

Items Made of Silver — A777

No. 2903: a, Pendant. b, Purse. c, Butterfly. d, Decorated case and cylinder with tip.
200 l, Open case and cylinder.

2011, Apr. 6 ***Perf. 13***

2903 A777 Block of 4, #a-d 4.25 4.25

Souvenir Sheet

2904 A777 200 l multi 4.25 4.25

Dated 2010.

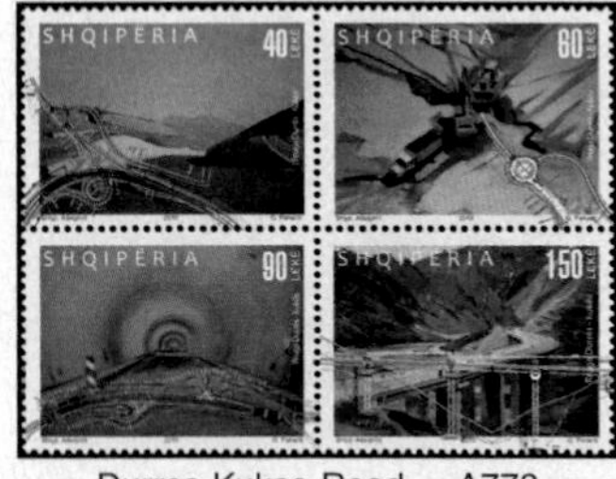

Durres-Kukes Road — A778

No. 2905 — Road design and: a, 40 l, Hills. b, 60 l, Construction equipment. c, 90 l, Tunnel. d, 150 l, Bridge.

2011, Apr. 11 ***Perf. 13x13¼***

2905 A778 Block of 4, #a-d 7.00 7.00

Dated 2010.

Miniature Sheet

Historic Center of Berati UNESCO World Heritage Site — A779

No. 2906: a, 10 l, Building. b, 20 l, Buildings on hillside, street light. c, 30 l, Bridge. d, 50 l, Archway, fence on wall, buildings. e, 60 l, Buildings on hillside. 80 l, Church.

2011, Apr. 11 ***Perf. 13x13¼***

2906 A779 Sheet of 6, #a-f 5.25 5.25

Europa — A780

Map of Europe with tree trunks and hills in: 200 l, Brown. 250 l, Green.

2011, July 30 ***Perf. 13¼x13***

2907 A780 200 l multi 4.25 4.25

Souvenir Sheet

2908 A780 250 l multi 5.25 5.25

Intl. Year of Forests.

Boxing — A781

No. 2909: a, 50 l, Boxers, boxer with red shirt at left. b, 100 l, Boxers, boxer with red shirt at right.
250 l, Boxer throwing punch.

2011, Aug. 26

2909 A781 Horiz. pair, #a-b 3.00 3.00

Souvenir Sheet

2910 A781 250 l multi 5.00 5.00

Multi-party Elections, 20h Anniv. — A782

2011, Sept. 1 ***Perf. 13x13¼***

2911 A782 150 l multi 3.00 3.00

Ismail Kadare, Writer A783

2011, Sept. 12 ***Perf. 13***

2912 A783 40 l multi .80 .80

Tourism — A784

No. 2913: a, 80 l, Valbona River and mountains. b, 120 l, Rocks in Valbona River.

2011, Sept. 27

2913 A784 Horiz. pair, #a-b 4.00 4.00

Albanian Red Cross, 90th Anniv. — A785

No. 2914 — Emblem and: a, 70 l + 10 l, Aid to pregnant woman, first aid. b, 120 l, Woman receiving two bags.

2011, Oct. 4

2914 A785 Horiz. pair, #a-b 4.00 4.00

Carrier Pigeons — A786

No. 2915 — Globe and: a, 10 l, Pigeon with mail bag. b, 1000 l, Pigeon without mail bag.

2011, Oct. 9

2915 A786 Horiz. pair, #a-b 19.50 19.50

Mosaics — A787

No. 2916 — Mosaic from: a, 20 l, St. Michael's Basilica, Arapaj. b, 60 l, Church, Antigone. c, 120 l, Mesaplikut Basilica.

2011, Oct. 14 **Litho.**

2916 A787 Horiz. strip of 3, #a-c 4.00 4.00

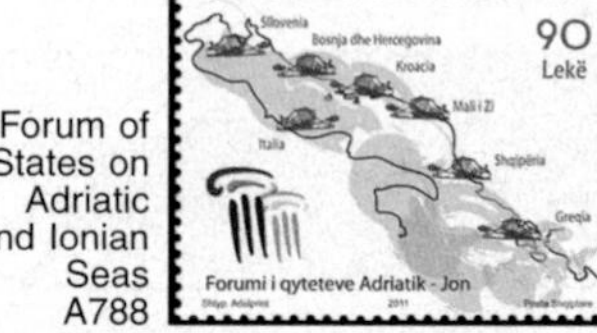

Forum of States on Adriatic and Ionian Seas A788

2011, Nov. 18 ***Perf. 13x13¼***

2917 A788 90 l multi 1.75 1.75

Flowers — A789

No. 2918: a, 30 l, Gymnospermium shqipetarum. b, 70 l, Viola kosaninii.c, 100 l, Aster albanicus subsp. paparisoi.

2011, Dec. 5 ***Perf. 13¼x13***

2918 A789 Horiz. strip of 3, #a-c 4.00 4.00

Academy of Arts, 45th Anniv. — A790

2011, Dec. 15 ***Perf. 13***

2919 A790 250 l multi 4.75 4.75

Nudes — A791

No. 2920 — Nude: a, 10 l, Painting by Vangjush Mio. b, 90 l, Painting by Abdurrahim Buza. c, 100 l, Scuplture by Janaq Paço.
250 l, Nude sculpture by Paço, diff.

2011, Dec. 22 ***Perf. 13x13¼***

2920 A791 Horiz. strip of 3, #a-c 3.75 3.75

Souvenir Sheet

2921 A791 250 l multi 4.75 4.75

Democracy in Albania, 20th Anniv. — A792

2012, Mar. 22 ***Perf. 13***

2922 A792 100 l multi 1.90 1.90

Europa — A793

No. 2923 — Various tourist attractions: a, 30 l. b, 250 l.

2012, Sept. 21 ***Perf. 13x13¼***

2923 A793 Horiz. pair, #a-b 5.25 5.25

2012 European Soccer Championships, Poland and Ukraine — A794

No. 2924 — Emblem, soccer ball, flags of European nations and large flag of: a, 100 l, Poland. b, 200 l, Ukraine.

2012, Sept. 28 ***Perf. 13***

2924 A794 Horiz. pair, #a-b 5.75 5.75

Kin Dushi (1922-94), Writer A795

2012, Oct. 3 ***Perf. 13x13¼***

2925 A795 150 l multi 2.75 2.75

Albanian Membership in Universal Postal Union, 90th Anniv. — A796

2012, Oct. 9 ***Perf. 13¼x12¾***

2926 A796 250 l multi 4.75 4.75

Revolts Against Ottoman Rule, Cent. — A797

No. 2927: a, 10 l, Rebel leader, row of rebels. b, 1000 l, Rebels.

2012, Oct. 19 *Perf. 13*
2927 A797 Horiz. pair, #a-b 18.50 18.50

Souvenir Sheet

Rock Art — A798

No. 2928 — Rock art at: a, 20 l, Rubik. b, 60 l, Boville. c, 150 l, Lepenice.

2012, Oct. 29 *Perf. 13¼x13*
2928 A798 Sheet of 3, #a-c 4.25 4.25

Linguists Who Have Studied Albanian Language A799

No. 2929: a, Eric Hamp. b, Norbert Jokl (1877-1942). c, Holger Pedersen (1867-1953).

2012, Nov. 16 *Perf. 13*
2929 Horiz. strip of 3 3.50 3.50
a. A799 50 l multi .95 .95
b. A799 60 l multi 1.10 1.10
c. A799 70 l multi 1.40 1.40

Dancers A800

No. 2930 — Dancers from: a, Tropoje. b, Tirana. c, Cameri. d, Lushnje.

2012, Nov. 23 *Perf. 13x13¼*
2930 Horiz. strip of 4 6.25 6.25
a. A800 20 l multi .40 .40
b. A800 40 l multi .75 .75
c. A800 120 l multi 2.25 2.25
d. A800 150 l multi 2.75 2.75

Independence, Cent. — A801

2012, Nov. 23 *Perf. 13¼x13*
2931 A801 40 l black & red .75 .75

Declaration of Independence, Cent. — A802

No. 2932: a, People, Albanian flag. b, People, Albanian flag, diff. c, Flags, United Nations Headquarters. d, Flags, NATO emblem.

2012, Nov. 28 *Perf. 13x13¼*
2932 Horiz. strip of 4 5.50 5.50
a. A802 50 l multi .95 .95
b. A802 60 l multi 1.10 1.10
c. A802 70 l multi 1.40 1.40
d. A802 100 l multi 1.90 1.90
e. Booklet pane of 4, #2932a-2932d 5.50 —
Complete booklet, #2932e 5.50

Albanian Army, Cent. — A803

No. 2933: a, 90 l, Soldiers in traditional costumes. b, 150 l, Soldiers wearing helmets.

2012, Dec. 4 **Litho.**
2933 A803 Horiz. pair, #a-b 4.50 4.50

Albanian Post, Telegraph and Telephone Administration, Cent. — A804

No. 2934 — Telephone, poles, wires, and: a, 80 l, Envelopes, mailbox. b, 200 l, Letter in open envelope.

2012, Dec. 5 *Perf. 13*
2934 A804 Horiz. pair, #a-b 5.25 5.25
c. Booklet pane of 2, #2934a-2934b, + 2 labels 5.25 —
Complete booklet, #2934c 5.25

Marine Life and Plants — A805

No. 2935: a, 10 l, Fish, sea grasses, diver. b, 250 l, Fish, sea grasses, coral.

2012, Dec. 14 *Perf. 13x12¾*
2935 A805 Horiz. pair, #a-b 5.00 5.00
c. Booklet pane of 2, #2935a-2935b 5.00 —
Complete booklet, #2935c 5.00

First Handstamped Envelope of Albania, Cent. — A806

No. 2936: a, 120 l, Front of addressed handstamped envelope. b, 150 l, Back of envelope, handstamp.

2013, May 5 *Perf. 13*
2936 A806 Horiz. pair, #a-b 5.25 5.25
c. Booklet pane of 2, #2936a-2936b 5.25 —
Complete booklet, #2936c 5.25

World Track and Field Championships, Moscow — A807

No. 2937: a, 30 l, Runner. b, 200 l, High jumper.
250 l, Pole vaulter.

2013, Aug. 27 **Litho.** *Perf. 13*
2937 A807 Horiz. pair, #a-b 4.50 4.50

Souvenir Sheet

2938 A807 250 l multi 4.75 4.75

Vedat Kokona (1913-98), Lexicographer — A808

2013, Aug. 30 **Litho.** *Perf. 13*
2939 A808 150 l multi 3.00 3.00

Europa — A809

No. 2940 — Globe, parcels, envelopes and: a, 80 l, Postal van and truck. b, 200 l, Airplane, train and ship.

2013, Oct. 4 **Litho.** *Perf. 13¼x13*
2940 A809 Horiz. pair, #a-b 5.50 5.50
c. Booklet pane of 2, #2940a-2940b 5.50 —
Complete booklet, #2940c 5.50

SEMI-POSTAL STAMPS

Nos. 148-151 Surcharged in Red and Black

1924, Nov. 1
B1 A18 5q + 5q yel grn 11.00 *30.00*
B2 A18 10q + 5q carmine 11.00 *30.00*
B3 A18 25q + 5q dark blue 11.00 *30.00*
B4 A18 50q + 5q dark grn 11.00 *30.00*
Nos. B1-B4 (4) 44.00 *120.00*

Nos. B1 to B4 with Additional Surcharge in Red and Black

1924
B5 A18 5q + 5q + 5q yel grn 11.00 26.00
B6 A18 10q + 5q + 5q car 11.00 26.00
B7 A18 25q + 5q + 5q dk bl 11.00 26.00
B8 A18 50q + 5q + 5q dk grn 11.00 26.00
Nos. B5-B8 (4) 44.00 *104.00*

Issued under Italian Dominion

Nurse and Child — SP1

Unwmk.

1943, Apr. 1 **Photo.** *Perf. 14*
B9 SP1 5q + 5q dark grn .75 *1.50*
B10 SP1 10q + 10q olive brn .75 *1.50*
B11 SP1 15q + 10q rose red .75 *1.50*
B12 SP1 25q + 15q saphire .75 *2.75*
B13 SP1 30q + 20q violet .75 *2.75*
B14 SP1 50q + 25q dk org 1.00 *2.75*
B15 SP1 65q + 30q grnsh blk 1.40 *4.00*
B16 SP1 1fr + 40q chestnut 3.00 *5.25*
Nos. B9-B16 (8) 9.15 *22.00*

The surtax was for the control of tuberculosis.
For surcharges see Nos. B24-B27.

Issued under German Administration

War Victims SP2

1944, Sept. 22
B17 SP2 5g + 5(q) dp grn 2.50 *17.00*
B18 SP2 10g + 5(q) dp brn 2.50 *17.00*
B19 SP2 15g + 5(q) car lake 2.50 *17.00*
B20 SP2 25g + 10(q) dp blue 2.50 *17.00*
B21 SP2 1fr + 50q dk olive 2.50 *17.00*
B22 SP2 2fr + 1(fr) purple 2.50 *17.00*
B23 SP2 3fr + 1.50(fr) dk org 2.50 *17.00*
Nos. B17-B23 (7) 17.50 *119.00*

Surtax for victims of World War II.

Independent State

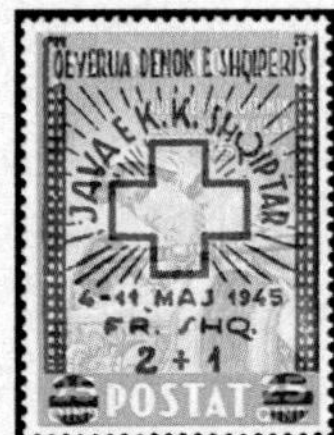

Nos. B9 to B12 Surcharged in Carmine

1945, May 4 **Unwmk.** *Perf. 14*
B24 SP1 30q +15q on 5q+5q 8.25 *13.00*
B25 SP1 50q +25q on 10q+10q 8.25 *13.00*
B26 SP1 1fr +50q on 15q+10q 21.00 *27.50*
B27 SP1 2fr +1fr on 25q+15q 29.00 *37.50*
Nos. B24-B27 (4) 66.50 91.00

The surtax was for the Albanian Red Cross.

People's Republic

Nos. 361 to 366 Overprinted in Red (cross) and Surcharged in Black

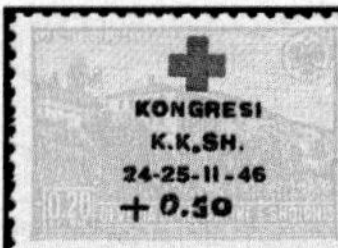

1946, July 16 *Perf. 11*

B28 A57 20q + 10q bluish grn 17.50 *30.00*
B29 A57 30q + 15q dp org 17.50 *30.00*
B30 A57 40q + 20q brown 17.50 *30.00*
B31 A57 60q + 30q red vio 17.50 *30.00*
B32 A57 1fr + 50q rose red 17.50 *30.00*
B33 A57 3fr + 1.50fr dk bl 17.50 *30.00*
Nos. B28-B33 (6) 105.00 *180.00*

To honor and benefit the Congress of the Albanian Red Cross.

Counterfeits: lithographed; genuine: typographed.

Catalogue values for unused stamps in this section, from this point to the end of the section, are for Never Hinged items.

SP3

First Aid and Red Cross: 25q+5q, Nurse carrying child on stretcher. 65q+25q, Symbolic blood transfusion. 80q+40q, Mother and child.

1967, Dec. 1 **Litho.** *Perf. 11½x12*

B34 SP3 15q + 5q blk, red & brn 1.00 .75
B35 SP3 25q + 5q multi 2.00 1.00
B36 SP3 65q + 25q multi 7.00 3.50
B37 SP3 80q + 40q multi 10.00 5.00
Nos. B34-B37 (4) 20.00 10.25

6th congress of the Albanian Red Cross.

SP4

1996, Aug. 5 **Litho.** *Perf. 13½x13*

B38 SP4 50 l +10 l multi 2.50 2.50

Albanian Red Cross, 75th anniv.

Nos. 2469-2470 Surcharged

Methods and Perfs as Before

2001, Mar. 12

B39 A567 80 l +10 l on 50 l multi 4.50 4.50
B40 A567 130 l +20 l on 100 l multi 7.50 7.50

AIR POST STAMPS

Airplane Crossing Mountains AP1

Wmk. 125

1925, May 30 **Typo.** *Perf. 14*

C1 AP1 5q green 2.25 *3.50*
C2 AP1 10q rose red 2.25 *3.50*
C3 AP1 25q deep blue 2.25 *3.50*
C4 AP1 50q dark green 3.50 *6.00*
C5 AP1 1fr dk vio & blk 6.25 *10.50*
C6 AP1 2fr ol grn & vio 10.50 *17.50*
C7 AP1 3fr brn org & dk grn 12.50 *17.50*
Nos. C1-C7 (7) 39.50 *62.00*

Nos. C1-C7 exist imperf. Value $3,000.
For overprint see Nos. C8-C28.

Nos. C1-C7 Overprinted

1927, Jan. 18

C8 AP1 5q green 5.25 *10.50*
  a. Dbl. overprint, one invtd. 50.00
C9 AP1 10q rose red 5.25 *10.50*
  a. Inverted overprint 45.00
  b. Dbl. overprint, one invtd. 50.00
C10 AP1 25q deep blue 4.75 *9.50*
C11 AP1 50q dark grn 3.25 *6.50*
  a. Inverted overprint 45.00
C12 AP1 1fr dk vio & blk 3.25 *6.50*
  a. Inverted overprint 45.00
  b. Double overprint 45.00
C13 AP1 2fr ol grn & vio 7.50 *10.50*
C14 AP1 3fr brn org & dk grn 10.50 *15.00*
Nos. C8-C14 (7) 39.75 *69.00*

Nos. C1-C7 Overprinted

1928, Apr. 21

C15 AP1 5q green 5.25 *10.50*
  a. Inverted overprint 70.00
C16 AP1 10q rose red 5.25 *10.50*
C17 AP1 25q deep blue 5.25 *10.50*
C18 AP1 50q dark green 10.00 *21.00*
C19 AP1 1fr dk vio & blk 55.00 *110.00*
C20 AP1 2fr ol grn & vio 55.00 *110.00*
C21 AP1 3fr brn org & dk grn 55.00 *110.00*
Nos. C15-C21 (7) 190.75 *382.50*

First flight across the Adriatic, Valona to Brindisi, Apr. 21, 1928.

The variety "SHQYRTARE" occurs once in the sheet for each value. Value 3 times normal.

Nos. C1-C7 Overprinted in Red Brown

1929, Dec. 1

C22 AP1 5q green 6.00 *8.75*
C23 AP1 10q rose red 6.00 *8.75*
C24 AP1 25q deep blue 6.00 *8.75*
C25 AP1 50q dk grn 125.00 *175.00*
C26 AP1 1fr dk vio & blk 225.00 *350.00*
C27 AP1 2fr ol grn 225.00 *350.00*
C28 AP1 3fr brn org & dk grn 225.00 *350.00*
Nos. C22-C28 (7) 818.00 *1,251.*

Excellent counterfeits exist.

King Zog and Airplane over Tirana AP2

AP3

1930, Oct. 8 **Photo.** **Unwmk.**

C29 AP2 5q yellow green 1.00 *1.75*
C30 AP2 15q rose red 1.00 *1.75*
C31 AP2 20q slate blue 1.00 *1.75*
C32 AP2 50q olive green 2.00 *2.75*
C33 AP3 1fr dark blue 3.00 *5.25*
C34 AP3 2fr olive brown 10.00 *17.50*
C35 AP3 3fr purple 22.50 17.50
Nos. C29-C35 (7) 40.50 *48.25*

For overprints and surcharges see Nos. C36-C45.

Nos. C29-C35 Overprinted

1931, July 6

C36 AP2 5q yellow grn 5.25 *10.50*
  a. Double overprint 140.00
C37 AP2 15q rose red 5.25 *10.50*
C38 AP2 20q slate blue 5.25 *10.50*
C39 AP2 50q olive grn 5.25 *10.50*
C40 AP3 1fr dark blue 30.00 *60.00*
C41 AP3 2fr olive brn 30.00 *60.00*
C42 AP3 3fr purple 30.00 *60.00*
  a. Inverted overprint 275.00
Nos. C36-C42 (7) 111.00 *222.00*

1st air post flight from Tirana to Rome.

Only a very small part of this issue was sold to the public. Most of the stamps were given to the Aviation Company to help provide funds for conducting the service.

Issued under Italian Dominion

Nos. C29-C30 Overprinted in Black

1939, Apr. 19 **Unwmk.** *Perf. 14*

C43 AP2 5q yel green 2.50 *7.00*
C44 AP2 15q rose red 2.50 *7.00*

No. C32 With Additional Surcharge

C45 AP2 20q on 50q ol grn 5.00 *11.50*
  a. Inverted overprint — —
Nos. C43-C45 (3) 10.00 *25.50*

See note after No. 309.

King Victor Emmanuel III and Plane over Mountains AP4

1939, Aug. 4 **Photo.**

C46 AP4 20q brown 32.50 15.00

Shepherds AP5

Map of Albania Showing Air Routes — AP6

Designs: 20q, Victor Emmanuel III and harbor view. 50q, Woman and river valley. 1fr, Bridge at Vezirit. 2fr, Ruins. 3fr, Women waving to plane.

1940, Mar. 20 **Unwmk.**

C47 AP5 5q green 1.25 *1.25*
C48 AP6 15q rose red 1.25 *1.90*
C49 AP5 20q deep blue 2.50 *3.25*
C50 AP6 50q brown 3.25 *9.50*
C51 AP5 1fr myrtle green 6.50 *12.50*
C52 AP6 2fr brown black 9.50 *19.00*
C53 AP6 3fr rose violet 16.00 *25.00*
Nos. C47-C53 (7) 40.25 *72.40*

People's Republic

Vuno-Himare AP12

Albanian Towns: 1 l, 10 l, Rozafat-Shkoder. 2 l, 20 l, Keshtjelle-Butrinto.

1950, Dec. 15 **Engr.** *Perf. 12½x12*

C54 AP12 50q gray black .25 *.80*
C55 AP12 1 l red brown .25 *.80*
C56 AP12 2 l ultra .50 *1.60*
C57 AP12 5 l deep green 1.75 *3.25*
C58 AP12 10 l deep blue 4.50 *5.50*
C59 AP12 20 l purple 9.00 8.00
Nos. C54-C59 (6) 16.25 *19.95*

Nos. C56-C58 Surcharged with New Value and Bars in Red or Black

1952-53

C60 AP12 50q on 2 l (R) 90.00 *150.00*
C61 AP12 50q on 5 l 22.50 *30.00*
C62 AP12 2.50 l on 5 l (R) 150.00 *175.00*
C63 AP12 2.50 l on 10 l 25.00 *45.00*
Nos. C60-C63 (4) 287.50 *400.00*

Issued: Nos. C60, C62, 12/26/52; Nos. C61, C63, 3/14/53.

Catalogue values for unused stamps in this section, from this point to the end of the section, are for Never Hinged items.

Banner with Lenin, Map of Stalingrad and Tanks — AP13

1963, Feb. 2 **Litho.** *Perf. 14*

C67 AP13 7 l grn & dp car 9.00 3.50

20th anniversary, Battle of Stalingrad.

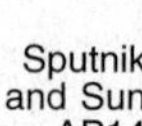

Sputnik and Sun AP14

Designs: 3 l, Lunik 4. 5 l, Lunik 3 photographing far side of the Moon. 8 l, Venus space probe. 12 l, Mars 1.

1963, Oct. 31 **Unwmk.** *Perf. 12*

C68 AP14 2 l org, yel & blk .50 .50
C69 AP14 3 l multi 1.00 .50
C70 AP14 5 l rose lil, yel & blk 1.50 .50
C71 AP14 8 l multi 2.50 1.00
C72 AP14 12 l blue & org 5.00 3.50
Nos. C68-C72 (5) 10.50 6.00

Russian interplanetary explorations.

Nos. C68 and C71 Overprinted: "Riccione 23-8-1964"

1964, Aug. 23

C73	AP14	2 l org, yel & blk	10.00	*20.00*
C74	AP14	8 l multicolored	20.00	*30.00*

Intl. Space Exhib. in Riccione, Italy.

Plane over Berat AP15

1975, Nov. 25 Litho. *Perf. 12*

C75	AP15	20q multi	.25	.25
C76	AP15	40q Gjirokaster	.50	.25
C77	AP15	60q Sarande	.80	.25
C78	AP15	90q Durres	1.50	.50
C79	AP15	1.20 l Kruje	2.00	1.00
C80	AP15	2.40 l Boga	4.00	2.00
C81	AP15	4.05 l Tirana	6.00	3.50
		Nos. C75-C81 (7)	15.05	7.75

SPECIAL DELIVERY STAMPS

Issued under Italian Dominion

King Victor Emmanuel III — SD1

1940 Unwmk. Photo. *Perf. 14*

E1	SD1	25q bright violet	4.50	*7.50*
E2	SD1	50q red orange	11.50	*18.00*

Issued under German Administration

No. E1 Overprinted in Carmine

1943

E3	SD1	25q bright violet	12.50	*24.00*

Proclamation of Albanian independence.

POSTAGE DUE STAMPS

Nos. 35-39 Handstamped in Various Colors

1914, Feb. 23 Unwmk. *Perf. 14*

J1	A3	2q org brn & buff (Bl)	10.50	4.50
J2	A3	5q green (R)	10.50	4.50
J3	A3	10q rose red (Bl)	15.00	4.50
J4	A3	25q dark blue (R)	17.50	4.50
J5	A3	50q vio & red (Bk)	26.00	14.00
		Nos. J1-J5 (5)	79.50	32.00

The two parts of the overprint are handstamped separately. Stamps exist with one or both handstamps inverted, double, omitted or in wrong color.

Nos. 48-51 Overprinted in Black

1914, Apr. 16

J6	A3 (a)	10pa on 5q green	5.25	4.50
J7	A3 (a)	20pa on 10q rose red	5.25	4.50
J8	A3 (b)	1gr on 25q blue	5.25	4.50
J9	A3 (b)	2gr on 50q vio & red	5.25	4.50
		Nos. J6-J9 (4)	21.00	18.00

Same Design as Regular Issue of 1919, Overprinted

1919, Feb. 10 *Perf. 11½, 12½*

J10	A8	(4)q on 4h rose	13.00	10.50
J11	A8	(10)q on 10k red, *grn*	13.00	10.50
J12	A8	20q on 2k org, *gray*	13.00	10.50
J13	A8	50q on 5k brn, *yel*	13.00	10.50
		Nos. J10-J13 (4)	52.00	42.00

Fortress at Scutari — D3

Post Horn Overprinted in Black

1920, Apr. 1 *Perf. 14x13*

J14	D3	4q olive green	.75	*4.50*
J15	D3	10q rose red	1.50	*6.50*
J16	D3	20q bister brn	1.50	*6.50*
J17	D3	50q black	4.00	*17.50*
		Nos. J14-J17 (4)	7.75	*35.00*

D5

Background of Red Wavy Lines

1922 *Perf. 12½, 11½*

J23	D5	4q black, *red*	1.10	*4.50*
J24	D5	10q black, *red*	1.10	*4.50*
J25	D5	20q black, *red*	1.10	*4.50*
J26	D5	50q black, *red*	1.10	*4.50*
		Nos. J23-J26 (4)	4.40	*18.00*

Same Overprinted in White

1925

J27	D5	4q black, *red*	1.90	*4.50*
J28	D5	10q black, *red*	1.90	*4.50*
J29	D5	20q black, *red*	1.90	*4.50*
J30	D5	50q black, *red*	1.90	*4.50*
		Nos. J27-J30 (4)	7.60	*18.00*

The 10q with overprint in gold was a trial printing. It was not put in use.

D7

Overprinted "QIND. AR" in Red

1926, Dec. 24 *Perf. 13½x13*

J31	D7	10q dark blue	.75	3.50
J32	D7	20q green	.75	3.50
J33	D7	30q red brown	1.50	*7.00*
J34	D7	50q dark brown	2.75	*13.00*
		Nos. J31-J34 (4)	5.75	*27.00*

Coat of Arms — D8

Wmk. Double Headed Eagle (220)

1930, Sept. 1 Photo. *Perf. 14, 14½*

J35	D8	10q dark blue	6.75	*21.00*
J36	D8	20q rose red	2.75	*13.00*
J37	D8	30q violet	2.75	*13.00*
J38	D8	50q dark green	2.75	*13.00*
		Nos. J35-J38 (4)	15.00	*60.00*

Nos. J36-J38 exist with overprint "14 Shtator 1943" (see Nos. 332-344) which is private and fraudulent on these stamps.

No. 253 Overprinted

1936 *Perf. 14*

J39	A34	10q carmine	15.00	*45.00*
a.		Hyphens on each side of "Takse" ('39)	100.00	*200.00*

Issued under Italian Dominion

Coat of Arms — D9

1940 Unwmk. Photo. *Perf. 14*

J40	D9	4q red orange	*37.50*	*75.00*
J41	D9	10q bright violet	*37.50*	*75.00*
J42	D9	20q brown	*37.50*	*75.00*
J43	D9	30q dark blue	*37.50*	*75.00*
J44	D9	50q carmine rose	*37.50*	*75.00*
		Nos. J40-J44 (5)	*187.50*	*375.00*

ALEXANDRETTA

ˌa-lig-ˌzan-ˈdre-tə

LOCATION — A political territory in northern Syria, bordering on Turkey
GOVT. — French mandate
AREA — 10,000 sq. mi. (approx.)
POP. — 270,000 (approx.)

Included in the Syrian territory mandated to France under the Versailles Treaty, the name was changed to Hatay in 1938. The following year France returned the territory to Turkey in exchange for certain concessions. See Hatay.

100 Centimes = 1 Piaster

Stamps of Syria, 1930-36, Overprinted or Surcharged in Black or Red

a

b

SANDJAK D'ALEXANDRETTE

c

d

Sandjak d'Alexandrette 2P.50

e

1938 Unwmk. *Perf. 12x12½*

1	A6 (a)	10c vio brn	3.50	3.50
2	A6 (a)	20c brn org	3.50	3.00
		Perf. 13½		
3	A9 (b)	50c vio (R)	4.50	3.50
4	A10 (b)	1p bis brn	4.50	3.00
5	A9 (b)	2p dk vio (R)	5.75	3.50
6	A13 (b)	3p yel grn (R)	9.00	7.00
7	A10 (b)	4p yel org	10.00	7.00
8	A16 (b)	6p grnsh blk (R)	12.00	8.00
9	A18 (b)	25p vio brn	25.00	25.00
10	A15 (c)	75c org red	9.00	9.00
11	A10 (d)	2.50p on 4p yel org	7.50	4.00
12	AP2 (e)	12.50p on 15p org red	20.00	15.00
		Nos. 1-12 (12)	114.25	91.50
		Set, never hinged	260.00	

Issue dates: Nos. 1-9, Apr. 14, Nos. 10-12, Sept. 2.

Nos. 4, 7, 10-12 Ovptd. in Black

1938, Nov. 10

13	A15	75c	57.50	57.50
14	A10	1p	35.00	35.00
15	A10	2.50p on 4p	30.00	30.00
16	A10	4p	35.00	35.00
17	AP2	12.50p on 15p	85.00	85.00
		Nos. 13-17 (5)	242.50	242.50
		Set, never hinged	425.00	

Death of Kemal Ataturk, pres. of Turkey.

AIR POST STAMPS

Air Post Stamps of Syria, 1937, Overprinted Type "b" in Red or Black

1938, Apr. 14 Unwmk. *Perf. 13*

C1	AP14	½p dark vio (R)	3.25	*3.75*
C2	AP15	1p black (R)	3.25	*3.75*
C3	AP14	2p blue grn (R)	4.50	*5.50*
C4	AP15	3p deep ultra	4.75	*6.00*
C5	AP14	5p rose lake	9.00	*14.00*
C6	AP15	10p red brown	9.50	*14.00*
C7	AP14	15p lake brown	12.50	*16.00*
C8	AP15	25p dk blue (R)	18.00	*22.50*
		Nos. C1-C8 (8)	64.75	*85.50*
		Set, never hinged	200.00	

POSTAGE DUE STAMPS

Postage Due Stamps of Syria, 1925-31, Ovptd. Type "b" in Black or Red

1938, Apr. 14 Unwmk. *Perf. 13½*

J1	D5	50c brown, *yel*	5.50	5.50
J2	D6	1p violet, *rose*	6.00	6.00
J3	D5	2p blk, *blue* (R)	7.50	7.50
J4	D5	3p blk, *red org*	9.00	9.00
J5	D5	5p blk, *bl grn* (R)	14.50	14.50
J6	D7	8p blk, *gray bl* (R)	20.00	20.00
		Nos. J1-J6 (6)	62.50	62.50
		Set, never hinged	200.00	

On No. J2, the overprint is vertical, reading up, other denominations, horizontal.

Stamps of Alexandretta were discontinued in 1938 and replaced by those of Hatay.

ALGERIA

al-'jir-ē-ə

LOCATION — North Africa
GOVT. — Republic
AREA — 919,595 sq. mi.
POP. — 29,300,000 (1998 est.)
CAPITAL — Algiers

The former French colony of Algeria became an integral part of France on Sept. 1, 1958, when French stamps replaced Algerian stamps. Algeria became an independent country July 3, 1962.

100 Centimes = 1 Franc
100 Centimes = 1 Dinar (1964)

Catalogue values for unused stamps in this country are for Never Hinged items, beginning with Scott 109 in the regular postage section, Scott B27 in the semi-postal section, Scott C1 in the air-post section, Scott CB1 in the air-post semi-postal section, and Scott J25 in the postage due section.

Stamps of France Overprinted in Red, Blue or Black

a

b

c

d

1924-26 Unwmk. *Perf. 14x13½*

No.	Type	Description	Unused	Used
1	A16(a)	1c dk gray (R)	.30	.30
2	A16(a)	2c violet brn	.35	.30
3	A16(a)	3c orange	.45	.30
4	A16(a)	4c yel brn (Bl)	.50	.30
5	A22(a)	5c orange (Bl)	.40	.30
6	A16(a)	5c green ('25)	.70	.55
7	A23(a)	10c green	.65	.40
b.		Booklet pane of 10	—	
		Complete booklet, 2 #7b	250.00	
8	A22(a)	10c green ('25)	.95	.40
a.		Pair, one without overprint	1,750.	
9	A20(a)	15c slate grn	.50	.30
10	A23(a)	15c green ('25)	1.10	.40
11	A22(a)	15c red brn (Bl) ('26)	.30	.30
12	A22(a)	20c red brn (Bl)	.50	.30
a.		Pair, one without overprint	1,750.	
13	A22(a)	25c blue (R)	.65	.30
a.		Booklet pane of 10	—	
		Complete booklet, 2 #13a	1,100.	
b.		Pair, one without overprint	2,100.	
14	A23(a)	30c red (Bl)	2.00	.65
15	A22(a)	30c cerise ('25)	1.20	.80
a.		"ALGERIE" double	225.00	150.00
16	A22(a)	30c lt bl (R) ('25)	.65	.40
a.		Booklet pane of 10	—	
		Complete booklet, 2 #16a	425.00	
17	A22(a)	35c violet	.70	.50
18	A18(b)	40c red & pale bl	1.00	.40
19	A22(a)	40c ol brn (R) ('25)	1.40	.85
20	A18(b)	45c grn & bl (R)	.90	.65
a.		Double overprint	350.00	
21	A23(a)	45c red (Bl) ('25)	1.25	.65
22	A23(a)	50c blue (R)	1.00	.65
23	A20(a)	60c lt violet	1.10	.65
a.		Inverted overprint		*3,900.*
24	A20(a)	65c rose (Bl)	.95	.65
25	A23(a)	75c blue (R)	1.25	.75
a.		Double overprint	325.00	325.00
26	A20(a)	80c ver ('26)	1.90	.90
27	A20(a)	85c ver (Bl)	1.60	.90
28	A18(b)	1fr cl & ol grn	1.90	.80
a.		Olive green omitted	325.00	325.00
29	A22(a)	1.05fr ver ('26)	1.75	.90
30	A18(c)	2fr org & pale bl	2.25	1.25
31	A18(b)	3fr vio & bl ('26)	4.50	2.00
a.		Blue omitted	350.00	
32	A18(d)	5fr bl & buff (R)	14.50	9.50
		Nos. 1-32 (32)	49.15	28.30

No. 15 was issued precanceled only. Values for precanceled stamps in first column are for those which have not been through the post and have original gum. Values in second column are for postally used, gumless stamps.

For surcharges see Nos. 75, P1.

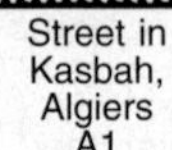

Street in Kasbah, Algiers A1

Mosque of Sidi Abd-er-Rahman A2

La Pêcherie Mosque — A3

Marabout of Sidi Yacoub A4

1926-39 Typo. *Perf. 14x13½*

No.	Type	Description	Unused	Used
33	A1	1c olive	.25	.25
a.		Imperforate	120.00	
34	A1	2c red brown	.25	.25
35	A1	3c orange	.25	.25
36	A1	5c blue green	.25	.25
37	A1	10c brt violet	.40	.25
a.		Booklet pane of 10	—	
		Complete booklet, 2 #37a	325.00	
38	A2	15c orange brn	.40	.25
a.		Imperforate	120.00	
b.		Booklet pane of 10	—	
		Complete booklet, 2 #38b	275.00	
39	A2	20c green	.40	.25
40	A2	20c deep rose	.25	.25
a.		Imperforate	130.00	
41	A2	25c blue grn	.40	.25
42	A2	25c blue ('27)	.65	.40
a.		Imperforate	130.00	
43	A2	25c vio bl ('39)	.25	.25
44	A2	30c blue	.55	.40
a.		Imperforate	130.00	
45	A2	30c bl grn ('27)	1.50	.80
46	A2	35c dp violet	1.90	1.40
47	A2	40c olive green	.55	.30
a.		Booklet pane of 10	—	
		Complete booklet, 2 #47a	250.00	
b.		Imperforate	140.00	
48	A3	45c violet brn	1.00	.40
49	A3	50c blue	.55	.40
a.		Booklet pane of 10	—	
		Complete booklet, 2 #49a	325.00	
b.		Imperforate	140.00	
c.		Vert. pair, #49 and 49b	225.00	
50	A3	50c dk red ('30)	.40	.25
a.		Booklet pane of 10	—	
		Complete booklet, 2 #50a	350.00	
b.		Imperforate	140.00	
51	A3	60c yellow grn	.55	.30
52	A3	65c blk brn ('27)	3.50	2.50
53	A1	65c ultra ('38)	.50	.30
a.		Booklet pane of 10	—	
		Complete booklet, 2 #53a	135.00	
54	A3	75c carmine	1.30	.70
a.		Imperforate	150.00	
b.		Vert. pair, #54 and 54a	240.00	
55	A3	75c blue ('29)	5.25	.75
56	A3	80c orange red	1.10	.75
57	A3	90c red ('27)	9.50	4.25
a.		Imperforate	130.00	
58	A4	1fr gray grn & red brn	1.30	.75
a.		Imperforate	180.00	
59	A3	1.05fr lt brown	1.20	.80
60	A3	1.10fr mag ('27)	9.50	3.50
61	A4	1.25fr dk bl & ultra	1.50	1.10
62	A4	1.50fr dk bl & ultra ('27)	6.25	1.00
a.		Imperforate	425.00	
63	A4	2fr prus bl & blk brn	4.50	1.00
a.		Imperforate	140.00	
64	A4	3fr violet & org	8.00	2.00
65	A4	5fr red & violet	14.50	5.00
66	A4	10fr ol brn & rose ('27)	85.00	45.00
a.		Imperforate	1,000.	
67	A4	20fr vio & grn ('27)	8.50	6.00
		Nos. 33-67 (35)	172.15	82.55

A 90c red, design A1, was prepared but not issued. Value, unused $1,000.

Type A4, 50c blue and rose red, inscribed "CENTENAIRE-ALGERIE" is France No. 255.

See design A24. For stamps and types surcharged see Nos. 68-74, 131, 136, 187, B1-B13, J27, P2.

Stamps of 1926 Surcharged

1927

No.	Type	Description	Unused	Used
68	A2	10c on 35c dp violet	.25	.25
69	A2	25c on 30c blue	.25	.25
70	A2	30c on 25c blue grn	.40	.25
71	A3	65c on 60c yel grn	1.75	1.25
72	A3	90c on 80c org red	1.50	1.10
73	A3	1.10fr on 1.05fr lt brn	1.00	.50
74	A4	1.50fr on 1.25fr dk bl & ultra	3.25	1.50
		Nos. 68-74 (7)	8.40	5.10

Bars cancel the old value on Nos. 68, 69, 73, 74.

No. 4 Surcharged

1927

No.	Type	Description	Unused	Used
75	A16	5c on 4c yellow brown	.50	.25
a.		Blue surcharge	1,400.	*1,650.*

Bay of Algiers A5

1930, May 4 Engr. *Perf. 12½*

No.	Type	Description	Unused	Used
78	A5	10fr red brown	22.50	22.50
a.		Imperf., pair	150.00	

Cent. of Algeria and for Intl. Phil. Exhib. of North Africa, May, 1930.

One example of No. 78 was sold with each 10fr admission.

Travel across the Sahara A6

Arch of Triumph, Lambese A7

Admiralty Building, Algiers A8

Kings' Tombs near Touggourt A9

El-Kebir Mosque, Algiers A10

Oued River at Colomb-Bechar A11

Sidi Bon Medine Cemetery at Tlemcen A13

View of Ghardaia A12

1936-41 Engr. *Perf. 13*

No.	Type	Description	Unused	Used
79	A6	1c ultra	.25	.25
80	A11	2c dk violet	.25	.25
81	A7	3c dk blue grn	.25	.25
82	A12	5c red violet	.25	.25
83	A8	10c emerald	.25	.25
84	A9	15c red	.25	.25
85	A13	20c dk blue grn	.55	.25
86	A10	25c rose vio	1.40	.50
87	A12	30c yellow grn	1.00	.25
88	A9	40c brown vio	.50	.25
89	A13	45c deep ultra	2.10	1.40
90	A8	50c red	1.00	.30
91	A6	65c red brn	7.50	4.25
92	A6	65c rose car ('37)	.85	.30
93	A6	70c red brn ('39)	.30	.30
94	A11	75c slate bl	.85	.30
95	A7	90c henna brn	2.50	1.40
96	A10	1fr brown	.85	.25
97	A8	1.25fr lt violet	1.45	.90
98	A8	1.25fr car rose ('39)	.80	.30
99	A11	1.50fr turq blue	2.60	.75
99A	A11	1.50fr rose ('40)	1.00	.60
100	A12	1.75fr henna brn	.55	.25
101	A7	2fr dk brown	.85	.25
102	A6	2.25fr yellow grn	24.50	15.00
103	A12	2.50fr dk ultra ('41)	.90	.60
104	A13	3fr magenta	1.20	.40
105	A10	3.50fr pck blue	6.50	5.00
106	A8	5fr slate blue	1.50	.50
107	A11	10fr henna brn	1.20	.65
108	A9	20fr turq blue	1.75	1.20
		Nos. 79-108 (31)	65.70	37.35

See Nos. 124-125, 162.

Nos. 82 and 100 with surcharge "E. F. M. 30frs" (Emergency Field Message) were used in 1943 to pay cable tolls for US and Canadian servicemen.

For other surcharges see Nos. 122, B27.

Catalogue values for unused stamps in this section, from this point to the end of the section, are for Never Hinged items.

Algerian Pavilion — A14

1937 *Perf. 13*

No.	Type	Value / Color	Unused	Used
109	A14	40c brt green	1.75	1.10
110	A14	50c rose carmine	1.75	.60
111	A14	1.50fr blue	2.50	1.20
112	A14	1.75fr brown black	2.50	1.75
		Nos. 109-112 (4)	8.50	4.65

Paris International Exposition.

Constantine in 1837 — A15

1937

No.	Type	Value / Color	Unused	Used
113	A15	65c deep rose	1.10	.85
114	A15	1fr brown	10.00	1.75
115	A15	1.75fr blue green	1.40	.85
116	A15	2.15fr red violet	1.75	.85
		Nos. 113-116 (4)	14.25	4.30

Taking of Constantine by the French, cent.

Ruins of a Roman Villa — A16

1938

No.	Type	Value / Color	Unused	Used
117	A16	30c green	1.75	.85
118	A16	65c ultra	.75	.40
119	A16	75c rose violet	1.75	.90
120	A16	3fr carmine rose	5.00	4.00
121	A16	5fr yellow brown	7.50	6.00
		Nos. 117-121 (5)	16.75	12.15

Centenary of Philippeville.

No. 90 Surcharged in Black

1938

No.	Type	Value / Color	Unused	Used
122	A8	25c on 50c red	.60	.35
a.		Double surcharge	110.00	65.00
b.		Inverted surcharge	75.00	50.00
c.		Pair, one without surcharge	425.00	

Types of 1936 Numerals of Value on Colorless Background

1939

No.	Type	Value / Color	Unused	Used
124	A7	90c henna brown	.90	.30
125	A10	2.25fr blue green	1.00	.65

For surcharge see No. B38.

American Export Liner Unloading Cargo A17

1939

No.	Type	Value / Color	Unused	Used
126	A17	20c green	2.60	1.25
127	A17	40c red violet	2.75	1.25
128	A17	90c brown black	1.60	.80
129	A17	1.25fr rose	9.00	3.00
130	A17	2.25fr ultra	2.75	2.10
		Nos. 126-130 (5)	18.70	8.40

New York World's Fair.

Type of 1926, Surcharged in Black

Two types of surcharge:
I — Bars 6mm
II — Bars 7mm

1939-40 *Perf. 14x13½*

No.	Type	Value / Color	Unused	Used
131	A1	1fr on 90c crimson (I)	.50	.35
a.		Booklet pane of 10	—	
		Complete booklet, 2 #131a	625.00	
b.		Double surcharge (I)	175.00	
c.		Inverted surcharge (I)	95.00	
d.		Pair, one without surch. (I)	*2,000.*	
e.		Type II ('40)	7.50	.80
f.		Inverted surcharge (II)	100.00	
g.		Pair, one without surch. (II)	*2,000.*	

View of Algiers — A18

1941 **Typo.**

No.	Type	Value / Color	Unused	Used
132	A18	30c ultra	.50	.30
133	A18	70c sepia	.50	.30
134	A18	1fr carmine rose	.50	.30
		Nos. 132-134 (3)	1.50	.90

See No. 163.

Marshal Pétain — A19

1941 **Engr.** *Perf. 13*

No.	Type	Value / Color	Unused	Used
135	A19	1fr dark blue	.50	.30

For stamp and type surcharged see Nos. B36-B37.

No. 53 Surcharged in Black — 136srch

1941 *Perf. 14x13½*

No.	Type	Value / Color	Unused	Used
136	A1	50c on 65c ultra	.70	.25
a.		Booklet pane of 10	—	
		Complete booklet, 2 #136a	120.00	
b.		Inverted surcharge	90.00	
c.		Pair, one without surch.	225.00	

Marshal Pétain — A20

1942 *Perf. 14x13*

No.	Type	Value / Color	Unused	Used
137	A20	1.50fr orange red	.30	.25

Four other denominations of type A20 exist but were not placed in use. Values: 4fr, $1,300; 5fr, $1,100; 10fr, 20fr, each $600.

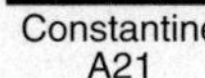

Constantine A21

Oran A22

Arms of Algiers — A23

Engraver's Name at Lower Left

1942-43 **Photo.** *Perf. 12*

No.	Type	Value / Color	Unused	Used
138	A21	40c dark vio ('43)	.70	.40
139	A22	60c rose ('43)	.55	.25
140	A21	1.20fr yel grn ('43)	.30	.25
141	A23	1.50fr car rose	.30	.25
142	A22	2fr sapphire	.80	.25
143	A21	2.40fr rose ('43)	.55	.25
144	A23	3fr sapphire	.90	.25
145	A21	4fr blue ('43)	.70	.25
146	A22	5fr yel grn ('43)	.65	.30
		Nos. 138-146 (9)	5.45	2.45

For type surcharged see No. 166.

No. 142 exists in green and violet. Value, each $60.

Imperforates

Nearly all of Algeria Nos. 138-285, B39-B96, C1-C12 and CB1-CB3 exist imperforate. See note after France No. 395.

Without Engraver's Name

1942-45 **Typo.** *Perf. 14x13½*

No.	Type	Value / Color	Unused	Used
147	A23	10c dull brn vio ('45)	.30	.25
148	A22	30c dp bl grn ('45)	.30	.25
149	A21	40c dull brn vio ('45)	.30	.25
150	A22	60c rose ('45)	.30	.25
151	A21	70c deep bl ('45)	.30	.25
152	A23	80c dk bl grn ('43)	1.20	.90
153	A21	1.20fr dp bl grn ('45)	.50	.30
154	A23	1.50fr brt rose ('43)	.30	.25
155	A22	2fr dp blue ('45)	.30	.25
156	A21	2.40fr rose ('45)	.80	.65
157	A23	3fr dp blue ('45)	.55	.40
158	A22	4.50fr brown vio	.30	.25
		Nos. 147-158 (12)	5.45	4.25

For surcharge see No. 190.

La Pêcherie Mosque — A24

1942 **Typo.**

No.	Type	Value / Color	Unused	Used
159	A24	50c dull red	.55	.25
a.		Booklet pane of 10	—	
		Complete booklet, 2 #159a	325.00	

1942 **Photo.** *Perf. 12*

No.	Type	Value / Color	Unused	Used
160	A24	40c gray green	.55	.25
161	A24	50c red	.55	.25

Types of 1936-41, Without "RF"

1942 **Engr.** *Perf. 13*

No.	Type	Value / Color	Unused	Used
162	A11	1.50fr rose	.55	.25

Typo. *Perf. 14x13½*

No.	Type	Value / Color	Unused	Used
163	A18	30c ultra	.55	.25

"One Aim Alone — Victory"
A25 A26

1943 **Litho.** *Perf. 12*

No.	Type	Value / Color	Unused	Used
164	A25	1.50fr deep rose	.55	.25
165	A26	1.50fr dark blue	.55	.25

Type of 1942-3 Surcharged with New Value in Black

1943 **Photo.**

No.	Type	Value / Color	Unused	Used
166	A22	2fr on 5fr red orange	.30	.25
a.		Surcharge omitted	325.00	

Summer Palace, Algiers A27

1944, Dec. 1 **Litho.**

No.	Type	Value / Color	Unused	Used
167	A27	15fr slate	2.00	1.75
168	A27	20fr lt blue grn	2.00	.80
169	A27	50fr dk carmine	1.60	.80
170	A27	100fr deep blue	4.00	2.50
171	A27	200fr dull bis brn	5.50	2.75
		Nos. 167-171 (5)	15.10	8.60

Marianne A28

Gallic Cock A29

1944-45

No.	Type	Value / Color	Unused	Used
172	A28	10c gray	.55	.30
173	A28	30c red violet	.30	.25
174	A29	40c rose car ('45)	.50	.30
175	A28	50c red	.50	.30
176	A28	80c emerald	.30	.25
177	A29	1fr green ('45)	.30	.25
178	A28	1.20fr rose lilac	.30	.25
179	A28	1.50fr dark blue	.30	.25
a.		Double impression	65.00	
180	A29	2fr red	.30	.25
a.		Double impression	80.00	
181	A29	2fr dk brown ('45)	.30	.25
182	A28	2.40fr rose red	.55	.25
183	A28	3fr purple	.55	.40
184	A29	4fr ultra ('45)	.30	.25
185	A28	4.50fr olive blk	.95	.70
186	A29	10fr grnsh blk ('45)	1.90	.95
		Nos. 172-186 (15)	7.90	5.20

No. 38 Surcharged in Black

1944 *Perf. 14x13½*

No.	Type	Value / Color	Unused	Used
187	A2	30c on 15c orange brn	1.20	.50
a.		Inverted surcharge	65.00	

This stamp exists precanceled only. See note below No. 32.

No. 154 Surcharged

1945

No.	Type	Value / Color	Unused	Used
190	A23	50c on 1.50fr brt rose	.55	.40
a.		Inverted surcharge	67.50	

Stamps of France, 1944, Overprinted Type "a" of 1924 in Black

1945-46

No.	Type	Value / Color	Unused	Used
191	A99	80c yellow grn	.65	.25
192	A99	1fr grnsh blue	.50	.25
193	A99	1.20fr violet	.70	.25
194	A99	2fr violet brown	.90	.25
195	A99	2.40fr carmine rose	1.20	.40
196	A99	3fr orange	1.00	.30
		Nos. 191-196 (6)	4.95	1.70

Stamps of France, 1945-47, Overprinted in Black, Red or Carmine

1945-47

No.	Type	Value / Color	Unused	Used
197	A145	40c lilac rose	.30	.25
198	A145	50c violet bl (R)	.30	.25
199	A146	60c brt ultra (R)	.95	.25
200	A146	1fr rose red ('47)	.50	.25
201	A146	1.50fr rose lilac ('47)	.50	.25
202	A147	2fr myr grn (R) ('46)	.30	.25
203	A147	3fr deep rose	.70	.25
204	A147	4.50fr ultra (C) ('47)	2.00	.25
205	A147	5fr lt green ('46)	.50	.25
206	A147	10fr ultra	1.75	.50
		Nos. 197-206 (10)	7.80	2.75

France No. 383 Surcharged and Overprinted in Black

1946

207 A99 2fr on 1.50fr henna brn .50 .25
a. Without "2F" 525.00

France Nos. 562 and 564 Overprinted in Carmine or Blue

1947

208 A153 10c dp ultra & blk (C) .30 .25
209 A155 50c brown, yel & red (Bl) .80 .30

Constantine A30

Algiers A31

Arms of Oran — A32

Perf. 14x13½

1947-49 Unwmk. Typo.

210 A30 10c dk grn & brt red .30 .25
211 A31 50c black & orange .30 .25
212 A32 1fr ultra & yellow .30 .25
213 A30 1.30fr blk & grnsh bl 1.90 1.25
214 A31 1.50fr pur & org yel .50 .25
215 A32 2fr blk & brt grn .30 .25
216 A30 2.50fr blk & brt red 1.20 .80
217 A31 3fr vio brn & grn .55 .25
218 A32 3.50fr lt grn & rose lil .55 .25
219 A30 4fr dk brn & brt grn .45 .25
220 A31 4.50fr ultra & scar .55 .25
221 A31 5fr blk & grnsh bl .30 .25
222 A32 6fr brown & scarlet 1.00 .30
223 A32 8fr choc & ultra ('48) .65 .25
224 A30 10fr car & choc ('48) 1.00 .40
225 A31 15fr black & red ('49) 1.10 .25
Nos. 210-225 (16) 10.95 5.75

See Nos. 274-280, 285.

Peoples of the World A33

1949, Oct. 24 Engr. *Perf. 13*

226 A33 5fr green 2.75 2.00
227 A33 15fr scarlet 3.50 2.00
228 A33 25fr ultra 6.00 5.25
Nos. 226-228 (3) 12.25 9.25

75th anniv. of the UPU.

Grapes — A34

25fr, Dates. 40fr, Oranges and lemons.

1950, Feb. 25

229 A34 20fr multicolored 2.75 .80
230 A34 25fr multicolored 3.25 1.25
231 A34 40fr multicolored 7.25 1.60
Nos. 229-231 (3) 13.25 3.65

Apollo of Cherchell — A35

Designs: 12fr, 18fr, Isis statue, Cherchell. 15fr, 20fr, Child with eagle.

1952 Unwmk. *Perf. 13*

240 A35 10fr gray black .65 .25
241 A35 12fr orange brn 1.25 .40
242 A35 15fr deep blue 1.10 .25
243 A35 18fr rose red 1.10 .40
244 A35 20fr deep green 1.60 .25
245 A35 30fr deep blue 1.90 .95
Nos. 240-245 (6) 7.60 2.50

War Memorial, Algiers — A38

1952, Apr. 11

246 A38 12fr dark green 2.00 .80

Issued to honor the French Africa Army.

Fossilized Nautilus — A39

Phonolite Dike A40

1952, Aug. 11

247 A39 15fr brt crimson 6.50 2.75
248 A40 30fr deep ultra 3.50 1.60

19th Intl. Geological Cong., Algiers, 9/8-15.

French and Algerian Soldiers and Camel — A41

1952, Nov. 30

249 A41 12fr chestnut brown 2.50 1.75

50th anniv. of the establishment of the Sahara Companies.

Eugène Millon A42

François C. Maillot — A43

Portrait: 50fr, Alphonse Laveran.

Unwmk.

1954, Jan. 4 Engr. *Perf. 13*

250 A42 25fr dk grn & choc 2.00 .80
251 A43 40fr org brn & brn car 3.00 1.20
252 A42 50fr ultra & indigo 3.00 .80
Nos. 250-252 (3) 8.00 2.80

Military Health Service.

Oranges — A44

1954, May 8

253 A44 15fr indigo & blue 2.00 1.20

3rd Intl. Cong. on Agronomy, Algiers, 1954.

Type of France, 1954 Overprinted type "a" in Black

Unwmk.

1954, June 6 Engr. *Perf. 13*

254 A240 15fr rose carmine 2.00 1.20

Liberation of France, 10th anniversary.

Darguinah Hydroelectric Works — A45

1954, June 19

255 A45 15fr lilac rose 1.60 1.20

Opening of Darguinah hydroelectric works.

Patio of Bardo Museum — A46

1954 Typo. *Perf. 14x13½*

257 A46 12fr red brn & brn org .80 .30
258 A46 15fr dk blue & blue .70 .25

See Nos. 267-271.

Type of France, 1954, Overprinted type "a" in Carmine

1954 Engr. *Perf. 13*

260 A247 12fr dark green 2.00 1.00

150th anniv. of the 1st Legion of Honor awards at Camp de Boulogne.

St. Augustine — A47

1954, Nov. 11

261 A47 15fr chocolate 1.60 1.25

1600th anniv. of the birth of St. Augustine.

Aesculapius Statue and El Kattar Hospital, Algiers A48

1955, Apr. 3 Unwmk. *Perf. 13*

262 A48 15fr red 1.60 .80

Issued to publicize the 30th French Congress of Medicine, Algiers, April 3-6, 1955.

Chenua Mountain and View of Tipasa A49

1955, May 31

263 A49 50fr brown carmine 1.50 .95

2000th anniv. of the founding of Tipasa.

Type of France, 1955 Overprinted type "a" in Red

1955, June 13

264 A251 30fr deep ultra 2.00 1.20

Rotary Intl., 50th anniv.

Marianne — A50

Perf. 14x13½

1955, Oct. 3 Typo. Unwmk.

265 A50 15fr carmine .80 .25

See No. 284.

Great Kabylia Mountains A51

1955, Dec. 17 Engr. *Perf. 13*

266 A51 100fr indigo & ultra 6.50 .80

Bardo Type of 1954, "Postes" and "Algerie" in White

Perf. 14x13½

1955-57 Unwmk. Typo.

267 A46 10fr dk brn & lt brn .80 .25
268 A46 12fr red brn & brn org ('56) .40 .25
269 A46 18fr crimson & ver ('57) 1.00 .30
270 A46 20fr grn & yel grn ('57) .90 .50
271 A46 25fr purple & brt purple 1.00 .25
Nos. 267-271 (5) 4.10 1.55

Marshal Franchet d'Esperey A52

1956, May 25 Engr. *Perf. 13*

272 A52 15fr sapphire & indigo 2.00 1.20

Birth cent. of Marshal Franchet d'Esperey.

Marshal Jacques Leclerc A53

1956, Nov. 29

273 A53 15fr red brown & sepia 2.00 1.60

Death of Marshal Leclerc.
For design surcharged see No. B90.

Type of 1947-49 and

Arms of Bône — A54

Arms: 2fr, Tizi-Quzou. 3fr, Mostaganem. 5fr, Tlemcen. 10fr, Setif. 12fr, Orleansville.

1956-58 Typo. *Perf. 14x13½*

274 A54 1fr green & ver .30 .25
275 A54 2fr ver & ultra ('58) 1.00 .55
276 A54 3fr ultra & emer ('58) 1.40 .30
277 A54 5fr ultra & yellow .80 .25
278 A31 6fr red & grn ('57) 1.40 .80
279 A54 10fr dp cl & emer ('58) 1.50 .90
280 A54 12fr ultra & red ('58) 1.75 .90
Nos. 274-280 (7) 8.15 3.95

Nos. 275 and 279 are inscribed "Republique Francaise." See No. 285.

View of Oran — A55

1956-58 Engr. *Perf. 13*

281 A55 30fr dull purple 1.20 .40
282 A55 35fr car rose ('58) 2.40 .80

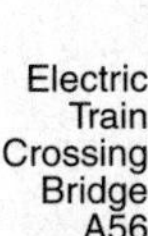

Electric Train Crossing Bridge A56

1957, Mar. 25

283 A56 40fr dk blue grn & emer 2.40 .55

Marianne Type of 1955 Inscribed "Algerie" Vertically
Perf. 14x13½

1957, Dec. 2 Typo. Unwmk.

284 A50 20fr ultra .95 .25

Arms Type of 1947-49 Inscribed "Republique Francaise"

1958, July

285 A31 6fr red & green 37.50 28.00

Independent State

France Nos. 939, 968, 945-946 & 1013 Ovptd. in Black or Red

1962, July 2
Typographed Overprint

286 A336 10c brt green .80 .50
287 A349 25c lake & gray .80 .50
288 A339 45c brt vio & ol gray 8.50 4.00
289 A339 50c sl grn & lt claret 8.50 4.00
290 A372 1fr dk bl, sl & bis 4.50 1.60
Nos. 286-290 (5) 23.10 10.60

Handstamped Overprint

286a A336 10c bright green .80 .50
287a A349 25c lake & gray .80 .50
288a A339 45c brt vio & ol gray 35.00 24.00
289a A339 50c sl grn & lt claret 35.00 24.00
290a A372 1fr dk bl, sl & bis 6.50 3.25
Nos. 286a-290a (5) 78.10 52.25

Post offices were authorized to overprint their stock of these 5 French stamps. The size of the letters was specified as 3x6mm each, but various sizes were used. The post offices had permission to make their own rubber stamps. Typography, pen or pencil were also used. Many types exist. Colors of handstamped overprints include black, red, blue, violet. "EA" stands for Etat Algérien.

Mosque, Tlemcen — A57

Roman Gates of Lodi, Médéa A58

5c, Kerrata Gorge. 10c, Dam at Foum el Gherza. 95c, Oil field, Hassi Messaoud.

1962, Nov. 1 Engr. *Perf. 13*

291 A57 5c Prus grn, grn & choc .25 .25
292 A58 10c ol blk & dk bl .25 .25
293 A57 25c sl grn, brn & ver .50 .25
294 A57 95c dk bl, blk & bis 3.00 1.00
295 A58 1fr green & blk 2.75 1.60
Nos. 291-295 (5) 6.75 3.35

The designs of Nos. 291-295 are similar to French issues of 1959-61 with "Republique Algerienne" replacing "Republique Francaise."

Flag, Rifle, Olive Branch — A59

Design: Nos. 300-303, Broken chain and rifle added to design A59.

1963, Jan. 6 Litho. *Perf. 12½*
Flag in Green and Red

296 A59 5c bister brown .25 .25
297 A59 10c blue .25 .25
298 A59 25c vermilion 2.10 .25
299 A59 95c violet 1.60 .80
300 A59 1fr green 1.50 .40
301 A59 2fr brown 3.75 .80
302 A59 5fr lilac 6.50 3.25
303 A59 10fr gray 25.00 15.00
Nos. 296-303 (8) 40.95 21.00

Nos. 296-299 for the successful revolution and Nos. 300-303 the return of peace.

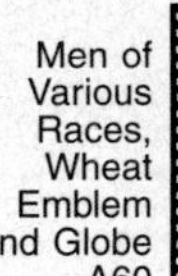

Men of Various Races, Wheat Emblem and Globe A60

1963, Mar. 21 Engr. *Perf. 13*

304 A60 25c maroon, dl grn & yel .65 .25

FAO "Freedom from Hunger" campaign.

Map of Algeria and Emblems — A61

1963, July 5 Unwmk. *Perf. 13*

305 A61 25c bl, dk brn, grn & red .65 .25

1st anniv. of Algeria's independence.

Physicians from 13th Century Manuscript — A62

1963, July 29 Engr.

306 A62 25c brn red, grn & bis 2.25 .60

2nd Congress of the Union of Arab physicians.

Orange and Blossom — A63

1963 *Perf. 14x13*

307 A63 8c gray grn & org .25 .25
308 A63 20c slate & org red .25 .25
309 A63 40c grnsh bl & org .70 .30
310 A63 55c ol grn & org red 1.25 .60
Nos. 307-310 (4) 2.45 1.40

Nos. 307-310 issued precanceled only. See note below No. 32.

Scales and Scroll A64

1963, Oct. 13 Unwmk. *Perf. 13*

311 A64 25c blk, grn & rose red .70 .35

Issued to honor the new constitution.

Guerrillas — A65

1963, Nov. 1

312 A65 25c dk brn, yel grn & car .70 .35

9th anniversary of Algerian revolution.

Centenary Emblem — A66

1963, Dec. 8 Photo. *Perf. 12*

313 A66 25c lt vio bl, yel & dk red 1.00 .65

Centenary of International Red Cross.

UNESCO Emblem, Scales and Globe — A67

1963, Dec. 16 Unwmk. *Perf. 12*

314 A67 25c lt blue & blk .70 .25

15th anniv. of the Universal Declaration of Human Rights.

Workers — A68

1964, May 1 Engr. *Perf. 13*

315 A68 50c dull red, red org & bl 1.50 .40

Issued for the Labor Festival.

Map of Africa and Flags A69

1964, May 25 Unwmk. *Perf. 13*

316 A69 45c blue, orange & car 1.00 .35

Africa Day on the 1st anniv. of the Addis Ababa charter on African unity.

Ramses II Battling the Hittites (from Abu Simbel) — A70

Design: 30c, Two statues of Ramses II.

1964, June 28 Engr. *Perf. 13*

317 A70 20c choc, red & vio bl .95 .40
318 A70 30c brn, red & grnsh bl 1.10 .55

UNESCO world campaign to save historic monuments in Nubia.

A71

5c, 25c, 85c, Tractors. 10c, 30c, 65c, Men working with lathe. 12c, 15c, 45c, Electronics center & atom symbol. 20c, 50c, 95c, Draftsman & bricklayer.

1964-65 Typo. *Perf. 14x13½*

319 A71 5c red lilac .25 .25
320 A71 10c brown .25 .25
321 A71 12c emerald ('65) .50 .25
322 A71 15c dk blue ('65) .30 .25
323 A71 20c yellow .50 .25
324 A71 25c red .50 .25
325 A71 30c purple ('65) .40 .25
326 A71 45c rose car .70 .25
327 A71 50c ultra .75 .25
328 A71 65c orange .80 .25
329 A71 85c green 1.60 .25
330 A71 95c car rose 1.90 .35
Nos. 319-330 (12) 8.45 3.10

For surcharges see Nos. 389, 424.

A72

1964, Aug. 30 Engr. *Perf. 13*
331 A72 85c Communications tower 2.00 .75

Inauguration of the Hertzian cable telephone line Algiers-Annaba.

Industrial & Agricultural Symbols — A73

1964, Sept. 26 Typo. *Perf. 13½x14*
332 A73 25c lt ultra, yel & red .60 1.25

1st Intl. Fair at Algiers, Sept. 26-Oct. 11.

Gas Flames and Pipes — A74

1964, Sept. 27
333 A74 30c violet, blue & yel .85 .50

Arzew natural gas liquification plant opening.

Planting Trees — A75

1964, Nov. 29 Unwmk.
334 A75 25c slate grn, yel & car .50 .25

National reforestation campaign.

Children and UNICEF Emblem — A76

1964, Dec. 13 *Perf. 13½x14*
335 A76 15c pink, vio bl & lt grn .50 .25

Issued for Children's Day.

Decorated Camel Saddle — A77

1965, May 29 Typo. *Perf. 13½x14*
336 A77 20c blk, red, emer & brn .70 .25

Handicrafts of Sahara.

ICY Emblem A78

1965, Aug. 29 Engr. *Perf. 13*
337 A78 30c blk, mar & bl grn 1.00 .40
338 A78 60c blk, brt bl & bl grn 1.40 .50

International Cooperation Year, 1965.

ITU Emblem A79

1965, Sept. 19
339 A79 60c purple, emer & buff 1.00 .50
340 A79 95c dk brn, mar & buff 1.40 .55

Cent. of the ITU.

Musicians A80

Miniatures by Mohammed Racim: 60c, Two female musicians. 5d, Algerian princess and antelope.

1965, Dec. 27 Photo. *Perf. 11½*
341 A80 30c multicolored 1.75 .65
342 A80 60c multicolored 2.50 1.25
343 A80 5d multicolored 14.00 7.50
Nos. 341-343 (3) 18.25 9.40

Bulls, Painted in 6000 B.C. — A81

Wall Paintings from Tassili-N-Ajjer, c. 6000 B.C.: No. 345, Shepherd, vert. 2d, Fleeing ostriches. 3d, Two girls, vert.

1966, Jan. 29 Photo. *Perf. 11½*
344 A81 1d brn, bis & red brn 4.25 2.75
345 A81 1d gray, blk, ocher & dk brn 4.25 2.75
346 A81 2d brn, ocher & red brn 10.00 4.75
347 A81 3d buff, blk, ocher & brn red 10.00 4.75
Nos. 344-347 (4) 28.50 15.00

See Nos. 365-368.

Pottery — A82

Handicrafts from Great Kabylia: 50c, Weaving, woman at loom, horiz. 70c, Jewelry.

1966, Feb. 26 Engr. *Perf. 13*
348 A82 40c Prus bl, brn red & blk .50 .35
349 A82 50c dk red, ol & ocher .65 .40
350 A82 70c vio bl, blk & red 1.40 .55
Nos. 348-350 (3) 2.55 1.30

Weather Balloon, Compass Rose and Anemometer — A83

1966, Mar. 23 Engr. Unwmk.
351 A83 1d claret, brt bl & grn 1.40 .50

World Meteorological Day.

Book, Grain, Cogwheel and UNESCO Emblem — A84

Design: 60c, Grain, cogwheel, book and UNESCO emblem.

1966, May 2 Typo. *Perf. 13x14*
352 A84 30c yellow bis & blk .50 .25
353 A84 60c dk red, gray & blk .70 .40

Literacy as basis for development.

WHO Headquarters, Geneva — A85

1966, May 30 Engr. *Perf. 13*
354 A85 30c multicolored .45 .35
355 A85 60c multicolored .85 .40

Inauguration of the WHO Headquarters, Geneva.

Algerian Scout Emblem — A86

Arab Jamboree Emblem — A87

1966, July 23 Photo. *Perf. 12x12½*
356 A86 30c multicolored .60 .40
357 A87 1d multicolored 1.75 .65

No. 356 commemorates the 30th anniv. of the Algerian Mohammedan Boy Scouts. No. 357, the 7th Arab Boy Scout Jamboree, held at Good Daim, Libya, Aug. 12.

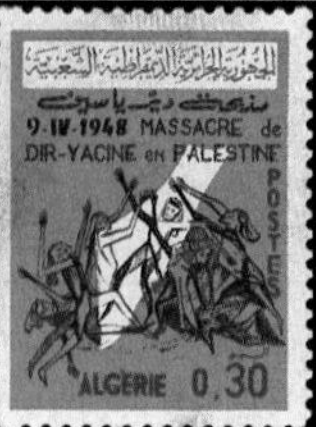
Map of Palestine and Victims A88

Abd-el-Kader A89

1966, Sept. 26 Typo. *Perf. 10½*
358 A88 30c red & black .70 .25

Deir Yassin Massacre, Apr. 9, 1948.

1966, Nov. 2 Photo. *Perf. 11½*
359 A89 30c multicolored .25 .25
360 A89 95c multicolored 1.10 .40

Transfer from Damascus to Algiers of the ashes of Abd-el-Kader (1807?-1883), Emir of Mascara. See Nos. 382-387.

UNESCO Emblem — A90

1966, Nov. 19 Typo. *Perf. 10½*
361 A90 1d multicolored 1.10 .40

20th anniv. of UNESCO.

Horseman A91

Miniatures by Mohammed Racim: 1.50d, Woman at her toilette. 2d, The pirate Barbarossa in front of the Admiralty.

1966, Dec. 17 Photo. *Perf. 11½*
Granite Paper
362 A91 1d multicolored 4.50 1.60
363 A91 1.50d multicolored 7.00 2.00
364 A91 2d multicolored 9.00 3.75
Nos. 362-364 (3) 20.50 7.35

Wall Paintings Type of 1966

Wall Paintings from Tassili-N-Ajjer, c. 6000 B.C.: 1d, Cow. No. 366, Antelope. No. 367, Archers. 3d, Warrior, vert.

1967, Jan. 28 Photo. *Perf. 11½*
365 A81 1d brn, bis & dl vio 4.50 2.00
366 A81 2d brn, ocher & red brn 7.00 4.00
367 A81 2d brn, yel & red brn 7.00 4.00
368 A81 3d blk, gray, yel & red brn 10.00 5.50
Nos. 365-368 (4) 28.50 15.50

Bardo Museum A92

La Kalaa Minaret — A93

Design: 1.30d, Ruins at Sedrata.

1967, Feb. 27 Photo. *Perf. 13*

369	A92	35c multicolored	.40	.25
370	A93	95c multicolored	.95	.50
371	A92	1.30d multicolored	1.50	.65
		Nos. 369-371 (3)	2.85	1.40

Moretti and International Tourist Year Emblem A94

Design: 70c, Tuareg riding camel, Tassili, and Tourist Year Emblem, vert.

1967, Apr. 29 Litho. *Perf. 14*

372	A94	40c multi	.70	.40
373	A94	70c multi	1.40	.60

International Tourist Year, 1967.

Spiny-tailed Agamid A95

Designs: 20c, Ostrich, vert. 40c, Slender-horned gazelle, vert. 70c, Fennec.

1967, June 24 Photo. *Perf. 11½*

374	A95	5c bister & blk	.70	.70
375	A95	20c ocher, blk & pink	1.40	.70
376	A95	40c ol bis, blk & red brn	2.10	1.00
377	A95	70c gray, blk & dp org	2.75	1.75
		Nos. 374-377 (4)	6.95	4.15

Dancers — A96

Typographed and Engraved

1967, July 4 *Perf. 10½*

378	A96	50c gray vio, yel & blk	.95	.40

National Youth Festival.

Map of the Mediterranean and Sport Scenes — A97

1967, Sept. 2 Typo. *Perf. 10½*

379	A97	30c black, red & blue	.70	.40

Issued to publicize the 5th Mediterranean Games, Tunis, Sept. 8-17.

Skiers — A98

Olympic Emblem and Sports A99

1967, Oct. 21 Engr. *Perf. 13*

380	A98	30c brt blue & ultra	1.00	.40
381	A99	95c brn org, pur & brt grn	1.75	.75

Issued to publicize the 10th Winter Olympic Games, Grenoble, Feb. 6-18, 1968.

Abd-el-Kader Type of 1966

Lithographed, Photogravure

1967-71 *Perf. 13½, 11½*

382	A89	5c dull pur ('68)	.25	.25
383	A89	10c green	.25	.25
383A	A89	10c sl grn (litho., '69)	.25	.25
383B	A89	25c orange ('71)	.35	.25
384	A89	30c black ('68)	.40	.25
385	A89	30c lt violet ('68)	.50	.25
386	A89	50c rose claret	.85	.25
387	A89	70c violet blue	1.00	.30
		Nos. 382-387 (8)	3.85	2.05

No. 383, 50c and 70c, issued Nov. 13, 1967, are on granite paper, photo. The 5c, No.383A, 25c and 30c are litho., perf. 13½; others, perf. 11½.

The three 1967 stamps (No. 383, 50c, 70c) have numerals thin, narrow and close together; the Arabic inscription at lower right is 2mm high. The 5 litho. stamps are redrawn, with numerals thicker and spaced more widely; Arabic at lower right 3mm high.

Boy Scouts Holding Jamboree Emblem A100

1967, Dec. 23 Engr. *Perf. 13*

388	A100	1d multicolored	2.00	.70

12th Boy Scout World Jamboree, Farragut State Park, Idaho, Aug. 1-9.

No. 324 Surcharged

1967 Typo. *Perf. 14x13½*

389	A71	30c on 25c red	.70	.25

Mandolin — A101

1968, Feb. 17 Photo. *Perf. 12½x13*

390	A101	30c shown	.60	.25
391	A101	40c Lute	.85	.40
392	A101	1.30d Rebec	3.00	1.10
		Nos. 390-392 (3)	4.45	1.75

Nememcha Rug — A102

Algerian Rugs: 70c, Guergour. 95c, Djebel-Amour. 1.30d, Kalaa.

1968, Apr. 13 Photo. *Perf. 11½*

393	A102	30c multi	1.10	.60
394	A102	70c multi	2.00	.95
395	A102	95c multi	3.25	2.00
396	A102	1.30d multi	3.75	1.50
		Nos. 393-396 (4)	10.10	5.05

Human Rights Flame A103

1968, May 18 Typo. *Perf. 10½*

397	A103	40c blue, red & yel	.70	.80

International Human Rights Year, 1968.

WHO Emblem A104

1968, May 18

398	A104	70c blk, lt bl & yel	.90	.40

20th anniv. of the WHO.

Welder — A105

1968, June 15 Engr. *Perf. 13*

399	A105	30c gray, brn & ultra	.50	.25

Algerian emigration to Europe.

Athletes, Olympic Flame and Rings — A106

50c, Soccer player. 1d, Mexican pyramid, emblem, Olympic flame, rings & athletes, horiz.

Perf. 12½x13, 13x12½

1968, July 4 Photo.

400	A106	30c green, red & yel	.70	.50
401	A106	50c rose car & multi	1.10	.60
402	A106	1d dk grn, org, brn & red	1.75	.95
		Nos. 400-402 (3)	3.55	2.05

19th Olympic Games, Mexico City, 10/12-27.

Scouts and Emblem — A107

Barbary Sheep — A108

1968, July 4 *Perf. 13*

403	A107	30c multicolored	.70	.25

8th Arab Boy Scout Jamboree, Algiers, 1968.

1968, Oct. 19 Photo. *Perf. 11½*

404	A108	40c shown	.85	.40
405	A108	1d Red deer	2.10	.65

Hunting Scenes, Djemila A109

"Industry" A110

Design: 95c, Neptune's chariot, Timgad, horiz. Both designs are from Roman mosaics.

Perf. 12½x13, 13x12½

1968, Nov. 23 Photo.

406	A109	40c gray & multi	.70	.25
407	A109	95c gray & multi	1.50	.55

1968, Dec. 14 *Perf. 11½*

Designs: No. 409, Miner with drill. 95c, "Energy" (circle and rays).

408	A110	30c dp orange & sil	.55	.25
409	A110	30c brown & multi	.55	.25
410	A110	95c silver, red & blk	1.40	.40
		Nos. 408-410 (3)	2.50	.90

Issued to publicize industrial development.

Opuntia Ficus Indica — A111

Flowers: 40c, Carnations. 70c, Roses. 95c, Bird-of-paradise flower.

1969, Jan. Photo. *Perf. 11½*

Flowers in Natural Colors

411	A111	25c pink & blk	.80	.50
412	A111	40c yellow & blk	1.25	.65
413	A111	70c gray & blk	2.00	.80
414	A111	95c brt blue & blk	3.00	1.25
		Nos. 411-414 (4)	7.05	3.20

See Nos. 496-499.

Irrigation Dam at Djorf Torba-Oued Guir — A112

Design: 1.50d, Truck on Highway No. 51 and camel caravan.

1969, Feb. 22 Photo. *Perf. 11½*

415	A112	30c multi	.60	.25
416	A112	1.50d multi	2.10	.80

Public works in the Sahara.

Mail Coach A113

1969, Mar. 22 Photo. *Perf. 11½*
417 A113 1d multicolored 2.75 .80

Issued for Stamp Day, 1969.

Capitol, Timgad — A114

1d, Septimius Temple, Djemila, horiz.

1969, Apr. 5 Photo. *Perf. 13x12½*
418 A114 30c gray & multi .60 .25
419 A114 1d gray & multi 1.40 .50

Second Timgad Festival, Apr. 4-8.

ILO Emblem A115

1969, May 24 Photo. *Perf. 11½*
420 A115 95c dp car, yel & blk 1.25 .50

50th anniv. of the ILO.

Arabian Saddle — A116

Algerian Handicrafts: 30c, Bookcase. 60c, Decorated copper plate.

1969, June 28 Photo. *Perf. 12x12½*
Granite Paper
421 A116 30c multicolored .40 .25
422 A116 60c multicolored .85 .35
423 A116 1d multicolored 1.50 .65
Nos. 421-423 (3) 2.75 1.25

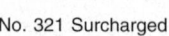

No. 321 Surcharged

1969 Typo. *Perf. 14x13½*
424 A71 20c on 12c emerald .55 .25

Pan-African Culture Festival Emblem — A117

1969, July 19 Photo. *Perf. 12½*
425 A117 30c multicolored .50 .25

1st Pan-African Culture Festival, Algiers, 7/21-8/1.

African Development Bank Emblem — A118

1969, Aug. 23 Typo. *Perf. 10½*
426 A118 30c dull blue, yel & blk .55 .25

5th anniv. of the African Development Bank.

Astronauts and Landing Module on Moon — A119

Perf. 12½x11½
1969, Aug. 23 Photo.
427 A119 50c gold & multi 1.25 .50

Man's 1st landing on the moon, July 20, 1969. US astronauts Neil A. Armstrong and Col. Edwin E. Aldrin, Jr., with Lieut. Col. Michael Collins piloting Apollo 11.

Algerian Women, by Dinet — A120

1.50d, The Watchmen, by Etienne Dinet.

1969, Nov. 29 Photo. *Perf. 14½*
428 A120 1d multi 2.25 .80
429 A120 1.50d multi 2.75 1.25

Mother and Child — A121

1969, Dec. 27 Photo. *Perf. 11½*
430 A121 30c multicolored .70 .40

Issued to promote mother and child protection.

Agricultural Growth Chart, Tractor and Dam A122

30c, Transportation and development. 50c, Abstract symbols of industrialization.

1970, Jan. 31 Photo. *Perf. 12½*
Size: 37x23mm
431 A122 25c dk brn, yel & org .25 .25

Litho. *Perf. 14*
Size: 49x23mm
432 A122 30c blue & multi .75 .25

Photo. *Perf. 12½*
Size: 37x23mm
433 A122 50c rose lilac & blk .50 .25
Nos. 431-433 (3) 1.50 .75

Four-Year Development Plan.

Old and New Mail Delivery — A123

Spiny Lobster — A124

1970, Feb. 28 Photo. *Perf. 11½*
Granite Paper
434 A123 30c multicolored .70 .25

Issued for Stamp Day.

1970, Mar. 28

Designs: 40c, Mollusks. 75c, Retepora cellulosa. 1d, Red coral.

435 A124 30c ocher & multi .70 .25
436 A124 40c multicolored 1.00 .40
437 A124 75c ultra & multi 1.75 .55
438 A124 1d lt blue & multi 2.50 .80
Nos. 435-438 (4) 5.95 2.00

Oranges, EXPO '70 Emblem A125

Designs (EXPO '70 Emblem and): 60c, Algerian pavilion. 70c, Grapes.

1970, Apr. 25 Photo. *Perf. 12½x12*
439 A125 30c lt blue, grn & org .70 .25
440 A125 60c multicolored .70 .40
441 A125 70c multicolored 1.40 .60
Nos. 439-441 (3) 2.80 1.25

EXPO '70 International Exhibition, Osaka, Japan, Mar. 15-Sept. 13, 1970.

Olives, Oil Bottle — A126

1970, May 16 Photo. *Perf. 12½x12*
442 A126 1d yellow & multi 2.00 .80

Olive Year, 1969-1970.

Common Design Types pictured following the introduction.

UPU Headquarters Issue
Common Design Type

1970, May 30 *Perf. 13*
Size: 36x26mm
443 CD133 75c multicolored 1.10 .40

Saber — A127

Designs: 40c, Guns, 18th century, horiz. 1d, Pistol, 18th century, horiz.

1970, June 27 Photo. *Perf. 12½*
444 A127 40c yellow & multi 1.25 .60
445 A127 75c red & multi 1.60 .80
446 A127 1d multicolored 2.40 1.10
Nos. 444-446 (3) 5.25 2.50

Map of Arab Countries and Arab League Flag A128

Typographed and Engraved
1970, July 25 *Perf. 10½*
447 A128 30c grn, ocher & lt bl .60 .25

25th anniversary of the Arab League.

Lenin — A129

1970, Aug. 29 Litho. *Perf. 11½x12*
448 A129 30c brown & buff 2.75 .40

Lenin (1870-1924), Russian communist leader.

Exhibition Hall and Algiers Fair Emblem — A130

1970, Sept. 11 Engr. *Perf. 14x13½*
449 A130 60c lt olive green .65 .30

New Exhibition Hall for Algiers Intl. Fair.

Education Year Emblem, Blackboard, Atom Symbol — A131

Koran Page — A132

1970, Oct. 24 Photo. *Perf. 14*
450 A131 30c pink, blk, gold & lt bl .50 .25
451 A132 3d multicolored 4.00 1.75

Issued for International Education Year.

Great Mosque, Tlemcen A133

Design: 40c, Ketchaoua Mosque, Algiers, vert. 1d, Mosque, Sidi-Okba, vert.

1970-71 Litho. *Perf. 14*

456 A133 30c multicolored .40 .25

457 A133 40c sepia & lemon ('71) .50 .25

458 A133 1d multicolored 1.00 .40

Nos. 456-458 (3) 1.90 .90

Symbols of the Arts A134

1970, Dec. 26 Photo. *Perf. 13x12½*

459 A134 1d grn, lt grn & org 1.10 .50

Main Post Office, Algiers A135

1971, Jan. 23 *Perf. 11½*

460 A135 30c multicolored 1.10 .40

Stamp Day, 1971.

Hurdling A136

40c, Vaulting, vert. 75c, Basketball, vert.

1971, Mar. 7 Photo. *Perf. 11½*

461 A136 20c lt blue & slate .50 .25

462 A136 40c lt ol grn & slate .60 .40

463 A136 75c salmon pink & slate 1.00 .60

Nos. 461-463 (3) 2.10 1.25

Mediterranean Games, Izmir, Turkey, Oct. 1971.

Symbolic Head — A137

1971, Mar. 27 *Perf. 12½*

464 A137 60c car rose, blk & sil .70 .30

Intl. year against racial discrimination.

Emblem and Technicians A138

1971, Apr. 24 Photo. *Perf. 12½x12*

465 A138 70c cl, org & bluish blk .75 .30

Founding of the Institute of Technology.

Woman from Aurès — A139

Regional Costumes: 70c, Man from Oran. 80c, Man from Algiers. 90c, Woman from Amour Mountains.

1971, Oct. 16 *Perf. 11½*

466 A139 50c gold & multi 1.25 .50

467 A139 70c gold & multi 1.50 .80

468 A139 80c gold & multi 2.00 .95

469 A139 90c gold & multi 2.40 1.00

Nos. 466-469 (4) 7.15 3.25

See Nos. 485-488, 534-537.

UNICEF Emblem, Birds and Plants — A140

1971, Dec. 6 *Perf. 11½*

470 A140 60c multicolored .80 .50

25th anniv. of UNICEF.

Lion of St. Mark A141

1.15d, Bridge of Sighs, Venice, vert.

1972, Jan. 24 Litho. *Perf. 12*

471 A141 80c multi 1.25 .55

472 A141 1.15d multi 2.50 .95

UNESCO campaign to save Venice.

Javelin — A142

Book and Book Year Emblem — A143

Designs: 25c, Bicycling, horiz. 60c, Wrestling. 1d, Gymnast on rings.

1972, Mar. 25 Photo. *Perf. 11½*

473 A142 25c maroon & multi .40 .25

474 A142 40c ocher & multi .50 .25

475 A142 60c ultra & multi 1.10 .50

476 A142 1d rose & multi 1.50 .55

Nos. 473-476 (4) 3.50 1.55

20th Olympic Games, Munich, 8/26-9/11.

1972, Apr. 15

477 A143 1.15d bister, brn & red .85 .50

International Book Year 1972.

Mailmen A144

Flowers A145

1972, Apr. 22

478 A144 40c gray & multi .70 .25

Stamp Day 1972.

1972, May 27

479 A145 50c Jasmine .65 .40

480 A145 60c Violets .65 .50

481 A145 1.15d Tuberose 1.75 .65

Nos. 479-481 (3) 3.05 1.55

Olympic Stadium, Chéraga A146

1972, June 10

482 A146 50c gray, choc & grn .70 .40

New Day, Algerian Flag — A147

1972, July 5

483 A147 1d green & multi 1.25 .65

10th anniversary of independence.

Festival Emblem — A148

1972, July 5 Litho. *Perf. 10½*

484 A148 40c grn, dk brn & org .60 .25

1st Arab Youth Festival, Algiers, July 5-11.

Costume Type of 1971

Regional Costumes: 50c, Woman from Hoggar. 60c, Kabyle woman. 70c, Man from Mzab. 90c, Woman from Tlemcen.

1972, Nov. 18 Photo. *Perf. 11½*

485 A139 50c gold & multi 1.60 .65

486 A139 60c gold & multi 1.75 .65

487 A139 70c gold & multi 2.25 .95

488 A139 90c gold & multi 2.50 1.10

Nos. 485-488 (4) 8.10 3.35

Mailing a Letter — A149

1973, Jan. 20 Photo. *Perf. 11*

489 A149 40c orange & multi .50 .25

Stamp Day.

Ho Chi Minh, Map of Viet Nam — A150

1973, Feb. 17 Photo. *Perf. 11½*

490 A150 40c multicolored .90 .35

To honor the people of Viet Nam.

Embroidery from Annaba A151

Designs: 60c, Tree of Life pattern from Algiers. 80c, Constantine embroidery.

1973, Feb. 24

491 A151 40c gray & multi .60 .30

492 A151 60c blue and multi .90 .50

493 A151 80c dk red, gold & blk 1.40 .65

Nos. 491-493 (3) 2.90 1.45

Stylized Globe and Wheat — A152

1973, Mar. 26 Photo. *Perf. 11½*

494 A152 1.15d brt rose lil, org & grn .90 .35

World Food Program, 10th anniversary.

Soldier and Flag A153

1973, Apr. 23 Photo. *Perf. 14x13½*

495 A153 40c multicolored .60 .25

Honoring the National Service.

Flower Type of 1969

30c, Opuntia ficus indica. 40c, Roses. 1d, Carnations. 1.15d, Bird-of-paradise flower.

1973, May 21 Photo. *Perf. 11½*

Flowers in Natural Colors

496 A111 30c pink & blk .70 .25

497 A111 40c gray & blk .80 .40

498 A111 1d yellow & multi 1.90 .65

499 A111 1.15d multi 2.50 .90

Nos. 496-499 (4) 5.90 2.20

For overprints and surcharges see Nos. 518-519, 531.

OAU Emblem — A154

1973, May 28 Photo. ***Perf. 12½x13***
500 A154 40c multicolored .60 .25

Org. for African Unity, 10th anniv.

Desert and Fruitful Land, Farmer and Family A155

1973, June 18 ***Perf. 11½***
501 A155 40c gold & multi .70 .25

Agricultural revolution.

Map of Africa, Scout Emblem — A156

1973, July 16 Litho. ***Perf. 10½***
502 A156 80c purple .70 .40

24th Boy Scout World Conference (1st in Africa), Nairobi, Kenya, July 16-21.

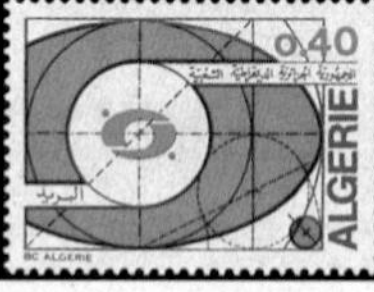

Algerian PTT Emblem A157

1973, Aug. 6 ***Perf. 14***
503 A157 40c blue & orange .50 .25

Adoption of new emblem for Post, Telegraph and Telephone System.

Conference Emblem — A158

Perf. 13½x12½
1973, Sept. 5 Photo.
504 A158 40c dp rose & multi .50 .30
505 A158 80c blue grn & multi .90 .40

4th Summit Conference of Non-aligned Nations, Algiers, Sept. 5-9.

Port of Skikda A159

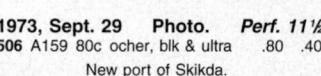

1973, Sept. 29 Photo. ***Perf. 11½***
506 A159 80c ocher, blk & ultra .80 .40

New port of Skikda.

Young Workers — A160

1973, Oct. 22 Photo. ***Perf. 13***
507 A160 40c multicolored .60 .25

Voluntary work service.

Arms of Algiers A161

1973, Dec. 22 Photo. ***Perf. 13***
508 A161 2d gold & multi 3.00 1.40

Millennium of Algiers.

Infant — A162

1974, Jan. 7 Litho. ***Perf. 10½x11***
509 A162 80c orange & multi .80 .50

Fight against tuberculosis.

Man and Woman, Industry and Transportation — A163

1974, Feb. 18 Photo. ***Perf. 11½***
510 A163 80c multicolored .85 .40

Four-year plan.

A164

1974, Feb. 25 Photo. ***Perf. 11½***
511 A164 1.50d multi 2.75 1.40

Millennium of the birth of abu-al-Rayhan al-Biruni (973-1048), philosopher and mathematician.

Map and Colors of Algeria, Tunisia, Morocco A165

1974, Mar. 4 Photo. ***Perf. 13***
512 A165 40c gold & multi .60 .25

Maghreb Committee for Coordination of Posts and Telecommunications.

Hand Holding Rifle — A166

Mother and Children — A167

1974, Mar. 25 ***Perf. 11½***
513 A166 80c red & black .75 .25

Solidarity with the struggle of the people of South Africa.

1974, Apr. 8 ***Perf. 13½***
514 A167 85c multicolored .75 .25

Honoring Algerian mothers.

Village A168

Designs: 80c, Harvest. 90c, Tractor and sun. Designs after children's drawings.

1974, June 15 **Size: 45x26mm**
515 A168 70c multicolored .70 .25

Size: 48x33mm

516 A168 80c multicolored .90 .40
517 A168 90c multicolored 1.10 .60
Nos. 515-517 (3) 2.70 1.25

Nos. 498-499 Overprinted "FLORALIES/1974"

1974, June 22 Photo. ***Perf. 11½***
518 A111 1d multi 1.75 .80
519 A111 1.15d multi 2.50 1.25

1974 Flower Show.

Stamp Vending Machine — A169

1974, Oct. 7 Photo. ***Perf. 13***
520 A169 80c multicolored 1.00 .25

Stamp Day 1974.

UPU Emblem and Globe A170

1974, Oct. 14 ***Perf. 14***
521 A170 80c multicolored 1.25 .40

Centenary of Universal Postal Union.

"Revolution" — A171

Soldiers and Mountains A172

Raising New Flag — A173

Design: 1d, Algerian struggle for independence (people, sun and fields).

1974, Nov. 4 Photo. ***Perf. 14***
522 A171 40c multicolored .60 .25
523 A172 70c multicolored .70 .25
524 A173 95c multicolored 1.10 .35
525 A171 1d multicolored 1.25 .40
Nos. 522-525 (4) 3.65 1.25

20th anniv. of the start of the revolution.

"Horizon 1980" — A174

1974, Nov. 23 Photo. ***Perf. 13***
526 A174 95c ocher, dk red & blk .70 .40

10-year development plan, 1971-1980.

Ewer and Basin — A175

1974, Dec. 21 ***Perf. 11½***

527	A175	50c shown	.65	.30
528	A175	60c Coffee pot	.85	.40
529	A175	95c Sugar bowl	1.15	.55
530	A175	1d Bath tub	1.60	.65
		Nos. 527-530 (4)	4.25	1.90

17th century Algerian copperware.

No. 497 Surcharged with New Value and Heavy Bar

1975, Jan. 4

531	A111	50c on 40c multi	3.00	.55

Mediterranean Games' Emblem — A176

1975, Jan. 27 ***Perf. 13½***

532	A176	50c purple, yel & grn	.50	.25
533	A176	1d orange, bl & mar	.90	.35

Mediterranean Games, Algiers, 1975.

Costume Type of 1971

Regional Costumes: No. 534, Woman from Hoggar. No. 535, Woman from Algiers. No. 536, Woman from Oran. No. 537, Man from Tlemcen.

1975, Feb. 22 **Photo.** ***Perf. 11½***

534	A139	1d gold & multi	1.60	.80
535	A139	1d gold & multi	1.60	.80
536	A139	1d gold & multi	1.60	.80
537	A139	1d gold & multi	1.60	.80
		Nos. 534-537 (4)	6.40	3.20

Map of Arab Countries, ALO Emblem A177

1975, Mar. 10 **Litho.** ***Perf. 10½x11***

538	A177	50c red brown	.60	.30

Arab Labor Organization, 10th anniversary.

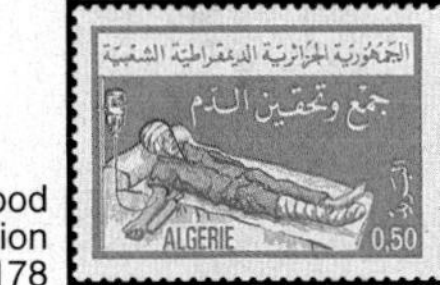

Blood Transfusion A178

1975, Mar. 15 ***Perf. 14***

539	A178	50c car rose & multi	.80	.40

Blood donation and transfusions.

Post Office, Al-Kantara A179

Policeman and Map of Algeria A180

1975, May 10 **Photo.** ***Perf. 11½***

Granite Paper

540	A179	50c multicolored	.70	.25

Stamp Day 1975.

1975, June 1 **Photo.** ***Perf. 13***

541	A180	50c multicolored	1.00	.40

Natl. Security and 10th Natl. Police Day.

Ground Receiving Station A181

Designs: 1d, Map of Algeria with locations of radar sites, transmission mast and satellite. 1.20d, Main and subsidiary stations.

1975, June 28 **Photo.** ***Perf. 13***

542	A181	50c blue & multi	.50	.25
543	A181	1d blue & multi	.85	.25
544	A181	1.20d blue & multi	1.10	.40
		Nos. 542-544 (3)	2.45	.90

National satellite telecommunications network.

Revolutionary with Flag — A182

1975, Aug. 20 **Photo.** ***Perf. 11½***

545	A182	1d multicolored	.70	.35

August 20th Revolutionary Movement (Skikda), 20th anniversary.

Swimming and Games' Emblem A183

Perf. 13x13½, 13½x13

1975, Aug. 23 **Photo.**

546	A183	25c shown	.25	.25
547	A183	50c Judo, map	.45	.25
548	A183	70c Soccer, vert.	.65	.30
549	A183	1d Running, vert.	.85	.40
550	A183	1.20d Handball, vert.	1.10	.60
a.		Souv. sheet, #546-550, perf 13	7.50	7.50
		Nos. 546-550 (5)	3.30	1.80

7th Mediterranean Games, Algiers, 8/23-9/46.

No. 550a sold for 4.50d. Exists imperf., same value.

Setif, Guelma, Kherrata — A184

1975 **Litho.** ***Perf. 13½x14***

551	A184	5c orange & blk	.25	.25
552	A184	10c emerald & brn	.25	.25
553	A184	25c dl blue & blk	.25	.25
554	A184	30c lemon & blk	.45	.25
555	A184	50c brt grn & blk	.45	.25
556	A184	70c fawn & blk	.50	.25
557	A184	1d vermilion & blk	.85	.35
		Nos. 551-557 (7)	3.00	1.85

30th anniv. of victory in World War II. Issued: 50c, 1d, Nov. 3; others, Dec. 17.

For surcharge see No. 611.

Map of Maghreb and APU Emblem A185

1975, Nov. 20 **Photo.** ***Perf. 11½***

558	A185	1d multicolored	.75	.40

10th Cong. of Arab Postal Union, Algiers.

Mosaic, Bey Constantine's Palace A186

Dey-Alger Palace — A187

Famous buildings: 2d, Prayer niche, Medersa Sidi-Boumediene, Tlemcen.

1975, Dec. 22

559	A186	1d lt blue & multi	1.20	.40
560	A186	2d buff & multi	2.50	.95
561	A187	2.50d buff & blk	3.25	1.40
		Nos. 559-561 (3)	6.95	2.75

Al-Azhar University A188

Perf. 11½x12½

1975, Dec. 29 **Litho.**

562	A188	2d multicolored	2.50	.80

Millennium of Al-Azhar University.

Red-billed Firefinch — A189

Birds: 1.40d, Black-headed bush shrike, horiz. 2d, Blue tit. 2.50d, Blackbellied sand-grouse, horiz.

1976, Jan. 24 **Photo.** ***Perf. 11½***

563	A189	50c multi	1.75	.70
564	A189	1.40d multi	3.00	1.25
565	A189	2d multi	3.50	1.40
566	A189	2.50d multi	4.00	2.00
		Nos. 563-566 (4)	12.25	5.35

See Nos. 595-598.

Telephones 1876 and 1976 — A190

1976, Feb. 23 **Photo.** ***Perf. 13½x13***

567	A190	1.40d rose, dk & lt bl	1.10	.55

Centenary of first telephone call by Alexander Graham Bell, Mar. 10, 1876.

Map of Africa with Angola and its Flag — A191

1976, Feb. 23 ***Perf. 11½***

568	A191	50c brown & multi	.65	.25

Algeria's solidarity with the People's Republic of Angola.

A192

Sahraoui flag and child, map of former Spanish Sahara.

1976, Mar. 15 **Photo.** ***Perf. 11½***

569	A192	50c multicolored	.60	.25

Algeria's solidarity with Sahraoui Arab Democratic Republic, former Spanish Sahara.

A193

1976, Mar. 22

570	A193	1.40d Mailman	1.10	.40

Stamp Day 1976.

Microscope, Slide with TB Bacilli, Patients A194

1976, Apr. 26 ***Perf. 13x13½***

571	A194	50c multicolored	1.00	.30

Fight against tuberculosis.

"Setif, Guelma, Kherrata" — A195

1976, May 24 **Photo.** ***Perf. 13½x13***

572	A195	50c blue & yellow	.60	.25
a.		Booklet pane of 6	7.00	
b.		Booklet pane of 10	10.50	

No. 572 was issued in booklets only.

Ram's Head over Landscape A196

1976, June 17 Photo. *Perf. 11½*
573 A196 50c multicolored .70 .25

Livestock breeding.

People Holding Torch, Map of Algeria — A197

1976, June 29 Photo. *Perf. 14x13½*
574 A197 50c multicolored .60 .25

National Charter.

Palestine Map and Flag — A198

1976, July 12 *Perf. 11½*
Granite Paper
575 A198 50c multicolored .65 .25

Solidarity with the Palestinians.

Map of Africa — A199

1976, Oct. 3 Litho. *Perf. 10½x11*
576 A199 2d dk blue & multi 1.75 .65

2nd Pan-African Commercial Fair, Algiers.

Blind Brushmaker A200

The Blind, by Dinet A201

1976, Oct. 23 Photo. *Perf. 14½*
577 A200 1.20d blue & multi 1.40 .50
578 A201 1.40d gold & multi 1.40 .65

Rehabilitation of the blind.

"Constitution 1976" — A202

1976, Nov. 19 Photo. *Perf. 11½*
579 A202 2d multicolored 1.75 .65

New Constitution.

Soldiers Planting Seedlings A203

1976, Nov. 25 Litho. *Perf. 12*
580 A203 1.40d multicolored 1.60 .55

Green barrier against the Sahara.

Ornamental Border and Inscription — A204

1976, Dec. 18 Photo. *Perf. 11½*
Granite Paper
581 A204 2d multicolored 1.60 .65

Re-election of Pres. Houari Boumediene. See No. 627.

Map with Charge Zones and Dials A205

People and Buildings A206

1977, Jan. 22 *Perf. 13*
582 A205 40c silver & multi .50 .25

Inauguration of automatic national and international telephone service.

1977, Jan. 29 Photo. *Perf. 11½*
583 A206 60c on 50c multi .60 .25

2nd General Population and Buildings Census. No. 583 was not issued without the typographed red brown surcharge, date, and bars.

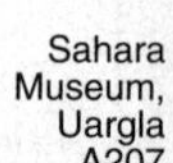

Sahara Museum, Uargla A207

1977, Feb. 12 Litho. *Perf. 14*
584 A207 60c multicolored .70 .40

El-Kantara Gorge — A208

Perf. 12½x13½

1977, Feb. 19 Photo.
585 A208 20c green & yellow .25 .25
a. Bklt. pane, 3 #585, 4 #586 + label 5.50
b. Bklt. pane, 5 #585, 2 #587 + label 5.75
586 A208 60c brt lilac & yel .25 .25
587 A208 1d brown & yellow .65 .25
Nos. 585-587 (3) 1.15 .75

National Assembly — A209

1977, Feb. 27 *Perf. 11½*
588 A209 2d multicolored 1.40 .55

People and Flag — A210

Soldier and Flag — A211

Perf. 13½, 11½ (3d)

1977, Mar. 12 Photo.
589 A210 2d multicolored 1.40 .55
590 A211 3d multicolored 2.25 .80

Solidarity with the peoples of Zimbabwe (Rhodesia), 2d; Namibia, 3d.

Winter, Roman Mosaic A212

The Seasons from Roman Villa, 2nd century A.D.: 1.40d, Fall. 2d, Summer. 3d, Spring.

1977, Apr. 21 Photo. *Perf. 11½*
Granite Paper
591 A212 1.20d multi 1.75 .80
592 A212 1.40d multi 1.75 .80
593 A212 2d multi 2.75 1.25
594 A212 3d multi 3.75 1.75
a. Souv. sheet, #591-594 15.00 15.00
Nos. 591-594 (4) 10.00 4.60

No. 594a sold for 8d and exists imperf.

Bird Type of 1976

Birds: 60c, Tristram's warbler. 1.40d, Moussier's redstart, horiz. 2d, Temminck's horned lark, horiz. 3d, Eurasian hoopoe.

1977, May 21 Photo. *Perf. 11½*
595 A189 60c multi 1.50 .70
596 A189 1.40d multi 2.25 1.00
597 A189 2d multi 3.50 1.60
598 A189 3d multi 5.00 2.00
Nos. 595-598 (4) 12.25 5.30

Horseman — A213

Design: 5d, Attacking horsemen, horiz.

1977, June 25 Photo. *Perf. 11½*
599 A213 2d multicolored 2.00 .80
600 A213 5d multicolored 5.00 2.00

Flag Colors, Games Emblem — A214

Wall Painting, Games Emblem A215

1977, Sept. 24 Photo. *Perf. 11½*
601 A214 60c multi .60 .25
602 A215 1.40d multi 1.40 .60

3rd African Games, Algiers 1978.

Village and Tractor A216

1977, Nov. 12 *Perf. 14x13*
603 A216 1.40d multi 1.00 .40

Socialist agricultural village.

Almohades Dirham, 12th Century — A217

Ancient Coins: 1.40d, Almohades coin, 12th century. 2d, Almoravides dinar, 11th century.

1977, Dec. 17 Photo. *Perf. 11½*
604 A217 60c ultra, sil & blk .60 .40
605 A217 1.40d grn, gold & brn 1.40 .60
606 A217 2d red brn, gold & brn 1.90 .90
Nos. 604-606 (3) 3.90 1.90

Flowering Trees — A218

1978, Feb. 11 Photo. ***Perf. 11½***

607 A218 60c Cherry .60 .25
608 A218 1.20d Peach 1.10 .70
609 A218 1.30d Almond 1.25 .75
610 A218 1.40d Apple 1.50 .80
Nos. 607-610 (4) 4.45 2.50

No. 555 Surcharged with New Value and Bar

1978, Feb. 11 Litho. ***Perf. 13½x14***

611 A184 60c on 50c .80 .25

Children with Traffic Signs and Car — A219

1978, Apr. 29 Photo. ***Perf. 11½***

612 A219 60c multicolored .80 .25

Road safety and protection of children.

Sports and Games Emblems A220

Designs (Games Emblem and): 40c, Volleyball. 60c, Rowing, vert. 1.20d, Basketball. 1.30d, Hammer throwing, vert. 1.40d, Map of Africa and boxers, vert.

1978, July 13 Photo. ***Perf. 11½***

613 A220 40c mul .25 .25
614 A220 60c multi .45 .25
615 A220 1.20d multi 1.00 .40
616 A220 1.30d multi 1.00 .50
617 A220 1.40d multi 1.40 .60
Nos. 613-617 (5) 4.10 2.00

3rd African Games, Algiers, July 13-28.

TB Patient Returning to Family — A221

1978, Oct. 5 Photo. ***Perf. 13½x14***

618 A221 60c multicolored .75 .25

Anti-tuberculosis campaign.

Holy Kaaba — A222

1978, Oct. 28 Photo. ***Perf. 11½***

619 A222 60c multicolored .80 .25

Pilgrimage to Mecca.

National Servicemen Building Road — A223

1978, Nov. 4

620 A223 60c multicolored .80 .25

African Unity Road from El Goleah to In Salah, inauguration.

Fibula A224

Pres. Boumediene A225

Jewelry: 1.35d, Pendant. 1.40d, Ankle ring.

1978, Dec. 21 Photo. ***Perf. 12x11½***

621 A224 1.20d multi 1.40 .55
622 A224 1.35d multi 1.60 .65
623 A224 1.40d multi 2.00 .80
Nos. 621-623 (3) 5.00 2.00

1979, Jan. 7 Photo. ***Perf. 12x11½***

624 A225 60c green, red & brown .55 .25

Houari Boumediene, pres. of Algeria 1965-1978.

Torch and Books A226

1979, Jan. 27 Photo. ***Perf. 11½***

625 A226 60c multicolored .60 .25

Natl. Front of Liberation Party Cong.

Pres. Boumediene — A227

1979, Feb. 4 Photo. ***Perf. 11½***

626 A227 1.40d multi 1.40 .55

40 days after death of Pres. Houari Boumediène.

Ornamental Type of 1976

Proclamation of new President.

1979, Feb. 10

627 A204 2d multicolored 1.75 .40

Election of Pres. Chadli Bendjedid.

A229

1979, Apr. 18 Photo. ***Perf. 11½***

628 A229 60c multicolored .50 .25

Sheik Abdul-Hamid Ben Badis (1889-1940).

A230

Designs: 1.20d, Telephone dial, map of Africa. 1.40d, Symbolic Morse key and waves.

1979, May 19 Photo. ***Perf. 13½x14***

629 A230 1.20d multi 1.00 .30
630 A230 1.40d multi 1.25 .50

Telecom '79 Exhib., Geneva, Sept. 20-26.

Harvest, IYC Emblem A231

1.40d, Dancers and IYC emblem, vert.

Perf. 11½x11, 11x11½

1979, June 21

631 A231 60c multi .50 .25
632 A231 1.40d multi 1.00 .50

International Year of the Child.

A232

1979, Oct. 20 Photo. ***Perf. 11½***

633 A232 1.40d Nuthatch 2.40 1.25

A233

Designs: 1.40d, Flag, soldiers and workers. 3d, Revolutionaries and emblem.

1979, Nov. 1 Photo. ***Perf. 12½***

634 A233 1.40d multi 1.00 .30

Size: 37x48mm

Perf. 11½

635 A233 3d multi 2.00 .85

November 1 revolution, 25th anniversary.

Hegira, 1500 Anniv. A234

1979, Dec. 2 Photo. ***Perf. 11½***

636 A234 3d multicolored 2.25 .80

Camels, Lion, Men and Slave — A235

Dionysian Procession (Setif Mosaic): 1.35d, Elephants, tigers and women. 1.40d, Men in tiger-drawn cart. No. 639a has continuous design.

Granite Paper

1980, Feb. 16 Photo. ***Perf. 11½***

637 A235 1.20d multi 1.50 .40
638 A235 1.35d multi 1.50 .55
639 A235 1.40d multi 1.75 .80
a. Strip of 3, #637-639 6.50 6.50

Science Day — A236

1980, Apr. 19 Photo. ***Perf. 12***

640 A236 60c multicolored .75 .25

Dam and Workers A237

1980, June 17 Photo. ***Perf. 11½***

641 A237 60c multicolored .50 .25

Extraordinary Congress of the National Liberation Front Party.

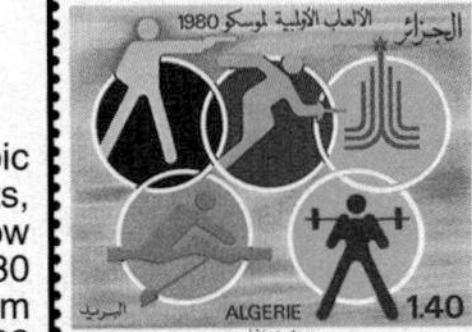

Olympic Sports, Moscow '80 Emblem A238

1980, June 28

642 A238 50c Flame, rings, vert. .50 .25
643 A238 1.40d shown 1.00 .50

22nd Summer Olympic Games, Moscow, July 19-Aug. 3.

20th Anniversary of OPEC — A239

Perf. 11x10½, 10½x11

1980, Sept. 15 **Engr.**

644	A239	60c Men holding OPEC emblem, vert.	.60	.25
645	A239	1.40d shown	1.40	.50

Aures Valley A240

1980, Sept. 25 **Litho.** ***Perf. 13½x14***

646	A240	50c shown	.45	.25
647	A240	1d El Oued Oasis	.85	.25
648	A240	1.40d Tassili Rocks	1.25	.40
649	A240	2d View of Algiers	2.10	.70
		Nos. 646-649 (4)	4.65	1.60

World Tourism Conf., Manila, Sept. 27.

Avicenna (980-1037), Philosopher and Physician A241

1980, Oct. 25 **Photo.** ***Perf. 12***

650	A241	2d multicolored	2.25	.80

Ruins of El Asnam A242

1980, Nov. 13 **Photo.** ***Perf. 12***

651	A242	3d multicolored	2.25	.55

Earthquake relief.

Crown A243

No. 652, Necklace, vert. No. 653, Earrings, bracelet, vert. No. 654, Crown.

Granite Paper

1980, Dec. 20 **Photo.** ***Perf. 12***

652	A243	60c multi	.65	.25
653	A243	1.40d multi	1.10	.50
654	A243	2d multi	1.75	.65
		Nos. 652-654 (3)	3.50	1.40

See Nos. 705-707.

1980-1984 Five-Year Plan — A244

1981, Jan. 29 **Litho.** ***Perf. 14***

655	A244	60c multicolored	.50	.25

Basket Weaving — A245

Granite Paper

1981, Feb. 19 **Photo.** ***Perf. 12½***

656	A245	40c shown	.40	.25
657	A245	60c Rug weaving	.50	.25
658	A245	1d Coppersmith	.85	.25
659	A245	1.40d Jeweler	1.25	.45
		Nos. 656-659 (4)	3.00	1.20

Cedar Tree A246

Arbor Day: 1.40d, Cypress tree, vert.

Granite Paper

1981, Mar. 19 **Photo.** ***Perf. 12***

660	A246	60c multi	.40	.25
661	A246	1.40d multi	1.10	.60

Mohamed Bachir el Ibrahimi (1869-1965) A247

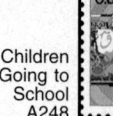

Children Going to School A248

1981, Apr. 16 **Granite Paper**

662	A247	60c multicolored	.50	.25
663	A248	60c multicolored	.50	.25

Science Day.

12th International Hydatidological Congress, Algiers — A249

1981, Apr. 23 ***Perf. 14x13½***

664	A249	2d multicolored	2.00	.50

13th World Telecommunications Day — A250

1981, May 14 **Photo.** ***Perf. 14x13½***

665	A250	1.40d multi	1.25	.25

Disabled People and Hand Offering Flower — A251

Perf. 12½x13, 13x12½

1981, June 20 **Litho.**

666	A251	1.20d Symbolic globe, vert.	.95	.25
667	A251	1.40d shown	1.10	.30

Intl. Year of the Disabled.

Papilio Machaon A252

1981, Aug. 20 **Photo.** ***Perf. 11½***

Granite Paper

668	A252	60c shown	.90	.35
669	A252	1.20d Rhodocera rhamni	1.60	.50
670	A252	1.40d Charaxes jasius	2.00	.90
671	A252	2d Papilio podalirius	2.50	.90
		Nos. 668-671 (4)	7.00	2.65

Monk Seal — A253

1981, Sept. 17 ***Perf. 14x13½***

672	A253	60c shown	.90	.40
673	A253	1.40d Macaque	1.90	.80

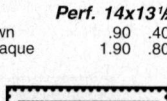

World Food Day — A254

1981, Oct. 16 **Photo.** ***Perf. 14x14½***

674	A254	2d multicolored	1.25	.50

Cave Drawings of Tassili — A255

Various cave drawings. 1.60d, 2d horiz.

1981, Nov. 21 ***Perf. 11½***

675	A255	60c multi	.50	.25
676	A255	1d multi	1.00	.40
677	A255	1.60d multi	1.40	.55
678	A255	2d multi	1.90	.80
		Nos. 675-678 (4)	4.80	2.00

Galley, 17-18th Cent. A256

1981, Dec. 17 **Photo.** ***Perf. 11½***

679	A256	60c shown	.70	.50
680	A256	1.60d Ship, diff.	1.90	.95

1982 World Cup Soccer A257

Designs: Various soccer players.

Perf. 13x12½x 12½x13

1982, Feb. 25 **Litho.**

681	A257	80c multi, vert.	.65	.25
682	A257	2.80d multi	2.00	.80

TB Bacillus Centenary A258

1982, Mar. 20 **Photo.** ***Perf. 14½x14***

683	A258	80c multi	.60	.25

Painted Stand A259

1982, Apr. 24 **Photo.** ***Perf. 11½***

Granite Paper

684	A259	80c Mirror, vert.	.50	.25
685	A259	2d shown	1.25	.45

Size: 48x33mm

686	A259	2.40d Chest	1.75	.60
		Nos. 684-686 (3)	3.50	1.30

Djamaael Djadid Mosque, Algiers A260

No. 688, Sidi Boumediene Mosque, Tlemcen. No. 689, Garden of Dey, Algiers.

1982, May 15 **Litho.** ***Perf. 14***

Size: 32x22mm

687	A260	80c brown	.50	.25
a.		Size: 30½x21mm	3.50	.75
688	A260	2.40d purple	1.50	.50
689	A260	3d slate	2.00	.60
a.		Size: 30½x21mm	5.00	1.25
		Nos. 687-689 (3)	4.00	1.35

See Nos. 731-734, 745-747, 774, 778-783.

A261

Medicinal plants: No. 690, Callitris articulata. No 691, Artemisia herba-alba. No. 692, Ricinus communis. No. 693, Thymus fontanesii.

1982, May 27 **Photo.** ***Perf. 11½***
Granite Paper

690 A261 50c multi .45 .25
691 A261 80c multi .65 .25
692 A261 1d multi 1.00 .40
693 A261 2.40d multi 2.00 .75
Nos. 690-693 (4) 4.10 1.65

A262

No. 694, Riflemen. No. 695, Soldiers, horiz. No. 696, Symbols, citizens, horiz. No. 697, Emblem.

1982, July 5 **Granite Paper**

694 A262 50c multi .45 .25
695 A262 80c multi .55 .25
696 A262 2d multi 1.40 .75
Nos. 694-696 (3) 2.40 1.25

Souvenir Sheet

697 A262 5d multi 5.50 5.50

Independence, 20th anniv.
No. 697 contains one 32x39mm stamp.

Soummam Congress A263

1982, Aug. 20 **Litho.**
698 A263 80c Congress building .60 .25

Scouting Year — A264

1982, Oct. 21 **Photo.**
Granite Paper
699 A264 2.80d multi 2.10 .60

Palestinian Child — A265

1982, Nov. 25 **Litho.** ***Perf. 10½***
700 A265 1.60d multi .95 .30

Chlamydotis Undulata — A266

Protected birds: No. 701, Geronticus eremita, horiz. No. 702, Chlamydotis Undulata. No. 703, Aguila rapax, horiz. No. 704, Gypaetus barbatus.

Perf. 15x14, 14x15
1982, Dec. 23 **Photo.**

701 A266 50c mutli .80 .50
702 A266 80c multi 1.25 .70
703 A266 2d multi 2.25 1.40
704 A266 2.40d multi 3.00 1.75
Nos. 701-704 (4) 7.30 4.35

Jewelry Type of 1980
1983, Feb. 10 ***Perf. 11½***
Granite Paper

705 A243 50c Picture frame .35 .25
706 A243 1d Flaska .60 .40
707 A243 2d Brooch, horiz. 1.25 .65
Nos. 705-707 (3) 2.20 1.30

A267

1983, Mar. 17 **Photo.**
Granite Paper

708 A267 80c Abies numidica, vert. .70 .25
709 A267 2.80d Acacia raddiana 2.25 .80

Intl. Arbor Day.

A268

Various minerals. 1.20d, 2.40d horiz.

Granite Paper
Perf. 12x12½, 12½x12
1983, Apr. 21 **Photo.**

710 A268 70c multi 1.25 .35
711 A268 80c multi 1.40 .50
712 A268 1.20d multi 1.60 .65
713 A268 2.40d multi 2.50 1.25
Nos. 710-713 (4) 6.75 2.75

30th Anniv. of Intl. Customs Cooperation Council A269

1983, May 14 **Photo.** ***Perf. 11½***
Granite Paper
714 A269 80c multi .70 .25

Emir Abdelkader Death Centenary — A270

1983, May 22 **Photo.** ***Perf. 12***
Granite Paper
715 A270 4d multi 2.25 .90

A271

Local mushrooms: No. 716, Amanita muscaria. No. 717, Amanita phalloides. No. 718, Pleurotus eryngii. No. 719, Tefezia leonis.

1983, July 21 ***Perf. 14x15***

716 A271 50c multi .85 .30
717 A271 80c multi 1.25 .75
718 A271 1.40d multi 2.50 1.10
719 A271 2.80d multi 4.00 1.75
Nos. 716-719 (4) 8.60 3.90

A272

1983, Sept. 1 **Photo.** ***Perf. 11½***
720 A272 80c multi .70 .25

ibn-Khaldun, historian, philosopher.

World Communications Year — A273

80c, Post Office, Algiers. 2.40d, Telephone, circuit box.

Perf. 11½x12½
1983, Sept. 22 **Litho.**

721 A273 80c multicolored .60 .25
722 A273 2.40d multicolored 1.50 .60

Goat and Tassili Mountains A274

1983, Oct. 20 **Litho.** ***Perf. 12½x13***

723 A274 50c shown .45 .25
724 A274 80c Tuaregs in native costume .55 .25
725 A274 2.40d Animals, rock painting 1.60 .55
726 A274 2.80d Rock formation 2.00 .75
Nos. 723-726 (4) 4.60 1.80

Sloughi Dog — A275

Perf. 14x14½, 14½x14
1983, Nov. 24 **Photo.**

727 A275 80c shown 1.00 .35
728 A275 2.40d Sloughi, horiz. 2.75 .95

Natl. Liberation Party, 5th Congress — A276

1983, Dec. 19 **Photo.** ***Perf. 11½***
729 A276 80c Symbols of development .80 .40

Souvenir Sheet

730 A276 5d Emblem 5.00 5.00

No. 730 contains one 32x38mm stamp.

View Type of 1982
1984, Jan. 26 **Litho.** ***Perf. 14***
Size: 32x22mm

731 A260 10c View of Oran, 1830 .25 .25
a. Size: 30½x21mm .80 .40
732 A260 1d Sidi Abderahman and Taalibi Mosques .50 .25
a. Size: 30½x21mm 1.50 .80
733 A260 2d Bejaia, 1830 1.00 .50
a. Size: 30½x21mm 3.00 1.50
734 A260 4d Constantine, 1830 2.50 .65
a. Size: 30½x21mm 6.00 1.50
Nos. 731-734 (4) 4.25 1.65

Pottery A278

Perf. 11½x12, 12x11½
1984, Feb. 23 **Photo.**
Granite Paper

735 A278 80c Jug, vert. .55 .25
736 A278 1d Platter .75 .40
737 A278 2d Oil lamp, vert. 1.60 .65
738 A278 2.40d Pitcher 2.00 .80
Nos. 735-738 (4) 4.90 2.10

Fountains of Old Algiers — A279

1984 Summer Olympics — A280

Various fountains.

1984, Mar. 22 **Photo.** ***Perf. 11½***
Granite Paper

739 A279 50c multi .25 .25
740 A279 80c multi .65 .40
741 A279 2.40d multi 1.60 .65
Nos. 739-741 (3) 2.50 1.30

1984, May 19 **Photo.** ***Perf. 11½***
Granite Paper
742 A280 1d multi 1.25 .40

Brown Stallion A281

1984, June 14 **Photo.** ***Perf. 11½***
Granite Paper

743 A281 80c shown .80 .40
744 A281 2.40d White mare 2.10 .95

View Type of 1982

1984 Litho. *Perf. 14*
Size: 32x22mm

745 A260 5c Mustapha Pacha .50 .25
a. Size: 30½x21mm .80 .40
746 A260 20c Bab Azzoun .50 .25
d. Size: 30½x21mm 1.00 .60
746A A260 30c Algiers .50 .25
d. Size: 30½x21mm 1.50 .50
746B A260 40c Kolea .50 .25
746C A260 50c Algiers .50 .25
e. Size: 30½x21mm 1.50 .50
747 A260 70c Mostaganem .60 .25
a. Size: 30½x21mm 2.00 1.00
Nos. 745-747 (6) 3.10 1.50

Issued: Nos. 745, 746, 747, 7/19; Nos. 746A-746C, 10/20.

Lute A282

Native musical instruments.

1984, Sept. 22 Litho. *Perf. 15x14*
748 A282 80c shown .60 .25
749 A282 1d Drum .90 .40
750 A282 2.40d Fiddle 1.75 .75
751 A282 2.80d Bagpipe 2.00 .95
Nos. 748-751 (4) 5.25 2.35

30th Anniv. of Algerian Revolution — A284

1984, Nov. 3 Photo. *Perf. 11½x12*
757 A284 80c Partisans .85 .25

Souvenir Sheet

758 A284 5d Algerian flags, vert. 5.50 5.50

M'Zab Valley A285

1984, Dec. 15 *Perf. 15x14, 14x15*
759 A285 80c Map of valley .75 .25
760 A285 2.40d Town of M'Zab, vert. 1.75 .60

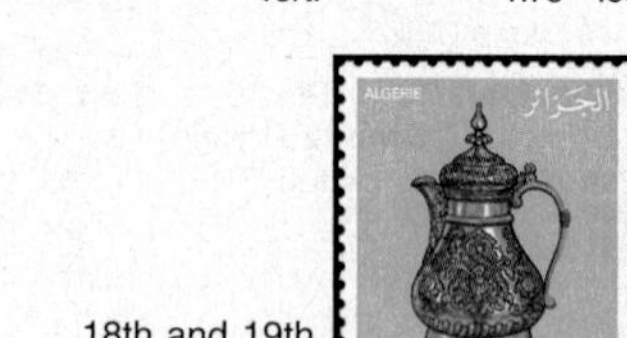
18th and 19th Century Metalware — A286

1985, Jan. 26 Photo. *Perf. 11½*
761 A286 80c Coffee pot .55 .25
762 A286 2d Bowl, horiz. 1.25 .60
763 A286 2.40d Covered bowl 1.60 .80
Nos. 761-763 (3) 3.40 1.65

Fish A287

1985, Feb. 23 Photo. *Perf. 15x14*
764 A287 50c Thunnus thynnus .55 .25
765 A287 80c Sparus aurata 1.00 .40
766 A287 2.40d Epinephelus guaza 2.40 1.10
767 A287 2.80d Mustelus mustelus 3.00 1.25
Nos. 764-767 (4) 6.95 3.00

National Games A288

1985, Mar. 28 *Perf. 11½x12*
Granite Paper

768 A288 80c Doves, emblem .80 .25

Environmental Conservation — A289

1985, Apr. 25 *Perf. 13½*
769 A289 80c Stylized trees .70 .25
770 A289 1.40d Stylized waves 1.00 .40

View Type of 1982 and

The Casbah — A290

View of Constantine A290a

Street Scene in Algiers A290b

Designs: 2.50d, Djamaael Djadid Mosque, Algiers. 2.90d, like No. 746. 5d, like No. 746A. 1.50d, like No. 746B. 4.20d, like No. 764.

Perf. 13½x12½, 13 (#774, 4.20d),
Perf. 13½x14 (#775)
Perf. 14½x14 (2d)

Photo., Litho. (2d, 6,20d, 7.50d, #775)

1985-94
771 A290 20c dk blue & buff .25 .25
772 A290 80c sage grn & buff .60 .25
773 A290a 1d dk olive grn .50 .25
a. Bklt. pane of 5 + label 4.00
774 A260 1.50d dull red .55 .25
775 A290b 1.50d red brn & brn .40 .25
a. Booklet pane of 6 2.75
776 A290b 2d dk bl & lt bl .40 .25
a. Booklet pane of 5 + label 3.00
777 A290 2.40d chestnut & buff 1.75 .25
a. Bklt. pane of 5 (20c, 3 80c, 2.40d) + label 5.75
778 A260 2.50d bluish green 1.00 .25
779 A260 2.90d slate 1.25 .25
780 A260 4.20d gray green 1.40 .35
781 A260 5d dp bis & blk 2.10 .40

Perf. 14
782 A260 6.20d like #731 1.10 .30
783 A260 7.50d like #745 1.75 .30
Nos. 771-783 (13) 13.05 3.60

Nos. 771-772, 777 issued only in booklet panes.

Issued: 20c, 80c, 2.40d, 6/1/85; 1d, 1/26/89; 2.50d, 2.90d, 5d, 2/23/89; No. 774, 4.20d, 3/21/91; No. 775, 5/20/92; 6.20d, 7.50d, 4/22/92; 2d, 10/21/93; No. 776a, 10/21/94.

See No. 1010.

UN, 40th Anniv. — A291

1985, June 26 Photo. *Perf. 14*
784 A291 1d Dove, emblem, 40 .90 .25

Natl. Youth Festival — A292

1985, July 5 Litho. *Perf. 13½*
785 A292 80c multicolored .70 .25

Intl. Youth Year A293

1985, July 5
786 A293 80c Silhouette, globe, emblem, vert. .55 .25
787 A293 1.40d Doves, globe .90 .40

World Map, OPEC — A294

1985, Sept. 14 Photo. *Perf. 12½x13*
788 A294 80c multicolored .80 .25

Organization of Petroleum Exporting Countries, 25th anniv.

Family Planning — A295

1985, Oct. 3 Litho. *Perf. 14*
789 A295 80c Mother and sons .55 .25
790 A295 1.40d Weighing infant .90 .40
791 A295 1.70d Breast-feeding 1.25 .50
Nos. 789-791 (3) 2.70 1.15

El-Meniaa Township — A296

1985, Oct. 24 Engr. *Perf. 13*
792 A296 80c Chetaibi Bay, horiz. .50 .25
793 A296 2d shown 1.40 .40
794 A296 2.40d Bou Noura Town, horiz. 1.60 .60
Nos. 792-794 (3) 3.50 1.25

The Palm Grove, by N. Dinet — A297

1985, Nov. 21 Photo. *Perf. 11½x12*
Granite Paper

795 A297 2d multi 1.60 .75
796 A297 3d multi, diff. 2.25 1.10

Tapestries A298

Various designs.

1985, Dec. 19 Granite Paper
797 A298 80c multi .75 .45
798 A298 1.40d multi 1.50 .70
799 A298 2.40d multi 2.10 1.10
800 A298 2.80d multi 2.75 1.50
Nos. 797-800 (4) 7.10 3.75

Wildcats A299

1986, Jan. 23 *Perf. 12x11½, 11½x12*
Granite Paper

801 A299 80c Felis margarita 1.40 .50
802 A299 1d Felis caracal 1.75 .65
803 A299 2d Felis sylvestris 2.50 1.00
804 A299 2.40d Felis serval, vert. 3.50 1.40
Nos. 801-804 (4) 9.15 3.55

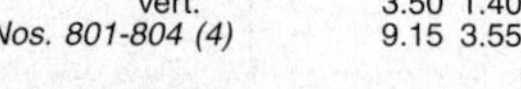

UN Child Survival Campaign — A300

Algerian General Worker's Union, 30th Anniv. — A301

1986, Feb. 13 Litho. *Perf. 13½*
805 A300 80c Oral vaccine .55 .25
806 A300 1.40d Mother, child, sun 1.10 .60
807 A300 1.70d Three children 1.60 .75
Nos. 805-807 (3) 3.25 1.60

1986, Feb. 24 *Perf. 12½*
Granite Paper

808 A301 2d multi 1.50 .55

National Charter — A302

Natl. Day of the Disabled — A303

1986, Mar. 6 Photo. *Perf. 11½*
Granite Paper

809 A302 4d multi 3.25 1.10

1986, Mar. 15 *Perf. 12½x13*

810 A303 80c multi .70 .30

A304

A305

1986, Apr. 17 Litho. *Perf. 14x15*

811 A304 80c multi .80 .40

Anti-Tuberculosis campaign.

1986, Apr. 24 *Perf. 14*

812 A305 2d Soccer ball, sombrero 1.40 .55
813 A305 2.40d Soccer players 1.60 .65

1986 World Cup Soccer Championships, Mexico.

Inner Courtyards — A306

1986, May 15 Photo. *Perf. 11½*
Granite Paper

814 A306 80c multi .70 .30
815 A306 2.40d multi, diff. 1.90 .95
816 A306 3d multi, diff. 2.40 1.25
Nos. 814-816 (3) 5.00 2.50

Blood Donation Campaign A307

1986, June 26 Litho. *Perf. 13½*

817 A307 80c multi 1.40 .40

Southern District Radio Communication Inauguration A308

1986, July *Perf. 13*

818 A308 60c multi .50 .25

Mosque Gateways A309

1986, Sept. 27 Photo. *Perf. 12x11½*
Granite Paper

819 A309 2d Door 1.40 .55
820 A309 2.40d Ornamental arch 1.60 .75

Intl. Peace Year A310

Perf. 13½x14½

1986, Oct. 16 Photo.

821 A310 2.40d multi 1.60 .55

Folk Dancing A311

1986, Nov. 22 Litho. *Perf. 14x13½*

822 A311 80c Woman, scarf .70 .25
823 A311 2.40d Woman, diff. 1.60 .60
824 A311 2.80d Man, sword 1.90 .80
Nos. 822-824 (3) 4.20 1.65

Flowers — A312

1986, Dec. 18 Photo. *Perf. 14*

825 A312 80c Narcissus tazetta .80 .30
826 A312 1.40d Iris unguicularis 1.25 .55
827 A312 2.40d Capparis spinosa 1.75 .90
828 A312 2.80d Gladiolus segetum 2.40 1.10
Nos. 825-828 (4) 6.20 2.85

See Nos. 936-938.

Abstract Paintings by Mohammed Issia Khem — A313

Perf. 11½x12, 12x11½

1987, Jan. 29 Litho.

829 A313 2d Man and woman, vert. 1.60 .75
830 A313 5d Man and books 3.75 2.00

Jewelry from Aures A314

1987, Feb. 27 Photo. *Perf. 12*
Granite Paper

831 A314 1d Earrings .80 .40
832 A314 1.80d Bracelets 1.25 .60
833 A314 2.90d Nose rings 1.75 1.10
834 A314 3.30d Necklace 2.25 1.25
Nos. 831-834 (4) 6.05 3.35

Nos. 831-833 vert.

Petroglyphs, Atlas — A315

1987, Mar. 26 Litho. *Perf. 12x11½*
Granite Paper

835 A315 1d Man and woman 1.10 .60
836 A315 2.90d Goat 2.50 1.40
837 A315 3.30d Horse, bull 2.75 1.40
Nos. 835-837 (3) 6.35 3.40

Syringe as an Umbrella — A316

1987, Apr. 7 *Perf. 11½*
Granite Paper

838 A316 1d multi .80 .25

Child Immunization Campaign, World Health Day.

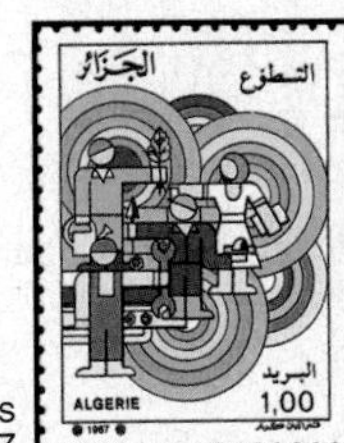
Volunteers A317

1987, Apr. 23 *Perf. 10½*

839 A317 1d multi .55 .30

Third General Census — A318

1987, May 21 *Perf. 13½*

840 A318 1d multi .60 .25

Algerian Postage, 25th Anniv. — A319

War Orphans' Fund label (1fr + 9fr) of 1962.

1987, July 5 Photo. *Perf. 11½x12*
Granite Paper

841 A319 1.80d multi 2.25 .60

A320

A321

1987, July 5 Granite Paper

842 A320 1d multi .60 .25

Souvenir Sheet

843 A321 5d multi 5.50 5.50

Natl. independence, 25th anniv.

Amateur Theater Festival, Mostaganem A322

1987, July 20 *Perf. 12x11½*
Granite Paper

844 A322 1d Actors on stage .55 .25
845 A322 1.80d Theater .95 .50
a. Pair, #844-845 1.50 1.50

No. 845a has continuous design.

Mediterranean Games, Latakia — A323

1987, Aug. 6 *Perf. 13x12½, 12½x13*

846 A323 1d Discus .55 .30
847 A323 2.90d Tennis, vert. 1.60 .75
848 A323 3.30d Team handball 1.90 .95
Nos. 846-848 (3) 4.05 2.00

Birds — A324

1987 Litho. *Perf. 13½*

849	A324	1d	Phoenicopterus ruber roseus	.90	.45
850	A324	1.80d	Porphyrio porphyrio	1.50	.90
851	A324	2.50d	Elanus caeruleus	2.40	1.10
852	A324	2.90d	Milvus milvus	2.75	1.40
			Nos. 849-852 (4)	7.55	3.85

Agriculture A325

Perf. 10½x11, 11x10½

1987, Nov. 26 Litho.

853	A325	1d	Planting	.65	.25
854	A325	1d	Reservoir	.65	.25
855	A325	1d	Harvesting crop, vert.	.65	.25
856	A325	1d	Produce, vert.	.65	.25
			Nos. 853-856 (4)	2.60	1.00

African Telecommunications Day — A326

1987, Dec. 7 *Perf. 10½*

857 A326 1d multi .80 .25

Transportation — A327

1987, Dec. 18 Litho. *Perf. 10½x11*

858	A327	2.90d	shown	1.50	.60
859	A327	3.30d	Diesel train	2.75	1.10

Algerian Universities A328

Various campuses.

1987, Dec. 26 *Perf. 10½x11, 11x10½*

860	A328	1d	shown	.55	.25
861	A328	2.50d	multi, diff.	1.40	.50
862	A328	2.90d	multi, diff.	1.60	.60
863	A328	3.30d	multi, diff., vert.	1.90	.70
			Nos. 860-863 (4)	5.45	2.05

Intl. Rural Development Fund, 10th Anniv. — A329

1988, Jan. 27 *Perf. 10½x11*

864 A329 1d multi .70 .25

Autonomy of State-owned Utilities — A330

1988, Feb. 27 Litho. *Perf. 11x10½*

865 A330 1d multi .60 .25

Intl. Women's Day — A331

1988, Mar. 10 Litho. *Perf. 11x10½*

866 A331 1d multi .70 .25

Arab Scouts, 75th Anniv. — A332

1988, Apr. 7 Litho. *Perf. 10½*

867 A332 2d multi 1.10 .50

1988 Summer Olympics, Seoul — A333

1988, July 23 Litho. *Perf. 10½*

868 A333 2.90d multi 1.60 .75

Hot Springs — A334

1988, July 16

869	A334	1d	shown	.55	.25
870	A334	2.90d	Caverns, horiz.	1.60	.55
871	A334	3.30d	Gazebo, fountain, horiz.	1.90	.65
			Nos. 869-871 (3)	4.05	1.45

World Wildlife Fund A335

Barbary apes, Macaca sylvanus.

1988, Sept. 17 Litho. *Perf. 10½*

872	A335	50c	Adult	1.10	.50
873	A335	90c	Family	1.40	.75
874	A335	1d	Close-up, vert.	2.10	1.00
875	A335	1.80d	Seated on branch, vert.	3.25	2.00
			Nos. 872-875 (4)	7.85	4.25

Intl. Literacy Day — A336

1988, Sept. 10 Photo. *Perf. 10½*

876 A336 2.90d multi 1.50 .75

WHO, 40th Anniv. — A337

1988, Oct. 15

877 A337 2.90d multi 1.40 .70

Fight Apartheid A338

1988, Nov. 19 Litho. *Perf. 10½x11*

878 A338 2.50d multi 1.25 .50

Natl. Front Congress — A339

1988, Nov. 29 *Perf. 11x10½*

879 A339 1d multi .50 .25

Agriculture A340

1988, Dec. 24 *Perf. 10½*

880	A340	1d	Irrigation	.50	.25
881	A340	1d	Orchard, fields, livestock	.50	.25

Natl. Goals — A342

Airports — A343

1989, Mar. 9 Litho. *Perf. 11½*

Granite Paper

886	A342	1d	shown	.55	.25
887	A342	1d	Ancient fort	.55	.25
888	A342	1d	Telecommunications	.55	.25
889	A342	1d	Modern buildings	.55	.25
			Nos. 886-889 (4)	2.20	1.00

Nos. 887-889 horiz.

1989, Mar. 23 *Perf. 10½x11, 11x10½*

890	A343	2.90d	Oran Es Senia, horiz.	1.25	.50
891	A343	3.30d	Tebessa, horiz.	1.50	.65
892	A343	5d	shown	2.25	1.10
			Nos. 890-892 (3)	5.00	2.25

Development of the South — A344

1989, Apr. 24 Litho. *Perf. 13½*

893	A344	1d	Irrigation	.45	.25
894	A344	1.80d	Building	.70	.40
895	A344	2.50d	Fossil fuel extraction, vert.	1.10	.55
			Nos. 893-895 (3)	2.25	1.20

Eradicate Locusts A345

1989, May 25 *Perf. 10½*

896 A345 1d multi .50 .25

National Service — A346

1989, May 11 Litho. *Perf. 13½*

897 A346 2d multicolored 1.50 .60

1st Moon Landing, 20th Anniv. A347

4d, Astronaut, lunar module, Moon's surface.

1989, July 23 Litho. *Perf. 13½*

898	A347	2.90d	shown	1.25	.55
899	A347	4d	multi, vert.	1.60	.75

Interparliamentary Union, Cent. — A348

1989, Sept. 4 ***Perf. 10½***

900 A348 2.90d gold, brt rose lil & blk	1.10	.40

Produce A349

1989, Sept. 23 **Litho.** ***Perf. 11½***

Granite Paper

901 Strip of 3	4.50	4.50
a. A349 2d multi, diff.	.75	.35
b. A349 3d multi, diff.	1.25	.50
c. A349 5d shown	1.90	1.25

Fish — A350

1989, Oct. 27 **Litho.** ***Perf. 13½***

902 A350 1d Sarda sarda	.80	.30
903 A350 1.80d Zeus faber	1.50	.50
904 A350 2.90d Pagellus bogaraveo	2.25	.70
905 A350 3.30d Xiphias gladius	2.75	.90
Nos. 902-905 (4)	7.30	2.40

Algerian Revolution, 35th Anniv. — A351

1989, Nov. 4 **Litho.** ***Perf. 13½***

906 A351 1d multicolored	.50	.25

African Development Bank, 25th Anniv. — A352

1989, Nov. 18 ***Perf. 10½***

907 A352 1d multicolored	.50	.25

Mushrooms A353

No. 908, Boletus satanas. No. 909, Psalliota xanthoderma. No. 910, Lepiota procera. No. 911, Lactarius deliciosus.

1989, Dec. 16 ***Perf. 13½***

908 A353 1d mutli	1.25	.30
909 A353 1.80d multi	1.90	.75
910 A353 2.90d multi	3.00	1.00
911 A353 3.30d multi	4.00	1.25
Nos. 908-911 (4)	10.15	3.30

A354

A355

1990, Jan. 18 **Litho.** ***Perf. 10½***

912 A354 1d multicolored	.50	.25

Pan-African Postal Union, 10th anniv.

1990, Feb. 22 **Litho.** ***Perf. 14***

913 A355 1d Energy conservation	.60	.25

A356

A357

1990, Mar. 2 **Photo.** ***Perf. 11½***

914 A356 3d multicolored	1.40	.50

African Soccer Championships.

1990, May 17 **Litho.** ***Perf. 13½***

917 A357 2.90d shown	1.10	.50
918 A357 5d Trophy	2.00	.90

World Cup Soccer Championships, Italy.

Rural Electrification — A358

1990, June 21

919 A358 2d multicolored	.90	.30

Youth A359

Youth Holding Rainbow — A360

1990, July 6 ***Perf. 13½***

920 A359 2d multicolored	.75	.30
921 A360 3d multicolored	1.25	.50

Maghreb Arab Union — A361

1990 ***Perf. 14x13½***

922 A361 1d multicolored	.50	.25

Vocations A362

1990, Apr. 26 **Litho.** ***Perf. 12½***

923 A362 2d Craftsmen	.85	.40
924 A362 2.90d Auto mechanics	1.10	.60
925 A362 3.30d Deep sea fishing	1.90	.70
Nos. 923-925 (3)	3.85	1.70

Organization of Petroleum Exporting Countries (OPEC), 30th Anniv. — A363

1990 ***Perf. 13½***

926 A363 2d multicolored	1.00	.30

Savings Promotion A364

1990, Oct. 31 **Litho.** ***Perf. 14***

927 A364 1d multicolored	.50	.25

Namibian Independence — A365

1990, Nov. 8

928 A365 3d multicolored	1.00	.30

A366

Farm animals.

1990, Nov. 29 ***Perf. 13½***

929 A366 1d Duck	.55	.25
930 A366 2d Rabbit, horiz.	1.10	.40
931 A366 2.90d Turkey	1.40	.60
932 A366 3.30d Rooster, horiz.	1.75	.75
Nos. 929-932 (4)	4.80	2.00

A367

1990, Dec. 11

933 A367 1d multicolored	.45	.25

Anti-French Riots, 30th anniv.

A368

1990, Dec. 20 ***Perf. 14***

934 A368 1d multicolored	.40	.25

Fight against respiratory diseases.

A369

1991, Feb. 24 **Litho.** ***Perf. 13½***

935 A369 1d multicolored	.35	.25

Constitution, 2nd anniv.

Flower Type of 1986

1991, May 23 **Litho.** ***Perf. 13½***

Size: 26x36mm

936 A312 2d Jasminum fruticans	.80	.30
937 A312 4d Dianthus crinitus	1.90	.70
938 A312 5d Cyclamen africanum	2.25	1.00
Nos. 936-938 (3)	4.95	2.00

Children's Drawings A370

1991, June 3 **Litho.** ***Perf. 13½***

939 A370 3d shown	1.25	.50
940 A370 4d Children playing	1.25	.50

Maghreb Arab Union Summit — A371

1991, June 10

941 A371 1d multicolored	.45	.25

Geneva Convention on Refugees, 40th Anniv. — A372

1991, July 28 Litho. ***Perf. 14½x13½***
942 A372 3d multicolored 1.00 .35

Postal Service A373

1991, Oct. 12 ***Perf. 14***
943 A373 1.50d shown .60 .25
944 A373 4.20d Expo emblem, vert. 1.25 .50

Telecom '91, 6th World Forum and Exposition on Telecommunications, Geneva, Switzerland (No. 944).

Butterflies A374

1991, Nov. 21 Litho. ***Perf. 11½***
Granite Paper
945 A374 2d Zerynthia rumina 1.00 .30
946 A374 4d Melitaea didyma 1.40 .45
947 A374 6d Vanessa atalanta 1.90 .70
948 A374 7d Nymphalis polychloros 2.25 1.00
Nos. 945-948 (4) 6.55 2.45

A375

1991, Dec. 21 ***Perf. 12***
Granite Paper
949 A375 3d Necklace .75 .30
950 A375 4d Jewelry of Southern Tuaregs .85 .45
951 A375 5d Brooch 1.00 .70
952 A375 7d Rings, horiz. 1.75 1.10
Nos. 949-952 (4) 4.35 2.55

A376

1992, Mar. 8 Litho. ***Perf. 14***
953 A376 1.50d Algerian Women .50 .25

Gazelles A377

Designs: 1.50d, Gazella dorcas. 6.20d, Gazella cuvieri. 8.60d, Gazella dama.

1992, May 13 ***Perf. 14½x13***
954 A377 1.50d multicolored .50 .25
955 A377 6.20d multicolored 1.10 .60
956 A377 8.60d multicolored 1.75 .80
Nos. 954-956 (3) 3.35 1.65

1992 Summer Olympics, Barcelona A379

1992, June 24 Litho. ***Perf. 14***
958 A379 6.20d Runners 1.50 .50

A381

1992, July 7 Litho. ***Perf. 14***
960 A381 5d multicolored 1.10 .30

Independence, 30th anniv.

A382

Medicinal plants: No. 961, Ajuga iva. No. 962, Rhamnus alaternus. No. 963, Silybum marianum. No. 964, Lavandula stoechas.

1992, Sept. 23 Litho. ***Perf. 14***
961 A382 1.50d multi .55 .25
962 A382 5.10d multi 1.25 .40
963 A382 6.20d multi 1.40 .55
964 A382 8.60d multi 1.75 .75
Nos. 961-964 (4) 4.95 1.95

Post Office Modernization A383

1992, Oct. 10 Litho. ***Perf. 14***
965 A383 1.50d multicolored .40 .25

Marine Life — A384

Designs: 1.50d, Hippocampus hippocampus. 2.70d, Caretta caretta. 6.20d, Muraena helena. 7.50d, Palinurus elephas.

1992, Dec. 23
966 A384 1.50d multicolored .55 .25
967 A384 2.70d multicolored .85 .25
968 A384 6.20d multicolored 1.75 .60
969 A384 7.50d multicolored 1.90 .75
Nos. 966-969 (4) 5.05 1.85

Pres. Mohammad Boudiaf (1919-92) — A385

1992, Nov. 3 Litho. ***Perf. 11½***
Granite Paper
970 A385 2d green & multi .45 .25
971 A385 8.60d blue & multi 1.90 .75

Coins A386

1992, Dec. 16 Litho. ***Perf. 11½***
Granite Paper
972 A386 1.50d Numidia, 2nd cent. BC .30 .25
973 A386 2d Dinar, 14th cent. .45 .25
974 A386 5.10d Dinar, 11th cent. 1.00 .35
975 A386 6.20d Abdelkader, 19th cent. 1.25 .50
Nos. 972-975 (4) 3.00 1.35

Door Knockers — A387

Flowering Trees — A388

1993, Feb. 17 Litho. ***Perf. 14***
976 A387 2d Algiers .30 .25
977 A387 5.60d Constantine .80 .40
978 A387 8.60d Tlemcen 1.50 .65
Nos. 976-978 (3) 2.60 1.30

1993, Mar. 17 ***Perf. 12x11½, 11½x12***
Granite Paper
979 A388 4.50d Neflier (medlar), horiz. .85 .40
980 A388 8.60d Cognassier (quince) 1.75 .75
981 A388 11d Abricotier (apricot) 2.25 .95
Nos. 979-981 (3) 4.85 2.10

Natl. Coast Guard Service, 20th Anniv. A389

1993, Apr. 3 Litho. ***Perf. 14***
982 A389 2d multicolored 1.00 .30

Traditional Grain Processing A390

1993, May 19 Litho. ***Perf. 14***
983 A390 2d Container .45 .25
984 A390 5.60d Millstone .90 .50
985 A390 8.60d Press 1.40 .65
Nos. 983-985 (3) 2.75 1.40

Royal Mausoleums — A391

1993, June 16 Litho. ***Perf. 14***
986 A391 8.60d Mauretania 1.10 .60
987 A391 12d El Khroub 1.90 .80

Ports A392

1993, Oct. 20 Litho. ***Perf. 14x13½***
988 A392 2d Annaba .35 .25
989 A392 8.60d Arzew 1.50 .55

Varanus Griseus A393

Design: 2d, Chamaeleo vulgaris, vert.

Perf. 13½x14, 14x13½
1993, Nov. 20
990 A393 2d multicolored .60 .25
991 A393 8.60d multicolored 1.90 .80

Tourism A394

1993, Dec. 18 Litho. ***Perf. 14x13½***
992 A394 2d Tipaza .35 .25
993 A394 8.60d Kerzaz 1.10 .50

A395

1994, Jan. 2 ***Perf. 13½x14***
994 A395 2d multicolored .60 .25

SONATRACH (Natl. Society for Research, Transformation, and Commercialization of Hydrocarbons), 30th anniv.

Chahid Day — A396

1994, Feb. 18 Litho. ***Perf. 13½x14***
995 A396 2d multicolored .60 .25

1994 World Cup Soccer Championships, US — A397

1994, Mar. 16 *Perf. 14x13½*
996 A397 8.60d multicolored 2.75 .80

A398

A399

Orchids: 5.60d, Orchis simia lam. 8.60d, Ophrys lutea cavan. 11d, Ophrys apifera huds.

1994, Apr. 20 **Litho.** *Perf. 11½*
Granite Paper

997 A398 5.60d multicolored 1.50 .60
998 A398 8.60d multicolored 1.75 .80
999 A398 11d multicolored 2.75 1.25
Nos. 997-999 (3) 6.00 2.65

1994, May 21 **Litho.** *Perf. 13x14*

Ancient petroglyphs.

1000 A399 3d Inscriptions 1.00 .25
1001 A399 10d Man on horse 2.25 .70

A400

1994, June 25
1002 A400 12d multicolored 2.10 .65

Intl. Olympic Committee, cent.

A401

1994, July 13
1003 A401 3d multicolored .50 .25

World Population Day.

Views of Algiers Type of 1992

Design: 3d, like No. 775.

1994, July 13 **Litho.** *Perf. 14*
1010 A290b 3d dk blue & lt blue .75 .25

Jewelry from Saharan Atlas Region A402

Perf. 13½x14, 14x13½
1994, Oct. 18 **Litho.**
1019 A402 3d Fibules, vert. .70 .25
1020 A402 5d Belt 1.00 .40
1021 A402 12d Bracelets 2.75 .95
Nos. 1019-1021 (3) 4.45 1.60

A403

1994, Nov. 3 **Litho.** *Perf. 13½x14*
1022 A403 3d multicolored .40 .25

Algerian Revolution, 40th anniv.

A404

1994, Nov. 16 **Litho.** *Perf. 13½x14*
1023 A404 3d Ladybugs .50 .25
1024 A404 12d Beetles 2.00 .75

Fight Against AIDS A405

1994, Dec. 1 **Litho.** *Perf. 14x13½*
1025 A405 3d multicolored 1.00 .25

Folk Dances — A406

1994, Dec. 17 **Litho.** *Perf. 13½x14*
1026 A406 3d Algeroise .50 .25
1027 A406 10d Constantinoise 1.25 .65
1028 A406 12d Alaoui 1.50 .80
Nos. 1026-1028 (3) 3.25 1.70

See Nos. 1170-1172.

Minerals — A407

1994, Sept. 21
1029 A407 3d Gres lite-erode .70 .25
1030 A407 5d Cipolin 1.10 .40
1031 A407 10d Marne a turitella 2.75 .95
Nos. 1029-1031 (3) 4.55 1.60

World Tourism Organization, 20th Anniv. — A408

1995, Jan. 28 **Litho.** *Perf. 14x13½*
1032 A408 3d multicolored .40 .25

Honey Bees — A409

1995, Feb. 22 *Perf. 13½x14, 14x13½*
1033 A409 3d shown .40 .25
1034 A409 13d On flower, horiz. 1.60 .80

Flowers — A410

Granite Paper

1995, Mar. 29 **Photo.** *Perf. 11½*
1035 A410 3d Dahlias .55 .25
1036 A410 10d Zinnias 1.60 .70
1037 A410 13d Lilacs 1.90 .85
Nos. 1035-1037 (3) 4.05 1.80

Decorative Stonework — A411

Various patterns.

1995, Apr. 19 *Perf. 14*
1039 A411 3d brown .35 .25
1040 A411 4d green .45 .25
1041 A411 5d deep claret .55 .30
Nos. 1039-1041 (3) 1.35 .80

End of World War II, 50th Anniv. A413

1995, May 3 *Perf. 14x13½*
1048 A413 3d multicolored .80 .25

Souvenir Sheet

VE Day, 50th Anniv. — A414

1995, May 10 **Litho.** *Perf. 13½x14*
1049 A414 13d multicolored 8.00 8.00

Volleyball, Cent. — A415

1995, June 14
1050 A415 3d multicolored .70 .25

Environmental Protection — A416

1995, June 5
1051 A416 3d Air, water pollution .40 .25
1052 A416 13d Air pollution 1.60 .85

General Electrification A417

1995, July 5 **Litho.** *Perf. 13½x14*
1053 A417 3d multicolored .45 .25

UN, 50th Anniv. A418

1995, Oct. 24 *Perf. 14x13½*
1054 A418 13d multicolored 2.50 1.00

Pottery — A419

10d, Pot, Lakhdaria. 20d, Pitcher, Aokas. 21d, Jar, Larbaa Nath Iraten. 30d, Vase, Ouadhia.

1995, Nov. 14 **Litho.** *Perf. 14*
1055 A419 10d dark brown 1.00 .50
1056 A419 20d dull maroon 2.10 1.00
1057 A419 21d golden brown 2.10 1.00
1058 A419 30d dark rose brown 3.25 1.50
Nos. 1055-1058 (4) 8.45 4.00

Aquatic Birds A420

1995, Dec. 20 **Litho.** *Perf. 14x13½*
1059 A420 3d Tadorna tadorna .60 .25
1060 A420 5d Gallinago gallinago 1.00 .40

1996 Summer Olympics, Atlanta A421

1996, Jan. 24 Litho. *Perf. 14x13½*
1061 A421 20d multicolored 2.25 1.00

Touareg Leather Crafts A422

Perf. 14x13½, 13½x14
1996, Feb. 14 Litho.
1062 A422 5d shown 1.25 .25
1063 A422 16d Saddle bag, vert. 2.00 .80

Pasteur Institute of Algeria — A423

1996, Mar. 20 Litho. *Perf. 13½x14*
1064 A423 5d multicolored .75 .25

Youm El Ilm — A424

Designs: 16d, Dove, stylus, vert. 23d, Open book showing pencil, stylus, compass, satellite in earth orbit, vert.

Perf. 14x13½,13½x14
1996, Apr. 16 Litho.
1065 A424 5d multicolored .55 .25
1066 A424 16d multicolored 1.40 .75
1067 A424 23d multicolored 2.50 1.10
Nos. 1065-1067 (3) 4.45 2.10

Minerals A425

Mineral, region: 10d, Iron, Djebel-Ouenza. 20d, Gold, Tirek-Amesmessa.

1996, May 6 Litho. *Perf. 14x13½*
1068 A425 10d multicolored 1.25 .50
1069 A425 20d multicolored 2.25 .90

Butterflies A426

Designs: 5d, Pandoriana pandora. 10d, Coenonympha pamphilus. 20d, Cynthia cardui. 23d, Melanargia galathea.

1996, June 12 Litho. *Perf. 11½*
Granite Paper
1070 A426 5d multicolored .80 .25
1071 A426 10d multicolored 1.40 .50
1072 A426 20d multicolored 3.00 1.00
1073 A426 23d multicolored 3.25 1.25
Nos. 1070-1073 (4) 8.45 3.00

Civil Protection A427

5d, Giving medical aid, ambulance. 23d, Prevention of natural disasters, vert.

Perf. 14x13½, 13½x14
1996, Oct. 9 Litho.
1074 A427 5d multicolored .50 .25
1075 A427 23d multicolored 2.25 1.25

World Day Against Use of Illegal Drugs A428

1996, June 26 Litho. *Perf. 14x13½*
1076 A428 5d multicolored .70 .25

UNICEF, 50th Anniv. — A429

Stylized designs: 5d, Two children, wreath, pencils, flowers. 10d, Five children, pencil, key, flower, flag, hypodermic.

1996, Nov. 20 Litho. *Perf. 13½x14*
1077 A429 5d multicolored .50 .25
1078 A429 10d multicolored .90 .35

4th General Census A430

1997, Feb. 12 Litho. *Perf. 14x13½*
1079 A430 5d multicolored .50 .25

Protest at Ouargla, 35th Anniv. — A431

1997, Feb. 27 *Perf. 13½x14*
1080 A431 5d multicolored .50 .25

Interior Courts of Algerian Dwellings A432

Designs: 5d, Palace of Hassan Pasha. 10d, Khedaouj El-Amia, Algiers. 20d, Palace of Light. 30d, Abdellatif Villa.

1996, Dec. 18 Litho. *Perf. 13½x14*
1081 A432 5d multicolored .35 .25
1082 A432 10d multicolored .80 .45
1083 A432 20d multicolored 1.60 1.00
1084 A432 30d multicolored 2.50 1.40
Nos. 1081-1084 (4) 5.25 3.10

Paintings by Ismail Samsom (1934-88) A433

20d, Woman with Pigeons. 30d, Interrogation.

1996, Dec. 25 *Perf. 14*
1085 A433 20d multicolored 1.50 1.00
1086 A433 30d multicolored 2.25 1.40

Victory Day, 35th Anniv. A434

1997, Mar. 19 *Perf. 14x13½*
1087 A434 5d multicolored .50 .25

Flowers — A435

Designs: 5d, Ficaria verna. 16d, Lonicera arborea. 23d, Papaver rhoeas.

1997, Apr. 23 Litho. *Perf. 13½x14*
1088 A435 5d multicolored .55 .25
1089 A435 16d multicolored 1.50 .80
1090 A435 23d multicolored 2.10 1.40
Nos. 1088-1090 (3) 4.15 2.45

World Day to Stop Smoking — A436

1997, May 31 Litho. *Perf. 13½x14*
1091 A436 5d multicolored .50 .25

Legislative Elections — A437

1997, June 4
1092 A437 5d multicolored .50 .25

Scorpions A438

Designs: 5d, Buthus occitanus tunetanus. 10d, Androctonus australis hector.

1997, June 18 *Perf. 14x13½*
1093 A438 5d multicolored .55 .25
1094 A438 10d multicolored .95 .55

Natl. Independence, 35th Anniv. — A439

Designs: 5d, Crowd celebrating, flags. 10d, Doves, broken chain, "35," flag.

1997, July 5 Litho. *Perf. 14x13½*
1095 A439 5d multicolored .50 .25

Souvenir Sheet
Perf. 14
1096 A439 10d multicolored 3.00 3.00

No. 1096 contains one 30x40mm stamp.

Wood Carvings — A440

Designs: 5d, Inscription, Nedroma Mosque. 23d, Door, Ketchaoua Mosque.

1997, Jan. 15 Litho. *Perf. 13½x14*
1097 A440 5d multicolored .50 .25
1098 A440 23d multicolored 1.75 1.00

Moufdi Zakaria (1908-77), poet. — A441

1997, Aug. 17 Litho. *Perf. 13½x14*
1099 A441 5d multicolored .50 .25

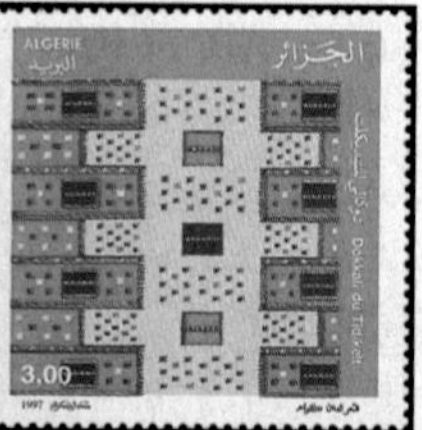

Textile Patterns A442

1997, Sept. 17 Litho. *Perf. 14*
1100 A442 3d Dokkali .30 .25
1101 A442 5d Tellis .50 .25
1102 A442 10d Bou-Taleb .80 .50
1103 A442 20d Ddil 1.60 1.10
Nos. 1100-1103 (4) 3.20 2.10

Natl. Police Force, 25th Anniv. A443

1997, Oct. 6 ***Perf. 14x13½***
1104 A443 5d multicolored .60 .25

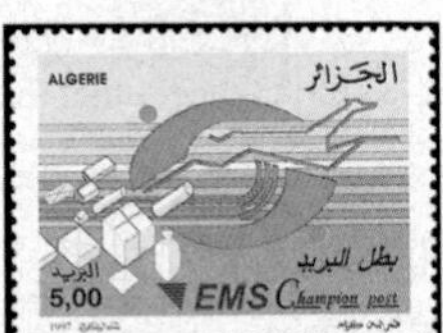

Express Mail Service A444

1997, Oct. 9
1105 A444 5d multicolored .60 .25

Local Elections — A445

1997, Oct. 23 ***Perf. 13½x14***
1106 A445 5d multicolored .50 .25

Lighthouses A446

Perf. 14x13½, 13½x14
1997, Nov. 5 **Litho.**
1107 A446 5d Tenes .60 .25
1108 A446 10d Cape Caxine, vert. 1.40 .60

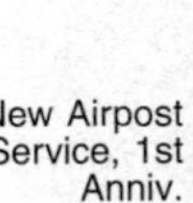

New Airpost Service, 1st Anniv. A447

1997, Nov. 17 ***Perf. 14x13½***
1109 A447 5d multicolored .60 .25

Shells A448

Designs: 5d, Chlamys varia. 10d, Bolinus brandaris. 20d, Hinia reticulata, vert.

Perf. 14x13½, 13½x14
1997, Dec. 17 **Litho.**
1110 A448 5d multicolored .90 .25
1111 A448 10d multicolored 1.50 .50
1112 A448 20d multicolored 3.00 1.00
Nos. 1110-1112 (3) 5.40 1.75

A449

1997, Dec. 25 ***Perf. 13½x14***
1113 A449 5d multicolored .50 .25

Election of the Natl. Council.

A450

Completion of Government Reforms: a, Natl. flag, people, book, ballot box. b, People, open book, torch. c, Ballot box. d, Flag, rising sun, flower. e, Ballots, building, flag.

1997, Dec. 30 **Litho.** ***Perf. 13½x14***
1114 A450 5d Strip of 5, #a.-e. 2.50 2.50

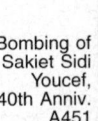

Bombing of Sakiet Sidi Youcef, 40th Anniv. A451

1998, Feb. 8 **Litho.** ***Perf. 14x13½***
1115 A451 5d multicolored .70 .25

National Archives A452

1998, Feb. 16
1116 A452 5d multicolored .50 .25

Intl. Women's Day A453

1998, Mar. 8 **Litho.** ***Perf. 14x13½***
1117 A453 5d multicolored .50 .25

Expo '98, Lisbon A454

1998, Jan. 21 **Litho.** ***Perf. 14x13½***
1118 A454 5d shown .50 .25

Size: 80x75mm

Imperf

1119 A454 24d Mosaic 3.25 3.25

1998 World Cup Soccer Championships, Paris — A455

1998, Apr. 15 **Litho.** ***Perf. 13½x14***
1120 A455 24d multi 2.40 1.10

Algiers Casbah A456

Designs: 5d, Aerial view, vert. 10d, Buildings, vert. 24d, Aerial view, diff.

1998, Apr. 22 ***Perf. 13½x14, 14x13½***
1121 A456 5d multi .40 .25
1122 A456 10d multi .75 .50
1123 A456 24d multi 2.00 1.10
Nos. 1121-1123 (3) 3.15 1.85

Zaatcha Resistance — A457

1998, May 20 ***Perf. 13¼x13***
1124 A457 5d multi .50 .25

Tourism A458

5d, Mountains, farm, desert, vert. 10d, Youths, modes of transportation. 24d, Taghit.

Perf. 13½x14, 14x13½
1998, June 4 **Litho.**
1125 A458 5d multi .40 .25
1126 A458 10d multi 1.00 .50
1127 A458 24d multi 2.00 1.10
Nos. 1125-1127 (3) 3.40 1.85

Arab Post Day A459

1998, Aug. 3 **Litho.** ***Perf. 14x13½***
1128 A459 5d multi .75 .25

Interpol, 75th Anniv. A460

1998, Sept. 7 **Litho.** ***Perf. 14x13½***
1129 A460 5d multi .60 .25

Creation of Provisional Government, 40th Anniv. — A461

1998, Sept. 19 ***Perf. 13¼x13***
1130 A461 5d multi .50 .25

Natl. Diplomacy Day A462

1998, Oct. 8 ***Perf. 14***
1131 A462 5d multi .50 .25

Algerian Olympic Committee, 35th Anniv. A463

1998, Oct. 18 ***Perf. 14x13½***
1132 A463 5d multi .60 .25

Birds A464

Designs: 5d, Pandion haliaetus. 10d, Larus audouinii. 24d, Phalacrocorax aristotelis, vert. 30d, Phalacrocorax carbo, vert.

Perf. 14x13½, 13½x14
1998, Nov. 11
1133 A464 5d multi .70 .25
1134 A464 10d multi 1.40 .50
1135 A464 24d multi 2.75 1.10
1136 A464 30d multi 3.50 1.50
Nos. 1133-1136 (4) 8.35 3.35

See Nos. 1204-1207, 1325-1326.

Universal Declaration of Human Rights, 50th Anniv. A465

1998, Dec. 10 **Litho.** ***Perf. 14x13½***
1137 A465 5d Profiles, emblem .70 .25
1138 A465 24d shown 2.25 1.00

Spinning and Weaving Tools A466

Designs: 5d, Comb, vert. 10d, Cards. 20d, Spindle, vert. 24d, Loom, vert.

1999, Jan. 20 ***Perf. 13½x14, 14x13½***
1139 A466 5d multi .55 .25
1140 A466 10d multi 1.00 .50
1141 A466 20d multi 2.10 1.00
1142 A466 24d multi 2.50 1.25
Nos. 1139-1142 (4) 6.15 3.00

Natl. Chahid Day — A467

1999, Feb. 18 ***Perf. 13x13¼***
1143 A467 5d multi .50 .25

Flowering Trees A468

1999, Mar. 17 ***Perf. 14x13½, 13½x14***
1144 A468 5d Pear .50 .25
1145 A468 10d Plum .90 .50
1146 A468 24d Orange, vert. 2.25 1.25
Nos. 1144-1146 (3) 3.65 2.00

Presidential Elections A469

1999, Apr. 15 ***Perf. 13x13¼***
1147 A469 5d multi .50 .25

Handicrafts A470

Designs: 5d, Tlemcen mosaic, 14th cent., vert. 10d, Mosaic, Al Qal'a of Beni Hammad, 11th cent, vert. 20d, Cradle. 24d, Table.

1999, Apr. 18 ***Perf. 13¼x14, 14x13¼***
1148 A470 5d multi .60 .25
1149 A470 10d multi 1.00 .60
1150 A470 20d multi 2.00 1.00
1151 A470 24d multi 2.40 1.25
Nos. 1148-1151 (4) 6.00 3.10

7th African Games, Johannesburg — A471

Stylized athletes and: 5d, Map of Africa, vert. 10d, South African flag.

1999, May 12 ***Perf. 13¼x14, 14x13¼***
1152 A471 5d multi .50 .25
1153 A471 10d multi .90 .50

A472

Rocks.

1999, June 6 ***Perf. 13¼x14***
1154 A472 5d Gneiss .50 .25
1155 A472 20d Granite 1.75 1.00
1156 A472 24d Schist 2.25 1.25
Nos. 1154-1156 (3) 4.50 2.50

A473

1999, July 12 ***Perf. 13x13¼***
1157 A473 5d multi .50 .25

Organization of African Unity, 35th summit.

A474

1999, July 12 ***Perf. 13¼x14***
1158 A474 5d multi .50 .25

Organization of African Unity Convention on Refugees.

A475

1999, July 22 ***Perf. 13x13¼***
1159 A475 5d Police Day 1.00 .25

Intl. Year of Culture and Peace (in 2000) A476

1999, Sept. 14 **Litho.** ***Perf. 14***
1160 A476 5d multi .50 .25

Fish A477

Designs: 5d, Dentex dentex. 10d, Mullus surmuletus. 20d, Dentex gibbosus. 24d, Diplodus sargus.

1999, Sept. 15 ***Perf. 14x13¼***
1161 A477 5d multi .65 .25
1162 A477 10d multi 1.25 .50
1163 A477 20d multi 2.25 1.00
1164 A477 24d multi 3.25 1.25
Nos. 1161-1164 (4) 7.40 3.00

Civil Peace Referendum A478

1999, Sept. 16 ***Perf. 13¼x14***
1165 A478 5d multi .50 .25

UPU, 125th Anniv. A479

1999, Oct. 9 ***Perf. 14x13¼***
1166 A479 5d multi .55 .25

World Post Day A480

1999, Oct. 9 **Litho.** ***Perf. 14x13½***
1167 A480 5d multi .55 .25

Intl. Rural Women's Day A481

1999, Oct. 14 **Litho.** ***Perf. 14x13¼***
1168 A481 5d multi .55 .25

Algerian Revolution, 45th Anniv. — A482

Soldiers and: a, Helicopters, burning flag. b, Burning flag.

1999, Nov. 1 ***Perf. 13x13¼***
1169 A482 5d Pair, #a.-b. 1.25 1.25

Folk Dances Type of 1994

1999, Dec. 15 ***Perf. 13¼x14***
1170 A406 5d Chaoui .60 .25
1171 A406 10d Targuie 1.10 .50
1172 A406 24d Mzab 2.25 1.25
Nos. 1170-1172 (3) 3.95 2.00

Millennium — A483

No. 1173: a, Doves, UN emblem. b, Sun, plant, trees. c, Umbrella over wheat and corn plants. d, Microscope and flasks. e, Crane, ship, truck. f, Train, Concorde, satellite dish, satellite, Moon. g, Windmills. h, Globe, ballot box. i, Apollo 15 astronauts on Moon. j, Film, inkwell, musical instrument and notes.

No. 1174: a, Dove with olive branch. b, Hand, flora, fauna. c, Satellites, computer, map of Africa and Europe. d, Heart, staff of Aesculapius, Red Cross, Red Crescent. e, Stylized globe and arrows. f, Animals, film, violin, painting, book. g, Flame, sun, water. h, Hand holding plant. i, symbols of democracy. j, Satellite, planets, space shuttle, astronaut.

Sawtooth Die Cut 6¼ Vert.

2000, Jan. 19 **Self-Adhesive**

Booklet Stamps

1173 Bklt. pane of 10 + 2 labels 10.00
a.-j. A483 5d any single .50 .25
1174 Bklt. pane of 10 + 2 labels 10.00
a.-j. A483 5d any single .50 .25

Birds A484

Designs: No. 1175, 5d, Canary (serin cini). No. 1176, 5d, Finch (pinson), vert. 10d, Bullfinch (bouvreuil). 24d, Goldfinch (chardonneret), vert.

Perf. 14x13¼, 13¼x14

2000, Jan. 19 **Litho.**
1175-1178 A484 Set of 4 5.50 5.50

Expo 2000, Hanover A485

2000, Feb. 16 **Litho.** ***Perf. 14x13¼***
1179 A485 5d multi .60 .30

2000 Summer Olympics, Sydney A486

2000, Mar. 22
1180 A486 24d multi 2.50 1.10

Telethon 2000 — A487

2000, Apr. 8 ***Perf. 13¼x14***
1181 A487 5d multi .75 .25

Civil Concord A488

Designs: 5d, Dove, handshake, crowd, vert. 10d, Handshake, hands releasing dove. 20d, Handshake, doves, flowers. 24d, Doves, flowers, handshake, vert.

Perf. 11½x11¾, 11¾x11½

2000, Apr. 15
1182-1185 A488 Set of 4 6.50 3.25

National Library — A489

2000, Apr. 16 *Perf. 13½x13*
1186 A489 5d multi .60 .25

Blood Donation — A490

2000, May 2 *Perf. 13¼x14*
1187 A490 5d multi .60 .25

Tuareg Handicrafts A491

Background colors: 5d, Rose. 10d, Buff, vert.

2000, May 17 *Perf. 14*
1188-1189 A491 Set of 2 1.60 .65

Famous Men — A492

No. 1190, Mohammed Dib (b. 1920), writer. No. 1191, Mustapha Kateb (1920-89), actor. No. 1192, Ali Maachi (1927-58), musician. No. 1193, Mohamed Racim (1896-1975), artist.

2000, June 8 *Perf. 13¼x13*
1190-1193 A492 10d Set of 4 4.50 2.00

Insects — A493

No. 1194, 5d, Hanneton. No. 1195, 5d, Anthrene. 10d, Vrillete du pain. 24d, Carabe.

2000, Sept. 20 *Perf. 13¼x14*
1194-1197 A493 Set of 4 5.25 2.50

Roman Cinerary Urns Found at Tipasa — A494

2000, Oct. 18 **Litho.** *Perf. 14*
1198-1200 A494 Set of 3, 5d, 10d, 24d 4.25 2.25

Orchids — A495

Designs: 5d, Limodorum abortivum. 10d, Orchis papilionacea. 24d, Orchis provincialis.

2000, Dec. 13 **Litho.** *Perf. 14*
1201-1203 A495 Set of 3 4.50 2.50

Bird Type of 1998

Designs: No. 1204, 5d, Anser anser. No. 1205, 5d, Recurvirostra avosetta, vert. 10d, Botaurus stellaris, vert. 24d, Numenius arquata.

2001, Jan. 24
1204-1207 A464 Set of 4 5.00 2.75

Handicrafts — A496

Designs: 5d, Skampla, vert. 10d, Etagere. 24d, Mirror, vert.

2001, Feb. 21
1208-1210 A496 Set of 3 4.50 2.50

National Parks A497

Designs: 5d, Belezma, vert. 10d, Gouraya. 20d, Théniet el Had. 24d, El Kala, vert.

2001, Mar. 21 *Perf. 13¼x14, 14x13¼*
1211-1214 A497 Set of 4 7.25 3.25

1st Intl. Colloquium on St. Augustine of Hippo — A498

Designs: 5d, Statue of St. Augustine (25x37mm). 24d, Mosaic.

Perf. 13¼x14, 13¼x13 (24d)

2001, Mar. 31
1215-1216 A498 Set of 2 3.50 1.60

Silver Coins — A499

Designs: 5d, 1830 Ryal boudjou. 10d, 1826 Double boudjou. 24d, 1771 Ryal drahem.

2001, Apr. 25 **Litho.** *Perf. 13½x13*
1217-1219 A499 Set of 3 4.50 2.25

Natl. Scouting Day — A500

2001, May 27 **Litho.** *Perf. 14*
1220 A500 5d multi .60 .25

Palestinian Intifada — A501

2001, June 2
1221 A501 5d multi .60 .25

Children's Games A502

Designs: No. 1222, 5d, Jacks. No. 1223, 5d, Hopscotch. No. 1224, 5d, Top spinning. No. 1225, 5d, Marbles.

2001, June 2
1222-1225 A502 Set of 4 2.50 .90

Natl. Asthma Day — A503

2001, June 9
1226 A503 5d multi .50 .25

14th Mediterranean Games, Tunis, Tunisia — A504

Designs: No. 1227, 5d, Map, "50." No. 1228, 5d, Runners, emblem.

2001, July 25 **Litho.** *Perf. 14*
1227-1228 A504 Set of 2 1.00 .50

15th World Festival of Youth and Students — A505

2001, Aug. 8
1229 A505 5d multi .50 .25

Natl. Mujahedeen Day — A506

2001, Aug. 20 *Perf. 13¼x14*
1230 A506 5d multi .50 .25

Intl. Teachers' Day — A507

2001, Oct. 6 **Litho.** *Perf. 13¼x14*
1231 A507 5d multi .50 .25

Year of Dialogue Among Civilizations A508

2001, Oct. 9
1232 A508 5d multi .75 .25

Natl. Emigration Day — A509

2001, Oct. 17 *Perf. 14x13¼*
1233 A509 5d multi .50 .25

19th Cent. Revolt Leaders — A510

Designs: No. 1234, 5d, Sheik El-Mokrani, 1871-73. No. 1235, 5d, Sheik Bouamama, 1881-1908.

2001, Nov. 1 *Perf. 13¼x14*
1234-1235 A510 Set of 2 1.10 .50

Jewelry From Aurès Region — A511

Designs: No. 1236, 5d, Fibula. No. 1237, 5d, Earring. 24d, Pendant.

2002, Jan. 23
1236-1238 A511 Set of 3 3.00 3.00

2002 World Cup Soccer Championships, Japan and Korea — A512

Designs: 5d, Goalie, ball, net, pagoda. 24d, Oriental man, ball, vert.

2002, Feb. 27 ***Perf. 14x13¼, 13¼x14***
1239-1240 A512 Set of 2 2.75 2.00

Ceasefire With French Forces, 40th Anniv. — A513

2002, Mar. 19 ***Perf. 13x13½***
1241 A513 5d multi .70 .40

Villages A514

Designs: No. 1242, 5d, Sidi-Ouali. No. 1243, 5d, Casbah of Ighzar.

2002, Apr. 17 Litho. ***Perf. 14x13¼***
1242-1243 A514 Set of 2 1.00 .80

World Basketball Championships, Indianapolis A515

2002, May 15 ***Perf. 13¼x14***
1244 A515 5d multi .70 .40

Children's Day — A516

Children's art: No. 1245, 5d, Shown. No. 1246, 5d, Two girls, one waving.

2002, June 1 ***Perf. 14x13¼***
1245-1246 A516 Set of 2 1.00 .80

Mohamed Temmam (1915-88), Artist — A517

Designs: No. 1247, 10d, Self-portrait. No. 1248, 10d, Tailor.

2002, June 8 ***Perf. 13x13¼***
1247-1248 A517 Set of 2 2.00 1.50

Independence, 40th Anniv. — A518

Designs: 5d, Emblem. 24d, People with flag.

2002, July 5 Litho. ***Perf. 14***
1249-1250 A518 Set of 2 2.50 2.00

Rocks and Minerals A519

Designs: No. 1251, 5d, Conglomerate rock. No. 1252, 5d, Galena. No. 1253, 5d, Calcite, vert. No. 1254, 5d, Feldspar, vert.

2002, July 24
1251-1254 A519 Set of 4 1.75 1.90

Lighthouses A520

Designs: 5d, Cherchell. 10d, Cap de Fer. 24d, Ile de Rachgoun.

2002, Sept. 11
1255-1257 A520 Set of 3 3.50 2.75

Reorganization of Postal Service — A521

2002, Oct. 9
1258 A521 5d multi .50 .40

Pottery — A522

Designs: No. 1259, 5d, Oil lamp. No. 1260, 5d, Jar with handles, Iraten. No. 1261, 5d, Jar, Miliana. No. 1262, 5d, Cooking pot and couscousier, Lakhdaria.

2002, Oct. 23
1259-1262 A522 Set of 4 2.00 2.00

Intl. Day for Tolerance A523

2002, Nov. 16 Litho. ***Perf. 14***
1263 A523 24d multi 2.00 2.00

Shells A524

Designs: No. 1264, 5d, Acanthocardia aculeata. No. 1265, 5d, Venus verrucosa. No. 1266, 5d, Epitonium commune. No. 1267, 5d, Xenophora crispa.

2002, Dec. 4 Litho. ***Perf. 14***
1264-1267 A524 Set of 4 2.50 1.90

Medicinal Plants — A525

Designs: 5d, Eucalyptus globulus. 10d, Malva sylvestris. 24d, Laurus nobilis.

2002, Dec. 21
1268-1270 A525 Set of 3 3.25 2.75

Algeria — France Year A526

Designs: 5d, Eiffel Tower, Paris and Martyr's Monument, Algiers, vert. 24d, Flags of Algeria and France.

2003, Feb. 19
1271-1272 A526 Set of 2 2.50 2.00

10th Arab Games A527

2003, Feb. 26
1273 A527 5d multi .40 .40

Intl. Year of Water A528

Designs: 5d, El Maadjen, Relizane. 10d, Well, M'zab Valley. 24d, Kesria, Timimoun.

2003, Mar. 22 Litho. ***Perf. 14***
1274-1276 A528 Set of 3 3.50 2.75

Vandal Tablets A529

Designs: 10d, Slave sale document, 494. 24d, Tablet for calculations, 493, vert.

Perf. 13x13¼, 13¼x13

2003, Apr. 23 Litho.
1277-1278 A529 Set of 2 3.00 2.25

Portions of the designs were applied by a thermographic process producing a shiny, raised effect.

Natl. Students Day — A530

2003, May 19 Litho. ***Perf. 14***
1279 A530 5d multi .40 .30

Snails — A531

Designs: 5d, Rumina decollata. 24d, Heix aspersa.

2003, May 21 Litho. ***Perf. 14***
1280-1281 A531 Set of 2 2.50 2.00

African Union, 1st Anniv. — A532

2003, July 9 ***Perf. 13¼x14***
1282 A532 5d multi .50 .30

Seaweeds — A533

Designs: 5d, Ulva lactuca. 24d, Gymnogongrus crenulatus.

2003, July 30 Litho. ***Perf. 14***
1283-1284 A533 Set of 2 2.50 1.75

Roman Mosaics — A534

Designs: 5d, Farm Work. 10d, Ulysses and the Sirens. 24d, Hunting Scene.

2003, Sept. 17 ***Perf. 13½x14***
1285-1287 A534 Set of 3 3.50 2.75

Algerian Olympic Committee, 40th Anniv. A535

2003, Oct. 18 Litho. ***Perf. 14x13½***
1288 A535 5d multi .50 .30

World Diabetes Prevention Day — A536

2003, Nov. 14 ***Perf. 13½x14***
1289 A536 5d multi .50 .30

Architectural Decorations A537

Designs: 5d, Door, Hassan Pacha Palace, Algiers. 10d, Window, Hassan Pacha Palace. 24d, Ceiling, Djamaa Edjedid, Algiers.

2003, Dec. 17 Litho. ***Perf. 13x13¼***
1290-1292 A537 Set of 3 3.50 3.50

Algeria — People's Republic of China Diplomatic Relations, 45th Anniv. A538

2003, Dec. 22 ***Perf. 12***
1293 A538 5d multi .50 .40

2004 Summer Olympics, Athens — A539

Olympic rings, Parthenon and: 5d, Hurdler. 10d, Torch bearer.

2004, Feb. 29 ***Perf. 13¼x14***
1294-1295 A539 Set of 2 1.50 1.00

Intl. Women's Day — A540

2004, Mar. 8
1296 A540 5d multi .50 .30

Arbor Day A541

Trees: 5d, Olive. 10d, Date palm, vert.

Perf. 14x13¼, 13¼x14
2004, Mar. 21 Litho.
1297-1298 A541 Set of 2 1.50 .75

Numidian Kings — A542

Designs: No. 1299, 5d, Massinissa (r. 203 BC-148 BC). No. 1300, 5d, Micipsa (r. 148 BC-118 BC). No. 1301, 5d, Jugurtha (r. 118 BC-105 BC). No. 1302, 5d, Juba I (r. 63 BC-50 to 46 BC). No. 1303, 5d, Juba II (r. 29 BC- 25 BC).

2004, Mar. 31 Litho. ***Perf. 13¼x14***
1299-1303 A542 Set of 5 2.50 1.75

2004 Presidential Elections — A543

Litho. & Embossed
2004, Apr. 8 ***Perf. 13¼x13***
1304 A543 24d multi 2.25 1.50

FIFA (Fédération Internationale de Football Association), Cent. — A544

"100" and: 5d, Goalie. 24d, Soccer balls, world map.

Perf. 14, 14x13¼ (24d)
2004, May 21 Litho.
1305-1306 A544 Set of 2 2.50 1.50

Dromedary A545

2004, June 9 Litho. ***Perf. 14x13¼***
1307 A545 24d multi 2.25 1.50

Blood Donation Day — A546

2004, June 14 ***Perf. 14***
1308 A546 5d multi .50 .30

Professional Training — A547

2004, June 23
1309 A547 5d multi .50 .30

Intl. Chess Federation (FIDE), 80th Anniv. — A548

2004, July 21 Litho. ***Perf. 14***
1310 A548 5d multi 1.00 .50

CNEP Bank, 40th Anniv. A549

Bank emblems and: 5d, Bank notes. 24d, Algiers.

2004, Aug. 10 Litho. ***Perf. 14***
1311-1312 A549 Set of 2 2.50 2.25

Roses — A550

2004, Oct. 20 Litho. ***Perf. 14***
Color of Rose
1313 A550 15d yellow 1.00 1.00
1314 A550 20d yellow, diff. 2.00 2.00
1315 A550 30d red 3.00 3.00
1316 A550 50d pink 4.00 4.00
Nos. 1313-1316 (4) 10.00 10.00

Sixth Pan-African Conference of Red Cross and Red Crescent, Algiers — A551

2004, Sept. 8 Litho. ***Perf. 14***
1317 A551 24d multi 2.25 1.25

Sahara Desert Landmarks A552

Designs: 5d, In Téhaq. 24d, Ekanassay, vert.

Perf. 14, 14¼x14 (24d)
2004, Sept. 15
1318-1319 A552 Set of 2 2.50 1.25

Revolutionary Committee of Unity and Action, 50th Anniv. — A553

2004, Nov. 1 Litho. ***Perf. 13¼x13***
1320 A553 15d multi 1.75 1.00

Souvenir Sheet

Start of Algerian Revolution, 50th Anniv. — A554

2004, Nov. 1 Litho. ***Perf. 13½x13***
1321 A554 30d multi 2.50 2.50

Launch of ALSAT 1 Satellite, 2nd Anniv. A555

2004, Nov. 28 Litho. ***Perf. 14x13½***
1322 A555 30d multi 2.50 2.50

Environmental Protection — A556

2004, Dec. 22
1323 A556 15d multi 1.25 1.25

Rabah Bitat (1925-2000), Politician — A557

2004, Dec. 29 Litho. ***Perf. 14x13½***
1324 A557 15d multi 1.25 1.25

Bird Type of 1998

Designs: 10d, Columba palumbus. 15d, Columba livia.

2005, Jan. 26 Litho. ***Perf. 14x13½***
1325-1326 A464 Set of 2 2.00 2.00

Flowers — A559

Designs: 15d, Echium australis. 30d, Borago officinalis.

2005, Feb. 23 Litho. ***Perf. 13½x14***
1327-1328 A559 Set of 2 3.50 3.50

Day of the Handicapped — A560

2005, Mar. 14 ***Perf. 14x13½***
1329 A560 15d multi 1.10 1.10

Arab League Emblem and Algerian Flag A561

Inscription commemorating: 15d, 17th Arab Summit, Algiers. 30d, Arab League, 60th anniv., vert.

2005, Mar. 22 ***Perf. 14x13½, 13½x14***
1330-1331 A561 Set of 2 3.50 3.50

National Reconciliation — A562

2005, Apr. 8 ***Perf. 14x13½***
1332 A562 15d multi 1.25 1.25

Madrases A563

Madras in: 10d, Algiers. 15d, Constantine. 30d, Tlemcen.

2005, Apr. 16
1333-1335 A563 Set of 3 4.50 4.50

Science Day.

Intl. Day of Intellectual Property A564

2005, Apr. 26
1336 A564 15d multi 1.25 1.25

Intl. Day of Work Safety and Health — A565

2005, Apr. 28 ***Perf. 13½x14***
1337 A565 15d multi 1.25 1.25

Massacres of May 8, 1945, 60th Anniv. A566

2005, May 8 Litho. ***Perf. 14x13¼***
1338 A566 15d multi 1.25 1.25

15th Mediterranean Games, Almeria, Spain — A567

Games emblem and: 15d, Medal, stylized athletes. 30d, Mediterranean Sea and "2005," horiz.

2005, May 28 ***Perf. 13¼x14, 14x13¼***
1339-1340 A567 Set of 2 3.50 3.50

Poets — A568

Designs: 10d, Lakhdar Ben Khlouf. 15d, Mohamed Ben M'sayeb. 20d, Si Mohand-Ou-M'hand. 30d, Aissa El-Djermouni.

2005, June 8 Litho. ***Perf. 13x13½***
1341-1344 A568 Set of 4 6.00 6.00

World Day Against Drug Abuse A569

2005, June 26 ***Perf. 14x13½***
1345 A569 15d multi 1.25 1.25

General Algerian Muslim Student's Union, 50th Anniv. — A570

2005, July 9 Litho. ***Perf. 13½x14***
1346 A570 15d multi 1.25 1.25

Leopards A571

Leopard: 15d, Sitting. 30d, Standing.

2005, July 21 ***Perf. 14x13½***
1347-1348 A571 Set of 2 3.00 3.00

World Summit on the Information Society, Tunis — A572

2005, July 27 ***Perf. 13½x14***
1349 A572 15d multi 1.50 1.50

Moudjahid Day — A573

2005, Aug. 20
1350 A573 15d multi 1.25 1.25

Uprising at Constantine and Philippeville, 50th anniv.

Intl. Year of Sports and Physical Education A574

2005, Sept. 7 Litho. ***Perf. 13¼x14***
1351 A574 30d multi 2.40 2.40

Forts A575

Designs: 10d, Lighthouse Fort, Algiers. 15d, Cap Matifou Fort, Algiers. 30d, Santa Cruz Fort, Oran.

2005, Sept. 15 ***Perf. 14x13¼***
1352-1354 A575 Set of 3 4.00 4.00

September 29, 2005 Referendum — A576

2005 Litho. ***Perf. 14x13½***
1355 A576 15d multi 1.10 1.10

Acquisition of Control of Broadcasting, 43rd Anniv. — A577

2005, Oct. 28
1356 A577 30d multi 2.25 2.25

Personal Effects of Emir Abdelkader (1808-83) A578

Designs: 15d, Saddle. 30d, Boots. 40d, Vest, vert. 50d, Signet, vert.

2005, Nov. 1 ***Perf. 14x13½, 13½x14***
1357-1360 A578 Set of 4 10.00 10.00

Miguel de Cervantes (1547-1616), Writer — A579

2005, Nov. 16 Litho. ***Perf. 13½x14***
1361 A579 30d multi 1.90 1.90

Public Destruction of Mines — A580

2005, Nov. Litho. *Perf. 13½x14*
1362 A580 30d multi 2.25 2.25

World AIDS Day — A581

2005, Dec. 1 Litho. *Perf. 13½x14*
1363 A581 30d multi 2.25 2.25

Numidian Kings — A582

Designs: 15d, Ptolemy of Mauretania, ruler from 23-40 A.D. 30d, Syphax, ruler from 220-203 B.C.

2005, Dec. 14 Litho. *Perf. 13¼x14*
1364-1365 A582 Set of 2 3.25 3.25

Emblem and Headquarters of Algeria Post — A583

2006, Jan. 14 *Perf. 14x13¼*
1366 A583 30d multi 1.90 1.90

Birds — A584

Designs: 10d, Ciconia ciconia. 15d, Ciconia nigra. 20d, Platalea leucorodia. 30d, Grus grus.

2006, Jan. 25 *Perf. 13x13½*
1367-1370 A584 Set of 4 5.50 5.50

2006 Winter Olympics, Turin A585

2006, Feb. 1 *Perf. 14x13¼*
1371 A585 15d multi 1.00 1.00

General Union of Algerian Workers, 50th Anniv. — A586

2006, Feb. 24 *Perf. 13¼x14*
1372 A586 15d multi 1.00 1.00

2006 World Cup Soccer Championships, Germany A587

2006, Mar. 22
1373 A587 30d multi 2.00 2.00

Opening of New Algiers Airport A588

2006, Apr. 8 *Perf. 14x13¼*
1374 A588 30d multi 2.00 2.00

Student's Day, 50th Anniv. — A589

2006, May 19 *Perf. 13x13½*
1375 A589 20d multi 1.40 1.40

World Environment Day — A590

2006, June 5 *Perf. 14*
1376 A590 30d multi 2.00 2.00

Soummam Congress, 50th Anniv. — A591

2006, Aug. 20 *Perf. 13x13½*
1377 A591 20d multi 1.40 1.40

16th Arab Scholars' Games — A592

2006, Sept. 2 *Perf. 13¼x14*
1378 A592 30d multi 2.25 2.25

Intl. Year of Deserts and Desertifcation — A593

Designs: No. 1379, 15d, Oasis. No. 1380, 15d, Oasis, sand dunes and water.

2006, Sept. 20 Litho. *Perf. 14*
1379-1380 A593 Set of 2 2.25 2.25

World Teachers Day A594

2006, Oct. 5
1381 A594 20d multi 1.40 1.40

Arbor Day — A595

Trees: 20d, Atlas pistachio. 30d, Pomagranate.

2006, Oct. 25
1382-1383 A595 Set of 2 3.50 3.50

Sino-African Cooperation Summit, Beijing — A596

2006, Nov. 4 *Perf. 12*
1384 A596 30d multi 2.25 2.25

19th Century Powder Flasks — A597

Background color: 15d, Pink. 20d, Pale green.

2006, Nov. 22 Litho. *Perf. 13½x14*
1385-1386 A597 Set of 2 2.50 2.50

Transitory Arab Parliament, 1st Anniv. — A598

2006, Dec. 17 *Perf. 13½x13*
1387 A598 15d multi 1.00 1.00

El Moudjahid Newspaper, 50th Anniv. — A599

2006, Dec. 18 *Perf. 14*
1388 A599 30d multi 2.25 2.25

Desalinization of Sea Water — A600

2006, Dec. 20
1389 A600 20d multi 1.40 1.40

A601

Algiers, 2007 Arab Cultural Capital — A602

2007, Jan. 12 Litho. *Perf. 13½x13*
1390 A601 15d multi 1.00 1.00
1391 A602 30d multi 2.00 2.00

Lighthouses — A603

Lighthouse at: 15d, Ilot d'Arzew. 20d, Cap Sigli. 38d, Ras-afia.

2007, Feb. 14 Litho. ***Perf. 14***
1392-1394 A603 Set of 3 5.25 5.25

Employment of Women — A604

2007, Mar. 8 Litho. ***Perf. 14***
1395 A604 15d multi 1.10 1.10

Sheikh Mohamed Ameziane Belhaddad (1790-1873), Leader of 1871 Rebellion A605

2007, Apr. 8 ***Perf. 13x13¼***
1396 A605 15d multi 1.10 1.10

Ksars A606

Village scenes: No. 1397, 15d, Kenadsa. No. 1398, 15d, Temacine, vert.

2007, Apr. 21 ***Perf. 13¼x13, 13x13¼***
1397-1398 A606 Set of 2 2.25 2.25

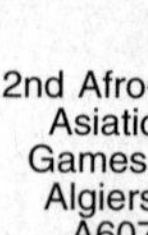

2nd Afro-Asiatic Games, Algiers A607

2007, May 18 Litho. ***Perf. 14***
1399 A607 15d multi 1.10 1.10

9th All-African Games, Algiers — A608

2007, May 18
1400 A608 15d multi 1.10 1.10

Gardens — A609

Designs: 15d, Landon Gardens, Biskra. 20d, Ibn Badis Gardens, Oran. 38d, Essai du Hamma Gardens, Algiers.

2007, June 5 ***Perf. 13½x13***
1401-1403 A609 Set of 3 5.25 5.25

National Gendarmerie, 45th Anniv. — A610

Designs: 15d, Gendarmerie emblem. 38d, Gendarmerie emblem, gendarme and automobile.

2007, June 25 Litho. ***Perf. 14***
1404-1405 A610 Set of 2 3.50 3.50

Independence, 45th Anniv. — A611

Designs: 15d, People, flags and dove. 20d, Anniversary emblem, vert.

2007, July 5 ***Perf. 13¼x13***
1406 A611 15d multi 1.25 1.25

Imperf

Size: 60x77mm

1407 A611 20d multi 2.00 2.00

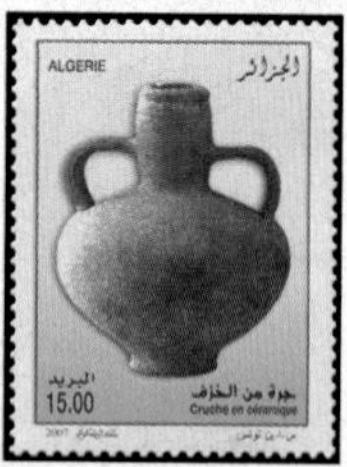

Ceramics A612

Designs: No. 1408, 15d, Jar with handles. No. 1409, 15d, Glazed jar without handles. 20d, Censer. 38d, Lamp, horiz.

2007, Aug. 5 Litho. ***Perf. 14***
1408-1411 A612 Set of 4 6.00 6.00

Endangered Animals — A613

Designs: 15d, Striped hyena. 38d, White-tailed fox.

2007, Sept. 12 ***Perf. 13¼x13***
1412-1413 A613 Set of 2 3.25 3.25

Theaters A614

Theater in: No. 1414, 15d, Setif. No. 1415, 15d, Oran. 20d, Annaba, horiz. 38d, Algiers.

Perf. 13x13¼, 13¼x13

2007, Oct. 24 Litho.
1414-1417 A614 Set of 4 5.75 5.75

Encyclopedia of Algerian Postage Stamps A615

2007, Nov. 1 ***Perf. 13x13¼***
1418 A615 15d multi 1.25 1.25

Bey Ahmed of Constantine (1784-1850), Leader of 1836-48 Resistance Against French A616

2007, Nov. 7
1419 A616 15d multi 1.25 1.25

National Artisan's Day — A617

2007, Nov. 9 ***Perf. 13¼x14***
1420 A617 15d multi 1.25 1.25

Tilapia A618

2007, Dec. 12 Litho. ***Perf. 14***
1421 A618 15d multi 1.10 1.10

Miniature Sheet

Emir Abdelkader (1808-83) — A619

No. 1422: a, Abdelkader seated. b, Abdelkader standing. c, Abdelkader, diff.

2007, Dec. 15
1422 A619 Sheet of 3 4.00 4.00
a.-b. 15d Either single .90 .90
c. 38d multi 2.25 2.25

Fifth General Census A620

2008, Jan. 16 ***Perf. 14x13¼***
1423 A620 15d multi 1.10 1.10

French Air Raid on Sakiet Sidi Youssef, Tunisia, 50th Anniv. — A621

2008, Feb. 8 Litho. ***Perf. 13x13¼***
1424 A621 15d multi 1.10 1.10

Miniature Sheet

Fountains — A621a

2008, Feb. 23 ***Perf. 14***
1425 A621a Sheet of 4 5.00 5.00
a. 10d Ain de la Grande Rue .60 .60
b. 15d Ain Bir Djebbah .90 .90
c. 20d Ain Sidi Abdellah 1.25 1.25
d. 38d Ain Bir Chebana 2.40 2.40

Miniature Sheet

Water and Sustainable Development — A622

No. 1428: a, Issakarssen Wetlands. b, Reghaia Wetlands. c, Guerbes Wetlands. d, Emblem of Expo Zaragoza 2008.

2008, Mar. 22 Litho. *Perf. 14*

1428 A622 Sheet of 4, #a-d		5.00	5.00
a.	10d multi	.60	.60
b.	15d multi	.90	.90
c.	20d multi	1.25	1.25
d.	38d multi	2.40	2.40

Souvenir Sheet

National Liberation Front Soccer Team, 50th Anniv. — A623

2008, Apr. 12 Litho. *Perf.*
1429 A623 38d multi 2.40 2.40

No. 1429 contains one 36mm diameter stamp.

Writers A624

No. 1430: a, Redha Houhou (1911-56). b, Abdelhamid Benhadouga (1925-96). c, Malek Bennabi (1905-73). d, Kateb Yacine (1929-89).

2008, Apr. 16 Litho. *Perf. 14x13½*
1430 Horiz. strip of 4 3.75 3.75
a.-d. A624 15d Any single .90 .90

Children and New Technologies A625

2008, June 1 *Perf. 13½x14*
1431 A625 15d multi .90 .90

Souvenir Sheet

Baya Mahieddine (1931-98), Artist — A626

No. 1432: a, 15d, Mahieddine. b, 38d, Painting by Mahieddine.

2008, June 8 *Perf. 14*
1432 A626 Sheet of 2, #a-b 3.25 3.25

Kassamen, Algerian National Anthem, by Moufdi Zakaria A627

2008, July 3 *Perf. 13x13¼*
1433 A627 15d multi .90 .90

Railway Stations A628

Station in: 10d, Algiers. 15d, Constantine. 20d, Oran. 38d, Skikda.

2008, July 9 *Perf. 14x13½*
1434-1437 A628 Set of 4 5.00 5.00

Ferhat Abbas (1899-1985), President of First Algerian Temporary Government A629

2008, Sept. 19 *Perf. 13x13¼*
1438 A629 15d multi 1.00 1.00

2008 Summer Olympics, Beijing A630

Designs: No. 1439, 15d, Fencing. No. 1440, 15d, Wrestling.

2008, July 23 Litho. *Perf. 14x13½*
1439-1440 A630 Set of 2 1.00 1.00

National Popular Army A631

2008, Nov. 1
1441 A631 15d multi .90 .90

12th Session of Government Postage Stamp Printers Assoc., Algiers — A632

2008, Nov. 5 *Perf. 13x13¼*
1442 A632 15d multi .95 .95

Miniature Sheet

Bridges in Constantine — A633

No. 1443: a, 10d, Sidi M'Cid Bridge. b, 15d, Sidi Rached Bridge. c, 20d, El Kantara Bridge. d, 38d, La Medersa Bridge.

2008, Nov. 26 *Perf. 14*
1443 A633 Sheet of 4, #a-d 5.00 5.00

Universal Declaration of Human Rights, 60th Anniv. A634

2008, Dec. 10 *Perf. 14x13½*
1444 A634 15d multi .95 .95

Cities A635

Designs: 10d, Tebessa. 15d, Saida. 20d, Miliana. 38d, Biskra.

2008, Dec. 18 *Perf. 13¼x13*
1445-1448 A635 Set of 4 5.00 5.00

Diplomatic Relations Between Algeria and People's Republic of China, 50th Anniv. A636

2008, Dec. 20 *Perf. 12*
1449 A636 15d multi 1.00 1.00

Louis Braille (1809-52), Educator of the Blind — A637

2009, Jan. 4 *Perf. 13½x14*
1450 A637 15d multi 1.00 1.00

Mausoleums A638

Mausoleum of: 15d, Sidi Abderrahmane, Algiers. 20d, Sidi Ibrahim El Atteuf, Ghardaia, horiz.

2009, Feb. 25 *Perf. 13½x14, 14x13½*
1451-1452 A638 Set of 2 2.00 2.00

Natl. Day of the Handicapped A639

Designs: 15d, Silhouettes of man with raised arm and man in wheelchair. 20d, Athlete in wheelchair, hand prints.

2009, Mar. 14 *Perf. 13½x14*
1453-1454 A639 Set of 2 2.00 2.00

Protection of Polar Regions and Glaciers — A640

2009, Mar. 28 Litho.
1455 A640 38d multi 2.25 2.25

Presidential Elections A641

2009, Apr. 9 *Perf. 13x13¼*
1456 A641 15d multi 1.00 1.00

Items in National Museum A642

Designs: 15d, Wooden sandals. 20d, Fragment of silver brooch. 30d, Vest.

2009, Apr. 18 *Perf. 14x13½*
1457-1459 A642 Set of 3 4.00 4.00

University of Algiers, Cent. A643

2009, May 11
1460 A643 15d multi 1.00 1.00

Jewelry of Southern Algeria — A644

Designs: 1d, Silver fibulas. 5d, Amulet necklace. 9d, Pectoral jewelry and chain. 10d, Circular fibula.

2009, May 13 ***Perf. 13¾***
1461-1464 A644 Set of 4 1.50 1.50

Protection of Children From Cyberspace Dangers — A645

2009, May 17 ***Perf. 14x13½***
1465 A645 15d multi 1.00 1.00

16th Mediterranean Games, Pescara, Italy — A646

Designs: 15d, Sailboarding. 20d, Equestrian, horiz.

Perf. 13½x14, 14x13½
2009, June 3 **Litho.**
1466-1467 A646 Set of 2 2.25 2.25

Roman Era Archaeological Sites — A647

Designs: 15d, Madaure archaeological site. 20d, Khemissa archaeological site. 30d, Old Theater, Guelma.

2009, June 14 ***Perf. 13½x14***
1468-1470 A647 Set of 3 4.00 4.00

Second Panafrican Cultural Festival of Algiers — A648

Designs: 15d, Shown. 20d, Map of Africa, antelope, geometric designs.

2009, July 4 ***Perf. 13¼x13***
1471-1472 A648 Set of 2 2.00 2.00

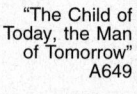

"The Child of Today, the Man of Tomorrow" A649

"I Love My Country" — A650

2009, June 26 ***Perf. 13½x14***
1473 A649 15d multi 1.00 1.00
1474 A650 20d multi 1.25 1.25

Algerian Electricity and Gas Company, 40th Anniv. — A651

2009, July 28
1475 A651 15d multi 1.00 1.00

Traffic Safety — A652

2009, Aug. 6
1476 A652 15d multi 1.00 1.00

Fishing Ports — A653

Designs: 15d, Bouharoun. 20d, Béni Saf. 30d, Stora.

2009, Sept. 2 **Litho.** ***Perf. 13½x13***
1477-1479 A653 Set of 3 4.00 4.00

Protection of the Aged — A654

2009, Oct. 10 ***Perf. 13½x14***
1480 A654 15d multi 1.00 1.00

National Armed Forces — A655

2009, Nov. 1 **Litho.** ***Perf. 13x13¼***
1481 A655 15d multi 1.00 1.00

Olive Oil Production — A656

Designs: 15d, Picking olives. 20d, Pressing olives, vert.

Perf. 13¼x13, 13x13¼
2009, Nov. 25
1482-1483 A656 Set of 2 2.00 2.00

Folktales A657

No. 1484: a, Loundja, la Fille de l'Ogre. b, Badra. c, La Fée Colombe. d, La Rose Rouge.

2009, Dec. 7 **Litho.** ***Perf. 13x13¼***
1484 Block or strip of 4 4.00 4.00
a.-d. A657 15d Any single .90 .90

Birds of Prey A658

Designs: 15d, Aquila chrysaetos. 20d, Falco biarmicus, vert. 30d, Falco peregrinus, vert.

2010, Jan. 27 ***Perf. 13¼x13, 13x13¼***
1485-1487 A658 Set of 3 4.00 4.00

Victims of French Nuclear Testing in Algeria — A659

2010, Feb. 10 ***Perf. 13¼x13***
1488 A659 15d multi 1.00 1.00

Forts A660

Designs: 15d, Fort de l'Empereur, Bordj Moulay Hassan, Algiers. 20d, Gouraya Fort, Béjaia.

2010, Feb. 15
1489-1490 A660 Set of 2 2.25 2.25

Expo 2010, Shanghai — A661

Designs: 15d, Stylized people, flowers, buildings. 38d, Algeria Pavilion.

2010, Mar. 24 **Litho.** ***Perf. 13¼x13***
1491-1492 A661 Set of 2 3.25 3.25

16th Intl. Conference on Liquified Gas, Oran — A662

Conference emblem, world map and: 15d, Gas plant. 20d, Port, horiz.

2010, Apr. 18 ***Perf. 13x13½, 13½x13***
1493-1494 A662 Set of 2 2.25 2.25

May 8, 1945 Massacres, 65th Anniv. — A663

2010, May 8 ***Perf. 13¼***
1495 A663 15d multi 1.00 1.00

2010 World Cup Soccer Championships, South Africa — A664

Designs: No. 1496, 15d, World Cup trophy, flags of participating countries. No. 1497, 15d, Player, crowd holding Algerian flags.

No. 1498: a, Fox playing soccer. b, Player, soccer ball.

2010, May 8 ***Perf. 13x13¼***
1496-1497 A664 Set of 2 2.00 2.00

Souvenir Sheet

Imperf

1498 A664 15d Sheet of 2, #a-b 2.00 2.00

Ahellil of Gourara UNESCO World Intangible Cultural Heritage — A665

2010, June 2 *Perf. 13¼x13*
1499 A665 15d multi 1.00 1.00

Martyr's Sanctuary, Algiers — A666

2010, June 20
1500 A666 (15d) multi 1.00 1.00

African Year of Peace and Security A667

2010, July 19 *Perf. 13x13¼*
1501 A667 15d multi 1.00 1.00

Caves A668

Designs: No. 1502, 15d, Béni Add Cave, Ain Fezza. No. 1503, 15d, Ziama Cave, Mansouriah.

2010, July 25 *Perf. 13¼x13*
1502-1503 A668 Set of 2 2.00 2.00

Organization of the Petroleum Exporting Countries, 50th Anniv. — A669

Designs: 15d, Emblem. 38d, Emblem, world map, oil tanker.

2010, Sept. 14 Litho. *Perf. 13¼x13*
1504-1505 A669 Set of 2 3.50 3.50

Mosques A670

Designs: 15d, El Hanafi Mosque, Blida. 20d, Sidi Ali Dib Mosque, Skikda. 30d, Grand Mosque, Nedroma.

2010, Sept. 15 *Perf. 13x13¼*
1506-1508 A670 Set of 3 4.50 4.50

Dates A671

Date varieties: No. 1509, 15d, Degla Beida. No. 1510, 15d, Akerbuch. No. 1511, 15d, Ghars, vert. No. 1512, 15d, Deglet Nour, vert.

2010, Oct. 6 *Perf. 13¼x13, 13x13¼*
1509-1512 A671 Set of 4 4.50 4.50

Handcrafted Items — A672

Designs: 15d, Candlestick holder. 20d, Quanoun (musical instrument). 30d, Leather-covered chest with handles, horiz.

Perf. 13¼x14, 14x13¼
2010, Nov. 30 Litho.
1513-1515 A672 Set of 3 4.50 4.50

Trees A673

Designs: 15d, Cork oak. 20d, Carob tree. 30d, Soapberry tree. 38d, Argan tree.

2011, Jan. 29 *Perf. 13¼x13*
1516-1519 A673 Set of 4 5.50 5.50

Tlemcen, 2011 Capital of Islamic Culture A674

Designs: 15d, Minaret of Mansoura. 20d, Door knocker, Side Boumedienne Mosque.

2011, Feb. 15 Litho. *Perf. 13x13¼*
1520-1521 A674 Set of 2 1.00 1.00

Snakes A675

Designs: No. 1522, 15d, Couleuvre a diademe (diadem snake). No. 1523, 15d, Vipere a cornes (Saharan horned viper).

2011, Mar. 13
1522-1523 A675 Set of 2 1.50 1.50

First Economic Census — A676

2011, Apr. 12 *Perf. 13½x14*
1524 A676 15d multi .75 .75

18th Cent. Tableware From Algiers — A677

Designs: 15d, Couscous dish. 30d, Butter dish.

2011, Apr. 19 *Perf. 13¼x13*
1525-1526 A677 Set of 2 2.25 2.25

Telecenters — A678

2011, May 17 *Perf. 14x13½*
1527 A678 15d multi .75 .75

Campaign Against Human Immunodeficiency Virus — A679

2011, June 30 *Perf. 13½x14*
1528 A679 15d multi .75 .75

Benyoucef Benkhedda (1920-2003), Politician A680

2011, Sept. 19 *Perf. 13x13¼*
1529 A680 15d multi .75 .75

A681

Comic Strips — A682

2011, Sept. 25 *Perf. 13¼x14*
1530 A681 15d multi .75 .75
1531 A682 15d multi .75 .75

World Post Day A683

Main post office in: No. 1532, 15d, Constantine. No. 1533, 15d, Oran.

2011, Oct. 9 *Perf. 14x13¼*
1532-1533 A683 Set of 2 .80 .80

Paris Massacre of Algerian Protestors, 50th Anniv. — A684

2011, Oct. 17 *Perf. 13x13¼*
1534 A684 15d multi .75 .75

Algerian Press Service, 50th Anniv. A685

2011, Oct. 25 *Perf. 14x13¼*
1535 A685 15d multi .75 .75

Army Museum — A686

2011, Nov. 1 ***Perf. 13¼x13***
1536 A686 15d multi .70 .70

Souvenir Sheet

Algiers Metro — A687

No. 1537: a, Train at station, people on platform. b, Train in tunnel.

2011, Nov. 14 ***Perf. 14***
1537 A687 15d Sheet of 2, #a-b .80 .80

Sheep — A688

Sheep breeds: No. 1538, 15d, Ouled Djallal. No. 1539, 15d, El Hamra.

2011, Nov. 16 ***Perf. 13¼x13***
1538-1539 A688 Set of 2 .80 .80

Ornamental Plants — A689

Designs: 15d, Bougainvillea. 20d, Glycine (wisteria). 30d, Mimosa, horiz. 38d, Galant de nuit (night-blooming cestrum), horiz.

2011, Dec. 26 ***Perf. 13x13¼, 13¼x13***
1540-1543 A689 Set of 4 5.00 5.00

Ceasefire Between Algeria and France, 50th Anniv. — A690

2012, Mar. 19 Litho. ***Perf. 13x13¼***
1544 A690 15d multi .40 .40

Expo 2012, Yeosu, South Korea — A691

2012, Mar. 21 ***Perf. 13¼x13***
1545 A691 15d multi .40 .40

Wainscoting A692

Designs: 15d, Door, Dar Aziza, Algiers. 20d, Ceiling, Dar Aziza. 30d, Window, Hassen Pacha Palace, Algiers.

2012, Mar. 26 ***Perf. 13x13¼***
1546-1548 A692 Set of 3 1.75 1.75

Snails — A693

Designs: 15d, Theba pisana. 20d, Eobania vermiculata.

2012, Mar. 28
1549-1550 A693 Set of 2 .95 .95

Ulemas A694

Designs: 15d, Sheikh Larbi Djedri Tebessi (1895-1957). 20d, Sheikh Embarek El-Mili (1898-1945). 30d, Sheikh Ahmed Hamani (1915-98).

2012, Apr. 16 Litho. ***Perf. 13x13¼***
1551-1553 A694 Set of 3 1.75 1.75

City Scenes A695

Designs: 15d, Casbah of Dellys. 20d, Saracen Gate, Bejaia. 30d, Casbah of Constantine.

2012, June 26
1554-1556 A695 Set of 3 1.60 1.60

2012 Summer Olympics, London A696

Designs: 15d, Judo, London Eye. 38d, Rowing, Tower Bridge, vert.

Perf. 14x13¼, 13¼x14
2012, June 27
1557-1558 A696 Set of 2 1.40 1.40

Algerian Armed Forces, 50th Anniv. A697

Designs: No. 1559, 15d, Gendarme on motorcycle. No. 1560, 15d, Tank. No. 1561, 15d, Missiles. No. 1562, 15d, Airplane in flight. No. 1563, 15d, Member of Republican Guard on horse. No. 1564, 15d, Naval vessel.

2012, July 5 ***Perf. 14***
Stamps With Year and Inscriptions At Bottom

1559-1564 A697 Set of 6 2.25 2.25
1561a Souvenir sheet of 3, #1559-1561, with year and inscriptions at bottom of stamp removed 1.10 1.10
1564a Souvenir sheet of 3, #1562-1564, with year and inscriptions at bottom of stamp removed 1.10 1.10

Souvenir Sheet

Algerian Independence, 50th Anniv. — A698

2012, July 5 ***Imperf.***
1565 A698 15d multi .40 .40

Wheat Varieties A699

Designs: 15d, Bousselam. 20d, Mohamed Ben Bachir. 30d, Hedba 03.

2012, Sept. 29 ***Perf. 13x13¼***
1566-1568 A699 Set of 3 1.75 1.75

Algerian Radio and Television, 50th Anniv. — A700

2012, Oct. 28 ***Perf. 13¼x13***
1569 A700 15d multi .40 .40

Postage Stamps of Independent Algeria, 50th Anniv. — A701

2012, Nov. 1
1570 A701 15d multi .40 .40

Medicinal Plants — A702

Designs: 15d, Globularia vulgaris. 20d, Glycyrrhiza glabra. 30d, Menyanthes trifoliata.

2012, Dec. 11 Litho. ***Perf. 13x13¼***
1571-1573 A702 Set of 3 1.75 1.75

Diplomatic Relations Between Algeria and Russia, 50th Anniv. — A703

2012, Dec. 18 Litho. ***Perf. 13¼x13***
1574 A703 15d multi .40 .40

Yennayer Festival (Berber New Year) — A705

2013, Jan. 12 Litho. *Perf. 13x13¼*

1577 A705 15d multi .40 .40

Fruit and Blossoms — A707

Designs: 15d, Apricots. 20d, Cherries.

2013, Mar. 3 Litho. *Perf. 13¼x13*

1581-1582 A707 Set of 2 .90 .90

National Copyright Office, 40th Anniv. — A709

2013, Apr. 26 Litho. *Perf. 13x13¼*

1585 A709 15d multi .40 .40

National Administration School — A710

2013, Apr. 29 Litho. *Perf. 13¼x13*

1586 A710 15d multi .40 .40

SEMI-POSTAL STAMPS

Regular Issue of 1926 Surcharged in Black or Red

1927 Unwmk. *Perf. 14x13½*

B1 A1 5c +5c bl grn 1.25 1.25
B2 A1 10c +10c lilac 1.25 1.25
B3 A2 15c +15c org brn 1.25 1.25
B4 A2 20c +20c car rose 1.25 1.25
B5 A2 25c +25c bl grn 1.25 1.25
B6 A2 30c +30c lt bl 1.25 1.25
B7 A2 35c +35c dp vio 1.25 1.25
B8 A2 40c +40c ol grn 1.25 1.25
B9 A3 50c +50c dp bl (R) 1.30 1.30
a. Double surcharge 475.00
B10 A3 80c +80c red org 1.30 1.30
B11 A4 1fr +1fr gray grn & red brn 1.30 1.30
B12 A4 2fr +2fr Prus bl & blk brn 30.00 30.00
B13 A4 5fr +5fr red & vio 40.00 40.00
Nos. B1-B13 (13) 83.90 83.90

The surtax was for the benefit of wounded soldiers. Government officials speculated in this issue.

Railroad Terminal, Oran SP1

Ruins at Djemila SP2

Mosque of Sidi Abd-er-Rahman SP3

Designs: 10c+10c, Rummel Gorge, Constantine. 15c+15c, Admiralty Buildings, Algiers. 25c+25c, View of Algiers. 30c+30c, Trajan's Arch, Timgad. 40c+40c, Temple of the North, Djemila. 75c+75c Mansourah Minaret, Tlemcen. 1f+1f, View of Ghardaia. 1.50f+1.50f, View of Tolga. 2f+2f, Tuareg warriors. 3f+3f, Kasbah, Algiers.

1930 Engr. *Perf. 12½*

B14 SP1 5c +5c orange 8.75 8.75
B15 SP1 10c +10c ol grn 9.50 9.50
B16 SP1 15c +15c dk brn 9.50 9.50
B17 SP1 25c +25c black 9.50 9.50
B18 SP1 30c +30c dk red 9.50 9.50
B19 SP1 40c +40c ap grn 9.50 9.50
B20 SP2 50c +50c ultra 9.50 9.50
B21 SP2 75c +75c red pur 9.50 9.50
B22 SP2 1fr +1fr org red 9.50 9.50
B23 SP2 1.50fr +1.50fr deep ultra 9.50 9.50
B24 SP2 2fr +2fr dk car 9.50 9.50
B25 SP2 3fr +3fr dk grn 9.50 9.50
B26 SP3 5fr +5fr grn & car 22.50 22.50
a. Center inverted 750.00
Nos. B14-B26 (13) 135.75 135.75

Centenary of the French occupation of Algeria. The surtax on the stamps was given to the funds for the celebration.

Nos. B14-B26 exist imperf. Value, set in pairs, $800.

Catalogue values for unused stamps in this section, from this point to the end of the section, are for Never Hinged items.

No. 102 Surcharged in Red

1938 *Perf. 13*

B27 A6 65c +35c on 2.25fr yel grn 1.50 1.10
a. Inverted surcharge 375.00
b. Pair, one without surcharge 1,875.

20th anniversary of Armistice.

No. 79 with surcharge is considered an essay. Value, $300.

René Caillié, Charles Lavigerie and Henri Duveyrier SP14

1939 Engr.

B28 SP14 30c +20c dk bl grn 2.40 1.60
B29 SP14 90c +60c car rose 2.40 1.60
B30 SP14 2.25fr +75c ultra 19.00 14.50
B31 SP14 5fr +5fr brn blk 40.00 30.00
Nos. B28-B31 (4) 63.80 47.70

Pioneers of the Sahara.

French and Algerian Soldiers SP15

1940 Photo. *Perf. 12*

B32 SP15 1fr +1fr bl & car 1.60 1.20
a. Double surcharge 625.00
B33 SP15 1fr +2fr brn rose & blk 1.60 1.20
B34 SP15 1fr +4fr dp grn & red 2.40 2.00
B35 SP15 1fr +9fr brn & car 3.25 2.00
Nos. B32-B35 (4) 8.85 6.40

The surtax was used to assist the families of mobilized men.

Nos. B32-B35 exist without surcharge. Value set, $290.

Type of Regular Issue, 1941 Surcharged in Carmine

1941 Engr. *Perf. 13*

B36 A19 1fr +4fr black .65 .30

No. 135 Surcharged in Carmine

B37 A19 1fr +4fr dark blue .65 .30

The surtax was for National Relief.

No. 124 Surcharged in Black

1942

B38 A7 90c +60c henna brn .55 .25
a. Double surcharge 175.00

The surtax was used for National Relief. The stamp could also be used as 1.50 francs for postage.

Mother and Child — SP16

1943, Dec. 1 Litho. *Perf. 12*

B39 SP16 50c +4.50fr brt pink 1.00 *1.30*
B40 SP16 1.50fr +8.50fr lt grn 1.00 *1.30*
B41 SP16 3fr +12fr dp bl 1.00 *1.30*
B42 SP16 5fr +15fr vio brn 1.00 *1.40*
Nos. B39-B42 (4) 4.00 *5.30*

The surtax was for the benefit of soldiers and prisoners of war.

Planes over Fields SP17

Unwmk.

1945, July 2 Engr. *Perf. 13*

B43 SP17 1.50fr +3.50fr lt ultra, red org & blk 1.10 .85

The surtax was for the benefit of Algerian airmen and their families.

France No. B192 Overprinted Type "a" of 1924 in Black

1945

B44 SP146 4fr +6fr dk vio brn 1.10 .85

The surtax was for war victims of the P.T.T.

Overprinted in Blue on Type of France, 1945

1945, Oct. 15

B45 SP150 2fr +3fr dk brn 1.10 .85

For Stamp Day.

Overprinted in Blue on Type of France, 1946

1946, June 29

B46 SP160 3fr +2fr red 1.60 1.25

For Stamp Day.

Children Playing by Stream SP18

Girl — SP19

Athlete — SP20

Repatriated Prisoner and Bay of Algiers SP21

1946, Oct. 2 Engr. *Perf. 13*

B47 SP18 3fr +17fr dark grn 2.75 2.25
B48 SP19 4fr +21fr red 2.75 2.25
B49 SP20 8fr +27fr rose lilac 7.25 6.25
B50 SP21 10fr +35fr dark blue 3.25 2.50
Nos. B47-B50 (4) 16.00 13.25

Type of France, 1947, Overprinted type "a" of 1924 in Carmine

1947, Mar. 15

B51 SP172 4.50fr +5.50fr dp ultra 1.75 1.25

For Stamp Day.

Same on Type of France, 1947, Surcharged Like No. B36 in Carmine

1947, Nov. 13

B52 A173 5fr +10fr dk Prus grn 1.60 1.25

Type of France, 1948, Overprinted in Dark Green — f

1948, Mar. 6
B53 SP176 6fr +4fr dk grn 1.75 1.25

For Stamp Day.

Type of France, 1948, Overprinted type "a" of 1924 in Blue and New Value

1948, May
B54 A176 6fr +4fr red 1.60 1.25

Battleship Richelieu and the Admiralty, Algiers SP22

Aircraft Carrier Arromanches — SP23

Unwmk.
1949, Jan. 15 Engr. *Perf. 13*
B55 SP22 10fr +15fr dp blue 10.00 8.00
B56 SP23 18fr +22fr red 10.00 8.00

The surtax was for naval charities.

Type of France, 1949, Overprinted in Blue — g

1949, Mar. 26
B57 SP180 15fr +5fr lilac rose 3.25 2.25

For Stamp Day, Mar. 26-27.

Type of France, 1950, Overprinted type "f" in Green

1950, Mar. 11
B58 SP183 12fr +3fr blk brn 3.25 2.75

For Stamp Day, Mar. 11-12.

Foreign Legionary — SP24

1950, Apr. 30
B59 SP24 15fr +5fr dk grn 3.00 2.40

Charles de Foucauld and Gen. J. F. H. Laperrine SP25

1950, Aug. 21 Unwmk. *Perf. 13*
B60 SP25 25fr +5fr brn ol & brn blk 8.00 6.25

50th anniversary of the presence of the French in the Sahara.

Emir Abd-el-Kader and Marshal T. R. Bugeaud — SP26

1950, Aug. 21
B61 SP26 40fr +10fr dk brn & blk brn 8.00 6.25

Unveiling of a monument to Emir Abd-el-Kader at Cacheron.

Col. Colonna d'Ornano and Fine Arts Museum, Algiers SP27

1951, Jan. 11
B62 SP27 15fr +5fr blk brn, vio brn & red brn 1.40 1.25

Death of Col. Colonna d'Ornano, 10th anniv.

Type of France, 1951, Overprinted type "a" of 1924 in Black

1951, Mar. 10
B63 SP186 12fr +3fr brown 2.75 2.50

For Stamp Day.

Type of France, 1952, Overprinted type "g" in Dark Blue

1952, Mar. 8 Unwmk. *Perf. 13*
B64 SP190 12fr +3fr dk bl 2.75 2.50

For Stamp Day.

French Military Medal — SP28

Unwmk.
1952, July 5 Engr. *Perf. 13*
B65 SP28 15fr +5fr grn, yel & brn 3.50 2.75

Centenary of the creation of the French Military Medal.

Type of France 1952, Surcharged type "g" and Surtax in Black

1952, Sept. 15
B66 A222 30fr +5fr dp ultra 4.00 3.25

10th anniv. of the defense of Bir-Hakeim.

View of El Oued SP29

Design: 12fr+3fr, View of Bou-Noura.

1952, Nov. 15 Engr.
B67 SP29 8fr +2fr ultra & red 3.25 3.00
B68 SP29 12fr +3fr red 6.50 4.75

The surtax was for the Red Cross.

Type of France, 1953, Overprinted type "a" of 1924 in Black

1953, Mar. 14 Engr.
B69 SP193 12fr +3fr purple 2.50 2.40

For Stamp Day. Surtax for Red Cross.

Victory of Cythera — SP30

Unwmk.
1953, Dec. 18 Engr. *Perf. 13*
B70 SP30 15fr +5fr blk brn & brn 1.60 1.25

The surtax was for army welfare work.

Type of France, 1954, Overprinted type "a" of 1924 in Black

1954, Mar. 20 Unwmk. *Perf. 13*
B71 SP196 12fr +3fr scarlet 2.25 2.00

For Stamp Day.

Soldiers and Flags SP31

Foreign Legionary SP32

1954, Mar. 27
B72 SP31 15fr +5fr dk brn 2.00 1.25

The surtax was for old soldiers.

1954, Apr. 30
B73 SP32 15fr +5fr dk grn 3.00 2.50

The surtax was for the welfare fund of the Foreign Legion.

Nurses and Verdun Hospital, Algiers SP33

15fr+5fr, J. H. Dunant & ruins at Djemila.

1954, Oct. 30
B74 SP33 12fr +3fr indigo & red 6.50 5.50
B75 SP33 15fr +5fr pur & red 7.50 6.25

The surtax was for the Red Cross.

Earthquake Victims and Ruins — SP34

First Aid — SP35

Design: Nos. B80-B81, Removing wounded.

1954, Dec. 5
B76 SP34 12fr +4fr dk vio brn 3.50 2.75
B77 SP34 15fr +5fr dp bl 3.50 2.75
B78 SP35 18fr +6fr lil rose 4.50 3.50
B79 SP35 20fr +7fr violet 4.50 3.50
B80 SP35 25fr +8fr rose brn 4.50 3.50
B81 SP35 30fr +10fr brt bl grn 4.50 3.50
Nos. B76-B81 (6) 25.00 19.50

The surtax was for victims of the Orleansville earthquake disaster of September 1954.

Type of France, 1955, Overprinted type "a" of 1924 in Black

1955, Mar. 19
B82 SP199 12fr +3fr dp ultra 2.75 2.25

For Stamp Day, Mar. 19-20.

Women and Children SP36

Cancer Victim SP37

1955, Nov. 5
B83 SP36 15fr +5fr blue & indigo 1.40 1.25

The tax was for war victims.

1956, Mar. 3 Unwmk. *Perf. 13*
B84 SP37 15fr +5fr dk brn 2.00 1.60

The surtax was for the Algerian Cancer Society. The male figure in the design is Rodin's "Age of Bronze."

Type of France, 1956, Overprinted type "a" of 1924 in Black

1956, Mar.
B85 SP202 12fr +3fr red 2.50 2.00

For Stamp Day, Mar. 17-18.

Foreign Legion Rest Home SP38

1956, Apr. 29
B86 SP38 15fr +5fr dk bl grn 2.50 2.00

Honoring the French Foreign Legion.

Type of France, 1957, Overprinted type "f" in Black

1957, Mar. 16 Engr. *Perf. 13*
B87 SP204 12fr +3fr dull purple 2.00 1.60

For Stamp Day and to honor the Maritime Postal Service.

Fennec SP39

Design: 15fr+5fr, Stork flying over roofs.

1957, Apr. 6
B88 SP39 12fr +3fr red brn & red 9.00 7.25
B89 SP39 15fr +5fr sepia & red 9.00 7.25

The surtax was for the Red Cross.

Regular Issue of 1956 Srchd. in Dark Blue

1957, June 18
B90 A53 15fr +5fr scar & rose red 2.50 1.60

17th anniv. of General de Gaulle's appeal for a Free France.

The Giaour, by Delacroix — SP40

On the Banks of the Oued, by Fromentin SP41

Design: 35fr+10fr, Dancer, by Chasseriau.

Unwmk.
1957, Nov. 30 Engr. *Perf. 13*

B91 SP40 15fr +5fr dk car	8.00	7.00
B92 SP41 20fr +5fr grn	8.00	7.00
B93 SP40 35fr +10fr dk bl	9.00	7.25
Nos. B91-B93 (3)	25.00	21.25

Surtax for army welfare organizations.

Type of France Overprinted type "f" in Blue

1958, Mar. 15 Unwmk. *Perf. 13*
B94 SP206 15fr +5fr org brn 2.00 1.60

For Stamp Day.

Bird-of-Paradise Flower — SP42

Arms & Marshal's Baton — SP43

1958, June 14 Engr. *Perf. 13*
B95 SP42 20fr +5fr grn, org & vio 5.50 4.00

The surtax was for Child Welfare.

1958, July 20
B96 SP43 20fr +5fr ultra, car & grn 2.50 2.00

Marshal de Lattre Foundation.

Independent State

Clasped Hands, Wheat, Olive Branch — SP44

Burning Books — SP45

1963, May 27 Unwmk. *Perf. 13*
B97 SP44 50c +20c sl grn, brt grn & car 1.10 .65

Surtax for the Natl. Solidarity Fund.

1965, June 7 Engr. *Perf. 13*
B98 SP45 20c +5c ol grn, red & blk .50 .40

Burning of the Library of Algiers, 6/7/62.

Soldiers and Woman Comforting Wounded Soldier — SP46

1966, Aug. 20 Photo. *Perf. 11½*

B99 SP46 30c +10c multi	1.25	.70
B100 SP46 95c +10c multi	1.75	1.25

Day of the Moudjahid (Moslem volunteers).

Red Crescent, Boy and Girl — SP47

1967, May 27 Litho. *Perf. 14*
B101 SP47 30c +10c brt grn, brn & car .80 .50

Algerian Red Crescent Society.

Flood Victims — SP48

Design: 95c+25c, Rescuing flood victims.

1969, Nov. 15 Typo. *Perf. 10½*
B102 SP48 30c +10c multi .70 .50

Litho.
B103 SP48 95c +25c multi 1.60 .95

Red Crescent Flag SP49

1971, May 17 Engr. *Perf. 10½*
B104 SP49 30c +10c slate grn & car .70 .40

Algerian Red Crescent Society.

Intl. Children's Day — SP50

1989, June 1 Litho. *Perf. 10½x11*
B105 SP50 1d +30c multi .70 .55

Surtax for child welfare.

Solidarity with Palestinians SP51

1990, Dec. 9 Litho. *Perf. 10½x11*
B106 SP51 1d +30c multi .70 .45

Natl. Solidarity with Education SP52

1995, Sept. 20 Litho. *Perf. 13x14*
B107 SP52 3d +50c multi .60 .30

Red Crescent Society SP53

1998, May 2 Litho. *Perf. 13x13¼*
B108 SP53 5d +1d multi .50 .30

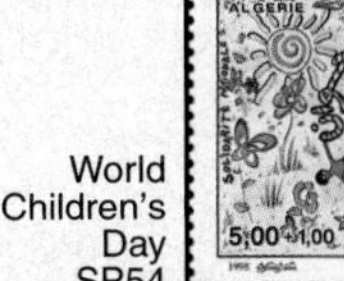
World Children's Day SP54

1998, June 1 *Perf. 14x13½, 13½x14*

B109 SP54 5d +1d shown	.50	.25
B110 SP54 5d +1d Flower, child, adult, vert.	.50	.25

Flood Victim Relief — SP55

2001, Dec. 24 Litho. *Perf. 13¼x14*
B111 SP55 5d +5d multi 1.00 .75

Earthquake Relief — SP56

2003, Dec. 3 Litho. *Perf. 13¼x14*
B112 SP56 5d +5d multi .90 .90

TeleFood SP57

Children's drawings with: No. B113, 5d+1d, Blue frame. No. B114, 5d+1d, Pink frame.

Perf. 14, 14x13½ (#B114)
2004, Oct. 16 Litho.
B113-B114 SP57 Set of 2 1.00 1.00

AIR POST STAMPS

Catalogue values for unused stamps in this section are for Never Hinged items.

Plane over Algiers Harbor AP1

Two types of 20fr:
Type I — Monogram "F" without serifs. "POSTE" indented 3mm.
Type II — Monogram "F" with serifs. "POSTE" indented 4½mm.

Unwmk.
1946, June 20 Engr. *Perf. 13*

C1 AP1 5fr red	.30	.25
C2 AP1 10fr deep blue	.30	.25
C3 AP1 15fr deep green	1.20	.40
C4 AP1 20fr brown (II)	1.10	.25
C4A AP1 20fr brown (I)	225.00	140.00
C5 AP1 25fr violet	1.40	.25
C6 AP1 40fr gray black	1.60	.65
Nos. C1-C4,C5-C6 (6)	5.90	2.05

For surcharges see Nos. C7, CB1-CB2.

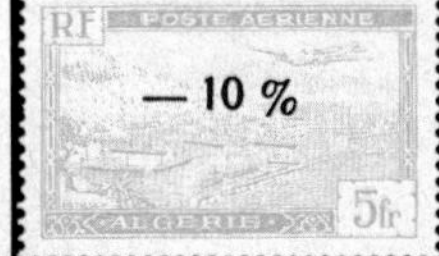

No. C1 Surcharged in Black

1947, Jan. 18

C7 AP1 (4.50fr) on 5fr red	.35	.25
a. Inverted surcharge	800.00	600.00
b. Double surcharge	1,000.	700.00
c. Pair, one without surcharge	1,200.	

Storks over Mosque — AP2

Plane over Village AP3

1949-53

C8 AP2 50fr green	4.50	.90
C9 AP3 100fr brown	3.50	.65
C10 AP2 200fr bright red	10.50	5.25
C11 AP3 500fr ultra ('53)	32.50	20.00
Nos. C8-C11 (4)	51.00	26.80

Beni Bahdel Dam — AP4

1957, July 1 Unwmk. *Perf. 13*

C12 AP4 200fr dark red 9.50 2.00

Independent State

Caravelle over Ghardaia — AP5

Designs: 2d, Caravelle over El Oued. 5d, Caravelle over Tipasa.

1967-68 Engr. *Perf. 13*

C13 AP5 1d lil, org brn & emer 1.40 .60
C14 AP5 2d brt bl, org brn & emer 3.25 1.40
C15 AP5 5d brt bl, grn & org brn ('68) 8.50 3.25
Nos. C13-C15 (3) 13.15 5.25

Plane over Casbah, Algiers — AP6

Designs: 3d, Plane over Oran. 4d, Plane over Rhumel Gorge.

1971-72 Photo. *Perf. 12½*

C16 AP6 2d grysh blk & multi 2.50 1.00
C17 AP6 3d violet & blk 3.75 1.60
C18 AP6 4d blk & multi 4.25 2.00
Nos. C16-C18 (3) 10.50 4.60

Issued: 2d, 6/12/71; 3d, 4d, 2/28/72.

Storks and Plane — AP7

1979, Mar. 24 Photo. *Perf. 11½*

C19 AP7 10d multi 6.50 2.50

Plane Approaching Coastal City — AP8

1991, Apr. 26 Litho. *Perf. 13½*

C20 AP8 10d shown 3.00 1.50
C21 AP8 20d Plane over city 6.00 3.00

Plane Over Djidjelli Corniche — AP9

1993, Sept. 25 Engr. *Perf. 13½x14*

C22 AP9 50d blue, grn & brn 6.75 3.25

AIR POST SEMI-POSTAL STAMPS

Catalogue values for unused stamps in this section are for Never Hinged items.

No. C2 Surcharged in Carmine

1947, June 18 *Perf. 13*

CB1 AP1 10fr +10fr deep blue 2.50 1.75

7th anniv. of Gen. Charles de Gaulle's speech in London, June 18, 1940.

No. C1 Surcharged in Blue

1948, June 18

CB2 AP1 5fr +10fr red 2.50 1.75

8th anniv. of Gen. Charles de Gaulle's speech in London, June 18, 1940.

Monument, Clock Tower and Plane — SPAP1

1949, Nov. 10 Engr. Unwmk.

CB3 SPAP1 15fr +20fr dk brn 7.00 5.25

25th anniv. of Algeria's 1st postage stamps.

POSTAGE DUE STAMPS

D1

Perf. 14x13½

1926-27 Typo. Unwmk.

J1 D1 5c light blue .40 .30
J2 D1 10c dk brn .40 .30
J3 D1 20c olive grn .85 .30
J4 D1 25c car rose .95 .70
J5 D1 30c rose red 1.50 .50
J6 D1 45c blue grn 1.90 .90
J7 D1 50c brn vio .40 .25
J8 D1 60c green ('27) 3.50 1.10
J9 D1 1fr red brn, *straw* .55 .30
J10 D1 2fr lil rose ('27) .90 .40
J11 D1 3fr deep blue ('27) .85 .40
Nos. J1-J11 (11) 12.20 5.45

See Nos. J25-J26, J28-J32. For surcharges, see Nos. J18-J20.

D2

1926-27

J12 D2 1c olive grn .40 .30
J13 D2 10c violet 1.50 .60
J14 D2 30c bister 1.50 .50
J15 D2 60c dull red 1.00 .50
J16 D2 1fr brt vio ('27) 20.00 4.25
J17 D2 2fr lt bl ('27) 17.50 1.60
Nos. J12-J17 (6) 41.90 7.75

See note below France No. J51. For surcharges, see Nos. J21-J24.

Stamps of 1926 Surcharged

1927

J18 D1 60c on 20c olive grn 2.25 .80
J19 D1 2fr on 45c blue grn 3.00 1.60
J20 D1 3fr on 25c car rose 1.75 .80
Nos. J18-J20 (3) 7.00 3.20

Recouvrement Stamps of 1926 Surcharged

1927-32

J21 D2 10c on 30c bis ('32) 5.00 4.00
J22 D2 1fr on 1c olive grn 3.25 1.75
J23 D2 1fr on 60c dl red ('32) 25.00 .95
J24 D2 2fr on 10c violet 16.00 12.00
Nos. J21-J24 (4) 49.25 18.70

Catalogue values for unused stamps in this section, from this point to the end of the section, are for Never Hinged items.

Type of 1926, Without "R F"

1942 Typo. *Perf. 14x13½*

J25 D1 30c dark red 1.25 1.25
J26 D1 2fr magenta 1.75 *2.75*

Type of 1926 Surcharged in Red

1944 *Perf. 14x13½*

J27 A2 50c on 20c yel grn 1.00 .70
a. Inverted surcharge 27.50
b. Double surcharge 70.00

No. J27 was issued precanceled only. See note after No. 32.

Type of 1926

1944 Litho. *Perf. 12*

J28 D1 1.50fr brt rose lilac 1.00 .50
J29 D1 2fr greenish blue 1.25 .90
J30 D1 5fr rose carmine 1.25 1.10
Nos. J28-J30 (3) 3.50 2.50

Type of 1926

1947 Typo. *Perf. 14x13½*

J32 D1 5fr green 2.50 1.25

France Nos. J80-J81 Overprinted in Carmine or Black

1947

J33 D5 10c sepia (C) .50 .25
J34 D5 30c bright red violet .65 .25

D3

Perf. 14x13

1947-55 Unwmk. Engr.

J35 D3 20c red .70 .35
J36 D3 60c ultra 1.00 .45
J37 D3 1fr dk org brn .50 .35
J38 D3 1.50fr dull green 1.50 1.10
J39 D3 2fr red .70 .35
J40 D3 3fr violet .75 .45
J41 D3 5fr ultra ('49) 1.10 .35
J42 D3 6fr black .85 .45
J43 D3 10fr lil rose 1.40 .45
J44 D3 15fr ol grn ('55) 1.40 1.25
J45 D3 20fr brt grn 1.10 .85
J46 D3 30fr red org ('55) 2.50 1.50
J47 D3 50fr indigo ('51) 4.75 2.75
J48 D3 100fr brt bl ('53) 17.50 8.50
Nos. J35-J48 (14) 35.75 19.15

Independent State

France Nos. J93-J97 Overprinted in Black

Perf. 14x13½

1962, July 2 Typo. Unwmk.

Handstamped Overprint

J49 D6 5c bright pink 7.25 7.25
J50 D6 10c red orange 7.25 7.25
J51 D6 20c olive bister 7.25 7.25
J52 D6 50c dark green 11.00 11.00
J53 D6 1fr deep green 14.50 14.50
Nos. J49-J53 (5) 47.25 47.25

Typographed Overprint

J49a D6 5c bright pink 26.00 17.00
J50a D6 10c red orange 26.00 17.00
J51a D6 20c olive bister 26.00 17.00
J52a D6 50c dark green 55.00 35.00
J53a D6 1fr deep green 80.00 55.00
Nos. J49a-J53a (5) 213.00 141.00

See note after No. 290.

Scales — D4

1963, June 25 *Perf. 14x13½*

J54 D4 5c car rose & blk .25 .25
J55 D4 10c olive & car .25 .25
J56 D4 20c ultra & blk .55 .30
J57 D4 50c bister brn & grn 1.25 .80
J58 D4 1fr lilac & org 2.25 2.00
Nos. J54-J58 (5) 4.55 3.60

No. J58 Surcharged with New Value & 3 Bars

1968, Mar. 28 Typo. *Perf. 14x13½*

J59 D4 60c on 1fr lilac & org .80 .65

Grain — D5

1972-93 Litho. *Perf. 13½x14*

J60 D5 10c bister .25 .25
J61 D5 20c deep brown .25 .25
J62 D5 40c orange .25 .25
J63 D5 50c dk vio blue .30 .25
J64 D5 80c dk olive gray .75 .30
J65 D5 1d green .90 .55
a. yel green, perf. 14¼x14 .25 .25
J66 D5 2d blue 1.75 1.00
a. Prus bl, perf. 14¼x14 .25 .25
J67 D5 3d violet .50 .25
J68 D5 4d lilac rose .65 .35
Nos. J60-J68 (9) 5.60 3.45

Issued: 3d, 4d, 1/21/93; others, 10/21/72.

Nos. J65a and J66a are inscribed "B ALGERIE" at bottom right.

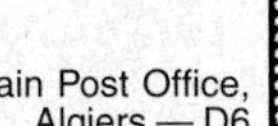

Main Post Office, Algiers — D6

2006, Mar. 28 Litho. ***Perf. 13¾x14***

No.	Type	Description	Unused	Used
J69	D6	5d green	.40	.40
J70	D6	10d blue	.70	.70

NEWSPAPER STAMPS

Nos. 1 and 33 Surcharged in Red

1924-26 Unwmk. ***Perf. 14x13½***

No.	Type	Description	Unused	Used
P1	A16	½c on 1c dk gray	.40	.40
a.		Triple surcharge	400.00	
P2	A1	½c on 1c olive ('26)	.45	.45

ALLENSTEIN

'a-lən-ˌshtin

LOCATION — In East Prussia
AREA — 4,457 sq. mi.
POP. — 540,000 (estimated 1920)
CAPITAL — Allenstein

Allenstein, a district of East Prussia, held a plebiscite in 1920 under the Versailles Treaty, voting to join Germany rather than Poland. Later that year, Allenstein became part of the German Republic.

100 Pfennig = 1 Mark

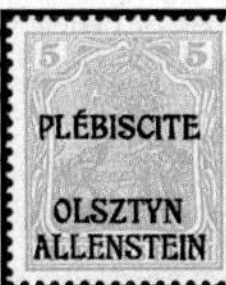

Stamps of Germany, 1906-20, Overprinted

Perf. 14, 14½, 14x14½, 14½x14

1920 Wmk. 125

No.	Type	Description	Unused	Used
1	A16	5pf green	.40	*.90*
2	A16	10pf carmine	.40	*.90*
3	A22	15pf dk vio	.40	*.90*
4	A22	15pf vio brn	5.50	*9.50*
5	A16	20pf bl vio	.40	*1.25*
6	A16	30pf org & blk, *buff*	.40	*1.25*
7	A16	40pf lake & blk	.40	*.90*
8	A16	50pf pur & blk, *buff*	.40	*.90*
9	A16	75pf grn & blk	.40	*.90*
10	A17	1m car rose	1.60	*3.75*
a.		Double overprint	—	—
11	A17	1.25m green	1.60	3.75
a.		Double overprint	—	—
12	A17	1.50m yel brn	.95	*3.25*
13	A21	2.50m lilac rose	2.40	*10.50*
14	A19	3m blk vio	2.40	*3.75*
a.		Double overprint	325.00	*1,150.*
		Never hinged	650.00	
b.		Inverted overprint	—	—
		Nos. 1-14 (14)	17.65	*42.40*
		Set, never hinged	45.00	

The 5pf brown (Germany No. 118), 10pf orange (No. 119), 20pf green (No. 121), 30pf blue (No. 123) and 40pf (No. 124) exist with this overprint but were not regularly issued. Value, each: $75 hinged, $145 never hinged.

Overprinted

No.	Type	Description	Unused	Used
15	A16	5pf green	.40	*.90*
16	A16	10pf carmine	.40	*.90*
17	A22	15pf dark vio	.40	*.90*
18	A22	15pf vio brn	20.00	*40.00*
19	A16	20pf blue vio	.65	*1.50*
20	A16	30pf org & blk, *buff*	.40	*.90*
21	A16	40pf lake & blk	.40	*.90*
22	A16	50pf pur & blk, *buff*	.40	*.90*
23	A16	75pf grn & blk	.65	*1.50*
24	A17	1m car rose	1.60	3.00
a.		Inverted overprint	600.00	*800.00*
		Never hinged	800.00	
25	A17	1.25m green	1.60	*3.00*
26	A17	1.50m yel brn	1.25	*3.00*
27	A21	2.50m lilac rose	2.75	*7.50*
28	A19	3m blk vio	1.75	3.00
a.		Inverted overprint	400.00	*975.00*
		Never hinged	725.00	
b.		Double overprint	200.00	*600.00*
		Never hinged	600.00	
		Nos. 15-28 (14)	32.65	*67.90*
		Set, never hinged	75.00	

The 40pf carmine rose (Germany No. 124) exists with this oval overprint, but it is doubtful whether it was regularly issued. Value $105 hinged, $210 never hinged.

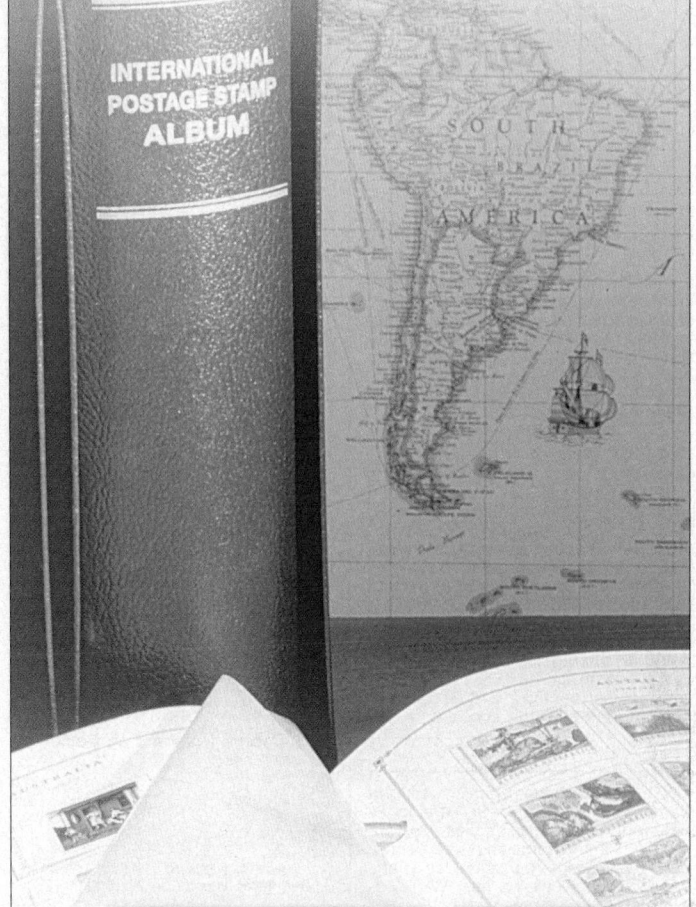

ANDORRA, SPANISH ADMINISTRATION

an-'dor-ə

LOCATION — On the southern slope of the Pyrenees Mountains between France and Spain.
GOVT. — Co-principality
AREA — 179 sq. mi.
POP. — 72,766 (July 1, 1996)
CAPITAL — Andorra la Vella

Andorra was subject to the joint control of France and the Spanish Bishop of Urgel and paid annual tribute to both. In 1993, Andorra became a constitutional coprincipality, governed by its own parliament.

100 Centimos = 1 Peseta
100 Centimes = 1 Franc
100 Cents = 1 Euro (2002)

Catalogue values for unused stamps in the Spanish Administration for this country are for Never Hinged items, beginning with Scott 50 in the regular postage section and Scott C2 in the airpost section; for the French Administration of this country, Never Hinged items begin at Scott 78 for regular postage, Scott B1 for the semi-postal section, Scott C1 for the airpost section, and Scott J21 for the postage due section.

A majority of the Spanish Andorra stamps issued to about 1950 are poorly centered. The fine examples that are valued will be somewhat off center. Very poorly centered examples (perfs cutting design) sell for less. Well centered very fine stamps are scarce and sell for approximately twice the values shown (Nos. 1-24, E1-E3), or 50% more (Nos. 25-49, E4-E5).

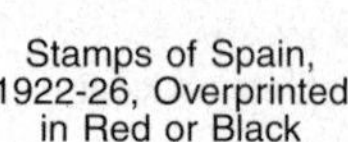

Stamps of Spain, 1922-26, Overprinted in Red or Black

Perf. 13½x12½, 12½x11½, 14

1928 **Unwmk.**

1	A49	2c olive green	.55	.55

Control Numbers on Back

2	A49	5c car rose (Bk)	.80	.80
3	A49	10c green	.80	.80
4	A49	15c slate blue	3.25	3.25
5	A49	20c violet	3.25	3.50
6	A49	25c rose red (Bk)	3.25	3.50
b.		Inverted ovpt., perf 14	160.00	—
7	A49	30c black brown	18.00	16.50
b.		Inverted ovpt., perf 12½x11½	160.00	50.00
8	A49	40c deep blue	18.00	11.00
9	A49	50c orange (Bk)	18.00	14.50
c.		Inverted ovpt., perf 14	160.00	—
10	A49a	1p blue blk	23.00	*23.50*
11	A49a	4p lake (Bk)	150.00	*175.00*
12	A49a	10p brown (Bk)	275.00	275.00
a.		Double overprint	*1,000.*	
		Nos. 1-12 (12)	513.90	527.90
		Set, never hinged	1,200.	

Counterfeit overprints exist.

Nos. 1-12 perf 14 are worth much more. See the *Scott Classic Specialized Catalogue.*

La Vall — A1

St. Juan de Caselles — A2

St. Julia de Loria — A3

St. Coloma — A4

General Council — A5

1929, Nov. 25 **Engr.** ***Perf. 14***

13	A1	2c olive green	1.10	.60

Control Numbers on Back

14	A2	5c carmine lake	3.50	1.25
15	A3	10c yellow green	3.50	*4.50*
16	A4	15c slate green	3.50	*4.50*
17	A3	20c violet	3.50	*4.50*
18	A4	25c carmine rose	7.75	6.25
19	A1	30c olive brown	115.00	*175.00*
20	A2	40c dark blue	4.50	3.00
21	A3	50c deep orange	5.50	4.50
22	A5	1p slate	12.50	14.50
23	A5	4p deep rose	90.00	*110.00*
24	A5	10p bister brown	100.00	*140.00*
		Nos. 13-24 (12)	350.35	*468.60*
		Set, never hinged	800.00	

Nos. 13-24 exist imperforate. Value, $950.

1931-38 ***Perf. 11½***

13a	A1	2c	6.25	.80

Control Numbers on Back

14a	A2	5c	10.00	2.25
15a	A3	10c	10.00	2.00
16a	A4	15c	30.00	25.00
17a	A3	20c	10.00	6.00
18a	A4	25c	10.00	6.00
19a	A1	30c ('33)	175.00	65.00
20a	A2	40c ('35)	17.00	13.00
22a	A5	1p ('38)	40.00	25.00
		Nos. 13a-22a (9)	308.25	145.05
		Set, never hinged	500.00	

Without Control Numbers

1936-43 ***Perf. 11½x11***

25	A1	2c red brown ('37)	2.00	1.60
26	A2	5c dark brown	2.00	1.60
27	A3	10c blue green	13.00	3.25
a.		10c yellow green	120.00	62.50
		Never hinged	165.00	
28	A4	15c blue green ('37)	7.50	3.50
a.		15c yellow green	8.00	5.75
29	A3	20c violet	7.00	3.50
30	A4	25c deep rose ('37)	3.25	*3.25*
31	A1	30c carmine	5.50	3.25
31A	A2	40c dark blue	*800.00*	—
		Never hinged	1,400.	
32	A1	45c rose red ('37)	2.00	1.60
33	A3	50c deep orange	10.00	5.75
34	A1	60c deep blue ('37)	7.00	3.50
34A	A5	1p slate	1,000.	—
		Never hinged	2,000.	
35	A5	4p deep rose ('43)	40.00	*47.50*
36	A5	10p bister brn ('43)	52.50	*57.50*
		Nos. 25-31,32-34,35-36 (12)	151.75	135.80
		Set, never hinged	325.00	

Exist imperforate. Value hinged, $290.

Beware of counterfeits of Nos. 31A and 34A. Purchase of stamps with certificates is strongly advised.

Edelweiss — A6

Provost — A7

Coat of Arms — A8

Plaza of Ordino — A9

Chapel of Meritxell — A10

Map — A11

1948-53 **Unwmk.** **Photo.** ***Perf. 12½***

37	A6	2c dark ol grn ('51)	.35	.35
38	A6	5c deep org ('53)	.35	.35
39	A6	10c deep blue ('53)	.35	.35

Engr. ***Perf. 9½x10***

40	A7	20c brown vio	4.25	2.75
41	A7	25c org, perf. 12½ ('53)	3.00	2.10
42	A8	30c dk slate grn	4.25	3.25
43	A9	50c deep green	5.00	4.75
44	A10	75c dark blue	6.50	4.75
45	A9	90c dp car rose	3.50	3.50
46	A10	1p brt orange ver	5.00	4.25
47	A8	1.35p dk blue vio	3.50	3.50

Perf. 10

48	A11	4p ultra ('53)	4.75	*8.50*
49	A11	10p dk vio brn ('51)	11.00	11.00
		Nos. 37-49 (13)	51.80	49.40
		Set, never hinged	110.00	

Catalogue values for unused stamps in this section, from this point to the end of the section, are for Never Hinged items.

Bridge of St. Anthony — A12

Madonna of Meritxell, 8th Century — A13

Designs: 70c, Aynos pasture. 1p, View of Canillo. 2p, St. Coloma. 2.50p, Arms of Andorra. 3p, Old Andorra, horiz. 5p, View of Ordino, horiz.

1963-64 **Unwmk.** **Engr.** ***Perf. 13***

50	A12	25c dk gray & sepia	.25	.25
51	A12	70c dk sl grn & brn blk	.35	.35
52	A12	1p slate & dull pur	.45	.45
53	A12	2p violet & dull pur	.50	.50
54	A12	2.50p rose claret	.70	.70
55	A12	3p blk & grnsh gray	1.10	.80
56	A12	5p dk brn & choc	2.00	1.25
57	A13	6p sepia & car	2.75	2.75
		Nos. 50-57 (8)	8.10	7.05

Issued: 25c-2p, 7/20/63; 2.50p-6p, 2/29/64.

Narcissus — A14

1966, June 10 **Engr.** ***Perf. 13***

58	A14	50c shown	.50	.50
59	A14	1p Pinks	.50	.50
60	A14	5p Jonquils	1.50	1.50
61	A14	10p Hellebore	1.00	1.00
		Nos. 58-61 (4)	3.50	3.50

Common Design Types pictured following the introduction.

Europa Issue 1972
Common Design Type

1972, May 2 **Photo.** ***Perf. 13***

Size: 25½x38mm

62	CD15	8p multicolored	*65.00*	*45.00*

Encamp Valley — A15

Tourist publicity: 1.50p, Massana (village). 2p, Skiing on De La Casa Pass. 5p, Pessons Lake, horiz.

1972, July 4 **Photo.** ***Perf. 13***

63	A15	1p multicolored	.35	.35
64	A15	1.50p multicolored	.45	.40
65	A15	2p multicolored	1.30	1.00
66	A15	5p multicolored	1.75	1.10
		Nos. 63-66 (4)	3.85	2.85

Butterfly Stroke A16

Design: 2p, Volleyball, vert.

1972, Oct. **Photo.** ***Perf. 13***

67	A16	2p lt blue & multi	.40	.40
68	A16	5p multicolored	.60	.60

20th Olympic Games, Munich, 8/26-9/11.

St. Anthony Singers A17

1.50p, Les Caramelles (boys' choir). 2p, Nativity scene. 5p, Man holding giant cigar, vert. 8p, Hermit of Meritxell, vert. 15p, Marratxa dancers.

1972, Dec. 5 **Photo.** ***Perf. 13***

69	A17	1p multicolored	.25	.25
70	A17	1.50p multicolored	.25	.25
71	A17	2p multicolored	.35	.35
72	A17	5p multicolored	.45	.45
73	A17	8p multicolored	.65	.50
74	A17	15p multicolored	1.35	1.10
		Nos. 69-74 (6)	3.30	2.90

Andorran customs. No. 71 is for Christmas.

Europa Issue 1973
Common Design Type and

Symbol of Unity A18

1973, Apr. 30 **Photo.** ***Perf. 13***

75	A18	2p ultra, red & blk	*.30*	*.25*

Size: 37x25mm

76	CD16	8p tan, red & blk	*.65*	*.55*

Nativity — A19

Christmas: 5p, Adoration of the Kings. Designs are from altar panels of Meritxell Parish Church.

1973, Dec. 14 **Photo.** ***Perf. 13***

77	A19	2p multicolored	.30	.30
78	A19	5p multicolored	1.00	1.00

Virgin of Ordino — A20

Europa: 8p, Les Banyes Cross.

1974, Apr. 29 Photo. *Perf. 13*

79 A20 2p multicolored *.90* *.70*
80 A20 8p slate & brt blue *2.75* *1.75*

Cupboard — A21 Crowns of Virgin and Child of Roser — A22

1974, July 30 Photo. *Perf. 13*

81 A21 10p multicolored 1.75 1.60
82 A22 25p dark red & multi 3.75 3.25

UPU Monument, Bern A23

1974, Oct. 9 Photo. *Perf. 13*

83 A23 15p multicolored 1.40 1.40

Centenary of Universal Postal Union.

Nativity A24

Christmas: 5p, Adoration of the Kings.

1974, Dec. 4 Photo. *Perf. 13*

84 A24 2p multicolored .90 .80
85 A24 5p multicolored 2.10 1.75

Mail Delivery, Andorra, 19th Century — A25

1975, Apr. 4 Photo. *Perf. 13*

86 A25 3p multicolored .45 .45

Espana 75 Intl. Philatelic Exhibition, Madrid, 4/4-13.

12th Century Painting, Ordino Church — A26

Design: 12p, Christ in Glory, 12th century Romanesque painting, Ordino church.

1975, Apr. 28 Photo. *Perf. 13*

87 A26 3p multicolored *1.25* *.70*
88 A26 12p multicolored *2.25* *1.40*

Urgel Cathedral and Document — A27

1975, Oct. 4 Photo. *Perf. 13*

89 A27 7p multicolored 1.35 1.10

Millennium of consecration of Urgel Cathedral, and Literary Festival 1975.

Nativity, Ordino A28

Christmas: 7p, Adoration of the Kings, Ordino.

1975, Dec. 3 Photo. *Perf. 13*

90 A28 3p multicolored .40 .40
91 A28 7p multicolored .85 .85

Caldron and CEPT Emblem — A29 Slalom and Montreal Olympic Emblem — A30

Europa: 12p, Chest and CEPT emblem.

1976, May 3 Photo. *Perf. 13*

92 A29 3p bister & multi *.30* .25
93 A29 12p yel & multi, horioz. *.90* .30

1976, July 9 Photo. *Perf. 13*

Design: 15p, One-man canoe and Montreal Olympic emblem, horiz.

94 A30 7p multicolored .45 .25
95 A30 15p multicolored .90 .35

21st Olympic Games, Montreal, Canada, July 17-Aug. 1.

Nativity A31

Christmas: 25p, Adoration of the Kings. Wall paintings in La Massana Church.

1976, Dec. 7 Photo. *Perf. 13*

96 A31 3p multicolored .55 .25
97 A31 25p multicolored 1.10 .35

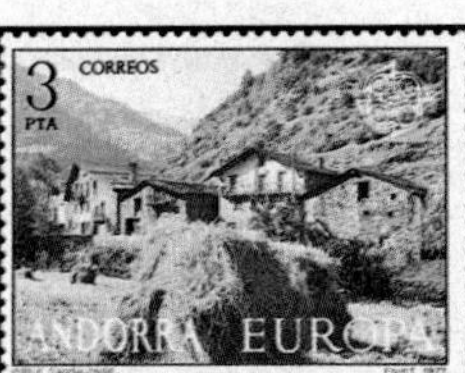

View of Ansalonge — A32

Europa: 12p, Xuclar, valley, mountains.

1977, May 2 Litho. *Perf. 13*

98 A32 3p multicolored *.35* .25
99 A32 12p multicolored *.90* .25

Cross of Terme — A33

Christmas: 12p, Church of St. Miguel d'Engolasters.

1977, Dec. 2 Photo. *Perf. 13x12½*

100 A33 5p multicolored .45 .35
101 A33 12p multicolored 1.10 .65

Souvenir Sheet

A34

Designs: 5p, Map of Post Offices. 10p, Mail delivery. 20p, Post Office, 1928. 25p, Andorran coat of arms.

1978, Mar. 31 Photo. *Perf. 13x13½*

102 Sheet of 4 1.40 1.40
a. A34 5p multicolored .30 .30
b. A34 10p multicolored .30 .30
c. A34 20p multicolored .30 .30
d. A34 25p multicolored .30 .30

Spanish postal service in Andorra, 50th anniv.

La Vall — A35

Europa: 12p, St. Juan de Caselles.

1978, May 2 *Perf. 13*

103 A35 5p multicolored *.25* .25
104 A35 12p multicolored *.80* .25

Crown, Bishop's Mitre and Staff A36

1978, Sept. 24 Photo. *Perf. 13*

105 A36 5p brown, car & yel .65 .30

700th anniversary of the signing of treaty establishing Co-Principality of Andorra.

Holy Family — A37

Christmas: 25p, Adoration of the Kings. Both designs after frescoes in the Church of St. Mary d'Encamp.

1978, Dec. 5 Photo. *Perf. 13*

106 A37 5p multicolored .25 .25
107 A37 25p multicolored .60 .30

Young Woman — A38

Designs: 5p, Young man. 12p, Bridegroom and bride riding mule.

1979, Feb. 14 Photo. *Perf. 13*

108 A38 3p multicolored .25 .25
109 A38 5p multicolored .25 .25
110 A38 12p multicolored .25 .25
Nos. 108-110 (3) .75 .75

Old Mail Truck A39

Europa: 12p, Stampless covers of 1846 & 1854.

1979, Apr. 30 Engr. *Perf. 13*

111 A39 5p yel grn & dk blue *.30* .25
112 A39 12p dk red & violet *.60* .25

Children Holding Hands A40

1979, Oct. 18 Photo. *Perf. 13*

113 A40 19p multicolored .80 .30

International Year of the Child.

St. Coloma's Church — A41

Christmas: 25p, Agnus Dei roundel, St. Coloma's Church.

1979, Nov. 28 Photo. *Perf. 13½*

114 A41 8p multicolored .25 .25
115 A41 25p multicolored .35 .25

Bishop Pere d'Arg A42

Bishops of Urgel: 5p, Josep Caixal. 13p, Joan Benlloch.

1979, Dec. 27 **Engr.**

116 A42 1p dk blue & brown .25 .25
117 A42 5p rose lake & purple .25 .25
118 A42 13p brown & dk green .25 .25
Nos. 116-118 (3) .75 .75

See Nos. 132-133, 159, 175, C4.

Antoni Fiter, Magistrate — A43

Europa: 19p, Francesc Cairat, magistrate.

1980, Apr. 28 Photo. ***Perf. 13x13½***

119 A43 8p bister, blk & brn *.35* .25
120 A43 19p lt green & blk *.70* .25

Boxing, Moscow '80 Emblem A44

1980, July 23 Photo. ***Perf. 13½x13***

121 A44 5p Downhill skiing .25 .25
122 A44 8p shown .25 .25
123 A44 50p Target shooting .80 .35
Nos. 121-123 (3) 1.30 .85

12th Winter Olympic Games, Lake Placid, NY, Feb. 12-24 (5p); 22nd Summer Olympic Games, Moscow, July 19-Aug. 3.

Nativity A45

1980, Dec. 12 Litho. ***Perf. 13***

124 A45 10p Nativity, vert. .25 .25
125 A45 22p shown .50 .25

Christmas 1980.

Children Dancing at Santa Anna Feast A46

Europa: 30p, Going to church on Aplec de la Verge de Canolich Day.

1981, May 7 Photo. ***Perf. 13***

126 A46 12p multicolored *.25* .25
127 A46 30p multicolored *.65* .30

50th Anniv. of Police Force A47

1981, July 2 Photo. ***Perf. 13½x13***

128 A47 30p multicolored .80 .25

Intl. Year of the Disabled A48

1981, Oct. 8 Photo. ***Perf. 13½***

129 A48 50p multicolored 1.10 .40

Christmas 1981 A49

Designs: Encamp Church retable.

1981, Dec. 3 Photo. ***Perf. 13½***

130 A49 12p Nativity .30 .25
131 A49 30p Adoration .50 .45

Bishops of Urgel Type of 1979

1981, Dec. 12 Engr. ***Perf. 13½***

132 A42 7p Salvador Casanas .30 .25
133 A42 20p Josep de Boltas .55 .25

Natl. Arms — A51

1982, Feb. 17 Photo. ***Perf. 13x13½***

134 A51 1p bright pink .25 .25
135 A51 3p bister brown .25 .25
136 A51 7p red orange .25 .25
137 A51 12p lake .25 .25
138 A51 15p ultra .30 .25
139 A51 20p blue green .35 .25
140 A51 30p crimson rose .45 .25

Perf. 13½x12½

1982, Sept. 30 **Engr.**

Size: 25½x30½mm

141 A51 50p dark green .90 .25
142 A51 100p dark blue 1.50 .60
Nos. 134-142 (9) 4.50 2.60

For type A51 without "PTA" see Nos. 192-198.

Europa 1982 A52

1982, May 12 Photo. ***Perf. 13***

143 A52 14p New Reforms, 1866, vert. *.30* .25
144 A52 33p Reform of Institutions, 1981 *.80* .25

1982 World Cup — A53

Designs: Various soccer players.

1982, June 13 Photo. ***Perf. 13x13½***

145 A53 14p multicolored .90 .90
146 A53 33p multicolored 1.60 1.60
a. Pair, #145-146 + label 2.75 2.75

A54

A55

Anniversaries: 9p, Permanent Spanish and French delegations, cent. 14p, 50th anniv. of Andorran stamps. 23p, St. Francis of Assisi (1182-1226). 33p, Anyos Pro-Vicarial District membership centenary (Relacio sobre la Vall de Andorra titlepage).

1982, Sept. 7 Engr. ***Perf. 13***

147 A54 9p dk blue & brown .25 .25
148 A54 14p black & green .45 .25
149 A54 23p dk blue & brown .30 .25
150 A54 33p black & olive grn .50 .35
Nos. 147-150 (4) 1.50 1.10

Perf. 13x13½, 13½x13

1982, Dec. 9 **Photo.**

Christmas: 14p, Madonna and Child, Andorra la Vieille Church, vert. 33p, El Tio de Nadal (children in traditional costumes striking hollow tree).

151 A55 14p multicolored .35 .25
152 A55 33p multicolored .60 .30

Europa 1983 A56

16, La Cortinada Church, architect, 12th cent. 38p, Water mill, 16th cent.

1983, June 7 Photo. ***Perf. 13***

153 A56 16p multicolored *.40* .25
154 A56 38p multicolored *.80* .35

Local Mushrooms — A57

1983, July 20 Photo. ***Perf. 13x12½***

155 A57 16p Lactarius sanguifluus .80 .60

See Nos. 165, 169, 172.

Universal Suffrage, 50th Anniv. A58

Photogravure and Engraved

1983, Sept. 6 ***Perf. 13***

156 A58 10p multicolored .30 .25

Visit of Monsignor Jacinto Verdaguer Bishop and Co-Prince A59

1983, Sept. 6

157 A59 50p multicolored .85 .55

Christmas 1983 — A60

Saint Cerni de Nagol, Romanesque fresco, Church of San Cerni de Nagol.

1983, Nov. 24 Photo. ***Perf. 13½***

158 A60 16p multicolored .45 .25

Bishops of Urgel Type of 1979

1983, Dec. 7 Engr. ***Perf. 13***

159 A42 26p Joan J. Laguarda Fenollera .45 .25

1984 Winter Olympics A62

1984, Feb. 17 Litho. ***Perf. 13½x14***

160 A62 16p Ski jumping .80 .25

ESPANA '84 — A63

1984, Apr. 27 Photo. ***Perf. 13***

161 A63 26p Emblems .50 .25

Europa (1959-84) A64

1984, May 5 **Engr.**

162 A64 16p brown *.55* .25
163 A64 38p blue *.80* *.35*

1984 Summer Olympics A65

1984, Aug. 9 Litho. ***Perf. 13½x14***

164 A65 40p Running .85 .40

Mushroom Type of 1983

1984, Sept. 27 Photo. ***Perf. 13x12½***

165 A57 11p Morchella esculenta *7.25* 2.00

Christmas 1984 A66

1984, Dec. 6 Photo. ***Perf. 13½***

166 A66 17p Nativity carving .50 .25

Europa 1985
A67

18p, Mossen Enric Arfany, composer, natl. hymn score. 45p, Musician Playing Viol, Romanesque fresco detail, La Cortinada Church, vert.

1985, May 3 Engr. *Perf. 13½*
167 A67 18p dk vio, grn & chocolate .45 .25
168 A67 45p green & chocolate *1.40* *.35*

Mushroom Type of 1983
Perf. 13½x12½
1985, Sept. 19 Photo.
169 A57 30p Gyromitra esculenta 1.10 .25

Pal Village — A68

1985, Nov. 7 Engr. *Perf. 13½*
170 A68 17p brt ultra & dk blue .50 .25

Christmas 1985
A69

Fresco: Angels Playing Trumpet and Psaltery, St. Bartholomew Chapel.

1985, Dec. 11 Photo. *Perf. 13½x13*
171 A69 17p multicolored .50 .25

Mushroom Type of 1983
Perf. 13½x12½
1986, Apr. 10 Photo.
172 A57 30p Marasmius oreades .70 .25

Europa 1986 — A70

1986, May 5 Engr. *Perf. 13*
173 A70 17p Water *.35* .25
174 A70 45p Soil and air *1.50* *.25*

Bishops of Urgel Type of 1979
1986, Sept. 11 Engr. *Perf. 13½*
175 A42 35p Justi Guitart .55 .25

A72

Santa Roma de Les Bons Church bell.

1986, Dec. 11 Litho. *Perf. 14*
176 A72 19p multicolored .50 .25

Christmas.

A73

Contemporary Natl. Coat of Arms.

1987, Mar. 27 Photo. *Perf. 14*
177 A73 48p multicolored .90 .30

Visit of the co-princes: the Bishop of Urgel and president of France, September 26, 1986.

Europa 1987
A74

Modern architecture: 19p, Meritxell Sanctuary interior. 48p, Sanctuary exterior, vert.

1987, May 15 Engr. *Perf. 14x13½*
178 A74 19p dark blue & brown *.35* .25
179 A74 48p dark blue & brown *1.60* .25

Souvenir Sheet

1992 Summer Olympics, Barcelona — A75

20p, House of the Valleys. 50p, Bell tower, Chapel of the Archangel Michael, and torchbearer.

1987, July 20 Photo. *Perf. 14*
180 Sheet of 2 3.00 3.00
a. A75 20p multicolored .90 .90
b. A75 50p multicolored 1.75 1.75

Local Mushrooms — A76

1987, Sept. 11 *Perf. 13½x12½*
181 A76 100p Boletus edulis 2.25 .60

Christmas
A77

Design: Detail from a Catalan manuscript, De Nativitat, by R. Llull.

1987, Nov. 18 Litho. *Perf. 14*
182 A77 20p multicolored .50 .25

Lance and Arrowhead (Bronze Age)
A78

1988, Mar. 25 Photo. *Perf. 14*
183 A78 50p multicolored .90 .30

Europa 1988 — A79

Pyrenean Mastiff — A80

Transport and communications: 20p, Les Bons, a medieval road. 45p, Trader and pack mules, early 20th cent.

1988, May 5 Engr. *Perf. 14x13½*
184 A79 20p dark bl & dark red *.45* .25
185 A79 45p dark bl & dark red *1.50* .25

1988, July 26 Litho. *Perf. 14x13½*
186 A80 20p multicolored .80 .25

Bishop of Urgel and Seigneur of Caboet Confirming Co-Principality, 700th Anniv. — A81

1988, Oct. 24 Litho. *Perf. 14x13½*
187 A81 20p gold, blk & int blue .50 .25

Christmas 1988
A82

1988, Nov. 30 Litho. *Perf. 14x13½*
188 A82 20p multicolored .30 .25

Arms Type of 1982 Without "PTA"
1988, Dec. 2 Photo. *Perf. 13x13½*
192 A51 20p brt blue green .45 .25

Size: 25x30½mm
Perf. 13½x12½
Engr.
194 A51 50p grnsh black .90 .25
196 A51 100p dark blue 1.90 .40
198 A51 500p dark brown 7.75 2.00
Nos. 192-198 (4) 11.00 2.90

Europa 1989
A83

Perf. 14x13½, 13½x14
1989, May 8 Litho. & Engr.
200 A83 20p Leapfrog, vert. *.55* .25
201 A83 45p Tug of war *1.50* .25

Santa Roma Church, Les Bons
A84

Litho. & Engr.
1989, June 20 *Perf. 13½x14*
202 A84 50p blk, dp bl & grn bl 1.10 .25

Anniv. Emblem — A85

1989, Oct. 26 Litho. *Perf. 14x13½*
203 A85 20p multicolored .70 .25

Intl. Red Cross and Red Crescent societies, 125th annivs.; Year for the Protection of Human Life.

Christmas — A86

The Immaculate Conception.

1989, Dec. 1
204 A86 20p multi .50 .25

Europa 1990
A87

Post offices.

Perf. 13½x14, 14x13½
1990, May 17 Photo.
205 A87 20p shown *.55* .25
206 A87 50p Post office, vert. *1.40* *.25*

Gomphidius Rutilus — A88

1990, June 21 Litho. *Perf. 13x13½*
207 A88 45p multicolored 1.10 .35

Plandolit House — A89

Christmas — A90

Litho. & Engr.

1990, Oct. 17 *Perf. 13x12½*
208 A89 20p brown & org yel .50 .25

1990, Nov. 26 Litho. *Perf. 14x13½*
209 A90 25p lake, brn & bister .50 .25

4th Games of the Small European States A91

1991, Apr. 29 Photo. *Perf. 13½x14*
210 A91 25p Discus *.55* .25
211 A91 45p High jump, runner *.90* *.30*

Europa — A92

Perf. 14x13½, 13½x14
1991, May 10 **Litho.**
212 A92 25p Olympus-1 satellite *.70* .25
213 A92 55p Olympus-1, horiz. *2.50* .35

A93

Christmas — A94

1991, Sept. 20 Litho. *Perf. 13x12½*
214 A93 45p Macrolepiota procera 1.10 .30

1991, Nov. 29 Photo. *Perf. 14x13½*
215 A94 25p multicolored .75 .25

Woman Carrying Water Pails A95

1992, Feb. 14 Photo. *Perf. 13½x14*
216 A95 25p multicolored .50 .25

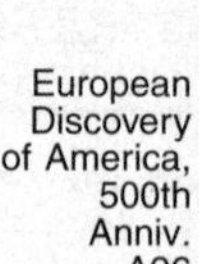

European Discovery of America, 500th Anniv. A96

Perf. 14x13½, 13½x14
1992, May 8 **Photo.**
217 A96 27p Santa Maria, vert. *.65* .25
218 A96 45p King Ferdinand *2.25* *.30*

Europa.

1992 Summer Olympics, Barcelona A97

1992, July 22 Photo. *Perf. 13½x14*
219 A97 27p Kayak .80 .25

Nativity Scene, by Fra Angelico — A98

1992, Nov. 18 Photo. *Perf. 14*
220 A98 27p multicolored .50 .25

Natl. Automobile Museum A99

Litho. & Engr.
1992, Sept. 10 *Perf. 13½x14*
221 A99 27p 1894 Benz 1.00 .25

Cantharellus Cibarius — A100

1993, Mar. 25 Photo. *Perf. 13½x14*
222 A100 28p multicolored .75 .40

Contemporary Paintings — A101

Europa: 28p, Upstream, by John Alan Morrison. 45p, Rhythm, by Angel Calvente, vert.

Perf. 13½x14, 14x13½
1993, May 20 **Litho.**
223 A101 28p multicolored *.55* .25
224 A101 45p multicolored *1.10* *.35*

Art and Literature Society, 25th Anniv. — A102

1993, Sept. 23 Litho. *Perf. 14*
225 A102 28p multicolored .75 .25

Christmas — A103

Litho. & Engr.
1993, Nov. 25 *Perf. 14x13½*
226 A103 28p multi .55 .25

Souvenir Sheet

Constitution, 1st Anniv. — A104

1994, Mar. 14 Photo. *Perf. 14*
227 A104 29p multicolored .75 .50

Sir Alexander Fleming (1881-1955), Co-discoverer of Penicillin — A105

1994, May 6 Photo. *Perf. 13½x14*
228 A105 29p Portrait *.50* *.30*
229 A105 55p AIDS virus *1.40* *.60*

Europa.

Hygrophorus Gliocyclus — A106

1994, Sept. 27 Photo. *Perf. 14*
230 A106 29p multicolored .75 .50

Christmas — A107

1994, Nov. 29 Photo. *Perf. 14x13½*
231 A107 29p multicolored .75 .50

Nature Conservation in Europe — A108

1995, Mar. 23 Photo. *Perf. 14*
232 A108 30p Farm in valley .70 .45
233 A108 60p Stone fence, valley 1.35 .75

Europa A109

1995, May 8 Photo. *Perf. 14*
234 A109 60p multicolored *1.60* *.70*

Christmas — A110

1995, Nov. 8 Photo. *Perf. 14*
235 A110 30p Flight to Egypt .65 .35

Entrance Into Council of Europe A111

1995, Nov. 10
236 A111 30p multicolored *1.10* .35

Mushrooms — A112

1996, Apr. 30 Photo. *Perf. 14*
237 A112 30p Ramaria aurea .90 .35
238 A112 60p Tuber melanosporum 1.60 .80

Isabelle Sandy (1884-1975), Writer — A113

1996, May 7
239 A113 60p brown & violet *1.50* *.65*

Europa.

Intl. Museum Day A114

Design: Antique coal-heated iron.

1996, Sept. 12 Photo. *Perf. 14*
240 A114 60p multicolored .90 .55

Christmas A115

The Annunciation, by Andrew Martin, 1753, St. Eulalia d'Encamp Church.

1996, Nov. 26 Photo. *Perf. 14*
241 A115 30p multicolored .75 .35

Museums of Andorra A116

Early bicycles designed by: 32p, Karl Drais, 1818. 65p, Pierre Michaux, 1861.

1997, Apr. 28 Photo. *Perf. 14*
242 A116 32p multicolored .45 .35
243 A116 65p multicolored .90 .70

See Nos. 248-249.

A117

UNESCO — A118

Europa (Stories and Legends): Hikers watching family of bears crossing over river on fallen tree.

1997, May 6 Photo. *Perf. 14*
244 A117 65p multicolored *1.25 .50*

1997, Sept. 30 Photo. *Perf. 14*
245 A118 32p multicolored .70 .35

Christmas — A119

1997, Nov. 25 Photo. *Perf. 14*
246 A119 32p multicolored .60 .35

1998 Winter Olympic Games, Nagano A120

1998, Feb. 23 Photo. *Perf. 14*
247 A120 35p Slalom skier .60 .35

Museums of Andorra Type of 1997

Early bicycles: 35p, Kangaroo, 1878. 70p, Hirondelle, 1889.

1998, Apr. 24 Photo. *Perf. 13½x14*
248 A116 35p multicolored .55 .35
249 A116 70p multicolored 1.10 .70

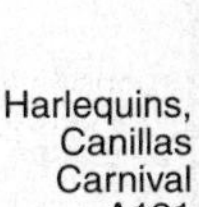

Harlequins, Canillas Carnival A121

1998, May 22 Photo. *Perf. 14*
250 A121 70p multicolored *1.35 .70*

Europa.

Manual Digest, 250th Anniv. — A122

1998, Sept. 30 Photo. *Perf. 14*
251 A122 35p multicolored .60 .40

Inauguration of the Postal Museum of Andorra — A123

1998, Nov. 19 Photo. *Perf. 14*
252 A123 70p multicolored 1.10 .75

Christmas A124

1998, Nov. 26
253 A124 35p multicolored .75 .40

Museums of Andorra A125

Early bicycles designed by: 35p, Salvo, 1878, vert. 70p, Rudge, 1883.

1999, Jan. 29 Photo. *Perf. 14*
254 A125 35p multicolored .70 .40
255 A125 70p multicolored 1.10 .75

Council of Europe, 50th Anniv. A126

1999, Apr. 29 Photo. *Perf. 14*
256 A126 35p multicolored .70 .35

Incles Valley A127

1999, May 6
257 A127 70p multicolored 1.60 .80

Europa.

Transporting Mail on Horseback — A128

1999, Feb. 18 Photo. *Perf. 14*
258 A128 35p black & sepia .60 .40

Restoration of Casa Rull, Sispony, La Massana A129

1999, Sept. 22 Photo. *Perf. 13½x14*
259 A129 35p multicolored .45 .35

Christmas — A130

St. Coloma's Church — A131

1999, Nov. 10 Engr. *Perf. 14x13½*
260 A130 35p orange brn & brn .60 .35

1999, Nov. 12 Photo.
261 A131 35p multicolored .60 .35

European heritage.

Europa, 2000

Common Design Type

2000, May 11 Photo. *Perf. 13¾*
262 CD17 70p multi *1.60 .70*

Angonella Lakes A132

2000, June 29 Photo. *Perf. 13¾x14*
263 A132 35p multi .65 .35

Casa Lacruz A133

2000, July 20 Photo. *Perf. 13¾x14*
264 A133 35p multi .65 .35

China, Areny-Plandolit Museum — A134

2000, July 27 *Perf. 14x13¾*
265 A134 70p multi 1.35 .70

2000 Summer Olympics, Sydney — A135

2000, Sept. 29 Photo. *Perf. 14x13½*
266 A135 70p multi 1.35 .65

European Convention on Human Rights, 50th Anniv. A136

2000, Nov. 3 *Perf. 13½x14*
267 A136 70p multi 1.35 .65

Natl. Archives, 25th Anniv. — A137

2000, Nov. 14 *Perf. 14x13½*
268 A137 35p multi .60 .30

Christmas — A138

2000, Nov. 22
269 A138 35p multi .75 .30

Rec de Solà — A139

2001, Mar. 30 Photo. *Perf. 14x13¾*
270 A139 40p multi .60 .60

Europa A140

2001, May 16 *Perf. 13¾x14*
271 A140 75p multi *1.35 .85*

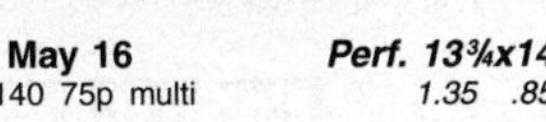

Casa Palau, Sant Julià de Lòria — A141

2001, June 20 Photo. ***Perf. 14x13¾***
272 A141 75p multi 1.00 1.10

Chapel of the Virgin of Meritxell, 25th Anniv. of Rebuilding — A142

2001, Sept. 7 Photo. ***Perf. 14x13¾***
273 A142 40p multi .65 .60

Natl. Auditorium, 10th Anniv. A143

2001, Sept. 20 ***Perf. 13¾x14***
274 A143 75p multi 1.35 1.00

Christmas A144

2001, Nov. 20 Photo. ***Perf. 13¾x14***
275 A144 40p multi .70 .55

100 Cents = 1 Euro (€)

Coat of Arms — A145

2002, Jan. 2 Photo. ***Perf. 12¾x13¼***
276 A145 25c brown orange .75 .60
277 A145 50c claret 1.25 1.10

Birds A146

Designs: 25c, Prunella collaris. 50c, Montifringilla nivalis.

2002, Mar. 27 ***Perf. 13¾x14***
278-279 A146 Set of 2 2.25 2.00

Intl. Year of Mountains A147

2002, Apr. 5
280 A147 50c multi 1.60 1.10

Europa A148

2002, May 9
281 A148 50c multi *11.50 1.75*

Architectural Heritage — A149

Designs: €1.80, Casa Fusilé, Escaldes-Engordany. €2.10, Farga Rossell Centre, La Massana.

2002, June 14 Photo. ***Perf. 14x13¾***
282-283 A149 Set of 2 10.00 9.00

Historic Automobiles A150

Designs: 25c, Pinette. 50c, Rolls-Royce, horiz.

2002, Oct. 8 ***Perf. 14x13¾, 13¾x14***
284-285 A150 Set of 2 2.25 2.00

Christmas A151

2002, Nov. 26 ***Perf. 13¾x14***
286 A151 25c multi .80 .70

Artistic Heritage — A152

Various religious murals from Santa Coloma Church: a, 25c. b, 75c. c, 50c.

2002, Nov. 28 ***Perf. 14x13¾***
287 A152 Horiz. strip of 3, #a-c 4.00 3.50

Sassanat Bridge A153

Perf. 13½x13¾
2003, Feb. 27 **Photo.**
288 A153 26c multi .70 .60

Constitution, 10th Anniv. — A154

2003, Mar. 14 Photo. ***Perf. 13¾x14***
289 A154 76c multi 2.00 1.75

Europa — A155

2003, Apr. 24 ***Perf. 14x13¾***
290 A155 76c multi *2.00 1.10*

Oenanthe Oenanthe — A156

2003, June 11 Photo. ***Perf. 14x13¾***
291 A156 26c multi .70 .60

Admission to United Nations, 10th Anniv. A157

2003, July 28 Photo. ***Perf. 13¾x14***
292 A157 76c multi 2.00 1.75

Automobiles — A158

Designs: 51c, 1908 Carter, vert. 76c, 1928 Peugeot.

2003, Oct. 15 ***Perf. 14x13¾, 13¾x14***
293-294 A158 Set of 2 7.75 7.75

Christmas A159

2003, Nov. 20 ***Perf. 13¾x14***
295 A159 26c multi .70 .60

Coat of Arms — A160

2004, Jan. 2 ***Perf. 12¾x13¼***
296 A160 27c bright blue .70 .60
297 A160 52c olive green 1.40 1.25
298 A160 77c red orange 2.00 1.75
Nos. 296-298 (3) 4.10 3.60

See Nos. 308-310, 319-320, 327-328.

Art by Joaquim Mir A161

Designs: 27c, Fira del Bestiar. 52c, L'Escorxador, vert.

2004 ***Perf. 13¾x14, 14x13¾***
299-300 A161 Set of 2 2.00 1.75

Issued: 27c, 2/20; 52c, 3/18.

Europa — A162

2004, Apr. 29 Photo. ***Perf. 14x13¾***
301 A162 77c black *2.00 1.60*

Fringilla Coelebs A163

2004, June 15 Photo. ***Perf. 13¾x14***
302 A163 27c multi .70 .60

Automobiles — A164

Designs: €1.90, 1939 Simca 508-C. €2.19, 1955 Messerschmitt KR-1.

2004, Oct. 15 Photo. ***Perf. 13¾x14***
303-304 A164 Set of 2 11.00 9.50

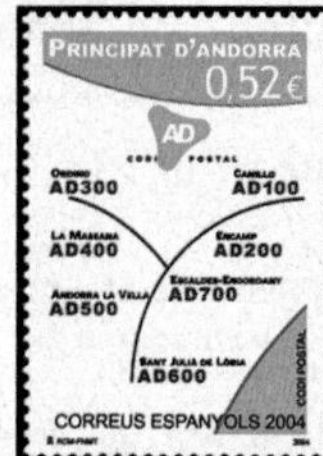

Postal Code — A165

2004, Oct. 25 ***Perf. 14x13¾***
305 A165 52c multi 1.40 1.25

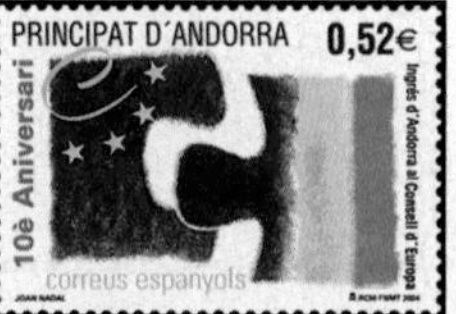

Admission to Council of Europe, 10th Anniv. A166

2004, Nov. 10 ***Perf. 13¾x14***
306 A166 52c multi 1.40 1.25

Christmas A167

2004, Nov. 22
307 A167 27c multi .75 .75

Arms Type of 2004

2005, Jan. 28 Litho. ***Perf. 12¾x13¼***
308 A160 28c blue .70 .65
309 A160 53c yel green 1.35 1.25
310 A160 78c brt pink 2.00 1.75
Nos. 308-310 (3) 4.05 3.65

Selection of Madriu-Peralita-Claror Valley as UNESCO World Heritage Site — A168

2005, Mar. 7 Photo. ***Perf. 14x13¾***
311 A168 28c multi .70 .70

Endless, Sculpture by Mark Brusse A169

2005, Mar. 14 ***Perf. 13¾x14***
312 A169 53c multi 1.35 1.35

Europa A170

2005, Apr. 15 Photo. ***Perf. 13¾x14***
313 A170 78c multi *2.00 1.60*

9th Games of Small European States — A171

2005, May 20 Photo. ***Perf. 14x13¾***
314 A171 €1.95 multi 5.00 4.25

Caritas Andorra, 25th Anniv. — A172

2005, June 15
315 A172 28c multi .70 .70

Cinclus Cinclus A173

2005, July 11 Photo. ***Perf. 13¾x14***
316 A173 €2.21 multi 5.75 5.75

Christmas A174

2005, Nov. 2 Photo. ***Perf. 13¾x14***
317 A174 28c blk & org .75 .65

2006 Winter Olympics, Turin A175

2006, Feb. 6
318 A175 29c multi .75 .70

Arms Type of 2004

2006, Mar. 1 Litho. ***Perf. 12¾x13¼***
319 A160 29c yel brown .75 .65
320 A160 57c blue 1.50 1.25

Earth, Fire, Water and Wind, Sculpture by Satoru Sato — A176

2006, Apr. 10 Photo. ***Perf. 14x13¾***
321 A176 78c multi 2.00 1.75

Europa A177

2006, May 16 ***Perf. 13¾x14***
322 A177 57c multi 1.45 1.35

Perdix Perdix A178

2006, June 6
323 A178 €2.39 multi 6.75 6.75

Fulbright Scholarships — A179

2006, Aug. 8 Photo. ***Perf. 13¾x14***
324 A179 57c multi 1.45 1.45

UNESCO, 60th Anniv., Andorran National UNESCO Committee, 10th Anniv. — A180

2006, Oct. 2 ***Perf. 14x13¾***
325 A180 €2.33 multi 6.75 6.75

Christmas A181

2006, Nov. 2 Photo. ***Perf. 13¾x14***
326 A181 29c multi .75 .75

Arms Type of 2004

2007, Jan. 19 Litho. ***Perf. 12¾x13¼***
327 A160 30c red .75 .75
328 A160 58c gray 1.50 1.50

Santa Eulalia d'Encamp Church, by Francesc Galobardes A182

2007, Feb. 12 Photo. ***Perf. 14x13¾***
329 A182 30c multi .75 .75

Europa — A183

2007, Apr. 23 Photo. ***Perf. 14x13¾***
330 A183 58c multi 1.50 1.50

Scouting, cent.

Jordino Family, Sculptures by Rachid Khimoune — A184

2007, May 21
331 A184 €2.43 multi 6.25 6.25

Tetrao Urogallus A185

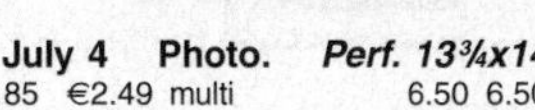

2007, July 4 Photo. ***Perf. 13¾x14***
332 A185 €2.49 multi 6.50 6.50

Casa de la Vall, by Francesc Galobardes — A186

2007, Sept. 10
333 A186 78c multi 2.00 2.00

Andorran Red Cross, 25th Anniv. A187

2007, Oct. 15 Photo. ***Perf. 13¾x14***
334 A187 30c black & red .80 .80

Christmas A188

2007, Nov. 2
335 A188 30c multi .80 .80

Gypaetus Barbatus A189

2008, Jan. 24 Photo. ***Perf. 13¾***
336 A189 31c multi .80 .80

Carro Votiu, Sculpture by Jordi Casamajor A190

2008, Jan. 24 ***Perf. 12¾x13***
337 A190 60c multi 1.60 1.60

Constitution, 15th Anniv. — A191

2008, Mar. 12 Photo. ***Perf. 14x13¾***
338 A191 31c multi .90 .90

Europa — A192

2008, Apr. 23
339 A192 60c black & deep blue 1.75 1.75

Andorran Science Society, 25th Anniv. — A193

2008, May 14
340 A193 78c blue & black 2.25 2.25

Souvenir Sheet

Expo Zaragoza 2008 — A194

2008, June 13 **Photo.** ***Perf. 13¾***
341 A194 €2.60 multi 7.50 7.50

2008 Summer Olympics, Beijing — A195

2008, July 8 **Litho.** ***Perf. 14x13¾***
342 A195 60c multi 1.90 1.90

Vall del Comapedrosa A196

2008, Sept. 15
343 A196 €2.44 multi 6.25 6.25

Sispony, by Carme Massana — A197

2008, Oct. 13 **Photo.** ***Perf. 12¾***
344 A197 31c multi .80 .80

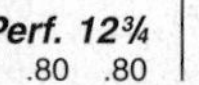

La Missa del Gallo, by Sergi Mas — A198

2008, Nov. 11
345 A198 31c multi .80 .80

Christmas.

Narcissus A199

Die Cut Perf. 13
2009, Jan. 17 **Litho.**
Self-Adhesive
346 A199 32c multi .85 .85

Andorran School, 25th Anniv. — A200

2009, Feb. 9 ***Perf. 14x13¾***
347 A200 62c multi 1.60 1.60

Mercè Rodoreda (1908-83), Writer — A201

2009, Mar. 6
348 A201 78c black 2.00 2.00

Council of Europe, 60th Anniv. — A202

2009, Apr. 6 **Litho.** ***Perf. 14x13¾***
349 A202 32c multi .90 .90

Europa — A203

2009, Apr. 23
350 A203 62c multi 1.75 1.75

Intl. Year of Astronomy.

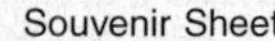
Souvenir Sheet

Madrid Bridge — A204

2009, May 18 **Photo.**
351 A204 €2.70 multi 7.00 7.00

Eurasian Sparrowhawk A205

2009, Sept. 10 **Photo.** ***Perf. 14x13¾***
352 A205 €2.47 multi 6.75 6.75

Paintings A206

Designs: 62c, El Tarter, by Francesc Galobardes. 78c, Contrallum a Canillo, by Carme Massana.

2009, Oct. 8 **Photo.** ***Perf. 13¾x14***
353-354 A206 Set of 2 4.00 4.00

Christmas A207

2009, Nov. 2 **Litho.**
355 A207 32c multi .95 .95

Pyrenees Iris A208

Die Cut Perf. 13
2010, Jan. 12 **Litho.**
Self-Adhesive
356 A208 34c multi .95 .95

Jacint Verdaguer (1845-1902), Poet — A209

Litho. & Engr.
2010, Feb. 8 ***Perf. 14x13¾***
357 A209 64c black & red 1.75 1.75

Paris Bridge, Andorra la Vella — A210

2010, Mar. 5 **Litho.**
358 A210 €2.75 multi 7.50 7.50

Europa — A211

2010, May 6 **Photo.** ***Perf. 13¼x13¾***
359 A211 64c multi 1.75 1.75

Bonfire A212

2010, June 1 ***Perf. 13¾x13¼***
360 A212 64c multi 1.60 1.60

2010 World Cup Soccer Championships, South Africa — A213

2010, June 1
361 A213 78c multi 1.90 1.90

Recycling A214

Perf. 13¾x13¼
2010, Sept. 6 **Photo.**
362 A214 €2.49 multi 6.50 6.50

Churches — A215

Nos. 363: a, Sant Joan de Caselles Church. b, Sant Romà de Les Bons Church, horiz.

Perf. 13¼x13, 13x13¼
2010, Oct. 6 **Engr.**
363 A215 78c Sheet of 2, #a-b 4.50 4.50

See Andorra, French Administration No. 679.

Christmas
A364

2010, Nov. 2 Photo. ***Perf. 13¾x13¼***
364 A216 34c multi .95 .95

Escaldes-Engordany Parish, 2011
Capital of Catalan Culture — A217

Die Cut Perf. 13
2011, Jan. 12 Litho.
Self-Adhesive
365 A217 35c multi .95 .95

Miquel Marti i Pol
(1929-2003),
Writer — A218

2011, Feb. 7 ***Perf. 14x13¾***
366 A218 65c black & gray 1.75 1.75

Europa — A219

2011, Apr. 4
367 A219 65c multi 1.90 1.90

Intl. Year of Forests.

Casa
Farràs
A220

2011, May 3 ***Perf. 13¾x14***
368 A220 80c multi 2.40 2.40

Painted
Keystone,
Sant
Esteve
Church
A221

2011, June 1
369 A221 €2.55 multi 7.50 7.50

Venice
Biennale
A222

Artwork by: 80c, Helena Guàrdia. €2.55, Francisco Sánchez.

2011, July 1
370-371 A222 Set of 2 9.50 9.50

Equality of the
Sexes — A223

2011, Sept. 8 ***Perf. 14x13¾***
372 A223 80c multi 2.25 2.25

America
Issue,
Mailbox
A224

2011, Oct. 11 ***Perf. 13¾x14***
373 A224 80c multi 2.25 2.25

Christmas
A225

2011, Nov. 3
374 A225 35c multi 1.00 1.00
a. Tete-beche pair 2.00 2.00

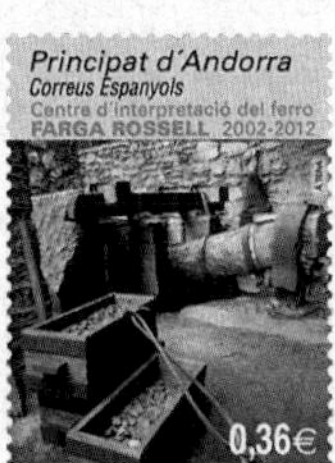

Rossell Forge
Interpretive
Center, La
Massana, 10th
Anniv, — A226

2012, Jan. 9 Litho. ***Die Cut Perf. 13***
Self-Adhesive
375 A226 36c multi .95 .95

Agustí Bartra
(1908-82),
Poet — A227

2012, Feb. 27 ***Perf. 14x13¾***
376 A227 51c black 1.40 1.40

Europa
A228

2012, Apr. 4 ***Perf. 13¾x14***
377 A228 70c multi 1.90 1.90

CIAM Building, Escaldes-
Engordany — A229

2012, May 3
378 A229 85c multi 2.25 2.25

Wood Carving,
Sant Marti de la
Cortinada
Church,
Ordino — A230

2012, June 1 ***Perf. 14x13¾***
379 A230 85c multi 2.25 2.25

A231

Art — A232

2012, July 2 ***Perf. 13¾x14***
380 A231 €2.90 multi 7.25 7.25
Perf. 14x13¾
381 A232 €2.90 multi 7.25 7.25

Civic
Values — A233

2012, Sept. 10 ***Perf. 14x13¾***
382 A233 85c multi 2.25 2.25

America Issue,
Cosmological
Legend — A234

2012, Oct. 11
383 A234 85c multi 2.25 2.25

Christmas — A235

2012, Nov. 5
384 A235 36c multi .95 .95

Salvador Espriu
(1913-85),
Poet — A236

2013, Jan. 10 ***Die Cut Perf. 13***
Self-Adhesive
385 A236 37c multi 1.00 1.00

Road Between Andorra and La Seu
d'Urgell, Spain, Cent.
A237

2013, Feb. 21 ***Perf. 13¾x14***
386 A237 75c multi 2.00 2.00

Areny-Plandolit
Museum,
Ordino — A238

2013, Mar. 4 ***Perf. 14x13¾***
387 A238 52c multi 1.40 1.40

Souvenir Sheet

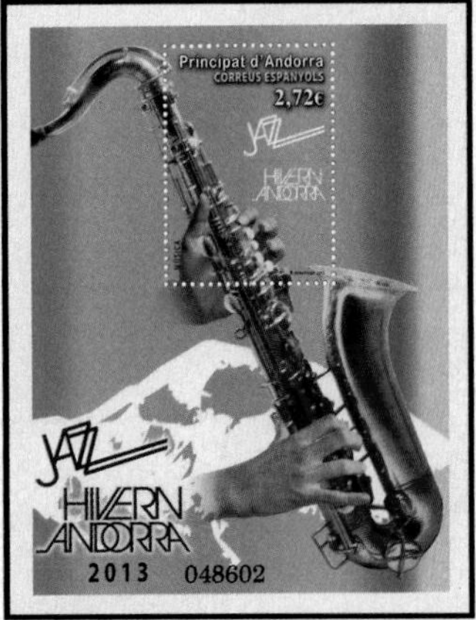

Winter Jazz Festival — A239

2013, Apr. 1 *Perf. 13¼x13¾*
388 A239 €2.72 multi 7.00 7.00

Europa
A240

2013, Apr. 23 *Perf. 13¾x13¼*
389 A240 75c multi 2.00 2.00

Women in Portuguese Costumes — A241

2013, May 6 *Perf. 13½x13¼*
390 A241 90c multi 2.40 2.40

Casa dels Russos
A242

2013, June 3
391 A242 75c multi 2.00 2.00

Souvenir Sheet

School Correspondence — A243

Perf. 13¼x13¾
2013, Sept. 16 **Litho.**
392 A243 €2.72 multi 7.50 7.50

AIR POST STAMPS

A set of 12 stamps, inscribed "CORREU AER / SOBRETAXA" was authorized in 1932 for a proposed private air service between Andorra and Barcelona. These stamps were prepared but not issued. Value, set $40. The stamps were also overprinted "FRANQUICIA DEL CONSELL" for official use. Value, set $140.

Catalogue values for unused stamps in this section are for Never Hinged items.

AP1

Unwmk.
1951, June 27 **Engr.** *Perf. 11*
C1 AP1 1p dark violet brown 17.50 4.25

AP2

AP3

Litho. & Engr.
1983, Oct. 20 *Perf. 13*
C2 AP2 20p brown & bis brn .30 .25

Jaime Sansa Nequi, Episcopal Church official.

1984, Oct. 25 **Photo.** *Perf. 13*
C3 AP3 20p multicolored .30 .25

Pyrenees Art Center.

Bishops of Urgel Type of 1979
1985, June 13 **Engr.** *Perf. 13½*
C4 A42 20p Ramon Iglesias .30 .25

SPECIAL DELIVERY STAMPS

Special Delivery Stamp of Spain, 1905 Overprinted

1928 **Unwmk.** *Perf. 14*
Without Control Number on Back
E1 SD1 20c red 80.00 *95.00*
Never hinged 150.00

With Control Number on Back
E2 SD1 20c pale red 50.00 *50.00*
Never hinged 90.00

Eagle over Mountain Pass — SD2

1929 *Perf. 14*
With Control Number on Back
E3 SD2 20c scarlet 25.00 20.00
Never hinged 35.00

Perf 11½ examples are numbered A000.000 and are specimens. Value, $400.

1937 *Perf. 11½x11*
Without Control Number on Back
E4 SD2 20c red 7.75 *9.50*
Never hinged 8.75

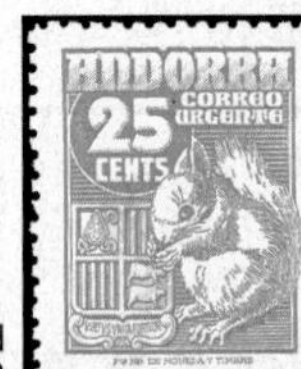

Arms and Squirrel — SD3

1949 **Unwmk.** **Engr.** *Perf. 10x9½*
E5 SD3 25c red 5.75 4.50
Never hinged 8.25

ANDORRA, FRENCH ADMINISTRATION

Stamps and Types of France, 1900-1929, Overprinted

Perf. 14x13½

1931, June 16 **Unwmk.**

No.	Type	Denom.	Color	Unused	Used
1	A16	1c	gray	1.25	*1.25*
a.			Double overprint	*2,000.*	*2,000.*
2	A16	2c	red brown	1.60	*1.60*
3	A16	3c	orange	1.60	*1.60*
4	A16	5c	green	2.40	*2.40*
5	A16	10c	lilac	4.00	*4.75*
6	A22	15c	red brown	5.50	5.50
7	A22	20c	red violet	8.75	*9.50*
8	A22	25c	yellow brn	9.50	*10.00*
9	A22	30c	green	9.50	*10.00*
10	A22	40c	ultra	10.00	*12.00*
11	A20	45c	lt violet	20.00	*21.50*
12	A20	50c	vermilion	13.50	*15.00*
a.			Pair, one without overprint	525.00	
13	A20	65c	gray green	28.00	28.00
14	A20	75c	rose lilac	32.50	28.00
15	A22	90c	red	40.00	*45.00*
16	A20	1fr	dull blue	40.00	*45.00*
17	A22	1.50fr	light blue	45.00	*47.50*

Overprinted

No.	Type	Denom.	Color	Unused	Used
18	A18	2fr	org & pale bl	87.50	*95.00*
19	A18	3fr	brt vio & rose	110.00	*125.00*
20	A18	5fr	dk bl & buff	135.00	*145.00*
21	A18	10fr	grn & red	275.00	*350.00*
22	A18	20fr	mag & grn	375.00	*575.00*
			Nos. 1-22 (22)	1,255.	*1,578.*

See No. P1 for ½c on 1c gray.

Nos. 9, 15 and 17 were not issued in France without overprint.

Chapel of Meritxell
A50

Bridge of St. Anthony
A51

St. Miguel d'Engolasters
A52

Gorge of St. Julia
A53

Old Andorra
A54

1932-43 **Engr.** *Perf. 13*

No.	Type	Denom.	Color	Unused	Used
23	A50	1c	gray blk	.55	*.65*
24	A50	2c	violet	.90	.90
25	A50	3c	brown	.90	*.95*
26	A50	5c	blue green	.90	*.95*
27	A51	10c	dull lilac	1.40	1.40
28	A50	15c	deep red	2.00	2.00
29	A51	20c	lt rose	13.50	11.00
30	A52	25c	brown	6.50	5.50
31	A51	25c	brn car ('37)	11.00	*14.00*
32	A51	30c	emerald	4.75	4.75
33	A51	40c	ultra	13.50	11.00
34	A51	40c	brn blk ('39)	1.25	1.25
35	A51	45c	lt red	13.50	11.00
36	A51	45c	bl grn ('39)	6.00	5.25
37	A52	50c	lilac rose	14.50	13.00
38	A51	50c	lt vio ('39)	6.00	5.50
38A	A51	50c	grn ('40)	2.40	2.40
39	A51	55c	lt vio ('38)	24.00	16.00
40	A51	60c	yel brn ('38)	1.60	1.60
41	A52	65c	yel grn	55.00	52.50
42	A51	65c	blue ('38)	18.50	14.50
43	A51	70c	red ('39)	2.40	2.40
44	A52	75c	violet	11.00	8.75
45	A51	75c	ultra ('39)	4.50	*4.75*
46	A51	80c	green ('38)	27.50	23.00
46A	A53	80c	bl grn ('40)	.40	.40
47	A53	90c	deep rose	6.50	6.50
48	A53	90c	dk grn ('39)	3.50	3.50
49	A53	1fr	blue grn	20.00	14.50
50	A53	1fr	scarlet ('38)	32.50	24.00
51	A53	1fr	dp ultra ('39)	.40	.40
51A	A53	1.20fr	brt vio ('42)	.40	.40
52	A50	1.25fr	rose car ('33)	55.00	45.00
52A	A50	1.25fr	rose ('38)	5.50	4.00
52B	A53	1.30fr	sepia ('40)	.40	.40
53	A54	1.50fr	ultra	24.00	19.50
53A	A53	1.50fr	crim ('40)	.40	.40
54	A53	1.75fr	violet ('33)	110.00	*120.00*
55	A53	1.75fr	dk bl ('38)	47.50	40.00
56	A53	2fr	red violet	13.00	11.50
56A	A50	2fr	rose red ('40)	1.60	1.60
56B	A50	2fr	dk bl grn ('42)	.40	.40
57	A50	2.15fr	dk vio ('38)	65.00	52.50
58	A50	2.25fr	ultra ('39)	8.75	8.75
58A	A50	2.40fr	red ('42)	.80	.40
59	A50	2.50fr	gray blk ('39)	8.00	8.00
59A	A50	2.50fr	dp ultra ('40)	2.75	2.75
60	A53	3fr	orange brn	13.50	10.50
60A	A50	3fr	red brn ('40)	.40	.40
60B	A50	4fr	sl bl ('42)	.40	.40
60C	A50	4.50fr	dp vio ('42)	2.00	2.00
61	A54	5fr	brown	.90	.80
62	A54	10fr	violet	1.00	.80
62B	A54	15fr	dp ultra ('42)	1.20	1.20
63	A54	20fr	rose lake	1.20	.80
63A	A51	50fr	turq bl ('43)	1.60	1.20
			Nos. 23-63A (56)	673.05	598.00

A 20c ultra exists but was not issued. Value: unused, $27,500; never hinged $42,500.

No. 37 Surcharged with Bars and New Value in Black

1935, Sept. 18
64 A52 20c on 50c lil rose 18.50 17.00
a. Double surcharge *6,000.*

Coat of Arms — A55

1936-42 *Perf. 14x13*

No.	Type	Denom.	Color	Unused	Used
65	A55	1c	black ('37)	.25	.25
66	A55	2c	blue	.25	*.25*
67	A55	3c	brown	.25	*.25*
68	A55	5c	rose lilac	.25	*.25*
69	A55	10c	ultra ('37)	.25	*.25*

70 A55 15c red violet 2.75 2.25
71 A55 20c emerald ('37) .25 .25
72 A55 30c cop red ('38) .80 .80
72A A55 30c blk brn ('42) .40 .40
73 A55 35c Prus grn ('38) 65.00 67.50
74 A55 40c cop red ('42) .80 .80
75 A55 50c Prus grn ('42) .80 .80
76 A55 60c turq bl ('42) .80 .80
77 A55 70c vio ('42) .80 .80
Nos. 65-77 (14) 73.65 75.65
Set, never hinged 135.00

Catalogue values for unused stamps in this section, from this point to the end of the section, are for Never Hinged items.

Coat of Arms — A56

1944

78 A56 10c violet .25 .25
79 A56 30c deep magenta .25 .25
80 A56 40c dull blue .25 .25
81 A56 50c orange red .25 .25
82 A56 60c black .25 .25
83 A56 70c brt red violet .25 .25
84 A56 80c blue green .25 .25
Nos. 78-84 (7) 1.75 1.75

See No. 114.

St. Jean de Caselles A57

La Maison des Vallees A58

Old Andorra A59

Provost A60

1944-47 ***Perf. 13***

85 A57 1fr brown violet .25 .25
86 A57 1.20fr blue .25 .25
87 A57 1.50fr red .25 .25
88 A57 2fr dk blue grn .25 .25
89 A58 2.40fr rose red .25 .25
90 A58 2.50fr rose red ('46) 7.25 .80
91 A58 3fr sepia .25 .25
92 A58 4fr ultra .40 .25
93 A59 4.50fr brown blk .40 .25
94 A58 4.50fr dk bl grn ('47) 9.50 5.50
95 A59 5fr ultra .35 .25
96 A59 5fr Prus grn ('46) 1.40 .50
97 A59 6fr rose car ('45) .35 .25
98 A59 10fr Prus green .35 .25
99 A59 10fr ultra ('46) 2.40 .40
100 A60 15fr rose lilac .95 .40
101 A60 20fr deep blue .95 .40
102 A60 25fr lt rose red ('46) 5.50 1.90
103 A60 40fr dk green ('46) 5.50 2.00
104 A60 50fr sepia 1.75 1.40
Nos. 85-104 (20) 38.55 16.05

1948-49

105 A58 4fr lt blue grn 1.60 .80
106 A59 6fr violet brn .80 .40
107 A59 8fr indigo 1.25 1.20
108 A59 12fr bright red 1.25 1.20
109 A59 12fr blue grn ('49) 1.50 .75
110 A59 15fr crimson ('49) 1.00 .55
111 A60 18fr deep blue 5.00 2.40
112 A60 20fr dark violet 3.50 2.00
113 A60 25fr ultra ('49) 2.50 1.20
Nos. 105-113 (9) 18.40 10.50

1949-51 ***Perf. 14x13, 13***

114 A56 1fr deep blue .95 .65
115 A57 3fr red ('51) 7.25 4.75
116 A57 4fr sepia 2.50 2.25
117 A58 5fr emerald 3.75 2.75
118 A58 5fr purple ('51) 13.50 4.75
119 A58 6fr blue grn ('51) 7.25 3.25
120 A58 8fr brown .95 .75
121 A59 15fr blk brn ('51) 13.50 2.40
122 A59 18fr rose red ('51) 27.50 11.00
123 A60 30fr ultra ('51) 35.00 13.50
Nos. 114-123 (10) 112.15 46.05

Les Escaldres Spa — A61

St. Coloma Belfry A62

Designs: 15fr-25fr, Gothic cross. 30fr-75fr, Village of Les Bons.

1955-58 Unwmk. Engr. ***Perf. 13***

124 A61 1fr dk gray bl .25 .25
125 A61 2fr dp green .35 .25
126 A61 3fr red .35 .25
127 A61 5fr chocolate .35 .25
128 A62 6fr dk bl grn .80 .80
129 A62 8fr rose brown .80 .80
130 A62 10fr brt violet 1.25 .80
131 A62 12fr indigo 1.60 .80
132 A61 15fr red 1.60 .85
133 A61 18fr blue grn 2.00 .85
134 A61 20fr dp purple 3.50 2.00
135 A61 25fr sepia 3.50 2.00
136 A62 30fr deep blue 40.00 19.50
137 A62 35fr Prus bl ('57) 12.00 7.25
138 A62 40fr dk green 47.50 28.00
139 A62 50fr cerise 4.50 3.25
140 A62 65fr purple ('58) 12.00 6.50
141 A62 70fr chestnut ('57) 7.25 6.50
142 A62 75fr violet blue 65.00 45.00
Nos. 124-142 (19) 204.60 125.90

Issued: 35fr, 70fr, 8/19; 65fr, 2/10; others, 2/15.

Coat of Arms — A63

Gothic Cross, Meritxell A64

65c, 85c, 1fr, Engolasters Lake.

1961, June 19 Typo. ***Perf. 14x13***

143 A63 5c brt green & blk .25 .25
144 A63 10c red, pink & blk .25 .25
145 A63 15c blue & black .30 .25
146 A63 20c yellow & brown .50 .30

Engr. ***Perf. 13***

147 A64 25c violet, bl & grn .75 .30
148 A64 30c mar, ol grn & brn .90 .50
149 A64 45c indigo, bl & grn 22.50 16.00
150 A64 50c pur, lt brn & ol grn 2.00 1.25
151 A64 65c bl, ol & brn 28.00 18.50
152 A64 85c rose lil, vio bl & brn 28.00 18.50
153 A64 1fr grnsh bl, ind & brn 2.00 1.25
Nos. 143-153 (11) 85.45 57.35

See Nos. 161-166A.

Imperforates
Most stamps of Andorra, French Administration, from 1961 onward exist imperforate in issued and trial colors, and also in small presentation sheets in issued colors.

Common Design Types pictured following the introduction.

Telstar Issue
Common Design Type

1962, Sept. 29 Engr.

154 CD111 50c ultra & purple 2.00 1.60

1st television connection of the US and Europe through the Telstar satellite, 7/11-12.

"La Sardane" A66

Charlemagne Crossing Andorra — A67

1fr, Louis le Debonnaire giving founding charter.

1963, June 22 Unwmk. ***Perf. 13***

155 A66 20c lil rose, cl & ol grn 5.00 5.00
156 A67 50c sl grn & dk car rose 8.50 8.50
157 A67 1fr red brn, ultra & dk grn 14.00 14.00
Nos. 155-157 (3) 27.50 27.50

Old Andorra Church and Champs-Elysées Palace — A68

1964, Jan. 20 Engr.

158 A68 25c vio brn, grn & blk 2.00 1.60

"PHILATEC," Intl. Philatelic and Postal Techniques Exhib., Paris, June 5-21, 1964.

Bishop of Urgel and Seigneur of Caboet Confirming Co-Principality, 1288 — A69

Design: 60c, Napoleon re-establishing Co-principality, 1806.

1964, Apr. 25 Engr. ***Perf. 13***

159 A69 60c dk brn, red brn & sl grn 22.50 22.50
160 A69 1fr brt bl, org brn & blk 22.50 22.50

Arms Type of 1961

1964, May 16 Typo. ***Perf. 14x13***

161 A63 1c dk blue & gray .25 .25
162 A63 2c black & orange .25 .25
163 A63 12c purple, emer & yel 1.10 1.00
164 A63 18c black, lil & pink 1.25 1.00
Nos. 161-164 (4) 2.85 2.50

Scenic Type of 1961

Designs: 40c, 45c, Gothic Cross, Meritxell. 60c, 90c, Pond of Engolasters.

1965-71 Engr. ***Perf. 13***

165 A64 40c dk brn, org brn & sl grn 1.00 .80
165A A64 45c vio bl, ol bis & slate 1.10 .80
166 A64 60c org brn & dk brn 1.60 1.25
166A A64 90c ultra, bl grn & bister 2.00 1.00
Nos. 165-166A (4) 5.70 3.85

Issued: 40c, 60c, Apr. 24, 1965. 45c, June 13, 1970. 90c, Aug. 28, 1971.

Syncom Satellite over Pleumeur-Bodou Station — A70

1965, May 17 ***Unwmk.***

167 A70 60c dp car, lil & bl 6.50 4.75

Cent. of the ITU.

Andorra House, Paris — A71

1965, June 5

168 A71 25c dk bl, org brn & ol gray 1.25 .80

Ski Lift — A72

Design: 25c, Chair lift, vert.

1966, Apr. 2 Engr. ***Perf. 13***

169 A72 25c brt bl, grn & dk brn 1.60 1.25
170 A72 40c mag, brt ultra & sep 2.40 1.60

Winter sports in Andorra.

FR-1 Satellite — A73

1966, May 7 ***Perf. 13***

171 A73 60c brt bl, grn & dk grn 2.10 1.60

Issued to commemorate the launching of the scientific satellite FR-1, Dec. 6, 1965.

Europa Issue, 1966
Common Design Type

1966, Sept. 24 Engr. ***Perf. 13***
Size: 21½x35½mm

172 CD9 60c brown *3.00 3.00*

Folk Dancers, Sculpture by Josep Viladomat — A74

1967, Apr. 29 Engr. *Perf. 13*
173 A74 30c ol grn, dp grn & slate 1.25 .80

Cent. (in 1966) of the New Reform, which reaffirmed and strengthened political freedom in Andorra.

Europa Issue, 1967
Common Design Type

1967, Apr. 29
Size: 22x36mm

174 CD10 30c bluish blk & lt bl *4.25 1.75*
175 CD10 60c dk red & brt pink *6.50 4.50*

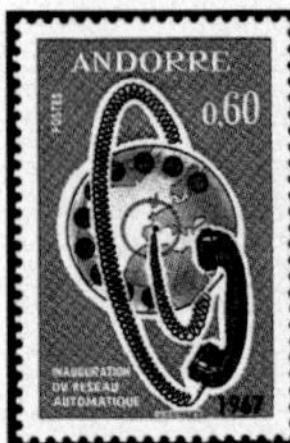

Telephone Encircling the Globe — A75

1967, Apr. 29
176 A75 60c dk car, vio & blk 2.00 1.25

Automatic telephone service.

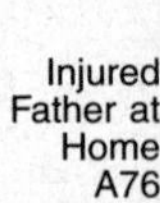

Injured Father at Home A76

1967, Sept. 23 Engr. *Perf. 13*
177 A76 2.30fr ocher, dk red brn & brn red 9.75 7.50

Introduction of Social Security System.

Jesus in Garden of Gethsemane — A77

Designs (from 16th century frescoes in La Maison des Vallees): 30c, The Kiss of Judas. 60c, The Descent from the Cross (Pieta).

1967, Sept. 23
178 A77 25c black & red brn .80 .80
179 A77 30c purple & red lilac .80 .80
180 A77 60c indigo & Prus blue 1.60 1.25
Nos. 178-180 (3) 3.20 2.85

See Nos. 185-187.

Downhill Skier — A78

1968, Jan. 27 Engr. *Perf. 13*
181 A78 40c org, ver & red lil 1.60 1.25

10th Winter Olympic Games, Grenoble, France, Feb. 6-18.

Europa Issue, 1968
Common Design Type

1968, Apr. 27 Engr. *Perf. 13*
Size: 36x22mm

182 CD11 30c gray & brt bl *6.50 3.00*
183 CD11 60c brown & lilac *10.00 7.00*

High Jump A79

1968, Oct. 12 Engr. *Perf. 13*
184 A79 40c brt blue & brn 1.75 1.25

19th Olympic Games, Mexico City, Oct. 12-27.

Fresco Type of 1967

Designs (from 16th century frescoes in La Maison des Vallees): 25c, The Scourging of Christ. 30c, Christ Carrying the Cross. 60c, The Crucifixion. (All horiz.)

1968, Oct. 12
185 A77 25c dk grn & gray grn .85 .80
186 A77 30c dk brown & lilac .85 .80
187 A77 60c dk car & vio brn 1.75 1.25
Nos. 185-187 (3) 3.45 2.85

Europa Issue, 1969
Common Design Type

1969, Apr. 26 Engr. *Perf. 13*
188 CD12 40c rose car, gray & dl bl *7.50 3.50*
189 CD12 70c indigo, dl red & ol *11.00 8.50*

10th anniv. of the Conf. of European Postal and Telecommunications Administrations.

Kayak on Isere River — A80

Drops of Water & Diamond — A80a

1969, Aug. 2 Engr. *Perf. 13*
190 A80 70c dk sl grn, ultra & ind 3.25 2.75

Intl. Canoe & Kayak Championships, Bourg-Saint-Maurice, Savoy, July 31-Aug. 6.

1969, Sept. 27 Engr. *Perf. 13*
191 A80a 70c blk, dp ultra & grnsh bl 5.50 4.00

European Water Charter.

St. John, the Woman and the Dragon A81

The Revelation (From the Altar of St. John, Caselles): 40c, St. John Hearing Voice from Heaven on Patmos. 70c, St. John and the Seven Candlesticks.

1969, Oct. 18
192 A81 30c brn, dp pur & brn red 1.00 1.00
193 A81 40c gray, dk brn & brn ol 1.40 1.40
194 A81 70c dk red, maroon & brt rose lilac 1.75 1.75
Nos. 192-194 (3) 4.15 4.15

See Nos. 199-201, 207-209, 214-216.

Field Ball — A82

1970, Feb. 21 Engr. *Perf. 13*
195 A82 80c multi 2.75 2.00

Issued to publicize the 7th International Field Ball Games, France, Feb. 26-Mar. 8.

Europa Issue, 1970
Common Design Type

1970, May 2 Engr. *Perf. 13*
Size: 36x22mm

196 CD13 40c orange *6.00 2.50*
197 CD13 80c violet blue *14.00 6.00*

Shot Put — A83

1970, Sept. 11 Engr. *Perf. 13*
198 A83 80c bl & dk brn 2.75 2.00

1st European Junior Athletic Championships, Colombes, France, Sept. 11-13.

Altar Type of 1969

The Revelation (from the Altar of St. John, Caselles): 30c, St. John recording angel's message. 40c, Angel erecting column symbolizing faithful in heaven. 80c, St. John's trial in kettle of boiling oil.

1970, Oct. 24
199 A81 30c dp car, dk brn & brt pur 1.00 1.00
200 A81 40c violet & slate grn 1.40 .95
201 A81 80c ol, dk bl & car rose 2.40 2.40
Nos. 199-201 (3) 4.80 4.35

Ice Skating A84

1971, Feb. 20 Engr. *Perf. 13*
202 A84 80c dk red, red lil & pur 2.50 2.00

World Figure Skating Championships, Lyons, France, Feb. 23-28.

Capercaillie — A85

Nature protection: No. 204, Brown bear.

1971, Apr. 24 Photo. *Perf. 13*
203 A85 80c multicolored 4.75 3.25

Engr.

204 A85 80c blue, grn & brn 3.50 2.40

Europa Issue, 1971
Common Design Type

1971, May 8 Engr. *Perf. 13*
Size: 35½x22mm

205 CD14 50c rose red *8.00 2.25*
206 CD14 80c lt blue green *12.00 5.50*

Altar Type of 1969

The Revelation (from the Altar of St. John, Caselles): 30c, St. John preaching, Rev. 1:3. 50c, "The Sign of the Beast . . ." Rev. 16:1-2. 90c, The Woman, Rev. 17:1.

1971, Sept. 18
207 A81 30c dl grn, ol & brt grn 1.25 1.00
208 A81 50c rose car, org & ol brn 1.60 1.25
209 A81 90c blk, dk pur & bl 2.40 2.00
Nos. 207-209 (3) 5.25 4.25

Europa Issue 1972
Common Design Type

1972, Apr. 29 Photo. *Perf. 13*
Size: 21½x37mm

210 CD15 50c brt mag & multi *7.50 2.50*
211 CD15 90c multicolored *13.50 4.50*

Golden Eagle A86

1972, May 27 Engr.
212 A86 60c dk grn, olive & plum 5.00 3.25

Nature protection.

Shooting A87

1972, July 8
213 A87 1fr dk purple 3.75 2.00

20th Olympic Games, Munich, 8/26-9/11.

Altar Type of 1969

The Revelation (from the Altar of St. John, Caselles): 30c, St. John, bishop and servant. 50c, Resurrection of Lazarus. 90c, Angel with lance and nails.

1972, Sept. 16 Engr. *Perf. 13*
214 A81 30c dk ol, gray & red lil 1.25 .85
215 A81 50c vio blue & slate 1.50 1.25
216 A81 90c dk Prus bl & sl grn 2.40 2.40
Nos. 214-216 (3) 5.15 4.50

De Gaulle as Coprince of Andorra — A88

90c, De Gaulle in front of Maison des Vallées.

1972, Oct. 23 Engr. *Perf. 13*
217 A88 50c violet blue 1.75 1.25
218 A88 90c dk carmine 2.50 2.00
a. Pair, #217-218 + label 5.75 5.75

Visit of Charles de Gaulle to Andorra, 5th anniv.
See Nos. 399-400.

Europa Issue 1973
Common Design Type

1973, Apr. 28 Photo. *Perf. 13*
Size: 36x22mm

219 CD16 50c violet & multi *9.00 3.00*
220 CD16 90c dk red & multi *11.00 8.00*

Virgin of Canolich A89

1973, June 16 Engr. *Perf. 13*

221 A89 1fr ol, Prus bl & vio 2.50 1.60

Lily — A90

45c, Iris. 50c, Columbine. 65c, Tobacco. No. 226, Pinks. No. 227, Narcissuses.

1973-74 Photo. *Perf. 13*

222	A90	30c car rose & multi	.80	.80
223	A90	45c yel grn & multi	.40	.40
224	A90	50c buff & multi	1.75	1.75
225	A90	65c gray & multi	.40	.40
226	A90	90c ultra & multi	1.50	1.50
227	A90	90c grnsh bl & multi	1.25	1.25
		Nos. 222-227 (6)	6.10	6.10

Issued: 30c, 50c, No. 226, 7/7/73. 45c, 65c, No. 227, 4/6/74.

See Nos. 238-240.

Blue Titmouse — A91

Nature protection: 60c, Citril finch and mistletoe. 80c, Eurasian bullfinch. 1fr, Lesser spotted woodpecker.

1973-74 Photo. *Perf. 13*

228	A91	60c buff & multi	4.00	1.75
229	A91	80c gray & multi	4.00	2.25
230	A91	90c gray & multi	2.75	1.25
231	A91	1fr yel grn & multi	2.75	1.60
		Nos. 228-231 (4)	13.50	6.85

Issued: 90c, 1fr, 10/27/73. 60c, 80c, 9/21/74.

Europa Issue 1974

Virgin of Pal — A92

90c, Virgin of Santa Coloma. Statues are polychrome 12th cent. carvings by rural artists.

1974, Apr. 27 Engr. *Perf. 13*

232 A92 50c multicolored *9.00 3.00*
233 A92 90c multicolored *12.50 7.00*

Arms of Andorra and Cahors Bridge — A93

1974, Aug. 24 Engr. *Perf. 13*

234 A93 1fr blue, vio & org 1.50 .80

First anniv. of meeting of the co-princes of Andorra: Pres. Georges Pompidou of France and Msgr. Juan Marti Alanis, Bishop of Urgel.

Mail Box, Chutes and Globe — A94

1974, Oct. 5 Engr. *Perf. 13*

235 A94 1.20fr multi 1.75 1.25

Centenary of Universal Postal Union.

Coronation of St. Marti, 16th Century — A95

Europa: 80c, Crucifixion, 16th cent., vert.

Perf. 11½x13, 13x11½

1975, Apr. 26 Photo.

236 A95 80c gold & multi *4.50 3.00*
237 A95 1.20fr gold & multi *6.50 4.00*

Flower Type of 1973

Designs: 60c, Gentian. 80c, Anemone. 1.20fr, Autumn crocus.

1975, May 10 Photo. *Perf. 13*

238	A90	60c olive & multi	.50	.40
239	A90	80c brt rose & multi	1.25	.80
240	A90	1.20fr green & multi	1.25	.80
		Nos. 238-240 (3)	3.00	2.00

Abstract Design — A96

1975, June 7 Engr. *Perf. 13*

241 A96 2fr bl, magenta & emer 2.00 1.50

ARPHILA 75 International Philatelic Exhibition, Paris, June 6-16.

A97 A98

1975, Aug. 23 Engr. *Perf. 13*

242 A97 80c violet bl & blk 1.00 1.00

Georges Pompidou (1911-74), pres. of France and co-prince of Andorra (1969-74).

1975, Nov. 8 Engr. *Perf. 13*

243 A98 1.20fr Costume, IWY Emblem 1.25 1.00

International Women's Year.

Skier and Snowflake A99

1976, Jan. 31 Engr. *Perf. 13*

244 A99 1.20fr multicolored 1.50 1.10

12th Winter Olympic Games, Innsbruck, Austria, Feb. 4-15.

Telephone and Satellite — A100

1976, Mar. 20 Engr. *Perf. 13*

245 A100 1fr multicolored 1.25 1.00

Centenary of first telephone call by Alexander Graham Bell, Mar. 10, 1976.

Catalan Forge A101

Europa: 1.20fr, Woolen worker.

1976, May 8 Engr. *Perf. 13*

246 A101 80c multi *3.25 1.00*
247 A101 1.20fr multi *4.75 1.75*

Thomas Jefferson A102

Trapshooting A103

1976, July 3 Engr. *Perf. 13*

248 A102 1.20fr multi 1.25 1.00

American Bicentennial.

1976, July 17 Engr. *Perf. 13*

249 A103 2fr multi 2.00 1.60

21st Olympic Games, Montreal, Canada, July 17-Aug. 1.

Meritxell Sanctuary and Old Chapel — A104

1976, Sept. 4 Engr. *Perf. 13*

250 A104 1fr multi 1.25 1.10

Dedication of rebuilt Meritxell Church, Sept. 8, 1976.

Apollo — A105

Ermine — A106

Design: 1.40fr, Morio butterfly.

1976, Oct. 16 Photo. *Perf. 13*

251 A105 80c black & multi 2.75 1.60
252 A105 1.40fr salmon & multi 4.75 2.40

Nature protection.

1977, Apr. 2 Photo. *Perf. 13*

253 A106 1fr vio bl, gray & blk 2.00 1.60

Nature protection.

St. Jean de Caselles A107

Manual Digest, 1748, Arms of Andorra A108

Europa: 1.40fr, Sant Vicens Castle.

1977, Apr. 30 Engr. *Perf. 13*

254 A107 1fr multi *4.00 1.25*
255 A107 1.40fr multi *6.25 2.50*

1977, June 11 Engr. *Perf. 13*

256 A108 80c grn, bl & brn 1.00 1.00

Establishment of Institute of Andorran Studies.

St. Romanus of Caesarea A109

1977, July 23 Engr. *Perf. 12½x13*

257 A109 2fr multi 2.00 1.60

Design from altarpiece in Church of St. Roma de les Bons.

General Council Chamber A110

Guillem d'Arény Plandolit — A111

1977, Sept. 24 Engr. *Perf. 13*

258 A110 1.10fr multi 1.60 1.25
259 A111 2fr car & dk brn 1.60 1.25

Andorran heritage. Guillem d'Arény Plandolit started Andorran reform movement in 1866.

Squirrel — A112

1978, Mar. 18 Engr. *Perf. 13*

260 A112 1fr multi 1.00 .80

Flag and Valira River Bridge — A113

1978, Apr. 8

261 A113 80c multi .80 .80

Signing of the treaty establishing the Co-Principality of Andorra, 700th anniv.

Pal Church A114

Europa: 1.40fr, Charlemagne's Castle, Charlemagne on horseback, vert.

1978, Apr. 29 Engr. *Perf. 13*

262 A114 1fr multi *3.00 1.50*
263 A114 1.40fr multi *5.50 2.75*

Virgin of Sispony A115

1978, May 20 Engr. *Perf. 12x13*

264 A115 2fr multi 1.60 1.25

Visura Tribunal A116

1978, June 24 Engr. *Perf. 13*

265 A116 1.20fr multi 1.25 .55

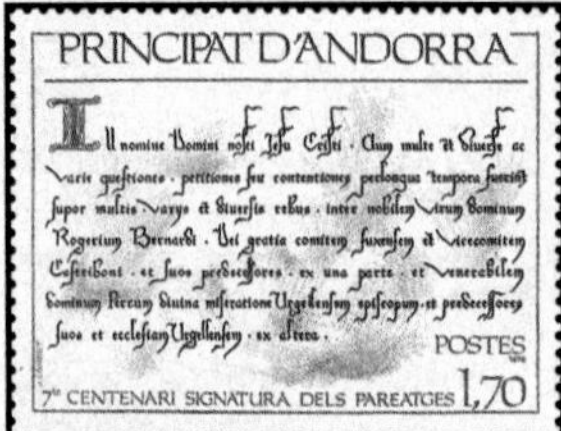
Preamble of 1278 Treaty — A117

1978, Sept. 2 Engr. *Perf. 13x12½*

266 A117 1.70fr multi 1.25 1.00

700th anniversary of the signing of treaty establishing Co-Principality of Andorra.

Pyrenean Chamois A118

White Partridges A119

1979, Mar. 26 Engr. *Perf. 13*

267 A118 1fr multi .70 .70

1979, Apr. 7 Photo. *Perf. 13*

268 A119 1.20fr multi 1.75 .90

Nature protection. See Nos. 288-289.

French Mailman, 1900 — A120

Europa: 1.70fr, 1st French p.o. in Andorra.

1979, Apr. 28 Engr. *Perf. 13*

269 A120 1.20fr multi *2.00 .75*
270 A120 1.70fr multi *4.00 1.25*

Falcon, Pre-Roman Painting A121

1979, June 2 Engr. *Perf. 12½x13*

271 A121 2fr multi 1.25 1.00

Child with Lambs, Church, IYC Emblem. — A122

1979, July 7 Photo. *Perf. 13*

272 A122 1.70fr multi 1.50 1.00

International Year of the Child.

Bas-relief, Trobada Monument. A123

1979, Sept. 29 Engr. *Perf. 13*

273 A123 2fr multi 1.25 1.00

Co-Principality of Andorra, 700th anniv

Judo Hold A124

Farm House, Cortinada A125

1979, Nov. 24 Engr. *Perf. 13*

274 A124 1.30fr multi 1.00 .80

World Judo Championships, Paris, Dec. 1979.

1980, Jan. 26 Engr. *Perf. 13*

275 A125 1.10fr multi 1.00 .80

Cross-Country Skiing — A126

1980, Feb. 9

276 A126 1.80fr ultra & lil rose 1.60 1.25

13th Winter Olympic Games, Lake Placid, NY, Feb. 12-24.

A128

1980, Aug. 30 Engr. *Perf. 13*

278 A128 1.20fr multi 1.25 .80

World Bicycling championships.

A129

Europa: 1.30fr, Charlemagne (742-814). 1.80fr, Napoleon I (1769-1821).

1980, Apr. 26 Engr. *Perf. 13*

279 A129 1.30fr multi *1.75 .60*
280 A129 1.80fr gray grn & brn *2.00 1.00*

Pyrenees Lily — A130

1980 Photo.

281 A130 1.10fr Dog-toothed violet .80 .55
282 A130 1.30fr shown .80 .65

Nature protection. Issue dates: 1.10fr, June 21; 1.30fr, May 17.

De La Vall House, 400th Anniversary of Restoration A131

1980, Sept. 6 Engr.

283 A131 1.40fr multi .80 .65

Angel, Church of St. Cerni de Nagol, Pre-Romanesque Fresco — A132

1980, Oct. 25 *Perf. 13x12½*

284 A132 2fr multi 1.60 1.25

Bordes de Mereig Mountain Village A133

1981, Mar. 21 Engr. *Perf. 13*

285 A133 1.40fr bl gray & dk brn .80 .80

Europa Issue 1981

Ball de l'Ossa, Winter Game A134

1981, May 16 Engr.

286 A134 1.40fr shown *1.50 .50*
287 A134 2fr El Contrapas dance *1.75 1.00*

Bird Type of 1979

1981, June 20 **Photo.**
288 A119 1.20fr Phylloscopus bonelli .80 .80
289 A119 1.40fr Tichodroma muraria 1.25 .80

World Fencing Championship, Clermont-Ferrand, July 2-13 — A135

1981, July 4 **Engr.**
290 A135 2fr bl & blk 1.00 .80

St. Martin, 12th Cent. Tapestry A136

1981, Sept. 5 **Engr.** ***Perf. 12x13***
291 A136 3fr multi 2.00 1.25

Intl. Drinking Water Decade A137

Intl. Year of the Disabled A138

1981, Oct. 17 ***Perf. 13***
292 A137 1.60fr multi 1.00 .65

1981, Nov. 7
293 A138 2.30fr multi 1.25 .80

Europa 1982 A139

1.60fr, Creation of Andorran govt., 1982. 2.30fr, Land Council, 1419.

1982, May 8 **Engr.** ***Perf. 13***
294 A139 1.60fr multi *1.50 .70*
295 A139 2.30fr multi *2.00 .70*

1982 World Cup — A140

Various soccer players.

1982, June 12 **Engr.** ***Perf. 13***
296 1.60fr red & dk brn .95 .65
297 2.60fr red & dk brn 1.20 .95
a. A140 Pair, #296-297 + label 2.50 2.00

Souvenir Sheet

No. 52 — A141

1982, Aug. 21 **Engr.**
298 A141 5fr blk & rose car 2.40 2.40

1st Andorran Stamp Exhib., 8/21-9/19.

Horse, Roman Wall Painting — A142

1982, Sept. 4 **Photo.** ***Perf. 13x12½***
299 A142 3fr multi 1.60 1.25

Wild Cat — A143

1982, Oct. 9 **Engr.** ***Perf. 13***
300 A143 1.80fr shown 1.60 1.25
301 A143 2.60fr Pine trees 1.25 1.25

TB Bacillus Centenary — A144

1982, Nov. 13
302 A144 2.10fr Koch, lungs 1.25 .80

St. Thomas Aquinas (1225-74) — A145

1982, Dec. 4
303 A145 2fr multi 1.00 .80

Manned Flight Bicentenary A146

1983, Feb. 26 **Engr.**
304 A146 2fr multi 1.00 .80

Nature Protection A147

1983, Apr. 16 **Engr.** ***Perf. 13***
305 A147 1fr Birch trees .65 .40
306 A147 1.50fr Trout .95 .80

See Nos. 325-3265

Europa 1983 A148

Catalane Gold Works.

1983, May 7 **Engr.** ***Perf. 13***
307 A148 1.80fr Exterior *1.25 .60*
308 A148 2.60fr Interior *2.00 1.00*

30th Anniv. of Customs Cooperation Council — A149

1983, May 14
309 A149 3fr Letter of King Louis XIII 1.60 1.25

First Arms of Valleys of Andorra A150

1983, Sept. 3 **Engr.** ***Perf. 13***
310 A150 5c olive grn & red .25 .25
311 A150 10c grn & olive grn .25 .25
312 A150 20c brt pur & red .25 .25
313 A150 30c brn vio & red .35 .35
314 A150 40c dk bl & vio .35 .35
315 A150 50c gray & red .25 .25
316 A150 1fr deep magenta .35 .25
317 A150 2fr org red & red brn 1.10 .40
318 A150 5fr dk brn & red 1.60 .80
Nos. 310-318 (9) 4.75 3.15

See Nos. 329-335, 380-385, 464-465.

Painting, Cortinada Church A151

1983, Sept. 24 ***Perf. 12x13***
319 A151 4fr multi 2.00 1.25

Plandolit House — A152

1983, Oct. 15 **Photo.** ***Perf. 13***
320 A152 1.60fr dp ultra & brn 1.00 .65

1984 Winter Olympics A153

1984, Feb. 18 **Engr.**
321 A153 2.80fr multicolored 1.40 1.00

Pyrenees Region Work Community (Labor Org.) A154

1984, Apr. 28 **Engr.** ***Perf. 13***
322 A154 3fr brt blue & sepia 1.40 1.00

Europa (1959-84) A155

1984, May 5 **Engr.**
323 A155 2fr brt grn *2.00 1.00*
324 A155 2.80fr rose car *3.50 1.75*

Nature Protection Type of 1983

1984, July 7 **Engr.** ***Perf. 13***
325 A147 1.70fr Chestnut tree 1.00 .50
326 A147 2.10fr Walnut tree 1.40 .75

Pyrenees Art Center — A155a

1984, Sept. 7 **Engr.**
327 A155a 3fr multi 1.40 1.00

Romanesque Fresco, Church of St. Cerni de Nagol — A156

1984, Nov. 17 ***Perf. 12x13***
328 A156 5fr multi 2.40 2.00

First Arms Type of 1983

1984-87 **Engr.** ***Perf. 13***
329 A150 1.90fr emerald 3.25 .80
330 A150 2.20fr red orange 1.40 .40
a. Bklt. pane, 2 #329, 6 #330 16.00
331 A150 3fr bl grn & red brn 2.00 1.25
332 A150 4fr brt org & brn 3.50 1.25
333 A150 10fr brn org & blk 3.50 1.60
334 A150 15fr grn & dk grn 5.00 2.40

335 A150 20fr brt bl & red brn 7.00 2.75
Nos. 329-335 (7) 25.65 10.45

Nos. 329-330 issued in booklets only.
Issued: 3fr, 20fr, 12/1/84; 10fr, 2/9/85; 4fr, 15fr, 4/19/86; 1.90fr, 2.20fr, 3/28/87.

Saint Julia Valley A157

1985, Apr. 13 **Engr.**
336 A157 2fr multi 1.25 .80

Europa 1985 — A158

Intl. Youth Year — A159

1985, May 4 **Engr.**
337 A158 2.10fr Le Val D'Andorre *2.50 1.00*
338 A158 3fr Instruments *6.00 1.75*

1985, June 8 **Engr.**
339 A159 3fr multi 1.40 1.00

Wildlife Conservation — A160

1.80fr, Anas platyrhynchos. 2.20fr, Carduelis carduelis.

1985, Aug. 3 **Photo.**
340 A160 1.80fr multicolored 1.00 .65
341 A160 2.20fr multicolored 1.50 .95

Two Saints, Medieval Fresco in St. Cerni de Nagol Church A161

1985, Sept. 14 **Engr.** ***Perf. 12½x13***
342 A161 5fr multi 2.40 2.00

Postal Museum Inauguration A162

1986, Mar. 22 **Engr.** ***Perf. 13***
343 A162 2.20fr like No. 269 1.25 .80

Europa 1986 A163

1986, May 3 **Engr.** ***Perf. 13***
344 A163 2.20fr Ansalonga *2.50 .90*
345 A163 3.20fr Isard *5.00 1.60*

1986 World Cup Soccer Championships, Mexico — A164

1986, June 14
346 A164 3fr multi 2.00 1.25

Angonella Lake A165

1986, June 28
347 A165 2.20fr multi 1.25 .80

Manual Digest Frontispiece, 1748 — A166

1986, Sept. 6 **Engr.**
348 A166 5fr chnt brn, gray ol & blk 2.50 1.60

Intl. Peace Year A167

1986, Sept. 27
349 A167 1.90fr bl gray & grnsh bl 1.25 .80

A168

1986, Oct. 18 **Engr.** ***Perf. 13½x13***
350 A168 1.90fr St. Vicenc D'Enclar 1.25 .80

Contemporary Natl. Coat of Arms — A169

1987, Mar. 27 **Litho.** ***Perf. 12½x13***
351 A169 2.20fr multi 2.00 2.00

Visit of the French co-prince.

Europa 1987 A170

1987, May 2 **Engr.** ***Perf. 13***
352 A170 2.20fr Meritxell Sanctuary *2.50 1.00*
353 A170 3.40fr Pleta D'Ordino *5.50 2.50*

Ransol Village — A171

1987, June 13 **Photo.**
354 A171 1.90fr multicolored 1.60 1.25

Nature A172

1987, July 4
355 A172 1.90fr Cavall rogenc 1.25 .80
356 A172 2.20fr Graellsia isabellae 1.60 1.25

Aryalsu, Romanesque Painting, La Cortinada Church — A173

Litho. & Engr.

1987, Sept. 5 ***Perf. 12½x13***
357 A173 5fr multi 2.50 1.60

Hiker Looking at Map A174

1987, Sept. 19 **Engr.** ***Perf. 13***
358 A174 2fr olive, grn & dark brn vio 1.25 .80

Medieval Iron Key, La Cortinada A175

1987, Oct. 17 **Litho.**
359 A175 3fr multi 1.60 1.25

Andorran Coat of Arms — A176

Booklet Stamp

1988, Feb. 6 **Engr.** ***Perf. 13***
360 A176 2.20fr red 2.00 .80
a. Bklt. pane of 5 10.00
Complete bklt., 2 #360a 20.00

See Nos. 386-388.

Shoemaker's Last from Roc de l'Oral — A177

1988, Feb. 13 **Photo.**
361 A177 3fr multi 1.60 1.25

Rugby A178

1988, Mar. 19 **Engr.** ***Perf. 13½x13***
362 A178 2.20fr emer grn, Prus grn & brn 1.60 1.25

Europa 1988 A179

Hot Springs, Escaldes A180

Transport and communication: 2.20fr, Broadcast tower. 3.60fr, Computer graphics.

1988, Apr. 30 **Engr.** ***Perf. 13***
363 A179 2.20fr multicolored *2.25 1.10*
364 A179 3.60fr multicolored *5.00 1.60*

1988, May 14 **Engr.**
365 A180 2.20fr Prus blue, org brn & emer 1.25 .80

Tor D'Ansalonga Farmhouse, Ansalonga Pass — A181

1988, June 11 **Engr.**
366 A181 2fr multi 1.25 .80

Sheepdog — A182

1988, July 2 **Photo.**
367 A182 2fr shown 1.75 .80
368 A182 2.20fr Hare 1.75 .80

Roman Fresco, 8th Cent., St. Steven's Church, Andorre-La-Vieille — A183

1988, Sept. 3 **Engr.** ***Perf. 13x12½***
369 A183 5fr multicolored 2.40 1.60

French Revolution, Bicent. — A184

1989, Jan. 1 **Litho.** ***Perf. 13***
370 A184 2.20fr red & vio bl 1.25 1.25

Poble de Pal Village A185

1989, Mar. 4 **Engr.** ***Perf. 13***
371 A185 2.20fr indigo & lilac 1.25 .80

Europa 1989 A186

Children's games.

1989, Apr. 29 **Engr.** ***Perf. 13***
372 A186 2.20fr Human tower *2.00 .80*
373 A186 3.60fr The handkerchief *2.50 1.75*

Red Cross A187

1989, May 6
374 A187 3.60fr multi 1.75 1.25

Visigothic — Merovingian Age Cincture from a Column, St. Vicenc D'Anclar — A188

1989, June 3 **Photo.**
375 A188 3fr multi 1.60 1.25

Wildlife A189

1989, Sept. 16 **Engr.** ***Perf. 13***
376 A189 2.20fr Wild boar 1.50 1.00
377 A189 3.60fr Newt 2.25 1.40

Scene of Salome from the Retable of St. Michael of Mosquera, Encamp — A190

1989, Oct. 14 ***Perf. 13x13½***
378 A190 5fr multi 3.00 1.60

La Margineda Bridge A191

1990, Feb. 26 **Engr.** ***Perf. 13***
379 A191 2.30fr multi 1.40 .65

Tourism.

Arms Types of 1983 and 1988

1990-93 **Engr.** ***Perf. 13***
380 A150 2.10fr green 1.40 .40
381 A150 2.20fr green 1.25 .40
382 A150 2.30fr vermilion 1.60 .40
383 A150 2.40fr green 1.40 .80
384 A150 2.50fr vermilion 1.50 .40
385 A150 2.80fr vermilion 1.60 .40
Nos. 380-385 (6) 8.75 2.80

Booklet Stamps

Perf. 13

386 A176 2.30fr red 2.00 .80
a. Booklet pane of 5 10.00
387 A176 2.50fr vermilion 2.00 .40
a. Booklet pane of 5 10.00
388 A176 2.80fr red 2.00 .40
c. Booklet pane of 5 10.00
Nos. 386-388 (3) 6.00 1.60

Issued: 2.20fr, #384, 10/26/91; #387, 10/21/91; 2.40fr, 2.80fr, 8/9/93; 2.10fr, 2.30fr, 1990.

Llorts Mines A193

1990, Apr. 21 **Engr.** ***Perf. 12½x13***
390 A193 3.20fr multicolored 2.00 1.25

Europa A194

Designs: 2.30fr, Early post office. 3.20fr, Modern post office.

1990, May 5 ***Perf. 13***
391 A194 2.30fr blk & scar *3.00 .75*
392 A194 3.20fr scar & vio *5.00 1.50*

Otter A195

1990, May 25 ***Perf. 12x13***
393 A195 2.30fr Roses, vert. 1.25 .55
394 A195 3.20fr shown 2.00 1.00

Censer of St. Roma of Les Bons A196

1990, June 25 ***Perf. 12½x13***
395 A196 3fr multicolored 1.60 .80

Tobacco Drying Sheds, Les Bons A197

1990, Sept. 15 **Engr.** ***Perf. 12½x13***
396 A197 2.30fr multi 1.25 .80

St. Coloma (Detail) A198

1990, Oct. 8 ***Perf. 12½x13***
397 A198 5fr multi 2.75 1.60

Coin from Church of St. Eulalia d'Encamp A199

1990, Oct. 27 **Litho.** ***Perf. 13***
398 A199 3.20fr multi 2.00 1.25

De Gaulle Type of 1972 Dated 1990

1990, Oct. 23 **Engr.** ***Perf. 13***
399 A88 2.30fr vio bl 1.25 .80
400 A88 3.20fr dk car 1.50 1.25
a. Pair, #399-400 + label 3.00 3.00

Birth centenary of De Gaulle.

4th Games of the Small European States — A200

1991, Apr. 8 **Photo.** ***Perf. 13***
401 A200 2.50fr multicolored 1.40 .80

Chapel of St. Roma Dels Vilars A201

1991, Mar. 9 **Engr.** ***Perf. 13***
402 A201 2.50fr multicolored 1.40 .80

Europa — A202

1991, Apr. 27 ***Perf. 13x12½, 12½x13***
403 A202 2.50fr TV satellite *3.75 2.00*
404 A202 3.50fr Telescope, horiz. *6.00 3.00*

Bottles from Tombs of St. Vincenc d'Enclar A203

1991, May 11 **Photo.** ***Perf. 13***
405 A203 3.20fr multicolored 2.00 1.25

Farm Animals A204

1991, June 22 **Engr.** ***Perf. 13***
406 A204 2.50fr Sheep 1.25 .80
407 A204 3.50fr Cow 2.00 1.25

Petanque World Championships — A205

1991, Sept. 14 **Engr.** ***Perf. 13***
408 A205 2.50fr multicolored 1.60 1.25

Wolfgang Amadeus Mozart, Death Bicent. A206

1991, Oct. 5
409 A206 3.40fr multicolored 2.00 1.25

Virgin and Child of St. Julia and St. Germa
A207

1991, Nov. 16 Engr. *Perf. 12½x13*

410 A207 5fr multicolored 3.00 1.60

1992 Winter Olympics, Albertville — A208

1992, Feb. 10 Litho. *Perf. 13*

411 A208 2.50fr Slalom skiing 1.60 1.25
412 A208 3.40fr Figure skating 1.60 1.25
a. Pair, #411-412 + label 3.75 3.75

Church of St. Andrew of Arinsal
A209

1992, Mar. 21 Engr. *Perf. 12x13*

413 A209 2.50fr black & tan 1.40 .65

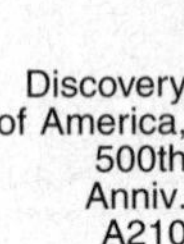

Discovery of America, 500th Anniv.
A210

1992, Apr. 25 *Perf. 13*

414 A210 2.50fr Columbus' fleet *3.00 1.25*
415 A210 3.40fr Landing in New World *6.00 2.50*

Europa.

1992 Summer Olympics, Barcelona
A211

European Globeflower
A212

1992, June 8 Litho. *Perf. 13*

416 A211 2.50fr Kayaking 1.60 1.25
417 A211 3.40fr Shooting 1.60 1.25
a. Pair, #416-417 + label 3.75 3.75

1992, July 6

Design: 3.40fr, Vulture, horiz.

418 A212 2.50fr multicolored 1.60 .80
419 A212 3.40fr multicolored 2.00 1.25

Martyrdom of St. Eulalia
A213

1992, Sept. 14 Photo. *Perf. 13*

420 A213 4fr multicolored 2.00 1.25

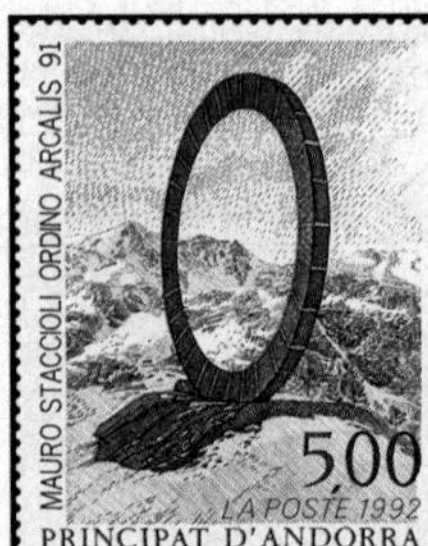

Sculpture by Mauro Staccioli
A214

1992, Oct. 5 Engr. *Perf. 12½x13*

421 A214 5fr multicolored 2.75 1.60

Ordino Arcalis '91.

Tempest in a Tea Cup, by Dennis Oppenheim — A215

1992, Nov. 14 Engr. *Perf. 13x12½*

422 A215 5fr multicolored 2.75 1.60

Skiing in Andorra — A216

Ski resorts: No. 423: a, 2.50fr, Soldeu El Tarter. b, 3.40fr, Arinsal.

No. 424: a, 2.50fr, Pas de la Casa-Grau Roig. b, 2.50fr, Ordino Arcalis. c, 3.40fr, Pal.

1993, Mar. 13 Litho. *Perf. 13*

423 A216 Pair, #a.-b. + label 3.50 3.50
424 A216 Strip of 3, #a.-c. 5.00 5.00

Sculptures — A217

Europa: 2.50fr, "Estructures Autogeneradores," by Jorge du Bon, vert. 3.40fr, Sculpture, "Fisicromia per Andorra," by Carlos Cruz-Diez.

1993, May 15 Engr. *Perf. 12½x13*

425 A217 2.50fr multicolored *1.60 1.25*

Litho.

Perf. 14x13½

426 A217 3.40fr multicolored *2.00 1.50*

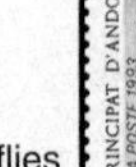

Butterflies
A218

1993, June 28 Litho. *Perf. 13*

427 A218 2.50fr Polymmatus icarus 1.40 .80
428 A218 4.20fr Nymphalidae 2.25 1.60

Tour de France Bicycle Race — A219

1993, July 20 Litho. *Perf. 13*

429 A219 2.50fr multicolored 1.60 .80

Andorra School, 10th Anniv.
A220

1993, Sept. 20 Litho. *Perf. 13*

430 A220 2.80fr multicolored 1.60 1.25

Un Lloc Paga, by Michael Warren
A221

1993, Oct. 18 Engr. *Perf. 12½x13*

431 A221 5fr blue & black 2.25 1.60

Sculpture, by Erik Dietman
A222

1993, Nov. 8 Engr. *Perf. 12½x13*

432 A222 5fr multicolored 2.40 1.60

1994 Winter Olympics, Lillehammer
A223

1994, Feb. 21 Litho. *Perf. 13*

433 A223 3.70fr multicolored 2.50 1.60

1st Anniversary of the Constitution — A224

Designs: 2.80fr, Monument, by Emili Armengol. 3.70fr, Stone tablet with inscription.

1994, Mar. 15 Litho. *Perf. 13*

434 A224 2.80fr multicolored 1.60 1.25
435 A224 3.70fr multicolored 1.60 1.25
a. Pair, #434-435 + label 3.75 3.75

European Discoveries
A225

Europa: 2.80fr, Discovery of AIDS virus. 3.70fr, Radio diffusion.

1994, May 7 Litho. *Perf. 13*

436 A225 2.80fr multicolored *2.00 1.10*
437 A225 3.70fr multicolored *3.00 1.40*

1994 World Cup Soccer Championships, US — A226

1994, June 20

438 A226 3.70fr multicolored 2.00 1.25

Tourist Sports — A227

Designs: No. 439, Mountain climbing. No. 440, Fishing. No. 441, Horseback riding. No. 442, Mountain biking.

1994, July 11

439 A227 2.80fr multicolored 1.60 1.25
440 A227 2.80fr multicolored 1.60 1.25
a. Pair, #439-440 + label 3.25 3.25
441 A227 2.80fr multicolored 1.60 1.25
442 A227 2.80fr multicolored 1.60 1.25
a. Pair, #441-442 + label 3.25 3.25
Nos. 439-442 (4) 6.40 5.00

Butterflies
A228

1994, Sept. 5 Litho. *Perf. 13*

443 A228 2.80fr Iphiclides podalirus 2.00 .80
444 A228 4.40fr Aglais urticae 2.75 1.25

A229

A230

1994, Oct. 22 Litho. *Perf. 13*
445 A229 2.80fr multicolored 1.25 .80

Meeting of the Co-Princes, 1st anniv.

1995, Feb. 27 Litho. *Perf. 13*
446 A230 2.80fr multicolored 1.60 .80

European Nature Conservation Year

1995 World Cup Rugby Championships — A231

1995, Apr. 24 Litho. *Perf. 13*
447 A231 2.80fr multicolored 1.60 .80

Peace & Freedom A232

Europa: 2.80fr, Dove with olive branch. 3.70fr, Flock of doves.

1995, Apr. 29
448 A232 2.80fr multicolored *1.75 .75*
449 A232 3.70fr multicolored *2.75 1.00*

Caritas in Andorra, 15th Anniv. A233

1995, May 15 Litho. *Perf. 13*
450 A233 2.80fr multicolored 1.60 .80

Caldea Health Spa — A234

1995, June 26 Litho. *Perf. 13*
451 A234 2.80fr multicolored 1.60 .80

Ordino Natl. Auditorium A235

1995, July 10 Litho. & Engr.
452 A235 3.70fr black & buff 2.00 1.25

Virgin of Meritxell — A236

1995, Sept. 11 Litho. *Perf. 14*
453 A236 4.40fr multicolored 2.40 1.25

Protection of Nature A237

Butterflies: 2.80fr, Papallona llimonera, vert. 3.70fr, Papallona melanargia galathea.

1995, Sept. 25 *Perf. 13*
454 A237 2.80fr multicolored 1.60 1.25
455 A237 3.70fr multicolored 2.00 1.50

UN, 50th Anniv. — A238

1995, Oct. 21 Litho. *Perf. 13*
456 A238 2.80fr Flag, emblem 1.60 1.25
457 A238 3.70fr Emblem, "50," flag 1.60 1.25
a. Pair, #456-457 + label 3.25 3.25

Andorra's Entrance into Council of Europe A239

1995, Nov. 4
458 A239 2.80fr multicolored 1.60 .80

World Skiing Championships, Ordino Arcalis — A240

1996, Jan. 29 Litho. *Perf. 13*
459 A240 2.80fr multicolored 1.60 .80

Basketball in Andorra — A241

1996, Jan. 29 Litho. *Perf. 13*
460 A241 3.70fr multicolored 2.40 1.25

Our Lady of Meritxell Special School, 25th Anniv. A242

1996, Feb. 17 Litho. *Perf. 13*
461 A242 2.80fr multicolored 1.60 1.25

Songbirds A243

1996, Mar. 25
462 A243 3fr Pit riog 1.60 .80
463 A243 3.80fr Mallarenga carbonera 2.00 1.60

First Arms Type of 1983

1996, Apr. 17 Engr. *Perf. 13*
464 A150 2.70fr green 1.25 .80
465 A150 3fr red 1.60 .40

Cross of St. James d'Engordany A244

1996, Apr. 20 Litho.
466 A244 3fr multicolored 1.60 .80

Censer of St. Eulalia d'Encamp A245

1996, Apr. 20
467 A245 3.80fr multicolored 2.00 1.60

Europa — A246

Chess — A247

1996, May 6
468 A246 3fr Ermessenda de Castellbo *2.25 1.25*

1996, June 8 Litho. *Perf. 13*
469 A247 4.50fr multicolored 2.75 1.25

1996 Summer Olympic Games, Atlanta A248

1996, June 29 Litho. *Perf. 13*
470 A248 3fr multicolored 1.60 .80

Arms of the Community of Canillo — A249

Serpentine Die Cut 7 Vert.

1996, June 10 Litho.

Self-Adhesive

471 A249 (3fr) multicolored 1.75 .45
a. Booklet of 10 17.50

Natl. Children's Choir, 5th Anniv. A250

1996, Sept. 14 *Perf. 13*
472 A250 3fr multicolored 1.60 .80

Livestock Fair A251

1996, Oct. 26 Engr. *Perf. 12x13*
473 A251 3fr multicolored 1.60 .80

Churches A252

Designs: No. 474, St. Romá de Les Bons. No. 475, St. Coloma.

1996, Nov. 16 Litho. *Perf. 13*
474 A252 6.70fr multicolored 3.50 1.75
475 A252 6.70fr multicolored 3.50 1.75

A253

A254

1997, Jan. 7 Litho. *Perf. 13*
476 A253 3fr multicolored 1.60 .80

Pres. Francois Mitterrand (1916-96).

Sawtooth Die Cut 7 Vert. x Straight Die Cut

1997, Feb. 24 Litho.

Self-Adhesive

477 A254 (3fr) Arms of Encamp 1.75 .45
a. Booklet pane of 10 17.50

By its nature, No. 477a is a complete booklet. The peelable paper backing serves as a booklet cover.

A255

A256

1997, Mar. 22 *Perf. 13*
478 A255 3fr Volleyball 1.60 .80

1997, June 10 **Litho.** *Perf. 13*
479 A256 3fr "The White Lady" *1.75 .90*

Europa (Stories and Legends).

Oreneta Cuablanca A257

1997, May 31 **Litho.** *Perf. 13*
480 A257 3.80fr multicolored 2.40 1.25

Paintings of Mills A258

1997, Sept. 15 **Litho.** *Perf. 13*
481 A258 3fr Cal Pal, vert. 1.60 .80
482 A258 4.50fr Mas d'en Sole 2.50 1.25

Religious Artifacts A259

Designs: 3fr, Monstrance of St. Iscle and St. Victoria. 15.50fr, Altar piece of St. Pierre d'Alxirivall.

1997, Oct. 27
483 A259 3fr multicolored 1.75 .80
484 A259 15.50fr multicolored 6.75 3.25
a. Pair, #483-484 + label 10.00 10.00

Legends — A260

Designs: No. 485, Legend of Meritxell. No. 486, The cross of seven arms. 3.80fr, The fountain of Esmelicat.

1997, Nov. 22 **Litho.** *Perf. 13*
485 A260 3fr multicolored 1.60 1.25
486 A260 3fr multicolored 1.60 1.25
487 A260 3.80fr multicolored 2.40 1.60
a. Strip of 3, #485-487 6.50 6.50

Monaco Intl. Philatelic Exhibition — A261

1997, Nov. 28 **Litho.** *Perf. 13*
488 A261 3fr Chapel of St. Miguel d'Engolasters 1.60 1.00

Happy Anniversary A262

1998 Winter Olympic Games, Nagano A263

1998, Jan. 3 **Litho.** *Perf. 13*
489 A262 3fr Juggling candles 1.60 .80

1998, Feb. 14
490 A263 4.40fr multicolored 2.50 1.25

Arms of Ordino — A264

Serpentine Die Cut Vert.
1998, Mar. 7 **Litho.**
Booklet Stamp
Self-Adhesive

491 A264 (3fr) multicolored 1.25 .30
a. Booklet pane of 10 12.50
Complete booklet, #491a 12.50

See Nos. 504, 518, 531.

Mesa de Vila Church — A265

1998, Mar. 28 *Perf. 13*
492 A265 4.50fr multicolored 3.00 2.40

Rotary Club of Andorra, 20th Anniv. — A265a

1998, Apr. 11
493 A265a 3fr multicolored 1.60 .90

Finch A266

1998 **Litho.** *Perf. 13*
494 A266 3.80fr multicolored 2.40 1.25

1998 World Cup Soccer Championships, France — A267

1998, June 6 **Litho.** *Perf. 13*
495 A267 3fr multicolored 1.60 1.25

For overprint see No. 499.

Music Festival A268

1998, June 20 **Litho.** *Perf. 13*
496 A268 3fr multicolored *1.50 .90*

Europa.

Expo '98, Lisbon A269

1998, July 6
497 A269 5fr multicolored 2.75 1.60

Chalice, House of the Valleys — A270

1998, Sept. 19 **Litho.** *Perf. 13*
498 A270 4.50fr multicolored 2.75 1.25

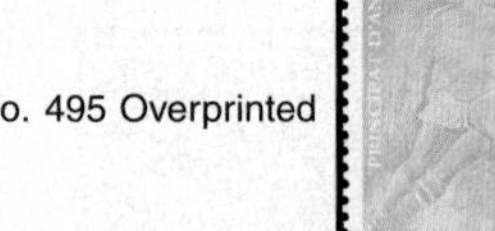
No. 495 Overprinted

1998, Nov. 16
499 A267 3fr multicolored 4.00 2.00

Early Maps of Andorra A271

1998, Nov. 16
500 A271 3fr 1717, vert. 2.00 1.25
501 A271 15.50fr 1777 8.00 3.50

Inauguration of the Postal Museum — A272

1998, Nov. 19 **Litho.** *Perf. 13*
502 A272 3fr multicolored 1.60 1.25

Manual Digest, 250th Anniv. A273

1998, Dec. 7
503 A273 3.80fr multicolored 2.00 1.25

Arms Type of 1998
Self-Adhesive
Serpentine Die Cut Vert.

1999, Jan. 18 **Booklet Stamp**
504 A264 (3fr) La Massana 1.25 .55
a. Booklet pane of 10 12.50

No. 504a is a complete booklet.

Recycling A274

1999, Mar. 13 **Litho.** *Perf. 13*
505 A274 5fr multicolored 2.75 1.60

Sorteny Valley — A275

1999, Apr. 10
506 A275 3fr multicolored *2.00 1.25*

Europa.

Council of Europe, 50th Anniv. A276

1999, May 5 **Litho.** *Perf. 13*
507 A276 3.80fr multicolored 2.40 1.25

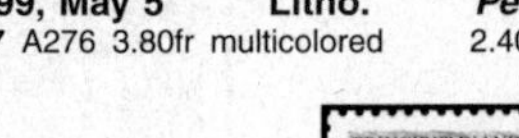

First Stage Coach — A277

1999, May 15
508 A277 2.70fr multi 1.60 1.25

1999 European National Soccer Championships — A278

1999, June 10 Photo. *Perf. 13*
509 A278 4.50fr multicolored 2.40 1.60

PhilexFrance 99 — A279

1999, July 2 Litho. *Perf. 13x13¼*
510 A279 3fr multicolored 1.60 .80

Historic View of Pal — A280

Perf. 13x13¼, 13¼x13
1999, July 10 Litho.
511 A280 3fr shown 1.60 .80
512 A280 3fr Different view, vert. 1.75 .80

International Federation of Photographic Art, 50th Anniv. — A281

1999, July 24 Litho. *Perf. 13*
513 A281 4.40fr multicolored 2.40 1.25

Casa Rull, Sispony A282

1999, Sept. 6 Litho. *Perf. 13x13¼*
514 A282 15.50fr multi 8.00 4.50

Chest With Six Locks — A283

1999, Oct. 9 Litho. *Perf. 13x13¼*
515 A283 6.70fr multicolored 3.50 2.00

Christmas A284

1999, Nov. 27 Litho. *Perf. 13*
516 A284 3fr multi 1.60 .80

Year 2000 A285

2000, Jan. 5 Litho. *Perf. 13x13¼*
517 A285 3fr multi 1.60 .80

Arms Type of 1998
Self-Adhesive
Serpentine Die Cut 6½ Vert.
2000, Feb. 26 Booklet Stamp
518 A264 (3fr) Andorra-la-Vielle 1.25 .40
a. Booklet pane of 10 12.50

No. 518a is a complete booklet.

Snowboarding A286

2000, Mar. 17 Litho. *Perf. 13*
519 A286 4.50fr multi 2.40 1.25

Montserrat Caballé Chant Competition A287

2000, Apr. 3 *Perf. 13x13¼*
520 A287 3.80fr multi 2.40 1.25

Campanula Cochlearifolia A288

2000, Apr. 17 Litho. *Perf. 13*
521 A288 2.70fr multi 1.60 .80

Europa, 2000
Common Design Type

2000, May 9 *Perf. 13½x13*
522 CD17 3fr multi *2.00 1.00*

Festivals A289

No. 523: a, Canòlic. b, Meritxell.

2000, May 27 Litho. *Perf. 13*
523 Pair + central label 4.00 4.00
a.-b. A289 3fr Any single 1.60 1.25

Pardal Comú — A290

2000, July 7 Litho. *Perf. 13*
524 A290 4.40fr multi 2.75 1.60

A291 A292

2000, Sept. 11 Litho. *Perf. 13*
525 A291 5fr multi 2.75 1.60

2000 Summer Olympics, Sydney.

2000, Sept. 28
526 A292 3fr multi 2.00 .80

World Tourism Day.

Expo 2000, Hanover A293

2000, Oct. 6 Litho. *Perf. 13*
527 A293 3fr multi 1.60 .80

"Europe, A Common Heritage" A294

2000, Nov. 4 Litho. *Perf. 13½x13*
528 A294 3.80fr multi 2.75 1.60

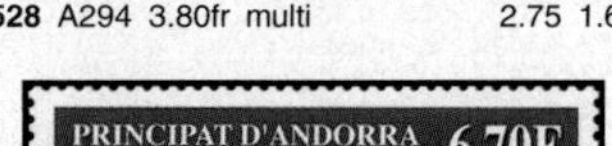

Prehistoric Pottery of Prats — A295

2000, Dec. 16 *Perf. 13x13¼*
529 A295 6.70fr multi 4.50 2.00

National Archives, 25th Anniv. — A296

2000, Dec. 22 *Perf. 13*
530 A296 15.50fr multi 9.50 5.50

Arms Type of 1998
Serpentine Die Cut 6½ Vert.
2001, Feb. 19 Litho.
Booklet Stamp
Self-Adhesive
531 A264 (3fr) Sant Julià de Lòria 1.25 .40
a. Booklet, 10 #531 12.50

Canillo Aliga Mountain Station — A297

2001, Feb. 10 Litho. *Perf. 13*
532 A297 4.50fr multi 2.40 2.00

Casa Cristo Museum A298

2001, Feb. 17 *Perf. 13¼x13*
533 A298 6.70fr multi 4.50 2.40

Andorran Heritage — A299

No. 534: a, Legend of Engolasters Lake. b, Foundation of Andorra.

2001, Mar. 23 *Perf. 13*
534 A299 3fr Pair, #a-b, with central label 5.00 4.50

Intl. Book Day — A300

Europa — A301

2001, Apr. 23 Litho. *Perf. 13*
535 A300 3.80fr multi 2.40 1.60

2001, Apr. 28
536 A301 3fr multi *2.00 1.00*

A302

2001, May 12
537 A302 3fr Raspberries, vert. 1.60 .80
538 A302 4.40fr shown 2.75 1.60

European Language Year A303

2001, June 16 Litho. *Perf. 13*
539 A303 3.80fr multi 3.00 1.60

Escaldes-Engordany Jazz Festival — A304

2001, July 7
540 A304 3fr multi 1.75 .80

General Council's Kitchen A305

2001, Aug. 10
541 A305 5fr multi 3.25 2.00

Chapel of the Virgin of Meritxell, 25th Anniv. of Rebuilding — A306

2001, Sept. 7 Litho. *Perf. 13*
542 A306 3fr multi 1.60 .80

Hotel Pla — A307

2001, Oct. 12
543 A307 15.50fr multi 8.50 4.00

Cross of Terme — A308

2001, Nov. 17 Litho. *Perf. 13½x13*
544 A308 2.70fr multi 2.25 1.00

100 Cents = 1 Euro (€)

National Arms — A309

Legends
A310 A311

Designs: 10c, Legend of Meritxell. 20c, Fountain of Esmelicat. 50c, The Cross with Seven Arms. €1, The Founding of Andorra. €2, Legend of Engolasters Lake. €5, The White Lady.

Perf. 13¼ (A309), 13¼x13
2002, Jan. 2 Photo. (A309), Litho.

545	A309	1c yel & multi	.25	.25
546	A309	2c tan & multi	.30	.25
547	A309	5c bl & multi	.40	.30
548	A310	10c multi	.50	.30
549	A310	20c multi	.75	.50
550	A309	(46c) red & multi	1.50	.40
551	A310	50c multi	2.25	.80
552	A311	€1 multi	3.50	1.25
553	A311	€2 multi	6.50	2.00
554	A311	€5 multi	16.00	7.00
		Nos. 545-554 (10)	31.95	13.05

See Nos. 577, 618, 635, 661-666, 680.

Traffic Safety Education in Schools — A312

2002, Jan. 25 Litho. *Perf. 13½x13*
555 A312 69c multi 2.50 1.25

2002 Winter Olympics, Salt Lake City — A313

2002, Feb. 2 Litho. *Perf. 13*
556 A313 58c multi 2.40 1.25

Hotel Rosaleda A314

2002, Mar. 16 Litho. *Perf. 13*
557 A314 46c multi 2.75 1.25

World Day for Water — A315

2002, Mar. 22 Litho. *Perf. 13*
558 A315 67c multi 2.75 2.00

Europa — A316

2002, May 10 Litho. *Perf. 13*
559 A316 46c multi *2.00 .40*

Bilberries — A317

2002, July 6 Litho. *Perf. 13*
560 A317 46c multi 1.60 .80

Seated Nude, Sculpture by Josep Viladomat — A318

2002, Aug. 24 Litho. *Perf. 13¼x13*
561 A318 €2.36 multi 7.50 3.75

Envalira Tunnel A319

2002, Sept. 2 *Perf. 13*
562 A319 46c multi 1.75 .80

Piper of Ordino — A320

2002, Sept. 27
563 A320 41c multi 1.75 .80

See No. 578.

Detail of Santa Coloma Wall Painting — A321

2002, Nov. 16 Litho. *Perf. 13*
564 A321 €1.02 multi 3.50 2.00

Comú d'Escaldes — Engordany Coat of Arms — A322

Serpentine Die Cut 6¾ Vert.
2003, Jan. 20 Photo.
Booklet Stamp
Self-Adhesive
565 A322 (46c) multi 1.40 .50
a. Booklet pane of 10 14.00

Legend of the Margineda Pine — A323

2003, Feb. 10 Litho. *Perf. 13*
566 A323 69c multi 3.50 2.00

See No. 579.

Constitution, 10th Anniv. A324

2003, Mar. 14 Litho. *Perf. 13x13½*
567 A324 €2.36 multi 7.75 4.00

Buildings, Les Bons — A325

2003, Mar. 31 ***Perf. 13***
568 A325 67c multi 3.50 2.00

Hotel Mirador A326

2003, Apr. 12 **Litho.** ***Perf. 13***
569 A326 €1.02 multi 4.00 2.40

Europa — A327

2003, May 17
570 A327 46c multi *1.75 .80*

Falles de San Joan A328

2003, June 23 **Litho.** ***Perf. 13***
571 A328 50c multi 1.60 .80

A329 A330

2003, July 5
572 A329 50c multi 1.75 .80

Tour de France bicycle race, cent.

2003, Aug. 8
573 A330 90c multi 3.50 2.00

World Track and Field Championships, Paris.

Sparassis Crispa A331

Currants A332

2003, Sept. 15 **Litho.** ***Perf. 13***
574 A331 45c multi 3.25 1.60
575 A332 75c multi 2.50 1.60

Telephones in Andorra, Cent. A333

2003, Oct. 30 **Litho.** ***Perf. 13***
576 A333 50c multi 2.00 .80

Types of 2002-03 Inscribed "Postes"

2003, Nov. 29 **Photo.** ***Perf. 13x13¼***
577 A309 (45c) green & multi 1.30 .80

Litho.

Perf. 13

578 A320 75c multi 3.25 2.00
579 A323 90c multi 3.25 2.25
Nos. 577-579 (3) 7.80 5.05

Maternity, by Paul Gauguin A334

2003, Nov. 29 **Litho.** ***Perf. 13¼x13***
580 A334 75c multi 4.00 2.25

St. Anthony's Auction — A335

2004, Jan. 17 **Litho.** ***Perf. 13***
581 A335 50c multi 1.75 .80

Children of the World — A336

2004, Mar. 20 **Litho.** ***Perf. 13***
582 A336 50c multi 1.75 .80

Hotel Valira A337

2004, Apr. 17 **Litho.** ***Perf. 13***
583 A337 €1.11 multi 4.00 3.25

Europa — A338

2004, May 7 **Litho.** ***Perf. 13***
584 A338 50c multi *1.75 .80*

A339 A340

2004, May 15
585 A339 45c multi 2.00 1.25

Legend of the Castle of St. Vincent.

2004, June 26
586 A340 75c multi 2.50 1.25

Madriu-Peralita-Claror Valley, UNESCO World Heritage Site candidate.

Poblet de Fontenada A341

2004, July 3
587 A341 50c multi 1.75 1.25

2004 Summer Olympics, Athens A342

2004, Aug. 7 **Litho.** ***Perf. 13***
588 A342 90c multi 3.00 2.25

Margineda Bridge — A343

No. 589: a, €1, Black and white sketch. b, €2, Full color painting.

2004, Oct. 2
589 A343 Horiz. pair, #a-b, + central label 10.00 10.00

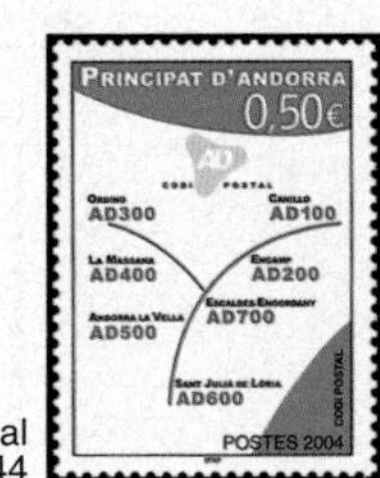

Postal Code — A344

2004, Oct. 23 ***Perf. 13¼x13***
590 A344 50c multi 2.00 1.00

Admission to Council of Europe, 10th Anniv. — A345

2004, Nov. 6
591 A345 €2.50 multi 8.00 5.50

Christmas — A346

2004, Dec. 4 ***Perf. 13***
592 A346 50c multi 2.00 .80

The Magi A347

2005, Jan. 5
593 A347 50c multi 2.00 .80

Selection of Madriu-Peralita-Claror Valley as UNESCO World Heritage Site — A348

2005, Jan. 22
594 A348 50c multi 1.75 1.40

Legend of Rat Pass A349

2005, Feb. 12
595 A349 48c multi 2.00 1.40

Aegolius Funereus — A350

2005, Apr. 6 **Litho.** ***Perf. 13***
596 A350 90c multi 3.00 2.60

Europa
A351

2005, May 7 Litho. ***Perf. 13x13¼***
597 A351 55c multi *1.60 1.40*

Souvenir Sheet

9th Games of Small European States — A352

No. 598: a, 53c, Shooting. b, 55c, Track and field. c, 82c, Swimming. d, €1, Basketball.

2005, May 28 ***Perf. 13¼x13***
598 A352 Sheet of 4, #a-d 10.00 10.00

Bordes d'Ensegur
A353

Police Motorcycle
A354

2005, June 11 Litho. ***Perf. 13***
599 A353 €2.50 multi 8.50 6.00

2005, July 2
600 A354 53c multi 2.00 1.50

Prats de Santa Coloma, by J. Mir — A355

2005, Aug. 10 ***Perf. 13x13¼***
601 A355 82c multi 3.00 2.50

Calones
Hostel
A356

2005, Sept. 10 Litho. ***Perf. 13***
602 A356 €1.98 multi 7.50 5.75

Josep Alsina
Photography
Business — A357

2005, Oct. 8 Litho. ***Perf. 13¼x13***
603 A357 53c multi 1.75 1.50

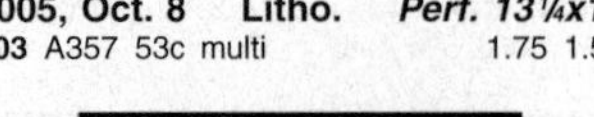

Rotary International, Cent. — A358

2005, Nov. 5 ***Perf. 13***
604 A358 55c multi 1.75 1.00

Adoration of the Shepherds, by Antoni Viladomat — A359

2005, Dec. 7 Litho. ***Perf. 13***
605 A359 €1.22 multi 4.00 3.50

Animals
A360

Designs: No. 606, 53c, Ursus arctos. No. 607, 53c, Rupicapra pyrenaica, vert.

2006, Jan. 16
606-607 A360 Set of 2 4.00 3.25

See Nos. 619-620, 633-634, 648-649, 670-671.

2006 Winter Olympics, Turin — A361

No. 608: a, 55c, Alpine skiing. b, 75c, Cross-country skiing.

2006, Feb. 4
608 A361 Horiz. pair, #a-b, + central label 4.50 4.50

Tobacco
Museum — A362

2006, Mar. 4 Litho. ***Perf. 13***
609 A362 82c multi 2.50 2.40

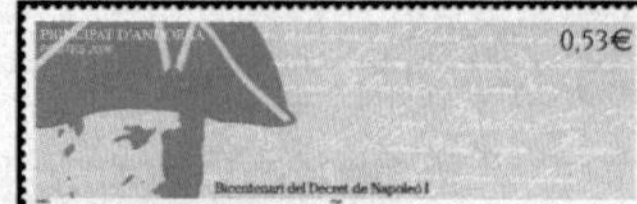

Decree of Napoleon I, Bicent. — A363

2006, Mar. 27
610 A363 53c multi 1.75 1.40

Legend of the Bear
Cave — A364

2006, Apr. 10 Litho. ***Perf. 13***
611 A364 48c multi 2.50 1.40

Europa
A365

2006, May 9 Litho. ***Perf. 13x13¼***
612 A365 53c multi 1.75 1.50

Sorteny Valley
Nature
Park — A366

2006, June 10 ***Perf. 13***
613 A366 55c multi 1.75 1.60

Pablo Casals (1876-1973),
Cellist — A367

2006, July 31 Litho. ***Perf. 13***
614 A367 90c multi 2.75 2.60

Ford
Model
T — A368

2006, Sept. 2 Litho. ***Perf. 13***
615 A368 85c multi 3.00 2.50

Montserrat Procession, by Josp Borrell — A369

2006, Nov. 4 Litho. ***Perf. 13¼x13***
616 A369 €1.30 multi 4.00 3.75

Retable,
St.
Martin's
Church,
Cortinada
A370

2006, Dec. 2 ***Perf. 13***
617 A370 54c multi 1.60 1.60

Arms Type of 2002 Inscribed "Postes"

2007, Jan. 13 ***Perf. 13x13¼***
618 A309 60c multi 1.75 1.75

Animals Type of 2006

Designs: 54c, Marmota marmota, vert. 60c, Sciurus vulgaris.

2007, Jan. 20 ***Perf. 13***
619-620 A360 Set of 2 4.00 3.25

Legend of the
Wolf's
Testament — A371

2007, Feb. 24
621 A371 49c multi 1.75 1.40

Predelle,
Prats
A372

2007, Mar. 17 Litho. ***Perf. 13¼x13***
622 A372 €1.30 multi 4.00 3.75

Compare with types A383, A396, A414 and A420.

National Arms — A373

Serpentine Die Cut 11
2007, Apr. 2 Litho.

Booklet Stamp
Self-Adhesive

623 A373 (54c) multi 1.60 1.60
a. Booklet pane of 10 16.00

Rose
A374

2007, Apr. 23 Photo. *Perf. 13¼*
624 A374 86c multi 2.75 2.50

Values are for stamps with surrounding selvage.

Europa — A375

2007, May 5 Litho. *Perf. 13¼x13*
625 A375 54c multi 1.75 1.60

Scouting, cent.

Joining of Meritxell and Sabart — A376

No. 626: a, Madonna and Child. b, Priest.

2007, June 2 Litho. *Perf. 13*
626 A376 54c Horiz. pair, #a-b, + central label 4.00 4.00

Engine
A377

2007, July 10
627 A377 60c multi 2.00 1.75

2007 Rugby World Cup, France
A378

2007, Sept. 1 Litho. *Perf. 13¼*
628 A378 85c multi 2.50 2.50

Values are for stamps with surrounding selvage.

Comapedrosa Valley — A379

2007, Oct. 6 Litho. *Perf. 13¼x13*
629 A379 €3.04 multi 10.00 8.75

Prehistoric People — A380

Prehistoric people at: 60c, Margineda Grotto. 85c, Cedre.

2007, Nov. 10
630-631 A380 Set of 2 5.00 4.25

Retable, St. Martin's Church, Cortinada
A381

2007, Dec. 3 Litho. *Perf. 13*
632 A381 54c multi 1.60 1.60

Animals Type of 2006

Designs: 54c, Vulpes vulpes. 60c, Sus scrofa, vert.

2008, Jan. 28
633-634 A360 Set of 2 4.00 3.50

Arms Type of 2002 Inscribed "Postes"

2008, Mar. 1 Photo. *Perf. 13x13¼*
635 A309 65c blue & multi 2.00 2.00

Legend of the Treasure of the Fountain of Manegó — A382

2008, Mar. 8 Litho. *Perf. 13*
636 A382 50c multi 1.75 1.60

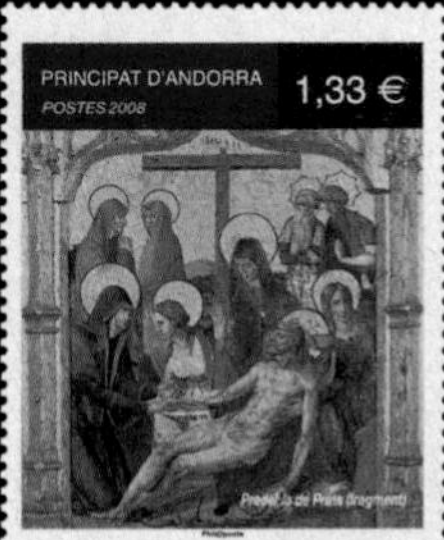

Predelle, Prats
A383

2008, Apr. 12 *Perf. 13¼x13*
637 A383 €1.33 multi 4.25 4.25

Compare with Types A372, A396, A414 and A420.

Cartercar Automobile
A384

2008, May 3 Litho. *Perf. 13*
638 A384 65c multi 2.25 2.00

Europa
A385

2008, May 17
639 A385 55c multi 1.75 1.75

Miniature Sheet

2008 Summer Olympics, Beijing — A386

No. 640: a, Kayaking. b, Running. c, Swimming. d, Judo.

2008, June 16 Litho. *Perf. 13x13½*
640 A386 55c Sheet of 4, #a-d 7.50 7.50

Olympex 2008 Philatelic Exhibition, Beijing (#640d).

Narcissus Poeticus — A387

2008, June 18 *Perf. 13¼x13*
641 A387 55c multi 1.75 1.75

No. 641 is impregnated with a narcissus scent.

Vall d'Incles
A388

2008, July 5 *Perf. 13*
642 A388 €2.80 multi 9.00 9.00

Universal Male Suffrage, 75th Anniv.
A389

2008, Aug. 30 Litho. *Perf. 13*
643 A389 55c multi 1.60 1.60

Sustainable Development — A390

2008, Oct. 4 Litho. *Perf. 13*
644 A390 88c multi 2.40 2.40

Roc d'Enclar — A391

2008, Nov. 8 *Perf. 13¼*
645 A391 85c multi 2.50 2.50

Retable of St. Mark and St. Mary — A392

2008, Dec. 13 *Perf. 13*
646 A392 55c multi 1.60 1.60

Louis Braille (1809-52), Educator of the Blind — A393

2009, Jan. 24 *Engr.*
647 A393 88c multi 2.50 2.50

Animals Type of 2006

Designs: 55c, Equus mulus, vert. 65c, Bos taurus.

2009, Feb. 14 Litho. *Perf. 13*
648-649 A360 Set of 2 3.50 3.50

Legend of the Devils of Aixirvall — A394

2009, Mar. 7
650 A394 51c multi 1.50 1.50

Souvenir Sheet

Protection of Polar Regions and Glaciers — A395

No. 651: a, 56c, Emperor penguins. b, 85c, Boat off shore in polar regions, vert.

Perf. 13x13¼, 13¼x13 (85c)

2009, Mar. 27 Litho. & Engr.

651 A395 Sheet of 2, #a-b, + label 4.50 4.50

Predelle, Prats A396

2009, Apr. 18 Litho. *Perf. 13¼x13*

652 A396 €1.35 multi 4.00 4.00

Compare with types A372, A383, A414 and A420.

Europa A397

2009, May 2 *Perf. 13*

653 A397 56c multi 1.75 1.75

Intl. Year of Astronomy.

Early Renault Automobile A398

2009, May 16

654 A398 70c multi 2.25 2.25

St. Joan de Caselles, by Maurice Utrillo — A399

2009, May 23 *Perf. 13x13¼*

655 A399 90c multi 2.75 2.75

Cercle des Pessons A400

2009, June 13 Litho. *Perf. 13*

656 A400 €2.80 multi 8.25 8.25

Tour de France Bicycle Race — A401

2009, July 11

657 A401 56c multi 1.75 1.75

Arts and Letters Circle, 40th Anniv. — A402

2009, Oct. 3 Litho. *Perf. 13*

658 A402 51c multi 1.75 1.75

Romanesque Art — A403

2009, Nov. 7 *Perf. 13¼x13*

659 A403 85c multi 2.60 2.60

Epiphany — A404

2009, Dec. 12 *Perf. 13*

660 A404 56c multi 1.60 1.60

Arms Type of 2002 Inscribed "POSTES"

2010, Jan. 4 Photo. *Perf. 13x13¼*

661	A309	1c yel & multi	.25	.25
662	A309	5c lt bl & multi	.25	.25
663	A309	10c org & multi	.30	.30
664	A309	20c lilac & multi	.55	.55
665	A309	50c ol grn & multi	1.40	1.40
666	A309	(70c) dk bl & multi	2.00	2.00
		Nos. 661-666 (6)	4.75	4.75

2010 Winter Olympics, Vancouver A405

2010, Jan. 23 Photo. *Perf. 13x13¼*

667 A405 85c multi 2.40 2.40

Casamanya Peak — A406

2010, Feb. 15 Litho. *Perf. 13*

668 A406 €2.80 multi 7.75 7.75

Rights of the Child Convention, 20th Anniv. — A407

2010, Mar. 2 Photo.

669 A407 56c multi 1.60 1.60

Animals Type of 2006

Designs: 56c, Gyps fulvus, vert. 90c, Ovis aries.

2010, Mar. 8 Litho. *Perf. 13*

670-671 A360 Set of 2 4.00 4.00

Andorran Embassy, Brussels — A408

2010, Apr. 12 Engr. *Perf. 13*

672 A408 70c multi + label 1.90 1.90

Legend of Charlemagne's Chair — A409

2010, Apr. 26 Litho. *Perf. 13*

673 A409 51c multi 1.40 1.40

Europa A410

Litho. & Embossed with Foil Application

2010, May 10 *Perf. 13¼*

674 A410 56c multi 1.40 1.40

Radio Andorra Building A411

2010, May 25 Litho. *Perf. 13*

675 A411 56c multi 1.40 1.40

1985 Ferrari 328 GTS A412

2010, June 21 Litho. *Perf. 13*

676 A412 70c multi 1.75 1.75

Still Life, by Carme Massana A413

2010, July 12 *Perf. 13¼x13*

677 A413 95c multi 2.50 2.50

Predelle, Prats A414

2010, Sept. 6 Litho. *Perf. 13¼x13*

678 A414 €1.40 multi 3.75 3.75

Compare with types A372, A383, A396 and A420.

Souvenir Sheet

Churches — A415

No. 679: a, Sant Joan de Caselles Church. b, Sant Romà de Les Bons Church, horiz.

Perf. 13¼x13, 13x13¼

2010, Oct. 4 Engr.

679 A415 58c Sheet of 2, #a-b 3.25 3.25

See Andorra, Spanish Administration No. 363.

Arms Type of 2002 Inscribed "POSTES"

2010, Oct. 18 Photo. *Perf. 13x13¼*

680 A309 (58c) red & multi 1.75 1.75

Feudal Andorra — A416

681 A416 87c multi 2.40 2.40

Christmas — A417

2010, Nov. 29 ***Perf. 13***
682 A417 58c multi 1.60 1.60

Legend of St. Joan de Caselles — A418

2011, Feb. 12 Litho. ***Perf. 13***
683 A418 €2.80 multi 8.00 8.00

Francophonia — A419

2011, Mar. 19 ***Perf. 13x13¼***
684 A419 87c multi 2.50 2.50

Predelle, Prats A420

2011, Apr. 9 ***Perf. 13¼x13***
685 A420 €1.40 multi 4.00 4.00

Compare with types A372, A383, A386 and A414.

Europa — A421

Silk-Screened on Wood Veneer
2011, May 7 ***Serpentine Die Cut 11***
Self-Adhesive
686 A421 58c black & white 1.75 1.75

Intl. Year of Forests.

Councilor, by Francesc Borràs (1891-1968) — A422

2011, May 21 Litho. ***Perf. 13***
687 A422 95c multi 2.75 2.75

Placeta de Sant Esteve — A423

2011, June 4 Engr.
688 A423 58c multi 1.75 1.75

Soriano-Pedroso Automobile — A424

2011, June 18 Litho.
689 A424 75c multi 2.10 2.10

Rugby A425

2011, July 9 Photo. ***Perf. 13***
690 A425 89c multi 2.40 2.40

Values are for stamps with surrounding selvage.

Souvenir Sheet

Dance of the Seven Parishes, Plaza Benlloch — A426

2011, July 16 Litho. & Engr.
691 A426 €1.45 multi 4.25 4.25

Flora — A427

Designs: 60c, Rhododendron ferrugineum. €1, Rosa sempervirens, horiz.

2011, Sept. 4 Litho. ***Perf. 13***
692-693 A427 Set of 2 4.50 4.50

See Nos. 706-707, 720-721.

Council of the Land A428

2011, Sept. 24 ***Perf. 13x13¼***
694 A428 89c multi 2.50 2.50

Leaf and Coat of Arms — A429

2011, Oct. 1 Photo. ***Perf. 13x13¼***
695 A429 (57c) multi 1.60 1.60

Angel From Santa Eulalia d'Encamp Retable — A430

2011, Nov. 26 Litho. ***Perf. 13***
696 A430 60c multi 1.60 1.60

Legend of the Shop of the Sorceresses A431

2012, Jan. 14
697 A431 €2.78 multi 7.50 7.50

Women's World Cup Alpine Skiing Races, Soldeu A432

2012, Feb. 11 ***Perf. 13x13¼***
698 A432 89c multi 2.40 2.40

Massana Valley, by Joaquim Mir (1873-1940) — A433

2012, Mar. 3
699 A433 €1 multi 2.60 2.60

Souvenir Sheet

Restoration of Casa de la Vall, 50th Anniv. — A434

No. 700 — Casa de la Vall in: a, 1962. b, 2012.

2012, Mar. 10 Litho. & Engr.
700 A434 60c Sheet of 2, #a-b 3.25 3.25

Bugatti 37 Race Car A435

2012, Apr. 14 Litho. ***Perf. 13***
701 A435 77c multi 2.10 2.10

Souvenir Sheet

Europa — A436

2012, May 5 Litho. ***Perf. 13¼x13***
702 A436 77c multi 2.00 2.00

Noi. 702 has die cut opening in center of stamp.

Placeta de la Consòrcia, Andorra la Vella — A437

2012, June 8 Engr. ***Perf. 13x12¾***
703 A437 60c multi 1.50 1.50

Judo — A438

2012, July 6 Litho. *Perf. 13*
704 A438 77c multi 1.90 1.90

Souvenir Sheet

Marratxa Dance — A439

Litho. & Engr.
2012, July 20 *Perf. 13x13¼*
705 A439 €1.45 multi 3.75 3.75

Flora Type of 2011

Designs: 60c, Sempervivum montanum. €1, Eryngium bourgatii.

2012, Sept. 14 Litho. *Perf. 13*
706-707 A427 Set of 2 4.25 4.25

Woman Suffrage, 42nd Anniv. — A440

2012, Oct. 5 *Perf. 13¼x13*
708 A440 89c multi 2.25 2.25

Andorran Presidency of the Council of Europe — A441

2012, Oct. 26
709 A441 €1 multi 2/6- 2.60

King Henri IV of France (1553-1610), Co-Prince of Andorra — A442

2012, Nov. 8 Engr. *Perf. 13x13¼*
710 A442 60c multi 1.60 1.60
a. Sheet of 10, 5 each #710, France #4297 16.00 16.00

See France No. 4297.

Angel From Roser d'Ordino Retable — A443

Legend of Moixella — A444

2012, Nov. 23 Litho. *Perf. 13*
711 A443 57c multi 1.50 1.50

2013, Jan. 12
712 A444 €2.78 multi 7.50 7.50

Souvenir Sheet

Bear Ball, Encamp — A445

Litho. & Engr.
2013, Feb. 23 *Perf. 13x13¼*
713 A445 €1.55 multi 4.00 4.00

Constitution, 20th Anniv. — A446

2013, Mar. 16 Litho. *Perf. 13*
714 A446 63c multi 1.60 1.60

Cord 810 Phaeton A447

2013, Apr. 13
715 A447 95c multi 2.50 2.50

Plaça Rebés, Andorra la Vella — A448

2013, May 11 Engr. *Perf. 12¾*
716 A448 63c multi 1.75 1.75

Europa A449

2013, May 18 Litho. *Perf. 13¼*
717 A449 80c multi 2.25 2.25

Flora Type of 2011

Designs: 58c, Papaver rhoeas. €1.05, Paeonia mascula, horiz.

2013, Sept. 7 Litho. *Perf. 13*
720-721 A427 Set of 2 4.50 4.50

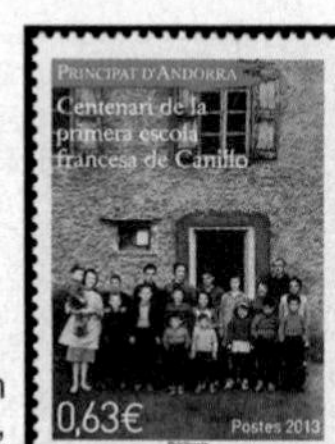

First French School in Canillo, Cent. — A452

2013, Oct. 2 Litho. *Perf. 13¼*
722 A452 63c multi 1.75 1.75

SEMI-POSTAL STAMP

Catalogue values for unused stamps in this section are for Never Hinged items.

Virgin of St. Coloma — SP1

Unwmk.
1964, July 25 Engr. *Perf. 13*
B1 SP1 25c + 10c multi 24.00 24.00

The surtax was for the Red Cross.

AIR POST STAMPS

Catalogue values for unused stamps in this section are for Never Hinged items.

Chamois AP1

Unwmk.
1950, Feb. 20 Engr. *Perf. 13*
C1 AP1 100fr indigo 87.50 60.00

East Branch of Valira River — AP2

1955-57

C2	AP2	100fr dark green	16.00	10.50
C3	AP2	200fr cerise	32.50	16.00
C4	AP2	500fr dp bl ('57)	120.00	65.00
		Nos. C2-C4 (3)	168.50	91.50

No. C3 in dark green was not regularly issued. Value, $3,500.

D'Inclès Valley AP3

1961-64 Unwmk. *Perf. 13*

C5	AP3	2fr red, ol gray & cl	1.25	1.25
C6	AP3	3fr bl, mar & slate grn	1.60	1.60
C7	AP3	5fr rose lil & red org	3.25	2.40
C8	AP3	10fr bl grn & slate grn	4.75	4.50
		Nos. C5-C8 (4)	10.85	9.75

Issued: 10fr, 4/25/64; others, 6/19/61.

POSTAGE DUE STAMPS

Postage Due Stamps of France, 1893-1931, Overprinted

On Stamps of 1893-1926

1931-33 Unwmk. *Perf. 14x13½*

J1	D2	5c blue	2.40	2.40
J2	D2	10c brown	2.40	2.40
J3	D2	30c rose red	1.60	1.60
J4	D2	50c violet brn	2.40	2.40
J5	D2	60c green	34.00	34.00
J6	D2	1fr red brn, *straw*	2.40	2.40
J7	D2	2fr brt violet	16.00	16.00
J8	D2	3fr magenta	3.25	3.25
		Nos. J1-J8 (8)	64.45	64.45

On Stamps of 1927-31

J9	D4	1c olive grn	3.25	3.25
J10	D4	10c rose	5.50	*6.50*
J11	D4	60c red	27.50	26.50
J12	D4	1fr Prus grn ('32)	110.00	*120.00*
J13	D4	1.20fr on 2fr bl	80.00	80.00
J14	D4	2fr ol brn ('33)	200.00	*225.00*
J15	D4	5fr on 1fr vio	120.00	120.00
		Nos. J9-J15 (7)	546.25	581.25

D5

D6

1935-41 Typo.

J16	D5	1c gray green	3.25	3.25
J17	D6	5c light blue ('37)	6.75	6.75
J18	D6	10c brown ('41)	4.00	*5.50*
J19	D6	2fr violet ('41)	11.00	8.75
J20	D6	5fr red orange ('41)	19.00	11.00
		Nos. J16-J20 (5)	44.00	35.25

Catalogue values for unused stamps in this section, from this point to the end of the section, are for Never Hinged items.

Wheat Sheaves — D7

1943-46 *Perf. 14x13½*

J21	D7	10c sepia	.80	.70
J22	D7	30c brt red vio	.90	.70
J23	D7	50c blue grn	1.25	1.10
J24	D7	1fr brt ultra	1.10	.90
J25	D7	1.50fr rose red	6.75	5.50
J26	D7	2fr turq blue	1.75	1.60
J27	D7	3fr brown org	2.00	1.90
J28	D7	4fr dp vio ('45)	6.25	5.50
J29	D7	5fr brt pink	4.25	3.75
J30	D7	10fr red org ('45)	6.50	5.50
J31	D7	20fr olive brn ('46)	7.75	6.50
		Nos. J21-J31 (11)	39.30	33.65

Inscribed: "Timbre Taxe"

1946-53

No.	Type	Description	Unused	Used
J32	D7	10c sepia ('46)	1.60	1.60
J33	D7	1fr ultra	.80	.80
J34	D7	2fr turq blue	1.25	1.25
J35	D7	3fr orange brn	2.75	2.75
J36	D7	4fr violet	3.50	3.50
J37	D7	5fr brt pink	2.75	2.75
J38	D7	10fr red orange	4.75	4.75
J39	D7	20fr olive brn	8.00	8.00
J40	D7	50fr dk green ('50)	47.50	47.50
J41	D7	100fr dp green ('53)	120.00	120.00
		Nos. J32-J41 (10)	192.90	192.90

Inscribed: "Timbre Taxe"

1961, June 19 ***Perf. 14x13½***

No.	Type	Description	Unused	Used
J42	D7	5c rose pink	4.00	4.00
J43	D7	10c red orange	8.00	8.00
J44	D7	20c olive	12.00	12.00
J45	D7	50c dark slate green	24.00	24.00
		Nos. J42-J45 (4)	48.00	48.00

D8

1964-71 **Typo.** ***Perf. 14x13½***

No.	Type	Description	Unused	Used
J46	D8	5c Centaury ('65)	.25	.25
J47	D8	10c Gentian ('65)	.25	.25
J48	D8	15c Corn poppy	.25	.25
J49	D8	20c Violets ('71)	.30	.25
J50	D8	30c Forget-me-not	.40	.30
J51	D8	40c Columbine ('71)	.55	.40
J52	D8	50c Clover ('65)	.65	.55
		Nos. J46-J52 (7)	2.65	2.25

D9

1985, Oct. 21 **Engr.** ***Perf. 13***

No.	Type	Description	Unused	Used
J53	D9	10c Holly	.25	.25
J54	D9	20c Blueberries	.25	.25
J55	D9	30c Raspberries	.25	.25
J56	D9	40c Bilberries	.30	.30
J57	D9	50c Blackberries	.30	.30
J58	D9	1fr Broom	.50	.50
J59	D9	2fr Rosehips	1.25	.80
J60	D9	3fr Nightshade	1.60	1.25
J61	D9	4fr Nabiu	2.00	1.60
J62	D9	5fr Strawberries	2.40	2.00
		Nos. J53-J62 (10)	9.10	7.50

NEWSPAPER STAMP

France No. P7 Overprinted

1931 **Unwmk.** ***Perf. 14x13½***

No.	Type	Description	Unused	Used
P1	A16	½c on 1c gray	1.25	1.25
a.		Double overprint	*3,000.*	
		Never Hinged	*4,000.*	

ANGOLA

aŋ-ˈgō-lə

LOCATION — S.W. Africa between Zaire and Namibia.
GOVT. — Republic
AREA — 481,351 sq. mi.
POP. — 11,177,537 (1999 est.)
CAPITAL — Luanda

Angola was a Portuguese overseas territory until it became independent November 11, 1975, as the People's Republic of Angola.

1000 Reis = 1 Milreis
100 Centavos = 1 Escudo (1913, 1954)
100 Centavos = 1 Angolar (1932)
10 Lweys = 1 Kwanza (1977)

Catalogue values for unused stamps in this country are for Never Hinged items, beginning with Scott 328 in the regular postage section, Scott C26 in the airpost section, Scott J31 in the postage due section, and Scott RA7 in the postal tax section.

Watermark

Wmk. 232 — Maltese Cross

Portuguese Crown — A1

Perf. 12½, 13½

1870-77 **Typo.** **Unwmk.**

Thin to Medium Paper

No.	Type	Description	Unused	Used
1	A1	5r gray black	3.00	1.75
2	A1	10r yellow	30.00	20.00
3	A1	20r bister	3.00	2.50
4	A1	25r red	15.00	11.00
5	A1	40r blue ('77)	150.00	100.00
6	A1	50r green	50.00	15.00
7	A1	100r lilac	8.00	5.00
8	A1	200r orange ('77)	7.00	3.25
9	A1	300r choc ('77)	8.00	5.00

1881-85 ***Perf. 12½, 13½***

No.	Type	Description	Unused	Used
10	A1	10r green ('83)	10.00	4.75
11	A1	20r carmine rose ('85)	21.00	17.50
12	A1	25r violet ('85)	14.00	5.00
13	A1	40r buff ('82)	13.00	4.75
15	A1	50r blue	52.50	14.00
		Nos. 10-15 (5)	110.50	46.00

Two types of numerals are found on #2, 11, 13, 15.

The cliche of 40r in plate of 20r error, was discovered before the stamps were issued. All examples were defaced by a blue pencil mark. Values, $2,100 unused; in pair with 20r, $2,400.

In perf. 12½, Nos. 1-4, 4a and 6, as well as 7a, were printed in 1870 on thicker paper and 1875 on normal paper. Stamps of the earlier printing sell for 2 to 5 times more than those of the 1875 printing.

Some reprints of the 1870-85 issues are on a smooth white chalky paper, ungummed and perf. 13½.

Other reprints of these issues are on thin ivory paper with shiny white gum and clear-cut perf. 13½.

King Luiz — A2

King Carlos — A3

1886 **Embossed** ***Perf. 12½***

No.	Type	Description	Unused	Used
16	A2	5r black	15.00	6.25
17	A2	10r green	15.00	6.25
18	A2	20r rose	22.50	12.50
19	A2	25r red violet	15.00	4.00
20	A2	40r chocolate	21.00	7.50
21	A2	50r blue	26.00	4.00
22	A2	100r yellow brn	35.00	10.00
23	A2	200r gray violet	50.00	13.00
24	A2	300r orange	50.00	14.00
		Nos. 16-24 (9)	249.50	77.50

For surcharges see Nos. 61-69, 172-174, 208-210.

Reprints of 5r, 20r & 100r have cleancut perf. 13½.

1893-94 **Typo.** ***Perf. 11½, 12½, 13½***

No.	Type	Description	Unused	Used
25	A3	5r yellow	3.75	1.50
26	A3	10r redsh violet	5.00	3.00
27a	A3	15r chocolate	7.00	3.00
28	A3	20r lavender	7.00	3.00
29c	A3	25r green	7.00	3.75
30b	A3	50r light blue	9.00	4.00
31	A3	75r carmine	17.50	12.00
32	A3	80r lt green	17.50	9.00
33	A3	100r brown, *buff*	17.50	9.00
34	A3	150r car, *rose*	27.50	17.50
35	A3	200r dk blue, *lt bl*	27.50	17.50
36	A3	300r dk blue, *sal*	30.00	17.50

For surcharges see Nos. 70-81, 175-179, 213-216, 234.

No. P1 Surcharged in Blue

1894, Aug.

No.	Type	Description	Unused	Used
37	N1	25r on 2½r brown	95.00	70.00

King Carlos — A5

1898-1903 ***Perf. 11½***

Name and Value in Black except 500r

No.	Type	Description	Unused	Used
38	A5	2½r gray	.65	.50
39	A5	5r orange	.65	.50
40	A5	10r yellow grn	.65	.50
41	A5	15r violet brn	3.00	1.60
42	A5	15r gray green ('03)	1.50	1.40
43	A5	20r gray violet	.60	.50
44	A5	25r sea green	1.60	.65
45	A5	25r car ('03)	.75	.45
46	A5	50r blue	2.75	1.00
47	A5	50r brown ('03)	8.00	3.75
48	A5	65r dull blue ('03)	12.00	5.75
49	A5	75r rose	11.00	6.00
50	A5	75r red violet ('03)	3.00	2.00
51	A5	80r violet	10.00	3.00
52	A5	100r dk blue, *blue*	2.00	1.25
53	A5	115r org brn, *pink* ('03)	13.00	7.50
54	A5	130r brn, *straw* ('03)	12.00	7.50
55	A5	150r brn, *straw*	11.00	6.00
56	A5	200r red vio, *pink*	8.00	1.75
57	A5	300r dk blue, *rose*	9.00	5.50
58	A5	400r dull bl, *straw* ('03)	9.00	3.50
59	A5	500r blk & red, *bl* ('01)	12.00	5.00
60	A5	700r vio, *yelsh* ('01)	35.00	17.50
		Nos. 38-60 (23)	167.15	83.10

For surcharges and overprints see Nos. 83-102, 113-117, 159-171, 181-183, 217-218, 221-225.

Stamps of 1886-94 Surcharged in Black or Red

Two types of surcharge:
I — 3mm between numeral and REIS.
II — 4½mm spacing.

1902 ***Perf. 12½***

No.	Type	Description	Unused	Used
61	A2	65r on 40r choc	12.00	7.50
62	A2	65r on 300r org, I	12.00	7.50
a.		Type II	12.00	7.50
63	A2	115r on 10r green	10.00	6.75
a.		Inverted surcharge	90.00	50.00
b.		Perf. 13½	75.00	45.00
64	A2	115r on 200r gray vio	11.00	6.75
65	A2	130r on 50r blue	15.00	5.75
66	A2	130r on 100r brown	10.00	5.75
67	A2	400r on 20r rose	110.00	65.00
a.		Perf. 13½	225.00	125.00
68	A2	400r on 25r violet	27.50	13.00
69	A2	400r on 5r black (R)	22.50	12.00
a.		Double surcharge	75.00	50.00
		Nos. 61-69 (9)	230.00	130.00

For surcharges see Nos. 172-174, 208-210.

Perf. 11½, 12½, 13½

No.	Type	Description	Unused	Used
70	A3	65r on 5r yel, I, perf. 11½	10.00	8.00
a.		Type II	10.00	10.00
71	A3	65r on 10r red vio, I, perf. 12½	9.00	6.75
a.		Type II	9.00	6.75
b.		Perf. 11½, I	14.00	8.00
c.		Perf. 11½, I	14.00	8.00
72	A3	65r on 20r lav, perf. 11½	12.50	7.50
73	A3	65r on 25r green, perf. 12½	9.00	6.50
b.		Perf. 13½	15.00	10.00
74	A3	115r on 80r lt grn, perf. 12½	18.00	10.00
75	A3	115r on 100r brn, *buff*, perf. 12½	17.50	9.00
b.		Perf. 13½	80.00	45.00
76	A3	115r on 150r car, *rose*, perf. 11½	22.50	15.00
a.		Perf. 13½	25.00	20.00
b.		Perf. 12½	29.00	20.00
77	A3	130r on 15r choc, perf. 12½	9.00	9.00
b.		Type II	11.00	6.00
78	A3	130r on 75r carmine, perf. 11½	12.00	9.00
a.		Perf. 13½	70.00	60.00
b.		Perf. 12½	14.00	10.00
79	A3	130r on 300r dk bl, *sal*, perf. 12½	25.00	20.00
a.		Perf. 13½	42.50	20.00
80	A3	400r on 50r lt bl, I, perf. 12½	14.00	7.00
a.		Perf. 11½	40.00	17.50
c.		Type II	10.00	10.00
81	A3	400r on 200r bl, *bl*, perf. 12½	12.00	11.00
a.		Perf. 13½	425.00	225.00
82	N1	400r on 2½r brn, I, perf. 12½	2.25	2.00
a.		Type II	2.25	2.00
		Nos. 70-82 (13)	167.75	120.75

For surcharges see Nos. 175-180, 211-216, 234-235.

Reprints of Nos. 65, 67, 68 and 69 have clean-cut perforation 13½.

For detailed listings of perforation and paper varieties, see *Scott Classic Specialized Catalogue of Stamps and Covers 1840-1940.*

Stamps of 1898 Overprinted — a

1902 ***Perf. 11½***

No.	Type	Description	Unused	Used
83	A5	15r brown	2.75	1.75
84	A5	25r sea green	2.25	1.00
85	A5	50r blue	5.00	2.25
86	A5	75r rose	8.00	6.00
		Nos. 83-86 (4)	18.00	11.00

For surcharge see No. 116.

No. 48 Surcharged in Black

1905

No.	Type	Description	Unused	Used
87	A5	50r on 65r dull blue	7.00	3.50

For surcharge see No. 183.

Stamps of 1898-1903 Overprinted in Carmine or Green — b

1911

No.	Type	Description	Unused	Used
88	A5	2½r gray	.60	.45
89	A5	5r orange yel	.60	.45
90	A5	10r light green	.60	.45
91	A5	15r gray green	.85	.70
92	A5	20r gray violet	1.00	.75
93	A5	25r car (G)	1.00	.75
94	A5	50r brown	3.75	2.00
95	A5	75r lilac	6.75	3.25

96 A5 100r dk blue, *bl* 6.75 4.00
97 A5 115r org brn, *pink* 4.25 2.25
98 A5 130r brn, *straw* 4.25 2.25
99 A5 200r red lil, *pnksh* 4.75 2.75
100 A5 400r dull bl, *straw* 4.75 2.00
101 A5 500r blk & red, *bl* 4.75 2.25
102 A5 700r violet, *yelsh* 4.75 2.50
Nos. 88-102 (15) 49.40 26.80

Inverted and double overprints of Nos. 88-102 were made intentionally.

For surcharges see Nos. 217-218, 221-222, 224.

King Manuel II — A6

Overprinted in Carmine or Green

1912 ***Perf. 11½x12***
103 A6 2½r violet .75 *.40*
104 A6 5r black .75 *.40*
105 A6 10r gray green .75 .40
106 A6 20r carmine (G) .75 .40
107 A6 25r violet brown .75 .40
108 A6 50r dk blue 1.75 1.25
109 A6 75r bister brown 2.00 1.75
110 A6 100r brown, *lt green* 3.50 2.25
111 A6 200r dk green, *salmon* 3.50 2.25
112 A6 300r black, *azure* 3.50 2.25
Nos. 103-112 (10) 18.00 11.75

For surcharges see Nos. 219-220, 226-227.

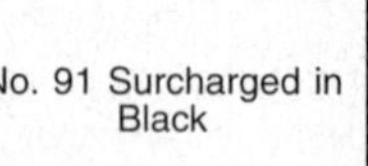

No. 91 Surcharged in Black

1912, June ***Perf. 11½***
113 A5 2½r on 15r gray green 5.50 3.25
114 A5 5r on 15r gray green 6.00 3.25
115 A5 10r on 15r gray green 4.50 3.25
Nos. 113-115 (3) 16.00 9.75

Inverted and double surcharges of Nos. 113-115 were made intentionally.

Nos. 86 and 50 Surcharged in Black and Overprinted in Violet — c

1912
116 A5 25r on 75r rose 100.00 55.00
117 A5 25r on 75r red violet 5.75 5.50
a. "REUPBLICA" 110.00 70.00
b. "25" omitted 110.00 70.00
c. "REPUBLICA" omitted 110.00 70.00

Ceres — A7

With Imprint
Chalky Paper

1914 ***Perf. 15x14***

Name and Value in Black

118 A7 ¼c olive brown 2.25 .80
119 A7 ½c black 2.25 .80
120 A7 1c blue green 2.25 .80
121 A7 1½c lilac brown 4.50 2.75
122 A7 2c carmine 8.00 3.75
123 A7 2½c violet 1.60 .70
124 A7 5c blue 3.50 .80
125 A7 7½c yellow brn 4.50 2.75
126 A7 8c slate 4.50 2.75
127 A7 10c orange brn 4.50 2.75
128 A7 15c brown rose 7.00 3.00
129 A7 20c yel green 3.50 1.75
130 A7 30c brown, *green* 2.75 2.50
131 A7 40c brown, *pink* 2.75 2.50
132 A7 50c orange, *sal* 11.00 7.50
133 A7 1e green, *blue* 8.00 5.00
Nos. 118-133 (16) 72.85 40.90

1915-22 **Ordinary Paper**
134 A7 ¼c olive brown .40 .35
135 A7 ½c black .40 .35
136 A7 1c blue green .40 .35
137 A7 1c yellow green ('18) .40 .35
138 A7 1½c lilac brown .40 .35
139 A7 2c carmine .40 .35
140 A7 2½c dark violet .35 .35
141 A7 3c orange 37.50 29.00
142 A7 4c dull rose ('21) .40 .35
143 A7 5c blue 1.50 1.25
144 A7 6c lilac ('21) .40 .35
145 A7 7c ultra ('21) .40 .35
146 A7 7½c yellow brn ('20) .40 .40
147 A7 8c slate .40 .40
148 A7 10c orange brn ('18) .40 .35
149 A7 12c olive brown ('21) .75 .50
150 A7 15c plum ('20) .60 .35
151 A7 15c brown rose ('21) .40 .35
152 A7 20c yel green ('18) 6.25 5.25
153 A7 30c gray green ('21) .60 .55
154 A7 80c pink ('21) 2.10 1.00
155 A7 2e dark violet ('22) 3.50 3.25
Nos. 134-155 (22) 58.35 46.15

1921-26 ***Perf. 12x11½***
156 A7 ¼c olive brown ('24) .40 .35
157 A7 ½c black .40 .35
158 A7 1c blue green ('24) .40 .35
158C A7 1½c lilac brown ('24) .40 .35
158D A7 2c carmine ('24) .40 .35
158E A7 2c gray ('25) .75 .55
158F A7 2½c lt violet ('24) .40 .35
158G A7 3c orange .35 .30
158H A7 4c dull rose .35 .30
158I A7 4½c gray .35 .30
158J A7 5c blue ('24) .35 .30
158K A7 6c lilac .35 .30
158L A7 7c ultra .35 .30
158M A7 7½c yellow brown ('24) .45 .40
158N A7 8c slate ('24) .45 .40
158O A7 10c orange brn ('24) .40 .35
158P A7 12c olive brn .75 .50
158Q A7 12c dp green ('25) .75 .50
158R A7 15c plum ('24) 1.00 .35
158S A7 20c yel green 2.00 1.60
158T A7 24c ultra ('25) 1.75 1.40
158U A7 25c choc ('25) 1.75 1.25
158V A7 30c gray grn .70 .55
158W A7 40c turq blue 1.40 .75
158X A7 50c lt violet ('25) 1.40 .70
158Y A7 60c dk blue ('22) 1.75 .90
158Z A7 60c dp rose ('26) 90.00 60.00
159A A7 80c pink ('22) 1.90 1.00
159B A7 1e rose ('22) 2.00 1.00
Nos. 156-159B (29) 113.30 76.20

Glazed Paper

1921-25 ***Perf. 12x11½***
159C A7 1e rose 2.10 1.00
159D A7 1e deep blue ('25) 3.50 2.00
159E A7 2e dark violet ('22) 2.75 2.00
159F A7 5e buff ('25) 16.50 12.50
159G A7 10e pink ('25) 75.00 27.50
159H A7 20e pale turq ('25) 150.00 75.00
Nos. 159C-159H (6) 249.85 120.00

For surcharges see Nos. 228-229, 236-239.

Stamps of 1898-1903 Overprinted type "c" in Red or Green

1914 ***Perf. 11½, 12***
159 A5 10r yel green (R) 6.50 5.25
160 A5 15r gray green (R) 6.00 5.25
161 A5 20r gray violet (G) 2.50 1.75
163 A5 75r red violet (G) 2.00 1.25
164 A5 100r blue, *blue* (R) 4.00 3.50
165 A5 115r org brn, *pink* (R) *125.00*
167 A5 200r red vio, *pnksh* (G) 2.50 1.75
169 A5 400r dl bl, *straw* (R) 47.50 47.50
170 A5 500r blk & red, *bl* (R) 6.00 5.50
171 A5 700r vio, *yelsh* (G) 40.00 25.00

Inverted and double overprints were made intentionally. No. 165 was not regularly issued. Red overprints on the 20r, 75r, 200r were not regularly issued. The 130r was not regularly issued without surcharge (No. 225).

On Nos. 63-65, 74-76, 78-79, 82
Perf. 11½, 12½, 13½

172 A2 115r on 10r (R) 17.00 17.00
a. Perf. 13½ 17.00 17.00
173 A2 115r on 200r (R) 24.00 24.00
174 A2 130r on 50r (R) 32.50 32.50
175 A3 115r on 80r (R) 225.00 225.00
176 A3 115r on 100r (R) 250.00 225.00
a. Perf. 11½ 300.00 300.00
b. Perf. 13½ 850.00 850.00
177 A3 115r on 150r (G) 250.00 210.00
a. Perf. 12½ 275.00 225.00
b. Perf. 13½ 825.00 825.00
178 A3 130r on 75r (G) 4.50 4.00
a. Perf. 12½ 9.00 7.50
179 A3 130r on 300r (R) 9.75 9.00
a. Perf. 12½ 17.50 16.00
180 N1 400r on 2½r (R) 1.00 .75
a. Perf. 11½ 4.75 4.00
Nos. 172-180 (9) 813.75 747.25

Nos. 85-87 Overprinted in Red or Green

On Stamps of 1902
Perf. 11½, 12

181 A5 50r blue (R) 2.50 2.00
182 A5 75r rose (G) 5.75 4.00

On No. 87

183 A5 50r on 65r dull blue (R) 5.50 3.50
Nos. 181-183 (3) 13.75 9.50

Inverted and double surcharges of Nos. 181-183 were made intentionally.

Common Design Types pictured following the introduction.

Vasco da Gama Issue of Various Portuguese Colonies

Common Design Types CD20-CD27 Srchd.

On Stamps of Macao

1913 ***Perf. 12½ to 16***
184 ¼c on ½a blue grn 2.75 2.25
185 ½c on 1a red 2.75 2.25
186 1c on 2a red violet 2.75 2.25
187 2½c on 4a yel green 2.25 1.60
188 5c on 8a dk blue 2.25 1.60
189 7½c on 12a vio brn 9.00 5.75
190 10c on 16a bister brn 3.25 2.50
191 15c on 24a bister 4.25 2.50
Nos. 184-191 (8) 29.25 20.70

On Stamps of Portuguese Africa
Perf. 14 to 15

192 ¼c on 2½r blue grn 1.25 .85
193 ½c on 5r red 1.25 .85
194 1c on 10r red violet 1.25 .85
195 2½c on 25r yel grn 1.25 .85
196 5c on 50r dk blue 1.25 .85
197 7½c on 75r vio brn 7.50 6.50
198 10c on 100r bister brn 3.00 2.00
199 15c on 150r bister 3.50 2.25
Nos. 192-199 (8) 20.25 15.00

On Stamps of Timor

200 ¼c on ½a blue grn 2.75 2.10
201 ½c on 1a red 2.75 2.10
202 1c on 2a red vio 2.75 2.10
203 2½c on 4a yel grn 2.25 1.50
204 5c on 8a dk blue 2.25 1.50
205 7½c on 12a vio brn 9.00 6.00
206 10c on 16a bis brn 3.25 2.40
207 15c on 24a bister 4.25 2.40
Nos. 200-207 (8) 29.25 20.10
Nos. 184-207 (24) 78.75 55.80

Provisional Issue of 1902 Overprinted in Carmine

1915 ***Perf. 11½, 12½, 13½***
208 A2 115r on 10r green 2.25 2.25
209 A2 115r on 200r gray vio 2.75 2.25
210 A2 130r on 100r brown 2.25 1.75
211 A3 115r on 80r lt green 2.00 1.75
212 A3 115r on 100r brn, *buff* 2.25 2.00
a. Perf. 11½ 100.00 95.00
b. Perf. 13½ 17.50 15.00
213 A3 115r on 150r car, *rose* 1.75 1.75
a. Perf. 12½ 4.25 3.50
b. Perf. 13½ 3.00 2.25
214 A3 130r on 15r choc 2.00 1.75
a. Perf. 12½ 9.00 8.00
215 A3 130r on 75r carmine 3.50 2.75
a. Perf. 13½ 6.00 4.75
216 A3 130r on 300r dk bl, *sal* 2.25 1.75
a. Perf. 13½ 4.50 2.75
Nos. 208-216 (9) 21.00 18.00

Stamps of 1911-14 Surcharged in Black

d

e

On Stamps of 1911

1919 ***Perf. 11½***
217 A5 (d) ½c on 75r red lilac 3.25 3.00
218 A5 (d) 2½c on 100r blue, *grysh* 3.50 3.00

On Stamps of 1912
Perf. 11½x12

219 A6 (e) ½c on 75r bis brn 2.00 2.00
220 A6 (e) 2½c on 100r brn, *lt grn* 3.50 3.00

On Stamps of 1914

221 A5 (d) ½c on 75r red lil 2.00 2.00
222 A5 (d) 2½c on 100r bl, *grysh* 2.75 2.50
Nos. 217-222 (6) 17.00 15.50

Inverted and double surcharges were made for sale to collectors.

Nos. 163, 98 and Type of 1914 Surcharged with New Values and Bars in Black

1921
223 A5 (c) 00.5c on 75r *350.00 350.00*
224 A5 (b) 4c on 130r (#98) 2.75 2.00
225 A5 (c) 4c on 130r brn, *straw* 8.00 7.50
a. Without surcharge *240.00*

Nos. 109 and 108 Surcharged with New Values and Bars in Black

226 A6 00.5c on 75r 2.00 1.75
227 A6 1c on 50r 2.25 2.00

Nos. 133 and 138 Surcharged with New Values and Bars in Black

228 A7 00.5c on 7½c 2.50 2.25
229 A7 04c on 15c 2.50 2.00
Nos. 224-229 (6) 20.00 17.50
Nos. 223-229 (7) *370.00 367.50*

The 04c surcharge exists on the 15c brown rose, perf 12x11½, No. 139.

Some authorities question the status of No. 223.

Nos. 81-82 Surcharged

1925 ***Perf. 12½***
234 A3 40c on 400r on 200r bl, *bl* 1.25 1.00
a. Perf. 13½ 6.75 4.50
235 N1 40c on 400r on 2½r brn .95 .95
a. Perf. 13½ .95 .95

Nos. 150-151, 154-155 Surcharged

1931 ***Perf. 12x 11½***
236 A7 50c on 60c deep rose 3.00 2.00
237 A7 70c on 80c pink 5.00 3.00
238 A7 70c on 1e deep blue 5.00 3.00
239 A7 1.40e on 2e dark violet 4.00 2.00
Nos. 236-239 (4) 17.00 10.00

Ceres — A14

Perf. 12x11½

1932-46 Typo. Wmk. 232

No.	Type	Description	Unused	Used
243	A14	1c bister brn	.30	.25
244	A14	5c dk brown	.35	.30
245	A14	10c dp violet	.35	.30
246	A14	15c black	.35	.30
247	A14	20c gray	.40	.30
248	A14	30c myrtle grn	.40	.30
249	A14	35c yel grn ('46)	9.25	4.25
250	A14	40c dp orange	.45	.25
251	A14	45c lt blue	1.75	1.40
252	A14	50c lt brown	.40	.25
253	A14	60c olive grn	1.00	.30
254	A14	70c orange brn	1.10	.30
255	A14	80c emerald	.75	.25
256	A14	85c rose	5.50	2.25
257	A14	1a claret	1.00	.30
258	A14	1.40a dk blue	11.50	2.25
258A	A14	1.75a dk blue ('46)	20.00	5.25
259	A14	2a dull vio	5.25	.60
260	A14	5a pale yel grn	11.50	2.00
261	A14	10a olive bis	22.50	5.75
262	A14	20a orange	57.50	5.75
		Nos. 243-262 (21)	151.60	32.90
		Set, never hinged	275.00	

For surcharges see Nos. 263-267, 271-273, 294A-300, J31-J36.

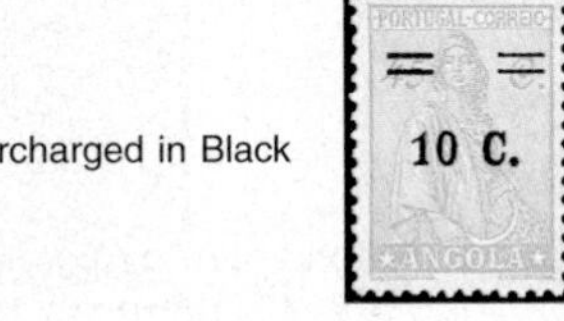

Surcharged in Black

5½mm between bars and new value.

1934

No.	Type	Description	Unused	Used
263	A14	10c on 45c lt bl	4.00	2.75
264	A14	20c on 85c rose	4.00	2.75
265	A14	30c on 1.40a dk bl	4.00	2.75
266	A14	70c on 2a dl vio	6.00	2.75
267	A14	80c on 5a pale yel grn	9.00	2.75
		Nos. 263-267 (5)	27.00	13.75
		Set, never hinged	45.00	

See Nos. 294A-300.

Nos. J26, J30 Surcharged in Black

1935 Unwmk. *Perf. 11½*

No.	Type	Description	Unused	Used
268	D2	5c on 6c lt brown	2.50	1.75
269	D2	30c on 50c gray	2.50	1.75
270	D2	40c on 50c gray	2.50	1.75
		Nos. 268-270 (3)	7.50	5.25
		Set, never hinged	14.00	

No. 255 Surcharged in Black

1938 Wmk. 232 *Perf. 12x11½*

No.	Type	Description	Unused	Used
271	A14	5c on 80c emerald	1.10	.60
272	A14	10c on 80c emerald	1.90	.90
273	A14	15c on 80c emerald	2.50	.90
		Nos. 271-273 (3)	5.50	2.40
		Set, never hinged	10.00	

Vasco da Gama Issue

Common Design Types

Engr.; Name & Value Typo. in Black

Perf. 13½x13

1938, July 26 Unwmk.

No.	Type	Description	Unused	Used
274	CD34	1c gray green	.30	.25
275	CD34	5c orange brn	.40	.35
276	CD34	10c dk carmine	.45	.35
277	CD34	15c dk violet brn	.45	.35
278	CD34	20c slate	.45	.35
279	CD35	30c rose violet	.55	.40
280	CD35	35c brt green	1.10	.80
281	CD35	40c brown	.40	.25
282	CD35	50c brt red vio	.55	.25
283	CD36	60c gray black	1.25	.35
284	CD36	70c brown vio	1.25	.35
285	CD36	80c orange	1.25	.35
286	CD36	1a red	1.25	.35
287	CD37	1.75a blue	2.25	1.00
288	CD37	2a brown car	3.50	1.10
289	CD37	5a olive grn	16.00	1.25
290	CD38	10a blue vio	32.50	1.25
291	CD38	20a red brown	45.00	4.00
		Nos. 274-291 (18)	108.90	13.35
		Set, never hinged	190.00	

For surcharges see Nos. 301-304.

Marble Column and Portuguese Arms with Cross — A20

1938, July 29 *Perf. 12½*

No.	Type	Description	Unused	Used
292	A20	80c blue green	3.75	2.25
293	A20	1.75a deep blue	22.50	6.25
294	A20	20a dk red brown	65.00	22.50
		Nos. 292-294 (3)	91.25	31.00
		Set, never hinged	175.00	

Visit of the President of Portugal to this colony in 1938.

Stamps of 1932 Surcharged with New Value and Bars

8mm between bars and new value.

1941-45 Wmk. 232 *Perf. 12x11½*

No.	Type	Description	Unused	Used
294A	A14	5c on 80c emer ('45)	1.00	.55
295	A14	10c on 45c lt blue	2.00	1.25
296	A14	15c on 45c lt blue	2.00	1.25
297	A14	20c on 85c rose	2.00	1.25
298	A14	35c on 85c rose	2.00	1.25
299	A14	50c on 1.40a dk blue	2.00	1.25
300	A14	60c on 1a claret	10.00	8.75
		Nos. 294A-300 (7)	21.00	15.55
		Set, never hinged	40.00	

Nos. 285 to 287 Surcharged with New Values and Bars in Black or Red

1945 Unwmk. *Perf. 13½x13*

No.	Type	Description	Unused	Used
301	CD36	5c on 80c org	.90	.50
302	CD36	50c on 1a red	.90	.50
303	CD37	50c on 1.75a bl (R)	.90	.50
304	CD37	50c on 1.75a bl	.90	.50
		Nos. 301-304 (4)	3.60	2.00
		Set, never hinged	4.75	

Sao Miguel Fort, Luanda — A21

John IV — A22

Designs: 10c, Our Lady of Nazareth Church, Luanda. 50c, Salvador Correia de Sa e Bene vides. 1a, Surrender of Luanda. 1.75a, Diogo Cao. 2a, Manuel Cerveira Pereira. 5a, Stone Cliffs, Yelala. 10a, Paulo Dias de Novais. 20a, Massangano Fort.

Perf. 14½

1948, May Unwmk. Litho.

No.	Type	Description	Unused	Used
305	A21	5c dk violet	.30	.25
306	A21	10c dk brown	.75	.35
307	A22	30c blue grn	.35	.25
308	A22	50c vio brown	.35	.25
309	A21	1a carmine	.75	.25
310	A22	1.75a slate blue	1.00	.25
311	A22	2a green	1.00	.25
312	A21	5a gray black	2.50	.70
313	A22	10a rose lilac	7.75	.90
314	A21	20a gray blue	17.50	5.25
a.		Sheet of 10, #305-314	100.00	100.00
		Never hinged	170.00	
		Nos. 305-314 (10)	32.25	8.70
		Set, never hinged	52.50	

300th anniv. of the restoration of Angola to Portugal. No. 314a sold for 42.50a.

Lady of Fatima Issue

Common Design Type

1948, Dec.

No.	Type	Description	Unused	Used
315	CD40	50c carmine	1.75	.90
316	CD40	3a ultra	7.75	3.00
317	CD40	6a red orange	24.00	6.00
318	CD40	9a dp claret	55.00	8.00
		Nos. 315-318 (4)	88.50	17.90
		Set, never hinged	125.00	

Our Lady of the Rosary at Fatima, Portugal.

Chiumbe River — A24

Black Rocks — A25

Designs: 50c, View of Luanda. 2.50a, Sa da Bandeira. 3.50a, Mocamedes. 15a, Cubal River. 50a, Duke of Bragança Falls.

1949 Unwmk. *Perf. 13½*

No.	Type	Description	Unused	Used
319	A24	20c dk slate blue	.60	.25
320	A25	40c black brown	.60	.25
321	A24	50c rose brown	.60	.25
322	A24	2.50a blue violet	3.25	.40
323	A24	3.50a slate gray	3.25	.60
323A	A24	15a dk green	21.00	2.75
324	A24	50a dp green	120.00	7.50
		Nos. 319-324 (7)	149.30	12.00
		Set, never hinged	250.00	

Sailing Vessel — A26

UPU Symbols — A27

1949, Aug. *Perf. 14*

No.	Type	Description	Unused	Used
325	A26	1a chocolate	6.00	.70
326	A26	4a dk Prus green	19.00	2.75
		Set, never hinged	37.50	

Centenary of founding of Mocamedes.

1949, Oct.

No.	Type	Description	Unused	Used
327	A27	4a dk grn & lt grn	11.00	3.00
		Never hinged	18.00	

75th anniv. of the UPU.

Catalogue values for unused stamps in this section, from this point to the end of the section, are for Never Hinged items.

Stamp of 1870 — A28

1950, Apr. 2 *Perf. 11½x12*

No.	Type	Description	Unused	Used
328	A28	50c yellow green	1.75	.55
329	A28	1a fawn	1.75	.85
330	A28	4a black	6.25	1.25
a.		Sheet of 3, #328-330	40.00	40.00
		Nos. 328-330 (3)	9.75	2.65

Angola's first philatelic exhibition, marking the 80th anniversary of Angola's first stamps.

No. 330a contains Nos. 328, 329 (inverted), 330, perf. 11½ and sold for 6.50a. All copies carry an oval exhibition cancellation in the margin but the stamps were valid for postage.

Holy Year Issue

Common Design Types

1950, May *Perf. 13x13½*

No.	Type	Description	Unused	Used
331	CD41	1a dull rose vio	1.60	.35
332	CD42	4a black	6.00	1.00

Dark Chanting Goshawk — A31

European Bee Eater — A32

10c, Racquet-tailed roller. 15c, Bataleur eagle. 50c, Giant kingfisher. 1a, Yellow-fronted barbet. 1.50a, Openbill (stork). 2a, Southern ground hornbill. 2.50a, African skimmer. 3a, Shikra. 3.50a, Denham's bustard. 4a, African golden oriole. 4.50a, Long-tailed shrike. 5a, Red-shouldered glossy starling. 6a, Sharp-tailed glossy starling. 7a, Red-shouldered widow bird. 10a, Half-colored kingfisher. 12.50a, White-crowned shrike. 15a, White-winged babbling starling. 20a, Yellow-billed hornbill. 25a, Amethyst starling. 30a, Orange-breasted shrike. 40a, Secretary bird. 50a, Rosy-faced lovebird.

Photogravure and Lithographed

1951 Unwmk. *Perf. 11½*

Birds in Natural Colors

No.	Type	Description	Unused	Used
333	A31	5c lt blue	.50	.50
334	A32	10c aqua	.50	.50
335	A32	15c salmon pink	.90	.50
336	A32	20c pale yellow	1.00	.75
337	A31	50c gray blue	1.00	.50
338	A31	1a lilac	1.00	.25
339	A31	1.50a gray buff	1.50	.25
340	A31	2a cream	4.75	.25
341	A32	2.50a gray	2.00	.25
342	A32	3a lemon yel	1.50	.25
343	A31	3.50a lt gray	2.25	.25
344	A31	4a rose buff	2.50	.25
345	A32	4.50a rose lilac	2.50	.25
346	A31	5a green	9.00	.65
347	A31	6a blue	13.00	1.50
348	A31	7a orange	14.00	2.00
349	A31	10a lilac rose	60.00	2.75
350	A32	12.50a slate gray	18.00	3.75
351	A31	15a pale olive	14.00	3.75
352	A31	20a pale bis brn	150.00	9.50
353	A31	25a lilac rose	55.00	8.00
354	A32	30a pale salmon	55.00	9.00
355	A31	40a yellow	80.00	13.00
356	A31	50a turquoise	175.00	29.00
		Nos. 333-356 (24)	664.90	87.65
		Set, hinged	300.00	

Holy Year Extension Issue

Common Design Type

1951, Oct. Litho. *Perf. 14*

No.	Type	Description	Unused	Used
357	CD43	4a orange + label	5.25	1.50

Sheets contain alternate vertical rows of stamps and labels bearing quotations from Pope Pius XII or the Patriarch Cardinal of Lisbon. Stamp without label attached sells for less.

Medical Congress Issue

Common Design Type

Design: Medical examination

1952, June *Perf. 13½*

No.	Type	Description	Unused	Used
358	CD44	1a vio blue & brn blk	1.25	.45

Head of Christ — A35

1952, Oct. Unwmk. *Perf. 13*

359 A35 10c dk blue & buff .25 .25
360 A35 50c dk ol grn & ol gray .95 .30
361 A35 2a rose vio & cream 3.50 .95
Nos. 359-361 (3) 4.70 1.50

Exhibition of Sacred Missionary Art, Lisbon, 1951.

Leopard — A36

Sable Antelope — A37

Animals: 20c, Elephant. 30c, Eland. 40c, African crocodile. 50c, Impala. 1a, Mountain zebra. 1.50a, Sitatunga. 2a, Black rhinoceros. 2.30a, Gemsbok. 2.50a, Lion. 3a, Buffalo. 3.50a, Springbok. 4a, Brindled gnu. 5a, Hartebeest. 7a, Wart hog. 10a, Defassa waterbuck. 12.50a, Hippopotamus. 15a, Greater kudu. 20a, Giraffe.

1953, Aug. 15 *Perf. 12½*

362 A36 5c multicolored .25 .25
363 A37 10c multicolored .25 .25
364 A37 20c multicolored .25 .25
365 A37 30c multicolored .25 .25
366 A36 40c multicolored .25 .25
367 A37 50c multicolored .25 .25
368 A37 1a multicolored .35 .25
369 A37 1.50a multicolored .40 .25
370 A36 2a multicolored .40 .25
371 A37 2.30a multicolored .45 .25
372 A37 2.50a multicolored .50 .25
373 A36 3a multicolored .55 .25
374 A37 3.50a multicolored .55 .25
375 A37 4a multicolored 20.00 .40
376 A37 5a multicolored 1.00 .35
377 A37 7a multicolored 1.50 .35
378 A37 10a multicolored 3.00 .35
379 A37 12.50a multicolored 7.50 4.00
380 A37 15a multicolored 10.00 4.00
381 A37 20a multicolored 13.00 1.10
Nos. 362-381 (20) 60.70 13.80
Set, hinged 20.00

Stamp of Portugal and Arms of Colonies — A38

1953, Nov. Photo. *Perf. 13*
Stamp and Arms Multicolored

382 A38 50c gray & dark gray 1.25 .60

Cent. of Portugal's 1st postage stamps.

Map and Plane — A39

Typographed and Lithographed
1954, May 27 *Perf. 13½*

383 A39 35c multicolored .25 .25
384 A39 4.50e multicolored 1.10 .65

Visit of Pres. Francisco H C. Lopes.

Sao Paulo Issue
Common Design Type

1954 Litho.

385 CD46 1e bister & gray .80 .50

Map of Angola — A41

Artur de Paiva — A42

1955, Aug. Unwmk. *Perf. 13½*

386 A41 5c multicolored .25 .25
387 A41 20c multicolored .25 .25
388 A41 50c multicolored .25 .25
389 A41 1e multicolored .25 .25
390 A41 2.30e multicolored .50 .35
391 A41 4e multicolored 2.50 .25
392 A41 10e multicolored 2.50 .25
393 A41 20e multicolored 4.00 .45
Nos. 386-393 (8) 10.50 2.30

For overprints see Nos. 593, 598, 604.

1956, Oct. 9 *Perf. 13½x12½*

394 A42 1e blk, dk bl & ocher .45 .30

Cent. of the birth of Col. Artur de Paiva.

Man of Malange — A43

Various Costumes in Multicolor; Inscriptions in Black Brown

1957, Jan. 1 Photo. *Perf. 11½*
Granite Paper

395 A43 5c gray .25 .25
396 A43 10c orange yel .25 .25
397 A43 15c lt blue grn .25 .25
398 A43 20c pale rose vio .25 .25
399 A43 30c brt rose .25 .25
400 A43 40c blue gray .25 .25
401 A43 50c pale olive .25 .25
402 A43 80c lt violet .45 .40
403 A43 1.50e buff 2.50 .40
404 A43 2.50e lt yel grn 3.25 .25
405 A43 4e salmon 2.00 .25
406 A43 10e salmon pink 3.00 .50
Nos. 395-406 (12) 12.95 3.55

Jose M. Antunes — A44

1957, Apr. *Perf. 13½*

407 A44 1e aqua & brown .90 .45

Birth cent. of Father Jose Maria Antunes.

Fair Emblem, Globe and Arms — A45

1958, July Litho. *Perf. 12x11½*

408 A45 1.50e multicolored .75 .35

World's Fair, Brussels, Apr. 17-Oct. 19.

Tropical Medicine Congress Issue
Common Design Type

Design: Securidaca longipedunculata.

1958, Dec. 15 *Perf. 13½*

409 CD47 2.50e multicolored 3.50 1.10

Medicine Man — A47

Designs: 1.50e, Early government doctor. 2.50e, Modern medical team.

1958, Dec. 18 *Perf. 11½x12*

410 A47 1e blue blk & brown .45 .25
411 A47 1.50e gray, blk & brown 1.40 .50
412 A47 2.50e multicolored 2.25 1.10
Nos. 410-412 (3) 4.10 1.85

75th anniversary of the Maria Pia Hospital, Luanda.

Welwitschia Mirabilis A48

1959, Oct. 1 Litho. *Perf. 14½*
Various Views of Plant and Various Frames

413 A48 1.50e lt brn, grn & blk 1.25 .65
414 A48 2.50e multicolored 1.75 .85
415 A48 5e multicolored 3.50 1.00
416 A48 10e multicolored 5.50 2.10
Nos. 413-416 (4) 12.00 4.60

Centenary of discovery of Welwitschia mirabilis, desert plant.

Map of West Africa, c. 1540, by Jorge Reinel — A49

1960, June 25 *Perf. 13½*

417 A49 2.50e multicolored .55 .25

500th anniv. of the death of Prince Henry the Navigator.

Distributing Medicines A50

1960, Oct. Litho. *Perf. 14½*

418 A50 2.50e multicolored .65 .35

10th anniv. of the Commission for Technical Co-operation in Africa South of the Sahara (C.C.T.A.).

Girl of Angola — A51

Various portraits.

1961, Nov. 30 Unwmk. *Perf. 13*

419 A51 10c multicolored .25 .25
420 A51 15c multicolored .25 .25
421 A51 30c multicolored .25 .25
422 A51 40c multicolored .25 .25
423 A51 60c multicolored .25 .25
424 A51 1.50e multicolored .25 .25
425 A51 2e multicolored 1.10 .25
426 A51 2.50e multicolored 1.10 .25
427 A51 3e multicolored 4.50 .30
428 A51 4e multicolored 2.00 .25
429 A51 5e multicolored 1.50 .30
430 A51 7.50e multicolored 2.00 .90
431 A51 10e multicolored 1.50 .70
432 A51 15e multicolored 2.50 .90
432A A51 25e multicolored 3.00 1.25
432B A51 50e multicolored 5.00 2.75
Nos. 419-432B (16) 25.70 9.35

Sports Issue
Common Design Type

Sports: 50c, Flying. 1e, Rowing. 1.50e, Water polo. 2.50e, Hammer throwing. 4.50e, High jump. 15e, Weight lifting.

1962, Jan. 18 *Perf. 13½*
Multicolored Design

433 CD48 50c lt blue .25 .25
434 CD48 1e olive bister 1.25 .25
435 CD48 1.50e salmon .90 .30
436 CD48 2.50e lt green 1.10 .30
437 CD48 4.50e pale blue 1.00 .60
438 CD48 15e yellow 2.00 1.50
Nos. 433-438 (6) 6.50 3.20

For overprint see No. 608.

Anti-Malaria Issue
Common Design Type

Design: Anopheles funestus.

1962, April Litho. *Perf. 13½*

439 CD49 2.50e multicolored 2.00 .90

Gen. Norton de Matos — A54

1962, Aug. 8 Unwmk. *Perf. 14½*

440 A54 2.50e multicolored .65 .40

50th anniv. of the founding of Nova Lisboa.

Locusts — A56

1963, June 2 Litho. *Perf. 14*

447 A56 2.50e multicolored 2.00 .95

15th anniv. of the Intl. Anti-Locust Organ.

Arms of Luanda A57

Vila de Santo Antonio do Zaire — A58

Coats of Arms (Provinces and Cities): 10c, Massangano. 15c, Sanza-Pombo. 25c, Ambriz. 30c, Muxima. 40c, Ambrizete. 50c, Carmona. 60c, Catete. 70c, Quibaxe. No. 458, Salazar. No. 459, Maquela do Zombo. 1.20e, Bembe. No. 461, Malanje. No. 462, Caxito. 1.80e, Dondo. 2e, Henrique de Carvalho. No. 465, Moçamedes. No. 466, Damba. 3e, Novo Redondo. 3.50e, S. Salvador do Congo. 4e, Cuimba. 5e, Luso. 6.50e, Negage. 7e, Quitexe. 7.50e, S. Filipe de Benguela. 8e, Mucaba. 9e, 31 de Janeiro. 10e, Lobito. 11e, Nova Caipemba. 12.50e, Gabela. 14e, Songo. 15e Sá da Bandeira. 17e, Quimbele. 17.50e, Silva Porto. 20e, Nova Lisboa. 22.50e, Cabinda. 25e, Noqui. 30e, Serpa Pinto. 35e, Santa Cruz. 50e, General Freire.

1963 *Perf. 13½*
Arms in Original Colors; Red and Violet Blue Inscriptions

448 A57 5c tan .25 .25
449 A57 10c lt blue .25 .25
450 A58 15c salmon .25 .25
451 A58 20c olive .25 .25
452 A58 25c lt blue .25 .25
453 A57 30c buff .25 .25

454 A58 40c gray .25 .25
455 A57 50c lt green .25 .25
456 A58 60c brt yellow .25 .25
457 A58 70c dull rose .25 .25
458 A57 1e pale lilac .75 .25
459 A58 1e dull yellow .30 .25
460 A58 1.20e rose .30 .25
461 A57 1.50e pale salmon 1.00 .25
462 A58 1.50e lt green .90 .25
463 A58 1.80e yel olive .90 .65
464 A57 2e lt yel green .75 .25
465 A57 2.50e lt gray 3.50 .30
466 A58 2.50e dull blue 3.00 .25
467 A57 3e yel olive .80 .25
468 A57 3.50e gray 1.10 .25
469 A58 4e citron .70 .30
470 A57 5e citron .80 .30
471 A58 6.50e tan .70 .40
472 A58 7e rose lilac 1.00 .90
473 A57 7.50e pale lilac 1.60 *.95*
474 A58 8e lt aqua 1.00 .80
475 A58 9e yellow 1.60 1.10
476 A57 10e dp salmon 1.50 .80
477 A58 11e dull yel grn 1.75 *5.00*
478 A57 12.50e pale blue 1.60 1.50
479 A58 14e lt gray 1.90 *2.00*
480 A57 15e lt blue 1.60 1.50
481 A58 17e pale blue 2.50 *6.00*
482 A57 17.50e dull yellow 2.50 2.40
483 A57 20e lt aqua 2.50 2.25
484 A57 22.50e gray 2.75 2.75
485 A58 25e citron 2.40 1.75
486 A57 30e yellow 3.25 3.25
487 A58 35e grysh blue 3.75 3.25
488 A58 50e dp yellow 4.75 2.40
Nos. 448-488 (41) 55.95 45.30

Pres. Américo Rodrigues Thomaz — A59

1963, Sept. 16 **Litho.**
489 A59 2.50e multicolored .65 .30

Visit of the President of Portugal.

Airline Anniversary Issue
Common Design Type

1963, Oct. 5 **Unwmk.** ***Perf. 14½***
490 CD50 1e lt blue & multi 1.25 .50

Cathedral of Sá da Bandeira — A61

Malange Cathedral A62

Churches: 20c, Landana. 30c, Luanda Cathedral. 40c, Gabela. 50c, St. Martin's Chapel, Baia dos Tigres. 1.50e, St. Peter, Chibia. 2e, Church of Our Lady, Benguela. 2.50e, Church of Jesus, Luanda. 3e, Camabatela. 3.50e, Mission, Cabinda. 4e, Vila Folgares. 4.50e, Church of Our Lady, Lobito. 5e, Church of Cabinda. 7.50e, Cacuso Church, Malange. 10e, Lubango Mission. 12.50e, Huila Mission. 15e, Church of Our Lady, Luanda Island.

1963, Nov. 1 **Litho.**
Multicolored Design and Inscription

491 A61 10c gray blue .25 .25
492 A61 20c pink .25 .25
493 A61 30c lt blue .25 .25
494 A61 40c tan .25 .25
495 A61 50c lt green .25 .25
496 A62 1e buff .25 .25
497 A61 1.50e lt vio blue .25 .25
498 A62 2e pale rose .35 .25
499 A61 2.50e gray .35 .25
500 A62 3e buff .35 .25
501 A61 3.50e olive .55 .25
502 A62 4e buff .55 .25
503 A62 4.50e pale blue .75 .30
504 A61 5e tan .75 .30
505 A62 7.50e gray 1.00 .55
506 A61 10e dull yellow 1.40 .75
507 A62 12.50e bister 1.60 1.25
508 A62 15e pale gray vio 2.40 1.40
Nos. 491-508 (18) 11.80 7.55

National Overseas Bank Issue
Common Design Type

Design: Antonio Teixeira de Sousa.

1964, May 16 ***Perf. 13½***
509 CD51 2.50e multicolored .90 .30

Commerce Building and Arms of Chamber of Commerce A64

1964, Nov. **Litho.** ***Perf. 12***
510 A64 1e multicolored .45 .25

Luanda Chamber of Commerce centenary.

ITU Issue
Common Design Type

1965, May 17 **Unwmk.** ***Perf. 14½***
511 CD52 2.50e gray & multi 1.25 .65

Plane over Luanda Airport — A65

1965, Dec. 3 **Litho.** ***Perf. 13***
512 A65 2.50e multicolored 1.25 .60

25th anniv. of DTA, Direccao dos Transportes Aereos.

Harquebusier, 1539 — A66

50c, Harquebusier, 1539. 1e, Harquebusier, 1640. 1.50e, Infantry officer, 1777. 2e, Standard bearer, infantry, 1777. 2.50e, Infantry soldier, 1777. 3e, Cavalry officer, 1783. 4e, Cavalry soldier, 1783. 4.50e, Infantry officer, 1807. 5e, Infantry soldier, 1807. 6e, Cavalry officer, 1807. 8e, Cavalry soldier, 1807. 9e, Infantry soldier, 1873.

1966, Feb. 25 **Litho.** ***Perf. 14½***
513 A66 50c multicolored .25 .25
514 A66 1e multicolored .25 .25
515 A66 1.50e multicolored .25 .25
516 A66 2e multicolored .25 .25
517 A66 2.50e multicolored .45 .25
518 A66 3e multicolored .45 .25
519 A66 4e multicolored .70 .25
520 A66 4.50e multicolored .75 .25
521 A66 5e multicolored .80 .30
522 A66 6e multicolored 1.10 .65
523 A66 8e multicolored 1.60 1.40
524 A66 9e multicolored 1.90 1.60
Nos. 513-524 (12) 8.75 5.95

National Revolution Issue
Common Design Type

Design: St. Paul's Hospital and Commercial and Industrial School.

1966, May 28 **Litho.** ***Perf. 12***
525 CD53 1e multicolored .45 .25

Emblem of Holy Ghost Society — A68

1966 **Litho.** ***Perf. 13***
526 A68 1e blue & multi .45 .25

Centenary of the Holy Ghost Society.

Navy Club Issue
Common Design Type

Designs: 1e, Mendes Barata and cruiser Dom Carlos I. 2.50e, Capt. Augusto de Castilho and corvette Mindelo.

1967, Jan. 31 **Litho.** ***Perf. 13***
527 CD54 1e multicolored 1.00 .25
528 CD54 2.50e multicolored 1.25 .75

Fatima Basilica — A70

1967, May 13 **Litho.** ***Perf. 12½x13***
529 A70 50c multicolored .45 .25

50th anniv. of the apparition of the Virgin Mary to 3 shepherd children at Fatima.

Angola Map, Manuel Cerveira Pereira — A71

1967, Aug. 15 **Litho.** ***Perf. 12½x13***
530 A71 50c multicolored .45 .25

350th anniv. of the founding of Benguela.

Administration Building, Carmona — A72

1967 **Litho.** ***Perf. 12***
531 A72 1e multicolored .25 .25

50th anniv. of the founding of Carmona.

Military Order of Valor — A73

50c, Ribbon of the Three Orders. 1.50e, Military Order of Avis. 2e, Military Order of Christ. 2.50e, Military Order of St. John of Espada. 3e, Order of the Empire. 4e, Order of Prince Henry. 5e, Order of Benemerencia. 10e, Order of Public Instruction. 20e, Order for Industrial & Agricultural Merit.

1967, Oct. 31 ***Perf. 14***
532 A73 50c lt gray & multi .25 .25
533 A73 1e lt green & multi .25 .25
534 A73 1.50e yellow & multi .25 .25
535 A73 2e multicolored .25 .25
536 A73 2.50e multicolored .35 .25
537 A73 3e lt olive & multi .25 .25
538 A73 4e gray & multi .45 .25
539 A73 5e multicolored .70 .25
540 A73 10e lilac & multi 1.10 .55
541 A73 20e lt blue & multi 2.50 1.40
Nos. 532-541 (10) 6.35 3.95

Our Lady of Hope — A74

1e, Belmonte Castle, horiz. 1.50e, St. Jerome's Convent. 2.50e, Cabral's Armada.

1968, Apr. 22 **Litho.** ***Perf. 14***
542 A74 50c yellow & multi .25 .25
543 A74 1e gray & multi .50 .25
544 A74 1.50e lt blue & multi .70 .25
545 A74 2.50e buff & multi 1.10 .35
Nos. 542-545 (4) 2.55 1.10

500th anniv. of the birth of Pedro Alvares Cabral, navigator who took possession of Brazil for Portugal.

Francisco Inocencio de Souza Coutinho — A75

1969, Jan. 7 **Litho.** ***Perf. 14***
546 A75 2e multicolored .45 .25

Founding of Novo Redondo, 200th anniv.

Admiral Coutinho Issue
Common Design Type

Design: Adm. Gago Coutinho and his first ship.

1969, Feb. 17 **Litho.** ***Perf. 14***
547 CD55 2.50e multicolored 1.00 .35

Compass Rose — A77

1969, Aug. 29 **Litho.** ***Perf. 14***
548 A77 1e multicolored .45 .25

500th anniv. of the birth of Vasco da Gama (1469-1524), navigator.

Administration Reform Issue
Common Design Type

1969, Sept. 25 **Litho.** ***Perf. 14***
549 CD56 1.50e multicolored .25 .25

Portal of St. Jeronimo's Monastery — A79

1969, Dec. 1 **Litho.** ***Perf. 14***
550 A79 3e multicolored .45 .25

500th anniv. of the birth of King Manuel I.

Angolasaurus Bocagei — A80

Fossils and Minerals: 1e, Ferrometeorite. 1.50e, Dioptase crystals. 2e, Gondwanidium. 2.50e, Diamonds. 3e, Estromatolite. 3.50e, Procarcharodon megalodon. 4e, Microceratodus angolensis. 4.50e, Moscovite. 5e, Barite. 6e, Nostoceras. 10e, Rotula orbiculus angolensis.

1970, Oct. 31 **Litho.** ***Perf. 13***
551 A80 50c tan & multi .50 .25
552 A80 1e multicolored .50 .25
553 A80 1.50e multicolored .75 .40
554 A80 2e multicolored .75 .40
555 A80 2.50e lt gray & multi .75 .40
556 A80 3e multicolored .75 .40

557 A80 3.50e blue & multi 1.00 .65
558 A80 4e lt gray & multi 1.00 .65
559 A80 4.50e gray & multi 1.25 .65
560 A80 5e gray & multi 1.25 .65
561 A80 6e pink & multi 2.00 .85
562 A80 10e lt blue & multi 4.00 1.00
Nos. 551-562 (12) 14.50 6.55

Marshal Carmona Issue
Common Design Type

1970, Nov. 15 ***Perf. 14***
563 CD57 2.50e multicolored .45 .25

Arms of Malanje, Cotton Boll and Field — A82

1970, Nov. 20 ***Perf. 13***
564 A82 2.50e multicolored .55 .35

Centenary of the municipality of Malanje.

Mail Ships and Angola No. 1 A83

4.50e, Steam locomotive and Angola No. 4.

1970, Dec. 1 ***Perf. 13½***
565 A83 1.50e multicolored .50 .30
566 A83 4.50e multicolored 2.75 .75

Cent. of stamps of Angola. See No. C36. For overprint see No. 616B.

Map of Africa, Diagram of Seismic Tests — A84

1971, Aug. 22 **Litho.** ***Perf. 13***
567 A84 2.50e multicolored .45 .25

5th Regional Conference of Soil and Foundation Engineers, Luanda, Aug. 22-Sept. 5.

Galleon on Congo River — A85

1972, May 25 **Litho.** ***Perf. 13***
568 A85 1e emerald & multi .65 .25

4th centenary of the publication of The Lusiads by Luiz Camoens.

Olympic Games Issue
Common Design Type

1972, June 20 ***Perf. 14x13½***
569 CD59 50c multicolored .65 .25

Lisbon-Rio de Janeiro Flight Issue
Common Design Type

1972, Sept. 20 **Litho.** ***Perf. 13½***
570 CD60 1e multicolored .35 .25

WMO Centenary Issue
Common Design Type

1973, Dec. 15 **Litho.** ***Perf. 13***
571 CD61 1e dk gray & multi .45 .25

Radar Station A89

1974, June 25 **Litho.** ***Perf. 13***
572 A89 2e multicolored .45 .25

Establishment of satellite communications network via Intelsat among Portugal, Angola and Mozambique.
For overprint see No. 616A.

Harpa Doris — A90

Designs: Sea shells.

1974, Oct. 25 **Litho.** ***Perf. 12x12½***
573 A90 25c shown .25 .25
574 A90 30c Murex melanamathos .25 .25
575 A90 50c Venus foliaceo lamellosa .30 .25
576 A90 70c Lathyrus filosus .35 .25
577 A90 1e Cymbium cisium .35 .25
578 A90 1.50e Cassis tesselata .40 .25
579 A90 2e Cypraea stercoraria .40 .25
580 A90 2.50e Conus prometheus .45 .25
581 A90 3e Strombus latus .65 .25
582 A90 3.50e Tympanotonus fuscatus .65 .45
583 A90 4e Cardium costatum .65 .45
584 A90 5e Natica fulminea .75 .45
585 A90 6e Lyropecten nodosus 1.25 .45
586 A90 7e Tonna galea 1.25 .45
587 A90 10e Donax rugosus 1.00 .45
588 A90 25e Cymatium trigonum 2.25 .90
589 A90 30e Olivancilaria acuminata 2.50 .90
590 A90 35e Semifusus morio 3.00 .90
591 A90 40e Clavatula lineata 3.50 1.10
592 A90 50e Solarium granulatum 5.00 1.75
Nos. 573-592 (20) 25.20 10.50

For overprints see Nos. 605-607, 617-630.

No. 386 Overprinted in Blue

1974, Dec. 21 **Litho.** ***Perf. 13½***
593 A41 5c multicolored .25 .25

Youth philately.

Republic

Star and Hand Holding Rifle — A91

1975, Nov. 11 **Litho.** ***Perf. 13x13½***
594 A91 1.50e red & multi .50 .25

Independence in 1975.

Diquiche Mask — A92

Design: 3e, Bui ou Congolo mask.

1976, Feb. 6 ***Perf. 13½***
595 A92 50c lt blue & multi .25 .25
596 A92 3e multicolored .55 .25

Workers — A93

1976, May 1 **Litho.** ***Perf. 12***
597 A93 1e red & multi .35 .25

International Workers' Day.

No. 392 Overprinted

1976, June 15 **Litho.** ***Perf. 13½***
598 A41 10e multicolored 1.10 .75

Stamp Day.

President Agostinho Neto — A94

1976, Nov. 11 **Litho.** ***Perf. 13***
599 A94 50c yel & dk brown .25 .25
600 A94 2e lt gray & plum .25 .25
601 A94 3e gray & indigo .40 .25
602 A94 5e buff & brown .40 .25
603 A94 10e tan & sepia .55 .25
a. Souv. sheet of 1, imperf. 5.00 5.00
Nos. 599-603 (5) 1.85 1.25

First anniversary of independence.

Nos. 393, 588-589, 592 Overprinted

1977, Feb. 9 ***Perf. 13½, 12x12½***
604 A41 20e multicolored 3.25 .30
605 A90 25e multicolored 3.75 .45
606 A90 30e multicolored 3.50 .65
607 A90 50e multicolored 7.00 .95
Nos. 604-607 (4) 17.50 2.35

Overprint in 3 lines on No. 604, in 2 lines on others.

No. 438 Overprinted

1976, Dec. 31 ***Perf. 13½***
608 CD48 15e multicolored 2.00 .65

Child and WHO Emblem — A95

1977 **Litho.** ***Perf. 10½***
609 A95 2.50k blk & lt blue .65 .25

Campaign for vaccination against poliomyelitis.

Map of Africa, Flag of Angola — A96

1977 **Photo.**
610 A96 6k blk, red & blue .60 .35

First Congress of Popular Movement for the Liberation of Angola.

Anti-Apartheid Emblem — A97

1979, June 20 **Litho.** ***Perf. 13½***
611 A97 1k multicolored .25 .25

Anti-Apartheid Year.

Human Rights Emblem — A98

1979, June 15 **Litho.** ***Perf. 13½***
612 A98 2.50k multicolored .35 .25

Declaration of Human Rights, 30th anniv. (in 1975).

Child Flowers, Globe, IYC Emblem — A99

1980, May 1 **Litho.** ***Perf. 14x14½***
613 A99 3.50k multicolored .45 .25

International Year of the Child (1979).

Running, Moscow '80 Emblem — A100

1980, Dec. 15 Litho. *Perf. 13½*

614 A100 9k shown .70 .25
615 A100 12k Swimming, horiz. .80 .25

22nd Summer Olympic Games, Moscow, July 19-Aug. 3.

5th Anniv. of Independence A101

1980, Nov. 11

616 A101 5.50k multicolored .45 .25

Nos. 572, 566 Overprinted

1980-81 Litho. *Perf. 13½x13*

616A A89 2e multi (bar only) 1.25 .25
616B A83 4.50e multicolored 2.75 1.50

Issued: 2e, 5/17/81; 4.50e, 6/15/80.
See No. C37.

Nos. 577-580, 582-591 Overprinted

1981, June 15 Litho. *Perf. 12x12½*

617 A90 1e multicolored .25 .25
618 A90 1.50e multicolored .25 .25
619 A90 2e multicolored .25 .25
620 A90 2.50e multicolored .25 .25
621 A90 3.50e multicolored .25 .25
622 A90 4e multicolored .40 .30
623 A90 5e multicolored .50 .30
624 A90 6e multicolored .70 .35
625 A90 7e multicolored .90 .45
626 A90 10e multicolored 1.10 .50
627 A90 25e multicolored 2.50 .75
628 A90 30e multicolored 3.00 1.00
629 A90 35e multicolored 4.00 1.25
630 A90 40e multicolored 5.00 1.75
Nos. 617-630 (14) 12.50 6.50

Man Walking with Canes, Tchibinda Ilunga Statue — A102

1981, Sept. 5 Litho. *Perf. 13½*

631 A102 9k multicolored .75 .30

Turipex '81 tourism exhibition.

M.P.L.A. Workers' Party Congress A103

1980, Dec. 23 Litho. *Perf. 14*

632 A103 50 l Millet .25 .25
633 A103 5k Coffee .35 .25
634 A103 7.50k Sunflowers .45 .25
635 A103 13.50k Cotton .75 .35
636 A103 14k Oil .90 .40
637 A103 16k Diamonds 1.10 .50
Nos. 632-637 (6) 3.80 2.00

People's Power — A104

1980, Nov. 11

638 A104 40k lt blue & blk 2.10 .75

Natl. Heroes' Day — A105

1980, Sept. 17 *Perf. 14x13½*

639 A105 4.50k Former Pres. Neto .25 .25
640 A105 50k Neto, diff. 3.50 1.00

Soweto Uprising, 5th Anniv. A106

1981

641 A106 4.50k multicolored .45 .25

2nd Central African Games A107

1981, Sept. 3 Litho. *Perf. 13½*

642 A107 50 l Bicycling, tennis .80 .25
643 A107 5k Judo, boxing .80 .25
644 A107 6k Basketball, volleyball 1.00 .25
645 A107 10k Handball, soccer 1.40 .35
Nos. 642-645 (4) 4.00 1.10

Souvenir Sheet

Imperf

646 A107 15k multicolored *5.00 5.00*

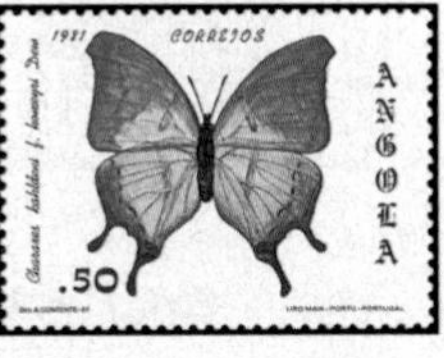

Charaxes Kahldeni A108

1982, Feb. 26 Litho. *Perf. 13½*

647 A108 50 l shown .65 .25
648 A108 1k Abantis zambesiaca .65 .25
649 A108 5k Catacroptera cloanthe .65 .25
650 A108 9k Myrina ficedula, vert. 1.25 .25
651 A108 10k Colotis danae 1.40 .25
652 A108 15k Acraea acrita 2.00 .35
653 A108 100k Precis hierta 10.00 3.00
a. Souvenir sheet 16.00 9.00
Nos. 647-653 (7) 16.60 4.60

No. 653a contains Nos. 647-653, imperf., and sold for 30k (stamps probably not valid individually).

5th Anniv. of UN Membership — A109

5.50k, The Silence of the Night, by Museque Catambor. 7.50k, Cotton picking, Catete.

1982, Sept. 22 Litho.

654 A109 5.50k multicolored .50 .25
655 A109 7.50k multicolored .60 .25

20th Anniv. of Engineering Laboratory A110

1982, Dec. 21 Litho. *Perf. 14*

656 A110 9k Lab .65 .35
657 A110 13k Worker, vert. .85 .45
658 A110 100k Equipment, vert. 8.00 3.00
Nos. 656-658 (3) 9.50 3.80

Local Flowers — A111

1983, Feb. 18 *Perf. 13½*

659 A111 5k Dichrostachys glomerata .40 .25
660 A111 12k Amblygonocarpus obtusangulus .90 .35
661 A111 50k Albizzia versicolor 4.50 1.40
Nos. 659-661 (3) 5.80 2.00

Women's Org., First Congress A112

1983 Litho. *Perf. 13½*

662 A112 20k multicolored 1.25 .50

Africa Day — A113

1983, June 30 *Perf. 13*

663 A113 6.5k multi .65 .35

World Communications Year — A114

1983, June 30 Litho. *Perf. 13½*

664 A114 6.5k M'pungi .75 .35
665 A114 12k Mondu 1.25 .55

BRASILIANA '83 Stamp Exhibition, Rio de Janeiro, July 29-Aug. 7 — A115

Crop-eating insects.

1983, July 29 Litho. *Perf. 13*

666 A115 4.5k Antestiopsis lineaticollis .70 .25
667 A115 6.5k Stephanoderes hampei ferr. 1.00 .45
668 A115 10k Zonocerus variegatus 1.50 .70
Nos. 666-668 (3) 3.20 1.40

25th Anniv. of Economic Commission for Africa — A116

1983, Aug. 2

669 A116 10k Map, emblem .80 .50

185th Anniv. of Post Office A117

1983, Dec. 7 Litho. *Perf. 13½*

670 A117 50 l Mail collection, vert. .25 .25
671 A117 3.5k Unloading mail plane .35 .25
672 A117 5k Sorting mail .60 .45
673 A117 15k Mailing letter, vert. 1.75 .90
674 A117 30k Post office box delivery 3.25 1.60
a. Min. sheet of 3, #671-672, 674 10.50 10.50
Nos. 670-674 (5) 6.20 3.45

No. 674a sold for 100k.

Local Butterflies A118

1984, Jan. 20 Litho. *Perf. 13½*

675 A118 50 l Parasa karschi .25 .25
676 A118 1k Diaphone angolensis .25 .25
677 A118 3.5k Choeropasis jucunda .65 .25
678 A118 6.5k Hespagarista rendalli .95 .35
679 A118 15k Euchromia guineensis 1.75 .90
680 A118 17.5k Mazuca roseistriga 2.50 1.00
681 A118 20k Utetheisa callima 3.75 1.25
Nos. 675-681 (7) 10.10 4.25

A119

1984, Apr. 11 Litho. *Perf. 13½*

682 A119 30k multicolored 3.00 1.75

First Natl. Worker's Union Congress, Apr. 11-16 .

A120

Local birds.

1984, Oct. 24 Litho. *Perf. 13½*

683 A120 10.50k Bucorvus leadbeateri .85 .50
684 A120 14k Gypohierax angolensis 1.25 .75
685 A120 16k Ardea goliath 1.60 .75
686 A120 19.50k Pelecanus onocrotalus 2.25 1.10
687 A120 22k Platalea alba 2.75 1.25
688 A120 26k Balearica pavonnia 4.50 1.50
Nos. 683-688 (6) 13.20 5.85

Local Animals A121

1984, Nov. 12

689 A121 1k Tragelaphus strepsiceros .50 .40
690 A121 4k Antidorcas marsupialis angolensis .90 .45
691 A121 5k Pan troglodytes 1.00 .55
692 A121 10k Syncerus caffer 2.00 1.10
693 A121 15k Hippotragus niger variani 2.75 1.25
694 A121 20k Orycteropus afer 3.00 1.75
695 A121 25k Crocuta crocuta 4.00 2.00
Nos. 689-695 (7) 14.15 7.50

Angolese Monuments A122

1985, Feb. 21 Litho. *Perf. 13½*

696 A122 5k San Pedro da Barra .55 .35
697 A122 12.5k Nova Oeiras 1.10 .60
698 A122 18k M'Banza Kongo 1.75 .90
699 A122 26k Massangano 2.50 1.25
700 A122 39k Escravatura Museum 3.75 1.90
Nos. 696-700 (5) 9.65 5.00

United Workers' Party, 25th Anniv. A123

1985, May Litho. *Perf. 12*

701 A123 77k XXV, red flags 10.00 4.50

Printed in sheets of 5.

A124

1985, May

702 A124 1k Flags .65 .65
703 A124 11k Oil drilling platform, Cabinda .80 .80
704 A124 57k Conference 3.50 3.50
a. Strip of 3, #702-704 7.25 7.25

Southern African Development Council, 5th anniv.

Medicinal plants — A125

No. 705, Lonchocarpus sericeus. No. 706, Gossypium. No. 707, Cassia occidentalis. No. 708, Gloriosa superba. No. 709, Cochlospermum angolensis.

Lithographed and Typographed

1985, July 5 *Perf. 11*

705 A125 1k multi .25 .25
706 A125 4k multi .40 .35
707 A125 11k multi 1.00 .55
708 A125 25.50k multi 2.00 1.00
709 A125 55k multi 5.00 2.50
Nos. 705-709 (5) 8.65 4.65

ARGENTINA '85 exhibition.

5th Natl. Heroes Day A126

Natl. flag and: 10.50k, Portrait of Agostinho Neto, party leader. 36.50k, Neto working.

1985 Litho. *Perf. 13½*

710 A126 10.50k multicolored 13.50 7.50
711 A126 36.50k multicolored 20.00 10.00

Ministerial Conference of Non-Aligned Countries, Luanda — A127

1985, Sept. 4 Photo. *Perf. 11*

712 A127 35k multicolored 3.50 1.75

UN, 40th Anniv. A128

1985, Oct. 29 Litho. *Perf. 11*

713 A128 12.50k multicolored 1.75 .95

Industry and Natural Resources — A129

1985, Nov. 11

714 A129 50 l Cement Factory .40 .25
715 A129 5k Logging .50 .35
716 A129 7k Quartz .60 .45
717 A129 10k Iron mine .90 .50
a. Souvenir sheet of 4, #714-717, imperf. 4.75 4.75
Nos. 714-717 (4) 2.40 1.55

Natl. independence, 10th anniv.

2nd Natl. Workers' Party Congress (MPLA) — A130

1985, Nov. 28 *Perf. 13½*

718 A130 20k multicolored 1.75 1.00

Demostenes de Almeida Clington Races, 30th Anniv. — A131

Various runners.

1985, Dec. 13

719 A131 50 l multicolored .50 .25
720 A131 5k multicolored .60 .35
721 A131 6.50k multicolored .70 .45
722 A131 10k multicolored .80 .50
Nos. 719-722 (4) 2.60 1.55

1986 World Cup Soccer Championships, Mexico — A132

Map, soccer field and various plays.

1986, May 6 Litho. *Perf. 11½x11*

723 A132 50 l multi .25 .25
724 A132 3.50k multi .50 .35
725 A132 5k multi .90 .45
726 A132 7k multi 1.00 .50
727 A132 10k multi 1.75 .90
728 A132 18k multi 3.00 1.60
Nos. 723-728 (6) 7.40 4.05

Struggle Against Portugal, 25th Anniv. A133

1986, May 6 *Perf. 11x11½*

729 A133 15k multicolored 1.90 .75

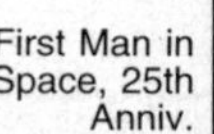

First Man in Space, 25th Anniv. A134

1986, Aug. 21 Litho. *Perf. 11x11½*

730 A134 50 l Skylab, US .25 .25
731 A134 1k Spacecraft .25 .25
732 A134 5k A. Leonov space-walking .55 .35
733 A134 10k Lunokhod on Moon 1.00 .55
734 A134 13k Apollo-Soyuz link-up 1.25 .70
Nos. 730-734 (5) 3.30 2.10

Admission of Angola to UN, 10th Anniv. A135

1986, Dec. 1 Litho. *Perf. 11x11½*

735 A135 22k multi 2.00 1.25

Liberation Movement, 30th Anniv. — A136

Angolese at work, fighting and: No. 736a, "1956." No. 736b, Congress emblem, "1980." No. 736c, Labor Party emblem, "1985."

1986, Dec. 3 *Perf. 11½x11*

736 A136 Strip of 3 2.00 2.00
a.-c. 5k any single .45 .30

Agostinho Neto University, 10th Anniv. A137

1986, Dec. 30 Litho. *Perf. 11x11½*

737 A137 50 l Mathematics .25 .25
738 A137 1k Law .65 .35
739 A137 10k Medicine 1.00 .60
Nos. 737-739 (3) 1.90 1.20

Tribal Hairstyles — A138

1987, Apr. 15 Litho. *Perf. 11½x11*

740 A138 1k Ouioca .30 .25
741 A138 1.50k Luanda .40 .30
742 A138 5k Humbe .80 .40
743 A138 7k Muila 1.00 .45
744 A138 20k Muila, diff. 2.75 1.75
745 A138 30k Dilolo 5.25 2.75
Nos. 740-745 (6) 10.50 5.90

Landscapes A139

Perf. 11½x12, 12x11½

1987, July 7 **Litho.**

746 A139 50 l Pambala Shore .25 .25
747 A139 1.50k Dala Waterfalls .25 .25
748 A139 3.50k Black Stones .25 .25
749 A139 5k Cuango River .50 .35
750 A139 10k Luanda coast 1.40 .75
751 A139 20k Hills of Leba 2.50 1.00
Nos. 746-751 (6) 5.15 2.85

Nos. 746-747, 749 and 751 horiz.

Lenin — A140

1987, Nov. 25 ***Perf. 12x12½***

752 A140 15k multi 1.60 .90

October Revolution, Russia, 70th anniv.

2nd Congress of the Organization of Angolan Women (OMA) — A141

1988, May 30 **Litho.** ***Perf. 13x13½***

753 A141 2k shown .40 .25
754 A141 10k Soldier, nurse, technician, student .80 .45

Victory Carnival, 10th Anniv. A142

Various carnival scenes.

1988, June 15 **Litho.** ***Perf. 13½x13***

755 A142 5k shown .60 .35
756 A142 10k multi, diff. .95 .45

Augusto N'Gangula (1956-1968), Youth Pioneer Killed by Portuguese Colonial Army — A143

Agostinho Neto Pioneers' Organization (OPA), 25th Anniv. — A144

1989, Oct. 2 **Litho.** ***Perf. 12x11½***

757 A143 12k multicolored 1.50 .90
758 A144 15k multicolored 1.75 1.00

Pioneer Day.

10th Natl. Soccer Championships, Benguela, May 1 — A145

1989, Oct. 16

759 A145 5k shown .75 .50
760 A145 5k Luanda, 3 years .75 .50
761 A145 5k Luanda, 5 years .75 .50
Nos. 759-761 (3) 2.25 1.50

Intl. Fund for Agricultural Development, 10th Anniv. — A146

1990, Feb. 15 **Litho.** ***Perf. 11½x12***

762 A146 10k multicolored 1.40 .90

Ingombotas' Houses — A147

Architecture: 2k, Alta Train Station. 5k, National Museum of Anthropology. 15k, Ana Joaquina Palace. 23k, Iron Palace. 36k, Meteorological observatory, vert. 50k, People's Palace.

1990, Feb. 20 ***Perf. 12x11½, 11½x12***

763 A147 1k shown .35 .35
764 A147 2k multicolored .35 .35
765 A147 5k multicolored .60 .60
766 A147 15k multicolored 1.25 1.25
767 A147 23k multicolored 2.00 2.00
768 A147 36k multicolored 3.00 3.00
769 A147 50k multicolored 4.75 4.75
Nos. 763-769 (7) 12.30 12.30

Luanda and Benguela Railways A148

Various maps and locomotives.

1990, Mar. 1 ***Perf. 12x11½***

770 A148 5k shown .70 .70
771 A148 12k Garrat T (left) 1.60 1.60
772 A148 12k Garrat T (right) 1.60 1.60
a. Pair, #771-772 4.00 4.00
773 A148 14k Mikado 2.10 2.10
Nos. 770-773 (4) 6.00 6.00

Souvenir Sheet

774 A148 25k Diesel electric 4.00 4.00

No. 772a has a continuous design.

Southern Africa Development Coordinating Conf. (SADCC), 10th Anniv. — A149

1990, Apr. 1 **Litho.** ***Perf. 14***

775 A149 5k shown .55 .55
776 A149 9k Floating oil rig 1.00 1.00

Pan-African Postal Union (PAPU), 10th Anniv. A150

1990, Apr. 6

777 A150 4k shown .75 .75
778 A150 10k Simulated stamp, map 1.25 1.25

Paintings by Raul Indipwo A151

1990, Apr. 24

779 A151 6k *Tres Gracas* .90 .90
780 A151 9k *Muxima*, vert. 1.10 1.10

Stamp World London 90.

Hippotragus Niger Variani, Adult Male and Female — A152

1990, May 9 ***Perf. 14x13½***

781 A152 5k Adult male 2.50 2.50
782 A152 5k shown 2.50 2.50
783 A152 5k Adult female 2.50 2.50
784 A152 5k Female, calf 2.50 2.50
Nos. 781-784 (4) 10.00 10.00

World Wildlife Fund. Various combinations available in blocks or strips of four.

Rosa de Porcelana A153

1990, June 2 **Litho.** ***Perf. 14***

785 A153 5k shown .60 .60
786 A153 8k Cravo burro .95 .95
787 A153 10k Alamandra 1.25 1.25
Nos. 785-787 (3) 2.80 2.80

Souvenir Sheet

788 A153 40k Hibiscus 6.00 6.00

Belgica '90.

Miniature Sheet

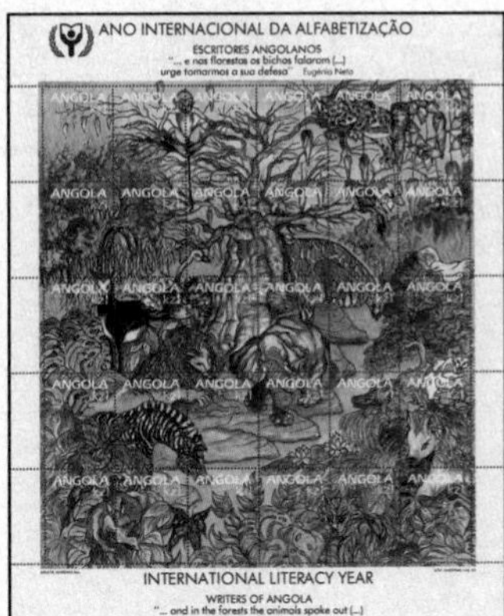

Intl. Literacy Year — A154

Various animals and forest scenes.

1990, July 26 **Litho.** ***Perf. 14***

789 A154 Sheet of 30 8.50 8.50
a.-ad. 1k any single .30 .30
790 A154 5k Zebra 1.00 1.00
791 A154 5k Butterfly 1.00 1.00
792 A154 5k Horse 1.00 1.00
a. Block of 3, #790-792 + label 4.00 4.00

People's Assembly, 10th Anniv. A155

1990, Nov. 11 ***Perf. 14***

793 A155 10k multicolored .90 .90

3rd Natl. Labor Congress A156

1990 **Litho.** ***Perf. 13½***

794 A156 14k multicolored 1.25 1.25

War of Independence, 30th Anniv. — A157

Uniforms.

1991, Feb. 28 **Litho.** ***Perf. 14***

795 A157 6k Machete, 1961 .85 .85
a. Perf. 13½ vert. 1.40 1.40
796 A157 6k Rifle, 1962-63 .85 .85
a. Perf. 13½ vert. 1.40 1.40
797 A157 6k Rifle, 1968 .85 .85
a. Perf. 13½ vert. 1.40 1.40
798 A157 6k Automatic rifle, 1972 .85 .85
a. Perf. 13½ vert. 1.40 1.40
b. Bklt. pane of 4, #795a-798a 7.00
Nos. 795-798 (4) 3.40 3.40

Musical Instruments A158

Designs: a, Marimba. b, Mucupela. c, Ngoma la Txina. d, Kissange.

1991, Apr. 5 **Litho.** ***Perf. 14***

799 A158 6k Block or strip of 4, #799a-799d 3.00 3.00

Tourism A159

Designs: 3k, Iona National Park. 7k, Kalandula Waterfalls. 35k, Lobito Bay. 60k, Weltwitschia Mirabilis plant.

1991, June 25 **Litho.** ***Perf. 14***

800 A159 3k multi .40 .40
801 A159 7k multi .55 .55
802 A159 35k multi 2.40 2.40
803 A159 60k multi 4.00 4.00
Nos. 800-803 (4) 7.35 7.35

Souvenir Sheet

Design: 30k, Map details.

1991, June 25 Litho. ***Perf. 13¼***
803A A159 30k multi *6.50 6.50*

Dogs A160

1991, July 5 Litho. ***Perf. 14***
804 A160 5k Kabir of dembos .65 .65
805 A160 7k Ombua .75 .75
806 A160 11k Kabir massongo 1.00 1.00
807 A160 12k Kawa tchowe 1.00 1.00
Nos. 804-807 (4) 3.40 3.40

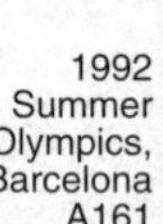

1992 Summer Olympics, Barcelona A161

1991, July 26 ***Perf. 13***
808 A161 4k Judo .25 .25
809 A161 6k Sailing .25 .25
810 A161 10k Running .45 .45
811 A161 100k Swimming 4.00 4.00
Nos. 808-811 (4) 4.95 4.95

Navigation Aids A162

1991, Nov. 8 Litho. ***Perf. 12***
812 A162 5k Quadrant .25 .25
813 A162 15k Astrolabe .70 .70
814 A162 20k Cross-staff .95 .95
815 A162 50k Portolano 2.40 2.40
Nos. 812-815 (4) 4.30 4.30

Iberex '91.

Rays A163

1992, Mar. 30 Litho. ***Perf. 14***
816 A163 40k Myliobatis aquila 1.10 1.10
817 A163 50k Aetobatus narinari 1.10 1.10
818 A163 66k Manta birostris 1.50 1.50
819 A163 80k Raja miraletus 2.10 2.10
Nos. 816-819 (4) 5.80 5.80

Souvenir Sheet

Perf. 13½
820 A163 25k Manta birostris, diff. 6.50 6.50

A164

Quioca masks.

1992, Apr. 30 Litho. ***Perf. 13½***
821 A164 60k Kalelwa .25 .25
822 A164 100k Mukixe Wa Kino .65 .60
823 A164 150k Cikunza .90 .80
824 A164 250k Mukixi Wa Mbwesu 1.75 1.50
Nos. 821-824 (4) 3.55 3.15

See Nos. 854-857, 868-871, 883-886, 895-898.

A165

Medicinal Plants: 200k, Ptaeroxylon obliquum. 300k, Spondias mombin. 500k, Parinari curatellifolia. 600k, Cochlospermum angolense.

1992, May 8 ***Perf. 14***
825 A165 200k brown & pale yel .95 .95
826 A165 300k brown & pale yel 1.40 1.40
827 A165 500k brown & pale yel 2.40 2.40
828 A165 600k brown & pale yel 2.75 2.75
a. Block or strip of 4, #825-828 8.25 8.25

Evangelization of Angola, 500th Anniv. — A166

1992, May 10 ***Perf. 13½***
829 A166 150k King, missionaries .75 .75
830 A166 420k Ruins of M'banza Congo 2.10 2.10
831 A166 470k Maxima Church 2.40 2.40
832 A166 500k Faces of people 2.50 2.50
Nos. 829-832 (4) 7.75 7.75

Traditional Houses — A167

Perf. 14, 13½ Vert. (#832A)

1992, May 22
832A A167 150k Dimbas 1.50 1.50
b. Bklt. pane of 4, #832A, 833a-835a 9.00
833 A167 330k Cokwe 1.60 1.60
a. Perf. 13½ vert. 1.75 1.75
834 A167 360k Mbali 1.90 1.90
a. Perf. 13½ vert. 1.90 1.90
835 A167 420k Ambwelas 2.25 2.25
a. Perf. 13½ vert. 2.10 2.10
836 A167 500k Upper Zambezi 4.00 4.00
Nos. 832A-836 (5) 11.25 11.25

Expo '92, Seville.

Agapornis Roseicollis A168

1992, June 2 ***Perf. 12x11½***
837 A168 150k Two birds on branch 1.25 1.25
838 A168 200k Birds feeding 1.75 1.75
839 A168 250k Hand holding bird 2.25 2.25
840 A168 300k Bird on perch 2.75 2.75
a. Strip of 4, #837-840 8.75 8.75

Expo '92, Seville.

Souvenir Sheet

Visit of Pope John Paul II to Angola — A169

Abstract paintings: a, 340k, The Crucifixion. b, 370k, The Resurrection.

1992, June 4 Litho. ***Perf. 13½***
841 A169 Sheet of 2, #a.-b. + 2 labels 6.00 6.00

1992 Summer Olympics, Barcelona A170

1992, July 30 ***Perf. 14***
842 A170 120k Hurdles .65 .65
843 A170 180k Cycling 1.10 1.10
844 A170 240k Roller hockey 1.25 1.25
845 A170 360k Basketball 2.10 2.10
Nos. 842-845 (4) 5.10 5.10

Native Fishing — A171

1992, Aug. 5 ***Perf. 11½x12***
846 A171 65k Building traps .65 .65
847 A171 90k Using nets .90 .90
848 A171 100k Laying traps 1.00 1.00
849 A171 120k Fisherman in boats 1.25 1.25
Nos. 846-849 (4) 3.80 3.80

Souvenir Sheet

Discovery of America, 500th Anniv. — A172

1992, Sept. 18 Litho. ***Perf. 12***
850 A172 500k multicolored 5.50 5.50

Genoa '92.

First Free Elections in Angola — A173

Designs: 120k, People voting. 150k, Map, ballot box, peace doves. 200k, People, dove, hand dropping ballot into ballot box.

1992, Oct. 27 Litho. ***Perf. 11½x12***
851 A173 120k multicolored .50 .50
852 A173 150k multicolored .65 .65
853 A173 200k multicolored .90 .90
Nos. 851-853 (3) 2.05 2.05

Quioca Mask Type of 1992

1992, Nov. 6 ***Perf. 13½***
854 A164 72k Cihongo .35 .35
855 A164 80k Mbwasu .40 .40
856 A164 120k Cinhanga .50 .50
857 A164 210k Kalewa .95 .95
Nos. 854-857 (4) 2.20 2.20

Inauguration of Express Mail Service — A174

1992, Dec. 14 Litho. ***Perf. 12x11½***
858 A174 450k Truck 2.10 2.10
859 A174 550k Airplane 2.25 2.25

Meteorological Instruments A175

1993, Mar. 23 Litho. ***Perf. 11½x12***
860 A175 250k Weather balloon 1.40 1.40
861 A175 470k Actinometer 2.40 2.40
862 A175 500k Rain gauge 2.75 2.75
Nos. 860-862 (3) 6.55 6.55

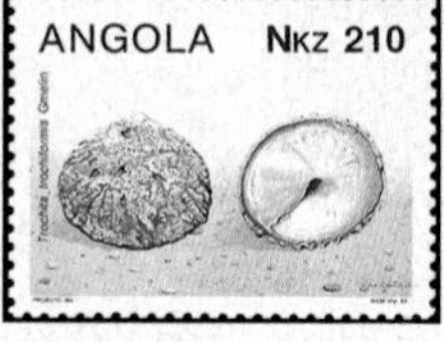

Seashells A176

1993, Apr. 6 ***Perf. 12x11½***
863 A176 210k Trochita trochiformis .75 .75
864 A176 330k Strombus latus 1.10 1.10
865 A176 400k Aporrhais pesgallinae 1.50 1.50
866 A176 500k Fusos aff. albinus 1.75 1.75
Nos. 863-866 (4) 5.10 5.10

Souvenir Sheet

867 A176 1000k Pusionella nifat 5.00 5.00

Quioca Art Type of 1992

1993, June 7 Litho. ***Perf. 12***
868 A164 72k Men with vehicles .40 .40
869 A164 210k Cavalier .95 .95
870 A164 420k Airplane 1.90 1.90
871 A164 600k Men carrying stretcher 2.50 2.50
Nos. 868-871 (4) 5.75 5.75

Flowering Plants — A177

1993, June 28 ***Perf. 11½x12***
872 A177 360k Sansevieria cylindrica 1.50 1.50
873 A177 400k Euphorbia tirucalli 1.75 1.75
874 A177 500k Opuntia ficus-indica 2.25 2.25
875 A177 600k Dracaena aubryana 2.75 2.75
Nos. 872-875 (4) 8.25 8.25

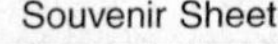

Souvenir Sheet

Africa Day — A178

1993, May 31 *Perf. 12*
876 A178 1500k Leopard 9.00 9.00

Tribal Pipes — A179

1993, Aug. 16 Litho. *Perf. 11½x12*
877 A179 72k Vimbundi .40 .40
878 A179 200k Vimbundi, diff. .95 .95
879 A179 420k Mutopa 1.90 1.90
880 A179 600k Pexi 2.75 2.75
Nos. 877-880 (4) 6.00 6.00

Souvenir Sheet

Union of Portuguese Speaking Capitals — A180

1993, July 30 *Perf. 12x11½*
881 A180 1500k multicolored 7.75 7.75

Turtles — A181

Designs: a, 180k, Chelonia mydas (b). b, 450k, Eretmochelys imbricata. c, 550k, Dermochelys coriacea. d, 630k, Caretta caretta.

1993, July 9 Litho. *Perf. 12½x12*
882 A181 Block of 4, #a.-d. 10.00 10.00

Quioca Art Type of 1992

1993, Sept. 1 Litho. *Perf. 12*
883 A164 300k Leopard 1.25 1.25
884 A164 600k Malhado 2.40 2.40
885 A164 800k Birds 3.25 3.25
886 A164 1000k Chickens 4.00 4.00
Nos. 883-886 (4) 10.90 10.90

Mushrooms A182

1993, Dec. 5 Litho. *Perf. 12*
887 A182 300k Tricholoma georgii 1.50 1.50
a. Perf. 11½ vert. 2.00 2.00
888 A182 500k Amanita phalloides 2.00 2.00
a. Perf. 11½ vert. 2.75 2.75
889 A182 600k Amanita vaginata 2.50 2.50
a. Perf. 11½ vert. 3.25 3.25
890 A182 1000k Macrolepiota procera 4.75 4.75
a. Perf. 11½ vert. 5.75 5.75
b. Booklet pane of 4, #887a-890a 14.00
Nos. 887-890 (4) 10.75 10.75

A183

Natl. Culture Day: 500k, Cinganji, wood carving of dancer. 1000k, Ohunya yo soma, staff with woman's face. 1200k, Ongende, sculpture of man on donkey. 2200k, Upi, corn pestle.

1994, Jan. 10 Litho. *Perf. 12*
891 A183 500k multicolored 1.00 1.00
892 A183 1000k multicolored 2.10 2.10
893 A183 1200k multicolored 2.40 2.40
894 A183 2200k multicolored 4.50 4.50
Nos. 891-894 (4) 10.00 10.00

Hong Kong '94.

Quioca Art Type of 1992

1994, Feb. 21 Litho. *Perf. 12*
895 A164 500k Bird on flower .50 .50
896 A164 2000k Plant with roots 3.00 3.00
897 A164 2500k Feto 3.75 3.75
898 A164 3000k Plant 4.75 4.75
Nos. 895-898 (4) 12.00 12.00

Social Responsibilities of AIDS — A184

500k, Mass of people. 1000k, Witchdoctor receiving AIDS through needle, people being educated. 3000k, Stylized man, woman.

1994, May 5 Litho. *Perf. 12*
899 A184 500k multicolored .90 .90
900 A184 1000k multicolored 1.50 1.50
901 A184 3000k multicolored 4.75 4.75
Nos. 899-901 (3) 7.15 7.15

1994 World Cup Soccer Championships, US — A185

1994, June 17 *Perf. 14*
902 A185 500k Large arrows, small ball .90 .90
903 A185 700k Small arrows, large ball 1.10 1.10
904 A185 2200k Ball in goal 3.50 3.50
905 A185 2500k Ball, foot 3.75 3.75
Nos. 902-905 (4) 9.25 9.25

Dinosaurs A186

1994, Aug. 16 Litho. *Perf. 12*
906 A186 1000k Brachiosaurus .35 .35
907 A186 3000k Spinosaurus .90 .90
908 A186 5000k Ouranosaurus 1.50 1.50
909 A186 10,000k Lesothosaurus 3.25 3.25
Nos. 906-909 (4) 6.00 6.00

Souvenir Sheet

910 A186 19,000k Lesothosaurus, map of Africa 10.00 10.00

PHILAKOREA '94, SINGPEX '94. No. 910 contains one 44x34mm stamp.

Tourism A187

2000k, Birds. 4000k, Wild animals. 8000k, Native women. 10,000k, Native men.

1994, Sept. 27 Litho. *Perf. 12x11½*
911 A187 2000k multi .75 .75
912 A187 4000k multi 1.25 1.25
913 A187 8000k multi 2.75 2.75
914 A187 10,000k multi 3.50 3.50
Nos. 911-914 (4) 8.25 8.25

Post Boxes — A188

Designs: 5000k, Letters, bundled mail wall box. 7500k, Wall box for letters. 10,000k, Pillar box. 21,000k, Multi-function units.

1994, Oct. 7 *Perf. 14½*
915 A188 5000k multicolored .95 .95
916 A188 7500k multicolored 1.50 1.50
917 A188 10,000k multicolored 1.75 1.75
918 A188 21,000k multicolored 4.00 4.00
Nos. 915-918 (4) 8.20 8.20

Cotton Pests — A189

Insects: 5000k, Heliothis armigera. 6000k, Bemisia tabasi. 10,000k, Dysdercus. 27,000k, Spodoptera exigua.

1994, Nov. 11 Litho. *Perf. 14*
919 A189 5000k multicolored 1.00 1.00
920 A189 6000k multicolored 1.10 1.10
921 A189 10,000k multicolored 2.10 2.10
922 A189 27,000k multicolored 5.50 5.50
Nos. 919-922 (4) 9.70 9.70

Intl. Olympic Committee, Cent. A190

1994, Dec. 15
923 A190 27,000k multicolored 6.00 6.00

Tribal Culture A191

Designs: 10,000k. Rubbing sticks to start fire. 15,000k, Extracting sap from tree. 20,000k, Smoking tribal pipe. 25,000k, Shooting bow & arrow. 28,000k, Mothers, children. 30,000k, Cave art.

1995, Jan. 6 Litho. *Perf. 14*
924 A191 10,000k multicolored .75 .75
925 A191 15,000k multicolored .95 .95
926 A191 20,000k multicolored 1.25 1.25
927 A191 25,000k multicolored 1.50 1.50
928 A191 28,000k multicolored 1.75 1.75
929 A191 30,000k multicolored 1.90 1.90
Nos. 924-929 (6) 8.10 8.10

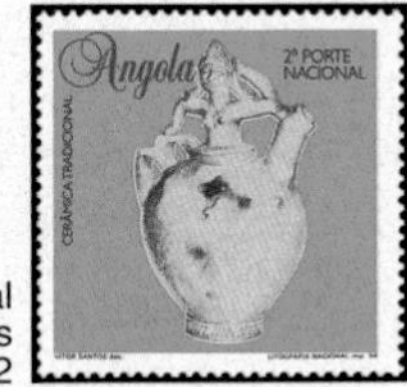

Traditional Ceramics A192

Designs: No. 930, Pitcher with bust of a woman as stopper. No. 931, Cone-shaped vase. No. 932, Bird-shaped vase. No. 933, Pitcher with bust of a man as stopper.

1995, Jan. 2 Litho. *Perf. 14½*
930 A192 (2) 2nd class natl. 1.00 .50
931 A192 (1) 1st class natl. 1.25 .75
932 A192 (2) 2nd class intl. 1.50 1.00
933 A192 (1) 1st class intl. 2.25 1.50
Nos. 930-933 (4) 6.00 3.75

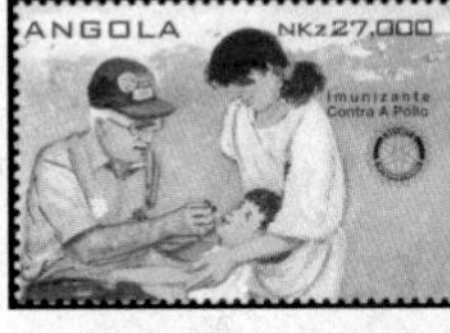

Rotary Intl., 90th Anniv. A193

a, Immunizing boy against polio. b, Medical examination. c, Immunizing girl against polio. No. 936, Dove over map.

1995, Feb. 23 Litho. *Perf. 14*
934 Strip of 3 8.25 8.25
a.-c. A193 27,000k any single 2.50 2.50
935 Strip of 3 8.25 8.25
a.-c. A193 27,000k any single 2.50 2.50

Souvenir Sheet

936 A193 81,000k multicolored 10.00 10.00
a. English inscription 10.00 10.00

No. 934 has Portuguese inscriptions. No. 935 has English inscriptions. Both were issued in sheets of 9 stamps.

No. 936 contains Portuguese inscription in sheet margin.

Rotary Intl., 90th Anniv. — A194

Litho. & Embossed

1995, Feb. 23 *Perf. 11½x12*
937 A194 81,000k gold 40.00

World Telecommunications Day — A195

Designs: No. 938, 1957 Sputnik 1. No. 939, Shuttle, Intelsat satellite.

1995 Litho. *Perf. 14*

938 A195 27,000k multicolored 3.00 3.00
939 A195 27,000k multicolored 3.00 3.00
a. Souvenir sheet, #938-939 6.50 6.50

Independence, 20th Anniv. — A196

1995, Nov. 11 Litho. *Perf. 14*

940 A196 2900k multicolored 2.10 2.10

4th World Conference on Women, Beijing — A197

Designs: 375k, Women working in fields. 1106k, Woman teaching, girls with book. 1265k, Woman in industry, career woman. 2900k, Woman in native headdress, vert.
1500k, Native mother, children, vert.

1996, Jan. 29 Litho. *Perf. 14*

941 A197 375k multicolored .25 .25
942 A197 1106k multicolored .80 .80
943 A197 1265k multicolored 1.50 1.50
944 A197 2900k multicolored 3.00 3.00
Nos. 941-944 (4) 5.55 5.55

Souvenir Sheet

945 A197 1500k multicolored 2.75 2.75

UN Assistance Programs — A198

Designs: 200k, Boy, highlift moving supplies. 1265k, Supply ship arriving. No. 948, Two high lifts. No. 949, Tractor-trailer traveling past vultures, native girl.
No. 950, Man, ship.

1996 Litho. *Perf. 14*

946 A198 200k multicolored .25 .25
947 A198 1265k multicolored 1.00 1.00
948 A198 2583k multicolored 2.25 2.25
949 A198 2583k multicolored 2.50 2.50
Nos. 946-949 (4) 6.00 6.00

Souvenir Sheet

950 A198 1265k multicolored *6.50 6.50*

Flora and Fauna A199

1500k, Verdant hawkmoth. 4400k, Water lily. 5100k, Panther toad. 6000k, African wild dog.
1500k: a, Western honey buzzard. b, Bateleuer. c, Common kestrel.
4400k; d, Red-crested turaco. e, Giraffe. f, Elephant.
5100k: g, Hippopotamus. h, Cattle egret. i, Lion.
6000k: j, Helmeted turtle. k, African pygmy goose. l, Egyptian plover.
12,000k, Spotted hyena.

1996, Apr. 20 Litho. *Perf. 14*

951-954 A199 Set of 4 5.00 5.00
955 A199 Sheet of 12, #a.-l. 10.00 10.00

Souvenir Sheet

956 A199 12,000k multicolored 3.00 3.00

Sheets of 12

Birds — A200

Fowl, each 5500k: No. 957a, California quail. b, Greater prairie chicken. c, Painted quail. d, Golden pheasant. e, Roulroul partridge. f, Ceylon sourfowl. g, Himalayan snowcock. h, Temminicks tragopan. i, Lady Amherst's pheasant. j, Great curassow. k, Red-legged partridge. l, Impeyan pheasant.
Hummingbirds, each 5500k: No. 958a, Anna's. b, Blue-throated. c, Broad-tailed. d, Costa's. e, White-eared. f, Calliope. g, Violet-crowned. h, Rufous. i, Crimson topaz. j, Broad-billed. k, Frilled coquette. l, Ruby-throated.
No. 959, 12,000k, Ring-necked pheasant. No. 960, 12,000k, Racquet-tail hummingbird.

1996, Apr. 20

957-958 A200 #a.-l., Set of 2 20.00 20.00

Souvenir Sheets

959-960 A200 Set of 2 5.50 5.50

Lubrapex '96 A201

Wild animals: a, 180k, Lions attacking zebra. b, 450k, Zebras, lions, diff. c, 180k, Zebras grazing, lions stalking. d, 450k, Panthera leo. e, 550k, Cheetah. f, 630k, Cheetah running. g, 550k, Cheetah chasing antilope. h, 630k, Cheetah attacking antelope. i, 180k, Antilope (gnu) being attacked by wild dogs. j, 450k, Antelope, wild dogs. k, 180k, Pack of wild dogs. l, 450k, Licaon pictus. m, 550k, Panthera pardus. n, 630k, Oryx. o, 550k, Oryx, diff. p, 630k, Leopard attacking oryx.

1996, Apr. 27

961 A201 Sheet of 16, #a.-p. 9.00 9.00

Sheets of 6

Ships — A202

Designs, each 6000k: No. 962a, Styrbjorn, Sweden, 1789. b, Constellation, US, 1797. c, Taureau, France, 1865. d, Bomb Ketch, France, 1682. e, Sardegna, Italy, 1881. f, HMS Glasgow, England, 1867.
No. 963a, Essex, US, 1812. b, HMS Inflexible, England, 1881. c, HMS Minotaur, England, 1863. d, Napoleon, France, 1854. e, Sophia Amalia, Denmark, 1650. f, Massena, France, 1887.
No. 964, 12,000k, HMS Tremendous, England, 1806, vert. No. 965, 12,000k, Royal Prince, England, 1666.

1996, May 4

962-963 A202 #a.-f., Set of 2 12.00 12.00

Souvenir Sheets

964-965 A202 Set of 2 10.00 10.00

UN, 50th Anniv. (in 1995) A203

Designs: No. 966, Boys pumping water. No. 967, Man, woman with girl.
8000k, Unloading supplies from ship.

1996, Apr. 27 Litho. *Perf. 14*

966 A203 3500k multicolored 1.25 1.25
967 A203 3500k multicolored 1.25 1.25

Souvenir Sheet

968 A203 8000k multicolored 2.75 2.75

Sonangol, 20th Anniv. A204

Face in traditional mask, costume, native birds, and: No. 969, Oil derricks. No. 970, Oil storage tanks, ship. 2500k, Refinery equipment. 5000k, Cargo shipment, jet.

1996, May 12

969 A204 1000k multicolored .25 .25
970 A204 1000k multicolored .25 .25
971 A204 2500k multicolored 1.60 1.60
972 A204 5000k multicolored 2.75 2.75
Nos. 969-972 (4) 4.85 4.85

Brapex '96 — A205

Designs: No. 973, Slaves in hold. No. 974, Slaves fleeing ship as it's overturned. No. 975, Slave boats approaching ship. No. 976, Slaves talking with captain.
50,000k, like No. 975.

1996, Oct. 19 Litho. *Perf. 14*

973 A205 20,000k multicolored 2.25 2.25
974 A205 20,000k multicolored 2.25 2.25
975 A205 30,000k multicolored 3.00 3.00
976 A205 30,000k multicolored 3.00 3.00
Nos. 973-976 (4) 10.50 10.50

Souvenir Sheet

977 A205 50,000k multicolored 8.00 8.00

Churches — A206

Designs: 5,000k, Mission, Huila. No. 979, Church of the Nazarene. No. 980, Church of Our Lady of Pó Pulo. 25,000k, St. Adriáo Church.

1996, Dec. 6 Litho. *Perf. 14*

978 A206 5,000k multicolored .40 .40
979 A206 10,000k multicolored .90 .90
980 A206 10,000k multicolored .90 .90
981 A206 25,000k multicolored 2.10 2.10
Nos. 978-981 (4) 4.30 4.30

1996 Summer Olympic Games, Atlanta A207

1996, Dec. 9

982 A207 5,000k Handball, vert. .60 .60
983 A207 10,000k Swimming 1.25 1.25
984 A207 25,000k Track & field, vert. 3.25 3.25
985 A207 35,000k Shooting 4.50 4.50
Nos. 982-985 (4) 9.60 9.60

Souvenir Sheet

986 A207 65,000k Basketball 6.00 6.00

MPLA (Liberation Movement), 40th Anniv. — A208

1996, Dec. 10 Litho. *Perf. 14*

987 A208 30,000k Dolphins, map *6.00 6.00*

Trains A209

Trains — A209a

No. 988: a, AVE, Spain. b, Bullet Train, Japan. c, GM F7 Warbonnet, US. d, Deltic, Great Britain. e, Eurostar, France/Great Britain. f, ETR 450, Italy.
No. 989: a, Class E1300, Morocco. b, ICE, Germany. c, X2000, Sweden. d, TGV Duplex, France.
No. 989E, each 250,000k: f, Steam engine. g, Garrat. h, General Electric.
No. 990, 110,000k, Canadian Pacific 4-4-0, Canada. No. 991, 110,000k, Via Rail Canadian, Canada.

1997, May 29 Litho. *Perf. 14*

Sheets of 6, 4 or 3

988 A209 100,000k #a.-f. *8.00 8.00*
989 A209 140,000k #a.-d. *8.00 8.00*
989E A209a Sheet of 3, #f.-h. *14.00 14.00*

Souvenir Sheets

Perf. 13½

990-991 A209 Set of 2 *8.00 8.00*

Nos. 990-991 contain one 38x50 or 50x38mm stamp, respectively.
PACIFIC 97.

Horses — A210

No. 992: a, Thoroughbred. b, Palomino, appaloosa. c, Arabians. d, Arabian colt. e, Thoroughbred colt. f, Mustang. g, Mustang, diff. h, Furioso.
No. 993: a, Thoroughbred. b, Arabian, palomino. c, Arabian, chincoteague. d, Pintos. e, Przewalski's horse. f, Thoroughbred colt. g, Arabians. h, New forest pony.
No. 994: a, Selle Francais. b, Fjord. c, Percheron. d, Italian heavy draft. e, Shagya Arab. f, Avelignese. g, Czechoslovakian warmblood. h, New forest pony.
215,000k, Thoroughbreds. 220,000k, Thoroughbreds, diff.

1997, July 5 Litho. *Perf. 14*

Sheets of 8

992 A210 100,000k #a.-h. *9.50 9.50*
993 A210 120,000k #a.-h. *11.50 11.50*
994 A210 140,000k #a.-h. *13.50 13.50*

Souvenir Sheets

995 A210 215,000k multi *6.00 6.00*
996 A210 220,000k multi *6.00 6.00*

PACIFIC 97.

1998 World Cup Soccer Championships, France — A211

Winners holding World Cup trophy: No. 997: a, Uruguay, 1930. b, Germany, 1954. c, Brazil, 1970. d, Argentina, 1986. e, Brazil, 1994.
Winning team pictures: No. 998a, Germany, 1954. b, Uruguay, 1958. c, Italy, 1938. d, Brazil, 1962. e, Brazil, 1970. f, Uruguay, 1930.
220,000k, Angolan team members standing. 250,000k, 1997 Angolan team picture.

1997, July 5 Litho. *Perf. 14*
Sheets of 5 or 6

997 A211 100,000k #a.-e. + label *9.00 9.00*
998 A211 100,000k #a.-f. *10.00 10.00*

Souvenir Sheets

999 A211 220,000k multi *5.50 5.50*
1000 A211 250,000k multi *5.50 5.50*

ENSA (Security System), 20th Anniv. — A212

"Star" emblem, and stylized protection of "egg," each 240,000k: No. 1001, Industry. No. 1002, Recreation. No. 1003, Homes, shelters. No. 1004, Accident prevention.
350,000k, Emblem.

1998 Litho. *Perf. 13½*

1001-1004 A212 Set of 4 *11.00 11.00*

Souvenir Sheet
Perf. 13½x13

1005 A212 350,000k multi *6.00 6.00*

No. 1005 contains one 60x40mm stamp.

GURN (Natl. Unity & Reconciliation Government), 1st Anniv. — A213

Emblem, portion of country map and: 100,000k, a, Sea, swordfish, ships, oil derrick. b, Sea, ships, swordfish. c, Sea, swordfish, ships, mining car on railroad track. d, Sea, power lines.
200,000k: e, Train on track, antelope. f, Mining cars on track, tractor pulling cart. g, Railroad track across rivers, tractor plowing. h, Power lines. i, UR corner of map, crystals. j, Train on track. k, Elephant, tree. l, Trunk of tree, bottom edge of map.

1998

1006 A213 Sheet of 12, #a.-l. 22.50 22.50

Souvenir Sheet

Education in Angola — A214

1998

1007 A214 400,000k multi *6.00 6.00*

Diana, Princess of Wales (1961-97) — A215

Various portraits, each 100,000k, color of sheet margin: No. 1008, pale green. No. 1009, pale yellow.
400,000k, Wearing protective clothing.

1998, May 21 Litho. *Perf. 14*
Sheets of 6, #a.-f.

1008-1009 A215 Set of 2 *22.50 22.50*

Souvenir Sheet

1010 A215 400,000k multi *6.00 6.00*

See No. 1028.

Expo '98, Lisbon A216

Marine life: No. 1011, 100,000k, Anemones. No. 1012, 100,000k, Sea urchin. No. 1013, 100,000k, Sea horses. No. 1014, 100,000k, Coral (Caravela). No. 1015, 240,000k, Sea slug. No. 1016, 240,000k, Worms (Tunicados).

1998, May 21 *Perf. 13½*

1011-1016 A216 Set of 6 11.00 11.00

Butterflies — A217

No. 1017, each 120,000k: a, Metamorpha stelene. b, Papilio glaucus. c, Danaus plexippus. d, Catonephele numili. e, Plebejus argus. f, Hypolimnas bolina.
No. 1018, each 120,000k: a, Terinos terpander. b, Bematistes aganice. c, Hebomoia glaucippe. d, Colias eurytheme. e, Pereute leucodrosime. f, Lycaena dispar.
No. 1019, each 120,000k, horiz.: a, Dynastor napolean. b, Zeuxidia amethystus. c, Battus philenor. d, Phoebis philea. e, Danaus chrysippus. f, Glaucopsyche alexis.
Each 250,000k: No. 1020, Euphaedra neophron. No. 1021, Thecla betulae, horiz. No. 1022, Uraneis ucubis, armillaria staminea.

1998, May 21 *Perf. 14*
Sheets of 6, #a.-f.

1017-1019 A217 Set of 3 *25.00 25.00*

Souvenir Sheets

1020-1022 A217 Set of 3 *18.00 18.00*

Cats and Dogs A218

Cats, each 140,000k: No. 1023a, British tortoiseshell. b, Chinchilla. c, Russian blue. d, Black Persian (longhair). e, British red tabby. f, Birman.
Dogs, each 140,000k: No. 1024a, West Highland terrier. b, Irish setter. c, Dachshund. d, St. John water dog. e, Shetland sheep dog. f, Dalmatian.
Each 500,000k: No. 1025, Turkish van (swimming cat). No. 1026, Labrador retriever.

1998, May 21 Litho. *Perf. 14x13½*
Sheets of 6

1023-1024 A218 #a.-f., Set of 2 *22.50 22.50*

Souvenir Sheets

1025-1026 A218 Set of 2 *13.00 13.00*

Wild Animals A219

100,000k: a, Panthera leo. b, Hippopotamus amphibius. c, Loxodonta africana. d, Giraffa camelopardalis.
220,000k: e, Syncerus caffer-caffer. f, Gorilla gorilla. g, Ceratotherim simum. h, Oryx gazella.

1998, July 24 Litho. *Perf. 14*

1027 A219 Sheet of 8, #a.-h. 13.00 13.00

Diana, Princes of Wales Type of 1998

Pictures showing Diana's campaign to ban land mines, each 150,000k: a, With girl. b, With two boys. c, Wearing protective clothing.

1998, Aug. 31 Litho. *Perf. 14*

1028 A215 Strip of 3, #a.-c. *7.00 7.00*

No. 1028 was issued in sheets of 6 stamps.

Intl. Year of the Ocean — A220

Marine life: No. 1029a, Pagurites. b, Callinectes marginatus. c, Thais forbesi. d, Ostrea tulipa. e, Balanus amohitrite. f, Uca tangeri.
No. 1030: a, Littorina angulifera. b, Semifusus morio. c, Thais coronata. d, Cerithium atratum (red branch). e, Ostrea tulipa. f, Cerithium atratum (green branch).
Each 300,000k: No. 1031, Goniopsis, horiz. No. 1032, Unidentified shell.

1998, Sept. 4
Sheets of 6

1029 A220 100,000k #a.-f. *5.00 5.00*
1030 A220 170,000k #a.-f. *8.00 8.00*

Souvenir Sheets

1031-1032 A220 Set of 2 *11.00 11.00*

Souvenir Sheet

Battle Against Polio in Angola — A221

1998, Aug. 28 Litho. *Perf. 13½*

1033 A221 500,000k multicolored *3.75 3.75*

Traditional Boats A222

Designs: No. 1034, 250,000k, Boat, Bimba. No. 1035, 250,000k, Canoe with sail, Ndongo. 500,000k, Constructing boat, Ndongo.

1998, Sept. 4 *Perf. 14*

1034-1036 A222 Set of 3 8.25 8.25

Titanic A223

Views of Titanic, each 350,000k: a, Under tow. b, Stern. c, Starboard side at night. d, At dock.

1998, Sept. 4

1037 A223 Sheet of 4, #a.-d. *12.00 12.00*

No. 1037c is 76x30mm, No. 1037d is 38x61mm.

Angolan Food A224

Various vegetables, fruits: No. 1038, 100,000k, 4 fruits. No. 1039, 100,000k, Squash sliced in half. No. 1040, 120,000k, Ears of corn. No. 1041, 120,000k, Green beans. No. 1042, 140,000k, Fruit with red seeds sliced in half. No. 1043, 140,000k, Sliced bananas.

1998

1038-1043 A224 Set of 6 7.75 7.75

Portugal '98.

Airplanes A225

No. 1044, IL-62 M. No. 1045, B737 100.
No. 1046: a, Ultralight. b, Gyroplane. c, Business jet. d, onvertible plane (e). e, Chuterplane (a, b, d). f, Twin rotors (e). g, Skycrane. h, Aerospatiale Concorde (i). i, Flying boat.
No. 1047: a, Pedal power (b). b, Sail plane (a, e). c, Aerobatic (f). d, Hang gliding (g). e, Balloon (h). f, Glidercraft (e, i). g, Model airplane. h, Air racing (i). i, Solar cells.
No. 1048, 1,000,000k, Boeing 777. No. 1049, 1,000,000k, Columbia Space Shuttle, vert. No. 1049A, 1,000,000k, Boeing 737-200. No. 1049B, 1,000,000k, Boeing 747-300.

1998-99 Litho. *Perf. 14*

1044 A225 200,000k multi *2.00 2.00*
1045 A225 200,000k multi *2.00 2.00*

Sheets of 9

1046 A225 150,000k #a.-i. *6.00 6.00*
1047 A225 250,000k #a.-i. *8.00 8.00*

Souvenir Sheets

1048-1049B A225 Set of 4 *30.00 30.00*

Nos. 1048-1049B each contain one 85x28mm stamp.
Issued: Nos. 1049A-1049B, 3/25/99; others 12/24/98.

Dinosaurs — A226

Designs, vert., each 120,000k: No. 1050, Parasaurolophus. No. 1051, Maiasaura. No. 1052, Iguanodon. No. 1053, Elaphosaurus.
No. 1054, vert, 120,000k: a, Brontosaurus. b, Plateosaurus. c, Brachiosaurus. d, Anatosaurus. e, Tyrannosaurus. f, Carnotaurus. g, Corythosaurus. h, Stegosaurus. i, Iguanodon, diff.
No. 1055, 120,000k: a, Hadrosaurus. b, Ouranosaurus. c, Hypsilophodon. d, Brachiosaurus. e, Shunosaurus. f, Amargasaurus. g,

Tuojiangosaurus. h, Monoclonius. i, Struthiosaurus.

Each 550,000k: No. 1056, Triceratops, vert. No. 1057, Tyrannosaurus, vert.

1998, Dec. 28

1050-1053 A226 Set of 4 *8.00 8.00*

Sheets of 9, #a.-i.

1054-1055 A226 Set of 2 *18.00 18.00*

Souvenir Sheets

1056-1057 A226 Set of 2 *9.00 9.00*

World Wildlife Fund — A227

Lesser flamingo: a, Facing left. b, Body facing forward. c, Head and neck. d, With wings spread.

Strip of 4

1999 Litho. *Perf. 14*

1058 A227 300,000k #a.-d. *5.50 5.50*

No. 1058 was issued in sheets of 16 stamps.

Fauna A228

Designs, each 300,000k: No. 1059, Equis caballus przewalski. No. 1060, Sphenisciformes, vert. No. 1061, Haliaeetus leucocephalus, vert. No. 1062, Anodorhynchus hyacinthinus.

No. 1063, 300,000k: a, Vulpes velox hebes. b, Odocoileus. c, Pongo pygmaeus. d, Leontopitecus rosalia. e, Panthera tigris. f, Tragelaphus eurycerus.

No. 1064, 300,000k: a, Tremarctos ornatus. b, Aphelocoma. c, Otus insularis. d, Balaeniceps rex. e, Lepidochelys kempii. f, Lutra canadensis.

Each 1,000,000k: No. 1065, Ailuropoda melanoleuca, vert. No. 1066, Ursus arctos horribilis.

1999

1059-1062 A228 Set of 4 *9.00 9.00*

Sheets of 6, #a.-f.

1063-1064 A228 Set of 2 *16.50 16.50*

Souvenir Sheets

1065-1066 A228 Set of 2 *13.00 13.00*

These Flora and Fauna stamps, formerly Nos. 1067-1078, were not authorized by Angola postal authorities.

Other items inscribed "Angola" that were not authorized but which have appeared on the market include sheets with the themes of Disney and History of Animation, Millennium, Animals, Trains, Flora, Muhammad Ali & Lennox Lewis, Bruce Lee, Albert Einstein / Moon Landing, Elvis Presley and other entertainers, Great Personalities, John Kennedy and Marilyn Monroe, Martin Luther King, Jr., Payne Stewart, Colin Montgomerie, Babe Ruth, Cardinal John O'Connor, Pope John Paul II / Mother Teresa and Queen Elizabeth II / Winston Churchill.

World Telecommunications Day — A230

1999, May 17 Litho. *Perf. 14*

1079 A230 500,000k multi *1.25 1.25*

Souvenir Sheet

Waterfalls — A231

a, Andulo. b, Chiumbo. c, Ruacaná. d, Coemba.

1999, June 5 Sheet of 4

1080 A231 500,000k #a.-d. *4.50 4.50*

A232

African Men's Basketball Championships — No. 1081: a, Poster. b, Basketball, hoop, tan background. c, Basketball, hoop, green background. d, Welwitschia plant holding basketball.

2,500,000k, Similar to No. 1081c.

1999, July 29 *Perf. 13½*

Sheet of 4

1081 A232 1,500,000k #a.-d. *4.50 4.50*

Souvenir Sheet

Perf. 13x13½

1082 A232 2,500,000k multi *3.50 3.50*

No. 1082 contains one 40x30mm stamp.

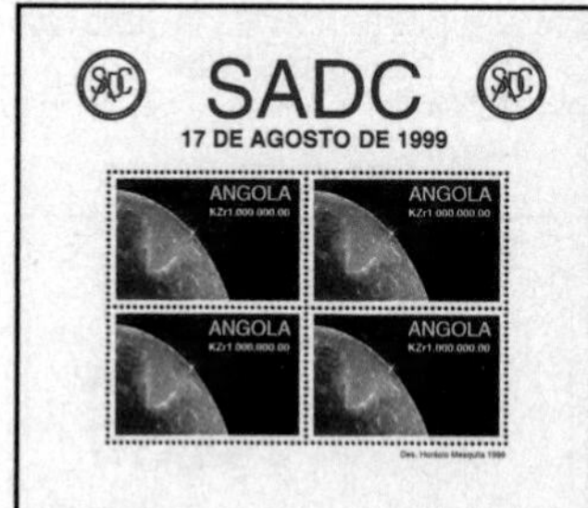

A233

1999, Aug. 17 *Perf. 14*

1083 A233 1,000,000k multi *1.50 1.50*

Southern African Development Community. Issued in sheets of 4. Value *$6.75.*

A234

Tribal kings — No. 782: a, Ekuikui II. b, Mvemba Nzinga. c, Mwata Yamvu Naweji II. d, Njinga Mbande.

1,000,000k, Mandume Ndemufayo.

1999, Sept. 17 Sheet of 4

1084 A234 500,000k #a.-d. *8.25 8.25*

Souvenir Sheet

1085 A234 1,000,000k multi *5.00 5.00*

A235

Queen Mother (b. 1900) — No. 1086: a, With King George VI. b, Wearing brooch. c, Wearing tiara. d, Wearing hat.

500,000k, Wearing academic gown.

Sheet of 4

1999, Sept. 17 Litho. *Perf. 14*

1086 A235 200,000k #a.-d. *9.00 9.00*

Souvenir Sheet

Perf. 13¾

1087 A235 500,000k multi *6.00 6.00*

No. 1087 contains one 38x51mm stamp.

Ships A236

No. 1088, each 950,000k: a, Egyptian bark, 1300 B.C. b, Flemish carrack, 1480. c, Beagle, 1830. d, North Star, 1852. e, Fram, 1892. f, Unyon Maru, 1909. g, Juan Sebastian de Elcano, 1927. h, Tovarishch, 1933.

No. 1089, each 950,000k: a, Bucentauro, 1728. b, Clermont, 1807. c, Savannah, 1819. d, Dromedary, 1844. e, Iberia, 1881. f, S.S. Gluckauf, 1886. g, City of Paris, 1888. h, Mauretania, 1906.

No. 1090, each 950,000k: a, Gloire, 1859. b, L'Ocean, 1868. c, Dandalo, 1876, stern of HMS Dreadnought, 1906. d, Bow of Dreadnought. e, Bismarck, 1939, stern of USS Cleveland, 1946. f, Bow of Cleveland. g, USS Boston, 1942, stern of USS Long Beach, 1959. h, Bow of Long Beach.

Each 5,000,000k: No. 1091, Chinese junk. No. 1092, Madre de Deus, 1609. No. 1093, Catamaran, 1861. No. 1094, Natchez, 1870.

1999, Sept. 23 Litho. *Perf. 14*

Sheets of 8

1088-1090 A236 Set of 3 *30.00 30.00*

Souvenir Sheets

1091-1094 A236 Set of 4 *24.00 24.00*

Mushrooms A237

No. 1095, Amanita caesarea. No. 1096, Psalliota xanthoderma. No. 1097, Hygrocybe conica. No. 1098, Boletus chrysenteron. No. 1099, Coprinus comatus. No. 1100, Boletus luteus.

No. 1101: a, Morchella crassipes. b, Boletus rufescens. c, Amanita phalloides. d, Collybia iocephala. e, Tricholoma aurantium. f, Cortinarius violaceus. g, Mycena polygramma. h, Psalliota augusta.

No. 1102: a, Amanita muscaria. b, Boletus aereus. c, Coprinus comatus. d, Amanita rubescens. e, Cortinarius collinitus. f, Boletus satanas. g, Lepiota procera. h, Clitocybe geotropa.

No. 1103: a, Russula nigricans. b, Boletus granulatus. c, Mycena strobilinoides. d, Amanita caesarea. e, Amanita muscaria. f, Boletus, crocipodius. g, Russula virescens. h, Lactarius deliciosus.

No. 1104, Psalliota haemorrhoidaria.

No. 1105, Mycena lilacifolia.

1999, Sept. 23 Litho. *Perf. 14*

1095 A237 1,250,000k multi 1.25 1.25

1096 A237 1,250,000k multi 1.25 1.25

1097 A237 1,250,000k multi 1.25 1.25

1098 A237 1,250,000k multi 1.25 1.25

1099 A237 1,250,000k multi 1.25 1.25

1100 A237 1,250,000k multi 1.25 1.25

Nos. 1095-1100 (6) 7.50 7.50

Sheets of 8

1101 A237 1,000,000k #a-h 8.75 8.75

1102 A237 1,000,000k #a-h 8.75 8.75

1103 A237 1,000,000k #a-h 8.75 8.75

Souvenir Sheets

1104 A237 5,000,000k multi 6.00 6.00

1105 A237 5,000,000k multi 6.00 6.00

A238

First Manned Moon Landing, 30th Anniv. A239

No. 1107: a, Astronaut spacewalking. b, Mariner 8. c, Viking 10. d, GINGA satellite. e, Soyuz 19. f, Voyager.

No. 1108, vert.: a, Space telescope. b, Space shuttle Atlantis. c, Uhuru satellite. d, Mir space station. e, Gemini 7. f, Venera 7.

No. 1109: a, Mercury, Venus. b, Jupiter. c, Neptune, Pluto. d, Earth, Mars. e, Saturn. f, Uranus.

No. 1110: a, Explorer 17. b, Intelsat 4A. c, GOES-D Satellite. d, Intelsat 2. e, Navstar. f, S.M.S.

No. 1111, 6,000,000k, Lunar rover, vert. No. 1112, 6,000,000k, Apollo 17 astronaut on moon, vert. No. 1113, 12,000,000k, Neil Armstrong, vert. No. 1114, 12,000,000k, Space shuttle Columbia. No. 1115, 12,000,000k, SBS-4, vert.

Perf. 13¾ (A238), 14 (A239)

1999, Nov. 15 Litho.

Sheets of 6, #a.-f.

1107-1108 A238 3,500,000k 11.00 11.00

1109-1110 A239 3,500,000k 10.00 10.00

Souvenir Sheets

1111-1112 A238 Set of 2 8.00 8.00

1113-1115 A239 Set of 3 18.00 18.00

Hokusai Paintings — A240

No. 1116, each 3,500,000k: a, Night attack. b, Usigafuchi No Kudan. c, Drawing of man and bowl. d, Wildlife. e, Pheasant. f, People on bridge.

No. 1117, each 3,500,000k: a, Tree and shoreline. b, Kabuki theater. c, Hen. d, Cooper. e, Trip to Enoshima. f, Sumida River landscape.

Each 12,000,000k: No. 1118, Yama-uba and Kintori, vert. No. 1119, Woman, vert.

1999, Dec. 13 Litho. *Perf. 13¾*

Sheets of 6, #a.-f.

1116-1117 A240 Set of 2 20.00 20.00

Souvenir Sheets

1118-1119 A240 Set of 2 13.00 13.00

On Dec. 13, the date of issue of these stamps, Angola devalued its currency, with approximately 1,000,000k being the equivalent of 1k after the devaluation.

Souvenir Sheets

PhilexFrance 99 — A241

No. 1120, 4-8-4 Linder Compound express. No. 1121, Hovertrain prototype.

2000, Mar. 13 Litho. *Perf. 13¾*
1120-1121 A241 12k Set of 2 12.00 12.00

A242

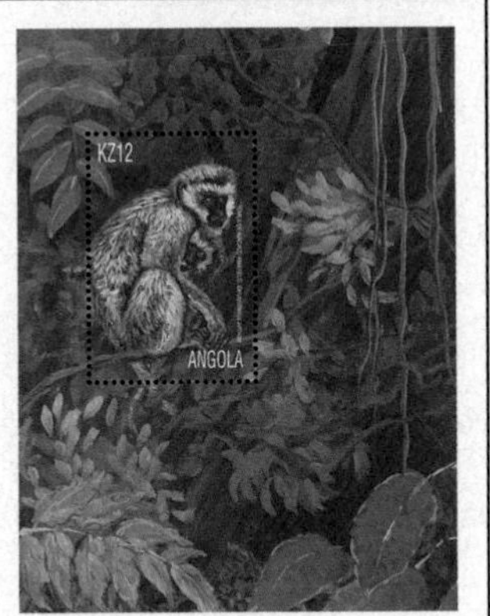

Wildlife — A243

1.50k, Zebra. 2k, Fruit bat. 3k, California condor. 5.50k, Lion.

No. 1126, horiz.: a, Equus zebra. b, Ploceus xanthops. c, Lycaon protus. d, Acinonyx jubatus. e, Oryx gazella. f, Nursing Otocyon megalotis. g, Giraffa camelopardalis. h, Canis adustus. i, Perodicticus potto. j, Panthera leo. k, Coracius caudata. l, Pair of Otocyon megalotis.

No. 1127, horiz.: a, Struthio camelus. b, Felis lybica. c, Aepyceros melampus. d, Cercopithecus aethiops. e, Diceros bicornis. f, Papio sp. g, Felis caracal. h, Sagittarius serpentarius. i, Phacochoerus aethiopicus. j, Arctocephalus pusillus. k, Alcedo cristata. l, Hippopotamus amphibius.

No. 1128: a, Deer. b, Turkey. c, Beaver. d, Frog. e, Manatee. f, Trout.

No. 1129: a, Macaque. b, Toucan. c, Bothriopsis bilineata. d, Hyla leucopyliata. e, Tamarin. f, Eagle.

No. 1130, vert.: a, Mountain gorilla. b, Rhinoceros. c, Water buffalo. d, Chameleon. e, Cobra. f, Meerkats.

No. 1131, vert.: a, Kangaroo. b, Koala. c, Kingfishers. d, Frog on tree root. e, Three fish. f, Turtle.

No. 1132, Sloth. No. 1133, Lemur, vert. No. 1134, Cheetah, vert. No. 1135, Orangutan, vert. No. 1136, Cercopithecus aethiops, diff. No. 1137, Loxodonta africana.

2000, Apr. 7 *Perf. 14*
1122-1125 A242 Set of 4 6.50 6.50

Sheets of 12

1126 A243 1.50k #a-l 10.50 10.50
1127 A243 2k #a-l 13.00 13.00

Sheets of 6, #a-f

1128-1131 A242 3.50k Set of 4 42.50 42.50

Souvenir Sheets

1132-1135 A242 12k Set of 4 26.00 26.00
1136-1137 A243 12k Set of 2 13.00 13.00

Birds of Prey A244

1.50k, Harpy eagle. 2k, Unidentified bird. 3k, Vulture, vert. 5.50k, King vulture, vert.

No. 1142: a, Accipiter gentilis. b, Surnia ulula. c, Falco peregrinus. d, Otus asio. e, Haliacetus vocifer. f, Herpetotheres cachinnans.

No. 1143: a, Falco sparverius. b, Pulsetrix perspicillata. c, Elemus leucurus. d, Ninox novaseelandiae. e, Polemaetus bellicosus. f, Polyborus plancus.

No. 1144: a, Verreaux's eagle. b, Aguia gigante. c, Aguia peixe.

No. 1145, vert.: a, Aguia despeida. b, Aguia dourada. c, Aguia devoradora de macacos.

No. 1146, King vulture, diff. No. 1147, Falcon, vert. No. 1148, Sagittarius serpentarius. No. 1149, Aquila chrysaetos.

2000, Apr. 10
1138-1141 A244 Set of 4 6.00 6.00

Sheets of 6, #a-f

1142-1143 A244 3.50k Set of 2 21.00 21.00

Sheets of 3, #a-c

1144-1145 A244 6.50k Set of 2 20.00 20.00

Souvenir Sheets

1146-1147 A244 12k Set of 2 13.00 13.00
1148-1149 A244 15k Set of 2 14.50 14.50

Millennium — A245

Highlights of the 16th Century: a, Paintings by Lai-Ji. b, The Last Judgment, by Luca Signorelli. c, Garden of Earthly Delights by Hieronymus Bosch. d, The Prince, written by Niccolò Machiavelli. e, Utopia, written by Sir Thomas More. f, Martin Luther. g, Charles I of Spain becomes Holy Roman Emperor Charles V. h, The School of Athens, by Raphael. i, Juan Sebastián de Elcano circumnavigates globe. j, Henry VIII of England. k, Spanish conquest of Aztecs and Incas. l, Placentia Cathedral. m, Potatoes introduced to Europe. n, Heliocentric theory of Copernicus. o, Portuguese reach Japan. p, Death of Albrecht Dürer (60x40mm). q, Bartolomé de Las Casas promotes rights for Indians.

2000, Oct. 2 Litho. *Perf. 12¾x12½*
1150 A245 2.50k Sheet of 17, #a-q, + label 26.50 26.50

War Damage in Angola A246

Designs: No. 1151, 3k, B.N.A. Building, Kuito. No. 1152, 3k, Kunje St., Kuito. No. 1153, 4k, Post office. No. 1154, 4k, Police headquarters. No. 1155, 5k, Apartment house. No. 1156, 5k, Independence Square. No. 1157, 6k, Child waving from upper floor of apartment house. No. 1158, 6k, Building, man carrying pack.

2000, Sept. 29 Litho. *Perf. 14*
1151-1158 A246 Set of 8 20.00 20.00

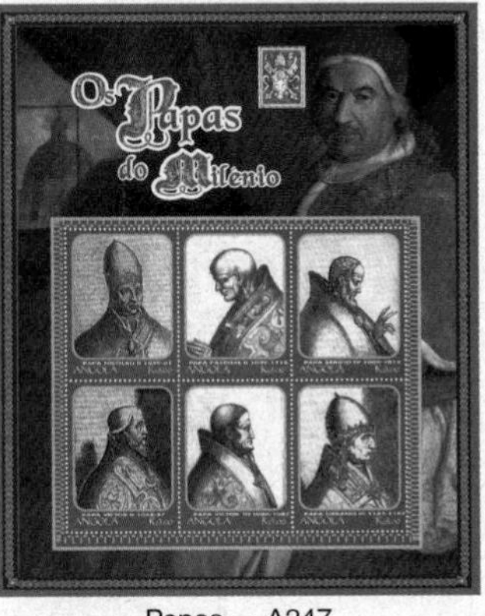

Popes — A247

Designs: No. 1159: a, Nicholas II, 1059-61. b, Paschal II, 1099-1118. c, Sergius IV, 1009-1012. d, Victor II, 1055-57. e, Victor III, 1086-87. f, Urban III, 1185-87.

No. 1160: a, Innocent II, 1130-43. b, John XIII, 965-72. c, Agapetus II, 946-55. d, John XV, 985-96. e, John XVIII, 1003-09. f, Lucius II, 1144-45.

No. 1161: a, Celestine II, 1143-44. b, Clement II, 1046-47. c, Clement III, 1187-91. d, Gelasius II, 1118-19. e, Benedict VII, 974-83. f, Gregory V, 996-99.

No. 1162, Leo IX, 1049-54. No. 1163, Gregory VII, 1073-85. No. 1164, Leo XIII, 1878-1903.

2000, Oct. 2 *Perf. 12x12¼*

Sheets of 6, #a-f

1159-1161 A247 Set of 3 30.00 30.00

Souvenir Sheets

1162-1164 A247 Set of 3 19.00 19.00

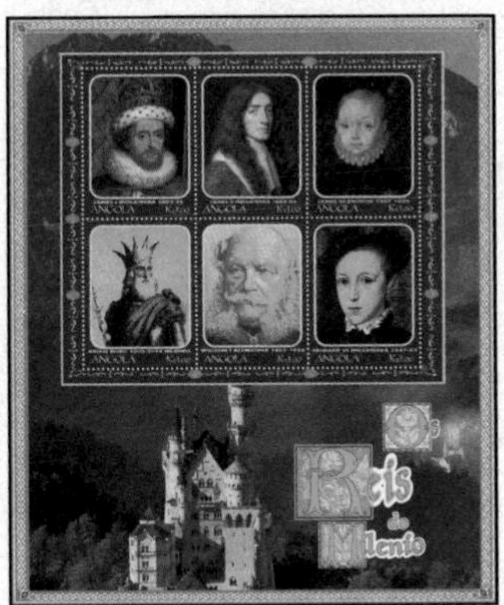

Monarchs — A248

Designs: No. 1165: a, Henry II, King of Germany and Holy Roman Emperor, 1002-24. b, Marina Mniszek, wife of false Russian czar Dmitri, 1605-06. c, Ivan IV of Russia, 1533-84. d, Ivan III of Russia, 1462-1505.

No. 1166: a, Charles II of Great Britain, 1660-85. b, Lady Jane Grey of England, 1533. c, Leopold III of Belgium, 1934-51. d, Louis XV of France, 1715-74.

No. 1167: a, James I of Great Britain, 1603-25. b, James II of Great Britain, 1685-88. c, James IV of Scotland, 1567-1625. d, Brian Boru of Ireland, 1002-14. e, Wilhelm I, King of Prussia and German Emperor, 1861-88. f, Edward VI of England, 1547-53.

No. 1168, Feodor I of Russia, 1584-98. No. 1169, False Russian czar Dmitri, 1605-06. No. 1170, William IV of Great Britain, 1830-37

2000, Oct. 2

Sheets of 4, #a-d

1165-1166 A248 Set of 2 13.00 13.00

Sheet of 6

1167 A248 #a-f 10.00 10.00

Souvenir Sheets

1168-1170 A248 Set of 3 19.00 19.00

Children's Drawings A249

Various designs. Denominations: 3k, 4k, 5k.

2000, Nov. 7 *Perf. 14*
1171-1173 A249 Set of 3 5.25 5.25

Post Office Buildings A250

Designs: No. 1174, 5k , Former Secretary of Communications Building, Luanda. No. 1175, 5k, Mbanza Congo Post Office. No. 1176, 5k, Namibe Post Office. No. 1177, 8k, Facade of Luanda Post Office. No. 1178, 8k, Luanda Post Office, diff. No. 1179, 8k, Lobito Post Office.

2000, Sept. 29 Litho. *Perf. 14*
1174-1179 A250 Set of 6 10.50 10.50

National Radio and Television, 25th Anniv. — A251

No. 1180, 9.50k: a, Woman at computer in newsroom. b, Reporter with tape recorder reporting on tank battle. c, Rescuing victims from airplane crash.

No. 1181, 9.50k: a, People and equipment in newsroom. b, Cameraman filming tank battle. c, Refugees.

No. 1182, 20k, Reporter with tape recorder. No. 1183, 20k, Cameraman, vert.

Perf. 13¼x13½, 13½x13¼
2000, Dec. 7

Sheets of 3, #a-c

1180-1181 A251 Set of 2 13.00 13.00

Souvenir Sheets

1182-1183 A251 Set of 2 9.00 9.00

Souvenir Sheet

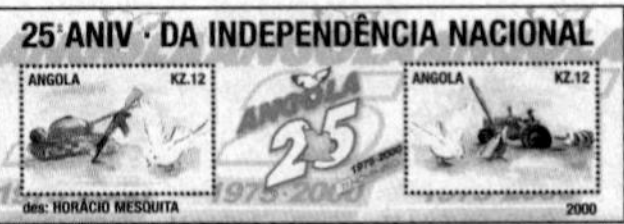

Independence, 25th Anniv. — A252

No. 1184: a, Tank, rifle, dove. b, Dove, hoe, tractor.

2001, Feb. 13 Litho. *Perf. 14¼x14*
1184 A252 12k Sheet of 2, #a-b 5.50 5.50

Africa Day A253

Designs: No. 1185, 10k, Shown. No. 1186, 10k, Xylophone.

30k, Map, musical instruments, native with mask, elephant, satellite dishes and computer.

2001, May 25 *Perf. 13x13¼*
1185-1186 A253 Set of 2 4.25 4.25

Souvenir Sheet

1187 A253 30k multi 6.50 6.50

Flowers
A254

Butterfly and: 8k, Nicolaia speciosa. 9k, Allamanda cathartica. No. 1190, 10k, Welwitschia mirabilis. No. 1191, 10k, Tagetes patula. 30k, Welwitschia mirabilis.

2001, June 9
1188-1191 A254 Set of 4 7.75 7.75

Souvenir Sheet

1192 A254 30k multi 6.50 6.50

Belgica 2001 Intl. Stamp Exhibition, Brussels (No. 1192).

Souvenir Sheet

Total Solar Eclipse, June 21 — A255

2001, June 21
1193 A255 30k multi 6.50 6.50

Fish
A256

Designs: 11k, Protopterus annectens. 17k, Protopterus amphibius. 18k, Tilapia ruweti. 36k, Tilapia rendalli.

Perf. 13½x13¼

2001, Sept. 28 **Litho.**
1194-1196 A256 Set of 3 *7.75 7.75*

Souvenir Sheet

Perf. 13x13¼

1197 A256 36k multi *6.00 6.00*

Traditional
Dances and
Costumes
A257

Designs: No. 1198, 11k, Massemba. No. 1199, 11k, Ovambo Efundula. 17k, Macolo Batuque. No. 1201, 18k, Humbi Puberty. No. 1202, 18k, Mukixi.
36k, Carneval.

2001, Nov. 12 ***Perf. 13x13¼***
1198-1202 A257 Set of 5 *12.00 12.00*

Souvenir Sheet

1203 A257 36k multi *6.00 6.00*

Souvenir Sheet

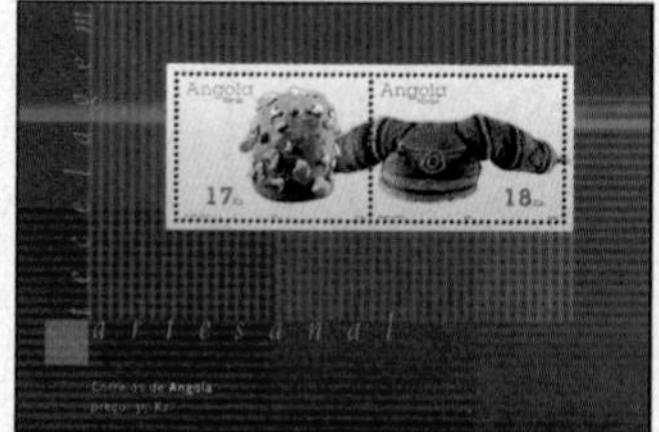
Handmade Weaving — A258

No. 1204: a, 17k, Banda. b, 18k, Kijinga.

2001, Dec. 7
1204 A258 Sheet of 2, #a-b *5.50 5.50*

Minerals
A259

Designs: No. 1205, 11k, Hematite. No. 1206, 11k, Malachite. No. 1207, 18k, Psilomelane. No. 1208, 18k, Diamond.

2001, Dec. 14 ***Perf. 13½x13¼***
1205-1208 A259 Set of 4 *9.25 9.25*

Masks — A260

Designs: 10k, Mwana Mpwevo. No. 1210, 11k, Mukixi. No. 1211, 11k, Mbunda. 17k, Mwana Pwo. 18k, Likisi-Cinganji.
36k, Ndemba, horiz.

2002, Jan. 8 ***Perf. 13¼x13½***
1209-1213 A260 Set of 5 *11.00 11.00*

Souvenir Sheet

Perf. 13x13¼

1214 A260 36k multi *6.00 6.00*

2002 World Cup Soccer Championships, Japan and Korea — A261

Two players and: 35k, Ball in air. 37k, Ball on ground.

2002, June 28 ***Perf. 13x13¼***
1215-1216 A261 Set of 2 *11.00 11.00*
1216a Souvenir sheet, #1215-1216 *11.00 11.00*

Meeting of
African
Committee
of
International
Socialists
A262

Designs: No. 1217, 10k, Fight against poverty (red and orange map of Africa). No. 1218, 10k, Abolition of the death penalty (man with target on chest). No. 1219, 10k, End to violence against women (stylized woman). No. 1220, 10k, Fight against poverty (masks). No. 1221, 10k, Annulment of foreign debt (map of Africa with dollar sign)

2002, July 12
1217-1221 A262 Set of 5 *8.25 8.25*
1221a Souvenir sheet, #1218-1221 *6.50 6.50*

National Peace and Reconciliation — A263

2002, Oct. 9
1222 A263 35k multi *3.00 3.00*

Reptiles
A264

Designs: 21k, Pithon anchietae. 35k, Lacerta sp. 37k, Naja nigricollis. 40k, Crocodylus niloticus.

2002, Oct. 15 ***Perf. 13x13¼***
1223-1226 A264 Set of 4 *11.00 11.00*

Lighthouses
and Buoys
A265

Designs: No. 1227, 45k, Tafe. No. 1228, 45k, Red buoy, Luanda Bay. No. 1229, 45k, Green buoy, Luanda Bay. No. 1230, 45k, Cabeça da Cobra. No. 1231, 45k, Barra do Dande. No. 1232, 45k, Moita Seca.

2002, Nov. 22
1227-1232 A265 Set of 6 *22.00 22.00*

Souvenir Sheet

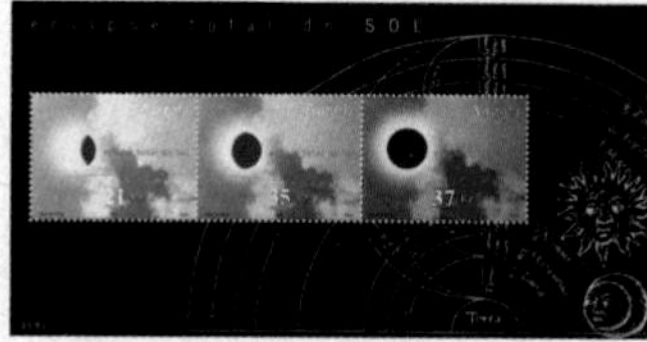
Dec. 4, 2002 Total Solar Eclipse — A266

No. 1233: a, 21k, Sun partially eclipsed. b, 35k, Sun mostly eclipsed. c, 37k, Sun totally eclipsed.

2002, Dec. 4
1233 A266 Sheet of 3, #a-c *7.75 7.75*

Angola -
Italy
Friendship
A267

António Manuel, Prince of N'Funta and Ambassador of Congo to Rome (d. 1608), and: 35k, Lion. 45k, Plaque with Italian inscription.

2002, Dec. 6
1234-1235 A267 Set of 2 *6.50 6.50*
1235a Souvenir sheet, #1234-1235 *6.50 6.50*

Pottery
A268

Designs: 27k, Omolingui. 45k, Mulondo. 47k, Ombya yo Tuma.
51k, Sanga.

2002, Dec. 7 **Litho.**

1236-1238 A268 Set of 3 *9.25 9.25*

Souvenir Sheet

1239 A268 51k multi *4.25 4.25*

United Nations 3rd Meeting on Science, Technology and Development — A269

2003, May 30 ***Perf. 13x13¼***
1240 A269 50k multi *4.00 4.00*

Powered
Flight, Cent.
A270

2003, Aug. 21 **Litho.** ***Perf. 13x13½***
1241 A270 25k multi *2.10 2.10*

Printed in sheets of 3 stamps + label.

Poets
A271

Designs: No. 1242, 27k, António Jacinto (1924-91) and poem. No. 1243, 45k, Agostinho Neto (1922-79) and poem.
No. 1244: a, 27k, Jacinto. b, 45k, Neto.

2003, Sept. 18 **Litho.** ***Perf. 13x13¼***
1242-1243 A271 Set of 2 *5.50 5.50*

Souvenir Sheet

1244 A271 Sheet of 2, #a-b 5.50 5.50

Hippotragus
Niger
A272

Designs: 27k, Pair with curved horns. 45k, Pair with straight horns. 47k, With herd in background.

2003, Oct. 9
1245-1247 A272 Set of 3 *9.25 9.25*

Women's Hairstyles — A273

No. 1248: a, Mbunda. b, Soyo. c, Huila. d, Humbi. e, Cabinda. f, Quipungu.

2003, Nov. 10 ***Perf. 13¼x13***
1248 A273 25k Sheet of 6, #a-f *12.00 12.00*

Whales
A274

Designs: 27k, Balaenoptera edeni. 45k, Cephalorhynchus heavisidii.
No. 1251: a, 47k, Giobiocephaia melaena.

2003, Dec. 5 ***Perf. 14¾x14¼***
1249-1250 A274 Set of 2 *5.50 5.50*

Souvenir Sheet

1251 A274 Sheet, #1249, 1251a *6.00 6.00*

Christmas — A275

No. 1252, 27k: a, The Ascension, attributed to Jorge Afonso. b, Adoration of the Shepherds, by André Reinoso.
No. 1253, 45k: a, Adoration of the Shepherds, detail showing Holy Family, by Josefa de Obidos. b, Adoration of the Shepherds, detail showing angels, by de Obidos.

2003, Dec. 5 ***Perf. 13¼x13¾***

Horiz. Pairs, #a-b

1252-1253 A275 Set of 2 *11.00 11.00*
1253c Souvenir sheet, #1252a-1252b, 1253a-1253b *11.00 11.00*

Chess — A276

No. 1254: a, Chess pieces. b, Chess pieces and board.

2003, Dec. 10
1254 A276 45k Horiz. pair, #a-b *7.25 7.25*

Eagles A277

Designs: No. 1255, 20k, Aquila rapax. No. 1256, 20k, Polemaetus bellicosus. No. 1257, 25k, Haliaeetus vocifer. No. 1258, 25k, Terathopius ecaudatus.
45k, Aquila verreauxi.

2003, Dec. 10 ***Perf. 14¾x14¼***
1255-1258 A277 Set of 4 *7.25 7.25*

Souvenir Sheet

1259 A277 45k multi *3.50 3.50*

Election of Pope John Paul II, 25th Anniv. — A278

No. 1260: a, Portrait. b, Pope waving.

2003, Dec. 15 ***Perf. 13¼x13¾***
1260 A278 27k Horiz. pair, #a-b, + central label *4.25 4.25*

Flora A279

Designs: No. 1261, 27k, Psidium guayava. No. 1262, 27k, Adansonia digitata. No. 1263, 45k, Cymbopogon citratus. No. 1264, 45k, Carica papaya.

2004, Aug. 17 Litho. ***Perf. 14x13½***
1261-1264 A279 Set of 4 *6.50 6.50*
1264a Souvenir sheet, #1261-1264 *6.50 6.50*

2004 Summer Olympics, Athens — A280

Designs: No. 1265, 27k, Handball. No. 1266, 27k, Basketball. No. 1267, 45k, Track. No. 1268, 45k, Volleyball.

2004, Sept. 30 ***Perf. 13¾***
1265-1268 A280 Set of 4 *6.50 6.50*

Marine Mammals A281

No. 1269: a, Megaptera novaeangliae. b, Cephalorhynchus heavisidii. c, Tursiops truncatus.
99k, Megaptera novaeangliae, diff.

2004, Oct. 9 ***Perf. 14x13½***
1269 Horiz. strip of 3 *4.25 4.25*
a.-b. A281 27k Either single *.65 .65*
c. A281 45k multi *1.10 1.10*

Souvenir Sheet

1270 A281 99k multi *4.50 4.50*

A sheetlet of eight hexagonal 15k depicting the national birds of South African Postal Operators Association (SAPOA) countries was produced in extremely limited quantities.

Trains A282

Designs: No. 1271, 27k, shown. No. 1272, 27k, Benguela Locomotive 225. No. 1273, 27k, Moçamedes locomotive.

2004, Nov. 30 ***Perf. 13¾***
1271-1273 A282 Set of 3 *3.50 3.50*

Fire Fighting A283

Telephone, emergency number and: No. 1274, 27k, Fire fighter with hose. No. 1275, 27k, Fire truck. 45k, Fire truck, diff.

2004, Nov. 30
1274-1276 A283 Set of 3 *4.25 4.25*
1276a Souvenir sheet, #1274-1276 *4.25 4.25*

FIFA (Fédération Internationale de Football Association), Cent. — A284

2004, Dec. 7
1277 A284 45k multi *2.10 2.10*

Christmas — A285

No. 1278: a, 27k, Magi. b, 45k Holy Family.

2004, Dec. 14 Litho. ***Perf. 13¾***
1278 A285 Horiz. pair, #a-b *3.25 3.25*

Worldwide Fund for Nature (WWF) — A286

No. 1279 — Colobus angolensis: a, Pair of adults. b, Adult and juvenile. c, Close-up of adult's face. d, Adult on rock.

2004, Dec. 29 Litho. ***Perf. 13¾***
1279 A286 27k Block of 4, #a-d *6.00 6.00*

Rotary International, Cent. — A287

Woman and: 45k, City. 51k, Ostriches.

2005, Feb. 23 Litho. ***Perf. 13x13¼***
1280-1281 A287 Set of 2 *6.50 6.50*
1281a Souvenir sheet, #1280-1281 *7.00 7.00*

Basketry A288

Designs: No. 1282, 27k, Kinda Kya Kuzambuila. No. 1283, 27k, Ngyendu. No. 1284, 45k, Ngombo Ya Cisuka. No. 1285, 45k, Silo.
90k, Kinda Kya Kuzambuila, diff.

2005, Sept. 6 Litho. ***Perf. 12x12½***
1282-1285 A288 Set of 4 *12.00 12.00*

Souvenir Sheet

1286 A288 90k multi *20.00 20.00*

Expo 2005, Aichi, Japan.

Independence, 30th Anniv. — A289

Designs: 27k, Capanda Hydroelectric Dam. 45k, Presidents Agostinho Neto and José Eduardo dos Santos, Angolan flag and dove.

2005, Nov. 8 Litho. ***Perf. 12x12½***
1287-1288 A289 Set of 2 *5.50 5.50*

Souvenir Sheet

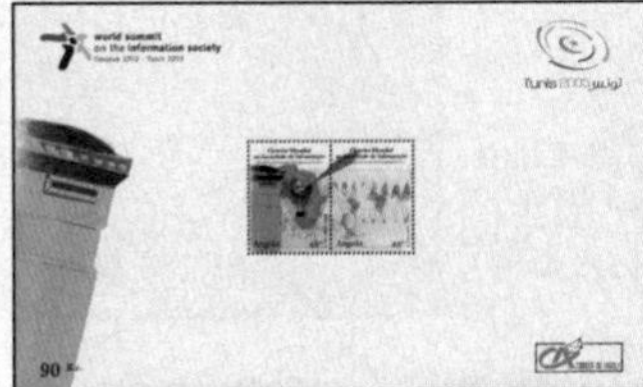

World Summit on the Information Society, Tunis — A290

No. 1289: a, Mail box, map of Africa, dish antenna, Angolan. b, Computer, world map, dish antenna.

2005, Nov. 14 Litho. ***Perf. 12***
1289 A290 45k Sheet of 2, #a-b *20.00 20.00*

Souvenir Sheet

23rd Ministerial Conference of the African Oil Producing Countries — A291

Design: 51p, Off-shore oil rig.

2006, Apr. 24 Litho. ***Perf. 12x12½***
1294 A291 51k multi — —

Four additional stamps were issued in this set. The editors would like to examine any examples.

A292

2006 World Cup Soccer Championships, Germany — A293

2006, Aug. 30 ***Perf. 12x11¾***
1295 A292 45k shown *3.00 3.00*
1296 A293 45k shown *3.00 3.00*

Souvenir Sheet

1297 A293 90k Player dribbling *4.50 4.50*

Nos. 1295-1297 lack country name.

Community of Portuguese Language Nations, 10th Anniv. — A294

Anniversary emblem, emblem of 2006 Lubrapex Intl. Stamp Exhibition and: 27k,

Dogs. No. 1299, 45k, Vultures. No. 1300, 45k, Parrots.

2006, Oct. 30 Litho. ***Perf. 12x11¾***
1298-1300 A294 Set of 3 *6.00 6.00*

Nos. 1298-1300 lack country name.

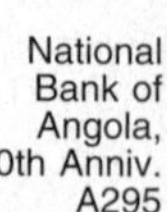

National Bank of Angola, 30th Anniv. A295

Designs: No. 1301, 27k, Bird in flight, people in boat, ship, Katanga cross currency. No. 1302, 27k, Men, cowrie shells. No. 1303, 45k, Early automobile, coins. No. 1304, 45k, Building, banknotes.
90k, Dome, luggage

2006, Nov. 7
1301-1304 A295 Set of 4 *7.50 7.50*

Souvenir Sheet

1305 A295 90k multi *7.00 7.00*

José Sayovo, First Angolan Paralympian Gold Medalist — A296

2006, Dec. 29 Litho. ***Perf. 12x11¾***
1306 A296 45k multi *1.10 1.10*

Peace, 5th Anniv. A297

2007, Apr. 20 Litho. ***Perf. 13x13½***
1307 A297 51k multi *1.75 1.75*

52nd Venice Art Biennale A298

Designs: 65k, Entire painting. 155k, Painting detail.

2007, Apr. 20 ***Perf. 13x13½***
1308 A298 65k multi *1.90 1.90*

Souvenir Sheet

Perf. 13½x13

1309 A298 155k multi *4.50 4.50*

No. 1309 contains one 60x40mm stamp.

Souvenir Sheet

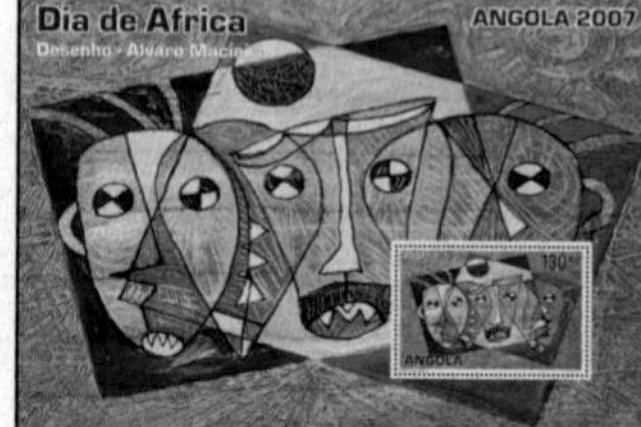

Africa Day — A299

2007, Apr. 20 ***Perf. 13½x13***
1310 A299 130k multi *3.75 3.75*

Scouting, Cent. — A300

No. 1311: a, 30k, Scouts sitting in fleur-de-lis pattern. b, 30k, Scouts sitting at desks. c, 55k, Scouts sitting on ground. d, 65k, Scouts saluting.
130k, Group of scouts standing on steps.

2007, June 1 ***Perf. 13x13½***
1311 A300 Sheet of 4, #a-d *5.50 5.50*

Souvenir Sheet

Perf. 13½x13

1312 A300 130k multi *4.00 4.00*

No. 1312 contains one 60x40mm stamp.

Souvenir Sheet

Southern African Development Community, 27th Anniv. — A301

2007, Aug. 17 ***Perf. 12½x13***
1313 A301 150k multi *8.00 8.00*

Souvenir Sheet

Sports — A302

Perf. 13¼ Syncopated

2007, Sept. 20
1314 A302 130k multi *4.00 4.00*

Souvenir Sheet

World Post Day — A303

No. 1315 — Post office at: a, Malange. b, Huamba.

2007, Oct. 9 ***Perf. 12¾x13½***
1315 A303 45k Sheet of 2, #a-b *2.75 2.75*

Sea Turtles — A304

No. 1316: a, 27k, Caretta caretta. b, 27k, Chelonia mydas. c, 45k, Eretmochelys imbricata. d, 45k, Lepidochelys olivacea.
130k, Dermochelys coriacea, vert.

2007, Nov. 11 ***Perf. 13x13¼***
1316 A304 Sheet of 4, #a-d *4.50 4.50*

Souvenir Sheet

Perf. 13¼ Syncopated

1317 A304 130k multi *4.00 4.00*

No. 1317 contains one 38x39mm stamp.

Angolan Cuisine A305

Various unnamed Angolan dishes: 37k, 40k, 59k, 153k.

2008, May 30 ***Perf. 13x13½***
1318-1320 A305 Set of 3 *7.00 7.00*

Souvenir Sheet

1321 A305 153k multi *13.00 13.00*

Water Resources A306

Designs: No. 1322, 37k, Kuebe River. No. 1323, 37k, Kuanza Rapids. No. 1324, 40k, Kuanza River. No. 1325, 40k, Mouth of Mbridge River.
153k, Kalandula Waterfalls.

2008, June 30 ***Perf. 13x13½***
1322-1325 A306 Set of 4 *8.00 8.00*

Souvenir Sheet

1326 A306 153k multi *8.00 8.00*

Miniature Sheet

Lwini Fund, 10th Anniv. — A307

No. 1327: a, 37k, Land mine removal, vert. b, 40k, Wooden box and books. c, 40k, Princess Diana and Angolan woman. d, 59k, Children in wheelchairs. e, 59k, Men making baskets.

Perf. 13½x13, 13x13½ (37k)

2008, June 30
1327 A307 Sheet of 5, #a-e, + label *10.00 10.00*

Water Jugs — A308

Designs: No. 1328, 37k, Jug with head on top. No. 1329, 37k, Two-handled jug. No. 1330, 40k, Jug with handle and spout. No. 1331, 40k, Jug with woman on top.

2008, July 30 ***Perf. 13½x13***
1328-1331 A308 Set of 4 *8.50 8.50*

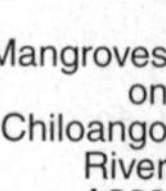

Mangroves on Chiloango River A309

Designs: No. 1332, 37k, Roots. No. 1333, 37k, Trees along river. 59k, Roots, diff.

2008, Aug. 30 ***Perf. 13x13½***
1332-1334 A309 Set of 3 *7.00 7.00*

Miniature Sheet

2008 Summer Olympics, Beijing — A310

No. 1335: a, Basketball. b, Handball. c, Running. d, Canoeing.

2008, Sept. 20 ***Perf. 12¾x13½***
1335 A310 30k Sheet of 4, #a-d *5.00 5.00*

Coffee — A311

Designs: 37k, Coffee berries. No. 1337, 45k, Woman picking berries, horiz. No. 1338, 45k, Tree with berries.

Perf. 13¼x13, 13x13¼

2009, Dec. 7 Litho.

Granite Paper

1336-1338 A311 Set of 3 *4.00 4.00*

Pres. Antonio Agostinho Neto (1922-79) — A312

Pres. Neto: 40k, Behind lectern. 50k, In army uniform.
150k, Pres. Neto with school children, horiz.

2009, Dec. 7 **Granite Paper**

1339-1340 A312 Set of 2 *2.75 2.75*

Souvenir Sheet

1341 A312 150k multi *4.25 4.25*

Souvenir Sheet

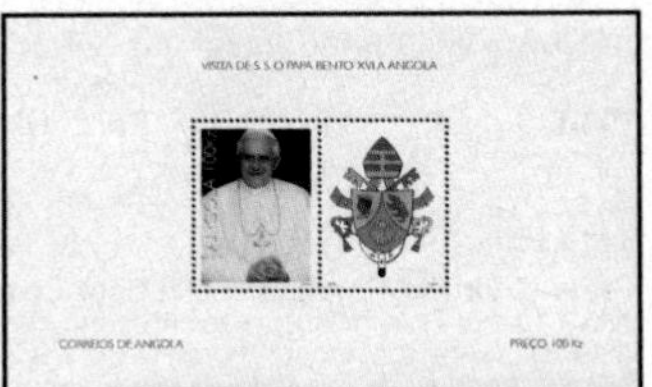

Pope Benedict XVI — A313

2009, Dec. 7 ***Perf. 13¼x13***

Granite Paper

1342 A313 100k multi + label *4.00 4.00*

2010 Africa Cup of Nations Soccer Tournament, Angola — A314

Stadiums in: No. 1343, 40k, Benguela. No. 1344, 40k, Cabinda. No. 1345, 50k, Luanda. No. 1346, 50k, Huilá.

2010, Jan. 8 ***Perf. 13x13¼***

Granite Paper

1343-1346 A314 Set of 4 *5.00 5.00*

Africa Day A315

Designs: 40k, People from Uige and Zaire Provinces. 60k, People from Lunda and Moxico Provinces.
120k, People from Luanda Province.

2010 ***Perf. 13x13¼***

1348-1349 A315 Set of 2 2.75 2.75

Souvenir Sheet

Perf. 13¼ Syncopated

1350 A315 120k multi 3.75 3.75

Expo 2010, Shanghai. No. 1350 contains one 50x39mm stamp.

African Women's Day — A316

Designs: No. 1351, 60k, Kwanhama woman. No. 1352, 60k, Quipungo woman.
150k, Mucubal woman.

2010 ***Perf. 13¼x13***

1351-1352 A316 Set of 2 3.25 3.25

Souvenir Sheet

Perf. 13¼ Syncopated

1353 A316 150k multi 4.00 4.00

Expo 2010, Shanghai. No. 1353 contains one 39x50mm stamp.

Intl. Children's Day A317

Children, flowers and wildlife with background color of: No. 1354, 40k, Green. No. 1355, 40k, Orange. No. 1356, 60k, Blue. No. 1357, 60k, Green.
150k, Orange.

2010 ***Perf. 13x13¼***

1354-1357 A317 Set of 4 5.00 5.00

Souvenir Sheet

Perf. 13¼ Syncopated

1358 A317 150k multi 4.25 4.25

Expo 2010, Shanghai. No. 1358 contains one 50x39mm stamp.

Organization of Petroleum Exporting Countries, 50th Anniv. — A318

50th anniversary emblem with Angolan flag and: 40k, Antelope. 50k, Statue. 60k, Off-shore oil drilling platform.
150k, Off-shore oil drilling platform and other equipment.

2010, Oct. ***Perf. 13x13¼***

1359-1361 A318 Set of 3 3.25 3.25

Souvenir Sheet

Perf. 13½ Syncopated

1362 A318 150k multi 3.25 3.25

No. 1362 contains one 50x39mm stamp.

Portuguese Agency for External Investment and Commerce, 20th Anniv. — A319

2010, Nov. ***Perf. 13x13¼***

1363 A319 60k multi 1.40 1.40

Worldwide Fund for Nature (WWF) A320

No. 1364: a, Two Cercopithecus cephus, one on rock at left. b, Three Cercopithecus ascanius. c, Two Cercopithecus ascanius. d, Two Cercopithecus cephus, one on branch at right.
350k, Cercopithecus cephus and Cercopithecus ascanius, vert.

2011, Aug. 31 ***Perf. 13x13¼***

1364 Strip of 4, #a-d 9.00 9.00
a.-d. A320 100k Any single 2.25 2.25
e. Souvenir sheet of 8, 2 each #1364a-1364d 18.00 18.00

Souvenir Sheet

Perf. 13¼

1365 A320 350k multi 7.50 7.50

No. 1365 contains one 39x45mm stamp.

A321

A322

A323

Southern African Development Community, 31st Anniv. — A324

Design: 150k, Emblem and map of Africa, diff.

2011, Aug. 12 ***Perf. 13x13¼***

1366 A321 50k multi 1.10 1.10
1367 A322 50k multi 1.10 1.10
1368 A323 50k multi 1.10 1.10
1369 A324 50k multi 1.10 1.10
Nos. 1366-1369 (4) 4.40 4.40

Souvenir Sheet

Perf. 13½

1370 A324 150k multi 3.25 3.25

Peonies — A325

No. 1371: a, Paeonia daurica. b, Paeonia mlokosewitschii. c, Paeonia veitchii. d, Paeonia broteri.
350k, Paeonia officinalis salmonea.

2011, Apr. 31 ***Perf. 13¼x13***

1371 Horiz. strip of 4 9.00 9.00
a.-d. A325 100k Any single 2.25 2.25
e. Souvenir sheet of 4, #1371a-1371d 9.00 9.00

Souvenir Sheet

Perf. 13½

1372 A325 350k multi 7.50 7.50

China 2011 International Stamp Exhibition, Wuxi. No. 1372 contains one 39x45mm stamp.

National Bank of Angola, 35th Anniv. A326

Emblem and: 40k, Ornamental planter. 50k, Crest on exterior wall. No. 1375, 60k, Roof ornament. No. 1376, 60k, Windows near corner of building.
150k, Aerial view of building.

2011, Nov. 4 ***Perf. 13x13¼***

1373-1376 A326 Set of 4 4.50 4.50

Souvenir Sheet

Perf. 13x13¼ Syncopated

1377 A326 150k multi 3.25 3.25

No. 1377 contains one 50x39mm stamp.

SEMI-POSTAL STAMPS

Angolan Red Cross — SP1

No. B1, Mother and child. No. B2, Zebra and foal.

1991, Sept. 19 **Litho.** ***Perf. 14***

B1 SP1 20k +5k multi 1.25 1.25
B2 SP1 40k +5k multi 2.25 2.25

AIR POST STAMPS

Plane Over Globe
Common Design Type

Perf. 13½x13

1938, July 26 **Engr.** **Unwmk.**

Name and Value in Black

C1	CD39	10c	red orange	.55	.45
C2	CD39	20c	purple	.55	.40
C3	CD39	50c	orange	.55	.45
C4	CD39	1a	ultra	.55	.45
C5	CD39	2a	lilac brn	1.25	.40
C6	CD39	3a	dk green	2.25	.75
C7	CD39	5a	red brown	5.75	1.00
C8	CD39	9a	rose carmine	8.50	2.00
C9	CD39	10a	magenta	12.50	3.00
	Nos. C1-C9 (9)			32.45	8.90

No. C7 exists with overprint "Exposicao Internacional de Nova York, 1939-1940" and Trylon and Perisphere. Value; used & unused $110., never hinged, $175.

AP2

1947, Aug. **Litho.** ***Rough Perf. 10½***

C10	AP2	1a	red brown	11.50	7.00
C11	AP2	2a	yellow grn	12.50	8.00
C12	AP2	3a	orange	12.50	8.00
C13	AP2	3.50a	orange	24.00	8.00
C14	AP2	5a	olive grn	110.00	30.00
C15	AP2	6a	rose	110.00	22.50
C16	AP2	9a	red	300.00	225.00
C17	AP2	10a	green	250.00	125.00
C18	AP2	20a	blue	375.00	125.00
C19	AP2	50a	black	500.00	300.00
C20	AP2	100a	yellow	825.00	700.00
	Nos. C10-C20 (11)			2,530.	1,558.

Planes Circling Globe — AP3

1949, May 1 **Photo.** ***Perf. 11½***

C21	AP3	1a	henna brown	.75	.25
C22	AP3	2a	red brown	1.50	.25
C23	AP3	3a	plum	2.00	.25

C24 AP3 6a dull green 4.00 .85
C25 AP3 9a violet brown 5.50 2.25
Nos. C21-C25 (5) 13.75 3.85
Set, Never Hinged 21.00

Catalogue values for unused stamps in this section, from this point to the end of the section, are for Never Hinged items.

Cambambe Dam AP4

Designs: 1.50e, Oil refinery, vert. 3e, Salazar Dam. 4e, Capt. Teófilo Duarte Dam. 4.50e, Craveiro Lopes Dam. 5e, Cuango Dam. 6e, Quanza River Bridge. 7e, Capt. Teófilo Duarte Bridge. 8.50e, Oliveira Salazar Bridge. 12.50e, Capt. Silva Carvalho Bridge.

Perf. 11½x12, 12x11½

1965, July 12 Litho. Unwmk.

C26 AP4 1.50e multicolored 2.50 .25
C27 AP4 2.50e multicolored 1.50 .25
C28 AP4 3e multicolored 2.50 .25
C29 AP4 4e multicolored 1.00 .25
C30 AP4 4.50e multicolored 1.00 .25
C31 AP4 5e multicolored 1.60 .25
C32 AP4 6e multicolored 1.60 .25
C33 AP4 7e multicolored 2.50 .25
C34 AP4 8.50e multicolored 3.25 1.40
C35 AP4 12.50e multicolored 3.75 1.60
Nos. C26-C35 (10) 21.20 5.00

Stamp Centenary Type

Design: 2.50e, Boeing 707 jet & Angola #2.

1970, Dec. 1 Litho. *Perf. 13½*

C36 A83 2.50e multicolored 2.00 .25
a. Souv. sheet of 3, #565-566, C36 16.00 16.00

No. C36a sold for 15e.

No. C36 Ovptd.

1980, June 15 Litho. *Perf. 13½*

C37 A83 2.50e multicolored 3.00 .55

POSTAGE DUE STAMPS

D1

1904 Unwmk. Typo. *Perf. 11½x12*

J1 D1 5r yellow grn .55 .45
J2 D1 10r slate .55 .45
J3 D1 20r yellow brn 1.00 .70
J4 D1 30r orange 1.00 .70
J5 D1 50r gray brown 1.40 1.00
J6 D1 60r red brown 11.50 7.00
J7 D1 100r lilac 5.00 3.50
J8 D1 130r dull blue 5.00 3.50
J9 D1 200r carmine 14.00 9.00
J10 D1 500r gray violet 12.00 7.75
Nos. J1-J10 (10) 52.00 34.05

Postage Due Stamps of 1904 Overprinted in Carmine or Green

1911

J11 D1 5r yellow grn .40 .35
J12 D1 10r slate .40 .35
J13 D1 20r yellow brn .40 .35
J14 D1 30r orange .55 .45
J15 D1 50r gray brown .55 .45
J16 D1 60r red brown 1.50 1.00
J17 D1 100r lilac 1.50 1.00
J18 D1 130r dull blue 1.75 1.25
J19 D1 200r carmine (G) 2.25 1.25
J20 D1 500r gray violet 2.50 2.25
Nos. J11-J20 (10) 11.80 8.70

D2

1921 *Perf. 11½*

J21 D2 ½c yellow green .40 .35
J22 D2 1c slate .40 .35
J23 D2 2c orange brown .40 .35
J24 D2 3c orange .40 .35
J25 D2 5c gray brown .40 .35
J26 D2 6c lt brown .40 .35
J27 D2 10c red violet .60 .40
J28 D2 13c dull blue 1.10 .95
J29 D2 20c carmine 1.10 .95
J30 D2 50c gray 1.10 .95
Nos. J21-J30 (10) 6.30 5.35

For surcharges see Nos. 268-270.

Catalogue values for unused stamps in this section, from this point to the end of the section, are for Never Hinged items.

Stamps of 1932 Surcharged in Black

1948 Wmk. 232 *Perf. 12x11½*

J31 A14 10c on 20c gray .45 .30
J32 A14 20c on 30c myrtle grn .75 .60
J33 A14 30c on 50c lt brown 1.40 .85
J34 A14 40c on 1a claret 2.25 1.25
J35 A14 50c on 2a dull vio 3.25 1.75
J36 A14 1a on 5a pale yel grn 4.75 2.75
Nos. J31-J36 (6) 12.85 7.50

Common Design Type

Photogravure and Typographed

1952 Unwmk. *Perf. 14*

Numeral in Red, Frame Multicolored

J37 CD45 10c red brown .35 .25
J38 CD45 30c olive green .35 .25
J39 CD45 50c chocolate .35 .25
J40 CD45 1a dk vio blue .80 .70
J41 CD45 2a red brown 1.10 .85
J42 CD45 5a black brown 1.10 .85
Nos. J37-J42 (6) 4.05 3.15

NEWSPAPER STAMP

N1

Perf. 11½, 12½, 13½

1893 Typo. Unwmk.

P1 N1 2½r brown 3.50 1.50

No. P1 was also used for ordinary postage.
For surcharges see Nos. 37, 82, 180, 235.

POSTAL TAX STAMPS

Pombal Issue

Common Design Types

1925, May 8 Unwmk. *Perf. 12½*

RA1 CD28 15c lilac & black 1.25 1.00
RA2 CD29 15c lilac & black 1.25 1.00
RA3 CD30 15c lilac & black 1.25 1.00
Nos. RA1-RA3 (3) 3.75 3.00

"Charity" PT1

Coat of Arms PT2

1929 Litho. *Perf. 11*

Without Gum

RA4 PT1 50c dark blue 7.25 2.25

1939 Without Gum *Perf. 10½*

RA5 PT2 50c turq green 3.75 .35
RA6 PT2 1a red 8.50 2.50

A 1.50a, type PT2, was issued for fiscal use. Value, $5.

Catalogue values for unused stamps in this section, from this point to the end of the section, are for Never Hinged items.

Old Man — PT3

Designs: 1e, Boy. 1.50e, Girl.

Imprint: "Foto-Lito-E.G.A.-Luanda"

Heads in dark brown

1955 Unwmk. *Perf. 13*

RA7 PT3 50c dk ocher .40 .25
RA8 PT3 1e orange ver .60 .30
RA9 PT3 1.50e brt yel grn 1.00 .35
Nos. RA7-RA9 (3) 2.00 .90

A 2.50e, type PT3 showing an old woman, was issued for revenue use. Value $2.
See Nos. RA16, RA19-RA21, RA25-RA27.

No. RA7 Surcharged in Red or Black

1957-58 Head in dark brown

RA11 PT3 10c on 50c dk ocher (R) .40 .40
RA12 PT3 10c on 50c dk ocher ('58) .40 .40
RA13 PT3 30c on 50c dk ocher .40 .40
Nos. RA11-RA13 (3) 1.20 1.20

Mother and Child — PT4

Design: 30c, Boy and girl.

1959 Litho. *Perf. 13*

RA14 PT4 10c orange & blk .30 .30
RA15 PT4 30c slate & blk .30 .30

Type of 1955 Redrawn

Design: 1e, Boy.

1961, Nov. *Perf. 13*

RA16 PT3 1e salmon pink & dk brn .35 .35

Denomination in italics.

Yellow, White and Black Men — PT5

1962, July 1 Typo. *Perf. 10½*

Without Gum

RA17 PT5 50c multicolored .50 .40
RA18 PT5 1e multicolored .75 .40

Issued for the Provincial Settlement Committee (Junta Provincial do Povoamento). The tax was used to promote Portuguese settlement in Angola, and to raise educational and living standards of recent immigrants.

Denominations higher than 1e were used for revenue purposes.

Head Type of 1955

Designs: 50c, Old man. 1e, Boy. 1.50e, Girl.

Without Imprint

Heads in dark brown

1964-65 Litho. *Perf. 11½*

RA19 PT3 50c orange .40 .25
RA20 PT3 1e dull red org ('65) .40 .25
RA21 PT3 1.50e yel grn ('65) .60 .35
Nos. RA19-RA21 (3) 1.40 .85

No. RA20 is the second redrawing of 1e, with bolder lettering. Space between "Assistencia" and denomination on RA20-RA21 is ½mm; on the 1955 issue space is 2¼mm and 1¾mm, respectively.

Map of Angola, Industrial and Farm Workers — PT6

1965, Sept. 1 Litho. *Perf. 13*

RA22 PT6 50c multicolored .35 .25
RA23 PT6 1e multicolored .50 .30

The 2e was used for revenue purposes. Value 50c.

Head Type of 1955

Designs: 50c, Old man. 1e, Boy. 1.50e, Girl.

Imprint: "I.N.A." or "INA" (1e)

1966 Heads in dark brown

RA25 PT3 50c dull orange .35 .25
RA26 PT3 1e dull brick red .35 .25
RA27 PT3 1.50e lt yel grn .55 .30
Nos. RA25-RA27 (3) 1.25 .80

Woman Planting Tree — PT7

1972 Litho. *Perf. 13*

RA28 PT7 50c shown .35 .35
RA29 PT7 1e Workers .35 .35
RA30 PT7 2e Produce .35 .35
Nos. RA28-RA30 (3) 1.05 1.05

POSTAL TAX DUE STAMPS

Pombal Issue

Common Design Types

1925, May 8 Unwmk. *Perf. 12½*

RAJ1 CD28 30c lilac & black 1.25 1.00
RAJ2 CD29 30c lilac & black 1.25 1.00
RAJ3 CD30 30c lilac & black 1.25 1.00
Nos. RAJ1-RAJ3 (3) 3.75 3.00

See note after Portugal No. RAJ4.

ANGRA

ˈaŋ-grə

LOCATION — An administrative district of the Azores, consisting of the islands of Terceira, Sao Jorge and Graciosa.
GOVT. — A district of Portugal
AREA — 275 sq. mi.
POP. — 70,000 (approx.)
CAPITAL — Angra do Heroismo

1000 Reis = 1 Milreis

King Carlos — A1

1892-93 Typo. Unwmk. *Perf. 12½*

No.	Type	Description	Unused	Used
1	A1	5r yellow	5.00	2.75
a.		Perf 11½	14.00	7.00
b.		Perf 13½	4.00	2.75
2	A1	10r redsh violet	5.00	2.75
a.		Perf 13½	5.75	4.00
3	A1	15r chocolate	7.00	4.00
a.		Perf 13½	7.00	4.00
4	A1	20r lavender	9.0	3.00
a.		Perf 13½	9.00	3.25
5	A1	25r green	5.00	.80
a.		Perf 13½	10.00	6.00
b.		Perf 11½	6.00	1.25
7	A1	50r blue	11.00	4.50
a.		Perf 13½	14.00	7.00
8	A1	75r carmine	12.00	6.00
9	A1	80r yellow green	15.00	11.50
10	A1	100r brown, *yel*, perf 13½ ('93)	55.00	16.00
a.		Perf 12½	175.00	150.00
11	A1	150r car, *rose* ('93)	65.00	45.00
a.		Perf 13½	75.00	60.00
12	A1	200r dk blue, *bl* ('93)	65.00	45.00
		Never hinged	90.00	
a.		Perf 13½	75.00	60.00
13	A1	300r dk blue, *sal* ('93)	65.00	45.00
		Never hinged	90.00	
a.		Perf 13½	75.00	60.00
		Nos. 1-13 (12)	319.00	186.30

Reprints of 50r, 150r, 200r and 300r, made in 1900, are perf. 11½ and ungummed. Value, each $50. Reprints of all values, made in 1905, have shiny white gum and clean-cut perf. Value, each $22.50.

King Carlos — A2

Name and Value in Black except Nos. 26 and 35

1897-1905 *Perf. 11½*

No.	Type	Description	Unused	Used
14	A2	2½r gray	.75	.50
15	A2	5r orange	.75	.50
a.		Diagonal half used as 2½r on newspaper or circular		32.50
16	A2	10r yellow grn	.75	.50
17	A2	15r brown	10.00	7.00
18	A2	15r gray grn ('99)	1.00	.70
19	A2	20r gray violet	2.00	1.50
20	A2	25r sea green	3.25	1.40
21	A2	25r car rose ('99)	.75	.70
22	A2	50r dark blue	6.00	2.00
23	A2	50r ultra ('05)	20.00	12.50
24	A2	65r slate bl ('98)	1.40	.70
25	A2	75r rose	4.00	1.90
26	A2	75r gray brn & car, *straw* ('05)	20.00	12.50
27	A2	80r violet	1.60	1.40
28	A2	100r dk blue, *bl*	3.50	2.00
29	A2	115r org brn, *pink* ('98)	4.00	2.25
30	A2	130r gray brn, *straw* ('98)	4.00	2.25
31	A2	150r lt brn, *straw*	3.50	2.00
32	A2	180r sl, *pnksh* ('98)	5.00	3.25
33	A2	200r red vio, *pnksh*	6.00	5.50
34	A2	300r blue, *rose*	12.00	8.00
35	A2	500r blk & red, *bl*	20.00	16.00
a.		Perf. 12½	35.00	20.00
		Nos. 14-35 (22)	130.25	85.05

Azores stamps were used in Angra from 1906 to 1931, when they were superseded by those of Portugal.

ANGUILLA

aŋ-ˌgwi-lə

LOCATION — In the West Indies southeast of Puerto Rico
GOVT. — British territory
AREA — 60 sq. mi.
POP. — 10,663 (est. 1997)
CAPITAL — The Valley

Anguilla separated unilaterally from the Associated State of St. Kitts-Nevis-Anguilla in 1967, formalized in 1980 following direct United Kingdom intervention some years before. A British Commissioner exercises executive authority.

100 Cents = 1 Eastern Caribbean Dollar

Catalogue values for all unused stamps in this country are for Never Hinged items.

St. Kitts-Nevis Nos. 145-160 Overprinted

On Type A14

On Type A15

Wmk. 314

1967, Sept. 4 Photo. *Perf. 14*

No.	Type	Description	Unused	Used
1	A14	½c blue & dk brn	85.00	32.50
2	A15	1c multicolored	100.00	11.00
3	A14	2c multicolored	85.00	2.75
4	A14	3c multicolored	85.00	7.25
5	A15	4c multicolored	100.00	9.00
6	A15	5c multicolored	375.00	35.00
7	A15	6c multicolored	160.00	14.50
8	A15	10c multicolored	90.00	11.00
9	A14	15c multicolored	180.00	22.50
10	A15	20c multicolored	425.00	40.00
11	A14	25c multicolored	300.00	75.00
12	A15	50c multicolored	*5,500.*	*800.00*
13	A14	60c multicolored	*6,500.*	*1,500.*
14	A14	$1 multicolored	*5,000.*	*750.00*
15	A15	$2.50 multicolored	*3,750.*	*475.00*
16	A14	$5 multicolored	*4,200.*	*500.00*
		Nos. 1-16 (16)	26,935.	4,285.

Counterfeit overprints exist.

Mahogany Tree, The Quarter — A1

Designs: 2c, Sombrero Lighthouse. 3c, St. Mary's Church. 4c, Valley Police Station. 5c, Old Plantation House, Mt. Fortune. 6c, Valley Post Office. 10c, Methodist Church, West End. 15c, Wall-Blake Airport. 20c, Plane over Sandy Ground. 25c, Island Harbor. 40c, Map of Anguilla. 60c, Hermit crab and starfish. $1, Hibiscus. $2.50, Coconut harvest. $5, Spiny lobster.

Perf. 12½x13

1967-68 Litho. Unwmk.

No.	Type	Description	Unused	Used
17	A1	1c orange & multi	.25	.80
18	A1	2c gray green & blk	.25	.90
19	A1	3c emerald & blk	.25	.25
20	A1	4c brt blue & blk	.25	.25
21	A1	5c lt blue & multi	.25	.25
22	A1	6c ver & black	.25	.25
23	A1	10c multicolored	.25	.25
24	A1	15c multicolored	2.00	.25
25	A1	20c multicolored	1.50	1.75
26	A1	25c multicolored	.80	.25
27	A1	40c blue & multi	1.10	1.75
28	A1	60c yellow & multi	5.00	4.50
29	A1	$1 lt green & multi	2.00	3.25
30	A1	$2.50 multicolored	2.75	4.50
31	A1	$5 multicolored	4.00	4.50
		Nos. 17-31 (15)	20.90	23.70

Issued: 1c, 5c, 10c, 20c, 25c, 40c, 11/27/67; 3c, 4c, 15c, 60c, $1, $5, 2/10/68; 2c, 6c, $2.50, 3/21/68.

For overprints see Nos. 53-67, 78-82.

Sailboats — A2

Designs: 15c, Boat building. 25c, Schooner Warspite. 40c, Yacht Atlantic Star.

1968, May 11 *Perf. 14*

No.	Type	Description	Unused	Used
32	A2	10c rose & multi	.45	.25
33	A2	15c olive & multi	.50	.25
34	A2	25c lilac rose & multi	.70	.35
35	A2	40c dull blue & multi	.80	.55
		Nos. 32-35 (4)	2.45	1.40

Purple-throated Carib — A3

Anguillan Birds: 15c, Bananaquit. 25c, Black-necked stilt, horiz. 40c, Royal tern, horiz.

1968, July 8

No.	Type	Description	Unused	Used
36	A3	10c dull yel & multi	1.25	.25
37	A3	15c yel green & multi	1.50	.30
38	A3	25c multicolored	1.90	.30
39	A3	40c multicolored	2.40	.40
		Nos. 36-39 (4)	7.05	1.25

Girl Guide Badge — A4

10c, Girl Guide badge, horiz. 25c, Badge and Headquarters, horiz. 40c, Merit Badges.

1968, Oct. 14 *Perf. 13x13½, 13½x13*

No.	Type	Description	Unused	Used
40	A4	10c lt green & multi	.25	.25
41	A4	15c lt blue & multi	.25	.25
42	A4	25c multicolored	.30	.25
43	A4	40c multicolored	.40	.25
		Nos. 40-43 (4)	1.20	1.00

Anguillan Girl Guides, 35th anniversary.

Three Kings — A5

Christmas: 10c, Three Kings seeing Star, vert. 15c, Holy Family, vert. 40c, Shepherds seeing Star. 50c, Holy Family and donkey.

1968, Nov. 18

No.	Type	Description	Unused	Used
44	A5	1c lilac rose & black	.25	.25
45	A5	10c blue & black	.25	.25
46	A5	15c brown & black	.25	.25
47	A5	40c brt ultra & black	.25	.25
48	A5	50c green & black	.40	.25
		Nos. 44-48 (5)	1.40	1.25

Bagging Salt — A6

Salt Industry: 15c, Packing salt. 40c, Salt pond. 50c, Loading salt.

1969, Jan. 4 *Perf. 13*

No.	Type	Description	Unused	Used
49	A6	10c red & multi	.30	.25
50	A6	15c lt blue & multi	.35	.25
51	A6	40c emerald & multi	.40	.25
52	A6	50c purple & multi	.45	.25
		Nos. 49-52 (4)	1.50	1.00

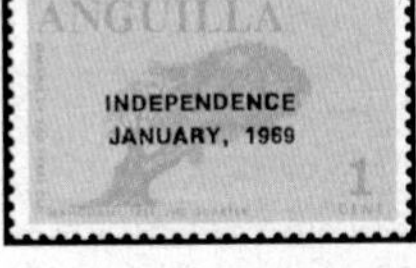

Nos. 17-31 Overprinted

1969, Jan. 9 *Perf. 12½x13*

No.	Type	Description	Unused	Used
53	A1	1c orange & multi	.25	.25
54	A1	2c gray green & blk	.25	.25
55	A1	3c emerald & blk	.25	.25
56	A1	4c brt blue & blk	.25	.25
57	A1	5c lt blue & multi	.25	.25
58	A1	6c vermilion & blk	.25	.25
59	A1	10c multicolored	.25	.25
60	A1	15c multicolored	.25	.30
61	A1	20c multicolored	.30	.35
62	A1	25c multicolored	.40	.50
63	A1	40c blue & multi	.70	*.75*
64	A1	60c yellow & multi	.95	*1.10*
65	A1	$1 lt green & multi	1.75	*1.90*
66	A1	$2.50 multicolored	4.75	*4.50*
67	A1	$5 multicolored	10.00	*9.50*
		Nos. 53-67 (15)	20.85	*20.65*

Crucifixion, School of Quentin Massys — A7

Easter: 40c, The Last Supper, ascribed to Roberti.

1969, Mar. 31 Litho. *Perf. 13½*

No.	Type	Description	Unused	Used
68	A7	25c multicolored	.30	.25
69	A7	40c multicolored	.50	.25

Amaryllis — A8

1969, June 10 *Perf. 14*

No.	Type	Description	Unused	Used
70	A8	10c shown	.25	.25
71	A8	15c Bougainvillea	.40	.35
72	A8	40c Hibiscus	.70	.60
73	A8	50c Cattleya orchid	2.25	1.40
		Nos. 70-73 (4)	3.60	2.60

Turban and Star Shells — A9

Sea Shells: 15c, Spiny oysters. 40c, Scotch, royal and smooth bonnets. 50c, Triton trumpet.

1969, Sept. 22

No.	Type	Description	Unused	Used
74	A9	10c multicolored	.30	.25
75	A9	15c multicolored	.40	.30
76	A9	40c multicolored	.80	.35
77	A9	50c multicolored	1.00	.40
		Nos. 74-77 (4)	2.50	1.30

Nos. 17, 25-28 Overprinted "CHRISTMAS 1969" and Various Christmas Designs

1969, Oct. 27 ***Perf. 12½x13***

No.	Type	Description	Unused	Used
78	A1	1c orange & multi	.25	.25
79	A1	20c multicolored	.25	.25
80	A1	25c multicolored	.25	.25
81	A1	40c blue & multi	.60	.25
82	A1	60c yellow & multi	1.25	.30
		Nos. 78-82 (5)	2.60	1.30

Red Goatfish A10

Designs: 15c, Blue-striped grunts. 40c, Mutton grouper. 50c, Banded butterfly-fish.

1969, Dec. 1 ***Perf. 14***

No.	Type	Description	Unused	Used
83	A10	10c multicolored	.35	.25
84	A10	15c multicolored	.45	.25
85	A10	40c multicolored	1.50	.55
86	A10	50c multicolored	1.90	.80
		Nos. 83-86 (4)	4.20	1.85

Morning Glory — A11

1970, Feb. 23

No.	Type	Description	Unused	Used
87	A11	10c shown	.55	.25
88	A11	15c Blue petrea	.75	.25
89	A11	40c Hibiscus	1.10	.30
90	A11	50c Flamboyant	1.40	.40
		Nos. 87-90 (4)	3.80	1.20

The Way to Calvary, by Tiepolo — A12

Easter: 20c, Crucifixion, by Masaccio, vert. 40c, Descent from the Cross, by Rosso Fiorentino, vert. 60c, Jesus Carrying the Cross, by Murillo.

1970, Mar. 26 ***Perf. 13½***

No.	Type	Description	Unused	Used
91	A12	10c multicolored	.25	.25
92	A12	20c multicolored	.25	.25
93	A12	40c multicolored	.40	.25
94	A12	60c multicolored	.60	.35
		Nos. 91-94 (4)	1.50	1.10

Anguilla Map, Scout Badge A13

Designs: 15c, Cub Scouts practicing first aid. 40c, Monkey bridge. 50c, Scout Headquarters, The Valley, and Lord Baden-Powell.

1970, Aug. 10 ***Perf. 13***

No.	Type	Description	Unused	Used
95	A13	10c multicolored	.25	.25
96	A13	15c multicolored	.30	.25
97	A13	40c multicolored	.40	.35
98	A13	50c multicolored	.60	.35
		Nos. 95-98 (4)	1.55	1.20

Anguilla Boy Scouts, 40th anniversary.

Boat Building A14

Designs: 2c, Road construction. 3c, Blowing Point dock. 4c, Radio announcer. 5c, Cottage Hospital extension. 6c, Valley secondary school. 10c, Hotel extension. 15c, Sandy Ground. 20c, Supermarket and movie house. 25c, Bananas and mangoes. 40c, Wall-Blake airport. 60c, Sandy Ground jetty. $1, Administration building. $2.50, Cow and calf. $5, Sandy Hill Bay.

1970, Nov. 23 **Litho.** ***Perf. 14***

No.	Type	Description	Unused	Used
99	A14	1c multicolored	.45	.40
100	A14	2c multicolored	.45	.40
101	A14	3c multicolored	.45	.25
102	A14	4c multicolored	.45	.55
103	A14	5c multicolored	.65	.55
104	A14	6c multicolored	.45	.55
105	A14	10c multicolored	.45	.30
106	A14	15c multicolored	.45	.30
107	A14	20c multicolored	.80	.30
108	A14	25c multicolored	.50	*1.10*
109	A14	40c multicolored	4.50	3.25
110	A14	60c multicolored	1.00	*3.50*
111	A14	$1 multicolored	1.90	1.25
112	A14	$2.50 multicolored	2.40	*4.00*
113	A14	$5 multicolored	4.75	4.00
		Nos. 99-113 (15)	19.65	20.70

Adoration of the Shepherds, by Guido Reni — A15

Christmas: 20c, Virgin and Child, by Benozzo Gozzoli. 25c, Nativity, by Botticelli. 40c, Santa Margherita Madonna, by Mazzola. 50c, Adoration of the Kings, by Tiepolo.

1970, Dec. 11 ***Perf. 13½***

No.	Type	Description	Unused	Used
114	A15	1c multicolored	.25	.25
115	A15	20c multicolored	.25	.25
116	A15	25c multicolored	.30	.25
117	A15	40c multicolored	.50	.35
118	A15	50c multicolored	.55	.45
		Nos. 114-118 (5)	1.85	1.55

Angels Weeping over the Dead Christ, by Guercino — A16

Easter: 10c, Ecce Homo, by Correggio, vert. 15c, Christ Appearing to St. Peter, by Carracci, vert. 50c, The Supper at Emmaus, by Caravaggio.

1971, Mar. 29

No.	Type	Description	Unused	Used
119	A16	10c pink & multi	.25	.25
120	A16	15c lt blue & multi	.25	.25
121	A16	40c yel green & multi	.45	.25
122	A16	50c violet & multi	.55	.25
		Nos. 119-122 (4)	1.50	1.00

Hypolimnas Misippus — A17

Butterflies: 15c, Junonia lavinia. 40c, Agraulis vanillae. 50c, Danaus plexippus.

1971, June 21 ***Perf. 14x14½***

No.	Type	Description	Unused	Used
123	A17	10c multicolored	2.75	1.00
124	A17	15c multicolored	2.75	1.25
125	A17	40c multicolored	3.25	1.75
126	A17	50c multicolored	3.25	2.25
		Nos. 123-126 (4)	12.00	6.25

Magnanime and Aimable in Battle — A18

Ships: 15c, HMS Duke and Agamemnon against Glorieux. 25c, HMS Formidable and Namur against Ville de Paris. 40c, HMS Canada. 50c, HMS St. Albans and wreck of Hector.

1971, Aug. 30 **Litho.** ***Perf. 14***

No.	Type	Description	Unused	Used
127	A18	10c multicolored	1.10	1.10
128	A18	15c multicolored	1.40	1.40
129	A18	25c multicolored	1.50	1.50
130	A18	40c multicolored	1.75	1.75
131	A18	50c multicolored	1.90	1.90
a.		Strip of 5, #127-131	8.50	8.50

West Indies sea battles.

Ansidei Madonna, by Raphael — A19

Christmas: 25c, Mystic Nativity, by Botticelli. 40c, Virgin and Child, School of Seville, inscribed Murillo. 50c, Madonna of the Iris, ascribed to Dürer.

1971, Nov. 29 ***Perf. 14x13½***

No.	Type	Description	Unused	Used
132	A19	20c green & multi	.25	.30
133	A19	25c blue & multi	.25	.30
134	A19	40c lilac rose & multi	.35	.40
135	A19	50c violet & multi	.40	.50
		Nos. 132-135 (4)	1.25	1.50

Map of Anguilla and St. Maarten, by Jefferys, 1775 — A20

Jesus Buffeted, Stained-glass Window — A21

Maps of Anguilla by: 15c, Samuel Fahlberg, 1814. 40c, Thomas Jefferys, 1775, horiz. 50c, Capt. E. Barnett, 1847, horiz.

1972, Jan. 24 ***Perf. 14x13½, 13½x14***

No.	Type	Description	Unused	Used
136	A20	10c lt blue & multi	.25	.25
137	A20	15c lt green & multi	.40	.30
138	A20	40c lt green & multi	.90	.60
139	A20	50c lt ultra & multi	1.10	.60
		Nos. 136-139 (4)	2.65	1.75

1972, Mar. 14 ***Perf. 14x13½***

Easter (19th cent. Stained-glass Windows, Bray Church): 15c, Jesus Carrying the Cross. 25c, Crucifixion. 40c, Descent from the Cross. 50c, Burial.

No.	Type	Description	Unused	Used
140	A21	10c multicolored	.30	.30
141	A21	15c multicolored	.40	.40
142	A21	25c multicolored	.40	.40
143	A21	40c multicolored	.45	.45
144	A21	50c multicolored	.55	.55
a.		Strip of 5, #140-144	2.50	2.50

Spear Fishing — A22

Sandy Ground — A23

1972-75 ***Perf. 13½***

No.	Type	Description	Unused	Used
145	A22	1c shown	.25	.50
146	A23	2c Loblolly tree, vert.	.25	.50
147	A23	3c shown	.25	.50
148	A23	4c Ferry, Blowing Point, vert.	1.90	.25
149	A23	5c Agriculture	.25	1.25
150	A23	6c St. Mary's Church, vert.	.35	.25
151	A23	10c St. Gerard's Church	.35	.50
152	A22	15c Cottage Hospital	.35	.40
153	A23	20c Public Library	.35	.45
154	A23	25c Sunset, Blowing Point	.50	*2.40*
155	A22	40c Boat building	5.50	1.75
156	A22	60c Hibiscus	4.75	4.50
157	A23	$1 Man-o-war bird	10.50	9.50
158	A23	$2.50 Frangipani	7.25	*12.00*
159	A23	$5 Brown pelican	19.00	20.00
160	A22	$10 Green-back turtle	18.00	21.50
		Nos. 145-160 (16)	69.80	*76.25*

Issued: $10, 5/20/75; others 10/30/72.

For overprints see Nos. 229-246.

Common Design Types pictured following the introduction.

Silver Wedding Issue, 1972

Common Design Type

Design: Queen Elizabeth II, Prince Philip, schooner and dolphin.

Perf. 14x14½

1972, Nov. 20 **Photo.** **Wmk. 314**

No.	Type	Description	Unused	Used
161	CD324	25c olive & multi	1.00	.75
162	CD324	40c maroon & multi	1.00	.75

Flight into Egypt — A24

Perf. 13½

1972, Dec. 4 **Litho.** **Unwmk.**

No.	Type	Description	Unused	Used
163	A24	1c shown	.25	.25
164	A24	20c Star of Bethlehem	.25	.25
165	A24	25c Nativity	.25	.25
166	A24	40c Three Kings	.25	*.25*
167	A24	50c Adoration of the Kings	.25	*.30*
a.		Vert. strip of 4, #164-167	1.00	1.00
		Nos. 163-167 (5)	1.25	1.30

Christmas.

Betrayal of Jesus — A25

1973, Mar. 26

No.	Type	Description	Unused	Used
168	A25	1c shown	.25	.25
169	A25	10c Man of Sorrow	.25	.25
170	A25	20c Jesus Carrying Cross	.25	.25
171	A25	25c Crucifixion	.25	.25
172	A25	40c Descent from Cross	.25	.25
173	A25	50c Resurrection	.25	.35
a.		Souvenir sheet of 6	1.25	*1.50*
b.		Vert. strip of 5, #169-173	1.00	1.00
		Nos. 168-173 (6)	1.50	1.60

Easter. No. 173a contains 6 stamps similar to Nos. 168-173 with bottom panel in lilac rose.

Santa Maria A26

20c, Old West Indies map. 40c, Map of voyages. 70c, Sighting land. $1.20, Columbus landing.

1973, Sept. 10

No.	Type	Description	Unused	Used
174	A26	1c multicolored	.25	.25
175	A26	20c multicolored	1.75	1.75
176	A26	40c multicolored	2.10	2.10
177	A26	70c multicolored	2.40	2.40
178	A26	$1.20 multicolored	3.25	3.25
a.		Souvenir sheet of 5, #174-178	9.25	*9.25*
b.		Horiz. strip of 4, #175-178	8.50	8.50
		Nos. 174-178 (5)	9.75	9.75

Discovery of West Indies by Columbus.

Princess Anne's Wedding Issue

Common Design Type

1973, Nov. 14 Wmk. 314 ***Perf. 13½***

No.	Type	Description	Unused	Used
179	CD325	60c blue grn & multi	.25	.25
180	CD325	$1.20 lilac & multi	.40	.30

Wedding of Princess Anne and Capt. Mark Phillips, Nov. 14, 1973.

Adoration of the Shepherds, by Guido Reni — A27

Paintings: 10c, Virgin and Child, by Filippino Lippi. 20c, Nativity, by Meester Van de Brunswijkse Diptiek. 25c, Madonna of the Meadow, by Bellini. 40c, Virgin and Child, by Cima. 50c, Adoration of the Kings, by Geertgen Tot Sint Jans.

1973, Dec. 2 **Unwmk.**

No.	Type	Description	Unused	Used
181	A27	1c multicolored	.25	.25
182	A27	10c multicolored	.25	.25
183	A27	20c multicolored	.25	.25
184	A27	25c multicolored	.25	.25
185	A27	40c multicolored	.25	.25
186	A27	50c multicolored	.25	.25
a.		Souvenir sheet of 6, #181-186	1.50	1.50
b.		Horiz. strip of 5, #182-186	1.00	1.00
		Nos. 181-186 (6)	1.50	1.50

Christmas.

Crucifixion, by Raphael — A28

Easter (Details from Crucifixion by Raphael): 15c, Virgin Mary and St. John. 20c, The Two Marys. 25c, Left Angel. 40c, Right Angel. $1, Christ on the Cross.

1974, Mar. 30

No.	Type	Description	Unused	Used
187	A28	1c lilac & multi	.25	.25
188	A28	15c gray & multi	.25	.25
189	A28	20c salmon & multi	.25	.25
190	A28	25c yel green & multi	.25	.25
191	A28	40c orange & multi	.25	.25
192	A28	$1 lt blue & multi	.25	.25
a.		Souvenir sheet of 6, #187-192	1.50	*1.75*
b.		Vert. strip of 5, #188-192	1.00	1.00
		Nos. 187-192 (6)	1.50	1.50

Churchill Making Victory Sign — A29

20c, Roosevelt, Churchill, US, British flags. 25c, Churchill broadcasting during the war. 40c, Blenheim Palace. 60c, Churchill Statue & Parliament. $1.20, Chartwell.

1974, June 24

No.	Type	Description	Unused	Used
193	A29	1c multicolored	.25	.25
194	A29	20c multicolored	.25	.25
195	A29	25c multicolored	.35	.35
196	A29	40c multicolored	.40	.40
197	A29	60c multicolored	.40	.40
198	A29	$1.20 multicolored	.50	.50
a.		Souvenir sheet of 6, #193-198	2.25	*2.50*
b.		Horiz. strip of 5, #194-198	2.25	2.25
		Nos. 193-198 (6)	2.15	2.15

Sir Winston Spencer Churchill (1874-1965).

UPU Emblem, Map of Anguilla — A30

1974, Aug. 27

No.	Type	Description	Unused	Used
199	A30	1c black & ultra	.25	.25
200	A30	20c black & orange	.25	.25
201	A30	25c black & yellow	.25	.25
202	A30	40c black & brt lilac	.25	.25
203	A30	60c black & lt green	.35	.35
204	A30	$1.20 black & blue	.55	.55
a.		Souvenir sheet of 6	1.75	*2.00*
b.		Horiz. strip of 5, #200-204	1.50	1.50
		Nos. 199-204 (6)	1.90	1.90

UPU, centenary. No. 204a contains one each of Nos. 199-204 with second row (40c, 60c, $1.20) perf. 15 at bottom.

Fishermen Seeing Star — A31

Christmas: 20c, Nativity. 25c, King offering gift. 40c, Star over map of Anguilla. 60c, Family looking at star. $1.20, Two angels with star and "Peace."

1974, Dec. 16 Litho. ***Perf. 14½***

No.	Type	Description	Unused	Used
205	A31	1c brt blue & multi	.25	.25
206	A31	20c dull grn & multi	.25	.25
207	A31	25c gray & multi	.25	.25
208	A31	40c car & multi	.25	.25
209	A31	60c dp blue & multi	.25	.25
210	A31	$1.20 ultra & multi	.25	.25
a.		Souvenir sheet of 6, #205-210	2.00	*2.25*
b.		Horiz. strip of 5, #206-210	1.25	1.25
		Nos. 205-210 (6)	1.50	1.50

Virgin Mary, St. John, Mary Magdalene A32

Paintings from Isenheim Altar, by Matthias Grunewald: 10c, Crucifixion. 15c, John the Baptist. 20c, St. Sebastian and Angels. $1, Burial of Christ, horiz. $1.50, St. Anthony, the Hermit.

1975, Mar. 25 ***Perf. 13½***

No.	Type	Description	Unused	Used
211	A32	1c multicolored	.25	.25
212	A32	10c multicolored	.25	.25
213	A32	15c multicolored	.25	.25
214	A32	20c multicolored	.25	.25
215	A32	$1 multicolored	.25	*.35*
216	A32	$1.50 multicolored	.30	*.45*
a.		Souvenir sheet of 6	1.75	*2.00*
b.		Horiz. strip of 5, #212-216	1.25	1.25
		Nos. 211-216 (6)	1.55	1.80

Easter. No. 216a contains 6 stamps similar to Nos. 211-216 with simulated perforations.

Statue of Liberty, N.Y. Skyline — A33

10c, Capitol, Washington, DC. 15c, Congress voting independence. 20c, Washington, map & his battles. $1, Boston Tea Party. $1.50, Bicentennial emblem, historic US flags.

1975, Nov. 10

No.	Type	Description	Unused	Used
217	A33	1c multicolored	.40	.40
218	A33	10c multicolored	.25	.25
219	A33	15c multicolored	.30	.25
220	A33	20c multicolored	.35	.25
221	A33	$1 multicolored	.60	.45
222	A33	$1.50 multicolored	.70	*.75*
a.		Souvenir sheet of 6	1.90	*2.50*
b.		Horiz. strip of 5, #218-222	2.00	*2.00*
		Nos. 217-222 (6)	2.60	2.35

American Bicentennial. No. 222a contains one each of Nos. 217-222 with second row (20c, $1, $1.50) perf. 15 at bottom.

Virgin and Child with St. John, by Raphael — A34

Paintings, Virgin and Child by: 10c, Cima. 15c, Dolci. 20c, Durer. $1, Bellini. $1.50, Botticelli.

1975, Dec. 8 ***Perf. 14x13½***

No.	Type	Description	Unused	Used
223	A34	1c ultra & multi	.25	.25
224	A34	10c Prus blue & multi	.25	.25
225	A34	15c plum & multi	.25	.25
226	A34	20c car rose & multi	.25	.25
227	A34	$1 brt grn & multi	.40	.25
228	A34	$1.50 blue grn & multi	.55	.40
a.		Souvenir sheet of 6, #223-228	2.75	2.75
b.		Horiz. strip of 5, #224-228	1.75	1.50
		Nos. 223-228 (6)	1.95	1.65

Christmas.

Nos. 145-146, 148, 150-160 Surcharged and/or Overprinted

(a)

(b)

1976 Litho. ***Perf. 13½***

No.	Type	Description	Unused	Used
229	A22 (a)	1c #145	.35	*.60*
230	A22 (b)	2c on 1c #145	.35	*.60*
231	A23 (a)	2c #146	8.25	2.75
232	A22 (b)	3c on 40c #155	.90	1.00
233	A23 (a)	4c #148	1.10	1.50
234	A22 (b)	5c on 40c #155	.35	*.70*
235	A23 (a)	6c #150	.35	*.70*
236	A23 (b)	10c on 20c #153	.35	*.70*
237	A23 (a)	10c #151	8.25	7.50
238	A22 (a)	15c #152	.35	*1.25*
239	A23 (a)	20c #153	.35	*.70*
240	A23 (a)	25c #154	.35	*.70*
241	A22 (a)	40c #155	1.10	1.00
242	A22 (a)	60c #156	.90	1.00
243	A23 (a)	$1 #157	7.75	3.25
244	A23 (a)	$2.50 #158	2.50	3.25
245	A23 (a)	$5 #159	9.50	*11.50*
246	A22 (a)	$10 #160	3.75	*9.25*
		Nos. 229-246 (18)	46.80	*47.95*

Flowering Trees — A35

1976, Feb. 16 ***Perf. 13½x14***

No.	Type	Description	Unused	Used
247	A35	1c Almond	.25	.25
248	A35	10c Clusia rosea	.35	.30
249	A35	15c Calabash	.35	.30
250	A35	20c Cordia	.35	.30
251	A35	$1 Papaya	.50	.40
252	A35	$1.50 Flamboyant	.70	.55
a.		Souvenir sheet of 6, #247-252	3.00	3.00
b.		Horiz. strip of 5, #248-252	2.50	2.50
		Nos. 247-252 (6)	2.50	2.10

The Three Marys — A36

Designs: 10c, Crucifixion. 15c, Two soldiers. 20c, Annunciation. $1, Altar tapestry, 1470, Monastery of Rheinau, Switzerland, horiz. $1.50, "Noli me Tangere" (Jesus and Mary Magdalene). Designs of vertical stamps show details from tapestry shown on $1 stamp.

1976, Apr. 5 ***Perf. 14x13½, 13½x14***

No.	Type	Description	Unused	Used
253	A36	1c multicolored	.25	.25
254	A36	10c multicolored	.25	.25
255	A36	15c multicolored	.25	.25
256	A36	20c multicolored	.25	.25
257	A36	$1 multicolored	.65	.65
258	A36	$1.50 multicolored	.80	.80
a.		Souvenir sheet of 6	2.50	*2.75*
b.		Horiz. strip of 5, #254-258	2.25	2.25
		Nos. 253-258 (6)	2.45	2.45

Easter. No. 258a contains 6 stamps similar to Nos. 253-258 with simulated perforations.

Le Desius and La Vaillante Approaching Anguilla — A37

Sailing Ships: 3c, Sailboat leaving Anguilla for Antigua to get help. 15c, HMS Lapwing in battle with frigate Le Desius and brig La Vaillante. 25c, La Vaillante aground off St. Maarten. $1, Lapwing. $1.50, Le Desius burning.

1976, Nov. 8 Litho. *Perf. 13½x14*

259 A37 1c multicolored .25 .25
260 A37 3c multicolored 1.40 .50
261 A37 15c multicolored 1.75 .70
262 A37 25c multicolored 1.75 .95
263 A37 $1 multicolored 2.10 1.40
264 A37 $1.50 multicolored 2.50 1.90
a. Souvenir sheet of 6, #259-264 8.50 8.50
b. Strip of 5, #260-264 9.75 9.75
Nos. 259-264 (6) 9.75 5.70

Bicentenary of Battle of Anguilla between French and British ships.

Christmas Carnival — A38

Children's Paintings: 3c, 3 children dreaming of Christmas gifts. 15c, Caroling. 25c, Candlelight procession. $1, Going to Church on Christmas Eve. $1.50, Airport, coming home for Christmas.

1976, Nov. 22

265 A38 1c multicolored .25 .25
266 A38 3c multicolored .25 .25
267 A38 15c multicolored .25 .25
268 A38 25c multicolored .25 .25
269 A38 $1 multicolored .35 .35
270 A38 $1.50 multicolored .50 .50
a. Souvenir sheet of 6, #265-270 2.75 *2.75*
b. Strip of 5, #266-270 1.70 1.50
Nos. 265-270 (6) 1.85 1.85

Christmas. For overprints and surcharges see Nos. 305-310a.

Prince Charles and HMS Minerva, 1973 — A39

Designs: 40c, Prince Philip landing at Road Bay, 1964. $1.20, Homage to Queen at Coronation. $2.50, Coronation regalia and map of Anguilla.

1977, Feb. 9

271 A39 25c multicolored .25 .25
272 A39 40c multicolored .25 .25
273 A39 $1.20 multicolored .25 .25
274 A39 $2.50 multicolored .35 .30
a. Souvenir sheet of 4, #271-274 1.00 *1.50*
Complete booklet, 2 each #271-274 3.00
Complete booklet, 2 each #271-274 with vert. selvage at right 5.00
Nos. 271-274 (4) 1.10 1.05

25th anniv. of reign of Queen Elizabeth II.
The booklets with thin vert. selvage at right were from a separate printing.
For overprints see Nos. 297-300.

Yellow-crowned Night Heron — A40

Designs: 2c, Great barracuda. 3c, Queen conch. 4c, Spanish bayonet (Yucca). 5c, Trunkfish. 6c, Cable and telegraph building. 10c, American sparrow hawk. 15c, Ground orchids. 20c, Parlorfish. 22c, Lobster fishing boat. 35c, Boat race. 50c Sea bean (flowers). $1, Sandy Island with palms. $2.50, Manchineel (fruit). $5, Ground lizard. $10, Red-billed tropic bird.

1977-78 Litho. *Perf. 13½x14*

275 A40 1c multicolored .40 *2.10*
276 A40 2c multicolored .40 *4.00*
277 A40 3c multicolored 2.75 *6.00*
278 A40 4c multicolored .55 *.70*
279 A40 5c multicolored 2.10 *.70*
280 A40 6c multicolored .40 *.70*
281 A40 10c multicolored 7.00 5.50
282 A40 15c multicolored 4.25 3.75
283 A40 20c multicolored 4.50 1.90
284 A40 22c multicolored .75 *1.40*
285 A40 35c multicolored 1.90 1.50
286 A40 50c multicolored 1.25 1.10
287 A40 $1 multicolored .85 1.10
288 A40 $2.50 multicolored 1.40 2.10
289 A40 $5 multicolored 2.75 4.00
290 A40 $10 multicolored 13.00 9.25
Nos. 275-290 (16) 44.25 45.80

Issued: Nos. 275-280, 290, 4/18/77; others 2/20/78.
For overprints and surcharges see Nos. 319-324, 337-342, 387-390, 402-404, 407-415, 417-423.

Crucifixion, by Quentin Massys — A41

Easter (Paintings): 3c, Betrayal of Christ, by Ugolino. 22c, Way to Calvary, by Ugolino. 30c, The Deposition, by Ugolino. $1, Resurrection, by Ugolino. $1.50, Crucifixion, by Andrea del Castagno.

1977, Apr. 25

291 A41 1c multicolored .25 .25
292 A41 3c multicolored .25 .25
293 A41 22c multicolored .25 .25
294 A41 30c multicolored .35 .30
295 A41 $1 multicolored .75 .65
296 A41 $1.50 multicolored 1.10 .90
a. Souvenir sheet of 6, #291-296 3.00 2.40
b. Strip of 5, #292-296 2.75 1.90
Nos. 291-296 (6) 2.95 2.60

Nos. 271-274, 274a Overprinted

1977, Oct. 26 Litho. *Perf. 13½x14*

297 A39 25c multicolored .25 .25
298 A39 40c multicolored .25 .25
299 A39 $1.20 multicolored .50 *.60*
300 A39 $2.50 multicolored 1.00 *1.25*
a. Souvenir sheet of 4 1.75 2.00
Nos. 297-300 (4) 2.00 *2.35*

Visit of Queen Elizabeth II to West Indies.

Suzanne Fourment in Velvet Hat, by Rubens — A42

Rubens Paintings: 40c, Helena Fourment with her Children. $1.20, Rubens with his wife. $2.50, Marchesa Brigida Spinola-Doria.

1977, Nov. 1 *Perf. 14x13½*

301 A42 25c black & multi .25 .25
302 A42 40c black & multi .30 .30
303 A42 $1.20 multicolored .90 .90
304 A42 $2.50 black & multi 1.25 *1.35*
a. Souvenir sheet of 4, #301-304 2.75 2.75
Nos. 301-304 (4) 2.70 2.80

Peter Paul Rubens, 400th birth anniv. Nos. 301-304 printed in sheets of 5 stamps and blue label with Rubens' portrait.
For overprint, see Nos. 311-314.

Nos. 265-270b Ovptd. & Srchd.

1977, Nov. 7 *Perf. 13½x14*

305 A38 1c multicolored .25 .25
306 A38 5c on 3c multi .25 .25
307 A38 12c on 15c multi .25 .25
308 A38 18c on 25c multi .30 .30
309 A38 $1 multicolored .70 .70
310 A38 $2.50 on $1.50 multi 1.50 1.50
a. Souvenir sheet of 6, #305-310 4.00 4.00
b. Strip of 5, #306-310 3.00 3.00
Nos. 305-310 (6) 3.25 3.25

Christmas. Stamps and souvenir sheets have "1976" and old denomination obliterated with variously shaped rectangles.

Nos. 301-304a Ovptd. in Gold

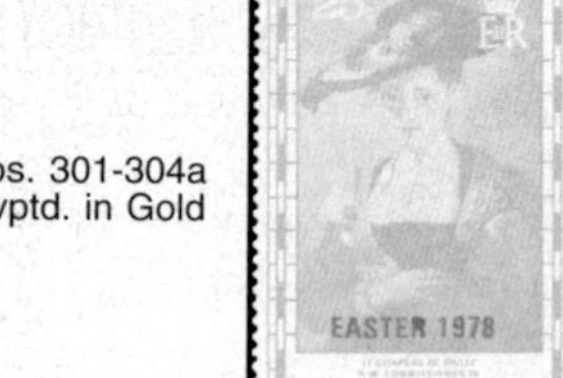

1978, Mar. 6 *Perf. 14x13½*

311 A42 25c black & multi .25 .25
312 A42 40c black & multi .25 .25
313 A42 $1.20 black & multi .70 .70
314 A42 $2.50 black & multi .80 .80
a. Souvenir sheet of 4, #311-314 2.50 *2.50*
Nos. 311-314 (4) 2.00 2.00

Buckingham Palace — A43

Designs: 50c, Coronation procession. $1.50, Royal family on balcony. $2.50, Royal coat of arms.

1978, Apr. 6 *Perf. 14*

315 A43 22c multicolored .25 .25
316 A43 50c multicolored .25 .25
317 A43 $1.50 multicolored .45 .45
318 A43 $2.50 multicolored .70 .70
a. Souvenir sheet of 4, #315-318 2.00 2.00
Complete booklet, 2 each #315-318 3.50
Complete booklet, 2 each #315-318 with thin vert. selvage at right 3.50
Nos. 315-318 (4) 1.65 1.65

25th anniv. of coronation of Queen Elizabeth II.
The booklets with thin vert. selvage at right were from a separate printing.

Nos. 284-285 and 288 Ovptd. and Surcharged

1978, Aug. 14 Litho. *Perf. 13½x14*

319 A40 22c multicolored .50 .50
320 A40 35c multicolored .85 .50
321 A40 $1.50 on $2.50 multi 1.90 1.90
Nos. 319-321 (3) 3.25 2.90

Valley Secondary School, 25th anniv. Surcharge on No. 321 includes heavy bar over old denomination.

Nos. 286-287, 289 Ovptd. and Surcharged

1978, Aug. 14

322 A40 50c multicolored 1.25 1.25
323 A40 $1 multicolored 1.50 1.50
324 A40 $1.20 on $5 multi 2.25 2.25
Nos. 322-324 (3) 5.00 5.00

Road Methodist Church, centenary. Surcharge on No. 324 includes heavy bar over old denomination.

Mother and Child — A44

Christmas: 12c, Christmas masquerade. 18c, Christmas dinner. 22c, Serenade. $1, Star over manger. $2.50, Family going to church.

1978, Dec. 11 Litho. *Perf. 13½*

325 A44 5c multicolored .25 .25
326 A44 12c multicolored .25 .25
327 A44 18c multicolored .25 .25
328 A44 22c multicolored .25 .25
329 A44 $1 multicolored .40 .40
330 A44 $2.50 multicolored .80 .80
a. Souvenir sheet of 6, #325-330 2.00 *2.25*
Nos. 325-330 (6) 2.20 2.20

Type A44 in Changed Colors with IYC Emblem and Inscription

1979, Jan. 15 Litho. *Perf. 13½*

331 A44 5c multicolored .25 .25
332 A44 12c multicolored .25 .25
333 A44 18c multicolored .25 .25
334 A44 22c multicolored .25 .25
335 A44 $1 multicolored .35 .35
336 A44 $2.50 multicolored .60 .60
a. Souvenir sheet of 4, #331-336 3.00 *3.25*
Nos. 331-336 (6) 1.95 1.95

Intl. Year of the Child. For overprint see No. 416

Nos. 275-278, 280-281 Surcharged

1979, Feb. 8 Litho. *Perf. 13½x14*

337 A40 12c on 2c multi *.75 .60*
338 A40 14c on 4c multi *.65 .75*
339 A40 18c on 3c multi *1.25 .95*
340 A40 25c on 6c multi *.85 .65*

341 A40 38c on 10c multi *3.50* *1.25*
342 A40 40c on 1c multi *3.50* *1.25*
Nos. 337-342 (6) *10.50* 5.45

Valley Methodist Church A45

Church Interiors: 12c, St. Mary's Anglican Church, The Valley. 18c, St. Gerard's Roman Catholic Church, The Valley. 22c, Road Methodist Church. $1.50, St. Augustine's Anglican Church, East End. $2.50, West End Methodist Church.

1979, Mar. 30 Litho. *Perf. 14*

343 A45 5c multicolored .25 .25
344 A45 12c multicolored .25 .25
345 A45 18c multicolored .25 .25
346 A45 22c multicolored .25 .25
347 A45 $1.50 multicolored .70 .70
348 A45 $2.50 multicolored .90 .90
a. Souvenir sheet of 6 2.25 2.25
b. Strip of 6, #343-348 2.00 2.00

Easter. No. 348a contains Nos. 343-348 in 2 horizontal rows of 3.

US No. C3a A46

No. 350, Cape of Good Hope #1. No. 351, Penny Black. No. 352, Germany #C36. No. 353, US #245. No. 354, Great Britain #93.

1979, Apr. 23 Litho. *Perf. 14*

349 A46 1c multicolored .25 .25
350 A46 1c multicolored .25 .25
351 A46 22c multicolored .25 .25
352 A46 35c multicolored .25 .25
353 A46 $1.50 multicolored .50 .50
354 A46 $2.50 multicolored .75 .75
a. Souvenir sheet of 6, #349-353 2.50 *2.75*
Complete booklet, 2 each #349-354 4.00
Nos. 349-354 (6) 2.25 2.25

Sir Rowland Hill (1795-1879), originator of penny postage.

Wright's Flyer A — A47

History of Aviation: 12c, Louis Bleriot landing at Dover, 1909. 18c, Vickers Vimy, 1919. 22c, Spirit of St. Louis, 1927. $1.50, LZ127 Graf Zeppelin, 1928. $2.50, Concorde, 1979.

1979, May 21 Litho. *Perf. 14*

355 A47 5c multicolored .25 .25
356 A47 12c multicolored .30 .25
357 A47 18c multicolored .35 .25
358 A47 22c multicolored .40 .30
359 A47 $1.50 multicolored 1.25 1.10
360 A47 $2.50 multicolored 3.75 1.50
a. Souvenir sheet of 6, #355-360 7.00 7.00
Nos. 355-360 (6) 6.30 3.65

Map of Anguilla, Map and View of Sombrero Island A48

Map of Anguilla, Map and View of: 12c, Anguillita Island. 18c, Sandy Island. 25c, Prickly Pear Cays. $1, Dog Island. $2.50, Scrub Island.

1979 Litho. *Perf. 14*

361 A48 5c multicolored .25 .25
362 A48 12c multicolored .25 .25
363 A48 18c multicolored .25 .25
364 A48 25c multicolored .25 .25
365 A48 $1 multicolored .50 *.55*
366 A48 $2.50 multicolored .90 *.95*
a. Souvenir sheet of 6, #361-366 3.50 3.25
Nos. 361-366 (6) 2.40 2.50

Anguilla's Outer Islands.

Red Poinsettia — A49

1979, Oct. 22 Litho. *Perf. 14½*

367 A49 22c shown .25 .25
368 A49 35c Kalanchoe .25 .25
369 A49 $1.50 Cream poinsettia .50 .50
370 A49 $2.50 White poinsettia .80 .80
a. Souvenir sheet of 4, #367-370 2.75 2.75
Nos. 367-370 (4) 1.80 1.80

Christmas.

Booths and Frames A50

Designs: 50c, Earls Court Exhibition Hall. $1.50, Penny Black, Great Britain #2. $2.50, Exhibition emblem.

1979, Dec. 10 Litho. *Perf. 13*

371 A50 35c multicolored .25 .25
372 A50 50c multicolored .25 .25
373 A50 $1.50 multicolored .45 .45
374 A50 $2.50 multicolored .80 .80
b. Souvenir sheet of 4, #371-374 2.25 2.25
Complete booklet, 2 each #371-374 4.00
Nos. 371-374 (4) 1.75 1.75

Perf. 14½

371a A50 35c .25 .25
372a A50 50c .25 .25
373a A50 $1.50 .45 .45
374a A50 $2.50 .80 .80
c. Souvenir sheet of 4, #371a-374a 2.25 2.25
Nos. 371a-374a (4) 1.75 1.75

London 1980 Intl. Stamp Exhibition, May 6-14, 1980.

Lake Placid and Olympic Rings — A51

Olympic Rings and: 18c, Ice Hockey. 35c, Figure skating. 50c, Bobsledding. $1, Downhill skiing. $2.50, Luge.

1980, Jan. Litho. *Perf. 13½, 14½*

375 A51 5c multicolored .25 .25
376 A51 18c multicolored .25 .25
377 A51 35c multicolored .25 .25
378 A51 50c multicolored .30 .25
379 A51 $1 multicolored .45 *.65*
380 A51 $2.50 multicolored .80 *1.10*
a. Souvenir sheet of 6, #375-380 2.25 *3.00*
Nos. 375-380 (6) 2.30 *2.75*

13th Winter Olympic Games, Lake Placid, NY, Feb. 12-24.

Salt Field A52

12c, Tallying salt. 18c, Unloading salt flats. 22c, Storage pile. $1, Bagging and grinding. $2.50, Loading onto boats.

1980, Apr. 14 Litho. *Perf. 14*

381 A52 5c multicolored .25 .25
382 A52 12c multicolored .25 .25
383 A52 18c multicolored .25 .25
384 A52 22c multicolored .25 .25
385 A52 $1 multicolored .40 .40
386 A52 $2.50 multicolored 1.00 1.00
a. Souvenir sheet of 6, #381-386 2.25 2.25
Nos. 381-386 (6) 2.40 2.40

Salt industry.

Nos. 281, 288 Overprinted

1980, Apr. 16 *Perf. 13½x14*

387 A40 10c multicolored 3.50 .30
388 A40 $2.50 multicolored 3.50 1.60

Nos. 283, 289 Overprinted

1980, Apr. 16 *Perf. 13½x14*

389 A40 20c multicolored 3.00 .30
390 A40 $5 multicolored 5.50 2.40

Rotary International, 75th anniversary.

Big Ben, Great Britain #643, London 1980 Emblem — A53

Designs: $1.50, Canada #756. $2.50, Statue of Liberty, US #1632.

1980, May

391 A53 50c multicolored .50 .50
392 A53 $1.50 multicolored .75 .75
393 A53 $2.50 multicolored 1.25 1.25
a. Souvenir sheet of 3, #391-393 2.75 2.75
Nos. 391-393 (3) 2.50 2.50

London 1980 International Stamp Exhibition, May 6-14.

Queen Mother Elizabeth, 80th Birthday — A54

1980, Aug. 4 Litho. *Perf. 14*

394 A54 35c multicolored .55 .35
395 A54 50c multicolored .70 .40
396 A54 $1.50 multicolored 1.25 1.00
397 A54 $3 multicolored 1.75 1.75
a. Souvenir sheet of 4, #394-397 6.00 4.25
Nos. 394-397 (4) 4.25 3.50

Pelicans — A55

22c, Great gray herons. $1.50, Swallows. $3, Hummingbirds.

1980, Nov. 10 Litho. *Perf. 14*

398 A55 5c multicolored .40 .25
399 A55 22c multicolored 1.10 .30
400 A55 $1.50 multicolored 2.40 .95
401 A55 $3 multicolored 3.00 2.10
a. Souvenir sheet of 4, #398-401 12.50 12.50
Nos. 398-401 (4) 6.90 3.60

Christmas. For overprints see Nos. 405-406.

Nos. 275, 278, 280-290, 334, 400-401 Overprinted

Perf. 13½x14, 14 (A55)

1980, Dec. 18 Litho.

402 A40 1c #275 .25 .80
403 A40 2c on 4c #278 .25 .80
404 A40 5c on 15c #282 1.25 .80
405 A55 5c on $1.50 #400 1.25 .80
406 A55 5c on $3 #401 1.25 .80
407 A40 10c #281 1.90 .80
408 A40 12c on $1 #287 .30 .80
409 A40 14c on $2.50 #288 .30 .80
410 A40 15c #282 1.50 .80
411 A40 18c on $5 #289 .35 .80
412 A40 20c #283 .35 .80
413 A40 22c #284 .35 .80
414 A40 25c on 15c #282 1.50 .95
415 A40 35c #285 .40 *.95*
416 A44 38c on 22c #334 .40 *.95*
417 A40 40c on 1c #275 .40 *.95*
418 A40 50c #286 .45 *1.10*
419 A40 $1 #287 .60 *1.40*
420 A40 $2.50 #288 1.50 *3.50*
421 A40 $5 #289 2.75 *4.50*
422 A40 $10 #290 6.25 *6.50*
423 A40 $10 on 6c #280 6.25 *6.50*
Nos. 402-423 (22) 29.80 36.90

Petition for Separation, 1825 — A56

22c, Referendum ballot, 1967. 35c, Airport blockade, 1967. 50c, Anguilla flag. $1, Separation celebration, 1980.

1980, Dec. 18 *Perf. 14*

424 A56 18c multicolored .25 .25
425 A56 22c multicolored .25 .25
426 A56 35c multicolored .30 .30
427 A56 50c multicolored .40 .35
428 A56 $1 multicolored .70 *.80*
a. Souvenir sheet of 5, #424-428 1.90 *2.00*
Nos. 424-428 (5) 1.90 1.95

Separation from St. Kitts-Nevis.

Nelson's Dockyard, by R. Granger Barrett A57

Ship Paintings: 35c, Agamemnon, Vanguard, Elephant, Captain and Victory, by Nicholas Pocock. 50c, Victory, by Monamy Swaine. $3, Battle of Trafalgar, by Clarkson

Stanfield. $5, Lord Nelson, by L.F. Abbott and Nelson's arms.

1981, Mar. 2 Litho. *Perf. 14*

429	A57	22c multicolored	2.10	.90
430	A57	35c multicolored	2.40	1.25
431	A57	50c multicolored	2.75	1.50
432	A57	$3 multicolored	3.75	*5.50*
		Nos. 429-432 (4)	11.00	*9.15*

Souvenir Sheet

433 A57 $5 multicolored 5.50 5.50

Lord Horatio Nelson (1758-1805), 175th death anniversary (1980).

Minnie Mouse A58

Easter: Various Disney characters in Easter outfits.

1981, Mar. 30 Litho. *Perf. 13½*

434	A58	1c multicolored	.25	.25
435	A58	2c multicolored	.25	.25
436	A58	3c multicolored	.25	.25
437	A58	5c multicolored	.25	.25
438	A58	7c multicolored	.25	.25
439	A58	9c multicolored	.25	.25
440	A58	10c multicolored	.25	.25
441	A58	$2 multicolored	1.75	1.75
442	A58	$3 multicolored	2.50	2.50
		Nos. 434-442 (9)	6.00	6.00

Souvenir Sheet

443 A58 $5 multicolored 6.75 6.75

Prince Charles, Lady Diana, St. Paul's Cathedral A59

1981, June 15 Litho. *Perf. 14*

444	A59	50c shown	.25	.25
a.		Souvenir sheet of 2	.30	.30
b.		Wmk. 380	.30	.30
c.		Booklet pane of 4 #444b	1.25	1.25
445	A59	$2.50 Althorp	.45	.60
a.		Souvenir sheet of 2	1.60	1.60
446	A59	$3 Windsor Castle	.55	.75
a.		Souvenir sheet of 2	2.00	2.00
b.		Wmk. 380	2.00	2.00
c.		Booklet pane of 4 #446b	8.00	8.00
		Complete booklet, #444c, 446c	9.50	
		Nos. 444-446 (3)	1.25	1.60

Souvenir Sheet

447 A59 $5 Buckingham Palace 2.00 2.00

Royal Wedding. Nos. 444a-446a contain stamps in different colors.

Boys Climbing Tree A60

10c, Boys sailing boats. 15c, Children playing instruments. $3, Children with animals. $4, Boys playing soccer, vert.

1981 Litho. *Perf. 14*

448	A60	5c multicolored	.25	.25
449	A60	10c multicolored	.30	.30
450	A60	15c multicolored	.40	*.45*
451	A60	$3 multicolored	3.00	*3.50*
		Nos. 448-451 (4)	3.95	4.50

Souvenir Sheet

452 A60 $4 multicolored 5.00 5.00

UNICEF, 35th anniv.
Issued: 5c-15c, July 31; $3-$4, Sept. 30.

"The Children were Nestled all Snug in their Beds" — A61

Christmas: Scenes from Walt Disney's The Night Before Christmas.

1981, Nov. 2 Litho. *Perf. 13½*

453	A61	1c multicolored	.25	.25
454	A61	2c multicolored	.25	.25
455	A61	3c multicolored	.25	.25
456	A61	5c multicolored	.30	.25
457	A61	7c multicolored	.30	.25
458	A61	10c multicolored	.30	.25
459	A61	12c multicolored	.30	.25
460	A61	$2 multicolored	4.00	2.10
461	A61	$3 multicolored	4.00	2.50
		Nos. 453-461 (9)	9.95	6.35

Souvenir Sheet

462 A61 $5 multicolored 8.50 8.50

Red Grouper — A62

No. 473

5c, Ferries, Blowing Point. 10c, Racing boats. 15c, Majorettes. 20c, Launching boat, Sandy Hill. 25c, Coral. 30c, Little Bay cliffs. 35c, Fountain Cave. 40c, Sandy Isld. 45c, Landing, Sombrero. 60c, Seine fishing. 75c, Boat race, Sandy Ground. $1, Bagging lobster, Island Harbor. $5, Pelicans. $7.50, Hibiscus. $10, Queen triggerfish.

1982, Jan. 1 Litho. *Perf. 14*

463	A62	1c multi	.25	*.90*
464	A62	5c multi	.35	*.90*
465	A62	10c multi	.25	*.90*
466	A62	15c multi	.25	*.90*
467	A62	20c multi	.45	*.90*
468	A62	25c multi	1.75	.90
469	A62	30c multi	.35	*1.10*
470	A62	35c multi	1.75	1.25
471	A62	40c multi	.35	*1.10*
472	A62	45c multi	.55	*1.25*
473	A62	50c on 45c, #472	.60	.55
474	A62	60c multi	3.50	3.75
475	A62	75c multi	1.10	*3.00*
476	A62	$1 multi	2.50	3.00
477	A62	$5 multi	18.00	18.00
478	A62	$7.50 multi	14.00	20.00
479	A62	$10 multi	18.00	24.00
		Nos. 463-479 (17)	64.00	82.40

For overprints & surcharges see Nos. 507-510, 546A-546D, 578-582, 606-608, 640-647.

Easter — A63

Designs: Butterflies on flowers.

1982, Apr. 5

480	A63	10c Zebra, anthurium	1.25	.25
481	A63	35c Caribbean buckeye	2.00	.55
482	A63	75c Monarch, allamanda	2.25	.80
483	A63	$3 Red rim, orchid	3.75	2.40
		Nos. 480-483 (4)	9.25	4.00

Souvenir Sheet

484 A63 $5 Flambeau, amaryllis 6.50 *7.00*

Princess Diana, 21st Birthday — A64

Designs: Portraits, 1961-1981.

1982, May 17

485	A64	10c 1961	.65	.25
486	A64	30c 1968	1.50	.25
487	A64	40c 1970	.80	.30
488	A64	60c 1974	.80	.40
489	A64	$2 1981	1.25	1.50
490	A64	$3 1981	6.25	2.10
a.		Souvenir sheet of 6, #485-490	12.00	12.00
		Complete booklet, 4 each #485, 487-489	10.00	
		Nos. 485-490 (6)	11.25	4.80

Souvenir Sheet

491 A64 $5 1981 11.50 11.50

For overprints see Nos. 639A-639G.

1982 World Cup — A65

Various Disney characters playing soccer.

1982, Aug. 3 Litho. *Perf. 11*

492	A65	1c multicolored	.25	.25
493	A65	3c multicolored	.25	.25
494	A65	4c multicolored	.25	.25
495	A65	5c multicolored	.25	.25
496	A65	7c multicolored	.25	.25
497	A65	9c multicolored	.25	.25
498	A65	10c multicolored	.25	.25
499	A65	$2.50 multicolored	3.50	2.40
500	A65	$3 multicolored	3.50	2.40
		Nos. 492-500 (9)	8.75	6.55

Souvenir Sheet
Perf. 14

501 A65 $5 multicolored 9.00 9.00

Scouting Year A66

1982, July 5

502	A66	10c Pitching tent	.65	.55
503	A66	35c Marching band	1.10	.80
504	A66	75c Sailing	1.60	1.40
505	A66	$3 Flag bearers	4.25	3.25
		Nos. 502-505 (4)	7.60	6.00

Souvenir Sheet

506 A66 $5 Camping 7.00 7.00

Nos. 465, 474-475, 477 Overprinted

1982, Oct. 18 Litho. *Perf. 14*

507	A62	10c multicolored	.30	.30
508	A62	60c multicolored	.75	.75
509	A62	75c multicolored	1.00	1.00
510	A62	$5 multicolored	5.50	5.50
		Nos. 507-510 (4)	7.55	7.55

12th Commonwealth Games, Brisbane, Australia, Sept. 30-Oct. 9.

Christmas — A67

Scenes from Walt Disney's Winnie the Pooh.

1982, Nov. 29

511	A67	1c multicolored	.25	.25
512	A67	2c multicolored	.25	.25
513	A67	3c multicolored	.25	.25
514	A67	5c multicolored	.45	.25
515	A67	7c multicolored	.45	.25
516	A67	10c multicolored	.55	.25
517	A67	12c multicolored	.70	.30
518	A67	20c multicolored	1.50	.35
519	A67	$5 multicolored	9.50	9.50
		Nos. 511-519 (9)	13.90	11.65

Souvenir Sheet

520 A67 $5 multicolored 14.00 14.00

Commonwealth Day (Mar. 14) — A68

10c, Carnival procession. 35c, Flags. 75c, Economic cooperation. $2.50, Salt pond. $5, Map showing Commonwealth.

1983, Feb. 28 Litho. *Perf. 14*

521	A68	10c multicolored	.25	.25
522	A68	35c multicolored	.45	.50
523	A68	75c multicolored	.85	1.00
524	A68	$2.50 multicolored	6.00	4.75
		Nos. 521-524 (4)	7.55	6.50

Souvenir Sheet

525 A68 $5 multicolored 7.50 7.50

Easter — A69

Ten Commandments.

1983, Mar. 31 Litho. *Perf. 14*

526	A69	1c multicolored	.25	.25
527	A69	2c multicolored	.25	.25
528	A69	3c multicolored	.25	.25
529	A69	10c multicolored	.25	.25
530	A69	35c multicolored	.55	.30
531	A69	60c multicolored	1.00	.50
532	A69	75c multicolored	1.10	.55
533	A69	$2 multicolored	3.00	2.10
534	A69	$2.50 multicolored	3.25	2.10
535	A69	$5 multicolored	5.25	3.25
		Nos. 526-535 (10)	15.15	9.80

Souvenir Sheet

536 A69 $5 Moses Taking Tablets 5.00 5.00

Local Turtles and World Wildlife Fund Emblem — A70

1983, Aug. 10 Litho. *Perf. 13½*

537 A70 10c Leatherback *4.50 2.10*
538 A70 35c Hawksbill *7.50 3.25*
539 A70 75c Green *11.00 4.75*
540 A70 $1 Loggerhead *12.50 6.50*
Nos. 537-540 (4) 35.50 16.60

Souvenir Sheet

541 A70 $5 Leatherback, diff. *30.00 8.25*

1983, Aug. 10 Litho. *Perf. 12*

537a A70 10c Leatherback *3.50 2.40*
538a A70 35c Hawksbill *11.00 4.75*
539a A70 75c Green *14.50 10.50*
540a A70 $1 Loggerhead *22.00 13.00*
Nos. 537a-540a (4) 51.00 30.65

Manned Flight Bicentenary A71

10c, Montgolfiere, 1783. 60c, Blanchard & Jeffries, 1785. $1, Giffard's airship, 1852. $2.50, Lilienthal's glider, 1890.
$5, Wright Brothers' plane, 1909.

1983, Aug. 22 *Perf. 14*

542 A71 10c multicolored .70 .40
543 A71 60c multicolored 2.10 .90
544 A71 $1 multicolored 2.50 1.10
545 A71 $2.50 multicolored 3.50 3.50
Nos. 542-545 (4) 8.80 5.90

Souvenir Sheet

546 A71 $5 multicolored 7.00 *8.25*

Nos. 465, 471, 476-477 Overprinted

1983, Oct. 24 Litho. *Perf. 14*

546A A62 10c Racing boats .30 .25
546B A62 40c Sandy Isld .45 .35
546C A62 $1 Bagging lobster, Island Harbor 1.10 .65
546D A62 $5 Pelicans 8.50 3.75
Nos. 546A-546D (4) 10.35 5.00

Jiminy Cricket A72

Designs: Various Disney productions.

1983, Nov. 14 *Perf. 13½*

547 A72 1c shown .25 .25
548 A72 2c Jiminy Cricket, kettle .25 .25
549 A72 3c Jiminy Cricket, toys .25 .25
550 A72 4c Mickey and Morty .25 .25
551 A72 5c Scrooge McDuck .25 .25
552 A72 6c Minnie and Goofy .25 .25
553 A72 10c Goofy and Elf .25 .25
554 A72 $2 Scrooge McDuck, diff. 5.25 3.50
555 A72 $3 Disney characters 6.50 3.25
Nos. 547-555 (9) 13.50 8.50

Souvenir Sheet

556 A72 $5 Scrooge McDuck 9.00 9.00

Boys' Brigade Centenary — A73

10c, Anguilla company, banner. $5, Marching with drummer.

1983, Sept. 12 Litho. *Perf. 14*

557 A73 10c multicolored .50 .50
558 A73 $5 multicolored 4.00 3.25
a. Souvenir sheet of 2, #557-558 5.00 5.00

1984 Olympics, Los Angeles — A74

Mickey Mouse Competing in Decathlon.

1984, Feb. 20 Litho. *Perf. 14*

559 A74 1c 100-meter run .25 .25
560 A74 2c Long jump .25 .25
561 A74 3c Shot put .25 .25
562 A74 4c High jump .25 .25
563 A74 5c 400-meter run .25 .25
564 A74 6c Hurdles .25 .25
565 A74 10c Discus .25 .25
566 A74 $1 Pole vault 4.25 3.00
567 A74 $4 Javelin 8.50 4.75
Nos. 559-567 (9) 14.50 9.50

Souvenir Sheet

568 A74 $5 1500-meter run 15.00 15.00

1984, Apr. 24 *Perf. 12½x12*

559a A74 1c .25 .25
560a A74 2c .25 .25
561a A74 3c .25 .25
562a A74 4c .25 .25
563a A74 5c .25 .25
564a A74 6c .25 .25
565a A74 10c .25 .25
566a A74 $1 5.50 3.75
567a A74 $4 8.00 *10.50*
Nos. 559a-567a (9) 15.25 16.00

Souvenir Sheet

568a A74 $5 With Olympic rings emblem 12.00 12.00

Nos. 559a-567a inscribed with Olympic rings emblem. Printed in sheets of 5 plus label.

Easter A75

Ceiling and Wall Frescoes, La Stanze della Segnatura, by Raphael (details).

1984, Apr. 19 Litho. *Perf. 13½x14*

569 A75 10c Justice .25 .25
570 A75 25c Poetry .30 .30
571 A75 35c Philosophy .40 .40
572 A75 40c Theology .40 .40
573 A75 $1 Abraham & Paul 1.10 1.10
574 A75 $2 Moses & Matthew 2.25 2.25
575 A75 $3 John & David 3.00 3.00
576 A75 $4 Peter & Adam 3.50 3.50
Nos. 569-576 (8) 11.20 11.20

Souvenir Sheet

577 A75 $5 Astronomy 6.25 6.25

Nos. 463, 469, 477-479 Surcharged

1984 Litho. *Perf. 14*

578 A62 25c on $7.50 #478 .85 .45
579 A62 35c on 30c #469 .70 .55
580 A62 60c on 1c #463 .75 .60
581 A62 $2.50 on $5 #477 4.00 1.90
582 A62 $2.50 on $10 #479 3.00 1.90
Nos. 578-582 (5) 9.30 5.40

Issue dates: 25c, May 17, others, Apr. 24.

Ausipex '84 — A76

Australian stamps.

1984, July 16 Litho. *Perf. 13½*

583 A76 10c No. 2 .65 .45
584 A76 75c No. 18 2.00 1.40
585 A76 $1 No. 130 2.75 1.90
586 A76 $2.50 No. 178 3.75 3.75
Nos. 583-586 (4) 9.15 7.50

Souvenir Sheet

587 A76 $5 Nos. 378, 379 7.50 7.50

Slavery Abolition Sesquicentennial — A77

Abolitionists and Vignettes: 10c, Thomas Fowell Buxton, planting sugar cane. 25c, Abraham Lincoln, cotton field. 35c, Henri Christophe, armed slave revolt. 60c, Thomas Clarkson, addressing Anti-Slavery Society. 75c, William Wilberforce, Slave auction. $1, Olaudah Equiano, slave raid on Benin coast. $2.50, General Gordon, slave convoy in Sudan. $5, Granville Sharp, restraining ship captain from boarding slave.

1984, Aug. 1 *Perf. 12*

588 A77 10c multicolored .25 .25
589 A77 25c multicolored .45 .45
590 A77 35c multicolored .60 .60
591 A77 60c multicolored .75 .75
592 A77 75c multicolored 1.00 1.00
593 A77 $1 multicolored 1.10 1.10
594 A77 $2.50 multicolored 2.10 2.10
595 A77 $5 multicolored 4.75 4.75
a. Miniature sheet of 8, #588-595 11.00 *12.00*
Nos. 588-595 (8) 11.00 11.00

For overprints see Nos. 688-695a.

Christmas — A78

Various Disney characters and celebrations.

Perf. 14, 12½x12 ($2)

1984, Nov. 12 Litho.

596 A78 1c multicolored .25 .25
597 A78 2c multicolored .25 .25
598 A78 3c multicolored .25 .25
599 A78 4c multicolored .25 .25
600 A78 5c multicolored .25 .25
601 A78 10c multicolored .25 .25
602 A78 $1 multicolored 4.50 3.00
603 A78 $2 multicolored 5.50 5.50
604 A78 $4 multicolored 8.00 *10.50*
Nos. 596-604 (9) 19.50 20.50

Souvenir Sheet

605 A78 $5 multicolored 10.00 10.00

Nos. 464-465, 477 Ovptd. or Srchd.

1984, Aug. 13

606 A62 5c #464 .35 .25
607 A62 20c on 10c #465 .50 .30
608 A62 $5 #477 7.50 4.25
Nos. 606-608 (3) 8.35 4.80

Intl. Civil Aviation Org., 40th Anniv. A79

60c, Icarus, by Hans Erni. 75c, Sun Princess, by Sadiou Diouf. $2.50, Anniv. emblem, vert.
$5, Map of the Caribbean.

1984, Dec. 3 Litho. *Perf. 14*

609 A79 60c multicolored 1.00 *1.10*
610 A79 75c multicolored 1.60 *1.75*
611 A79 $2.50 multicolored 4.50 *4.75*
Nos. 609-611 (3) 7.10 7.60

Souvenir Sheet

612 A79 $5 multicolored 6.50 7.50

Audubon Birth Bicent. — A80

Illustrations by artist and naturalist J. J. Audubon (1785-1851) — 10c, Hirundo rustica. 60c, Mycteria americana. 75c, Sterna dougallii. $5, Pandion haliaetus.
No. 617, Vireo solitarus, horiz. No. 618, Piranga ludoviciana, horiz.

1985, Apr. 30 Litho. *Perf. 14*

613 A80 10c multicolored 1.40 1.10
614 A80 60c multicolored 2.40 2.40
615 A80 75c multicolored 2.40 2.40
616 A80 $5 multicolored 8.50 8.50
Nos. 613-616 (4) 14.70 14.40

Souvenir Sheets

617 A80 $4 multicolored 7.50 7.50
618 A80 $4 multicolored 7.50 7.50

Queen Mother 85th Birthday — A81

Photographs: 10c, Visiting the children's ward at King's College Hospital. $2, Inspecting Royal Marine Volunteer Cadets at Deal. $3, Outside Clarence House in London. $5, In an open carriage at Ascot.

1985, July 2

619 A81 10c multicolored .25 .25
620 A81 $2 multicolored 1.40 1.40
621 A81 $3 multicolored 2.25 2.25
Nos. 619-621 (3) 3.90 3.90

Souvenir Sheet

622 A81 $5 multicolored 3.00 3.00

Nos. 619-621 printed in sheetlets of 5.

Birds A82

1985-86 Litho. *Perf. 13½x14*

623 A82 5c Brown pelican 3.00 2.00
624 A82 10c Turtle dove 3.00 2.00
625 A82 15c Man-o-war 3.00 2.00
626 A82 20c Antillean crested hummingbird 3.00 2.00
627 A82 25c White-tailed tropicbird 3.00 2.50
628 A82 30c Caribbean elaenia 3.00 2.50
629 A82 35c Black-whiskered vireo 13.00 10.00
629A A82 35c Lesser Antillean bullfinch ('86) 3.00 2.50
630 A82 40c Yellow-crowned night heron 3.00 2.50
631 A82 45c Pearly-eyed thrasher 3.00 2.50
632 A82 50c Laughing bird 3.00 2.50
633 A82 65c Brown booby 3.00 2.50
634 A82 80c Gray kingbird 4.00 5.00
635 A82 $1 Audubon's shearwater 4.00 5.00
636 A82 $1.35 Roseate tern 3.00 *5.00*
637 A82 $2.50 Bananaquit 10.00 11.00
638 A82 $5 Belted kingfisher 7.75 *13.50*
639 A82 $10 Green heron 13.00 17.50
Nos. 623-639 (18) 87.75 *92.50*

Issued: 25c, 65c, $1.35, $5, 7/22; 45c, 50c, 80c, $1, $10, 9/30; 5c-20c, 30c, No. 629, 40c, $2.50, 11/11; No. 629A, 3/10.

For overprints & surcharges see Nos. 678-682, 713-716, 723-739, 750-753, 764-767, 783-786.

Nos. 485-491 Overprinted

1985, Oct. 31 Litho. *Perf. 14*

639A A64 10c multicolored .25 .25
639B A64 30c multicolored .25 .25
639C A64 40c multicolored .30 .30
639D A64 60c multicolored .45 .45
639E A64 $2 multicolored 1.50 1.50
639F A64 $3 multicolored 4.25 4.25
h. Souv. sheet of 6, #639A-639F 4.80 4.80
Complete booklet, 4 each #639A, 639C-639E 11.00
Nos. 639A-639F (6) 7.00 7.00

Souvenir Sheet

639G A64 $5 multicolored 5.00 5.00

Nos. 464, 469, 475 and 477 Ovptd.

1985, Oct. 14 Litho. *Perf. 14*

640 A62 5c multicolored .45 .25
641 A62 30c multicolored .75 .55
642 A62 75c multicolored 1.10 .90
643 A62 $5 multicolored 11.75 11.75
Nos. 640-643 (4) 14.05 13.45

Nos. 465 and 469 Ovptd. or Srchd.

1985, Nov. 18

644 A62 10c multicolored .65 .25
645 A62 35c on 30c multi 1.40 .50

Nos. 476, 469 Srchd. or Ovptd.

1985, Nov. 18

646 A62 $1 multicolored 2.25 1.25
647 A62 $5 on 30c multi 7.25 7.25

Brothers Grimm — A83

Christmas: Disney characters in Hansel and Gretel.

1985, Nov. 11 Litho. *Perf. 14*

648 A83 5c multicolored .60 .55
649 A83 50c multicolored 1.90 .80
650 A83 90c multicolored 2.50 1.25
651 A83 $4 multicolored 5.00 5.00
Nos. 648-651 (4) 10.00 7.60

Souvenir Sheet

652 A83 $5 multicolored 9.00 9.00

Mark Twain (1835-1910), Author — A84

Disney characters in Huckleberry Finn.

1985, Nov. 11

653 A84 10c multicolored .80 .35
654 A84 60c multicolored 2.50 1.25
654A A84 $1 multicolored 3.25 1.90
655 A84 $3 multicolored 4.75 4.75
Nos. 653-655 (4) 11.30 8.25

Souvenir Sheet

656 A84 $5 multicolored 10.00 10.00

Christmas. No. 654A printed in sheets of 8.

Statue of Liberty Centennial A85

10c, Danmark, Denmark. 20c, Eagle, USA. 60c, Amerigo Vespucci, Italy. 75c, Sir Winston Churchill, G.B. $2, Nippon Maru, Japan. $2.50, Gorch, Germany.
$5, Statue of Liberty, vert.

1985, Nov. 25

657 A85 10c multicolored 1.00 .70
658 A85 20c multicolored 1.50 .95
659 A85 60c multicolored 2.00 1.60
660 A85 75c multicolored 2.00 1.50
661 A85 $2 multicolored 2.00 *2.40*
662 A85 $2.50 multicolored 2.40 *2.75*
Nos. 657-662 (6) 10.90 *9.90*

Souvenir Sheet

663 A85 $5 multicolored 10.00 10.00

Easter — A86

Stained glass windows.

1986, Mar. 27 Litho. *Perf. 14*

664 A86 10c multicolored .30 .30
665 A86 25c multicolored .60 .60
666 A86 45c multicolored 1.10 1.10
667 A86 $4 multicolored 5.75 5.75
Nos. 664-667 (4) 7.75 7.75

Souvenir Sheet

668 A86 $5 multi, horiz. 8.25 8.25

Halley's Comet A87

A88

Designs: 5c, Johannes Hevelius (1611-1687), Mayan temple observatory. 10c, US Viking probe landing on Mars, 1976. 60c, Theatri Cosmicum (detail), 1668. $4, Sighting, 1835. $5, Comet over Anguilla.

1986, Mar. 24

669 A87 5c multicolored .45 .45
670 A87 10c multicolored .50 .50
671 A87 60c multicolored 1.50 1.10
672 A87 $4 multicolored 6.25 6.25
Nos. 669-672 (4) 8.70 8.30

Souvenir Sheet

673 A88 $5 multicolored 5.25 *7.25*

Queen Elizabeth II, 60th Birthday
Common Design Type

20c, Inspecting guards, 1946. $2, Garter Ceremony, 1985. $3, Trooping the color.
$5, Christening, 1926.

1986, Apr. 21

674 CD339 20c multicolored .25 .25
675 CD339 $2 multicolored 1.75 1.75
676 CD339 $3 multicolored 2.50 2.50
Nos. 674-676 (3) 4.50 4.50

Souvenir Sheet

677 CD339 $5 multicolored 4.50 4.50

Nos. 623, 631, 635, 637 and 639 Ovptd.

1986, May 22 *Perf. 13½x14*

678 A82 5c multicolored 1.00 *1.10*
679 A82 45c multicolored 2.25 .90
680 A82 $1 multicolored 4.00 1.90
681 A82 $2.50 multicolored 5.00 *5.00*
682 A82 $10 multicolored 11.00 *12.00*
Nos. 678-682 (5) 23.25 20.90

Wedding of Prince Andrew and Sarah Ferguson — A89

1986, July 23 Litho. *Perf. 14*

683 A89 10c Couple .25 *.25*
684 A89 35c Andrew .30 *.35*
685 A89 $2 Sarah 1.25 *1.90*
686 A89 $3 Couple, diff. 2.00 *3.00*
Nos. 683-686 (4) 3.80 *5.50*

Souvenir Sheet

687 A89 $6 Westminster Abbey 6.00 6.00

Perf. 12

683a A89 10c Couple .40 *.25*
684a A89 35c Andrew .65 *.30*
685a A89 $2 Sarah 1.60 *1.25*
686a A89 $3 Couple, diff. 2.00 *1.90*
Nos. 683a-686a (4) 4.65 *3.70*

Souvenir Sheet

687a A89 $6 Westminster Abbey 6.00 6.00

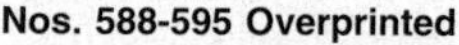
Nos. 588-595 Overprinted

1986, Sept. 29 Litho. *Perf. 12*

688 A77 10c multicolored .65 .35
689 A77 25c multicolored 1.00 .55
690 A77 35c multicolored 1.25 .65
691 A77 60c multicolored 2.00 .95
692 A77 75c multicolored 2.00 1.25
693 A77 $1 multicolored 2.00 1.40
694 A77 $2.50 multicolored 3.50 *5.00*
695 A77 $5 multicolored 4.75 *6.50*
a. Miniature sheet, #688-695 20.00 *21.00*
Nos. 688-695 (8) 17.15 *16.65*

Ships A90

1986, Nov. 29 Litho. *Perf. 14*

696 A90 10c Trading Sloop 1.75 .45
697 A90 45c Lady Rodney 3.25 .60
698 A90 80c West Derby 4.50 3.00
699 A90 $3 Warspite 7.75 6.00
Nos. 696-699 (4) 17.25 10.05

Souvenir Sheet

700 A90 $6 Boat Race Day, vert. 22.50 22.50

Christmas.

Discovery of America, 500th Anniv. (in 1992) — A91

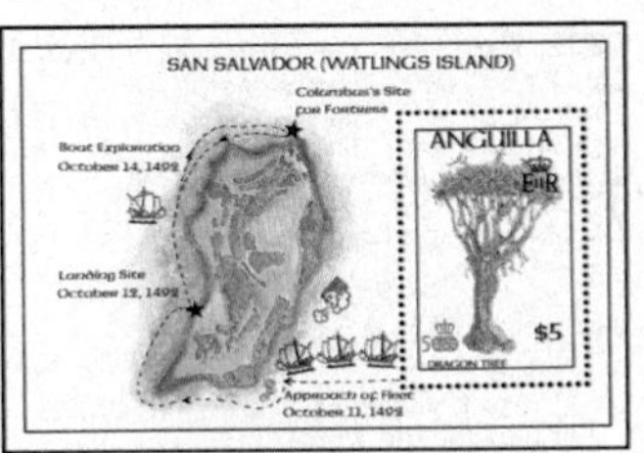

Dragon Tree — A92

5c, Christopher Columbus, astrolabe. 10c, Aboard ship. 35c, Santa Maria. 80c, Ferdinand, Isabella. $4, Indians. No. 707, Caribbean manatee.

1986, Dec. 22

701 A91 5c multi .90 *.90*
702 A91 10c multi 1.50 .90
703 A91 35c multi 3.00 1.60
704 A91 80c multi, horiz. 2.25 *2.25*
705 A91 $4 multi 5.00 *5.00*
Nos. 701-705 (5) 12.65 *10.65*

Souvenir Sheets

706 A92 $5 shown 10.00 10.00
707 A92 $5 multi, horiz. 10.00 10.00

Butterflies A93

1987, Apr. 14 Litho. *Perf. 14*

708 A93 10c Monarch 2.00 .90
709 A93 80c White peacock 5.50 2.75
710 A93 $1 Zebra 6.50 3.25
711 A93 $2 Caribbean buck-eye 10.00 *11.00*
Nos. 708-711 (4) 24.00 *17.90*

Souvenir Sheet

712 A93 $6 Flambeau 20.00 20.00

Easter.

Nos. 629A, 631, 634 and 639 Ovptd in Red

1987, May 25 Litho. *Perf. 13½x14*

713 A82 35c on No. 629A 2.25 1.00
714 A82 45c on No. 631 2.25 1.10
715 A82 80c on No. 634 3.25 1.60
716 A82 $10 on No. 639 12.00 *16.00*
Nos. 713-716 (4) 19.75 *19.70*

Separation from St. Kitts and Nevis, 20th Anniv. — A94

10c, Old goose iron, electric iron. 35c, Old East End School, Albena Lake-Hodge Comprehensive College. 45c, Old market place, People's Market. 80c, Old ferries & modern ferry at Blowing Point. $1, Old & new cable & wireless offices. $2, Public meeting at Burrowes Park, House of Assembly.

1987, May 25 *Perf. 14*

717 A94 10c multicolored .75 .50
718 A94 35c multicolored .85 .65
719 A94 45c multicolored 1.00 .80
720 A94 80c multicolored 2.25 1.00
721 A94 $1 multicolored 1.75 1.25
722 A94 $2 multicolored 2.50 *2.75*
a. Souvenir sheet of 6, #717-722 14.50 14.50
Nos. 717-722 (6) 9.10 6.95

Nos. 623, 625-628, 629A-639 Ovptd. in Red or Srchd. in Red & Black

1987, Sept. 4 Litho. *Perf. 13½x14*

723 A82 5c No. 623 3.00 2.50
724 A82 10c on 15c No. 625 3.00 2.50
725 A82 15c No. 625 3.50 3.00
726 A82 20c No. 626 3.50 3.00
727 A82 25c No. 627 3.50 3.00
728 A82 30c No. 628 3.50 3.00
729 A82 35c No. 629A 3.50 3.00
730 A82 40c No. 630 3.50 3.00
731 A82 45c No. 631 3.50 3.00
732 A82 50c No. 632 3.50 3.00
733 A82 65c No. 633 3.50 3.00
734 A82 80c No. 634 3.50 3.00
735 A82 $1 No. 635 4.00 *4.00*
736 A82 $1.35 No. 636 4.75 *4.75*
737 A82 $2.50 No. 637 5.25 *6.00*
738 A82 $5 No. 638 7.25 *8.25*
739 A82 $10 No. 639 11.00 *13.50*
Nos. 723-739 (17) 73.25 *71.50*

Cricket World Cup — A95

Various action scenes.

1987, Oct. 5 *Perf. 14*

740 A95 10c multicolored 1.90 .90
741 A95 35c multicolored 2.75 .90
742 A95 45c multicolored 2.75 .95
743 A95 $2.50 multicolored 5.50 6.00
Nos. 740-743 (4) 12.90 8.75

Souvenir Sheet

744 A95 $6 multicolored 16.00 16.00

Sea Shells, Crabs A96

1987, Nov. 2

745 A96 10c West Indian top shell 1.90 .70
746 A96 35c Ghost crab 2.50 1.10
747 A96 50c Spiny Caribbean vase 4.25 2.10
748 A96 $2 Great land crab 6.25 *10.50*
Nos. 745-748 (4) 14.90 *14.40*

Souvenir Sheet

749 A96 $6 Queen conch 15.00 15.00

Christmas.

Nos. 629A, 635-636 and 639 Ovptd. in Scarlet

1987, Dec. 14 Litho. *Perf. 13½x14*

750 A82 35c multicolored .30 .30
751 A82 $1 multicolored .70 .75
752 A82 $1.35 multicolored 1.00 1.00
753 A82 $10 multicolored 7.00 7.50
Nos. 750-753 (4) 9.00 9.55

Easter (Lilies) — A97

1988, Mar. 28 Litho. *Perf. 14*

754 A97 30c Crinum erubescens .75 .35
755 A97 45c Hymenocallis caribaea .95 .35
756 A97 $1 Crinum macowanii 2.50 1.00
757 A97 $2.50 Hemerocallis fulva 3.00 *4.00*
Nos. 754-757 (4) 7.20 *5.70*

Souvenir Sheet

758 A97 $6 Lilium longiflorum 7.00 *7.25*

1988 Summer Olympics, Seoul — A98

1988, July 25 Litho. *Perf. 14*

759 A98 35c 4x100-Meter relay .70 .35
760 A98 45c Windsurfing .80 .50
761 A98 50c Tennis 2.25 1.60
762 A98 80c Basketball 5.50 4.25
Nos. 759-762 (4) 9.25 6.70

Souvenir Sheet

763 A98 $6 Women's 200 meters 6.50 6.50

Nos. 629A, 634-635 and 637 Ovptd.

1988, Dec. 14 Litho. *Perf. 13½x14*

764 A82 35c multicolored 2.10 .85
765 A82 80c multicolored 3.00 1.75
766 A82 $1 multicolored 3.00 2.10
767 A82 $2.50 multicolored 5.25 *5.75*
Nos. 764-767 (4) 13.35 *10.45*

Marine Life — A99

1988, Dec. 5 Litho. *Perf. 14*

768 A99 35c Common sea fan 1.50 .45
769 A99 80c Coral crab 2.25 .95
770 A99 $1 Grooved brain coral 3.25 1.60
771 A99 $1.60 Old wife 3.75 *4.50*
Nos. 768-771 (4) 10.75 7.50

Souvenir Sheet

772 A99 $6 West Indies spiny lobster 7.75 7.75

Christmas.

Lizards — A100

1989, Feb. 20 Litho. *Perf. 13½x14*

773 A100 45c Wood slave 1.50 .70
774 A100 80c Slippery back 2.40 1.25
775 A100 $2.50 Iguana 5.50 *7.00*
Nos. 773-775 (3) 9.40 *8.95*

Souvenir Sheet

776 A100 $6 Tree lizard 16.00 16.00

Easter — A101

Paintings: 35c, Christ Crowned with Thorns, by Hieronymous Bosch (c. 1450-1516. 80c, Christ Bearing the Cross, by David. $1, The Deposition, by David. $1.60, Pieta, by Rogier van der Weyden (1400-1464). $6, Crucified Christ with the Virgin Mary and Saints, by Raphael.

1989, Mar. 23 Litho. *Perf. 14x13½*

777 A101 35c multicolored .55 *.35*
778 A101 80c multicolored 1.00 *.75*
779 A101 $1 multicolored 1.10 .80
780 A101 $1.60 multicolored 1.75 *2.00*
Nos. 777-780 (4) 4.40 *3.90*

Souvenir Sheet

781 A101 $6 multicolored 4.75 *5.50*

University of the West Indies, 40th Anniv. — A102

1989, Apr. 24 Litho. *Perf. 14x13½*

782 A102 $5 Coat of arms 4.00 *5.00*

Nos. 634-636 and 638 Ovptd.

1989, July 3 Litho. *Perf. 13½X14*

783 A82 80c multicolored 2.75 1.25
784 A82 $1 multicolored 2.75 1.60
785 A82 $1.35 multicolored 3.25 2.50
786 A82 $5 multicolored 9.25 *12.00*
Nos. 783-786 (4) 18.00 17.35

Christmas — A103

Well-known and historic houses.

1989, Dec. 4 Litho. *Perf. 13½x14*

787	A103	5c	Lone Star, 1930	.45	*.75*
788	A103	35c	Whitehouse, 1906	.80	.55
789	A103	45c	Hodges House	.95	.65
790	A103	80c	Warden's Place	1.75	2.10
			Nos. 787-790 (4)	3.95	4.05

Souvenir Sheet

791	A103	$6	Wallblake House, 1787	5.50	5.50

Fish A104

1990, Apr. 2 Litho. *Perf. 13½x14*

792	A104	5c	Blear eye	1.10	*1.00*
793	A104	10c	Redman	1.10	*1.00*
794	A104	15c	Speckletail	1.10	.90
795	A104	25c	Grunt	1.25	*1.10*
796	A104	30c	Amber jack	1.25	*1.10*
797	A104	35c	Red hind	1.25	1.10
798	A104	40c	Goatfish	1.50	1.10
799	A104	45c	Old wife	1.50	.80
800	A104	50c	Butter fish	1.75	1.25
801	A104	65c	Shell fish	2.25	1.25
802	A104	80c	Yellowtail snapper	2.10	1.50
803	A104	$1	Katy	2.25	1.50
804	A104	$1.35	Mutton grouper	2.50	2.25
805	A104	$2.50	Doctor fish	4.00	*4.75*
806	A104	$5	Angelfish	5.75	*7.75*
807	A104	$10	Barracuda	9.25	*12.00*
			Nos. 792-807 (16)	39.90	*40.35*

Inscribed "1992"

792a	A104	5c	Blear eye	.90	*.90*
793a	A104	10c	Redman	.90	*.90*
797a	A104	35c	Red hind	1.00	1.00
			Nos. 792a-797a (3)	2.80	*2.80*

For overprints and surcharge see Nos. 821-824, 849. For booklet see No. 890.

Easter — A105

1990, Apr. 2 *Perf. 14x13½*

811	A105	35c	Last Supper	1.25	.25
812	A105	45c	Trial	1.25	.35
813	A105	$1.35	Calvary	3.00	3.00
814	A105	$2.50	Empty tomb	3.75	3.75
			Nos. 811-814 (4)	9.25	7.35

Souvenir Sheet

815	A105	$6	The Resurrection	11.50	11.50

See Nos. 834-838.

Cape of Good Hope #7 A106

Stamps of Great Britain and exhibition emblem: 25c, #1, vert. 50c, #2, vert. $2.50, #93. $6, #1-2.

1990, Apr. 30 *Perf. 14*

816	A106	25c	multicolored	1.00	.40
817	A106	50c	multicolored	1.75	.70
818	A106	$1.50	shown	3.25	3.00
819	A106	$2.50	multicolored	4.25	*4.75*
			Nos. 816-819 (4)	10.25	*8.85*

Souvenir Sheet

820	A106	$6	multicolored	13.50	*14.00*

Stamp World London '90, Penny Black 150th anniv.

Nos. 803-806 Overprinted

a

b

c

d

1990, Sept. 24 Litho. *Perf. 13½x14*

821	A104(a)	$1	Katy	2.25	1.40
822	A104(b)	$1.35	Mutton grouper	2.50	1.60
823	A104(c)	$2.50	Doctor fish	6.00	6.00
824	A104(d)	$5	Angelfish	11.50	*11.50*
			Nos. 821-824 (4)	22.25	*20.50*

Christmas — A107

Birds.

1990, Dec. 3 *Perf. 14*

825	A107	10c	Laughing gull	.95	.55
826	A107	35c	Brown booby	1.60	.55
827	A107	$1.50	Bridled tern	3.00	3.00
828	A107	$3.50	Brown pelican	5.50	5.50
			Nos. 825-828 (4)	11.05	9.60

Souvenir Sheet

829	A107	$6	Least tern	11.00	11.00

Flags A108

1990, Nov. 5 Litho. *Perf. 13½x14*

830	A108	50c	Mermaid	1.75	.65
831	A108	80c	New Anguilla official	2.75	1.25
832	A108	$1	Three dolphins	2.90	1.50
833	A108	$5	Governor's official	8.25	7.75
			Nos. 830-833 (4)	15.65	*11.15*

Nos. 811-815 Inscribed or Overprinted

1991, Apr. 30 Litho. *Perf. 14x13½*

834	A105	35c	like #811	1.25	.75
835	A105	45c	like #812	1.50	.75
836	A105	$1.35	like #813	3.00	3.00
837	A105	$2.50	like #814	5.25	5.25
			Nos. 834-837 (4)	11.00	9.75

Souvenir Sheet

838	A105	$6	like #815	14.00	14.00

Easter. "1990" obliterated by black bar in souvenir sheet margin.

Christmas — A109

Perf. 14x13½, 13½x14

1991, Dec. Litho.

839	A109	5c	Angel, vert.	.75	.90
840	A109	35c	Santa, vert.	2.00	.75
841	A109	80c	shown	3.00	2.75
842	A109	$1	Palm trees, poinsettias	3.00	2.75
			Nos. 839-842 (4)	8.75	7.15

Souvenir Sheet

843	A109	$5	Homes, holly	10.00	10.00

Easter A110

Designs: 35c, Church, angels holding palms, vert. 45c Church, angels singing, vert. 80c, Village. $1, People going to church, vert. $5, People at beach, sailboats.

1992 Litho. *Perf. 14*

844	A110	35c	multicolored	1.25	.65
845	A110	45c	multicolored	1.60	.65
846	A110	80c	multicolored	2.75	1.10
847	A110	$1	multicolored	2.75	1.60
848	A110	$5	multicolored	7.25	*12.00*
			Nos. 844-848 (5)	15.60	*16.00*

No. 796 Surcharged

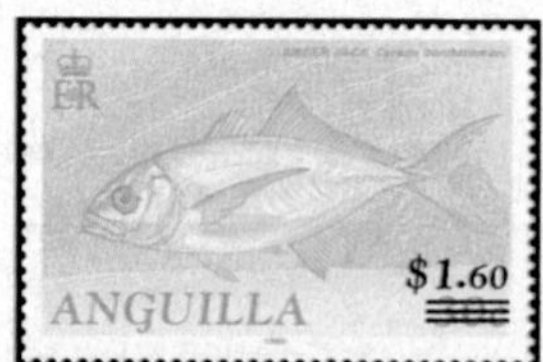

1992, June 10 Litho. *Perf. 13½x14*

849	A104	$1.60	on 30c #796	3.75	2.75

No. 849 inscribed "1992."

Independence, 25th Anniv. — A111

1992, Aug. 10 Litho. *Perf. 14*

850	A111	80c	Official seal, flag	2.50	1.50
851	A111	$1	Official seal	2.50	1.50
852	A111	$1.60	Flags, airport	4.75	4.75
853	A111	$2	First seal	4.75	4.75
			Nos. 850-853 (4)	14.50	12.50

Souvenir Sheet

854	A111	$10	#1, 8-11, 15-16	15.00	15.00

No. 854 contains one 85x85mm stamp. For booklet see No. 970.

Sailboat Racing — A112

Designs: 20c, On course. 35c, Stylized boat poster. 45c, Start of race. No. 858, Blue Bird, 1971, vert. No. 859, Construction plans for Blue Bird, vert. $1, Stylized boat poster, diff. $6, Like Nos. 855 & 857.

Perf. 13½x14, 14x13½

1992, Oct. 12 Litho.

855	A112	20c	multicolored	1.90	.60
856	A112	35c	multicolored	2.40	.50
857	A112	45c	multicolored	2.75	.50
858	A112	80c	multicolored	3.75	*4.00*
859	A112	80c	multicolored	3.75	*4.00*
a.			Pair, #858-859	*8.00*	*10.00*
860	A112	$1	multicolored	3.75	2.50
			Nos. 855-860 (6)	18.30	12.10

Souvenir Sheet

861	A112	$6	multicolored	11.00	11.00

No. 861 contains one 96x31mm stamp.

Discovery of America, 500th Anniv. A113

1992, Dec. 15 Litho. *Perf. 14*

862	A113	80c	Landfall	3.25	1.75
863	A113	$1	Columbus, vert.	3.25	1.75
864	A113	$2	Fleet	5.25	*5.50*
865	A113	$3	Pinta	6.00	*7.00*
			Nos. 862-865 (4)	17.75	*16.00*

Souvenir Sheet

866	A113	$6	Map of voyage, vert.	15.50	15.50

Christmas A114

Various Christmas trees and: 20c, Mucka Jumbie on stilts. 70c, Masquerading house to house. $1.05, Christmas baking, old oven style. $2.40, $5, Collecting presents.

1992, Dec. 7

867	A114	20c	multicolored	.90	.65
868	A114	70c	multicolored	2.00	.95
869	A114	$1.05	multicolored	2.25	1.75
870	A114	$2.40	multicolored	4.25	*6.00*
			Nos. 867-870 (4)	9.40	*9.35*

Souvenir Sheet

871	A114	$5	Sheet of 1 + 3 labels	7.50	7.50

Labels on No. 871 are similar to Nos. 867-869, but without denomination.

Easter — A115

Children's drawings: 20c, Kite flying. 45c, Cliff top village service. 80c, Morning devotion on Sombrero. $1.50, Hilltop church service. $5, Good Friday kites.

1993, Mar. 29 Litho. *Perf. 14*

872	A115	20c multicolored	1.75	.90
873	A115	45c multicolored	2.75	.90
874	A115	80c multicolored	4.00	2.10
875	A115	$1.50 multicolored	5.50	*7.00*
		Nos. 872-875 (4)	14.00	*10.90*

Souvenir Sheet

876	A115	$5 multicolored	9.50	9.50

No. 876 contains one 42x56mm stamp.

Native Industries A116

1993, June 23 Litho. *Perf. 14*

877	A116	20c Salt	3.25	1.10
878	A116	80c Tobacco	3.25	1.75
879	A116	$1 Cotton	3.25	1.75
880	A116	$2 Sugar cane	4.75	*6.50*
		Nos. 877-880 (4)	14.50	*11.10*

Souvenir Sheet

881	A116	$6 Fishing	14.50	14.50

Coronation of Queen Elizabeth II, 40th Anniv. — A117

Designs: 80c, Lord Great Chamberlain presents the spurs of chivalry. $1, The benediction. $2, Queen Elizabeth II, coronation photograph. $3, St. Edward's Crown. $6, Queen, Prince Philip in Gold State Coach.

1993, Aug. 16 Litho. *Perf. 14*

882	A117	80c multicolored	2.25	1.00
883	A117	$1 multicolored	2.50	1.10
884	A117	$2 multicolored	3.25	3.25
885	A117	$3 multicolored	3.75	*4.75*
		Nos. 882-885 (4)	11.75	*10.10*

Souvenir Sheet

886	A117	$6 multicolored	15.00	*16.00*

Anguilla Carnival — A118

1993, Aug. 23 Litho. *Perf. 14*

887	A118	20c Pan musician	.70	.50
888	A118	45c Pirates	1.25	.50
889	A118	80c Stars	2.40	1.10
890	A118	$1 Playing mas	2.40	1.25
		Booklet, 5 ea #796, 890	13.75	
891	A118	$2 Masqueraders	3.75	*5.50*
892	A118	$3 Commandos	4.50	*6.25*
		Nos. 887-892 (6)	15.00	*15.10*

Souvenir Sheet

893	A118	$5 Carnival fantasy	15.00	15.00

Christmas A119

Traditional Christmas customs: 20c, Mucka Jumbies. 35c, Serenaders. 45c, Baking. $3, Five-fingers Christmas tree. $4, Mucka Jumbies and serenaders.

1993, Dec. 7 Litho. *Perf. 14x13½*

894	A119	20c multicolored	1.10	.90
895	A119	35c multicolored	1.50	.90
896	A119	45c multicolored	1.75	.90
897	A119	$3 multicolored	6.25	*8.00*
		Nos. 894-897 (4)	10.60	*10.70*

Souvenir Sheet

Perf. 14

898	A119	$4 multicolored	5.50	5.50

No. 898 contains one 54x42mm stamp.

Mail Delivery — A120

Designs: 20c, Traveling Branch mail van, Sandy Ground, horiz. 45c, Mail boat, Betsy R, The Forest. 80c, Old post office, horiz. $1, Mail by jeep, Island Harbor. $4, New post office, 1993, horiz.

1994, Feb. 11 Litho. *Perf. 14*

899	A120	20c multicolored	2.00	.95
900	A120	45c multicolored	2.75	.95
901	A120	80c multicolored	3.50	1.90
902	A120	$1 multicolored	3.50	1.90
903	A120	$4 multicolored	5.50	*8.75*
		Nos. 899-903 (5)	17.25	*14.45*

Royal Visits — A121

1994, Feb. 18

904	A121	45c Princess Alexandra	2.00	.80
905	A121	50c Princess Alice	2.25	.80
906	A121	80c Prince Philip	3.00	1.75
907	A121	$1 Prince Charles	3.50	1.75
908	A121	$2 Queen Elizabeth II	4.75	*5.50*
a.		Souvenir sheet of 4, #904-908	15.00	*15.00*
		Nos. 904-908 (5)	15.50	*10.60*

Easter — A122

Stained glass windows: 20c, Crucifixion. 45c, Empty tomb. 80c, Resurrection. $3, Risen Christ with disciples.

1994, Apr. 6 Litho. *Perf. 14x15*

909	A122	20c multicolored	.90	.65
910	A122	45c multicolored	1.10	.80
911	A122	80c multicolored	2.10	1.10
912	A122	$3 multicolored	5.50	*6.25*
		Nos. 909-912 (4)	9.60	*8.80*

Christmas — A123

Designs: 20c, Adoration of the shepherds. 30c, Magi, shepherds. 35c, The Annunciation. 45c, Nativity Scene. $2.40, Flight into Egypt.

1994, Nov. 22 Litho. *Perf. 14*

913	A123	20c multicolored	1.00	.80
914	A123	30c multicolored	1.25	.80
915	A123	35c multicolored	1.25	.80
916	A123	45c multicolored	1.50	.80
917	A123	$2.40 multicolored	4.50	*5.50*
		Nos. 913-917 (5)	9.50	*8.70*

1994 World Cup Soccer Championships, US — A124

Soccer player and: 20c, Pontiac Silverdome, Detroit. 70c, Foxboro Stadium, Boston. $1.80, RFK Memorial Stadium, Washington. $2.40, Soldier Field, Chicago.

$6, Two players.

1994, Oct. 3 Litho. *Perf. 13½x14*

918	A124	20c multicolored	1.00	.50
919	A124	70c multicolored	1.50	1.10
920	A124	$1.80 multicolored	3.00	*3.25*
921	A124	$2.40 multicolored	3.50	*4.00*
		Nos. 918-921 (4)	9.00	*8.85*

Souvenir Sheet

922	A124	$6 multicolored	14.00	14.00

Easter A125

Turtle dove: 45c, One on tree branch. 50c, One on nest, one on branch. $5, Mother with young.

1995, Apr. 10 Litho. *Perf. 14*

923	A125	20c multicolored	.70	.60
924	A125	45c multicolored	1.10	.90
925	A125	50c multicolored	1.25	1.10
926	A125	$5 multicolored	8.00	*11.00*
		Nos. 923-926 (4)	11.05	*13.60*

UN, 50th Anniv. A126

Secretaries general and: 20c, Trygve Lie (1946-53), general assembly. 80c, UN flag, UN headquarters with "50" (no portrait). $1, Dag Hammarskjold (1953-61), charter, U Thant (1961-71). $5, UN complex, New York, vert. (no portrait).

Perf. 13½x14, 14x13½

1995, June 26 Litho.

927	A126	20c multicolored	.40	.40
928	A126	80c multicolored	.80	.80
929	A126	$1 multicolored	1.00	1.00
930	A126	$5 multicolored	5.25	5.25
		Nos. 927-930 (4)	7.45	7.45

Caribbean Development Bank, 25th Anniv. — A127

Designs: 45c, Emblem, map of Anguilla. $5, Local headquarters along waterfront.

1995, Aug. 15 Litho. *Perf. 13½x14*

931	A127	45c multicolored	2.75	2.75
932	A127	$5 multicolored	5.50	5.50
a.		Pair, #931-932	8.50	8.50

Whales — A128

20c, Blue whale. 45c, Right whale, vert. $1, Sperm whale. $5, Humpback whale.

Perf. 13½x14, 14x13½

1995, Nov. 24 Litho.

933	A128	20c multi	2.75	.95
934	A128	45c multi	3.00	.80
935	A128	$1 multi	3.75	2.10
936	A128	$5 multi	10.50	*11.50*
		Nos. 933-936 (4)	20.00	*15.35*

Christmas A129

1995, Dec. 12 *Perf. 14½*

937	A129	10c Palm tree	.80	.80
938	A129	25c Fish net floats	1.10	.65
939	A129	45c Sea shells	1.25	.65
940	A129	$5 Fish	10.00	*12.00*
		Nos. 937-940 (4)	13.15	*14.10*

Corals A130

20c, Deep water gorgonia. 80c, Common sea fan. $5, Venus sea fern.

1996, June 21 Litho. *Perf. 14x14½*

941	A130	20c multi	2.00	.95
942	A130	80c multi	3.25	1.40
943	A130	$5 multi	9.50	*11.25*
		Nos. 941-943 (3)	14.75	*13.60*

A131

1996 Summer Olympic Games, Atlanta: 20c, Running. 80c, Javelin, wheelchair basketball. $1, High jump. $3.50, Olympic torch, Greek, US flags.

1996, Dec. 12 Litho. *Perf. 14*

944 A131	20c multicolored	.95	.75
945 A131	80c multicolored	3.25	1.50
946 A131	$1 multicolored	2.25	1.50
947 A131	$3.50 multicolored	6.00	*7.00*
	Nos. 944-947 (4)	12.45	*10.75*

A132

Battle for Anguilla, bicent.: 60c, Sandy Hill Fort, HMS Lapwing. 75c, French troops destroy church, horiz. $1.50, HMS Lapwing defeats Valiant, Decius, horiz. $4, French troops land, Rendezvous Bay.

1996, Dec. 12

948 A132	60c multicolored	1.25	1.25
949 A132	75c multicolored	1.25	1.25
950 A132	$1.50 multicolored	2.50	2.50
951 A132	$4 multicolored	4.25	*4.25*
	Nos. 948-951 (4)	9.25	*9.25*

Fruits and Nuts A133

1997, Apr. 30 Litho. *Perf. 14*

952 A133	10c Gooseberry	.25	*.50*
953 A133	20c West Indian cherry	.25	*.40*
954 A133	40c Tamarind	.35	*.40*
955 A133	50c Pommesurette	.55	.50
956 A133	60c Sea almond	.65	*.60*
957 A133	75c Sea grape	.90	.80
958 A133	80c Banana	.95	.90
959 A133	$1 Genip	1.25	1.25
960 A133	$1.10 Coco plum	1.50	*1.75*
961 A133	$1.25 Pope	1.75	*1.90*
962 A133	$1.50 Papaya	1.90	*1.90*
963 A133	$2 Sugar apple	2.50	*2.50*
964 A133	$3 Soursop	4.00	*4.00*
965 A133	$4 Pomegrante	5.25	*5.50*
966 A133	$5 Cashew	6.25	*6.00*
967 A133	$10 Mango	10.00	*10.50*
	Nos. 952-967 (16)	38.30	*39.40*

Iguanas — A134

World Wildlife Fund: a, 20c, Baby iguanas emerging from eggs, juvenile iguana. b, 50c, Adult on rock. c, 75c, Two iguanas on tree limbs. d, $3, Adult up close, adult on tree branch.

1997, Oct. 13 Litho. *Perf. 13½x14*

968 A134	Strip of 4, #a.-d.	10.00	9.75

Diana, Princess of Wales (1961-97) A135

Designs: a, 15c, In red & white. b, $1, In yellow. c, $1.90, Wearing tiara. d, $2.25, Wearing blouse with Red Cross emblem.

1998, Apr. 14 Litho. *Perf. 14*

969 A135	Strip of 4, #a.-d.	12.00	11.00

No. 969 was issued in sheets of 16 stamps.

Fountain Cavern Carvings A136

30c, Rainbow Deity (Juluca). $1.25, Lizard. $2.25, Solar Chieftan. $2.75, Creator.

1997, Nov. 17 Litho. *Perf. 14x14½*

970 A136	30c multicolored	.70	.55
	Booklet, 5 ea #851, 970	12.00	
971 A136	$1.25 multicolored	1.50	1.50
972 A136	$2.25 multicolored	2.40	2.40
973 A136	$2.75 multicolored	3.25	3.25
	Nos. 970-973 (4)	7.85	7.70

1998 Intl. Arts Festival A137

Paintings: 15c, "Treasure Island." 30c, "Posing in the Light." $1, "Pescadores de Anguilla." $1.50, "Fresh Catch." $1.90, "The Bell Tower of St. Mary's."

1998, Aug. 24 Litho. *Perf. 14*

974 A137	15c multi	.65	.65
975 A137	30c multi, vert.	.80	.80
976 A137	$1 multi, vert.	1.40	1.40
	Booklet, 5 ea #975-976	10.00	
977 A137	$1.50 multi	1.60	1.60
978 A137	$1.90 multi, vert.	2.00	2.00
	Nos. 974-978 (5)	6.45	6.45

Christmas A138

Paintings of "Hidden beauty of Anguilla:" 15c, Woman cooking over open fire, girl seated on steps. $1, Person looking over fruits and vegetables. $1.50, Underwater scene. $3, Cacti growing along shore.

1998

979 A138	15c multicolored	.50	.50
980 A138	$1 multicolored	1.00	1.00
981 A138	$1.50 multicolored	1.40	1.40
982 A138	$3 multicolored	2.10	2.10
	Nos. 979-982 (4)	5.00	5.00

Royal Air Force, 80th Anniv. A139

Designs: 30c, Sopwith Camel, Bristol F2B. $1, Supermarine Spitfire II, Hawker Hurricane Mk1. $1.50, Avro Lancaster. $1.90, Harrier GR7, Panavia Tornado F3.

1998 Litho. *Perf. 13½*
Granite Paper (No. 983)

983 A139	30c multicolored	1.25	.60
984 A139	$1 multicolored	2.00	1.00
985 A139	$1.50 multicolored	2.50	2.25
986 A139	$1.90 multicolored	4.00	3.25
	Complete booklet, 5each #983-984	16.50	
	Nos. 983-986 (4)	9.75	7.10

University of the West Indies, 50th Anniv. — A140

Designs: $1.50, Anguilla campus. $1.90, Anguilla campus, torchbearer, University arms.

1998 Litho. *Perf. 13¼*
Granite Paper (#988)

987-988 A140	Set of 2	3.00	*3.25*

First Manned Moon Landing, 30th Anniv. — A141

Designs: 30c, Lift-off of Apollo 11, Command and Service Modules in lunar orbit. $1, Buzz Aldrin on Moon, footprint. $1.50, Lunar Module leaving Moon. $1.90, Splashdown.

1999, May 6 Litho. *Perf. 13¾*

989 A141	30c multi	.90	.50
990 A141	$1 multi	1.60	.90
991 A141	$1.50 multi	1.75	1.75
992 A141	$1.90 multi	2.75	*3.25*
	Nos. 989-992 (4)	7.00	*6.40*

Heroes of Anguilla's Revolution A142

Designs: 30c, Albena Lake Hodge (1920-85). $1, Collins O. Hodge (1926-78). $1.50, Edwin W. Rey (1906-80). $1.90, Walter G. Hodge (1920-89).

1999, July 5 *Perf. 14½x14¼*

993 A142	30c multi	.50	.30
994 A142	$1 multi	.90	.60
995 A142	$1.50 multi	1.25	*1.25*
996 A142	$1.90 multi	1.90	*2.00*
	Nos. 993-996 (4)	4.55	*4.15*

Modern Architecture A143

Designs: No. 997, 30c, Library and resource center. No. 998, 65c, Parliamentary building and court house. No. 999, $1, Caribbean Commercial Bank. No. 999A, $1.50, Police headquarters. No. 1000, $1.90, Post office.

1999 Litho. *Perf. 14x14½*

997-1000 A143	Set of 5	7.50	*7.75*

Christmas and Millennium Celebrations — A144

Designs: 30c, Fireworks display and barbecue. $1, Globe, musicians. $1.50, Family dinner. $1.90, Decorated tree.

1999 Litho. *Perf. 13¼*

1001 A144	30c multi	.55	.50
1002 A144	$1 multi	1.40	.90
1003 A144	$1.50 multi	2.10	2.10
1004 A144	$1.90 multi	2.25	*3.75*
	Nos. 1001-1004 (4)	6.30	*7.25*

Beaches — A145

1005, 15c, Shoal Bay. 1006, 30c, Maundys Bay. 1007, $1, Rendezvous Bay. 1008, $1.50, Meads Bay. 1009, $1.90, Little Bay. 1010, $2, Sandy Ground.

1999 *Perf. 12*

1005-1010 A145	Set of 6	8.75	8.75
a.	Sheet of 6, #1005-1010	8.75	*8.75*
b.	As "a," with show emblem in margin	8.00	*8.25*

The Stamp Show 2000, London (No. 1010b). Issued: No. 1010b, 5/22/00.

Easter A146

Toys: 25c, Banjo. 30c, Top. $1.50, Slingshot. $1.90, Roller. $2.50, Killy ban.
No. 1016: a, 75c, Rag doll. b, $1, Kite. c, $1.25, Cricket ball. d, $4, Pond boat.

2000 *Perf. 13¼*

1011 A146	25c multi	.25	.25
1012 A146	30c multi	.40	.40
1013 A146	$1.50 multi	1.50	1.50
1014 A146	$1.90 multi	2.00	*2.25*
1015 A146	$2.50 multi	2.75	*3.00*
	Nos. 1011-1015 (5)	6.90	7.40

Souvenir Sheet

1016 A146	Sheet of 4, #a-d	6.75	6.75

100th Test Match at Lord's Ground — A147

$2, Lanville Harrigan. $4, Cardigan Connor. $6, Lord's Ground, horiz.

2000, May 5 Litho. *Perf. 13¾x13¼*

1017-1018 A147	Set of 2	7.75	7.75

Souvenir Sheet

1018A A147	$6 multi	12.00	12.00

HRH PRINCE WILLIAM - 18th Birthday
ANGUILLA 30c

Prince William, 18th Birthday — A148

Prince William and: 30c, Queen Elizabeth II, Princes Philip and Charles. $1, Princess Diana, Princes Harry and Charles. $1.90, Princes Harry and Charles. $2.25, Princes Charles and Harry, in winter wear.

2000, July 20 ***Perf. 13¼***
1019-1022 A148 Set of 4 9.25 9.25

Souvenir Sheet

1023 A148 $8 Prince William, vert. 9.75 *10.00*

Queen Mother, 100th Birthday — A149

Queen Mother and: 30c, Prince William. $1.50, Anguilla shoreline. $1.90, Clarence House. $5, Castle of Mey.

2000, Aug. 4
1024-1027 A149 Set of 4 9.00 9.00

Intl. Arts Festival A150

Artwork: 15c, Anguilla Montage, by Weme Caster. 30c, Serenity, by Damien Carty. 65c, Inter-island Cargo, by Paula Walden. $1.50, Rainbow City Where Spirits Find Form, by Fiona Percy. $1.90, Sailing Silver Seas, by Valerie Carpenter.

$7, Historic Anguilla, by Melsadis Fleming.

2000, Sept. 21 ***Perf. 14¼x14½***
1028-1032 A150 Set of 5 5.65 5.65

Souvenir Sheet

Perf. 14¼

1033 A150 $7 multi 7.25 7.25

No. 1033 contains one 43x28mm stamp.

Christmas A151

Flower and Garden Show flower arrangements by: 15c, Rowena Carty. 25c, Yvonda Hodge. 30c, Carty, diff. $1, Simon Rogers. $1.50, Lady Josephine Gumbs. $1.90, Carty, diff.

2000, Nov. 22 ***Perf. 13¼***
1034-1039 A151 Set of 6 7.75 *8.25*

Natl. Bank of Anguilla, 15th Anniv. — A152

Designs: 30c, Soccer team in annual primary school tournament. $1, Sponsored sailboat, De Chan, vert. $1.50, Bank's crest, vert. $1.90, New bank building.

2000, Nov. 27
1040-1043 A152 Set of 4 5.50 *6.00*

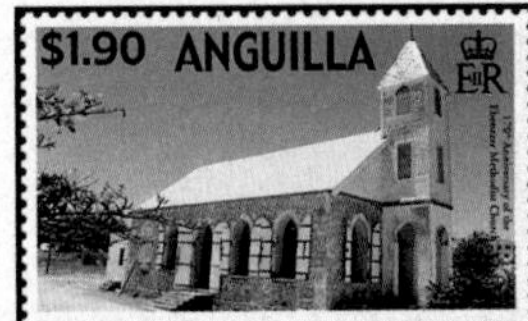

Ebenezer Methodist Church, 170th Anniv. — A153

Church in: 30c, Sepia tones. $1.90, Full color.

2000, Dec. 4
1044-1045 A153 Set of 2 3.00 *3.25*

UN Women's Human Rights Campaign — A154

Designs: 25c, Soroptimist Day Care Center. 30c, Britannia Idalia Gumbs, vert. $2.25, Woman, vert.

2001 **Litho.** ***Perf. 13¼***
1046-1048 A154 Set of 3 3.50 *4.00*

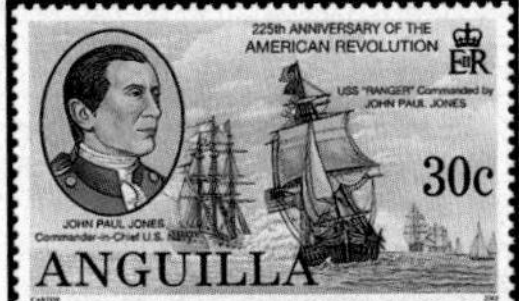

American Revolution, 225th Anniv. — A155

Designs: 30c, John Paul Jones, USS Ranger. $1, George Washington, Battle of Yorktown. $1.50, Thomas Jefferson, Submission of Declaration of Independence. $1.90, John Adams, Adams and Benjamin Franklin signing peace treaty.

2001, July 4 **Litho.** ***Perf. 13¼***
1049-1052 A155 Set of 4 7.75 *8.00*

Birds A156

Designs: 30c, White-cheeked pintail. $1, Black-faced grassquits, vert. $1.50, Brown noddy. $2, Black-necked stilts, vert. $3, Snowy plovers.

No. 1058: a, 25c, Snowy egret. b, 65c, Red-billed tropicbird. $1.35, Greater yellowlegs. $2.25, Sooty tern.

2001, Aug. 7
1053-1057 A156 Set of 5 12.00 12.00

Souvenir Sheet

1058 A156 Sheet of 4, #a-d 8.00 8.00

Year of Dialogue Among Civilizations A157

2001, Oct. 9 ***Perf. 13¼x13***
1059 A157 $1.90 multi 2.25 *2.40*

Christmas — A158

Musical instruments: 15c, Triangle. 25c, Maracas. 30c, Guiro, vert. $1.50, Marimba. $1.90, Tambu, vert. $2.50, Bath pan, vert.

No. 1066, vert.: a, 75c, Banjo. b, $1, Quatro. c, $1.25, Ukulele. d, $3, Cello.

2001, Nov. 5 **Litho.** ***Perf. 13¼***
1060-1065 A158 Set of 6 8.75 *8.75*

Souvenir Sheet

1066 A158 Sheet of 4, #a-d 7.75 *8.25*

Sombrero Lighthouse — A159

Designs: 30c, Lighthouse in 1960s, vert. $1.50, Comparison of old and new lighthouses. $1.90, New lighthouse, 2001, vert.

2002, Apr. 2 **Litho.** ***Perf. 13¼***
1067-1069 A159 Set of 3 6.50 6.50

Social Security Board, 20th Anniv. — A160

Social Security: 30c, Community service, vert. 75c, Benefits all ages, vert. $2.50, Benefits employees.

2002, May 28 **Litho.** ***Perf. 13¼***
1070-1072 A160 Set of 3 5.00 5.00

Royal Navy Ships A161

Designs: 30c, HMS Antrim, 1967. 50c, HMS Formidable, 1939. $1.50, HMS Dreadnought, 1906. $2, HMS Warrior, 1860.

$7, HMS Ark Royal, 1981, vert.

2002, June 24 **Litho.** ***Perf. 13¼***
1073-1076 A161 Set of 4 6.25 6.25

Souvenir Sheet

1077 A161 $7 multi 10.00 10.00

Reign of Queen Elizabeth II, 50th Anniv. — A162

Designs: 30c, Holding baby. $1.50, Wearing white dress. $1.90, Wearing tiara. $5, Wearing yellow hat.

$8, At desk.

2002, Oct. 14 **Litho.** ***Perf. 13¼***
1078-1081 A162 Set of 4 8.50 8.50

Souvenir Sheet

1082 A162 $8 multi 8.50 *10.00*

Pan-American Health Organization, Cent. — A163

Designs: 30c, The Valley Health Center. $1.50, Emblem, "100."

2002, Nov. 11
1083-1084 A163 Set of 2 2.50 2.50

Ships A164

2003, June 10 **Litho.** ***Perf. 14***

1085	A164	15c	Finance	.25	.25
1086	A164	30c	Tiny Gull	.25	.25
1087	A164	65c	Lady Laurel	.65	.65
1088	A164	75c	Spitfire	.85	.75
1089	A164	$1	Liberator	1.00	1.00
1090	A164	$1.35	Excelsior	1.50	1.50
1091	A164	$1.50	Rose Millicent	1.75	1.60
1092	A164	$1.90	Betsy R	2.00	1.90
1093	A164	$2	Sunbeam R	2.25	2.00
1094	A164	$2.25	New London	3.00	2.50
1095	A164	$3	Ismay	3.25	3.25
1096	A164	$10	Warspite	10.00	*11.00*
	Nos. 1085-1096 (12)			26.75	26.65

Artifacts — A165

Designs: 30c, Stone pestle. $1, Frog-shaped shell ornament. $1.50, Pottery. $1.90, Mask.

2003, Aug. 18 **Litho.** ***Perf. 13¼***
1097-1100 A165 Set of 4 5.25 5.25

Hotels A166

Designs: 75c, Frangipani Beach Club. $1, Pimms, Cap Juluca. $1.35, Cocoloba Beach Resort. $1.50, Malliouhana Hotel. $1.90, Carimar Beach Club. $3, Covecastles.

2003 **Litho.** ***Perf. 13¼***
1101-1106 A166 Set of 6 8.50 8.50

2002 International Arts Festival — A167

Paintings: 15c, Eudice's Garden, by Eunice Summer. 30c, Hammocks, by Lisa Davenport. $1, Conched Out, by Richard Shaffett. $1.50, Island Rhythms, by Carol Gavin. $1.90, Party at the Beach, by Jean-Pierre Ballagny. $3, Shoal Bay Before Luis, by Jacqueline Mariethoz, vert.

Perf. 13½x13¼, 13¼x13½

2004, Aug. 23 **Litho.**

1107-1112 A167 Set of 6 11.00 11.00

2004 Summer Olympics, Athens — A168

2004 Athens Olympics emblem and: 30c, Runners. $1, Yachting. $1.50, Gymnastics. $1.90, Acropolis, Pierre de Coubertin, Dimitrios Vikelas, horiz.

Perf. 13½x13¼, 13¼x13½

2004, Sept. 20 **Litho.**

1113-1116 A168 Set of 4 6.25 6.25

Goats A169

Various goats: 30c, 50c, $1, $1.50, $1.90, $2.25. $1, $1.90 are vert.

Perf. 13¼x13½, 13½x13¼

2004, Oct. 4

1117-1122 A169 Set of 6 9.50 9.50

Development of the Telephone A170

Types of telephones: 30c, Cordless. $1, Touch-tone. $1.50, Cellular. $1.90, Rotary dial, horiz. $3.80, Magneto.

Perf. 13¼x13, 13x13¼

2004, Nov. 8 **Litho.**

1123-1127 A170 Set of 5 8.00 8.00

Christmas A171

Santa Claus: 30c, Baking with rock oven. $1.50, Climbing coconut tree. $1.90, With string band. $3.80, Delivering gifts by donkey. $8, Delivering gifts by boat.

2004, Nov. 15 ***Perf. 13x13¼***

1128-1131 A171 Set of 4 6.75 6.75

Souvenir Sheet

1132 A171 $8 multi 7.00 7.00

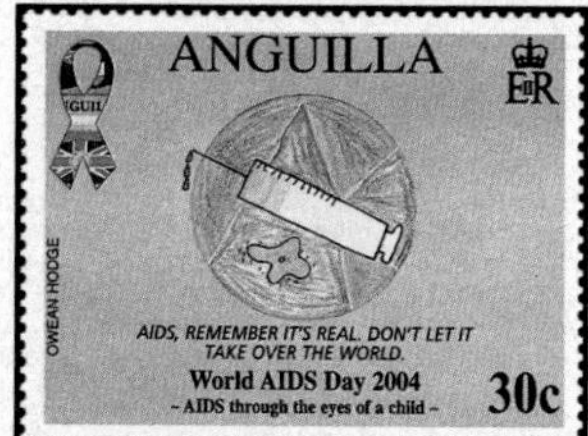

World AIDS Day — A172

Children's drawings by: 30c, Owean Hodge. $1.50, Lydia Fleming. $1.90, Nina Rodriguez.

No. 1136: a, 15c, Kenswick Richardson. b, 75c, Toniquewah Ruan. c, $1, Elizabeth Anne Orchard. d, $2, Tricia Watty-Beard.

2004, Dec. 1 ***Perf. 13***

1133-1135 A172 Set of 3 4.00 4.00

Souvenir Sheet

1136 A172 Sheet of 4, #a-d 4.00 4.00

Rotary International, Cent. — A173

Designs: 30c, Emblem of Anguilla Rotary Club. $1, Pelican and palm tree. $1.50, Rotary International founder Paul Harris. $1.90, Children at playground.

2005 **Litho.** ***Perf. 14¾x14¼***

1137-1140 A173 Set of 4 4.25 4.25

Dogs A174

Designs: 30c, Dog in field. $1.50, Two dogs sitting, vert. $1.90, Dog sitting, vert. $2.25, Dog.

2005 ***Perf. 14¼x14¾, 14¾x14¼***

1141-1144 A174 Set of 4 5.00 5.00

Commercial Airplanes — A175

Designs: 30c, Air Anguilla Cessna 402. 40c, LIAT DHC Dash 8. 60c, Winair Foxtrot-DHC Twin Otter. $1, Anguilla Airways Piper Aztec. $1.50, St. Thomas Air Transport Piper Aztec. $1.90, Carib Air Service Piper Aztec.

2006, Mar. 13 **Litho.** ***Perf. 13¼***

1145-1150 A175 Set of 6 6.50 6.50

Butterflies — A176

Designs: 30c, Appias drusillia. $1.50, Danaus plexippus megalippe. $1.90, Phoebis sennae. $2.75, Papilio demoleus.

No. 1155: a, 40c, Aphrissa statira. b, 60c, Eurema elathea. c, $1, Danaus plexippus megalippe, diff. d, $3, Agraulis vanillae.

2006, Oct. 9 **Litho.** ***Perf. 13¼***

1151-1154 A176 Set of 4 6.75 6.75

Miniature Sheet

1155 A176 Sheet of 4, #a-d 5.25 5.25

Anguilla Soroptomist Club, 25th Anniv. — A177

Designs: $1.90, Soroptomist International emblem. $2.75, Alecia Ballin.

2007, Jan. 29

1156-1157 A177 Set of 2 4.75 4.75

Bronze Devotional Medallions From El Buen Consuelo Shipwreck A178

Medallions depicting: 30c, St. Bruno. $1.50, Our Lady of Sorrows. $1.90, Five Wounds of Jesus. $2.75, Virgin and Child.

2007, Mar. 19 **Litho.** ***Perf. 13¼***

1158-1161 A178 Set of 4 5.75 5.75

Anguilla Revolution, 40th Anniv. — A179

Participants: 30c, Hyacinth Carty. $1, Edward Duncan. $1.50, Connell Harrigan. $1.90, Rev. Leonard Carty. $2.25, Jeremiah Gumbs. $3.75, Atlin Harrigan.

2007, July 18 **Litho.** ***Perf. 13¼***

1162-1167 A179 Set of 6 9.25 9.25

Historical Architecture — A180

Designs: 30c, Building with lean-to and gabled roof, by Melsadis Fleming. $1, Building with lean-to and gabled roof, by Daryl Thompson. $1.25, Building with double-hipped roof, by Fleming. $1.50, Building with hipped roof, by Susan Croft. $1.90, Building with double-gabled roof, by Fleming. $2.40, Building with double-hipped roof, by Fleming, diff. $2.75, Building with hipped roof, by Fleming. $3.75, Building with gabled roof, by Fleming.

2008, Oct. 6 ***Perf. 14x14¾***

1168-1175 A180 Set of 8 9.00 9.00

Traditional Household Items — A181

Designs: 30c, Three-legged pot. $1, Mortar and pestle. $1.50, Gas and coal irons. $1.90, Oil and gas lamps. $2, Coal pots. $2.25, Enamel and aluminum utensils.

2009, June 18 ***Perf. 13¼***

1176-1181 A181 Set of 6 6.75 6.75

Wild Flowers — A182

Designs: 30c, Tabebulia heterophylla. $1, Argemone mexicana. $1.50, Catharanthus roseus. $1.90, Datura stramonium. $2, Centrosena virginiatum. $2.25, Tetramicra canaliculata.

2009, Sept. 12

1182-1187 A182 Set of 6 6.75 6.75

Endemic Flora and Fauna — A183

Designs: $1.50, Sombrero Island ground lizard. $2, Little Scrub Island ground lizard. $2.25, Anguilla bush.

2010, Aug. 10 ***Perf. 13¼***

1188-1190 A183 Set of 3 4.50 4.50

Wedding of Prince William and Catherine Middleton A184

Designs: $4, Couple. $5, Couple, horiz. $6, Couple, diff. $10, Couple and royal arms, horiz.

2011, June 20 **Litho.** ***Perf. 13¼***

1191-1194 A184 Set of 4 18.50 18.50

Anguilla Revolutionary Coins — A185

Designs: 15c, 1967 Liberty dollar counterstruck on Panamanian balboa. 40c, 1967 Liberty dollar counterstruck on Mexican peso. $2.50, Obverse and reverse of 1968 silver $25 coin commemorating first year of Independence. $5, Ship, reverse of 1969 $4 coin.

2012, Feb. 28 ***Perf. 13½x13¼***

1195-1198 A185 Set of 4 6.00 6.00

Royal Anguilla Police Force, 40th Anniv. — A186

Designs: 30c, Old Valley Police Station. $1, Police on parade. $1.50, Police headquarters. $1.90, Past and present police crests. $5, Lt. Col. Claudius M. Roberts, first Chief of Police, vert.

2012, Nov. 26 ***Perf. 13¼***
1199-1203 A186 Set of 5 7.25 7.25

Methodism on Anguilla, 200th Anniv. — A187

Designs: 40c, Old Methodist Manse, Sandy Ground. 65c, Map of Anguilla, 200th anniversary emblem. $10, Montage of Ebenezer and Bethel Churches, by Aileen Lamond-Smith.

2013, Nov. 11 Litho. ***Perf. 13¼***
1204-1206 A187 Set of 3 8.25 8.25

Ship Captains — A188

Captains: 15c, George Richardson (1919-2003). 50c, James Woods (1908-98). 75c, Fritz Ericson Hughes (1891-1970). $1.35, Christopher John Connor (1925-94). $2, Herchel Gumbs (1884-1965). $2.25, Zilphus Fleming (1915-92). $2.50, Walter Hodge (1920-89). $5, John Franklin (1912-98).

2013, Nov. 25 Litho. ***Perf. 13¼***
1207-1214 A188 Set of 8 11.00 11.00
1214a Sheet of 8, #1207-1214 11.00 11.00

ANJOUAN

'an-jü-wän

LOCATION — One of the Comoro Islands in the Mozambique Channel between Madagascar and Mozambique.
GOVT. — French colony.
AREA — 89 sq. mi.
POP. — 20,000 (approx. 1912)
CAPITAL — Mossamondu

See Comoro Islands.

100 Centimes = 1 Franc

Navigation and Commerce — A1

Perf. 14x13½

1892-1907 Typo. Unwmk.

Name of Colony in Blue or Carmine

1 A1 1c black, *blue* 1.75 1.75
2 A1 2c brown, *buff* 2.75 1.75
3 A1 4c claret, *lav* 5.50 4.00
4 A1 5c green, *grnsh* 9.50 6.25
5 A1 10c blk, *lavender* 11.50 6.75
6 A1 10c red ('00) 37.50 30.00
7 A1 15c blue, quadrille paper 17.00 11.50
8 A1 15c gray, *lt gray*('00) 27.50 22.50
9 A1 20c red, *green* 17.50 11.00
10 A1 25c black, *rose* 17.50 14.00
11 A1 25c blue ('00) 30.00 22.50
12 A1 30c brn, *bister* 35.00 22.50
13 A1 35c blk, *yel* ('06) 18.00 10.00
14 A1 40c red, *straw* 37.50 32.50
15 A1 45c blk, *gray grn* ('07) 140.00 115.00
16 A1 50c car, *rose* 42.50 32.50
17 A1 50c brn, *az* ('00) 32.50 32.50
18 A1 75c vio, *orange* 37.50 27.50
19 A1 1fr brnz grn, *straw* 85.00 77.50
Nos. 1-19 (19) 606.00 482.00

Perf. 13½x14 stamps are counterfeits.

Issues of 1892-1907 Surcharged in Black or Carmine

1912

20 A1 5c on 2c brn, *buff* 1.25 1.25
21 A1 5c on 4c cl, *lav* (C) 1.40 *1.50*
a. Pair, one without surcharge *1,000. 1,100.*
22 A1 5c on 15c blue (C) 1.40 1.40
a. Pair, one without surcharge *1,100. 1,000.*
23 A1 5c on 20c red, *green* 1.40 1.40
a. Pair, one without surcharge *1,100. 1,100.*
24 A1 5c on 25c blk, *rose* (C) 1.50 *1.75*
25 A1 5c on 30c brn, *bis* (C) 2.00 *2.10*
26 A1 10c on 40c red, *straw* 2.00 *2.25*
27 A1 10c on 45c black, *gray green* (C) 2.40 2.40
28 A1 10c on 50c car, *rose* 5.75 *6.50*
29 A1 10c on 75c vio, *org* 4.00 *4.50*
30 A1 10c on 1fr brnz grn, *straw* 5.25 *5.75*
a. Pair, one without surcharge *1,250. 1,200.*
Nos. 20-30 (11) 28.35 30.80

Two spacings between the surcharged numerals are found on Nos. 20-30. See the *Scott Classic Specialized Catalogue of Stamps and Covers* for detailed listings.

Nos. 20-30 were available for use in Madagascar and the Comoro archipelago.

The stamps of Anjouan were superseded by those of Madagascar, and in 1950 by those of Comoro Islands.

ANNAM & TONKIN

a-'nam and 'tän-'kin

LOCATION — In French Indo-China bordering on the China Sea on the east and Siam on the west.
GOVT. — French Protectorate
AREA — 97,503 sq. mi.
POP. — 14,124,000 (approx. 1890)
CAPITAL — Annam: Hue; Tonkin: Hanoi

For administrative purposes, the Protectorates of Annam, Tonkin, Cambodia, Laos and the Colony of Cochin-China were grouped together and were known as French Indo-China.

100 Centimes = 1 Franc

Catalogue values for unused stamps are for examples without gum as most stamps were issued in that condition.

Stamps of French Colonies, 1881-86 Handstamped Surcharged in Black

Perf. 14x13½

1888, Jan. 21 Unwmk.

1 A9 1c on 2c brn, *buff* 47.50 *50.00*
a. Inverted surcharge 200.00 *200.00*
b. Sideways surcharge 200.00 *210.00*
2 A9 1c on 4c claret, *lav* 37.50 35.00
a. Inverted surcharge 200.00 *210.00*
b. Double surcharge 275.00 225.00
c. Sideways surcharge 200.00 *210.00*
3 A9 5c on 10c blk, *lav* 47.50 37.50
a. Inverted surcharge 200.00 200.00
b. Double surcharge 225.00 225.00

Hyphen between "A" and "T"

7 A9 1c on 2c brn, *buff* 325.00 *400.00*
a. Inverted surcharge 750.00 *775.00*
b. Sideways surcharge 750.00 *775.00*
c. Pair, Nos. 1, 7 9,000.
8 A9 1c on 4c claret, *lav* 525.00 *625.00*
9 A9 5c on 10c blk, *lav* 220.00 *240.00*

A 5c on 2c was prepared but not issued. Value $8,500.

In these surcharges there are different types of numerals and letters.

There are numerous other errors in the placing of the surcharges, including double one inverted, double both inverted, double one sideways, and pair one without surcharge. Such varieties command substantial premiums.

These stamps were superseded in 1892 by those of Indo-China.

ANTIGUA

an-ˈtēg-ˌwə

LOCATION — In the West Indies, southeast of Puerto Rico
GOVT. — Independent state
AREA — 171 sq. mi.
POP. — 64,246 (est. 1999)
CAPITAL — St. John's

Antigua was one of the presidencies of the former Leeward Islands colony until becoming a Crown Colony in 1956. It became an Associated State of the United Kingdom in 1967 and an independent nation on November 1, 1981, taking the name of Antigua and Barbuda.

Antigua stamps were discontinued in 1890 and resumed in 1903. In the interim, stamps of Leeward Islands were used. Between 1903-1956, stamps of Antigua and Leeward Islands were used concurrently.

12 Pence = 1 Shilling
20 Shillings = 1 Pound
100 Cents = 1 Dollar (1951)

Catalogue values for unused stamps in this country are for Never Hinged items, beginning with Scott 96.

Watermark

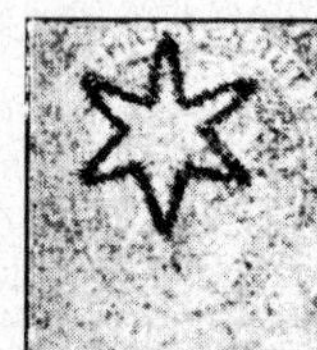

Wmk. 5 — Star

Values for unused stamps are for examples with original gum as defined in the catalogue introduction. Any exceptions will be noted. Very fine examples of Nos. 1-8, 11, 18-20 will have perforations touching the design on at least one frameline due to the narrow spacing of the stamps on the plates. Stamps with perfs clear of the framelines on all four sides are extremely scarce and will command higher prices.

Queen Victoria
A1 A2

Rough Perf. 14-16

1862 Engr. Unwmk.

1	A1 6p blue green	950.00	600.00
a.	Perf. 11-13	*7,750.*	
b.	Perf. 11-13x14-16	*3,500.*	
c.	Perf. 11-13 compound with 14-16	*3,500.*	

There is a question whether Nos. 1a-1c ever did postal duty.

Values for No. 1 are for stamps with perfs. cutting into the design. Values for No. 1b are for examples without gum.

1863-67 Wmk. 5

2	A1 1p dull rose	140.00	70.00
a.	Vert. pair, imperf. btwn.	*32,500.*	
b.	Imperf., pair		2,750.
c.	1p lilac rose	150.00	65.00
3	A1 1p vermilion ('67)	275.00	32.50
a.	Horiz. pair, imperf. btwn.	*32,500.*	
4	A1 6p green	700.00	30.00
a.	6p yellow green	*4,500.*	105.00
b.	Pair, imperf. btwn.		—

1872 Wmk. 1 *Perf. 12½*

5	A1 1p lake	200.00	22.50
6	A1 1p vermilion	225.00	25.00
7	A1 6p blue green	575.00	12.00

1873-79 *Perf. 14*

8	A1 1p lake	225.00	11.50
a.	Half used as ½p on cover		*8,000.*

Typo.

9	A2 2½p red brown ('79)	700.00	210.00
10	A2 4p blue ('79)	290.00	18.00

Engr.

11	A1 6p blue green ('76)	500.00	19.00

1882-86 Typo. Wmk. 2

12	A2 ½p green	4.00	*20.00*
13	A2 2½p red brown	225.00	67.50
14	A2 2½p ultra ('86)	8.50	*17.00*
15	A2 4p blue	350.00	19.00
16	A2 4p brown org ('86)	2.50	*3.75*
17	A2 1sh violet ('86)	175.00	175.00

Engr.

18	A1 1p carmine ('84)	2.50	*4.50*
19	A1 6p deep green	77.50	*150.00*

No. 18 was used for a time in St. Christopher and is identified by the "A12" cancellation.

1884 *Perf. 12*

20	A1 1p rose red	65.00	19.00

Seal of the Colony — A3

King Edward VII — A4

1903 Typo. Wmk. 1 *Perf. 14*

21	A3 ½p blue grn & blk	4.00	*7.50*
a.	Bluish paper ('09)	100.00	100.00
22	A3 1p car & black	11.00	1.50
a.	Bluish paper ('09)	92.50	92.50
23	A3 2p org brn & vio	8.25	*27.50*
24	A3 2½p ultra & black	14.00	*19.00*
25	A3 3p ocher & gray green	12.00	*24.00*
26	A3 6p black & red vio	35.00	*60.00*
27	A3 1sh violet & ultra	55.00	*65.00*
28	A3 2sh pur & gray green	90.00	*120.00*
29	A3 2sh6p red vio & blk	27.50	*65.00*
30	A4 5sh pur & gray green	110.00	*160.00*
	Nos. 21-30 (10)	366.75	*549.50*

The 2½p, 1sh and 5sh exist on both ordinary and chalky paper.

1908-20 Wmk. 3

31	A3 ½p green	4.75	*5.25*
32	A3 1p carmine	11.00	2.75
33	A3 2p org brn & dull vio ('12)	5.25	*35.00*
34	A3 2½p ultra	21.00	*19.00*
35	A3 3p ocher & grn ('12)	7.00	*21.00*
36	A3 6p blk & red vio ('11)	8.25	*47.50*
37	A3 1sh vio & ultra	24.00	*80.00*
38	A3 2sh vio & green ('12)	110.00	*130.00*
	Nos. 31-38 (8)	191.25	*340.50*

Nos. 33, 35 to 38 are on chalky paper.
For overprints see Nos. MR1-MR3.

George V — A6

1913

41	A6 5sh violet & green	95.00	*150.00*

St. John's Harbor — A7

1921-29 Wmk. 4

42	A7 ½p green	3.25	.60
43	A7 1p rose red	4.50	.60
44	A7 1p dp violet ('23)	6.50	1.75
45	A7 1½p orange ('22)	6.00	*8.00*
46	A7 1½p rose red ('26)	10.00	2.00
47	A7 1½p fawn ('29)	3.25	.75
48	A7 2p gray	4.50	.90
49	A7 2½p ultra	7.50	5.00
50	A7 2½p orange ('23)	2.75	*20.00*

Chalky Paper

51	A7 3p violet, *yel* ('25)	11.00	9.50
52	A7 6p vio & red vio	7.00	6.00
53	A7 1sh black, *emer* ('29)	6.50	5.75
54	A7 2sh vio & ultra, *blue* ('27)	12.00	*65.00*
55	A7 2sh6p blk & red, *blue* ('27)	47.50	*35.00*
56	A7 3sh grn & vio ('22)	52.50	*105.00*
57	A7 4sh blk & red ('22)	52.50	*77.50*
	Nos. 42-57 (16)	237.25	*343.35*

Wmk. 3

Chalky Paper

58	A7 3p violet, *yel*	5.00	*14.00*
59	A7 4p black & red, *yel* ('22)	2.50	*6.50*
60	A7 1sh black, *emerald*	4.75	*10.50*
61	A7 2sh vio & ultra, *bl*	14.50	*27.50*
62	A7 2sh6p blk & red, *bl*	19.00	*65.00*
63	A7 5sh grn & red, *yel* ('22)	9.25	*60.00*
64	A7 £1 vio & black, *red* ('22)	275.00	*425.00*
	Nos. 58-64 (7)	330.00	*608.50*

Old Dockyard, English Harbour — A8

Govt. House, St. John's — A9

Nelson's "Victory," 1805 — A10

Sir Thomas Warner's Ship, 1632 — A11

Perf. 12½

1932, Jan. 27 Engr. Wmk. 4

67	A8 ½p green	4.50	*8.75*
68	A8 1p scarlet	6.00	*8.75*
69	A8 1½p lt brown	3.75	*5.50*
70	A9 2p gray	7.50	*26.00*
71	A9 2½p ultra	7.50	*9.75*
72	A9 3p orange	7.50	*14.00*
73	A10 6p violet	16.00	14.00
74	A10 1sh olive green	21.00	*32.50*
75	A10 2sh6p claret	55.00	*77.50*
76	A11 5sh red brown & black	110.00	*150.00*
	Nos. 67-76 (10)	238.75	*346.75*
	Set, never hinged	600.00	

Tercentenary of the colony.

Forged cancellations abound, especially dated "MY 18 1932."

Common Design Types pictured following the introduction.

Silver Jubilee Issue

Common Design Type

1935, May 6 *Perf. 13½x14*

77	CD301 1p car & blue	2.50	*2.75*
78	CD301 1½p gray blk & ultra	3.00	1.25
79	CD301 2½p blue & brn	7.00	1.75
80	CD301 1sh brt vio & ind	9.00	*17.00*
	Nos. 77-80 (4)	21.50	*22.75*
	Set, never hinged	35.00	

Coronation Issue

Common Design Type

1937, May 12 *Perf. 11x11½*

81	CD302 1p carmine	.50	*1.25*
82	CD302 1½p brown	.50	*1.25*
83	CD302 2½p deep ultra	1.00	*2.00*
	Nos. 81-83 (3)	2.00	*4.50*
	Set, never hinged	3.25	

English Harbour — A14

Nelson's Dockyard — A15

Fort James — A16

St. John's Harbor — A17

1938-51 Engr. *Perf. 12½*

84	A14 ½p yel green	.30	*1.50*
85	A15 1p scarlet	2.50	2.50
86	A15 1½p red brown ('43)	2.00	*2.25*
87	A14 2p gray	.70	*1.00*
88	A15 2½p ultra ('43)	.75	*.90*
89	A16 3p pale orange ('44)	.75	*1.10*
90	A17 6p purple	2.75	1.40
91	A17 1sh brown & blk	3.75	2.00
92	A16 2sh6p dp claret ('42)	18.00	18.00
93	A17 5sh grayish olive green ('44)	10.00	10.00
94	A15 10sh red vio ('48)	12.00	*35.00*
95	A16 £1 Prussian blue ('48)	22.50	*55.00*
	Nos. 84-95 (12)	76.00	*130.65*
	Set, never hinged	120.00	

See Nos. 107-113, 115-116, 118-121, 136-142, 144-145.
For overprint see Nos. 125-126.

Catalogue values for unused stamps in this section, from this point to the end of the section, are for Never Hinged items.

Peace Issue

Common Design Type

1946, Nov. 1 Wmk. 4 *Perf. 13½x14*

96	CD303 1½p brown	.25	.25
97	CD303 3p dp orange	.25	*.55*

Silver Wedding Issue

Common Design Types

1949, Jan. 3 Photo. *Perf. 14x14½*

98	CD304 2½p bright ultra	1.00	*2.75*

Engraved; Name Typographed

Perf. 11½x11

99	CD305 5sh dk brown olive	14.00	11.50

UPU Issue
Common Design Types
Perf. 13½, 11x11½

1949, Oct. 10			Wmk. 4
	Engr.; Name Typo. on 3p and 6p		
100 CD306	2½p deep ultra	.45	*.60*
101 CD307	3p orange	2.00	*2.75*
102 CD308	6p purple	.75	*2.00*
103 CD309	1sh red brown	.75	*1.25*
	Nos. 100-103 (4)	3.95	*6.60*

University Issue
Common Design Types
Perf. 14x14½

1951, Feb. 16	Engr.		Wmk. 4
104 CD310	3c chocolate & blk	.45	*1.50*
105 CD311	12c purple & blk	.90	*1.75*

Coronation Issue
Common Design Type

1953, June 2	*Perf. 13½x13*		
106 CD312	2c dk green & blk	.50	*.75*

Types of 1938 with Portrait of Queen Elizabeth II

Martello Tower — A24

Perf. 13x13½, 13½x13

1953-56			Wmk. 4
107 A16	½c dk red brn ('56)	.35	*.35*
108 A14	1c gray	.30	*1.25*
109 A15	2c deep green	.30	.25
110 A15	3c yellow & blk	.50	.25
111 A14	4c rose red (shades)	1.25	.25
112 A15	5c dull vio & blk	2.25	.45
113 A16	6c orange	2.25	.25
114 A24	8c deep blue	2.50	.25
115 A17	12c violet	2.50	.25
116 A17	24c chocolate & blk	4.25	.25
117 A24	48c dp bl & rose lil	9.00	2.75
118 A16	60c claret	8.00	.75
119 A17	$1.20 olive green	3.50	.90
120 A15	$2.40 magenta	16.00	11.50
121 A16	$4.80 greenish blue	21.00	*24.50*
	Nos. 107-121 (15)	73.95	*44.20*

See No. 143. For overprint see No. 125-126.

West Indies Federation
Common Design Type
Perf. 11½x11

1958, Apr. 22	Engr.		Wmk. 314
122 CD313	3c green	1.50	.30
123 CD313	6c blue	1.90	*2.75*
124 CD313	12c carmine rose	2.40	.75
	Nos. 122-124 (3)	5.80	3.80

Nos. 110 and 115 Overprinted in Red or Black: "Commemoration Antigua Constitution 1960"
Perf. 13x13½, 13½x13

1960, Jan. 1			Wmk. 4
125 A15	3c yellow & black	.25	.25
126 A17	12c violet (Blk)	.25	.25

Constitutional reforms effective Jan. 1, 1960.

Lord Nelson and Nelson's Dockyard A26

Perf. 11½x11

1961, Nov. 14			Wmk. 314
127 A26	20c brown & lilac	1.60	1.60
128 A26	30c dk blue & green	1.75	*2.00*

Completion of the restoration of Lord Nelson's headquarters, English Harbour.

Stamp of 1862 and Royal Mail Steam Packet in English Harbour A27

1962, Aug. 1	Engr.		*Perf. 13*
129 A27	3c dull green & pur	.70	.25
130 A27	10c dull green & ultra	.80	.25
131 A27	12c dull green & blk	.90	.25
132 A27	50c dull grn & brn org	1.50	*2.00*
	Nos. 129-132 (4)	3.90	2.75

Centenary of first Antigua postage stamp.

Freedom from Hunger Issue
Common Design Type
Perf. 14x14½

1963, June 4	Photo.		Wmk. 314
133 CD314	12c green	.35	.35

Red Cross Centenary Issue
Common Design Type

1963, Sept. 2	Litho.		*Perf. 13*
134 CD315	3c black & red	.25	.25
135 CD315	12c ultra & red	.85	1.25

Types of 1938-53 with Portrait of Queen Elizabeth II
Perf. 13x13½, 13½x13

1963-65	Engr.		Wmk. 314
136 A16	½c brown ('65)	2.50	.75
137 A14	1c gray ('65)	1.25	1.00
138 A15	2c deep green	.70	.30
139 A15	3c orange yel & blk	.40	.30
140 A14	4c brown red	.35	*2.00*
141 A15	5c dull vio & black	.30	.25
142 A16	6c orange	.60	.35
143 A24	8c deep blue	.35	.25
144 A17	12c violet	1.00	.25
145 A17	24c choc & black	5.00	.90
	Nos. 136-145 (10)	12.45	6.35

For surcharge see No. 152.

Shakespeare Issue
Common Design Type
Perf. 14x14½

1964, Apr. 23	Photo.		Wmk. 314
151 CD316	12c red brown	.40	.25

No. 144 Surcharged with New Value and Bars
Perf. 13½x13

1965, Apr. 1	Engr.		Wmk. 314
152 A17	15c on 12c violet	.30	.30

ITU Issue
Common Design Type
Perf. 11x11½

1965, May 17	Litho.		Wmk. 314
153 CD317	2c blue & ver	.25	.25
154 CD317	50c orange & vio bl	1.40	1.10

Intl. Cooperation Year Issue
Common Design Type

1965, Oct. 25			*Perf. 14½*
155 CD318	4c blue grn & claret	.25	.25
156 CD318	15c lt vio & green	.35	.25

Churchill Memorial Issue
Common Design Type

1966, Jan. 24	Photo.		*Perf. 14*
	Design in Black, Gold and Carmine Rose		
157 CD319	½c bright blue	.25	*1.50*
158 CD319	4c green	.30	.25
159 CD319	25c brown	1.25	.30
160 CD319	35c violet	1.25	.50
	Nos. 157-160 (4)	3.05	2.55

Royal Visit Issue
Common Design Type

1966, Feb. 4	Litho.		*Perf. 11x12*
	Portraits in Black		
161 CD320	6c violet blue	1.90	1.10
162 CD320	15c dark car rose	1.90	1.50

World Cup Soccer Issue
Common Design Type

1966, July 1	Wmk. 314		*Perf. 14*
163 CD321	6c multicolored	.25	.25
164 CD321	35c multicolored	.60	.25

WHO Headquarters Issue
Common Design Type

1966, Sept. 20			*Perf. 14*
165 CD322	2c multicolored	.25	.25
166 CD322	15c multicolored	.80	.30

Nelson's Dockyard A35

Designs: 1c, Old post office, St. John's. 2c, Health Center. 3c, Teachers' Training College. 4c, Martello Tower, Barbuda. 5c, Ruins of officers quarters, Shirley Heights. 6c, Government House, Barbuda. 10c, Princess Margaret School. 15c, Air terminal. 25c, General post office. 35c, Clarence House. 50c, Government House. 75c, Administration building. $1, Court House, St. John's. $2.50, Magistrates' Court. $5, St. John's Cathedral.

Perf. 11½x11

1966, Nov. 1	Engr.		Wmk. 314
167 A35	½c green & blue	.25	1.00
168 A35	1c purple & rose	.25	.30
169 A35	2c slate & org	.25	.25
170 A35	3c rose red & blk	.30	.30
171 A35	4c dull vio & brn	1.00	.25
172 A35	5c vio bl & olive	.25	.25
173 A35	6c dp org & pur	1.00	.30
174 A35	10c brt grn & rose red	.25	.25
175 A35	15c brn & blue	1.50	.25
	Complete booklet, 4 ea. #172, 174, 175	11.00	
176 A35	25c slate & brn	.55	.25
177 A35	35c dp rose & sep	1.50	.55
178 A35	50c green & black	2.00	2.00
179 A35	75c Prus bl & vio blue	3.50	2.25
180 A35	$1 dp rose & olive	8.00	2.50
181 A35	$2.50 black & rose	6.50	6.75
182 A35	$5 ol grn & dl vio	9.00	6.50
	Nos. 167-182 (16)	36.10	23.95

For surcharge see No. 231.

1969			*Perf. 13½*
167a A35	½c	.25	*2.00*
168a A35	1c	.25	*1.00*
169a A35	2c	.25	*.65*
170a A35	3c	.25	.25
171a A35	4c	.25	.25
172b A35	5c	.25	.25
173a A35	6c	.25	*.80*
174b A35	10c	.25	.25
175b A35	15c	.55	.25
176a A35	25c	.45	.25
177a A35	35c	.60	*1.00*
178a A35	50c	.75	*2.25*
180a A35	$1	1.25	*5.00*
181a A35	$2.50	1.50	*8.00*
182a A35	$5	11.50	*24.00*
	Nos. 167a-182a (15)	18.60	*46.20*

The ½c, 3c, 6c are on ordinary paper. The 15c through $5 on glazed paper. The others exist on both papers.

UNESCO Anniversary Issue
Common Design Type

1966, Dec. 1	Litho.		*Perf. 14*
183 CD323	4c "Education"	.25	.25
184 CD323	25c "Science"	.40	.25
185 CD323	$1 "Culture"	1.25	*2.00*
	Nos. 183-185 (3)	1.90	*2.50*

Independent State

Flag of Antigua, Spiny Lobster, Maps of Antigua and Barbuda A37

Designs: 15c, 35c, Flag of Antigua. 25c, Flag and Premier's Office Building.

1967, Feb. 27	Photo.		*Perf. 14*
186 A37	4c multicolored	.25	.25
187 A37	15c multicolored	.25	.25
188 A37	25c multicolored	.25	.25
189 A37	35c multicolored	.25	.25
	Nos. 186-189 (4)	1.00	1.00

Antigua's independence, Feb. 27, 1967.

Gilbert Memorial Church, Antigua — A38

25c, Nathaniel Gilbert's House. 35c, Map of the Caribbean and Central America.

Perf. 14x13½

1967, May 18	Photo.		Wmk. 314
190 A38	4c brt red & black	.25	.25
191 A38	25c emerald & black	.25	.25
192 A38	35c ultra & black	.25	.25
	Nos. 190-192 (3)	.75	.75

Attainment of autonomy by the Methodist Church in the Caribbean and the Americas, and the opening of headquarters near St. John's, Antigua, May 1967.

Antiguan and British Royal Arms — A39

1967, July 21			*Perf. 14½x14*
193 A39	15c dark green & multi	.25	.25
194 A39	35c deep blue & multi	.25	.25

Granting of a new coat of arms to the State of Antigua; 300th anniv. of the Treaty of Breda.

Sailing Ship, 17th Century A40

Design: 6c, 35c, Map of Barbuda from Jan Blaeu's Atlas, 1665.

Perf. 11½x11

1967, Dec. 14	Engr.		Wmk. 314
195 A40	4c dark blue	.35	.25
196 A40	6c deep plum	.35	*.90*
197 A40	25c green	.50	.25
198 A40	35c black	.50	.30
	Nos. 195-198 (4)	1.70	*1.70*

Resettlement of Barbuda, 300th anniv.

Dow Hill Antenna — A41

Designs: 15c, Antenna and rocket blasting off. 25c, Nose cone orbiting moon. 50c, Reentry of space capsule.

Perf. 14½x14

1968, Mar. 29	Photo.		Wmk. 314
199 A41	4c dk blue, org & black	.25	.25
200 A41	15c dk blue, org & black	.25	.25
201 A41	25c dk blue, org & black	.25	.25
202 A41	50c dk blue, org & black	.25	.25
	Nos. 199-202 (4)	1.00	1.00

Dedication of the Dow Hill tracking station in Antigua for the NASA Apollo project.

Beach and Sailfish
A42

Designs: ½c, 50c, Limbo dancer, flames and dancing girls. 15c, Three girls on a beach and water skier. 35c, Woman scuba diver, corals and fish.

1968, July 1 Photo. *Perf. 14*

No.	Type	Denom.	Description	Unused	Used
203	A42	½c	red & multi	.25	.25
204	A42	15c	sky blue & multi	.25	.25
205	A42	25c	blue & multi	.35	.25
206	A42	35c	brt blue & multi	.35	.25
207	A42	50c	multicolored	.60	*.90*
			Nos. 203-207 (5)	1.80	*1.90*

Issued for tourist publicity.

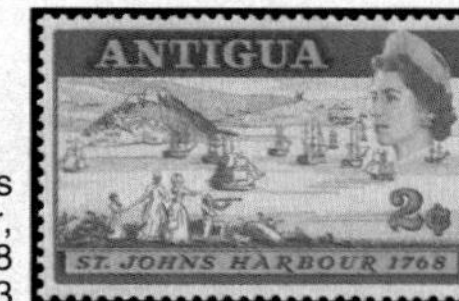

St. John's Harbor, 1768
A43

St. John's Harbor: 15c, 1829. 25c, Map of deep-sea harbor, 1968. 35c, Dock, 1968. 2c, Like $1.

Engr. & Litho.; Engr. ($1)

1968, Oct. 31 Wmk. 314 *Perf. 13*

No.	Type	Denom.	Description	Unused	Used
208	A43	2c	dp car & lt blue	.25	*.30*
209	A43	15c	sepia & yel grn	.40	.25
210	A43	25c	dk blue & yel	.50	.25
211	A43	35c	dp green & sal	.55	.25
212	A43	$1	black	.95	*1.50*
			Nos. 208-212 (5)	2.65	*2.55*

Opening of St. John's deep-sea harbor.

Mace and Parliament
A44

Mace and: 15c, Mace bearer. 25c, House of Representatives, interior. 50c, Antigua coat of arms and great seal.

1969, Feb. 3 Photo. *Perf. 12½*

No.	Type	Denom.	Description	Unused	Used
213	A44	4c	crimson & multi	.25	.25
214	A44	15c	crimson & multi	.25	.25
215	A44	25c	crimson & multi	.25	.25
216	A44	50c	crimson & multi	.30	*1.00*
			Nos. 213-216 (4)	1.05	*1.75*

300th anniversary of Antigua Parliament.

CARIFTA Cargo — A45

4c, 15c, Ship, plane and trucks, horiz.

Perf. 13½x13, 13x13½

1969, Apr. 14 Litho. Wmk. 314

No.	Type	Denom.	Description	Unused	Used
217	A45	4c	blk & brt lilac rose	.25	.25
218	A45	15c	blk & brt grnsh blue	.25	.25
219	A45	25c	bister & black	.25	.25
220	A45	35c	tan & black	.25	.25
			Nos. 217-220 (4)	1.00	1.00

1st anniv. of CARIFTA (Caribbean Free Trade Area).

Map of Redonda Island
A46

25c, View of Redonda from the sea & seagulls.

1969, Aug. 1 Photo. *Perf. 13x13½*

No.	Type	Denom.	Description	Unused	Used
221	A46	15c	ultra & multi	.25	.25
222	A46	25c	multicolored	.25	.25
223	A46	50c	salmon & multi	.40	*.50*
			Nos. 221-223 (3)	.90	*1.00*

Centenary of Redonda phosphate industry.

Adoration of the Kings, by Gugliemo Marcillat
A47

Christmas: 10c, 50c, Holy Family, by anonymous German artist, 15th century.

1969, Oct. 15 Litho. *Perf. 13x14*

No.	Type	Denom.	Description	Unused	Used
224	A47	6c	bister brn & multi	.25	.25
225	A47	10c	fawn & multi	.25	.25
226	A47	35c	gray olive & multi	.25	.25
227	A47	50c	gray blue & multi	.30	.25
			Nos. 224-227 (4)	1.05	1.00

Arms of Antigua — A48

Coil Stamps

Wmk. 314 upright

1970, Jan. 30 Photo. *Perf. 14½x14*

No.	Type	Denom.	Description	Unused	Used
228	A48	5c	bright blue	.25	.25
a.			Wmk. 373 ('77)	*7.00*	
229	A48	10c	bright green	.25	.25
a.			Wmk. 373, invtd. ('77)	—	*2.00*
230	A48	25c	deep magenta	.25	.25
a.			Wmk. 373 ('77)	*12.50*	
			Nos. 228-230 (3)	.75	.75

Glazed Paper

1973, Mar. 5 Wmk. 314 sideways

No.	Type	Denom.	Description	Unused	Used
228b	A48	5c	bright blue	1.00	1.00
229b	A48	10c	bright green	1.00	1.00
230b	A48	25c	deep magenta	1.25	1.25
			Nos. 228b-230b (3)	3.25	3.25

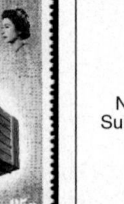

No. 176 Surcharged

1970, Jan. 2 Engr. *Perf. 11½x11*

No.	Type	Denom.	Description	Unused	Used
231	A35	20c	on 25c slate & brown	.35	.25

Sikorsky S-38
A49

Aircraft: 20c, Dornier DO-X. 35c, Hawker Siddeley 748. 50c, Douglas C-124C Globemaster II. 75c, Vickers VC 10.

1970, Feb. 16 Litho. *Perf. 14½*

No.	Type	Denom.	Description	Unused	Used
232	A49	5c	brt green & multi	.75	.25
233	A49	20c	ultra & multi	1.25	.25
234	A49	35c	blue grn & multi	1.50	.25
235	A49	50c	blue & multi	1.50	1.50
236	A49	75c	vio blue & multi	2.00	2.00
			Nos. 232-236 (5)	7.00	4.25

40th anniversary of air service.

Dickens and Scene from "Pickwick Papers"
A50

Charles Dickens (1812-1870), English novelist and Scene from: 5c, "Nicholas Nickleby." 35c, "Oliver Twist." $1, "David Copperfield."

Wmk. 314

1970, May 19 Litho. *Perf. 14*

No.	Type	Denom.	Description	Unused	Used
237	A50	5c	olive & sepia	.25	.25
238	A50	20c	aqua & sepia	.25	.25
239	A50	35c	violet & sepia	.30	.25
240	A50	$1	scarlet & sepia	.75	.60
			Nos. 237-240 (4)	1.55	1.35

Carib Indian and War Canoe
A51

Ships: 1c, Columbus and "Nina." 2c, Sir Thomas Warner's arms and sailing ship. 3c, Viscount Hood and "Barfleur." 4c, Sir George Rodney and "Formidable." 5c, Capt. Horatio Nelson and "Boreas." 6c, King William IV and "Pegasus." 10c, Blackbeard (Edward Teach) and pirate ketch. 15c, Capt. Cuthbert Collingwood and "Pelican." 20c, Admiral Nelson and "Victoria." 25c, Paddle steamer "Solent" and Steam Packet Company emblem. 35c, King George V and corvette "Canada." 50c, Cruiser "Renown" and royal badge. 75c, S.S. "Federal Maple" and maple leaf. $1, Racing yacht "Sol-Quest" and Gallant 53 class emblem. $2.50, Missile destroyer "London" and her emblem. $5, Tug "Pathfinder" and arms of Antigua.

Wmk. 314 Sideways

1970, Aug. 19 Litho. *Perf. 14*

No.	Type	Denom.	Description	Unused	Used
241	A51	½c	ocher & multi	.25	*1.25*
242	A51	1c	Prus bl & multi	.30	*1.25*
243	A51	2c	yel grn & multi	.35	*3.00*
244	A51	3c	ol bis & multi	.35	*2.50*
245	A51	4c	bl gray & multi	.40	*2.75*
246	A51	5c	fawn & multi	.50	.40
247	A51	6c	rose lil & multi	1.50	*3.50*
248	A51	10c	brn org & multi	.80	.25
249	A51	15c	ultra & multi	7.50	1.00
250	A51	20c	ol grn & multi	1.25	.40
251	A51	25c	olive & multi	1.25	.40
252	A51	35c	dull red brn & multi	1.75	.80
253	A51	50c	lt brn & multi	3.75	5.25
254	A51	75c	beige & multi	5.00	*5.25*
255	A51	$1	Prus green & multi	5.00	1.75
256	A51	$2.50	gray & multi	7.00	*7.00*
257	A51	$5	yel & multi	3.00	*6.00*
			Nos. 241-257 (17)	39.95	*42.75*

1972-74 Wmk. 314 Upright

No.	Type	Denom.	Unused	Used
241a	A51	½c	.30	*.45*
242a	A51	1c	.40	*1.00*
244a	A51	3c	.80	*1.00*
245a	A51	4c	.55	*1.75*
246a	A51	5c	.60	.40
247a	A51	6c	.90	*2.75*
248a	A51	10c	.60	*.60*
249a	A51	15c	7.00	.90
254a	A51	75c	7.00	3.00
255a	A51	$1	3.00	1.75
256a	A51	$2.50	2.75	*6.50*
257a	A51	$5	4.00	*10.00*
		Nos. 241a-257a (12)	27.90	*30.10*

For surcharge see No. 368.

1975, Jan. 21 Wmk. 373

No.	Type	Denom.	Description	Unused	Used
257b	A51	$5	yellow & multi	4.50	*12.00*

Nativity, by Albrecht Dürer — A52

Christmas: 10c, 50c, Adoration of the Magi, by Albrecht Dürer.

Engr. & Litho.

1970, Oct. 28 *Perf. 13½x14*

No.	Type	Denom.	Description	Unused	Used
258	A52	3c	brt grnsh blue & blk	.25	.25
259	A52	10c	pink & plum	.25	.25
260	A52	35c	brick red & black	.25	.25
261	A52	50c	lilac & violet	.35	.25
			Nos. 258-261 (4)	1.10	1.00

Private, 4th West India Regiment, 1804 — A53

Military Uniforms: ½c, Drummer Boy, 4th King's Own Regiment, 1759. 20c, Grenadier Company Officer, 60th Regiment, The Royal American, 1809. 35c, Light Company Officer, 93rd Regiment, The Sutherland Highlanders, 1826-1834. 75c, Private, 3rd West India Regiment, 1851.

Perf. 14x13½

1970, Dec. 1 Litho. Wmk. 314

No.	Type	Denom.	Description	Unused	Used
262	A53	½c	lake & multi	.25	.25
263	A53	10c	brn org & multi	.50	.25
264	A53	20c	Prus grn & multi	1.00	.25
265	A53	35c	dl pur & multi	1.25	.25
266	A53	75c	dk ol grn & multi	2.50	2.00
a.			Souv. sheet, #262-266 + label	8.00	*8.00*
			Nos. 262-266 (5)	5.50	3.00

See Nos. 274-278, 283-287, 307-311, 329-333.

Market Woman Voting — A54

Voting by: 20c, Businessman. 35c, Mother (and child). 50c, Workman.

Perf. 14½x14

1971, Feb. 1 Photo. Wmk. 314

No.	Type	Denom.	Description	Unused	Used
267	A54	5c	brown	.25	.25
268	A54	20c	olive black	.25	.25
269	A54	35c	rose magenta	.25	.25
270	A54	50c	violet blue	.25	.25
			Nos. 267-270 (4)	1.00	1.00

Adult suffrage, 20th anniversary.

Last Supper, from The Small Passion, by Dürer — A55

Woodcuts by Albrecht Dürer: 35c, Crucifixion from Eichstatt Missal. 75c, Resurrection from The Great Passion.

Perf. 14x13½

1971, Apr. 7 Litho. Wmk. 314

No.	Type	Denom.	Description	Unused	Used
271	A55	5c	gray, red & black	.25	.25
272	A55	35c	gray, violet & black	.25	.25
273	A55	75c	gray, gold & black	.25	.25
			Nos. 271-273 (3)	.75	.75

Easter.

Uniform Type of 1970

Military Uniforms: ½c, Private, Suffolk Regiment, 1704. 10c, Grenadier, South Staffordshire, 1751. 20c, Fusilier, Royal Northumberland, 1778. 35c, Private, Northamptonshire. 1793, 75c, Private, East Yorkshire, 1805.

1971, July 12 Litho. Wmk. 314

274 A53 ½c gray grn & multi .25 .25
275 A53 10c bluish blk & multi .50 .25
276 A53 20c dk pur & multi 1.25 .25
277 A53 35c dk ol & multi 1.50 .25
278 A53 75c brown & multi 2.00 2.75
a. Souv. sheet, #274-278 + label 8.00 8.00
Nos. 274-278 (5) 5.50 3.75

Virgin and Child, by Veronese — A56

Christmas: 5c, 50c, Adoration of the Shepherds, by Bonifazio Veronese.

1971, Oct. 4 *Perf. 14x13½*

279 A56 3c multicolored .25 .25
280 A56 5c multicolored .25 .25
281 A56 35c multicolored .25 .25
282 A56 50c multicolored .40 .35
Nos. 279-282 (4) 1.15 1.05

Uniform Type of 1970

Military Uniforms: ½c, Officer, King's Own Borderers Regiment, 1815. 10c, Sergeant, Buckinghamshire Regiment, 1837. 20c, Private, South Hampshire Regiment, 1853. 35c, Officer, Royal Artillery, 1854. 75c, Private, Worcestershire Regiment, 1870.

1972, July 1

283 A53 ½c ol brn & multi .25 .25
284 A53 10c dp grn & multi .70 .25
285 A53 20c brt vio & multi 1.25 .25
286 A53 35c mar & multi 1.50 .30
287 A53 75c dk vio bl & multi 2.00 *3.00*
a. Souvenir sheet of 5, #283-287 + label 8.75 8.75
Nos. 283-287 (5) 5.70 *4.05*

Reticulated Helmet Cowrie — A57

Sea Shells: 5c, Measled cowrie. 35c, West Indian fighting conch. 50c, Hawkwing conch.

1972, Aug. 1 *Perf. 14½x14*

288 A57 3c multicolored .60 .25
289 A57 5c ver & multi .60 .25
290 A57 35c lt vio & multi 1.75 .25
291 A57 50c rose red & multi 2.00 *2.50*
Nos. 288-291 (4) 4.95 *3.25*

St. John's Cathedral, 1745-1843 — A58

Christmas: 50c, Interior of St. John's. 75c, St. John's rebuilt.

1972, Nov. 6 Litho. *Perf. 14*

292 A58 35c org brn & multi .25 .25
293 A58 50c vio & multi .30 .30
294 A58 75c multicolored .50 *.50*
a. Souv. sheet, #292-294, perf 15 1.00 *1.25*
Nos. 292-294 (3) 1.05 *1.05*

Silver Wedding Issue, 1972
Common Design Type

1972, Nov. 20 Photo. *Perf. 14x14½*

295 CD324 20c ultra & multi .25 .25
296 CD324 35c steel blue & multi .25 .25

Map of Antigua, Batsman Driving Ball — A60

Designs: 35c, Batsman and wicketkeeper. $1, Emblem of Rising Sun Cricket Club.

1972, Dec. 15 *Perf. 13½x14*

297 A60 5c multicolored .25 .25
298 A60 35c multicolored .75 .30
299 A60 $1 multicolored 2.25 *2.50*
a. Souvenir sheet of 3, #297-299 5.75 5.75
Nos. 297-299 (3) 3.25 *3.05*

Rising Sun Cricket Club, St. John's, 50th anniv.

Map of Antigua and Yacht — A61

1972, Dec. 29 *Perf. 14½*

300 A61 35c shown .25 .25
301 A61 50c Racing yachts .25 .25
302 A61 75c St. John's G.P.O. .40 .25
303 A61 $1 Statue of Liberty .35 .25
a. Souvenir sheet of 2, #301, 303 1.25 1.25
Nos. 300-303 (4) 1.25 1.00

Opening of Antigua and Barbuda Information Office in New York City.

Window with Episcopal Coat of Arms — A62

Stained glass windows from Cathedral of St. John: 35c, Crucifixion. 75c, Arm of Rt. Rev. D.G. Davis, 1st bishop of Antigua.

1973, Apr. 16 Litho. *Perf. 13½*

304 A62 5c yellow & multi .25 .25
305 A62 35c brt lilac & multi .25 .25
306 A62 75c blue & multi .35 .25
Nos. 304-306 (3) .85 .75

Easter.

Uniform Type of 1970

Military Uniforms: ½c, Private, Col. Zacharia Tiffin's Regiment, 1701. 10c, Private, 63rd Regiment, 1759. 20c, Officer, 35th Sussex Regiment, 1828. 35c, Private, 2nd West India Regiment, 1853. 75c, Sergeant, Princess of Wales Regiment, Hertfordshire, 1858.

Perf. 14x13½

1973, July 1 Wmk. 314

307 A53 ½c dp ultra & multi .25 .25
308 A53 10c rose lilac & multi .35 .25
309 A53 20c gray & multi .50 .25
310 A53 35c multicolored .70 .25
311 A53 75c multicolored 1.50 1.25
a. Souv. sheet, #307-311 + label 4.50 4.25
Nos. 307-311 (5) 3.30 2.25

Butterfly Costumes — A63

Designs: 20c, Carnival revelers. 35c, Costumed group. 75c, Carnival Queen.

Perf. 13½x14

1973, July 30 Unwmk.

312 A63 5c multicolored .25 .25
313 A63 20c multicolored .25 .25
314 A63 35c multicolored .25 .25
315 A63 75c multicolored .30 .25
a. Souvenir sheet of 4, #312-315 1.10 *1.25*
Nos. 312-315 (4) 1.05 1.00

Carnival, July 29-Aug. 7.

Virgin of the Porridge, by David — A64

Christmas: 5c, Adoration of the Kings, by Stomer. 20c, Virgin of the Grand Duke, by Raphael. 35c, Nativity with God the Father and Holy Ghost, by Tiepolo. $1, Madonna and Child, by Murillo.

Perf. 14½

1973, Oct. 15 Photo. Unwmk.

316 A64 3c brt blue & multi .25 .25
317 A64 5c emerald & multi .25 .25
318 A64 20c gold & multi .25 .25
319 A64 35c violet & multi .25 .25
320 A64 $1 red & multi .35 *.40*
a. Souvenir sheet of 5, #316-320 1.50 1.50
Nos. 316-320 (5) 1.35 1.40

Princess Anne and Mark Phillips — A65

Design: $2, different border.

1973, Nov. 14 Litho. *Perf. 13½*

321 A65 35c dull ultra & multi .25 .25
322 A65 $2 yel grn & multi .25 .25
a. Souvenir sheet of 2, #321-322 .75 .75

Wedding of Princess Anne and Capt. Mark Phillips.

Nos. 321-322 were issued in sheets of 5 plus label.

Nos. 321-322 and 322a Ovptd.

1973, Dec. 15 Litho. *Perf. 13½*

323 A65 35c multicolored .25 .25
324 A65 $2 multicolored .50 .50
a. Souvenir sheet of 2, #323-324 .75 .75

Visit of Princess Anne and Mark Phillips to Antigua, Dec. 16. Same overprint in sheet margins of Nos. 323-324 and 324a.

Overprint lithographed. Also exists typographed.

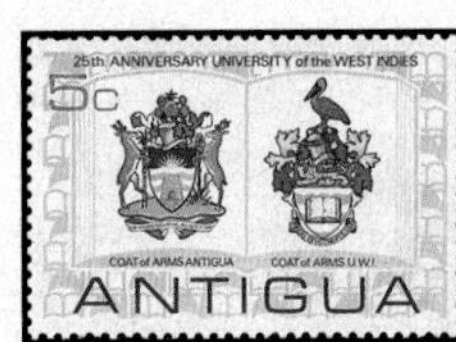

Arms of Antigua and U.W.I. A66

Designs: 20c, Dancers. 35c, Antigua campus. 75c, Chancellor Sir Hugh Wooding.

1974, Feb. 18 Wmk. 314

325 A66 5c multicolored .25 .25
326 A66 20c multicolored .25 .25
327 A66 35c multicolored .25 .25
328 A66 75c multicolored .25 .25
Nos. 325-328 (4) 1.00 1.00

University of the West Indies, 24th anniv.

Uniform Type of 1970

Military Uniforms: ½c, Officer, 59th Foot, 1797. 10c, Gunner, Royal Artillery, 1800. 20c, Private, 1st West India Regiment, 1830. 35c, Officer, Gordon Highlanders, 1843. 75c, Private, Royal Welsh Fusiliers, 1846.

1974, May 1 *Perf. 14x13½*

329 A53 ½c dull grn & multi .25 .25
330 A53 10c ocher & multi .40 .25
331 A53 20c multicolored .75 .25
332 A53 35c gray bl & multi .90 .25
333 A53 75c dk gray & multi 1.25 *1.75*
a. Souvenir sheet of 5, #329-333 3.75 3.00
Nos. 329-333 (5) 3.55 2.75

English Mailman and Coach, Helicopter — A67

UPU, Cent.: 1c, English bellman, 1846; Orinoco mailboat, 1851; telecommunications satellite. 2c, English mailtrain guard, 1852; Swiss post passenger bus, 1906; Italian hydrofoil. 5c, Swiss messenger, 16th century; Wells Fargo coach, 1800; Concorde. 20c, German position, 1820; Japanese mailmen, 19th century; carrier pigeon. 35c, Contemporary Antiguan mailman; radar station; aquaplane. $1, Medieval French courier; American train, 1884; British Airways jet.

1974, July 15 Litho. *Perf. 14½*

334 A67 ½c multicolored .25 .25
335 A67 1c multicolored .25 .25
336 A67 2c multicolored .25 .25
337 A67 5c multicolored .60 .40
338 A67 20c multicolored .35 .25
339 A67 35c multicolored .45 .25
340 A67 $1 multicolored 1.75 1.75
a. Souvenir sheet of 7, #334-340 + label, perf. 13 4.50 3.50
Nos. 334-340 (7) 3.90 3.40

For surcharges see Nos. 365-367.

Traditional Steel Band A68

Carnival 1974 (Steel Bands): 5c, Traditional players, vert. 35c, Modern steel band. 75c, Modern players, vert.

1974, Aug. 1, Wmk. 314 *Perf. 14*

341 A68 5c rose red, dk red & blk .25 .25
342 A68 20c ocher, brn & blk .25 .25
343 A68 35c yel grn, grn & blk .25 .25
344 A68 75c dl bl, dk bl & blk .25 *.50*
a. Souvenir sheet of 4, #341-344 .75 .75
Nos. 341-344 (4) 1.00 *1.25*

For surcharge see No. 364.

Soccer — A69

Designs: Games' emblem and soccer.

1974, Sept. 23 Unwmk. *Perf. 14½*

345 A69 5c multicolored .25 .25
346 A69 35c multicolored .25 .25
347 A69 75c multicolored .25 .25

348	A69	$1 multicolored	.35	.35
a.		Souvenir sheet of 4	1.25	1.25
		Nos. 345-348 (4)	1.10	1.10

World Cup Soccer Championship, Munich, June 13-July 7. Nos. 345-348 issued in sheets of 5 plus label showing Soccer Cup. No. 348a contains one each of Nos. 345-348, perf. 13½, and 2 labels.

For overprints and surcharges see Nos. 361-363.

Winston Churchill (1874-1965) at Harrow — A70

Designs: 35c, St. Paul's during bombing and Churchill portrait. 75c, Churchill's coat of arms and catafalque. $1, Churchill during Boer war, warrant for arrest and map of his escape route.

1974, Oct. 20 Unwmk. *Perf. 14½*

349	A70	5c multicolored	.25	.25
350	A70	35c multicolored	.25	.25
351	A70	75c multicolored	.25	*.30*
352	A70	$1 multicolored	.35	*.50*
a.		Souvenir sheet of 4, #349-352	1.25	*1.75*
		Nos. 349-352 (4)	1.10	*1.30*

Virgin and Child, by Giovanni Bellini — A71

Christmas: Paintings of the Virgin and Child.

1974, Nov. 18 Litho. *Perf. 14½*

353	A71	½c shown	.25	.25
354	A71	1c Raphael	.25	.25
355	A71	2c Van der Weyden	.25	.25
356	A71	3c Giorgione	.25	.25
357	A71	5c Andrea Mantegna	.25	.25
358	A71	20c Alvise Vivarini	.25	.25
359	A71	35c Bartolommeo Montagna	.25	.25
360	A71	75c Lorenzo Costa	.35	*.60*
a.		Souv. sheet, #357-360, perf 13½	1.25	*1.50*
		Nos. 353-360 (8)	2.10	2.35

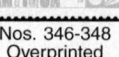

Nos. 346-348 Overprinted

No. 344 Surcharged and Overprinted

1974, Oct. 16 Litho. *Perf. 14½, 14*

361	A69	35c multicolored	.35	.30
362	A69	75c multicolored	.50	.35
363	A69	$1 multicolored	.60	.45
364	A68	$5 on 75c multi	2.00	2.00
		Nos. 361-364 (4)	3.45	3.10

Earthquake of Oct. 8, 1974.

Nos. 338-340 and 254a Surcharged

1974-75 Wmk. 314 *Perf. 14½*

365	A67	50c on 20c	1.40	*2.10*
366	A67	$2.50 on 35c	3.00	*6.25*
367	A67	$5 on $1	6.50	*8.00*

Perf. 14

368	A51	$10 on 75c	3.00	8.75
		Nos. 365-368 (4)	13.90	*25.10*

Carib War Canoe, English Harbour A72

Designs (Nelson's Dockyard): 15c, Raising ship, 1770. 35c, Lord Nelson and "Boreas." 50c, Yachts arriving for Sailing Week, 1974. $1, "Anchorage" in Old Dockyard, 1970.

1975, Mar. 17 Unwmk. *Perf. 14½*

369	A72	5c multicolored	.30	.25
370	A72	15c multicolored	1.00	.25
371	A72	35c multicolored	1.50	.25
372	A72	50c multicolored	1.75	1.75
373	A72	$1 multicolored	2.00	2.00
		Nos. 369-373 (5)	6.55	4.50

Souvenir Sheet

Perf. 13½

373A	A72	Sheet of 5, #369-373	7.00	7.00

Stamps in No. 373A are 43x28mm.

Lady of the Valley Church A73

Churches of Antigua: 20c, Gilbert Memorial. 35c, Grace Hill Moravian. 50c, St. Phillip's. $1, Ebenezer Methodist.

1975, May 19 Litho. *Perf. 14½*

374	A73	5c multicolored	.25	.25
375	A73	20c multicolored	.25	.25
376	A73	35c multicolored	.25	.25
377	A73	50c multicolored	.25	.25
378	A73	$1 multicolored	.25	.25
a.		Souvenir sheet of 3, #376-378, perf. 13½	1.00	*1.50*
		Nos. 374-378 (5)	1.25	1.25

Antigua, Senex's Atlas, 1721, and Hevelius Sextant, 1640 A74

Maps of Antigua: 20c, Jeffery's Atlas, 1775, and 18th century engraving of ship. 35c, Barbuda and Antigua, 1775 and 1975. $1, St. John's and English Harbour, 1973.

1975, July 21 Wmk. 314

379	A74	5c multicolored	.40	.25
380	A74	20c multicolored	.75	.25
381	A74	35c multicolored	.95	.25
382	A74	$1 multicolored	1.90	1.90
a.		Souvenir sheet of 4, #379-382	5.25	3.50
		Nos. 379-382 (4)	4.00	2.65

Bugler and Sunset A75

Nordjamb 75 Emblem and: 20c, Black and white Scouts, tents and flags. 35c, Lord Baden-Powell and tents. $2, Dahomey dancers.

Unwmk.

1975, Aug. 26 Litho. *Perf. 14*

383	A75	15c multicolored	.30	.25
384	A75	20c multicolored	.40	.25
385	A75	35c multicolored	.60	.30
386	A75	$2 multicolored	2.25	2.10
a.		Souvenir sheet of 4, #383-386	4.75	4.75
		Nos. 383-386 (4)	3.55	2.90

Nordjamb 75, 14th Boy Scout Jamboree, Lillehammer, Norway, July 29-Aug. 7.

Eurema Elathea A76

Butterflies: 1c, Danaus plexippus. 2c, Phoebis philea. 5c, Marpesia petreus thetys. 20c, Eurema proterpia. 35c, Papilio polydamas. $2, Vanessa cardui.

1975, Oct. 30 Litho. *Perf. 14*

387	A76	½c multicolored	.25	.25
388	A76	1c multicolored	.25	.25
389	A76	2c multicolored	.25	.25
390	A76	5c multicolored	.30	.25
391	A76	20c multicolored	1.25	.50
392	A76	35c multicolored	1.75	.90
393	A76	$2 multicolored	5.00	5.00
a.		Miniature sheet of 4, #390-393	9.50	9.50
		Nos. 387-393 (7)	9.05	7.40

Virgin and Child, by Correggio — A77

Christmas: Virgin and Child paintings.

1975, Nov. 17 Unwmk.

394	A77	½c shown	.25	.25
395	A77	1c El Greco	.25	.25
396	A77	2c Durer	.25	.25
397	A77	3c Antonello	.25	.25
398	A77	5c Bellini	.25	.25
399	A77	10c Durer	.25	.25
400	A77	35c Bellini	.40	.25
401	A77	$2 Durer	.75	.60
a.		Souvenir sheet of 4, #398-401	2.25	2.25
		Nos. 394-401 (8)	2.65	2.35

West Indies Team A78

Designs: 5c, Batsman I.V.A. Richards and cup, vert. 35c, Bowler A.M.E. Roberts and cup, vert.

1975, Dec. 15 Litho. *Perf. 14*

402	A78	5c multicolored	1.25	.25
403	A78	35c multicolored	2.25	.55
404	A78	$2 multicolored	4.75	*7.25*
		Nos. 402-404 (3)	8.25	*8.05*

World Cricket Cup, victory of West Indies team.

A number of unissued items, imperfs., part perfs., missing color varieties, etc., were made available when the Format International inventory was liquidated. Imperfs of some or all of the Antigua stamps in the following sets are included: #405-422, 503-507, 515-517, 703-707, 745-749, 755-759, 808-816, 819-826, 905-909, 934-937.

See footnote after #962.

Antillean Crested Hummingbird — A79

Irrigation System, Diamond Estate — A80

Designs: 1c, Imperial parrot. 2c, Zenaida dove. 3c, Loggerhead kingbird. 4c, Red-necked pigeon. 5c, Rufous-throated solitaire. 6c, Orchid tree. 10c, Bougainvillea. 15c, Geiger tree. 20c, Flamboyant. 25c, Hibiscus. 35c, Flame of the Woods. 50c, Cannon at Fort James. 75c, Premier's Office. $1, Potworks Dam. $5, Government House. $10, Coolidge International Airport.

1976, Jan. 19 Litho. *Perf. 15*

405	A79	½c multicolored	.35	*.50*
406	A79	1c multicolored	1.00	.50
407	A79	2c multicolored	1.00	.50
408	A79	3c multicolored	1.00	.55
409	A79	4c multicolored	1.10	1.25
410	A79	5c multicolored	1.50	.25
411	A79	6c multicolored	.30	*1.25*
412	A79	10c multicolored	.30	.25
413	A79	15c multicolored	.35	.25
414	A79	20c multicolored	.35	.35
415	A79	25c multicolored	.35	.25
416	A79	35c multicolored	.35	.35
417	A79	50c multicolored	.50	.50
418	A79	75c multicolored	.60	*1.25*
419	A79	$1 multicolored	.75	*.85*

Perf. 13½x14

420	A80	$2.50 rose & multi	1.50	*3.75*
421	A80	$5 lilac & multi	2.50	*5.00*
422	A80	$10 multicolored	4.25	*6.50*
		Nos. 405-422 (18)	18.05	*24.10*

Inscribed "1978"

1978

405a	A79	½c multicolored	.55	*.75*
406a	A79	1c multicolored	1.25	1.00
407a	A79	2c multicolored	1.25	1.00
408a	A79	3c multicolored	1.25	1.00
409a	A79	4c multicolored	1.40	1.00
410a	A79	5c multicolored	1.50	.60
411a	A79	6c multicolored	.35	*1.25*
412a	A79	10c multicolored	.35	.35
413a	A79	15c multicolored	.30	.35
414a	A79	20c multicolored	.30	*1.00*
415a	A79	25c multicolored	.35	*.55*
416a	A79	35c multicolored	.35	*.55*
417a	A79	50c multicolored	.55	*1.00*
418a	A79	75c multicolored	.55	*1.10*
419a	A79	$1 multicolored	.75	*1.25*

Perf. 13½x14

420a	A80	$2.50 rose & multi	1.75	*5.50*
421a	A80	$5 lilac & multi	1.90	*6.50*
422a	A80	$10 multicolored	6.50	*8.50*
		Nos. 405a-422a (18)	21.20	*33.25*

For overprints see Nos. 607-617.

Privates, Clark's Illinois Regiment — A81

1c, Riflemen, Pennsylvania Militia. 2c, Decorated American powder horn. 5c, Water bottle of Maryland troops. 35c, "Liberty Tree" and "Rattlesnake" flags. $1, American privateer Montgomery. $2.50, Congress Flag. $5, Continental Navy sloop Ranger.

1976, Mar. 17 Litho. *Perf. 14½*

423	A81	½c multicolored	.25	.25
424	A81	1c multicolored	.25	.25
425	A81	2c multicolored	.25	.25
426	A81	5c multicolored	.25	.25
427	A81	35c multicolored	.55	.25
428	A81	$1 multicolored	1.50	.30
429	A81	$5 multicolored	2.75	2.75
		Nos. 423-429 (7)	5.80	4.30

Souvenir Sheet

Perf. 13

430	A81	$2.50 multicolored	2.10	2.10

American Bicentennial.

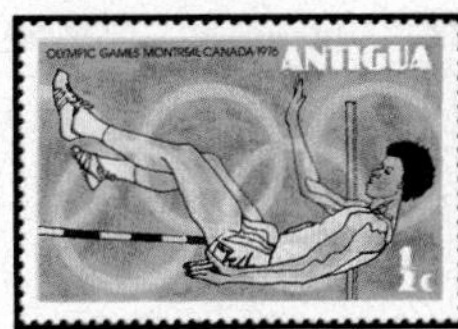

High Jump, Olympic Rings A82

Olympic Rings and: 1c, Boxing. 2c, Pole vault. 15c, Swimming. 30c, Running. $1, Bicycling. $2, Shot put.

1976, July 12 Litho. *Perf. 14½*

431 A82 ½c yellow & multi .25 .25
432 A82 1c purple & multi .25 .25
433 A82 2c emerald & multi .25 .25
434 A82 15c brt blue & multi .25 .25
435 A82 30c olive & multi .30 .25
436 A82 $1 orange & multi .50 .25
437 A82 $2 red & multi 1.50 1.50
a. Souvenir sheet of 4 2.50 *3.25*
Nos. 431-437 (7) 3.30 3.00

21st Olympic Games, Montreal, Canada, July 17-Aug. 1. No. 437a contains one each of Nos. 434-437, perf. 13½.

Water Skiing A83

Water Sports: 1c, Sailfish sailing. 2c, Snorkeling. 20c, Deep-sea fishing. 50c, Scuba diving. $2, Swimming.

1976, Aug. 26 *Perf. 14*

438 A83 ½c yel grn & multi .25 .25
439 A83 1c sepia & multi .25 .25
440 A83 2c gray & multi .25 .25
441 A83 20c multicolored .25 .25
442 A83 50c brt vio & multi .45 .50
443 A83 $2 lt gray & multi 1.25 1.40
a. Souvenir sheet of 3, #441-443 2.25 2.25
Nos. 438-443 (6) 2.70 2.90

French Angelfish — A84

1976, Oct. 4 Litho. *Perf. 13½x14*

444 A84 15c shown .50 .25
445 A84 30c Yellowfish grouper .85 .25
446 A84 50c Yellowtail snappers 1.00 .45
447 A84 90c Shy hamlet 1.50 .75
Nos. 444-447 (4) 3.85 1.70

The Annunciation A85

Christmas: 10c, Flight into Egypt. 15c, Three Kings. 50c, Shepherds and star. $1, Kings presenting gifts to Christ Child.

1976, Nov. 15 Litho. *Perf. 14*

448 A85 8c multicolored .25 .25
449 A85 10c multicolored .25 .25
450 A85 15c multicolored .25 .25
451 A85 50c multicolored .25 .25
452 A85 $1 multi .25 .25
Nos. 448-452 (5) 1.25 1.25

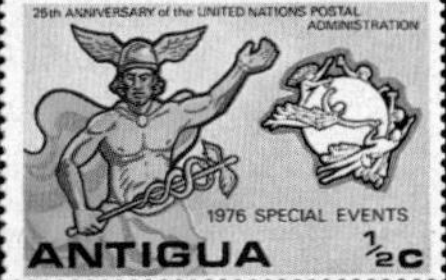

Mercury and UPU Emblem A86

Designs: 1c, Alfred Nobel, symbols of prize categories. 10c, Viking spacecraft. 50c, Vivi Richards (batsman) and Andy Roberts (bowler). $1, Alexander G. Bell, telephones, 1876 and 1976. $2, Schooner Freelance.

1976, Dec. 28 Litho. *Perf. 14*

453 A86 ½c multicolored .25 .25
454 A86 1c multicolored .25 .25
455 A86 10c multicolored .35 .25
456 A86 50c multicolored 3.75 1.75
457 A86 $1 multicolored 1.00 1.25
458 A86 $2 multicolored 2.25 3.00
a. Souvenir sheet of 4, #455-458 8.25 8.25
Nos. 453-458 (6) 7.85 6.75

Special 1976 Events: UN Postal Admin., 25th anniv. (½c); Nobel Prize, 75th anniv. (1c); Viking Space Mission to Mars (10c); World Cricket Cup victory (50c); Telephone cent. ($1); Operation Sail, American Bicent. ($2).

Royal Family — A87

Designs: 30c, Elizabeth II and Prince Philip touring Antigua. 50c, Queen enthroned. 90c, Queen wearing crown. $2.50, Queen and Prince Charles. $5, Queen and Prince Philip.

1977, Feb. 7 *Perf. 13½x14*

459 A87 10c multicolored .25 .25
460 A87 30c multicolored .25 .25
461 A87 50c multicolored .25 .25
462 A87 90c multicolored .25 .25
463 A87 $2.50 multicolored .25 .40
Nos. 459-463 (5) 1.25 1.40

Souvenir Sheet

464 A87 $5 multicolored .80 1.00
Complete booklet, 6 #461 var., 1 #464 var., self-adhesive and in changed colors 4.50

Reign of Queen Elizabeth II, 25th anniv.
Nos. 459-463 were printed in sheets of 40. Sheets of 5 plus label, perf. 12, probably were not sold by the Antigua Post Office.
For overprints see Nos. 477-482.

Scouts Camping A88

Boy Scout Emblem and: 1c, Scouts on hike. 2c, Rock climbing. 10c, Cutting logs. 30c, Map and compass reading. 50c, First aid. $2, Scouts on raft.

1977, May 23 Litho. *Perf. 14*

465 A88 ½c multicolored .25 .25
466 A88 1c multicolored .25 .25
467 A88 2c multicolored .25 .25
468 A88 10c multicolored .25 .25
469 A88 30c multicolored .35 .25
470 A88 50c multicolored .60 .35
471 A88 $2 multicolored 1.25 1.25
a. Souvenir sheet of 3, #469-471 3.50 3.50
Nos. 465-471 (7) 3.20 2.85

Caribbean Boy Scout Jamboree, Jamaica.

Carnival Queen Holding Horseshoe — A89

30c, Carnival Queen in feather costume. 50c, Butterfly costume. 90c, Carnival Queen with ornaments. $1, Carnival King, Queen.

1977, July 18 Litho. *Perf. 14*

472 A89 10c multicolored .25 .25
473 A89 30c multicolored .25 .25
474 A89 50c multicolored .25 .25
475 A89 90c multicolored .45 .40
476 A89 $1 multicolored .50 .50
a. Souvenir sheet of 4, #473-476 1.75 *1.75*
Nos. 472-476 (5) 1.70 1.65

21st Summer Carnival.

Nos. 459-464 Overprinted

Perf. 13½x14, 12

1977, Oct. 17 Litho.

477 A87 10c multicolored .25 .25
478 A87 30c multicolored .25 .25
479 A87 50c multicolored .25 .25
480 A87 90c multicolored .35 .30
481 A87 $2.50 multicolored .50 .40
Nos. 477-481 (5) 1.60 1.45

Souvenir Sheet

482 A87 $5 multicolored 1.75 1.75

Visit of Queen Elizabeth II, Oct. 28.

Virgin and Child, by Cosimo Tura — A90

Virgin and Child by: 1c, $2, Carlo Crivelli (different). 2c, 25c, Lorenzo Lotto (different). 8c, Jacopo da Pontormo. 10c, Tura.

1977, Nov. 15 Litho. *Perf. 14*

483 A90 ½c multicolored .25 .25
484 A90 1c multicolored .25 .25
485 A90 2c multicolored .25 .25
486 A90 8c multicolored .25 .25
487 A90 10c multicolored .25 .25
488 A90 25c multicolored .25 .25
489 A90 $2 multicolored .85 .80
a. Souvenir sheet of 4, #486-489 1.50 *2.00*
Nos. 483-489 (7) 2.35 2.30

Christmas.

Pineapple A91

10th anniv. of Statehood: 15c, Flag of Antigua. 50c, Police band. 90c, Prime Minister V. C. Bird. $2, Coat of Arms.

1977, Dec. 28 Litho. *Perf. 13x13½*

490 A91 10c multicolored .25 .25
491 A91 15c multicolored .50 .25
492 A91 50c multicolored 2.50 .75
493 A91 90c multicolored .50 .75
494 A91 $2 multicolored .90 *1.50*
a. Souv. sheet, #491-494, perf 14 3.50 3.50
Nos. 490-494 (5) 4.65 3.50

Wright Glider III, 1902 A92

1c, Flyer I in air, 1903. 2c, Weight and derrick launch system and Wright engine, 1903. 10c, Orville Wright, vert. 50c, Flyer III, 1905. 90c, Wilbur Wright, vert. $2, Wright Model B, 1910. $2.50, Flyer I, 1903, on ground.

1978, Mar. 28 *Perf. 14*

495 A92 ½c multicolored .25 .25
496 A92 1c multicolored .25 .25
497 A92 2c multicolored .25 .25
498 A92 10c multicolored .35 .25
499 A92 50c multicolored .55 .25
500 A92 90c multicolored .80 .30
501 A92 $2 multicolored 1.10 .80
Nos. 495-501 (7) 3.55 2.35

Souvenir Sheet

502 A92 $2.50 multicolored 2.25 *2.75*

1st powered flight by Wright brothers, 75th anniv.

Sunfish Regatta A93

Sailing Week 1978: 50c, Fishing and work boat race. 90c, Curtain Bluff race. $2, Powerboat rally. $2.50, Guadeloupe-Antigua race.

1978, Apr. 29 Litho. *Perf. 14½*

503 A93 10c multicolored .30 .25
504 A93 50c multicolored .40 .25
505 A93 90c multicolored .75 .40
506 A93 $2 multicolored 1.50 .75
Nos. 503-506 (4) 2.95 1.65

Souvenir Sheet

507 A93 $2.50 multicolored 2.25 2.25

25th Anniv. of the Coronation of Queen Elizabeth II — A94

Designs: 10c, Elizabeth II and Prince Philip. 30c, Coronation. 50c, State coach. 90c, Elizabth II and Archbishop. $2.50, Elizabeth II. $5, Elizabeth II, Prince Philip, Prince Charles and Princess Anne as children.

1978, June 2 Litho. *Perf. 14, 12*

508 A94 10c multicolored .25 .25
509 A94 30c multicolored .25 .25
510 A94 50c multicolored .25 .25
511 A94 90c multicolored .25 .25
512 A94 $2.50 multicolored .40 .40
Nos. 508-512 (5) 1.40 1.40

Souvenir Sheet

513 A94 $5 multicolored 1.40 1.40

25th anniv. of coronation of Queen Elizabeth II.
Nos. 508-512 were printed in sheets of 50 (2 panes of 25), perf. 14, and in sheets of 3 plus label, perf. 12, with frames in changed colors.

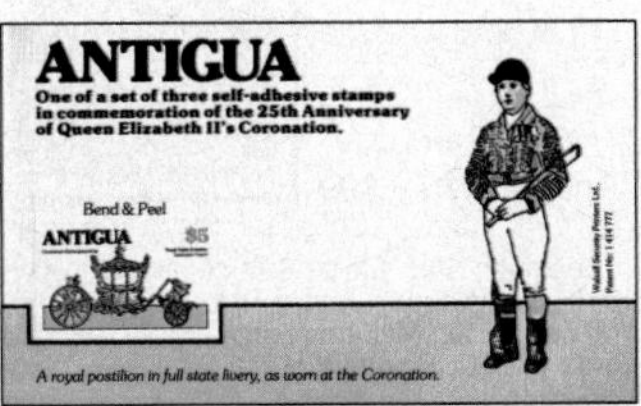

Glass Coach — A95

Royal Coaches: 50c, Irish state coach. $5, Coronation coach.

1978, June 2 Litho. *Imperf.*

Self-adhesive

514 Souvenir booklet 2.50
a. A95 Bklt. pane, 3 each 25c, 50c 1.00
b. A95 Bklt. pane, 1 $5 1.40

25th anniversary of coronation of Queen Elizabeth II. No. 514 contains 2 booklet panes printed on peelable paper backing showing royal processions.

Soccer — A96

Purple Wreath — A97

Designs: Various soccer scenes. Stamps in souvenir sheet horizontal.

1978, Aug. 18 Litho. *Perf. 15*

515 A96 10c multicolored .25 .25
516 A96 15c multicolored .25 .25
517 A96 $3 multicolored 1.75 1.75
Nos. 515-517 (3) 2.25 2.25

Souvenir Sheet

518 Sheet of 4 4.25 4.25
a. A96 25c multicolored .30 .30
b. A96 30c multicolored .45 .45
c. A96 50c multicolored .80 .80
d. A96 $2 multicolored 2.25 2.25

11th World Cup Soccer Championship, Argentina, June 1-25.

1978, Oct. Litho. *Perf. 14*

519 A97 25c shown .30 .25
520 A97 50c Sunflowers .45 .25
521 A97 90c Frangipani .75 .30
522 A97 $2 Passionflower 1.60 1.50
Nos. 519-522 (4) 3.10 2.30

Souvenir Sheet

523 A97 $2.50 Red hibiscus 2.00 *2.00*

St. Ildefonso Receiving Chasuble, by Rubens A98

Christmas: 25c, *Flight of St. Barbara*, by Rubens. $2, *Madonna and Child with Ss. Joseph and John and a Donor*, by Sebastiano del Piombo. $4, Annunciation, by Rubens.

1978, Oct. 30 Litho. *Perf. 14*

524 A98 8c multicolored .25 .25
525 A98 25c multicolored .25 .25
526 A98 $2 multicolored .65 .55
Nos. 524-526 (3) 1.15 1.05

Souvenir Sheet

527 A98 $4 multicolored 2.10 *2.10*

No. 526 is incorrectly attributed to Rubens.

Antigua #2 — A99

Designs: 50c, Great Britain Penny Black, 1840. $1, Woman posting letter in pillar box, and coach. $2, Mail train, ship, plane and Concorde. $2.50, Rowland Hill.

1979, Aug. 27 Litho. *Perf. 14*

528 A99 25c multicolored .25 .25
529 A99 50c multicolored .25 .25
530 A99 $1 multicolored .35 .25
531 A99 $2 multicolored .85 .50
Nos. 528-531 (4) 1.70 1.25

Souvenir Sheet

532 A99 $2.50 multicolored 1.25 *1.40*

Sir Rowland Hill (1795-1879), originator of penny postage.

Nos. 528-531 were printed in sheets of 50 (2 panes of 25), perf. 14, and in sheets of 5 plus label, perf. 12, with frames in changed colors.

For overprints, see Nos. 571A-571D.

Crucifixion, by Durer — A100

Designs (after Dürer): 10c, Deposition. $2.50, Crucifixion. $4, Man of Sorrows.

1979, Mar. 15

533 A100 10c multicolored .25 .25
534 A100 50c multicolored .50 .25
535 A100 $4 multicolored 1.25 1.10
Nos. 533-535 (3) 2.00 1.60

Souvenir Sheet

536 A100 $2.50 multicolored 1.25 1.25

Easter.

Child Playing with Sailboat — A101

IYC emblem, child's hand holding toy: 50c, Rocket. 90c, Automobile. $2, Train. $5, Plane.

1979, Apr. 9 Litho. *Perf. 14*

537 A101 25c multicolored .25 .25
538 A101 50c multicolored .25 .25
539 A101 90c multicolored .40 .30
540 A101 $2 multicolored 1.10 1.00
Nos. 537-540 (4) 2.00 1.80

Souvenir Sheet

541 A101 $5 multicolored 2.10 2.10

International Year of the Child.

Yellowjacks — A102

Sport Fish: 50c, Bluefin tunas. 90c, Sailfish. $2.50, Barracuda. $3, Wahoos.

1979, May Litho. *Perf. 14½*

542 A102 30c multicolored .35 .25
543 A102 50c multicolored .50 .30
544 A102 90c multicolored 1.00 .40
545 A102 $3 multicolored 3.00 2.00
Nos. 542-545 (4) 4.85 2.95

Souvenir Sheet

546 A102 $2.50 multicolored 2.25 2.25

Capt. Cook and his Birthplace at Marton — A103

Capt. James Cook (1728-1779) and: 50c, HMS Endeavour. 90c, Marine timekeeper. $2.50, HMS Resolution. $3, Landing at Botany Bay.

1979, July 2 Litho. *Perf. 14*

547 A103 25c multicolored .60 .30
548 A103 50c multicolored .95 .40
549 A103 90c multicolored .70 .70
550 A103 $3 multicolored 1.60 *2.50*
Nos. 547-550 (4) 3.85 *3.90*

Souvenir Sheet

551 A103 $2.50 multicolored 2.75 2.75

Holy Family — A104

Stained-glass Windows: 25c, Flight into Egypt. 50c, Shepherd and star. $3, Angel with trumpet. $4, Three Kings offering gifts.

1979, Oct. 1 Litho. *Perf. 14*

552 A104 8c multicolored .25 .25
553 A104 25c multicolored .25 .25
554 A104 50c multicolored .30 .30
555 A104 $4 multicolored .90 *2.00*
Nos. 552-555 (4) 1.70 *2.80*

Souvenir Sheet

Perf. 12x12½

556 A104 $3 multicolored 1.25 *2.00*

Christmas.

Javelin, Olympic Rings — A105

1980, Feb. 7 Litho. *Perf. 14*

557 A105 10c shown .25 .25
558 A105 25c Running .30 .30
559 A105 $1 Pole vault .60 .60
560 A105 $2 Hurdles .70 .70
Nos. 557-560 (4) 1.85 1.85

Souvenir Sheet

561 A105 $3 Boxing, horiz. 1.40 *1.40*

22nd Summer Olympic Games, Moscow, July 19-Aug. 3.

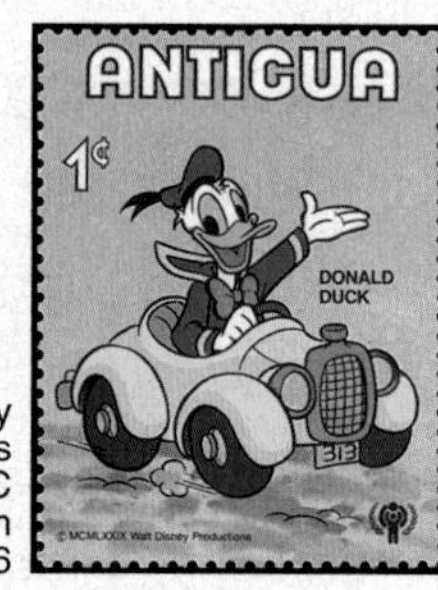

Disney Characters and IYC Emblem A106

Designs: Transportation scenes. ½c, 2c, 3c, 4c, 5c, $1, $2.50, horiz.

1980, Mar. 24 Litho. *Perf. 11*

562 A106 ½c Mickey, plane .25 .25
563 A106 1c Donald, car .25 .25
564 A106 2c Goofy driving taxi .25 .25
565 A106 3c Mickey, Minnie in sidecar .25 .25
566 A106 4c Huey, Dewey and Louie .25 .25
567 A106 5c Grandma Duck .25 .25
568 A106 10c Mickey in jeep .25 .25
569 A106 $1 Chip and Dale sailing 1.50 1.50
570 A106 $4 Donald on train 3.75 *4.00*
Nos. 562-570 (9) 7.00 *7.25*

Souvenir Sheet

571 A106 $2.50 Goofy in glider 7.50 7.50

Nos. 528-531 in Changed Colors & Overprinted

1980, May 6 Litho. *Perf. 12*

571A A99 25c multicolored .35 .35
571B A99 50c multicolored .45 .45
571C A99 $1 multicolored .75 .75
571D A99 $2 multicolored 3.25 3.25
Nos. 571A-571D (4) 4.80 4.80

London '80 Intl. Stamp Exhib., May 6-14.

Birth of Venus, by Botticelli — A106a

10c, David, by Donatello. 50c, Reclining Couple, sarcophagus, Cerveteri. 90c, The Garden of Earthly Delights, by Hieronymus Bosch. $1, Portinari Altarpiece, by Hugo van der Goes. $4, Eleanora of Toledo and her Son Giovanni de Medici, by Bronzino. $5, The Holy Family, by Rembrandt.

Perf. 13½x14, 14x13½

1980, June 23 Litho.

572 A106a 10c multi, vert. .25 .25
573 A106a 30c multi .40 .25
574 A106a 50c multi .55 .40
575 A106a 90c multi .75 .75
576 A106a $1 multi .85 .85
577 A106a $4 multi, vert. 2.25 *3.00*
Nos. 572-577 (6) 5.05 5.50

Souvenir Sheet

Perf. 14

578 A106a $5 multicolored 3.25 3.25

Anniversary Emblem, Intl. Headquarters, Evanston, IL — A107

1980, July 21 Litho. *Perf. 14*

579 A107 30c shown .35 .25
580 A107 50c Antigua club banner .40 .40
581 A107 90c Map of Antigua .60 .60
582 A107 $3 Paul. P. Harris, emblem 2.00 *2.50*
Nos. 579-582 (4) 3.35 *3.75*

Souvenir Sheet

583 A107 $5 Emblems, Antigua flags 2.00 2.00

Rotary International, 75th anniv.

A108

1980, Sept. 15

584 A108 10c multicolored .25 .25
585 A108 $2.50 multicolored 1.25 *1.75*

Souvenir Sheet

Perf. 12

586 A108 $3 multicolored 1.50 *2.00*

Queen Mother Elizabeth, 80th birthday.

A109

No. 587, Ringed Kingfisher. No. 588, Plain pigeon. No. 889, Green-throated carib. No. 890, Black-necked stilt.
No. 591, Roseate tern.

1980, Nov. 3 Litho. *Perf. 14*
587 A109 10c multi .90 .30
588 A109 30c multi 1.25 .50
589 A109 $1 multi 1.75 1.75
590 A109 $2 multi 2.50 *3.50*
Nos. 587-590 (4) 6.40 *6.05*

Souvenir Sheet

591 A109 $2.50 multi 7.50 7.50

Sleeping Beauty and the Prince — A110

Christmas: Various scenes from Walt Disney's Sleeping Beauty. $4 vert.

1980, Dec. 23 *Perf. 11, 13½x14 ($4)*
592 A110 ½c multicolored .25 .25
593 A110 1c multicolored .25 .25
594 A110 2c multicolored .25 .25
595 A110 4c multicolored .25 .25
596 A110 8c multicolored .25 .25
597 A110 10c multicolored .25 .25
598 A110 25c multicolored .30 .30
599 A110 $2 multicolored 2.50 2.50
600 A110 $2.50 multicolored 2.75 2.75
Nos. 592-600 (9) 7.05 7.05

Souvenir Sheet

601 A110 $4 multicolored 7.25 7.25

Sugar-cane Railway Diesel Locomotive No. 15 — A111

1981, Jan. 12 *Perf. 14*
602 A111 25c shown .25 .25
603 A111 50c Narrow-gauge steam locomotive .40 .40
604 A111 90c Diesels #1, #10 .75 .75
605 A111 $3 Hauling sugar-cane 2.75 2.75
Nos. 602-605 (4) 4.15 4.15

Souvenir Sheet

606 A111 $2.50 Sugar factory, train yard 3.00 3.00

Nos. 411-412, 414-422 Overprinted

1981, Mar. 31 Litho.
607 A79 6c multicolored .25 .25
608 A79 10c multicolored .25 .25
609 A79 20c multicolored .25 .25
610 A79 25c multicolored .25 .25
611 A79 35c multicolored .30 .30
612 A79 50c multicolored .55 .55
613 A79 75c multicolored .65 .65
614 A79 $1 multicolored .95 *1.25*
615 A80 $2.50 multicolored 1.60 *2.25*
616 A80 $5 multicolored 2.75 *3.75*
617 A80 $10 multicolored 5.75 *8.00*
Nos. 607-617 (11) 13.55 *17.75*

Pipes of Pan, by Picasso — A112

Paintings by Pablo Picasso (1881-1973): 50c, Seated Harlequin. 90c, Paulo as Harlequin. $4, Mother and Child. $5, Three Musicians.

1981, May 5 Litho. *Perf. 14*
618 A112 10c multicolored .25 .25
619 A112 50c multicolored .40 .40
620 A112 90c multicolored .75 .75
621 A112 $4 multicolored 2.75 2.75
Nos. 618-621 (4) 4.15 4.15

Souvenir Sheet
Perf. 14x14½

622 A112 $5 multicolored 2.75 *2.75*

Royal Wedding Issue
Common Design Type

1981, June 16 Litho. *Perf. 14*
623 CD331a 25c Couple .25 .25
624 CD331a 50c Glamis Castle .25 .25
625 CD331a $4 Charles .80 .80
Nos. 623-625 (3) 1.30 1.30

Souvenir Sheet

626 CD331 $5 Glass coach 1.25 1.25
627 CD331 Booklet 5.00
a. Pane of 6 (2x25c, 2x$1, 2x$2), Charles 3.00
b. Pane of 1, $5, Couple 2.00

No. 627 contains imperf., self-adhesive stamps.
Nos. 623-625 also printed in sheets of 5 plus label, perf. 12 in changed colors.
For surcharges see Nos. 792, 795, 802, 805.

Campfire Sing A113

1981, Oct. 28 Litho. *Perf. 15*
628 A113 10c Irene Joshua .25 .25
629 A113 50c shown .45 .25
630 A113 90c Sailing .75 .55
631 A113 $2.50 Milking cow 1.75 1.75
Nos. 628-631 (4) 3.20 2.80

Souvenir Sheet

632 A113 $5 Flag raising 6.25 6.25

Girl Guides, 50th anniv.

A114

1981, Nov. 1 Litho. *Perf. 15*
633 A114 10c Arms .30 .25
634 A114 50c Flag 1.00 .50
635 A114 90c Prime Minister Bird .60 .60
636 A114 $2.50 St. John's Cathedral, horiz. 1.60 *2.25*
Nos. 633-636 (4) 3.50 *3.60*

Souvenir Sheet

637 A114 $5 Map 4.75 4.75

Independence.
No. 637 contains one 41x41mm stamp.

A115

Christmas (Virgin and Child Paintings by): 8c, Holy Night, by Jacques Stella (1596-1657). 30c Julius Schnorr von Carolsfeld (1794-1872). $1, Alonso Cano (1601-1667). $3, Lorenzo de Credi (1459-1537). $5, Holy Family, by Pieter von Avoni (1600-1652).

1981, Nov. 16
638 A115 8c multicolored .30 .25
639 A115 30c multicolored .60 .25
640 A115 $1 multicolored 1.40 1.40
641 A115 $3 multicolored 2.00 *3.50*
Nos. 638-641 (4) 4.30 *5.40*

Souvenir Sheet

642 A115 $5 multicolored 4.25 *4.50*

On No. 639, the artist's name is misspelled as "Carolfeld."

Intl. Year of the Disabled A116

1981, Dec. 1 Litho. *Perf. 15*
643 A116 10c Swimming .25 .25
644 A116 50c Discus .30 *.30*
645 A116 90c Archery .45 *.50*
646 A116 $2 Baseball 1.25 *1.40*
Nos. 643-646 (4) 2.25 *2.45*

Souvenir Sheet

647 A116 $4 Basketball 5.00 5.00

1982 World Cup Soccer A117

Designs: Various soccer players.

1982, Apr. 15 Litho. *Perf. 14*
648 A117 10c multicolored .30 .25
649 A117 50c multicolored .55 .30
650 A117 90c multicolored 1.10 .65
651 A117 $4 multicolored 3.50 3.50
Nos. 648-651 (4) 5.45 4.70

Souvenir Sheet

652 A117 $5 multicolored 7.75 7.75

Also issued in sheetlets of 5 + label in changed colors, perf. 12.

A118

No. 653, A-300 Airbus. No. 654, Hawker-Siddeley 748. No. 655, De Havilland Twin Otter DCH6. No. 656, Britten-Norman Islander.
No. 657, Jet, horiz.

1982, June 17 Litho. *Perf. 14½*
653 A118 10c multi .25 .25
654 A118 50c multi .35 .35
655 A118 90c multi .75 .75
656 A118 $2.50 multi 2.25 2.25
Nos. 653-656 (4) 3.60 3.60

Souvenir Sheet

657 A118 $5 multi 4.25 4.25

Coolidge Intl. Airport opening.

A119

No. 658, Cordia, vert. No. 659, Golden spotted mongoose. No. 660, Corallita, vert. No. 661, Bulldog bats.
No. 662, Caribbean monk seals.

1982, June 28 Litho. *Perf. 14½*
658 A119 10c multi .35 .25
659 A119 50c multi .70 .40
660 A119 90c multi 1.10 .75
661 A119 $3 multi 2.50 *3.25*
Nos. 658-661 (4) 4.65 *4.65*

Souvenir Sheet

662 A119 $5 multi 7.75 7.75

Charles Darwin's death centenary.

Princess Diana Issue
Common Design Type

1982, July 1 Litho. *Perf. 14½x14*
663 CD332 90c Greenwich Palace .80 .80
664 CD332 $1 Wedding .90 .90
665 CD332 $4 Diana 3.50 3.50
Nos. 663-665 (3) 5.20 5.20

Souvenir Sheet

666 CD332 $5 Diana, diff. 4.50 4.50

For overprints and surcharges see Nos. 672-675, 797, 799, 803, 806.

Scouting Year A120

Designs: Independence Day celebration.

1982, July 15 *Perf. 14*
667 A120 10c Decorating buildings .30 .25
668 A120 50c Helping woman .60 .45
669 A120 90c Princess Margaret .95 .65
670 A120 $2.20 Cub Scout giving directions 1.75 *2.25*
Nos. 667-670 (4) 3.60 *3.60*

Souvenir Sheet

671 A120 $5 Baden-Powell 6.75 6.75

Nos. 663-666 Overprinted

1982, Aug. 30 Litho. *Perf. 14½x14*
672 CD332 90c multicolored .45 .45
673 CD332 $1 multicolored .55 .55
674 CD332 $4 multicolored 2.25 1.90
Nos. 672-674 (3) 3.25 2.90

Souvenir Sheet

675 CD332 $5 multicolored 3.00 3.00

For surcharges see Nos. 798, 800, 804, 807.

Roosevelt Driving by "The Little White House" A121

1982, Sept. 20 *Perf. 15*
676 A121 10c shown .25 .25
677 A121 25c Washington as blacksmith .40 .25

678 A121 45c Churchill, Roosevelt, Stalin 1.50 .35
679 A121 60c Washington cross-ing Delaware, vert. 1.00 .35
680 A121 $1 Roosevelt on train, vert. 1.25 .90
681 A121 $3 Roosevelt, vert. 1.40 *2.50*
Nos. 676-681 (6) 5.80 *4.60*

Souvenir Sheets

682 A121 $4 Washington, vert. 3.75 3.75
683 A121 $4 Eleanor and Frank-lin 3.75 3.75

George Washington's 250th birth anniv. and Franklin D. Roosevelt's birth centenary.

Christmas — A122

Raphael Paintings.

1982, Nov. **Litho.** ***Perf. 14***

684 A122 10c Annunciation .25 .25
685 A122 30c Adoration of the Magi .25 .25
686 A122 $1 Presentation at the Temple .50 .50
687 A122 $4 Coronation of the Virgin 2.50 *2.50*
Nos. 684-687 (4) 3.50 *3.50*

Souvenir Sheet

688 A122 $5 Marriage of the Virgin 3.50 3.25

500th Birth Anniv. of Raphael — A123

1983, Jan. 28. **Litho.** ***Perf. 14½***

689 A123 45c Galatea taking Reins of Dol-phins, vert. .30 .30
690 A123 50c Sea Nymphs car-ried by Tritons, vert. .40 .40
691 A123 60c Winged Angel Steering Dolphins .45 .45
692 A123 $4 Cupids Shooting Arrows 2.50 2.50
Nos. 689-692 (4) 3.65 3.65

Souvenir Sheet

693 A123 $5 Galatea 4.50 4.50

A124

1983, Mar. 14 ***Perf. 14***

694 A124 25c Pineapple crop .25 .25
695 A124 45c Carnival .25 .25
696 A124 60c Tourists, sailboat .35 .35
697 A124 $3 Control Tower 1.10 1.10
Nos. 694-697 (4) 1.95 1.95

Commonwealth Day.

World Communications Year — A125

1983, Apr. 5 **Litho.** ***Perf. 14***

698 A125 15c TV screen, cam-era .50 .25
699 A125 50c Police radio, car 2.10 1.25
700 A125 60c Long distance phone call 2.25 1.40
701 A125 $3 Dish antenna, planets 4.25 *5.00*
Nos. 698-701 (4) 9.10 7.90

Souvenir Sheet

702 A125 $5 Comsat satellite 3.50 3.50

Imperforates
See note following No. 404.

Bottlenose Dolphin A126

1983, May 9 **Litho.** ***Perf. 15***

703 A126 15c shown .85 .25
704 A126 50c Finback whale 1.75 1.25
705 A126 60c Bowhead whale 2.00 1.25
706 A126 $3 Spectacled por-poise 3.75 4.25
Nos. 703-706 (4) 8.35 7.00

Souvenir Sheet

707 A126 $5 Unicorn whale 8.75 8.75

Cashew Nut A127

1983, July 11 ***Perf. 14***

708 A127 1c shown .25 *.90*
709 A127 2c Passion fruit .25 *.90*
710 A127 3c Mango .25 *.90*
711 A127 5c Grapefruit .25 .50
712 A127 10c Pawpaw .40 .25
713 A127 15c Breadfruit .75 .25
714 A127 20c Coconut .45 .25
715 A127 25c Oleander .75 .35
716 A127 30c Banana .55 .40
717 A127 40c Pineapple .75 .40
718 A127 45c Cordia .85 .55
719 A127 50c Cassia .90 .60
720 A127 60c Poui 1.75 .90
721 A127 $1 Frangipani 2.25 1.25
722 A127 $2 Flamboyant 3.50 3.50
723 A127 $2.50 Lemon 3.75 5.00
724 A127 $5 Lignum vitae 6.00 11.00
725 A127 $10 Arms 9.00 16.00
Nos. 708-725 (18) 32.65 43.90

1985 ***Perf. 12½x12***

708a	A127	1c	.25	*.55*
709a	A127	2c	.25	*.55*
710a	A127	3c	.25	*.55*
711a	A127	5c	.30	.45
712a	A127	10c	.35	.25
713a	A127	15c	.50	.25
714a	A127	20c	.60	.25
715a	A127	25c	.60	.25
716a	A127	30c	.70	.30
717a	A127	40c	.75	.30
718a	A127	45c	.80	.45
719a	A127	50c	1.20	.45
720a	A127	60c	1.75	1.10
721a	A127	$1	2.00	1.25
722a	A127	$2	3.75	3.75
723a	A127	$2.50	4.25	5.00
724a	A127	$5	6.75	*10.00*
725a	A127	$10	11.00	*16.00*
Nos. 708a-725a (18)			36.05	*41.70*

Issue dates: $2-$5, Dec; others Mar.

Manned Flight Bicentenary — A128

1983, Aug. 15 ***Perf. 15***

726 A128 30c Dornier DoX 1.00 .30
727 A128 50c Supermarine S-6B 1.25 .60
728 A128 60c Curtiss F9C, USS Akron 1.50 .75
729 A128 $4 Pro Juventute bal-loon 3.75 *5.00*
Nos. 726-729 (4) 7.50 *6.65*

Souvenir Sheet

730 A128 $5 Graf Zeppelin 4.00 4.00

Christmas — A129

Raphael Paintings: 10c, 30c, $1, $4, Sybils and Angels details. $5, Vision of Ezekiel.

1983, Oct. 4 **Litho.** ***Perf. 14***

731 A129 10c Angel flying with scroll .40 .25
732 A129 30c Angel, diff. .75 .40
733 A129 $1 Inscribing tablet 1.60 1.25
734 A129 $4 Angel showing tab-let 3.25 *4.50*
Nos. 731-734 (4) 6.00 *6.40*

Souvenir Sheet

735 A129 $5 multicolored 1.90 1.90

Methodist Church, Anniv. — A130

1984 Olympics, Los Angeles — A131

Designs: 15c, John Wesley founder of Methodism. 50c, Nathaniel Gilbert, Antiguan founder. 60c, St. John's Methodist Church Steeple. $3, Ebenezer Methodist Church.

1983, Nov. **Litho.** ***Perf. 14***

736 A130 15c multicolored .35 .25
737 A130 50c multicolored .95 .45
738 A130 60c multicolored 1.00 .60
739 A130 $3 multicolored 2.75 *3.75*
Nos. 736-739 (4) 5.05 *5.05*

1984, Jan. **Litho.** ***Perf. 15***

740 A131 25c Discus .25 .25
741 A131 50c Gymnastics .30 .25
742 A131 90c Hurdling .60 *.60*
743 A131 $3 Bicycling 2.40 *3.00*
Nos. 740-743 (4) 3.55 *4.10*

Souvenir Sheet

744 A131 $5 Volleyball, horiz. 3.50 *4.00*

Booker Vanguard A132

1984, June 4 **Litho.** ***Perf. 15***

745 A132 45c shown 1.25 .45
746 A132 50c Canberra 1.50 .70
747 A132 60c Yachts 1.75 .85
748 A132 $4 Fairwind 3.50 *6.00*
Nos. 745-748 (4) 8.00 *8.00*

Souvenir Sheet

749 A132 $5 Man-of-war, vert. 3.00 *4.00*

Local Flowers — A133

1984, June 25 **Litho.** ***Perf. 15***

755 A133 15c multicolored .50 .25
756 A133 50c multicolored 1.00 .75
757 A133 60c multicolored 1.00 1.00
758 A133 $3 multicolored 3.50 *5.50*
Nos. 755-758 (4) 6.00 *7.50*

Souvenir Sheet

759 A133 $5 multicolored 4.25 4.25

US Presidents — A134

1984, July 18 **Litho.** ***Perf. 14***

760 A134 10c Lincoln .25 .25
761 A134 20c Truman .25 .25
762 A134 30c Eisenhower .30 .25
763 A134 40c Reagan .50 .45
764 A134 90c Lincoln, diff. 1.00 .80
765 A134 $1.10 Truman, diff. 1.25 1.10
766 A134 $1.50 Eisenhower, diff. 1.75 1.50
767 A134 $2 Reagan, diff. 2.00 1.75
Nos. 760-767 (8) 7.30 6.35

Slavery Abolition Sesquicentennial — A135

40c, Moravian Mission. 50c, Antigua Courthouse, 1823. 60c, Sugar cane planting. $3, Boiling House, Delaps' Estate.
$5, Willoughby Bay.

1984, Aug. 1

768 A135 40c multicolored .95 .45
769 A135 50c multicolored 1.00 .60
770 A135 60c multicolored 1.10 .70
771 A135 $3 multicolored 4.25 4.25
Nos. 768-771 (4) 7.30 6.00

Souvenir Sheet

772 A135 $5 multicolored 7.25 7.25

Song Birds — A136

1984, Aug. 15 ***Perf. 15***

773 A136 40c Rufous-sided towhee 1.50 .70
774 A136 50c Parula warbler 1.75 .90
775 A136 60c House wren 2.00 1.90
776 A136 $2 Ruby-crowned kinglet 2.25 *1.50*
777 A136 $3 Yellow-shafted flicker 2.50 *4.00*
Nos. 773-777 (5) 10.00 *9.00*

Souvenir Sheet

778 A136 $5 Yellow-breasted chat 5.25 5.25

AUSIPEX '84 — A137

1984, Sept. 21 ***Perf. 15***

779 A137 $1 Grass skiing 1.40 1.40

780 A137 $5 Australian rules football 4.50 4.50

Souvenir Sheet

781 A137 $5 Boomerang 3.75 3.75

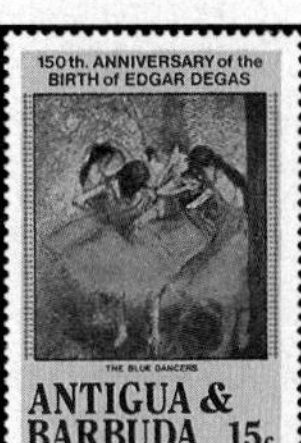

The Blue Dancers, by Degas — A137a

Paintings by Correggio: 25c, Virgin and Infant with Angels and Cherubs. 60c, The Four Saints. 90c, Saint Catherine. $3, The Campori Madonna. No. 790, St. John the Baptist.

Paintings by Degas: 50c, The Pink Dancers. 70c, Two Dancers. $4, Dancers at the Bar. No. 791, Folk Dancers.

1984, Oct. Litho. *Perf. 15*

782 A137a 15c multicolored .40 .25
783 A137a 25c multicolored .45 .25
784 A137a 50c multicolored 1.00 .50
785 A137a 60c multicolored 1.00 .40
786 A137a 70c multicolored 1.25 .70
787 A137a 90c multicolored 1.25 .75
788 A137a $3 multicolored 2.75 *3.50*
789 A137a $4 multicolored 3.00 *4.00*
Nos. 782-789 (8) 11.10 *10.35*

Souvenir Sheets

790 A137a $5 multicolored 3.75 3.75
791 A137a $5 multi, horiz. 3.75 3.75

Nos. 623-626, 663-666, 672-675, 694-697 Surcharged in Black or Gold

(CD331)

(A124)

(CD332)

1984, June *Perf. 14, 14½x14*

792 CD331 $2 on 25c #623 3.50 3.50
793 A124 $2 on 25c #694 2.75 1.50
794 A124 $2 on 45c #695 2.75 1.50
795 CD331 $2 on 50c #624 3.50 3.50
796 A124 $2 on 60c #696 2.75 2.75
797 CD332 $2 on 90c #663 (G) 3.00 2.75
798 CD332 $2 on 90c #672 (G) 3.00 2.75
799 CD332 $2 on $1 #664 (G) 3.00 2.75
800 CD332 $2 on $1 #673 (G) 3.00 2.75
801 A124 $2 on $3 #697 2.75 1.50
802 CD331 $2 on $4 #625 3.50 3.50
803 CD332 $2 on $4 #665 (G) 3.00 2.75
804 CD332 $2 on $4 #674 (G) 3.00 2.75
Nos. 792-804 (13) 39.50 34.25

Souvenir Sheets

805 CD331 $2 on $5 #626 9.50 9.50
806 CD332 $2 on $5 #666 8.25 8.25
807 CD332 $2 on $5 #675 8.25 8.25

Nos. 797-800, 803-804 exist with silver surcharge.

Christmas 1984 and 50th Anniv. of Donald Duck A138

Scenes from various Donald Duck comics.

1984, Nov. Litho. *Perf. 11*

808 A138 1c multicolored .25 .25
809 A138 2c multicolored .25 .25
810 A138 3c multicolored .25 .25
811 A138 4c multicolored .25 .25
812 A138 5c multicolored .25 .25
813 A138 10c multicolored .25 .25
814 A138 $1 multicolored 2.00 1.00
815 A138 $2 multicolored 2.25 2.25
816 A138 $5 multicolored 4.25 4.25
Nos. 808-816 (9) 10.00 9.00

Souvenir Sheets

Perf. 14

817 A138 $5 multi, horiz. 6.50 6.50
818 A138 $5 Donald on beach 6.50 6.50

20th Century Leaders A139

No. 819, John F. Kennedy (1917-1963), vert. No. 820, Winston Churchill (1874-1965), vert. No. 821, Mahatma Gandhi (1869-1948), vert. No. 822, Mao Tse-Tung (1883-1976), vert. No. 823, Kennedy in Berlin. No. 824, Churchill in Paris. No. 825, Gandhi in Great Britain. No. 826, Mao in Peking.

No. 827, Flags of Great Britain, India, China, USA.

1984, Nov. 19 Litho. *Perf. 15*

819 A139 60c multicolored 1.30 1.30
820 A139 60c multicolored 1.30 1.30
821 A139 60c multicolored 1.30 1.30
822 A139 60c multicolored 1.30 1.30
823 A139 $1 multicolored 1.40 1.40
824 A139 $1 multicolored 1.40 1.40
825 A139 $1 multicolored 1.40 1.40
826 A139 $1 multicolored 1.40 1.40
Nos. 819-826 (8) 10.80 10.80

Souvenir Sheet

827 A139 $5 multicolored 9.25 9.25

Statue of Liberty Centennial A140

25c, Torch on display, 1885. 30c, Restoration, 1984-1986, vert. 50c, Bartholdi supervising construction, 1876. 90c, Statue on Liberty Island. $1, Dedication Ceremony, 1886, vert. $3, Operation Sail, 1976, vert.

$5, Port of New York.

1985, Jan. 7

828 A140 25c multicolored .25 .25
829 A140 30c multicolored .25 .25
830 A140 50c multicolored .40 .30
831 A140 90c multicolored .80 .50
832 A140 $1 multicolored 1.60 1.10
833 A140 $3 multicolored 2.25 2.25
Nos. 828-833 (6) 5.55 4.65

Souvenir Sheet

834 A140 $5 multicolored 5.00 5.00

Traditional Scenes A141

15c, Ceramics, Arawak pot shard. 50c, Tatooing, body design. 60c, Harvesting Manioc, god Yocahu. $3, Caribs in battle, war club.

$5, Tainos worshiping.

1985, Jan. 21

835 A141 15c multicolored .30 .25
836 A141 50c multicolored .50 .40
837 A141 60c multicolored .65 .50
838 A141 $3 multicolored 2.00 *2.50*
Nos. 835-838 (4) 3.45 *3.65*

Souvenir Sheet

839 A141 $5 multicolored 3.50 3.50

Invention of the Motorcycle, Cent. — A142

10c, Triumph 2HP Jap, 1903. 30c, Indian Arrow, 1949. 60c, BMW R100RS, 1976. $4, Harley Davidson Model II, 1916.

$5, Laverda Jota, 1975.

1985, Mar. 7 *Perf. 14*

840 A142 10c multicolored .70 .40
841 A142 30c multicolored 1.25 .50
842 A142 60c multicolored 1.60 1.25
843 A142 $4 multicolored 6.00 6.00
Nos. 840-843 (4) 9.55 8.15

Souvenir Sheet

844 A142 $5 multicolored 7.00 7.00

John J. Audubon, 200th Birth Anniv. A143

1985, Mar. 25 *Perf. 14*

845 A143 90c Horned grebe 1.75 1.10
846 A143 $1 Least petrel 2.00 1.10
847 A143 $1.50 Great blue heron 2.75 2.75
848 A143 $3 Double-crested cormorant 4.50 *5.25*
Nos. 845-848 (4) 11.00 *10.20*

Souvenir Sheet

849 A143 $5 White-tailed tropic bird, vert. 9.50 9.50

See Nos.910-914.

Butterflies A144

1985, Apr. 16 *Perf. 14*

850 A144 25c Polygrapha cyanea 1.40 .25
851 A144 60c Leodonta dysoni 2.50 1.00
852 A144 90c Junea doraete 3.25 1.10
853 A144 $4 Prepona xenagoras 8.00 *9.00*
Nos. 850-853 (4) 15.15 11.35

Souvenir Sheet

854 A144 $5 Caerois gerdrudtus 7.25 7.25

Cessna 172 A145

1985, Apr. 30

855 A145 30c shown 1.25 .25
856 A145 90c Fokker DVII 2.50 1.25
857 A145 $1.50 Spad VII 3.50 3.25
858 A145 $3 Boeing 747 5.25 *6.00*
Nos. 855-858 (4) 12.50 *10.75*

Souvenir Sheet

859 A145 $5 Twin Otter, Coolidge Intl. Airport 5.75 5.75

40th anniv. of the ICAO. Nos. 855, 858-859 show the ICAO and UN emblems.

Maimonides (1135-1204), Judaic Philosopher and Physician — A146

1985, June 17 Litho. *Perf. 14*

860 A146 $2 yellow green 4.00 3.25

Souvenir Sheet

861 A146 $5 deep brown 7.25 6.00

Intl. Youth Year A147

1985, July 1

862 A147 25c Agriculture .25 .25
863 A147 50c Hotel management .35 .30
864 A147 60c Environmental studies 1.00 .75
865 A147 $3 Windsurfing 2.25 *3.25*
Nos. 862-865 (4) 3.85 *4.55*

Souvenir Sheet

866 A147 $5 Youths, national flag 3.75 3.75

Queen Mother, 85th Birthday — A148

Designs: 90c, $1, Attending a church service. No. 867A, $1.50, Touring the London Gardens, children in a sandpit. $2.50, $3, Photograph (1979). $5, With Prince Edward at the wedding of Prince Charles and Lady Diana Spencer.

Perf. 14, 12x12½ (90c, $1, $3)

1985, July 15

866A A148 90c multi ('86) .65 .65
867 A148 $1 multi .75 .75
867A A148 $1 multi ('86) .75 .75
868 A148 $1.50 multi 1.10 1.10
869 A148 $2.50 multi 1.75 1.75
869A A148 $3 multi ('86) 2.00 2.00
Nos. 866A-869A (6) 7.00 7.00

Souvenir Sheet

870 A148 $5 multicolored 4.50 4.50

Nos. 866A, 867A, 869A issued in sheets of 5 plus label on Jan. 13, 1986.

Marine Life — A149

1985, Aug. 1 *Perf. 14*

871 A149 15c Fregata magnificens 1.00 .25
872 A149 45c Diploria labyrinthi-formis 2.00 .75
873 A149 60c Oreaster reticulatus 2.25 1.50

874 A149 $3 Gymnothorax moringa 7.00 *7.50*
Nos. 871-874 (4) 12.25 *10.00*

Souvenir Sheet

875 A149 $5 Acropora palmata 8.75 8.75

Johann Sebastian Bach — A150

1985, Aug. 26 Litho. *Perf. 14*

876 A150 25c Bass trombone 1.10 .40
877 A150 50c English horn 1.40 .90
878 A150 $1 Violino piccolo 2.75 1.50
879 A150 $3 Bass rackett 6.50 6.50
Nos. 876-879 (4) 11.75 9.30

Souvenir Sheet

880 A150 $5 Portrait 6.25 6.25

Girl Guides, 75th Anniv. A151

Public service and growth-oriented activities.

1985, Sept. 10

881 A151 15c Public service .75 .25
882 A151 45c Guides meeting 1.40 .40
883 A151 60c Lord and Lady Baden-Powell 1.75 .60
884 A151 $3 Nature study 4.50 4.50
Nos. 881-884 (4) 8.40 5.75

Souvenir Sheet

885 A151 $5 Barn swallow 5.75 5.75

State Visit of Elizabeth II, Oct. 24 — A152

1985, Oct. 24 Litho. *Perf. 14½*

886 A152 60c National flags 1.00 .45
887 A152 $1 Elizabeth II, vert. 1.50 .90
888 A152 $4 HMY Britannia 3.50 *5.00*
Nos. 886-888 (3) 6.00 *6.35*

Souvenir Sheet

889 A152 $5 Map of Antigua 4.00 4.00

Mark Twain — A153

Disney characters in Roughing It.

1985, Nov. 4 *Perf. 14*

890 A153 25c Cowboys and Indians 1.00 .25
891 A153 50c Canoeing 1.25 .40
892 A153 $1.10 Pony Express 2.00 1.25
893 A153 $1.50 Buffalo hunt in Missouri 2.50 2.50
894 A153 $2 Nevada silver mine 3.25 3.25
Nos. 890-894 (5) 10.00 7.65

Souvenir Sheet

895 A153 $5 Stagecoach on Kansas plains 8.75 8.75

Jacob and Wilhelm Grimm, Fabulists and Philologists — A154

Disney characters in Spindle, Shuttle and Needle.

1985, Nov. 11

896 A154 30c multicolored 1.00 .30
897 A154 60c multicolored 1.50 .55
898 A154 70c multicolored 1.75 .90
899 A154 $1 multicolored 2.00 1.40
900 A154 $3 multicolored 4.50 *5.00*
Nos. 896-900 (5) 10.75 *8.15*

Souvenir Sheet

900A A154 $5 multicolored 8.75 8.75

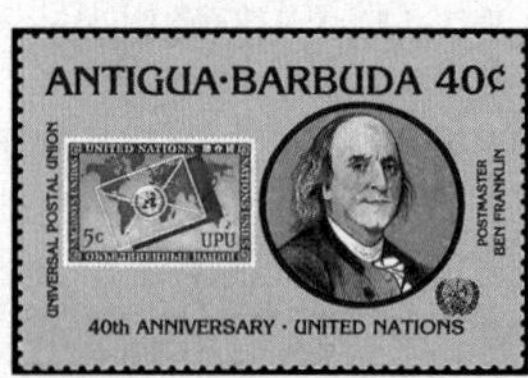

UN 40th Anniv. A155

Stamps of UN and portraits: 40c, No. 18 and Benjamin Franklin. $1, No. 391 and George Washington Carver, agricultural chemist. $3, No. 299 and Charles Lindbergh. $5, Marc Chagall, artist, vert.

1985, Nov. 18 *Perf. 13½x14*

901 A155 40c multicolored .90 .50
902 A155 $1 multicolored 1.75 1.25
903 A155 $3 multicolored 4.75 *5.75*
Nos. 901-903 (3) 7.40 *7.50*

Souvenir Sheet

Perf. 14x13½

904 A155 $5 multicolored 7.25 7.25

Christmas — A156

Religious paintings: 10c, Madonna and Child, by De Landi. 25c, Madonna and Child, by Bonaventura Berlinghieri (d. 1244). 60c, The Nativity, by Fra Angelico (1400-1455). $4, Presentation in the Temple, by Giovanni di Paolo Grazia (c.1403-1482). $5, The Nativity, by Antoniazzo Romano.

1985, Dec. 30 *Perf. 15*

905 A156 10c multicolored .35 .25
906 A156 25c multicolored .75 .25
907 A156 60c multicolored 1.00 .45
908 A156 $4 multicolored 2.25 *3.25*
Nos. 905-908 (4) 4.35 *4.20*

Souvenir Sheet

909 A156 $5 multicolored 3.75 *3.75*

Audubon Type of 1985

Illustrations of North American ducks.

1986, Jan. 6 *Perf. 12½x12*

910 A143 60c Mallard 2.25 1.00
911 A143 90c Dusky duck 2.75 1.50
912 A143 $1.50 Common pintail 3.50 3.50
913 A143 $3 Widgeon 4.75 *5.25*
Nos. 910-913 (4) 13.25 11.25

Souvenir Sheet

Perf. 14

914 A143 $5 Common eider 7.75 7.75

1986 World Cup Soccer Championships, Mexico — A157

1986, Mar. 17 Litho. *Perf. 14*

915 A157 30c shown 1.50 .25
916 A157 60c Heading the ball 1.75 .60
917 A157 $1 Referee 2.25 1.40
918 A157 $4 Goal 6.00 6.00
Nos. 915-918 (4) 11.50 8.25

Souvenir Sheet

919 A157 $5 Action 8.50 7.50

Nos. 916-917 vert.

For overprints see Nos. 963-967.

A158

Halley's Comet — A159

Designs: 5c, Edmond Halley, Greenwich Observatory. 10c, Me 163B Komet. German WWII fighter plane. 60c, Montezuma sighting comet, 1517. $4, Pocahontas saving Capt. John Smith's life, 1607 sighting as sign for Powhatan Indians to raid Jamestown. $5, Comet over Antigua.

1986, Mar. 24

920 A158 5c multicolored .35 .25
921 A158 10c multicolored .40 .25
922 A158 60c multicolored 1.75 .50
923 A158 $4 multicolored 5.25 5.25
Nos. 920-923 (4) 7.75 6.25

Souvenir Sheet

924 A159 $5 multicolored 5.00 5.00

For overprints see Nos. 973-977.

Queen Elizabeth II, 60th Birthday

Common Design Type

1986, Apr. 21

925 CD339 60c Wedding, 1947 .45 .45
926 CD339 $1 Trooping the color .70 .70
927 CD339 $4 Visiting Scotland 2.10 2.10
Nos. 925-927 (3) 3.25 3.25

Souvenir Sheet

928 CD339 $5 Held by Queen Mary, 1927 3.50 3.50

Boats — A160

1986, May 15

929 A160 30c Tugboat .30 .25
930 A160 60c Fishing boat .55 .30
931 A160 $1 Sailboat 2056 1.00 .50
932 A160 $4 Lateen-rigged sailboat 3.75 3.75
Nos. 929-932 (4) 5.60 4.80

Souvenir Sheet

933 A160 $5 Boatbuilding 3.75 *4.00*

A number of unissued items, imperfs., part perfs., missing color varieties, etc., were made available when the Format International inventory was liquidated. Imperfs of some or all of the Antigua stamps in the following sets are included: Nos. 405-422, 503-507, 515-517, 703-707, 745-749, 755-759, 808-816, 819-826, 905-909, 934-937.

See footnote after No. 962.

AMERIPEX '86 — A161

American trains.

1986, May 22 *Perf. 15*

934 A161 25c Hiawatha 1.25 .30
935 A161 50c Grand Canyon 1.50 .60
936 A161 $1 Powhattan Arrow 2.00 1.75
937 A161 $3 Empire State 3.25 *5.00*
Nos. 934-937 (4) 8.00 *7.65*

Souvenir Sheet

938 A161 $5 Daylight 8.00 8.00

Wedding of Prince Andrew and Sarah Ferguson

Common Design Type

1986, July 23 *Perf. 14*

939 CD340 45c Couple .30 .30
940 CD340 60c Prince Andrew .45 .45
941 CD340 $4 Princes Andrew, Philip 3.75 *3.75*
Nos. 939-941 (3) 4.50 *4.50*

Souvenir Sheet

942 CD340 $5 Couple, diff. 3.75 3.75

Conch Shells — A162

1986, Aug. 6 Litho. *Perf. 15*

943 A162 15c Say fly-specked cerith .90 .35
944 A162 45c Gmelin smooth scotch bonnet 2.10 1.25
945 A162 60c Linne West Indian crown conch 2.25 2.25
946 A162 $3 Murex ciboney 6.75 *8.00*
Nos. 943-946 (4) 12.00 *11.85*

Souvenir Sheet

947 A162 $5 Atlantic natica 7.50 7.50

Flowers A163

1986, Aug. 25 Litho. *Perf. 15*

948 A163 10c Water lily .30 .25
949 A163 15c Queen of the night .30 .25
950 A163 50c Cup of gold .60 .45
951 A163 60c Beach morning glory .75 .55
952 A163 70c Golden trumpet .85 .65
953 A163 $1 Air plant 1.00 1.00
954 A163 $3 Purple wreath 2.25 *2.50*
955 A163 $4 Zephyr lily 2.75 *3.50*
Nos. 948-955 (8) 8.80 *9.15*

Souvenir Sheets

956 A163 $4 Dozakie 3.00 *3.25*
957 A163 $5 Four o'clock 3.75 *4.00*

Fungi — A164

1986, Sept. 15

958 A164 10c Hygrocybe occidentalis scarletina .35 .25
959 A164 50c Trogia buccinalis .75 .55
960 A164 $1 Collybia subpruinosa 1.50 1.25
961 A164 $4 Leucocoprinus brebissonii 3.75 *4.50*
Nos. 958-961 (4) 6.35 6.55

Souvenir Sheet

962 A164 $5 Pyrrhoglossum pyrrhum 11.00 11.00

An unissued $3 stamp and No. 961 inscribed "4$" were made available when the Format International inventory was liquidated.

Nos. 915-919 Ovptd. in Gold in 2 or 3 lines

1986, Sept. 15 *Perf. 14*

963 A157 30c multicolored 1.10 .35
964 A157 60c multicolored 1.60 .70
965 A157 $1 multicolored 2.25 1.10
966 A157 $4 multicolored 5.50 4.50
Nos. 963-966 (4) 10.45 6.65

Souvenir Sheet

967 A157 $5 multicolored 6.00 6.00

Automobile, Cent. — A165

Carl Benz and classic automobiles.

1986, Oct. 20

968 A165 10c 1933 Auburn Speedster .25 .25
968A A165 15c 1986 Mercury Sable .30 .25
969 A165 50c 1959 Cadillac .65 .25
970 A165 60c 1950 Studebaker .80 .30
970A A165 70c 1939 Lagonda V-12 .90 .40
970B A165 $1 1930 Adler Standard 1.25 .55
970C A165 $3 1956 DKW 3.00 3.00
971 A165 $4 1936 Mercedes 500K 3.50 3.50
Nos. 968-971 (8) 10.65 8.50

Souvenir Sheets

972 A165 $5 1921 Mercedes Knight 4.50 4.00
972A A165 $5 1896 Daimler 4.50 4.00

Nos. 920-924 Ovptd. in Black or Silver

1986, Oct. 22 Litho. *Perf. 14*

973 A158 5c multicolored .25 .25
974 A158 10c multicolored .25 .25
975 A158 60c multicolored 1.25 .60
976 A158 $4 multicolored 5.50 4.00
Nos. 973-976 (4) 7.25 5.10

Souvenir Sheet

977 A159 $5 multicolored (S) 6.50 6.50

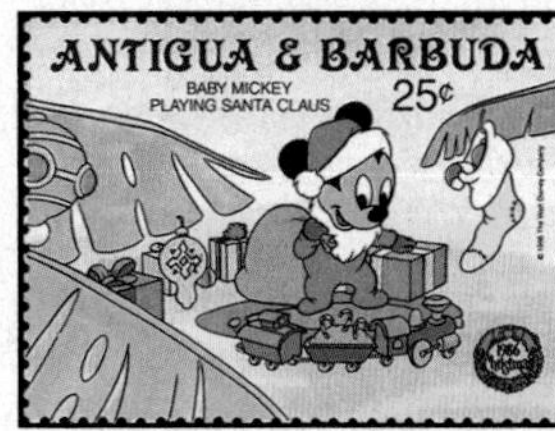

Christmas — A166

Disney characters as children.

1986, Nov. 4 *Perf. 11*

978 A166 25c Mickey .60 .25
979 A166 30c Mickey, Minnie .75 .30
980 A166 40c Aunt Matilda, Goofy .85 .35
981 A166 60c Goofy, Pluto 1.00 .65
982 A166 70c Pluto, Donald, Daisy 1.25 1.00
983 A166 $1.50 Stringing popcorn 2.00 2.00
984 A166 $3 Grandma Duck, Minnie 3.00 *3.75*
985 A166 $4 Donald, Pete 3.50 *4.00*
Nos. 978-985 (8) 12.95 *12.30*

Souvenir Sheets

Perf. 14

986 A166 $5 Playing with presents 7.00 7.00
987 A166 $5 Reindeer 7.00 7.00

Nos. 985 printed in sheets of 8.

Coat of Arms A167

Natl. Flag A168

1986, Nov. 25 Litho. *Perf. 14x14½*

988 A167 10c bright blue 1.00 .90
989 A168 25c orange 1.75 1.25

Marc Chagall (1887-1985), Artist A169

Designs: No. 990, The Profile, 1957. No. 991, Portrait of the Artist's Sister, 1910. No. 992, Bride with Fan, 1911. No. 993, David in Profile, 1914. No. 994, Fiancee with Bouquet, 1977. No. 995, Self-portrait with Brushes, 1909. No. 996, The Walk, 1973. No. 997, Candles, 1938. No. 998, Fall of Icarus, 1975. No. 999, Myth of Orpheus, 1977.

1987, Mar. 30 Litho. *Perf. 13½x14*

990 A169 10c multicolored .45 .25
991 A169 30c multicolored .60 .30
992 A169 40c multicolored .80 .35
993 A169 60c multicolored .90 .40
994 A169 90c multicolored 1.00 .55
995 A169 $1 multicolored 1.00 .60
996 A169 $3 multicolored 2.50 2.50
997 A169 $4 multicolored 2.75 2.75

Size: 110x95mm

Imperf

998 A169 $5 multicolored 5.75 5.75
999 A169 $5 multicolored 5.75 5.75
Nos. 990-999 (10) 21.50 19.20

A170

America's Cup — A171

1987, Feb. 5 *Perf. 15*

1000 A170 30c Canada I, 1981 .55 .25
1001 A170 60c Gretel II, 1970 .70 .35
1002 A170 $1 Sceptre, 1958 1.25 1.00
1003 A170 $3 Vigilant, 1893 2.75 *3.00*
Nos. 1000-1003 (4) 5.25 *4.60*

Souvenir Sheet

1004 A171 $5 Australia II, Liberty, 1983 6.25 6.25

Fish, World Wildlife Fund A172

Marine Birds A173

1987, Feb. 23 Litho. *Perf. 14*

1005 A172 15c Bridled burrfish 3.00 .40
1006 A173 30c Brown noddy 6.00 .45
1007 A172 40c Nassau grouper 3.75 .55
1008 A173 50c Laughing gull 6.75 1.25
1009 A172 60c French angelfish 4.00 1.25
1010 A172 $1 Porkfish 4.00 1.50
1011 A173 $2 Royal tern 9.00 4.75
1012 A173 $3 Sooty tern 9.00 7.00
Nos. 1005-1012 (8) 45.50 17.15

Souvenir Sheets

1013 A172 $5 Banded butterfly fish 11.00 11.00
1014 A173 $5 Brown booby 11.00 11.00

The 30c, 50c, $2, $3 and Nos. 1013-1014 do not picture the WWF emblem.
For overprints see Nos. 1137-1139A.

Statue of Liberty, Cent. A174

Photographs by Peter B. Kaplan.

1987, Apr. 20 *Perf. 14*

1015 A174 15c Lee Iacocca .25 .25
1016 A174 30c Statue at dusk .25 .25
1017 A174 45c Crown, head .40 .40
1018 A174 50c Iacocca, torch .45 .45
1019 A174 60c Crown observatory .45 .45
1020 A174 90c Interior restoration .65 .65
1021 A174 $1 Head .75 .75
1022 A174 $2 Statue at sunset 1.50 1.50
1023 A174 $3 Men on scaffold, flag 1.60 *2.00*
1024 A174 $5 Statue at night 2.75 *3.50*
Nos. 1015-1024 (10) 9.05 *10.20*

Nos. 1015-1018, 1021-1022, 1024 vert.

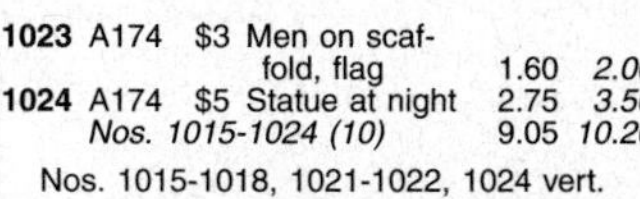

A175

Transportation Innovations — A175a

10c, Spirit of Australia, 1978. 15c, Siemens' Electric locomotive, 1879. 30c, USS Triton, 1960. 50c, Trevithick, 1801. 60c, USS New Jersey, 1942. 70c, Draisine bicycle, 1818. 90c, SS United States, 1952. $1.50, Cierva C-4, 1923. $2, Curtiss NC-4, 1919. $3, Queen Elizabeth II, 1969.

1987, Apr. 19 *Perf. 15*

1025 A175 10c multi .85 .25
1026 A175a 15c multi 1.10 .30
1027 A175 30c multi 1.10 .35
1028 A175a 50c multi 1.25 .45
1029 A175 60c multi 1.25 .50
1030 A175a 70c multi 1.25 .65
1031 A175 90c multi 1.25 .75
1032 A175a $1.50 multi 1.90 *1.90*
1033 A175a $2 multi 2.10 *2.10*
1034 A175 $3 multi 3.25 *3.25*
Nos. 1025-1034 (10) 15.30 *10.50*

Reptiles and Amphibians — A176

1987, June 15 *Perf. 14*

1035 A176 30c Eleutherodactylus martinicensis .55 .25
1036 A176 60c Thecadactylus rapicauda .85 .35
1037 A176 $1 Anolis bimaculatus leachi 1.10 .65
1038 A176 $3 Geochelone carbonaria 2.25 *2.75*
Nos. 1035-1038 (4) 4.75 *4.00*

Souvenir Sheet

1039 A176 $5 Ameiva griswoldi 5.50 5.50

Entertainers A177

1987, May 11

1040 A177 15c Grace Kelly 1.00 .30
1041 A177 30c Marilyn Monroe 2.75 .60
1042 A177 45c Orson Welles 1.00 .40
1043 A177 50c Judy Garland 1.00 .45
1044 A177 60c John Lennon 4.00 1.00
1045 A177 $1 Rock Hudson 1.50 .90
1046 A177 $2 John Wayne 2.75 1.50
1047 A177 $3 Elvis Presley 9.00 4.00
Nos. 1040-1047 (8) 23.00 9.15

No. 1047 Overprinted

1987, Sept. 9 Litho. *Perf. 14*

1047A A177 $3 multicolored 8.50 8.50

1988 Summer Olympics, Seoul A178

1987, Mar. 23

1048 A178 10c Basketball .60 .30
1049 A178 60c Fencing .90 .40
1050 A178 $1 Women's gymnastics 1.25 1.00
1051 A178 $3 Soccer 3.00 *4.00*
Nos. 1048-1051 (4) 5.75 *5.70*

Souvenir Sheet

1052 A178 $5 Boxing glove 4.75 *4.75*

16th World Scout Jamboree, Australia, 1987-88 A179

1987, Nov. 2 Litho. *Perf. 15*

1053 A179 10c Campfire, red kangaroo .75 .25
1054 A179 60c Kayaking, blue-winged kookaburra 1.50 .65
1055 A179 $1 Obstacle course, ring-tailed rock wallaby 1.25 .75
1056 A179 $3 Field kitchen, koalas 2.00 *3.50*
Nos. 1053-1056 (4) 5.50 *5.15*

Souvenir Sheet

1057 A179 $5 Flags 4.00 4.00

US Constitution Bicent. — A180

Designs: 15c, Virginia House of Burgesses exercising right of freedom of speech. 45c, Connecticut state seal. 60c, Delaware state seal. $4, Gouverneur Morris (1752-1816), principal writer of the Constitution, vert. $5, Roger Sherman (1721-1793), jurist and statesman, vert.

1987, Nov. 16 Litho. *Perf. 14*

1058 A180 15c multicolored .25 .25
1059 A180 45c multicolored .30 .30
1060 A180 60c multicolored .35 .35
1061 A180 $4 multicolored 2.75 *3.00*
Nos. 1058-1061 (4) 3.65 *3.90*

Souvenir Sheet

1062 A180 $5 multicolored 4.00 4.00

A181

Christmas (Paintings): 45c, Madonna and Child, by Bernardo Daddi (1290-1355). 60c, Joseph, detail from The Nativity, by Sano Di Pietro (1406-1481). $1, Mary, detail from Di Pietro's The Nativity. $4, Music-making Angel, by Melozzo Da Forli (1438-1494). $5, The Flight into Egypt, by Di Pietro.

1987, Dec. 1

1063 A181 45c multicolored .35 .25
1064 A181 60c multicolored .45 .35
1065 A181 $1 multicolored .75 .55
1066 A181 $4 multicolored 2.10 *3.00*
Nos. 1063-1066 (4) 3.65 *4.15*

Souvenir Sheet

1067 A181 $5 multicolored 3.75 3.75

A182

No. 1068, Wedding portrait. No. 1069, Elizabeth II, c. 1970. No. 1070, Christening of Charles, 1948. No. 1071, Elizabeth II, c. 1980. No. 1072, Royal family, c. 1951.

1988, Feb. 8 Litho. *Perf. 14*

1068 A182 25c multi .25 .25
1069 A182 60c multi .50 .40
1070 A182 $2 multi 1.10 1.10
1071 A182 $3 multi 1.75 1.75
Nos. 1068-1071 (4) 3.60 3.50

Souvenir Sheet

1072 A182 $5 multi 3.25 3.25

40th wedding anniv. of Queen Elizabeth II and Prince Philip.

Tropical Birds A183

1988, Mar. 1

1073 A183 10c Great blue heron, vert. .55 .35
1074 A183 15c Ringed kingfisher .60 .30
1075 A183 50c Bananaquit 1.10 .40
1076 A183 60c Purple gallinule 1.10 .40
1077 A183 70c Blue-hooded euphonia 1.25 .50
1078 A183 $1 Caribbean parakeet, vert. 1.50 .60
1079 A183 $3 Troupial 3.00 *3.50*
1080 A183 $4 Hummingbird 3.00 *3.50*
Nos. 1073-1080 (8) 12.10 9.55

Souvenir Sheets

1081 A183 $5 Roseate flamingo, vert. 4.75 4.75
1082 A183 $5 Brown pelicans, vert. 4.75 4.75

Salvation Army — A184

25c, Day-care, Antigua. 30c, Penicillin inoculation, Indonesia. 40c, Day-care Center, Bolivia. 45c, Rehabilitation, India. 50c, Training the blind, Kenya. 60c, Infant care, Ghana. $1, Job training, Zambia. $2, Food distribution, Sri Lanka.

$5, General Eva Burrows.

1988, Mar. 7

1083 A184 25c multicolored .90 .45
1084 A184 30c multicolored .90 .45
1085 A184 40c multicolored 1.00 .55
1086 A184 45c multicolored 1.00 .55
1087 A184 50c multicolored 1.25 1.10
1088 A184 60c multicolored 1.40 1.25
1089 A184 $1 multicolored 1.75 1.50
1090 A184 $2 multicolored 2.50 *3.00*
Nos. 1083-1090 (8) 10.70 *8.85*

Souvenir Sheet

1091 A184 $5 multicolored 5.50 5.50

A185

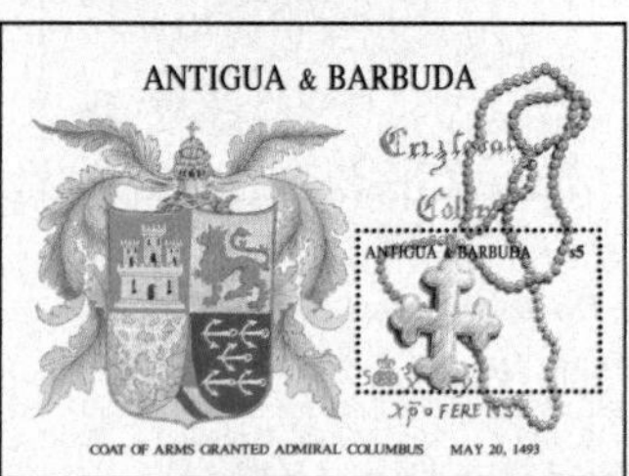

Discovery of America, 500th Anniv. (in 1992) — A186

Anniv. emblem and: 10c, Fleet. 30c, View of fleet in harbor from Paino Indian village. 45c, Caravel anchored in harbor, Paino village. 60c, Columbus, 3 Indians in canoe. 90c, Indian, parrot, Columbus. $1, Columbus in longboat. $3, Spanish guard, fleet in harbor. $4, Ships under full sail. No. 1100, Stone cross given to Columbus by Queen Isabella. No. 1101, Gold excelente.

1988, Mar. 14 Litho. *Perf. 14*

1092 A185 10c multicolored .75 .30
1093 A185 30c multicolored .75 .35
1094 A185 45c multicolored .85 .35
1095 A185 60c multicolored .85 .35
1096 A185 90c multicolored 1.50 .80
1097 A185 $1 multicolored 1.50 .80
1098 A185 $3 multicolored 2.50 *3.00*
1099 A185 $4 multicolored 2.75 *3.25*
Nos. 1092-1099 (8) 11.45 9.20

Souvenir Sheets

1100 A186 $5 multicolored 4.50 4.50
1101 A186 $5 multicolored 4.50 4.50

Paintings by Titian A187

Details: 30c, Bust of Christ. 40c, Scourging of Christ. 45c, Madonna in Glory with Saints. 50c, The Averoldi Polyptych. $1, Christ Crowned with Thorns. $2, Christ Mocked. $3, Christ and Simon of Cyrene. $4, Crucifixion with Virgin and Saints. No. 1110, Ecce Homo. No. 1111, Noli Me Tangere.

1988, Apr. 11 Litho. *Perf. 13½x14*

1102 A187 30c shown .55 .25
1103 A187 40c multicolored .65 .30
1104 A187 45c multicolored .65 .30
1105 A187 50c multicolored .65 .45
1106 A187 $1 multicolored 1.00 .65
1107 A187 $2 multicolored 1.25 1.25
1108 A187 $3 multicolored 2.00 2.00
1109 A187 $4 multicolored 2.50 *2.75*
Nos. 1102-1109 (8) 9.25 *7.95*

Souvenir Sheets

1110 A187 $5 multicolored 4.25 4.25
1111 A187 $5 multicolored 4.25 4.25

Sailing Week A188

1988, Apr. 18 *Perf. 15*

1112 A188 30c Canada I, 1980 .25 .25
1113 A188 60c Gretel II, Australia, 1970 .50 .45
1114 A188 $1 Sceptre, GB, 1958 .70 .60
1115 A188 $3 Vigilant, US, 1893 1.50 *2.25*
Nos. 1112-1115 (4) 2.95 *3.55*

Souvenir Sheet

1116 A188 $5 Australia II, 1983 3.50 3.50

Walt Disney Animated Characters and Epcot Center, Walt Disney World — A189

1988, May 3 *Perf. 14x13½, 13½x14*

1116A A189 1c like 25c .25 .25
1116B A189 2c like 30c .25 .25
1116C A189 3c like 40c .25 .25
1116D A189 4c like 60c .25 .25
1116E A189 5c like 70c .25 .25
1116F A189 10c like $1.50 .25 .25
1117 A189 25c The Living Seas .50 .25
1118 A189 30c World of Motion .50 .25
1119 A189 40c Spaceship Earth .60 .25
1120 A189 60c Universe of Energy .85 .35
1121 A189 70c Journey to Imagination .95 .40
1122 A189 $1.50 The Land 1.75 1.75
1123 A189 $3 Communicore 2.50 2.50
1124 A189 $4 Horizons 2.50 2.50
Nos. 1116A-1124 (14) 11.65 9.75

Souvenir Sheets

1125 A189 $5 Epcot Center 4.50 4.50
1126 A189 $5 The Contemporary Resort Hotel 4.50 4.50

30c, 40c, $1.50, $3 and No. 1126 are vert.

Flowering Trees — A190

1988, May 16 *Perf. 14*

1127 A190 10c Jacaranda .30 .25
1128 A190 30c Cordia .35 .25
1129 A190 50c Orchid tree .50 .40
1130 A190 90c Flamboyant .60 .50
1131 A190 $1 African tulip tree .75 .60
1132 A190 $2 Potato tree 1.40 1.40
1133 A190 $3 Crepe myrtle 1.75 *2.00*
1134 A190 $4 Pitch apple 2.00 *2.50*
Nos. 1127-1134 (8) 7.65 *7.90*

Souvenir Sheets

1135 A190 $5 Cassia 3.75 *4.00*
1136 A190 $5 Chinaberry 3.75 *4.00*

Nos. 1135-1136 are continuous designs.

Nos. 1011-1012, 1014 and 1013 Ovptd. in Black for Philatelic Exhibitions

a

b

c

d

1988, May 9 Litho. *Perf. 14*
1137 A173 (a) $2 multi 8.50 8.50
1138 A173 (b) $3 multi 9.00 9.00

Souvenir Sheets

1139 A173 (c) $5 multi 15.00 15.00
1139A A172 (d) $5 multi 15.00 15.00

1988 Summer Olympics, Seoul A192

1988, June 10
1140 A192 40c Gymnastic rings, vert. .40 .30
1141 A192 60c Weight lifting, vert. .45 .30
1142 A192 $1 Water polo .90 .45
1143 A192 $3 Boxing 1.75 *2.25*
Nos. 1140-1143 (4) 3.50 *3.30*

Souvenir Sheet

1144 A192 $5 Torch-bearer, vert. 3.75 3.75

Butterflies A193

1c, Monarch. 2c, Jamaican clearwing. 3c, Yellow-barred ringlet. 5c, Cracker. 10c,Jamaican mestra. 15c, Mimic. 20c, Silver spot. 25c, Zebra. 30c, Fiery sulphur. 40c, Androgeus swallowtail. 45c, Giant brimstone. 50c, Orbed sulphur. 60c, Blue-backed skipper. $1, Common white skipper. $2, Baracoa skipper. $2.50, Mangrove skipper. $5, Silver king. $10, Pygmy skipper. $20, Parides lycimenes.

1988-90 Litho. *Perf. 14*
1145 A193 1c multi .50 *.90*
1146 A193 2c multi .65 *.90*
1147 A193 3c multi .65 *.90*
1148 A193 5c multi .80 *.90*
1149 A193 10c multi .95 .35
1150 A193 15c multi 1.25 .35
1151 A193 20c multi 1.40 .35
1152 A193 25c multi 1.40 .35
1153 A193 30c multi 1.40 .35
1154 A193 40c multi 1.40 .35
1155 A193 45c multi 1.40 .35
1156 A193 50c multi 1.50 .45
1157 A193 60c multi 1.60 .60
1158 A193 $1 multi 2.00 1.00
1159 A193 $2 multi 3.00 3.00
1160 A193 $2.50 multi 4.00 4.00
1161 A193 $5 multi 5.00 5.00
1161A A193 $10 multi 7.00 *11.00*
1162 A193 $20 multi 18.00 *20.00*
Nos. 1145-1162 (19) 53.90 *51.10*

Issued: $20, Feb. 19, 1990; others, Aug. 29.

John F. Kennedy A194

1988, Nov. 22 Litho. *Perf. 14*
1162A A194 1c like 30c .25 .25
1162B A194 2c like $4 .25 .25
1162C A194 3c like $1 .25 .25
1162D A194 4c like 60c .25 .25
1163 A194 30c First family .40 .25
1164 A194 60c Motorcade, Mexico .80 .40
1165 A194 $1 Funeral procession .90 .65
1166 A194 $4 Aboard PT109 2.50 2.50
Nos. 1162A-1166 (8) 5.60 4.80

Souvenir Sheet

1167 A194 $5 Taking Oath of Office 4.25 4.25

Miniature Sheet

Christmas, Mickey Mouse 60th Anniv. — A195

Walt Disney characters: No. 1168: a, Morty and Ferdie. b, Goofy. c, Chip-n-Dale. d, Huey and Dewey. e, Minnie Mouse. f, Pluto. g, Mickey Mouse. h, Donald Duck and Louie.

No. 1169, Goofy driving Mickey and Minnie in a horse-drawn carriage. No. 1170, Characters on roller skates, caroling.

1988, Dec. 1 *Perf. 13½x14, 14x13½*
1168 A195 Sheet of 8 9.50 9.50
a.-h. $1 any single 1.00 1.00

Souvenir Sheets

1169 A195 $7 multicolored 5.75 5.75
1170 A195 $7 multi, horiz. 5.75 5.75

1988, Dec. 1 Litho. *Perf. 14*
1171 A195 10c like No. 1168e .25 .25
1172 A195 25c like No. 1168f .25 .25
1173 A195 30c like No. 1168g .30 .30
1174 A195 70c like No. 1168h .70 .70
Nos. 1171-1174 (4) 1.50 1.50

Arawak Indian Whip Dance — A196

UPAE and discovery of America emblems and: a, Five adults. b, Eight adults. c, Seven adults. d, Three adults, three children.

1989, May 16 Litho. *Perf. 14*
1175 Strip of 4 5.50 5.50
a.-d. A196 $1.50 any single 1.00 1.00

Souvenir Sheet

1176 A196 $6 Arawak chief 4.50 4.50

Discovery of America 500th anniv. (in 1992), pre-Columbian societies and customs.

Jet Flight, 50th Anniv. A197

Various jet aircraft.

1989, May 29 Litho. *Perf. 14x13½*
1177 A197 10c DeHavilland Comet 4 1.00 .35
1178 A197 30c Messerschmitt Me262 1.50 .35
1179 A197 40c Boeing 707 1.50 .35
1180 A197 60c Canadair F-86 Sabre 1.75 .50
1181 A197 $1 Lockheed F-104 Starfighter 1.90 .75
1182 A197 $2 McDonnell Douglas DC-10 2.75 2.75
1183 A197 $3 Boeing 747 3.00 *3.25*
1184 A197 $4 McDonnell F-4 Phantom 3.00 *3.25*
Nos. 1177-1184 (8) 16.40 *11.55*

Souvenir Sheets

1185 A197 $7 Grumman F-14 Tomcat 6.00 6.00
1186 A197 $7 Concorde 6.00 6.00

Caribbean Cruise Ships A198

1989, June 20 Litho. *Perf. 14*
1187 A198 25c TSS Festivale 1.30 .35
1188 A198 45c M.S. Southward 1.50 .35
1189 A198 50c M.S. Sagafjord 1.50 .35
1190 A198 60c MTS Daphne 1.50 .40
1191 A198 75c M.V. Cunard Countess 1.75 .90
1192 A198 90c M.S. Song of America 2.00 1.00
1193 A198 $3 M.S. Island Princess 4.00 *5.00*
1194 A198 $4 S.S. Galileo 4.00 *5.50*
Nos. 1187-1194 (8) 17.55 *13.85*

Souvenir Sheets

1195 A198 $6 S.S. Norway 5.00 *5.50*
1196 A198 $6 S.S. Oceanic 5.00 *5.50*

Paintings by Hiroshige — A199

Designs: 25c, *Fish Swimming by Duck Half-submerged in Stream.* 45c, *Crane and Wave.* 50c, *Sparrows and Morning Glories.* 60c, *Crested Blackbird and Flowering Cherry.* $1, *Great Knot Sitting among Water Grass.* $2, *Goose on a Bank of Water.* $3, *Black Paradise Flycatcher and Blossoms.* $4, *Sleepy Owl Perched on a Pine Branch.* No. 1205, *Bullfinch Flying Near a Clematis Branch.* No. 1206, *Titmouse on a Cherry Branch.*

1989, July 3 *Perf. 14x13½*
1197 A199 25c multicolored .90 .30
1198 A199 45c multicolored 1.10 .40
1199 A199 50c multicolored 1.25 .40
1200 A199 60c multicolored 1.25 .50
1201 A199 $1 multicolored 1.60 .65
1202 A199 $2 multicolored 2.50 2.50
1203 A199 $3 multicolored 3.00 3.00
1204 A199 $4 multicolored 3.00 3.00
Nos. 1197-1204 (8) 14.60 10.75

Souvenir Sheets

1205 A199 $5 multicolored 6.00 6.00
1206 A199 $5 multicolored 6.00 6.00

Hirohito (1901-1989) and enthronement of Akihito as emperor of Japan.

PHILEXFRANCE '89 — A200

Walt Disney characters, French landmarks: 1c, Helicopter over the Seine. 2c, Arc de Triomphe. 3c, Painting Notre Dame Cathedral. 4c, Entrance to the Metro. 5c, Fashion show. 10c, Follies. No. 1213, Shopping stalls on the Seine. $6, Sidewalk cafe, Left Bank. No. 1215, Hot air balloon *Ear Force One.* No. 1216, Dining.

1989, July 7 *Perf. 14x13½*
1207 A200 1c multicolored .25 .25
1208 A200 2c multicolored .25 .25
1209 A200 3c multicolored .25 .25
1210 A200 4c multicolored .25 .25
1211 A200 5c multicolored .25 .25
1212 A200 10c multicolored .25 .25
1213 A200 $5 multicolored 8.50 8.50
1214 A200 $6 multicolored 8.50 8.50
Nos. 1207-1214 (8) 18.50 18.50

Souvenir Sheets

1215 A200 $5 multicolored 7.00 7.00
1216 A200 $5 multicolored 7.00 7.00

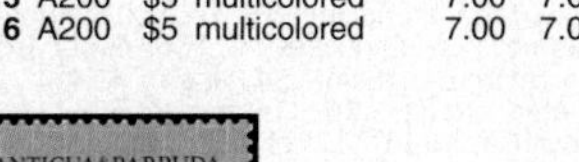

1990 World Cup Soccer Championships, Italy — A201

Natl. flag, various actions of a defending goalie.

1989, Aug. 21 *Perf. 14*
1217 A201 15c multicolored .90 .25
1218 A201 25c multicolored 1.00 .25
1219 A201 $1 multicolored 1.50 1.00
1220 A201 $4 multicolored 2.50 *4.25*
Nos. 1217-1220 (4) 5.90 *5.75*

Souvenir Sheets

1221 A201 $5 2 players, horiz. 4.25 4.25
1222 A201 $5 3 players, horiz. 4.25 4.25

For overprints see Nos. 1344-1349.

Mushrooms — A202

1989, Oct. 12 Litho. *Perf. 14*
1223 A202 10c Lilac fairy helmet .85 .35
1224 A202 25c Rough psathyrella, vert. 1.25 .30
1225 A202 50c Golden tops 1.75 .50
1226 A202 60c Blue cap, vert. 1.75 .60
1227 A202 75c Brown cap, vert. 2.00 1.10
1228 A202 $1 Green gill, vert. 2.00 1.25
1229 A202 $3 Red pinwheel 3.25 *3.75*
1230 A202 $4 Red chanterelle 3.25 *3.75*
Nos. 1223-1230 (8) 16.10 11.60

Souvenir Sheets

1231 A202 $6 Slender stalk 8.50 8.50
1232 A202 $6 Paddy straw mushroom 8.50 8.50

Nos. 1224, 1226-1228, 1231 vert.

Wildlife A203

1989, Oct. 19 Litho. *Perf. 14*
1233 A203 25c Hutia .80 .35
1234 A203 45c Caribbean monk seal 2.50 .75
1235 A203 60c Mustache bat, vert. 1.50 .75
1236 A203 $4 Manatee, vert. 3.50 *4.25*
Nos. 1233-1236 (4) 8.30 *6.10*

Souvenir Sheet

1237 A203 $5 West Indies giant rice rat 8.50 8.50

American Philatelic Soc. Emblem, Stamps on Stamps and Walt Disney Characters Promoting Philately
A204

Designs: 1c, Israel #150, printing press. 2c, Italy #1238, first day cancel. 3c, US #143L4, Pony Express recruits. 4c, Denmark #566, early radio broadcast. 5c, German Democratic Republic #702, television. 10c, Great Britain #1, stamp collector. $4, Japan #1414, integrated circuits. $6, Germany #B667, boom box. No. 1246, US #1355, C3a, and Jenny biplane over Disneyland, horiz. No. 1247, US #940, 1421 and stamps for the wounded.

1989, Nov. 2 ***Perf. 13½x14, 14x13½***

1238 A204 1c multicolored .25 .25
1239 A204 2c multicolored .25 .25
1240 A204 3c multicolored .25 .25
1241 A204 4c multicolored .25 .25
1242 A204 5c multicolored .25 .25
1243 A204 10c multicolored .25 .25
1244 A204 $4 multicolored 4.50 4.50
1245 A204 $6 multicolored 5.50 5.50
Nos. 1238-1245 (8) 11.50 11.50

Souvenir Sheets

1246 A204 $5 multicolored 6.50 6.50
1247 A204 $5 multicolored 6.50 6.50

Locomotives and Walt Disney Characters — A205

Perf. 14x13½, 13½x14

1989, Nov. 17

1248 A205 25c John Bull, 1831 1.00 .40
1249 A205 45c Atlantic, 1832 1.10 .40
1250 A205 50c William Crook's, 1861 1.10 .40
1251 A205 60c Minnetonka, 1869 1.10 .60
1252 A205 $1 Thatcher Perkins, 1863 1.40 .75
1253 A205 $2 Pioneer, 1848 2.00 2.00
1254 A205 $3 Peppersass, 1869 2.50 *3.00*
1255 A205 $4 Gimbels Flyer 2.75 *3.00*
Nos. 1248-1255 (8) 12.95 10.55

Souvenir Sheets

1256 A205 $6 #6100 Class S-1 & 1835 Thomas Jefferson 6.50 6.50
1257 A205 $6 Jupiter & #119 6.50 6.50

New York World's Fair, 50th anniv., and World Stamp Expo '89, Washington, DC.

1st Moon Landing, 20th Anniv.
A206

1989, Nov. 24 **Litho.** ***Perf. 14***

1258 A206 10c Apollo 11 liftoff .60 .25
1259 A206 45c Aldrin walking on Moon 1.50 .25
1260 A206 $1 Eagle ascending from Moon 1.75 .85
1261 A206 $4 Recovery after splashdown 2.75 *3.75*
Nos. 1258-1261 (4) 6.60 *5.10*

Souvenir Sheet

1262 A206 $5 Armstrong 6.25 6.25

Nos. 1258-1259 and 1262, vert.

Souvenir Sheet

Smithsonian Institution, Washington, DC — A207

1989, Nov. 17 **Litho.** ***Perf. 14***

1263 A207 $4 multicolored 3.75 3.75

World Stamp Expo '89.

Christmas — A208

Religious paintings: 10c, *The Small Cowper Madonna*. 25c, *Madonna of the Goldfinch*. 30c, *The Alba Madonna*. 50c, *Bologna Altarpiece* (attendant). 60c, *Bologna Altarpiece* (heralding angel). 70c, *Bologna Altarpiece* (archangel). $4, *Bologna Altarpiece* (saint holding ledger). No. 1271, *Madonna of Foligno*. No. 1272, *The Marriage of the Virgin*. No. 1273, *Bologna Altarpiece* (Madonna and Child).

Bologna Altarpiece by Giotto. Other paintings by Raphael.

1989, Dec. 11 **Litho.** ***Perf. 14***

1264 A208 10c multicolored .35 .25
1265 A208 25c multicolored .45 .25
1266 A208 30c multicolored .45 .25
1267 A208 50c multicolored .70 .40
1268 A208 60c multicolored .75 .45
1269 A208 70c multicolored .85 .50
1270 A208 $4 multicolored 3.00 *3.50*
1271 A208 $5 multicolored 3.00 *4.25*
Nos. 1264-1271 (8) 9.55 *9.85*

Souvenir Sheets

1272 A208 $5 multicolored 5.50 5.50
1273 A208 $5 multicolored 5.50 5.50

America Issue — A210

UPAE, discovery of America 500th anniv. emblems and marine life: 10c, Star-eyed hermit crab. 20c, Spiny lobster. 25c, Magnificent banded fanworm. 45c, Cannonball jellyfish. 60c, Red-spiny sea star. $2, Peppermint shrimp. $3, Coral crab. $4, Branching fire coral. No. 1283, Common sea fan. No. 1284, Portuguese man-of-war.

1990, Mar. 26 **Litho.** ***Perf. 14***

1275 A210 10c multicolored .50 .25
1276 A210 20c multicolored .75 .25
1277 A210 25c multicolored .80 .25
1278 A210 45c multicolored 1.00 .30
1279 A210 60c multicolored 1.25 .50
1280 A210 $2 multicolored 2.00 2.00
1281 A210 $3 multicolored 2.25 *3.00*
1282 A210 $4 multicolored 2.25 *3.00*
Nos. 1275-1282 (8) 10.80 *9.55*

Souvenir Sheets

1283 A210 $5 multicolored 4.75 4.75
1284 A210 $5 multicolored 4.75 4.75

Orchids — A211

No. 1285, Vanilla mexicana. No. 1286, Epidendrum ibaguense. No. 1287, Epidendrum secundum. No. 1288, Maxillaria conferta. No. 1289, Oncidium altissimum. No. 1290, Spiranthes lanceolata. No. 1291, Tonopsis utricularioides. No. 1292, Epidendrum nocturnum.

No. 1293, Octomeria graminifolia. No. 1294, Rodriguezia lanceolata.

1990, Apr. 17 ***Perf. 14***

1285 A211 15c multicolored .90 .35
1286 A211 45c multicolored 1.25 .35
1287 A211 50c multicolored 1.40 .40
1288 A211 60c multicolored 1.50 .40
1289 A211 $1 multicolored 1.60 .85
1290 A211 $2 multicolored 2.00 2.00
1291 A211 $3 multicolored 2.50 2.50
1292 A211 $5 multicolored 3.25 *3.75*
Nos. 1285-1292 (8) 14.40 10.60

Souvenir Sheets

1293 A211 $6 multicolored 4.50 4.50
1294 A211 $6 multicolored 4.50 4.50

EXPO '90, Osaka.

Fish
A212

1990, May 21 ***Perf. 14***

1295 A212 10c Flamefish .80 .45
1296 A212 15c Coney 1.10 .45
1297 A212 50c Squirrelfish 1.50 .55
1298 A212 60c Sergeant major 1.60 .55
1299 A212 $1 Yellowtail snapper 1.75 .75
1300 A212 $2 Rock beauty 2.50 2.50
1301 A212 $3 Spanish hogfish 3.00 3.00
1302 A212 $4 Striped parrotfish 3.25 3.25
Nos. 1295-1302 (8) 15.50 11.50

Souvenir sheets

1303 A212 $5 Blackbar soldierfish 6.75 6.75
1304 A212 $5 Foureye butterflyfish 6.75 6.75

Victoria and Elizabeth II — A213

1990, May 3 **Litho.** ***Perf. 15x14***

1305 A213 45c green 1.00 .30
1306 A213 60c bright rose 1.40 .50
1307 A213 $5 bright ultra 4.25 *4.75*
Nos. 1305-1307 (3) 6.65 5.55

Souvenir Sheet

1308 A213 $6 black 5.50 5.50

Penny Black, 150th anniv.

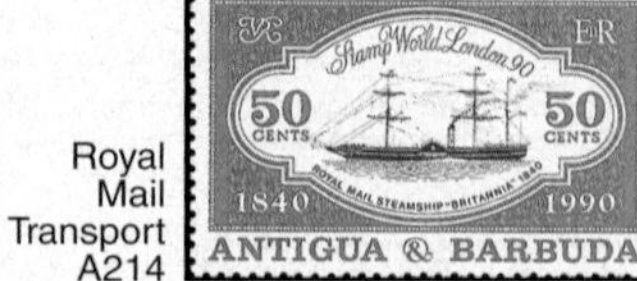

Royal Mail Transport
A214

Designs: 50c, Steam packet *Britannia*, 1840. 75c, Railway mail car, 1892. $4, *Centaurus* seaplane, 1938. $6, Subway, 1927.

1990, May 3 ***Perf. 13½***

1309 A214 50c red & deep green 1.25 .30
1310 A214 75c red & vio brn 1.50 1.00
1311 A214 $4 red & brt ultra 4.00 *5.00*
Nos. 1309-1311 (3) 6.75 6.30

Souvenir Sheet

1312 A214 $6 red & black 5.50 5.50

Stamp World London '90.

Miniature Sheet

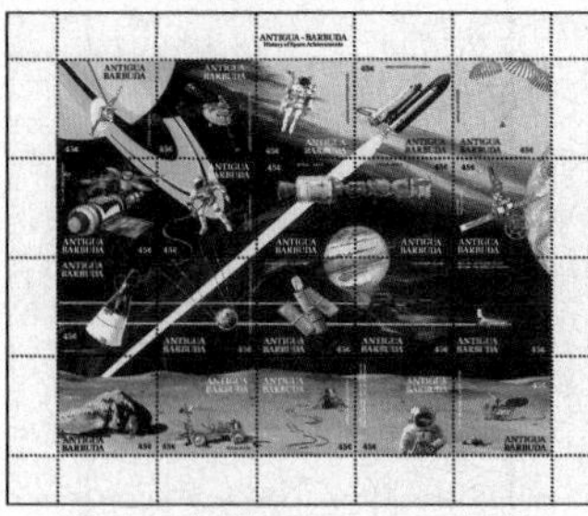

Space Achievements — A215

Designs: a, *Voyager 2* passing Saturn. b, *Pioneer 11* photographing Saturn. c, Manned maneuvering unit. d, *Columbia* space shuttle. e, Splashdown of Apollo 10 command module. f, *Skylab*. g, Ed White space walking, Gemini 4 mission. h, Apollo module, Apollo-Soyuz mission. i, Soyuz module, Apollo-Soyuz mission. j, *Mariner 1* passing Venus. k, Gemini 4 module. l, *Sputnik*. m, Hubble Space Telescope. n, X-15 rocket plane. o, Bell X-1 breaking sound barrier. p, Astronaut, Apollo 17 mission. r, American lunar rover. r, Lunar module, Apollo 14 mission. s, First men on the Moon, Apollo 11 mission. t, Lunokhod, Soviet lunar rover.

1990, June 11 **Litho.** ***Perf. 14***

1313 A215 Sheet of 20 16.00 16.00
a.-t. 45c any single .75 .75

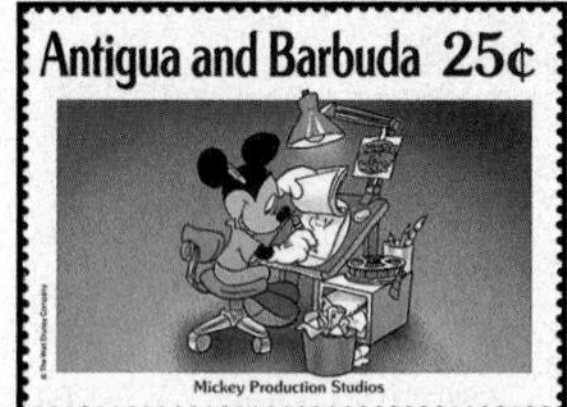

Mickey Production Studios — A216

Walt Disney characters in Hollywood: 45c, Minnie Mouse reading script. 50c, Director Mickey Mouse, take 1 of Minnie. 60c, Make-up artist Daisy Duck. $1, Clarabelle as Cleopatra. $2, Mickey, Goofy, Donald Duck. $3, Goofy destroying set. $4, Mickey, Donald editing film. No. 1322, Mickey directs surfing film. No. 1323, Minnie, Daisy, Clarabelle in musical.

1990, Sept. 3 **Litho.** ***Perf. 14x13½***

1314 A216 25c shown .80 .25
1315 A216 45c multicolored .90 .25
1316 A216 50c multicolored 1.00 .25
1317 A216 60c multicolored 1.25 .30
1318 A216 $1 multicolored 1.40 .60
1319 A216 $2 multicolored 1.75 1.75
1320 A216 $3 multicolored 2.25 2.25
1321 A216 $4 multicolored 2.25 2.25
Nos. 1314-1321 (8) 11.60 7.90

Souvenir Sheets

1322 A216 $5 multicolored 4.75 4.75
1323 A216 $5 multicolored 4.75 4.75

A217

1990, Aug. 27 Litho. *Perf. 14*
1324 A217 15c multicolored .50 .25
1325 A217 35c multi, diff. .75 .25
1326 A217 75c multi, diff. 1.25 .65
1327 A217 $3 multi, diff. 2.25 *3.00*
Nos. 1324-1327 (4) 4.75 4.15

Souvenir Sheet

1328 A217 $6 multi, diff. 5.50 5.50

Queen Mother, 90th birthday.

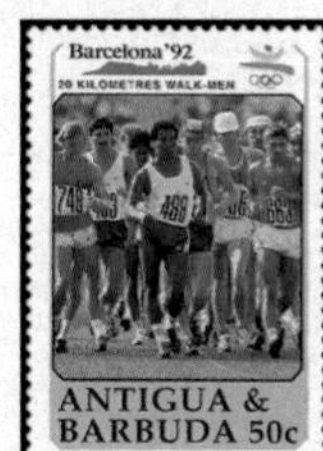

A218

No. 1329, 20-Kilometer Walk. No. 1330, Triple jump. No. 1331, 10,000 meter run. No. 1332, Javelin.

No. 1333, Opening ceremony, Los Angeles, 1984.

1990, Oct. 1 Litho. *Perf. 14*
1329 A218 50c multicolored 1.00 .30
1330 A218 75c multicolored 1.25 .60
1331 A218 $1 multicolored 1.50 .70
1332 A218 $5 multicolored 3.75 *4.50*
Nos. 1329-1332 (4) 7.50 6.10

Souvenir Sheet

1333 A218 $6 multicolored 6.50 6.50

1992 Summer Olympics, Barcelona.

Intl. Literacy Year — A219

Walt Disney characters in scenes from books by Charles Dickens: 15c, Huey and Dewey, Christmas Stories. 45c, Donald Duck, Bleak House. 50c, Dewey, Bad Pete, Oliver Twist. 60c, Daisy Duck, Old Curiosity Shop. $1, Little Nell. $2, Scrooge McDuck, Pickwick Papers. $3, Mickey and Minnie Mouse, Dombey and Son. $5, Minnie, Our Mutual Friend. No. 1342, Mickey and friends, David Copperfield. No. 1343, Pinocchio, Oliver Twist.

1990, Oct. 15 Litho. *Perf. 14*
1334 A219 15c multicolored .75 .25
1335 A219 45c multicolored 1.00 .35
1336 A219 50c multicolored 1.10 .40
1337 A219 60c multicolored 1.25 .45
1338 A219 $1 multicolored 1.50 .70
1339 A219 $2 multicolored 2.00 2.00
1340 A219 $3 multicolored 2.25 2.25
1341 A219 $5 multicolored 3.00 *3.50*
Nos. 1334-1341 (8) 12.85 9.90

Souvenir Sheets

1342 A219 $6 multicolored 6.50 6.50
1343 A219 $6 multicolored 6.50 6.50

Nos. 1217-1222 Overprinted

1990, Nov. 11
1344 A201 15c multicolored .85 .30
1345 A201 25c multicolored .85 .30
1346 A201 $1 multicolored 2.00 1.50
1347 A201 $4 multicolored 3.75 4.25
Nos. 1344-1347 (4) 7.45 6.35

Souvenir Sheets

1348 A201 $5 on #1221 6.00 6.00
1349 A201 $5 on #1222 6.00 6.00

Overprint on Nos. 1348-1349 is 32x13mm.

Birds A220

1990, Nov. 19
1350 A220 10c Pearly-eyed thrasher .50 .35
1351 A220 25c Purple-throated carib .60 .40
1352 A220 50c Common yellowthroat .70 .45
1353 A220 60c American kestrel 1.10 .75
1354 A220 $1 Yellow-bellied sapsucker 1.25 .80
1355 A220 $2 Purple gallinule 2.25 2.25
1356 A220 $3 Yellow-crowned night heron 2.50 2.50
1357 A220 $4 Blue-hooded euphonia 2.75 2.75
Nos. 1350-1357 (8) 11.65 10.25

Souvenir Sheets

1358 A220 $6 Brown pelican 8.00 8.00
1359 A220 $6 Frigate bird 8.00 8.00

Christmas — A221

Paintings: 25c, Madonna and Child with Saints by del Piombo. 30c, Virgin and Child with Angels by Grunewald, vert. 40c, Holy Family and a Shepherd by Titian. 60c, Virgin and Child by Fra Filippo Lippi, vert. $1, Jesus, St. John and Two Angels by Rubens. $2, Adoration of the Shepherds by Catena. $4, Adoration of the Magi by Giorgione. $5, Virgin and Child Adored by a Warrior by Catena. No. 1368, Allegory of the Blessings of Jacob by Rubens, vert. No. 1369, Adoration of the Magi by Fra Angelico, vert.

Perf. 14x13½, 13½x14

1990, Dec. 10 Litho.
1360 A221 25c multicolored .85 .40
1361 A221 30c multicolored .85 .40
1362 A221 40c multicolored 1.00 .45
1363 A221 60c multicolored 1.25 .50
1364 A221 $1 multicolored 1.50 1.00
1365 A221 $2 multicolored 2.25 2.25
1366 A221 $4 multicolored 3.50 3.50
1367 A221 $5 multicolored 3.50 3.50
Nos. 1360-1367 (8) 14.70 12.00

Souvenir Sheets

1368 A221 $6 multicolored 4.50 4.50
1369 A221 $6 multicolored 4.50 4.50

Peter Paul Rubens (1577-1640), Painter — A222

Entire paintings or different details from: 25c, Rape of the Daughters of Leucippus. 45c, $2, $4, Bacchanal. 50c, $1, $3, Rape of the Sabine Women. 60c, Battle of the Amazons. No. 1378, Rape of Hippodameia. No. 1379, Battle of the Amazons.

1991, Jan. 21 Litho. *Perf. 14*
1370 A222 25c multicolored 1.00 .30
1371 A222 45c multicolored 1.25 .45
1372 A222 50c multicolored 1.25 .50
1373 A222 60c multicolored 1.50 .65
1374 A222 $1 multicolored 1.75 1.00
1375 A222 $2 multicolored 2.00 *2.25*
1376 A222 $3 multicolored 2.50 *3.00*
1377 A222 $4 multicolored 2.75 *3.50*
Nos. 1370-1377 (8) 14.00 11.65

Souvenir Sheets

1378 A222 $6 multicolored 4.75 4.75
1379 A222 $6 multicolored 4.75 4.75

World War II Milestones A223

Designs: 10c, US troops enter Germany, Sept. 11, 1944. 15c, All axis forces surrender in North Africa, May 12, 1943. 25c, US troops invade Kwajalein, Jan. 31, 1944. 45c, Roosevelt and Churchill meet in Casablanca, Jan. 14, 1943. 50c, Marshal Badoglio signs agreement with allies, Sept. 1, 1943. $1, Mountbatten appointed Supreme Allied Commander, Southeast Asia Command, Aug. 25, 1943. $2, Major Greek tactical victory, Koritza, Nov. 22, 1940. $4, Britain and USSR sign mutual assistance pact, July 12, 1941. $5, Operation Torch, Nov. 8, 1942. No. 1389, Japanese attack on Pearl Harbor, Dec. 7, 1941. No. 1390, American bombing attack on Schweinfurt, Oct. 14, 1943.

1991, Mar. 11 Litho. *Perf. 14*
1380 A223 10c multicolored 1.10 .60
1381 A223 15c multicolored 1.25 .50
1382 A223 25c multicolored 1.25 .50
1383 A223 45c multicolored 2.50 .65
1384 A223 50c multicolored 1.50 .65
1385 A223 $1 multicolored 2.75 1.50
1386 A223 $2 multicolored 3.00 2.75
1387 A223 $4 multicolored 3.00 3.00
1388 A223 $5 multicolored 3.25 3.25
Nos. 1380-1388 (9) 19.60 13.40

Souvenir Sheets

1389 A223 $6 multicolored 6.75 6.75
1390 A223 $6 multicolored 6.75 6.75

Cog Railways of the World A224

Designs: 25c, Prince Regent, Middleton Colliery, 1812. 30c, Snowdon Mountain Railway, Wales. 40c, 1st Railcar at Hell Gate, Manitou and Pike's Peak Railway. 60c, PNKA Rack Railway, Amberawa, Java. $1, Green Mountain Railway, Mt. Desert Island, Maine, 1883. $2, Cog locomotive, Pike's Peak, 1891. $4, Vitznau-Rigi Cog Railway, Lake Lucerne. $5, Leopoldina Railway, Brazil. No. 1399, Electric Cog Donkey Engines, Panama Canal. No. 1400, Gornergratbahn, 1st electric cog railway in Switzerland, vert.

1991, Mar. 18 Litho. *Perf. 14*
1391 A224 25c multicolored 1.10 .35
1392 A224 30c multicolored 1.25 .35
1393 A224 40c multicolored 1.25 .45
1394 A224 60c multicolored 1.50 .50
1395 A224 $1 multicolored 2.00 .75
1396 A224 $2 multicolored 2.75 2.75
1397 A224 $4 multicolored 3.25 3.25
1398 A224 $5 multicolored 3.25 3.25
Nos. 1391-1398 (8) 16.35 11.65

Souvenir Sheets

1399 A224 $6 multicolored 7.50 7.50
1400 A224 $6 multicolored 7.50 7.50

Butterflies A225

1991, Apr. 15 Litho. *Perf. 14*
1401 A225 10c Zebra .70 .35
1402 A225 35c Southern daggertail 1.10 .35
1403 A225 50c Red anartia 1.25 .45
1404 A225 75c Malachite 1.50 .85
1405 A225 $1 Polydamas swallowtail 1.75 1.00
1406 A225 $2 Orion 2.25 2.25
1407 A225 $4 Mimic 3.00 3.00
1408 A225 $5 Cracker 3.00 *3.75*
Nos. 1401-1408 (8) 14.55 12.00

Souvenir Sheets

Caterpillars

1409 A225 $6 Monarch, vert. 8.00 8.00
1410 A225 $6 Painted lady, vert. 8.00 8.00

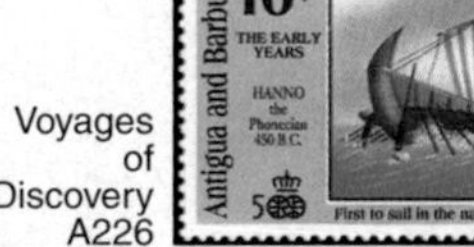

Voyages of Discovery A226

Designs: 10c, Hanno, Phoenicia, c. 450 B.C. 15c, Pytheas, Greece, 325 B.C. 45c, Eric the Red, Viking, A.D. 985. 60c, Leif Erikson, Viking, A.D. 1000. $1, Scylax, Greece, A.D. 518. $2, Marco Polo, A.D. 1259. $4, Queen Hatsheput, Egypt, 1493 B.C. $5, St. Brendan, Ireland, 500 A.D. No. 1419, Columbus, bareheaded. No. 1420, Columbus, wearing hat.

1991, Apr. 22
1411 A226 10c multicolored .85 .35
1412 A226 15c multicolored .95 .35
1413 A226 45c multicolored 1.25 .40
1414 A226 60c multicolored 1.50 .55
1415 A226 $1 multicolored 2.00 .90
1416 A226 $2 multicolored 2.25 2.25
1417 A226 $4 multicolored 3.00 3.00
1418 A226 $5 multicolored 3.00 *4.00*
Nos. 1411-1418 (8) 14.80 11.80

Souvenir Sheets

1419 A226 $6 multicolored 4.75 4.75
1420 A226 $6 multicolored 4.75 4.75

Discovery of America, 500th anniv. (in 1992).

Paintings by Vincent Van Gogh A227

Designs: 5c, Portrait of Camille Roulin. 10c, Portrait of Armand Roulin. 15c, Young Peasant Woman with Straw Hat Sitting in the Wheat. 25c, Portrait of Adeline Ravoux. 30c, The Schoolboy (Camille Roulin). 40c, Portrait of Doctor Gachet. 50c, Portrait of a Man. 75c, Two Children. $2, Portrait of Postman Joseph Roulin. $3, The Seated Zouave. $4, L'arlesienne: Madame Ginoux with Books. No. 1432, Self Portrait, November/December 1888. No. 1433, Flowering Garden. No. 1434, Farmhouse in Provence. $6, The Bridge at Trinquetaille.

1991, May 13 *Perf. 13½*
1421 A227 5c multicolored .60 .75
1422 A227 10c multicolored .60 .55
1423 A227 15c multicolored .70 .45
1424 A227 25c multicolored .80 .45
1425 A227 30c multicolored .80 .45
1426 A227 40c multicolored .90 .45
1427 A227 50c multicolored 1.00 .45
1428 A227 75c multicolored 1.60 .75
1429 A227 $2 multicolored 2.50 2.50
1430 A227 $3 multicolored 3.00 2.75
1431 A227 $4 multicolored 3.50 3.50
1432 A227 $5 multicolored 3.50 3.50
Nos. 1421-1432 (12) 19.50 16.55

Size: 102x76mm

Imperf

1433 A227 $5 multicolored 5.00 5.00
1434 A227 $5 multicolored 5.00 5.00
1435 A227 $6 multicolored 6.00 6.00

Phila Nippon '91 — A228

Walt Disney characters demonstrating Japanese martial arts: 10c, Mickey as champion sumo wrestler, vert. 15c, Goofy using tonfa.

45c, Ninja Donald in full field dress. 60c, Mickey using weapon in kung fu, vert. $1, Goofy tries kendo, vert. $2, Mickey, Donald demonstrating special technique of aikido. $4, Mickey flips Donald with judo throw. $5, Mickey demonstrates yabusame (target shooting from running horse), vert. No. 1444, Mickey using karate. No. 1445, Mickey demonstrating tamashiwara (powerbreaking), vert.

Perf. 13½x14, 14x13½

1991, June 29 **Litho.**

1436 A220 10c multicolored .75 .25
1437 A228 15c multicolored .85 .25
1438 A228 45c multicolored 1.50 .45
1439 A220 60c multicolored 2.00 .60
1440 A228 $1 multicolored 2.50 1.25
1441 A220 $2 multicolored 3.00 3.00
1442 A220 $4 multicolored 4.00 4.00
1443 A228 $5 multicolored 4.00 4.00
Nos. 1436-1443 (8) 18.60 13.80

Souvenir Sheets

1444 A228 $6 multicolored 6.50 6.50
1445 A228 $6 multicolored 6.50 6.50

Royal Family Birthday, Anniversary

Common Design Type

1991, July 8 **Litho.** ***Perf. 14***

1446 CD347 10c multicolored .50 .25
1447 CD347 15c multicolored .35 .25
1448 CD347 20c multicolored .35 .25
1449 CD347 40c multicolored 1.00 .30
1450 CD347 $1 multicolored 1.25 .75
1451 CD347 $2 multicolored 1.75 1.75
1452 CD347 $4 multicolored 2.75 2.75
1453 CD347 $5 multicolored 4.50 4.50
Nos. 1446-1453 (8) 12.45 10.80

Souvenir Sheets

1454 CD347 $4 Elizabeth, Philip 3.75 3.75
1455 CD347 $4 Charles, Diana, sons 5.75 5.75

10c, 40c, $1, $5, No. 1455, Charles and Diana, 10th wedding anniversary. Others, Queen Elizabeth II, 65th birthday.

Walt Disney Characters Playing Golf — A229

Designs: 10c, Daisy Duck teeing off. 15c, Goofy using 3-Wood. 45c, Mickey using 3-Iron. 60c, Mickey missing ball using 6-Iron. $1, Donald trying 8-Iron to get out of pond. $2, Minnie using 9-Iron. $4, Donald digging hole with sand wedge. $5, Goofy trying new approach with putter. No. 1464, Grandma Duck using pitching wedge. No. 1465, Mickey cheering Minnie as she uses her 5-Wood, horiz.

Perf. 13½x14, 14x13½

1991, Aug. 7 **Litho.**

1456 A229 10c multicolored .75 .40
1457 A229 15c multicolored .85 .40
1458 A229 45c multicolored 1.25 .40
1459 A229 60c multicolored 1.75 .50
1460 A229 $1 multicolored 2.00 1.10
1461 A229 $2 multicolored 2.50 2.50
1462 A229 $4 multicolored 3.25 3.25
1463 A229 $5 multicolored 3.50 *4.00*
Nos. 1456-1463 (8) 15.85 12.55

Souvenir Sheets

1464 A229 $6 multicolored 6.50 6.50
1465 A229 $6 multicolored 6.50 6.50

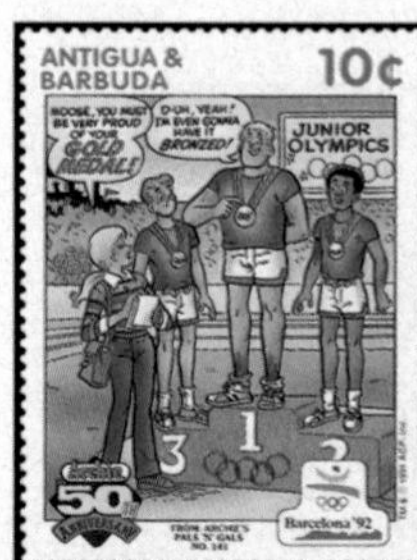

1992 Summer Olympics, Barcelona A230

Archie Comics, 50th anniv.: 10c, Moose receiving gold medal. 25c, Archie, Veronica, Mr. Lodge, polo match, horiz. 40c, Archie & Betty, fencing. 60c, Archie, women's volleyball. $1, Archie, tennis. $2, Archie, marathon race. $4, Archie, judging women's gymnastics, horiz. $5, Archie, Betty, Veronica, basketball. No. 1474, Archie, soccer. No. 1475, Archie, Betty, baseball, horiz.

Perf. 13½x14, 14x13½

1991, Aug. 19

1466 A230 10c multicolored .65 .30
1467 A230 25c multicolored 1.00 .30
1468 A230 40c multicolored 1.25 .35
1469 A230 60c multicolored 1.50 .45
1470 A230 $1 multicolored 1.75 1.00
1471 A230 $2 multicolored 2.50 2.50
1472 A230 $4 multicolored 3.75 3.75
1473 A230 $5 multicolored 4.00 *5.00*
Nos. 1466-1473 (8) 16.40 13.65

Souvenir Sheets

1474 A230 $6 multicolored 6.25 6.25
1475 A230 $6 multicolored 6.25 6.25

Charles de Gaulle, Birth Cent. A231

Charles de Gaulle: 10c, and Pres. Kennedy, families, 1961. 15c, and Pres. Roosevelt, 1945, vert. 45c, and Chancellor Adenauer, 1962, vert. 60c, Liberation of Paris, 1944, vert. $1, Crossing the Rhine, 1945. $2, In Algiers, 1944. $4, and Pres. Eisenhower, 1960. $5, Returning from Germany, 1968, vert. No. 1484, and Churchill at Casablanca, 1943. No. 1485, and Citizens.

1991, Sept. 11 **Litho.** ***Perf. 14***

1476 A231 10c multicolored .90 .35
1477 A231 15c multicolored 1.00 .35
1478 A231 45c multicolored 1.40 .40
1479 A231 60c multicolored 1.50 .50
1480 A231 $1 multicolored 1.75 .90
1481 A231 $2 multicolored 2.75 2.75
1482 A231 $4 multicolored 3.25 3.25
1483 A231 $5 multicolored 3.50 *4.00*
Nos. 1476-1483 (8) 16.05 12.50

Souvenir Sheets

1484 A231 $6 multicolored 6.50 6.50
1485 A231 $6 multicolored 6.50 6.50

Independence, 10th Anniv. — A232

Designs: 10c, Island maps, government building. $6, Old P. O., St. Johns, #1 & #635.

1991, Oct. 28

1486 A232 10c multicolored .85 .50

Souvenir Sheet

1487 A232 $6 multicolored 7.50 7.50

No. 1487 contains one 50x38mm stamp.

Miniature Sheet

Attack on Pearl Harbor, 50th Anniv. — A233

Designs: No. 1488a, Bow of Nimitz class carrier, Ticonderoga class cruiser. b, Tourist boat to Arizona Memorial. c, USS Arizona Memorial. d, Aircraft salute to missing men. e, White tern. f, Japanese Kate torpedo bombers. g, Japanese Zero fighters. h, Battleship row in flames. i, USS Nevada breaking out. j, Zeros returning to carriers.

1991, Dec. 9 ***Perf. 14½x15***

1488 A233 $1 Sheet of 10, #a.-j. 22.50 22.50

Inscription for No. 1488f incorrectly describes torpedo bombers as Zekes.

3rd Antigua Methodist Cub Scout Pack, 60th Anniv. A234

Designs: $2, Lord Robert Baden-Powell, scouts, vert. $3.50, Scouts around campfire. $5, Antigua & Barbuda flag, Jamboree emblem, vert.

1991, Dec. 9 ***Perf. 14***

1489 A234 75c multicolored 1.75 .90
1490 A234 $2 multicolored 6.50 5.50
1491 A234 $3.50 multicolored 5.50 5.50
Nos. 1489-1491 (3) 13.75 11.90

Souvenir Sheet

1492 A234 $5 multicolored 5.25 5.25

17th World Scout Jamboree, Korea.

Wolfgang Amadeus Mozart, Death Bicent. A235

Portrait of Mozart and: $1.50, Scene from opera, Don Giovanni. $4, St. Peter's Cathedral, Salzburg.

1991, Dec. 9

1493 A235 $1.50 multicolored 4.00 2.75
1494 A235 $4 multicolored 7.50 6.50

Anniversaries and Events — A236

Designs: $2, Otto Lilienthal's glider No. 5. $2.50, Locomotive cab, vert.

1991, Dec. 9 **Litho.** ***Perf. 14***

1495 A236 $2 multicolored 4.00 2.75
1496 A236 $2.50 multicolored 7.25 4.00

First glider flight, cent. (No. 1495). Trans-Siberian Railway, cent. (No. 1496). Numbers have been reserved for additional values in this set.

Brandenburg Gate, Bicent. — A237

25c, Demonstrators in autos, German flag. $2, Statue. $3, Portions of decorative frieze.

1991, Dec. 9 **Litho.** ***Perf. 14***

1499 A237 25c multicolored .25 .25
1500 A237 $2 multicolored 1.25 1.50
1501 A237 $3 multicolored 2.25 2.25
Nos. 1499-1501 (3) 3.75 4.00

Souvenir Sheet

1502 A237 $4 multicolored 5.25 5.25

Christmas A238

Paintings by Fra Angelico: 10c, The Annunciation. 30c, Nativity. 40c, Adoration of the Magi. 60c, Presentation in the Temple. $1, Circumcision. $3, Flight into Egypt. $4, Massacre of the Innocents. $5, Christ Teaching in the Temple. No. 1511, Adoration of the Magi, diff. No. 1512, Adoration of the Magi (Cook Tondo).

1991, Dec. 12 ***Perf. 12***

1503 A238 10c multicolored .40 .25
1504 A238 30c multicolored .65 .25
1505 A238 40c multicolored .80 .30
1506 A238 60c multicolored 1.00 .45
1507 A238 $1 multicolored 1.25 .75
1508 A238 $3 multicolored 2.50 2.50
1509 A238 $4 multicolored 2.75 2.75
1510 A238 $5 multicolored 3.00 *3.75*
Nos. 1503-1510 (8) 12.35 11.00

Souvenir Sheets

1511 A238 $6 multicolored 7.00 7.00
1512 A238 $6 multicolored 7.00 7.00

Queen Elizabeth II's Accession to the Throne, 40th Anniv.

Common Design Type

Queen Elizabeth II and various island scenes.

1992, Feb. 6 **Litho.** ***Perf. 14***

1513 CD348 10c multicolored .90 .30
1514 CD348 30c multicolored 1.10 .30
1515 CD348 $1 multicolored 1.25 .75
1516 CD348 $5 multicolored 2.75 2.75
Nos. 1513-1516 (4) 6.00 4.10

Souvenir Sheets

1517 CD348 $6 Beach 5.00 5.00
1518 CD348 $6 Flora 5.00 5.00

Mushrooms A239

1992 **Litho.** ***Perf. 14***

1519 A239 10c Amanita caesarea .75 .35
1520 A239 15c Collybia fusipes .90 .35
1521 A239 30c Boletus aereus 1.25 .35
1522 A239 40c Laccaria amethystina 1.25 .45
1523 A239 $1 Russula virescens 2.25 1.00
1524 A239 $2 Tricholoma auratum 3.00 3.00
1525 A239 $4 Calocybe gambosa 3.75 3.75
1526 A239 $5 Panus tigrinus 3.75 *4.25*
Nos. 1519-1526 (8) 16.90 13.50

Souvenir Sheet

1527 A239 $6 Auricularia auricula 7.50 7.50
1528 A239 $6 Clavariadelphus truncatus 7.50 7.50

Issued: 10c, 30c, $1, $5, No. 1528, May 18; others, Mar.

Disney Characters at Summer Olympics, Barcelona A240

Designs: 10c, Mickey presenting gold medal to mermaid for swimming. 15c, Dewey and Huey watching Louie in kayak. 30c, Uncle McScrooge, Donald yachting. 50c, Donald, horse trying water polo. $1, Big Pete weight lifting. $2, Donald, Goofy fencing. $4, Mickey, Donald playing volleyball. $5, Goofy vaulting over horse.

No. 1537, $6, Mickey playing basketball, horiz. No. 1538, $6, Minnie Mouse on uneven parallel bars, horiz. No. 1539, $6, Mickey, Goofy, and Donald judging Minnie's floor exercise, horiz. No. 1540, $6, Mickey running after soccer ball.

1992, Mar. 16 *Perf. 13*

1529	A240	10c multicolored	.65	.25
1530	A240	15c multicolored	.75	.25
1531	A240	30c multicolored	.95	.30
1532	A240	50c multicolored	1.50	.50
1533	A240	$1 multicolored	1.75	.85
1534	A240	$2 multicolored	2.75	2.75
1535	A240	$4 multicolored	3.50	3.50
1536	A240	$5 multicolored	3.50	3.50
		Nos. 1529-1536 (8)	15.35	11.90

Souvenir Sheets

1537-1540	A240	Set of 4	17.50	17.50

Dinosaurs A241

1992, Apr. 6 *Perf. 14*

1541	A241	10c Pteranodon	.70	.35
1542	A241	15c Brachiosaurus	.75	.35
1543	A241	30c Tyrannosaurus rex	.95	.35
1544	A241	50c Parasaurolophus	1.10	.45
1545	A241	$1 Deinonychus	1.50	.80
1546	A241	$2 Triceratops	2.25	2.25
1547	A241	$4 Protoceratops	2.50	2.50
1548	A241	$5 Stegosaurus	2.50	*4.00*
		Nos. 1541-1548 (8)	12.25	11.05

Souvenir Sheets

1549	A241	$6 Apatosaurus	5.50	5.50
1550	A241	$6 Allosaurus	5.50	5.50

Nos. 1541-1544 are vert.

Easter — A242

Paintings: 10c, Supper at Emmaus, by Caravaggio. 15c, The Vision of St. Peter, by Francisco de Zurbaran. 30c, $1, Christ Driving the Money Changers from the Temple, by Tiepolo (detail on $1). 40c, Martyrdom of St. Bartholomew (detail), by Jusepe de Ribera. $2, Crucifixion (detail), by Albrecht Altdorfer. $4, $5, The Deposition (diff. detail), by Fra Angelico. No. 1559, Crucifixion, by Albrecht Altdorfer, vert. No. 1560, The Last Supper, by Vicente Juan Masip.

1992 *Perf. 14x13½*

1551	A242	10c multicolored	.55	.25
1552	A242	15c multicolored	.75	.25
1553	A242	30c multicolored	1.00	.35
1554	A242	40c multicolored	1.25	.50
1555	A242	$1 multicolored	2.25	1.00
1556	A242	$2 multicolored	3.25	3.25
1557	A242	$4 multicolored	4.25	4.25
1558	A242	$5 multicolored	4.25	4.25
		Nos. 1551-1558 (8)	17.55	14.10

Souvenir Sheet

Perf. 13½x14

1559	A242	$6 multicolored	6.00	6.00
1560	A242	$6 multicolored	6.00	6.00

Spanish Art — A243

Designs: 10c, The Miracle at the Well, by Alonso Cano. 15c, The Poet Luis de Gongora y Argote, by Velazquez. 30c, The Painter Francisco Goya, by Vincente Lopez Portana. 40c, Maria de Las Nieves Michaela Fourdiniere, by Luis Paret y Alcazar. $1, Charles III Eating before His Court, by Paret y Alcazar, horiz. $2, A Rain Shower in Granada, by Antonio Munoz Degrain, horiz. $4, Sarah Bernhardt, by Santiago Rusinol y Prats. $5, The Hermitage Garden, by Joaquin Mir Trinxet. No. 1569, Olympus: Battle with the Giants, by Francisco Bayeu y Subias. No. 1570, The Ascent of Monsieur Boucle's Montgolfier Balloon in the Gardens of Aranjuez, by Antonio Carnicero.

1992, May 11

1561	A243	10c multicolored	.45	.25
1562	A243	15c multicolored	.65	.30
1563	A243	30c multicolored	.90	.35
1564	A243	40c multicolored	1.00	.50
1565	A243	$1 multicolored	1.60	.90
1566	A243	$2 multicolored	2.50	2.50
1567	A243	$4 multicolored	3.75	3.75
1568	A243	$5 multicolored	4.25	4.50

Size: 120x95mm

Imperf

1569	A243	$6 multicolored	7.50	7.50
1570	A243	$6 multicolored	7.50	7.50
		Nos. 1561-1570 (10)	30.10	28.05

Granada '92.

Discovery of America, 500th Anniv. A244

Designs: 15c, San Salvador Island. 30c, Martin Alonzo Pinzon, captain of Pinta. 40c, Columbus, signature, coat of arms. $1, Pinta. $2, Nina. $4, Santa Maria. No. 1577, Sea monster. No. 1578, Map, sailing ship.

1992, May 25 **Litho.** *Perf. 14*

1571	A244	15c multicolored	.35	.25
1572	A244	30c multicolored	.45	.25
1573	A244	40c multicolored	.60	.35
1574	A244	$1 multicolored	2.25	2.25
1575	A244	$2 multicolored	2.50	2.50
1576	A244	$4 multicolored	3.00	3.50
		Nos. 1571-1576 (6)	9.15	9.10

Souvenir Sheets

1577	A244	$6 multicolored	6.00	6.00
1578	A244	$6 multicolored	6.00	6.00

World Columbian Stamp Expo '92, Chicago.

Hummel Figurines — A245

Designs 15c, No. 1587a, $1.50, Boy sitting on rock pointing to flower in cap. 30c, No. 1587b, $1.50, Girl sitting on fence. 40c, No. 1587c, $1.50, Boy holding binoculars. 50c, No. 1587d, $1.50, Boy carrying umbrella. $1, No. 1588a, $1.50, Two boys looking up at direction marker. $2, No. 1588b, $1.50, Boy carrying basket on back, walking with stick. $4, No. 1588c, $1.50, Two girls, goat. $5, No. 1588d, $1.50, Boy carrying walking stick.

1993, Jan. 6 **Litho.** *Perf. 14*

1579	A245	15c multicolored	.40	.25
1580	A245	30c multicolored	.65	.25
1581	A245	40c multicolored	.80	.30
1582	A245	50c multicolored	.90	.40
1583	A245	$1 multicolored	1.50	.75
1584	A245	$2 multicolored	1.75	1.75
1585	A245	$4 multicolored	2.75	2.75
1586	A245	$5 multicolored	2.75	*3.75*
		Nos. 1579-1586 (8)	11.50	10.20

Souvenir Sheets

1587	A245	$1.50 Sheet of 4, #a.-d.	8.50	8.50
1588	A245	$1.50 Sheet of 4, #a.-d.	8.50	8.50

Hummingbirds and Flowers — A246

Designs: 10c, Antillean crested, wild plantain. 25c, Green mango, parrot's plantain. 45c, Purple-throated carib, lobster claws. 60c, Antillean mango, coral plant. $1, Vervain, cardinal's guard. $2, Rufous breasted hermit, heliconia. $4, Blue-headed, red ginger. $5, Green-throated carib, ornamental banana. No. 1597, Bee, jungle flame. No. 1598, Western streamertails, bignonia.

1992, Aug. 10 **Litho.** *Perf. 14*

1589	A246	10c multicolored	.45	.45
1590	A246	25c multicolored	.60	.30
1591	A246	45c multicolored	.80	.35
1592	A246	60c multicolored	.90	.45
1593	A246	$1 multicolored	1.25	.75
1594	A246	$2 multicolored	2.00	2.00
1595	A246	$4 multicolored	3.25	3.25
1596	A246	$5 multicolored	3.50	3.50
		Nos. 1589-1596 (8)	12.75	11.05

Souvenir Sheets

1597	A246	$6 multicolored	6.50	6.50
1598	A246	$6 multicolored	6.50	6.50

Genoa '92.

Discovery of America, 500th Anniv. — A247

1992 **Litho.** *Perf. 14½*

1599	A247	$1 Coming ashore	1.10	.75
1600	A247	$2 Natives, ships	1.90	1.90

Organization of East Caribbean States.

Souvenir Sheet

Madison Square Garden, NYC — A248

1992 **Litho.** *Perf. 14*

1601	A248	$6 multicolored	5.50	5.50

Postage Stamp Mega-Event, Jacob Javits Center, New York City.

Elvis Presley (1935-1977) A249

Various pictures of Elvis Presley.

1992 *Perf. 13½x14*

1602	A249	$1 Sheet of 9, #a.-i.	15.00	15.00

Inventors and Pioneers A250

Designs: 10c, Ts'ai Lun, paper. 25c, Igor I. Sikorsky, 4-engine airplane. 30c, Alexander Graham Bell, telephone. 40c, Johannes Gutenberg, printing press. 60c, James Watt, steam engine. $1, Anton van Leeuwenhoek, microscope. $4, Louis Braille, Braille printing. $5, Galileo, telescope. No. 1607, Phonograph. No. 1608, Steamboat.

1992, Oct. 19 **Litho.** *Perf. 14*

1603	A250	10c multicolored	.25	.25
1604	A250	25c multicolored	1.50	.35
1605	A250	30c multicolored	.60	.40
1605A	A250	40c multicolored	.60	.40
1605B	A250	60c multicolored	3.75	1.00
1605C	A250	$1 multicolored	2.00	1.25
1605D	A250	$4 multicolored	4.50	4.50
1606	A250	$5 multicolored	4.75	4.50
		Nos. 1603-1606 (8)	17.95	12.65

Souvenir Sheet

1607	A250	$6 multicolored	6.00	6.00
1608	A250	$6 multicolored	6.00	6.00

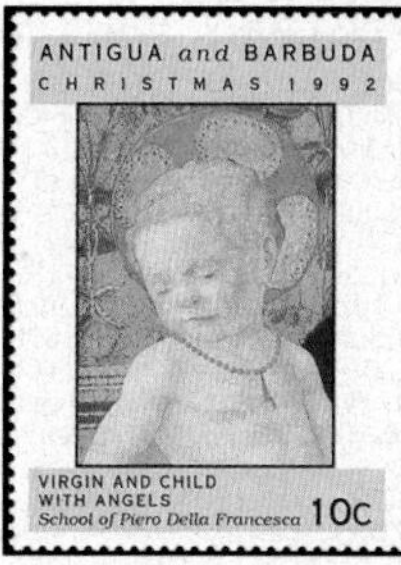

Christmas A251

Details from Paintings: 10c, Virgin and Child with Angels, by School of Piero Della Francesca. 25c, Madonna Degli Alberelli, by Giovanni Bellini. 30c, Madonna and Child with St. Anthony Abbot and St. Sigismund, by Neroccio di Landi. 40c, Madonna and the Grand Duke, by Raphael. 60c, The Nativity, by George de la Tour. $1, Holy Family, by Jacob Jordaens. $4, Madonna and Child Enthroned, by Margaritone. $5, Madonna and Child on a Curved Throne, by Byzantine artist. No. 1617, Madonna and Child, by Domenico Ghirlandaio (both names misspelled). No. 1618, The Holy Family, by Pontormo.

1992 *Perf. 13½x14*

1609	A251	10c multicolored	.65	.25
1610	A251	25c multicolored	1.00	.25
1611	A251	30c multicolored	1.10	.25
1612	A251	40c multicolored	1.25	.30
1613	A251	60c multicolored	1.75	.60
1614	A251	$1 multicolored	2.00	1.00
1615	A251	$4 multicolored	4.00	4.00
1616	A251	$5 multicolored	4.00	4.00
		Nos. 1609-1616 (8)	15.75	10.65

Souvenir Sheet

1617	A251	$6 multicolored	6.50	6.50
1618	A251	$6 multicolored	6.50	6.50

A252

A253

Anniversaries and Events: 10c, Cosmonauts. 40c, Graf Zeppelin, Goodyear blimp. 45c, Right Rev. Daniel C. Davis, St. John's Cathedral. 75c, Konrad Adenauer. $1, Bus Mosbacher, Weatherly. $1.50, Rain forest. No. 1625, Felis tigris. No. 1626, Flag, emblems, plant. No. 1627, Women acting on stage. $2.25, Women carrying baskets of food on their heads. $3, Lions Club emblem, club member. No. 1630, West German, NATO flags. No. 1631, China's Long March Booster Rocket. No. 1632, Dr. Hugo Eckener.

No. 1633, $6, The Hindenburg. No. 1634, $6, Brandenburg Gate, German flag. No. 1635, $6, Monarch butterfly. No. 1636, $6, Hermes Shuttle, Columbus Space Station.

1992 Litho. *Perf. 14*

1619	A252	10c multicolored	.80	.50
1620	A252	40c multicolored	1.75	.55
1621	A253	45c multicolored	.75	.35
1622	A252	75c multicolored	.90	.60
1623	A252	$1 multicolored	1.25	.75
1624	A252	$1.50 multicolored	1.75	1.10
1625	A252	$2 multicolored	4.25	2.00
1626	A253	$2 multicolored	2.75	1.50
1627	A253	$2 multicolored	2.50	1.75
1628	A252	$2.25 multicolored	2.50	2.50
1629	A252	$3 multicolored	3.75	3.75
1630	A252	$4 multicolored	3.75	3.75
1631	A252	$4 multicolored	4.25	4.25
1632	A252	$6 multicolored	4.00	4.00
		Nos. 1619-1632 (14)	34.95	27.35

Souvenir Sheets

1633-1636	A252	Set of 4	22.00	22.00

Intl. Space Year (Nos. 1619, 1631, 1636). Count Zeppelin, 75th anniv. of death (Nos. 1620, 1632-1633). Diocese of Northeast Caribbean and Aruba District, 150th anniv. (No. 1621). Konrad Adenauer, 25th anniv. of death (Nos. 1622, 1630, 1634). 1962 winner of America's Cup (No. 1623). Earth Summit, Rio (Nos. 1624-1625, 1635). Inter-American Institute for Cooperation on Agriculture, 50th anniv. (No. 1626). Cultural Development, 40th anniv. (No. 1627). WHO Intl. Conf. on Nutrition, Rome (No. 1628). Lions Club, 75th anniv. (No. 1629).

Issued: Nos. 1619, 1621-1623, 1626-1631, 1634, 1636, Nov.; Nos. 1624-1625, 1635, Dec. 14.

Euro Disney, Paris — A254

Disney characters: 10c, Golf course. 25c, Davy Crockett Campground. 30c, Cheyenne Hotel. 40c, Santa Fe Hotel. $1, New York Hotel. $2, In car, map showing location. $4, Pirates of the Caribbean. $5, Adventureland.

No. 1645, $6, Mickey Mouse on map with star, vert. No. 1646, $6, Roof turret at entrance, Mickey Mouse in uniform. No. 1646A, $6, Mickey Mouse, colored spots on poster, vert. No. 1646B, $6, Mickey on poster, vert., diff.

1992-93 Litho. *Perf. 14x13½*

1637	A254	10c multicolored	.70	.25
1638	A254	25c multicolored	.90	.25
1639	A254	30c multicolored	.90	.25
1640	A254	40c multicolored	1.00	.30
1641	A254	$1 multicolored	2.00	.75
1642	A254	$2 multicolored	2.75	2.75
1643	A254	$4 multicolored	3.75	3.00
1644	A254	$5 multicolored	3.75	3.75
		Nos. 1637-1644 (8)	15.75	11.30

Souvenir Sheets

Perf. 13½x14

1645-1646B	A254	Set of 4	19.00	19.00

Issued: Nos. 1638-1639, 1642-1643, 1646-1646B, 2/22/93; others, 12/1992.

Miniature Sheets

Louvre Museum, Bicent. — A255

Details or entire paintings, by Peter Paul Rubens: No. 1647a, Destiny of Marie de' Medici. b, Birth of Marie de'Medici. c, Marie's Education. d, Destiny of Marie de'Medici, diff. e, Henry IV Receives the Portrait. f, The Meeting at Lyons. g, The Marriage. h, The Birth of Louis XIII.

No. 1648a, The Capture of Juliers. b, The Exchange of Princesses. c, The Happiness of the Regency. d, The Majority of Louis XIII. e, The Flight from Blois. f, The Treaty of Angouleme. g, The Peace of Angers. h, The Queen's Reconciliation with Her Son.

$6, Helene Fourment Au Carosse.

1993, Mar. 22 Litho. *Perf. 12*

1647	A255	$1 Sheet of 8, #a.-h., + label	7.50	7.50
1648	A255	$1 Sheet of 8, #a.-h., + label	7.50	7.50

Souvenir Sheet

Perf. 14½

1649	A255	$6 multicolored	7.75	7.75

No. 1649 contains one 55x88mm stamp.

Flowers — A256

1993, Mar. 15 Litho. *Perf. 14*

1650	A256	15c Cardinal's guard	.95	.30
1651	A256	25c Giant granadilla	1.10	.30
1652	A256	30c Spider flower	1.10	.35
1653	A256	40c Gold vine	1.10	.35
1654	A256	$1 Frangipani	2.10	.90
1655	A256	$2 Bougainvillea	2.75	2.75
1656	A256	$4 Yellow oleander	4.00	4.00
1657	A256	$5 Spicy jatropha	4.00	4.50
		Nos. 1650-1657 (8)	17.10	13.45

Souvenir Sheets

1658	A256	$6 Bird lime tree	6.00	6.00
1659	A256	$6 Fairy lily	6.00	6.00

Endangered Species — A257

Designs: No. 1660a, St. Lucia parrot. b, Cahow. c, Swallow-tailed kite. d, Everglades kite. e, Imperial parrot. f, Humpback whale. g, Puerto Rican plain pigeon. h, St. Vincent parrot. i, Puerto Rican parrot. j, Leatherback turtle. k, American crocodile. l, Hawksbill turtle.

No. 1662, West Indian manatee.

1993, Apr. 5

1660	A257	$1 Sheet of 12, #a.-l.	13.00	13.00

Souvenir Sheets

1661	A257	$6 like #1660f	5.25	5.25
1662	A257	$6 multicolored	5.25	5.25

Philatelic Publishing Personalities — A258

Portrait, stamp: No. 1663, J. Walter Scott (1842-1919), US "#C3a," Antigua #1. No. 1664, Theodore Champion, France #8, Antigua #1. No. 1665, E. Stanley Gibbons (1856-1913), cover of his first price list and catalogue, Antigua #1. No. 1666, Hugo Michel (1866-1944), Bavaria #1, Antigua #1. No. 1667, Alberto (1877-1944) and Giulio (1902-1987) Bolaffi, Sardinia #1, Great Britain #3. No. 1668, Richard Borek (1874-1947), Brunswick #24, Bavaria #1.

Front pages, Mekeel's Weekly Stamp News: No. 1669a, Jan. 7, 1890. b, Feb. 12, 1993.

1993, June 14

1663	A258	$1.50 multicolored	2.10	2.10
1664	A258	$1.50 multicolored	2.10	2.10
1665	A258	$1.50 multicolored	2.10	2.10
1666	A258	$1.50 multicolored	2.10	2.10
1667	A258	$1.50 multicolored	2.10	2.10
1668	A258	$1.50 multicolored	2.10	2.10
		Nos. 1663-1668 (6)	12.60	12.60

Souvenir Sheet

1669	A258	$3 Sheet of 2, #a.-b.	7.50	7.50

Mekeel's Weekly Stamp News, cent. (in 1891; No. 1669).

Miniature Sheets

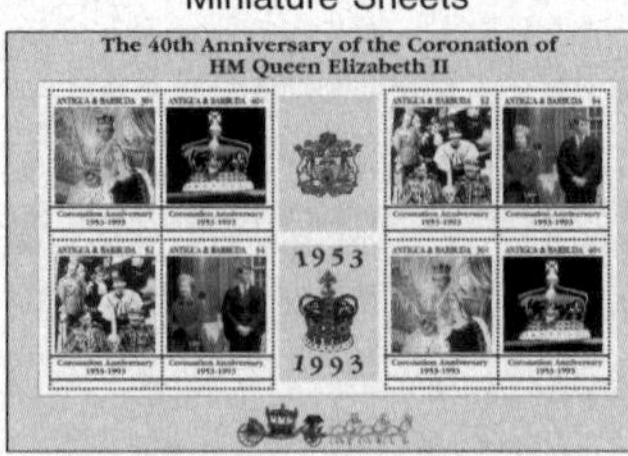

Coronation of Queen Elizabeth II, 40th Anniv. — A259

No. 1670 — Coronation: a, 30c, Official photograph. b, 40c, Crown of Queen Elizabeth, the Queen Mother. c, $2, Dignataries attending ceremony. d, $4, Queen, Prince Edward.

No. 1671, $1 — First decade, 1953-1963: a, Wedding photograph of Princess Margaret and Antony Armstrong-Jones. b, Queen opening Parliament, Prince Philip. c, Queen holding infant. d, Royal family. e, Queen Elizabeth II, formal portrait. f, Queen, Charles de Gaulle. g, Queen, Pope John XXIII. h, Queen inspecting troops.

No. 1672, $1 — Second decade, 1963-1973: a, Investiture of Charles as Prince of Wales. b, Queen opening Parliament, Prince Philip, diff. c, Queen holding infant, diff. d, Queen, Prince Philip, children. e, Wearing blue robe, diadem. f, Prince Philip, Queen seated. g, Prince Charles, Queen at microphone. h, Queen conversing, model airplane.

No. 1673, $1 — Third decade, 1973-1983: a, Wedding photograph of Prince Charles and Princess Diana. b, Queen opening Parliament, Prince Philip, diff. c, Princess Diana with infant. d, Princess Anne with infant. e, Portrait of Queen. f, Queen waving, Prince Philip. g, Queen, Pope John Paul II. h, Wedding portrait of Mark Phillips and Princess Anne.

No. 1674, $1 — Fourth decade, 1983-1993: a, Wedding photograph of Sarah Ferguson and Prince Andrew. b, Queen opening Parliament, Prince Philip, diff. c, Princess Diana holding infant, diff. d, Sarah Ferguson, infant. e, Queen wearing blue dress. f, Queen waving from carriage, Prince Philip. g, Queen wearing military uniform. h, Queen Mother.

$6, Portrait, by Denis Fildes.

1993, June 2 Litho. *Perf. 13½x14*

1670	A259	Sheet, 2 each #a.-d.	11.50	11.50

Sheets of 8, #a-h

1671-1674	A259	Set of 4	37.50	37.50

Souvenir Sheet

Perf. 14

1675	A259	$6 multicolored	5.75	5.75

No. 1675 contains one 28x42mm stamp.

Wedding of Japan's Crown Prince Naruhito and Masako Owada A260

Cameo photos of couple and: 40c, Crown Prince. $3, Princess.

$6, Princess wearing white coat, vert.

1993, Aug. 16 Litho. *Perf. 14*

1676	A260	40c multicolored	.75	.40
1677	A260	$3 multicolored	2.50	2.25

Souvenir Sheet

1678	A260	$6 multicolored	6.00	6.00

Picasso (1881-1973) — A261

Paintings: 30c, Cat and Bird, 1939. 40c, Fish on a Newspaper, 1957. $5, Dying Bull, 1934.

$6, Woman with a Dog, 1953.

1993, Aug. 16 Litho. *Perf. 14*

1679	A261	30c multicolored	1.00	.40
1680	A261	40c multicolored	1.00	.40
1681	A261	$5 multicolored	4.00	4.00
		Nos. 1679-1681 (3)	6.00	4.80

Souvenir Sheet

1682	A261	$6 multicolored	6.50	6.50

Copernicus (1473-1543) A262

Designs: 40c, Astronomical devices. $4, Photograph of supernova.

$5, Copernicus.

1993, Aug. 16

1683	A262	40c multicolored	.75	.50
1684	A262	$4 multicolored	3.50	3.50

Souvenir Sheet

1685	A262	$5 multicolored	6.00	6.00

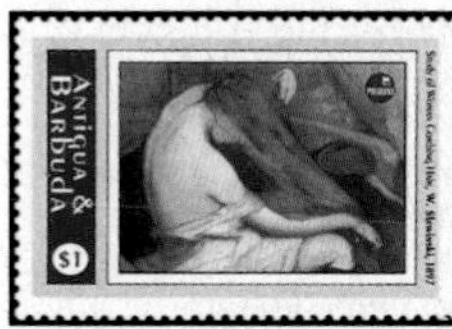

Willy Brandt (1913-1992), German Chancellor — A263

Designs: 30c, Helmut Schmidt, George Leber, Brandt. $4, Brandt, newspaper headlines.

$6, Brandt at Warsaw Ghetto Memorial, 1970.

1993, Aug. 16

1686 A263 30c multicolored 1.00 .35
1687 A263 $4 multicolored 4.25 4.25

Souvenir Sheet

1688 A263 $6 multicolored 6.25 6.25

Polska '93 A264

Paintings: $1, Study of a Woman Combing Her Hair, by Wladyslaw Slewinski, 1897. $3, Artist's Wife with Cat, by Konrad Kryzanowski, 1912.

$6, General Confusion, by S. I. Witkiewicz, 1930, vert.

1993, Aug. 16

1689 A264 $1 multicolored 1.00 1.00
1690 A264 $3 multicolored 2.50 2.50

Souvenir Sheet

1691 A264 $6 multicolored 6.00 6.00

Inauguration of Pres. William J. Clinton — A265

Designs: $5, Pres. Clinton driving car. $6, Pres. Clinton, inauguration ceremony, vert.

1993, Aug. 16

1692 A265 $5 multicolored 3.75 3.75

Souvenir Sheet

1693 A265 $6 multicolored 6.00 6.00

No. 1693 contains one 43x57mm stamp.

1994 World Cup Soccer Championships, US — A267

English soccer players: No. 1697, $2, Gordon Banks. Nos. 1698, $2, Bobby Moore. No. 1699, $2, Peter Shilton. No. 1700, $2, Nobby Stiles. No. 1701, $2, Bryan Robson. No. 1702, $2, Geoff Hurst. No. 1703, $2, Gary Lineker. No. 1704, $2, Bobby Charlton. No. 1705, $2, Martin Peters. No. 1706, $2, John Barnes. No. 1707, $2, David Platt. No. 1708, $2, Paul Gascoigne.

No. 1709, $6, Bobby Moore. No. 1710, $6, Player holding 1990 Fair Play Winners Trophy.

1993, July 30 Litho. *Perf. 14*

1697-1708 A267 Set of 12 19.00 19.00

Souvenir Sheets

1709-1710 A267 Set of 2 11.50 11.50

Nos. 1697-1708 issued in sheets of five plus label identifying player.

Aviation Anniversaries — A268

Designs: 30c, Dr. Hugo Eckener, Dr. Wm. Beckers, zeppelin over Lake George, NY. No. 1712, Chicago Century of Progress Exhibition seen from zeppelin. No. 1713, George Washington, Blanchard's balloon, vert. No. 1714, Gloster E.28/39, first British jet plane. $4, Pres. Wilson watching take-off of first scheduled air mail plane. No. 1716, Hindenburg over Ebbets Field, Brooklyn, NY, 1937. No. 1717, Gloster Meteor in combat.

No. 1718, Eckener, vert. No. 1719, Alexander Hamilton, Pres. Washington, John Jay, gondola of Blanchard's balloon. No. 1720, PBY-5.

1993, Oct. 11

1711 A268 30c multicolored 1.00 .60
1712 A268 40c multicolored 1.00 1.00
1713 A268 40c multicolored 1.00 1.00
1714 A268 40c multicolored 1.00 1.00
1715 A268 $4 multicolored 4.00 4.00
1716 A268 $5 multicolored 4.00 4.00
1717 A268 $5 multicolored 5.75 5.75
Nos. 1711-1717 (7) 17.75 17.35

Souvenir Sheets

1718 A268 $6 multicolored 5.50 5.50
1719 A268 $6 multicolored 6.25 6.25
1720 A268 $6 multicolored 6.25 6.25

Dr. Hugo Eckener, 125th anniv. of birth (Nos. 1711-1712, 1716, 1718). First US balloon flight, bicent. (Nos. 1713, 1715, 1719). Royal Air Force, 75th anniv. (Nos. 1714, 1717, 1720).

No. 1720 contains one 57x43mm stamp.

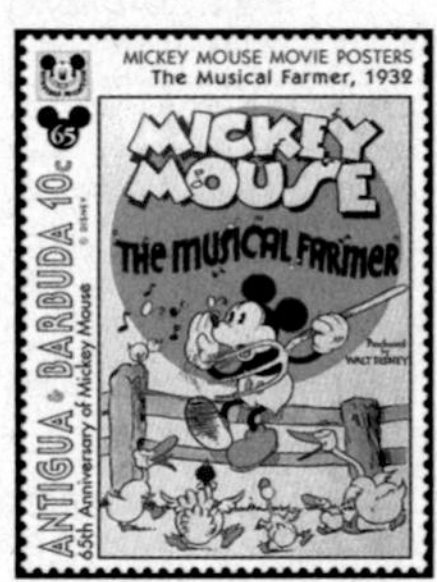

Mickey Mouse Movie Posters A269

Nos. 1721-1729: 10c, The Musical Farmer, 1932. 15c, Little Whirlwind, 1941. 30c, Pluto's Dream House, 1940. 40c, Gulliver Mickey, 1934. 50c, Alpine Climbers, 1936. $1, Mr. Mouse Takes a Trip, 1940. $2, The Nifty Nineties, 1941. $4, Mickey Down Under, 1948. $5, The Pointer, 1939.

No. 1730, $6, The Simple Things, 1953. No. 1731, $6,The Prince and the Pauper, 1990.

1993, Oct. 25 Litho. *Perf. 13½x14*

1721-1729 A269 Set of 9 15.50 15.50

Souvenir Sheets

1730-1731 A269 Set of 2 15.00 15.00

St. John's Lodge #492, 150th Anniv. A270

Designs: 10c, W.K. Heath, Grand Inspector 1961-82, vert. 30c, Present Masonic Hall. 40c, 1st Masonic Hall. 60c, J.L.E. Jeffery, Grand Inspector 1953-61, vert.

1993, Aug. 16 Litho. *Perf. 14*

1732-1735 A270 Set of 4 11.00 11.00

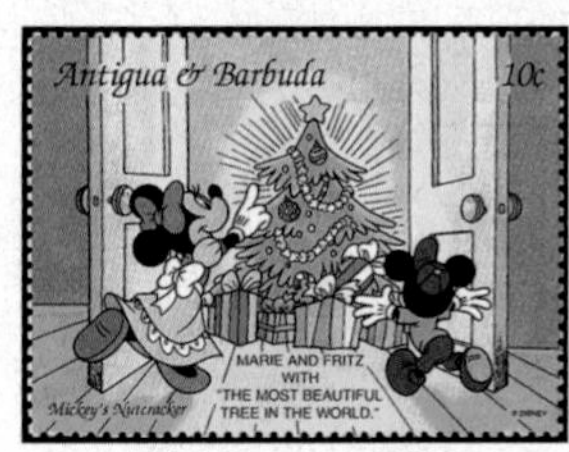

First Ford Engine and Benz's First 4-Wheel Car, Cent. A271

30c, Lincoln Continental. 40c, 1914 Mercedes racing car. $4, 1966 Ford GT40. $5, 1954 Mercedes Benz gull wing coupe, street version.

No. 1740, $6, Mustang emblem. No. 1741, $6, US #1286A, Germany #471.

1993, Oct. 11 Litho. *Perf. 14*

1736-1739 A271 Set of 4 10.00 10.00

Souvenir Sheets

1740-1741 A271 Set of 2 12.50 12.50

Christmas — A272

Nos. 1742-1750, Disney characters in The Nutcracker: 10c, 15c, 20c, 30c, 40c, 50c, 60c, $3, $6.

No. 1751, $6, Minnie and Mickey. No. 1752, $6, Mickey, vert.

1993, Nov. 8 *Perf. 14x13½, 13½x14*

1742-1750 A272 Set of 9 14.50 14.50

Souvenir Sheets

1751-1752 A272 Set of 2 13.00 13.00

Fine Art — A273

Paintings by Rembrandt: No. 1753, 15c, Hannah and Samuel. No. 1755, Isaac & Rebecca (The Jewish Bride). No. 1756, Jacob Wrestling with the Angel. No. 1760, Moses with the Tablets of the Law.

Paintings by Matisse: No. 1754, 15c, Guitarist. No. 1757, Interior with a Goldfish Bowl. No. 1758, Portrait of Mlle. Yvonne Landsberg. No. 1759, The Toboggan, Plate XX from Jazz.

No. 1761, $6, The Blinding of Samson by the Philistines, by Rembrandt. No. 1762, $6, The Three Sisters, by Matisse.

1993, Nov. 22 *Perf. 13½x14*

1753-1760 A273 Set of 8 11.50 11.50

Souvenir Sheets

1761-1762 A273 Set of 2 13.00 13.00

A274

Hong Kong '94 — A275

Stamps, fishing boats at Shau Kei Wan: No. 1763, Hong Kong #370, bow of boat. No. 1764, Stern of boat, #1300.

Museum of Qin figures, Shaanxi Province, Tomb of Qin First Emperor: No. 1765a, Inside museum. b, Cavalryman, horse. c, Warriors in battle formation. d, Painted bronze horses, chariot. e, Pekingese dog (not antiquity). f, Chin warrior figures, horses.

1994, Feb. 18 Litho. *Perf. 14*

1763 A274 40c multicolored .80 .80
1764 A274 40c multicolored .80 .80
a. Pair, #1763-1764 1.75 1.75

Miniature Sheet

1765 A275 40c Sheet of 6, #a.-f. 5.75 5.75

Nos. 1763-1764 issued in sheets of 5 pairs. No. 1764a is a continuous design.

New Year 1994 (Year of the Dog) (No. 1765e).

Hong Kong '94 — A276

Disney characters: 10c, Mickey's "Pleasure Junk." 15c, Mandarin Minnie. 30c, Donald, Daisy journey by house boat. 50c, Mickey, Birdman of Mongkok. $1, Pluto encounters a good-luck dog. $2, Minnie, Daisy celebrate Bun Festival. $4, Goofy, the noodle maker. $5, Goofy pulls Mickey in a rickshaw.

No. 1774, $5, Mickey celebrating New Year with Dragon Dance, horiz. No. 1775, $5, View of Hong Kong Harbor, horiz.

1994, Feb. 18 Litho. *Perf. 13½x14*

1766-1773 A276 Set of 8 15.00 15.00

Souvenir Sheets

Perf. 14x13½

1774-1775 A276 $5 Set of 2 10.00 10.00

Sierra Club, Cent. — A277

No. 1776: a, Bactrian camel, emblem UR. b, Bactrian camel, emblem UL. c, African elephant, emblem UL. d, African elephant, emblem UR. e, Leopard, blue background. f, Leopard, emblem UR. g, Leopard, emblem UL. h, Club emblem.

No. 1777: a, Sumatran rhinoceros, lying on ground. b, Sumatran rhinoceros, looking straight ahead. c, Ring-tailed lemur standing. d, Ring-tailed lemur sitting on branch. e, Red-fronted brown lemur on branch. f, Red-fronted brown lemur. g, Red-fronted brown lemur, diff.

No. 1778, $1.50, Sumatran rhinoceros, horiz. No. 1779, $1.50, Ring-tailed lemur, horiz. No. 1780, $1.50, Bactrian camel, horiz. No. 1781, $1.50, African elephant, horiz.

1994, Mar. 1 Litho. *Perf. 14*

1776 A277 $1.50 Sheet of 8, #a.-h. 12.00 12.00

1777 A277 $1.50 Sheet of 8, #a.-g, #1776h 12.00 12.00

Souvenir Sheets

1778-1781 A277 Set of 4 7.00 7.00

New Year 1994 (Year of the Dog) — A278

Small breeds of dogs: No. 1782a, West highland white terrier. b, Beagle. c, Scottish terrier. d, Pekingese. e, Dachshund. f, Yorkshire terrier. g, Pomeranian. h, Poodle. i, Shetland sheepdog. j, Pug. k, Shih tzu. l, Chihuahua.

Large breeds of dogs: No. 1783a, Mastiff. b, Border collie. c, Samoyed. d, Airedale terrier. e, English setter. f, Rough collie. g, Newfoundland. h, Weimaraner. i, English springer spaniel. j, Dalmatian. k, Boxer. l, Old English sheepdog.

No. 1784, $6, Welsh corgi. No. 1785, $6, Labrador retriever.

1994, Apr. 5 *Perf. 14*

1782 A278 50c Sheet of 12, #a.-l. 7.50 7.50

1783 A278 75c Sheet of 12, #a.-l. 11.00 11.00

Souvenir Sheets

1784-1785 A278 Set of 2 11.00 11.00

Orchids — A279

Designs: 10c, Spiranthes lanceolata. 20c, Ionopsis utricularioides. 30c, Tetramicra canaliculata. 50c, Oncidium picturatum. $1, Epidendrum difforme. $2, Epidendrum ciliare. $4, Epidendrum ibaguense. $5, Epidendrum nocturnum.

No. 1794, $6, Encyclia cochleata. No. 1795, $6, Rodriguezia lanceolata.

1994, Apr. 11 *Perf. 14*

1786-1793 A279 Set of 8 17.50 17.50

Souvenir Sheets

1794-1795 A279 Set of 2 12.50 12.50

Butterflies — A280

Designs: 10c, Monarch. 15c, Florida white. 30c, Little sulphur. 40c, Troglodyte. $1, Common long-tail skipper. $2, Caribbean buckeye. $4, Polydamas swallowtail. $5, Zebra.

No. 1804, $6, Cloudless sulphur. No. 1805, $6, Hanno blue.

1994, June 27 *Perf. 14*

1796-1803 A280 Set of 8 18.50 18.50

Souvenir Sheets

1804-1805 A280 Set of 2 12.50 12.50

Marine Life — A281

No. 1806: a, Bottlenose dolphin. b, Killer whale (a). c, Spinner dolphin (b). d, Ocean sunfish (a). e, Caribbean reef shark, short fin pilot whale (d, f). f, Butterfly fish. g, Moray eel. h, Trigger fish. i, Red lobster (h).

No. 1807, $6, Blue marlin, horiz. No. 1808, $6, Sea horse.

1994, July 21 Litho. *Perf. 14*

1806 A281 50c Sheet of 9, #a.-i. 7.75 7.75

Souvenir Sheets

1807-1808 A281 Set of 2 13.00 13.00

Intl. Year of the Family A282

1994, Aug. 4

1809 A282 90c multicolored 1.10 1.10

D-Day, 50th Anniv. A283

Designs: 40c, Short Sunderland attacks U-boat. $2, Lockheed P-38 Lightning attacks train. $3, B-26 Marauders of 9th Air Force.

$6, Hawker Typhoon Fighter Bombers.

1994, Aug. 4

1810-1812 A283 Set of 3 7.00 7.00

Souvenir Sheet

1813 A283 $6 multicolored 6.75 6.75

A284

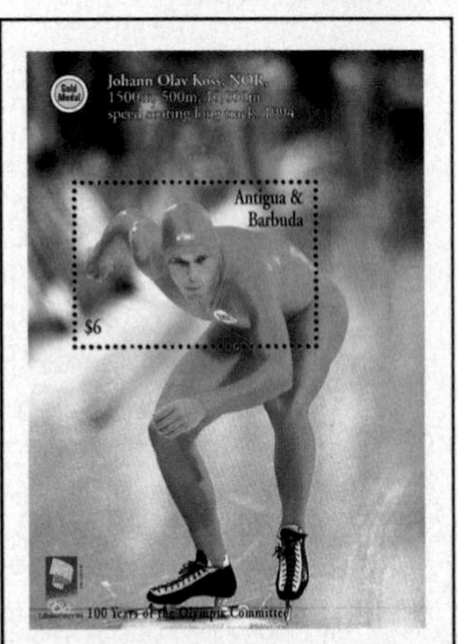

Intl. Olympic Committee, Cent. — A285

Designs: 50c, Edwin Moses, US, hurdles, 1984. $1.50, Steffi Graf, Germany, tennis, 1988. $6, Johann Olav Koss, Norway, speed skating, 1994.

1994, Aug. 4

1814 A284 50c multicolored .40 .30

1815 A284 $1.50 multicolored 2.00 2.00

Souvenir Sheet

1816 A285 $6 multicolored 6.25 6.25

English Touring Cricket, Cent. A286

35c, M.A. Atherton, England, Wisden Trophy. 75c, I.V.A. Richards, Leeward Islands, vert. $1.20, R.B. Richardson, Leeward Islands, Wisden Trophy.

$3, First English team, 1895.

1994, Aug. 4

1817-1819 A286 Set of 3 6.00 6.00

Souvenir Sheet

1820 A286 $3 multicolored 3.25 3.25

First Manned Moon Landing, 25th Anniv. A287

No. 1821, $1.50: a, Edwin E. Aldrin, Jr. b, First footprint on Moon. c, Neil A. Armstrong. d, Aldrin descending to lunar surface. e, Aldrin deploys ALSEP (spelled ALSET in error on stamp). f, Aldrin, US flag, Tranquility Base.

No. 1822, $1.50: a, Scientific research, Tranquility Base. b, Plaque on Moon. c, Eagle ascending to docking. d, Command module in lunar orbit. e, US No. C76 made from die carried to Moon. f, Pres. Nixon, Apollo 11 crew.

$6, Armstrong, Aldrin, Postmaster General Blount.

1994, Aug. 4

Sheets of 6, #a-f

1821-1822 A287 Set of 2 22.50 22.50

Souvenir Sheet

1823 A287 $6 multicolored 5.75 5.75

A288

PHILAKOREA '94 — A289

40c, Entrance bridge, Songgwangsa Temple. 90c, Song-op Folk Village, Cheju. $3, Panoramic view, Port Sogwip'o.

Ceramics, Koryo & Choson Dynasties: No. 1827a, Long-necked bottle. b, Jar. c, Jar, diff. d, Ewer in form of bamboo shoot. e, Jar, diff. f, Pear-shaped bottle. g, Porcelain jar with dragon design. h, Porcelain jar with bonsai design.

$4, Ox, ox herder, vert.

1994, Aug. 4 *Perf. 14, 13½ (#1827)*

1824-1826 A288 Set of 3 3.25 3.25

1827 A289 75c Sheet of 8, #a.-h. 6.50 6.50

Souvenir Sheet

1828 A288 $4 multicolored 4.75 4.75

Stars of Country & Western Music — A290

No. 1829, 75c: a, Patsy Cline. b, Tanya Tucker. c, Dolly Parton. d, Anne Murray. e, Tammy Wynette. f, Loretta Lynn. g, Reba McEntire. h, Skeeter Davis.

No. 1830, 75c: a, Travis Tritt. b, Dwight Yoakam. c, Billy Ray Cyrus. d, Alan Jackson. e, Garth Brooks. f, Vince Gill. g, Clint Black. h, Eddie Rabbit.

No. 1831, 75c: a, Hank Snow. b, Gene Autry. c, Jimmie Rogers. d, Ernest Tubb. e, Eddy Arnold. f, Willie Nelson. g, Johnny Cash. h, George Jones.

No. 1832, $6, Kitty Wells, horiz. No. 1833, $6, Hank Williams, Sr. No. 1834, $6, Hank Williams, Jr.

1994, Aug. 18 Litho. *Perf. 14*

Sheets of 8, #a-h

1829-1831 A290 Set of 3 16.50 16.50

Souvenir Sheets

1832-1834 A290 Set of 3 16.50 16.50

1994 World Cup Soccer Championships, US — A291

Designs: 15c, Hugo Sanchez, Mexico. 35c, Juergen Klinsmann, Germany. 65c, Antigua player. $1.20, Cobi Jones, US. $4, Roberto Baggio, Italy. $5, Bwalya Kalusha, Zambia.

No. 1841, $6, FIFA World Cup Trophy, vert. No. 1842, $6, Maldive Islands player, vert.

1994, Sept. 19

1835-1840 A291 Set of 6 14.50 14.50

Souvenir Sheets

1841-1842 A291 Set of 2 9.75 9.75

Order of the Caribbean Community — A292

First award recipients: 65c, Sir Shridath Ramphal, statesman, Guyana. 90c, William Demas, economist, Trinidad & Tobago. $1.20, Derek Walcott, writer, St. Lucia.

1994, Sept. 26

1843-1845 A292 Set of 3 3.50 3.50

Herman E. Sieger (1902-54) A293

Germany #C35, Graf Zeppelin, Sieger.

1994 Litho. *Perf. 14*

1846 A293 $1.50 multicolored 4.25 4.25

Birds A294

Designs: 10c, Magnificent frigate birds. 15c, Bridled quail dove. 30c, Magnificent frigate bird hatchling. 40c, Purple-throated carib, vert. No. 1851, $1, Antigua broad-wing hawk, vert. No. 1852, $1, Magnificent frigate bird, vert. $3, Magnificent frigate bird, white head. $4, Yellow warbler.

No. 1855, $6, West Indian Whistling duck. No. 1856, $6, Magnificent frigate bird, diff., vert.

1994, Dec. 12 Litho. *Perf. 14*

1847-1854 A294 Set of 8 11.00 11.00

Souvenir Sheets

1855-1856 A294 Set of 2 9.25 9.25

World Wildlife Fund (Nos. 1847, 1849, 1852-1853).

Christmas A295

Paintings of Madonnas: 15c, The Virgin and Child by the Fireside, by Robert Campin. 35c, The Reading Madonna, by Giorgione. 40c, Madonna and Child, by Giovanni Bellini. 45c, The Litta Madonna, by da Vinci. 65c, The Virgin and Child Under the Apple Tree, by Lucas Cranach the Elder. 75c, Madonna and Child, by Master of the Female Half-Lengths. $1.20, An Allegory of the Church, by Alessandro Allori. $5, Madonna and Child Wreathed with Flowers, by Jacob Jordaens.

No. 1865, $6, The Virgin Enthroned with Child, by Bohemian Master. No. 1866, $6, Madonna and Child with (painting's) Commissioners, by Palma Vecchio.

1994, Dec. 12 *Perf. 13½x14*

1857-1864 A295 Set of 8 15.00 15.00

Souvenir Sheets

1865-1866 A295 Set of 2 10.00 10.00

Birds — A296

Designs: 15c, Magnificent frigate bird. 25c, Blue-hooded euphonia. 35c, Meadowlark. 40c, Red-billed tropic bird. 45c, Greater flamingo. 60c, Yellow-faced grassquit. 65c, Yellow-billed cuckoo. 70c, Purple-throated carib. 75c, Bananaquit. 90c, Painted bunting. $1.20, Red-legged honeycreeper. $2, Jacana. $5, Greater antillean bullfinch. $10, Caribbean elaenia. $20, Trembler.

1995, Feb. 6 *Perf. 14½x14*

1867 A296 15c multicolored .25 .25
1868 A296 25c multicolored .25 .25
1869 A296 35c multicolored .25 .25
1870 A296 40c multicolored .30 .30
1871 A296 45c multicolored .40 .40
1872 A296 60c multicolored .45 .45
1873 A296 65c multicolored .60 .60
1874 A296 70c multicolored .60 .60
1875 A296 75c multicolored .65 .65
1876 A296 90c multicolored .80 .80
1877 A296 $1.20 multicolored 1.00 1.00
1878 A296 $2 multicolored 1.75 1.75
1879 A296 $5 multicolored 4.75 4.75
1880 A296 $10 multicolored 9.50 9.50
1881 A296 $20 multicolored 19.00 19.00
Nos. 1867-1881 (15) 40.55 40.55

See Nos. 2693-2694.

Prehistoric Animals A297

Designs, vert: 15c, Pachycephalosaurus. 20c, Afrovenator. 65c, Centrosaurus. 90c, Pentaceratops. $1.20, Tarbosaurus. $5, Styracosaur.

No. 1888: a, Kronosaur. b, Ichthyosaur. c, Plesiosaur. d, Archelon. e, Two tyrannosaurs. f, One tyrannosaur. g, One parasaurolophus. h, Two parasaurolophuses. i, Oviraptor. j, Protoceratops with eggs. k, Pteranodon, protoceratops. l, Protoceratops.

No. 1889, $6, Carnotaurus. No. 1890, $6, Corythosaurus.

1995, May 15 Litho. *Perf. 14*

1882-1887 A297 Set of 6 7.50 7.50
1888 A297 75c Sheet of 12, #a.-l. 8.50 8.50

Souvenir Sheets

1889-1890 A297 Set of 2 14.50 14.50

1996 Summer Olympics, Atlanta A298

Gold medalists: 15c, Al Oerter, US, discus. 20c, Greg Louganis, US, diving. 65c, Naim Suleymanoglu, Turkey, weight lifting. 90c, Louise Ritter, US, high jump. $1.20, Nadia Comaneci, Romania, gymnastics. $5, Olga Bondarenko, USSR, 10,000-meter run.

No. 1897, $6, Lutz Hessilch, Germany, 1000-meter sprint cycling, vert. No. 1898, $6, US team, eight-oared shell, 800-, 1500-meters.

1995, June 6 Litho. *Perf. 14*

1891-1896 A298 Set of 6 7.25 7.25

Souvenir Sheets

1897-1898 A298 Set of 2 13.50 13.50

End of World War II, 50th Anniv. A299

No. 1899: a, Chiang Kai-Shek. b, Gen. MacArthur. c, Gen. Chennault. d, Brigadier Orde C. Wingate. e, Gen. Stilwell. f, Field Marshall William Slim.

No. 1900: a, Map of Germany showing battle plan. b, Tanks, infantry advance. c, Red Army at gates of Berlin. d, German defenses smashed. e, Airstrikes on Berlin. f. German soldiers give up. g, Berlin falls to Russians. h, Germany surrenders.

$3, Plane, ship, Adm. Chester Nimitz. $6, Gen. Konev at command post outside Berlin, vert.

1995, July 20

1899 A299 $1.20 Sheet of 6, #a.-f. + label 7.00 7.00
1900 A299 $1.20 Sheet of 8, #a.-h. + label 10.50 10.50

Souvenir Sheets

1901 A299 $3 multicolored 4.00 4.00
1902 A299 $6 multicolored 6.00 6.00

UN, 50th Anniv. — A300

FAO, 50th Anniv. — A301

No. 1903: a, 75c, Earl of Halifax, signatures. b, 90c, Virginia Gildersleeve. c, $1.20, Harold Stassen.

$6, Franklin D. Roosevelt.

1995, July 20 Litho. *Perf. 14*

1903 A300 Strip of 3, #a.-c. 2.50 2.50

Souvenir Sheet

1904 A300 $6 multicolored 4.75 4.75

No. 1903 is a continuous design.

1995, July 20

No. 1905 — Street market scene: a, 75c, Two women, bananas. b, 90c, Women, crates, produce. c, $1.20, Women talking, one with box of food on head.

$6, Tractor.

1905 A301 Strip of 3, #a.-c. 2.50 2.50

Souvenir Sheet

1906 A301 $6 multicolored 4.75 4.75

No. 1905 is a continuous design.

Rotary Intl., 90th Anniv. — A302

1995, July 20

1907 A302 $5 shown 5.00 5.00

Souvenir Sheet

1908 A302 $6 Natl. flag, Rotary emblem 5.00 5.00

Queen Mother, 95th Birthday A303

No. 1909: a, Drawing. b, White & dark pink hat. c, Formal portrait. d, Blue green hat, dress.

$6, Light blue dress, pearls.

1995, July 20 *Perf. 13½x14*

1909 A303 $1.50 Strip or block of 4, #a.-d. 5.75 5.75

Souvenir Sheet

1910 A303 $6 multicolored 6.00 6.00

No. 1909 was issued in sheets of 2 each.

Sheets of 1909-1910 exist with black frame overprinted in margin, with text "In Memoriam/1900-2002."

Ducks — A304

No. 1911: a, Ring-necked duck. b, Ruddy duck. c, Green-winged teal (d). d, Wood duck. e, Hooded merganser (f). f, Lesser scaup (g). g, West Indian tree duck (h, k, l). h, Fulvous whistling duck (l). i, Bahama pintail. j, Shoveler (i). k, Masked duck (l). l, American widgeon.

$6, Blue-winged teal.

1995, Aug. 31 Litho. *Perf. 14*

1911 A304 75c Sheet of 12, #a.-l. 11.00 11.00

Souvenir Sheet

1912 A304 $6 multicolored 7.50 7.50

Bees A305

Designs: 90c, Mining bee. $1.20, Solitary bee. $1.65, Leaf-cutter. $1.75, Honey bee.

$6, Solitary mining bee.

1995, Sept. 7

1913-1916 A305 Set of 4 6.75 6.75

Souvenir Sheet

1917 A305 $6 multicolored 6.00 6.00

Domestic Cats A306

Designs: a, Somali. b, Persian. c, Devon rex. d, Turkish angora. e, Himalayan. f, Maine coon. g, Nonpedigree. h, American wirehair. i, British shorthair. j, American curl. k, Black nonpedigree. l, Birman.

$6, Siberian, vert.

1995, Sept. 7

1918 A306 45c Sheet of 12, #a.-l. 9.50 9.50

Souvenir Sheet

1919 A306 $6 multicolored 6.75 6.75

Tourism A307

Stylized paintings depicting: a, Caring. b, Marketing. c, Working. d, Enjoying life.

1995, July 31 Litho. *Perf. 14*

1920 A307 $2 Sheet of 4, #a.-d. 7.25 7.25

Date of issue is in question. First day cover of Aug. 10, 1995, has been seen.

Greenbay Moravian Church, 150th Anniv. — A308

Designs: 20c, 1st structure, wood & stone. 60c, 1st stone, concrete building, 3/67. 75c, $2, Present structure. 90c, John A. Buckley, 1st minister of African descent. $1.20, John Ephraim Knight, longest serving minister. $6, Front of present structure.

1995, Sept. 4

1921-1926 A308 Set of 6 9.00 9.00

Souvenir Sheet

1927 A308 $6 multicolored 6.00 6.00

Flowers — A309

No. 1928: a, Narcissus. b, Camellia. c, Iris. d, Tulip. e, Poppy. f, Peony. g, Magnolia. h, Oriental lily. i, Rose. j, Pansy. k, Hydrangea. l, Azaleas.

$6, Bird of paradise, calla lily.

1995, Sept. 7

1928 A309 75c Sheet of 12, #a.-l. 9.50 9.50

Souvenir Sheet

1929 A309 $6 multicolored 6.00 6.00

1995 Boy Scout Jamboree, Netherlands — A310

No. 1930, $1.20: a, Explorer tent. b, Camper tent. c, Wall tent.
No. 1931, $1.20: a, Trail tarp. b, Miner's. c, Voyager.
No. 1932, $6, Scout with camping equipment, vert. No. 1933, $6, Scout making camp fire.

1995, Oct. 5

Strips of 3, #a-c

1930-1931 A310 Set of 2 9.50 9.50

Souvenir Sheets

1932-1933 A310 Set of 2 11.00 11.00

For overprints see Nos. 1963-1966.

Trains A311

Designs: 35c, Gabon. 65c, Canadian. 75c, US. 90c, British high-speed. No. 1938, $1.20, French high-speed. No. 1939, American high-speed (Amtrak).
No. 1940: a, Australian diesel. b, Italian high-speed. c, Thai diesel. d, US steam. e, South African steam. f, Natal steam. g, US war train. h, British steam. i, British steam, diff.
No. 1941, $6, Australian diesel, vert. No. 1942, $6, Asian steam, vert.

1995, Oct. 23 Litho. *Perf. 14*

1934-1939 A311 Set of 6 11.50 11.50
1940 A311 $1.20 Sheet of 9, #a.-i. 13.50 13.50

Souvenir Sheets

1941-1942 A311 Set of 2 15.00 15.00

Birds — A312

No. 1943: a, Purple-thoated carib. b, Antillean crested hummingbird. c, Bananaquit (d). d, Mangrove cuckoo. e, Troupial. f, Green-throated carib (e, g). g, Yellow warbler (h). h, Blue-hooded Euphonia. i, Scally-breasted thrasher. j, Burrowing owl (i). k, Caribbean crackle (k). l, Adelaide's warbler.
$6, Purple gallinule.

1995

1943 A312 75c Sheet of 12, #a.-l. 10.00 10.00

Souvenir Sheet

1944 A312 $6 multicolored 7.50 7.50

Miniature Sheets of 9

Establishment of Nobel Prize Fund, Cent. — A313

No. 1945, $1: a, S.Y. Agnon, literature, 1966. b, Kipling, literature, 1907. c, Aleksandr Solzhenitsyn, literature, 1970. d, Jack Steinberger, physics, 1988. e, Andrei Sakharov, peace, 1975. f, Otto Stern, physics, 1943. g, Steinbeck, literature, 1962. h, Nadine Gordimer, literature, 1991. i, Faulkner, literature, 1949.

No. 1946, $1: a, Hammarskjold, peace, 1961. b, Georg Wittig, chemistry, 1979. c, Wilhelm Ostwald, chemistry, 1909. d, Koch, physiology or medicine, 1945. e, Karl Ziegler, chemistry, 1963. f, Fleming, physiology or medicine, 1945. g, Hermann Staudinger, chemistry, 1953. h, Manfred Eigen, chemistry, 1967. i, Arno Penzias, physics, 1978.
No. 1947, $6, Elie Wiesel, peace, 1986, vert. No. 1948, $6, Dalai Lama, peace, 1989, vert.

1995, Nov. 8

Sheets of 9, #a-i, + label

1945-1946 A313 Set of 2 22.00 22.00

Souvenir Sheets

1947-1948 A313 Set of 2 11.00 11.00

Christmas A314

Details or entire paintings: 15c, Rest on the Flight into Egypt, by Veronese. 35c, Madonna with The Child, by Van Dyck. 65c, Sacred Conversation Piece, by Veronese. 75c, Vision of Saint Anthony, by Van Dyck. 90c, The Virgin and the Infant, by Van Eyck. No. 1954, The Immaculate Conception, by Tiepolo.
$5, Christ Appearing to His Mother, by Van Der Weyden. $6, Infant Jesus and the Young St. John, by Murillo.

1995, Dec. 18 Litho. *Perf. 13½x14*

1949-1954 A314 Set of 6 8.00 8.00

Souvenir Sheets

1955 A314 $5 multicolored 4.50 4.50
1956 A314 $6 multicolored 6.00 6.00

Elvis Presley (1935-77) A315

Nos. 1957-1958, Various portraits depicting Presley's life.

1995, Dec. 8 *Perf. 14*

1957 A315 $1 Sheet of 9, #a.-i. 11.50 11.50

Souvenir Sheet

1958 A315 $6 multicolored 7.50 7.50

John Lennon (1940-80), Entertainer — A316

45c, 50c, 65c, 75c, Various portraits of Lennon.

1995, Dec. 8

1959-1962 A316 Set of 4 3.25 3.25

Souvenir Sheet

1962A A316 $6 like 75c 7.25 7.25

Nos. 1959-1962 were each issued in miniature sheets of 16.
No. 1962A has a continuous design.

Nos. 1930-1933 Ovptd.

1995, Dec. 14

1963 A310 $1.20 Strip of 3, #a-c (#1930) 3.75 3.75
1964 A310 $1.20 Strip of 3, #a-c (#1931) 3.75 3.75

Souvenir Sheets

1965 A310 $6 multi (#1932) 7.00 7.00
1966 A310 $6 multi (#1933) 7.00 7.00

Size and location of overprint varies.

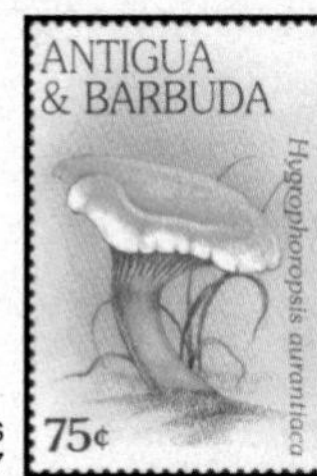
Mushrooms A317

No. 1967, 75c: a, Hygrophoropsis aurantiaca. b, Hygrophorus bakerensis. c, Hygrophorus conicus. d, Hygrophorus miniatus.
No. 1968, 75c: a, Suillus brevipes. b, Suillus luteus. c, Suillus granulatus. d, Suillus caerulescens.
No. 1969, $6, Conocybe filaris. No. 1970, $6, Hygrocybe flavescens.

1996, Apr. 22 Litho. *Perf. 14*

Strips of 4, #a-d

1967-1968 A317 Set of 2 6.75 6.75

Souvenir Sheets

1969-1970 A317 Set of 2 10.00 10.00

Nos. 1967-1968 were each issued in sheets of 12 stamps.

Sailing Ships A318

Designs: 15c, Resolution. 25c, Mayflower. 45c, Santa Maria. No. 1970D, 75c, Aemilia, Holland, 1630. No. 1970E, 75c, Sovereign of the Seas, England, 1637. 90c, HMS Victory, England, 1765.
No. 1971 — Battleships: a, Aemila, Holland, 1630. b, Sovereign of the Seas, England, 1637. c, Royal Louis, France, 1692. d, HMS Royal George, England, 1715. e, Le Protecteur, France, 1761. f, HMS Victory, England, 1765.
No. 1972 — Ships of exploration: a, Santa Maria. b, Victoria. c, Golden Hinde. d, Mayflower. e, Griffin. f, Resolution.
No. 1973, $6, Grande Hermine. No. 1974, $6 USS Constitution, 1797.

1996, Apr. 25

1970A-1970F A318 Set of 6 3.50 3.50
1971 A318 $1.20 Sheet of 6, #a.-f. 8.50 8.50
1972 A318 $1.50 Sheet of 6, #a.-f. 10.00 10.00

Souvenir Sheets

1973-1974 A318 Set of 2 12.50 12.50

1996 Summer Olympics, Atlanta A319

Designs: 65c, Florence Griffith Joyner, women's track, vert. 75c, Olympic Stadium, Seoul, 1988. 90c, Allison Jolly, yachting. $1.20, 2000m Tandem cycling,

No. 1979, 90c — Medalists: a, Wolfgang Nordwig, pole vault. b, Shirley Strong, women's 100m hurdles. c, Sergei Bubka, pole vault. d, Filbert Bayi, 3000m steeplechase. e, Victor Saneyev, triple jump. f, Silke Renk, women's javelin. g, Daley Thompson, decathlon. h, Bob Richards, pole vault. i, Parry O'Brien, shot put.
No. 1980, 90c — Diving medalists: a, Ingrid Kramer, women's platform. b, Kelly McCormick, women's springboard. c, Gary Tobian, men's springboard. d, Greg Louganis, men's diving. e, Michelle Mitchell, women's platform. f, Zhou Jihong, women's platform. g, Wendy Wyland, women's platform. h, Xu Yanmei, women's platform. i, Fu Mingxia, women's platform.
$5, Bill Toomey, decathlon. $6, Mark Lenzi, men's springboard.

1996, May 6

1975-1978 A319 Set of 4 2.75 2.75

Sheets of 9, #a-i

1979-1980 A319 90c Set of 2 14.00 14.00

Souvenir Sheets

1981 A319 $5 multicolored 5.00 5.00
1982 A319 $6 multicolored 6.00 6.00

Sea Birds A320

No. 1983, 75c: a, Black skimmer. b, Black-capped petrel. c, Sooty tern. d, Royal tern.
No. 1984, 75c: a, Pomarina jaegger. b, White-tailed tropicbird. c, Northern gannet. d, Laughing gull.
$5, Great frigatebird. $6, Brown pelican.

1996, May 13

Vertical Strips of 4, #a-d

1983-1984 A320 Set of 2 6.00 6.00

Souvenir Sheets

1985 A320 $5 multicolored 5.00 5.00
1986 A320 $6 multicolored 6.00 6.00

Nos. 1983-1984 were each issued in sheets of 12 stamps with each strip in sheet having a different order.

Disney Characters In Scenes from Jules Verne's Science Fiction Novels — A321

Designs: 1c, Around the World in Eighty Days. 2c, Journey to the Center of the Earth. 5c, Michel Strogoff. 10c, From the Earth to the Moon. 15c, Five Weeks in a Balloon. 20c, Around the World in Eighty Days, diff. $1, The Mysterious Island. $2, From the Earth to the Moon, diff. $3, Captain Grant's Children. $5, Twenty Thousand Leagues Under the Sea.
No. 1997, $6, Twenty Thousand Leagues Under the Sea, diff. No. 1998, $6, Journey to the Center of the Earth, diff.

1996, June 6 Litho. *Perf. 14x13½*

1987-1996 A321 Set of 10 14.00 14.00

Souvenir Sheets

1997-1998 A321 Set of 2 14.00 14.00

Bruce Lee (1940-73), Martial Arts Expert — A322

Various portraits.

1996, June 13 ***Perf. 14***
1999 A322 75c Sheet of 9, #a.-i. 7.25 7.25

Souvenir Sheet

2000 A322 $5 multicolored 6.25 6.25

China '96 (No. 1999).

Queen Elizabeth II, 70th Birthday — A323

Designs: a, In blue dress, pearls. b, Carrying bouquet of flowers. c, In uniform.
$6, Painting as younger woman.

1996, July 17 ***Perf. 13½x14***
2001 A323 $2 Strip of 3, #a.-c. 4.25 4.25

Souvenir Sheet

2002 A323 $6 multicolored 5.25 5.25

No. 2001 was issued in sheets of 9 stamps.

Traditional Cavalry A324

No. 2003: a, Ancient Egyptian. b, 13th cent. English. c, 16th cent. Spanish. d, 18th cent. Chinese.
$6, 19th cent. French.

1996, July 24 **Litho.** ***Perf. 14***
2003 A324 60c Block of 4, #a.-d. 2.75 2.75

Souvenir Sheet

2004 A324 $6 multicolored 5.25 5.25

No. 2003 was issued in sheets of 16 stamps.

UNICEF, 50th Anniv. — A325

Designs: 75c, Girl. 90c, Children. $1.20, Woman holding baby. $6, Girl, diff.

1996, July 30
2005-2007 A325 Set of 3 3.25 3.25

Souvenir Sheet

2008 A325 $6 multicolored 4.75 4.75

Jerusalem, 3000th Anniv. — A326

Site, flower: 75c, Tomb of Zachariah, verbascum sinuatum. 90c, Pool of Siloam, hyacinthus orientalis. $1.20, Hurva Synagogue, ranunculus asiaticus.
$6, Model of Herod's Temple.

1996, July 30
2009-2011 A326 Set of 3 2.50 2.50

Souvenir Sheet

2012 A326 $6 multicolored 7.00 7.00

Radio, Cent. A327

Entertainers: 65c, Kate Smith. 75c, Dinah Shore. 90c, Rudy Vallee. $1.20, Bing Crosby.
$6, Jo Stafford.

1996, July 30
2013-2016 A327 Set of 4 3.75 3.75

Souvenir Sheet

2017 A327 $6 multicolored 4.75 4.75

Christmas A328

Details or entire paintings, by Filippo Lippi: 60c, Madonna Enthroned. 90c, Adoration of the Child and Saints. $1, Annunciation. $1.20, Birth of the Virgin. $1.60, Adoration of the Child. $1.75, Madonna and Child.
No. 2024, $6, Madonna and Child, diff. No. 2025, $6, Circumcision.

1996, Nov. 25 ***Perf. 13½x14***
2018-2023 A328 Set of 6 8.00 8.00

Souvenir Sheets

2024-2025 A328 Set of 2 11.50 11.50

Disney Pals — A329

Designs: 1c, Goofy, Wilbur. 2c, Donald, Goofy. 5c, Donald, Panchito, Jose Carioca. 10c, Mickey, Goofy. 15c, Dale, Chip. 20c, Pluto, Mickey. $1, Daisy, Minnie at ice cream shop. $2, Daisy, Minnie. $3, Gus Goose, Donald.
No. 2035, $6, Donald, vert. No. 2036, $6, Goofy.

1997, Feb. 17 **Litho.** ***Perf. 14x13½***
2026-2034 A329 Set of 9 6.00 6.00

Souvenir Sheets

Perf. 13½x14, 14x13½

2035-2036 A329 Set of 2 10.00 10.00

Salute to Broadway A330

No. 2037 — Stars, show: a, Robert Preston, The Music Man. b, Michael Crawford, Phantom of the Opera. c, Zero Mostel, Fiddler on the Roof. d, Patti Lupone, Evita. e, Raul Julia, Threepenny Opera. f, Mary Martin, South Pacific. g, Carol Channing, Hello Dolly. h, Yul Brynner, The King and I. i, Julie Andrews, My Fair Lady.
$6, Mickey Rooney, Sugar Babies.

1997 ***Perf. 14***
2037 A330 $1 Sheet of 9, #a.-i. 8.75 8.75

Souvenir Sheet

2038 A330 $6 multicolored 6.00 6.00

Butterflies — A331

Designs: 90c, Charaxes porthos. $1.20, Aethiopana honorius. $1.60, Charaxes hadrianus. $1.75, Precis westermanni.
No. 2043, $1.10: a, Charaxes protoclea. b, Byblia ilithyia. c, Black-headed tchagra (bird). d, Charaxes nobilis. e, Pseudacraea boisduvali. f, Charaxes smaragdalis. g, Charaxes lasti. h, Pseudacraea poggei. i, Graphium colonna.
No. 2044, $1.10: a, Carmine bee-eater (bird). b, Pseudacraea eurytus. c, Hypolimnas monteironis. d, Charaxes anticlea. e, Graphium leonidas. f, Graphium illyris. g, Nepheronia argia. h, Graphium policenes. i, Papilio dardanus.
No. 2045, $6, Euxanthe tiberius, horiz. No. 2046, $6, Charaxes lactitinctus, horiz. No. 2047, $6, Euphaedra neophron.

1997, Mar. 10
2039-2042 A331 Set of 4 5.75 5.75

Sheets of 9, #a-i

2043-2044 A331 Set of 2 18.50 18.50

Souvenir Sheets

2045-2047 A331 Set of 3 14.50 14.50

UNESCO, 50th Anniv. — A332

World Heritage Sites: 60c, Convent of the Companions of Jesus, Morelia, Mexico. 90c, Fortress, San Lorenzo, Panama, vert. $1, Canaima Natl. Park, Venezuela, vert. $1.20, Huascarán Natl. Park, Peru, vert. $1.60, Church of San Francisco, Guatemala, vert. $1.75, Santo Domingo, Dominican Republic, vert.
No. 2054, vert, each $1.10: a-c, Guanajuato, Mexico. d, Jesuit missions of the Chiquitos, Bolivia. e, Huascarán Natl. Park, Peru. f, Jesuit missions, La Santisima, Paraguay. g, Cartagena, Colombia. h, Old Havana fortification, Cuba.
No. 2055, each $1.65: a, Tikal Natl. Park, Guatemala. b, Rio Platano Reserve, Honduras. c, Ruins of Copán, Honduras. d, Church of El Carmen, Antigua, Guatemala. e, Teotihuacán, Mexico.
No. 2056, $6, Teotihuacán, Mexico, diff. No. 2057, $6, Tikal Natl. Park, Guatemala, diff.

1997, Apr. 10 **Litho.** ***Perf. 14***
2048-2053 A332 Set of 6 5.00 5.00
2054 A332 Sheet of 8, #a.-h. + label 8.50 8.50
2055 A332 Sheet of 5, #a.-e. + label 8.00 8.00

Souvenir Sheets

2056-2057 A332 Set of 2 10.50 10.50

Fauna — A333

No. 2058, each $1.20: a, Red bishop. b, Yellow baboon. c, Superb starling. d, Ratel. e, Hunting dog. f, Serval.
No. 2059, each $1.65: a, Okapi. b, Giant forest squirrel. c, Masked weaver. d, Common genet. e, Yellow-billed stork. f, Red-headed agama.
No. 2060, $6, Malachite kingfisher. No. 2061, $6, Gray crowned crane. No. 2062, $6, Bat-eared fox.

1997, Apr. 24
2058 A333 Sheet of 6, #a.-f. 8.00 8.00
2059 A333 Sheet of 6, #a.-f. 10.00 10.00

Souvenir Sheets

2060-2062 A333 Set of 3 17.50 17.50

Charlie Chaplin (1889-1977), Comedian, Actor A334

Various portraits.

1997, Feb. 24 **Litho.** ***Perf. 14***
2063 A334 $1 Sheet of 9, #a.-i. 7.25 7.25

Souvenir Sheet

2064 A334 $6 multicolored 5.75 5.75

Paul P. Harris (1868-1947), Founder of Rotary, Intl. — A335

Designs: $1.75, Service above self, James Grant, Ivory Coast, 1994, portrait of Harris.
$6, Group study exchange, New Zealand.

1997, June 12 **Litho.** ***Perf. 14***
2065 A335 $1.75 multicolored 1.75 1.75

Souvenir Sheet

2066 A335 $6 multicolored 5.00 5.00

Heinrich von Stephan (1831-97) A336

No. 2067, each $1.75, Portrait of Von Stephan and: a, Kaiser Wilhelm I. b, UPU emblem. c, Pigeon Post.
$6, Von Stephan, Basel messenger, 1400's.

1997, June 12
2067 A336 Sheet of 3, #a.-c. 4.00 4.00

Souvenir Sheet

2068 A336 $6 multicolored 5.50 5.50

PACIFIC 97.

Queen Elizabeth II, Prince Philip, 50th Wedding Anniv. A337

No. 2069: a, Queen. b, Royal arms. c, Queen, Prince in royal attire. d, Queen, King riding in open carriage. e, Balmoral Castle. f. Prince Philip.

$6, Early portrait of Queen, King in royal attire.

1997, June 12

2069 A337 $1 Sheet of 6, #a.-f. 6.75 6.75

Souvenir Sheet

2070 A337 $6 multicolored 5.75 5.75

Grimm's Fairy Tales A338

Scenes from "Cinderella", each $1.75: No. 2071: a, Mother, stepsisters. b, Cinderella, fairy godmother. c, Cinderella, Prince Charming.

$6, Prince trying shoe on Cinderella.

1997, June 13 ***Perf. 13½x14***

2071 A338 Sheet of 3, #a.-c. 5.00 5.00

Souvenir Sheet

2072 A338 $6 multicolored 5.75 5.75

Chernobyl Disaster, 10th Anniv. A339

Designs: $1.65, UNESCO. $2, Chabad's Children of Chernobyl.

1997, June 12

2073 A339 $1.65 multicolored 1.60 1.60
2074 A339 $2 multicolored 1.90 1.90

Mushrooms — A340

Designs: 45c, Marasmius rotula. 65c, Cantharellus cibarius. 70c, Lepiota cristata. 90c, Auricularia mesenterica. $1, Pholiota alnicola. $1.65, Leccinum aurantiacum.

No. 2081, each $1.75: a, Entoloma serrulatum. b, Panaeolus sphinctrinus. c, Volvariella bombycina. d, Conocybe percincta. e, Pluteus cervinus. f, Russula foetens.

No. 2082, $6, Panellus serotinus. No. 2083, $6, Amanita cothurnata.

1997, Aug. 12 **Litho.** ***Perf. 14***

2075-2080 A340 Set of 6 4.50 4.50
2081 A340 Sheet of 6, #a.-f. 8.75 8.75

Souvenir Sheets

2082-2083 A340 Set of 2 11.00 11.00

Orchids — A341

Designs: 45c, Odontoglossum cervantesii. 65c, Medford star. 75c, Motes resplendent. 90c, Debutante. $1, Apple blossom. $2, Dendrobium.

No. 2090, $1.65: a, Angel lace. b, Precious stones. c, Orange theope butterfly. d, Promenaea xanthina. e, Lycaste macrobulbon. f, Amesiella philippinensis. g, Machu Picchu. h, Zuma urchin.

No. 2091, $1.65: a, Sophia Martin. b, Dogface butterfly. c, Mini purple. d, Showgirl. e, Mem. Dorothy Bertsch. f, Black II. g, Leeanum. h, Paphiopedilum macranthum.

No. 2092, $6, Seine. No. 2093, $6, Paphiopedilum gratrixianum.

1997, Aug. 19 **Litho.** ***Perf. 14***

2084-2089 A341 Set of 6 6.25 6.25

Sheets of 8, #a-h

2090-2091 A341 Set of 2 19.00 19.00

Souvenir Sheets

2092-2093 A341 Set of 2 11.00 11.00

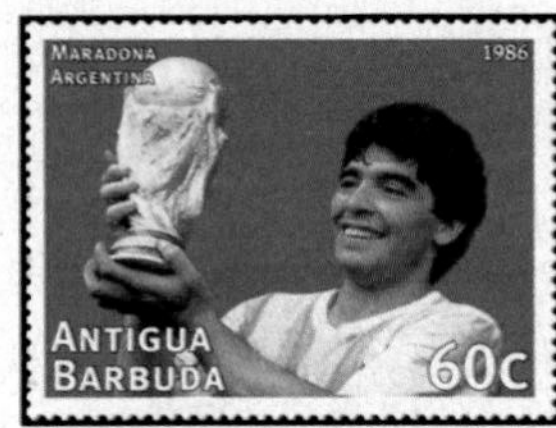

1998 World Cup Soccer Championships, France — A342

Designs: 60c, Maradona, Argentina, 1986. 75c, Fritz Walter, W. Germany, 1954. 90c, Zoff, Italy, 1982. $1.20, Moore, England, 1966. $1.65, Alberto, Brazil, 1970. $1.75, Matthäus, W. Germany.

No. 2100, vert: a, Ademir, Brazil, 1950. b, Eusebio, Portugal, 1966. c, Fontaine, France, 1958. d, Schillaci, Italy, 1990. e, Leonidas, Brazil, 1938. f, Stabile, Argentina, 1930. g, Nejedly, Czechoslovakia, 1934. h, Muller, W. Germany, 1970.

No. 2101, $6, Players, W. Germany, 1990. No. 2102, $6, Bebeto, Brazil, vert.

1997, Oct. 6 **Litho.** ***Perf. 14***

2094-2099 A342 Set of 6 5.75 5.75
2100 A342 $1 Sheet of 8, #a.-h., + label 5.75 5.75

Souvenir Sheets

2101-2102 A342 Set of 2 9.25 9.25

Domestic Animals A343

No. 2103, $1.65 — Dogs: a, Dachshund. b, Staffordshire terrier. c, Sharpei. d, Beagle. e, Norfolk terrier. f, Golden retriever.

No. 2104, $1.65 — Cats: a, Scottish fold. b, Japanese bobtail. c, Tabby manx. d, Bicolor American shorthair. e, Sorrel abyssinian. f, Himalayan blue point.

No. 2105, $6, Siberian husky, vert. No. 2106, $6, Red tabby American shorthair kitten, vert.

1997, Oct. 27 **Litho.** ***Perf. 14***

Sheets of 6, #a-f

2103-2104 A343 Set of 2 19.50 19.50

Souvenir Sheets

2105-2106 A343 Set of 2 11.00 11.00

Early Trains A344

No. 2107, $1.65: a, Original Trevithick drawing, 1804. b, "Puffing Billy," William Hedley, 1860. c, Crampton locomotive, Northern Railway, France, 1858. d, Twenty-five ton locomotive, Lawrence Machine Shop, 1860's. e, First locomotive, "Mississippi," built in England. f, "Coppernob," locomotive by Edward Bury, Furness Railway.

No. 2108, $1.65: a, "Jenny Lind," by David Joy for E.B. Wilson. b, "Atlantic" type locomotive, by Schenectady Locomotive Works, 1899. c, British built tank engine, Japan, by Kisons of Leeds, 1881. d, Express freight locomotive, 4-8-2 type, Pennsylvania Railroad. e, Four-cylinder locomotive, by Karl Golsdorf, Austria. f, "E" series 0-10-0 locomotive, produced by Lugansk Works, Russia, 1930.

No. 2109, $6, "Patente" George Stephenson, 1843. No. 2110, $6, Brunel's Trestle, Lynher River.

1997, Nov. 10

Sheets of 6, #a-f

2107-2108 A344 Set of 2 20.00 20.00

Souvenir Sheets

2109-2110 A344 Set of 2 11.00 11.00

Christmas A345

Entire paintings or details: 15c, The Angel Leaving Tobias and His Family, by Rembrandt. 25c, The Resurrection, by Martin Knoller. 60c, Astronomy, by Raphael. 75c, Music-making Angel, by Melozzo da Forli. 90c, Amor, by Parmigianino. $1.20, Madonna and Child with Saints John the Baptist, Anthony, Stephen and Jerome, by Rosso Fiorentino.

No. 2117, $6, The Portinari Altarpiece, by Hugo Van Der Goes. No. 2118, $6, The Wedding of Tobiolo, by Gianantonio and Francesco Guardi.

1997, Dec. 2 **Litho.** ***Perf. 14***

2111-2116 A345 $6 Set of 6 4.00 4.00

Souvenir Sheets

2117-2118 A345 $6 Set of 2 10.00 10.00

Diana, Princess of Wales (1961-97) — A346

Various portraits, color of sheet margin: No. 2119, $1.65, Pale green. No. 2120, $1.65, Pale pink.

No. 2121, $6,With her sons (in margin). No. 2122, $6, With Pope John Paul II (in margin).

1998, Jan. 19 **Litho.** ***Perf. 14***

Sheets of 6, #a-f

2119-2120 A346 Set of 2 13.50 13.50

Souvenir Sheets

2121-2122 A346 Set of 2 9.75 9.75

Fish A347

Designs: 75c, Yellow damselfish. 90c, Barred hamlet. $1, Jewelfish. $1.20, Bluehead wrasse. $1.50, Queen angelfish. $1.75, Queen triggerfish.

No. 2129, $1.65: a, Jack-knife fish. b, Cuban hogfish. c, Sergeant major. d, Neon goby. e, Jawfish. f, Flamefish.

No. 2130, $1.65: a, Rock beauty. b, Yellowtail snapper. c, Creole wrasse. d, Slender filefish. e, Squirrel fish. f, Fairy basslet.

No. 2131, $6, Black-capped gramma. No. 2132, $6, Porkfish.

1998, Feb. 19

2123-2128 A347 Set of 6 4.75 4.75

Sheets of 6, #a-f

2129-2130 A347 Set of 2 14.00 14.00

Souvenir Sheets

2131-2132 A347 Set of 2 11.00 11.00

Cedar Hall Moravian Church, 175th Anniv. A348

Designs: 20c, First church, manse, 1822-40. 45c, Cedar Hall School, 1840. 75c, Hugh A. King, former minister. 90c, Present structure. $1.20, Water tank, 1822. $2, Former manse demolished, 1978.

$6, Present structure, diff.

1998, Mar. 16 **Litho.** ***Perf. 14***

2133-2138 A348 Set of 6 4.25 4.25

Souvenir Sheet

2139 A348 $6 multicolored 5.00 5.00

No. 2139 contains one 50x37mm stamp.

Lighthouses — A349

Lighthouse, location: 45c, Trinity, Europa Point, Gibraltar, vert. 65c, Tierra Del Fuego, Argentina. 75c, Point Loma, California, US. 90c, Groenpoint, South Africa, vert. $1, Youghal, County Cork, Ireland, vert. $1.20, Launceston, Tasmania, Australia, vert. $1.65, Point Abino, Ontario, Canada. $1.75, Great Inagua, Bahamas.

$6, Capa Hatteras, North Carolina, US.

1998, Apr. 20

2140-2147 A349 Set of 8 8.25 8.25

Souvenir Sheet

2148 A349 $6 multi, vert. 8.00 8.00

Winnie the Pooh A350

No. 2149, $1: a, Pooh, Tigger in January. b, Pooh, Piglet in February. c, Piglet in March. d, Tigger, Pooh, Piglet in April. e, Kanga, Roo in May. f, Pooh, Owl in June.

No. 2150, $1,: a, Pooh, Eeyore, Tigger, Piglet in July. b, Pooh, Piglet in August. c, Christopher Robin in September. d, Eeyore in October. e, Pooh, Rabbit in November. f, Pooh, Piglet in December.

No. 2151, $6, Pooh, Rabbit holding blanket, Spring. No. 2152, $6, Pooh holding hand to mouth, Summer. No. 2153, $6, Pooh holding rake, Fall. No. 2154, $6, Eeyore, Pooh, Winter.

1998, May 11 **Litho.** ***Perf. 13½x14***

Sheets of 6, #a-f

2149-2150 A360 Set of 2 13.50 13.50

Souvenir Sheet

2151-2154 A350 Set of 4 20.00 20.00

Thomas Oliver Robinson Memorial High School, Cent. A351

Designs: 20c, $6, Nellie Robinson (1880-1972), founder, vert. 45c, School picture, 1985. 65c, Former building, 1930-49. 75c, Students with present headmistress, Natalie Hurst. 90c, Ina Loving (1908-96), educator, vert. $1.20, Present building, 1950.

1998, July 23 Litho. *Perf. 14*

2155-2160 A351 Set of 6 4.00 4.00

Souvenir Sheet

2161 A351 $6 multicolored 4.25 4.25

No. 2161 is a continuous design.

Intl. Year of the Ocean A352

No. 2162 — Marine life, "20,000 Leagues Under the Sea": a, Spotted eagle ray. b, Manta ray. c, Hawksbill turtle. d, Jellyfish. e, Queen angelfish. f, Octopus. g, Emperor angelfish. h, Regal angelfish. i, Porkfish. j, Raccoon butterfly fish. k, Atlantic barracuda. l, Sea horse. m, Nautilus. n, Trumpet fish. o, White tip shark. p, Spanish galleon. q, Black tip shark. r, Long-nosed butterfly fish. s, Green moray eel. t, Captain Nemo. u, Treasure chest. v, Hammerhead shark. w, Divers. x, Lion fish. y, Clown fish.

No. 2163 — Wildlife and birds: a, Maroon tailed conure. b, Cocoi heron. c, Common tern. d, Rainbow lorikeet. e, Saddleback butterfly fish. f, Goatfish, cat shark. g, Blue shark, stingray. h, Majestic snapper. i, Nassau grouper. j, Black-cap gramma, blue tang. k, Stingrays. l, Stingrays, giant starfish.

No. 2164, $6, Fiddler ray. No. 2165, $6, Humpback whale.

1998, Aug. 17

2162 A352 40c Sheet of 25, #a.-y. 8.75 8.75

2163 A352 75c Sheet of 12, #a.-l. 8.25 8.25

Souvenir Sheets

2164-2165 A352 Set of 2 10.00 10.00

Ships A353

No. 2166, each $1.75: a, Savannah. b, Viking ship. c, Greek warship.

No. 2167, each $1.75: a, Clipper. b, Dhow. c, Fishing cat.

No. 2168, $6, Dory, vert. No. 2169, $6, Baltimore clipper. No. 2170, $6, English warship, 13th cent.

1998, Aug. 18 *Perf. 14x14½*

Sheets of 3, #a-c

2166-2167 A353 Set of 2 7.50 7.50

Souvenir Sheets

Perf. 14

2168-2170 A353 $6 Set of 3 16.50 16.50

CARICOM, 25th Anniv. — A354

1998, Aug. 20 Litho. *Perf. 13½*

2171 A354 $1 multicolored 1.50 1.50

Antique Automobiles — A355

No. 2172 $1.65: a, 1911 Torpedo. b, 1913 Mercedes 22. c, 1920 Rover. d, 1956 Mercedes Benz. e, 1934 Packard V12. f, 1924 Opel.

No. 2173, $1.65 — Fords: a, 1896. b, 1903 Model A. c, 1928 Model T. d, 1922 Model T. e, 1929 Blackhawk. f, 1934 Sedan.

No. 2174, $6, 1908 Ford. No. 2175, $6, 1929 Ford.

1998, Sept. 1 *Perf. 14*

Sheets of 6, #a-f

2172-2173 A355 Set of 2 15.50 15.50

Souvenir Sheets

2174-2175 A355 Set of 2 9.50 9.50

Nos. 2174-2175 each contain one 60x40mm stamp.

Aircraft A356

No. 2176, $1.65: a, NASA Space Shuttle. b, Saab Grippen. c, Eurofighter EF2000. d. Sukhoi SU 27. e, Northrop B-2. f, Lockheed F-117 Nighthawk.

No. 2177, $1.65: a, Lockheed-Boeing General Dynamics Yf-22. b, Dassault-Breguet Rafale BO 1. c, MiG 29. d, Dassault-Breguet Mirage 2000D. e, Rockwell B-1B Lancer. f, McDonnell-Douglas C-17A.

No. 2178, $6, Sukhoi SU 35. No. 2179, $6, F-18 Hornet.

1998, Sept. 21

Sheets of 6, #a-f

2176-2177 A356 Set of 2 15.50 15.50

Souvenir Sheets

2178-2179 A356 Set of 2 11.00 11.00

Inventors and Inventions — A357

No. 2180 $1: a, Rudolf Diesel (1858-1913). b, Internal combustion, diesel engines. c, Zeppelin war balloon, Intrepid. d, Ferdinand von Zeppelin (1838-1917). e, Wilhelm Conrad Röntgen (1845-1923). f, X-ray machine. g, Saturn rocket. h, Wernher von Braun (1912-77).

No. 2181, $1: a, Carl Benz (1844-1929). b, Internal combustion engine, automobile. c, Atomic bomb. d, Albert Einstein. e, Leopold Godowsky, Jr. (1901-83) and Leopold Damrosch Mannes (1899-1964). f, Kodachrome film. g, First turbo jet airplane. h, Hans Pabst von Ohain (1911-98).

No. 2182, $6, Hans Geiger (1882-1945), inventor of the Geiger counter. No. 2183, $6, William Shockley (1910-89), developer of transistors.

1998, Nov. 10 Litho. *Perf. 14*

Sheets of 8, #a-h

2180-2181 A357 Set of 2 17.00 17.00

Souvenir Sheets

2182-2183 A357 Set of 2 10.50 10.50

Nos. 2180b-2180c, 2180f-2180g, 2181b-2181c, 2181f-2181g are 53x38mm.

Diana, Princess of Wales (1961-97) A358

1998, Nov. 18

2184 A358 $1.20 multicolored 1.25 1.25

No. 2184 was issued in sheets of 6.

Gandhi — A359

Portraits: 90c, Up close, later years. $1, Seated with hands clasped. $1.20, Up close, early years. $1.65, Primary school, Rajkot, age 7. $6, With stick, walking with boy (in margin).

1998, Nov. 18

2185-2188 A359 Set of 4 6.00 6.00

Souvenir Sheet

2189 A359 $6 multicolored 5.25 5.25

Picasso — A360

Paintings: $1.20, Figures on the Seashore, 1931, horiz. $1.65, Three Figures Under a Tree, 1907. $1.75, Two Women Running on the Beach, 1922, horiz.

$6, Bullfight, 1900, horiz.

1998, Nov. 18

2190-2192 A360 Set of 3 3.25 3.25

Souvenir Sheet

2193 A360 $6 multicolored 5.00 5.00

1998 World Scouting Jamboree, Chile A361

90c, Handshake. $1, Scouts hiking. $1.20, Sign.

$6, Lord Baden-Powell.

1998, Oct. 8 Litho. *Perf. 14*

2194-2196 A361 Set of 3 2.50 2.50

Souvenir Sheet

2197 A361 $6 multicolored 4.75 4.75

Organization of American States, 50th Anniv. A362

1998, Nov. 18 *Perf. 13½*

2198 A362 $1 multicolored .85 .85

Enzo Ferrari (1898-1988), Automobile Manufacturer — A363

No. 2199, each $1.75: a, Top view of Dino 246 GT-GTS. b, Front view of Dino 246 GT-GTS. c, 1977 365 GT4 BB.

$6, Dino 246 GT-GTS.

1998, Nov. 18 *Perf. 14*

2199 A363 Sheet of 3, #a.-c. 8.00 8.00

Souvenir Sheet

2200 A363 $6 multicolored 8.00 8.00

No. 2200 contains one 92x35mm stamp.

Royal Air Force, 80th Anniv. A364

No. 2201, each $1.75: a, McDonnell Douglas Phantom FGR1. b, Sepecat Jaguar GR1A. c, Panavia Tornado F3. d, McDonnell Douglas Phantom FGR2.

No. 2202, $6, Eurofighter 2000, Hurricane. No. 2203, $6, Hawk, biplane.

1998, Nov. 18

2201 A364 Sheet of 4, #a.-d. 6.25 6.25

Souvenir Sheets

2202-2203 A364 Set of 2 11.50 11.50

Sea Birds A365

Designs: 15c, Brown pelican. 25c, Dunlin. 45c, Atlantic puffin. 90c, Pied cormorant.

No. 2208: a, King eider. b, Inca tern. c, Dovekie. d, Ross's gull. e, Brown noddy. f, Marbled murrelet. g, Northern gannet. h, Razorbill. i, Long-tailed jaeger. j, Black guillemot. k, Whimbrel. l, Oystercatcher.

No. 2209, $6, Rhynchops niger. No. 2210, $6, Diomedea exulans.

1998, Nov. 24

2204-2207 A365 Set of 4 2.00 2.00

2208 A365 75c Sheet of 12, #a.-l. 9.00 9.00

Souvenir Sheets

2209-2210 A365 Set of 2 11.50 11.50

Christmas A366

Dogs with Christmas decorations: 15c, Border collie. 25c, Dalmatian. 65c, Weimaraner.

75c, Scottish terrier. 90c, Long-haired dachshund. $1.20, Golden retriever. $2, Pekingese.
No. 2218, $6, Dalmatian, diff. No. 2219, $6, Jack Russell terrier.

1998, Dec. 10

2211-2217 A366 Set of 7 7.25 7.25

Souvenir Sheet

2218-2219 A366 Set of 2 9.50 9.50

Disney Characters in Water Sports A367

No. 2220, $1 — Water skiing: a, Goofy, maroon skis. b, Mickey. c, Goofy, Mickey. d, Donald. e, Goofy, blue skis. f, Minnie.
No. 2221, $1 — Surfing: a, Goofy running with board. b, Mickey. c, Donald holding board. d, Donald, riding board. e, Minnie. f, Goofy in water.
No. 2221G, Sailing & sailboarding: h, Mickey wearing cap. i, Mickey, Goofy, counterbalancing boat. j, Goofy sailboarding. k, Mickey, seagull overhead. l, Goofy puffing at sail. m, Mickey sailboarding.
No. 2222, Mickey. No. 2223, Minnie. No. 2224, Goofy. No. 2225, Donald.

1999, Jan. 11 Litho. *Perf. 13½x14*

Sheets of 6, #a-f

2220-2221 A367 Set of 2 11.00 11.00
2221G A367 $1 Sheet of 6, #h.-m. 5.50 5.50

Souvenir Sheets

2222-2225 A367 Set of 4 19.50 19.50

Mickey Mouse, 70th anniv.

Hell's Gate Steel Orchestra, 50th Anniv. A368

Designs: 20c, Nelson's Dockyard, 1996. 60c, Holiday Inn, Rochester, New York, 1992. 75c, Early years, 1950. 90c, World's Fair, 1964, Eustace Henry (AKA Manning). $1.20, Alston Henry playing double tenor.
No. 2231, $4, Like #2229, vert. No. 2232, $4, The early years, vert.

1999, Feb. 1 Litho. *Perf. 14*

2226-2230 A368 Set of 5 3.25 3.25

Souvenir Sheets

2231-2232 A368 Set of 2 6.75 6.75

Flowers A369

Designs, vert: 60c, Tulip. 75c, Fuschia. $1.20, Calla lily. $1.65, Sweet pea.
No. 2237: a, Morning glory. b, Geranium. c, Blue hibiscus. d, Marigolds. e, Sunflower. f, Impatiens. g, Petunia. h, Pansy. i, Saucer magnolia.
No. 2238: a, Primrose. b, Bleeding heart. c, Pink dogwood. d, Peony. e, Rose. f, Hellebores. g, Lily. h, Violet. i, Cherry blossoms.
No. 2239, $6, Lily, vert. No. 2240, $6, Zinnias, vert.

1999, Apr. 19 Litho. *Perf. 14*

2233-2236 A369 Set of 4 3.25 3.25
2237 A369 90c Sheet of 9, #a.-i. 6.50 6.50
2238 A369 $1 Sheet of 9, #a.-i. 7.50 7.50

Souvenir Sheets

2239-2240 A369 Set of 2 9.25 9.25

Elle Macpherson, Model — A370

Various portraits, each $1.20.

1999, Apr. 26 *Perf. 13½*

2241 A370 Sheet of 8, #a.-h. 8.50 8.50

Australia '99 World Stamp Expo.

John Glenn's Space Flight — A371

Space Exploration A372

No. 2242 — John Glenn, 1962, each $1.75: a, Climbing into Mercury Capsule. b, Formal portrait. c, Having helmet adjusted. d, Entering pressure chamber.
No. 2243, $1.65: a, Luna 2. b, Mariner 2. c, Giotto space probe. d, Rosat. e, Intl. Ultraviolet Explorer. f, Ulysses Space Probe.
No. 2244, $1.65: a, Mariner 10. b, Luna 9. c, Advanced X-ray Astrophysics Facility. d, Magellan Spacecraft. e, Pioneer-Venus 2. f, Infra-red Astronomy Satellite.
No. 2245, $6, Salyut 1, horiz. No. 2246, $6, MIR, horiz.

1999, May 6 Litho. *Perf. 14*

2242 A371 Sheet of 4, #a.-d. 6.50 6.50

Sheets of 6, #a-f

2243-2244 A372 Set of 2 15.00 15.00

Souvenir Sheets

2245-2246 A372 Set of 2 9.00 9.00

Nos. 2245-2246 are incorrectly inscribed.

Prehistoric Animals A373

Designs: 65c, Brachiosaurus. 75c, Oviraptor, vert. $1, Homotherium. $1.20, Macrauchenia, vert.
No. 2251, each $1.65: a, Leptictidium. b, Ictitherium. c, Plesictis. d, Hemicyon. e, Diacodexis. f, Stylinodon. g, Kanuites. h, Chriacus. i, Argyrolagus.
No. 2252, each $1.65: a, Struthiomimus. b, Corythosaurus. c, Dsungaripterus. d, Compognathus. e, Prosaurolophus. f, Montanoceratops. g, Stegosaurus. h, Deinonychus. i, Ouranosaurus.
No. 2253, each $6, Pteranodon. No. 2254, $6, Eurhinodelphus.

1999, May 26

2247-2250 A373 Set of 4 3.50 3.50

Sheets of 9, #a-i

2251-2252 A373 Set of 2 23.00 23.00

Souvenir Sheets

2253-2254 A373 Set of 2 9.25 9.25

Illustrations on Nos. 2247-2248 are switched.

IBRA'99, World Stamp Exhibition, Nuremberg — A374

Exhibition emblem, Leipzig-Dresden Railway and: No. 2255, $1, Caroline Islands #19. No. 2257, $1.65, Caroline Islands #4.
Emblem, Gölsdorf 4-4-0 and: No. 2256, $1.20, Caroline Islands #16. No. 2258, $1.90, Caroline Islands #8, #10.
$6, Registered label on cover.

1999, June 24 Litho. *Perf. 14*

2255-2258 A374 Set of 4 5.00 5.00

Souvenir Sheet

2259 A374 $6 multicolored 4.75 4.75

Paintings by Hokusai (1760-1849) — A375

No. 2260, $1.65 — Details or entire paintings: a, Asakusa Honganji. b, Dawn at Isawa in Kai Province. c, Samurai with Bow and Arrow (bows level). d, Samurai with Bow and Arrow (bows at different angles). e, Kajikazawa in Kai Province. f, A Great Wave.
No. 2261, $1.65: a, People on the Balcony of the Sazaido. b, Nakahara in Sagami Province. c, Defensive Positions (2 men). d, Defensive Positions (3 men). e, Mount Fuji in Clear Weather. f, Nihonbashi in Edo.
No. 2262, $6, Gotenyama At Shinagawa on Tokaido Highway, vert. No. 2263, $6, A Netsuke Workshop, vert.

1999, June 24

Sheets of 6, #a-f

2260-2261 A375 Set of 2 15.00 15.00

Souvenir Sheets

2262-2263 A375 Set of 2 9.25 9.25

Johann Wolfgang von Goethe (1749-1832), Poet — A376

No. 2264, each $1.75: a, Three archangels in "Faust." b, Portraits of Goethe and Friedrich von Schiller (1759-1805). c, Faust reclining in landscape with spirits.
$6, Profile portrait of Goethe.

1999, June 24 Litho. *Perf. 14*

2264 A376 Sheet of 3, #a.-c. 4.50 4.50

Souvenir Sheet

2265 A376 $6 multicolored 4.50 4.50

Souvenir Sheets

Philexfrance '99, World Philatelic Exhibition — A377

Locomotives: No. 2266, Crampton 1855-69. No. 2267, 232-U1 4-Cylinder Compound 4-6-4, 1949.

1999, June 24 *Perf. 13¾*

2266 A377 $6 multicolored 5.00 5.00
2267 A377 $6 multicolored 5.00 5.00

A378

Wedding of Prince Edward and Sophie Rhys-Jones — No. 2268: a, Sophie. b, Sophie, Edward. c, Edward.
$6, Horse and carriage, couple.

1999, June 24 *Perf. 13½*

2268 A378 $3 Sheet of 3, #a.-c. 6.75 6.75

Souvenir Sheet

2269 A378 $6 multicolored 5.00 5.00

A379

Various white kittens: 35c, 45c, 60c, 75c, 90c, $1.
No. 2276, $1.65: a, One holding paw on another. b, Black & white. c, White kitten, black kitten. d, One with yarn. e, Two in basket. f, One looking up.
No. 2277, $1.65: a, One playing with red yarn. b, Two long-haired. c, Yellow tabby. d, One with mouse. e, Yellow tabby on pillow. f, Black & gray tabby.
No. 2278, $6, Tabby cat carrying kitten. No. 2279, $6, Yellow kitten in tree.

1999, May 25 Litho. *Perf. 14½x14*

2270-2275 A379 Set of 6 3.00 3.00

Sheets of 6

2276-2277 A379 Set of 2 15.00 15.00

Souvenir Sheets

2278-2279 A379 Set of 2 9.25 9.25

Australia '99, World Stamp Expo (Nos. 2276-2279).

A380

UN Rights of the Child Convention, 10th Anniv. — No. 2280: a, Three children. b, Adult hand taking child's hand, silhouette of mother holding infant. c, UN Building, member flags, dove.
$6, Dove.

1999, June 22 *Perf. 14*

2280 A380 $3 Sheet of 3, #a.-c. 6.75 6.75

Souvenir Sheet

2281 A380 $6 multicolored 5.00 5.00

Boats — A381

Designs: 25c, Missa Ferdie. 45c, Sailboats. 60c, Jolly Roger Pirate Ship. 90c, $4, Freewinds. $1.20, Monarch of the Seas.

1999, June 24 Litho. *Perf. 13x11*

2282-2286 A381 Set of 5 3.25 3.25
2286a Souvenir sheet, #2282-2286 3.75 3.75

Souvenir Sheet

Perf. 13¾

2287 A381 $4 multicolored 3.75 3.75

No. 2287 contains one 51x38mm stamp.

A382

Butterflies: 65c, Fiery jewel. 75c, Hewitson's blue hairstreak. $1.20, Scarce bamboo page, horiz. $1.65, Paris peacock, horiz.

No. 2292, horiz.: a, California dog face. b, Small copper. c, Zebra swallowtail. d, White M hairstreak. e, Old world swallowtail. f, Buckeye. g, Apollo. h, Sonoran blue. i, Purple emperor.

No. 2293, $6, Monarch. No. 2294, $6, Cairns birdwing, horiz.

1999, Aug. 16 *Perf. 14*

2288-2291 A382 Set of 4 3.75 3.75
2292 A382 $1 Sheet of 9, #a.-i. 8.50 8.50

Souvenir Sheets

2293-2294 A382 Set of 2 11.00 11.00

Christmas A383

15c, Madonna and child in a Wreath of Flowers by Peter Paul Rubens. 25c, Shroud of Christ Held by Two Angels, by Albrecht Dürer. 45c, Madonna and Child Enthroned Between Two Saints, by Raphael. 60c, Holy Family with the Lamb, by Raphael. $2, The Transfiguration, by Raphael. $4, Three Putti Holding a Coat of Arms, by Dürer.

$6, The Coronation of the Holy St. Catherine, by Rubens.

1999, Nov. 22 Litho. *Perf. 13¾*

2295-2300 A383 Set of 6 6.50 6.50

Souvenir Sheet

2301 A383 $6 multicolored 5.50 5.50

Famous Elderly People A384

Designs: a, Katharine Hepburn. b, Martha Graham. c, Eubie Blake. d, Agatha Christie. e, Eudora Welty. f, Helen Hayes. g, Vladimir Horowitz. h, Katharine Graham. i, Pablo Casals. j, Pete Seeger. k, Andres Segovia. l, Frank Lloyd Wright.

2000, Jan. 18 Litho. *Perf. 14*

2302 A384 90c Sheet of 12, #a-l 8.00 8.00

Charlie Chaplin A385

Designs: a, "Modern Times," street scene. b, "The Gold Rush," with other actor. c, Unidentified film. d, "Modern Times," on gears. e, "The Gold Rush," arms akimbo. f, "The Gold Rush," with cane.

2000, Jan. 18 *Perf. 13¾*

2303 A385 $1.65 Sheet of 6, #a-f 7.25 7.25

Sir Cliff Richard, Rock Musician A386

2000, Jan. 18 *Perf. 13¼*

2304 A386 $1.65 multi 1.25 1.25

Issued in sheets of 6.

Birds A387

Designs: 75c, Streamertail. 90c, Yellow-bellied sapsucker. $1.20, Rufous-tailed jacamar. $2, Spectacled owl.

No. 2309, $1.20: a, Ground dove. b, Wood stork. c, Saffron finch. d, Green-backed heron. e, Lovely cotinga. f, St. Vincent parrot. g, Cuban grassquit. h, Red-winged blackbird.

No. 2310, $1.20: a, Scarlet macaw. b, Yellow-fronted amazon. c, Queen-of-Bavaria. d, Nanday conure. e, Jamaican tody. f, Smooth-billed ani. g, Puerto Rican woodpecker. h, Ruby-throated hummingbird.

No. 2311, $6, Vermilion flycatcher. No. 2312, $6, Red-capped manakin, vert.

2000, Apr. 17 Litho. *Perf. 14*

2305-2308 A387 Set of 4 4.00 4.00

Sheets of 8, #a-h

Perf. 13¾x14

2309-2310 A387 Set of 2 15.00 15.00

Souvenir Sheets

Perf. 13¾

2311-2312 A387 Set of 2 9.25 9.25

The Stamp Show 2000, London (Nos. 2309-2312). Size of stamps: Nos. 2309-2310, 48x31mm; No. 2311, 50x38mm; No. 2312, 38x50mm.

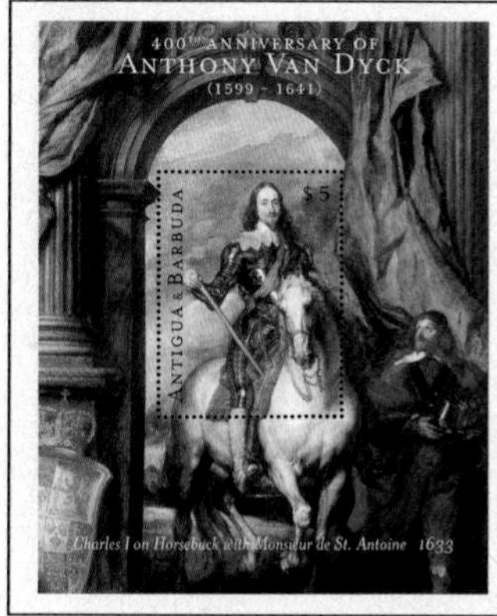

Paintings of Anthony Van Dyck — A388

No. 2313, $1.20: a, Arthur Goodwin. b, Sir Thomas Wharton. c, Mary Villers (as Venus), Daughter of the Duke of Buckingham. d, Christina Bruce, Countess of Devonshire. e, James Hamilton, 3rd Marquis and 1st Duke of Hamilton. f, Henry Danvers, Earl of Danby.

No. 2314, $1.20: a, Charles I in Robes of State. b, Henrietta Maria. c, Queen Henrietta Maria with Her Dwarf Sir Jeffrey Hudson. d, Charles I in Armor. e, Henrietta Maria in Profile, facing right. f. Queen Henrietta Maria.

No. 2315, $1.20: a, Marie de Raet, Wife of Philippe le Roy. b, Jacomo de Cachiopin. c, Princess Henrietta of Lorraine Attended by a Page. d, Portrait of a Man. e, Portrait of a Woman. f, Philippe le Roy, Seigneur de Ravels.

No. 2316, $5, Charles I on Horseback with Monsieur de St. Antoine. No. 2317, $5, Le Roi a La Chasse (Charles I hunting). No. 2318, $5, Charles I in Three Positions. No. 2319, $5, Charles I and Queen Henrietta.

No. 2320, $6, Portrait of Two Young English Gentlemen, Sons of the Duke of Lenox. No. 2321, $6, George, Lord Digby, and William, Lord Russell.

Illustration reduced.

2000, May 15 *Perf. 13¾*

Sheets of 6, #a-f

2313-2315 A388 Set of 3 15.00 15.00

Souvenir Sheets

2316-2319 A388 Set of 4 15.50 15.50
2320-2321 A388 Set of 2 9.25 9.25

Butterflies — A389

No. 2322, $1.65: a, Orange theope. b, Sloane's urania. c, Gold-drop helicopis. d, Papilio velovis. e, Graphium androcles. f, Cramer's mesene.

No. 2323, $1.65, horiz.: a, Euploea miniszeki. b, Doris. c, Evenus coronata. d, Anchisiades swallowtail. e, White-spotted tadpole. f, Morpho patroclus.

No. 2324, $1.65, horiz.: a, Mesosemia loruhama. b, Bia actorion. c, Ghost brimstone. d, Blue tharops. e, Catasticta manco. f, White-tailed page.

No. 2325, $6, Reakirt's blue. No. 2326, $6, Graphium encelades, horiz. No. 2327, $6, Graphium milon, horiz.

Illustration reduced.

2000, May 29 *Perf. 14*

Sheets of 6, #a-f

2322-2324 A389 Set of 3 22.50 22.50

Souvenir Sheets

2325-2327 A389 Set of 3 14.00 14.00

Prince William, 18th Birthday — A390

Prince William — No. 2328: a, With checked shirt, waving. b, In jacket and white shirt. c, With arms clasped. d, In striped shirt, waving.

$6, With Prince Harry, Princess Diana and unidentified man.

2000, June 21 *Perf. 14*

2328 A390 $1.65 Sheet of 4, #a-d 4.75 4.75

Souvenir Sheet

Perf. 13¾

2329 A390 $6 multi 4.25 4.25

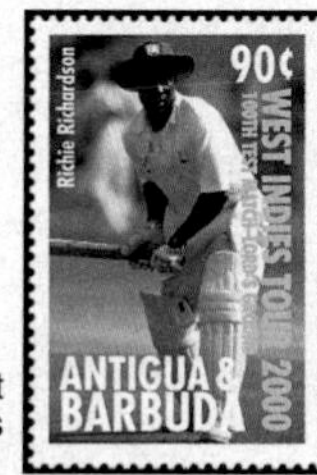

100th Test Cricket Match at Lord's Ground — A391

90c, Richie Richardson. $5, Viv Richard. $6, Lord's Ground, horiz.

2000, June 26 *Perf. 14*

2330-2331 A391 Set of 2 4.50 4.50

Souvenir Sheet

2332 A391 $6 multi 4.50 4.50

Souvenir Sheet

2000 Summer Olympics, Sydney — A392

Designs: a, Cyclist. b, Diver. c, Italian flag, Flaminio Stadium, Rome. d, Ancient Greek javelin thrower.

2000, June 26

2333 A392 $2 Sheet of 4, #a-d 6.00 6.00

First Zeppelin Flight, Cent. — A393

No. 2334: a, LZ-1. b, LZ-2. c, LZ-3.
$6, LZ-7.

2000, June 26 ***Perf. 13½***

2334 A393 $3 Sheet of 3, #a-c 6.75 6.75

Souvenir Sheet

Perf. 14¼

2335 A393 $6 multi 4.25 4.25

No. 2334 contains three 45x27mm stamps.

Cats — A394

No. 2336: a, Long-haired blue & white. b, Snow shoe. c, Persian. d, Chocolate lynx point. e, Brown & white sphynx. f, White tortoiseshell.
$6, Lavender tortie.

2000, May 29 **Litho.** ***Perf. 14***

2336 A394 $1.65 Sheet of 6, #a-f 7.50 7.50

Souvenir Sheet

2337 A394 $6 multi 4.50 4.50

Souvenir Sheet

Public Railways, 175th Anniv. — A395

No. 2338: a, Locomotion No. 1, George Stephenson. b, John Bull.

2000, June 26

2338 A395 $3 Sheet of 2, #a-b 4.50 4.50

The Stamp Show 2000, London.

Souvenir Sheet

Johann Sebastian Bach (1685-1750) — A396

2000, June 26

2339 A396 $6 multi 4.25 4.25

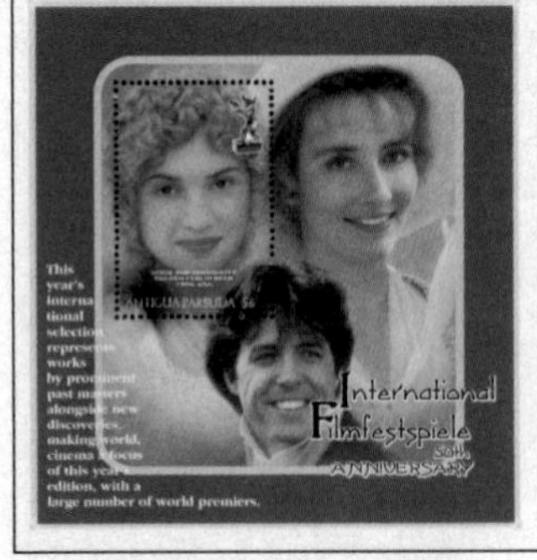

Berlin Film Festival, 50th Anniv. — A397

No. 2340: a, Une Femme Est Une Femme. b, Carmen Jones. c, Die Ratten. d, Die Vier im Jeep. e, Lilies of the Field. f, Invitation to the Dance.
$6, Sense and Sensibility.

2000, June 26

2340 A397 $1.65 Sheet of 6, #a-f 7.25 7.25

Souvenir Sheet

2341 A397 $6 multi 4.50 4.50

Flowers — A398

Designs: 45c, Epidendrum pseudepidndrum. 65c, Odontoglossum cervantesii. 75c, Cattleya dowiana. 90c, Beloperone guttata. $1, Colliandra haematocephala. $1.20, Brassavola nodosa.

No. 2348, $1.65: a, Masdevallia coccinea. b, Paphinia cristata. c, Vanilla planifolia. d, Cattleya forbesii. e, Lycaste skinneri. f, Cattleya percivaliana.

No. 2349, $1.65: a, Anthurium andreanum. b, Doxantha unguiscati. c, Hibiscus rosasinensis. d, Canna indica. e, Heliconius umilis. f, Strelitzia reginae.

No. 2350, $1.65: a, Pseudocalymna alliaceum. b, Datura candida. c, Ipomoea tuberosa. d, Allamanda cathartica. e, Aspasia epidendroides. f, Maxillaria cucullata.

No. 2351, $6, Strelitzia reginae. No. 2352, $6, Cattleya leopoldii. No. 2353, $6, Rossioglossum grande.

2000, May 29 **Litho.** ***Perf. 14***

2342-2347 A398 Set of 6 3.50 3.50

Sheets of 6, #a-f

2348-2350 A398 Set of 3 22.50 22.50

Souvenir Sheets

2351-2353 A398 Set of 3 13.00 13.00

Dogs — A399

Designs: 90c, Boxer. $1, Wire-haired pointer (inscribed Alaskan malamute). $2, Alaskan malamute (inscribed Wire-haired pointer). $4, Saluki.

No. 2358: a, Bearded collie. b, Cardigan Welsh corgi. c, Saluki. d, Basset hound. e, Standard poodle. f, Boston terrier.
$6, Cavalier King Charles Spaniel.

2000, May 29

2354-2357 A399 Set of 4 5.50 5.50

2358 A399 $1.65 Sheet of 6, #a-f 7.00 7.00

Souvenir Sheet

2359 A399 $6 multi 4.50 4.50

Space Achievements — A400

No. 2360, $1.65: a, Sputnik 1. b, Explorer 1. c, Mars Express. d, Luna 1. e, Ranger 7. f, Mariner 4.

No. 2361, $1.65: a, Mariner 10. b, Soho. c, Mariner 2. d, Giotto. e, Exosat. f, Pioneer.

No. 2362, $6, Hubble Space Telescope. No. 2363, $6, Vostok 1.

2000, June 26

Sheets of 6, #a-f

2360-2361 A400 Set of 2 14.00 14.00

Souvenir Sheets

2362-2363 A400 Set of 2 9.00 9.00

World Stamp Expo 2000, Anaheim.

Apollo-Soyuz Mission, 25th Anniv. — A401

No. 2364: a, Alexei Leonov. b, Soyuz 19. c, Valeri Kubasov.
$6, Leonov and Thomas Stafford.

2000, June 26

2364 A401 $3 Sheet of 3, #a-c 6.50 6.50

Souvenir Sheet

2365 A401 $6 multi 4.25 4.25

Souvenir Sheet

Albert Einstein (1879-1955) — A402

2000, June 26 ***Perf. 14¼***

2366 A402 $6 multi 4.25 4.25

Girls' Brigade A403

Designs: 20c, Outreach program to Sunshine Home for Girls. 60c, Ullida Rawlins Gill, Intl. vice-president, vert. 75c, Officers and girls. 90c, Raising the flag, vert. $1.20, Members with 8th Antigua Company flag.
$5, Emblem, vert.

2000, July 13 ***Perf. 14***

2367-2371 A403 Set of 5 2.75 2.75

Souvenir Sheet

2372 A403 $5 multi 3.75 3.75

A404

Queen Mother, 100th Birthday — A405

No. 2373: a, As child. b, In 1940. c, With Princess Anne, 1951. d, In Canada, 1989.
$6, Inspecting the troops. $20, In gardens.

Litho., Margin Embossed

2000, Aug. 4 ***Perf. 14***

2373 A404 $2 Sheet of 4, #a-d, + label 6.00 6.00

Souvenir Sheet

Perf. 13¾

2374 A404 $6 multi 4.50 4.50

Without Gum

Litho. & Embossed

Die Cut 8¾x9

2375 A405 $20 gold & multi

No. 2374 contains one 38x51mm stamp.
See Nos. 2536-2537.

Popes — A406

No. 2376, $1.65: a, Alexander VI, 1492-1503, hands clasped. b, Benedict XIII, 1724-30. c, Boniface IX, 1389-1404. d, Alexander

VI, no hands. e, Clement VIII, 1592-1605. f, Clement VI, 1342-52.

No. 2377, $1.65: a, John Paul II, 1978-present. b, Benedict XV, 1914-22. c, John XXIII, 1958-63. d, Pius XI, 1922-39. e, Pius XII, 1939-58. f, Paul VI, 1963-78.

No. 2378, $6, Pius II, 1458-1464. No. 2379, $6, Pius VII, 1800-23.

2000, Aug. 21 Litho. *Perf. 13¾*

Sheets of 6, #a-f

2376-2377 A406 Set of 2 15.00 15.00

Souvenir Sheets

2378-2379 A406 Set of 2 9.25 9.25

Monarchs — A407

No. 2380, $1.65: a, Donaldbane of Scotland, 1093-97. b, Duncan I of Scotland, 1034-40. c, Duncan II of Scotland, 1094. d, Macbeth of Scotland, 1040-57. e, Malcolm III of Scotland, 1057-93. f, Edgar of Scotland, 1097-1107.

No. 2381, $1.65: a, Charles I of Great Britain, 1625-49. b, Charles II of Great Britain, 1660-85. c, Charles Edward Stuart, the "Young Pretender," 1720-1788. d, James II of Great Britain, 1685-89. e, James II of Scotland, 1437-60. f, James III of Scotland, 1460-88.

No. 2382, $6, Robert I of Scotland, 1306-29. No. 2383, $6, Anne of Great Britain, 1702-14. Illustration reduced.

2000, Aug. 21

Sheets of 6, #a-f

2380-2381 A407 Set of 2 15.00 15.00

Souvenir Sheets

2382-2383 A407 Set of 2 9.25 9.25

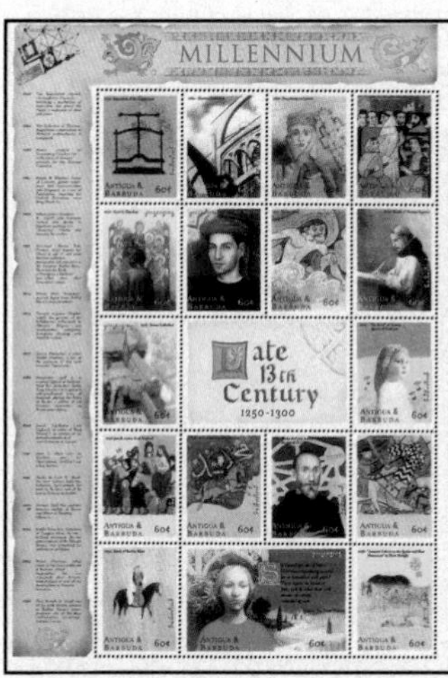

Millennium (#2385) — A408

No. 2384 — Chinese paintings: a, Admonitions of the Instructress to the Court Ladies, attributed to Ku K'ai-chih. b, Ink drawing on silk, 3rd cent. B.C. c, Ink and color drawing on silk, 2nd cent. B.C. d, Scholars of the Northern Qi Collating Texts (detail), attributed to Yang Zihua. e, Spring Outing (detail), attributed to Zhan Ziqian. f, Portrait of the Emperors (detail), attributed to Yen Liben. g, Sailing Boats and a Riverside Mansion, attributed to Li Sixun. h, Two Horses and a Groom (detail), by Han Kan. i, King's Portrait (detail), attributed to Wu Daozi. j, Court Ladies Wearing Flowered Headdresses (detail), attributed to Zhou Fang. k, Wintry Groves and Layered Banks, by Dong Yuan. l, Mount Kuanglu, by Jing Hao. m, Pheasant and Small Birds by a Jujube Shrub, by Huang Jucai. n, Deer Among Red Maples, by anonymous painter. o, Wintry Groves and Layered Banks, diff., by Dong Yuan. p, Literary Gathering, by Han Huang (60x40mm). q, Sketches of Birds and Insects (detail), by Huang Quan.

Perf. 12¾x12½

2000, Aug. 21 Litho.

2384 A408 25c Sheet of 17, #a-q, + label 5.00 5.00

Highlights of 1250-1300: a, Expansion of the Inquisition. b, Chartres Cathedral. c, Sculptures in Naumburg Cathedral. d, 1st English Parliament. e, The Madonna in Majesty (Maestà), by Cimabue. f, Marco Polo. g Divine wind. h, Death of St. Thomas Aquinas. i, Arezzo Cathedral. j, Margaret, Queen of Scotland. k, Jewish exodus from England. l, Fall of Acre to Muslims. m, Moses de León writes much of The Zohar. n, German Civil War. o, Death of Kublai Khan. p, Dante writes La Vita Nuova (60x40mm). q, Chao Meng-fu paints Autumn Colors on the Quiao and Hua Mountains.

2000, Aug. 21

2385 A408 60c Sheet of 17, #a-q + label 9.00 9.00

Battle of Britain, 60th Anniv. — A409

No. 2386, $1.20: a, Bristol Blenheim. b, Winston Churchill. c, Bristol Blenheim and barrage balloon. d, Heinkel. e, Spitfire. f, German rescue vessel. g, Messerschmitt 109. h, RAF air and sea rescue launch.

No. 2387, $1.20: a, German lookout. b, Children being evacuated. c, Youngsters evacuated from hospitals. d, Hurricane. e, Rescue workers. f, British political cartoon. g, King George VI and Queen Elizabeth inspect wreckage. h, Barrage balloon over Tower Bridge.

No. 2388, $6, Spitfires. No. 2389, $6, Junkers 87B.

2000, Oct. 16 Litho. *Perf. 14*

Sheets of 8, #a-h

2386-2387 A409 Set of 2 14.50 14.50

Souvenir Sheets

2388-2389 A409 Set of 2 9.25 9.25

Rainforest Fauna — A410

Designs: 75c, Agouti. 90c, Capybara. $1.20, Basilisk lizard. $2, Heliconid butterfly.

No. 2394, $1.65: a, Green violet-ear hummingbird. b, Harpy eagle. c, Three-toed sloth. d, White uakari monkey. e, Anteater. f, Coati.

No. 2395, $1.75: a, Red-eyed tree frog. b, Black spider monkey. c, Emerald toucanet. d, Kinkajou. e, Spectacled bear. f, Tapir.

No. 2396, $6, Keel-billed toucan, horiz. No. 2397, $6, Scarlet macaw, horiz.

2000, Sept. 25 Litho. *Perf. 14*

2390-2393 A410 Set of 4 3.75 3.75

Sheets of 6, #a-f

2394-2395 A410 Set of 2 15.00 15.00

Souvenir Sheets

2396-2397 A410 Set of 2 9.25 9.25

Submarines — A411

Designs: 65c, Sea Cliff. 75c, Beaver Mark IV. 90c, Reef Ranger. $1, Cubmarine. $1.20, Alvin. $3, Argus.

No. 2404, $2: a, Revenge. b, Walrus. c, Los Angeles. d, Daphne. e, USS Ohio. f, USS Skipjack.

No. 2405, $6, Trieste. No. 2406, $6, German Type 209.

2000, Oct. 2

2398-2403 A411 Set of 6 5.50 5.50

2404 A411 $2 Sheet of 6, #a-f 8.75 8.75

Souvenir Sheets

2405-2406 A411 Set of 2 9.00 9.00

Paintings from the Prado — A412

No. 2407, $1.65: a, Three men. b, Man's head. c, Three women. d, Man on white horse. e, Man on brown horse. f, Man leading horse. a-c from Family Portrait, by Adriaen Thomasz Key. d-f from The Devotion of Rudolf I, by Peter Paul Rubens and Jan Wildens.

No. 2408, $1.65: a, Seated man. b, Man with sash. c, Group of men. d, Laureated figure. e, Men working at anvil. f, Two workers. a-c from The Defense of Cadiz Against the English by Francisco de Zurbaran. d-f from Vulcan's Forge, by Diego Velázquez

No. 2409, $1.65: a, Mandolin player. b, Woman with fan. c, Two men. d, Bald man. e, Two Magi. f, Jesus, Mary and Joseph. a-c from The Concert, by Vicente Palmaroli y Gonzalez. d-f from The Adoration of the Magi, by Juan Bautista Maino

No. 2410, $6, The Seller of Fans, by José del Castillo. No. 2411, $6, Portrait of a Family in a Garden, by Jan van Kessel, the Younger. No. 2412, $6, The Deliverance of St. Peter, by José de Ribera, horiz.

Illustration reduced.

2000, Oct. 6 *Perf. 12x12¼, 12¼x12*

Sheets of 6, #a-f

2407-2409 A412 Set of 3 20.00 20.00

Souvenir Sheets

2410-2412 A412 Set of 3 13.00 13.00

España 2000 Intl. Philatelic Exhibition.

Christmas — A413

Designs (background): 25c, No. 2417a, Angels, full body (blue). 45c, No. 2417b, Angel's heads (orange). 90c, No. 2417c, Angel's heads (blue). $5, No. 2417d, Angels, full body (yellow).

2000, Dec. 4 *Perf. 14*

2413-2416 A413 Set of 4 4.50 4.50

2417 A413 $1.75 Sheet of 4, #a-d 5.25 5.25

Souvenir Sheet

2418 A413 $6 Jesus 4.50 4.50

Rijksmuseum, Amsterdam, Bicent. (in 2000) — A414

No. 2419, $1: a, Dr. Ephraim Bueno, by Rembrandt. b, Woman Writing a Letter, by Frans van Mieris, the Elder. c, Mary Magdalene, by Jan van Scorel. d, Portrait of a Woman (inscribed Anna Coddle), by Maarten van Heemskerck. e, Cleopatra's Banquet, by Gerard Lairesse. f, Titus van Rijn in Friar's Habit, by Rembrandt.

No. 2420, $1.20: a, Saskia van Uylenburgh, by Rembrandt. b, In the Month of July, by Paul Joseph Constantin Gabriel. c, Maria Trip, by Rembrandt. d, Still Life with Flowers, by Jan van Huysum. e, Hesje van Cleyburgh, by Rembrandt. f, Girl in a White Kimono, by George Hendrik Breitner.

No. 2421, $1.65: a, Man and woman at spinning wheel, by Pieter Pietersz. b, Self-portrait, by Rembrandt. c, Jeremiah Lamenting the Destruction of Jerusalem, by Rembrandt. d, The Jewish Bride, by Rembrandt. e, Tobit and Anna with a Kid, by Rembrandt. f, The Prophetess Anna, by Rembrandt.

No. 2422, $6, Doubting Thomas, by Hendrick ter Bruggen. No. 2423, $6, Still Life with Cheeses, by Floris van Dijck. No. 2424, $6, Isaac Blessing Jacob, by Govert Flinck.

2001, Jan. 15 Litho. *Perf. 13¾*

Sheets of 6, #a-f

2419-2421 A414 Set of 3 17.00 17.00

Souvenir Sheets

2422-2424 A414 Set of 3 13.50 13.50

Pokémon — A415

No. 2425: a, Starmie. b, Misty. c, Brock. d, Geodude. e, Krabby. f, Ash.

2001, Feb. 13

2425 A415 $1.75 Sheet of 6, #a-f 7.25 7.25

Souvenir Sheet

2426 A415 $6 Charizard 4.25 4.25

Mushrooms A416

Designs: 25c, Blue-toothed entoloma. 90c, Common morel. $1, Red cage fungus. $1.75, Fawn shield-cap.

No. 2431, $1.65: a, Lilac bonnet. b, Silky volvar. c, Poplar field cap. d, St. George's mushroom. e, Red-stemmed tough shank. f, Fly agaric.

No. 2432, $1.65: a, Copper trumpet. b, Meadow mushroom. c, Green-gilled parasol. d, Panther. e, Death cap. f, King bolete.

No. 2433, $6, Yellow parasol. No. 2434, Mutagen milk cap.

2001, Mar. 26 *Perf. 13¾x13¼*

2427-2430 A416 Set of 4 3.00 3.00

Sheets of 6, #a-f

2431-2432 A416 Set of 2 15.00 15.00

Souvenir Sheets

2433-2434 A416 Set of 2 9.25 9.25

Hong Kong 2001 Stamp Exhibition (2431-2434).

Population and Housing Census — A417

Map of Antigua with various graphs. Denominations: 15c, 25c, 65c, 90c.

2001, Apr. 2 ***Perf. 13¾***
2435-2438 A417 Set of 4 1.50 1.50

Souvenir Sheet

2439 A417 $6 Map, emblem 4.50 4.50

Phila Nippon '01, Japan — A418

Designs: 45c Two women facing right, from Yuna (Bath-house Women). 60c, Woman facing left, from Yuna. 65c, Two women, from Yuna. 75c, Man with stringed instrument at top, from Hikone Screen. $1, Woman with stringed instrument at bottom, from Hikone Screen. $1.20, Two people, from Hikone Screen.

No. 2446 — Namban Screen, by Naizen Kano, each $1.65: a, Ship's stern. b, Ship's bow. c, Man with closed umbrella. d, Man with open umbrella.

No. 2447 — Merry Making Under the Cherry Blossoms, by Naganobu Kano, each $1.65: a, Steps. b, Tree. c, Four people near building. d, Four people, mountains. e, Three people. f, One person.

No. 2448, $6, Visiting a Shrine on a Rainy Night, by Harunobu Suzuki. No. 2449, $6, Courtesan on a Veranda Upstairs, by Kokan Shiba. No. 2450, $6, Daruma, by Tsujo Kano.

2001, May 28 **Litho.** ***Perf. 14¼x14***
2440-2445 A418 Set of 6 3.50 3.50
2446 A418 Sheet of 4, #a-d 5.00 5.00
2447 A418 Sheet of 6, #a-f 7.50 7.50

Souvenir Sheets

Perf. 13¾

2448-2450 A418 Set of 3 12.50 12.50

Nos. 2448-2450 each contain one 38x51mm stamp.

No. 2449 is incorrectly inscribed. It actually depicts "Courtesan on a Veranda Upstairs," by Kokan.

Orchids A419

Designs: 45c, Hintleya burtii. 75c, Neomoovea irrovata. 90c, Comparettia speciosa. $1, Cypripedium crapeanum.

No. 2455, $1.20, vert.: a, Trichoceuos muralis. b, Dracula rampira. c, Psychopsis papilio. d, Lycaste clenningiana. e, Telipogon nevuosus. f, Masclecallia ayahbacana.

No. 2456, $1.65, vert.: a, Rhyncholaelia glanca. b, Oncidium barbatum. c, Phaius tankervillege. d, Ghies brechtiana. e, Angraecum leonis. f, Cychnoches loddigesti.

No. 2457, $1.65, vert.: a, Cattleya dowiana. b, Dendrobium cruentum. c, Bulbophyllum lobbi. d, Chysis laevis. e, Ancistrochilus rothschildicanus. f, Angraecum sororium.

No. 2458, $6, Trichopilia fragrans, vert. No. 2459, $6, Symphalossum sanguinem, vert.

2001, June 11 ***Perf. 14***
2451-2454 A419 Set of 4 2.40 2.40

Sheets of 6, #a-f

2455-2457 A419 Set of 3 19.00 19.00

Souvenir Sheets

2458-2459 A419 Set of 2 9.00 9.00

Souvenir Sheets

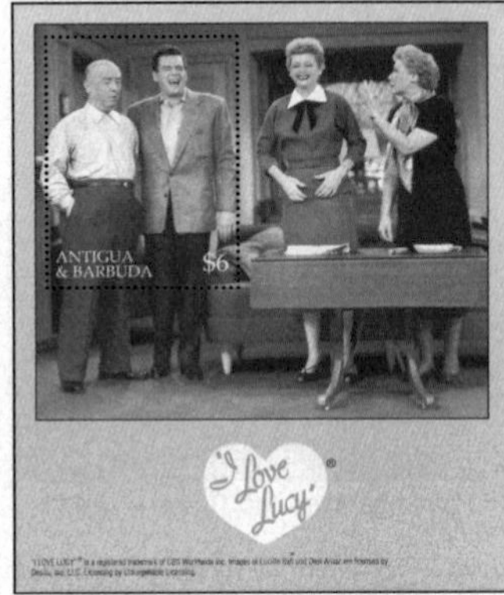

I Love Lucy — A420

Designs: No. 2460, $6, Fred and Ricky. No. 2461, $6, Lucy and Ethel. No. 2462, $6, Lucy and fireplace. No. 2463, $6, Lucy and open door.

2001, Mar. 5 **Litho.** ***Perf. 13¾***
2460-2463 A420 Set of 4 18.00 18.00

See Nos. 2522-2525.

Marine Life and Birds A421

Designs: 25c, Yellowtail damselfish. 45c, Indigo hamlet. 65c, Great white shark. No. 2467, 90c, Bottlenose dolphin. No. 2468, 90c, Palette surgeonfish. $1, Octopus.

No. 2470, $1.20: a, Common dolphin. b, Franklin's gull. c, Rock beauty. d, Bicolor angelfish. e, Beaugregory. f, Banded butterflyfish.

No. 2471, $1.20: a, Common tern. b, Flying fish. c, Queen angelfish. d, Blue-striped grunt. e, Porkfish. f, Blue tang.

No. 2472, $1.65: a, Dugong. b, White-tailed tropicbird. c, Bull shark and Spanish grunt. d, Manta ray. e, Green turtle. f, Spanish grunt.

No. 2473, $1.65: a, Red-footed booby. b, Bottlenose dolphin. c, Hawksbill turtle. d, Monk seal. e, Bull shark and coral. f, Lemon shark.

No. 2474, $5, Sailfish. No. 2475, $5, Beaugregory and brown pelican, vert. No. 2476, $6, Hawksbill turtle. No. 2477, $6, Queen triggerfish.

2001, June 11 ***Perf. 14***
2464-2469 A421 Set of 6 3.25 3.25

Sheets of 6, #a-f

2470-2473 A421 Set of 4 24.00 24.00

Souvenir Sheets

2474-2477 A421 Set of 4 16.00 16.00

Ship Freewinds — A422

Designs: 30c, Maiden voyage anniversary in Antigua. 45c, In St. Barthelemy. 75c, In Caribbean at sunset. 90c, In Bonaire. $1.50, In Bequia.

No. 2483, $4, With lights on during eclipse. No. 2484, $4, In Curacao.

2001, June 15
2478-2482 A422 Set of 5 3.00 3.00

Souvenir Sheets

2483-2484 A422 Set of 2 6.00 6.00

Toulouse-Lautrec Paintings — A423

No. 2485: a, Monsieur Georges-Henri Manuel Standing. b, Monsieur Louis Pascal. c, Roman Coolus. d, Monsieur Fourcade.

$5, Dancing at the Moulin de la Galette.

2001, July 3 ***Perf. 13¾***
2485 A423 $2 Sheet of 4, #a-d 6.00 6.00

Souvenir Sheet

2486 A423 $5 multi 3.75 3.75

Giuseppe Verdi (1813-1901), Opera Composer — A424

No. 2487: a, Verdi in hat. b, Character and score from Don Carlos. c, Conductor and score for Aida. d, Musicians and score for Rigoletto.

2001, July 3 ***Perf. 14***
2487 A424 $2 Sheet of 4, #a-d 6.00 6.00

Souvenir Sheet

2488 A424 $5 Verdi, score 3.75 3.75

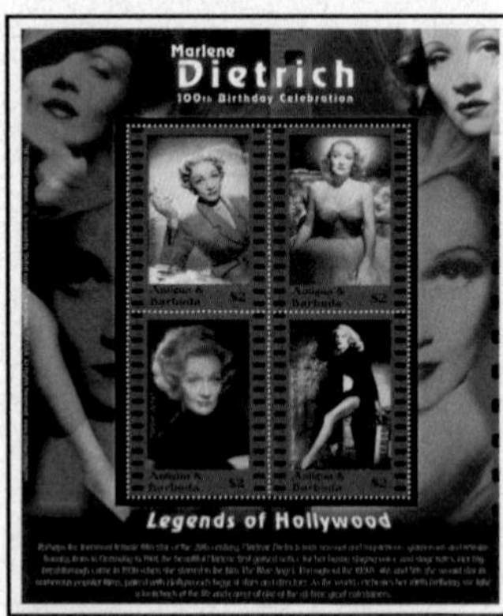

Marlene Dietrich — A425

No. 2489: a, With cigarette. b, On sofa. c, Color photograph. d, With piano.

2001, July 3 ***Perf. 13¾***
2489 A425 $2 Sheet of 4, #a-d 6.00 6.00

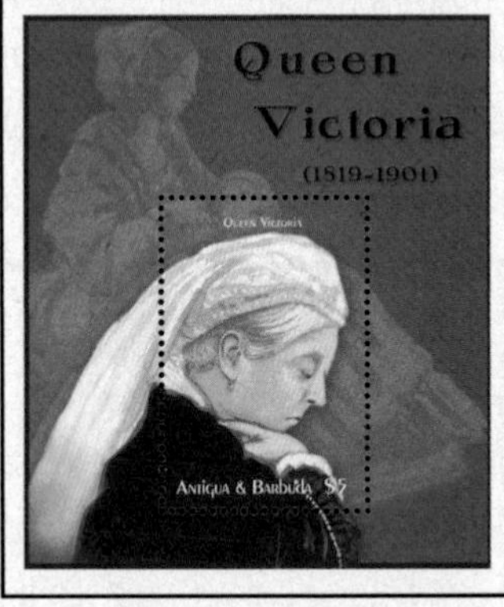

Queen Victoria (1819-1901) — A426

No. 2490: a, Blue dress. b, Red hat. c, Crown. d, Crown and blue sash.

2001, July 3 ***Perf. 14***
2490 A426 $2 Sheet of 4, #a-d 6.00 6.00

Souvenir Sheet

2491 A426 $5 As old woman 3.75 3.75

Queen Elizabeth II, 75th Birthday — A427

No. 2492: a, At birth, 1926. b, In 1938. c, In 1939. d, At coronation, 1953. e, In 1956. f, In 1985.

2001, July 3
2492 A427 $1 Sheet of 6, #a-f 3.75 3.75

Souvenir Sheet

2493 A427 $6 In 1940 4.50 4.50

Photomosaic of Queen Elizabeth II — A428

2001, July 3 **Litho.** ***Perf. 14***
2494 A428 $1 multi .75 .75

Queen Elizabeth II, 75th birthday. Issued in sheets of 8.

Monet Paintings — A429

No. 2495, horiz.: a, Water Lilies. b, Rose Portals, Giverny. c, The Water Lily Pond, Harmony in Green. d, The Artist's Garden, Irises.

$5, Jerusalem Artichokes.

2001, July 3 *Perf. 13¾*
2495 A429 $2 Sheet of 4, #a-d 6.00 6.00

Souvenir Sheet

2496 A429 $5 multi 3.75 3.75

Endangered Animals — A430

Designs: 25c, Collared peccary. 30c, Baird's tapir. 45c, Agouti. 75c, Bananaquit. 90c, Six-banded armadillo. $1, Roseate spoonbill.

No. 2503, each $1.80: a, Mouse opossum. b, Magnificent black frigatebird. c, Northern jacana. d, Painted bunting. e, Haitian solenodon. f, St. Lucia iguana.

No. 2504, each $2.50: a, West Indian iguana. b, Scarlet macaw. c, Cotton-topped tamarin. d, Kinkajou.

No. 2505, $6, Ocelot, vert. No. 2506, $6, King vulture, vert.

2001, Sept. 10 *Perf. 14*
2497-2502 A430 Set of 6 2.50 2.50
2503 A430 Sheet of 6, #a-f 8.00 8.00
2504 A430 Sheet of 4, #a-d 7.00 7.00

Souvenir Sheets

2505-2506 A430 Set of 2 9.00 9.00

Rudolph Valentino (1895-1926), Actor — A431

No. 2507, $1: a, Blood and Sand. b, Eyes of Youth. c, All Night. d, Last known photo of Valentino. e, Camille. f, Cobra.

No. 2508, $1: a, The Son of the Sheik. b, The Young Rajah. c, The Eagle. d, The Sheik. e, A Sainted Devil. f, Monsieur Beaucaire.

No. 2509, $6, The Four Horsemen of the Apocalypse. No. 2510, $6, Valentino with Natasha Rambova.

2001, Oct. 2 *Perf. 13¾*

Sheets of 6, #a-f

2507-2508 A431 Set of 2 9.00 9.00

Souvenir Sheets

2509-2510 A431 Set of 2 9.00 9.00

Scenes From Shirley Temple Movies — A432

No. 2511, $1.65 — Scenes from Baby, Take a Bow, with Temple: a, In polka-dot dress. b, With man on steps. c, With man holding gun. d, With woman.

No. 2512, $1.80, horiz. — Scenes from The Little Princess, with Temple: a, With man. b, Washing floor. c, With woman and child. d, With old woman.

No. 2513, $1.50 — Scenes from The Little Princess, with Temple: a, With woman. b, In pink dress. c, Holding doll. d, On throne. e, With man. f, With birthday cake.

No. 2514, $1.65, horiz. — Scenes from Baby, Take a Bow, with Temple: a, With woman and five children. b, With arms around man. c, Being tucked in bed. d, With man. e, Standing with man and woman. f, Looking in cradle.

No. 2515, $6, In polka-dot dress, from Baby, Take a Bow. No. 2516, With soldiers, from The Little Princess.

2001, Oct. 2 **Sheets of 4, #a-d**
2511-2512 A432 Set of 2 10.50 10.50

Sheets of 6, #a-f

2513-2514 A432 Set of 2 14.00 14.00

Souvenir Sheets

2515-2516 A432 Set of 2 8.00 8.00

Nobel Prizes, Cent. — A433

No. 2517, $1.50 — Chemistry laureates: a, Melvin Calvin, 1961. b, Linus C. Pauling, 1954. c, Vincent du Vigneaud, 1955. d, Richard Synge, 1952. e, Archer Martin, 1952. f, Alfred Werner, 1913.

No. 2518, $1.50 — Chemistry laureates: a, Robert F. Curl, Jr., 1996. b, Alan J. Heeger, 2000. c, Michael Smith, 1993. d, Sidney Altman, 1989. e, Elias James Corey, 1990. f, William Francis Giauque, 1949.

No. 2519, $6, Ernest Rutherford, Chemistry, 1908. No. 2520, $6, International Red Cross, Peace, 1944. No. 2521, $6, Ernst Otto Fischer, Chemistry, 1973.

2001, Nov. 29 *Perf. 14*

Sheets of 6, #a-f

2517-2518 A433 Set of 2 13.50 13.50

Souvenir Sheets

2519-2521 A433 Set of 3 13.50 13.50

I Love Lucy Type of 2001

Designs: No. 2522, $6, Fred at desk. No. 2523, $6, Lucy and Fred. No. 2524, $6, Lucy, closed door. No. 2525, $6, Fred and Ricky at desk, horiz.

2001 *Perf. 13¾*
2522-2525 A420 Set of 4 18.00 18.00

Christmas — A434

Paintings: 25c, Madonna and Child with Angels, by Filippo Lippi. 45c, Madonna of Corneto Tarquinia, by Lippi. 50c, Madonna and Child, by Domenico Ghirlandaio. 75c, Madonna and Child, by Lippi. $4, Madonna del Ceppo, by Lippi.

$6, Madonna Enthroned with Angels and Saints, by Lippi.

2001, Dec. 4 **Litho.** *Perf. 14*
2526-2530 A434 Set of 5 4.50 4.50

Souvenir Sheet

2531 A434 $6 multi 4.50 4.50

2002 World Cup Soccer Championships, Japan and Korea — A435

No. 2532, $1.50: a, Scene from final game, 1950. b, Ferenc Puskas, 1954. c, Raymond Kopa, 1958. d, Mauro, 1962. e, Gordon Banks, 1966. f, Pelé, 1970.

No. 2533, $1.50: a, Daniel Passarella, 1978. b, Karl-Heinz Rummenigge, 1982. c, World Cup trophy, 1986. d, Diego Maradona, 1990. e, Roger Milla, 1994. f, Zinedine Zidane, 1998.

No. 2534, $6, Head from Jules Rimet Cup, 1930. No. 2535, $6, Head and globe from World Cup trophy, 2002.

2001, Dec. 17 *Perf. 13¾x14¼*

Sheets of 6, #a-f

2532-2533 A435 Set of 2 12.00 12.00

Souvenir Sheets

Perf. 14¼

2534-2535 A435 Set of 2 8.00 8.00

Queen Mother Type of 2000 Redrawn

No. 2536, each $2: a, As child. b, In 1940. c, With Princess Anne, 1951. d, In Canada, 1989.

$6, Inspecting the troops.

2001, Dec. *Perf. 14*

Yellow Orange Frames

2536 A404 Sheet of 4, #a-d, + label 6.00 6.00

Souvenir Sheet

Perf. 13¾

2537 A404 $6 multi 4.50 4.50

Queen Mother's 101st birthday. No. 2537 contains one 38x51mm stamp with a darker appearance than that found on No. 2374. Sheet margins of Nos. 2536-2537 lack embossing and gold arms found on Nos. 2373-2374.

US Civil War — A436

No. 2538: a, Battle of Nashville. b, Battle of Atlanta. c, Battle of Spotsylvania. d, Battle of the Wilderness. e, Battle of Chickamauga Creek. f, Battle of Gettysburg. g, Battle of Chancellorsville. h, Battle of Fredericksburg. i, Battle of Antietam. j, Second Battle of Bull Run. k, Battle of Five Forks. l, Seven Days' Battle. m, Battle of Bull Run. n, Battle of Shiloh. o, Battle of Seven Pines. p, Battle of Fort Sumter. q, Battle of Chattanooga. r, Surrender at Appomattox.

No. 2539, vert.: a, Gen. Ulysses S. Grant. b, Pres. Abraham Lincoln. c, Confederate Pres. Jefferson Davis. d, Gen. Robert E. Lee. e, Gen. George A. Custer. f, Adm. Andrew Hull Foote. g, General Thomas "Stonewall" Jackson. h, Gen. J.E.B. Stuart. i, Gen. George G. Meade. j, Gen. Philip H. Sheridan. k, Gen. James Longstreet. l, Gen. John S. Mosby.

No. 2540, $6, Monitor. No. 2541, $6, Merrimack.

2002, Jan. 28 *Perf. 14¾*
2538 A436 45c Sheet of 18, #a-r 10.00 10.00
2539 A436 50c Sheet of 12, #a-l 8.00 8.00

Souvenir Sheets

Perf. 14½x14¾ (#2540), 13¾

2540-2541 A436 Set of 2 11.00 11.00

No. 2541 contains one 50x38mm stamp.

Reign of Queen Elizabeth II, 50th Anniv. — A437

No. 2542: a, Striped dress. b, Green patterned dress. c, Orange patterned dress. d, White jacket.

$6, Queen with Princess Margaret.

2002, Feb. 6 *Perf. 14¼*
2542 A437 $2 Sheet of 4, #a-d 7.00 7.00

Souvenir Sheet

2543 A437 $6 multi 4.50 4.50

United We Stand — A438

2002, Feb. 11 *Perf. 13½x13¼*
2544 A438 $2 multi 1.50 1.50

Printed in sheets of 4.

Cricket Player Sir Vivian Richards, 50th Birthday — A439

Designs: 25c, Raising bat. 30c, Receiving gift. 50c, With arms raised. 75c, At bat. $1.50, Wearing sash, with woman. $1.80, Standing next to photograph of himself.

No. 2551, $6, Holding sword. No. 2552, $6, With Antigua color guard.

2002, Mar. 7 *Perf. 13½x13¼*
2545-2550 A439 Set of 6 4.00 4.00

Souvenir Sheets

2551-2552 A439 Set of 2 9.00 9.00

Flora and Fauna A440

Designs: 50c, Thick-billed parrot. 75c, Lesser long-nosed bat. $1.50, Montserrat oriole. $1.80, Miss Perkin's blue butterfly.

No. 2557, 90c: a, Quetzals. b, Two-toed sloth. c, Lovely cotinga. d, Giant hairstrak butterfly. e, Magenta-throated woodstar. f, Bull's-eye silk moth. g, Golden toads. h, Collared peccaries. i, Tamandua anteater.

No. 2558, $1: a, St. Lucia parrot. b, Cuban kite. c, West Indian whistling duck. d, Poey's sulphur butterfly. e, Scarlet ibis. f, Black-capped petrel. g, St. Lucia whiptail. h, Cuban

Solenodon. i, False androgeus swallowtail butterfly.
No. 2559, $6, Margay. No. 2560, $6, Olive Ridley turtle.

2002, Apr. 8 ***Perf. 14***
2553-2556 A440 Set of 4 3.50 3.50

Sheets of 9, #a-i

2557-2558 A440 Set of 2 14.00 14.00

Souvenir Sheets

2559-2560 A440 Set of 2 9.00 9.00

Antigua Community Players, 50th Anniv. — A441

Various photos: 20c, 25c, 30c, 75c, 90c, $1.50, $1.80.
No. 2568, $4, Former Pres. Edie Hill-Thibou, vert. No. 2569, $4, Acting Pres. and Music Director Yvonne Maginley, vert.

Perf. 13½x13¾

2002, June 11 **Litho.**
2561-2567 A441 Set of 7 4.25 4.25

Souvenir Sheets

Perf. 14

2568-2569 A441 Set of 2 6.00 6.00

Endangered Animals — A442

No. 2570, each $1.50: a, Red-billed tropicbird. b, Brown pelican. c, Magnificent frigatebird. d, Ground lizard. e, West Indian whistling duck. f, Antiguan racer snake. g, Spiny lobster. h, Hawksbill turtle. i, Queen conch.

2002, July 12 ***Perf. 14***
2570 A442 Sheet of 9, #a-i 9.00 9.00

2002 Winter Olympics, Salt Lake City — A443

Designs: No. 2571, $2, Cross-country skiing. No. 2572, $2, Pairs figure skating.

2002, July 15 ***Perf. 13½x13¼***
2571-2572 A443 Set of 2 3.00 3.00
2572a Souvenir sheet, #2571-2572 3.00 3.00

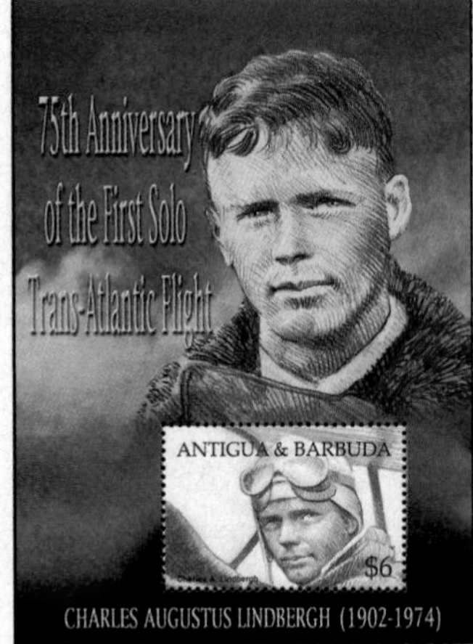

First Solo Transatlantic Flight, 75th Anniv. — A444

No. 2573, each $2.50: a, Charles Lindbergh and The Spirit of St. Louis. b, Arrival at Le Bourget Airport, Paris. c, Lindbergh receiving hero's welcome, New York.
$6, Lindbergh in airplane.

2002, July 15 ***Perf. 13¼x13½***
2573 A444 Sheet of 3, #a-c 5.75 5.75

Souvenir Sheet

2574 A444 $6 multi 4.50 4.50

Intl. Year of Mountains — A445

No. 2575: a, Mt. Fuji. b, Machu Picchu. c, Matterhorn.

2002, July 15 ***Perf. 13½x13¼***
2575 A445 $2 Sheet of 3, #a-c 4.50 4.50

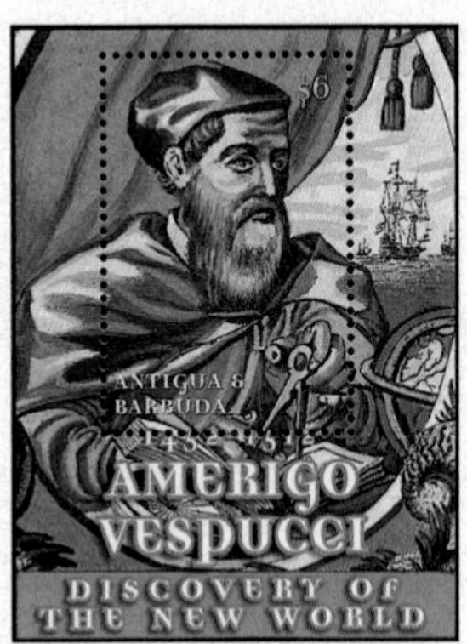

Amerigo Vespucci (1454-1512), Explorer — A446

No. 2576, horiz., each $2.50: a, Vespucci with gray head covering. b, Vespucci with red head covering. c, Hands and map.
$6, Vespucci and compass.

Perf. 13¼x13½, 13½x13¼

2002, July 15
2576 A446 Sheet of 3, #a-c 6.00 6.00

Souvenir Sheet

2577 A446 $6 multi 4.50 4.50

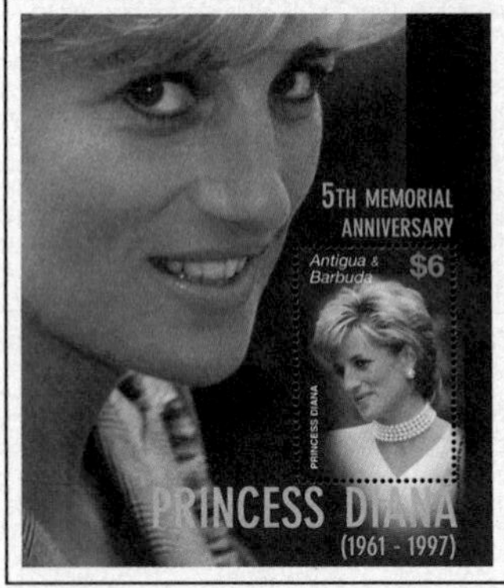

Princess Diana (1961-97) — A447

No. 2578: a, Wearing seven-strand pearl necklace. b, Wearing tiara and white dress. c, Wearing hat. d, Wearing earrings and black dress. e, Wearing tiara, no dress seen. f, Wearing earrings, no dress seen.
$6, Wearing white dress.

2002, July 29 ***Perf. 14***
2578 A447 $1.80 Sheet of 6, #a-f 7.50 7.50

Souvenir Sheet

2579 A447 $6 multi 4.50 4.50

Presidents John F. Kennedy and Ronald Reagan — A448

No. 2580, $1.50, horiz.: a, John, Robert and Edward Kennedy. b, Kennedy with Danny Kaye. c, Kennedy addressing nation. d, With wife, Jacqueline. e, Shaking hands with young Bill Clinton. f, Family members at funeral.
No. 2581, $1.50, horiz.: a, Reagan with wife, Nancy, and Pope John Paul II. b, As George Gipp in movie *Knute Rockne, All American.* c, With Gen. Matthew Ridgeway at Bitburg Cemetery. d, With Vice-president George H. W. Bush and Mikhail Gorbachev. e, With Presidents Ford, Carter, and Nixon. f, On horseback, with Queen Elizabeth II.
No. 2582, $6, Kennedy and flag. No. 2583, $6, Reagan.

2002, July 29 **Litho.**

Sheets of 6, #a-f

2580-2581 A448 Set of 2 13.50 13.50

Souvenir Sheets

2582-2583 A448 Set of 2 9.00 9.00

Elvis Presley (1935-77) A449

2002, Aug. 20 ***Perf. 13¾***
2584 A449 $1 multi .90 .90

Printed in sheets of 9.

Teddy Bears, Cent. — A450

No. 2585: a, Cheerleader bear. b, Figure skater bear. c, Ballet dancer bear. d, Aerobics instructor bear.

2002, Aug. 26
2585 A450 $2 Sheet of 4, #a-d 6.00 6.00

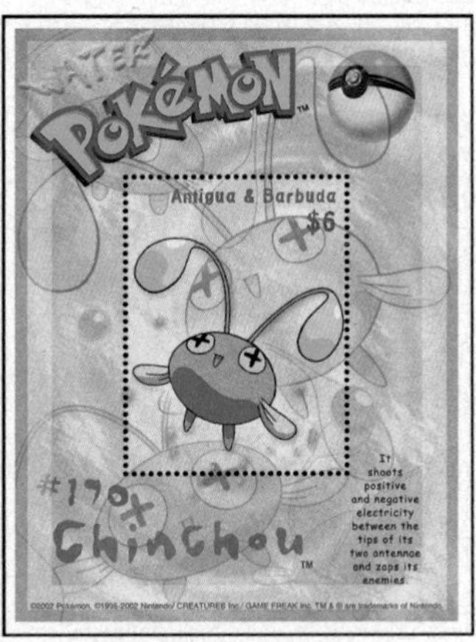

Pokémon — A451

No. 2586: a, Croconau. b, Mantine. c, Feraligatr. d, Quilfish. e, Remoraid. f, Quagsire.
$6, Chinchou.

2002, Aug. 26
2586 A451 $1.50 Sheet of 6, #a-f 6.75 6.75

Souvenir Sheet

2587 A451 $6 multi 4.50 4.50

Lee Strasberg (1901-82), Movie Actor and Director — A452

2002, Sept. 16 ***Perf. 14***
2588 A452 $1 multi .75 .75

Printed in sheets of 9.

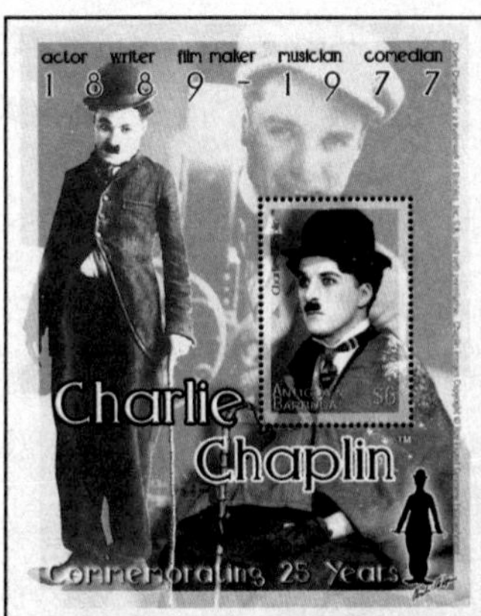

Charlie Chaplin (1889-1977), Actor — A453

No. 2589: a, Wearing bowler hat, facing forward. b, Wearing suit and vest. c, Wearing top hat. d, Wearing bowler hat, profile. e, Wearing bow tie and suit. f, With hand at chin.
$6, Wearing bowler hat, diff.

2002, Sept. 16
2589 A453 $1.80 Sheet of 6, #a-f 8.25 8.25

Souvenir Sheet

2590 A453 $6 multi 4.50 4.50

Marlene Dietrich (1901-92), Actress — A454

No. 2591: a, With hands at side of face. b, Wearing top hat. c, Faciing forward. d, With hand on chin. e, Wearing black hat. f, Wearing gloves.
$6, Facing forward, diff.

2002, Sept. 16
2591 A454 $1.50 Sheet of 6, #a-f 6.75 6.75

Souvenir Sheet

2592 A454 $6 multi 4.50 4.50

Bob Hope — A455

No. 2593: a, Wearing red cap. b, Wearing hat with strap. c, Wearing top hat. d, Wearing black cap. e, Wearing camouflage. f, Wearing white cap.

2002, Sept. 16
2593 A455 $1.50 Sheet of 6, #a-f 7.50 7.50

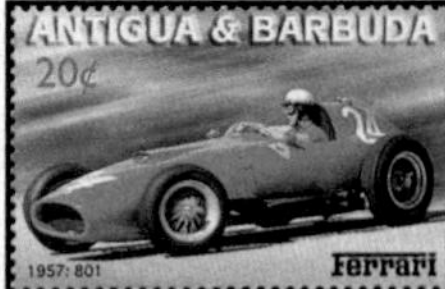

Ferrari Race Cars A456

Designs: 20c, 1957 801. 25c, 1959 256 F1. 30c, 1960 246P F1. 90c, 1966 246 F1. $1, 1971 312 B2. $1.50, 1969 312 F1. $2, 1997 F310B. $4, 2002 F2002.

2002, Oct. 14 **Litho.**
2594-2601 A456 Set of 8 7.75 7.75

Independence, 21st Anniv. — A457

Designs: 25c, Flag. 30c, Arms, vert. $1.50, Mt. St. John's Hospital nearing completion. $1.80, Parliament Building.
No. 2606, $6, Prime Minister Lester B. Bird, vert. No. 2607, $6, Sir Vere C. Bird, vert.

2002, Oct. 31 ***Perf. 14***
2602-2605 A457 Set of 4 3.50 3.50

Souvenir Sheets

2606-2607 A457 Set of 2 9.00 9.00

Nos. 2606-2607 each contain one 38x50mm stamp.

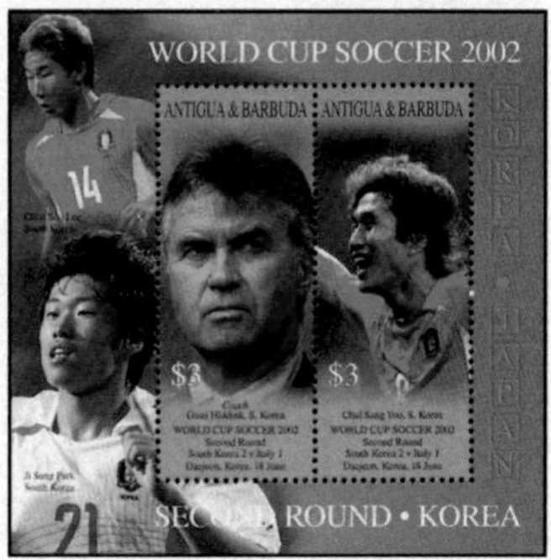

Second Round of World Cup Soccer Championships — A458

No. 2608, $1.65: a, Pyo Lee. b, Ji Sung Park. c, Jung Hwan Ahn. d, Filippo Inzaghi. e, Paolo Maldini. f, Damiano Tommasi.
No. 2609, $1.65: a, Juan Valeron. b, Iker Casillas. c, Fernando Hierro. d, Gary Kelly. e, Damien Duff. f, Matt Holland.
No. 2610, $3: a, South Korean coach Guus Hiddink. b, Chul Sang Yoo.
No. 2611, $3: a, Francesco Totti. b, Italy coach Giovanni Trapattoni.
No. 2612, $3: a, Spain coach Jose Antonio Camacho. b, Carlos Gamarra.
No. 2613, $3: a, Robbie Keane. b, Ireland coach Mick McCarthy.

2002, Nov. 4 ***Perf. 13½x13¼***

Sheets of 6, #a-f

2608-2609 A458 Set of 2 15.00 15.00

Souvenir Sheets, #a-b

2610-2613 A458 Set of 4 18.00 18.00

Christmas A459

Designs: 25c, Coronation of the Virgin, by Domenico Ghirlandaio. 45c, Adoration of the Magi (detail), by Ghirlandaio. 75c, Annunciation (detail), by Simone Martini, vert. 90c, Adoration of the Magi (detail, diff.) by Ghirlandaio. $5, Madonna and Child, by Giovanni Bellini.
$6, Madonna and Child, by Martini.

2002, Nov. 18 ***Perf. 14***
2614-2618 A459 Set of 5 5.50 5.50

Souvenir Sheet

2619 A459 $6 multi 4.50 4.50

Worldwide Fund for Nature (WWF) A460

Antiguan racer snake: a, Head. b, Snake with head near tail. c, Snake and dried leaves. d, Snake on rocks.

2002, Nov. 25
2620 Strip of 4 3.75 3.75
a.-d. A460 $1 Any single .90 .90

Printed in sheets of 4 strips.

Flora & Fauna — A461

No. 2621, $1.50: a, Magnificent frigatebird. b, Sooty tern. c, Bananaquit. d, Yellow-crowned night heron. e, Greater flamingo. f, Belted kingfisher.
No. 2622, $1.50: a, Killer whale. b, Sperm whale. c, Minke whale. d, Blainville's beaked whale. e, Blue whale. f, Cuvier's beaked whale.
No. 2623, $1.80: a, Hieroglyphic moth. b, Hypocrita dejanira. c, Snowy eupseudosoma moth. d, Composia credula. e, Giant silkworm moth. f, Diva moth.
No. 2624, $1.80: a, Epidendrum fragrans. b, Dombeya. c, Yellow poul. d, Milky wave plant. e, Cinderella plant. f, Coral orchid.
No. 2625, $5, Snowy egret. No. 2626, $5, Rothschildia orizaba. No. 2627, $6, Humpback whale. No. 2628, $6, Ionopsis utricularoides.

2002, Nov. 25 **Litho.**

Sheets of 6, #a-f

2621-2624 A461 Set of 4 30.00 30.00

Souvenir Sheets

2625-2628 A461 Set of 4 17.50 17.50

Souvenir Sheet

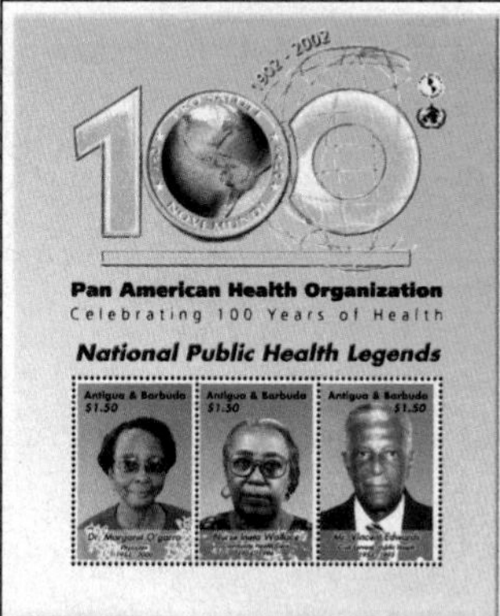

Pan-American Health Organization, Cent. — A462

No. 2629: a, Dr. Margaret O'Garro. b, Nurse Ineta Wallace. c, Public Health Worker Vincent Edwards.

2002, Dec. 2
2629 A462 $1.50 Sheet of 3, #a-c 3.50 3.50

Souvenir Sheets

Science Fiction — A463

No. 2630, $6, Writings of Nostradamus. No. 2631, $6, *2001: A Space Odyssey*, by Arthur C. Clarke. No. 2632, $6, Are We Alone?

2002, Dec. 12 ***Perf. 13¾***
2630-2632 A463 Set of 3 13.50 13.50

A464

20th World Scout Jamboree, Thailand — A465

No. 2633, horiz.: a, Lord Robert Baden-Powell. b, Ernest Thompson Seton, first Chief Scout. c, First black troop.
No. 2634: a, Brownie with broad neckerchief "X." b, Brownie with narrow neckerchief "X." c, Brownie with incomplete neckerchief "X."
No. 2635, Seton. No. 2636, Scout salute.

2002, Dec. 12 **Litho.** ***Perf. 14***
2633 A464 $3 Sheet of 3, #a-c 7.00 7.00
2634 A465 $3 Sheet of 3, #a-c 7.00 7.00

Souvenir Sheet

2635 A464 $6 multi 4.50 4.50
2636 A465 $6 multi 4.50 4.50

Ram, by Liu Jiyou — A466

2003, Feb. 10 *Perf. 13¾*

2637 A466 $1.80 multi 1.40 1.40

New Year 2003 (Year of the Ram). Issued in sheets of 4.

A467

Coronation of Queen Elizabeth II, 50th Anniv. — A468

No. 2638, each $3: a, In uniform. b, With tan jacket. c, With white dress and hat.
$6, With white dress.

2003 **Litho.** *Perf. 14*

2638 A467 Sheet of 3, #a-c 6.75 6.75

Souvenir Sheet

2639 A467 $6 multi 4.50 4.50

Miniature Sheet

Litho. & Embossed

Perf. 13¼x13

2640 A468 $20 gold & multi 17.50 17.50

Issued: Nos. 2638-2639, 5/14; No. 2640, 2/10.

Paintings of Lucas Cranach the Elder (1472-1553) A469

Designs: 75c, Lucretia. 90c, Venus and Cupid. $1, Judith with the Head of Holofernes, c. 1530. $1.50, Portrait of a Young Lady.

No. 2645: a, Portrait of the Wife of a Jurist. b, Portrait of a Jurist. c, Johannes Cuspinian. d, Portrait of Anna Cuspinian.
$6, Judith with the Head of Holofernes, c. 1532.

2003, Apr. 30 **Litho.** *Perf. 14¼*

2641-2644 A469 Set of 4 3.25 3.25
2645 A469 $2 Sheet of 4, #a-d 6.00 6.00

Souvenir Sheet

2646 A469 $6 multi 4.50 4.50

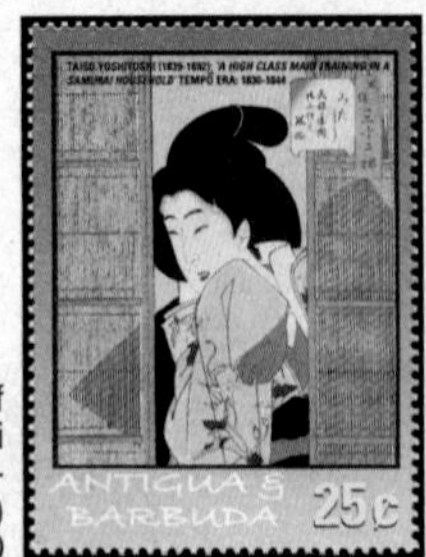

Paintings of Yoshitoshi Taiso (1839-92) A470

Designs: 25c, A High Class Maid Training in a Samurai Household. 50c, A Castle-Toppler Known as "Keisei": A Beautiful Woman Able to Seduce a Ruler So That He Forgets the Affairs of the State. $1, Stylish Young Geisha Battling a Snowstorm on Her Way to Work. $5, A Lady in Distress Being Treated With Moxa.

No. 2651: a, A Lady of the Imperial Court Wearing Four Layers of Robes. b, Young Mother Adoring Her Infant Son. c, Lady-in-waiting Looking Amused Over a Veranda in the Household of a Great Lord. d, A High-ranking Courtesan Known as "Oiran" Waiting For a Private Assignation.
$6, A Girl Teasing Her Cat.

2003, Apr. 30

2647-2650 A470 Set of 4 5.00 5.00
2651 A470 $2 Sheet of 4, #a-d 6.00 6.00

Souvenir Sheet

2652 A470 $6 multi 4.50 4.50

Paintings of Raoul Dufy (1877-1953) — A471

Designs: 90c, Boats at Martigues. $1, Harvesting. $1.80, Sailboats in the Port of Le Havre. $5, The Big Bather, vert.

No. 2657: a, The Beach and the Pier at Trouville. b, Port With Sailing Ships. c, Black Cargo. d, Nice, the Bay of Anges.

No. 2658, $6, The Interior With an Open Window. No. 2659, $6, Vence.

2003, Apr. 30

2653-2656 A471 Set of 4 6.50 6.50
2657 A471 $2 Sheet of 4, #a-d 6.00 6.00

Size: 96x76mm

Imperf

2658-2659 A471 Set of 2 9.00 9.00

Prince William, 21st Birthday — A472

No. 2660: a, With yellow and black shirt. b, With polo helmet. c, With blue shirt.
$6, In suit.

2003, May 14 *Perf. 14*

2660 A472 $3 Sheet of 3, #a-c 7.00 7.00

Souvenir Sheet

2661 A472 $6 multi 4.50 4.50

Salvation Army in Antigua, Cent. — A473

Designs: 30c, Emblem, Tamarind tree, Parham, vert. 90c, Salvation Army Pre-school, vert. $1, Meals on Wheels. $1.50, St. John's Citadel Band. $1.80, Salvation Army Citadel.
$6, Tamarind tree, Parham, vert.

2003, May 19 *Perf. 14¼*

2662-2666 A473 Set of 5 4.25 4.25

Souvenir Sheet

2667 A473 $6 multi 4.50 4.50

Antigua & Barbuda Scouts Association, 90th Anniv. — A474

Designs: 30c, First Anglican Scout troop, 1931. $1, National Scout Camp, 2002. $1.50, Woodbadge Training Course, 2000, horiz. $1.80, Men visiting National Scout Camp, 1986, horiz.

No. 2672: a, Edris George. b, Theodore George. c, Edris James.
$6, Scout with semaphore flags.

2003, June 9 *Perf. 14*

2668-2671 A474 Set of 4 3.75 3.75
2672 A474 90c Sheet of 3, #a-c 2.25 2.25

Souvenir Sheet

2673 A474 $6 multi 4.75 4.75

Tour de France Bicycle Race, Cent. — A475

No. 2674, $2: a, Cesar Garin, 1903. b, Henri Cornet, 1904. c, Louis Trousselier, 1905. d, René Pottier, 1906.

No. 2675, $2: a, Lucien Petit-Breton, 1907. b, Petit-Breton, 1908. c, François Faber, 1909. d, Octave Lapize, 1910.

No. 2676, $2: a, Gustave Garrigou, 1911. b, Odile Defraye, 1912. c, Philippe Thys, 1913. d, Thys, 1914.

No. 2677, $6, Pierre Giffard. No. 2678, $6, Henri Desgrange. No. 2679, $6, Comte de Dion.

2003, June 9 *Perf. 13¼*

Sheets of 4, #a-d

2674-2676 A475 Set of 3 18.00 18.00

Souvenir Sheets

2677-2679 A475 Set of 3 13.50 13.50

Caribbean Community, 30th Anniv. — A476

2003, July 4 *Perf. 14*

2680 A476 $1 multi .80 .80

Intl. Year of Fresh Water — A477

No. 2681, horiz.: a, Chutes de Carbet and rocks. b, Chutes de Carbet and foliage at left and right. c, Rocks at base of Chutes de Carbet.
$6, Ocho Rios Waterfall.

2003, July 14 *Perf. 13¼*

2681 A477 $2 Sheet of 3, #a-c 5.25 5.25

Souvenir Sheet

2682 A477 $6 multi 5.00 5.00

General Motors Automobiles — A478

No. 2683, $2 — Cadillacs: a, 1955 Eldorado convertible. b, 1937 Series 60. c, 1959 Eldorado. d, 2002 Eldorado.

No. 2684, $2 — Chevrolet Corvettes: a, 1954 convertible. b, 1964 Sting Ray. c, 1964 Sting Ray convertible. d, 1998 convertible.

No. 2685, $6, 1953 Cadillac Eldorado. No. 2686, $6, 1956 Corvette convertible.

2003, July 14 *Perf. 13¼x13½*

Sheets of 4, #a-d

2683-2684 A478 Set of 2 12.00 12.00

Souvenir Sheets

2685-2686 A478 Set of 2 9.00 9.00

Cadillac, cent.; Corvette, 50th anniv.

History of Aviation — A479

No. 2687, $2: a, First Wright Brothers flight, 1903. b, First free flight in helicopter by Paul Cornu, 1907. c, First landing on ship, by E. B. Ely. d, Curtiss A-1, first hydroplane, 1911.

No. 2688, $2: a, Bell X-5, 1951. b, Convair XFY-1, 1954. c, North American X-15, 1959 . d, Alexei Leonov, first man to walk in space, 1965.

No. 2689, $2: a, Concorde, 1969. b, Martin X-24, 1969. c, Apollo-Soyuz space mission, 1975. d, Mars probe Viking, 1976.

No. 2690, $6, Boeing Model 200 Monomail, 1930. No. 2691, $6, Breaking of sound barrier by Bell X-1, 1947. No. 2692, $6, Grumman X-29, 1984.

2003, July 28 *Perf. 14*

Sheets of 4, #a-d

2687-2689 A479 Set of 3 20.00 20.00

Souvenir Sheets

2690-2692 A479 Set of 3 13.50 13.50

Bird Type of 1995

Designs: $5, Montezuma oropendola. $10, Green jay.

2003, Aug. 11 Litho. *Perf. 15x14*

2693 A296 $5 multi 3.75 3.75
2694 A296 $10 multi 7.50 7.50

Circus Performers — A480

No. 2695, $1.80 — Clowns: a, Apes. b, Mo Lite. c, Gigi. d, "Buttons" McBride.

No. 2696, $1.80 — Perfomers: a, Chun Group. b, Casselly Sisters. c, Oliver Groszer. d, Keith Nelson.

2003, Sept. 1 *Perf. 14*

Sheets of 4, #a-d

2695-2696 A480 Set of 2 11.00 11.00

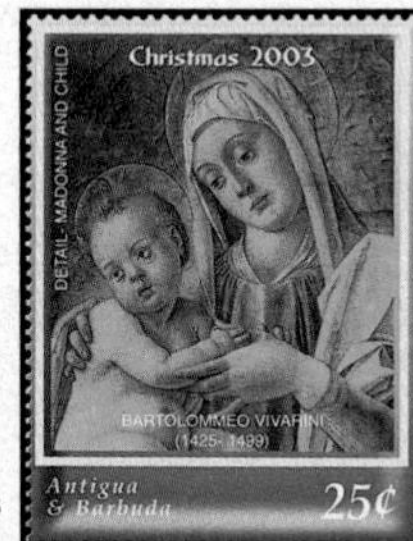

Christmas A481

Designs: 25c, Madonna and Child, by Bartolomeo Vivarini. 30c, Holy Family, by Pompeo Girolamo Batoni. 45c, Madonna and Child, by Benozzo Gozzoli. 50c, Madonna and Child (Calci Parish Church), by Gozzoli. 75c, Madonna and Child Giving Blessings, by Gozzoli. 90c, Madonna and Child, by Master of the Female Half-figures. $2.50, Benois Madonna, by Leonardo da Vinci.

$6, The Virgin and Child with Angels, by Rosso Fiorentino.

2003, Nov. 10 Litho. *Perf. 14¼*

2697-2703 A481 Set of 7 4.25 4.25

Souvenir Sheet

2704 A481 $6 multi 4.50 4.50

Orchids — A482

No. 2705, $2.50, vert.: a, Psychopsis papilio. b, Amesiella philippinensis. c, Maclellanara Pagan Dove Song. d, Phalaenopsis Little Hal.

No. 2706, $2.50: a, Daeliocattleya Amber Glow. b, Hygrochilus parishii. c, Dendrobium crystallinum. d, Disa hybrid.

$5, Cattleya deckeri.

2003, Dec. 8 *Perf. 13½*

Sheets of 4, #a-d

2705-2706 A482 Set of 2 15.00 15.00

Souvenir Sheet

2707 A482 $5 multi 4.00 4.00

Birds — A483

No. 2708, $2.50, vert.: a, Blue and gold macaw. b, Green-winged macaw. c, Green-naped lorikeet. d, Lesser sulfur-crested cockatoo.

No. 2709, $2.50: a, Severe macaw. b, Blue-headed parrot. c, Budgerigar. d, Sun conure.

$5, Bald ibis.

2003, Dec. 8

Sheets of 4, #a-d

2708-2709 A483 Set of 2 17.00 17.00

Souvenir Sheet

2710 A483 $5 multi 4.00 4.00

Butterflies — A484

No. 2711, $2: a, Esmerelda. b, Tiger pierid. c, Blue night. d, Charaxes nobilis.

No. 2712, $2.50: a, Orange-barred sulphur. b, Scarce bamboo page. c, Charaxes latona. d, Hewitson's blue hairstreak.

$5, Diaethia meridionalis.

2003, Dec. 8

Sheets of 4, #a-d

2711-2712 A484 Set of 2 14.50 14.50

Souvenir Sheet

2713 A484 $5 multi 4.00 4.00

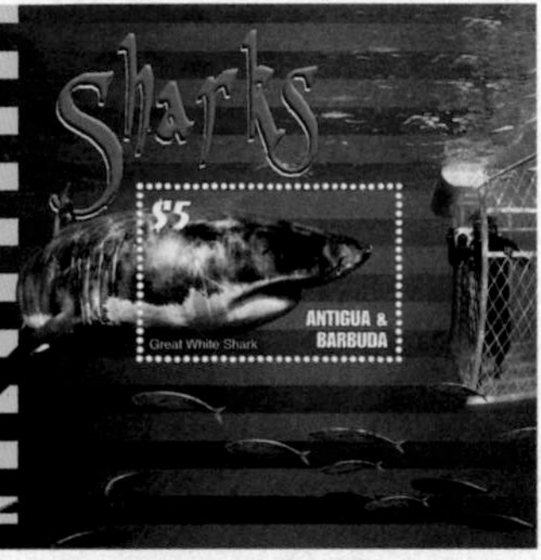

Sharks — A485

No. 2714: a, Bull. b, Gray reef. c, Black tip. d, Leopard.

$5, Great white.

2003, Dec. 8

2714 A485 $2 Sheet of 4, #a-d 6.50 6.50

Souvenir Sheet

2715 A485 $5 multi 3.75 3.75

New Year 2004 (Year of the Monkey) — A486

No. 2716, each $1.50: a, Monkey with black face and white chest. b, Monkey with brown face and white chest. c, Monkey with black, gray and yellow face. d, Red brown monkey on branch.

2004, Jan. 19 *Perf. 14*

2716 A486 Sheet of 4, #a-d 5.00 5.00

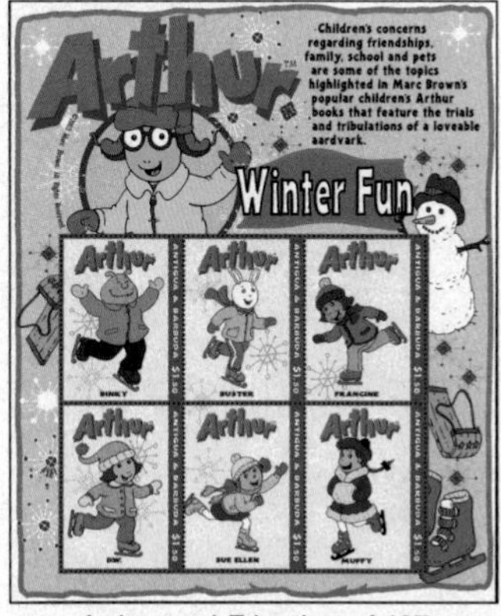

Arthur and Friends — A487

No. 2717, each $1.50: a, Binky. b, Buster. c, Francine. d, D.W. e, Sue Ellen. f, Muffy.

No. 2718, each $1.80: a, Binky. b, Muffy. c, Francine. d, Buster.

No. 2719, each $2.50: a, Arthur hitting baseball. b, Sue Ellen. c, Binky. d, Arthur with foot on home plate.

2004, Feb. 16 *Perf. 13¼*

2717 A487 Sheet of 6, #a-f 6.75 6.75

Sheets of 4, #a-d

2718-2719 A487 Set of 2 13.00 13.00

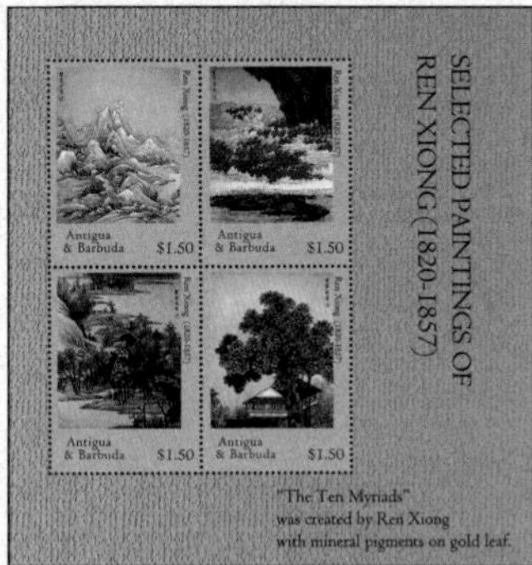

Paintings by Ren Xiong (1820-57) — A488

No. 2720, each $1.50: a, Purple hills. b, Cliffside waves. c, Hills at left, trees, Chinese text at right. d, House and tree.

No. 2721, each $1.50: a, Rocky pinnacles. b, Rocks at left and right. c, Hills, trees and bridge, Chinese text at top right. d, Waterfall at right, Chinese text at top left. e, Waterfalls, Chinese text at left. f, Rocks and flowers, Chinese text at top left.

No. 2722, each $1.50: a, Bird on flowering tree. b, Bird in tree.

2004, Feb. 16

2720 A488 Sheet of 4, #a-d 4.50 4.50
2721 A488 Sheet of 6, #a-f 6.75 6.75
2722 A488 Sheet of 2, #a-b 4.00 4.00

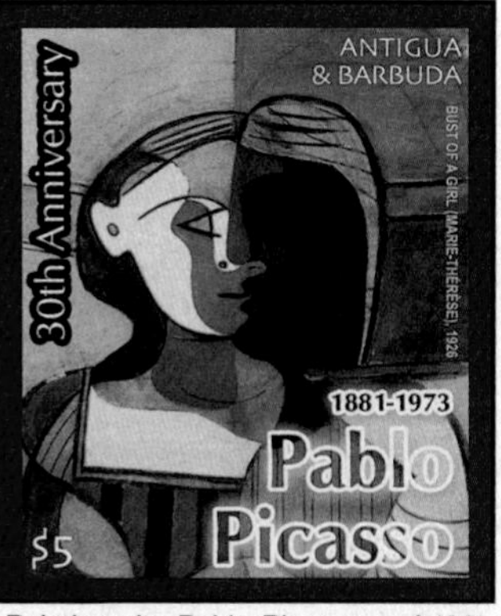

Paintings by Pablo Picasso — A489

No. 2723: a, Woman with a Flower. b, Marie-Thérèse Seated. c, The Red Armchair (Marie-Thérèse) Seated. d, The Dream (Marie-Thérèse) Seated.

$5, Bust of a Girl (Marie-Thérèse).

2004, Mar. 8 *Perf. 14¼*

2723 A489 $2 Sheet of 4, #a-d 6.50 6.50

Imperf

2724 A489 $5 shown 4.00 4.00

No. 2723 contains four 38x50mm stamps.

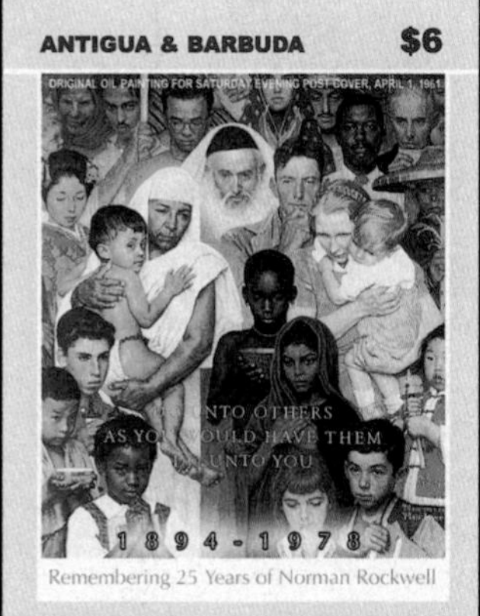

Paintings by Norman Rockwell — A490

No. 2725: a, Freedom of Speech. b, Freedom to Worship. c, Freedom from Want. d, Freedom from Fear.

$5, Painting for cover of Apr. 1, 1961 Saturday Evening Post.

2004, Mar. 8

2725 A490 $2 Sheet of 4, #a-d 6.00 6.00

Imperf

2726 A490 $6 shown 4.50 4.50

No. 2725 contains four 38x50mm stamps.

Paintings by Paul Gauguin (1848-1903) — A491

Designs: 25c, Vaite Goupil, vert. 30c, Autoportrait prés de Golgotha, vert. 75c, Le Moulin David à Pont-Aver. $2.50, Moisson en Bretagne, vert.

$4, Cavaliers sur la Plage.

2004, Mar. 8 Litho. *Perf. 14¼*

2727-2730 A491 Set of 4 3.00 3.00

Imperf

Size: 77x63mm

2731 A491 $4 multi 4.75 4.75

Paintings by Joan Miró (1893-1983) — A492

Designs: 75c, The Smile of Flaming Wings. 90c, The Bird's Song in the Dew of the Moon. $1, Dancer II, vert. $4, Painting, 1954, vert.

No. 2736, $2 — Painting Based on a Collage, description in: a, LL. b, LR. c, UL. d, UR.

$5, Bather. $6, Flame in Space and Nude Woman, vert.

2004, Mar. 8 Litho. *Perf. 14¼*

2732-2735 A492 Set of 4 5.50 5.50
2736 A492 $2 Sheet of 4, #a-d 6.50 6.50

Imperf

Size: 102x83mm

2737 A492 $5 multi 4.00 4.00

Size: 83x102mm

2738 A492 $6 multi 5.00 5.00

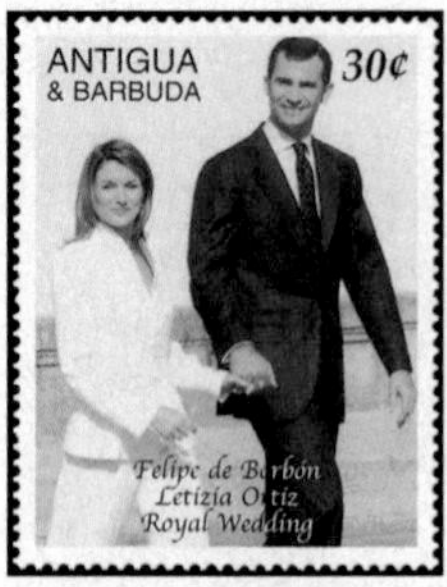

Wedding of Prince Felipe de Borbón of Spain and Letizia Ortiz A493

Designs: 30c, Couple. 50c, Couple, diff. 75c, Letizia. 90c, Prince Felipe. $1, Couple, diff. No. 2744, $5, Couple, diff.

No. 2745: a, Spanish royal family. b, Flags and Prince Felipe in uniform. c, Prince Felipe, his grandfather, Juan de Borbón y Battenberg, and his father, King Juan Carlos. d, Letizia, Prince Felipe, King Juan Carlos and Queen Sophia, horiz. e, Similar to 75c. f, Similar to 90c.

No. 2746, $5, Couple, diff. No. 2747, $5, Similar to #2745a. No. 2748, $5, Similar to #2745c. No. 2749, $6, Letizia, map of Europe. No. 2750, $6, Similar to #2745b. No. 2751, $6, Similar to #2745d, horiz.

2004, May 21 *Perf. 13¼*

2739-2744 A493 Set of 6 6.50 6.50
2745 A493 $1.80 Sheet of 6, #a-f 8.50 8.50

Souvenir Sheets

2746-2751 A493 Set of 6 25.00 25.00

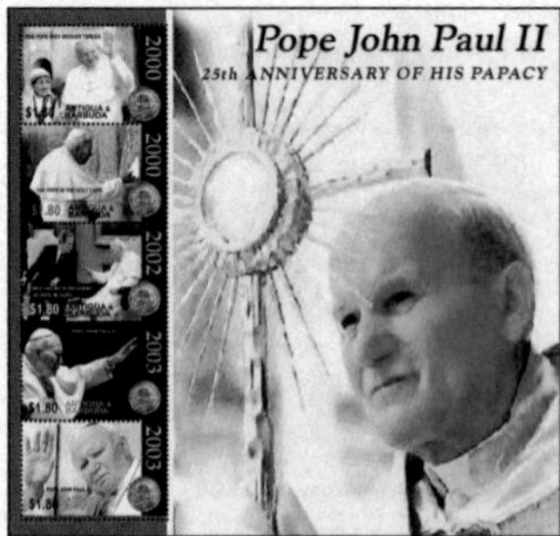

Election of Pope John Paul II, 25th Anniv. (in 2003) — A494

No. 2752: a, Pope with Mother Teresa. b, Pope in the Holy Land. c, Pope meeting with Pres. George W. Bush. d, Pope waving, dark background. e, Pope waving, light background.

2004, June 17 *Perf. 14*

2752 A494 $1.80 Sheet of 5, #a-e 7.25 7.25

Inscription of "2000" on No. 2752a is incorrect.

Intl. Year of Peace — A495

No. 2753 Dove and: a, Intl. Year of Peace emblem. b, Earth. c, UN emblem.

2004, June 17

2753 A495 $3 Sheet of 3, #a-c 6.75 6.75

2004 Summer Olympics, Athens A496

Designs: $1, Poster for 1964 Tokyo Olympics. $1.65, Commemorative medal for 1964 Tokyo Olympics. $1.80, Fencing, horiz. $2, Wrestlers, horiz.

2004, June 17 *Perf. 14¼*

2754-2757 A496 Set of 4 5.00 5.00

European Soccer Championships, Portugal — A497

No. 2758: a, Milan Galic. b, Slava Metreveli. c, Igor Netto. d, Parc des Princes.

$6, 1960 USSR team.

2004, June 17 *Perf. 14*

2758 A497 $2 Sheet of 4, #a-d 7.50 7.50

Souvenir Sheet

Perf. 14¼

2759 A497 $6 multi 5.00 5.00

No. 2758 contains four 28x42mm stamps.

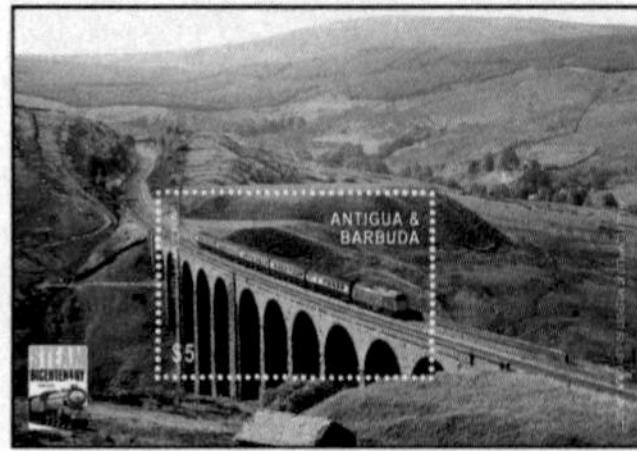

Locomotives, Signals and Stations — A498

No. 2760, $1: a, Evening Star. b, Indian Railways XC Pacific. c, German Kreigslokomotive. d, Bulleid Light Pacific. e, G. W. R. copper cap chimney. f, Tallylyn Railway. g, Preservation volunteers. h, N. E. R. Y7 0-4-0T. h, Breda 0-4-0 WT, locomotive shed, Asmara, Eritrea.

No. 2761, $1, vert.: a, King Class 4-6-0. b, Argentinian 11B Class 2-8-0. c, Baldwin Mikado. d, Round trackside signal with red horizontal band. e, Wooden box with button signal. f, Signal house, signals with red and yellow arms. g, Signal house, signal with two red arms. h, Window of signal house. i, Signal lights.

No. 2762, $1, vert.: a, 2-4-0T on Douglas to Port Erin line, Isle of Man. b, South African Railways 4-8-2S. c, China Railways SY Class 2-8-2. d, St. Pancras Station. e, Ulverston Station, f, Bolton Station. g, Liverpool St. Station. h, Cannon St. Station. i, Malvern Station.

No. 2763, $5, Settle-Carlisle line. No. 2764, $6, Douro Valley Railway. No. 2765, $6, Train over Lake Egridir, Turkey.

2004, June 17 *Perf. 14*

Sheets of 9, #a-i

2760-2762 A498 Set of 3 21.00 21.00

Souvenir Sheets

2763-2765 A498 Set of 3 14.00 14.00

D-Day, 60th Anniv. A499

Designs: 30c, Derrick Tysoe. 45c, Lt. Gen. Walter Bedell Smith. $1.50, Les Perry. $3, Maj. Gen. Percy Hobart.

No. 2770, $2: a, Tiger II tank. b, Standartenfuhrer Kurt Meyer. c, Canadian infantry. d, British infantry.

No. 2771, $2: a, Hamilcar disgorges Tetrarch tank. b, Horsa glider unloads cargo. c, Beachheads established. d, Liberation begins.

No. 2772, $6, Sherman tank. No. 2773, $6, Mulberry Harbor.

2004, July 26 *Perf. 14¼*

Stamp + Label (#2766-2769)

2766-2769 A499 Set of 4 4.00 4.00

Sheets of 4, #a-d

2770-2771 A499 Set of 2 12.00 12.00

Souvenir Sheets

2772-2773 A499 Set of 2 9.00 9.00

Miniature Sheet

Queen Juliana of the Netherlands (1909-2004) — A500

No. 2774 — Netherlands flag and: a, Juliana. b, Juliana and Prince Bernhard. c, Juliana and Princess Beatrix. d, Juliana and Princess Irene. e, Juliana and Princess Margriet. f, Juliana and Princess Christina.

2004, June 17 Litho. *Perf. 13¼*

2774 A500 $2 Sheet of 6, #a-f 9.00 9.00

Miniature Sheet

National Basketball Association Players — A501

No. 2775: a, Mike Bibby, Sacramento Kings. b, Jim Jackson, Houston Rockets. c, Tracy McGrady, Houston Rockets. d, Chris Webber, Sacramento Kings. e, Peja Stojakovic, Sacramento Kings. f, Yao Ming, Houston Rockets.

2004, Nov. 8 *Perf. 12*

2775 A501 $1.50 Sheet of 6, #a-f 6.75 6.75

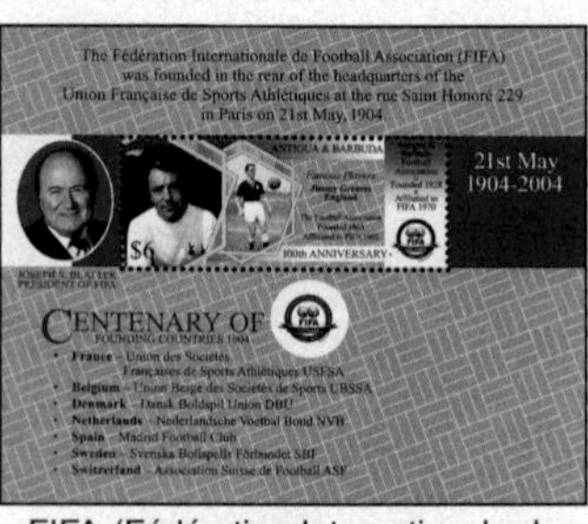

FIFA (Fédération Internationale de Football Association), Cent. — A502

No. 2776: a, Zinedine Zidane. b, Roberto Baggio. c, Franz Beckenbauer. d, Ossie Ardiles.

$6, Jimmy Greaves.

2004, Nov. 8 *Perf. 12¾x12½*

2776 A502 $2 Sheet of 4, #a-d 6.00 6.00

Souvenir Sheet

2777 A502 $6 multi 4.50 4.50

Miniature Sheet

John Denver (1943-97), Singer — A503

No. 2778, each $1.50: a, At microphone. b, Tuning guitar. c, With arm extended. d, Facing left, playing guitar.

2004, Nov. 22 *Perf. 14*

2778 A503 Sheet of 4, #a-d 4.50 4.50

Miniature Sheet

George Herman "Babe" Ruth (1895-1948), Baseball Player — A504

No. 2779, each $1.80: a, Wearing blue cap. b, Wearing crown. c, Wearing pinstriped cap. d, Holding bat.

2004, Nov. 22

2779 A504 Sheet of 4, #a-d 5.50 5.50

The Family Circus, Comic Strip by Bil and Jeff Keane — A505

No. 2780, $2: a, "Billy attackled me too hard," purple panel. b, "His ears came from where his eyes are." c, "Tennessee!" d, "One candy or one bowl?"

No. 2781, $2: a, "If you had wider shoulders, Daddy, you could be a two-seater." b, "Billy attackled me too hard," red panel. c, "Who tee-peed the mummies?" d, "Looking out there makes me realize it's indeed the little things that count."

No. 2782, $2: a, "Someday I might travel to another planet, but I'm not sure why." b, "Adam and Eve were lucky. They didn't have any history to learn." c, "My backpack is too full. Will somebody help me stand up?" d, "I tripped because one foot tried to hug the other foot."

No. 2783, $2: a, "If you don't put enough stamps on it the mailman will only take it part way." b, "Gee, Grandma, you have a lot of thoughts on your wall." c, "Shall I play for you pa-rum-pa-pum-pummm. . .?" d, "You have to do that when you're married."

No. 2784, $2: a, Billy. b, Jeffy. c, PJ. d, Dolly.

Perf. 13¼, 14¼(#2784)

2004, Nov. 22

Sheets of 4, #a-d

2780-2784 A505 Set of 5 30.00 30.00

World AIDS Day A506

2004, Dec. 1 ***Perf. 14***

2785 A506 $2 multi 1.75 1.75

Christmas A507

Designs: 20c, Madonna in Floral Wreath, by Jan Breughel the Elder and Peter Paul Rubens. 25c, Madonna and Child, by Jan Gossaert. 30c, Santa Claus on skis. 45c, Santa Claus with raised arms. 50c, Santa Claus, reindeer on roof. $1, Floral Wreath with Virgin and Child, by Daniel Seghers. $1.80, Madonna and Child, by Andrea Mantegna.

$6, Madonna in a Floral Wreath, by Seghers.

2004, Dec. 13 ***Perf. 12¼x12***

2786-2792 A507 Set of 7 3.50 3.50

Souvenir Sheet

2793 A507 $6 multi 5.00 5.00

Dogs — A508

Designs: 30c, American pit bull terrier. 90c, Maltese. $1.50, Rottweiler. $3, Australian terrier.

$6, German shepherd, horiz.

2005, May 23 **Litho.** ***Perf. 12¾***

2794-2797 A508 Set of 4 7.00 7.00

Souvenir Sheet

2798 A508 $6 multi 5.50 5.50

Cats — A509

Designs: 75c, Golden Persian. $1, Calico shorthair. $1.50, Siamese. $3, Tabby Persian.

$5, Turkish.

2005, May 23

2799-2802 A509 Set of 4 5.00 5.00

Souvenir Sheet

2803 A509 $5 multi 4.00 4.00

Insects — A510

No. 2804, horiz.: a, Figure-of-eight butterfly. b, Honeybee. c, Migratory grasshopper. d, Hercules beetle.

$5, Cramer's Mesene butterfly.

2005, May 23

2804 A510 $2 Sheet of 4, #a-d 6.50 6.50

Souvenir Sheet

2805 A510 $5 multi 3.75 3.75

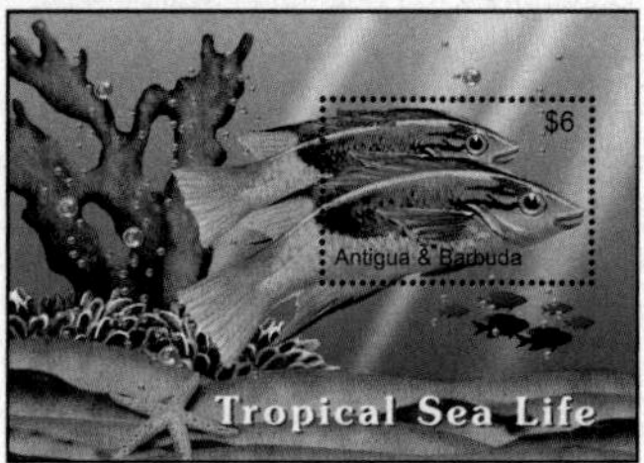

Marine Life — A511

No. 2806: a, Yellowtail damselfish. b, French angelfish. c, Horseshoe crab. d, Emerald mithrax crab.

$6, Spanish hogfish.

2005, May 23

2806 A511 $2 Sheet of 4, #a-d 6.00 6.00

Souvenir Sheet

2807 A511 $6 multi 4.75 4.75

Prehistoric Animals — A512

No. 2808, $2: a, Mammuthus imperator. b, Brontops. c, Hyracotherium. d, Propaleotherium.

No. 2809, $2.50: a, Ceratosaur. b, Coelurosaurs. c, Ornitholestes. d, Baryonyx.

No. 2810, $3: a, Plateosaurus. b, Yangchuanosaurus. c, Ceolophysis. d, Lystrosaurus.

No. 2811, $4, Triceratops. No. 2812, $5, Stegoasurus, vert. No. 2813, $6, Coelodonta.

2005, May 23

Sheets of 4, #a-d

2808-2810 A512 Set of 3 25.00 25.00

Souvenir Sheets

2811-2813 A512 Set of 3 12.00 12.00

Miniature Sheet

Pres. Ronald Reagan (1911-2004) — A513

No. 2814 — Background colors: a, Gray blue. b, Gray brown. c, Pink. d, White. e, Gray green. f, Buff.

2005, June 15 ***Perf. 14***

2814 A513 $1.50 Sheet of 6, #a-f 7.50 7.50

New Year 2005 (Year of the Rooster) A514

Mother Hen and Her Brood, by Wang Ning: $1, Detail. $4, Entire painting.

2005, June 15 ***Perf. 14¼***

2815 A514 $1 multi .75 .75

Souvenir Sheet

2816 A514 $4 multi 4.00 4.00

No. 2815 printed in sheets of 4.

Friedrich von Schiller (1759-1805), Writer — A515

No. 2817: a, Bust of Schiller, by C. L. Richter, Central Park, New York. b, Actors in "Kabale und Liebe." c, Schiller's birthplace, Marbach, Germany.

$6, Sculpture of Schiller, by Ernst Rau, Lincoln Park, Chicago.

2005, June 15 ***Perf. 14***

2817 A515 $3 Sheet of 3, #a-c 6.75 6.75

Souvenir Sheet

2818 A515 $6 multi 5.25 5.25

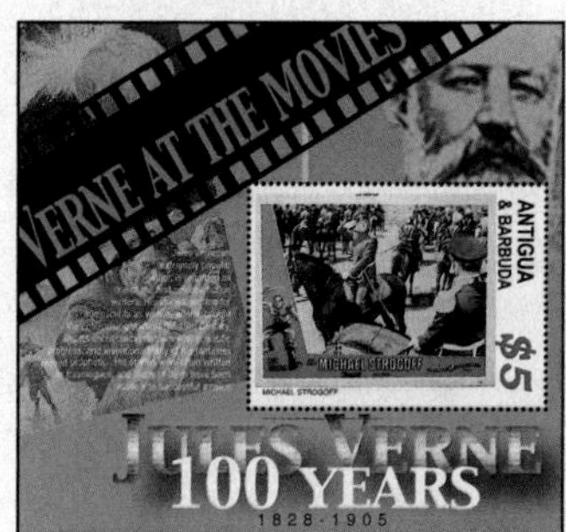

Jules Verne (1828-1905), Writer — A516

No. 2819, vert. — Movie posters for Verne works: a, Monster Island, 1961. b, Journey to the Center of the Earth, 1961. c, From the Earth to the Moon, 1956. d, Sea Devils, 1961.

$5, Michael Strogoff, 1956.

2005, June 15

2819 A516 $2 Sheet of 4, #a-d 6.00 6.00

Souvenir Sheet

2820 A516 $5 multi 3.75 3.75

No. 2819 contains four 28x42mm stamps.

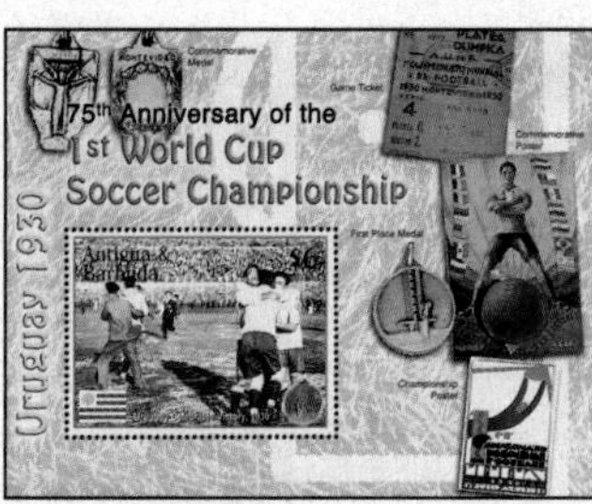

World Cup Soccer Championships, 75th Anniv. — A517

No. 2821, each $1.50 — Uruguayan flag, first place medal and: a, 1930 Uruguay team. b, Hector Castro scoring goal against Argentina. c, Crowd in Estadio Centenario. d, Hector Castro.

$6, Uruguay team celebrating 1930 victory.

2005, June 15 ***Perf. 14¼***

2821 A517 Sheet of 4, #a-d 8.00 8.00

Souvenir Sheet

2822 A517 $6 multi 4.50 4.50

End of World War II, 60th Anniv. — A518

No. 2823, $1.50: a, Soldiers in Red Square, Moscow, May 9, 1945. b, Gen. Bernard Law Montgomery. c, Marshal Georgi K. Zhukov. d, Gen. Omar N. Bradley.

No. 2824, $2, horiz.: a, Winston Churchill, Franklin D. Roosevelt and Joseph Stalin at Yalta Summit. b, Raising of US flag on Mount Suribachi. c, Gen. Douglas MacArthur signing Japanese surrender documents. d, Japanese officials at surrender ceremony.

2005, June 15 *Perf. 14*

Sheets of 4, #a-d

2823-2824 A518 Set of 2 10.50 10.50

Battle of Trafalgar, Bicent. — A519

Various ships in battle: 90c, $1, $1.50, $1.80.

$6, The Victory firing during the Battle of Trafalgar.

2005, June 15 *Perf. 14¼*

2825-2828 A519 Set of 4 6.75 6.75

Souvenir Sheet

2829 A519 $6 multi 7.75 7.75

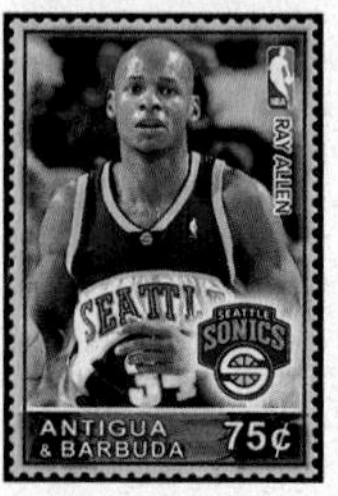

National Basketball Association Players — A520

Designs: No. 2830, 75c, Ray Allen, Seattle Supersonics. No. 2831, 75c, Lucious Harris, Cleveland Cavaliers. No. 2832, 75c, Dwight Howard, Orlando Magic. No. 2833, 75c, Antonio McDyess, Detroit Pistons. No. 2834, 75c, Emeka Okafor, Charlotte Bobcats.

2005 *Perf. 14*

2830-2834 A520 Set of 5 3.00 3.00

Pope John Paul II (1920-2005) and Meir Lau, Chief Rabbi of Israel — A521

2005, Oct. 10 *Perf. 13½x13¼*

2835 A521 $3 multi 4.25 4.25

Printed in sheets of 6.

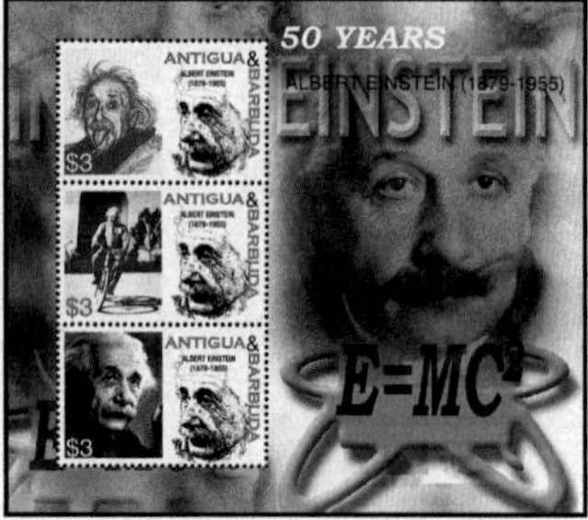

Albert Einstein (1879-1955), Physicist — A522

No. 2836 — Photograph of Einstein in: a, Brown. b, Olive green. c, Black.

2005, Oct. 10 Litho. *Perf. 13¼x13½*

2836 A522 $3 Sheet of 3, #a-c 6.75 6.75

Hans Christian Andersen (1805-75), Author — A523

No. 2837: a, Portrait of Andersen. b, Statue of Andersen, Central Park, New York City. c, Andersen's gravesite.

$6, Andersen seated.

2005, Oct. 10 *Perf. 13½x13¼*

2837 A523 $3 Sheet of 3, #a-c 6.75 6.75

Souvenir Sheet

2838 A523 $6 multi 5.25 5.25

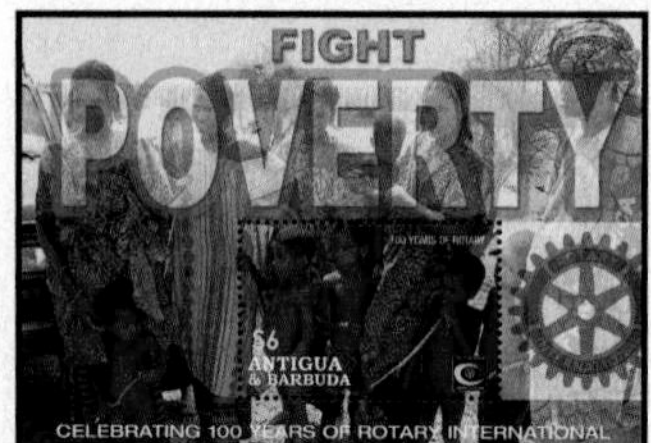

Rotary International, Cent. — A524

No. 2839, vert.: a, Italy #1372. b, Paul Harris Medallion. c, Paul P. Harris, first Rotary President.

$6, Children.

2005, Oct. 10 *Perf. 13½x13¼*

2839 A524 $3 Sheet of 3, #a-c 7.25 7.25

Souvenir Sheet

Perf. 13¼x13½

2840 A524 $6 multi 6.00 6.00

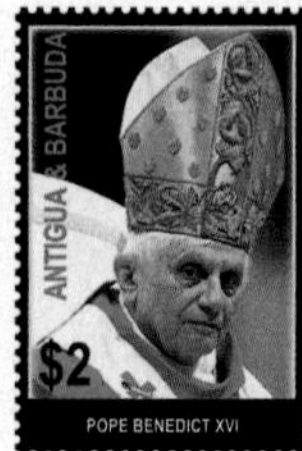

Pope Benedict XVI — A525

2005, Nov. 21 *Perf. 13½x13¼*

2841 A525 $2 multi 1.75 1.75

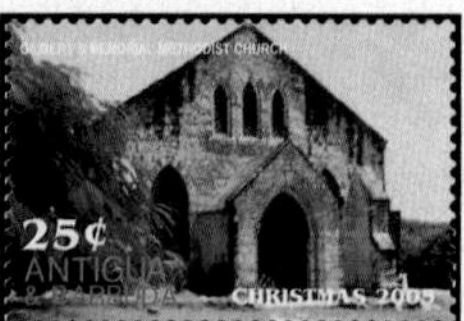

Christmas — A526

Churches: 25c, Gilbert's Memorial Methodist Church. No. 2843, 30c, People's Church, Barbuda. No. 2844, 30c, Tyrell's Roman Catholic Church. 45c, St. Barnabas Anglican Church. 50c, St. Peter's Anglican Church. No. 2847, 75c, Spring Gardens Moravian Church. No. 2848, 75c, St. Steven's Anglican Church. No. 2849, 90c, Holy Family Catholic Cathedral. No. 2850, 90c, Pilgrim Holiness Church, vert. $1, Ebenezer Methodist Church.

No. 2852, $5, St. John's Cathedral. No. 2853, $5, Worship service, Spring Gardens Moravian Church, vert.

2005, Dec. 19 *Perf. 12¾*

2842-2851 A526 Set of 10 6.75 6.75

Souvenir Sheets

2852-2853 A526 Set of 2 8.00 8.00

Elvis Presley (1935-77) — A527

Serpentine Die Cut 8¾x9

2005 Litho. & Embossed

2854 A527 $20 gold & multi 16.00 16.00

National Parks A528

Designs: No. 2855, 20c, Joiner's Loft, Nelson's Dockyard Natl. Park. No. 2856, 20c, Pay Office, Nelson's Dockyard Natl. Park, vert. No. 2857, 30c, Admiral's House Museum, Nelson's Dockyard Natl. Park. No. 2858, 30c, Bakery, Nelson's Dockyard Natl. Park. No. 2859, 75c, Devil's Bridge Natl. Park. No. 2860, 75c, View from Shirley Heights Lookout, Nelson's Dockyard Natl. Park. No. 2861, 90c, Green Castle Hill Natl. Park. No. 2862, 90c, Fort Berkeley, Nelson's Dockyard Natl. Park. No. 2863, $1.50, Pigeon Point Beach, Nelson's Dockyard Natl. Park. No. 2864, $1.50, Half Moon Bay Natl. Park. $1.80, Cannon at Ft. Berkeley.

No. 2866, $5, Codrington Lagoon Natl. Park. No. 2867, $5, Museum, Nelson's Dockyard Natl. Park, vert.

2006, Jan. 9 *Perf. 14*

2855-2865 A528 Set of 11 7.00 7.00

Souvenir Sheets

2866-2867 A528 Set of 2 9.50 9.50

National Parks of the United States — A529

No. 2868: a, Yellowstone. b, Olympic. c, Glacier. d, Grand Canyon. e, Yosemite. f, Great Smoky Mountains.

$6, Mount Rainier.

2006, Jan. 6 *Perf. 14¼*

2868 A529 $1.50 Sheet of 6, #a-f 7.50 7.50

Souvenir Sheet

Perf. 14

2869 A529 $6 multi 4.75 4.75

No. 2868 contains six 50x38mm stamps.

Moravian Church Antigua Conference, 250th Anniv. — A530

Designs: 30c, Bishop John Ephraim Knight. $1, John Andrew Buckley. $1.50, Old Spring Gardens Moravian Church, horiz.

No. 2873, $5, Sandbox tree. No. 2874, $5, Westerby Memorial. No. 2875, $5, Spring Gardens Teachers College, horiz.

2006, Apr. 3 *Perf. 12¾*

2870-2872 A530 Set of 3 2.25 2.25

Souvenir Sheets

2873-2875 A530 Set of 3 13.00 13.00

Marilyn Monroe (1926-62), Actress — A531

2006, Apr. 10 *Perf. 13¼*

2876 A531 $3 multi 2.25 2.25

Printed in sheets of 4.

Queen Elizabeth II, 80th Birthday — A532

No. 2877: a, As young woman (black and white photo). b, Wearing pearl necklace. c, Wearing white blouse. d, Wearing crown.

$6, Wearing crown, diff.

2006, Apr. 10

2877 A532 $2 Sheet of 4, #a-d 6.50 6.50

Souvenir Sheet

2878 A532 $6 multi 4.75 4.75

2006 Winter Olympics, Turin — A533

Designs: No. 2879, 75c, Austria #715. No. 2880, 75c, Poster for 1972 Sapporo Winter Olympics, vert. No. 2881, 90c, Austria #714. No. 2882, 90c, Japan #1103, vert. $2, Austria #717. $3, Poster for 1964 Innsbruck Winter Olympics, vert.

2006, May 11 Litho. *Perf. 14¼*

2879-2884 A533 Set of 6 7.00 7.00

Miniature Sheets

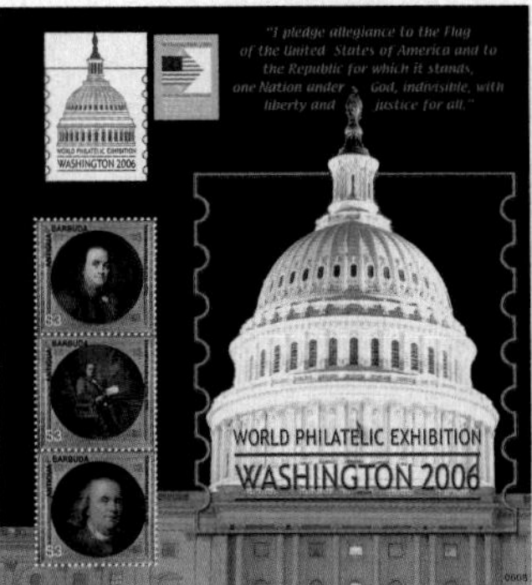

A534

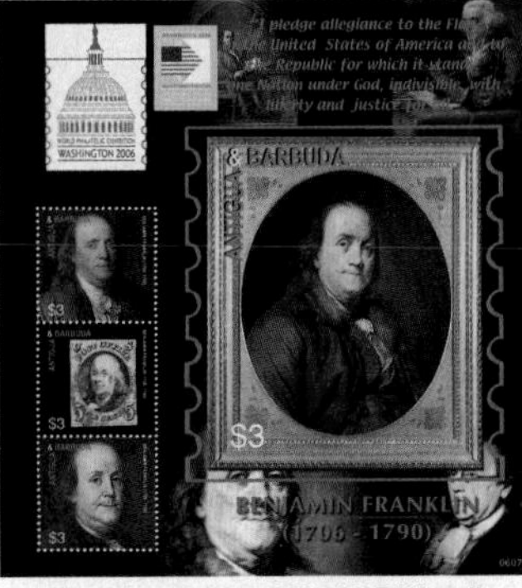

Washington 2006 World Philatelic Exhibition — A535

No. 2885: a, Framed circular portrait of Benjamin Franklin wearing red jacket with fur collar. b, Framed circular portrait of Franklin seated. c, Framed circular portrait of Franklin wearing gray jacket.

No. 2886: a, Unframed portrait of Franklin wearing jacket with fur collar. b, US #1. c, Unframed portrait of Franklin wearing black coat. d, Framed oval portrait like #2885a (73x87mm).

2006, May 29 ***Perf. 11½***

2885 A534 $3 Sheet of 3, #a-c 7.50 7.50

Perf. 11½, Imperf. (#2886d)

2886 A535 $3 Sheet of 4, #a-d 9.50 9.50

Miniature Sheet

Wolfgang Amadeus Mozart (1756-91), Composer — A536

No. 2887: a, Mozart's viola. b, Mozart at age 11. c, Young Mozart. d, Mozart in Verona, 1770.

2006, July 3 ***Perf. 12¾***

2887 A536 $3 Sheet of 4, #a-d 11.00 11.00

Miniature Sheet

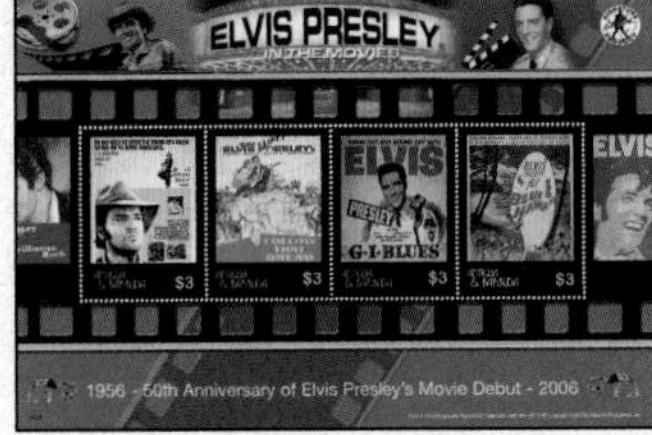

Posters of Elvis Presley Movies — A537

No. 2888: a, Charro! b, Follow That Dream. c, G.I. Blues. d, Blue Hawaii.

2006, July 12 ***Perf. 13¼***

2888 A537 $3 Sheet of 4, #a-d 10.00 10.00

Antigua and Barbuda Girl Guides, 75th Anniv. — A538

Designs: 25c, Leaders after garbage collection race, 2002. 30c, Girl Guides color party, horiz. 45c, Uniformed and non-uniformed members. 50c, Girl Guides marching band, horiz. $1, Leeward Islands leaders training camp, 1946.

No. 2894, $5, Assistant Commissioner Lisa Simon. No. 2895, $5, Girl Guides gathering at Fort James, 1935, horiz. No. 2896, $5, Enrollment ceremony, 2006, horiz.

2006, July 17 ***Perf. 12¾***

2889-2893 A538 Set of 5 2.75 2.75

Souvenir Sheets

2894-2896 A538 Set of 3 12.50 12.50

Leeward Islands Air Transport, 50th Anniv. A539

Designs: 30c, HS-748 Hawker Siddely Avro. No. 2898, 50c, BN2 Islanders. No. 2899, 50c, BN2 Norman Islander. No. 2900, 50c, Beechcraft Twin Bonanza, vert. $1.50, BAC 111, HS-748. $2.50, DH8-300 de Havilland.

$5, Sir Frank Delisle, LIAT founder, and Beechcraft Twin Bonanza, vert.

2006, Oct. 2 **Litho.** ***Perf. 14¼***

2897-2902 A539 Set of 6 6.25 6.25

Souvenir Sheet

2903 A539 $5 multi 5.25 5.25

Independence, 25th Anniv. — A540

Designs: 30c, Pineapple. $1, Flag. $1.50, Coat of arms.

No. 2907: a, One magnificent frigatebird. b, Two fallow deer. c, One fallow deer. d, Two magnificent frigatebirds.

$5, New Parliament Building, vert.

2006, Oct. 30 ***Perf. 12¾***

2904-2906 A540 Set of 3 2.50 2.50

2907 A540 25c Sheet of 4, #a-d 1.50 1.50

Souvenir Sheet

2908 A540 $5 multi 5.50 5.50

No. 2908 contains one 38x50mm stamp.

Civil Rights Leaders — A541

No. 2909, $2: a, Dalai Lama. b, Pres. Abraham Lincoln. c, Susan B. Anthony. d, Harriet Tubman.

No. 2910, $2: a, Mahatma Gandhi. b, Nelson Mandela. c, Rosa Parks.

$5, Dr. Martin Luther King, Jr.

2006, Nov. 20 ***Perf. 12, 12½ (#2910)***

2909 Horiz. strip of 4 8.00 8.00

a.-d. A541 $2 Any single 1.75 1.75

2910 A541 $2 Sheet of 3, #a-c 5.00 5.00

Souvenir Sheet

2911 A541 $5 multi 5.50 5.50

Rembrandt (1606-69), Painter A542

Designs: 50c, Landscape with the Baptism of the Eunuch. 75c, Landscape with a Coach. $1, River Landscape with Ruins. $2, Landscape with a Castle.

No. 2916, $2: a, The Holy Family (Joseph at table). b, The Good Samaritan Arriving at the Inn. c, Rebecca Taking Leave of Her Family. d, The Holy Family (Madonna and Child).

No. 2917, $2 — Samson Posting the Riddle to the Wedding Guests: a, Woman with beads in hair. b, Three men. c, Two men. d, Woman holding glass.

No. 2918, $5, Self-portrait. No. 2919, $5, Rembrandt's Mother.

2006, Dec. 20 ***Perf. 12¼x12***

2912-2915 A542 Set of 4 5.00 5.00

Sheets of 4, #a-d

2916-2917 A542 Set of 2 13.50 13.50

Imperf

Size: 70x100mm

2918-2919 A542 Set of 2 9.00 9.00

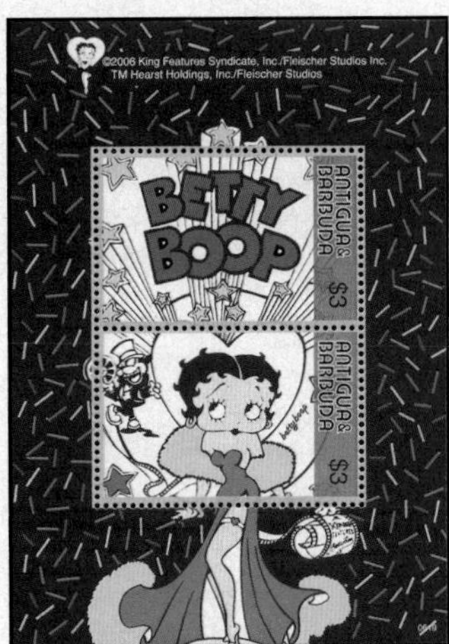

Betty Boop — A543

No. 2920, vert. — Background color: a, Yellow. b, Green. c, Red violet. d, Orange. e, Blue green. f, Purple.

No. 2921: a, Text, "Betty Boop" and stars. b, Betty Boop and cat.

2006, Dec. 20 ***Perf. 14¼***

2920 A543 $1.50 Sheet of 6, #a-f 7.50 7.50

Souvenir Sheet

2921 A543 $3 Sheet of 2 5.00 5.00

Space Achievements — A544

No. 2922: a, JSC Shuttle mission simulator. b, STS-1 prime crew in classroom. c, STS-1 Columbia on launch pad. d, Launch of Columbia. e, Columbia landing at Edwards Air Force Base. f, Columbia on runway.

No. 2923, $3: a, Molniya 8K78M launch vehicle. b, Luna 9 flight apparatus. c, Moon images transmitted by Luna 9. d, Luna 9 capsule.

No. 2924, $3: a, Apollo crew boards transfer van. b, Handshake after Apollo-Soyuz linkup. c, Display of Apollo-Soyuz plaque. d, Recovery of Apollo command module.

No. 2925, $6, Artist's conception of NASA spaceship to orbit Moon. No. 2926, $6, Calipso Satellite. No. 2927, $6, Space Station Mir.

2006 ***Perf. 12¾***

2922 A544 $2 Sheet of 6, #a-f 10.00 10.00

Sheets of 4, #a-d

2923-2924 A544 Set of 2 21.00 21.00

Souvenir Sheets

2925-2927 A544 Set of 3 16.00 16.00

Christmas — A545

Ornaments: 30c, Ball. 90c, Star. $1, Bell. $1.50, Christmas tree.

No. 2932: a, Ball. b, Star. c, Bell. d, Christmas tree.

$6, Santa Claus at beach.

2006 ***Perf. 13½***

2928-2931 A545 Set of 4 3.00 3.00

2932 A545 $2 Sheet of 4, #a-d 6.75 6.75

Souvenir Sheet

2933 A545 $6 multi 6.00 6.00

Scouting, Cent. — A546

Scout emblem at: $4, UL. $6, LR.

2007, Jan. 18 ***Perf. 13½***

2934 A546 $4 multi 4.00 4.00

Souvenir Sheet

2935 A546 $6 multi 6.00 6.00

No. 2934 was printed in sheets of 3.

Christopher Columbus (1451-1506), Explorer — A547

Designs: 75c, Map of North and South America, Columbus on bended knee. 90c, Portrait of Columbus. $2, Portrait, diff. $3, Portrait, diff.

$6, Columbus and ships.

2007, Jan. 18 ***Perf. 13¼***

2936-2939 A547 Set of 4 7.00 7.00

Souvenir Sheet

2940 A547 $6 multi 6.00 6.00

Miniature Sheets

Pres. John F. Kennedy (1917-63) — A548

No. 2941, $3: a, Wearing naval ensign dress uniform. b, With crew. c, On PT-109. d, Wearing light jacket in South Pacific.

No. 2942, $3: a, Campaigning on crutches. b, Wearing t-shirt. c, With John F. Fitzgerald and Joseph P. Kennedy. d, Celebrating victory with sister.

2007, Jan. 18 **Litho.**

Sheets of 4, #a-d

2941-2942 A548 Set of 2 22.00 22.00

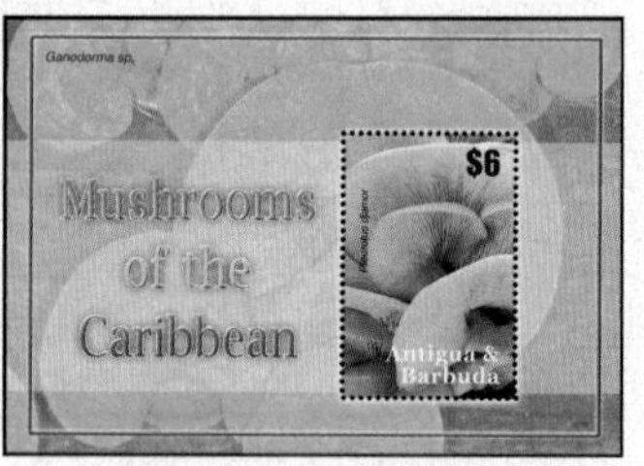

Mushrooms — A549

No. 2943: a, Cantharellus cibarius. b, Auricularia auricula-judae. c, Mycena acicula. d, Peziza vesiculosa.

$6, Pleurotus djamor.

2007, Apr. 2 **Litho.** ***Perf. 14¼***

2943 A549 $2 Sheet of 4, #a-d 8.00 8.00

Souvenir Sheet

2944 A549 $6 multi 6.00 6.00

Butterflies — A550

Designs: 75c, Figure-of-eight. 90c, Tiger pierid. $1, Purple mort bleu. $4, Mosaic.

No. 2949: a, Small lacewing. b, Clorinde. c, Common morpho. d, White peacock.

$5, Grecian shoemaker.

2007, Apr. 2

2945-2948 A550 Set of 4 7.00 7.00

2949 A550 $2 Sheet of 4, #a-d 6.00 6.00

Souvenir Sheet

2950 A550 $5 multi 5.75 5.75

Flowers — A551

Designs: 75c, Allamanda. 90c, Bidens sulphurea. $1, Alstromeria caryophyflacea. $4, Bougainvillea.

No. 2955, $2, horiz.: a, Canna limbata. b, Gazania rigens. c, Gloriosa rothschildiana. d, Hibiscus sinensis.

No. 2956, $3, horiz.: a, Oncidium flexuosum. b, Paphiopedilum pinocchio. c, Cattleyopsis lindenii. d, Cattleyopsis cubensis.

No. 2957, $6, Caesalpinia pulcherrima. No. 2958, $6, Osmoglossum pulchellum.

2007, Apr. 2

2951-2954 A551 Set of 4 7.00 7.00

Sheets of 4, #a-d

2955-2956 A551 Set of 2 19.00 19.00

Souvenir Sheets

2957-2958 A551 Set of 2 11.00 11.00

Cricket Players — A552

Designs: 25c, Kenneth Benjamin. 30c, Anderson Roberts. 90c, Ridley Jacobs. $1, Curtly Ambrose. $1.50, Richard Richardson. $5, Sir Vivian Richards.

2007, Apr. 5 ***Perf. 12¾***

2959-2963 A552 Set of 5 3.75 3.75

Souvenir Sheet

2964 A552 $5 multi 6.00 6.00

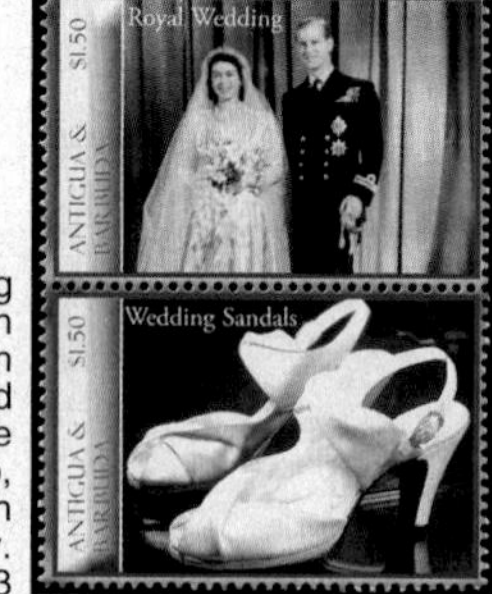

Wedding of Queen Elizabeth II and Prince Philip, 60th Anniv. A553

No. 2965: a, Couple. b, Wedding sandals.

$6, Couple, vert.

2007, May 1 ***Perf. 14***

2965 A553 $1.50 Pair, #a-b 3.00 3.00

Souvenir Sheet

2966 A553 $6 multi 6.00 6.00

No. 2965 was printed in sheets containing three of each stamp.

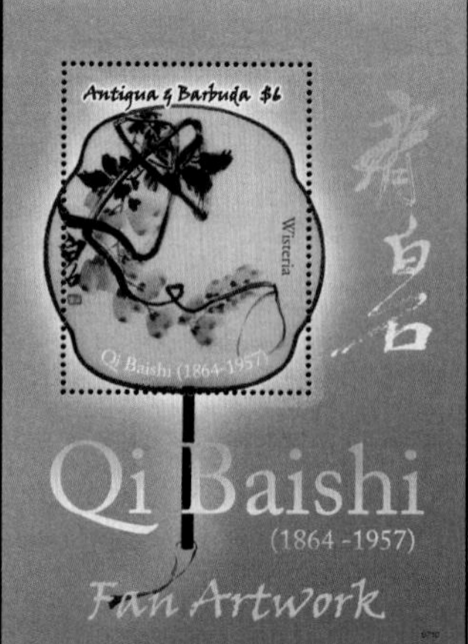

Painted Fans by Qi Baishi (1864-1957) — A554

No. 2967, horiz.: a, Camellias and butterfly. b, Two Shrimp and Arrowhead Leaves. c, Gourd and Ladybug. d, Bird. e, Landscape. f, Five Shrimp.

No. 2968: a, Chrysanthemums. b, Maple Leaves.

$6, Wisteria.

2007, May 1 ***Perf. 14¼***

2967 A554 $1.50 Sheet of 6, #a-f 7.50 7.50

2968 A554 $3 Sheet of 2, #a-b 6.00 6.00

Souvenir Sheet

2969 A554 $6 multi 6.00 6.00

Miniature Sheet

Ferrari Automobiles — A555

No. 2970: a, 1969 365 GTS4. b, 2005 Superamerica. c, 1990 F1 90. d, 1976 400 Automatic. e, 1954 250 GT Coupe. f, 1960 156 F2. g, 1972 312 P. h, 1956 D 50.

2007, June 4 ***Perf. 13¼***

2970 A555 $1.40 Sheet of 8, #a-h 10.00 10.00

Concorde — A556

No. 2971, $1.50 — Concorde O1: a, On ground, red frame. b, In air, green frame. c, On ground, blue violet frame. d, In air, red frame. e, On ground, green frame. f, In air, blue violet frame.

No. 2972, $1.50 — Concorde in flight and: a, Millennium Wheel, green denomination. b, Sydney Opera House, black denomination. c, Millennium Wheel, red violet denomination. d, Sydney Opera House, red orange denomination. e, Millennium Wheel, black denomination. f, Sydney Opera House, blue denomination.

2007, June 20 ***Perf. 12¾***

Sheets of 6, #a-f

2971-2972 A556 Set of 2 17.50 17.50

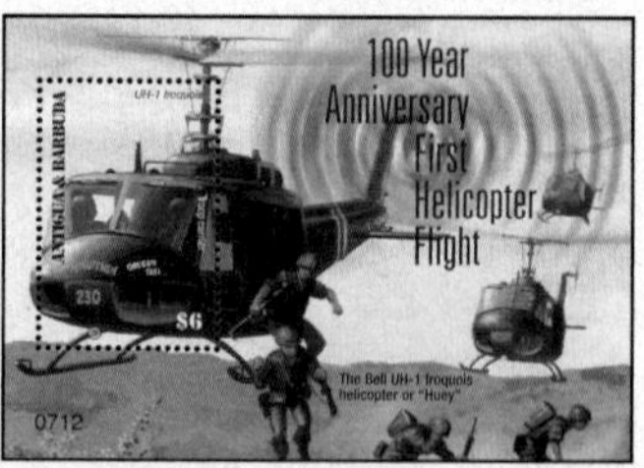

First Helicopter Flight, Cent. — A557

No. 2973, horiz.: a, NH 90. b, BO 105, black denomination at LR. c, NH 90. d, AS-61 over water. e, BO 105, black denomination at LL. f, AS-61 from below.

$6, UH-1 Iroquiois.

2007, June 20 ***Perf. 12¾***

2973 A557 $1.50 Sheet of 6, #a-f 9.25 9.25

Souvenir Sheet

2974 A557 $6 multi 6.75 6.75

Pope Benedict XVI — A558

2007, July 30 ***Perf. 13¾***

2975 A558 $1.40 multi 1.50 1.50

Printed in sheets of 8.

Miniature Sheet

Elvis Presley (1935-77) — A559

No. 2967 — Presley: a, Wearing black jacket. b, Facing left, wearing striped shirt, brown background. c, Wearing jacket and holding guitar. d, Facing forward, wearing striped shirt, brown background. e, Wearing red shirt. f, Holding guitar, purple background.

2007, July 30 ***Perf. 13¼***

2976 A559 $1.50 Sheet of 6, #a-f 11.00 11.00

Princess Diana (1961-97) — A560

No. 2977 — Princess Diana wearing: a, Beige suit. b, Lilac dress. c, Purple jacket with black-edged collar. d, Hat.

$6, White robe.

2007, July 30

2977 A560 $2 Sheet of 4, #a-d 7.50 7.50

Souvenir Sheet

2978 A560 $6 multi 5.75 5.75

Flora — A561

Designs: 15c, Bird of paradise. 20c, Seaside mahoe. 30c, Hibiscus. 50c, Agave. 70c, Barringtonia tree. 75c, Coconut tree. 90c, Mesquite tree, horiz. $1, Tamarind tree. $1.50, Black willow flowers, horiz. $1.80, Baobab tree, horiz. $2, Petrea volubilis. $2.50, Opuntia cochenillifera, horiz. $5, Locust fruit, horiz. $10, Barbuda black warri. $20, Castor oil plant.

Perf. 12½x13¼, 13¼x12½

2007, Oct. 1 **Litho.**

2979	A561	15c multi	.25	.25
2980	A561	20c multi	.25	.25
2981	A561	30c multi	.30	.25
2982	A561	50c multi	.45	.40
2983	A561	70c multi	.70	.55
2984	A561	75c multi	.75	.60
2985	A561	90c multi	.90	.70
2986	A561	$1 multi	1.00	.75
2987	A561	$1.50 multi	1.40	1.10
2988	A561	$1.80 multi	1.75	1.40
2989	A561	$2 multi	2.25	1.50
2990	A561	$2.50 multi	2.75	1.90
2991	A561	$5 multi	5.00	3.75
2992	A561	$10 multi	8.00	7.50
2993	A561	$20 multi	19.00	15.00
		Nos. 2979-2993 (15)	44.75	35.90

Miniature Sheet

Intl. Holocaust Remembrance Day — A562

No. 2994 — United Nations delegates, each $1.40: a, John W. Ashe, Antigua & Barbuda. b, Alfred Capelle, Marshall Islands. c, Masao Nakayama, Micronesia. d, Gilles Noghes, Monaco. e, Baatar Choisuren, Mongolia. f, Filipe Chidumo, Mozambique. g, Marlene Moses, Nauru. h, Franciscus Majoor, Netherlands.

2007, Oct. 25 *Perf. 13¼*

2994 A562 Sheet of 8, #a-h 10.00 10.00

Christmas A563

Designs: 30c, Stylized map of Antigua & Barbuda, sailboat, candy canes. 90c, Dancers, sailboat, decorated palm tree. $1, Decorated cake. $1.50, Woman in costume.

2007, Nov. 5 *Perf. 14¾x14*

2995-2998 A563 Set of 4 2.75 2.75

Hospice and Palliative Care A564

Emblem of Hospice Antigua & Barbuda and: No. 2999, 30c, Clock. No. 3000, 30c, Hands.

2007, Dec. 27 *Perf. 13¼*

2999-3000 A564 Set of 2 .85 .85

National Heroes — A565

Designs: No. 3001, 90c, King Court (1691-1736), slave rebellion leader. No. 3002, 90c, Dame Georgianna E. (Nellie) Robinson (1880-1972), educator. $1, Sir Vivian Richards, cricket player. $1.50, Sir Vere Cornwall Bird, Sr. (1909-99), first Prime Minister.

2008, Mar. 7 **Litho.** *Perf. 12¾*

3001-3004 A565 Set of 4 4.00 4.00

World Glaucoma Day — A566

Designs: 30c, Person applying glaucoma eyedrops. 50c, Normal and glaucomatous optic nerves. $1, Braille writing.

2008, Mar. 7 *Perf. 13¼*

3005-3007 A566 Set of 3 2.25 2.25

32nd America's Cup Yacht Races, Off Valencia, Spain — A567

No. 3008 — Various yachts with text "32nd America's Cup" in: a, $1.20, Yellow. b, $1.80, White. c, $3, Blue. d, $5, Orange.

2008, Mar. 25 *Perf. 12½*

3008 A567 Block of 4, #a-d 8.25 8.25

Miniature Sheet

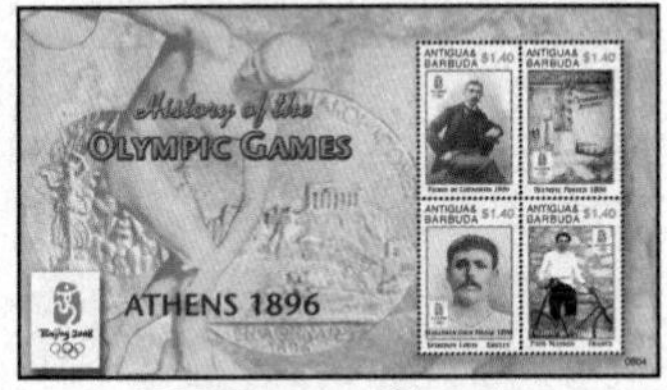

2008 Summer Olympics, Beijing — A568

No. 3009, each $1.40: a, Pierre de Coubertin. b, Poster for 1896 Athens Olympic Games. c, Spiridon Louis, 1896 marathon gold medalist. d, Paul Masson, 1896 cycling gold medalist.

2008, Mar. 25 *Perf. 12¾*

3009 A568 Sheet of 4, #a-d 4.25 4.25

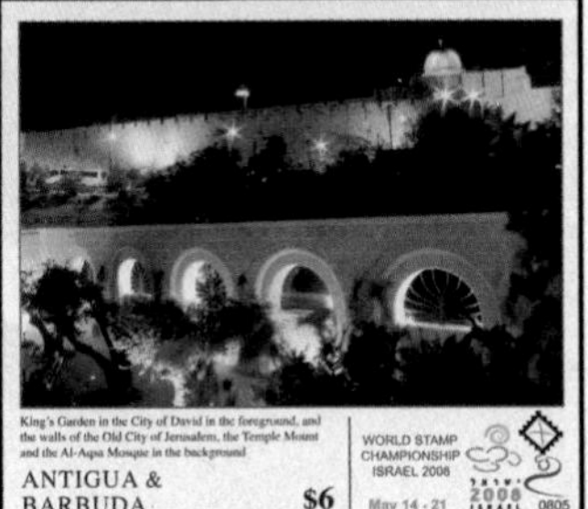

2008 World Stamp Championship, Israel — A569

2008, May 14 *Imperf.*

3010 A569 $6 multi 4.75 4.75

Visit of Pope Benedict XVI to United States A570

2008, June 18 *Perf. 13¼*

3011 A570 $2 multi 1.75 1.75

Printed in sheets of 4.

Miniature Sheet

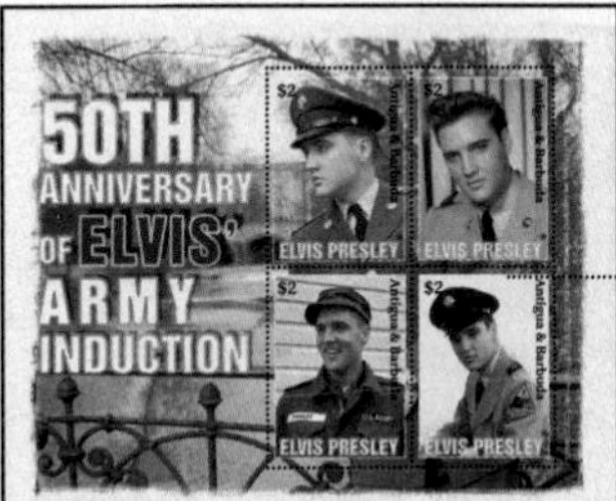

Army Induction of Elvis Presley, 50th Anniv. — A571

No. 3012 — Presley wearing: a, Dress uniform and cap. b, Dress uniform, no cap. c, Army fatigues and cap. d, Dress uniform with shoulder insignia and cap.

2008, June 18

3012 A571 $2 Sheet of 4, #a-d 6.50 6.50

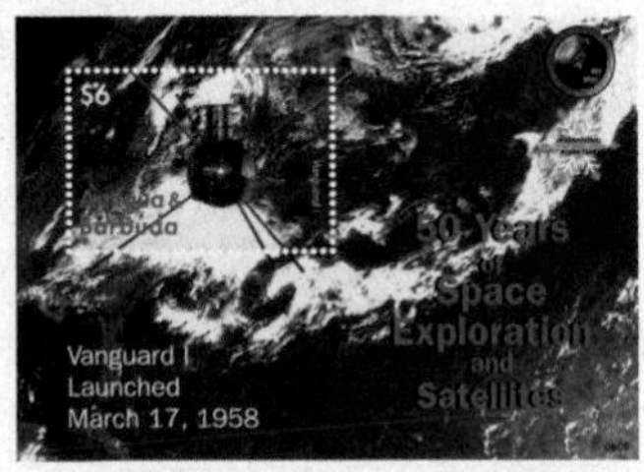

Space Achievements — A572

No. 3013, $1.50, vert. — Vanguard I: a, Against black background, with five rods showing. b, Against white and green background. c, Against black background, with six rods showing.

No. 3014, $1.50: a, Explorer III and equipment, vert. b, Explorer III and Earth, vert. c, Diagram of Van Allen radiation belts.

No. 3015, $2, vert. — Vanguard I and: a, Black background. b, Multicolored background.

No. 3016, $2, vert. — Explorer III and: a, Red and green background. b, Black background.

No. 3017, $6, Vanguard I. No. 3018, $6, Explorer III.

2008, July 29 *Perf. 13¼*

Horiz. Strips of 3, #a-c

3013-3014 A572 Set of 2 9.00 9.00

Pairs, #a-b

3015-3016 A572 Set of 2 8.00 8.00

Souvenir Sheets

3017-3018 A572 Set of 2 12.00 12.00

Nos. 3013-3014 were each printed in sheets containing two strips. Nos. 3015-3016 were each printed in sheets containing two pairs.

Miniature Sheets

Muhammad Ali, Boxer — A573

No. 3019 — Ali with words or letters in background: a, "ws" at UR. b, "learned" above denomination. c, "is so ugly" at UR. d, "should donate" at UR. e, "greates" at UR. f, "hat" at UR.

No. 3020 — Ali, each $2: a, Hitting punching bag. b, Wearing robe. c, With bare shoulders. d, Wearing protective headgear.

2008, Sept. 29 *Perf. 11½*

3019 A573 $1.50 Sheet of 6, #a-f 7.50 7.50

Perf. 13¼

3020 A573 Sheet of 4, #a-d 6.50 6.50

No. 3020 contains four 37x50mm stamps.

Star Trek — A574

No. 3021: a, Capt. James Kirk and Mr. Spock. b, Chief Engineer Scott, Dr. Leonard McCoy, Kirk and Spock. c, Lt. Uhura, Spock. d, Actors on planetary city set. e, Uhura. f, Scott.

No. 3022: a, McCoy. b, Spock. c, Kirk. d, Hikaru Sulu.

2008, Sept. 29 *Perf. 11½*

3021 A574 $1.50 Sheet of 6, #a-f 8.00 8.00

Perf. 13¼

3022 A574 $2 Sheet of 4, #a-d 7.50 7.50

No. 3022 contains four 50x37mm stamps.

Miniature Sheet

Pres. John F. Kennedy (1917-63) — A575

No. 3023 — Kennedy: a, Looking right. b, Looking forward, curtains in background. c, Looking forward, smiling with teeth showing. d, Looking right with hand at chin.

2008, Dec. 18 *Perf. 13¼*

3023 A575 $2 Sheet of 4, #a-d 6.75 6.75

Miniature Sheet

Marilyn Monroe (1926-62), Actress — A576

No. 3024 — Monroe wearing: a, Orange sweater, with arm raised. b, Orange sweater, arms at side. c, Pink sweater. d, Purple sweater.

2008, Dec. 18
3024 A576 $2 Sheet of 4, #a-d 8.50 8.50

Christmas A577

Stained-glass windows: 30c, Holy Family. 90c, Infant Jesus in manger. $1, Madonna and Child, vert. $1.50, Sts. Elizabeth and John the Baptist, vert.

2009, Jan. 2 ***Perf. 14¾x14, 14x14¾***
3025-3028 A577 Set of 4 3.00 3.00

Miniature Sheet

China 2009 World Stamp Exhibition — A578

No. 3029: a, Baseball. b, Beach volleyball. c, Artistic gymnastics. d, Judo.

2009, Jan. 5 ***Perf. 11¼x11½***
3029 A578 $1.40 Sheet of 4, #a-d 4.50 4.50

Miniature Sheet

Pres. Abraham Lincoln (1809-65) — A579

No. 3030: a, Lincoln's first inaugural address, 1861. b, Lincoln, flag. c, Lincoln's second inaugural address, 1865. d, Lincoln at right, crowd at second inaugural.

2009, Jan. 5 ***Perf. 11½x11¼***
3030 A579 $2 Sheet of 4, #a-d 7.25 7.25

Inauguration of US Pres. Barack Obama — A580

Pres. Obama facing: $2.75, Right. $10, Left.

2009, Jan. 20 ***Perf. 12¼x11¾***
3031 A580 $2.75 multi 2.75 .275

Souvenir Sheet

Perf. 13¼x13½

3032 A580 $10 multi 7.75 7.75

No. 3031 was printed in sheets of 4. No. 3032 contains one 37x51mm stamp.

New Year 2009 (Year of the Ox) A581

2009, Jan. 26 ***Perf. 11½x12***
3033 A581 $1 multi 1.25 1.25

Printed in sheets of 4.

A582

A583

2009, Apr. 10 ***Perf. 13½x13¼***
3034 A582 $1 multi 1.10 1.10

Souvenir Sheet

Perf. 13

3035 A583 $5 multi 4.75 4.75

No. 3034 was printed in sheets of 8.

Miniature Sheet

Elvis Presley (1935-77) — A584

No. 3036 — Presley wearing: a, Hat. b, Suit with handkerchief in pocket. c, Black shirt and pants. d, Pink, white and black windbreaker. e, Blue shirt and lei. f, Suit without handkerchief.

2009, Apr. 14 ***Perf. 14x14¼***
3036 A584 $1.50 Sheet of 6, #a-f 7.75 7.75

Miniature Sheets

A585

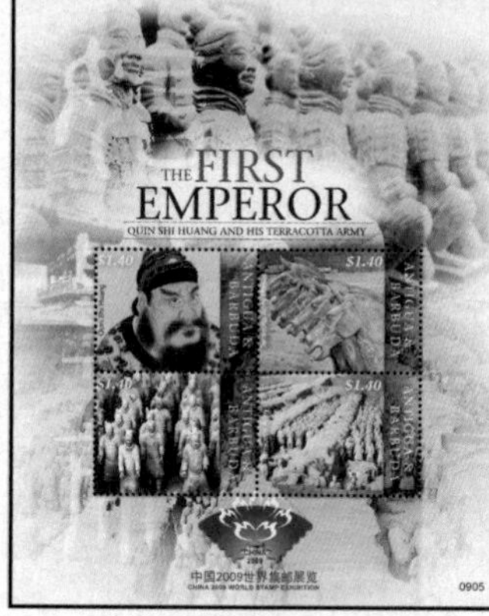

China 2009 World Stamp Exhibition — A586

No. 3037 — Landmarks in China: a, Bell Tower, Xian. b, St. Sophia Church, Harbin. c, Great Hall of the People, Chongqing. d, Fenghua Bridge, Tianjin.

No. 3038 — First emperor of China: a, Qin Shi Huang (259-210 B.C.). b, Horses of Terracotta Army. c, Soldiers of Terracotta Army. d, Excavated Terracotta Army.

2009, June 29 **Litho.** ***Perf. 12***
3037 A585 $1.40 Sheet of 4, #a-d 5.50 5.50

Perf. 12½x12¾

3038 A586 $1.40 Sheet of 4, #a-d 5.50 5.50

A587

2009, July 9 ***Perf. 14x15***
3039 A587 $4 multi 3.50 3.50

Miniature Sheets

Dogs — A588

No. 3040, $2.50 — Labrador retrievers: a, Puppy in canoe. b, Two puppies at window. c, Two puppies with stick. d, Puppy in bucket.

No. 3041, $2.50 — Dachshunds: a, Dog and carrying case. b, Dog and flowers. c, Two dogs in flower box. d, Dog near flower pot.

2009, Aug. 13 ***Perf. 12***

Sheets of 4, #a-d

3040-3041 A588 Set of 2 19.00 19.00

A589

Michael Jackson (1958-2009), Singer — A590

No. 3042 — Jackson: a, Holding microphone, wearing black coat with gold trim. b, Wearing black coat with gold trim, not holding microphone. c, Wearing red and black shirt. d, Wearing jacket with eagle and shield.

No. 3043 — Jackson: a, Wearing black pants, white above red orange frame at top of stamp. b, Wearing pants with buckles along leg, white above red orange frame at top of stamp. c, As "b," with black above red orange frame. d, As "a," with black above red orange frame.

$6, Jackson singing.

2009 **Litho.** ***Perf. 11¼x11½***
3042 A589 $2.50 Sheet of 4, #a-d 9.50 9.50

Perf. 12x11½

3043 A590 $2.50 Sheet of 4, #a-d 9.50 9.50

Souvenir Sheet

Perf. 13¼

3044 A590 $6 multi 4.75 4.75

Issued: Nos. 3042-3043, 9/30; No. 3044, 12/3. No. 3044 contains one 37x50mm stamp.

Meeting of US Pres. Barack Obama and Pope Benedict XVI — A591

No. 3045, vert.: a, Pres. Obama. b, Pope Benedict XVI. c, Michelle Obama.
$6, Pope Benedict XVI and Pres. Obama.

2009, Nov. 4 ***Perf. 11¼x11½***
3045 A591 $2.75 Sheet of 3, #a-c 7.50 7.50

Souvenir Sheet
Perf. 11½x12
3046 A591 $6 multi 5.75 5.75

Chinese Aviation, Cent. — A592

No. 3047 — Aerobatic team: a, Six airplanes with blue, white and red contrails. b, Six airplanes flying right in double triangle formation. c, Six airplanes flying left in diagonal line formation. d, Five airplanes.
$6, J-7GB.

2009, Nov. 12 ***Perf. 14***
3047 A592 $2 Sheet of 4, #a-d 6.75 6.75

Souvenir Sheet
Perf. 14¼
3048 A592 $6 multi 5.00 5.00

Aeropex 2009 Intl. Philatelic Exhibition, Beijing. No. 3048 contains one 50x37mm stamp.

First Man on the Moon, 40th Anniv. — A593

No. 3049: a, Apollo 11 patch, US flag on Moon. b, Lunar Module on Moon. c, Passive seismic experiment package. d, Apollo 11 on launch pad.
$6, Apollo 11 Command and Service Modules.

2009, Nov. 13 ***Perf. 12¾x12½***
3049 A593 $2.50 Sheet of 4, #a-d 9.50 9.50

Souvenir Sheet
Perf. 12¾x13
3050 A593 $6 multi 5.50 5.50

Intl. Year of Astronomy.

Souvenir Sheets

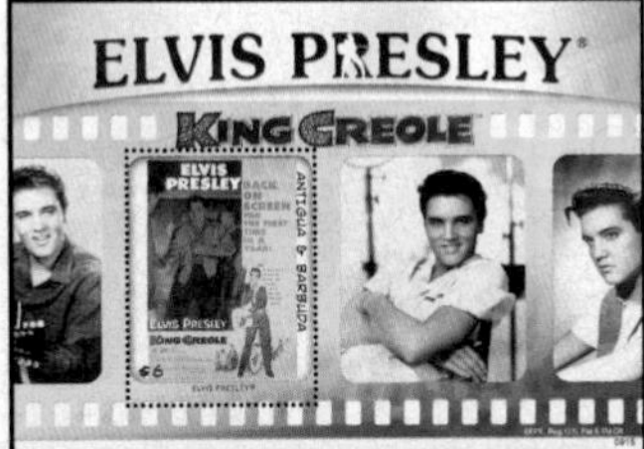

A594

A595

A596

Elvis Presley (1935-77) — A597

2009, Nov. 26 ***Perf. 13¼***
3051 A594 $6 multi 5.50 5.50
3052 A595 $6 multi 5.50 5.50
3053 A596 $6 multi 5.50 5.50
3054 A597 $6 multi 5.50 5.50
Nos. 3051-3054 (4) 22.00 22.00

Worldwide Fund for Nature (WWF) — A598

No. 3055 — Caribbean coots: a, Pair in water. b, Pair taking off. c, Pair and chick. d, Adult and chick.

2009, Dec. 3 ***Perf. 13¼***
3055 Strip of 4 8.50 8.50
a.-d. A598 $2.65 Any single 2.00 2.00
e. Miniature sheet, 2 each #3055a-3055d 20.00 20.00

Christmas A599

Christmas light displays: 90c, Candles. $1, Palm tree and reindeer. $1.80, Bells. $3, Nativity scene, horiz.

2009, Dec. 3 ***Perf. 14x14¾, 14¾x14***
3056-3059 A599 Set of 4 5.00 5.00

Sir Vere Cornwall Bird, Sr. (1909-99), First Chief Minister, Premier and Prime Minister — A600

Bird: 30c, In chair. 75c, With blue, white and red stripes in background. 90c, Wearing red hat. $1.50, With building in background.
No. 3064: a, Like 75c. b, Like 30c. c, Like 90c. d, Like $1.50.
$6, Bird, map of Antigua with flag.

2009, Dec. 8 ***Perf. 11¼x11½***
3060-3063 A600 Set of 4 3.00 3.00
3064 A600 $2.50 Sheet of 4, #a-d 8.00 8.00

Souvenir Sheet
Perf. 12x11½
3065 A600 $6 multi 5.00 5.00

Birds A601

Designs: $1.20, Glossy ibis. $1.80, Green-winged teal. No. 3068, $3, California clapper rail. $5, Cattle egret, vert.
No. 3070: a, Green heron. b, Common ground dove. c, White-tailed hawk. d, Black-faced grassquit.
No. 3071, $3: a, Bananaquit. b, Osprey.

Perf. 11½x11¼, 11¼x11½
2009, Dec. 8
3066-3069 A601 Set of 4 8.75 8.75

Perf. 11½x12
3070 A601 $2.50 Sheet of 4, #a-d 8.00 8.00

Souvenir Sheet
3071 A601 $3 Sheet of 2, #a-b 5.00 5.00

Souvenir Sheet

New Year 2010 (Year of the Tiger) — A602

No. 3072 — Chinese bronze tigers of: a, Western Han Dynasty. b, Shang Dynasty.

2010, Jan. 4 ***Perf. 11½x12***
3072 A602 $5 Sheet of 2, #a-b 7.75 7.75

Ferrari Automobiles and Their Parts — A603

No. 3073, $1.25: a, Engine of 1960 246 P F1. b, 1960 246 P F1.
No. 3074, $1.25: a, Engine of 1964 158 F1. b, 1964 158 F1.
No. 3075, $1.25: a, Interior of 1966 365P Speciale. b, 1966 365P Speciale.
No. 3076, $1.25: a, Air foil and rear wheel of 1968 312 F1-68. b, 1968 312 F1-68.

2010, Feb. 22 ***Perf. 12***
Vert. Pairs, #a-b
3073-3076 A603 Set of 4 8.25 8.25

Whales and Dolphins A604

Designs: $1.20, Risso's dolphin. $1.80, Common dolphin. $3, Humpback whale. $5, Sperm whale.
No. 3081: a, Shortsnout dolphin. b, Spotted dolphin. c, Cuvier's beaked whale. d, Shortfin pilot whale. e, Gulf Stream beaked whale. f, Rough-toothed dolphin.

2010, Feb. 23 **Litho.**
3077-3080 A604 Set of 4 9.00 9.00
3081 A604 $2 Sheet of 6, #a-f 10.00 10.00

Miniature Sheets

A605

A606

Princess Diana (1961-97) — A607

No. 3082 — Diana wearing: a, White dress. b, Pink dress. c, Lilac suit. d, White dress, holding flowers.

No. 3083 — Diana wearing tiara and: a, White dress, two earrings visible. b, Red dress, earring with black stone. c, Red dress, pearl earring. d, White dress with high collar.

No. 3084 — Diana wearing: a, Lei. b, Lilac dress. c, Blue and white dress and hat. d, Red orange hat and dress.

2010 Litho. *Perf. 12x11½*

3082 A605 $2 Sheet of 4, #a-d 6.50 6.50
3083 A606 $2.75 Sheet of 4, #a-d 8.25 8.25
3084 A607 $2.75 Sheet of 4, #a-d 8.25 8.25
Nos. 3082-3084 (3) 23.00 23.00

Issued: No. 3082, 2/23; Nos. 3083-3084, 5/10.

Butterflies A608

Designs: $1.20, Common buckeye. $1.80, Red postman. $3, Red admiral. $5, Zebra longwing.

No. 3089: a, Orange sulfur. b, Blue morpho. c, Queen butterfly. d, Zebra swallowtail. e, Malachite. f, Gatekeeper butterfly.

2010, Apr. 14 *Perf. 14*

3085-3088 A608 Set of 4 9.00 9.00

Perf. 14¾x14

3089 A608 $2 Sheet of 6, #a-f 9.50 9.50

No. 3089 contains six 40x30mm stamps.

Sharks A609

Designs: $1.20, Nurse shark. $1.80, Caribbean reef shark. $3, Tiger shark. $5, Whale shark.

No. 3094: a, Caribbean sharpnose shark. b, Blacktip shark. c, Oceanic whitetip shark. d, Bull shark.

2010, Apr. 14 *Perf. 14*

3090-3093 A609 Set of 4 9.25 9.25

Perf. 14¾x14

3094 A609 $2.75 Sheet of 4, #a-d 9.00 9.00

No. 3094 contains four 40x30mm stamps.

Pope John Paul II (1920-2005) A610

2010, May 10 *Perf. 11¼x11½*

3095 A610 $2.75 multi 2.10 2.10

Printed in sheets of 4, with each stamp having slight differences in background.

Boy Scouts of America, Cent. — A611

No. 3096, $2.50: a, Scout at lectern. b, Scouts canoeing.

No. 3097, $2.50: a, Statue of Liberty giving Scout salute. b, Scouts using map and compass.

2010, May 10 *Perf. 13¼*

Pairs, #a-b

3096-3097 A611 Set of 2 7.50 7.50

Nos. 3096 and 3097 each were printed in sheets containing two pairs.

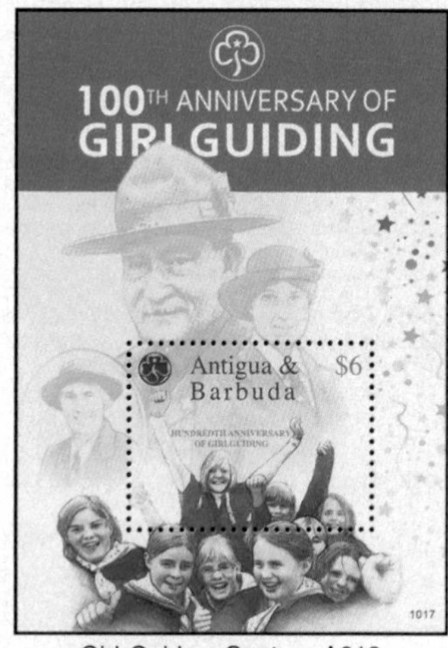

Girl Guides, Cent. — A612

No. 3098: a, Rainbows. b, Brownies. c, Guides. d, Senior Section.

$6, Girl Guides, diff.

2010, May 10 *Perf. 11½x12*

3098 A612 $2.75 Sheet of 4, #a-d 8.50 8.50

Souvenir Sheet

Perf. 11½

3099 A612 $6 multi 4.75 4.75

Miniature Sheet

Expo 2010, Shanghai — A613

No. 3100: a, Dancers, Shanghai Intl. Culture and Art Festival. b, China National Grand Theater, Beijing. c, Rice terraces, Guangxi Province, China. d, Dance performance, Beijing.

2010, May 10 *Perf. 11½*

3100 A613 $1.50 Sheet of 4, #a-d 4.50 4.50

Miniature Sheet

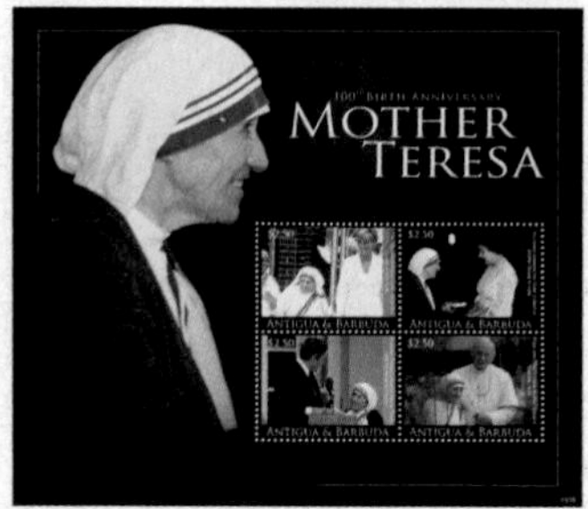

Mother Teresa (1910-97), Humanitarian — A614

No. 3101 — Mother Teresa and: a, Princess Diana. b, Queen Elizabeth II. c, Pres. Ronald Reagan. d, Pope John Paul II.

2010, May 10 *Perf. 11½x12*

3101 A614 $2.50 Sheet of 4, #a-d 7.50 7.50

Miniature Sheet

Pres. John F. Kennedy (1917-63) — A615

No. 3102: a, Sitting in limousine. b, Standing. c, Sitting in rocking chair. d, Behind microphones.

2010, May 10 *Perf. 11¼x11½*

3102 A615 $2.75 Sheet of 4, #a-d 8.25 8.25

Miniature Sheet

Awarding of Nobel Peace Prize to Pres. Barack Obama — A616

No. 3103 — Pres. Obama: a, Holding diploma and medal, blue curtain in background. b, At lectern, with hand closed. c, At lectern, with hand open. d, Holding diploma and medal.

2010, May 10 *Perf. 12x11½*

3103 A616 $2.75 Sheet of 4, #a-d 8.25 8.25

Miniature Sheets

A617

Pres. Abraham Lincoln (1809-65) — A618

Various photographs of Lincoln.

2010, May 10 *Perf. 11¼x11½*

3104 A617 $2.75 Sheet of 4, #a-d 8.25 8.25
3105 A618 $2.75 Sheet of 4, #a-d 8.25 8.25

Miniature Sheets

A619

Elvis Presley (1935-77) — A620

No. 3106: a, Wearing rhinestone-studded jacket, microphone in front of mouth. b, Wearing black open-neck shirt. c, Two portraits. d, Wearing white jacket with lapels and pockets with dark trim.

No. 3107: a, Presley holding guitar, parts of "E" and "L" in background. b, Presley holding guitar, parts of "L" and "V" in background. c, Presley holding guitar, parts of "V" and "7" in background. d, Three portraits.

2010, May 10 *Perf. 13¼*

3106 A619 $2.75 Sheet of 4, #a-d 8.25 8.25
3107 A620 $2.75 Sheet of 4, #a-d 8.25 8.25

Miniature Sheet

Chinese Zodiac Animals — A621

No. 3108: a, Rat. b, Ox. c, Tiger. d, Rabbit. e, Dragon. f, Snake. g, Horse. h, Goat. i, Monkey. j, Cock. k, Dog. l, Pig.

2010, Jan. 4 Litho. *Perf. 12¼*
3108 A621 60c Sheet of 12, #a-l 5.50 5.50

Miniature Sheet

The Three Stooges — A622

No. 3109: a, Moe and Larry with cowboy hats, Curly with pick. b, Moe, Larry and Curly in painter's coveralls. c, Moe and Larry in surgical garb examining Curly. d, Moe and Larry squeezing Curly's neck in giant nutcracker.

2010, Sept. 27 Litho. *Perf. 11½x12*
3109 A622 $2.50 Sheet of 4, #a-d 7.50 7.50

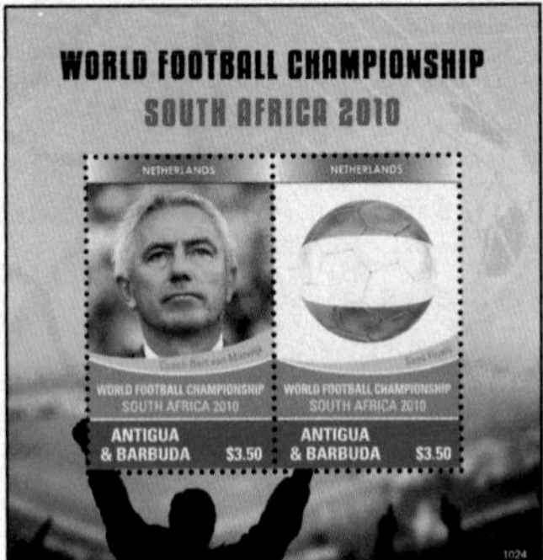

2010 World Cup Soccer Championships, South Africa — A623

No. 3110: a, Maximiliano Pereira. b, John Heitinga. c, Edinson Cavani. d, Mark Van Bommel. e, Martin Caceres. f, Giovanni van Bronckhorst.

No. 3111, $3.50: a, Netherlands Coach Bert van Marwijk. b, Netherlands flag on soccer ball.

No. 3112, $3.50: a, Uruguay Coach Oscar Tabarez. b, Uruguay flag on soccer ball.

2010, Oct. 18 *Perf. 12*
3110 A623 $1.50 Sheet of 6, #a-f 7.75 7.75

Souvenir Sheets of 2, #a-b
3111-3112 A623 Set of 2 11.00 11.00

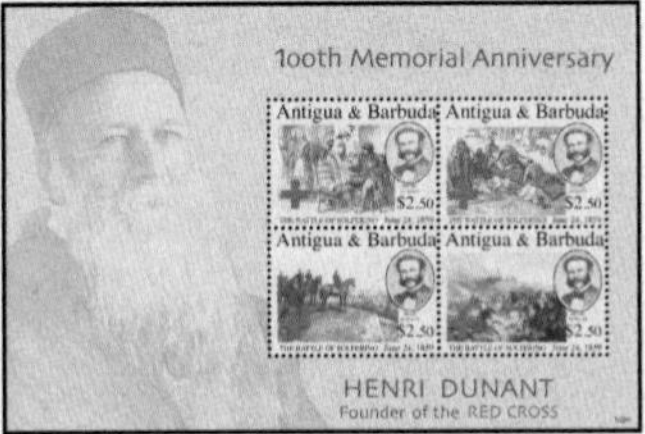

Henri Dunant (1828-1910), Founder of Red Cross — A624

No. 3113 — Red Cross, scenes from Battle of Solferino and portrait of Dunant in: a, Blue green. b, Brown. c, Lilac. d, Blue gray.

$6, Red Cross, Battle of Solferino, Dunant in lilac.

2010, Dec. 20
3113 A624 $2.50 Sheet of 4, #a-d 8.00 8.00

Souvenir Sheet
3114 A624 $6 multi 4.75 4.75

Cats — A625

No. 3115: a, California spangled cat. b, Siamese cat. c, British shorthair cat. d, Norwegian forest cat. e, Egyptian Mau cat. f, American curl longhair cat.

$6, Manx cat.

2010, Dec. 20
3115 A625 $2.50 Sheet of 6, #a-f 12.00 12.00

Souvenir Sheet
3116 A625 $6 multi 4.50 4.50

No. 3115 contains six 30x40mm stamps.

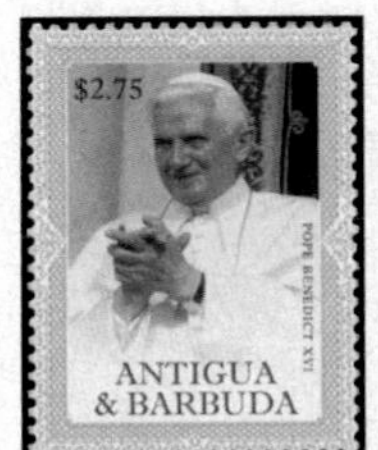

A626

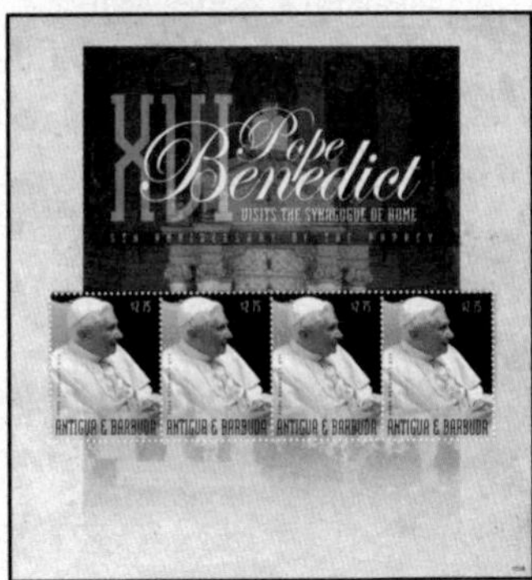

Pope Benedict XVI — A627

No. 3118 — Pope Benedict XVI and: a, Buff area below "G" in "Antigua," brown area below "U" in "Antigua." b, Red brown area below "IG" of "Antigua," buff area below first "A" in "Antigua." c, Dark brown areas below "ANTIG" of "Antigua." d, Buff areas below first and second "A" of "Antigua."

2010, Dec. 20 Litho. *Perf. 12*
3117 A626 $2.75 multi 2.10 2.10
3118 A627 $2.75 Sheet of 4, #a-d 8.50 8.50

No. 3117 issued in sheets of 4.

Souvenir Sheet

New Year 2011 (Year of the Rabbit) — A628

No. 3119: a, Rabbit. b, Chinese character for "rabbit."

2011, Jan. 3
3119 A628 $4 Sheet of 2, #a-b 6.00 6.00

Pandas — A629

No. 3120: a, Panda with mouth open. b, Head of panda. c, Panda eating, large leaf partially covering head. d, Panda eating, diff.

$5, Panda, diff.

2011, Jan. 3
3120 A629 $2 Sheet of 4, #a-d 7.00 7.00

Souvenir Sheet
3121 A629 $5 multi 4.25 4.25

Beijing 2010 Intl. Philatelic Exhibition.

Christmas 2010 — A630

Designs: 30c, Casini Madonna, by Tommaso Masaccio. 75c, Madonna of the Stars, by Tintoretto. 90c, Wall mosaic, Basilica of Sant'Apollinaire Nuovo, Ravenna, Italy. $1.50, The Annunciation, by Fra Angelico.

2011, Jan. 17 *Perf. 12¾x12½*
3122-3125 A630 Set of 4 2.60 2.60

Engagement of Prince William and Catherine Middleton — A631

Design: No. 3126, Couple.

No. 3127: a, Prince William. b, Middleton.

No. 3128, $6, Prince William wearing striped shirt and necktie, vert. No. 3129, $6, Prince William wearing white shirt and bow tie, vert.

2011, Feb. 14 *Perf. 13 Syncopated*
3126 A631 $2.50 multi 1.90 1.90
3127 A631 $2.50 Horiz. pair, #a-b 3.75 3.75

Souvenir Sheets
3128-3129 A631 Set of 2 9.00 9.00

No. 3126 printed in sheets of 4. No. 3127 printed in sheets of 2 pairs.

Miniature Sheets

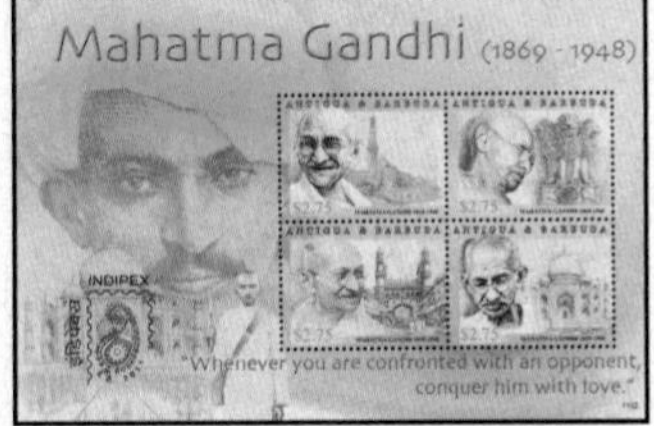

A632

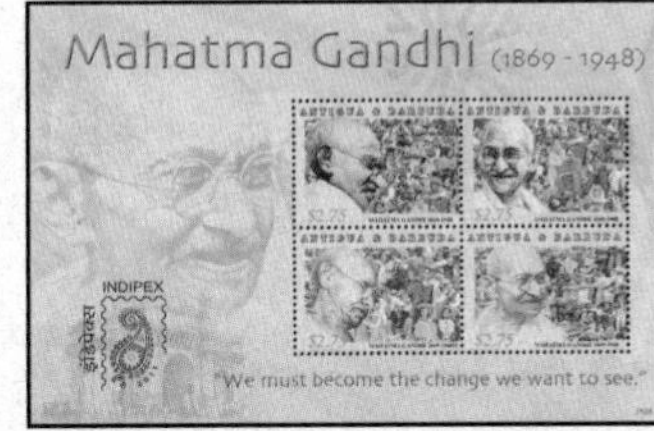

Mohandas K. Gandhi (1869-1948), Indian Nationalist — A633

No. 3130 — Gandhi and: a, Qutub Minar Tower, Delhi. b, Asoka pillar. c, Hyderabad Mosque. d, Taj Mahal.

No. 3131 — Crowd and: a, Profile of Gandhi, robe visible. b, Gandhi looking forward. c, Profile of Gandhi, robe not visible. d, Gandhi looking right.

2011, Mar. 1 *Perf. 12*
3130 A632 $2.75 Sheet of 4, #a-d 8.25 8.25
3131 A633 $2.75 Sheet of 4, #a-d 8.25 8.25

2011 Indipex Intl. Philatelic Exhibition, New Delhi

Beatification of Pope John Paul II — A634

No. 3132 — Pope John Paul II: a, Holding crucifix. b, Wearing red stole.

$6, Head of Pope John Paul II.

2011, Apr. 4 *Perf. 13 Syncopated*
3132 A634 $2 Pair, #a-b 3.00 3.00

Souvenir Sheet
Perf. 12
3133 A634 $6 multi 4.50 4.50

Miniature Sheets

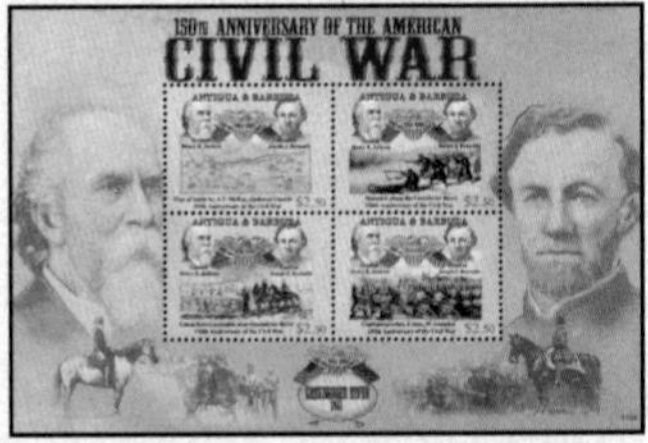

United States Civil War, 150th Anniv. — A635

No. 3134, $2.50 — Eagle, shield, flags, Generals Henry R. Jackson and Joseph J. Reynolds of Battle of Greenbrier River, Oct. 3, 1861, and: a, Battle map by A. T. McRae, Quitman Guards. b, Skirmish along the Greenbrier river. c, Union forces assembling near Greenbrier River. d, Battle scene.

No. 3135, $2.50 — Eagle, shield, flags, Confederate Secretary of the navy Stephen Mallory, Union Lt. Commander Alexander Murray of Battle of Cockle Creek, Oct. 5, 1861, and: a, Warships of the Atlantic Blockading Squadron. b, Flotilla of Union warships. c, Confederate privateers near Delaware Bay. d, USS Minnesota.

No. 3136, $2.50 — Eagle, shield, flags, Confederate Brigadier General Richard H. Anderson, Union Colonel Harvey Brown of Battle of Santa Rosa Island, Oct. 9, 1861, and: a, Fort Pickens. b, Drawing of Fight at Santa Rosa Island, by John Volck. c, Boats cutting off confederate dispatch galley. d, Col. Brown commanding 3rd U.S. Infantry.

2011, Apr. 4 *Perf. 12*
Sheets of 4, #a-d
3134-3136 A635 Set of 3 22.50 22.50

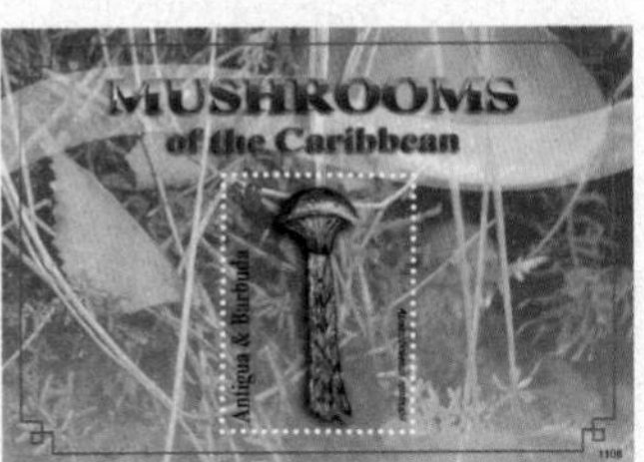

Mushrooms — A636

No. 3137: a, Tylopilus potamogeton. b, Amanita campinaranae. c, Cantharellus altratus. d, Tylopilus orsonianus. e, Boletellus ananas. f, Amanita craseoderma.

No. 3138: a, Amanita cyanopus. b, Phyllobolites miniatus. c, Chroogomphus jamaicensis. d, Coltricia cf. montagnei.
No. 3139, $6, Austroboletus rostrupii. No. 3140, $6, Austroboletus festivus.

2011, May 9 **Litho.**

3137 A636 $2 Sheet of 6, #a-f 10.00 10.00
3138 A636 $2.50 Sheet of 4, #a-d 7.50 7.50

Souvenir Sheets

3139-3140 A636 Set of 2 9.00 9.00

1997 Visit of Princess Diana To Barbuda — A637

Designs: No. 3141, $10, Princess Diana, her sons, family friend and airplane. No. 3142, $10, Princess Diana.
$50, Princess Diana, horiz.

2011, July 12 ***Perf. 12***

3141-3142 A637 Set of 2 17.00 17.00

Souvenir Sheet

3143 A637 $50 multi 37.50 37.50

Nos. 3141-3142 each were issued in sheets of 5.

Wedding of Prince William and Catherine Middleton — A638

No. 3144: a, Prince William wearing cap. b, Middleton, name at left in one line. c, Couple.
No. 3145: a, Prince William waving. b, Middleton, name at top in two lines. c, Couple kissing.
$6, Couple, diff.

2011, Aug. 15 ***Perf. 13x13¼***

3144 A638 $2.50 Sheet of 4, #3144a-3144b, 2 #3144c 7.50 7.50
3145 A638 $2.50 Sheet of 4, #3145a-3145b, 2 #3145c 7.50 7.50

Souvenir Sheet

Perf. 12

3146 A638 $6 multi 4.50 4.50

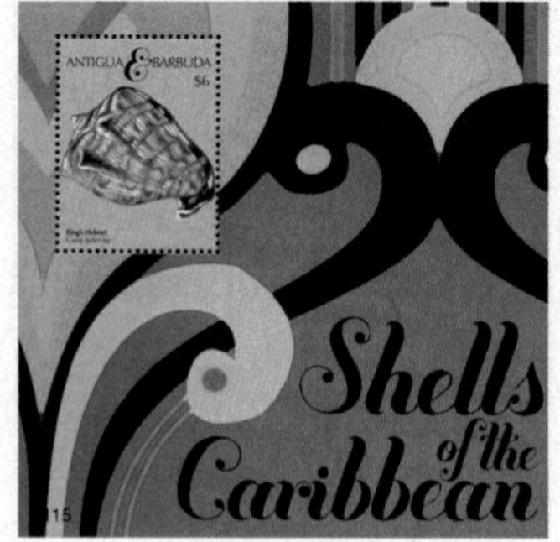

Shells — A639

No. 3147: a, Bleeding tooth nerite. b, Pen shell. c, Banded tulip shell. d, Chank shell. e, Flame helmet. f, Atlantic partridge tun.
No. 3148: a, Pink conch. b, Sunrise tellin. c, Flamingo tongue. d, Queen's helmet.
No. 3149, $6, King's helmet. No. 3150, $6, Triton's trumpet, horiz.

Perf. 13¼x13, 13x13¼

2011, Aug. 15

3147 A639 $2 Sheet of 6, #a-f 9.00 9.00
3148 A639 $2.75 Sheet of 4, #a-d 8.25 8.25

Souvenir Sheets

3149-3150 A639 Set of 2 9.00 9.00

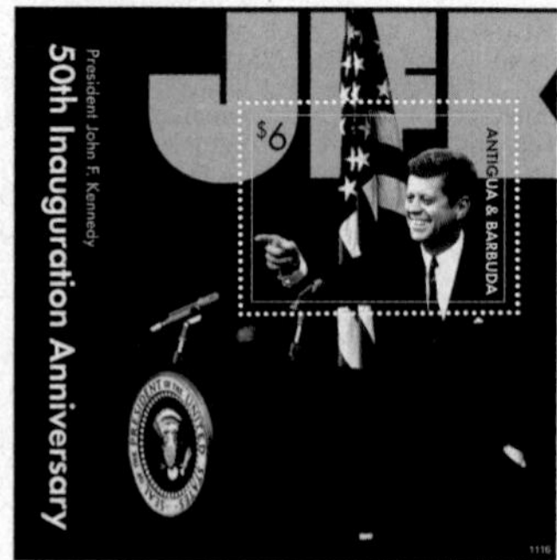

Pres. John F. Kennedy (1917-63) — A640

No. 3151, vert. — Pres. Kennedy: a, Inspecting Mercury capsule, Feb. 22, 1962. b, On Cape Canaveral tour, Nov. 16, 1963. c, At Saturn rocket briefing, Nov. 16, 1963. d, At Cape Canaveral, pointing, Nov. 16, 1963.
$6, Kennedy and flag.

2011, Sept. 9 ***Perf. 12***

3151 A640 $2.75 Sheet of 4, #a-d 8.25 8.25

Souvenir Sheet

Perf. 12¾

3152 A640 $6 multi 4.50 4.50

No. 3151 contains four 30x40mm stamps.

Pres. Barack Obama, 50th Birthday — A641

No. 3153 — Pres. Obama: a, Looking right, wearing dark tie and flag lapel pin. b, Wearing light patterned tie, standing in front of microphone. c, Wearing dark patterned tie, standing in front of microphones. d, Looking left.
$6, Pres. Obama, diff.

2011, Sept. 9 ***Perf. 13 Syncopated***

3153 A641 $2.75 Sheet of 4, #a-d 8.25 8.25

Souvenir Sheet

3154 A641 $6 multi 5.00 5.00

Princess Diana (1961-97) — A642

No. 3155 — Princess Diana: a, Seated on sofa. b, Wearing beige and white dress. c, Wearing white dress. d, With Prince Charles.
$6, Princess Diana, horiz.

2011, Sept. 9 ***Perf. 12***

3155 A642 $2.75 Sheet of 4, #a-d 8.25 8.25

Souvenir Sheet

Perf. 12¾

3156 A642 $6 multi 4.50 4.50

No. 3156 contains one 51x38mm stamp.

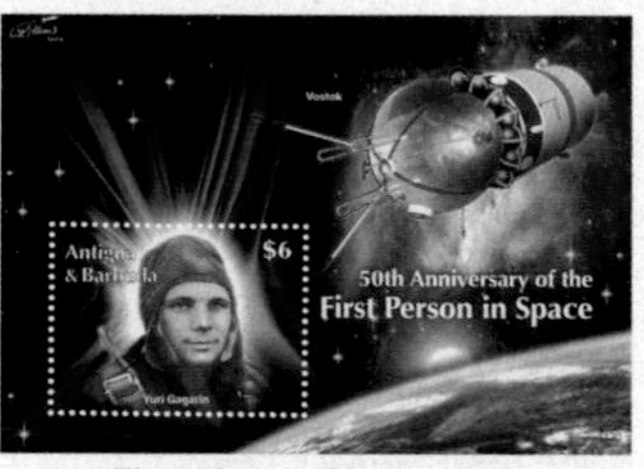

First Man in Space, 50th Anniv. — A643

No. 3157, $2.75: a, Liftoff of Vostok 1. b, Russian tracking ship named after Yuri Gagarin. c, Vostok 1 mission emblem. d, Alan Shepard, first American astronaut.
No. 3158, $2.75: a, Map of Gagarin's flightpath. b, Vostok 8K72K rocket. c, Gagarin, first cosmonaut. d, Virgil "Gus" Grissom, American astronaut, and rocket.
No. 3159, $6, Gagarin, diff. No. 3160, $6, Vostok spacecraft and Earth.

2011, Sept. 9 ***Perf. 12***

Sheets of 4, #a-d

3157-3158 A643 Set of 2 16.50 16.50

Souvenir Sheets

3159-3160 A643 Set of 2 9.00 9.00

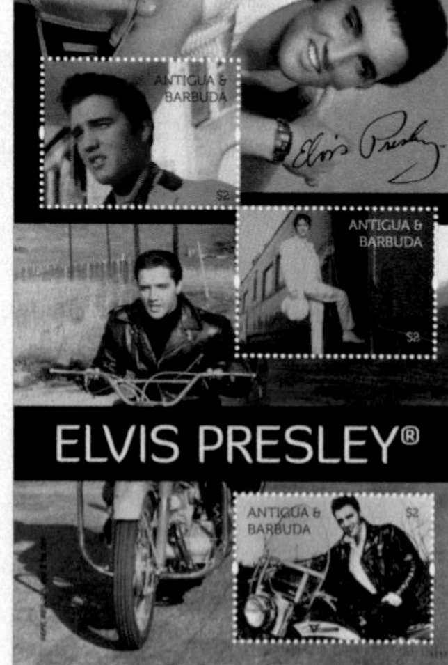

A644

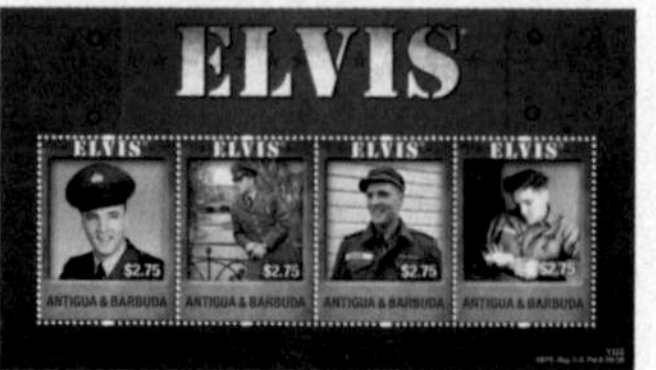

A645

A646

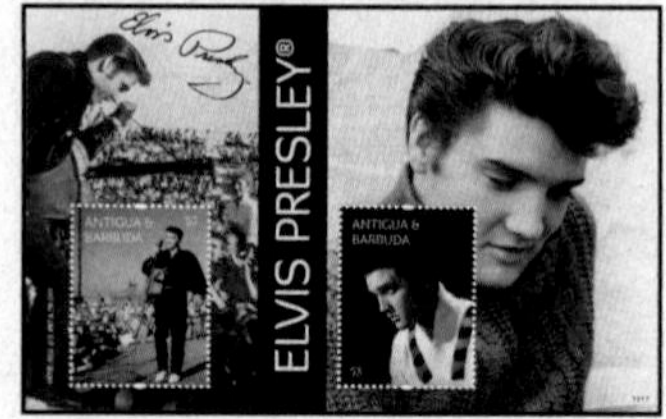

Elvis Presley (1935-77) — A647

No. 3161 — Presley: a, With building in background. b, On train steps. c, On motorcycle.
No. 3162 — Presley wearing: a, Army dress uniform. b, Dress uniform, standing next to railing. c, Battle fatigues. d, Battle fatigues, reading letter.
No. 3163 — Presley wearing: a, Glasses and red shirt. b, Suit, facing right. c, Sequined suit, facing forward. d, Suit, facing left.
No. 3164 — Presley: a, On stage. b, Wearing sweater.

2011, Sept. 9 ***Perf. 13 Syncopated***

3161 A644 $2 Sheet of 3, #a-c 4.50 4.50
3162 A645 $2.75 Sheet of 4, #a-d 8.25 8.25
3163 A646 $2.75 Sheet of 4, #a-d 8.25 8.25
Nos. 3161-3163 (3) 21.00 21.00

Souvenir Sheet

3164 A647 $3 Sheet of 2, #a-b 4.50 4.50

Miniature Sheets

A648

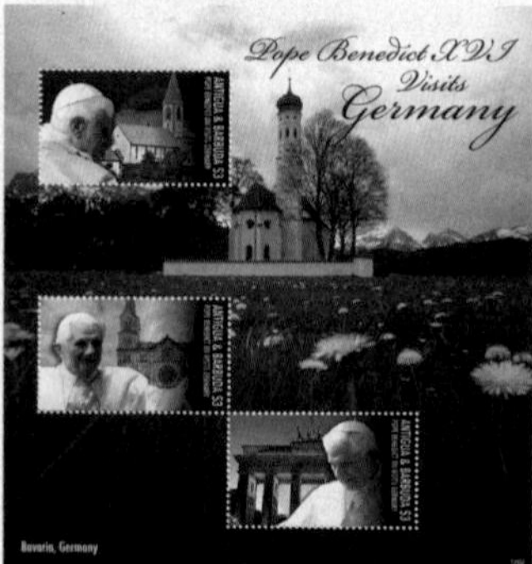

Visit of Pope Benedict XVI to Germany — A649

No. 3165 — Pope Benedict XVI: a, With church spires behind head. b, With arm extended, crucifix visible, hand in front of church steeple. c, With mountain behind head, chuch steeple and building with flowers at right.
No. 3166 — Pope Benedict XVI: a, Facing right, church with red roof at right. b, With arm

extended, no crucifix visible, chuch at right.c, With Brandenburg Gate at left.

2011, Aug. 3 Litho. *Perf. 12*
3165 A648 $3 Sheet of 3, #a-c 6.75 6.75
3166 A649 $3 Sheet of 3, #a-c 6.75 6.75

Fish — A650

No. 3167, $3.50: a, Queen angelfish. b, Ocean surgeonfish. c, Rock beauty. d, Gray angelfish.
No. 3168, $3.50: a, Foureye butterflyfish. b, French grunt. c, French angelfish. d, Spotfin butterflyfish.
No. 3169, $9, Great barracuda (80x30mm). No. 3170, $9, Banded butterflyfish (40x40mm).

2011, Sept. 30 *Perf. 12*
Sheets of 4, #a-d
3167-3168 A650 Set of 2 21.00 21.00
Souvenir Sheets
3169-3170 A650 Set of 2 13.50 13.50

Hu Jintao, President of People's Republic of China — A651

Pres. Hu and flag of People's Republic of China: $3, At lower left. $6, In background.

2011, Oct. 24
3171 A651 $3 multi 2.25 2.25
Souvenir Sheet
3172 A651 $6 multi 4.50 4.50

China 2011 Intl. Philatelic Exhibition, Wuxi (No. 3172).

Christmas A652

Paintings: 30c, Madonna and Child with Angels, by Giottino. 75c, The Annunciation and Two Saints, by Simone Martini. $1.50, Paradise, by Giusto de' Menabuoi. $3, Madonna, by Vitale da Bologna.

2011, Nov. 15 *Perf. 14*
3173-3176 A652 Set of 4 4.25 4.25

Miniature Sheet

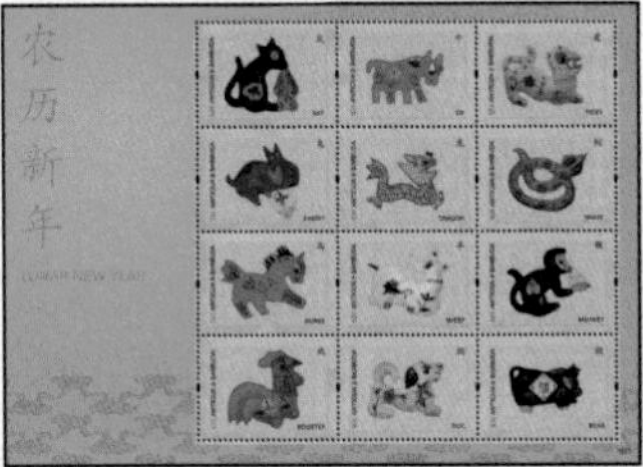

Chinese Zodiac Animals — A653

No. 3177: a, Rat. b, Ox. c, Tiger. d, Rabbit. e, Dragon. f, Snake. g, Horse. h, Sheep. i, Monkey. j, Rooster. k, Dog. l, Boar.

Litho. With Foil Application
2011, Nov. 15 *Perf. 13 Syncopated*
3177 A653 65c Sheet of 12, #a-l 5.75 5.75

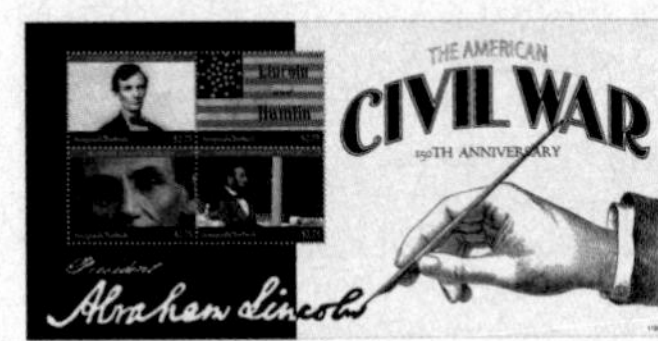

Pres. Abraham Lincoln (1809-65) — A654

No. 3178: a, Lincoln without beard. b, Campaign poster for Lincoln and Hannibal Hamlin. c, Eyes and nose of Lincoln. d, Linoln with beard.
$6, Lincoln, vert.

2011, Dec. 19 Litho. *Perf. 12*
3178 A654 $2.75 Sheet of 4, #a-d 8.25 8.25
Souvenir Sheet
3179 A654 $6 multi 4.50 4.50

No. 3179 contains one 30x50mm stamp.

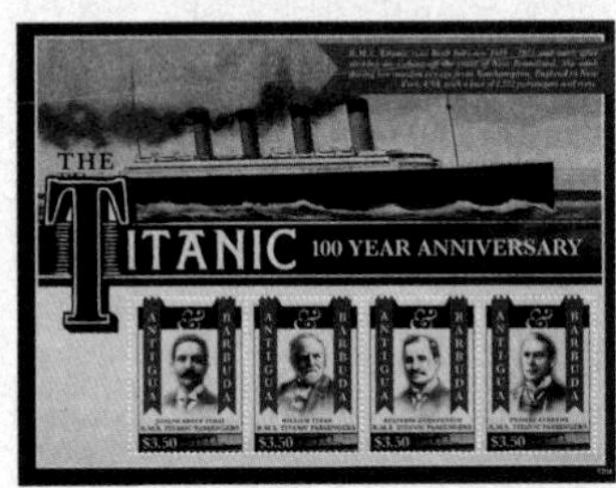

Sinking of the Titanic, Cent. — A655

No. 3180 — Titanic passengers: a, Joseph Bruce Ismay (1862-1937), chairman of White Star Line. b, William Stead (1849-1912), journalist. c, Benjamin Guggenheim (1865-1912), businessman. d, Thomas Andrews (1873-1912), naval architect of Titanic.
$9, Titanic, horiz.

2012, Jan. 25
3180 A655 $3.50 Sheet of 4, #a-d 10.50 10.50
Souvenir Sheet
3181 A655 $9 multi 6.75 6.75

No. 3181 contains one 50x30mm stamp.

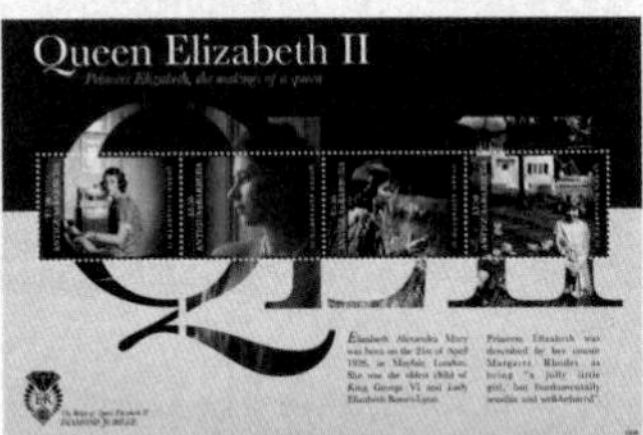

Reign of Queen Elizabeth II, 60th Anniv. — A656

No. 3182 — Queen Elizabeth II as young girl: a, At piano. b, Color photograph, looking left. c, In meadow, looking right. d, Near house and flowers.
$9, Queen Elizabeth II and flowers, vert.

2012, Mar. 26
3182 A656 $3.50 Sheet of 4, #a-d 10.50 10.50
Souvenir Sheet
3183 A656 $9 multi 6.75 6.75

First Wedding Anniversary of the Duke and Duchess of Cambridge — A657

No. 3184 — Duke and Duchess, rose and background color of: a Dark red violet. b, Red. c, Rose. d, Pink.
No. 3185: a, Rose and Duke of Cambridge. b, Rose and Duchess of Cambridge.

2012, May 3 *Perf. 13 Syncopated*
3184 A657 $3.50 Sheet of 4, #a-d 10.50 10.50
Souvenir Sheet
3185 A657 $4.50 Sheet of 2, #a-b 6.75 6.75

Miniature Sheet

2012 Summer Olympics, London — A658

No. 3186: a, Rhythmic gymnastics. b, Hurdles. c, Judo. d, Three runners.

2012, June 18 *Perf. 12*
3186 A658 $2.20 Sheet of 4, #a-d 6.50 6.50

Charles Dickens (1812-70), Writer — A659

No. 3187: a, Illustration from *Great Expectations*. b, Illustration from *Oliver Twist*. c, Sketch of Dickens. d, Photograph of Dickens. e, Illustration from *David Copperfield*. f, Illustration from *A Christmas Carol*.
$9, Illustration from *A Tale of Two Cities*, horiz.

2012, July 30 *Perf. 14*
3187 A659 $2.75 Sheet of 6, #a-f 12.50 12.50
Souvenir Sheet
Perf. 12
3188 A659 $9 multi 6.75 6.75

Princess Diana (1961-97) — A660

No. 3189 — Princess Diana wearing: a, White gown, denomination at UL. b, White jacket, denomination at UL. c, Red dress. d, White dress and necklace, denomination at UR.
$9, Princess Diana and school children.

2012, July 30 *Perf. 14*
3189 A660 $3.50 Sheet of 4, #a-d 10.50 10.50
Souvenir Sheet
3190 A660 $9 multi 6.75 6.75

Miniature Sheet

Seahorses — A661

Various seahorses.

2012, Sept. 24 *Perf. 14*
3191 A661 $3 Sheet of 5, #a-e 11.50 11.50

War of 1812 — A662

No. 3192: a, HMS Shannon Leading Her Prize The American Frigate Chesapeake into Halifax Harbor, by Louis Haghe. b, Action Between USS Constitution and HMS Guerriere, by Michele F. Corne. c, Portrait of Pres. James Madison, by John Vanderlyn. d, Portrait of Pres. Andrew Jackson, by Ralph E. W. Earl. e, The U.S. Capitol After Burning by the British, by George Munger. f, Battle of Lake Erie, by William H. Powerll.
$9, A View of the Bombardment of Fort McHenry, Near Baltimore, by John Bower.

2012, Nov. 12 *Perf. 12*
3192 A662 $2.75 Sheet of 6, #a-f 12.50 12.50
Souvenir Sheet
3193 A662 $9 multi 6.75 6.75

Christmas A663

Paintings: 30c, Adoration of the Child, by Antonio da Correggio. 75c, Madonna and Child with Two Angels, by Fra Filippo Lippi. $1.50, Virgin and Child, by Peter Paul Rubens. $2, Madonna and Child, by Parmigianino. $3, The Grand Duke's Madonna, by Raphael. $3.25, Adoration of the Magi, by Sandro Botticelli.

2012, Nov. 19 *Perf. 12¾*
3194-3199 A663 Set of 6 8.00 8.00

Miniature Sheet

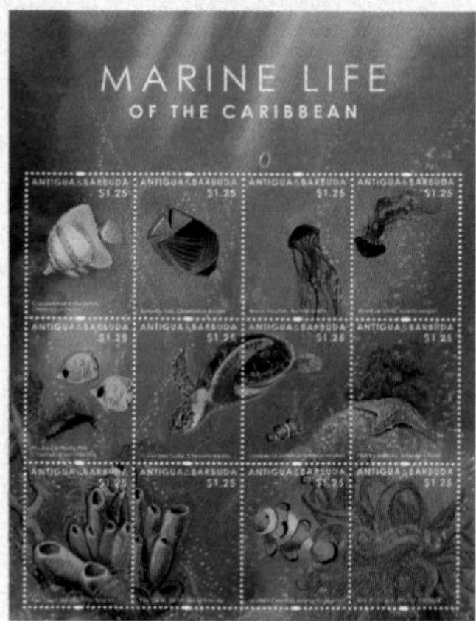

Marine Life — A664

No. 3200: a, Copperband butterflyfish. b, Butterfly fish. c, Moon jellyfish, tentacles at bottom. d, Moon jellyfish, tentacles at top. e, Masked butterflyfish. f, Head of Green sea turtle. g, Rear of Green sea turtle, Ocellaris clownfish. h, Forbes sea star. i, Fan coral, red coral at left. j, Fan coral at left. k, Ocellaris clownfish and sea anemone. l, Sea anemone.

2012, Dec. 3 ***Perf. 13 Syncopated***
3200 A664 $1.25 Sheet of 12, #a-l 11.50 11.50

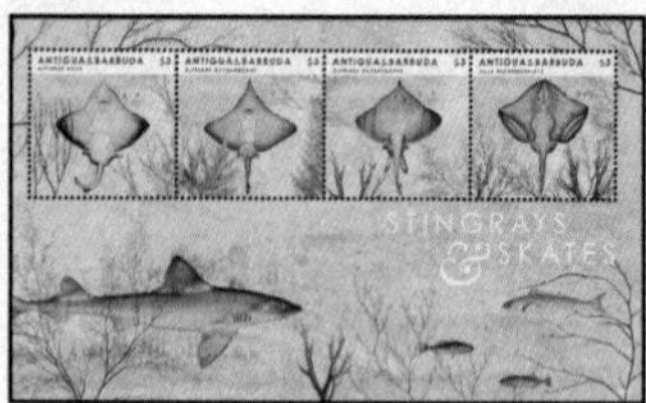

Stingrays and Skates — A665

No. 3201: a, Dipturus batis. b, Dipturus oxyrhynchus without long appendages near tail. c, Dipturus oxyrhynchus with long appendages near tail. d, Raja microocellata.
$9, Leucoraja naevus, vert.

2012, Dec. 3 ***Perf. 13¾***
3201 A665 $3 Sheet of 4, #a-d 9.00 9.00

Souvenir Sheet
Perf. 12¾

3202 A665 $9 multi 6.75 6.75

No. 3202 contains one 38x51mm stamp.

Turtles — A666

No. 3203: a, Chelonia mydas. b, Trachemys decorata. c, Dermochelys coriacea. d, Chelonoidis carbonaria.
$9, Chelus fimbriatus.

2012, Dec. 3 ***Perf. 14***
3203 A666 $3.50 Sheet of 4, #a-d 10.50 10.50

Souvenir Sheet
Perf. 12

3204 A666 $9 multi 6.75 6.75

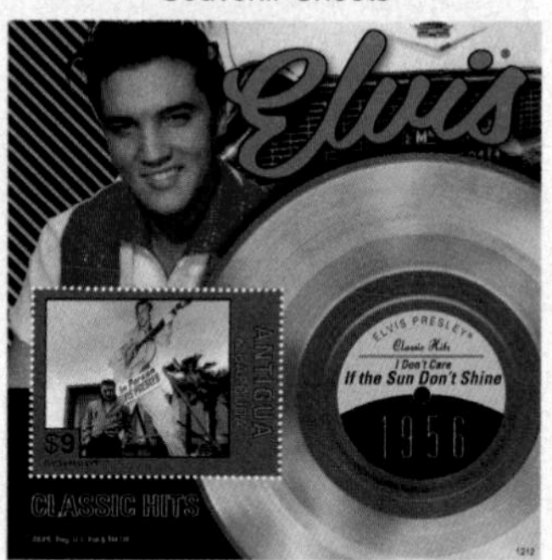

Paintings by Raphael — A667

No. 3205: a, Andrea Navagero. b, La Muta. c, Self-portrait. d, La Fornarina.
$9, Portrait of a Cardinal.

2013, Feb. 20 ***Perf. 12½***
3205 A667 $3.25 Sheet of 4, #a-d 9.75 9.75

Souvenir Sheet

3206 A667 $9 multi 6.75 6.75

Souvenir Sheets

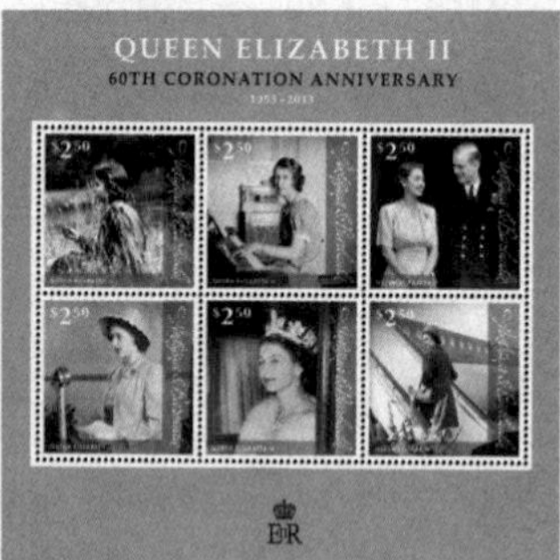

Elvis Presley (1935-77) — A668

Presley: No. 3207, $9, Standing in front of sign depicting him playing guitar, purple frame. No. 3208, $9, Wearing suit and tie, black frame. No. 3209, $9, Holding microphone, red frame. No. 3210, $9, With guitar on back, looking at music stand, red frame. No. 3211, $9, With Pres. Richard M. Nixon, gray frame.

2013, Feb. 20
3207-3211 A668 Set of 5 34.00 34.00

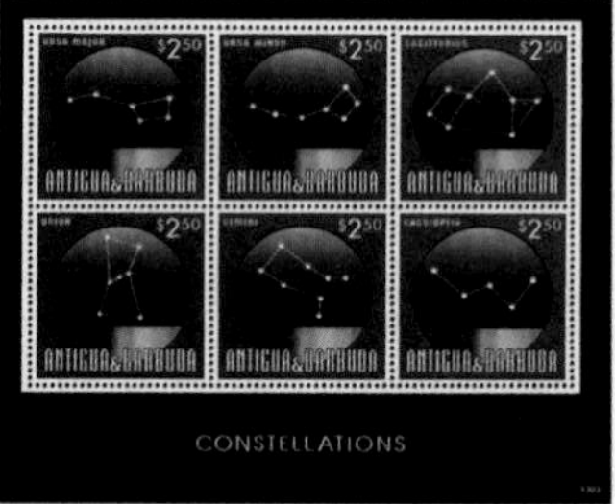

Coronation of Queen Elizabeth II, 60th Anniv. — A669

No. 3212 — Queen Elizabeth II: a, As young woman in field. b, As young woman at piano. c, With Prince Philip. d, Behind microphone. e, Wearing tiara. f, Boarding ariplane.
$9, Queen Eliazbeth II wearing hat, vert.

2013, May 13 **Litho.** ***Perf. 13¾***
3212 A669 $2.50 Sheet of 6, #a-f 11.50 11.50

Souvenir Sheet
Perf. 12½

3213 A669 $9 multi 6.75 6.75

No. 3213 contains one 38x51mm stamp.

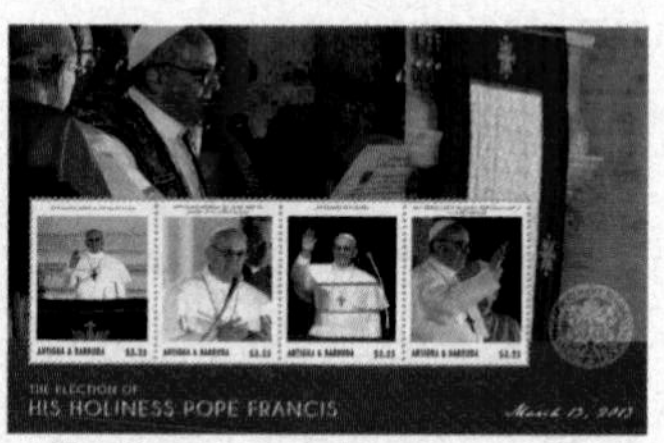

Constellations — A670

No. 3214: a, Ursa Major. b, Ursa Minor. c, Sagittarius. d, Orion. e, Gemini. f, Cassiopeia.
$9, Canis Major, vert.

2013, May 13 **Litho.** ***Perf. 13¾***
3214 A670 $2.50 Sheet of 6, #a-f 11.50 11.50

Souvenir Sheet
Perf. 12½

3215 A670 $9 multi 6.75 6.75

No. 3215 contains one 38x51mm stamp.

Election of Pope Francis — A671

No. 3216 — Pope Francis: a, Waving, orange background. b, Behind microphone, cardinal in background. c, Waving, behind lectern and microphone. d, Facing right, waving, cardinals in background.
$9, Pope Francis waving, diff.

Perf. 13¼x12½
2013, June 19 **Litho.**
3216 A671 $3.25 Sheet of 4, #a-d 9.75 9.75

Souvenir Sheet
Perf. 13½

3217 A671 $9 multi 6.75 6.75

No. 3217 contains one 38x51mm stamp.

Dolphins — A672

No. 3218: a, Bottlenose dolphins. b, Spotted dolphins. c, Striped dolphins. d, Fraser's dolphins.
$9, Pygmy killer whale.

Perf. 12½x13¼
2013, June 19 **Litho.**
3218 A672 $3.25 Sheet of 4, #a-d 9.75 9.75

Souvenir Sheet
Perf. 12½x12

3219 A672 $9 multi 6.75 6.75

WAR TAX STAMPS

No. 31 and Type A3 Overprinted in Black or Red

1916-18 **Wmk. 3** ***Perf. 14***

MR1	A3	½p green	3.50	3.25
MR2	A3	½p green (R) ('17)	1.60	*3.25*
MR3	A3	1½p orange ('18)	1.10	*1.60*
		Nos. MR1-MR3 (3)	6.20	*8.10*

ARGENTINA

ˌär-jən-ˈtē-nə

LOCATION — In South America
GOVT. — Republic
AREA — 1,084,120 sq. mi.
POP. — 36,737,664 (est. 1999)
CAPITAL — Buenos Aires

100 Centavos = 1 Peso (1858, 1992)
100 Centavos = 1 Austral (1985)

Catalogue values for unused stamps in this country are for Never Hinged items, beginning with Scott 587 in the regular postage section, Scott B12 in the semi-postal section, Scott C59 in the airpost section, Scott CB1 in the airpost semi-postal section and Scott O79 in the officials section.

Watermarks

Wmk. 84 — Italic RA

Wmk. 85 — Small Sun, 4½mm

Wmk. 86 — Large Sun, 6mm

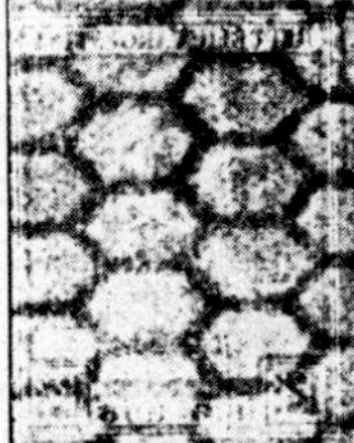
Wmk. 87 — Honeycomb

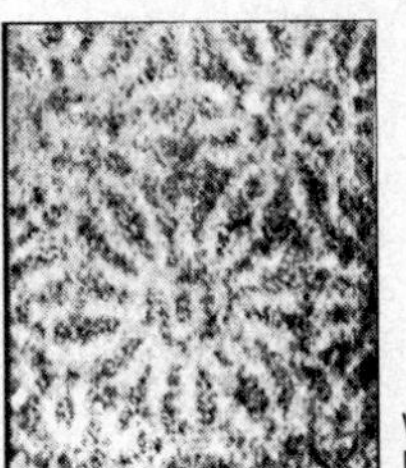
Wmk. 88 — Multiple Suns

Wmk. 89 — Large Sun

In this watermark the face of the sun is 7mm in diameter, the rays are heavier than in the large sun watermark of 1896-1911 and the watermarks are placed close together, so that parts of several frequently appear on one stamp. This paper was intended to be used for fiscal stamps and is usually referred to as "fiscal sun paper."

Wmk. 90 — RA in Sun

In 1928 watermark 90 was slightly modified, making the diameter of the Sun 9mm instead of 10mm. Several types of this watermark exist.

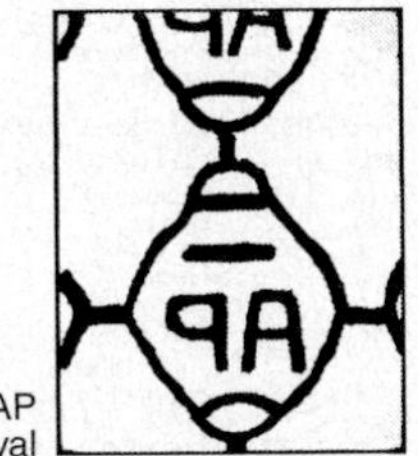
Wmk. 205 — AP in Oval

The letters "AP" are the initials of "AHORRO POSTAL." This paper was formerly used exclusively for Postal Savings stamps.

Wmk. 287 — Double Circle and Letters in Sheet

Wmk. 288 — RA in Sun with Straight Rays

Wmk. 365 — Argentine Arms, "Casa de Moneda de la Nacion" & "RA" Multiple

Values for Unused
Unused values for Nos. 5-17 are for examples without gum. Examples with original gum command higher prices. Unused values of Nos. 1-4B and stamps after No. 17 are for examples with original gum as defined in the catalogue introduction.

Argentine Confederation

Symbolical of the Argentine Confederation
A1 A2

Unwmk.

1858, May 1 Litho. *Imperf.*

1	A1	5c red	1.50	*40.00*
a.		Colon after "5"	1.75	*35.00*
b.		Colon after "V"	1.75	*35.00*
2	A1	10c green	2.50	*90.00*
f.		Diagonal half used as 5c on cover		*725.00*
3	A1	15c blue	18.00	*250.00*
c.		Horiz. third used as 5c on cover		*10,000.*
		Nos. 1-3 (3)	22.00	*380.00*

There are nine varieties of Nos. 1, 2 and 3. Counterfeits and forged cancellations of Nos. 1-3 are plentiful.

1860, Jan.

4	A2	5c red	3.25	*100.00*
4A	A2	10c green	7.00	
4B	A2	15c blue	30.00	
		Nos. 4-4B (3)	40.25	

Nos. 4A and 4B were never placed in use. Some compostitions of Nos. 4-4B contain 8 different types across the sheet. Other settings exist with minor variations. Counterfeits and forged cancellations of Nos. 4-4B are plentiful.

Argentine Republic

Seal of the Republic — A3

Broad "C" in "CENTAVOS," Accent on "U" of "REPUBLICA"

1862, Jan. 11

5	A3	5c rose	49.00	37.50
6	A3	10c green	175.00	80.00
b.		Diagonal half used as 5c on cover		*7,000.*
7	A3	15c blue	350.00	225.00
a.		Without accent on "U"	*8,000.*	*5,000.*
b.		Tete beche pair	*150,000.*	*120,000.*
i.		15c ultramarine	500.00	350.00
j.		Diagonal third used as 5c on cover		*12,000.*

Only one used example of No. 7b is known. It has faults. Two unused examples are known. One is sound with origional gum, the other is in a block, without gum, and has tiny faults.

Broad "C" in "CENTAVOS," No Accent on "U"

1863

7C	A3	5c rose	20.00	*21.00*
d.		5c rose lilac	200.00	250.00
m.		Worn plate (rose)	500.00	52.50
7F	A3	10c yellow green	1,000.	250.00
g.		10c olive green	*1,500.*	400.00
q.		10c green, ribbed paper	1,200.	350.00
r.		Worn plate (green)	1,200.	375.00
s.		Worn plate (olive green)	650.00	500.00

Narrow "C" in "CENTAVOS," No Accent on "U"

1864

7H	A3	5c rose red	225.00	32.50

The so-called reprints of 10c and 15c are counterfeits. They have narrow "C" and straight lines in shield. Nos. 7C and 7H have been extensively counterfeited.

Rivadavia Issue

Bernardino Rivadavia
A4 A5

Rivadavia — A6

1864-67 Engr. Wmk. 84 *Imperf.*

Clear Impressions

8	A4	5c brown rose	*2,500.*	*250.*
a.		5c orange red ('67)	*2,500.*	*250.*
9	A5	10c green	*3,000.*	*1,750.*
10	A6	15c blue	*13,500.*	*6,500.*

Perf. 11½

Dull to Worn Impressions

11	A4	5c brown rose ('65)	40.00	16.00
11B	A4	5c lake	100.00	22.50
12	A5	10c green	150.00	70.00
a.		Diagonal half used as 5c on cover		*2,000.*
b.		Vert. half used as 5c on cover		*3,000.*
c.		Horiz. pair, imperf vert.		*5,000.*
13	A6	15c blue	450.00	150.00

1867-72 Unwmk. *Imperf.*

14	A4	5c carmine ('72)	350.	100.
15	A4	5c rose	350.	100.
15A	A5	10c green	*3,000.*	*3,200.*
16	A6	15c blue	*3,000.*	*2,700.*

Nos. 15A-16 issued without gum.

1867 *Perf. 11½*

17	A4	5c carmine	1,000.	200.00

Nos. 14, 15 and 17 exist with part of papermaker's wmk. Unused values, $1,200, $2,000 and $2,000, respectively.

Rivadavia A7

Manuel Belgrano A8

Jose de San Martin — A9

Groundwork of Horizontal Lines

1867-68 *Perf. 12*

18	A7	5c vermilion	225.00	17.50
18A	A8	10c green	50.00	7.50
b.		Diag. half used as 5c on cover		*2,500.*
19	A9	15c blue	100.00	22.50

Groundwork of Crossed Lines

20	A7	5c vermilion	15.00	1.25
21	A9	15c blue	120.00	15.00

See Nos. 27, 33-34, 39 and types A19, A33, A34, A37. For surcharges and overprints see Nos. 30-32, 41-42, 47-51, O6-O7, O26.

Gen. Antonio G. Balcarce A10

Mariano Moreno A11

Carlos Maria de Alvear A12

Gervasio Antonio Posadas A13

Cornelio Saavedra — A14

1873

22	A10	1c purple	6.00	2.25
a.		1c gray violet	10.00	2.25
23	A11	4c brown	6.00	.75
a.		4c red brown	15.00	2.00
24	A12	30c orange	140.00	25.00
a.		Vert. pair, imperf horiz.	*4,000.*	
25	A13	60c black	160.00	5.00
26	A14	90c blue	60.00	3.00
		Nos. 22-26 (5)	372.00	36.00

For overprints see Nos. O5, O12-O14, O19-O21, O25, O29.

Four examples of No. 24a are known. Three examples of No. 26 are known on cover.

1873 — **Laid Paper**

27	A8	10c green	325.00	32.50

Nos.18, 18A Surcharged in Black

Nos. 30-31

No. 32

1877, Feb. — **Wove Paper**

30	A7	1c on 5c vermilion	75.00	25.00
a.		Inverted surcharge	1,000.	300.00
31	A7	2c on 5c vermilion	125.00	75.00
a.		Inverted surcharge	1,200.	750.00
32	A8	8c on 10c green	160.00	40.00
b.		Inverted surcharge	2,500.	1,000.
		Nos. 30-32 (3)	360.00	140.00

Varieties also exist with double and triple surcharges, surcharge on reverse, 8c on No. 27, all made clandestinely from the original cliches of the surcharges.

Forgeries of these surcharges include the inverted and double varieties.

1876-77 — ***Rouletted***

33	A7	5c vermilion	200.00	85.00
34	A7	8c lake ('77)	35.00	.65

Belgrano A17

Dalmacio Vélez Sarsfield A18

San Martín — A19

1878 — ***Rouletted***

35	A17	16c green	12.00	1.10
36	A18	20c blue	20.00	2.25
37	A19	24c blue	30.00	3.50
		Nos. 35-37 (3)	62.00	6.85

See No. 56. For overprints see Nos. O9-O10, O15-O17, O22, O28.

Vicente Lopez — A20

Alvear — A21

1877-80 — ***Perf. 12***

38	A20	2c yellow green	5.00	.75
39	A7	8c lake ('80)	4.50	.75
a.		8c brown lake	*52.50*	.75
40	A21	25c lake ('78)	30.00	6.00
		Nos. 38-40 (3)	39.50	7.50

For overprints see Nos. O4, O11, O18, O24.

No. 18 Surcharged in Black

Large "P"

Small "P"

1882

41	A7	½c on 5c ver	2.75	2.75
a.		Double surcharge	100.00	100.00
b.		Inverted surcharge	50.00	50.00
c.		"PROVISORIO" omitted	110.00	110.00
d.		Fraction omitted	100.00	
e.		"PROVISOBIO"	50.00	50.00
f.		Pair, one without surcharge	250.00	
g.		Small "P" in "PROVISORIO"	2.75	2.75
h.		As "a," small "P" in "PROVISORIO"	50.00	50.00
i.		As "b," small "P" in "PROVISORIO"	75.00	75.00
j.		As "d," small "P" in "PROVISORIO"	30.00	30.00

Perforated across Middle of Stamp

42	A7	½c on 5c ver	6.00	6.00
a.		"PROVISORIQ"	50.00	50.00
b.		Large "P" in "PROVISORIO"	40.00	30.00

A23

1882 — **Typo.** — ***Perf. 12½***

43	A23	½c brown	2.25	1.50
a.		Imperf., pair	100.00	80.00
44	A23	1c red	15.00	6.00
45	A23	12c ultra	90.00	14.00

Perf. 14¼

44A	A23	1c red	3.50	1.50
45A	A23	12c ultra	65.00	12.00

Engr.

46	A23	12c grnsh blue	225.00	16.00
		Nos. 43-46 (6)	400.75	51.00

See type A29. For overprints see Nos. O2, O8, O23, O27.

No. 21 Surcharged in Red

a

b

c

1884 — **Engr.** — ***Perf. 12***

47	A9 (a)	½c on 15c blue	3.00	2.00
a.		Groundwork of horiz. lines	150.00	90.00
b.		Inverted surcharge	35.00	25.00
48	A9 (b)	1c on 15c blue	22.50	16.50
a.		Groundwork of horiz. lines	13.00	11.50
b.		Inverted surcharge	100.00	62.50
c.		Double surcharge	50.00	40.00
d.		Triple surcharge	400.00	

Nos. 20-21 Surcharged in Black

49	A7 (a)	½c on 5c ver	5.00	4.50
a.		Inverted surcharge	200.00	150.00
b.		Date omitted	200.00	—
c.		Pair, one without surcharge	500.00	
d.		Double surcharge	550.00	
50	A9 (a)	½c on 15c blue	15.00	12.00
a.		Groundwork of horiz. lines	50.00	35.00
b.		Inverted surcharge	90.00	70.00
c.		Pair, one without surcharge	400.00	
51	A7 (c)	4c on 5c ver	12.00	9.00
a.		Inverted surcharge	35.00	28.00
b.		Double surcharge	700.00	350.00
c.		Pair, one without surcharge but with "4" in manuscript	750.00	650.00
d.		Pair, one without surcharge	400.00	
		Nos. 47-51 (5)	57.50	44.00

A29

1884-85 — **Engr.** — ***Perf. 12***

52	A29	½c red brown	1.50	.65
a.		Horiz. pair, imperf vert.		*1,200.*
53	A29	1c rose red	7.00	.65
a.		Horiz. pair, imperf vert.	*300.00*	*250.00*
54	A29	12c deep blue	35.00	1.50
a.		12c grnsh blue ('85)	50.00	1.50
b.		Horiz. pair, imperf vert.	*300.00*	*250.00*
		Nos. 52-54 (3)	43.50	2.80

For overprints see Nos. O1, O3, O9.

San Martin Type of 1878

1887 — **Engr.**

56	A19	24c blue	20.00	1.40

Justo Jose de Urquiza — A30

Lopez — A31

Miguel Juarez Celman — A32

Rivadavia (Large head) — A33

Rivadavia (Small head) A34

Domingo F. Sarmiento A35

Nicolas Avellaneda — A36

San Martin — A37

Julio A. Roca — A37a

Belgrano — A37b

Manuel Dorrego — A38

Moreno — A39

Bartolome Mitre — A40

CINCO CENTAVOS.

A33 — Shows collar on left side only.

A34 — Shows collar on both sides. Lozenges in background larger and clearer than in A33.

1888-90 — **Litho.** — ***Perf. 11½***

57	A30	½c blue	1.75	.75
b.		Vert. pair, imperf. horiz.	200.00	200.00
c.		Horiz. pair, imperf. vert.	200.00	200.00
58	A31	2c yel grn	20.00	10.00
b.		Vert. pair, imperf. horiz.	130.00	
c.		Horiz. pair, imperf. vert.	250.00	
59	A32	3c blue green	3.50	1.50
b.		Horiz. pair, imperf. vert.	60.00	
c.		Horiz. pair, imperf. btwn.	130.00	
d.		Vert. pair, imperf. btwn.	25.00	25.00
60	A33	5c carmine	18.00	.75
b.		Vert. pair, imperf. horiz.	175.00	
61	A34	5c carmine	26.00	2.25
b.		Vert. pair, imperf. btwn.	*200.00*	
c.		Vert. pair, imperf. horiz.		400.00
62	A35	6c red	50.00	20.00
b.		Vert. pair, imperf. btwn.	*150.00*	
c.		Perf. 12	100.00	50.00
63	A36	10c brown	26.00	1.50
64	A37	15c orange	27.50	2.25
d.		Vert. pair, imperf. btwn.		600.00
64A	A37a	20c green	25.00	1.50
64B	A37b	25c purple	45.00	4.00
65	A38	30c brown	40.00	4.00
b.		30c reddish chocolate brown	400.00	80.00
c.		Horiz. pair, imperf. btwn.	700.00	500.00
66	A39	40c slate, perf. 12	150.00	3.00
a.		Perf. 11½	300.00	4.00
b.		Horiz. pair, imperf. btwn. (#66)		800.00
67	A40	50c blue	350.00	20.00
		Nos. 57-67 (13)	782.75	71.50

In this issue there are several varieties of each value, the difference between them being in the relative position of the head to the frame.

Imperf., Pairs

57a	A30	½c	85.00	67.50
58a	A31	2c	100.00	
59a	A32	3c	45.00	27.50
61a	A34	5c		*100.00*
62a	A35	6c	*150.00*	150.00
63a	A36	10c	*55.00*	
64c	A37	15c		*200.00*
65a	A38	30c	*325.00*	*225.00*

Urquiza A41

Velez Sarsfield A42

Miguel Juarez Celman
A43

Rivadavia (Large head)
A44

Sarmiento
A45

Juan Bautista Alberdi
A46

1888-89 Engr. *Perf. 11½, 11½x12*

No.	Type	Description	Unused	Used
68	A41	½c ultra	.75	.45
a.		Vert. pair, imperf. horiz.	—	—
b.		Imperf., pair	30.00	—
69	A42	1c brown	1.50	.75
a.		Vert. pair, imperf. horiz.	65.00	
b.		Vert. pair, imperf. btwn.	—	
c.		Imperf., pair	30.00	
d.		Horiz. pair, imperf. btwn.	100.00	
70	A43	3c blue green	6.00	1.75
71	A44	5c rose	4.50	.75
a.		Imperf., pair	50.00	—
72	A45	6c blue black	3.00	.90
b.		Perf. 11½x12	15.00	4.50
73	A46	12c blue	8.75	3.75
a.		Imperf., pair	45.00	
b.		bluish paper	9.50	3.75
c.		Perf. 11½	14.00	3.00
		Nos. 68-73 (6)	24.50	8.35

Nos. 69-70 exist with papermakers' watermarks.

See No. 77, types A50, A61. For surcharges see Nos. 83-84.

Jose Maria Paz — A48

Santiago Derqui — A49

Rivadavia (Small head)
A50

Avellaneda
A51

Moreno
A53

Mitre
A54

Posadas — A55

1890 Engr. *Perf. 11½*

No.	Type	Description	Unused	Used
75	A48	¼c green	.65	.45
76	A49	2c violet	1.50	.75
a.		2c purple	2.00	.75
b.		2c slate	2.00	.75
c.		Horiz. pair, imperf. btwn.	30.00	25.00
d.		Imperf., pair	37.50	
e.		Perf. 11½x12	9.00	.75
77	A50	5c carmine	3.50	.45
a.		Imperf., pair	70.00	32.50
b.		Perf. 11½x12	10.00	1.25
c.		Vert. pair, imperf. btwn.	75.00	60.00
d.		Horiz. pair, imperf. btwn.	75.00	60.00
78	A51	10c brown	4.50	.75
b.		Imperf., pair	150.00	
c.		Vert. pair, imperf. btwn.	225.00	
80	A53	40c olive green	8.00	1.50
a.		Imperf., pair	55.00	
b.		Horiz. pair, imperf. btwn.		*250.00*

No.	Type	Description	Unused	Used
81	A54	50c orange	9.00	1.50
a.		Imperf., pair	80.00	
b.		Perf. 11½x12	40.00	3.00
82	A55	60c black	20.00	4.50
a.		Imperf., pair	—	
b.		Vert. pair, imperf. btwn.	125.00	100.00
		Nos. 75-82 (7)	47.15	9.90

Type A50 differs from type A44 in having the head smaller, the letters of "Cinco Centavos" not as tall, and the curved ornaments at sides close to the first and last letters of "Republica Argentina."

Lithographed Surcharge on No. 73 in Black or Red

1890 *Perf. 11½x12*

No.	Type	Description	Unused	Used
83	A46	¼c on 12c blue	.75	.75
a.		Perf. 11½	50.00	40.00
b.		Double surcharge	75.00	47.50
c.		Inverted surcharge	100.00	
84	A46	¼c on 12c blue (R)	.75	.75
a.		Double surcharge	55.00	50.00
b.		Perf. 11½	8.00	6.00

Surcharge is different on Nos. 83 and 84.

Nos. 83-84 exist as pairs, one without surcharge. These were privately produced.

Rivadavia
A57

Jose de San Martin
A58

Gregorio Araoz de Lamadrid
A59

Admiral Guillermo Brown
A60

1891 Engr. *Perf. 11½*

No.	Type	Description	Unused	Used
85	A57	8c carmine rose	1.50	.65
a.		Imperf., pair	130.00	
86	A58	1p deep blue	50.00	12.00
87	A59	5p ultra	325.00	45.00
88	A60	20p green	500.00	100.00
		Nos. 85-88 (4)	876.50	157.65

A 10p brown and a 50p red were prepared but not issued. Values: 10p $1,500 for fine, 50p $1,200 with rough or somewhat damaged perfs.

Velez Sarsfield
A61

"Santa Maria," "Nina" and "Pinta"
A62

1890 *Perf. 11½*

No.	Type	Description	Unused	Used
89	A61	1c brown	1.25	.65
b.		Horiz. pair, imperf. btwn.		*550.00*

Type A61 is a re-engraving of A42. The figure "1" in each upper corner has a short horizontal serif instead of a long one pointing downward. In type A61 the first and last letters of "Correos y Telegrafos" are closer to the curved ornaments below than in type A42. Background is of horizontal lines (cross-hatching on No. 69).

1892, Oct. 12 Wmk. 85 *Perf. 11½*

No.	Type	Description	Unused	Used
90	A62	2c light blue	8.50	3.00
a.		Double impression	225.00	
91	A62	5c dark blue	9.50	4.00

Discovery of America, 400th anniv. Counterfeits of Nos. 90-91 are litho.

Rivadavia
A63

Belgrano
A64

San Martin — A65

1892-95 Wmk. 85 *Perf. 11½*

No.	Type	Description	Unused	Used
92	A63	½c dull blue	1.00	.35
a.		½c bright ultra	80.00	40.00
93	A63	1c brown	.65	.50
94	A63	2c green	1.00	.35
95	A63	3c orange ('95)	1.75	.35
96	A63	5c carmine	1.75	.35
b.		5c green (error)	700.00	700.00
98	A64	10c carmine rose	13.50	.60
99	A64	12c deep blue ('93)	10.00	.60
100	A64	16c gray	16.50	.65
101	A64	24c gray brown	16.50	.65
102	A64	50c blue green	27.50	.75
103	A65	1p lake ('93)	12.00	1.00
a.		1p red brown	20.00	5.00
104	A65	2p dark green	27.50	3.50
105	A65	5p dark blue	37.50	3.50
		Nos. 92-105 (13)	167.15	13.15

Perf. 12

No.	Type	Description	Unused	Used
92E	A63	½c dull blue	6.00	1.00
93E	A63	1c brown	10.00	2.00
94E	A63	2c green	10.00	3.00
95E	A63	3c orange ('95)	30.00	5.00
96E	A63	5c carmine	35.00	1.00
98E	A64	10c carmine rose	21.00	3.50
99E	A64	12c deep blue ('93)	40.00	4.00
100E	A64	16c gray	40.00	4.00
101E	A64	24c gray brown	30.00	17.00
102E	A64	50c blue green	30.00	6.00
104E	A65	2p dark green	125.00	40.00
		Nos. 92E-104E (11)	377.00	86.50

Perf. 11½x12

No.	Type	Description	Unused	Used
92F	A63	½c dull blue	18.00	10.00
93F	A63	1c brown	15.00	8.00
94F	A63	2c green	40.00	15.00
95F	A63	3c orange ('95)	55.00	22.50
96F	A63	5c carmine	20.00	4.00
98F	A64	10c carmine rose	30.00	7.50
99F	A64	12c deep blue ('93)	60.00	27.50
100F	A64	16c gray	60.00	27.50
102F	A64	50c blue green	60.00	10.00
103F	A64	1p red brown	60.00	10.00
104F	A65	2p dark green	175.00	75.00
		Nos. 92F-104F (11)	593.00	217.00

The high values of this and succeeding issues are frequently punched with the word "INUTILIZADO," parts of the letters showing on each stamp. These punched stamps sell for only a small fraction of the catalogue values.

Examples of No. 95 in yellow shades are changelings.

Reprints of No. 96b have white gum. The original stamp has yellowish gum. Value $125.

Imperf., Pairs

No.	Type	Value	Unused	Used
92b	A63	½c	60.00	
93a	A63	1c	60.00	
94a	A63	2c	30.00	
96a	A63	5c	30.00	
98a	A64	10c	60.00	
99a	A64	12c	60.00	
100a	A64	16c	60.00	
101a	A64	24c	60.00	
102a	A64	50c	60.00	
103b	A65	1p	60.00	
105a	A65	5p	150.00	

Nos. 102a, 103b and 105a exist only without gum; the other imperfs are found with or without gum, and values are the same for either condition.

Vertical Pairs, Imperf. Between

No.	Type	Value	Unused	Used
92c	A63	½c	125.00	
93b	A63	1c	100.00	
94b	A63	2c	50.00	
95a	A63	3c	250.00	
96c	A63	5c	45.00	—
98b	A64	10c	100.00	
99b	A64	12c	100.00	

Horizontal Pairs, Imperf. Between

No.	Type	Value	Unused	Used
93c	A63	1c	110.00	
94c	A63	2c	55.00	
96d	A63	5c	55.00	45.00
98c	A64	10c	110.00	

1896-97 Wmk. 86 *Perf. 11½*

No.	Type	Description	Unused	Used
106	A63	½c slate	.65	.30
a.		½c gray blue	.65	.30
b.		½c indigo	.65	.30
107	A63	1c brown	.65	.30
108	A63	2c yellow green	.65	.30
109	A63	3c orange	.65	.30
110	A63	5c carmine	.65	.30
a.		Imperf., pair	100.00	
111	A64	10c carmine rose	10.00	.30
112	A64	12c deep blue	5.00	.30
a.		Imperf., pair	—	
113	A64	16c gray	13.50	.90
114	A64	24c gray brown	13.50	1.25
a.		Imperf., pair	100.00	—
115	A64	30c orange ('97)	13.50	.70
116	A64	50c blue green	13.50	.70
117	A64	80c dull violet	20.00	.90
118	A65	1p lake	30.00	1.60
119	A65	1p20c black ('97)	13.50	3.50
120	A65	2p dark green	20.00	10.00
121	A65	5p dark blue	135.00	13.50
		Nos. 106-121 (16)	290.75	35.15

Perf. 12

No.	Type	Description	Unused	Used
106E	A63	½c slate	2.00	1.00
a.		½c gray blue	10.00	4.00
b.		½c indigo	10.00	4.00
107E	A63	1c brown	1.75	1.00
108E	A63	2c yellow green	2.50	1.00
109E	A63	3c orange	45.00	2.00
110E	A63	5c carmine	3.50	1.00
111E	A64	10c carmine rose	15.00	1.00
112E	A64	12c deep blue	11.00	2.00
113E	A64	16c gray	35.00	5.50
114E	A64	24c gray brown	52.50	11.00
115E	A64	30c orange ('97)	52.50	2.50
116E	A64	50c blue green	65.00	.80
117E	A64	80c dull violet	65.00	22.50
118E	A65	1p lake	65.00	3.50
119E	A65	1p20c black ('97)	65.00	22.50
121E	A65	5p dark blue	800.00	20.00
		Nos. 106E-121E (15)	1,280.	97.30

Perf. 11½x12

No.	Type	Description	Unused	Used
106F	A63	½c slate	20.00	11.00
107F	A63	1c brown	30.00	25.00
108F	A63	2c yellow green	20.00	11.00
109F	A63	3c orange	13.00	8.00
110F	A63	5c carmine	26.00	4.50
111F	A64	10c carmine rose	45.00	18.00
112F	A64	12c deep blue	47.50	15.00
113F	A64	16c gray	60.00	20.00
115F	A64	30c orange ('97)	—	75.00
116F	A64	50c blue green	—	75.00
117F	A64	80c dull violet	—	75.00
119F	A65	1p20c black ('97)	100.00	60.00
		Nos. 106F-119F (12)	361.50	397.50

Vertical Pairs, Imperf. Between

No.	Type	Value	Unused	Used
106c	A63	½c	200.00	
107a	A63	1c	125.00	
108a	A63	2c	125.00	
109a	A63	3c	200.00	
110b	A63	5c	125.00	125.00
112b	A64	12c	125.00	100.00

Horizontal Pairs, Imperf. Between

No.	Type	Value	Unused	Used
107b	A63	1c	125.00	
108b	A63	2c	125.00	
110c	A63	5c	125.00	80.00
111a	A64	10c	125.00	
112c	A64	12c	125.00	

Allegory, Liberty Seated
A66 A67

1899-1903 *Perf. 11½*

No.	Type	Description	Unused	Used
122	A66	½c yellow brown	.40	.30
123	A66	1c green	.60	.30
124	A66	2c slate	.60	.30
125	A66	3c orange ('01)	.80	.50
126	A66	4c yellow ('03)	1.40	.60
127	A66	5c carmine rose	.60	.30
128	A66	6c black ('03)	.90	.60
129	A66	10c dark green	1.40	.40
130	A66	12c dull blue	.95	.60
131	A66	12c olive grn ('01)	.95	.60
132	A66	15c sea green ('01)	2.50	.60
132B	A66	15c dull blue ('01)	2.50	.60
133	A66	16c orange	8.00	8.00
134	A66	20c claret	1.90	.30
135	A66	24c violet	4.00	1.00

136 A66 30c rose 7.25 .60
137 A66 30c vermilion ('01) 4.00 .50
a. 30c scarlet 47.50 3.00
138 A66 50c brt blue 4.50 .50
139 A67 1p bl & blk 15.00 1.25
a. Center inverted *2,000.* *1,000.*
b. Perf. 12 500.00 160.00
140 A67 5p orange & blk 57.50 11.00
Punch cancellation 3.00
a. Center inverted *2,750.* 2,500.
141 A67 10p green & blk 70.00 18.00
Punch cancellation 3.00
a. Center inverted *5,000.*
Punch cancellation 675.00
142 A67 20p red & black 200.00 35.00
Punch cancellation 3.00
a. Center invtd. (punch cancel) *4,000.*
Nos. 122-142 (22) 385.75 81.85

Nos. 139-142 used are valued with violet oval or black boxed parcel cancels. Examples with letter cancels are worth ⅓rd more.

Perf. 12

122E A66 ½c yellow brown 1.50 1.20
123E A66 1c green 2.00 .60
124E A66 2c slate 1.50 .60
125E A66 3c orange ('01) 3.50 1.75
126E A66 4c yellow ('03) 10.00 3.50
127E A66 5c carmine rose 5.25 .60
128E A66 6c black ('03) 8.50 2.00
129E A66 10c dark green 8.50 1.75
130E A66 12c dull blue 8.50 2.00
131E A66 12c olive grn ('01) 8.50 2.00
132E A66 15c sea green ('01) 17.00 1.75
133E A66 16c orange 10.00 9.50
134E A66 20c claret 12.00 9.50
135E A66 24c violet 11.00 8.50
136E A66 30c rose 28.00 3.50
137E A66 30c vermilion ('01) 60.00 4.00
a. 30c scarlet 47.50 3.00
138E A66 50c brt blue 27.50 3.50
139E A67 1p bl & blk 500.00 160.00
Nos. 122E-139E (18) 723.25 216.25

Perf. 11½x12

122F A66 ½c yellow brown 25.00 15.00
Never hinged 37.50
On cover, single franking 20.00
123F A66 1c green 25.00 15.00
Never hinged 37.50
On cover 1.00
124F A66 2c slate 12.00 3.00
Never hinged 18.00
On cover 1.00
125F A66 3c orange ('01) 47.50 18.00
Never hinged 72.50
On cover 1.50
127F A66 5c carmine rose 12.00 6.00
Never hinged 18.00
On cover 1.00
128F A66 6c black ('03) 32.50 20.00
Never hinged 13.00
On cover 2.00
129F A66 10c dark green 30.00 6.50
Never hinged 45.00
On cover 1.50
130F A66 12c dull blue 50.00 15.00
Never hinged 75.00
On cover 2.00
131F A66 12c olive grn ('01) 50.00 10.00
Never hinged 75.00
On cover 2.00
132F A66 15c sea green ('01) 50.00 8.00
Never hinged 75.00
On cover 2.50
134F A66 20c claret 60.00 12.00
Never hinged 90.00
On cover 1.00
135F A66 24c violet 50.00 10.00
Never hinged 75.00
On cover 5.00
136F A66 30c rose 120.00 20.00
Never hinged 175.00
On cover 5.00
137F A66 30c vermilion ('01) 140.00 25.00
Never hinged 210.00
On cover 5.00
138F A66 50c brt blue 120.00 20.00
Never hinged 175.00
On cover 10.00
Nos. 122F-138F (15) 824.00 203.50

Imperf., Pairs

122a A66 ½c 35.00
123a A66 1c 50.00
124a A66 2c 17.50
125a A66 3c 325.00
127a A66 5c 17.50
128a A66 6c 60.00
129a A66 10c 50.00
132a A66 15c 50.00

Vertical Pairs, Imperf. Between

122b A66 ½c 10.00 9.50
123b A66 1c 10.00 9.50
124b A66 2c 5.00 4.50
125b A66 3c 325.00 200.00
126a A66 4c 400.00 275.00
127b A66 5c 4.50 2.50
128b A66 6c 13.50 10.00
129b A66 10c 85.00
132c A66 15c 15.00 10.00

Horizontal Pairs, Imperf. Between

122c A66 ½c 30.00 19.00
123c A66 1c 47.50 27.50
124c A66 2c 10.00 5.00
125c A66 3c 325.00 200.00
126b A66 4c 400.00
127c A66 5c 10.00 5.00
128c A66 6c 17.00 10.00
129c A66 10c 17.00 10.00
132d A66 15c 40.00 23.00
138a A66 50c 165.00

River Port of Rosario A68

1902, Oct. 26 *Perf. 11½, 11½x12*

143 A68 5c deep blue 4.75 2.00
a. Imperf., pair 95.00
b. Vert. pair, imperf. btwn. 60.00
c. Horiz. pair, imperf. btwn. 90.00

Completion of port facilities at Rosario.

San Martin
A69 A70

1908-09 **Typo.** *Perf. 13½x12½*

144 A69 ½c violet .50 .30
145 A69 1c brnsh buff .50 .30
146 A69 2c chocolate .60 .30
147 A69 3c green .65 .40
148 A69 4c redsh violet 1.25 .40
149 A69 5c carmine .60 .30
150 A69 6c olive bister .75 .40
151 A69 10c gray green 1.75 .30
152 A69 12c yellow buff 1.00 .60
153 A69 12c dk blue ('09) 1.75 .30
155 A69 20c ultra 1.25 .30
156 A69 24c red brown 3.50 .60
157 A69 30c dull rose 6.00 .60
158 A69 50c black 6.00 .50
159 A70 1p sl bl & pink 18.00 2.50
Nos. 144-159 (15) 44.10 8.10

The 1c blue was not issued. Value $500.

Wmk. 86 appears on ½, 1, 6, 20, 24 and 50c. Other values have similar wmk. with wavy rays.

Stamps lacking wmk. are from outer rows printed on sheet margin.

Perf. 13½

146A A69 2c chocolate 1.20 .25
147A A69 3c green 2.00 1.00
148A A69 4c redsh violet 1.30 .50
149A A69 5c carmine 1.00 .30
151A A69 10c gray green 6.25 2.25
152A A69 12c yellow buff 1.20 .70
153A A69 12c dk blue ('09) 4.25 1.00
154A A69 15c apple green .60 .50
156A A69 24c red brown 4.75 1.30
157A A69 30c dull rose 9.50 1.30
159A A70 1p sl bl & pink 20.00 3.00

Pyramid of May — A71

Nicolas Rodriguez Pena and Hipolito Vieytes — A72

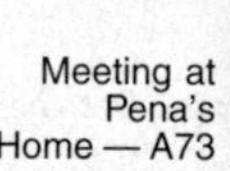
Meeting at Pena's Home — A73

Designs: 3c, Miguel de Azcuenaga (1754-1833) and Father Manuel M. Alberti (1763-1811). 4c, Viceroy's house and Fort Buenos Aires. 5c, Cornelio Saavedra (1759-1829). 10c, Antonio Luis Beruti (1772-1842) and French distributing badges. 12c, Congress building. 20c, Juan Jose Castelli (1764-1812) and Domingo Matheu (1765-1831). 24c, First council. 30c, Manuel Belgrano (1770-1820) and Juan Larrea (1782-1847). 50c, First meeting of republican government, May 25, 1810. 1p, Mariano Moreno (1778-1811) and Juan Jose Paso (1758-1833). 5p, Oath of the Junta. 10p, Centenary Monument. 20p, Jose Francisco de San Martin (1778-1850).

Inscribed "1810 1910"
Various Frames

1910, May 1 **Engr.** *Perf. 11½*

160 A71 ½c bl & gray bl .30 .25
161 A72 1c blue grn & blk .30 .30
b. Horiz. pair, imperf. btwn. *65.00*
162 A73 2c olive & gray .25 .30
163 A72 3c green .70 .40
164 A73 4c dk blue & grn .70 .40
165 A71 5c carmine .40 .25
166 A73 10c yel brn & blk 1.10 .50
167 A73 12c brt blue 1.10 .50
168 A72 20c gray brn & blk 3.25 .60
169 A73 24c org brn & bl 1.75 1.25
170 A72 30c lilac & blk 1.75 1.00
171 A71 50c carmine & blk 4.50 1.25
172 A72 1p brt blue 9.50 3.25
173 A73 5p orange & vio 72.50 35.00
Punch cancel 5.00
174 A71 10p orange & blk 90.00 62.50
Punch cancel 10.00
175 A71 20p dp blue & ind 150.00 100.00
Punch cancel 15.00
Nos. 160-175 (16) 338.10 207.75

Centenary of the republic.

Center Inverted

160a A71 ½c *1,000.*
161a A72 1c *1,000.*
162a A73 2c *800.00*
164a A73 4c *650.00*
167a A73 12c *1,000.*
171a A71 50c *1,000.*
173a A73 5p *750.00*

Domingo F. Sarmiento A87

Agriculture A88

1911, May 15 **Typo.** *Perf. 13½*

176 A87 5c gray brn & blk .80 .40

Domingo Faustino Sarmiento (1811-88), pres. of Argentina, 1868-74.

Size: 19x25mm

Wmk. 86, without Face

1911 **Engr.** *Perf. 12*

177 A88 5c vermilion .40 .25
178 A88 12c deep blue 5.00 .50

Size: 18x23mm

Wmk. 86, with Face

1911 **Typo.** *Perf. 13½x12½*

179 A88 ½c violet .50 .30
180 A88 1c brown ocher .30 .30
181 A88 2c chocolate .30 .25
a. Perf. 13½ 15.00 4.00
b. Imperf., pair *40.00*
182 A88 3c green .50 .50
183 A88 4c brown violet .50 .30
184 A88 10c gray green .50 .30
185 A88 20c ultra 4.00 .95
186 A88 24c red brown 6.00 3.75
187 A88 30c claret 3.00 .50
188 A88 50c black 6.00 .80
Nos. 179-188 (10) 21.60 7.95

The 5c dull red is a proof. In this issue Wmk. 86 comes: straight rays (4c, 20c, 24c) and wavy rays (2c). All other values exist with both forms.

Wmk. 87 (Horiz. or Vert.)

1912-14 *Perf. 13½x12½*

189 A88 ½c violet .30 .30
190 A88 1c ocher .30 .30
191 A88 2c chocolate .50 .30
192 A88 3c green .50 .50
193 A88 4c brown violet .50 .60
194 A88 5c red .40 .30
195 A88 10c deep green 1.75 .30
196 A88 12c deep blue .60 .30
197 A88 20c ultra 3.00 .50
198 A88 24c red brown 6.00 2.00
199 A88 30c claret 5.00 7.00
200 A88 50c black 9.00 .90
Nos. 189-200 (12) 27.85 13.30

See Nos. 208-212. For overprints see Nos. OD1-OD8, OD47-OD54, OD102-OD108, OD146-OD152, OD183-OD190, OD235-OD241, OD281-OD284, OD318-OD323.

Perf. 13½

189a A88 ½c 1.00 .30
190a A88 1c 1.00 .30
191a A88 2c 1.00 .30
192a A88 3c 150.00 30.00
193a A88 4c 2.50 1.25
194a A88 5c .90 .30
196a A88 12c 3.50 1.50
197a A88 20c 9.00 .90
Nos. 189a-197a (8) 168.90 34.85

A89

1912-13 *Perf. 13½*

201 A89 1p dull bl & rose 10.00 1.10
Punch cancel .30
202 A89 5p slate & ol grn 19.00 7.00
Punch cancel 1.00
203 A89 10p violet & blue 75.00 17.50
Punch cancel 1.40
204 A89 20p blue & claret 210.00 80.00
Punch cancel 2.00
Nos. 201-204 (4) 314.00 105.60

1915 **Unwmk.** *Perf. 13½x12½*

208 A88 1c ocher .50 .30
209 A88 2c chocolate .90 .30
212 A88 5c red .50 .30
Nos. 208-212 (3) 1.90 .90

Only these denominations were printed on paper without watermark.

Other stamps of the series are known unwatermarked but they are from the outer rows of sheets the other parts of which are watermarked.

Francisco Narciso de Laprida A90

Declaration of Independence A91

A92 A92a
Jose de San Martin

Perf. 13½, 13½x12½

1916, July 9 **Litho.** **Wmk. 87**

215 A90 ½c violet .60 .30
216 A90 1c buff .50 .30

Perf. 13½x12½

217 A90 2c chocolate .60 .30
218 A90 3c green .60 .60
219 A90 4c red violet .60 .60

Perf. 13½

220 A91 5c red .50 .30
a. Imperf., pair *40.00*
221 A91 10c gray green 1.50 .30
222 A92 12c blue .90 .35
223 A92 20c ultra .70 .70
224 A92 24c red brown 2.75 1.40
225 A92 30c claret 2.75 1.60
226 A92 50c gray black 6.75 1.60
227 A92a 1p slate bl & red 10.00 10.00
Punch cancel .50
a. Imperf., pair *325.00*
228 A92a 5p black & gray grn 100.00 80.00
Punch cancel 15.00
229 A92a 10p violet & blue 150.00 135.00
Punch cancel 9.00
230 A92a 20p dull blue & cl 150.00 100.00
Punch cancel 7.00
a. Imperf., pair 650.00
Nos. 215-230 (16) 428.75 333.35

Cent. of Argentina's declaration of independence of Spain, July 9, 1816.

The watermark is either vert. or horiz. on Nos. 215-220, 222; only vert. on No. 221, and only horiz. on Nos. 223-230.

For overprints see Nos. OD9, OD55-OD56, OD109, OD153, OD191-OD192, OD285, OD324.

A93

A94

A94a

1917 *Perf. 13½*

231 A93 ½c violet .30 .30
a. Imperf. pair 70.00
232 A93 1c buff .30 .30
a. Imperf. pair 70.00
233 A93 2c brown .30 .30
a. Imperf. pair 70.00
234 A93 3c lt green .70 .30
a. imperf. pair 70.00
235 A93 4c red violet .70 .30
a. Imperf. pair 70.00
236 A93 5c red .30 .30
Never hinged .45
a. Imperf. pair *15.00*
237 A93 10c gray green .30 .30
a. Imperf. pair 70.00
Nos. 231-237 (7) 2.90 2.10

Perf. 13½x12½

231B A93 ½c violet .30 .30
232B A93 1c buff .40 .40
233B A93 2c brown .40 .40
234B A93 3c lt green .70 .30
235B A93 4c red violet .70 .30
236B A93 5c red .30 .30
237B A93 10c gray green .30 .30
Nos. 231B-237B (7) 3.10 2.30

Perf. 13½

238 A94 12c blue 1.00 .25
239 A94 20c ultra 2.50 .30
240 A94 24c red brown 6.00 3.00
241 A94 30c claret 6.00 1.50
242 A94 50c gray black 6.00 .60
243 A94a 1p slate bl & red 6.00 .60
244 A94a 5p black & gray grn 19.00 3.00
Punch cancel 1.50
245 A94a 10p violet & blue 47.50 12.00
Punch cancel 1.50
246 A94a 20p dull blue & cl 90.00 50.00
Punch cancel 1.00
a. Center inverted 1,500. 1,500.
Nos. 231-246 (16) 186.90 73.35

The watermark is either vert. or horiz. on Nos. 231-236, 238 and 231B-236B, 238B; only vert. on No. 237 and 237B, and only horiz. on Nos. 239-246.

All known examples of No. 246a are off-center to the right.

Juan Gregorio Pujol — A95

1918, June 15 **Litho.** *Perf. 13½*

247 A95 5c bister & gray .60 .30

Cent. of the birth of Juan G. Pujol (1817-61), lawyer and legislator.

1918-19 **Unwmk.** *Perf. 13½*

248 A93 ½c violet .30 .25
249 A93 1c buff .30 .25
a. Imperf., pair 14.00
250 A93 2c brown .30 .25
251 A93 3c lt green .50 .25
252 A93 4c red violet .50 .25
253 A93 5c red .30 .25
254 A93 10c gray green .80 .25
255 A94 12c blue 1.25 .25
256 A94 20c ultra 1.40 .25
257 A94 24c red brown 2.40 .25
258 A94 30c claret 3.00 .30
259 A94 50c gray black 6.00 .50
Nos. 248-259 (12) 17.05 3.30

Perf. 13½x12½

248B A93 ½c violet .30 .25
249B A93 1c buff .30 .25
250B A93 2c brown .30 .25
251B A93 3c lt green .50 .25
252B A93 4c red violet .50 .25
253B A93 5c red .30 .25
254B A93 10c gray green 1.10 .25
Nos. 248B-254B (7) 3.30 1.75

The stamps of this issue sometimes show letters of papermakers' watermarks.

There were two printings, in 1918 and 1923, using different ink and paper.

1920 **Wmk. 88**

264 A93 ½c violet .50 .25
265 A93 1c buff .50 .25
266 A93 2c brown .50 .25
267 A93 3c green 1.50 1.00
268 A93 4c red violet 2.00 1.50
269 A93 5c red .50 .25
270 A93 10c gray green 4.50 .25

Perf. 13½

264A A93 ½c violet .80 .30
265A A93 1c buff .80 .30
266A A93 2c brown 1.00 .30
267A A93 3c green 2.00 1.00
269A A93 5c red 4.00 .30
270A A93 10c gray green 55.00 15.00
271 A94 12c blue 3.00 .30
272 A94 20c ultra 4.25 .40
274 A94 30c claret 15.00 3.00
275 A94 50c gray black 10.00 3.00
Nos. 264-275 (17) 105.85 27.65

See Nos. 292-300, 304-307A, 310-314, 318, 322.

For overprints see Nos. OD10-OD20, OD57-OD71, OD74, OD110-OD121, OD154-OD159, OD161-OD162, OD193-OD207, OD209-OD211, OD242-OD252, OD254-OD255, OD286-OD290, OD325-OD328, OD330.

Belgrano's Mausoleum A96

Creation of Argentine Flag A97

Gen. Manuel Belgrano — A98

1920, June 18

280 A96 2c red 1.00 .30
a. Perf. 13½x12½ 2.00 .50
281 A97 5c rose & blue 1.00 .30
282 A98 12c green & blue 2.00 1.00
Nos. 280-282 (3) 4.00 1.60

Belgrano (1770-1820), Argentine general, patriot and diplomat.

Gen. Justo Jose de Urquiza — A99

Bartolome Mitre — A100

1920, Nov. 11

283 A99 5c gray blue .60 .30

Gen. Justo Jose de Urquiza (1801-70), pres. of Argentina, 1854-60. See No. 303.

1921, June 26 **Unwmk.**

284 A100 2c violet brown .50 .30
285 A100 5c light blue .50 .30

Bartolome Mitre (1821-1906), pres. of Argentina, 1862-65.

Allegory, Pan-America — A101

1921, Aug. 25 *Perf. 13½*

286 A101 3c violet .55 .30
287 A101 5c blue 2.00 .30
288 A101 10c vio brown 2.50 .50
289 A101 12c rose 3.00 1.00
Nos. 286-289 (4) 8.05 2.10

Inscribed "Buenos Aires-Agosto de 1921" A102

Inscribed "Republica Argentina" A103

1921, Oct. *Perf. 13½x12½*

290 A102 5c rose .60 .30
291 A103 5c rose 2.50 .30

Perf. 13½

290A A102 5c rose 6.00 .50
291A A103 5c rose 2.50 .30

1st Pan-American Postal Cong., Buenos Aires, Aug., 1921.

See Nos. 308-309, 319. For overprints see Nos. OD72, OD160, OD208, OD253, OD329.

1920 **Wmk. 89** *Perf. 13½x12½*

292 A93 ½c violet 1.60 .80
293 A93 1c buff 4.50 1.50
294 A93 2c brown 3.50 .50
297 A93 5c red 4.50 .35
298 A93 10c gray green 4.50 .35

Perf. 13½

294A A93 2c brown 7.00 1.50
297A A93 5c red 52.50 9.00
298A A93 10c gray green 40.00 2.00
299 A94 12c blue *3,000.* 200.00
300 A94 20c ultra 12.00 1.00

1920

303 A99 5c gray blue 450.00 300.00

1922-23 **Wmk. 90** *Perf. 13½*

304 A93 ½c violet .60 .25
305 A93 1c buff 1.00 .30
306 A93 2c brown 1.00 .30
307 A93 3c green .60 .40
307A A93 4c red violet 1.50 1.00
308 A102 5c rose 10.00 3.00
309 A103 5c red 5.00 .80
310 A93 10c gray green 9.00 1.00
311 A94 12c blue 1.00 .40
312 A94 20c ultra 2.00 .50
313 A94 24c red brown 20.00 10.00
314 A94 30c claret 10.00 1.00

Perf. 13½x12½

304B A93 ½c violet .50 .30
305B A93 1c buff .50 .30
306B A93 2c brown .50 .30
307B A93 3c green 1.00 .80
307B A93 4c red violet 22.50 10.00
308B A102 5c rose 3.00 .60
309B A103 5c red .50 .25
310B A93 10c gray green 2.25 .25
Nos. 304-310B (20) 92.45 31.75

Paper with Gray Overprint RA in Sun

1922-23 **Unwmk.** *Perf. 13½*

318 A93 2c brown 3.00 1.00
319 A103 5c red 10.00 1.00
322 A94 20c ultra 30.00 1.50

Perf. 13½x12½

318A A93 2c brown 3.00 1.00
319A A103 5c red 3.00 .30

A104

San Martín — A105

With Period after Value

Perf. 13½x12½

1923, May **Litho.** **Wmk. 90**

323 A104 ½c red violet .50 .30
324 A104 1c buff .50 .30
325 A104 2c dark brown .50 .30
326 A104 3c lt green .50 .40
327 A104 4c red brown .50 .40
328 A104 5c red .50 .30
329 A104 10c dull green 3.50 .30
330 A104 12c deep blue .50 .30
331 A104 20c ultra 1.50 .30
332 A104 24c lt brown 3.50 3.00
333 A104 30c claret 15.00 .50
334 A104 50c black 7.50 .50

Perf. 13½

323A A104 ½c red violet .50 .30
324A A104 1c buff .50 .30
325A A104 2c dark brown .50 .30
326A A104 3c lt green .50 .40
327A A104 4c red brown .50 .40
328A A104 5c red .50 .30
329A A104 10c dull green 3.50 .30
330A A104 12c deep blue .50 .30
331A A104 20c ultra 1.50 .30
332A A104 24c lt brown 3.50 3.00
333A A104 30c claret 15.00 .50
334A A104 50c black 7.50 .50

Without Period after Value

Wmk. 87

Perf. 13½

335 A105 1p blue & red 10.00 .50
336 A105 5p gray lilac & grn 30.00 6.00
Punch cancel 1.00
337 A105 10p claret & blue 90.00 15.00
Punch cancel 2.00
338 A105 20p sl & brn lake 120.00 45.00
Punch cancel 1.25
a. Center inverted
Nos. 323-338 (28) 319.00 80.30

Nos. 335-338 and 353-356 canceled with round or oval killers in purple (revenue cancelations) sell for one-fifth to one-half as much as postally used copies.

For overprints see Nos. 399-404.

Design of 1923
Without Period after Value

Perf. 13½x12½

1923-24 **Litho.** **Wmk. 90**

340 A104 ½c red violet .50 .30
341 A104 1c buff .50 .30
342 A104 2c dk brown .50 .30
343 A104 3c green .60 .30
a. Imperf., pair 8.00
344 A104 4c red brown .60 .30
345 A104 5c red .50 .30
346 A104 10c dull green .50 .30
347 A104 12c deep blue .60 .30
348 A104 20c ultra .90 .30
349 A104 24c lt brown 2.50 1.25
350 A104 25c purple 1.25 .30
351 A104 30c claret 2.50 .30
352 A104 50c black 6.00 .30

Perf. 13½

340B A104 ½c red violet 125.00 40.00
345B A104 5c red 55.00 22.50
346B A104 10c dull green 55.00 22.50
349B A104 24c lt brown 92.50 30.00
353 A105 1p blue & red 6.00 .30
354 A105 5p dk vio & grn 30.00 1.50
355 A105 10p claret & blue 75.00 6.00
356 A105 20p slate & lake 105.00 15.00
Nos. 340-356 (21) 560.85 142.65

1931-33 **Typo.**

343b A104 3c 3.00 .50
345a A104 5c 4.50 .50
346a A104 10c 7.50 .50
347a A104 12c 15.00 3.00
348a A104 20c 50.00 2.50
350a A104 25c 40.00 1.75
351a A104 30c 21.00 1.25
Nos. 343b-351a (7) 141.00 10.00

The typographed stamps were issued only in coils and have a rough impression with heavy shading about the eyes and nose. Nos. 343 and 346 are known without watermark.

Nos. 341-345, 347-349, 351a may be found in pairs, one with period.

See note after No. 338. See Nos. 362-368. For overprints see Nos. OD21-OD33, OD75-OD87, OD122-OD133, OD163-OD175, OD212-OD226, OD256-OD268, OD291-OD304, OD331-OD345.

Rivadavia — A106

1926, Feb. 8 ***Perf. 13½***

357	A106	5c rose	.60	.30

Presidency of Bernardino Rivadavia, cent.

Rivadavia A108

San Martin A109

General Post Office, 1926 — A110

General Post Office, 1826 — A111

1926, July 1 ***Perf. 13½x12½***

358	A108	3c gray green	.40	.30
359	A109	5c red	.40	.30

Perf. 13½

360	A110	12c deep blue	1.25	.40
361	A111	25c chocolate	1.60	.25
a.		"1326" for "1826"	15.00	5.00
		Nos. 358-361 (4)	3.65	1.25

Centenary of the Post Office.

For overprints see Nos. OD34, OD88, OD134, OD227-OD228, OD269, OD305, OD346.

Type of 1923-31 Issue Without Period after Value

1927 **Wmk. 205** ***Perf. 13½x12½***

362	A104	½c red violet	.50	.50
a.		Pelure paper	2.50	2.50
363	A104	1c buff	.50	.50
364	A104	2c dark brown	.50	.30
a.		Pelure paper	.70	.70
365	A104	5c red	.50	.30
a.		Period after value	9.00	6.00
b.		Pelure paper	.70	.70
366	A104	10c dull green	5.00	3.00
367	A104	20c ultra	47.50	4.75

Perf. 13½

368	A105	1p blue & red	36.00	6.00
		Nos. 362-368 (7)	90.50	15.35

Arms of Argentina and Brazil A112

Wmk. RA in Sun (90)

1928, Aug. 27 ***Perf. 12½x13***

369	A112	5c rose red	1.50	.40
370	A112	12c deep blue	2.50	.70

Cent. of peace between the Empire of Brazil and the United Provinces of the Rio de la Plata.

Allegory, Discovery of the New World — A113

"Spain" and "Argentina" — A114

"America" Offering Laurels to Columbus A115

1929, Oct. 12 **Litho.** ***Perf. 13½***

371	A113	2c lilac brown	2.00	.40
372	A114	5c light red	2.00	.40
373	A115	12c dull blue	6.00	1.00
		Nos. 371-373 (3)	10.00	1.80

Discovery of America by Columbus, 437th anniv.

Spirit of Victory Attending Insurgents — A116

March of the Victorious Insurgents A117

Perf. 13½x12½ (A116), 12½x13 (A117)

1930

374	A116	½c violet gray	1.00	.50
375	A116	1c myrtle green	1.00	.50
376	A117	2c dull violet	1.00	.50
377	A116	3c green	.50	.50
378	A116	4c violet	.80	.70
379	A116	5c rose red	.70	.30
380	A116	10c gray black	1.00	.70
381	A117	12c dull blue	1.50	.70
382	A117	20c ocher	1.50	.80
383	A117	24c red brown	5.00	2.00
384	A117	25c green	6.00	2.00
385	A117	30c deep violet	8.00	3.00
386	A117	50c black	10.00	4.00
387	A117	1p sl bl & red	24.00	8.00
388	A117	2p black & org	30.00	12.00
389	A117	5p dull grn & blk	92.50	35.00
390	A117	10p dp red brn & dull blue	120.00	40.00
391	A117	20p yel grn & dl bl	210.00	90.00
392	A117	50p dk grn & vio	750.00	650.00
		Nos. 374-390 (17)	304.50	111.20

Revolution of 1930.

Nos. 387-392 with oval (parcel post) cancellation sell for less.

For overprint see No. 405.

1931 ***Perf. 12½x13***

393	A117	½c red violet	.50	.50
394	A117	1c gray black	1.50	1.00
395	A117	3c green	1.50	.70
396	A117	4c red brown	.80	.50
397	A117	5c red	.70	.50
a.		Plane omitted, top left corner	3.00	1.50
398	A117	10c dull green	1.50	.70
		Nos. 393-398 (6)	6.50	3.90

Revolution of 1930.

Stamps of 1924-25 Overprinted in Red or Green

1931, Sept. 6 ***Perf. 13½, 13½x12½***

399	A104	3c green	.40	.40
400	A104	10c dull green	.60	.60
401	A104	30c claret (G)	4.50	2.50
402	A104	50c black	4.50	3.00

Overprinted in Blue

403	A105	1p blue & red	5.50	3.00
404	A105	5p dk violet & grn	60.00	20.00

No. 388 Overprinted in Blue

Perf. 12½x13

405	A117	2p black & orange	10.00	7.50
		Nos. 399-405 (7)	85.50	37.00

1st anniv. of the Revolution of 1930.
See Nos. C30-C34.

Refrigeration Compressor — A118

Perf. 13½x12½

1932, Aug. 29 **Litho.**

406	A118	3c green	1.00	.50
407	A118	10c scarlet	2.00	.40
408	A118	12c gray blue	7.00	1.10
		Nos. 406-408 (3)	10.00	2.00

6th Intl. Refrigeration Congress.

Port of La Plata A119

Pres. Julio A. Roca — A120

Municipal Palace A121

Cathedral of La Plata — A122

Dardo Rocha A123

Perf. 13½x13, 13x13½ (10c)

1933, Jan.

409	A119	3c green & dk brn	.40	.30
410	A120	10c orange & dk vio	.60	.30
411	A121	15c dk bl & dp bl	2.50	1.50
412	A122	20c violet & yel brn	1.75	.90
413	A123	30c dk grn & vio brn	13.00	6.00
		Nos. 409-413 (5)	18.25	9.00

50th anniv. of the founding of the city of La Plata, Nov. 19th, 1882.

Christ of the Andes — A124

Buenos Aires Cathedral A125

1934, Oct. 1 ***Perf. 13x13½, 13½x13***

414	A124	10c rose & brown	1.00	.30
415	A125	15c dark blue	3.00	.60

32nd Intl. Eucharistic Cong., Oct. 10-14.

"Liberty" with Arms of Brazil and Argentina A126

Symbolical of "Peace" and "Friendship" A127

1935, May 15 ***Perf. 13x13½***

416	A126	10c red	1.00	.30
417	A127	15c blue	2.00	.60

Visit of Pres. Getulio Vargas of Brazil.

Belgrano A128

Sarmiento A129

Urquiza — A130

Louis Braille — A131

San Martin — A132

Brown — A133

Moreno A134

Alberdi A135

Nicolas Avellaneda
A136

Rivadavia
A137

Mitre
A138

Bull (Cattle Breeding)
A139

Agriculture
A141

Martin Güemes
A140

Merino Sheep (Wool)
A142

Sugar Cane
A143

Oil Well (Petroleum) — A144

Map of South America
A145 A146

Fruit — A147

Iguacu Falls (Scenic Wonders)
A148

Grapes (Vineyards)
A149

Cotton — A150

Two types of A140:
Type I — Inscribed Juan Martin Guemes.
Type II — Inscribed Martin Güemes.

Perf. 13, 13½x13, 13x13½

1935-51 Litho. Wmk. 90

No.	Type	Denom.	Color	Unused	Used
418	A128	½c	red violet	.30	.25
419	A129	1c	buff	.30	.25
a.			Typo.	.80	.25
420	A130	2c	dark brown	.50	.25
421	A131	2½c	black ('39)	.30	.25
422	A132	3c	green	.50	.25
423	A132	3c	lt gray ('39)	.50	.25
424	A134	3c	lt gray ('46)	.50	.25
425	A133	4c	lt gray	.50	.25
426	A133	4c	sage green ('39)	.40	.25
427	A134	5c	yel brn, typo.	.25	.25
a.			Tete beche pair, typo.	20.00	10.00
b.			Booklet pane of 8, typo.		
c.			Booklet pane of 4, typo.		
d.			Litho.	5.00	.50
428	A135	6c	olive green	.40	.25
429	A136	8c	orange ('39)	.40	.25
430	A137	10c	car, perf. 13½ (typo.)	.25	.25
a.			Perf. 13½x13	2.00	.25
431	A137	10c	brown ('42)	.25	.25
432	A138	12c	brown	1.00	.25
433	A138	12c	red ('39)	.25	.25
434	A139	15c	slate bl ('36)	1.50	.25
435	A139	15c	pale ultra ('39)	1.00	.25
436	A140	15c	lt gray bl (II) ('42)	45.00	2.00
437	A140	20c	lt ultra (I)	1.00	.25
438	A140	20c	lt ultra (II) ('36)	1.00	.25
439	A140	20c	bl gray (II) ('39)	.35	.25
439A	A139	20c	dk bl & pale bl, ('42) 22x33mm	1.00	.25
440	A139	20c	blue ('51)	.25	.25
a.			Typo.	.25	.25
441	A141	25c	car & pink ('36)	.50	.25
442	A142	30c	org brn & yel brown ('36)	.80	.25
443	A143	40c	dk vio ('36)	.70	.25
444	A144	50c	red & org ('36)	.70	.25
445	A145	1p	brn blk & lt bl ('36)	25.00	1.00
446	A146	1p	brn blk & lt bl ('37)	15.00	.30
a.			Chalky paper	100.00	2.00
447	A147	2p	brn lake & dk ultra ('36)	1.00	.25
448	A148	5p	ind & ol grn ('36)	3.00	.25
449	A149	10p	brn lake & blk	15.00	1.00
450	A150	20p	bl grn & brn ('36)	25.00	3.00
			Nos. 418-450 (34)	144.40	14.55

See Nos. 485-500, 523-540, 659, 668. For overprints see Nos. O37-O41, O43-O51, O53-O56, O58-O78, O108, O112, OD35-OD46, OD89-OD101, OD135-OD145, OD176-OD182C, OD229-OD234F, OD270-OD280, OD306-OD317, OD347-OD357.

No. 439A exists with attached label showing medallion. Value $42.50 unused, $22.50 used.

Souvenir Sheet

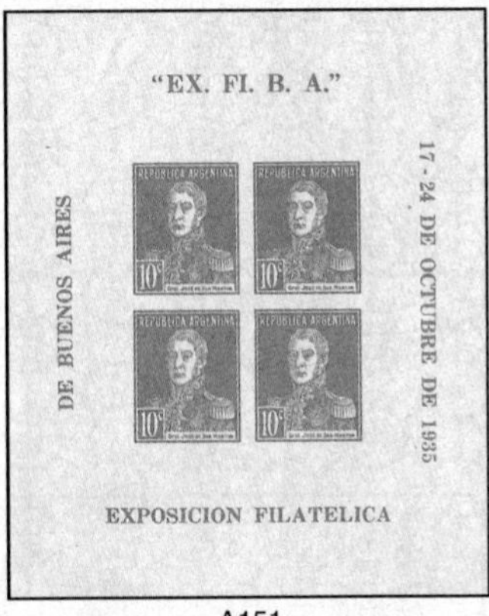

A151

Without Period after Value

1935, Oct. 17 Litho. *Imperf.*

No.	Type	Description	Unused	Used
452	A151	Sheet of 4	75.00	35.00
a.		10c dull green	16.50	7.50

Phil. Exhib. at Buenos Aires, Oct. 17-24, 1935. The stamps were on sale during the 8 days of the exhibition only. Sheets measure 83x101mm.

Plaque — A152

1936, Dec. 1 *Perf. 13x13½*

No.	Type	Denom.	Color	Unused	Used
453	A152	10c	rose	.80	.40

Inter-American Conference for Peace.

Domingo Faustino Sarmiento — A153

1938, Sept. 5

No.	Type	Denom.	Color	Unused	Used
454	A153	3c	sage green	.50	.50
455	A153	5c	red	.50	.50
456	A153	15c	deep blue	1.00	.50
457	A153	50c	orange	4.00	1.00
			Nos. 454-457 (4)	6.00	2.50

50th anniv. of the death of Domingo Faustino Sarmiento, pres., educator and author.

"Presidente Sarmiento" — A154

1939, Mar. 16

No.	Type	Denom.	Color	Unused	Used
458	A154	5c	greenish blue	.50	.30

Final voyage of the training ship "Presidente Sarmiento."

Allegory of the UPU — A155

Coat of Arms — A157

Post Office, Buenos Aires — A156

Iguacu Falls — A158

Bonete Hill, Nahuel Huapi Park — A159

Allegory of Modern Communications
A160

Argentina, Land of Promise
A161

Lake Frias, Nahuel Huapi Park — A162

Perf. 13x13½, 13½x13

1939, Apr. 1 Photo.

No.	Type	Denom.	Color	Unused	Used
459	A155	5c	rose carmine	.70	.25
460	A156	15c	grnsh black	.70	.40
461	A157	20c	brt blue	.70	.25
462	A158	25c	dp blue grn	1.10	.40
463	A159	50c	brown	1.60	.90
464	A160	1p	brown violet	4.25	2.40
465	A161	2p	magenta	18.50	15.00
466	A162	5p	purple	42.50	30.00
			Nos. 459-466 (8)	70.05	49.60

Universal Postal Union, 11th Congress.

Souvenir Sheets

A163

A164

1939, May 12 Wmk. 90 *Imperf.*

467 A163 Sheet of 4 6.50 5.00
a. 5c rose carmine (A155) 1.40 1.00
b. 20c bright blue (A157) 1.40 1.00
c. 25c deep blue green (A158) 1.40 1.00
d. 50c brown (A159) 1.40 1.00
468 A164 Sheet of 4 6.50 5.00

Issued in four forms:

a. Unsevered horizontal pair of sheets, type A163 at left, A164 at right 27.50 16.00
b. Unsevered vertical pair of sheets, type A163 at top, A164 at bottom 27.50 16.00
c. Unsevered block of 4 sheets, type A163 at left, A164 at right 55.00 55.00
d. Unsevered block of 4 sheets, type A163 at top, A164 at bottom 55.00 55.00

11th Cong. of the UPU and the Argentina Intl. Phil. Exposition (C.Y.T.R.A.).
No. 468 contains Nos. 467a-467d.

Family and New House A165

Perf. 13½x13

1939, Oct. 2 Litho. Wmk. 90

469 A165 5c bluish green .50 .25

1st Pan-American Housing Congress.

Bird Carrying Record A166

Head of Liberty and Arms of Argentina A167

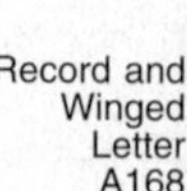

Record and Winged Letter A168

Perf. 13x13½, 13½x13 (#472)

1939, Dec. 11 Photo.

470 A166 1.18p indigo 14.00 10.00
471 A167 1.32p bright blue 14.00 10.00
472 A168 1.50p dark brown 52.50 35.00
Nos. 470-472 (3) 80.50 55.00

These stamps were issued for the recording and mailing of flexible phonograph records.

Map of the Americas — A169

1940, Apr. 14 *Perf. 13x13½*

473 A169 15c ultramarine .50 .25

50th anniv. of the Pan American Union.

Souvenir Sheet

Reproductions of Early Argentine Stamps — A170

Wmk. RA in Sun (90)

1940, May 25 Litho. *Imperf.*

474 A170 Sheet of 5 11.00 8.00
a. 5c dark blue (Corrientes A2) 1.75 1.50
b. 5c red (Argentina A1) 1.75 1.50
c. 5c dark blue (Cordoba #1) 1.75 1.50
d. 5c red (Argentina A3) 1.75 1.50
e. 10c dark blue (Buenos Aires A1) 1.75 1.50

100th anniv. of the first postage stamp.

General Domingo French and Colonel Antonio Beruti A171

1941, Feb. 20

Perf. 13½x13

475 A171 5c dk gray blue & lt blue .35 .25

Issued in honor of General French and Colonel Beruti, patriots.

Marco M. de Avellaneda — A172

1941, Oct. 3 *Perf. 13x13½*

476 A172 5c dull slate blue .35 .25

Avellaneda, (1814-41), army leader and martyr.

Statue of Gen. Julio Roca — A173

1941, Oct. 19 Photo. Wmk. 90

477 A173 5c dark olive green .35 .25

Dedication of a monument to Lt. Gen. Julio Argentino Roca (1843-1914).

Carlos Pellegrini and Bank of the Nation A174

1941, Oct. 26 *Perf. 13½x13*

478 A174 5c brown carmine .35 .25

Founding of the Bank of the Nation, 50th anniv.

Gen. Juan Lavalle — A175

1941, Dec. 5 *Perf. 13x13½*

479 A175 5c bright blue .35 .25

Gen. Juan Galo de Lavalle (1797-1841).

National Postal Savings Bank A176

1942, Apr. 5 Litho. *Perf. 13½x13*

480 A176 1c pale olive .35 .25

Jose Manuel Estrada — A177

1942, July 13 *Perf. 13x13½*

481 A177 5c brown violet .45 .25

Jose Estrada (1842-1894), writer and diplomat.
Exists imperf. Value, pair $45.
No. 481 exists with label, showing medallion, attached. Value, pair $11.

Types of 1935-51

Perf. 13, 13x13½, 13½x13

1942-50 Litho. Wmk. 288

485 A128 ½c brown violet 9.00 1.50
486 A129 1c buff ('50) .30 .30
487 A130 2c dk brown ('50) .40 .25
488 A132 3c lt gray 16.00 1.25
489 A134 3c lt gray ('49) .25 .25
490 A137 10c red brn ('49) .25 .25
491 A138 12c red .25 .25
492 A140 15c lt gray blue (II) .30 .25
493 A139 20c dk sl bl & pale bl 4.00 .30
494 A141 25c dull rose ('49) 1.00 .25
495 A142 30c org brn ('49) 1.50 .25
496 A143 40c violet ('49) 10.00 1.00
497 A144 50c red & org ('49) 10.00 .40
498 A146 1p brn blk & lt bl 10.00 .30
499 A147 2p brn lake & bl ('49) 20.00 2.00
500 A148 5p ind & ol grn ('49) 60.00 3.00
Nos. 485-500 (16) 143.25 11.80

No. 493 measures 22x33mm.

Post Office, Buenos Aires — A178

Inscribed: "Correos y Telegrafos."

1942, Oct. 5 Litho. *Perf. 13*

503 A178 35c lt ultra 4.25 .25

See Nos. 541-543.

Proposed Columbus Lighthouse A179

1942, Oct. 12 Wmk. 288

504 A179 15c dull blue 3.00 .50

Wmk. 90

505 A179 15c dull blue 65.00 8.00

450th anniv. of the discovery of America by Columbus.

Jose C. Paz — A180

Books and Argentine Flag — A181

1942, Dec. 15 Wmk. 288

506 A180 5c dark gray .35 .25

Cent. of the birth of Jose C. Paz, stateman and founder of the newspaper La Prensa.

1943, Apr. 1 Litho. *Perf. 13*

507 A181 5c dull blue .30 .25

1st Book Fair of Argentina.

Arms of Argentina Inscribed "Honesty, Justice, Duty" — A182

1943-50 Wmk. 288 *Perf. 13*

Size: 20x26mm

508 A182 5c red ('50) 4.50 .25

Wmk. 90

509 A182 5c red .30 .25
a. 5c dull red, unsurfaced paper 5.00 .25
510 A182 15c green .60 .25

Perf. 13x13½

Size: 22x33mm

511 A182 20c dark blue .95 .25
Nos. 508-511 (4) 6.35 1.00

Change of political organization, 64/43.

Independence House, Tucuman A183

Liberty Head and Savings Bank A184

1943-51 Wmk. 90 *Perf. 13*

512 A183 5c blue green .95 .25

Wmk. 288

513 A183 5c blue green ('51) .45 .25

Restoration of Independence House.

1943, Oct. 25 Wmk. 90

514 A184 5c violet brown .45 .25

Wmk. 288

515 A184 5c violet brown 47.50 6.00

1st conference of National Postal Savings.

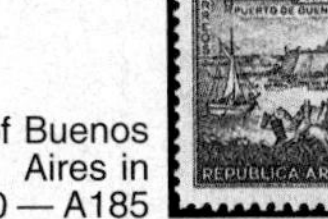

Port of Buenos Aires in 1800 — A185

1943, Dec. 11 **Wmk. 90**
516 A185 5c gray black .45 .25

Day of Exports.

Warship, Merchant Ship and Sailboat A186

Arms of Argentine Republic A187

1944, Jan. 31 ***Perf. 13***
517 A186 5c blue .45 .25

Issued to commemorate Sea Week.

1944, June 4
518 A187 5c dull blue .45 .35

1st anniv. of the change of political organization in Argentina.

St. Gabriel A188

Cross at Palermo A189

1944, Oct. 11
519 A188 3c yellow green .45 .25
520 A189 5c deep rose .45 .25

Fourth national Eucharistic Congress.

Allegory of Savings A190

Reservists A191

1944, Oct. 24
521 A190 5c gray .25 .25

20th anniv. of the National Savings Bank.

1944, Dec. 1
522 A191 5c blue .25 .25

Day of the Reservists.

Types of 1935-51

Perf. 13x13½, 13½x13

1945-47	**Litho.**	**Unwmk.**	
523 A128	½c brown vio ('46)	.25	.25
524 A129	1c yellow brown	.25	.25
525 A130	2c sepia	.25	.25
526 A132	3c lt gray (San Martin)	.60	.25
527 A134	3c lt gray (Moreno) ('46)	.25	.25
528 A135	6c olive grn ('47)	.35	.35
529 A137	10c brown ('46)	1.60	.30
530 A140	15c lt gray bl (II)	.70	.25
531 A139	20c dk sl bl & pale bl	1.60	.25
532 A141	25c dull rose	.75	.25
533 A142	30c orange brown	.70	.25
534 A143	40c violet	1.75	.35
535 A144	50c red & orange	2.00	.25
536 A146	1p brn blk & lt bl	2.75	.25
537 A147	2p brown lake & bl	27.50	1.00
538 A148	5p ind & ol grn ('46)	40.00	4.00
539 A149	10p dp cl & int blk	10.00	2.00
540 A150	20p bl grn & brn ('46)	9.00	2.00
	Nos. 523-540 (18)	100.30	12.75

No. 531 measures 22x33mm.

Post Office Type Inscribed: "Correos y Telecommunicaciones"

1945 **Unwmk.** ***Perf. 13x13½***
541 A178 35c lt ultra 1.75 .25

Wmk. 90

542 A178 35c lt ultra 1.00 .25

Wmk. 288

543 A178 35c lt ultra .35 .25
Nos. 541-543 (3) 3.10 .75

Nos. 541 and 543 exist imperf. Value, each, pair $10.

Bernardino Rivadavia
A192 A193

Mausoleum of Rivadavia A194

Perf. 13½x13

1945, Sept. 1 **Litho.** **Unwmk.**
544 A192 3c blue green .25 .25
545 A193 5c rose .25 .25
546 A194 20c blue .35 .25
Nos. 544-546 (3) .85 .75

Cent. of the death of Bernardino Rivadavia, Argentina's first president.
No. 546 exists imperf. Value, pair $20.
No. 546 exists with mute label attached. Value, pair, $4.50.

San Martin — A195

1945-46 **Wmk. 90** **Typo. or Litho.**
547 A195 5c carmine .25 .25
a. Litho. ('46) .25 .25

Wmk. 288

548 A195 5c carmine, litho. 100.00 30.00

Unwmk.

549 A195 5c carmine ('46) .65 .25
a. Litho. ('46) .25 .25

Nos. 547 and 547a exist imperf. Values, pairs: No. 547, $17.50; No. 547a, $10.
For overprints see Nos. O42, O57.

Monument to Army of the Andes, Mendoza — A196

1946, Jan. 14 **Litho.** ***Perf. 13½x13***
550 A196 5c violet brown .25 .25

Issued to honor the Unknown Soldier of the War for Independence.

Franklin D. Roosevelt — A197

1946, Apr. 12
551 A197 5c dark blue .25 .25

A198

Liberty Administering Presidential Oath.

1946, June 4 ***Perf. 13x13½***
552 A198 5c blue .25 .25

Inauguration of Pres. Juan D. Perón, 6/4/46.

Argentina Receiving Popular Acclaim A199

1946, Oct. 17 ***Perf. 13½x13***
553 A199 5c rose violet .35 .30
554 A199 10c blue green .40 .40
555 A199 15c dark blue .55 .60
556 A199 50c red brown .40 .50
557 A199 1p carmine rose 1.00 1.20
Nos. 553-557 (5) 2.70 3.00

First anniversary of the political organization change of Oct. 17, 1945.

Coin Bank and World Map — A200

1946, Oct. 31 **Unwmk.**
558 A200 30c dk rose car & pink .45 .30

Universal Day of Savings, October 31, 1946.

Argentine Industry — A201

1946, Dec. 6 ***Perf. 13x13½***
559 A201 5c violet brown .25 .25

Day of Argentine Industry, Dec. 6.

International Bridge Connecting Argentina and Brazil A202

1947, May 21 **Litho.** ***Perf. 13½x13***
560 A202 5c green .25 .25

Opening of the Argentina-Brazil International Bridge, May 21, 1947.

Map of Argentine Antarctic Claims — A203

1947-49 **Unwmk.** ***Perf. 13x13½***
561 A203 5c violet & lilac .35 .25
562 A203 20c dk car rose & rose .70 .25

Wmk. 90

563 A203 20c dk car rose & rose 1.40 .30

Wmk. 288

564 A203 20c dk car rose & rose ('49) 4.25 .50
Nos. 561-564 (4) 6.70 1.30

1st Argentine Antarctic mail, 43rd anniv.
Nos. 561 and 563 exist imperf. Values, pairs: No. 561, $13.50; No. 563, $27.50.

Justice — A204

1947, June 4 **Unwmk.**
565 A204 5c brn vio & pale yel .25 .25

1st anniversary of the Peron government.

Icarus Falling A205

1947, Sept. 25 ***Perf. 13½x13***
566 A205 15c red violet .25 .25

Aviation Week.

Training Ship Presidente Sarmiento — A206

1947, Oct. 5 ***Perf. 13x13½***
567 A206 5c blue .25 .25

50th anniv. of the launching of the Argentine training frigate "Presidente Sarmiento."

Cervantes and Characters from Don Quixote A207

Perf. 13½x13

1947, Oct. 12 **Photo.** **Wmk. 90**
568 A207 5c olive green .25 .25

400th anniv. of the birth of Miguel de Cervantes Saavedra, playwright and poet.
Exists imperf. Value, pair $10.

Gen. Jose de San Martin A208

Perf. 13½x13

1947-49 Unwmk. Litho.

569 A208 5c dull green .25 .25

Wmk. 288

570 A208 5c dull green ('49) .35 .25

Transfer of the remains of Gen. Jose de San Martin's parents.
Nos. 569 and 570 exist imperf. Value for pair, each $10.

School Children — A209

Statue of Araucanian Indian — A210

1947-49 Unwmk. ***Perf. 13x13½***

571 A209 5c green .25 .25

Wmk. 90

574 A209 20c brown .35 .25

Wmk. 288

575 A209 5c green ('49) .30 .25
Nos. 571-575 (3) .90 .75

Argentine School Crusade for World Peace.
Nos. 571 and 574 exist imperf. Value for pair, each $10.

1948, May 21 Wmk. 90

576 A210 25c yellow brown .25 .25

American Indian Day, Apr. 19.
No. 576 exists imperf. Value, pair $10.

Cap of Liberty — A211

Manual Stop Signal — A212

1948, July 16

577 A211 5c ultra .25 .25

Revolution of June 4, 1943, 5th anniv.

1948, July 22

578 A212 5c chocolate & yellow .25 .25

Traffic Safety Day, June 10.
No. 578 exists imperf. Value, pair $10.

Post Horn and Oak Leaves — A213

Argentine Farmers — A214

1948, July 22 Unwmk.

579 A213 5c lilac rose .25 .25

200th anniversary of the establishment of regular postal service on the Plata River.
No. 579 exists imperf. Value, pair $10.

Perf. 13x13½

1948, Sept. 20 Wmk. 288

580 A214 10c red brown .25 .25

Agriculture Day, Sept. 8, 1948.

Liberty and Symbols of Progress — A215

Perf. 13x13½

1948, Nov. 23 Photo. Wmk. 287

581 A215 25c red brown .30 .25

3rd anniversary of President Juan D. Peron's return to power, October 17, 1945.
No. 581 exists imperf. Value, pair $10.

Souvenir Sheets

A216

15c, Mail coach. 45c, Buenos Aires in 18th cent. 55c, 1st train, 1857. 85c, Sailing ship, 1767.

1948, Dec. 21 Unwmk. ***Imperf.***

582 A216 Sheet of 4 5.50 4.50
a. 15c dark green 1.00 .75
b. 45c orange brown 1.00 .75
c. 55c lilac brown 1.00 .75
d. 85c ultramarine 1.00 .75

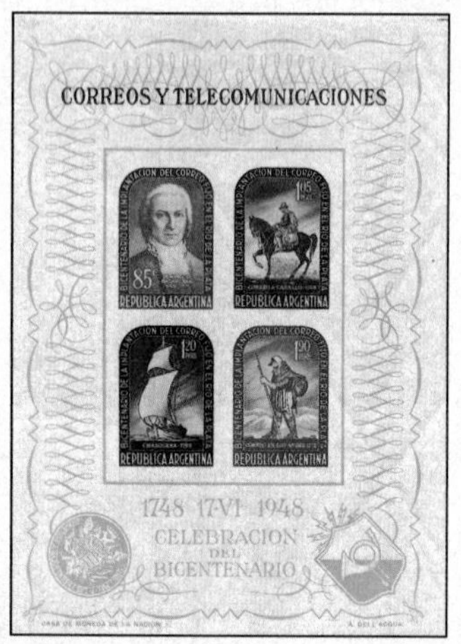

A217

Designs: 85c, Domingo de Basavilibaso (1709-75). 1.05p, Postrider. 1.20p, Sailing ship, 1798. 1.90p, Courier in the Andes, 1772.

583 A217 Sheet of 4 26.50 15.00
a. 85c brown 4.75 3.25
b. 1.05p dark green 4.75 3.25
c. 1.20p dark blue 4.75 3.25
d. 1.90p red brown 4.75 3.25

200th anniversary of the establishment of regular postal service on the Plata River.

Winged Wheel — A218

Perf. 13½x13

1949, Mar. 1 Wmk. 288

584 A218 10c blue .25 .25

Railroad nationalization, 1st anniv.

Liberty A219

1949, June 20 Engr. Wmk. 90

585 A219 1p red & red violet .70 .30

Ratification of the Constitution of 1949.

Allegory of the UPU A220

1949, Nov. 19

586 A220 25c dk grn & yel grn .25 .25

75th anniv. of the UPU.

Catalogue values for unused stamps in this section, from this point to the end of the section, are for Never Hinged items.

Gen. Jose de San Martin — A221

San Martin at Boulogne sur Mer — A222

Mausoleum of San Martin — A223

20c, 50c, 75c, Different portraits of San Martin. 1p, House where San Martin died.

Engr., Photo. (25c, 1p, 2p)

1950, Aug. 17 Wmk. 90 ***Perf. 13½***

587 A221 10c indigo & dk pur .35 .25
588 A221 20c red brn & dk brn .35 .25
589 A222 25c brown .35 .30
590 A221 50c dk green & ind .60 .30
591 A221 75c choc & dk grn .90 .30
a. Souv. sheet of 4, #587, 588, 590, 591, imperf. 4.00 2.50
592 A222 1p dark green 2.00 .40
593 A223 2p dp red lilac 2.50 .50
Nos. 587-593 (7) 7.05 2.30

Death cent. of General Jose de San Martin.

Map Showing Antarctic Claims — A224

1951, May 21 Litho. ***Perf. 13x13½***

594 A224 1p choc & lt blue .60 .25

For overprint see No. O52.
No. 594 exists imperf. Value, pair $25.

Pegasus and Train A225

Communications Symbols — A226

Design: 25c, Ship and dolphin.

1951, Oct. 17 Photo. ***Perf. 13½***

595 A225 5c dark brown .35 .25
596 A225 25c Prus green .50 .30
597 A226 40c rose brown .60 .30
Nos. 595-597 (3) 1.45 .85

Close of Argentine Five Year Plan.

Woman Voter and "Argentina" A227

1951, Dec. 14 ***Perf. 13½x13***

598 A227 10c brown violet .35 .25

Granting of women's suffrage.

Eva Peron
A228 A229

Litho. or Engraved (#605)

1952, Aug. 26 Wmk. 90 ***Perf. 13***

599 A228 1c orange brown .35 .25
600 A228 5c gray .35 .25
601 A228 10c rose lilac .35 .25
602 A228 20c rose pink .35 .25
603 A228 25c dull green .40 .25
604 A228 40c dull violet .50 .25
605 A228 45c deep blue .50 .25
606 A228 50c dull brown .75 .25

Photo.

607 A229 1p dark brown .90 .30
608 A229 1.50p deep green 4.00 .30
609 A229 2p brt carmine .90 .30
610 A229 3p indigo 1.60 .30
Nos. 599-610 (12) 10.95 3.20

For overprints see Nos. O79-O85.

Nos. 599, 601-604 and 606 exist imperf. Value for set of 6 pairs, $235.

Inscribed: "Eva Peron"

1952-53 ***Perf. 13x13½***

611	A229	1p	dark brown	.90	.35
612	A229	1.50p	deep green	2.00	.35
613	A229	2p	brt car ('53)	2.00	.40
614	A229	3p	indigo	4.00	.90

Engr.

Perf. 13½x13

Size: 30x40mm

615	A229	5p	red brown	4.75	1.75
616	A228	10p	red	8.00	3.75
617	A229	20p	green	17.50	8.50
618	A228	50p	ultra	40.00	17.50
			Nos. 611-618 (8)	79.15	33.50

For overprints see Nos. O86-O93.

Indian Funeral Urn — A230

1953, Aug. 28 Photo. ***Perf. 13x13½***

619 A230 50c blue green .35 .25

Founding of Santiago del Estero, 400th anniv.

Rescue Ship "Uruguay" — A231

1953, Oct. 8 ***Perf. 13½***

620 A231 50c ultra 1.75 .50

50th anniv. of the rescue of the Antarctic expedition of Otto C. Nordenskjold.

Planting Argentine Flag in the Antarctic A232

1954, Jan. 20 Engr. ***Perf. 13½x13***

621 A232 1.45p blue 1.40 .50

50th anniv. of Argentina's 1st antarctic p.o. and the establishing of the La Hoy radio p.o. in the South Orkneys.

Wired Communications A233

Television A234

Perf. 13x13½, 13½x13

1954, Apr. Photo. Wmk. 90

622	A233	1.50p	shown	.50	.30
623	A233	3p	Radio	2.00	.30
624	A234	5p	shown	3.00	.40
			Nos. 622-624 (3)	5.50	1.00

Intl. Plenipotentiary Conf. of Telecommunications, Buenos Aires, 1952.

Pediment, Buenos Aires Stock Exchange A235

1954, July 13 ***Perf. 13½x13***

625 A235 1p dark green .50 .25

Cent. of the establishment of the Buenos Aires Stock Exchange.

Eva Peron — A236

1954 **Wmk. 90**

626 A236 3p dp car rose 3.00 .50

Wmk. 288

627 A236 3p dp car rose 250.00 50.00

2nd anniv. of the death of Eva Peron.

Jose de San Martin — A237

Wheat — A238

Industry — A238a

Eva Peron Foundation Building A239

Cliffs of Humahuaca — A240

Gen. Jose de San Martin — A241

Designs: 50c, Buenos Aires harbor. 1p, Cattle ranch (Ganaderia). 3p, Nihuil Dam. 5p, Iguacu Falls, vert. 20p, Mt. Fitz Roy, vert.

Engraved (#632, 638-642), Photogravure (#634-637)

Perf. 13½, 13x13½ (80c), 13½x13 (#639, 641-642)

1954-59 **Wmk. 90**

628	A237	20c	brt red, typo.	.25	.25
629	A237	20c	red, litho. ('55)	1.00	.25
630	A237	40c	red, litho. ('56)	.25	.25
631	A237	40c	brt red, typo. ('55)	.25	.25
632	A239	50c	blue ('56)	.30	.25
633	A239	50c	bl, litho. ('59)	.60	.25
634	A238	80c	brown	.40	.25
635	A239	1p	brown ('58)	.40	.25
636	A238a	1.50p	ultra ('58)	.40	.25
637	A239	2p	dk rose lake	.50	.25
638	A239	3p	violet brn ('56)	.50	.25
639	A240	5p	gray grn ('55)	8.00	.25
a.			Perf. 13½	10.00	.25
640	A240	10p	yel grn ('55)	8.00	.25
641	A240	20p	dull vio ('55)	11.00	.50
a.			Perf. 13½	14.00	1.50
642	A241	50p	ultra & ind ('55)	12.00	1.50
a.			Perf. 13½	15.00	1.00
			Nos. 628-642 (15)	43.85	5.25

See Nos. 699-700. For similar designs inscribed "Republica Argentina" see Nos. 823-827, 890, 935, 937, 940, 990, 995, 1039, 1044, 1048.

For overprints see Nos. O94-O106, O142, O153-O157.

Allegory A242

1954, Aug. 26 Typo. ***Perf. 13½***

643 A242 1.50p slate black .80 .25

Cent. of the establishment of the Buenos Aires Grain Exchange.

Clasped Hands and Congress Medal — A243

1955, Mar. 21 Photo. ***Perf. 13½x13***

644 A243 3p red brown 1.50 .30

Issued to publicize the National Productivity and Social Welfare Congress.

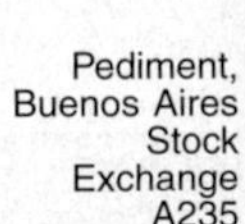

Allegory of Aviation — A244

Argentina Breaking Chains — A245

1955, June 18 Wmk. 90 ***Perf. 13½***

645 A244 1.50p olive gray 1.00 .25

Commercial aviation in Argentina, 25th anniv.

1955, Oct. 16 **Litho.**

647 A245 1.50p olive green .50 .25

Liberation Revolution of Sept. 16, 1955.

Army Navy and Air Force Emblems A246

Perf. 13½x13

1955, Dec. 31 Photo. Wmk. 90

648 A246 3p blue .50 .25

"Brotherhood of the Armed Forces."

A247

1956, Feb. 3 ***Perf. 13½***

649 A247 1.50p Justo Jose de Urquiza .40 .25

Battle of Caseros, 104th anniversary. No. 649 exists imperf. Value, pair $30.

A248

1956, July 28 Engr. ***Perf. 13½x13***

650 A248 2p Coin and die .40 .25

75th anniversary of the Argentine Mint.

1856 Stamp of Corrientes A249

Juan G. Pujol — A250

Design: 2.40p, Stamp of 1860-78.

1956, Aug. 21

651 A249 40c dk grn & blue .40 .25
652 A249 2.40p brn & lil rose .40 .25

Photo.

653 A250 4.40p brt blue 1.10 .30
a. Souv. sheet, #651-653, imperf. 9.00 3.75
Nos. 651-653 (3) 1.90 .80

Centenary of Argentine postage stamps.
No. 653a for the Argentine stamp cent. and Philatelic Exhib. for the Cent. of Corrientes Stamps, Oct. 12-21. The 4.40p is photo., the other two stamps and border litho. Colors of 40c and 2.40p differ slightly from engraved stamps.

Felling Trees, La Pampa A251

Maté Herb and Gourd, Misiones — A252

1p, Cotton plant and harvest, Chaco.

1956, Sept. 1 ***Perf. 13½***

654 A251 50c ultra .35 .25
655 A251 1p magenta .35 .25
656 A252 1.50p green .40 .25
Nos. 654-656 (3) 1.10 .75

Elevation of the territories of La Pampa, Chaco and Misiones to provinces.

"Liberty" A253

Florentino Ameghino A254

Perf. 13½

1956, Sept. 15 Wmk. 90 Photo.

657 A253 2.40p lilac rose .45 .25

1st anniv. of the Revolution of Liberation.

1956, Nov. 30

658 A254 2.40p brown .40 .25

Issued to honor Florentino Ameghino (1854-1911), anthropologist.
For overprint see No. O110.

Adm. Brown Type of 1935-51

Two types:
I. Bust touches upper frame line of name panel at bottom.
II. White line separates bust from frame line.

Size: 19½-20½x26-27mm

1956 Litho. ***Perf. 13***

659 A133 20c dull purple (I) .25 .25
a. Type II .25 .25
b. Size 19½x25¼mm (I) .25 .25

For overprint see No. O108.

Benjamin Franklin A255

1956, Dec. 22 Photo. ***Perf. 13½***

660 A255 40c intense blue .50 .25

250th anniv. of the birth of Benjamin Franklin.

Frigate "Hercules" A256

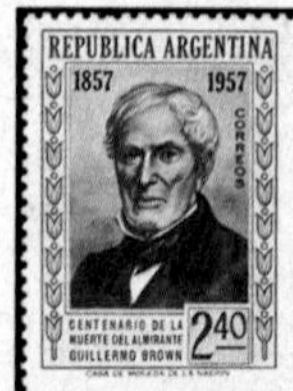

Guillermo Brown A257

1957, Mar. 2

661 A256 40c brt blue .40 .25
662 A257 2.40p gray black .50 .25
Nos. 661-662,C63-C65 (5) 1.75 1.25

Admiral Guillermo (William) Brown (1777-1857), founder of the Argentine navy.

Roque Saenz Pena (1851-1914) A258

Church of Santo Domingo, 1807 A259

1957, Apr. 1

663 A258 4.40p grnsh gray .45 .25

Roque Saenz Pena, pres. 1910-14.
For overprint see No. O111.

1957, July 6 **Wmk. 90**

664 A259 40c brt blue green .30 .25

150th anniv. of the defense of Buenos Aires.

"La Portena" A260

1957, Aug. 31 Wmk. 90 ***Perf. 13½***

665 A260 40c pale brown .50 .25

Centenary of Argentine railroads.

Esteban Echeverria A261

"Liberty" A262

1957, Sept. 2 ***Perf. 13x13½***

666 A261 2p claret .30 .25

Esteban Echeverria (1805-1851), poet.

For overprint see No. O109.

1957, Sept. 28 ***Perf. 13½***

667 A262 40c carmine rose .40 .25

Constitutional reform convention.

Portrait Type of 1935-51

1957, Oct. 28 Litho. ***Perf. 13½***

Size: 16½x22mm

668 A128 5c Jose Hernandez .25 .25

For overprint see No. O112.

Oil Derrick and Hands Holding Oil — A263

Perf. 13½

1957, Dec. 21 Wmk. 90 Photo.

669 A263 40c bright blue .40 .25

50th anniv. of the national oil industry.
No. 669 exists imperf. Value, pair $30.

Museum, La Plata — A264

1958, Jan. 11

670 A264 40c dark gray .35 .25

City of La Plata, 75th anniversary.

A265

A266

40c, Locomotive & arms of Argentina & Bolivia. 1p, Map of Argentine-Bolivian boundary & plane.

1958, Apr. 19 Wmk. 90 ***Perf. 13½***

671 A265 40c slate & dp car .35 .25
672 A266 1p dark brown .35 .25

Argentine-Bolivian friendship. No. 671 for the opening of the Jacuiba-Santa Cruz railroad; No. 672, the exchange of presidential visits.

Symbols of the Republic A267

1958, Apr. 30 Photo. & Engr.

673 A267 40c multicolored .35 .25
674 A267 1p multicolored .35 .25
675 A267 2p multicolored .50 .25
Nos. 673-675 (3) 1.20 .75

Transmission of Presidential power.

Flag Monument — A268

1958, June 21 Litho. Wmk. 90

676 A268 40c blue & violet bl .35 .25

1st anniv. of the Flag Monument of Rosario.
Exists imperf. Value, pair $40.

Map of Antarctica — A269

1958, July 12 ***Perf. 13½***

677 A269 40c car rose & blk .70 .40

International Geophysical Year, 1957-58.
Exists imperf. Value, pair $80.

Stamp of Cordoba and Mail Coach A270

1958, Oct. 18

678 A270 40c pale blue & slate .25 .25
Nos. 678,C72-C73 (3) .75 .75

Centenary of Cordoba postage stamps.

"Slave" by Michelangelo and UN Emblem — A271

Engraved and Lithographed

1959, Mar. 14 Wmk. 90 ***Perf. 13½***

679 A271 40c violet brn & gray .35 .25

10th anniv. (in 1958) of the signing of the Universal Declaration of Human Rights. No UN Emblem (error) Value, $200.
Exists imperf. Value, pair $50.

Orchids and Globe — A272

1959, May 23 Photo. ***Perf. 13½***

680 A272 1p dull claret .40 .25

1st International Horticulture Exposition.
Exists imperf. Value, pair $50.

Pope Pius XII — A273

1959, June 20 Engr. *Perf. 13½*

681	A273	1p yellow & black	.50	.25

Pope Pius XII, 1876-1958.
Exists imperf. Value, pair $50.

William Harvey — A274

1p, Claude Bernard. 1.50p, Ivan P. Pavlov.

1959, Aug. 8 Litho. Wmk. 90

682	A274	50c green	.30	.25
683	A274	1p dark red	.30	.25
684	A274	1.50p brown	.70	*2.00*
		Nos. 682-684 (3)	1.30	2.50

21st Intl. Cong. of Physiological Sciences, Buenos Aires.

Type of 1958 and

Domestic Horse — A275

Jose de San Martin — A276

Tierra del Fuego A277

Inca Bridge, Mendoza — A278

Ski Jumper A279

Mar del Plata A280

Designs: 10c, Cayman. 20c, Llama. 50c, Puma. No. 690, Sunflower. 3p, Zapata Slope, Catamarca. 12p, 23p, 25p, Red Quebracho tree. 20p, Nahuel Huapi Lake. 22p, "Industry" (cogwheel and factory).
Two overall paper sizes for 1p, 5p:
I — 27x37½mm or 37½x27mm.
II — 27x39mm or 39x27mm.

Perf. 13x13½

1959-70 Litho. Wmk. 90

685	A275	10c	slate green	.25	.25
686	A275	20c	dl red brn ('61)	.25	.25
687	A275	50c	bister ('60)	.25	.25
688	A275	50c	bis, typo. ('60)	.30	.25
689	A275	1p	rose red	.25	.25

Perf. 13½

690	A278	1p	brn, photo., I ('61)	.25	.25
a.			Paper II ('69)	1.00	.25
690B	A278	1p	brown, I	.80	.25
691	A276	2p	rose red ('61)	.40	.25
692	A276	2p	red, typo. (19½ x 26mm) ('61)	.50	.25
a.			Redrawn (19½ x 25mm)	4.00	.25
693	A277	3p	dk bl, photo. ('60)	.25	.25
694	A276	4p	red, typo ('62)	1.00	.25
694A	A276	4p	red ('62)	.60	.25
695	A277	5p	gray brn, photo., I	.30	.25
e.			5p dark brown, paper II ('70)	8.00	4.00
695A	A276	8p	ver ('65)	1.25	.25
695B	A276	8p	red, typo. ('65)	.30	.25
695C	A276	10p	ver ('66)	.65	.25
695D	A276	10p	red, typo. ('66)	.50	.25

Photo.

696	A278	10p	lt red brn ('60)	.50	.25
697	A278	12p	dk brn vio ('62)	1.00	.25
697A	A278	12p	dk brn, litho. ('64)	12.00	.30
698	A278	20p	Prus grn ('60)	3.00	.25
698A	A276	20p	red, typo. ('67)	.25	.25
699	A238a	22p	ultra ('62)	1.75	.25
700	A238a	22p	ultra, litho. ('62)	25.00	.30
701	A278	23p	green ('65)	5.00	.25
702	A278	25p	dp vio ('66)	1.50	.25
703	A278	25p	pur, litho. ('66)	3.00	.25
704	A279	100p	blue ('61)	8.00	.25
705	A280	300p	dp vio ('62)	5.00	.25
			Nos. 685-705 (29)	74.10	7.35

Imperf and imperf between examples of some numbers exist.
See Nos. 882-887, 889, 892, 923-925, 928-930, 938, 987-989, 991.
For overprints and surcharges see Nos. 1076, C82-C83, O113-O118, O122-O124, O126-O141, O143-O145, O163.
The 300p remained on sale as a 3p stamp after the 1970 currency exchange.

Symbolic Sailboat — A281

1959, Oct. 3 Litho. *Perf. 13½*

706	A281	1p blk, red & bl	.30	.25

Red Cross sanitary education campaign.

Child Playing with Doll — A282

1959, Oct. 17

707	A282	1p red & blk	.30	.25

Issued for Mother's Day, 1959.

Buenos Aires 1p Stamp of 1859 — A283

1959, Nov. 21 Wmk. 90 *Perf. 13½*

708	A283	1p gray & dk bl	.30	.25

Issued for the Day of Philately.

Bartolomé Mitre and Justo José de Urquiza — A284

1959, Dec. 12 Photo. *Perf. 13½*

709	A284	1p purple	.35	.25

Treaty of San Jose de Flores, centenary.
Exists imperf. Value, pair $40.

WRY Emblem — A285

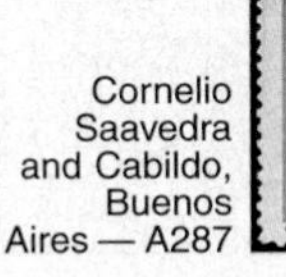

Abraham Lincoln — A286

1960, Apr. 7 Litho. Wmk. 90

710	A285	1p bister & car	.35	.25
711	A285	4.20p apple grn & dp claret	.50	.50

World Refugee Year, July 1, 1959-June 30, 1960. See No. B25.

1960, Apr. 14 Photo. *Perf. 13½*

712	A286	5p ultra	.45	.25

Sesquicentennial (in 1959) of the birth of Abraham Lincoln.
Exists imperf. Value, pair $70.

Cornelio Saavedra and Cabildo, Buenos Aires — A287

"Cabildo" and: 2p, Juan José Paso. 4.20p, Manuel Alberti and Miguel Azcuénaga. 10.70p, Juan Larrea and Domingo Matheu.

Perf. 13½

1960, May 28 Wmk. 90 Photo.

713	A287	1p rose lilac	.30	.25
714	A287	2p bluish grn	.30	.25
715	A287	4.20p gray & grn	.30	.25
716	A287	10.70p gray & ultra	.45	.25
		Nos. 713-716,C75-C76 (6)	1.95	1.50

150th anniversary of the May Revolution.
Souvenir sheets are Nos. C75a and C76a.

Luis Maria Drago — A288

Juan Bautista Alberdi — A289

1960, July 8

717	A288	4.20p brown	.35	.25

Centenary of the birth of Dr. Luis Maria Drago, statesman and jurist.
Exists imperf. Value, pair $40.

1960, Sept. 10 Wmk. 90 *Perf. 13½*

718	A289	1p green	.30	.25

150th anniversary of the birth of Juan Bautista Alberdi, statesman and philosopher.
Exists imperf. Value, pair $40.

Map of Argentina and Antarctic Sector — A290

1960, Sept. 24 Litho. *Perf. 13½*

719	A290	5p violet	.60	.25

National census of 1960.
Exists imperf. Value, pair $70.

Caravel and Emblem A291

1960, Oct. 1 Photo.

720	A291	1p dk olive grn	.40	.25
721	A291	5p brown	.50	.50
		Nos. 720-721,C78-C79 (4)	2.10	1.35

8th Congress of the Postal Union of the Americas and Spain.

Virgin of Luján, Patroness of Argentina A292

Argentine Boy Scout Emblem A293

1960, Nov. 12 Wmk. 90 *Perf. 13½*

722	A292	1p dark blue	.75	.25

First Inter-American Marian Congress.
Exists imperf. Value, pair $30.

1961, Jan. 17 Litho.

723	A293	1p car rose & blk	.50	.25

International Patrol Encampment of the Boy Scouts, Buenos Aires.
Exists imperf. Value, pair $70.

"Shipment of Cereals," by Quinquela Martin — A294

1961, Feb. 11 Photo. *Perf. 13½*
724 A294 1p red brown .40 .25

Export drive: "To export is to advance."
Exists imperf. Value, pair $40.

Naval Battle of San Nicolás — A295

1961, Mar. 2 *Perf. 13½*
725 A295 2p gray .50 .25

Naval battle of San Nicolas, 150th anniv.
Exists imperf. Value, pair $67.50.

Mariano Moreno by Juan de Dios Rivera A296

1961, Mar. 25 *Perf. 13½*
726 A296 2p blue .35 .25

Mariano Moreno (1778-1811), writer, politician, member of the 1810 Junta.
Exists imperf. Value, pair $40.

Emperor Trajan Statue — A297

Rabindranath Tagore — A298

1961, Apr. 11
727 A297 2p slate green .35 .25

Visit of Pres. Giovanni Gronchi of Italy to Argentina, April 1961.
Exists imperf. Value, pair $40.

1961, May 13 Photo. *Perf. 13½*
728 A298 2p purple, *grysh* .40 .25

Centenary of the birth of Rabindranath Tagore, Indian poet.

San Martin Statue, Madrid A299

1961, May 24 Wmk. 90
729 A299 1p olive gray .35 .25

Unveiling of a statue of General José de San Martin in Madrid.
Exists imperf. Value, pair $40.

Manuel Belgrano A300

1961, June 17 *Perf. 13½*
730 A300 2p violet blue .40 .25

Erection of a monument by Hector Rocha, to General Manuel Belgrano in Buenos Aires.
Exists imperf. Value, pair $40.

Explorers, Sledge and Dog Team A301

1961, Aug. 19 Photo. Wmk. 90
731 A301 2p black .85 .30

10th anniversary of the General San Martin Base, Argentine Antarctic.
Exists imperf. Value, pair $75.

Spanish Conquistador and Sword — A302

Sarmiento Statue by Rodin, Buenos Aires — A303

1961, Aug. 19 Litho.
732 A302 2p red & blk .35 .25

First city of Jujuy, 400th anniversary.
Exists imperf. Value, pair $40.

1961, Sept. 9 Photo.
733 A303 2p violet .35 .25

Domingo Faustino Sarmiento (1811-88), political leader and writer.
Exists imperf. Value, pair $40.

Symbol of World Town Planning A304

1961, Nov. 25 Litho. *Perf. 13½*
734 A304 2p ultra & yel .30 .25

World Town Planning Day, Nov. 8.

Manuel Belgrano Statue, Buenos Aires — A305

Grenadier, Flag and Regimental Emblem — A306

1962, Feb. 24 Photo.
735 A305 2p Prus blue .30 .25

150th anniversary of the Argentine flag.
Exists imperf. Value, pair $40.

1962, Mar. 31 Wmk. 90 *Perf. 13½*
736 A306 2p carmine rose .30 .25

150th anniversary of the San Martin Grenadier Guards regiment.
Exists imperf. Value, pair $40.

Mosquito and Malaria Eradication Emblem A307

1962, Apr. 7 Litho.
737 A307 2p vermilion & blk .35 .25

WHO drive to eradicate malaria.

Church of the Virgin of Lujàn — A308

Bust of Juan Jufrè — A309

1962, May 12 *Perf. 13½*
738 A308 2p org brn & blk .30 .25

75th anniversary of the pontifical coronation of the Virgin of Lujan.

1962, June 23 Photo.
739 A309 2p Prus blue .30 .25

Founding of San Juan, 4th cent.
Exists imperf. Value, pair $40.

"Soaring into Space" — A310

Juan Vucetich — A311

1962, Aug. 18 Litho. *Perf. 13½*
740 A310 2p maroon, blk & bl .30 .25

Argentine Air Force, 50th anniversary.
Exists imperf. Value, pair $40.

1962, Oct. 6 Photo. Wmk. 90
741 A311 2p green .30 .25

Juan Vucetich (1864-1925), inventor of the Argentine system of fingerprinting.
Exists imperf. Value, pair $40.

Domingo F. Sarmiento — A312

Design: 4p, Jose Hernandez.

1962-66 Photo. *Perf. 13½*
742 A312 2p deep green .85 .25

Litho.
742A A312 2p lt green ('64) .65 .25

Photo.
742B A312 4p dull red ('65) .60 .25

Litho.
742C A312 4p rose red ('66) 1.25 .25
Nos. 742-742C (4) 3.35 1.00

No. 742A exists imperf. Value, pair $40.
See No. 817-819. For overprints see Nos. O119-O121, O125, O149.

February 20th Monument, Salta — A313

1963, Feb. 23 Photo. Wmk. 90
743 A313 2p dark green .60 .25

150th anniversary of the Battle of Salta, War of Independence.
Exists imperf. Value, pair $40.

Gear Wheels A314

1963, Mar. 16 Litho. *Perf. 13½*
744 A314 4p gray, blk & brt rose .35 .25

Argentine Industrial Union, 75th anniv.
Exists imperf. Value, pair $40.

National College, Buenos Aires — A315

Child Draining Cup — A316

1963, Mar. 16 Wmk. 90
745 A315 4p dull org & blk .40 .25

National College of Buenos Aires, cent.
Exists imperf. Value, pair $40.

1963, Apr. 6
746 A316 4p multicolored .40 .25

FAO "Freedom from Hunger" campaign.
Exists imperf. Value, pair $40.

Frigate "La Argentina," 1817, by Emilio Biggeri A317

1963, May 18 Photo.
747 A317 4p bluish green .60 .25

Issued for Navy Day, May 17.
Exists imperf. Value, pair $40.

Seat of 1813 Assembly and Official Seal — A318

1963, July 13 Litho. *Perf. 13½*
748 A318 4p lt blue & blk .30 .25

150th anniversary of the 1813 Assembly.
Exists imperf. Value, pair $40.

Battle of San Lorenzo, 1813 A319

1963, Aug. 24
749 A319 4p grn & blk, *grnsh* .30 .25

Sesquicentennial of the Battle of San Lorenzo.

Queen Nefertari Offering Papyrus Flowers, Abu Simbel A320

1963, Sept. 14 ***Perf. 13½***
750 A320 4p ocher, blk & bl grn .30 .25

Campaign to save the historic monuments in Nubia.
Exists imperf. Value, pair $40.

Government House, Buenos Aires — A321

1963, Oct. 12 Wmk. 90 ***Perf. 13½***
751 A321 5p rose & brown .45 .25

Inauguration of President Arturo Illia.
Exists imperf. Value, pair $40.

"Science" A322

Francisco de las Carreras, Supreme Court Justice A323

1963, Oct. 16 **Litho.**
752 A322 4p org brn, bl & blk .35 .25

10th Latin-American Neurosurgery Congress.
Exists imperf. Value, pair $40.

1963, Nov. 23 Photo. ***Perf. 13½***
753 A323 5p bluish green .35 .25

Centenary of judicial power.
Exists imperf. Value, pair $40.

Blackboards A324

1963, Nov. 23 **Litho.**
754 A324 5p red, blk & bl .35 .25

Issued to publicize "Teachers for America" through the Alliance for Progress program.
Exists imperf. Value, pair $40.

Kemal Atatürk A325

"Payador" by Juan Carlos Castagnino A326

1963, Dec. 28 Photo. ***Perf. 13½***
755 A325 12p dark gray .50 .25

25th anniversary of the death of Kemal Atatürk, president of Turkey.
Exists imperf. Value, pair $40.

1964, Jan. 25 **Litho.**
756 A326 4p ultra, blk & lt bl .35 .25

Fourth National Folklore Festival.
Exists imperf. Value, pair $40.

Maps of South Georgia, South Orkney and South Sandwich Islands A327

4p, Map of Argentina & Antarctic claims, vert.

1964, Feb. 22 Wmk. 90 ***Perf. 13½***
Size: 33x22mm
757 A327 2p lt & dk bl & bister .75 .30
Size: 30x40mm
758 A327 4p lt & dk bl & ol grn 1.25 .40
Nos. 757-758,C92 (3) 4.75 1.45

Argentina's claim to Antarctic territories, 60th anniv.
Exist imperf. Value, set of 3 pairs, $150.

Jorge Newbery in Cockpit A328

1964, Feb. 23 **Photo.**
759 A328 4p deep green .40 .25

Newbery, aviator, 50th death anniv.
Exists imperf. Value, pair $40.

John F. Kennedy A329

1964, Apr. 14 Engr. Wmk. 90
760 A329 4p claret & dk bl .50 .25

President John F. Kennedy (1917-63).
Exists imperf. Value, pair $100.

José Brochero by José Cuello — A330

1964, May 9 Photo. ***Perf. 13½***
761 A330 4p light sepia .35 .25

50th anniversary of the death of Father Jose Gabriel Brochero.
Exists imperf. Value, pair $50.

Soldier of Patricios Regiment A331

1964, May 29 Litho. Wmk. 90
762 A331 4p blk, ultra & red .50 .25

Issued for Army Day. Later Army Day stamps, inscribed "Republica Argentina," are of type A340a.
Exists imperf. Value, pair $40.

Pope John XXIII — A332

1964, June 27 **Engr.**
763 A332 4p orange & blk .40 .25

Issued in memory of Pope John XXIII.
Exists imperf. Value, pair $50.

University of Cordoba Arms — A333

Pigeons and UN Building, NYC — A334

1964, Aug. 22 Litho. Wmk. 90
764 A333 4p blk, ultra & yel .30 .25

350th anniv. of the University of Cordoba.

1964, Oct. 24 ***Perf. 13½***
765 A334 4p dk blue & lt blue .35 .25

Issued for United Nations Day.
Exists imperf. Value, pair $40.

Joaquin V. Gonzalez A335

Julio Argentino Roca A336

1964, Nov. 14 **Photo.**
766 A335 4p dk rose carmine .35 .25

Centenary (in 1963) of the birth of Joaquin V. Gonzalez, writer.
Exists imperf. Value, pair $40.

1964, Dec. 12 ***Perf. 13½***
767 A336 4p violet blue .35 .25

General Julio A. Roca, (1843-1914), president of Argentina, (1880-86, 1898-1904).
Exists imperf. Value, pair $40.

Market at Montserrat Square, by Carlos Morel — A337

1964, Dec. 19 **Photo.**
768 A337 4p sepia .50 .25

19th century Argentine painter Carlos Morel.
Exists imperf. Value, pair $40.

Icebreaker General San Martin A338

2p, General Belgrano Base, Antarctica.

1965 ***Perf. 13½***
769 A338 2p dull purple .75 .30
770 A338 4p ultra 1.25 .40

Issued to publicize the natl. territory of Tierra del Fuego, Antarctic and South Atlantic Isles.
Issue dates: 4p, Feb. 27; 2p, June 5.
No. 769 exists imperf. Value, pair $50.

Girl with Piggy Bank — A339

1965, Apr. 3 **Litho.**
771 A339 4p red org & blk .35 .25

National Postal Savings Bank, 50th anniv.
Exists imperf. Value, pair $40.

Sun and Globe A340

1965, May 29
772 A340 4p blk, org & dl bl .35 .30
Nos. 772,C98-C99 (3) 2.30 1.15

International Quiet Sun Year, 1964-65.
Exists imperf. Value, pair $40.

Hussar of Pueyrredon Regiment — A340a

1965, June 5 Wmk. 90 *Perf. 13½*
773 A340a 8p dp ultra, blk & red .60 .25

Issued for Army Day. See Nos. 796, 838, 857, 893, 944, 958, 974, 1145.
Exists imperf. Value, pair $50.

Ricardo Rojas (1882-1957) A341

Portraits: No. 775, Ricardo Guiraldes (1886-1927). No. 776, Enrique Larreta (1873-1961). No. 777, Leopoldo Lugones (1874-1938). No. 778, Roberto J. Payro (1867-1928).

1965, June 26 Photo.

774 A341 8p brown	.40	.30
775 A341 8p brown	.40	.30
776 A341 8p brown	.40	.30
777 A341 8p brown	.40	.30
778 A341 8p brown	.40	.30
Nos. 774-778 (5)	2.00	1.50

Issued to honor Argentine writers. Printed se-tenant in sheets of 100 (10x10); 2 horizontal rows of each design with Guiraldes in top rows and Rojas in bottom rows.
Nos. imperf. Value, strip of 5, $250.

Hipolito Yrigoyen A342

1965, July 3 Litho.
779 A342 8p pink & black .35 .25

Hipolito Yrigoyen (1852-1933), president of Argentina 1916-22, 1928-30.

Children Looking Through Window A343

1965, July 24 Photo.
780 A343 8p salmon & blk .35 .25

International Seminar on Mental Health.
Exists imperf. Value, pair $40.

Child's Funerary Urn and 16th Century Map A344

1965, Aug. 7 Litho.
781 A344 8p lt grn, dk red, brn & ocher .35 .25

City of San Miguel de Tucuman, 400th anniv.
Exists imperf. Value, pair $40.

Cardinal Cagliero — A345

Dante Alighieri — A346

1965, Aug. 21 Photo.
782 A345 8p violet .35 .25

Juan Cardinal Cagliero (1839-1926), missionary to Argentina and Bishop of Magida. Exists imperf. Value, pair $40.

1965, Sept. 16 Wmk. 90 *Perf. 13½*
783 A346 8p light ultra .35 .25

Dante Alighieri (1265-1321), Italian poet. Exists imperf. Value, pair $40.

Clipper "Mimosa" and Map of Patagonia A347

1965, Sept. 25 Litho.
784 A347 8p red & black .50 .25

Centenary of Welsh colonization of Chubut, and the founding of the city of Rawson. Exists imperf. Value, pair $40.

Map of Buenos Aires, Cock and Compass Emblem of Federal Police A348

1965, Oct. 30 Photo. *Perf. 13½*
785 A348 8p carmine rose .40 .25

Issued for Federal Police Day. Exists imperf. Value, pair $40.

Child's Drawing of Children A349

1965, Nov. 6 Litho. Wmk. 90
786 A349 8p lt yel grn & blk .35 .25

Public education law, 81st anniversary. Exists imperf. Value, pair $40.

Church of St. Francis, Catamarca A350

Ruben Dario A351

1965, Dec. 8
787 A350 8p org yel & red brn .35 .25

Brother Mamerto de la Asuncion Esquiu, preacher, teacher and official of 1885 Provincial Constitutional Convention.

Litho. and Photo.

1965, Dec. 22 *Perf. 13½*
788 A351 15p bl vio, *gray* .40 .25

Ruben Dario (pen name of Felix Ruben Garcia Sarmiento, 1867-1916), Nicaraguan poet, newspaper correspondent and diplomat.
Exists imperf. Value, pair $40.

"The Orange Seller" A352

Pueyrredon Paintings: No. 790, "Stop at the Grocery Store." No. 791, "Landscape at San Fernando" (sailboats). No. 792, "Bathing Horses at River Plata."

1966, Jan. 29 Photo. *Perf. 13½*

789 A352 8p bluish green	.70	.50
790 A352 8p bluish green	.70	.50
791 A352 8p bluish green	.70	.50
792 A352 8p bluish green	.70	.50
a. Block of 4, #789-792 + 2 labels	5.00	5.00

Prilidiano Pueyrredon (1823-1870), painter.

Sun Yat-sen, Flags of Argentina and China — A353

1966, Mar. 12 Wmk. 90 *Perf. 13½*
793 A353 8p dk red brown .70 .30

Dr. Sun Yat-sen (1866-1925), founder of the Republic of China. Exists imperf. Value, pair $100.

Souvenir Sheet

Rivadavia Issue of 1864 — A354

Wmk. 90

1966, Apr. 20 Litho. *Imperf.*

794 A354 Sheet of 3	1.10	1.10
a. 4p gray & red brown	.25	.25
b. 5p gray & green	.25	.25
c. 8p gray & dark blue	.25	.25

2nd Rio de la Plata Stamp Show, Buenos Aires, Mar. 16-24. Exists with flags omitted (error). Value, $150.

People of Various Races and WHO Emblem A355

1966, Apr. 23 *Perf. 13½*
795 A355 8p brown & black .35 .25

Opening of the WHO Headquarters, Geneva. Exists imperf. Value, pair $40.

Soldier Type of 1965

Army Day: 8p, Cavalryman, Guemes Infernal Regiment.

1966, May 28 Litho.
796 A340a 8p multicolored .40 .30

Exists imperf. Value, pair $40.

Coat of Arms — A356

Arms: a, National. b, Buenos Aires. c, La Rioja. d, Catamarca. e, Cordoba. f, Corrientes. g, Chaco. h, Chubut. i, Entre Rios. j, Formosa. k, Jujuy. l, La Pampa. m, Federal Capital. n, Mendoza. o, Misiones. p, Neuquen. q, Salta. r, San Juan. s, San Luis. t, Santa Cruz. u, Santa Fe. v, Santiago del Estero. w, Tucuman. x, map of Rio Negro. y, Map of Tierra del Fuego, Antarctica, South Atlantic Islands.

1966, July 30 Wmk. 90 *Perf. 13½*

797 Sheet of 25	35.00	
a.-y. A356 10p black & multi	1.00	1.00

150th anniv. of Argentina's Declaration of Independence. Exists imperf. Value, sheet $2,000.

Three Crosses, Caritas Emblem A357

1966, Sept. 10 Litho. *Perf. 13½*
798 A357 10p ol grn, blk & lt bl .35 .25

Caritas, charity organization.

Hilario Ascasubi (1807-75) — A358

Portraits: No. 800, Estanislao del Campo (1834-80). No. 801, Miguel Cane (1851-1905). No. 802, Lucio V. Lopez (1848-94). No. 803, Rafael Obligado (1851-1920). No. 804, Luis Agote (1868-1954), M.D. No. 805, Juan B. Ambrosetti (1865-1917), naturalist and archaeologist. No. 806, Miguel Lillo (1862-1931), botanist and chemist. No. 807, Francisco P. Moreno (1852-1919), naturalist and paleontologist. No. 808, Francisco J. Muñiz (1795-1871), physician.

1966 Photo. Wmk. 90

799 A358 10p dk blue green	.40	.30
800 A358 10p dk blue green	.40	.30
801 A358 10p dk blue green	.40	.30
802 A358 10p dk blue green	.40	.30
803 A358 10p dk blue green	.40	.30
804 A358 10p deep violet	.40	.30
805 A358 10p deep violet	.40	.30
806 A358 10p deep violet	.40	.30
807 A358 10p deep violet	.40	.30
808 A358 10p deep violet	.40	.30
Nos. 799-808 (10)	4.00	3.00

Nos. 799-803 issued Sept. 17 to honor Argentine writers. Printed se-tenant in sheets of 100 (10x10); 2 horizontal rows of each portrait. Nos. 804-808 issued Oct. 22 to honor Argentine scientists; 2 horizontal rows of each portrait. Scientists set has value at upper left, frame line with rounded corners.

Anchor A359

1966, Oct. 8 Litho.
809 A359 4p multicolored .30 .25

Argentine merchant marine. Exists imperf. Value, pair $40.

Flags and Map of the Americas — A360

1966, Oct. 29 ***Perf. 13½***
810 A360 10p gray & multi .40 .25

7th Conference of American Armies.

Argentine National Bank — A361

1966, Nov. 5 **Photo.**
811 A361 10p brt blue green .35 .25

75th anniv. of the Argentine National Bank. Exists imperf. Value, pair $40.

La Salle Monument and College, Buenos Aires — A362

1966, Nov. 26 **Litho.** ***Perf. 13½***
812 A362 10p brown org & blk .35 .25

75th anniv. of the Colegio de la Salle, Buenos Aires, and to honor Saint Jean Baptiste de la Salle (1651-1719), educator. Exists imperf. Value, pair $125.

Map of Argentine Antarctica and Expedition Route — A363

1966, Dec. 10 **Wmk. 90**
813 A363 10p multicolored .60 .35

1965 Argentine Antarctic expedition, which planted the Argentine flag on the South Pole. Exists imperf. Value, pair $70.

See No. 851.

Juan Martin de Pueyrredon — A364

1966, Dec. 17 **Photo.** ***Perf. 13½***
814 A364 10p dull red brn .35 .25

Issued to honor Juan Martin de Pueyrredon (1777-1850), Governor of Cordoba and of the United Provinces of the River Plata.

Gen. Juan de Las Heras — A365

1966, Dec. 17 **Engr.**
815 A365 10p black .35 .25

Issued to honor Gen. Juan Gregorio de Las Heras (1780-1866), Peruvian field marshal and aide-de-camp to San Martin.

Inscribed "Republica Argentina" Types of 1955-61 and

Jose Hernandez — A366

Designs: 50p, Gen. Jose de San Martin. 90p, Guillermo Brown. 500p, Red deer in forest.

Two overall paper sizes for 6p, 50p (No. 827) and 90p:
I — 27x37½mm
II — 27x39mm

Perf. 13½
1965-68 **Wmk. 90** **Photo.**
817 A366 6p rose red, litho, I ('67) 1.50 .25
818 A366 6p rose red ('67), II 4.00 .25
819 A366 6p brn, 15x22mm ('68) .30 .25
823 A238a 43p dk car rose 7.00 .25
824 A238a 45p brn ('66) 4.25 .25
825 A238a 45p brn, litho ('67) 8.00 .25
826 A241 50p dk bl, 29x40mm 8.00 .40
827 A241 50p dk bl, 22x31½mm, I ('67) 4.75 .25
a. Paper II 2.25 .25
828 A366 90p ol bis, I ('67) 3.00 .25
a. Paper II 12.00 2.00

See Nos. 888, 891.

Trout Leaping in National Park — A366a

Engr.
829 A495 500p yellow grn ('66) 2.50 .30
829A A366a 1,000p vio bl ('68) 8.50 1.50
Nos. 817-829A (11) 51.80 4.20

The 500p and 1,000p remained on sale as 5p and 10p stamps after the 1970 currency exchange.

See Nos. 888, 891, 939, 941, 992, 1031, 1040, 1045-1047. For surcharge and overprints see Nos. 1077, O153-O158, O162.

Pre-Columbian Pottery — A367

1967, Feb. 18 **Litho.** ***Perf. 13½***
830 A367 10p multicolored .40 .25

20th anniv. of UNESCO. Exists imperf. Value, pair $40.

"The Meal" by Fernando Fader — A368

1967, Feb. 25 **Photo.** **Wmk. 90**
831 A368 10p red brown .35 .25

Issued in memory of the Argentine painter Fernando Fader (1882-1935). Exists imperf. Value, pair $40.

Col. Juana Azurduy de Padilla (1781-1862), Soldier — A369

Famous Argentine Women: No. 833, Juana Manuela Gorriti, writer. No. 834, Cecilia Grierson (1858-1934), physician. No. 835, Juana Paula Manso (1819-75), writer and educator. No. 836, Alfonsina Storni (1892-1938), writer and educator.

1967, May 13 **Photo.** ***Perf. 13½***
832 A369 6p dark brown .40 .25
833 A369 6p dark brown .40 .25
834 A369 6p dark brown .40 .25
835 A369 6p dark brown .40 .25
836 A369 6p dark brown .40 .25
Nos. 832-836 (5) 2.00 1.25

Printed se-tenant in sheets of 100 (10x10); 2 horizontal rows of each portrait.

Schooner "Invencible," 1811 — A370

1967, May 20 **Litho.**
837 A370 20p multicolored .70 .35

Issued for Navy Day. Exists imperf. Value, pair $50.

Soldier Type of 1965

Army Day: 20p, Highlander (Arribeños Corps).

1967, May 27
838 A340a 20p multicolored .60 .30

Exists imperf. Value, pair $50.

Souvenir Sheet

Manuel Belgrano and José Artigas — A371

1967, June 22 ***Imperf.***
839 A371 Sheet of 2 .50 .50
a. 6p gray & brown .25 .25
b. 22p brown & gray .25 .25

Third Rio de la Plata Stamp Show, Montevideo, Uruguay, June 18-25.

Peace Dove and Valise — A372

PADELAI Emblem — A373

1967, Aug. 5 **Litho.** ***Perf. 13½***
840 A372 20p multicolored .35 .25

Issued for International Tourist Year 1967.

1967, Aug. 12 **Litho.**
841 A373 20p multicolored .35 .25

75th anniv. of the Children's Welfare Association (Patronato de la Infancia-PADELAI).

Stagecoach and Modern City — A374

1967, Sept. 23 **Wmk. 90** ***Perf. 13½***
842 A374 20p rose, yel & blk .35 .25

Centenary of Villa Maria, Cordoba.

San Martin by Ibarra — A375

"Battle of Chacabuco" by P. Subercaseaux — A376

1967, Sept. 30 **Litho.**
843 A375 20p blk brn & pale yel .45 .25

Engr.
844 A376 40p blue black .85 .30

Battle of Chacabuco, 150th anniversary.

Exhibition Rooms — A377

1967, Oct. 11 **Photo.**
845 A377 20p blue gray .35 .25

Government House Museum, 10th anniv.

Pedro L. Zanni, Fokker and 1924 Flight Route A378

1967, Oct. 21 **Litho.** ***Perf. 13½***
846 A378 20p multicolored .40 .25

Issued for Aviation Week and to commemorate the 1924 flight of the Fokker seaplane "Province of Buenos Aires" from Amsterdam, Netherlands, to Osaka, Japan.

Training Ship General Brown, by Emilio Biggeri A379

1967, Oct. 28 **Wmk. 90**
847 A379 20p multicolored .70 .35

Issued to honor the Military Naval School.

Ovidio Lagos and Front Page — A380

1967, Nov. 11 **Photo.**
848 A380 20p sepia .35 .25

Centenary of La Capital, Rosario newspaper. Imperf pair $40.

St. Barbara A381

1967, Dec. 2 ***Perf. 13½***
849 A381 20p rose red .35 .25

St. Barbara, patron saint of artillerymen.

Portrait of his Wife, by Eduardo Sivori — A382

1968, Jan. 27 **Photo.** ***Perf. 13½***
850 A382 20p blue green .35 .25

Eduardo Sivori (1847-1918), painter.

Antarctic Type of 1966 and

Admiral Brown Scientific Station A383

Planes over Map of Antarctica — A384

6p, Map showing radio-postal stations 1966-67.

1968, Feb. 17 **Litho.** **Wmk. 90**
851 A363 6p multicolored .75 .30
852 A383 20p multicolored .85 .40
853 A384 40p multicolored 1.50 .60
Nos. 851-853 (3) 3.10 1.30

Issued to publicize Argentine research projects in Argentine Antarctica.

The Annunciation, by Leonardo da Vinci — A385

Man in Wheelchair and Factory — A386

1968, Mar. 23 **Photo.** ***Perf. 13½***
854 A385 20p lilac rose .35 .25

Issued for the Day of the Army Communications System and its patron saint, Gabriel. Exists imperf. Value, pair $40.

1968, Mar. 23 **Litho.**
855 A386 20p green & black .35 .25

Day of Rehabilitation of the Handicapped.

Children and WHO Emblem — A387

1968, May 11 **Wmk. 90** ***Perf. 13½***
856 A387 20p dk vio bl & ver .35 .25

20th anniv. of WHO.

Soldier Type of 1965

Army Day: 20p, Uniform of First Artillery Regiment "General Iriarte."

1968, June 8 **Litho.**
857 A340a 20p multicolored .60 .30

Frigate "Libertad," Painting by Emilio Biggeri — A388

1968, June 15 **Wmk. 90**
858 A388 20p multicolored .75 .30

Issued for Navy Day. Exists imperf. Value, pair $40.

Guillermo Rawson and Old Hospital A389

1968, July 20 **Photo.** ***Perf. 13½***
859 A389 6p olive bister .35 .25

Cent. of Rawson Hospital, Buenos Aires.

Student Directing Traffic for Schoolmates A390

1968, Aug. 10 **Litho.** ***Perf. 13½***
860 A390 20p lt bl, blk, buff & car .40 .25

Traffic safety and education.

O'Higgins Joining San Martin at Battle of Maipu, by P. Subercaseaux — A391

1968, Aug. 15 **Engr.**
861 A391 40p bluish black .65 .30

Sesquicentennial of the Battle of Maipu.

Osvaldo Magnasco (1864-1920), Lawyer, Professor of Law and Minister of Justice — A392

1968, Sept. 7 **Photo.** ***Perf. 13½***
862 A392 20p brown .40 .25

Grandmother's Birthday, by Patricia Lynch — A393

The Sea, by Edgardo Gomez — A394

1968, Sept. 21 **Litho.**
863 A393 20p multicolored .35 .25
864 A394 20p multicolored .35 .25

The designs were chosen in a competition among kindergarten and elementary school children.

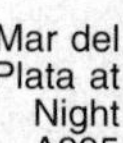

Mar del Plata at Night A395

1968, Oct. 19 **Litho.** ***Perf. 13½***
865 A395 20p black, ocher & bl .35 .25
Nos. 865,C113-C114 (3) 2.35 1.05

4th Plenary Assembly of the Intl. Telegraph and Telephone Consultative Committee, Mar del Plata, Sept. 23-Oct. 25.

Frontier Gendarme A396

Patrol Boat A397

1968, Oct. 26
866 A396 20p multicolored .50 .25
867 A397 20p blue, vio bl & blk .50 .25

No. 866 honors the Gendarmery; No. 867 the Coast Guard.

Aaron de Anchorena and Pampero Balloon A398

1968, Nov. 2 **Photo.**
868 A398 20p blue & multi .40 .25

22nd Aeronautics and Space Week.

St. Martin of Tours, by Alfredo Guido — A399

1968, Nov. 9 **Litho.**
869 A399 20p lilac & dk brn .35 .25

St. Martin of Tours, patron saint of Buenos Aires.

Municipal Bank Emblem A400

1968, Nov. 16

870 A400 20p multicolored .35 .25

Buenos Aires Municipal Bank, 90th anniv.

Anniversary Emblem A401

1968, Dec. 14 Wmk. 90 ***Perf. 13½***

871 A401 20p car rose & dk grn .35 .25

ALPI (Fight Against Polio Assoc.), 25th anniv.

Shovel and State Coal Fields Emblem — A402

Pouring Ladle and Army Manufacturing Emblem — A403

1968, Dec. 21 **Litho.**

872 A402 20p orange, bl & blk .35 .25
873 A403 20p dl vio, dl yel & blk .35 .25

Issued to publicize the National Coal and Steel industry at the Rio Turbio coal fields and the Zapla blast furnaces.

Woman Potter, by Ramon Gomez Cornet — A404

1968, Dec. 21 Photo. ***Perf. 13½***

874 A404 20p carmine rose .50 .40

Centenary of the Witcomb Gallery.

View of Buenos Aires and Rio de la Plata by Ulrico Schmidl A405

1969, Feb. 8 Litho. Wmk. 90

875 A405 20p yellow, blk & ver .50 .35

Ulrico Schmidl (c. 1462-1554) who wrote "Journey to the Rio de la Plata and Paraguay."

Types of 1955-67

Designs: 50c, Puma. 1p, Sunflower. 3p, Zapata Slope, Catamarca. 5p, Tierra del Fuego. 6p, José Hernandez. 10p, Inca Bridge, Mendoza. 50p, José de San Martin. 90p, Guillermo Brown. 100p, Ski jumper.

Photo.; Litho. (50c, 3p, 10p)

1969-70 Wmk. 365 ***Perf. 13½***

882 A275 50c bister ('70) 1.25 .60
883 A277 5p brown 1.40 .90
884 A279 100p blue 26.00 8.00

Unwmk.

885 A278 1p brown ('70) .40 .25
886 A277 3p dk blue ('70) .65 .25
a. Wmk. 90 10.00 3.00
887 A277 5p brown ('70) .75 .25
888 A366 6p red brn, 15x22mm ('70) .90 .25
889 A278 10p dull red ('70) .50 .25
a. Wmk. 90 475.00 60.00
890 A241 50p dk bl, 22x31½mm ('70) 1.25 .25
891 A366 90p ol brn, 22x32mm ('70) 3.50 .50
892 A279 100p blue ('70) 11.00 1.00
Nos. 882-892 (11) 47.60 12.50

For surcharges see Nos. 1076-1077.

Soldier Type of 1965

Army Day: 20p, Sapper (gastador) of Buenos Aires Province, 1856.

Wmk. 365

1969, May 31 Litho. ***Perf. 13½***

893 A340a 20p multicolored .85 .35

Frigate Hercules, by Emilio Biggeri — A406

1969, May 31

894 A406 20p multicolored .75 .30

Issued for Navy Day.

"All Men are Equal" — A407

ILO Emblem — A408

1969, June 28 Wmk. 90

895 A407 20p black & ocher .35 .25

International Human Rights Year.

1969, June 28 Litho. Wmk. 365

896 A408 20p lt green & multi .35 .25

50th anniv. of the ILO. Exists imperf. Value, pair $100.

Pedro N. Arata (1849-1922), Chemist — A409

Radar Antenna, Balcarce Station and Satellite — A410

Portraits: No. 898, Miguel Fernandez (1883-1950), zoologist. No. 899, Angel P. Gallardo (1867-1934), biologist. No. 900, Cristobal M. Hicken (1875-1933), botanist. No. 901, Eduardo Ladislao Holmberg, M.D. (1852-1937), natural scientist.

1969, Aug. 9 Wmk. 365 ***Perf. 13½***

897 A409 6p Arata .45 .30
898 A409 6p Fernandez .45 .30
899 A409 6p Gallardo .45 .30
900 A409 6p Hicken .45 .30
901 A409 6p Holmberg .45 .30
Nos. 897-901 (5) 2.25 1.50

Argentine scientists. See No. 778 note.

1969, Aug. 23 Wmk. 99

902 A410 20p yellow & blk .40 .25

Communications by satellite through Intl. Telecommunications Satellite Consortium (INTELSAT). Exists imperf. Value, pair $40.

See No. C115.

Nieuport 28, Flight Route and Map of Buenos Aires Province A411

1969, Sept. 13 Litho. Wmk. 90

903 A411 20p multicolored .50 .25

50th anniv. of the first Argentine airmail service from El Palomar to Mar del Plata, flown Feb. 23-24, 1919, by Capt. Pedro L. Zanni.

Military College Gate and Emblem A412

1969, Oct. 4 Wmk. 365 ***Perf. 13½***

904 A412 20p multicolored .35 .25

Cent. of the National Military College, El Palomar (Greater Buenos Aires).

Gen. Angel Pacheco — A413

1969, Nov. 8 Photo. Wmk. 365

905 A413 20p deep green .35 .25

Gen. Angel Pacheco (1795-1869).

La Farola, Logotype of La Prensa — A414

Design: No. 907, Bartolomé Mitre & La Nacion logotype.

1969, Nov. 8 Litho. ***Perf. 13½***

906 A414 20p orange, yel & blk .70 .30
907 A414 20p brt green & blk .70 .30

Cent. of newspapers La Prensa and La Nacion.

Julian Aguirre — A415

Musicians: No. 909, Felipe Boero. No. 910, Constantino Gaito. No. 911, Carlos Lopez Buchardo. No. 912, Alberto Williams.

Wmk. 365

1969, Dec. 6 Photo. ***Perf. 13½***

908 A415 6p Aguirre .50 .30
909 A415 6p Boero .50 .30
910 A415 6p Gaito .50 .30
911 A415 6p Buchardo .50 .30
912 A415 6p Williams .50 .30
Nos. 908-912 (5) 2.50 1.50

Argentine musicians. See No. 778 note.

Lt. Benjamin Matienzo and Nieuport Plane — A416

1969, Dec. 13 Litho.

913 A416 20p multicolored .70 .35

23rd Aeronautics and Space Week.

High Power Lines and Map A417

Design: 20p, Map of Santa Fe Province and schematic view of tunnel.

1969, Dec. 13

914 A417 6p multicolored .50 .25
915 A417 20p multicolored 1.00 .25

Completion of development projects: 6p for the hydroelectric dams on the Limay and Neuquen Rivers, the 20p the tunnel under Rio Grande from Sante Fe to Parana. Set exists imperf.©

Lions Emblem A418

1969, Dec. 20 Wmk. 365 ***Perf. 13½***

916 A418 20p black, emer & org .70 .25

Argentine Lions Intl. Club, 50th anniv.

Madonna and Child, by Raul Soldi — A419

1969, Dec. 27 Litho.

917 A419 20p multicolored .70 .30

Christmas 1969.

Manuel Belgrano, by Jean Gericault A420

The Creation of the Flag, Bas-relief by Jose Fioravanti — A421

Perf. 13½

1970, July 4 Unwmk. Photo.

918 A420 20c deep brown .40 .25

Litho. *Perf. 12½*

919 A421 50c bister, blk & bl .85 .50

Gen. Manuel Belgrano (1770-1820), Argentine patriot.

San Jose Palace A422

1970, Aug. 9 Litho. *Perf. 13½*

920 A422 20c yellow grn & multi .40 .25

Gen. Justo Jose de Urquiza (1801-70), pres. of Argentina, 1854-60.

Schooner "Juliet" — A423

1970, Aug. 8 Unwmk.

921 A423 20c multicolored .75 .40

Issued for Navy Day.

Receiver of 1920 and Waves A424

1970, Aug. 29

922 A424 20c lt blue & multi .50 .30

50th anniv. of Argentine broadcasting.

Types of 1955-67 Inscribed "Republica Argentina" and

Belgrano A425

Lujan Basilica A426

Designs: 1c, Sunflower. 3c, Zapata Slope, Catamarca. 5c, Tierra del Fuego. 8c, No. 931, Belgrano. 10c, Inca Bridge, Mendoza. 25c, 50c, 70c, Jose de San Martin. 65c, 90c, 1.20p, San Martin. 1p, Ski jumper. 1.15p, 1.80p, Adm. Brown.

1970-73 Photo. Unwmk. *Perf. 13½*

923	A278	1c	dk green ('71)	.25	.25
924	A277	3c	car rose ('71)	.25	.25
925	A277	5c	blue ('71)	.25	.25
926	A425	6c	deep blue	.25	.25
927	A425	8c	green ('72)	.25	.25
928	A278	10c	dull red ('71)	.40	.25
929	A278	10c	brn, litho. ('71)	.60	.25
930	A278	10c	org brn ('72)	.45	.25
931	A425	10c	brown ('73)	.25	.25
932	A426	18c	yel & dk brn, litho ('73)	.25	.25
933	A425	25c	brown ('71)	.50	.25
934	A425	50c	scarlet ('72)	.90	.25
935	A241	65c	brn, 22x31½mm, paper II ('71)	1.25	.25
936	A425	70c	dk blue ('73)	.30	.25
937	A241	90c	emer, 22x31½mm ('72)	3.25	.25
938	A279	1p	brn, 22½x29½mm ('71)	4.00	.25
939	A366	1.15p	dk bl, 22½x32mm ('71)	1.50	.25
940	A241	1.20p	org, 22x31½mm ('73)	1.25	.25
941	A366	1.80p	brown ('73)	.65	.25
			Nos. 923-941 (19)	16.80	4.75

The imprint "Casa de Moneda de la Nacion" (in capitals) appears on 3c, 5c, Nos. 928-929; 65c, 90c, 1p, 1.20p.

On type A425 only the 6c is inscribed "Ley 18.188" below denomination.

Fluorescent paper was used in printing the 25c, 50c, and 70c. The 3c, 5c, 8c, No. 931 and 65c were issued on both ordinary and fluorescent paper.

See Nos. 987-996, 1032-1038, 1042-1043, 1089-1107. For overprint and surcharge see Nos. 1010, 1078.

Soldier Type of 1965

Galloping messenger of Field Army, 1879.

1970, Oct. 17 Litho. *Perf. 13½*

944 A340a 20c multicolored .80 .30

Dome of Cathedral of Cordoba A430

1970, Nov. 7 Unwmk.

945 A430 50c gray & blk 1.00 .40

Bishopric of Tucuman, 400th anniv. See No. C131.

People Around UN Emblem A431

1970, Nov. 7

946 A431 20c tan & multi .40 .30

25th anniversary of the United Nations.

State Mint and Medal A432

1970, Nov. 28 Unwmk. *Perf. 13½*

947 A432 20c gold, grn & blk .40 .30

Inauguration of the State Mint Building, 25th anniversary.

St. John Bosco and Dean Funes College A433

1970, Dec. 19 Litho.

948 A433 20c olive & blk .40 .30

Honoring the work of the Salesian Order in Patagonia.

Nativity, by Horacio Gramajo Gutierrez — A434

1970, Dec. 19

949 A434 20c multicolored .55 .35

Christmas 1970.

Argentine Flag, Map of Argentine Antarctica A435

1971, Feb. 20 Litho. *Perf. 13½*

950 A435 20c multicolored 1.25 .50

Argentine South Pole Expedition, 5th anniv.

Phosphorescent Sorting Code and Albert Einstein — A436

1971, Apr. 30 Unwmk. *Perf. 13½*

951 A436 25c multicolored .50 .30

Electronics in postal development.

Symbolic Road Crossing A437

1971, May 29 Litho.

952 A437 25c blue & blk .50 .25

Inter-American Regional Meeting of the Intl. Federation of Roads, Buenos Aires, 3/28-31.

Elias Alippi — A438

Actors: No. 954, Juan Aurelio Casacuberta. No. 955, Angelina Pagano. No. 956, Roberto Casaux. No. 957, Florencio Parravicini. See No. 778 note.

1971, May 29 Litho.

953	A438	15c	Alippi	.50	.30
954	A438	15c	Casacuberta	.50	.30
955	A438	15c	Pagano	.50	.30
956	A438	15c	Casaux	.50	.30
957	A438	15c	Parravicini	.50	.30
			Nos. 953-957 (5)	2.50	1.50

Soldier Type of 1965

Army Day, May 29: Artilleryman, 1826.

1971, July 3 Unwmk. *Perf. 13½*

958 A340a 25c multicolored 1.25 .50

Bilander "Carmen," by Emilio Biggeri — A439

1971, July 3

959 A439 25c multicolored 1.25 .40

Navy Day

Peruvian Order of the Sun A440

1971, Aug. 28

960 A440 31c multicolored .60 .30

Sesquicentennial of Peru's independence.

Güemes in Battle, by Lorenzo Gigli A441

Design: No. 962, Death of Güemes, by Antonio Alice.

1971, Aug. 28 Size: 39x29mm

961 A441 25c multicolored .50 .30

Size: 84x29mm

962 A441 25c multicolored 1.00 .40

Sesquicentennial of the death of Martin Miguel de Güemes, leader in Gaucho War,

Governor and Captain General of Salta Province.

Stylized Tulip — A442

1971, Sept. 18
963 A442 25c tan & multi .50 .30

3rd Intl. and 8th Natl. Horticultural Exhib.

Father Antonio Saenz, by Juan Gut — A443

1971, Sept. 18
964 A433 25c gray & multi .40 .30

Sesquicentennial of University of Buenos Aires, and to honor Father Antonio Saenz, first Chancellor and Rector.

Fabricaciones Militares Emblem — A444

1971, Oct. 16 Unwmk. *Perf. 13½*
965 A444 25c brn, gold, bl & blk .35 .25

30th anniv. of military armament works.

Cars and Trucks A445

Design: 65c, Tree converted into paper.

1971, Oct. 16
966 A445 25c dull bl & multi .50 .25
967 A445 65c green & multi 1.25 .50
Nos. 966-967,C134 (3) 2.55 1.05

Nationalized industries.

Luis C. Candelaria and his Plane, 1918 — A446

1971, Nov. 27
968 A446 25c multicolored .50 .30

25th Aeronautics and Space Week.

Observatory and Nebula of Magellan — A447

1971, Nov. 27
969 A447 25c multicolored .75 .25

Cordoba Astronomical Observatory, cent.

Christ in Majesty A448

1971, Dec. 18 Litho.
970 A448 25c blk & multi .50 .30

Christmas 1971. Design is from a tapestry by Horacio Butler in Basilica of St. Francis, Buenos Aires.

Mother and Child, by J. C. Castagnino A449

1972, May 6 Unwmk. *Perf. 13½*
971 A449 25c fawn & black .40 .25

25th anniv. (in 1971) of UNICEF.

Mailman's Bag — A450

1972, Sept. 2 Litho. *Perf. 13½*
972 A450 25c lemon & multi .40 .25

Bicentenary of appointment of first Argentine mailman.

Adm. Brown Station, Map of Antarctica — A451

1972, Sept. 2
973 A451 25c blue & multi .75 .40

10th anniv. (in 1971) of Antarctic Treaty.

Soldier Type of 1965

Army Day: 25c, Sergeant, Negro and Mulatto Corps, 1806-1807.

1972, Sept. 23
974 A340a 25c multicolored .75 .35

Brigantine "Santisima Trinidad" — A452

1972, Sept. 23
975 A452 25c multicolored .75 .35

Navy Day. See No. 1006.

A453

1972, Sept. 30 Litho. *Perf. 13½*
976 A453 45c Oil pump .90 .40

50th anniv. of the organ. of the state oil fields (Yacimientos Petroliferos Fiscales).

A454

1972, Sept. 30
977 A454 25c Sounding balloon .40 .25

Cent. of Natl. Meteorological Service.

Trees and Globe — A455

1972, Oct. 14 *Perf. 13x13½*
978 A455 25c bl, blk & lt bl .60 .30

7th World Forestry Congress, Buenos Aires, Oct. 4-18.

Arms of Naval School, Frigate "Presidente Sarmiento" — A456

1972, Oct. 14
979 A456 25c gold & multi .70 .40

Centenary of Military Naval School.

Early Balloon and Plane, Antonio de Marchi — A457

1972, Nov. 4 *Perf. 13½*
980 A457 25c multicolored .60 .30

Aeronautics and Space Week, and in honor of Baron Antonio de Marchi (1875-1934), aviation pioneer.

Bartolomé Mitre — A458

1972, Nov. 4 Engr.
981 A458 25c dark blue .50 .30

Pres. Bartolome Mitre (1821-1906), writer, historian, soldier.

Flower and Heart — A459

1972, Dec. 2 Litho. *Perf. 13½*
982 A459 90c lt bl, ultra & blk .60 .35

"Your heart is your health," World Health Day.

"Martin Fierro," by Juan C. Castagnino A460

"Spirit of the Gaucho," by Vicente Forte — A461

1972, Dec. 2 Litho. *Perf. 13½*
983 A460 50c multicolored .40 .25
984 A461 90c multicolored .65 .35

Intl. Book Year 1972, and cent. of publication of the poem, Martin Fierro, by Jose Hernandez (1834-86).

Iguacu Falls and Tourist Year Emblem — A462

1972, Dec. 16 ***Perf. 13x13½***
985 A462 45c multicolored .40 .25

Tourism Year of the Americas.

King, Wood Carving, 18th Century A463

1972, Dec. 16 ***Perf. 13½***
986 A463 50c multicolored .60 .30

Christmas 1972.

Types of 1955-73 Inscribed "Republica Argentina" and

Moon Valley, San Juan Province — A463a

Designs: 1c, Sunflower. 5c, Tierra del Fuego. 10c, Inca Bridge, Mendoza. 50c, Lujan Basilica. 65c, 22.50p, San Martin. 1p, Ski jumper. 1.15p, 4.50p, Guillermo Brown. 1.80p, Manuel Belgrano.

Litho.; Photo. (1c, 65c, 1p)
Perf. 13½, 12½ (1.80p)

1972-75			**Wmk. 365**	
987	A278	1c dk green	.25	.25
988	A277	5c dark blue	.25	.25
989	A278	10c bister brn	.25	.25
989A	A426	50c dull pur ('75)	.30	.25
990	A241	65c gray brown	3.25	.25
991	A279	1p brown	4.00	.25
992	A366	1.15p dk gray bl	1.50	.50
993	A425	1.80p blue ('75)	.30	.25
994	A366	4.50p green ('75)	.70	.25
995	A241	22.50p vio bl ('75)	1.50	.40
996	A463a	50p multi ('75)	3.00	.30
		Nos. 987-996 (11)	15.30	3.20

Paper size of 1c is 27½x39mm; others of 1972, 37x27, 27x37mm.
Size of 22.50p, 50p: 26½x38½mm.
See Nos. 1050, 1108.

Cock (Symbolic of Police) — A464

1973, Feb. 3 **Litho.** **Unwmk.**
997 A464 50c lt green & multi .35 .25

Sesqui. of Federal Police of Argentina.

First Coin of Bank of Buenos Aires — A465

1973, Feb. 3 ***Perf. 13½***
998 A465 50c purple, yel & brn .40 .30

Sesquicentennial of the Bank of Buenos Aires Province.

DC-3 Planes Over Antarctica — A466

1973, Apr. 28 **Litho.** ***Perf. 13½***
999 A466 50c lt blue & multi 1.00 .50

10th anniversary of Argentina's first flight to the South Pole.

Rivadavia's Chair, Argentine Arms and Colors — A467

1973, May 19 **Litho.** ***Perf. 13½***
1000 A467 50c multicolored .35 .25

Inauguration of Pres. Hector J. Campora, May 25, 1973.

San Martin, by Gil de Castro — A468

San Martin and Bolivar A469

1973, July 7 **Litho.** ***Perf. 13½***
1001 A468 50c lt green & multi .35 .25
1002 A469 50c yellow & multi .35 .30

Gen. San Martin's farewell to the people of Peru and his meeting with Simon Bolivar at Guayaquil July 26-27, 1822.

Eva Peron A470

1973, July 26 **Litho.** ***Perf. 13½***
1003 A470 70c black, org & bl .40 .30

Maria Eva Duarte de Peron (1919-1952), political leader.

House of Viceroy Sobremonte, by Hortensia de Virgilion — A471

1973, July 28 ***Perf. 13x13½***
1004 A471 50c blue & multi .35 .25

400th anniversary of the city of Cordoba.

Woman, by Lino Spilimbergo A472

1973, Aug. 28 **Litho.** ***Perf. 13½***
1005 A472 70c multicolored .70 .50

Philatelists' Day. See Nos. B60-B61.

Ship Type of 1972

Navy Day: 70c, Frigate "La Argentina."

1973, Oct. 27 **Litho.** ***Perf. 13½***
1006 A452 70c multicolored .70 .35

New and Old Telephones — A473

1973, Oct. 27
1007 A473 70c brt blue & multi .40 .25

Natl. telecommunications system, 25th anniv.

Plume Made of Flags of Participants A474

1973, Nov. 3 ***Perf. 13½***
1008 A474 70c yellow bis & multi .35 .25

12th Cong. of Latin Notaries, Buenos Aires.

No. 940 Overprinted

1973, Nov. 30 **Photo.**
1010 A241 1.20p orange .85 .30

Assumption of presidency by Juan Peron, Oct. 12.

Virgin and Child, Window, La Plata Cathedral A476

Christmas: 1.20p, Nativity, by Bruno Venier, b. 1914.

1973, Dec. 15 **Litho.** ***Perf. 13½***
1011 A476 70c gray & multi .40 .30
1012 A476 1.20p black & multi .80 .40

The Lama, by Juan Battle Planas — A477

Paintings: 50c, Houses in Boca District, by Eugenio Daneri, horiz. 90c, The Blue Grotto, by Emilio Pettoruti, horiz.

1974, Feb. 9 **Litho.** ***Perf. 13½***
1013 A477 50c multicolored .50 .25
1014 A477 70c multicolored .50 .30
1015 A477 90c multicolored .60 .30
Nos. 1013-1015,B64 (4) 1.95 1.10

Argentine painters.

Mar del Plata A478

1974, Feb. 9
1016 A478 70c multicolored .35 .25

Centenary of Mar del Plata.

Weather Symbols — A479

1974, Mar. 23 **Litho.** ***Perf. 13½***
1017 A479 1.20p multicolored .35 .25

Cent. of intl. meteorological cooperation.

Justo Santa Maria de Oro — A480

1974, Mar. 23

1018 A480 70c multicolored .35 .25

Bicentenary of the birth of Brother Justo Santa Maria de Oro (1772-1836), theologian, patriot, first Argentine bishop.

Belisario Roldan (1873-1922), Writer — A481

1974, June 29 Photo. Unwmk.

1019 A481 70c bl & brn .35 .25

Poster with Names of OAS Members — A482

1974, June 29 Litho.

1020 A482 1.38p multicolored .35 .25

Organization of American States, 25th anniv.

ENCOTEL Emblem — A483

1974, Aug. 10 Litho. *Perf. 13*

1021 A483 1.20p blue, gold & blk .50 .25

ENCOTEL, Natl. Post and Telegraph Press.

Flags of Argentina, Bolivia, Brazil, Paraguay, Uruguay A484

1974, Aug. 16 *Perf. 13½*

1022 A484 1.38p multicolored .35 .25

6th Meeting of Foreign Ministers of Rio de la Plata Basin Countries.

El Chocon Hydroelectric Complex, Limay River — A485

Somisa Steel Mill, San Nicolas A486

Gen. Belgrano Bridge, Chaco-Corrientes — A487

Perf. 13½, 13x13½ (4.50p)

1974, Sept. 14

1023 A485 70c multicolored .50 .25

1024 A486 1.20p multicolored .60 .30

1025 A487 4.50p multicolored 1.25 .60

Nos. 1023-1025 (3) 2.35 1.15

Development projects.

Brigantine Belgrano, by Emilio Biggeri — A488

1974, Oct. 26 Litho. *Perf. 13½*

1026 A488 1.20p multicolored .75 .35

Departure into exile in Chile of General San Martin, Sept. 22, 1822.

Alberto R. Mascias and Bleriot Plane — A489

1974, Oct. 26 Unwmk.

1027 A489 1.20p multicolored .60 .35

a. Wmk 365 — —

Air Force Day, Aug. 10, and to honor Alberto Roque Garcias (1878-1951), aviation pioneer.

Hussar, 1812, by Eleodoro Marenco A490

1974, Oct. 26

1028 A490 1.20p multicolored .60 .30

Army Day.

Post Horn and Flags A491

1974, Nov. 23 Unwmk. *Perf. 13½*

1029 A491 2.65p multicolored .70 .35

a. Wmk 365 *50.00 10.00*

Centenary of Universal Postal Union.

Franciscan Monastery — A492

1974, Nov. 23 Litho.

1030 A492 1.20p multicolored .40 .25

400th anniversary, city of Santa Fe.

Trout Type of 1968

1974 Engr. Unwmk.

1031 A366a 1000p vio bl 4.00 .80

Due to a shortage of 10p stamps a quantity of this 1,000p was released for use as 10p.

Types of 1954-73 Inscribed "Republica Argentina" and

Red Deer in Forest — A495

Congress Building — A497

Designs: 30c, 60c, 1.80p, Manuel Belgrano. 50c, Lujan Basilica. 1.20p, 2p, 6p, San Martin (16x22½mm). 2.70p, 7.50p, 22.50p, San Martin (22x31½mm). 4.50p, 13.50p, Guillermo Brown. 10p, Leaping trout.

1974-76 Unwmk. Photo. *Perf. 13½*

1032 A425 30c brown vio .30 .25

1033 A426 50c blk & brn red .30 .25

1034 A426 50c bister & bl .25 .25

1035 A425 60c ocher .30 .25

1036 A425 1.20p red .30 .25

1037 A425 1.80p deep blue .30 .25

1038 A425 2p dark purple .40 .30

1039 A241 2.70p dk bl, 22x31½mm .50 .40

1040 A366 4.50p green 1.50 .50

1041 A495 5p yel green .40 .25

1042 A425 6p red orange .30 .25

1043 A425 6p emerald .40 .25

1044 A241 7.50p grn, 22x31½mm 1.00 .25

1045 A366a 10p violet blue 2.00 .25

1046 A366 13.50p scar, 16x22½mm .85 .25

1047 A366 13.50p scar, 22x31½mm 1.50 .40

1048 A241 22.50p dp bl, 22x31½mm 1.00 .30

1049 A497 30p yel & dk red brn 3.50 .25

1050 A463a 50p multicolored 2.00 .25

Nos. 1032-1050 (19) 17.10 5.40

Issued: 10p, 5/74; 30c, 1.20p, 2.70p, 5/15/74; 5p, 11/20/74; 30p, 12/10/74; 2p, 3/1/75; 60c, 7.50p, 4/30/75; 4.50p, 7/21/75; 1.80p, Nos. 1042, 1047, 22.50p, 8/14/75; No. 1046, 10/10/75; No. 1034, 10/30/75; No. 1043, 11/6/75; 50p, 2/76.

Fluorescent paper was used in printing No. 1036, 2p, Nos. 1044 and 1047. The 30p was issued on both ordinary and fluorescent paper.

See No. 829. For type of A495 overprinted see No. 1144.

Miniature Sheet

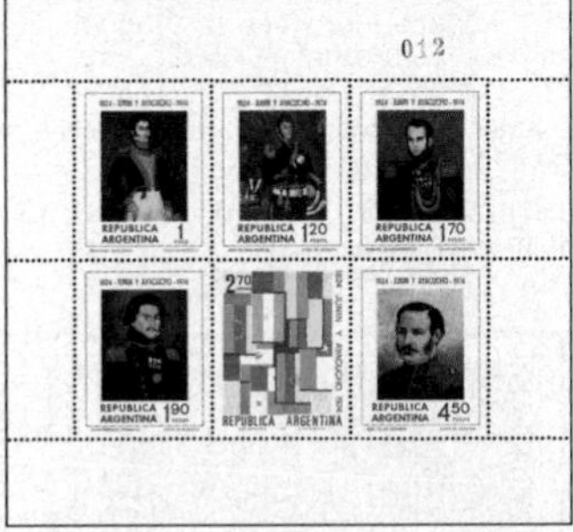

A498

1974, Dec. 7 Litho. *Perf. 13½*

1052 A498 Sheet of 6 3.50 2.75

a. 1p Mariano Necochea .25 .25

b. 1.20p Jose de San Martin .25 .25

c. 1.70p Manuel Isidoro Suarez .35 .25

d. 1.90p Juan Pascual Pringles .40 .30

e. 2.70p Latin American flags .65 .35

f. 4.50p Jose Felix Bogado 1.10 .50

Sesqui. of Battles of Junin and Ayacucho.

Dove, by Vito Campanella — A499

St. Anne, by Raul Soldi — A500

1974, Dec. 21 Litho. *Perf. 13½*

1053 A499 1.20p multicolored .70 .25

1054 A500 2.65p multicolored .80 .30

Christmas 1974.

Boy Looking at Stamp — A501

1974, Dec. 21

1055 A501 1.70p black & yel .40 .25

World Youth Philately Year.

Space Monsters, by Raquel Forner — A502

Argentine modern art: 4.50p, Dream, by Emilio Centurion.

1975, Feb. 22 Litho. *Perf. 13½*

1056 A502 2.70p multi .90 .30
1057 A502 4.50p multi 1.75 .40

Indian Woman and Cathedral, Catamarca — A503

Tourist Publicity: No. 1059, Carved chancel and street scene. No. 1060, Logging operations and monastery yard. No. 1061, Painted pottery and power station. No. 1062, Farm cart and colonial mansion. No. 1063, Perito Moreno glacier and spinning mill. No. 1064, Lake Lapataia and scientific surveyor. No. 1065, Los Alerces National Park and oil derrick.

1975 Litho. *Perf. 13½*
Unwmk., Wmk 365 (6p)

1058 A503 1.20p shown .35 .25
1059 A503 1.20p Jujuy .35 .25
1060 A503 1.20p Salta .35 .25
1061 A503 1.20p Santiago del Estero .35 .25
1062 A503 1.20p Tucuman .35 .25
1063 A503 6p Santa Cruz .50 .25
1064 A503 6p Tierra del Fuego .50 .25
1065 A503 6p Chubut .50 .25
Nos. 1058-1065 (8) 3.25 2.00

Issue dates: 1.20p, Mar. 8; 6p, Dec. 20.

"We Have Been Inoculated" A504

1975, Apr. 26 Unwmk. *Perf. 13½*

1066 A504 2p multi .45 .25

Children's inoculation campaign (child's painting).

Hugo A. Acuña and South Orkney Station — A505

Designs: No. 1068, Francisco P. Moreno and Lake Nahuel Huapi. No. 1069, Lt. Col. Luis Piedra Buena and cutter, Luisito. No. 1070, Ensign José M. Sobral and Snow Hill House. No. 1071, Capt. Carlos M. Moyano and Cerro del Toro (mountain).

1975, June 28 Litho. *Perf. 13*

1067 A505 2p grnsh bl & multi .40 .30
1068 A505 2p yel grn & multi .40 .30
1069 A505 2p lt vio & multi .40 .30
1070 A505 2p gray bl & multi .40 .30
1071 A505 2p pale grn & multi .40 .30
Nos. 1067-1071 (5) 2.00 1.50

Pioneers of Antarctica.

Frigate "25 de Mayo" A506

1975, Sept. 27 Unwmk. *Perf. 13½*

1072 A506 6p multi .50 .30

Navy Day 1975.

Eduardo Bradley and Balloon A507

1975, Sept. 27 Wmk. 365

1073 A507 6p multi .50 .30

Air Force Day.

Declaration of Independence, by Juan M. Blanes — A508

1975, Oct. 25

1074 A508 6p multi .50 .25

Sesquicentennial of Uruguay's declaration of independence.

Flame A509

1975, Oct. 17 Unwmk.

1075 A509 6p gray & multi .40 .25

Loyalty Day, 30th anniversary of Pres. Peron's accession to power.

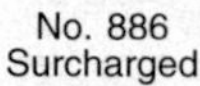
No. 886 Surcharged

No. 891 Surcharged

No. 932 Surcharged

1975 Lithographed, Photogravure

1076 A277 6c on 3p .25 .25
1077 A366 30c on 90p .30 .25
1078 A426 5p on 18c .50 .25
Nos. 1076-1078 (3) 1.05 .75

Issued: 6c, 10/30; 30c, 11/20; 5p, 10/24.
The 6c also exists on No. 886a. Value, $50.

International Bridge, Flags of Argentina & Uruguay — A510

1975, Oct. 25 Litho. Wmk. 365

1081 A510 6p multi .50 .25

Post Horn, Surcharged A511

1975, Nov. 8

1082 A511 10p on 20c multi .50 .25

Introduction of postal code. Not issued without surcharge.

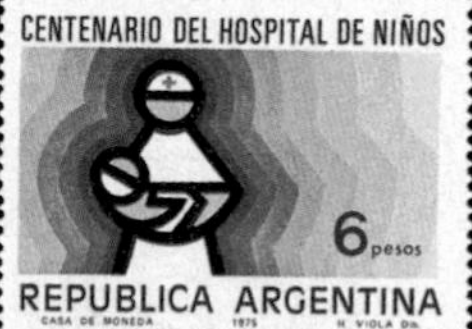

Nurse Holding Infant A512

1975, Dec. 13 Litho. *Perf. 13½*

1083 A512 6p multi .50 .25

Children's Hospital, centenary.

Nativity, Nueva Pompeya Church — A513

1975, Dec. 13 Litho. Unwmk.

1084 A513 6p multicolored .50 .25

Christmas 1975.

Types of 1970-75 and

Church of St. Francis, Salta — A515

Designs: 3p, No. 1099, 60p, 90p, Manuel Belgrano. 12p, 15p, 20p, 30p, No. 1100, 100p, 110p, 120p, 130p, San Martin. 15p, 70p, Guillermo Brown. 300p, Moon Valley (lower inscriptions italic). 500p, Adm. Brown Station, Antarctica.

1976-78 Photo. Unwmk. *Perf. 13½*

1089 A425 3p slate .50 .25
1090 A425 12p rose red .40 .25

Perf. 12½x13
Litho. Wmk. 365

1091 A425 12p rose red .40 .25
1092 A425 12p emerald .40 .25

Perf. 13½
Photo. Unwmk.

1093 A425 12p emer ('77) .40 .25
1094 A425 15p rose red .30 .25
1095 A425 15p vio bl ('77) .35 .25
1097 A425 20p rose red ('77) .35 .25
1098 A425 30p rose red ('77) .50 .25
1099 A425 40p dp grn 1.00 .25
1100 A425 40p rose red ('77) .35 .25
1101 A425 60p dk bl ('77) 1.50 .25
1102 A425 70p dk bl ('77) 1.50 .30
1103 A425 90p emer ('77) 1.00 .30
1104 A425 100p red 1.00 .25
1105 A425 110p rose red ('78) .65 .25
1106 A425 120p rose red ('78) .60 .25
1107 A425 130p rose red ('78) .70 .25

Litho.

1108 A463a 300p multi 3.50 1.50
a. Wmk 365 20.00 5.00
1109 A515 500p multi ('77) 10.00 1.40
a. Wmk 365 120.00 20.00
1110 A515 1000p multi ('77) 11.00 2.00
Nos. 1089-1110 (21) 36.40 9.50

Fluorescent paper was used in printing both 12p rose red, 15p rose red, 20p, 30p, 40p rose red, 100p, 110p, 120p, 130p.

No. 1099 and the 300p were issued on both ordinary and fluorescent paper.

Nos. 1108 and 1109 exist imperf. Values, pairs: No. 1108 $250; No. 1109 $120.

See Nos. B73-B74.

A516

1976 Photo. Unwmk. *Perf. 13½*

1112 A516 12c gray & blk .25 .25
1113 A516 50c gray & grn .25 .25
1114 A516 1p red & blk .25 .25
1115 A516 4p bl & blk .25 .25
1116 A516 5p org & blk .30 .25
1117 A516 6p dp brn & blk .25 .25
1118 A516 10p gray & vio bl .50 .25
1119 A516 27p lt grn & blk .80 .25
1120 A516 30p lt bl & blk .90 .25
1121 A516 45p yel & blk 1.00 .25
1122 A516 50p dl grn & blk 1.25 .25
1123 A516 100p brt grn & red 1.50 .25

Perf. 13x12½
1976 Litho. Wmk. 365

1124 A516 5p org & blk .25 .25
1125 A516 27p lt grn & blk .50 .25
1126 A516 45p yel & blk 1.25 .25
Nos. 1112-1126 (15) 9.50 3.75

The 1p, 6p, 10p, 50p and No. 1116 were issued on both ordinary and fluorescent paper.

Jet and Airlines Emblem — A517

Perf. 13x13½

1976, Apr. 24 Litho. Unwmk.

1130 A517 30p bl, lt bl & dk bl 1.00 .50

Argentine Airlines, 25th anniversary.

Frigate Heroina & Map of Falkland Islands — A518

1976, Apr. 26

1131 A518 6p multi 1.00 .40

Argentina's claim to Falkland Islands.

Louis Braille — A519

Wmk. 365

1976, May 22 Engr. *Perf. 13½*

1132 A519 19.70 deep blue .40 .30

Sesquicentennial of the invention of the Braille system of writing for the blind by Louis Braille (1809-1852).

Private, 7th Infantry Regiment A520

1976, May 29 Litho. Unwmk.

1133 A520 12p multi .40 .30

Army Day.

Schooner Rio de la Plata, by Emilio Biggeri — A521

1976, June 19

1134 A521 12p multi .70 .30

Navy Day.

Dr. Bernardo Houssay — A522

Argentine Nobel Prize Winners:
10p, Bernardo Houssay, medicine and physiology, 1947. 15p, Luis F. Leloir, chemistry, 1970. 20p, Carlos Saavedra Lamas, peace, 1936.

1976, Aug. 14 Litho. *Perf. 13½*

1135 A522 10p org & blk .35 .25
1136 A522 15p yel & blk .40 .25
1137 A522 20p ocher & blk .50 .40
Nos. 1135-1137 (3) 1.25 .90

Rio de la Plata International Bridge — A523

1976, Sept. 18 Litho. *Perf. 13½*

1138 A523 12p multi .50 .25

Inauguration of International Bridge connecting Puerte Unzue, Argentina, and Fray Bentos, Uruguay.

Pipelines & Cooling Tower, Gen. Mosconi Plant A524

1976, Nov. 20 Litho. *Perf. 13½*

1139 A524 28p multi .50 .30

Pablo Teodoro Fels & Bleriot Monoplane, 1910 — A525

1976, Nov. 20

1140 A525 15p multi .60 .30

Air Force Day.

Nativity A526

1976, Dec. 18 Litho. *Perf. 13½*

1141 A526 20p multi .70 .30

Christmas. Painting by Edith Chiapetto.

Water Conference Emblem — A527

1977, Mar. 19 Litho. *Perf. 13½*

1142 A527 70p multi .50 .30

UN Water Conf., Mar del Plata, Mar. 14-25.

Dalmacio Velez Sarsfield — A528

1977, Mar. 19 Engr.

1143 A528 50p blk & red brn .50 .30

Dalmacio Velez Sarsfield (1800-1875), author of Argentine civil code.

Red Deer Type of 1974 Surcharged

1977, July 30 Photo. *Perf. 13½*

1144 A495 100p on 5p brn 1.50 .35

Sesquicentennial of Uruguayan postal service. Not issued without surcharge.

Soldier, 16th Lancers A529

1977, July 30

1145 A529 30p multi .50 .30

Army Day.

Schooner Sarandi, by Emilio Biggeri — A530

1977, July 30

1146 A530 30p multi .60 .30

Navy Day.

Soccer Games' Emblem A531

70p, Argentina '78 emblem, flags & soccer field.

1977, May 14

1147 A531 30p multi .50 .30
1148 A531 70p multi .70 .40

11th World Cup Soccer Championship, Argentina, June 1-25, 1978.

The Visit, by Horacio Butler A532

Consecration, by Miguel P. Caride — A533

1977, Mar. 26 Litho.

1149 A532 50p multi .50 .30
1150 A533 70p multi .65 .40

Argentine artists.

Sierra de la Ventana — A534

Views: No. 1152, Civic Center, Santa Rosa. No. 1153, Skiers, San Martin de los Andes. No. 1154, Boat on Lake Fonck, Rio Negro.

1977, Oct. 8 Litho. *Perf. 13x13½*

1151 A534 30p multi .40 .25
1152 A534 30p multi .40 .25
1153 A534 30p multi .40 .25
1154 A534 30p multi .40 .25
Nos. 1151-1154 (4) 1.60 1.00

Guillermo Brown, by R. del Villar — A535

1977, Oct. 8 *Perf. 13½*

1155 A535 30p multi .40 .25

Adm. Guillermo Brown (1777-1857), leader in fight for independence, bicentenary of birth.

Jet A536

Double-decker, 1926 — A537

1977 Litho. *Perf. 13½*

1156	A536	30p	multi	.35	.25
1157	A537	40p	multi	.40	.30

50th anniversary of military plane production (30p); Air Force Day (40p).
Issue dates: 30p, Dec. 3; 40p, Nov. 26.

Adoration of the Kings — A538

1977, Dec. 17

1158	A538	100p	multi	.75	.30

Christmas 1977.

Historic City Hall, Buenos Aires — A539

Chapel of Rio Grande Museum, Tierra del Fuego A540

5p, 20p, La Plata Museum. 10p, Independence Hall, Tucuman. 40p, City Hall, Salta. No. 1165, City Hall, Buenos Aires. 100p, Columbus Theater, Buenos Aires. 200p, flag Monument, Rosario. 280p, 300p, Chapel of Rio Grande Museum, Tierra del Fuego. 480p, 520p, 800, Ruins of Jesuit Mission Church of San Ignacio, Misiones. 500p, Candonga Chapel, Cordoba. 1000p, G.P.O., Buenos Aires. 2000p, Civic Center, Bariloche, Rio Negro.

Three types of 10p: I. Nine vertical window bars; small imprint "E. MILIAVACA Dib." II. Nine bars; large imprint "E. MILIAVACA DIB." III. Redrawn; 5 bars; large imprint.

1977-81 Photo. Unwmk. *Perf. 13½*
Size: 32x21mm, 21x32mm

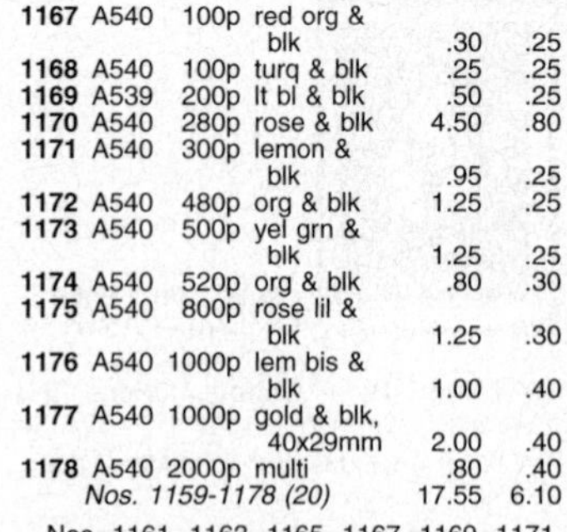

1159	A540	5p	gray & blk	.25	.25
1160	A540	10p	lt ultra & blk, I	.25	.25
a.			Type II	.30	.25
1161	A540	10p	lt bl & blk, III	.25	.25
1162	A540	20p	citron & blk, litho.	.25	.25
1163	A540	40p	gray bl & blk	.30	.25
1164	A539	50p	yel & blk	.50	.25
1165	A540	50p	citron & blk	.50	.25
1166	A540	100p	org & blk, litho.	.40	.25
a.			Wmk. 365	100.00	24.00
1167	A540	100p	red org & blk	.30	.25
1168	A540	100p	turq & blk	.25	.25
1169	A539	200p	lt bl & blk	.50	.25
1170	A540	280p	rose & blk	4.50	.80
1171	A540	300p	lemon & blk	.95	.25
1172	A540	480p	org & blk	1.25	.25
1173	A540	500p	yel grn & blk	1.25	.25
1174	A540	520p	org & blk	.80	.30
1175	A540	800p	rose lil & blk	1.25	.30
1176	A540	1000p	lem bis & blk	1.00	.40
1177	A540	1000p	gold & blk, 40x29mm	2.00	.40
1178	A540	2000p	multi	.80	.40
			Nos. 1159-1178 (20)	17.55	6.10

Nos. 1161, 1163, 1165, 1167, 1169, 1171, 1173, 1176, 1177 were issued on both ordinary and fluorescent paper. No. 1174 was issued only on fluorescent paper. All others were issued only on ordinary paper.
Issued: No. 1164, 5/30/77; 280p, 12/15/77; No. 1160, 3/14/78; 480p, 5/22/78; 5p, 7/25/78; 20p, 500p, 9/8/78; No. 1166, 9/20/78; No. 1177, 9/28/78; 520p, 9/30/78; 300p, 10/5/78; 40p, 12/1/78; No. 1161, 1979; No. 1165, 1/8/79; 800p, 3/20/79; No. 1167, 4/25/79; 200p, 6/23/79; No. 1176, 12/15/79; 2000p, 6/25/80; No. 1168, 5/26/81.
For overprints see Nos. 1253, 1315.

Soccer Games' Emblem A544

1978, Feb. 10 Photo. *Perf. 13½*

1179	A544	200p	yel grn & bl	.50	.30
a.			Wmk 365	*100.00*	*80.00*

11th World Cup Soccer Championship, Argentina, June 1-25.

View of El Rio, Rosario — A545

Designs (Argentina '78 Emblem and): 100p, Rio Tercero Dam, Cordoba. 150p, Cordillera Mountains, Mendoza. 200p, City Center, Mar del Plata. 300p, View of Buenos Aires.

1978, May 6 Litho. *Perf. 13*

1180	A545	50p	multi	.50	.30
1181	A545	100p	multi	.50	.30
1182	A545	150p	multi	.50	.30
1183	A545	200p	multi	.50	.30
1184	A545	300p	multi	.75	.35
			Nos. 1180-1184 (5)	2.75	1.55

Sites of 11th World Cup Soccer Championship, June 1-25.

Children — A546

1978, May 20

1185	A546	100p	multi	.50	.30

50th anniversary of Children's Institute.

Labor Day, by B. Quinquela Martin — A547

Design: No. 1187, Woman's torso, sculpture by Orlando Pierri.

1978, May 20 *Perf. 13½*

1186	A547	100p	multi	.50	.30
1187	A547	100p	multi	.50	.30

Argentina, Hungary, France, Italy and Emblem — A548

Stadium — A549

Teams and Argentina '78 Emblem: 200p, Poland, Fed. Rep. of Germany, Tunisia, Mexico. 300p, Austria, Spain, Sweden, Brazil. 400p, Netherlands, Iran, Peru, Scotland.

1978 Litho. *Perf. 13*

1188	A548	100p	multi	.50	.30
1189	A548	200p	multi	.65	.30
1190	A548	300p	multi	1.00	.40
1191	A548	400p	multi	1.25	.40
			Nos. 1188-1191 (4)	3.40	1.40

Souvenir Sheet
Lithographed and Engraved
Perf. 13½

1192	A549	700p	buff & blk	1.75	1.50

11th World Cup Soccer Championship, Argentina, June 1-25. Issued: Nos. 1188-1191, 6/6; No. 1192, 6/3.

Stadium Type of 1978 Inscribed in Red

Lithographed and Engraved
1978, Sept. 2 *Perf. 13½*

1193	A549	1000p	buff, blk & red	3.25	2.25

Argentina's victory in 1978 Soccer Championship. No. 1193 has margin similar to No. 1192 with Rimet Cup emblem added in red.

Young Tree Nourished by Old Trunk, UN Emblem — A550

1978 Sept. 2 Litho.

1194	A550	1000p	multi	.40	.25

Technical Cooperation among Developing Countries Conf., Buenos Aires, Sept. 1978.

Emblems of Buenos Aires & Bank — A551

1978, Sept. 16

1195	A551	100p	multi	.40	.25

Bank of City of Buenos Aires, centenary.

General Savio & Steel Production — A552

1978, Sept. 16

1196	A552	100p	multi	.40	.25

Gen. Manuel N. Savio (1892-1948), general manager of military heavy industry.

San Martin — A553

1978, Oct. Engr.

1197	A553	2000p	grnsh blk	2.50	.35

1979 Wmk. 365

1198	A553	2000p	grnsh blk	3.50	.35

Gen Jose de San Martin (1778-1850), soldier and statesman. See No. 1292.

Globe & Argentine Flag — A554

1978, Oct. 7 Litho. *Perf. 13½*

1199	A554	200p	multi	.80	.30

12th Intl. Cancer Cong., Buenos Aires, Oct. 5-11.

Chessboard, Queen & Pawn — A555

1978, Oct. 7

1200	A555	200p	multi	2.00	.65

23rd National Chess Olympics, Buenos Aires, Oct. 25-Nov. 12.

Correct Positioning of Stamps A557

50p, Use correct postal code number.

1978 **Photo.** ***Perf. 13½***

1201	A557	20p ultra	.25	.25
1203	A557	50p carmine	.40	.25

No. 1201 issued on both ordinary and fluorescent paper.

A558

A559

1978-82 **Photo.** ***Perf. 13½***

1204	A558	150p bl & ultra	.35	.25
1205	A558	180p bl & ultra	.35	.25
1206	A558	200p bl & ultra	.35	.25
1207	A559	240p ol bis & bl ('79)	.35	.25
1208	A559	260p blk & lt bl ('79)	.35	.25
1209	A559	290p brn & lt bl ('79)	.35	.25
1210	A559	310p mag & bl ('79)	.35	.25
1211	A559	350p ver & bl ('79)	.35	.25
1212	A559	450p ultra & bl	.65	.25
1213	A559	600p grn & bl ('80)	.65	.25
1214	A559	700p blk & bl ('80)	.65	.25
1215	A559	800p red & bl ('81)	.65	.25
1216	A559	1100p gray & bl ('81)	.75	.25
1217	A559	1500p blk & bl ('81)	.65	.25
1218	A559	1700p grn & bl ('82)	.65	.25
		Nos. 1204-1218 (15)	7.45	3.75

No. 1204 issued on fluorescent and ordinary paper. No. 1206 issued only on fluorescent paper.

For overprint see No. 1338.

Balsa "24" A561

Ships: 200p, Tug Legador. 300p, River Parana tug No. 34. 400p, Passenger ship Ciudad de Parana.

1978, Nov. 4 **Litho.** ***Perf. 13½***

1220	A561	100p multi	.40	.30
1221	A561	200p multi	.50	.30
1222	A561	300p multi	.70	.40
a.		Pair, #1221-1222	1.50	
1223	A561	400p multi	.95	.50
a.		Pair, #1220, 1223	1.50	
		Nos. 1220-1223 (4)	2.55	1.50

20th anniversary of national river fleet. Issued on fluorescent paper.

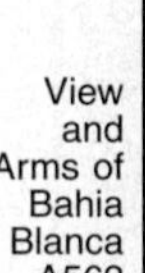

View and Arms of Bahia Blanca A562

1978, Nov. 25 **Litho.** ***Perf. 13½***

1224	A562	20p multi	.50	.25

Sesquicentennial of Bahia Blanca.

"Spain," (Queen Isabella and Columbus) by Arturo Dresco — A563

1978, Nov. 25

1225	A563	300p multi	2.50	.60

Visit of King Juan Carlos and Queen Sofia of Spain to Argentina, Nov. 26.

Virgin and Child, San Isidro Cathedral A564

1978, Dec. 16

1226	A564	200p gold & multi	.55	.30

Christmas 1978.

Slope at Chacabuco, by Pedro Subercaseaux — A565

Painting: 1000p, The Embrace of Maipu (San Martin and O'Higgins), by Pedro Subercaseaux, vert.

1978, Dec. 16 **Litho.** ***Perf. 13½***

1227	A565	500p multi	2.00	.40
1228	A565	1000p multi	3.00	.60

José de San Martin, 200th birth anniversary.

Adolfo Alsina A566

Design: No. 1230, Mariano Moreno.

1979, Jan. 20

1229	A566	200p lt bl & blk	.50	.30
1230	A566	200p yel red & blk	.50	.30

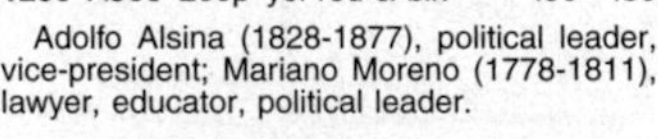
Adolfo Alsina (1828-1877), political leader, vice-president; Mariano Moreno (1778-1811), lawyer, educator, political leader.

Argentina No. 37 and UPU Emblem — A567

1979, Jan. 20

1231	A567	200p multi	.50	.30

Centenary of Argentina's UPU membership.

Still-life, by Carcova A568

Painting: 300p, The Laundresses, by Faustino Brughetti.

1979, Mar. 3

1232	A568	200p multi	.60	.30
1233	A568	300p multi	1.00	.40

Ernesto de la Carcova (1866-1927) and Faustino Brughetti (1877-1956), Argentine painters.

A569

1979, Mar. 3

1234	A569	200p Balcarce Earth station	.40	.30

Third Inter-American Telecommunications Conference, Buenos Aires, March 5-9.

A570

1979

1235	A570	30p Stamp collecting	.25	.25

Printed on ordinary and fluorescent paper.

European Olive — A571

1979, June 2 **Litho.** ***Perf. 13½***

1236	A571	100p shown	.50	.30
1237	A571	200p Tea	.70	.30
1238	A571	300p Sorghum	1.00	.40
1239	A571	400p Common flax	1.25	.55
		Nos. 1236-1239 (4)	3.45	1.55

Laurel and Regimental Emblem A572

1979, June 9

1240	A572	200p gold & multi	.50	.30

Founding of Subteniente Berdina Village in memory of Sub-lieutenant Rodolfo Hernan Berdina, killed by terrorists in 1975.

"75" and Automobile Club Emblem — A573

1979, June 9

1241	A573	200p gold & multi	.50	.30

Argentine Automobile Club, 75th anniv.

Exchange Building and Emblem — A574

1979, June 9

1242	A574	200p bl, blk & gold	.40	.30

Grain Exchange, 125th anniversary.

Cavalry Officer, 1817 — A575

1979, July 7 **Litho.** ***Perf. 13½***

1243	A575	200p multi	1.00	.30

Army Day.

Corvette Uruguay and Navy Emblem — A576

Design: No. 1245, Hydrographic service ship & emblem.

1979 ***Perf. 13***

1244	A576	250p multi	1.10	.35
1245	A576	250p multi	1.00	.35

Navy Day; Cent. of Naval Hydrographic Service. Issued: No. 1244, July 28; No. 1245, July 7.

Tree and Man — A577

1979, July 28 ***Perf. 13½***

1246	A577	250p multi	.60	.30

Protection of the Environment Day, June 5.

"Spad" Flying over Andes, and Vicente Almandos Almonacid — A578

1979, Aug. 4
1247 A578 250p multi .80 .30

Air Force Day.

Gen. Julio A. Roca Occupying Rio Negro, by Juan M. Blanes — A579

1979, Aug. 4
1248 A579 250p multi .70 .30

Conquest of Rio Negro Desert, centenary.

Rowland Hill — A580

1979, Sept. 29 Litho. *Perf. 13½*
1249 A580 300p gray red & blk .90 .30

Sir Rowland Hill (1795-1879), originator of penny postage.

Viedma Navarez Monument A581

1979, Sept. 29
1250 A581 300p multi .65 .30

Viedma and Carmen de Patagones towns, bicentenary.

Pope Paul VI — A582

Design: No. 1252, Pope John Paul I.

1979, Oct. 27 Engr. *Perf. 13½*
1251 A582 500p black 1.25 .40
1252 A582 500p sepia 1.25 .40

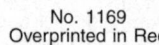

No. 1169 Overprinted in Red

1979, Nov. 10 Photo. *Perf. 13½*
1253 A539 200p lt blue & blk .50 .30

Rosario Philatelic Society, 75th anniversary.

A583

1979, Nov. 10 Litho.
1254 A583 300p multi .70 .30

Frontier resettlement.

A584

1979, Dec. 1 Litho. *Perf. 13½*
1255 A584 300p multi .70 .40

Military Geographic Institute centenary.

Christmas 1979 — A585

1979, Dec. 1
1256 A585 300p multi .50 .30

General Mosconi Birth Centenary — A586

1979, Dec. 15 Engr. *Perf. 13½*
1257 A586 1000p blk & bl 1.10 .40

Rotary Emblem and Globe A587

1979, Dec. 29 Litho.
1258 A587 300p multi 1.25 .40

Rotary International, 75th anniversary.

Child and IYC Emblem A588

Family, by Pablo Menicucci — A589

1979, Dec. 29
1259 A588 500p lt bl & sepia .65 .40
1260 A589 1000p multi 1.00 .40

International Year of the Child.

Microphone, Waves, ITU Emblem — A590

1980, Mar. 22 Litho. *Perf. 13x13½*
1261 A590 500p multi 1.00 .40

Regional Administrative Conference on Broadcasting by Hectometric Waves for Area 2, Buenos Aires, Mar. 10-29.

Guillermo Brown — A591

1980 Engr. *Perf. 13½*
1262 A591 5000p black 2.50 .30

See No. 1372.

Argentine Red Cross Centenary — A592

1980, Apr. 19 Litho. *Perf. 13½*
1263 A592 500p multi 1.00 .40

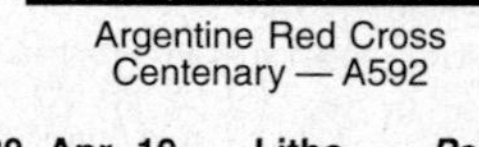

OAS Emblem A593

1980, Apr. 19
1264 A593 500p multi .55 .40

Day of the Americas, Apr. 14.

Dish Antennae, Balcarce — A594

1980, Apr. 26 Litho. & Engr.
1265 A594 300p shown .60 .30
1266 A594 300p Hydroelectric Station, Salto Grande .60 .30
1267 A594 300p Bridge, Zarate-Brazo Largo .60 .30
Nos. 1265-1267 (3) 1.80 .90

Capt. Hipolito Bouchard, Frigate "Argentina" — A595

1980, May 31 Litho. *Perf. 13x13½*
1268 A595 500p multicolored .80 .40

Navy Day.

"Villarino," San Martin, by Theodore Gericault — A596

1980, May 31
1269 A596 500p multicolored .80 .40

Return of the remains of Gen. Jose de San Martin to Argentina, centenary.

Buenos Aires Gazette, 1810, Signature — A597

1980, June 7 *Perf. 13½*
1270 A597 500p multicolored .55 .30

Journalism Day.

Miniature Sheet

Coaches in Victoria Square — A598

1980 June 14

1271	Sheet of 14	11.00	11.00
a.-n.	A598 500p any single	.75	.50

Buenos Aires, 400th anniv. No. 1271 shows ceramic mural of Victoria Square by Rodolfo Franco in continuous design. See No. 1285.

Gen. Pedro Aramburu A599

1980, July 12 Litho. *Perf. 13½*

1272	A599 500p yel & blk	.45	.30

Gen. Pedro Eugenio Aramburu (1903-1970), provisional president, 1955.

Army Day A600

1980, July 12

1273	A600 500p multicolored	.60	.30

Gen. Juan Gregorio de Las Heras (1780-1866), Hero of 1817 War of Independence — A601

Grandees of Argentina Bicentenary: No. 1275, Rivadavia. No. 1276, Brig. Gen Jose Matias Zapiola (1780-1874), naval commander and statesman.

1980, Aug. 2 Litho. *Perf. 13½*

1274	A601 500p tan & blk	.55	.30
1275	A601 500p multicolored	.55	.30
1276	A601 500p lt lilac & blk	.55	.30
	Nos. 1274-1276 (3)	1.65	.90

Avro "Gosport" Biplane, Maj. Francisco de Artega — A602

1980, Aug. 16 *Perf. 13*

1277	A602 500p multicolored	.70	.40

Air Force Day. Artega (1882-1930) was first director of Military Aircraft Factory where Avro "Gosport" was built (1927).

University of La Plata, 75th Anniversary — A603

1980, Aug. 16 *Perf. 13½*

1278	A603 500p multi	.55	.30

Souvenir Sheets

A604

A605

No. 1279 (A604): a, King penguin. b, Bearded penguin. c, Adelie penguins. d, Papua penguins. e, Sea elephants. f, Puerto Soledad, 1829. g, Puerto Soledad harbor, 1829. h, Fur seals. i, Giant petrels. j, Blue-eyed cororants. k, Stormy petrels. l, Antarctic doves.

1980, Sept. 27 Litho. *Perf. 13½*

1279	Sheet of 12	11.00	11.00
a.-l.	A604 500p, any single	.75	.60
1280	Sheet of 12	11.00	11.00
a.	A605 500p South Orkneys Base	.75	.60
b.	A605 500p Boat in Harbor	.75	.60

75th anniv. of Argentina's presence in the South Orkneys and 150th anniv. of political and military command in the Falkland Islands. Nos. 1279-1280 each contain 12 stamps (4x3) with landscape designs in center of sheets. Silhouettes of Argentine exploration ships in margins. No. 1280 contains Nos. 1279a-1279e, 1279h-1279m, 1280a-1280b.

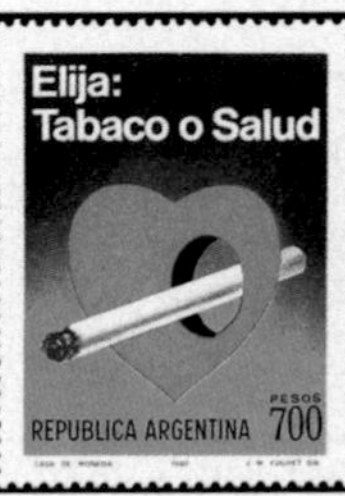

Anti-smoking Campaign A608

1980, Oct. 11

1282	A608 700p multi	.60	.40

National Census — A609

1980, Sept.

1283	A609 500p blk & bl	1.25	.25

Madonna and Child (Congress Emblem) — A610

1980, Oct. 1 Litho.

1284	A610 700p multi	.60	.40

National Marian Cong., Mendoza, Oct. 8-12

Mural Type of 1980

Miniature Sheet

1980, Oct. 25

1285	Sheet of 14	10.00	10.00
a.-n.	A598 500p, any single	.65	.50

Buenos Aires, 400th anniv./Buenos Aires '80 Stamp Exhib., Oct. 24-Nov. 2. No. 1285 shows ceramic mural Arte bajo la Ciudad by Alfredo Guido in continuous design.

Technical Military Academy, 50th Anniversary A611

1980, Nov. 1

1286	A611 700p multi	.50	.30

Amateur Radio Operation A612

1980, Nov. 1

1287	A612 700p multi	.50	.30

Medal — A613

Lujan Cathedral Floor Plan — A614

1980, Nov. 29 Litho. *Perf. 13½*

1288	A613 700p multi	.60	.40
1289	A614 700p olive & brn	.60	.40

Christmas 1980. 150th anniv. of apparition of Holy Virgin to St. Catherine Laboure, Paris (No. 1288), 350th anniv. of apparition at Lujan.

150th Death Anniversary of Simon Bolivar — A615

1980, Dec. 13

1290	A615 700p multi	.75	.40

Soccer Gold Cup Championship, Montevideo, 1980 — A616

1981, Jan. 3 Litho.

1291	A616 1000p multi	1.25	.40

San Martin Type of 1978

1981, Jan. 20 Engr. *Perf. 13½*

1292	A553 10,000p dark blue	6.00	.30

Landscape in Lujan, by Marcos Tiglio — A617

Paintings: No. 1304, Expansion of Light along a Straight Line, by Miguel Angel Vidal, vert.

1981, Apr. 11 Litho.

1303	A617 1000p multi	.85	.40
1304	A617 1000p multi	.85	.45

Intl. Sports Medicine Congress, June 7-12 — A618

1981, June 6 Litho. *Perf. 13½*

1305	A618 1000p bl & dk brn	.65	.30

Esperanza Base, Antarctica — A619

Cargo Plane, Map of Vice-Commodore Marambio Island — A620

Perf. 13½, 13x13½ (No. 1308)

1981, June 13

1306 A619 1000p shown 2.00 1.00
1307 A619 2000p Almirante Irizar 3.00 1.00
1308 A620 2000p shown 3.00 1.00
Nos. 1306-1308 (3) 8.00 3.00

Antarctic Treaty 20th anniv.

Antique Pistols (Military Club Centenary) — A621

1981, June 27 ***Perf. 13½***

1309 A621 1000p Club building .80 .30
1310 A621 2000p shown .80 .30

Gen. Juan A. Alvarez de Arenales (1770-1831) A622

Famous Men: No. 1312, Felix G. Frias (1816-1881), writer. No. 1313, Jose E. Uriburu (1831-1914), statesman.

1981, Aug. 8 Litho. ***Perf. 13½***

1311 A622 1000p multi .70 .30
1312 A622 1000p multi .70 .30
1313 A622 1000p multi .70 .30
Nos. 1311-1313 (3) 2.10 .90

Naval Observatory Centenary — A623

1981, Aug. 15 Litho. ***Perf. 13x13½***

1314 A623 1000p multi 1.00 .40

No. 1176 Overprinted in Red

1981, Aug. 15 Photo. ***Perf. 13½***

1315 A540 1000p lem & blk 2.00 1.00

50th anniv. of Bahia Blanca Philatelic and Numismatic Society.

St. Cayetano, Stained-glass Window, Buenos Aires — A624

1981, Sept. 5 Litho. ***Perf. 13½***

1316 A624 1000p multi .70 .30

St. Cayetano, founder of Teatino Order, 500th birth anniv.

Pablo Castaibert (1883-1909) and his Monoplane (Air Force Day) — A625

1981, Sept. 5 ***Perf. 13x13½***

1317 A625 1000p multi 1.10 .40

Intl. Year of the Disabled A626

1981, Sept. 10 ***Perf. 13½***

1318 A626 1000p multi .55 .30

22nd Latin-American Steelmakers' Congress, Buenos Aires, Sept. 21-23 — A627

1981, Sept. 19

1319 A627 1000p multi .55 .30

Army Regiment No. 1 (Patricios), 175th Anniv. — A628

1981, Oct. 10 Litho. ***Perf. 13½***

1320 1500p Natl. arms .60 .30
1321 1500p shown .60 .30
a. A628 Pair, #1320-1321 1.60 1.50

A629

San Martin as artillery Captain in Battle of Bailen, 1808.

1981, Oct. 5

1322 Sheet of 8 + 4 labels 4.75 4.75
a. A629 1000p multi .35 .30
b. A629 1500p multi .50 .35

Espamer '81 Intl. Stamp Exhib. (Americas, Spain, Portugal), Buenos Aires, Nov. 13-22.

No. 1322 contains 2 each se-tenant pairs with label between.

A630

1981, Oct. 5

1323 A630 1000p multi 4.00 .40

Anti-indiscriminate whaling.

Espamer '81 Emblem and Ship A631

1981

1324 A631 1300p multi 1.00 .40

No. 1324 Overprinted in Blue

1981, Nov. 7 Photo. ***Perf. 13½***

1325 A631 1300p multi 1.25 .40

Postal Administration philatelic training course.

Soccer Players A632

Designs: Soccer players.

1981, Nov. 13 Litho.

1326 Sheet of 4 + 2 labels 8.00 8.00
a. A632 2000p multi 1.50 1.25
b. A632 3000p multi 1.75 1.50
c. A632 5000p multi 2.00 1.75
d. A632 15,000p multi 2.25 2.00

Espamer '81.

"Peso" Coin Centenary — A633

1981, Nov. 21

1327 A633 2000p Patacon, 1881 .55 .30
1328 A633 3000p Argentine Oro, 1881 .55 .30

Christmas 1981 — A634

1981, Dec. 12

1329 A634 1500p multi 2.00 .40

Traffic Safety A635

1981, Dec. 19 Litho.

1330 A635 1000p Observe traffic lights, vert. 1.50 .50
1331 A635 2000p Drive carefully, vert. 1.10 .50
1332 A635 3000p Cross at white lines 1.10 .70
1333 A635 4000p Don't shine headlights 1.10 .80
Nos. 1330-1333 (4) 4.80 2.50

Francisco Luis Bernardez, Ciuda Laura — A636

Writers and title pages from their works: 2000p, Lucio V. Mansilla, Excursion a los indios ranqueles. 3000p, Conrado Nale Roxlo, El Grillo. 4000p, Victoria Ocampo, Sur.

1982, Mar. 20 Litho.

1334 A636 1000p shown 1.50 .50
1335 A636 2000p multi 1.10 .50
1336 A636 3000p multi 1.10 .70
1337 A636 4000p multi 1.10 .80
Nos. 1334-1337 (4) 4.80 2.50

No. 1218 Overprinted

1982, Apr. 17 Photo. ***Perf. 13½***

1338 A559 1700p green & blue .70 .25

Argentina's claim on Falkland Islands.

Robert Koch — A637

1982, Apr. 17 Litho. Wmk. 365

1339 A637 2000p multi 1.10 .40

TB bacillus centenary and 25th Intl. Tuberculosis Conference.

American Airforces Commanders' 22nd Conf. — A638

1982, Apr. 17
1340 A638 2000p multi 1.00 .40

Stone Carving, City Founder's Signature (Don Hernando de Lerma) — A639

1982, Apr. 17
1341 A639 2000p multi 1.00 .40

Souvenir Sheet

1342 A639 5000p multi 2.50 2.50

City of Salta, 400th anniv. No. 1342 contains one 43x30mm stamp.

Naval Center Centenary — A640

1982, Apr. 24 ***Perf. 13x13½***
1343 A640 2000p multi .80 .40

Chorisia Speciosa — A641

1982 Unwmk. Photo. ***Perf. 13½***
1344 A641 200p Zinnia peruviana .30 .25
1345 A641 300p Ipomoea purpurea .30 .25
1346 A641 400p Tillandsia aeranthos .25 .25
1347 A641 500p shown .25 .25
1348 A641 800p Oncidium bifolium .25 .25
1349 A641 1000p Erythrina crista-galli .30 .25
1350 A641 2000p Jacaranda mimosi-folia .30 .25
1351 A641 3000p Bauhinia candicans 1.00 .25
1352 A641 5000p Tecoma stans .60 .25
1353 A641 10,000p Tabebuia ipe 1.00 .25
1354 A641 20,000p Passiflora coerulea 1.25 .35
1355 A641 30,000p Aristolochia littoralis 2.25 .50
1356 A641 50,000p Oxalis en-neaphylla 5.25 .75
Nos. 1344-1356 (13) 13.30 4.10

Nos. 1344-1346, 1348-1350 issued on fluorescent paper. Nos. 1353-1356 issued on ordinary paper. Others issued on both fluorescent and ordinary paper.

Issued: 500p, 2000p, 5000p, 10,000p, 5/22; 200p, 300p, 1000p, 20,000p, 9/25; 400p, 800p, 30,000p, 50,000p, 12/4; 3000p, 12/18.

See Nos. 1429-1443A, 1515-1527, 1683-1691. For overprint see No. 1382.

10th Death Anniv. of Gen. Juan C. Sanchez — A641a

1982, May 29 Litho. Wmk. 365
1364 A641a 5000p grn & blk .90 .40

Luis Venet, First Commander A641b

1982, June 12
1365 A641b 5000p org & blk 2.00 1.25

Size: 83x28mm

1366 A641b 5000p Map 1.00 .85
a. Pair, Nos. 1365-1366 3.50 2.50

153rd Anniv. of Malvinas Political and Military Command District.
Compare with No. 1411.

Visit of Pope John Paul II — A641c

1982, June 12
1367 A641c 5000p multi 1.75 .55

Organ Grinder, by Aldo Severi (b. 1928) — A641d

3000p, Still Life, by Santiago Cogorno (b. 1915).

1982, July 3 Wmk. 365
1368 A641d 2000p shown 1.00 .40
1369 A641d 3000p multi 1.00 .40

Guillermo Brown Type of 1980 and

Jose de San Martin — A641e

Litho. and Engr.

1982 Unwmk. ***Perf. 13½***
1372 A591 30,000p blk & bl 2.75 .40
1376 A641e 50,000p sepia & car 6.00 .75

Issue dates: 30,000p, June; 50,000p, July.

Scouting Year — A641f

Wmk. 365

1982, Aug. 7 Litho. ***Perf. 13½***
1380 A641f 5000p multi 1.75 .50

Alconafta Fuel Campaign — A641g

1982, Aug. 7 Wmk. 365
1381 A641g 2000p multi .60 .25

No. 1352 Overprinted

1982, Aug. 7 Photo. Unwmk.
1382 A641 5000p multi 2.00 1.25

Rio III Central Nuclear Power Plant, Cordoba A642

Wmk. 365

1982, Sept. 4 Litho. ***Perf. 13½***
1383 A642 2000p shown .50 .30
1384 A642 2000p Control room .50 .30

Namibia Day — A643

1982, Sept. 4
1385 A643 5000p Map .75 .40

Formosa Cathedral — A644

Churches and Cathedrals of the Northeast: 2000p, Our Lady of Itati, Corrientes, vert. 3000p, Resistencia Cathedral, Chaco, vert. 10,000p, St. Ignatius Church ruins, Misiones.

1982, Sept. 18 Litho. & Engr.
1386 A644 2000p dk grn & blk .50 .50
1387 A644 3000p dk brn & brn .75 .50
1388 A644 5000p dk bl & brn 1.00 .50
1389 A644 10,000p dp org & blk 1.50 .75
Nos. 1386-1389 (4) 3.75 2.25

Tension Sideral, by Mario Alberto Agatiello A645

Sculpture (Espamer '81 and Juvenex '82 Exhibitions): 3000p, Sugerencia II, by Eduardo Mac Entyre. 5000p, Storm, by Carlos Silva.

1982, Oct. 2 Litho. ***Perf. 13½***
1390 A645 2000p multi 1.00 .40
1391 A645 3000p multi 1.40 .50
1392 A645 5000p multi 1.75 .75
Nos. 1390-1392 (3) 4.15 1.65

Santa Fe Bridge A646

1982, Oct. 16 Litho. & Engr.
1393 A646 2000p bl & blk .65 .30

2nd Southern Cross Games, Santa Fe and Rosario, Nov. 26-Dec. 5.

10th World Men's Volleyball Championship — A647

1982, Oct. 16 Litho. Wmk. 365
1394 A647 2000p multi .50 .30
1395 A647 5000p multi .75 .40

Los Andes Newspaper Centenary — A648

Design: Army of the Andes Monument, Hill of Glory, Mendoza.

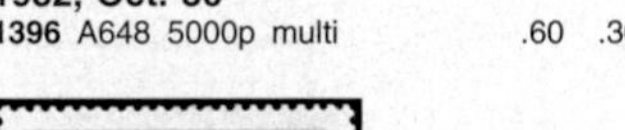

1982, Oct. 30
1396 A648 5000p multi .60 .30

A649

1982, Oct. 30 Wmk. 365
1397 A649 5000p Signs .60 .30

50th Anniv. of Natl. Roads, Administration.

A650

A650a

La Plata City Cent., each 2500p: No. 1400: a, Cathedral, diff. b, Head, top. c, Observatory. d, City Hall, diff. e, Head, bottom. f, University.

1982, Nov. 20 **Litho.**
1398 A650 5000p Cathedral .75 .30
1399 A650 5000p City Hall .75 .30
1400 A650a Sheet of 6 2.25 2.25
a.-f. 2500p Any single .35 .30

Well, Natl. Hydrocarbon Congress Emblem — A651

1982, Nov. 20
1401 A651 5000p multi .80 .30

Oil Discovery, Comodoro Rivadavia, 75th anniv.

Jockey Club of Buenos Aires Centenary A652

Design: No. 1403, Carlos Pellegrini, first president.

1982, Dec. 4 **Litho.**
1402 A652 5000p Emblem .75 .30
1403 A652 5000p multi .75 .30

Christmas A653

1982, Dec. 18 ***Perf. 13½***
1404 A653 3000p St. Vincent de Paul 1.75 .50

Size: 29x38mm

1405 A653 5000p St. Francis of Assisi 1.25 .40

Pedro B. Palacios (1854-1917), Writer — A654

Writers: 2000p, Leopoldo Marechal (1900-1970). 3000p, Delfina Bunge de Galvez (1881-1952). 4000p, Manuel Galvez (1882-1962). 5000p, Evaristo Carriego (1883-1912).

1983, Mar. 26 **Litho.** ***Perf. 13½***
1406 A654 1000p multi .50 .30
1407 A654 2000p multi .50 .30
1408 A654 3000p multi .50 .30
1409 A654 4000p multi .50 .30
1410 A654 5000p multi .50 .30
a. Strip of 5, #1406-1410 3.00 3.00

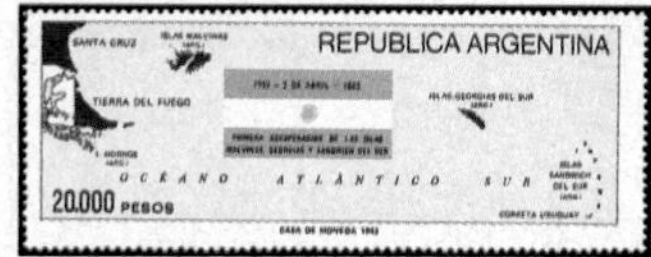

Recovery of the Malvinas (Falkland Islands) — A655

1983, Apr. 9 **Litho.** ***Perf. 13½***
1411 A655 20,000p Map, flag 1.75 .50

Compare No. 1411 with No. 1366.

Telecommunications Systems — A656

1983, Apr. 16 **Wmk. 365**
1412 A656 5000p SITRAM 1.10 .50
1413 A656 5000p ARPAC network 1.10 .50

Naval League Emblem A657

1983, May 14 **Litho.** ***Perf. 13½***
1414 A657 5000p multi .60 .30

Navy Day and 50th anniv. of Naval League.

Allegory, by Victor Rebuffo A658

1983, May 14
1415 A658 5000p multi .60 .40

Natl. Arts Fund, 25th Anniv.

75th Anniv. of Colon Opera House, Buenos Aires — A659

1983, May 28 **Wmk. 365**
1416 A659 5000p Main hall .60 .40
1417 A659 10000p Stage .90 .50

Protected Species — A660

1983, July 2 **Litho.** ***Perf. 13½***
1418 A660 1p Chrysocyon brachtyurus .75 .40
1419 A660 1.50p Ozotocerus bezoarticus .75 .40
1420 A660 2p Myrmecophaga tridactyla .90 .40
1421 A660 2.50p Leo onca 1.25 .40
Nos. 1418-1421 (4) 3.65 1.60

City of Catamarca, 300th Anniv. — A661

Foundation of the City of Catamarca, by Luis Varela Lezana (1900-1982).

1983, July 16 **Litho.** ***Perf. 13½***
1422 A661 1p multi .50 .40

Mamerto Esquiu (1826-1883) A662

1983, July 16
1423 A662 1p multi .50 .40

Bolivar, by Herrera Toro — A663

Bolivar, Engraving by Kepper — A664

Perf. 13 (A663), 13½ (A664)

1983 **Unwmk.**
1424 A663 1p multi .45 .35
1425 A664 2p blk & maroon .65 .40
1426 A664 10p San Martin 3.00 .75
Nos. 1424-1426 (3) 4.10 1.50

Issue dates: 1p, 2p, July 23. 10p, Aug. 20.
See Nos. 1457-1462B.

Gen. Toribio de Luzuriaga (1782-1842) A665

1983, Aug. 20 **Litho.** ***Perf. 13½***
1427 A665 1p multi .60 .40

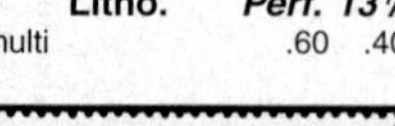

50th Anniv. of San Martin National Institute A666

1983, Aug. 20 **Engr.** **Unwmk.**
1428 A666 2p sepia .60 .40

Flower Type of 1982 in New Currency

1983-85 **Photo.** ***Perf. 13½***
1429 A641 5c like #1347 .50 .25
1430 A641 10c like #1349 .25 .25
1431 A641 20c like #1350 .30 .25
1432 A641 30c like #1351 .30 .25
1433 A641 40c Eichhornia crassipes .40 .25
1434 A641 50c like #1352 .25 .25
1435 A641 1p like #1353 .30 .25
1435A A641 1.80p Mutisia retusa .30 .25
1436 A641 2p like #1354 .30 .25
1437 A641 3p like #1355 .40 .25
1438 A641 5p like #1356 .40 .25
1439 A641 10p Alstroemeria aurantiaca 1.10 .80
1440 A641 20p like #1345 .50 .25
1441 A641 30p Embothrium coccineum .40 .25
1442 A641 50p like #1346 .60 .40
1443 A641 100p like #1348 1.00 .50
1443A A641 300p Cassia carnaval 2.00 .25
Nos. 1429-1443A (17) 9.30 5.20

Issued: 20p, 8/27/84; 50p, 10/19/84; 100p, 12/84; 300p, 6/15/85.

Nos. 1429, 1433, 1435A issued on fluorescent paper. Nos. 1443, 1443A issued on ordinary paper. Others issued on both ordinary and fluorescent paper.

For overprint and surcharge see Nos. 1489, 1530.

Intl. Rotary South American Regional Conference, Buenos Aires, Sept. 25-28 — A667

1983, Sept. 24 **Litho.**

1444 A667 1p multi .75 .35

9th Pan American Games, Caracas, Aug. 13-28 — A668

1983, Sept. 24

1445 A668 1p Track .45 .35
1446 A668 2p Emblem .60 .40

World Communications Year — A669

1983, Oct. 8 ***Perf. 13½***

1447 A669 2p multi .60 .40

Squash Peddler by Antonio Berni (1905-1981) A670

2p, Figure in Yellow by Luis Seoane (1910-79).

1983, Oct. 15 ***Perf. 13½***

1448 A670 1p multi .50 .35
1449 A670 2p multi .60 .40

World Communications Year — A671

Designs: 1p, Wagon, 18th cent. 2p, Post chaise, 19th cent. 4p, Steam locomotive, 1857. 5p, Tramway, 1910.

1983, Nov. 19 **Litho.** ***Perf. 13½***

1450 A671 1p multi .50 .35
1451 A671 2p multi .60 .40
1452 A671 4p multi 1.00 .50
1453 A671 5p multi 1.25 .60
Nos. 1450-1453 (4) 3.35 1.85

World Communications Year — A672

1983, Nov. 26 **Litho.** ***Perf. 12½x12***

1454 A672 2p General Post Office .45 .30

Return to Elected Government A673

1983, Dec. 10 **Photo.** ***Perf. 13½***

1455 A673 2p Coin, 1813 .60 .40

Eudyptes Crestatus A674

Designs: b, Diomedea exulans. c, Diomedea melanophris. d, Eudyptes chrysolophus. e, Luis Piedra Buena. f, Carlos Maria Moyano. g, Luis Py. h, Augusto Lasserre. i, Phoebetria palpebrata. j, Hydrurga leptonyx. k, Lobodon carcinophagus. l, Leptonychotes weddelli.

1983, Dec. 10 **Litho.**

1456 Sheet of 12 7.25 7.25
a.-l. A674 2p any single .50 .45

Southern pioneers and fauna. Margin depicts various airplanes and emblems.

Bolivar Type of 1983

Famous men: 10p, Angel J. Carranza (1834-99), historian. No. 1458, 500p, Guillermo Brown. No. 1459, Estanislao del Campo (1834-80), poet. 30p, Jose Hernandez (1834-86), author. 40p, Vicente Lopez y Planes (1784-1856), poet and patriot. 50p, San Martin. 200p, Belgrano.

1983-85 **Litho. & Engr.** ***Perf. 13½***

1457 A664 10p pale bl & dk bl .50 .40
1458 A664 20p dk bl & blk 1.25 .60
1459 A664 20p dl brn ol & ol blk .50 .40
1460 A664 30p pale bl & bluish blk .70 .40
1461 A664 40p lt bl grn & blk .90 .40
1462 A664 50p Prus grn & choc 3.50 .50
1462A A664 200p int bl & blk 2.00 .60
1462B A664 500p brn & int bl 2.50 .50
Nos. 1457-1462B (8) 11.85 3.80

Issued: No. 1458, 10/6; 10p, No. 1459, 30p, 40p, 3/23/85; 50p, 4/23/85; 200p, 11/2/85; 500p, 5/2/85.

Christmas 1983 — A675

Nativity Scenes: 2p, Tapestry, by Silke. 3p, Stained-glass window, San Carlos de Bariloche's Wayn Church, vert.

1983, Dec. 17 **Litho.** ***Perf. 13½***

1463 A675 2p multi .60 .40
1464 A675 3p multi .80 .40

Centenary of El Dia Newspaper A676

1984, Mar. 24 **Litho.**

1465 A676 4p Masthead, printing roll .40 .40

Alejandro Carbo Teachers' College Centenary — A677

1984, June 2 **Litho.** ***Perf. 13½***

1466 A677 10p Building .45 .40

1984 Olympics A678

Designs: No. 1468, Weightlifting, discus, shot put. No. 1469, Javelin, fencing. No. 1470, Bicycling, swimming.

1984, July 28 **Litho.** ***Perf. 13½***

1467 A678 5p shown .65 .40
1468 A678 5p multicolored .65 .40
1469 A678 10p multicolored .65 .40
1470 A678 10p multicolored .65 .40
Nos. 1467-1470 (4) 2.60 1.60

Rosario Stock Exchange Centenary A679

1984, Aug. 11

1471 A679 10p multicolored .45 .30

Wheat A680

1984, Aug. 11

1472 A680 10p shown .50 .30
1473 A680 10p Corn .50 .30
1474 A680 10p Sunflower .50 .30
Nos. 1472-1474 (3) 1.50 .90

18th FAO Regional Conference for Latin America and Caribbean (No. 1472); 3rd Natl. Corn Congress (No. 1473); World Food Day (No. 1474).

Wildlife Protection — A681

1984, Sept. 22 **Litho.** ***Perf. 13½***

1475 A681 20p Hippocamelus bisulcus .80 .40
1476 A681 20p Vicugna vicugna .80 .40
1477 A681 20p Aburria jacutinga .80 .40
1478 A681 20p Mergus octosetaceus .80 .40
1479 A681 20p Podiceps gallardoi .80 .40
Nos. 1475-1479 (5) 4.00 2.00

First Latin American Theater Festival, Cordoba, Oct. — A682

1984, Oct. 13 **Litho.** ***Perf. 13½***

1480 A682 20p Mask .40 .40

Intl. Eucharistic Congress, 50th Anniv. — A683

Apostles' Communion, by Fra Angelico.

1984, Oct. 13

1481 A683 20p multicolored .40 .40

Glaciares Natl. Park (UNESCO World Heritage List) — A684

1984, Nov. 17 **Litho.**

1482 A684 20p Sea .70 .40
1483 A684 30p Glacier .80 .40

City of Puerto Deseado Centenary — A685

1984, Nov. 17 *Perf. 13½*
1484 A685 20p shown .70 .40
1485 A685 20p Ushuaia centenary .70 .40

Childrens' Paintings, Christmas 1984 — A686

1984, Dec. 1 **Litho.** *Perf. 13½*
1486 A686 20p Diego Aguero .50 .40
1487 A686 30p Leandro Ruiz .70 .40
1488 A686 50p Maria Castillo, vert. .80 .50
Nos. 1486-1488 (3) 2.00 1.30

No. 1439 Overprinted

1984, Dec. 1 **Photo.** *Perf. 13½*
1489 A641 10p multicolored .40 .40

Buenos Aires Philatelic Center, 50th anniv.

Vista Del Jardin Zoologico, by Fermin Eguia — A687

Paintings: No. 1491, El Congreso Iluminado, by Francisco Travieso. No. 1492, Galpones (La Boca), by Marcos Borio.

1984, Dec. 15 *Perf. 13½*
1490 A687 20p multi .50 .40
1491 A687 20p multi, vert. .50 .40
1492 A687 20p multi, vert. .50 .40
Nos. 1490-1492 (3) 1.50 1.20

Gen. Martin Miguel de Guemes (1785-1821) — A688

1985, Mar. 23 **Litho.** *Perf. 13½*
1493 A688 30p multicolored .65 .35

ARGENTINA '85 Exhibition — A689

First airmail service from: 20p, Buenos Aires to Montevideo, 1917. 40p, Cordoba to Villa Dolores, 1925. 60p, Bahia Blanca to Comodoro Rivadavia, 1929. 80p, Argentina to Germany, 1934. 100p, naval service to the Antarctic, 1952.

1985, Apr. 27
1494 A689 20p Bleriot Gnome .65 .35
1495 A689 40p Junker F-13L .65 .35
1496 A689 60p Latte 25 .65 .40
1497 A689 80p L.Z. 127 Graf Zeppelin .70 .45
1498 A689 100p Consolidated PBY Catalina .85 .50
Nos. 1494-1498 (5) 3.50 2.05

Central Bank, 50th Anniv. A690

1985, June 1
1499 A690 80p Bank Bldg., Buenos Aires .70 .35

Jose A. Ferreyra (1889-1943), Director of Munequitas Portenas — A691

Famous directors and their films: No. 1501, Leopoldo Torre Nilsson (1924-1978), scene from Martin Fierro.

1985, June 1
1500 A691 100p shown .70 .35
1501 A691 100p multi .70 .35

Carlos Gardel (1890-1935), Entertainer A692

Paintings: No. 1502, Gardel playing the guitar on stage, by Carlos Alonso (b. 1929). No. 1503, Gardel in a wide-brimmed hat, by Hermenegildo Sabat (b. 1933). No. 1504, Portrait of Gardel in an ornamental frame, by Aldo Severi (b. 1928) and Martiniano Arce (b. 1939).

1985, June 15
1502 A692 200p multi .75 .40
1503 A692 200p multi .75 .40
1504 A692 200p multi .75 .40
Nos. 1502-1504 (3) 2.25 1.20

The Arrival, by Pedro Figari A693

A Halt on the Plains, by Prilidiano Pueyrredon — A693a

Oil paintings (details): 30c, The Wagon Square, by C. B. de Quiros.

1985, July 6 **Litho.** *Perf. 13½*
1505 A693 20c multi 1.00 .40
1506 A693 30c multi 1.25 .40

Souvenir Sheet

Perf. 12

1507 A693a Sheet of 2 2.75 2.75
a. 20c Pilgrims, vert. .50 .50
b. 30c Wagon .75 .75

ARGENTINA '85. No. 1507 contains 2 30x40mm stamps. See No. 1542.

Buenos Aires to Montevideo, 1917 Teodoro Fels Flight — A694

Historic flight covers: No. 1509, Villa Dolores to Cordoba, 1925. No. 1510, Buenos Aires to France, 1929 St. Exupery flight. No. 1511, Buenos Aires to Bremerhaven, 1934 Graf Zeppelin flight. No. 1512, 1st Antarctic flight, 1952.

1985, July 13 *Perf. 12x12½*
1508 A694 10c emer & multi .50 .40
1509 A694 10c ultra & multi .50 .40
1510 A694 10c lt choc & multi .50 .40
1511 A694 10c chnt & multi .50 .40
1512 A694 10c ap grn & multi .50 .40
Nos. 1508-1512 (5) 2.50 2.00

ARGENTINA '85.

Illuminated Fruit, by Fortunato Lacamera (1887-1951) — A695

Paintings: 20c, Woman with Bird, by Juan del Prete, vert.

1985, Sept. 7 *Perf. 13½*
1513 A695 20c multi .75 .40
1514 A695 30c multi .75 .40

Flower Types of 1982-85

Designs: 1a, Begonia micranthera var. hieronymi. 5a, Gymnocalycium bruchii.

1985-88 **Photo.** *Perf. 13½*
1515 A641 ½c like #1356 .80 .25
1516 A641 1c like #1439 .30 .25
1517 A641 2c like #1345 .30 .25
1518 A641 3c like #1441 .30 .25
1519 A641 5c like #1346 .80 .25
1520 A641 10c like #1348 .60 .25
1521 A641 20c like #1347 .50 .25
1522 A641 30c like #1443A .50 .30
1523 A641 50c like #1344 .80 .30
1524 A641 1a multi 1.00 .35
1525 A641 2a like #1351 .40 .25
1526 A641 5a multi .90 .40

Size: 15x23mm

1527 A641 8½c like #1349 .30 .25
Nos. 1515-1527 (13) 7.50 3.60

Issued: ½c, 1c, 12/16; 2c, 8½c, 30c, 9/18; 3c, 5c, 10c, 50c, 1a, 9/7; 20c, 10/17; 5a, 3/21/87; 2a, 12/5/88.

No. 1435 Surcharged

1986, Nov. 4 **Photo.** *Perf. 13½*
1530 A641 10c on 1p No. 1435 1.00 .50

Folk Musical Instruments A699

1985, Sept. 14 **Litho.** *Perf. 13½*
1531 A699 20c Frame drum .60 .40
1532 A699 20c Long flute .60 .40
1533 A699 20c Jew's harp .60 .40
1534 A699 20c Pan flutes .60 .40
1535 A699 20c Musical bow .60 .40
Nos. 1531-1535 (5) 3.00 2.00

Juan Bautista Alberdi (1810-1884), Historian, Politician A700

Famous men: 20c, Nicolas Avellaneda (1836-1885), President in 1874. 30c, Fr. Luis Beltran (1784-1827), military and naval engineer. 40c, Ricardo Levene (1885-1959), historian, author.

1985, Oct. 5
1536 A700 10c multi .50 .40
1537 A700 20c multi .50 .40
1538 A700 30c multi .65 .45
1539 A700 40c multi .75 .50
Nos. 1536-1539 (4) 2.40 1.75

Type of 1985 and

Skaters A701

Deception, by J. H. Rivoira — A702

1985, Oct. 19 **Litho.** *Perf. 13½*
1540 A701 20c multi .70 .40
1541 A702 30c multi .80 .40

Size: 147x75mm

Imperf

1542 A693a 1a multi 2.75 2.75

IYY. No. 1542 is inscribed in silver with the UN 40th anniversary and IYY emblems.

Provincial Views — A703

Designs: No. 1543, Rock Window, Buenos Aires. No. 1544, Forclaz Windmill, Entre Rios. No. 1545, Lake Potrero de los Funes, San Luis. No. 1546, Mission church, north-east province. No. 1547, Penguin colony, Punta

Tombo, Chubut. No. 1548, Water Mirrors, Cordoba.

1985, Nov. 23 *Perf. 13½*

1543 A703 10c multi	.65	.50
1544 A703 10c multi	.65	.50
1545 A703 10c multi	.65	.50
1546 A703 10c multi	.65	.50
1547 A703 10c multi	.65	.50
1548 A703 10c multi	.65	.50
Nos. 1543-1548 (6)	3.90	3.00

Christmas 1985 — A704

Designs: 10c, Birth of Our Lord, by Carlos Cortes. 20c, Christmas, by Hector Viola.

1985, Dec. 7

1549 A704 10c multi	.50	.40
1550 A704 20c multi	1.00	.40

Natl. Campaign for the Prevention of Blindness — A705

1985, Dec. 7

1551 A705 10c multi	.40	.30

Rio Gallegos City, Cent. — A716

1985, Dec. 21 **Litho.** *Perf. 13½*

1552 A716 10c Church	1.25	.45

Natl. Grape Harvest Festival, 50th Anniv. A717

1986, Mar. 15

1553 A717 10c multi	.50	.40

Exists with Wmk. 265, Value $20.

Historical Architecture in Buenos Aires — A718

Designs: No. 1554, Valentin Alsina House, Italian Period, 1860-70. No. 1555, House on Cerrito Street, French influence, 1880-1900. No. 1556, House on the Avenida de Mayo y Santiago del Estero, Art Nouveau, 1900-10. No. 1557, Customs Building, academic architecture, 1900-15. No. 1558, Isaac Fernandez Blanco Museum, house of architect Martin Noel, natl. restoration, 1910-30. Nos. 1554-1556 vert.

1986, Apr. 19

1554 A718 20c multi	.60	.40
1555 A718 20c multi	.60	.40
1556 A718 20c multi	.60	.40
1557 A718 20c multi	.60	.40
1558 A718 20c multi	.60	.40
Nos. 1554-1558 (5)	3.00	2.00

Antarctic Bases, Pioneers and Fauna — A719

Designs: a, Base, Jubany. b, Arctocephalus gazella. c, Otaria byronia. d, Gen. Belgrano Base. e, Daption capensis. f, Diomedia melanophris. g, Apterodytes patagonica. h, Macronectes giganteus. i, Hugo Alberto Acuna (1885-1953). j, Spheniscus magellanicus. k, Gallinago gallinage. l, Capt. Agustin del Castillo (1855-89).

1986, May 31

1559 Sheet of 12	13.00	11.00
a.-l. A719 10c any single	.90	.85

Famous People — A720

Designs: No. 1560, Dr. Alicia Moreau de Justo, human rights activist. No. 1561, Dr. Emilio Ravignani (1886-1954), historian. No. 1562, Indira Gandhi.

1986, July 5 **Litho.** *Perf. 13½*

1560 A720 10c multi	.55	.40
1561 A720 10c multi	.55	.40
1562 A720 30c multi	.90	.65
Nos. 1560-1562 (3)	2.00	1.45

Statuary, Buenos Aires — A721

20c, Fountain of the Nereids, by Dolores Lola Mora (1866-1936). 30c, Lamenting at Work, by Rogelio Yrurtia (1879-1950), horiz.

1986, July 5

1563 A721 20c multi	1.00	.45
1564 A721 30c multi	1.00	.45

Famous Men — A722

Designs: No. 1565, Francisco N. Laprida (1786-1829), politician. No. 1566, Estanislao Lopez (1786-1838), brigadier general. No. 1567, Francisco Ramirez (1786-1821), general.

1986, Aug. 9 **Litho.** *Perf. 13*

1565 A722 20c dl yel, brn & blk	.50	.40
1566 A722 20c dl yel, brn & blk	.50	.40
1567 A722 20c dl yel, brn & blk	.50	.40
Nos. 1565-1567 (3)	1.50	1.20

Fr. Ceferino Namuncura (1886-1905) A723

1986, Aug. 30 *Perf. 13½*

1568 A723 20c multi	.50	.40

Miniature Sheets

Natl. Team Victory, 1986 World Cup Soccer Championships, Mexico — A724

Designs: No. 1569a-1569d, Team. Nos. 1569e-1569h, Shot on goal. Nos. 1570a-1570d, Action close-up. Nos. 1570e-1570h, Diego Maradona holding soccer cup.

1986, Nov. 8 **Litho.** *Perf. 13½*

1569 A724 Sheet of 8	12.00	*12.00*
a.-h. 75c any single	1.25	*1.25*
1570 A724 Sheet of 8	12.00	*12.00*
a.-h. 75c any single	1.25	*1.25*

San Francisco (Cordoba), Cent. — A725

1986, Nov. 8

1571 A725 20c Municipal Building	.50	.35

Trelew City (Chubut), Cent. — A726

1986, Nov. 22 **Litho.** *Perf. 13½*

1572 A726 20c Old railroad station, 1865	.50	.35

Mutualism Day — A727

1986, Nov. 22

1573 A727 20c multi	.60	.40

Christmas — A728

Designs: 20c, Naif retable, by Aniko Szabo (b. 1945). 30c, Everyone's Tree, by Franca Delacqua (b. 1947).

1986, Dec. 13 **Litho.** *Perf. 13½*

1574 A728 20c multicolored	.75	.50
1575 A728 30c multicolored	.85	.50

Santa Rosa de Lima, 400th Birth Anniv. — A729

1986, Dec. 13

1576 A729 50c multicolored	1.25	.50

Rio Cuarto Municipal Building A730

1986, Dec. 20

1577 A730 20c shown	.65	.40
1578 A730 20c Court Building, Cordoba	.65	.40

Rio Cuarto City, bicent. Court Building, Cordoba, 50th anniv.

Antarctic Treaty, 25th Anniv. — A731

1987, Mar. 7 **Litho.** *Perf. 13½*

1579 A731 20c Marine biologist	1.00	.50
1580 A731 30c Ornithologist	1.25	.50

Souvenir Sheet

Perf. 12

1581 Sheet of 2	5.50	5.50
a. A731 20c like No. 1579	2.00	1.50
b. A731 30c like No. 1580	3.00	2.00

No. 1581 contains 2 stamps, size: 40x50mm. Exist imperf. Value $500.

Natl. Mortgage Bank, Cent. — A732

1987, Mar. 21 ***Perf. 13½***

1582 A732 20c multicolored .60 .40

Natl. Cooperative Associations Movement — A733

1987, Mar. 21

1583 A733 20c multicolored .60 .40

Second State Visit of Pope John Paul II — A734

Engr., Litho. (No. 1585)

1987, Apr. 4 ***Perf. 13½***

1584 A734 20c shown .75 .40
1585 A734 80c Papal blessing 1.25 .60

Souvenir Sheet

Perf. 12

1586 A734 1a like 20c 3.50 3.50

No. 1586 contains one 40x50mm stamp.

Intl. Peace Year A735

30c, Pigeon, abstract sculpture by Victor Kaniuka.

1987, Apr. 11 **Litho.**

1587 A735 20c multicolored .85 .50
1588 A735 30c multicolored .85 .50

Low Handicap World Polo Championships A736

Polo Players, painting by Alejandro Moy.

1987, Apr. 11

1589 A736 20c multicolored 1.00 .50

Miniature Sheet

ICOM '86 — A737

Designs: a, Emblem. b, Family crest, National History Museum, Buenos Aires. c, St. Bartholomew, Enrique Larreta Museum of Spanish Art, Buenos Aires. d, Zoomorphic club, Patagonian Museum, San Carlos de Bariloche. e, Supplication, anthropomorphic sculpture, Natural Sciences Museum, La Plata. f, Wrought iron lattice from the house of J. Urquiza, president of the Confederation of Argentina, Entre Rios History Museum, Parana. g, St. Joseph, 18th cent. wood figurine, Northern History Museum, Salta. h, Funerary urn, Provincial Archaeological Museum, Santiago del Estero.

1987, May 30

1590 Sheet of 8 5.00 5.00
a.-h. A737 25c any single .50 .50

Intl. Council of Museums, 14th general conf.

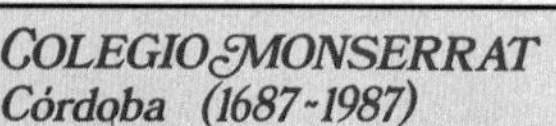
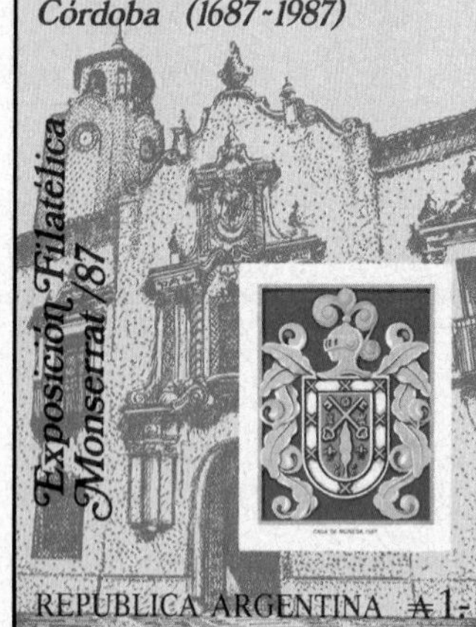

Natl. College of Monserrat, Cordoba, 300th Anniv. — A738

1987, July 4 ***Imperf.***

1591 A738 1a multicolored 1.75 1.25

Monserrat '87 Philatelic Exposition.

Fight Drug Abuse A739

The Proportions of Man, by da Vinci.

1987, Aug. 15 ***Perf. 13½***

1592 A739 30c multicolored .90 .35

Famous Men A740

Portraits and quotations: 20c, Jorge Luis Borges (1899-1986), writer. 30c, Armando Discepolo (1887-1971), playwright. 50c, Carlos A. Pueyrredon (1887-1962), professor, Legion of Honor laureate.

1987, Aug. 15

1593 A740 20c multicolored .45 .35
1594 A740 30c multicolored .60 .35
1595 A740 50c multicolored .75 .50
Nos. 1593-1595 (3) 1.80 1.20

Pillar Boxes
A741 A742

1987 **Photo.** ***Perf. 13½***

1596 A741 (30c) yel, blk & dark red 2.00 .25
Booklet with 10 stamps 25.00
1597 A742 (33c) lt blue grn, blk & yel 2.50 .25
Complete booklet, 10 #1597 30.00

Issue dates: (30c), June 8; (33c), July 13.

The Sower, by Julio Vanzo A743

1987, Sept. 12

1598 A743 30c multicolored .75 .35

Argentine Agrarian Federation, 75th anniv.

10th Pan American Games, Indianapolis, Aug. 7-25 — A744

1987, Sept. 26

1599 A744 20c Basketball .55 .35
1600 A744 30c Rowing .75 .40
1601 A744 50c Yachting .85 .45
Nos. 1599-1601 (3) 2.15 1.20

Children Playing Doctor, WHO Emblem A745

1987, Oct. 7

1602 A745 30c multi .50 .35

Vaccinate every child campaign.

Heroes of the Revolution A746

Signing of the San Nicolas Accord, 1852, by Rafael del Villar A747

Independence anniversaries and historic events: No. 1603, Maj.-Col. Ignacio Alvarez Thomas (1787-1857). No. 1604, Col. Manuel Crispulo Bernabe Dorrego (1787-1829). No. 1606, 18th cent. Spanish map of the Falkland Isls., administered by Jacinto de Altolaguirre.

1987, Oct. 17

1603 A746 25c shown .65 .35
1604 A746 25c multi .65 .35
1605 A747 50c shown .65 .35
1606 A747 50c multi .65 .35
Nos. 1603-1606 (4) 2.60 1.40

Museum established in the House of the San Nicholas Accord, 50th anniv. (No. 1605); Jacinto de Altolaguirre (1754-1787), governor the Malvinas Isls. for the King of Spain (No. 1606).

Celedonio Galvan Moreno, 1st Director — A748

1987, Nov. 21

1607 A748 50c multicolored .65 .35

Postas Argentinas magazine, 50th anniv.

LRA National Radio, Buenos Aires, 50th Anniv. — A749

1987, Nov. 21

1608 A749 50c multicolored .60 .35

Natl. Philatelic Society, Cent. A750

1987, Nov. 21

1609 A750 1a Jose Marco del Pont .90 .40

Christmas A751

Tapestries: 50c, *Navidad*, by Alisia Frega. 1a, *Vitral*, by Silvina Trigos.

1987, Dec. 5

1610 A751 50c multicolored .60 .35
1611 A751 1a multicolored .80 .45

Natl. Parks — A752

1987, Dec. 19 ***Perf. 13x13½***

1612 A752 50c Baritu .70 .35
1613 A752 50c Nahuel Huapi .70 .35
1614 A752 50c Rio Pilcomayo .70 .35
1615 A752 50c Tierra del Fuego .70 .35
1616 A752 50c Iguacu .70 .35
Nos. 1612-1616 (5) 3.50 1.75

See Nos. 1647-1651, 1715-1719, 1742-1746.

Landscapes in Buenos Aires Painted by Jose Cannella — A753

1988-89 **Litho.** ***Perf. 13½***

1617 A753 5a Caminito 1.90 .50
1618 A753 10a Viejo Almacen 3.50 .50
1618A A753 10a like No. 1618 1.90 .50
1618B A753 50a like No. 1617 1.90 .50
c. Wmk 365 *125.00* 20.00
Nos. 1617-1618B (4) 9.20 2.00

No. 1618 inscribed "Viejo Almacen"; No. 1618A inscribed "El Viejo Almacen."

Issue dates: 5a, No. 1618, 3/15; No. 1618A, 10/20; 50a, 5/30/89.

For overprint see No. 1635.

Minstrel in a Tavern, by Carlos Morel A754

Paintings: No. 1620, Interior of Curuzu, by Candido Lopez.

1988, Mar. 19 **Litho.** ***Perf. 13½***

1619 A754 1a shown .70 .35
1620 A754 1a multicolored .70 .35

See Nos. 1640-1641.

Argentine-Brazilian Economic Cooperation and Integration Program for Mutual Growth — A755

1988, Mar. 19

1621 A755 1a multicolored .65 .35

Cities of Alta Gracia and Corrientes, 400th Annivs. — A756

1988, Apr. 9 **Litho.** ***Perf. 13½***

1622 A756 1a Alta Gracia Church .70 .40
1623 A756 1a Chapel of St. Anne, Corrientes .70 .40

Labor Day — A757

Grain Carriers, a tile mosaic by Alfredo Guido, Line D of Nueve de Julio station, Buenos Aires subway: a, (UL). b, (UR). c, (LL). d, (LR).

1988, May 21

1624 A757 Block of 4 4.00 2.25
a.-d. 50c any single .70 .40

1988 Summer Olympics, Seoul — A758

1988, July 16 **Litho.** ***Perf. 13½***

1625 A758 1a Running .75 .50
1626 A758 2a Soccer .75 .50
1627 A758 3a Field hockey 1.25 .50
1628 A758 4a Tennis 1.40 .65
Nos. 1625-1628 (4) 4.15 2.15

Mendoza Bank, Cent. — A759

Natl. Gendarmerie, Cent. — A760

1988, Aug. 13

1629 A759 2a multicolored .60 .35
1630 A760 2a multicolored .60 .35

Sarmiento and Cathedral School to the North, Buenos Aires — A761

1988, Sept. 10 **Litho.** ***Perf. 13½***

1631 A761 3a multicolored .60 .35

Domingo Faustino Sarmiento (1811-1888), educator, politician.

St. Cayetano, Patron of Workers A762

El Amor, by Antonio Berni, Pacific Gallery, Buenos Aires — A763

1988, Sept. 10 **Litho.**

1632 A762 2a multicolored .65 .35
1633 A762 3a Our Lady of Carmen, Cuyo .65 .45

Souvenir Sheet

Perf. 12

1634 A763 5a multicolored 2.40 2.40

Liniers Philatelic Circle and the Argentine Western Philatelic Institution (IFADO), 50th annivs.

No. 1634 contains one 40x30mm stamp.

No. 1617 Ovptd.

1988, Oct. 29 **Litho.** ***Perf. 13½***

1635 A753 5a multicolored 5.50 1.50

21st Congress of the Intl. Urology Soc.

Tourism — A763a

1988, Nov. 1 **Litho.** ***Perf. 13½***

1635A A763a 3a Purmamarca, Jujuy .50 .30

Size: 28½x38mm

1635B A763a 20a Ushuaia 2.00 .50

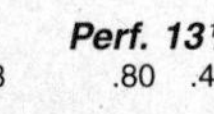
Buenos Aires Subway, 75th Anniv. A764

1988, Dec. 17 **Litho.** ***Perf. 13½***

1636 A764 5a Train, c. 1913 .80 .40

Christmas A765

Frescoes in Ucrania Cathedral, Buenos Aires: No. 1637, *Virgin Patron.* No. 1638, *Virgin of Tenderness.*

1988, Dec. 17

1637 A765 5a multicolored 1.00 .45
1638 A765 5a multicolored 1.00 .45

St. John Bosco (1815-1888), Educator, and Church in Ushuaia — A766

1989, Apr. 8 **Litho.** ***Perf. 13½***

1639 A766 5a multicolored .90 .40

Dated 1988.

Art Type of 1988

Paintings: No. 1640, *Blancos,* by Fernando Fader (1882-1935). No. 1641, *Rincon de los Areneros,* by Justo Lynch (1870-1953).

1989, Apr. 8

1640 A754 5a multicolored 1.00 .35
1641 A754 5a multicolored 1.00 .35

Holy Week A767

Sculpture and churches: No. 1642, *The Crown of Thorns,* Calvary of Tandil, and Church of Our Lady Carmelite, Tandil. No. 1643, *Jesus the Nazarene* and Metropolitan Cathedral, Buenos Aires. No. 1644, *Jesus Encounters His Mother* (scene of the crucifixion), La Quebrada Village, San Luis. No. 1645, *Our Lady of Sorrow* and Church of Humahuaca, Jujuy.

1989, Apr. 22 **Litho.** ***Perf. 13½***

1642 A767 2a multicolored .50 .35
1643 A767 2a multicolored .50 .35
1644 A767 3a multicolored .50 .35
1645 A767 3a multicolored .50 .35
a. Block of 4 + 2 labels 2.50 2.00
Nos. 1642-1645 (4) 2.00 1.40

Printed in sheets of 16+4 labels containing blocks of 4 of each design. Labels picture Jesus's arrival in Jerusalem (Palm Sunday).

Prevent Alcoholism — A768

1989, Apr. 22

1646 A768 5a multicolored .75 .50

Natl. Park Type of 1987

1989, May 6 ***Perf. 13x13½***

1647 A752 5a Lihue Calel .70 .35
1648 A752 5a El Palmar .70 .35
1649 A752 5a Calilegua .70 .35
1650 A752 5a Chaco .70 .35
1651 A752 5a Los Glaciares .70 .35
Nos. 1647-1651 (5) 3.50 1.75

Admission of Argentina to the ITU, Cent. — A769

1989, May 6 *Perf. 13½*

1652 A769 10a multicolored .70 .40

World Model Aircraft Championships — A770

1989, May 27 **Litho.** *Perf. 13½*

1653 A770 5a F1A glider .50 .35
1654 A770 5a F1B rubber band motor .50 .35
1655 A770 10a F1C gas motor .65 .35
Nos. 1653-1655 (3) 1.65 1.05

French Revolution, Bicent. — A771

Designs: 10a, "All men are born free and equal." 15a, French flag and *La Marianne,* by Gandon. 25a, *Liberty Guiding the People,* by Delacroix.

1989, July 1 **Litho.** *Perf. 13½*

1656 A771 10a shown .60 .60
1657 A771 15a multicolored .60 .50

Souvenir Sheet

Perf. 12

1658 A771 25a multicolored 1.50 1.50

No. 1658 contains one 40x30mm stamp.

The Republic, a Bronze Bust in the Congreso de la Nacion, Buenos Aires — A772

1989, Aug. 12 **Litho.** *Perf. 13½*

1659 A772 300a on 50a multi 1.25 .50

Peaceful transition of power (presidential office). Not issued without surcharge.

Immigration to Argentina — A773

1989, Aug. 19 *Perf. 13½*

1660 A773 150a S.S. *Weser,* 1889 .85 .40
1661 A773 200a Immigrant hotel, 1889 .95 .50

Souvenir Sheet

Perf. 12

1662 Sheet of 2 2.75 2.75
a. A773 150a like No. 1660 1.25 1.25
b. A773 200a like No. 1661 1.25 1.25

No. 1662 contains 40c30mm stamps.

Famous Men A774

Designs: No. 1663, Fr. Guillermo Furlong (1889-1974), historian, and title page of *The Jesuits.* No. 1664, Dr. Gregorio Alvarez (1889-1986), physician, and title page of *Canto a Chos Malal.* 200a, Brig.-Gen. Enrique Martinez (1789-1870) and lithograph *La Batalla de Maipu,* by Teodoro Gericault.

1989, Oct. 7 **Litho.** *Perf. 13½*

1663 A774 150a multicolored .65 .35
1664 A774 150a multicolored .65 .35
1665 A774 200a multicolored .65 .35
Nos. 1663-1665 (3) 1.95 1.05

America Issue — A775

Emblem of the Postal Union of the Americas and Spain (PUAS) and pre-Columbian art from Catamarca Province: 200a, Wooden mask from Atajo, Loma Morada. 300a, Urn of the Santa Maria Culture (Phase 3) from Punta de Balastro, Santa Maria Department.

1989, Oct. 14

1666 A775 200a multicolored 1.25 .50
1667 A775 300a multicolored 1.35 .70

Federal Police Week — A776

Children's drawings: No. 1668, Diego Molinari, age 13. No. 1669, Carlos Alberto Sarago, age 8. No. 1670, Roxana Andrea Osuna, age 7. No. 1671, Pablo Javier Quaglia, age 9.

1989, Oct. 28 **Litho.** *Perf. 13½*

1668 A776 100a multi .65 .35
1669 A776 100a multi .65 .35
1670 A776 150a multi .65 .35
1671 A776 150a multi .65 .35
Nos. 1668-1671 (4) 2.60 1.40

Battle of Vuelta de Obligado, 1845 — A777

1989, Dec. 2 **Litho.** *Perf. 13x13½*

1672 A777 300a multicolored 1.00 .35

Paintings — A778

Cristo de los Cerros, Sculpture by Chipo Cespedes A779

1989, Dec. 2 *Perf. 13½*

1673 A778 200a Gato Frias .75 .50
1674 A778 200a Maria Carballido .75 .50
1675 A779 300a shown .90 .50
Nos. 1673-1675 (3) 2.40 1.50

Christmas.

Buenos Aires Port, Cent. — A780

1990, Mar. 3 **Litho.** *Perf. 13½*

1676 A780 Strip of 4 8.50 6.25
a.-d. 200a any single 1.75 1.00

Aconcagua Intl. Fair, Mendoza — A781

Design: Aconcagua mountain, Los Horcones Lagoon and fair emblem.

1990, Mar. 3

1677 A781 Pair, #a.-b. 2.00 1.25

Natl. Savings and Insurance Fund, 75th Anniv. — A782

1990, May 5 **Litho.** *Perf. 13½*

1678 A782 1000a multicolored .60 .40

Miniature Sheet

1990 World Cup Soccer Championships, Italy — A783

Designs: a, Athlete's torso (striped jersey). b, Athlete's torso (solid jersey). c, Players' feet, soccer ball. d, Player (knee to waist).

1990, May 5

1679 A783 Sheet of 4 9.00 9.00
a.-d. 2500a multicolored 1.50 1.00

Carlos Pellegrini, Commercial High School Founder, Cent. — A784

1990, June 2 **Litho.** *Perf. 13½*

1680 A784 2000a multicolored .80 .50

Youth Against Drugs A785

1990, June 2

1681 A785 2000a multicolored .80 .50

Intl. Literacy Year A786

1990, July 14 **Litho.** *Perf. 13½*

1682 A786 2000a multicolored .80 .50

Flower Type of 1982 in New Currency

1989-90 **Photo.** *Perf. 13½*

1683 A641 10a like #1433 .30 .25
1684 A641 20a like #1435A .30 .25
1685 A641 50a like #1354 .30 .25
1686 A641 100a like #1439 .30 .25
1687 A641 300a like #1345 .35 .25
1688 A641 500a like #1441 .40 .25
1689 A641 1000a like #1355 .50 .25
1690 A641 5000a like #1349 3.00 .25
1691 A641 10,000a like #1350 10.00 .50
Nos. 1683-1691 (9) 15.45 2.50

Issued: 20a, 100a, 300a, 500a, 8/1/89; 10a, 8/24/89; 50a, 8/30/89; 1000, 3/8/90; 5000a, 4/6/90; 10,000a, 7/2/90.

World Basketball Championships A787

1990, Aug. 11 **Litho.** *Perf. 13½*

1703 A787 2000a multicolored 1.25 .60

Souvenir Sheet

Perf. 12

1704 A787 5000a Jump ball 6.50 6.50

Postal Union of the Americas and Spain, 14th Congress — A788

1990, Sept. 15 Litho. *Perf. 13½*

1705 A788 3000a Arms, seal 1.25 .60
1706 A788 3000a Sailing ships 1.25 .60
1707 A788 3000a Modern freighter 1.25 .60
1708 A788 3000a Van, cargo plane 1.25 .60
Nos. 1705-1708 (4) 5.00 2.40

America Issue A789

No. 1709, Iguacu Falls, hamelia erecta. No. 1710, Puerto Deseado, elephant seal.

1990, Oct. 13

1709 A789 3000a multicolored 2.00 1.25
1710 A789 3000a multicolored 2.00 1.25

Natl. Park Type of 1987

1990, Oct. 27 *Perf. 13x13½*

1715 A752 3000a Lanin 1.25 .90
1716 A752 3000a Laguna Blanca 1.25 .90
1717 A752 3000a Perito Moreno 1.25 .90
1718 A752 3000a Puelo 1.25 .90
1719 A752 3000a El Rey 1.25 .90
Nos. 1715-1719 (5) 6.25 4.50

Stamp Day A790

1990, Oct. 27 *Perf. 13½*

1720 A790 3000a multicolored 1.25 .55

Salvation Army, Cent. — A793

Designs: No. 1722, Natl. University of the Littoral, Santa Fe, cent.

1990, Dec. 1 Litho. *Perf. 13½*

1721 A793 3000a multicolored 1.75 .90
1722 A793 3000a multicolored 1.75 .90
a. Pair, #1721-1722 + label 7.50 6.50

Miniature Sheets

Christmas — A794

Stained glass windows: No. 1723, The Immaculate Conception. No. 1724, The Nativity. No. 1725, Presentation of Jesus at the Temple.

1990, Dec. 1 *Perf. 13½x13*
Sheets of 4

1723 A794 3000a #a.-d. 6.75 6.75
1724 A794 3000a #a.-d. 6.75 6.75
1725 A794 3000a #a.-d. 6.75 6.75

Landscapes — A795

Paintings: No. 1726, Los Sauces, by Atilio Malinverno. No. 1727, Paisaje, by Pio Collivadino, vert.

1991, May 4 Litho. *Perf. 13½*

1726 A795 4000a multicolored 1.00 .60
1727 A795 4000a multicolored 1.00 .60

Return of Remains of Juan Manuel de Rosas (1793-1877) A796

1991, June 1 Litho. *Perf. 13½*

1728 A796 4000a multicolored 1.00 .60

Swiss Confederation, 700th Anniv. — A797

1991, Aug. 3 Litho. *Perf. 13½*

1729 A797 4000a multicolored 1.25 .60

Miniature Sheet

Cartoons — A798

Designs: a, Hernan, the Corsair by Jose Luis Salinas. b, Don Fulgencio by Lino Palacio. c, Medical Rules of Salerno by Oscar Esteban Conti. d, Buenos Aires Undershirt by Alejandro del Prado. e, Girls! by Jose A.G. Divito. f, Langostino by Eduardo Carlos Ferro. g, Mafalda by Joaquin Salvador Lavoro. h, Mort Cinder by Alberto Breccia.

1991, Aug. 3

1730 A798 4000a Sheet of 8, #a.-h. 17.00 17.00

City of La Rioja, 400th Anniv. — A799

1991, Sept. 14 Litho. *Perf. 13½*

1731 A799 4000a multicolored 1.25 .60

First Balloon Flight over the Andes, 75th Anniv. — A800

1991, Sept. 14

1732 A800 4000a multicolored 1.25 .60

America Issue A801

Designs: No. 1733, Magellan's caravel, Our Lady of Victory. No. 1734, Ships of Juan Diaz de Solis.

1991, Nov. 9 Litho. *Perf. 13½*

1733 A801 4000a multicolored 1.75 .70
1734 A801 4000a multicolored 1.75 .70

Anniversaries — A802

Designs: a, Johann Heinrich Pestalozzi, Swiss pedagogue and educational reformer, whose Argentine school, the *Colegio Pestalozzi*, was associated with the anti-fascist newspaper *Argentinisches Tageblatt*. b, Leandro N. Alem, founder of Radical People's Party. c, Man with rifle, emblem of Argentine Federal Shooting Club. d, Dr. Nicasio Etchepareborda, emblem of College of Odontology. e, Dalmiro Huergo, emblem of Graduate School of Economics.

1991, Nov. 30

1735 A802 4000a Strip of 5, #a.-e. 7.00 7.00

Christmas — A803

Stained glass windows from Our Lady of Lourdes Basilica, Buenos Aires: Nos. 1736a-1736b, Top and bottom portions of Virgin of the Valley, Catamarca. Nos. 1736c-1736d, Top and bottom portions of Virgin of the Rosary of the Miracle, Cordoba.

1991, Nov. 30

1736 A803 4000a Block of 4, #a.-d. 5.00 3.50
a. Sheet of 16, 4 ea #a-d, + 4 labels 25.00 20.00

The four labels of No. 1736a form a nativity scene across the middle of the sheet.

Famous Men A804

Designs: a, Gen. Juan de Lavalle (1797-1841), Peruvian medal of honor. b, Brig. Gen. Jose Maria del Rosario Ciriaco Paz (1791-1854), medal. c, Marco Manuel de Avellaneda (1813-1841), lawyer. d, Guillermo Enrique Hudson (1841-1922), author.

1991, Dec. 14 Litho. *Perf. 13½*

1737 A804 4000a Block of 4, #a.-d. 5.00 3.75

Birds — A805

1991, Dec. 28

1738 A805 4000a Pterocnemia pennata 1.50 1.00
1739 A805 4000a Morphnus guianensis 1.50 1.00
1740 A805 4000a Ara chloroptera 1.50 1.00
Nos. 1738-1740 (3) 4.50 3.00

Miniature Sheet

Arbrafex '92, Argentina-Brazil Philatelic Exhibition — A806

Traditional costumes: a, Gaucho, woman. b, Gaucho, horse. c, Gaucho in store. d, Gaucho holding lariat.

1992, Mar. 14 Litho. *Perf. 13½*
1741 A806 38c Sheet of 4, #a.-d. 5.00 4.00

Natl. Park Type of 1987

1992, Apr. 4 Litho. *Perf. 13x13½*
1742 A752 38c Alerces 1.40 .70
1743 A752 38c Formosa Nature Reserve 1.40 .70
1744 A752 38c Petrified Forest 1.40 .70
1745 A752 38c Arrayanes 1.40 .70
1746 A752 38c Laguna de los Pozuelos 1.40 .70
Nos. 1742-1746 (5) 7.00 3.50

Mushrooms — A807

1992-94 Photo. *Perf. 13½*
1748 A807 10c Psilocybe cubensis .70 .30
1749 A807 25c Coprinus atramentarius 1.00 .35
a. Wmk. 365 12.50 4.00
1750 A807 38c like #1748 1.75 .30
1751 A807 48c like #1749 2.00 .75
1752 A807 50c Suillus granulatus 2.00 .30
1753 A807 51c Morchella esculenta 2.00 1.00
1754 A807 61c Amanita muscaria 2.75 1.25
1755 A807 68c Coprinus comatus 2.75 1.25
1756 A807 1p like #1754 3.00 .80
1757 A807 1.25p like #1752 4.00 1.25
1758 A807 1.77p Stropharia oeruginosa 5.50 3.50
1759 A807 2p like #1753 7.00 1.50
Nos. 1748-1759 (12) 34.45 12.55

No. 1758 not issued without overprint "Centro Filatelico de Neuquen y Rio Negro 50th Aniversario."

Issued: 38c, 4/4/92; 48c, 51c, 61c, 8/1/92; 1.77p, 11/7/92; 25c, 50c, 8/17/93; 1p, 2p, 8/26/93; 10c, 1/11/94; 68c, 1.25p, 10/10/92; No. 1749a, 1997.

See design A838.

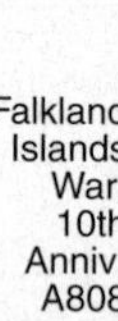

Falkland Islands War, 10th Anniv. A808

1992, May 2 Litho. *Perf. 13½*
1767 A808 38c Pucara 1A-58 1.40 .75
1768 A808 38c Cruiser Gen. Belgrano 1.40 .75
1769 A808 38c Soldier and truck 1.40 .75
Nos. 1767-1769 (3) 4.20 2.25

Miniature Sheet

Preserve the Environment — A809

a, Deer. b, Geese. c, Butterflies. d, Whale.

1992, June 6 Litho. *Perf. 12*
1770 A809 38c Sheet of 4, #a.-d. 6.75 5.50

Paintings by Florencio Molina Campos — A810

1992, June 6 *Perf. 13½*
1771 A810 38c A La Sombra 1.40 .60
1772 A810 38c Tileforo Areco, vert. 1.40 .60

Famous Men A811

Designs: No. 1773, Gen. Lucio N. Mansilla (1792-1871). No. 1774, Jose Manuel Estrada (1842-1894), writer. No. 1775, Brig. Gen. Jose I. Garmendia (1842-1915).

1992, July 4 Litho. *Perf. 13½*
1773 A811 38c multicolored 1.00 .60
1774 A811 38c multicolored 1.00 .60
1775 A811 38c multicolored 1.00 .60
Nos. 1773-1775 (3) 3.00 1.80

Fight Against Drugs — A812

1992, Aug. 1 *Perf. 13½x13*
1776 A812 38c multicolored 1.25 .60

Col. Jose M. Calaza, 140th Birth Anniv. A813

1992, Sept. 5 Litho. *Perf. 13½*
1777 A813 38c multicolored 1.25 .70

Discovery of America, 500th Anniv. — A814

Designs: a, Columbus, castle, ship. b, Native drawings, Columbus.

1992, Oct. 10 Litho. *Perf. 13½*
1778 A814 38c Pair, #a.-b. 3.50 3.50

Argentine Film Posters A815

1992, Nov. 7 Litho. *Perf. 13½*
1779 A815 38c Dios Se Lo Pague, 1948 1.25 .70
1780 A815 38c Las Aguas Bajan Turbias, 1952 1.25 .70
1781 A815 38c Un Guapo Del 900, 1960 1.25 .70
1782 A815 38c La Tregua, 1974 1.25 .70
1783 A815 38c La Historia Oficial, 1984 1.25 .70
Nos. 1779-1783 (5) 6.25 3.50

Christmas A816

1992, Nov. 28
1784 A816 38c multicolored 1.25 .60

Miniature Sheet

Iberoprenfil '92 — A817

Lighthouses: a, Punta Mogotes. b, Rio Negro. c, San Antonio. d, Cabo Blanco.

1992, Dec. 5
1785 A817 38c Sheet of 4, #a.-d. 8.50 7.00

Fight Against AIDS
A818 A819

1992, Dec. 12 Litho. *Perf. 13½*
1786 A818 10c multicolored 2.00 1.00
1787 A819 26c multicolored 3.00 1.75

Intl. Space Year A820

1992, Dec. 19
1788 A820 38c multicolored 1.50 .70

Souvenir Sheet

Miraculous Lord Crucifix, 400th Anniv. of Arrival in America — A821

1992, Dec. 26 *Perf. 12*
1789 A821 76c multicolored 4.50 4.50

Jujuy City, 400th Anniv. — A822

1993, Apr. 24 Litho. *Perf. 13½*
1790 A822 38c multicolored 1.25 .60

Argentina Soccer Assoc., Cent. — A823

1993, Mar. 27
1791 A823 38c multicolored 1.50 .60

Souvenir Sheet

Intl. Philatelic Exhibitions — A824

Designs: a, 38c, City Hall, Poznan, Poland. b, 48c, Statue of Christ the Redeemer, Rio de Janeiro, Brazil. c, 76c, Royal Palace, Bangkok, Thailand.

1993, May 8 Litho. ***Perf. 12***
1792 A824 Sheet of 3, #a.-c. 6.00 5.50

Polska '93 (No. 1792a), Brasiliana '93 (No. 1792b), Bangkok '92 (No. 1792c).

Luis C. Candelaria's Flight Over Andes Mountains, 75th Anniv. — A825

1993, June 26 Litho. ***Perf. 13x13½***
1793 A825 38c multicolored 1.50 .60

Order of San Martin, 50th Anniv. — A826

National History Academy, Cent. — A827

1993, May 29 ***Perf. 13½***
1794 A826 38c multicolored 1.25 .60
1795 A827 38c multicolored 1.25 .60

Armed Forces Memorial Day — A828

1993, June 12
1796 A828 38c Natl. Gendarmerie 1.50 .60
1797 A828 38c Coast Guard 1.50 .60

Paintings — A829

Designs: No. 1798, Old House, by Norberto Russo. No. 1799, Pa'las Casas, by Adriana Zaefferer.

1993, Aug. 14 Litho. ***Perf. 13½***
1798 A829 38c multicolored 1.50 .60
1799 A829 38c multicolored 1.50 .60

Pato — A830

1993, Aug. 28 Litho. ***Perf. 12***
1800 A830 1p multicolored 3.25 1.25

Nut-Bearing Trees — A831

Designs: No. 1801, Enterolobium contortisiliquum. No. 1802, Prosopis alba. No. 1803, Magnolia grandiflora. No. 1804, Erythrina falcata.

1993, Sept. 25 Litho. ***Perf. 13x13½***
1801 A831 75c multicolored 1.75 .75
1802 A831 75c multicolored 1.75 .75
1803 A831 1.50p multicolored 3.75 1.25
1804 A831 1.50p multicolored 3.75 1.25
Nos. 1801-1804 (4) 11.00 4.00

America Issue A832

Whales: 50c, Eubalaena australis. 75c, Cephalorhynchus commersonii.

1993, Oct. 9 ***Perf. 13½***
1805 A832 50c multicolored 1.75 .80
1806 A832 75c multicolored 2.50 1.25

Miniature Sheet

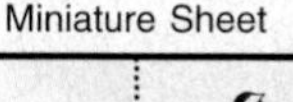

Christmas, New Year — A833

Denomination at: a, UL. b, UR. c, LL. d, LR.

1993, Dec. 4 Litho. ***Perf. 13½***
1807 A833 75c Sheet of 4, #a.-d. 8.00 7.50

Cave of the Hands, Santa Cruz — A834

1993, Dec. 18
1808 A834 1p multicolored 3.00 .90

New Emblem, Argentine Postal Service — A835

1994, Jan. 8 ***Perf. 11½***
1809 A835 75c multicolored 6.00 .60

A836

Players from: 25c, Germany, 1990. 50c, Brazil, 1970. 75c, 1.50p, Argentina, 1986. 1p, Italy, 1982.

1994, June 11 Litho. ***Perf. 13½***
1810 A836 25c multicolored .75 .40
1811 A836 50c multicolored 1.50 .50
1812 A836 75c multicolored 2.00 .60
1813 A836 1p multicolored 2.75 1.00
Nos. 1810-1813 (4) 7.00 2.50

Souvenir Sheet

Perf. 12

1814 A836 1.50p multicolored 4.50 4.00

No. 1814 contains one 40x50mm stamp with continuous design.

1994 World Cup Soccer Championships, US — A837

Drawings of championships by: No. 1815, Julian Lisenberg. No. 1816, Matias Taylor, vert. No. 1817, Torcuato S. Gonzalez Agote, vert. No. 1818, Maria Paula Palma.

1994, July 23 ***Perf. 13½***
1815 A837 75c multicolored 2.25 .75
1816 A837 75c multicolored 2.25 .75
1817 A837 75c multicolored 2.25 .75
1818 A837 75c multicolored 2.25 .75
Nos. 1815-1818 (4) 9.00 3.00

Issued in sheet containing a block of 4 of each stamp + 4 labels.

A838

Molothrus Badius — A838a

1994-95 Litho. ***Perf. 13½***
1819 A838 10c like #1748 .50 .35
1820 A838 25c like #1749 .70 .35
1823 A838 50c like #1752 1.25 .40
1828 A838 1p like #1754 2.75 .50
1832 A838 2p like #1753 5.75 .60
1835 A838a 9.40p multicolored 20.00 1.00
Nos. 1819-1835 (6) 30.95 3.20

See designs A807, A849.
Issued: 10c, 25c, 50c, 1p, 2p, 6/14/94; 9.40p, 4/12/95.

Wildlife of Falkland Islands A839

Designs: 25c, Melanodera melanodera. 50c, Pygoscelis papua. 75c, Tachyeres brachypterus. 1p, Mirounga leonina.

1994, Aug 6
1839 A839 25c multicolored 1.00 .55
1840 A839 50c multicolored 2.00 .55
1841 A839 75c multicolored 2.50 .55
1842 A839 1p multicolored 3.00 .55
Nos. 1839-1842 (4) 8.50 2.20

City of San Luis, 400th Anniv. — A840

1994, Aug. 20
1843 A840 75c multicolored 1.60 .80

Province of Tierra del Fuego, Antarctica and South Atlantic Islands A841

1994, Aug. 20

1844	A841	75c multicolored	2.00	.80

Argentine Inventors — A842

Designs: No. 1845, Ladislao Jose Biro (1899-1985), ball point pen. No. 1846, Raul Pateras de Pescara (1890-1966), helicopter. No. 1847, Quirino Cristiani (1896-1984), animated drawings. No. 1848, Enrique Finochietto (1881-1948), surgical instruments.

1994, Oct. 1

1845	A842	75c multicolored	1.60	.70
1846	A842	75c multicolored	1.60	.70
1847	A842	75c multicolored	1.60	.70
1848	A842	75c multicolored	1.60	.70
a.		Block of 4, #1845-1848	6.00	6.00

Issued in sheets containing 4 No. 1848a + 4 labels.

UNICEF Christmas A843

1994, Nov. 26 Litho. *Perf. 11½*

1849	A843	50c shown	1.25	.50
1850	A843	75c Bell, bulb, star, diff.	1.75	.70

Take Care of Our Planet A844

Children's paintings: No. 1851, Boy, girl holding earth, vert. No. 1852, Children outdoors, vert. No. 1853, World as house. No. 1854, People around "world" table.

1994, Dec. 3 *Perf. 13½*

1851	A844	25c multicolored	.75	.35
1852	A844	25c multicolored	.75	.35
1853	A844	50c multicolored	1.25	.70
1854	A844	50c multicolored	1.25	.70
		Nos. 1851-1854 (4)	4.00	2.10

Christmas — A845

1994, Dec. 10

1855	A845	50c Annunciation	1.25	.60
1856	A845	75c Madonna & Child	1.75	.60

Nos. 1855-1856 each issued in sheets of 20 + 5 labels.

12th Pan American Games, Mar del Plata — A846

1995 Litho. *Perf. 13½*

1857	A846	75c Running	1.75	.65
1858	A846	75c Cycling	1.75	.65
1859	A846	75c Diving	1.75	.65
1860	A846	1.25p Gymnastics, vert.	2.75	.75
1861	A846	1.25p Soccer, vert.	2.75	.75
		Nos. 1857-1861 (5)	10.75	3.45

Issued: No. 1857, 2/18; others, 3/11.

Natl. Constitution — A847

Design: 75c, Natl. Congress Dome, woman from statue The Republic Triumphant.

1995, Apr. 8

1862	A847	75c multicolored	1.75	.70

21st Intl. Book Fair — A848

1995, Apr. 8

1863	A848	75c multicolored	1.60	.70

Birds A849

1995 Litho. *Perf. 13½*

1876	A849	5p Carduelis magellanica	10.00	1.00
1880	A849	10p Zonotrichia capensis	26.50	2.00

Issued: 5p, 10p, 5/23/95.

A850

1995, Mar. 25 Litho. *Die Cut*

Self-Adhesive

1883A	A850	25c multicolored	10.00	.50
1884	A850	75c multicolored	3.00	.50
a.		Booklet pane, 2 #1883A, 6 #1884	40.00	
		Complete booklet, #1884a	50.00	
b.		Booklet pane, 4 #1883A, 12 #1884	77.50	
		Complete booklet, #1884b	85.00	

See Nos. 1921A-1921B.

Argentine Engineers' Center, Cent. — A851

1995, June 3 *Perf. 13½*

1885	A851	75c multicolored	1.50	.60

Jose Marti (1853-95) — A852

No. 1887, Antonio Jose de Sucre (1795-1830).

1995, Aug. 12 Litho. *Perf. 13½*

1886	A852	1p multicolored	2.25	.75
1887	A852	1p multicolored	2.25	.75

Fauna — A853

1995, Sept. 1 Litho. *Perf. 13½*

1888	A853	5c Ostrich	1.00	.25
1889	A853	25c Penguin	.65	.35
1890	A853	50c Toucan	1.25	.35
1891	A853	75c Condor	1.75	.35
1892	A853	1p Owl	3.50	.35
1893	A853	2p Bigua	5.00	.35
1894	A853	2.75p Tero	8.50	.35

Booklet Stamps

Perf. 13½ on 2 or 3 Sides

1895	A853	25c Alligator	.65	.40
1896	A853	50c Fox	1.25	.70
1897	A853	75c Anteater	1.75	1.00
1898	A853	75c Deer	1.75	1.00
1899	A853	75c Whale	1.75	1.00
a.		Booklet pane, 1 each Nos. 1889-1891, 1895-1899	10.00	10.00
		Complete booklet, #1899a	11.00	
		Nos. 1888-1899 (12)	28.80	6.45

See Nos. 1958, 2004-2004A.

Native Heritage — A854

a, Cave drawings, shifting sands. b, Stone mask. c, Anthropomorphous vessel. d, Woven textile.

1995, Sept. 9

1900	A854	75c Block of 4, #a.-d.	7.00	5.50

Sunflower, Postal Service Emblem — A855

1995, Oct. 7

1901	A855	75c multicolored	7.00	.50

Juan D. Peron (1895-1974) — A856

1995, Oct. 7

1902	A856	75c lt ol bis & dk bl	2.00	.60

Miniature Sheet

Anniversaries — A857

Annivs: a, UN, 50th. b, ICAO, 50th (in 1994). c, FAO, 50th. d, ILO, 75th (in 1994).

1995, Oct. 14 *Perf. 12*

1903	A857	75c Sheet of 4, #a.-d.	7.00	5.00

Christmas and New Year — A858

Designs: Nos. 1904, 1908, Christmas tree, presents. No. 1905, "1996." No. 1906, Champagne glasses. No. 1907, Present.

1995, Nov. 25 Litho. *Perf. 13½*

1904	A858	75c multicolored	2.00	.45

Booklet Stamps

Perf. 13½ on 1 or 2 Sides

1905	A858	75c multicolored	3.00	.75
1906	A858	75c multicolored	3.00	.75
1907	A858	75c multicolored	3.00	.75
1908	A858	75c multicolored	3.00	.75
a.		Booklet pane, #1905-1908 + label	12.00	
		Complete booklet, #1908a	20.00	
		Nos. 1904-1908 (5)	14.00	3.45

No. 1908a is a continuous design. Ribbon extends from edge to edge on No. 1908 and stops at edge of package on No. 1905.

Miniature Sheet

Motion Pictures, Cent. — A859

Black and white film clips, director: a, The Battleship Potemkin, Sergei Eisenstein (Soviet Union). b, Casablanca, Michael Curtiz (US). c, Bicycle Thief, Vittorio De Sica (Italy). d, Limelights, Charles Chaplin (England). e, The 400 Blows, Francois Truffaut (France). f, Chronicle of the Lonely Child, Leonardo Favio (Argentina).

1995, Dec. 2 ***Perf. 13½***

1909 A859 75c Sheet of 6, #a.-f. 17.50 17.50

The Sky — A860

1995, Dec. 16 ***Perf. 13½ on 3 Sides***

Booklet Stamps

1910 A860 25c Dirigible .50 .35
1911 A860 25c Kite .50 .35
1912 A860 25c Hot air balloon .50 .35
1913 A860 50c Balloons 1.10 .35
1914 A860 50c Paper airplane 1.10 .35
1915 A860 75c Airplane 1.60 .35
1916 A860 75c Helicopter 1.60 .35
1917 A860 75c Parachute 1.60 .35
a. Booklet pane, #1910-1917 + label 10.00
Complete booklet, No. 1917a 20.00

Nos. 1910-1917 do not appear in Scott number order in No. 1917a, which has a continuous design.

America Issue A861

Postal vehicles from Postal &Telegraph Museum: No. 1918, Horse & carriage. No. 1919, Truck.

1995, Dec. 16 ***Perf. 13½***

1918 A861 75c multicolored 1.60 .75
1919 A861 75c multicolored 1.60 .75

Olympic Games, Cent. A862

1996, Mar. 30 **Litho.** ***Perf. 13½***

1920 A862 75c Running 1.75 .75
1921 A862 1p Discus 2.50 .90

Type of 1995

Country Name and Denomination in Blue

Self-Adhesive

Coil Stamps

1996 **Litho.** ***Die Cut***

1921A A850 25c multi *5.00 2.00*
1921B A850 75c multi *7.50 3.00*

Physicians A863

Designs: a, Francisco J. Muniz (1795-1871). b, Ricardo Gutierrez (1838-96). c, Ignacio Pirovano (1844-95). d, Esteban L. Maradona (1895-1995).

1996, Apr. 20 **Litho.** ***Perf. 12***

1922 A863 50c Sheet of 4 6.00 6.00
a.-d. Any single 1.00 1.00

Jerusalem, 3000th Anniv. — A864

7th cent. mosaic maps of city, denomination at: No. 1923, LL. No. 1924, LR.

1996, May 18 **Litho.** ***Perf. 13½***

1923 A864 75c multicolored 1.50 .75
1924 A864 75c multicolored 1.50 .75
a. Pair, #1923-1924 6.00 4.00

No. 1924a is a continuous design and was issued in sheets of 8 + 4 labels.

Endangered Fauna — A865

1996, June 15 **Litho.** ***Perf. 13½***

1925 A865 75c Capybara 1.75 .75
1926 A865 75c Guanaco 1.75 .75
a. Pair, #1925-1926 4.50 3.50

America Issue.

Summer Olympic Games A866

Designs: 75c, Torch bearer, Buenos Aires, candidate for 2004 Games. 1p, Men's eight with coxswain, Atlanta, 1996.

1996, July 6

1927 A866 75c multicolored 1.75 .70
1928 A866 1p multicolored 2.50 .90

National Parks — A867

Wildlife, national park: No. 1929, Mountain turkey, Diamante. No. 1930, Parrot, San Antonio Nature Reserve. No. 1931, Deer, Otamendi Natl. Reserve. No. 1932, Rabbit, El Leoncito Nature Reserve.

1996, Aug. 24 **Litho.** ***Perf. 13x13½***

1929 A867 75c multicolored 1.60 .70
1930 A867 75c multicolored 1.60 .70
1931 A867 75c multicolored 1.60 .70
1932 A867 75c multicolored 1.60 .70
Nos. 1929-1932 (4) 6.40 2.80

Central Post Office, Buenos Aires — A868

1996, Oct. 5 **Litho.** ***Die Cut***

Self-Adhesive

Size: 25x35mm

1933 A868 75c multicolored 8.50 1.00

Vignette of No. 1933 is broken by circular and rectangular die cut areas to guard against reuse.

See Nos. 1983-1984.

Carousel Figures — A869

Designs: No. 1934, Hand-carved decorative ornaments. No. 1935, Child on carousel horse. No. 1936, Carousel. No. 1937, Heads of horses. No. 1938, Child in airplane. No. 1939, Carousel pig. No. 1940, Boy in car.

1996, Oct. 5 ***Perf. 13½ Horiz.***

Booklet Stamps

1934 A869 25c multicolored .50 .30
1935 A869 25c multicolored .50 .30
1936 A869 25c multicolored .50 .30
1937 A869 50c multicolored 1.00 .60
1938 A869 50c multicolored 1.00 .60
1939 A869 50c multicolored 1.00 .60
1940 A869 75c multicolored 1.50 .70
a. Booklet pane, #1934-1940 7.00
Complete booklet, #1940a 9.00

Sequence of stamps in No. 1940a: No. 1940, 1934, 1937, 1935, 1938, 1936, 1939.

Port Belgrano Naval Base, Cent. — A870

Designs: 25c, LST "San Antonio." 50c, Corvette *Rosales.* 75c, Destroyer *Hercules.* 1p, Aircraft carrier, "25th of May."

1996-97 **Litho.** ***Perf. 13½***

1941 A870 25c multicolored 1.00 .50
1942 A870 50c multicolored 1.50 .50
1943 A870 75c multicolored 2.25 .75
1944 A870 1p multicolored 2.75 1.00
Nos. 1941-1944 (4) 7.50 2.75

Issued: 25c, 1p, 10/5/96; 50c, 75c, 2/1/97.

Christmas — A871

Tapestries: 75c, Nativity, by Gladys Angelica Rinaldi, vert. 1p, Candles, by Norma Bonet de Maekawa.

1996, Nov. 30 **Litho.** ***Perf. 13½***

1945 A871 75c multicolored 1.50 .75
1946 A871 1p multicolored 2.25 1.00

Exploration of Antarctica — A872

Designs: 75c, Melchior Base. 1.25p, Icebreaker ARA Alte. Irizar.

1996, Nov. 30

1947 A872 75c multicolored 1.50 .75
1948 A872 1.25p multicolored 2.75 1.25

National Gallery, Cent. A873

Paintings of women by: 75c, Paul Gauguin, vert. No. 1950, Edouard Monet, vert. No. 1951, Amedeo Modigiliani, vert. 1.25p, Pablo Picasso.

1996, Dec. 14

1949 A873 75c multicolored 1.75 .60
1950 A873 1p multicolored 2.25 .90
1951 A873 1p multicolored 2.25 .90
1952 A873 1.25p multicolored 3.50 1.10
Nos. 1949-1952 (4) 9.75 3.50

Mining Industry — A874

1997, Feb. 1 **Litho.** ***Perf. 13½***

1953 A874 75c Granite 1.75 .75
1954 A874 1.25p Borax 3.00 1.10

Traditional Costumes — A875

1997, Feb. 22 **Litho.** ***Perf. 13½***

1955 A875 75c multicolored 1.60 .75

America issue.

Repatriation of the Curved Sword of Gen. San Martin, Cent. — A876

1997, Mar. 15 **Litho.** ***Perf. 13½***

1956 A876 75c multicolored 1.60 .60

29th Youth Rugby World Championships — A877

1997, Mar. 22
1957 A877 75c multicolored 1.75 .75

Fauna Type of 1995

1997, Feb. 22 Litho. *Perf. 13½*
1958 A853 10c Reddish sandpiper 1.40 .25

Buenos Aires-Rio de Janeiro Regatta, 50th Anniv. — A879

1997, Apr. 5 Litho. *Perf. 13½*
1960 A879 75c Fortuna II 1.75 .75

Natl. History Museum, Cent. — A880

1997, May 17
1961 A880 75c multicolored 1.60 .75

La Plata Natl. University, Cent. — A881

1997, May 17
1962 A881 75c multicolored 1.60 .75

Lighthouses A882

a, Cabo Virgenes. b, Isla Pingüino. c, San Juan de Salvamento. d, Punta Delgada.

1997, May 31
1963 A882 75c Sheet of 4, #a.-d. 9.50 7.50

Ramón J. Cárcano (1860-1946), Developer of Postal and Telegraph System A883

1997, May 31
1964 A883 75c multicolored 1.60 .75

Buenos Aires, Candidate for 2004 Summer Olympics — A884

1997, June 21
1965 A884 75c multicolored 1.60 .50

First Electric Tram in Buenos Aires, Cent. A885

Designs: a, Lacroze Suburban Service Tram Co, 1912. b, Lacroze Urban Service Tram Co., 1907. c, Anglo Argentina Tram Co., 1930. d, Buenos Aires City Transportation Corp., 1942. e, Military Manufacture Tram, 1956. f, South Electric Tram, 1908.

1997, July 12 Sheet of 6
1966 A885 75c #a.-f. + 2 labels 10.00 10.00

Monument to Joaquín V. González (1863-1923), La Rioja — A886

1997, Aug. 9
1967 A886 75c multicolored 1.60 .75

Musicians and Composers A887

Paintings: No. 1968, Alberto Ginastera (1916-83), by Carlos Nine. No. 1969, Astor Piazzolla (1921-92), by Carlos Alonso. No. 1970, Anibal Troilo (1914-75), by Hermenegildo Sabat. No. 1971, Atahualpa Yupanqui (b. 1908), by Luis Scafati.

1997, Aug. 9
1968 A887 75c multicolored 1.60 .70
1969 A887 75c multicolored 1.60 .70
1970 A887 75c multicolored 1.60 .70
1971 A887 75c multicolored 1.60 .70
Nos. 1968-1971 (4) 6.40 2.80

Argentine Authors — A888

Designs: No. 1972, Jorge Luis Borges (1899-1986), maze. No. 1973, Julio Cortázar (1914-84), hop scotch game.

1997, Aug. 30 Litho. *Perf. 13*
1972 A888 1p multicolored 2.25 1.00
1973 A888 1p multicolored 2.25 1.00

Women's Political Rights Law, 50th Anniv. A889

1997, Sept. 6 Litho. *Perf. 13½*
1974 A889 75c Eva Perón 2.50 1.00

Mercosur (Common Market of Latin America) A890

1997, Sept. 27 Litho. *Perf. 13½*
1975 A890 75c multicolored 1.60 .60

See Bolivia No. 1019, Brazil No. 2646, Paraguay No. 2564, Uruguay No. 1681.

Launching of Frigate President Sarmiento, Cent. — A891

Designs: No. 1976, Painting of ship by Hugo Leban.
No. 1977: a, Ship. b, Ship's figurehead, vert.

1997, Oct. 4
1976 A891 75c multicolored 1.75 .75

Souvenir Sheet
Perf. 12
1977 A891 75c Sheet of 2, #a.-b. 5.00 4.00

No. 1977 contains two 40x30mm stamps.

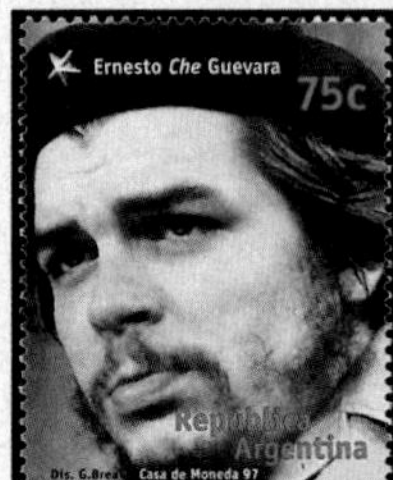
Ernesto "Che" Guevara (1928-67) A892

1997, Oct. 18
1978 A892 75c multicolored 5.00 .75

Ecology on Stamps — A893

Children's drawings: No. 1979, Animal, by J. Chiapparo, vert. No. 1980, Vicuna, by L.L. Portal, vert. No. 1981, Seal, by A. Lloren. No. 1982, Bird in flight, by J. Saccone.

1997, Nov. 8 Litho. *Perf. 13½*
1979 A893 50c multicolored 1.10 .50
1980 A893 50c multicolored 1.10 .50
1981 A893 75c multicolored 1.60 .75
1982 A893 75c multicolored 1.60 .75
Nos. 1979-1982 (4) 5.40 2.50

Central Post Office, Buenos Aires, Type of 1996

1997, July 24 Litho. *Die Cut*
Self-Adhesive
Size: 23x35mm
1983 A868 25c multicolored *12.00* .75
1984 A868 75c multicolored *5.00* .75
a. Bklt. pane, 2 #1983, 6 #1984 *55.00*
Complete booklet, #1984a *60.00*

Nos. 1983-1984 are broken at both the top and bottom of each stamp by three lines of wavy die cutting.

Christmas — A893a

Nativity scene tapestries by: Nos. 1984B, 1984G, Mary José. No. 1984C, Elena Aguilar. No. 1984D, Silvia Pettachi. No. 1984E, Ana Escobar. No. 1984F, Alejandra Martinez. No. 1984H, Nidia Martinez.

1997, Nov. 22 Litho. *Perf. 13½*
1984B A893a 75c multicolored 1.75 .75

Booklet Stamps
Self-Adhesive
Size: 44x27mm
Die Cut
1984C A893a 25c multicolored .75 .50
1984D A893a 25c multicolored 1.00 .50
1984E A893a 50c multicolored 1.50 .75
1984F A893a 50c multicolored 1.50 .75
1984G A893a 75c multicolored 2.00 .75
1984H A893a 75c multicolored 2.00 .75
i. Booklet pane, #1984C-1984H 10.00

Nos. 1984C-1984H are broken at upper right by three die cut chevrons. By its nature, No. 1984Hi is a complete booklet.

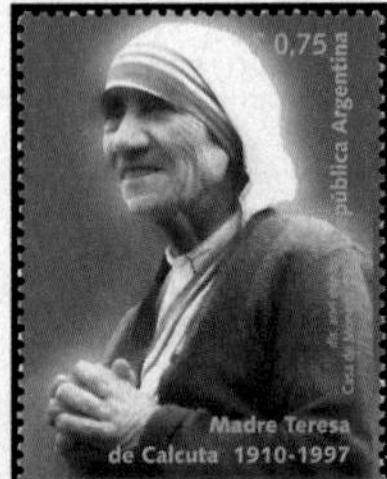
Mother Teresa (1910-97) — A893b

1997, Dec. 27
1984J A893b 75c multicolored 2.00 .75

Dr. Bernardo A. Houssay (1887-1971), 1947 Nobel Prize Winner in Medicine — A894

1998, Jan. 31 Litho. *Perf. 13½*
1985 A894 75c multicolored 1.50 .60

First Ascension of Mount Aconcagua, Cent. — A895

1998, Feb. 14 *Perf. 12*
1986 A895 1.25p multicolored 3.00 1.10

Founding of San Martin de los Andes, Cent. — A896

1998, Mar. 14 Litho. *Perf. 13½*
1987 A896 75c multicolored 1.60 .75

Regimental Quarters of Gen. San Martin's Mounted Grenadiers A897

Designs: a, Statue. b, Large jar with painting of San Martin. c, Regimental seal. d, Regimental quarters.

1998, Mar. 21 Litho. *Perf. 13½*
1988 A897 75c Block of 4, #a.-d. 7.50 6.50

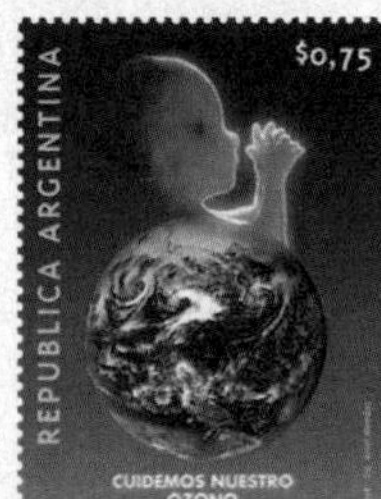

Protection of the Ozone — A898

1998, Mar. 28 Litho. *Perf. 13½*
1989 A898 75c multicolored 1.60 .75

America Issue — A899

Letter carriers: No. 1990, Wearing white uniform. No. 1991, Carrying letter bag with shoulder strap.

1998, Apr. 4
1990 A899 75c multicolored 1.60 .75
1991 A899 75c multicolored 1.60 .75

Characters from Stories by Maria Elena Walsh — A900

Designs: No. 1992, El Reino Del Reves. No. 1993, Zoo Loco. No. 1994, Dailan Kifki. No. 1995, Manuelita.

1998, Apr. l7 Litho. *Die Cut*
Booklet Stamps
Self-Adhesive

1992 A900 75c multicolored 3.75 3.00
1993 A900 75c multicolored 3.75 3.00
1994 A900 75c multicolored 3.75 3.00
1995 A900 75c multicolored 3.75 3.00
a. Complete booklet, #1992-1995 20.00

Historic Chapels A901

Designs: No. 1996, San Pedro de Fiambalá, Catamarca. No. 1997, Huacalera, Jujuy. No. 1998, Santo Domingo, La Rioja. No. 1999, Tumbaya, Jujuy.

1998, Apr. 25 Litho. *Perf. 13x13½*
1996 A901 75c multicolored 1.60 .75
1997 A901 75c multicolored 1.60 .75
1998 A901 75c multicolored 1.60 .75
1999 A901 75c multicolored 1.60 .75
Nos. 1996-1999 (4) 6.40 3.00

White Helmets, A Commitment to Humanity — A902

1998, May 23 Litho. *Perf. 13½*
2000 A902 1p multicolored 2.50 1.00

Beginning with No. 2001, many Argentine stamps are inscribed "Correo Oficial," but these are not Official stamps (i.e., for government use only). The addition of "Correo Oficial" distinguishes these stamps, which are products of the Argentine Postal Service, from other stamps from a private post, OCA, which are also inscribed "Republica Argentina."

1998 World Cup Soccer Championships, France — A903

Stylized players representing: a, Argentina. b, Croatia. c, Jamaica. d, Japan.

1998, May 30
2001 A903 75c Block of 4, #a.-d. 6.50 6.50

Journalist's Day — A904

1998, June 20
2002 A904 75c multicolored 1.60 .75

Creation of Argentine Postal System, 250th Anniv. — A905

a, Corrientes design A2, peso coin. b, Building, post box.

1998, June 27
2003 A905 75c Pair, #a.-b. 3.25 3.25

Fauna Type of 1995

1998 Litho. *Die Cut*
Self-Adhesive (#2004)

2004 A853 60c Picaflor 2.25 .50

Perf. 13½

2004A A853 3.25p Tero 10.00 .50

No. 2004 is broken at bottom right by 3 or 5 lines of wavy die cutting.
Issued: 60c, 12/12; 3.25p, 7/22.

Ruins, Mission St. Ignacio A906

1998, July 25 Litho. *Perf. 13½*
2005 A906 75c multicolored 2.00 .75

Mercosur.

Cattle A907

1998, Aug. 1
2006 A907 25c Brahman .65 .50
2007 A907 25c Aberdeen-Angus .65 .50
2008 A907 50c Hereford 1.25 .50
2009 A907 50c Criolla 1.25 .50
2010 A907 75c Holland-Argentina 1.75 1.00
2011 A907 75c Shorthorn 1.75 1.00
Nos. 2006-2011 (6) 7.30 4.00

Deception Island Base, Antarctica, 50th Anniv. — A908

1998, Aug. 15 Litho. *Perf. 14½*
2012 A908 75c multicolored 2.00 1.00

State of Israel, 50th Anniv. A909

1998, Sept. 5 Litho. *Perf. 13½*
2013 A909 75c multicolored 1.75 .75

Argentina-Japan Friendship Treaty, Cent. — A910

1998, Oct. 3
2014 A910 75c multicolored 1.75 .75

Post Office Building, Buenos Aires, 70th Anniv. A911

Designs: No. 2015, Building, clock, tile. No. 2016, Column ornamentation, tile, bench.

1998, Oct. 3
2015 A911 75c multicolored 1.60 .75
2016 A911 75c multicolored 1.60 .75
a. Pair, #2015-2016 6.25 6.25

Cartoons — A912

Designs: a, Patoruzu, by Quinterno. b, Matias, by Sendra. c, Clemente, by Caloi. d, El Eternauta, by Oesterheld and López. e, Loco Chavez, by Trillo and Altuna. f, Inodoro Pereyra, by Fontanarrosa. g, Tia Vicenta, by Landrú. h, Gaturro, by Nik.

1998, Oct. 17 Litho. *Perf. 13¾x13¼*
2017 A912 75c Sheet of 8, #a.-h. 20.00 17.50

Dr. Pedro de Elizalde's Children's Hospital, 220th Anniv. — A913

1998, Oct. 24 Litho. *Perf. 13½*
2025 A913 75c multicolored 1.60 .75

Raoul Wallenberg (1912-47), Humanitarian — A914

1998, Nov. 21
2026 A914 75c multicolored 1.60 .75

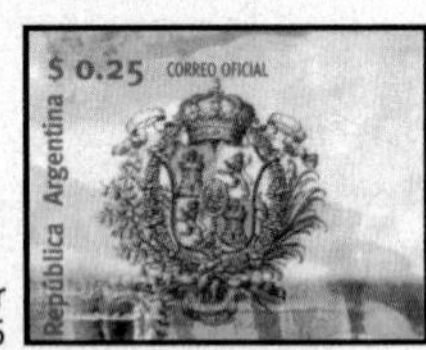

Espamer '98 — A915

25c, Spanish flags, arms. 75c, 18th cent. schooner. 75c+75c, Brigantine, gray sails. 1.25p+1.25p, Brigantine, white sails.

1998, Nov. 21 *Die Cut*
Booklet Stamps
Self-Adhesive

2027 A915 25c multicolored 1.00 .75
2028 A915 75c multicolored 2.00 2.00
2029 A915 75c +75c multi 4.00 4.00
2030 A915 1.25p +1.25p multi 4.00 3.25
a. Booklet pane, #2027-2030 17.50

Nos. 2027-2030 are broken at top right of each stamp by four lines of wavy die cutting. No. 2030a is a complete booklet.

Organization of American States, 50th Anniv. — A916

1998, Nov. 28 *Perf. 13½*
2031 A916 75c multicolored 1.60 .75

Dinosaurs of Argentina — A917

Designs: a, Eoraptor. b, Gasparinisaura. c, Giganotosaurus. d, Patagosaurus.

1998, Nov. 28
2032 A917 75c Sheet of 4, #a.-d. 10.00 9.00

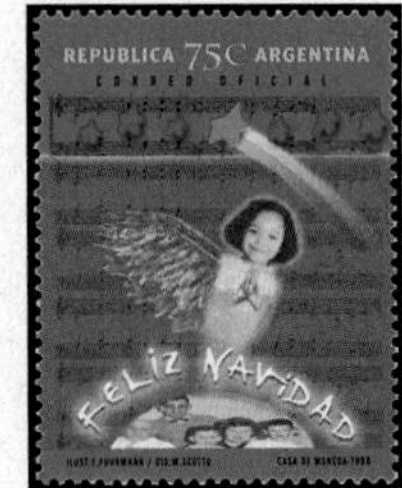

Christmas A918

1998, Dec. 5
2033 A918 75c multicolored 1.60 .75

Newspaper El Liberal, Cent. A919

1998, Dec. 5
2034 A919 75c Juan A. Figueroa 1.60 .75

La Nueva Provincia, Daily Newspaper, Cent. A920

1998, Dec. 12
2035 A920 75c Enrique Julio 1.60 .75

Universal Declaration of Human Rights, 50th Anniv. — A921

1998, Dec. 12
2036 A921 75c multicolored 1.60 .75

Holocaust Memorial, Cathedral of Buenos Aires — A922

1998, Dec. 12
2037 A922 75c multicolored 1.75 1.00

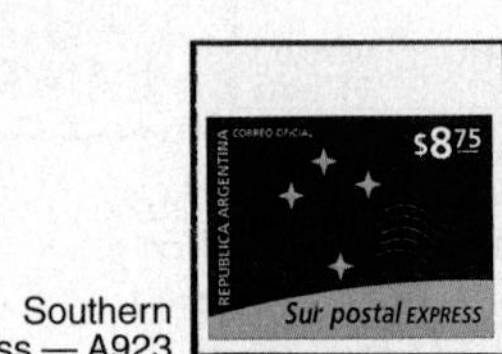

Southern Cross — A923

Inscriptions: 8.75p, Sur postal express. 17.50p, Sur postal 24.

1999-2000 Litho. *Die Cut*
Self-Adhesive

2038 A923 8.75p bl & silver 17.50 15.00
2039 A923 17.50p bl & gold 35.00 30.00

Issued: 8.75p, 7/1/99; 17.50p, 3/2/00. Nos. 2038-2039 are broken at right by five wavy lines of die cutting.

National Fund for the Arts, 40th Anniv. A925

1999, Mar. 6 Litho. *Perf. 13½*
2042 A925 75c multicolored 1.50 .75

Intl. Year of the Ocean (in 1998) A926

1999, Mar. 6
2043 A926 50c Penguin, vert. 1.50 1.00
2044 A926 75c Dolphins 1.60 1.00

Postmen — A927

Designs: 25c, Early postman, city scene. 50c, Early postman, people on bicycles, factory. 75c, Modern postman, city buildings.

1998-2001 Litho. *Die Cut*
Self-Adhesive

2045 A927 25c multicolored *30.00* .75
2046 A927 75c multicolored *15.00* .50
a. Strip of 4, 1 #2045, 3 #2046 *75.00*

Booklet Stamps
Serpentine Die Cut 6

2047 A927 25c multicolored *27.00* 1.00
2048 A927 75c multicolored *10.00* 1.00
a. Bklt. pane, 2 #2047, 6 #2048 *115.00*
Complete booklet, #2048a *120.00*

Serpentine Die Cut 11

2048B A927 25c multi *1.00* .25
2048C A927 75c multi *3.00* .50
d. Booklet pane, 2 #2048B, 6 #2048C *22.00*
Complete booklet, 2 #2048Cd *44.00*
Complete booklet, 4 #2048Cd *88.00*

Size: 21x27mm
Die Cut

2049 A927 25c multicolored 3.50 .50
2050 A927 50c multicolored 3.50 1.00
2051 A927 75c multicolored 3.50 1.75
a. Bklt. pane, 2 ea #2049-2051 21.00
Complete booklet, #2051a 30.00

Nos. 2045-2048C are broken at lower right by five lines of wavy die cutting. Nos. 2049-2051 are broken in center by five wavy lines of die cutting. Nos. 2045-2046 have darker vignettes than Nos. 2047-2048.

Issued: Nos. 2045-2048, 12/9/98. Nos. 2049-2051, 2/2/99. Nos. 2048B-2048C, Feb. 2001.

25th Book Fair A928

Designs: a, Book. b, Obelisk, readers.

1999, Apr. 17 Litho. *Perf. 13¾x13½*
2052 A928 75c Pair, a.-b. 3.25 3.25

Argentine Rugby Union, Cent. — A929

75c, Player, balls. 1.50p, Old, modern players.

1999, Apr. 24 Litho. *Perf. 13¾x13½*
2054 A929 75c multicolored 1.75 1.00

Souvenir Sheet

2055 A929 1.50p multi + 3 labels 6.50 4.00

Cafes of Buenos Aires — A930

Designs: a, Mug, Giralda Dairy. b, Two glasses, Homero Manzi Cafe. c, Hat hanging on rack, Ideal Sweet Shop. d, Cup and saucer, Tortoni Cafe.

Serpentine Die Cut
1999, Apr. 30 Litho.
Self-Adhesive

2056 Booklet pane of 4 10.00 *10.00*
a. A930 25c multicolored .50 .50
b.-c. A930 75c multi, each 1.50 1.00
d. A930 1.25p multicolored 2.50 1.25
Complete booklet, #2056 13.50

Argentine Olympic Committee, 75th Anniv. — A931

1999, May 15 *Perf. 14x13¼*
2057 A931 75c Pierre de Coubertin 1.60 .70

Enrico Caruso (1873-1921), Opera Singer — A932

Designs: a, Portrait of Caruso. b, Singer, various musical instruments. c, Outside of Colon Theatre, Buenos Aires. d, Scene from opera, "El Matrero."

1999, May 15 *Perf. 13½*
2058 A932 75c Sheet of 4, #a.-d. 7.75 7.75

Famous Women A933

Designs: a, Rosario Vera Penaloza (1873-1950), educator. b, Julieta Lanteri (1862-1932), physician.

1999, June 5 *Perf. 14x13¼*

2059 A933 75c Pair, #a.-b. 3.25 2.00

Souvenir Sheets

Paintings from Natl. Museum of Art, Buenos Aires — A934

No. 2060: a, Anarchy of Year 20, by Luis Felipe Noé. b, Retrato de L.E.S., by Carlos Alonso.

No. 2061: a, Typical Orchestra, by Antonio Berni. b, Untitled, (Woman seated), by Aída Carballo.

1999, June 5 *Perf. 14*

Sheets of 2

2060 A934 75c #a.-b. 4.75 3.25
2061 A934 75c #a.-b. 4.75 3.25

No. 2060b is 40x40mm, No. 2061a, 70x50mm, No. 2061b, 40x50mm.

Carrier Pigeon A935

1999, June 12 *Perf. 13¾x13½*

2062 A935 75c multicolored 2.00 .75

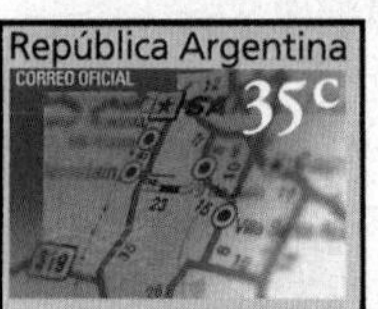

Maps — A936

1999, June 12 *Die Cut*

Self-Adhesive

2063 A936 35c Local highway 1.25 .50
2064 A936 40c City street 2.00 .50
2065 A936 50c Regional highway 2.25 .50
Nos. 2063-2065 (3) 5.50 1.50

Nos. 2063-2065 are broken at lower left by five wavy lines of die cutting.

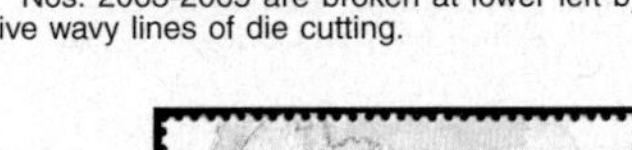

Dogs A937

Designs: a, 25c, Boxer. b, 25c, English sheepdog. c, 50c, Collie. d, 50c, St. Bernard. e, 75c, German shepherd. f, 75c, Siberian husky.

1999, July 24 Litho. *Perf. 13½*

2066 A937 Sheet of 6, #a.-f. 9.00 6.50

Natl. Telecommunications Day — A938

1999, July 24 *Perf. 13½x13¾*

2067 A938 75c multicolored 1.60 .75

Justo José de Urquiza School, Concepcion del Uruguay, 150th Anniv. — A939

1999, Aug. 7 *Perf. 13¾x13½*

2068 A939 75c multicolored 1.60 .75

Otto Krause Technical School, Buenos Aires, Cent. — A940

1999, Aug. 7 *Perf. 13½x13¾*

2069 A940 75c multicolored 1.60 .75

Bethlehem 2000 Project — A941

1999, Aug. 21 *Perf. 13½*

2070 A941 75c multicolored 1.60 .75

America Issue, A New Millennium Without Arms — A942

Perf. 13½x13¾, 13¾x13½

1999, Aug. 21

2071 A942 75c shown 1.60 .75
2072 A942 75c Tree of hands, vert. 1.60 .75

National Parks — A943

Parks and animals: No. 2073, Mburucuyá, coypu. No. 2074, Quebrada de Los Condoritos, condor. No. 2075, San Guillermo, vicuna. No. 2076, Sierra de las Quijadas, puma. No. 2077, Talampaya, gray fox.

1999, Sept. 25 Litho. *Perf. 14x13½*

2073 A943 50c multicolored 1.10 .60
2074 A943 50c multicolored 1.10 .60
2075 A943 50c multicolored 1.10 .60
2076 A943 75c multicolored 1.60 .75
2077 A943 75c multicolored 1.60 .75
Nos. 2073-2077 (5) 6.50 3.30

Inter-American Development Bank, 40th Anniv. — A944

1999, Oct. 9 Litho. *Perf. 13½x13¾*

2078 A944 75c multi 1.60 1.00

UPU, 125th Anniv. A945

1999, Oct. 9 *Perf. 13¾x13½*

2079 A945 1.50p multi 3.00 1.50

Trees — A946

a, Nothofagus pumilio. b, Prosopis caldenia. c, Schinopsis balansae. d, Cordia trichotoma.

1999, Oct. 16 *Perf. 13½x13¾*

2080 A946 75c Strip of 4, #a-d 6.50 6.50

Sinking of A.R.A. Fournier, 50th Anniv. A947

1999, Oct. 16 *Perf. 13¾x13½*

2081 A947 75c multi 1.60 .75

Aviation Anniversaries — A948

Designs: No. 2082, Late 25 airplane. No. 2083, Parachutists.

1999, Oct. 30 *Perf. 13¾x13½*

2082 A948 75c multi 1.50 .75
2083 A948 75c multi 1.50 .75

First Argentine airmail flight, 70th anniv. (No. 2082), Hundred consecutive jumps by Argentine Parachute Club, 50th anniv.

Souvenir Sheets

Millennium — A949

No. 2084: a, 75c, Head of soccer player. b, 50c, Machine as soccer player.

No. 2085: a, 50c, Cane, vert. b, 75c, Head of Jorge Luis Borges (1899-1986), writer.

No. 2086: a, 50c, Accordion player on bed, vert. b, 75c, Stylized tango dancers.

1999, Oct. 30 *Perf. 14*

2084 A949 Sheet of 2, #a.-b. 2.75 2.75
2085 A949 Sheet of 2, #a.-b. 2.75 2.75
2086 A949 Sheet of 2, #a.-b. 2.75 2.75

Size of 75c stamps: 40x40mm.

Argentine Soccer Teams — A950

Designs: No. 2087, Banner and flags of River Plate team. No. 2088, Banner of Boca Juniors team, balloons.

River Plate team (red and white team colors) — No. 2089: a, Stadium, emblem, soccer balls. b, Team on field. c, Fans. d, Emblem. e, Trophy. f, Banner in stadium. g, Player, ball.

Boca Juniors team (blue and yellow team colors) — No. 2090: a, Two players, ball. b, Emblem. c, Four players celebrating. d, Fans, balloons. e, Banner in stadium. f, Blurred shot of players in action. g, Blurred shot of players, diff.

1999 *Perf. 13½x13¼*

2087 A950 75c multi 1.60 .50
2088 A950 75c multi 1.60 .50

Self-Adhesive

Die Cut

2089 Pane of 7 37.50
a. A950 25c multi 2.50 2.00
b.-c. A950 50c any single 2.50 2.00
d.-f. A950 75c any single 5.50 5.50
g. A950 1.50p multi 11.00 10.00
2090 Pane of 7 37.50
a. A950 25c multi 2.50 2.00
b.-c. A950 50c any single 3.50 2.00
d.-f. A950 75c any single 5.50 5.00
g. A950 1.50p multi 11.00 10.00

Issued: Nos. 2087-2088, 11/13; Nos. 2089-2090, 11/15.

Sizes: Nos. 2089a-2089f, 2090a-2090f, 37x27mm; No. 2089g, 2090g, 37x37mm.

Canonization of Brother Héctor Valdivielso Sáez — A951

1999, Nov. 20 *Perf. 13¾x13½*

2091 A951 75c multi 1.75 .75

Manuel Belgrano National Naval School, Bicent. A952

1999, Nov. 27

2092 A952 75c multi 1.60 .75

Souvenir Sheet

Launch of Corvette Uruguay, 125th Anniv. — A953

1999, Nov. 27 Litho. *Perf. 14*
2093 A953 1.50p multi 4.50 4.00

A954

Christmas
A955

No. 2094, Figurines of Holy Family.
No. 2095: a, Magus. b, Bell. c, Two Magi, camels. d, Leaf. e, Angel with star. f, Nativity scene. g, Star. h, Ornaments.

1999, Dec. 4 *Perf. 13¾x13½*
2094 A954 75c multi 1.25 .60

Perf. 14

2095	Sheet of 8	12.50	10.00
a.-b.	A955 25c any single	.75	.50
c.-d.	A955 50c any single	1.25	1.00
e.-h.	A955 75c any single	1.50	1.25

Sizes: Nos. 2095a, 2095b, 2095g, 2095h, 30x30mm.

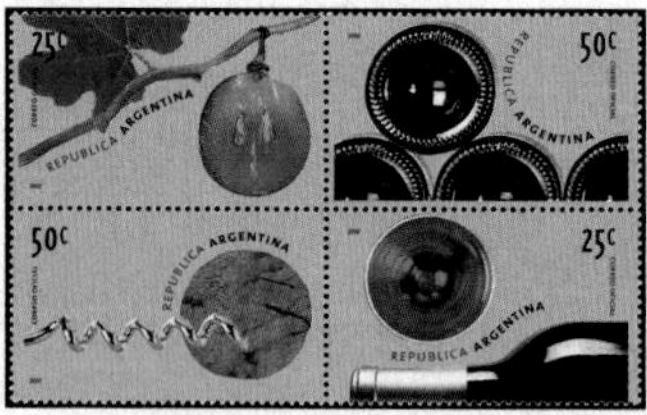

Viticulture — A956

Designs: a, 25c, Grape on vine. b, 50c, Bottoms of wine bottles. c, 50c, Cork and corkscrew. d, 25c, Glass of wine, wine bottle.

2000, Feb. 26 Litho. *Perf. 13¼*
2096 A956 Block of 4, #a-d 6.00 4.50

World Mathematics Year — A957

2000, Mar. 18 *Perf. 13¾x13½*
2097 A957 75c multi 1.25 .60

Birds
A958

a, Leptotila verrauxi. b, Columba picazuro. c, Columbina picni. d, Zenaida auriculata.

2000, Mar. 18 *Die Cut*

Self-Adhesive

2098 Booklet of 4 10.00
a.-d. A958 75c any single 2.00 1.50

Souvenir Sheet

Bangkok 2000 Stamp Exhibition — A959

Designs: a, 25c, Vanda coerulea. b, 75c, Erythrina crista-galli.

2000, Mar. 25 *Perf. 14*
2099 A959 Sheet of 2, #a-b 3.50 2.50

Miniature Sheet

Libraries — A960

Designs: a, 25c, National Public Library Protection Commission. b, 50c, Jujuy Public Library. c, 75c, Argentine Library for the Blind. d, Argentine National Library.

Litho., Litho. & Embossed (#2100c)
2000, Apr. 15 *Perf. 13½*
2100 A960 Sheet of 4, #a-d 6.75 5.50

Gen. Luis Maria Campos Military School, Cent.
A961

2000, Apr. 29 *Perf. 13¾x13½*
2101 A961 75c multi 1.60 1.00

Discovery of Brazil, 500th Anniv. — A962

a, 75c, Pedro Cabral, 1558 map of Brazil coastline. b, 25c, Compass rose and ship.

2000, Apr. 29
2102 A962 Pair, #a-b 3.25 2.50

Souvenir Sheet

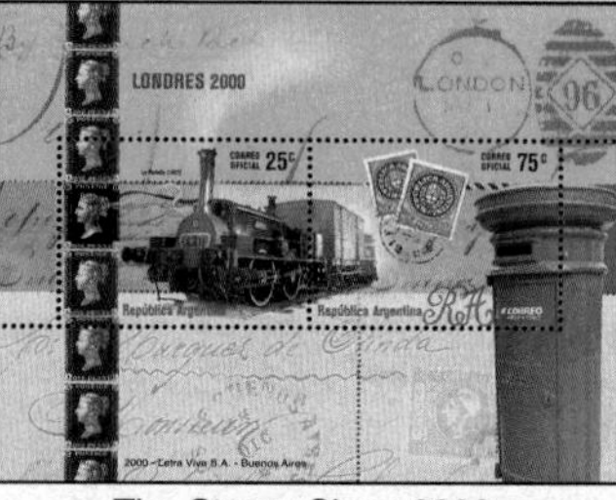

The Stamp Show 2000, London — A963

Designs: a, 25c, Great Britain #1 and design A1, La Porteña, 1st locomotive in Argentina. b, 75c, Argentina No. 7, mail box.

2000, May 20 *Perf. 14*
2103 A963 Sheet of 2, #a-b 3.50 2.50

91st Intl. Convention of Rotary International, Buenos Aires — A964

2000, June 3 Litho. *Perf. 13½x13¾*
2104 A964 75c multi 1.50 1.00

Stampin' the Future — A965

Children's Stamp Design Contest Winners: 25c, Rocío Casado. 50c, Carolina Cáceres, vert. 75c, Valeria A. Pizarro. 1p, Cristina Ayala Castro, vert.

Perf. 13½x13¼, 13¼x13½
2000, June 24
2105-2108 A965 Set of 4 5.25 4.00

America Issue
A966

AIDS Prevention: No. 2109, Handshake. No. 2110, Heart and hands.

2000, July 8 *Perf. 13¾x13½*
2109-2110 A966 75c Set of 2 3.25 2.00

Antoine de Saint-Exupéry (1900-44), Pilot, Writer — A967

Designs: Nos. 2111, 2115, Potez 25. Nos. 2112, 2116, Late 28. No. 2113, Saint-Exupéry. No. 2114, Henri Guillaumet, Vicente A. Almonacid and Jean Mermoz. No. 2117, Map of southern Argentina, tail of Late 25 plane. 1p, Nose of Late 25 plane, cover from 1st airmail flight to Trelew.

2000, July 29 *Perf. 13½*
2111 A967 25c multi .50 .40
2112 A967 50c multi 1.10 .80

Booklet Stamps

Perf. 14

Size: 30x30mm

2113 A967 25c multi 1.00 .50
2114 A967 50c multi 1.50 1.10

Size: 60x20mm

2115 A967 25c multi 1.00 .50
2116 A967 50c multi 1.50 1.10
a. Booklet pane, #2113-2116 5.50

Size: 40x30mm

2117 A967 50c multi 1.50 1.10
2118 A967 1p multi 2.10 1.75
a. Booklet pane, #2117-2118 4.00
Booklet, #2116a, 2118a 10.00
Nos. 2111-2118 (8) 10.20 7.25

Argentine airmail service, 73rd anniv., Aerofila 2000 Philatelic Exhibition, Buenos Aires (No. 2118a).

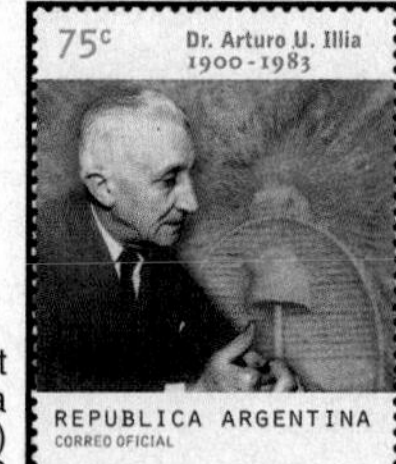

President Arturo U. Illia (1900-82)
A968

2000, Aug. 5 *Perf. 13½x13¼*
2119 A968 75c multi 1.50 1.00

José de San Martín (1778-1850)
A969

2000, Aug. 26 *Perf. 13½*
2120 A969 75c multi 1.50 1.00

Dalmacio Vélez Sarsfield (1800-75), Writer of Civil Code — A970

Perf. 13½x13¼
2000, Sept. 23 Litho.
2121 A970 75c multi 1.60 1.00

2000 Summer Olympic, Sydney — A971

No. 2122: a, Windsurfing. b, Field hockey. c, Volleyball. d, Pole vault.

2000, Sept. 23 *Perf. 13½*
2122 A971 75c Block of 4, #a-d 6.50 6.50

Horses
A972

No. 2123: a, Argentine Petiso. b, Argentine Carriage Horse. c, Peruvian. d, Criolla. e, Argentine Saddle Horse. f, Argentine Polo.
No. 2124: a, Horse-drawn mail coach. b, Horse's head.

2000, Oct. 7 ***Perf. 13¾x13½***

2123 Sheet of 6 + 2 labels 6.50 6.50
a.-b. A972 25c Any single .85 .50
c.-d. A972 50c Any single 1.00 .85
e.-f. A972 75c Any single 1.60 1.25

Souvenir Sheet

Perf. 14

2124 Sheet of 2 3.50 2.75
a. A972 25c multi 1.25 1.00
b. A972 75c mutli 1.75 1.50

España 2000 Intl. Philatelic Exhibition.

Archaeological Artifacts — A973

Designs: 10c, Ceremonial hatchet, Santa Maria culture. 25c, Musical pipes. 50c, Loom, Mapuche culture. 60c, Poncho. 75c, Funerary mask, Tafi culture. 1p, Basket, Mbayá Indians. 2p, Drum, Mapuche culture. 3.25p, Ceremonial mask, Chané culture. 5p, Funerary urn, Belén culture. 9.40p, Rhea-feather costume.

Perf. 13½x13¾ Syncopated

2000 **Litho.**

2125	A973	10c multi	.25	.25
2126	A973	25c multi	.55	.50
2127	A973	50c multi	1.00	.80
2128	A973	60c multi	1.25	1.00
2129	A973	75c multi	1.50	1.25
2130	A973	1p multi	2.00	1.75
2131	A973	2p multi	4.00	3.00
2132	A973	3.25p multi	7.50	5.50
2133	A973	5p multi	10.00	7.00
2134	A973	9.40p multi	19.00	9.50
		Nos. 2125-2134 (10)	47.05	30.55

Issued: 10c, 60c, 11/16; 25c, 50c, 75c, 9.40p, 10/26; 1p, 2p, 9/13; 3.25p, 5p, 8/30.
See Nos. 2495, 2670-2672.

Natl. Atomic Energy Commission, 50th Anniv.
A974

2000, Nov. 11 **Litho.** ***Perf. 13½***

2135 A974 75c multi 1.60 1.00

Fileteado Art Style and the Tango — A975

No. 2136: a, Left side of Fileteado design. b, Right side of Fileteado design. c, Musicians. d, Tango dancers.

2000, Nov. 11 ***Perf. 13¾x13½***

2136 A975 75c Block of 4, #a-d 10.00 6.50

Organ Donation Campaign
A976

2000, Nov. 25 ***Perf. 13½***

2137 A976 75c multi 1.60 1.00

Christmas
A977

2000, Nov. 25

2138 A977 75c multi 1.75 1.00

Medicinal Plants — A978

Designs: No. 2139, 75c, Mirabilis jalapa. No. 2140, 75c, Senna corymbosa. No. 2141, 75c, Eugenia uniflora. No. 2142, 75c, Commelina erecta.

2000, Nov. 25

2139-2142 A978 Set of 4 6.50 4.50

Pre-Columbian Art — A979

Various artifacts. Background colors: a, Bright orange. b, Red orange. c, Green. d, Red violet.

2000, Dec. 9

2143 A979 75c Block of 4, #a-d 8.50 6.50

A979a

Serpentine Die Cut 11¼x11

2001, Feb. 6 **Litho.**

Self-Adhesive

Background Color

2143E	A979a	10c blue green	2.75	.25
2143F	A979a	25c brt green	4.00	.55
2143G	A979a	60c orange	5.00	1.40
2143H	A979a	75c red	6.75	1.60
2143I	A979a	1p blue	10.00	2.10
2143J	A979a	3p red brown	27.50	6.50
2143K	A979a	3.25p yel green	35.00	7.00
2143L	A979a	5.50p rose	40.00	12.00
		Nos. 2143E-2143L (8)	131.00	31.40

Nos. 2143E-2143L are broken at right by five die cut wavy lines. Sold at Unidad Postal outlets. See Nos. 2217-2224A.

Miniature Sheet

Cenozoic Mammals — A980

No. 2144: a, Megaterio (Megatherium americanum). b, Gliptodonte (Doedicurus clavicaudatus). c, Macrauquenia (Macrauchenia patachonica). d, Toxodonte (Toxodon platensis).

2001, Mar. 10 ***Perf. 13¾x13½***

2144 A980 75c Sheet of 4, #a-d 10.00 6.50

Antarctic Bases, 50th Anniv. — A981

Map and: No. 2145, 75c, Cormorant, Base Brown. No. 2146, 75c, Skua, Base San Martín.

Perf. 13¾x13½

2001, Mar. 24 **Litho.**

2145-2146 A981 Set of 2 3.25 2.50

Apiculture — A982

No. 2147: a, Bee on flower. b, Bees on honeycomb. c, Bees, apiarist, and hives. d, Honey, pollen.

2001, Apr. 7 ***Perf. 13½x13¼***

2147 Block of 4 10.00 6.50
a.-d. A982 75c Any single 1.60 1.00

Souvenir Sheet

Argentine Antarctic Institute, 50th Anniv. — A983

No. 2148: a, Scientist with fossils. b, Scientist with mapping equipment.

2001, Apr. 21 ***Perf. 14***

2148 A983 75c Sheet of 2, #a-b 8.00 5.00

Spain to Argentina Flight of Plus Ultra Seaplane, 75th Anniv. — A984

2001, Apr. 28 ***Perf. 13¾x13½***

2149 A984 75c multi 1.60 1.25

Art in Silver — A985

No. 2150: a, Bridle (Freno). b, Stirrups (Estribos). c, Spurs (Espuelas). d, Gaucho's ornament (Rastra).

2001, May 19 **Litho.** ***Perf. 13¾x13½***

2150 A985 75c Block of 4, #a-d 10.00 6.50

World Youth Soccer Championships — A986

Designs: No. 2151, 75c, Player kicking ball. No. 2152, 75c, Goalie catching ball.

2001, June 16

2151-2152 A986 Set of 2 3.25 2.50

Souvenir Sheet

Belgica 2001 Intl. Stamp Exhibition, Brussels — A987

No. 2153: a, 25c, Washerwoman by the Banks of the Belgrano, by Prilidiano Pueyrredón. b, 75c, The Hay Harvest, by Pieter Breughel, the Elder.

2001, June 16 ***Perf. 14***
2153 A987 Sheet of 2, #a-b 3.50 2.50

2001 Census — A988

Perf. 13½x13¾ Syncopated
2001, July 14
2154 A988 75c multi 1.60 1.00

SAC-C Satellite, Birds and Flowers A989

2001, July 14 ***Perf. 13¾x13½***
2155 A989 75c multi 1.60 1.25

Environmental protection.

Bandoneón Recital — 1990, by Aldo Severi — A990

2001, July 28 ***Perf. 13½x13¾***
2156 A990 75c multi 1.60 1.25

The tango in art.

Souvenir Sheet

Phila Nippon '01, Japan — A991

No. 2157: a, Tango dancers, musical score. b, Kabuki dancer.

2001, July 28 ***Perf. 14***
2157 A991 75c Sheet of 2, #a-b 5.00 3.50

Exists imperf. Value, pair $200.

Miniature Sheet

Wild Cats — A992

No. 2158: a, 25c, Puma. b, 25c, Jaguar. c, 50c, Jaguarundi and young. d, 50c, Ocelot. e, 75c, Mountain cat. f, 75c, Huiña.

2001, July 28 ***Perf. 13¾x13½***
2158 A992 Sheet of 6, #a-f, +2 labels 10.00 6.50

Enrique Santos Discépolo (1901-51), Tango Lyricist — A993

2001, Aug. 4 ***Perf. 13½x13¾***
2159 A993 75c multi 1.60 1.25

America Issue — UNESCO World Heritage — A994

No. 2160 — Buildings and artifacts from Jesuit Block and Estancias of Cordoba: a, Denomination at UL. b, Denomination at UR.

2001, Aug. 11 ***Perf. 13¾x13½***
2160 A994 75c Horiz. pair, #a-b 8.50 4.00

Prevention of Breast Cancer — A995

2001, Sept. 1 ***Perf. 13½x13¾***
2161 A995 75c multi 1.60 1.25

World Championship Race Cars of Juan Manuel Fangio — A996

No. 2162 — Cars and track layouts: a, Alfa Romeo 159 Alfetta, Barcleona, 1951. b, Mercedes-Benz W196, Reims, France, 1954. c, Lancia-Ferrari D50, Monte Carlo, Monaco, 1956. d, Maserati 250F, Nürburgring, Germany, 1957.

2001, Oct. 6 ***Perf. 13¾x13½***
2162 A996 75c Block of 4, #a-d 10.00 6.50

Politicians — A997

Designs: No. 2163, 75c, Roque Sáenz Peña (1851-1914). No. 2164, 75c, Justo José de Urquiza (1801-70).

2001, Oct. 20
2163-2164 A997 Set of 2 3.25 2.50

Bulnesia Sarmientoi A998

2001, Oct. 20 Litho. ***Perf. 13½x13¾***
2165 A998 75c multi 1.50 1.25

Souvenir Sheet

Hafnia 01 Philatelic Exhibition, Copenhagen — A999

No. 2166: a, 25c, Argentine post rider, 18th cent. b, 75c, European post rider, 17th cent.

2001, Oct. 27 Litho. ***Perf. 14***
2166 A999 Sheet of 2, #a-b 3.50 2.75

Items in Argentine Museums A1000

Designs: No. 2167, 75c, Ammonite, skeleton of Carnotaurus sastrei, from Argentine Naural Science Museum. No. 2168, 75c, Letter from Buenos Aires, stagecoach "La Pobladora," from Enrique Udaondo Graphic Museum Complex. No. 2169, 75c, Icons from Averias culture, funerary urn from Las Mercedes culture, from Emilio and Duncan Wagner Museum of Anthropological and Natural Sciences, vert. No. 2170, 75c, Crucifix of Juan Martin de Pueyrredon, and detail, from Pueyrredon Museum, vert.

Perf. 13¾x13½, 13½x13¾
2001, Nov. 10 **Litho.**
2167-2170 A1000 Set of 4 7.50 6.00

Aviators and Their Airplanes A1001

Designs: No. 2171, 75c, Carola Lorenzini (1899-1941) and Focke Wulf 44-J. No. 2172, 75c, Jean Mermoz (1901-36) and "Arc-en-Ciel."

2001, Nov. 24 ***Perf. 13¾x13½***
2171-2172 A1001 Set of 2 3.00 2.50

No. 2171 exists imperf. Value, pair $150.

Christmas A1002

2001, Nov. 24 ***Perf. 13½x13¾***
2173 A1002 75c multi 1.50 1.25

Dances A1003

No. 2174: a, Flamenco. b, Waltz. c, Zamba. d, Tango.

Perf. 13¾x13½
2001, Nov. 29 **Litho.**
2174 Booklet pane of 4 6.00 —
a.-d. A1003 75c Any single 1.50 1.50
Booklet, #2174 6.00

Dancers' Day A1004

2001, Dec. 1 Litho. ***Perf. 13¾x13½***
2175 A1004 75c multi 1.50 1.25

Argentine Television, 50th Anniv. — A1005

No. 2176: a, Television, camera, microphone, test pattern. b, Televisions and videotape reels. c, Television, astronaut and satellite dish. d, Televisions, cables and VCR remote control.

2001, Dec. 1 ***Perf. 13¾x13½***
2176 A1005 75c Block of 4, #a-d 7.00 6.00

Argentina in the Antarctic A1006

Designs: No. 2177, 75c, Esperanza Base, 50th anniv. No. 2178, 75c, First air and sea courier service, 50th anniv.

2002, Mar. 9
2177-2178 A1006 Set of 2 3.00 2.50

America Issue — Education A1007

No. 2179: a, School and Argentine flag. b, Children playing hop scotch.

2002, Mar. 23
2179 A1007 75c Vert. pair, #a-b 3.00 2.50

Falkland Islands Birds A1008

Designs: No. 2180, 50c, Charadrius falklandicus. No. 2181, 50c, Larus scoresbii. No. 2182, 75c, Chloephaga rubidiceps, vert. No. 2183, 75c, Aptenodytes patagonicus, vert.

Perf. 13¾x13½, 13½x13¾
2002, Apr. 13 **Litho.**
2180-2183 A1008 Set of 4 6.00 4.00

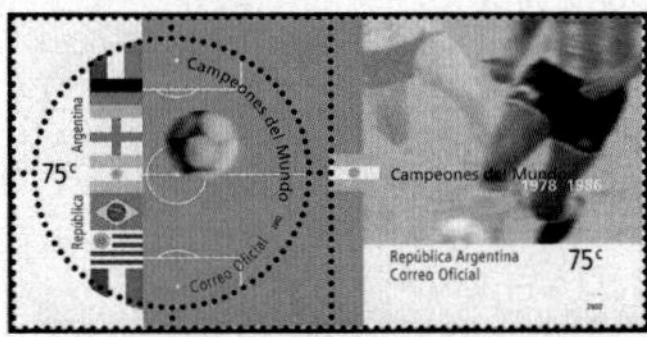

2002 World Cup Soccer Championships, Japan and Korea — A1009

No. 2184: a, Flags, soccer ball and field (38mm diameter). b, Soccer players, years of Argentinian championships.

2002, Apr. 27 **Litho.** ***Perf. 12¾***
2184 A1009 75c Horiz. pair, #a-b 3.00 2.50

See Brazil No. 2840, France No. 2891, Germany No. 2163, Italy No. 2526, Uruguay No. 1946.

Anniversaries — A1010

No. 2185, 25c: a, Rosario riverfront, Ship on Paraná River, arms. b, Rosario riverfront, National Flag Monument.
No. 2186, 50c: a, Mt. Fitzroy, Nahuel Huapi Natl. Park. b, Dr. Francisco P. Moreno.
No. 2187, 75c: a, Flower, aerial view of San Carlos de Bariloche. b, Church and town map.

2002, May 11 **Litho.** ***Perf. 13½x13¾***
Horiz. Pairs, #a-b
2185-2187 A1010 Set of 3 6.00 4.00

Pan-American Health Organization, Cent. — A1011

2002, June 1
2188 A1011 75c multi 1.50 1.00

Doctors — A1012

No. 2189: a, Cosme Mariano Argerich (1758-1820), founder of Military Health Service. b, José María Ramos Mejía (1849-1914), psychiatric educator. c, Salvador Mazza (1886-1946), Chagas' disease specialist. d, Carlos Arturo Gianantonio (1926-95), pediatrician.

Perf. 13¾x13½
2002, June 15 **Litho.**
2189 A1012 50c Block of 4, #a-d 4.00 3.00

Landscapes — A1013

No. 2190: a, Seven-colored Mountain, Jujuy Province. b, Iguaçu Falls, Misiones Province. c, Talampaya Natl. Park, La Rioja Province. d, Mt. Aconcagua, Mendoza Province. e, Rose Garden, Buenos Aires. f, San Jorge Lighthouse, Chubut. g, Perito Moreno Glacier, Santa Cruz Province. h, Lapataia Bay, Tierra del Fuego Province.

2002, July 29 ***Perf. 14x13½***
2190 Block of 8 12.00 6.00
a.-h. A1013 75c Any single 1.50 .60

Eva Perón (1919-52) A1014

No. 2191: a, Official portrait. b, Embossed profile. c, At microphone. d, Painting by Nicolas Garcia Uriburu.

Litho., Litho & Embossed (#2191b)
2002, July 27 ***Perf. 13½x13¾***
2191 Horiz. strip of 4 6.00 4.00
a.-d. A1014 75c Any single 1.25 .60

Worldwide Fund for Nature (WWF) — A1015

No. 2192: a, Ozotoceros bezoarticus. b, Vicugna vicugna. c, Pudu puda. d, Catagonus wagneri.

2002, July 27 **Litho.** ***Perf. 13¾x13½***
2192 A1015 $1 Block of 4, #a-d 6.00 4.50

Souvenir Sheet

Philakorea 2002 World Stamp Exhibition, Seoul — A1016

No. 2193: a, Argentine soccer player (blue and white shirt). b, Korean soccer player (red shirt).

2002, Aug. 10 ***Perf. 14***
2193 A1016 1.50p Sheet of 2, #a-b 6.00 4.50

Sports — A1016a

Perf. 13½x13¾ Syncopated
2002, Sept. 6 **Litho.**

2193C	A1016a	10c Cycling	1.75	.25
2193D	A1016a	25c Tennis	1.75	.25
2193E	A1016a	50c Auto racing	1.75	.30
2193F	A1016a	75c Parachuting	3.00	.50
2193G	A1016a	1p Horse racing	3.00	.70
2193H	A1016a	2p Golf	5.00	1.40
2193I	A1016a	5p Sailing	7.25	3.50
	Nos. 2193C-2193I (7)		23.50	6.90

Nos. 2193C-2193I were sold only to customers who met certain mailing requirements but could be used on mail by anyone without restrictions.

Valdés Peninsula Tourism — A1017

Whale breaching: a, Head. b, Tail.

2002, Sept. 14 ***Perf. 13½x13¾***
2194 A1017 75c Horiz. pair, #a-b 3.00 2.00

Insects A1018

Designs: 25c, Edessa meditabunda. 50c, Elaechlora viridis. 75c, Chrysodina aurata. 1p, Steirastoma breve.

2002, Sept. 21 ***Perf. 13¾x13½***
2195-2198 A1018 Set of 4 5.25 3.00

Men's Volleyball World Championships A1019

Various players with background colors of: No. 2199, 75c, Blue green (shown). No. 2200, 75c, Light blue. No. 2201, 75c, Yellow green. No. 2202, 75c, Orange.

Perf. 13½x13¾
2002, Sept. 28 **Litho.**
2199-2202 A1019 Set of 4 6.00 4.00

On Nos. 2199-2202 portions of the design were applied by a thermographic process producing a shiny, raised effect.

Argentine Highway Association, 50th Anniv. — A1020

2002, Oct. 5 ***Perf. 13¾x13½***
2203 A1020 75c multi 1.50 .75

Argentine Personalities — A1021

Designs: No. 2204, 75c, Roberto Arlt (1900-42), novelist. No. 2205, 75c, Beatriz Guido (1924-88), writer. No. 2206, 75c, Niní Marshall (1903-96), actress. No. 2207, 75c, Luis Sandrini (1905-80), actor.

2002, Oct. 19
2204-2207 A1021 Set of 4 6.00 3.00

Immigrant Agricultural Colonies A1022

Flags of France, Switzerland, Spain and Italy and: a, Hotel for immigrants, mother and son, stamped passport. b, Two immigrants and ship. c, Two immigrants, Provisory Hotel for immigrants, French immigrant instruction book. d, Farmer plowing field, family of immigrants.

2002, Oct. 19 Litho. *Perf. 13½x13¾*

2208	Horiz. strip of 4		6.00	4.00
a.-d.	A1022 75c Any single		1.50	.75

Argentine Federation of Philatelic Entities, 50th Anniv. — A1023

Designs: No. 2209, 75c, Stamped cover, stagecoach, EXFICEC '56 exhibition cancel, Head of Ceres from Corrientes issue. No. 2210, 75c, ESPAMER '98 Cancel, postman, ship and map, coat of arms.

2002, Nov. 2 *Perf. 13¾x13½*

2209-2210	A1023	Set of 2	3.00	1.50

Christmas — A1024

2002, Nov. 16

2211	A1024 75c multi		1.50	.75

Folk Musicians A1025

Designs: No. 2212, 75c, Gustavo "Cuchi" Leguizamón (1917-2000). No. 2213, 75c, Armando Tejada Gómez (1929-92). No. 2214, 75c, Carlos Vega (1898-1966). No. 2215, 75c, Andrés Chazarreta (1876-1960).

2002, Dec. 7 *Perf. 13½x13¾*

2212-2215	A1025	Set of 4	6.00	3.00

Puppets A1026

No. 2216: a, Marionette of woman. b, King and fish hand puppets. c, Rod puppet of man. d, Shadow theater.

2002, Dec. 7 *Perf. 13¾x13½*

2216	Booklet pane of 4		6.00	4.00
a.-d.	A1026 75c Any single		1.50	.75
	Booklet, #2216		8.50	

Unidad Postal Type of 2001
Perf. 13¾x13½ Syncopated
2002 Litho.
Size: 35x24mm (10p, 35x25mm)
Background Color

2217	A979a	10c blue green	1.00	.25
2218	A979a	25c brt green	1.00	.25
2219	A979a	50c tan	1.25	.35
2220	A979a	75c red	1.75	.55
2221	A979a	1p blue	2.25	.75
2222	A979a	2p gray	4.50	1.50
2223	A979a	3p brown	6.50	1.75
2224	A979a	5p olive bister	9.50	2.25
2224A	A979a	10p yellow	18.50	3.00
	Nos. 2217-2224A (9)		46.25	10.65

Issue dates: Nos. 2217-2224, 6/02; 10p, 8/16/02.

Nos. 2217-2224A were sold only at Unidad Postal outlets.

Communal Vegetable Gardens — A1027

Designs: No. 2225, 75c, Cabbage. No.2226, 75c, Corn, vert.

Perf. 13¾x13½, 13½x13¾
2003, Mar. 8

2225-2226	A1027	Set of 2	3.00	1.50

Native Handicrafts — A1028

Designs: No. 2227, 75c, Sieve, by Mbyá people, fork and spoon by Wichi people. No. 2228, 75c, Woven waistband of Pilagal'ek people, Bag by Nam Qom people.

2003, Mar. 8 *Perf. 13¾x13½*

2227-2228	A1028	Set of 2	3.00	1.50

National Parks — A1029

Animals and parks: No. 2229, 50c, Lama guanicoe, Los Cardones National Park. No. 2230, 50c, Piaya cayana, Colonia Benítez Natural Reserve. No. 2231, 50c, Mazama gouazoupira, Copo National Park. No. 2232, 75c, Tinamotis pentlandii, Campo de los Alisos National Park. No. 2233, 75c, Spheniscus magellanicus, Monte León, planned National Park.

2003, Mar. 22 *Perf. 14x13½*

2229-2233	A1029	Set of 5	6.00	3.00

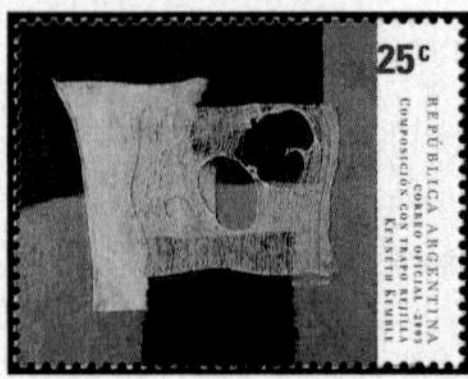
Paintings A1030

Designs: No. 2234, 25c, Composición con Trapo Rejilla, by Kenneth Kemble. No. 2235, 25c, Pintura, by Roberto Aizenberg, vert. 50c, Pantalla, by Rómulo Macció, vert. No. 2237, 75c, La Giaconda, by Guillermo Roux. No. 2238, 75c, Hacerse Humo, by Antonio Seguí. 1p, San P., by Xul Solar (with attached label).

Perf. 13¾x13½, 13½x13¾
2003, Apr. 12

2234-2239	A1030	Set of 6	7.50	3.75

Nos. 2234-2238 were each printed in sheets of 4; No. 2239 was printed in sheets of 2 + 2 labels.

Argentina, Champions of 2002 Intl. Sporting Events — A1031

Designs: No. 2240, 75c, Women's field hockey. No. 2241, 75c, Soccer for blind players.

Litho., Litho. & Embossed (#2241)
2003, May 3 *Perf. 13¾x13½*

2240-2241	A1031	Set of 2	3.00	2.00

Comic Strips — A1032

No. 2242: a, 25c, Mago Fafa, by Alberto Bróccoli. b, 25c, Astronaut, by Crist (Cristóbal Reinoso). c, 50c, Hijitus, by Manuel García Ferré. d, 50c, Savarese, by Domingo Mandrafina and Robin Wood. e, 75c, Sónoman, by Oswal (Oswaldo Walter Viola). f, 75c, El Tipito, by Daniel Paz and Rudy (Marcelo E. Rudaeff). g, 75c, La Vaca Aurora, by Domingo Mirco Repetto. h, 75c, Diógenes y el Linyera, by Tabaré (Gómez Laborde), Jorge Guinzberg and Carlos Abrevaya.

2003, May 17 Litho. *Perf. 13½x13¾*

2242	A1032	Sheet of 8, #a-h	9.00	5.00

Silver Tableware — A1033

No. 2243: a, Soup bowl with lid (sopera). b, Kettle and burner, maté kettle and drinking tube. c, Chocolate pot and jar with handle. d, Sugar bowl (azucarera).

2003, May 24 *Perf. 13¾x13½*

2243	A1033	75c Block of 4, #a-d	6.00	3.00

Food — A1034

Designs: Nos. 2244a, 2245a, Empanadas (red denomination). Nos. 2244b, 2245b, Locro (orange denomination) Nos. 2244c, 2246a, Parrillada (green denomination) Nos. 2244d, 2246b, Pastelitos (blue denomination).

2003, June 7 *Perf. 13¾x13½*

2244	A1034	75c Horiz strip of 4, #a-d, + 4 labels	6.00	2.25

Booklet Panes
Perf. 14

2245	A1034	75c Pane of 2, #a-b, + 2 labels	4.00	2.00
2246	A1034	75c Pane of 2, #a-b, + 2 labels	4.00	2.00
	Complete booklet, #2245-2246		8.50	

Size of stamps in booklet panes: 40x30mm.

Miniature Sheet

Children's Games — A1035

No. 2247: a, El Elástico. b, La escondida (hide and seek). c, La mancha (tag). d, Martín Pescador.

2003, July 12 *Perf. 13¾x13½*

2247	A1035	50c Sheet of 4, #a-d	6.00	3.00

Landscapes — A1036

No. 2248: a, Mbiguá Marsh, Formosa Province. b, Dead Man's Salt Flats, Catamarca Province. c, Quilmes Ruins, Tucumán Province. d, Iberá Marshes, Corrientes Province. e, Ischigualasto Provincial Park, San Juan Province. f, Mar del Plata, Buenos Aires Province. g, Caleu Caleu Department, La Pampa Province. h, Lanín National Park, Nequén Province.

2003, July 19 *Perf. 14x13¾*

2248	A1036	75c Block of 8, #a-h	12.00	6.00

Opening of Nuestra Señora del Rosario Bridge and Roadway, Rosario-Victoria — A1037

No. 2249: a, 25c, Bridge, map of roadway. b, 75c, Bridge and cross-section.

Perf. 13½x13¾

2003, Aug. 23 **Litho.**
2249 A1037 Horiz. pair, #a-b 2.75 1.75

Argentine History A1038

Designs: No. 2250, 75c, Dr. Vicente Fidel López (1815-1903), Education minister, headquarters of Province of Buenos Aires Bank. No. 2251, 75c, First page of constitution, medal and signature of Juan Bautista Alberdi. No. 2252, 75c, Emblem and squadron of General San Martín Mounted Grenadiers Regiment. No. 2253, 75c, Presidential sash and staff, Casa Rosada. No. 2254, 75c, Arms of Río Negro Province, vert.

Perf. 13¾x13½, 13½x13¾

2003, Sept. 6
2250-2254 A1038 Set of 5 7.25 4.00

Constitution, 150th anniv. (No. 2251), Revival of General San Martín Mounted Grenadiers Regiment, cent. (No. 2252), Presidential inauguration (No. 2253).

Souvenir Sheet

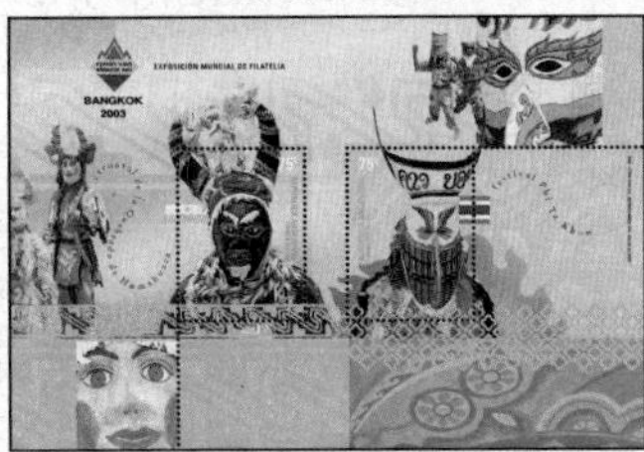

Bangkok 2003 World Philatelic Exhibition — A1039

No. 2255: a, Quebrada de Humahuacha black demon mask, Argentine flag. b, Phi Ta Khon Festival mask, Thailand flag.

Litho. with Foil Application

2003, Oct. 4 ***Perf. 14***
2255 A1039 75c Sheet of 2, #a-b 3.75 2.75

America Issue — Flora and Fauna A1040

Designs: No. 2256, 75c, Nothofagus pumilio. No. 2257, 75c, Vultur gryphus.

2003, Oct. 11 Litho. ***Perf. 13¾x13½***
2256-2257 A1040 Set of 2 3.00 2.00

Jubany Base, Antarctica, 50th Anniv. — A1041

2003, Oct. 18
2258 A1041 75c multi 1.50 1.00

Rescue of Swedish Scientific Expedition by A. R. A. Uruguay, Cent. — A1042

Designs: No. 2259, Welcome, (ship and penguins) by Eduardo De Martino.

No. 2260: a, A. R. A. Uruguay. b, A. R. A. Uruguay and Lt. Julián Irízar.

2003, Oct. 18 ***Perf. 13¾x13½***
2259 A1042 75c multi 1.50 1.00

Souvenir Sheet

Perf. 14

2260 A1042 75c Sheet of 2, #a-b 4.00 3.00

No. 2260 contains two 40x30mm stamps.

Agricultural and Industrial Products — A1043

Designs: No. 2261, 75c, Cattle. No. 2262, 75c, Soybeans. No. 2263, 75c, Aluminum. No. 2264, 75c, Teradi 800 cobalt therapy machine.

2003, Oct. 18 ***Perf. 13¾x13½***
2261-2264 A1043 Set of 4 6.00 3.00

Christmas A1044

Designs: No. 2265, 75c, Purmamarca clay creche figures. No. 2266, 75c, Gaucho Birth, carved wood creche figures by Eloy López.

2003, Nov. 8 ***Perf. 13½x13¾***
2265-2266 A1044 Set of 2 3.00 1.50

20th Century Architecture A1045

Designs: No. 2267, 75c, Barolo Palace, Buenos Aires, by Mario Palanti, 1923. No. 2268, 75c, Tucumán Province Bank Building, San Miguel de Tucumán, by Alejandro Virasoro, 1928. No. 2269, 75c, Córdoba Province Savings Bank Building, Córdoba, by Jaime Roca, 1929. No. 2270, 75c, Minetti Palace, Rosario, by Juan B. Durand, Leopoldo Schwarz and José Gerbino, 1930.

2003, Nov. 8
2266-2270 A1045 Set of 4 6.00 3.00

Orcadas Base, Antarctica, Cent. — A1046

Designs: No. 2271, Helicopter, Orcadas Base.

No. 2272: a, #127 with 1904 South Orcadas cancel, vert. b, Meteorological observatory and weather vane.

2004, Feb. 21 ***Perf. 13¾x13½***
2271 A1046 75c multi 1.50 1.00

Souvenir Sheet

Perf. 14

2272 A1046 75c Sheet of 2, #a-b 4.00 3.00

No. 2272 contains one 30x40mm and one 40x30mm stamp.

Quebrada de Humahuaca UNESCO World Heritage Site — A1047

No. 2273 — View of Rio Grande Valley and: a, Decorated llama, rock painting, person in front of door. b, Santa Rosa de Lima Church, costumed carnival participants.

2004, Mar. 27 ***Perf. 13½x13¾***
2273 A1047 75c Horiz. pair, #a-b 3.00 2.00

America Issue — Forest Conservation — A1048

No. 2274 — Forest and timeline charting hectares of forest with years: a, 1914, 1956. b, 1989, 2004.

2004, Mar. 27
2274 A1048 75c Horiz. pair, #a-b 3.00 2.00

No. 2274b has large hole in center of stamp.

La Voz del Interior Newspaper, Cent. — A1049

2004, Apr. 17 ***Perf. 13¾x13½***
2275 A1049 75c multi 1.50 .75

Landscapes — A1050

No. 2276: a, Molinos, Salta Province. b, Pampa del Indio Provincial Park, Chaco Province. c, Rio Hondo Dam, Santiago del Estera Province. d, Bridge, Santa Fe de la Vera Cruz, Santa Fe Province. e, San Roque Lake, Córdoba Province. f, El Palmar National Park, Entre Rios Province. g, Potrero de los Funes, San Luis Province. h, Mt. Tronador, Río Negro Province.

2004, Apr. 17 ***Perf. 14x13½***
2276 A1050 75c Block of 8, #a-h 10.00 7.50

FIFA (Fédération Internationale de Football Association), Cent. — A1051

Paintings of soccer players by Rubén Ramonda: No. 2277, 75c, The Tunnel (blue background). No. 2278, 75c, El Picado (orange background).

2004, May 22 Litho. ***Perf. 13¾x13½***
2277-2278 A1051 Set of 2 3.00 1.50

Souvenir Sheet

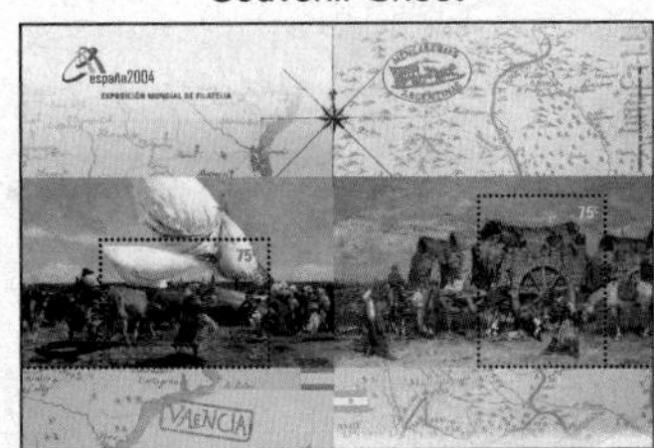

España 2004 World Philatelic Exhibition — A1052

No. 2279: a, Return of the Fishing Fleet, by Joaquín Sorolla y Bastida. b, A Stop in the Pampas, by Angel Della Valle, vert.

2004, May 22 ***Perf. 14***
2279 A1052 75c Sheet of 2, #a-b 3.75 2.75

Naval Hydrographic Service, 125th Anniv. — A1053

No. 2280 — Nautical chart and: a, Binnacle. b, Sextant. c, Cabo Vírgenes Lighthouse. d, Oceanographic ship Puerto Deseado.

2004, June 5 ***Perf. 13¾x13½***
2280 A1053 75c Block of 4, #a-d 6.00 3.00

Printed in sheets of four blocks separated by a central column of labels.

Souvenir Sheet

Circus — A1054

No. 2281: a, Trained dogs. b, Clown on stilts, trapeze artist. c, Clown juggling on unicycle. d, Bareback rider.

2004, June 12
2281 A1054 50c Sheet of 4, #a-d 4.00 3.00

Characters From Comic Strip "Patoruzito," by Dante Quinterno — A1055

No. 2282: a, 25c, Isidorito. b, 25c, Upita. c, 50c, Patoruzito. d, 50c, Malén. e, 75c, Pamperito. f, 75c, Chacha.
No. 2283: a, Patoruzito (20x60mm). b, Pamperito (20x60mm). c, Isidorito (30x30mm)
No. 2284: a, Malén (30x40mm). b, Upita (30x40mm). c, Chacha (30x40mm)

2004, July 10 Litho. ***Perf. 13½x13¾***
2282 A1055 Sheet of 6 + 2 labels 3.75 2.75

Booklet Panes

Perf. 14

2283 Booklet pane of 3 + label 4.00 3.50
a.-c. A1055 75c Any single 1.25 .75
2284 Booklet pane of 3 + label 4.00 3.50
a.-c. A1055 75c Any single 1.25 .75
Complete booklet, #2283-2284 8.50

Fish of the Falkland Islands Area A1056

Designs: No. 2285, 75c, Salilota australis. No. 2286, 75c, Patagonotothen ramsayi. No. 2287, 75c, Dissostichus eleginoides. No. 2288, 75c, Bathyraja griseocauda.

2004, July 17 Litho. ***Perf. 13¾x13½***
2285-2288 A1056 Set of 4 6.00 3.00

Assistance Dogs — A1057

Designs: No. 2289, 75c, Rescue dog. No. 2290, 75c, Seeing-eye dog, vert.

Perf. 13¾x13½, 13½x13¼

2004, July 17
2289-2290 A1057 Set of 2 3.00 1.50

2004 Summer Olympics, Athens — A1058

No. 2291: a, Cycling. b, Judo. c, Swimming. d, Tennis.

2004, Aug. 7 ***Perf. 13¾x13½***
2291 A1058 75c Block of 4, #a-d 5.00 3.50

Legends A1059

Designs: No. 2292, 75c, El Pehuén. No. 2293, 75c, La Yacumama. No. 2294, 75c, La Pachamama. No. 2295, 75c, La Difunta Correa.

2004, Aug. 21
2292-2295 A1059 Set of 4 5.00 3.50

Souvenir Sheet

World Stamp Championship 2004, Singapore — A1060

No. 2296: a, Mangifera indica. b, Syagrus romanzoffiana.

2004, Aug. 21 ***Perf. 14***
2296 A1060 75c Sheet of 2, #a-b 3.00 1.50

Centenaries — A1061

Designs: No. 2297, 75c, Agronomy and Veterinary Science Institute for Higher Learning, Buenos Aires. No. 2298, 75c, City of Neuquén. No. 2299, 75c, Philatelic Association of Rosario.

2004, Sept. 11 ***Perf. 13¾x13½***
2297-2299 A1061 Set of 3 3.50 1.50

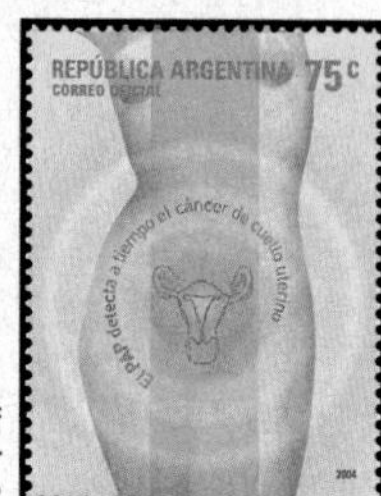

Prevention of Uterine Cancer A1062

2004, Sept. 18 ***Perf. 13½x13¾***
2300 A1062 75c multi 1.25 .65

Preservation of Water Resources — A1063

No. 2301: a, Hourglass with clean water. b, Hourglass with polluted water.

2004, Sept. 18 ***Perf. 13¾x13½***
2301 A1063 75c Vert. tete beche pair, #a-b 3.00 1.50

Landmarks in Argentina — A1063a

Designs: 25c, Ruins of San Ignacio Miní, Misiones Province. 50c, Iruya. 1p, Buenos Aires. 2p, Aconcagua Provincial Park. 3p, Valdes Peninsula. 5p, Mina Clavero. 10p, Ushuaia.

Perf. 13¾x13½ Syncopated

2004, Sept. 24 **Litho.**
2301C A1063a 25c multi .25 .25
2301D A1063a 50c multi .35 .35
2301E A1063a 1p multi .70 .70
2301F A1063a 2p multi 1.40 1.40
2301G A1063a 3p multi 2.10 2.10
2301H A1063a 5p multi 3.50 3.50
j. With label 2.60 2.60
2301I A1063a 10p multi 6.75 6.75
Nos. 2301D-2301I (6) 14.80 14.80

Issued: No. 2301Hj, 5/11/10.
See Nos. 2357, 2586-2587, 2678-2679.

The Nativity A1064

Virgin Mary — A1065

2004, Oct. 16 Litho. ***Perf. 13½x13¾***
2302 A1064 75c multi 1.25 .65
2303 A1065 75c multi 1.25 .65

Christmas, Stained glass windows, St. Felicitas Church, Buenos Aires.

Numismatics — A1066

No. 2304 — Halves of 1813 silver 1 real coin and 1813 gold 8 escudos coin: a, Obverse (sun). b, Reverse (coat of arms).

2004, Oct. 23
2304 A1066 75c Horiz. pair, #a-b 2.50 1.25

Andrés Bello and Front Page of Spanish Grammar for Americans — A1067

2004, Nov. 6 ***Perf. 13¾x13½***
2305 A1067 75c multi 1.25 .65

Third Intl. Spanish Language Congress, Rosario.

Buenos Aires Commodities Exchange, 150th Anniv. — A1068

2004, Nov. 6
2306 A1068 75c multi 1.25 .65

Medicinal Plants A1069

Designs: No. 2307, 75c, Aloysia citriodora. No. 2308, 75c, Minthostachys mollis. No. 2309, 75c, Lippia turbinata. No. 2310, 75c, Tagetes minuta.

2004, Nov. 20 ***Perf. 13½x13¾***
2307-2310 A1069 Set of 4 5.00 3.75

12th Pan-American Scout Jamboree — A1070

2005, Jan. 15 ***Perf. 13¾x13½***
2311 A1070 75c multi 1.25 .65

Argentina — Thailand Diplomatic Relations, 50th Anniv.
A1071

Designs: No. 2312, 75c, Tango dancers, Argentina. No. 2313, 75c, Tom-tom dancers, Thailand.

2005, Feb. 5 ***Perf. 13½x13¾***
2312-2313 A1071 Set of 2 2.50 1.25

Paintings by Antonio Berni (1905-81)
A1072

Designs: No. 2314, Woman with a Red Sweater.
No. 2315 — Details from Manifestation: a, 75c, Bearded man, man looking up (40x50mm). b, 75c, Child, two men with hats in foreground, horiz. (50x40mm).

2005, Mar. 12 ***Perf. 13½x13¾***
2314 A1072 75c shown 1.00 .55

Souvenir Sheet
Perf. 14
2315 A1072 Sheet of 2, #a-b 3.00 2.00

Rotary International, Cent. — A1073

2005, Mar. 19 ***Perf. 13¾x13½***
2316 A1073 75c multi 1.00 .55

Writers
A1074

Designs: No. 2317, 75c, Silvina Ocampo (1903-93). No. 2318, 75c, Ezequiel Martínez Estrada (1895-1964).

2005, Mar. 19 ***Perf. 13½x13¾***
2317-2318 A1074 Set of 2 2.00 1.10

Argentine Motor Vehicles — A1075

Designs: No. 2319, 75c, Graciela sedan. No. 2320, 75c, Justicialista Sport. No. 2321, 75c, Rastrojero Diesel truck. No. 2322, 75c, Siam Di Tella 1500. No. 2323, 75c, Torino 380 W.

2005, Apr. 9 **Litho.** ***Perf. 13¾x13½***
2319-2323 A1075 Set of 5 5.00 2.75

A portion of the design of each stamp is coated with a glossy varnish.

Intl. Year of Physics
A1076

Designs: No. 2324, 75c, José Antonio Balseiro, founder of Balseiro Institute, nuclear reactor. No. 2325, 75c, Albert Einstein, front page of Einstein's theory of relativity.

2005, Apr. 23 **Litho.** ***Perf. 13¾x13½***
2324-2325 A1076 Set of 2 2.00 1.10

Balseiro Institute, 50th anniv.

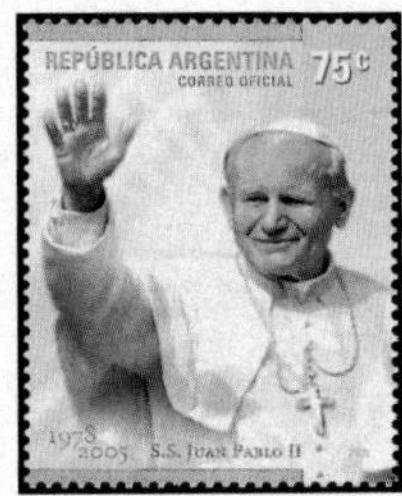

Pope John Paul II (1920-2005)
A1077

Designs: No. 2326, Pope waving.
No. 2327: a, Pope with crucifix, Papal arms. b, Pope and crowd.

2005, Apr. 23 ***Perf. 13½x13¾***
2326 A1077 75c shown 1.00 .55

Souvenir Sheet
Perf. 14
2327 A1077 75c Sheet of 2, #a-b 3.75 2.75

No. 2327 contains two 40x50mm stamps.

General Workers Confederation, 75th Anniv.
A1078

La Capital Newspaper, Mar del Plata, Cent. — A1079

Sunday Blue Law No. 4661, Cent. — A1080

2005, May 21 **Litho.** ***Perf. 13½x13¾***
2328 A1078 75c multi 1.00 .55
2329 A1079 75c multi 1.00 .55
2330 A1080 75c multi 1.00 .55
Nos. 2328-2330 (3) 3.00 1.65

César Milstein (1927-2002), 1984 Nobel Laureate in Physiology or Medicine — A1081

2005, June 4 ***Perf. 13¾x13½***
2331 A1081 75c multi 1.00 .55

Volunteer Firefighters
A1082

Designs: No. 2332, 75c, Orestes Liberti (1860-1936), first commander of volunteer firefighter brigade, horse-drawn fire engine. No. 2333, 75c, Fire fighters in action, fire truck.

2005, June 4 ***Perf. 13½x13¾***
2332-2333 A1082 Set of 2 2.00 1.10

Argentine Red Cross, 125th Anniv. — A1083

2005, June 11 ***Perf. 13¾x13½***
2334 A1083 75c multi 1.00 .55

Juan Filloy (1894-2000), Writer — A1084

2005, July 16
2335 A1084 75c multi 1.00 .55

Miniature Sheet

Cats — A1085

No. 2336: a, 25c, Birman. b, 25c, Siamese. c, 50c, Oriental. d, 50c, Persian. e, 75c, Abyssinian. f, 75c, European.

2005, July 16
2336 A1085 Sheet of 6, #a-f, + 2 labels 5.00 3.50

Wine Regions — A1086

Glass of wine, map, vineyard in: No. 2337, 75c, Salta Province, Torrontés grapes. No. 2338, 75c, Mendoza Province, Malbec grapes. No. 2339, 75c, San Juan Province, Syrah grapes. No. 2340, 75c, Río Negro Province, Merlot grapes.

2005, July 16 ***Perf. 14x13½***
2337-2340 A1086 Set of 4 4.00 2.10

Historic Houses of Worship
A1087

Designs: No. 2341, 75c, Our Lady of the Rosary of Candonga Chapel, Sierra Chicas. No. 2342, 75c, Al Ahmad Mosque, Buenos Aires. No. 2343, 75c, Temple of the Israelite Congregation, Buenos Aires. No. 2344, 75c, Vision of the Middle Buddhist Temple, Buenos Aires.

2005, Aug. 6 ***Perf. 13¾x13½***
2341-2344 A1087 Set of 4 4.00 2.10

Local Grocery Stores
A1088

Designs: No. 2345, 75c, Pulpería de Cacho di Catarina, Mercedes. No. 2346, 75c, Pulpería El Torito, Baradero. No. 2347, 75c, Pulpería Perucho, General Lavalle. No. 2348, 75c, Pulpería Impini, Larroque.

2005, Sept. 10
2345-2348 A1088 Set of 4 4.00 2.10

Antarctic Science A1089

Designs: No. 2349, Iceberg, Antarctic Treaty emblem

No. 2350: a, Major General Hernán Pujato and members of First Argentine Polar Expedition air crew. b, Divers, raft, iceberg.

2005, Sept. 24 ***Perf. 13¾x13½***

2349 A1089 75c multi 1.00 .75

Souvenir Sheet

Perf. 14

2350 A1089 75c Sheet of 2, #a-b 3.50 2.75

No. 2350 contains two 40x30mm stamps.

Colón Theater Companies, 80th Anniv. — A1090

No. 2351: a, Dancer Julio Bocca, ballet dancers, Colón Theater building. b, Orchestra, choir, opera singers.

2005, Sept. 24 ***Perf. 13½x13¾***

2351 A1090 75c Horiz. pair, #a-b 2.00 1.10

Alternative Energy Sources A1091

Designs: 75c, Solar power. 4p, Wind power.

2005, Oct. 15

2352-2353 A1091 Set of 2 5.75 3.25

Christmas A1092

Details from altarpiece by Elena Storni: No. 2354, Madonna and Child.

No. 2355: a, The Annunciation, Mary and Elizabeth. b, Nativity. c, Magi. d, Presentation of Jesus in the Temple.

2005, Oct. 15 ***Perf. 13½x13¾***

2354 A1092 75c shown 1.00 .50

Souvenir Sheet

Perf. 14

2355 A1092 75c Sheet of 4, #a-d 4.00 3.00

No. 2355 contains four 40x40mm stamps.

Fourth Summit of the Americas, Mar del Plata — A1093

2005, Oct. 29 Litho. ***Perf. 13¾x13½***

2356 A1093 75c multi 1.00 .50

Landmarks Type of 2004

Design: Perito Moreno Glacier

Perf. 13¾x13½ Syncopated

2005, Nov. 18

2357 A1063a 4p multi 2.75 2.75

Immigrants to Argentina — A1095

Designs: No. 2358, 75c, German immigrants in Cañada de Gómez, bandoneon. No. 2359, 75c, Slovakian immigrants in Buenos Aires, weather indicator. No. 2360, 75c, Welsh immigrants, Chubut Central Railway train, railway lantern. No. 2361, 75c, Jewish settlers, Moisés Ville, wheat.

2005, Nov. 19 ***Perf. 13¾x13½***

2358-2361 A1095 Set of 4 4.00 2.00

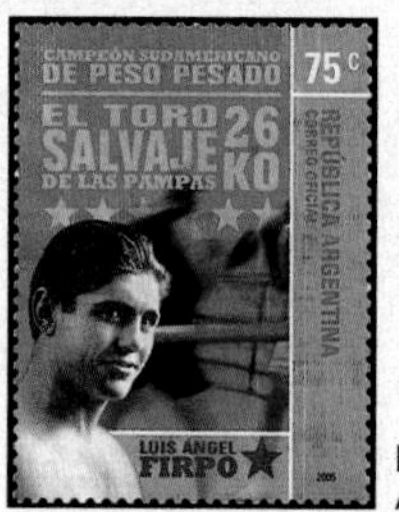

Boxers A1096

Designs: No. 2362, 75c, Lius Angel Firpo (1894-1960). No. 2363, 75c, Nicolino Locche (1939-2005).

2005, Dec. 17 ***Perf. 13½x13¾***

2362-2363 A1096 Set of 2 2.00 1.00

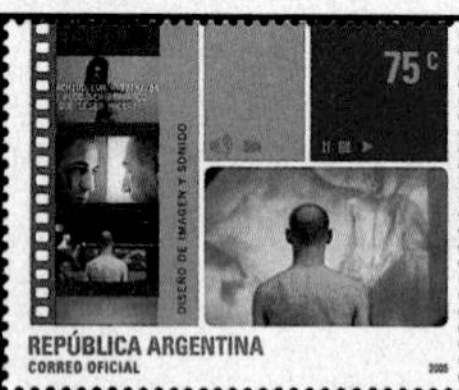

Argentine Design — A1097

Designs: No. 2364, 75c, Image and sound design. No. 2365, 75c, Clothes and textile design, vert. No. 2366, 75c, Industrial design, vert. No. 2367, 75c, Graphic design.

Perf. 13¾x13½, 13½x13¾

2005, Dec. 17

2364-2367 A1097 Set of 4 4.00 2.00

Pres. Bartolomé Mitre (1821-1906) — A1098

2006, Jan. 21 ***Perf. 13¾x13½***

2368 A1098 75c multi 1.00 .50

Esquel, Cent. A1099

2006, Feb. 18

2369 A1099 75c multi 1.00 .50

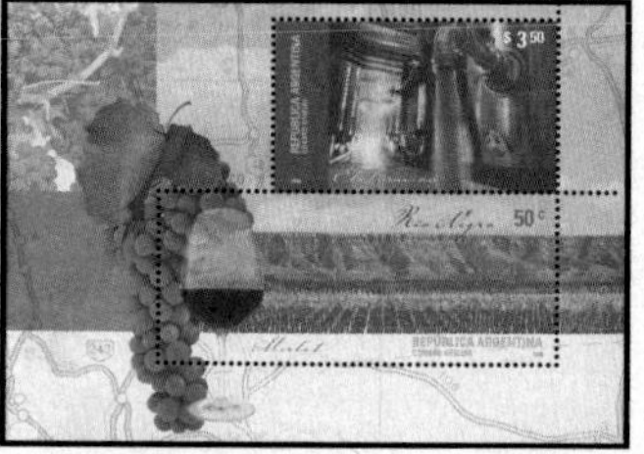

Wine Producing Regions — A1100

No. 2370: a, Merlot grapes and wine, Alto Valle, Río Negro (70x30mm). b, Wine flowing from vat (50x30mm).

No. 2371: a, Wine barrels (50x30mm). b, Torrontés grapes and wine, Cafayate, Salta (70x30mm).

No. 2372: a, Grape harvesters (50x30mm). b, Syrah grapes and wine, Valle del Zonda, San Juan (70x30mm).

No. 2373: a, Malbec grapes and wine, Valle del Tupungato, Mendoza (70x30mm). b, Wine in glass and bottle (50x30mm).

2006, Mar. 3 Litho. ***Perf. 14***

2370 A1100 Booklet pane of 2 5.00 —
a. 50c multi .60 .35
b. 3.50p multi 4.00 2.25
Complete booklet, #2370 5.50

2371 A1100 Booklet pane of 2 5.00 —
a. 75c multi .90 .50
b. 3.25p multi 3.75 2.10
Complete booklet, #2371 5.50

2372 A1100 Booklet pane of 2 5.00 —
a. 1p multi 1.25 .70
b. 3p multi 3.50 1.90
Complete booklet, #2372 5.50

2373 A1100 Booklet pane of 2 5.00 —
a. 1.25p multi 1.50 .85
b. 2.75p multi 3.25 1.75
Complete booklet, #2373 5.50

Nos. 2370-2373 (4) 20.00

Dr. Ramón Carrillo (1906-56), Neurologist — A1101

Perf. 13¾x13½

2006, Mar. 11 **Litho.**

2374 A1101 75c multi 1.00 .50

Musical Instruments A1102

Designs: 75c, Charango. 3.50p, Drum.

2006, Mar. 11 ***Perf. 13½x13¾***

2375-2376 A1102 Set of 2 5.00 2.75

Miniature Sheet

Lighthouses — A1103

No. 2377: a, Primero de Mayo. b, Año Nuevo. c, El Rincón. d, Recalada a Bahía Blanca.

2006, Mar. 18

2377 A1103 75c Sheet of 4, #a-d 4.50 2.25

Souvenir Sheet

Start of Military Dictatorship, 30th Anniv. — A1104

No. 2378: a, Man, left side of Navy Mechanics School. b, Flower, right side of Navy Mechanics School.

2006, Mar. 25 ***Perf. 14***

2378 A1104 75c Sheet of 2, #a-b 2.00 1.00

Silver Religious Objects — A1105

No. 2379: a, Crown. b, Candelabra. c, Chalice. d, Viaticum.

2006, Apr. 8 ***Perf. 13¾x13½***

2379 A1105 75c Block of 4, #a-d 4.00 2.00

Auto Racing A1106

Races and winning automobiles: No. 2380, 75c, Rally Nacional A8, Toyota Corolla WRC. No. 2381, 75c, Turismo Carretera, Ford Falcon. No. 2382, 75c, Turismo Competición 2000, Ford Focus. No. 2383, 75c, Class 3 Turismo Nacional, Ford Escort.

2006, May 6
2380-2383 A1106 Set of 4 4.00 2.00

Miniature Sheet

Dogs — A1107

No. 2384: a, 25c, Springer spaniel. b, 25c, Yorkshire terrier. c, 50c, Argentino dog. d, 50c, Miniature schnauzer. e, 75c, Poodle. f. 75c, Chow chow.

2006, May 20
2384 A1107 Sheet of 6 #a-f, + 2 labels 5.00 3.50

A1108

2006 World Cup Soccer Championships — A1109

No. 2386: a, Serbia & Montenegro player. b, Argentina player, blue and white background.

No. 2387: a, Ivory Coast player. b, Netherlands player.

2006, May 20 Litho. ***Perf. 13¾x13½***
2385 A1108 4p shown 4.75 2.75

Booklet Panes

Perf. 14¼

2386	Pane of 2	2.25	—
a.-b.	A1109 1p Either single	1.00	.70
2387	Pane of 2	2.25	—
a.-b.	A1109 1p Either single	1.00	.70
	Complete booklet, #2386-2387	5.00	

Souvenir Sheet

2388 A1109 1.50p shown 2.50 2.50

World No Tobacco Day — A1110

2006, May 27 Litho. ***Perf. 14x13½***
2389 A1110 75c multi 1.00 .50

Intl. Year of Deserts and Desertification — A1111

Designs: No. 2390, 75c, Lizard and plant. No. 2391, 75c, Impression of lizard in sand, dead plant.

Perf. 13¾x13½

2006, June 10 Litho.
2390-2391 A1111 Set of 2 2.00 1.00

Famous Men — A1112

Designs: No. 2392, 75c, Tato Bores (1927-96), television actor. No. 2393, 75c, Rodolfo Walsh (1927-77), kidnapped journalist.

2006, June 10 ***Perf. 13½x13¾***
2392-2393 A1112 Set of 2 2.00 1.00

Winter Sports — A1113

No. 2394: a, Alpine skiing. b, Snowboarding. c, Cross-country skiing. d, Biathlon.

2006, June 17 ***Perf. 13¾x13½***
2394 A1113 75c Block of 4, #a-d 4.00 2.00

Tango Dancing A1114

Designs: 75c, Musician. 4p, Dancers.

2006, June 24
2395-2396 A1114 Set of 2 4.75 3.25

See France Nos. 3224-3225.

Patoruzito Riding Pamperito — A1115

2006, July 8
2397 A1115 75c multi 1.00 .50

Endangered Animals — A1116

Designs: No. 2398, 75c, Eubalaena australis. No. 2399, 75c, Hippocamelus bisulcus. No. 2400, 75c, Hippocamelus antisensis. No. 2401, 75c, Panthera onca.

2006, July 8 ***Perf. 14x13¾***
2398-2401 A1116 Set of 4 4.00 2.00

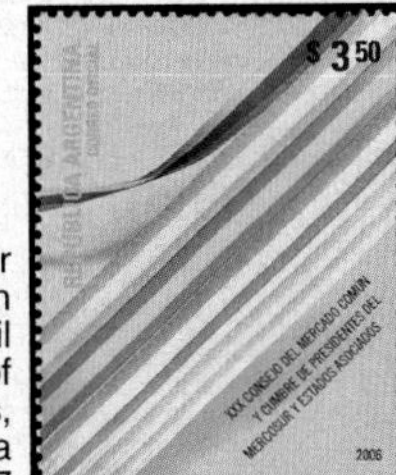

30th Mercosur Common Market Council and Summit of Presidents, Córdoba A1117

2006, July 22 ***Perf. 13¾x13½***
2402 A1117 3.50p multi 3.75 2.50

Souvenir Sheet

First British Invasion of Buenos Aires and Reconquest, Bicent. — A1118

2006, July 22 ***Perf. 14***
2403 A1118 1.50p multi 2.50 2.00

Energy Conservation — A1119

Winning designs in children's art contest: No. 2404, 75c, Light bulb, house and electrical cord, by Florencia Tovi. No. 2405, 75c, Plant in sunlight, unplugged lamp, by Camila Suárez.

2006, July 22 ***Perf. 13¾x13½***
2404-2405 A1119 Set of 2 2.00 1.00

First Postage Stamps of Corrientes, 150th Anniv. — A1120

Designs: 75c, August 21, 1856 Corrientes cancel. 1.50p, Corrientes #1.

Litho. & Embossed

2006, Aug. 19 ***Perf. 13¾x13½***
2406 A1120 75c multi 1.00 .50

Souvenir Sheet

Litho.

Perf. 14

2407 A1120 1.50p multi 2.50 2.00

No. 2407 contains one 40x40mm stamp.

Interjurisdictional Committee on the Colorado River, 50th Anniv. — A1121

Perf. 13½x13¾

2006, Aug. 26 Litho.
2408 A1121 75c multi 1.00 .50

Patricios Infantry Corps, Bicent. A1122

2006, Sept. 9
2409 A1122 75c multi 1.00 .50

Grapes, Wines and Vineyards — A1123

Designs: No. 2410, 75c, Syrah grapes and wine, Catamarca vineyards. No. 2411, 75c, Torrontés Riojano grapes and wine, La Rioja vineyards. No. 2412, 75c, Pinot Noir grapes and wine, Neuquén vineyards.

2006, Sept. 16 ***Perf. 14x13½***
2410-2412 A1123 Set of 3 2.50 1.50

Col. Ramón L. Falcón Federal Police Cadet School, Cent. A1124

2006, Oct. 14 Litho. ***Perf. 13¾x13½***
2413 A1124 75c multi 1.00 .50

Border Bridges — A1125

Designs: No. 2414, 75c, Pres. Tancredo Neves Intl. Bridge. No. 2415, 75c, San Roque González de Santa Cruz Intl. Bridge.

2006, Oct. 14 ***Perf. 14x13¾***
2414-2415 A1125 Set of 2 2.00 1.00

Christmas A1126

Paintings by Alfredo Guttero: No. 2416, 75c, Madonna and Dove. No. 2417, 75c, The Annunciation, horiz.

Perf. 13½x13¾, 13¾x13½
2006, Oct. 21
2416-2417 A1126 Set of 2 1.00 1.00

Natl. Institute of Agricultural and Cattle Ranching Technology, 50th Anniv. — A1127

Perf. 13¾x13½
2006, Nov. 11 **Litho.**
2418 A1127 75c multi 1.00 .50

Rock Musicians A1128

Designs: No. 2419, 75c, Tanguito (1945-72). No. 2420, 75c, Luca Prodan (1953-87). No. 2421, 75c, Miguel Abuelo (1946-88). No. 2422, 75c, Pappo (1950-2005).

2006, Nov. 18 ***Perf. 13½x13¾***
2419-2422 A1128 Set of 4 4.00 2.00

Caciques A1129

Designs: No. 2423, 75c, Valentín Sayhueque (1823-1903), Huilliche cacique. No. 2424, 75c, Casimiro Biguá, Tehuelche cacique.

2006, Dec. 2
2423-2424 A1129 Set of 2 2.00 1.00

Frigate Hercules, Detail From *Battle of Martín García Island,* by Emilio Biggeri — A1130

2007, Mar. 10 ***Perf. 13¾x13½***
2425 A1130 75c multi 1.00 .50

Adm. Guillermo Brown (1777-1857).

Wine-Growing Regions — A1131

No. 2426: a, Hand picking bunch of grapes. b, Vineyard, grapes, bottle of Pinot Noir, Neuquén Region (60x30mm).

No. 2427: a, Harvester cutting grapes from vine. b, Vineyard, grapes, bottle of Torrontés Riojano, La Rioja Region (60x30mm).

No. 2428: a, Harvester inspecting grapes on vine. b, Vineyard, grapes, bottle of Syrah, Catamarca Region (60x30mm).

2007, Mar. 10 **Litho.** ***Perf. 14***

2426	Booklet pane of 2	4.00	—
a.	A1131 75c multi	.75	.50
b.	A1131 3.25p multi	3.00	2.25
	Complete booklet, #2426	4.25	
2427	Booklet pane of 2	4.00	—
a.	A1131 75c multi	.75	.50
b.	A1131 3.25p multi	3.00	2.25
	Complete booklet, #2427	4.25	
2428	Booklet pane of 2	4.00	—
a.	A1131 75c multi	.75	.50
b.	A1131 3.25p multi	3.00	2.25
	Complete booklet, #2428	4.25	

Complete booklets include a plastic wine bottle spout.

Falkland Islands War, 25th Anniv. A1132

Map of the Falkland Islands and: No. 2429, 75c, Argentina #C90 in changed colors with Islas Malvinas cancel. No. 2430, 75c, IAI Dagger fighters. No. 2431, 75c, Battle cruiser ARA General Belgrano. No. 2432, 75c, Decorated war veteran. No. 2433, 75c, War decoration, vert.

Perf. 13¾x13½, 13½x13¾
2007, Mar. 31 **Litho.**
2429-2433 A1132 Set of 5 6.00 4.00

Postal and Telecommunications Workers Federation, 50th Anniv. — A1133

2007, Apr. 14 ***Perf. 13¾x13½***
2434 A1133 75c multi .90 .50

Map of Antarctica, Icebreaker Almirante Irízar — A1134

No. 2436 — Antarctic fauna: a, Phalacrocorax atriceps. b, Leptonychotes weddellii. c, Sterna vittata, denomination at UR. d, Sterna vittata, denomination at UL. e, Pygoscelis adeliae. f, Chionis alba. g, Pygoscelis papua, denomination at UR. h, Pygoscelis papua, denomination at UL.

2007, Apr. 21

2435	A1134 4p shown	3.75	2.75
2436	Sheet of 8	4.00	4.00
a.-h.	A1134 75c Any single	.50	.50

Miniature Sheet

Toys — A1135

No. 2437: a, Rocking horse. b, Tea set. c, Toy train and stations. d, Toy soldiers.

2007, May 5 **Litho.** ***Perf. 13¾x13½***

2437	A1135 Sheet of 4	4.00	4.00
a.-d.	75c Any single	.90	.90

Museums — A1136

Designs: 75c, Latin American Art Museum, Buenos Aires. 3.25p, High Mountain Archaeological Museum, Salta.

2007, May 5
2438-2439 A1136 Set of 2 4.75 3.25

Road Safety Year — A1137

2007, May 19 **Litho.** ***Perf. 13½x13¾***
2440 A1137 75c red & silver .90 .50

Souvenir Sheet

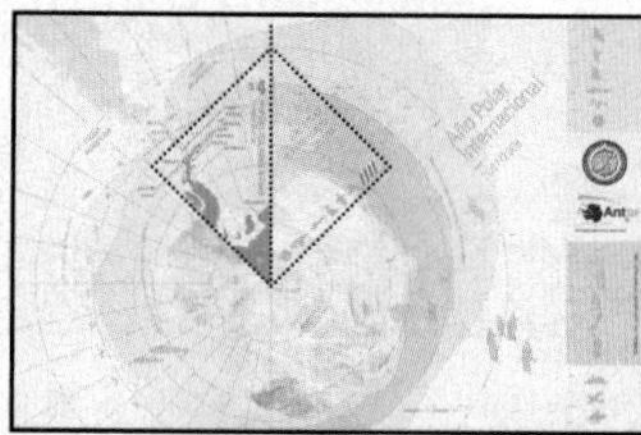

Intl. Polar Year — A1138

2007, June 2 ***Perf. 14***
2441 A1138 4p multi + label 4.00 3.00

Defense of Buenos Aires From British Attack, Bicent. A1139

Perf. 13¾x13½
2007, June 23 **Litho.**
2442 A1139 75c multi .90 .50

Pierre Auger Observatory A1140

2007, July 14 **Litho.** ***Perf. 13½x13¾***
2443 A1140 75c multi .90 .50

St. Joseph Calasanctius (1557-1648) A1141

2007, July 14
2444 A1141 1p multi 1.00 .65

Souvenir Sheet

Campo del Cielo Meteorite — A1142

2007, July 28 ***Perf. 14***
2445 A1142 6p multi 8.00 8.00

No. 2445 was sold with, but unattached to, a booklet cover, and 3-D glasses.

Homero Manzi (1907-51), Political Leader, Tango Lyricist A1143

Perf. 13½x13¾

2007, Aug. 11 **Litho.**

2446 A1143 1p multi .90 .65

Tourism Along Route 40 — A1144

No. 2447: a, Road to San Carlos de Bariloche (30x30mm). b, El Acay Pass (40x30mm). c, Road to Perito Moreno (70x30mm). d, La Trochita locomotive (40x30mm). e, Lanin Volcano (40x30mm). f, Rio Grande (50x30mm). g, Animals on road, San José Jachal (40x30mm). h, Cuesta de Miranda (50x30mm) i, Nuestra Senora del Tránsito Chapel (30x30mm). j, Quilmes Ruins (30x30mm). k, Road to Oratorio (40x30mm).

2007, Aug. 25 **Litho.** *Perf. 14*

2447 Sheet of 11 10.00 10.00
a.-b. A1144 50c Either single .45 .30
c.-k. A1144 1p Any single .90 .65

Souvenir Sheet

Diplomatic Relations Between Argentina and Germany, 150th Anniv. — A1145

2007, Sept. 8

2448 A1145 4p multi 3.75 2.75

Prevention of Carbon Monoxide Accidents — A1146

Children's art by: No. 2449, 1p, Julieta Saavedra Barragán. No. 2450, 1p, Leandro Ventancour. No. 2451, 1p, Efraín Osvaldo Rost, vert. No. 2452, 1p, Camila M. Alvarez Petrone, vert.

Perf. 13¾x13½, 13½x13¾

2007, Sept. 8

2449-2452 A1146 Set of 4 3.60 2.60

San Lorenzo de Almagro Athletic Club, Cent. — A1147

2007, Sept. 22 *Perf. 13½x13¾*

2453 A1147 1p multi .90 .65

Beatification of Ceferino Namuncurá (1886-1905) — A1148

2007, Oct. 13 **Litho.** *Perf. 13¾x13½*

2454 A1148 1p multi .90 .65

Contemporary Art — A1149

Designs: No. 2455, 1p, Corrientes Esquina Uruguay, photograph by Horacio Coppola. No. 2456, 1p, 0611, painting by Pablo Siquier. No. 2457, 1p, Diálogo, digital photograph by Liliana Porter, vert. No. 2458, 1p, Imaginando el Estupor, mosaic by Marta Minujin, vert.

Perf. 13¾x13½, 13½x13¾

2007, Oct. 27

2455-2458 A1149 Set of 4 3.60 2.60

Nos. 2455-2458 each were printed in sheets of 4.

Christmas A1150

Designs: 25c, Adoration of the Magi. 1p, Holy Family.

2007, Nov. 10 *Perf. 13½x14*

2459-2460 A1150 Set of 2 1.80 1.30

First Balloon Crossing of Río de la Plata, Cent. A1151

Perf. 13¾x13½

2007, Nov. 24 **Litho.**

2461 A1151 1p multi .90 .65

Discovery of Oil and Gas in Argentina, Cent. — A1152

2007, Nov. 24

2462 A1152 1p multi .90 .65

2007 Presidential Inauguration A1153

2007, Dec. 15 *Perf. 13½x13¾*

2463 A1153 1p multi .90 .65

Festivals A1154

Designs: No. 2464, 1p, National Chamamé Festival, Corrientes Province. No. 2465, 1p, National Poncho Festival, Catamarca Province. No. 2466, 1p, National Festival of Dressage and Folklore, Jesús María, Cordoba Province. No. 2467, 1p, National Snow Festival, San Carlos de Bariloche, Río Negro Province.

2007, Dec. 15

2464-2467 A1154 Set of 4 3.60 2.60

2008 Summer Olympics, Beijing A1155

Designs: No. 2468, 50c, Mountain biking. No. 2469, 50c, Taekwondo. 1p, Basketball. 4p, Pole vault.

Perf. 13½x13¾

2008, Mar. 29 **Litho.**

2468-2471 A1155 Set of 4 5.00 4.00

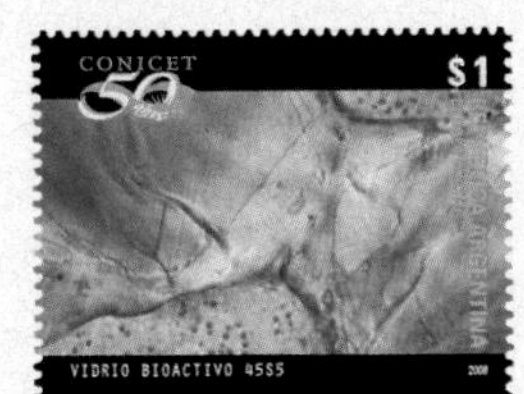

Natl. Scientific and Technical Research Council, 50th Anniv. — A1156

Designs: No. 2472, 1p, Bone tissue bridges with 45S5 bioactive glass particles. No. 2473, 1p, Pollen grain of Polygonum sp. No. 2474, 1p, Remnants of Supernova W44. No. 2475, 1p, Cave paintings, Epuyén River Valley. No. 2476, 1p, Gas heater device.

2008, Apr. 12 *Perf. 13¾x13½*

2472-2476 A1156 Set of 5 4.50 3.25

Association of Argentine Private Radio Stations, 50th Anniv. — A1157

2008, Apr. 26

2477 A1157 1p multi .90 .65

Pres. Arturo Frondizi (1908-95), Oil Pumps — A1158

2008, Apr. 26

2478 A1158 1p multi .90 .65

Birds — A1159

Male and female: 1p, Sturnella loyca. 4p, Xanthopsar flavus.

2008, Apr. 26 *Perf. 13½x13¾*

2479-2480 A1159 Set of 2 4.75 3.25

Argentine Aero Club, Cent. — A1160

2008, May 10 *Perf. 14x13½*

2481 A1160 1p multi .90 .65

Colón Theater, Buenos Aires, Cent. — A1161

2008, May 24

2482 A1161 1p multi .90 .65

Aimé Bonpland (1773-1858), Founder of Corrientes Natural Sciences Museum — A1162

2008, May 24 *Perf. 13¾x13½*

2483 A1162 1p multi .90 .65

Dr. Marcos Sastre (1808-87), Textbook Writer, and Text from Reading Book, Anagnosia — A1163

Perf. 13¾x13½

2008, June 21 **Litho.**

2484 A1163 1p multi .90 .70

Luciano-Honorato Valette (1880-1957), Antarctic Naturalist — A1164

Disappearance of Rescue Ship ARA Guaraní, 50th Anniv. — A1165

2008, June 28

2485 A1164 1p multi .90 .70

2486 A1165 1p multi .90 .70

Characters From "The Mail Song," by Maria Elena Walsh A1166

Character From "Big Brother," by Silvia Schujer A1167

Characters From "Letters to Santa Claus," by Luis María Pescetti — A1168

Character From "Mammarachos por Carta," by Ricardo Mariño — A1169

Perf. 13½x13¾, 13¾x13½

2008, July 26

2487 A1166 1p multi .65 .65

2488 A1167 1p multi .65 .65

2489 A1168 1p multi .65 .65

2490 A1169 1p multi .65 .65

Nos. 2487-2490 (4) 2.60 2.60

Children's songs and literature.

Scenes From "The Mail Song," by María Elena Walsh — A1170

Scenes From "Mamarrachos por Carta," by Ricardo Mariño — A1171

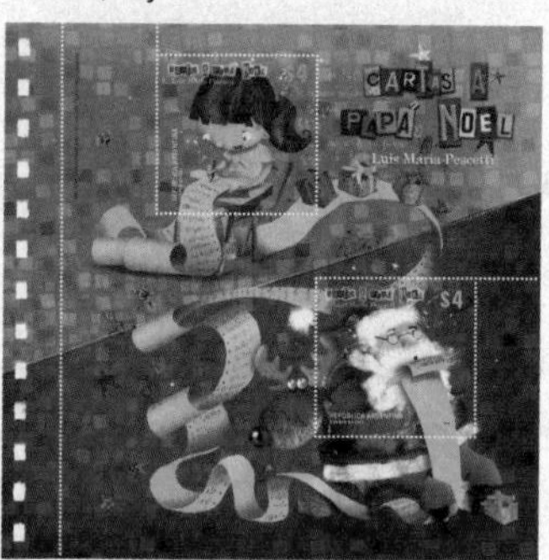

Characters From "Letters to Santa Claus," by Luis María Pescetti — A1172

Characters From "Big Brother," by Silvia Schujer — A1173

No. 2491: a, Bird holding Argentina #2216b in beak. b, Mailbox. c, Paper airplane, letters. d, Post office, letters. e, Smokestacks behind open envelope with letter. f, Philatelic office, Argentina #2236, #2239 and its adjacent label.

No. 2492: a, Postman holding letter. b, Postman and woman reading letter. c, Bird reading letter. d, Man with pipe. e, Birds on mail box. f, Monkey with banana.

No. 2493: a, Child writing letter to Santa Claus. b, Santa Claus reading letter from child.

No. 2494: a, Girl at table playing card game (40x50mm). b, Boy and mother, horiz. (70x40mm).

2008, July 26 **Litho.** *Perf. 13½x13¾*

Booklet Stamps

2491 A1170 Block of 6 4.00 4.00

a.-f. 1p Any single .65 .65

g. Booklet pane, 2 #2491 8.00 —

2492 A1171 Block of 6 4.00 4.00

a.-f. 1p Any single .65 .65

g. Booklet pane, 2 #2492 8.00 —

Perf. 14¼

2493 A1172 Booklet pane of 2 5.25 —

a.-b. 4p Either single 2.60 2.60

Perf. 14

2494 A1173 Booklet pane of 2 5.25 —

a.-b. 4p Either single 2.60 2.60

Complete booklet, #2491g, 2492g, 2493, 2494 26.50

Complete booklet is a spiral-bound book containing the four booklet panes, postal cards, text pages and pieces for a children's card game.

Archaeological Artifacts Type of 2000

Design: Jar, Yocavil culture.

Perf. 13½x13¾ Syncopated

2008, Aug. 2

2495 A973 10p multi 6.75 6.75

Souvenir Sheet

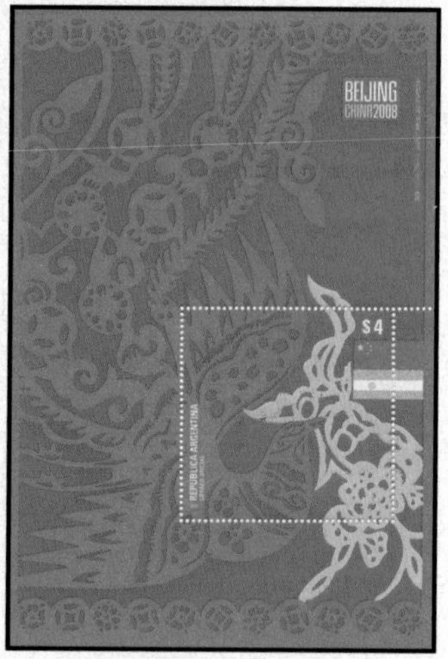

Olympex 2008 World Stamp Exhibition, Beijing — A1174

Litho. With Foil Application

2008, Aug. 2 *Perf. 14*

2496 A1174 4p multi 5.00 4.00

Immigrants to Argentina — A1175

Designs: No. 2497, 1p, Cherry blossoms, koi, immigrants from Japan. No. 2498, 1p, Metal decorative plates and immigrants from Lebanon. No. 2499, 1p, Tiles, guitar and immigrants from Portugal. No. 2500, 1p, Wooden decorative box, embroidered silk, Ugaritic alphabet and immigrants from Syria.

Perf. 13¾x13½

2008, Sept. 20 **Litho.**

2497-2500 A1175 Set of 4 2.60 2.60

Souvenir Sheets

National Flower Festival — A1176

Designs: No. 2501, 5p, Gerbera daisy, gardenia and rose (shown). No. 2502, 5p, Carnation, gold-banded lily and delphinium.

2008, Sept. 27 ***Perf. 14***
2501-2502 A1176 Set of 2 6.50 6.50

Nos. 2501-2502 are impregnated with a floral scent.

Souvenir Sheets

Sports Personalities — A1177

Designs: No. 2503, 5p, Hand of Manu Ginobili, basketball and hoop. No. 2504, 5p, Rugby football kicked by Hugo Porta, goal posts, silhouettes of rugby player kicking ball. No. 2505, 5p, Silhouette of golfer putting, foot of Roberto De Vicenzo, vert. No. 2506, 5p, Juan Manuel Fangio in race car, vert.

2008, Oct. 11 ***Perf. 14***
2503-2506 A1177 Set of 4 12.00 12.00

See Nos. 2541-2544, 2632-2635.

Science Teaching Year — A1178

2008, Oct. 25 ***Perf. 13¾x13½***
2507 A1178 1p multi .60 .60

Flowers A1179

Designs: No. 2508, 1p, Ceiba chodatii. No. 2509, 1p, Nelumbo nucifera.

2008, Oct. 25
2508-2509 A1179 Set of 2 1.25 1.25

See Viet Nam Nos. 3343-3344.

Souvenir Sheet

First Stamps of Argentina, Buenos Aires and Cordoba,150th Anniv. — A1180

No. 2510: a, Cordoba #2 (30x30mm). b, Buenos Aires #4 (40x30mm). c, Argentina #3 (30x40mm).

2008, Nov. 1 ***Perf. 14***
2510 A1180 1p Sheet of 3, #a-c 1.90 1.90

Christmas A1181

2008, Nov. 15 ***Perf. 13½x13¾***
2511 A1181 1p multi .60 .60

Dances A1182

Designs: No. 2512, 1p, Malambo sureño dancer, Argentina. No. 2513, 1p, Hoy-nazan dancers, Armenia.

2008, Nov. 22 **Litho.**
2512-2513 A1182 Set of 2 1.25 1.25

See Armenia Nos. 790-791.

El Cronista Comercial Newspaper, Cent. — A1183

2008, Dec. 13 ***Perf. 13¾x13½***
2514 A1183 1p multi .60 .60

School of Forestry, 50th Anniv. A1184

2008, Dec. 13 ***Perf. 13½x3¾***
2515 A1184 1p multi .60 .60

Festivals A1185

Designs: No. 2516, 1p, Chaya Festival, La Rioja Province. No. 2517, 1p, Natl. Grape Harvest Festival, Mendoza Province. No. 2518, 1p, Natl. Cherry Festival, Los Antiguos, Santa Cruz Province. No. 2519, 1p, Natl. Sea Festival, Mar del Plata, Buenos Aires Province.

2009, Feb. 14 ***Perf. 13½x13¾***
2516-2519 A1185 Set of 4 2.25 2.25

Souvenir Sheet

Preservation of Polar Regions and Glaciers — A1186

No. 2520: a, Retreat of Piedras Blancas Glacier. b, Retreat of Argentine Antarctic Territory ice.

2009, Mar. 7 ***Perf. 14***
2520 A1186 5p Sheet of 2, #a-b 5.50 5.50

Bishop Colombres Memorial Experimental Agribusiness, Cent. — A1187

2009, Mar. 21 ***Perf. 13¾x13½***
2521 A1187 1p multi .55 .55

Souvenir Sheet

New Year 2009 (Year of the Ox) — A1188

Litho. & Embossed, Margin With Foil Application

2009, Apr. 4 ***Perf. 14***
2522 A1188 5p multi 2.75 2.75

China 2009 World Stamp Exhibition, Luoyang.

Holy Cross Exaltation Parish, Puerto Santa Cruz, Cent. — A1189

2009, Apr. 18 Litho. ***Perf. 13½x13¾***
2523 A1189 1p multi .55 .55

Argentine Exports — A1190

Designs: 1p, Wine. 5p, Agricultural machines.

2009, Apr. 18 ***Perf. 13¾x13½***
2524-2525 A1190 Set of 2 3.25 3.25

Endangered Species A1191

Designs: No. 2526, 1p, Harpyhaliaetus coronatus. No. 2527, 1p, Chelonoidis chilensis, horiz.

Perf. 13½x13¾, 13¾x13½
2009, Apr. 18
2526-2527 A1191 Set of 2 1.10 1.10

Pres. Raúl Ricardo Alfonsín (1927-2009) A1192

2009, May 9 ***Perf. 13½x13¾***
2528 A1192 1p multi .55 .55

Children of the Holy Virgin of the Garden Congregation in Argentina, 150th Anniv. A1193

2009, May 23
2529 A1193 1p multi .55 .55

Raúl Scalabrini Ortiz (1898-1959), Writer — A1194

2009, May 23
2530 A1194 1p multi .55 .55

Political and Military Command of the Malvinas (Falkland Islands), 180th Anniv. A1195

Paintings: 1p, Luis Vernet, governor of the Malvinas, by Luisa Vernet Lavalle Lloveras. 5p, Ship and houses near cliff, by Vernet, map of Malvinas.

2009, June 13 ***Perf. 13½x13¾***
2531 A1195 1p multi .55 .55

Souvenir Sheet

Perf. 14

2532 A1195 5p multi 2.75 2.75

No. 2532 contains one 70x30mm stamp.

Water — A1196

No. 2533: a, Droplets. b, Drops, clouds and hand, vert.

2009, June 27 ***Perf. 14***
2533 Sheet of 2, unscratched 5.50 5.50
a. A1196 5p multi 2.75 2.75
b. A1196 5p multi, unscratched 2.75 2.75
c. As "b," scratched 2.75

No. 2533b and sheet margin have scratch-off panels.

Flora and Fauna A1197

Designs: No. 2534, 1p, Polybetes pythagoricus. No. 2535, 1p, Passiflora caerulea.

2009, July 25 ***Perf. 13¾x13½***
2534-2535 A1197 Set of 2 1.10 1.10

Amusement Park Rides — A1198

No. 2536: a, Bumper cars. b, Roller coaster. c, Ferris wheel. d, Ghost train.

2009, Aug. 1
2536 Horiz. strip of 4 + flanking label 2.25 2.25
a.-d. A1198 1p Any single .55 .55

Miniature Sheet

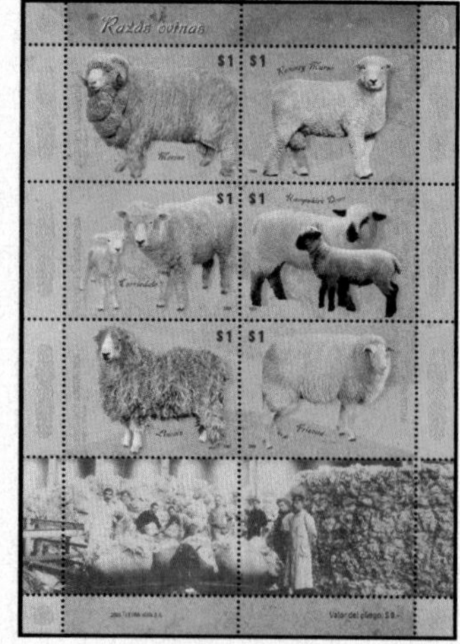

Sheep — A1199

No. 2537: a, Merino ram. b, Romney Marsh yearling. c, Corriedale ewe and lamb. d, Hampshire Down ewe and lamb. e, Lincoln ewe. f, Frisian ewe.

2009, Aug. 22
2537 A1199 1p Sheet of 6, #a-f, + 2 labels 3.25 3.25

Soil Erosion — A1200

No. 2538 — Erosion by: a, Water. b, Wind.

2009, Sept. 12 ***Perf. 14x13½***
2538 Horiz. pair 1.10 1.10
a.-b. A1200 1p Either single .55 .55

A1201

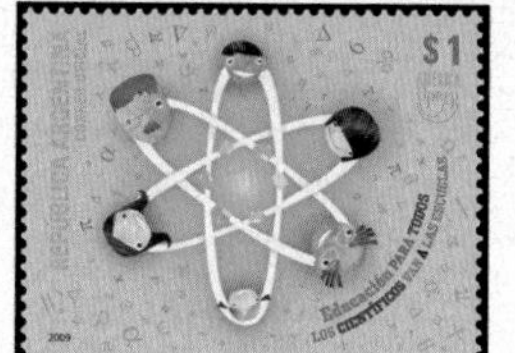

America Issue, Education For All — A1202

Perf. 13¾x13½

2009, Sept. 12 **Litho.**
2539 A1201 1p multi .55 .55
2540 A1202 1p multi .55 .55

Sports Personalities Type of 2008

Designs: No. 2541, 5p, Delfo Cabrera running in 1948 Summer Olympics, vert. No. 2542, 5p, Tennis ball and shorts of Guillermo Vilas (38mm diameter). No. 2543, 10p, Field hockey players, stick of Luciana Aymar, vert. No. 2544, 10p, Cyclists chasing Juan Curuchet, vert.

Perf. 14, Perf. (No. 2542)

2009, Sept. 26 **Litho.**
2541-2544 A1177 Set of 4 16.00 16.00

The tennis ball on No 2542 is covered with flocking.

National Technological University, 50th Anniv. A1203

2009, Oct. 17 ***Perf. 13½x13¾***
2545 A1203 1p multi .55 .55

Souvenir Sheets

A1204

Italia 2009 Intl. Philatelic Exhibition, Rome — A1205

No. 2546: a, La Scala Theater, Milan. b, Colon Theater, Buenos Aires.
No. 2547: a, Froilán González racing in Ferrari 375 (85x30mm rhomboid) b, Ferrari F60 race car (60x20mm).

2009, Oct. 24 **Litho.** ***Perf. 14***
2546 A1204 6p Sheet of 2, #a-b 6.50 6.50
2547 A1205 6p Sheet of 2, #a-b 6.50 6.50

Intl. Year of Astronomy — A1206

Designs: 1p, Telescope, National University of Córdoba Astronomical Observatory.
10p, Galileo Galilei (1564-1642), diagram of solar system orbits.

2009, Oct. 24 **Litho.** ***Perf. 13¾x13½***
2548 A1206 1p multi .55 .55

Souvenir Sheet

Perf. 14

2549 A1206 10p multi 5.25 5.25

No. 2549 contains one 80x20mm stamp.

Children's Art — A1207

Winning art in "I Can Slow TB Down" children's stamp design contest: No. 2550, 1p, Boxing gloves hitting "TB," by Alberto Penayo Pardo. No. 2551, 1p, Lungs with bandage, by Candela Alemany Fiandrino. No. 2552, 1p, Boy coughing, doctor holding sign, by Rocío Cabrera, vert. No. 2553, 1p, Hands holding lungs, by Juliana Benzo, vert.

Perf. 13¾x13½, 13½x13¾

2009, Nov. 14 **Litho.**
2550-2553 A1207 Set of 4 2.10 2.10

Christmas A1208

2009, Nov. 21 ***Perf. 13½x14***
2554 A1208 1p multi .55 .55

Historic Buildings — A1209

No. 2555, 1p — San Martín Mansion, 1910: a, Exterior. b, Interior.
No. 2556, 1p — Ortiz Basualdo Mansion, 1918: a, Exterior. b, Interior.
No. 2557, 1p — Fernandez-Anchorena Mansion, 1909: a, Exterior. b, Interior.
No. 2558, 1p — Duhau Mansion, 1934: a, Exterior. b, Interior.

Perf. 13¾x13½

2009, Dec. 12 **Litho.**

Horiz. Pairs, #a-b

2555-2558 A1209 Set of 4 4.25 4.25

Nos. 2555-2558 each were printed in sheets containing 8 pairs and 4 labels.

Festivals A1210

Designs: No. 2559, 1.50p, National Apple Festival, General Roca, Río Negro Province. No. 2560, 1.50p, National Sun Festival, San Juan, San Juan Province. No. 2561, 1.50p, National Students Festival, San Salvador de Jujuy, Jujuy Province. No. 2562, 1.50p, National Tradition Festival, San Antonio de Areco, Buenos Aires Province.

2010, Feb. 20 ***Perf. 13½x13¾***
2559-2562 A1210 Set of 4 3.25 3.25

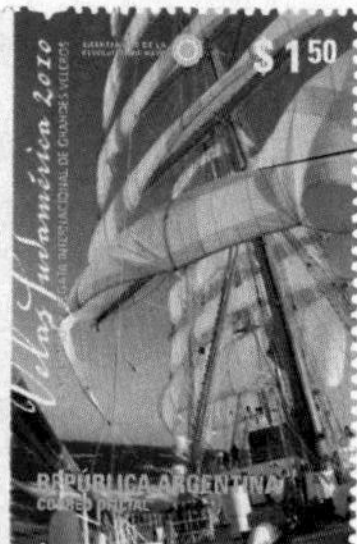

South American Sails 2010 Regatta A1211

Designs: 1.50p, Argentine Navy frigate Libertad.
No. 2564: a, Chilean Navy schooner Esmeralda. b, Libertad, diff.

Perf. 13¾x13½ Syncopated

2010, Feb. 20

2563 A1211 1.50p multi .80 .80

Souvenir Sheet

Perf. 14

2564 A1211 6p Sheet of 2, #a-b, + 12 labels 6.25 6.25

No. 2564 contains two 40x50mm stamps.

May Revolution, Bicent. — A1212

Perf. 13½x13¾ Syncopated

2010, Mar. 6

2565 A1212 1.50p multi .80 .80

National Symbols A1213

Designs: No. 2566, 1.50p, Coat of arms. No. 2567, 1.50p, Flag, horiz.

Perf. 13½x13¾, 13¾x13½

2010, Mar. 27

2566-2567 A1213 Set of 2 1.60 1.60

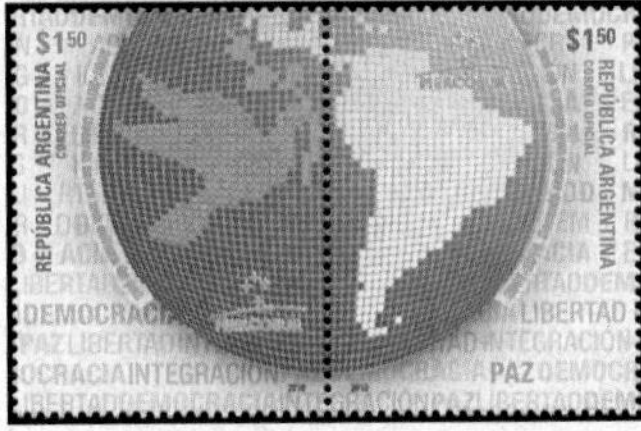

A Culture of Peace — A1214

No. 2568: a, Dove. b, Map of South America.

2010, Apr. 24 Litho. *Perf. 13½x13¾*

2568 A1214 1.50p Horiz. pair, #a-b 1.60 1.60

Buenos Aires City Symphony, Cent. — A1215

2010, Apr. 24 *Perf. 14x13½*

2569 A1215 1.50p multi .80 .80

Argentine Army, Bicent. A1216

2010, May 8 *Perf. 13½x13¾*

2570 A1216 1.50p multi .80 .80

Argentine Naval Command, Bicent. — A1217

2010, May 29 *Perf. 13¾x13½*

2571 A1217 1.50p multi .80 .80

Bicentenary Mural — A1218

No. 2572: a, Cabildo, Buenos Aires (30x50mm). b, General Manuel Belgrano, flag of Argentina on pole, Casa de Tucumán, San Miguel de Tucumán (30x50mm). c, Gen. José de San Martín on horseback, raising sword (40x80mm). d, National Constitution (30x50mm). e, Ships unloading immigrants (30x50mm). f, Sword battle, people voting, "1910," horiz. (70x30mm). g, National Congress, Blind Justice (30x50mm). h, Trolley, film set, bridge, horiz. (40x30mm). i, Palm tree, crowd, banners, men with feet in fountain, baby with umbilical cord (30x60mm). j, Military with guns, cardinal, man smoking cigar, eyes, "the disappeared" in pit (30x40mm). k, Mothers of the Plaza de Mayo holding pictures of the disappeared, May Pyramid statue (40x60mm). l, Motorcyclist, men with briefcases holding cellular phones, man on computer, airplanes (40x60mm).

2010, May 29 Litho. *Perf. 14*

2572 Sheet of 12 9.75 9.75

a.-l. A1218 1.50p Any single .80 .80

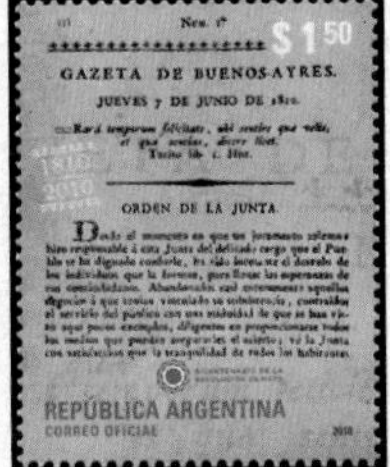

Gazeta de Buenos-Ayres, Bicent. A1219

2010, June 5 Litho. *Perf. 13½x13¾*

2573 A1219 1.50p multi .80 .80

A1220

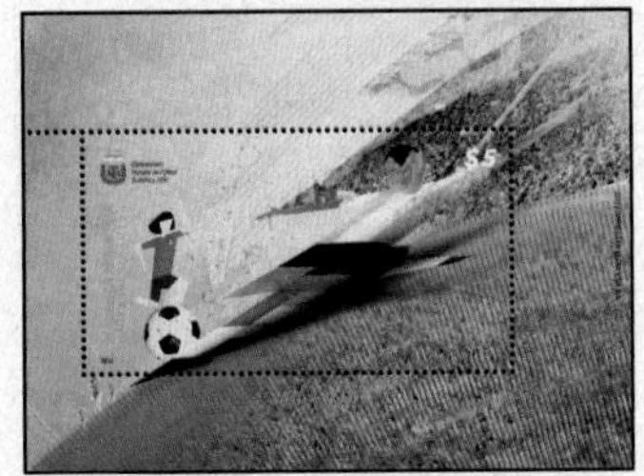

2010 World Cup Soccer Championships, South Africa — A1221

2010 World Cup emblem and stylized player from: No. 2574, 1.50p, Nigeria. No. 2575, 1.50p, Greece, vert. 5p, South Korea. 7p, Argentina, vert.

No. 2578, 5p, Argentina player sliding to kick ball. No. 2579, 5p, Argentina player heading ball into net. No. 2580, 5p, Argentina player making scissor kick. No. 2581, 5p, Goalie making save, vert.

Perf. 13¾x13½, 13½x13¾

2010, June 5

2574-2577 A1220 Set of 4 7.75 7.75

Souvenir Sheets

Perf. 14

2578-2581 A1221 Set of 4 10.50 10.50

Nos. 2578-2579 each contain one 70x40mm stamp, No. 2580 contains one 60x40mm stamp, and No. 2581 contains one 40x60mm stamp.

World Junior Rugby Championships, Argentina — A1222

2010, June 19 *Perf. 13¾x13½*

2582 A1222 1.50p multi .80 .80

Souvenir Sheet

First Government Junta, Bicent. — A1223

2010, July 24 *Perf. 14*

2583 A1223 5p multi 2.60 2.60

Miniature Sheet

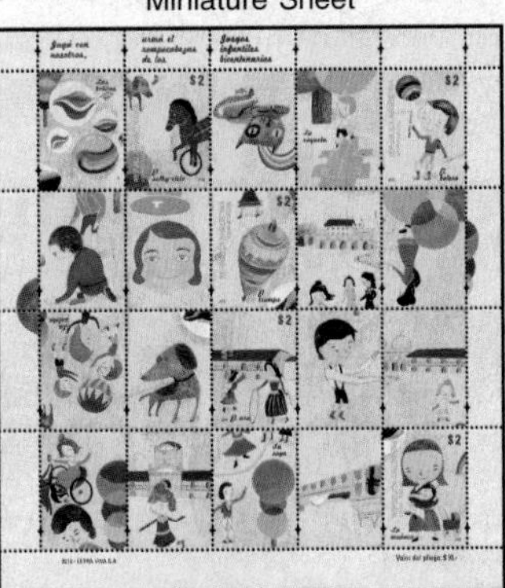

Toys and Games — A1224

No. 2584: a, Sulky-cycle (sulky-ciclo). b, Cup and ball (balero). c, Top (trompo). d, Hoop (aro). e, Doll (muñeca).

Perf. 13½x13¾ Syncopated

2010, July 24 Litho.

2584 A1224 2p Sheet of 5, #a-e, + 15 labels 5.25 5.25

The stamps and labels of No. 2584 are puzzle pieces that when separated and rearranged form a picture.

Jorge Luis Borges (1899-1986), Writer A1225

Perf. 13¾x13½ Syncopated

2010, Aug. 14 Litho.

2585 A1225 7p multi 3.50 3.50

2010 Frankfurt Book Fair. See Germany No. 2585.

Landmarks Type of 2004

Designs: 1.50p, Parana River, Corrientes. 6p, Les Eclaireurs Lighthouse, Tierra del Fuego.

Perf. 13¾x13½ Syncopated

2010 Litho.

2586 A1063a 1.50p multi + label .80 .80

2587 A1063a 6p multi 3.25 3.25

Issued: 1.50p, 5/11; 6p, 2/12.

Mountain Lakes — A1226

Flags of Romania and Argentina and: 1.50p, Lake Ballea, Romania. 7p, Lake Nahuel Huapi, Argentina.

2010, Aug. 14 *Perf. 13¾x13½*

2588-2589 A1226 Set of 2 4.50 4.50

See Romania Nos. 5201-5202.

Women's Field Hockey World Cup Championships, Rosario — A1227

2010, Aug. 28

2590 A1227 1.50p multi .80 .80

Games A1228

Designs: No. 2591, 1.50p, Truco (card game). No. 2592, 1.50p, Bocce.

2010, Aug. 28 *Perf. 13½x13¾*

2591-2592 A1228 Set of 2 1.60 1.60

2010 Census A1229

Perf. 13¾x13½ Syncopated

2010, Sept. 18

2593 A1229 1.50p multi .75 .75

Juan Bautista Alberdi (1810-84), Lawyer and Diplomat A1230

2010, Sept. 18 *Perf. 13½x13¾*

2594 A1230 1.50p multi .75 .75

National Library, Bicent. A1231

Perf. 13¾x13½

2010, Sept. 18 **Litho.**

2595 A1231 1.50p multi .75 .75

Souvenir Sheet

Weather Stations in Austria and Argentina — A1232

No. 2596 — Weather station in: a, Stadtpark, Vienna. b, Buenos Aires Botanical Garden.

2010, Oct. 16 *Perf. 14*

2596 A1232 5p Sheet of 2, #a-b 5.25 5.25

See Austria No. 2283.

The Child of Bethlehem, by Aldo Severi — A1233

2010, Nov. 13 *Perf. 13¾x13½*

2597 A1233 1.50p multi .75 .75

Christmas.

Federal Electric Power Council, 50th Anniv. A1234

2010, Nov. 27 *Perf. 13½x13¾*

2598 A1234 1.50p multi .75 .75

Souvenir Sheets

Lighthouses — A1235

Portuguese Ceramic Tile — A1236

No. 2599: a, Querandí Lighthouse, Argentina. b, Santa Marta Lighthouse, Portugal.

2010, Sept. 25 *Perf. 14*

2599 A1235 5p Sheet of 2, #a-b 5.25 5.25

2600 A1236 10p multi 5.25 5.25

Portugal 2010 Intl. Philatelic Exhibition, Lisbon. Portions of the designs of Nos. 2599a-2599b were applied by a thermographic process producing a shiny, raised effect.

World Post Day — A1237

2010, Oct. 9 **Litho.** *Perf. 13½x13¾*

2601 A1237 1.50p multi .75 .75

A Song to Work, Sculpture by Rogelio Yrurtia — A1238

2010, Oct. 16 *Perf. 14x13½*

2602 A1238 1.50p multi .75 .75

Dakar Rally in Argentina — A1239

No. 2603 — Photographs of 2009 and 2010 Rallies: a, Starting line of Rally, Buenos Aires (60x40mm). b, Motorcycle No. 107 (50x50mm). c, Car No. 300 on dirt road (60x40mm). d, Truck No. 502 on dirt road, (50x50mm). e, Vehicles on dirt road (50x50mm). f, Quad No. 251 (40x80mm). g, Quad No. 277 (40x80mm).

No. 2604: a, Car No. 375 on dirt road (60x50mm). b, Two quad riders in sand near hill (60x40mm). c, Car No. 377 in air (60x40mm). d, Motorcycle No. 1 (40x50mm). e, Tree near Laguna del Pescado (40x50mm). f, White clouds over mountain near Tucumán (40x50mm). g, Road and bridge near Jujuy (40x50mm). h, Truck No. 500 in water (70x50mm).

2010, Dec. 11 *Perf. 14*

2603	Booklet pane of 7	9.75	—
a.-e.	A1239 1.50p Any single	.75	.75
f.	A1239 5p multi	2.50	2.50
g.	A1239 7p multi	3.50	3.50
2604	Booklet pane of 8	10.50	—
a.-g.	A1239 1.50p Any single	.75	.75
h.	A1239 10p multi	5.00	5.00
	Complete booklet, #2603-2604 + post card	20.50	

Intl. Year of Forests A1240

2011, Mar. 19 *Perf. 13½x13¾*

2605 A1240 2p multi 1.00 1.00

Postal Union of the Americas, Spain and Portugal (UPAEP), Cent. — A1241

2011, Mar. 19 *Perf. 13¾x13½*

2606 A1241 8p multi 4.00 4.00

Buenos Aires, 2010 World Book Capital — A1242

No. 2607 — Stylized buildings spelling: a, "Buenos Aires Capital." b, "Mundial del Libro 2011."

2011, Apr. 16 *Perf. 14x13½*

2607 Horiz. pair 2.00 2.00

a.-b. A1242 2p Either single 1.00 1.00

A1243

Antarctic Treaty, 50th Anniv. — A1244

Designs: 2p, Iceberg and Antarctic Treaty emblem.

No. 2609: a, Pygoscelis papua. b, Scientist and equipment.

2011, Apr. 16 *Perf. 13¾x13½*

2608 A1243 2p multi 1.00 1.00

Souvenir Sheet

Perf. 14

2609 A1244 8p Sheet of 2, #a-b 8.00 8.00

34th Antarctic Treaty Consultative Meeting, Buenos Aires.

Mariano Moreno (1778-1811), Politician — A1245

2011, May 21 *Perf. 13¾x13½*

2610 A1245 2p multi 1.00 1.00

World Blood Donor Day — A1246

Perf. 13¾x13½ Syncopated

2011, May 21

2611 A1246 5p multi 2.50 2.50

Year of Decent Labor, Health and Safety for Workers A1247

2011, June 4 *Perf. 13¾x13½*

2612 A1247 2p multi 1.00 1.00

Pres. Domingo Faustino Sarmiento (1811-88) A1248

2011, June 25 *Perf. 13½x13¾*

2613 A1248 2.50p multi 1.25 1.25

May Pyramid, Buenos Aires, Bicent. — A1249

2011, June 25 *Perf. 13½x14*

2614 A1249 2.50p multi 1.25 1.25

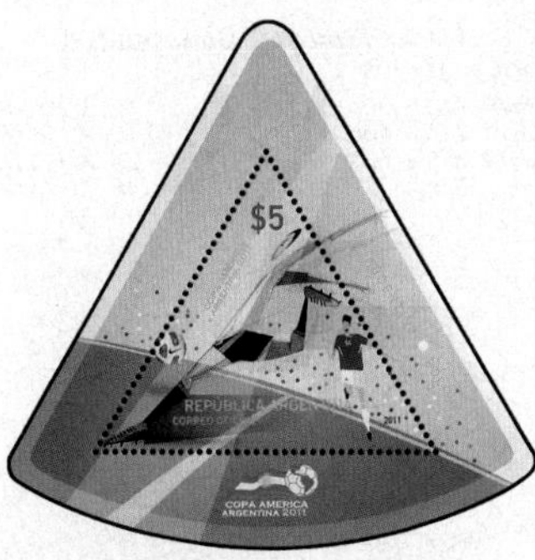

America Cup Soccer Tournament — A1250

No. 2615 — Players from Group A teams: a, Argentina and Bolivia. b, Colombia and Costa Rica.

No. 2616 — Players from Group B teams: a, Venezuela and Brazil. b, Paraguay and Ecuador.

No. 2617 — Players from Group C teams: a, Peru and Uruguay. b, Mexico and Chile.

2011, June 25 *Perf. 14*

2615 Wheel with 2 sheets 5.00 —
a.-b. A1250 5p Either sheet 2.50 2.50
2616 Wheel with 2 sheets 5.00 —
a.-b. A1250 5p Either sheet 2.50 2.50
2617 Wheel with 2 sheets 5.00 —
a.-b. A1250 5p Either sheet 2.50 2.50
Nos. 2615-2617 (3) 15.00

Nos. 2615a-2615b, 2616a-2616b and 2617a-2617b are attached to wheels with a metal grommet at the center of the wheels.

Launch of SAC-D/Aquarius Satellite — A1251

2011, July 23 Litho. *Perf. 13¾x13½*
2618 A1251 2.50p multi 1.25 1.25

Mailboxes — A1252

Designs: No. 2619, 2.50p, Corneta type mailbox, cancel. No. 2620, 2.50p, Pillar box, handwritten letter, vert.

Perf. 13¾x13½, 13½x13¾

2011, Aug. 20
2619-2620 A1252 Set of 2 2.40 2.40

Festivals A1253

Designs: No. 2621, 2.50p, National Beer Festival, Villa General Belgrano. No. 2622, 2.50p, National Horse Festival, San Cristóbal. No. 2623, 2.50p, Foreign Communities Fair, Comodoro Rivadavia. No. 2624, 2.50p, National Tea Festival, Campo Viera.

2011, Sept. 10 *Perf. 13½x13¾*
2621-2624 A1253 Set of 4 4.75 4.75

Orchids A1254

Designs: No. 2625, 2.50p, Zygopetalum maxillare. No. 2626, 2.50p, Sacoila lanceolata, vert.

Perf. 13¾x13½, 13½x13¾

2011, Sept. 24
2625-2626 A1254 Set of 2 2.40 2.40

Train on the Clouds — A1255

No. 2627: a, Train cars, bridge (yellow orange panel). b, Locomotive, bridge (blue panel). c, Train on curved bridge (orange panel). d, Train on curved bridge, diff. (red panel).

2011, Sept. 24 *Perf. 14*
2627 Sheet of 4 9.75 9.75
a.-d. A1255 5p Any single 2.40 2.40

Argentine Pediatric Society, Cent. — A1256

2011, Oct. 22 *Perf. 13¾x13½*
2628 A1256 2.50p multi 1.25 1.25

Miniature Sheet

Pig Breeds — A1257

No. 2629: a, Landrace. b, Hampshire. c, Pietrain. d, Duroc Jersey. e, Spotted Poland. f, Yorkshire.

2011, Oct. 29 **Litho.**
2629 A1257 2.50p Sheet of 6, #a-f, + 2 labels 7.25 7.25

Christmas A1258

Litho. With Glitter Affixed

2011, Oct. 29 *Perf. 13¾ Syncopated*
2630 A1258 2.50p multi 1.25 1.25

Souvenir Sheet

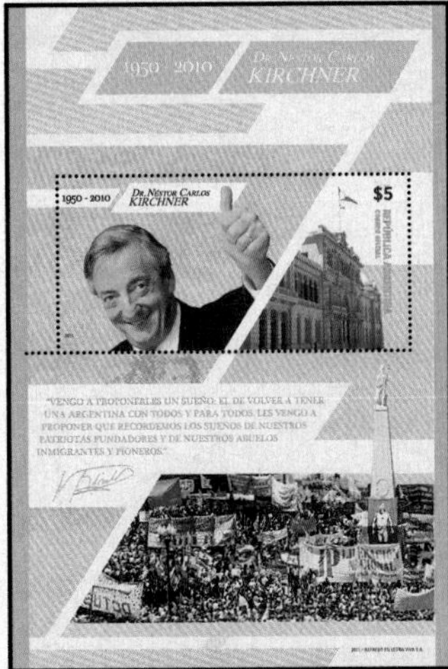

Pres. Néstor Carlos Kirchner (1950-2010), and Casa Rosada — A1259

2011, Nov. 26 Litho. *Perf. 14*
2631 A1259 5p multi 2.40 2.40

Sports Personalities Type of 2008

Souvenir Sheets

Designs: No. 2632, 10p, Horse and mallet of Adolfo Cambiaso, polo player, vert. No. 2633, 10p, Chessboard and Miguel Najdorf (1910-97), chess player, vert. (50x60mm). No. 2634, 10p, Sailboard of Carlos Espinola, sailboarder, vert. (50x60mm). No. 2635, 10p, Roller skates of Nora Vega, roller skater (60x40mm).

2011, Nov. 12
2632-2635 A1177 Set of 4 19.00 19.00

Rights of the Child — A1260

Winning art in children's stamp design contest by: No. 2636, 2.50p, Nicolás Agustín Bernachea (blue panels). No. 2637, 2.50p, Sofía Panagópulo (pink panels). No. 2638, 2.50p, Ezequiel Catalano Segesso (yellow green panels). No. 2639, 2.50p, Laura Florencia Martinessi (orange panels).

2011, Nov. 26 *Perf. 13½x13¾*
2636-2639 A1260 Set of 4 4.75 4.75

Souvenir Sheet

Creation of Argentine Flag and Pledge of Allegiance, Bicent. — A1261

2012, Mar. 3 Litho. *Perf. 14*
2640 A1261 5p multi 2.25 2.25

First Argentine Flight Landing at South Pole, 50th Anniv. — A1262

2012, Mar. 3 Litho. *Perf. 13¾x13½*
2641 A1262 2.50p multi 1.25 1.25

Monument to Gen. Manuel Belgrano, Buenos Aires, and Argentine Flag — A1263

2012, Mar. 31 *Perf. 14x13¾*
2642 A1263 2.50p multi 1.25 1.25

Argentine Claims of Sovereignty Over British South Atlantic Islands — A1264

Argentine flag and map of: No. 2643, 2.50p, Falkland Islands (Isla Gran Malvina and Isla Soledad). No. 2644, 2.50p, South Georgia (Isla San Pedro). No. 2645, 2.50p, South Sandwich Islands (Islas Traverse, Islas Candelaria, Isla Saunders, Isla Jorge, Isla Blanca and Grupo Tule del Sur), vert. (28x67mm).

Perf. 13¾x13½, 13¾x14 (#2645)

2012, Mar. 31
2643-2645 A1264 Set of 3 3.50 3.50

Presidential Staff and Argentine Flag — A1265

2012, Apr. 14 *Perf. 13½x13¾*
2646 A1265 2.50p multi 1.25 1.25

Presidential mandate of Cristina Fernández Kirchner for 2011-15.

Monument to Gen. José de San Martín, First Deed of Río Gallegos Town Council — A1266

2012, Apr. 14 ***Perf. 14x13¾***
2647 A1266 2.50p multi 1.25 1.25

Río Gallegos Town Council, cent.

Alernative Energies — A1267

Designs: 2.50p, Biogas, biomass and biocombustibles. 9.50p, Solar, wind and hydroelectric energy.

2012, Apr. 28 Litho. ***Perf. 14x13½***
2648-2649 A1267 Set of 2 5.50 5.50

Argentine Natural History Museum, Bicent. A1268

Museum emblem and: No. 2650, 2.50p, Skeleton of Dahlia the Elephant. No. 2651, 2.50p, Skull of Bonatitan reigi (dinosaur). No. 2652, 2.50p, Agrias narcissus butterflies, horiz. No. 2653, 2.50p, Display in Hall of Birds, horiz.

Perf. 13½x13¾, 13¾x13½
2012, Apr. 28
2650-2653 A1268 Set of 4 4.50 4.50

Intl. Year of Cooperatives — A1269

2012, June 16 ***Perf. 13¾x13½***
2654 A1269 2.50p multi 1.10 1.10

Passage of Sáenz Peña Universal Male Suffrage Law, Cent. — A1270

2012, June 16 ***Perf. 13½x13¾***
2655 A1270 2.50p multi 1.10 1.10

Paintings of Historical Events of 1812 — A1271

Painting of: No. 2656, 2.50p, Jujuy Exodus, by unknown artist. No. 2657, 2.50p, Battle of Tucuman, by Tomas del Villar.

2012, June 16 ***Perf. 13¾x13½***
2656-2657 A1271 Set of 2 2.25 2.25

Argentine School of Military Aviation, Cent. — A1272

2012, July 21 ***Perf. 14x13½***
2658 A1272 2.75p multi 1.25 1.25

Operation Southern Cross for Naval Assistance in Antarctica — A1273

2012, July 21 ***Perf. 13¾x13½***
2659 A1273 5p multi 2.25 2.25

Souvenir Sheet

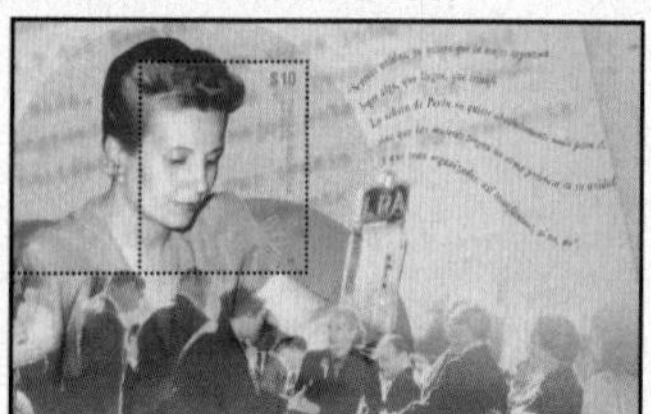

Eva Perón, (1919-52) — A1274

2012, Sept. 1 ***Perf. 14***
2660 A1274 10p multi 4.50 4.50

Alzheimer's Disease Awareness A1275

2012, Sept. 15 ***Perf. 13½x13¾***
2661 A1275 3p multi 1.40 1.40

Festivals A1276

Designs: No. 2662, 3p, National Artisans Festival, Colón. No. 2663, 3p, Maní National Festival, Hernando. No. 2664, 3p, National Orange Festival, Bella Vista. No. 2665, 3p, National Calf Festival and Branding Day, Ayacucho.

2012, Sept. 25
2662-2665 A1276 Set of 4 5.25 5.25

General San Martín Mounted Grenadiers Regiment, 200th Anniv. — A1277

2012, Oct. 13 ***Perf. 13¾x13½***
2666 A1277 3p multi 1.25 1.25

Christmas A1278

2012, Nov. 17 ***Perf. 13½x13¾***
2667 A1278 3p multi 1.25 1.25

Miniature Sheet

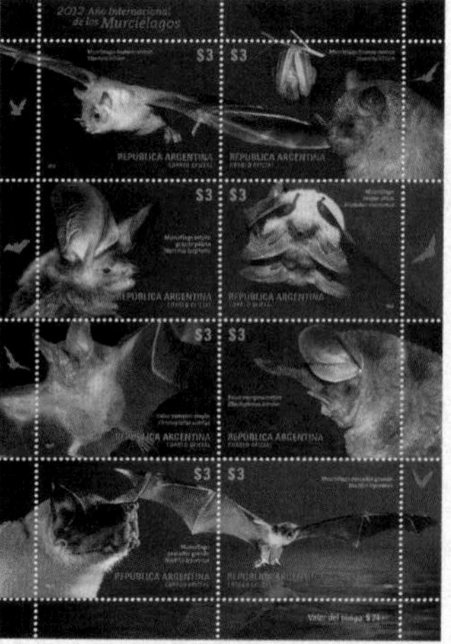

Bats — A1279

No. 2668: a, Sturnira lillium in flight. b, Sturnira lillium hanging and close-up of head. c, Histiotus laephotis. d, Histiotus montanus. e, Chrotopterus auritus in flight. f, Head of Chrotopterus auritus. g, Head of Noctilio leporinus. h, Noctilio leporinus in flight.

2012, Dec. 22 ***Perf. 13¾x13½***
2668 A1279 3p Sheet of 8, #a-h 9.75 9.75

Battle of Salta, 200th Anniv. — A1280

2013, Feb. 23 ***Perf. 14x13½***
2669 A1280 3.50p multi 1.40 1.40

Archaeological Artifacts Type of 2000

Designs: 30p, Ceremonial hatchet, Tehuelche culture. 40p, Basket with handle, Selk'nam culture. 50p, Basket with handle and lid, Wichi culture.

Perf. 13½x13¾ Syncopated
2013, Mar. 1

2670 A973 30p multi	12.00	12.00
2671 A973 40p multi	16.00	16.00
2672 A973 50p multi	20.00	20.00
Nos. 2670-2672 (3)	48.00	48.00

General Constituent Assembly of 1813, 200th Anniv. A1281

2013, Mar. 9 ***Perf. 13½x13¾***
2673 A1281 3.50p multi 1.40 1.40

Festivals A1282

Designs: No. 2674, 3.50p, National Folklore Festival, Cosquín. No. 2675, 3.50p, National Trout Festival, Junín de los Andes. No. 2676, 3.50p, National Lemon Festival, Tafí Viejo, vert. No. 2677, 3.50p, National Petroleum Festival, Comodoro Rivadavia, vert.

Perf. 13¾x13½, 13½x13¾
2013, Mar. 23
2674-2677 A1282 Set of 4 5.50 5.50

Landmarks Type of 2004

Designs: 3.50p, Cancha de Bochas, Ischigualasto National Park. 30p, Hill of Seven Colors, Jujuy.

Perf. 13¾x13½ Syncopated
2013, Mar.

2678 A1063a 3.50p multi	1.40	1.40
2679 A1063a 30p multi	12.00	12.00

Souvenir Sheet

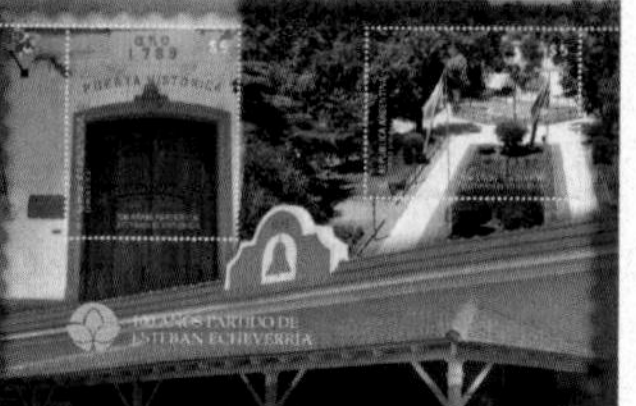

Partido de Esteban Echeverría Area of Buenos Aires, Cent. — A1283

No. 2680: a, Door on building built in 1789. b, Plaza and flags, horiz.

2013, Apr. 13 Litho. ***Perf. 14***
2680 A1283 Sheet of 2 4.00 4.00
a.-b. 5p Either single 2.00 2.00

National University of Córdoba, 400th Anniv. — A1284

2013, Apr. 27 ***Perf. 14x13½***
2681 A1284 3.50p multi 1.40 1.40

Election of Pope Francis A1285

No. 2682 — Arms of Pope Francis and: a, Pope Francis, flags of Vatican City, Italy and Argentina. b, Pope Francis in profile, flags of Vatican City and Argentina. c, Pope Francis waving, flags of Vatican City and Argentina. d, Pope Francis holding cross, flags of Vatican City and Argentina.

2013, May 2 ***Perf. 13¾x13½***

2682	Vert. strip of 4	12.50	12.50
a.-b.	A1285 3.50p Either single	1.40	1.40
c.	A1285 10p multi	4.00	4.00
d.	A1285 14p multi	5.50	5.50

See Italy No. 3179, Vatican City Nos. 1523-1526.

SEMI-POSTAL STAMPS

Samuel F. B. Morse — SP1

Globe — SP2

Landing of Columbus SP5

Map of Argentina SP6

Designs: 10c+5c, Alexander Graham Bell. 25c+15c, Rowland Hill.

Wmk. RA in Sun (90)

1944, Jan. 5 **Litho.** ***Perf. 13***

B1	SP1 3c +2c lt vio & sl bl	1.00	1.50
B2	SP2 5c +5c dl red & sl bl	.80	.50
B3	SP1 10c +5c org & slate bl	1.50	.50
B4	SP1 25c +15c red brn & sl bl	2.25	1.10
B5	SP5 1p +50c lt grn & sl bl	9.50	10.00
	Nos. B1-B5 (5)	15.05	13.60

The surtax was for the Postal Employees Benefit Association.

1944, Feb. 17 **Wmk. 90** ***Perf. 13***

B6	SP6 5c +10c ol yel & slate	1.10	.50
B7	SP6 5c +50c vio brn & slate	5.00	1.50
B8	SP6 5c +1p dl org & slate	13.50	7.00
B9	SP6 5c +20p dp bl & slate	30.00	30.00
	Nos. B6-B9 (4)	49.60	39.00

The surtax was for the victims of the San Juan earthquake.

Souvenir Sheets

National Anthem and Flag — SP7

1944, July 17 ***Imperf.***

B10	SP7 5c +1p vio brn & lt bl	9.00	5.00
B11	SP7 5c +50p bl blk & lt bl	425.00	275.00

Surtax for the needy in the provinces of La Rioja and Catamarca.

Catalogue values for unused stamps in this section, from this point to the end of the section, are for Never Hinged items.

Stamp Designing SP8

1950, Aug. 26 **Photo.** ***Perf. 13½***

B12	SP8 10c +10c violet	.35	.35
	Nos. B12,CB1-CB5 (6)	21.05	15.50

Argentine Intl. Philatelic Exhibition, 1950.

Poliomyelitis Victim — SP9

1956, Apr. 14 ***Perf. 13½x13***

B13	SP9 20c +30c slate	.50	.25

The surtax was for the poliomyelitis fund. Head in design is from Correggio's "Antiope," Louvre.

Stamp of 1858 and Mail Coach on Raft — SP10

Designs: 2.40p+1.20p, Album, magnifying glass and stamp of 1858. 4.40p+2.20p, Government seat of Confederation, Parana.

1958, Mar. 29 **Litho.** ***Perf. 13½***

B14	SP10 40c +20c brt grn & dl pur	.60	.60
B15	SP10 2.40p +1.20p ol gray & bl	.75	.75
B16	SP10 4.40p +2.20p lt bl & dp claret	1.00	1.00
	Nos. B14-B16,CB8-CB12 (8)	7.05	6.35

Surtax for Intl. Centennial Philatelic Exhibition, Paraná, Entre Rios, Apr. 19-27. Nos. B14-B16 exist imperf. Value, set of pairs, $200.

View of Flooded Land — SP11

1958, Oct. 4 **Photo.** ***Perf. 13½***

B17	SP11 40c +20c brown	.50	.25
	Nos. B17,CB13-CB14 (3)	1.80	1.30

The surtax was for flood victims in the Buenos Aires district. Exists imperf. Value, pair $37.50.

Child Receiving Blood — SP12

1958, Dec. 20 **Litho.** **Wmk. 90**

B18	SP12 1p +50c blk & rose red	.75	.25

The surtax went to the Anti-Leukemia Foundation. Exists imperf. Value, pair $25.

Runner SP13

Designs: 50c+20c, Basketball players, vert. 1p+50c, Boxers, vert.

1959, Sept. 5 ***Perf. 13½***

B19	SP13 20c +10c emer & blk	.25	.25
B20	SP13 50c +20c yel & blk	.25	.25
B21	SP13 1p +50c mar & blk	.25	.25
	Nos. B19-B21,CB15-CB16 (5)	1.75	1.50

3rd Pan American Games, Chicago, Aug. 27-Sept. 7, 1959.

Condor — SP14

Birds: 50c+20c, Fork-tailed flycatchers. 1p+50c, Magellanic woodpecker.

1960, Feb. 6

B22	SP14 20c +10c dk bl	.40	.25
B23	SP14 50c +20c dp vio bl	.40	.25
B24	SP14 1p +50c brn & buff	.40	.25
	Nos. B22-B24,CB17-CB18 (5)	2.15	1.35

The surtax was for child welfare work. See Nos. B30, CB29.

Souvenir Sheet

Uprooted Oak Emblem — SP15

1960, Apr. 7 **Wmk. 90** ***Imperf.***

B25	SP15 Sheet of 2	1.75	1.75
a.	1p + 50c bister & carmine	.75	.75
b.	4.20p + 2.10p apple grn & dp claret	.75	.75

WRY, July 1, 1959-June 30, 1960. The surtax was for aid to refugees.

Jacaranda — SP16

Flowers: 1p+1p, Passionflower. 3p+3p, Orchid. 5p+5p, Tabebuia.

1960, Dec. 3 **Photo.** ***Perf. 13½***

B26	SP16 50c +50c deep blue	.25	.25
B27	SP16 1p +1p bluish grn	.25	.25
B28	SP16 3p +3p henna brn	.55	.35
B29	SP16 5p +5p dark brn	.95	.60
	Nos. B26-B29 (4)	2.00	1.45

"TEMEX 61" (Intl. Thematic Exposition). For overprints see Nos. B31-B34.

Type of 1960

Bird: 4.20p+2.10p, Blue-eyed shag.

1961, Feb. 25 **Wmk. 90** ***Perf. 13½***

B30	SP14 4.20p +2.10p chestnut brn	.65	.35

Surtax for child welfare work. See No. CB29.

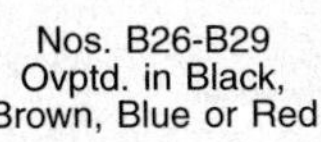

Nos. B26-B29 Ovptd. in Black, Brown, Blue or Red

1961, Apr. 15

B31	SP16 50c +50c deep blue	.35	.25
B32	SP16 1p +1p bluish grn (Brn)	.35	.25
B33	SP16 3p +3p henna brn (Bl)	.65	.25
B34	SP16 5p +5p dk brn (R)	.95	.40
	Nos. B31-B34 (4)	2.30	1.15

Day of the Americas, Apr. 14.

Cathedral, Cordoba SP17

Stamp of 1862 SP18

Flight into Egypt, by Ana Maria Moncalvo SP19

Design: 10p+10p, Cathedral, Buenos Aires.

Perf. 13½

1961, Oct. 21 **Wmk. 90** **Photo.**

B35	SP17 2p +2p rose claret	.30	.25
B36	SP18 3p +3p green	.40	.25
B37	SP17 10p +10p brt blue	.95	.60
a.	Souvenir sheet of 3	3.00	2.00
	Nos. B35-B37 (3)	1.65	1.10

1962 International Stamp Exhibition.
No. B37a contains three imperf. stamps similar to Nos. B35-B37 in dark blue.

1961, Dec. 16 **Litho.**

B38	SP19 2p +1p lilac & blk brn	.25	.25
B39	SP19 10p +5p light & deep claret	.50	.25

The surtax was for child welfare.

Mimus Saturninus Modulator SP20

Design: 12p+6p, Zonotrichia capensis hypoleuca.

1962, Dec. 29 *Perf. 13½*
B40 SP20 4p +2p bis, brn & bl grn 1.25 .65
B41 SP20 12p +6p gray, yel, grn & brn 2.00 1.25

The surtax was for child welfare. See Nos. B44, B47, B48-B50, CB32, CB35-CB36.

Soccer — SP21

Perf. 13½

1963, May 18
B42 SP21 4p +2p multi .25 .25
B43 SP21 12p +6p Horseman-ship .50 .35
a. Dark carmine (jacket) omitted *15.00*
Nos. B42-B43,CB31 (3) 1.35 1.10

4th Pan American Games, Sao Paulo.

Bird Type of 1962

1963, Dec. 21 **Litho.**
B44 SP20 4p +2p Pyrocephalus rubineus rubineus .60 .30

The surtax was for child welfare. See No. CB32.

Fencers — SP22

4p+2p, National Stadium, Tokyo, horiz.

1964, July 18 **Wmk. 90** *Perf. 13½*
B45 SP22 4p +2p red, ocher & brn .25 .25
B46 SP22 12p +6p bl grn & blk .50 .30
Nos. B45-B46,CB33 (3) 1.75 1.55

18th Olympic Games, Tokyo, Oct. 10-25, 1964. See No. CB33.

Bird Type of 1962

1964, Dec. 23 **Litho.**
B47 SP20 4p +2p Cardinal paroaria coronata 1.10 .75

The surtax was for child welfare. See No. CB35.

SP22a

Designs: 8p+4p, Belonopterus cayennensis lampronotus. 10p+5p, Amblyramphus holosericeus, horiz. 20p+10p, Chloroceryle amazona.

1966-67 *Perf. 13½*
B48 SP22a 8p +4p blk, ol, brt grn & red .80 .35
B49 SP22a 10p +5p blk, bl, org & grn .80 .55
B50 SP22a 20p +10p blk, yel, bl & pink .40 .35
Nos. B48-B50,CB36,CB38-CB39 (6) 5.00 3.50

The surtax was for child welfare.
Issue dates: 8p+4p, Mar. 26, 1966. 10p+5p, Jan. 14, 1967. 20p+10p, Dec. 23, 1967.

Grandmother's Birthday, by Patricia Lynch; Lions Emblem — SP23

Perf. 12½x13½

1968, Dec. 14 **Litho.** **Wmk. 90**
B51 SP23 40p + 20p multi .45 .40

1st Lions Intl. Benevolent Phil. Exhib. Surtax for the Children's Hospital Benevolent Fund.

White-faced Tree Duck — SP24

1969, Sept. 20 **Wmk. 365** *Perf. 13½*
B52 SP24 20p + 10p multi .50 .35

Surtax for child welfare. See No. CB40.

Slender-tailed Woodstar (Hummingbird) SP25

1970, May 9 **Wmk. 365** *Perf. 13½*
B53 SP25 20c + 10c multi .45 .40

The surtax was for child welfare. See Nos. CB41, B56-B59, B62-B63.

Dolphinfish — SP26

1971, Feb. 20 **Unwmk.** *Perf. 12½*
Size: 75x15mm
B54 SP26 20c + 10c multi .50 .45

Surtax for child welfare. See No. CB42.

Children with Stamps, by Mariette Lydis — SP27

1971, Dec. 18 **Litho.** *Perf. 13½*
B55 SP27 1p + 50p multi .50 .30

2nd Lions Intl. Solidarity Stamp Exhib.

Bird Type of 1970

Birds: 25c+10c, Saffron finch. 65c+30c, Rufous-bellied thrush, horiz.

1972, May 6 **Unwmk.** *Perf. 13½*
B56 SP25 25c + 10c multi .30 .25
B57 SP25 65c + 30c multi .45 .30

Surtax was for child welfare.

Bird Type of 1970

Birds: 50c+25c, Southern screamer (chaja). 90c+45c, Saffron-cowled blackbird, horiz.

1973, Apr. 28
B58 SP25 50c + 25c multi .55 .30
B59 SP25 90c + 45c multi .75 .55

Surtax was for child welfare.

Painting Type of Regular Issue

Designs: 15c+15c, Still Life, by Alfredo Guttero, horiz. 90c+90c, Nude, by Miguel C. Victorica, horiz.

1973, Aug. 28 **Litho.** *Perf. 13½*
B60 A472 15c + 15c multi .35 .25
B61 A472 90c + 90c multi 1.10 .75

Bird Type of 1970

Birds: 70c+30c, Blue seed-eater. 1.20p+60c, Hooded siskin.

1974, May 11 **Litho.** *Perf. 13½*
B62 SP25 70c + 30c multi .60 .35
B63 SP25 1.20p + 60c multi 1.00 .50

Surtax was for child welfare.

Painting Type of 1974

Design: 70c+30c, The Lama, by Juan Batlle Planas.

1974, May 11 **Litho.** *Perf. 13½*
B64 A477 70c + 30c multi .35 .25

PRENFIL-74 UPU, Intl. Exhib. of Phil. Periodicals, Buenos Aires, Oct. 1-12.

Plushcrested Jay — SP28

Designs: 13p+6.50p, Golden-collared macaw. 20p+10p, Begonia. 40p+20p, Teasel.

1976, June 12 **Litho.** *Perf. 13½*
B65 SP28 7p + 3.50p multi .60 .30
B66 SP28 13p + 6.50p multi .70 .35
B67 SP28 20p + 10p multi .80 .40
B68 SP28 40p + 20p multi 1.10 .60
Nos. B65-B68 (4) 3.20 1.65

Argentine philately.

Telegraph, Communications Satellite — SP29

Designs: 20p+10p, Old and new mail trucks. 60p+30p, Old, new packet boats. 70p+35p, Biplane and jet.

1977, July 16 **Litho.** *Perf. 13½*
B69 SP29 10p + 5p multi .30 .25
B70 SP29 20p + 10p multi .60 .60
B71 SP29 60p + 30p multi 1.25 .85
B72 SP29 70p + 35p multi 1.40 .90
Nos. B69-B72 (4) 3.55 2.60

Surtax was for Argentine philately.
No. B70 exists with wmk. 365.

Church of St. Francis Type, 1977

Inscribed "EXPOSICION ARGENTINA '77"

1977, Aug. 27
B73 A515 160p + 80p multi 2.50 2.00

Surtax was for Argentina '77 Philatelic Exhibition. Issued in sheets of 4. Value $12

No. B73 Overprinted with Soccer Cup Emblem

1978, Feb. 4 **Litho.** *Perf. 13½*
B74 A515 160p + 80p multi 4.50 4.25
a. Souvenir sheet of 4 22.50 20.00

11th World Cup Soccer Championship, Argentina, June 1-25.

Spinus Magellanicus SP30

Birds: No. B76, Variable seedeater. No. B77, Yellow thrush. No. B78, Pyrocephalus rubineus. No. B79, Great kiskadee.

1978, Aug. 5 **Litho.** *Perf. 13½*
B75 SP30 50p + 50p multi 1.00 .80
B76 SP30 100p + 100p multi 1.25 1.00
B77 SP30 150p + 150p multi 1.75 1.50
B78 SP30 200p + 200p multi 2.25 1.75
B79 SP30 500p + 500p multi 8.50 6.00
Nos. B75-B79 (5) 14.75 11.05

ARGENTINA '78, Inter-American Philatelic Exhibition, Buenos Aires, Oct. 27-Nov. 5. Nos. B75-B79 issued in sheets of 4 with marginal inscriptions commemorating Exhibition and 1978 Soccer Championship. Value, set $62.50.

Caravel "Magdalena," 16th Century — SP31

Sailing Ships: 500+500p, 3 master "Rio de la Plata," 17th cent. 600+600p, Corvette "Descubierta," 18th cent. 1500+1500p, Naval Academy yacht "A.R.A. Fortuna," 1979.

1979, Sept. 8 **Litho.** *Perf. 13½*
B80 SP31 400p +400p multi 4.00 2.25
B81 SP31 500p +500p multi 4.75 2.50
B82 SP31 600p +600p multi 6.25 3.25
B83 SP31 1500p +1500p multi 15.00 8.00
Nos. B80-B83 (4) 30.00 16.00

Buenos Aires '80, Intl. Philatelic Exhibition, 10/24-11/2/80. Issued in sheets of 4. Value, set $125.

Purmamarca Church SP32

Churches: 200p + 100p, Molinos. 300p + 150p, Animana. 400p + 200p, San Jose de Lules.

1979, Nov. 3 Litho. *Perf. 13½*

B84 SP32 100p + 50p multi	.35	.25
B85 SP32 200p + 100p multi	.55	.25
B86 SP32 300p + 150p multi	.80	.30
B87 SP32 400p + 200p multi	1.10	.50
Nos. B84-B87 (4)	2.80	1.30

Buenos Aires No. 3, Exhibition and Society Emblems — SP33

Argentine Stamps: 750p+750p, type A580. 1000p+1000p, No. 91. 2000p+2000p, type A588.

1979, Dec. 15 Litho. *Perf. 13½*

B88 SP33 250p + 250p	1.50	1.25
B89 SP33 750p + 750p	2.75	2.25
B90 SP33 1000p + 1000p	4.75	4.00
B91 SP33 2000p + 2000p	6.75	6.00
Nos. B88-B91 (4)	15.75	13.50

PRENFIL '80, Intl. Philatelic Literature and Publications Exhib., Buenos Aires, Nov. 7-16, 1980.

Minuet, by Carlos E. Pellegrini SP34

Paintings: 700p+350p, Media Cana, by Carlos Morel. 800p+400p, Cielito, by Pellegrini. 1000p+500p, El Gato, by Juan Leon Palliere.

1981, July 11 Litho. *Perf. 13½*

B92 SP34 500p + 250p multi	.85	.45
B93 SP34 700p + 350p multi	1.10	.80
B94 SP34 800p + 400p multi	1.25	1.00
B95 SP34 1000p + 500p multi	1.60	1.40
Nos. B92-B95 (4)	4.80	3.65

Espamer '81 Intl. Stamp Exhib. (Americas, Spain, Portugal), Buenos Aires, Nov. 13-22.

Canal, by Beatrix Bongliani (b. 1933) — SP35

Tapestries: 1000p+500p, Shadows, by Silvia Sieburger, vert. 2000p+1000p, Interpretation of a Rectangle, by Silke R. de Haupt, vert. 4000p+2000p, Tilcara, by Tana Sachs.

1982, July 31 Litho. *Perf. 13½*

B96 SP35 1000p + 500p multi	.40	.40
B97 SP35 2000p + 1000p multi	.50	.50
B98 SP35 3000p + 1500p multi	.70	.70
B99 SP35 4000p + 2000p multi	1.10	1.10
Nos. B96-B99 (4)	2.70	2.70

Boy Playing Marbles SP36

1983, July 2 Litho. *Perf. 13½*

B100 SP36 20c + 10c shown	.35	.35
B101 SP36 30c + 15c Jumping rope	.45	.40
B102 SP36 50c + 25c Hopscotch	.90	.75
B103 SP36 1p + 50c Flying kites	1.10	.90
B104 SP36 2p + 1p Spinning top	1.60	1.25
Nos. B100-B104 (5)	4.40	3.65

Surtax was for natl. philatelic associations. See Nos. B106-B110.

Compass, 15th Cent. — SP37

ARGENTINA '85 Intl. Stamp Show: b, Arms of Spain, Argentina. c, Columbus' arms. d-f, Columbus' arrival at San Salvador Island. Nos. B105d-B105f in continuous design; ships shown on singles range in size, left to right, from small to large. Surtax was for exhibition.

1984, Apr. 28 Litho. *Perf. 13½*

B105 Block of 6	4.50	4.50
a.-f. SP37 5p + 2.50p, any single	.60	.40

Children's Game Type of 1983

1984, July 7 Litho. *Perf. 13½*

B106 SP36 2p + 1p Blind Man's Buff	.35	.25
B107 SP36 3p + 1.50p The Loop	.50	.40
B108 SP36 4p + 2p Leap Frog	.55	.45
B109 SP36 5p + 2.50p Rolling the loop	.75	.60
B110 SP36 6p + 3p Ball Mold	.90	.75
Nos. B106-B110 (5)	3.05	2.45

Butterflies — SP38

1985, Nov. 9 Litho. *Perf. 13½*

B111 SP38 5c + 2c Rothschildia jacobaeae	1.10	.75
B112 SP38 10c + 5c Heliconius erato phyllis	1.10	.85
B113 SP38 20c + 10c Precis evarete hilaris	1.60	.95
B114 SP38 25c + 13c Cyanopepla pretiosa	2.25	1.75
B115 SP38 40c + 20c Papilio androgeus	3.25	2.50
Nos. B111-B115 (5)	9.30	6.80

Children's Drawings — SP39

1986, Aug. 30 Litho.

B116 SP39 5c + 2c N. Pastor	.30	.30
B117 SP39 10c + 5c T. Valleistein	.45	.45
B118 SP39 20c + 10c J.M. Flores	.65	.65
B119 SP39 25c + 13c M.E. Pezzuto	.85	.85
B120 SP39 40c + 20c E. Diehl	1.25	1.25
Nos. B116-B120 (5)	3.50	3.50

Surtax for natl. philatelic associations.

Miniature Sheets

Fresh-water Fish — SP40

No. B121: a, Metynnis maculatus. b, Cynolebias nigripinnis. c, Leporinus solarii. d, Aphyocharax rathbuni. e, Corydoras aeneus. f, Thoracocharax securis. g, Cynolebias melanotaenia. h, Cichlasoma facetum.

No. B122: a, Tetragonopterus argenteus. b, Hemigrammus caudovittatus. c, Astyanax bimaculatus. d, Gymnocorymbus ternetzi. e, Hoplias malabaricus. f, Aphyocharax rubripinnis. g, Apistogramma agassizi. h, Pyrrhulina rachoviana.

1987, June 27

B121 Sheet of 8	3.00	3.00
a.-h. SP40 10c +5c, any single	.35	.25
B122 Sheet of 8	4.50	4.50
a.-h. SP40 20c +10c, any single	.55	.40

PRENFIL '88, Intl. Philatelic Literature and Media Exhibition, Buenos Aires, Nov. 25-Dec. 2 — SP41

Locomotives and railroad car: No. B123, Yatay locomotive, 1888. No. B124, FCCA electric passenger car, 1914. No. B125, B-15 locomotive, 1942. No. B126, GT-22 No. 200 locomotive, 1988.

1988, June 4 Litho. *Perf. 13½*

B123 SP41 1a +50c multi	.90	.65
B124 SP41 1a +50c multi	.90	.65
B125 SP41 1a +50c multi	.90	.65
B126 SP41 1a +50c multi	.90	.65
Nos. B123-B126 (4)	3.60	2.60

Nos. B123-B125 each issued in sheets of 4. Value, set $16.

Horses SP42

Paintings: No. B127, *The Waiting,* by Gustavo Solari. No. B128, *Mare and Foal,* by E. Castro. No. B129, *Saint Isidor,* by Castro. No. B130, *At Lagoon's Edge,* by F. Romero Carranza. No. B131, *Under the Tail,* by Castro.

1988, Oct. 29 Litho. *Perf. 13½*

B127 SP42 2a +1a multi	1.50	1.50
B128 SP42 2a +1a multi	1.50	1.50
B129 SP42 2a +1a multi	1.50	1.50
B130 SP42 2a +1a multi	1.50	1.50
B131 SP42 2a +1a multi	1.50	1.50
Nos. B127-B131 (5)	7.50	7.50

PRENFIL '88 — SP43

Covers of philatelic magazines: No. B132, *Cronaca Filatelica,* Italy. No. B133, *CO-FI,* Brazil. No. B134, *References de la Poste,* France. No. B135, *Postas Argentinas.*

1988, Nov. 26 Litho. *Perf. 13½*

B132 SP43 1a +1a multi	.80	.55
B133 SP43 1a +1a multi	.80	.55
B134 SP43 1a +1a multi	.80	.55
B135 SP43 2a +2a multi	.80	.55
Nos. B132-B135 (4)	3.20	2.20

Nos. B132-B135 printed in sheets of 4. Value, set $14.

Souvenir Sheet

ARBRAPEX '88 — SP44

Designs: No. B136a, *Candel Delivery at San Ignacio,* by Leonie Matthis, Cornelio Saavedra Museum, Buenos Aires. No. B136b, *Immaculate Conception,* a statue in the Isaac Fernandez Blanco Museum, Buenos Aires.

1988, Nov. 26 *Perf. 12*

B136 SP44 Sheet of 2	3.00	3.00
a. 2a +2a multi	1.00	.75
b. 3a +3a multi	1.75	1.25

Fish SP45

Designs: No. B137, Diplomystes viedmensis. No. B138, Haplochiton taeniatus. No. B139, Percichthys trucha. No. B140, Galaxias platei. No. B141, Salmo fario.

1989, June 24 Litho. *Perf. 13½*

B137 SP45 10a +5a multi	.60	.50
B138 SP45 10a +5a multi	.60	.50
B139 SP45 10a +5a multi	.60	.50
B140 SP45 10a +5a multi	.60	.50
B141 SP45 10a +5a multi	.60	.50
Nos. B137-B141 (5)	3.00	2.50

Nos. B137-B141 printed in sheets of 4. Value, set $15.

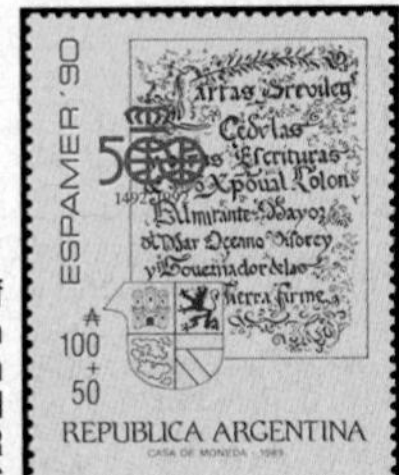

Discovery of America 500th Anniv. (in 1992) and ESPAMER '90 — SP46

Documents and chronicles: No. B142, Columbus's coat of arms, *Book of Privileges* title page. No. B143, Illustration from *New Chronicle and Good Government,* by Guaman Poma de Ayala. No. B144, Illustration from *Discovery and Conquest of Peru,* by Pedro de Cieza de Leon. No. B145, Illustration from *Travel to the River Plate,* by Ulrico Schmidl.

1989, Sept. 16 Litho. *Perf. 13½*
Yellow, Rose Violet & Black

B142 SP46 100a +50a 1.00 .85
B143 SP46 150a +50a 1.00 .85
B144 SP46 200a +100a 1.00 .85
B145 SP46 250a +100a 1.00 .85
Nos. B142-B145 (4) 4.00 3.40

Nos. B142-B145 printed in sheets of 4. Value, set $17.

Insects SP47

Designs: No. B146, *Podisus nigrispinus.* No. B147, *Adalia bipunctata.* No. B148, *Nabis punctipennis.* No. B149, *Hippodamia convergens.* No. B150, *Calleida suturalis.*

1990, June 30 Litho. *Perf. 13½*

B146 SP47 1000a +500a multi 1.10 .95
B147 SP47 1000a +500a multi 1.10 .95
B148 SP47 1000a +500a multi 1.10 .95
B149 SP47 1000a +500a multi 1.10 .95
B150 SP47 1000a +500a multi 1.10 .95
Nos. B146-B150 (5) 5.50 4.75

Nos. B146-B150 printed in sheets of 4. Value, set $24.

Souvenir Sheet

First Natl. Exposition of Aerophilately — SP48

a, Lieut. Marcos A. Zar, Macchi seaplane. b, Capt. Antonio Parodi, Ansaldo SVA biplane.

1990, July 14 Litho. *Perf. 12*

B151 SP48 Sheet of 2 8.50 6.50
a. 2000a +2000a multi 3.50 2.75
b. 3000a +3000a multi 3.50 2.75

Souvenir Sheet

1992 Summer Olympics, Barcelona — SP49

Designs: a, Shot put. b, High jump. c, Hurdles. d, Pole vault.

1990, Dec. 15 Litho. *Perf. 13½*

B152 Sheet of 4 11.00 11.00
a.-d. SP49 2000a +2000a multi 2.50 2.50

Espamer '91 Philatelic Exhibition.
See No. B155.

Souvenir Sheet

Discovery of America, 500th Anniv. (in 1992) — SP50

Voyage of Alesandro Malaspina, 1789-1794: a, Sailing ship. b, Malaspina. c, Indian, hut. d, Indian, horse, artist drawing.

1990, Oct. 13 Litho. *Perf. 13½*

B153 Sheet of 4 8.00 8.00
a.-d. SP50 2000a +1000a, any single 1.60 1.60

Espamer '91, Buenos Aires.

Souvenir Sheet

Race Cars and Drivers — SP51

Designs: a, Juan Manuel Fangio. b, Juan Manuel Bordeu. c, Carlos Alberto Reutemann. d, Oscar and Juan Galvez.

1991 Litho. *Perf. 13½*

B154 SP51 Sheet of 4 6.50 6.50
a.-d. 2500a +2500a, any single 1.40 1.25

Espamer '91.

1992 Summer Olympics Type of 1990
Souvenir Sheet

Women's gymnastics routines: a, Floor exercise. b, Uneven parallel bars. c, Balance beam. d, Rhythmic gymnastics.

1991, June 29 Litho. *Perf. 13½*

B155 Sheet of 4 6.50 6.50
a.-d. SP49 2500a +2500a, any single 1.40 1.25

Espamer '91.

Iberoprenfil '92 — SP52

Designs: No. B156, Castor missile. No. B157, Satellite LUSAT 1.

1991, Dec. 28 Litho. *Perf. 13½*

B156 SP52 4000a +4000a multi 3.00 3.00
B157 SP52 4000a +4000a multi 3.00 3.00

Dinosaurs SP53

No. B158, Carnotaurus. No. B159, Amargasaurus.

1992, May 2 Litho. *Perf. 13½*

B158 SP53 38c +38c multi 2.00 2.00
B159 SP53 38c +38c multi 2.00 2.00
a. Pair, #B158-B159 6.00 6.00

Iberoprenfil '92, Buenos Aires — SP54

Paintings by Raul Soldi (b. 1905): No. B160, The Fiesta. No. B161, Church of St. Anne of Glew.

1992, Sept. 5 Litho. *Perf. 13½*

B160 SP54 76c +76c multi 3.75 3.75
B161 SP54 76c +76c multi 3.75 3.75

Parafil '92 — SP55

1992, Nov. 21 Litho. *Perf. 13½*

B162 SP55 76c +76c multi 3.75 3.75

2nd Argentine-Paraguayan Philatelic Exhibition, Buenos Aires.

Souvenir Sheet

Birds — SP56

a, Egretta thula. b, Amblyramphus holosericeus. c, Paroaria coronata. d, Chloroceryle amazona.

1993, July 17 Litho. *Perf. 13½*

B163 SP56 38c +38c Sheet of 4 8.00 8.00

Souvenir Sheet

Latin American Air Post Philatelic Exhibition — SP57

Designs: a, 25c+25c, Antoine de Saint-Exupery (1940-44), pilot, author. b, 75c+75c, "The Little Prince," vert.

1995, June 3 Litho. *Perf. 12*

B164 SP57 Sheet of 2, #a.-b. 7.50 7.50

For overprint see No. B180.

Souvenir Sheet

Exploration of Antarctica — SP58

75c+25c, Transport ship ARA Bahia Aguirre. 1.25p+75c, Argentine Air Force Hercules C-130.

1995, July 8

B165 SP58 Sheet of 2, #a.-b. 9.00 9.00

Aerofila '96 SP59

Historic airplanes, pilots: No. B166, "Plus ultra," Ramón Franco Bahamonde (1896-1938). No. B167, 14 Bis, Alberto Santos-Dumont (1873-1932). No. B168, Spirit of St. Louis, Charles A. Lindbergh (1902-1974). No. B169, Buenos Aires, Eduardo A. Olivero (1896-1966).

1996, July 13 Litho. *Perf. 13½*

B166 SP59 25c +25c multi 1.50 1.50
B167 SP59 25c +25c multi 1.50 1.50
B168 SP59 50c +50c multi 3.00 3.00
B169 SP59 50c +50c multi 3.00 3.00
Nos. B166-B169 (4) 9.00 9.00

Ceramic Murals from Buenos Aires Subway SP60

1996, Sept. 21 Litho. *Perf. 13½*

B170 SP60 1p +50c Dragon 4.00 4.00
B171 SP60 1.50p +1p Bird 7.00 7.00

MEVIFIL '97, 1st Intl. Exhibition of Audio-Visual and Philatelic Information Media — SP61

Designs: No. B172, France Type A1. No. B173, Spain Type A3. No. B174, Argentina Type A4. No. B175, Buenos Aires Type A1.

1997, May 10 Litho. *Perf. 13½*

B172 SP61 50c +50c multi 2.25 2.25
B173 SP61 50c +50c multi 2.25 2.25
B174 SP61 50c +50c multi 2.25 2.25
B175 SP61 50c +50c multi 2.25 2.25
a. Block of 4, #B172-B175 9.50 9.50

Issued in sheets of 16 stamps + 4 labels.

Trains — SP62

Designs: No. B176, Las Nubes (Train to the Clouds), Salta. No. B177, Historical train, Buenos Aires. No. B178, Old Patagonian Express, Rio Negro-Chubut. No. B179, Southern Fueguino Railway, Tierra Del Fuego.

1997, Sept. 6 Litho. *Perf. 13*

B176 SP62 50c +50c multi 3.00 3.00
B177 SP62 50c +50c multi 3.00 3.00
B178 SP62 50c +50c multi 3.00 3.00
B179 SP62 50c +50c multi 3.00 3.00
Nos. B176-B179 (4) 12.00 12.00

No. B164 Overprinted in Red Violet

1997, Sept. 27 Litho. *Perf. 12*
B180 SP57 Sheet of 2 7.50 7.50

Cartography — SP63

Maps of the Buenos Aires area from: 25c+25c, 1546. No. B182, 17th century. No. B183, 1910. 75c+75c, 1999.

Perf. 13¾x13½
1999, Nov. 20 Litho.

B181 SP63 25c + 25c multi 1.00 1.00
B182 SP63 50c + 50c multi 2.00 2.00
B183 SP63 50c + 50c multi 2.00 2.00
B184 SP63 75c + 75c multi 3.00 3.00
a. Block of 4, #B181-B184 13.00 13.00

Methods of Transportation — SP64

No. B185: a, Bicycle. b, Graf Zeppelin. c, Train. d, Trolley.

2000, Oct. 21 Litho. *Perf. 14x13½*
B185 Block of 4 10.00 10.00
a. SP64 25c +25c multi 1.00 1.00
b.-c. SP64 50c +50c Any single 2.00 2.00
d. SP64 75c +75c multi 3.00 3.00

Cetaceans — SP65

No. B186: a, Burmeister's porpoise (Mariposa espinosa). b, River Plate dolphin. c, Minke whale. d, Humpback whale (Yubarta).

2001, Sept. 15 Litho. *Perf. 14x13½*
B186 Block of 4 11.00 11.00
a. SP65 25c +25c multi 1.00 1.00
b.-c. SP65 50c +50c Any single 2.00 2.00
d. SP65 75c +75c multi 3.00 3.00

Reptiles — SP66

No. B187: a, Boa constrictor occidentalis. b, Caiman yacare. c, Tupinambis merianae. d, Chelonoidis carbonaria.

2002, Aug. 24 Litho. *Perf. 14x13½*
B187 Block of 4 6.00 6.00
a. SP66 25c +25c multi .75 .75
b.-c. SP66 50c +50c Either single 1.25 1.25
d. SP66 75c +75c multi 2.00 2.00

Bicycles — SP67

No. B188: a, Velocipede, 1855, Cycling Club champions, 1902. b, Velocipede, 1867, postman with delivery tricycle. c, Coventry Eagle touring bicycle, 1949, cyclists in park. d, Racing bicycle, 1960s, Palermo Velodrome, 1902.

2003, Aug. 9 Litho. *Perf. 14x13¾*
B188 Block of 4 5.50 5.50
a. SP67 25c+25c multi .50 .50
b.-c. SP67 50c+50c Either single 1.00 1.00
d. SP67 75c+75c multi 1.50 1.50

Ships — SP68

No. B189: a, A. R. A. Villarino. b, A. R. A. Pampa. c, A. R. A. Bahia Thetis. d, A. R. A. Cabo de Hornos.

2004, Aug. 21 Litho. *Perf. 14x13½*
B189 Block of 4 4.25 4.25
a. SP68 25c +25c multi .45 .45
b.-c. SP68 50c +50c either single .80 .80
d. SP68 75c +75c multi 1.25 1.25

Merchant Ships — SP69

No. B190: a, Río de la Plata. b, Libertad. c, Campo Durán. d, Isla Soledad.

2005, Sept. 24 Litho. *Perf. 14x13½*
B190 Block of 4 3.75 3.75
a. SP69 25c +25c multi .40 .40
b.-c. SP69 50c +50c either single .75 .75
d. SP69 75c +75c multi 1.10 1.10

River Boats — SP70

No. B191: a, Ciudad de Buenos Aires. b, Lambaré. c, Madrid. d, Rawson.

2006, Aug. 19 Litho. *Perf. 14x13½*
B191 Block of 4 3.50 3.50
a. SP70 25c +25c multi .40 .40
b.-c. SP70 50c +50c either single .75 .75
d. SP70 75c +75c multi 1.10 1.10

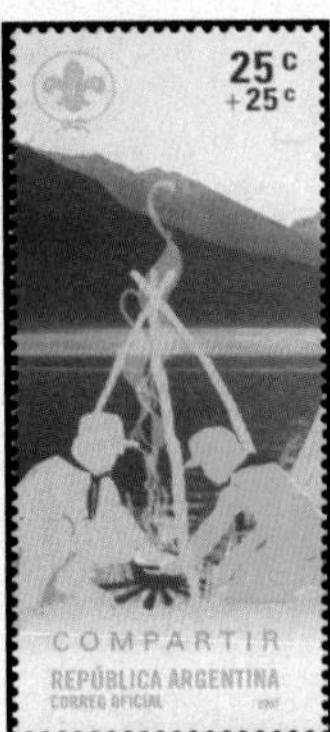

Scouting, Cent. — SP71

No. B192: a, Scouts at campfire. b, Scout saluting near tent. c, Scout saluting, Scout with patrol flag. d, Scouts pulling rope.

2007, July 28 Litho. *Perf. 13½x14*
B192 Horiz. strip of 4 4.00 4.00
a. SP71 25c +25c multi .35 .35
b. SP71 50c +50c multi .70 .70
c. SP71 75c +75c multi 1.00 1.00
d. SP71 1p +1p multi 1.25 1.25

Shells — SP72

Designs: 25c+25c, Calliostoma militaris. 50c+50c, Epitonium fabrizioi. 75c+75c, Odontocymbiola magellanica. 1p+1p, Trophon geversianus.

Perf. 13½x13¾
2008, Aug. 23 Litho.
B193-B196 SP72 Set of 4 4.00 4.00

Astronomical Observatories — SP73

Designs: No. B197, 50c+50c, Radio telescope, Argentine Institute of Radioastronomy. No. B198, 50c+50c, Telescope, La Plata Astronomical Observatory. No. B199, 1p+1p, El Lioncito Astronomical Complex. No. B200, 1p+1p, Telescope, Félix Aguilar Astronomical Observatory.

2009, Aug. 22 Litho. *Perf. 14x13½*
B197-B200 SP73 Set of 4 3.25 3.25

Girl Guides and Girl Scouts, Cent. — SP74

Designs: No. B201, 75c+75c, Girl Scout salute. No. B202, 75c+75c, Hands of five Girl Scouts joined. No. B203, 1p+1p, Hands of Girl Scouts joined, campfire. No. B204, 1p+1p, Hand on shoulder of Girl Scout.

2010, Aug. 21 Litho. *Perf. 13½x14*
B201-B204 SP74 Set of 4 3.75 3.75

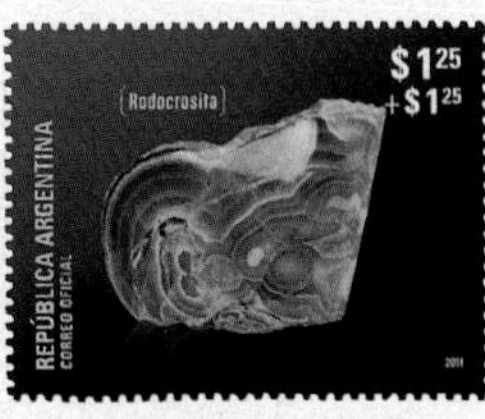

Minerals SP75

Designs: No. B205, 1.25p+1.25p, Rhodochrosite (rodocrisita). No. B206, 1.25p+1.25p, Sulphur (azufre). No. B207, 1.25p+1.25p, Pyrite (pirita). No. B208, 1.25p+1.25p, Quartz (cuarzo).

2011, Aug. 20 *Perf. 13¾x13½*
B205-B208 SP75 Set of 4 4.75 4.75

Minerals Type of 2011

Designs: No. B209, 1.50p+1.50p, Agate (agata). No. B210, 1.50p+1.50p, Amethyst (amatista). No. B211, 1.50p+1.50p, Fluorite (fluorita). No. B212, 1.50p+1.50p, Malachite (malaquita).

2012, Aug. 25
B209-B212 SP75 Set of 4 5.25 5.25

AIR POST STAMPS

Airplane Circles the Globe — AP1

Eagle — AP2

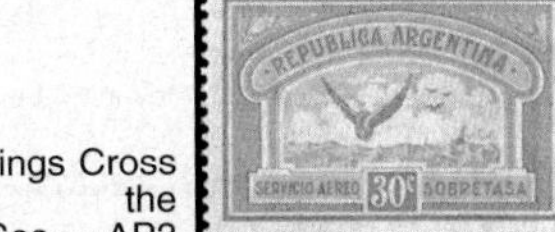

Wings Cross the Sea — AP3

Condor on Mountain Crag — AP4

Perforations of Nos. C1-C37 vary from clean-cut to rough and uneven, with many skipped perfs.

Perf. 13x13½, 13½x13
1928, Mar. 1 Litho. Wmk. 90

C1 AP1 5c lt red 1.50 .60
C2 AP1 10c Prus blue 2.50 1.10
C3 AP2 15c lt brown 2.50 1.00
C4 AP1 18c lilac gray 4.00 3.00
a. 18c brown lilac 4.50 3.00
b. Double impression *375.00*
C5 AP2 20c ultra 3.00 1.00
C6 AP2 24c deep blue 5.00 3.00
C7 AP3 25c brt violet 5.00 1.60
C8 AP3 30c rose red 6.00 1.25
C9 AP4 35c rose 5.00 1.10
C10 AP1 36c bister brn 3.00 1.60
C11 AP4 50c gray black 5.00 .75
C12 AP2 54c chocolate 5.00 2.25
C13 AP2 72c yellow grn 6.00 2.25
a. Double impression *350.00*
C14 AP3 90c dk brown 11.00 2.00
C15 AP3 1p slate bl & red 13.00 .90
C16 AP3 1.08p rose & dk bl 18.00 5.00
C17 AP4 1.26p dull vio & grn 25.00 10.00
C18 AP4 1.80p blue & lil rose 25.00 10.00
C19 AP4 3.60p gray & blue 50.00 22.00
Nos. C1-C19 (19) 195.50 70.40

The watermark on No. C4a is larger than on the other stamps of this set, measuring 10mm across Sun.

Zeppelin First Flight

Air Post Stamps of 1928 Overprinted in Blue

1930, May

C20	AP2	20c ultra	10.00	5.00
C21	AP4	50c gray black	20.00	10.00
a.		Inverted overprint	*475.00*	
C22	AP3	1p slate bl & red	25.00	12.50
a.		Inverted overprint	*650.00*	
C23	AP4	1.80p blue & lil rose	70.00	30.00
C24	AP4	3.60p gray & blue	200.00	90.00
		Nos. C20-C24 (5)	325.00	147.50

Overprinted in Green

C25	AP2	20c ultra	13.00	8.00
C26	AP4	50c gray black	15.00	10.00
C27	AP3	90c dark brown	13.00	8.00
C28	AP3	1p slate bl & red	25.00	15.00
C29	AP4	1.80p blue & lil rose	700.00	500.00
a.		Thick paper	*850.00*	
		Nos. C25-C29 (5)	766.00	541.00

Air Post Stamps of 1928 Overprinted in Red or Blue

On AP1-AP2

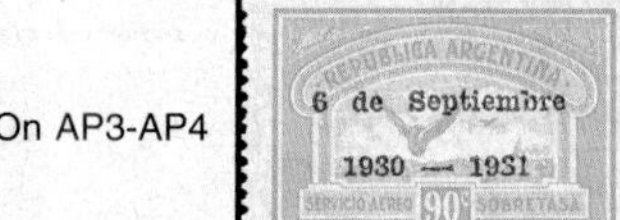

On AP3-AP4

1931

C30	AP1	18c lilac gray	2.00	1.50
C31	AP2	72c yellow green	14.00	10.50
C32	AP3	90c dark brown	14.00	10.50
C33	AP4	1.80p bl & lil rose (Bl)	30.00	22.50
C34	AP4	3.60p gray & blue	57.50	40.00
		Nos. C30-C34 (5)	117.50	85.00

1st anniv. of the Revolution of 1930.

Zeppelin Issue

Nos. C1, C4, C4a, C14 Overprinted in Blue or Red

On AP1

On AP3

1932, Aug. 4

C35	AP1	5c lt red (Bl)	3.00	2.00
C36	AP1	18c lilac gray (R)	12.50	9.00
a.		18c brown lilac (R)	100.00	60.00
C37	AP3	90c dark brown (R)	32.50	26.00
		Nos. C35-C37 (3)	48.00	37.00

Plane and Letter — AP5

Mercury — AP6

Plane in Flight — AP7

Perf. 13½x13, 13x13½

1940, Oct. 23 Photo. Wmk. 90

C38	AP5	30c deep orange	5.00	.25
C39	AP6	50c dark brown	7.50	.25
C40	AP5	1p carmine	1.75	.25
C41	AP7	1.25p deep green	.50	.25
C42	AP5	2.50p bright blue	1.25	.25
		Nos. C38-C42 (5)	16.00	1.25

Plane and Letter — AP8

Mercury and Plane — AP9

Perf. 13½x13, 13x13½

1942, Oct. 6 Litho. Wmk. 90

C43	AP8	30c orange	.25	.25
C44	AP9	50c dull brn & buff	.40	.25

No. C43 exists imperf. Value, pair $20.
See Nos. C49-C52, C57, C61.

Plane over Iguaçu Falls — AP10

Plane over the Andes — AP11

Perf. 13½x13

1946, June 10 Unwmk.

C45	AP10	15c dull red brn	.25	.25
C46	AP11	25c gray green	.25	.25

See Nos. C53-C54.

Allegory of Flight AP12

Astrolabe — AP13

Perf. 13½x13, 13x13½

1946, Sept. 25 Litho. Unwmk.

Surface-Tinted Paper

C47	AP12	15c sl grn, *pale grn*	.55	.25
C48	AP13	60c vio brn, *ocher*	.55	.35

Types of 1942

1946-48 Unwmk. *Perf. 13½x13*

C49	AP8	30c orange	1.40	.25
C50	AP9	50c dull brn & buff	2.50	.25
C51	AP8	1p carmine ('47)	1.25	.25
C52	AP8	2.50p brt blue ('48)	5.50	.75
		Nos. C49-C52 (4)	10.65	1.50

No. C51 exists imperf. Value, pair $30.

Types of 1946

1948 Wmk. 90

C53	AP10	15c dull red brn	.25	.25
C54	AP11	25c gray green	.25	.25

Atlas (National Museum, Naples) — AP14

Map of Argentine Republic, Globe and Caliper — AP15

Perf. 13½x13, 13x13½

1948-49 Photo. Wmk. 288

C55	AP14	45c dk brown ('49)	.40	.25
C56	AP15	70c dark green	.70	.40

4th Pan-American Reunion of Cartographers, Buenos Aires, Oct.-Nov., 1948.

Mercury Type of 1942

1949 Litho. *Perf. 13x13½*

C57	AP9	50c dull brn & buff	.40	.25

Marksmanship Trophy — AP16

1949, Nov. 4 Photo.

C58	AP16	75c brown	.75	.25

World Rifle Championship, 1949.

Catalogue values for unused stamps in this section, from this point to the end of the section, are for Never Hinged items.

Douglas DC-3 and Condor AP17

Perf. 13x13½

1951, June 20 Wmk. 90

C59	AP17	20c dk olive grn	.50	.25

10th anniversary of the State air lines.

Douglas DC-6 and Condor — AP18

1951, Oct. 17 *Perf. 13½*

C60	AP18	20c blue	.50	.25

End of Argentine 5-year Plan.

Plane-Letter Type of 1942

1951 Litho. *Perf. 13½x13*

C61	AP8	1p carmine	.40	.25

No. C61 exists imperf. Value, pair $20.

Jesus by Leonardo da Vinci (detail, "Virgin of the Rocks") AP19

Perf. 13½x13

1956, Sept. 29 Photo. Wmk. 90

C62	AP19	1p dull purple	.80	.25

Issued to express the gratitude of the children of Argentina to the people of the world for their help against poliomyelitis.

Battle of Montevideo AP20

Leonardo Rosales and Tomas Espora AP21

Guillermo Brown — AP22

1957, Mar. 2 *Perf. 13½*

C63	AP20	60c blue gray	.25	.25
C64	AP21	1p brt pink	.30	.25
C65	AP22	2p brown	.30	.25
		Nos. C63-C65 (3)	.85	.60

Cent. of the death of Admiral Guillermo Brown, founder of the Argentine navy.

Map of Americas & Arms of Buenos Aires — AP23

1957, Aug. 16

C66	AP23	2p rose violet	.50	.25

Issued to publicize the Inter-American Economic Conference in Buenos Aires.

Modern locomotive AP24

1957, Aug. 31 Wmk. 90 *Perf. 13½*
C67 AP24 60c gray .45 .25

Centenary of Argentine railroads.

AP25

No. C68, Globe, Flag,Compass Rose. No. C69, Key.

1957, Sept. 14
C68 AP25 1p multi .25 .25
C69 AP25 2p multi .30 .25

1957 International Congress for Tourism.

Birds Carrying Letters AP26

1957, Nov. 6
C70 AP26 1p bright blue .35 .25

Issued for Letter Writing Week, Oct. 6-12.

Early Plane AP27

1958, May 31 *Perf. 13½*
C71 AP27 2p maroon .25 .25

50th anniv. of the Argentine Aviation Club.

Stamp Anniv. Type

Designs: 80c, Stamp of Buenos Aires and view of the Plaza de la Aduana. 1p, Stamp of 1858 and "The Post of Santa Fe."

1958 Litho. *Perf. 13½*
C72 A270 80c pale bis & sl bl .25 .25
C73 A270 1p red org & dk bl .25 .25

Cent. of the 1st postage stamps of Buenos Aires & the Argentine Confederation.
Issue dates: 80c, Oct. 18; 1p, Aug. 23.

Comet Jet over World Map AP29

1959, May 16 *Perf. 13½*
C74 AP29 5p black & olive .40 .25

Inauguration of jet flights by Argentine Airlines.

Type of Regular Issue, 1960

"Cabildo" and: 1.80p, Mariano Moreno. 5p, Manuel Belgrano and Juan Jose Castelli.

Perf. 13½
1960, May 28 Wmk. 90 Photo.
C75 A287 1.80p red brown .25 .25
a. Souvenir sheet of 3 1.40 .95
C76 A287 5p buff & purple .35 .25
a. Souvenir sheet of 3 2.00 1.50

Souvenir sheets are imperf. No. C75a contains one No. C75 and 1p and 2p resembling Nos. 713-714; stamps in reddish brown. No. C76a contains one No. C76 and 4.20p and 10.70p resembling Nos. 715-716; stamps are in green.

Symbolic of New Provinces — AP30

1960, July 8 Litho.
C77 AP30 1.80p dp car & blue .30 .25

Elevation of the territories of Chubut, Formosa, Neuquen, Rio Negro and Santa Cruz to provinces.

Type of Regular Issue, 1960

1960, Oct. 1 Photo. *Perf. 13½*
C78 A291 1.80p rose lilac .50 .25
C79 A291 10.70p brt grnsh blue .70 .35

UNESCO Emblem AP31

1962, July 14 Litho.
C80 AP31 13p ocher & brown .40 .25

15th anniv. of UNESCO.

Mail Coach AP32

1962, Oct. 6 Wmk. 90 *Perf. 13½*
C81 AP32 5.60p gray brn & blk .75 .25

Mailman's Day, Sept. 14, 1962.

No. 695 and Type of 1959 Surcharged in Green

1962, Oct. 31 Photo.
C82 A277 5.60p on 5p brown .30 .25
C83 A277 18p on 5p brn, *grnsh* 1.00 .25

UPAE Emblem — AP33

1962, Nov. 24 Photo. *Perf. 13½*
C84 AP33 5.60p dark blue .40 .25

50th anniv. of the founding of the Postal Union of the Americas and Spain, UPAE.

Skylark — AP34

Design: 11p, Super Albatros.

1963, Feb. 9 Litho.
C85 AP34 5.60p blue & black .25 .25
C86 AP34 11p blue, blk & red .40 .25

9th World Gliding Championships.

Symbolic Plane AP35

1963-65 Wmk. 90 *Perf. 13½*

C87	AP35	5.60p dk pur, car & brt grn	.40	.25
C88	AP35	7p black & bis ('64)	.55	.25
C88A	AP35	7p black & bis ('65)	5.00	1.00
C89	AP35	11p blk, dk pur & grn	.60	.25
C90	AP35	18p dk pur, red & vio bl	1.25	.35
C91	AP35	21p brown, red & gray	1.75	.40
		Nos. C87-C91 (6)	9.55	2.50

"Argentina" reads down on No. C88, up on No. C88A. See Nos. C101-C104, C108-C111, C123-C126, C135-C141. For overprint and surcharges see Nos. C96, C146-C150.

Type of Regular Issue, 1964

Map of Falkland Islands (Islas Malvinas).

1964, Feb. 22 *Perf. 13½*
Size: 33x22mm
C92 A327 18p lt & dk bl & ol grn 2.75 .75

UPU Monument, Bern, and UN Emblem AP36

1964, May 23 Engr. *Perf. 13½*
C93 AP36 18p red & dk brown .60 .25

15th UPU Cong., Vienna, Austria, 5-6/64.

Discovery of America, Florentine Woodcut AP37

1964, Oct. 10 Litho.
C94 AP37 13p tan & black .90 .35

Day of the Race, Columbus Day.

Lt. Matienzo Base, Antarctica AP38

1965, Feb. 27 Photo. *Perf. 13½*
C95 AP38 11p salmon pink .50 .25

Issued to publicize the national territory of Tierra del Fuego, Antarctic and South Atlantic Isles.

No. C88A Overprinted in Silver

1965, Mar. 17 Litho.
C96 AP35 7p black & bister .30 .25

1st Rio de la Plata Stamp Show, sponsored jointly by the Argentine and Uruguayan Philatelic Associations, Montevideo, Mar. 19-28.

ITU Emblem — AP39

1965, May 11 Wmk. 90 *Perf. 13½*
C97 AP39 18p slate, blk & red .40 .25

Centenary of the ITU.

Ascending Rocket — AP40

Design: 50p, Earth with trajectories and magnetic field, horiz.

1965, May 29 Photo. *Perf. 13½*
C98 AP40 18p vermilion .70 .30
C99 AP40 50p dp violet blue 1.25 .55

6th Symposium on Space Research, held in Buenos Aires, and to honor the Natl. Commission of Space Research.

Type of 1963-65 Inscribed "Republica Argentina"

1965, Oct. 13 Litho. Wmk. 90

C101	AP35	12p dk car rose & brn	1.40	.25
C102	AP35	15p vio blue & dk red	1.50	.50
C103	AP35	27.50p dk bl grn & gray	2.50	1.00
C104	AP35	30.50p dk brown & dk bl	3.00	1.50
		Nos. C101-C104 (4)	8.40	3.25

Argentine Antarctica Map and Centaur Rocket AP41

1966, Feb. 19 *Perf. 13½*

C105 AP41 27.50p bl, blk & dp org 1.10 .85

Launchings of sounding balloons and of a Gamma Centaur rocket in Antarctica during February, 1965.

Sea Gull and Southern Cross AP42

1966, May 14 *Perf. 13½*

C106 AP42 12p Prus blue, blk & red .40 .25

50th anniv. of the Naval Aviation School.

Blériot Plane Flown by Fels, 1917 — AP43

1967, Sept. 2 Litho. *Perf. 13½*

C107 AP43 26p olive, bl & blk .30 .25

Flight by Theodore Fels from Buenos Aires to Montevideo, Sept. 2, 1917, allegedly the 1st intl. airmail flight.

Type of 1963-65 Inscribed "Republica Argentina" Reading Down

1967, Dec. 20 *Perf. 13½*

C108	AP35	26p brown	.60	.25
C109	AP35	40p violet	5.25	.30
C110	AP35	68p blue green	3.50	.45
C111	AP35	78p ultra	1.50	.60
		Nos. C108-C111 (4)	10.85	1.60

Vito Dumas and Ketch "Legh II" AP44

1968, July 27 Litho. Wmk. 90

C112 AP44 68p bl, blk, red & vio bl .65 .40

Issued to commemorate Vito Dumas's one-man voyage around the world in 1943.

Type of Regular Issue and

Assembly Emblem — AP45

40p, Globe and map of South America.

1968, Oct. 19 Litho. *Perf. 13½*

C113 A395 40p brt pink, lt bl & blk .75 .30
C114 AP45 68p bl, lt bl, gold & blk 1.25 .50

4th Plenary Assembly of the Intl. Telegraph and Telephone Consultative Committee, Mar del Plata, Sept. 23-Oct. 25.

Radar Antenna, Balcarce Station AP46

Perf. 13½

1969, Aug. 23 Wmk. 90 Photo.

C115 AP46 40p blue gray .70 .25

Communications by satellite through Intl. Telecommunications Consortium (INTELSAT).

Atucha Nuclear Center AP47

1969, Dec. 13 Litho. Wmk. 365

C116 AP47 26p blue & multi 2.00 .80

Completion of Atucha Nuclear Center.

Type of 1963-65 Inscribed "Republica Argentina" Reading Down

1969-71 *Perf. 13½*

C123	AP35	40p violet	5.75	.40
C124	AP35	68p dk blue grn ('70)	2.10	.60

Unwmk.

C125	AP35	26p yellow brn ('71)	.35	.25
C126	AP35	40p violet ('71)	3.00	.40
		Nos. C123-C126 (4)	11.20	1.65

Old Fire Engine and Fire Brigade Emblem AP48

1970, Aug. 8 Litho. Unwmk.

C128 AP48 40c green & multi 1.50 .30

Centenary of the Fire Brigade.

Education Year Emblem AP49

1970, Aug. 29 *Perf. 13½*

C129 AP49 68c blue & blk .80 .30

Issued for International Education Year.

Fleet Leaving Valparaiso, by Antonio Abel — AP50

1970, Oct. 17 Litho. *Perf. 13½*

C130 AP50 26c multicolored 1.00 .35

150th anniv. of the departure for Peru of the liberation fleet from Valparaiso, Chile.

Sumampa Chapel — AP51

1970, Nov. 7 Photo.

C131 AP51 40c multicolored 1.00 .40

Bishopric of Tucuman, 400th anniversary.

Buenos Aires Planetarium — AP52

1970, Nov. 28 Litho. *Perf. 13½*

C132 AP52 40c multicolored .75 .25

Jorge Newbery and Morane Saulnier Plane AP53

1970, Dec. 19

C133 AP53 26c bl, blk, yel & grn .45 .25

24th Aeronautics and Space Week.

Industries Type of Regular Issue

Design: 31c, Refinery.

1971, Oct. 16 Litho. *Perf. 13½*

C134 A445 31c red, blk & yel .80 .30

Type of 1963-65 Inscribed "Republica Argentina" Reading Down

1971-74 Unwmk.

C135	AP35	45c brown	3.50	.25
C136	AP35	68c red	.50	.25
C137	AP35	70c vio blue ('73)	2.75	.50
C138	AP35	90c emerald ('73)	2.75	.50
C139	AP35	1.70p blue ('74)	.60	.25
C140	AP35	1.95p emerald ('74)	.60	.25
C141	AP35	2.65p dp claret ('74)	.60	.25
		Nos. C135-C141 (7)	11.30	2.25

Fluorescent paper was used for Nos. C135-C136, C138-C141. The 70c was issued on both papers. Value, 70c on fluorescent paper $5.50

Don Quixote, Drawing by Ignacio Zuloaga AP54

1975, Apr. 26 Photo. *Perf. 13½*

C145 AP54 2.75p yellow, blk & red .60 .35

Day of the Race and for Espana 75 Intl. Philatelic Exhibition, Madrid, Apr. 4-13.

No. C87 Surcharged

1975, Sept. 15 Litho. Wmk. 90

C146	AP35	9.20p on 5.60p	.90	.25
C147	AP35	19.70p on 5.60p	1.25	.45
C148	AP35	100p on 5.60p	5.50	2.25
		Nos. C146-C148 (3)	7.65	2.95

No. C87 Surcharged

1975, Oct. 15

C149	AP35	9.20p on 5.60p	.90	.30
C150	AP35	19.70p on 5.60p	1.50	.60

Argentine State Airline, 50th Anniv. — AP55

1990, Sept. 15 Litho. *Perf. 13½*

C151	AP55	2500a Junkers JU52-3M	1.50	.90
C152	AP55	2500a Grumman SA-16	1.50	.90
C153	AP55	2500a Fokker F-27	1.50	.90
C154	AP55	2500a Fokker F-28	1.50	.90
		Nos. C151-C154 (4)	6.00	3.60

AIR POST SEMI-POSTAL STAMPS

Catalogue values for unused stamps in this section are for Never Hinged items.

Philatelic Exhibition Type

Designs: No. CB1, Stamp engraving. No. CB2, Proofing stamp die. No. CB3, Sheet of stamps. No. CB4, The letter. No. CB5, Gen. San Martin.

Perf. 13½

1950, Aug. 26 Wmk. 90 Photo.

CB1	SP8	45c + 45c vio bl	.35	.25
CB2	SP8	70c + 70c dk brn	.60	.40
a.		Souv. sheet of 3, #B12, CB1, CB2, imperf.	5.00	3.00
CB3	SP8	1p + 1p cerise	1.25	1.25
CB4	SP8	2.50p + 2.50p ol gray	8.50	6.00
CB5	SP8	5p + 5p dull grn	10.00	7.25
		Nos. CB1-CB5 (5)	21.45	15.40

Argentine Intl. Philatelic Exhib., 1950.

Pieta by Michelangelo SPAP2

1951, Dec. 22 ***Perf. 13½x13***
CB6 SPAP2 2.45p +7.55p grnsh blk 22.50 14.00

Surtax as for the Eva Peron Foundation.

Flower and Child's Head SPAP3

1958, Mar. 15 ***Perf. 13½***
CB7 SPAP3 1p +50c deep claret .30 .30

Surtax for National Council for Children.

Stamp of 1858 — SPAP4

1958, Mar. 29 Litho. Wmk. 90
CB8 SPAP4 1p + 50c gray ol & bl .45 .35
CB9 SPAP4 2p + 1p rose lilac & vio .55 .45
CB10 SPAP4 3p + 1.50p green & brown .60 .55
CB11 SPAP4 5p + 2.50p gray ol & car rose 1.10 .90
CB12 SPAP4 10p + 5p gray ol & brn 2.00 1.75
Nos. CB8-CB12 (5) 4.70 4.00

The surtax was for the Intl. Centennial Philatelic Exhibition, Buenos Aires, Apr. 19-27.

Type of Semi-Postal Issue, 1958

Designs: 1p+50c, Flooded area. 5p+2.50p, House and truck under water.

1958, Oct. 4 Photo. ***Perf. 13½***
CB13 SP11 1p + 50c dull purple .30 .25
CB14 SP11 5p + 2.50p grnsh blue 1.00 .80

The surtax was for victims of a flood in the Buenos Aires district.

Type of Semi-Postal Issue

1959, Sept. 5 Litho. ***Perf. 13½***
CB15 SP13 2p + 1p Rowing .40 .25
CB16 SP13 3p + 1.50p Woman diver .60 .50

Bird Type of Semi-Postal Issue

2p+1p, Rufous tinamou. 3p+1.50p, Rhea.

1960, Feb. 6 ***Perf. 13½***
CB17 SP14 2p + 1p rose car & sal .45 .25
CB18 SP14 3p + 1.50p slate green .50 .35

The surtax was for child welfare work. See No. CB29.

Buenos Aires Market Place, 1810 SPAP5

6p+3p, Oxcart water carrier. 10.70p+5.30p, Settlers landing. 20p+10p, The Fort.

1960, Aug. 20 Photo. Wmk. 90
CB19 SPAP5 2 + 1p rose brown .25 .25
CB20 SPAP5 6 + 3p gray .35 .25
CB21 SPAP5 10.70 + 5.30p blue .60 .50
CB22 SPAP5 20 + 10p bluish grn 1.00 .85
Nos. CB19-CB22 (4) 2.20 1.85

Inter-American Philatelic Exhibition EFIMAYO 1960, Buenos Aires, Oct. 12-24, held to for the sesquicentennial of the May Revolution of 1810.
No. CB22 exists imperf. Value, pair $40.
For overprints see Nos. CB25-CB28.

Seibo, National Flower — SPAP6

#CB24, Copihue, Chile's national flower.

1960, Sept. 10 ***Perf. 13½***
CB23 SPAP6 6 + 3p lilac rose .50 .30
CB24 SPAP6 10.70 + 5.30p ver .70 .40

The surtax was for earthquake victims in Chile. Nos. CB23-CB24 exist imperf. Value, each pair $40.

Nos. CB19-CB22 Overprinted

1960, Oct. 8
CB25 SPAP5 2 + 1p rose brown .25 .25
CB26 SPAP5 6 + 3p gray .30 .30
CB27 SPAP5 10.70 + 5.30p blue .50 .40
CB28 SPAP5 20 + 10p bluish green 1.00 .75
Nos. CB25-CB28 (4) 2.05 1.70

United Nations Day, Oct. 24, 1960.

Type of Semi-Postal Issue, 1960

Design: Emperor penguins.

1961, Feb. 25 Photo. Wmk. 90
CB29 SP14 1.80p + 90c gray .40 .25

The surtax was for child welfare work. Exists imperf. Value, pair $50.

Stamp of 1862 — SPAP7

1962, May 19 Litho.
CB30 SPAP7 6.50p + 6.50p Prus bl & grnsh bl .70 .65

Opening of the "Argentina 62" Philatelic Exhibition, Buenos Aires, May 19-29. Exists imperf. Value, pair $40.

Type of Semi-Postal Issue, 1963

1963, May 18 Wmk. 90 ***Perf. 13½***
CB31 SP21 11p + 5p Bicycling .60 .50

Exists imperf. Value, pair $40.

Type of Semi-Postal Issue, 1962

1963, Dec. 21 ***Perf. 13½***
CB32 SP20 11p + 5p Pitangus sulphuratus bolivianus 1.10 .60

The surtax was for child welfare.

Type of Semi-Postal Issue, 1964

1964, July 18 Litho.
CB33 SP22 11p + 5p Sailboat 1.00 1.00

Exists imperf. Value, pair $50.

Crutch, Olympic Torch and Rings — SPAP8

1964, Sept. 19 Litho. ***Perf. 13½***
CB34 SPAP8 18p + 9p bluish grn, blk, red & yel .60 .60

13th "Olympic" games for the handicapped, Tokyo, 1964. Exists imperf. Value, pair $50.

Bird Type of Semi-Postal Issue, 1962

1964, Dec. 23 Litho. Wmk. 90
CB35 SP20 18p + 9p Iridoprocne leucopyga 1.10 .85

The surtax was for child welfare.

Furnarius Rufus Rufus — SP22a

1966, Mar. 26 ***Perf. 13½***
CB36 SP22a 27.50p + 12.50p bl, ocher, yel & grn 1.10 .85

The surtax was for child welfare.

Coat of Arms — SPAP9

1966, June 25 Litho. ***Perf. 13½***
CB37 SPAP9 10p + 10p multi 1.75 1.40

ARGENTINA '66 Philatelic Exhibition held in connection with the sesquicentennial celebration of the Declaration of Independence, Buenos Aires, July 16-23. The surtax was for the Exhibition. Issued in sheets of 4.

Designs: 15p+7p, Thraupis bonariensis. 26p+13p, Ramphastos toco.

1967 Litho. Wmk. 90
CB38 SP22a 15p + 7p blk, bl, grn & yel 1.40 1.00
CB39 SP22a 26p + 13p blk, org, yel & bl .50 .40

The surtax was for child welfare.
Issued: 15p+7p, Jan. 14; 26p+13p, Dec. 23.

Bird Type of Semi-Postal Issue, 1969

1969, Sept. 20 Wmk. 365 ***Perf. 13½***
CB40 SP24 26p + 13p Cephloeus lineatus .75 .40

The surtax was for child welfare.

Bird Type of Semi-Postal Issue, 1970

1970, May 9 Litho. Wmk. 365
CB41 SP25 40c + 20c Phoenicopterus ruber chilensis .75 .40

The surtax was for child welfare.

Fish Type of Semi-Postal Issue, 1971

1971, Feb. 20 Unwmk. ***Perf. 12½***
Size: 75x15mm
CB42 SP26 40c + 20c Odostethes platensis .50 .40

The surtax was for child welfare.

OFFICIAL STAMPS

Regular Issues Overprinted in Black — a

1884-87 Unwmk. ***Perf. 12, 14***
O1 A29 ½c brown *40.00 25.00*
O2 A23 1c red 12.00 8.00
b. Perf. 12 100.00 80.00
O3 A29 1c red 1.00 .50
b. Double overprint 100.00 100.00
O4 A20 2c green 1.00 .50
b. Double overprint 120.00 120.00
O5 A11 4c brown 1.00 .50
O6 A7 8c lake 1.00 1.00
O7 A8 10c green 100.00 50.00
O8 A23 12c ultra (#45) 1.50 1.00
a. Perf. 14 1,000. 250.00
O9 A29 12c grnsh blue 1.50 1.00
O10 A19 24c blue 2.00 1.50
O11 A21 25c lake 30.00 25.00
O12 A12 30c orange 80.00 70.00
O13 A13 60c black 50.00 40.00
O14 A14 90c blue 30.00 25.00
b. Double overprint 120.00 120.00
Nos. O1-O14 (14) 351.00 249.00

Inverted Overprint

O1a A29 ½c 30.00 20.00
O2a A23 1c Perf. 14 100.00 80.00
c. Perf. 12 75.00 —
O3a A29 1c 2.50 1.25
O4a A20 2c 120.00 120.00
O5a A11 4c 60.00 50.00
O6a A7 8c (Inverted overprint on reverse) *500.00* —
O8b A23 12c Perf. 12 — —
O9a A29 12c 300.00 250.00
O10a A19 24c 6.00 5.00
O13a A13 60c 150.00 120.00
O14a A14 90c 120.00 120.00

1884 ***Rouletted***
O15 A17 16c green 3.00 2.00
a. Double overprint 25.00 —
b. Inverted overprint 300.00
O16 A18 20c blue 15.00 12.00
a. Inverted overprint 120.00 80.00
O17 A19 24c blue 2.00 1.50
a. Inverted overprint 6.00 5.00
b. Double ovpt., one inverted 250.00 —
Nos. O15-O17 (3) 20.00 15.50

Overprinted Diagonally in Red

1885 ***Perf. 12***
O18 A20 2c green 3.00 2.00
a. Inverted overprint 100.00 100.00
O19 A11 4c brown 3.00 2.00
a. Inverted overprint 100.00 —
b. Double overprint 100.00 100.00
O20 A13 60c black 50.00 40.00
O21 A14 90c blue 450.00 275.00

1885 ***Rouletted***
O22 A19 24c blue 27.50 20.00

On all of these stamps, the overprint is found reading both upwards and downwards.
Counterfeits exist of No. O21 overprint and others.

Regular Issues Handstamped Horizontally in Black — b

1884 *Perf. 12, 14*

O23 A23 1c red 100.00 50.00
a. Perf. 12 400.00 300.00
O24 A20 2c green, diagonal overprint 60.00 40.00
a. Horizontal overprint 450.00 300.00
O25 A11 4c brown 25.00 20.00
O26 A7 8c lake 25.00 10.00
O27 A23 12c ultra 60.00 50.00

Overprinted Diagonally

O28 A19 24c bl, rouletted 50.00 35.00
O29 A13 60c black 30.00 15.00

Counterfeit overprints exist.

Liberty Head — O1

Perf. 11½, 12 and Compound

1901, Dec. 1 **Engr.**

O31 O1 1c gray .40 .25
b. Vert. pair, imperf. horiz. 50.00
c. Horiz. pair, imperf. vert. 50.00
O32 O1 2c orange brown .40 .25
O33 O1 5c red .45 .25
b. Vert. pair, imperf. horiz. 50.00
O34 O1 10c dark green .90 .25
O35 O1 30c dark blue 5.00 1.60
O36 O1 50c orange 3.00 1.40
Nos. O31-O36 (6) 10.15 4.00

Imperf, Pairs

O31a O1 1c 80.00
O32a O1 2c 80.00
O33a O1 5c 100.00
O34a O1 10c 80.00
O35a O1 30c 100.00
O36a O1 50c 150.00

Regular Stamps of 1935-51 Overprinted in Black — c

Perf. 13x13½, 13½x13, 13

1938-54 **Wmk. RA in Sun (90)**

O37 A129 1c buff ('40) .40 .25
O38 A130 2c dk brn ('40) .40 .25
O39 A132 3c grn ('39) 1.00 .25
O40 A132 3c lt gray ('39) .40 .25
O41 A134 5c yel brn .40 .25
O42 A195 5c car ('53) .40 .25
O43 A137 10c carmine .55 .25
O44 A137 10c brn ('39) .45 .25
O45 A140 15c lt gray bl, type II ('47) .40 .25
O46 A139 15c slate blue .75 .25
O47 A139 15c pale ultra ('39) .45 .25
O48 A139 20c blue ('53) 1.10 .40
O49 A141 25c carmine .40 .25
a. Overprint 11mm .55 .25
O49B A143 40c dk violet 1.50 .35
O50 A144 50c red & org .40 .25
a. Overprint 11mm .40 .25
O51 A146 1p brn blk & lt bl ('40) .45 .25
a. Overprint 11mm .45 .40
O52 A224 1p choc & lt bl ('51) 1.50 .25
a. Overprint 11mm .40 .25
O53 A147 2p brn lake & dk ultra (ovpt. 11mm) ('54) 1.50 .25
Nos. O37-O53 (18) 12.45 4.75

Overprinted in Black on Stamps and Types of 1945-47

Perf. 13x13½, 13½x13

1945-46 **Unwmk.**

O54 A130 2c sepia 3.00 1.75
O55 A132 3c lt gray 2.50 1.10
O56 A134 5c yel brn .65 .25
O57 A195 5c dp car .25 .25
O58 A137 10c brown .25 .25
a. Double overprint
O59 A140 15c lt gray bl, type II .30 .25
O61 A141 25c dull rose .25 .25
O62 A144 50c red & org .55 .25
O63 A146 1p brn blk & lt bl .25 .25
O64 A147 2p brn lake & bl .40 .25
O65 A148 5p ind & ol grn .25 .25
O66 A149 10p dp cl & int blk .45 .25
O67 A150 20p bl grn & brn 1.00 .80
Nos. O54-O67 (13) 10.10 6.15

Overprinted in Black on Stamps and Types of 1942-50

Perf. 13, 13x13½

1944-51 **Wmk. 288**

O73 A132 3c lt gray 3.25 1.25
O74 A134 5c yellow brown .70 .40
O75 A137 10c red brown .35 .25
O76 A140 15c lt gray bl, type II .25 .25
O77 A144 50c red & org (overprint 11 mm) 3.25 1.25
O78 A146 1p brn blk & lt bl (overprint 11mm) 3.25 1.25
Nos. O73-O78 (6) 11.05 4.65

Catalogue values for unused stamps in this section, from this point to the end of the section, are for Never Hinged items.

Nos. 600-606 Overprinted in Black — d

1953 **Wmk. 90** ***Perf. 13***

O79 A228 5c gray .40 .25
O80 A228 10c rose lilac .40 .25
O81 A228 20c rose pink .40 .25
O82 A228 25c dull green .40 .25
O83 A228 40c dull violet .40 .25
O84 A228 45c deep blue .55 .30
O85 A228 50c dull brown .40 .25

Nos. 611-617 Overprinted in Blue — e

Perf. 13x13½, 13½x13

O86 A229 1p dk brown .50 .25
O87 A229 1.50p dp green .50 .25
O88 A229 2p brt carmine .50 .25
O89 A229 3p indigo .60 .35

Size: 30x40mm

O90 A229 5p red brown .95 .55
O91 A228 10p red 5.00 4.00
O92 A228 20p green 50.00 30.00
Nos. O79-O92 (14) 61.00 37.45

No. 612 Overprinted in Blue — f

O93 A229 1.50p dp grn 1.50 .45

Regular Issues of 1954-59 Variously Overprinted in Black or Blue

g

SERVICIO OFICIAL

h

Perf. 13½, 13x13½, 13½x13

1955-61 **Litho.** **Wmk. 90**

O94 A237(c) 20c red (#629) .40 .25
O95 A237(d) 20c red (#629) .40 .25
O96 A237(d) 40c red, ovpt. 15mm (#630) .40 .25

Engr.

O97 A239(g) 50c bl (#632) .40 .25

Photo.

O98 A239(h) 1p brn (#635) .40 .25
O99 A239(e) 1p brn (Bl, #635) .40 .25
O100 A239(e) 1p brn (Bk, #635) .40 .25

Engr.

O101 A239(h) 3p vio brn (#638) .40 .25
O102 A240(h) 5p gray grn (#639) .40 .25
O103 A240(e) 10p yel grn (#640) .85 .25
O104 A240(f) 20p dl vio (#641) 1.00 .50
O105 A240(h) 20p dl vio (#641) 1.00 .50
a. Perf 13½ (#641a) 1.00 .50
O106 A241(e) 50p ultra & ind (#642) 2.50 1.00
Nos. O94-O106 (13) 8.95 4.50

The overprints on Nos. O99-O100 & O103-O104 are horizontal; that on No. O106 is vertical. On No. O106 overprint measures 23mm.

Issued: No. O102, 1957; Nos. O97, O101, O103, O105, 1958; Nos. O98-O99, O104, 1959; No. O100, 1960; No. O106, 1961.

No. 659 Overprinted Type "d"

1957 **Wmk. 90** **Litho.** ***Perf. 13***

O108 A133 20c dl pur (ovpt. 15mm) .40 .25

Nos. 666, 658 and 663 Variously Overprinted

1957 **Photo.** ***Perf. 13x13½, 13½***

O109 A261(g) 2p claret .30 .25
O110 A254(e) 2.40p brown .40 .25
O111 A258(c) 4.40p grnsh gray .40 .25
Nos. O109-O111 (3) 1.10 .75

Nos. 668, 685-687, 690-691, 693-705, 742, 742C and Types of 1959-65 Overprinted in Black, Blue or Red Types "e," "g," or

i

S. OFICIAL

j

k

S. OFICIAL

m

n

Lithographed; Photogravure

1960-68 ***Perf. 13x13½, 13½***

O112 A128(g) 5c buff (vert. ovpt.) .35 .25
O113 A275(j) 10c sl grn .35 .25
O114 A275(j) 20c dl red brn .35 .25
O115 A275(i) 50c bister .35 .25
O116 A278(k) 1p brn .45 .25
O117 A278(j) 1p brn, photo. (vert. ovpt.) .45 .25
O117A A278(j) 1p brn, litho., (down) .40 .25
O118 A276(j) 2p rose red .35 .25
O119 A312(m) 2p dp grn .50 .25
O120 A312(j) 2p brt grn (up) .45 .25
O121 A312(j) 2p grn litho. (down) .50 .25
O122 A277(e) 3p dk bl (horiz.) .35 .25
O123 A277(j) 3p dk blue .35 .25
O124 A276(j) 4p red, litho. .60 .25
O125 A312(j) 4p rose red, litho. (down) .45 .25
O126 A277(e) 5p brn (Bl) (horiz.) .60 .25
O127 A277(e) 5p brn (Bk) (horiz.) .45 .25
O128 A277(j) 5p sepia .45 .25
O129 A277(e) 5p sepia (horiz. ovpt.) .55 .25
O130 A276(j) 8p red .35 .25
O131 A278(i) 10p lt red brn .45 .25
O132 A276(j) 10p vermilion .45 .25
O133 A278(j) 10p brn car (up) 2.25 1.00
O133A A278(j) 10p brn car (down) 90.00 30.00
O134 A278(m) 12p dk brn vio (horiz.) .40 .25
O135 A278(k) 20p Prus grn .50 .25
O136 A278(j) 20p Prus grn (up) .50 .25
O137 A276(j) 20p red, litho. .45 .25
O138 A276(m) 20p red, litho. (horiz.) .60 .25
O139 A278(j) 23p grn (vert. ovpt.) 1.10 .40
O140 A278(j) 25p dp vio, photo. (R) (up) 1.00 .45
O141 A278(j) 25p pur, litho. (R) (down) 1.75 .75
O142 A241(n) 50p dk blue 3.50 1.00
O143 A279(m) 100p bl (horiz. ovpt.) 2.50 1.00
O144 A279(m) 100p blue (up) 2.50 1.00
O145 A280(m) 300p dp violet (horiz.) 7.50 3.50
Nos. O112-O133,O134-O145 (35) 34.10 15.85

The "m" overprint measures 15½mm on 2p; 14½mm on 12p, 100p and 300p; 13mm on 20p.

Issued: Nos. O122, O127, O135, 1961; Nos. O112-O114, O116, O118, 1962; No. O124, 1963; Nos. O119, O134, O143, 1964; Nos. O117, O125, O130, O139, O144, 1965; Nos. O120, O128, O132-O133, O136, O140, O142, O145, 1966; Nos. O121, O129, O137-O138, O141, 1967; No. O117A, 1968.

Nos. 699, 823-825, 827-829, and Type of 1962 Overprinted in Black or Red Types "j," "m," or "o"

o

Inscribed: "Republica Argentina"

Litho., Photo., Engr.

1964-67 Wmk. 90 *Perf. 13½*

O149 A312(j) 6p rose red (down) .55 .30
O153 A238a(m) 22p ultra 1.00 .45
O154 A238a(j) 43p dk car rose (down) 2.00 1.00
O155 A238a(j) 45p brn, photo. (up) 2.00 1.00
O156 A238a(j) 45p brn, litho. (up) 3.00 1.00
O157 A241(j) 50p dk bl (up) (R) 5.00 1.10
O158 A366(j) 90p ol bis (up) 6.00 2.75
O162 A495(o) 500p yel grn 12.50 5.50
Nos. O149-O162 (8) 32.05 13.10

Issued: No. O153, 1964; No. O155, 1966; Nos. O149, O156-O162, 1967.

Type of 1959-67 Ovptd. Type "j"

1969 Litho. Wmk. 365 *Perf. 13½*

O163 A276 20p vermilion .50 .25

Beginning with No. 2001, many Argentine stamps are inscribed "Correo Official," but are not official stamps.

OFFICIAL DEPARTMENT STAMPS

Regular Issues of 1911-38 Overprinted in Black Ministry of Agriculture

No. OD1

1913 Type I *Perf. 13½x12½*

OD1 A88 2c chocolate (#181) .50 .25
OD2 A88 1c ocher (#190) .50 .25
OD3 A88 2c chocolate (#191) 1.00 .50
OD4 A88 5c red (#194) 1.00 .50
a. Perf. 13½ (#194a) 3.00 1.00
OD5 A88 12c deep blue (#196) 1.00 .50
a. Perf. 13½ (#196a) 3.00 .50
Nos. OD2-OD5 (4) 3.50 1.75

1915

OD6 A88 1c ocher (#208) 1.50 .50
OD7 A88 2c chocolate (#209) 1.00 .50
OD8 A88 5c red (#212) 1.00 .50
Nos. OD6-OD8 (3) 3.50 1.50

No. OD9

1916 *Perf. 13½*

OD9 A91 5c red (#220) .50 .25

No. OD11

No. OD15

1918

OD10 A94 12c blue (#238) 1.50 .50
OD11 A93 1c buff (#249) .50 .25
OD12 A93 2c brown (#250) .50 .25
OD13 A93 5c red (#253) .50 .25
OD14 A94 12c blue (#255) .50 .25
OD15 A94 20c ultra (#256) .50 .25
Nos. OD10-OD15 (6) 4.00 1.75

1920 *Perf. 13½, 13½x12½*

OD16 A93 1c buff (13½x12½) (#265) 1.00 .50
OD17 A93 2c brown (#266A) 4.00 1.00
OD18 A93 5c red (#269A) .70 .30
a. Perf. 13½x12½ (#269) .70 .30
Nos. OD16-OD18 (3) 5.70 1.80

1922 *Perf. 13½*

OD19 A94 12c blue (#311) 2.00 .75
OD20 A94 20c ultra (#312) 75.00

No. OD23

1923 *Perf. 13½x12½*

OD21 A104 1c buff (#324) 1.00 .50
a. Perf. 13½ (#324A) 5.00 2.00
OD22 A104 2c dark brown (#325) .50 .25
OD23 A104 5c red (#328) .50 .25
a. Perf. 13½ (#328A) 1.00 .50
OD24 A104 12c deep blue (#330) .80 .25
OD25 A104 20c ultra (#331) .80 .25
a. Perf. 13½ (#331A) 6.00 2.00
Nos. OD21-OD25 (5) 3.60 1.50

1924

OD26 A104 1c buff (#341) .50 .25
a. Inverted ovpt. 20.00 15.00
OD27 A104 2c dk brown (#342) .50 .25
OD29 A104 5c red (#345) .50 .25
OD30 A104 10c dull green (#346) .50 .25
OD31 A104 12c deep blue (#347) .50 .25
OD32 A104 20c deep blue (#348) .50 .25
a. Inverted ovpt. 80.00 60.00
Nos. OD26-OD32 (6) 3.00 1.50

No. OD34

1926

OD34 A110 12c deep blue (#360) .50 .25

No. OD28B

Type II

1931-36 *Perf. 13x13½, 13½x13*

OD27B A104 2c dark brown (#342) 5.00 2.00
OD28B A104 3c green (#343) .50 .25
OD29B A104 5c red (#345) .50 .25
OD30B A104 10c dull green (#346) .50 .25
c. Typo (coil) (#346a) .50 .25
OD32B A104 20c ultra (#348) 1.00 .50
c. Typo (coil) (#348a) .50 .25
OD33B A104 30c claret (#351) .50 .25
c. Typo (coil) (#351a) .50 .25

No. OD36

1936-38 Litho.

OD35 A129 1c buff (#419) .50 .25
OD36 A130 2c dark brown (#420) .50 .25
OD37 A132 3c green (#422) .50 .25
OD38 A134 5c yel brn (#427) .50 .25
OD40 A139 15c lt gray bl (#436) 2.50 .30
OD41 A140 20c lt ultra (#437) 3.00 .30
OD42 A140 20c lt ultra (#438) .80 .25
OD43 A141 25c car & pink (#441), perf. 13x13½ .50 .25
OD44 A142 30c org brn & yel brown (#442) .50 .25
OD45 A145 1p brn blk & Lt bl (#445) 3.50 1.50
OD46 A146 1p brn blk & lt bl (#446) .60 .30
Nos. OD35-OD46 (11) 13.40 4.15

Typo. *Perf. 13½*

OD38A A134 5c yel brn (#427) .50 .25
OD39A A137 10c carmine (#430) .50 .25
b. Perf. 13½x13 (#430a) 1.00 .50

Ministry of War

No. OD47

1913 Type I *Perf. 13½x12½*

OD47 A88 2c chocolate (#181) .80 .30
OD48 A88 1c ocher (#190) .30 .25
OD49 A88 2c chocolate (#191) 4.00 .50
a. Perf. 13½ (#191a) 15.00 5.00
OD50 A88 5c red (#194) 1.00 .50
a. Inverted ovpt. 50.00 —
OD51 A88 12c deep blue (#196) .50 .25
a. Perf. 13½ (#196a) 5.00 1.00
Nos. OD48-OD51 (4) 5.80 1.50

1915

OD52 A88 1c ocher (#208) 30.00 6.00
OD53 A88 2c chocolate (#209) 4.00 .80
OD54 A88 5c red (#212) 4.00 .80
Nos. OD52-OD54 (3) 38.00 7.60

1916 *Perf. 13½*

OD55 A91 5c red (#220) 3.00 .50
OD56 A92 12c chocolate (#222) 3.00 .50

1918

OD57 A93 1c buff (#232) 1.00 .50
a. Perf. 13½x12½ (#232B) 8.00 3.00
OD58 A93 2c brown (#233) 5.00 .80
a. Perf. 13½x12½ (#233B) 1.50 .50
OD59 A93 5c red (#236B) (Perf. 13½x12½) 1.50 .50
OD60 A94 12c blue (#238) 2.00 .80
Nos. OD57-OD60 (4) 9.50 2.60

1918

OD61 A93 1c buff (#249) 1.50 .50
a. Perf. 13½x12½ (#249B) 6.00 5.00
OD62 A93 2c brown (#250) .50 .25
a. Perf. 13½x12½ (#250B) 1.00 .50
OD63 A93 5c red (#253) 1.00 .50
a. Perf. 13½x12½ (#253B) .50 .25
OD64 A94 12c blue (#255) 1.50 .50
OD65 A94 20c ultra (#256) 4.00 .60
Nos. OD61-OD65 (5) 8.50 2.35

1920

OD66 A93 2c brown (#266A) 2.50 .50
a. Perf. 13½x12½ (#266) .50 .25
OD67 A93 5c red (#269A) 1.50 .50
a. Perf. 13½x12½ (#269) 1.00 .25
OD68 A94 12c blue (#271) 1.00 .50
Nos. OD66-OD68 (3) 5.00 1.50

1921

OD69 A94 12c blue (#299) 5.00 1.00

No. OD72

1922

OD70 A93 1c buff (#305) 3.00 .30
OD71 A93 2c brown (13½x12½) (#306B) 5.00 1.00
OD72 A103 5c red (#309) 2.00 .50
OD73 A94 20c ultra (#312) 1.00 .50
Nos. OD70-OD73 (4) 11.00 2.30

Perf. 13½x12½

OD74 A93 2c brown (#318A) 5.00 1.00

1923 *Perf. 13½x12½*

OD75 A104 1c buff (#324) 1.00 .50
a. Inverted ovpt. 20.00 18.00
b. Perf. 13½ (#324A) 5.00 1.50
OD76 A104 2c dark brown (#325) .50 .25
a. Perf. 13½ (#325A) 2.00 .50
OD77 A104 5c red (#328) .50 .25
a. Inverted ovpt. 20.00 18.00
b. Perf. 13½ (#328A) 1.50 .50
OD78 A104 12c deep blue (#330) 1.00 .50
OD79 A104 20c ultra (#331) 2.00 .50
a. Perf. 13½ (#331A) 3.00 .25
b. As "a.," inverted ovpt. 20.00 18.00
Nos. OD75-OD79 (5) 5.00 2.00

1924

OD80 A104 1c buff (#341) 5.00 1.00
OD81 A104 2c dark brown (#342) .50 .25
OD82 A104 3c green (#343) .80 .25
OD83 A104 5c red (#345) .50 .25
OD84 A104 10c dull green (#346) 2.00 .25
OD85 A104 20c ultra (#348) .50 .25
OD86 A104 30c claret (#351) 5.00 .50
OD87 A105 1p blue & red (#353) 5.00 .30
Nos. OD80-OD87 (8) 19.30 3.05

No. OD88

1926

OD88 A109 5c red (#359) 1.50 .25

No. OD82B

Type II

1931-36 *Perf. 13½x12½, 13*

OD82B A104 3c green (#343) 1.50 .50
OD83B A104 5c red (#345) .60 .25
c. Inverted ovpt. — *60.00*
OD84B A104 10c dull green (#346) .50 .25
c. Typo (coil) (346a) 1.50 .50
OD85B A104 20c ultra (#348) 1.00 .30
c. Typo (coil) (#348a) 5.00 .50
OD86B A104 30c claret (#351) .80 .25
c. Typo (coil) (#351a) 2.00 .50
OD87B A105 1p blue & red (#353) (Perf. 13) 5.00 .30
Nos. OD82B-OD87B (6) 9.40 1.85

No. OD90

1936-38 Litho.

OD89 A129 1c buff (#419) .50 .25
OD90 A130 2c dark brown (#420) .50 .25

OD91 A132 3c green (#422) .50 .25
OD92 A134 5c yel brn (#427) .50 .25
OD93 A137 10c carmine (#430) .50 .25
OD94 A139 15c slate bl (#434) .80 .25
OD95 A140 20c lt ultra (#437) 7.00 .50
OD96 A140 20c lt ultra (#438) .50 .25
OD97 A141 25c car & pink (#441) .50 .25
OD98 A142 30c org brn & yel brown (#442) .50 .25
OD99 A144 50c red & org (#444) .70 .25
OD100 A145 1p brn blk & lt bl (#445) 2.00 .60
OD101 A146 1p brn blk & lt bl (#446) 1.00 .50
Nos. OD89-OD101 (13) 15.50 4.10

Typo. ***Perf. 13½***
OD92B A134 5c yel brn (#427) .50 .25
c. Inverted ovpt. 20.00 15.00
OD93B A137 10c car (#430) .50 .25
c. Inverted ovpt. 50.00 35.00
d. Perf. 13½x13 (#430a) 1.00 .50

Ministry of Finance

No. OD102

1913 **Type I** ***Perf. 13½x12½***
OD102 A88 2c chocolate (#181) .50 .25
OD103 A88 1c ocher (#190) .50 .25
OD104 A88 2c chocolate (#191) .50 .25
OD105 A88 5c red (#194) .50 .25
OD106 A88 12c deep blue (#196) .50 .25
a. Perf. 13½ (#196a) 90.00 35.00
Nos. OD103-OD106 (4) 2.00 1.00

1915
OD107 A88 2c chocolate (#209) .50 .25
OD108 A88 5c red (#212) .50 .25

1916 ***Perf. 13½***
OD109 A91 5c red (#220) .70 .30

1917
OD110 A93 2c brown (#233) .50 .25
OD111 A93 5c red (#236) 4.00 .50
OD112 A94 12c blue (#238) .50 .25
Nos. OD110-OD112 (3) 5.00 1.00

1918
OD113 A93 2c brown (#250) 100.00
OD114 A93 5c red (#253) .50 .25
a. Perf. 13½x12½ (#253B) .70 .25
OD115 A94 12c blue (#255) .70 .25
OD116 A94 20c ultra (#256) 1.00 .50
Nos. OD113-OD116 (4) 2.20 101.00

1920
OD117 A93 1c buff (#265) 3.00 1.00
OD118 A93 2c brown (#266) 4.50 1.50
OD119 A93 5c #269 6.00 1.50
a. Perf. 13½ (#269A) 1.50 .30
OD120 A94 12c blue (perf. 13½) (#271) 1.50 .30
Nos. OD117-OD120 (4) 15.00 4.30

1922
OD121 A94 20c ultra (#312) 40.00 7.00

1923 ***Perf. 13½x12½, 13½***
OD122 A104 1c buff (#324) 20.00 10.00
a. Perf. 13½ (#324A) 2.00 1.00
OD123 A104 2c dark brown (#325) .50 .25
a. Perf. 13½ (#325A) 10.00 1.00
OD124 A104 5c red (#328) .50 .25
a. Inverted ovpt. — 35.00
b. Perf. 13½ (#328A) 1.00 .50
OD125 A104 12c deep blue (#330) .70 .25
a. Perf. 13½ (#330A) 3.00 .30
OD126 A104 20c ultra (#331) .50 .25
a. Perf. 13½ (#331A) 2.50 .30
Nos. OD122-OD126 (5) 22.20 11.00

1924 ***Perf. 13½x12½***
OD127 A104 2c dark brown (#342) 250.00 250.00
OD128 A104 5c red (#345) 1.00 .25
OD130 A104 12c deep blue (#347) 40.00 17.50
OD131 A104 20c ultra (#348) .50 .25
Nos. OD127-OD131 (4) 291.50 268.00

1926
OD134 A110 12c deep blue (#360) 30.00 12.50

No. OD129B

No. OD133B

1931-36 **Type II**
OD127B A104 3c green (#343) 25.00 10.00
OD129B A104 10c dull green (#346) .50 .25
c. Typo (coil) (#346a) .60 .25
OD131B A104 20c ultra (#348) 1.00 .50
c. Typo (coil) (#348a) .50 .25
OD132B A104 30c claret (#351) .50 .25
c. Typo (coil) (#351a) 1.50 .25

Perf. 13
OD133B A105 1p blue & red (#353) 1.00 .50
Nos. OD127B-OD133B (5) 28.00 11.50

No. OD135

1936-38 **Litho.** ***Perf. 13½x13***
OD135 A129 1c buff (#419) .50 .25
OD136 A130 2c dark brown (#420) .50 .25
OD137 A132 3c green (#422) .50 .25
OD138 A134 5c yel brn (Perf. 13½) (#427d) .50 .25
OD139 A137 10c carmine (#430) .50 .30
OD140 A139 15c slate blue (#434) ('36) 2.00 .80
a. Inverted ovpt. — 80.00
OD141 A140 20c lt ultra (#437) 2.50 .25
OD142 A140 20c lt ultra (#438) .50 .25
OD143 A142 30c org brn & yel brown (#442) .50 .25
OD144 A145 1p brn blk & lt bl (#445) 5.00 1.50
OD145 A146 1p brn blk & lt bl (#446) .60 .30
Nos. OD135-OD145 (11) 13.60 4.65

Typo. ***Perf. 13½***
OD138A A134 5c yel brn (#427) .50 .25
b. Inverted ovpt. *50.00 50.00*
OD139A A137 10c car (#430) .50 .25
b. Perf. 13½x13 (#430a) 18.00 1.50

Ministry of the Interior

No. OD147

1913 **Type I** ***Perf. 13½x12½***
OD146 A88 2c chocolate (#181) .90 .30
OD147 A88 1c ocher (#190) .50 .25
OD148 A88 2c chocolate (#191) 2.50 .50
OD149 A88 5c red (#194) 1.00 .40
OD150 A88 12c deep blue (#196) 1.20 .50
a. Perf. 13½ (#196a) 6.00 1.50
Nos. OD146-OD150 (5) 6.10 1.95

1915
OD151 A88 2c chocolate (#209) 2.00 .60
OD152 A88 5c red (#212) 2.00 .60

1916 ***Perf. 13½***
OD153 A91 5c red (#220) 2.00 .80

1918
OD154 A93 5c red (#236B) 5.00 .50
OD155 A93 2c brown (#250) .50 .25
OD156 A93 5c red (#253) .70 .30
a. Perf. 13½x12½ (#253B) .50 .25
Nos. OD154-OD156 (3) 6.20 1.05

1920
OD157 A93 1c buff (13½x12½) (#265) 10.00 3.00
OD158 A93 5c red (#269) 5.00 1.00

1922 ***Perf. 13½***
OD160 A103 5c red (#309) 6.00 2.00
OD161 A94 12c blue (#311) 2.00 .50
OD162 A94 20c ultra (#312) 2.00 .50
Nos. OD160-OD162 (3) 10.00 3.00

1923 ***Perf. 13½x12½***
OD163 A104 1c buff (#324) 1.50 .50
a. Perf. 13½ (#324A) 1.00 .50
OD164 A104 2c dark brown (#325) .50 .25
a. Perf. 13½ (#325A) 50.00 30.00
OD165 A104 5c red (#328) .60 .25
a. Perf. 13½ (#328A) 4.00 .50
OD166 A104 12c deep blue (#330) 6.00 .80
a. Perf. 13½ (#330A) 45.00 20.00
OD167 A104 20c ultra (#331) 9.00 1.00
a. Perf. 13½ (#331A) 7.00 1.00
Nos. OD163-OD167 (5) 17.60 2.80

1924
OD168 A104 1c buff (#341) .50 .25
OD169 A104 2c dk brown (#342) .50 .25
OD170 A104 3c green (#343) 3.00 .60
OD171 A104 5c red (#345) .50 .25
OD173 A104 12c deep blue (#347) 1.00 .25
OD174 A104 20c ultra (#348) 10.00 8.00
Nos. OD168-OD174 (6) 15.50 9.60

No. OD172B

Type II

1931-36 ***Perf. 13½x12½***
OD170B A104 3c green (#343) .70 .25
OD171B A104 5c red (#345) .70 .25
OD172B A104 10c dull green (#346) .50 .25
c. Typo (coil) (#346a) .50 .25
OD174B A104 20c ultra (#348) .50 .25
c. Typo (coil) (#348a) 1.00 .50
OD175B A104 30c claret (#351) 3.00 .50
c. Typo (coil) (#351a) 6.00 2.00
Nos. OD170B-OD175B (5) 5.40 1.50

No. OD182A

1936-38 **Litho.** ***Perf. 13½x13***
OD176 A129 1c buff (#419) .50 .25
OD177 A130 2c dark brown (#420) .50 .25
OD178 A132 3c green (#422) .50 .25
OD178A A134 5c yel brn (#427d) .50 .25
OD180 A139 15c slate bl (#434) ('36) .70 .30
OD181 A140 20c lt ultra (#437) 3.00 .50
OD182 A140 20c lt ultra (#438) .50 .25
OD182A A142 30c org brn & yel brown (#442) .50 .25
OD182B A145 1p brn blk & lt blue (#445) 5.00 2.00
OD182C A146 1p brn blk & lt bl (#446) ('37) .60 .30
Nos. OD176-OD182C (10) 12.30 4.60

Typo. ***Perf. 13½***
OD178D A134 5c yel brn (#427) .60 .25
e. Inverted ovpt. *75.00*
OD179D A137 10c car (#430) .80 .30
e. Perf. 13½x13 (#430a) .50 .25

Ministry of Justice and Instruction

No. OD184

1913 **Type I** ***Perf. 13½x12½***
OD183 A88 2c chocolate (#181) 3.00 .50
OD184 A88 1c ocher (#190) 4.00 .50
OD185 A88 2c chocolate (#191) 2.50 .50
a. Perf. 13½ (#191a) 30.00 10.00
OD186 A88 5c red (#194) 1.00 .50
OD187 A88 12c deep blue (#196) 1.50 .50
Nos. OD184-OD187 (4) 9.00 2.00

1915
OD188 A88 1c ocher (#208) 1.00 .50
OD189 A88 2c chocolate (#209) 1.00 .50
OD190 A88 5c red (#212) 2.00 .80
Nos. OD188-OD190 (3) 4.00 1.80

1916 ***Perf. 13½***
OD191 A91 5c red (#220) 1.00 .50
OD192 A92 12c blue (#222) 2.00 .80

1918
OD193 A93 1c buff (#232) 1.00 .50
a. Perf. 13½x12½ (#232B) 1.00 .50
OD194 A93 2c brown (#233) 4.00 .50
a. Perf. 13½x12½ (#233B) 2.00 .50
OD195 A93 5c red (#236) 9.00 1.00
a. Perf. 13½x12½ (#236B) 1.00 .50
OD196 A94 12c blue (#238) 45.00 10.00
Nos. OD193-OD196 (4) 59.00 12.00

OD197 A93 1c buff (#249) .60 .30
a. Perf. 13½x12½ (#249B) 20.00 7.00
OD198 A93 2c brown (#250) .30 .25
a. Perf. 13½x12½ (#250B) .50 .25
OD199 A93 5c red (#253) .50 .25
a. Perf. 13½x12½ (#253B) .60 .30
OD200 A94 12c blue (#255) .50 .25
OD201 A94 20c ultra (#256) .70 .30
Nos. OD197-OD201 (5) 2.60 1.35

1920 ***Perf. 13½x12½***
OD202 A93 1c buff (#265) .70 .25
OD203 A93 2c brown (#266) .50 .25
OD204 A93 5c red (#269) .50 .25
a. Perf. 13½ (#269A) 8.00 2.50
OD205 A94 12c blue (Perf. 13½) (#271) 1.00 .50
Nos. OD202-OD205 (4) 2.70 1.25

1922 ***Perf. 13½***
OD206 A93 1c buff (#305) 3.00 1.00
a. Perf. 13½x12½ (#305B) .70 .25
OD207 A93 2c brown, perf. 13½x12½ (#306B) 4.00 1.00
OD208 A103 5c red (#309) .70 .25
a. Perf. 13½x12½ (#309B) .50 .25
OD209 A94 12c blue (#311) 20.00 4.00
OD210 A94 20c ultra (#312) 4.00 .60
Nos. OD206-OD210 (5) 31.70 6.85

1922 ***Perf. 13½x12½***
OD211 A93 2c brown (#318A) 3.50 .70

1923
OD212 A104 1c buff (#324) .60 .25
a. Perf. 13½ (#324A) 1.20 .50
OD213 A104 2c dark brown (#325) .50 .25
a. Perf. 13½ (#325A) 1.00 .50
b. As "a," inverted ovpt. 25.00 20.00
OD214 A104 5c red (#328) .50 .25
a. Perf. 13½ (#328A) .50 .25
OD215 A104 12c deep blue (#330) .50 .25
OD216 A104 20c ultra (#331) .50 .25
a. Perf. 13½ (#331A) 1.20 .30
Nos. OD212-OD216 (5) 2.60 1.25

1924
OD218 A104 1c buff (#341) .50 .25
OD219 A104 2c dark brown (#342) .50 .25
OD220 A104 3c green (#343) .60 .25
OD221 A104 5c red (#345) .50 .25
OD222 A104 10c dull green (#346) 1.00 .50
OD223 A104 12c deep blue (#347) .50 .25
OD224 A104 20c ultra (#348) .50 .25
Nos. OD218-OD224 (7) 4.10 2.00

1926
OD227 A109 5c red (#359) .50 .25
a. Inverted ovpt. 35.00 30.00
OD228 A110 12c deep blue (#360) .50 .25

No. OD217B

Type II

1931-36 *Perf. 13½x12½, 13*

OD217B A104 ½c red violet (#340) 5.00 2.00
OD218B A104 1c buff (#341) .50 .25
OD220B A104 3c green (#343) .50 .25
c. Typo (coil) (#343b) .50 .25
OD221B A104 5c red (#345) .50 .25
OD222B A104 10c dull green (#346) .50 .25
c. Typo (coil) (#346a) .50 .25
OD223B A104 12c deep blue (#347) 1.20 .30
OD224B A104 20c ultra (#348) .50 .25
c. Typo (coil) (#348a) .50 .25
OD225B A104 30c claret (#351) .50 .25
c. Typo (coil) (#351a) 1.30 .50
OD226B A105 1p blue & red (Perf. 13½) (#353) 1.00 .50
Nos. OD217B-OD226B (9) 10.20 4.30

No. OD229

1936-38 *Perf. 13½x13*

OD229 A129 1c buff (#419) .50 .25
OD230 A130 2c dark brown (#420) .50 .25
OD231 A132 3c green (#422) .50 .25
OD232 A134 5c yel brn (#427d) .50 .25
OD234 A139 15c slate bl (#434) 1.00 .25
OD234A A140 20c lt ultra (#437) .50 .25
OD234B A140 20c lt ultra (#438) .60 .25
OD234C A141 25c car & pink (#441) .50 .25
OD234D A142 30c org brn & yel brown (#442) .50 .25
OD234E A145 1p brn blk &l lt bl (#445) 2.00 .60
OD234F A146 1p brn blk &l lt bl (#446) 3.00 .30
Nos. OD229-OD234F (11) 10.10 3.15

Typo. *Perf. 13½*

OD232A A134 5c yel brn (#427) .50 .25
OD233 A137 10c car (#430) .50 .25
a. Perf. 13½x13 (#430a) .50 .25

Ministry of Marine

No. OD236

1913 **Type I** *Perf. 13½x12½*

OD235 A88 2c chocolate (#181) .60 .25
a. Perf. 13½ (#181a) 150.00 75.00
OD236 A88 1c ocher (#190) .50 .25
OD237 A88 2c chocolate (#191) 8.00 .50
OD238 A88 5c red (#194) .50 .25
a. Perf. 13½ (#194a) 40.00 8.00
OD239 A88 12c deep blue (#196) .60 .30
Nos. OD236-OD239 (4) 9.60 1.30

1915

OD240 A88 2c chocolate (#209) 3.00 .50
OD241 A88 5c red (#212) 2.00 .25

1918

OD242 A93 1c buff (#232) .70 .30
OD243 A93 2c brown (#233) .70 .25
OD244 A93 5c red (#236) .70 .25
a. Perf. 13½ (#236B) 1.00 .50
Nos. OD242-OD244 (3) 2.10 .80

1920 *Perf. 13½*

OD245 A93 1c buff (#249) .50 .25
OD246 A93 2c brown (#250) .70 .25
a. Perf. 13½x12½ (#250) 1.00 .50
OD247 A93 5c red (#253) 3.50 .25
a. Perf. 13½x12½ (#253B) .60 .25
OD248 A94 12c blue (#255) 2.50 .30
OD249 A94 20c ultra (#256) 8.00 1.50
Nos. OD245-OD249 (5) 15.20 2.55

1920

OD250 A93 1c buff Perf. 13½x12½ (#265A) .50 .25
OD251 A93 2c brown (#266A) .70 .30
a. Perf. 13½x12½ (#266) .80 .30
OD252 A93 5c red (#269A) .80 .25
Nos. OD250-OD252 (3) 2.00 .80

1922

OD253 A103 5c red (#309) 3.00 .50
a. Perf. 13½x12½ (#309B) 1.50 .30
OD254 A94 12c blue (#311) 30.00 10.00
OD255 A94 20c ultra (#312) 45.00 8.00
Nos. OD253-OD255 (3) 78.00 18.50

1923 *Perf. 13½x12½*

OD256 A104 1c buff (#324) .50 .25
a. Perf. 13½ (#324A) 87.50 50.00
OD257 A104 2c dark brown (#325) 1.00 .50
a. Inverted overprint — 75.00
b. Perf. 13½ (#325A) 1.00 .50
OD258 A104 5c red (#328) 2.50 .25
a. Inverted overprint — 75.00
b. Perf. 13½ (#328A) 15.00 2.00
c. As "b," inverted overprint — 75.00
OD259 A104 12c deep blue (#330) 1.20 .40
a. Perf. 13½ (#330A) 10.00 1.50
OD260 A104 20c ultra (#331) 2.00 .40
a. Perf. 13½ (#331A) 3.50 1.00
Nos. OD256-OD260 (5) 7.20 1.80

1924

OD261 A104 1c buff (#341) 3.00 1.00
OD262 A104 2c dk brown (#342) .50 .25
OD264 A104 5c red (#345) .50 .25
OD266 A104 20c ultra (#348) 3.50 .25
Nos. OD261-OD266 (4) 7.50 1.75

1926

OD269 A109 5c red (#359) .50 .25

No. OD264B

Type II

1931-36 *Perf. 13½x12½, 13*

OD263B A104 3c green (#343) 1.50 .40
OD264B A104 5c red (#345) 1.50 .25
OD265B A104 10c dull green (#346) 2.00 .50
c. Typo (coil) (#346a) .60 .25
OD266B A104 20c ultra (#348) 7.00 1.00
c. Typo (coil) (#348a) 5.00 .50
OD267B A104 30c claret (#351) 3.00 .50
OD268B A105 1p blue & red (Perf. 13½) (#353) 40.00 20.00

No. OD270

1936-38 *Perf. 13½x13*

OD270 A129 1c buff (#419) .50 .25
OD271 A130 2c dark brown (#420) .50 .25
OD272 A132 3c green (#422) .50 .25
OD273 A134 5c yel brn (#427d) .50 .25
OD275 A139 15c slate bl (#434) ('36) 1.00 .30
OD276 A140 20c lt ultra (#437) 1.20 .30
OD277 A140 20c lt ultra (#438) 1.00 .30
OD278 A142 30c org brn & yel brn (#442) ('36) .60 .25
OD279 A145 1p brn blk & lt bl (#445) ('36) 8.00 2.00
OD280 A146 1p brn blk & lt bl (#446) ('37) 2.00 .50
Nos. OD270-OD280 (10) 15.80 4.65

Typo. *Perf. 13½*

OD273A A134 5c yel brn (#427) .50 .25
b. Inverted overprint 25.00 25.00
OD274A A137 10c car (#430) 2.00 .25
b. Perf. 13½x13 (#430a) .60 .25

Ministry of Public Works

No. OD281

1913 **Type I** *Perf. 13½x12½*

OD281 A88 2c chocolate (#181) 1.00 .25
a. Perf. 13½ (#181a) 4.00 1.00
OD282 A88 1c ocher (#190) 1.00 .25
OD283 A88 5c red (#194) .80 .25
OD284 A88 12c deep blue (#196) 5.00 1.00
a. Perf. 13½ (#196a) 15.00 6.00
Nos. OD282-OD284 (3) 6.80 1.50

1916 *Perf. 13½*

OD285 A91 5c red (#220) 35.00 10.00

1918 *Perf. 13½x12½*

OD286 A93 2c brown (#233) 30.00 20.00
OD287 A93 5c red (#236) 18.00 9.00

1920 *Perf. 13½*

OD288 A93 2c brown (#266) 35.00 8.00
OD289 A93 5c red (#269) 5.00 1.00
OD290 A94 12c blue (#271) 50.00 20.00
Nos. OD288-OD290 (3) 90.00 29.00

1923 *Perf. 13½x12½*

OD291 A104 1c buff (#324) .60 .25
a. Perf. 13½ (#324A) 40.00 15.00
OD292 A104 2c dark brown (#325) .50 .25
a. Perf. 13½ (#325A) .80 .25
OD293 A104 5c red (#328) .60 .30
a. Perf. 13½ (#328A) .80 .25
OD294 A104 12c deep blue (#330) .80 .30
a. Perf. 13½ (#330A) 2.00 .50
OD295 A104 20c ultra #331 2.00 .50
a. Perf. 13½ (#331A) 2.50 .50
Nos. OD291-OD295 (5) 4.50 1.60

No. OD299

1924

OD296 A104 1c buff (#341) .50 .25
OD297 A104 2c dk brown (#342) .50 .25
OD299 A104 5c red (#345) .50 .25
OD301 A104 12c deep blue (#347) 30.00 8.00
OD302 A104 20c ultra (#348) .50 .25
Nos. OD296-OD302 (5) 32.00 9.00

1926

OD305 A109 5c red (#359) .60 .25

Type II

1931-36 *Perf. 13½x12½, 13*

OD298B A104 3c green (#343) .50 .25
c. Typo (coil) (#343b) 25.00 5.00
OD299B A109 5c red (#345) .60 .25
OD300B A104 10c dull green (#346) .60 .25
c. Typo (coil) (#346a) 2.00 .25
OD301B A104 20c ultra typo (coil) (#348b) 50.00 10.00
OD303B A104 30c claret (#351) 1.00 .25
OD304B A105 1p blue & red (13½) (#353) 70.00 20.00
Nos. OD298B-OD304B (6) 122.70 31.00

No. OD307

1936-38 *Perf. 13½x13*

OD306 A129 1c buff (#419) .50 .25
OD307 A130 2c dark brown (#420) .50 .25
OD308 A132 3c green (#422) .50 .25
OD309 A134 5c yel brn (#427d) .50 .25
OD311 A139 15c slate bl (#434) 1.50 .25
OD312 A140 20c lt ultra (#437) 2.00 .30
OD313 A140 20c lt ultra (#438) .50 .25
OD314 A142 30c org brn & yel brown (#442) ('36) .60 .25
OD315 A144 50c red & org (#444) ('36) .60 .30
OD316 A145 1p brn blk & lt bl (#445) ('36) 4.00 1.00
OD317 A146 1p brn blk & lt bl (#446) ('37) 1.20 .40
Nos. OD306-OD317 (11) 12.40 3.75

Typo. *Perf. 13½*

OD309A A134 5c yel brn (#427) .60 .25
b. Inverted overprint — 75.00
OD310 A137 10c car (#430) 1.00 .30
a. Perf. 13½x13 (#430a) 1.00 .30

Ministry of Foreign Affairs and Religion

No. OD318

1913 **Type I** *Perf. 13½x12½*

OD318 A88 2c chocolate (#181) 45.00 9.00
OD319 A88 1c ocher (#190) .50 .25
OD320 A88 2c chocolate (#191) .50 .25
OD321 A88 5c red (#194) 1.20 .30
OD322 A88 12c deep blue (#196) .60 .25
a. Perf. 13½ (#196a) 50.00 20.00
Nos. OD319-OD322 (4) 2.80 1.05

1915

OD323 A88 5c red (#212) 1.00 .50

1916 *Perf. 13½*

OD324 A91 5c red (#220) 1.20 .50

1918

OD325 A94 20c ultra (#256) 5.00 2.00

1922

OD326 A93 1c buff, perf. 13½x12½ (#265) 1.00 .40
OD327 A93 5c red (#269) .50 .30

1922-23 *Perf. 13½x12½*

OD328 A93 2c brown (#306) 40.00 15.00
OD329 A103 5c red (#309B) 100.00

Perf. 13½

OD330 A93 12c blue (#311) 100.00
OD330A A94 20c ultra (#312) 100.00

1923 *Perf. 13½x12½*

OD331 A104 1c buff (#324) .60 .30
a. Perf. 13½ (#324A) 25.00 10.00
OD332 A104 2c dark brown (#325) .50 .25
a. Perf. 13½ (#325A) 5.00 2.00
OD333 A104 5c red (#328) .50 .25
a. Perf. 13½ (#328A) 2.00 .30
OD334 A104 12c deep blue (#330) .50 .25
a. Perf. 13½ (#330A) 1.50 .50
OD335 A104 20c ultra (#331) .50 .25
Nos. OD331-OD335 (5) 2.60 1.30

No. OD344

1924

OD337 A104 1c buff (#341) .60 .25
OD338 A104 2c dark brown (#342) .50 .25
OD339 A104 3c green (#343) .50 .25
OD340 A104 5c red (#345) .50 .25
OD341 A104 10c dull green (#346) 4.00 .50
OD342 A104 12c deep blue (#347) .60 .30
OD343 A104 20c ultra (#348) .60 .30
OD344 A104 30c claret (#351) .70 .30
Nos. OD337-OD344 (8) 8.00 2.40

1926

OD346 A110 12c deep blue (#360) .50 .25

Type II

1931-36 ***Perf. 13½x12½, 13½***

OD336B A104 ½c red violet (#340) 2.50 1.00
OD341B A104 10c dull green (#346) .60 .30
OD343B A104 20c ultra (typo, coil) (#348a) .60 .30
OD344B A104 30c claret (typo, coil) (#351a) .60 .30
OD345B A105 1p blue & red, perf. 13½ (#353) .60 .30
Nos. OD336B-OD345B (5) 4.90 2.20

No. OD347

1935-37 **Typo.** ***Perf. 13x13½***

OD347 A129 1c buff (#419) .50 .25
OD348 A130 2c dark brown (#420) .50 .25
OD349 A132 3c green (#422) .50 .25
OD350 A134 5c yel brn #427d .50 .25
OD352 A139 15c slate bl (#434) .70 .30
OD353 A140 20c lt ultra (#437) 1.00 .50
OD354 A140 20c lt ultra #438 .50 .25
OD355 A142 30c org brown & yel brown (#442) .50 .25
OD356 A145 1p brn blk & lt bl (#445) 6.00 2.50
OD357 A146 1p brn blk & lt bl (#446) .70 .50
Nos. OD347-OD357 (10) 11.40 5.30

Typo. ***Perf. 13½***

OD350B A134 5c yel brn (#427) .60 .25
OD351B A137 10c car (#430) .50 .25
c. Perf. 13½x13 (#430a) 2.00 .25

PARCEL POST STAMPS

PP1

Postal Service Headquarters, Buenos Aires — PP2

2001 **Litho.** ***Serpentine Die Cut 11***
Self-Adhesive

Q1 PP1 1p red & black *20.00 20.00*

Die Cut

Q1A PP1 1p red & black *40.00 20.00*
Q2 PP2 7p blue & black *25.00 20.00*
Q3 PP2 11p brown & black *35.00 30.00*
Nos. Q1-Q3 (3) *80.00 70.00*

Nos. Q1-Q3 were sold only at Unidas Postal outlets. No. Q3 is inscribed "Caja Envio 2."

Stamps of Type PP2 lacking "U.P." in denominations of 7p, 11p, 16p, and 23p were issued in 1999, but were applied by postal workers to packages brought to post offices by customers with large mailings (Grandes Clientes). These stamps were not to be given to any customers purchasing them. Value, set unused $180.

The same sale and use restrictions applied to three other non-denominated stamps for use by "Grandes Clientes," which are inscribed "Caja Normalizada," have blue, brown violet and ocher frames, and were issued in 1995. Value, set unused $550.

Nos. Q2 and Q3, though inscribed "Grandes Clientes," apparently were available for purchase by any customers, at Unidas Postal outlets.

BUENOS AIRES

The central point of the Argentine struggle for independence. At intervals Buenos Aires maintained an independent government but after 1862 became a province of the Argentine Republic.

8 Reales = 1 Peso

Values of Buenos Aires Nos. 1-8 vary according to condition. Quotations are for fine examples. Very fine to superb specimens sell at much higher prices, and inferior or poor stamps sell at reduced values, depending on the condition of the individual specimen.

Nos. 1-8 are normally found without gum, and the values below are for such items. Examples with original gum sell for higher prices.

Steamship — A1

1858 **Unwmk.** **Typo.** ***Imperf.***

1 A1 1 (in) pesos lt brn *500.00* *300.*
a. Double impression 700.
2 A1 2 (dos) pesos blue 300.00 150.
b. Diag. half used as 1p on cover *7,500.*
3 A1 3 (tres) pesos grn 1,500. *950.*
a. 3p dark green 2,000. *1,500.*
4 A1 4 (cuatro) pesos ver 5,000. *4,500.*
a. Half used as 2p on cover *25,000.*
b. 4p chestnut brown (error) *30,000.* *40,000.*
5 A1 5 (cinco) pesos org 5,000. *3,000.*
a. 5p ocher 5,000. *3,000.*
b. 5p olive yellow 5,000. *3,000.*

Issued: Nos. 2-5, Apr. 29; No. 1, Oct. 26.

1858, Oct. 26

6 A1 4 (cuatro) reales brown 350.00 300.
a. 4r gray brown 400.00 300.
b. 4r chestnut 350.00 300.

1859, Jan. 1

7 A1 1 (in) pesos blue 200. *100.*
a. 1p indigo 300. *150.*
b. Impression on reverse of stamp in blue *28,500.*
c. Double impression 2,800. *700.*
d. Vert. tête-bêche pair *675,000.*
e. Horiz. tête-bêche pair —
f. Half used as 4r on cover *7,500.*
8 A1 1 (to) pesos blue 600. 325.

No. 7e is valued with faults.

Nos. 1, 2, 3 and 7 have been reprinted on very thick, hand-made paper. The same four stamps and No. 8 have been reprinted on thin, hard, white wove paper.

Counterfeits of Nos. 1-8 are plentiful.

Liberty Head — A2

1859, Sept. 3

9 A2 4r green, *bluish* 400.00 275.00
10 A2 1p blue, fine impression 40.00 30.00
d. Double impression 600.00 400.00
e. Partial double impression 325.00 175.00
11 A2 2p vermilion, fine impression 500.00 300.00
a. 2p red, blurred impression 375.00 125.00
b. Vert. half used as 1p on cover *4,000.*

Both fine and blurred impressions of these stamps may be found. They have generally been called Paris and Local prints, respectively, but the opinion now obtains that the differences are due to the impression and that they do not represent separate issues. Values are for fine impressions. Rough or blurred impressions sell for less.

Many shades exist of Nos. 1-11.

1862, Oct. 4

12 A2 1p rose 350.00 150.00
13 A2 2p blue 350.00 90.00

All three values have been reprinted in black, brownish black, blue and red brown on thin hard white paper. The 4r has also been reprinted in green on bluish paper.

Values are for fine impressions. Rough or blurred impressions sell for less.

No. 13 exists with papermaker's wmk.

CORDOBA

A province in the central part of the Argentine Republic.

100 Centavos = 1 Peso

Arms of Cordoba — A1

Unwmk.

1858, Oct. 28 **Litho.** ***Imperf.***
Laid Paper

1 A1 5c blue 150.
2 A1 10c black *3,000.*

Cordoba stamps were printed on laid paper, but stamps from edges of the sheets sometimes do not show any laid lines and appear to be on wove paper. Counterfeits are plentiful.

CORRIENTES

The northeast province of the Argentine Republic.

1 Real M(oneda) C(orriente) =
12½ Centavos M.C. = 50 Centavos
100 Centavos Fuertes = 1 Peso Fuerte

Nos. 1-2 were issued without gum. Nos. 3-8 were issued both with and without gum (values the same).

Ceres

A1 A2

Unwmk.

1856, Aug. 21 **Typo.** ***Imperf.***

1 A1 1r black, *blue* 100.00 *40.00*

No. 1 used is valued with pen cancellation.

Pen Stroke Through "Un Real"

1860, Feb. 8

2 A1 (3c) black, *blue* 600.00 *120.00*

No. 2 used is valued with pen cancellation.

1860-80

3 A2 (3c) black, *blue* 9.50 *30.00*
4 A2 (2c) blk, *yel grn* ('64) 50.00 *100.00*
a. (2c) black, *blue green* 92.50 *150.00*
5 A2 (2c) blk, *yel* ('67) 7.50 *19.00*
6 A2 (3c) blk, *dk bl* ('71) 3.00 *19.00*
7 A2 (3c) blk, *rose red* ('76) 150.00 70.00
a. (3c) black, *lil rose* ('75) 200.00 100.00
8 A2 (3c) blk, *dk rose* ('79) 8.00 *35.00*
a. (3c) black, *red vio* ('77) 75.00 50.00
Nos. 3-8 (6) 228.00 273.00

Pen canceled examples of Nos. 3-8 that do not indicate the town of origin sell for much less.

Printed from settings of 8 varieties, 3 or 4 impressions constituting a sheet. Some impressions were printed inverted and tete beche pairs may be cut from adjacent impressions.

From Jan. 1 to Feb. 24, 1864, No. 4 was used as a 5 centavos stamp but examples so used can only be distinguished when they bear dated cancellations.

The reprints show numerous spots and small defects which are not found on the originals. They are printed on gray blue, dull blue, gray green, dull orange and light magenta papers.

ARMENIA

är-'mē-nē-ə

LOCATION — South of Russia bounded by Georgia, Azerbaijan, Iran and Turkey
GOVT. — Republic
AREA — 11,490 sq. mi.
POP. — 3,409,234 (est. 1999)
CAPITAL — Yerevan

With Azerbaijan and Georgia, Armenia made up the Transcaucasian Federation of Soviet Republics.

Stamps of Armenia were replaced in 1923 by those of Transcaucasian Federated Republics.

With the breakup of the Soviet Union on Dec. 26, 1991, Armenia and ten former Soviet republics established the Commonwealth of Independent States.

100 Kopecks = 1 Ruble
100 Luma = 1 Dram (1993)

Catalogue values for unused stamps in this country are for Never Hinged items, beginning with Scott 430 in the regular postage section.

Counterfeits abound of all overprinted and surcharged stamps.

Watermark

Wmk. 171 — Diamonds

Perforations
Perforations are the same as the basic Russian stamps.

National Republic

Russian Stamps of 1902-19 Handstamped

At least thirteen types exist of both framed and unframed overprints ("a" and "c"). The device is the Armenian "H," initial of Hayasdan (Armenia). Inverted and double overprints are found.

Surcharged

Type I — Without periods (two types).
Type II — Periods after 1st "K" and "60."

Black Surcharge

1919 Unwmk. *Perf. 14x14½*

1 A14 60k on 1k orange (II) 2.75 2.75
a. Imperf. (I) 5.00 5.00
b. Imperf. (II) 1.25 1.25

Violet Surcharge

2 A14 60k on 1k orange (II) 1.00 1.00

Handstamped in Violet
a

Perf.

6 A15 4k carmine 3.50 3.50
7 A14 5k claret, imperf. 9.00 9.00
a. Perf. 8.00 6.00
9 A14 10k on 7k lt blue 6.00 6.00
10 A11 15k red brn & bl 3.50 3.50
11 A8 20k blue & car 2.50 2.50
13 A11 35k red brn & grn 4.75 4.75
14 A8 50k violet & green 4.25 4.25
15 A14 60k on 1k orange (II) 3.50 3.50
a. Imperf. (I) 6.00 6.00
b. Imperf. (II) 10.00 10.00
18 A13 5r dk bl, grn & pale bl 18.00 18.00
a. Imperf. 9.00 9.00
19 A12 7r dk green & pink 35.00 15.00
20 A13 10r scar, yel & gray 40.00 15.00

Handstamped in Black

31 A14 2k green, imperf. 3.00 3.00
a. Perf. 6.00 6.00
32 A14 3k red, imperf. 3.00 3.00
a. Perf. 10.00 10.00
33 A15 4k carmine 5.00 5.00
a. Imperf. 10.00 10.00
34 A14 5k claret 1.25 1.25
a. Imperf. 10.00 10.00
36 A15 10k dark blue 2.50 2.50
37 A14 10k on 7k lt blue 2.00 *5.00*
38 A11 15k red brn & bl 1.00 *5.00*
a. Imperf. 5.00 *15.00*
39 A8 20k blue & car 2.00 *5.00*
40 A11 25k green & gray vio 2.00 *5.00*
41 A11 35k red brn & grn 2.00 *4.00*
42 A8 50k violet & green 3.00 *5.00*
43 A14 60k on 1k orange (II) 5.00 5.00
43A A11 70k brown & org 3.00 3.00
b. Imperf. 2.00 *4.00*
44 A9 1r pale brn, dk brn & org 3.00 *5.00*
a. Imperf. 8.00 8.00
45 A12 3½r mar & lt grn, imperf. 3.00 *6.00*
a. Perf. 6.00 6.00
46 A13 5r dk bl, grn & pale bl 6.00 6.00
a. Imperf. 10.00 10.00
47 A12 7r dk green & pink 7.25 7.25
48 A13 10r scar, yel & gray 35.00 *50.00*

Handstamped in Violet
c

Unwmk. *Perf.*
Wove Paper

62 A14 2k green, imperf. 12.00 12.00
a. Perf. 18.00 18.00
63 A14 3k red, imperf. 2.50 2.50
a. Perf. 15.00 15.00
64 A15 4k carmine 10.00 10.00
65 A14 5k claret 3.50 3.50
a. Imperf. 3.50 3.50
67 A15 10k dark blue 5.00 *10.00*
68 A14 10k on 7k lt bl 3.50 3.50
69 A11 15k red brn & bl 3.00 *5.00*
70 A8 20k blue & car 3.00 *5.00*
71 A11 25k grn & gray vio 7.50 *15.00*
72 A11 35k red brn & grn 15.00 14.00
73 A8 50k violet & grn 5.00 *10.00*
74 A14 60k on 1k org (II) 6.00 *8.00*
a. Imperf. (I) 6.00 *8.00*
b. Imperf. (II) 6.00 *8.00*
75 A9 1r pale brn, dk brn & org 12.50 12.50
a. Imperf. 10.00 10.00
76 A12 3½r mar & lt grn, imperf. 5.00 5.00
a. Perf. 6.00 6.00
77 A13 5r dk bl, grn & pale bl, imperf. 12.50 12.50
a. Perf. 8.00 8.00
78 A12 7r dk green & pink 20.00 20.00
79 A13 10r scar, yel & gray 20.00 20.00

Imperf

85 A11 70k brown & org 6.00 6.00

Handstamped in Black

Perf.

90 A14 1k orange 8.00 8.00
a. Imperf. 10.00 10.00
91 A14 2k green, imperf. 1.25 1.25
a. Perf. 8.00 8.00
92 A14 3k red, imperf. 5.00 *10.00*
a. Perf. 2.00 2.00
93 A15 4k carmine 3.00 3.00
94 A14 5k claret 1.25 1.25
a. Imperf. 3.50 *5.00*
95 A14 7k light blue 10.00 *15.00*
96 A15 10k dark blue 10.00 *15.00*
97 A14 10k on 7k lt bl 1.00 *2.00*
98 A11 15k red brn & bl 2.00 *4.00*
99 A8 20k blue & car 1.75 *3.00*
100 A11 25k grn & gray vio 2.00 *5.00*
101 A11 35k red brn & grn 2.00 *4.00*
102 A8 50k violet & grn 2.00 *5.00*
102A A14 60k on 1k org, imperf. (I) 5.00 *5.00*
b. Imperf. (II) 5.00 *10.00*
c. Perf. (II) 5.00 5.00
103 A9 1r pale brn, dk brn & org 2.00 *5.00*
a. Imperf. 2.00 *5.00*
104 A12 3½r maroon & lt grn 4.75 8.00
a. Imperf. 15.00 15.00
105 A13 5r dk bl, grn & pale bl 15.00 15.00
a. Imperf. 6.00 6.00
106 A12 7r dk green & pink 5.00 *10.00*
107 A13 10r scar, yel & gray 20.00 *45.00*

Imperf

113 A11 70k brown & org 2.50 *4.00*

Handstamped in Violet or Black

f

g

Violet Surcharge, Type f

1920 *Perf.*

120 A14 3r on 3k red, imperf. 10.00 15.00
a. Perf. 10.00 15.00
121 A14 5r on 3k red 10.00 10.00
122 A15 5r on 4k car 10.00 *12.00*
123 A14 5r on 5k claret, imperf. 5.00 *12.00*
a. Perf. 12.00 *20.00*
124 A15 5r on 10k dk blue 20.00 *30.00*
125 A14 5r on 10k on 7k lt bl 20.00 *30.00*
126 A8 5r on 20k bl & car 10.00 *15.00*

Imperf

127 A14 5r on 2k green 12.00 12.00
128 A11 5r on 35k red brn & grn 12.00 12.00

Black Surcharge, Type f or Type g (#130)

Perf.

130 A14 1r on 1k orange 10.00 12.00
a. Imperf. 15.00 15.00
131 A14 3r on 3k red 10.00 10.00
a. Imperf. 5.00 5.00
132 A15 3r on 4k carmine 25.00 25.00
133 A14 5r on 2k grn, imperf. 2.50 2.50
a. Perf. 5.00 5.00
134 A14 5r on 3k red 10.00 10.00
a. Imperf. 5.00 5.00
135 A15 5r on 4k carmine 4.00 4.00
a. Imperf. 10.00 10.00
136 A14 5r on 5k claret 4.00 4.00
a. Imperf. 2.00 2.00
137 A14 5r on 7k lt blue 3.00 3.00
138 A15 5r on 10k dk blue 2.00 2.00
139 A14 5r on 10k on 7k lt bl 2.00 2.00
140 A11 5r on 14k bl & rose 2.50 2.50
141 A11 5r on 15k red brn & blue 1.00 1.00
a. Imperf. 2.50 2.50
142 A8 5r on 20k bl & car 1.00 *5.00*
a. Imperf. 30.00 30.00
143 A11 5r on 20k on 14k bl & rose 75.00 *100.00*
144 A11 5r on 25k grn & gray vio 10.00 *15.00*

Black Surcharge, Type g or Type f (#148A, 151)

145 A14 10r on 1k org, imperf. 1.10 1.10
a. Perf. *125.00 125.00*
146 A14 10r on 3k red *175.00 175.00*
147 A14 10r on 5k claret 18.00 18.00
a. Imperf. 15.00
148 A8 10r on 20k bl & car 15.00 15.00
148A A11 10r on 25k grn & gray vio 10.00 10.00
149 A11 10r on 25k grn & gray vio 5.00 *6.00*
a. Imperf. 10.00 *20.00*
150 A11 10r on 35k red brn & grn 2.00 2.00
151 A8 10r on 50k brn vio & grn 50.00 50.00
152 A8 10r on 50k brn vio & grn 3.00 *4.00*
152A A11 10r on 70k brn & org, imperf. 5.00 5.00
b. Perf. *240.00 240.00*
152C A8 25r on 20k bl & car 4.75 4.75
153 A11 25r on 25k grn & gray vio 5.00 5.00
154 A11 25r on 35k red brn & grn 20.00 20.00
a. Imperf. 4.00 4.00
155 A8 25r on 50k vio & grn 5.00 5.00
a. Imperf. 6.00 6.00
156 A11 25r on 70k brn & org 8.00 8.00
a. Imperf. 5.00 5.00
157 A9 50r on 1r pale brn, dk brn & org, imperf. 2.00 2.00
a. Perf. 10.00 *15.00*
158 A13 50r on 5r dk bl, grn & lt bl 25.00 25.00
a. Imperf. 45.00 45.00
159 A12 100r on 3½r mar & lt grn 10.00 *15.00*
a. Imperf. 10.00 10.00
160 A13 100r on 5r dk bl, grn & pale bl 12.00 12.00
a. Imperf. 25.00 25.00
161 A12 100r on 7r dk grn & pink 12.00 15.00
a. Imperf. 42.00 42.00
162 A13 100r on 10r scar, yel & gray 15.00 20.00

Wmk. Wavy Lines (168)
Perf. 11½
Vertically Laid Paper

163 A12 100r on 3½r blk & gray *120.00 120.00*
164 A12 100r on 7r blk & yel *120.00 120.00*

1920 Unwmk. *Imperf.*
Wove Paper

166 A14 (g) 1r on 60k on 1k org (I) 12.00 14.50
168 A14 (f) 5r on 1k orange 12.00 12.00
173 A11 (f) 5r on 35k red brn & grn 12.00 12.00
177 A11 (g) 50r on 70k brn & org 6.00 10.00
179 A12 (g) 50r on 3½r mar & lt grn 20.00 20.00
181 A9 (g) 100r on 1r pale brn, dk brn & org 20.00 20.00

Romanov Issues Surcharged Type g or Type f (#185-187, 190) on Stamps of 1913

1920 *Perf. 13½*

184 A16 1r on 1k brn org 175.00 175.00
185 A18 3r on 3k rose red 24.00 24.00
186 A19 5r on 4k dull red 12.00 12.00
187 A22 5r on 14k blue grn 50.00 50.00
187A A19 10r on 4k dull red 40.00
187B A26 10r on 35k gray vio & dk grn
187C A19 25r on 4k dull red 20.00 20.00
188 A26 25r on 35k gray vio & dk grn 3.25 3.25
189 A28 25r on 70k yel grn & brn 3.25 3.25
190 A31 50r on 3r dk vio 2.50 2.50
190A A16 100r on 1k brn org 125.00 125.00
190B A17 100r on 2k green 125.00 125.00
191 A30 100r on 2r brown 12.50 12.50
192 A31 100r on 3r dk vio 12.50 12.50

On Stamps of 1915, Type g
Thin Cardboard
Inscriptions on Back
Perf. 12

193 A21 100r on 10k blue 20.00
194 A23 100r on 15k brn 20.00
195 A24 100r on 20k ol grn 18.00

On Stamps of 1916, Type f
Perf. 13½

196 A20 5r on 10k on 7k brown 8.00 8.00
197 A22 5r on 20k on 14k bl grn 15.00 25.00

Srch. Type f or Type g (#204-205A, 207-207C, 210-211) over Type c
Type c in Violet
Perf.

200 A15 5r on 4k car 6.00 *8.00*
201 A15 5r on 10k dk bl 25.00 25.00
202 A11 5r on 15k red brn & bl 5.00 5.00
203 A8 5r on 20k blue & car 10.00 10.00
204 A11 10r on 25k grn & gray vio 12.00 12.00
205 A11 10r on 35k red brn & grn 3.50 3.50
205A A8 10r on 50k brn vio & grn 12.00 12.00
206 A8 25r on 50k brn vio & grn 150.00 150.00
207 A9 50r on 1r pale brn, dk brn & org, imperf. 30.00 30.00
a. Perf. 30.00 30.00
207B A12 100r on 3½r mar & lt grn 50.00 50.00
207C A12 100r on 7r dk grn & pink 60.00 60.00

Imperf

208 A14 5r on 2k green 30.00 30.00
209 A14 5r on 5k claret 30.00 30.00
210 A11 25r on 70k brn & org 40.00 *50.00*
211 A13 100r on 5r dk bl, grn & pale bl 100.00 *110.00*

Surcharged Type g or Type f (212-213, 215, 219-219A, 221-222) over Type c

Type c in Black

Perf.

No.	Type	Description	Unused	Used
212	A14	5r on 7k lt bl	150.00	150.00
213	A14	5r on 10k on 7k lt bl	6.00	6.00
214	A11	5r on 15k red brn & bl	5.00	*7.00*
215	A8	5r on 20k blue & car	3.50	3.50
215A	A11	10r on 5r on 25k grn & gray vio	50.00	50.00
216	A11	10r on 35k red brn & grn	50.00	*60.00*
217	A8	10r on 50k brn vio & grn	12.00	*15.00*
217A	A9	50r on 1r pale brn, dk brn & org	35.00	*50.00*
b.		Imperf.	40.00	*50.00*
217C	A12	100r on 3½r mar & lt grn	30.00	30.00
218	A13	100r on 5r dk bl, grn & pale bl	35.00	*40.00*
a.		Imperf.	45.00	*55.00*
219	A12	100r on 7r dk grn & pink	35.00	*50.00*
219A	A13	100r on 10r scar, yel & gray	45.00	*55.00*

Imperf

No.	Type	Description	Unused	Used
220	A14	1r on 60k on 1k org (I)	35.00	35.00
221	A14	5r on 2k green	6.00	6.00
222	A14	5r on 5k claret	10.00	*12.00*
223	A11	10r on 70k brn & org	30.00	*40.00*
224	A11	25r on 70k brn & org	25.00	*30.00*

Surcharged Type g or Type f (#233) over Type a

Type a in Violet

Imperf

No.	Type	Description	Unused	Used
231	A9	50r on 1r pale brn, dk brn & org	170.00	170.00
232	A13	100r on 5r dk bl, grn & pale bl	100.00	*110.00*

Type a in Black

Perf.

No.	Type	Description	Unused	Used
233	A8	5r on 20k blue & car	6.00	6.00
233A	A11	10r on 25k grn & gray vio	20.00	20.00
234	A11	10r on 35k red brn & grn	175.00	175.00
235	A12	100r on 3½r mar & lt grn	10.00	10.00
a.		Imperf.	10.00	10.00

Imperf

No.	Type	Description	Unused	Used
237	A14	5r on 2k green	150.00	150.00
237A	A11	10r on 70k brn & org		

Surcharged Type a and New Value

Type a in Violet

Perf.

No.	Type	Description	Unused	Used
238	A11	10r on 15k red brn & blue	30.00	30.00

Type a in Black

No.	Type	Description	Unused	Used
239	A8	5r on 20k blue & car	4.00	5.00
239A	A8	10r on 20k blue & car	*20.00*	*20.00*
239B	A8	10r on 50k brn red & grn	*30.00*	*40.00*

Imperf

No.	Type	Description	Unused	Used
240	A12	100r on 3½r mar & lt grn	50.00	*60.00*

Surcharged Type c and New Value

Type c in Black

1920

Perf.

No.	Type	Description	Unused	Used
241	A15	5r on 4k red	6.00	*8.00*
242	A11	5r on 15k red brn & bl	4.00	*6.00*
243	A8	10r on 20k blue & car	*20.00*	*20.00*
243A	A11	10r on 25k grn & gray vio	12.00	*15.00*
244	A11	10r on 35k red brn & grn	45.00	*50.00*
a.		With additional surch. "5r"	—	—
245	A12	100r on 3½r mar & lt grn	10.00	*15.00*

Imperf

No.	Type	Description	Unused	Used
247	A14	3r on 3k red	10.00	*15.00*
248	A14	5r on 2k green	3.00	*7.00*
249	A9	50r on 1r pale brn, dk brn & org	20.00	20.00

Type c in Violet

No.	Type	Description	Unused	Used
249A	A14	5r on 2k green	8.00	12.00

Russia AR1-AR3 Surcharged

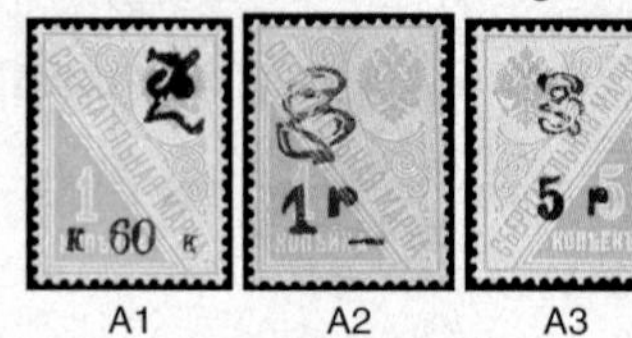

A1 A2 A3

Perf. 14½x15

Wmk. 171

No.	Type	Description	Unused	Used
250	A1	60k on 1k red & buff	60.00	60.00
251	A2	1r on 1k red & buff	60.00	60.00
252	A3	5r on 5k green & buff	60.00	60.00
253	A3	5r on 10k brn & buff	60.00	60.00

Russian Semi-Postal Stamps of 1914-18 Surcharged with Armenian Monogram and New Values like Regular Issues

On Stamps of 1914

Unwmk. ***Perf.***

No.	Type	Description	Unused	Used
255	SP5	25r on 1k red brn & dk grn, *straw*	72.50	72.50
256	SP5	25r on 3k mar & gray grn, *pink*	72.50	72.50
257	SP5	50r on 7 dk brn & dk grn, *buff*	90.00	90.00
258	SP5	100r on 1k red brn & dk grn, *straw*	90.00	90.00
259	SP5	100r on 3k mar & gray grn, *pink*	90.00	90.00
260	SP5	100r on 7k dk brn & dk grn, *buff*	90.00	90.00

On Stamps of 1915-19

No.	Type	Description	Unused	Used
261	SP5	25r on 1k org brn & gray	100.00	100.00
262	SP5	25r on 3k car & gray	90.00	90.00
263	SP5	50r on 10k dk bl & brn	50.00	50.00
264	SP5	100r on 1k org brn & gray	90.00	90.00
265	SP5	100r on 10k dk bl & brn	90.00	90.00

These surcharged semi-postal stamps were used for ordinary postage.

A set of 10 stamps in the above designs was prepared in 1920, but not issued for postal use, though some were used fiscally. Value of set, $10. Exist imperf with "SPECIMEN" overprint. Value of set, $40. Reprints exist.

Soviet Socialist Republic

Hammer and Sickle — A7

Mythological Monster — A8

Symbols of Soviet Republics on Designs from old Armenian Manuscripts A9

Ruined City of Ani — A10

Mythological Monster — A11

Armenian Soldier — A12

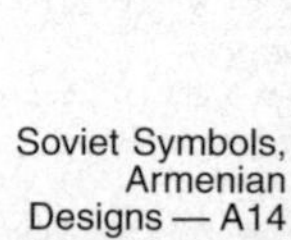

Mythological Monster A13

Soviet Symbols, Armenian Designs — A14

Mt. Alagöz and Plain of Shirak A15

Fisherman on River Aras — A16

Post Office in Erevan and Mt. Ararat A17

Ruin in City of Ani — A18

Street in Erevan — A19

Lake Sevan and Sevan Monastery — A20

Mythological Subject from old Armenian Monument — A21

Mt. Ararat — A22

1921 **Unwmk.** ***Perf. 11½, Imperf.***

No.	Type	Description	Unused	Used
278	A7	1r gray green	.50	
279	A8	2r slate gray	.50	
280	A9	3r carmine	.50	
281	A10	5r dark brown	.50	
282	A11	25r gray	.50	.50
283	A12	50r red	.30	
284	A13	100r orange	.30	
285	A14	250r dark blue	.30	
286	A15	500r brown vio	.30	
287	A16	1000r sea green	.40	
288	A17	2000r bister	1.75	
289	A18	5000r dark brown	1.00	
290	A19	10,000r dull red	1.00	
291	A20	15,000r slate blue	1.25	
292	A21	20,000r lake	1.50	
293	A22	25,000r gray blue	2.00	
294	A22	25,000r brown olive	8.00	
		Nos. 278-294 (17)	20.60	

Except the 25r, Nos. 278-294 were not regularly issued and used. Counterfeits exist.

For surcharges see Nos. 347-390.

Russian Stamps of 1909-17 Surcharged

Wove Paper

Lozenges of Varnish on Face

1921, Aug. ***Perf. 13½***

No.	Type	Description	Unused	Used
295	A9	5000r on 1r	*25.00*	
296	A12	5000r on 3½r	*25.00*	
297	A13	5000r on 5r	*25.00*	

No.	Type	Description	Unused
298	A12	5000r on 7r	25.00
299	A13	5000r on 10r	25.00
		Nos. 295-299 (5)	*125.00*

Nos. 295-299 were not officially issued. Counterfeits abound.

A23

Mt. Ararat & Soviet Star — A24

Soviet Symbols — A25

Crane — A26

Peasant — A27

Harpy — A28

Peasant Sowing — A29

Soviet Symbols — A30

Forging — A31

Plowing A32

1922 ***Perf. 11½***

No.	Type	Description	Unused
300	A23	50r green & red	.85
301	A24	300r slate bl & buff	1.00
302	A25	400r blue & pink	1.00
303	A26	500r vio & pale lil	1.00
304	A27	1000r dull bl & pale bl	1.00
305	A28	2000r black & gray	1.25
306	A29	3000r black & grn	1.25
307	A30	4000r black & lt brn	1.25
308	A31	5000r blk & dull red	1.25
309	A32	10,000r black & pale rose	1.25
a.		Tête-bêche pair	42.50
		Nos. 300-309 (10)	11.10

Nos. 300-309 were not issued without surcharge.

Stamps of types A23 to A32, printed in other colors than Nos. 300 to 309, are essays.

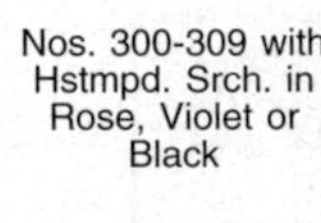

Nos. 300-309 with Hstmpd. Srch. in Rose, Violet or Black

1922

No.	Description	Unused	Used
310	10,000 on 50r (R)	*90.00*	*90.00*
311	10,000 on 50r (V)	*60.00*	*60.00*
312	10,000 on 50r	*30.00*	*30.00*
313	15,000 on 300r (R)	*120.00*	*120.00*
314	15,000 on 300r (V)	*90.00*	*90.00*
315	15,000 on 300r	*30.00*	*30.00*
316	25,000 on 400r (V)	*60.00*	*60.00*
317	25,000 on 400r	*30.00*	*30.00*
318	30,000 on 500r (R)	*120.00*	*120.00*
319	30,000 on 500r (V)	*60.00*	*60.00*
320	30,000 on 500r	*30.00*	*30.00*
321	50,000 on 1000r (R)	*120.00*	*120.00*
322	50,000 on 1000r (V)	*60.00*	*60.00*
323	50,000 on 1000r	*25.00*	*25.00*
324	75,000 on 3000r	*30.00*	*30.00*
325	100,000 on 2000r (R)	*120.00*	*275.00*
326	100,000 on 2000r (V)	*60.00*	*60.00*
327	100,000 on 2000r	*25.00*	*25.00*
328	200,000 on 4000r (V)	*12.00*	*12.00*
329	200,000 on 4000r	*12.00*	*12.00*
330	300,000 on 5000r (V)	*60.00*	*60.00*
331	300,000 on 5000r	*25.00*	*25.00*
332	500,000 on 10,000r (V)	*60.00*	*60.00*
333	500,000 on 10,000r	*12.00*	*12.00*
	Nos. 310-333 (24)	*1,341.*	*1,496.*

Forgeries exist.

Goose — A33

Armenian Woman at Well — A35

Armenian Village Scene A34

Mt. Ararat A36

Mt. Ararat A37

New Values in Gold Kopecks, Handstamped Surcharge in Black

1922 ***Imperf.***

No.	Type	Description	Unused	Used
334	A33	1(k) on 250r rose	18.00	18.00
335	A33	1(k) on 250r gray	24.00	24.00
336	A34	2(k) on 500r rose	10.00	10.00
337	A34	3(k) on 500r gray	10.00	10.00
338	A35	4(k) on 1000r rose	10.00	10.00
339	A35	4(k) on 1000r gray	18.00	18.00
340	A36	5(k) on 2000r gray	10.00	10.00
341	A36	10(k) on 2000r rose	10.00	10.00
342	A37	15(k) on 5000r rose	62.50	62.50
343	A37	20(k) on 5000r gray	10.00	10.00
		Nos. 334-343 (10)	182.50	182.50

Nos. 334-343 were issued for postal tax purposes.

Nos. 334-343 exist without surcharge but are not known to have been issued in that condition. Counterfeits exist of both sets.

Regular Issue of 1921 Handstamped with New Values in Black or Red
Short, Thick Numerals

1922 ***Imperf.***

No.	Type	Description	Unused	Used
347	A8	2(k) on 2r (R)	60.00	60.00
350	A11	4(k) on 25r (R)	100.00	100.00
353	A13	10(k) on 100r (R)	24.00	24.00
354	A14	15(k) on 250r	3.50	3.50
355	A15	20(k) on 500r	18.00	18.00
a.		With "k" written in red	12.00	12.00
357	A22	50(k) on 25,000r bl (R)	300.00	300.00
358	A22	50(k) on 25,000r brn ol (R)	150.00	150.00
359	A22	50(k) on 25,000r brn ol		
		Nos. 347-358 (7)	655.50	655.50

Perf. 11½

No.	Type	Description	Unused	Used
360	A7	1(k) on 1r, imperf.	*75.00*	*75.00*
a.		Perf.	*50.00*	*50.00*
361	A7	1(k) on 1r (R)	*45.00*	*45.00*
a.		Imperf.	*50.00*	*70.00*
362	A8	2(k) on 2r, imperf.	*47.50*	47.50
a.		Perf.	*50.00*	*50.00*
363	A15	2(k) on 500r	*100.00*	125.00
a.		Imperf.	*100.00*	*100.00*
364	A15	2(k) on 500r (R)	150.00	150.00
365	A11	4(k) on 25r, imperf.	*30.00*	*30.00*
a.		Perf.	*50.00*	*50.00*
366	A12	5(k) on 50r, imperf.	24.00	*36.00*
a.		Perf.	*100.00*	*100.00*
367	A13	10(k) on 100r	*24.00*	*24.00*
a.		Imperf.	*50.00*	*50.00*
368	A21	35(k) on 20,000r, imperf.	*90.00*	*100.00*
a.		With "k" written in violet	*90.00*	*90.00*
b.		Perf.	*90.00*	*90.00*
c.		As "a," perf.	*90.00*	*90.00*
d.		With "kop" written in violet, imperf.		
		Nos. 360-368 (9)	*585.50*	*632.50*

Manuscript Surcharge in Red

Perf. 11½

No.	Type	Description	Unused	Used
371	A14	1k on 250r dk bl	*50.00*	*50.00*

Handstamped in Black or Red
Tall, Thin Numerals

No. 381

Imperf

No.	Type	Description	Unused	Used
377	A11	4(k) on 25r (R)	5.00	5.00
379	A13	10(k) on 100r	90.00	*100.00*
380	A15	20(k) on 500r	7.25	7.25
381	A22	50k on 25,000r bl	*20.00*	*90.00*
a.		Surcharged "50" only	60.00	60.00
382	A22	50k on 25,000r bl (R)	14.50	14.50
382A	A22	50k on 25,000r brn ol	29.00	29.00
		Nos. 377-382A (6)	*165.75*	*245.75*

On Nos. 381, 382 and 382A the letter "k" forms part of the surcharge.

Perf. 11½

No.	Type	Description	Unused	Used
383	A7	1(k) on 1r (R)	*40.00*	*40.00*
a.		Imperf.	100.00	
384	A14	1(k) on 250r	60.00	60.00
385	A15	2(k) on 500r	10.00	10.00
a.		Imperf.	24.00	24.00
386	A15	2(k) on 500r (R)	24.00	24.00
387	A9	3(k) on 3r	35.00	35.00
a.		Imperf.	40.00	40.00
388	A21	3(k) on 20,000r, imperf.	12.00	12.00
a.		Perf.	60.00	60.00
389	A11	4(k) on 25r	30.00	30.00
a.		Imperf.	120.00	120.00
390	A12	5(k) on 50r, imperf.	*12.00*	*12.00*
a.		Perf.	*18.00*	*75.00*
		Nos. 383-390 (8)	*223.00*	*223.00*

Catalogue values for unused stamps in this section, from this point to the end of the section, are for Never Hinged items.

Mt. Ararat — A45

a, 20k. b, 2r. c, 5r.

1992, May 28 **Litho.** ***Perf. 14***

No.	Type	Description	Unused	Used
430	A45	Strip of 3, #a.-c.	4.25	4.25

Souvenir Sheet

No.	Type	Description	Unused	Used
431	A45	7r Eagle & Mt. Ararat	*50.00*	*50.00*

AT & T Communications System in Armenia—A45a

1992, July 1 **Litho.** ***Perf. 13x13½***

No.	Type	Description	Unused	Used
431A	A45a	50k multicolored	5.00	5.00

A46

1992 Summer Olympics, Barcelona: a, 40k, Ancient Greek wrestlers. b, 3.60r, Boxing. c, 5r, Weight lifting. d, 12r, Gymnastics.

1992, July 25 **Litho.** ***Perf. 14***

No.	Type	Description	Unused	Used
432	A46	Strip of 4, #a.-d.	3.50	3.50

A47

20k, Natl. flag. 1r, Goddess Waroubini, Orgov radio telescope. 2r, Yerevan Airport. No. 436, Goddess Anahit. No. 437, Runic message, 7th cent B.C. 5r, UPU emblem. 20r, Silver cup.

1992-93 Litho. *Perf. 14½, 15x14½*

433	A47	20k multicolored	.30	.30
434	A47	1r gray green	.30	.30
435	A47	2r blue	.40	.40
436	A47	3r brown	.60	.60
437	A47	3r bronze	.30	.30
438	A47	5r brown black	.90	.90
439	A47	20r gray	.70	.70
		Nos. 433-439 (7)	3.50	3.50

No. 435 is airmail. See Nos. 464-471, 521-524.

Issued: No. 436, 20k, 2r, 5r, 8/25/92; others, 5/12/93.

Religious Artifacts — A50

David of Sassoun, by Hakop Kojoian A50a

1993, May 23 Litho. *Perf. 14*

448	A50	40k Marker	.25	.25
449	A50	80k Gospel page	.40	.30
450	A50	3.60r Bas-relief, 13th cent.	1.25	1.00
451	A50	5r Icon of the Madonna	2.25	2.00
		Nos. 448-451 (4)	4.15	3.55

Souvenir Sheet

Perf. 14x13½

451A	A50a	12r multicolored	10.00	10.00

Scenic Views — A51

Designs: 40k, Garni Canyon, vert. 80k, Shaki Waterfall, Zangezur, vert. 3.60r, Arpa River Canyon, vert. 5r, Lake Sevan. 12r, Mount Aragats.

1993, May 24 *Perf. 14*

452	A51	40k multicolored	.25	.25
453	A51	80k multicolored	.25	.25
454	A51	3.60r multicolored	.50	.50
455	A51	5r multicolored	.70	.70
456	A51	12r multicolored	1.75	1.75
		Nos. 452-456 (5)	3.45	3.45

Yerevan '93 — A52

1993, May 25 *Perf. 14½*

457	A52	10r multicolored	.95	.95
a.		Min. sheet of 6 + 2 labels	5.75	5.75

For surcharges see Nos. 485-486.

Souvenir Sheet

Noah's Descent from Mt. Ararat, by Hovhannes Aivazovsky — A52a

1993, Aug. 4 Litho. *Perf. 14½*

458	A52a	7r multicolored	4.50	4.50

Religious Relics, Echmiadzin — A53

Designs: 3r, Wooden panel, descent from cross, 9th cent. 5r, Gilded silver reliquary for Holy Cross of Khotakerats. 12r, Cross depicting right hand of St. Karapet, 14th cent. 30r, Reliquary for arm of St. Thaddeus the Apostle, 17th cent. 50r, Gilded silver vessel for consecrated ointment, 1815.

1994, Aug. 4 Litho. *Perf. 14x14½*

459	A53	3d multicolored	.25	.25
460	A53	5d multicolored	.25	.25
461	A53	12d multicolored	.85	.85
462	A53	30d multicolored	1.75	1.75
463	A53	50d multicolored	2.40	2.40
		Nos. 459-463 (5)	5.50	5.50

Artifacts and Landmarks Type of 1993

Gods of Van (Urartu): 10 l, Shivini, god of the sun. 50 l, Tayshaba, god of elements. 10d, Khaldi, supreme god.
25d, Natl. arms.

1994, Aug. 4 *Perf. 14½*

464	A47	10 l black & brown	.25	.25
465	A47	50 l black & red brown	.25	.25
469	A47	10d black & gray	1.00	1.00
471	A47	25d red & bister	2.25	2.25
		Nos. 464-471 (4)	3.75	3.75

A54

1994, Dec. 31 Litho. *Perf. 14½x14*

479	A54	16d No. 1a	.60	.60

First Armenian postage stamp, 75th anniv.

A54a

A54b

1994, Dec. 30 Litho. *Perf. 14x14½*

480	A54a	30d Early printing press	.80	.80

First Armenian periodical, 200th anniv.

1994, Dec. 30 Litho. *Perf. 14x14½*

481	A54b	30d Natl. arms, stadium	.75	.75

Natl. Olympic Committee.

A54c

1994, Dec. 30 Litho. *Perf. 14x14½*

482	A54c	40d Olympic rings	1.25	1.25

Intl. Olympic Committee, Cent.

A54d

1994, Dec. 31 Litho. *Perf. 14x14½*

483	A54d	50d multi + label	.85	.85

Ervand Otian (1869-1926)

A54e

1994, Dec. 31 Litho. *Perf. 14½x14*

484	A54e	50d multi + label	.85	.85

Levon Shant (1869-1951).

No. 457 Surcharged in Blue or Red Brown

a b

1994, Sept. 10 Litho. *Perf. 14*

485	A52(a)	40d on 10r (Bl)	6.50	6.50
486	A52(b)	40d on 10r (RB)	6.50	6.50

Yerevan '94.

A55

Christianity in Armenia: 60d, Cross, 10th-11th cent. No. 488, Kings Abgar & Trdat, 1836. No. 489, St. Bartholomew, St. Thaddeus. 80d, St. Gregory, the Illuminator. 90d, Baptism of the Armenian people, 1892. 400d, Plan of Echmiadzin, c. 1660, engr. by Jakob Peeters.

1995, Apr. 3 Litho. *Perf. 14x15*

487	A55	60d multicolored	.95	.95
488	A55	70d multicolored	1.00	1.00
489	A55	70d multicolored	1.00	1.00
490	A55	80d multicolored	1.25	1.25
491	A55	90d multicolored	1.40	1.40
		Nos. 487-491 (5)	5.60	5.60

Souvenir Sheet

492	A55	400d multicolored	5.50	5.50

Nos. 488-489 are 45x44mm.

A56

1995, Apr. 3

493	A56	150d gray & black	2.10	2.10

Vazgen I (1908-94), Catholikos of All Armenians.

Armenia Fund A57

1995, Apr. 27 *Perf. 15x14*

494	A57	90d multicolored	1.25	1.25

UN, 50th Anniv. A58

1995, Apr. 28

495	A58	90d multicolored	1.20	1.20

Cultural Artifacts — A59

Designs: 30d, Black polished pottery, 14th-13th cent. B.C. 60d, Silver cup, 5th cent. B.C. 130d, Gohar carpet, 1700 A.D.

1995, Apr. 27 *Perf. 15x14*

496	A59	30d multicolored	.50	.50
497	A59	60d multicolored	.80	.80
498	A59	130d multicolored	2.00	2.00
		Nos. 496-498 (3)	3.30	3.30

Birds — A60

1995, Apr. 27 ***Perf. 14***

499 A60 40d Milvus milvus .65 .65
500 A60 60d Aquila chrysaetos .95 .95

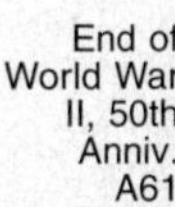

End of World War II, 50th Anniv. A61

Designs: No. 501, P. Kitsook, 408th Armenian Rifle Division. No. 502, A. Sargissin, N. Safarian, 89th Taman Armenian Triple Order-Bearer Division. No. 503, B. Chernikov, N. Tavartkeladze, V. Penkovsky, 76th Armenian Alpine Rifle Red Banner (51st Guards) Division. No. 504, S. Zakian, H. Babayan, I. Lyudnikov, 390th Armenian Rifle Division. No. 505, A. Vasillian, M. Dobrovolsky, Y. Grechany, G. Sorokin, 409th Armenian Rifle Division.

No. 506, vert.: a, Marshal Hovhannes Baghramian. b, Adm. Hovhannes Issakov. c, Marshal Hamazasp Babajanian. d, Marshal Sergey Khoudyakov.

No. 507: Return of the Hero, by Mariam Aslamazian.

1995, Sept. 30 Litho. ***Perf. 15x14***

501 A61 60d multicolored .80 .80
502 A61 60d multicolored .80 .80
503 A61 60d multicolored .80 .80
504 A61 60d multicolored .80 .80
505 A61 60d multicolored .80 .80
Nos. 501-505 (5) 4.00 4.00

Miniature Sheet

Perf. 15x14½

506 A61 60d Sheet of 4, #a.-d. 3.25 3.25

Souvenir Sheet

Perf. 15x14

507 A61 300d multicolored 4.00 4.00

Authors A62

Designs: No. 508, Ghevond Alishan (1820-1901). No. 509, Gregor Artsruni (1845-92), vert. No. 510, Franz Werfel (1890-1945).

1995, Oct. 5 Litho. ***Perf. 15x14***

508 A62 90d blue & black 1.00 1.00
509 A62 90d multicolored 1.00 1.00
510 A62 90d blue & maroon 1.00 1.00
Nos. 508-510 (3) 3.00 3.00

Nos. 508-510 issued with se-tenant label.

A64

Prehistoric artifacts: 40d, Four-wheeled carriages, 15th cent. BC. 60d, Bronze model of geocentric solar system, 11-10th cent. BC, vert. 90d, Tombstone, Red Tufa, 7-6th cent. BC, vert.

1995, Dec. 5 ***Perf. 14½x15, 15x14½***

512 A64 40d multicolored .40 .40
513 A64 60d multicolored .80 .80
514 A64 90d multicolored 1.20 1.20
Nos. 512-514 (3) 2.40 2.40

A65

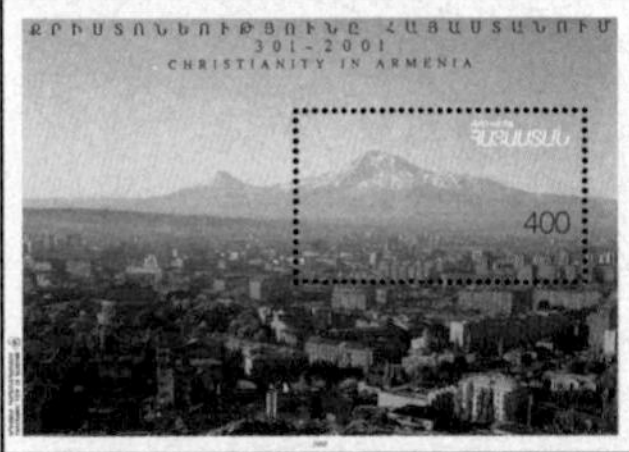

Christianity in Armenia — A66

Views of Yerevan: 60d, Brandy distillery, wine cellars. 80d, Abovian Street. 90d, Sports and concert complex. 100d, Baghramian Avenue. 120d, Republic Square.

400d, Panoramic photograph of Yerevan.

1995, Dec. 5 ***Perf. 15x14***

515 A65 60d salmon & black .55 .55
516 A65 80d pale org & blk .65 .65
517 A65 90d buff & black .75 .75

Size: 61x24mm

518 A65 100d pale yel bis & blk 1.20 1.20
519 A65 120d dull org & blk 1.50 1.50
Nos. 515-519 (5) 4.65 4.65

Souvenir Sheet

520 A66 400d multicolored 5.00 5.00

No. 464 Surcharged in Green, Red, Blue Violet, or Red Brown

1996, Mar. 30 Litho. ***Perf. 14½***

521 A47 40d on 10l (G) 1.75 1.75
522 A47 100d on 10l (R) 4.00 4.00
523 A47 150d on 10l (BV) 6.50 6.50
524 A47 200d on 10l (RB) 9.50 9.50
Nos. 521-524 (4) 21.75 21.75

Alexandre Griboyedov (1795-1829), Writer — A67

1996, Apr. 24 Litho. ***Perf. 14x14½***

525 A67 90d multi + label .90 .90

Khrimian Hayrik (1820-1907), Catholicos of All Armenians — A68

1996, Apr. 30 ***Perf. 14½x14***

526 A68 90d brown & blue 1.10 1.10

No. 526 is printed se-tenant with label.

Admiral Lazar Serbryakov (1795-1862) — A69

1996, Apr. 30

527 A69 90d multi + label 1.10 1.10

Armenian Red Cross, 75th Anniv. — A70

1996, May 4 ***Perf. 14x14½***

528 A70 60d multicolored .80 .80

Motion Pictures, Cent. A71

1996, May 4 ***Perf. 14½x14***

529 A71 60d multicolored .90 .90

No. 529 exists imperf. Value $45.

Endangered Fauna — A72

1996, May 3 ***Perf. 14***

530 A72 40d Carpa aegagrus .70 .70
531 A72 60d Panthera pardus 1.10 1.10

1996 Summer Olympics, Atlanta — A73

Designs: a, 40d, Cyclist. b, 60d, Athletic event. c, 90d, Wrestling.

1996, July 25

532 A73 Strip of 3, #a.-c. 2.10 2.10

Modern Olympic Games, Cent. — A74

1996, July 25 ***Perf. 14x14½***

533 A74 60d multicolored .80 .80

Fridtjof Nansen (1861-1930), Arctic Explorer — A75

1996, May 20 Litho. ***Perf. 14x14½***

534 A75 90d multicolored 1.00 1.00

32nd Chess Olympiad, Yerevan — A76

Designs: No. 535, Petrosian-Botvinnik, World Championship match, Moscow, 1963. No. 536, Kasparov-Karpov, World Championship Match, Leningrad, 1986. No. 537, G. Kasparian, first prize winner, Contest of the Shakhmati v SSSR magazine, 1939. No. 538, 32nd Chess Olympiad, Yerevan.

1996, Sept. 15 Litho. ***Perf. 14***

535 A76 40d multicolored .70 .70
536 A76 40d multicolored .70 .55
537 A76 40d multicolored .70 .70
538 A76 40d multicolored .70 .70
a. Booklet pane, #535-538 *3.00*
Complete booklet, 2 #538a *7.50*
Nos. 535-538 (4) 2.80 2.65

No. 538a issued 9/24.

Nos. 535-538 also exist imperf. Value $30.

Tigran Petrosian, World Chess Champion, Chess House, Yerevan — A77

1996, Sept. 20 ***Perf. 14x15***

539 A77 90d multicolored 1.20 1.20

No. 539 also exists imperf. Value $20.

Capra Aegagrus A78

World Wildlife Fund: 70d, Two running. 100d, One standing. 130d, One holding head down. 350d, Two facing forward.

1996, Oct. 20 Litho. ***Perf. 14½x14***

540 A78 70d multicolored .85 .85
541 A78 100d multicolored .95 .95
542 A78 130d multicolored 1.25 1.25
543 A78 350d multicolored 4.00 4.00
a. Block of 4, #540-543 7.25 7.25
b. Booklet pane, 2 #543a 14.50 14.50
Complete booklet, #543b 20.00 20.00

Issued in sheets of 16 stamps.

Christianity in Armenia, 1700th Anniv. — A79

Armenian churches: No. 544, St. Catherine Church, St. Petersburg, 1780. No. 545, Church of the Holy Mother, Kishinev, 1803. No. 546, Church of the Holy Mother, Samarkand, 1903. No. 547, Armenian Church, Lvov, 1370. No. 548, St. Hripsime Church, Yalta, 1913.

500d, Church of St. Gevorg of Etchmiadzin, Tbilisi, 1805.

1996 Litho. ***Perf. 14x15***

544 A79 100d multicolored 1.50 1.50
545 A79 100d multicolored 1.50 1.50
546 A79 100d multicolored 1.50 1.50
547 A79 100d multicolored 1.50 1.50
548 A79 100d multicolored 1.50 1.50
Nos. 544-548 (5) 7.50 7.50

Souvenir Sheet

549 A79 500d multicolored 5.00 5.00

First Armenian Printing Press, Etchmiadzin, 225th Anniv. — A80

1997, Mar. 26 Litho. *Perf. 15x14*
550 A80 70d multicolored 1.00 1.00

Armenian Entertainers — A81

Designs: No. 551, Folk singer, Jivani (1846-1909). No. 552, Arno Babajanian (1921-83), composer, vert.

1997, Mar. 26 *Perf. 15x14, 14x15*
551 A81 90d multicolored 1.00 1.00
552 A81 90d multicolored 1.00 1.00

Paintings from Natl. Gallery of Armenia A82

Designs: No. 553, "One of my Dreams," by Eghishe Tadevossian. No. 554, "Countryside," by Gevorg Bashinjaghian. No. 555, "Portrait of Natalia Tehumian," by Hakob Hovnatanian. No. 556, "Salomé," by Vardges Sureniants.

1997, May 28 Litho. *Perf. 15x14*
553 A82 150d multi 1.25 1.25
554 A82 150d multi 1.25 1.25
555 A82 150d multi, vert. 1.25 1.25
556 A82 150d multi, vert. 1.25 1.25
Nos. 553-556 (4) 5.00 5.00

See Nos. 573-575.

Rouben Mamulian (1897-1987), Motion Picture Director — A83

1997, Oct. 8 Litho. *Perf. 15x14*
557 A83 150d multicolored 1.10 1.10

Moscow '97, World Philatelic Exhibition — A84

1997, Oct. 17 *Perf. 14x15*
558 A84 170d St. Basil's Cathedral 1.75 1.75

Eghishe Charents (1897-1937), Poet — A85

1997, Oct. 19 *Perf. 15x14*
559 A85 150d multicolored 1.25 1.25

A86

A87

Europa (Stories and Legends): 170d, Hayk, the Progenitor of the Armenians. 250d, Vahagn, the Dragon Slayer.

1997, Oct. 18 *Perf. 14x15*
560 A86 170d multicolored *3.50 3.50*
561 A86 250d multicolored *4.00 4.00*

1997, Dec. 19 Litho. *Perf. 14*
562 A87 40d Iris lycotis .45 .45
563 A87 170d Iris elegantissima 1.40 1.40

Religious Buildings A88

Christmas A89

Designs: No. 564, San Lazzaro, the Mekhitarian Congregation, Venice. No. 565, St. Gregory the Illuminator Cathedral, Anthelias. No. 566, St. Khach Armenian Church, Rostov upon Don. No. 567, St. James Monastery, Jerusalem. No. 568, Nercissian School, Tbilisi.
500d, Lazarian Seminary, Moscow.

1997, Dec. 22 *Perf. 15x14, 14x15*
564 A88 100d multi, horiz. .80 .80
565 A88 100d multi .80 .80
566 A88 100d multi .80 .80
567 A88 100d multi, horiz. .80 .80

Size: 60x21mm

568 A88 100d multi, horiz. .80 .80
Nos. 564-568 (5) 4.00 4.00

Souvenir Sheet

569 A88 500d multicolored 4.75 4.75

Christianity in Armenia, 1700th anniv. (in 2001).

1997, Dec. 26 *Perf. 14x15*
570 A89 40d multicolored .60 .60

Diana, Princess of Wales (1961-97) A90

1998, Apr. 8 Litho. *Perf. 15x14*
571 A90 250d multicolored 2.50 2.50

No. 571 was issued in sheets of 5 + label.

Karabakh Movement, 10th Anniv. — A91

1998, Feb. 20 Litho. *Perf. 13½x14*
572 A91 250d multicolored 3.50 3.50

Paintings from Natl. Gallery of Armenia Type of 1997

Designs: No. 573, "Tartar Women's Dance," by Alexander Bazhbeouk-Melikian. No. 574, "Family. Generations," by Yervand Kochar. No. 575, "Spring in Our Yard," by Haroutiun Kalents.

1998, Feb. 21 *Perf. 15x14, 14x15*
573 A82 150d multi 1.40 1.40
574 A82 150d multi, vert. 1.40 1.40
575 A82 150d multi, vert. 1.40 1.40
Nos. 573-575 (3) 4.20 4.20

1998 World Cup Soccer Championships, France — A92

1998, June 10 Litho. *Perf. 14x15*
576 A92 250d multicolored 2.75 2.75

No. 576 was issued in sheets of 10 and sheets of 8 + 2 labels. Value, sheet of 8 + 2 labels $55.

National Holidays and Festivals A93

Europa: 170d, Couple jumping over fire, Trndez. 250d, Girls taking part in traditional ceremony, Ascension Day.

1998, June 24 Litho. *Perf. 15x14*
577 A93 170d multicolored *2.50 2.50*
578 A93 250d multicolored *5.00 5.00*

Butterflies A94

National Costumes A95

1998, June 26 *Perf. 14*
579 A94 170d Papilio alexanor 1.25 1.25
580 A94 250d Rethera komarovi 2.25 2.25

1998, July 16 Litho. *Perf. 14x13½*
581 A95 170d Ayrarat 1.50 1.50
582 A95 250d Vaspurakan 2.50 2.50

See Nos. 591-592.

Christianity in Armenia, 1700th Anniv. (in 2001) — A96

Churches: a, St. Forty Children's, 1958, Milan. b, St. Sargis, London, 1923. c, St. Vardan Cathedral, 1968, New York. d, St. Hovannes Cathedral, 1902, Paris. e, St. Gregory the Illuminator Cathedral, 1938, Buenos Aires.

1998, Sept. 25 Litho. *Perf. 11½*
583 A96 100d Sheet of 5, #a.-e. 5.00 5.00

Memorial to Armenian Earthquake Victims A97

1998, Sept. 26 *Perf. 15x14*
584 A97 250d multicolored 2.75 2.75

No. 584 was issued in sheets of 10 and sheets of 8 + 2 labels. Value, sheet of 8 + 2 labels $35.

Minerals A98

1998, Oct. 23
585 A98 170d Pyrite 1.75 1.75
586 A98 250d Agate 2.25 1.75

See Nos. 616-617.

Valery Bryusov (1873-1924), Writer — A99

1998, Dec. 1 *Perf. 14x15*
587 A99 90d multicolored .90 .90

Souvenir Sheet

Sergei Parajanov, Film Director, 75th Birth Anniv. — A100

1999, Apr. 19 Litho. *Perf. 14x14¾*
588 A100 500d multicolored 4.75 4.75
a. IBRA 99 emblem in margin 5.50 5.50

State Reserves A101

1999, Apr. 22 *Perf. 14¾x14¼*
589 A101 170d Khosrov *1.50 1.50*
590 A101 250d Kilijan *2.50 2.50*

Europa.

National Costumes Type of 1998

1999, Apr. 20 Litho. *Perf. 14x13½*
591 A95 170d Karin 1.90 1.90
592 A95 250d Zangezour 2.40 2.40

Council of Europe, 50th Anniv. — A102

1999, June 12
593 A102 170d multicolored 5.50 5.50

Cilician Ships A103

1999, Aug. 12 Litho. *Perf. 14¾x14*

Sail Colors

594 A103 170d orange & blue 2.25 2.25
595 A103 250d red & white 2.25 2.25

With PhilexFrance 99 Emblem at LR

596 A103 250d red & white 2.75 2.75
Nos. 594-596 (3) 7.25 7.25

Domesticated Animals — A104

1999, Aug. 19 ***Perf. 13¼x13¾***

597 A104 170d Armenian gampr dog 2.00 2.00
598 A104 250d Van cat 2.50 2.50

With China 1999 World Philatelic Exhibition Emblem at LR

599 A104 250d Van cat 3.00 3.00
Nos. 597-599 (3) 7.50 7.50

Souvenir Sheet

First Pan-Armenian Games — A105

1999, Aug. 28 ***Perf. 14¾x14***

600 A105 250d multicolored 4.00 4.00

Souvenir Sheet

Christianity in Armenia, 1700th Anniv. (in 2001) — A106

Churches: a, St. Gregory the Illuminator, Cairo. b, St. Gregory the Illuminator, Singapore. c, St. Khach, Suceava, Romania. d, St. Savior, Worcester, Mass. e, Church of the Holy Mother, Madras, India.

1999, Aug. Litho. ***Perf. 13¼x13¾***

601 A106 70d Sheet of 5, #a.-e. + label 7.50 7.50

UPU, 125th Anniv. A107

1999, Oct. ***Perf. 14¾x14¼***

602 A107 270d multicolored 3.25 3.25

Politicians Assassinated Oct. 27, 1999 — A108

Designs: No. 603, Parliament Speaker Karen Demirchyan, Parliament building. No. 604, Prime Minister Vazgen Sargsyan, troops. 540d, Demirchyan, Sargsyan, Yuri Bakhshyan, Ruben Miroyan, Henrik Abrahamyan, Armenak Armenakyan, Leonard Petrossyan and Mikael Kotanyan.

Perf. 14¾x14¼

2000, Feb. 21 **Litho.**

603 A108 250d multi 3.00 3.00
604 A108 250d multi 3.00 3.00
a. Sheet, 5 each #603-604 *85.00 85.00*

Imperf

Size: 60x44mm

605 A108 540d multi 6.00 6.00

Fish — A109

Designs: 50d, Salmo ischchan. 270d, Barbus goktschaicus.

2000, May 23 Litho. ***Perf. 13¼x13¾***

606 A109 50d multi 1.00 1.00
607 A109 270d multi 2.00 2.00

Fairy Tales A110

2000, May 25 ***Perf. 14¾x14¼***

608 A110 70d The Liar Hunter .75 .75
609 A110 130d The King and the Peddler 1.50 1.50

Europa, 2000

Common Design Type

2000, June 19 ***Perf. 14¼x14¾***

610 CD17 40d multi *.75 .75*
611 CD17 500d multi *8.25 8.25*

Christianity as State Religion, 1700th Anniv. — A111

No. 612: a, St. Gayane Church, Vagharshapat. b, Etchmiadzin Cathedral, Vagharshapat. c, Church of the Holy Mother, Khor Virap. d, St. Shoghakat Church, Vagharshapat. e, St. Hripsime Church, Vagharshapat.

2000, July 10 Litho. ***Perf. 13¼x13¾***

612 A111 70d Sheet of 5, #a-e, + label 5.25 5.25

2000 Summer Olympics, Sydney — A112

Designs: 10d, Basketball. 30d, Tennis. 500d, Weight lifting.

2000, July 11 ***Perf. 13½x13¾***

613-615 A112 Set of 3 6.00 6.00

Mineral Type of 1998

Designs: 170d, Quartz. 250d, Molybdenite.

2000, Sept. 4 ***Perf. 14¾x14***

616-617 A98 Set of 2 4.00 4.00

A113 A114

2000, Sept. 11 ***Perf. 14x14¾***

618 A113 270d multi 2.50 2.50

Nerses Shnorhali (1100-73), poet and musician.

2000, Sept. 15

619 A114 170d multi 1.60 1.60

Christmas.

Avetik Issahakian (1875-1957), Poet — A115

2000, Sept. 17 ***Perf. 14¾x14***

620 A115 130d multi 1.10 1.10

Musical Instruments A116

Designs: 170d, Dhol. 250d, Duduk.

2000, Dec. 22 Litho. ***Perf. 14x13¼***

621-622 A116 Set of 2 3.50 3.50

Famous Armenians — A117

No. 623: a, Viktor Hambartsoumian (1908-96), cosmologist. b, Abraham Alikhanov (1904-70), physicist. c, Andranik Iossifian (1905-93), engineer. d, Sargis Saltikov (1905-83), metallurgist. e, Samuel Kochariants (1909-87), nuclear weapons scientist. f, Atrem Mikoyan (1905-70), aircraft designer. g, Norayr Sissakian (1907-66), biologist. h, Ivan Knunyants (1906-90), chemist. i, Nikoghayos Yenikolopian (1924-93), chemist.

No. 624: a, Nikoghayos Adonts (1871-1942), historian. b, Manouk Abeghian (1865-1944), grammarian. c, Hovhannes Toumanian (1869-1923), poet. d, Hrachya Ajarian (1876-1953), linguist. e, Gevorg Emin (1918-98), writer. f, Yervand Lalayan (1864-1931), anthropologist. g, Daniel Varoujan (1884-1915), poet. h, Paruyr Sevak (1924-71), writer. i, William Saroyan (1908-81), writer.

No. 625: a, Hamo Beknazarian (1892-1965), actor. b, Alexandre Tamanian (1878-1936), architect. c, Vahram Papazian (1888-1968), actor. d, Vassil Tahirov (1859-1938), viticulturist. e, Leonid Yengibarian (1935-72), mime. f, Haykanoush Danielian (1893-1958), singer. g, Sergo Hambartsoumian (1910-83) "Strongest man on Earth". h, Hrant Shahinian (1923-96), gymnast. i, Toros Toramanian (1864-1934), architectural historian.

No. 626: a, Komitas (1869-1935), composer. b, Aram Khachatourian (1903-78), composer. c, Martiros Sarian (1880-1972), artist. d, Avet Terterian (1929-94), composer. e, Alexandre Spendiarian (1871-1928), composer. f, Arshile Gorky (1904-48), artist. g, Minas Avetissian (1928-75), artist. h, Levon Orbeli (1882-1958), physiologist. i, Hripsimeh Simonian (1916-98), artist.

2000, Dec. 23 ***Perf. 14¾x14¼***

623 Booklet pane of 9 8.75 8.75
a.-i. A117 110d Any single .90 .90
624 Booklet pane of 9 8.75 8.75
a.-i. A117 110d Any single .90 .90
625 Booklet pane of 9 8.75 8.75
a.-i. A117 110d Any single .90 .90
626 Booklet pane of 9 8.75 8.75
a.-i. A117 110d Any single .90 .90
Booklet, #623-626 45.00

Souvenir Sheet

Battle of Avarayr, 1550th Anniv. — A118

No. 627: a, 170d, St. Vardan Mamikonian (388-451). b, 270d, Battle of Avarayr, 451.

2001, June 7 Litho. ***Perf. 14x14¾***

627 A118 Sheet of 2, #a-b 4.50 4.50

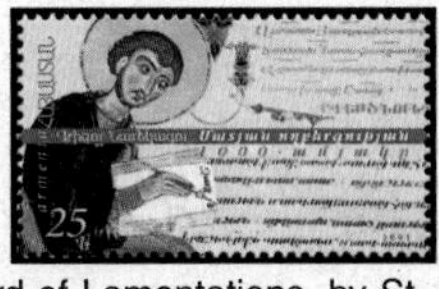

Record of Lamentations, by St. Grigor Narekatzi, 1000th Anniv. — A119

2001, June 8 Litho. ***Perf. 14¾x14***

628 A119 25d multi 2.00 2.00

Europa A120

Designs: 50d, Lake Sevan. 500d, Spandarian Reservoir.

2001, June 9

629-630 A120 Set of 2 *5.75 5.75*

Armenian Admission to Council of Europe A121

2001, June 11

631 A121 240d multi 2.50 2.50

Worldwide Fund for Nature (WWF) — A122

Sciurus persicus: a, 40d, On branch. b, 50d, Eating. c, 80d, Close-up. d, 120d, Digging.

Perf. 13¼x13¾

2001, Aug. 25 **Litho.**

632 A122 Block of 4, #a-d 4.75 4.75

Souvenir Sheet

Second Pan-Armenian Games — A123

2001, Aug. 18 Litho. ***Perf. 14¾x14***
633 A123 300d multi 4.50 4.50

Souvenir Sheet

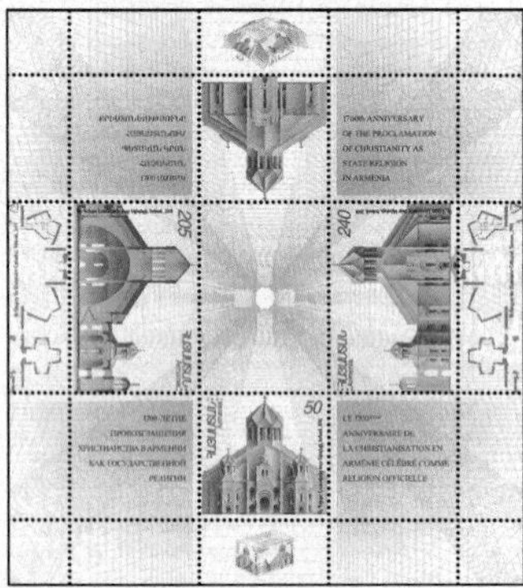

Christianity in Armenia, 1700th Anniv. — A124

Views of St. Gregory the Illuminator Cathedral, Yerevan: a, 50d, Front. b, 205d, Side (45x30mm). c, 240d, Side, diff. (45x30mm).

Perf. 13¾x13¼, 13¼x13¾

2001, Aug. 27
634 A124 Sheet of 3, #a-c, + 6 labels 10.00 10.00
d. As No. 634, with brown inscriptions in margins *65.00 65.00*

Marginal inscriptions on No. 634d read "INTERNATIONAL / PHILATELIC EXHIBITION / ARMENIA '01/ 10-16 September, 2001, Yerevan," in English, Armenian, Russian and French. Souvenir sheet can be formed into a box which shows cathedral from various angles.

Ivan Lazarev (1735-1801) and Institute of Eastern Languages, Moscow — A125

2001, Sept. 26 Litho. ***Perf. 14¾x14***
635 A125 300d multi 8.00 8.00

See Russia No. 6665.

Native Costumes — A126

Man and woman from: 50d, Javakhch. 250r, Artzakh.

2001, Sept. 27 ***Perf. 14x13½***
636-637 A126 Set of 2 3.00 3.00

6th World Wushu Championships A127

2001, Oct. 3 ***Perf. 13¼x13¾***
638 A127 180d black 2.75 2.75

Year of Dialogue Among Civilizations — A128

2001, Oct. 9 ***Perf. 14x14¾***
639 A128 275d multi 6.00 6.00

Commonwealth of Independent States, 10th Anniv. — A129

2001, Nov. 29
640 A129 205d multi 2.25 2.25

European Year of Languages A130

2001, Dec. 21 ***Perf. 14¾x14***
641 A130 350d multi 5.00 5.00

Independence, 10th Anniv. — A131

2001, Dec. 22
642 A131 300d multi 2.75 2.75

Transportation A132

Designs: 180d, Cart. 205d, Phaeton.

2001, Dec. 24 ***Perf. 13½x14***
643-644 A132 Set of 2 3.75 3.75

Medicinal Plants — A133

Designs: 85d, Hypericum perforatum. 205d, Thymus serpyllum.

2001, Dec. 25 ***Perf. 13¼x13¾***
645-646 A133 Set of 2 3.50 3.50

Eagle — A134

2002, Mar. 28 Litho. ***Perf. 14¾x14***
647 A134 10d brown .60 .60
648 A134 25d green .75 .75
649 A134 50d dk blue 1.00 1.00
Nos. 647-649 (3) 2.35 2.35

See Nos. 674-676.

Industries A135

Designs: 120d, Calendar belt, 2nd cent. B.C., copper smelter. 350d, Containers, 7th cent. B.C., hops, barley, beer kettles.

2002, Apr. 26
650-651 A135 Set of 2 6.50 6.50

National Gallery Artworks — A136

Designs: No. 652, 200d, Lily, by Edgar Chahine. No. 653, 200d, Salomé, sculpture by Hakob Gurjian.

2002, Apr. 29 ***Perf. 14x14¾***
652-653 A136 Set of 2 3.50 3.50

2002 World Cup Soccer Championships, Japan and Korea — A137

2002, May 2 ***Perf. 14¾x14***
654 A137 350d multi 3.00 3.00

Souvenir Sheet

Hovsep Pushman (1877-1906), Artist — A138

2002, May 9
655 A138 650d multi 5.25 5.25

Hovhannes Tevossian (1902-58), Engineer — A139

2002, May 14
656 A139 350d multi 3.00 3.00

Europa — A140

Designs: 70d, Magician's hat. 500d, Clown.

2002, July 30 Litho. ***Perf. 14x14¾***
657-658 A140 Set of 2 *4.50 4.50*

Artemy Aivazian, Composer, Cent. of Birth A141

2002, July 31 ***Perf. 14¾x14***
659 A141 600d multi 4.75 4.75

Souvenir Sheet

Cathedral of Ani, 1000th Anniv. (in 2001) — A142

Perf. 13¼x13¾

2002, Sept. 24 Litho.
660 A142 550d multi 4.50 4.50

Intl. Year of Mountains A143

2002-03 ***Perf. 14¾x14***
661 A143 350d multi 3.00 3.00
661a Booklet pane of 3 9.00 9.00

Issued: No. 661, 9/26/02. No. 661a, 2003.

Reptiles — A144

Designs: 170d, Lacerta armeniaca. 220d, Vipera raddei.

2002-03 ***Perf. 13¼x13¾***
662-663 A144 Set of 2 4.25 4.25
663a Booklet pane, 2 each #662-663 8.50 8.50

Issued: Nos. 662-663, 9/27/02. No. 663a, 2003.

Women for Peace A145

2002, Dec. 20 Litho. ***Perf. 14¾x14***
664 A145 220d multi 2.25 2.25

Alexandrapol — Yeravan Railway, Cent. — A146

2002, Dec. 21
665 A146 350d multi 3.25 3.25

Flowers — A147

Designs: 150d, Galanthus artjuschenkoae. 200d, Merendera mirzoevae.

2002, Dec. 23 ***Perf. 13¼x13¾***
666-667 A147 Set of 2 3.50 3.50
667a Booklet pane, 2 each #666-667 7.00 —
Complete booklet, #661a, 663a, 667a 24.50

Issued: No. 667a, 2003.

Space Research A148

Designs: 120d, Cosmic ray research. 220d, Orion 1 and Orion 2 space observatories.

2002, Dec. 24 ***Perf. 14¾x14***
668-669 A148 Set of 2 3.50 3.50

Europa — A149

Poster art: 170d, Handle With Care!, by Artak Bagdassaryan. 250d, Armenia, Our Home, by Karen Koyojan.

Perf. 13½x13¼
2003, June 24 **Litho.**
670-671 A149 Set of 2 3.50 3.50
671a Booklet pane, 4 each #670-671 14.00 14.00

No. 671a was sold with booklet cover, but was unattached to it.

Aram Khatchaturian (1903-78), Composer — A150

Perf. 13½x13¼
2003, June 25 **Litho.**
672 A150 350d multi 3.00 3.00

Larus Armenicus A151

2003, June 26 ***Perf. 12½***
673 A151 220d multi 1.60 1.60

Eagle Type of 2002
Perf. 13¼x13½
2003, Sept. 23 **Litho.**
674 A134 70d red .70 .70
675 A134 300d dk blue 2.50 2.50
676 A134 500d bister brn 5.00 5.00
Nos. 674-676 (3) 8.20 8.20

Souvenir Sheet

Transport Corridor Europe — Caucausus — Asia (TRACECA), 10th Anniv. — A152

2003, Oct. 9 ***Perf. 13***
677 A152 480d multi 6.50 6.50

First Armenian Postal Dispatch, 175th Anniv. A153

2003, Nov. 24 ***Perf. 13¼x13½***
678 A153 70d multi 1.00 1.00

Introduction of Dram Currency, 10th Anniv. — A154

2003, Nov. 25
679 A154 170d multi 2.25 2.25

A155

2003, Nov. 25 ***Perf. 13½x13¼***
680 A155 350d multi 5.25 5.25

Siamanto (1878-1915), poet.

A156

2003, Nov. 27
681 A156 200d multi 2.75 2.75

Vahan Tekeyan (1878-1945), poet.

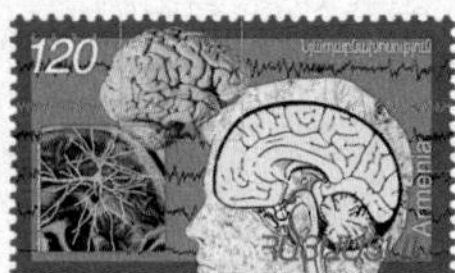

Neurophysiology — A157

2003, Nov. 28 ***Perf. 13¼x13½***
682 A157 120d multi 1.50 1.50

Souvenir Sheet

Third Pan-Armenian Games, Yerevan — A158

2003, Nov. 28
683 A158 350d multi 5.00 5.00

Souvenir Sheet

The Baptism, Miniature From Gospel of Ejmiatsin — A159

2003, Nov. 28 ***Perf. 13½x13¼***
684 A159 550d multi 7.25 7.25

A160

Paintings in Museum of Russian Art: 200d, Still Life, by Alexander Shevchenko. 220d, In a Restaurant, by Konstantin Roudakov.

2004, Sept. 6 **Litho.** ***Perf. 13½x13¼***
685-686 A160 Set of 2 5.50 5.50

A161

2004, Sept. 9
687 A161 350d multi 5.00 5.00

FIFA (Fédération Internationale de Football Association), Cent.

Grapes — A162

Grape color: 170d, Yellow. 220d, Purple.

2004, Sept. 8 ***Perf. 12½***
688-689 A162 Set of 2 4.50 4.50

Souvenir Sheet

Armenian Settlement of New Julfa, 400th Anniv. — A163

2004, Sept. 9 ***Perf. 13***
690 A163 590d multi 7.50 7.50

Animated Films A164

Designs: 70d, Cat and Dog, 1937. 120d, Foxbook, 1975.

2004, Sept. 10 ***Perf. 13¼x13½***
691-692 A164 Set of 2 2.75 2.75

Aramayis Yerzinkyan (1879-1931), Statesman — A165

2004, Sept. 11 ***Perf. 13½x13¼***
693 A165 220d multi 3.00 3.00

Karabakh Horse — A166

2005, Feb. 14 Litho. ***Perf. 12½***
694 A166 350d multi 4.50 4.50

Dated 2004.

2004 Summer Olympics, Athens — A167

Hand: 70d, With Olympic Rings. 170d, As runner. 350d, As pistol.

2005, Feb. 14
695-697 A167 Set of 3 *12.50 12.50*

Dated 2004.

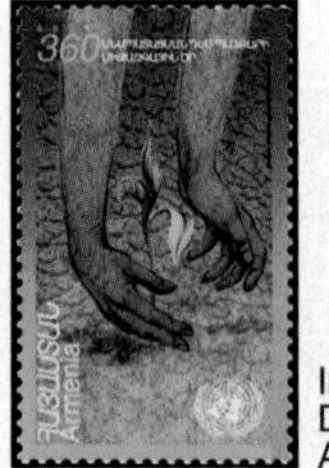

Intl. Day Against Desertification A168

2005, Feb. 21 ***Perf. 13½x13¼***
698 A168 360d multi 3.50 3.50

Dated 2004.

Heart, Molecule and Chemistry Apparatus A169

2005, Feb. 22
699 A169 220d multi 3.25 3.25

Dated 2004.

Michael Nalbandian (1829-66), Writer — A170

2005, Feb. 23
700 A170 220d multi 3.25 3.25

Dated 2004.

Mouratsan (1854-1908), Writer — A171

2005, Feb. 24
701 A171 350d multi 5.00 5.00

Dated 2004.

Tigran Petrosian (1929-84), Chess Champion A172

2005, Feb. 25
702 A172 220d multi 4.00 4.00

Europa
A173 A174

2005, Mar. 16 ***Perf. 13½x13¼***
703 A173 70d multi .90 .90
704 A174 350d multi 4.75 4.75

Dated 2004.

Souvenir Sheet

Goshavank Monastery — A175

2005, Mar. 17 ***Perf. 12½***
705 A175 480d multi 6.00 6.00

Dated 2004.

Armen Tigranian (1879-1950), Composer — A176

2005, Mar. 18 ***Perf. 13¼x13½***
706 A176 220d multi 3.00 3.00

Dated 2004.

A177 A178

2005, Apr. 21 ***Perf. 13½x13¼***
707 A177 350d multi 3.50 3.50

Armenian genocide, 90th anniv.

2005, Apr. 29
708 A178 350d multi 4.00 4.00

End of World War II, 60th anniv.
No. 708 was issued in sheets of 10 and sheets of 8 + 2 labels. Value, sheet of 8 + 2 labels $425.

Anushavan Arzumanian (1904-65), Educator — A179

2005, May 2 ***Perf. 13¼x13½***
709 A179 220d multi 2.25 2.25

Dated 2004.

Paintings by Martiros Sarian (1880-1972)
A180 A181

2005, May 10 ***Perf. 13½x13¼***
710 A180 170d Self-portrait 1.75 1.75
711 A181 200d Mount Aragats 2.00 2.00

Mother's Day A182

2005, Oct. 4 Litho. ***Perf. 13¼x13½***
712 A182 350d multi 3.50 3.50

A183 A184

Europa: 70d, Bread. 350d, Porridge.

2005, Oct. 4 ***Perf. 13½x13¼***
713-714 A183 Set of 2 5.00 5.00
714a Booklet pane, 4 each #713-714 20.00 —

No. 714a was sold with booklet cover, but unattached to it.

2005, Oct. 5
715 A184 70d multi .75 .75

Armenian alphabet, 1600th anniv.

A185 A186

2005, Oct. 5
716 A185 70d multi .80 .80

Vardan Ajemian (1905-77), theater director.

2005, Oct. 5
717 A186 170d multi 2.50 2.50

Anania Shirakatsi (605-85), scientist.

Mher Mkrtchian (1930-93), Actor — A187

2005, Oct. 6 ***Perf. 13¼x13½***
718 A187 120d multi 1.40 1.40

Artem Mikoyan (1905-70), Aircraft Designer, and MiG Fighters — A188

2005, Oct. 6
719 A188 350d multi 4.25 4.25

Rugs — A189

Rugs from: 60d, 19th cent. 350d, 1904. 480d, 18th cent.

2005, Oct. 6 ***Perf. 13½x13¼***
720-721 A189 Set of 2 4.50 4.50

Souvenir Sheet

722 A189 480d multi 6.00 6.00

No. 722 contains one 28x42mm stamp.

Armenia Year in Russia — A190

2006, Jan. 22 Litho. ***Perf. 11¼***
723 A190 350d multi 3.00 3.00

See Russia No. 6938.

Alexander Melik-Pashaev (1905-64), Conductor — A191

2006, Mar. 27 ***Perf. 13¼x13½***
724 A191 70d multi 1.00 1.00

Dated 2005.

St. Mary's Russian Orthodox Cathedral, Yerevan — A192

2006, Mar. 27
725 A192 170d multi 2.50 2.50

Dated 2005.

Vakhtang Ananyan (1805-80), Writer — A193

2006, Mar. 27
726 A193 170d multi 2.25 2.25

Dated 2005.

Raphael Patkanian (1830-92), Writer — A194

2006, Mar. 27 ***Perf. 13½x13¼***
727 A194 220d multi 2.50 2.50

Dated 2005.

2006 Winter Olympics, Turin — A195

Mountains and: 120d, 2006 Winter Olympics emblem. 170d, Emblem, map of Italy on snowboard.

2006, Mar. 27 ***Perf. 12½x12¾***
728-729 A195 Set of 2 4.00 4.00
729a Miniature sheet, 5 each #728-729 *30.00 30.00*

Dated 2005.

Spiridon Melikian (1880-1933), Musician — A196

2006, Mar. 28 ***Perf. 13½x13¼***
730 A196 350d multi 5.00 5.00

Dated 2005.

Souvenir Sheet

Miniature Art Depicting Nativity and Adoration of the Magi — A197

2006, Mar. 28 ***Perf. 13¼x13½***
731 A197 480d multi 6.50 6.50

Dated 2005.

Native Costumes — A198

Costumes from: 170d, Sassoun. 200d, Shatakhk.

2006, Mar. 28 ***Perf. 13½x13¼***
732-733 A198 Set of 2 4.00 4.00

Dated 2005.

Insects — A199

Designs: 170d, Porphyrophora hamelii. 350d, Procerus scabrosus fallettianus.

2006, Mar. 28 ***Perf. 12¾x12½***
734-735 A199 Set of 2 6.50 6.50

Dated 2005.

Europa Stamps, 50th Anniv. — A200

Designs: Nos. 736, 740a, 70d, Orange panel and "C." Nos. 737, 740b, 70d, Blue panel and "E." Nos. 738, 740c, 70d, Red panel and "P." Nos. 739, 740d, 70d, Green panel and "T."

2006, Mar. 28 ***Perf. 12¾x12½***

Stamps With "Europa 1956-2006" Inscription

736-739 A200 Set of 4 4.00 4.00

Souvenir Sheet

Stamps Without "Europa 1956-2006" Inscription

740 A200 70d Sheet of 4, #a-d 4.00 4.00

Dated 2005.

Souvenir Sheet

Independence, 15th Anniv. — A201

2006, Sept. 19 Litho. ***Perf. 12¾***
741 A201 480d multi 6.25 6.25

World Peace — A202

2006, Oct. 16 ***Perf. 13½x13¼***
742 A202 50d multi .65 .65

Souvenir Sheet

Gospel of Haghpat to Jerusalem — A203

2006, Oct. 16
743 A203 220d multi 2.50 2.50

2006 World Cup Soccer Championships, Germany — A204

2006, Oct. 17 ***Perf. 13¼x13½***
744 A204 350d multi 3.75 3.75

Europa A205

Designs: 200d, Gears and clock hands. 350d, Keys.

2006, Oct. 17
745-746 A205 Set of 2 5.25 5.25

Sergei Merkyurov (1881-1952), Sculptor — A206

2006, Oct. 18
747 A206 230d multi 2.50 2.50

Souvenir Sheet

Armenian General Benevolent Union, Cent. — A207

No. 748: a, Boghos Nubar (1851-1930). b, Signed document. c, Alex Manoogian (1901-96).

2006, Oct. 18 ***Perf. 13½x13¼***
748 A207 120d Sheet of 3, #a-c 3.75 3.75

On Nov. 30, 2006, the Armenian Postal Service was sold to a Dutch-owned firm, HayPost CJSC, affiliated with the Netherlands Postal Corporation. The items illustrated below were released in early 2007 by the stamp producer for the Armenian Postal Service prior to this sale, but as of December 2007, were never put on sale at any HayPost CJSC post office and were not valid for postage. HayPost CJSC acquired the remaining stock of these items from the producer and is negotiating with the Armenian government to place these items on sale and make the items valid for postage. All valid postage stamps from 2007, starting with No. 749 below are inscribed "Post." The items illustrated below do not have this inscription.

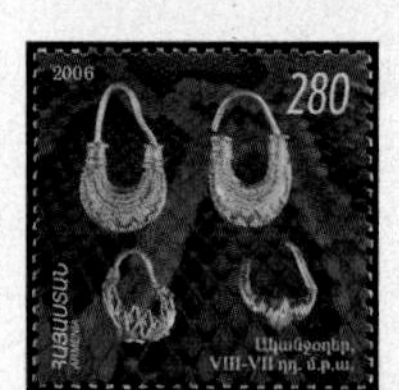

Smile of Reims, France — A208

Nativity, 15th Cent. Miniature, Armenia — A209

2007, May 22 Litho. *Perf. 13¼x13*

749 A208 70d multi 1.00 1.00
750 A209 350d multi 4.25 4.25

See France Nos. 3335-3336.

Apricot — A210

2007, July 6 *Perf. 13¼x13¾*

751 A210 350d multi 4.00 4.00

King Tigran the Great (c. 140-55 B.C.) — A211

2007, July 19 *Perf. 14¾x14*

Background Color

752 A211 50d red .60 .60
753 A211 60d olive green .75 .75
754 A211 70d green .90 .90
755 A211 120d blue 1.50 1.50
Nos. 752-755 (4) 3.75 3.75

See Nos. 780-783. Compare with types A240, A256, A271-A272.

Europa A212

2007, Sept. 12

756 A212 350d multi 4.25 4.25

Scouting, cent.

Gusan Sheram (1857-1938), Composer — A213

2007, Sept. 13 *Perf. 14x14¾*

757 A213 280d multi 3.25 3.25

Margar Sedrakyan (1907-73), Cognac Producer A214

2007, Sept. 14 *Perf. 14¾x14*

758 A214 170d multi 2.00 2.00

Souvenir Sheet

Genocide Memorial, Tsitsernakaberd — A215

2007, Oct. 9 *Perf. 14x14¾*

759 A215 480d multi 4.50 4.50

Children's Art A216

2007, Oct. 24 *Perf. 14¾x14*

760 A216 35d multi .55 .55

Rural Landscape, by Gevorg Bashinjaghyan (1857-1925) — A217

Kazbek, by Bashinjaghyan — A218

2007, Oct. 24 Litho.

761 A217 160d multi 1.75 1.75
762 A218 220d multi 2.50 2.50

Souvenir Sheet

Fourth Pan-Armenian Games, Yerevan — A219

2007, Oct. 25 *Perf. 14x14¾*

763 A219 360d multi 4.00 4.00

Jean Garzou (1907-2000), Painter — A220

Seda, by Garzou — A221

2007, Oct. 25 *Perf. 14¾x14*

764 A220 180d multi 1.75 1.75
765 A221 220d multi 2.25 2.25

Norayr Sisakyan (1907-66), Biochemist A222

2007, Oct. 26 *Perf. 14¾x14*

766 A222 120d multi 1.50 1.50

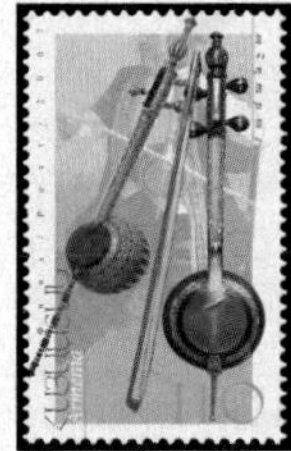

Kamancha — A223

2007, Oct. 27 *Perf. 14x14¾*

767 A223 110d multi 1.40 1.40

Birds — A224

Designs: 120d, Pelecanus crispus. 200d, Aegypius monachus.

2007, Oct. 27 *Perf. 13¼x13¾*

768-769 A224 Set of 2 4.00 4.00

Matenadaran Ancient Book Depository — A225

2007, Oct. 29 *Perf. 14¾x14*

770 A225 200d multi 2.50 2.50

Bagrat Nalbandyan (1902-90), Communications Administrator — A226

2007, Oct. 29 Litho.

771 A226 230d multi 2.50 2.50

N. Baghdasaryan (1907-88), Photojournalist A227

2007, Oct. 31 *Perf. 14x14¾*

772 A227 200d multi 2.50 2.50

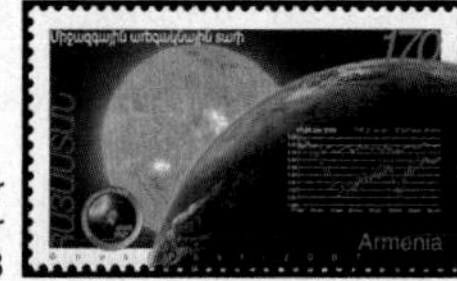

Intl. Solar Year A228

2007, Nov. 7 *Perf. 14¾x14*

773 A228 170d multi 2.00 2.00

Busts of Goddesses — A229

Designs: 70d, Greek Goddess Aphrodite. 350d, Armenian Goddess Anahit.

2007, Dec. 14 Litho. *Perf. 14x113½*

774-775 A229 Set of 2 5.00 5.00

See Greece Nos. 2328-2329.

2008 Summer Olympics, Beijing — A230

Perf. 13¼x13¾

2008, June 11 Litho.

776 A230 350d multi 4.25 4.25

Wood Carving — A231

2008, June 17 *Perf. 14x14¾*

777 A231 120d multi 1.50 1.50

Europa A232

2008, June 18 *Perf. 14¾x14*

778 A232 350d multi 4.25 4.25

Alexander Shirvanzade (1858-1935), Writer — A233

2008, June 19 ***Perf. 14x14¾***
779 A233 280d multi 3.25 3.25

King Tigran the Great Type of 2007

2008, June 20 ***Perf. 14¾x14***

Background Color

780	A211	10d bright blue	.25	.25
781	A211	20d orange brn	.25	.25
782	A211	50d rose lilac	.60	.60
783	A211	1100d purple	11.50	11.50
		Nos. 780-783 (4)	12.60	12.60

Flowers — A234

Designs: 120d, Anemone fasciculata. 280d, Scabiosa caucasica.

2008, Oct. 9 **Litho.** ***Perf. 13¼x14***
784-785 A234 Set of 2 4.75 4.75

Yerevan State University of Architecture and Construction, 75th Anniv. — A235

2008, Oct. 28 ***Perf. 14¾x14***
786 A235 220d multi 2.50 2.50

William Saroyan (1908-81), Writer — A236

2008, Oct. 29 ***Perf. 14x14¾***
787 A236 350d multi 4.00 4.00

Victor Hambardzumyan (1908-96), Astrophysicist — A237

2008, Oct. 20 ***Perf. 14¾x14***
788 A237 120d multi 1.50 1.50

Famous Men — A238

No. 789: a, Peyo Yavorov (1878-1914), Bulgarian poet. b, Andranik Ozanian (1865-1927), Armenian general who participated in Balkan Wars.

2008, Nov. 10 ***Perf. 13***

789	Horiz. pair	4.00	4.00
a.	A238 70d multi	.60	.60
b.	A238 350d multi	3.40	3.40

See Bulgaria No. 4492.

Dances — A239

Designs: 70d, Malambo sureño dancer, Argentina. 350d, Hoy-nazan dancers, Armenia.

2009, Apr. 4 ***Perf. 12½x12¾***
790-791 A239 Set of 2 3.75 3.75

See Argentina Nos. 2512-2513.

King Tigran the Great (c. 140-55 B.C.) — A240

2009, Apr. 8 ***Perf. 13¼***

Granite Paper

Background Color

792	A240	10d olive green	.25	.25
793	A240	25d yel bister	.25	.25
794	A240	50d cerise	.45	.45
795	A240	70d brown	.65	.65
796	A240	120d purple	1.10	1.10
797	A240	220d dark blue	2.10	2.10
798	A240	280d dk bl violet	2.60	2.60
799	A240	350d plum	3.25	3.25
		Nos. 792-799 (8)	10.65	10.65

Numerals are in a different font than on Type A211. Compare with types A256, A271-A272.

Van, Ancient Armenian Capital A241

2009, Apr. 29 ***Perf. 14¾x14***
800 A241 220d multi 2.25 2.25

Europa — A242

2009, July 1 ***Perf. 13¼x13¾***
801 A242 350d multi 3.25 3.25

Intl. Year of Astronomy.

38th Chess Olympiad, Dresden, Germany A243

Designs: 70d, Chess board, Armenian players holding flag. 280d, Chess pieces, Armenian flag.

2009, July 29 ***Perf. 13¾x13¼***

802-803 A243	Set of 2	3.50	3.50
803a	Miniature sheet of 10, 5 each #802-803	25.00	25.00

European Court of Human Rights, 50th Anniv. A244

Perf. 12¾x13¼

2009, Nov. 13 **Litho.**
804 A244 70d multi 5.00 5.00

Council of Europe, 60th Anniv. — A245

2009, Nov. 13 ***Perf. 13¼x12¾***
805 A245 280d multi 7.00 7.00

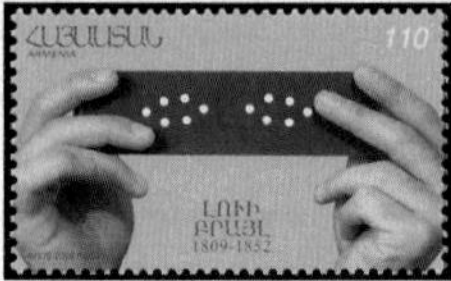

Louis Braille (1809-52), Educator of the Blind A246

2009, Nov. 24 **Litho.** ***Perf. 14¾x14***
806 A246 110d multi 1.10 1.10

No. 806 was issued in sheets of 10 and sheets of 8 + 2 labels. Value, sheet of 8 + 2 labels $12.

Daniel Varuzhan (1884-1915), Poet — A247

2009, Dec. 8 ***Perf. 13¼x12¾***
807 A247 230d multi 2.00 2.00

Souvenir Sheet

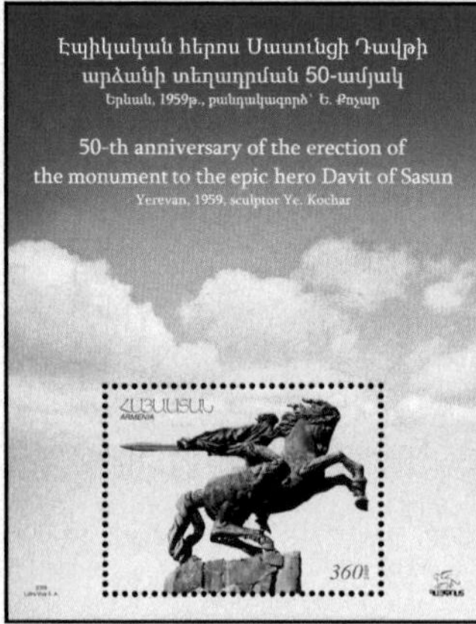

Davit of Sasun Monument, Yerevan, 50th Anniv. — A248

2009, Dec. 11 ***Perf. 14***
808 A248 360d multi 3.00 3.00

Souvenir Sheet

Olympic Champions — A249

No. 809: a, 70d, Hrant Shahinyan, gymnastics, 1952. b, 120d, Igor Novikov, pentathlon, 1956, 1964. c, 160d, Albert Azaryan, gymnastics, 1956, 1960.

2009, Dec. 11 **Litho.**
809 A249 Sheet of 3, #a-c 3.25 3.25

Khachatur Abovyan (1809-48), Writer A250

2009, Dec. 15 ***Perf. 12¾x13¼***
810 A250 170d multi 1.75 1.75

Animals — A251

Designs: 120d, Lutra lutra meridionalis. 160d, Ursus arctos syriacus.

2009, Dec. 16 ***Perf. 14***

811-812 A251	Set of 2	2.75	2.75
812a	Miniature sheet of 10, 5 each #811-812	14.50	14.50

Paintings in the National Gallery — A252

Designs: No. 813, 200d, Autumn. A Corner in Yerevan, by Sedrak Arakelyan. No. 814, 200d, Panna Paskevich, by Georgi Yakulov.

Perf. 13¼x12¾

2009, Dec. 16 **Litho.**
813-814 A252 Set of 2 3.75 3.75

Vagharshapat Churches on UNESCO World Heritage List — A253

No. 815: a, Zvarnots Church. b, St. Hripsime Church. c, Mother See of Holy Etchmiadzin Church. d, St. Gayane Church.

2009, Dec. 18 ***Perf. 14***
815 A253 70d Sheet of 4, #a-d 4.50 4.50

Christmas A254

Madonna and Child with: 280d, Country name in white. 650d, Country name in black.

Perf. 13½x13¾

2009, Dec. 18 **Litho.**

816 A254 280d multi 2.50 2.50

No. 816 was issued in sheets of 9 and sheets of 6 + 3 labels.

Souvenir Sheet

Perf. 14

817 A254 650d multi 5.75 5.75

No. 817 contains one 30x60mm stamp.

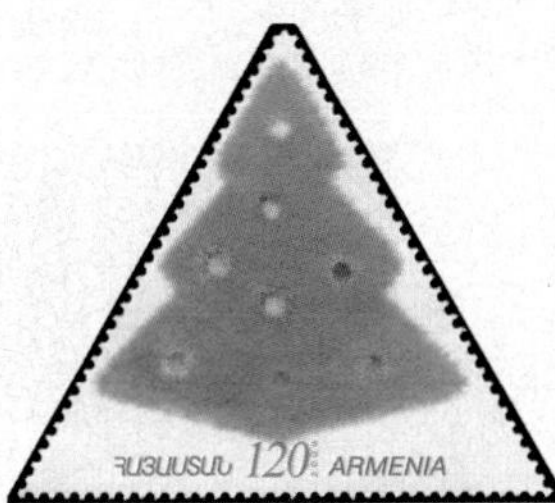

New Year 2010 — A255

Litho. with Flocking

2009, Dec. 18 *Perf. 14*

818 A255 120d multi 3.75 3.75

King Tigran the Great (c. 140-55 B.C.) — A256

2010, Jan. 29 **Litho.** *Perf. 13x13¼*

Background Color

819	A256	10d	cerise	.25	.25
820	A256	25d	dark blue	.25	.25
821	A256	50d	yel bister	.50	.50
822	A256	70d	vermilion	.65	.65
823	A256	100d	brown	.85	.85
824	A256	120d	maroon	1.00	1.00
825	A256	200d	gray	1.75	1.75
826	A256	220d	purple	2.00	2.00
827	A256	280d	red brown	2.50	2.50
828	A256	650d	yel green	6.00	6.00
			Nos. 819-828 (10)	15.75	15.75

Self-Adhesive

Serpentine Die Cut 11¼

829	A256	10d	cerise	.25	.25
830	A256	25d	dark blue	.25	.25
831	A256	50d	yel bister	.40	.40
832	A256	70d	vermilion	.55	.55
833	A256	100d	brown	.75	.75
834	A256	120d	maroon	.90	.90
835	A256	200d	gray	1.50	1.50
836	A256	220d	purple	1.75	1.75
837	A256	280d	red brown	2.10	2.10
838	A256	650d	yel green	5.00	5.00
			Nos. 829-838 (10)	13.45	13.45

Type A256 has no lettering below king's neck. The country name is smaller than that found on types A211 and A240. Compare with types A271-A272.

Henrik Kasparyan (1910-95), Chess Player — A257

2010, Feb. 27 *Perf. 14*

839 A257 870d multi 9.00 9.00

Victory in World War II, 65th Anniv. — A258

2010, May 6 *Perf. 13¼x12¾*

840 A258 350d multi 3.25 3.25

Cemetery for Russian Officers, Gyumri — A259

2010, Aug. 20 **Litho.** *Perf. 13¼x13*

Background Color

841 A259 350d light blue 3.00 3.00

Souvenir Sheet

842 A259 650d maroon 5.75 5.75

Mt. Ararat A260

Flag of Armenia — A261

2010, Sept. 21 *Perf. 12½x13*

843 A260 350d multi 3.00 3.00

Perf. 13¼

844 A261 650d multi 5.75 5.75

Independence Day.

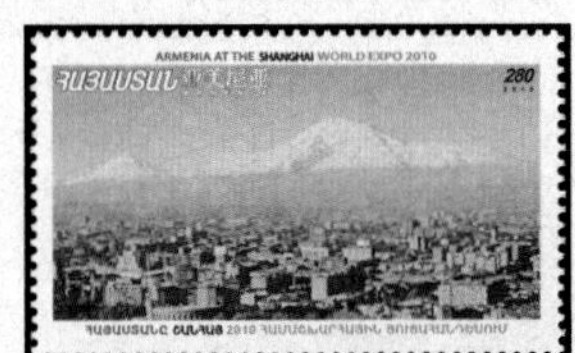

Yerevan and Mt. Ararat — A262

Armenian Pavilion at Expo 2010, Shanghai — A263

2010, Sept. 22 *Perf. 14*

845 A262 280d multi 2.50 2.50

Perf. 12½x13

846 A263 280d multi 2.50 2.50

Expo 2010, Shanghai.

Europa — A264

2010, Oct. 8 *Perf. 13¼*

847 A264 350d multi 3.00 3.00

2010 Youth Olympics, Singapore A265

2010, Nov. 26 *Perf. 12½x13*

848 A265 870d multi 7.75 7.75

2010 World Cup Soccer Championships, South Africa — A266

2010, Nov. 26 **Litho.**

849 A266 1100d multi 9.50 9.50

Souvenir Sheet

Olympic Champions — A267

No. 850: a, Vladimir Yengibaryan, boxing gold medalist, 1956. b, Faina Melnik, discus gold medalist, 1972. c, Yuri Vardanyan, weight lifting gold medalist, 1980.

2010, Nov. 26 *Perf. 13¼*

850 A267 160d Sheet of 3, #a-c 4.25 4.25

Souvenir Sheet

2010 Winter Olympics, Vancouver — A268

No. 851 — Skiers and 2010 Winter Olympics emblem at: a, 350d, Upper left. b, 500d, Center. c, 500d, Upper right.

2010, Nov. 26

851 A268 Sheet of 3, #a-c 13.00 6.50

Arakel Babakhanyan (1860-1932), Historian — A269

2010, Dec. 27 *Perf. 12½x13*

852 A269 220d multi 2.00 2.00

Raffi (Hakob Melik Hakobyan) (1835-88), Writer — A270

2010, Dec. 27 *Perf. 13x12½*

853 A270 220d multi 2.00 2.00

King Tigran the Great (c. 140-55 B.C.)

A271 A272

2011, Feb. 1 **Litho.** *Perf. 13¼*

Granite Paper

Background Color

854	A271	10d	dark blue	.25	.25
855	A272	35d	gray brn	.30	.30
856	A272	50d	green	.45	.45
857	A272	70d	blue green	.65	.65
858	A272	120d	org brown	1.10	1.10
859	A272	160d	maroon	1.50	1.50
860	A272	220d	dark red	2.00	2.00
861	A272	280d	purple	2.50	2.50
862	A272	350d	bister	3.25	3.25
863	A272	1100d	dk brown	10.00	10.00
			Nos. 854-863 (10)	22.00	22.00

Nos. 854-863 lack the word "Post." Compare with Types A211, A240 and A256.

Ruben Sevak (1885-1915), Writer — A273

2011, Feb. 2 *Perf. 13¼*

864 A273 280d multi 2.50 2.50

Dated 2010.

A274

2011, Feb. 2 *Perf. 13¼*

865 A274 280d multi 2.50 2.50

Vahan Teryan (1885-1920), writer. Dated 2010.

A275

Paintings in National Gallery: No. 866, 450d, Portrait of Actress Khmara, by Haroutyun Kalents. No. 867, 450d, Catholicos Mkrtich Khrimyan, by Vardghes Sourenyants.

2011, Feb. 2 *Perf. 13x12½*

866-867 A275 Set of 2 8.00 8.00

Dated 2010.

Souvenir Sheet

Pepo, First Armenian Film With Sound, 75th Anniv. (in 2010) — A276

No. 868: a, 170d, Actors Avet Avetisyan and Davit Malyan. b, 200d, Actor Hrachya Nercissyan. c, 500d, Actress Tatiana Makhmuryan.

2011, Feb. 2 ***Perf. 13¼***
868 A276 Sheet of 3, #a-c 7.25 7.25

Dated 2010.

Leonid Yenigbarov (1935-72), Circus Clown — A277

2011, Feb. 2 Litho. ***Perf. 13x12½***
869 A277 220d multi 1.75 1.75

Flora — A278

Designs: No. 870, 280d, Fritillaria armena. No. 871, 280d, Sambucus tigranii.

2011, Feb. 2 ***Perf. 13¼***
870-871 A278 Set of 2 4.75 4.75

Souvenir Sheet

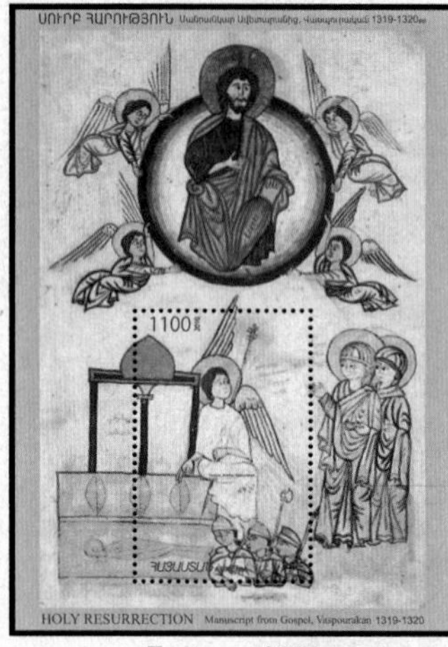

Easter — A279

2011, Apr. 15 Litho. ***Perf. 12½x13***
872 A279 1100d multi 8.50 8.50

Andranik Iossifian (1905-93), Designer of Meteorological Satellites — A280

First Man in Space, 50th Anniv. A281

2011, Apr. 18 ***Perf. 13x12½***
873 A280 200d multi 1.50 1.50

Perf. 12½x13
874 A281 350d multi 2.50 2.50

Capitals of Belarus and Armenia — A282

No. 875 — Buildings and arms of: a, Minsk, Belarus. b, Yerevan, Armenia.

2011, June 1 Litho. ***Perf. 13***
875 A282 200d Horiz. pair, #a-b 3.50 3.50

See Belarus No. 771.

Souvenir Sheet

Communications Regional Commonwealth, 20th Anniv. — A283

2011, June 1
876 A283 200d multi 1.75 1.75

Writers — A284

Designs: 120d, Hovhannes Tumanian (1869-1923). 230d, Valery Bryusov (1873-1924).

2011, June 1 ***Perf. 12¾***
877-878 A284 Set of 2 3.00 3.00
878a Vert. pair, #877-878 3.00 3.00

Nos. 877-878 each were printed in sheets of 9 + label. No. 878a was printed in sheets containing five pairs.

See Russia Nos. 7273-7274.

Souvenir Sheet

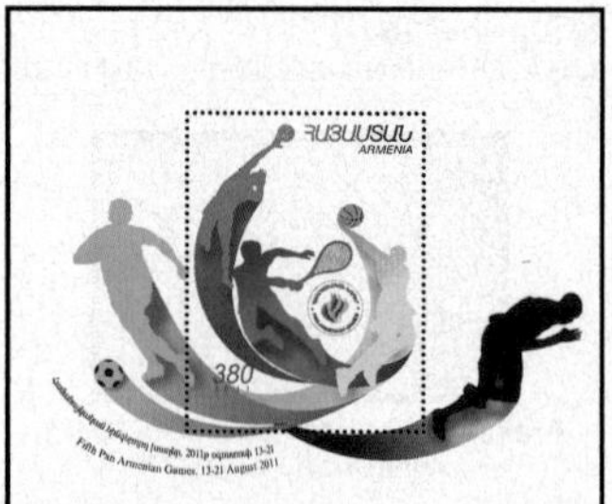

Fifth Pan-Armenian Games — A285

2011, Aug. 20
879 A285 380d multi 3.50 3.50

Birds — A286

Designs: 230d, Luscinia svecica. 330d, Parus major.

2011, Sept. 5 ***Perf. 13¼***
880 A286 230d multi 2.00 2.00
881 A286 330d multi 3.00 3.00
a. Horiz. pair, #880-881 5.00 5.00

Independence of Nagorno Karabakh From Azerbaijan, 20th Anniv. — A287

2011, Sept. 13 ***Perf. 13x13¼***
882 A287 330d multi 3.00 3.00

Independence of Armenia, 20th Anniv. — A288

2011, Sept. 13
883 A288 380d multi 3.00 3.00

Fridtjof Nansen (1861-1930), Polar Explorer, Diplomat Assisting in Alleviating Armenian Refugee Crisis A289

2011, Nov. 9 ***Perf. 13½***
884 A289 350d olive bister 3.00 3.00

Commonwealth of Independent States, 20th Anniv. — A290

2011, Dec. 1 ***Perf. 13x12½***
885 A290 280d multi 2.40 2.40

Souvenir Sheet

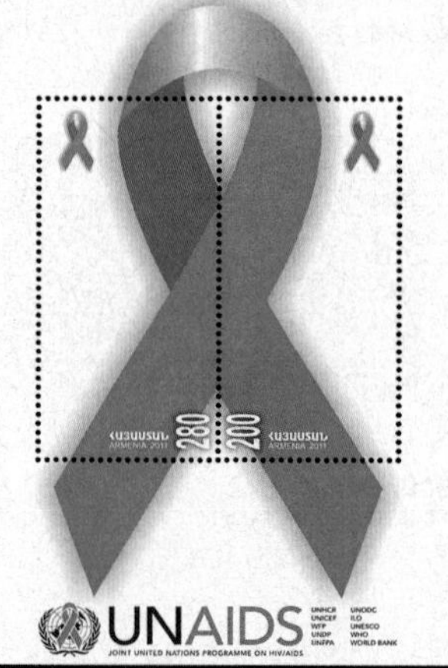

Joint United Nations Program on AIDS — A291

No. 886 — AIDS ribbons: a, 200d. b, 280d.

2011, Dec. 1 ***Perf. 13¼***
886 A291 Sheet of 2, #a-b 4.25 4.25

2011 Junior Eurovision Song Contest, Yerevan — A292

2011, Dec. 3 ***Perf. 13¼x13***
887 A292 230d multi 2.00 2.00
a. Souvenir sheet of 4 8.00 8.00

No. 887 was printed in sheets of 8.

Europa A293

Photographs of forest in Dilijan Reserve with denominations at: No. 888, 350d, LL. No. 889, 350d, LR.

2011, Dec. 14 ***Perf. 12½x13***
888-889 A293 Set of 2 6.00 6.00

Intl. Year of Forests.

Grigor Zohrap (1861-1915), Lawyer and Writer — A294

2011, Dec. 23 ***Perf. 13¼x13***
890 A294 170d multi 1.40 1.40

Children — A295

No. 891: a, 100d, Girl holding grapes and bird, flag of Armenia. b, 120d, Boy holding wheat stalks, flag of Nagorno Karabakh.

2011, Dec. 27 **Litho.**
891 A295 Horiz. pair, #a-b 1.90 1.90

Youth philately. No. 891 was printed in sheets containing two pairs.

Souvenir Sheet

UNESCO World Heritage Sites — A296

No. 892: a, 230d, Sanahin Monastery. b, 330d, Haghpat Monastery.

2011, Dec. 27 ***Perf. 13¼x13***
892 A296 Sheet of 2, #a-b 4.75 4.75

Christmas and New Year's Day — A297

2011, Dec. 27 ***Perf. 13¼***
893 A297 220d multi 1.90 1.90

Armenian Army, 20th Anniv. — A298

Army coat of arms and: 200d, Soldiers, tank, military vehicle, airplanes. 280d, Armenian flag.

2012, Feb. 9 ***Perf. 13¼x13***
894-895 A298 Set of 2 4.25 4.25

Admission to United Nations, 20th Anniv, A299

2012, Mar. 23 Litho. ***Perf. 13x13¼***
896 A299 350d multi 3.00 3.00

Souvenir Sheet

Yerevan, World Book Capital — A300

2012, Apr. 22
897 A300 560d multi 5.00 5.00

Garegin Nzhdeh (1886-1955), Statesman A301

2012, May 3 ***Perf. 13¼***
898 A301 200d multi 1.90 1.90

Misak Metsarents (1886-1908), Poet — A302

2012, May 3 ***Perf. 13¼x13***
899 A302 280d black 2.50 2.50

Armenian Alphabet — A303

First seven letters of Armenian alphabet in capital and lower-case.

2012, May 14 ***Perf. 13x13¼***

Color of Panel at Left

900	A303	10d dull rose	.25	.25
901	A303	25d yel green	.25	.25
902	A303	50d gray blue	.45	.45
903	A303	70d dull blue	.60	.60
904	A303	100d greenish gray	.90	.90
905	A303	120d dull blue	1.10	1.10
906	A303	280d lilac rose	2.50	2.50
		Nos. 900-906 (7)	6.05	6.05

See Nos. 940-946.

Khachkars — A304

Khachkar: 200d, By Master Poghos, Goshavank, 1291. 280d, Arinj, 13th cent.

2012, June 14 ***Perf. 13¼***
907-908 A304 Set of 2 4.00 4.00

Souvenir Sheet

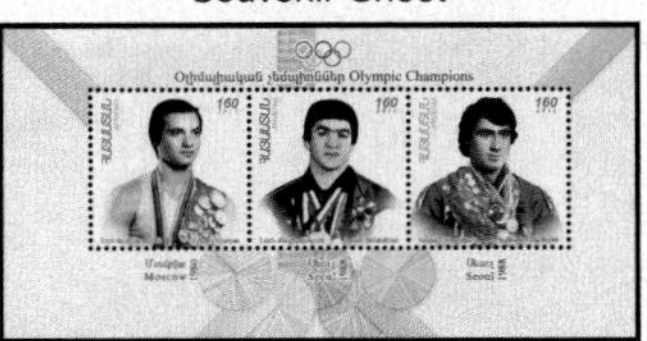

Armenian Olympic Gold Medalists — A305

No. 909: a, Eduard Azaryan. b, Levon Julfalakyan. c, Hoksen Mirzoyan.

2012, June 15
909 A305 160d Sheet of 3, #a-c 4.00 4.00

Souvenir Sheet

Mesrop Mashtots (361-440), Monk — A306

2012, June 19 ***Perf. 14½x14¼***
910 A306 560d multi 4.50 4.50

Hagigadar Monastery — A307

2012, Aug. 11 ***Perf. 13¼***
911 A307 380d multi 3.25 3.25
a. Souvenir sheet of 2 + 2 labels 6.50 6.50

See Romania No. 5383.

Armenian Membership in Organization for Security and Cooperation in Europe, 20th Anniv. — A308

2012, Sept. 7 ***Perf. 13x13¼***
912 A308 330d multi 2.75 2.75

Ancient Artashat, Capital of Kingdom of Armenia, 185 B.C.-120 A.D. A309

2012, Oct. 30
913 A309 220d multi 1.90 1.90

Mount Ararat and Alexander Misnikyan (1886-1925), Bolshevik Leader — A310

2012, Oct. 30
914 A310 230d multi 2.00 2.00

Samvel Kocharyants (1909-93), Nuclear Physicist — A311

2012, Nov. 30 ***Perf. 14x13½***
915 A311 350d multi 3.00 3.00

2012 Summer Olympics, London — A312

2012, Nov. 30 ***Perf. 13¼***
916 Horiz. strip of 3 5.25 5.25
a. A312 170d Boxing 1.50 1.50
b. A312 200d Weight lifting 1.75 1.75
c. A312 230d Wrestling 2.00 2.00

Miniature Sheet

Armenian Olympic Gold Medalists — A313

No. 917: a, Hrachya Petikyan, shooting, 1992. b, Israyel Militosyan, weight lifting, 1992. c, Mnatsakan Iskandaryan, boxing, 1992. d, Armen Nazaryan, boxing, 1996.

2012, Nov. 30
917 A313 120d Sheet of 4, #a-d 4.25 4.25

Perch Proshyan (1837-1907), Writer — A314

2012, Dec. 4 **Litho.**
918 A314 170d multi 1.50 1.50

Lusine Zakaryan (1937-92), Opera Singer A315

2012, Dec. 4 ***Perf. 13x13¼***
919 A315 220d multi 1.90 1.90

Religious Treasures of Etchmiadzin — A316

No. 920: a, 200d, Reliquary of Geghard, 1687. b, 220d, Cross with relic, 1746. c, 450d, Reliquary, Argadsz, St. Nshan, 13th cent.

2012, Dec. 4 ***Perf. 13¼x13***
920 A316 Horiz. strip of 3, #a-c 7.50 7.50

Ashot Hovhannisyan (1887-1977), First Secretary of Armenian Communist Party — A317

2012, Dec. 5 ***Perf. 13x13¼***
921 A317 170d black 1.50 1.50

A318 A319

2012, Dec. 5 ***Perf. 13¼x13***
922 A318 280d multi 2.50 2.50

Hovsep Orbeli (1887-1961), President of Armenian Academy of Arts and Sciences.

2012, Dec. 5
923 A319 280d multi 2.50 2.50

Hayk Bzhishkyants (1887-1937), military leader.

Tigran Tchoukhadjian (1837-98), Composer — A320

2012, Dec. 6 **Litho.**
924 A320 330d multi 3.00 3.00

Hayastan All-Armenian Fund, 20th Anniv. — A321

2012, Dec. 12 ***Perf. 13x13¼***
925 A321 380d multi 3.50 3.50

Collective Security Treaty Organization, 20th Anniv. — A322

2012, Dec. 17 ***Perf. 13¼x13***
926 A322 230d multi 2.10 2.10

Tadevos Minasyants (1912-82), Minister of Communications — A323

2012, Dec. 27 ***Perf. 13x13¼***
927 A323 170d multi 1.60 1.60

Tatev Monastery — A324

2012, Dec. 27 **Litho.**
928 A324 350d multi 3.25 3.25
a. Sheet of 4 + 2 labels 13.00 13.00

Europa.

Paintings in National Gallery of Armenia — A325

Designs: 220d, Dacha, by Marc Chagall. 280d, Self-portrait, by Rudolf Khachatryan.

2012, Dec. 27 ***Perf. 13¼x13***
929-930 A325 Set of 2 4.50 4.50

Souvenir Sheet

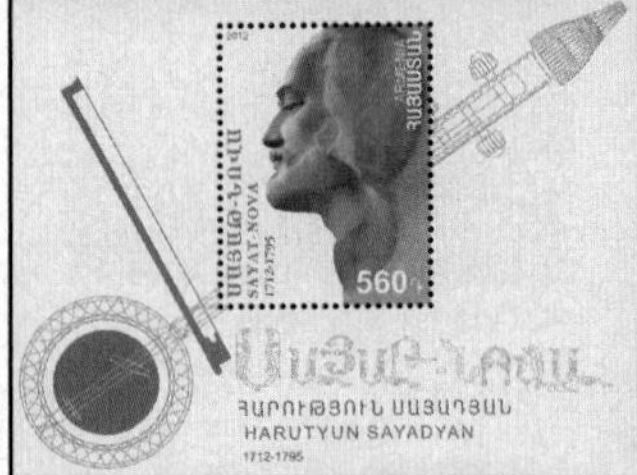

Sayat-Nova (1712-95), Musician — A326

2012, Dec. 27
931 A326 560d multi 5.00 5.00

Children's Art — A327

Designs: 100d, Trees. 120d, Soccer player.

2012, Dec. 28 ***Perf. 13¾***
932-933 A327 Set of 2 2.00 2.00

Mammals A328

Designs: 230d, Allactaga elater. 330d, Ovis orientalis gmelinii.

2012, Dec. 28 ***Perf. 12½***
934 A328 230d multi 2.00 2.00
935 A328 330d multi 3.00 3.00
a. Horiz. pair, #934-935 5.00 5.00

Christmas and New Year's Day A329

2012, Dec. 28 ***Perf. 13x13¼***
936 A329 220d multi 2.00 2.00

St. Sargis's Day — A330

2013, Jan. 29 ***Perf. 13¼x13***
937 A330 280d multi 2.50 2.50

Souvenir Sheet

Churches — A331

No. 938: a, 160d, Holy Trinity Church, Yerevan. b, 200d, Church of Holy Archangels, St. Etchmiadzin. c, 200d, Church of St. Hakob of Msbin, Gyumri.

2013, Apr. 4 ***Perf. 13¼***
938 A331 Sheet of 3, #a-c 4.50 4.50

Brandy Production in Armenia A332

2013, June 18 ***Perf. 13x13¼***
939 A332 300d multi 2.50 2.50

No. 939 was printed in sheets of 8 + 2 labels.

Armenian Alphabet Type of 2012

Second seven letters of Armenian alphabet in capital and lower-case.

2013, July 30 ***Perf. 13x13¼***
Color of Panel at Left

940	A303	10d	olive bister	.25	.25
941	A303	35d	salmon rose	.35	.35
942	A303	50d	green	.50	.50
943	A303	60d	blue	.60	.60
944	A303	70d	rose	.70	.70
945	A303	100d	greenish blue	1.00	1.00
946	A303	120d	gray blue	1.25	1.25
			Nos. 940-946 (7)	4.65	4.65

Europa A333

2013, Aug. 15 **Litho.**
947 A333 350d multi 3.50 3.50
a. Souvenir sheet of 4 14.00 14.00

Johannes Lepsius (1858-1926), Documenter of Armenian Genocide — A334

James Bryce (1838-1922), Documenter of Armenian Genocide — A335

2013, Aug. 16 ***Perf. 13x13¼***
948 A334 280d multi 2.75 2.75

Perf. 13¼x13
949 A335 330d multi 3.25 3.25

Armenian Genocide, cent. (in 2015).

Souvenir Sheet

Church of St. Grigor, Kecharis Monastery, Tsakhkadsor — A336

2013, Aug. 24 **Litho.** ***Perf. 13¼x13***
950 A336 480d multi 4.75 4.75

Souvenir Sheet

Aurora Mardiganian (1901-94), Writer of Memoir "Ravished Armenia" — A337

Perf. 14¼x14½
2013, Sept. 24 **Litho.**
951 A337 480d multi 4.75 4.75

SEMI-POSTAL STAMPS

International Children's Day — SP1

2008, June 1 **Litho.** ***Perf. 14¾x14***
B1 SP1 70d +30d multi 1.10 1.10

Surtax (on sheet margin) was for UNICEF.

AIR POST STAMPS

AP1

Design: 90d, Artiom Katsian (1886-1943), world record holding pilot on range and altitude in 1909.

1995, Dec. 5 **Litho.** ***Perf. 14x15***
C1 AP1 90d multicolored 1.50 1.50

AP2

1996, Apr. 30 **Litho.** ***Perf. 14x14½***
C2 AP2 90d multicolored 1.25 1.25

Nelson Stepanian (1913-44), WWII fighter ace.

ARUBA

ə-ˈrü-bə

LOCATION — West Indies, north of Venezuela
AREA — 78 sq. mi.
POP. — 67,014
CAPITAL — Oranjestad

On Jan. 1, 1986 Aruba, formerly part of Netherlands Antilles, achieved a separate status within the Kingdom of the Netherlands.

100 Cents = 1 Gulden

Catalogue values for all unused stamps in this country are for Never Hinged items.

Used values are for CTO or stamps removed from first day covers. Postally used examples sell for more.

Traditional House — A1

Perf. 14x13

1986-87		**Litho.**	**Unwmk.**	
1	A1	5c shown	.40	.25
2	A1	15c King William III Tower	.85	.40
3	A1	20c Loading crane	.60	.30
4	A1	25c Lighthouse	1.00	.35
5	A1	30c Snake	1.25	.70
6	A1	35c Owl	1.25	.70
7	A1	45c Shell	1.25	.70
8	A1	55c Frog	1.40	.80
9	A1	60c Water skier	1.50	1.00
10	A1	65c Net fishing	1.50	1.00
11	A1	75c Music box	1.50	1.10
12	A1	85c Pre-Columbian bisque pot	1.60	1.00
13	A1	90c Bulb cactus	2.00	1.25
14	A1	100c Grain	2.00	1.25
15	A1	150c Watapana tree	4.00	2.00
16	A1	250c Aloe plant	5.25	4.00
		Nos. 1-16 (16)	27.35	16.80

Issued: 5c, 30c, 60c, 150c, 1/1; 15c, 35c, 65c, 250c, 2/5; 20c, 45c, 75c, 100c, 4/7/87; 25c, 55c, 85c, 90c, 7/17/87.

Independence A2

1986, Jan. 1		***Perf. 14x13, 13x14***		
18	A2	25c Map	1.50	.50
19	A2	45c Coat of arms, vert.	2.00	1.00
20	A2	55c Natl. anthem, vert.	2.50	1.50
21	A2	100c Flag	3.00	2.50
		Nos. 18-21 (4)	9.00	5.50

Intl. Peace Year — A3

1986, Aug. 29		**Litho.** ***Perf. 14x13***		
22	A3	60c shown	2.00	1.00
23	A3	100c Barbed wire	4.75	1.75

Princess Juliana and Prince Bernhard, 50th Wedding Anniv. — A4

1987, Jan. 7		**Photo.** ***Perf. 13x14***		
24	A4	135c multicolored	4.00	2.25

State Visit of Queen Beatrix and Prince Claus of the Netherlands A5

1987, Feb. 16		**Litho.** ***Perf. 14x13***		
25	A5	55c shown	2.00	1.00
26	A5	60c Prince William-Alexander	2.00	1.00

Tourism — A6

1987, June 5		**Litho.**		
27	A6	60c Beach and sea	2.00	1.25
28	A6	100c Rock and cacti	2.75	1.50

Aloe Vera Plant — A7

Coins — A8

1988, Jan. 27		**Litho.** ***Perf. 13x14***		
29	A7	45c Field	1.75	.90
30	A7	60c Plant	2.00	1.25
31	A7	100c Harvest	2.50	1.40
		Nos. 29-31 (3)	6.25	3.55

1988, Mar. 16		**Litho.** ***Perf. 13x14***		
32	A8	25c 25-cent	1.25	.40
33	A8	55c 50-cent	1.75	.90
34	A8	65c 5 and 10-cent	2.00	1.25
35	A8	150c 1-florin	3.50	2.25
		Nos. 32-35 (4)	8.50	4.80

Love Issue — A9

A10

1988, May 4				
36	A9	70c shown	1.75	1.00
37	A9	135c Seashells, coastal scenery	2.50	1.75

1988, Aug. 24				
38	A10	35c shown	1.50	.75
39	A10	100c Emblems	2.50	1.40

Aruba, the 162nd member of the Intl. Olympic Committee (35c), 1988 Summer Olympics, Seoul (100c).

Carnival A11

1989, Jan. 5		***Perf. 14x13***		
40	A11	45c Two children	2.00	.90
41	A11	60c Girl	2.00	.90
42	A11	100c Entertainer	2.50	1.25
		Nos. 40-42 (3)	6.50	3.05

Maripampun, *Omphalophalmum Rubrum* — A12

1989, Mar. 16		**Litho.** ***Perf. 14x13***		
43	A12	35c Leaves	1.50	.70
44	A12	55c Pods	1.50	.90
45	A12	200c Blossom	4.00	2.75
		Nos. 43-45 (3)	7.00	4.35

New Year 1990 — A13

UPU — A14

Dande band members playing instruments or singing: 25c, Violin, tambor, cuatro, marimba. 70c, Lead singer, guitar. 150c, Accordion, urri, guitar.

1989, Nov. 16		**Litho.** ***Perf. 13x14***		
46	A13	25c multicolored	1.00	.50
47	A13	70c multicolored	1.40	.90
48	A13	150c multicolored	2.75	1.90
		Nos. 46-48 (3)	5.15	3.30

1989, June 8		**Litho.** ***Perf. 13x14***		
49	A14	250c multicolored	5.25	3.00

Crotalus durissus unicolor A15

1989, Aug. 24		***Perf. 14x13***		
50	A15	45c shown	1.50	.75
51	A15	55c multi, diff.	1.75	.90
52	A15	60c multi, diff.	1.75	.90
		Nos. 50-52 (3)	5.00	2.55

Snake species in danger of extinction.

Man Living in Harmony with Nature — A16

1990, Feb. 7		***Perf. 13x14, 14x13***		
53	A16	45c The land	1.25	.90
54	A16	55c shown	1.50	.90
55	A16	100c The sea	2.50	1.75
		Nos. 53-55 (3)	5.25	3.55

Environmental protection. Nos. 53, 55 horiz.

Marine Life — A17

Designs: 60c, Giant caribbean anemone, Pederson's cleaning shrimp. 70c, Queen angelfish, red and orange coral. 100c, Banded coral shrimp, fire sponge, yellow boring sponge.

1990, Apr. 4		**Litho.** ***Perf. 14x13***		
56	A17	60c multicolored	1.50	.90
57	A17	70c multicolored	2.00	1.25
58	A17	100c multicolored	2.75	2.25
		Nos. 56-58 (3)	6.25	4.40

A18

A19

1990, May 30		**Litho.** ***Perf. 13x14***		
59	A18	35c multicolored	1.25	.75
60	A18	200c Character trademark	4.00	2.75

World Cup Soccer Championships, Italy.

1990, Sept. 12				
61	A19	45c Tools	1.25	.90
62	A19	60c Stone figure	1.50	.90
63	A19	100c Jar	2.75	1.40
		Nos. 61-63 (3)	5.50	3.20

Archeological discoveries.

Landscapes A20

1991, Jan. 31		**Litho.** ***Perf. 14x13***		
64	A20	55c Seashore	1.40	.90
65	A20	65c Desert	1.60	1.25
66	A20	100c Cactus, ocean view	2.25	1.90
		Nos. 64-66 (3)	5.25	4.05

Working Women — A21

Medicinal Plants — A22

Designs: 35c, Taking care of others. 70c, Housewife. 100c, Women in society.

1991, Mar. 28		**Litho.** ***Perf. 13x14***		
67	A21	35c multicolored	1.00	.45
68	A21	70c multicolored	1.50	1.25
69	A21	100c multicolored	2.00	1.75
		Nos. 67-69 (3)	4.50	3.45

Style of inscriptions varies.

1991, May 29				
70	A22	65c Ocimum sanctum	1.50	.90
71	A22	75c Jatropha gossypifolia	1.75	1.25
72	A22	95c Croton flavens	2.00	1.40
		Nos. 70-72 (3)	5.25	3.55

A23

A24

Aruban Handicrafts: 35c, Fish net, wood float, wooden needle. 250c, Straw hat, hat block.

1991, July 31		**Litho.** ***Perf. 13x14***		
73	A23	35c lt bl, dk bl & blk	1.00	.75
74	A23	250c pink, lil rose & blk	4.50	3.50

1991, Nov. 29 Litho. *Perf. 13x14*

75 A24 35c Toucan 1.00 .90
76 A24 70c People shaking hands 1.50 .90
77 A24 100c Windmill 2.50 1.75
Nos. 75-77 (3) 5.00 3.55

Welcome to Aruba.

Aruba Postal Service, Cent. — A25

60c, Government decree, 1892, vert. 75c, First post office. 80c, Current post office.

Perf. 13x14, 14x13

1992, Jan. 31 Litho.

78 A25 60c multicolored 1.25 .90
79 A25 75c multicolored 1.50 .90
80 A25 80c multicolored 2.00 1.25
Nos. 78-80 (3) 4.75 3.05

Equality Day — A26

1992, Mar. 25 Litho. *Perf. 14x13*

81 A26 100c People of five races 2.00 1.40
82 A26 100c Woman, man, scales 2.00 1.40

Discovery of America, 500th Anniv. — A27

1992, July 30 Litho. *Perf. 13x14*

83 A27 30c Columbus 1.25 .50
84 A27 40c Sailing ship 1.50 .75
85 A27 50c Natives, map 1.75 .95
Nos. 83-85 (3) 4.50 2.20

Natural Bridges in Aruba — A28

Designs: 70c, Seroe Colorado Bridge, south coast. 80c, Natural Bridge, north coast.

1992, Nov. 30 Litho. *Perf. 14x13*

86 A28 70c multicolored 1.50 .90
87 A28 80c multicolored 1.75 1.40

A29

A30

1993, Jan. 29 Litho. *Perf. 13x14*

88 A29 200c multicolored 4.00 2.75

Express mail service.

1993, Mar. 31 Litho. *Perf. 13x14*

Various rock formations found in Districts of Ayo and Casibari.

89 A30 50c multicolored 1.00 .90
90 A30 60c multicolored 1.25 .90
91 A30 100c multicolored 2.00 1.75
Nos. 89-91 (3) 4.25 3.55

Folklore — A31

Sailing Sports — A32

40c, String instruments, drum. 70c, Traditional music & games. 80c, Dera Gai song lyrics.

1993, May 28 Litho. *Perf. 13x14*

92 A31 40c multicolored 1.00 .90
93 A31 70c multicolored 1.25 .90
94 A31 80c multicolored 1.50 1.40
Nos. 92-94 (3) 3.75 3.20

1993, July 30 Litho. *Perf. 13x14*

95 A32 50c Sailboating 1.10 .90
96 A32 65c Land sailing 1.40 .90
97 A32 75c Wind surfing 1.60 1.10
Nos. 95-97 (3) 4.10 2.90

Iguana Iguana — A33

Perf. 14x13, 13x14

1993, Sept. 1 Litho.

98 A33 35c Young 1.25 .75
99 A33 60c Almost grown 1.50 1.25
100 A33 100c Mature, vert. 2.25 1.90
Nos. 98-100 (3) 5.00 3.90

Burrowing Owl — A34

Perf. 14x13, 13x14

1994, Jan. 28 Litho.

101 A34 5c Two adults 1.50 .50
102 A34 10c Two adults, young 1.50 .75
103 A34 35c Adult with prey, vert. 2.00 1.00
104 A34 40c Adult, vert. 2.00 1.50
Nos. 101-104 (4) 7.00 3.75

World Wildlife Fund.

A35

A36

Intl. Olympic Committee, Cent.: 90c, Baron Pierre de Coubertin (1863-1937), founder of modern Olympics.

1994, Mar. 29 Litho. *Perf. 13x14*

105 A35 50c multicolored 1.25 1.00
106 A35 90c multicolored 1.75 1.40

1994, July 7 Litho. *Perf. 13x14*

107 A36 65c shown 1.50 1.25
108 A36 150c Mascot, soccer ball 2.75 2.50

1994 World Cup Soccer Championships, US.

Wild Fruit — A37

Designs: 40c, Malpighia punicifolia. 70c, Cordia sebestena. 85c, Pithecellobium unguis-cati. 150c, Coccoloba uvifera.

1994, Sept. 28 Litho. *Perf. 13x14*

109 A37 40c multicolored 1.00 .90
110 A37 70c multicolored 1.50 .90
111 A37 85c multicolored 1.75 1.40
112 A37 150c multicolored 3.25 2.50
Nos. 109-112 (4) 7.50 5.70

Architectural Landmarks A38

Designs: 35c, Government building, 1888. 60c, Ecury residence, 1929, vert. 100c, Protestant Church, 1846, vert.

1995, Jan. 27 Litho. *Perf. 14x13*

113 A38 35c multicolored .80 .70

Perf. 13x14

114 A38 60c multicolored 1.25 .85
115 A38 100c multicolored 2.10 1.75
Nos. 113-115 (3) 4.15 3.30

UN, 50th Anniv. — A39

Interpaso Horses — A40

Designs: 30c, Flags, sea, UN emblem, dove, text from UN charter. 200c, World with flags, doves, UN emblem.

1995, Mar. 29 Litho. *Perf. 13x14*

116 A39 30c multicolored 1.25 .75
117 A39 200c multicolored 3.75 3.00

1995, May 26 *Perf. 14x13, 13x14*

Designs: 25c, 10-time champion Casanova II, ribbons, horiz. 75c, Paso Fino, horiz. 80c, Horse doing figure 8. 90c, Girl on horse.

118 A40 25c multicolored .75 .45
119 A40 75c multicolored 1.50 1.25
120 A40 80c multicolored 1.50 1.40
121 A40 90c multicolored 1.75 1.40
Nos. 118-121 (4) 5.50 4.50

Vegetables — A41

1995, July 28 Litho. *Perf. 13x14*

122 A41 25c Vigna sinensis .75 .45
123 A41 50c Cucumis anguria 1.25 .90
124 A41 70c Hibiscus esculentus 1.40 1.25
125 A41 85c Cucurbita moschata 1.60 1.50
Nos. 122-125 (4) 5.00 4.10

Turtles — A42

1995, Sept. 27 Litho. *Perf. 14x13*

126 A42 15c Hawksbill 1.40 .55
127 A42 50c Green 1.75 .90
128 A42 95c Loggerhead 2.25 1.50
129 A42 100c Leatherback 2.50 1.50
Nos. 126-129 (4) 7.90 4.45

Separate Status, 10th Anniv. — A43

Statesmen and politicians: No. 130, Jan Hendrik Albert Eman (1887-1957). No. 131, Juan Enrique Irausquin (1904-62). No. 132, Cornelis Albert Eman (1916-67). No. 133, Gilberto Francois Croes (1938-85).

1996, Jan. 1 Litho. *Perf. 13x14*

130 A43 100c multicolored 1.75 1.40
131 A43 100c multicolored 1.75 1.40
132 A43 100c multicolored 1.75 1.40
133 A43 100c multicolored 1.75 1.40
Nos. 130-133 (4) 7.00 5.60

The 1986 date on No. 133 is in error.

America Issue — A44

National dresswear: 65c, Woman wearing long, full dress, apron, vert. 70c, Man wearing hat, bow tie, white shirt, black pants, vert. 100c, Couple dancing.

Perf. 13x14, 14x13

1996, Mar. 25 Litho.

134 A44 65c multicolored 2.00 .95
135 A44 70c multicolored 2.00 .95
136 A44 100c multicolored 2.75 1.60
Nos. 134-136 (3) 6.75 3.50

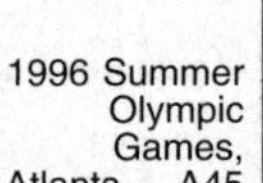

1996 Summer Olympic Games, Atlanta — A45

1996, May 28 Litho. *Perf. 14x13*

137 A45 85c Runners 2.00 1.25
138 A45 130c Cyclist 2.75 2.10

A46

A47

Famous Women: No. 139, Livia (Mimi) Ecury (1920-91), nurse. No. 140, Lolita Euson (1914-94), poet. No. 141, Laura Wernet-Paskel (1911-62), teacher.

1996, Sept. 27 Litho. *Perf. 13x14*

139 A46 60c multicolored 1.40 1.25
140 A46 60c multicolored 1.40 1.25
141 A46 60c multicolored 1.40 1.25
Nos. 139-141 (3) 4.20 3.75

1997, Jan. 23 Litho. *Perf. 13x14*

Year of Papiamento 1997: 50c, Sign promoting use of Papiamento language, children playing on beach, people in water, boat. 140c, "Papiamento," sunrise.

142 A47 50c multicolored 1.00 1.00
143 A47 140c multicolored 2.50 2.50

Mailman on Bicycle, 1936-57 A48

America issue: 70c, Mailman handing mail to woman, jeep, 1957-88. 80c, Mailman on motor scooter placing mail in mailbox, 1995.

1997, Mar. 27 Litho. *Perf. 14x13*

144 A48 60c multicolored 2.40 1.40
145 A48 70c multicolored 2.50 1.50
146 A48 80c multicolored 3.00 1.60
Nos. 144-146 (3) 7.90 4.50

Aruban Architectrue A49

30c, Decorated cunucu house. 65c, Steps with "popchi's." 100c, Arends's Building, vert.

1997, May 22 Litho. *Perf. 14x13*

147 A49 30c multicolored .90 .75
148 A49 65c multicolored 1.75 1.25

Perf. 13x14

149 A49 100c multicolored 2.00 1.75
Nos. 147-149 (3) 4.65 3.75

Marine Life — A50

Designs: a, Marlin jumping out of water, lighthouse. b, Dolphin jumping out of water, trees, plants on beach. c, Iguana on rock, beach. d, Dolphin, fish. e, Two dolphins, fish. f, Fish, turtles, owl on beach. g, Various fish among coral. h, Diver, shipwreck, fish, coral. i, Various fish.

1997, May 29 Litho. *Perf. 12½x13*

150 A50 90c Sheet of 9, #a.-i. 25.00 25.00

PACIFIC 97.

Cruise Tourism A51

Designs: 35c, Ship at pier, tourists walking toward ship. 50c, Ship with gangway lowered, tourists. 150c, Ship out to sea, small boat.

1997, July 24 Litho. *Perf. 14x13*

151 A51 35c multicolored 1.00 .85
152 A51 50c multicolored 1.25 1.10
153 A51 150c multicolored 3.00 2.50
Nos. 151-153 (3) 5.25 4.45

Aruban Wild Flowers A52

50c, Erythrina velutina. 60c, Cordia dentata. 70c, Tabebuia billbergii. 130c, Guaiacum officinale.

1997, Sept. 25

154 A52 50c multicolored 1.25 .95
155 A52 60c multicolored 1.50 1.25
156 A52 70c multicolored 1.75 1.25
157 A52 130c multicolored 2.75 2.00
Nos. 154-157 (4) 7.25 5.45

Fort Zoutman, Bicent. — A53

1998, Jan. 13 Litho. *Perf. 14x13*

158 A53 30c sepia & multi 1.00 .75
159 A53 250c gray & multi 4.25 3.75

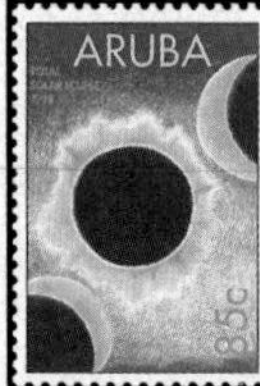

Total Solar Eclipse, 1998 — A54

1998, Feb. 26 Litho. *Perf. 13x14*

160 A54 85c shown 2.75 1.50
161 A54 100c Map, track of eclipse 3.50 2.00

Native Birds — A55

50c, Mimus gilvus. 60c, Falco sparverius. 70c, Icterus icterus. 150c, Coereba flaveola.

Perf. 14x13, 13x14

1998, July 10 Litho.

162 A55 50c multi 1.60 1.00
163 A55 60c multi, vert. 2.00 1.25
164 A55 70c multi, vert. 2.25 1.25
165 A55 150c multi 3.50 2.75
Nos. 162-165 (4) 9.35 6.25

World Stamp 1998 — A56

1998, Sept. 8 Litho. *Perf. 14x13*

166 A56 225c multicolored 5.50 4.25

Endangered Animals A57

Equus asinus: 40c, Two standing on hill. 65c, Three standing, rocks, cacti, tree. 100c, Adult, foal standing among rocks, cacti.

1999, June 21 Litho. *Perf. 14x13*

167 A57 40c multicolored 1.40 .75
168 A57 65c multicolored 1.60 1.25
169 A57 100c multicolored 2.40 1.90
Nos. 167-169 (3) 5.40 3.90

Cacti — A58

Designs: 50c, Opuntia wentiana. 60c, Lemaireocereus griseus. 70c, Cephalocereus lanuginosus. 75c, Cephalocereus lanuginosus (in bloom).

1999, Mar. 31 Litho. *Perf. 14x13*

170 A58 50c multicolored 1.25 .85
171 A58 60c multicolored 1.50 1.00
172 A58 70c multicolored 1.50 1.25
173 A58 75c multicolored 1.75 1.40
Nos. 170-173 (4) 6.00 4.50

Dogs — A59

Various dogs, background: 40c, Trees. 60c, Cactus, aloe plant, rocks. 80c, Tree, sea. 165c, Sky, clouds.

1999, May 31 Litho. *Perf. 13x14*

174 A59 40c multicolored 1.50 1.00
175 A59 60c multicolored 1.75 1.25
176 A59 80c multicolored 2.00 1.50
177 A59 165c multicolored 3.25 2.75
Nos. 174-177 (4) 8.50 6.50

Discovery of Aruba, 500th Anniv. — A60

1999, Aug. 9 Litho. *Perf. 14x13*

178 A60 150c shown 2.50 2.25
179 A60 175c Abstract paintings 3.00 2.50
a. Souvenir sheet, #178-179 6.00 5.75

Natl. Library, 50th Anniv. — A61

1999, Aug. 20

180 A61 70c shown 1.50 1.40
181 A61 100c Original building 2.10 1.75

Christmas — A62

Die Cut Perf. 13x13½

1999, Dec. 1 Litho.

Self-Adhesive Coil Stamps

182 A62 40c Magi on shore 1.60 1.00
183 A62 70c Magi in desert 2.25 1.25
184 A62 100c Holy Family 2.75 1.75
Nos. 182-184 (3) 6.60 4.00

Tourist Attractions A62a

Reptiles A63

Tourist Attractions: 25c, Guadirikiri Cave. 55c, Cactus landscape. 85c, Hooiberg. 500c, Conchi. Reptiles: 40c, Norops lineatus. 60c, Iguana iguana, vert. 75c, Leptodeira annulata, vert. 150c, Cnemidophorus murinus.

2000 Litho. *Perf. 14x13, 13x14*

185 A62a 25c multi 1.00 .50
186 A63 40c multi 1.25 .75
187 A62a 55c multi 1.40 1.00
188 A63 60c multi 1.40 1.25
189 A63 75c multi 1.60 1.25
190 A62a 85c multi 1.75 1.50
191 A63 150c multi 3.25 2.25
192 A62a 500c multi 8.50 7.25
Nos. 185-192 (8) 20.15 15.75

Issued: 40c, 60c, 75c, 150c, 1/31; 25c, 55c, 85c, 500c, 6/5.

See Nos. 197-204.

America Issue, Campaign Against AIDS — A64

Perf. 14x13, 13x14

2000, Mar. 2 Litho.

193 A64 75c Flags 2.25 2.25
194 A64 175c Ribbon on globe, vert. 4.50 4.50

Organization Anniversaries A65

Designs: 150c, Aruba Bank N.V., 75th anniv. 165c, Alto Vista Church, 250th anniv.

2000, Apr. 20 Litho. *Perf. 14x13*

195 A65 150c multi 2.75 2.25
196 A65 165c multi 3.00 2.50

Type of 2000

Animals: 5c, Cat. 15c, Shells. 30c, Tortoise. 35c, Mud house, vert. 50c, Rabbit. 100c, Balashi gold smelter, vert. 200c, Parakeet. 250c, Rock crystals.

Perf. 14x13, 13x14 (#200, 202)

2001 Litho.

197 A63 5c multi 1.00 .40
198 A62a 15c multi .50 .40
199 A63 30c multi 1.00 .85
200 A62a 35c multi .90 .85
201 A63 50c multi 1.75 1.60
202 A62a 100c multi 2.75 2.10
203 A63 200c multi 4.25 4.00
204 A62a 250c multi 4.75 4.50
Nos. 197-204 (8) 16.90 14.70

Issued: 5c, 30c, 50c, 200c, 1/31. 15c, 35c, 100c, 250c, 8/6.

Mascaruba, 40th Anniv. — A66

Actors on stage and audience in: 60c: Background. 150c, Foreground.

2001, Mar. 26 Litho. *Perf. 14x13*

205-206 A66 Set of 2 4.00 3.50

Classic Motor Vehicles A67

Designs: 25c, 1930 Ford Crown Victoria Leatherback. 40c, 1933 Citroen Commerciale. 70c, 1948 Plymouth pickup truck. 75c, 1959 Ford Edsel.

2001, May 31

207-210 A67 Set of 4 7.00 5.00

Year of Dialogue Among Civilizations A68

2001, Oct. 9 Litho. *Perf. 14x13*

211 A68 175c multi 3.50 3.00

Airport Views — A69

Designs: 30c, Dakota Airport, 1950. 75c, Queen Beatrix Airport, 1972. 175c, Queen Beatrix Airport, 2000.

2002, Jan. 31 Litho. *Perf. 14x13*

212-214 A69 Set of 3 6.00 4.75

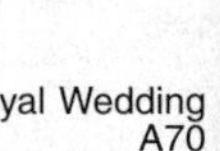

Royal Wedding A70

Prince Willem-Alexander, Maxima Zorreguieta and: 60c, Royal palace, golden coach. 300c, Bourse of Berlage, New Church.

2002, Feb. 2
215-216 A70 Set of 2 6.25 6.00

Water and Energy Company, 70th Anniv. — A71

Designs: 60c, Faucet and water drop, vert. 85c, Pipeline. 165c, Meter and meter-reading equipment, vert.

Perf. 13x14, 14x13
2002, June 3 Litho.
217-219 A71 Set of 3 5.50 5.25

America Issue — Youth, Education and Literacy — A72

Designs: 25c, Hand writing letters with quill pen. 100c, Child looking over wall of letters.

2002, July 15 Litho. *Perf. 14x12¾*
220-221 A72 Set of 2 4.00 2.75

Aruba in World War II — A73

Designs: 60c, Attack on Lago Oil Refinery by German U-boat U-156. 75c, Torpedoing of ships by U-156. 150c, Statue of "Boy" Ecury, Aruban resistance fighter, Aruban militiaman, vert.

Perf. 14x13, 13x14
2002, Sept. 9 Litho.
222-224 A73 Set of 3 8.50 6.50

Mud Houses — A74

Various houses with frame color of: 40c, Yellow green. 60c, Blue green. 75c, Red.

2003, Jan. 31 Litho. *Perf. 14x13*
225-227 A74 Set of 3 3.25 3.00

De Trupialen Performing Organization, 50th Anniv. — A75

Designs: 30c, Trupialen Boys' Choir. 50c, Play handbills. 100c, Emblems.

2003, Mar. 31 Litho. *Perf. 14x13*
228-230 A75 Set of 3 3.25 3.00

Orchids — A76

Designs: 75c, Schomburgkia humboldtii. 500c, Brassavola nodosa.

2003, May 30 Litho. *Perf. 14x13*
231-232 A76 Set of 2 10.00 10.00

Butterflies A77

Designs: 40c, Orange-barred sulphur. 75c, Monarch. 85c, Hairstreak. 175c, Gulf fritillary.

2003, July 31
233-236 A77 Set of 4 7.50 7.00

Endangered Animals A78

Turtles: 25c, Eretmochelys imbricata, vert. 60c, Dermochelys coriacea. 75c, Chelonia mydas, vert. 150c, Caretta caretta.

Perf. 13x14, 14x13
2003, Sept. 30 Litho.
237-240 A78 Set of 4 6.00 5.25

Carnival, 50th Anniv. — A79

Designs: 60c, Masks. 75c, Carnival Queen, vert. 150c, Aruba flag, Carnival participants.

Perf. 14x13, 13x14
2004, Jan. 30 Litho.
241-243 A79 Set of 3 3.75 3.75

Birds — A80

Designs: 70c, Sterna sandvicensis. 75c, Pelecanus occidentalis. 80c, Fregata magnificens. 90c, Larus atricilla.

2004, Mar. 31 *Perf. 13x14*
244-247 A80 Set of 4 5.50 4.50

Fish — A81

Designs: 40c, Parrotfish. 60c, Queen angelfish. 75c, Squirrelfish. 100c, Smallmouth grunt.

2004, May 31 Litho. *Perf. 14x13*
248-251 A81 Set of 4 4.75 3.75

Christmas and New Year's Day — A82

Designs: 50c, Children, Christmas tree, gifts. 85c, Choir, stained glass window, candle, gifts. 125c, Fireworks display.

2004, Dec. 1 Litho. *Perf. 13x14*
252-254 A82 Set of 3 3.25 3.25

Kingdom Statutes, 50th Anniv. — A83

Designs: 160c, Collage of Netherlands Antilles islands. 165c, Kingdom Statute Monument.

2004, Dec. 15 *Perf. 14x13*
255-256 A83 Set of 2 3.75 3.75

Greetings A84

Designs: 60c, Sun, flower (Thank you). 75c, Cacti and rabbits (Love). 135c, Fish (Get well soon). 215c, Balloons and flag (Congratulations).

2005, Jan. 31 Litho. *Perf. 14x13*
257-260 A84 Set of 4 6.25 6.25

Drag Racing A85

Drag racers: 60c, One car going airborne. 85c, One car with chute deployed. 185c, Cars at start line.

2005, Mar. 16
261-263 A85 Set of 3 4.25 4.00

Souvenir Sheet

Reign of Queen Beatrix, 25th Anniv. — A86

No. 264: a, 30c, At coronation, 1980. b, 60c, Making speech, 1991. c, 75c, With Nelson Mandela, 1999. d, 105c, Visiting Aruba and the Netherlands Antilles, 1999. e, 215c, Speaking before European Parliament, 2004.

2005, Apr. 30 Litho. *Perf. 13¼x13¾*
264 A86 Sheet of 5, #a-e 6.50 6.50

Sunsets — A87

Designs: 60c, Birds and cacti. 100c, Palm tree. 205c, Pelicans and pilings.

2005, May 31 *Perf. 13x14*
265-267 A87 Set of 3 4.75 4.75

Birds of Prey — A88

Designs: 60c, Falco sparverius. 75c, Athene cunicularia. 135c, Pandion haliaetus. 200c, Polyborus plancus.

2005, July 29 Litho. *Perf. 14x13*
268-271 A88 Set of 4 7.00 6.50
271a Souvenir sheet, #268-271 7.00 7.00

A89

A90

Corals: 60c, Staghorn coral. 75c, Blade fire coral. 100c, Deepwater sea fan. 215c, Smooth brain coral.

2005, Sept. 30 Litho. *Perf. 13x14*
272-275 A89 Set of 4 6.00 6.00

2005, Oct. 31

Children and philately: 75c, Girl, stamps. 85c, Boy with magnifying glass and stamp album. 125c, Boy with tongs and stock book.

276-278 A90 Set of 3 4.50 4.50

Paintings A91

Designs: 60c, House at Savaneta, by Jean Georges Pandellis. 75c, Haf di Rei, by Mateo Hayde. 185c, Landscape, by Julie Q. Oduber.

2006, Feb. 6 Litho. *Perf. 14x13*
279-281 A91 Set of 3 5.00 5.00

Aruba YMCA, 50th Anniv. — A92

Designs: 75c, YMCA emblem. 205c, Children in playground, horiz.

Perf. 13x14, 14x13
2006, Apr. 3 Litho.
282-283 A92 Set of 2 4.25 4.25

Souvenir Sheet

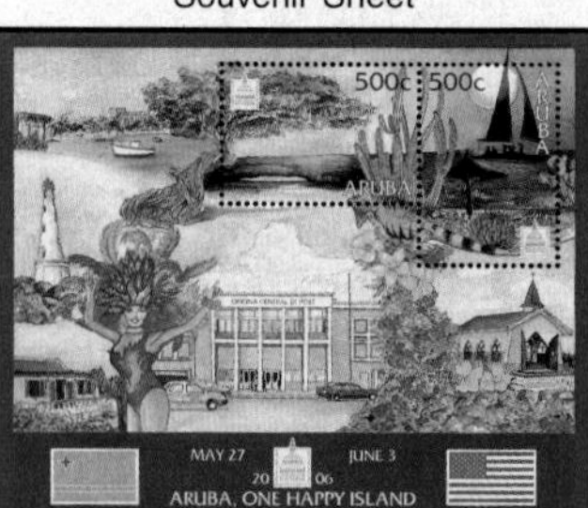

Washington 2006 World Philatelic Exhibition — A93

No. 284 — Exhibition emblem and: a, Natural Bridge, head of iguana, tree and cactus. b, Cacti, tail of iguana, sailboat, vert.

2006, May 27 Litho. *Perf. 12¾*
284 A93 500c Sheet of 2, #a-b 12.50 12.50

2006 World Cup Soccer Championships, Germany — A94

Designs: 75c, Children's drawing of goalie. 215c, Goalie's gloves and ball.

2006, June 5 **Litho.** ***Perf. 14x13***
285-286 A94 Set of 2 4.25 4.25

Hi-Winds Windsurfing Regatta, 20th Anniv. — A95

Designs: 60c, Hotel, windsurfers, kitesurfer, and fishing boats. 100c, Kitesurfers, windsurfer and flag in water. 125c, Windsurfers.

2006, July 3 **Litho.** ***Perf. 14x13***
287-289 A95 Set of 3 3.50 3.50

Fire Prevention A96

Designs: 60c, Fire prevention, safety and extinguishing strategies. 100c, Firemen at house fire. 205c, Fire trucks.

2006, Sept. 29 **Litho.** ***Perf. 14x13***
290-292 A96 Set of 3 4.50 4.50

Arikok National Park — A97

Designs: 75c, Cas di Torto, goat and garden, Cunucu Arikok. 100c, View of Miralamar, vert. 200c, Dunes of Boca Prins.

2006, Oct. 31 **Litho.** ***Perf. 14x13***
293-295 A97 Set of 3 4.50 4.50

Souvenir Sheet

New Year 2007 (Year of the Pig) — A98

No. 296: a, 205c, Pig. b, 215c, Dragon, vert.

2007, Feb. 15 **Litho.** ***Perf. 12¾***
296 A98 Sheet of 2, #a-b 5.25 5.25

Casa Cuna Children's Home Foundation, 50th Anniv. — A99

Designs: 50c, Original Casa Cuna building, Luciana Maria Koolman. 125c, Children in hands. 150c, New Casa Cuna building.

2007, Apr. 4 ***Perf. 14x13***
297-299 A99 Set of 3 4.25 4.25

Museums in Oranjestad A100

Designs: 70c, Museum of Antiquities. 85c, Numismatic Museum. 100c, Archaeological Museum. 135c, Historical Museum.

2007, July 2 **Litho.** ***Perf. 14x13***
300-303 A100 Set of 4 5.00 5.00

Souvenir Sheet

Wrecks and Reefs — A101

No. 304: a, 200c, Pipeline system of wrecked oil tanker Pedernalis. b, 300c, Convair 400 airplane near Sonesta Island. c, 500c, Sea turtle, wreck of freighter Jane. d, 500c, Fish, wreck of freighter Antilla.

2007, Sept. 3 **Litho.** ***Perf. 14x13***
304 A101 Sheet of 4, #a-d 17.00 17.00

Christmas and New Year's Day — A102

Designs: 70c, Infant and mother. 100c, Girl with toys and gift box. 150c, Boy at New Year's celebration.

2007, Oct. 17
305-307 A102 Set of 3 4.00 4.00

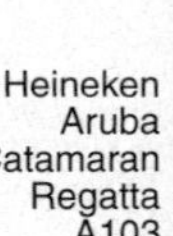

Heineken Aruba Catamaran Regatta A103

Designs: 40c, Catamarans on beach. 80c, Catamarans racing near race buoy. 125c, Competitor leaning off side of catamaran. 130c, Row of catamarans in race.

2007, Nov. 8
308-311 A103 Set of 4 4.50 4.50

Alto Vista Church — A103a

2007-09 **Litho.** ***Perf. 14x13***

Frame Color

311A	A103a	5c	pink	.25	.25
311B	A103a	10c	blue	.25	.25
311C	A103a	25c	lt bl grn	.30	.30
311D	A103a	50c	yel green	.55	.55
311E	A103a	85c	green	.95	.95
311F	A103a	90c	lt grnsh bl	1.00	1.00
311G	A103a	100c	salmon	1.10	1.10
311H	A103a	125c	violet	1.40	1.40
311I	A103a	130c	lt blue	1.50	1.50
311J	A103a	135c	beige	1.50	1.50
311K	A103a	140c	violet	1.60	1.60
311L	A103a	200c	dull org	2.25	2.25
311M	A103a	215c	gray	2.40	2.40
311N	A103a	220c	gray	2.50	2.50
	Nos. 311A-311N (14)			17.45	17.45

Issued: 5c, 50c, 85c, 100c, 200c, 7/30/07; 135c, 9/3/08, 90c, 130c, 140c, 220c, 3/9/09. Others, 2007.

Queen Beatrix, 70th Birthday — A104

Queen Beatrix: 75c, As one-year old with Dutch dignitaries. 125c, With Prince Claus and newborn Crown Prince Willem Alexander. 250c, In royal robes on day of accession to throne. 300c, With family of Crown Prince Willem Alexander.

2008, Jan. 31 ***Perf. 13x14***
312-315 A104 Set of 4 8.50 8.50

Aruban Cultural Year — A105

Designs: 80c, Carnival participants. 130c, Organ grinders. 205c, Dera Gai celebration. 275c, Dande musicians visiting home.

2008, Mar. 18 **Litho.** ***Perf. 14x13***
316-319 A105 Set of 4 7.75 7.75

2008 Summer Olympics, Beijing A106

Designs: 50c, Running. 75c, Synchronized swimming. 100c, Men's rings, vert. 125c, Judo.

2008, Apr. 1 ***Perf. 14x13, 13x14***
320-323 A106 Set of 4 5.00 5.00

Athene Cunicularia Arubensis — A107

Aruban burrowing owl: 100c, Entire bird. 150c, Two birds, horiz. 350c, Head of bird.

Perf. 13x14, 14x13

2008, June 2 **Litho.**
324-326 A107 Set of 3 7.50 7.50

Harley-Davidson Motorcycles — A108

Designs: 175c, FRX Super Glide Big Boy. 225c, Knucklehead. 305c, Roadking.

2008, July 4 **Litho.** ***Perf. 14x13***
327-329 A108 Set of 3 8.00 8.00

Aruban Culture A109

Designs: No. 330, Poem by Federico Oduber. No. 331, 240c, Watapana Magazine covers, vert. No. 332, Henry Habibe and poem by Habibe, vert.

2008, July 8 **Litho.** ***Perf. 13¾***

330	A109 240c multi		4.25	4.25
331	A109 240c multi		4.25	4.25
332	A109 240c multi		4.25	4.25
a.	Souvenir sheet of 5, #330-332, Netherlands #1311, Netherlands Antilles #1187, + etiquette		17.50	17.50
	Nos. 330-332 (3)		12.75	12.75

No. 332a sold for 10g. No. 330 also was available on Netherlands Nos. 1313a and 1313b and Netherlands Antilles No. 1189a.

Flowers — A110

No. 333: a, 100c, Calatropis procera. b, 215c, Passiflora foetida.

No. 334: a, 185c, Thespesia populnea. b, 200c, Cryptostegia grandiflora.

2008, Aug. 8 **Litho.** ***Perf. 13½***
333 A110 Pair, #a-b 3.50 3.50
334 A110 Pair, #a-b 4.50 4.50

Drawings by Rembrandt (1606-69) — A111

Designs: 350c, Self-portrait, 1652. 425c, Self-portrait, 1630. 500c, Beggars at door, 1648.

2008, Sept. 30 **Litho.** ***Perf. 13x14***
335-337 A111 Set of 3 14.50 14.50

Aruba in the Past — A112

Designs: 100c, Carting of potable water. 200c, Clay houses. 215c, Processing of aloe resin.

2008, Nov. 3 **Litho.** ***Perf. 14x13***
338-340 A112 Set of 3 5.75 5.75

Louis Braille (1809-52), Educator of the Blind — A113

Designs: 200c, Braille. 215c, Walking stick for the blind.

2009, Jan. 5 **Litho.** ***Perf. 13x14***
341-342 A113 Set of 2 5.50 5.50

Miniature Sheet

Carnival, 55th Anniv. — A114

No. 343: a, 75c, Miss Carnival on float. b, 100c, Clown on float. c, 175c, Float with "55" and champagne bottle. d, 225c, Carnival dancers.

2009, Feb. 6 Litho. ***Perf. 13¼x13¾***
343 A114 Sheet of 4, #a-d 8.50 8.50

Caves A115

Designs: 175c, Tunnel of Love Cave. 200c, Fountain Cave. 225c, Guadirikiri Cave.

2009, Apr. 1 ***Perf. 14x13***
344-346 A115 Set of 3 6.75 6.75

Souvenir Sheet

Global Warming — A116

No. 347: a, 200c, Hurricane over map of Caribbean. b, 250c, Map of polar regions, mountains, parched earth. c, 250c, Pollution from industry and vehicles. d, 300c, Fluorescent light bulb, recycling symbols, windmill.

2009, June 2
347 A116 Sheet of 4, #a-d 11.50 11.50

Souvenir Sheet

Architecture — A117

No. 348: a, 175c, California Lighthouse. b, 250c, Plaza Daniel Leo, horiz. c, 275c, Henriquez Building, horiz. d, 325c, Ecury Complex main building.

2009, July 3 ***Perf. 12¾***
348 A117 Sheet of 4, #a-d 11.50 11.50

National Library, 60th Anniv. — A118

Book reader: 185c, Girl. 300c, Woman.

2009, Aug. 20 Litho. ***Perf. 13x14***
349-350 A118 Set of 2 5.50 5.50
350a Vert. pair, #349-350 5.50 5.50

Dolphins A119

Designs: 125c, Stenella frontalis. 200c, Steno bredanensis. 300c, Two Stenella frontalis. 325c, Group of Steno bredanensis at surface.

2009, Sept. 30 ***Perf. 14x13***
351-354 A119 Set of 4 14.00 14.00

Christmas A120

Designs: 75c Madonna and Child. 120c, Angel and stars. 125c, Hands, globe, stars, "2009." 210c, Shepherds and sheep.

2009, Oct. 19
355-358 A120 Set of 4 6.00 6.00

Miniature Sheet

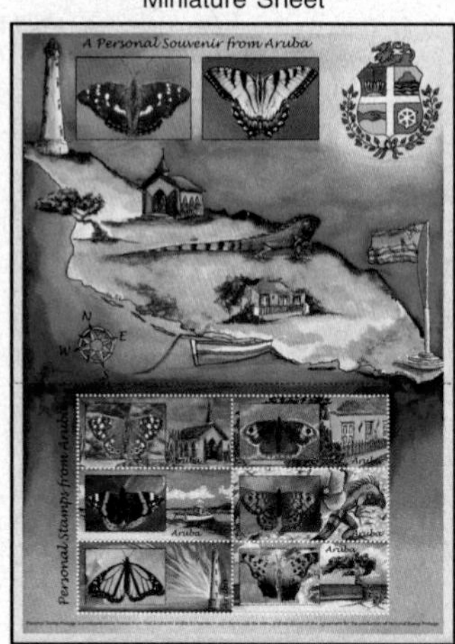

Personalized Stamps — A120a

No. 358A: b, Church. c, House. d, Boat. e, Lizard and flower. f, Lighthouse. g, Tree.

2009, Dec. 18 Litho. ***Perf. 13¼x14***
358A A120a (295c) Sheet of 6, #b-g 20.00 20.00

No. 358A sold for 1770c or $20 in U.S. currency. Stamps could be personalized. Butterfly images shown are generic.

Recycling A121

Various works of art from recycled materials: 90c, Island landscape. 180c, Post office, tree, and animal. 325c, Fish.

2010, Jan. 22 Litho. ***Perf. 13¼***
359-361 A121 Set of 3 6.75 6.75

Historic Airplanes — A122

No. 362: a, 250c, Seaplane. b, 500c, Seaplane and lighthouse.

2010, Mar. 26 ***Perf. 13¼x13***
362 A122 Horiz. pair, #a-b 8.50 8.50

Scouting in Aruba, 10th Anniv. — A123

No. 363: a, 85c, Scouts observing nature. b, 95c, Scouts building fire. c, 135c, Scout near tent. d, 180c, Scouts playing drums.

2010, Apr. 1 Litho.
363 A123 Block of 4, #a-d 5.50 5.50

End of World War II, 65th Anniv. A124

No. 364: a, 140c, Large cannon. b, 200c, Beached torpedo. 275c, Equipment and ramp.

2010, May 4 Litho. ***Perf. 13¼x13***
364 A124 Vert. strip of 3, #a-c 7.00 7.00

Parrots — A125

No. 365 — Various parrots: a, 85c. b, 90c. c, 180c.

2010, June 2 ***Perf. 13x13¼***
365 A125 Horiz. strip of 3, #a-c 4.00 4.00

Paintings by Vincent Van Gogh — A126

No. 366: a, 200c, Self-portrait with Gray Felt Hat. b, 250c, Still Life: Vase with Fifteen Sunflowers. c, 305c, Starry Night. d, 500c, Wheat Field with Crows.

2010, July 29 ***Perf. 13¼x13***
366 A126 Block of 4, #a-d 14.00 14.00

Rum Shops A127

No. 367: a, 100c, Essoville Rum Shop. b, 200c, Aruba Rum Shop. c, 255c, Caribbean Store.

2010, Sept. 13
367 A127 Vert. strip of 3, #a-c 7.50 7.50

Flowers — A128

No. 368: a, Caesalpinia pulcherrima. b, Dipladenia sanderi. c, Hibiscus. d, Adenium obesum. e, Bougainvillea. f, Ixora. g, Eichhornia crassipes. h, Passiflora caerulea. i, Allamanda cathartica. j, Nerium oleander.

2010, Sept. 29 ***Perf. 14***
368 Block of 10 22.50 22.50
a.-j. A128 200c Any single 2.25 2.25

Houses of Worship — A129

No. 369: a, 85c, Synagogue. b, 90c, Church. c, 135c, Church, diff. d, 240c, Church interior.

2010, Oct. 28 ***Perf. 13x13¼***
369 A129 Block of 4, #a-d 6.25 6.25

Birds — A130

No. 370: a, Falco sparverius. b, Icterus icterus. c, Mimus gilvus. d, Egretta alba. e, Aratinga pertinax. f, Pelecanus occidentalis. g, Athene cunicularia arubensis. h, Coerba flaveola. i, Polyborus plancus. j, Colibri thalassinus.

2010, Nov. 17 Litho. ***Perf. 14***
370 Block of 10 22.50 22.50
a.-j. A130 200c Any single 2.25 2.25

Briareus Caribbean Reef Octopus — A131

No. 371 — Various depictions of octopus: a, 100c. b, 175c. c, 255c. d, 300c.

2010, Nov. 30 ***Perf. 13¼x13***
371 A131 Block of 4, #a-d 9.25 9.25

Butterflies — A132

No. 372: a, Zuleika. b, Blue morpho. c, Monarch. d, White peacock. e, Sulphur. f, Zebra. g, Malachite. h, Owl. i, Postman. j, Gulf fritillary.

2010, Dec. 22 ***Perf. 14***
372 Block of 10 22.50 22.50
a.-j. A132 200c Any single 2.25 2.25

Separate Political Status, 25th Anniv. — A133

No. 373 — Curved lines and: a, 200c, Star. b, 300c, "Status Aparte." c, 300c, F. B. Tromp, first governor of Aruba, and J. H. A. Eman, first prime minister of Aruba, country name in white at UL. d, 400c, A. J. Booi, first president of Parliament, and G. F. Croes, political party leader, country name in red at LR.

2011, Jan. 1
373 A133 Block of 4, #a-d 13.50 13.50

Flowers A134

No. 374: a, Catharanthus roseus. b, Echinopsis lageniformis. c, Allamanda cathartica. d, Cordia sebestena. e, Ipomoea pes-caprae. f, Hibiscus rosa-sinensis. g, Cassia fistula. h, Bougainvillea glabra. i, Delonix regia. j, Nerium oleander.

2011, Feb. 16 ***Perf. 14***
374 Block of 10 18.00 18.00
a.-j. A134 160c Any single 1.75 1.75

America Issue A135

No. 375 — Hands with flags of: a, 200c, Portugal, United States, Cuba and Brazil. b, 250c, Honduras, Canada, Colombia and Chile. c, 350c, United States, Brazil, Aruba and Panama. d, 400c, Suriname, Colombia, Chile and Spain.
No. 376: a, Like No. 375a. b, Like No. 375b. c, Like No. 375c. d, Like No. 375d.

2011, Mar. 23
375 Vert. strip of 4 13.50 13.50
a. A135 200c multi 2.25 2.25
b. A135 250c multi 2.75 2.75
c. A135 350c multi 4.00 4.00
d. A135 400c multi 4.50 4.50

Miniature Sheet

376 A135 300c Sheet of 4, #a-d 13.50 13.50

Postal Union of the Americas, Spain and Portugal (UPAEP), cent.

Bank Notes A136

No. 377: a, 1964 Indonesia 25 sen note. b, 1986 Bhutan 2 ngultrum note. c, 1949 Philippines 50 centavo note. d, 1987 Sudan 25 piastre note. e, 1976 Mozambique 100 escudo note. f, 1993 Haiti 25 gourde note. g, 1917 Göttingen 25 pfennig note. h, 1997 Turkey 250,000 lira note. i, 1977 Solomon Islands 10 dollar note. j, 1915 Lille 25 centime note. k, 1985 Egypt 25 piastre note. l, 1976 Albania 100 lek note.

2011, Apr. 4
377 Block of 12 23.00 23.00
a.-l. A136 167c Any single 1.90 1.90

Maastricht Paper Money Fair.

Peonies — A137

No. 378 — Color of flowers: a, Dark red. b, Yellow. c, White. d, Pink.
350c, Pink peony.

2011, May 11 Litho. ***Perf. 14***
378 A137 110c Sheet of 4, #a-d 5.00 5.00

Souvenir Sheet

379 A137 350c multi 4.00 4.00

Fish — A138

No. 380: a, Holacanthus ciliaris. b, Chaetodon capistratus. c, Sparisoma viride. d, Pomacanthus paru. e, Balistes vetula. f, Lactophrys triqueter. g, Holocentrus rufus. h, Chaetodon striatus. i, Diodon holocanthus. j, Equetus punctatus.

2011, June 15
380 Block of 10 14.00 14.00
a.-j. A138 120c Any single 1.40 1.40

Chess — A139

No. 381 — Positions of chess pieces at end of 1956 match between Donald Byrne and winner Bobby Fischer: a, White queen on tan square. b, Black king on tan square. c, White knight on tan square, d, Black bishop on tan square. e, White pawn on tan square. f, Black bishop on green square. g, Black knight on tan square. h, Black rook on green square. i, White pawn on green square. j, White king on tan square. k, Black pawn on green square.

2011, July 22
381 Sheet of 15, #a-j, 5 #k + 49 labels 30.00 30.00
a.-k. A139 180c Any single 2.00 2.00

Mail Boxes of the World — A140

No. 382: a, Dark red rectangular pillar box. b, Orange red Estonian Post mail box. c, Yellow mail box. d, Blue USPS mail box. e, Yellow mail box inscribed "Postbriefkasten." f, Blue mail box with Cyrillic letters. g, Green pillar box with Chinese inscriptions. h, Red mail box inscribed "Brieven Drukwerken." i, Green mail box with two legs. j, Red hexagonal British pillar box.

2011, Aug. 19
382 Block of 10 17.50 17.50
a.-j. A140 150c Any single 1.75 1.75

Paintings by Jan Vermeer (1632-75) — A141

No. 383: a, Girl with a Red Hat (red frame). b, The Milkmaid (blue frame). c, The Lacemaker (brown frame). d, Girl with a Pearl Earring (red frame).

2011, Sept. 21 Litho. ***Perf. 14***
383 Vert. strip of 4 11.50 11.50
a. A141 200c multi 2.25 2.25
b.-c. A141 250c Either single 2.75 2.75
d. A141 300c multi 3.50 3.50

Ships — A142

No. 384 — Various tall ships with panel color of: a, 200c, Blue violet. b, 225c, Maroon, horiz. c, 250c, Blue violet, horiz. d, 250c, Maroon, horiz. e, 275c, Maroon, horiz. f, 300c, Blue violet.

2011, Oct. 25
384 A142 Block of 6, #a-f 17.00 17.00

Butterflies A143

Designs: No. 385, 160c, Diaethria neglecta. No. 386, 160c, Lycaena cupreus lapidicola. No. 387, 160c, Pyrrhogyra edocla. No. 388, 160c, Anartia amathea amathea. No. 389, 160c, Anglais urticae. No. 390, 160c, Morpho aega. No. 391, 160c, Junonia coenia coenia (red violet background). No. 392, 160c, Junonia coenia coenia (dark purple background). No. 393, 160c, Dione juno juno. No. 394, 160c, Lycaena heteronea austin.

2011, Dec. 1
385-394 A143 Set of 10 18.00 18.00

Nos. 385-394 were printed in sheets containing two of each stamp + a central label.

Birds — A144

No. 395: a, Pithecophaga jeffreyi. b, Harpia harpyja. c, Morphnus guaianensis. d, Caracara plancus. e, Lophaetus occipitalis. f, Stephanoaetus coronatus. g, Haliaeetus leucocephalus. h, Vultur gryphus. i, Aquila chrysaetos. j, Falco sparverius.

2012, Jan. 19
395 Block of 10 17.50 17.50
a.-j. A144 150c Any single 1.75 1.75

Aruban Goats — A145

No. 396: a, Three goats on rocks. b, Two goats on rocks, horiz. c, Goat, horiz. d, Goat and cactus.

2012, Feb. 21
396 Strip of 4 11.00 11.00
a. A145 175c multi 2.00 2.00
b. A145 225c multi 2.50 2.50
c. A145 275c multi 3.00 3.00
d. A145 300c multi 3.50 3.50

2012 Summer Olympics, London — A146

No. 397: a, Torch. b, Swimmer, horiz. c, Hurdler, horiz. d, "Olympia."

2012, Apr. 27
397 A146 500c Block of 4, #a-d 22.50 22.50
e. Souvenir sheet of 4, #397a-397d 22.50 22.50

Whales
A147

No. 398: a, Delphinapterus leucas. b, Kogia breviceps. c, Balaena mysticetus. d, Orcinus orca. e, Physeter macrocephalus. f, Balaenoptera musculus. g, Globicephala macrorhynchus. h, Mesoplodon europaeus. i, Balaenoptera edeni. j, Megaptera novaeangliae.

2012, May 15

398	Block of 10	14.00	14.00
a.-j.	A147 120c Any single	1.40	1.40

Women's Dresses — A148

No. 399: a, 175c, Woman. b, 200c, Woman with Aruban flag. c, 200c, Two women dancing. d, 250c, Two women, diff.

2012, June 21

399 A148 Block of 4, #a-d 9.25 9.25

2012 Rembrandt Regatta — A149

No. 400 — Various sailboats: a, 150c, Horiz. b, 150c, Vert. c, 175c, Horiz. d, 175c, Vert. e, 200c, Horiz. f, 200c, Vert.

2012, Aug. 7

400 A149 Block of 6, #a-f 12.00 12.00

A150

A151

A152

A153

A154

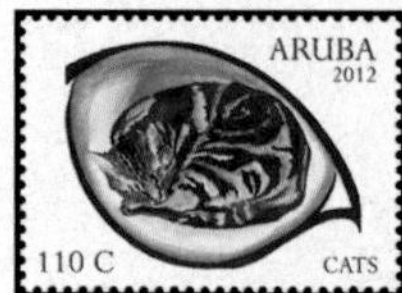

A155

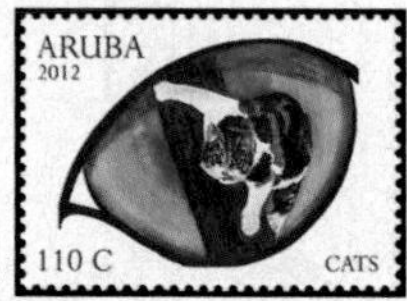

A156

Cats — A157

2012, Sept. 20

401	A150	110c multi	1.25	1.25
402	A151	110c multi	1.25	1.25
403	A152	110c multi	1.25	1.25
404	A153	110c multi	1.25	1.25
405	A154	110c multi	1.25	1.25
406	A155	110c multi	1.25	1.25
407	A156	110c multi	1.25	1.25
408	A157	110c multi	1.25	1.25
		Nos. 401-408 (8)	10.00	10.00

Nos. 401-408 were printed in sheets containing two of each stamp and two labels.

Christmas and New Year's Day — A158

No. 409: a, 75c, Ornaments and tree. b, 120c, Gifts and Nativity manger. c, 125c, Candles. d, 210c, Fireworks and champagne flutes.

2012, Oct. 18

409 A158 Block of 4, #a-d 6.00 6.00

A159

A160

A161

A162

A163

A164

A165

A166

A167

Underwater Exploration
A168

2012, Nov. 15

410	Block of 10	11.00	11.00
a.	A159 100c multi	1.10	1.10
b.	A160 100c multi	1.10	1.10
c.	A161 100c multi	1.10	1.10
d.	A162 100c multi	1.10	1.10
e.	A163 100c multi	1.10	1.10
f.	A164 100c multi	1.10	1.10
g.	A165 100c multi	1.10	1.10
h.	A166 100c multi	1.10	1.10
i.	A167 100c multi	1.10	1.10
j.	A168 100c multi	1.10	1.10

Orchids — A169

No. 411: a, Laelia xanthina. b, Dendrobium. c, Dendrobium convolutum. d, Brassavola nodosa. e, Rossioglossum grande. f, Cattleya aclandiae. g, Cattleya. h, Epidendrum cinnabarinum. i, Phragmipedium cardinale. j, Phragmipedium. k, Phalaenopsis. l, Cattleya gaskelliana.

2012, Dec. 20

411 A169 200c Block of 12, #a-l 27.00 27.00

Butterflies — A170

Designs: No. 412, 150c, Graphium sarpedon. No. 413, 150c, Danaus plexippus. No. 414, 150c, Danis danis. No. 415, 150c, Pseudacraea boisduvali. No. 416, 150c, Morpho peleides. No. 417, 150c, Scoptes alphaeus. No. 418, 150c, Jumonia oritya. No. 419, 150c, Palla ussheri. No. 420, 150c, Eryphanis polyxena. No. 421, 150c, Diaethria clymena. No. 422, 150c, Colias eurytheme. No. 423, 150c, Anthocharis cardamis.

2013, Jan. 16

412-423 A170 Set of 12 20.00 20.00

Nos. 412-423 were printed in sheets of 24 containing two of each stamp + a central label.

Wedding Dresses — A171

No. 424: a, Brown and green dress. b, Blue gray strapless dress. c, Brown dress with white veil. d, Lilac dress with sash. e, White dress with black ribbon. f, Red dress with gray collar.

2013, Feb. 28

424 A171 200c Block of 6, #a-f 13.50 13.50

Aruban Bank Notes — A172

No. 425: a, 10-florin banknote. b, 25-florin banknote. c, 50-florin banknote. d, 100-florin banknote. e, 500-florin banknote.

2013, Apr. 5

425	Horiz. strip of 5	11.50	11.50
a.-e.	A172 200c Any single	2.25	2.25

Printed in sheets containing two tete-beche strips.

A173

A174

A175

A176

Cruise Ships — A177

2013, May 16

426	Horiz. strip of 5	14.00	14.00
a.	A173 250c multi	2.75	2.75
b.	A174 250c multi	2.75	2.75
c.	A175 250c multi	2.75	2.75
d.	A176 250c multi	2.75	2.75
e.	A177 250c multi	2.75	2.75

No. 426 was printed in sheets containing two tete-beche strips.

A178

Paintings by Frans Hals (c. 1582-1666) — A179

Designs: Nos. 427a, 428a, Jester with a Lute. Nos. 427b, 428b, Singing Boy with a Flute.

2013, June 17

427	A178 500c Horiz. pair, #a-b	11.50	11.50

Souvenir Sheet

428	A179 500c Sheet of 2, #a-b	11.50	11.50

Birds — A180

No. 429: a, Coereba flaveola. b, Aratinga pertinax arubensis. c, Anas bahamensis. d, Zonotrichia capensis. e, Colinus cristatus. f, Columbigallina passerina. g, Egretta thula. h, Icterus icterus. i, Mimus gilvus. j, Pelecanus occidentalis. k, Sterna eurygnatha. l, Athene cunicularia.

2013, Aug. 1

429	A180 167c Block of 12, #a-l	22.50	22.50

Flowers — A181

No. 430: a, Passiflora. b, Canna. c, Bougainvillea. d, Aramyllis. e, Hibiscus. f, Ipomoea. g, Strelitzia. h, Lillium. i, Allamanda. j, Lantana.

2013, Sept. 5 Litho. *Perf. 14*

430	Block of 10	22.50	22.50
a.-j.	A181 200c Any single	2.25	2.25

Printed in sheets containing two blocks that are tete-beche in relationship to each other.

Shells — A182

No. 431: a, 200c, Tonna maculosa. b, 200c, Nerita versicolor. c, 250c, Tellina radiata. d, 275c, Cymatium caribbaeum. e, 275c, Oliva caribaeensis. f, 300c, Voluta musica.

2013, Oct. 4 Litho. *Perf. 14*

431	A182 Block of 6, #a-f	17.00	17.00

SEMI-POSTAL STAMPS

Surtax for child welfare organizations unless otherwise stated.

Solidarity SP1

1986, May 7 Litho. *Perf. 14x13*

B1	SP1 30c + 10c shown	1.75	.90
B2	SP1 35c + 15c Three ropes	1.75	.90
B3	SP1 60c + 25c One rope	2.50	1.40
	Nos. B1-B3 (3)	6.00	3.20

Surtax for social and cultural projects.

Child Welfare SP2

1986, Oct. 29 Litho. *Perf. 14x13*

B4	SP2 45c + 20c Boy, caterpillar	2.50	1.00
B5	SP2 70c + 25c Boy, cocoon	2.75	1.75
B6	SP2 100c + 40c Girl, butterfly	3.50	2.25
	Nos. B4-B6 (3)	8.75	5.00

Christmas (Child Welfare) SP3

1987, Oct. 27 Litho. *Perf. 14x13*

B7	SP3 25c +10c Boy on beach	1.50	.75
B8	SP3 45c +20c Drawing Christmas tree	2.00	.90
B9	SP3 70c +30c Child, creche figures	2.75	1.40
	Nos. B7-B9 (3)	6.25	3.05

Solidarity SP4

YMCA emblem in various geometric designs.

1988, Aug. 3 Litho. *Perf. 14x13*

B10	SP4 45c +20c shown	2.00	.90
B11	SP4 60c +25c multi, diff.	2.00	1.40
B12	SP4 100c +50c multi, diff.	2.50	1.90
	Nos. B10-B12 (3)	6.50	4.20

11th YMCA world council.
Surtax for social and cultural projects.

Children's Toys (Child Welfare) — SP5

1988, Oct. 26 *Perf. 13x14*

B13	SP5 45c +20c Jacks	2.00	1.00
B14	SP5 70c +30c Top	2.00	1.40
B15	SP5 100c +50c Kite	3.00	1.90
	Nos. B13-B15 (3)	7.00	4.30

Child Welfare SP6

1989, Oct. 26 *Perf. 14x13*

B16	SP6 45c +20c Baby spoon	1.75	1.00
B17	SP6 60c +30c Chasing a ball	2.00	1.00
B18	SP6 100c +50c Adult & child holding hands	3.00	1.90
	Nos. B16-B18 (3)	6.75	3.90

Solidarity SP7

1990, July 25

B19	SP7 55c +25c shown	2.00	1.50
B20	SP7 100c +50c Family, house	3.50	2.50

Surtax for social and cultural projects.

Child Welfare — SP8

Child Welfare — SP9

Christmas song.

1990, Oct. 24 Litho. *Perf. 13x14*

B21	SP8 45c +20c Wind surfboards	1.50	.90
B22	SP8 60c +30c shown	2.00	1.25
B23	SP8 100c +50c Kites, lizard	3.00	2.25
	Nos. B21-B23 (3)	6.50	4.40

1991, Oct. 25 Litho. *Perf. 13x14*

Literacy: 45c+25c, Discovery of reading. 60c+35c, Pointing to letter. 100c+50c, Child reading.

B24	SP9 45c +25c multi	1.50	1.25
B25	SP9 60c +35c multi	2.00	1.40
B26	SP9 100c +50c multi	3.00	2.25
	Nos. B24-B26 (3)	6.50	4.90

Solidarity SP10

55c+30c, Girl scouts, flag & emblem. 100c+50c, Hand holding cancer fund emblem, people.

1992, May 27 Litho. *Perf. 14x13*

B27	SP10 55c +30c multi	2.00	1.50
B28	SP10 100c +50c multi	3.00	2.25

Surtax for social and cultural projects.

Postal Services of Aruba, Cent. (Child Welfare) SP11

Designs: 50c+30c, Heart. 70c+35c, Airplane, letters. 100c+55c, Pigeon with letter in beak, vert.

1992, Oct. 30 Litho. *Perf. 14x13*

B29	SP11 50c +30c multi	1.75	1.25
B30	SP11 70c +35c multi	2.00	1.40

Perf. 13x14

B31	SP11 100c +50c multi	2.75	2.25
	Nos. B29-B31 (3)	6.50	4.90

Youth Foreign Study Programs (Child Welfare) SP12

Abstract designs of: 50c+30c, Landscapes. 75c+40c, Young man, scenes of other countries, vert. 100c+50c, Integrating cultures.

1993, Oct. 27 *Perf. 14x13, 13x14*

B32	SP12 50c +30c multi	1.50	1.25
B33	SP12 75c +40c multi	2.00	1.90
B34	SP12 100c +50c multi	2.50	2.25
	Nos. B32-B34 (3)	6.00	5.40

Solidarity SP13

Intl. Year of the Family: 50c+35c, Family seated, reading, studying. 100c+50c, Family playing in front of house.

1994, May 30 Litho. *Perf. 14x13*

B35	SP13	50c +35c multi	1.50	1.25
B36	SP13	100c +50c multi	2.75	2.50

Surtax for social and cultural projects.

Child Welfare SP14

Designs: 50c+30c, Children on anchor with umbrella. 80c+35c, Children inside Sun. 100c+50c, Child riding owl.

1994, Oct. 27 Litho. *Perf. 14x13*

B37	SP14	50c +30c multi	1.75	1.40
B38	SP14	80c +35c multi	2.25	1.90
B39	SP14	100c +50c multi	2.50	2.40
		Nos. B37-B39 (3)	6.50	5.70

Child Welfare SP15

Solidarity SP16

Children's drawings: 50c+25c, Children with balloons, house. 70c+35c, Three people with picnic basket on sunny day. 100c+50c, People gardening on sunny day.

1995, Oct. 26 Litho. *Perf. 13x14*

B40	SP15	50c +25c multi	1.50	1.10
B41	SP15	70c +35c multi	2.00	1.60
B42	SP15	100c +50c multi	3.00	2.25
		Nos. B40-B42 (3)	6.50	4.95

1996, July 26 Litho. *Perf. 13x14*

El Sol Naciente Lodge, 75th Anniv.: 60c+30c, Masonic emblems. 100c+ 50c, Columns, terrestrial and celestial globes.

B43	SP16	60c +30c multi	2.50	1.50
B44	SP16	100c +50c multi	3.50	2.50

Surtax for social and cultural projects (Solidarity)

Child Welfare SP17

Cartoons: 50c+25c, Mother, baby rabbit waiting at school bus stop. 70c+35c, Mother, baby owl, outside school. 100c+50c, Children flying kite.

1996, Oct. 24 Litho. *Perf. 14x13*

B45	SP17	50c +25c multi	1.75	1.25
B46	SP17	70c +35c multi	2.25	1.75
B47	SP17	100c +50c multi	2.50	2.40
		Nos. B45-B47 (3)	6.50	5.40

Child Welfare SP18

Designs: 50c+25c, Girl sitting among aloe plants. 70c+35c, Boy, butterfly, cactus, vert. 100c+50c, Girl swimming under water, fish, coral.

Perf. 14x13, 13x14

1997, Oct. 23 Litho.

B48	SP18	50c +25c multi	1.50	1.10
B49	SP18	70c +35c multi	2.25	1.90
B50	SP18	100c +50c multi	2.50	2.40
		Nos. B48-B50 (3)	6.25	5.40

Solidarity SP19

Service Organizations: 60c+30c, Globe, emblem of Lions Intl., wheelchair balanced on map of Aruba. 100c+50c, Child reading book, emblem of Rotary Intl., woman in rocking chair.

1998, May 29 Litho. *Perf. 14x13*

B51	SP19	60c +30c multi	2.50	1.50
B52	SP19	100c +50c multi	3.50	2.75

Surtax for social and cultural projects.

Child Welfare — SP20

50c+25c, Girl performing traditional ribbon dance. 80c+40c, Boy playing a cuarta. 100c+50c, Two boys playing basketball.

1998, Oct. 22 Litho. *Perf. 13x14*

B53	SP20	50c +25c multi	1.50	1.10
B54	SP20	80c +40c multi	2.25	2.10
B55	SP20	100c +50c multi	3.00	2.40
		Nos. B53-B55 (3)	6.75	5.60

Child Welfare SP21

Designs: 60c+30c, Child on beach with man with fishing net. 80c+40c, Adult reading to children. 100c+50c, Mother, child, vert.

Perf. 14x13, 13x14

1999, Oct. 21 Litho.

B56	SP21	60c +30c multi	1.50	1.25
B57	SP21	80c +40c multi	2.25	1.90
B58	SP21	100c +50c multi	2.75	2.40
		Nos. B56-B58 (3)	6.50	5.55

Solidarity SP22

75c+35c, Children on playground equipment. 100c+50c, Children playing in sand.

2000, Aug. 28 Litho. *Perf. 14x13*

B59-B60	SP22	Set of 2	5.00	4.00

Child Welfare SP23

Children's art: 60c+30c, House with solar collectors. 80c+40c, House, girl, garbage can. 100c+50c, Flying automobiles.

2000, Oct. 26

B61-B63	SP23	Set of 3	7.00	5.75

Child Welfare — SP24

Intl. Volunteers Year: 40c+20c, Children at crosswalk. 60c+30c, Boys walking dog. 100c+50c, Children depositing trash in can at beach.

2001, Oct. 31 Litho. *Perf. 13x14*

B64-B66	SP24	Set of 3	6.25	4.75

Child Welfare — SP25

Designs: 40c+20c, Boy, iguana and goat. 60c+30c, Girl, hawksbill turtle, red crab, horiz. 100c+50c, Boy, pelicans, parakeet, conch shell.

Perf. 13x14, 14x13

2002, Oct. 31 Litho.

B67-B69	SP25	Set of 3	6.50	5.00

Child Welfare SP26

Children playing: 40c+20c, Baseball. 60c+30c, Volleyball. 100c+50c, Soccer.

2003, Oct. 31 Litho. *Perf. 14x13*

B70-B72	SP26	Set of 3	6.00	6.00

Children's Welfare — SP27

Children playing: 60c+30c, Maracas. 85c+40c, Steel drum. 100c+50c, Tambourine, wiri.

2004, Oct. 29 Litho. *Perf. 13x14*

B73-B75	SP27	Set of 3	5.00	5.00

ASCENSION

ə-ˈsen‸t‸-shən

LOCATION — An island in the South Atlantic Ocean, 900 miles from Liberia

GOVT. — A part of the British Crown Colony of St. Helena

AREA — 34 sq. mi.

POP. — 1,117 (1993)

In 1922 Ascension was placed under the administration of the Colonial Office and annexed to the British Crown Colony of St. Helena. The only post office is at Georgetown.

12 Pence = 1 Shilling
20 Shillings = 1 Pound
100 Pence = 1 Pound (1971)

Catalogue values for unused stamps in this country are for Never Hinged items, beginning with Scott 50.

Stamps and Types of St. Helena, 1912-22 Overprinted in Black or Red

1922 Wmk. 4 *Perf. 14*

1	A9	½p	green & blk	6.50	*26.00*
2	A10	1p	green	6.50	*25.00*
3	A10	1½p	rose red	21.00	*60.00*
4	A9	2p	gray & blk	21.00	16.00
5	A9	3p	ultra	16.00	*26.00*
6	A10	8p	dl vio & blk	34.00	*62.50*
7	A10	2sh	ultra & blk, *blue*	120.00	*150.00*
8	A10	3sh	vio & blk	175.00	*200.00*

Wmk. 3

9	A9	1sh	blk, *gray grn* (R)	35.00	*60.00*
			Nos. 1-9 (9)	435.00	*625.50*
			Set, never hinged	675.00	

Seal of Colony — A3

1924-33 Typo. Wmk. 4 *Perf. 14*

Chalky Paper

10	A3	½p	black & gray	6.00	*19.00*
11	A3	1p	green & blk	7.00	*12.50*
12	A3	1½p	rose red	10.00	*42.50*
13	A3	2p	bluish gray & gray	21.00	12.00
14	A3	3p	ultra	10.00	*19.00*
15	A3	4p	blk & gray, *yel*	60.00	*100.00*
16	A3	5p	ol & lil ('27)	19.00	*29.00*
17	A3	6p	rose lil & gray	62.50	*125.00*
18	A3	8p	violet & gray	19.00	*52.50*
19	A3	1sh	brown & gray	25.00	*62.50*
20	A3	2sh	ultra & gray, *blue*	75.00	*110.00*
21	A3	3sh	blk & gray, *blue*	100.00	*110.00*
			Nos. 10-21 (12)	414.50	*694.00*
			Set, never hinged	675.00	

View of Georgetown — A4

Map of Ascension — A5

Sooty Tern Breeding Colony A9

Designs: 1½p, Pier at Georgetown. 3p, Long Beach. 5p, Three Sisters. 5sh, Green Mountain.

1934, July 2 Engr.

23	A4	½p	violet & blk	1.10	1.00
24	A5	1p	lt grn & blk	2.25	1.60
25	A4	1½p	red & black	2.25	*2.75*
26	A5	2p	org & black	2.25	*3.00*
27	A4	3p	ultra & blk	2.25	1.90
28	A4	5p	blue & black	2.75	*4.00*
29	A5	8p	dk brn & blk	5.25	*6.00*
30	A9	1sh	carmine & blk	22.50	11.00
31	A5	2sh6p	violet & blk	57.50	47.50
32	A4	5sh	brown & blk	62.50	*70.00*
			Nos. 23-32 (10)	160.60	*148.75*
			Set, never hinged	240.00	

Common Design Types pictured following the introduction.

Silver Jubilee Issue
Common Design Type

1935, May 6 *Perf. 11x12*

33 CD301 1½p car & dk blue 3.50 *10.50*
34 CD301 2p blk & ultra 11.00 *30.00*
35 CD301 5p ind & grn 22.50 *32.50*
36 CD301 1sh brn vio & indigo 24.00 *40.00*
Nos. 33-36 (4) 61.00 *113.00*
Set, never hinged 100.00

25th anniv. of the reign of King George V.

Coronation Issue
Common Design Type

1937, May 19 *Perf. 13½x14*

37 CD302 1p deep green .75 1.50
38 CD302 2p deep orange 1.00 .65
39 CD302 3p bright ultra 1.00 .60
Nos. 37-39 (3) 2.75 *2.75*
Set, never hinged 3.50

Georgetown — A11

Designs: No. 41, 41A, 2p, 4p, Green Mountain. No. 41D, 6p, 10sh, Three Sisters. 1½p, 2sh6p, Pier at Georgetown. 3p, 5sh, Long Beach.

Perf. 13, 13½ (#41, 44, 45), 14 (#43C)
1938-53 **Center in Black**

40 A11 ½p violet ('44) .70 *3.25*
Never hinged 1.40
a. Perf. 13½ 3.00 *3.25*
Never hinged 6.00
41 A11 1p green 25.00 13.00
Never hinged 52.50
41A A11 1p org yel, ('42) .25 *.60*
Never hinged .50
b. Perf. 14 ('49) .40 *16.00*
Never hinged .70
c. Perf. 13½ 7.00 *9.00*
Never hinged 14.00
41D A11 1p green ('49) .35 *1.50*
Never hinged .60
42 A11 1½p red, ('44) .45 *.80*
Never hinged .95
a. Perf. 14 ('49) 1.30 *12.50*
Never hinged 2.50
b. Perf. 13½ 2.50 1.40
Never hinged 4.75
42C A11 1½p lilac rose ('53) .30 *6.50*
Never hinged .55
d. Perf. 14 ('49) .75 *1.00*
Never hinged 1.50
e. 1½p carmine, perf 14 6.00 6.50
Never hinged 12.00
43 A11 2p orange ('44) .40 .40
Never hinged .85
a. Perf. 14 ('49) 1.50 *45.00*
Never hinged 2.75
b. Perf. 13½ 3.50 1.00
Never hinged 7.00
43C A11 2p red ('49) .65 *2.00*
Never hinged 1.25
44 A11 3p ultra 55.00 29.00
Never hinged 125.00
44A A11 3p black, ('44) .35 *.80*
Never hinged .85
c. Perf. 13½ ('40) 10.00 3.50
Never hinged 20.00
44B A11 4p ultra, ('44) 2.50 3.00
Never hinged 5.00
d. Perf. 13½ 9.00 3.25
Never hinged 17.50
45 A11 6p gray blue 5.50 2.50
Never hinged 10.00
a. Perf. 13 ('44) 6.00 7.00
Never hinged 12.00
46 A11 1sh dk brn ('44) 3.25 2.00
Never hinged 5.50
a. Perf. 13½ 11.00 2.25
Never hinged 22.00
47 A11 2sh6p car ('44) 19.00 *35.00*
Never hinged 37.50
a. Perf. 13½ 29.00 10.50
Never hinged 50.00
b. Frame printed doubly, one albino *3,750.*
Never hinged *5,250.*
48 A11 5sh yel brn ('44) 25.00 40.00
Never hinged 50.00
a. Perf. 13½ 60.00 9.50
Never hinged 100.00
49 A11 10sh red vio ('44) 30.00 *60.00*
Never hinged 45.00
a. Perf. 13½ 72.50 47.50
Never hinged 115.00
b. 10sh brt analine red pur, perf 13 60.00 47.50
Never hinged 110.00
Nos. 40-49 (16) 168.70 *200.35*
Set, never hinged 350.00

Catalogue values for unused stamps in this section, from this point to the end of the section, are for Never Hinged items.

Peace Issue
Common Design Type
Perf. 13½x14

1946, Oct. 21 **Engr.** **Wmk. 4**

50 CD303 2p deep orange .45 1.10
51 CD303 4p deep blue .45 .65

Silver Wedding Issue
Common Design Types

1948, Oct. 20 **Photo.** *Perf. 14x14½*

52 CD304 3p black .65 .60

Engraved; Name Typographed
Perf. 11½x11

53 CD305 10sh red violet 57.50 *60.00*

The stamps formerly listed as Nos. 54-56 have been merged into the rest of the George VI definitive series as Nos. 41//43C.

UPU Issue
Common Design Types

Engr.; Name Typo. on Nos. 58, 59
1949, Oct. 10 *Perf. 13½, 11x11½*

57 CD306 3p rose carmine 1.40 *1.75*
58 CD307 4p indigo 4.75 1.25
59 CD308 6p olive 1.75 2.75
60 CD309 1sh slate 3.00 2.00
Nos. 57-60 (4) 10.90 7.75

Coronation Issue
Common Design Type

1953, June 2 **Engr.** *Perf. 13½x13*

61 CD312 3p gray & black 1.25 1.25

Reservoir A16

Designs: 1p, Map of Ascension. 1½p, Georgetown. 2p, Map showing Ascension between South America and Africa and cable lines. 2½p, Mountain road. 3p, Yellow-billed tropic bird. 4p, Longfinned tuna. 6p, Waves. 7p, Young green turtles. 1sh, Land crab. 2sh6p, Sooty tern (wideawake). 5sh, Perfect Crater. 10sh, View from Northwest.

1956, Nov. 19 **Wmk. 4** *Perf. 13*
Center in Black

62 A16 ½p brown .25 .45
63 A16 1p lilac rose 2.75 1.75
64 A16 1½p orange .85 .85
65 A16 2p carmine 3.00 1.75
66 A16 2½p org brown 1.50 *2.00*
67 A16 3p blue 3.75 1.10
68 A16 4p turq blue 1.25 *1.75*
69 A16 6p dark blue 1.25 *2.00*
70 A16 7p olive 2.50 1.10
71 A16 1sh scarlet 1.10 1.10
72 A16 2sh6p brown violet 30.00 8.25
73 A16 5sh bright green 40.00 20.00
74 A16 10sh purple 55.00 42.50
Nos. 62-74 (13) 143.20 84.60

Brown Booby — A17

Birds: 1½p, Black tern. 2p, Fairy tern. 3p, Red-billed tropic bird in flight. 4½p, Brown noddy. 6p, Sooty tern. 7p, Frigate bird. 10p, Blue-faced booby. 1sh, Yellow-billed tropic bird. 1sh6p, Red-billed tropic bird. 2sh6p, Madeiran storm petrel. 5sh, Red-footed booby (brown phase). 10sh, Frigate birds. £1, Red-footed booby (white phase).

Perf. 14x14½
1963, May 23 **Photo.** **Wmk. 314**

75 A17 1p multicolored 1.25 .30
76 A17 1½p multicolored 2.00 .90
b. Blue omitted 110.00
77 A17 2p multicolored 1.60 .30
78 A17 3p multicolored 1.75 .30
79 A17 4½p multicolored 1.75 .30
80 A17 6p multicolored 1.60 .30
81 A17 7p multicolored 1.60 .30
82 A17 10p multicolored 1.60 .30
83 A17 1sh multicolored 1.60 .30
84 A17 1sh6p multicolored 5.00 2.00
Complete booklet, 4 each #75, 76, 77, 78, 80 and 84, in blocks of 4 90.00
85 A17 2sh6p multicolored 9.00 10.00
86 A17 5sh multicolored 9.00 10.00
87 A17 10sh multicolored 16.00 11.00
88 A17 £1 multicolored 24.50 13.00
Nos. 75-88 (14) 78.25 49.30

Freedom from Hunger Issue
Common Design Type

1963, June 4 **Wmk. 314**

89 CD314 1sh6p car rose 1.00 1.00

Red Cross Centenary Issue
Common Design Type

1963, Sept. 2 **Litho.** *Perf. 13*

90 CD315 3p black & red 3.00 .95
91 CD315 1sh6p ultra & red 5.25 1.75

ITU Issue
Common Design Type
Perf. 11x11½

1965, May 17 **Litho.** **Wmk. 314**

92 CD317 3p mag & violet .50 .40
93 CD317 6p grnsh bl & brn org 1.40 1.10

Intl. Cooperation Year Issue
Common Design Type

1965, Oct. 25 **Wmk. 314** *Perf. 14½*

94 CD318 1p bl grn & claret .40 .50
95 CD318 6p lt vio & green .90 1.00

Churchill Memorial Issue
Common Design Type

1966, Jan. 24 **Photo.** *Perf. 14*
Design in Black, Gold and Carmine Rose

96 CD319 1p bright blue .50 .25
97 CD319 3p green 1.75 .90
98 CD319 6p brown 2.25 1.50
99 CD319 1sh6p violet 5.50 4.50
Nos. 96-99 (4) 10.00 7.15

World Cup Soccer Issue
Common Design Type

1966, July 1 **Litho.** *Perf. 14*

100 CD321 3p multicolored 1.00 .55
101 CD321 6p multicolored 1.50 1.25

WHO Headquarters Issue
Common Design Type

1966, Sept. 20 **Litho.** *Perf. 14*

102 CD322 3p multicolored 2.10 1.10
103 CD322 1sh6p multicolored 4.50 2.40

Apollo Satellite Station, Ascension — A18

Wmk. 314
1966, Nov. 7 **Photo.** *Perf. 14*

104 A18 4p purple & black .25 .25
105 A18 8p blue grn & blk .25 .25
106 A18 1sh3p brn ol & blk .25 .25
107 A18 2sh6p brt grnsh blue & black .40 .40
Nos. 104-107 (4) 1.15 1.15

Opening of the Apollo communications satellite-earth station, part of the US Apollo program.

UNESCO Anniversary Issue
Common Design Type

1967, Jan. 3 **Litho.** *Perf. 14*

108 CD323 3p "Education" 2.50 1.25
109 CD323 6p "Science" 3.50 1.90
110 CD323 1sh6p "Culture" 5.00 3.00
Nos. 108-110 (3) 11.00 6.15

BBC Emblem A19

Photo.; Gold Impressed
1967, Dec. 1 **Wmk. 314** *Perf. 14½*

111 A19 1p ultra & gold .25 .25
112 A19 3p dk green & gold .25 .25
113 A19 6p brt purple & gold .25 .25
114 A19 1sh6p brt red & gold .35 .35
Nos. 111-114 (4) 1.10 1.10

Opening of the British Broadcasting Company's South Atlantic Relay Station on Ascension Island.

Human Rights Flame and Chain — A20

Perf. 14½x14
1968, July 8 **Litho.** **Wmk. 314**

115 A20 6p org, car & blk .25 .25
116 A20 1sh6p gray, mag & blk .30 .30
117 A20 2sh6p brt grn, plum & blk .40 .40
Nos. 115-117 (3) .95 .95

International Human Rights Year.

Blackfish A21

Fish: No. 119, Sailfish. 6p, Oldwife. 8p, Leather jackets. 1sh6p, Yellowtails. 1sh9p, Tuna. 2sh3p, Mako sharks. 2sh11p, Rock hind (jack).

Perf. 13x12½
1968-69 **Wmk. 314** **Litho.**

118 A21 4p brt grnsh bl & blk .30 .25
119 A21 4p red & multi .35 .35
120 A21 6p yel olive & multi .40 .40
121 A21 8p brt rose lil & multi .60 .45
122 A21 1sh6p brown & multi 2.00 1.90
123 A21 1sh9p emer & multi 1.25 .95
124 A21 2sh3p ocher & multi 1.90 1.25
125 A21 2sh11p dp org & multi 3.75 3.25
Nos. 118-125 (8) 10.55 8.80

Issue dates: No. 119, 6p, 1sh6p, 2sh11p, Mar. 3, 1969; others, Oct. 23, 1968.
See Nos. 130-133.

Arms of R.N.S. Rattlesnake A22

Coats of Arms of Royal Naval Ships: 9p, Weston. 1sh9p, Undaunted. 2sh3p, Eagle.

Perf. 14x14½
1969, Oct. 1 **Photo.** **Wmk. 314**

126 A22 4p multicolored .65 .50
127 A22 9p multicolored .75 .60
128 A22 1sh9p multicolored 1.25 .75

129 A22 2sh3p multicolored 1.40 .85
a. Min. sheet of 4, #126-129 9.00 9.00
Nos. 126-129 (4) 4.05 2.70

See Nos. 134-137, 152-159, 166-169.

Fish Type of 1968

Deep-sea fish: 4p, Wahoo. 9p, Coalfish. 1sh9p, Dolphinfishes. 2sh3p, Soldierfish.

1970, Apr. 6 Litho. *Perf. 14*

130 A21 4p bluish grn & multi 4.25 2.75
131 A21 9p org & multi 3.25 1.90
132 A21 1sh9p ultra & multi 5.50 3.00
133 A21 2sh3p gray & multi 5.50 3.00
Nos. 130-133 (4) 18.50 10.65

Naval Arms Type of 1969

4p, Penelope. 9p, Carlisle. 1sh6p, Amphion. 2sh6p, Magpie.

Perf. 12½x12

1970, Sept. 7 Photo. Wmk. 314

134 A22 4p ultra, gold & blk 1.25 .30
135 A22 9p lt bl, blk, gold & red 1.50 .55
136 A22 1sh6p grnsh bl, gold & blk 1.60 1.50
137 A22 2sh6p lt grnsh bl, gold & blk 2.25 2.10
a. Miniature sheet of 4, #134-137 11.00 12.50
Nos. 134-137 (4) 6.60 4.45

Decimal Currency Issue

Tycho Brahe's Observatory, Quadrant and Supernova, 1572 — A23

Man into Space: ½p, Chinese rocket, 1232, vert. 1p, Medieval Arab astronomers, vert. 2p, Galileo, his telescope and drawing of moon, 1609. 2½p, Isaac Newton, telescope and apple. 3½p, Harrison's chronometer and ship, 1735. 4½p, First American manned orbital flight (Project Mercury, 1962, vert.). 5p, Reflector of Palomar telescope and ring nebula in Lyra, Messier 57. 7½p, Jodrell Bank telescope. 10p, Mariner 7, 1969, and telescopic view of Mars. 12½p, Sputnik 2 and dog Laika, 1957. 25p, Astronaut walking in space, 1965 (Gemini 4; vert.). 50p, US astronauts and moon landing module, 1969. £1, Future space research station.

1971, Feb. 15 Litho. *Perf. 14½*

138 A23 ½p multicolored .25 .25
139 A23 1p multicolored .25 .25
140 A23 1½p multicolored .30 .30
141 A23 2p multicolored .35 .35
142 A23 2½p multicolored 1.10 .90
143 A23 3½p multicolored 2.25 .90
Complete booklet, 4 each #138-143 30.00
144 A23 4½p multicolored 1.50 .95
145 A23 5p multicolored 1.25 .90
146 A23 7½p multicolored 4.00 2.10
147 A23 10p multicolored 4.00 3.50
148 A23 12½p multicolored 5.00 3.75
149 A23 25p multicolored 6.00 3.50
150 A23 50p multicolored 5.00 4.00
151 A23 £1 multicolored 5.00 5.00
Nos. 138-151 (14) 36.25 26.65

For overprints see Nos. 189-191.
Booklet also exists with a date of 5/71 on the back cover. Value, $45.

Arms of H.M.S. Phoenix — A24

Coats of Arms of Royal Naval Ships: 4p, Milford. 9p, Pelican. 15p, Oberon.

1971, Nov. 15 Photo. *Perf. 13½x13*

152 A24 2p gold & multi 1.10 .25
153 A24 4p gold & multi 1.25 .45
154 A24 9p gold & multi 1.75 1.10
155 A24 15p gold & multi 1.90 1.75
a. Souvenir sheet of 4, #152-155 9.50 9.50
Nos. 152-155 (4) 6.00 3.55

Naval Arms Type of 1969

1½p, Lowestoft. 3p, Auckland. 6p, Nigeria. 17½p, Bermuda.

1972, May 22 Litho. *Perf. 14x14½*

156 A22 1½p bl, gold & blk .85 .65
157 A22 3p grnsh bl, gold & blk .95 .70
158 A22 6p grn, gold, blk & bl 1.00 1.00
159 A22 17½p lil, gold, blk & red 1.50 *1.75*
a. Miniature sheet of 4, #156-159 4.50 4.50
Nos. 156-159 (4) 4.30 4.10

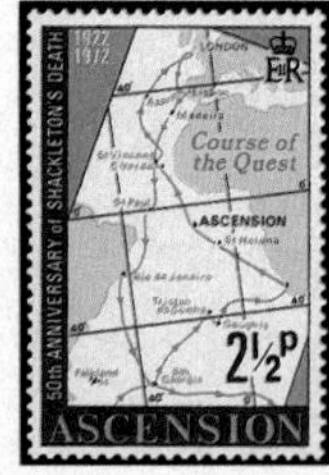

Course of Quest — A25

Designs: 4p, Shackleton and "Quest", horiz. 7½p, Shackleton's cabin and Quest in pack ice, horiz. 11p, Shackleton statue, London, and memorial cairn, South Georgia.

1972, Aug. 2 *Perf. 14*

160 A25 2½p multicolored .55 .50
161 A25 4p multicolored .60 .65
162 A25 7½p multicolored .60 .70
163 A25 11p multicolored .75 .90
a. Souvenir sheet of 4, #160-163 3.00 3.00
Nos. 160-163 (4) 2.50 2.75

Sir Ernest Henry Shackleton (1874-1922), explorer of Antarctica.

Silver Wedding Issue, 1972
Common Design Type

Design: Queen Elizabeth II, Prince Philip, land crab and shark.

1972, Nov. 20 Photo. *Perf. 14x14½*

164 CD324 2p violet & multi .25 .25
165 CD324 16p car rose & multi .55 .55

Naval Arms Type of 1969

2p, Birmingham. 4p, Cardiff. 9p, Penzance. 13p, Rochester.

1973, May 28 Litho. Wmk. 314

166 A22 2p blue & multi 2.40 1.50
167 A22 4p yel grn & multi 3.00 1.50
168 A22 9p lt blue & multi 3.75 1.75
169 A22 13p violet & multi 4.25 1.75
a. Min. sheet of 4, #166-169 26.00 18.00
Nos. 166-169 (4) 13.40 6.50

Turtles — A26

1973, Aug. 28 *Perf. 13½*

170 A26 4p Green 2.75 1.10
171 A26 9p Loggerhead 3.50 2.25
172 A26 12p Hawksbill 5.00 3.50
Nos. 170-172 (3) 11.25 6.85

Light Infanty Marine Sergeant, 1900 — A27

Uniforms (Royal Marines): 6p, Private, 1816. 12p, Officer, Light Infantry, 1880. 20p, Color Sergeant, Artillery, 1910.

1973, Oct. 31 *Perf. 14½*

173 A27 2p multicolored 2.00 1.50
174 A27 6p lt green & multi 3.00 1.90
175 A27 12p lt blue & multi 3.50 2.75
176 A27 20p lt lilac & multi 4.00 3.00
Nos. 173-176 (4) 12.50 9.15

Departure of the Royal Marines from Ascension, 50th anniv.

Princess Anne's Wedding Issue
Common Design Type

1973, Nov. 14 *Perf. 14*

177 CD325 2p ocher & multi .25 .25
178 CD325 18p multicolored .40 .40

Letter and UPU Emblem A29

UPU Cent.: 9p, Emblem and Mercury.

Wmk. 314

1974, Mar. 27 Litho. *Perf. 14½*

179 A29 2p multicolored .25 .25
180 A29 9p vio blue & multi .50 .50

Young Churchill and Blenheim Palace A30

25p, Churchill and UN Headquarters, NYC.

1974, Nov. 30 Litho. Unwmk.

181 A30 5p slate grn & multi .25 .25
182 A30 25p purple & multi .80 .80
a. Souvenir sheet of 2, #181-182 2.00 2.25

Sir Winston Churchill (1874-1965).

Skylab over Photograph of Ascension Taken by Skylab 3 — A31

Skylab Space Station: 18p, Command module and photo of Ascension from Skylab 4.

1975, Mar. 20 Wmk. 314 *Perf. 14½*

183 A31 2p multicolored .25 .25
184 A31 18p multicolored .80 .80

US Air Force C-141A Starlifter — A32

Aircraft: 5p, Royal Air Force C-130 Hercules. 9p, Vickers VC-10. 24p, U.S. Air Force C-5A Galaxy.

Perf. 13½x14

1975, June 19 Litho. Wmk. 314

185 A32 2p multicolored 1.25 .60
186 A32 5p multicolored 1.75 .75
187 A32 9p multicolored 1.75 1.90
188 A32 24p multicolored 2.75 3.75
a. Souvenir sheet of 4, #185-188 16.00 16.00
Nos. 185-188 (4) 7.50 7.00

Wideawake Airfield, Ascension Island.

Nos. 144, 148-149 Overprinted

1975, Aug. 18 Litho. *Perf. 14½*

189 A23 4½p multicolored .30 .30
190 A23 12½p multicolored .40 .40
191 A23 25p multicolored .60 .60
Nos. 189-191 (3) 1.30 1.30

Apollo Soyuz space test project (Russo-American cooperation), launching July 15; link-up, July 17.

HMS Peruvian and Zenobia Arriving Oct. 22, 1815 A33

Designs: 5p, Water Supply, Dampiers Drip. 9p, First Landing, Oct. 1815. 15p, The Garden on Green Mountain. All designs after paintings by Isobel McManus.

1975, Oct. 22 Wmk. 373 *Perf. 14½*

192 A33 2p lt blue & multi .25 .25
193 A33 5p lt blue & multi .30 .25
194 A33 9p red & multi .45 .40
195 A33 15p red & multi .90 .75
Nos. 192-195 (4) 1.90 1.65

British occupation, 160th anniv.

Canaries A34

2p, Fairy tern, vert. 3p, Waxbills. 4p, Black noddy. 5p, Brown noddy. 6p, Common mynah. 7p, Madeira storm petrels. 8p, Sooty terns. 9p, White booby. 10p, Red-footed booby. 15p, Red-throated francolin. 18p, Brown booby. 25p, Red-billed bo'sun bird. 50p, Yellow-billed bo'sun bird. £1, Ascension frigatebird. £2, Boatswain Island Bird Sanctuary and birds.

Perf. 14x14½, 14½x14

1976, Apr. 26 Litho. Wmk. 373

Size: 35x27mm, 27x35mm

196 A34 1p multi .45 *2.10*
197 A34 2p multi .50 *2.10*
198 A34 3p multi .50 *2.10*
199 A34 4p multi, vert. .55 *2.10*
200 A34 5p multi .70 *2.10*
201 A34 6p multi .70 *2.10*
202 A34 7p multi, vert. .70 *2.10*
203 A34 8p multi .70 *2.10*
204 A34 9p multi, vert. .70 *2.10*
205 A34 10p multi .70 *2.10*
206 A34 15p multi, vert. 1.40 *2.10*
207 A34 18p multi, vert. 1.40 *2.10*
208 A34 25p multi 1.50 *2.10*
209 A34 50p multi 2.00 *3.25*
210 A34 £1 multi, vert. 2.50 4.00

Perf. 13½

Size: 46x33mm

211 A34 £2 multicolored 5.00 *5.00*
Nos. 196-211 (16) 20.00 39.55

Great Britain Type A1 with Ascension Cancel — A35

9p, Ascension #1, vert. 25p, Freighter Southampton Castle.

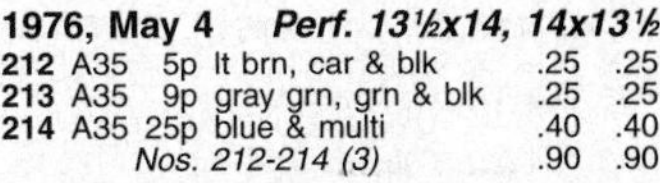

1976, May 4 ***Perf. 13½x14, 14x13½***

212 A35 5p lt brn, car & blk .25 .25
213 A35 9p gray grn, grn & blk .25 .25
214 A35 25p blue & multi .40 .40
Nos. 212-214 (3) .90 .90

Festival of Stamps 1976. See Tristan da Cunha No. 208a for souvenir sheet that contains one each of Ascension #214, St. Helena #297 and Tristan da Cunha #208.

US Base A36

Designs: 9p, NASA Station, Devil's Ashpit. 25p, Viking satellite landing on Mars.

Wmk. 373

1976, July 4 **Litho.** ***Perf. 13½***

215 A36 8p black & multi .30 .30
216 A36 9p black & multi .40 .40
217 A36 25p black & multi .80 *1.25*
Nos. 215-217 (3) 1.50 *1.95*

American Bicentennial. No. 215 also for the 20th anniv. of Bahamas Long Range Proving Ground (extension) Agreement.

Queen in Coronation Coach — A37

Designs: 8p, Prince Philip on Ascension Island, 1957, vert. 12p, Queen leaving Buckingham Palace in coronation coach.

Perf. 14x13½, 13½x14

1977, Feb. 7 **Litho.** **Wmk. 373**

218 A37 8p multicolored .25 .25
219 A37 12p multicolored .25 .25
220 A37 25p multicolored .45 .45
Nos. 218-220 (3) .95 .95

Reign of Queen Elizabeth II, 25th anniv.

Water Pipe in Tunnel — A38

5p, Breakneck Valley wells. 12p, Break tank in pipe line, horiz. 25p, Dam & reservoir, horiz.

1977, June 27 **Litho.** ***Perf. 14½***

221 A38 3p multicolored .25 .25
222 A38 5p multicolored .25 .25
223 A38 12p multicolored .40 .30
224 A38 25p multicolored .75 .60
Nos. 221-224 (4) 1.65 1.40

Water supplies constructed by Royal Marines, 1832 and 1881.

Mars Bay Site, 1877 A39

Designs: 8p, Mars Bay and instrument sites. 12p, Prof. and Mrs. Gill before their tent. 25p, Map of Ascension.

Perf. 13½x14

1977, Oct. 3 **Litho.** **Wmk. 373**

225 A39 3p multicolored .25 .25
226 A39 8p multicolored .30 .25
227 A39 12p multicolored .40 .40
228 A39 25p multicolored .75 .75
Nos. 225-228 (4) 1.70 1.65

Centenary of visit of Prof. David Gill (1843-1914), astronomer, to Ascension.

Elizabeth II Coronation Anniversary Issue

Souvenir Sheet

Common Design Types

Unwmk.

1978, May 21 **Litho.** ***Perf. 15***

229 Sheet of 6 2.50 2.50
a. CD326 25p Lion of England .40 .40
b. CD327 25p Elizabeth II .40 .40
c. CD328 25p Green turtle .40 .40

No. 229 contains 2 se-tenant strips of Nos. 229a-229c, separated by horizontal gutter with commemorative and descriptive inscriptions and showing central part of coronation procession with coach.

East Crater (Broken Tooth) — A40

Volcanoes: 5p, Hollands Crater (Hollow Tooth). 12p, Bears Back. 15p, Green Mountain. 25p, Two Boats village.

1978, Sept. 4 **Litho.** ***Perf. 14½***

230 A40 3p multicolored .25 .25
231 A40 5p multicolored .25 .25
232 A40 12p multicolored .40 .40
233 A40 15p multicolored .50 .50
234 A40 25p multicolored .80 .80
a. Souvenir sheet, 2 each #230-234 3.00 *4.25*
b. Strip of 5, #230-234 2.00 2.00

No. 234b shows panoramic view of volcanic terrain.

Resolution A41

Capt. Cook's voyages: 8p, Cook's chronometer. 12p, Green turtle. 25p, Cook after Flaxman/Wedgwood medallion.

Litho.; Litho. & Embossed. (25p)

1979, Jan. 8 ***Perf. 11***

235 A41 3p multicolored .25 .25
236 A41 8p multicolored .30 .30
237 A41 12p multicolored .55 .55
238 A41 25p multicolored .75 *1.00*
Nos. 235-238 (4) 1.85 *2.10*

St. Mary's Church, Georgetown — A42

Designs: 12p, Old map of Ascension Island. 50p, Ascension, by Rembrandt.

Wmk. 373

1979, May 24 **Litho.** ***Perf. 14½***

239 A42 8p multicolored .25 .25
240 A42 12p multicolored .25 .25
241 A42 50p multicolored .40 .40
Nos. 239-241 (3) .90 .90

Ascension Day.

Landing Cable at Comfortless Cove — A43

Eastern Telegraph Co., 80th anniv.: 8p, Cable Ship Anglia. 12p, Map showing cables across the Atlantic, vert. 15p, Cable-laying ship. 25p, Cable and earth station.

1979, Sept. 15

242 A43 3p rose car & black .25 .25
243 A43 8p dk yel grn & black .25 .25
244 A43 12p yel bister & black .30 .30
245 A43 15p violet & black .40 .40
246 A43 25p deep org & black .50 .50
Nos. 242-246 (5) 1.70 1.70

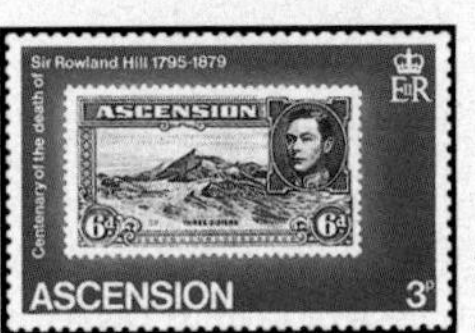

Ascension No. 45 — A44

1979, Dec. 17 **Wmk. 373** ***Perf. 14***

247 A44 3p shown .25 .25
248 A44 8p No. 73 .25 .25
249 A44 12p No. 14 .25 .25
250 A44 50p Hill portrait, vert. .55 *.75*
Nos. 247-250 (4) 1.30 1.50

Sir Rowland Hill (1795-1879), originator of penny postage.

Anogramma Ascensionis A45

1980, Feb. 18 **Litho.** ***Perf. 14½***

251 A45 3p shown .25 .25
252 A45 6p Xiphopteris ascensionense .25 .25
253 A45 8p Sporobolus caespitosus .25 .25
254 A45 12p Sporobolus durus, vert. .25 .25
255 A45 18p Dryopteris ascensionis, vert. .30 .30
256 A45 24p Marattia purpurascens, vert. .40 .40
Nos. 251-256 (6) 1.70 1.70

17th Century Bottle Post, London 1980 Emblem A46

1980, May 1 **Wmk. 373** ***Perf. 14***

257 A46 8p shown .25 .25
258 A46 12p 36-gun frigate, 19th century .30 .30
259 A46 15p "Garth Castle," 1863 .35 .35
260 A46 50p "St. Helena," Lockheed C141 .75 .75
a. Souvenir sheet of 4, #257-260 1.75 *2.25*
Nos. 257-260 (4) 1.65 1.65

London 1980 Intl. Stamp Exhib., May 6-14.

Queen Mother Elizabeth Birthday

Common Design Type

1980, Aug. 11 **Litho.** ***Perf. 14***

261 CD330 15p multicolored .50 .50

Lubbock's Yellowtail A47

1980, Sept. 15 **Litho.** ***Perf. 13½x14***

262 A47 3p shown .40 .40
263 A47 10p Resplendent angelfish .50 .50
264 A47 25p Hedgehog butterflyfish 1.00 .90
265 A47 40p Marmalade razorfish 1.25 *1.50*
Nos. 262-265 (4) 3.15 *3.30*

Tortoisen, by Thomas Maxon A48

Map of South Atlantic Ridge and Contintental Drift — A49

15p, Wideawake Fair, by Linton Palmer, 1866.

1980, Nov. 17 ***Perf. 13½, 14 (60p)***

266 A48 10p multicolored .25 *.40*
267 A48 15p multicolored .35 *.50*
268 A49 60p multicolored 1.00 *1.40*
Nos. 266-268 (3) 1.60 *2.30*

Royal Geographical Soc., 50th anniv.

Green Mountain Farm, 1881 — A50

Designs: 15p, Two Boats, 1881. 20p, Green Mountain and Two Boats farms, 1981. 30p, Green Mountain Farm, 1981.

1981, Feb. 15 **Litho.** ***Perf. 14***

269 A50 12p multicolored .25 .25
270 A50 15p multicolored .30 .30
271 A50 20p multicolored .30 .30
272 A50 30p multicolored .40 .40
Nos. 269-272 (4) 1.25 1.25

Cable and Wireless Earth Station A51

1981, Apr. 27 **Litho.** ***Perf. 14***

273 Sheet of 10 4.00 4.00
a. A51 15p multicolored .40 .40

Flight of Columbia space shuttle. Gutter contains story of Ascension and space shuttle; margin shows craft and dish antenna.

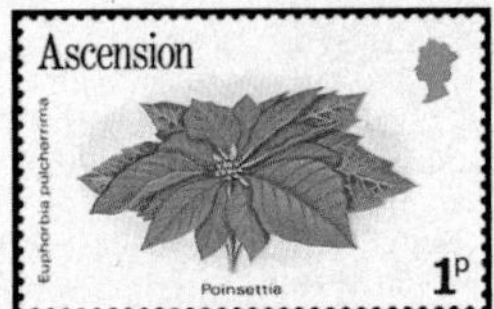

Poinsettia — A52

1981, May 11 **Wmk. 373** ***Perf. 13½***

274 A52 1p shown .90 .90
275 A52 2p Clustererd wax flower .70 .95
276 A52 3p Kolanchoe, vert. .70 .95
277 A52 4p Yellow pops 1.00 .95
278 A52 5p Camel's foot creeper 1.00 .95
279 A52 8p White oleander 1.00 1.00

280 A52 10p Ascension lily, vert. .65 .95
281 A52 12p Coral plant, vert. 2.00 1.10
282 A52 15p Yellow allamanda .75 .95
Complete booklet, 4 ea. #275, 276, 280 and 282, in blocks of 4 15.00
283 A52 20p Ascention euphorbia 1.25 .95
284 A52 30p Flame of the forest, vert. 1.50 1.60
285 A52 40p Bougainvillea 1.50 *3.25*

Size: 42x53mm

286 A52 50p Solanum 1.60 *3.50*
287 A52 £1 Ladies petticoat 2.40 *4.00*
288 A52 £2 Red hibiscus 4.00 *7.00*
Nos. 274-288 (15) 20.95 29.00

1982, Aug. 27 Inscribed "1982"

275a A52 2p Clustererd wax flower .60 1.25
276a A52 3p Kolanchoe, vert. .60 1.25
280a A52 10p Ascension lily, vert. .55 .75
282a A52 15p Yellow allamanda .60 .75
283a A52 20p Ascention euphorbia 1.25 .75
287a A52 £1 Ladies petticoat 2.25 *3.00*
Nos. 275a-287a (6) 5.85 7.75

For overprints see Nos. 321-322.

Linschoten's Map of Ascension, 1599. — A53

Maxwell's Map of Ascension, 1793 — A54

Designs: Old maps of Ascension.

1981, May 22 Perf. 14½

289 A53 Sheet of 4 .60 .60
a.-d. 5p any single .25 .25
290 A54 10p shown .25 .25
291 A54 12p Maxwell, 1793, diff. .35 .35
292 A54 15p Eckberg & Chapman, 1811 .40 .40
293 A54 40p Campbell, 1819 .75 .75
Nos. 289-293 (5) 2.35 2.35

Royal Wedding Issue

Common Design Type

1981, July 22 Wmk. 373 Perf. 14

294 CD331 10p Bouquet .25 .25
295 CD331 15p Charles .30 .30
296 CD331 50p Couple .75 .75
Nos. 294-296 (3) 1.30 1.30

Nos. 294-296 each se-tenant with label.

Man Shining Cannon — A55

1981, Sept. 14 Litho. Perf. 14

297 A55 5p shown .25 .25
298 A55 10p Mountain climbing .25 .25
299 A55 15p First aid treatment .30 .30
300 A55 40p Duke of Edinburgh .60 .60
Nos. 297-300 (4) 1.40 1.40

Duke of Edinburgh's Awards, 25th anniv.

Scouting Year A56

1982, Feb. 22 Litho. Perf. 14

301 A56 10p Parallel rope walking .25 *.35*
302 A56 15p 1st Ascension scout flag .40 *.50*
303 A56 25p Radio operators .60 *.75*
304 A56 40p Baden-Powell .75 *1.10*
a. Souvenir sheet of 4 2.25 2.25
Nos. 301-304 (4) 2.00 *2.70*

No. 304a contains stamps in designs of Nos. 301-304 (30x30mm, perf. 14½, diamond-shape).

Sesquicentennial of Charles Darwin's Visit — A57

1982, Apr. 19

305 A57 10p Portrait .30 .30
306 A57 12p Pistols .40 .40
307 A57 15p Rock crab .55 .55
308 A57 40p Beagle 1.00 1.00
Nos. 305-308 (4) 2.25 2.25

40th Anniv. of Wideawake Airfield — A58

1982, June 15 Litho. Perf. 14

309 A58 5p Fairey Swordfish .95 .95
310 A58 10p North American B25C Mitchell 1.10 1.10
Complete booklet, 4 ea. #309 and 310, in blocks of 4 8.50
311 A58 15p Boeing EC-135N Aria 1.40 1.40
312 A58 50p Lockheed Hercules 2.25 2.25
Nos. 309-312 (4) 5.70 5.70

The cover of the booklet containing Nos. 309 and 310 exists with both brown and blue inscriptions. Same value.

Princess Diana Issue

Common Design Type

Perf. 14½x14

1982, July 1 Wmk. 373

313 CD333 12p Arms .60 .60
314 CD333 15p Diana .60 .60
315 CD333 25p Wedding 1.00 1.00
316 CD333 50p Portrait 1.75 1.75
Nos. 313-316 (4) 3.95 3.95

Christmas and 50th Anniv. of BBC Overseas Broadcasting — A59

Anniv. Emblem and: 5p, Bush House (London headquarters). 10p, Atlantic relay station. 25p, Lord Reith, first director general. 40p, King George V delivering Christmas address, 1932.

1982, Dec. 20 Litho. Perf. 14

317 A59 5p multicolored .25 .25
318 A59 10p multicolored .30 .30
319 A59 25p multicolored .70 .70
320 A59 40p multicolored 1.10 1.10
Nos. 317-320 (4) 2.35 2.35

Nos. 282a-283a Overprinted: "1st PARTICIPATION / COMMONWEALTH GAMES 1982"

1982 Litho. Perf. 13½

321 A52 15p multicolored .35 .35
322 A52 20p multicolored .45 .45

12th Commonwealth Games, Brisbane, Australia, Sept. 30-Oct. 9.

A60

1983, Mar. 1 Perf. 14

323 A60 7p Marasmius echinosphaerus .60 .30
324 A60 12p Chlorophyllum molybdites .90 .50
325 A60 15p Leucocoprinus cepaestipes 1.00 .60
326 A60 20p Lycoperdon marginatum 1.25 .70
327 A60 50p Marasmiellus distantifolius 1.60 *1.75*
Nos. 323-327 (5) 5.35 *3.85*

View of Georgetown A61

1983, May 12 Litho. Perf. 14

328 A61 12p shown .25 .25
329 A61 15p Farm, Green Mountain .25 .25
330 A61 20p Boatswain Bird Isld. .35 .35
331 A61 60p Telemetry Hill 1.00 1.00
Nos. 328-331 (4) 1.85 1.85

See Nos. 359-362.

Manned Flight Bicentenary — A62

Military Aircraft.

1983, Aug. 1 Wmk. 373 Perf. 14

332 A62 12p Wessex Five helicopter 1.00 .75
333 A62 15p Vulcan B2 1.25 .85
334 A62 20p Nimrod MR2P 1.25 .80
335 A62 60p Victor K2 2.00 1.40
Nos. 332-335 (4) 5.50 3.80

Introduced Species A63

1983, Sept. Litho. Wmk. 373

336 A63 12p Iguanid .45 .40
337 A63 15p Rabbit .55 .50
338 A63 20p Cat .65 .60
339 A63 60p Donkey 1.50 1.50
Nos. 336-339 (4) 3.15 3.00

Tellina Antonii Philippi A64

1983, Nov. 28 Litho. Perf. 14½

340 A64 7p shown .25 .25
341 A64 12p Nodipecten nodosus .35 .35
342 A64 15p Cypraea lurida oceanica .45 .45
343 A64 20p Nerita ascensionis gmelin .60 .60
344 A64 50p Micromelo undatus 1.25 1.25
Nos. 340-344 (5) 2.90 2.90

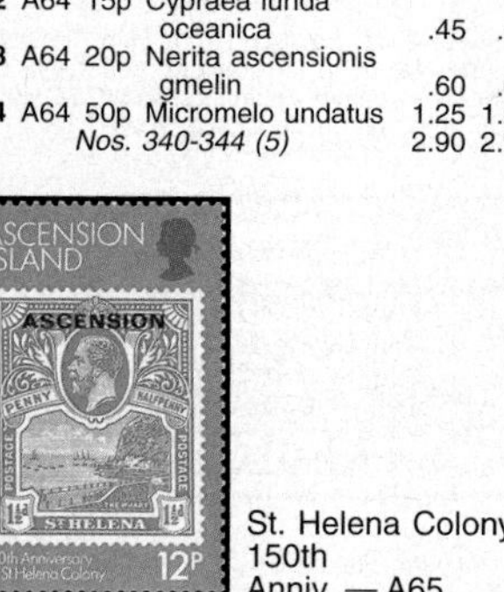

St. Helena Colony, 150th Anniv. — A65

Designs: First issue inscribed Ascension instead of overprinted.

1984, Jan. 10 Litho. Perf. 14

345 A65 12p No. 3 .30 .30
346 A65 15p No. 4 .40 .40
347 A65 20p No. 6 .55 .55
348 A65 60p No. 9 1.25 1.25
Nos. 345-348 (4) 2.50 2.50

Souvenir Sheet

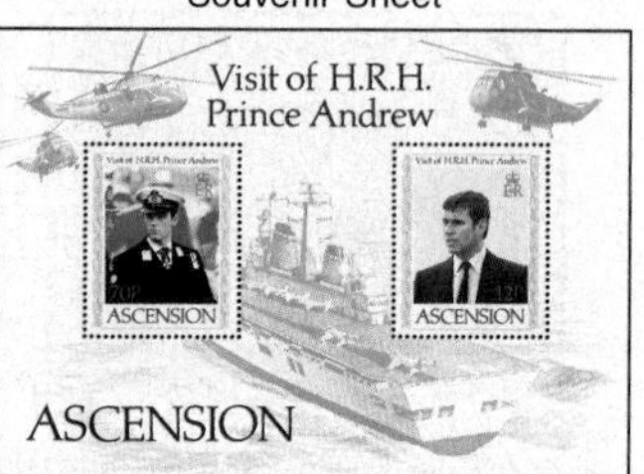

Visit of Prince Andrew — A66

1984, Apr. 10 Perf. 14½x14

349 Sheet of 2 2.00 2.00
a. A66 12p Andrew .25 .25
b. A66 70p In naval uniform 1.50 1.50

Lloyd's List Issue

Common Design Type

1984, May 28

351 CD335 12p Naval semaphore .50 .25
352 CD335 15p "Southampton Castle" .60 .35
353 CD335 20p Pier Head .70 .45
354 CD335 70p Dane 1.50 1.50
Nos. 351-354 (4) 3.30 2.55

1984 Coins and Wildlife A67

1984, June Perf. 14

355 A67 12p One penny, yellowfin tuna .80 .80
356 A67 15p Two pence, donkeys 1.00 1.00
357 A67 20p Fifty pence, green turtle 1.00 1.00
358 A67 70p One pound, sooty terns 1.75 *2.50*
Nos. 355-358 (4) 4.55 5.30

View Type of 1983

1984, Oct. Litho. Wmk. 373

359 A61 12p Devil's Riding School .25 .25
360 A61 15p St. Mary's Church .35 .35
361 A61 20p Two Boats Village .50 .50
362 A61 70p Ascension Isld. 1.75 1.75
Nos. 359-362 (4) 2.85 2.85

Trees — A68

1985, Mar. 8 Litho. *Perf. 14½x14*

363 A68 7p Bermuda cypress .65 .55
364 A68 12p Norfolk Island pine .70 .60
365 A68 15p Screwpine .85 .70
366 A68 20p Eucalyptus .90 .90
367 A68 65p Spore tree 2.25 2.25
Nos. 363-367 (5) 5.35 5.00

Military Firearms A69

Large guns and insignia: 12p, Thirty-two pounder small bore muzzle loader, c. 1820; Royal Marines hat plate, c. 1816. 15p, Seven-inch rifled muzzle loader, c. 1866; royal cipher. 20p, Seven-pounder rifled muzzle loader, c. 1877; Royal Artillery badge. 70p, HMS Hood 5.5-inch gun; ship crest.

1985, July 21 Wmk. 373 *Perf. 14½*

368 A69 12p multicolored .65 .65
369 A69 15p multicolored 1.00 1.00
370 A69 20p multicolored 1.00 1.00
371 A69 70p multicolored 2.50 2.50
Nos. 368-371 (4) 5.15 5.15

Queen Mother 85th Birthday
Common Design Type

12p, With Duke of York, Balmoral, 1924. 15p, With Princes Andrew and Edward. 20p, At Ascot. 70p, Christening of Prince Henry, Windsor Castle. 75p, Leaving the QEII, 1968.

Perf. 14½x14
1985, June 7 Wmk. 384

372 CD336 12p multicolored .55 .55
373 CD336 15p multicolored .55 .55
374 CD336 20p multicolored .75 .75
375 CD336 70p multicolored 1.75 1.75
Nos. 372-375 (4) 3.60 3.60

Souvenir Sheet

376 CD336 75p multicolored 1.75 1.75

Intl. Youth Year, Girl Guides 75th Anniv. — A70

1985, Oct. 4 Wmk. 373

377 A70 12p Guides' banner .60 .60
378 A70 15p First aid .65 .55
379 A70 20p Camping .75 .65
380 A70 70p Lady Baden-Powell 2.00 2.00
Nos. 377-380 (4) 4.00 3.80

Wildflowers — A71

Wmk. 384
1985, Dec. 6 Litho. *Perf. 14*

381 A71 12p Clerodendrum fragrans .50 .50
382 A71 15p Shell ginger .60 .60
383 A71 20p Cape daisy .70 .70
384 A71 70p Ginger lily 1.40 *1.75*
Nos. 381-384 (4) 3.20 3.55

Halley's Comet — A72

Designs: 12p, Newton's reflector telescope. 15p, Edmond Halley, Old Greenwich Observatory. 20p, Short's Gregorian telescope, comet, 1759. 70p, ICE space probe, Ascension satellite tracking station.

1986, Mar. 7

385 A72 12p multicolored .60 .60
386 A72 15p multicolored .70 .70
387 A72 20p multicolored .75 .75
388 A72 70p multicolored 2.00 *2.50*
Nos. 385-388 (4) 4.05 4.55

Queen Elizabeth II 60th Birthday
Common Design Type

Designs: 7p, Infant photograph, 1926. 15p, 1st worldwide Christmas broadcast, 1952. 20p, Garter Ceremony, Windsor Castle, 1983. 35p, Royal Tour, New Zealand, 1981. £1, Visiting Crown Agents' offices, 1983.

1986, Apr. 21 *Perf. 14x14½*

389 CD337 7p scarlet, blk & sil .25 .25
390 CD337 15p ultra, blk & sil .35 .35
391 CD337 20p green & multi .45 .45
392 CD337 35p violet & multi .50 .50
393 CD337 £1 rose vio & multi 1.25 1.25
Nos. 389-393 (5) 2.80 2.80

For overprints see Nos. 431-435.

AMERIPEX '86 — A73

1986, May 22 *Perf. 14½*

394 A73 12p No. 183 .40 .40
395 A73 15p No. 260 .60 .60
396 A73 20p No. 215 .75 .75
397 A73 70p No. 310 1.50 1.50
Nos. 394-397 (4) 3.25 3.25

Souvenir Sheet

398 A73 75p Statue of Liberty, New York Harbor 3.50 3.50

Statue of Liberty, cent.

Royal Wedding Issue, 1986
Common Design Type

Designs: 15p, Couple kissing. 35p, Andrew in navy uniform, helicopter.

Wmk. 384
1986, July 23 Litho. *Perf. 14*

399 CD338 15p multicolored .45 .45
400 CD338 35p multicolored 1.00 1.00

Ships A74

1986, Oct. 14 Wmk. 384 *Perf. 14½*

401 A74 1p Ganymede, c. 1811 .90 *1.10*
402 A74 2p Kangaroo, c. 1811 1.00 *1.10*
403 A74 4p Trinculo, c. 1811 1.00 *1.10*
404 A74 5p Daring, c. 1811 1.00 *1.10*
405 A74 9p Thais, c. 1811 1.10 *1.10*
406 A74 10p Pheasant, 1819 1.10 *1.10*
407 A74 15p Myrmidon, 1819 1.25 *1.50*
408 A74 18p Atholl, 1825 1.25 *1.50*
409 A74 20p Medina, 1830 1.25 *1.50*
410 A74 25p Saracen, 1840 1.25 *1.75*
411 A74 30p Hydra, c. 1845 1.25 *1.75*
412 A74 50p Sealark, 1840 1.75 *2.40*
413 A74 70p Rattlesnake, 1868 2.50 2.75
414 A74 £1 Penelope, 1889 3.50 3.75
415 A74 £2 Monarch, 1897 6.50 7.00
Nos. 401-415 (15) 26.60 30.50

For surcharges see Nos. 502-504.

Edible Bush Fruits A75

1987, Jan. 29 *Perf. 14*

416 A75 12p Cape gooseberry .90 .90
417 A75 15p Prickly pear 1.00 1.00
418 A75 20p Guava 1.10 1.10
419 A75 70p Loquat 2.00 *2.00*
Nos. 416-419 (4) 5.00 5.00

1st American Manned Orbital Space Flight, 25th Anniv. — A76

Military Uniforms, 1815-20 — A77

1987, Mar. 30

420 A76 15p Ignition .85 .85
421 A76 18p Lift-off .95 .95
422 A76 25p Reentry 1.25 1.25
423 A76 £1 Splashdown 4.00 4.00
Nos. 420-423 (4) 7.05 7.05

Souvenir Sheet

424 A76 70p Friendship 7 capsule 2.50 2.50

1987, June 29

Designs: a, Captains in full dress, 1st landing on Ascenion. b, Surgeon and sailors at campsite. c, Seaman returning from Dampier's Drip with water supply. d, Midshipman at lookout post. e, Commander and surveyor.

425 Strip of 5 5.00 5.00
a.-e. A77 25p multicolored .85 .85

See Nos. 458, 482, 507.

Butterflies A78

1987, Aug. 10 *Perf. 14½*

426 A78 15p Painted lady 1.25 1.25
427 A78 18p Monarch 1.25 1.25
428 A78 25p Diadem 1.75 1.75
429 A78 £1 Long-tailed blue 4.50 4.50
Nos. 426-429 (4) 8.75 8.75

See Nos. 436-439, 459-462.

Birds — A79

Designs: a, Ascension frigatebirds (males). b, Brown booby, frigatebird, white boobies. c, Frigatebird, white booby. d, Ascension frigatebirds (females). e, Adult frigatebird feeding young.

1987, Oct. 8 Wmk. 373 *Perf. 14*

430 Strip of 5 12.00 12.00
a.-e. A79 25p any single 2.00 2.00

No. 430 has continuous design.
See No. 453.

Nos. 389-393 Ovptd. "40TH WEDDING ANNIVERSARY" in Silver

Perf. 14x14½
1987, Dec. 9 Litho. Wmk. 384

431 CD337 7p scar, blk & sil .25 .25
432 CD337 15p ultra, blk & sil .30 .30
433 CD337 20p green & multi .50 .50
434 CD337 35p violet & multi .75 .75
435 CD337 £1 rose vio & multi 2.00 2.00
Nos. 431-435 (5) 3.80 3.80

40th wedding anniv. of Queen Elizabeth II and Prince Philip.

Insects Type of 1987

1988, Jan. 18 *Perf. 14½*

436 A78 15p Field cricket .80 .80
437 A78 18p Bush cricket .90 .90
438 A78 25p Ladybug 1.25 1.25
439 A78 £1 Burnished brass moth 4.25 4.25
Nos. 436-439 (4) 7.20 7.20

Capt. William Bate (d. 1838), 1st Garrison Commander and Colonial Founder of Ascension A80

Designs: 9p, Bate's Memorial, St. Mary's Church. 15p, Commodore's Cottage, Cross Hill. 18p, North East or Bate's Cottage, 1833. 25p, Landmarks on map. 70p, Bate and 3 soldiers.

1988, Apr. 14 Litho. *Perf. 14*

440 A80 9p multicolored .30 .30
441 A80 15p multicolored .50 .50
442 A80 18p multicolored .60 .60
443 A80 25p multicolored .85 .85
444 A80 70p multicolored 2.00 2.00
Nos. 440-444 (5) 4.25 4.25

Australia Bicentennial Emblem and Ships Named HMS Resolution — A81

1988, June 23 Litho. *Perf. 14*

445 A81 9p 3-Masted square-rigger, 1667 1.25 .50
446 A81 18p 3-Masted square-rigger, 1772 1.75 .80
447 A81 25p Navy cruiser, 1892 2.00 1.10
448 A81 65p Battleship, 1916 3.50 2.50
Nos. 445-448 (4) 8.50 4.90

Australia bicentennial.

Nos. 445-448 Overprinted

Wmk. 384
1988, July 30 Litho. *Perf. 14*

449 A81 9p multicolored .75 .55
450 A81 18p multicolored 1.25 .90
451 A81 25p multicolored 1.25 .95
452 A81 65p multicolored 2.50 2.50
Nos. 449-452 (4) 5.75 4.90

SYDPEX '88, July 30-Aug. 7.

Bird Type of 1987

Behaviors of the wideawake tern, Sterna fuscata: a, Two adults, flock overhead. b, Nesting (two birds). c, Nesting (three birds). d, Adult and young. e, Tern flapping its wings.

1988, Aug. 15 *Perf. 14*

453	Strip of 5	10.00	10.00
a.-e.	A79 25p any single	1.90	1.90

No. 453 has continuous design.

Lloyds of London, 300th Anniv.

Common Design Type

8p, Lloyd's Coffee House, Tower Street, 1688. 18p, Cable ship Alert, horiz. 25p, Satellite recovery in space, horiz. 65p, Ship Good Hope Castle on fire off Ascension, 1973.

Wmk. 373

1988, Oct. 17 Litho. *Perf. 14*

454	CD341 8p multicolored	.40	.40
455	CD341 18p multicolored	.85	.85
456	CD341 25p multicolored	1.25	1.25
457	CD341 65p multicolored	2.50	2.50
	Nos. 454-457 (4)	5.00	5.00

Military Uniforms Type of 1987

Uniforms of the Royal Marines: a, Marines arrive in Ascension (marines), 1821. b, Semaphore station (officer, marine), 1829. c, Octagonal tank (sergeant), 1831. d, Water pipe tunnel (officers), 1833. e, Constructing barracks (officer), 1834.

1988, Nov. 21

458	Strip of 5	8.50	8.50
a.-e.	A77 25p multicolored	1.50	1.50

Insect Type of 1987

Wmk. 384

1989, Jan. 16 Litho. *Perf. 14½*

459	A78 15p Plume moth	1.40	.85
460	A78 18p Green bottle	1.40	.95
461	A78 25p Weevil	1.10	1.10
462	A78 £1 Paper wasp	5.25	3.50
	Nos. 459-462 (4)	9.15	6.40

Land Crabs, Gecarcinus Lagostoma — A82

1989, Apr. 17

463	A82 15p multicolored	.75	.75
464	A82 18p multi, diff.	.80	.80
465	A82 25p multi, diff.	1.25	1.25
466	A82 £1 multi, diff.	4.25	4.25
	Nos. 463-466 (4)	7.05	7.05

Background designs continuous

467	A82 15p multicolored	.55	.55
467A	A82 18p multi, diff.	.75	.75
467B	A82 25p multi, diff.	.95	.95
467C	A82 £1 multi, diff.	4.25	4.25
d.	Souvenir sheet of 4, #467-467C	8.00	8.00

Moon Landing, 20th Anniv.

Common Design Type

Apollo 7: 15p, Tracking Station, Ascension Is. 18p, Launch, Cape Kennedy. 25p, Mission emblem. 70p, Expended Saturn IVB stage. £1, Lunar landing profile for the Apollo 11 mission.

1989, July 20 *Perf. 14x13½*

Size of Nos. 469-470: 29x29mm

468	CD342 15p multicolored	.90	.65
469	CD342 18p multicolored	1.00	.75
470	CD342 25p multicolored	1.25	.95
471	CD342 70p multicolored	2.25	2.25
	Nos. 468-471 (4)	5.40	4.60

Souvenir Sheet

472	CD342 £1 multicolored	3.75	3.75

Souvenir Sheet

A83

1989, July 7 *Perf. 14x13½*

473	A83 75p Emblems, No. 60	4.50	4.50

Miniature Sheet

World Stamp Expo '89, Washington, DC, and PHILEXFRANCE '89, Paris — A84

The Statue of Liberty and scenes from the centenary celebrations, 1986: a, Operation Sail. b, Face. c, Upper body. d, Three crown points. e, Ships in harbor, view of lower Manhattan. f, Ship in port, New York City.

1989, Aug. 21 **Wmk. 373**

474	Sheet of 6	5.25	5.25
a.-f.	A84 15p any single	.75	.75

Devil's Ashpit Tracking Station A85

1989, Sept. 30 Wmk. 384 *Perf. 14*

475	Sheet, 5 each #a.-b.	10.50	10.50
a.	A85 18p shown	.70	.70
b.	A85 25p US space shuttle launch	1.10	1.10

Termination of NASA tracking operations, begun in 1965, at the station.

Shells and Mollusks A86

Designs: 8p, Strombus latus. 18p, Tonna galea. 25p, Harpa doris. £1, Charonia variegata.

Wmk. 384

1989, Nov. 6 Litho. *Perf. 14*

476	A86 8p multicolored	.70	.45
477	A86 18p multicolored	1.25	.65
478	A86 25p multicolored	1.75	.90
479	A86 £1 multicolored	4.50	3.75
	Nos. 476-479 (4)	8.20	5.75

Donkeys — A87

Perf. 14 on 3 Sides

1989, Nov. 17 Litho. Wmk. 384

Booklet Stamps

480	A87 18p shown	.80	1.00
a.	Booklet pane of 6	5.00	
481	A87 25p Green turtle	1.00	1.00
a.	Booklet pane of 4	4.25	

No. 480a sold for £1.

Military Type of 1987

Royal Navy equipment, c. 1815-1820: a, Seaman's pistol, hat, cutlass. b, Midshipman's belt buckle, button, sword, hat. c, Surgeon's hat, sword, instrument chest. d, Captain's hat, telescope, sword. e, Admiral's epaulet, megaphone, hat, pocket.

1990, Feb. 12 Litho. *Perf. 14*

482	Strip of 5	6.50	6.50
a.-e.	A77 25p any single	1.10	1.10

World Wildlife Fund — A88

Frigate birds *(Fregata aquila)*: 9p, Family group. 10p, Chick. 11p, Male in flight. 15p, Female and immature in flight.

Perf. 14½x14

1990, Mar. 5 Litho. Wmk. 373

483	A88 9p multicolored	*4.00*	*1.25*
484	A88 10p multicolored	*4.00*	*1.50*
485	A88 11p multicolored	*4.00*	*1.75*
486	A88 15p multicolored	*4.00*	*2.25*
	Nos. 483-486 (4)	*16.00*	*6.75*

Great Britain Nos. 1-2 A89

Exhibition emblem and: 18p, Early Ascension cancellations. 25p, Unloading mail at Wideawake Airfield. £1, Main P.O., Royal Mail van.

1990, May 3 Litho. *Perf. 14*

487	A89 9p shown	.50	.50
488	A89 18p multicolored	.80	.80
489	A89 25p multicolored	1.10	1.10
490	A89 £1 multicolored	4.00	4.00
	Nos. 487-490 (4)	6.40	6.40

Penny Black 150th anniv., Stamp World London '90.

Queen Mother, 90th Birthday

Common Design Types

1990, Aug. 4 Wmk. 384 *Perf. 14x15*

491	CD343 25p Portrait, 1940	1.25	1.40

Perf. 14½

492	CD344 £1 King, Queen with soldiers	3.50	4.25

Garth Castle, 1910 — A90

Designs: 18p, RMS St. Helena, 1982. 25p, Launching new RMS St. Helena, 1989. 70p, Duke of York launching new RMS St. Helena. £1, New RMS St. Helena.

Wmk. 373

1990, Sept. 13 Litho. *Perf. 14½*

493	A90 9p multicolored	1.40	1.40
494	A90 18p multicolored	1.75	1.75
495	A90 25p multicolored	2.75	2.75
496	A90 70p multicolored	4.75	4.75
	Nos. 493-496 (4)	10.65	10.65

Souvenir Sheet

497	A90 £1 multicolored	7.50	7.50

See St. Helena Nos. 535-539, Tristan da Cunha Nos. 482-486.

Christmas — A91

Sculpture (8p) and paintings of Madonna and Child by: 8p, Felici. 18p, Unknown artist. 25p, Gebhard. 65p, Gritti.

1990, Oct. 24 *Perf. 14*

498	A91 8p multicolored	1.10	.80
499	A91 18p multicolored	1.90	1.40
500	A91 25p multicolored	2.75	1.90
501	A91 65p multicolored	4.25	4.25
	Nos. 498-501 (4)	10.00	8.35

Nos. 410, 412 & 414 Ovptd. in Silver "BRITISH FOR 175 YEARS"

1991, Feb. 5 Wmk. 384 *Perf. 14½*

502	A74 25p on #410	3.00	3.00
503	A74 50p on #412	3.50	3.50
504	A74 £1 on #414	4.75	4.75
	Nos. 502-504 (3)	11.25	11.25

Elizabeth & Philip, Birthdays

Common Design Types

1991, June 18

505	CD345 25p multicolored	1.40	*1.60*
506	CD346 25p multicolored	1.40	*1.60*
a.	Pair, #505-506 + label	3.50	3.75

Military Uniforms Type of 1987

Royal Marines Equipment 1821-1844: a, Officer's shako, epaulettes, belt plate, button. b, Officer's cap, sword, epaulettes, belt plate. c, Drum Major's shako with cords, staff. d, Sergeant's shako, chevrons, belt plate, canteen. e, Drummer's drum, sticks, shako.

1991, Aug. 1 Wmk. 373 *Perf. 14*

507	A77 25p Strip of 5, #a.-e.	10.00	10.00

Atlantic Relay Station, 25th Anniv. A92

15p, BBC Atlantic relay station. 18p, English Bay transmitters. 25p, Satellite receiving station. 70p, Antenna support tower.

1991, Sept. 17 Wmk. 384 *Perf. 14½*

508	A92 15p multi	1.40	1.40
509	A92 18p multi	1.60	1.60
510	A92 25p multi, vert.	2.00	2.00
511	A92 70p multi, vert.	4.50	4.50
	Nos. 508-511 (4)	9.50	9.50

Christmas A93

Designs: 8p, St. Mary's Church, exterior. 18p, St. Mary's Church, interior. 25p, Grotto of Our Lady of Ascension, exterior. 65p, Grotto of Our Lady of Ascension, interior.

1991, Oct. 1 *Perf. 14*

512	A93 8p multicolored	.95	.80
513	A93 18p multicolored	1.75	1.40
514	A93 25p multicolored	2.25	1.75
515	A93 65p multicolored	4.25	*5.00*
	Nos. 512-515 (4)	9.20	8.95

Fish A94

Wmk. 373

1991, Dec. 10 Litho. *Perf. 14*

516 A94 1p Blackfish .70 .70
517 A94 2p Five finger 1.00 .75
518 A94 4p Resplendent angelfish 1.10 .95
519 A94 5p Silver fish 1.10 .95
520 A94 9p Gurnard 1.50 1.10
521 A94 10p Blue dad 1.50 1.10
522 A94 15p Cunning fish 2.00 1.10
523 A94 18p Grouper 2.00 1.25
524 A94 20p Moray eel 2.00 1.50
525 A94 25p Hardback soldierfish 2.00 1.60
526 A94 30p Blue marlin 2.00 1.75
527 A94 50p Wahoo 2.50 2.50
528 A94 70p Yellowfin tuna 3.25 *4.00*
529 A94 £1 Blue shark 3.75 *4.50*
530 A94 £2.50 Bottlenose dolphin 7.50 *9.50*
Nos. 516-530 (15) 33.90 *33.25*

Queen Elizabeth II's Accession to the Throne, 40th Anniv.
Common Design Type

Wmk. 373

1992, Feb. 6 Litho. *Perf. 14*

531 CD349 9p multicolored .45 .45
532 CD349 15p multicolored .75 .75
533 CD349 18p multicolored .90 .90
534 CD349 25p multicolored 1.25 1.25
535 CD349 70p multicolored 3.00 3.00
Nos. 531-535 (5) 6.35 6.35

Discovery of America, 500th Anniv. — A95

Wmk. 373

1992, Feb. 18 Litho. *Perf. 14*

536 A95 9p STV Eye of the Wind 1.50 .65
537 A95 18p STV Soren Larsen 2.50 .95
538 A95 25p Pinta, Santa Maria, & Nina 3.00 1.25
539 A95 70p Columbus, Santa Maria 5.75 2.75
Nos. 536-539 (4) 12.75 5.60

World Columbian Stamp Expo '92, Chicago and Genoa '92 Intl. Philatelic Exhibitions.

Wideawake Airfield, 50th Anniv. — A96

Wmk. 373

1992, May 5 Litho. *Perf. 14*

540 A96 15p Control tower .95 .95
541 A96 18p Nose hangar 1.25 1.25
542 A96 25p Construction work 1.50 1.50
543 A96 70p Laying fuel pipeline 3.75 3.75
Nos. 540-543 (4) 7.45 7.45

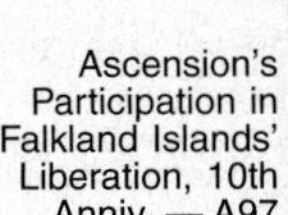

Ascension's Participation in Falkland Islands' Liberation, 10th Anniv. — A97

Designs: No. 548a, 15p + 3p like #544. b, 18p + 4p like #545. c, 25p + 5p like #546. d, 65p + 13p like #547.

Wmk. 373

1992, June 12 Litho. *Perf. 14*

544 A97 15p Nimrod Mk.2 1.25 1.10
545 A97 18p VC10 1.25 1.10
546 A97 25p Wessex HU Mk.5 helicopter 1.90 1.50
547 A97 65p Vulcan B2 3.00 3.50
Nos. 544-547 (4) 7.40 7.20

Souvenir Sheet

548 A97 Sheet of 4, #a.-d. 8.50 8.50

Surtax for Soldiers', Sailors' and Airmen's Families Association.

Christmas A98

Children's drawings: 8p, Snowman, rocks, candle. 18p, Underwater Santa, Christmas tree. 25p, Hello, bells. 65p, Nativity Scene, angel.

Wmk. 384

1992, Oct. 13 Litho. *Perf. 14*

549 A98 8p multicolored 1.10 .90
550 A98 18p multicolored 1.60 1.25
551 A98 25p multicolored 1.90 1.50
552 A98 65p multicolored 3.75 3.75
Nos. 549-552 (4) 8.35 7.40

Yellow Canary — A99

Wmk. 373

1993, Jan. 12 Litho. *Perf. 14½*

553 A99 15p Singing male 1.25 1.25
554 A99 18p Adult male, female 1.40 1.40
555 A99 25p Young calling for food 1.75 1.75
556 A99 70p Mixed flock 4.50 4.50
Nos. 553-556 (4) 8.90 8.90

Royal Air Force, 75th Anniv.
Common Design Type

Designs: 20p, Sopwith Snipe. No. 558, Supermarine Southampton. 30p, Avro Anson. 70p, Vickers Wellington 1C.

No. 561a, Westland Lysander. b, Gloster Meteor. c, DeHavilland Comet. d, British Aerospace Nimrod.

Wmk. 373

1993, Apr. 1 Litho. *Perf. 14*

557 CD350 20p multicolored 1.90 1.40
558 CD350 25p multicolored 1.90 1.40
559 CD350 30p multicolored 2.00 1.50
560 CD350 70p multicolored 3.50 3.50
Nos. 557-560 (4) 9.30 7.80

Souvenir Sheet

561 CD350 25p Sheet of 4, #a.-d. 6.25 6.25

South Atlantic Cable Company, 25th Anniv. A100

Designs: 20p, Map showing cable route. 25p, Cable ship laying cable. 30p, Map of Ascension. 70p, Cable ship off Ascension.

Perf. 14x14½

1993, June 8 Litho. Wmk. 384

562 A100 20p multicolored 1.25 1.25
563 A100 25p multicolored 1.50 1.50
564 A100 30p multicolored 1.75 1.75
565 A100 70p multicolored 4.00 4.00
Nos. 562-565 (4) 8.50 8.50

Flowers A101

Perf. 14x14½

1993, Aug. 3 Litho. Wmk. 384

566 A101 20p Lantana camara 1.50 .75
567 A101 25p Moonflower 1.75 .97
568 A101 30p Hibiscus 1.75 1.10
569 A101 70p Frangipani 4.00 3.50
Nos. 566-569 (4) 9.00 6.32

Christmas A102

Designs: 12p, Child mailing Christmas card. 20p, Mail loaded onto Tristar. 25p, Plane in flight. 30p, Mail unloaded at Wideawake Airfield. 65p, Child reading card, Georgetown.

Perf. 14½x14

1993, Oct. 19 Litho. Wmk. 373

570 A102 12p multicolored .75 .40
571 A102 20p multicolored 1.25 .45
572 A102 25p multicolored 1.40 .50
573 A102 30p multicolored 2.25 2.25
574 A102 65p multicolored 2.75 2.75
a. Souvenir sheet of 5, #570-574 12.00 12.00
Nos. 570-574 (5) 8.40 6.35

Stamps from No. 574a show a continuous design, while Nos. 570-574 have white borders on sides.

Prehistoric Aquatic Reptiles — A103

1994, Jan. 25 Wmk. 373 *Perf. 14*

575 A103 12p Ichthyosaurus 1.10 1.10
576 A103 20p Metriorhynchus 1.35 1.35
577 A103 25p Mosasaurus 1.60 1.60
578 A103 30p Elasmosaurus 1.60 1.60
579 A103 65p Plesiosaurus 3.00 3.00
Nos. 575-579 (5) 8.65 8.65

Ovptd. with Hong Kong '94 Emblem

1994, Feb. 18

580 A103 12p on #575 1.10 1.10
581 A103 20p on #576 1.75 1.75
582 A103 25p on #577 1.75 1.75
583 A103 30p on #578 1.90 1.90
584 A103 65p on #579 3.25 3.25
Nos. 580-584 (5) 9.75 9.75

Green Turtle A104

20p, Four on beach. 25p, Crawling in sand. No. 587, Crawling from sea. 65p, Swimming.

No. 589a, Side view, crawling from sea. b, Digging nest. c, Hatchlings heading to sea. d, Digging nest, diff.

1994, Mar. 22

585 A104 20p multicolored 2.25 2.25
586 A104 25p multicolored 2.75 2.75
587 A104 30p multicolored 2.75 2.75
588 A104 65p multicolored 4.25 4.00
Nos. 585-588 (4) 12.00 11.75

Souvenir Sheet

589 A104 30p Sheet of 4, #a.-d. 14.00 14.00

Civilian Ships A105

Ships serving during Falkland Islands War, 1982: 20p, Tug Yorkshireman. 25p, Minesweeper support ship RMS St. Helena. 30p, Oil tanker British ESK. 65p, Cruise liner Uganda, hospital ship.

1994, June 14

590 A105 20p multicolored 2.75 2.75
591 A105 25p multicolored 3.00 3.00
592 A105 30p multicolored 3.00 3.00
593 A105 65p multicolored 5.25 5.25
Nos. 590-593 (4) 14.00 14.00

Sooty Tern A106

1994, Aug. 16

594 A106 20p Chick 1.50 1.50
595 A106 25p Juvenile 1.60 1.60
596 A106 30p Brooding adult 1.90 1.90
597 A106 65p Displaying male 3.00 3.00
Nos. 594-597 (4) 8.00 8.00

Souvenir Sheet

598 A106 £1 Dread 7.25 7.25

Christmas A107

Donkeys: 12p, Mare with foal. 20p, Young adult. 25p, Foal. 30p, Adult, egrets. 65p, Adult.

1994, Oct. 11 *Perf. 14x14½*

599 A107 12p multicolored 1.40 1.00
600 A107 20p multicolored 1.90 1.40
601 A107 25p multicolored 1.90 1.40
602 A107 30p multicolored 2.10 1.50
603 A107 65p multicolored 4.00 4.00
Nos. 599-603 (5) 11.30 9.30

Flowers A108

20p, Leonurus japonicus. 25p, Periwinkle. 30p, Four o'clock. 65p, Blood flower.

1995, Jan. 10 *Perf. 14*

604 A108 20p multi, vert. 2.50 2.50
605 A108 25p multi 2.50 2.50
606 A108 30p multi, vert. 3.50 3.50
607 A108 65p multi 4.50 4.50
Nos. 604-607 (4) 13.00 13.00

Island Scenes, c. 1895 A109

Designs: 12p, Horse-drawn wagon, Two Boats, Green Mountain. 20p, Island stewards' store. 25p, Royal Navy headquarters, barracks. 30p, Police office. 65p, Pier head.

1995, Mar. 7 Wmk. 384 *Perf. 14½*

608 A109 12p sepia .80 .80
609 A109 20p sepia 1.10 1.10
610 A109 25p sepia 1.50 1.50
611 A109 30p sepia 2.75 2.75
612 A109 65p sepia 3.00 3.00
Nos. 608-612 (5) 9.15 9.15

End of World War II, 50th Anniv.
Common Design Types

Designs: 20p, 5.5-inch guns taken from HMS Hood, 1941. 25p, Fairey Swordfish, first aircraft to land at Ascension. 30p, HMS Dorsetshire patrolling South Atlantic. 65p, HMS Devonshire patrolling South Atlantic.
£1, Reverse of War Medal, 1939-45.

1995, May 8 Wmk. 373 *Perf. 14*

613 CD351 20p multicolored 2.00 2.00
614 CD351 25p multicolored 2.25 2.25
615 CD351 30p multicolored 2.75 2.50
616 CD351 65p multicolored 4.50 4.50
Nos. 613-616 (4) 11.50 11.25

Souvenir Sheet

617 CD352 £1 multicolored 8.25 8.25
Nos. 613-617 (5) 19.75 19.50

Butterflies — A110

1995, Sept. 1 Wmk. 384

618 A110 20p Long-tailed blue 2.10 2.10
619 A110 25p Painted lady 2.40 2.40
620 A110 30p Diadem 2.50 2.50
621 A110 65p African monarch 4.00 4.00
Nos. 618-621 (4) 11.00 11.00

Souvenir Sheet

622 A110 £1 Red admiral 9.00 9.00

Singapore '95 (No. 622).

Christmas A111

Designs based on children's drawings:
12p, Santa on boat. 20p, Santa on wall. 25p, Santa in chimney. 30p, Santa on dolphin. 65p, South Atlantic run.

1995, Oct. 10 Wmk. 373

623 A111 12p multicolored 1.10 1.10
624 A111 20p multicolored 1.40 1.40
625 A111 25p multicolored 1.50 1.50
626 A111 30p multicolored 1.75 1.75
627 A111 65p multicolored 3.00 3.00
Nos. 623-627 (5) 8.75 8.75

Mollusks A112

12p, Cypraea lurida. 25p, Cypraea spurca. 30p, Harpa doris. 65p, Umbraculum umbraculum.

Wmk. 384

1996, Jan. 10 Litho. *Perf. 14*

628 A112 12p multicolored 2.25 2.25
629 A112 25p multicolored 2.75 2.75
630 A112 30p multicolored 3.00 3.00
631 A112 65p multicolored 3.75 3.75
a. Strip of 4, #628-631 14.00 14.00

Queen Elizabeth II, 70th Birthday
Common Design Type

Various portraits of Queen, scenes of Ascension:
20p, St. Marys Church. 25p, The Residency. 30p, Roman Catholic Grotto. 65p, The Exiles Club.

Wmk. 384

1996, Apr. 22 Litho. *Perf. 13½*

632 CD354 20p multicolored .90 .90
633 CD354 25p multicolored 1.00 1.00
634 CD354 30p multicolored 1.25 1.25
635 CD354 65p multicolored 2.75 2.75
Nos. 632-635 (4) 5.90 5.90

CAPEX '96 A113

Island transport: 20p, US Army Jeep. 25p, 1924 Citreon 7.5HP two seater. 30p, 1930 Austin Ten-four Tourer. 65p, Series 1 Land Rover.

Wmk. 384

1996, June 8 Litho. *Perf. 14*

636 A113 20p multicolored 1.25 1.25
637 A113 25p multicolored 1.40 1.40
638 A113 30p multicolored 1.50 1.50
639 A113 65p multicolored 2.75 2.75
Nos. 636-639 (4) 6.90 6.90

Birds and Their Young — A114

1p, Madeiran storm petrel. 2p, Red-billed tropicbird. 4p, Indian mynah. 5p, House sparrow. 7p, Common waxbill. 10p, White tern. 12p, Francolin. 15p, Brown noddy. 20p, Yellow canary. 25p, Black noddy. 30p, Red-footed booby. 40p, Yellow-billed tropicbird. 65p, Brown booby. £1, Masked booby. £2, Sooty tern. £3, Ascension frigate bird.

Wmk. 373

1996, Aug. 12 Litho. *Perf. 13*

640 A114 1p multicolored .25 .25
641 A114 2p multicolored .25 .25
642 A114 4p multicolored .25 .25
643 A114 5p multicolored .25 .25
644 A114 7p multicolored .25 .25
645 A114 10p multicolored .35 .45
646 A114 12p multicolored .40 .50
647 A114 15p multicolored .50 .65
648 A114 20p multicolored .75 .90
649 A114 25p multicolored .90 1.00
650 A114 30p multicolored 1.10 1.25
651 A114 40p multicolored 1.50 1.60
652 A114 65p multicolored 2.50 2.75
a. Sheet of 1, perf. 14 4.50 4.50
653 A114 £1 multicolored 3.75 4.50
a. Souvenir sheet of 1 4.50 4.50
654 A114 £2 multicolored 7.75 9.25
655 A114 £3 multicolored 10.00 11.50
Nos. 640-655 (16) 30.75 35.60

No. 652a for Hong Kong '97. Issued 2/3/97.
No. 653a for return of Hong Kong to China. Issued 7/1/97.

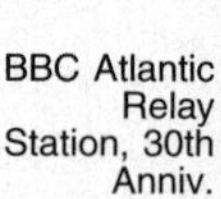

BBC Atlantic Relay Station, 30th Anniv. A115

Various views of relay station: 20p, 25p, Towers. 30p, Towers, buildings. 65p, Satellite dish, towers, beach.

1996, Sept. 9 Wmk. 384 *Perf. 14*

656 A115 20p multicolored .95 .95
657 A115 25p multicolored 1.10 1.10
658 A115 30p multicolored 1.25 1.25
659 A115 65p multicolored 2.75 2.75
Nos. 656-659 (4) 6.05 6.05

Christmas A116

Santa Claus: 12p, On satellite dish. 20p, Playing golf. 25p, By beach. 30p, On RAF Tristar. 65p, Aboard RMS St. Helena.

Perf. 14x14½

1996, Sept. 23 Litho. Wmk. 373

660 A116 12p multicolored .55 .55
661 A116 20p multicolored 1.00 1.00
662 A116 25p multicolored 1.00 1.00
663 A116 30p multicolored 1.25 1.10
664 A116 65p multicolored 2.75 2.50
Nos. 660-664 (5) 6.55 6.15

UNICEF, 50th anniv.

A117

Wmk. 373

1997, Jan. 7 Litho. *Perf. 14½*

665 A117 20p Date palm .85 .85
666 A117 25p Mauritius hemp 1.10 1.10
667 A117 30p Norfolk Island pine 1.25 1.25
668 A117 65p Dwarf palm 2.25 2.25
Nos. 665-668 (4) 5.45 5.45

Hong Kong '97.

A118

Flag, ship or aircraft: 12p, Great Britain Red Ensign, tanker Maserk Ascension. 25p, RAF Ensign, Tristar. 30p, NASA emblem, Space Shuttle Atlantis. 65p, Royal Navy White Ensign, HMS Northumberland.

Wmk. 373

1997, Apr. 1 Litho. *Perf. 14½*

669 A118 12p multicolored 1.10 1.10
670 A118 25p multicolored 1.60 1.60
671 A118 30p multicolored 1.75 1.75
672 A118 65p multicolored 3.50 3.50
Nos. 669-672 (4) 7.95 7.95

Herbs A119

Designs: a, Solanum sodomaeum. b, Ageratum conyzoides. c, Leonurus sibricus. d, Cerastium vulgatum. e, Commelina diffusa.

Perf. 14x14½

1997, June 7 Litho. Wmk. 373

673 A119 30p Strip of 5, #a.-e. 8.50 8.50

A120

Queen Elizabeth II and Prince Philip, 50th Wedding Anniv.: No. 674, Queen Elizabeth II. No. 675, Prince Philip playing polo. No. 676, Queen petting horse. No. 677, Prince Philip. No. 678, Prince Philip, Queen Elizabeth II. No. 679, Prince Harry, Prince William riding horses.
£1.50, Queen Elizabeth, Prince Philip riding in open carriage.

Wmk. 384

1997, July 10 Litho. *Perf. 13½*

674 A120 20p multicolored 1.50 1.50
675 A120 20p multicolored 1.50 1.50
a. Pair, #674-675 3.75 3.75
676 A120 25p multicolored 1.60 1.60
677 A120 25p multicolored 1.60 1.60
a. Pair, #676-677 4.00 4.00
678 A120 30p multicolored 1.75 1.75
679 A120 30p multicolored 1.75 1.75
a. Pair, #678-679 4.25 4.25
Nos. 674-679 (6) 9.70 9.70

Souvenir Sheet

680 A120 £1.50 multicolored 9.00 9.00

Birds — A121

Booklet Stamps

Perf. 14 on 3 Sides

1997, Sept. 1 Litho. Wmk. 373

681 A121 15p like #644 2.50 2.50
682 A121 35p like #648 3.25 3.25
a. Booklet pane, 2 ea #681-682 8.00
Complete booklet, #682a 8.00

Game Fish — A122

Perf. 14x14½

1997, Sept. 3 Litho. Wmk. 373

683 A122 12p Black marlin .90 .90
684 A122 20p Atlantic sailfish 1.40 1.40
685 A122 25p Swordfish 1.50 1.50
686 A122 30p Wahoo 1.60 1.60
687 A122 £1 Yellowfin tuna 4.25 4.25
Nos. 683-687 (5) 9.65 9.65

A123 A124

St. Mary's Church (Christmas): 15p, Interior view. 35p, Stained glass window, Madonna and Child. 40p, Stained glass window, Falklands, 1982. 50p, Stained glass window.

Wmk. 384

1997, Oct. 1 Litho. *Perf. 14*

688 A123 15p multicolored .90 .90
689 A123 35p multicolored 1.75 1.75
690 A123 40p multicolored 1.90 1.90
691 A123 50p multicolored 2.50 2.50
Nos. 688-691 (4) 7.05 7.05

Wmk. 373

1998, Feb. 10 Litho. *Perf. 14*

Insects: 15p, Cactoblastis cactorum. 35p, Teleonemia scrupulosa. 40p, Neltumius arizonensis. 50p, Algarobius prosopis.

692 A124 15p multicolored 1.90 1.90
693 A124 35p multicolored 2.50 2.50
694 A124 40p multicolored 3.25 3.25
695 A124 50p multicolored 3.25 3.25
Nos. 692-695 (4) 10.90 10.90

Diana, Princess of Wales (1961-97)
Common Design Type

a, In polka-dotted dress. b, In yellow blouse. c, With longer hair style. d, Holding flowers.

Perf. 14½x14

1998, Mar. 31 Litho. Wmk. 373

696 CD355 35p Sheet of 4, #a.-d. 5.50 5.50

No. 696 sold for £1.40 + 20p, with surtax from international sales being donated to the Princess Diana Memorial Fund and surtax from national sales being donated to designated local charity.

Royal Air Force, 80th Anniv.
Common Design Type of 1993
Re-inscribed

15p, Fairey Fawn. 35p, Vickers Vernon. 40p, Supermarine Spitfire F-22. 50p, Bristol Britannia C2.
No. 701: a, Blackburn Kangaroo. b, SE5a. c, Curtiss Kittyhawk III. d, Boeing Fortress II (B-17).

Wmk. 384

1998, Apr. 1 Litho. *Perf. 14*
697 CD350 15p multicolored 1.10 1.10
698 CD350 35p multicolored 2.25 2.25
699 CD350 40p multicolored 2.50 2.50
700 CD350 50p multicolored 3.00 3.00
Nos. 697-700 (4) 8.85 8.85

Souvenir Sheet

701 CD350 50p Sheet of 4, #a.-d. 8.50 8.50

Birds — A125

Island Sports — A126

Wmk. 373

1998, June 15 Litho. *Perf. 14*
702 A125 15p Swallow 1.10 1.10
703 A125 25p House martin 1.60 1.60
704 A125 35p Cattle egret 1.90 1.90
705 A125 40p Swift 1.90 1.90
706 A125 50p Allen's gallinule 2.25 2.25
Nos. 702-706 (5) 8.75 8.75

Wmk. 373

1998, Aug. 17 Litho. *Perf. 14*
707 A126 15p Cricket 2.25 .80
708 A126 35p Golf 3.00 1.50
709 A126 40p Soccer 2.25 1.50
710 A126 50p Trapshooting 2.25 1.50
Nos. 707-710 (4) 9.75 5.30

Christmas A127

Designs: 15p, Children's nativity play. 35p, Santa arriving on Ascension. 40p, Santa arriving at a party. 50p, Carol singers.

Wmk. 373

1998, Oct. 1 Litho. *Perf. 14*
711 A127 15p multicolored 1.25 1.25
712 A127 35p multicolored 2.00 2.00
713 A127 40p multicolored 2.25 2.25
714 A127 50p multicolored 2.25 2.25
Nos. 711-714 (4) 7.75 7.75

World War II Aircraft A128

15p, Curtiss C-46 Commando. 35p, Douglas C-47 Dakota. 40p, Douglas C-54 Skymaster. 50p, Consolidated Liberator Mk.V. £1.50, Consolidated Liberator LB-30.

Wmk. 373

1999, Jan. 20 Litho. *Perf. 14*
715 A128 15p multicolored 1.25 1.25
716 A128 35p multicolored 2.00 2.00
717 A128 40p multicolored 2.25 2.25
718 A128 50p multicolored 2.25 2.25
Nos. 715-718 (4) 7.75 7.75

Souvenir Sheet

719 A128 £1.50 multicolored 12.50 12.50

Winston Churchill, 125th birth anniv.

Australia '99, World Stamp Expo A129

Union Castle Mail Ships: 15p, SS Glengorm Castle. 35p, SS Gloucester Castle. 40p, SS Durham Castle. 50p, SS Garth Castle. £1, HMS Endeavour.

Perf. 14½x14

1999, Mar. 5 Litho. Wmk. 373
720 A129 15p multicolored 1.25 1.25
721 A129 35p multicolored 2.25 2.25
722 A129 40p multicolored 2.40 2.40
723 A129 50p multicolored 2.40 2.40
Nos. 720-723 (4) 8.30 8.30

Souvenir Sheet

724 A129 £1 multicolored 7.25 7.25

World Wildlife Fund — A130

Fairy tern: No. 725, Two on branch. No. 726, One on branch. No. 727, Adult feeding chick. No. 728, Two in flight.

Wmk. 384

1999, Apr. 27 Litho. *Perf. 14½*
725 A130 10p multicolored .50 .40
726 A130 10p multicolored .50 .40
727 A130 10p multicolored .50 .40
728 A130 10p multicolored .50 .40
a. Sheet of 16, 4 each #725-728 8.00 8.00
Nos. 725-728 (4) 2.00 1.60

Wedding of Prince Edward and Sophie Rhys-Jones
Common Design Type

Perf. 13¾x14

1999, June 19 Litho. Wmk. 384
729 CD356 50p Separate portraits 1.90 1.90
730 CD356 £1 Couple 4.00 4.00

1st Manned Moon Landing, 30th Anniv.
Common Design Type

Designs: 15p, Command and service modules. 35p, Moon from Apollo 11. 40p, Devil's Ashpit Tracking Station. 50p, Lunar module lifts off moon.
£1.50, Looking at earth from moon.

Perf. 14x13¾

1999, July 20 Litho. Wmk. 384
731 CD357 15p multicolored 1.40 1.40
732 CD357 35p multicolored 1.75 1.75
733 CD357 40p multicolored 1.75 1.75
734 CD357 50p multicolored 1.75 1.75
Nos. 731-734 (4) 6.65 6.65

Souvenir Sheet
Perf. 14

735 CD357 £1.50 multicolored 7.25 7.25

No. 735 contains one 40mm circular stamp.

Queen Mother's Century
Common Design Type

Queen Mother: 15p, With King George VI, Winston Churchill. 35p, With Prince Charles. 40p, At Clarence House, 88th birthday. 50p, With drummers at Clarence House.
£1.50, With Titanic.

Wmk. 384

1999, Aug. 20 Litho. *Perf. 13½*
736 CD358 15p multicolored 1.25 1.25
737 CD358 35p multicolored 1.75 1.75
738 CD358 40p multicolored 2.00 2.00
739 CD358 50p multicolored 2.50 2.50
Nos. 736-739 (4) 7.50 7.50

Souvenir Sheet

740 CD358 £1.50 black 9.50 9.50

Christmas A131

Wmk. 384

1999, Oct. 6 Litho. *Perf. 13¾*
741 A131 15p 3 children 1.25 1.25
742 A131 35p 2 children, hats 2.25 2.25
743 A131 40p 2 children, bed 2.25 2.25
744 A131 50p 4 children 2.25 2.25
Nos. 741-744 (4) 8.00 8.00

Cable and Wireless, Cent. A132

Perf. 13¼x13¾

1999, Dec. 13 Litho. Wmk. 373
745 A132 15p CS Anglia 1.75 1.75
746 A132 35p CS Cambria 2.50 2.50
747 A132 40p Map 2.50 2.50
748 A132 50p CS Colonia 2.75 2.75
Nos. 745-748 (4) 9.50 9.50

Souvenir Sheet

749 A132 £1.50 CS Seine 9.50 9.50

Turtle Project — A133

15p, Young turtles. 35p, Turtle, trail at left. 40p, Turtle with tracking device on beach. 50p, Turtle with tracking device heading to sea.
No. 754: a, Turtle head, rock. b, Like 15p. c, Turtle on beach, sea. d, Turtle in surf.

2000, Mar. 8 Litho. *Perf. 13¾*
750 A133 15p multi 1.10 1.10
751 A133 35p multi 1.90 1.90
752 A133 40p multi 1.90 1.90
753 A133 50p multi 2.10 2.10
Nos. 750-753 (4) 7.00 7.00

Souvenir Sheet
Perf. 14

754 A133 25p Sheet of 4, #a-d 8.50 8.50
e. With Stamp Show 2000 emblem in margin 8.50 8.50

No. 754 contains four 40x26mm stamps.
No. 754e issued 5/8.

Prince William, 18th Birthday
Common Design Type

William: 15p, As toddler, vert. 35p, Wearing suit and wearing cap, vert. 40p, Holding flowers, and in parka. 50p, In suit and in checked shirt.

Perf. 13¾x14¼, 14¼x13¾

2000, June 21 Litho. Wmk. 373

Stamps With White Border

755 CD359 15p multi 1.00 1.00
756 CD359 35p multi 1.75 1.75
757 CD359 40p multi 2.50 2.50
758 CD359 50p multi 3.00 3.00
Nos. 755-758 (4) 8.25 8.25

Souvenir Sheet
Stamps Without White Border
Perf. 14¼

759 Sheet of 5 9.50 9.50
a. CD359 10p multi .60 .60
b. CD359 15p multi .90 .90
c. CD359 35p multi 1.75 1.75
d. CD359 40p multi 2.00 2.00
e. CD359 50p multi 2.75 2.75

Forts A134

Designs: 15p, 1815 fortifications. 35p, Fort Thornton, 1817. 40p, Fort Hayes, 1860. 50p, Fort Bedford, 1940.

Wmk. 373

2000, Aug. 14 Litho. *Perf. 14*
760-763 A134 Set of 4 11.00 11.00

Christmas — A135

Carols: 15p, I Saw Three Ships. 25p, Silent Night. 40p, Away in a Manger. 90p, Hark, the Herald Angels Sing.

2000, Oct. 16 Wmk. 384
764-767 A135 Set of 4 11.00 11.00

Souvenir Sheet

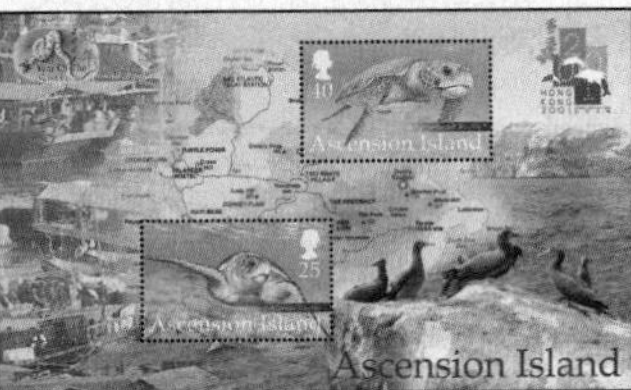

New Year 2001 (Year of the Snake) — A136

Turtles: a, 25p, Green. b, 40p, Loggerhead.

Wmk. 373

2001, Feb. 1 Litho. *Perf. 14½*
768 A136 Sheet of 2, #a-b 5.25 5.25

Hong Kong 2001 Stamp Exhibition.

Sinking of the Roebuck, Tercentenary A137

Designs: 15p, Capt. William Dampier. 35p, Drawing of the Roebuck, horiz. 40p, Cave dwelling at Dampier's Drip, horiz. 50p, Map.

2001, Feb. 25 Litho. *Perf. 14*
769-772 A137 Set of 4 11.00 11.00

Discovery of Ascension Island, 500th Anniv. — A138

Designs: 15p, Alfonso de Albuquerque. 35p, Portuguese caravel. 40p, Cantino map. 50p, Rear admiral Sir George Cockburn.

Perf. 14¾x14¼

2001, Mar. 25 Litho. Wmk. 384
773-776 A138 Set of 4 12.00 12.00

The Age of Victoria A139

Designs: 15p, Great Britain Type A1 with Ascension cancel, vert. 25p, Parade, 1901. 35p, HMS Phoebe. 40p, The Red Lion, 1863. 50p, Queen Victoria, vert. 65p, Sir Joseph Dalton Hooker, botanist, vert.
£1.50, Queen Victoria's Funeral.

Wmk. 373

2001, May 24 Litho. *Perf. 14*
777-782 A139 Set of 6 12.00 12.00

Souvenir Sheet

783 A139 £1.50 multi 10.00 10.00

Souvenir Sheet

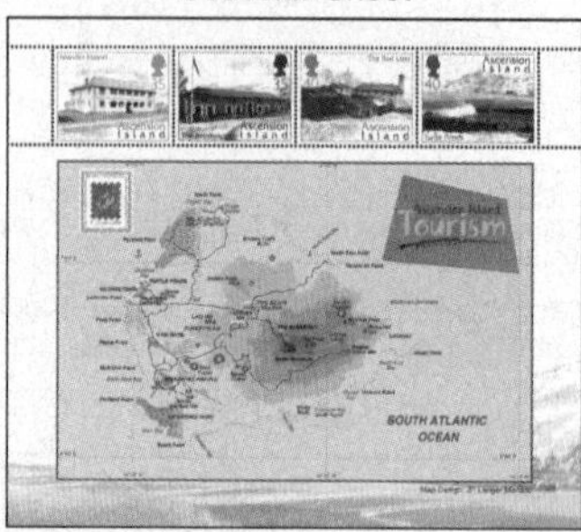

Belgica 2001 Intl. Stamp Exhibition, Brussels — A140

Ascension tourist sites: a, 35p, Islander Hostel. b, 35p, The Residency. c, 40p, The Red Lion. d, 40p, Turtle Ponds.

Wmk. 373

2001, June 9 Litho. *Perf. 14¼*
784 A140 Sheet of 4, #a-d 11.00 11.00

Birdlife International World Bird Festival A141

Ascension frigate bird: 15p, On rock with wings outstretched, vert. 35p, Chick, with mouth open, vert. 40p, Pair in flight. 50p, Close-up of bird.

Perf. 13¾x14¼, 14¼x13¾

2001, Oct. 1 Litho. Wmk. 373
785-788 A141 Set of 4 8.50 8.50

Souvenir Sheet

789 Sheet, #785-788, 789a, perf. 14¼ 9.00 9.00
a. A141 10p Two birds on rock 1.25 1.25

Reign Of Queen Elizabeth II, 50th Anniv. Issue

Common Design Type

Designs: Nos. 790, 794a, 15p, Princess Elizabeth with dog. Nos. 791, 794b, 35p, In 1978. Nos. 792, 794c, 40p, In 1946. Nos. 793, 794d, 50p, In 1998. No. 794e, 60p, 1955 portrait by Annigoni (38x50mm).

Perf. 14¼x14½, 13¾ (#794e)

2002, Feb. 6 Litho. Wmk. 373

With Gold Frames

790 CD360 15p multicolored 1.25 1.25
791 CD360 35p multicolored 1.75 1.75
792 CD360 40p multicolored 2.00 2.00
793 CD360 50p multicolored 2.25 2.25
Nos. 790-793 (4) 7.25 7.25

Souvenir Sheet

Without Gold Frames

794 CD360 Sheet of 5, #a-e 10.00 10.00

Falkland Islands War, 20th Anniv. A142

Designs: 15p, Troops landing at English Bay. 35p, Weapons testing at Ascension. 40p, HMS Hermes and helicopter. 50p, Vulcan bomber at Wideawake Airfield.

Wmk. 373

2002, June 14 Litho. *Perf. 14*
795-798 A142 Set of 4 6.50 6.50

Queen Mother Elizabeth (1900-2002)

Common Design Type

Designs: 35p, Wearing flowered bonnet (sepia photograph). 40p, Wearing pink hat.
No. 801: a, 50p, Wearing hat (sepia photograph). b, £1, Wearing blue hat.

Wmk. 373

2002, Aug. 5 Litho. *Perf. 14¼*

With Purple Frames

799 CD361 35p multicolored 1.25 1.25
800 CD361 40p multicolored 2.00 2.00

Souvenir Sheet

Without Purple Frames

Perf. 14½x14¼

801 CD361 Sheet of 2, #a-b 6.50 6.50

Flowers and Local Scenes A143

Designs: 10p, Vinca, Travellers palm. 15p, Mexican poppy, Broken Tooth. 20p, Ascension lily, St. Mary's Church. 25p, Goatweed, Boatswain Bird Island. 30p, Mauritius hemp, Cannon. 35p, Frangipani, Guest House. 40p, Ascension spurge, Wideawake tern. 50p, Lovechaste, Pier head. 65p, Yellowboy, Sisters Peak. 90p, Persian lilac, Two Boats School. £2, Wild currant, Green turtle. £5, Coral tree, Wideawake Airfield.

Wmk. 373

2002, Aug. 28 Litho. *Perf. 14*
802 A143 10p multi .35 .45
803 A143 15p multi .60 .70
804 A143 20p multi .80 .95
805 A143 25p multi 1.00 1.10
806 A143 30p multi 1.25 1.25
807 A143 35p multi 1.50 1.80
808 A143 40p multi 1.60 1.90
809 A143 50p multi 2.00 2.40
810 A143 65p multi 2.75 3.25
811 A143 90p multi 3.50 4.00
812 A143 £2 multi 7.00 8.00
813 A143 £5 multi 17.50 20.00
Nos. 802-813 (12) 39.85 45.80

Christmas — A144

Paintings: 15p, Ecce Ancilla Dominii, by Dante Gabriel Rossetti. 25p, The Holy Family and a Shepherd, by Titian, horiz. 35p, Christ Carrying the Cross, by Ambrogio Bergognone. 75p, Sketch for "The Ascension," by Benjamin West.

Perf. 14x14¼, 14¼x14

2002, Oct. 9 Litho. Wmk. 373
814-817 A144 Set of 4 7.00 7.00

Ariane Downrange Tracking Station — A145

Designs: 35p, Ariane 4 on launchpad, vert. 40p, Map of downrange tracking stations. 65p, Automated Transfer vehicle in space. 90p, Ariane 5 launch, vert.

2003, Jan. 13 Litho. *Perf. 14½*
818-821 A145 Set of 4 10.00 10.00
821a Souvenir sheet, #818-821 10.00 10.00

Head of Queen Elizabeth II

Common Design Type

Wmk. 373

2003, June 2 Litho. *Perf. 13¾*
822 CD362 £3 multi 13.50 13.50
Nos. 822 (1) 13.50 13.50

Coronation of Queen Elizabeth II, 50th Anniv.

Common Design Type

Designs: Nos. 823, 825a, 40p, Queen in carriage. Nos. 824, 825b, £1, Queen with crown at coronation.

Perf. 14¼x14½

2003, June 2 Litho. Wmk. 373

Vignettes Framed, Red Background

823 CD363 40p multicolored 1.75 1.75
824 CD363 £1 multicolored 5.00 5.00

Souvenir Sheet

Vignettes Without Frame, Purple Panel

825 CD363 Sheet of 2, #a-b 6.75 6.75

Prince William, 21st Birthday

Common Design Type

No. 826: a, Color photograph at right. b, Color photograph at left.

Wmk. 373

2003, June 21 Litho. *Perf. 14¼*
826 Horiz. pair 7.50 7.50
a.-b. CD364 75p Either single 3.00 3.00

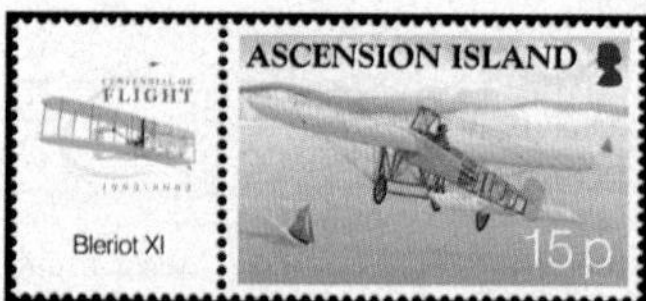

Powered Flight, Cent. — A146

Designs: 15p, Bleriot XI. 20p, Vickers VC-10. 35p, BAe Harrier FRS Mk 1. 40p, Westland Sea King HAS Mk 4. 50p, Rockwell Space Shuttle. 90p, General Dynamics F-16.
£1.50, Fairey Swordfish Mk II.

Wmk. 373

2003, Aug. 12 Litho. *Perf. 14*

Stamp + Label

827-832 A146 Set of 6 12.00 12.00

Souvenir Sheet

833 A146 £1.50 multi 8.50 8.50

Democracy, 1st Anniv., and Christmas — A147

Dove and: 15p, Casting ballot. 25p, Island council session. 40p, Higher education. £1, Government headquarters.

Wmk. 373

2003, Nov. 1 Litho. *Perf. 14*
834-837 A147 Set of 4 8.25 8.25

Birdlife International A148

Masked booby: 15p, Adult and chick. 35p, Two adults, vert. 40p, Adult in flight, vert. 50p, Adult with neck and wings extended. 90p, Adult.

Perf. 14¼x13¾, 13¾x14¼

2004, Feb. 6 Litho. Wmk. 373
838-842 A148 Set of 5 11.00 11.00
842a Souvenir sheet, #838-842, perf. 14¼ 11.00 11.00

Royal Horticultural Society, Bicent. — A149

Flora: 15p, Bougainvillea glabra (red flowers). 35p, Bougainvillea glabra (red violet flowers). 40p, Bougainvillea glabra (white flowers). 90p, Bougainvillea spectabilis.
£1.50, Pteris adscensionis.

Wmk. 373

2004, May 25 Litho. *Perf. 14*
843-846 A149 Set of 4 8.50 8.50

Souvenir Sheet

847 A149 £1.50 multi 7.25 7.25

Fish A150

Designs: 15p, Blue marlin underwater. 35p, Swordfish. 40p, Sailfish. 90p, White marlin.
£1.50, Blue marlin breaching surface.

Wmk. 373

2004, July 26 Litho. *Perf. 13¾*
848-851 A150 Set of 4 8.50 8.50

Souvenir Sheet

852 A150 £1.50 multi 7.25 7.25

The Moon — A151

Designs: 15p, Lunar eclipse from Hummock Point. 25p, Lunar eclipse from Sister's Peak. 35p, Lunar eclipse from Daly's Craggs. £1.25, Moon and birds from Mars Bay.

Wmk. 373

2004, Oct. 28 Litho. *Perf. 13½*
853-856 A151 Set of 4 9.50 9.50
856a Souvenir sheet of 1 6.25 6.25

Merchant Ships A152

Designs: 15p, MV Ascension. 35p, RMS St. Helena. 40p, RMS Caronia. £1.25, MV Maersk Gannet.

2004, Nov. 26 *Perf. 13¼*
857-860 A152 Set of 4 9.75 9.75

Battle of Trafalgar, Bicent. — A153

Designs: 15p, British carronade on sliding carriage. 25p, Royal Marine drummer boy, 1805, vert. 35p, HMS Britannia, vert. 40p, Horatio Nelson, by Jean Frances Rigaud. 50p, HMS Neptune and Santissima Trinidad. 90p, HMS Victory.

No. 867, vert.: a, Horatio Nelson, by Lemuel Francis Abbott. b, HMS Ajax.

Wmk. 373, Unwmkd. (#866)

2005, Apr. 29 Litho. *Perf. 13½*

861-866 A153 Set of 6 10.50 10.50

Souvenir Sheet

867 A153 £1 Sheet of 2, #a-b 9.00 9.00

No. 866 has particles of wood from the HMS Victory embedded in the areas covered by a thermographic process that produces a shiny, raised effect.

Birdlife International A154

Birds: 15p, Fairy tern. 35p, White-tailed tropicbird. 40p, Brown booby. 50p, Brown noddy. £1.25, Red-billed tropicbird.

Wmk. 373

2005, May 27 Litho. *Perf. 13¾*

868-872 A154 Set of 5 11.00 11.00

872a Souvenir sheet, #868-872 11.50 11.50

Tuna Fish A155

Designs: 35p, Three yellowfin tunas. 40p, Skipjack tunas. 50p, Albacore tunas. £1.25, Bigeye tunas.
£1.50, Yellowfin tuna jumping.

Wmk. 373

2005, July 22 Litho. *Perf. 13¾*

873-876 A155 Set of 4 10.00 10.00

Souvenir Sheet

877 A155 £1.50 multi 6.75 6.75

Pope John Paul II (1920-2005) A156

Wmk. 373

2005, Aug. 18 Litho. *Perf. 14*

878 A156 40p multi 2.25 2.25

Battle of Trafalgar, Bicent. — A157

Designs: 40p, HMS Victory. 65p, Ships in battle, horiz. 90p, Admiral Horatio Nelson.

Perf. 13¼

2005, Oct. 21 Litho. Unwmk.

879-881 A157 Set of 3 9.00 9.00

Christmas — A158

Stories by Hans Christian Andersen (1805-75): 15p, The Little Fir Tree. 25p, The Mailcoach Passengers. 35p, The Little Match Girl. £1.25, The Snow Man.

2005, Oct. 3 Wmk. 373 *Perf. 14*

882-885 A158 Set of 4 9.50 9.50

Fish A159

Designs: 20p, Black jack. 35p, Almaco jack. 50p, Horse-eye jack. £1, Rainbow runner. £1.50, Longfin crevalle jack.

Wmk. 373

2006, Jan. 24 Litho. *Perf. 13¾*

886-889 A159 Set of 4 9.50 9.50

Souvenir Sheet

890 A159 £1.50 multi 6.50 6.50

Queen Elizabeth II, 80th Birthday A160

"80" and Queen: 20p, As child. 40p, Wearing tiara. 50p, Wearing tiara, diff. £1.30, Wearing hat.

No. 895: a, Wearing tiara, diff. b, Without head covering.

Wmk. 373

2006, Apr. 21 Litho. *Perf. 14¼*

891-894 A160 Set of 4 11.00 11.00

Souvenir Sheet

895 A160 £1 Sheet of 2, #a-b 9.50 9.50

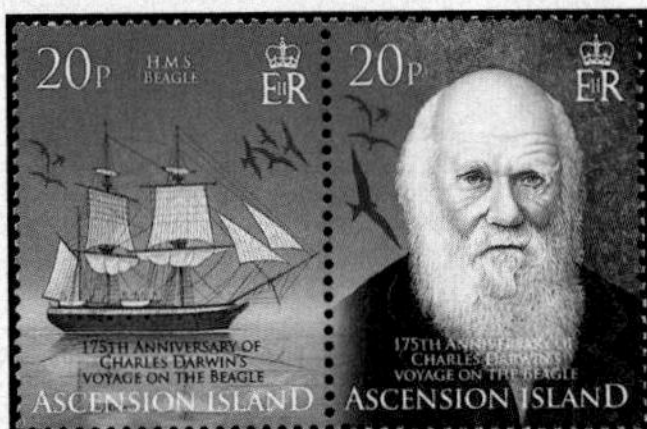

Anniversaries — A161

No. 896, 20p: a, HMS Beagle. b, Charles Darwin.

No. 897, 35p: a, SS Great Britain. b, Isambard Kingdom Brunel.

No. 898, 40p: a, Niña. b, Christopher Columbus.

No. 899, 50p: a, Map with lines of magnetic variation of the compass. b, Edmond Halley.

Perf. 13x13¼

2006, July 24 Litho. Wmk. 373

Horiz. Pairs, #a-b

896-899 A161 Set of 4 14.00 14.00

Darwin's voyage on the Beagle, 175th anniv., birth of Brunel, 200th anniv., death of Columbus, 500th anniv., birth of Halley, 350th anniv.

Greetings A162

Designs: 15p, Long Beach (Greetings from Ascension). 25p, Sunset over lava flow (Merry Christmas). 35p, Dewpond (Seasons Greetings). £1.25, Boatswain Bird Island (Happy New Year).

Wmk. 373

2006, Oct. 30 Litho. *Perf. 14¼*

900-903 A162 Set of 4 10.00 10.00

Worldwide Fund for Nature (WWF) A163

Resplendent angelfish: 35p, Three fish. 40p, Seven fish. 50p, Three fish, diff. £1.25, Four fish.

Perf. 13¾

2007, Mar. 23 Litho. Unwmk.

904-907 A163 Set of 4 8.00 8.00

907a Sheet, 4 each #904-907 32.50 32.50

Falkland Islands War, 25th Anniv. A164

Designs: Nos. 908, 913a, 35p, Handley Page Victor K Mk 2 tanker plane. Nos. 909, 912b, 40p, HMS Dumbarton Castle and Chinook helicopter. Nos. 910, 912c, 50p, HMS Fearless, landing craft and helicopters. Nos. 911, 913d, £1.25, Vulcan XM607 leaving Wideawake Airfield.

No. 912: a, 35p, RFA Tidespring refueling HMS Antrim. d, £1.25, Atlantic Conveyor and Harrier jet.

No. 913: b, 40p, Vickers VC 10 transport plane. c, 50p, Nimrod MR2 maritime reconnaisance plane.

2007, May 25 *Perf. 13¼x13*

Stamps With White Frames

908-911 A164 Set of 4 12.00 12.00

Stamps Without White Frames

912 A164 Sheet of 4, #a-d 12.00 12.00

913 A164 Sheet of 4, #a-d 12.00 12.00

Scouting, Cent. A165

Lord Robert Baden-Powell blowing kudu horn and: 35p, Fleur-de-lis of scouts. 40p, Scouts rescuing turtle. 50p, Scouts on gun of HMS Hood. £1.25, Scouts on Land Rover.

2007, July 9 *Perf. 14*

914-917 A165 Set of 4 12.00 12.00

Mother Teresa (1910-97) and Princess Diana (1961-97) — A166

2007, Aug. 31

918 A166 50p multi 2.50 2.50

Wedding of Queen Elizabeth II and Prince Philip, 60th Anniv. — A167

No. 919: a, 35p, Couple in 1947. b, 90p, Wedding program. c, £1.25, Couple in 2006.

2007, Nov. 20 Litho. *Perf. 14¼*

919 A167 Horiz. strip of 3, #a-c 14.00 14.00

British Ornithological Union Expedition, 50th Anniv. — A168

No. 920, 15p: a, British Ornithological Union base. b, Drawing of extinct rail.

No. 921, 25p: a, Scientist recording sounds of Wideawake tern. b, Wideawake terns.

No. 922, 40p: a, Boatswainbird Island outpost. b, Masked booby.

No. 923, 50p: a, Scientist pushing dinghy in surf. b, Red-footed booby.

2007, Dec. 10 *Perf. 14¼*

Horiz. Pairs, #a-b

920-923 A168 Set of 4 14.00 14.00

Oviparous Creatures — A169

Creature and eggs: 15p, Long-tailed blue butterfly. 20p, Ladybird beetle. 25p, Spiny lobster. 30p, Desert locust. 35p, Green turtle. 40p, Land crab. 50p, Red-footed booby. 65p, Coconut palm gecko. 90p, Common waxbill. £1, Yellowtail damselfish. £2.50, Madeiran storm petrel. £5, Red-necked francolin.

2008, Feb. 5 Litho. *Perf. 14¼*

924	A169	15p multi	.60	.60
925	A169	20p multi	.80	.80
926	A169	25p multi	1.00	1.00
927	A169	30p multi	1.25	1.25
928	A169	35p multi	1.40	1.40
929	A169	40p multi	1.60	1.60
930	A169	50p multi	2.00	2.00
931	A169	65p multi	2.60	2.60
932	A169	90p multi	3.75	3.75
933	A169	£1 multi	4.00	4.00
934	A169	£2.50 multi	10.00	10.00
935	A169	£5 multi	20.00	20.00
		Nos. 924-935 (12)	49.00	49.00

Sharks A170

Designs: 35p, Bluntnose sixgill shark. 40p, Scalloped hammerhead shark. 50p, Shortfin mako shark. £1.25, Whale shark.
£1.50, Bigeye thresher shark.

2008, Mar. 14 Litho. *Perf. 14*

936-939 A170 Set of 4 12.50 12.50

939a Sheet of 16, 4 each #936-939 40.00 40.00

Souvenir Sheet

940 A170 £1.50 multi 7.50 7.50

National Aeronautical and Space Administration, 50th Anniv. — A171

Designs: No. 941, 35p, Bell X-1E airplane. No. 942, 35p, Apollo 11 Moon walk. 40p, Apollo 17 Lunar Rover. 50p, Space Shuttle Columbia. 65p, Hubble Space Telescope. 90p, International Space Station.

2008, May 23 Litho. *Perf. 14*
941-946 A171 Set of 6 12.50 12.50

Royal Air Force, 90th Anniv. A172

Airplanes: 15p, Sopwith 7F.1 Snipe. 35p, Vickers Wellington Mk 1C. 40p, Supermarine Spitfire Mk IX. 50p, Gloster Meteor F. IV. 65p, BAe Hawk. 90p, Typhoon F-2 Eurofighter.

Unwmk.

2008, June 20 Litho. *Perf. 14*
947-952 A172 Set of 6 14.50 14.50

Botanists and Flowers — A173

Designs: 35p, Valerius Cordus (1515-44), and Cordia sebestena. 40p, Nehemiah Grew (1641-1712), and Grewia occidentalis. 50p, Charles Plumier (1646-1704), and Plumeria rubra. £2, Carl Peter Thunberg (1743-1828), and Thunbergia grandiflora.

2008, Aug. 28 Litho. *Perf. 14*
953-956 A173 Set of 4 14.50 14.50

Christmas — A174

Santa Claus: 15p, Holding microphone. 25p, With reindeer in surf. 50p, On inflatable lounger in water. £2, Piloting flying sleigh.

2008, Nov. 22
957-960 A174 Set of 4 14.00 14.00

Longest-Reigning British Monarchs — A175

Designs: 35p, King Henry III and Tower of London. 40p, King James I and Stirling Castle. 50p, King George III and Windsor Castle. 65p, Queen Victoria and Osborne House. £1.25, Queen Elizabeth II and Buckingham Palace.

2008, Dec. 15
961-965 A175 Set of 5 12.00 12.00

Marine Mammals — A176

Designs: 35p, Bottlenose dolphins. 40p, Pantropical spotted dolphins. 50p, Sperm whale. £1.25, Gervais' beaked whales. £2, Humpback whale.

2009, Mar. 23 *Perf. 14x14¾*
966-969 A176 Set of 4 7.50 7.50
969a Sheet, 4 each #966-969 30.00 30.00

Souvenir Sheet

970 A176 £2 multi 6.00 6.00

Naval Aviation, Cent. — A177

No. 971, 35p: a, Flight Sub-lieutenant Rex Warneford and Victoria Cross. b, Moraine-Saulnier L destroys Zeppelin LZ-37.

No. 972, 35p: a, Squadron Commander Richard Bell Davies and Victoria Cross. b, Nieuport 10 taking off.

No. 973, 40p: a, Lieutenant Commander Eugene Esmonde and Victoria Cross. b, Fairey Swordfish attacking German warships.

No. 974, 50p: a, Lieutenant Robert Hampton Gray and Victoria Cross. b, Corsair bombing Japanese warships.

2009, May 7 *Perf. 14*
Horiz. Pairs, #a-b
971-974 A177 Set of 4 12.00 12.00

Botany A178

Designs: No. 975, 35p, Raspberry. No. 976, 35p, Blue water lily. 40p, Prickly pear. 50p, Ascension lily. 65p, Yellowboy. 90p, Joseph Dalton Hooker (1817-1911), botanist.

2009, Sept. 7 *Perf. 14*
975-980 A178 Set of 6 12.00 12.00

Turtle Research and Conservation — A179

No. 981, 15p: a, Early turtle tracking and head of turtle. b, Dr. Archie Carr (1909-87) and map of Ascension.

No. 982, 35p: a, Turtle laying eggs and head of turtle. b, Turtle hatchlings and map of Ascension.

No. 983, 40p: a, Beach raking and head of turtle. b, Population monitoring and map of Ascension.

No. 984, 65p: a, Turtle rescue and head of turtle. b, Turtle rescue and map of Ascension.

2009, Oct. 1 *Perf. 13¾*
Horiz. Pairs, #a-b
981-984 A179 Set of 4 10.00 10.00

Charles Darwin (1809-82), Naturalist — A180

Darwin and: 35p, Woodpecker finch. 40p, Marine iguanas. 50p, Galapagos tortoise. £2, Galapagos penguins.

2009, Nov. 9 Unwmk. *Perf. 14*
985-988 A180 Set of 4 13.00 13.00

White-tailed Tropicbird — A181

Designs: 35p, Bird in rock crevice. 40p, Bird on rock. 50p, Juvenile in flight. £1.25, Adult in flight.

2009, Dec. 4 Litho. *Perf. 14*
989-992 A181 Set of 4 12.00 12.00
992a Sheet, 4 each #989-992 48.00 48.00

Reef Fish — A182

Designs: 35p, Hardback soldier. 40p, Grouper. 50p, Five fingers. £1.25, Rock bullseye. £2, Softback soldier.

2010, Mar. 19 *Perf. 13¾*
993-996 A182 Set of 4 12.00 12.00
996a Sheet, 4 each #993-996 48.00 48.00

Souvenir Sheet

997 A182 £2 multi 8.50 8.50

A183

Girl Guides, Cent. — A184

Designs: 40p, Girl Guides wearing clown noses. 50p, Girl Guides and fish. 90p, Leaders holding cake. £1.25, Girl Guide climbing rock.

No. 1002: a, Olave Baden-Powell (1889-1977). b, Agnes Baden-Powell (1858-1945). c, Lord Robert Baden-Powell (1857-1941).

2010, Apr. 10 *Perf. 14*
998-1001 A183 Set of 4 12.00 12.00

Souvenir Sheet

1002 A184 £1 Sheet of 3, #a-c 12.00 12.00

Miniature Sheet

Battle of Britain, 70th Anniv. — A185

No. 1003: a, Supermarine Spitfire R6803. b, Hawker Hurricane V7383. c, Supermarine Spitfire X4036. d, Hawker Hurricane R4175. e, Supermarine Spitfire R6885. f, Hawker Hurricane V6684. g, Supermarine Spitfire K9998. h, Hawker Hurricane R4118.

2010, May 7 *Perf. 14*
1003 A185 50p Sheet of 8 #a-h 15.00 15.00

London 2010 Festival of Stamps.

Yellow Canary — A186

Designs: 15p, Juvenile. 35p, Adult male on branch. 60p, Adult female. 90p, Adult male on ground.

2010, Oct. 11 *Perf. 13¾*
1004-1007 A186 Set of 4 8.50 8.50
1007a Miniature sheet of 16, 4 each #1004-1007 35.00 35.00

Christmas — A187

Designs: 15p, Christmas lunch. 40p, Christmas parade. 50p, Christingle. £1.25, Nativity play.

2010, Nov. 17 *Perf. 14*
1008-1011 A187 Set of 4 9.00 9.00

Rediscovery of the Parsley Fern — A188

Ascension National Park emblem and: 15p, HMS Erebus and HMS Terror approaching Ascension, 1843. 15p, Parsley fern. 35p, Parsley fern in situ. 40p, Parsley fern seedlings in pots. £1, Parsley fern cultivation at Kew Gardens.

2011, Feb. 16 *Perf. 13¾*
1012-1016 A188 Set of 5 9.00 9.00

Service of Queen Elizabeth II and Prince Philip — A189

Designs: 15p, Queen Elizabeth II. 25p, Queen and Prince Philip. 35p, Queen and Prince Philip, diff. 40p, Queen and Prince Philip, diff. 60p, Queen and Prince Philip, diff. £1.25, Prince Philip.
£2, Queen and Prince Philip, diff.

2011, Mar. 23 *Perf. 13¼*
1017-1022 A189 Set of 6 10.00 10.00
1022a Sheet of 6, #1017-1022, + 3 labels 10.00 10.00

Souvenir Sheet

1023 A189 £2 multi 6.75 6.75

Royal Air Force Search and Rescue, 70th Anniv. — A190

Emblem and Sea King helicopter: 35p, On airplane's cargo ramp. 40p, Flying near Ascension. 90p, Approaching HMS Dumbarton Castle. £1, Approaching HMS Spartan submarine.
£2.50, Sea King helicopter in flight.

2011, May 19
1024-1027 A190 Set of 4 8.75 8.75

Souvenir Sheet

1028 A190 £2.50 multi 8.25 8.25

Miniature Sheet

Peonies — A191

No. 1029 — Peony color: a, Red. b, Gray lilac. c, Light orange. d, White.

2011, June 22 *Perf. 13¾*
1029 A191 50p Sheet of 4, #a-d 6.50 6.50

Wedding of Prince William and Catherine Middleton — A192

Couple, with Middleton: 35p, Wearing hat. 90p, Without hat. £1.25, Seated in coach in wedding dress.
£2, Couple standing on wedding day, vert.

2011, July 20 *Perf. 14*
1030-1032 A192 Set of 3 8.25 8.25

Souvenir Sheet

Perf. 14¾x14

1033 A192 £2 multi 6.50 6.50

No. 1033 contains one 29x45mm stamp.

Worldwide Fund for Nature (WWF) — A193

Phaethon aethereus: Nos. 1034, 1038a, 35p, Bird in rock crevice. Nos. 1035, 1038b, 40p, Two birds in flight. Nos. 1036, 1038c, 50p, Adult and juvenile in rock crevice. Nos. 1037, 1038d, £1.25, Bird in flight.

2011, Aug. 31

Stamps With White Frames

1034-1037 A193 Set of 4 8.00 8.00

Stamps Without White Frames

1038 A193 Strip of 4, #a-d 8.00 8.00

Nos. 1038a-1038d were printed in sheets of 16 stamps containing four strips.

Christmas A194

Pantomimes: 15p, Mother Goose. 40p, Jack and the Beanstalk. 50p, Aladdin. £1.25, Cinderella.

2011, Nov. 16 *Perf. 14*
1039-1042 A194 Set of 4 7.25 7.25

Reign of Queen Elizabeth II, 60th Anniv. — A195

Photographs of Queen Elizabeth II taken in: 15p, 2011. 25p, 1998. 35p, 1988. 40p, 1975. 60p, 1961. £1.25, 1953.
£2, 1977.

2012, Feb. 6 *Perf. 13¼*
1043-1048 A195 Set of 6 9.50 9.50
1048a Sheet of 6, #1043-1048, + 3 labels 9.50 9.50

Souvenir Sheet

1049 A195 £2 multi 6.50 6.50

Reef Fish A196

Designs: 35p, Trumpetfish. 40p, Peacock flounder. 90p, Queen triggerfish. £1, Scrawled filefish.
£2, Yellow goatfish.

2012, Apr. 15 **Litho.** *Perf. 13¾*
1050-1053 A196 Set of 4 8.75 8.75
1053a Sheet, 4 each #1050-1053 35.00 35.00

Souvenir Sheet

1054 A196 £2 multi 6.50 6.50

Sinking of the Titanic, Cent. A197

Designs: 20p, The departure. 45p, The boat deck. 50p, The iceberg. £1, The sinking.
£2, Abandoning ship.

2012, Aug. 1 *Perf. 14*
1055-1058 A197 Set of 4 6.75 6.75

Souvenir Sheet

1059 A197 £2 multi 6.25 6.25

Shackleton-Rowett Antarctic Expedition, 90th Anniv. — A198

No. 1060, 45p: a, Sir Ernest Shackleton (36x36mm). b, John Quiller Rowett (18x36mm). c, Frank Wild (36x36mm).
No. 1061, 50p: a, Quest leaving London (36x36mm). b, Quest at Ascension (18x36mm). c, Quest in ice (36x36mm).

2012, Sept. 17 *Perf. 13¼*

Horiz. Strips of 3, #a-c

1060-1061 A198 Set of 2 9.25 9.25

Christmas A199

Scenes from *A Christmas Carol,* by Charles Dickens: 25c, Ebenezer Scrooge passing Christmas carolers. 40p, Ghost visiting Scrooge. 50p, Scrooge carrying Tiny Tim, vert. £1.25, Scrooge watching boy deliver turkey, vert.

2012, Nov. 15 *Perf. 13¼x13½*
1062-1065 A199 Set of 4 7.75 7.75

Miniature Sheet

Wideawake Airfield, 70th Anniv. — A200

No. 1066: a, 45p, Wideawake tern. b, 50p, Douglas DC-3 Dakota. c, £1, Eurofighter Typhoon. d, £1.45, Masked booby.

2012, Dec. 5 *Perf. 13¼*
1066 A200 Sheet of 4, #a-d 11.00 11.00

Aircraft A201

Designs: 15p, Fairey Swordfish. 20p, North American B-25 Mitchell. 25p, Lockheed C-130K Hercules. 30p, Hawker Siddeley Nimrod MR2. 40p, BAE Sea Harrier FRS1. 45p, Lockheed C-5 Galaxy. 50p, Douglas DC-3 Dakota. 65p, Avro Vulcan. 90p, McDonnell Douglas Phantom F-4. £1, Eurofighter Typhoon. £2.50, Lockheed C-121. £5, Shorts Belfast.

2013, Jan. 15 *Perf. 13¾*

1067	A201	15p multi	.50	.50
1068	A201	20p multi	.65	.65
1069	A201	25p multi	.80	.80
1070	A201	30p multi	.95	.95
1071	A201	40p multi	1.25	1.25
1072	A201	45p multi	1.40	1.40
1073	A201	50p multi	1.60	1.60
1074	A201	65p multi	2.10	2.10
1075	A201	90p multi	3.00	3.00
1076	A201	£1 multi	3.25	3.25
1077	A201	£2.50 multi	8.00	8.00
1078	A201	£5 multi	16.00	16.00
	Nos. 1067-1078 (12)		39.50	39.50

Items Commemorating British Coronations — A202

Coronation of Queen Elizabeth II, 60th Anniv. — A203

Various items commemorating the coronation of: 45p, Queen Victoria. 50p, King Edward VII. 70p, King George V. £1.10, King George VI. £1.25, Queen Elizabeth II.

2013, Feb. 6 *Perf. 14*
1079-1083 A202 Set of 5 12.00 12.00

Souvenir Sheet

Perf. 14¾x14¼

1084 A203 £2 multi 6.00 6.00

British Settlement of Ascension, Bicent. (in 2015) — A204

Imprisonment of Napoleon Bonaparte on Ascension: 45p, Joséphine Bonaparte at Malmaison, by François Pascal Simon. 50p, Bonaparte at the Bridge of Arcole, by Antoine-Jean Gros. 60p, Napoleon and his General Staff, by Jean-Léon Gérôme. £1.45, Napoleon as First Consul, detail of painting by Jean-Baptiste Isabey.

2013, May 21 *Perf. 13¾*
1085-1088 A204 Set of 4 9.50 9.50

Lady Margaret Thatcher (1925-2013), British Prime Minister — A205

Photographs of Thatcher: 45p, Giving "Victory" sign, 1976. 50p, In cockpit of Sea Harrier jet, 1982. 60p, Holding teacup during visit to Ascension, 1992. £1.45, At Order of the Garter ceremony, 1995.

2013, June 14

1089-1092 A205	Set of 4	9.50	9.50

Ascension Frigatebirds — A206

Designs: 20p, Male and female. 45p, Male on egg. 50p, Chick. 60p, Female and chick. £1.10, Juvenile. £1.45, Male in flight.

2013, Aug. 16 ***Perf. 13¼x13½***

1093-1098 A206	Set of 6	14.00	14.00

Shallow Marine Surveys Group A207

Marine life: Nos. 1099, 1103a, 45p, Fire worm. Nos. 1100, 1103b, 50p, Black bar soldier fish. Nos. 1101, 1103c, 60p, Endemic white hawk fish. Nos. 1102, 1103d, £1.45, Atlantic blue tang.

No. 1104a, £1, Anemone, vert.

2013, Aug. 29 ***Perf. 13¼x13½***

Stamps With White Frames

1099-1102 A207	Set of 4	9.75	9.75

Stamps Without White Frames

1103 A230	Strip of 4, #a-d	9.75	9.75

Souvenir Sheet

Perf. 13½x13¼

1104 A207	Sheet of 3 (see footnote)	9.75	9.75
a.	A207 £1 multi	3.25	3.25

No. 1104 contains No. 1104a, Falkland Islands No. 1107a and South Georgia and South Sandwich Islands No. 485a. This sheet was sold in Ascension, Falkland Islands and South Georgia and South Sandwich Islands.

Churches A208

Stained-Glass Windows A209

Designs: 45p, Grotto of Our Lady Catholic Church. 50p, Window depicting Madonna and Child. 60p, St. Mary's Anglican Church. £1, Window depicting St. Michael.

2013, Nov. 18 **Litho.** ***Perf. 13¼***

Stamps With White Frames

1105 A208	45p multi	1.50	1.50
1106 A209	50p multi	1.75	1.75
1107 A208	60p multi	2.00	2.00
1108 A209	£1 multi	3.25	3.25
	Nos. 1105-1108 (4)	8.50	8.50

Stamps Without White Frames

1109	Horiz. strip of 4	8.50	8.50
a.	A208 45p multi	1.50	1.50
b.	A209 50p multi	1.75	1.75
c.	A208 60p multi	2.00	2.00
d.	A209 £1 multi	3.25	3.25

Christmas.

POSTAGE DUE STAMPS

Outline Map of Ascension — D1

1986 **Litho.** ***Perf. 15x14***

J1	D1	1p beige & brown	.25	.25
J2	D1	2p orange & brown	.25	.25
J3	D1	5p org ver & brn	.25	.25
J4	D1	7p violet & black	.25	*.40*
J5	D1	10p ultra & black	.35	*.50*
J6	D1	25p pale green & blk	.75	*1.00*
		Nos. J1-J6 (6)	2.10	*2.65*

AUSTRALIAN STATES

NEW SOUTH WALES

'nü sauth 'wā̦ə̦lz

LOCATION — Southeast coast of Australia in the South Pacific Ocean
GOVT. — British Crown Colony
AREA — 309,432 sq. mi.
POP. — 1,500,000 (estimated, 1900)
CAPITAL — Sydney

In 1901 New South Wales united with five other British colonies to form the Commonwealth of Australia. Stamps of Australia are now used.

12 Pence = 1 Shilling
20 Shillings = 1 Pound

Watermarks

Wmk. 12 — Crown and Single-lined A

Wmk. 13 — Large Crown and Double-lined A

Wmk. 49 — Double-lined Numerals Corresponding with the Value

Wmk. 50 — Single-lined Numeral

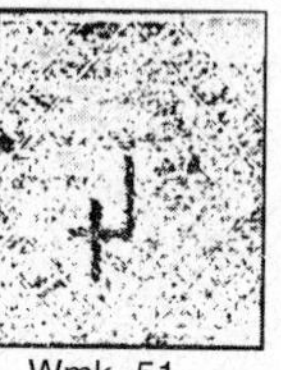

Wmk. 51 — Single-lined Numeral

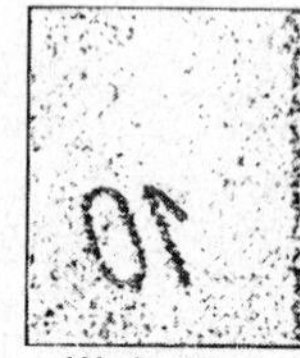

Wmk. 52 — Single-lined Numeral

Wmk. 53 — 5/-

Wmk. 54 — Small Crown and NSW

Wmk. 55 — Large Crown and NSW

Wmk. 56 — NSW

Wmk. 57 — 5/- NSW in Diamond

Wmk. 58 — 20/- NSW in Circle

Wmk. 70 — V and Crown

Wmk. 199 — Crown and A in Circle

Values for unused stamps are for examples with original gum as defined in the catalogue introduction except for Nos. 1-20 which are rarely found with gum and are valued without gum. Very fine examples of Nos. 35-100, F3-F5, J1-J10 and O1-O40 will have perforations touching the framelines or design on one or more sides due to the narrow spacing of the stamps on the plates and imperfect perforation methods. Stamps with perfs clear of the design on all four sides are scarce and will command higher prices.

Seal of the Colony
A1 A2

A1 has no clouds. A2 has clouds added to the design, except in pos. 15.

1850 **Unwmk.** **Engr.** ***Imperf.***

1	A1 1p red, *yelsh wove*	9,500.	725.00
b.	1p red, *bluish wove*	9,500.	725.00
2	A2 1p red, *yelsh wove*	7,000.	600.00
b.	A2 1p carmine red, *yellowish laid*	10,000.	800.00
c.	A3 1p carmine red, *bluish wove*	5,000.	750.00
e.	1p carmine red, *bluish laid*		
f.	Hill unshaded	10,500.	925.00
g.	No clouds	10,500.	925.00
h.	No trees	10,500.	925.00

Printed in panes of 25 (5x5). Twenty-five varieties.

Stamps from early impressions of the plate sell at considerably higher prices.

No. 1 was reproduced by the collotype process in a souvenir sheet distributed at the London International Stamp Exhibition 1950. The paper is white.

Plate I — A3

Plate II — A4

Plate I: Vertically lined background.

Plate I re-touched: Lines above and below "POSTAGE" and "TWO PENCE" deepened. Outlines of circular band around picture also deepened.

Plate II (First re-engraving of Plate I): Horizontally lined background; the bale on the left side is dated and there is a dot in the star in each corner.

Plate II retouched: Dots and dashes added in lower spandrels.

Plate I

Late (worn plate) Impressions

3	A3 2p blue, *yelsh wove*	4,500.	300.00
a.	Early impression	12,500.	550.00

Printed in panes of 24 (12x2). Twenty-four varieties.

Plate I, Retouched

4	A3 2p blue, *yelsh wove*	6,500.	400.00

Twelve varieties.

Plate II

Late (worn plate) Impressions

5	A4 2p blue, *yelsh wove*	4,500.	165.00
b.	2p 2p blue, *grayish wove*	4,250.	165.00
c.	"CREVIT" omitted	—	575.00
d.	Pick and shovel omitted	—	450.00
e.	No whip	*6,500.*	325.00
h.	Early impression	8,500.	375.00
5F	A4 2p blue, *bluish wove*	6,000.	300.00
g.	No whip	—	475.00
i.	"CREVIT" omitted		1,500.

Eleven varieties.

Plate III A5

Plate IV A6

Plate III (Second re-engraving of Plate I): The bale is not dated and, with the exception of Nos. 7, 10 and 12, it is single-lined. There are no dots in the stars.

Plate IV (Third re-engraving of Plate I): The bale is double-lined and there is a circle in the center of each star.

1850-51 Wove Paper

6 A5 2p bl, *grayish wove* 6,000. 300.00
- a. Fan with 6 segments — 650.00
- b. Double-lined bale — 500.00
- c. No whip — 475.00

7 A6 2p blue, *bluish wove* ('51) 5,500. 250.00
- a. 2p blue, *bluish wove* 4,250. 165.00
- b. 2p blue, *grayish wove* 5,750. 275.00
- c. Fan with 6 segments (Pos. 2/8) — 425.00
- d. No clouds (Pos. 2/10) — 425.00

Twenty-four varieties.

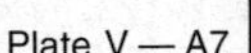

Plate V — A7

A8

Plate V (Fourth re-engraving of Plate I): There is a pearl in the fan-shaped ornament below the central design.

1850-51

8 A7 2p blue, *grayish wove* ('51) 5,500. 300.00
- a. 2p ultra, *yellowish laid* 8,500. 425.00
- b. Fan with 6 segments (Pos. 2/8) — 500.00
- c. Pick and shovel omitted (Pos. 2/5) — 525.00

9 A8 3p green, *bluish wove* 6,250. 325.00
- a. 3p green, *yellowish wove* 7,000. 3575.00
- b. 3p green, *yellowish laid* 12,000. 925.00
- c. 3p green, *bluish laid* 12,000. 925.00
- e. No whip — 600.00

Twenty-four varieties of No. 8, twenty-five of No. 9.

Queen Victoria
A9 A10

TWO PENCE
Plate I — Background of wavy lines.
Plate II — Stars in corners.
Plate III (Plate I re-engraved) — Background of crossed lines.

SIX PENCE
Plate I — Background of fine lines.
Plate II (Plate I re-engraved) — Background of coarse lines.

1851 Yellowish Wove Paper

10 A9 1p carmine 4,000. 400.00
- b. No leaves to right of "SOUTH" *5,500.* 1,000.
- c. Two leaves to right of "SOUTH" *5,500.* 1,100.
- d. "WALE" *5,500.* 1,100.

11 A9 2p ultra, Plate I 1,600. 125.00

1852 Bluish Laid Paper

12 A9 1p orange brown 6,000. 600.00
- b. As "a," no leaves to right of "SOUTH" 1,250.
- c. As "a," two leaves to right of "SOUTH" 1,300.
- d. As "a," "WALE" 1,300.

1852-55

Bluish or Grayish Wove Paper

13 A9 1p red 1,750. 200.00
- a. 1p carmine 1,900. 200.00
- d. As "c," no leaves to right of "SOUTH" 4,000. 400.00
- e. As "c," two leaves to right of "SOUTH" 475.00
- f. As "c," "WALE" 550.00

14 A9 2p blue, Plate I 1,150. 45.00
- a. 2p ultramarine 1,350. 45.00
- b. 2p slate 1,750. 45.00

15 A10 2p blue, Plate II ('53) 2,000. 125.00
- a. "WAEES" *3,000.* 550.00

16 A9 2p blue, Plate III ('55) 925.00 90.00

17 A9 3p green 2,600. 210.00
- a. 3p emerald 3,750. 300.00
- b. As "a," "WACES" 900.00

18 A9 6p brown, Plate I 3,200. 450.00
- a. "WALLS" *4,500.* 1,500.
- b. 6p black brown 4,500. 1,250.

19 A9 6p brown, Plate II 3,600. 425.00
- a. 6p bister brown 3,500. 425.00

20 A9 8p yellow ('53) 10,000. 1,100.
- a. 8p orange 9,500. 1,100.
- b. No leaves to right of "SOUTH" — 2,250.

The plates of the 1, 2, 3 and 8p each contained 50 varieties and those of the 6p 25 varieties.

The 2p, plate II, 6p, plate II, and 8p have been reprinted on grayish blue wove paper. The reprints of the 2p have the spandrels and background much worn. Most of the reprints of the 6p have no floreate ornaments to the right and left of "South." On all the values the wreath has been retouched.

Type of 1851 and

A11 A12

A13 A14

1854-55 Wmk. 49 *Imperf.*

23 A9 1p orange 450.00 57.50
- a. No leaves to right of "SOUTH" 975.00 225.00
- b. Two leaves to right of "SOUTH" 1,125. 240.00
- c. "WALE" 1,150. 240.00

24 A9 2p blue 400.00 27.50
- a. 2p ultramarine 400.00 27.50

25 A9 3p green 525.00 57.50
- a. "WACES" *1,400.* 225.00
- b. Watermarked "2" 6,000. 2,250.

Value for No. 25b is for copy with the design cut into.

26 A11 5p green 1,600. 800.00
27 A12 6p sage green 1,600. 125.00
28 A12 6p brown 900.00 42.50
- a. Watermarked "8" 4,600. 175.00

29 A12 6p gray 1,250. 125.00
- f. As "e," watermarked "8" *4,500.* 175.00

30 A13 8p orange ('55) *15,500.* 1,900.
- a. 8p yellow *16,750.* 1,600.

31 A14 1sh pale red brown 2,250. 140.00
- a. 1sh red 2,200. 110.00
- c. As "b," watermarked "8" *6,500.* 250.00

See Nos. 38-42, 56, 58, 65, 67.

Nos. 38-42 exist with wide margins. Stamps with perforations trimmed are often offered as Nos. 26, 30, and 30a.

A15

1856 *Imperf.*

32 A15 1p red 400.00 57.50
- a. 1p orange red 400.00 57.50
- b. As "a," printed on both sides *4,200.* *2,500.*
- c. Watermarked "2" *8,000.*

33 A15 2p blue 325.00 27.50
- a. Watermarked "1" *8,750.*
- b. Watermarked "5" 1,000. 110.00
- c. Watermarked "8" *8,250.*

34 A15 3p green 1,350. 125.00
- a. 3p yellow green 1,350. 125.00
- b. Watermarked "2" *5,000.*

Nos. 32-34 (3) 2,075. 210.00

The two known examples of No. 33c are in museums. Both are used.

The 1p has been reprinted in orange on paper watermarked Small Crown and NSW, and the 2p in deep blue on paper watermarked single lined "2." These reprints are usually overprinted "SPECIMEN."

See Nos. 34C-37, 54, 63, 90.

1859 Litho.

34C A15 2p light blue — 1,250.

1860-63 Engr. Wmk. 49 *Perf. 13*

35 A15 1p red 175.00 20.00
- a. 1p orange 225.00 42.50
- b. Perf. 12x13 *2,100.*
- c. Perf. 12 325.00 42.50

36 A15 2p blue, perf. 12 325.00 29.00
- a. Watermarked "1" *4,500.*
- c. Perf. 12x13 *3,400.* 250.00

37 A15 3p blue green 100.00 29.00
- a. 3p yellow green 140.00 25.00
- b. 3p deep green 140.00 24.00
- c. Watermarked "6" 225.00 32.50
- d. Perf. 12 1,300. 92.50

38 A11 5p dark green 110.00 29.00
- a. 5p yellow green 200.00 87.50
- b. Perf. 12 400.00 175.00

39 A12 6p brown, perf. 12 750.00 97.50
- a. 6p gray, perf. 12 750.00 110.00

40 A12 6p violet 325.00 14.00
- a. 6p aniline lilac 1,600. 170.00
- b. Watermarked "5" 850.00 65.00
- c. Watermarked "12" 850.00 32.50
- e. Perf. 12 775.00 32.50

41 A13 8p yellow 450.00 92.50
- a. 8p orange 500.00 92.50
- b. As "a," perf. 12 6,000. 1,450.
- c. 8p red orange 500.00 92.50
- d. As "c," perf 12 6,000. 1,450.

42 A14 1sh rose 325.00 20.00
- a. 1sh carmine 275.00 22.50
- b. As "a," perf. 12 1,350. 100.00

Nos. 35-42 (8) 2,560. 331.00

1864 Wmk. 50 *Perf. 13*

43 A15 1p red 100.00 40.00

A16

1861-80 Wmk. 53 *Perf. 13*

44 A16 5sh dull violet 350.00 77.50
- a. 5sh purple 450.00 105.00
- b. 5sh dull violet, perf. 12 2,100. 400.00
- c. 5sh purple, perf. 12 — 110.00
- d. 5sh purple, perf. 10 325.00 110.00
- e. 5sh purple, perf. 12x10 475.00 110.00

See No. 101. For overprint see No. O11.

Reprints are perf. 10 and overprinted "REPRINT" in black.

A17 A18

1862-65 Typo. Unwmk. *Perf. 13*

45 A17 1p red ('65) 200.00 60.00
- a. Perf. 14 200.00 90.00

46 A18 2p blue 160.00 29.00
- a. Perf. 14 175.00 105.00

1863-64 Wmk. 50 *Perf. 13*

47 A17 1p red 57.50 20.00
- a. Watermarked "2" 225.00 35.00
- e. Horiz. pair, imperf between 1,500.

48 A18 2p blue 35.00 6.00
- a. Watermarked "1" 375.00 13.00

1862 Wmk. 49 *Perf. 13*

49 A18 2p blue 140.00 20.00
- a. Watermarked "5" 200.00 25.00
- b. Perf. 12x13 *975.00* 500.00
- c. Perf. 12 400.00 85.00

See Nos. 52-53, 61-62, 70-71.

A19 A20

1867, Sept. Wmk. 51, 52 *Perf. 13*

50 A19 4p red brown 105.00 10.50
- a. Imperf.

51 A20 10p lilac 32.50 10.50
- b. Horiz. pair, imperf between *2,500.*

See Nos. 55, 64, 91, 97, 117, 129.

A21 A22

A23

Typo.; Engr. (3p, 5p, 8p)

1871-84 Wmk. 54 *Perf. 13*

52 A17 1p red 22.50 2.50
- a. Perf. 10 375.00 57.50
- b. Perf. 13x10 35.00 1.90
- c. Horiz. pair, imperf between *2,250.*

53 A18 2p blue 30.00 2.25
- a. Imperf.
- b. Horiz. pair, imperf vert. *2,500.*
- c. Perf. 10 525.00 42.50
- d. Perf. 13x10 30.00 1.75
- e. Perf. 12x13
- f. Perf. 11x12 450.00 72.50

54 A15 3p green ('74) 60.00 9.50
- a. Perf. 11 250.00 140.00
- b. Perf. 12 — 400.00
- c. Perf. 10x12 250.00 57.50
- d. Perf. 11x12 200.00 45.00
- e. Perf. 10 175.00 17.50
- f. Perf. 13x10 200.00 25.00

55 A19 4p red brown ('77) 125.00 20.00
- a. Perf. 10 275.00 105.00
- b. Perf. 13x10 175.00 12.00

56 A11 5p dk grn, perf. 10 ('84) 35.00 29.00
- a. Horiz. pair, imperf between 2,250.
- b. Perf. 12 375.00 200.00
- c. Perf. 10x12 250.00 92.50
- d. Perf. 10x13

57 A21 6p lilac ('72) 105.00 3.50
- a. Imperf.
- b. Perf. 13x10 125.00 3.50
- c. Perf. 10 325.00 21.00

58 A13 8p yellow ('77) 250.00 35.00
- a. Imperf.
- b. Perf. 10 625.00 50.00
- c. Perf. 13x10 400.00 47.50

59 A22 9p on 10p red brown, perf. 12 (Bk) 32.50 13.00
- a. Double surcharge, blk & bl 325.00
- b. Perf. 12x10 525.00 400.00
- c. Perf. 10 25.00 11.00
- d. Perf. 12x11 35.00 12.00
- e. Perf. 11x12 — —
- f. Perf. 13 65.00 15.00
- g. Perf. 11 72.50 15.00
- h. Perf. 10x11 105.00 25.00

60 A23 1sh black ('76) 80.00 3.75
- b. Perf. 13x10 425.00 14.00
- c. Perf. 10 450.00 35.00
- d. Perf. 11 — —
- e. Vert. pair, imperf between *2,250.*
- f. Pair, imperf *2,000.*

Nos. 52-60 (9) 740.00 118.50

The surcharge on No. 59 measures 15mm.

See Nos. 66, 68. For overprints see Nos. O1-O10.

Typo.; Engr. (3p, 5p, 8p)

1882-91 Wmk. 55 *Perf. 11x12*

61 A17 1p red 13.00 1.10
- a. Perf. 10 19.00 1.25
- b. Perf. 10x13 240.00 14.00
- c. Perf. 10x12 525.00 140.00
- d. Perf. 12x11 250.00
- e. Perf. 10x11 *1,100.* 225.00
- f. Perf. 11 350.00
- g. Perf. 13 1,100. 475.00
- h. Perf. 13x10 87.50 3.50
- i. Perf. 12x10 525.00 135.00
- j. Perf. 11x10 1,100. 225.00
- k. Horiz. pair, imperf between *2,100.*

62 A18 2p blue 24.00 1.10
- a. Perf. 10 45.00 1.25
- b. Perf. 13x10 140.00 6.25
- c. Perf. 13 1,100. 250.00
- d. Perf. 12x10 750.00 140.00
- e. Perf. 11 250.00
- f. Perf. 12x11 950.00 250.00
- g. Perf. 11x10 1,100. 325.00
- h. Perf. 12 525.00

63 A15 3p green 18.00 7.00
- a. Imperf., pair 700.00
- b. Vert. pair, imperf. btwn. —
- c. Horiz. pair, imperf. vert. 700.00
- d. Double impression —
- e. Perf. 10 21.00 5.00
- f. Perf. 11 21.00 5.00
- g. Perf. 12 24.00 5.25
- h. Perf. 12x11 22.50 5.00
- i. Perf. 10x12 97.50 9.25
- m. Perf. 10x11 50.00 6.50
- n. Perf. 12x10 97.50 9.25

64 A19 4p red brown 95.00 5.75
- a. Perf. 10 105.00 8.00
- b. Perf. 10x12 425.00 125.00
- c. Perf. 12 700.00 400.00

65 A11 5p dk blue green 21.00 3.50
- a. Imperf., pair 625.00
- b. Perf. 11 22.50 3.50
- c. Perf. 10 32.50 3.50
- d. Perf. 12 42.50 4.25
- e. Perf. 10x12 57.50
- f. 5p green, perf. 12x11 15.00 2.50
- g. 5p green, perf. 11x10 105.00 13.25
- h. 5p green, perf. 12x10 240.00 140.00
- i. 5p green, perf. 10x11 120.00 10.50
- j. 5p green, perf. 11 16.00 2.50

66 A21 6p lilac, perf. 10 105.00 5.25
- a. Horiz. pair, imperf. between *2,000.*
- b. Perf. 10x12 105.00 5.75
- c. Perf. 11x12 200.00 25.00
- d. Perf. 12 200.00 20.00
- e. Perf. 11x10 140.00 6.25

f. Perf. 11 200.00 18.00
g. Perf. 10x13 700.00
67 A13 8p yellow, perf. 10 200.00 32.50
a. Perf. 11 200.00 42.50
b. Perf. 12 350.00 57.50
c. Perf. 10x12 250.00 100.00
68 A23 1sh black 175.00 18.00
a. Perf. 10x13 — —
b. Perf. 10 175.00 14.00
c. Perf. 11 450.00 29.00
d. Perf. 10x12 — 525.00
Nos. 61-68 (8) 651.00 74.20

Nos. 63 and 65 exist with two types of watermark 55 — spacings of 1mm or 2mm between crown and NSW.

See No. 90. For surcharges and overprints see Nos. 92-94, O12-O19.

The 1, 2, 4, 6, 8p and 1sh have been reprinted on paper watermarked Large Crown and NSW. The 1, 2, 4p and 1sh are perforated 11x12, the 6p is perforated 10 and the 8p 11. All are overprinted "REPRINT," the 1sh in red and the others in black.

Perf. 11x12

1886-87 Typo. Wmk. 56

Bluish Revenue Stamp Paper

70 A17 1p scarlet 13.00 6.00
a. Perf. 10 35.00 13.00
71 A18 2p dark blue 32.50 6.00
a. Perf. 10 105.00 15.00

For overprint, see No. O20.

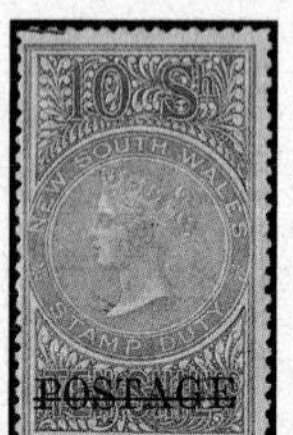
A24

Perf. 12 (#73-75), 12x10 (#72, 75A) and Compound

1885-86 "POSTAGE" in Black

72 A24 5sh green & vio 850.00 125.00
a. Perf. 10 — —
73 A24 10sh rose & vio 1,750. 275.00
74 A24 £1 rose & vio 9,000. —
a. Perf. 13 — 5,250.

"POSTAGE" in Blue

Bluish Paper

75 A24 10sh rose & vio 325.00 80.00
b. Perf. 10 1,350. 300.00
c. Perf. 12x11 — —

White Paper

75A A24 £1 rose & vio 6,750. *4,250.*

For overprints, see Nos. O21-O23.

The 5sh with black overprint and the £1 with blue overprint have been reprinted on paper watermarked NSW. They are perforated 12x10 and are overprinted "REPRINT" in black.

"POSTAGE" in Blue

1894 White Paper

76 A24 10sh rose & violet, perf 12 450.00 105.00
a. Double overprint
b. 10sh mauve & claret, perf 10 850.00 275.00
c. 10sh mauve & violet, perf 11 750.00 190.00
d. 10sh mauve & violet, perf 12x11 425.00 125.00

See No. 108B.

View of Sydney A25

Emu A26

Captain Cook — A27

Victoria and Coat of Arms — A28

Lyrebird A29

Kangaroo A30

1888-89 Wmk. 55 *Perf. 11x12*

77 A25 1p violet 10.00 1.40
a. Perf. 12 14.00 1.10
b. Perf. 12x11½ 42.50 2.40
78 A26 2p blue 16.00 1.40
a. Imperf., pair 400.00
b. Perf. 12 25.00 .95
c. Perf. 12x11½ 29.00 .95
79 A27 4p brown 25.00 8.75
a. Perf. 12x11½ 87.50 20.00
b. Perf. 12 72.50 10.00
c. Perf. 11 700.00 200.00
d. Imperf.
80 A28 6p carmine rose 57.50 8.75
a. Perf. 12 47.50 15.00
b. Perf. 12x11½ 57.50 8.75
81 A29 8p red violet 42.50 9.50
a. Perf. 12 42.50 9.50
b. Perf. 12x11½ 75.00 20.00
82 A30 1sh maroon ('89) 57.50 8.75
a. Imperf., pair 1,000.
b. Perf. 12x11½ 57.50 4.25
c. Perf. 12 72.50 4.25
Nos. 77-82 (6) 208.50 38.55

First British settlement in Australia, cent.

For overprints see Nos. O24-O29.

1888 Wmk. 56 *Perf. 11x12*

83 A25 1p violet 35.00 4.00
84 A26 2p blue 115.00 6.00

See Nos. 104B-106C, 113-115, 118, 125-127, 130.

Map of Australia — A31

Governors Capt. Arthur Phillip (above) and Lord Carrington — A32

1888-89 Wmk. 53 *Perf. 10*

85 A31 5sh violet ('89) 475.00 105.00
86 A32 20sh ultra 600.00 225.00

See Nos. 88, 120. For overprints see Nos. O30-O31.

1890 Wmk. 57 *Perf. 10*

87 A31 5sh violet 400.00 77.50
a. Perf. 11 450.00 100.00
b. Perf. 10x11 550.00 77.50
c. Perf. 12 700.00 115.00
f. Horiz. pair, imperf btwn. —

Perf. 11x12, 12x11

Wmk. 58

88 A32 20sh ultra 225.00 90.00
a. Perf. 11 275.00 90.00
b. Perf. 12 700.00 275.00
c. 20sh cobalt blue, perf 10 525.00 275.00

For overprints see Nos. O32-O33.

"Australia" — A33

1890, Dec. 22 Wmk. 55 *Perf. 11x12*

89 A33 2½p ultra 14.00 5.75
a. Perf. 12 29.00 5.75
b. Perf. 12x11½ 87.50 —

For overprint see No. O35.

Type of 1856

1891 Engr. Wmk. 52 *Perf. 10*

90 A15 3p green 15.00 *100.00*
a. Double impression —

Type of 1867

1893 Typo. *Perf. 11*

91 A20 10p lilac 35.00 11.50
a. Perf. 10 42.50 14.00
b. Perf. 11x10 or 10x11 47.50 18.00
c. Perf. 12x11 250.00 35.00

Types of 1862-84 Surcharged in Black

a

b

1891, Jan. 5 Wmk. 55 *Perf. 11x12*

92 A17(a) ½p on 1p gray 21.00 *14.00*
a. Imperf.
b. Surcharge omitted —
c. Double surcharge *550.00*
93 A21(b) 7½p on 6p brown 21.00 14.00
a. Perf. 10 21.00 14.00
b. Perf. 11 20.00 11.50
c. Perf. 12 24.00 14.00
d. Perf. 10x12 24.00 14.00

Perf. 12x11½

94 A23(b) 12½p on 1sh red 14.00 12.00
a. Perf. 11x12 22.50 22.50
b. Perf. 10 29.00 25.00
c. Perf. 11 30.00 25.00
d. Perf. 12 35.00 25.00
Nos. 92-94 (3) 56.00 40.00

For overprints see Nos. O34, O36-O37.

Victoria — A37

1892-97 *Perf. 11x12*

95 A37 ½p slate ('97) 5.75 .85
a. Perf. 12x11½ 5.75 .85
b. Perf. 12 5.50 .85
c. As #95, horiz. pair, imperf between *1,350.*
d. ½p gray, perf. 10 80.00 7.25
e. As "d," perf. 10x12 140.00 18.00
f. As "d," perf. 11 160.00 14.00
g. As "d," perf. 11x12 2.25 .50

See Nos. 102, 109, 121. For overprint see No. O38.

Types of 1867-71

1897 *Perf. 11x12*

96 A22 9p on 10p red brn (Bk) 20.00 17.50
a. 9p on 10p org brn (Bk) 20.00 17.50
b. Surcharge omitted —
c. Double surcharge 375.00 375.00
d. Perf. 11 25.00 24.00
e. Perf. 12 25.00 22.50
97 A20 10p violet 25.00 16.00
a. Perf. 12x11½ 25.00 16.00
b. Perf. 11 47.50 22.50
c. Perf. 12 35.00 17.50

The surcharge on No. 96 measures 13½mm.

For overprints see Nos. O39-O40.

Seal A38

Victoria A39

A40

ONE PENNY:

Die I — The first pearl in the crown at the left is merged into the arch, the shading under the fleur-de-lis is indistinct, and the "s" of "WALES" is open.

Die II — The first pearl is circular, the vertical shading under the fleur-de-lis is clear, and the "s" of "WALES" not so open.

2½ PENCE:

Die I — There are 12 radiating lines in the star on the Queen's breast.

Die II — There are 16 radiating lines in the star. The eye is nearly full of color.

1897 *Perf. 12*

98 A38 1p rose red, II 4.75 .50
a. Die I, perf. 11x12 5.75 .50
b. Imperf., pair —
c. Imperf. horiz., pair 700.00
d. Die I, perf. 12x11½ 5.50 .50
e. Die I, perf. 12 11.50 1.75
f. Die II, perf. 12x11½ 4.75 .50
g. Die II, perf. 11x12 4.75 .50
99 A39 2p deep blue 13.50 .65
a. Perf. 11x12 9.00 .65
b. Perf. 12x11½ 7.75 .65
100 A40 2½p dp purple, II 20.00 4.25
a. Die I, perf. 12x11 22.50 4.75
b. Die I, perf. 11 25.00 7.75
c. Die I, perf. 11½x12 25.00 4.25
d. Die II, perf. 11x12 21.00 4.25
e. Die II, perf. 11½x12 25.00 4.25
Nos. 98-100 (3) 38.25 5.40

Sixtieth year of Queen Victoria's reign.

See Nos. 103-104, 110-112, 122-124.

Type of 1861

1897 Engr. Wmk. 53 *Perf. 11*

101 A16 5sh red violet 105.00 29.00
a. Horiz. pair, imperf. btwn. *11,000.*
b. Perf. 11x12 or 12x11 130.00 42.50
c. Perf. 12 140.00 52.50

Perf. 12x11½, 11½x12

1899, Oct. Typo. Wmk. 55

HALF PENNY:

Die I — Narrow "H" in "HALF."

102 A37 ½p blue green, I 3.50 .95
a. Imperf., pair 190.00 *325.00*
103 A39 2p ultra 5.75 .95
a. Imperf., pair 325.00
104 A40 2½p dk blue, II 8.00 3.25
a. Imperf., pair 325.00
104B A27 4p org brown 22.50 13.50
d. As "c," imperf. pair 750.00
105 A28 6p emerald 135.00 52.50
a. Imperf., pair 600.00
106 A28 6p orange 29.00 6.75
a. 6p yellow 26.00 10.75
b. Imperf., pair 475.00
106C A29 8p magenta 42.50 8.00
Nos. 102-106C (7) 246.25 85.90

Lyrebird A41

"Australia" A42

1903 *Perf. 12x11½*

107 A41 2sh6p blue green 87.50 42.50

See Nos. 119, 131.

1903 Wmk. 70 *Perf. 12½*

108 A42 9p org brn & ultra 29.00 7.25
a. Perf. 11 5,250. 1,850.

See No. 128.

Type of 1885-86

1904 Wmk. 56 *Perf. 12x11*

"POSTAGE" in Blue

108B A24 10sh brt rose & vio 325.00 125.00
c. Perf. 11 525.00 200.00
d. Perf. 14 400.00 135.00
e. 10sh aniline crimson & violet, perf 12 650.00 200.00
f. As "e," perf 12x11 475.00 130.00
g. 10sh claret & violet, chalky paper, perf 12x11 475.00 175.00

The watermark (NSW) of No. 108B is 20x7mm, with rounded angles in "N" and "W." On No. 75, the watermark is 21x7mm, with sharp angles in the "N" and "W."

HALF PENNY:

Die II — Wide "H" in "HALF."

Perf. 11, 11x12½, 12x11½ and Compound

1905-06 Wmk. 12

109 A37 ½p blue grn, II 6.00 1.10
a. ½p blue green, I 6.25 1.10
b. Booklet pane of 12 —
110 A38 1p car rose, II 4.75 .50
a. Booklet pane of 6 —
b. Booklet pane of 12 —
111 A39 2p deep ultra 4.75 .50
112 A40 2½p dk blue, II 9.00 5.25
113 A27 4p org brown 21.00 8.75
114 A28 6p orange 29.00 6.00
a. 6p yellow 35.00 6.00
b. Perf. 11 525.00
115 A29 8p magenta 52.50 11.00
117 A20 10p violet 32.50 10.00
118 A30 1sh vio brown 57.50 5.75
119 A41 2sh6p blue green 77.50 40.00

Wmk. 199

Perf. 12x11 or 11x12

120 A32 20sh ultra 225.00 87.50
Nos. 109-115,117-120 (11) 519.50 176.35

1906-07 **Wmk. 13**

121 A37	½p green, I	8.75	3.25
122 A38	1p rose, II	17.00	2.25
123 A39	2p ultra	17.00	2.25
124 A40	2½p blue, II	110.00	*200.00*
125 A27	4p org brown	29.00	25.00
126 A28	6p orange	67.50	37.50
127 A29	8p red violet	42.50	37.50
128 A42	9p org brn & ultra, perf. 12x12½ ('06)	22.50	4.50
a.	Perf. 11	175.00	140.00
129 A20	10p violet	62.50	*87.50*
130 A30	1sh vio brown	92.50	18.00
131 A41	2sh6p blue green	125.00	105.00
	Nos. 121-131 (11)	594.25	522.75

Portions of some of the sheets on which the above are printed show the watermark "COMMONWEALTH OF AUSTRALIA." Stamps may also be found from portions of the sheet without watermark.

SEMI-POSTAL STAMPS

SP1

Allegory of Charity SP2

1897, June **Wmk. 55** ***Perf. 11***

B1 SP1	1p (1sh) grn & brn	72.50	72.50
B2 SP2	2½p (2sh6p) rose, bl & gold	350.00	350.00

Diamond Jubilee of Queen Victoria.

The difference between the postal and face values of these stamps was donated to a fund for a home for consumptives.

REGISTRATION STAMPS

Queen Victoria — R1

Unwmk.

1856, Jan. 1 **Engr.** ***Imperf.***

F1 R1	(6p) orange & blue	1,400.	250.00
F2 R1	(6p) red & blue	1,400.	210.00
a.	Frame printed on back	*7,000.*	*4,000.*

1860 ***Perf. 12, 13***

F3 R1	(6p) orange & blue	900.00	190.00
F4 R1	(6p) red & blue	625.00	90.00

Nos. F1 to F4 exist also on paper with papermaker's watermark in sheet.

1863 **Wmk. 49**

F5 R1	(6p) red & blue	250.00	47.50
c.	Double impression of frame	—	*800.00*

Fifty varieties.

Nos. F1-F2 were reprinted on thin white wove unwatermarked paper and on thick yellowish wove unwatermarked paper; the former are usually overprinted "SPECIMEN."

No. F4 was reprinted on thin white wove unwatermarked paper; perf. 10 and overprinted "REPRINT" in black.

POSTAGE DUE STAMPS

D1

Perf. 10, 11, 11½, 12 and Compound

1891-92 **Typo.** **Wmk. 55**

J1 D1	½p green, perf 10	10.00	10.00
J2 D1	1p green	21.00	3.75
a.	Perf 12	45.00	9.00
J3 D1	2p green	29.00	5.75
a.	Perf 12x10	47.50	7.00
J4 D1	3p green	47.50	21.00
J5 D1	4p green	42.50	11.50
J6 D1	6p green, perf 10	27.50	17.50
J7 D1	8p green, perf 10	160.00	42.50
J8 D1	5sh green, perf 10	325.00	105.00
a.	Perf 11	575.00	175.00
b.	Perf 11x12	—	300.00

Perf. 12x10

J9 D1	10sh green	600.00	300.00
a.	Perf. 10	600.00	140.00
J10 D1	20sh green	700.00	300.00
a.	Perf. 10	1,000.	225.00
b.	Perf. 12	1,050.	
	Nos. J1-J10 (10)	1,962.	817.00

Nos. J1-J5 exist on both ordinary and chalky paper.

Used values for Nos. J8-J10 are for c-t-o stamps.

OFFICIAL STAMPS

Regular Issues Overprinted in Black or Red

Perf. 10, 11, 12, 13 and Compound

1879-80 **Wmk. 54**

O1 A17	1p red	30.00	5.75
a.	Perf. 10	350.00	65.00
b.	Perf. 10x13	72.50	9.50
O2 A18	2p blue	47.50	5.25
a.	Perf. 11x12		525.00
b.	Perf. 10	525.00	77.50
O3 A15	3p green (R)	1,200.	700.00
O4 A15	3p green	350.00	60.00
a.	Watermarked "6"	—	925.00
b.	Double overprint		
c.	3p yel grn, perf 10	350.00	60.00
d.	3p yel grn, perf 12	425.00	175.00
O5 A19	4p red brown	400.00	21.00
a.	Perf. 10x13	450.00	190.00
O6 A11	5p dark green	42.50	27.50
O7 A21	6p lilac	600.00	20.00
a.	Perf. 10	800.00	75.00
b.	Perf. 13x10	450.00	90.00
O8 A13	8p yellow (R)	*1,500.*	400.00
O9 A13	8p yellow	—	52.50
a.	Perf. 10	625.00	175.00
O10 A23	1sh black (R)	600.00	17.50
a.	Perf. 10	—	35.00
b.	Perf. 10x13	—	77.50
c.	Perf. 13x10	—	29.00

1880 **Wmk. 53**

O11 A16	5sh lilac, perf. 11	475.00	175.00
a.	Double overprint	4,500.	*2,400.*
b.	Perf. 10	1,150.	375.00
c.	Perf. 12x10	1,000.	250.00
d.	Perf. 13	1,350.	225.00
e.	Perf. 10x12		—

1881 **Wmk. 55**

O12 A17	1p red	35.00	6.00
a.	Perf. 10x13		200.00
O13 A18	2p blue	21.00	2.40
a.	Perf. 10x13	400.00	200.00
O14 A15	3p green	17.50	8.50
a.	Double overprint		1,200.
b.	Perf. 12	325.00	200.00
c.	Perf. 11		
O15 A19	4p red brown	35.00	7.50
a.	Perf. 10x12	350.00	200.00
b.	Perf. 12	350.00	350.00
O16 A11	5p dark green	32.50	*35.00*
a.	Perf. 12	250.00	
b.	Perf. 12x10	—	—
O17 A21	6p lilac	50.00	11.50
a.	Perf. 12		105.00
b.	Perf. 11x12	—	—
c.	Perf. 12x11 ('85)	100.00	27.50
O18 A13	8p yellow	57.50	25.00
a.	Double overprint	—	
b.	Perf. 12	350.00	525.00
O19 A23	1sh black (R)	72.50	*21.00*
a.	Double overprint		525.00
b.	Perf. 10x13		140.00
c.	Perf. 11x12, comb.	57.50	21.00
	Nos. O12-O19 (8)	321.00	116.90

Beware of other red overprints on watermark 55 stamps.

No. O14 exists with two overprint types: "O" and "S" 7mm and 5.5mm apart. For detailed listings, see the Scott Classic Specialized catalogue.

1881 **Wmk. 56**

O20 A17	1p red	105.00	17.50

1887-90

O21 A24	10sh on #75	—	*3,200.*
O22 A24	£1 on #75A	*19,500.*	*9,250.*

No. 75 Overprinted

1889

O23 A24	10sh rose & vio	*4,500.*	*1,500.*
a.	Perf. 10	*7,000.*	*2,750.*

Overprinted

1888-89 **Wmk. 55**

O24 A25	1p violet	6.25	2.00
a.	Overprinted "O" only		
O25 A26	2p blue	9.50	1.40
O26 A27	4p red brown	25.00	9.50
O27 A28	6p carmine	18.00	12.00
O28 A29	8p red lilac	47.50	32.50
O29 A30	1sh vio brown	45.00	9.50
a.	Double overprint		
	Nos. O24-O29 (6)	151.25	66.90

Wmk. 53

O30 A31	5sh violet (R)	*1,500.*	*650.00*
O31 A32	20sh ultra	*3,750.*	1,100.

1890 **Wmk. 57**

O32 A31	5sh violet	*425.00*	175.00
a.	5sh, dull lilac, perf. 12	1,200.	325.00

Wmk. 58

O33 A32	20sh ultra	*4,000.*	*3,500.*

Centenary of the founding of the Colony (Nos. O24-O33).

1891 **Wmk. 55**

O34 A17(a)	½p on 1p gray & black	125.00	125.00
a.	Double overprint		
O35 A33	2½p ultra	24.00	14.00
O36 A21(b)	7½p on 6p brn & black	72.50	85.00
O37 A23(b)	12½p on 1sh red & black	125.00	*140.00*

1892

O38 A37	½p gray, perf 11x12	12.50	*24.00*
a.	Perf 10	16.00	*27.50*
b.	Perf 12	15.00	*20.00*
c.	Perf 12x11½	27.50	22.50

1894 **Wmk. 54**

O39 A22	9p on 10p red brn	800.00	675.00

Wmk. 52

O40 A20	10p lilac, perf. 13	325.00	*175.00*
a.	Perf. 11x10 or 10x11	475.00	*450.00*
b.	Perf 10	400.00	

The official stamps became obsolete on Dec. 31, 1894. In Aug., 1895, sets of 32 varieties of "O.S." stamps, together with some envelopes and postal cards, were placed on sale at the Sydney post office at £2 per set.

These sets contained most of the varieties listed above and a few which are not known in the original issues. An obliteration consisting of the letters G.P.O. or N.S.W. in three concentric ovals was lightly applied to the center of each block of four stamps.

It is understood that the earlier stamps and many of the overprints were reprinted to make up these sets.

QUEENSLAND

'kwēnz-,land

LOCATION — Northeastern part of Australia
GOVT. — British Crown Colony
AREA — 670,500 sq. mi.
POP. — 498,129 (1901)
CAPITAL — Brisbane

Originally a part of New South Wales, Queensland was constituted a separate colony in 1859. It was one of the six British Colonies that united in 1901 to form the Commonwealth of Australia.

12 Pence = 1 Shilling
20 Shillings = 1 Pound

Values for unused stamps are for examples with original gum as defined in the catalogue introduction. Very fine examples of Nos. 4-73, 84-125, 128-140, and F1-F3b will have perforations touching the design on at least one or more sides due to the narrow spacing of the stamps on the plates. Stamps with perfs clear of the design on all four sides are scarce and will command higher prices.

Watermarks

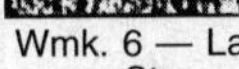

Wmk. 5 — Small Star

Wmk. 6 — Large Star

Wmk. 12 — Crown and Single-lined A

Wmk. 13 — Crown and Double-lined A

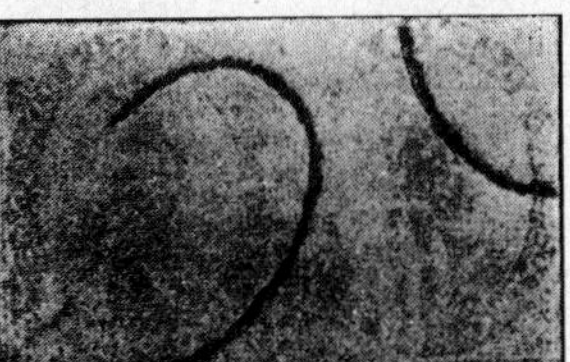

Wmk. 65 — "Queensland Postage Stamps" in Sheet in Script Capitals

Wmk. 66

Wmks. 66 & 67 — "Queensland" in Large Single-lined Roman Capitals in the Sheet and Short-pointed Star to Each Stamp (Stars Vary Slightly in Size and Shape)

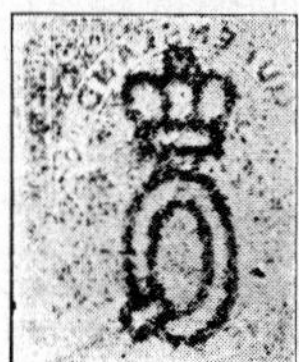

Wmk. 68 — Crown and Q

Wmk. 69 — Large Crown and Q

There are two varieties of the watermark 68, differing slightly in the position and shape of the crown and the tongue of the "Q."

Wmk. 70 — V and Crown

Queen Victoria — A1

Wmk. 6

1860, Nov. 1 Engr. *Imperf.*
1 A1 1p deep rose 4,500. 1,050.
2 A1 2p deep blue 12,000. 2,250.
3 A1 6p deep green 8,500. 1,050.

Clean-Cut Perf. 14 to 16
4 A1 1p deep rose 2,750. 375.
5 A1 2p deep blue 1,050. 140.
a. Horiz. pair, imperf between — 4,250.
6 A1 6p deep green 1,050. 110.

Clean-Cut Perf. 14 to 16

1860-61 Wmk. 5
6A A1 2p blue 925.00 135.00
b. Horiz. pair, imperf. vert 4,000.
6D A1 3p brown ('61) 550.00 110.00
6E A1 6p deep green 1,000. 95.00
6F A1 1sh gray violet 1,050. 120.00

Regular Perf. 14
6H A1 1p rose 225.00 62.50
6I A1 2p deep blue 625.00 105.00

Rough Perf. 14 to 16
7 A1 1p deep rose 115.00 57.50
8 A1 2p blue 185.00 52.50
a. Horiz. pair, imperf between 5,250. —
9 A1 3p brown ('61) 105.00 60.00
a. Horiz. pair, imperf. vert. 5,250. —
10 A1 6p deep green 275.00 52.50
a. 6p yellow green 400.00 42.50
11 A1 1sh dull violet 800.00 140.00

Thick Yellowish Paper

Square Perf. 12½ to 13

1862-67 Unwmk.
12 A1 1p Indian red 575.00 115.00
13 A1 1p orange ('63) 140.00 22.50
a. Perf. 13, round holes ('67) 160.00 42.50
b. Horiz. pair, imperf. between —
c. Imperf., pair — 2,000.
14 A1 2p deep blue 100.00 15.00
a. 2p pale blue 200.00 60.00
b. Perf. 13, round holes ('67) 100.00 27.50
c. Imperf., pair — 2,000.
e. Horiz. pair, imperf. between 2,400.
f. Vert. pair, imperf. between 4,500.
15 A1 3p brown ('63) 105.00 62.50
a. Imperf.
b. Perf. 13, round holes ('67) 130.00 60.00
16 A1 6p yellow grn ('63) 195.00 32.50
a. 6p green 240.00 100.00
b. Perf. 13, round holes ('67) 200.00 32.50
c. Imperf., pair — 2,400.
d. Horiz. pair, imperf. between — 2,400.
17 A1 1sh gray ('63) 500.00 47.50
b. Imperf. horizontally
c. Horiz. pair, imperf. between — 3,500.
d. Perf. 13, round holes ('67) 500.00 47.50
e. Vert. pair, imperf between —

White Wove Paper

1865 Wmk. 5 *Rough Perf. 13*
18 A1 1p orange 120.00 40.00
a. Horiz. pair, imperf. between 1,600.
19 A1 2p light blue 130.00 30.00
a. Vert. pair, imperf. between 2,750.
b. Half used as 1p on cover 4,500.
20 A1 6p yellow green 180.00 45.00
Nos. 18-20 (3) 430.00 115.00

1865 *Perf. 12½x13*
18B A1 1p orange vermilion 140.00 75.00
19C A1 2p blue 175.00 75.00

Perf. 13, Round Holes

1866 Wmk. 65
21 A1 1p orange vermilion 250.00 52.50
22 A1 2p blue 100.00 32.50
b. Diagonal half used as 1p on cover —

1865 *Perf. 12½x13*
21A A1 1p orange vermilion 250.00 75.00
22C A1 2p blue 250.00 75.00

1866 Unwmk. Litho. *Perf. 13*
23 A1 4p lilac 240.00 42.50
a. 4p slate 325.00 42.50
24 A1 5sh pink 975.00 250.00
b. Vert. pair, imperf between 3,500.

Wmk. 66, 67

1868-74 Engr. *Perf. 13*
25 A1 1p orange ('71) 87.50 9.25
26 A1 2p blue 72.50 6.00
27 A1 3p grnsh brn ('71) 175.00 12.50
a. 3p brown 115.00 11.50
b. 3p olive brown 180.00 11.50
28 A1 6p yel green ('71) 250.00 14.00
a. 6p deep green 325.00 35.00
30 A1 1sh grnsh gray ('72) 750.00 175.00
31 A1 1sh violet ('74) 400.00 37.50
a. 1sh brownish gray 750.00 175.00

Perf. 12
32 A1 1p orange 600.00 47.50
33 A1 2p blue 140.00 75.00
34 A1 3p brown 875.00 325.00
35 A1 6p deep green 1,600. 52.50
36 A1 1sh violet 900.00 87.50

Perf. 13x12
36A A1 1p orange 250.00
37 A1 2p blue 1,600. 50.00
37A A1 3p brown 1,250.

The reprints are perforated 13 and the colors differ slightly from those of the originals.

1868-75 Wmk. 68 *Perf. 13*
38 A1 1p orange 115.00 8.75
a. Imperf pair 575.00
39 A1 1p rose ('74) 105.00 17.00
40 A1 2p blue 62.50 4.00
a. Vert. pair, imperf between —
b. Imperf., pair 725.00
41 A1 3p brown ('75) 140.00 21.00
42 A1 6p yel green ('69) 185.00 14.00
a. 6p apple green 240.00 17.50
b. 6p deep green 225.00 17.50
c. As "a," imperf pair 725.00
43 A1 1sh violet ('75) 375.00 87.50
Nos. 38-43 (6) *982.50* 152.25

1876-78 *Perf. 12*
44 A1 1p orange 72.50 9.50
a. Imperf. 775.00
c. Vert. pair, imperf between —
45 A1 1p rose 90.00 20.00
a. 1p salmon 115.00 20.00
46 A1 2p blue 70.00 2.40
a. 2p pale blue 160.00 29.00
47 A1 3p brown 125.00 17.50
48 A1 6p yellow green 250.00 9.50
a. 6p apple green 300.00 15.50
b. 6p deep green 250.00 16.00
49 A1 1sh violet 75.00 17.50
m. Vert. pair, imperf between —
Nos. 44-49 (6) 682.50 76.40

Nos. 44, 49 exist in vertical pairs, imperf. between.

Perf. 13x12
49B A1 1p orange 300.00
49C A1 2p blue *1,500.* 325.00
49D A1 4p yellow 575.00
49E A1 6p deep green 575.00

Perf. 12½x13
49G A1 1p orange vermilion 700.00
49H A1 2p deep blue 700.00

The reprints are perforated 12 and are in paler colors than the originals.

1879 Unwmk. *Perf. 12*
50 A1 6p pale emerald 450.00 40.00
a. Horiz. pair, imperf. vert. 2,250.

A2

1875-81 Litho. Wmk. 68 *Perf. 13*
50B A1 4p yellow ('75) 1,250. 100.00

Perf. 12
51 A1 4p buff ('76) 1,000. 30.00
a. 4p yellow 1,000. 32.00
52 A1 2sh pale blue ('81) 180.00 57.50
Fiscal cancellation 5.75
a. 2sh deep blue 200.00 57.50
b. Imperf. —
53 A2 2sh6p lt red ('81) 325.00 175.00
Fiscal cancellation 5.75
54 A1 5sh orange brn ('81) 425.00 200.00
Fiscal cancellation 7.00
a. 5sh fawn 425.00 200.00
55 A1 10sh brown ('81) 875.00 400.00
Fiscal cancellation 7.00
a. Imperf., pair *1,750.*
56 A1 20sh rose ('81) 2,900. 675.00
Fiscal cancellation 9.25
Nos. 50B-56 (7) 6,955. 1,637.

Nos. 53-56, 62-64, 74-83 with pen (revenue) cancellations removed are often offered as unused.

A3

1879-81 Typo. Wmk. 68 *Perf. 12*
57 A3 1p rose red 62.50 14.00
a. 1p red orange 87.50 21.00
b. 1p brown orange 115.00 29.00
c. "QOEENSLAND" 1,375. 225.00
d. Imperf. —
e. Vert. pair, imperf. horiz. 1,100.
58 A3 2p gray blue 115.00 7.25
a. 2p deep ultra 120.00 7.25
b. Imperf. —
c. "PENGE" 800.00 125.00
d. "TW" joined 87.50 7.25
e. Vert. pair, imperf. horiz. 1,750.
59 A3 4p orange yellow 350.00 42.50
a. Imperf. —
60 A3 6p yellow green 125.00 12.50
a. Imperf. —
61 A3 1sh pale violet ('81) 140.00 15.00
a. 1sh deep violet 125.00 14.00
Nos. 57-61 (5) 792.50 91.25

The stamps of type A3 were electrotyped from plates made up of groups of four types, differing in minor details. Two dies were used for the 1p and 2p, giving eight varieties for each of those values.

Nos. 59-60 exist imperf. vertically.

For surcharge see No. 65.

Moiré on Back

1878-79 Unwmk.
62 A3 1p brown org ('79) 725.00 100.00
a. "QOEENSLAND" 2,000.
63 A3 2p deep ultra ('79) 650.00 57.50
a. "PENGE" 4,750. 900.00
64 A1 1sh red violet 250.00 115.00
Nos. 62-64 (3) 1,625. 272.50

No. 57b Surcharged Vertically in Black

1880 Wmk. 68
65 A3 ½p on 1p brn org 600.00 1,850.
a. "QOEENSLAND" 2,000. 1,100.

On No. 65, the surcharge reads from bottom to top. Stamps with surcharges reading downward are fakes.

A4

1882-83 Typo. *Perf. 12*
66 A4 1p pale red 8.50 1.10
a. 1p rose 9.00 1.10
b. Imperf. pair —
67 A4 2p gray blue 12.00 1.10
a. 2p deep ultra 13.00 1.10
b. Horiz. pair, imperf between —
68 A4 4p yellow ('83) 35.00 4.75
a. "PENGE" 325.00 70.00
b. Imperf., single —
69 A4 6p yellow green 26.50 3.25
70 A4 1sh violet ('83) 35.00 7.25
Nos. 66-70 (5) 117.00 17.45

There are eight minor varieties of the 1p, twelve of the 2p and four each of the other values. On the 1p there is a period after "PENNY." On all values the lines of shading on the neck extend from side to side.

Compare design A4 with A6, A10, A11, A15, A16.

1883 *Perf. 9½x12*
71 A4 1p rose 250.00 77.50
72 A4 2p gray blue 850.00 92.50
73 A4 1sh pale violet 425.00 95.00
Nos. 71-73 (3) 1,525. 265.00

Beware of faked perfs.

See Nos. 94, 95, 100.

A5

Wmk. 68 Twice Sideways

1882-85 Engr. *Perf. 12*

Thin Paper
74 A5 2sh ultra 225.00 60.00
75 A5 2sh6p vermilion 160.00 32.50
76 A5 5sh car rose ('85) 125.00 35.00
77 A5 10sh brown 425.00 110.00
78 A5 £1 dk grn ('83) 650.00 250.00
Nos. 74-78 (5) 1,585. 487.50

The 2sh, 5sh and £1 exist imperf.

There are two varieties of the watermark on Nos. 74-78, as in the 1879-81 issue.

Stamps with revenue cancels sell for $3.25-6.50.

1886 Wmk. 69 *Perf. 12*

Thick Paper
79 A5 2sh ultra 250.00 52.50
80 A5 2sh6p vermilion 87.50 35.00
81 A5 5sh car rose 80.00 62.50
82 A5 10sh dark brown 185.00 70.00
83 A5 £1 dark green 425.00 125.00
Nos. 79-83 (5) 1,027. 345.00

High value stamps with cancellations removed are offered as unused.

Stamps with revenue cancels sell for $3.25-6.50.

See Nos. 126-127, 141-144.

A6

Redrawn

1887-89 Typo. Wmk. 68 *Perf. 12*
84 A6 1p orange 9.50 1.40
85 A6 2p gray blue 14.00 1.40
a. 2p deep ultra 18.00 1.75
b. Half used as 1c on cover —
86 A6 2sh red brown ('89) 130.00 72.50

Perf. 9½x12

88 A6 2p deep ultra 775.00 125.00
Nos. 84-88 (4) 928.50 200.30

The 1p has no period after the value.

In the redrawn stamps the shading lines on the neck are not completed at the left, leaving an irregular white line along that side.

Variety "LA" joined exists on Nos. 84-86, 88, 90, 91, 93, 97, 98, 102.

On No. 88 beware of faked perfs.

A7

A8

1890-92 ***Perf. 12½, 13***

89 A7 ½p green 9.50 3.25
90 A6 1p orange red 6.25 1.00
a. Imperf, pair 275.00 275.00
b. Double impression 650.00
91 A6 2p gray blue 11.50 .70
92 A8 2½p rose carmine 24.00 7.25
93 A6 3p brown ('92) 17.50 5.75
94 A4 4p orange 27.50 4.75
a. "PENGE" for "PENCE" 125.00 42.50
b. 4p orange yellow 37.50 4.75
c. As "b," "PENGE" for "PENCE" 160.00 42.50
d. 4p yellow 42.50 4.75
e. As "d," "PENGE" for "PENCE" 180.00 52.50
95 A4 6p green 21.00 3.25
96 A6 2sh red brown 105.00 57.50
Nos. 89-96 (8) 222.25 83.45

The ½p and 3p exist imperf.

1895 Wmk. 69 ***Perf. 12½, 13***

Thick Paper

98 A6 1p orange 8.75 .95
99 A6 2p gray blue 4.50 .50

Perf. 12

100 A4 1sh pale violet 25.00 11.50
Nos. 98-100 (3) 38.25 12.95

A9

A10

Moiré on Back

1895 Unwmk. ***Perf. 12½, 13***

101 A9 ½p green 8.75 4.50
a. Without moire 80.00
102 A6 1p orange 4.75 1.10
a. "PE" missing 350.00 350.00
b. 1p reddish vermilion 4.75 1.10

Wmk. 68

103 A9 ½p green 4.50 2.00
a. ½p deep green 4.50 2.00
b. Printed on both sides 200.00
c. Double impression —
104 A10 1p orange 4.75 .70
105 A10 2p gray blue 14.00 1.40

Wmk. 69

Thick Paper

106 A9 ½p green, perf 12½ 6.00 3.75
a. Perf 13 6.00 3.25
b. Perf 12 27.50

1895-96 Unwmk. Thin Paper

Crown and Q Faintly Impressed

107 A9 ½p green 4.50 4.50
108 A10 1p orange 6.00 3.75
108A A6 2p gray blue 22.50 *250.00*

A11

A12

A13

1895-96 Wmk. 68

109 A11 1p red 11.50 1.05
110 A12 2½p rose 27.50 9.25
111 A13 5p violet brown 35.00 9.25
111A A11 6p yellow green *22,500.*

Only a few used examples of No. 111A are known, and readable cancels are from 1902. It is suggested that this otherwise unissued design was accidentally included in the plate of No. 120.

A14

A15

A16

A17

A18

A19

TWO PENCE:

Type I — Point of bust does not touch frame.

Type II — First redrawing. The top of the crown, the chignon and the point of the bust touch the frame. The forehead is completely shaded.

Type III — Second redrawing. The top of crown does not touch the frame, though the chignon and the point of the bust do. The forehead and the bridge of the nose are not shaded.

1897-1900 ***Perf. 12½, 13***

112 A14 ½p deep green 10.00 10.00
a. Perf. 12 225.00
113 A15 1p red 4.75 .60
a. Perf. 12 15.00 5.75
114 A16 2p gray blue (I) 6.25 .60
a. Perf. 12 1,000. 7.00
115 A17 2½p rose 47.50 37.50
116 A17 2½p violet, *blue* 18.00 4.50
117 A15 3p brown 21.00 4.50
118 A15 4p bright yellow 21.00 4.50
119 A18 5p violet brown 17.50 4.50
120 A15 6p yellow green 17.50 4.50
121 A19 1sh lilac 26.00 4.75
a. 1sh light violet 32.50 7.25
122 A19 2sh turq blue 65.00 45.00
Nos. 112-122 (11) 254.50 120.95

See Nos. 130-140.

1898 ***Serrated Roulette 13***

123 A15 1p scarlet 12.00 7.75
a. Serrated and perf. 13 16.00 11.50
b. Serrated in black 24.00 17.50
c. Serrated without color and in black 24.00 *35.00*
d. Same as "b," and perf. 13 125.00 *175.00*
e. Same as "c," and perf. 13 125.00 175.00

Victoria — A20

1899 Typo. ***Perf. 12, 12½, 13***

124 A20 ½p blue green 5.25 4.00

Unwatermarked stamps are proofs.

"Australia" — A21

NINE PENCE:
Type I — "QUEENSLAND" 18x1½mm.
Type II — "QUEENSLAND" 17½x1¼mm.

1903 Wmk. 70 ***Perf. 12½***

125 A21 9p org brn & ultra, II 35.00 7.75
a. Type I 35.00 7.75

See No. 128.

Type of 1882

1903-06 Wmk. 68 ***Perf. 12, 12½-13***

Typographed, Perf. 12½-13 Irreg. ('03)

125B A5 5sh rose 200.00 92.50
125C A5 £1 dark green 2,250. 750.00

Lithographed, Perf. 12 ('05-'06)

126 A5 5sh rose 120.00 92.50
127 A5 £1 dark green 550.00 140.00
c. Perf. 12½-13 Irreg. 1,250. 210.00

1907 Typo. Wmk. 13 ***Perf. 12½***

128 A21 9p yel brn & ultra, I 25.00 6.50
a. Type II 77.50 7.75
b. Perf. 11, type II 5,500. 750.00

1907 Wmk. 68 ***Perf. 12½, 13***

129 A16 2p ultra, type II 17.50 7.25
129A A18 5p dark brown 16.00 6.50
b. 5p olive brown 12.50 4.75

1907-09 Wmk. 12

130 A20 ½p deep green 3.50 *5.75*
131 A15 1p red 5.75 .85
a. Imperf., pair 475.00
132 A16 2p ultra, II 14.00 2.40
133 A16 2p ultra, III 7.25 .75
134 A15 3p pale brown 24.00 4.50
135 A15 4p bright yellow 21.00 5.75
136 A15 4p gray black ('09) 32.50 9.00
137 A18 5p brown 20.00 11.50
a. 5p olive brown 25.00 12.50
138 A15 6p yellow green 21.00 7.75
139 A19 1sh violet 22.50 6.00
140 A19 2sh turquoise bl 55.00 37.50

Wmk. 12 Sideways

Litho.

141 A5 2sh6p deep orange 77.50 60.00
142 A5 5sh rose 120.00 82.50
143 A5 10sh dark brown 225.00 120.00
144 A5 £1 blue green 400.00 140.00
Nos. 130-144 (15) 1,049. 494.25

POSTAL FISCAL STAMPS

Authorized for postal use from Jan. 1, 1880. Authorization withdrawn July 1, 1892.

Used values are for examples with postal cancellations used from Jan. 1, 1880 through June 30, 1892.

Beware of stamps with a pen cancellation removed and a fake postmark added.

Queen Victoria
PF1 PF2

1866-74 Engr. Unwmk. ***Perf. 13***

AR1 PF1 1p blue 105.00 47.50
AR2 PF1 6p violet 250.00 175.00
AR3 PF1 1sh green 240.00 140.00
AR4 PF1 2sh brown 260.00 140.00
AR5 PF1 2sh 6p red 475.00 275.00
AR6 PF1 5sh yellow 925.00 375.00
AR7 PF1 6sh yellow *1,250.*
AR8 PF1 10sh yellow green 925.00 325.00
AR9 PF1 20sh rose 1,250. *500.00*

Wmk. 68

AR10 PF1 1p blue 52.50 *47.50*
AR11 PF1 6p violet 115.00 *115.00*
AR12 PF1 6p blue 425.00 325.00
AR13 PF1 1sh green 125.00 92.50
AR14 PF1 2sh brown 200.00 110.00
AR15 PF1 5sh yellow 650.00 225.00
AR16 PF1 10sh yellow green 925.00 *325.00*
AR17 PF1 20sh rose 1,250. *500.00*

1872-73 Wmk. 69 ***Perf. 13***

AR18 PF2 1p lilac 35.00 29.00
AR19 PF2 6p brown 175.00 87.50
AR20 PF2 1sh green 200.00 105.00
AR21 PF2 2sh blue 325.00 140.00
AR22 PF2 2sh 6p vermilion 400.00 200.00
AR23 PF2 5sh orange brown 275.00 120.00
AR24 PF2 10sh brown 600.00 *225.00*
AR25 PF2 20sh rose 1,100. *325.00*

Perf. 12

AR26 PF2 1p lilac 35.00 29.00
AR27 PF2 6p brown 175.00 87.50
AR28 PF2 2sh blue 325.00 140.00
AR29 PF2 2sh 6p vermilion 200.00 100.00
AR30 PF2 5sh orange brown 275.00 125.00
AR31 PF2 10sh brown 600.00 *225.00*
AR32 PF2 20sh rose 1,100. *325.00*

Unwmk.

Perf. 13

AR33 PF2 1p lilac 40.00 20.00
AR34 PF2 6p lilac 200.00 100.00
AR35 PF2 6p brown 175.00 77.50
AR36 PF2 1sh green 115.00 47.50
AR37 PF2 2sh blue 140.00 *115.00*
AR38 PF2 2sh 6p vermilion 250.00 125.00
AR39 PF2 5sh orange brown 400.00 140.00
AR40 PF2 10sh brown 650.00 225.00
AR41 PF2 20sh rose 1,100. 325.00

Perf. 12

AR42 PF2 1p lilac 40.00 20.00
AR43 PF2 6p lilac 200.00 100.00
AR44 PF2 6p brown 175.00 77.50
AR45 PF2 1sh green 115.00 47.50
AR46 PF2 2sh blue 140.00 115.00
AR47 PF2 2sh 6p vermilion 250.00 125.00
AR48 PF2 5sh orange brown 400.00 140.00
AR49 PF2 10sh brown 650.00 225.00
AR50 PF2 20sh rose 1,100. 325.00

Queen Victoria — PF3

1878-79 Engr. Unwmk. ***Perf. 12***

AR51 PF3 1p violet 275.00 140.00

Wmk. 68

AR52 PF3 1p violet 175.00 105.00

SEMI-POSTAL STAMPS

Queen Victoria, Colors and Bearers — SP1

SP2

Perf. 12, 12½

1900, June 19 Wmk. 68

B1 SP1 1p red lilac 225.00 200.00
B2 SP2 2p deep violet 600.00 525.00

These stamps were sold at 1sh and 2sh respectively. The difference was applied to a patriotic fund in connection with the Boer War.

REGISTRATION STAMPS

R1

Clean-Cut Perf. 14 to 16

1861 Wmk. 5 Engr.

F1 R1 (6p) olive yellow 675.00 125.00
a. Horiz. pair, imperf. vert. *8,000.*

Rough Perf. 14 to 16

F2 R1 (6p) dull yellow 110.00 72.50

1864 ***Perf. 12½ to 13***

F3 R1 (6p) golden yellow 125.00 50.00
a. Imperf.
b. Double impression 2,750. 2,750.

The reprints are watermarked with a small truncated star and perforated 12.

SOUTH AUSTRALIA

'sauth o-'strāl-yə

LOCATION — Central part of southern Australia
GOVT. — British Colony
AREA — 380,070 sq. mi.
POP. — 358,346 (1901)
CAPITAL — Adelaide

South Australia was one of the six British colonies that united in 1901 to form the Commonwealth of Australia.

12 Pence = 1 Shilling
20 Shillings = 1 Pound

Values for unused stamps are for examples with original gum as defined in the catalogue introduction.

Very fine examples of Nos. 10-60 and O1-O60 will have perforations slightly cutting into the framelines or design on one or more sides due to the narrow spacing of the stamps on the plates.

Stamps with perfs clear on all sides are scarce to rare and will command higher to substantially higher prices.

Watermarks

Wmk. 6 — Star with Long Narrow Points

Wmk. 7 — Star with Short Broad Points

Wmk. 70 — Crown and V

Wmk. 72 — Crown and SA

Wmk. 73 — Crown and SA, Letters Close

Wmk. 74 — Crown and Single-lined A

Queen Victoria — A1

1855-56 Engr. Wmk. 6 ***Imperf.***
London Print

1 A1 1p dark green 7,500. 525.
2 A1 2p dull carmine 750. 100.
3 A1 6p deep blue 2,800. 200.
4 A1 1sh violet ('56) *15,000.*

1856-59 Local Print

5 A1 1p deep yel grn ('58) *10,000.* 675.00
a. 1p yellow green ('58) *8,500.* 800.00
6 A1 2p blood red 2,250. 90.00
a. Printed on both sides *1,100.*
b. 2p orange red ('56) 2,250. 97.50
7 A1 2p pale red ('57) 800. 55.00
a. Printed on both sides *900.00*
8 A1 6p slate blue ('57) 3,750. 210.00
9 A1 1sh orange ('57) 7,500. 500.00
a. Printed on both sides — —
b. 1sh red orange — 625.00

1858-59 ***Rouletted***

10 A1 1p yellow grn ('59) 1,150. 110.00
a. Horiz. pair, imperf. between — —
b. 1p pale yellow green ('59) 1,150. 115.00
11 A1 2p pale red ('59) 180.00 37.50
a. Printed on both sides *1,150.*
12 A1 6p slate blue 650.00 70.00
13 A1 1sh orange ('59) 1,500. 55.00
c. Printed on both sides *1,600.*

See Nos. 14-16, 19-20, 25-26, 28-29, 32, 35-36, 41-43, 47, 51-52, 69-70, 73, 113, 118. For overprints see Nos. O1-O2, O5, O7, O9, O11-O13, O17, O20, O27, O30, O32, O39-O40, O42, O52, O76, O85.

A2

A3

Surcharge on #22-24, 34, 49-50

1860-69 ***Rouletted***

14 A1 1p dull blue green 100.00 57.50
a. 1p deep green 525.00 92.50
b. 1p bright green 110.00 47.50
15 A1 1p sage green 130.00 57.50
16 A1 2p vermilion ('62) 120.00 7.25
a. Horiz. pair, imperf. btwn. 3,100. 650.00
b. Rouletted and perf. all around *2,100.* *550.00*
d. As "c," printed on both sides — 750.00
18 A2 4p dull violet ('67) 130.00 40.00
19 A1 6p grnsh bl ('63) 140.00 7.25
20 A1 6p dull blue 200.00 11.50
a. 6p sky blue 200.00 11.50
b. 6p Prussian blue 1,100. 90.00
c. Horiz. pair, imperf btwn. *2,000.*
d. 6p ultramarine 140.00 7.25
e. Horiz. pair, imperf. btwn. (#20f) — *1,600.*
f. 6p indigo blue — 100.00
g. Rouletted and perf. all around (#20f) *575.00*
21 A3 9p gray lilac ('69) 100.00 16.00
a. Double impression —
b. Horiz. pair, imperf between 2,500.
c. Rouletted and perf. all around *2,150.* *250.00*
22 A3 10p on 9p red org (Bl) ('66) 350.00 62.50
23 A3 10p on 9p yel (Bl) ('67) 625.00 47.50
24 A3 10p on 9p yel (Blk) ('69) 2,800. 72.50
a. Inverted surcharge — *5,000.*
c. Printed on both sides — *1,250.*
d. Rouletted x perf. 10 —
24E A1 1sh yellow ('61) 900.00 52.50
f. Vert. pair, imperf. btwn. — 2,700.
25 A1 1sh lake brn ('65) 200.00 21.50
a. Horiz. pair, imperf. btwn. — *1,300.*
26 A1 1sh brown ('63) 275.00 35.00
a. 1sh chestnut ('64) 290.00 16.00
27 A2 2sh carmine ('67) 350.00 52.50
a. Vert. pair, imperf. btwn. *1,600.*

There are six varieties of the surcharge "TEN PENCE" in this and subsequent issues.

Nos. 16b, 20g, 21c, 28a, 32c, 33a are rouletted remainders that were later perforated.

See Nos. 31, 33, 46, 48, 53, 63, 68, 72, 74, 112, 113B, 119-120. For surcharges & overprints see Nos. 34, 44-45, 49-50, 59, 67, 71, O4, O6, O8, O10, O16-O19, O18, O21, O26, O28-O29, O31, O33, O36-O38, O41, O41B, O43, O53. Compare with design A6a.

1867-72 ***Perf. 11½ to 12½xRoulette***

28 A1 1p blue green 475.00 77.50
a. Rouletted and perf. all around 975.00
29a A1 1p bright green 345.00 45.00
31 A2 4p dull violet ('68) 2,250. 185.00
a. 4p purple ('69) — 185.00
32 A1 6p Prus blue 750.00 35.00
a. 6p sky blue 900.00 35.00
b. Printed on both sides — —
c. Rouletted and perf. all around — *475.00*
d. 6p indigo blue ('69) 1,000. 47.50
33 A3 9p gray lilac ('72) — *525.00*
34 A3 10p on 9p yel (Bl) ('68) 975.00 62.50
a. Printed on both sides — *1,100.*
35 A1 1sh chestnut ('68) 475.00 32.50
36 A1 1sh lake brown ('69) 475.00 35.00
a. Rouletted and perf. all around — —

Nos. 44-45 Surcharged

Perf. 10, 11½, 12½ and Compond

1867-74

41 A1 1p yellow green 130.00 40.00
42 A1 1p blue green 140.00 40.00
a. Printed on both sides
b. Horiz. pair, imperf between 2,400.
43 A1 2p vermilion 1,250.
44 A2 3p on 4p sky blue (Blk) ('70) 550.00 22.50
a. 3p on 4p ultra, black surcharge 140.00 16.00
b. Surcharge omitted *30,000.* *15,000.*
c. Double surcharge 4,500.
d. Surcharged on both sides 3,500.
45 A2 3p on 4p sl bl (Red) ('70) 1,050. 160.00
46 A2 4p dull violet 115.00 14.00
47 A1 6p Prussian blue 200.00 10.00
a. 6p sky blue 450.00 15.00
b. Imperf. vert., pair —
48 A3 9p red lilac ('72) 100.00 14.00
a. 9p violet 200.00 14.00
b. 9p red violet 200.00 11.50
c. Printed on both sides 925.00
49 A3 10p on 9p yel (Bl) ('68) *1,600.* 50.00
50 A3 10p on 9p yel (Blk) ('69) 350.00 55.00
51 A1 1sh deep brown 185.00 21.00
52 A1 1sh red brown 155.00 21.00
a. 1sh chestnut 225.00 29.00
53 A2 2sh carmine 125.00 18.00
a. Printed on both sides 700.00
b. Horiz. pair, imperf. vert. —

See Nos. 67, O14, O28, O36.

A6

A6a

1868 Typo. Wmk. 72 ***Rouletted***

54 A6a 2p orange red 125.00 4.00
a. Imperf.
b. Printed on both sides 725.00
c. Horiz. pair, imperf. btwn. 1,100.

1869 ***Perf. 11½ to 12½xRoulette***

55 A6a 2p orange red 250.00

1870 ***Perf. 10xRoulette***

56 A6a 2p orange red 700.00 47.50

Perf. 10, 11½, 12½ and Compound

1868-75

57 A6 1p bl grn ('75) 82.50 10.00
58 A6a 2p orange red 22.50 1.90
a. Printed on both sides 575.00
b. Horiz. pair, imperf. vert.

Engr.

59 A3 10p on 9p yel (Bl) *1,550.*

1869 Typo. Wmk. 6 ***Rouletted***

60 A6a 2p orange red 140.00 32.50
a. Imperf.
b. Printed on both sides

Perf. 11½ to 12½xRoulette

61 A6a 2p orange red *2,500.* 125.00

Perf. 11½ to 12½

61B A6a 2p orange red — *1,350.*

See Nos. 62, 64-66, 97-98, 105-106, 115-116, 133-134, 145-146. For surcharges & overprints see Nos. 75, O3, O22-O25, O34-O35, O44-O47, O49, O55-O56, O62-O63, O68-O69, O74, O78-O79.

1871 Wmk. 70 ***Perf. 10***

62 A6a 2p orange red 140.00 40.00

Engr.

63 A2 4p dull violet 3,750. 325.00
a. Printed on both sides *4,500.*

Examples of the 4p from edge of sheet sometimes lack watermark.

Perf. 10, 11½, 12½ and Compound

1876-80 Typo. Wmk. 73

64 A6 1p green 27.50 .95
65 A6a 2p orange 29.00 .70
66 A6a 2p blood red ('80) 325.00 7.75
Nos. 64-66 (3) 381.50 9.40

See Nos. 97-98, 105-106, 115-116, 133-134, 145-146.

No. 71

No. 75

1876-84 Engr. Wmk. 7

67 A2 3p on 4p ultra (Blk) 140.00 35.00
a. 3p on 4p deep blue 140.00 22.50
b. Double surcharge *1,850.*
68 A2 4p reddish violet 110.00 10.00
a. 4p dull violet 110.00 12.00
69 A1 6p deep blue 130.00 7.00
a. Horiz. pair, imperf. between —
b. Imperf.
70 A1 6p pale ultra ('84) 95.00 3.75
71 A3 8p on 9p bister brn 160.00 12.00
a. 8p on 9p yellow brown 140.00 12.00
b. 8p on 9p gray brown ('80) 130.00 12.00
d. Double surcharge 1,950.
e. Vert. pair, imperf between 1,850.
72 A3 9p rose lilac 20.00 5.75
a. Printed on both sides 700.00
73 A1 1sh red brown 72.50 4.50
a. 1sh brown 92.50 6.00
c. As "b," horiz. pair, imperf. btwn. 400.00
74 A2 2sh carmine 70.00 9.25
a. Horiz. pair, imperf. vert. *2,000.*
b. Imperf., pair

For overprint see No. O41.

1882 Wmk. 73 ***Perf. 10***
Black Surcharge

75 A6 ½p on 1p green 22.50 15.00

A9

A10

A11

A12

Perf. 10, 11½, 12½ and Compound

1883-93 **Typo.**

76 A9 ½p chocolate brown 11.50 2.50
a. ½p red brown ('89) 7.50 2.25
b. ½p bister brown 6.25 2.25
78 A10 3p deep green ('93) 17.00 4.75
a. 3p olive green ('90) 24.00 4.75
b. 3p sage green ('86) 24.00 3.25
79 A11 4p violet ('90) 37.50 4.50
80 A12 6p pale blue ('87) 37.50 3.50
Nos. 76-80 (4) 103.50 15.25

See Nos. 96, 100-101, 104, 108-109, 111. For surcharges & overprints see Nos. 94-95, 99, O48, O50-O51, O54, O57-O61, O64, O66-O67, O71, O73, O75, O81-O82.

A13

1886-96 ***Perf. 10, 11½ to 12½***

81 A13 2sh6p violet 67.50 12.50
82 A13 5sh rose 85.00 22.50
83 A13 10sh green 210.00 60.00
84 A13 15sh buff 675.00 225.00
85 A13 £1 blue 475.00 160.00
86 A13 £2 red brown 2,500. 475.00
87 A13 50sh rose red 3,250. 550.00
88 A13 £3 olive green 3,500. 550.00
89 A13 £4 lemon 5,750. 1,000.
90 A13 £5 gray *6,000.*
90A A13 £5 brown ('96) *4,300.* 1,000.
91 A13 £10 bronze *5,000.* *1,100.*
92 A13 £15 silver *19,000.* 1,850.
93 A13 £20 lilac *22,000.* 2,000.

For overprints see Nos. O83-O84.

#94, 99

#95

Perf. 10, 11½x12½ and Compound

1891 **Brown Surcharge**

94 A11 2½p on 4p green 14.00 4.00
a. "½" nearer the "2" 47.50 35.00
b. Pair, imperf. between 2,150.
c. Fraction bar omitted 175.00 130.00

Carmine Surcharge

95 A12 5p on 6p red brn 24.00 9.25
a. No period after "D" 300.00

See No. 99. For overprints see Nos. O48, O57, O59.

Many stamps of the issues of 1855-91 have been reprinted; they are all on paper watermarked Crown and SA, letters wide apart, and are overprinted "REPRINT."

1893 **Typo.** ***Perf. 15***

96 A9 ½p brown 9.50 2.00
a. Horiz. pair, imperf. btwn 290.00
b. Pair, perf. 12 btwn; perf. 15 around 350.00 87.50
97 A6 1p green 24.00 2.00
98 A6a 2p orange 22.50 1.40
a. Vert. pair, imperf. between 700.00
99 A11 2½p on 4p green 42.50 5.25
a. "½" nearer the "2" 110.00 42.50
b. Fraction bar omitted

100 A11 4p gray violet 35.00 4.75
101 A12 6p blue 72.50 6.25
Nos. 96-101 (6) 206.00 21.65

Kangaroo, Palm — A16

Coat of Arms — A17

1894, Mar. 1

102 A16 2½p blue violet 42.50 4.75
103 A17 5p dull violet 37.50 4.75

See Nos. 107, 110, 117, 135-136, 147, 151. For overprints see Nos. O65, O70, O72, O80.

1895-97 ***Perf. 13***

104 A9 ½p pale brown 5.25 .60
105 A6 1p green 14.00 .70
a. Vert. pair, imperf. between
106 A6a 2p orange 11.50 .35
107 A16 2½p blue violet 35.00 1.60
108 A10 3p olive green ('97) 12.00 3.50
109 A11 4p bright violet 11.50 1.00
110 A17 5p dull violet 13.00 2.00
111 A12 6p blue 14.00 2.75
Nos. 104-111 (8) 116.25 12.50

Some authorities regard the so-called redrawn 1p stamps with thicker lettering (said to have been issued in 1897) as impressions from a new or cleaned plate.

Perf. 11½, 12½, Clean-Cut, Compound

1896 **Engr.** **Wmk. 7**

112 A3 9p lilac rose 18.00 8.75
113 A1 1sh dark brown 45.00 7.50
a. Horiz. pair, imperf. vert. 350.00
c. Vert. pair, imperf. btwn. 475.00
113B A2 2sh carmine 57.50 12.00
Nos. 112-113B (3) 120.50 28.25

Adelaide Post Office — A18

1899 **Typo.** **Wmk. 73** ***Perf. 13***

114 A18 ½p yellow green 5.25 1.25
115 A6 1p carmine 9.00 .70
a. 1p scarlet 7.75 .85
116 A6a 2p purple 7.55 .40
117 A16 2½p dark blue 11.50 3.50
Nos. 114-117 (4) 33.30 5.85

See Nos. 132, 144. For overprint see No. O77.

Perf. 11½, 12½

1901 **Engr.** **Wmk. 72**

118 A1 1sh dark brown 40.00 18.00
a. 1sh red brown 45.00 25.00
b. Horiz. pair, imperf. vert.
119 A2 2sh carmine 45.00 17.50

1902

120 A3 9p magenta 25.00 25.00

A19

A20

Perf. 11½, 12½ and Compound

1902-03 **Typo.** **Wmk. 73**

121 A19 3p olive green 12.00 2.75
a. 3p olive grn (20mm), perf 12 24.00 3.50
b. Wmk sideways *1,900.*
122 A19 4p red org 20.00 3.50
123 A19 6p blue green 14.00 2.60
124 A19 8p ultra (value 19mm long) 15.00 13.00
124A A19 8p ultra (value 16½mm long) ('03) 18.00 15.00
b. "EIGNT" 2,000. *3,000.*
125 A19 9p claret 15.00 8.75
a. Vert. pair, imperf. between 1,750.
b. Horiz. pair, imperf. between
126 A19 10p org buff 22.50 14.00
127 A19 1sh brn ('03) 30.00 8.75
a. Horiz. pair, imperf. btwn.
b. Vert. pair, imperf. btwn. 1,850.
c. "Postage" and denomination in red brown 1,100. 1,000.
128 A19 2sh6p purple 37.50 24.00
a. 2sh6p pale violet 72.50 45.00
129 A19 5sh rose 130.00 82.50
130 A19 10sh grn ('03) 180.00 130.00
131 A19 £1 blue 525.00 290.00
Nos. 121-131 (12) 1,019. 594.85

1904 ***Perf. 12x11½***

132 A18 ½p yellow green 7.50 2.40
133 A6 1p rose 11.50 .85
134 A6a 2p purple 12.00 1.40
135 A16 2½p dark blue 15.00 4.50
136 A17 5p dull violet 25.00 3.75
Nos. 132-136 (5) 71.00 12.90

1904-08 ***Perf. 12 and 12x11½***

137 A20 6p blue green 27.50 5.75
a. Vert. pair, imperf. between *4,250.*
138 A20 8p ultra ('06) 17.50 15.00
139 A20 9p claret 25.00 9.00
139A A20 10p org buff ('07) 30.00 24.00
b. Vert. pair, imperf. between 3,750.
c. Horiz. pair, imperf. between 2,000. 1,850.
140 A20 1sh brown 35.00 5.75
a. Vert. pair, imperf between 1,750.
b. Horiz. pair, imperf between 2,000.
141 A20 2sh6p purple ('05) 110.00 32.50
142 A20 5sh scarlet 100.00 60.00
142B A20 10sh green ('08) 225.00 *260.00*
143 A20 £1 deep blue 350.00 200.00
Nos. 137-143 (9) 920.00 612.00

See Nos. 148-150, 152-157.

1906-12 **Wmk. 74**

144 A18 ½p green 10.50 1.60
145 A6 1p carmine 9.25 .60
146 A6a 2p purple 8.75 .60
a. Horiz. pair, imperf. between 2,500.
147 A16 2½p dk blue ('11) 17.50 11.50
148 A20 3p ol grn (value 19mm long) 22.50 6.25
a. Horiz. pair, imperf. between *5,500.*
149 A20 3p ol grn (value 17mm long) ('09) 13.00 6.25
150 A20 4p red orange 18.00 4.75
151 A17 5p dull vio ('08) 30.00 7.25
152 A20 6p blue grn ('07) 14.00 4.75
a. Vert. pair, imperf. between 1,850. 1,750.
153 A20 8p ultra ('09) 20.00 *22.50*
154 A20 9p claret 20.00 8.75
a. Vert. pair, imperf. between 1,600.
b. Horiz. pair, imperf. between 4,250.
155 A20 1sh brown 21.00 9.00
a. Horiz. pair, imperf. between 3,100.
b. Vert. pair, imperf. between 2,500.
156 A20 2sh6p purple ('09) 105.00 25.00
157 A20 5sh lt red ('12) 140.00 105.00
Nos. 144-157 (14) 449.50 213.80

OFFICIAL STAMPS

For Departments
Regular Issues Overprinted in Red, Black or Blue:

A. (Architect), A. G. (Attorney General), A. O. (Audit Office), B. D. (Barracks Department), B. G. (Botanical Gardens), B. M. (Bench of Magistrates), C. (Customs), C. D. (Convict Department), C. L. (Crown Lands), C. O. (Commissariat Officer), C. S. (Chief Secretary), C. Sgn. (Colonial Surgeon), C. P. (Commissioner of Police), C. T. (Commissioner of Titles), D. B. (Destitute Board), D. R. (Deed Registry), E. (Engineer), E. B. (Education Board),

G. P. (Government Printer), G. S. (Government Storekeeper), G. T. (Goolwa Tramway), G. F. (Gold Fields), H. (Hospital), H. A. (House of Assembly), I. A. (Immigration Agent), I. E. (Intestate Estates), I. S. (Inspector of Sheep), L. A. (Lunatic Asylum), L. C. (Legislative Council), L. L. (Legislative Library), L. T. (Land Titles), M. (Military), M. B. (Marine Board), M. R. (Manager of Railways), M. R. G. (Main Roads Gambierton), N. T. (Northern Territory),

O. A. (Official Assignee), P. (Police), P. A. (Protector of Aborigines), P. O. (Post Office), P. S. (Private Secretary), P. W. (Public Works), R. B. (Road Board), R. G. (Registrar General of Births, &c.), S. (Sheriff), S. C. (Supreme Court), S.G. (Surveyor General), S. M. (Stipendiary Magistrate), S. T. (Superintendent of Telegraph), T. (Treasurer), T. R. (Titles Registry), V. (Volunteers), V. A. (Valuator), V. N. (Vaccination), W. (Waterworks).

1868-74 **Wmk. 6** ***Rouletted***

O1 A1 1p green *350.00*
O2 A1 2p pale red *275.00*
O3 A6a 2p vermilion *120.00*
O4 A2 4p dull violet *275.00*
O5 A1 6p slate blue *275.00*
O6 A3 9p gray lilac *500.00*
O7 A1 1sh brown *275.00*
O8 A2 2sh carmine *275.00*

Perf. 11½ to 12½ x Roulette

O9 A1 1p green *275.00*
O10 A2 4p dull violet *850.00*
O11 A1 6p blue *210.00*
O12 A1 1sh brown *200.00*

Perf. 10, 11½, 12½ and Compound

O13 A1 1p green *160.00*
O14 A2 3p on 4p slate blue (Red) *750.00*
O15 A2 3p on 4p slate blue (Blk) *275.00*
O16 A2 4p dull violet *200.00*
O17 A1 6p deep blue *275.00*
O18 A3 9p violet *500.00*
O19 A3 10p on 9p yellow (Blk) *500.00*
O20 A1 1sh brown *140.00* *160.00*
O21 A2 2sh carmine *100.00*

Rouletted
Wmk. 72

O22 A6a 2p orange *120.00*

Perf. 11 ½ x Roulette

O23 A6a 2p orange *160.00*
a. Perf 10 x Roulette *275.00*

Perf. 10, 11½, 12½ and Compound

O24 A6a 2p orange *22.50*

Wmk. 70
Perf. 10

O25 A6a 2p orange *110.00*
O26 A2 4p dull violet *275.00*

For General Use

Overprinted in Black

Perf. 10, 11½, 12½ and Compound

1874 **Wmk. 6**

O27 A1 1p green — *400.00*
a. 1p dp yel green, perf 11½-12½x10 2,500. *400.00*
b. As "a," printed on both sides 1,100.
O28 A2 3p on 4p ultra 6,750. 2,150.
a. No period after "S" 3,000.
O29 A2 4p dull violet 92.50 17.50
a. Inverted overprint
b. No period after "S" 62.50
c. Perf. 11½-12½x10 2,000. 400.00
O30 A1 6p deep blue 175.00 24.00
a. No period after "S" 95.00
b. 6p Prussian blue, perf 11½-12½x10 130.00 15.00
O31 A3 9p violet 3,000. 1,200.
a. No period after "S" 4,000. 1,750.
O32 A1 1sh red brown 130.00 16.00
a. Double overprint 225.00
b. No period after "S" 350.00 95.00
O33 A2 2sh carmine 275.00 30.00
a. Double overprint
b. No period after "S" 125.00
c. 2sh carmine, perf 11½-12½x10 175.00

1874-75 **Wmk. 72**

O34 A6 1p blue green 175.00 42.50
a. Inverted overprint
O35 A6a 2p orange 40.00 6.00

1876-86 **Wmk. 7**

O37	A2	4p dull violet	130.00	12.00
O38	A2	4p reddish vio	57.50	5.25
a.		Double overprint		
b.		Inverted overprint		225.00
c.		Dbl. ovpt., one inverted		
O39	A1	6p dark blue	1,350.	10.00
a.		Double overprint		140.00
b.		Inverted overprint		
O40	A1	6p ultramarine	130.00	8.75
a.		Double overprint		
b.		Inverted overprint		
O41B	A3	9p violet	*7,500.*	
O42	A1	1sh red brown	70.00	14.00
a.		Inverted overprint	625.00	180.00
b.		Double overprint		
O43	A2	2sh carmine	225.00	15.00
a.		Double overprint		225.00
b.		Inverted overprint		250.00
c.		No period after "S"		175.00

1880-91 **Wmk. 73**

O44	A6	1p blue green	27.50	2.00
a.		Inverted overprint		95.00
b.		Double overprint	130.00	85.00
c.		Dbl. ovpt., one inverted		*750.00*
O45	A6	1p yellow green	35.00	2.00
O46	A6a	2p orange	17.00	2.00
a.		Inverted overprint		42.50
b.		Double overprint	130.00	62.50
c.		Overprinted sideways		
d.		Dbl. ovpt., one inverted		
e.		Dbl. ovpt., both inverted		240.00
O47	A6a	2p blood red	110.00	22.50
O48	A11	2½p on 4p green	130.00	14.00
a.		"½" nearer the "2"		100.00
b.		Double overprint		
c.		Pair, one without ovpt.		
		Nos. O44-O48 (5)	319.50	42.50

1882-90 ***Perf. 10***

O49	A6	½p on 1p green	130.00	30.00
a.		Inverted overprint		
O50	A11	4p violet	135.00	9.25
O51	A12	6p blue	37.50	2.40
a.		Double overprint		
b.		No period after "S"		
		Nos. O49-O51 (3)	302.50	41.65

Overprinted in Black

Perf. 10, 11½, 12½ and Compound

1891 **Wmk. 7**

O52	A1	1sh red brown	70.00	10.50
a.		No period after "S"		115.00
b.		1sh lake brown, perf 11½-12½	105.00	27.50
O53	A2	2sh carmine	140.00	20.00
a.		Double overprint		
b.		No period after "S"		

1891-95 **Wmk. 73**

O54	A9	½p brown	40.00	10.50
a.		No period after "S"	87.50	52.50
O55	A6	1p blue green	45.00	3.75
a.		Double overprint	140.00	77.50
b.		No period after "S"	75.00	17.50
O56	A6a	2p orange	42.50	3.25
a.		No period after "S"		45.00
O57	A11	2½p on 4p green	77.50	25.00
a.		"½" nearer the "2"	175.00	57.50
b.		Inverted overprint	400.00	
O58	A11	4p violet	92.50	6.50
a.		Double overprint		
O59	A12	5p on 6p red brn	80.00	35.00
O60	A12	6p blue	40.00	4.50
a.		Double overprint		
b.		No period after "S"		
		Nos. O54-O60 (7)	417.50	88.50

1893 ***Perf. 15***

O61	A9	½p brown	77.50	18.00
O62	A6	1p green	24.00	2.40
O63	A6a	2p orange	27.50	.85
a.		Inverted overprint		40.00
b.		Double overprint		57.50
O64	A11	4p gray violet	115.00	8.75
a.		Double overprint	375.00	77.50
O65	A17	5p dull violet	125.00	22.50
O66	A12	6p blue	52.50	5.75
		Nos. O61-O66 (6)	421.50	58.25

1896 ***Perf. 13***

O67	A9	½p brown	40.00	11.50
a.		Triple overprint	375.00	
O68	A6	1p green	42.50	1.10
a.		No period after "S"	125.00	18.00
O69	A6a	2p orange	42.50	1.10
a.		No period after "S"	115.00	18.00
O70	A16	2½p blue violet	75.00	9.50
a.		No period after "S"		70.00
O71	A11	4p brt violet	100.00	5.75
a.		Double overprint	300.00	57.50
b.		No period after "S"	300.00	42.50
O72	A17	5p dull violet	130.00	27.50
a.		No period after "S"		
O73	A12	6p blue	62.50	3.75
a.		No period after "S"	180.00	105.00
		Nos. O67-O73 (7)	492.50	60.20

On No. O67a, one overprint is upright, two sideways.

Same Overprint in Dark Blue

1891-95 ***Perf. 10***

O74	A6	1p green	375.00	1,100.
O75	A12	6p blue		

Black Overprint

Perf. 11½, 12½, Clean-Cut

1897 **Wmk. 7**

O76	A1	1sh brown	62.50	11.00
a.		Double overprint		
b.		No period after "S"		375.00

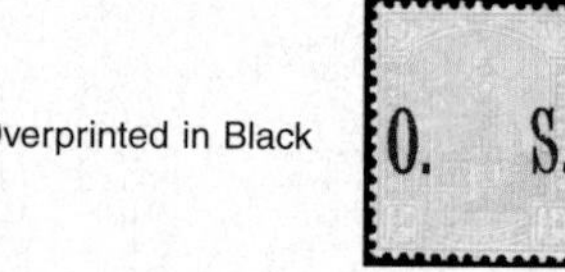

Overprinted in Black

1900 **Wmk. 73** ***Perf. 13***

O77	A18	½p yellow green	22.50	11.50
a.		Inverted overprint	110.00	
b.		No period after "S"	62.50	
c.		As "b," inverted overprint		—
O78	A6	1p carmine rose	27.50	2.25
a.		Inverted overprint	115.00	72.50
b.		Double overprint		475.00
c.		No period after "S"	82.50	22.50
O79	A6a	2p purple	35.00	1.40
a.		Inverted ovpt.	95.00	72.50
b.		No period after "S"	77.50	21.00
O80	A16	2½p dark blue	105.00	35.00
a.		Inverted overprint		140.00
b.		No period after "S"	225.00	
O81	A11	4p violet	92.50	10.50
a.		Inverted overprint	325.00	
b.		No period after "S"	200.00	
O82	A12	6p blue	42.50	10.50
a.		No period after "S"	110.00	
		Nos. O77-O82 (6)	325.00	71.15

1901 ***Perf. 10***

O83	A13	2sh6p violet	*6,000.*	*5,000.*
O84	A13	5sh rose	*6,000.*	*5,000.*

On Nos. O77-O82 the letters "O.S." are 11½mm apart; on Nos. O83-O84, 14½mm apart.

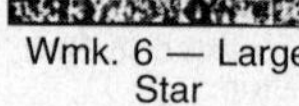
Overprinted in Black

1903 **Wmk. 72** ***Perf. 11½, 12½***

O85	A1	1sh red brown	105.00	27.50

TASMANIA

taz-ˈmā-nē-ə

LOCATION — An island off the south-eastern coast of Australia
GOVT. — British Colony
AREA — 26,215 sq. mi.
POP. — 172,475 (1901)
CAPITAL — Hobart

Tasmania was one of the six British colonies that united in 1901 to form the Commonwealth of Australia. The island was originally named Van Diemen's Land by its discoverer, Abel Tasman, the present name having been adopted in 1853. Stamps of Australia are now used.

12 Pence = 1 Shilling
20 Shillings = 1 Pound

Watermarks

Wmk. 6 — Large Star

Wmk. 49 Double-lined Numeral

Wmk. 75 Double-lined Numeral

Wmk. 50 Single-lined "2"

Wmk. 51 Single-lined "4"

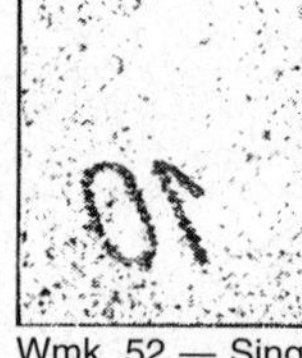
Wmk. 52 — Single-lined "10"

Wmk. 70 — V and Crown

Wmk. 13 — Crown & Double-lined A

Wmk. 76 — TAS

Wmk. 77 — TAS

Wmk. 78 — Multiple TAS

Values for unused stamps are for examples with original gum as defined in the catalogue introduction except for Nos. 1-2b and 10 which are valued without gum as few examples exist with any remaining original gum. Very fine examples of Nos. 17-75a will have perforations touching the design on one or more sides due to the narrow spacing of the stamps on the plates. Stamps with perfs clear of the design on all four sides are scarce and command higher prices.

Queen Victoria
A1 A2

Unwmk.

1853, Nov. 1 **Engr.** ***Imperf.***

1a	A1	1p blue, blurred impression, hard paper	7,500.	1,200.
2	A2	4p red orange	3,750.	550.00
a.		4p yellow orange	3,500.	450.00
		Cut to shape		25.00

Twenty-four varieties of each.

The 4p on vertically laid paper is believed to be a proof. Value, unused, $7,500.

The reprints are made from defaced plates and show marks across the face of each stamp. They are on thin and thick, unwatermarked paper and thin cardboard; only the first are perforated. Nearly all the reprints of Tasmania may be found with and without the overprint "REPRINT."

Nos. 1-47A with pen or revenue cancellations sell for a small fraction of the price of postally used examples. Stamps are found with pen cancellation removed.

Queen Victoria — A3

1855 **Wmk. 6** **Wove Paper**

4	A3	1p dark carmine	9,000.	1,000.
5	A3	2p green	4,000.	550.00
a.		2p deep green	4,000.	625.00
6	A3	4p deep blue	3,250.	125.00

1856-57 **Unwmk.**

7	A3	1p pale red	10,500.	750.00
8	A3	2p emerald ('57)	13,000.	1,100.
9	A3	4p blue ('57)	1,700.	135.00

1856 **Pelure Paper**

10	A3	1p brown red	7,250.	925.00

1857-69 **Wmk. 49, 75**

11	A3	1p carmine ('67)	180.00	72.50
a.		1p orange red ('65)	325.00	57.50
b.		1p brown red	650.00	52.50
c.		Double impression	860.00	300.00
e.		Wmk. 50 (error) ('69)		—
12	A3	2p sage green ('60)	275.00	115.00
a.		2p yellow green	750.00	160.00
b.		2p green	—	95.00
d.		As "b," double impression		325.00
13	A3	4p pale blue	275.00	42.50
a.		4p blue	290.00	45.00
b.		Printed on both sides		—
d.		As "a," double impression		275.00
		Nos. 11-13 (3)	730.00	230.00

See Nos. 17-19, 23-25, 29-31, 35-37, 39-41, 45-47A.

A4

A4a

1858-67

14	A4	6p gray lilac ('63)	375.00	85.00
a.		6p red violet ('67)	875.00	180.00
b.		Double impression ('63)		450.00
15	A4	6p blue gray ('65)	700.00	135.00
16	A4a	1sh vermilion	675.00	90.00
		Nos. 14-16 (3)	1,750.	310.00

No. 15 watermarked large star was not regularly issued.

Issued: No. 14c, 16, 1/58; No. 14, 4/63; No. 15, 2/65; No. 14a, 4/67.

1864 ***Rouletted***

17	A3	1p carmine	750.00	275.00
a.		1p brick red	—	425.00
18	A3	2p yellow grn	—	1,250.
19	A3	4p blue	—	400.00
21	A4	6p gray lilac	—	475.00
22	A4a	1sh vermilion	—	1,300.

Values for Nos. 17-22 are for stamps showing rouletting on two or three sides. Examples with full roulettes on all four sides are rare.

1864-69 ***Perf. 10***

23	A3	1p brick red	140.00	62.50
a.		1p carmine	125.00	55.00
b.		1p orange red	140.00	45.00
c.		As "b," double impression		—
24	A3	2p yellow green	800.00	225.00
a.		2p sage green	625.00	275.00

No.	Type	Description	Unused	Used
25	A3	4p blue	275.00	27.50
a.		Double impression		240.00
26	A4	6p lilac	425.00	40.00
a.		6p red lilac	600.00	140.00
27	A4	6p slate blue	650.00	125.00
28	A4a	1sh vermilion	325.00	40.00
a.		Horiz. pair, imperf. vert.		
		Nos. 23-28 (6)	2,615.	520.00

1864-91 ***Perf. 12, 12½***

No.	Type	Description	Unused	Used
29	A3	1p carmine	130.00	27.50
a.		1p orange red	115.00	40.00
b.		1p brick red	140.00	62.50
c.		Double impression		—
d.		Wmkd. "2"		*2,750.*
		As "d," pen cancel		275.00
30	A3	2p yellow green	400.00	115.00
a.		2p dark green	475.00	240.00
b.		2p sage green	475.00	240.00
31	A3	4p blue	225.00	40.00
a.		4p deep blue	225.00	35.00
b.		4p cobalt blue	—	92.50
32	A4	6p red lilac	130.00	57.50
a.		Horiz. pair, imperf between		—
b.		Vert. pair, imperf between		—
c.		6p violet	260.00	40.00
d.		As "c," Vert. pair, imperf between		—
e.		6p purple ('84)	175.00	57.50
g.		6p dull claret ('91)	45.00	20.00
33	A4	6p slate blue	625.00	175.00
34	A4a	1sh vermilion	325.00	175.00
a.		Double impression	—	325.00
b.		Horiz. pair, imperf. vert.		—

The reprints are on unwatermarked paper, perforated 11½, and on thin cardboard, imperforate and perforated.

Perf. Pin-perf. 5½ to 9½, 13½ to 14½

1867

No.	Type	Description	Unused	Used
35	A3	1p carmine	1,000.	250.00
36	A3	2p yellow green		975.00
37	A3	4p blue		475.00
38	A4	6p gray		450.00
38A	A4	6p red lilac		1,250.
38B	A4a	1sh vermilion		—

Oblique Roulette 14-15

No.	Type	Description	Unused	Used
39	A3	1p carmine		850.00
40	A3	2p yellow green		1,150.
41	A3	4p blue		850.00
42	A4	6p gray		1,450.
43	A4	6p red lilac		—
44	A4a	1sh vermilion		1,800.

1868 ***Serrate Perf. 19***

No.	Type	Description	Unused	Used
45	A3	1p carmine	575.00	200.00
46	A3	2p yellow green		800.00
47	A3	4p blue	1,350.	200.00
47A	A3	6p purple	—	1,150.
47B	A3	1sh vermilion		—

Queen Victoria — A5

1870-71 Typo. Wmk. 50 ***Perf. 11½***

No.	Type	Description	Unused	Used
48	A5	2p blue green	130.00	8.75
a.		Double impression	4,500.	1,750.
b.		Perf. 12	155.00	13.00
c.		2p green	250.00	13.00
d.		As "c," perf. 12	140.00	13.00
e.		As "d," imperf, pair		—

See Nos. 49-75, 98, 108-109.

Wmk. 51

No.	Type	Description	Unused	Used
49	A5	1p rose ('71)	110.00	27.50
a.		Imperf., pair	1,300.	1,300.
50	A5	4p blue	1,100.	525.00

Wmk. 52

No.	Type	Description	Unused	Used
51	A5	1p rose	75.00	17.50
a.		Imperf. pair	1,300.	1,300.
c.		Perf. 11½	1,400.	
52	A5	10p black	42.50	42.50
a.		Imperf. pair	625.00	
b.		Perf. 11½	47.50	47.50

The reprints are on unwatermarked paper. The 4p has also been reprinted on thin cardboard, imperf and perf.

1871-76 Wmk. 76 ***Perf. 11½***

No.	Type	Description	Unused	Used
53	A5	1p rose	14.00	1.90
a.		Imperf.		
c.		Perf. 12	185.00	22.50
53B	A5	1p vermilion ('73)	375.00	130.00
54	A5	2p deep green ('72)	62.50	2.40
a.		2p yellow green	300.00	5.75
b.		2p blue green	57.50	2.25
c.		Imperf. pair		1,700.
d.		2p green, perf. 12	1,050.	260.00
e.		Double impression		
55	A5	3p brown	90.00	6.00
a.		3p purple brown	90.00	7.25
b.		As "a," imperf. pair		1,150.
56	A5	3p red brown ('71)	90.00	7.50
a.		3p indian red	90.00	7.75
b.		Imperf. pair	140.00	
c.		Vert. pair, imperf. horiz.		
d.		Perf. 12	175.00	30.00
57	A5	4p dull yellow ('76)	120.00	32.50
a.		Perf. 12	450.00	32.50
58	A5	9p blue	32.50	14.00
a.		Imperf. pair	450.00	
b.		Perf. 12	52.50	52.50
59	A5	5sh bright violet	450.00	240.00
a.		Imperf.		
b.		Horiz. pair, imperf. vert.		
c.		Perf. 12	650.00	475.00
		Nos. 53-59 (8)	1,234.	434.30

The reprints are on unwatermarked paper, the 5sh has also been reprinted on thin cardboard; all are perforated.

1878 Wmk. 77 ***Perf. 14***

No.	Type	Description	Unused	Used
60	A5	1p rose	7.50	3.00
61	A5	2p deep green	9.00	3.00
62	A5	8p violet brown	30.00	14.00
		Nos. 60-62 (3)	46.50	20.00

The 8p has been reprinted on thin unwatermarked paper, perforated 11½.

1880-83 ***Perf. 12, 11½***

No.	Type	Description	Unused	Used
63	A5	3p indian red, perf. 12	20.00	6.50
a.		Imperf. pair	400.00	
b.		Horiz. pair, imperf. between	1,750.	
c.		Perf. 11½	25.00	7.75
64	A5	4p lem, perf. 11½ ('83)	87.50	42.50
a.		4p olive yellow, perf. 11½	175.00	35.00
b.		Printed on both sides	1,100.	
c.		Imperf.		
d.		4p deep yellow, perf. 12	105.00	20.00

Type of 1871 Surcharged in Black

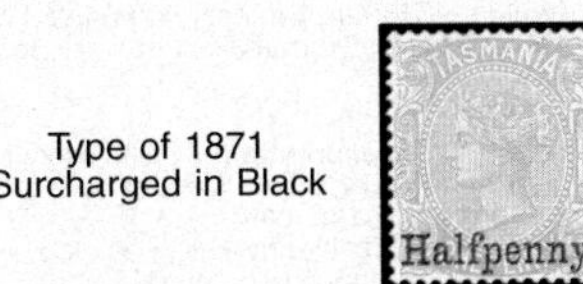

1889 ***Perf. 14***

No.	Type	Description	Unused	Used
65	A5	½p on 1p carmine	27.50	*27.50*
a.		"al" sideways in surcharge	1,450.	*1,200.*

No. 65 has been reprinted on thin cardboard, perforated 12, with the surcharge "Halfpenny" 19mm long.

1889-96 ***Perf. 11½***

No.	Type	Description	Unused	Used
66	A5	½p red orange	5.75	5.25
a.		½p yellow orange	5.75	5.25
b.		Perf. 12	5.25	*7.25*
67	A5	1p dull red	11.50	4.50
a.		1p vermilion	10.50	4.50
68	A5	1p car, perf. 12	25.00	6.00
a.		1p pink, perf. 12	29.00	9.00
b.		1p salmon rose, perf. 12	32.50	7.75
c.		Imperf. pair	350.00	*375.00*

Perf. 12

No.	Type	Description	Unused	Used
69	A5	4p bister ('96)	29.00	20.00
70	A5	9p chalky bl ('96)	15.00	5.75
		Nos. 66-70 (5)	86.25	41.50

1891 Wmk. 76 ***Perf. 11½***

No.	Type	Description	Unused	Used
71	A5	½p orange	57.50	35.00
a.		½p brown orange	45.00	22.50
b.		Imperf. pair	240.00	
c.		Perf. 12	47.50	35.00
72	A5	1p salmon rose	32.50	15.00
a.		1p carmine, perf. 12	40.00	29.00
73	A5	4p ol bis, perf. 12	32.50	21.00
		Nos. 71-73 (3)	122.50	71.00

See Nos. 98, 108-109.

Surcharged in Black

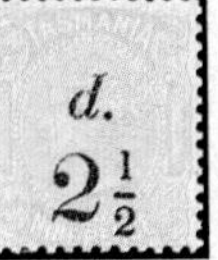

1891 Wmk. 77 ***Perf. 11½***

Surcharge 14mm High

No.	Type	Description	Unused	Used
74	A5	2½p on 9p lt blue	17.50	9.25
a.		Dbl. surcharge, one invtd.	850.00	*950.00*
b.		Imperf. pair		—

Perf. 12

Surcharge 15mm High

No.	Type	Description	Unused	Used
75	A5	2½p on 9p lt blue	8.50	7.75
a.		Surcharged in blue	10.00	6.50

No. 74 has been reprinted on thin unwatermarked paper, imperforate. There is also a reprint on thin cardboard, in deep ultramarine, with surcharge 16½mm high, and perforated 12.

A8

A9

1892-99 Typo. ***Perf. 14***

No.	Type	Description	Unused	Used
76	A8	½p orange & vio	4.25	4.25
77	A9	2½p magenta	7.25	7.25
78	A8	5p pale bl & brn	11.50	7.25
79	A8	6p blue vio & blk	15.00	7.25
80	A8	10p red brn & grn ('99)	29.00	21.00
81	A8	1sh rose & green	15.00	7.25
82	A8	2sh6p brown & blue	47.50	35.00
83	A8	5sh brn vio & red	92.50	42.50
84	A8	10sh brt vio & brn	160.00	115.00
85	A8	£1 green & yel	700.00	450.00
		Nos. 76-85 (10)	1,082.	696.75

No. 80 shows the numeral on white tablet.
See Nos. 99, 110-111.

Lake Marion — A10

Mt. Wellington — A11

View of Hobart — A12

Tasman's Arch — A13

Spring River, Port Davey — A14

Russell Falls — A15

Mt. Gould and Lake St. Clair — A16

Dilston Falls — A17

1899-1900 Engr. Wmk. 78 ***Perf. 14***

No.	Type	Description	Unused	Used
86	A10	½p dark green	16.00	12.00
87	A11	1p carmine	10.50	3.00
88	A12	2p violet	25.00	3.50
89	A13	2½p dark blue	35.00	17.50
90	A14	3p dark brown	18.00	9.00
91	A15	4p ocher	42.50	12.00
92	A16	5p ultramarine	47.50	29.00
93	A17	6p lake	45.00	37.50
		Nos. 86-93 (8)	239.50	123.50

See Nos. 94-97, 102-107, 114-117.

Perf. 11, 12½, 11x12½

1902-03 Litho., Typo. Wmk. 70

No.	Type	Description	Unused	Used
94	A10	½p green	8.00	2.75
95	A11	1p carmine	15.00	2.40
96	A11	1p dull red	22.50	3.00
97	A12	2p violet	14.00	1.40
98	A5	9p blue	15.00	7.25
a.		9p ultramarine	750.00	
b.		9p indigo	240.00	
c.		Perf. 11	15.00	15.00
99	A8	1sh rose & green	32.50	10.50
a.		Perf. 11	75.00	75.00
		Nos. 94-99 (6)	107.00	27.30

Nos. 94, 97 are litho., Nos. 96, 98-99 typo. No. 95 was printed both ways.

No. 78 Surcharged in Black

1904 Wmk. 77 ***Perf. 14***

No.	Type	Description	Unused	Used
100	A8	1½p on 5p blue & brn	2.75	2.75

Perf. 11, 12, 12½ and Compound

1905-08 Typo. Wmk. 13

No.	Type	Description	Unused	Used
102	A10	½p dull green	4.25	.95
a.		Booklet pane of 12		
103	A11	1p carmine	3.50	.60
a.		Booklet pane of 18		
104	A12	2p violet	18.00	.80
105	A14	3p dark brown	15.00	9.00
106	A15	4p ocher	25.00	7.25
107	A17	6p lake	70.00	12.50
108	A5	8p violet brown	35.00	16.00
109	A5	9p blue	130.00	8.00
110	A8	1sh rose & green	24.00	9.25
111	A8	10sh brt vio & brn	325.00	*350.00*
a.		Perf. 11	475.00	475.00
		Nos. 102-111 (10)	649.75	414.35

Nos. 104-107 also printed litho.

1911 **Redrawn**

No.	Type	Description	Unused	Used
114	A12	2p bright violet	15.00	7.50
115	A15	4p dull yellow	72.50	72.50
116	A17	6p lake	35.00	*55.00*
		Nos. 114-116 (3)	122.50	135.00

The redrawn 2p measures 33½x25mm instead of 32½x24½mm. There are many slight changes in the clouds and other parts of the design.

The 4p is much lighter, especially the waterfall and trees above it. This appears to be a new or cleaned plate rather than a redrawn one.

In the redrawn 6p there are more colored lines in the waterfall and the river and more white dots in the trees.

No. 114 Surcharged in Red

1912

No.	Type	Description	Unused	Used
117	A12	1p on 2p bright violet	2.75	2.75

POSTAL FISCAL STAMPS

Authorized for postal use by Act of November 1, 1882. Authorization withdrawn Nov. 30, 1900.

Used values are for examples with postal cancellations used from Nov. 1, 1882 through Nov. 30, 1900.

Beware of stamps with a pen cancellation removed, often regummed or with a fake postmark added.

PF1

PF2

St. George and the Dragon
PF3 PF4

1863-80 Engr. Wmk. 139 ***Imperf.***

AR1 PF1 3p green 450.00 200.00
AR2 PF2 2sh 6p car 450.00 180.00
AR3 PF3 5sh green 525.00 250.00
AR4 PF3 5sh brown 900.00 550.00
AR5 PF4 10sh salmon ('80) 900.00 575.00
a. 10sh orange 1,200. 550.00

For overprint see No. AR32.

Perf. 10

AR6 PF1 3p green 475.00 300.00
AR7 PF2 2sh 6p car 450.00
AR8 PF3 5sh brown 650.00 475.00
AR9 PF4 10sh orange 525.00

Perf. 12

AR10 PF1 3p green 500.00 375.00
AR11 PF2 2sh 6p car 500.00 425.00
AR12 PF3 5sh green 500.00 350.00
AR13 PF3 5sh brown 950.00
AR14 PF4 10sh orange 600.00 375.00

Perf. 12½

AR15 PF1 3p green 800.00
AR16 PF2 2sh 6p car 375.00
AR17 PF3 5sh brown 650.00
AR18 PF4 10sh orange 575.00

Perf. 11½

AR19 PF1 3p green
AR20 PF2 2sh 6p car 750.00 425.00
AR21 PF3 5sh green 300.00 200.00
AR22 PF4 10sh salmon 350.00 300.00
a. 10sh orange 300.00 140.00

Wmk. 77

Perf. 12

AR23 PF2 2sh 6p car 72.50 52.50

For overprint see No. AR33.

Duck-billed Platypus — PF5

1880 Engr. Wmk. 77 ***Perf. 14***

AR24 PF5 1p slate 42.50 12.00
AR25 PF5 3p brown 29.00 7.75
AR26 PF5 6p lilac 140.00 21.00
AR27 PF5 1sh rose 200.00 35.00

For overprints see Nos. AR28-AR31.

Nos. AR24-AR27, AR2, AR23, 85 Overprinted "REVENUE"

1900, Nov. 15

AR28 PF5 1p slate 42.50 42.50
AR29 PF5 3p brown 42.50 45.00
AR30 PF5 6p lilac 300.00 140.00
AR31 PF5 1sh rose 500.00 240.00
AR32 PF2 2sh 6p car (#AR2) 675.00 525.00
AR33 PF2 2sh 6p car (#AR23) 450.00
AR34 PF4 10sh orange 950.00 950.00
AR35 A8 £1 grn & yel (#85) 375.00 350.00

Nos. AR28-AR35 were not supposed to be postally used. Because of imprecise terminology, postal use was tolerated until all postal use of revenues ceased on Nov. 30, 1900.

Other denominations and watermarks were overprinted after postal use was no longer allowed.

VICTORIA

vik-'tōr-ē-ə

LOCATION — In the extreme south-eastern part of Australia
GOVT. — British Colony
AREA — 87,884 sq. mi.
POP. — 1,201,341 (1901)
CAPITAL — Melbourne

Victoria was one of the six former British colonies which united on Jan. 1, 1901, to form the Commonwealth of Australia.

12 Pence = 1 Shilling
20 Shillings = 1 Pound

Unused values for Nos. 1-16 are for stamps without gum as these stamps are seldom found with original gum. Otherwise, unused values are for stamps with original gum as defined in the catalogue introduction.

Very fine examples of all rouletted, perforated and serrate perforated stamps from Nos. 9-109 and F2 will have roulettes, perforations or serrate perforations touching the design. Examples clear on four sides range from scarce to rare and will command higher prices.

Watermarks

Wmk. 6 — Large Star

Wmk. 80

Wmk. 50

Wmk. 80a

Wmk. 81

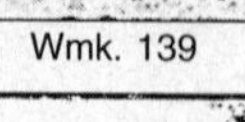
Wmk. 139

Wmk. 49

Wmk. 75

Wmk. 70 — V and Crown

Wmk. 13 — Crown & Double-lined A

Queen Victoria — A1

A1 TYPES

1p:

Type I — "VICTORIA" very close to top of design, with very thin line of color between "VICTORIA" and frameline.

Type II — Thicker line of color between "VICTORIA" and frameline at top.

2p:

Type I — Border, two sets of nine wavy lines crisscrossing. Background, 22 groups of wavy triple lines below "VICTORIA."

Type II — Border, same. Background, 15 groups of wavy triple lines below "VICTORIA."

Type III — Border, two sets of five wavy lines crisscrossing. Background, same as type II.

3p:

Type I — Orb poorly defined, with white area at right and thicker at left. Central band of orb does not protrude at left.

Type II — Orb clearly defined, with white outlines at left and right. Central band of orb protrudes at left.

1850 Litho. Unwmk. ***Imperf.***

1 A1 1p dull red, II 3,750. 225.00
a. 1p dull org ver, II 5,000. 750.00
b. 1p brownish red, II ('51) 1,500. 210.00
c. 1p dull brown, I 19,000. 2,500.
d. 1p orange vermilion, I 30,000. 5,500.
e. 1p orange brown, I 2,100.
2 A1 1p rose, II 3,000. 200.00
a. 1p pink, II 1,750. 190.00
b. 1p reddish brown, II ('51) 5,000. 190.00
3 A1 3p blue, I 6,000. 450.00
a. 3p light blue, II ('52) 2,100. 110.00
b. 3p bright blue, I 7,250. 625.00
4 A1 3p indigo, II 3,000. 100.00
a. 3p pale grnsh blue, II ('52) 3,500. 210.00
Nos. 1-4 (4) 15,750. 975.00

Nos. 1-4 exist with and without frame line.

5 A1 2p lilac, I 7,500. 550.00
a. 2p brn lilac, I 7,000. 550.00
b. 2p orange brown, I 2,500.
6 A1 2p brn lilac, II 2,500. 250.00
a. 2p gray lilac, II 6,000. 200.00
7 A1 2p brn lilac, III 7,250. 200.00
a. 2p gray lilac, III 11,000. 500.00
b. Value omitted, III 17,500.
8 A1 2p yel brn, III 3,000. 200.00

Rouletted 7

9 A1 1p vermilion 3,350.
10 A1 3p blue 2,500. 250.00
a. 3p deep blue 2,500. 300.00

Perf. 12

12 A1 3p blue 2,000. 175.00
a. 3p deep blue 2,000. 175.00

Victoria on Throne — A2

1852 Engr. ***Imperf.***

14 A2 2p reddish brn 400.00 45.00
a. 2p chestnut 175.00
b. 2p purple brown 575.00 30.00

No. 14 was reprinted on paper with watermark 70, imperf. & perf. 12½, overprinted "REPRINT."

1854 Litho.

15 A2 2p gray brown 450.00 45.00
16 A2 2p brown lilac 300.00 40.00
a. 2p red lilac — 37.50
b. As "a," "TVO" for "TWO" 10,000. 1,500.

Fifty varieties.

A3

A4

1854-58 **Typo.**

17 A3 6p yellow orange 375.00 32.50
a. 6p dull orange 375.00 32.50
b. 6p reddish brown 725.00 72.50

See Nos. 19-20, 22-24A, 26-28

Lithographed

18 A4 1sh blue 1,100. 35.00
a. 1sh greenish blue 1,250. 35.00
b. 1sh indigo blue — 180.00

See Nos. 21, 25.

Typographed

19 A3 2sh green 3,000. 250.00

1857-58 ***Rouletted 7, 9½***

20 A3 6p orange — 87.50
a. 6p yellow orange — 100.00
b. 6p reddish brown — 115.00

Lithographed

21 A4 1sh blue — 160.00
a. 1sh greenish blue — 160.00

Typographed

22 A3 2sh green ('58) 7,000. 675.00

Small Serrate Perf. 19

23 A3 6p orange — 125.00

Large Serpentine Perf. 10½

24 A3 6p orange — 125.00

Serrate x Serpentine Perf.

24A A3 6p orange — 200.00

1859 Litho. ***Perf. 12***

25 A4 1sh blue 250.00 25.00
a. 1sh greenish blue 275.00 27.50
b. 1sh indigo blue — 52.50

Typographed

26 A3 2sh green 525.00 70.00

1861 Wmk. "SIX PENCE" (80)

27 A3 6p black 300.00 80.00

Wmk. Single-lined "2" (50)

1864 ***Perf. 12, 13***

28 A3 2sh blue, *green* 350.00 13.00

A5

Wmk. Large Star (6)

1856, Oct. Engr. ***Imperf.***

29 A5 1p green 250.00 42.50

1858 ***Rouletted 5½-6½***

30 A5 6p blue 350.00 28.00
a. 6p light blue 450.00 45.00

Nos. 29 and 30 have been reprinted on paper watermarked V and Crown. They are imperforate and overprinted "REPRINT."

A6

1857-61 Typo. ***Imperf.***

Wove Paper

31 A6 1p yellow green 175.00 25.00
a. Printed on both sides 2,750.
32 A6 4p vermilion 450.00 15.00
a. Printed on both sides 2,750.
33 A6 4p rose 375.00 15.00

Rouletted 7 to 9½

34 A6 1p yellow green 625.00 140.00
35 A6 4p rose — 57.50
35A A6 4p vermilion 575.00

Perf. 12

36 A6 1p yellow green — 500.00

Unwmk. ***Imperf.***

37	A6	1p blue green	425.00	22.50
38	A6	2p lilac	400.00	21.00
39	A6	4p rose	*575.00*	47.50

Examples of No. 39 printed in dull carmine on thin paper are regarded as printer's waste and of little value. They are also found printed on both sides.

Rouletted 7 to 9½

40	A6	1p emerald green	575.00	37.50
41	A6	2p lilac	1,150.	725.00
42	A6	4p rose pink	400.00	11.50
a.		Vert. pair, imperf. btwn.		*750.00*
b.		4p reddish pink		20.00

Perf. 12

43	A6	1p blue green	225.00	20.00
a.		1p yellow green	325.00	24.00
b.		Horiz. pair, imperf. btwn.		—
44	A6	2p lilac		450.00
45	A6	4p rose	300.00	8.00
b.		Vert. pair, imperf. btwn.		—

Rouletted 5½-6½

45C	A6	4p dull rose		1,250.

Serrate Rouletted 19

45A	A6	2p lilac	1,100.	600.00

Laid Paper

Imperf

46	A6	4p rose	825.00	35.00

Rouletted 5 to 7

47	A6	2p violet	275.00	10.50
a.		2p brown lilac	225.00	15.00
b.		2p dark lilac	300.00	25.00
48	A6	4p rose	250.00	7.25

Serrate Rouletted 19

48D	A6	4p rose red		*825.00*

Perf. 12

49	A6	1p green	300.00	25.00
50	A6	4p rose	200.00	15.00

Wove Paper

1860 Wmk. Value in Words (80)

51	A6	1p pale yellowish green	130.00	10.50
a.		Wmk. "FOUR PENCE" (error)		*9,750.*
52	A6	2p gray lilac	200.00	10.00
a.		2p brown lilac ('61)	—	52.50

Wmk. "THREE PENCE" (80)

53	A6	2p bluish gray ('63)	225.00	25.00

Single-lined "2" (50)

54	A6	2p lilac	300.00	18.00
a.		2p gray lilac	275.00	22.50
b.		2p brown lilac	225.00	21.00
c.		As "a," wmkd. single-lined "6"		*7,750.*

A7

1860 Unwmk. Laid Paper

56	A7	3p deep blue	625.00	77.50

Wmk. Value in Words (80)

Perf. 11½ to 12

1860-64 Wove Paper

57	A7	3p blue ('63)	240.00	12.50
a.		"TRREE" instead of "THREE" in watermark		800.00
58	A7	3p claret	180.00	37.50
a.		Perf. 13	240.00	47.50
59	A7	4p rose	200.00	7.75
60	A7	6p orange	*5,750.*	350.00
61	A7	6p black	250.00	10.50

Wmk. "FIVE SHILLINGS" (80)

62	A7	4p rose	*3,000.*	30.00

Wmk. Single-lined "4" (80a)

1863 ***Imperf.***

63	A7	4p rose	—	*175.00*

Rouletted

64	A7	4p rose	*3,250.*	350.00

Perf. 11½ to 12

65	A7	4p rose	180.00	10.50

1863 Unwmk. ***Perf. 12***

66	A7	4p rose	625.00	30.00

A8

A9

1861-63 Wmk. 80 ***Perf. 11½ to 12***

67	A8	1p green	140.00	17.00
68	A9	6p black	140.00	15.00

Wmk. Double-lined "1" (139)

69	A8	1p green	250.00	18.00
b.		Horiz. pair, imperf between		—

Wmk. Single-lined Figures (50)

70	A8	1p green	115.00	11.50
71	A9	6p gray black	140.00	10.00

The 1p and 6p of 1861-63 are known on paper without watermark but were probably impressions on the margins of watermarked sheets.

A10

A11

A12

A13

Wmk. Single-lined Figures (50, 80a, 81)

1863-67 ***Perf. 11½ to 13***

74	A10	1p green	120.00	8.50
a.		Double impression		1,500.
75	A10	2p gray lilac	120.00	15.00
a.		2p violet	115.00	11.50
76	A10	4p rose	140.00	5.00
a.		Double impression		1,500.
77	A11	6p blue	115.00	4.25
78	A10	8p orange	700.00	115.00
79	A12	10p brn, *rose*	200.00	10.50
80	A13	1sh blue, *blue*	200.00	6.50
		Nos. 74-80 (7)	1,595.	164.75

See Nos. 81-82, 84-96, 99-101, 108-112, 115-119, 124-126, 144, 188. Compare type A11 with type A54.

A14

Wmk. Double-lined "1" (139)

81	A10	1p green	125.00	7.00
82	A10	2p gray lilac	325.00	10.50
83	A14	3p lilac	325.00	100.00
84	A11	6p blue	115.00	9.50
		Nos. 81-84 (4)	890.00	127.00

See Nos. 97, 113, 114, 155, 186. Compare type A14 with type A51.

Wmk. Double-lined "2" (49)

85	A11	6p blue		*4,250.*

Wmk. Single-lined "4" (80a)

86	A10	1p green	200.00	30.00
87	A10	2p gray lilac	250.00	10.50
88	A11	6p blue		*2,750.*

Wmk. Double-lined "4" (75)

89	A10	1p green	2,500.	160.00
90	A10	2p gray lilac	250.00	8.00
91	A10	4p rose	300.00	9.50
92	A11	6p blue	325.00	35.00

Wmk. Single-lined "6" (50)

93	A10	1p green	325.00	42.50
94	A10	2p gray lilac	350.00	11.50

Wmk. Single-lined "8" (50)

95	A10	1p green	300.00	27.50
96	A10	2p gray lilac	325.00	10.50
97	A14	3p lilac	250.00	57.50
99	A12	10p slate	1,000.	200.00

Wmk. "SIX PENCE" (80)

100	A10	1p green	1,150.	57.50
100A	A10	2p slate gray		*16,000.*
101	A11	6p blue	800.00	42.50

All values of the 1864-67 series except the 3p and 8p are known on unwatermarked paper. They are probably varieties from watermarked sheets which have been so placed on the printing press that some of the stamps escaped the watermark.

One example of the 2p gray lilac, type A10, is reported to exist with only "PENCE" of watermark 80 showing. Some believe this is part of the "SIX PENCE" watermark.

1870 Wmk. "THREE PENCE" (80)

108	A11	6p blue	475.00	17.50

Wmk. "FOUR PENCE" (80)

109	A11	6p blue	800.00	52.50

A15

1867-78 Wmk. (70) ***Perf. 11½ to 13***

110	A10	1p green	115.00	5.75
111	A10	2p lilac	110.00	5.25
a.		2p gray lilac	125.00	9.50
112	A10	2p lilac, *lilac*	130.00	14.00
113	A14	3p red lilac	400.00	65.00
a.		3p lilac	475.00	72.50
114	A14	3p orange	47.50	6.50
a.		3p yellow	77.50	7.75
115	A10	4p rose	130.00	11.50
116	A11	6p blue	60.00	4.75
117	A11	6p ultra	72.50	5.00
a.		6p lilac blue	130.00	17.50
118	A10	8p brn, *rose*	140.00	10.50
119	A13	1sh bl, *blue*	325.00	17.50
120	A15	5sh bl, *yel*	3,250.	500.00
121	A15	5sh bl & rose	400.00	32.50
a.		Without blue line under crown	375.00	30.00
122	A15	5sh ultra & rose	325.00	42.50

See Nos. 126, 144, 188. For surcharge see No. 124.

For additional stamps of type A15, see No. 191. Compare type A15 with type A58.

A16

1870 ***Perf. 13***

123	A16	2p lilac	115.00	2.60
a.		Perf. 12	125.00	3.50

No. 110 Surcharged in Red

1873, July 19 ***Perf. 13, 12***

124	A10	½p on 1p green	100.00	24.00

No. 79 Surcharged in Blue

1871 Wmk. Single-lined "10" (81)

125	A12	9p on 10p brn, *rose*	650.00	25.00
a.		Double surcharge		*2,500.*

A19

1873-78 Typo.

126	A10	8p brown, *rose* ('78)	175.00	10.50
127	A19	9p brown, *rose*	175.00	27.50

For additional stamps of type A19, see Nos. 128-129, 174-175. Compare type A19 with type A55.

1875 Wmk. V and Crown (70)

128	A19	9p brown, *rose*	200.00	27.50

No. 128 Surcharged in Blue

1876

129	A19	8p on 9p brn, *rose*	350.00	32.50

A21

A22

A23

A24

A25

1873-81 ***Perf. 13, 12***

130	A21	½p rose ('74)	24.00	2.00
131	A21	½p rose, *rose* ('78)	70.00	42.50
132	A22	1p grn ('75)	52.50	3.25
133	A22	1p grn, *gray* ('78)	240.00	110.00
134	A22	1p grn, *yel* ('78)	160.00	30.00
135	A23	2p violet	77.50	1.30
136	A23	2p vio, *grnsh* ('78)	325.00	40.00
137	A23	2p vio, *buff* ('78)	300.00	40.00
137A	A23	2p vio, *lil* ('78)	—	*1,200.*
138	A24	1sh bl, *bl* ('76)	130.00	6.75
139	A25	2sh bl, *grn* ('81)	240.00	35.00

See Nos. 140, 156A-158, 184, 189-190. Compare design A21 with design A46, A24 with A56, A25 with A57.

1878 Double-lined Outer Oval

140	A23	2p violet	77.50	3.75
b.		Vert. pair, lower stamp imperf horiz.		*3,000.*

A26

A27

A28

1880-84 ***Perf. 12½***

141	A26	1p green ('84)	140.00	22.50
142	A27	2p brown	50.00	1.40
143	A27	2p lilac	37.50	2.25
144	A10	4p car rose	260.00	15.00
145	A28	4p car rose ('81)	115.00	10.00
		Nos. 141-145 (5)	602.50	51.15

See Nos. 156, 185, 187. Compare design A26 with design A47, A27 with A49, A28 with A52.

A29 A30 A31 A32 A33 A34

1884-86

146	A29	½p rose	22.50	2.25
147	A30	1p green	29.00	2.40
148	A31	2p violet	32.50	1.25
a.		2p lilac rose	32.50	1.25
149	A30	3p bister	20.00	2.40
a.		3p ocher	20.00	2.40
150	A32	4p magenta	110.00	6.25
a.		4p violet (error)	*6,000.*	*1,250.*
151	A30	6p bright blue ('85)	125.00	5.00
a.		6p ultramarine ('85)	85.00	4.75
b.		6p gray blue ('85)	82.50	4.75
152	A33	8p rose, *rose*	52.50	14.00
153	A34	1sh blue, *yel*	175.00	24.00
154	A33	2sh olive, *grn*	115.00	6.25
		Nos. 146-154 (9)	681.50	63.80

See Nos. 177-178, 192A. Compare designs A31-A32 with designs A37-A38.

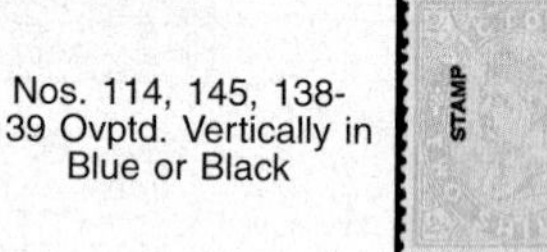

Nos. 114, 145, 138-139 Ovptd. Vertically in Blue or Black

1885

155	A14	3p orange (Bl)	115.00	47.50
156	A28	4p car rose (Bl)	105.00	72.50
156A	A24	1sh bl, *bl* (Bl)		*3,500.*
		Revenue cancel		*1,250.*
157	A24	1sh bl, *bl* (Bk)	175.00	37.50
158	A25	2sh bl, *grn* (Bk)	175.00	35.00
		Nos. 155-156,157-158 (4)	570.00	192.50

Reprints of 4p and 1sh have brighter colors than originals. They lack the overprint "REPRINT."

A35 A36 A37 A38 A39 A40

1886-87 ***Perf. 12½***

159	A35	½p lilac	37.50	9.50
160	A35	½p rose	17.50	1.40
160A	A35	½p scarlet	7.75	1.40
161	A36	1p green	16.00	2.25
162	A37	2p violet	20.00	.55
a.		2p red lilac	11.50	.70
b.		Imperf.		*1,100.*
163	A38	4p red	22.50	2.40
164	A39	6p blue	37.50	3.25
165	A39	6p ultra	32.50	1.10
166	A40	1sh lilac brown	37.50	3.75
		Nos. 159-166 (9)	228.75	25.60

See No. 180.

A41

1889

167	A41	1sh6p blue	260.00	140.00
168	A41	1sh6p orange	35.00	15.00

A42

Southern Cross — A43

Queen Victoria — A44

1890-95 ***Perf. 12½***

169	A42	1p org brn	10.00	.75
a.		1p chocolate brown	12.50	1.10
170	A42	1p yel brn	12.50	.55
171	A42	1p brn org, *pink* ('91)	10.50	4.50
172	A43	2½p brn red, *yel*	19.00	1.75
173	A44	5p choc ('91)	15.00	3.75
174	A19	9p green ('92)	45.00	16.00
175	A19	9p rose red	32.50	6.00
a.		9p rose ('95)	37.50	11.50
176	A40	1sh deep claret	37.50	2.40
a.		1sh red brown	32.50	1.40
b.		1sh maroon	87.50	5.25
177	A33	2sh yel grn	37.50	17.50
178	A33	2sh emerald	35.00	19.00
		Nos. 169-178 (10)	254.50	72.20

In 1891 many stamps of the early issues were reprinted. They are on paper watermarked V and Crown, perforated 12, 12½, and overprinted "REPRINT."

See Nos. 181, 183, 192. Compare type A43 with type A50, A44 with A53.

A45

1897

179	A45	1½p yellow green	6.00	*6.50*

See No. 182. Compare type A45 with type A48.

1899

180	A35	½p emerald	25.00	5.75
181	A42	1p brt rose	11.50	.55
182	A45	1½p red, *yel*	5.75	3.50
183	A43	2½p dark blue	15.00	15.00
		Nos. 180-183 (4)	57.25	24.80

1901

184	A21	½p blue green	3.75	3.25
a.		"VICTCRIA"	110.00	62.50
185	A27	2p violet	14.00	3.00
186	A14	3p brown org	22.50	50.00
187	A28	4p bister	42.50	25.00
188	A11	6p emerald	17.50	13.00
189	A24	1sh orange yel	87.50	65.00
190	A25	2sh blue, *rose*	72.50	55.00
191	A15	5sh rose red & bl	90.00	72.50
		Nos. 184-191 (8)	350.25	286.75

1901

192	A42	1p olive green	11.50	7.50
192A	A30	3p sage green	40.00	19.00

Nos. 192-192A were available for postal use until June 30, 1901, and thereafter restricted to revenue use.

A46 A47

A48 A49

A50 A51

A52 A53

A54 A55

A56

A57

A58

1901 ***Perf. 11, 12½ and Compound***

193	A46	½p blue green	5.75	1.40
194	A47	1p rose red	4.50	.65
a.		1p rose	14.00	1.00
195	A48	1½p red, *yellow*	3.75	1.25
a.		Perf. 11	110.00	110.00
196	A49	2p violet	21.00	1.10
197	A50	2½p blue	15.00	1.10
198	A51	3p brown org	15.00	2.50
199	A52	4p bister	10.50	1.25
200	A53	5p chocolate	17.50	1.10
201	A54	6p emerald	21.00	2.40
202	A55	9p rose	26.00	4.00
203	A56	1sh org yel	29.00	5.00
204	A57	2sh blue, *rose*	40.00	5.00
205	A58	5sh rose red & bl	110.00	35.00
a.		5sh carmine & blue	110.00	26.00
		Nos. 193-205 (13)	319.00	61.75

See Nos. 209-229, 232.

King Edward VII
A59 A60

1901-05

206	A59	£1 deep rose	350.00	150.00
a.		Perf. 11 ('05)	475.00	225.00
208	A60	£2 dk blue ('02)	700.00	450.00
a.		Perf. 11 ('05)	2,250.	1,400.

See Nos. 230-231.

1903 **Redrawn**

209	A56	1sh yellow	35.00	5.75
a.		1sh orange	32.50	4.75

No. 209 has the network lighter than No. 203. In the latter the "P" and "E" of "POSTAGE" are in a position more nearly horizontal than on No. 209.

Perf. 11, 12x12½, 12½, 12½x11

1905-10 **Wmk. 13**

218	A46	½p blue green	4.75	.75
219	A47	1p rose red	2.40	.35
a.		1p carmine rose	15.00	3.00
220	A49	2p violet	9.25	.75
a.		2p purple	10.00	.90
221	A50	2½p blue	5.75	1.00
222	A51	3p brown org	15.00	3.00
a.		3p dull yellow	17.50	3.00
223	A52	4p bister	12.50	1.75
224	A53	5p chocolate	12.50	4.75
225	A54	6p emerald	24.00	2.00
226	A55	9p orange brown	24.00	5.00
a.		9p brown rose	26.00	5.25
227	A55	9p car rose	17.50	3.00
228	A56	1sh yellow ('08)	24.00	4.50
229	A58	5sh orange red & ultra	130.00	26.00
a.		5sh rose red & ultra	140.00	32.50
230	A59	£1 pale red ('07)	450.00	240.00
a.		£1 rose ('10)	350.00	240.00
231	A60	£2 dull blue	1,150.	725.00
		Nos. 218-229 (12)	281.65	52.85

No. 220 Surcharged in Red

1912, July 1

232	A49	1p on 2p violet	1.75	1.25

POSTAL-FISCAL STAMPS

On Jan. 1, 1884, all postage and fiscal stamps were made available for either purpose. Fiscal stamps became invalid after June 30, 1901.

Used values are for examples with postal cancellations used from Jan. 1, 1884 through June 30, 1901.

Beware of stamps with a pen cancellation removed, often regummed or with a fake postmark added.

Stamps inscribed "Stamp Duty" that were issued primarily in postal rates in the normal postage stamp size are listed in the postage section (Nos. 146-178, 180-183, 192-192A). The stamps meeting primarily fiscal rates and in the larger fiscal stamp size, are listed here in the Postal-Fiscal section.

Stamps Inscribed "Stamp Statute"

Victoria — PF1

PF1a (AR3)

PF1b (AR5)

PF1c (AR6)

Coat of Arms — PF2

PF3

Wmk. V and Crown (70)

1870-83		Typo.		Perf. 13
AR1	PF1a	1p green	90.00	75.00
		Revenue cancel		7.25
a.		Perf. 12½	140.00	120.00
AR2	PF1	3p lilac	1,150.	600.00
		Revenue cancel		140.00
AR3	PF1a	4p red	1,000.	500.00
		Revenue cancel		125.00
AR4	PF1a	6p blue	125.00	45.00
		Revenue cancel		14.00
a.		Perf. 12	140.00	35.00
		Revenue cancel		10.50
AR5	PF1b	1sh blue, *blue*	140.00	45.00
		Revenue cancel		14.00
a.		Perf. 12	140.00	50.00
		Revenue cancel		17.50
b.		Perf. 12½	140.00	45.00
		Revenue cancel		14.00
c.		Wmk. 50, perf. 13	140.00	32.50
		Revenue cancel		11.50
d.		Wmk. 50, perf. 12	160.00	37.50
		Revenue cancel		13.00
AR6	PF1c	2sh blue, *grn*	225.00	130.00
		Revenue cancel		30.00
a.		Perf. 12	225.00	—
		Revenue cancel		35.00
b.		Wmk. 50, perf. 13	300.00	125.00
		Revenue cancel		17.50
c.		Wmk. 50, perf. 12	325.00	125.00
		Revenue cancel		21.00
AR7	PF2	2sh 6p orange, *yel*	650.00	260.00
		Revenue cancel		72.50
a.		Perf. 12	650.00	260.00
		Revenue cancel		72.50
b.		Perf. 12½	—	300.00
		Revenue cancel		87.50
AR8	PF1a	5sh blue, *yel*	600.00	140.00
		Revenue cancel		72.50
a.		Perf. 12	650.00	—
b.		Perf. 12½	650.00	140.00
		Revenue cancel		72.50
AR9	PF1a	10sh brn, *rose*	1,600.	375.00
		Revenue cancel		90.00
a.		Perf. 12		—
b.		Wmk. 50, perf. 13	1,600.	350.00
		Revenue cancel		75.00
c.		Wmk. 50, perf. 12		
AR10	PF1a	£1 lilac, *yel*	1,250.	350.00
		Revenue cancel		90.00
a.		Perf. 12	1,150.	325.00
		Revenue cancel		90.00
b.		Perf. 12½	1,150.	325.00
		Revenue cancel		90.00
AR11	PF3	£5 black, *grn*	10,000.	1,900.
		Revenue cancel		135.00
a.		Perf. 12		—
b.		Perf. 12½	10,000.	1,900.
		Revenue cancel		150.00

Nos. AR1-AR12 distributed for postal use from Jan. 1, 1884 through Apr. 23, 1884.

No. AR1 Surcharged "½d/HALF"

1879-96				
AR12	PF1	½p on 1p grn	120.00	105.00
		Revenue cancel		42.50

Stamps Inscribed "Stamp Duty"

PF4

PF5

PF6

PF7

PF8

PF9

PF10

PF11

PF12

PF13

PF14

PF15

PF16

PF17

PF18

PF19

PF20

PF21

PF22

PF23

PF24

PF25

PF26

PF27

PF28

Wmk. V and Crown (70)

1879-96		Litho.		Perf. 13
AR13	PF4	1p green	140.00	45.00
		Revenue cancel		14.00
a.		Perf. 12	140.00	45.00
		Revenue cancel		14.00
b.		Perf. 12½	—	—
AR14	PF8	1sh 6p pink	375.00	50.00
		Revenue cancel		21.00
a.		Perf. 12	—	65.00
		Revenue cancel		26.00
b.		Perf. 12½	—	—
AR15	PF11	3sh violet, *blue*	875.00	85.00
		Revenue cancel		21.00
a.		Perf. 12	1,000.	100.00
		Revenue cancel		21.00
b.		Perf. 12½	—	—
AR16	PF12	4sh orange	175.00	35.00
		Revenue cancel		11.00
a.		Perf. 12	175.00	35.00
		Revenue cancel		11.00
b.		Perf. 12½	—	—
AR17	PF14	6sh green	575.00	70.00
		Revenue cancel		12.50
a.		Perf. 12½	—	—
AR18	PF15	10sh brown, *pink*	925.00	175.00
		Revenue cancel		62.50
a.		Perf. 12	—	—
b.		Perf. 12½	—	—
AR19	PF16	15sh lilac	1,750.	325.00
		Revenue cancel		125.00
AR20	PF17	£1 orange	800.00	110.00
		Revenue cancel		25.00
a.		Perf. 12½	800.00	110.00
AR21	PF18	£1 5sh pink	2,400.	450.00
		Revenue cancel		125.00
AR22	PF19	£1 10sh olive	2,750.	275.00
		Revenue cancel		75.00
AR23	PF20	35sh lilac	*10,000.*	
		Revenue cancel		350.00
AR24	PF21	£2 blue	—	240.00
		Revenue cancel		37.50
AR25	PF22	45sh violet	5,000.	425.00
		Revenue cancel		92.50
AR26	PF23	£5 rose	9,000.	1,000.
		Revenue cancel		125.00
AR27	PF24	£6 blue, *pink*	—	1,500.
		Revenue cancel		175.00
AR28	PF25	£7 violet, *blue*	—	1,500.
		Revenue cancel		175.00
AR29	PF26	£8 scarlet, *yel*	—	1,700.
		Revenue cancel		200.00
AR30	PF27	£9 green, *grn*	—	1,700.
		Revenue cancel		200.00

Typo.

AR31	PF4	1p green	105.00	45.00
		Revenue cancel		8.75
a.		Perf. 12	105.00	45.00
		Revenue cancel		8.75
b.		Perf. 12½	—	—
AR32	PF5	1p brown	40.00	7.75
		Revenue cancel		1.40
a.		Perf. 12	40.00	9.25
		Revenue cancel		1.40
b.		Perf. 12½	—	—
AR33	PF6	6p blue	140.00	22.50
		Revenue cancel		5.75
a.		Perf. 12	140.00	37.50
		Revenue cancel		5.75
b.		Perf. 12½	—	—
AR34	PF7	1sh blue, *blue*	140.00	11.50
		Revenue cancel		5.75
a.		Perf. 12	140.00	14.00
		Revenue cancel		5.75
b.		Perf. 12½	140.00	13.00
		Revenue cancel		5.75
AR35	PF7	1sh blue, *yel,* perf 12½	200.00	45.00
		Revenue cancel		17.50
AR36	PF8	1sh 6p pink	260.00	50.00
		Revenue cancel		17.50

AR37 PF9 2sh blue, *grn* 325.00 45.00
Revenue cancel 13.00
a. Perf. 12 — 50.00
Revenue cancel 13.00
b. Perf. 12½ 350.00 52.50
Revenue cancel 13.00
AR38 PF10 2sh 6p org, perf 12½ 175.00 37.50
a. 2sh6p yellow ('85) 115.00 17.50
b. 2sh6p lemon yellow ('92) 115.00 18.00
Revenue cancel 5.75
AR39 PF11 3sh violet, *bl,* perf 12½ 700.00 65.00
Revenue cancel 14.00
AR40 PF11 3sh bister 125.00 29.00
Revenue cancel 21.00
AR41 PF12 4sh org, perf 12½ 140.00 26.00
Revenue cancel 7.25
AR42 PF13 5sh claret, *yel* 110.00 11.50
Revenue cancel 5.75
a. Perf. 12 125.00 22.50
Revenue cancel 5.75
b. Perf. 12½ 100.00 22.50
Revenue cancel 5.75
AR43 PF13 5sh car rose 140.00 35.00
Revenue cancel 7.25
AR44 PF14 6sh green 200.00 85.00
Revenue cancel 16.00
AR45 PF15 10sh brn, *pink* — 175.00
Revenue cancel 57.50
a. Perf. 12 — —
b. Perf. 12½ — —
AR46 PF15 10sh green 325.00 65.00
Revenue cancel 20.00
AR47 PF16 15sh brown 1,200. 145.00
Revenue cancel 42.50
AR48 PF17 £1 org, *yel,* perf 12½ 875.00 80.00
Revenue cancel 25.00
a. Perf. 12 1,100. 95.00
Revenue cancel 30.00
AR49 PF18 £1 5sh pink 2,250. 160.00
Revenue cancel 75.00
AR50 PF19 £1 10sh olive 1,750. 135.00
Revenue cancel 50.00
AR51 PF21 £2 blue 1,350. 125.00
Revenue cancel 27.50
a. Perf. 12 — 200.00
Revenue cancel 27.50
AR52 PF22 45sh gray lilac 5,000. 180.00
Revenue cancel 62.50
AR53 PF23 £5 rose, perf. 12 — 900.00
Revenue cancel 105.00
a. perf. 12½ — 1,100.
Revenue cancel 150.00
AR54 PF28 £10 lilac 5,500. 210.00
Revenue cancel 62.50
a. Perf. 12 5,500. 325.00
Revenue cancel 62.50

Nos. AR49-AR52, AR54, used, are valued cto.

PF29

PF30

PF31

Wmk. V and Crown (70)

1879-1900 Engr. *Perf. 12½*

AR55 PF29 £25 green — 900.00
Revenue cancel 110.00
a. Perf. 13 —
b. Perf. 12 —
AR56 PF30 £50 violet — 975.00
Revenue cancel 125.00
a. Perf. 13 —
AR57 PF31 £100 red — 1,000.
Revenue cancel 225.00
a. Perf. 13 —
b. Perf. 12 —
Revenue cancel 225.00

Typo.

AR58 PF29 £25 green — 325.00
a. Lithographed —
Revenue cancel 100.00
AR59 PF30 £50 violet — 500.00
a. Lithographed —
Revenue cancel 140.00
AR60 PF31 £100 red — 650.00
a. Lithographed —
Revenue cancel 225.00

Nos. AR55-AR60, used, are valued cto.

PF32

1887-90 Typo.

AR61 PF32 £5 cl & ultra *4,000.* 175.00
Revenue cancel 82.50
AR62 PF32 £6 blue & yel *5,000.* 200.00
Revenue cancel 90.00
AR63 PF32 £7 blk & red *5,500.* 225.00
Revenue cancel 110.00
AR64 PF32 £8 org & lil *6,000.* 250.00
Revenue cancel 110.00
AR65 PF32 £9 red & green *6,500.* 275.00
Revenue cancel 135.00

Nos. AR61-AR65, used, are valued cto.

SEMI-POSTAL STAMPS

SP1

Queen Victoria and Figure of Charity SP2

Wmk. V and Crown (70)

1897, Oct. Typo. *Perf. 12½*

B1 SP1 1p deep blue 27.50 27.50
B2 SP2 2½p red brown 140.00 110.00

These stamps were sold at 1sh and 2sh6p respectively. The premium was given to a charitable institution.

Victoria Cross — SP3

Scout Reporting SP4

1900

B3 SP3 1p brown olive 125.00 75.00
B4 SP4 2p emerald 225.00 225.00

These stamps were sold at 1sh and 2sh respectively. The premium was given to a patriotic fund in connection with the South African War.

REGISTRATION STAMPS

R1

Unwmk.

1854, Dec. 1 Typo. *Imperf.*

F1 R1 1sh rose & blue 2,500. 225.00

1857 *Rouletted 7*

F2 R1 1sh rose & blue 8,750. 425.00

LATE FEE STAMP

LF1

Unwmk.

1855, Jan. 1 Typo. *Imperf.*

I1 LF1 6p lilac & green 1,900. 275.00

POSTAGE DUE STAMPS

D1

Wmk. V and Crown (70)

1890 Typo. *Perf. 12½*

J1 D1 ½p claret & blue 8.00 7.00
J2 D1 1p claret & blue 11.50 2.60
J3 D1 2p claret & blue 18.00 3.25
J4 D1 4p claret & blue 27.50 4.75
J5 D1 5p claret & blue 26.00 3.50
J6 D1 6p claret & blue 27.50 6.50
J7 D1 10p claret & blue 140.00 90.00
J8 D1 1sh claret & blue 90.00 14.00
J9 D1 2sh claret & blue 200.00 92.50
J10 D1 5sh claret & blue 300.00 140.00
Nos. J1-J10 (10) 848.50 364.10

1891-94

J11 D1 ½p lake & blue 5.50 *7.75*
J12 D1 1p brown red & blue ('93) 15.00 2.75
J13 D1 2p brown red & blue ('93) 26.00 2.00
J14 D1 4p lake & blue ('94) 22.50 11.50
Nos. J11-J14 (4) 69.00 24.00

1894-96

J15 D1 ½p bl grn & rose 9.50 3.00
J16 D1 1p bl grn & rose 9.00 3.00
J17 D1 2p bl grn & rose 18.00 3.50
J18 D1 4p bl grn & rose 18.00 3.00
J19 D1 5p bl grn & rose 22.50 22.50
J20 D1 6p bl grn & rose 20.00 14.00
J21 D1 10p bl grn & rose 45.00 20.00
J22 D1 1sh bl grn & rose 32.50 6.00
J23 D1 2sh yel green & rose 115.00 37.50
J24 D1 5sh yel green & rose 200.00 75.00
Nos. J15-J24 (10) 489.50 187.50

1905-09 Wmk. 13

J25 D1 ½p yel grn & rose 10.00 *13.00*
J26 D1 1p yel grn & rose 12.00 4.50
J27 D1 2p yel grn & rose 29.00 5.25
J28 D1 4p yel grn & rose 35.00 21.00
Nos. J25-J28 (4) 86.00 43.75

A 5p with wmk. 13 exists but was not issued.

WESTERN AUSTRALIA

'wes-tərn o-'strāl-yə

LOCATION — Western part of Australia, occupying about a third of that continent
GOVT. — British Colony
AREA — 975,920 sq. mi.
POP. — 184,124 (1901)
CAPITAL — Perth

Western Australia was one of the six British colonies that united on January 1, 1901, to form the Commonwealth of Australia.

12 Pence = 1 Shilling
20 Shillings = 1 Pound

Unused values for Nos. 1-10 are for stamps without gum as these stamps are seldom found with original gum. Otherwise, unused values are for stamps with original gum as defined in the catalogue introduction.

Very fine examples of all rouletted and perforated stamps from Nos. 6-34 have roulettes or perforations touching the design. Examples clear on all four sides range from scarce to rare and will command higher prices.

Watermarks

Wmk. 82 — Swan

Wmk. 83 — Crown and W A

Wmk. 70 — V and Crown

Wmk. 13 — Crown & Double-lined A

Wmk. 74 — Crown and Single-lined A

Swan

A1 A2

1854-57 Engr. Wmk. 82 *Imperf.*
1 A1 1p black 1,350. 275.

Litho.

2 A2 2p brown, *red* ('57) 4,000. 800.
a. 2p brown, *deep red* ('57) 4,250. 1,100.
b. Printed on both sides 4,250. 950.

See Nos. 4, 6-7, 9, 14-39, 44-52, 54, 59-61. For surcharges see Nos. 41, 55-56.

A3 A4

3 A3 4p blue 450. 275.
a. Frame inverted 95,000.
As "a," cut to shape 27,500.
b. 4p slate blue 3,750. 1,350.
4 A2 6p bronze ('57) *6,000.* *900.*
5 A4 1sh pale brown 550. 400.
a. 1sh dark brown 700. 450.
b. 1sh dark red brown 2,250. 1,000.
c. 1sh pale red brown 26,500. 4,000.

Engraved

Rouletted

6 A1 1p black 3,200. 750.

Lithographed

7 A2 2p brown, *red* ('57) *9,500.* 1,900.
a. Printed on both sides 2,300.
8 A3 4p blue — 675.
9 A2 6p bronze ('57) *12,500.* 2,000.
10 A4 1sh brown 4,750. 1,000.

The 1p, 2p, 4p and 6p are known with pin-perforation but this is believed to be unofficial. No. 7a is only recorded used and with pin perforations.

1860 Engr. *Imperf.*
14 A1 2p vermilion 140.00 130.00
a. 2p pale orange 140.00 130.00
15 A1 4p blue 325. *2,000.*
16 A1 6p dull green 2,100. 875.00

Rouletted

17 A1 2p vermilion 800.00 250.00
a. 2p pale orange 650.00 250.00
18 A1 4p deep blue 5,000. —
19 A1 6p dull green 4,500. 750.00

1861 *Clean-Cut Perf. 14 to 16*
20 A1 1p rose 700.00 200.00
a. Imperf.
21 A1 2p blue 140.00 45.00
a. Imperf., pair
b. Horiz. pair, imperf. vert.
22 A1 4p vermilion 1,550. *2,400.*
a. Imperf.
23 A1 6p purple brn 525.00 92.50
a. Imperf.
24 A1 1sh green 875.00 140.00
a. Imperf.

Rough Perf. 14 to 16

24B A1 1p rose 300.00 65.00
24C A1 6p pur brn, *blu-ish* 3,500. 525.00
24D A1 1sh deep green 2,500. 425.00

Perf. 14

25 A1 1p rose 400.00 110.00
25A A1 2p blue 180.00 72.50
25B A1 4p vermilion 450.00 300.00

Unwmk. *Perf. 13*
26 A1 1p lake 115.00 7.75
28 A1 6p violet 240.00 77.50

1865-79 Wmk. 1 *Perf. 12½*
29 A1 1p bister 110.00 10.00
30 A1 1p yel ocher 130.00 15.00
31 A1 2p yellow 125.00 4.75
a. 2p lilac (error) ('79) *20,000.* *17,500.*
32 A1 4p carmine 120.00 8.75
a. Double impression *42,500.*
33 A1 6p violet 160.00 11.50
a. 6p lilac 300.00 11.50
b. 6p red lilac 300.00 11.50
c. Double impression *27,500.*
34 A1 1sh bright green 200.00 21.00
a. 1sh sage green 525.00 45.00
Nos. 29-34 (6) 845.00 71.00

1872-78 *Perf. 14*
35 A1 1p bister 180.00 7.25
36 A1 1p yellow ocher 115.00 5.00
37 A1 2p yellow 115.00 2.40
38 A1 4p carmine 750.00 140.00
39 A1 6p lilac 200.00 6.50
Nos. 35-39 (5) 1,360. 161.15

A5

1872 Typo.
40 A5 3p red brown 72.50 7.25
a. 3p brown 72.50 8.50

See Nos. 53, 92. For surcharges see Nos. 57, 69-72A.

No. 31 Surcharged in Green

1875 Engr. *Perf. 12½*
41 A1 1p on 2p yellow 625.00 80.00
a. Pair, one without surcharge
b. "O" of "ONE" omitted
c. Triple surcharge *5,500.*

Forged surcharges exist.

1882 Wmk. 2 *Perf. 12*
44 A1 1p ocher yellow 125.00 8.00
46 A1 2p yellow 160.00 7.75
47 A1 4p carmine 300.00 60.00
48 A1 6p pale violet 575.00 60.00
Nos. 44-48 (4) 1,160. 135.75

1882 *Perf. 14*
49 A1 1p ocher yellow 45.00 3.00
50 A1 2p yellow 50.00 3.00
51 A1 4p carmine 180.00 17.50
52 A1 6p pale violet 140.00 5.25
a. 6p violet 140.00 6.50

Typographed

53 A5 3p red brown 14.00 4.50
a. 3p brown 29.00 4.50
Nos. 49-53 (5) 429.00 33.25

1883 Engr. *Perf. 12x14*
54 A1 1p ocher yellow 4,000. 300.00

Nos. 44 and 49 Surcharged in Red

1884 *Perf. 12*
55 A1 ½p on 1p ocher yel 18.00 *32.50*

Perf. 14

56 A1 ½p on 1p ocher yel 30.00 *40.00*

No. 40 Surcharged in Green

1885 Typo. Wmk. 1
57 A5 1p on 3p red brown 87.50 26.00
a. 1p on 3p brown 115.00 27.50
b. "1" with straight top 240.00 75.00

A8

Wmk. Crown and C A (2)

1885 Typo. *Perf. 14*
58 A8 ½p green 7.25 1.25

See No. 89.

1888 Engr.
59 A1 1p rose 35.00 5.75
60 A1 2p slate 90.00 2.75
61 A1 4p red brown 130.00 37.50
Nos. 59-61 (3) 255.00 46.00

A9

A10

A11

A12

1890-93 Typo.
62 A9 1p carmine rose 35.00 2.00
63 A10 2p slate 37.50 3.00
64 A11 2½p blue 20.00 3.25
65 A12 4p orange brown 14.00 2.75
66 A12 5p bister 15.00 5.00
67 A12 6p violet 21.00 6.50
68 A12 1sh olive green 26.00 7.50
Nos. 62-68 (7) 168.50 30.00

See Nos. 73-74, 76, 80, 90, 94.

Nos. 40 and 53a Surcharged in Green

1893 Wmk. Crown and C C (1)
69 A5 1p on 3p red brown 16.00 7.75
a. 1p on 3p brown 16.00 7.50
b. Double surcharge *1,600.*

Wmkd. Crown and C A (2)

70 A5 1p on 3p brown 77.50 10.50

Nos. 40a and 53a Surcharged in Green

1895 Wmk. Crown and C C (1)
71 A5 ½p on 3p brown 13.00 *35.00*
a. Double surcharge *1,250.*

No. 72 Surcharged in Green and Red

72 A5 ½p on 3p brown 140.00 *350.00*

Wmk. Crown and C A (2)

72A A5 ½p on 3p brown 100.00 *225.00*

After the supply of paper watermarked Crown and C C was exhausted, No. 72A was printed. Ostensibly this was to provide samples for Postal Union distribution, but a supply for philatelic demands was also made.

Types of 1890-93 and

A15

1899-1901 Typo. Wmk. 83
73 A9 1p carmine rose 7.75 1.75
74 A10 2p yellow 29.00 3.50
75 A15 2½p blue ('01) 14.00 4.75
Nos. 73-75 (3) 50.75 10.00

A16

A17

A18

A19

A20

A21

A22

Southern Cross — A23

Queen Victoria

A24 A25

Perf. 12½, 12x12½

1902-05 Wmk. 70
76 A9 1p car rose 22.00 1.00
a. 1p salmon —
b. Perf. 11 400.00 35.00
c. Perf. 12½x11 1,200. 675.00
77 A16 2p yellow 22.50 4.75
a. Perf. 11 400.00 57.50
b. Perf. 12½x11 *1,750.* *1,100.*
79 A17 4p orange brn 29.00 4.00
a. Perf. 11 1,400. 450.00
80 A12 5p ol bis, perf 12½ ('05) 175.00 115.00
a. Perf. 11 90.00 *100.00*
81 A18 8p pale yel grn 30.00 4.75
82 A19 9p orange 50.00 17.50
b. Perf. 11 175.00 *185.00*
83 A20 10p red 57.50 13.00
84 A21 2sh orange red, *yel* ('06) 115.00 32.50
a. Perf. 11 500.00 225.00
b. 2sh orange brown, *yel* ('11) 77.50 19.00
c. 2sh bright red 130.00 19.00
d. As "c," perf. 11 350.00 200.00
85 A22 2sh6p dk bl, *rose* 77.50 14.00
86 A23 5sh blue green 125.00 45.00
87 A24 10sh violet 300.00 130.00
a. 10sh bright purple 725.00 400.00
88 A25 £1 brown org 450.00 225.00
a. £1 orange 750.00 425.00
Nos. 76-88 (12) 1,453. 606.50

Perf. 12½, 12x12½

1905-12 Wmk. 13
89 A8 ½p dp green ('10) 8.00 *9.25*
a. Perf 11 *2,750.*
90 A9 1p rose 18.00 1.75
e. Perf. 11 55.00 21.00
f. Perf. 12½x11 *1,100.* 475.00
91 A16 2p yellow 11.50 3.25
a. Perf. 11 65.00 32.50
b. Perf. 12½x11 *925.00* 525.00
92 A5 3p brown 37.50 4.75
a. Perf. 11 29.00 9.50
b. Perf. 12½x11 — 1,200.
93 A17 4p orange brn 35.00 12.00
a. 4p bister brown 37.50 13.00
b. Perf. 11 1,100. 290.00
94 A12 5p olive bis 29.00 15.00
a. Perf. 11, pale olive bister 52.50 18.00
b. Perf. 11, olive green 32.50 24.00
95 A18 8p pale yel grn ('12) 32.50 *82.50*
96 A19 9p orange 45.00 8.75
b. Perf. 11 200.00 *240.00*
97 A20 10p red orange 37.50 35.00
98 A23 5s blue green 240.00 180.00
Nos. 89-98 (10) 494.00 352.25

For surcharge see No. 103.

A26

A27

1906-07 Wmk. 83 *Perf. 14*

99	A26	6p bright violet	40.00	3.25
100	A27	1sh olive green	50.00	6.50

1912 Wmk. 74 *Perf. 11½x12*

101	A26	6p bright violet	21.00	19.00
102	A27	1sh gray green	45.00	29.00
a.		Perf. 12½		*2,750.*

No. 91 Surcharged

1912 Wmk. 13 *Perf. 12½*

103	A16	1p on 2p yellow	2.00	*2.50*
a.		Perf compound 12½x11	*750.00*	*500.00*

Stamps of Western Australia were replaced by those of Australia.

POSTAL-FISCAL STAMPS

Postal use of the 1p telegraph stamp was authorized beginning Oct. 25, 1886.

Used values are for examples with postal cancellations.

Beware of stamps with a pen cancellation removed and a fake postmark added.

PF1

1886 Wmk. 1 *Perf. 14*

AR1	PF1	1p bister	65.00	9.25
		Perf. 12½		
AR2	PF1	1p bister	65.00	7.75

Authorized for postal use by the Post and Telegraph Act of Sept. 5, 1893 were the current revenue stamps through the 1sh value.

Beware of stamps with a pen cancellation removed and a fake postmark added.

Because the Act specified current stamps, postally used examples from the provisional issue of of 1881 are not included here.

PF2

1882 Wmk. 2 *Perf. 14*

AR3	PF2	1p purple	26.00	4.00
AR4	PF2	2p purple	260.00	100.00
AR5	PF2	3p purple	90.00	5.75
AR6	PF2	6p purple	105.00	7.75
AR7	PF2	1sh purple	180.00	15.00

The 6p is known postally used but was not authorized.

Wmk. 83

AR8	PF2	1p purple	22.50	4.50
AR9	PF2	3p purple	85.00	5.75
AR10	PF2	6p purple	85.00	6.00
AR11	PF2	1sh purple	180.00	22.50

Nos. AR7, AR11 have a rectangular outer frame and a circular frame around the swan.

Higher values are known with postal cancels, some postally used, but these were not authorized.

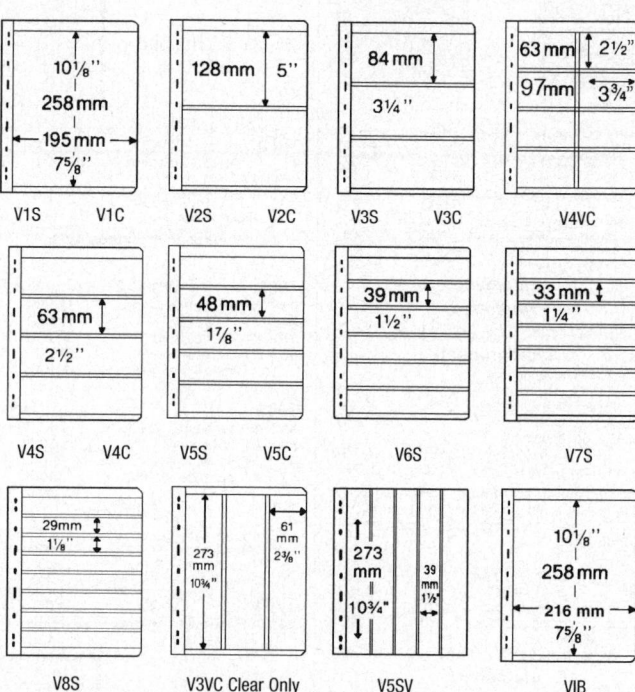

AUSTRALIA

o-'strāl-yə

LOCATION — Oceania, south of Indonesia, bounded on the west by the Indian Ocean
GOVT. — Self-governing dominion of the British Commonwealth
AREA — 2,967,909 sq. mi.
POP. — 17,892,423 (1996)
CAPITAL — Canberra

Australia includes the former British colonies of New South Wales, Victoria, Queensland, South Australia, Western Australia and Tasmania.

12 Pence = 1 Shilling
20 Shillings = 1 Pound
100 Cents = 1 Dollar (1966)

Catalogue values for unused stamps in this country are for Never Hinged items, beginning with Scott 197 in the regular postage section, Scott B1 in the semi-postal section, Scott C6 in the air post section, Scott J71 in the postage due section, and all of the Australian Antarctic Territory.

Watermarks

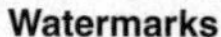

Wmk. 8 — Wide Crown and Wide A

Wmk. 9 — Wide Crown and Narrow A

Wmk. 10 — Narrow Crown and Narrow A

Wmk. 11 — Multiple Crown and A

Wmk. 12 — Crown and Single-lined A

Wmk. 13 — Large Crown and Double-lined A

Wmk. 55 — Large Crown and NSW

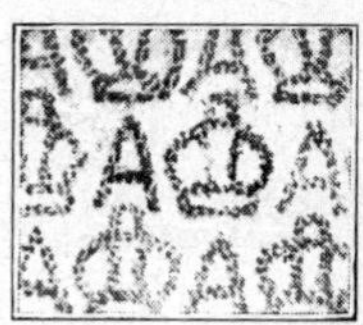

Wmk. 203 — Small Crown and A Multiple

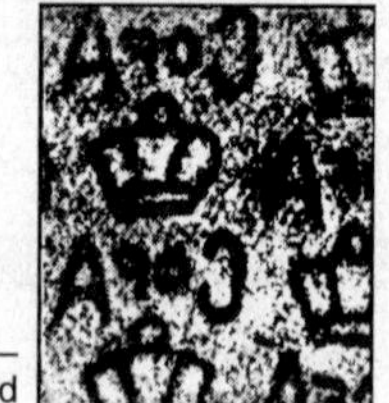

Wmk. 228 — Small Crown and C of A Multiple

Kangaroo and Map — A1

Die I — The inside frameline has a break at left, even with the top of the letters of the denomination.

Die II — The frameline does not show a break (repaired die).

Die III — The left inside frameline shows a break opposite the face of the kangaroo.

Die IV — As Die III, with a break in the top outside frameline above the "ST" of "AUSTRALIA." The upper right inside frameline has an incomplete corner.

Dies are only indicated when there are more than one for any denomination.

1913 Typo. Wmk. 8 *Perf. 11½, 12*

1	A1	½p green	11.50	7.50
		Never hinged	17.00	
2	A1	1p car (I)	15.00	1.75
		Never hinged	24.00	
h.		1p carmine (III)	24.00	2.25
		Never hinged	40.00	
3	A1	2p gray	70.00	10.00
		Never hinged	175.00	
4	A1	2½p dark blue	70.00	22.50
		Never hinged	190.00	
5	A1	3p ol bis, die I	140.00	17.50
		Never hinged	310.00	
a.		Die II	450.00	225.00
		Never hinged	*850.00*	
6	A1	4p orange	150.00	40.00
		Never hinged	700.00	
7	A1	5p orange brown	150.00	50.00
		Never hinged	375.00	
8	A1	6p ultra (II)	140.00	30.00
		Never hinged	450.00	
b.		As #8, (III)	*4,000.*	*1,300.*
9	A1	9p purple	160.00	37.50
		Never hinged	575.00	
10	A1	1sh blue green	130.00	29.00
		Never hinged	700.00	
11	A1	2sh brown	300.00	140.00
		Never hinged	1,250.	
12	A1	5sh yellow & gray	550.00	260.00
		Never hinged	2,000.	
13	A1	10sh pink & gray	1,600.	800.00
		Never hinged	4,250.	
14	A1	£1 ultra & brown	4,000.	2,400.
		Never hinged	9,250.	
15	A1	£2 dp rose & blk	8,500.	3,750.
		Never hinged	16,000.	
		Nos. 1-12 (12)	1,886.	645.75

On No. 4, "2½d" is colorless in solid blue background.

See Nos. 38-59, 96-102, 121-129, 206.

King George V
A2

Kookaburra (Kingfisher)
A3

1913-14 Unwmk. Engr. *Perf. 11*

17	A2	1p carmine	5.25	*7.00*
		Never hinged	8.00	
a.		Vert. pair, imperf. between	*3,250.*	
18	A3	6p lake brown ('14)	115.00	70.00
		Never hinged	260.00	

See No. 95.

A4

ONE PENNY

Die I — Normal die, having outside the oval band with "AUSTRALIA" a white line and a heavy colored line.

Die Ia — As die I with a small white spur below the right serif at foot of the "1" in left tablet.

Die II — A heavy colored line between two white lines back of the emu's neck. A white scratch crossing the vertical shading lines at the lowest point of the bust.

TWO PENCE

Die I — The numeral "2" is thin. The upper curve is 1mm. across and a very thin line connects it with the foot of the figure.

Die II — The "2" is thicker than in die I. The top curve is 1½mm across and a strong white line connects it with the foot of the figure. There are thin vertical lines across the ends of the groups of short horizontal lines at each side of "TWO PENCE."

THREE PENCE

Die I — The ends of the thin horizontal lines in the background run into the solid color of the various parts of the design. The numerals are thin and the letters of "THREE PENCE" are thin and irregular.

Die II — The oval about the portrait, the shields with the numerals, etc., are outlined by thin white lines which separate them from the horizontal background lines. The numerals are thick and the letters of "THREE PENCE" are heavy and regular.

FIVE PENCE

Die I — The top of the flag of the "5" is slightly curved.

Die II — The top of the flag of the "5" is flat. There are thin white vertical lines across the ends of the short horizontal lines at each side of "FIVE PENCE."

1914-24 Typo. Wmk. 9 *Perf. 14*

19	A4	½p emerald ('15)	3.75	1.75
		Never hinged	8.50	
a.		Thin "½" at right	*20,000.*	*5,750.*
20	A4	½p orange ('23)	4.00	4.00
		Never hinged	7.00	
21	A4	1p red (I)	9.00	1.75
		Never hinged	15.00	
a.		1p carmine rose (I)	22.50	4.00
		Never hinged	40.00	
b.		1p red (Ia)	550.00	9.75
		Never hinged	1,150.	
c.		1p carmine (II) ('18)	85.00	35.00
		Never hinged	175.00	
d.		1p scar (I), rough paper	22.50	9.75
e.		1p rose red (Ia), rough paper	800.00	29.00
f.		1p brt rose (Ia), rough paper	750.00	115.00
22	A4	1p vio (I) ('22)	7.00	1.75
		Never hinged	11.50	
a.		1p red violet	10.50	5.25
		Never hinged	14.00	
23	A4	1p green (I) ('24)	5.75	2.50
		Never hinged	10.50	
24	A4	1½p choc ('18)	7.50	2.25
		Never hinged	12.50	
a.		1½p red brown	8.00	2.50
		Never hinged	18.00	
b.		1½p black brown	7.00	2.50
		Never hinged	11.50	
25	A4	1½p emerald ('23)	7.50	2.75
		Never hinged	12.50	
a.		Rough paper	260.00	160.00
26	A4	1½p scarlet ('24)	4.25	1.10
		Never hinged	7.00	
27	A4	2p brn org (I) ('20)	17.50	3.25
		Never hinged	32.50	
a.		2p orange (I) ('20)	17.50	2.50
		Never hinged	32.50	
b.		Booklet pane of 6		
28	A4	2p red (I) ('22)	17.50	3.25
		Never hinged	30.00	
29	A4	2p red brn (I) ('24)	22.50	12.50
		Never hinged	37.50	
30	A4	3p ultra (I) ('24)	32.50	7.75
		Never hinged	70.00	
31	A4	4p orange ('15)	45.00	4.00
		Never hinged	92.50	
a.		4p yellow	140.00	32.50
		Never hinged	600.00	
32	A4	4p violet ('21)	22.50	21.00
		Never hinged	37.50	
33	A4	4p lt ultra ('22)	67.50	13.00
		Never hinged	140.00	
34	A4	4p ol bis ('24)	35.00	13.00
		Never hinged	70.00	
35	A4	4½p violet ('24)	27.50	6.75
		Never hinged	60.00	
36	A4	5p org brn (I) ('15)	37.50	6.75
		Never hinged	110.00	
37	A4	1sh4p lt blue ('20)	140.00	35.00
		Never hinged	475.00	
		Nos. 19-37 (19)	513.75	144.10

See Nos. 60-76, 113-120, 124.

1915 *Perf. 11½, 12*

38	A1	2p gray	160.00	17.00
		Never hinged	325.00	
39	A1	2½p dark blue	140.00	37.50
		Never hinged	300.00	
40	A1	6p ultra (II)	325.00	29.00
		Never hinged	875.00	
a.		Die III	*4,250.*	1,450.
41	A1	9p violet	325.00	60.00
		Never hinged	1,400.	
42	A1	1sh blue green	275.00	35.00
		Never hinged	1,250.	
43	A1	2sh brown	1,050.	125.00
		Never hinged	4,750.	
44	A1	5sh yellow & gray	1,500.	475.00
		Never hinged	3,250.	
		Nos. 38-44 (7)	3,775.	778.50

1915-24 Wmk. 10

45	A1	2p gray (I)	37.50	10.50
		Never hinged	62.50	
a.		Die II, shiny paper	45.00	17.50
		Never hinged	62.50	
46	A1	2½p dark blue	30.00	17.50
		Never hinged	47.50	
a.		"1" of fraction omitted	*45,000.*	*50,000.*
47	A1	3p olive bister (I)	37.50	9.50
		Never hinged	72.50	
a.		Die II	175.00	57.50
		Never hinged	325.00	
b.		3p lt olive (IV)	52.50	14.00
		Never hinged	92.50	
48	A1	6p ultra (II)	120.00	17.50
		Never hinged	275.00	
a.		6p chalky blue (III)	125.00	22.50

Never hinged 250.00
c. 6p ultra (IV) 120.00 20.00
Never hinged 250.00
49 A1 6p yel brn (IV, '23) 32.50 7.25
Never hinged 62.50
50 A1 9p violet (IV) 80.00 22.50
Never hinged 190.00
a. 9p lilac (II) 82.50 22.50
Never hinged 200.00
51 A1 1sh blue grn (II, '16) 72.50 14.00
Never hinged 190.00
b. Die IV 75.00 14.00
52 A1 2sh brown ('16) 325.00 27.50
Never hinged 975.00
53 A1 2sh vio brn (II, '24) 140.00 37.50
Never hinged 325.00
54 A1 5sh yel & gray ('18) 325.00 125.00
Never hinged 850.00
55 A1 10sh brt pink & gray ('17) 1,050. 400.00
Never hinged 1,750.
56 A1 £1 ultra & brn org ('16) 3,450. 2,100.
Never hinged 9,250.
a. £1 ultra & brn ('16) 3,250. 2,100.
Never hinged 10,500.
57 A1 £1 gray (IV, '24) 900.00 425.00
Never hinged 2,250.
58 A1 £2 dp rose & blk ('19) 7,000. 3,250.
Never hinged 14,000.
59 A1 £2 rose & vio brn ('24) 5,250. 3,250.
Never hinged 12,500.
Nos. 45-54 (10) 1,200. 288.75

Perf. 14, 14½, 14½x14

1918-23 Wmk. 11

60 A4 ½p emerald 3.50 3.25
Never hinged 8.00
a. Thin "½" at right 140.00 160.00
61 A4 1p rose (I) 27.50 19.00
Never hinged 45.00
62 A4 1p dl grn (I) ('24) 9.25 9.25
Never hinged 17.50
63 A4 1½p choc ('19) 8.00 4.25
Never hinged 17.50
a. 1½p red brown ('19) 12.50 4.50
Never hinged 26.00
Nos. 60-63 (4) 48.25 35.75

1924 Unwmk. *Perf. 14*

64 A4 1p green (I) 5.75 6.25
Never hinged 12.50
65 A4 1½p carmine 9.25 7.50
Never hinged 17.50

Perf. 14, 13½x12½

1926-30 Wmk. 203

66 A4 ½p orange 3.75 2.25
Never hinged 7.00
a. Perf. 14 ('27) 7.50 8.25
Never hinged 11.50
67 A4 1p green (I) 3.75 1.10
Never hinged 8.00
a. 1p green (Ia) 55.00 *70.00*
Never hinged 75.00
b. Perf. 14 4.50 1.75
Never hinged 9.25
68 A4 1½p rose red ('27) 4.50 2.00
Never hinged 9.25
c. Perf. 14 ('26) 11.50 2.00
Never hinged 22.50
69 A4 1½p red brn ('30) 6.25 4.50
Never hinged 9.75
70 A4 2p red brn (II, '28) 9.25 5.75
Never hinged 20.00
a. Perf. 14 (I, '27) 45.00 29.00
Never hinged 85.00
71 A4 2p red (II) ('30) 11.50 3.25
Never hinged 22.50
a. Tête bêche pair 175,000.
c. Unwmkd. (II) ('31) *2,000.* *2,500.*
72 A4 3p ultra (II) ('29) 35.00 5.50
Never hinged 57.50
a. 3p ultra (I) 70.00 22.50
Never hinged 150.00
b. Perf. 14 45.00 11.50
Never hinged 80.00
73 A4 4p ol bis ('29) 29.00 6.75
Never hinged 52.50
a. Perf. 14 ('28) 125.00 50.00
Never hinged 300.00
74 A4 4½p dk vio ('27) 26.00 10.50
Never hinged 45.00
a. Perf. 13½x12½ ('28) 85.00 32.50
Never hinged 150.00
75 A4 5p brn buff (II) ('30) 45.00 14.00
Never hinged 85.00
76 A4 1sh4p pale turq bl ('28) 200.00 37.50
Never hinged 500.00
a. Perf. 14 ('27) 260.00 140.00
Never hinged 775.00
Nos. 66-76 (11) 374.00 93.10

For surcharges & overprints see Nos. 106-107, O3-O4.

Parliament House, Canberra A5

Unwmk.

1927, May 9 Engr. *Perf. 11*

94 A5 1½p brown red 1.10 1.10
Never hinged 2.00
a. Vert. pair, imperf. btwn. *4,500.* *4,250.*
b. Horiz. pair, imperf. btwn. *7,500.* *7,500.*

Opening of Parliament House at Canberra.

Melbourne Exhibition Issue

Kookaburra Type of 1914

1928, Oct. 29

95 A3 3p deep blue 5.50 8.00
Never hinged 8.25
a. Pane of 4 200.00 *260.00*
Never hinged 300.00

No. 95a was issued at the Melbourne Intl. Phil. Exhib. No marginal inscription. Printed in sheets of 60 stamps (15 panes). No. 95a exists imperf. Value, $300,000.

No. 95 was printed in sheets of 120 and issued Nov. 2 throughout Australia.

Kangaroo-Map Type of 1913

Perf. 11½, 12

1929-30 Wmk. 203 Typo.

96 A1 6p brown 35.00 22.50
Never hinged 57.50
97 A1 9p violet 75.00 26.00
Never hinged 160.00
98 A1 1sh blue green 70.00 14.50
Never hinged 165.00
99 A1 2sh red brown 150.00 29.00
Never hinged 425.00
100 A1 5sh yel & gray 475.00 150.00
Never hinged 1,000.
101 A1 10sh pink & gray 1,000. 725.00
Never hinged 2,000.
102 A1 £2 dl red & blk ('30) 5,250. 925.00
Never hinged 11,500.
Nos. 96-102 (7) 7,055. 1,892.

For overprint see No. O5.

Black Swan — A6

Unwmk.

1929, Sept. 28 Engr. *Perf. 11*

103 A6 1½p dull red 1.60 2.00
Never hinged 2.75

Centenary of Western Australia.

Capt. Charles Sturt — A7

1930, June 2

104 A7 1½p dark red 1.25 1.25
Never hinged 2.50
105 A7 3p dark blue 7.50 *10.00*
Never hinged 11.00

Capt. Charles Sturt's exploration of the Murray River, cent.

Nos. 68 and 74a surcharged

1930 Wmk. 203 *Perf. 13½x12½*

106 A4 2p on 1½p rose red 1.90 1.25
Never hinged 3.50
107 A4 5p on 4½p dark violet 11.00 *14.00*
Never hinged 18.00

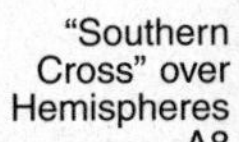

"Southern Cross" over Hemispheres A8

Perf. 11, 11½

1931, Mar. 19 Unwmk.

111 A8 2p dull red 1.25 1.25
Never hinged 2.50
112 A8 3p blue 6.25 6.25
Never hinged 10.00
Nos. 111-112,C2 (3) 15.50 15.50

Trans-oceanic flights (1928-1930) of Sir Charles Edward Kingsford-Smith (1897-1935).

See No. C3 for similar design. For overprints see Nos. CO1, O1-O2.

Types of 1913-23 Issues

Perf. 13½x12½

1931-36 Typo. Wmk. 228

113 A4 ½p orange ('32) 7.50 7.50
Never hinged 11.50
114 A4 1p green (I) 2.50 .40
Never hinged 4.50
115 A4 1½p red brn ('36) 8.00 15.00
Never hinged 12.50
116 A4 2p red (II) 2.50 .30
Never hinged 4.50
117 A4 3p ultra (II) ('32) 32.50 2.25
Never hinged 75.00
118 A4 4p ol bis ('33) 29.00 2.25
Never hinged 55.00
120 A4 5p brn buff (II) ('32) 22.50 2.25
Never hinged 35.00

Perf. 11½, 12; 13½x12½ (1sh4p)

121 A1 6p yel brn ('36) 30.00 *37.50*
Never hinged 52.50
122 A1 9p violet ('32) 42.50 9.00
Never hinged 115.00
124 A4 1sh4p lt blue ('32) 115.00 11.00
Never hinged 160.00
125 A1 2sh red brn ('35) 7.50 5.25
Never hinged 12.50
126 A1 5sh yel & gray ('32) 350.00 27.50
Never hinged 925.00
127 A1 10sh pink & gray ('32) 600.00 225.00
Never hinged 2,000.
128 A1 £1 gray ('35) 1,400. 375.00
Never hinged 2,500.
129 A1 £2 dl rose & blk ('34) 4,500. 800.00
Never hinged 9,250.
Nos. 113-129 (15) 7,149. 1,520.

For redrawn 2sh see No. 206. For overprints see Nos. O6-O11.

Sydney Harbor Bridge — A9

Unwmk.

1932, Mar. 14 Engr. *Perf. 11*

130 A9 2p red 4.50 *5.25*
Never hinged 7.00
131 A9 3p blue 7.50 *9.50*
Never hinged 11.50
132 A9 5sh gray green 575.00 350.00
Never hinged 1,600.

Wmk. 228

Perf. 10½

Typo.

133 A9 2p red 4.00 2.25
Never hinged 5.75

Opening of the Sydney Harbor Bridge on Mar. 19, 1932.

Value for 5sh, used, is for CTO examples.

For overprints see Nos. O12-O13.

Kookaburra — A14

1932, June 1 *Perf. 13½x12½*

139 A14 6p light brown 17.00 1.10
Never hinged 27.50

Male Lyrebird — A16

1932, Feb. 15 Unwmk. *Perf. 11*

Size: 21½x25mm

141 A16 1sh green 42.50 4.50
Never hinged 110.00

See No. 175, 300. For overprint see No. O14.

Yarra Yarra Tribesman, Yarra River and View of Melbourne A17

Wmk. 228

1934, July 2 Engr. *Perf. 10½*

142 A17 2p vermilion 3.00 1.75
Never hinged 4.50
a. Perf. 11½ 10.50 4.50
Never hinged 20.00
143 A17 3p blue 4.00 *6.50*
Never hinged 10.00
a. Perf. 11½ 5.00 *9.00*
Never hinged 9.00
144 A17 1sh black 55.00 27.50
Never hinged 110.00
a. Perf. 11½ 65.00 32.50
Never hinged 120.00
Nos. 142-144 (3) 62.00 35.75

Centenary of Victoria.

Merino Sheep — A18

1934, Nov. 1 ***Perf. 11½***

147 A18 2p copper red 8.00 2.00
Never hinged 11.50
a. Die II 15.00 5.75
Never hinged 29.00
148 A18 3p dark blue 15.00 *19.00*
Never hinged 20.00
149 A18 9p dark violet 35.00 *50.00*
Never hinged 75.00
Nos. 147-149 (3) 58.00 71.00

Capt. John Macarthur (1767-1834), "father of the New South Wales woolen industry."

Two dies of 2p: I, shading on hill in background uneven from light to dark. II, shading is uniformly dark.

Cenotaph in Whitehall, London — A19

George V on His Charger "Anzac" — A20

1935, Mar. 18 ***Perf. 13½x12½***

150 A19 2p red 2.50 .50
Never hinged 5.25

Perf. 11

151 A19 1sh black 50.00 45.00
Never hinged 100.00

Anzacs' landing at Gallipoli, 20th anniv.

The 1sh perf 13½x12½ is a plate proof. Value, unused $2,250, mint never hinged $3,500.

1935, May 2 ***Perf. 11½***

152 A20 2p red 2.75 .35
Never hinged 5.00
153 A20 3p blue 8.00 *12.50*
Never hinged 17.50
154 A20 2sh violet 35.00 *47.50*
Never hinged 85.00
Nos. 152-154 (3) 45.75 60.35

25th anniv. of the reign of King George V.

Amphitrite Joining Cables between Australia and Tasmania A21

1936, Apr. 1

157 A21 2p red 1.25 .60
Never hinged 2.75
158 A21 3p dark blue 3.75 3.50
Never hinged 5.50

Australia/Tasmania telephone link.

Proclamation Tree and View of Adelaide, 1936 — A22

1936, Aug. 3

159 A22 2p red 1.00 .60
Never hinged 2.25
160 A22 3p dark blue 3.75 3.75
Never hinged 5.75
161 A22 1sh green 14.00 10.00
Never hinged 27.50
Nos. 159-161 (3) 18.75 14.35

Centenary of South Australia.

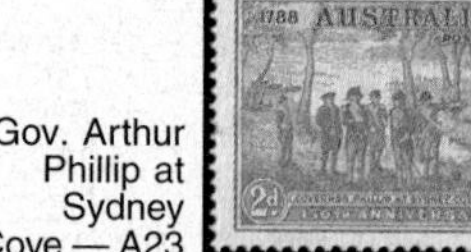
Gov. Arthur Phillip at Sydney Cove — A23

1937, Oct. 1 ***Perf. 13x13½***

163 A23 2p red 1.00 .45
Never hinged 3.25
164 A23 3p ultra 3.75 3.25
Never hinged 6.50
165 A23 9p violet 15.00 13.00
Never hinged 25.00
Nos. 163-165 (3) 19.75 16.70

150th anniversary of New South Wales.

Kangaroo A24

Queen Elizabeth A25

King George VI A26 A27

Koala — A28

Merino Sheep — A29

Kookaburra (Kingfisher) A30

Platypus A31

Queen Elizabeth and King George VI in Coronation Robes
A32 A33

King George VI and Queen Elizabeth A34

Type I

Type II

Two Types of A25 and A26:

Type I — Highlighted background. Lines around letters of Australia Postage and numerals of value.

Type II — Background of heavy diagonal lines without the highlighted effect. No lines around letters and numerals.

Perf. 13½x14, 14x13½

1937-46 **Engr.** **Wmk. 228**

166 A24 ½p org, perf. 15x14 ('42) .85 .70
Never hinged 2.25
a. Perf. 13½x14 ('38) 1.40 .60
Never hinged 3.50
167 A25 1p emerald (I) 1.10 1.00
Never hinged 2.25
168 A26 1½p dull red brn (II) 6.25 5.75
Never hinged 11.50
a. Perf. 15x14 ('41) 4.75 14.00
Never hinged 8.00
169 A26 2p scarlet (I) 1.10 .60
Never hinged 2.25
170 A27 3p ultramarine 40.00 24.00
Never hinged 75.00
a. 3p dp ultra, thin paper ('38) 40.00 4.50
Never hinged 75.00
171 A28 4p grn, perf. 15x14 ('42) 1.10 .30
Never hinged 2.25
a. Perf. 13½x14 ('38) 3.25 3.00
Never hinged 9.00
172 A29 5p pale rose vio, perf. 14x15 ('46) 1.40 1.10
Never hinged 2.25
a. Perf. 14x13½ ('38) 3.00 .90
Never hinged 4.50
173 A30 6p vio brn, perf. 15x14 ('42) 1.25 .30
Never hinged 3.00
a. Perf. 13½x14 12.50 2.25
Never hinged 26.00
b. 6p chocolate, perf. 15x14 1.40 .55
Never hinged 2.25
174 A31 9p sep, perf. 14x15 ('43) 2.00 .45
Never hinged 3.00
a. Perf. 14x13½ ('38) 4.50 2.25
Never hinged 9.75
175 A16 1sh gray grn, perf. 15x14 ('41) 1.40 .40
Never hinged 2.00
a. Perf. 13½x14 27.50 3.50
Never hinged 72.50
176 A27 1sh4p magenta ('38) 1.60 *3.25*
Never hinged 3.50

Perf. 13½

177 A32 5sh dl red brn ('38) 9.75 4.50
Never hinged 26.00
178 A33 10sh dl gray vio ('38) 35.00 20.00
Never hinged 57.50
179 A34 £1 bl gray ('38) 70.00 42.50
Never hinged 115.00
Nos. 166-179 (14) 172.80 104.85

No. 175 measures 17½x21½mm.

See Nos.223A, 293, 295, 298, 300. For surch. & overprints see Nos. 190, M1, M4-M5, M7.

1938-42 ***Perf. 15x14***

180 A25 1p emerald (II) 1.00 .70
181 A25 1p dl red brn (II) ('41) .70 .60
181B A26 1½p bl grn (II) ('41) .70 *2.25*
182 A26 2p scarlet (II) 1.00 .30
182B A26 2p red vio (II) ('41) .40 .30
183 A27 3p dk ultra ('40) 29.00 4.50
Never hinged 57.50
183A A27 3p dk vio brn ('42) .40 .30
Nos. 180-183A (7) 33.20 8.95
Set, never hinged 72.50

No. 183 differs from Nos. 170-170a in the shading lines on the king's left eyebrow which go downward, left to right, instead of the reverse. Also, more of the left epaulette shows.

For surcharges & ovpt. see Nos. 188-189, M3.

Coil Perforation

A special perforation was applied to stamps intended for use in coils to make separation easier. It consists of small and large holes (2 small, 10 large, 2 small) on the stamps' narrow side. Some of the stamps so perforated were sold in sheets.

This coil perforation may be found on Nos. 166, 181, 182, 182B, 193, 215, 223A, 231, 257, 315-316, 319, 319a and others.

Nurse, Sailor, Soldier and Aviator — A35

Perf. 13½x13

1940, July 15 **Engr.** **Wmk. 228**

184 A35 1p green 1.10 *3.25*
Never hinged 2.50
185 A35 2p red 1.10 *1.90*
Never hinged 2.50
186 A35 3p ultra 8.00 *12.50*
Never hinged 16.00
187 A35 6p chocolate 17.00 *27.50*
Never hinged 32.50
Nos. 184-187 (4) 27.20 45.15

Australia's participation in WWII.

No. 182 Surcharged in Blue

1941, Dec. 10 ***Perf. 15x14***

188 A26 2½p on 2p red .75 *1.00*
Never hinged 1.50

No. 183 Surcharged in Black and Yellow

189 A27 3½p on 3p dk ultra .90 *2.25*
Never hinged 1.75

No. 172a Surcharged in Purple

Perf. 14x13½

190 A29 5½p on 5p pale rose vio 3.25 *6.50*
Never hinged 5.00
Nos. 188-190 (3) 4.90 9.75

Queen Elizabeth
A36 A37

King George VI
A38 A39

George VI and Blue Wrens A40

Emu A41

1942-44 **Engr.** ***Perf. 15x14***

191 A36 1p brown vio ('43) .45 .25
192 A37 1½p green .70 .25
193 A38 2p lt rose vio ('44) .70 .25
194 A39 2½p red .70 .30

195	A40 3½p ultramarine		.95	.70
196	A41 5½p indigo		1.75	.35
	Nos. 191-196 (6)		5.25	2.10
	Set, never hinged		9.00	

See Nos. 224-225. For overprint see No. M2.

Catalogue values for unused stamps in this section, from this point to the end of the section, are for Never Hinged items.

Duke and Duchess of Gloucester A42

1945, Feb. 19 Engr. *Perf. 14½*

197	A42 2½p brown red	.30	.25
198	A42 3½p bright ultra	.45	*1.25*
199	A42 5½p indigo	.55	*1.25*
	Nos. 197-199 (3)	1.30	*2.75*

Inauguration of the Duke of Gloucester as Governor General.

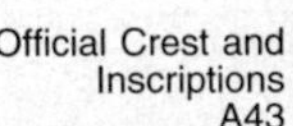

Official Crest and Inscriptions A43

Dove and Australian Flag A44

Angel of Peace; "Motherhood" and "Industry" A45

1946, Feb. 18 Wmk. 228 *Perf. 14½*

200	A43 2½p carmine	.25	.25
201	A44 3½p deep ultra	.65	*1.75*
202	A45 5½p deep yellow green	.70	*1.00*
	Nos. 200-202 (3)	1.60	*3.00*

End of WWII. See Nos. 1456-1458.

Sir Thomas Mitchell and Map of Queensland A46

1946, Oct. 14

203	A46 2½p dark carmine	.25	.25
204	A46 3½p deep ultra	.75	1.60
205	A46 1sh olive green	.75	.60
	Nos. 203-205 (3)	1.75	2.45

Sir Thomas Mitchell's exploration of central Queensland, cent.

Kangaroo-Map Type of 1913 Redrawn

1945, Dec. Typo. *Perf. 11½*

206	A1 2sh dk red brown	5.50	5.50

The R and A of AUSTRALIA are separated at the base and there is a single line between the value tablet and "Two Shillings." On No. 125 the tail of the R touches the A, while two lines appear between value tablet and "Two Shillings." There are many other minor differences in the design.

For overprint see No. M6.

John Shortland A47

Pouring Steel A48

Loading Coal — A49

1947, Sept. Engr. *Perf. 14½x14*

207	A47 2½p brown red	.35	.25

Perf. 14½

208	A48 3½p deep blue	.65	*1.50*
209	A49 5½p deep green	.65	*.75*
	Nos. 207-209 (3)	1.65	2.50

150th anniv. of the discovery of the Hunter River estuary, site of Newcastle by Lieut. John Shortland. By error the 2½p shows his father, Capt. John Shortland.

Princess Elizabeth — A50

Perf. 14x14½

1947, Nov. 20 Wmk. 228

210	A50 1p brown violet	.40	.45

See No. 215.

Hereford Bull A51

Crocodile A52

1948, Feb. 16 *Perf. 14½*

211	A51 1sh3p violet brown	2.25	1.40
212	A52 2sh chocolate	2.25	.35

See No. 302.

William J. Farrer — A53

Design: No. 214, Ferdinand von Mueller.

1948 *Perf. 14½x14*

213	A53 2½p red	.50	.25
214	A53 2½p dark red	.45	.25

William J. Farrer (1845-1906), wheat researcher, and Ferdinand von Mueller (1825-1896), German-born botanist.

Issue dates: No. 213, July 12. No. 214, Sept. 13.

Elizabeth Type of 1947

1948, Aug. Unwmk. *Perf. 14x14½*

215	A50 1p brown violet	.40	.25

Scout in Uniform — A55

Arms of Australia — A56

1948, Nov. 15 Engr. Wmk. 228

216	A55 2½p brown red	.45	.25

Pan-Pacific Scout Jamboree, Victoria, Dec. 29, 1948 to Jan. 9, 1949. See No. 249.

1949-50 Wmk. 228 *Perf. 14x13½*

218	A56 5sh dark red	4.50	.85
219	A56 10sh red violet	29.00	2.00
220	A56 £1 deep blue	45.00	8.50
221	A56 £2 green ('50)	200.00	26.00
	Nos. 218-221 (4)	278.50	37.35

Henry Hertzberg Lawson (1867-1922), Author and Poet — A57

Perf. 14½x14

1949, June 17 Unwmk.

222	A57 2½p rose brown	.50	.25

Outback Mail Carrier and Plane — A58

1949, Oct. 10

223	A58 3½p violet blue	.60	.55

UPU, 75th anniv.

Types of 1938, 1942-44 and

Aborigine — A59

1948-50 Unwmk. *Perf. 14½x14*

223A	A24 ½p orange ('49)	.45	.25
224	A37 1½p green ('49)	.35	.45
225	A38 2p lt rose violet	1.00	.55

Wmk. 228

226	A59 8½p dark brown ('50)	.55	.45
	Nos. 223A-226 (4)	2.35	1.70

Issued: 2p, Dec.; ½p, Sept.; 1½p, 8/29; 8½p, 8/14.

See Nos. 248, 303.

John Forrest — A60

1949, Nov. 28 Wmk. 228

227	A60 2½p brown red	.50	.25

Forrest (1847-1918), explorer & statesman.

New South Wales A61

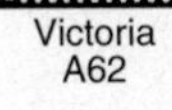

Victoria A62

First stamp designs.

Perf. 14½x14

1950, Sept. 27 Unwmk.

228	A61 2½p rose brown	.45	.25
229	A62 2½p rose brown	.45	.25
a.	Pair, #228-229	1.40	1.10

Cent. of Australian adhesive postage stamps. Issued in sheets of 160 stamps containing alternate copies of Nos. 228 and 229.

Elizabeth A63

George VI A64

1950-51 Engr. Unwmk.

230	A63 1½p deep green	.85	.75
231	A63 2p yellow grn ('51)	.30	.25
232	A64 2½p violet brn ('51)	.30	*.45*
233	A64 3p dull green ('51)	.35	.25
	Nos. 230-233 (4)	1.80	1.70

Issued: 1½p, 6/19; 2p, 3/28; 2½p, 5/23; 3p, 11/14.

A65

A66

1950-52 Wmk. 228

234	A64 2½p red	.25	.25
235	A64 3p red ('51)	.35	*.45*
236	A65 3½p red brown ('51)	.35	.25
237	A65 4½p scarlet ('52)	.45	*.90*
238	A65 6½p choc ('52)	.35	.55
238A	A65 6½p blue green ('52)	.45	.25
239	A66 7½p deep blue ('51)	.50	.55
	Nos. 234-239 (7)	2.70	3.20

Issued: 2½p, 4/12; 3p, 2/28; 7½p, 10/31; 3½p, 11/28; 4½p, No. 238, 2/20; No. 238A, 4/9.

A67

Founding of the Commonwealth of Australia, 50th Anniv. — A68

Designs: No. 240, Sir Edmund Barton. No. 241, Sir Henry Parkes. 5½p, Duke of York opening first Federal Parliament. 1sh6p, Parliament House, Canberra.

Perf. 14½x14

1951, May 1 Engr. Unwmk.

240	3p carmine	1.60	.25
241	3p carmine	1.60	.25
a.	A67 Pair, #240, 241	3.50	3.50
242	A68 5½p deep blue	.90	*3.00*
243	A68 1sh6p red brown	1.40	1.40
	Nos. 240-243 (4)	5.50	4.90

Edward Hammond Hargraves — A69

Design: No. 245, Charles Joseph Latrobe (1801-1875), first governor of Victoria.

1951, July 2

244	A69 3p rose brown	1.00	.25
245	A69 3p rose brown	1.00	.25
a.	Pair, #244, 245	2.50	2.50

Discovery of gold in Australia, cent. (No. 244); Establishment of representative government in Victoria, cent. (No. 245). Sheets contain alternate rows of Nos. 244 and 245.

King George VI — A70

1952, Mar. 19 Wmk. 228 *Perf. 14½*

247 A70 1sh½p slate blue 2.50 .85

Aborigine Type of 1950 Redrawn
Size: 20½x25mm

248 A59 2sh6p dark brown 5.75 1.10

Portrait as on A59; lettering altered and value repeated at lower left. See No. 303.

Scout Type of 1948
Dated "1952-53"
Perf. 14x14½

1952, Nov. 19 Wmk. 228

249 A55 3½p red brown .45 .25

Pan-Pacific Scout Jamboree, Greystanes, Dec. 30, 1952, to Jan. 9, 1953.

Modern Dairy, Butter Production — A71

Perf. 14½

1953, Feb. 11 Unwmk. Typo.

250 A71 3p shown .90 .40
251 A71 3p Wheat .90 .40
252 A71 3p Beef .90 .40
a. Strip of 3, #250-252 8.00 9.25
253 A71 3½p shown .90 .40
254 A71 3½p Wheat .90 .40
255 A71 3½p Beef .90 .40
a. Strip of 3, #253-255 5.75 *7.50*
Nos. 250-255 (6) 5.40 2.40

Both the 3p and 3½p were printed in panes of 50 stamps: 17 Butter, 17 Wheat and 16 Beef. The stamps were issued to encourage food production.

Queen Elizabeth II — A72

Perf. 14½x14

1953-54 Unwmk. Engr.

256 A72 1p purple .30 .30
256A A72 2½p deep blue ('54) .45 .30
257 A72 3p dark green .45 .25

Wmk. 228

258 A72 3½p dark red .55 .45
258B A72 6½p orange ('54) 3.25 .75
Nos. 256-258B (5) 5.00 2.05

Issued: 3½p, 4/21; 3p, 6/17; 1p, 8/19; 2½p, 6½p, 6/23.
See Nos. 292, 296.

Coronation Issue

Queen Elizabeth II A73

1953, May 25 Unwmk.

259 A73 3½p rose red .60 .25
260 A73 7½p violet 1.00 1.00
261 A73 2sh dull green 3.00 2.00
Nos. 259-261 (3) 4.60 3.25

Boy and Girl with Calf — A74

1953, Sept. 3 *Perf. 14½*

262 A74 3½p dp green & red brn .50 .25

Official establishment of Young Farmers' Clubs, 25th anniv.

Lieut. Gov. David Collins A75

Tasmania Stamp of 1853 A77

Sullivan Cove, Hobart A76

Design: No. 264, Lieut. Gov. William Paterson (facing left).

1953, Sept. 23 *Perf. 14½x14*

263 A75 3½p red brown .45 .25
264 A75 3½p red brown .60 .25
a. Pair, #263-264 1.50 1.50
265 A76 2sh green 3.50 2.25
Nos. 263-265 (3) 4.55 2.75

Settlement in Tasmania, 150th anniv. Sheets contain alternate rows of Nos. 263 and 264.

1953, Nov. 11 *Perf. 14½*

266 A77 3p red .35 .45

Tasmania's first postage stamps, cent.

Elizabeth II and Duke of Edinburgh — A78

Elizabeth II — A79

Telegraph Pole and Key — A80

1954, Feb. 2 *Perf. 14½x14, 14x14½*

267 A78 3½p rose red .35 .25
268 A79 7½p purple .40 *.90*
269 A78 2sh green 1.60 .75
Nos. 267-269 (3) 2.35 1.90

Visit of Queen Elizabeth II and the Duke of Edinburgh, 1954.

1954, Apr. 7 Engr. *Perf. 14*

270 A80 3½p dark red .45 .25

Inauguration of the telegraph in Australia, cent.

Red Cross and Globe — A81

Swan — A82

1954, June 9 *Perf. 14½x14*

271 A81 3½p deep blue & red .40 .25

Australian Red Cross Society.

1954, Aug. 2 Unwmk. *Perf. 14½*

274 A82 3½p black .40 .25

Western Australia's first postage stamp, cent.

Diesel and Early Steam Locomotives A83

1954, Sept. 13 *Perf. 14x14½*

275 A83 3½p red brown .45 .25

Centenary of Australian railroads.

Antarctic Flora and Fauna and Map — A84

1954, Nov. 17 *Perf. 14*

276 A84 3½p black .40 .25

Australia's interest in the Antarctic continent.

Olympic Circles and Arms of Melbourne — A85

1954, Dec. 1

277 A85 2sh dark blue 3.00 2.00

16th Olympic Games to be held in Melbourne Nov.-Dec. 1956. See No. 286.

Globe, Flags and Rotary Emblem — A86

1955, Feb. 23 *Perf. 14x14½*

278 A86 3½p carmine .40 .25

Rotary International, 50th anniv.

Elizabeth II — A87

1955, Mar. 9 Wmk. 228 *Perf. 14½*

279 A87 1sh½p dk gray blue 2.75 1.00

See No. 301.

Top of US Monument, Canberra — A88

1955, May 4 Unwmk. *Perf. 14x14½*

280 A88 3½p deep ultra .50 .25

Friendship between Australia and the US.

Cobb and Company Mail Coach A89

1955, July 6 *Perf. 14½x14*

281 A89 3½p dark brown .50 .25
282 A89 2sh brown 2.25 2.25

Pioneers of Australia's coaching era.

World Map, YMCA Emblem A90

Engr. and Typo.

1955, Aug. 10 *Perf. 14*

283 A90 3½p Prus green & red .40 .25
a. Red omitted *25,000.*

Centenary of YMCA.

Florence Nightingale and Modern Nurse — A91

Queen Victoria — A92

1955, Sept. 21 Engr. *Perf. 14x14½*

284 A91 3½p red violet .40 .25

Centenary of Florence Nightingale's work in the Crimea and of the founding of modern nursing.

1955, Oct. 17 *Perf. 14½*

285 A92 3½p green .40 .25

South Australia's first postage stamps, cent.

Olympic Type of 1954

1955, Nov. 30 Unwmk. *Perf. 14*

286 A85 2sh deep green 2.25 2.00

16th Olympic Games at Melbourne, Nov. 22-Dec. 8, 1956.

Queen Victoria, Queen Elizabeth II and Badges of Victoria, New South Wales and Tasmania A93

1956, Sept. 26 *Perf. 14½x14*

287 A93 3½p brown carmine .40 .25

Centenary of responsible government in Victoria, New South Wales and Tasmania.

Melbourne Coat of Arms — A94

Southern Cross, Olympic Torch — A95

Collins Street, Melbourne A96

Design: 2sh, Melbourne across Yarra River.

1956, Oct. 31	**Engr.**	***Perf. 14½, 14***		
288 A94	4p	dark carmine	.50	.25
289 A95	7½p	ultramarine	.75	*1.00*

Photo.

Perf. 14x14½

290 A96	1sh	multicolored	.95	.50

Perf. 12x11½

Granite Paper

291 A96	2sh	multicolored	1.60	1.25
		Nos. 288-291 (4)	3.80	3.00

16th Olympic Games, Melbourne, 11/22-12/8.

A lithographed souvenir sheet incorporating reproductions of Nos. 288-291 in reduced size was of private origin and not postally valid.

Types of 1938-55 and

Queen Elizabeth II — A97

Perf. 14½x14, 14x15, 15x14, 14½

1956-57		**Engr.**		**Unwmk.**	
292	A72	3½p	dark red	1.40	.55
293	A28	4p	green	2.00	.45
294	A97	4p	claret ('57)	.45	.25
a.			Booklet pane of 6 ('57)	12.50	
295	A30	6p	brown violet	3.50	.55
296	A72	6½p	orange	3.50	.25
297	A97	7½p	violet ('57)	1.75	.55
298	A31	9p	sepia	17.00	2.00
299	A97	10p	gray blue ('57)	1.10	.55
300	A16	1sh	gray green	7.25	1.10
301	A87	1sh7p	redsh brn ('57)	5.50	.70
302	A52	2sh	chocolate	14.00	1.10
303	A59	2sh6p	brown ('57)	10.50	1.10
			Nos. 292-303 (12)	67.95	9.15

No. 300 measures 17½x21½mm. No. 303 measures 20½x25mm and is the redrawn type of 1952.

Issued: 3½p, 7/2; 2sh, 7/21; No. 293, 6p, 8/18; 6½p, Sept. 9p, 1sh, 12/13; 2sh6p, 1/30; 10p, 3/6; No. 294, 1sh7p, 3/13; 7½p, 11/13.

South Australia Coat of Arms — A99

1957, Apr. 17	**Unwmk.**	***Perf. 14½***		
304 A99	4p	brown red	.40	.25

Centenary of responsible government in South Australia.

There are two types of No. 304.

Caduceus and Map of Australia A100

1957, Aug. 21		***Perf. 14½x14***		
305 A100	7p	violet blue	.60	.30

Royal Flying Doctor Service of Australia.

Star of Bethlehem and Praying Child A101

1957, Nov. 6		**Engr.**		
306 A101	3½p	dull rose	.35	.25
307 A101	4p	pale purple	.35	.25

Christmas.

Canberra War Memorial, Sailor and Airman A102

Design: No. 309, As No. 308 with soldier and service woman. Printed in alternate rows in sheet.

1958, Feb. 10		**Unwmk.**		
308 A102	5½p	brown carmine	1.00	.70
309 A102	5½p	brown carmine	1.00	.70
a.		Pair, #308-309	3.50	3.50

Sir Charles Kingsford-Smith and "Southern Cross" — A103

1958, Aug. 27		***Perf. 14x14½***		
310 A103	8p	brt violet blue	1.00	1.00

1st air crossing of the Tasman Sea, 30th anniv. See New Zealand No. 321.

Broken Hill Mine — A104

1958, Sept. 10		***Perf. 14½x14***		
311 A104	4p	brown	.40	.25

Broken Hill mining field, 75th anniv.

Nativity — A105

1958, Nov. 5		***Perf. 14½x15***		
312 A105	3½p	dark red	.30	.25
313 A105	4p	dark purple	.30	.25

Christmas.

A106

A107

A108

A109

A110

Platypus A111

Tasmanian Tiger A112

Flannel Flower — A113

Aboriginal Stockman Cutting Out a Steer A114

Designs: 3p, Queen Elizabeth II facing right. 6p, Banded anteater. 8p, Tiger cat. 9p, Kangaroos. 11p, Rabbit bandicoot. 1sh6p, Christmas bells (flower). 2sh3p, Wattle (flower). 2sh5p, Banksia (flower). 3sh, Waratah (flower).

FIVE PENCE

Die I — Four short lines inside "5" at right of ball; six short lines left of ball; full length line above ball is seventh from bottom. Odd numbered horizontal rows in each sheet are in Die I.

Die II — Five short lines inside "5" at right of ball; seven at left; full length line above ball is eighth from bottom. Even numbered horizontal rows in each sheet are in Die II.

Perf. 14½x14, 14x14½, 14½

1959-64		**Engr.**		**Unwmk.**	
314	A106	1p	dull violet	.25	.25
315	A107	2p	red brown	.70	.45
316	A108	3p	bluish green	.35	.25
317	A108	3½p	dark green	.25	.25
318	A109	4p	carmine	2.25	.25
a.			Booklet pane of 6	29.00	
319	A110	5p	dark blue (I)	1.10	.25
a.			5p dark blue (II)	1.10	.25
b.			Booklet pane of 6 ('60)	17.00	
320	A111	6p	chocolate	2.25	.25
321	A111	8p	red brown	2.25	.25
322	A111	9p	brown black	2.25	.85
323	A111	11p	dark blue	2.25	.25
324	A111	1sh	slate green	4.50	.70
325	A112	1sh2p	dk purple	2.25	.35
326	A113	1sh6p	red, *yellow*	3.50	1.40
327	A113	2sh	dark blue	2.25	.25
328	A113	2sh3p	green, *yel*	2.25	.25
328A	A113	2sh3p	yellow grn	7.00	2.25
329	A113	2sh5p	brown, *yellow*	7.50	1.10
330	A113	3sh	crimson	2.25	.45

Wmk. 228

331	A114	5sh	red brown	24.00	2.25
			Nos. 314-331 (19)	69.40	12.30

Issued: 1p, 4p, 2/2; 3½p, 3/18; 2sh, 4/8; 3p, 5/20; 3sh, 7/15; 1sh, No. 328, 9/9; 5p, 10/1; 9p, 10/21; 1sh6p, 2/3/60; 2sh5p, 3/16/60; 8p, 5/11/60; 6p, 9/30/60; 11p, 5/3/61; 5sh, 7/26/61; 2p, 1sh2p, 3/21/62; No. 328A, 10/28/64.

Luminescent Printings

Paper with an orange red phosphorescence (surface coating), was used for some printings of the Colombo Plan 1sh, No. 340, the Churchill 5p, No. 389, and several regular postage stamps. These include 2p, 3p, 6p, 8p, 9p, 11p, 1sh2p, 1sh6p and 2sh3p (Nos. 315, 316, 365, 367, 321, 368, 323, 325, 369, 328A).

Stamps printed only on phosphorescent paper include the Monash 5p, Hargrave 5p, ICY 2sh3p and Christmas 5p (Nos. 388, 390-393) and succeeding commemoratives; the 2sh, 2sh6p and 3sh regular birds (Nos. 370, 372, 373); and most of the regular series in decimal currency.

Ink with a phosphorescent content was used in printing most of the 5p red, No. 366, almost all of the 5p red booklets, No. 366a, most of the decimal 4c regular, No. 397, and its booklet pane, No. 397a, and all of No. 398.

Postmaster Isaac Nichols Boarding Vessel to Receive Mail — A115

1959, Apr. 22		***Perf. 14½x14***		
332 A115	4p	dark gray blue	.40	.25

First post office, Sydney, 150th anniv.

Parliament House, Brisbane, and Queensland Arms — A116

1959, June 5		***Perf. 14x14½***		
333 A116	4p	dk green & violet	.40	.25

Cent. of Queensland self-government.

Approach of the Magi — A117

1959, Nov. 4		***Perf. 15x14½***		
334 A117	5p	purple	.40	.25

Christmas.

Girl Guide and Lord Baden-Powell — A118

1960, Aug. 18		***Perf. 14½x14***		
335 A118	5p	dark blue	.45	.25

50th anniversary of the Girl Guides.

The Overlanders by Sir Daryl Lindsay — A119

1960, Sept. 21		***Perf. 14½***		
336 A119	5p	lilac rose	.40	.25

Exploration of Australia's Northern Territory, cent.

Melbourne Cup and Archer, 1861 Winner — A120

1960, Oct. 12 **Unwmk.**
337 A120 5p sepia .40 .25

Centenary of the Melbourne Cup.

Queen Victoria A121

Open Bible and Candle A122

1960 Nov. 2 **Engr.** ***Perf. 14½***
338 A121 5p dark green .40 .25

Centenary of the first Queensland stamps.

1960, Nov. 9 **Unwmk.**
339 A122 5p maroon .40 .25

Christmas; beginning of 350th anniv. year of the publication of the King James translation of the Bible.

Colombo Plan Emblem — A123

1961, June 30 ***Perf. 14x14½***
340 A123 1sh red brown .85 .30

Colombo Plan for the peaceful development of South East Asia countries, 10th anniv.

Dame Nellie Melba, by Sir Bertram Mackennal — A124

1961, Sept. 20 ***Perf. 14½***
341 A124 5p deep blue .45 .30

Dame Nellie Melba, singer, birth cent.

Page from Book of Hours, 15th Century A125

1961, Nov. 8 ***Perf. 14½x14***
342 A125 5p reddish brown .40 .25

Christmas; end of the 350th anniv. year of the publication of the King James translation of the Bible.

John McDouall Stuart — A126

1962, July 25 **Unwmk.** ***Perf. 14½***
345 A126 5p carmine .40 .25

First south-north crossing of Australia by John McDouall Stuart, cent.

Nurse and Rev. Flynn's Grave — A127

1962, Sept. 5 **Photo.** ***Perf. 13½***
346 A127 5p multicolored .50 .30
a. Red omitted *450.00*

Australian Inland Mission founded by Rev. John Flynn, 50th anniv.

Woman and Globe — A128

Madonna and Child — A129

1962, Sept. 26 **Engr.** ***Perf. 14x14½***
347 A128 5p dark green .40 .25

World Conf. of the Associated Country Women of the World, Melbourne, Oct. 2-12.

1962, Oct. 17 ***Perf. 14½***
348 A129 5p deep violet .40 .25

Christmas.

View of Perth and Kangaroo Paw — A130

Arms of Perth A131

1962, Nov. 1 **Photo.** ***Perf. 14***
349 A130 5p multicolored .65 .25
a. Red omitted *5,500.*

Perf. 14½x14

350 A131 2sh3p emer, blk, red & ultra 3.50 3.50

British Empire and Commonwealth Games, Perth, Nov. 22-Dec. 1.

Perf 14x14¾ examples of Nos. 349-350 are from a booklet pane issued for the 2006 Commonwealth Games. These stamps were not valid for postage.

Elizabeth II — A132

Elizabeth II and Prince Philip — A133

1963, Feb. 18 **Engr.** ***Perf. 14½***
351 A132 5p dark green .50 .25
352 A133 2sh3 red brown 3.00 3.00

Visit of Elizabeth II and Prince Philip.

Perf 14½x14 lithographed examples of Nos. 351-352 come from the booklet footnoted under No. 2507. These stamps were not valid for postage.

Walter Burley Griffin and Arms of Canberra A134

1963, Mar. 8 **Unwmk.** ***Perf. 14½x14***
353 A134 5p dark green .40 .25

50th anniv. of Canberra; Walter Burley Griffin, American architect, who laid out plan for Canberra.

Red Cross Centenary Emblem — A135

1963, May 8 **Photo.** ***Perf. 13½x13***
354 A135 5p dk blue, red & gray .50 .25

Centenary of the International Red Cross.

Explorers Blaxland, Lawson and Wentworth Looking West from Mt. York — A136

1963, May 28 **Engr.** ***Perf. 14½x14***
355 A136 5p dark blue .40 .25

1st crossing of the Blue Mts., 150th anniv.

Globe, Ship, Plane and Map of Australia A137

1963, Aug. 28 **Unwmk.**
356 A137 5p red .40 .25

Importance of exports to Australian economy.

Elizabeth II A138

Black-backed Magpie and Eucalyptus A139

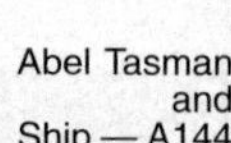

Abel Tasman and Ship — A144

George Bass, Whaleboat — A145

Designs: 6p, Yellow-tailed thornbill, horiz. 1sh6p, Galah on tree stump. 2sh, Golden whistler. 2sh5p, Blue wren and bracken fern. 2sh6p, Scarlet robin, horiz. 3sh, Straw-necked ibis. 5sh, William Dampier and "Roebuck" sailing ship. 7sh6p, Capt. James Cook. 10sh, Matthew Flinders and three-master "Investigator." £2, Admiral Philip Parker King.

Perf. 15x14

1963-65 **Unwmk.** **Engr.**
365 A138 5p green 1.10 .25
a. Booklet pane of 6 ('64) 35.00
b. Pair, imperf. btwn. 2.00 2.00
366 A138 5p red 1.10 .25
a. Booklet pane of 6 45.00

Photo.

Perf. 13½

367 A139 6p multi 1.10 .50
a. Vert. pair, imperf. btwn.
368 A139 9p multi 2.00 *2.75*
369 A139 1sh6p multi 1.75 *1.40*
370 A139 2sh multi 2.25 .55
371 A139 2sh5p multi 5.25 *3.50*
372 A139 2sh6p multi 4.75 3.25
a. Red omitted *12,000.* *12,000.*
373 A139 3sh multi 4.75 1.75

Engr.

Perf. 14½x14, 14½x15

374 A144 4sh violet blue 3.75 .95

Wmk. 228

375 A145 5sh red brown 4.50 2.50
376 A144 7sh6p olive green 21.00 16.00
377 A144 10sh deep claret 35.00 5.75
378 A145 £1 purple 57.50 30.00
379 A145 £2 brn blk 105.00 92.50
Nos. 365-379 (15) 250.80 161.90

No. 365a was printed in sheets of 288 which were sold intact by the Philatelic Bureau. These sheets have been broken to obtain pairs and blocks which are imperf. between (see No. 365b).

Issued: No. 365, 4sh, 10/9/63; 10sh, £1, 2/26/64; 9p, 1sh6p, 2sh5p, 3/11/64; 6p, 8/19/64; 7sh6p, £2, 8/26/64; 5sh, 11/25/64; 2sh, 2sh6p, 3sh, 4/21/65; No. 366, 6/30/65.

See Nos. 400-401, 406-417, 1727-1728.

Star of Bethlehem — A146

1963, Oct. 25 **Unwmk.** ***Perf. 14½***
380 A146 5p blue .40 .25

Christmas.

Cable Around World and Under Sea — A147

1963, Dec. 3 **Photo.** ***Perf. 13½***
381 A147 2sh3p gray, ver, blk & blue 3.50 3.50

Opening of the Commonwealth Pacific (telephone) cable service (COMPAC).

See New Zealand No. 364.

Bleriot 60 Plane, 1914 — A148

1964, July 1 **Engr.** ***Perf. 14½x14***
382 A148 5p olive green .40 .25
383 A148 2sh3p red 3.25 3.25

50th anniv. of the first air mail flight in Australia; Maurice Guillaux, aviator.

Child Looking at Nativity Scene — A149

1964, Oct. 21 Photo. *Perf. 13½*

384 A149 5p bl, blk, red & buff .40 .25
a. Red omitted *4,750. 2,750.*
b. Black omitted *2,750.*
c. Buff omitted *3,500.*

Christmas.

No. 384a used is valued on cover. The red ink can be removed from No. 384 by bleaching.

"Simpson and His Donkey" by Wallace Anderson — A150

1965, Apr. 14 Engr. *Perf. 14x14½*

385 A150 5p olive bister .50 .25
386 A150 8p dark blue .90 .80
387 A150 2sh3p rose claret 3.00 3.00
Nos. 385-387 (3) 4.40 4.05

50th anniv. of the landing of the Australian and New Zealand Army Corps (ANZAC) at Gallipoli, Turkey, Apr. 25, 1915. Private John Simpson Kirkpatrick saved the lives of many wounded soldiers. The statue erected in his honor stands in front of Melbourne's Shrine of Remembrance.

Radio Mast and Satellite Orbiting Earth A151

Winston Churchill A152

1965, May 10 Photo. *Perf. 13½*

388 A151 5p multicolored .65 .25
a. Gray omitted *5,000. 5,000.*

ITU, cent.

1965, May 24

389 A152 5p lt bl, pale gray, dk gray & blk .40 .25
a. Pale gray omitted (white face) *5,500.*
b. Dark gray ("Australia") omitted *7,500.*

Sir Winston Spencer Churchill (1874-1965), statesman and WWII leader.

Two examples of No. 389b recorded, one damaged. Value is for sound example.

See New Zealand No. 371.

John Monash and Transmission Tower — A153

1965, June 23 Photo. *Perf. 13½*

390 A153 5p red, yel, blk & lt brn .40 .25

Birth cent. of General Sir John Monash (1865-1931), soldier, Vice-Chancellor of University of Melbourne and chairman of the Victoria state electricity commission.

Lawrence Hargrave and Sketch for 1902 Seaplane A154

1965, Aug. 4 Unwmk. *Perf. 13½*

391 A154 5p multicolored .40 .25
a. Purple (5d) omitted *600.00 600.00*

50th anniv. of the death of Lawrence Hargrave (1850-1915), aviation pioneer.

ICY Emblem — A155

Nativity — A156

1965, Sept. 1 Photo. *Perf. 13½*

392 A155 2sh3p lt blue & green 3.25 3.00

International Cooperation Year.

1965, Oct. 20 Unwmk. *Perf. 13½*

393 A156 5p multicolored .40 .25
a. Gold omitted *5,500.*
b. Ultramarine omitted *1,000.*
c. Brown omitted (white faces) *5,000.*

Christmas.

Types of 1963-65 and

Elizabeth II — A157

Humbug Fish — A158

Designs: No. 400, Yellow-tailed thornbill, horiz. 6c, blue-faced honeyeater, horiz. 8c, Coral fish. 9c, Hermit crab. 10c Anemone fish. 13c, Red-necked avocet. 15c, Galah on tree stump. 20c, Golden whistler. 24c Azure kingfisher, horiz. 25c, Scarlet robin, horiz. 30c Straw-necked ibis. 40c Abel Tasman and ship. 50c, William Dampier and "Roebuck" sailing ship. 75c, Capt. James Cook. $1, Matthew Flinders and three-master "Investigator." $2, George Bass and whaleboat. $4, Admiral Philip Parker King.

Perf. 14½x14 (A157); 13½ (A158, A139)

Engr. (A157), Photo. (A158, A139)

1966-71

394 A157 1c red brown .45 .25
395 A157 2c olive green .75 .25
396 A157 3c Prus green .75 .25
397 A157 4c red .30 .25
a. Booklet pane of 5 + label 35.00
398 A157 5c on 4c red ('67) .40 .25
a. Booklet pane of 5 + label ('67) 7.00
399 A157 5c dk blue ('67) .75 .25
a. Booklet pane of 5 + label 12.50
400 A139 5c lt grn, blk, brn & yel .55 .25
a. Brown omitted *3,500.* —
401 A139 6c gray, blk, lem & bl .80 .35
b. Blue omitted *2,500.*
401A A157 6c orange ('70) .55 .25
402 A158 7c brn, ver, blk & gray .85 .25
402A A157 7c dp rose lilac ('71) .75 .25
403 A158 8c multicolored .85 .55
404 A158 9c multicolored .85 .35
405 A158 10c lt brn, blk, org & bl .85 .25
a. Orange omitted *4,250.*
b. Blue omitted *3,000. 2,000.*
406 A139 13c lt bl grn, blk, gray & red 2.25 .45
a. Red omitted *2,250.*
b. Gray omitted *2,100.*
407 A139 15c lt grn, blk, gray & rose 2.25 1.10
a. Rose omitted *4,500.*
b. Gray omitted *2,750. 750.00*
408 A139 20c pink, blk, yel & gray 3.25 .30
a. Yellow omitted *2,900.*
b. Gray omitted *750.00*
409 A139 24c tan, blk, vio bl & org 1.10 *1.10*
410 A139 25c gray, grn, blk & red 3.75 .55
a. Red omitted *5,750.*
411 A139 30c lt grn, buff, blk & red 12.50 .85
a. Red omitted *3,000.*

Engr.

Perf. 14½x14, 14½x15

412 A144 40c violet blue 5.75 .25
413 A145 50c brown red 7.50 .25
414 A144 75c olive green 1.60 1.40
415 A144 $1 deep claret 2.60 .45
a. Perf 15x14 125.00 32.50
416 A145 $2 purple 8.00 2.25
417 A145 $4 sepia 7.00 7.00
Nos. 394-417 (26) 67.00 19.95

No. 398 issued in booklets only.

Booklet panes of 10 of No. 399, and of 5 No. 400, are torn from sheets. They were issued for the use of "Australian Defence Forces," as the covers read, in Viet Nam.

Issued: Nos. 398, 399, 9/29/67; No. 401A, 9/28/70; No. 402A, 10/1/71; No. 415a, 1973; others, 2/14/66.

Coil Stamps

1966-67 Photo. *Perf. 15 Horiz.*

418 A157 3c emerald, blk & buff .85 .55
419 A157 4c org red, blk & buff .70 .55
420 A157 5c blue, black & buff .85 .25
Nos. 418-420 (3) 2.40 1.35

Issued: 5c, 9/29/67; others, 2/14/66.

Rescue A159

1966, July 6 Photo. *Perf. 13½*

421 A159 4c blue, ultra & black .30 .25

Royal Life Saving Society, 75th anniv.

Adoration of the Shepherds A160

1966, Oct. 19 Photo. *Perf. 13½*

422 A160 4c olive & black .30 .25
a. Olive omitted *7,250.*

Christmas.

Dutch Sailing Ship, 17th Century — A161

Hands Reaching for Bible — A162

1966, Oct. 24 Photo. *Perf. 13½*

423 A161 4c bl, blk, dp org & gold .30 .25
a. Deep orange omitted *6,000.*
b. Gold omitted *2,000.*

350th anniv. of Dirk Hartog's discovery of the Australian west coast, and his landing on the island named after him.

1967, Mar. 7 Photo. *Perf. 13½*

424 A162 4c multicolored .30 .25

British and Foreign Bible Soc., 150th anniv.

Combination Lock and Antique Keys — A163

1967, Apr. 5 Photo. *Perf. 13½*

425 A163 4c emerald, blk & lt blue .30 .25

150th anniv. of banking in Australia (Bank of New South Wales).

Lions Intl., 50th Anniv. — A164

1967, June 7 Photo. *Perf. 13½*

426 A164 4c ultra, black & gold .30 .25

YWCA Emblems and Flags A165

1967, Aug. 21 Photo. *Perf. 13½*

427 A165 4c dk blue, lt bl & lilac .30 .25

World Council Meeting of the YWCA, Monash University, Victoria, Aug. 14-Sept. 1.

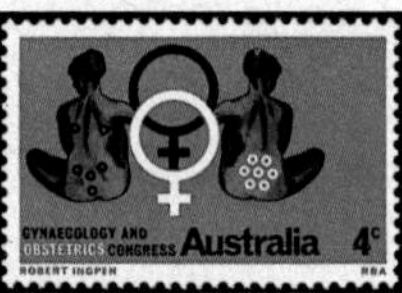

Seated Women Symbolizing Obstetrics and Gynecology, Female Symbol A166

1967, Sept. 20 Photo. *Perf. 13½*

428 A166 4c lilac, dk blue & blk .30 .25

5th World Congress of Gynecology and Obstetrics, Sydney, Sept. 23-30.

Gothic Arches and Christmas Bell Flower A167

Cross, Stars of David and Yin Yang Forming Mandala — A168

1967 Photo. *Perf. 13½*

429 A167 5c multicolored .30 .25
430 A168 25c multicolored 2.00 2.00

Christmas.

Issue dates: 5c, Oct. 18; 25c, Nov. 27.

Satellite Orbiting Earth — A169

Satellite and Antenna, Moree, N.S.W. — A170

Design: 20c, World weather map connecting Washington, Moscow and Melbourne, and computer and teleprinter tape spools.

1968, Mar. 20 Photo. *Perf. 13½*

431 A169 5c dull yel, red, bl & dk blue .50 .25
432 A169 20c blue, blk & red 2.25 2.25
a. Red omitted *3,000.*

433 A170 25c Prus blue, blk & lt green 2.25 2.25
Nos. 431-433 (3) 5.00 4.75

Use of satellites for weather observations and communications.

Kangaroo Paw, Western Australia — A171

State Flowers: 13c, Pink heath, Victoria. 15c, Tasmanian blue gum, Tasmania. 20c, Sturt's desert pea, South Australia. 25c, Cooktown orchid, Queensland. 30c, Waratah, New South Wales.

1968, July 10 Photo. *Perf. 13½*
Flowers in Natural Colors

434 A171 6c multicolored .55 .65
435 A171 13c multicolored .65 .55
436 A171 15c multicolored 1.00 .45
437 A171 20c multicolored 5.00 .75
438 A171 25c multicolored 2.25 .75
439 A171 30c multicolored .75 .25
a. Green omitted *3,750.*
Nos. 434-439 (6) 10.20 3.40

A 1971 reprinting of No. 439 shows more areas of white in the pink petals. This is scarcer than the first printing. Value, $4.75.

Sturt's Desert Rose, Northern Territory — A171a

Designs: 5c, Golden wattle, national flower. 7c, 10c, Sturt's desert pea.

Coil Stamps

1970-75 *Perf. 14½ Horiz.*

439A A171a 2c dk grn & multi .25 .25
i. Lettering and value bolder .25 .25
439B A171a 4c gray & multi .70 .45
439C A171a 5c gray & multi .25 .25
439D A171a 6c gray & multi 1.40 .55
h. Green omitted *2,250.*
439E A171a 7c blk, red & grn .40 .25
f. Green omitted 110.00
439G A171a 10c blk, red & grn .35 .25
Nos. 439A-439G (6) 3.35 2.00

Issued: 4c, 5c, 4/27; 6c, 10/28; 2c, 7c, 10/1/71; 10c, 1/15/75; No. 439Ai, 11/73.

Soil Testing Through Chemistry & by Computer A172

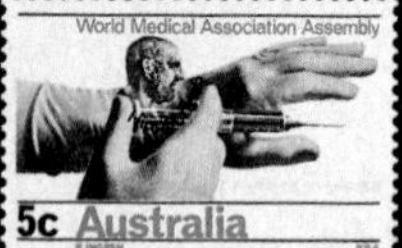

Hippocrates & Hands Holding Hypodermic A173

1968, Aug. 6 Photo. *Perf. 13½*

440 A172 5c multicolored .30 .25
441 A173 5c multicolored .30 .25

9th Intl. Congress of Soil Science, University of Adelaide, Aug. 6-16 (No. 440); General Assembly of World Medical Associations, Sydney, Aug. 6-9 (No. 441). Nos. 440-441 printed in sheets of 100 in two separate panes of 50 connected by a gutter. Each sheet contains 10 gutter pairs.

Runner and Aztec Calendar Stone — A174

Symbolic House and Money — A175

Design: 25c, Aztec calendar stone and Mexican flag, horiz.

1968, Oct. 2

442 A174 5c multicolored .55 .25
443 A174 25c multicolored 1.75 1.75
a. Green omitted *3,500.*

19th Olympic Games, Mexico City, Oct. 12-27. Nos. 442-443 printed in sheets of 100 in two separate panes of 50 connected by a gutter. Each sheet contains 10 gutter pairs.

1968, Oct. 16

444 A175 5c multicolored .35 .35

11th Triennial Congress of the Intl. Union of Building Societies and Savings Associations, Sydney, Oct. 20-27.

View of Bethlehem and Church Window — A176

1968, Oct. 23 Photo. *Perf. 13½*

445 A176 5c lt bl, red, grn & gold .30 .25
a. Red omitted *3,500.* *2,000.*
b. Gold omitted *850.00* *500.00*

Christmas.

Edgeworth David (1858-1934), Geologist A177

Sir Edmund Barton (1849-1920) A178

Famous Australians: No. 447, Caroline Chisholm (1808-77), social worker, reformer. No. 448, Albert Namatjira (1902-59), aborigine, artist. No. 449, Andrew Barton (Banjo) Paterson 1864-1941), poet, writer.

1968, Nov. 6 Engr. *Perf. 15x14*

446 A177 5c green, *greenish* .90 .35
a. Booklet pane of 5 + label 4.75
447 A177 5c purple, *pink* .90 .35
a. Booklet pane of 5 + label 4.75
448 A177 5c dark brown, *buff* .90 .35
a. Booklet pane of 5 + label 4.75
449 A177 5c indigo, *lt blue* .90 .35
a. Booklet pane of 5 + label 4.75
Nos. 446-449 (4) 3.60 1.40

1969, Oct. 22 Engr. *Perf. 15x14*

Prime Ministers: No. 451, Alfred Deakin (1856-1919). No. 452, John C. Watson (1867-1941). No. 453, Sir George H. Reid (1845-1918).

450 A178 5c indigo, *greenish* .90 .35
a. Booklet pane of 5 + label 4.75
451 A178 5c indigo, *greenish* .90 .35
a. Booklet pane of 5 + label 4.75
452 A178 5c indigo, *greenish* .90 .35
a. Booklet pane of 5 + label 4.75
453 A178 5c indigo, *greenish* .90 .35
a. Booklet pane of 5 + label 4.75
Nos. 450-453 (4) 3.60 1.40

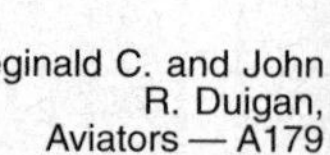

Reginald C. and John R. Duigan, Aviators — A179

Famous Australians: No. 455, Lachlan Macquarie (1761-1824), Governor of New South Wales. No. 456, Adam Lindsay Gordon (1833-70), poet. No. 457, Edward John Eyre (1815-1901), explorer.

1970, Nov. 16 Engr. *Perf. 15x14*

454 A179 6c dark blue .90 .35
a. Booklet pane of 5 + label 4.75
455 A179 6c dk brn, *salmon* .90 .35
a. Booklet pane of 5 + label 4.75
456 A179 6c magenta, *brt pink* .90 .35
a. Booklet pane of 5 + label 4.75
457 A179 6c brown red, *salmon* .90 .35
a. Booklet pane of 5 + label 4.75
Nos. 454-457 (4) 3.60 1.40

Nos. 446-457 were issued in booklet panes only; all stamps have 1 or 2 straight edges.

Macquarie Lighthouse — A180

1968, Nov. 27 Engr. *Perf. 14½x13½*

458 A180 5c indigo, *buff* .45 .50

Macquarie Lighthouse, Outer South Head, Sydney, 150th anniv.

Surveyor George W. Goyder and Assistants, 1869; Building in Darwin, 1969 — A181

1969, Feb. 5 Photo. *Perf. 13½*

459 A181 5c black brn & dull yel .30 .25

First permanent settlement of the Northern Territory of Australia, cent.

Melbourne Harbor Scene A182

1969, Feb. 26 Photo. *Perf. 13½*

460 A182 5c dull blue & multi .30 .25

6th Biennial Conference of the Intl. Assoc. of Ports and Harbors, Melbourne, March 3-8.

Overlapping Circles A183

1969, June 5 Photo. *Perf. 13½*

461 A183 5c gray, vio bl, bl & gold .30 .25
a. Gold omitted *3,000.*

ILO, 50th anniv.

Sugar Cane — A184

Primary industries: 15c, Eucalyptus (timber). 20c, Wheat. 25c, Ram, ewe, lamb (wool).

1969, Sept. 17 *Perf. 13½x13*

462 A184 7c blue & multi .75 1.10
463 A184 15c emerald & multi 3.00 3.00
a. Black omitted *1,750.* —
464 A184 20c org brn & multi 1.00 .75
465 A184 25c gray, black & yel 1.25 1.10
Nos. 462-465 (4) 6.00 5.95

Nativity — A185

Tree of Life — A186

Perf. 13½x13, 13x13½

1969, Oct. 15 Photo.

466 A185 5c multicolored .30 .25
a. Yellow omitted *1,800.*
b. Magenta omitted *1,800.*
467 A186 25c multicolored 2.25 2.25

Christmas.

Vickers Vimy Flown by Ross Smith, England to Australia A187

Designs: No. 469, B.E. 2E plane, automobile, spectators. No. 470, Ford truck, surveyors Lieuts. Hudson Fysh & P.J. McGinness.

1969, Nov. 12 *Perf. 13x13½*

468 A187 5c bl, blk, cop red & ol .55 .35
469 A187 5c bl, blk, cop red & ol .55 .35
470 A187 5c cop red, black & ol .55 .35
a. Strip of 3, #468-470 3.25 3.25
Nos. 468-470 (3) 1.65 1.05

1st England to Australia flight by Capt. Ross Smith & Lieut. Keith Smith, 50th anniv.

No. 470a has various combinations possible.

Diesel Locomotive and New Track Linking Melbourne, Sydney and Brisbane with Perth A188

1970, Feb. 11 Photo. *Perf. 13x13½*

471 A188 5c multicolored .35 .25

Completion of the standard gauge railroad between Sydney and Perth.

EXPO '70 Australian Pavilion A189

Design: 20c, Southern Cross and Japanese inscription: "From the country of the south with warm feeling."

1970, Mar. 16 Photo. *Perf. 13x13½*

472 A189 5c bl, blk, red & brnz .30 .25
473 A189 20c red & black .75 .45

EXPO '70 Intl. Exhib., Osaka, Japan, Mar. 15-Sept. 13.

Queen Elizabeth II and Prince Philip A190

Australian Flag — A191

1970, Mar. 31
474 A190 5c yel bister & black .50 .30
475 A191 30c vio blue & multi 1.25 1.25

Visit of Queen Elizabeth II, Prince Philip and Princess Anne to Australia.

Steer, Alfalfa and Native Spear Grass A192

1970, Apr. 13 Photo. ***Perf. 13x13½***
476 A192 5c emerald & multi .30 .35

11th Intl. Grasslands Congress, Surfers Paradise, Queensland, Apr. 13-23.

Capt. James Cook and "Endeavour" — A193

Designs: No. 478, Sextant, "Endeavour." No. 479, "Endeavour," landing party, kangaroo. No. 480, Daniel Charles Solander, Sir Joseph Banks, Cook, map, botanical drawing. No. 481, Cook taking possession with Union Jack; "Endeavour," coral. 30c, Cook, "Endeavour," sextant, kangaroo, aborigines.

1970, Apr. 20 ***Perf. 13½x13***

Size: 24x35½mm

477 A193 5c org brn & multi .35 .25
478 A193 5c org brn & multi .35 .25
479 A193 5c org brn & multi .35 .25
480 A193 5c org brn & multi .35 .25
481 A193 5c org brn & multi .35 .25
a. Strip of 5, #477-481 1.75 1.75

Size: 62x29mm

482 A193 30c org brn & multi 1.75 1.75
a. Souv. sheet, #477-482, imperf 11.00 11.00
Nos. 477-482 (6) 3.50 3.00

Cook's discovery and exploration of the eastern coast of Australia, 200th anniv.

No. 481a has continuous design.

No. 482a with brown marginal overprint "Souvenir Sheet ANPEX 1970. . ." is of private origin. Value $25.

Snowy Mountains Hydroelectric Project A194

Designs: 8c, Ord River hydroelectric project (dam, cotton plant and boll). 9c, Bauxite and aluminum production (mine, conveyor belt and aluminum window frame). 10c, Oil and natural gas (off-shore drilling rig and pipelines).

1970, Aug. 31 Photo. ***Perf. 13x13½***
483 A194 7c multicolored .50 .40
484 A194 8c multicolored .25 .25
485 A194 9c multicolored .25 .25
486 A194 10c multicolored .35 .30
Nos. 483-486 (4) 1.35 1.20

Australian economic development.

Flame Symbolizing Democracy and Freedom of Speech — A195

1970, Oct. 2 Photo. ***Perf. 13½x13***
487 A195 6c green & multi .30 .25

16th Commonwealth Parliamentary Assoc. Conference, Canberra, Oct. 2-9.

Herd of Illawarra Shorthorns and Laboratory A196

1970, Oct. 7 ***Perf. 13x13½***
488 A196 6c multicolored .30 .25

18th Intl. Dairy Cong., Sydney, Oct. 12-16.

Madonna and Child, by William Beasley A197

UN Emblem, Dove and Symbols A198

1970, Oct. 14 ***Perf. 13½x13***
489 A197 6c multicolored .30 .25

Christmas.

1970, Oct. 19
490 A198 6c blue & multi .30 .25

25th anniversary of the United Nations.

Qantas Boeing 707, and Avro 504 — A199

30c, Sunbeam Dyak powered Avro 504 on ground and Qantas Boeing 707 in the air.

1970, Nov. 2 ***Perf. 13x13½***
491 A199 6c multicolored .40 .25
492 A199 30c multicolored 1.25 1.25

Qantas, Australian overseas airlines, 50th anniv.

Japanese Noh Actor, Australian Dancer and Chinese Opera Character — A200

15c, Chinese pipe, trumpet, Australian aboriginal didgeridoo, Thai fiddle, Indian double oboe, Tibetan drums. 20c, Red Sea dhow, Chinese junk, Australian lifeguard's surfboat, Malaysian & South Indian river boats.

1971, Jan. 6 Photo. ***Perf. 13½x13***
493 A200 7c multicolored .45 *.55*
494 A200 15c multicolored .70 *.70*
495 A200 20c multicolored .70 *.70*
Nos. 493-495 (3) 1.85 1.95

Link between Australia and Asia; 28th Intl. Congress of Orientalists, Canberra, Jan. 6-12.

Southern Cross A201

1971, Apr. 21 Photo. ***Perf. 13x13½***
496 A201 6c multicolored .30 .25

Australian Natives Assoc., cent.

Symbolic Market Graphs — A202

1971, May 5 ***Perf. 13½x13***
497 A202 6c silver & multi .30 .25

Centenary of Sydney Stock Exchange.

Rotary Emblem A203

1971, May 17 ***Perf. 13x13½***
498 A203 6c multicolored .30 .25

First Intl. Rotary Convention held in Australia, Sydney, May 16-20.

DH-9A, Australian Mirage Jet Fighters — A204

1971, June 9 ***Perf. 13½x13***
499 A204 6c multicolored .55 .25

Royal Australian Air Force, 50th anniv.

RSPCA Centenary — A205

Designs: 12c, Man and lamb (animal science). 18c, Kangaroo (fauna conservation). 24c, Seeing eye dog (animals' aid to man).

1971, July 5 Photo. ***Perf. 13½x13***
500 A205 6c blk, brown & org .25 .25
501 A205 12c blk, dk grn & yel .45 .25
502 A205 18c brown & multi .65 .35
a. Litho., perf. 14¾x14, dated "2013" (#1003b) .45 .45
503 A205 24c blue & multi .70 .70
Nos. 500-503 (4) 2.05 1.55

Royal Society for Prevention of Cruelty to Animals in Australia, cent.

Issued: No. 502a, 5/10/2013.

Longnecked Tortoise, Painted on Bark — A206

Aboriginal Art: 25c, Mourners' body paintings, Warramunga tribe. 30c, Cave painting, Western Arnhem Land, vert. 35c, Graveposts, Bathurst and Melville Islands, vert.

Perf. 13x13½, 13½x13

1971, Sept. 29
504 A206 20c multicolored .45 .30
505 A206 25c multicolored .45 .45
506 A206 30c multicolored 1.00 .45
507 A206 35c multicolored .45 .45
Nos. 504-507 (4) 2.35 1.65

Three Kings and Star — A207

1971, Oct. 13 Photo. ***Perf. 13½x13***
508 Block of 7 35.00 35.00
a. A207 7c brt grn, dk bl (Kings) & lil 2.00 .70
b. A207 7c lil, red brn, grn & dk bl 2.00 .70
c. A207 7c red brown & lilac 5.00 1.25
d. A207 7c lilac, red brn & brt grn 2.00 .70
e. A207 7c red brown & dark blue 2.00 .70
f. A207 7c lilac, green & dk blue 15.00 2.25
g. A207 7c brt grn, dk bl & lilac (Kings) 2.00 .70

Christmas. Nos. 508a-508g printed se-tenant in sheets of 50. Each sheet contains 2 green crosses formed by 4 No. 508g and three No. 508a.

Andrew Fisher (1862-1928) A208

Cameo Brooch A209

Prime Ministers: No. 515, Joseph Cook (1860-1947). No. 516, William Morris Hughes (1864-1952). No. 517, Stanley Melbourne Bruce (1883-1967).

1972, Mar. 8 Engr. ***Perf. 15x14***
514 A208 7c dark blue .70 .40
a. Booklet pane of 5 + label 3.50
515 A208 7c dark red .70 .40
a. Booklet pane of 5 + label 3.50
516 A208 7c dark blue .70 .40
a. Booklet pane of 5 + label 3.50
517 A208 7c dark red .70 .40
a. Booklet pane of 5 + label 3.50
Nos. 514-517 (4) 2.80 1.60

Nos. 514-517 were issued in booklets only; all stamps have one or two straight edges.

1972, Apr. 18 Photo. ***Perf. 13½***
518 A209 7c multicolored .35 .25

Country Women's Assoc., 50th anniv.

Apple and Banana A210

1972, June 14
519 A210 20c shown 1.50 1.50
520 A210 25c Rice 1.50 1.50
521 A210 30c Fish 1.50 1.50
522 A210 35c Cattle 3.00 3.00
Nos. 519-522 (4) 7.50 7.50

Worker in Sheltered Workshop — A211

18c, Amputee assembling electrical circuit. 24c, Boy wearing Toronto splint, playing ball.

1972, Aug. 2 ***Perf. 13½x13***
523 A211 12c grn & brn .30 .25
524 A211 18c org & ol, horiz. 1.25 .60
525 A211 24c brn & ultra .50 .25
Nos. 523-525 (3) 2.05 1.10

Rehabilitation of the handicapped.

Overland Telegraph Line — A212

1972, Aug. 22 Photo. ***Perf. 13x13½***
526 A212 7c dk red, blk & lemon .30 .30

Centenary of overland telegraph line.

Athlete, Olympic Rings — A213

1972, Aug. 28 ***Perf. 13½x13***
527 A213 7c shown .45 .45
528 A213 7c Swimming .45 .45
529 A213 7c Rowing .45 .45
530 A213 35c Equestrian 2.75 2.75
Nos. 527-530 (4) 4.10 4.10

20th Olympic Games, Munich, 8/26-9/11.

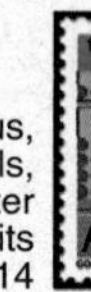

Abacus, Numerals, Computer Circuits A214

1972, Oct. 16 Photo. ***Perf. 13x13½***
531 A214 7c multicolored .30 .30

10th Intl. Congress of Accountants.

19th Cent. Combine Harvester A215

Perf. 13½x13, 13x13½
1972, Nov. 15 **Photo.**
532 A215 5c Pioneer family, vert. .25 .25
533 A215 10c Water pump, vert. .35 .25
534 A215 15c shown .30 .25
535 A215 40c Pioneer house .55 .25
536 A215 50c Cobb & Co. coach .80 .25
537 A215 60c Early Morse key, vert. .80 .55
538 A215 80c Paddle-wheel steamer 1.00 .55
Nos. 532-538 (7) 4.05 2.35

Australian pioneer life.

Jesus and Children A216

Dove, Cross and "Darkness into Light" — A217

Metric Conversion, Mass — A218

Perf. 14½x14, 13½x13
1972, Nov. 29
539 A216 7c tan & multi .35 .25
540 A217 35c blue & multi 6.50 6.50

Christmas.

1973, Mar. 7 Photo. ***Perf. 14x14½***

Metric conversion: No. 542, Temperature, horiz. No. 543, Length. No. 544, Volume.

541 A218 7c pale vio & multi .50 .30
542 A218 7c yellow & multi .50 .30
543 A218 7c yel green & multi .50 .30
544 A218 7c brt rose & multi .50 .30
Nos. 541-544 (4) 2.00 1.20

Conversion to metric system.

Stylized Caduceus and Laurel A219

1973, Apr. 4 Photo. ***Perf. 14½x14***
545 A219 7c dk bl, emer & lil rose .40 .30

WHO, 25th anniv.

Dame Mary Gilmore, Writer A220

Shipping Industry A221

Famous Australians: No. 547, William Charles Wentworth, explorer. No. 548, Sir Isaac Isaacs, lawyer, 1st Australian-born Governor-General. No. 549, Marcus Clarke, writer.

Engr. & Litho.
1973, May 16 ***Perf. 15x14***
546 A220 7c bister & black .65 .30
547 A220 7c bister & black .65 .30
548 A220 7c black & violet .65 .30
549 A220 7c black & violet .65 .30
a. Block of 4, #546-549 3.25 3.25

1973, June 6 Photo. ***Perf. 13½x13***

Designs: 25c, Iron ore and steel. 30c, Truck convoy (beef road). 35c, Aerial mapping.

550 A221 20c ultra & multi 1.50 1.40
551 A221 25c red & multi 1.50 1.40
552 A221 30c ol brn & multi 1.50 1.40
553 A221 35c olive & multi 2.00 1.75
Nos. 550-553 (4) 6.50 5.95

Australian economic development.

Banded Coral Shrimp — A222

Chrysoprase A223

Helichrysum Thomsonii A223a

Wombat A224

Radio Astronomy A225

Red Gums of the Far North, by Hans Heysen — A226

Coming South (Immigrants), by Tom Roberts — A226a

Paintings: $1, Sergeant of Light Horse, by George Lambert. No. 575, On the Wallaby Track. $4, Shearing the Rams, by Tom Roberts. No. 577, McMahon's Point, by Arthur Streeton. No. 578, Mentone.

Perf. 14x15, 15x14 (A222, A223, A223a); Perf. 14x14½ (A224); Perf. 13x13½ (A225, A226, $1)
1973-84 **Photo.**
554 A222 1c shown .25 .25
555 A222 2c Fiddler crab .25 .25
556 A222 3c Coral crab .25 .25
557 A222 4c Mauve stinger .25 .25
558 A223 6c shown .25 .25
559 A223 7c Agate .30 .25
560 A223 8c Opal .30 .25
561 A223 9c Rhodonite .30 .25
562 A223 10c Star sapphire ('74) .35 .25
563 A225 11c Atomic absorption spectrophotometry ('75) .65 .30
564 A223a 18c shown ('75) .60 .25
565 A224 20c shown ('74) .45 .25
566 A225 24c shown ('75) 1.10 .45
567 A224 25c Spiny anteater ('74) 1.40 .40
568 A224 30c Brushtail possum ('74) .80 .25
569 A225 33c Immunology ('75) 1.10 1.10
570 A223a 45c Callistemon teretifolius, horiz. ('75) .95 .35
571 A225 48c Oceanography ('75) 2.00 1.25
572 A224 75c Feather-tailed glider ('74) 1.60 .85
573 A226a $1 multi ('74) 2.00 .35
574 A226 $2 shown ('74) 3.75 .60
575 A226 $2 multi ('81) 3.75 .50
576 A226 $4 multi ('74) 7.50 3.25

Litho.
Perf. 14½
577 A226a $5 multi ('79) 9.50 2.60
578 A226 $5 multi ('84) 9.50 1.40
579 A226a $10 shown ('77) 15.00 3.75
Nos. 554-579 (26) 64.15 20.15

Issued: 1c-9c, 7/11; 20c, 25c, 30c, 75c, 2/13; $1, No. 574, $4, 4/24; 10c, 10/16; 11c, 24c, 33c, 48c, 5/14; 18c, 45c, 8/27; $10, 10/19; No. 577, 3/14; No. 575, 6/17; No. 578, 4/4.

No. 560 Surcharged in Red

Perf. 15x14
580 A223 9c on 8c multi ('74) .30 .35

Hand Protecting Playing Children A227

1973, Sept. 5 Photo. ***Perf. 13x13½***
581 A227 7c bis brn, grn & plum .30 .25

50th anniv. of Legacy, an ex-servicemen's organization concerned with the welfare of widows and children of servicemen.

Baptism of Christ A228

The Good Shepherd A229

1973, Oct. 3 ***Perf. 14x14½***
582 A228 7c gold & multi .30 .25
a. Perf. 14x15 3.00 .75

Perf. 13½
583 A229 30c gold & multi 2.25 2.25

Christmas.

Buchanan's Hotel, Townsville A230

St. James' Church, Sydney — A231

Designs: 7c, Opera House, Sydney. 40c, Como House, Melbourne.

1973, Oct. 17 Photo. ***Perf. 14½x14***
584 A230 7c lt blue & ultra .35 .25
a. Perf. 15x14 4.50 .90
585 A230 10c bister & black .50 .35

Perf. 13x13½, 13½x13
586 A230 40c dl pink, gray & blk .65 .75
587 A231 50c gray & multi 1.50 1.25
Nos. 584-587 (4) 3.00 2.60

Australian architecture; opening of the Sydney Opera House, Oct. 14, 1973 (No. 584).

Radio and Gramophone Speaker A232

1973, Nov. 21 Photo. ***Perf. 13½x13***
588 A232 7c dull blue, blk & brn .35 .25

Broadcasting in Australia, 50th anniv.

Supreme Court Judge on Bench A233

Australian Football A234

1974, May 15 Photo. *Perf. 14x14½*

589 A233 7c multicolored .35 .25

150th anniv. of the proclamation of the Charter of Justice in New South Wales and Van Diemen's Land (Australia's Third Charter).

1974, July 24 Photo. *Perf. 14x14½*

590 A234 7c shown .35 .25
591 A234 7c Cricket .35 .25
a. Booklet pane of 1, litho., perf. 14¾x14, dated "2007" .25 —
592 A234 7c Golf .35 .25
593 A234 7c Surfing .35 .25
594 A234 7c Tennis .35 .25
595 A234 7c Bowls, horiz. .35 .25
596 A234 7c Rugby, horiz. .35 .25
Nos. 590-596 (7) 2.45 1.75

No. 591a issued 11/14/2007.

Carrier Pigeon A235

Designs: 30c, Carrier pigeons, vert.

1974, Oct. 9 Photo. *Perf. 14½x14*

597 A235 7c multicolored .35 .25
a. Perf. 15x14 .60 .35

Perf. 13½x13

598 A235 30c multicolored 1.10 1.10

UPU, cent. A booklet containing a strip of 5 each of Nos. 597-598 was produced and sold for $4 Australian by the National Stamp Week Promotion Council with government approval.

William Charles Wentworth A236

Adoration of the Kings, by Dürer A237

Typo. & Litho.

1974, Oct. 9 *Perf. 14x15*

599 A236 7c bister & black .40 .25
a. Perf. 14x14½ 1.60 *.40*

Sesquicentennial of 1st Australian independent newspaper. W. C. Wentworth and Dr. Robert Wardell were the editors and the "A" is type from masthead of "The Australian."

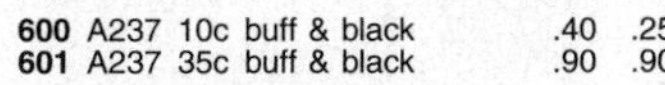

1974, Nov. 13 Engr. *Perf. 14x14½*

Christmas: 35c, Flight into Egypt, by Albrecht Dürer.

600 A237 10c buff & black .40 .25
601 A237 35c buff & black .90 .90

Pre-school Education A238

Correspondence Schools — A239

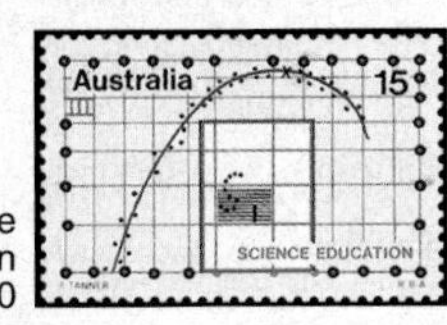

Science Education A240

Advanced Education — A241

Perf. 13x13½, 13½x13

1974, Nov. 20 Photo.

602 A238 5c multicolored .30 .25
603 A239 11c multicolored .30 .25
604 A240 15c multicolored .40 .30
605 A241 60c multicolored .75 .75
Nos. 602-605 (4) 1.75 1.55

"Avoid Pollution" A242

"Road Safety" — A243

Design: No. 607, "Avoid bush fires."

1975, Jan. 29 Photo. *Perf. 14½x14*

606 A242 10c multicolored .55 .45
a. Perf. 15x14 7.50 5.00
607 A242 10c multicolored .55 .45
a. Perf. 15x14 1.75 1.10

Perf. 14x14½

608 A243 10c multicolored .55 .45
Nos. 606-608 (3) 1.65 1.35

Environmental dangers.

Symbols of Womanhood, Sun, Moon A244

Joseph B. Chifley (1885-1951) A245

1975, Mar. 12 Photo. *Perf. 14x14½*

609 A244 10c dk vio blue & grn .35 .25

International Women's Year.

1975, Mar. 26

610 A245 10c shown .30 .25
611 A245 10c John Curtin, 1885-1945 .30 .25
612 A245 10c Arthur W. Fadden, 1895-1973 .30 .25
613 A245 10c Joseph A. Lyons, 1879-1939 .30 .25
614 A245 10c Earle Page, 1880-1963 .30 .25
615 A245 10c John H. Scullin, 1876-1953 .30 .25
Nos. 610-615 (6) 1.80 1.50

Australian Prime Ministers.

Australian Postal Commission A246

Design: No. 617, Australian Telecommunications Commission.

1975, July 1 Photo. *Perf. 14½x14*

616 A246 10c red, black & gray .65 .45
a. Perf. 15x14 .85 .45
617 A246 10c yel, black & gray .65 .45
a. Pair, #616-617 1.60 1.25
b. Perf. 15x14 .85 .45
c. Pair, #616a, 617b 3.50 3.50

Formation of Australian Postal and Telecommunications Commissions. Printed checkerwise.

Edith Cowan, Judge and Legislator A247

Truganini, Last Tasmanian Aborigine A248

Portraits: No. 619, Louisa Lawson (1848-1920), journalist. No. 620, Ethel Florence (Henry Handel) Richardson (1870-1946), novelist. No. 621, Catherine Spence (1825-1910), teacher, journalist, voting reformer. No. 622, Emma Constance Stone (1856-1902), first Australian woman physician.

1975, Aug. 6 Photo. *Perf. 14x14½*

618 A247 10c olive grn & multi .45 .30
a. Perf. 14x15 .45 .30
619 A247 10c yel bister & multi .45 .30
a. Perf. 14x15 .45 .30
620 A248 10c olive & multi .45 .30
a. Perf. 14x15 .45 .30
621 A248 10c gray & multi .45 .30
a. Perf. 14x15 .45 .30
622 A247 10c violet & multi .45 .30
a. Perf. 14x15 .45 .30
623 A248 10c brown & multi .45 .30
a. Perf. 14x15 .45 .30
Nos. 618-623 (6) 2.70 1.80

Famous Australian women.

Spirit House (PNG) and Sydney Opera House — A249

Bird in Flight and Southern Cross A250

1975, Sept. 16 Photo. *Perf. 13½*

624 A249 18c multicolored .45 .25
625 A250 25c multicolored .80 .65

Papua New Guinea independence, Sept. 16, 1975.

Adoration of the Kings — A251

"The Light Shineth in the Darkness" A252

1975, Oct. 29 Photo. *Perf. 14½x14*

626 A251 15c multicolored .40 .25
627 A252 45c silver & multi 1.50 1.50

Christmas.

Australian Coat of Arms A253

Type I

Type II

Type I — Kangaroo: eye is dot, right paw has 1 toe, left foot has 1 toe. Emu: feet have 1 toe.

Type II — Kangaroo: eye is line, right paw has 3 toes, left foot has 2 toes. Emu: feet have 2 toes.

Other differences exist.

1976, Jan. 5 Photo. *Perf. 14½x14*

628 A253 18c multicolored, type I .40 .25
a. Type II .95 .40

"Williams' Coffin" Telephone, 1878 — A254

1976, Mar. 10 Photo. *Perf. 13½*

629 A254 18c buff & multi .40 .30

Centenary of first telephone call by Alexander Graham Bell, Mar. 10, 1876.

John Oxley A255

Designs: Australian explorers.

1976, June 9 Photo. *Perf. 13½*

630 A255 18c shown .35 .25
631 A255 18c Hamilton Hume and William Hovell .35 .25
632 A255 18c John Forrest .35 .25
633 A255 18c Ernest Giles .35 .25
634 A255 18c Peter Warburton .35 .25
635 A255 18c William Gosse .35 .25
Nos. 630-635 (6) 2.10 1.50

Survey Rule, Graph, Punched Tape — A256

1976, June 15 ***Perf. 15x14***
636 A256 18c multicolored .40 .25

Commonwealth Scientific and Industrial Research Organization, 50th anniv.

Soccer Goalkeeper A257

Olympic Rings and: No. 638, Woman gymnast, vert. 25c, Woman diver, vert. 40c, Bicycling.

Perf. 13x13½, 13½x13
1976, July 14 **Photo.**
637 A257 18c multicolored .30 .25
638 A257 18c multicolored .30 .25
639 A257 25c multicolored .40 .40
640 A257 40c multicolored .60 .50
Nos. 637-640 (4) 1.60 1.40

21st Olympic Games, Montreal, Canada, July 17-Aug. 1.

Richmond Bridge, Tasmania A258

Mt. Buffalo, Victoria — A259

Designs: 25c, Broken Bay, New South Wales. 35c, Wittenoom Gorge, Western Australia. 70c, Barrier Reef, Queensland. 85c, Ayers Rock, Northern Territory.

Perf. 14½x14, 14x14½
1976, Aug. 25 **Photo.**
641 A258 5c multicolored .30 .25
642 A258 25c multicolored .45 .25
643 A258 35c multicolored .50 .30
644 A259 50c multicolored .70 .30
645 A258 70c multicolored .85 .40
646 A258 85c multicolored 1.00 .70
Nos. 641-646 (6) 3.80 2.20

Blamire Young and Australia No. 59 — A260

1976, Sept. 27 **Photo.** ***Perf. 13½***
647 A260 18c apple grn & multi .40 .25

Miniature Sheet

648 Sheet of 4 2.00 2.00
a. A260 18c yellow & dark brown .50 .50
b. A260 18c rose, dk brown & yel .50 .50
c. A260 18c bl, dk brn, rose & yel .50 .50

Natl. Stamp Week, Sept. 27-Oct. 3. Blamire Young (1862-1935), designer of Australia's 1st issue. No. 648 shows different stages of 4-color printing. The 4th stamp in sheet is identical with No. 647.

Virgin and Child, after Simone Cantarini A261

Holly, Toy Koala, Christmas Tree and Decoration, Partridge A262

1976, Nov. 1 **Photo.** ***Perf. 14½x14***
649 A261 15c brt car & lt blue .40 .25

Perf. 13½

650 A262 45c multicolored .80 .80

Christmas.

John Gould (1804-1881) Ornithologist A263

Famous Australians: No. 652, Thomas Laby (1880-1946), nuclear scientist. No. 653, Sir Baldwin Spencer (1860-1929), anthropologist (aborigines). No. 654, Griffith Taylor (1880-1963), geographer and antarctic explorer.

1976, Nov. 10 ***Perf. 15x14***
651 A263 18c shown .35 .25
652 A263 18c Laby .35 .25
653 A263 18c Spencer .35 .25
654 A263 18c Taylor .35 .25
Nos. 651-654 (4) 1.40 1.00

Violinists — A264

1977, Jan. 19 **Photo.** ***Perf. 14x14½***
655 A264 20c shown .30 .25
656 A264 30c Dramatic scene .35 .25
657 A264 40c Dancer .45 .30
658 A264 60c Opera singer .90 .40
Nos. 655-658 (4) 2.00 1.20

Performing arts in Australia.

Elizabeth II — A265

Design: 45c, Elizabeth II and Prince Philip.

1977, Feb. 2 ***Perf. 14x14½***
659 A265 18c multicolored .40 .30
660 A265 45c multicolored .75 .75

Reign of Queen Elizabeth II, 25th anniv.
Perf 14½x14 examples of Nos. 659-660 are from a booklet pane containing 2 of each stamp, found in the booklet footnoted under No. 2507.

Wicket Keeper, Slip Fieldsman — A266

Cricket match, 19th century: No. 662, Umpire and batsman. No. 663, Two fieldsmen. No. 664, Batsman and umpire. No. 665, Bowler and fieldsman. 45c, Batsman facing bowler.

1977, Mar. 9 **Photo.** ***Perf. 13½***
661 A266 18c gray & multi .45 .45
a. Litho., perf. 14¾x14, dated "2007" .55 .55
662 A266 18c gray & multi .45 .45
a. Litho., perf. 14¾x14, dated "2007" .55 .55
663 A266 18c gray & multi .45 .45
a. Litho., perf. 14¾x14, dated "2007" .55 .55
664 A266 18c gray & multi .45 .45
a. Litho., perf. 14¾x14, dated "2007" .55 .55
665 A266 18c gray & multi .45 .45
a. Strip of 5, #661-665 3.00 3.00
b. Litho., perf. 14¾x14, dated "2007" .55 .55
666 A266 45c gray & multi 1.00 1.00
a. Litho., imperf., dated "2007" 1.25 1.25
b. Booklet pane of 6, #661a, 662a, 663a, 664a, 665b, 666a 4.00 —
Nos. 661-666 (6) 3.25 3.25

Nos. 661a, 662a, 663a, 664a, 665b, 666a, 666b issued 11/14/2007.

Parliament House, Canberra A267

1977, Apr. 13 ***Perf. 14½x14***
667 A267 18c multicolored .40 .25

Parliament House, Canberra, 50th anniv.

Trade Union Workers A268

1977, May 9 **Photo.** ***Perf. 13***
668 A268 18c multicolored .40 .25

Australian Council of Trade Unions (ACTU), 50th anniv.

Surfing Santa — A269

Virgin and Child — A270

1977, Oct. 31 **Photo.** ***Perf. 14x14½***
669 A269 15c multicolored .40 .25

Perf. 13½x13

670 A270 45c multicolored .75 .75

Christmas.

Australian Flag — A271

1978, Jan. 26 **Photo.** ***Perf. 13x13½***
671 A271 18c multicolored .40 .30

Australia Day, 190th anniversary of first permanent settlement in New South Wales.

Harry Hawker and Sopwith "Camel" A272

Australian Aviators and their Planes: No. 673, Bert Hinkler and Avro Avian. No. 674, Charles Kingsford-Smith and Fokker "Southern Cross." No. 675, Charles Ulm and "Southern Cross."

1978, Apr. 19 **Litho.** ***Perf. 15½***
672 A272 18c ultra & multi .40 .30
673 A272 18c blue & multi .40 .30
674 A272 18c orange & multi .40 .30
675 A272 18c yellow & multi .40 .30
a. Souv. sheet, 2 each #674-675, imperf. 1.60 1.50
Nos. 672-675 (4) 1.60 1.20

No. 675a for 50th anniv. of first Trans-Pacific flight from Oakland, Cal., to Brisbane.

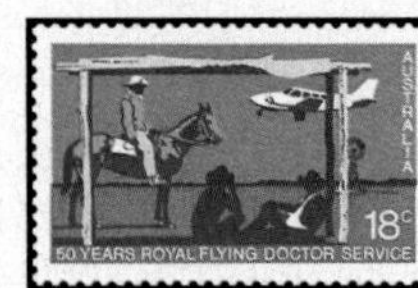

Beechcraft Baron Landing A273

1978, May 15 **Photo.** ***Perf. 13½***
676 A273 18c multicolored .40 .30

Royal Flying Doctor Service, 50th anniv.

Illawarra Flame Tree A274

Sturt's Desert Rose, Map of Australia A275

Australian trees: 25c, Ghost gum. 40c, Grass tree. 45c, Cootamundra wattle.

1978, June 1
677 A274 18c multicolored .25 .25
678 A274 25c multicolored .50 .50
679 A274 40c multicolored .65 .65
680 A274 45c multicolored .70 .70
Nos. 677-680 (4) 2.10 2.10

1978, June 19 **Litho.** ***Perf. 15½***
681 A275 18c multicolored .40 .25

Establishment of Government of the Northern Territory.

Hooded Dotterel — A276

Australian birds: 20c, Little grebe. 25c, Spur-wing Plover. 30c, Pied oystercatcher. 55c, Lotus bird.

1978 **Photo.** ***Perf. 13½***
682 A276 5c multicolored .25 .25
683 A276 20c multicolored .40 .25
684 A276 25c multicolored .45 .25
685 A276 30c multicolored .70 .35
686 A276 55c multicolored .90 .60
Nos. 682-686 (5) 2.70 1.70

Issued: Nos. 683, 686, July 3; others, July 17. See Nos. 713-718, 732-739, 768.

Australia No. 95 on Album Page — A277

1978, Sept. 25 **Litho.** ***Perf. 15½***
687 A277 20c multicolored .40 .25
a. Miniature sheet of 4 1.10 1.10

National Stamp Week; 50th anniv. of Melbourne Intl. Phil. Exhib., Oct. 1928.

Virgin and Child, by Simon Marmion — A278

Paintings from National Gallery, Victoria: 15c, Virgin and Child, after Van Eyck. 55c, Holy Family, by Perino del Vaga.

1978 ***Perf. 15***

688 A278 15c multicolored .40 .25
689 A278 25c multicolored .55 .55
690 A278 55c multicolored 1.00 .80
Nos. 688-690 (3) 1.95 1.60

Christmas. Issued: 25c, 10/3; others, 11/1.

Tulloch A279

Race horses: 35c, Bernborough, vert. 50c, Phar Lap, vert. 55c, Peter Pan.

Perf. 15x14, 14x15

1978, Oct. 18 **Photo.**

691 A279 20c multicolored .40 .30
692 A279 35c multicolored .70 .55
693 A279 50c multicolored .90 .85
694 A279 55c multicolored 1.00 .95
Nos. 691-694 (4) 3.00 2.65

Australian horse racing.

Flag Raising at Sydney Cove — A280

1979, Jan. 26 **Litho.** ***Perf. 15½***

695 A280 20c multicolored .40 .30

Australia Day, Jan. 26.

Passenger Steamer Canberra A281

Ferries and Murray River Steamers: 35c, M.V. Lady Denman. 50c, P.S. Murray River Queen. 55c, Hydrofoil Curl Curl.

Perf. 13½, 15x14 (20c)

1979, Feb. 14 **Photo.**

696 A281 20c multicolored .35 .30
697 A281 35c multicolored .70 .55
698 A281 50c multicolored .90 .90
699 A281 55c multicolored 1.00 .95
Nos. 696-699 (4) 2.95 2.70

Port Campbell A282

Designs: Australian National Parks.

1979, Apr. 9 **Litho.** ***Perf. 15½***

700 A282 20c shown .35 .35
701 A282 20c Uluru .35 .35
702 A282 20c Royal .35 .35
703 A282 20c Flinders Ranges .35 .35
704 A282 20c Namburg .35 .35
a. Strip of 5, #700-704 2.00 2.00
705 A282 20c Girraween, vert. .35 .35
706 A282 20c Mount Field, vert. .35 .35
a. Pair, #705-706 .75 .75
Nos. 700-706 (7) 2.45 2.45

Double Fairlie A283

Australian steam locomotives: 35c, Puffing Billy. 50c, Pichi Richi. 55c, Zig Zag.

Perf. 13½, 15x14 (20c)

1979, May 16 **Photo.**

707 A283 20c multicolored .40 .30
708 A283 35c multicolored .75 .55
709 A283 50c multicolored .90 .85
710 A283 55c multicolored 1.00 .95
Nos. 707-710 (4) 3.05 2.65

"Black Swan" A284

1979, June 6 **Photo.** ***Perf. 13½***

711 A284 20c multicolored .40 .25

150th anniversary of Western Australia.

Children Playing, IYC Emblem A285

1979, Aug. 13 **Litho.** ***Perf. 13½x13***

712 A285 20c multicolored .40 .25

International Year of the Child.

Bird Type of 1978

Australian birds: 1c, Zebra finch. 2c, Crimson finch. 15c, Forest kingfisher, vert. 20c, Eastern yellow robin. 40c, Lovely wren, vert. 50c, Flame robin, vert.

1979, Sept. 17 **Photo.** ***Perf. 13½***

713 A276 1c multicolored .25 .25
714 A276 2c multicolored .25 .25
715 A276 15c multicolored .35 .25
716 A276 20c multicolored .45 .25
717 A276 40c multicolored .75 .35
718 A276 50c multicolored 1.00 .40
Nos. 713-718 (6) 3.05 1.75

Christmas Letters, Flag-wrapped Parcels — A286

Trout Fishing — A287

Christmas: 15c, Nativity, icon. 55c, Madonna and Child, by Buglioni.

1979 **Litho.** ***Perf. 13***

719 A286 15c multicolored .35 .25
720 A286 25c multicolored .45 .30
721 A286 55c multicolored 1.00 .90
Nos. 719-721 (3) 1.80 1.45

Issue dates: 25c, Sept. 24. Others, Nov. 1.

1979, Oct. 24 **Photo.** ***Perf. 14x14½***

Sport fishing: 35c, Angler. 50c, Black marlin fishing. 55c, Surf fishing.

722 A287 20c multicolored .35 .30
723 A287 35c multicolored .70 .55
724 A287 50c multicolored .90 .75
725 A287 55c multicolored 1.00 .85
Nos. 722-725 (4) 2.95 2.45

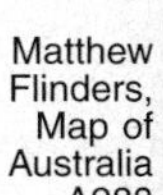

Matthew Flinders, Map of Australia A288

1980, Jan. 23 **Litho.** ***Perf. 13½***

726 A288 20c multicolored .40 .25

Australia Day, Jan. 28.

Dingo A289

1980, Feb. 20 **Photo.** ***Perf. 13½x13***

727 A289 20c shown .35 .25
728 A289 25c Border collie .45 .45
729 A289 35c Australian terrier .65 .65
730 A289 50c Australian cattle dog .90 .85
731 A289 55c Australian kelpie 1.00 .90
Nos. 727-731 (5) 3.35 3.10

Bird Type of 1978

Perf. 13x12½ (10c, 28c, 35c, 60c, $1), 14x15 (22c), 12½x13 (45c, 80c)

1980 **Litho., Photo. (22c)**

732 A276 10c Golden-shoulder parrot, vert. .30 .25
a. Perf. 14½x14 1.40 .45
733 A276 22c White-tailed kingfisher, vert. .45 .30
734 A276 28c Rainbow bird, vert. .55 .45
735 A276 35c Regent bower bird, vert. .70 .45
736 A276 45c Masked woodswallow .95 .60
a. Perf. 14x14½ 2.50 1.80
737 A276 60c King parrot, vert. 1.25 .60
738 A276 80c Rainbow pitta 1.60 1.00
739 A276 $1 Western magpie, vert. 2.00 .45
Nos. 732-739 (8) 7.80 4.10

Issued: Nos. 733, 734, 737, 3/31; others, 7/1.

Queen Elizabeth II, 54th Birthday — A290

1980, Apr. 21 **Litho.** ***Perf. 13x13½***

740 A290 22c multicolored .35 .25

Wanderer A291

High Court Building, Canberra A292

1980, May 7 **Litho.** ***Perf. 13x13½***

741 Strip of 5 2.00 2.00
a. A291 22c shown .35 .35
b. A291 22c Stealing sheep .35 .35
c. A291 22c Squatter on horseback .35 .35
d. A291 22c Three troopers .35 .35
e. A291 22c Wanderer's ghost .35 .35

"Waltzing Matilda", poem by Andrew Barton Patterson (1864-1941). No. 741 in continuous design.

1980, May 19

742 A292 22c multicolored .40 .25

Opening of High Court of Australia Building, Canberra, May 26.

Salvation Army Officers A294

Perf. 13x13½, 13½x13

1980, Aug. 11

747 A294 22c shown .40 .30
748 A294 22c St. Vincent de Paul Society, vert. .40 .30
749 A294 22c Meals on Wheels, vert. .40 .30
750 A294 22c "Life. Be in it." (Joggers, bicyclists) .40 .30
Nos. 747-750 (4) 1.60 1.20

Mailman c. 1900 — A295

Holy Family, by Prospero Fontana — A296

1980, Sept. 29 **Litho.** ***Perf. 13x13½***

751 A295 22c Mailbox .40 .25
752 A295 22c shown .40 .25
753 A295 22c Mail truck .40 .25
754 A295 22c Mailman, mailbox .40 .25
755 A295 22c Mailman, diff. .40 .25
a. Souvenir sheet of 3 1.50 1.50
b. Strip of 5, #751-755 2.00 2.00
Nos. 751-755 (5) 2.00 1.25

Natl. Stamp Week, Sept. 29-Oct. 5. Nos. 755a contains stamps similar to #751, 753, 755.

No. 755a overprinted "SYDPEX 80" was privately produced.

1980 ***Perf. 13x13½***

Christmas: 15c, Virgin Enthroned, by Justin O'Brien. 60c, Virgin and Child, by Michael Zuern the Younger, 1680.

756 A296 15c multicolored .30 .25
757 A296 28c multicolored .55 .45
758 A296 60c multicolored 1.10 .65
Nos. 756-758 (3) 1.95 1.35

Issued: 15c, 60c, Nov. 3; 28c, Oct. 1.

CA-6 Wackett Trainer, 1941 — A297

Designs: Australian military training planes.

1980, Nov. 19 ***Perf. 13½x14***

759 A297 22c shown .40 .30
760 A297 40c Winjeel, 1955 .75 .55
761 A297 45c Boomerang, 1944 .80 .60
762 A297 60c Nomad, 1975 1.10 .80
Nos. 759-762 (4) 3.05 2.25

Bird Type of 1978

1980, Nov. 17 **Litho.** ***Perf. 13½***

768 A276 18c Spotted catbird, vert. .50 .25

Flag on Map of Australia A298

1981, Jan. 21 ***Perf. 13½x13***

771 A298 22c multicolored .40 .25

Australia Day, Jan. 21.

Jockey Darby Munro (1913-1966), by Tony Rafty — A299

Australian sportsmen (Caricatures by Tony Rafty): 35c, Victor Trumper (1877-1915), cricket batsman. 55c, Norman Brookes (1877-1968), tennis player. 60c, Walter Lindrum (1898-1960), billiards player.

1981, Feb. 18 ***Perf. 14x13½***

772 A299 22c multicolored .40 .25
773 A299 35c multicolored .65 .60
a. Booklet pane of 1, perf. 14¾x14, dated "2007" 1.10 —
774 A299 55c multicolored 1.00 .90
775 A299 60c multicolored 1.10 1.00
Nos. 772-775 (4) 3.15 2.75

No. 773a issued 11/14/2007.

Australia No. C2 and Cover A300

Perf. 13x13½, 13½x13

1981, Mar. 25 **Litho.**

776 A300 22c Australia No. C2, vert. .45 .45
777 A300 60c shown 1.10 .80

Australia-United Kingdom official airmail service, 50th anniv.

Map of Australia, APEX Emblem A301

1981, Apr. 6 **Photo.** ***Perf. 13x13½***

778 A301 22c multicolored .40 .25

50th anniv. of APEX (young men's service club).

Queen Elizabeth's Personal Flag of Australia A302

1981, Apr. 21 **Litho.** ***Perf. 13***

779 A302 22c multicolored .40 .25

Queen Elizabeth II, 55th birthday.

Perf 14x14¾ examples in a booklet pane of 4 come from the booklet footnoted under No. 2507.

License Inspected, Forrest Creek, by S.T. Gill — A303

Gold Rush Era (Sketches by S.T. Gill): No. 781, Puddling. No. 782, Quality of Washing Stuff. No. 783, Diggers on Route to Deposit Gold.

1981, May 20 ***Perf. 13x13½***

780 A303 22c multicolored .40 .30
781 A303 22c multicolored .40 .30
782 A303 22c multicolored .40 .30
783 A303 22c multicolored .40 .30
Nos. 780-783 (4) 1.60 1.20

Lace Monitor — A303a

Tasmanian Tiger — A304

Two Types of A304:

Type I — Indistinct line at right of ear, stripes even with base of tail.

Type II — Heavy line at right of ear, stripes longer.

1981-83 **Litho.**

784 A303a 1c shown .25 .25
785 A303a 3c Corroboree frog .25 .25
786 A304 5c Queensland hairy-nosed wombat, vert. .35 .35
b. Imperf., dated "2007" .25 .25
787 A303a 15c Eastern snake-necked tortoise .35 .25
788 A304 24c Type I, photo. & litho. .60 .40
a. Shown, type II, litho. .70 .40
b. Imperf., dated "2007" .50 .50
789 A304 25c Greater bilby, vert. .70 .45
b. Imperf., dated "2007" .60 .60
790 A303a 27c Blue Mountains tree frog .60 .25
791 A304 30c Bridled nail-tailed wallaby, vert. .90 .60
a. Imperf., dated "2007" .70 .70
792 A303a 40c Smooth knob-tailed gecko .85 .45
793 A304 50c Leadbeater's opossum 1.10 .70
b. Imperf., dated "2007" 1.10 1.10
c. Booklet pane, 2 each #788b, 793b 3.50 —
794 A304 55c Stick-nest rat, vert. 1.10 .70
a. Imperf., dated "2007" 1.25 1.25
b. Booklet pane, #786b, 789b, 791a, 794a 2.75 —
795 A303a 65c Yellow-faced whip snake 1.40 .70
796 A303a 70c Crucifix toad 1.40 .75
797 A303a 75c Eastern water dragon 1.60 .75
798 A303a 85c Centralian blue-tongued lizard 1.90 1.10
799 A303a 90c Freshwater crocodile 1.90 .90
800 A303a 95c Thorny devil 2.00 1.10
Nos. 784-800 (17) 17.25 9.95

Perfs: 1c, 70c, 85c, 95c, 13½; 3c, 15c, 27c, 40c, 50c, 65c, 75c, 90c, 12½x13; 5c, 25c, 30c, 55c, 13x12½; 24c, 13x13½.

Issued: 24c, 7/1/81; 5c, 25c, 30c, 50c, 55c, 7/15/81; 3c, 27c, 65c, 75c, 4/19/82; 15c, 40c, 90c, 6/16/82. 1c, 70c, 85c, 95c, 2/2/83.

Nos. 786b, 788b, 789b, 791a, 793b. 793c, 794a, 794b issued 6/26/07. No. 788b has wider spacing between text lines than on the original stamps.

1982-84 ***Perf. 14x14½, 14½x14***

785a	A303a	3c ('84)	.70	.45
786a	A304	5c ('84)	1.40	.50
787a	A303a	15c ('84)	1.25	.60
789a	A304	25c ('83)	1.40	.60
790a	A303a	27c	1.10	.30
792a	A303a	40c ('84)	3.00	1.10
793a	A304	50c ('83)	2.25	1.10
795a	A303a	65c ('84)	2.25	1.40
797a	A303a	75c ('84)	2.60	1.40
Nos. 785a-797a (9)			15.95	7.45

Prince Charles and Lady Diana A305

1981, July 29 **Litho.** ***Perf. 13***

804 A305 24c multicolored .45 .25
805 A305 60c multicolored 1.25 *1.50*

Royal Wedding.

Fungi — A306

Intl. Year of the Disabled — A307

1981, Aug. 19 **Litho.** ***Perf. 13***

806 A306 24c Cortinarius cinnabarinus .55 .40
807 A306 35c Coprinus comatus .70 .70
808 A306 55c Armillaria luteobubalina 1.00 1.00
809 A306 60c Cortinarius austrovenetus 1.10 1.10
Nos. 806-809 (4) 3.35 3.20

1981, Sept. 16 ***Perf. 14x13½***

810 A307 24c multicolored .45 .30

Christmas Bush for His Adorning A308

Globe A309

Christmas (Carols by William James and John Wheeler): 30c, The Silver Stars are in the Sky. 60c, Noeltime.

1981 **Litho.** ***Perf. 13x13½***

811 A308 18c multicolored .35 .25
812 A308 30c multicolored .60 .55
813 A308 60c multicolored 1.10 1.00
Nos. 811-813 (3) 2.05 1.80

Issue dates: 30c, Sept. 28; others, Nov. 2.

1981, Sept. 30

814 A309 24c multicolored .55 .40
815 A309 60c multicolored 1.00 1.00

Commonwealth Heads of Government Meeting, Melbourne, Sept. 30-Oct. 7.

Yacht — A310

1981, Oct. 14 **Litho.** ***Perf. 13x13½***

816 A310 24c Ocean racer .45 .30
817 A310 35c Lightweight sharpie .65 .50
818 A310 55c 12-Meter 1.00 .90
819 A310 60c Sabot 1.10 1.00
Nos. 816-819 (4) 3.20 2.70

Australia Day, Jan. 26 A311

1982, Jan. 20 **Litho.** ***Perf. 13x13½***

820 A311 24c multicolored .45 .30

Sperm Whale A312

1982, Feb. 17 ***Perf. 13x13½, 13½x13***

821 A312 24c shown .60 .55
822 A312 35c Southern right whale, vert. .80 .70
823 A312 55c Blue whale, vert. 1.00 1.00
824 A312 60c Humpback whale 1.10 1.10
Nos. 821-824 (4) 3.50 3.35

A trial printing of No. 824 exists with a greenish blue background and no white streaks at the UL. A small number of these stamps were sold by mistake.

Elizabeth II, 56th Birthday — A313

Roses — A314

1982, Apr. 21 ***Perf. 13½***

825 A313 27c multicolored .50 .40

1982, May 19 ***Perf. 13x13½***

826 A314 27c Marjorie Atherton .50 .30
827 A314 40c Imp .75 .60
828 A314 65c Minnie Watson 1.10 1.00
829 A314 75c Satellite 1.25 1.10
Nos. 826-829 (4) 3.60 3.00

50th Anniv. of Australian Broadcasting Commission A315

1982, June 16 ***Perf. 13½x13***

830 A315 27c Announcer, microphone .45 .35
831 A315 27c Emblem .45 .35
a. Pair, #830-831 1.00 1.00

Nos. 830-831 se-tenant in continuous design.

Alice Springs Post Office, 1872 — A316

1982, Aug. 4 ***Perf. 13½x14, 14x13½***

832 A316 27c shown .50 .30
833 A316 27c Kingston, 1869 .50 .30
834 A316 27c York, 1893 .50 .30
835 A316 27c Flemington, 1890, vert. .50 .30
836 A316 27c Forbes, 1881, vert. .50 .30
837 A316 27c Launceston, 1889, vert. .50 .30
838 A316 27c Rockhampton, 1892, vert. .50 .30
Nos. 832-838 (7) 3.50 2.10

Christmas — A317

1st Australian Christmas cards, 1881. 21c, horiz.

1982 **Litho.** ***Perf. 14½***

839 A317 21c multicolored .35 .25
840 A317 35c multicolored .65 .40
841 A317 75c multicolored 1.25 1.00
Nos. 839-841 (3) 2.25 1.65

Issue dates: 35c, Sept. 15; others, Nov. 1.

12th Commonwealth Games, Brisbane, Sept. 30-Oct. 9 — A318

1982, Sept. 22 Litho. *Perf. 14x14½*

842 A318 27c Archery .50 .40
843 A318 27c Boxing .50 .40
844 A318 27c Weightlifting .50 .40
a. Souvenir sheet of 3, #842-844 1.75 1.75
845 A318 75c Pole vault 1.25 1.25
a. Booklet pane of 4, #842-845, perf. 14x14¾ ('06) 3.00 —
Nos. 842-845 (4) 2.75 2.45

Nos. 842-842 are perf 14½. No. 844a is perf 13½x13.

No. 845a issued 3/1/2006.

Natl. Stamp Week A319

1982, Sept. 27 *Perf. 13x13½*

846 A319 27c No. 132 .50 .30

A320

A321

Design: Gurgurr (Moon Spirit), Bark Painting by Yirawala Gunwinggu Tribe.

1982, Oct. 12 *Perf. 14½*

847 A320 27c multicolored .50 .30

Opening of Natl. Gallery, Canberra.

Perf. 12½x13½

1982, Nov. 17 Photo.

Designs: Various eucalypts (gum trees).

848 A321 1c Pink-flowered marri .25 .25
849 A321 2c Gungurru .25 .25
850 A321 3c Red-flowering gum 1.00 *1.50*
851 A321 10c Tasmanian blue gum 1.00 *1.75*
852 A321 27c Forrest's marlock .55 .50
a. Bklt. pane, #850-851, 2 #848-849, 3 #852 + label 4.00
b. Bklt. pane, 2 ea #848-849, 852 2.10
Nos. 848-852 (5) 3.05 4.25

Nos. 848-852 issued in booklets only.

Mimi Spirits Singing and Dancing, by David Milaybuma A322

Aboriginal Bark Paintings: Music and dance of the Mimi Spirits, Gunwinggu Tribe.

1982, Nov. 17 Litho. *Perf. 13½x14*

853 A322 27c shown .50 .30
854 A322 40c Lofty Nabardayal .75 .70
855 A322 65c Jimmy Galareya 1.10 .60
856 A322 75c Dick Nguleingulei Murrumurru 1.25 1.00
Nos. 853-856 (4) 3.60 2.60

Historic Fire Engines A323

1983, Jan. 12 *Perf. 13½x14*

857 A323 27c Shand Mason Steam, 1891 .50 .30
858 A323 40c Hotchkiss, 1914 .75 .60
859 A323 65c Ahrens-Fox PS2, 1929 1.10 .90
860 A323 75c Merryweather Manual, 1851 1.25 1.00
Nos. 857-860 (4) 3.60 2.80

Australia Day — A324

1983, Jan. 26 Litho. *Perf. 14½*

861 A324 27c Sirius .50 .45
862 A324 27c Supply .50 .45
a. Pair, #861-862 1.10 1.10

A325

A326

1983, Feb. 2 *Perf. 14x13½*

863 A325 27c multicolored .50 .30
863a Perf. 14¾x14, dated "2013" (#1003b) .70 .70

Australia-New Zealand Closer Economic Relationship agreement (ANZCER).

Issued: No. 863a, 5/10/2013.

1983, Mar. 9 Litho. *Perf. 14½*

864 A326 27c Equality, dignity .50 .30
865 A326 27c Social justice, co-operation .50 .30
866 A326 27c Liberty, freedom .50 .30
867 A326 75c Peace, harmony 1.40 1.00
Nos. 864-867 (4) 2.90 1.90

Commonwealth day.

Queen Elizabeth II, 57th Birthday A327

1983, Apr. 20 *Perf. 14½*

868 A327 27c Britannia .50 .35

World Communications Year — A328

1983, May 18 Litho. *Perf. 13½x14*

869 A328 27c multicolored .50 .35

50th Anniv. of Australian Jaycees Youth Organization A329

1983, June 8

870 A329 27c multicolored .50 .35

St. John Ambulance Cent. — A330

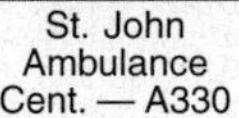

Regent Skipper — A331

1983, June 8 *Perf. 13½x14*

871 A330 27c multicolored .50 .35

1983 *Perf. 13½, 14½x14 (30c)*

872 A331 4c shown .30 .25
873 A331 10c Cairn's birdwing .30 .25
874 A331 20c Macleay's swallowtail .45 .25
875 A331 27c Ulysses .65 .25
875A A331 30c Chlorinda hairstreak .85 .25
876 A331 35c Blue tiger .70 .35
877 A331 45c Big greasy 1.00 .45
878 A331 60c Wood white 1.40 .55
879 A331 80c Amaryllis azure 1.90 .80
880 A331 $1 Sword grass brown 2.40 .90
Nos. 872-880 (10) 9.95 4.30

Issue dates: 30c, Oct. 24; others, June 15.

The Sentimental Bloke, by C.J. Dennis, 1909 — A332

Folktale scenes: a, The bloke. b, Doreen-the intro. c, The stror at coot. d, Hitched. e, The mooch of life.

1983, Aug. 3 *Perf. 14½*

881 Strip of 5 2.50 2.50
a.-e. A332 27c multi, any single .45 .40

Kookaburra Bird Wearing Santa Hat — A333

1983 Litho. *Perf. 13½x14*

882 A333 24c Nativity .40 .30
883 A333 35c multicolored .60 .35
884 A333 85c Holiday beach scene 1.50 .90
Nos. 882-884 (3) 2.50 1.55

Christmas. Issued: No. 883, 9/14; Nos. 882, 884, 11/2.

Inland Explorers — A334

Clay sculptures by Dianne Quinn: No. 885, Ludwig Leichhardt (1813-48). No. 886, William John Wills (1834-61), Robert O'Hara Burke (1821-61). No. 887, Paul Edmund de Strzelecki (1797-1873). No. 888, Alexander Forrest (1849-1901).

1983, Sept. 26 *Perf. 14½*

885 A334 30c multicolored .50 .35
886 A334 30c multicolored .50 .35
887 A334 30c multicolored .50 .35
888 A334 30c multicolored .50 .35
Nos. 885-888 (4) 2.00 1.40

Australia Day — A335

1984, Jan. 26 Litho. *Perf. 13½x14*

889 A335 30c Cooks' Cottage .50 .30

50th Anniv. of Official Air Mail Service — A336

Pilot Charles Ulm (1898-1934); his plane, "Faith in Australia," and different flight covers.

1984, Feb. 22 Litho. *Perf. 13½*

890 A336 45c Australia-New Zealand 1.00 *1.25*
891 A336 45c Australia-Papua New Guinea 1.00 *1.25*
a. Pair, #890-891 2.25 *3.00*

Thomson, 1898 — A337

Australian-made vintage cars: b, Tarrant, 1906. c, Australian Six, 1919. d, Summit, 1923. e, Chic, 1924.

1984, Mar. 14 *Perf. 14½*

892 Strip of 5 3.00 3.00
a.-e. A337 30c any single .45 .45

Queen Elizabeth II, 58th Birthday A338

1984, Apr. 18 *Perf. 14½*

893 A338 30c multicolored .55 .30

Clipper Ships A339

1984, May 23 *Perf. 14x13½, 13½x14*

894 A339 30c Cutty Sark, 1869, vert. .55 .45
895 A339 45c Orient, 1853 .85 .80
896 A339 75c Sobraon, 1866 1.25 1.10
897 A339 85c Thermopylae, 1868, vert. 1.50 1.25
Nos. 894-897 (4) 4.15 3.60

Freestyle Skiing — A340

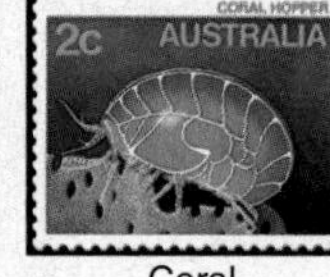

Coral Hopper — A341

1984, June 6 Litho. *Perf. 14½*

898 A340 30c shown .50 .35
899 A340 30c Slalom, horiz. .50 .35
900 A340 30c Cross-country, horiz. .50 .35
901 A340 30c Downhill .50 .35
Nos. 898-901 (4) 2.00 1.40

Perf. 13½, 14x14½ (30c, 33c)

1984-86 **Litho.**

902 A341 2c shown .25 .25
903 A341 3c Jimble .25 .25
904 A341 5c Tasseled anglerfish .25 .25
905 A341 10c Stonefish .25 .25
906 A341 20c Red handfish .45 .35
907 A341 25c Orange-tipped cowrie .60 .35
908 A341 30c Choat's wrasse .65 .25
909 A341 33c Leafy sea dragon .70 .25
910 A341 40c Red velvet fish .85 .60
911 A341 45c Texile cone shell .90 .70
912 A341 50c Blue-lined surgeonfish 1.00 .70
913 A341 55c Bennett's nudibranch 1.10 .90
914 A341 60c Lionfish 1.25 .90
915 A341 65c Stingray 1.25 .90
916 A341 70c Blue-ringed octopus 1.40 1.00
917 A341 80c Pineapple fish 1.60 1.00
918 A341 85c Regal angelfish 1.75 1.10
919 A341 90c Crab-eyed goby 1.75 1.10
920 A341 $1 Crown of thorns starfish 2.00 1.10
Nos. 902-920 (19) 18.25 12.20

Issued: 2c, 25c, 30c, 50c, 55c, 85c, 6/18; 33c, 1/20/85; 5c, 20c, 40c, 80c, 90c, 6/12/85; 3c, 10c, 45c, 60c, 65c, 70c, $1, 6/11/86.

1984 Summer Olympics A342

Event stages.

Perf. 13½x14, 14x13½

1984, July 25 **Litho.**

922 A342 30c Start (facing down) .60 .35
923 A342 30c Competing (facing right) .60 .35
924 A342 30c Finish, vert. .60 .35
Nos. 922-924 (3) 1.80 1.05

Ausipex '84 A343

Christmas A344

Designs: No. 926: a, Victoria #3. b, New South Wales #1. c, Tasmania #1. d, South Australia #1. e, Western Australia #1. f, Queensland #3.

1984 **Litho.** ***Perf. 14½***

925 A343 30c No. 2 .50 .35

Souvenir Sheet

926 Sheet of 7 4.00 4.00
a.-f. A343 30c any single .50 .40

No. 926 contains Nos. 925, 926a-926f. Issued: No. 925, Aug. 22; No. 926, Sept. 21.

1984 **Litho.** ***Perf. 14x13½***

927 A344 24c Angel and Child .45 .25
928 A344 30c Veiled Virgin and Child .55 .30
929 A344 40c Angel .75 .65
930 A344 50c Three Kings .90 .90
931 A344 85c Madonna and Child 1.50 1.25
Nos. 927-931 (5) 4.15 3.35

Stained-glass windows. Issue dates: 40c, Sept. 17; others, Oct. 30.

European Settlement Bicentenary A345

Design: No. 932, Bicentennial Emblem.

Rock paintings: No. 933, Stick figures, Cobar Region, New South Wales. No. 934, Bunjil's Cave, Grampians, Western Victoria. No. 935, Quinkan Gallery, Cape York, Queensland. No. 936, Wandjina Spirit and Snake Babies, Gibb River, Western Australia. No. 937, Rock Python, Western Australia. No. 938, Silver Barramundi, Kakadu Natl. Park, Northern Territory. 85c, Rock Possum, Kakadu Natl. Park.

1984, Nov. 7 **Litho.** ***Perf. 14½***

932 A345 30c multicolored .55 .30
933 A345 30c multicolored .55 .30
934 A345 30c multicolored .55 .30
935 A345 30c multicolored .55 .30
936 A345 30c multicolored .55 .30
937 A345 30c multicolored .55 .30
938 A345 30c multicolored .55 .30
939 A345 85c multicolored 1.75 *2.00*
Nos. 932-939 (8) 5.60 4.10

Settlement of Victoria Sesquicentenary A346

1984, Nov. 19

940 A346 30c Helmeted honeyeater .50 .50
941 A346 30c Leadbeater's possum .50 .50
a. Pair, #940-941 1.25 1.25

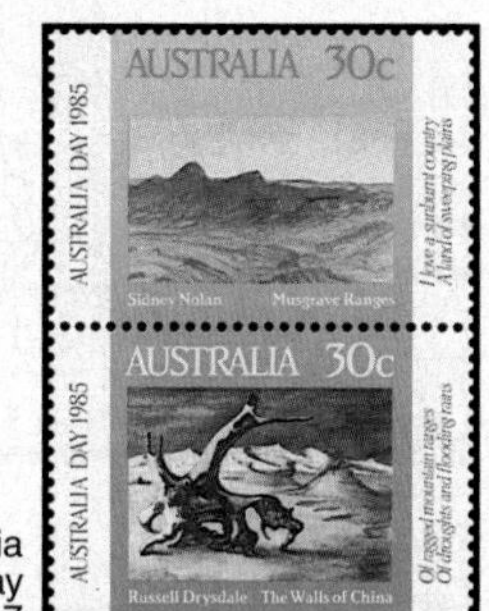

Australia Day A347

1985, Jan. 25 **Litho.**

942 30c Musgrave Ranges, by Sidney Nolan .55 .55
a. Pair, #942 tete-beche 2.50 2.50
943 30c The Walls of China, by Russell Drysdale .55 .55
a. A347 Pair, #942-943 1.50 1.50
b. Pair, #943 tete-beche 2.50 2.50

Intl. Youth Year — A348

1985, Feb. 13 **Litho.** ***Perf. 14x13½***

944 A348 30c multicolored .55 .40

Royal Victorian Volunteer Artillery A349

District Nursing Service Centenary A350

Colonial military uniforms: b, Western Australian Pinjarrah Cavalry. c, New South Wales Lancers. d, New South Wales Contingent to the Sudan. e, Victorian Mounted Rifles.

1985, Feb. 25 ***Perf. 14½***

945 Strip of 5 3.25 3.25
a.-e. A349 33c any single .55 .30

1985, Mar. 13

946 A350 33c multicolored .60 .40

Australian Cockatoo — A351

Perf. 14 Horiz. on 1 or 2 sides

1985, Mar. 13

947 A351 1c apple grn, yel & buff 3.00 *4.00*
948 A351 33c apple grn, yel, & lt grnsh blue 1.25 *1.00*
a. Bklt. pane, 1 #947, 3 #948 6.50

Issued in booklets only.

A352

1985, Apr. 10 ***Perf. 13***

949 A352 33c Abel Tasman, explorer .65 .45
950 A352 33c The Eendracht .65 .45
951 A352 33c William Dampier .65 .45
952 A352 90c Globe and hand 1.90 *2.25*
a. Souvenir sheet of 4, #949-952 5.50 5.50
Nos. 949-952 (4) 3.85 3.60

Queen Elizabeth II, 59th Birthday — A353

1985, Apr. 22 ***Perf. 14x13½***

953 A353 33c Queen's Badge, Order of Australia .65 .45
a. Perf. 14¾x14, dated "2013" (#1003b) .85 .85

Issued: No. 953a, 5/10/2013.

A354

A356

1985, May 15 **Litho.** ***Perf. 14x13***

954 A354 33c Soil .60 .25
955 A354 50c Air .90 *.75*
956 A354 80c Water 1.50 1.00
957 A354 90c Energy 1.60 1.25
Nos. 954-957 (4) 4.60 3.25

Environmental conservation.

1985, July 17 **Litho.** ***Perf. 14½***

Illustrations from classic children's books: a, Elves & Fairies, by Annie Rentoul. b, The Magic Pudding, text and illustrations by Norman Lindsay. c, Ginger Meggs, by James Charles Bancks. d, Blinky Bill, by Dorothy Wall. e, Snugglepot and Cuddlepie, by May Gibbs.

960 Strip of 5 3.00 3.00
a.-e. A356 33c any single .50 .40

Electronic Mail — A357

1985, Sept. 18 **Litho.**

961 A357 33c multicolored .55 .30

Christmas A358

Angel in a ship, detail from a drawing by Albrecht Durer (1471-1528).

1985, Sept. 18 **Litho.**

962 A358 45c multicolored .80 .35

See Nos. 967-970.

Coastal Shipwrecks A359

Salvaged antiquities: 33c, Astrolabe from Batavia, 1629. 50c, German beardman (Bellarmine) jug from Vergulde Draeck, 1656. 90c, Wooden bobbins from Batavia, and scissors from Zeewijk, 1727. $1, Silver buckle from Zeewijk.

1985, Oct. 2 **Litho.** ***Perf. 13***

963 A359 33c multicolored .65 .25
964 A359 50c multicolored 1.00 .95
965 A359 90c multicolored 1.90 1.75
966 A359 $1 multicolored 2.60 2.25
Nos. 963-966 (4) 6.15 5.20

Christmas Type of 1985

Illustrations by Scott Hartshorne.

1985, Nov. 1 **Litho.** ***Perf. 14***

967 A358 27c Angel with trumpet .50 .25
968 A358 33c Angel with bells .60 .40
969 A358 55c Angel with star 1.00 .90
970 A358 90c Angel with ornament 1.50 1.50
Nos. 967-970 (4) 3.60 3.05

Australia Day — A360

AUSSAT — A361

1986, Jan. 24 **Litho.** ***Perf. 14½***

971 A360 33c Aboriginal painting .55 .35

1986, Jan. 24

Various communications satellites.

972 A361 33c multicolored .65 .30
973 A361 80c multicolored 1.60 1.60

South Australia, Sesquicent. A362

1986, Feb. 12 ***Perf. 13½x14***

974 A362 33c Sailing ship Buffalo .50 .45
975 A362 33c City Sign, sculpture by O.H. Hajek .50 .45
a. Pair, #974-975 1.50 1.50

Cook's New Holland Expedition A363

1986, Mar. 12 *Perf. 13*

976 A363 33c Hibiscus merankensis .65 .35
977 A363 33c Banksia serrata .65 .35
978 A363 50c Dillenia alata 1.10 *1.25*
979 A363 80c Corria reflexa 1.60 1.40
980 A363 90c Parkinson 1.75 1.75
981 A363 90c Banks 1.75 1.75
Nos. 976-981 (6) 7.50 6.85

Australian bicentennial. Sydney Parkinson (d. 1775), artist. Sir Joseph Banks (1743-1820), naturalist.

Halley's Comet — A364

Elizabeth II, 60th Birthday — A365

1986, Apr. 9 *Perf. 14x13½*

982 A364 33c Radio telescope, trajectory diagram .65 .40

1986, Apr. 21 *Perf. 14½*

983 A365 33c multicolored .65 .40

Horses A366

1986, May 21

984 A366 33c Brumbies .60 .30
985 A366 80c Stock horse mustering 1.50 1.50
986 A366 90c Show-jumping 1.60 1.60
987 A366 $1 Australian pony 1.75 1.75
Nos. 984-987 (4) 5.45 5.15

Click Go the Shears, Folk Song — A366a

Lines from the song: b, Old shearer stands. c, Ringer looks around. d, Boss of the board. e, Tar-boy is there. f, Shearing is all over.

1986, July 21 **Litho.** *Perf. 14½*

987A Strip of 5 3.00 3.00
b.-f. A366a 33c, any single .50 .40

Amalgamated Shearers' Union, predecessor of the Australian Workers' Union, cent.

Australia Bicentennial A367

Settling of Botany Bay penal colony: No. 988, King George III, c. 1767, by A. Ramsay. No. 989, Lord Sydney, secretary of state, 1783-1789, by Gilbert Stuart. No. 990, Capt. Arthur Phillip, 1st penal colony governor, by F. Wheatley, 1786. $1, Capt. John Hunter, governor, 1795-1800, by W. B. Bennett, 1815.

1986, Aug. 6 **Litho.** *Perf. 13*

988 A367 33c multicolored .85 .70
989 A367 33c multicolored .85 .70
990 A367 33c multicolored .85 .70
991 A367 $1 multicolored 2.25 2.25
Nos. 988-991 (4) 4.80 4.35

Wildlife A368

Alpine Wildflowers A369

Designs: a, Red kangaroo. b, Emu. c, Koala. d, Kookaburra. e, Platypus.

1986, Aug. 13 *Perf. 14½x14*

992 Strip of 5 3.50 3.50
a.-e. A368 36c any single .70 .60

Rouletted 9½ Vert. on 1 or 2 sides

1986, Aug. 25 **Booklet Stamps**

993 A369 3c Royal bluebell 1.10 *1.25*
994 A369 5c Alpine marsh marigold 2.40 *2.60*
995 A369 25c Mount Buffalo sunray 2.40 *2.25*
996 A369 36c Silver snow daisy 1.00 .70
a. Bklt. pane, #993, #994, 2 #996 5.75
b. Bklt. pane, #993, #995, 2 #996 6.00
Nos. 993-996 (4) 6.90 6.80

Orchids — A370

America's Cup Triumph '83 — A371

1986, Sept. 18 *Perf. 14½*

997 A370 36c Elythranthera emarginata .75 .25
998 A370 55c Dendrobium nindii 1.10 1.10
999 A370 90c Caleana major 1.90 1.90
1000 A370 $1 Thelymitra variegata 2.25 2.25
Nos. 997-1000 (4) 6.00 5.50

1986, Sept. 26 *Perf. 14x13½*

1001 A371 36c Australia II crossing finish line .65 .50
1002 A371 36c Trophy .65 .50
1003 A371 36c Boxing kangaroo .65 .50
a. Perf. 14¾x14, dated "2013" (#1003b) .95 .95
b. Booklet pane of 4, #502a, 863a, 953a, 1003a 3.50 —
Nos. 1001-1003 (3) 1.95 1.50

Issued: Nos. 1003a, 1003b, 5/10/2013. No. 1003b was issued in a booklet also containing Nos. 1284b, 3534d and 3918.

Intl. Peace Year — A372

1986, Oct. 22 **Litho.** *Perf. 14x13½*

1004 A372 36c multicolored .65 .35

Christmas A373

Kindergarten nativity play: No. 1005, Holy Family, vert. No. 1006, Three Kings, vert. No. 1007, Angels. No. 1008a, Angels, peasants. No. 1008b, Holy Family, angels, vert. No. 1008c, Shepherd, angels, vert. No. 1008d, Three Kings. No. 1008e, Shepherds.

1986, Nov. 3 **Litho.**

1005 A373 30c multicolored .60 .35
a. Perf 14x13½ 1.25 1.25
1006 A373 36c multicolored .70 .55
1007 A373 60c multicolored 1.25 1.25
Nos. 1005-1007 (3) 2.55 2.15

Souvenir Sheet

1008 Sheet of 5 3.25 3.25
a.-e. A373 30c any single .60 .60

Perfs: Nos. 1005-1006, 1008c, 15x14½; Nos. 1007, 1008a 1008e, 14½x15.
No. 1008b, 15x14½x15x15; No. 1008d, 14½x15x14½x14½.

Australia Day — A374

1987, Jan. 23 **Litho.** *Perf. 13½x14*

1009 A374 36c Flag, circuit board .70 .40
1010 A374 36c Made in Australia campaign emblem .70 .40

America's Cup — A375

Fruits — A376

Views of yachts racing.

1987, Jan. 28 *Perf. 15x14½*

1011 A375 36c multicolored .70 .30
1012 A375 55c multicolored 1.10 *1.25*
1013 A375 90c multicolored 1.75 *1.90*
1014 A375 $1 multicolored 2.00 1.75
Nos. 1011-1014 (4) 5.55 5.20

1987, Feb. 11 *Perf. 14x13½*

1015 A376 36c Melons, grapes .70 .30
1016 A376 65c Tropical fruit 1.25 1.25
1017 A376 90c Pears, apples, oranges 1.75 1.40
1018 A376 $1 Berries, peaches 2.00 1.75
Nos. 1015-1018 (4) 5.70 4.70

Agricultural Shows — A377

1987, Apr. 10 **Litho.** *Perf. 14x13½*

1019 A377 36c Livestock .70 .30
1020 A377 65c Produce 1.25 1.25
1021 A377 90c Carnival 1.75 1.75
1022 A377 $1 Farmers 2.25 2.25
Nos. 1019-1022 (4) 5.95 5.55

Queen Elizabeth II, 61st Birthday A378

1987, Apr. 21 *Perf. 13½x14*

1023 A378 36c multicolored .70 .40

First Fleet Leaving England A379

Continuous design: No. 1024a, Convicts awaiting transportation. b, Capt. Arthur Phillip, Mrs. Phillip, longboat on shore. c, Sailors relaxing and working. d, Longboats heading from and to fleet. 4e, Fleet in harbor.
No. 1025a, Longboat approaching Tenerife, The Canary Isls. b, Fishing in Tenerife Harbor. $1, Fleet, dolphins.

1987 *Perf. 13*

1024 Strip of 5 3.50 3.50
a.-e. A379 36c any single .70 .40
1025 Pair 1.50 1.50
a.-b. A379 36c any single .70 .40
1026 A379 $1 multicolored 2.25 2.25
Nos. 1024-1026 (3) 7.25 7.25

Australia bicent.; departure of the First Fleet, May 13, 1787; arrival at Tenerife, June 1787.
Issued: No. 1024, 5/13; Nos. 1025-1026, 6/3.

1987, Aug. 6

First Fleet arrives at Rio de Janeiro, Aug. 1787: a, Whale, storm in the Atlantic. b, Citrus grove. c, Market. d, Religious procession. e, Fireworks over harbor.

1027 Strip of 5 3.50 3.50
a.-e. A379 37c any single .65 .40

No. 1027 has a continuous design.

1987, Oct. 13

First Fleet arrives at Cape of Good Hope, Oct. 1787: No. 1028a, British officer surveys livestock and supplies, Table Mountain. No. 1028b, Ships anchored in Table Bay. No. 1029, Fishermen pull in nets as the Fleet approaches the Cape.

1028 Pair 1.50 1.50
a.-b. A379 37c any single .75 .75
1029 A379 $1 multicolored 2.25 1.40

No. 1028 has a continuous design.

1988, Jan. 26

Arrival of the First Fleet, Sydney Cove, Jan. 1788: a, Five aborigines on shore. b, Four aborigines on shore. c, Kangaroos. d, White cranes. e, Flag raising.

1030 Strip of 5 3.75 3.75
a.-e. A379 37c any single .75 .45

Printed se-tenant in a continuous design.

The Early Years: Sydney Cove and Parramatta Colonies A380

Details from panorama "View of Sydney from the East Side of the Cove," 1808, painted by convict artist John Eyre to illustrate The Present Picture of New South Wales, published in London in 1811, and paintings in British and Australian museums: a, Government House, 1790, Sydney, by midshipman George Raper. b, Government Farm, Parramatta, 1791, attributed to the Port Jackson Painter. c, Parramatta Road, 1796, attributed to convict artist Thomas Watling. d, The Rocks and Sydney Cove, 1800, an aquatint engraving by Edward Dayes. e, Sydney Hospital, 1803, by George William Evans, an explorer and surveyor-general of New South Wales. Printed se-tenant in a continuous design.

1988, Apr. 13 **Litho.** *Perf. 13*

1031 Strip of 5 3.50 3.50
a.-e. A380 37c any single .65 .40

Australia Bicentennial.

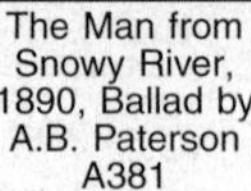

The Man from Snowy River, 1890, Ballad by A.B. Paterson
A381

Fauna
A382

Excerpts: a, At the station. b, Mountain bred. c, Terrible descent. d, At their heels. e, Brought them back.

1987, June 24 ***Perf. 14x13½***

1034 Strip of 5 3.50 3.50
a.-e. A381 36c any single .70 .50

Printed se-tenant in a continuous design.

1987, July 1 ***Perf. 14½x14***

Designs: a, Possum. b, Cockatoo. c, Wombat. d, Rosella. e, Echidna.

1035 Strip of 5 3.75 3.75
a.-e. A382 37c any single .75 .45

Printed se-tenant in a continuous design.

Technology — A383

1987, Aug. 19 ***Perf. 14½***

1036 A383 37c Bionic ear .75 .30
1037 A383 53c Microchips 1.10 .75
1038 A383 63c Robotics 1.25 1.10
1039 A383 68c Zirconia ceramics 1.40 1.25
Nos. 1036-1039 (4) 4.50 3.40

Children
A384

1987, Sept. 16

1040 A384 37c Crayfishing .75 .25
1041 A384 55c Cat's cradle 1.10 *1.25*
1042 A384 90c Eating meat pies 1.75 1.75
1043 A384 $1 Playing with a jo-ey 2.25 2.25
Nos. 1040-1043 (4) 5.85 5.50

Christmas
A385

Carolers: a, Woman, two girls. b, Man, two girls. c, Four children. d, Man, two women, boy. e, Six youths. 37c, three women, two men. Nos. 1044a-1044e are vert.

1987, Nov. 2 **Litho.** ***Perf. 14½***

1044 Strip of 5 3.25 3.25
a.-e. A385 30c any single .60 .55

Perf. 13½x14

1045 A385 37c multicolored .75 .45
1046 A385 63c shown 1.75 1.10
Nos. 1044-1046 (3) 5.75 4.80

Carols by Candlelight, Christmas Eve, Sidney Myer Bowl, Melbourne.

Aboriginal Crafts — A386

Designs: 3c, Spearthrower, Western Australia. 15c, Shield, New South Wales. No. 1049, Basket, Queensland. No. 1050, Bowl, Central Australia. No. 1051, Belt, Northern Territory.

Perf. 15½ Horiz.

1987, Oct. 13 **Photo.**

1047 A386 3c multicolored 1.25 1.25
1048 A386 15c multicolored 4.50 4.50
1049 A386 37c multicolored 1.25 1.25
a. Bklt. pane, 2 ea #1047, 1049 5.75
1050 A386 37c multicolored 1.10 1.10
1051 A386 37c multicolored 1.25 1.25
a. Bklt. pane, #1048, 3 #1050, 2 #1051 11.50
Nos. 1047-1051 (5) 9.35 9.35

Issued only in booklets.

Caricature of Australian Koala and American Bald Eagle — A387

1988, Jan. 26 ***Perf. 13***

1052 A387 37c multicolored .75 .40

Australia bicentennial. See No. 1086 and US No. 2370.

Living Together — A388

Cartoons.

1988 ***Perf. 14***

1053 A388 1c Religion .25 .25
1054 A388 2c Industry .25 .25
1055 A388 3c Local government .25 .25
1056 A388 4c Trade unions .25 .25
1057 A388 5c Parliament .25 .25
1058 A388 10c Transportation .25 .25
1059 A388 15c Sports .35 .25
1060 A388 20c Commerce .40 .25
1061 A388 25c Housing .50 .25
1062 A388 30c Welfare .60 .25
1063 A388 37c Postal services .75 .25
a. Booklet pane of 10 7.50
1063B A388 39c Tourism .80 .35
c. Booklet pane of 10 8.00
1064 A388 40c Recreation .80 .45
1065 A388 45c Health .90 .65
1066 A388 50c Mining 1.00 .60
1067 A388 53c Primary industry 1.75 1.00
1068 A388 55c Education 1.10 .75
1069 A388 60c Armed Forces 1.50 .90
1070 A388 63c Police 2.00 1.75
1071 A388 65c Telecommunications 1.50 1.10
1072 A388 68c The media 2.00 1.75
1073 A388 70c Science and technology 1.50 .95
1074 A388 75c Visual arts 1.60 .95
1075 A388 80c Performing arts 1.75 1.10
1076 A388 90c Banking 2.00 1.40
1077 A388 95c Law 2.00 1.10
1078 A388 $1 Rescue and emergency services 2.25 1.40
Nos. 1053-1078 (27) 28.55 18.95

Issued: 1c, 2c, 3c, 5c, 30c, 40c, 55c, 60c, 63c, 65c, 68c, 75c, 95c, 3/16; 39c, 9/28; others, 2/17.

Queen Elizabeth II, 62nd Birthday
A389

1988, Apr. 21 ***Perf. 14½***

1079 A389 37c multicolored 1.00 .50

EXPO '88, Brisbane, Apr. 30-Oct. 30 — A390

1988, Apr. 29 ***Perf. 13***

1080 A390 37c multicolored 1.00 .50

Opening of Parliament House, Canberra
A391

1988, May 9 ***Perf. 14½***

1081 A391 37c multicolored 1.00 .50

Australia Bicentennial
A392

Designs: No. 1082, Colonist, clipper ship. No. 1083, British and Australian parliaments, Queen Elizabeth II. No. 1084, Cricketer W.G. Grace. No. 1085, John Lennon (1940-1980), William Shakespeare (1564-1616) and Sydney Opera House. Nos. 1083a, 1085a have continuous design picturing flag of Australia.

1988, June 21 **Litho.** ***Perf. 13***

1082 A392 37c multicolored .85 .50
1083 A392 37c multicolored .85 .50
a. Pair, #1082-1083 1.75 1.75
1084 A392 $1 multicolored 2.25 *3.25*
a. Booklet pane of 1, imperf., dated "2007" 3.25 —
1085 A392 $1 multicolored 2.25 *3.25*
a. Pair, #1084-1085 4.50 6.25
Nos. 1082-1085 (4) 6.20 7.50

No. 1084a issued 11/14/2007.
See Great Britain Nos. 1222-1225.

Caricature Type of 1988

Design: Caricature of an Australian koala and New Zealand kiwi.

1988, June 21 **Litho.** ***Perf. 13½***

1086 A387 37c multicolored 1.10 .60

Australia bicentennial. See New Zealand No. 907.

"Dream" Lore on Art of the Desert
A393

Aboriginal paintings from Papunya Settlement in the Flinders University Art Museum: 37c, Bush Potato Country, by Turkey Tolsen Tjupurrula with by David Corby Tjapaltjarri. 55c, Courtship Rejected, by Limpi Puntungka Tjapangati. 90c, Medicine Story, anonymous. $1, Ancestor Dreaming, by Tim Leura Tjapaltjarri.

1988, Aug. 1 **Litho.** ***Perf. 13***

1087 A393 37c multicolored 1.00 .60
1088 A393 55c multicolored 1.40 1.40
1089 A393 90c multicolored 2.00 *2.25*
1090 A393 $1 multicolored 2.25 2.25
Nos. 1087-1090 (4) 6.65 6.50

1988 Summer Olympics, Seoul — A394

1988, Sept. 14 ***Perf. 14½***

1091 A394 37c Basketball 1.00 .85
1092 A394 65c Running 1.60 1.60
1093 A394 $1 Rhythmic gymnastics 2.60 2.60
Nos. 1091-1093 (3) 5.20 5.05

34th Commonwealth Parliamentary Conference, Canberra — A395

1988, Sept. 19

1094 A395 37c Scepter and mace 1.00 .50

Works in the Contemporary Decorative Arts Collection at the Natl. Gallery — A396

Roulette 9 Horiz.

1988, Sept. 28 **Litho.**

1095 A396 2c "Australian Fetish," by Peter Tully 3.75 *6.00*
1096 A396 5c Vase by Colin Levy 4.25 *6.00*
1097 A396 39c Teapot by Frank Bauer 1.60 .40
a. Bklt. pane of 3 (2c, 2 39c) 7.00
b. Bklt. pane of 6 (5c, 5 39c) 12.50
Nos. 1095-1097 (3) 9.60 12.40

Nos. 1095-1097 issued in booklets only.

Views — A397

1988, Oct. 17 **Photo.** ***Perf. 13***

1098 A397 39c The Desert 1.00 1.00
1099 A397 55c The Top End 1.60 1.60
1100 A397 65c The Coast 1.75 1.75
1101 A397 70c The Bush 1.90 1.90
Nos. 1098-1101 (4) 6.25 6.25

Christmas
A398

Children's design contest winning drawings: 32c, Nativity scene, by Danielle Hush, age 7.

39c, Koala wearing a Santa hat, by Kylie Courtney, age 6. 63c, Cockatoo wearing a Santa hat, by Benjamin Stevenson, age 10.

1988, Oct. 31 ***Perf. 13½x13***

1102 A398 32c multicolored .80 .30
1103 A398 39c multicolored 1.00 .60
1104 A398 63c multicolored 1.60 1.60
Nos. 1102-1104 (3) 3.40 2.50

Sir Henry Parkes (1815-1896), Advocate of the Federation of the Six Colonies — A399

1989, Jan. 25 Litho. ***Perf. 14x13½***

1105 A399 39c multicolored 1.00 .50

Australia Day.

Sports — A400

1989, Feb. 13 ***Perf. 14x14½***

1106 A400 1c Bowls .30 .25
a. Perf. 13¼x13¾ ('90) .40 .35
1107 A400 2c Bowling .25 .25
a. Perf. 13¼x13¾ ('91) .25 .25
1108 A400 3c Football .35 .25
1109 A400 39c Fishing 1.10 .35
a. Booklet pane of 10 11.00
d. Perf. 13¼x13¾ on sides ('90) 2.25 *3.00*
e. Booklet pane of 10, #1109d 22.50
1109B A400 41c Cycling 1.10 .25
c. Booklet pane of 10 11.00
1110 A400 55c Kite-flying 1.10 .85
1111 A400 70c Cricket 2.25 1.10
a. Imperf., dated "2007" (from booklet pane No. 1302b) 2.25 2.25
1112 A400 $1.10 Golf 2.25 1.40

No. 1109d also exists perfed on 4 sides from sheets. These are scarcer. Value, unused or used $17.50.

No. 1111a issued 11/14/2007.

1990-94

1114 A400 5c Kayaking, canoeing 1.40 1.10
a. Perf. 13¼x13¾ .35 .25
1115 A400 10c Windsurfing 2.00 1.10
a. Perf. 13¼x13¾ .70 .70
1116 A400 20c Tennis 2.00 .60
a. Perf. 13¼x13¾ .60 .35
1117 A400 65c Rock climbing 2.60 2.25
a. Perf. 13¼x13¾ 1.40 1.40
1118 A400 $1 Running 2.25 2.25
a. Perf. 13¼x13¾ 4.75 3.50

Issued: Nos. 1114a, 1115a, 1116a, 1117a, 1118, 1/17/90; No. 1118a, 1/91; Nos. 1115, 1117, 2/92; No. 1116, 7/93; No. 1114, 3/94.

The 1990 year date on the original printing of No. 1117 is in serif type. The date on the 4 koala reprint of 2005 is in san-serif type.

1990, Aug. 27

1119 A400 43c Skateboarding .85 .25
a. Booklet pane of 10 8.50

Perf. 13½

1120 A400 $1.20 Hang-gliding 2.60 1.10

1991, Aug. 22 ***Perf. 14x14½***

1121 A400 75c Netball 1.50 .90
1122 A400 80c Squash 1.60 .85
1123 A400 85c Diving 1.75 .95
1124 A400 90c Soccer 1.75 1.10
Nos. 1106-1124 (19) 29.00 17.15

For self-adhesive stamps see Nos. 1185-1186.

Botanical Gardens — A401

Designs: $2, Nooroo, New South Wales. $5, Mawarra, Victoria. $10, Palm House, Adelaide Botanical Garden. $20, A View of the Artist's House and Garden in Mills Plains, Van Diemen's Land by John Glover.

1989-90 Litho. & Engr. ***Perf. 14***

1132 A401 $2 multicolored 4.00 1.00
a. Perf. 13¼x13¾ ('91) 10.00 4.00
1133 A401 $5 multicolored 10.00 2.25
a. Perf. 13¼x13¾ 20.00 9.25
1134 A401 $10 multicolored 20.00 4.50

Litho with Foil Application

Perf. 14½x14

1135 A401 $20 multicolored 40.00 11.00
Nos. 1132-1135 (4) 74.00 18.75

Issued: $10, 4/12; $2, $5, 9/13; $20, 8/15/90.

Sheep A402

1989, Feb. 27 Litho. ***Perf. 13½x14***

1136 A402 39c Merino .80 .80
1137 A402 39c Poll Dorset .80 .80
1138 A402 85c Polwarth 1.75 1.75
1139 A402 $1 Corriedale 2.10 2.10
Nos. 1136-1139 (4) 5.45 5.45

World Sheep and Wool Congress, Tasmania, Feb. 27-Mar. 6.

Queen Elizabeth II, 63rd Birthday — A403

1989, Apr. 21 Litho. ***Perf. 14½***

1140 A403 39c Statue by John Dowie 1.00 .40

Colonial Australia A404

Pastoral Era: a, Immigrant ship in port, c. 1835. b, Pioneer's hut, wool bales in dray. c, Squatter's homestead. d, Shepherds. e, Explorers.

1989, May 10

1141 Strip of 5 4.00 4.00
a.-e. A404 39c any single .80 .65

Stars of Stage and Screen — A405

Performers and directors: 39c, Gladys Moncrieff and Roy Rene, the stage, 1920's. 85c, Charles Chauvel and Chips Rafferty, talking films. $1, Nellie Stewart and James Cassius Williamson, the stage, 1890's. $1.10, Lottie Lyell and Raymond Longford, silent films.

1989, July 12 Litho. ***Perf. 14½***

1142 A405 39c multicolored 1.10 .25
a. Perf. 14x13½ 11.50 11.50
1143 A405 85c multicolored 2.00 *2.25*
1144 A405 $1 multicolored 2.10 1.75
1145 A405 $1.10 multicolored 2.25 2.00
Nos. 1142-1145 (4) 7.45 6.25

Impressionist Paintings A406

Paintings by Australian artists: No. 1146, *Impression for Golden Summer,* by Sir Arthur Streeton. No. 1147, *All on a Summer's Day,* by Charles Conder, vert. No. 1148, *Petit Dejeuner,* by Frederick McCubbin. No. 1149, *Impression,* by Tom Roberts.

Perf. 13½x14, 14x13½

1989, Aug. 23 **Litho.**

1146 A406 41c shown .80 .65
1147 A406 41c multicolored .80 .65
1148 A406 41c multicolored .80 .65
1149 A406 41c multicolored .80 .65
Nos. 1146-1149 (4) 3.20 2.60

The Urban Environment — A407

1989, Sept. 1 Litho. ***Perf. 15½***

Booklet Stamps

1150 A407 41c Freeways .80 .80
1151 A407 41c Architecture .80 .80
1152 A407 41c Commuter train .80 .80
a. Bklt. pane, 2 ea #1150, 1152, 3 #1151 5.50
Nos. 1150-1152 (3) 2.40 2.40

No. 1152a sold for $3.

Australian Youth Hostels, 50th Anniv. A408

1989, Sept. 13 ***Perf. 14½***

1153 A408 41c multicolored 1.00 .50

Street Cars — A409

Designs: No. 1154, Horse-drawn tram, Adelaide, 1878. No. 1155, Steam tram, Sydney, 1884. No. 1156, Cable car, Melbourne, 1886. No. 1157, Double-deck electric tram, Hobart, 1893. No. 1158, Combination electric tram, Brisbane, 1901.

1989, Oct. 11 Litho. ***Perf. 13½x14***

1154 A409 41c multicolored .90 .80
1155 A409 41c multicolored .90 .80
1156 A409 41c multicolored .90 .80
a. Perf. 14½ on 3 sides 3.25 3.25
b. Booklet pane of 10, #1156a 32.50
1157 A409 41c multicolored .90 .80
1158 A409 41c multicolored .90 .80
Nos. 1154-1158 (5) 4.50 4.00

Purchase of booklet containing No. 1156b included STAMPSHOW '89 admission ticket and a Melbourne one-day transit pass. Sold for $8.

Christmas A410

Radio Australia, 50th Anniv. A411

Illuminations: 36c, Annunciation, from the Nicholai Joseph Foucault Book of Hours, c. 1510-20. 41c, Annunciation to the Shepherds, from the Wharncliffe Hours, c. 1475. 80c, Adoration of the Magi, from Parisian Book of Hours, c. 1490-1500.

1989, Nov. 1 ***Perf. 14x13½***

1159 A410 36c multicolored .70 .40
a. Booklet pane of 10 7.00

Perf. 15x14½

1160 A410 41c multicolored .85 .65
1161 A410 80c multicolored 1.90 1.90
Nos. 1159-1161 (3) 3.45 2.95

1989, Nov. 1 ***Perf. 14x13½***

1162 A411 41c multicolored 1.00 .60

Australia Day A412

Special Occasions A413

1990, Jan. 17 Litho. ***Perf. 15x14½***

1163 A412 41c Golden wattle 1.00 .50

1990, Feb. 7 ***Perf. 14x13½***

1164 A413 41c Thinking of You .90 .50
a. Booklet pane of 10 9.00
b. Perf. 14½ on 3 sides 3.50 1.10
c. Booklet pane of 10, #1164b 35.00

See No. 1193.

Women Practicing Medicine in Australia, Cent. A414

1990, Feb. 7 ***Perf. 14½x15***

1165 A414 41c Constance Stone .80 .50

Dr. Constance Stone, Australia's first woman doctor.

A415

A416

Fauna of the High Country.

1990, Feb. 21 ***Perf. 14x13½***

1166 A415 41c Greater glider .85 .50
1167 A415 65c Spotted-tailed quoll 1.40 1.40
1168 A415 70c Mountain pygmy-possum 1.60 1.60
1169 A415 80c Brush-tailed rock-wallaby 1.90 1.90
Nos. 1166-1169 (4) 5.75 5.40

1990, Mar. 14

1170 A416 41c Quit smoking .80 .55
1171 A416 41c Don't drink and drive .80 .55
1172 A416 41c Eat right .80 .55
1173 A416 41c Medical check-ups .80 .55
Nos. 1170-1173 (4) 3.20 2.20

Community health.

A417

A418

Scenes from WW II, 1940-41: No. 1174, Anzacs at the front. No. 1175, Women working in factories, aircraft at the ready. 65c, Veterans and memorial parade. $1, Helicopters picking up wounded, cemetery. $1.10, Anzacs reading mail from home, 5 women watching departure of 2 ships.

1990-2005 Litho. *Perf. 14½*

1174 A417 41c shown .85 .35
1175 A417 41c multicolored .85 .35
1176 A417 65c multicolored 1.40 1.40
a. Booklet pane of 2, perf. 14½x14 ('05) 3.00 —
1177 A417 $1 multicolored 2.10 2.10
1178 A417 $1.10 multicolored 2.25 2.25
Nos. 1174-1178 (5) 7.45 6.45

Australia and New Zealand Army Corps (ANZAC).
Issued: Nos. 1174-1178, 4/12/90. No. 1176a, Apr. 2005.

1990, Apr. 19 *Perf. 14½*

1179 A418 41c multicolored 1.00 .50

Queen Elizabeth's 64th birthday.

Penny Black, 150th Anniv. A419

Stamps on stamps: a, New South Wales #44. b, South Australia #4. c, Tasmania #2. d, Victoria #120. e, Queensland #111A. f, Western Australia #3a.

1990, May 1 *Perf. 13½x14*

1180 Block of 6 5.50 5.50
a.-f. A419 41c any single .80 .50
g. Souvenir sheet of 6 5.75 5.75
h. As "g," with Stamp World London '90 emblem ovpt. in silver in sheet margin *14.50 14.50*

No. 1180h issued 5/3.

The Gold Rush — A420

a, Off to the diggings. b, The diggings. c, Panning for gold. d, Commissioner's tent. e, Gold escort.

1990, May 16 *Perf. 13*

1181 Strip of 5 4.00 4.00
a.-e. A420 41c any single .80 .50

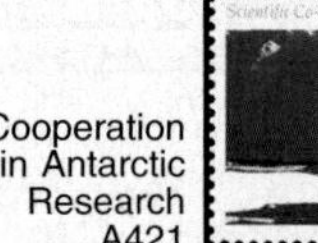

Cooperation in Antarctic Research A421

1990, June 13 Litho. *Perf. 14½x14*

1182 A421 41c Glaciology .80 .45
1183 A421 $1.10 Krill (marine biology) 2.25 1.10
a. Min. sheet of 2, #1182-1183 3.25 3.25
b. #1183a overprinted 8.00 8.00

No. 1183 is overprinted in gold, in sheet margin only, for NZ 1990 International Stamp Exhibition, Auckland, Aug. 24-Sept. 2, 1990.
See Russia Nos. 5902-5903.

Colonial Australia A422

Boom Time: a, Land boom. b, Building boom. c, Investment boom. d, Retail boom. e, Factory boom.

1990, July 12 Litho. *Perf. 13*

1184 Strip of 5 4.00 4.00
a.-e. A422 41c any single .80 .55

Sports Type of 1989

1990-91 Typo. *Die Cut Perf. 11½*
Self-Adhesive

1185 A400 41c Cycling 1.00 .75
1186 A400 43c Skateboarding 1.00 .25
a. Litho. 1.00 .25

Blue background has large dots on No. 1186 and smaller dots on No. 1186a. No. 1186 is on waxed paper backing printed with 0 to 4 koalas. No. 1186a is on plain paper backing printed with one kangaroo.
Issued: 41c, 5/16; No. 1186, 8/27; No. 1186a, 1991.

Salmon Gums by Robert Juniper — A423

43c, The Blue Dress by Brian Dunlop.

Perf. 15½ Vert.
1990, Sept. 3 Litho.
Booklet Stamps

1191 A423 28c multicolored 3.75 3.50
a. Perf. 14½ vert. 2.50 2.25
1192 A423 43c multicolored 1.00 .85
a. Bklt. pane, #1191, 4 #1192 6.00
b. Perf. 14½ vert. .90 .60
c. Bklt. pane, #1191a, 4 #1192b 4.50

Thinking Of You Type

1990, Sept. 3 *Perf. 14½*

1193 A413 43c multicolored .85 .50
a. Booklet pane of 10 8.50

Christmas A424

1990, Oct. 31 Litho. *Perf. 14½*

1194 A424 38c Kookaburras .75 .35
a. Booklet pane of 10 7.50
1195 A424 43c Nativity, vert. .85 .45
a. Perf. 14¾x14, additionally dated "2013" (#3534b) 1.10 1.10
1196 A424 80c Opossum 1.60 1.60
Nos. 1194-1196 (3) 3.20 2.40

Issued: No. 1195a, 5/10/2013.

Local Government in Australia, 150th Anniv. — A425

1990, Oct. 31

1197 A425 43c Town Hall, Adelaide 1.00 .50

Flags A426

1991, Jan. 10 Litho. *Perf. 14½*

1199 A426 43c National flag .85 .45
1200 A426 90c White ensign 1.75 1.75
1201 A426 $1 Air Force ensign 2.00 2.00
1202 A426 $1.20 Red ensign 2.40 2.40
Nos. 1199-1202 (4) 7.00 6.60

Australia Day.

Water Birds — A427

1991, Feb. 14

1203 A427 43c Black swan .95 .45
1204 A427 43c Black-necked stork, vert. .95 .45
1205 A427 85c Cape Barren goose, vert. 2.00 2.00
1206 A427 $1 Chestnut teal 2.50 2.50
Nos. 1203-1206 (4) 6.40 5.40

Women's Wartime Services, 50th Anniv. A428

50th Anniv: No. 1208, Siege of Tobruk. $1.20, Australian War Memorial, Canberra.

1991-2005 Litho. *Perf. 14½*

1207 A428 43c shown .90 .45
a. Booklet pane of 4, perf. 14x14½ ('05) 3.75 —
1208 A428 43c multicolored .90 .45
1209 A428 $1.20 multicolored 2.50 2.50
Nos. 1207-1209 (3) 4.30 3.40

Issued: Nos. 1207-1209, 3/14/91. No. 1207a, Apr. 2005.

Queen Elizabeth II's 65th Birthday — A429

1991, Apr. 11 Litho. *Perf. 14½*

1210 A429 43c multicolored 1.00 .80

Insects A430

1991, Apr. 11

1211 A430 43c Hawk moth .95 .70
1212 A430 43c Cotton harlequin bug .95 .70
1213 A430 80c Leichhardt's grasshopper 2.25 2.25
1214 A430 $1 Jewel beetle 2.25 2.00
Nos. 1211-1214 (4) 6.40 5.65

Australian Photography, 150th Anniv. — A431

Designs: No. 1215a, Bondi, by Max Dupain, 1939. No. 1215b, Gears for the Mining Industry, Vickers Ruwolt Melbourne, by Wolfgang Sievers, 1967. 70c, Wheel of Youth, by Harold Cazneaux, 1929. $1.20, Teacup Ballet, by Olive Cotton, 1935.

1991, May 13 Litho. *Perf. 14½*

1215 Pair 1.75 1.75
a.-b. A431 43c any single .85 .75
1216 A431 70c blk, olive & cl 1.40 1.25
1217 A431 $1.20 blk, gray & Prus bl 2.40 2.25
Nos. 1215-1217 (3) 5.55 5.25

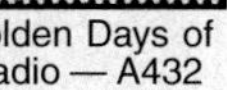

Golden Days of Radio — A432

Pets — A433

1991, June 13 Litho. *Perf. 14½*

1218 A432 43c Music & variety shows .90 .55
1219 A432 43c Soap operas .90 .55
1220 A432 85c Quiz shows 1.75 1.75
1221 A432 $1 Children's stories 2.10 1.90
Nos. 1218-1221 (4) 5.65 4.75

1991, July 25 Litho. *Perf. 14½*

1222 A433 43c Puppy 1.00 .70
1223 A433 43c Kitten 1.00 .70
1224 A433 70c Pony 1.75 1.75
1225 A433 $1 Cockatoo 2.25 2.00
Nos. 1222-1225 (4) 6.00 5.15

George Vancouver (1757-1798) and Edward John Eyre (1815-1901), Explorers — A434

1991, Sept. 26 Litho. *Perf. 14½*

1226 A434 $1.05 multicolored 2.25 .65
a. Souvenir sheet of 1 2.25 2.25
b. As "a," overprinted in gold 3.50 3.50

Vancouver's visit to Western Australia, 200th anniv. and Eyre's journey to Albany, Western Australia, 150th anniv.
No. 1226b overprinted in sheet margin with show emblem and: "PHILANIPPON / WORLD STAMP / EXHIBITION / TOKYO / 16-24 NOV 1991" followed by Japanese inscription.
Issued: No. 1226b, Nov. 16.

Australian Literature of the 1890's A435

Designs: 43c, Seven Little Australians by Ethel Turner. 75c, On Our Selection by Steele Rudd. $1, Clancy of the Overflow by A.B. "Banjo" Paterson, vert. $1.20, The Drover's Wife by Henry Lawson, vert.

1991, Oct. 10

1227 A435 43c multicolored .85 .40
1228 A435 75c multicolored 1.50 1.50
1229 A435 $1 multicolored 2.00 1.60
1230 A435 $1.20 multicolored 2.40 2.40
Nos. 1227-1230 (4) 6.75 5.90

Christmas A436

1991, Nov. 1

1231 A436 38c Shepherd .75 .45
a. Booklet pane of 20 15.00
1232 A436 43c Baby Jesus .85 .50
1233 A436 90c Wise man, camel 1.90 1.75
Nos. 1231-1233 (3) 3.50 2.70

Thinking of You — A437

1992, Jan. 2 Litho. *Perf. 14½*

1234 A437 45c Wildflowers .90 .30
a. Booklet pane of 10 9.00

Threatened Species — A438

Designs: Nos. 1235a, 1241, Parma wallaby. Nos. 1235b, 1242, Ghost bat. Nos. 1235c, 1243, Long-tailed dunnart. Nos. 1235d, 1244, Little pygmy possum. Nos. 1235e, 1245, Dusky hopping mouse. Nos. 1235f, 1246, Squirrel glider.

1992, Jan. 2 Litho. *Perf. 14x14½*

1235 Block of 6 5.50 5.50
a.-f. A438 45c any single .90 .70

Die Cut
Perf. 11½
Self-Adhesive
Size: 31x22mm

1241 A438 45c multi 1.40 .85
a. Typo. 1.10 .85
1242 A438 45c multi 1.40 .85
a. Typo. 1.10 .85
1243 A438 45c multi 1.40 .85
a. Typo. 1.10 .85
1244 A438 45c multi 1.40 .85
a. Typo. 1.10 .85
1245 A438 45c multi 1.40 .85
a. Typo. 1.10 .85
1246 A438 45c multi 1.40 .85
a. Typo. 1.10 .85
b. Bklt. pane, 2 each #1241-1244, 1 each #1245-1246 14.00
c. Pane of 5, #1242-1246 11.50
d. Strip of 6, #1241-1246 8.50
e. Strip of 6, #1241a-1246a 7.00
f. #1246c overprinted 11.50
g. As "f," no die cutting 210.00
Nos. 1241-1246 (6) 8.40 5.10

Litho. stamps are sharper in appearance than typo. stamps, most notably on the black lettering. Nos. 1246b and 1246c have tagging bars which make the right portion of the stamps appear toned.

No. 1246f — overprinted in Gold on sheet margin of No. 1246c with emblem of "WORLD COLUMBIAN / STAMP EXPO '92 / MAY 22-31, 1992 - CHICAGO." Issued in May.

See Nos. 1271-1293.

Wetlands A439

Perf. 14½ Horiz.

1992, Jan. 2 Litho.
Booklet Stamps

1247 A439 20c Noosa River, Queensland 1.10 .85
a. Perf. 14 horiz. 1.10 .85
1248 A439 45c Lake Eildon, Victoria 1.10 .85
a. Bklt. pane, #1247, 4 #1248 5.75
Complete booklet, #1248a 5.75
b. Perf. 14 horiz. .90 .65
c. Bklt. pane, #1247a, 4 #1248b 4.75
Complete booklet, #1248c 4.75

Sailing Ships A440

1992, Jan. 15 Litho. *Perf. 14½*

1249 A440 45c Young Endeavour .90 .50
1250 A440 45c Britannia, vert. .90 .50
1251 A440 $1.05 Akarana, vert. 2.10 2.10
1252 A440 $1.20 John Louis 2.25 2.25
a. Sheet of 4, #1249-1252 6.75 6.75
b. As "a," overprinted 9.25 9.25
c. As "a," overprinted 10.50 10.50
Nos. 1249-1252 (4) 6.15 5.35

Australia Day. Discovery of America, 500th anniv. (No. 1252a).

Overprint in gold on sheet margin of No. 1252b contains emblem and "WORLD COLUMBIAN / STAMP EXPO '92 / MAY 22-31, 1992-CHICAGO." No. 1252b issued in May.

Overprint in gold on sheet margin of No. 1252c contains emblem and "GENOVA '92 / 18-27 SEPTEMBER." No. 1252c issued in Sept.

Australian Battles, 1942 — A441

1992-2005 Litho. *Perf. 14½*

1253 A441 45c Bombing of Darwin .90 .45
1254 A441 75c Milne Bay 1.50 1.25
1255 A441 75c Kokoda Trail 1.50 1.25
1256 A441 $1.05 Coral Sea 2.10 2.10
a. Booklet pane, #1253-1256, perf. 14x14½ ('05) 6.00 —
1257 A441 $1.20 El Alamein 2.40 1.90
Nos. 1253-1257 (5) 8.40 6.95

No. 1256a issued Apr. 2005.

Intl. Space Year — A442

1992, Mar. 19

1258 A442 45c Helix Nebula .90 .45
1259 A442 $1.05 The Pleiades 2.10 1.40
1260 A442 $1.20 Spiral Galaxy NGC 2997 2.40 1.60
a. Sheet of 3, #1258-1260 6.25 6.25
b. As "a," overprinted 14.00 14.00
Nos. 1258-1260 (3) 5.40 3.45

Overprint on sheet margin of No. 1260b contains emblem of "WORLD COLUMBIAN / STAMP EXPO '92 / MAY 22-31, 1992-CHICAGO." No. 1260b issued in May.

Queen Elizabeth II, 66th Birthday A443

1992, Apr. 9 *Perf. 14x14½*

1261 A443 45c Wmk. 228 & #258 .90 .25

Vineyard Regions A444

Designs: No. 1262, Hunter Valley New South Wales. No. 1263, North Eastern Victoria. No. 1264, Barossa Valley South Australia. No. 1265, Coonawarra South Australia. No. 1266, Margaret River Western Australia.

1992, Apr. 9

1262 A444 45c multicolored .90 .80
1263 A444 45c multicolored .90 .80
1264 A444 45c multicolored .90 .80
1265 A444 45c multicolored .90 .80
1266 A444 45c multicolored .90 .80
Nos. 1262-1266 (5) 4.50 4.00

Land Care — A445

a, Salt action. b, Farm planning. c, Erosion control. d, Tree planting. e, Dune care.

1992, June 11 Litho. *Perf. 14½x14*

1267 Strip of 5 4.50 4.50
a.-e. A445 45c Any single .90 .45

1992 Summer Olympics and Paralympics, Barcelona A446

1992, July 2 *Perf. 14½*

1268 A446 45c Cycling 1.40 .60
1269 A446 $1.20 Weight lifting 2.50 2.50
1270 A446 $1.20 High jump 2.50 2.50
Nos. 1268-1270 (3) 6.40 5.60

Threatened Species Type of 1992

Designs: 30c, Saltwater crocodile. 35c, Echidna. 40c, Platypus. No. 1274, Kangaroo. No. 1275, Adult kangaroo with joey. No. 1276, Two adult kangaroos. No. 1277, Four koalas. No. 1278, Koala walking. No. 1279, Koala in tree. 50c, Koala. 60c, Common brushtail possum. 70c, Kookaburra. Nos. 1283, 1283A, Pelican. 90c, Eastern gray kangaroo. 95c, Common wombat. $1.20, Pink cockatoo. $1.35, Emu.

1992-98 Litho. *Perf. 14x14½*

1271 A438 30c multi .60 .25
1272 A438 35c multi .70 .35
1273 A438 40c multi .80 .30
1274 A438 45c orange & multi .90 .80
a. Brown panel 1.25 .90
b. Bright orange panel 1.25 .90
c. Additionally dated "2013" (#1284b) 1.25 1.25
1275 A438 45c orange & multi .90 .80
a. Brown panel 1.25 .90
b. Bright orange panel 1.25 .90
c. Additionally dated "2013" (#1284b) 1.25 1.25
1276 A438 45c orange & multi .90 .80
a. Sheet of 3, #1274-1276 2.75 2.75
b. Brown panel 1.25 1.25
c. Bright orange panel 1.25 1.25
d. Additionally dated "2013" (#1284b) 1.25 1.25
1277 A438 45c orange & multi .90 .80
a. Brown panel 1.25 1.25
b. Bright orange panel 1.25 1.25
1278 A438 45c orange & multi .90 .80
a. Brown panel 1.25 1.25
b. Bright orange panel 1.25 1.25
1279 A438 45c orange & multi .90 .80
a. Block of 6, #1274-1279 5.50 5.50
b. Souv. sheet, #1274-1279 15.00 15.00
c. Brown panel 1.25 1.25
d. Block, #1274a-1275a, 1276b, 1277a-1278a, 1279c 7.75 7.75
e. Bright orange panel 1.25 1.25
f. Block, #1274b-1275b, 1276c, 1277b-1278b, 1279e 7.75 7.75

On No. 1279a Australia and denomination are orange, "KANGAROO" is 9mm long, and date is 1½mm long. Date is 1mm long and "KANGAROO" 8mm long on Nos. 1279d and 1279f. No. 1279d comes from 2 Koala printing. No. 1279f comes from 3 Koala printing.

1280 A438 50c multi 1.00 .40
1281 A438 60c multi 1.25 .55
1282 A438 70c multi 1.40 .55
a. "Australia 70c" in brn ('96) 1.60 1.40
1283 A438 85c peach panel at bottom 1.75 .80
1283A A438 85c yellow panel at bottom 1.90 1.60
1284 A438 90c multi 1.75 .80
a. Additionally dated "2013" (#1284b) 2.25 2.25
b. Booklet pane of 4, #1274c, 1275c, 1276d, 1284a 6.00 —
1285 A438 95c multi 1.90 .80
1286 A438 $1.20 multi 2.40 2.25
a. "Australia $1.20" in brown ('98) 4.25 3.25
1287 A438 $1.35 multi 2.75 2.00
Nos. 1271-1287 (18) 23.60 15.45

PHILAKOREA '94 (No. 1279b).

"Australia" and denominations on Nos. 1282, 1286 are in orange.

No. 1276a inscribed in sheet margin with "CHINA '96 — 9th Asian International Exhibition" in Chinese and English and exhibition emblems.

No. 1282a comes from 3 Koala or 1 Kangaroo and 1 Koala printing. No. 1286a comes from 1 Kangaroo printing.

No. 1283A is from the three koala printing.

Issued: 35c, 50c, 60c, 95c, 8/13; 40c, 70c, 90c, $1.20, 8/12/93; 30c, 85c, $1.35, 3/10/94; 45c, 5/12/94; No. 1279b, 8/94; No. 1282a, 3/96; No. 1276a, 5/18/96; No. 1283A, 1997; No. 1286a, 12/98; Nos. 1274c, 1275c, 1276d, 1284a, 1284b, 5/10/13. No. 1284b was issued in a booklet also containing Nos. 1003b, 3534d and 3918.

Die Cut Perf. 11

1994, May 12 Litho.
Self-Adhesive

1288 A438 45c like #1274 1.75 .75
1289 A438 45c like #1275 1.75 .75
1290 A438 45c like #1276 1.75 .75
1291 A438 45c like #1277 1.75 .75
1292 A438 45c like #1278 1.75 .75
1293 A438 45c like #1279 1.75 .75
a. Bklt. pane, #1290, 1293, 2 each #1288-1289, 1291-1292 17.50
b. Strip of 6, #1288-1293 11.50
Nos. 1288-1293 (6) 10.50 4.50

Serpentine Die Cut 11½

1995 Typo. Self-Adhesive
Coil Stamps

1294 A438 45c Like #1274 1.00 .55
1294A A438 45c Like #1275 1.00 .55
1294B A438 45c Like #1276 1.00 .55
1294C A438 45c Like #1277 1.00 .55
1294D A438 45c Like #1278 1.00 .55
1295 A438 45c Like #1279 1.00 .55
a. Strip of 6, #1294, 1294A-1294D, 1295 8.00
Nos. 1294-1295 (6) 6.00 3.30

Nos. 1294-1295 come from the third through seventh Koala printings by Pemara.

Opening of Sydney Harbor Tunnel, August 29 — A447

Sydney Harbor Bridge and Tunnel: a, Left side. b, Right side.

1992, Aug. 28 Litho. *Perf. 14½*

1296 A447 45c Pair, #a.-b. 8.50 8.50
c. Pair, #d.-e., perf 15½ 3.50 3.50

Buildings in Western Australia Goldfield Towns A448

Designs: No. 1297, Warden's Courthouse, Coolgardie. No. 1298, Post Office, Kalgoorlie. $1.05, York Hotel, Kalgoorlie. $1.20, Town Hall, Kalgoorlie.

1992, Sept. 17 Litho. *Perf. 14x14½*

1297 A448 45c multicolored .90 .50
1298 A448 45c multicolored .90 .50
1299 A448 $1.05 multicolored 2.10 2.10
1300 A448 $1.20 multicolored 2.40 2.40
Nos. 1297-1300 (4) 6.30 5.50

Sheffield Shield Cricket Competition, Cent. — A449

Cricket match, 1890s: 45c, Bowler. $1.20, Batsman, wicket keeper.

1992, Oct. 15 Litho. *Perf. 14½*

1301 A449 45c multicolored 1.10 .55
a. Perf. 14¾x14, dated "2007" 1.40 1.40
1302 A449 $1.20 multicolored 2.60 2.60
a. Perf. 14¾x14, dated "2007" 3.75 3.75
b. Booklet pane of 3, #1111a, 1301a, 1302a 7.50 —

Nos. 1301a, 1302a, 1302b issued 11/14/2007.

Christmas A450

Designs: 40c, Children dressed as Mary and Joseph with baby carriage. 45c, Boy jumping from bed Christmas morning. $1, Boy and girl singing Christmas carol.

1992, Oct. 30 Litho. ***Perf. 14x14½***

1303 A450 40c multicolored .80 .50
a. Booklet pane of 20 16.00
1304 A450 45c multicolored .90 .35
1305 A450 $1 multicolored 2.00 1.75
Nos. 1303-1305 (3) 3.70 2.60

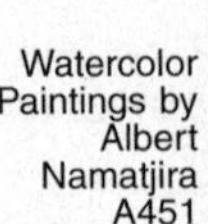

Watercolor Paintings by Albert Namatjira A451

Designs: No. 1306a, Ghost Gum, Central Australia. b, Across the Plain to Mount Giles.

1993, Jan. 14 Litho. ***Perf. 14x15***

1306 A451 45c Pair, #a.-b. 2.25 2.25

Australia Day.

Dreamings — A452

Aboriginal paintings: 45c, Wild Onion Dreaming, by Pauline Nakamarra Woods. 75c, Yam Plants, by Jack Wunuwun, vert. 85c, Goose Egg Hunt, by George Milpurrurru, vert. $1, Kalumpiwarra-Ngulalintji, by Rover Thomas.

Perf. 14x14½, 14½x14

1993, Feb. 4 Litho.

1307 A452 45c red & multi .90 .75
1308 A452 75c org yel & multi 1.50 1.25
1309 A452 85c buff & multi 1.75 1.50
1310 A452 $1 salmon & multi 2.00 1.75
Nos. 1307-1310 (4) 6.15 5.25

World Heritage Sites in Australia — A453

1993, Mar. 4 Litho. ***Perf. 14½x14***

1311 A453 45c Uluru (Ayers Rock) .90 .60
1312 A453 85c Fraser Island 1.75 1.60
1313 A453 95c Shark Bay 1.90 1.60
1314 A453 $2 Kakadu 4.00 2.75
Nos. 1311-1314 (4) 8.55 6.55

See Nos. 1485-1488.

World War II Ships A454

45c, Cruiser HMAS Sydney II. 85c, Corvette HMAS Bathurst. $1.05, Destroyer HMAS Arunta. $1.20, Hospital Ship Centaur.

1993-2005 Litho. ***Perf. 14x14½***

1315 A454 45c multicolored .90 .60
1316 A454 85c multicolored 1.75 1.60
1317 A454 $1.05 multicolored 2.10 2.10
a. Booklet pane, #1315, 1317 ('05) 3.25 —
1318 A454 $1.20 multicolored 2.40 2.40
Nos. 1315-1318 (4) 7.15 6.70

Issued: Nos. 1315-1318, 4/7/93. No. 1317a, April 2005.

A455

A456

1993, Apr. 7 ***Perf. 14½x14***

1319 A455 45c multicolored .90 .50

Queen Elizabeth II, 67th birthday.

1993, May 7 Litho. ***Perf. 14½x14***

Designs based on 19th cent. trade union banners: No. 1320, Baker, shoe maker. No. 1321, Stevedore, seamstresses. $1, Blacksmith, telephone operator, cook. $1.20, Carpenters.

1320 A456 45c multicolored .90 .70
1321 A456 45c multicolored .90 .70
1322 A456 $1 multicolored 2.00 1.60
1323 A456 $1.20 multicolored 2.40 2.25
Nos. 1320-1323 (4) 6.20 5.25

Working life in the 1890s.

Trains A457

Designs: No. 1324, Centenary Special, Tasmania. No. 1325, Spirit of Progress. No. 1326, Western Endeavour. No. 1327, Silver City Comet. No. 1328, Kuranda Tourist Train. No. 1329, The Ghan.

1993, June 1 ***Perf. 14x14½***

1324 A457 45c multicolored 1.25 1.10
1325 A457 45c multicolored 1.25 1.10
1326 A457 45c multicolored 1.25 1.10
1327 A457 45c multicolored 1.25 1.10
1328 A457 45c multicolored 1.25 1.10
1329 A457 45c multicolored 1.25 1.10
a. Block of 6, #1324-1329 7.75 7.75
Nos. 1324-1329 (6) 7.50 6.60

Die Cut Perf. 12x11½

Self-Adhesive

1330 A457 45c like No. 1324 2.25 .70
1331 A457 45c like No. 1325 2.25 .70
1332 A457 45c like No. 1326 2.25 .70
1333 A457 45c like No. 1327 2.25 .70
1334 A457 45c like No. 1328 2.25 .70
1335 A457 45c like No. 1329 2.25 .70
a. Strip of 6, #1330-1335 14.00
b. Bklt. pane, #1332, 1335, 2 ea #1330-1331, 1333-1334 14.00
Nos. 1330-1335 (6) 13.50 4.20

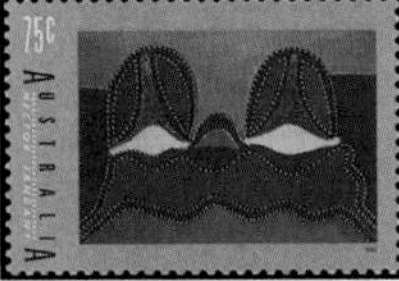

Aboriginal Art — A458

Aboriginal paintings: 45c, Black Cockatoo Feather, by Fiona Foley, vert. 75c, Ngarrgooroon Country, by Hector Jandany. $1, Ngak Ngak, by Ginger Riley. $1.05, Untitled work, by Robert Cole, vert.

Perf. 14½x14, 14x14½

1993, July 1 Litho.

1336 A458 45c henna brown & multi .90 .35
1337 A458 75c brown & multi 1.50 1.10
1338 A458 $1 gray & multi 2.00 1.75
1339 A458 $1.05 olive & multi 2.10 1.75
Nos. 1336-1339 (4) 6.50 4.95

Dame Enid Lyons, MP, and Sen. Dorothy Tangney A459

No. 1340, Stylized globe, natl. arms, Inter-Parliamentary Conf. emblem.

1993, Sept. 2 Litho. ***Perf. 14½***

1340 A459 45c multicolored 1.10 .90
1341 A459 45c multicolored 1.10 .90
a. Pair, #1340-1341 2.25 2.25

90th Inter-Parliamentary Union Conference (No. 1340). First women in Australian Federal Parliament, 50th anniv. (No. 1341). Nos. 1340-1341 printed in panes of 25 with 16 #1340 and 9 #1341. Panes with 16 #1341 and 9 #1340 were issued Nov. 19, but were available only through Philatelic Agency.

A460

A461

Dinosaurs: Nos. 1342, 1348, Ornithocheirus. Nos. 1343, 1349, Leaellynasaura. No. 1344, Allosaurus. No. 1345, Timimus. No. 1346, Muttaburrasaurus. No. 1347, Minmi.

1993, Oct. 1 ***Perf. 14x14½, 14½x14***

1342 A460 45c multi, horiz. .90 .70
1343 A460 45c multi .90 .70
1344 A461 45c multi .90 .70
1345 A461 45c multi .90 .70

Size: 30x50mm

1346 A461 75c multi 1.50 1.00
1347 A461 $1.05 multi horiz. 2.10 2.10
a. Souvenir sheet of 6, #1342-1347, perf. 14¼ 8.25 8.25
b. As "a," overprinted 10.00 10.00
c. As "a," overprinted 10.00 10.00
Nos. 1342-1347 (6) 7.20 5.90

Self-Adhesive

Die Cut Perf. 11½

1348 A460 45c multi horiz. 3.25 2.25
1349 A460 45c multi 3.25 2.25
a. Bklt. pane, 5 each #1348-1349 32.50

Overprint in gold on sheet margin of No. 1347b contains "BANGKOK 1993" show emblem and "WORLD PHILATELIC / EXHIBITION / BANGKOK 1-10 OCTOBER 1993."

Overprint in gold on sheet margin of No. 1347c contains dinosaur and "Sydney / STAMP & COIN / SHOW / 15-17 October 1993."

Christmas — A462

1993, Nov. 1 Litho. ***Perf. 14½x14***

1354 A462 40c Goodwill .80 .40
a. Booklet pane of 20 16.00
1355 A462 45c Joy .90 .50
1356 A462 $1 Peace 2.00 1.60
Nos. 1354-1356 (3) 3.70 2.50

Australia Day — A463

Landscape paintings: 45c, Shoalhaven River Bank-Dawn, by Arthur Boyd. 85c, Wimmera (from Mt. Arapiles), by Sir Sidney Nolan. $1.05, Lagoon, Wimmera, by Nolan. $2, White Cockatoos in Paddock with Flame Trees, by Boyd, vert.

Perf. 14½x14, 14x14½

1994, Jan. 13 Litho.

1357 A463 45c multicolored .90 .45
1358 A463 85c multicolored 1.75 1.75
1359 A463 $1.05 multicolored 2.10 2.10
1360 A463 $2 multicolored 4.00 3.75
Nos. 1357-1360 (4) 8.75 8.05

See Nos.1418-1421, 1476-1479, 1572-1574.

Royal Life Saving Society, Cent. A464

1994, Jan. 20 Litho. ***Perf. 14x14½***

1361 A464 45c Vigilance .90 .70
1362 A464 45c Education .90 .70
1363 A464 95c Drill 1.90 1.90
1364 A464 $1.20 Fitness 2.40 2.10
Nos. 1361-1364 (4) 6.10 5.40

Die Cut Perf. 11½

Self-Adhesive

1365 A464 45c like #1361 2.60 1.10
1366 A464 45c like #1362 2.60 1.10
a. Pair, #1365-1366 5.75
b. Booklet pane, 5 #1366a 29.00

Thinking of You — A465

1994, Feb. 3 Litho. ***Perf. 14½x14***

1367 A465 45c Rose .90 .50
1368 A465 45c Tulips .90 .50
1369 A465 45c Poppies .90 .50
a. Pair, #1368-1369 1.75 1.75
b. Booklet pane, 5 #1369a 8.75
Nos. 1367-1369 (3) 2.70 1.50

A466

A467

1994, Apr. 8 Litho. ***Perf. 14½***

1370 A466 45c multicolored 1.00 .55

Queen Elizabeth II, 68th birthday.

1994, Apr. 8 ***Perf. 14½x14***

1371 A467 95c multicolored 1.90 1.90

Opening of Friendship Bridge, Thailand-Laos.

Intl. Year of the Family A468

Children's paintings of their families: 45c, Bobbie Lea Blackmore. 75c, Kathryn Teoh. $1, Maree McCarthy.

1994, Apr. 14 Litho. ***Perf. 14x14½***

1372 A468 45c multicolored .90 .55
1373 A468 75c multicolored 1.50 1.50
1374 A468 $1 multicolored 2.00 2.00
Nos. 1372-1374 (3) 4.40 4.05

Australian Women's Right to Vote, Cent. A469

1994, June 9 Litho. ***Perf. 14x14½***

1375 A469 45c multicolored 1.00 .55

Bunyips Folklore Creatures A470

Types of Bunyips: No. 1376, Aboriginal legend. No. 1377, Nature Spirit. 90c, Berkeley's Creek. $1.35, Natural history.

1994, July 14 Litho. *Perf. 14x14½*

1376 A470 45c multicolored 1.10 1.10
1377 A470 45c multicolored 1.10 1.10
a. Pair, #1376-1377 2.25 2.25
1378 A470 90c multicolored 2.25 2.25
1379 A470 $1.35 multicolored 3.00 3.00
Nos. 1376-1379 (4) 7.45 7.45

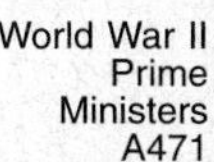

World War II Prime Ministers A471

Designs: a, Robert Menzies. b, Arthur Fadden. c, John Curtin. d, Francis (Frank) Forde. e, Joseph Benedict (Ben) Chifley.

1994-2005

1380 Strip of 5 6.50 6.50
a.-e. A471 45c any single 1.10 .90
f. Booklet pane, #1380a, 1380c ('05) 2.60 —

Issued: No. 1380, 8/11/94. No. 1380f, April 2005.

Aviation Pioneers — A472

Designs: No. 1381, Lawrence Hargrave, box kites. No. 1382, Ross and Keith Smith, Vickers Vimy. $1.35, Ivor McIntyre, Stanley Goble, Fairey IIID A10-3 seaplane. $1.80, Freda Thompson, DeHavilland Moth Major.

1994, Aug. 29 Engr. *Perf. 12*

1381 A472 45c multicolored 1.00 1.00
1382 A472 45c multicolored 1.00 1.00
1383 A472 $1.35 multicolored 2.75 2.75
1384 A472 $1.80 multicolored 3.75 3.75
Nos. 1381-1384 (4) 8.50 8.50

First England-Australia flight within 30-day time span (No. 1382). First aerial circumnavigation of Australia (No. 1383). First woman to fly solo from England-Australia (No. 1384).

A473

Australian Zoo Animals — A474

Perf. 14x14½, 14½x14

1994, Sept. 28 Litho.

1385 A473 45c Scarlet macaw 1.00 .90
1386 A473 45c Cheetah, vert. 1.00 .90
1387 A474 45c Fijian crested iguana 1.00 .90
1388 A474 45c Orangutan 1.00 .90

Size: 50x30mm

Perf. 14½x14

1389 A473 $1 Asian elephant 2.60 2.60
a. Souv. sheet of 5, #1385-1389, perf. 14½ 10.50 10.50
b. As "a," ovptd. 10.50 10.50
c. As "a," ovptd. 10.50 10.50
d. As "a," ovptd. 10.50 10.50
e. As "a," ovptd. 10.50 10.50
Nos. 1385-1389 (5) 6.60 6.20

Self-Adhesive

Die Cut Perf. 11½

1390 A473 45c like #1385 3.00 2.25
1391 A473 45c like #1386 3.00 2.25
a. Bklt. pane, 6 #1390, 4 #1391 30.00

Denomination is in LL corner on No. 1391.

Overprint in gold on sheet margin:

No. 1389b, show emblem and "Brisbane Stamp Show Zoos / October 21-23, 1994."

No. 1389c, show emblem and "SYDNEY / STAMP / AND / COIN / SHOW / 30/9/94 TO 2/10/94."

No. 1389d, show emblem and "Stampshow '94 Melbourne October 27-30 / National/State Centennial Exhibition 1894-1994."

No. 1389e, show emblem and "STAMP SHOW 94 / Fremantle Convention Centre / 5-6 November 1994."

Christmas A475

Details from Adoration of the Magi, by Giovanni Toscani: 40c, Madonna and Child, vert. 45c, One of Magi, horse and groom. $1, Joseph receiving frankincense from Magi. $1.80, Entire painting.

1994, Oct. 31 Litho. *Perf. 14½x14*

1392 A475 40c multicolored .80 .50
a. Booklet pane of 20 16.00
Complete booklet, #1392a 16.00

Perf. 14x14½

1393 A475 45c multicolored .90 .55
1394 A475 $1 multicolored 2.00 2.00

Size: 50x30mm

1395 A475 $1.80 multicolored 3.50 3.50
Nos. 1392-1395 (4) 7.20 6.55

50th Sydney-Hobart Yacht Race — A476

Designs: a, Yachts bow-on, Sydney Opera House, Harbor Bridge. b, Two yachts abeam.

1994, Oct. 31 *Perf. 14½*

1396 Pair 3.50 3.50
a.-b. A476 45c any single 1.10 1.10

Self-Adhesive

Die Cut Perf. 11½

1397 A476 45c like #1396a 3.50 3.50
1397A A476 45c like #1396b 3.50 3.50

A477

Self-Adhesive Booklet Stamps Background Color

Die Cut Perf. 17

1994, Nov. 2 Litho.

1398 A477 45c bluish green 1.40 1.40
1399 A477 45c blue 1.40 1.40
1400 A477 45c purple 1.40 1.40
1401 A477 45c yellow green 1.40 1.40
1402 A477 45c pale yel green 1.40 1.40
1403 A477 45c pale red brown 1.40 1.40
1404 A477 45c rose 1.40 1.40
1405 A477 45c orange yellow 1.40 1.40
a. Booklet pane of 20 28.00
Nos. 1398-1405 (8) 11.20 11.20

No. 1405a contains 3 each of Nos.1399, 1401, 1403, 1405 and 2 each of Nos. 1398, 1400, 1402, 1404. No. 1405a was sold in ATM machines, at the Natl. Philatelic Center, and Australian Philatelic Bureau.

Two printings differ slightly in shade and advertisement on back of pane.

Nos. 1406-1417 were deleted from the 2003 Standard catalogue. These self-adhesive stamps of design No. A438 have computer-generated denominations and exist with a large variety of different inscriptions for shows and other purposes.

Australia Day Type of 1994

Paintings: No. 1418, Back Verandah, by Russell Drysdale. No. 1419, Skull Springs Country, by Guy Grey-Smith. $1.05, Outcamp, by Robert Juniper. $1.20, Kite Flying, by Ian Fairweather.

1995, Jan. 12 Litho. *Perf. 15x14½*

1418 A463 45c multicolored 1.00 .60
1419 A463 45c multicolored 1.00 .60
1420 A463 $1.05 multicolored 2.10 1.90
1421 A463 $1.20 multicolored 2.40 2.10
Nos. 1418-1421 (4) 6.50 5.20

St. Valentine's Day — A478

Various designs: a, Red heart. b, Red & gold heart. c, Gold heart.

1995, Feb. 6 Litho. *Perf. 14½x14*

1422 Strip of 3 3.50 2.25
a.-c. A478 45c any single 1.10 .55

See No. 1480.

Endeavour A479

No. 1423: a, Captain Cook's Endeavour. b, Replica.

1995, Feb. 9 Litho. *Perf. 14x14½*

1423 Pair 3.75 3.75
a.-b. A479 45c any single 1.10 .90

Booklet Stamps

Size: 44x26mm

Perf. 14 Horiz.

1424 A479 20c like #1423b 3.00 2.60
1425 A479 45c like #1423a 1.40 .70
a. Bklt. pane, #1424, 4 #1425 8.50
Complete booklet, #1425a 8.50

Natl. Trust, 50th Anniv. A480

Designs: No. 1426a, Coalport plate, Regency style bracket clock. No. 1426b, 15th-16th cent. x-frame Italian style chair, 19th cent. Steiner doll. $1, Advance Australia teapot, neo-classical parian-ware statuette. $2, China urn, silver bowl.

1995, Mar. 16 Engr. *Perf. 14x14½*

1426 Pair 2.25 2.25
a.-b. A480 45c any single 1.00 .55
1427 A480 $1 red brn & bl 2.10 1.90
1428 A480 $2 blue & green 4.00 4.00
Nos. 1426-1428 (3) 8.35 8.15

Opals — A481

1995, Apr. 5 Litho. *Perf. 14½x14*

1429 A481 $1.20 Light opal 3.00 3.00
1430 A481 $2.50 Black opal 5.25 5.25

Nos. 1429-1430 each contain a holographic image. Soaking in water may affect the hologram.

See Nos. 1554-1555.

A482

1995, Apr. 20 Litho. *Perf. 14½*

1431 A482 45c multicolored 1.00 .55

Queen Elizabeth II, 69th birthday.

A483

Famous Australians from World War II.

1995, Apr. 20 Litho. *Perf. 14½x14*

1432 A483 45c Sir Edward Dunlop 1.10 1.10
1433 A483 45c Mrs. Jessie Vasey 1.10 1.10
1434 A483 45c Tom Derrick 1.10 1.10
1435 A483 45c Rawdon Hume Middleton 1.10 1.10
a. Block of 4, #1432-1435 4.75 4.75
Nos. 1432-1435 (4) 4.40 4.40

Self-Adhesive

Die Cut Perf. 11½

1436 A483 45c like #1432 2.25 .85
1437 A483 45c like #1433 2.25 .85
1438 A483 45c like #1434 2.25 .85
1439 A483 45c like #1435 2.25 .85
a. Booklet pane, 4 #1436, 2 each #1437-1439 22.50
b. Strip of 4, #1436-1439 9.75
Nos. 1436-1439 (4) 9.00 3.40

See Nos. 1452-1455.

UN, 50th Anniv. A484

1995, May 11 Litho. *Perf. 14x14½*

1440 A484 45c + label, multi 1.10 .55
a. Block of 4 + 4 labels 5.75 4.50

No. 1440 was issued se-tenant with label in blocks of 4 + 4 labels in four designs. In alternating rows, labels appear on left or right side of stamp.

A485

Poster, scene from: No. 1441, The Story of the Kelly Gang, 1906. No. 1442, On Our Selection, 1932. No. 1443, Jedda, 1955. No. 1444, Picnic at Hanging Rock, 1970s. No. 1445, Strictly Ballroom, 1992.

1995, June 8 Litho. *Perf. 14½x14*

1441 A485 45c multicolored 1.25 1.00
1442 A485 45c multicolored 1.25 1.00
1443 A485 45c multicolored 1.25 1.00
1444 A485 45c multicolored 1.25 1.00
1445 A485 45c multicolored 1.25 1.00
a. Strip of 5, #1441-1445 7.00 7.00
Nos. 1441-1445 (5) 6.25 5.00

Self-Adhesive

Die Cut Perf. 11½

1446 A485 45c like #1441 3.25 .85
1447 A485 45c like #1442 3.25 .85
1448 A485 45c like #1443 3.25 .85
1449 A485 45c like #1444 3.25 .85
1450 A485 45c like #1445 3.25 .85
a. Strip of 5, #1446-1450 20.00
b. Bklt. pane, 2 ea #1446-1450 32.50
Nos. 1446-1450 (5) 16.25 4.25

Motion Pictures, cent.

By its nature No. 1450b constitutes a complete booklet. The peelable backing serves as a booklet cover.

A486

People with Disabilities: No. 1451a, Person flying kite from wheelchair. b, Blind person playing violin, guide dog.

1995, July 13 Litho. *Perf. 14½x14*
1451 Pair 2.25 2.25
a.-b. A486 45c any single 1.00 .55

Famous Australians from World War II Type of 1995

1995-2005 Litho. *Perf. 14½x14*
1452 A483 45c Leon Goldsworthy 1.25 .85
a. Booklet pane, #1432, 1434, 1435, 1452 ('05) 5.75 —
1453 A483 45c Len Waters 1.25 .85
1454 A483 45c Ellen Savage 1.25 .85
a. Booklet pane, #1433, 1454 ('05) 3.00 —
1455 A483 45c Percy Collins 1.25 .85
a. Block of 4, #1452-1455 5.25 4.50
Nos. 1452-1455 (4) 5.00 3.40

Issued: Nos. 1452-1455, 8/10/95. Nos 1452a and 1454a, April 2005.

Peace Types of 1946

Perf. 14x14½, 14½x14

1995, Aug. 10 Engr.
1456 A43 45c red brown 1.25 1.00
1457 A45 45c dark green 1.25 1.00
1458 A44 $1.50 dark blue 3.50 3.50
Nos. 1456-1458 (3) 6.00 5.50

End of World War II, 50th anniv.

Wildlife A487

Designs: a, Koalas. b, Pandas.

1995, Sept. 1 Litho. *Perf. 14*
1459 Pair 2.25 2.25
a.-b. A487 45c any single 1.10 1.10
c. Souv. sheet #1459a, perf. 11x11½ 2.25 2.25
d. Souv. sheet #1459b, perf. 11x11½ 2.25 2.25
e. #1459c Ovptd. in sheet margin 4.50 4.50
f. #1459d Ovptd. in sheet margin 4.50 4.50

Overprints read: No. 1459e: "AUSTRALIAN STAMP EXHIBITION." No. 1459f: "INTERNATIONAL STAMP & COIN EXPO. / BEIJING '95."

Issued: No. 1459f, 9/14/95.

See People's Republic of China Nos. 2597-2598.

Australian Medical Discoveries A488

Designs: No. 1461a, Joseph Slattery, Thomas Lyle, Walter Filmer, x-ray pioneers. No. 1461b, Jean Macnamara, Macfarlane Burnet, viruses and immunology. No. 1461C, Fred Hollows, eye care, vert. $2.50, Howard Florey, co-discoverer of penicillin, vert.

1995, Sept. 7 *Perf. 14x14½, 14½x14*
1461 Pair 1.90 1.60
a.-b. A488 45c any single .85 .80
1461C A488 45c multicolored 1.10 .55
1461D A488 $2.50 multicolored 5.75 5.75
Nos. 1461-1461D (3) 8.75 7.90

No. 1461D exists in sheetlets of 10.

The World Down Under A489

Designs: Nos. 1462a, 1465a, Flatback turtle. Nos. 1462b, 1465b, Flame angelfish, nudibranch. Nos. 1463a, 1465c, Potato cod, giant maori wrasse. Nos. 1463b, 1465d, Giant trevally. Nos. 1464a, 1465e, Black marlin. Nos. 1464b, 1465f, Mako & tiger sharks.

1995, Oct. 3 Litho. *Perf. 14x14½*
1462 Pair 2.25 2.25
a.-b. A489 45c any single 1.10 .90
1463 Pair 2.25 2.25
a.-b. A489 45c any single 1.10 .90
1464 Pair 2.25 2.25
a.-b. A489 45c any single 1.10 .90
Nos. 1462-1464 (3) 6.75 6.75

Miniature Sheet of 6

1465 A489 45c #a.-f. 7.00 7.00
g. Ovptd. in sheet margin 8.00 8.00
h. Ovptd. in sheet margin 8.00 8.00
i. Ovptd. in sheet margin 8.00 8.00
j. Ovptd. in sheet margin 8.00 8.00
k. Ovptd. in sheet margin 8.00 8.00

Nos. 1462-1464 have pale blue border on three sides. No. 1465 is a continuous design and does not have the pale border. Fish on No. 1465 are printed with additional phosphor ink producing a glow-in-the-dark effect under ultraviolet light.

Overprints in gold in sheet margin of No. 1465 include show emblems and text:

No. 1465g: "ADELAIDE / STAMP AND / COLLECTIBLES / FAIR / 14/10/95 - / 15/10/95."

No. 1465h: "SYDNEY / CENTREPOINT 95 / STAMPSHOW."

No. 1465i: "Brisbane Stamp Show / 20-22 October 1995."

No. 1465j: "Melbourne Stamp & Coin Fair / 27-29 October 1995."

No. 1465k: "Swanpex WA / 28-29 October 1995."

Booklet Stamps
Self-Adhesive

Die Cut Perf. 11½

1466 A489 45c like #1462a 1.10 .55
1467 A489 45c like #1462b 1.10 .55
1468 A489 45c like #1463a 1.10 .55
1469 A489 45c like #1463b 1.10 .55
1470 A489 45c like #1464a 1.10 .55
1471 A489 45c like #1464b 1.10 .55
a. Booklet pane, #1470-1471, 2 each #1466-1469 14.00
b. Strip of 6, #1466-1471 14.00
Nos. 1466-1471 (6) 6.60 3.30

By its nature, No. 1471a constitutes a complete booklet. The peelable backing serves as a booklet cover.

Christmas — A490

Stained glass windows, Our Lady Help of Christians Church, Melbourne: 40c, Madonna and Child. 45c, Angel carrying banner. $1, Three rejoicing angels.

1995, Nov. 1 Litho. *Perf. 14½x14*
1472 A490 40c multicolored 1.00 .70
1473 A490 45c multicolored 1.25 .75
1474 A490 $1 multicolored 2.25 2.00
Nos. 1472-1474 (3) 4.50 3.45

Booklet Stamp
Self-Adhesive

Die Cut Perf. 11½

1475 A490 40c multicolored 1.40 .45
a. Booklet pane of 20 28.00

Madonna and Child on No. 1475 are printed with additional phosphor ink giving parts of the stamp a rough texture.

By its nature, No. 1475a constitutes a complete booklet. The peelable backing serves as a booklet cover, which also contains 20 labels. The complete booklet is available with backing showing two different advertisements.

Australia Day Type of 1994

Paintings by Australian women: 45c, West Australian Banksia, by Margaret Preston, vert. 85c, The Babe is Wise, by Lina Bryans, vert. $1, The Bridge in Curve, by Grace Cossington Smith. $1.20, Beach Umbrellas, by Vida Lahey.

Perf. 14x14½, 14½x14

1996, Jan. 16 Litho.
1476 A463 45c multicolored 1.00 .35
1477 A463 85c multicolored 1.90 1.60
1478 A463 $1 multicolored 2.10 1.90
1479 A463 $1.20 multicolored 2.40 2.10
Nos. 1476-1479 (4) 7.40 5.95

Heart and Roses A491

1996, Jan. 30 *Perf. 14x14½*
1480 A491 45c gold & multi 1.00 .55

See No. 1422.

Military Aviation A492

Airplanes: No. 1481, Firefly, Sea Fury. No. 1482, Beaufighter, Kittyhawk. No. 1483, Hornet. No. 1484, Kiowa.

1996-2005 Litho. *Perf. 14x14½*
1481 A492 45c multicolored .90 .90
1482 A492 45c multicolored .90 .90
a. Booklet pane, #1481, 1482 ('05) 1.90 —
1483 A492 45c multicolored .90 .90
1484 A492 45c multicolored .90 .90
a. Block of 4, #1481-1484 4.00 4.00

Issued: 1481-1484, 2/26/96. No. 1482a, April 2005.

Australian World Heritage Sites Type of 1993

Designs: 45c, Tasmanian Wilderness. 75c, Willandra Lakes. 95c, Fossil Cave, Naracoorte. $1, Lord Howe Island.

1996, Mar. 14 Litho. *Perf. 14½x14*
1485 A453 45c multicolored 1.10 .95
1486 A453 75c multicolored 1.90 1.60
1487 A453 95c multicolored 2.00 2.00
1488 A453 $1 multicolored 2.25 1.90
a. Booklet pane, #1311, 1314, 1485, 1488 ('06) 8.25 —
Nos. 1485-1488 (4) 7.25 6.45

No. 1488a issued 3/15/2006.

Indonesian Bear Cuscus — A493

No. 1489, Australian Spotted Cuscus.

1996, Mar. 22
1489 A493 45c multicolored 1.00 .80
1490 A493 45c multicolored 1.00 .80
a. Pair, Nos. 1489-1490 2.50 2.50
b. Souvenir sheet, No. 1490a 4.00 4.00
c. As "b," with World Philatelic Youth Exhibition emblem in sheet margin 9.25 9.25

No. 1490a has continuous design.

See Indonesia Nos. 1640-1642.

Queen Elizabeth II, 70th Birthday A494

Litho. & Engr.

1996, Apr. 11 *Perf. 14x14½*
1491 A494 45c multicolored 1.00 .55

North Melbourne Kangaroos A495

Brisbane Bears A496

Sydney Swans — A497

Carlton Blues — A498

Adelaide Crows — A499

Fitzroy Lions — A500

Richmond Tigers — A501

St. Kilda Saints — A502

Melbourne Demons — A503

Collingwood Magpies — A504

Fremantle Dockers — A505

Footscray Bulldogs — A506

West Coast Eagles A507

Essendon Bombers A508

Geelong Cats — A509

Hawthorn Hawks — A510

1996, Apr. 23 Litho. *Perf. 14½x14*

1492	A495 45c multicolored		1.25	1.10
1493	A496 45c multicolored		1.25	1.10
1494	A497 45c multicolored		1.25	1.10
1495	A498 45c multicolored		1.25	1.10
1496	A499 45c multicolored		1.25	1.10
1497	A500 45c multicolored		1.25	1.10
1498	A501 45c multicolored		1.25	1.10
1499	A502 45c multicolored		1.25	1.10
1500	A503 45c multicolored		1.25	1.10
1501	A504 45c multicolored		1.25	1.10
1502	A505 45c multicolored		1.25	1.10
1503	A506 45c multicolored		1.25	1.10
1504	A507 45c multicolored		1.25	1.10
1505	A508 45c multicolored		1.25	1.10
1506	A509 45c multicolored		1.25	1.10
1507	A510 45c multicolored		1.25	1.10
a.	Min. sheet of 16, #1492-1507		20.00	
	Nos. 1492-1507 (16)		20.00	17.60

Booklet Stamps

Self-Adhesive

Serpentine Die Cut 11½

1508	A495 45c multicolored	1.40	.70
a.	Booklet pane of 10	14.00	
1509	A496 45c multicolored	1.40	.70
a.	Booklet pane of 10	14.00	
1510	A497 45c multicolored	1.40	.70
a.	Booklet pane of 10	14.00	
1511	A498 45c multicolored	1.40	.70
a.	Booklet pane of 10	14.00	
1512	A499 45c multicolored	1.40	.70
a.	Booklet pane of 10	14.00	
1513	A500 45c multicolored	1.40	.70
a.	Booklet pane of 10	14.00	
1514	A501 45c multicolored	1.40	.70
a.	Booklet pane of 10	14.00	
1515	A502 45c multicolored	1.40	.70
a.	Booklet pane of 10	14.00	
1516	A503 45c multicolored	1.40	.70
a.	Booklet pane of 10	14.00	
1517	A504 45c multicolored	1.40	.70
a.	Booklet pane of 10	14.00	
1518	A505 45c multicolored	1.40	.70
a.	Booklet pane of 10	14.00	
1519	A506 45c multicolored	1.40	.70
a.	Booklet pane of 10	14.00	
1520	A507 45c multicolored	1.40	.70
a.	Booklet pane of 10	14.00	
1521	A508 45c multicolored	1.40	.70
a.	Booklet pane of 10	14.00	
1522	A509 45c multicolored	1.40	.70
a.	Booklet pane of 10	14.00	
1523	A510 45c multicolored	1.40	.70
a.	Booklet pane of 10	14.00	
	Nos. 1508-1523 (16)	22.40	11.20

By their nature, Nos. 1508a-1523a are complete booklets. The peelable paper backing serves as a booklet cover.

Australian Football League, cent.

Flora and Fauna — A511

Designs: 5c, Leadbeater's possum. 10c, Powerful owl. 20c, Saltwater crocodile, Kangkong flower. 25c, Northern dwarf tree frog, red lily. No. 1528, Little kingfisher. No. 1529, Jacana. No. 1530, Jabiru. No. 1531, Brolga. $1, Big greasy butterfly, water lily. $2, Blackwood wattle. $5, Mountain ash, fern. $10, Kakadu Wetlands during lightning storm, great egret, red lily.

Perf. 14x14½, 14½x14 (#1535)

1996-99 Litho.

1524	A511	5c multi	.25	.25
1525	A511	10c multi	.30	.25
1526	A511	20c multi	.40	.40
1527	A511	25c multi	.55	.55
1528	A511	45c multi	.95	.95
1529	A511	45c multi	.95	.95
1530	A511	45c multi	.95	.95
1531	A511	45c multi	.95	.95
a.		Block of 4, #1528-1531	4.00	4.00
b.		Souvenir sheet of 2, #1530-1531	1.60	
1532	A511	$1 multi	2.10	1.40
1533	A511	$2 multi	4.00	2.50

Size: 30x50mm

1534	A511	$5 multi, vert.	10.00	6.50

Size: 50x30mm

1535	A511	$10 multi	20.00	12.00
a.		Souvenir sheet of 1	22.50	18.00
b.		As "a," ovptd. in sheet margin	35.00	30.00
c.		As "a," ovptd in sheet margin	25.00	25.00
d.		As "a," ovptd in sheet margin	21.00	21.00
		Nos. 1524-1535 (12)	41.40	27.65

Self-Adhesive

Serpentine Die Cut 11½, 11¼ (#1539i)

1536	A511	45c like #1529	1.00	.55
1537	A511	45c like #1528	1.00	.55
1538	A511	45c like #1531	1.00	.55
1539	A511	45c like #1530	1.00	.55
a.		Booklet pane, 3 ea #1536, #1538, 2 ea #1537, #1539	10.50	
b.		Strip of 4, #1536-1539	4.50	
h.		Sheet of 5, #1537-1539, 2 #1536	5.75	
i.		Booklet pane, 5 each #1536-1539	20.00	

Serpentine Die Cut 12½x13

1539C	A511	45c like #1529	1.00	.55
1539D	A511	45c like #1528	1.00	.55
1539E	A511	45c like #1531	1.00	.55
1539F	A511	45c like #1530	1.00	.55
g.		Strip of 4, #1539C-1539F	4.50	
		Nos. 1536-1539F (8)	8.00	4.40

Nos. 1536-1539 are booklet stamps.

No. 1531b is inscribed in sheet margin with Shanghai '97 emblem and "International Stamp & Coin Exposition Shanghai '97" in Chinese and English.

No. 1535b is overprinted in silver in sheet margin with PACIFIC 97 emblem and "Australia Post Exhibition Sheet No. 4."

No. 1535c is overprinted in sheet margin for "Italia '98" in Milan.

No. 1535d is overprinted in copper in sheet margin with "PHILA NIPPON '01" and show emblem. Issued: No. 1535c, 8/1/01.

By its nature No. 1539a is a complete booklet. The peelable backing serves as a booklet cover.

Issued: 5c, 10c, $2, $5, 5/9/96; 20c, 25c, $1, $10, #1538a, 4/10/97; #1528-1531, 1536-1539, 6/2/97; #1531b, 11/17/97; #1539C-1539F, 11/13/99; No. 1539i, 9/1/98.

No. 1539i is a complete booklet.

See Nos. 1734-1746L, 1984-1995, 2060-2063, 2111-2114, 2159-2170, 2235-2238.

Modern Olympic Games, Cent. A512

Designs: No. 1540, Edwin Flack, 1st Australian gold medalist, runners. No. 1541, Fanny Durack, 1st Australian woman gold medalist, swimmers. $1.05, Paralympics, Atlanta.

Litho. & Engr.

1996, June 6 *Perf. 14x14½*

1540	A512	45c multicolored	1.00	.30
1541	A512	45c multicolored	1.00	.30
a.		Pair, #1540-1541	2.25	1.75
1542	A512	$1.05 multicolored	2.50	2.10
		Nos. 1540-1542 (3)	4.50	2.70

Transfer of Olympic Flag from Atlanta to Sydney A513

1996, July 22 Litho.

1543	A513	45c multicolored	1.10	.50

Issued in sheets of 10.

Children's Book Council, 50th Anniv. A514

Covers from "Book of the Year" books: No. 1544, "Animalia." No. 1545, "Greetings from Sandy Beach." No. 1546, "Who Sank the Boat?" No. 1547, "John Brown, Rose and the Midnight Cat."

1996, July 4 Litho. *Perf. 14x14½*

1544	A514	45c multicolored	1.00	1.00
1545	A514	45c multicolored	1.00	1.00
1546	A514	45c multicolored	1.00	1.00
1547	A514	45c multicolored	1.00	1.00
a.		Block of 4, #1544-1547	4.50	4.50
		Nos. 1544-1547 (4)	4.00	4.00

Serpentine Die Cut 11½

Self-Adhesive

1548	A514	45c like #1544	1.40	.70
1549	A514	45c like #1546	1.40	.70
1550	A514	45c like #1547	1.40	.70
1551	A514	45c like #1545	1.40	.70
a.		Booklet pane, 4 #1548, 2 each #1549-1551	15.50	
b.		Strip of 4, #1548-1551	7.00	
		Nos. 1548-1551 (4)	5.60	2.80

By its nature, No. 1551a is a complete booklet. The peelable paper backing serves as a booklet cover.

National Council of Women, Cent. — A515

Designs: 45c, Margaret Windeyer (1866-1939), honorary life president. $1, Rose Scott (1847-1925), founding executive member.

1996, Aug. 8 Litho. *Perf. 14½x14*

1552	A515	45c claret & yellow	.95	.30
1553	A515	$1 blue & yellow	2.10	2.10

Gems Type of 1995

1996, Sept. 5 Litho. *Perf. 14½x14*

1554	A481	45c Pearl	1.10	.30
1555	A481	$1.20 Diamond	3.00	3.00

No. 1555 contains a round foil design. Soaking in water may affect the design.

Arts Councils in Regional Australia A516

Silhouettes of performing artists, outdoor scene: 20c, Ballet dancer, violinist, field, bales, trees. 45c, Violinist, hand holding flower, dancer, tree in field.

Perf. 14 Horiz.

1996, Sept. 12 Litho.

Booklet Stamps

1556	A516	20c multicolored	1.75	1.25
1557	A516	45c multicolored	.95	.85
a.		Bklt. pane, #1556, 4 #1557	5.75	
		Complete booklet, #1557a	5.75	

A517

Pets — A518

1996-97 *Perf. 14x14½, 14½x14*

1558	A517	45c Cockatoo	1.10	1.10
1559	A517	45c Ducks, vert.	1.10	1.10
1560	A517	45c Dog, cat, vert.	1.10	1.10
a.		Pair, #1559-1560	2.60	2.60
1561	A518	45c Dog, puppy	1.10	1.10
1562	A518	45c Kittens	1.10	1.10
a.		Pair, #1561-1562	2.60	2.60

Size: 30x50mm

1563	A518	45c Pony mare, foal	1.10	.55
a.		Souvenir sheet, #1558-1563, perf. 14¼	7.75	7.75
b.		As "a," ovptd.	8.00	8.00
c.		As "a," ovptd.	8.00	8.00
d.		As "a," ovptd.	8.00	8.00
e.		As "a," ovptd.	8.00	8.00
f.		As "a," ovptd.	8.00	8.00
g.		As "a," ovptd.	8.00	8.00
h.		As "a," ovptd.	8.00	8.00
		Nos. 1558-1563 (6)	6.60	6.05

Self-Adhesive

Serpentine Die Cut 11½

1564	A518	45c like #1561	2.25	1.10
1565	A518	45c like #1562	2.25	1.10
a.		Bklt. pane, 6 #1564, 4 #1565	22.50	

No. 1563a is a continuous design.

Overprints in gold on sheet margin: No. 1563b, show emblem and "10TH ASIAN INTERNATIONAL PHILATELIC EXHIBITION 1996" in Chinese and English. No. 1563c, pets emblem and, "ASDA CENTREPOINT '96 STAMP AND COIN SHOW / 5-7 October 1996." No. 1563d, pets emblem and "ST PETERS STAMP & COLLECTIBLE FAIR / 12-13 OCTOBER 1996." No. 1563e, pets emblem and "MELBOURNE '96 NATIONAL PHILATELIC EXHIBITION / 17-20 OCTOBER 1996." No. 1563f, pets emblem and "QUEENSLAND SPRING STAMP AND COIN SHOW / 25-27 OCTOBER 1996." No. 1563g, pets emblem and "SWANPEX '96 / 26-27 OCTOBER 1996." No. 1563h: Hong Kong '97 emblem and "11TH ASIAN INTERNATIONAL STAMP EXHIBITION / 12-16 FEBRUARY 1997."

By its nature, No. 1565a is a complete booklet. The peelable paper backing serves as a booklet cover.

Issued: Nos. 1558-1563, 1563a, 1564-1565, 10/1/96; Nos. 1563b-1563g, 10/3/96; No. 1563h, 2/12/97.

Baron Ferdinand von Mueller (1825-96), Botanist — A519

1996, Oct. 9 *Perf. 14*

1566	A519	$1.20 multicolored	2.50	2.50

See Germany No. 1949.

Christmas — A520

1996, Nov. 1 *Perf. 14½x14*

1567	A520	40c Madonna and Child	.80	.80
1568	A520	45c Wise man	.90	.90
1569	A520	$1 Shepherd boy, lamb	2.00	2.00
		Nos. 1567-1569 (3)	3.70	3.70

Self-Adhesive

Serpentine Die Cut 12

1570	A520	40c like #1567	2.25	.55
a.		Booklet pane of 20	45.00	

By its nature, No. 1570a is a complete booklet. The peelable paper backing serves as a booklet cover.

Exploration of Australian Coast & Christmas Island by Willem de Vlamingh, 300th Anniv. — A521

Portrait of a Dutch Navigator, by Jan Verkolje.

1996, Nov. 1 ***Perf. 14x14½***

1571 A521 45c multicolored .90 .30

a. Pair, #1571 & Christmas Is. #404 2.25 2.25

Australia Day Type of 1994

Paintings: 85c, Landscape '74, by Fred Williams. 90c, The Balcony 2, by Brett Whiteley. $1.20, Fire Haze at Gerringong, by Lloyd Rees.

1997, Jan. 16 Litho. ***Perf. 14½x14***

1572 A463 85c multicolored 1.90 1.90

1573 A463 90c multicolored 2.00 2.00

1574 A463 $1.20 multicolored 3.00 3.00

Nos. 1572-1574 (3) 6.90 6.90

Sir Donald Bradman, Cricketer A522

1997, Jan. 23 Litho. ***Perf. 14¼***

1575 A522 45c Portrait 1.10 .55

a. Without gold highlights, dated "2007" 1.40 1.40

1576 A522 45c At bat 1.10 .55

a. Pair, No. 1575-1576 2.25 2.25

b. Booklet pane, #1575-1576 1.90 —

c. Without gold highlights, dated "2007" 1.40 1.40

No. 1576b issued 1/24/07. Nos. 1575a, 1576c issued 11/14/2007.

See Nos. 1634-1646, 1719-1722, 1800-1807, 1933-1936, 1941-1942, 2021-2030, 2125-2132, 2207-2210.

Greetings — A523

1997, Jan. 29 ***Perf. 14½x14***

1577 A523 45c Rose .90 .90

Serpentine Die Cut 11½

Booklet Stamp

Self-Adhesive

1578 A523 45c like #1577 1.25 .30

a. Booklet pane of 10 12.50

By its nature, No. 1578a is a complete booklet. The peelable paper backing, which also contains 12 labels, serves as a booklet cover.

Classic Cars — A524

Automobiles: No. 1579, 1934 Ford Coupe Utility. No. 1580, 1948 GMH Holden 48-215 (FX). No. 1581, 1958 Austin Lancer. No. 1582, 1962 Chrysler Valiant R Series.

1997, Feb. 27 Litho. ***Perf. 14x14½***

1579 A524 45c multicolored .90 .90

a. Booklet pane of 4 3.75

1580 A524 45c multicolored .90 .90

a. Booklet pane of 4 3.75

1581 A524 45c multicolored .90 .90

a. Booklet pane of 4 3.75

1582 A524 45c multicolored .90 .90

a. Booklet pane of 4 3.75

b. Block of 4, #1579-1582 4.50 4.50

Complete booklet, #1579a, 1580a, 1581a, 1582a 19.00

Nos. 1579-1582 (4) 3.60 3.60

Complete booklet contains 2 postal cards and 16 self-adhesive labels.

Serpentine Die Cut 12

Booklet Stamps

Self-Adhesive

1583 A524 45c like #1579 1.25 .55

1584 A524 45c like #1580 1.25 .55

1585 A524 45c like #1581 1.25 .55

1586 A524 45c like #1582 1.25 .55

a. Bklt. pane, 2 ea #1583, 1585, 3 ea #1584, 1586 14.00

b. Strip of 4, #1583-1586 8.00

Nos. 1583-1586 (4) 5.00 2.20

By its nature, No. 1586a is a complete booklet. The peelable backing serves as a booklet cover. The backing for No. 1586b is inscribed with a 3x8mm black vertical box and "SNP CAMBEC."

Circuses in Australia, 150th Anniv. — A525

Designs: No. 1591, Queen of the Arena, May Wirth (1894-1978). No. 1592, Wizard of the Wire, Con Colleano (1899-1973). No. 1593, Clowns. No. 1594, Tumblers.

1997, Mar. 13 Litho. ***Perf. 14½x14***

1591 A525 45c multicolored 1.00 .70

1592 A525 45c multicolored 1.00 .70

1593 A525 45c multicolored 1.00 .70

1594 A525 45c multicolored 1.00 .70

a. Block of 4, #1591-1594 4.50 4.50

Nos. 1591-1594 (4) 4.00 2.80

Queen Elizabeth II, 71st Birthday, 50th Wedding Anniv. A526

1997, Apr. 17 Engr. ***Perf. 14x14½***

1595 A526 45c Design A50 1.00 .55

A527

A528

1997, Apr. 17 ***Perf. 14½x14***

1596 A527 45c multicolored 1.00 .55

Lions Clubs of Australia, 50th anniv.

1997, May 8 Litho. ***Perf. 14½x14***

Dolls and Teddy Bears: No. 1597, Doll wearing red hat. No. 1598, Bear standing. No. 1599, Doll wearing white dress holding teddy bear. No. 1600, Doll in brown outfit. No. 1601, Teddy bear seated.

1597 A528 45c multicolored 1.10 1.10

1598 A528 45c multicolored 1.10 1.10

1599 A528 45c multicolored 1.10 1.10

1600 A528 45c multicolored 1.10 1.10

1601 A528 45c multicolored 1.10 1.10

a. Strip of 5, #1597-1601 5.50 5.50

Nos. 1597-1601 (5) 5.50 5.50

Nos. 1597-1601 were printed in sheets containing two strips of five. Some sheets exist overprinted in margin with picture of teddy bear and inscription "Brisbane Stamp & Coin Expo / 7-9 June 1997."

Emergency Services A529

Designs: No. 1602, Disaster victim evacuated. No. 1603, Police rescue hiker. $1.05, Rapid response saves home. $1.20, Ambulance dash saves life.

1997, July 10 Litho. ***Perf. 14x14½***

1602 A529 45c multicolored 1.00 .80

1603 A529 45c multicolored 1.00 .80

a. Pair, #1602-1603 2.25 2.25

1604 A529 $1.05 multicolored 2.10 2.00

1605 A529 $1.20 multicolored 2.40 2.10

Nos. 1602-1605 (4) 6.50 5.70

Arrival of Merino Sheep in Australia, Bicent. A530

Designs: No. 1606, George Peppin, Junior (1827-76), breeder, Merino sheep. No. 1607, "Pepe" chair, uses of wool.

1997, Aug. 7 Litho. ***Perf. 14x14½***

1606 A530 45c multicolored 1.00 .75

1607 A530 45c multicolored 1.00 .75

a. Pair, #1606-1607 2.25 2.25

Scenes from "The Dreaming," Animated Stories for Children A531

Designs: 45c, Dumbi the Owl. $1, The Two Willy-Willies. $1.20, How Brolga Became a Bird. $1.80, Tuggan-Tuggan.

1997, Aug. 21 ***Perf. 14½***

1608 A531 45c multicolored .90 .70

1609 A531 $1 multicolored 2.00 1.50

1610 A531 $1.20 multicolored 2.40 2.40

1611 A531 $1.80 multicolored 3.50 3.50

Nos. 1608-1611 (4) 8.80 8.10

Prehistoric Animals — A532

Designs: No. 1612, Rhoetosaurus brownei. No. 1613, Mcnamaraspis kaprios. No. 1614, Ninjemys oweni. No. 1615, Paracyclotosaurus davidi. No. 1616, Woolungasaurus glendowerensis.

1997, Sept. 4 Litho. ***Perf. 14½x14***

1612 A532 45c multicolored .90 .65

1613 A532 45c multicolored .90 .65

1614 A532 45c multicolored .90 .65

1615 A532 45c multicolored .90 .65

1616 A532 45c multicolored .90 .65

a. Strip of 5, #1612-1616 4.75 4.75

Nos. 1612-1616 (5) 4.50 3.25

Printed in sheets of 10 stamps.

A533

Nocturnal Animals — A534

Perf. 14½x14, 14x14½

1997, Oct. 1 **Litho.**

1617 A533 45c Barking owl .90 .80

1618 A533 45c Spotted-tailed quoll .90 .80

a. Pair, #1617-1618 2.25 2.25

1619 A534 45c Platypus .90 .80

1620 A534 45c Brown antechinus .90 .80

1621 A534 45c Dingo .90 .80

a. Strip of 3, #1619-1621 3.25 3.25

Size: 50x30mm

1622 A534 45c Yellow-bellied glider 1.40 1.40

a. Souvenir sheet, #1617-1622, perf. 14¼ 8.00 8.00

Nos. 1617-1622 (6) 5.90 5.40

No. 1622a is printed with additional phosphor ink revealing a glow-in-the-dark spider and web under ultraviolet light.

Size: 21x32mm

Serpentine Die Cut Perf. 11½

Self-Adhesive

1623 A533 45c like #1617 2.25 .50

1624 A533 45c like #1618 2.25 .50

a. Booklet pane, 5 each #1623-1624 22.50

b. Pair, #1623-1624 4.50

By its nature No. 1624a is a complete booklet. The peelable paper backing serves as a booklet cover.

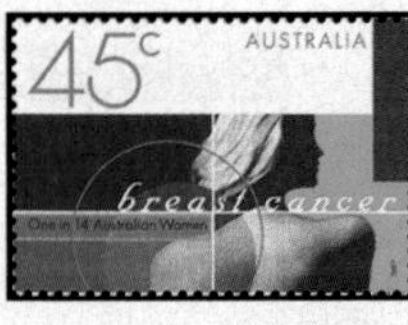

Breast Cancer Awareness A535

1997, Oct. 27 Litho. ***Perf. 14x14½***

1625 A535 45c multicolored 1.00 .55

Christmas A536

Children in Christmas Nativity pageant: 40c, Angels. 45c, Mary holding Baby Jesus. $1, Three Wise Men.

1997, Nov. 3

1626 A536 40c multicolored .85 .65

1627 A536 45c multicolored 1.10 .85

1628 A536 $1 multicolored 2.10 2.10

Nos. 1626-1628 (3) 4.05 3.60

Booklet Stamps

Serpentine Die Cut Perf. 11½

Self-Adhesive

1629 A536 40c multicolored 1.10 .55

a. Booklet pane of 20 22.00

By its nature No. 1629a is a complete booklet. The peelable paper backing serves as a booklet cover, which also contains 20 labels.

Maritime Heritage — A537

1998, Jan. 15 Litho. ***Perf. 14½x14***

1630 A537 45c Flying Cloud .90 .70

a. Pane of 10 9.00 9.00

1631 A537 85c Marco Polo 1.75 1.40

a. Sheet of 2, #1631 perf. 13½ & Canada #1779b 3.75 3.75

1632 A537 $1 Chusan 2.10 2.40

1633 A537 $1.20 Heather Belle 2.40 2.40

Nos. 1630-1633 (4) 7.15 6.90

Australia '99 (No. 1630a). World Stamp Expo. (No. 1631a).

See Canada No. 1779a.

Issued: No. 1630a, 6/17/98; No. 1631a, 3/19/99.

Legends Type of 1997

Olympians: No. 1634: a, Betty Cuthbert. b, Cuthbert running. c, Herb Elliott. d, Elliott running. e, Dawn Fraser. f, Fraser swimming. g, Marjorie Jackson. h, Jackson running. i, Murray Rose. j, Rose swimming. k, Shirley Strickland. l, Strickland clearing hurdle.

1998, Jan. 21 ***Perf. 14x14½***

Size: 34x26mm

1634 Sheet of 12 14.00 14.00

a.-l. A522 45c any single 1.10 1.10

m. Booklet pane, #1634a-1634d 5.50 —

n. Booklet pane, #1634e-1634h 5.50 —

o. Booklet pane, #1634i-1634l 5.50 —

Booklet Stamps
Self-Adhesive
Serpentine Die Cut 11½
Size: 34x25mm

1635 A522 45c like #1634a 1.10 .65
1636 A522 45c like #1634b 1.10 .65
1637 A522 45c like #1634c 1.10 .65
1638 A522 45c like #1634d 1.10 .65
1639 A522 45c like #1634e 1.10 .65
1640 A522 45c like #1634f 1.10 .65
1641 A522 45c like #1634g 1.10 .65
1642 A522 45c like #1634h 1.10 .65
1643 A522 45c like #1634i 1.10 .65
1644 A522 45c like #1634j 1.10 .65
1645 A522 45c like #1634k 1.10 .65
1646 A522 45c like #1634l 1.10 .65
a. Bklt. pane of 12, #1635-1646 13.50
Nos. 1635-1646 (12) 13.20 7.80

By its nature, No. 1646a is a complete booklet. The peelable backing serves as a booklet cover.

Nos. 1634m-1634o issued 1/24/07.

Greetings — A538

1998, Feb. 12 Litho. ***Perf. 14½x14***
1647 A538 45c Champagne roses 1.10 .65

Booklet Stamp
Self-Adhesive
Serpentine Die Cut 11½

1648 A538 45c like #1647 1.10 .65
a. Booklet pane of 10 11.00

By its nature No. 1648a is a complete booklet. The peelable paper backing, which contains 12 labels, serves as a booklet cover.

Queen Elizabeth II, 72nd Birthday A539

1998, Apr. 9 Litho. ***Perf. 14x14½***
1649 A539 45c multicolored 1.10 .65

Royal Australian Navy Fleet Air Arm, 50th Anniv. A540

1998, Apr. 9
1650 A540 45c multicolored 1.10 .65

Farming in Australia A541

Designs: No. 1651, Sheep for producing wool. No. 1652, Sheaves of wheat. No. 1653, Herding cattle on horseback. No. 1654, Harvesting sugar cane. No. 1655, Dairy cattle, man on motorcycle.

1998, Apr. 21
1651 A541 45c multicolored .90 .75
1652 A541 45c multicolored .90 .75
1653 A541 45c multicolored .90 .75
1654 A541 45c multicolored .90 .75
1655 A541 45c multicolored .90 .75
a. Strip of 5, #1651-1655 4.75 4.75
Nos. 1651-1655 (5) 4.50 3.75

Booklet Stamps
Self-Adhesive
Serpentine Die Cut 11½
Size: 37x25mm

1656 A541 45c like #1651 1.75 .90
1657 A541 45c like #1652 1.75 .90
1658 A541 45c like #1653 1.75 .90
1659 A541 45c like #1654 1.75 .90
1660 A541 45c like #1655 1.75 .90
a. Bklt. pane, 2 ea #1656-1660 17.50
Nos. 1656-1660 (5) 8.75 4.50

The peelable backing of No. 1660a serves as a booklet cover.

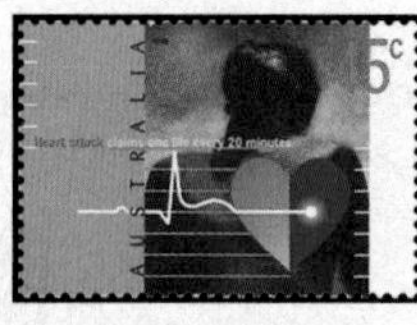
Heart Health A542

1998, May 4 Litho. ***Perf. 14x14½***
1661 A542 45c multicolored 1.10 .65

Rock and Roll in Australia A543

a, "The Wild One," by Johnny O'Keefe, 1958. b, "Oh Yeah Uh Huh," by Col Joye and the Joye Boys, 1959. c, "He's My Blonde-headed Stompie Wompie Real Gone Surfer Boy," by Little Pattie, 1963. d, "Shakin' All Over," by Normie Rowe, 1965. e, "She's So Fine," by The Easybeats, 1965. f, "The Real Thing," by Russell Morris, 1969. g, "Turn Up Your Radio," by The Masters Apprentices, 1970. h, "Eagle Rock," by Daddy Cool, 1971. i, "Most People I Know Think That I'm Crazy," by Billy Thorpe & the Aztecs, 1972. j, "Horror Movie," by Skyhooks, 1974. k, "It's a Long Way to the Top," by AC/DC, 1975. l, "Howzat," by Sherbet, 1976.

1998, May 26
1662 A543 Sheet of 12 11.50 11.50
a.-l. 45c any single .90 .80

Coil Stamps
Self-Adhesive
Serpentine Die Cut 11½
Size: 37x25mm

1663 A543 45c like #1662a 1.25 .70
1664 A543 45c like #1662b 1.25 .70
1665 A543 45c like #1662c 1.25 .70
1666 A543 45c like #1662d 1.25 .70
1667 A543 45c like #1662e 1.25 .70
1668 A543 45c like #1662f 1.25 .70
1669 A543 45c like #1662g 1.25 .70
1670 A543 45c like #1662h 1.25 .70
1671 A543 45c like #1662i 1.25 .70
1672 A543 45c like #1662j 1.25 .70
1673 A543 45c like #1662k 1.25 .70
1674 A543 45c like #1662l 1.25 .70
a. Strip of 12 + label 15.00
Nos. 1663-1674 (12) 15.00 8.40

Endangered Birds — A544

World Wildlife Fund: No. 1675, Helmeted honeyeater. No. 1676, Orange-bellied parrot. No. 1677, Red-tailed black cockatoo. No. 1678, Gouldian finch.

1998, June 25 ***Perf. 14x14½***
1675 A544 5c multicolored .80 .60
1676 A544 5c multicolored .80 .60
a. Pair, #1675-1676 2.60 2.00
1677 A544 45c multicolored 1.40 1.10
1678 A544 45c multicolored 1.40 1.10
a. Pair, #1677-1678 3.50 3.50

Performing and Visual Arts — A545

Young people: No. 1679, Playing French horn. No. 1680, Dancing.

1998, July 16 Litho. ***Perf. 14x14½***
1679 A545 45c multicolored 1.00 .80
1680 A545 45c multicolored 1.00 .80
a. Pair, #1679-1680 2.25 2.25

Orchids — A546

Designs: 45c, Phalaenopsis rosenstromii. 85c, Arundina graminifolia. $1, Grammatophyllum speciosum. $1.20, Dendrobium phalaenopsis.

1998, Aug. 6 Litho. ***Perf. 14½x14***
1681 A546 45c multicolored .90 .70
1682 A546 85c multicolored 1.75 1.60
1683 A546 $1 multicolored 2.00 1.90
1684 A546 $1.20 multicolored 2.40 2.10
a. Souvenir sheet, #1681-1684 7.25 7.25
Nos. 1681-1684 (4) 7.05 6.30

See Singapore Nos. 858-861b.

The Teapot of Truth, by Cartoonist Michael Leunig A547

Designs: No. 1685, Angel carrying teapot, bird with flower. No. 1686, Birds perched on heart-shaped vine. No. 1687, Characters using their heads to pour tea into cup. $1, Stylized family. $1.20, Stylized teapot with face & legs.

1998, Aug. 13 ***Perf. 14x14½***
1685 A547 45c multicolored 1.10 .55
a. Booklet pane of 4 4.50
1686 A547 45c multicolored 1.10 .55
a. Booklet pane of 4 4.50
1687 A547 45c multicolored 1.10 .55
a. Booklet pane of 4 4.50

Size: 30x25mm

1688 A547 $1 multicolored 2.60 2.60
a. Booklet pane of 2 5.25
1689 A547 $1.20 multicolored 3.25 3.25
a. Booklet pane of 2 6.25
Complete booklet, #1685a, 1686a, 1687a, 1688a, 1689a, 1 postal card & 16 self-adhesive labels 25.00
Nos. 1685-1689 (5) 9.15 7.50

A548

Butterflies — No. 1690, Red lacewing. No. 1691, Dull oakblue. No. 1692, Meadow argus. No. 1693, Ulysses. No. 1694, Common red-eye.

1998, Sept. 3 Litho. ***Perf. 14½x14***
1690 A548 45c multicolored 1.10 .85
1691 A548 45c multicolored 1.10 .85
1692 A548 45c multicolored 1.10 .85
1693 A548 45c multicolored 1.10 .85
1694 A548 45c multicolored 1.10 .85
a. Strip of 5, #1690-1694 5.75 5.25
b. Souv. sheet of 5, #1690-1694 8.50 8.50
Nos. 1690-1694 (5) 5.50 4.25

No. 1694b for China 1999 World Philatelic Exhibition. Issued 8/21/99.

Self-Adhesive
Serpentine Die Cut 11½

1695 A548 45c like #1690 1.25 .70
1696 A548 45c like #1691 1.25 .70
1697 A548 45c like #1692 1.25 .70
1698 A548 45c like #1693 1.25 .70
1699 A548 45c like #1694 1.25 .70
a. Strip of 5, #1695-1699 6.75
Nos. 1695-1699 (5) 6.25 3.50

A549

Designs: No. 1700, Sextant, map of Bass Strait. No. 1701, Telescope, map of Van Diemen's Land (Tasmania).

1998, Sept. 10
1700 A549 45c multicolored 1.10 .70
1701 A549 45c multicolored 1.10 .70
a. Pair, #1700-1701 2.25 2.25

Circumnavigation of Tasmania by George Bass (1771-c. 1803) and Matthew Flinders (1774-1814), bicent.

A550

Marine Life — A551

Designs: No. 1702, Fiery squid. No. 1703, Manta ray. No. 1704, Bottlenose dolphin. No. 1705, Weedy seadragon. No. 1706, Southern right whale. No. 1707, White pointer shark.

Perf. 14½x14, 14x14½
1998, Oct. 1 Litho.
1702 A550 45c multi 1.10 .85
1703 A550 45c multi, horiz. 1.10 .85
1704 A551 45c multi 1.10 .85
1705 A551 45c multi 1.10 .85
a. Pair, #1704-1705 2.25 2.25

Size: 50x30mm

1706 A551 45c multi, horiz. 1.10 .85
1707 A551 45c multi 1.10 .85
a. Souvenir sheet, #1702-1707 7.00 5.75
Nos. 1702-1707 (6) 6.60 5.10

Booklet Stamps
Self-Adhesive
Serpentine Die Cut Perf. 11½

1708 A551 45c like #1704 1.10 .55
1709 A551 45c like #1705 1.10 .55
a. Bklt. pane, 5 ea #1708-1709 11.00

No. 1709a is a complete booklet. The peelable paper backing serves as a booklet cover.

Nos. 1708-1709 also exist in coils, issued in rolls of 100 with surrounding selvage removed. Value, set of singles $4.50.

Universal Declaration of Human Rights, 50th Anniv. — A552

1998, Oct. 22 Litho. ***Perf. 14½x14***
1712 A552 45c multicolored 1.10 .70

Christmas A553

40c, Magi. 45c, Nativity. $1, Journey to Bethlehem.

1998, Nov. 2 ***Perf. 14x14½***
1713 A553 40c multicolored .80 .55
1714 A553 45c multicolored .90 .80
1715 A553 $1 multicolored 2.00 2.00
Nos. 1713-1715 (3) 3.70 3.35

Booklet Stamp
Self-Adhesive
Serpentine Die Cut Perf. 11½

1716	A553	40c multicolored	1.10	.55
a.		Booklet pane of 20	22.00	

No. 1716a is a complete booklet.

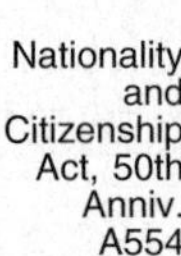

Nationality and Citizenship Act, 50th Anniv. A554

1999, Jan. 14 Litho. *Perf. 14x14½*

1717	A554	45c multicolored	1.10	.80

Die Cut Perf. 11¾
Self-Adhesive

1718	A554	45c multicolored	1.10	.55

Legends Type of 1997

Designs: Nos. 1719, 1721, Arthur Boyd, artist. Nos. 1720, 1722, "Nebuchadnezzar on Fire Falling over a Waterfall," by Boyd.

1999, Jan. 22 Litho. *Perf. 14x14½*

1719	A522	45c multicolored	1.10	.85
1720	A522	45c multicolored	1.10	.85
a.		Pair, #1719-1720	2.25	2.25
b.		Booklet pane, #1719-1720	*3.00*	—

Booklet Stamps
Self-Adhesive
Serpentine Die Cut Perf. 11½

1721	A522	45c multicolored	1.10	.55
1722	A522	45c multicolored	1.10	.55
a.		Bklt. pane, 5 ea #1721-1722	11.00	

No. 1722a is a complete booklet.
No. 1720b issued 1/24/07.

Love — A555

1999, Feb. 4 *Perf. 14x14½*

1723	A555	45c Red roses	1.00	.75

Booklet Stamp
Self-adhesive
Serpentine Die Cut Perf. 11½

1724	A555	45c like #1723	1.10	.55
a.		Booklet pane of 10	11.00	

No. 1724a is a complete booklet.

Intl. Year of Older Persons A556

Designs: No. 1725, Woman walking with girl, man up close. No. 1726, Woman up close, man playing soccer with boy.

1999, Feb. 11 *Perf. 14x14½*

1725	A556	45c multicolored	.90	.65
1726	A556	45c multicolored	.90	.65
a.		Pair, #1725-1726	2.25	2.25

Early Navigators Type of 1963

No. 1727: a, like #374. b, like #376. c, like #377.

No. 1728: a, like #375. b, like #379. c, like #378.

Perf. 14x14½, 14½x14

1999, Mar. 19 Litho.

1727		Sheet of 3	3.25	3.25
a.-c.	A144	45c any single	1.00	1.00
d.		As #1727, imperf.	16.00	16.00
e.		As #1727, perfin "A99" in sheet margin	40.00	40.00
1728		Sheet of 3	3.25	3.25
a.-c.	A145	45c any single	1.00	1.00
d.		As #1728, imperf.	16.00	16.00
e.		As #1728, perfin "A99" in sheet margin	40.00	40.00

Australia '99, World Stamp Expo.

Nos. 1727e-1728e were made from Nos. 1727d-1728d at Australia '99. Examples different perforations or with the perforating and "A99" inverted were intentionally misperfed personally by patrons of the show.

Sailing Ships — A557

1999, Mar. 19 *Perf. 14½x14*

1729	A557	45c Polly Woodside	.90	.55
a.		Perf 14x14½	3.00	3.00
b.		Souvenir sheet of 2, #1729a, Ireland #1173a	7.00	7.00
1730	A557	85c Alma Doepel	1.75	1.75
1731	A557	$1 Enterprize	2.00	2.00
1732	A557	$1.05 Lady Nelson	2.10	2.10
		Nos. 1729-1732 (4)	6.75	6.40

Australia '99, World Stamp Expo (No. 1729a). See Ireland No. 1173.

No. 1729 was issued in sheets of 20 with a se-tenant label showing Australia '99 logo. Panes of 10 No. 1729 with labels were sold only at the show, where patrons could have their photos printed on the label.

Olympic Torch — A558

1999, Mar. 22

1733	A558	$1.20 #289	2.40	2.40

Flora & Fauna Type of 1996

Flowers: Nos. 1734, 1742A, 1743, 1746B, 1746I Correa reflexa. Nos. 1735, 1744, 1746C, Hibbertia scandens. Nos. 1736, 1745, 1746D, Ipomoea pes-caprae. Nos. 1737, 1746, 1746E, Wahlenbergia stricta.

70c, Humpback whales, zebra volute. No. 1739, Brahminy kite, checkerboard helmet shell. No. 1740, Fraser Island, chambered nautilus. $1.05, Loggerhead turtle, baler. $1.20, White-bellied sea eagle, Campbell's stromb.

1999 Litho. *Perf. 14x14½*

1734	A511	45c multicolored	.90	.75
1735	A511	45c multicolored	.90	.75
1736	A511	45c multicolored	.90	.75
1737	A511	45c multicolored	.90	.75
a.		Block of 4, #1734-1737	3.75	3.75
1738	A511	70c multicolored	1.40	1.40
1739	A511	90c multicolored	1.75	1.75
1740	A511	90c multicolored	1.75	1.75
a.		Pair, #1739-1740	3.50	3.50
1741	A511	$1.05 multicolored	2.10	1.90
1742	A511	$1.20 multicolored	2.40	2.40
		Nos. 1734-1742 (9)	13.00	12.20

Booklet Stamps
Serpentine Die Cut 11, 11¼ (#1742Df)
Self-Adhesive

1742A	A511	45c like #1734	1.10	.55
1742B	A511	45c like #1735	1.10	.55
1742C	A511	45c like #1736	1.10	.55
1742D	A511	45c like #1737	1.10	.55
e.		Booklet pane, 3 each #1742A, 1742C, 2 each #1742B, 1742D	11.00	
f.		Booklet pane, 5 each #1742A-1742D	22.50	

Die Cut perf. 12½x12¾

1743	A511	45c like #1734	1.10	.55
1744	A511	45c like #1735	1.10	.55
1745	A511	45c like #1736	1.10	.55
1746	A511	45c like #1737	1.10	.55
a.		Booklet pane, 3 each #1743, 1745, 2 each #1744, #1746	11.00	
g.		Strip of 4, #1743-1746	4.50	
		Nos. 1742A-1746 (8)	8.80	4.40

Nos. 1742De, 1746a are complete booklets.

Coil Stamps
Serpentine Die Cut 11½

1746B	A511	45c like #1734	1.10	.55
1746C	A511	45c like #1735	1.10	.55
1746D	A511	45c like #1736	1.10	.55
1746E	A511	45c like #1737	1.10	.50
f.		Strip of 4, #1746B-1746E	4.50	
h.		Pane, #1746B, 1746D-1746E, 2 #1746C	5.50	

Serpentine Die Cut 13

1746I	A511	45c like #1734	1.10	.55
1746J	A511	45c like #1735	1.10	.55
1746K	A511	45c like #1736	1.10	.55
1746L	A511	45c like #1737	1.10	.55
m.		Strip of 4, #1746I-1746K	4.50	
		Nos. 1746B-1746L (8)	8.80	4.35

Issued: Nos. 1738-1742, 7/8; 1746B-1746E, 4/8.

No. 1742Df is a complete booklet.

Queen Mother and Queen Elizabeth II — A559

1999, Apr. 15 *Perf. 14x14½*

1747	A559	45c multicolored	1.00	.75

Queen Elizabeth II, 73rd birthday.

Children's Television Programs — A560

Designs: Nos. 1748, 1753, "Here's Humphrey." Nos. 1749, 1754, "Bananas in Pajamas." Nos. 1750, 1755, "Mr. Squiggle." Nos. 1751, 1756, Teddy bears from "Play School." Nos. 1752, 1757, Clock, dog, boy from "Play School."

1999, May 6 Litho. *Perf. 14½x14*

1748	A560	45c multicolored	1.25	1.10
1749	A560	45c multicolored	1.25	1.10
1750	A560	45c multicolored	1.25	1.10
1751	A560	45c multicolored	1.25	1.10
1752	A560	45c multicolored	1.25	1.10
a.		Strip of 5, #1748-1752	6.75	6.75
		Nos. 1748-1752 (5)	6.25	5.50

Self-Adhesive
Serpentine Die Cut 11½x11¼

1753	A560	45c like #1748	1.50	.80
1754	A560	45c like #1749	1.50	.80
1755	A560	45c like #1750	1.50	.80
1756	A560	45c like #1751	1.50	.80
1757	A560	45c like #1752	1.50	.80
a.		Bklt. pane, 2 ea #1753-1757	15.00	
		Nos. 1753-1757 (5)	7.50	4.00

No. 1757a is a complete booklet.

Perth Mint, Cent. A561

1999, May 13 Litho. *Perf. 14¼x14*

1758	A561	$2 gold & multi	4.00	4.00

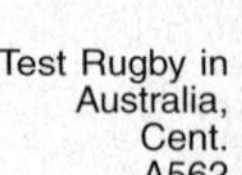

Test Rugby in Australia, Cent. A562

Designs: Nos. 1759, 1763, Kicking ball, vert. Nos. 1760, 1764, Catching ball. $1, Diving with ball. $1.20, Being tackled.

1999, June 8 Litho. *Perf. 14½x14*

1759	A562	45c multi	1.10	.85
1760	A562	45c multi, vert.	1.10	.85
a.		Pair, #1759-1760	2.25	2.25

Perf. 14x14½

1761	A562	$1 multi	2.25	2.25
1762	A562	$1.20 multi	2.50	2.50

Serpentine Die Cut 11½
Self-Adhesive
Coil Stamps

1763	A562	45c like #1759	1.75	.60
1764	A562	45c like #1760	1.75	.60
a.		Pair, #1763-1764	3.50	

Snowy Mountains Hydroelectric Projects, 50th Anniv. A563

Designs: No. 1765, Rock bolters at Tumut 2 Power Station Hall, driller at Tooma-Tumut Tunnel. No. 1766, English class for migrant workers at Cooma. No. 1767, Eucumbene Dam, Tumut 2 Tailwater Tunnel. No. 1768, Island Bend Dam, German carpenters.

1999, Aug. 12 Litho. *Perf. 14x14½*

1765	A563	45c multicolored	1.10	.85
1766	A563	45c multicolored	1.10	.85
1767	A563	45c multicolored	1.10	.85
1768	A563	45c multicolored	1.10	.85
a.		Block of 4, #1765-1768	4.50	4.50
		Nos. 1765-1768 (4)	4.40	3.40

Self-Adhesive
Coil Stamps
Litho.
Serpentine Die Cut 11¾

1769	A563	45c Like #1765	1.25	.60
1770	A563	45c Like #1766	1.25	.60
1771	A563	45c Like #1767	1.25	.60
1772	A563	45c Like #1768	1.25	.60
a.		Strip of 4, #1769-1772	5.25	5.25
		Nos. 1769-1772 (4)	5.00	2.40

Teddy Bear — A564

Birthday cake — A564a

Roses, Rings — A564b

Pen, Letter — A564c

Christmas Ornament — A564d

Koala — A564e

1999-2003 Litho. *Perf. 14½x14*

1773	A564	45c multicolored	.90	.65
1774	A564a	45c multicolored	.90	.65
1775	A564b	45c multicolored	.90	.65
a.		Booklet pane of 4 + 4 labels ('02)	3.75	—
		Booklet, 5 #1775a	19.00	

Booklet Stamp
Serpentine Die Cut 11¾

1924 A591 40c multi .85 .70
a. Booklet of 20 + 20 stickers 17.25

Tourist Attractions Type of 2000

2000, Nov. 1 *Perf. 14½x14*
1925 A581 80c Byron Bay 1.75 1.40

No. 1778 Digitally Overprinted in Dark Blue

2001, Jan. Litho. *Perf. 14½x14*
1926 A564 $1 multi + label *14.50 14.50*

Federation of Australia, Cent. — A592

Designs: Nos. 1927, 1931, Federation Arch, Sydney. Nos. 1928, 1932, Sir Edmund Barton, first prime minister. No. 1929, National celebrations, horiz (50x30mm). No. 1930, State banquet (30x50mm).

Perf. 14¾x14, 14x14¾
2001, Jan. 1 **Litho.**
1927 A592 49c multi 1.10 1.00
1928 A592 49c multi 1.10 1.00
a. Pair, #1927-1928 3.00 2.50
1929 A592 $2 multi 4.25 4.25
1930 A592 $2 multi 4.25 4.25
a. Souvenir sheet, #1927-1930, perf. 14½ 11.25 11.25
Nos. 1927-1930 (4) 10.70 10.50

Self-Adhesive
Booklet Stamps
Serpentine Die Cut 11½x11

1931 A592 49c multi 1.10 .30
a. Serpentine die cut 11½x11¾ — —
1932 A592 49c multi 1.10 .30
a. Booklet, 5 each # 1931-1932 11.50

Australian Legends Type of 1997

Slim Dusty, musician: Nos. 1933, 1935, With guitar. Nos. 1934, 1936, Wearing blue shirt.

2001, Jan. 25 *Perf. 14x14¾*
Size: 34x26mm
1933 A522 45c multi 1.10 1.00
1934 A522 45c multi 1.10 1.00
a. Pair, #1933-1934 2.75 2.75
b. Booklet pane, #1933-1934 *3.00* —

Self-Adhesive
Booklet Stamps
Serpentine Die Cut 11x11½

1935 A522 45c multi 1.10 .75
1936 A522 45c multi 1.10 .75
a. Booklet, 5 each #1935-1936 11.50
Nos. 1933-1936 (4) 4.40 3.50

No. 1934b issued 1/24/07.

Australian Army, Cent. A593

Rising Sun badge and: No. 1937, Light Horse Brigade, 1940, soldiers in New Guinea, 1943. No. 1938, Soldier in UN peacekeeping mission carrying Rwandan child, 1995, soldiers on commando officer selection course, 1997.

2001-05 *Perf. 14x14¾*
1937 A593 45c multi 1.25 .85
a. Additionally dated "2013" (#1938d) 1.10 1.10
1938 A593 45c multi 1.25 .85
a. Pair, #1937-1938 2.75 2.75
b. Booklet pane, #1937-1938 *3.00* —
c. Additionally dated "2013" (#1938d) 1.10 1.10
d. Booklet pane of 2, #1937a, 1938c 2.25 —
Complete booklet, #1176a, 1207a, 1256a, 1317a, 1380f, 1452a, 1454a, 1482a, 1938b 40.00

Issued: Nos. 1937-1938, 2/15/01. No. 1938b, 4/05. Complete booklet sold for $14.95.

Issued: Nos. 1937a, 1938c, 1938d, 3/5/13. No. 1938d was issued in booklet along with Nos. 2710c, 2869e, 3107c, 3349b and 3877a.

Opening of National Museum, Canberra A594

Designs: No. 1939, Museum floor plan. No. 1940, Pangk (wallaby sculpture), by George MacNaught and Joe Ngallametta.

2001, Mar. 8
1939 A594 49c multi 1.00 .85
1940 A594 49c multi 1.00 .85
a. Pair, #1939-1940 2.25 2.25

Australian Legends Type of 1997

Similar to Nos. 1575-1576, but with cropped designs and "1908-2001" inscription added.

2001, Mar. 13 *Perf. 14¼*
1941 A522 45c Like #1575 1.00 .85
a. Without gold highlights, dated "2007" 1.40 1.40
1942 A522 45c Like #1576 1.00 .85
a. Pair, #1941-1942 2.25 2.25
b. Without gold highlights, dated "2007" 1.40 1.40

Nos. 1941a, 1942b issued 11/14/07.

Rock Music A595

Designs: Nos. 1943a, 1953, Khe Sanh, by Cold Chisel, 1978. Nos. 1943b, 1952, Down Under, by Men at Work, 1981. Nos. 1943c, 1951, Power and the Passion, by Midnight Oil, 1983. Nos. 1943d, 1950, Original Sin, by INXS. Nos. 1943e, 1949, You're the Voice, by John Farnham, 1986. Nos. 1943f, 1948, Don't Dream It's Over, by Crowded House, 1986. Nos. 1943g, 1947, Treaty, by Yothu Yindi, 1991. Nos. 1943h, 1946, Tomorrow, by Silverchair, 1994. Nos. 1943i, 1945, Confide in Me, by Kylie Minogue, 1994. Nos. 1943j, 1944, Truly, Madly, Deeply, by Savage Garden, 1997.

2001, Mar. 20 Litho. *Perf. 14x14¾*
1943 Sheet of 10 10.00 10.00
a.-j. A595 45c Any single 1.00 1.00

Self-Adhesive
Serpentine Die Cut 11¼x11½

1944 A595 45c multi 1.25 .80
1945 A595 45c multi 1.25 .80
1946 A595 45c multi 1.25 .80
1947 A595 45c multi 1.25 .80
1948 A595 45c multi 1.25 .80
1949 A595 45c multi 1.25 .80
1950 A595 45c multi 1.25 .80
1951 A595 45c multi 1.25 .80
1952 A595 45c multi 1.25 .80
1953 A595 45c multi 1.25 .80
a. Horiz. strip of 10, #1944-1953 13.75
b. Booklet, #1944-1953 13.75
Nos. 1944-1953 (10) 12.50 8.00

Queen Elizabeth II, 75th Birthday — A596

2001, Apr. 12 Litho. *Perf. 14¾x14*
1954 A596 45c multi 1.00 .75

Flower — A597

Balloons — A598

Streamers — A599

Kangaroos — A600

Bayulu Banner — A601

Litho., Litho with Hologram (#1957)

2001-03 *Perf. 14½x14*
1955 A597 45c multi + label .95 .95
1956 A598 45c multi + label .95 .95
1957 A599 45c multi + label .95 .95
1958 A600 $1 multi + label 2.25 2.25
a. Booklet pane of 4 + 4 labels 9.25 —
Complete booklet, 2 #1958a 19.00
1959 A601 $1.50 multi + label 3.50 3.50
Nos. 1955-1959 (5) 8.60 8.60

Issued: Nos. 1955-1959, 4/24/01. No. 1958a, 10/31/03.

The complete booklet, which sold for $10.95, contains two panes of No. 1958a with different margins.

Federal Parliament, Cent. — A602

Designs: No. 1960, The Opening of the First Federal Parliament, 9 May 1901, by Charles Nuttall. No. 1961, Opening of the First Parliament of the Commonwealth of Australia by H.R.H. The Duke of Cornwall and York (Later King George V), May 9, 1901, by Tom Roberts.

2001, May 3 Litho. *Perf. 14¼*
1960 A602 45c multi 1.10 .85
a. Souvenir sheet of 1 1.25 1.25
1961 A602 $2.45 multi 5.25 5.25
a. Souvenir sheet of 1 5.50 5.50

Outback Services A603

Designs: Nos. 1962, 1967, 1972, Telecommunications. Nos. 1963, 1968, 1973, Transport. Nos. 1964, 1969, 1974, School of the Air. Nos. 1965, 1970, 1975, Postal service. Nos., 1966, 1971, 1976, Royal flying Doctor Service.

2001, June 5 *Perf. 14x14½*
1962 A603 45c multi 1.00 1.00
1963 A603 45c multi 1.00 1.00
1964 A603 45c multi 1.00 1.00
1965 A603 45c multi 1.00 1.00
1966 A603 45c multi 1.00 1.00
a. Horiz. strip, #1962-1966 5.75 5.75
Nos. 1962-1966 (5) 5.00 5.00

Self-Adhesive
Coil Stamps
Serpentine Die Cut 11¼

1967 A603 45c multi 1.10 .95
1968 A603 45c multi 1.10 .95
1969 A603 45c multi 1.10 .95
1970 A603 45c multi 1.10 .95
1971 A603 45c multi 1.10 .95
a. Horiz. strip, #1967-1971 5.75

Booklet Stamps
Serpentine Die Cut 11¾

1972 A603 45c multi 1.10 .95
1973 A603 45c multi 1.10 .95
1974 A603 45c multi 1.10 .95
1975 A603 45c multi 1.10 .95
1976 A603 45c multi 1.10 .95
a. Booklet, 2 each #1972-1976 11.50
Nos. 1967-1976 (10) 11.00 9.50

Dragon Boat Races A604

Dragon boats and: 45c, Hong Kong Convention and Exhibition Center. $1, Sydney Opera House.

2001, June 25 *Perf. 14x14½*
1977 A604 45c multi 1.10 .85
1978 A604 $1 multi 2.25 2.25
a. Souvenir sheet, #1977-1978 3.50 3.50

See Hong Kong Nos. 938-939.

Tourist Attraction Type of 2000

Designs: 50c, Blue Mountains. $1, Murrumbidgee River. $1.50, Port Douglas. $20, Uluru.

Litho., Litho with Foil Application ($20)

2001, July 12 *Perf. 14½x14*
1979 A581 50c multi .90 .90
1980 A581 $1 multi 1.90 1.90
1981 A581 $1.50 multi 2.75 2.75

Size: 56x25mm
Perf. 14x14½

1982 A581 $20 multi 23.00 25.75
Nos. 1979-1982 (4) 28.55 31.30

Booklet Stamp
Self-Adhesive
Serpentine Die Cut 11¼x10½

1983 A581 50c multi 1.10 1.00
a. Booklet, 10 #1983 11.50

Flora & Fauna Type of 1996

Birds: Nos. 1984, 1988, 1992, Variegated fairy wren. Nos. 1985, 1989, 1993, Painted firetail. Nos. 1986, 1990, 1994, Crimson chat. Nos. 1987, 1991, 1995, Budgerigar.

2001-02 Litho. *Perf. 14x14½*
1984 A511 45c multi 1.00 .90
1985 A511 45c multi 1.00 .90
1986 A511 45c multi 1.00 .90
1987 A511 45c multi 1.00 .90
a. Block of 4, #1984-1987 4.25 4.25
Nos. 1984-1987 (4) 4.00 3.60

Self-Adhesive
Coil Stamps
Die Cut Perf. 12½x12¾

1988 A511 45c multi 1.25 .75
1989 A511 45c multi 1.25 .75
1990 A511 45c multi 1.25 .75
1991 A511 45c multi 1.25 .75
a. Horiz. strip of 4, #1988-1991 5.25 5.25

Booklet Stamps

Serpentine Die Cut 11¼

1992 A511 45c multi 1.25 .75
1993 A511 45c multi 1.25 .75
1994 A511 45c multi 1.25 .75
1995 A511 45c multi 1.25 .75
a. Booklet pane, #1993, 1995 2.75
b. Booklet pane, #1992-1995, rouletted at bottom 5.75
Booklet, #1995a, 2 #1995b 11.50
c. Booklet pane, #1992-1995, rouletted at side 5.75
Booklet, 5 #1995c 28.75
d. Pane, #1992-1994, 2 #1995 6.25
e. Coil strip, #1992-1995 5.75
f. As "d," with Philakorea 2002 ovpt. in margin ('02) 9.00
g. As "d," with China 2002 Stamp & Coin Expo ovpt. in margin ('02) 9.00
h. As "d," with Hafnia '01 ovpt. in margin 19.00
Nos. 1988-1995 (8) 10.00 6.00

Issued: No. 1995f, 8/2/02; No. 1995g, 9/28/02. No. 1995h, 10/16/01. Rest of set, 8/9/01.

Daniel Solander (1733-82), Botanist on Endeavour A605

Designs: 45c, Barringtonia calyptrata and Solander. $1.50, Cachlospermum gillivraei and Endeavour.

Perf. 12½x12¾

2001, Aug. 16 Litho. & Engr.

1996 A605 45c multi 1.00 .75
1997 A605 $1.50 multi 3.50 3.50

See Sweden No. 2419.

Commonwealth Heads of Government Meeting, Brisbane — A606

2001, Sept. 4 Litho. ***Perf. 14½x14***

1998 A606 45c Southern Cross 1.00 .85
1999 A606 45c Australia on globe 1.00 .85
a. Pair, #1998-1999 2.25 2.25

Christmas — A607

2001, Sept. 4 ***Perf. 14½x14***

Stamp + Label

2000 A607 40c Christmas tree .85 .85
2001 A607 80c Star 1.75 1.75

Nos. 2000-2001 were each printed in sheets of 20 + 20 labels. The labels could be personalized.

Birds of Prey — A608

Designs: No. 2002, Wedge-tailed eagle. No. 2003, Nankeen kestrel. No. 2004, Red goshawk, vert. No. 2005, Spotted harrier, vert.

Perf. 14x14½, 14½x14

2001, Sept. 11

2002 A608 49c multi 1.10 .85
2003 A608 49c multi 1.10 .85
a. Pair, #2002-2003 2.50 2.50
2004 A608 98c multi 2.25 2.25
2005 A608 98c multi 2.25 2.25
a. Pair, #2004-2005 5.00 5.00
Nos. 2002-2005 (4) 6.70 6.20

Caricatures of Australian Wildlife by Roland Harvey — A609

Designs: Nos. 2006, 2012, Bilby and antechinus musicians, dancing cockatoo. Nos. 2007, 2013, Koala with birthday cake. Nos. 2008, 2014, Ring-tailed possums with drinks and food. Nos. 2009, 2015, Bilbies, crocodile, emu, koala and gifts. Nos. 2010, 2016, Wombat and ladder. Nos. 2011, 2017, Wallabies, echidnas, platypus and ladder.

2001, Oct. 2 ***Perf. 14½x14***

2006 A609 45c multi 1.10 .80
2007 A609 45c multi 1.10 .80
2008 A609 45c multi 1.10 .80
a. Horiz. strip of 3, #2006-2008 3.50 3.50
b. Souvenir sheet, #2006-2008 3.50 3.50
2009 A609 45c multi 1.10 .80
2010 A609 45c multi 1.10 .80
2011 A609 45c multi 1.10 .80
a. Horiz. strip, #2009-2011 3.50 3.50
b. Souvenir sheet, #2009-2011 3.50 3.50
Nos. 2006-2011 (6) 6.60 4.80

Self-Adhesive

Serpentine Die Cut 11½x11

2012 A609 45c multi 1.25 .80
2013 A609 45c multi 1.25 .80
2014 A609 45c multi 1.25 .80
2015 A609 45c multi 1.25 .80
2016 A609 45c multi 1.25 .80
2017 A609 45c multi 1.25 .80
a. Coil strip, 2012-2017 9.25
b. Booklet, #2014-2015, 2 each #2012-2013, 2016-2017 12.75
Nos. 2012-2017 (6) 7.50 4.80

Christmas — A610

Illuminations from the Wharncliffe Hours, by Maitre Francois: 40c, Adoration of the Magi. 45c, Flight into Egypt.

2001, Nov. 1 ***Perf. 14½x14***

2018 A610 40c multi 1.10 .60
2019 A610 45c multi 1.10 .65

Self-Adhesive

Serpentine Die Cut 11½x11¼

2020 A610 40c multi 1.10 .25
a. Booklet of 20 + 20 labels 24.00

Australian Legends Type of 1997

Medical researchers: Nos. 2021, 2026, Sir Gustav Nossal. Nos. 2022, 2027, Nancy Mills. No. 2023, 2028, Peter Doherty. Nos. 2024, 2029, Fiona Stanley. Nos. 2025, 2030, Donald Metcalf.

2002, Jan. 23 Litho. ***Perf. 14x14¾***

Size: 34x26mm

2021 A522 45c multi .95 .75
2022 A522 45c multi .95 .75
2023 A522 45c multi .95 .75
2024 A522 45c multi .95 .75
2025 A522 45c multi .95 .75
a. Vert. strip, #2021-2025 5.25 5.25
b. Booklet pane, #2021-2025 *8.00 8.00*
Nos. 2021-2025 (5) 4.75 3.75

Booklet Stamps

Self-Adhesive

Serpentine Die Cut 11x11½

2026 A522 45c multi 1.10 1.00
2027 A522 45c multi 1.10 1.00
2028 A522 45c multi 1.10 1.00
2029 A522 45c multi 1.10 1.00
2030 A522 45c multi 1.10 1.00
a. Booklet, 2 each #2026-2030 12.50
Nos. 2026-2030 (5) 5.50 5.00

No. 2025b issued 1/24/07.

Reign of Queen Elizabeth II, 50th Anniv. — A611

Queen: 45c, As young woman. $2.45, In 2000.

2002, Feb. 6 ***Perf. 14¾x14***

2031 A611 45c multi .95 .70
2032 A611 $2.45 multi 5.25 5.25
a. Souvenir sheet, #2031-2032 6.25 6.25

A booklet pane containing 2 each of Nos. 2031-2032 is found in the booklet footnoted under No. 2507.

Gold Medalists at 2002 Winter Olympics, Salt Lake City — A612

Designs: No. 2033, Steven Bradbury. No. 2034, Alisa Camplin.

2002 ***Perf. 14¼***

2033 A612 45c multi 1.10 1.00
2034 A612 45c multi 1.10 1.00

Issued: No. 2033, 2/20; No. 2034, 2/22.

Race Cars — A613

Designs: Nos. 2035, 2041, Victoria Austin 7 and Bugatti Type 40, Phillip Island, Victoria, 1928. Nos. 2036, 2042, Jaguar Mark II, Mallala, South Australia, 1963. Nos. 2037, 2043, Repco-Brabham, Sandown, Victoria, 1966. Nos. 2038, 2044, Holden Torana XU1 and Ford Falcon XY GTHO, Bathurst, New South Wales, 1972. Nos. 2039, 2045, Williams FW07 Ford, Calder, Victoria, 1980. Nos. 2040, 2046, Benetton-Renault, Albert Park, Victoria, 2001.

2002, Feb. 27 ***Perf. 14x14¾***

2035 A613 45c multi 1.10 1.10
2036 A613 45c multi 1.10 1.10
2037 A613 45c multi 1.10 1.10
2038 A613 45c multi 1.10 1.10
2039 A613 45c multi 1.10 1.10
2040 A613 45c multi 1.10 1.10
a. Block of 6, #2035-2040 7.00 7.00
Nos. 2035-2040 (6) 6.60 6.60

Self-Adhesive

Serpentine Die Cut 11¼x11½

2041 A613 45c multi 1.10 .80
2042 A613 45c multi 1.10 .80
2043 A613 45c multi 1.10 .80
2044 A613 45c multi 1.10 .80
2045 A613 45c multi 1.10 .80
2046 A613 45c multi 1.10 .80
a. Coil strip, #2041-2046 7.00
b. Booklet, #2045-2046, 2 each #2041-2044 11.50
Nos. 2041-2046 (6) 6.60 4.80

Lighthouses and Maps — A614

Designs: 45c, Macquarie, New South Wales. Nos. 2048, 2051, Troubridge Island, South Australia. Nos. 2049, 2052, Cape Naturaliste, Western Australia. $1.50, Cape Bruny, Tasmania.

2002, Mar. 12 ***Perf. 14½x14***

2047 A614 45c multi 1.40 .60
a. Booklet pane of 4 5.75 —
2048 A614 49c multi 1.40 1.10
a. Booklet pane of 2 2.75 —
2049 A614 49c multi 1.40 1.10
a. Horiz. pair, #2048-2049 2.75 2.75
b. Booklet pane of 2 2.75 —
2050 A614 $1.50 multi 3.50 3.50
a. Booklet pane of 2 7.00 —
b. Booklet pane, #2047-2050 7.75 —
Booklet, #2047a, 2048a, 2049b, 2050a, 2050b 25.75

Booklet Stamps

Self-Adhesive

Serpentine Die Cut 11¾

2051 A614 49c multi 1.40 .85
2052 A614 49c multi 1.40 .85
a. Booklet, 5 each #2051-2052 14.50
Nos. 2047-2052 (6) 10.50 8.00

Booklet containing Nos. 2047a-2050b sold for $9.95.

Encounter of Matthew Flinders and Nicolas Baudin, Bicent. A615

Map, ship and: 45c, Baudin and kangaroo. $1.50, Flinders and Port Lincoln parrot.

2002, Apr. 4 ***Perf. 14x14¾***

2053 A615 45c multi .95 .85
2054 A615 $1.50 multi 3.25 3.25

See France Nos. 2882-2883.

Tourist Attractions Type of 2000

Designs: 50c, Walker Flat. $1, Mt. Roland. $1.50, Cape Leveque.

2002, May 1 ***Perf. 14½x14***

2055 A581 50c multi 1.10 1.00
2056 A581 $1 multi 2.25 2.25
2057 A581 $1.50 multi 3.25 3.25

Booklet Stamps

Self-Adhesive

Serpentine Die Cut 11¼x10½

2058 A581 50c multi 1.40 .85
2059 A581 $1 multi 2.25 2.00
a. Booklet, 6 #2058, 4 #2059 18.00
Nos. 2055-2059 (5) 10.25 9.35

Flora & Fauna Type of 1996

Designs: 50c, Desert star flower. $1, Bilby. $1.50, Thorny devil. $2, Great Sandy Desert.

2002, June 4 Litho. ***Perf. 14x14½***

2060 A511 50c multi 1.00 1.00
2061 A511 $1 multi 2.25 2.25
2062 A511 $1.50 multi 3.25 3.25

Perf. 14½x14

Size: 50x30mm

2063 A511 $2 multi 4.25 4.25
Nos. 2060-2063 (4) 10.75 10.75

See Nos. 2112-2114 for self-adhesive versions of 50c stamp.

Paintings by Albert Namatjira (1902-59) A616

Designs: Nos. 2064, 2068, Ghost Gum Mt. Sonder, MacDonnel Ranges. Nos. 2065, 2069, Mt. Hermannsburg. Nos. 2066, 2070, Glen Helen Country. Nos. 2067, 2071, Simpsons Gap.

2002, July 2 Litho. ***Perf. 14x14¾***

2064 A616 45c multi .95 .95
a. Booklet pane of 4 4.00 4.00
2065 A616 45c multi .95 .95
a. Booklet pane of 4 4.00 4.00
2066 A616 45c multi .95 .95
a. Booklet pane of 4 4.00 4.00
2067 A616 45c multi .95 .95
a. Block of 4, #2064-2067 4.25 4.25
b. Souvenir sheet of 4, #2064-2067 4.25 4.25
c. Booklet pane of 4 4.00 4.00
d. Booklet pane, #2067b 4.25 4.25
Booklet, #2064a, 2065a, 2066a, 2067c, 2067d 20.75
Nos. 2064-2067 (4) 3.80 3.80

Serpentine Die Cut 11x11½

Self-Adhesive

2068 A616 45c multi 1.10 1.10
2069 A616 45c multi 1.10 1.10
2070 A616 45c multi 1.10 1.10

2071 A616 45c multi 1.10 1.10
a. Booklet pane of 10, 3 each #2068-2069, 2 each #2070-2071 12.50
b. Coil strip of 4, #2068-2071 5.25
Nos. 2068-2071 (4) 4.40 4.40

Australia — Thailand Diplomatic Relations, 50th Anniv. A617

Designs: 45c, Nelumbo nucifera. $1, Nymphaea immutabilis.

2002, Aug. 6 Litho. ***Perf. 14x14½***
2072 A617 45c multi 1.10 .85
2073 A617 $1 multi 2.25 2.00
a. Souvenir sheet, #2072-2073 4.00 3.50
b. As "a," overprinted in gold in margin 8.00 8.00

Overprint on margin of No. 2073b has IFSDA and APTA emblems and text reading "50th Anniversary International Federation / of Stamp Dealers Associations."
See Thailand Nos. 2028-2029.

Christmas — A618

Koala A619

Puja, by Ngarralja Tommy May — A620

2002 ***Perf. 14¼x14***
2074 A618 90c multi + label 1.90 1.90
2075 A619 $1.10 multi + label 2.25 2.25
2076 A620 $1.65 multi + label 3.50 3.50
a. Booklet pane of 4 + 4 labels 13.75 —
Complete booklet, 3 #2076a 42.00
Nos. 2074-2076 (3) 7.65 7.65

Issued: 2074-2076, 8/23. No. 2076a, 10/31.
Nos. 2074-2076 were each printed in sheets of 20 stamps + 20 labels. Labels on some sheets could be personalized for an additional fee.
The complete booklet, which sold for $20.75, contains three panes of No. 2076a with different margins.

Tourist Attractions Type of 2000

Designs: $1.10, Coonawarra. $1.65, Gariwerd-Grampians Natl. Park. $2.20, National Library. $3.30, Cape York.

2002, Aug. 23 Litho. ***Perf. 14½x14***
2077 A581 $1.10 multi 2.25 2.25
2078 A581 $1.65 multi 3.50 3.50
2079 A581 $2.20 multi 4.50 4.50
2080 A581 $3.30 multi 7.00 7.00
Nos. 2077-2080 (4) 17.25 17.25

Aboriginal Food Plants — A621

Designs: Nos. 2081, 2088, Murnong. Nos. 2082, 2087, Acacia seeds. Nos. 2083, 2086, Quandong. Nos. 2084, 2090, Honey grevillea. Nos. 2085, 2089, Lilly-pilly.

2002, Sept. 3 Litho. ***Perf. 14¾x14***
2081 A621 49c multi 1.10 1.10
2082 A621 49c multi 1.10 1.10
2083 A621 49c multi 1.10 1.10
2084 A621 49c multi 1.10 1.10
2085 A621 49c multi 1.10 1.10
a. Horiz. strip of 5, #2081-2085 5.75 5.75
b. Tete beche block of 10, 2 each # 2081-2085 11.50 11.50
Nos. 2081-2085 (5) 5.50 5.50

Booklet Stamps
Self-Adhesive
Serpentine Die Cut 11¾

2086 A621 49c multi 1.10 .90
2087 A621 49c multi 1.10 .90
2088 A621 49c multi 1.10 .90
2089 A621 49c multi 1.10 .90
2090 A621 49c multi 1.10 .90
a. Booklet pane, 2 each #2086-2090 11.50
Nos. 2086-2090 (5) 5.50 4.50

Bunyip — A622

Fairy — A623

Gnome — A624

Goblin — A625

Wizard — A626

Sprite — A627

2002, Sept. 25 ***Perf. 14¾x14***
2091 A622 45c multi 1.10 1.10
2092 A623 45c multi 1.10 1.10
2093 A624 45c multi 1.10 1.10
a. Horiz. strip of 3, #2091-2093 3.50 3.50
2094 A625 45c multi 1.10 1.10
2095 A626 45c multi 1.10 1.10
2096 A627 45c multi 1.10 1.10
a. Horiz. strip of 3, #2094-2096 3.50 3.50
b. Souvenir sheet, #2091-2096 5.75 5.75
Nos. 2091-2096 (6) 6.60 6.60

Self-Adhesive
Serpentine Die Cut 11½x11

2097 A622 45c multi 1.10 .85
2098 A623 45c multi 1.10 .85
2099 A624 45c multi 1.10 .85
2100 A625 45c multi 1.10 .85
2101 A626 45c multi 1.10 .85
2102 A627 45c multi 1.10 .85
a. Vert. coil strip of 6, #2097-2102 7.00
b. Booklet pane, #2097, 2102, 2 each #2098-2101 11.50
Nos. 2097-2102 (6) 6.60 5.10

Characters from The Magic Rainforest, by John Marsden.

Race Horses A628

2002, Oct. 15 Litho. ***Perf. 14x14½***
2103 A628 45c Wakeful 1.10 .80
2104 A628 45c Rising Fast 1.10 .80
2105 A628 45c Manikato 1.10 .80
2106 A628 45c Might and Power 1.10 .80
2107 A628 45c Sunline 1.10 .80
a. Horiz. strip of 5, #2103-2107 5.75 5.75
Nos. 2103-2107 (5) 5.50 4.00

Christmas — A629

2002, Nov. 1 ***Perf. 14½x14***
2108 A629 40c Nativity 1.10 1.10
2109 A629 45c Magi 1.10 .70

Self-Adhesive
Booklet Stamp
Serpentine Die Cut 11¼

2110 A629 40c Nativity 1.10 .70
a. Booklet pane of 20 + 20 labels 23.00
Nos. 2108-2110 (3) 3.30 2.50

Flora and Fauna Type of 1996

Designs: 50c, Desert star flower. $1.45, Blue orchid.

2003 Litho. ***Perf. 14x14½***
2111 A511 $1.45 multi 3.50 3.50

Self-Adhesive
Coil Stamps
Serpentine Die Cut 11¼

2112 A511 50c multi 1.10 .75

Serpentine Die Cut 12¾

2113 A511 50c multi 1.10 .75

Booklet Stamp
Serpentine Die Cut 11¼x11

2114 A511 50c multi 1.10 .75
a. Booklet pane of 10 11.50
b. Booklet pane of 20 23.00
Nos. 2111-2114 (4) 6.80 5.75

Issued: 50c, 1/7; $1.45, 2/11.

Flowers — A630

Roses and Wedding Rings — A631

Roses and Hearts — A632

Birthday Cake, Balloons and Gifts — A633

Teddy Bear A634

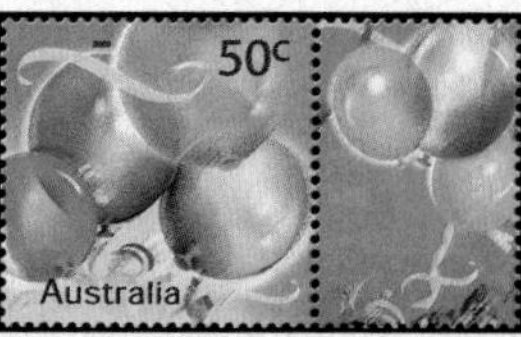
Balloons and Streamers — A635

Kangaroo and Australian Flag — A636

Australia on Globe — A637

Automobile — A638

Rose and Wedding Rings — A639

2003 ***Perf. 14½x14***
2115 A630 50c multi + label 1.00 .85
a. Booklet pane of 4 + 4 labels 4.25
Booklet, 5 #2115a 21.50
2116 A631 50c multi + label 1.00 .85
a. Booklet pane of 4 + 4 labels 4.25
Booklet, 5 #2116a 21.50
2117 A632 50c multi + label 1.00 .85
a. Booklet pane of 4 + 4 labels 4.25
Booklet, 5 #2117a 22.00
b. Strip of 3, #2115-2117, + 3 labels 3.25
2118 A633 50c multi + label 1.00 .85
a. Booklet pane of 4 + 4 labels 4.25
Booklet, 5 #2118a 22.00
2119 A634 50c multi + label 1.00 .85
a. Booklet pane of 4 + 4 labels 4.25 —
Complete booklet, 5 #2119a 22.00
2120 A635 50c multi + label 1.00 .85
a. Booklet pane of 4 + 4 labels 4.25
Booklet, 5 #2120a 22.00
b. Strip of 3, #2118-2120, + 3 labels 3.25
2121 A636 50c multi + label 1.00 .85
2122 A637 50c multi + label 1.00 .85
a. Booklet pane of 4 + 4 labels 4.25 —
Complete booklet, 5 #2122a 22.00
2123 A638 50c multi + label 1.00 .85
a. Strip of 3, #2121-2123, + 3 labels 3.25
2124 A639 $1 multi + label 2.25 2.25
a. Booklet pane of 4 + 4 labels 9.00
Booklet, 5 #2124a 45.00
Nos. 2115-2124 (10) 11.25 9.90

Issued: No. 2119a, 10/31/03; No. 2122a, 3/16/04. Rest of set, 1/7/03.
Panes of 20 stamps containing the same design could have labels personalized. The personalized panes sold for a higher price.
Nos. 2115a, 2116a, 2117a, 2118a, 2119a, 2120a, 2122a and 2124a come in complete booklets, each containing 5 panes, each pane having different margins. Some panes are found in a number of different booklets.

Australian Legends Type of 1997

Tennis players: Nos. 2125, 2129, Margaret Court with Wimbledon trophy. Nos. 2126, 2131, Court in action. Nos. 2127, 2130, Rod Laver with Wimbledon trophy. Nos. 2128, 2132, Laver in action.

2003, Jan. 24 ***Perf. 14x14¾***
Size: 34x26mm
2125 A522 50c multi 1.00 1.00
2126 A522 50c multi 1.00 1.00
2127 A522 50c multi 1.00 1.00

2128 A522 50c multi 1.00 1.00
a. Block of 4, #2125-2128 5.25 5.25
b. Booklet pane, #2125-2128 *6.00* —
Nos. 2125-2128 (4) 4.00 4.00

Self-Adhesive

Booklet Stamps

Serpentine Die Cut 11x11½

2129 A522 50c multi 1.25 .80
2130 A522 50c multi 1.25 .80
2131 A522 50c multi 1.25 .80
2132 A522 50c multi 1.25 .80
a. Booklet pane, 3 each #2129-2130, 2 each #2131-2132 12.50
Nos. 2129-2132 (4) 5.00 3.20

No. 2128b issued 1/24/07.

Fish A640

2003, Feb. 11 ***Perf. 14½x14***

2133 A640 50c Snapper 1.10 .90
2134 A640 50c Murray cod 1.10 .90
2135 A640 50c Brown trout 1.10 .90
2136 A640 50c Yellowfin tuna 1.10 .90
2137 A640 50c Barramundi 1.10 .90
a. Horiz. strip of 5, #2133-2137 5.75 5.75
Nos. 2133-2137 (5) 5.50 4.50

Australian Cultivars — A641

Designs: Nos. 2138, 2143, Hari Withers camellia. Nos. 2139, 2144, Victoria Gold rose. Nos. 2140, 2145, Superb grevillea. Nos. 2141, 2146, Bush Tango kangaroo paw. Nos. 2142, 2147, Midnight rhododendron.

2003, Mar. 25 ***Perf. 14¾x14***

2138 A641 50c multi 1.00 .95
2139 A641 50c multi 1.00 .95
2140 A641 50c multi 1.00 .95
2141 A641 50c multi 1.00 .95
2142 A641 50c multi 1.00 .95
a. Horiz. strip of 5, #2138-2142 5.25 5.25
Nos. 2138-2142 (5) 5.00 4.75

Self-Adhesive

Serpentine Die Cut 11½x11¼

2143 A641 50c multi 1.10 .75
2144 A641 50c multi 1.10 .75
2145 A641 50c multi 1.10 .75
2146 A641 50c multi 1.10 .75
2147 A641 50c multi 1.10 .75
a. Coil strip of 5, #2143-2147 5.75
b. Booklet pane, 2 each #2143-2147 11.00
Nos. 2143-2147 (5) 5.50 3.75

Paintings — A642

Designs: No. 2148, Ned Kelly, by Sidney Nolan. No. 2149, Family Home, Suburban Exterior, by Howard Arkley. $1.45, Cord Drawn Long, Expectant, by Robert Jacks. $2.45, Girl, by Joy Hester.

2003, May 6 Litho. ***Perf. 14½x14***

2148 A642 $1 multi 2.25 2.00
2149 A642 $1 multi 2.25 2.00
a. Horiz. pair, #2148-2149 3.50 3.50
2150 A642 $1.45 multi 3.25 3.25
2151 A642 $2.45 multi 5.25 5.25
Nos. 2148-2151 (4) 13.00 12.50

Coronation of Queen Elizabeth II, 50th Anniv. — A643

Designs: 50c, Queen Elizabeth II, 1953. $2.45, St. Edward's Crown.

2003, June 2 Litho. ***Perf. 14¾x14***

2152 A643 50c multi 1.00 1.00
2153 A643 $2.45 multi 5.25 5.25
a. Souvenir sheet, #2152-2153 6.50 6.50

Booklet Stamp

Self-Adhesive

Serpentine Die Cut 11½x11¼

2154 A643 50c multi 1.00 .85
a. Booklet pane of 10 10.25
Nos. 2152-2154 (3) 7.25 7.10

Papunya Tula Aboriginal Art A644

Untitled works by: $1.10, Ningura Napurrula. $1.65, Naata Nungurrayi. $2.20, Graham Tjupurrula. $3.30, Dini Campbell Tjampitjinpa.

2003, June 17 ***Perf. 14½x14***

2155 A644 $1.10 multi 2.25 2.25
2156 A644 $1.65 multi 3.50 3.50

Size: 56x25mm

Perf. 14x14½

2157 A644 $2.20 multi 4.50 4.50
2158 A644 $3.30 multi 7.00 7.00
Nos. 2155-2158 (4) 17.25 17.25

Flora & Fauna Type of 1996

Designs: Nos. 2159, 2163, 2167, Orange-thighed tree frog. Nos. 2160, 2164, 2168, Green-spotted triangle butterfly. Nos. 2161, 2165, 2169, Striped possum. Nos. 2162, 2166, 2170, Yellow-bellied sunbird.

2003, July 8 Litho. ***Perf. 14x14¼***

2159 A511 50c multi 1.00 .90
2160 A511 50c multi 1.00 .90
2161 A511 50c multi 1.00 .90
2162 A511 50c multi 1.00 .90
a. Block of 4, #2159-2162 4.50 4.50
Nos. 2159-2162 (4) 4.00 3.60

Self-Adhesive

Serpentine Die Cut 11¼

2163 A511 50c multi 1.00 .80
2164 A511 50c multi 1.00 .80
a. Booklet pane of 2, #2163-2164 2.25
2165 A511 50c multi 1.00 .80
2166 A511 50c multi 1.00 .80
a. Booklet pane of 4, #2163-2166, rouletted at bottom 4.50
Complete booklet, #2164a, 2 #2166a 10.25
b. Booklet pane of 4, #2163-2166, rouletted at side 4.50
Complete booklet, 5 #2166b 23.00
c. Coil strip of 4, #2163-2166 4.50

Coil Stamps

Serpentine Die Cut 12¾

2167 A511 50c multi 1.10 .80
2168 A511 50c multi 1.10 .80
2169 A511 50c multi 1.10 .80
2170 A511 50c multi 1.10 .80
a. Strip of 4, #2167-2170 5.25
Nos. 2163-2170 (8) 8.40 6.40

Genetics A645

Map of Australia and: No. 2171, DNA molecule. No. 2172, Kangaroo chromosomes in cell division.

2003, July 8 Litho. ***Perf. 14x14¾***

2171 A645 50c red & multi 1.00 .80
2172 A645 50c grn & multi 1.00 .80
a. Horiz. pair, #2171-2172 2.25 1.75

Murray River Shipping, 150th Anniv. A646

Murray River vessels: Nos. 2173, 2178, Oscar W. Nos. 2174, 2179, Marion. Nos. 2175, 2180, Ruby. Nos. 2176, 2181, Pyap. Nos. 2177, 2182, Adelaide.

2003, Aug. 5 Litho. ***Perf. 14x14¾***

2173 A646 50c multi 1.00 .90
a. Booklet pane of 4 4.25 —
2174 A646 50c multi 1.00 .90
a. Booklet pane of 4 4.25 —
2175 A646 50c multi 1.00 .90
a. Booklet pane of 4 4.25 —
2176 A646 50c multi 1.00 .90
a. Booklet pane of 4 4.25 —
2177 A646 50c multi 1.00 .90
a. Booklet pane of 4 4.25 —
Complete booklet, #2173a-2177a 29.00
b. Horiz. strip of 5, #2173-2177 7.50 7.50
Nos. 2173-2177 (5) 5.00 4.50

Self-Adhesive

Serpentine Die Cut 11¼x11½

2178 A646 50c multi 1.10 .80
2179 A646 50c multi 1.10 .80
2180 A646 50c multi 1.10 .80
2181 A646 50c multi 1.10 .80
2182 A646 50c multi 1.10 .80
a. Horiz. coil strip of 5, #2178-2182 5.75
b. Booklet pane, 2 each #2178-2182 11.00
Nos. 2178-2182 (5) 5.50 4.00

The booklet containing Nos. 2173a-2177a sold for $10.95.

Christmas — A647

2003, Aug. 5 Litho. ***Perf. 14½x14***

2183 A647 50c Christmas tree 1.00 .90
a. Sheet of 20 + 20 labels 35.00 —
2184 A647 90c Star 1.90 1.75
a. Sheet of 20 + 20 labels 50.00 —

Labels on Nos. 2183a and 2184a could be personalized. No. 2183a sold for $23 on day of issue; No. 2184a for $32.

High Court of Australia, Cent. A648

Designs: 50c, Sir Samuel Griffith (1845-1920), first Chief Justice, text from Constitution about High Court. $1.45, "Justice," names of significant cases.

2003, Sept. 2 Litho. ***Perf. 14x14¾***

2185 A648 50c multi 1.00 .85
2186 A648 $1.45 multi 3.25 3.25
a. Souvenir sheet, #2185-2186 4.25 4.25

Insects A649

Designs: Nos. 2187, 2198, Ulysses butterfly. Nos. 2188, 2197, Leichhardt's grasshopper. Nos. 2189, 2196, Vedalia ladybird. Nos. 2190, 2195, Green mantid and damselfly. Nos. 2191, 2194, Emperor gum moth caterpillar. Nos. 2192, 2193, Fiddler beetle.

2003, Sept. 24 ***Perf. 14x14¾***

2187 A649 50c multi 1.00 .90
2188 A649 50c multi 1.00 .90
2189 A649 50c multi 1.00 .90
a. Horiz. strip, #2187-2189 3.50 3.50
2190 A649 50c multi 1.00 .90
2191 A649 50c multi 1.00 .90
2192 A649 50c multi 1.00 .90
a. Horiz. strip, #2190-2192 3.50 3.50
b. Souvenir sheet, #2187-2192 5.75 5.75
c. As "b," with Bangkok 2003 emblem in margin in gold 8.00 8.00
Nos. 2187-2192 (6) 6.00 5.40

Self-Adhesive

Serpentine Die Cut 11x11¼

2193 A649 50c multi 1.10 .90
2194 A649 50c multi 1.10 .90
2195 A649 50c multi 1.10 .90
2196 A649 50c multi 1.10 .90
2197 A649 50c multi 1.10 .90
2198 A649 50c multi 1.10 .90
a. Horiz. coil strip, #2193-2198 7.50
b. Booklet pane, #2193-2194, 2 each #2195-2198 12.00
Nos. 2193-2198 (6) 6.60 5.40

No. 2193c issued 10/4.

2003 Rugby World Cup — A650

Designs: 50c, Players running with ball, hands and ball. $1.10, Webb Ellis Cup, Telstra Stadium. $1.65, Player kicking at goal, ball in hand.

2003, Oct. 8 Litho. ***Perf. 14½x14***

2199 A650 50c multi 1.00 .85
a. Booklet pane of 3 3.50 —
2200 A650 $1.10 multi 2.25 2.25
a. Booklet pane of 3 7.00 —
2201 A650 $1.65 multi 3.50 3.50
a. Booklet pane of 3 10.50 —
Complete booklet, #2199a, 2200a, 2201a 21.00
b. Souvenir sheet, #2199-2201 7.00 7.00
Nos. 2199-2201 (3) 6.75 6.60

Booklet sold for $10.95.

Active With Asthma A651

2003, Oct. 14 ***Perf. 14x14½***

2202 A651 50c multi 1.00 .70

Christmas — A652

Designs: 45c, Madonna and Child with Angels. 50c, Three Wise Men. 90c, Angel Appearing to the Shepherds.

2003, Oct. 31 ***Perf. 14½x14***

2203 A652 45c multi .95 .95
2204 A652 50c multi 1.00 1.00
2205 A652 90c multi 1.90 1.90

Booklet Stamp

Self-Adhesive

Serpentine Die Cut 11½x11¼

2206 A652 45c multi 1.00 .60
a. Booklet pane of 20 + 20 labels 21.00
Nos. 2203-2206 (4) 4.85 4.45

Australian Legends Type of 1997

Dame Joan Sutherland, opera singer: Nos. 2207, 2209, In costume. Nos. 2208, 2210, In black and red dress.

2004, Jan. 23 Litho. ***Perf. 14x14¾***

Size: 37x26mm

2207 A522 50c multi 1.00 .90
2208 A522 50c multi 1.00 .90
a. Horiz. pair, #2207-2208 2.25 2.25
b. Booklet pane, #2207-2208 *3.00* —

Booklet Stamps

Self-Adhesive

Serpentine Die Cut 11x11½

2209 A522 50c multi 1.00 .80
2210 A522 50c multi 1.00 .80
a. Booklet pane, 5 each #2209-2210 10.50
Nos. 2207-2210 (4) 4.00 3.40

No. 2208b issued 1/24/07.

Settlement of Hobart Town, Tasmania, Bicent. A653

Segment of shell necklace, map of Tasmania and: No. 2211, Cheshunt House, Deloraine. No. 2212, Complete shell necklace. No. 2213, Mount Wellington. No. 2214, Hobart Town from Kangaroo Point, by John Glover.

2004, Feb. 3 Litho. *Perf. 14x14½*

2211 A653 50c multi 1.00 .80
2212 A653 50c multi 1.00 .80
a. Pair, #2211-2212 2.25 2.25
2213 A653 $1 multi 2.25 2.00
2214 A653 $1 multi 2.25 2.00
a. Pair, #2213-2214 4.50 4.50
b. Souvenir sheet, #2211-2214 7.00 7.00
c. As "b," ovptd. for Paris Ex-hib. 2004 *35.00 35.00*
d. As "b," ovptd. for China 2005 exhibition *10.00 10.00*
Nos. 2211-2214 (4) 6.50 5.60

Historic Bridges A654

Designs: Nos. 2215, 2220, Ross Bridge, Tasmania, 1836. Nos. 2216, 2221, Lockyer Creek Bridge, Queensland, 1911. Nos. 2217, 2222, Sydney Harbour Bridge, 1932. Nos. 2218, 2223, Birkenhead Bridge, Adelaide, 1940. Nos. 2219, 2224, Bolte Bridge, Melbourne, 1999.

2004, Mar. 2 Litho. *Perf. 14x14½*

2215 A654 50c multi 1.00 .90
a. Booklet pane of 4 4.25 —
2216 A654 50c multi 1.00 .90
a. Booklet pane of 4 4.25 —
2217 A654 50c multi 1.00 .90
a. Booklet pane of 4 4.25 —
2218 A654 50c multi 1.00 .90
a. Booklet pane of 4 4.25 —
2219 A654 50c multi 1.00 .90
a. Booklet pane of 4 4.25 —
Complete booklet, #2215a, 2216a, 2217a, 2218a, 2219a 21.00
b. Horiz. strip of 5, #2215-2219 5.25 5.25
c. Booklet pane of 6 ('06) 6.25 —
Nos. 2215-2219 (5) 5.00 4.50

The complete booklet No. 2219a sold for $10.95.

No. 2219c issued 3/1/06.

Self-Adhesive

Serpentine Die Cut 11x11½

2220 A654 50c multi 1.40 .90
2221 A654 50c multi 1.40 .90
2222 A654 50c multi 1.40 .90
2223 A654 50c multi 1.40 .90
2224 A654 50c multi 1.40 .90
a. Horiz. coil strip of 5, #2220-2224 7.25
b. Booklet pane, 2 each #2220-2224 14.50
Nos. 2220-2224 (5) 7.00 4.50

Southern Cross — A655

2004-05 *Perf. 14½x14*

2225 A655 50c multi 1.00 .80
a. Booklet pane of 4 + 4 labels 4.25 —
Complete booklet, 5 #2225a 22.00

Issued: No. 2225, 3/16/04. No. 2225a, Jan. 2005. No. 2225a was issued in a variety of complete booklets, each containing 5 panes with different margins. Each complete booklet sold for $10.95.

Renewable Energy A656

Designs: Nos. 2226, 2230, Solar energy. Nos. 2227, 2231, Wind energy. Nos. 2228, 2232, Hydroelectric energy. Nos. 2229, 2233, Biomass energy.

2004, Mar. 30 *Perf. 14x14½*

2226 A656 50c multi 1.00 1.00
2227 A656 50c multi 1.00 1.00
2228 A656 50c multi 1.00 1.00
2229 A656 50c multi 1.00 1.00
a. Block of 4, #2226-2229 4.25 4.25
Nos. 2226-2229 (4) 4.00 4.00

Coil Stamps

Self-Adhesive

Serpentine Die Cut 11x11½

2230 A656 50c multi 1.10 .85
2231 A656 50c multi 1.10 .85
2232 A656 50c multi 1.10 .85
2233 A656 50c multi 1.10 .85
a. Horiz. strip of 4, #2230-2233 4.50
Nos. 2230-2233 (4) 4.40 3.40

Royal Visit, 50th Anniv. — A657

2004, Apr. 13 *Perf. 14½x14*

2234 A657 50c multi 1.00 .85
a. Booklet pane of 4 4.25 —
Complete booklet, 5 #2234a 21.50

The booklet, which contains five panes with different margins, sold for $10.95. Another booklet pane, with a different margin, is found in the booklet footnoted under No. 2507.

Flora & Fauna Type of 1996

Designs: 5c, Red lacewing butterfly. 10c, Blue-banded eggfly butterfly. 75c, Cruiser butterfly. $2, Butterflies, Daintree National Park rainforest.

2004, May 4 Litho. *Perf. 14x14½*

2235 A511 5c multi .25 .25
2236 A511 10c multi .25 .25
2237 A511 75c multi 1.60 .95

Size: 50x30mm

Perf. 14½x14

2238 A511 $2 multi 4.25 4.25
Nos. 2235-2238 (4) 6.35 5.70

Australian Innovations A658

Designs: Nos. 2239, 2248, Black box flight recorder, 1961. Nos. 2240, 2247, Ultrasound imaging equipment, 1976. Nos. 2241, 2246, Racecam television sports coverage, 1979. Nos. 2242, 2245, Baby safety capsule, 1984. Nos. 2243, 2244, Polymer banknotes, 1988.

2004, May 18 *Perf. 14x14½*

2239 A658 50c multi 1.10 .90
2240 A658 50c multi 1.10 .90
2241 A658 50c multi 1.10 .90
2242 A658 50c multi 1.10 .90
2243 A658 50c multi 1.10 .90
a. Horiz. strip, #2239-2243 5.00 5.00
Nos. 2239-2243 (5) 5.50 4.50

Booklet Stamps

Self-Adhesive

Serpentine Die Cut 11x11½

2244 A658 50c multi 1.10 .90
2245 A658 50c multi 1.10 .90
2246 A658 50c multi 1.10 .90
2247 A658 50c multi 1.10 .90
2248 A658 50c multi 1.10 .90
a. Booklet pane, 2 each #2244-2248 12.00
Nos. 2244-2248 (5) 5.50 4.50

Passenger Ship Travel Posters — A659

Designs: 50c, Shaw Savill Lines. $1, Awatea, Union Steam Ship Co. $1.45, Orient Line. $2, Aberdeen & Commonwealth Line.

2004, June 1 Litho. *Perf. 14½x14*

2249 A659 50c multi 1.00 .80
2250 A659 $1 multi 2.25 1.40
2251 A659 $1.45 multi 3.00 3.00
2252 A659 $2 multi 4.25 4.25
Nos. 2249-2252 (4) 10.50 9.45

Serpentine Die Cut 11½x11¼ Syncopated

2252A A659 50c Like #2249, *2005* 1.00 .80

Booklet Stamp

Self-Adhesive

Serpentine Die Cut 11½x11¼

2253 A659 50c multi 1.00 .90
a. Booklet pane of 10 10.25

Issued: Nos. 2249-2252, 2253, 6/1/04. No. 2252A, 2/22/05. No. 2252A issued in sheet of 10.

Eureka Stockade, 150th Anniv. A660

Designs: 50c, Eureka flag. $2.45, Peter Lalor (1827-89), leader of rebellious gold diggers.

2004, June 29 *Perf. 14x14½*

2254 A660 50c multi 1.00 .85
a. Booklet pane of 2 2.25 —
2255 A660 $2.45 multi 5.25 5.25
a. Booklet pane of 2 10.25 —
b. Booklet pane, #2254-2255 6.25
Complete booklet, #2255a, 2255b, 2 #2254a 25.00
c. Souvenir sheet, #2254-2255 7.00 7.00

No. 2255b has perfs that extend to the right margin. No. 2255c does not have perfs that extend through the margin. The margin is larger on No. 2255b than on No. 2255c. The complete booklet sold for $10.95.

Tourist Attractions — A661

Designs: No. 2256, Koala, Eastern Australia, vert. No. 2257, Little penguin, Phillip Island, vert. $1.45, Clown anemonefish, Great Barrier Reef. $2.45, Beach, Gold Coast.

Perf. 14x14½, 14½x14

2004, July 13 Litho.

2256 A661 $1 multi 2.25 1.75
2257 A661 $1 multi 2.25 1.75
a. Horiz. pair, #2256-2257 4.50 4.50
2258 A661 $1.45 multi 3.00 2.00

Litho. With Foil Application

2259 A661 $2.45 multi 5.25 5.25
Nos. 2256-2259 (4) 12.75 10.75

2004 Summer Olympics and Paralympics, Athens A662

2004, Aug. 3 Litho. *Perf. 14x14½*

2260 A662 50c Swimmer 1.00 .90
2261 A662 $1.65 Runner 3.50 3.50
2262 A662 $1.65 Cyclist 3.50 2.75
Nos. 2260-2262 (3) 8.00 7.15

Gold Medalists at 2004 Summer Olympics, Athens A663

Designs: No. 2263, Ian Thorpe, Men's swimming 400m freestyle. No. 2264, Women's 4x100m medley relay swimming team. No. 2265, Sara Carrigan, Women's cycling road race. No. 2266, Petria Thomas, Women's swimming 100m butterfly. No. 2267, Suzanne Balogh, Women's trap shooting. No. 2268, Ian Thorpe, Men's swimming 200m freestyle. No. 2269, Jodie Henry, Women's swimming 100m freestyle. No. 2270, Anna Meares, Women's cycling 500m time trial. No. 2271, James Tomkins and Drew Ginn, Men's rowing pairs. No. 2272, Grant Hackett, Men's swimming 1500m freestyle. No. 2273, Women's 4x100 freestyle relay swimming team. No. 2274, Chantelle Newbery, Women's diving 10m platform. No. 2275, Men's 4000m team pursuit cycling team. No. 2276, Ryan Bayley, Men's cycling individual sprint. No. 2277, Graeme Brown and Stuart O'Grady, Men's cycling Madison. No. 2278, Ryan Bayley, Men's cycling Keirin. No. 2279, Men's field hockey team.

2004 Litho. *Perf. 14¼*

2263 A663 50c multi 1.00 .90
2264 A663 50c multi 1.00 .90
2265 A663 50c multi 1.00 .90
2266 A663 50c multi 1.00 .90
2267 A663 50c multi 1.00 .90
2268 A663 50c multi 1.00 .90
2269 A663 50c multi 1.00 .90
2270 A663 50c multi 1.00 .90
2271 A663 50c multi 1.00 .90
2272 A663 50c multi 1.00 .90
2273 A663 50c multi 1.00 .90
2274 A663 50c multi 1.00 .90
2275 A663 50c multi 1.00 .90
2276 A663 50c multi 1.00 .90
2277 A663 50c multi 1.00 .90
2278 A663 50c multi 1.00 .90
2279 A663 50c multi 1.00 .90
Nos. 2263-2279 (17) 17.00 15.30

Issued: Nos. 2263-2264, 8/16; Nos. 2265-2266, 8/17; Nos. 2267-2268, 8/18; Nos. 2269-2273, 8/23; No. 2274, 8/24; No. 2275, 8/25; No. 2276. 8/26; Nos. 2277-2278, 8/27; No. 2279, 8/30.

A sheet containing Nos. 2263-2279 was available only in the Australia Post annual collection. Value, $50.

Tourist Attractions Type of 2000

Designs: $1.20, Entrance Beach, Broome, Western Australia. $1.80, Mt. William National Park, Tasmania. $2.40, Potato Point, Bodalla, New South Wales. $3.60, Point Gibbon, South Australia.

2004, Sept. 6 *Perf. 14½x14*

2280 A581 $1.20 multi 2.50 1.75
2281 A581 $1.80 multi 3.75 2.75
2282 A581 $2.40 multi 5.25 4.00
2283 A581 $3.60 multi 7.50 6.25
Nos. 2280-2283 (4) 19.00 14.75

Block of £2 Kangaroo & Map Stamps from Australia Post Archives — A664

2004, Sept. 7 *Perf. 14¼*

2284 A664 $5 multi 11.00 9.25

Souvenir Sheet

Self-Adhesive

Serpentine Die Cut 11¼

2285 A664 $5 multi 11.00 11.00

Australian Railways, 150th Anniv. A665

Designs: Nos. 2286, 2291, Melbourne to Sandridge line, 1854. Nos. 2287, 2292, Sydney to Parramatta line, 1855. Nos. 2288, 2293, Helidon to Toowoomba line, 1867. Nos. 2289, 2294, Kalgoorlie to Port Augusta line, 1917. Nos. 2290, 2295, Alice Springs to Darwin line, 2004.

2004, Sept. 7 *Perf. 14x14¾*

2286	A665 50c multi	1.00	.90
a.	Booklet pane of 4	4.25	—
2287	A665 50c multi	1.00	.90
a.	Booklet pane of 4	4.25	—
2288	A665 50c multi	1.00	.90
a.	Booklet pane of 4	4.25	—
2289	A665 50c multi	1.00	.90
a.	Booklet pane of 4	4.25	—
2290	A665 50c multi	1.00	.90
a.	Booklet pane of 4	4.25	—
	Complete booklet, #2286a-2290a	22.00	
b.	Horiz. strip, #2286-2290	5.25	5.25
	Nos. 2286-2290 (5)	5.00	4.50

Complete booklet of Nos. 2286a-2290a sold for $10.95.

Self-Adhesive

With Designs Lightened at Stamp Edges

Serpentine Die Cut 11¼x11½

2291	A665 50c multi	1.10	1.00
2292	A665 50c multi	1.10	1.00
2293	A665 50c multi	1.10	1.00
2294	A665 50c multi	1.10	1.00
2295	A665 50c multi	1.10	1.00
a.	Horiz. coil strip, #2291-2295	6.25	
b.	Booklet pane, 2 each #2291-2295	12.50	
	Nos. 2291-2295 (5)	5.50	5.00

Cats and Dogs — A666

Designs: Nos. 2296, 2302, Cat (fish background). Nos. 2297, 2304, Cat (mouse background). Nos. 2298, 2301, Labrador retriever puppy (ball background). Nos. 2299, 2303, West Highland terriers (paw print background). $1, Jack Russell terrier (bone background).

2004, Sept. 21 *Perf. 14¾x14*

2296	A666 50c multi	1.00	.90
a.	Booklet pane of 4	4.25	—
2297	A666 50c multi	1.00	.90
a.	Horiz. pair, #2296-2297	2.25	2.25
b.	Booklet pane of 4	4.25	—
c.	Booklet pane, 2 each #2296-2297	4.50	—
	Complete booklet, #2296a, 2297b, 3 #2297c	21.00	
2298	A666 50c multi	1.00	.90
a.	Booklet pane of 4	4.25	—
2299	A666 50c multi	1.00	.90
a.	Horiz. pair, #2298-2299	2.25	2.25
b.	Booklet pane of 4	4.25	—
c.	Booklet pane, 2 each #2298-2299	4.50	—
2300	A666 $1 multi	2.25	2.00
a.	Booklet pane of 2	4.25	—
	Complete booklet, #2298a, 2299b, 2300a, 2 #2299c	21.00	
b.	Souvenir sheet, #2296-2300	5.50	5.50
	Nos. 2296-2300 (5)	6.25	5.60

The complete booklets each sold for $10.95. The Cat booklet contains three examples of No. 2297c, each with different margins and stamp arrangements. The Dog booklet contains two examples of No. 2299c with different margins and stamp arrangements.

Self-Adhesive

Booklet Stamps

Serpentine Die Cut 11¼ Syncopated

2301	A666 50c multi	1.00	.90
2302	A666 50c multi	1.00	.90
2303	A666 50c multi	1.00	.90
a.	Booklet pane, 3 #2301, 2 #2303	5.25	
2304	A666 50c multi	1.00	.90
a.	Booklet pane, 3 each #2301-2302, 2 each #2303-2304	10.25	
b.	Booklet pane, 3 #2302, 2 #2304	5.25	
2305	A666 $1 multi	2.25	.90
a.	Booklet pane of 5	11.00	
	Nos. 2301-2305 (5)	6.25	4.50

Grand Prix Motorcycle Racing A667

Designs: Nos. 2306, 2311, Mick Doohan (motorcycle #1, red panel). Nos. 2307, 2312, Wayne Gardner (motorcycle #1, blue panel). Nos. 2308, 2313, Troy Bayliss (motorcycle #12, orange red panel). Nos. 2309, 2314, Daryl Beattie (motorcycle #4, green panel). Nos. 2310, 2315, Garry McCoy (motorcycle #8, yellow orange panel).

2004, Oct. 12 Litho. *Perf. 14x14¾*

2306	A667 50c multi	1.00	.90
2307	A667 50c multi	1.00	.90
2308	A667 50c multi	1.00	.90
2309	A667 50c multi	1.00	.90
2310	A667 50c multi	1.00	.90
a.	Horiz. strip of 5, #2306-2310	5.25	5.25
	Nos. 2306-2310 (5)	5.00	4.50

Self-Adhesive

Serpentine Die Cut 11¼ Syncopated

2311	A667 50c multi	1.10	1.00
2312	A667 50c multi	1.10	1.00
2313	A667 50c multi	1.10	1.00
2314	A667 50c multi	1.10	1.00
2315	A667 50c multi	1.10	1.00
a.	Horiz. coil strip, #2311-2315	6.25	
b.	Booklet pane, 2 each #2311-2315	12.50	
	Nos. 2311-2315 (5)	5.50	5.00

Christmas — A668

Designs: 45c, Madonna and Child. 50c, Shepherds. $1, Magi, horiz.

2004, Nov. 1 *Perf. 14¾x14, 14x14¾*

2316	A668 45c multi	.95	.85
2317	A668 50c multi	1.00	.90
2318	A668 $1 multi	2.25	1.90
	Nos. 2316-2318 (3)	4.20	3.65

Self-Adhesive

Booklet Stamps

Serpentine Die Cut 11¼ Syncopated

2319	A668 45c multi	.95	.85
a.	Booklet pane of 20 + 20 etiquettes	20.00	
2320	A668 $1 multi	2.25	1.75
a.	Booklet pane of 5	11.00	

Australian Tennis Open, Cent. A669

Designs: 50c, Male player, tennis court and stands, 1905. $1.80, Female player, tennis court and stands, 2005.

2005, Jan. 11 Litho. *Perf. 14x14¾*

2321	A669 50c multi	1.00	.85
a.	Booklet pane of 2	2.25	—
2322	A669 $1.80 multi	3.75	3.00
a.	Booklet pane of 2	7.50	—
	Complete booklet, 2 each #2321a, 2322a	20.00	

The complete booklet contains two examples of Nos. 2321a and 2322a, each with different margins.

Australian Legends — Fashion Designers — A670

Designs: Nos. 2323, 2329, Prue Acton. Nos. 2324, 2330, Jenny Bannister. Nos. 2325, 2331, Collette Dinnigan. Nos. 2326, 2332, Akira Isogawa. Nos. 2327, 2333, Joe Saba. Nos. 2328, 2334, Carla Zampatti.

2005, Jan. 21 *Perf. 14¾x14*

2323	A670 50c multi	1.00	.95
2324	A670 50c multi	1.00	.95
a.	Horiz. pair, #2323-2324	2.25	2.00
b.	Booklet pane, #2323-2324	*3.00*	—
2325	A670 50c multi	1.00	.95
2326	A670 50c multi	1.00	.95
a.	Horiz. pair, #2325-2326	2.25	2.00
b.	Booklet pane, #2325-2326	*3.00*	—
2327	A670 50c multi	1.00	.95
2328	A670 50c multi	1.00	.95
a.	Horiz. pair, #2327-2328	2.25	2.00
b.	Booklet pane, #2327-2328	*3.00*	—
	Nos. 2323-2328 (6)	6.00	5.70

Self-Adhesive

Booklet Stamps

Serpentine Die Cut 11¼ Syncopated

2329	A670 50c multi	1.00	.95
2330	A670 50c multi	1.00	.95
a.	Booklet pane, 5 each #2329-2330	10.00	
2331	A670 50c multi	1.00	.95
2332	A670 50c multi	1.00	.95
a.	Booklet pane, 5 each #2331-2332	10.00	
2333	A670 50c multi	1.00	.95
2334	A670 50c multi	1.00	.95
a.	Booklet pane, 5 each #2333-2334	10.00	
	Nos. 2329-2334 (6)	6.00	5.70

Nos. 2324b, 2326b, 2328b, 1/24/07.

Parrots — A671

Designs: Nos. 2335, 2340, Princess parrot. Nos. 2336, 2344, Rainbow lorikeet. Nos. 2337, 2343, Green rosella. Nos. 2338, 2342, Red-capped parrot. Nos. 2339, 2341, Purple-crowned lorikeet.

2005, Feb. 8 *Perf. 14¾x14*

2335	A671 50c multi	1.25	.95
2336	A671 50c multi	1.25	.95
2337	A671 50c multi	1.25	.95
2338	A671 50c multi	1.25	.95
2339	A671 50c multi	1.25	.95
a.	Horiz. strip of 5, #2335-2339	6.25	6.25
	Nos. 2335-2339 (5)	6.25	4.75

A sheet containing Nos. 2335-2339 + 4 labels was available only with purchase of the "2005 Collection of Australian Stamps." Value $24.

Self-Adhesive

Coil Stamps

Serpentine Die Cut 11¼ Syncopated

2340	A671 50c multi	1.25	.85
2341	A671 50c multi	1.25	.85
2342	A671 50c multi	1.25	.85
2343	A671 50c multi	1.25	.85
2344	A671 50c multi	1.25	.85
a.	Vert. strip of 5, #2340-2344	6.25	
	Nos. 2340-2344 (5)	6.25	4.25

Sports Memorabilia A672

Designs: No. 2345, Sir Donald Bradman's cricket cap. No. 2346, Lionel Rose's boxing gloves. No. 2347, Marjorie Jackson's running spikes. No. 2348, Racing silks of Phar Lap's jockeys.

2005, Mar. 8 Litho. *Perf. 14¾x14*

2345	A672 50c multi	1.00	.95
a.	Booklet pane of 5, #1575a, 1576c, 1941a, 1942b, 2345 dated "2007"	7.50	—
2346	A672 50c multi	1.00	.95
a.	Horiz. pair, #2345-2346	2.25	2.00
2347	A672 $1 multi	2.25	2.00
2348	A672 $1 multi	2.25	2.00
a.	Horiz. pair, #2347-2348	4.50	4.50
	Nos. 2345-2348 (4)	6.50	5.90

No. 2345a issued 11/14/2007.

Child's Plush Toy — A673

Red Roses — A674

Gifts A675

Kangaroos A676

White Roses — A677

Yellow Roses and Woman's Hand — A678

Koala — A679

Shell on Beach — A680

Sydney Opera House — A681

2005, Mar. 22 *Perf. 14¾x14*

2349	A673 50c multi	1.00	1.00
2350	A674 50c multi	1.00	1.00
2351	A675 50c multi	1.00	1.00
2352	A676 50c multi	1.00	1.00
a.	Additionally dated "2013" (#3534d)	1.25	1.25
2353	A677 50c multi	1.00	1.00
a.	Horiz. strip, #2349-2353	5.25	5.25
2354	A678 $1 multi	2.25	2.00
2355	A679 $1.10 multi	2.25	2.25
2356	A680 $1.20 multi	2.40	2.40
2357	A681 $1.80 multi	3.75	3.75
	Nos. 2349-2357 (9)	15.65	15.40

Issued: No. 2352a, 5/10/2013.

Booklet Stamps

Self-Adhesive

Serpentine Die Cut 11x11¼ Syncopated

2358	A673 50c multi	2.25	*2.25*
a.	Booklet pane of 4	9.25	
	Complete booklet, 5 #2358a	45.00	
2359	A674 50c multi	2.25	*2.25*
a.	Booklet pane of 4	9.25	
	Complete booklet, 5 #2359a	45.00	
2360	A675 50c multi	2.25	*2.25*
a.	Booklet pane of 4	9.25	
	Complete booklet, 5 #2360a	45.00	
2361	A677 50c multi	2.75	*2.75*
a.	Booklet pane of 4	11.50	
	Complete booklet, 5 #2361a	57.50	
2362	A678 $1 multi	5.75	*5.75*
a.	Booklet pane of 4	23.00	
	Complete booklet, 5 #2362a	115.00	
2363	A679 $1.10 multi	8.00	*8.00*
a.	Booklet pane of 4	32.00	
	Complete booklet, 2 #2363a	65.00	

2364 A680 $1.20 multi 9.00 *9.00*
a. Booklet pane of 2 18.00
2365 A681 $1.80 multi 13.00 *13.00*
a. Booklet pane of 2 26.00
Complete booklet, 2 each #2364a, 2365a 88.00
Nos. 2358-2365 (8) 45.25 45.25

Each pane in the various complete booklets has a different margin. The complete booklets containing Nos. 2358-2361 each sold for $10.95, the complete booklet containing No. 2362 sold for $20.95, and the complete booklets containing Nos. 2363-2365 sold for $12.95.

See Nos. 2439-2447.

First Australian Coin, 150th Anniv. A682

1855 One sovereign coin: Nos. 2366, 2368a, Obverse. Nos. 2367, 2368b, Reverse.

2005, Apr. 21 Litho. *Perf. 14x14¾*
2366 A682 50c multi 1.00 1.00
2367 A682 $2.45 multi 5.25 5.25
a. Booklet pane, #2366-2367 7.75 —

Litho. & Embossed with Foil Application

2368 Sheet of 2 7.00 7.00
a. A682 50c multi 1.00 1.00
b. A682 $2.45 multi 5.25 5.25

UNESCO World Heritage Sites in Australia and Great Britain — A683

Designs: No. 2369, Wet Tropics of Queensland, Australia. No. 2370, Stonehenge, England. No. 2371, Greater Blue Mountains Area, New South Wales, Australia. No. 2372, Blenheim Castle, England. No. 2373, Purnululu National Park, Western Australia. No. 2374, Heart of Neolithic Orkney, Scotland. No. 2375, Ayers Rock, Uluru-Kata Tjuta National Park, Northern Territory, Australia. No. 2376, Hadrian's Wall, England.

2005, Apr. 21 Litho. *Perf. 14¼*
2369 A683 50c multi 1.00 .95
2370 A683 50c multi 1.00 .95
a. Horiz. pair, #2369-2370 2.25 2.25
2371 A683 50c multi 1.00 .95
2372 A683 50c multi 1.00 .95
a. Horiz. pair, #2371-2372 2.25 2.25
2373 A683 $1 multi 2.25 2.00
2374 A683 $1 multi 2.25 2.00
a. Horiz. pair, #2373-2374 4.50 4.50
b. Booklet pane, #2369-2370, 2373-2374, + 4 labels 7.75 —
2375 A683 $1.80 multi 3.75 3.50
2376 A683 $1.80 multi 3.75 3.50
a. Horiz. pair, #2375-2376 7.50 7.50
b. Booklet pane, #2371-2372, 2375-2376, + 4 labels 11.50 —
Nos. 2369-2376 (8) 16.00 14.80

See Great Britain Nos. 2280-2287.

Creatures of the Slime A684

2005, Apr. 21 *Perf. 14x14¾*
2377 A684 50c Tribrachidium 1.00 .95
2378 A684 50c Dickinsonia 1.00 .95
2379 A684 50c Spriggina 1.00 .95
2380 A684 50c Kimberella 1.00 .95
2381 A684 50c Inaria 1.00 .95
a. Horiz. strip of 5, #2377-2381 5.25 5.25
2382 A684 $1 Charnodiscus 2.25 2.00
a. Souvenir sheet, #2377-2382 7.50 7.50
b. Booklet pane, #2377-2382 9.00 —
Nos. 2377-2382 (6) 7.25 6.75

Rotary International, Cent. — A685

2005, Apr. 21 *Perf. 14¾x14*
2383 A685 50c multi 1.00 .90
a. Imperf. 5.75 5.75

Self-Adhesive
Serpentine Die Cut 11½x11¼ Syncopated

2384 A685 50c multi 1.00 .90
a. Booklet pane of 10 10.25
b. Booklet pane of 1 1.40 —
Complete booklet, #2367a, 2374b, 2376b, 2382b, 2384b 37.50

No. 2383a was sold at the Pacific Explorer Intl. Philatelic Exhibition 2005.

Queen Elizabeth II, 79th Birthday A686

2005, May 10 *Perf. 14x14¾*
2385 A686 50c multi 1.40 1.10
a. Booklet pane of 4 5.75 —
Complete booklet, 5 #2385a 29.00

2006 Commonwealth Games, Melbourne. No. 2385a was issued in a booklet that sold for $10.95, with the 5 panes having different margins.

Bush Wildlife A687

2005, June 7 *Perf. 14x14¾*
2386 A687 $1 Superb lyrebird 2.25 1.75
2387 A687 $1.10 Laughing kookaburra 2.25 2.00
2388 A687 $1.20 Koala 2.40 2.25
2389 A687 $1.80 Red kangaroo 3.75 3.75
Nos. 2386-2389 (4) 10.65 9.75

Serpentine Die Cut 11¼x11½ Syncopated
Self-Adhesive
Booklet Stamps

2390 A687 $1.10 Laughing kookaburra 2.25 2.00
a. Booklet pane of 5 11.50
2391 A687 $1.20 Koala 2.40 2.25
a. Booklet pane of 5 12.00
2392 A687 $1.80 Red kangaroo 3.75 3.75
a. Booklet pane of 5 19.00
Nos. 2390-2392 (3) 8.40 8.00

Wild Flowers — A688

Designs: Nos. 2393, 2397, 2401, Sturt's desert pea. Nos. 2394, 2398, 2402, Coarse-leaved mallee. Nos. 2395, 2399, 2403, Common fringe lily. Nos. 2396, 2400, 2404, Swamp daisy.

2005, July 5 *Perf. 14x14½*
2393 A688 50c multi 1.40 1.00
2394 A688 50c multi 1.40 1.00
2395 A688 50c multi 1.40 1.00
2396 A688 50c multi 1.40 1.00
a. Horiz. strip of 4, #2393-2396 5.75 5.75
Nos. 2393-2396 (4) 5.60 4.00

Self-Adhesive
Serpentine Die Cut 11¼x11

2397 A688 50c multi 1.40 .90
2398 A688 50c multi 1.40 .90
2399 A688 50c multi 1.40 .90
2400 A688 50c multi 1.40 .90
a. Horiz. coil strip of 4, #2397-2400 5.75
b. Booklet pane of 10, 3 each #2397-2398, 2 each #2399-2400 15.00
c. Booklet pane of 20, 5 each #2397-2400 30.00
d. Booklet pane of 5, #2398-2400, 2 #2397 7.25

Coil Stamps
Die Cut Perf. 12¾

2401 A688 50c multi 1.40 .90
2402 A688 50c multi 1.40 .90
2403 A688 50c multi 1.40 .90
2404 A688 50c multi 1.40 .90
a. Horiz. coil strip of 4, #2401-2404 5.75
Nos. 2397-2404 (8) 11.20 7.20

Australian Wine — A689

Designs: Nos. 2405, 2410, Grapevine, vineyard. Nos. 2406, 2411, Grapes, grape leaves. No. 2407, Grape pickers, basket of grapes, wine bottle. No. 2408, Wine bottle, corkscrew, wine barrels. $1.45, Wine glasses, cheese.

2005, July 19 *Perf. 14x14¾*
2405 A689 50c multi 1.00 1.00
2406 A689 50c multi 1.00 1.00
a. Horiz. pair, #2405-2406 2.25 2.25
b. Booklet pane, #2406a 2.25 —
c. Booklet pane, 2 #2406a 4.50 —
2407 A689 $1 multi 2.25 2.25
2408 A689 $1 multi 2.25 2.25
a. Horiz. pair, #2407-2408 4.50 4.50
b. Booklet pane, 2 #2408a 9.25 —
2409 A689 $1.45 multi 3.25 3.25
a. Booklet pane of 2 6.25 —
Complete booklet, #2406b, 2406c, 2408b, 2409a 22.50
Nos. 2405-2409 (5) 9.75 9.75

Booklet Stamps
Self-Adhesive
Serpentine Die Cut 11¼x11½ Syncopated

2410 A689 50c multi 1.25 1.25
2411 A689 50c multi 1.25 1.25
a. Booklet pane, 5 each #2410-2411 12.50

Complete booklet sold for $10.95.

Trees A690

Designs: Nos. 2412, 2417, Snowgum. Nos. 2413, 2418, Wollemi pine. Nos. 2414, 2419, Boab. Nos. 2415, 2420, Karri. Nos. 2416, 2421, Moreton Bay fig.

2005, Aug. 8 *Perf. 14x14¾*
2412 A690 50c multi 1.10 1.10
2413 A690 50c multi 1.10 1.10
2414 A690 50c multi 1.10 1.10
2415 A690 50c multi 1.10 1.10
2416 A690 50c multi 1.10 1.10
a. Horiz. strip of 5, #2412-2416 5.50 5.50
Nos. 2412-2416 (5) 5.50 5.50

Coil Stamps
Serpentine Die Cut 11¼x11½ Syncopated

2417 A690 50c multi 1.10 1.00
2418 A690 50c multi 1.10 1.00
2419 A690 50c multi 1.10 1.00
2420 A690 50c multi 1.10 1.00
2421 A690 50c multi 1.10 1.00
a. Horiz. strip of 5, #2417-2421 7.00
Nos. 2417-2421 (5) 5.50 5.00

Nos. 2417-2421 have "frames" that are faded portions of the design.

Portion of Specimen Pane of New South Wales No. 86 from Australia Post Archives — A691

2005, Sept. 6 Litho. *Perf. 14¼*
2422 A691 $5 multi 10.50 10.50

No. 2422 exists imperf.

Southern Cross — A692

Southern Cross and: 45c, Christmas tree. 50c, Map of Oceania and East Asia.

2005 *Perf. 14½x14*
2423 A692 45c multi 1.25 1.10
a. Booklet pane of 4 5.25 —
Complete booklet (see footnote) 23.00
2424 A692 50c multi 1.40 1.25

Issued: Nos. 2423, 2424, 9/6. No. 2423a, 11/1. No. 2423a exists with three different margins, each of which appear in a booklet also containing two examples of Christmas Island No. 452a. The complete booklet sold for $9.95.

Southern Cross With Personalized Picture — A692a

Serpentine Die Cut 11½x11¼ Syncopated
2005, Sept. 6 Litho.
Self-Adhesive

2425 A692a 45c Like #2423 2.50 2.50
2426 A692a 50c Like #2424 2.50 2.50

Nos. 2425-2426 were sold in sheets of 20 and have personalized pictures and a straight edge at right, and lack separations between the stamp and the picture. Sheets of 20 of No. 2425 sold for $22, and of No. 2426, $23.

Down on the Farm — A693

Designs: Nos. 2427, 2433, Hen and chicks. Nos. 2428, 2434, Lambs and insects. Nos. 2429, 2437, Goats and rabbit. Nos. 2430, 2435, Pigs and frog. Nos. 2431, 2436, Cow and bird. $1, Horse, dogs, birds, lizard.

2005, Oct. 4 Litho. *Perf. 14x14¾*
2427 A693 50c multi 1.00 .95
a. Booklet pane of 1 1.40 —
2428 A693 50c multi 1.00 .95
a. Booklet pane of 1 1.40 —
2429 A693 50c multi 1.00 .95
a. Booklet pane of 1 1.40 —
2430 A693 50c multi 1.00 .95
a. Booklet pane of 1 1.40 —
2431 A693 50c multi 1.00 .95
a. Booklet pane of 1 1.40 —
b. Horiz. strip of 5, #2427-2431 5.25 5.25
2432 A693 $1 multi 2.25 2.00
a. Booklet pane of 1 2.50 —
b. Souvenir sheet, #2427-2432 8.00 8.00

c.	Booklet pane of 1 #2432b (120x190mm)	8.50	—
	Complete booklet, #2427a-2432a, 2432c	18.50	
	Nos. 2427-2432 (6)	7.25	6.75

The complete booklet containing Nos. 2427a-2432a and 2432c sold for $9.95.

Booklet Stamps
Self-Adhesive
Serpentine Die Cut 11¼ Syncopated

2433	A693 50c multi	1.25	.90
2434	A693 50c multi	1.25	.90
2435	A693 50c multi	1.25	.90
2436	A693 50c multi	1.25	.90
2437	A693 50c multi	1.25	.90
a.	Booklet pane of 5, #2433-2437	6.25	—
b.	Booklet pane of 10, 2 each #2433-2437	12.50	
c.	Booklet pane of 20, 4 each #2433-2437	25.00	
2438	A693 $1 multi	1.90	1.50
a.	Booklet pane of 5	9.50	—
	Nos. 2433-2438 (6)	8.15	6.00

Greetings Types of 2005 With Personalized Photo at Right Like Type A692a
Serpentine Die Cut 11½x11¼ Syncopated

2005 Self-Adhesive

2439	A673 50c multi	2.75	2.75
2440	A674 50c multi	2.75	2.75
2441	A675 50c multi	2.75	2.75
2442	A676 50c multi	2.75	2.75
2443	A677 50c multi	2.75	2.75
2444	A678 $1 multi	4.25	4.25
2445	A679 $1.10 multi	4.50	4.50
2446	A680 $1.20 multi	5.00	5.00
2447	A681 $1.80 multi	6.25	6.25
	Nos. 2439-2447 (9)	33.75	33.75

Nos. 2439-2447 were sold in sheets of 20 and have personalized pictures and a straight edge at right, and lack separations between the stamp and the picture. Sheets of 20 of Nos. 2439-2443 sold for $23 each, of No. 2444, $33.50, of No. 2445, $35, of No. 2446, $37, of No. 2447, $48.

Christmas — A694

Designs: Nos. 2448, 2450, Madonna and Child. Nos. 2449, 2451, Angel, horiz.

2005, Nov. 1 Litho. *Perf. 14½x14*

2448	A694 45c multi	.95	.85

Perf. 14x14½

2449	A694 $1 multi	2.25	2.00

Booklet Stamps
Self-Adhesive
Serpentine Die Cut 11½x11¼ Syncopated

2450	A694 45c multi	.95	.85
a.	Booklet pane of 20	19.50	

Serpentine Die Cut 11¼x11½ Syncopated

2451	A694 $1 multi	2.25	2.00
a.	Booklet pane of 5	11.00	
	Nos. 2448-2451 (4)	6.40	5.70

Emblem of 2006 Commonwealth Games, Melbourne — A695

Commonwealth Games Athletes — A696

Highlights of Commonwealth Games — A697

Medalists at Commonwealth Games — A698

"Equality, Humanity, Destiny" — A699

"Destiny, Equality, Humanity" — A700

"Humanity, Destiny, Equality" — A701

Designs: Nos. 2455, 2458, Runner crouching before race. $1.25, Cyclist. $1.85, Athlete holding ball.

No. 2459 — Sheet #1: a, Trolley car with wings. b, Fish sculpture. c, Cat and mouse puppets. d, Queen Elizabeth II. e, Opening ceremony crowd and fireworks.

No. 2460 — Sheet #2: a, Anna Meares. b, Equality, Humanity, destiny. c, Stephanie Rice swimming. d, Destiny, Equality, Humanity. e, Ben Kersten.

No. 2461 — Sheet #3: a, Ryan Bayley holding flag. b, Adam Vella & Michael Diamond. c, Sean Finning. d, Deserie Baynes & Suzanne Balogh. e, Danni Miatke. f, Women's Artistic Gymnastics team. g, Kate Bates. h, Leisel Jones wearing swim cap and waving. i, David Moore & Daniel Repacholi.

No. 2462 — Sheet #4: a, Brad Kahlfeldt. b, Libby Lenton, lane marker in background. c, Josh Jefferis on pommel horse. d, Emma Snowsill.

No. 2463 — Sheet #5: a, Leisel Jones wearing sweatsuit. b, Ryan Bayley wearing cycling helmet. c, Matthew Cowdrey in water. d, Chloe Sims. e, Sophie Edington in water. f, Women's 4x200m freestyle swim team. g, Ben Turner.

No. 2464 — Sheet #6: a, Katie Mactier. b, Russell Mark & Craig Trembath. c, Jessicah Schipper in water. d, Kerryn McCann. e, Lalita Yauhleuskaya & Dina Aspandiyarova.

No. 2465 — Sheet #7: a, Lauryn Mark & Natalia Rahman. b, Jane Saville. c, Libby Lenton, pushing on lane marker. d, Nathan Deakes in 20km walk. e, Lisa McIntosh.

No. 2466 — Sheet #8: a, Leisel Jones with fist raised. b, Men's triples lawn bowling team. c, Sophie Edington holding medal. d, Matthew Cowdrey wearing sweatsuit. e, Brooke Krueger-Billett. f, Josh Jefferis kissing medal. g, Natalie Grinham. h, Women's 4x100m freestyle swim team. i, Joanna Fargus.

No. 2467 — Sheet #9: a, Alex Karapetyan. b, Jessicah Schipper wearing sweatsuit. c, Nathan O'Neill. d, Lalita Yauhleuskaya holding medal.

No. 2468 — Sheet #10: a, Hollie Dykes. b, Men's 4x100m medley swim team. c, Oenone Wood. d, Women's 4x100m medley swim team. e, Stephanie Rice with arm raised. f, Damian Istria. g, Deborah Lovely.

No. 2469 — Sheet #11: a, Chantelle Newbery & Loudy Tourky. b, John Steffensen. c, Bree Cole & Sharleen Stratton. d, Lynsey Armitage & Karen Murphy.

No. 2470 — Sheet #12: a, Heath Francis. b, Jana Pittman. c, Lalita Yauhleuskaya wearing sight. d, Scott Martin. e, Loudy Tourky. f, Women's basketball team. g, Chris Rae. h, Bruce Scott.

No. 2471 — Sheet #13: a, Nathan Deakes in 50km walk. b, Bronwyn Thompson. c, Robert Newbery & Mathew Helm. d, Steven Hooker. e, Stuart Rendell. f, Kelvin Kerkow. g, Men's basketball team.

No. 2472 — Sheet #14: a, Women's 4x400m relay team. b, Kym Howe. c, Women's field hockey team. d, Mathew Helm. e, Men's 4x400m relay team. f, Bradley Pitt. g, Jarrod Fletcher.

No. 2473 — Sheet #15: a, Natalie Bates. b, Natalie Grinham & Joe Kneipp. c, Men's field hockey team. d, Rachael Grinham & Natalie Grinham. e, Mathew Hayman.

No. 2474 — Sheet #16: a, Dancer on hoops. b, Women wearing hats. c, Dancer. d, Lit-up stadium and fireworks. e, Darkened stadium and fireworks.

No. 2475 — Sheet #17 — Kerryn McCann: a, Running, with opponents in background. b, Drinking from water bottle. c, Running past opponent, profile. d, Running on track with opponent. e, With hands over mouth. f, Collapsed on track. g, With both arms raised. h, Holding flag. i, Raising flower bouquet. j, Holding medal.

2006 Litho. *Perf. 14¾x14*

2452	A695 50c shown	1.00	1.00
a.	Sheet of 9 + 9 labels	27.50	—
b.	Booklet pane of 4	4.25	—

Self-Adhesive (#2453-2454)
Serpentine Die Cut 11¼ Syncopated

2453	A695 50c multi	1.00	1.00
a.	Booklet pane of 4	4.50	

With Personalized Photo at Right Like Type A692a
Booklet Stamp
Serpentine Die Cut 11½x11¼ on 3 Sides, Syncopated

2454	A695 50c multi	4.50	*5.75*
a.	Booklet pane of 4	18.50	

Perf. 14x14¾

2455	A696 50c shown	1.00	1.00
2456	A696 $1.25 multi	2.50	2.50
2457	A696 $1.85 multi	3.75	3.75
a.	Souvenir sheet, #2455-2457, 142x75mm sheet	7.75	7.75
b.	Booklet pane, #2455-2457, in 168x118mm pane	7.75	—
	Complete booklet, #1488a, 2457b, 2 each #2453a, 2454a, + 3 postal cards	42.50	
c.	Booklet pane, #2455-2457, in 156x103mm pane	7.75	—
	Complete booklet, #845a, 2219c, 2452b, 2457c	22.00	
	Nos. 2455-2457 (3)	7.25	7.25

Booklet Stamp
Self-Adhesive
Serpentine Die Cut 11¼ Syncopated

2458	A696 50c multi	1.00	1.00
a.	Booklet pane of 10	10.25	

Miniature Sheets
Perf. 14½x14

2459	Sheet of 5	7.25	*15.00*
a.-e.	A697 50c any single	1.40	*3.00*
2460	Sheet of 5	7.25	*11.00*
a.	A698 50c multi	1.40	*3.00*
b.	A699 50c multi	1.40	1.00
c.	A698 50c multi	1.40	*3.00*
d.	A700 50c multi	1.40	1.00
e.	A698 50c multi	1.40	*3.00*
2461	Sheet of 10, #2460b, 2461a-2461i	14.50	*28.00*
a.-i.	A698 50c any single	1.40	*3.00*
2462	Sheet of 5, #2460b, 2462a-2462d	7.25	*13.00*
a.-d.	A698 50c any single	1.40	*3.00*
2463	Sheet of 10, #2460b, 2460d, 2461a-2461h	14.50	*24.00*
a.-g.	A698 50c any single	1.40	*3.00*
h.	A701 50c multi	1.40	1.00
2464	Sheet of 5	7.25	*15.00*
a.-e.	A698 50c any single	1.40	*3.00*
2465	Sheet of 5	7.25	*15.00*
a.-e.	A698 50c any single	1.40	*3.00*
2466	Sheet of 10, #2460b, 2466a-2466i	14.50	*28.00*
a.-i.	A698 50c any single	1.40	*3.00*
2467	Sheet of 5, #2460b, 2467a-2467d	7.25	*13.00*
a.-d.	A698 50c any single	1.40	*3.00*
2468	Sheet of 10, #2460b, 2460d, 2463h, 2468a-2468g	14.50	*24.00*
a.-g.	A698 50c any single	1.40	*3.00*
2469	Sheet of 5, #2460b, 2469a-2469d	7.25	*13.00*
a.-d.	A698 50c any single	1.40	*3.00*
2470	Sheet of 10, #2460b, 2460d, 2470a-2470h	14.50	*26.00*
a.-h.	A698 50c any single	1.40	*3.00*
2471	Sheet of 10, #2460b, 2460d, 2463h, 2471a-2471g	14.50	*24.00*
a.-g.	A698 50c any single	1.40	*3.00*
2472	Sheet of 10, #2460b, 2460d, 2463h, 2472a-2472g	14.50	*24.00*
a.-g.	A698 50c any single	1.40	*3.00*
2473	Sheet of 5	7.25	*15.00*
a.-e.	A698 50c any single	1.40	*3.00*
2474	Sheet of 5	7.25	*15.00*
a.-e.	A697 50c any single	1.40	*3.00*
2475	Sheet of 10	14.50	*30.00*
a.-j.	A697 50c any single	1.40	*3.00*
	Nos. 2459-2475 (17)	181.25	*333.00*

Issued: Nos. 2452-2453, 1/12; Nos. 2454, 2457b, 3/15; Nos. 2452b, 2455-2458, 2457c, 3/1; No. 2459, 3/16; No. 2460, 3/17; No. 2461, 3/18; Nos. 2462, 2463, 3/19; No. 2464, 3/20; Nos. 2465, 2466, 3/21; Nos. 2467, 2468, 3/22; No. 2469, 3/23; No. 2470, 3/24; No. 2471, 3/25; No. 2472, 3/26; Nos. 2473, 2474, 3/27; No. 2475, 3/28.

No. 2452a sold for $15.95. Labels could be personalized.

Complete booklet containing No. 2454 sold for $19.95. Labels could be personalized.

Complete booklet containing No. 2457c sold for $10.95 and included a booklet pane with perf. 14x14¾ lithographed examples of Nos. 349-350 which were not valid for postage.

A booklet issued 2/1, containing #2452b, an imperf booklet pane of 4 #2452, a booklet pane of 2 #2453, a booklet pane of 1 #2453 and four 50c coins, sold for $24.95.

Dame Edna Everage in 2004 A702

Barry Humphries A703

Inscriptions: Nos. 2476, 2481, Mrs. Norm Everage, 1969. Nos. 2477, 2482, Mrs. Edna Everage, 1973. Nos. 2478, 2483, Dame Edna Everage, 1982.

2006, Jan. 20 Litho. *Perf. 14½x14*

2476	A702 50c multi	1.00	1.00
2477	A702 50c multi	1.00	1.00
2478	A702 50c multi	1.00	1.00
2479	A702 50c shown	1.00	1.00
2480	A703 50c shown	1.00	1.00
a.	Horiz. strip of 5, #2476-2480	5.25	5.25
b.	Booklet pane, #2476-2480	5.25	—
	Complete booklet	45.00	
	Nos. 2476-2480 (5)	5.00	5.00

Booklet Stamps
Self-Adhesive
Serpentine Die Cut 11¼ Syncopated

2481	A702 50c multi	1.00	.90
2482	A702 50c multi	1.00	.90
2483	A702 50c multi	1.00	.90
a.	Booklet pane, 4 #2481, 3 each #2482-2483	10.25	
2484	A702 50c multi	1.00	.90
2485	A703 50c multi	1.00	.90
a.	Booklet pane, 5 each #2484-2485	10.25	
	Nos. 2481-2485 (5)	5.00	4.50

Edna Everage, stage character played by Barry Humphries.

No. 2480b issued 1/24/07. Complete booklet, which sold for $22.95, contains Nos. 1576b, 1634m, 1634n, 1634o, 1720b, 1803b, 1934b, 2025b, 2128b, 2208b, 2324b, 2326b, 2328b, and 2480b.

Rose A704

2006, Jan. 27 Litho. *Perf. 14x14¾*

2486	A704 50c multi	1.00	1.00

With White Border
Self-Adhesive
Litho. & Typo.
Serpentine Die Cut 11¼ Syncopated
2487 A704 50c multi 1.00 .90

Booklet Stamp
Litho.
2488 A704 50c multi 1.00 .90
a. Booklet pane of 10 8.50

No. 2487 has a scratch-and-sniff area with a rose scent applied to the center of the rose, has a denomination composed of small black dots, and was printed in sheets of 10. No. 2488 lacks the scrach and sniff panel and has a solid gray denomination.

Flowers — A705

Designs: $1, Pincushion hakea. $2, Donkey orchid. $5, Mangles kangaroo paw. $10, Waratah.

2006, Feb. 7 Litho. *Perf. 14x14½*
2489 A705 $1 multi 2.25 1.40
2490 A705 $2 multi 4.25 2.75

Perf. 14½x14
Size:50x30mm
2491 A705 $5 multi 10.25 7.00
2492 A705 $10 multi 20.75 11.00
Nos. 2489-2492 (4) 37.50 22.15

Souvenir Sheet
Litho. & Embossed
2493 A705 $10 multi 22.00 22.00

Dale Begg-Smith, Men's Moguls Gold Medalist at 2006 Winter Olympics, Turin — A706

2006, Feb. 15 Litho. *Perf. 14½*
2494 A706 50c multi 1.00 1.00

Animals A707

Royal Exhibition Building, Melbourne — A708

Designs: 2495, 5c, Platypus. 2496, 25c, Short-beaked echidna. No. 2497, $1.25, Common wombat. Nos. 2498, $1.25, Koala, vert. No. 2499, $1.85, Tasmanian devil. 2501, $2.50, Greater bilby. 2502, $3.70, Dingo.

2006 *Perf. 14x14¾, 14¾x14*
2495 A707 5c multi .25 .25
2496 A707 25c multi .50 .35
2497 A707 $1.25 multi 2.50 2.50
2498 A707 $1.25 multi 2.50 2.50
a. Souvenir sheet of 1, with China 2006 emblem and Great Wall of China in sheet margin 2.25 2.25
b. As "a," with Sydney landmarks in sheet margin 2.25 2.25
2499 A707 $1.85 multi 3.75 3.75
2500 A708 $1.85 multi 3.75 3.75
2501 A707 $2.50 multi 5.25 5.25
2502 A707 $3.70 multi 7.75 7.75
Nos. 2495-2502 (8) 26.25 26.10

Self-Adhesive
Booklet Stamps
Serpentine Die Cut 11¼ Syncopated
2503 A707 $1.25 multi 2.50 2.50
a. Booklet pane of 5 12.75
b. Booklet pane of 2 5.75
Complete booklet, 4 #2503b 23.00
c. As "a," with Washington 2000 Exhib. emblem added to lower right margin of bklt. pane 13.75
2504 A708 $1.85 multi 3.75 3.75
a. Booklet pane of 5 19.00
b. Booklet pane of 2 7.50
Complete booklet, 4 #2504b 30.00

Issued: Nos. 2498, 2500, 2503, 2504, 5/2; No. 2503c, 5/27; others, 3/6.

Each of the four panes of Nos. 2503b and 2504b in the complete booklets have different margins. The complete booklet containing No. 2503b sold for $12.95; the booklet containing No. 2504b sold for $14.95.

Nos. 2498a-2498b issued 10/26.

See Nos. 2542-2543, 2674, 2676, 2678.

Queen Elizabeth II, 80th Birthday
A709 A710

2006, Apr. 19 *Perf. 14¾x14*
2505 A709 50c multi 1.00 1.00
a. Booklet pane of 2 2.25 —
b. Dated "2010" 2.00 1.00
2506 A710 $2.45 multi 5.25 5.25
a. Booklet pane of 2 10.25 —
b. Booklet pane, #2505-2506, 153x104mm pane size 6.25 —
Complete booklet, #2506a, 2506b, 2 #2505a 21.00
c. Souvenir sheet, #2505-2506, 105x70mm sheet size 7.00 7.00

Self-Adhesive
Booklet Stamp
Serpentine Die Cut 11¼ Syncopated
2507 A709 50c multi 1.10 .90
a. Booklet pane of 10 11.50

Complete booklet containing Nos. 2505-2506 sold for $10.95.

A booklet commemorating royal visits to Australia containing a booklet pane of 2 each of lithographed, perf. 14x14¾ example of Nos. 474-475, a booklet pane of 4 lithographed, perf. 14x14¾ examples of No. 779, a booklet pane of 2 each of lithographed perf. 14½x14 examples of Nos. 659-660, a booklet pane of 2 each Nos. 2031-2032, a booklet pane of No. 2234a with a different margin, a booklet pane of 2 each of perf. 14½x14 examples of Nos. 351-352 (not valid for postage), and a 50c coin was released in 2006. It sold for $15.95.

Lighthouses A711

Designs: Nos. 2508, 2513, Point Lonsdale Lighthouse, Victoria. Nos. 2509, 2514, Cape Don Lighthouse, Northern Territory. Nos. 2510, 2515, Wollongong Head Lighthouse, New South Wales. Nos. 2511, 2516, Casuarina Point Lighthouse, Western Australia. Nos. 2512, 2517, Point Cartwright Lighthouse, Queensland.

2006, May 2 *Perf. 14¾x14*
2508 A711 50c multi 1.00 1.00
2509 A711 50c multi 1.00 1.00
2510 A711 50c multi 1.00 1.00
a. Booklet pane, #2509, 2510, 2 #2508 4.25 —
b. Booklet pane, #2508, 2509, 2 #2510 4.25 —
2511 A711 50c multi 1.00 1.00
2512 A711 50c multi 1.00 1.00
a. Horiz. strip, #2508-2512 5.25 4.50
b. Booklet pane, #2511, 2512, 2 #2509 4.25 —
c. Booklet pane, #2510, 2512, 2 #2511 4.25 —
d. Booklet pane, #2508, 2511, 2 #2512 4.25 —
Complete booklet, #2510a, 2510b, 2512b, 2512c, 2512d 20.00
Nos. 2508-2512 (5) 5.00 5.00

Coil Stamps
Self-Adhesive
Serpentine Die Cut 11¼ Syncopated
2513 A711 50c multi 1.10 .90
2514 A711 50c multi 1.10 .90
2515 A711 50c multi 1.10 .90
2516 A711 50c multi 1.10 .90
2517 A711 50c multi 1.10 .90
a. Vert. strip, #2513-2517 5.75

Complete booklet sold for $10.95.

2006 World Cup Soccer Championships, Germany — A712

Soccer player, 2006 World Cup emblem and word: Nos. 2518, 2522, "Play." Nos. 2519, 2523, "Goal." $1.25, "Save." $1.85, "Shot."

2006, May 9 *Perf. 14x14¾*
2518 A712 50c multi 1.00 1.00
2519 A712 50c multi 1.00 1.00
a. Horiz. pair, #2518-2519 2.25 2.25
2520 A712 $1.25 multi 2.50 2.50
2521 A712 $1.85 multi 3.75 3.75
a. Souvenir sheet, #2518-2521 8.50 8.50
b. As "a," with 2006 Paris Exhib. ovpt. 9.25 9.25
Nos. 2518-2521 (4) 8.25 8.25

Booklet Stamps
Self-Adhesive
Serpentine Die Cut 11¼ Syncopated
2522 A712 50c multi 1.10 1.10
2523 A712 50c multi 1.10 1.10
a. Booklet pane, 5 each #2522-2523 11.50

No. 2521b issued 6/17.

Postie Kate — A713

Kate: Nos. 2524, 2529, Writing address on letter. Nos. 2525, 2530, On motorcycle, delivering letter. Nos. 2526, 2531, With van, delivering package. Nos. 2527, 2532, Riding motorcycle in rain. Nos. 2528, 2533, Waving.

2006, June 1 Litho. *Perf. 14x14¾*
2524 A713 50c multi 1.00 1.00
a. Booklet pane of 1 1.75 —
2525 A713 50c multi 1.00 1.00
a. Booklet pane of 1 1.75 —
2526 A713 50c multi 1.00 1.00
a. Booklet pane of 1 1.75 —
2527 A713 50c multi 1.00 1.00
a. Booklet pane of 1 1.75 —
2528 A713 50c multi 1.00 1.00
a. Horiz. strip of 5, #2524-2528 5.25 5.25
b. Booklet pane of 1 1.75 —
Nos. 2524-2528 (5) 5.00 5.00

Booklet Stamps
Self-Adhesive
Serpentine Die Cut 11¼ Syncopated
2529 A713 50c multi 1.10 .90
2530 A713 50c multi 1.10 .90
2531 A713 50c multi 1.10 .90
2532 A713 50c multi 1.10 .90
2533 A713 50c multi 1.10 .90
a. Booklet pane, 2 each #2529-2533 11.50
b. Booklet pane, 4 each #2529-2533 22.50
c. Booklet pane, #2529-2533 5.75
Complete booklet, #2524a, 2525a, 2526a, 2527a, 2528b, 2533c 20.00
Nos. 2529-2533 (5) 5.50 4.50

Complete booklet sold for $9.95.

Worldwide Fund for Nature (WWF) A714

Designs: Nos. 2534, 2538, Humpback whale. Nos. 2535, 2539, Blue whale. $1.25, Fin whale. $1.85, Southern bottlenose whale.

2006, June 6 *Perf. 14x14¾*
2534 A714 50c multi 1.10 1.00
2535 A714 50c multi 1.10 1.00
a. Horiz. pair, #2534-2535 2.25 2.25
2536 A714 $1.25 multi 2.75 2.25
2537 A714 $1.85 multi 4.00 3.50
a. Souvenir sheet, #2534-2537 9.50 9.50
Nos. 2534-2537 (4) 8.95 7.75

Self-Adhesive
Serpentine Die Cut 11¼ Syncopated
Coil Stamps
2538 A714 50c multi 1.10 .95
2539 A714 50c multi 1.10 .95
a. Horiz. pair, #2538-2539 2.25

Booklet Stamps
2540 A714 $1.25 multi 2.75 2.25
a. Booklet pane of 5 14.50
2541 A714 $1.85 multi 4.00 3.50
a. Booklet pane of 5 20.00
Nos. 2538-2541 (4) 8.95 7.65

Types of 2006 With Personalized Photo at Right Like Type A692a

Designs: $1.25, Koala. $1.85, Royal Exhibition Building.

Serpentine Die Cut 11½x11¼ Syncopated
2006 Litho.
Self-Adhesive
2542 A707 $1.25 multi 3.75 3.75
2543 A708 $1.85 multi 4.50 4.50

Nos. 2542-2543 were sold in sheets of 20 and have personalized pictures and a straight edge at right, and lack separations between the stamp and the pictures. Sheets of 20 of No. 2542 sold for $38, and of No. 2543, $49.

Extreme Sports A715

Designs: 50c, Surfing. $1, Snowboarding. $1.45, Skateboarding. $2, Freestyle motocross.

2006, July 18 Litho. *Perf. 14x14¾*
2544 A715 50c multi 1.00 .90
2545 A715 $1 multi 2.25 1.75
2546 A715 $1.45 multi 3.25 2.75
2547 A715 $2 multi 4.25 4.25
Nos. 2544-2547 (4) 10.75 9.65

Cars and Trucks A716

Designs: Nos. 2548, 2553, 1917 Ford TT Truck. Nos. 2549, 2554, 1956 Holden FE. Nos. 2550, 2555, 1961 Morris 851. Nos. 2551, 2556, 1976 Holden Sandman HX. Nos. 2552, 2557, 1985 Toyota Land Cruiser FJ60.

2006, Aug. 15 *Perf. 14x14¾*
2548 A716 50c multi 1.00 1.00
a. Booklet pane of 4 4.25 —
2549 A716 50c multi 1.00 1.00
a. Booklet pane of 4 4.25 —
2550 A716 50c multi 1.00 1.00
a. Booklet pane of 4 4.25 —
2551 A716 50c multi 1.00 1.00
a. Booklet pane of 4 4.25 —
2552 A716 50c multi 1.00 1.00
a. Booklet pane of 4 4.25 —
Complete booklet, #2548a-2552a 22.50
b. Horiz. strip of 5, #2548-2552 5.25 5.25
Nos. 2548-2552 (5) 5.00 5.00

Booklet Stamps
Self-Adhesive
Serpentine Die Cut 11¼ Syncopated

2553 A716 50c multi 1.10 .90
a. Booklet pane of 10 11.50
b. Missing 2006 date
2554 A716 50c multi 1.10 .90
a. Booklet pane of 10 11.50
2555 A716 50c multi 1.10 .90
a. Booklet pane of 10 11.50
2556 A716 50c multi 1.10 .90
a. Booklet pane of 10 11.50
2557 A716 50c multi 1.10 .90
a. Booklet pane of 10 11.50
b. Booklet pane, 2 each #2553-2557 11.50
Nos. 2553-2557 (5) 5.50 4.50

Complete booklet containing Nos. 2548a-2552a sold for $10.95.

Rock Posters — A717

Designs: Nos. 2558a, 2559a, Sunbury Rock Festival, 1972. Nos. 2558b, 2559b, Magic Dirt Tour, 2002. Nos. 2558c, 2559c, The Masters Apprentices Parramatta concert, 1972. Nos. 2558d, 2559d, Goanna's Spirit of Place album, 1983. Nos. 2558e, 2559e, Angels, Sports and Paul Kelly and the Dots Latrobe concert, 1979. Nos. 2558f, 2559f, Midnight Oil, 1979. Nos. 2558g, 2559g, Big Day Out Festival, 2003. Nos. 2558h, 2559h, Apollo Bay Music Festival, 1999. Nos. 2558i, 2559i, Rolling Stones Australian Tour, 1973. Nos. 2558j, 2559j, Mental as Anything's Another Falcon Tour, 1990.

2006, Sept. 12 Litho. *Perf. 14½x14*

2558 Sheet of 10 10.00 10.00
a.-j. A717 50c Any single 1.00 1.00
k. Booklet pane of 2 #2558a 2.25 —
l. Booklet pane of 2 #2558b 2.25 —
m. Booklet pane of 2 #2558c 2.25 —
n. Booklet pane of 2 #2558d 2.25 —
o. Booklet pane of 2 #2558e 2.25 —
p. Booklet pane of 2 #2558f 2.25 —
q. Booklet pane of 2 #2558g 2.25 —
r. Booklet pane of 2 #2558h 2.25 —
s. Booklet pane of 2 #2558i 2.25 —
t. Booklet pane of 2 #2558j 2.25 —
Complete booklet, #2558k-2558t 22.00

Self-Adhesive
Serpentine Die Cut 11½x11¼ Syncopated

2559 Booklet pane of 10 10.50
a.-j. A717 50c Any single 1.00 1.00

Complete booklet containing Nos. 2558k-2558t sold for $10.95.

Dangerous Australian Wildlife A718

Designs: Nos. 2560, 2566, White shark. Nos. 2561, 2567, Eastern brown snake. Nos. 2562, 2568, Box jellyfish. Nos. 2563, 2569, Saltwater crocodile. Nos. 2564, 2570, Blue-ringed octopus. Nos. 2565, 2571, Yellow-bellied sea snake.

2006, Oct. 3 Litho. *Perf. 14x14¾*

2560 A718 50c multi 1.00 1.00
a. Booklet pane of 2 2.25 —
2561 A718 50c multi 1.00 1.00
2562 A718 50c multi 1.00 1.00
a. Booklet pane of 2 2.25 —
2563 A718 50c multi 1.00 1.00
a. Booklet pane of 2 2.25 —
2564 A718 50c multi 1.00 1.00
a. Horiz. strip of 5, #2560-2564 5.25 5.25
b. Booklet pane of 2 2.25 —
2565 A718 $1 multi 2.25 2.25
a. Booklet pane, 2 each #2561, 2565 6.50 —
b. Booklet pane, #2560-2565 (page 26) 7.50 —
c. Souvenir sheet, #2560-2565 7.75 7.75
Complete booklet, #2560a, 2562a, 2563a, 2564b, 2565a, 2565b 25.00
Nos. 2560-2565 (6) 7.25 7.25

Self-Adhesive
Serpentine Die Cut 11 Syncopated

2566 A718 50c multi 1.00 .90
2567 A718 50c multi 1.00 .90
2568 A718 50c multi 1.00 .90
2569 A718 50c multi 1.00 .90
2570 A718 50c multi 1.00 .90
a. Horiz. coil strip of 5, #2566-2570 5.25
b. Booklet pane, #2566-2570 5.25
2571 A718 $1 multi 2.25 1.75
a. Booklet pane of 5 11.00
Nos. 2566-2571 (6) 7.25 6.25

Complete booklet sold for $10.95. A souvenir sheet similar to No. 2565c containing partially perforated examples of Nos. 2560-2564 and a stamp that is assumed to be invalid depicting a red-back spider sold for $9.95. Value $20.

Television in Australia, 50th Anniv. A719

Television shows: Nos. 2572, 2577, IMT (In Melbourne Tonight). Nos. 2573, 2578, Homicide. Nos. 2574, 2579, Dateline. Nos. 2575, 2580, Neighbours. Nos. 2576, 2581, Kath & Kim.

2006, Oct. 24 Litho. *Perf. 14x14¾*

2572 A719 50c multi .90 .90
2573 A719 50c multi .90 .90
2574 A719 50c multi .90 .90
2575 A719 50c multi .90 .90
2576 A719 50c multi .90 .90
a. Horiz. strip of 5, #2572-2576 4.50 4.50
Nos. 2572-2576 (5) 4.50 4.50

Self-Adhesive
Serpentine Die Cut 11¼x11½ Syncopated

2577 A719 50c multi .90 .30
a. Booklet pane of 10 #2577 9.00
2578 A719 50c multi .90 .30
2579 A719 50c multi .90 .30
2580 A719 50c multi .90 .30
2581 A719 50c multi .90 .30
a. Booklet pane of 10 #2581 9.25
b. Booklet pane of 10, 2 each #2577-2581 9.25
c. Horiz. coil strip of 5, #2577-2581 4.50
Nos. 2577-2581 (5) 4.50 1.50

Melbourne Summer Olympics, 50th Anniv. A720

1956 Melbourne Olympics emblem and: No. 2582, Australia #291, Olympic torch. No. 2583, View of Melbourne across Yarra River, 2006, Olympic torch. No. 2584, Australia #290, runners. No. 2585, Collins Street, Melbourne, 2006, runners.

2006, Nov. 1 *Perf. 14¾x14*

2582 A720 50c multi .90 .70
2583 A720 50c multi .90 .70
a. Horiz. pair, #2582-2583 1.90 1.40
2584 A720 $1 multi 1.90 1.40
2585 A720 $1 multi 1.90 1.40
a. Horiz. pair, #2584-2585 3.75 2.75
Nos. 2582-2585 (4) 5.60 4.20

Christmas — A721

Designs: 45c, Madonna and Child. 50c, Magus with gift. $1.05, Shepherd and lamb.

2006, Nov. 1 *Perf. 14¾x14*

2586 A721 45c multi .80 .80
2587 A721 50c multi .90 .70
2588 A721 $1.05 multi 1.90 1.90
Nos. 2586-2588 (3) 3.60 3.40

Self-Adhesive
Booklet Stamps
Serpentine Die Cut 11½x11¼ Syncopated

2589 A721 45c multi .80 .30
a. Booklet pane of 20 16.00
2590 A721 $1.05 multi 1.90 .30
a. Booklet pane of 5 9.25

Australian Victory in 2006 Ashes Cricket Match — A722

Designs: 50c, Players celebrating. $1.85, Players with Ashes Urn.

2007, Jan. 16 Litho. *Perf. 14½x14*

2591 A722 50c multi .85 .85
a. Imperf. 1.60 1.60
2592 A722 $1.85 multi 3.50 3.50
a. Souvenir sheet, #2591-2592 4.50 4.50
b. Imperf. *15.00 12.00*
c. Booklet pane of 2, #2591a, 2592b 7.50 —
Complete booklet, #591a, 666b, 773a, 1084a, 1302b, 2345a, 2592c 32.00

Booklet Stamps
Self-Adhesive
Serpentine Die Cut 10¾x11¼ Syncopated

2593 A722 50c multi .90 .30
a. Booklet pane of 5 4.50
2594 A722 $1.85 multi 3.50 1.75
a. Booklet pane of 5 17.50
Nos. 2591-2594 (4) 8.75 6.40

Nos. 2591a, 2592b, 2592c issued 11/14/07. Complete booklet sold for $14.95 and was not made available to foreign addresses.

Horse Racing Personalities A723

Designs: Nos. 2595, 2607, Scobie Breasley, jockey, in silks. No. 2596, Breasley on horse. Nos. 2597, 2608, Bart Cummings, horse trainer, with binoculars. No. 2598, Cummings holding trophy. No. 2599, Roy Higgins, jockey, in silks. Nos. 2600, 2609, Higgins on horse. No. 2601, Bob Ingham, horse breeder. Nos. 2602, 2610, Ingham with horse. Nos. 2603, 2611, George Moore, jockey, in silks. No. 2604, Moore on horse. Nos. 2605, 2612, John Tapp, horse race announcer. No. 2606, Tapp with binoculars.

2007, Jan. 24 *Perf. 14½x14*

2595 A723 50c multi .90 .90
2596 A723 50c multi .90 .90
2597 A723 50c multi .90 .90
2598 A723 50c multi .90 .90
a. Block of 4, #2595-2598 3.75 3.75
2599 A723 50c multi .90 .90
2600 A723 50c multi .90 .90
2601 A723 50c multi .90 .90
2602 A723 50c multi .90 .90
a. Block of 4, #2599-2602 3.75 3.75
2603 A723 50c multi .90 .90
2604 A723 50c multi .90 .90
2605 A723 50c multi .90 .90
2606 A723 50c multi .90 .90
a. Block of 4, #2603-2606 3.75 3.75
Nos. 2595-2606 (12) 10.80 10.80

Booklet Stamps
Self-Adhesive
Serpentine Die Cut 11x11¼ Syncopated

2607 A723 50c multi .90 .30
2608 A723 50c multi .90 .30
a. Booklet pane of 10, 5 each #2607-2608 9.25
2609 A723 50c multi .90 .30
2610 A723 50c multi .90 .30
a. Booklet pane of 10, 5 each #2609-2610 9.25
2611 A723 50c multi .90 .30
2612 A723 50c multi .90 .30
a. Booklet pane of 10, 5 each #2611-2612 9.25
Nos. 2607-2612 (6) 5.40 1.80

Flowers — A724

Designs: Nos. 2613, 2617, 2621, Tasmanian Christmas bell. Nos. 2614, 2618, 2622, Green spider flower. Nos. 2615, 2619, 2623, Sturt's desert rose. Nos. 2616, 2620, 2624, Phebalium whitei.

2007, Feb. 13 Litho. *Perf. 14x14½*

2613 A724 50c multi .90 .90
2614 A724 50c multi .90 .90
2615 A724 50c multi .90 .90
2616 A724 50c multi .90 .90
a. Horiz. strip of 4, #2613-2616 3.75 3.75
Nos. 2613-2616 (4) 3.60 3.60

Self-Adhesive
Serpentine Die Cut 11¼

2617 A724 50c multi .90 .30
2618 A724 50c multi .90 .30
2619 A724 50c multi .90 .30
2620 A724 50c multi .90 .30
a. Horiz. coil strip of 4, #2617-2620 3.75
b. Booklet pane of 10, 3 each #2617-2618, 2 each #2619-2620 9.25
c. Booklet pane of 20, 5 each #2617-2620 18.50

Coil Stamps
Die Cut Perf. 12¾

2621 A724 50c multi .90 .30
2622 A724 50c multi .90 .30
2623 A724 50c multi .90 .30
2624 A724 50c multi .90 .30
a. Horiz. strip of 4, #2621-2624 3.75
Nos. 2617-2624 (8) 7.20 2.40

12th FINA World Swimming Championships, Melbourne — A725

2007, Feb. 20 *Perf. 14½x14*

2625 A725 50c multi .90 .90

Coil Stamp
Self-Adhesive
Serpentine Die Cut 11¼ Syncopated

2626 A725 50c multi .90 .30

Islands A726

Designs: 10c, Maria Island, Tasmania. 30c, Rottnest Island, Western Australia. $1.30, Green Island, Queensland. $1.95, Fraser Island, Queensland. $2.60, Kangaroo Island, South Australia. $3.85, Lord Howe Island, New South Wales.

2007, Mar. 5 *Perf. 14x14½*

2627 A726 10c multi .25 .25
2628 A726 30c multi .60 .30
2629 A726 $1.30 multi 2.25 2.25
2630 A726 $1.95 multi 3.50 3.50
2631 A726 $2.60 multi 4.50 2.25
2632 A726 $3.85 multi 7.00 3.50
Nos. 2627-2632 (6) 18.10 12.05

Booklet Stamps
Self-Adhesive
Serpentine Die Cut 11¼ Syncopated

2633 A726 $1.30 multi 2.25 .30
a. Booklet pane of 5 11.50
2634 A726 $1.95 multi 3.50 .30
a. Booklet pane of 5 17.50

Surf Life Saving Australia, Cent. A727

Designs: Nos. 2635, 2639, Female lifeguard. Nos. 2536, 2540, Male lifeguards. $1, Surf boat crew. $2, Nippers (junior lifeguards). $2.45, Inflatable rescue boat and crew, vert. (30x50mm).

2007, Mar. 6 Litho. *Perf. 14x14½*

2635 A727 50c multi .90 .90
a. Booklet pane of 1 1.25 —
2636 A727 50c multi .90 .90
a. Horiz. pair, #2635-2636 1.90 1.90
b. Booklet pane of 1 1.25 —
2637 A727 $1 multi 1.90 1.40
a. Booklet pane of 1 2.50 —

2638 A727 $2 multi 3.75 2.75
a. Booklet pane of 1 5.25 —
Nos. 2635-2638 (4) 7.45 5.95

Self-Adhesive
Coil Stamps (#2639-2640)
Serpentine Die Cut 11¼ Syncopated

2639 A727 50c multi .90 .30
2640 A727 50c multi .90 .30
a. Horiz. pair, #2639-2640 1.90

Litho. With Three-Dimensional Plastic Affixed

2641 A727 $2.45 multi 4.25 4.25
a. Souvenir sheet of 2 8.50
b. Booklet pane, as "a," with rouletting at left of pane 12.50
Complete booklet, #2635a, 2636b, 2637a, 2638a, 2641b 23.00

Complete booklet sold for $12.95. No. 2641a does not have rouletting at left side of sheet.

Signs of the Zodiac — A728

Designs: Nos. 2642, 2654, 2665B, Aries. Nos. 2643, 2655, 2665C, Taurus. Nos. 2644, 2656, 2665D, Gemini. Nos. 2645, 2657, 2665E, Cancer. Nos. 2646, 2658, 2665F, Leo. Nos. 2647, 2659, 2665G, Virgo. Nos. 2648, 2660, 2665H, Libra. Nos. 2649, 2661, 2665I, Scorpio. Nos. 2650, 2662, 2665J, Sagittarius. Nos. 2651, 2663, 2665K, Capricorn. Nos. 2652, 2664, 2665L, Aquarius. Nos. 2653, 2665, 2665M, Pisces.

2007, Apr. 3 Litho. *Perf. 14½x14*

2642 A728 50c multi .95 .95
2643 A728 50c multi .95 .95
2644 A728 50c multi .95 .95
2645 A728 50c multi .95 .95
a. Block of 4, #2642-2645 4.00
2646 A728 50c multi .95 .95
2647 A728 50c multi .95 .95
2648 A728 50c multi .95 .95
2649 A728 50c multi .95 .95
a. Block of 4, #2646-2649 4.00
2650 A728 50c multi .95 .95
2651 A728 50c multi .95 .95
2652 A728 50c multi .95 .95
2653 A728 50c multi .95 .95
a. Block of 4, #2650-2653 4.00
Nos. 2642-2653 (12) 11.40 11.40

Booklet Stamps
Self-Adhesive
Serpentine Die Cut 11¼ Syncopated

2654 A728 50c multi 1.00 .30
a. Booklet pane of 10 10.50
2655 A728 50c multi 1.00 .30
a. Booklet pane of 10 10.50
2656 A728 50c multi 1.00 .30
a. Booklet pane of 10 10.50
2657 A728 50c multi 1.00 .30
a. Booklet pane of 10 10.50
2658 A728 50c multi 1.00 .30
a. Booklet pane of 10 10.50
2659 A728 50c multi 1.00 .30
a. Booklet pane of 10 10.50
2660 A728 50c multi 1.00 .30
a. Booklet pane of 10 10.50
2661 A728 50c multi 1.00 .30
a. Booklet pane of 10 10.50
2662 A728 50c multi 1.00 .30
a. Booklet pane of 10 10.50
2663 A728 50c multi 1.00 .30
a. Booklet pane of 10 10.50
2664 A728 50c multi 1.00 .30
a. Booklet pane of 10 10.50
2665 A728 50c multi 1.00 .30
a. Booklet pane of 10 10.50
Nos. 2654-2665 (12) 12.00 3.60

With Personalized Photo at Right Like Type A692a
Serpentine Die Cut 11½x11¼ Syncopated
Self-Adhesive

2665B A728 50c multi 2.50 *2.50*
2665C A728 50c multi 2.50 *2.50*
2665D A728 50c multi 2.50 *2.50*
2665E A728 50c multi 2.50 *2.50*
2665F A728 50c multi 2.50 *2.50*
2665G A728 50c multi 2.50 *2.50*
2665H A728 50c multi 2.50 *2.50*
2665I A728 50c multi 2.50 *2.50*
2665J A728 50c multi 2.50 *2.50*
2665K A728 50c multi 2.50 *2.50*
2665L A728 50c multi 2.50 *2.50*
2665M A728 50c multi 2.50 *2.50*
Nos. 2665B-2665M (12) 30.00 *30.00*

Nos. 2665B-2665M were sold in sheets of 20 and have personalized pictures and a straight edge at right, and lack separations between the stamp and the pictures. Sheets of 20 of Nos. 2665B-2665M each sold for $23.

Travel Posters of the 1930s — A729

Designs: 50c, At the Beach, by Percy Trompf. $1, Fishing, by John Vickery. $2, Riding in the Country, by James Northfield. $2.45, Winter Sport, by Northfield.

2007, Apr. 10 *Perf. 14½x14*

2666 A729 50c multi .95 .75
2667 A729 $1 multi 2.00 1.60
a. Booklet pane of 2, #2666-2667 3.25 —
2668 A729 $2 multi 4.00 3.00
2669 A729 $2.45 multi 5.00 3.75
a. Booklet pane of 4, #2666-2669 12.00 —
b. Booklet pane of 2, #2666, 2669 6.00 —
Complete booklet, #2667a, 2669a, 2669b 21.00
Nos. 2666-2669 (4) 11.95 9.10

Queen Elizabeth II, 81st Birthday A730

2007, Apr. 18 *Perf. 14x14½*

2670 A730 50c multi .95 .75

Shipwrecks A731

Designs: 50c, Admella, 1859. $1, Loch Ard, 1878. $2, Dunbar, 1857.

2007, May 1 Litho. *Perf. 14x14½*

2671 A731 50c multi .95 .70
2672 A731 $1 multi 2.00 1.60
2673 A731 $2 multi 4.00 3.25
Nos. 2671-2673 (3) 6.95 5.55

Animals Type of 2006 and

Sydney Harbour Bridge — A732

Design: $1.30, Yellow-footed rock wallaby, vert.

2007 Litho. *Perf. 14½x14*

2674 A707 $1.30 multi 2.50 2.50
2675 A732 $1.95 multi 3.75 3.75
a. Imperf. x perf. 14 x imperf. x imperf. 3.75 3.75
b. Souvenir sheet, #2675, 2675a 7.50 7.50
c. Souvenir sheet, 2 #2675 7.75 7.75
d. As "b," with Sberatel Exhib., Prague ovpt. 9.75 9.75
e. As "c," with Bangkok 2007 Exhib. ovpt. 9.75 9.75

Self-Adhesive
Booklet Stamps
Serpentine Die Cut 11¼ Syncopated

2676 A707 $1.30 multi 3.25 3.25
a. Booklet pane of 2 6.25
Complete booklet, 4 #2676a 25.00
2677 A732 $1.95 multi 4.00 4.00
a. Booklet pane of 1 4.00
b. Booklet pane of 2 8.00
Complete booklet, #2677a, 3 #2677b 29.00

With Personalized Photo at Right Like Type A692a
Serpentine Die Cut 11½x11¼

2678 A707 $1.30 multi 4.50 4.50
2679 A732 $1.95 multi 5.75 5.75

Issued: Nos. 2674-2679, 5/8; No. 2675b, 6/15. Complete booklet containing No. 2676 sold for $12.95. It contains four different examples of No. 2676a. The booklet containing No. 2677 sold for $14.95, and it contains three different examples of No. 2677b.

No. 2675c issued 6/15. Margin of No. 2675c is overprinted in gold with emblem for Sydney Philatelic Show.

Nos. 2678-2679 were sold in sheets of 20 and have personalized pictures and a straight edge at right, and lack separations between the stamp and the picture. A sheet of 20 of No. 2678 sold for $39; of No. 2679, $51.

Circus Performers — A733

Circus acts: Nos. 2680, 2685, 2690, Torch juggler. Nos. 2681, 2686, 2691, Contortionist. Nos. 2682, 2687, 2692, Trapeze artists. Nos. 2683, 2688, 2693, Acrobats. Nos. 2684, 2689, 2694, Human cannonball.

2007, May 15 Litho. *Perf. 14½x14*

2680 A733 50c multi .95 .95
2681 A733 50c multi .95 .95
a. Booklet pane of 2 2.50 —
2682 A733 50c multi .95 .95
a. Booklet pane of 2 2.50 —
2683 A733 50c multi .95 .95
a. Booklet pane of 2 2.50 —
2684 A733 50c multi .95 .95
a. Horiz. strip of 5, #2680-2684 5.00 5.00
b. Booklet pane, #2680-2684 6.25 —
c. Booklet pane, 2 each # 2680, 2684 5.25 —
Nos. 2680-2684 (5) 4.75 4.75

Booklet Stamps
Self-Adhesive
Serpentine Die Cut 11¼ Syncopated

2685 A733 50c multi 1.10 .40
2686 A733 50c multi 1.10 .40
2687 A733 50c multi 1.10 .40
2688 A733 50c multi 1.10 .40
2689 A733 50c multi 1.10 .40
a. Booklet pane, 2 each #2685-2689 11.50

Litho. With Foil Application

2690 A733 50c multi 1.40 1.40
2691 A733 50c multi 1.40 1.40
2692 A733 50c multi 1.40 1.40
2693 A733 50c multi 1.40 1.40
2694 A733 50c multi 1.40 1.40
a. Booklet pane, #2690-2694 7.25
Complete booklet, #2681a, 2682a, 2683a, 2684b, 2684c, 2694a 25.00
Nos. 2685-2694 (10) 12.50 9.00

Complete booklet sold for $12.95. Nos. 2690-2694 each have gold stars and a portion of stamp covered by varnish.

Tourist Attractions — A734

Designs: Nos. 2695, 2700, Big Guitar, Tamworth, New South Wales. Nos. 2696, 2701, Big Lobster, Kingston Southeast, South Australia. Nos. 2697, 2702, Big Banana, Coffs Harbour, New South Wales. Nos. 2698, 2703, Big Merino Sheep, Goulburn, New South Wales. Nos. 2699, 2704, Big Pineapple, Nambour, Queensland.

2007, June 5 *Perf. 14½x14*

2695 A734 50c multi .95 .95
2696 A734 50c multi .95 .95
2697 A734 50c multi .95 .95
2698 A734 50c multi .95 .95
2699 A734 50c multi .95 .95
a. Horiz. strip of 5, #2695-2699 5.00 5.00
Nos. 2695-2699 (5) 4.75 4.75

Booklet Stamps
Self-Adhesive
Serpentine Die Cut 11¼ Syncopated

2700 A734 50c multi 1.10 .40
2701 A734 50c multi 1.10 .40
2702 A734 50c multi 1.10 .40
2703 A734 50c multi 1.10 .40
2704 A734 50c multi 1.10 .40
a. Booklet pane, 2 each #2700-2704 11.50
Nos. 2700-2704 (5) 5.50 2.00

Endangered Animals — A735

Designs: No. 2705, Gray-headed flying fox. No. 2706, Mountain pygmy possum. $1.25, Flatback turtle, horiz. $1.30, Wandering albatross, horiz.

2007, June 26 *Perf. 14½x14*

2705 A735 50c multi .95 .70
a. Booklet pane of 2 #2705 2.25 —
2706 A735 50c multi .95 .70
a. Horiz. pair, #2705-2706 2.00 1.40
b. Booklet pane of 2 #2706 2.25 —

Perf. 14x14½

2707 A735 $1.25 multi 2.40 1.90
a. Booklet pane of 2 5.75 —
2708 A735 $1.30 multi 2.50 2.00
a. Booklet pane of 2 6.00 —
Complete booklet, #793c, 794b, 2705a, 2706b, 2707a, 2708a 23.00

Complete booklet sold for $10.95.

Modern Architecture A736

Designs: No. 2709, Former ICI House, Melbourne. No. 2710, Academy of Science, Canberra. $1, Council House, Perth. $2.45, Sydney Opera House.

2007, July 10 *Perf. 14x14¾*

2709 A736 50c multi .95 .70
2710 A736 50c multi .95 .70
a. Horiz. pair, #2709-2710 2.00 1.40
b, Additionally dated "2013" (#2710c) 1.10 1.10
c. Booklet pane of 2 of #2710b 2.25 —
2711 A736 $1 multi 2.00 1.60
2712 A736 $2.45 multi 5.00 3.75
a. Souvenir sheet, #2709-2712 9.00 9.00

Due to the arrangement of the stamps on No. 2712a, the left side of the top row of perfs on each of the stamps is perf. 14 and the right side of the top row is perf. 14¾.

No. 2712a exists imperf from a telephone drawing at a substantial premium over face value. Value for single souvenir sheet, $17.50.

Issued: Nos. 2710b, 2710c, 3/5/13. No. 2710c was issued in booklet along with Nos. 1939c, 2869e, 3107c, 3349b and 3877a.

Markets — A737

Designs: Nos. 2713, 2718, Queen Victoria Market, Melbourne. Nos. 2714, 2719, Rusty's Market, Cairns. Nos. 2715, 2720, Sydney Fish Market. Nos. 2716, 2721, Adelaide Central Market. Nos. 2717, 2722, Hume Murray Farmers Market, Albury Wodonga.

2007, July 24 *Perf. 14½x14*

2713 A737 50c multi .95 .95
2714 A737 50c multi .95 .95
2715 A737 50c multi .95 .95
2716 A737 50c multi .95 .95
2717 A737 50c multi .95 .95
a. Horiz. strip of 5, #2713-2717 5.00 5.00
Nos. 2713-2717 (5) 4.75 4.75

Booklet Stamps
Self-Adhesive
Serpentine Die Cut 11¼ Syncopated

2718 A737 50c multi 1.10 .40
a. Booklet pane of 10 11.50
2719 A737 50c multi 1.10 .40
a. Booklet pane of 10 11.50
2720 A737 50c multi 1.10 .40
a. Booklet pane of 10 11.50
2721 A737 50c multi 1.10 .40
a. Booklet pane of 10 11.50
2722 A737 50c multi 1.10 .40
a. Booklet pane of 10 11.50
Nos. 2718-2722 (5) 5.50 2.00

Asia-Pacific Economic Cooperation Forum, Sydney A738

2007, Aug. 28 ***Perf. 14x14½***
2723 A738 50c multi .95 .95

Coil Stamp
Self-Adhesive
Serpentine Die Cut 11¼x11½ Syncopated

2724 A738 50c multi .95 .30

Special Air Service, 50th Anniv. A739

2007, Sept. 4 ***Perf. 14x14½***
2725 A739 50c multi .95 .75

This stamp exists with "SAS" insignia embossed with gold foil. This was a restricted issue sold at far more than face value by the Philatelic Bureau.

Botanical Gardens A740

Designs: Nos. 2726, 2731, Brisbane Botanic Gardens, Mt. Coot-tha. Nos. 2727, 2732, Kings Park and Botanic Gardens, Perth. Nos. 2728, 2733, Royal Botanic Gardens and Domain, Sydney. Nos. 2729, 2734, Royal Botanic Gardens, Melbourne. Nos. 2730, 2735, Botanic Gardens of Adelaide.

2007, Sept. 12 ***Perf. 14x14½***
2726 A740 50c multi .95 .95
a. Booklet pane of 4 4.25 —
2727 A740 50c multi .95 .95
a. Booklet pane of 4 4.25 —
2728 A740 50c multi .95 .95
a. Booklet pane of 4 4.25 —
2729 A740 50c multi .95 .95
a. Booklet pane of 4 4.25 —
2730 A740 50c multi .95 .95
a. Booklet pane of 4 4.25 —
Complete booklet, #2726a-2730a 22.00
b. Horiz. strip of 5, #2726-2730 5.00 5.00
Nos. 2726-2730 (5) 4.75 4.75

Self-Adhesive
Serpentine Die Cut 11¼x11½ Syncopated

2731 A740 50c multi .95 .30
2732 A740 50c multi .95 .30
2733 A740 50c multi .95 .30
2734 A740 50c multi .95 .30
2735 A740 50c multi .95 .30
a. Horiz. coil strip of 5, #2731-2735 5.00
b. Booklet pane of 20, 5 each #2731-2735, + 10 labels 19.50
Nos. 2731-2735 (5) 4.75 1.50

Complete booklet sold for $10.95.

Space Age, 50th Anniv. — A741

Designs: Nos. 2736, 2743, Sputnik, 1957. Nos. 2737, 2744, First space walk, 1965. Nos. 2738, 2745, First Moon walk, 1969. Nos. 2739, 2746, Voyager, 1977. Nos. 2740, 2747, International Space Station, 1998. Nos. 2741, 2742a, Hubble Space Telescope, 1990, horiz.

2007, Oct. 2 Litho. ***Perf. 14½x14***
2736 A741 50c multi 1.00 1.00
a. Booklet pane of 2 2.40 —
2737 A741 50c multi 1.00 1.00
a. Booklet pane of 2 2.40 —
2738 A741 50c multi 1.00 1.00
a. Booklet pane of 2 2.40 —
2739 A741 50c multi 1.00 1.00
a. Booklet pane of 2 2.40 —
2740 A741 50c multi 1.00 1.00
a. Horiz. strip of 5, #2736-2740 5.25 5.25
b. Booklet pane of 2 2.40 —
c. Booklet pane of 5, #2736-2740 6.00 —
2741 A741 $1 multi, 50x30mm 2.25 2.25
a. Booklet pane of 2 5.00 —
Complete booklet, #2736a, 2737a, 2738a, 2739a, 2740b, 2740c, 2741a 23.00
Nos. 2736-2741 (6) 7.25 7.25

Souvenir Sheet

2742 Sheet of 6, #2736-2740, 2742a 7.50 7.50
a. A741 $1 multi, 52x43mm 2.25 2.25

A souvenir sheet in the 50c denomination exists. It was sold in a restricted sale with a normal souvenir sheet and a coin at a price far in advance of face value.

Self-Adhesive
Booklet Stamps
Serpentine Die Cut 11¼ Syncopated

2743 A741 50c multi 1.00 .30
2744 A741 50c multi 1.00 .30
2745 A741 50c multi 1.00 .30
2746 A741 50c multi 1.00 .30
2747 A741 50c multi 1.00 .30
a. Coil strip of 5, #2743-2747 5.25
b. Booklet pane, 2 each #2743-2747 10.00
Nos. 2743-2747 (5) 5.00 1.50

Complete booklet sold for $10.95.

Trailer Campers A742

People and trailer campers from: Nos. 2748, 2753, 1950s. Nos. 2749, 2754, 1960s. Nos. 2750, 2755, 1970s. Nos. 2751, 2756, 1980s. Nos. 2752, 2757, Today.

2007, Oct. 16 ***Perf. 14x14½***
2748 A742 50c multi 1.10 1.10
a. Booklet pane of 4 5.00 —
2749 A742 50c multi 1.10 1.10
a. Booklet pane, 2 each #2748-2749 5.00 —
2750 A742 50c multi 1.10 1.10
a. Booklet pane of 4 5.00 —
2751 A742 50c multi 1.10 1.10
a. Booklet pane, 2 each #2750-2751 5.00 —
2752 A742 50c multi 1.10 1.10
a. Horiz. strip of 5, #2748-2752 5.50 5.50
b. Booklet pane of 4 5.00 —
Complete booklet, #2748a, 2749a, 2750a, 2751a, 2752b 25.00
Nos. 2748-2752 (5) 5.50 5.50

Self-Adhesive
Booklet Stamps
Serpentine Die Cut 11¼ Syncopated

2753 A742 50c multi 1.10 .30
a. Booklet pane of 10 11.00 —
2754 A742 50c multi 1.10 .30
a. Booklet pane of 10 11.00 —
2755 A742 50c multi 1.10 .30
a. Booklet pane of 10 11.00 —
2756 A742 50c multi 1.10 .30
a. Booklet pane of 10 11.00 —
2757 A742 50c multi 1.10 .30
a. Booklet pane of 10 11.00 —
b. Booklet pane, 2 each #2753-2757 11.00 —
Nos. 2753-2757 (5) 5.50 1.50

Complete booklet sold for $10.95.

Christmas — A743

Designs of past Australian Christmas stamps with original denominations removed: Nos. 2758, 2763, 2768, #669. Nos. 2759, 2764, 2769, #1195. Nos. 2760, 2765, #1567. Nos. 2761, 2766, #306, horiz. Nos. 2762, 2767, 2770, #931.

Perf. 14½x14, 14x14½
2007, Nov. 1 **Litho.**
2758 A743 45c multi .95 .95
a. Booklet pane of 4 4.25 —
2759 A743 45c multi .95 .95
a. Booklet pane of 4 4.25 —
2760 A743 45c multi .95 .95
a. Horiz. pair, #2759-2760 2.00 2.00
b. Booklet pane of 4 4.25 —
2761 A743 50c multi 1.10 1.10
a. Booklet pane of 2 2.25 —
2762 A743 $1.10 multi 2.40 2.40
a. Booklet pane of 1 2.50 —
Nos. 2758-2762 (5) 6.35 6.35

Self-Adhesive
Serpentine Die Cut 11¼ Syncopated

2763 A743 45c multi .95 .30
a. With varnish block over stamp vignette .95 .30
2764 A743 45c multi .95 .30
a. Booklet pane of 20 20.00
2765 A743 45c multi .95 .95
a. Booklet pane of 20 20.00
2766 A743 50c multi 1.10 1.10
a. Booklet pane of 5 5.50
2767 A743 $1.10 multi 2.40 2.40
a. Booklet pane of 5 12.00
b. Souvenir sheet, #2763-2767 6.50
c. Booklet pane, #2763-2767 7.00
Complete booklet, #2758a, 2759a, 2760b, 2761a, 2762a, 2767c 25.00
Nos. 2763-2767 (5) 6.35 5.05

Complete booklet sold for $10.95. Size of No. 2767b is 156x100mm. Size of No. 2767c is 156x104mm.

With Personalized Photo at Right Like Type A692a
Serpentine Die Cut 11½x11¼ Syncopated

2768 A743 45c multi 2.40 2.40
2769 A743 45c multi 2.40 2.40
2770 A743 $1.10 multi 3.75 3.75
Nos. 2768-2770 (3) 8.55 8.55

Nos. 2768-2770 were sold in sheets of 20 and have personalized pictures and a straight edge at right, and lack separations between the stamp and the pictures. Sheets of 20 of Nos. 2768 and 2769 sold for $22, and of No. 2770, $35.

A booklet entitled "Behind the Stamp," which contained four panes, sold for $19.95. The panes were in two designs, one containing Nos. 740, 1164, 1193, 1891 and a litho. reproduction of No. 277, the other containing Nos. 400, 616-617, 882, 1063 and a reproduction of No. 367. The stamps within both panes were dated "2007" and the panes were either perforated at a different gauge than the original stamps or imperforate.

Red Rose — A744

2008, Jan. 15 Litho. ***Perf. 14***
2771 A744 50c multi 1.00 1.00

Litho. With Foil Application
Serpentine Die Cut 11¼ Syncopated
Self-Adhesive

2772 A744 50c multi 1.00 .30

Booklet Stamp
Litho.

2773 A744 50c multi 1.10 .30
a. Booklet pane of 4 4.50
Complete booklet, 5 #2773a 22.50

With Personalized Photo at Right Like Type A692a
Serpentine Die Cut 11½x11¼ Syncopated

2774 A744 50c multi 2.40 2.40

No. 2772 was printed in a sheet of 10 + 10 labels, having rose-scented scratch and sniff areas on the rose and the labels. No. 2773 lacks the scratch and sniff areas. The complete booklet, which sold for $10.95, contains five examples of No. 2773a, each with a different margin.

No. 2774 was sold in sheets of 20 for $23 and have personalized pictures and a straight edge at right, and lack separations between the stamp and the personalized photo.

Philanthropists A745

Designs: Nos. 2775, 2782, Dame Elisabeth Murdoch. Nos. 2776, 2781, Victor and Loti Smogron. Nos. 2777, 2780, Lady Mary Fairfax. Nos. 2778, 2779, Frank Lowy.

2008, Jan. 23 Litho. ***Perf. 14¾x14***
2775 A745 50c multi 1.25 1.25
2776 A745 50c multi 1.25 1.25
2777 A745 50c multi 1.25 1.25
2778 A745 50c multi 1.25 1.25
a. Horiz. strip of 4, #2775-2778 5.00 5.00
Nos. 2775-2778 (4) 5.00 5.00

Coil Stamps
Self-Adhesive
Serpentine Die Cut 11¼ Syncopated

2779 A745 50c multi 1.00 .30
2780 A745 50c multi 1.00 .30
2781 A745 50c multi 1.00 .30
2782 A745 50c multi 1.00 .30
a. Vert. strip of 4, #2779-2782 4.00
Nos. 2779-2782 (4) 4.00 1.20

Organ and Tissue Donation — A746

2008, Feb. 5 ***Perf. 14¾x14***
2783 A746 50c multi 1.10 1.10

Booklet Stamp
Self-Adhesive
Serpentine Die Cut 11¼ Syncopated

2784 A746 50c multi 1.10 .30
a. Booklet pane of 10 11.00

Scouting in Australia, Cent. A747

Australian Scouting emblem and: 50c, Four scouts near tent. $1.35, Scouts from various nations. $2, Lord Robert Baden-Powell.

2008, Feb. 19 ***Perf. 14***
2785 A747 50c multi 1.10 1.10
2786 A747 $1.35 multi 2.75 2.75
2787 A747 $2 multi 4.25 4.25
a. Perf. 14x14½ 4.25 4.25
b. Souvenir sheet, 2 #2787a 8.50 8.50
Nos. 2785-2787 (3) 8.10 8.10

Self-Adhesive
Serpentine Die Cut 11¼ Syncopated
Coil Stamp

2788 A747 50c multi 1.10 .30

Booklet Stamps

2789 A747 $1.35 multi 2.75 1.40
a. Booklet pane of 5 14.50
2790 A747 $2 multi 4.25 2.25
a. Booklet pane of 5 22.00
Nos. 2788-2790 (3) 8.10 3.95

Canberra Stamp Show (No. 2787b).

Gorges — A748

Designs: $1.35, Grose River Gorge, New South Wales. $2, Walpa Gorge, Northern Territory. $2.70, Katherine Gorge, Northern Territory, horiz. $4, Geikie Gorge, Western Australia.

2008, Mar. 3 Litho. *Perf. 14*

2791 A748 $1.35 multi 2.75 2.75
2792 A748 $2 multi 4.25 4.25
2793 A748 $2.70 multi 5.75 2.75
2794 A748 $4 multi 8.50 4.25
Nos. 2791-2794 (4) 21.25 14.00

Booklet Stamps (#2795-2796)
Self-Adhesive
Serpentine Die Cut 11½x11¼ Syncopated

2795 A748 $1.35 multi 7.50 5.00
a. Booklet pane of 5 37.50
b. Booklet pane of 2 15.00 —
Complete booklet, 4 #2795b 68.00
2796 A748 $2 multi 9.00 7.50
a. Booklet pane of 5 45.00
b. Booklet pane of 2 18.00 —
Complete booklet, 4 #2796b 72.00

With Personalized Photo at Right Like Type A692a

2797 A748 $1.35 multi *8.00 8.00*
2798 A748 $2 multi *12.00 12.00*

Nos. 2797-2798 each were sold in sheets of 20 and have personalized pictures and a straight edge at right, and lack separations between the stamp and the personalized photo. Sheets of 20 of No. 2797 sold for $40, and of No. 2798, $52.

Complete booklet containing No. 2795b sold for $10.95, and containing No. 2796b, $16.95. Each booklet contains four panes with differing margins.

World Youth Day — A749

Various depictions of Pope Benedict XVI with "08" in: 50c, Light blue. $1.35, Pink. $2, Light green.

2008, Mar. 4 *Perf. 14*

2799 A749 50c multi 1.10 .85
2800 A749 $1.35 multi 2.75 2.75
2801 A749 $2 multi 4.25 4.25
Nos. 2799-2801 (3) 8.10 7.85

Booklet Stamps (#2802-2803)
Self-Adhesive
Serpentine Die Cut 11½x11¼ Syncopated

2802 A749 $1.35 multi 2.75 .30
a. Booklet pane of 5 14.25
2803 A749 $2 multi 4.25 2.25
a. Booklet pane of 5 22.00

With Personalized Photo at Right Like Type A692a

2804 A749 50c multi 3.00 3.00
2805 A749 $1.35 multi 6.00 6.00
2806 A749 $2 multi 8.50 8.50
Nos. 2804-2806 (3) 17.50 17.50

Nos. 2804-2806 each were sold in sheets of 20 and have personalized pictures and a straight edge at right, and lack separations between the stamp and the personalized photo. Sheets of 20 of No. 2804 sold for $23, No. 2805, sold for $40, and No. 2806 sold for $52.

Rugby League, Cent. — A750

Players and teams: Nos. 2807, 2823, Andrew Ryan, Bulldogs. Nos. 2808, 2824, Scott Prince, Titans. Nos. 2809, 2825, Brett Kimmorley, Sharks. Nos. 2810, 2826, Danny Buderus, Knights. Nos. 2811, 2827, Johnathan Thurston, Cowboys. Nos. 2812, 2828, Darren Lockyer, Broncos. Nos. 2813, 2829, Matt Orford, Sea Eagles. Nos. 2814, 2830, Cameron Smith, Storm. Nos. 2815, 2831, Craig Fitzgibbon, Roosters. Nos. 2816, 2832, Alan Tongue, Raiders. Nos. 2817, 2833, Dean Widders, Rabbitohs. Nos. 2818, 2834, Tony Puletua, Panthers. Nos. 2819, 2835, Mark Gasnier, Dragons. Nos. 2820, 2836, Nathan Cayless, Eels. Nos. 2821, 2837, Robbie Farah, Wests Tigers. Nos. 2822, 2838, Steve Price, Warriors.

2008, Mar. 24 *Perf. 14*

2807 A750 50c multi 1.10 1.10
2808 A750 50c multi 1.10 1.10
2809 A750 50c multi 1.10 1.10
2810 A750 50c multi 1.10 1.10
a. Block of 4, #2807-2810 4.50 4.50
2811 A750 50c multi 1.10 1.10
2812 A750 50c multi 1.10 1.10
2813 A750 50c multi 1.10 1.10
2814 A750 50c multi 1.10 1.10
a. Block of 4, #2811-2814 4.50 4.50
2815 A750 50c multi 1.10 1.10
2816 A750 50c multi 1.10 1.10
2817 A750 50c multi 1.10 1.10
2818 A750 50c multi 1.10 1.10
a. Block of 4, #2815-2818 4.50 4.50
2819 A750 50c multi 1.10 1.10
2820 A750 50c multi 1.10 1.10
2821 A750 50c multi 1.10 1.10
2822 A750 50c multi 1.10 1.10
a. Block of 4, #2819-2822 4.50 4.50
Nos. 2807-2822 (16) 17.60 17.60

Booklet Stamps
Self-Adhesive
Serpentine Die Cut 11 Syncopated

2823 A750 50c multi 1.10 .30
a. Booklet pane of 10 11.00
2824 A750 50c multi 1.10 .30
a. Booklet pane of 10 11.00
2825 A750 50c multi 1.10 .30
a. Booklet pane of 10 11.00
2826 A750 50c multi 1.10 .30
a. Booklet pane of 10 11.00
2827 A750 50c multi 1.10 .30
a. Booklet pane of 10 11.00
2828 A750 50c multi 1.10 .30
a. Booklet pane of 10 11.00
2829 A750 50c multi 1.10 .30
a. Booklet pane of 10 11.00
2830 A750 50c multi 1.10 .30
a. Booklet pane of 10 11.00
2831 A750 50c multi 1.10 .30
a. Booklet pane of 10 11.00
2832 A750 50c multi 1.10 .30
a. Booklet pane of 10 11.00
2833 A750 50c multi 1.10 .30
a. Booklet pane of 10 11.00
2834 A750 50c multi 1.10 .30
a. Booklet pane of 10 11.00
2835 A750 50c multi 1.10 .30
a. Booklet pane of 10 11.00
2836 A750 50c multi 1.10 .30
a. Booklet pane of 10 11.00
2837 A750 50c multi 1.10 .30
a. Booklet pane of 10 11.00
2838 A750 50c multi 1.10 .30
a. Booklet pane of 10 11.00
b. Booklet pane of 20, #2823-2829, 2831-2838, 5 #2830 22.00
Nos. 2823-2838 (16) 17.60 4.80

A booklet containing one Rugby League dollar coin, and panes containing Nos. 2810a, 2814a, 2818a, 2822a, and four No. 2814, each in perf. 14½x14, sold for $15.95.

Heavy Haulers — A751

Designs: Nos. 2839, 2844, 2849, Excavator. Nos. 2840, 2845, 2850, Dump truck. Nos. 2841, 2846, 2851, Road train. Nos. 2842, 2847, 2852, Locomotive and ore cars. Nos. 2843, 2848, 2853, Ore carrier MS Berge Stahl.

2008, Apr. 1 *Perf. 14*
Without White Frames

2839 A751 50c multi 1.10 1.10
2840 A751 50c multi 1.10 1.10
2841 A751 50c multi 1.10 1.10
2842 A751 50c multi 1.10 1.10
2843 A751 50c multi 1.10 1.10
a. Horiz. strip of 5, #2839-2843 5.50 5.50
Nos. 2839-2843 (5) 5.50 5.50

Booklet Stamps
Self-Adhesive
Serpentine Die Cut 11 Syncopated

2844 A751 50c multi 1.10 .60
2845 A751 50c multi 1.10 .60
2846 A751 50c multi 1.10 .60
2847 A751 50c multi 1.10 .60
2848 A751 50c multi 1.10 .60
a. Booklet pane, 4 each #2844-2848 22.00

Coil Stamps
With White Frames

2849 A751 50c multi 1.10 .60
2850 A751 50c multi 1.10 .60
2851 A751 50c multi 1.10 .60
2852 A751 50c multi 1.10 .60
2853 A751 50c multi 1.10 .60
a. Vert. strip of 5, #2849-2853 5.50
Nos. 2844-2853 (10) 11.00 6.00

ANZAC Day — A752

Designs: Nos. 2854, 2863, Veterans marching. Nos. 2855, 2862, Laying of wreaths at memorial. Nos. 2856, 2861, Buglers. Nos. 2857, 2860, Veteran holding child. Nos. 2858, 2859, Young people at Gallipoli.

2008, Apr. 16 *Perf. 14*

2854 A752 50c multi 1.10 1.10
a. Perf. 14¾x14 1.10 1.10
b. Booklet pane, 4 #2854a 5.00 —
2855 A752 50c multi 1.10 1.10
a. Perf. 14¾x14 1.10 1.10
b. Booklet pane, 4 #2855a 5.00 —
c. Souvenir sheet, 2 each #2854-2855, perf. 14 4.50 4.50
2856 A752 50c multi 1.10 1.10
a. Perf. 14¾x14 1.10 1.10
b. Booklet pane, 4 #2856a 5.00 —
c. Souvenir sheet of 4 #2856a 4.50 4.50
d. Souvenir sheet, 2 each #2855-2856, perf. 14 4.50 4.50
2857 A752 50c multi 1.10 1.10
a. Perf. 14¾x14 1.10 1.10
b. Booklet pane, 4 #2857a 5.00 —
2858 A752 50c multi 1.10 1.10
a. Perf. 14¾x14 1.10 1.10
b. Booklet pane, 4 #2858a 5.00 —
Complete booklet, #2854b-2858b 25.00
c. Souvenir sheet, #2854a-2858a 5.50
d. Horiz. strip of 5, #2854-2858 5.50 5.50
Nos. 2854-2858 (5) 5.50 5.50

Coil Stamps
Self-Adhesive
Serpentine Die Cut 11 Syncopated

2859 A752 50c multi 1.10 .60
2860 A752 50c multi 1.10 .60
2861 A752 50c multi 1.10 .60
2862 A752 50c multi 1.10 .60
2863 A752 50c multi 1.10 .60
a. Vert. strip of 5, #2859-2863 5.50
Nos. 2859-2863 (5) 5.50 3.00

Complete booklet sold for $10.95.

2008 World Stamp Championships, Israel (No. 2856c). Issued: No. 2855c, 11/3; No. 2856d, 11/5.

Queen's Birthday — A753

Designs: 50c, Queen Elizabeth II. $2, Order of Australia badge.

2008, Apr. 18 *Perf. 14*

2864 A753 50c multi 1.10 .85
a. Perf. 14¾x14 1.10 .85
b. Dated "2010" 2.00 1.00
2865 A753 $2 multi 4.25 2.25
a. Perf. 14¾x14 4.25 2.25
b. Souvenir sheet, #2864a, 2865a 5.50 5.50

First Hot-air Balloon Flight in Australia, 150th Anniv. A754

Hot-air balloons over: Nos. 2866, 2870, Sydney Harbour Bridge and Sydney Opera House. Nos. 2867, 2871, Mount Feathertop, Victoria (red denomination). Nos. 2868, 2873, Western MacDonnell Ranges, Northern Territory (lilac denomination). Nos. 2869, 2872, Canberra.

2008, May 6 Litho. *Perf. 14x14¾*

2866 A754 50c multi 1.10 1.10
a. Booklet pane of 4 5.00 —
2867 A754 50c multi 1.10 1.10
a. Booklet pane of 4 5.00 —
2868 A754 50c multi 1.10 1.10
a. Booklet pane of 4 5.00 —
2869 A754 50c multi 1.10 1.10
a. Booklet pane of 4 5.00 —
b. Booklet pane of 4, #2866-2869 5.00 —
Complete booklet, #2866a-2869a, 2869b 25.00
c. Horiz. strip of 4, #2866-2869 4.50 4.50
d. Additionally dated "2013" (#2869e) 1.10 1.10
e. Booklet pane of 2 #2869d 2.25 —
Nos. 2866-2869 (4) 4.40 4.40

Issued: Nos. 2869d, 2869e, 3/5/13. No. 2869e was issued in booklet along with Nos. 1939c, 2710c, 3107c, 3349b and 3877a.

Booklet Stamps
Self-Adhesive
Serpentine Die Cut 11 Syncopated

2870 A754 50c multi 1.10 .30
2871 A754 50c multi 1.10 .30
2872 A754 50c multi 1.10 .30
2873 A754 50c multi 1.10 .30
a. Booklet pane, 4 #2870, 2 each #2871-2873 11.00
Nos. 2870-2873 (4) 4.40 1.20

Complete booklet sold for $10.95.

Working Dogs — A755

Designs: Nos. 2874, 2879, German shepherd. Nos. 2875, 2880, Australian cattle dog. Nos. 2876, 2881, Beagle. Nos. 2877, 2882, Border collie. Nos. 2878, 2883, Labrador retriever.

2008, June 10 Litho. *Perf. 14¾x14*

2874 A755 50c multi 1.10 1.10
a. Booklet pane of 4 5.00 —
2875 A755 50c multi 1.10 1.10
a. Booklet pane of 4 5.00 —
2876 A755 50c multi 1.10 1.10
a. Booklet pane of 4 5.00 —
2877 A755 50c multi 1.10 1.10
a. Booklet pane of 4 5.00 —
2878 A755 50c multi 1.10 1.10
a. Booklet pane of 4 5.00 —
Complete booklet, #2874a-2878a 25.00
b. Horiz. strip of 5, #2874-2878 5.50 5.50
Nos. 2874-2878 (5) 5.50 5.50

Booklet Stamps
Self-Adhesive
Serpentine Die Cut 11 Syncopated

2879 A755 50c multi 1.10 .30
a. Booklet pane of 10 + 5 stickers 11.00
2880 A755 50c multi 1.10 .30
a. Booklet pane of 10 + 5 stickers 11.00
2881 A755 50c multi 1.10 .30
a. Booklet pane of 10 + 5 stickers 11.00
2882 A755 50c multi 1.10 .30
a. Booklet pane of 10 + 5 stickers 11.00
2883 A755 50c multi 1.10 .30
a. Booklet pane of 10 + 5 stickers 11.00
b. Booklet pane of 10, 2 each #2879-2883, + 5 stickers 11.00
Nos. 2879-2883 (5) 5.50 1.50

Complete booklet sold for $10.95.

2008 Summer Olympics, Beijing — A756

2008, June 24 ***Perf. 14¾x14***

2884 A756 50c multi 1.10 1.10

Coil Stamp

Self-Adhesive

Serpentine Die Cut 11 Syncopated

2885 A756 50c multi 1.10 .30

Ecology A757

Slogans: Nos. 2886, 2890, Save water. Nos. 2887, 2891, Reduce waste. Nos. 2888, 2892, Travel smart. Nos. 2889, 2893, Save energy.

2008, July 8 **Litho.** ***Perf. 14x14¾***

2886 A757 50c multi 1.10 1.10
2887 A757 50c multi 1.10 1.10
2888 A757 50c multi 1.10 1.10
2889 A757 50c multi 1.10 1.10
a. Block of 4, #2886-2889 4.50 4.50
Nos. 2886-2889 (4) 4.40 4.40

Self-Adhesive

Serpentine Die Cut 11¼x11 Syncopated

2890 A757 50c multi 1.10 .30
a. Booklet pane of 2 2.25
2891 A757 50c multi 1.10 .30
a. Booklet pane of 2 2.25
2892 A757 50c multi 1.10 .30
a. Booklet pane of 2 2.25
2893 A757 50c multi 1.10 .30
a. Booklet pane of 2 2.25
b. Booklet pane of 4, #2890-2893 4.50
c. Double-sided booklet pane of 8, 2 each #2890-2893 9.25
Complete booklet, #2890a, 2891a, 2892a, 2893a, 2893b, 2893c 24.00
d. Double-sided booklet of 20, 5 each #2890-2893 22.00
e. Horiz. coil strip of 4, #2890-2893 4.50
Nos. 2890-2893 (4) 4.40 1.20

Complete booklet sold for $10.95.

A758

A759

2008, July 15 ***Perf. 14¾x14***

2894 A758 50c multi 1.10 1.10

Coil Stamp

Self-Adhesive

Serpentine Die Cut 11x11¼ Syncopated

2895 A758 50c multi 1.10 .30

Quarantine laws, cent.

2008, July 29 ***Perf. 14¾x14***

2896 A759 50c multi 1.10 .85

Australian Football, 150th anniv.

2008 Summer Olympics, Beijing — A760

2008, Aug. 1

2897 A760 50c Basketball 1.10 .85
2898 A760 $1.30 Cycling 2.75 2.75
2899 A760 $1.35 Rhythmic gymnastics 2.75 2.75
Nos. 2897-2899 (3) 6.60 6.35

Olympics Type of 2008

Serpentine Die Cut 11¼ Syncopated

2008, Aug. 1 **Litho.**

Booklet Stamps

Self-Adhesive

2900 A760 $1.30 Cycling 2.75 .30
a. Booklet pane of 5 14.00
2901 A760 $1.35 Rhythmic gymnastics 2.75 .30
a. Booklet pane of 5 14.50

Scenes From World Youth Day — A761

Designs: No. 2902, Pilgrims at opening mass. No. 2903, Papal welcome. No. 2904, Stations of the Cross. No. 2905, Pilgrimage walk. No. 2906, Pope Benedict XVI at final mass.

2008, July 24 **Litho.** ***Perf. 14½x14***

2902 A761 50c multi 2.00 *2.00*
2903 A761 50c multi 2.00 *2.00*
2904 A761 50c multi 2.00 *2.00*
2905 A761 50c multi 2.00 *2.00*
2906 A761 50c multi 2.00 *2.00*
a. Vert. strip of 5, #2902-2906 10.00 *10.00*
Nos. 2902-2906 (5) 10.00 10.00

Aircraft A762

Designs: No. 2907, Bristol Tourer. No. 2908, Short S.30 Empire Flying Boat. No. 2909, Lockheed Super Constellation. $2, Airbus A380.

2008, Aug. 5 ***Perf. 14***

2907 A762 50c multi 1.00 .80
a. Perf. 14x14¾ 1.25 1.25
b. Booklet pane of 2, #2907a 2.50 —
2908 A762 50c multi 1.00 .80
a. Perf. 14x14¾ 1.25 1.25
b. Booklet pane of 2, #2907a 2.50 —
2909 A762 50c multi 1.00 .80
a. Perf. 14x14¾ 1.25 1.25
b. Booklet pane of 2, #2907a 2.50 —
c. Horiz. strip of 3, #2907-2909 3.00 2.40
2910 A762 $2 multi 4.00 2.00
a. Perf. 14x14¾ 5.50 5.50
b. Booklet pane of 1, #2907a 5.50 —
c. Booklet pane of 4, #2907a-2910a 9.50 —
Complete booklet, #2907b, 2908b, 2909b, 2910b, 2910c 23.00
d. Souvenir sheet, 2 each #2868, 2910a 9.50 9.50
Nos. 2907-2910 (4) 7.00 4.40

Booklet Stamp

Self-Adhesive

Serpentine Die Cut 11¼ Syncopated

2911 A762 $2 multi 4.00 2.00
a. Booklet pane of 5 20.00

Complete booklet sold for $10.95. Issued: No./ 2910d, 8/22. SunStamp 2008 Philatelic Exhibition, Brisbane (No. 2910d).

Gold Medalists at 2008 Summer Olympics, Beijing A763

Designs: No. 2912, Stephanie Rice, Women's swimming 400m individual medley. No. 2913, Lisbeth Trickett, Women's swimming 100m butterfly. No. 2914, Leisel Jones, Women's swimming, 100m breaststroke. No. 2915, Stephanie Rice, Women's swimming 200m individual medley. No. 2916, Women's 4x200m freestyle relay swimming team. No. 2917, Drew Ginn and Duncan Free, Men's rowing pairs. No. 2918, David Crawshay and Scott Brennan, Men's rowing double sculls. No. 2919, Women's 4x100m medley relay swimming team. No. 2920, Emma Snowsill, Women's triathlon. No. 2921, Malcolm Page and Nathan Wilmot, Men's sailing 470 crew. No. 2922, Tessa Parkinson and Elise Rechichi, Women's sailing 470 crew. No. 2923, Ken Wallace, Men's single kayak 500m. No. 2924, Steven Hooker, Men's pole vault. No. 2925, Matthew Mitcham, Men's 10m platform diving.

2008, Aug. **Litho.** ***Perf. 14¼***

2912 A763 50c multi .95 .75
2913 A763 50c multi .95 .75
2914 A763 50c multi .95 .75
2915 A763 50c multi .95 .75
2916 A763 50c multi .95 .75
2917 A763 50c multi .95 .75
2918 A763 50c multi .95 .75
2919 A763 50c multi .95 .75
2920 A763 50c multi .95 .75
2921 A763 50c multi .95 .75
2922 A763 50c multi .95 .75
2923 A763 50c multi .95 .75
2924 A763 50c multi .95 .75
2925 A763 50c multi .95 .75
Nos. 2912-2925 (14) 13.30 10.50

Issued: Nos. 2912, 8/11; No. 2913, 8/12; No. 2914, 8/13; No. 2915, 8/14; No. 2916, 8/15; Nos. 2917-2919, 8/18; Nos. 2920-2922, 8/19; Nos. 2923-2925, 8/25. Nos. 2912-2925 were printed in sheets of 10. Digitally printed versions of Nos. 2912-2925 were printed in Beijing in sheets of 10. The digitally printed stamps were only available in complete sets of 14 sheets to collectors in Australia who preordered the sets, and purchasers at the Olympex Stamp Exhibition in China. The digitally printed stamps have a larger dot pattern, most evident in the background and the Olympic rings, and a browner cast to the orange background.

Waterfalls — A764

Designs: $1.40, Russell Falls, Tasmania. $2.05, Jim Jim Falls, Northern Territory. $2.80, Spa Pool, Hammersley Gorge, Western Australia. $4.10, Mackenzie Falls, Victoria.

2008, Sept. 8 **Litho.** ***Perf. 14¾x14***

2926 A764 $1.40 multi 2.50 2.50
2927 A764 $2.05 multi 3.75 3.75
2928 A764 $2.80 multi 5.25 2.50
2929 A764 $4.10 multi 7.50 3.75
Nos. 2926-2929 (4) 19.00 12.50

Booklet Stamps

Self-Adhesive

Serpentine Die Cut 11¼ Syncopated

2930 A764 $1.40 multi 2.50 .30
a. Booklet pane of 5 13.00
b. Booklet pane of 2 5.50
Complete booklet, 4 #2930b 22.00
2931 A764 $2.05 multi 3.75 1.90
a. Booklet pane of 5 19.00
b. Booklet pane of 2 7.75
Complete booklet, 4 #2931b 30.00

With Personalized Photo at Right Like Type A692a

Serpentine Die Cut 11½x11¼ Syncopated

Self-Adhesive

2932 A764 $1.40 multi 3.75 3.75
2933 A764 $2.05 multi 5.00 5.00

Complete booklet containing No. 2930 sold for $11.95; booklet containing No. 2931, $16.95. Margins for each pane in the complete booklets differ.

Nos. 2932-2933 each were sold in sheets of 20 and have personalized pictures and a straight edge at right, and lack separations between the stamp and the personalized photo. Sheets of 20 of No. 2932 sold for $41, and No. 2933 sold for $53.

Tourist Areas of Cities — A765

Designs: Nos. 2934, 2941, 2945, Luna Park, Melbourne. Nos. 2935, 2942, 2946, South Bank, Brisbane. Nos. 2936, 2943, 2947, The Rocks, Sydney. Nos. 2937, 2944, 2948, Fishermans Wharf, Fremantle. $1.10, Foreshore, Cairns. $1.65, Salamanca Place, Hobart. $2.75, Glenelg, Adelaide (50x30mm).

2008, Sept. 8 **Litho.** ***Perf. 14x14½***

2934 A765 55c multi .95 .95
2935 A765 55c multi .95 .95
2936 A765 55c multi .95 .95
2937 A765 55c multi .95 .95
a. Block of 4, #2934-2937 4.00 4.00
b. Sheet of 4, #2934-2937 4.00 4.00
c. Block of 4, #2934-2937, perf. 13½x14 *18.00* *18.00*
2938 A765 $1.10 multi 2.00 1.60
2939 A765 $1.65 multi 3.00 2.25

Perf. 14½x14

2940 A765 $2.75 multi 5.00 2.40
Nos. 2934-2940 (7) 13.80 10.05

Self-Adhesive

Coil Stamps

Die Cut Perf. 12¾

2941 A765 55c multi .95 .30
2942 A765 55c multi .95 .30
2943 A765 55c multi .95 .30
2944 A765 55c multi .95 .30
a. Horiz. strip of 4, #2941-2944 4.00

Booklet Stamps

Serpentine Die Cut 11¼

2945 A765 55c multi .95 .30
a. Booklet pane of 10 9.75
2946 A765 55c multi .95 .30
a. Booklet pane of 10 9.75
2947 A765 55c multi .95 .30
a. Booklet pane of 10 9.75
2948 A765 55c multi .95 .30
a. Booklet pane of 10 9.75
b. Booklet pane of 20, 5 each #2945-2948 20.00
Nos. 2941-2948 (8) 7.60 2.40

Issued: No. 2937b, 5/14/09. Hong Kong 2009 Intl. Stamp Exhibition (No. 2937b).

Australia and Southern Cross — A766

Balloons — A767

Bird and Beach — A768

Stylized Map A769

Sparklers A770

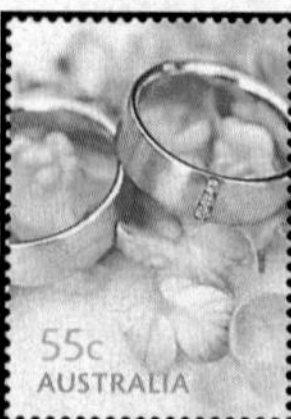

Flowers and Silver Wedding Rings — A771

Gold Wedding Rings — A772

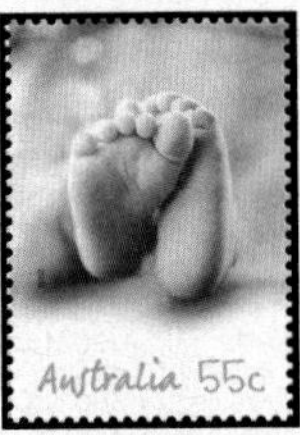

Baby's Feet — A773

Heart and Roses — A774

Roses and Wedding Gown — A775

2008, Sept. 23 *Perf. 14½x14*

2949 A766 55c multi .95 .95

Perf. 14¾x14

2950 A767 55c multi .95 .95
2951 A768 55c multi .95 .95
2952 A769 55c multi .95 .95
a. Souvenir sheet of 2 + 2 labels, Chips Rafferty in margin 4.25 4.25
b. As "a," Errol Flynn in margin 4.25 4.25
2953 A770 55c multi .95 .95
a. Block of 4, #2950-2953 4.00 4.00
2954 A771 55c multi .95 .95
2955 A772 55c multi .95 .95
2956 A773 55c multi .95 .95
2957 A774 55c multi .95 .95
a. Block of 4, #2954-2957 4.00 4.00
2958 A775 $1.10 multi 2.00 1.60
Nos. 2949-2958 (10) 10.55 10.15

Nos. 2952a and 2952b were sold with Nos. 3009b and 3010d in a set for $12.95.

Booklet Stamps
Self-Adhesive
Serpentine Die Cut 11¼ Syncopated

2959 A767 55c multi 1.00 .30
a. Booklet pane of 4 4.25
Complete booklet, 5 #2959a 22.00
b. Booklet pane of 10 10.50
2960 A770 55c multi 1.00 .30
a. Booklet pane of 4 4.25
Complete booklet, 5 #2960a 22.00
b. Booklet pane of 10 10.50
2961 A771 55c multi 1.00 .30
a. Booklet pane of 4 4.25
Complete booklet, 5 #2961a 22.00
2962 A772 55c multi 1.00 .30
a. Booklet pane of 4 4.25
Complete booklet, 5 #2962a 22.00
b. Booklet pane of 10 10.50
2963 A773 55c multi 1.00 .30
a. Booklet pane of 4 4.25
Complete booklet, 5 #2963a 22.00
b. Booklet pane of 10 10.50
2964 A774 55c multi 1.00 .30
a. Booklet pane of 4 4.25
Complete booklet, 5 #2964a 22.00
2965 A775 $1.10 multi 2.00 2.00
a. Booklet pane of 4 8.00
Complete booklet, 5 #2965a 41.00
b. Booklet pane of 10 20.00
Nos. 2959-2965 (7) 8.00 3.80

With Personalized Photo at Right Like Type A692a
Serpentine Die Cut 11½x11¼ Syncopated
Self-Adhesive

2966 A767 55c multi 2.25 2.25
2967 A768 55c multi 2.25 2.25
2968 A769 55c multi 2.25 2.25
2969 A770 55c multi 2.25 2.25
2970 A771 55c multi 2.25 2.25
2971 A772 55c multi 2.25 2.25
2972 A773 55c multi 2.25 2.25
2973 A774 55c multi 2.25 2.25
2974 A775 $1.10 multi 3.25 3.25
Nos. 2966-2974 (9) 21.25 21.25

Issued: Nos. 2959b, 2960b, 2962b, 2963b, 2965b, 3/2/09.

Complete booklet containing No. 2965 sold for $22.95; booklets containing Nos. 2959-2964 each sold for $11.95. Each booklet contained panes with five different margins.

Nos. 2966-2974 each were sold in sheets of 20 and have personalized pictures and a straight edge at right, and lack separations between the stamp and the personalized photo. Sheets of 20 of Nos. 2966-2973 each sold for $24, and No. 2974 sold for $35.

Large Extinct Animals — A776

Designs: Nos. 2975, 2981, Genyornis. Nos. 2976, 2982, Diprotodon. Nos. 2977, 2983, Thylacoleo. Nos. 2978, 2984, Thylacine. No. 2979, Megalania, horiz. (52x37mm). No. 2980, Procoptodon, horiz. (52x37mm).

2008, Oct. 1 **Litho.** *Perf. 14½x14*

2975 A776 55c multi .95 .95
a. Perf. 14 .95 .95
b. Booklet pane of 2 #2975 2.25 —
2976 A776 55c multi .95 .95
a. Perf. 14 .95 .95
b. Booklet pane of 2 #2976 2.25 —
2977 A776 55c multi .95 .95
a. Perf. 14 .95 .95
b. Booklet pane of 2 #2977 2.25 —
2978 A776 55c multi .95 .95
a. Perf. 14 .95 .95
b. Horiz. strip of 4, #2975-2978 4.00 4.00
c. Booklet pane of 2 #2978 2.25 —
d. Booklet pane of 4, #2975-2978 4.25 —
2979 A776 $1.10 multi 2.00 1.60
a. Perf. 14 .95 .95
b. Booklet pane of 2 #2979 4.25 —
2980 A776 $1.10 multi 2.00 1.60
a. Perf. 14 .95 .95
b. Horiz. pair, #2979-2980 4.00 4.00
c. Souvenir sheet, #2975a-2980a 8.00 8.00
d. Booklet pane of 2 #2980 4.25 —
e. Booklet pane of 2, #2979-2980 4.25 —
Complete booklet, #2975b, 2976b, 2977b, 2978c, 2978d, 2979b, 2980d, 2980e 26.50
f. As "c," overprinted with Beijing 2008 Stamp Exposition emblem in margin 7.00 7.00
Nos. 2975-2980 (6) 7.80 7.00

Self-Adhesive
Serpentine Die Cut 11¼ Syncopated

2981 A776 55c multi .95 .30
2982 A776 55c multi .95 .30
2983 A776 55c multi .95 .30
2984 A776 55c multi .95 .30
a. Vert. coil strip of 4, #2981-2984 4.00
b. Booklet pane of 10, 3 each #2981-2982, 2 each #2983-2984 9.75
Nos. 2981-2984 (4) 3.80 1.20

Complete booklet sold for $13.95. Issued: No. 2980f, 10/24.

Matthew Cowdrey, Paralympian of the Year — A777

2008, Oct. 24 **Litho.** *Perf. 14¼*

2985 A777 55c multi .85 .70

Christmas
A778 A779

Star of Bethlehem and: Nos. 2987, 2992, 2995, Madonna and child. No. 2988, 2996, Angel. Nos. 2989, 2993, Magus.

2008, Oct. 31 **Litho.** *Perf. 14¾x14*

2986 A778 50c multi .80 .80
2987 A779 50c multi .80 .80
2988 A779 55c multi .85 .70
2989 A779 $1.20 multi 1.90 1.90
Nos. 2986-2989 (4) 4.35 4.20

Booklet Stamps
Self-Adhesive
Litho. & Typo.
Serpentine Die Cut 11¼ Syncopated

2990 A778 50c multi .80 .30
a. Booklet pane of 10 8.00

Litho.

2991 A778 50c multi .80 .30
a. Booklet pane of 20 16.00
2992 A779 50c multi .80 .30
a. Booklet pane of 20 16.00
2993 A779 $1.20 multi 1.90 .30
a. Booklet pane of 5 9.25
Nos. 2990-2993 (4) 4.30 1.20

With Personalized Photo at Right Like Type A692a
Serpentine Die Cut 11½x11¼ Syncopated
Self-Adhesive

2994 A778 50c multi 1.75 1.75
2995 A779 50c multi 1.75 1.75
2996 A779 55c multi 1.75 1.75
Nos. 2994-2996 (3) 5.25 5.25

Nos. 2994-2996 each were sold in sheets of 20 and have personalized pictures and a straight edge at right, and lack separations between the stamp and the personalized photo. Sheets of 20 of Nos. 2994-2995 each sold for $23, and No. 2996 sold for $24.

Posters for Popular Australian Films — A780

Poster for: Nos. 2997, 3002, The Adventures of Priscilla, Queen of the Desert. Nos. 2998, 3003, The Castle. Nos. 2999, 3004, Muriel's Wedding. Nos. 3000, 3005, Lantana. Nos. 3001, 3006, Gallipoli.

2008, Nov. 3 **Litho.** *Perf. 14¾x14*

2997 A780 55c multi .85 .85
2998 A780 55c multi .85 .85
2999 A780 55c multi .85 .85
3000 A780 55c multi .85 .85
3001 A780 55c multi .85 .85
a. Horiz. strip of 5, #2997-3001 4.25 4.25
Nos. 2997-3001 (5) 4.25 4.25

Self-Adhesive
Serpentine Die Cut 11¼ Syncopated

3002 A780 55c multi .85 .30
a. Booklet pane of 10 8.50
3003 A780 55c multi .85 .30
a. Booklet pane of 10 8.50
3004 A780 55c multi .85 .30
a. Booklet pane of 10 8.50
3005 A780 55c multi .85 .30
a. Booklet pane of 10 8.50
3006 A780 55c multi .85 .30
a. Booklet pane of 10 8.50
b. Booklet pane of 10, 2 each #3002-3006 8.50
c. Vert. coil strip of 5, #3002-3006 4.25
d. Souvenir sheet of 10, 1 ea #3002, 3004-3006, 6 #3003 11.00
Nos. 3002-3006 (5) 4.25 1.50

Academy Award-winning Actors and Actresses — A781

Designs: Nos. 3007, 3015, Nicole Kidman. Nos. 3008, 3016, Russell Crowe. Nos. 3009, 3018, Geoffrey Rush. Nos. 3010, 3017, Cate Blanchett. Nos. 3011, 3020, Crowe in *Gladiator*. Nos. 3012, 3019, Kidman in *Moulin Rouge!* Nos. 3013, 3021, Blanchett in *Elizabeth: The Golden Age*. Nos. 3014, 3022, Rush in *Shine*.

2009, Jan. 22 **Litho.** *Perf. 14¾x14*

3007 A781 55c multi .80 .80
a. Booklet pane of 4 4.25 —
3008 A781 55c multi .80 .80
a. Booklet pane of 4 4.25 —
b. Sheet of 10 + 10 labels 14.00 14.00
3009 A781 55c multi .80 .80
a. Booklet pane of 4 4.25 —
b. Souvenir sheet of 4 8.25 8.25
3010 A781 55c multi .85 .85
a. Booklet pane of 4 4.25 —
b. Block of 4, #3007-3010 3.50 3.50
c. Booklet pane of 4, #3007-3010 4.25 —
d. Souvenir sheet of 4, #3007-3010 8.25 8.25
3011 A781 55c multi .85 .85
a. Booklet pane of 4 4.25 —
b. Booklet pane of 4, 2 each #3008, 3011 4.25 —
Complete booklet, #3008a, 3010c, 3011a, 3011b 17.00
3012 A781 55c multi .85 .85
a. Booklet pane of 4 4.25 —
b. Booklet pane of 4, 2 each #3007, 3012 4.25 —
Complete booklet, #3007a, 3010c, 3012a, 3012b 17.00
3013 A781 55c multi .85 .85
a. Booklet pane of 4 4.25 —
b. Booklet pane of 4, 2 each #3010, 3013 4.25 —
Complete booklet, #3010a, 3010c, 3013a, 3013b 17.00
3014 A781 55c multi .85 .85
a. Booklet pane of 4 4.25 —
b. Booklet pane of 4, 2 each #3009, 3014 4.25 —
Complete booklet, #3009a, 3010c, 3014a, 3014b 17.50
c. Block of 4, #3011-3014 3.50 3.50
Nos. 3007-3014 (8) 6.65 6.65

Issued: No. 3008b, 5/6/10. Two sheets of 3008b, each sheet having different labels, were sold together as a set for $13.50. Nos. 3009b and 3010d were sold with Nos. 2952a and 2952b in a set for $12.95.

Self-Adhesive
Booklet Stamps
Serpentine Die Cut 11¼ Syncopated

3015 A781 55c multi .85 .30
3016 A781 55c multi .85 .30
3017 A781 55c multi .85 .30
3018 A781 55c multi .85 .30
3019 A781 55c multi .85 .30
a. Booklet pane of 10, 5 each #3015, 3019 8.50
3020 A781 55c multi .85 .30
a. Booklet pane of 10, 5 each #3016, 3020 8.50
3021 A781 55c multi .85 .30
a. Booklet pane of 10, 5 each #3017 3021 8.50
3022 A781 55c multi .85 .30
a. Booklet pane of 20, 3 each #3015-3018, 2 each #3019-3022 17.00
b. Booklet pane of 10, 5 each #3019, 3022 8.50
Nos. 3015-3022 (8) 6.80 2.40

Each complete booklet sold for $10.95.

Roses — A782

Heart — A783

Flowers With Heart-Shaped Petals — A784

2009, Feb. 3 **Litho.** *Perf. 14¾x14*

3023 A782 55c multi .80 .80
3024 A783 55c gray blue .80 .80
3025 A784 55c multi .80 .80
a. Pair, #3024-3025 1.60 1.60
Nos. 3023-3025 (3) 2.40 2.40

Booklet Stamps
Self-Adhesive
Serpentine Die Cut 11¼ Syncopated

3026 A782 55c multi .80 .80
a. Booklet pane of 10 8.00
3027 A783 55c gray blue .80 .80
a. Booklet pane of 10 8.00
3028 A784 55c multi .80 .80
a. Booklet pane of 10 8.00

Litho. With Foil Application

3029 A784 55c multi .80 .80

Litho. With Flocking

3030 A783 55c gray blue .80 .80
a. Booklet pane of 10, 2 each #3029-3030 8.00
Nos. 3026-3030 (5) 4.00 4.00

With Personalized Photo at Right Like Type A692a

Syncopated Die Cut 11½x11¼ Syncopated

Self-Adhesive

3031 A782 55c multi 1.75 1.75
3032 A783 55c multi 1.75 1.75
3033 A784 55c multi 1.75 1.75
Nos. 3031-3033 (3) 5.25 5.25

Nos. 3031-3033 each were sold in sheets of 20 and have personalized pictures and a straight edge at right and lack separations between the stamp and the personalized photo. Sheets of 20 of each stamp sold for $24.

Australian Inventions — A785

Designs: Nos. 3034, 3039, Esky (insulated cooler), wine cask. Nos. 3035, 3040, Hills hoist (rotatable clothes line frame). Nos. 3036, 3041, Speedos (swim wear), zinc oxide cream. Nos. 3037, 3042, Ute (utility vehicle), B&D Roll-A-Door (garage door). Nos. 3038, 3043, Victa rotary lawnmower.

2009, Feb. 19 Litho. *Perf. 14¾x14*

3034 A785 55c multi .80 .80
a. Booklet pane of 4 4.00 —
b. As #3034, perf. 14 .80 .80
3035 A785 55c multi .80 .80
a. Booklet pane of 4 4.00 —
b. As #3035, perf. 14 .80 .80
3036 A785 55c multi .80 .80
a. Booklet pane of 4 4.00 —
b. As #3036, perf. 14 .80 .80
3037 A785 55c multi .80 .80
a. Booklet pane of 4 4.00 —
b. As #3037, perf. 14 .80 .80
3038 A785 55c multi .80 .80
a. Booklet pane of 4 4.00 —
Complete booklet, #3034a, 3035a, 3036a, 3037a, 3038a 19.50
b. As #3038, perf. 14 .80 .80
c. Souvenir sheet, #3034b-3038b 4.00 4.00
d. Horiz. strip of 5, #3034-3038 4.00 4.00
Nos. 3034-3038 (5) 4.00 4.00

Self-Adhesive

Serpentine Die Cut 11¼ Syncopated

3039 A785 55c multi .80 .30
3040 A785 55c multi .80 .30
3041 A785 55c multi .80 .30
3042 A785 55c multi .80 .30
3043 A785 55c multi .80 .30
a. Vert. coil strip of 5, #3039-3043 4.00
b. Booklet pane of 10, 2 each #3039-3043 8.00
Nos. 3039-3043 (5) 4.00 1.50

Complete booklet sold for $12.95.

Earth Hour — A786

Animals and slogan: Nos. 3044, 3047, Lights out. No. 3045, 3048, Switch off. $2.05, Save energy.

2009, Mar. 11 *Perf. 14¾x14*

3044 A786 55c multi .90 .90
3045 A786 55c multi .90 .90
a. Horiz. pair, #3044-3045 1.90 1.90
3046 A786 $2.05 multi 3.50 3.50
Nos. 3044-3046 (3) 5.30 5.30

Booklet Stamps

Self-Adhesive

Serpentine Die Cut 11¼ Syncopated

3047 A786 55c multi .90 .30
3048 A786 55c multi .90 .30
a. Booklet pane of 20, 10 each #3047-3048 18.50

Australia Post, Bicent. — A787

Inscriptions: Nos. 3049a, 3050, First postmaster. Nos. 3049b, 3051, Early post office. Nos. 3049c, 3052, Early posting box. Nos. 3049d, 3053, News from home. Nos. 3049e, 3054, Early air mail. Nos. 3049f, 3055, Home delivery. Nos. 3049g, 3056, Post-war immigration. Nos. 3049h, 3057, Retail post shop. Nos. 3049i, 3058, Express post. Nos. 3049j, 3059, Part of every day.

2009, Mar. 25 *Perf. 14¾x14*

3049 Sheet of 10 9.25 9.25
a.-j. A787 55c Any single .90 .90
k. Booklet pane of 10, #3049a-3049j 11.00 —
l. As "k," imperf. 11.00
Complete booklet, #3049l, 2 #3049k 32.50

Self-Adhesive

Serpentine Die Cut 11¼ Syncopated

3050 A787 55c multi .90 .30
3051 A787 55c multi .90 .30
3052 A787 55c multi .90 .30
3053 A787 55c multi .90 .30
3054 A787 55c multi .90 .30
3055 A787 55c multi .90 .30
3056 A787 55c multi .90 .30
3057 A787 55c multi .90 .30
3058 A787 55c multi .90 .30
3059 A787 55c multi .90 .30
a. Vert. coil strip of 10, #3050-3059 9.00
b. Booklet pane of 10, #3050-3059 9.00
Nos. 3050-3059 (10) 9.00 3.00

Complete booklet sold for $19.95. Compare with type A806.

Aboriginal Art — A788

Designs: No. 3060, Mamu, by Nura Rupert. No. 3061, All the Jila, by Jan Billycan. No. 3062, Mina Mina, by Judy Napangardi Watson. $1.40, Untitled work from the Mission Series, by Elaine Russell. $2.05, Natjula, by Tjuruparu Watson.

2009, Apr. 1 *Perf. 14x14¾*

3060 A788 55c multi .90 .70
3061 A788 55c multi .90 .70
3062 A788 55c multi .90 .70
a. Horiz. strip of 3, #3060-3062 2.75 2.00
3063 A788 $1.40 multi 2.25 1.10
3064 A788 $2.05 multi 3.50 1.75
Nos. 3060-3064 (5) 8.45 4.95

Self-Adhesive

Booklet Stamps

Serpentine Die Cut 11¼ Syncopated

3065 A788 $1.40 multi 2.25 1.10
a. Booklet pane of 5 11.50
3066 A788 $2.05 multi 3.50 1.75
a. Booklet pane of 5 17.50

Queen's Birthday — A789

Queen Elizabeth II: 55c, In uniform. $2.05, Wearing green coat and hat.

2009, Apr. 15 *Perf. 14¾x14*

3067 A789 55c multi .90 .70
a. Booklet pane of 2 2.25 —
b. Dated "2010" 2.00 1.00
3068 A789 $2.05 multi 3.50 1.75
a. Booklet pane of 2 8.50 —
b. Souvenir sheet of 2, #3067-3068 4.50 2.40
c. Booklet pane, #3068b 5.25 —
Complete booklet, #3068a, 3068c, 2 #3067a 18.50

Complete booklet sold for $10.95.

Eponymous Desserts A790

Designs: Nos. 3069, 3073, Anna Pavlova and Pavlova. Nos. 3070, 3074, Dame Nellie Melba and Peach Melba. Nos. 3071, 3075, Baron and Lady Lamington and Lamingtons. Nos. 3072, 3076, ANZAC soldiers and ANZAC biscuits.

2009, May 15 Litho. *Perf. 14x14¾*

3069 A790 55c multi 1.00 1.00
a. Booklet pane of 4 5.25 —
3070 A790 55c multi 1.00 1.00
a. Booklet pane of 4 5.25 —
3071 A790 55c multi 1.00 1.00
a. Booklet pane of 4 5.25 —
3072 A790 55c multi 1.00 1.00
a. Booklet pane of 4 5.25 —
Complete booklet, #3069a-3072a 20.75
b. Horiz. strip of 4, #3069-3072 4.25 4.25
Nos. 3069-3072 (4) 4.00 4.00

Booklet Stamps

Self-Adhesive

Serpentine Die Cut 11¼ Syncopated

3073 A790 55c multi 1.00 .30
3074 A790 55c multi 1.00 .30
3075 A790 55c multi 1.00 .30
3076 A790 55c multi 1.00 .30
a. Booklet pane of 10, 3 each #3073-3074, 2 each #3075-3076 11.00
Nos. 3073-3076 (4) 4.00 1.20

Complete booklet sold for $10.95.

Worldwide Fund for Nature (WWF) A791

Designs: 55c, Spotted bottlenose dolphins. $1.35, Hourglass dolphins. $1.40, Southern right whale dolphins. $2.05, Dusky dolphins.

2009, May 26 *Perf. 14x14¾*

3077 A791 55c multi 1.00 .80
3078 A791 $1.35 multi 2.50 2.50
3079 A791 $1.40 multi 2.50 2.50
3080 A791 $2.05 multi 3.75 3.75
a. Souvenir sheet, #3077-3080 10.00 10.00
Nos. 3077-3080 (4) 9.75 9.55

Booklet Stamps

Self-Adhesive

Serpentine Die Cut 11¼ Syncopated

3081 A791 $1.35 multi 2.50 2.50
a. Booklet pane of 5 13.00
3082 A791 $1.40 multi 2.50 2.50
a. Booklet pane of 5 13.00
3083 A791 $2.05 multi 3.75 3.75
a. Booklet pane of 5 19.00
Nos. 3081-3083 (3) 8.75 8.75

Queensland, 150th Anniv. — A792

Designs: 55c, Queensland Parliament, windmill. $2.75, Great Barrier Reef, red-eyed tree frog.

2009, June 9 Litho. *Perf. 14¾x14*

3084 A792 55c multi 1.00 .80
3085 A792 $2.75 multi 5.25 4.00
a. Souvenir sheet, #3084-3085 6.25 6.25

Australia's Favorite Stamps A793

Designs: Nos. 3086, 3091, 3095B, Australia #15. Nos. 3087, 3092, Australia #132. Nos. 3088, 3093, Australia #200. Nos. 3089, 3094, Australia #226. Nos. 3090, 3095, Australia #18.

2009, June 26 Litho. *Perf. 14x14¾*

3086 A793 55c multi 1.00 1.00
a. Booklet pane of 4 4.50 —
3087 A793 55c multi 1.00 1.00
a. Booklet pane of 4 4.50 —
3088 A793 55c multi 1.00 1.00
a. Booklet pane of 4 4.50 —
3089 A793 55c multi 1.00 1.00
a. Booklet pane of 4 4.50 —
3090 A793 55c multi 1.00 1.00
a. Booklet pane of 4 4.50 —
Complete booklet, #3086a-3090a 23.00
b. Horiz. strip of 5, #3086-3090 5.25 5.25
Nos. 3086-3090 (5) 5.00 5.00

Self-Adhesive

Serpentine Die Cut 11¼ Syncopated

3091 A793 55c multi 1.00 .30
3092 A793 55c multi 1.00 .30
3093 A793 55c multi 1.00 .30
3094 A793 55c multi 1.00 .30
3095 A793 55c multi 1.00 .30
a. Horiz. coil strip of 5, #3091-3095 5.25
Nos. 3091-3095 (5) 5.00 1.50

Litho. & Embossed

Serpentine Die Cut 11¼ Syncopated

Self-Adhesive

3095B A793 55c multi 1.00 .30
c. Sheet of 13, #3091-3095, 8 #3095B 14.00

The complete booklet sold for $12.95. Nos. 3091-3095 each were printed by two different printers. There is no noticeable difference between single coil stamps, but Pemara-printed stamps are slightly closer to each other on the strip compared to the McKellar Renown-printed stamps.

Marsupials and Their Young — A794

Designs: $1.45, Koalas. $2.10, Eastern gray kangaroos. $2.90, Brushtail possums, horiz. $4.20, Common wombats, horiz.

2009, July 1 *Perf. 14¾x14*

3096 A794 $1.45 multi 2.75 2.75
3097 A794 $2.10 multi 4.00 4.00
a. Additionally dated "2013" (#3534d) 5.50 5.50

Perf. 14x14¾

3098 A794 $2.90 multi 5.50 2.75
3099 A794 $4.20 multi 7.75 4.00
Nos. 3096-3099 (4) 20.00 13.50

Issued: No. 3097a, 5/10/13.

Booklet Stamps

Self-Adhesive

Serpentine Die Cut 11¼ Syncopated

3100 A794 $1.45 multi 2.75 1.40
a. Booklet pane of 5 14.00
3101 A794 $2.10 multi 4.00 2.00
a. Booklet pane of 5 20.00

With Personalized Photo at Right Like Type A692a

Serpentine Die Cut 11¼ Syncopated

Self-Adhesive

3102 A794 $1.45 multi 4.00 4.00
3103 A794 $2.10 multi 5.25 5.25

Nos. 3102-3103 each were sold in sheets of 20 and have personalized pictures and a straight edge at right and lack separations between the stamp and the personalized photo. Sheets of 20 of No. 3102 sold for $42; No. 3103, for $54.

Parks and Gardens A795

Designs: Nos. 3104, 3109, Fitzroy Gardens, Melbourne. Nos. 3105, 3110, Roma Street Parkland, Brisbane. Nos. 3106, 3111, St. David's Park, Hobart. Nos. 3107, 3112, Commonwealth Park, Canberra. Nos. 3108, 3113, Hyde Park, Sydney.

2009, July 14 Litho. ***Perf. 14x14¾***

3104 A795 55c multi 1.10 1.10
a. Booklet pane of 4 5.25 —
b. Sheet of 4, #3072, 3086, 3090, 3104 4.25 4.25
3105 A795 55c multi 1.10 1.10
a. Booklet pane of 4 5.25 —
3106 A795 55c multi 1.10 1.10
a. Booklet pane of 4 5.25 —
3107 A795 55c multi 1.10 1.10
a. Booklet pane of 4 5.25 —
b. Additionally dated "2013" (#3107c) 1.25 1.25
c. Booklet pane of 2 #3107b 2.50 —
3108 A795 55c multi 1.10 1.10
a. Booklet pane of 4 5.25 —
Complete booklet, #3104a-3108a 26.00
b. Horiz. strip of 5, #3104-3108 5.50 5.50
Nos. 3104-3108 (5) 5.50 5.50

Issued: Nos. 3107b, 3107c, 3/5/13. No. 3107c was issued in booklet along with Nos. 1939c, 2710c, 2869e, 3349b and 3877a.

Coil Stamps

Self-Adhesive

Serpentine Die Cut 11¼ Syncopated

3109 A795 55c multi 1.10 .30
3110 A795 55c multi 1.10 .30
3111 A795 55c multi 1.10 .30
3112 A795 55c multi 1.10 .30
3113 A795 55c multi 1.10 .30
a. Horiz. strip of 5, #3109-3113 5.25
b. Booklet pane of 10, 2 each # 3109-3113 11.00
Nos. 3109-3113 (5) 5.50 1.50

The complete booklet sold for $12.95.

Issued: No. 3104b, 7/23. Melbourne Stamp Show 09 (No. 3104b).

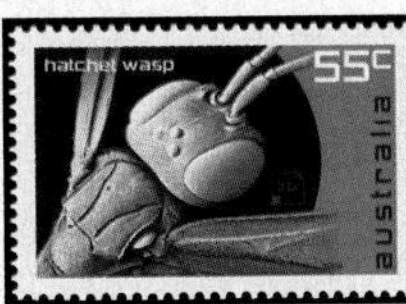

Insects and Spiders A796

Designs: Nos. 3114, 3120a, 3121, Hatchet wasp. Nos. 3115, 3120b, 3122, Praying mantis. Nos. 3116, 3120c, 3123, Ground beetle. Nos. 3117, 3120d, 3124, Jumping spider. Nos. 3118, 3120e, 3125, Ant. $1.10, Weevil.

2009, July 28 Litho. ***Perf. 14x14¾***

3114 A796 55c multi 1.10 1.10
3115 A796 55c multi 1.10 1.10
3116 A796 55c multi 1.10 1.10
3117 A796 55c multi 1.10 1.10
3118 A796 55c multi 1.10 1.10
b. Horiz. strip of 5, #3114-3118 5.25 5.25
3119 A796 $1.10 multi 2.25 1.60
Nos. 3114-3119 (6) 7.75 7.10

Miniature Sheet

With Square of Thermochromic Ink Covering Magnification Squares

3120 Sheet of 6 7.75 7.75
a.-e. A796 55c Any single 1.10 1.10
f. A796 $1.10 multi 2.25 2.25

Coil Stamps

Self-Adhesive

Serpentine Die Cut 11¼ Syncopated

3121 A796 55c multi 1.10 .30
3122 A796 55c multi 1.10 .30
3123 A796 55c multi 1.10 .30
3124 A796 55c multi 1.10 .30
3125 A796 55c multi 1.10 .30
a. Horiz. strip of 5, #3121-3125 5.25
Nos. 3121-3125 (5) 5.50 1.50

Endangered Wildlife — A797

Designs: Nos. 3126, 3132, Bridled nailtail wallaby. Nos. 3127, 3133, Norfolk Island green parrot. Nos. 3128, 3134, Subarctic fur seal. Nos. 3129, 3135, Christmas Island blue-tailed skink. Nos. 3130, 3136, Green turtle.

2009, Aug. 4 Litho. ***Perf. 14¾x14***

"Australia" Above Denomination

3126 A797 55c multi 1.10 1.10
3127 A797 55c multi 1.10 1.10
3128 A797 55c multi 1.10 1.10
3129 A797 55c multi 1.10 1.10
3130 A797 55c multi 1.10 1.10
a. Horiz. strip of 5, #3126-3130 5.25 5.25
Nos. 3126-3130 (5) 5.50 5.50

3131 A797 55c Sheet of 5, #3126, 3128-3130, Norfolk Island #980 5.25 5.25

Booklet Stamps

Self-Adhesive

Serpentine Die Cut 11¼ Syncopated

3132 A797 55c multi 1.10 .30
3133 A797 55c multi 1.10 .30
3134 A797 55c multi 1.10 .30
3135 A797 55c multi 1.10 .30
3136 A797 55c multi 1.10 .30
a. Booklet pane of 20, 4 each #3132-3136 22.00
Nos. 3132-3136 (5) 5.50 1.50

Inscribed on the left side of Nos. 3128 and 3134 is "Australian Antarctic Territory"; on Nos. 3129 and 3135, "Christmas Island"; and on Nos. 3130 and 3136, "Cocos (Keeling) Islands." All recent stamps of the Australian possessions of Australian Antarctic Territory, Christmas Island and Cocos Islands are doubly-inscribed with "Australia" and the territory's name, and all stamps inscribed "Australia," "Australian Antarctic Territory," "Christmas Island," or "Cocos Islands," are valid for postage anywhere in those four areas. However, because Nos. 3128-3130 and 3134-3136 have the territorial inscriptions at the side rather than above the denomination like similar Norfolk Island stamps, Nos. 979-983, they will be listed here only and not in the listings for each of these territories. No. 3131 is identical to Norfolk Island No. 984. Norfolk Island No. 980 has "Norfolk Island" above the denomination, which differentiates it from Australia No. 3127.

Corrugated Iron Water Tank, Fleurieu Peninsula, South Australia A798

Corrugated Iron House, Broken Hill, New South Wales A799

Corrugated Iron Shearing Shed, Bushy Park Cattle Station, Queensland A800

Magney House, Bingie Bingie Point, New South Wales A801

2009, Aug. 11 ***Perf. 14x14¾***

3137 A798 55c multi 1.10 1.10
a. Booklet pane of 4 5.25 —
3138 A799 55c multi 1.10 1.10
a. Booklet pane of 4 5.25 —
3139 A800 55c multi 1.10 1.10
a. Booklet pane of 4 5.25 —
3140 A801 55c multi 1.10 1.10
a. Booklet pane of 4 5.25 —
Complete booklet, #3137a-3140a 22.00
b. Horiz. strip of 4, #3137-3140 4.50 4.50
Nos. 3137-3140 (4) 4.40 4.40

Self-Adhesive

Serpentine Die Cut 11¼ Syncopated

3141 A798 55c multi 1.10 .30
3142 A799 55c multi 1.10 .30
3143 A800 55c multi 1.10 .30
3144 A801 55c multi 1.10 .30
a. Horiz. coil strip of 4, #3141-3144 4.50
b. Booklet pane of 20, 5 each #3141-3144 22.00
Nos. 3141-3144 (4) 4.40 1.20

Complete booklet sold for $10.95.

Intl. Year of Astronomy A802

Designs: 55c, Sombrero Galaxy (M104). $1.45, Reflection Nebula (M78). $2.10, Spiral Galaxy (M83).

2009, Aug. 25 ***Perf. 14x14¾***

3145 A802 55c multi 1.10 .85
3146 A802 $1.45 multi 2.75 2.25
3147 A802 $2.10 multi 4.00 3.00
a. Souvenir sheet, #3145-3147 8.00 6.00
Nos. 3145-3147 (3) 7.85 6.10

No. 31347a exists imperf from a telephone drawing at a substantial premium over face value. Value for a single sheet, $22.

Birds — A803 Toys — A804

Designs: 55c, Green catbird. $1.10, Noisy scrub-bird. $1.65, Mangrove golden whistler. $2.75, Scarlet honeyeater.

2009, Sept. 9 Litho. ***Perf. 14¾x14***

3148 A803 55c multi 1.10 1.10
a. Additionally dated "2013" 1.10 1.10
3149 A803 $1.10 multi 2.25 1.60
a. Booklet pane of 2, #3148-3149 4.25 —
b. Additionally dated "2013" 2.10 2.10
3150 A803 $1.65 multi 3.50 2.50
a. Booklet pane of 2, #3149-3150 7.25 —
b. Booklet pane of 2, #3148, 3150 6.75 —
c. Additionally dated "2013" 3.25 3.25
3151 A803 $2.75 multi 5.50 4.25
a. Booklet pane of 2, #3148, 3151 8.50 —
Complete booklet, #3149a, 3150a, 3150b, 3151a 26.00
b. Additionally dated "2013" 5.50 5.50
c. Booklet pane of 4, #3148a, 3149b, 3150c, 3151d 12.00 —
Nos. 3148-3151 (4) 12.35 9.45

Issued: Nos. 3148a, 3149b, 3150c, 3151b, 3151c, 5/11/13. No. 3151c was issued in a booklet also containing Nos. 3376b, 3665b and 3925a.

Self-Adhesive

Serpentine Die Cut 11¼ Syncopated

3152 A803 55c multi .95 .25
a. Booklet pane of 20 19.00

Complete booklet sold for $12.95.

2009, Sept. 25 ***Perf. 14¾x14***

Children and: Nos. 3153, 3158, Cyclops pedal car. Nos. 3154, 3159, Test Match board game. Nos. 3155, 3160, Barbie doll. Nos. 3156, 3161, Malvern Star Dragstar bicycle. Nos. 3157, 3162, Cabbage Patch Kids doll.

3153 A804 55c multi 1.10 1.10
a. Booklet pane of 4 5.25 —
3154 A804 55c multi 1.10 1.10
a. Booklet pane of 4 5.25 —
3155 A804 55c multi 1.10 1.10
a. Booklet pane of 4 5.25 —
b. Sheet of 10 #3155 + 10 labels 22.00 22.00
3156 A804 55c multi 1.10 1.10
a. Booklet pane of 4 5.25 —
3157 A804 55c multi 1.10 1.10
a. Booklet pane of 4 5.25 —
Complete booklet, #3153a, 3154a, 3155a, 3156a, 3157a 26.00
b. Horiz. strip of 5, #3153-3157 5.50 5.50
Nos. 3153-3157 (5) 5.50 5.50

No. 3155b sold for $10.95.

Booklet Stamps

Self-Adhesive

Serpentine Die Cut 11¼ Syncopated

3158 A804 55c multi 1.10 .30
3159 A804 55c multi 1.10 .30
3160 A804 55c multi 1.10 .30
3161 A804 55c multi 1.10 .30
3162 A804 55c multi 1.10 .30
a. Booklet pane of 10, 2 each #3158-3162 11.00
Nos. 3158-3162 (5) 5.50 1.50

Complete booklet sold for $12.95.

Children Playing Sports — A805

"Let's get active" and children playing: Nos. 3163, 3169, Australian rules football. Nos. 3164, 3170, Basketball. Nos. 3165, 3171, Soccer. Nos. 3166, 3172, Netball. Nos. 3167, 3173, Cricket. Nos. 3168, 3174, Tennis.

2009, Oct. 6 ***Perf. 14¾x14***

3163 A805 55c multi 1.10 1.10
3164 A805 55c multi 1.10 1.10
3165 A805 55c multi 1.10 1.10
3166 A805 55c multi 1.10 1.10
3167 A805 55c multi 1.10 1.10
3168 A805 55c multi 1.10 1.10
a. Block of 6, #3163-3168 7.00 7.00
b. Souvenir sheet, #3163-3168 7.00 7.00
Nos. 3163-3168 (6) 6.60 6.60

Booklet Stamps

Self-Adhesive

Serpentine Die Cut 11¼ Syncopated

3169 A805 55c multi 1.10 .30
a. Booklet pane of 10 11.50
3170 A805 55c multi 1.10 .30
a. Booklet pane of 10 11.50
3171 A805 55c multi 1.10 .30
a. Booklet pane of 10 11.50
3172 A805 55c multi 1.10 .30
a. Booklet pane of 10 11.50
3173 A805 55c multi 1.10 .30
a. Booklet pane of 10 11.50
3174 A805 55c multi 1.10 .30
a. Booklet pane of 10 11.50
b. Booklet pane of 10, #3172, 3174, 2 each #3169-3171, 3173 11.50
Nos. 3169-3174 (6) 6.60 1.80

Miniature Sheet

Australia Post Employees — A806

No. 3175: a, Patrica Crabb (with white blouse with red dots). b, Shirley Freeman (at counter, with brochures at left). c, Vinko Romank (lifting mail tubs). d, Valda Knott (sorting boxes in background). e, Gordon Morgan (motorcycle in background). f, Vongpradith Phongsavan (with conveyor belt in background). g, Norma Thomas (with contractor delivery automobile). h, John Marsh (with blue shirt and tie). i, Anne Brun (at desk, with computer keyboard at left). j, Russell Price (with beard).

2009, Oct. 13 ***Perf. 14¾x14***

3175 A806 Sheet of 10 11.50 8.50
a.-j. 55c Any single 1.10 .85

Australia Post, bicent. Compare with Type A787.

Christmas

A807 A808

Designs: Nos. 3176, 3183, Madonna and Child. Nos. 3177, 3184, 3190, 3195, Candles in star frame. Nos. 3178, 3185, 3191, 3196, Tree ornaments in Christmas tree frame. Nos. 3179, 3186, 3192, 3197, Gifts in stocking cap frame. Nos. 3180, 3187, 3193, 3198, Ornaments in bell frame. Nos. 3181, 3188, 3194, 3199, Candy canes in stocking frame. $1.25, Magi.

2009, Nov. 2 Litho. ***Perf. 14¾x14***

3176 A807 50c multi 1.10 1.10
3177 A808 50c multi 1.10 1.10
3178 A808 50c multi 1.10 1.10

3179 A808 50c multi 1.10 1.10
3180 A808 50c multi 1.10 1.10
3181 A808 50c multi 1.10 1.10
a. Horiz. strip of 5, #3177-3181 5.50 5.50
3182 A807 $1.25 multi 2.75 2.75
a. Souvenir sheet of 2, #3176, 3182 4.00 4.00
Nos. 3176-3182 (7) 9.35 9.35

Booklet Stamps (#3183-3194)
Self-Adhesive
Serpentine Die Cut 11¼ Syncopated

3183 A807 50c multi 1.10 .30
a. Booklet pane of 20 22.00
3184 A808 50c multi 1.10 .30
3185 A808 50c multi 1.10 .30
3186 A808 50c multi 1.10 .30
3187 A808 50c multi 1.10 .30
3188 A808 50c multi 1.10 .30
a. Booklet pane of 10, 2 each #3184-3188 11.00
3189 A807 $1.25 multi 2.75 .30
a. Booklet pane of 5 14.00

Litho. With Foil Application
Frames in Gold

3190 A808 50c multi 1.10 .30
3191 A808 50c multi 1.10 .30
3192 A808 50c multi 1.10 .30
3193 A808 50c multi 1.10 .30
3194 A808 50c multi 1.10 .30
a. Booklet pane of 10, 2 each #3190-3194 11.00
Nos. 3183-3194 (12) 14.85 3.60

With Personalized Photo at Right Like Type A692a

3195 A808 50c multi 2.40 2.40
3196 A808 50c multi 2.40 2.40
3197 A808 50c multi 2.40 2.40
3198 A808 50c multi 2.40 2.40
3199 A808 50c multi 2.40 2.40
Nos. 3195-3199 (5) 12.00 12.00

Nos. 3195-3199 were sold in sheets of 20 containing 4 of each stamp, have personalized pictures and a straight edge at right and lack separations between the stamp and the personalized photo. Sheets of 20 of sold for $23.

No. 3197 exists without "Australia" and the denomination.

Authors — A809

Designs: Nos, 3200, 3212, Color photograph of Peter Carey. No. 3201, Black-and-white photograph of Carey. No. 3202, Black-and-white photograph of David Malouf. Nos. 3203, 3213, Color photograph of Malouf. Nos, 3204, 3214, Color photograph of Colleen McCullough. No. 3205, Black-and-white photograph of McCullough. No. 3206, Black-and-white photograph of Bryce Courtenay. Nos. 3207, 3215, Color photograph of Courtenay. Nos, 3208, 3216, Color photograph of Thomas Keneally. No. 3209, Black-and-white photograph of Keneally. No. 3210, Black-and-white photograph of Tim Winton. Nos. 3211, 3217, Color photograph of Winton.

2010, Jan. 21 Litho. *Perf. 14¾x14*

3200 A809 55c multi 1.10 1.10
3201 A809 55c black & gray 1.10 1.10
3202 A809 55c black & gray 1.10 1.10
3203 A809 55c multi 1.10 1.10
a. Block of 4, #3200-3203 4.50 4.50
b. Booklet pane of 4, #3203-3203 8.50 —
c. As "b," with color separations of stamps 8.50 —
3204 A809 55c multi 1.10 1.10
3205 A809 55c black & gray 1.10 1.10
3206 A809 55c black & gray 1.10 1.10
3207 A809 55c multi 1.10 1.10
a. Block of 4, #3204-3207 4.50 4.50
b. Booklet pane of 4, #3204-3207 8.50 —
c. As "b," with color separations of stamps 8.50 —
3208 A809 55c multi 1.10 1.10
3209 A809 55c black & gray 1.10 1.10
3210 A809 55c black & gray 1.10 1.10
3211 A809 55c multi 1.10 1.10
a. Block of 4, #3208-3211 4.50 4.50
b. Booklet pane of 4, #3208-3211 8.50 —
c. As "b," with color separations of stamps 8.50 —
Complete booklet, #3203b, 3203c, 3207b, 3207c, 3211b, 3211c 52.00
Nos. 3200-3211 (12) 13.20 13.20

Booklet Stamps
Self-Adhesive
Serpentine Die Cut 11¼ Syncopated

3212 A809 55c multi 1.10 .30
3213 A809 55c multi 1.10 .30
3214 A809 55c multi 1.10 .30
3215 A809 55c multi 1.10 .30
3216 A809 55c multi 1.10 .30
3217 A809 55c multi 1.10 .30
a. Booklet pane of 20, 5 #3214, 3 each #3212-3213, 3215-3217 23.00
Nos. 3212-3217 (6) 6.60 1.80

Complete booklet sold for $24.95. Color separations were not valid for postage.

Rule of Governor Lachlan Macquarie, Bicent. A810

Designs: No. 3218, Macquarie (1762-1824) and north view of Sydney. No. 3219, Port Jackson and Sydney Town. No. 3220, Parramatta Female Penitentiary. No. 3221, Governor's Sydney Stables.

2010, Feb. 16 *Perf. 14x14¾*

3218 A810 55c multi 1.10 .85
a. Booklet pane of 4 5.75 —
3219 A810 55c multi 1.10 .85
a. Booklet pane of 4 5.75 —
3220 A810 55c multi 1.10 .85
a. Booklet pane of 4 5.75 —
3221 A810 55c multi 1.10 .85
a. Booklet pane of 4 5.75 —
Complete booklet, #3218a-3221a 23.00
b. Block of 4, #3218-3221 4.50 3.50
Nos. 3218-3221 (4) 4.40 3.40

Complete booklet sold of $10.95.

Coinage of the Australian Commonwealth, Cent. — A811

1910 two shilling coin: Nos. 3222, 3224a, Reverse depicting Australian coat of arms. Nos. 3223, 3224b, Obverse depicting King Edward VII.

2010, Feb. 23 Litho. *Perf. 14x14¾*

3222 A811 55c multi 1.10 .85
3223 A811 $2.75 multi 5.75 2.75

Souvenir Sheet
Litho. & Embossed With Foil Application

3224 Sheet of 2 7.00 3.75
a. A811 55c multi 1.10 .85
b. A811 $2.75 multi 5.75 2.75

No. 3224 exists imperf from a telephone drawing at a substantial premium over face value. Value for single souvenir sheet, $14.

Gold Medalists at 2010 Winter Olympics, Vancouver A812

Designs: No. 3225, Torah Bright, Snowboard halfpipe. No. 3226, Lydia Lassila, Freestyle skiing aerials.

2010 Litho. *Perf. 14¼*

3225 A812 55c multi 1.10 .85
3226 A812 55c multi 1.10 .85

Issued: No. 3225, 2/25; No. 3226, 3/3.

Powered Flight in Australia, Cent. (in 2009) A813

Airplane of: 55c, Colin Defries. $1.45, John Duigan. $2.10, Harry Houdini.

2010, Mar. 9 *Perf. 14x14¾*

3227 A813 55c multi 1.10 .85
3228 A813 $1.45 multi 3.25 1.60
a. Souvenir sheet, #3218, 3223, 3227, 3228 11.00 11.00
b. Sheet of 4, 2 each #3227-3228 9.00 6.75
3229 A813 $2.10 multi 4.50 2.25
Nos. 3227-3229 (3) 8.85 4.70

Booklet Stamps
Self-Adhesive
Serpentine Die Cut 11¼ Syncopated

3230 A813 $1.45 multi 3.25 1.60
a. Booklet pane of 5 16.00
3231 A813 $2.10 multi 4.50 2.25
a. Booklet pane of 5 23.00

2010 Canberra Stamp Show (No. 3228a). London 2010 Festival of Stamps (No. 3228b). Issued: No. 3228a, 3/12. No. 3228b, 5/8.

Agricultural Shows — A814

Designs: Nos. 3232, 3237, Prize bull. Nos. 3233, 3238, Cake decorating competition. Nos. 3234, 3239, Horse competition. Nos. 3235, 3240, Wood chopping competition. Nos. 3236, 3241, Dog show.

2010, Mar. 23 Litho. *Perf. 14¾x14*

3232 A814 55c multi 1.10 1.10
a. Booklet pane of 4 5.50 —
3233 A814 55c multi 1.10 1.10
a. Booklet pane of 4 5.50 —
3234 A814 55c multi 1.10 1.10
a. Booklet pane of 4 5.50 —
3235 A814 55c multi 1.10 1.10
a. Booklet pane of 4 5.50 —
3236 A814 55c multi 1.10 1.10
a. Booklet pane of 4 5.50 —
Complete booklet, #3232a-3236a 27.50
b. Horiz. strip of 5, #3232-3236 5.75 5.75
c. Souvenir sheet, #3232-3236 5.75 5.75
Nos. 3232-3236 (5) 5.50 5.50

Booklet Stamps
Self-Adhesive
Serpentine Die Cut 11¼ Syncopated

3237 A814 55c multi 1.10 .30
3238 A814 55c multi 1.10 .30
3239 A814 55c multi 1.10 .30
3240 A814 55c multi 1.10 .30
3241 A814 55c multi 1.10 .30
a. Booklet pane of 10, 2 each #3237-3241 11.50 —
Nos. 3237-3241 (5) 5.50 1.50

Complete booklet sold for $12.95.

Queen's Birthday — A815

2010, Apr. 6 *Perf. 14¾x14*

3242 A815 55c multi 1.25 1.25
a. Sheet of 4, #2505b, 2864b, 3067b, 3242 8.00 4.00

Booklet Stamp
Self-Adhesive
Serpentine Die Cut 11¼ Syncopated

3243 A815 55c multi 1.25 .30
a. Booklet pane of 10 12.75

Issued: No. 3242a, 5/8. London 2010 Festival of Stamps (No. 3242a).

Kokoda Campaign, 68th Anniv. — A816

Designs: Nos. 3244, 3249, Soldiers in battle. Nos. 3245, 3250, Injured Australian soldier, Papuan natives. Nos. 3246, 3251, Veterans of Kokoda Campaign, Papuan houses. Nos. 3247, 3252, Tourists at Kokoda. $1.45, Veterans at Kokoda Campaign Memorial, Isurava, Papua New Guinea.

2010, Apr. 20 *Perf. 14¾x14*

3244 A816 55c multi 1.10 1.10
3245 A816 55c multi 1.10 1.10
a. Booklet pane of 4, 2 each #3244-3245 6.25 —
3246 A816 55c multi 1.10 1.10
3247 A816 55c multi 1.10 1.10
a. Booklet pane of 4 6.25 —
b. Horiz. strip of 4, #3244-3247 4.50 4.50
3248 A816 $1.45 multi 3.25 2.40
a. Booklet pane of 4, 2 each #3246, 3248 11.50
Complete booklet, #3245a, 3247a, 3248a 24.00
b. Souvenir sheet, #3244-3248 7.75 7.75
Nos. 3244-3248 (5) 7.65 6.80

Self-Adhesive
Serpentine Die Cut 11¼ Syncopated

3249 A816 55c multi 1.10 .30
3250 A816 55c multi 1.10 .30
3251 A816 55c multi 1.10 .30
3252 A816 55c multi 1.10 .30
a. Vert. coil strip of 4, #3249-3252 4.50
b. Booklet pane of 10, 2 each #3250, 3252, 3 each #3249, 3251 11.50
Nos. 3249-3252 (4) 4.40 1.20

Complete booklet sold for $10.95. See Papua New Guinea Nos. 1455-1456.

Queen Victoria ("Chalon Head" Portrait of Tasmania and Queensland Stamps) — A817

2010, May 7 Litho. *Perf. 14x13½*

3253 A817 $5 multi 10.00 5.25
a. Souvenir sheet of 1 10.00 5.25
b. As "a," with London 2010 emblem in gold in sheet margin 8.25 8.25

No. 3253 has simulated toning. A souvenir sheet with a litho. and engraved stamp sold for $15.

Issued: No. 3253b, 5/8.

Railway Journeys A818

Designs: Nos. 3254, 3258, The Ghan. Nos. 3255, 3259, West Coast Wilderness Railway, Tasmania. Nos. 3256, 3260, The Indian Pacific. $2.10, Kuranda Scenic Railway, Queensland (50x30mm).

2010, May 7 *Perf. 14x14¾*

3254 A818 55c multi 1.10 1.10
3255 A818 55c multi 1.10 1.10
3256 A818 55c multi 1.10 1.10
a. Booklet pane of 4, #3254, 3255, 2 #3256 6.50 —
b. Booklet pane of 4, #3255, 3256, 2 #3254 6.50 —
c. Booklet pane of 4, #3254, 3256, 2 #3255 6.50 —

Perf. 13½x14

3257 A818 $2.10 multi 4.25 2.25
a. Booklet pane of 1 6.25 —
Complete booklet, #3256a-3256c, 3257a 26.50
b. Souvenir sheet of 1 4.25 2.25

c. As "b," with London 2010 emblem in gold in sheet margin 3.50 3.50
Nos. 3254-3257 (4) 7.55 5.55

Self-Adhesive

Serpentine Die Cut 11¼ Syncopated

3258 A818 55c multi 1.10 .30
3259 A818 55c multi 1.10 .30
3260 A818 55c multi 1.10 .30
a. Horiz. coil strip of 3, #3258-3260 3.50
b. Booklet pane of 20, 8 each #3258-3259, 4 #3260 23.00

Serpentine Die Cut 11¼

3261 A818 $2.10 multi 4.25 2.25
a. Booklet pane of 5 22.00
Nos. 3258-3261 (4) 7.55 3.15

No. 3257a has blue panels at the sides. Complete booklet sold for $12.95.
Issued: No. 3257c, 5/8.

Expo 2010, Shanghai — A819

Designs: No. 3262, Australian Pavilion. No. 3263, Australian kookaburra mascot, Peng Peng.

2010, May 18 ***Perf. 14¾x14***

3262 A819 55c multi 1.00 .80
3263 A819 55c multi 1.00 .80
a. Pair, #3262-3263 2.00 1.60

UNESCO World Heritage Sites in Australia — A820

Designs: Nos. 3264, 3268, Purnululu National Park. Nos. 3265, 3269, Kakadu National Park. No. 3266, Gondwana Rainforests, horiz. No. 3267, Tasmanian Wilderness, horiz.

2010, May 25 ***Perf. 14¾x14***

3264 A820 55c multi 1.00 1.00
3265 A820 55c multi 1.00 1.00
a. Horiz. pair, #3264-3265 2.00 2.00

Perf. 14x14¾

3266 A820 $1.10 multi 2.25 1.60
3267 A820 $1.10 multi 2.25 1.60
a. Horiz. pair, #3266-3267 4.50 3.25
Nos. 3264-3267 (4) 6.50 5.20

Self-Adhesive

Serpentine Die Cut 11¼ Syncopated

3268 A820 55c multi 1.00 1.00
3269 A820 55c multi 1.00 1.00
a. Vert. coil pair, #3268-3269 2.00
b. Booklet pane of 10, 5 each #3268-3269 10.00

Fish — A821

Designs: 5c, Coral rabbitfish. Nos. 3271, 3278, 3283, Clown triggerfish. Nos. 3272, 3279, 3284, Spotted sweetlips. Nos. 3273, 3280, 3285, Golden damsel. Nos. 3274, 3281, 3286, Regal angelfish. $1.20, Saddle butterflyfish. $1.80, Chevron butterflyfish. $3, Orangefin anemonefish.

2010, June 21 Litho. ***Perf. 14x14½***

3270 A821 5c multi .25 .25
3271 A821 60c multi 1.00 .25
3272 A821 60c multi 1.00 .25
a. Souvenir sheet, #3271, 3272, 2 #3270 2.40 2.40
3273 A821 60c multi 1.00 .25
3274 A821 60c multi 1.00 .25
a. Block or strip of 4, #3271-3274 4.00 1.00
3275 A821 $1.20 multi 2.00 1.00
3276 A821 $1.80 multi 3.00 1.50

Perf. 14½x14

Size: 50x30mm (#3277)

3277 A821 $3 multi 5.00 2.50
Nos. 3270-3277 (8) 14.25 6.25

Coil Stamps

Self-Adhesive

Die Cut Perf. 12¾

3278 A821 60c multi 1.00 .25
3279 A821 60c multi 1.00 .25
3280 A821 60c multi 1.00 .25
3281 A821 60c multi 1.00 .25
a. Horiz. strip of 4, #3278-3281 4.00

Booklet Stamps

Serpentine Die Cut 11¼

3282 A821 5c multi .25 .25
a. Booklet pane of 20 4.00
3283 A821 60c multi 1.00 .25
3284 A821 60c multi 1.00 .25
3285 A821 60c multi 1.00 .25
3286 A821 60c multi 1.00 .25
a. Booklet pane of 10, 3 each #3283-3284, 2 each #3285-3286 10.00
b. Booklet pane of 20, 5 each #3283-3286 20.00
Nos. 3278-3286 (9) 8.25 2.25

Issued: No. 3272a, 8/4/10. Bangkok 2010 Intl. Stamp Exhibition (No. 3272a).

Beaches — A822

Designs: $1.50, Bay of Fires, Tasmania. $2.20, Cape Tribulation, Queensland. $4.30, Hellfire Bay, Western Australia, horiz.

2010, June 28 ***Perf. 14¾x14***

3287 A822 $1.50 multi 2.50 1.25
3288 A822 $2.20 multi 3.75 1.90

Size: 50x30mm (#3289)

Perf. 14½x14

3289 A822 $4.30 multi 7.25 3.75
Nos. 3287-3289 (3) 13.50 6.90

Booklet Stamps

Self-Adhesive

Serpentine Die Cut 11¼ Syncopated

3290 A822 $1.50 multi 2.50 1.25
a. Booklet pane of 5 12.50
3291 A822 $2.20 multi 3.75 1.90
a. Booklet pane of 5 19.00

With Personalized Photo at Right Like Type A692a

Serpentine Die Cut 11½x11¼ Syncopated

3292 A822 $1.50 multi 3.75 3.75
3293 A822 $2.20 multi 4.75 4.75

Nos. 3292-3293 each were printed in sheets of 20 and have personalized pictures and a straight edge at right, and lack separations between the stamp and the personalized photo. Sheets of 20 of No. 3292 sold for $43, and No. 3293 sold for $56.

Adopted Dogs — A823

Designs: Nos. 3294, 3299, Piper. Nos. 3295, 3300, Jessie. Nos. 3296, 3301, Buckley. Nos. 3297, 3302, Daisy. Nos. 3298, 3303, Tigger.

2010, June 29 ***Perf. 14¾x14***

3294 A823 60c multi 1.00 1.00
3295 A823 60c multi 1.00 1.00
3296 A823 60c multi 1.00 1.00
3297 A823 60c multi 1.00 1.00
3298 A823 60c multi 1.00 1.00
a. Horiz. strip of 5, #3294-3298 5.00 5.00
Nos. 3294-3298 (5) 5.00 5.00

Self-Adhesive

Serpentine Die Cut 11¼ Syncopated

3299 A823 60c multi 1.00 .25
3300 A823 60c multi 1.00 .25
3301 A823 60c multi 1.00 .25
3302 A823 60c multi 1.00 .25
3303 A823 60c multi 1.00 .25
a. Vert. coil strip of 5, #3299-3303 5.00
b. Booklet pane of 10, 2 each #3299-3303 10.00
Nos. 3299-3303 (5) 5.00 1.25

No. 3303a was produced by two different printers, Pemara and McKellar Renown. The stamps have the printer's name on the backing paper, but are essentially identical to each other.

Emergency Services — A824

000 Emergency Services emblem and: Nos. 3304, 3308, "Stay Focused, Stay Relevant, Stay on Line." Nos. 3305, 3309, Police Helicopter. Nos. 3306, 3310, Fire. Nos. 3307, 3311, Ambulance Cross.

2010, July 13 ***Perf. 14¾x14***

3304 A824 60c multi 1.10 1.10
3305 A824 60c multi 1.10 1.10
3306 A824 60c multi 1.10 1.10
3307 A824 60c multi 1.10 1.10
a. Horiz. strip of 4, #3304-3307 4.40 4.40
Nos. 3304-3307 (4) 4.40 4.40

Self-Adhesive

Serpentine Die Cut 11¼ Syncopated

3308 A824 60c multi 1.10 .25
3309 A824 60c multi 1.10 .25
3310 A824 60c multi 1.10 .25
3311 A824 60c multi 1.10 .25
a. Vert. coil strip of 4, #3308-3311 4.40
b. Booklet pane of 20, 5 each #3308-3311 22.00
Nos. 3308-3311 (4) 4.40 1.00

Southern Cross — A825

2010, July 19 ***Perf. 14½x14***

3312 A825 60c Blue sky 1.10 1.10
a. Sheet of 20 + 20 labels 27.00 27.00
3313 A825 60c Purple & orange sky 1.10 1.10
a. Horiz. pair, #3312-3313 2.25 2.25
b. Sheet of 20 + 20 labels 27.00 27.00
c. Perf. 14x14½, + label at bottom 1.40 1.40

Nos. 3312a and 3313b each sold for $12.95 and have labels depicting various National Rugby League and Australian Football League team emblems that could not be personalized. No. 3313c was issued in sheet of 10 + 10 labels depicting race horse Black Caviar that were sold in groups of 2 sheets that sold for $12.95.

Balloons — A826

Teddy Bear — A827

Wattle — A828

Flowers — A829

Tulips — A830

Roses — A831

Flowers and Champagne Flutes — A832

Wedding Rings — A833

2010, July 19 ***Perf. 14¾x14***

3314 A826 60c multi 1.10 1.10
3315 A827 60c multi 1.10 1.10
3316 A828 60c multi 1.10 1.10
a. Horiz. strip of 3, #3314-3316 3.30 3.30
3317 A829 60c multi 1.10 1.10
3318 A830 60c multi 1.10 1.10
3319 A831 60c multi 1.10 1.10
3320 A832 60c multi 1.10 1.10
a. Block of 4, #3317-3320 4.40 4.40
3321 A833 $1.20 multi 2.25 2.25
Nos. 3314-3321 (8) 9.95 9.95

Booklet Stamps

Self-Adhesive

Serpentine Die Cut 11¼ Syncopated

3322 A826 60c multi 1.10 .25
a. Booklet pane of 10 11.00
3323 A827 60c multi 1.10 .25
a. Booklet pane of 10 11.00
3324 A828 60c multi 1.10 .25
a. Booklet pane of 10 11.00
3325 A830 60c multi 1.10 .25
a. Booklet pane of 10 11.00
3326 A831 60c multi 1.10 .25
a. Booklet pane of 10 11.00
3327 A833 $1.20 multi 2.25 1.10
a. Booklet pane of 10 22.50
Nos. 3322-3327 (6) 7.75 2.35

With Personalized Photo at Right Like Type A692a

Serpentine Die Cut 11½x11¼ Syncopated

3328 A826 60c multi 2.25 2.25
3329 A827 60c multi 2.25 2.25
3330 A828 60c multi 2.25 2.25
3331 A829 60c multi 2.25 2.25
3332 A830 60c multi 2.25 2.25
3333 A831 60c multi 2.25 2.25
3334 A832 60c multi 2.25 2.25
3335 A833 $1.20 multi 3.50 3.50
Nos. 3328-3335 (8) 19.25 19.25

Nos. 3328-3335 each were printed in sheets of 20 and have personalized pictures and a straight edge at right, and lack separations between the stamp and the personalized photo. Sheets of 20 of Nos. 3328-3334 each sold for $25, and No. 3335 sold for $37.
See No. 3401.

Australian Taxation Office, Cent. A834

2010, July 27 Litho. ***Perf. 14x14¾***

3336 A834 60c multi 1.10 .85

Burke and Wills Expedition, 150th Anniv. A835

Designs: Nos. 3337, 3341, Explorers Robert Burke (1820-61) and William J. Wills (1834-61). Nos. 3338, 3342, Burke and Wills on horses leaving Melbourne. No. 3339, Expedition members returning from Gulf of Carpenteria. No. 3340, Expedition members heading towards Mt. Hopeless.

2010, Aug. 3 Litho. *Perf. 14x14¾*

3337 A835 60c multi 1.10 1.10
a. Booklet pane of 4 5.00 —
3338 A835 60c multi 1.10 1.10
a. Horiz. pair, #3337-3338 2.20 2.20
b. Booklet pane of 4 5.00 —
3339 A835 $1.20 multi 2.25 2.25
a. Booklet pane of 2 5.00 —
3340 A835 $1.20 multi 2.25 2.25
a. Horiz. pair, #3339-3340 4.50 4.50
b. Booklet pane of 2 5.00 —
Complete booklet, #3337a, 3338b, 3339a, 3340b 20.00
Nos. 3337-3340 (4) 6.70 6.70

Coil Stamps
Self-Adhesive
Serpentine Die Cut 11¼ Syncopated

3341 A835 60c multi 1.10 .25
3342 A835 60c multi 1.10 .25
a. Horiz. pair, #3341-3342 2.20

Complete booklet sold for $10.95.
See Australian Antarctic Territory No. L149b.

Girl Guides, Cent. A836

Emblem, early Girl Guides and: 60c, Girl Guide with helmet and climbing rope. $1.50, Girl Guides wearing hats. $2.20, Olave Baden-Powell.

2010, Aug. 31 Litho. *Perf. 14x14¾*

3343 A836 60c multi 1.10 1.10
3344 A836 $1.50 multi 2.75 2.75
3345 A836 $2.20 multi 4.00 4.00
Nos. 3343-3345 (3) 7.85 7.85

Self-Adhesive
Serpentine Die Cut 11¼ Syncopated

3346 A836 60c multi 1.10 .25
a. Booklet pane of 20 22.00

Booklet Stamps

3347 A836 $1.50 multi 2.75 1.40
a. Booklet pane of 5 14.00
3348 A836 $2.20 multi 4.00 2.00
a. Booklet pane of 5 20.00
Nos. 3346-3348 (3) 7.85 3.65

Dedication of National Service Memorial, Canberra A837

2010, Sept. 8 Litho. *Perf. 14x14¾*

3349 A837 60c multi 1.10 1.10
a. Additionally dated "2013" (#3349b) 1.25 1.25
b. Booklet pane of 4 #3349a 5.00 —

Issued: Nos. 3349a, 3349b, 3/5/13. No. 3349b was issued in booklet along with Nos. 1939c, 2710c, 2869e, 3107c and 3877a.

Booklet Stamp
Self-Adhesive
Serpentine Die Cut 11¼ Syncopated

3350 A837 60c multi 1.10 .25
a. Booklet pane of 10 11.00

Long Weekend Vacations A838

People on weekend vacations: Nos. 3351, 3356, Boating at beach, 1950s. Nos. 3352, 3357, Camping, 1960s. Nos. 3353, 3358, Surfing at beach, 1970s. Nos. 3354, 3359, Houseboating on river, 1980s. Nos. 3355, 3360, At winter resort, 1990s.

2010, Sept. 22 *Perf. 14x14¾*

3351 A838 60c multi 1.25 1.25
a. Booklet pane of 4 5.50 —
3352 A838 60c multi 1.25 1.25
a. Booklet pane of 4 5.50 —
3353 A838 60c multi 1.25 1.25
a. Booklet pane of 4 5.50 —
3354 A838 60c multi 1.25 1.25
a. Booklet pane of 4 5.50 —
3355 A838 60c multi 1.25 1.25
a. Booklet pane of 4 5.50 —
Complete booklet, #3351a-3355a 27.50
b. Horiz. strip of 5, #3351-3355 6.25 6.25
Nos. 3351-3355 (5) 6.25 6.25

Self-Adhesive
Serpentine Die Cut 11¼ Syncopated

3356 A838 60c multi 1.25 .25
3357 A838 60c multi 1.25 .25
3358 A838 60c multi 1.25 .25
3359 A838 60c multi 1.25 .25
3360 A838 60c multi 1.25 .25
a. Horiz. coil strip of 5, #3356-3360 6.25
b. Booklet pane of 10, 2 each #3356-3360 12.50
Nos. 3356-3360 (5) 6.25 1.25

Complete booklet sold for $13.95.

Care for Wildlife — A839

Designs: Nos. 3361, 3367, Common wombat. Nos. 3362, 3368, Eastern gray kangaroo. Nos. 3363, 3369, Koala. Nos. 3364, 3370, Gray-headed flying fox. Nos. 3365, 3371, Southern boobook. $1.20, Ringtail possum.

2010, Oct. 5 Litho. *Perf. 14¾x14*
Denomination Color

3361 A839 60c orange brown 1.25 1.25
3362 A839 60c blue 1.25 1.25
3363 A839 60c green 1.25 1.25
3364 A839 60c red brown 1.25 1.25
3365 A839 60c bister 1.25 1.25
a. Horiz. strip of 5, #3361-3365 6.25 6.25
3366 A839 $1.20 red 2.40 1.75
a. Souvenir sheet of 6, #3361-3366 8.75 8.75
Nos. 3361-3366 (6) 8.65 8.00

Self-Adhesive
Serpentine Die Cut 11¼ Syncopated

3367 A839 60c orange brown 1.25 .25
3368 A839 60c blue 1.25 .25
3369 A839 60c green 1.25 .25
3370 A839 60c red brown 1.25 .25
3371 A839 60c bister 1.25 .25
a. Vert. coil strip of 5, #3367-3371 6.25
b. Booklet pane of 10, 2 each #3367-3371 12.50
Nos. 3367-3371 (5) 6.25 1.25

Canonization of St. Mary MacKillop (1842-1909) A840

2010, Oct. 18 *Perf. 14¾x14*

3372 A840 60c multi 1.25 .95

Kingfishers A841

Designs: 60c, Red-backed kingfisher. $1.20, Sacred kingfisher. $1.80, Blue-winged kookaburra. $3, Yellow-billed kingfisher.

2010, Oct. 26 *Perf. 14¾x14*

3373 A841 60c multi 1.25 1.25
a. Additionally dated "2013" 1.25 1.25
3374 A841 $1.20 multi 2.50 1.90
a. Additionally dated "2013" 2.40 2.40
3375 A841 $1.80 multi 3.75 1.90
a. Additionally dated "2013" 3.50 3.50
3376 A841 $3 multi 6.25 3.25
a. Additionally dated "2013" 5.75 5.75
b. Booklet pane of 4, #3373a, 3374a, 3375a, 3376a 13.00 —
Nos. 3373-3376 (4) 13.75 8.30

Issued: Nos. 3373a, 3374a, 3375a, 3376a, 3376b, 5/11/13. No. 3376b was issued in a booklet also containing Nos. 3151c, 3665b and 3925a.

Self-Adhesive
Serpentine Die Cut 11¼ Syncopated

3377 A841 60c multi 1.25 .25
a. Booklet pane of 10 12.50

150th Running of the Melbourne Cup Horse Race — A842

Designs: No. 3378, Melbourne Cup. Nos. 3379, 3382, Carbine, 1890 winner, horiz. Nos. 3380, 3383, Phar Lap, 1930 winner, horiz. Nos. 3381, 3384, Saintly, 1996 winner, horiz.

2010, Nov. 1 Litho. *Perf. 14¾x14*

3378 A842 60c multi 1.25 .95
a. Booklet pane of 4 7.25 —

Perf. 14x14¾

3379 A842 60c multi 1.25 1.25
a. Booklet pane of 4 7.25 —
3380 A842 60c multi 1.25 1.25
a. Booklet pane of 4 7.25 —
3381 A842 60c multi 1.25 1.25
a. Booklet pane of 4 7.25 —
Complete booklet, #3378a, 3379a, 3380a, 3381a 29.00
b. Souvenir sheet, #3378-3381 5.00 5.00
Nos. 3378-3381 (4) 5.00 4.70

No. 3381b exists imperf from a telephone drawing at a substantial premium over face value. Value for single souvenir sheet, $15.

Booklet Stamps
Self-Adhesive
Serpentine Die Cut 11¼ Syncopated

3382 A842 60c multi 1.25 .25
3383 A842 60c multi 1.25 .25
3384 A842 60c multi 1.25 .25
a. Booklet pane of 20, 7 each #3382-3383, 6 #3384 25.00
Nos. 3382-3384 (3) 3.75 75.00

Complete booklet sold for $13.95 and also included imperforate and gummed lithographed pages reproducing pairs of Nos. 337, 693, 694, 2104 and 2106 that were not valid for postage.

Christmas
A843 A844

Designs: Nos. 3385, 3390, 3393, 3396, Girl writing letter to Santa Claus. Nos. 3386, 3389, 3394, 3395, Santa Claus reading letter. Nos. 3387, 3391, Adoration of the Magi. $1.30, Adoration of the Shepherds.

2010, Nov. 1 Litho. *Perf. 14¾x14*

3385 A843 55c multi 1.10 1.10
3386 A843 55c multi 1.10 1.10
a. Horiz. pair, #3385-3386 2.25 2.25
3387 A844 55c multi 1.10 1.10
3388 A844 $1.30 multi 2.75 2.75
Nos. 3385-3388 (4) 6.05 6.05

Booklet Stamps
Self-Adhesive
Serpentine Die Cut 11¼ Syncopated

3389 A843 55c multi 1.10 .25
3390 A843 55c multi 1.10 .25
a. Booklet pane of 20, 10 each #3389-3390 22.00
3391 A844 55c multi 1.10 .25
a. Booklet pane of 20 22.00
3392 A844 $1.30 multi 2.75 1.40
a. Booklet pane of 5 14.00

Litho. With Foil Application

3393 A843 55c multi 1.10 .25
a. Booklet pane of 10 11.00
3394 A843 55c multi 1.10 .25
a. Booklet pane of 10 11.00
Nos. 3389-3394 (6) 8.25 2.65

With Personalized Photo at Right Like Type A692a
Litho.
Self-Adhesive
Serpentine Die Cut 11½x11¼ Syncopated

3395 A843 55c multi 2.50 2.50
3396 A843 55c multi 2.50 2.50

Nos. 3395-3396 were printed together in sheets of 20 (10 of each design), and have personalized pictures and a straight edge at right and lack separations between the stamp and the personalized photo. Sheets of 20 sold for $24.

Champagne Flutes Type of 2010 and

Roses — A845

Hearts and Flowers — A846

2011, Jan. 18 *Perf. 14¾x14*

3397 A845 60c multi 1.25 1.25
3398 A846 60c multi 1.25 1.25
a. Horiz. pair, #3397-3398 2.50 2.50

Booklet Stamps
Self-Adhesive
Serpentine Die Cut 11¼ Syncopated

3399 A845 60c multi 1.25 .25
a. Booklet pane of 12 12.50
3400 A846 60c multi 1.25 .25
a. Booklet pane of 12 12.50
3401 A832 60c multi 1.25 .60
a. Booklet pane of 12 12.50
Nos. 3399-3401 (3) 3.75 1.10

With Personalized Photo at Right Like Type A692a
Serpentine Die Cut 11½x11¼ Syncopated

3402 A845 60c multi 2.50 2.50
3403 A846 60c multi 2.50 2.50

Nos. 3395-3396 each were printed in sheets of 20 and have personalized pictures and a straight edge at right and lack separations between the stamp and the personalized photo. Sheets of 20 of Nos. 3402-3403 each sold for $25.
No. 3401 dated 2010.

Famous Women — A848

Designs: Nos. 3404, 3408, Eva Cox, feminist. Nos. 3405, 3409, Germaine Greer, writer on feminist topics. Nos. 3406, 3410, Elizabeth Evatt, jurist. Nos. 3407, 3411, Anne Summers, writer.

2011, Jan. 20 *Perf. 14¾x14*

3404 A848 60c multi 1.25 1.25
3405 A848 60c multi 1.25 1.25
3406 A848 60c multi 1.25 1.25
3407 A848 60c multi 1.25 1.25
a. Horiz. strip of 4, #3404-3407 5.00 5.00
Nos. 3404-3407 (4) 5.00 5.00

Booklet Stamps
Self-Adhesive
Serpentine Die Cut 11¼ Syncopated

3408 A848 60c multi 1.25 .25
3409 A848 60c multi 1.25 .25
3410 A848 60c multi 1.25 .25
3411 A848 60c multi 1.25 .25
a. Booklet pane of 20, 5 each #3408-3411 25.00
Nos. 3408-3411 (4) 5.00 1.00

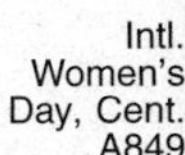

Intl. Women's Day, Cent. A849

2011, Feb. 15 ***Perf. 14x14¾***

3412 A849 60c multi 1.25 .95
a. Miniature sheet of 10 12.50 12.50

Military Aircraft A850

Designs: Nos. 3413, 3417, F-111. Nos. 3414, 3418, F/A-18F. $1.20, Wedge Tail. $3, C-17.

2011, Feb. 22 ***Perf. 14x14¾***

3413 A850 60c multi 1.25 1.25
3414 A850 60c multi 1.25 1.25
3415 A850 $1.20 multi 2.40 1.90
a. Souvenir sheet of 4, #3337, 3339, 3413, 3415 7.75 7.75
3416 A850 $3 multi 6.00 4.50
a. Souvenir sheet of 4, #3413-3416 11.00 11.00
Nos. 3413-3416 (4) 10.90 8.90

Booklet Stamps
Self-Adhesive
Serpentine Die Cut 11¼ Syncopated

3417 A850 60c multi 1.25 .25
3418 A850 60c multi 1.25 .25
a. Booklet pane of 10, 5 each #3417-3418 12.50

Issued: No. 3415a, 3/31. Sydney Stamp Expo 2011 (No. 3415a).

Flowers — A851

Designs: Nos. 3419, 3424, Gerbera daisy. Nos. 3420, 3425, Jacarandas. Nos. 3421, 3426, Australian everlasting. Nos. 3422, 3427, Violet. Nos. 3423, 3428, Tulip.

2011, Mar. 8 **Litho.** ***Perf. 14¾x14***

3419 A851 60c multi 1.25 1.25
a. Booklet pane of 4 5.25 —
3420 A851 60c multi 1.25 1.25
a. Booklet pane of 4 5.25 —
3421 A851 60c multi 1.25 1.25
a. Booklet pane of 4 5.25 —
3422 A851 60c multi 1.25 1.25
a. Booklet pane of 4 5.25 —
3423 A851 60c multi 1.25 1.25
a. Booklet pane of 4 5.25 —
Complete booklet, #3419a, 3420a, 3421a, 3422a, 3423a 27.00
b. Horiz. strip of 5, #3419-3423 6.25 6.25
Nos. 3419-3423 (5) 6.25 6.25

Self-Adhesive
Serpentine Die Cut 11¼ Syncopated

3424 A851 60c multi 1.25 .25
3425 A851 60c multi 1.25 .25
3426 A851 60c multi 1.25 .25
3427 A851 60c multi 1.25 .25
3428 A851 60c multi 1.25 .25
a. Vert. coil strip of 5, #3424-3428 6.25
b. Booklet pane of 20, 4 each #3424-3428 25.00
Nos. 3424-3428 (5) 6.25 1.25

Complete booklet sold for $12.95.

Paintings of Flowers in National Gallery of Victoria A852

Paintings: Nos. 3429, 3434, A Bunch of Flowers, by Nora Heysen. Nos. 3430, 3435, Camellias, by Arnold Shore. Nos. 3431, 3436, Fruit and Flowers, by Vida Lahey. Nos. 3432, 3437, Still Life, Zinnias, by Roy de Maistre. Nos. 3433, 3438, A Cottage Bunch, by Hans Heysen.

2011, Mar. 22 ***Perf. 14x14¾***

3429 A852 60c multi 1.25 1.25
3430 A852 60c multi 1.25 1.25
3431 A852 60c multi 1.25 1.25
3432 A852 60c multi 1.25 1.25
3433 A852 60c multi 1.25 1.25
a. Horiz. strip of 5, #3429-3433 6.25 6.25
Nos. 3429-3433 (5) 6.25 6.25

Self-Adhesive
Serpentine Die Cut 11¼ Syncopated

3434 A852 60c multi 1.25 .25
3435 A852 60c multi 1.25 .25
3436 A852 60c multi 1.25 .25
3437 A852 60c multi 1.25 .25
3438 A852 60c multi 1.25 .25
a. Horiz. coil strip of 5, #3434-3438 6.25
b. Booklet pane of 10, 2 each #3434-3438 12.50
Nos. 3434-3438 (5) 6.25 1.25

Lake Eyre — A853

Lake Eyre: 60c, In dry season. $1.55, With new growth. $2.25, Bird life. $3.10, In flood.

2011, Apr. 4 ***Perf. 14½x14***

3439 A853 60c multi 1.25 .65
3440 A853 $1.55 multi 3.25 3.25
3441 A853 $2.25 multi 4.75 4.75
3442 A853 $3.10 multi 6.50 3.25
Nos. 3439-3442 (4) 15.75 11.90

Booklet Stamps
Self-Adhesive
Serpentine Die Cut 11¼

3443 A853 $1.55 multi 3.25 1.60
a. Booklet pane of 5 16.50
3444 A853 $2.25 multi 4.75 2.40
a. Booklet pane of 5 24.00

A854

Portraits of Queen Elizabeth II by: 60c, Brian Dunlop, 1984. $2.25, Rolf Harris, 2005.

2011, Apr. 5 ***Perf. 14¾x14***

3445 A854 60c multi 1.25 .65
3446 A854 $2.25 multi 4.75 2.40
a. Souvenir sheet of 2, #3445-3446 6.00 6.00

Queen Elizabeth II, 85th birthday.

A855

Background color: 60c, Pale olive green. $2.25, White.

2011, Apr. 12 ***Perf. 14¾x14***

3447 A855 60c multi 1.25 1.25
3448 A855 $2.25 multi 4.75 2.40
a. Souvenir sheet of 2, #3447-3448 6.00 6.00

Booklet Stamp
Self-Adhesive
Serpentine Die Cut 11¼ Syncopated

3449 A855 60c multi 1.25 .25
a. Booklet pane of 10 12.50

Wedding of Prince William and Catherine Middleton.

Wedding Photograph of Prince Willliam and Wife Catherine A856

2011, May 4 ***Perf. 14¼***

3450 A856 60c multi 1.25 1.25

Booklet Stamp
Self-Adhesive
Serpentine Die Cut 11¼ Syncopated

3451 A856 60c multi 1.25 .25
a. Booklet pane of 10 12.50

Dame Nellie Melba (1861-1931), Operatic Soprano — A857

2011, May 10 ***Perf. 14¾x14***

3452 A857 60c multi 1.25 1.25

Booklet Stamp
Self-Adhesive
Serpentine Die Cut 11¼ Syncopated

3453 A857 60c multi 1.25 .25
a. Booklet pane of 20 25.00

Native Agricultural Products A858

Designs: Nos. 3454, 3458, Eucalyptus oil. Nos. 3455, 3459, Australian honey. Nos. 3456, 3460, Macadamia nuts. Nos. 3457, 3461, Tea tree oil.

2011, May 17 ***Perf. 14x14¾***

3454 A858 60c multi 1.25 1.25
3455 A858 60c multi 1.25 1.25
3456 A858 60c multi 1.25 1.25
3457 A858 60c multi 1.25 1.25
a. Horiz. strip of 4, #3454-3457 5.00 5.00
Nos. 3454-3457 (4) 5.00 5.00

Self-Adhesive
Serpentine Die Cut 11¼ Syncopated

3458 A858 60c multi 1.25 .25
3459 A858 60c multi 1.25 .25
3460 A858 60c multi 1.25 .25
3461 A858 60c multi 1.25 .25
a. Horiz. coil strip of 4, #3458-3461 5.00
b. Booklet pane of 10, 4 #3458, 2 each #3459-3461 12.50
Nos. 3458-3461 (4) 5.00 1.00

Southern Cross With Sports Team Emblem — A859

Booklet Stamps
Self-Adhesive
Blue Sky
With Emblem of Australian Rules Football Team
Adelaide Crows

Serpentine Die Cut 10¾x11¼ Syncopated

2011, Apr. 12 **Litho.**

3462 A859 60c Emblem at R 1.50 .75
3463 A859 60c Emblem at L 1.50 .75
a. Booklet pane of 10, 5 each #3462-3463 15.00

Carlton Blues

3464 A859 60c Emblem at R 1.50 .75
3465 A859 60c Emblem at L 1.50 .75
a. Booklet pane of 10, 5 each #3464-3465 15.00

Essendon Bombers

3466 A859 60c Emblem at R 1.50 .75
3467 A859 60c Emblem at L 1.50 .75
a. Booklet pane of 10, 5 each #3466-3467 15.00

Geelong Cats

3468 A859 60c Emblem at R 1.50 .75
3469 A859 60c Emblem at L 1.50 .75
a. Booklet pane of 10, 5 each #3468-3469 15.00

Gold Coast Suns

3470 A859 60c Emblem at R 1.50 .75
3471 A859 60c Emblem at L 1.50 .75
a. Booklet pane of 10, 5 each #3470-3471 15.00

North Melbourne Kangaroos

3472 A859 60c Emblem at R 1.50 .75
3473 A859 60c Emblem at L 1.50 .75
a. Booklet pane of 10, 5 each #3472-3473 15.00

Port Adelaide Power

3474 A859 60c Emblem at R 1.50 .75
3475 A859 60c Emblem at L 1.50 .75
a. Booklet pane of 10, 5 each #3474-3475 15.00

West Coast Eagles

3476 A859 60c Emblem at R 1.50 .75
3477 A859 60c Emblem at L 1.50 .75
a. Booklet pane of 10, 5 each #3476-3477 15.00

Western Bulldogs

3478 A859 60c Emblem at R 1.50 .75
3479 A859 60c Emblem at L 1.50 .75
a. Booklet pane of 10, 5 each #3478-3479 15.00

Purple & Orange Sky
Brisbane Lions

3480 A859 60c Emblem at R 1.50 .75
3481 A859 60c Emblem at L 1.50 .75
a. Booklet pane of 10, 5 each #3480-3481 15.00

Collingwood Magpies

3482 A859 60c Emblem at R 1.50 .75
3483 A859 60c Emblem at L 1.50 .75
a. Booklet pane of 10, 5 each #3482-3483 15.00

Fremantle Dockers

3484 A859 60c Emblem at R 1.50 .75
3485 A859 60c Emblem at L 1.50 .75
a. Booklet pane of 10, 5 each #3484-3485 15.00

Hawthorn Hawks

3486 A859 60c Emblem at R 1.50 .75
3487 A859 60c Emblem at L 1.50 .75
a. Booklet pane of 10, 5 each #3486-3487 15.00

Melbourne Demons

3488 A859 60c Emblem at R 1.50 .75
3489 A859 60c Emblem at L 1.50 .75
a. Booklet pane of 10, 5 each #3488-3489 15.00

Richmond Tigers

3490 A859 60c Emblem at R 1.50 .75
3491 A859 60c Emblem at L 1.50 .75
a. Booklet pane of 10, 5 each #3490-3491 15.00

St. Kilda Saints

3492 A859 60c Emblem at R 1.50 .75
3493 A859 60c Emblem at L 1.50 .75
a. Booklet pane of 10, 5 each #3492-3493 15.00

Sydney Swans

3494 A859 60c Emblem at R 1.50 .75
3495 A859 60c Emblem at L 1.50 .75
a. Booklet pane of 10, 5 each #3494-3495 15.00

Blue Sky With National Rugby League Emblems

North Queensland Cowboys

3496 A859 60c Emblem at R 1.50 .75
3497 A859 60c Emblem at L 1.50 .75
a. Booklet pane of 10, 5 each #3496-3497 15.00

St. George Illawarra Dragons

3498 A859 60c Emblem at R 1.50 .75
3499 A859 60c Emblem at L 1.50 .75
a. Booklet pane of 10, 5 each #3498-3499 15.00

Parramatta Eels

3500 A859 60c Emblem at R 1.50 .75
3501 A859 60c Emblem at L 1.50 .75
a. Booklet pane of 10, 5 each #3500-3501 15.00

Newcastle Knights

3502 A859 60c Emblem at R 1.50 .75
3503 A859 60c Emblem at L 1.50 .75
a. Booklet pane of 10, 5 each #3502-3503 15.00

Penrith Panthers

3504 A859 60c Emblem at R 1.50 .75
3505 A859 60c Emblem at L 1.50 .75
a. Booklet pane of 10, 5 each #3504-3505 15.00

Canberra Raiders

3506 A859 60c Emblem at R 1.50 .75
3507 A859 60c Emblem at L 1.50 .75
a. Booklet pane of 10, 5 each #3506-3507 15.00

Sydney Roosters

3508 A859 60c Emblem at R 1.50 .75
3509 A859 60c Emblem at L 1.50 .75
a. Booklet pane of 10, 5 each #3508-3509 15.00

Cronulla Sutherland Sharks

3510 A859 60c Emblem at R 1.50 .75
3511 A859 60c Emblem at L 1.50 .75
a. Booklet pane of 10, 5 each #3510-3511 15.00

Gold Coast Titans

3512 A859 60c Emblem at R 1.50 .75
3513 A859 60c Emblem at L 1.50 .75
a. Booklet pane of 10, 5 each #3512-3513 15.00

Purple & Orange Sky Brisbane Broncos

3514 A859 60c Emblem at R 1.50 .75
3515 A859 60c Emblem at L 1.50 .75
a. Booklet pane of 10, 5 each #3514-3515 15.00

Canterbury-Bankstown Bulldogs

3516 A859 60c Emblem at R 1.50 .75
3517 A859 60c Emblem at L 1.50 .75
a. Booklet pane of 10, 5 each #3516-3517 15.00

South Sydney Rabbitohs

3518 A859 60c Emblem at R 1.50 .75
3519 A859 60c Emblem at L 1.50 .75
a. Booklet pane of 10, 5 each #3518-3519 15.00

Manly Warringah Sea Eagles

3520 A859 60c Emblem at R 1.50 .75
3521 A859 60c Emblem at L 1.50 .75
a. Booklet pane of 10, 5 each #3520-3521 15.00

Melbourne Storm

3522 A859 60c Emblem at R 1.50 .75
3523 A859 60c Emblem at L 1.50 .75
a. Booklet pane of 10, 5 each #3522-3523 15.00

New Zealand Warriors

3524 A859 60c Emblem at R 1.50 .75
3525 A859 60c Emblem at L 1.50 .75
a. Booklet pane of 10, 5 each #3524-3525 15.00

Wests Tigers

3526 A859 60c Emblem at R 1.50 .75
3527 A859 60c Emblem at L 1.50 .75
a. Booklet pane of 10, 5 each #3526-3527 15.00
Nos. 3462-3527 (66) 99.00 49.50

Each booklet, Nos. 3463a-3527a, sold for $6.95. Stamps with team emblem at right have straight edge at right, and stamps with team emblem at left have straight edge at left.

Australian Navy, Cent. A860

Sailor and: Nos. 3528, 3530, HMAS Australia and biplane. Nos. 3529, 3531, HMAS Sydney and helicopter.

2011, June 14 *Perf. 14x14¾*
3528 A860 60c multi 1.40 1.40
3529 A860 60c multi 1.40 1.40
a. Horiz. pair, #3528-3529 2.80 2.80

Booklet Stamps Self-Adhesive

Serpentine Die Cut 11¼ Syncopated

3530 A860 60c multi 1.40 .25
3531 A860 60c multi 1.40 .25
a. Booklet pane of 20, 10 each #3530-3531 28.00

A861

A862

Baby animals: 60c, Bilby. $1.60, Dingo. $1.65, Kangaroo. $2.35, Koala. $4.70, Sugar glider.

2011, July 1 Litho. *Perf. 14¾x14*
3532 A861 60c multi 1.40 1.10
3533 A861 $1.60 multi 3.50 1.75
a. Souvenir sheet of 1 3.50 3.50
3534 A861 $1.65 multi 3.50 3.50
a. Souvenir sheet of 2, #3533-3534 7.00 7.00
b. Souvenir sheet of 1 3.50 3.50
c. Additionally dated "2013" 4.25 4.25
d. Booklet pane of 4, #1195a, 2352a, 3097a, 3534c 12.50 —
3535 A861 $2.35 multi 5.00 5.00
a. Souvenir sheet of 2 9.75 9.75
3536 A861 $4.70 multi 10.00 5.00
Nos. 3532-3536 (5) 23.40 16.35

Issued: No. 3534a, 7/28; No. 3535a, 6/18/12. Nos. 3533a, 3534b, 11/11. PhilaNippon '11 World Stamp Exhibition, Yokohama (No. 3534a). 2012 World Stamp Championship, Indonesia (No. 3535a). China 2011 Intl. Stamp Exhibition, Wuxi (Nos. 3533a, 3534b). Nos. 3534c, 3534d, 5/10/13. No. 3534d was issued in a booklet also containing Nos. 1003b, 1284b, and 3918.

Booklet Stamps Self-Adhesive

Serpentine Die Cut 11¼ Syncopated

3537 A861 $1.65 multi 3.50 1.75
a. Booklet pane of 5 17.50
3538 A861 $2.35 multi 5.00 2.50
a. Booklet pane of 5 25.00

With Personalized Photo at Right Like Type A692a

Serpentine Die Cut 11½x11¼ Syncopated

3539 A861 $1.60 multi 4.75 4.75
3540 A861 $1.65 multi 5.00 5.00
3541 A861 $2.35 multi 11.50 11.50
Nos. 3539-3541 (3) 21.25 21.25

Nos. 3539-3541 each were printed in sheets of 20 and have personalized pictures and at straight edge at right, and lack separations between the stamp and the personalized photo. Sheets of 20 of No. 3539 sold for $45; No. 3540, $46; No. 3541, $106.

2011, July 5 *Perf. 14¾x14*
3542 A862 60c yellow & black 1.40 1.10

Amnesty International, 50th anniv.

Living Australian A863

Photographs of Australian scenes: Nos. 3543, 3548, Boy and dog on beach. Nos. 3544, 3549, Children with flags painted on faces hugging. Nos. 3545, 3550, Reflection in sunglasses of sports fans in stadium. Nos. 3546, 3551, Aboriginal boy performing wedge tail eagle dance. Nos. 3547, 3552, Kangaroo resting on beach.

2011, July 5 *Perf. 14x14¾*

Denomination Color

3543 A863 60c orange 1.40 1.40
3544 A863 60c purple 1.40 1.40
3545 A863 60c green 1.40 1.40
3546 A863 60c red violet 1.40 1.40
3547 A863 60c blue 1.40 1.40
a. Horiz. strip of 5, #3543-3547 7.00 7.00

Self-Adhesive

Serpentine Die Cut 11¼ Syncopated

3548 A863 60c orange 1.40 .25
3549 A863 60c purple 1.40 .25
3550 A863 60c green 1.40 .25
3551 A863 60c red violet 1.40 .25
3552 A863 60c blue 1.40 .25
a. Horiz. coil strip of 5, #3548-3552 7.00
b. Booklet pane of 10, 2 each #3548-3552 14.00
Nos. 3548-3552 (5) 7.00 1.25

Skiing — A864

Designs: 60c, Child learning to ski. $1.60, Snowboarder, horiz. $1.65, Downhill skier, horiz.

2011, July 19 *Perf. 14¾x14*
3553 A864 60c multi 1.25 1.25

Perf. 14x14¾

3554 A864 $1.60 multi 3.50 3.50
3555 A864 $1.65 multi 3.50 3.50
Nos. 3553-3555 (3) 8.25 8.25

Self-Adhesive Coil Stamp

Serpentine Die Cut 11¼ Syncopated

3556 A864 60c multi 1.25 .25

Booklet Stamps

3557 A864 $1.60 multi 3.50 1.75
a. Booklet pane of 5 17.50
3558 A864 $1.65 multi 3.50 1.75
a. Booklet pane of 5 17.50
Nos. 3556-3558 (3) 8.25 3.75

Items Depicted on Australian States Stamps — A865

Designs: No. 3559, Kangaroo and lyrebird. No. 3560, Black swan and Southern Cross.

2011, July 28 *Perf. 14x13½*
3559 A865 $2 pale grn & blue 4.25 2.10
3560 A865 $2 pink & blue 4.25 2.10
a. Pair, #3559-3560 8.50 4.25
b. Souvenir sheet of 2, #3559-3560 8.50 4.25

A limited edition of No. 3560b with a gold overprint in the sheet margin exists.

Worldwide Fund for Nature (WWF), 50th Anniv. A866

Designs: No. 3561, Quokka. No. 3562, Southern elephant seal. No. 3563, Dugong. No. 3564, Christmas Island shrew.

2011, Aug. 30 Litho. *Perf. 14x14¾*
3561 A866 60c multi 1.25 .95
3562 A866 60c multi 1.25 .95
3563 A866 60c multi 1.25 .95
3564 A866 60c multi 1.25 .95
a. Block of 4, #3561-3564 5.00 4.00
b. Souvenir sheet of 4, #3561-3564, #3561 at UL 5.00 5.00
c. Souvenir sheet of 4, #3561-3564, #3562 at UL 5.00 5.00
d. Souvenir sheet of 4, #3561-3564, #3563 at UL 5.00 5.00
e. Souvenir sheet of 4, #3561-3564, #3564 at UL 5.00 5.00
Nos. 3561-3564 (4) 5.00 3.80

Along with the "Australia" inscription at left, inscribed at the bottom above the animal's name is "Australian Antarctic Territory" on No. 3562, "Cocos (Keeling) Islands" on No. 3563, and "Christmas Island" on No. 3564. All recent stamps of the Australian possessions of Australian Antarctic Territory, Cocos Islands and Christmas Island are doubly-inscribed with "Australia" and the possession's name, and all stamps inscribed "Australia," "Australian Antarctic Territory," "Cocos Islands," or "Christmas Island" are valid for postage anywhere in those four areas. As there was no attempt to make the stamps bearing the names of these possessions in this set available separately in those locations they will be listed here only and not in the listings for each of the possessions.

2011 Presidents Cup Golf Tournament, Melbourne — A867

Designs: Nos. 3565, 3570, Hand on golf club. Nos. 3566, 3569B, 3571, Presidents Cup. Nos. 3567, 1572, Golf shoes, glove and ball. $1.65, Golf club and ball. $2.35, Clubs in golf bag.

2011, Sept. 27 *Perf. 14¾x14*
3565 A867 60c multi 1.25 1.25
3566 A867 60c multi 1.25 1.25
3567 A867 60c multi 1.25 1.25
a. Horiz. strip of 3, #3565-3567 3.75 3.75
3568 A867 $1.65 multi 3.25 3.25
3569 A867 $2.35 multi 4.75 4.75
a. Souvenir sheet of 5, #3565-3569 12.00 12.00
Nos. 3565-3569 (5) 11.75 11.75

Litho. & Embossed With Foil Application

3569B A867 60c multi 1.25 1.25

No. 3569B was printed in sheets of 15 that sold for $9.45.

Litho. Self-Adhesive

Serpentine Die Cut 11¼ Syncopated

3570 A867 60c multi 1.25 .25
3571 A867 60c multi 1.25 .25
3572 A867 60c multi 1.25 .25
a. Booklet pane of 10, 4 each # 3570-3571, 2 #3572 12.50
b. Vert. coil strip of 3, #3570-3572 3.75
3573 A867 $1.65 multi 3.25 1.60
a. Booklet pane of 5 16.50
3574 A867 $2.35 multi 4.75 2.40
a. Booklet pane of 5 24.00
Nos. 3570-3574 (5) 11.75 4.75

Mythical Creatures — A868

Designs: Nos. 3575, 3581, Fairy. Nos. 3576, 3582, Troll. Nos. 3577, 3583, Mermaid. Nos. 3578, 3584, Griffin. Nos. 3579, 3585, Unicorn. $1.20, Dragon.

2011, Oct. 4 Litho. *Perf. 14¾x14*
3575 A868 60c multi 1.25 1.25
3576 A868 60c multi 1.25 1.25
3577 A868 60c multi 1.25 1.25
3578 A868 60c multi 1.25 1.25
3579 A868 60c multi 1.25 1.25
a. Horiz. strip of 5, #3575-3579 6.25 6.25
3580 A868 $1.20 multi 2.40 1.90
a. Souvenir sheet of 6, #3575-3580 8.75 8.75
Nos. 3575-3580 (6) 8.65 8.15

Booklet Stamps Self-Adhesive

Serpentine Die Cut 11¼ Syncopated

3581 A868 60c multi 1.25 .25
3582 A868 60c multi 1.25 .25
3583 A868 60c multi 1.25 .25
3584 A868 60c multi 1.25 .25
3585 A868 60c multi 1.25 .25
a. Booklet pane of 10, 2 each #3581-3585 12.50
b. Booklet pane of 20, 4 each #3581-3585 25.00
Nos. 3581-3585 (5) 6.25 1.25

Commonwealth Heads of Government Meeting, Perth — A869

2011, Oct. 18 ***Perf. 14½x14***
3586 A869 60c multi 1.25 .95

Diplomatic Relations Between Australia and South Korea, 50th Anniv. — A870

Designs: 60c, Korean woman playing haegeum. $1.65, Australian aborigine playing didgeridoo.

2011, Oct. 31 ***Perf. 13¼x13***
3587 A870 60c multi 1.25 .95
3588 A870 $1.65 multi 3.50 1.75

Booklet Stamp
Self-Adhesive
Serpentine Die Cut 11¼ Syncopated

3589 A870 $1.65 multi 3.50 1.75
a. Booklet pane of 5 17.50

See South Korea No. 2373.

Christmas
A871 A872

Designs: Nos. 3590, 3595, Madonna and Child. Nos. 3591, 3596, 3599, 3601, Star on Christmas tree. Nos. 3592, 3597, 3600, 3602, Star and gift. 60c, Star and fruit tree branches. $1.50, Magi and camels, horiz.

2011, Oct. 31 **Litho.** ***Perf. 14¾x14***
3590 A871 55c multi 1.10 1.10
3591 A872 55c multi 1.10 1.10
3592 A872 55c multi 1.10 1.10
a. Horiz. pair, #3591-3592 2.20 2.20
3593 A872 60c multi 1.25 1.25

Perf. 14x14¾

3594 A871 $1.50 multi 3.25 3.25
Nos. 3590-3594 (5) 7.80 7.80

Booklet Stamps
Self-Adhesive
Serpentine Die Cut 11¼ Syncopated

3595 A871 55c multi 1.10 .25
a. Booklet pane of 20 + 20 etiquettes 22.00
3596 A872 55c multi 1.10 .25
3597 A872 55c multi 1.10 .25
a. Booklet pane of 20, 10 each #3596-3597 + 20 etiquettes 22.00
3598 A871 $1.50 multi 3.25 1.60
a. Booklet pane of 5 16.50

Litho. With Foil Application

3599 A872 55c multi 1.10 .25
a. Booklet pane of 10 11.00
3600 A872 55c multi 1.10 .25
a. Booklet pane of 10 11.00
Nos. 3595-3600 (6) 8.75 2.85

Litho.
With Personalized Photo at Right Like Type A692a
Serpentine Die Cut 11½x11¼ Syncopated

3601 A872 55c multi 2.50 2.50
3602 A872 55c multi 2.50 2.50
3603 A872 60c multi 2.60 2.60
Nos. 3601-3603 (3) 7.60 7.60

Nos. 3601-3603 each were printed in sheets of 20 and have personalized pictures and a straight edge at right, and lack separations between the stamp and the personalized photo. Sheets of 20 of Nos. 3601 and 3602 each sold for $24, for No. 3603, $25.

Remembrance Day — A873

Lines from "In Flanders Fields," poem by John McCrae, and: 60c, Poppy, bugler. $1.20, Two poppies, two soldiers.

2011, Nov. 2 **Litho.** ***Perf. 14x14¾***
3604 A873 60c multi 1.25 1.25
3605 A873 $1.20 multi 2.50 1.90
a. Souvenir sheet of 2, #3604-3605 3.75 3.25

Self-Adhesive
Serpentine Die Cut 11¼ Syncopated

3606 A873 60c multi 1.25 .25
a. Booklet pane of 10 12.50

No. 3606 was issued in coils and booklets.

Australian Lieutenant General Sydney F. Rowell, New Zealand Major General William Gentry, and U.S. Admiral Arthur Radford
A874

2011, Nov. 16 ***Perf. 14x14¾***
3607 A874 60c multi 1.25 .95

ANZUS Treaty, 60th anniv.

Cupcake and Birthday Candle — A875

Teddy Bear — A876

Balloons and Streamers
A877

"Love" and Hearts
A878

Birds — A879

Rose — A880

2012, Jan. 17 ***Perf. 14¾x14***
3608 A875 60c multi 1.25 1.25
3609 A876 60c multi 1.25 1.25
3610 A877 60c multi 1.25 1.25
3611 A878 60c multi 1.25 1.25
3612 A879 60c multi 1.25 1.25
a. Horiz. strip of 5, $3608-3612 6.25 6.25
3613 A880 $1.20 multi 2.60 2.60
Nos. 3608-3613 (6) 8.85 8.85

Booklet Stamps
Self-Adhesive
Serpentine Die Cut 11¼ Syncopated

3614 A875 60c multi 1.25 .25
a. Booklet pane of 10 + 5 stickers 12.50
3615 A876 60c multi 1.25 .25
a. Booklet pane of 10 + 5 stickers 12.50
3616 A877 60c multi 1.25 .25
a. Booklet pane of 10 + 5 stickers 12.50
3617 A878 60c multi 1.25 .25
a. Booklet pane of 10 + 5 stickers 12.50
3618 A879 60c multi 1.25 .25
a. Booklet pane of 10 + 5 stickers 12.50
3619 A880 $1.20 multi 2.75 1.40
a. Booklet pane of 4 11.00
Complete booklet, 5 #3619a 55.00
Nos. 3614-3619 (6) 9.00 2.65

With Personalized Photo at Right Like Type A692a
Serpentine Die Cut 11½x11¼ Syncopated

3620 A875 60c multi 2.75 2.75
3621 A876 60c multi 2.75 2.75
3622 A877 60c multi 2.75 2.75
3623 A878 60c multi 2.75 2.75
3624 A879 60c multi 2.75 2.75
3625 A880 $1.20 multi 4.00 4.00
Nos. 3620-3625 (6) 17.75 17.75

Complete booklet sold for $24.95 and contains five booklet panes of No. 3619a, each with a different margin.

Nos. 3620-3625 each were printed in sheets of 20 and have personalized pictures and a straight edge at right, and lack separations between the stamp and the personalized photo. Sheets of 20 of Nos. 3620-3624 each sold for $25, for No. 3625, $37.

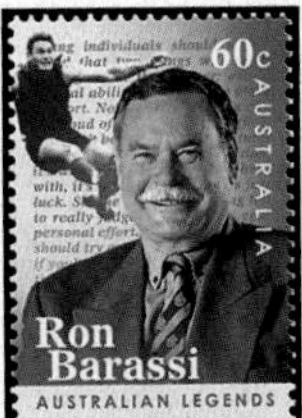

Athletes — A881

Designs: Nos. 3626, 3634, Ron Barassi, Australian Rules Football player. Nos. 3627, 3635, Gary Ablett, Jr., Australian Rules Football player. Nos. 3628, 3636, John Raper, Rugby League player. Nos. 3629, 3637, Billy Slater, Rugby League player. Nos. 3630, 3638, David Campese, Rugby Union player. Nos. 3631, 3639, David Pocock, Rugby Union player. Nos. 3632, 3640, Joe Marston, soccer player. Nos. 3633, 3641, Mark Schwarzer, soccer player.

2012, Jan. 20 ***Perf. 14¾x14***
3626 A881 60c multi 1.25 1.25
a. Booklet pane of 4 5.50 —
3627 A881 60c multi 1.25 1.25
a. Booklet pane of 4 5.50 —
3628 A881 60c multi 1.25 1.25
a. Booklet pane of 4 5.50 —
3629 A881 60c multi 1.25 1.25
a. Booklet pane of 4 5.50 —
3630 A881 60c multi 1.25 1.25
a. Booklet pane of 4 5.50 —
3631 A881 60c multi 1.25 1.25
a. Booklet pane of 4 5.50 —
3632 A881 60c multi 1.25 1.25
a. Booklet pane of 4 5.50 —
3633 A881 60c multi 1.25 1.25
a. Booklet pane of 4 5.50 —
Complete booklet, #3626a-3633a 44.00
Nos. 3626-3633 (8) 10.00 10.00

Booklet Stamps
Self-Adhesive
Serpentine Die Cut 11¼ Syncopated

3634 A881 60c multi 1.25 .25
a. Booklet pane of 10 12.50
3635 A881 60c multi 1.25 .25
a. Booklet pane of 10 12.50
3636 A881 60c multi 1.25 .25
a. Booklet pane of 10 12.50
3637 A881 60c multi 1.25 .25
a. Booklet pane of 10 12.50
3638 A881 60c multi 1.25 .25
a. Booklet pane of 10 12.50
3639 A881 60c multi 1.25 .25
a. Booklet pane of 10 12.50
3640 A881 60c multi 1.25 .25
a. Booklet pane of 10 12.50
3641 A881 60c multi 1.25 .25
a. Booklet pane of 10 12.50
Nos. 3634-3641 (8) 10.00 2.00

Complete booklet sold for $19.95.

Technological Changes Through the Years — A882

Designs: Nos. 3642, 3647, Woman on pay telephone, 4G phone. Nos. 3643, 3648, Man carrying ice to icebox, modern refrigerator. Nos. 3644, 3649, Family watching black-and-white television, flat-screen television. Nos. 3645, 3650, Man with vinyl records and record player, digital media player. Nos. 3646, 3651, Man reading paper road map, global positioning system.

2012, Feb. 7 ***Perf. 14x14¾***
3642 A882 60c multi 1.40 1.40
3643 A882 60c multi 1.40 1.40
3644 A882 60c multi 1.40 1.40
3645 A882 60c multi 1.40 1.40
3646 A882 60c multi 1.40 1.40
a. Horiz. strip of 5, #3642-3646 7.00 7.00
b. Souvenir sheet of 5, #3642-3646 7.00 7.00

Self-Adhesive
Serpentine Die Cut 11¼ Syncopated

3647 A882 60c multi 1.40 .25
3648 A882 60c multi 1.40 .25
3649 A882 60c multi 1.40 .25
3650 A882 60c multi 1.40 .25
3651 A882 60c multi 1.40 .25
a. Horiz. coil strip of 5, #3647-3651 7.00
b. Booklet pane of 10, 2 each #3647-3651 14.00
Nos. 3647-3651 (5) 7.00 1.25

Transportation in State Capitals — A883

Designs: Nos. 3652, 3657, O-Bahn bus system, Adelaide. Nos. 3653, 3658, Ferry in Sydney Harbor. Nos. 3654, 3659, Train in Perth. Nos. 3655, 3660, St. Kilda-bound tram, Melbourne. Nos. 3656, 3661, North Sydney-bound double-decker train, Sydney.

2012, Feb. 21 ***Perf. 14x14¾***
3652 A883 60c multi 1.40 1.40
a. Booklet pane of 4 5.75 —
3653 A883 60c multi 1.40 1.40
a. Booklet pane of 4 5.75 —
3654 A883 60c multi 1.40 1.40
a. Booklet pane of 4 5.75 —
3655 A883 60c multi 1.40 1.40
a. Booklet pane of 4 5.75 —
3656 A883 60c multi 1.40 1.40
a. Booklet pane of 4 5.75 —
Complete booklet, #3652a-3656a 29.00
b. Horiz. strip of 5, #3652-3656 7.00 7.00

Booklet Stamps
Self-Adhesive
Serpentine Die Cut 11¼ Syncopated

3657 A883 60c multi 1.40 .25
3658 A883 60c multi 1.40 .25
3659 A883 60c multi 1.40 .25
3660 A883 60c multi 1.40 .25
3661 A883 60c multi 1.40 .25
a. Booklet pane of 20, 4 each #3657-3661 28.00
Nos. 3657-3661 (5) 7.00 1.25

Complete booklet sold for $12.95.

Ducks
A884

Designs: Nos. 3662, 3666, Radjah shelduck. Nos. 3663, 3667, Pink-eared duck. $1.65, Australian shelduck. $2.35, Plumed whistling duck.

2012, Mar. 6 ***Perf. 14x14¾***
3662 A884 60c multi 1.25 1.25
a. Additionally dated "2013" 1.25 1.25
3663 A884 60c multi 1.25 1.25
a. Additionally dated "2013" 1.25 1.25
3664 A884 $1.65 multi 3.50 3.50
a. Additionally dated "2013" 3.25 3.25

3665 A884 $2.35 multi 5.00 5.00
a. Additionally dated "2013" 4.50 4.50
b. Booklet pane of 4, #3662a, 3663a, 3664a, 3665a 10.50 —
Nos. 3662-3665 (4) 11.00 11.00

Issued: Nos. 3662a, 3663a, 3664a, 3665a, 3665b, 5/11/13. No. 3665b was issued in a booklet also containing Nos. 3151c, 3376b and 3925a.

Self-Adhesive

Serpentine Die Cut 11¼ Syncopated

3666 A884 60c multi 1.25 .25
3667 A884 60c multi 1.25 .25
a. Horiz. coil pair, #3666-3667 2.50
b. Booklet pane of 10, 5 each #3666-3667 25.00

Booklet Stamps

3668 A884 $1.65 multi 3.50 1.75
a. Booklet pane of 5 17.50
3669 A884 $2.35 multi 5.00 2.50
a. Booklet pane of 5 25.00
Nos. 3666-3669 (4) 11.00 4.75

Farm Products — A885

Designs: 10c, Dairy cows. 20c, Pineapples. $1, Wine grapes. $3, Sunflowers. $5, Apples.

2012, Mar. 20 ***Perf. 14x14½***

3670 A885 10c multi .25 .25
3671 A885 20c multi .40 .25
a. As No. 3671, with part of design and 1mm wide white space separating designs at left side 1.10 1.10

Size: 50x30mm

Perf. 14½x14

3672 A885 $1 multi 2.10 1.10
3673 A885 $3 multi 6.25 3.25
3674 A885 $5 multi 10.50 5.25
Nos. 3670-3674 (5) 19.50 10.10

No. 3671 has a white margin extending to the perforation tips at left. Four of the five stamps in the bottom row of the bottom pane in the sheet of 100 stamps (composed of two panes of 50) are No. 3671a.

See Nos. 3712-3723.

Compulsory Voting Enrollment, Cent. — A886

2012, Mar. 27 Litho. ***Perf. 14¾x14***

3675 A886 60c multi 1.25 .95

Reign of Queen Elizabeth II, 60th Anniv. — A887

Photograph of Queen Elizabeth II in: 60c, 1952. $2.35, 2012.

2012, Apr. 3 ***Perf. 14¾x14***

3676 A887 60c multi 1.25 .95
3677 A887 $2.35 multi 5.00 5.00
a. Souvenir sheet of 2, #3676-3677 6.25 6.00

Booklet Stamp
Self-Adhesive

Serpentine Die Cut 11¼ Syncopated

3678 A887 $2.35 multi 5.00 2.50
a. Booklet pane of 5 25.00

Medical Doctors — A888

Designs: Nos. 3679, 3684, Dr. Jane Stocks Greig (1872-1939), public health specialist. Nos. 3680, 3685, Dame Kate Campbell (1899-1986), pediatrician. Nos. 3681, 3686, Dr. Victor Chang (1936-91), cardiac surgeon. Nos. 3682, 3687, Dr. Fred Hollows (1929-93), ophthalmologist. Nos. 3683, 3688, Dr. Chris O'Brien (1952-2009), surgeon.

2012, Apr. 10 ***Perf. 14¾x14***

3679 A888 60c multi 1.25 1.25
3680 A888 60c multi 1.25 1.25
3681 A888 60c multi 1.25 1.25
3682 A888 60c multi 1.25 1.25
3683 A888 60c multi 1.25 1.25
Nos. 3679-3683 (5) 6.25 6.25

Coil Stamps
Self-Adhesive

Serpentine Die Cut 11¼ Syncopated

3684 A888 60c multi 1.25 .25
3685 A888 60c multi 1.25 .25
3686 A888 60c multi 1.25 .25
3687 A888 60c multi 1.25 .25
3688 A888 60c multi 1.25 .25
a. Vert. coil strip of 5, #3684-3688 6.25
Nos. 3684-3688 (5) 6.25 1.25

Rising Sun Badge A889

Rising Sun Badge in use from: Nos. 3689, 3694, 1902-04. Nos. 3690, 3695, 1904-49. Nos. 3691, 3696, 1954-69. Nos. 3692, 3697, 1969-91. Nos. 3693, 3698, 1991-present.

2012, Apr. 17 ***Perf. 14x14¾***

3689 A889 60c multi 1.25 1.25
3690 A889 60c multi 1.25 1.25
3691 A889 60c multi 1.25 1.25
3692 A889 60c multi 1.25 1.25
3693 A889 60c multi 1.25 1.25
a. Horiz. strip of 5, #3689-3693 6.25 6.25
b. Souvenir sheet of 5, #3689-3693 6.25 6.25

Booklet Stamps
Self-Adhesive

Serpentine Die Cut 11¼ Syncopated

3694 A889 60c multi 1.25 .25
3695 A889 60c multi 1.25 .25
3696 A889 60c multi 1.25 .25
3697 A889 60c multi 1.25 .25
3698 A889 60c multi 1.25 .25
a. Booklet pane of 10, 2 each #3694-3698 12.50
Nos. 3694-3698 (5) 6.25 1.25

Limited editions of Nos. 3693b (part-perforate) and 3698a with a gold overprint in the margin exist.

Nudibranchs A890

Designs: Nos. 3699, 3705, Chromodoris westraliensis. Nos. 3700, 3706, Godiva sp. Nos. 3701, 3707, Flabellina rubrolineata. No. 3702, Phyllidia ocellata. No. 3703, Thorunna florens. $1.80, Nembrotha purpureolineata.

2012, May 8 ***Perf. 14x14¾***

3699 A890 60c multi 1.25 1.25
a. Booklet pane of 4 5.25 —
3700 A890 60c multi 1.25 1.25
a. Booklet pane of 4 5.25 —
3701 A890 60c multi 1.25 1.25
a. Booklet pane of 4 5.25 —
3702 A890 $1.20 multi 2.40 1.90
3703 A890 $1.20 multi 2.40 1.90
a. Booklet pane of 4, #3699-3702 6.50 —
3704 A890 $1.80 multi 3.75 1.90
a. Booklet pane of 4, #3699-3701, 3704 7.75 —
Complete booklet, #3699a, 3700a, 3701a, 3703a, 3704a 30.00
b. Souvenir sheet of 6, #3699-3704 12.50 12.50
Nos. 3699-3704 (6) 12.30 9.45

Booklet Stamps
Self-Adhesive

Serpentine Die Cut 11¼ Syncopated

3705 A890 60c multi 1.25 .25
3706 A890 60c multi 1.25 .25
3707 A890 60c multi 1.25 .25
a. Booklet pane of 20, 7 each #3705-3706, 6 #3707 25.00
Nos. 3705-3707 (3) 3.75 .75

Complete booklet sold for $14.95.

Australian Flag, Olympic Rings, London Tourist Attractions — A891

2012, June 5 ***Perf. 14¾x14***

3708 A891 60c multi 1.25 1.25

Self-Adhesive

Serpentine Die Cut 11¼ Syncopated

3709 A891 60c multi 1.25 .25
a. Booklet pane of 10 12.50

2012 Summer Olympics, London.

Colonial Heritage — A892

Designs: No. 3710, Redrawn vignette of New South Wales #1. No. 3710, Redrawn vignette of Tasmania #88.

2012, June 19 ***Perf. 14x14½***

3710 A892 $2 yellow & blue 4.25 2.10
a. Perf. 14x13½ 4.25 2.10
3711 A892 $2 lt blue & blue 4.25 2.10
a. Perf. 14x13½ 4.25 2.10
b. Horiz. pair, #3710-3711 8.50 4.25
c. Souvenir sheet of 2, #3710a, 3711a 8.50 4.25

Farm Products Type of 2012

Designs: Nos. 3712, 3716, 3720, Beef cattle. Nos. 3713, 3717, 3721, Oranges. Nos. 3714, 3718, 3722, Sugar. Nos. 3715, 3719, 3723, Wool.

2012, June 26 Litho. ***Perf. 14x14½***

3712 A885 60c multi 1.25 .25
3713 A885 60c multi 1.25 .25
3714 A885 60c multi 1.25 .25
3715 A885 60c multi 1.25 .25
a. Block of 4, #3712-3715 5.00 2.50
Nos. 3712-3715 (4) 5.00 1.00

Coil Stamps
Self-Adhesive

Serpentine Die Cut 12¾

3716 A885 60c multi 1.25 .25
3717 A885 60c multi 1.25 .25
3718 A885 60c multi 1.25 .25
3719 A885 60c multi 1.25 .25
a. Horiz. strip of 4, #3716-3719 5.00

Booklet Stamps

Serpentine Die Cut 11¼

3720 A885 60c multi 1.25 .25
3721 A885 60c multi 1.25 .25
3722 A885 60c multi 1.25 .25
3723 A885 60c multi 1.25 .25
a. Booklet pane of 10, 2 each #3720, 3722-3723, 4 #3721 12.50
b. Booklet pane of 20, 5 each #3720-3723 25.00
Nos. 3716-3723 (8) 10.00 2.00

Inland Exploration A893

Designs: No. 3724, Explorers crossing Blue Mountains, 1813. No. 3725, Explorers William Lawson, William Charles Wentworth and Gregory Blaxland. No. 3726, Explorer John McDouall Stuart. No. 3727, Stuart Overland Crossing Expedition planting flag on Indian Ocean coast.

2012, July 3 ***Perf. 14x14¾***

3724 A893 60c multi 1.25 .95
3725 A893 60c multi 1.25 .95
a. Horiz. pair, #3724-3725 2.50 1.90
3726 A893 $1.20 multi 2.50 2.00
3727 A893 $1.20 multi 2.50 2.00
a. Horiz. pair, #3726-3727 5.00 4.00
b. Souvenir sheet of 4, #3724-3727 7.50 6.00
Nos. 3724-3727 (4) 7.50 5.90

Sports of the Summer Olympics A894

Designs: 60c, Swimming. $1.60, Pole vault. $2.30, Rowing.

2012, July 17 ***Perf. 14x14¾***

3728 A894 60c multi 1.25 1.25
3729 A894 $1.60 multi 3.50 3.50
3730 A894 $2.35 multi 5.00 5.00
Nos. 3728-3730 (3) 9.75 9.75

Coil Stamp
Self-Adhesive

Serpentine Die Cut 11¼ Syncopated

3731 A894 60c multi 1.25 .25

Booklet Stamps

3732 A894 $1.60 multi 3.50 1.75
a. Booklet pane of 5 17.50
3733 A894 $2.35 multi 5.00 2.50
a. Booklet pane of 5 25.00
Nos. 3731-3733 (3) 9.75 4.50

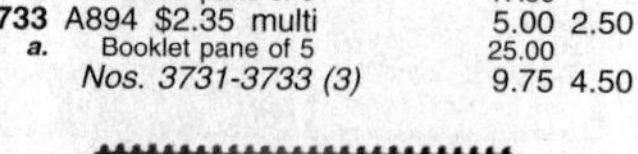

Photographs of Everyday Life in Australia — A895

Designs: Nos. 3734, 3740, Little Wonders, by Ann Clark (children on beach). Nos. 3735, 3742, The Godfathers, by Chevelle Williams (sheep in pen). Nos. 3736, 3741, Is There a Letter for Me?, by Wanda Lach (row of mailboxes in rural area). Nos. 3737, 3743, Lunch on the Harbor, by Damian Madden (seagull with French fry in beak). Nos. 3738, 3739, Fuel Ask at the Store Across the Road, by Ronald Rockman (rural gas station).

2012, July 24 ***Perf. 14x14¾***

3734 A895 60c multi 1.25 1.25
3735 A895 60c multi 1.25 1.25
3736 A895 60c multi 1.25 1.25
3737 A895 60c multi 1.25 1.25
3738 A895 60c multi 1.25 1.25
a. Horiz. strip of 5, #3734-3738 6.25 6.25
Nos. 3734-3738 (5) 6.25 6.25

Booklet Stamps
Self-Adhesive

Serpentine Die Cut 11¼ Syncopated

3739 A895 60c multi 1.25 .25
3740 A895 60c multi 1.25 .25
3741 A895 60c multi 1.25 .25
3742 A895 60c multi 1.25 .25
3743 A895 60c multi 1.25 .25
a. Booklet pane of 20, 4 each #3739-3742 25.00
Nos. 3739-3743 (5) 6.25 1.25

Souvenir Sheet

Emblem of Australia 2013 World Stamp Expo and Royal Exhibition Building, Melbourne — A896

2012, June 18 Litho. ***Perf. 14¾x14***

3744 A896 $1.85 multi 3.75 1.90

A limited edition of No. 3744 with a gold overprint in the sheet margin exists.

Australian Gold Medalists at 2012 Summer Olympics, London A897

Designs: No. 3745, Women's 4x100 meter freestyle swimming relay team. No. 3746, Tom Slingsby, men's Laser class sailing. No. 3747, Anna Meares, women's sprint cycling. No. 3748, Iain Jensen and Nathan Outteridge, men's 49er class sailing. No. 3749, Sally Pearson, women's 100 meter hurdles. No. 3750, Men's 1000 meter kayak fours team. No. 3751, Mathew Belcher and Malcolm Page, men's 470 class sailing.

2012 ***Perf. 14¼***

3745 A897 60c multi 1.25 .95
3746 A897 60c multi 1.25 .95
3747 A897 60c multi 1.25 .95
3748 A897 60c multi 1.25 .95
3749 A897 60c multi 1.25 .95
3750 A897 60c multi 1.25 .95
3751 A897 60c multi 1.25 .95
Nos. 3745-3751 (7) 8.75 6.65

Nos. 3745-3751 each were printed in sheets of 10. Issued: No. 3745, 7/31; No. 3746, 8/9; No. 3747, 8/10; others, 8/13.

Portraits of Autralian Nobel Prize Winners — A898

Portrait of: Nos. 3752, 3757, Sir Frank Macfarlane Burnet, by Clifton Pugh. Nos. 3753, 3758, Sir John Carew Eccles, by Judy Cassab. Nos. 3754, 3759, Patrick White, by Brett Whiteley. Nos. 3755, 3760, Sir Howard Walter Florey, by Allan Gwynne-Jones. Nos. 3756, 3761, William Lawrence Bragg, by Sir William Dargie.

2012, Aug. 28 Litho. ***Perf. 14¾x14***

3752 A898 60c multi 1.25 1.25
3753 A898 60c multi 1.25 1.25
3754 A898 60c multi 1.25 1.25
3755 A898 60c multi 1.25 1.25
3756 A898 60c multi 1.25 1.25
a. Horiz. strip of 5, #3752-3756 6.25 6.25
Nos. 3752-3756 (5) 6.25 6.25

Self-Adhesive

Serpentine Die Cut 11¼ Syncopated

3757 A898 60c multi 1.25 .25
3758 A898 60c multi 1.25 .25
3759 A898 60c multi 1.25 .25
3760 A898 60c multi 1.25 .25
3761 A898 60c multi 1.25 .25
a. Vert. coil strip of 5, #3757-3761 6.25
b. Booklet pane of 10, 2 each #3757-3761 12.50
Nos. 3757-3761 (5) 6.25 1.25

Road Trips — A899

Designs: Nos. 3762, 3769, Station wagon at Port Arthur, Tasmania. Nos. 3763, 3767, Volkswagen Bus at Great Barrier Reef, Queensland. Nos. 3764, 3768, Motorcyclists picnicking near Margaret River, Western Australia. $1.65, Station wagon at Phillip Island, Victoria. $2.35, Car at camel race, Alice Springs, Northern Territory.

2012, Sept. 18 ***Perf. 14¼***

3762 A899 60c multi 1.25 1.25
3763 A899 60c multi 1.25 1.25
3764 A899 60c multi 1.25 1.25
a. Horiz. strip of 3, #3762-3764 3.75 3.75
3765 A899 $1.65 multi 3.50 1.75
3766 A899 $2.35 multi 4.75 2.40
a. Souvenir sheet of 5, #3762-3766 12.00 12.00
Nos. 3762-3766 (5) 12.00 7.90

Booklet Stamps
Self-Adhesive

Serpentine Die Cut 11¼ Syncopated

3767 A899 60c multi 1.25 .25
3768 A899 60c multi 1.25 .25
3769 A899 60c multi 1.25 .25
a. Booklet pane of 10, 3 each #3767, 3769, 4 #3768 12.50
3770 A899 $1.65 multi 3.50 1.75
a. Booklet pane of 5 17.50
3771 A899 $2.35 multi 4.75 2.40
a. Booklet pane of 5 24.00
Nos. 3767-3771 (5) 12.00 4.90

Compare with type A933.

Wilderness Areas — A900

Designs: $1.65, Nullarbor Plain, Western Australia. $2.35, Daintree National Park, Queensland. $4.50, Cradle Mountain, Tasmania.

2012, Sept. 25 ***Perf. 14¾x14***

3772 A900 $1.65 multi 3.50 1.75
3773 A900 $2.35 multi 4.75 2.40
3774 A900 $4.50 multi 9.25 4.75
Nos. 3772-3774 (3) 17.50 8.90

Booklet Stamps
Self-Adhesive

Serpentine Die Cut 11¼ Syncopated

3775 A900 $1.65 multi 3.50 1.75
a. Booklet pane of 5 17.50
3776 A900 $2.35 multi 4.75 2.40
a. Booklet pane of 5 24.00

Animals in Australian Zoos — A901

Designs: No. 3777, Sumatran tiger, Melbourne Zoo, Victoria. Nos. 3778, 3789, Wedge-tailed hawk, Healesville Sanctuary, Victoria. Nos. 3779, 3787. Sumatran orangutan, Perth Zoo, Western Australia. Nos. 3780, 3786, Giant panda, Adelaide Zoo, South Australia. Nos. 3781, 3785, Giraffe, Taronga Zoo, Sydney, New South Wales. Nos. 3782, 3788, Saltwater crocodile, Australia Zoo, Sunshine Coast, Queensland. Nos. 3783, 3784, Black rhinoceros, Taronga Western Plains Zoo, Dubbo, New South Wales.

2012, Sept. 28 ***Perf. 13¾x14***

3777 A901 60c multi 1.25 .95

Size: 37x26mm

Perf. 14x14¾

3778 A901 60c multi 1.25 1.25
3779 A901 60c multi 1.25 1.25
3780 A901 60c multi 1.25 1.25
3781 A901 60c multi 1.25 1.25
3782 A901 60c multi 1.25 1.25
3783 A901 60c multi 1.25 1.25
a. Souvenir sheet of 7, #3777-3783 8.75 8.75
Nos. 3777-3783 (7) 8.75 8.45

Self-Adhesive

Serpentine Die Cut 11¼ Syncopated

3784 A901 60c multi 1.25 .25
3785 A901 60c multi 1.25 .25
3786 A901 60c multi 1.25 .25
3787 A901 60c multi 1.25 .25
3788 A901 60c multi 1.25 .25
3789 A901 60c multi 1.25 .25
a. Horiz. coil strip of 6, #3784-3789 7.50
b. Booklet pane of 20, 4 each #3784-3785, 3 each #3786-3789 25.00
Nos. 3784-3789 (6) 7.50 1.50

Auto Racing at Bathurst, 50th Anniv. A902

Designs: Nos. 3790, 3794, Race car, country name in red. Nos. 3791, 3797, Mount Panorama Race Track, country name in yellow green. Nos. 3792, 3796, Race car, country name in blue. Nos. 3793, 3795, Race car, country name in yellow.

2012, Oct. 2 ***Perf. 14x14¾***

3790 A902 60c multi 1.25 1.25
3791 A902 60c multi 1.25 1.25
3792 A902 60c multi 1.25 1.25
3793 A902 60c multi 1.25 1.25
a. Block of 4, #3790-3793 5.00 5.00
b. Souvenir sheet of 4, #3790-3793 5.00 5.00
Nos. 3790-3793 (4) 5.00 5.00

Booklet Stamps
Self-Adhesive

Serpentine Die Cut 11¼ Syncopated

3794 A902 60c multi 1.25 .25
3795 A902 60c multi 1.25 .25
3796 A902 60c multi 1.25 .25
3797 A902 60c multi 1.25 .25
a. Booklet pane of 10, 2 each #3794-3796, 4 #3797 12.50
Nos. 3794-3797 (4) 5.00 1.00

Susie O'Neill, Swimmer — A903

O'Neill: No. 3798, Wearing black jacket. No. 3799, Swimming in pool.

2012, Oct. 12 ***Perf. 14¾x14***

3798 A903 60c multi 1.25 .95
3799 A903 60c multi 1.25 .95
a. Pair, #3798-3799 2.50 1.90

Australian Ballet, 50th Anniv. — A904

Designs: Nos. 3800, 3802, One dancer. Nos. 3801, 3803, Two dancers.

2012, Oct. 16 ***Perf. 14¾x14***

3800 A904 60c multi 1.25 1.25
3801 A904 60c multi 1.25 1.25
a. Pair, #3800-3801 2.50 2.50

Coil Stamps
Self-Adhesive

Serpentine Die Cut 11¼ Syncopated

3802 A904 60c multi 1.25 .25
3803 A904 60c multi 1.25 .25
a. Vert. pair, #3802-3803 2.50

Lawn Bowling A905

Designs: 60c, Female bowlers. $1.20, Male bowlers.

2012, Nov. 1 ***Perf. 14x14¾***

3804 A905 60c multi 1.25 .95
3805 A905 $1.20 multi 2.50 1.90
a. Souvenir sheet of 2, #3804-3805 3.75 3.00

Christmas
A906 A907

Designs: Nos. 3806, 3811, Detail of Madonna and Child from Adoration of the Magi tapestry. Nos. 3807, 3812, 3815, 3817, Reindeer. Nos. 3808, 3813, 3816, 3818, Gifts. 60c, Bells. $1.60, Entire Adoration of the Magi tapestry (50x30mm), horiz.

2012, Nov. 1 ***Perf. 14¾x14***

3806 A906 55c multi 1.25 1.25
3807 A907 55c multi 1.25 1.25
3808 A907 55c multi 1.25 1.25
3809 A907 60c multi 1.25 .60

Perf. 14½x14

3810 A906 $1.60 multi 3.50 1.75
Nos. 3806-3810 (5) 8.50 6.10

Booklet Stamps
Self-Adhesive

Serpentine Die Cut 11¼ Syncopated

3811 A906 55c multi 1.25 .25
a. Booklet pane of 20 25.00
3812 A907 55c multi 1.25 .25
3813 A907 55c multi 1.25 .25
a. Booklet pane of 20, 10 each #3812-3813 25.00
3814 A906 $1.60 multi 3.50 1.75
a. Booklet pane of 5 17.50

Litho. With Foil Application

3815 A907 55c multi 1.25 .25
a. Booklet pane of 10 12.50

Litho. & Embossed With Foil Application

3816 A907 55c multi 1.25 .25
a. Booklet pane of 10 12.50
Nos. 3811-3816 (6) 9.75 3.00

With Personalized Photo at Right Like Type A692a
Litho.

Serpentine Die Cut 11½x11¼ Syncopated

3817 A907 55c multi 2.50 2.50
3818 A907 55c multi 2.50 2.50

Nos. 3817-3818 each were printed in sheets of 20 and have personalized pictures and straight edge at right, and lack separations between the stamp an the personalized photo. Sheets of 20 of each stamp sold for $24.

Jacqueline Freney, Paralympian of the Year — A908

2012, Nov. 9 ***Perf. 14¼***

3819 A908 60c multi 1.25 .95

Musical Legends — A909

Designs: Nos. 3820, 3830, AC/DC (rock band). Nos. 3821, 3831, Cold Chisel (rock band). Nos. 3822, 3832, INXS (rock band). Nos. 3823, 3833, John Farnham (singer). Nos. 3824, 3834, Kylie Minogue (singer). Nos. 3825, 3835, Men At Work (rock band). Nos. 3826, 3836, Ian "Molly" Meldrum (record producer). Nos. 3827, 3837, Olivia Newton-John (singer). No. 3828, 3838, Paul Kelly (singer). Nos. 3829, 3839, The Seekers (rock band).

2013, Jan. 18 ***Perf. 14¾x14***

3820 A909 60c multi 1.25 1.25
a. Booklet pane of 4 5.25 —
3821 A909 60c multi 1.25 1.25
a. Booklet pane of 4 5.25 —
b. Horiz. pair, #3820-3821 2.50 2.50
3822 A909 60c multi 1.25 1.25
a. Booklet pane of 4 5.25 —
3823 A909 60c multi 1.25 1.25
a. Booklet pane of 4 5.25 —
3824 A909 60c multi 1.25 1.25
a. Booklet pane of 4 5.25 —
3825 A909 60c multi 1.25 1.25
a. Booklet pane of 4 5.25 —
3826 A909 60c multi 1.25 1.25
a. Booklet pane of 4 5.25 —
b. Horiz. pair, #3824, 3826 2.50 2.50
3827 A909 60c multi 1.25 1.25
a. Booklet pane of 4 5.25 —
b. Horiz. pair, #3823, 3827 2.50 2.50
3828 A909 60c multi 1.25 1.25
a. Booklet pane of 4 5.25 —
b. Horiz. pair, #3822, 3828 2.50 2.50
3829 A909 60c multi 1.25 1.25
a. Booklet pane of 4 5.25 —
b. Horiz. pair, #3825, 3829 2.50 2.50
Complete booklet, #3820a-3829a 52.50
Nos. 3820-3829 (10) 12.50 12.50

Booklet Stamps
Self-Adhesive

Serpentine Die Cut 11¼ Syncopated

3830 A909 60c multi 1.25 .25
a. Booklet pane of 10 12.50
3831 A909 60c multi 1.25 .25
a. Booklet pane of 10 12.50
3832 A909 60c multi 1.25 .25
a. Booklet pane of 10 12.50
3833 A909 60c multi 1.25 .25
a. Booklet pane of 10 12.50
3834 A909 60c multi 1.25 .25
a. Booklet pane of 10 12.50
3835 A909 60c multi 1.25 .25
a. Booklet pane of 10 12.50
3836 A909 60c multi 1.25 .25
a. Booklet pane of 10 12.50
3837 A909 60c multi 1.25 .25
a. Booklet pane of 10 12.50
3838 A909 60c multi 1.25 .25
a. Booklet pane of 10 12.50
3839 A909 60c multi 1.25 .25
a. Booklet pane of 10 12.50
Nos. 3830-3839 (10) 12.50 2.50

Complete booklet sold for $24.95.

Eucalyptus Leaves — A910

Map of Australia — A911

Rose Petal — A912

Orchid — A913

Gifts and Champagne Flutes — A914

2013, Feb. 5 **Litho.** ***Perf. 14¾x14***

3840 A910 60c multi 1.25 1.25
3841 A911 60c blue & multi 1.25 1.25
3842 A911 60c org & multi 1.25 1.25
3843 A912 60c multi 1.25 1.25
3844 A913 60c multi 1.25 1.25
a. Horiz. strip of 5, #3840-3844 6.25 6.25
3845 A914 $1.20 multi 2.50 2.50
Nos. 3840-3845 (6) 8.75 8.75

Booklet Stamps
Self-Adhesive

Serpentine Die Cut 11¼ Syncopated

3846 A910 60c multi 1.25 .25
a. Booklet pane of 10 + 5 stickers 12.50
3847 A911 60c blue & multi 1.25 .25
3848 A911 60c org & multi 1.25 .25
a. Booklet pane of 10, 5 each #3847-3848, + 5 stickers 12.50
3849 A912 60c multi 1.25 .25
a. Booklet pane of 10 + 5 stickers 12.50
3850 A913 60c multi 1.25 .25
a. Booklet pane of 10 + 5 stickers 12.50
3851 A914 $1.20 multi 2.50 1.25
a. Booklet pane of 10 + 5 stickers 25.00
b. Booklet pane of 4 10.50
Complete booklet, 5 #3851b 52.50
Nos. 3846-3851 (6) 8.75 2.50

Complete booklet sold for $24.95 and contains five examples of No. 3851b, each with a different image in pane margin.

Women and Surfboards A915

Surfer and Stylized Waves A916

Surfboards on Automobile Roof — A917

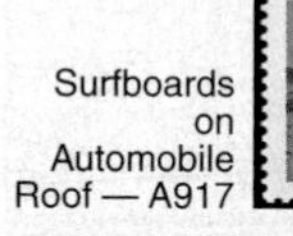

Surfer A918

2013, Feb. 12 **Litho.** ***Perf. 14x14¾***

3858 A915 60c multi 1.25 1.25
a. Booklet pane of 4 5.25 —
3859 A916 60c multi 1.25 1.25
a. Booklet pane of 4 5.25 —
3860 A917 60c multi 1.25 1.25
a. Booklet pane of 4 5.25 —
3861 A918 60c multi 1.25 1.25
a. Booklet pane of 4 5.25 —
b. Booklet pane of 4, #3858-3861, #3859 in UL 5.25 —
Complete booklet, #3858a, 3859a, 3860a, 3861a, 3861b 26.50
c. Block of 4, #3851-3861 5.00 5.00
d. Souvenir sheet of 4, #3858-3861, #3858 in UL 5.00 5.00
Nos. 3858-3861 (4) 5.00 5.00

Self-Adhesive

Serpentine Die Cut 11¼ Syncopated

3862 A915 60c multi 1.25 .25
3863 A916 60c multi 1.25 .25
3864 A917 60c multi 1.25 .25
3865 A918 60c multi 1.25 .25
a. Horiz. coil strip of 4, #3862-3865 5.00
b. Booklet pane of 10, 3 each #3862, 3865, 2 each #3863-3864 12.50
Nos. 3862-3865 (4) 5.00 1.00

Complete booklet sold for $12.95.

Dogs — A919

Designs: Nos. 3866, 3871, Miniature schnauzer. Nos. 3867, 3872, Miniature dachshund. Nos. 3868, 3873, Cavalier King Charles spaniel. Nos. 3869, 3874, Pug. Nos. 3870, 3875, Australian terrier.

2013, Feb. 19 ***Perf. 14¾x14***

3866 A919 60c multi 1.25 1.25
3867 A919 60c multi 1.25 1.25
3868 A919 60c multi 1.25 1.25
3869 A919 60c multi 1.25 1.25
3870 A919 60c multi 1.25 1.25
a. Horiz. strip of 5, #3866-3870 6.25 6.25
Nos. 3866-3870 (5) 6.25 6.25

Booklet Stamps
Self-Adhesive

Serpentine Die Cut 11¼ Syncopated

3871 A919 60c multi 1.25 .25
a. Booklet pane of 10 + 5 stickers 12.50
3872 A919 60c multi 1.25 .25
a. Booklet pane of 10 + 5 stickers 12.50
3873 A919 60c multi 1.25 .25
a. Booklet pane of 10 + 5 stickers 12.50
3874 A919 60c multi 1.25 .25
a. Booklet pane of 10 + 5 stickers 12.50
3875 A919 60c multi 1.25 .25
a. Booklet pane of 10 + 5 stickers 12.50
Nos. 3871-3875 (5) 6.25 1.25

Canberra, Cent. A920

Map and: 60c, National Portrait Gallery. $2.35, Parliament House.

2013, Mar. 5 ***Perf. 14x14¾***

3876 A920 60c multi 1.25 1.25
3877 A920 $2.35 multi 4.75 2.40
a. Booklet pane of 4, 2 each #3876-3877 13.00 —
Complete booklet, #1938d, 2710c, 2869e, 3107c, 3349b, 3877a 27.50

Self-Adhesive

Serpentine Die Cut 11¼ Syncopated

3878 A920 60c multi 1.25 .25
a. Booklet pane of 20 25.00

Complete booklet sold for $12.95. No. 3878 was issued in coils and booklet panes.

Paintings in National Gallery of Australia — A921

Designs: Nos. 3879, 3884, Dandenong Ranges from 'Beleura,' by Eugene von Guérard. Nos. 3880, 3885, In the Flinders - Far North, by Hans Heysen. Nos. 3881, 3886, Land of the Golden Fleece, by Arthur Streetson. Nos. 3882, 3887, Mr. Robinson's House on the Derwent, Van Diemen's Land, by John Glover. Nos. 3883, 3888, Studley Park at Sunrise, by Nicholas Chevalier.

2013, Mar. 19 ***Perf. 14¾x14***

3879 A921 60c multi 1.25 1.25
3880 A921 60c multi 1.25 1.25
3881 A921 60c multi 1.25 1.25
3882 A921 60c multi 1.25 1.25
3883 A921 60c multi 1.25 1.25
a. Horiz. strip of 5, #3879-3883 6.25 6.25
Nos. 3879-3883 (5) 6.25 6.25

Booklet Stamps
Self-Adhesive

Serpentine Die Cut 11¼ Syncopated

3884 A921 60c multi 1.25 .25
3885 A921 60c multi 1.25 .25
3886 A921 60c multi 1.25 .25
3887 A921 60c multi 1.25 .25
3888 A921 60c multi 1.25 .25
a. Booklet pane of 10, 2 each #3884-3888 12.50
Nos. 3884-3888 (5) 6.25 1.25

Baby Animals — A922

Designs: $1.70, Kookaburra. $1.75, Wombat. $2.60, Echidna. $4.65, Platypus. $6.45, Possum.

2013, Apr. 2 ***Perf. 14¾x14***

3889 A922 $1.70 multi 3.50 3.50
3890 A922 $1.75 multi 3.75 3.75
3891 A922 $2.60 multi 5.50 5.50
3892 A922 $4.65 multi 9.75 7.50
3893 A922 $6.45 multi 13.50 10.00
Nos. 3889-3893 (5) 36.00 30.25

Booklet Stamps
Self-Adhesive

Serpentine Die Cut 11¼ Syncopated

3894 A922 $1.70 multi 3.50 1.75
a. Booklet pane of 5 17.50
3895 A922 $1.75 multi 3.75 1.90
a. Booklet pane of 5 19.00
3896 A922 $2.60 multi 5.50 2.75
a. Booklet pane of 5 27.50
Nos. 3894-3896 (3) 12.75 6.40

Coach — A923

Queen Elizabeth II — A924

2013, Apr. 9 **Litho.** ***Perf. 14¾x14***

3900 A923 60c multi 1.25 .95
a. Booklet pane of 1 1.25 —
3901 A924 $2.60 multi 5.50 5.50
a. Souvenir sheet of 2, #3900-3901 6.75 6.75
b. Booklet pane of 1 5.50 —
c. Booklet pane of 3 16.50 —
Complete booklet, #3901b, 2 each #3900a, 3901c, + 50c coin 41.00

Complete booklet sold for $19.95.

Booklet Stamp
Self-Adhesive

Serpentine Die Cut 11¼ Syncopated

3902 A924 $2.60 multi 5.50 2.75
a. Booklet pane of 5 27.50

Coronation of Queen Elizabeth II, 60th anniv. Examples of No. 3901a with an overprint for the Australia 2013 World Stamp Expo were made given to the show organizers and sold only by them.

Botanical Gardens A925

Designs: Nos. 3904, 3909, Royal Tasmanian Botanical Gardens, Hobart. Nos. 3905,

3910, Australian National Botanic Gardens, Canberra. Nos. 3906, 3911, Blue Mountains Botanic Garden, Mount Tomah, New South Wales. Nos. 3907, 3912, Darwin Botanic Gardens, Darwin, Northern Territory. No. 3908, 3913, Royal Botanic Gardens, Cranbourne, Victoria.

2013, Apr. 23 Litho. ***Perf. 14x14¾***

3904 A925 60c multi 1.25 1.25
a. Booklet pane of 4 + 2 labels 5.50 —
3905 A925 60c multi 1.25 1.25
a. Booklet pane of 4 + 2 labels 5.50 —
3906 A925 60c multi 1.25 1.25
a. Booklet pane of 4 + 2 labels 5.50 —
3907 A925 60c multi 1.25 1.25
a. Booklet pane of 4 + 2 labels 5.50 —
3908 A925 60c multi 1.25 1.25
a. Booklet pane of 4 + 2 labels 5.50 —
Complete booklet, #3904a, 3905a, 3906a, 3907a, 3908a 27.50
b. Horiz. strip of 5, #3904-3908 6.25 6.25
Nos. 3904-3908 (5) 6.25 6.25

Coil Stamps
Self-Adhesive

Serpentine Die Cut 11¼ Syncopated

3909 A925 60c multi 1.25 .25
3910 A925 60c multi 1.25 .25
3911 A925 60c multi 1.25 .25
3912 A925 60c multi 1.25 .25
3913 A925 60c multi 1.25 .25
a. Horiz. strip of 5, #3909-3913 6.25
Nos. 3909-3913 (5) 6.25 1.25

Complete booklet sold for $12.95. Examples of complete booklets with overprints for the Australia 2013 World Stamp Expo were made given to the show organizers and sold only by them.

Battle of Beersheba, 96th Anniv. A926

Designs: 60c, Statue of Australian Light Horseman, by Peter Corlett, Beersheva, Israel. $2.60, Australian Light Horsemen, photograph of battle re-enactment.

2013, May 10 ***Perf. 13x13½***

3914 A926 60c multi 1.25 .95
3915 A926 $2.60 multi 5.00 3.75

See Israel Nos. 1975-1976.

Black Caviar, Undefeated Racehorse — A927

2013, May 10 ***Perf. 14¾x14***

3916 A927 60c multi 1.25 1.25

Booklet Stamp
Self-Adhesive

Serpentine Die Cut 11¼ Syncopated

3917 A927 60c multi 1.25 .25
a. Booklet pane of 10 12.50

Stamps like No. 3916 but with a white frame were printed in limited-quantity sheets of 10 that were sold in special packages only at the Australia 2013 World Stamp Expo.

Stamps Depicting Kangaroos — A928

2013, May 10 Litho. ***Imperf.***

3918 A928 $1.62 Booklet pane 3.50 —
Complete booklet, #1003b, 1284b, 3534d, 3918 25.00

No. 3918 contains imperforate examples of Nos. 992a, 1030c, 1063B and 2121, but these stamps were not valid for postage individually as cutouts from the entire booklet pane. Complete booklet sold for $12.95, and also contains a perforated booklet pane containing lithographed reproductions of Nos. 166 and 322 that is invalid for postage.

Kangaroo and Map Stamps, Cent. — A929

2013, May 10 Litho. ***Perf. 14¼x14***

3919 A929 $10 red 19.00 9.50
a. Souvenir sheet of 1 19.00 9.50

A booklet containing an imperforate example of No. 3919 sold for $24.95.

First Commonwealth of Australia Banknotes, Cent. — A930

Designs: 60c, Scene from ceremony for numbering first banknote. $2.60, Arms of Australia.

2013, May 11 Litho. ***Perf. 14x13½***

3920 A930 60c multi 1.25 .95
3921 A930 $2.60 multi 5.00 3.75
a. Souvenir sheet of 2, #3920-3921 6.25 4.75

Examples of No. 3921a overprinted in the margin with the emblem of the 2013 Melbourne World Stamp Expo were sold by the exhibitions organizers for $15.

Pardalotes A931

Designs: 60c, Forty-spotted pardalote. $1.20, Spotted pardalotes. $1.80, Red-browed pardalote. $3, Striated pardalote.

2013, May 11 Litho. ***Perf. 14x14¾***

3922 A931 60c multi 1.25 1.25
3923 A931 $1.20 multi 2.25 2.25
3924 A931 $1.80 multi 3.50 2.60
3925 A931 $3 multi 5.75 4.50
a. Booklet pane of 4, #3922-3925 13.00 —
Complete booklet, #3151c, 3376b, 3665b, 3925a 48.50
Nos. 3922-3925 (4) 12.75 10.60

Coil Stamp
Self-Adhesive

Serpentine Die Cut 11¼ Syncopated

3926 A931 60c multi 1.25 .25

Booklet Stamp

3927 A931 $1.20 multi 2.25 .50
a. Booklet pane of 5 11.50

Complete booklet sold for $24.95.

State Government Houses A932

Government House of: Nos. 3928, 3932, South Australia. Nos. 3929, 3933, Western Australia. Nos. 3930, 3934, New South Wales. Nos. 3931, 3935, Tasmania.

2013, June 11 Litho. ***Perf. 14x14¾***

3928 A932 60c multi 1.25 1.25
3929 A932 60c multi 1.25 1.25
3930 A932 60c multi 1.25 1.25
3931 A932 60c multi 1.25 1.25
a. Block of 4, #3928-3931 5.00 5.00
Nos. 3928-3931 (4) 5.00 5.00

Self-Adhesive

Serpentine Die Cut 11¼ Syncopated

3932 A932 60c multi 1.25 .25
3933 A932 60c multi 1.25 .25
3934 A932 60c multi 1.25 .25
3935 A932 60c multi 1.25 .25
a. Horiz. coil strip of 4, #3932-3935 5.00
b. Booklet pane of 20, 5 each #3932-3935 25.00
Nos. 3932-3935 (4) 5.00 1.00

Road Trips — A933

Designs: Nos. 3936, 3942, Utility vehicle in Sydney. Nos. 3937, 3941, Station wagon in Melbourne. Nos, 3938, 3945, Car on roller coaster tracks, Gold Coast. Nos. 3939, 3943, Utility vehicle and camper in Adelaide. Nos. 3940, 3944, Car and camper in Canberra.

2013, July 2 Litho. ***Perf. 14¼***

3936 A933 60c multi 1.10 1.10
3937 A933 60c multi 1.10 1.10
3938 A933 60c multi 1.10 1.10
3939 A933 60c multi 1.10 1.10
3940 A933 60c multi 1.10 1.10
a. Souvenir sheet of 5, #3936-3940 5.50 5.50
Nos. 3936-3940 (5) 5.50 5.50

Booklet Stamps
Self-Adhesive

Serpentine Die Cut 11¼ Syncopated

3941 A933 60c multi 1.10 .25
3942 A933 60c multi 1.10 .25
a. Booklet pane of 10, 5 each #3941-3942 11.00
3943 A933 60c multi 1.10 .25
3944 A933 60c multi 1.10 .25
3945 A933 60c multi 1.10 .25
a. Booklet pane of 20, 7 each #3943, 3945, 6 #3944 22.00
Nos. 3941-3945 (5) 5.50 1.25

Aboriginal Leaders — A934

Designs: Nos. 3946, 3951, Shirley Smith (1921-98), justice and welfare advocate. Nos. 3947, 3952, Neville Bonner (1922-99), first Aboriginal member of Australian Parliament. Nos. 3948, 3953, Oodgeroo Noonuccal (1920-93), poet. Nos. 3949, 3954, Eddie "Koiki" Mabo (1936-92), plaintiff in historic Aboriginal land rights lawsuit. Nos. 3950, 3955, Charles Perkins (1936-2000), Secretary of the Department of Aboriginal Affairs.

2013, July 9 Litho. ***Perf. 14¾x14***

3946 A934 60c multi 1.10 1.10
a. Booklet pane of 4 4.75 —
3947 A934 60c multi 1.10 1.10
a. Booklet pane of 4 4.75 —
3948 A934 60c multi 1.10 1.10
a. Booklet pane of 4 4.75 —
3949 A934 60c multi 1.10 1.10
a. Booklet pane of 4 4.75 —
3950 A934 60c multi 1.10 1.10
a. Booklet pane of 4 4.75 —
Complete booklet, #3946a, 3947a, 3948a, 3949a, 3950a 24.00
b. Horiz. strip of 5, #3946-3950 5.50 5.50
Nos. 3946-3950 (5) 5.50 5.50

Coil Stamps
Self-Adhesive

Serpentine Die Cut 11¼ Syncopated

3951 A934 60c multi 1.10 .25
3952 A934 60c multi 1.10 .25
3953 A934 60c multi 1.10 .25
3954 A934 60c multi 1.10 .25
3955 A934 60c multi 1.10 .25
a. Vert. coil strip of 5, #3951-3955 5.50
Nos. 3951-3955 (5) 5.50 1.25

Complete booklet sold for $12.95.

Birth of Prince George of Cambridge A935

2013, July 22 Litho. ***Perf. 14¼***

3956 A935 60c multi 1.10 1.10

Booklet Stamp
Self-Adhesive

Serpentine Die Cut 11¼ Syncopated

3957 A935 60c multi 1.10 .25
a. Booklet pane of 10 11.00

Headline News — A936

News stories of: Nos. 3958, 3962, August 15, 1945 (end of World War II). Nos. 3959, 3963, July 21, 1969 (first man on the Moon). Nos. 3960, 3964, December 25, 1974 (destruction of Darwin by Cyclone Tracy). Nos. 3961, 3965, September 27, 1983 (victory of Australia in America's Cup yacht races).

2013, July 23 Litho. ***Perf. 14¾x14***

3958 A936 60c multi 1.10 1.10
3959 A936 60c multi 1.10 1.10
3960 A936 60c multi 1.10 1.10
3961 A936 60c multi 1.10 1.10
a. Block of 4, #3958-3961 4.40 4.40
b. Souvenir sheet of 4, #3958-3961 4.40 4.40
Nos. 3958-3961 (4) 4.40 4.40

Self-Adhesive

Serpentine Die Cut 11¼ Syncopated

3962 A936 60c multi 1.10 .25
3963 A936 60c multi 1.10 .25
3964 A936 60c multi 1.10 .25
3965 A936 60c multi 1.10 .25
a. Vert. coil strip of 4, #3962-3965 4.40
b. Booklet pane of 20, 5 each #3962-3965 22.00
Nos. 3962-3965 (4) 4.40 1.00

Carnivorous Plants — A937

Designs: Nos. 3966, 3970, Cephalotus follicularis and ants. Nos. 3967, 3971, Drosera rupicola and fly. Nos. 3968, 3972, Drosera lowriei and butterfly. Nos. 3969, 3973, Nepenthes rowanae and frog.

2013, Aug. 13 Litho. ***Perf. 14¾x14***

3966 A937 60c multi 1.10 1.10
3967 A937 60c multi 1.10 1.10
3968 A937 60c multi 1.10 1.10
3969 A937 60c multi 1.10 1.10
a. Block of 4, #3966-3969 4.40 4.40
Nos. 3966-3969 (4) 4.40 4.40

Booklet Stamps
Self-Adhesive

Serpentine Die Cut 11¼ Syncopated

3970 A937 60c multi 1.10 .25
3971 A937 60c multi 1.10 .25
3972 A937 60c multi 1.10 .25
3973 A937 60c multi 1.10 .25
a. Booklet pane of 10, 3 each #3970, 3972, 2 each #3971, 3973 11.00
Nos. 3970-3973 (4) 4.40 1.00

Coral Reefs A938

Designs: Nos. 3974, 3979, Underwater view of Ningaloo Reef, Western Australia. Nos. 3975, 3978, Underwater view of Great Barrier Reef, Queensland. Nos. 3976, 3981, Aerial veiw of Ningaloo Reef. Nos. 3977, 3980, Aerial view of Great Barrier Reef.

2013, Aug. 20 Litho. *Perf. 14½x14*

3974 A938 60c multi 1.10 1.10
a. Perf. 13½x14 1.10 1.10
3975 A938 60c multi 1.10 1.10
a. Horiz. pair, #3974-3975 2.20 2.20
b. Perf. 13½x14 1.10 1.10
3976 A938 $1.20 multi 2.25 2.25
a. Perf. 13½x14 2.25 2.25
3977 A938 $1.20 multi 2.25 2.25
a. Horiz. pair, #3976-3977 4.50 4.50
b. Perf. 13½x14 2.25 2.25
c. Souvenir sheet of 4, #3974a, 3975b, 3976a, 3977b 6.75 6.75
Nos. 3974-3977 (4) 6.70 6.70

Booklet Stamps
Self-Adhesive
Serpentine Die Cut 10½ Syncopated

3978 A938 60c multi 1.10 .25
3979 A938 60c multi 1.10 .25
a. Booklet pane of 20, 10 each #3978-3979 22.00
3980 A938 $1.20 multi 2.25 .50
3981 A938 $1.20 multi 2.25 .50
a. Booklet pane of 5, 3 #3980, 2 #3981 11.50
Nos. 3978-3981 (4) 6.70 1.50

Poultry Breeds — A939

Designs: No. 3982, Australian Game hen and rooster. No. 3983, Australian Pit Game hen and chicks. Nos. 3984, 3985, Australorp hens (37x26mm).

2013, Sept. 3 Litho. *Perf. 14x13½*

3982 A939 60c multi 1.10 .85
a. Booklet pane of 4 4.75 —
3983 A939 60c multi 1.10 .85
a. Booklet pane of 4 4.75 —
b. Booklet pane of 4, 2 each #3982-3983 4.75 —

Perf. 14x14¾

3984 A939 60c multi 1.10 1.10
a. Booklet pane of 4 4.75 —
b. Souvenir sheet of 3, #3982-3984 3.30 3.30
Complete booklet, #3982a, 3983a, 3983b, 2 #3984a 24.00
Nos. 3982-3984 (3) 3.30 2.80

Booklet Stamp
Self-Adhesive
Serpentine Die Cut 11¼ Syncopated

3985 A939 60c multi 1.10 .25
a. Booklet pane of 10 11.00

Complete booklet sold for $12.95 and contains two examples of No. 3984a having different margins.

Dinosaurs — A940

Designs: Nos. 3986, 3992, Koolasuchus. Nos. 3987, 3995, Serendipaceratops (26x37mm). No. 3988, Timimus (30x50mm). Nos. 3989, 3993, Diamantinasaurus, horiz. No. 3990, Qantassaurus, horiz. (50x30mm). Nos. 3991, 3994, Australovenator (26x37mm).

2013, Sept. 24 Litho. *Perf. 14½x14*

3986 A940 60c multi 1.25 1.25
a. Booklet pane of 4 5.00 —
b. Perf. 14½ 1.25 1.25

Perf. 14¾x14

3987 A940 60c multi 1.25 1.25
a. Booklet pane of 4 5.00 —
b. Perf. 14½ 1.25 1.25

Perf. 14x14½

3988 A940 60c multi 1.25 1.25
a. Perf. 14x13½ 1.25 1.25
b. Booklet pane of 2 #3988a 2.50 —
c. Perf. 14½ 1.25 1.25

Perf. 14x14½

3989 A940 60c multi 1.25 1.25
a. Booklet pane of 4 5.00 —
b. Perf. 14½ 1.25 1.25

Perf. 14½x14

3990 A940 60c multi 1.25 1.25
a. Perf. 13½x14 1.25 1.25
b. Booklet pane of 2 #3990a 2.50 —
c. Perf. 14½ 1.25 1.25

Perf. 14¾x14

3991 A940 60c multi 1.25 1.25
a. Booklet pane of 4 5.00 —
Complete booklet, #3986a, 3987a, 3988b, 3989a, 3990b, 3991a 25.00
b. Perf. 14½ 1.25 1.25
c. Souvenir sheet of 6, #3986b, 3987b, 3988c, 3989b, 3990c, 3991b 7.50 7.50
Nos. 3986-3991 (6) 7.50 7.50

Booklet Stamps
Self-Adhesive
Serpentine Die Cut 11¼

3992 A940 60c multi 1.25 .25
3993 A940 60c multi 1.25 .25
a. Booklet pane of 10, 5 each #3992-3993 12.50

Serpentine Die Cut 11¼ Syncopated

3994 A940 60c multi 1.25 .25
3995 A940 60c multi 1.25 .25
a. Booklet pane of 20, 10 each #3994-3995 25.00
Nos. 3992-3995 (4) 5.00 1.00

Complete booklet sold for $12.95.

Historic Railroad Stations A941

Station at: Nos. 3996, 4000, Maryborough, Victoria. Nos. 3997, 4001, Quorn, South Australia. Nos. 3998, 4002, Hay, New South Wales. Nos. 3999, 4003, Normanton, Queensland.

2013, Oct. 8 Litho. *Perf. 14x14¾*

3996 A941 60c multi 1.25 1.25
3997 A941 60c multi 1.25 1.25
3998 A941 60c multi 1.25 1.25
3999 A941 60c multi 1.25 1.25
a. Block of 4, #3996-3999 5.00 5.00
Nos. 3996-3999 (4) 5.00 5.00

Self-Adhesive
Serpentine Die Cut 11¼ Syncopated

4000 A941 60c multi 1.25 .25
4001 A941 60c multi 1.25 .25
4002 A941 60c multi 1.25 .25
4003 A941 60c multi 1.25 .25
a. Horiz. coil strip of 4, #4000-4003 5.00
b. Booklet pane of 10, 3 each #4000-4001, 2 each #4002-4003 12.50
Nos. 4000-4003 (4) 5.00 1.00

Ludwig Leichhardt (1813-48), Explorer of Outback Region A942

2013, Oct. 15 Litho. *Perf. 14¼*

4004 A942 60c multi 1.25 .95

See Germany No. 2752.

Early Australian Coinage A943

Designs: 60c, Holey dollar and dumps. $3, Holey dollars.

2013, Oct. 22 Litho. *Perf. 14x14¾*

4005 A943 60c multi 1.25 .95
4006 A943 $3 multi 5.75 4.50

Souvenir Sheet
Litho. & Embossed With Foil Application

4007 Sheet of 2 7.00 7.00
a. A943 60c multi 1.25 .95
b. A943 $3 multi 5.75 4.50

Christmas
A944 A945

Designs: Nos. 4008, 4014, Madonna and Child. Nos. 4009, 4015, 4019, Christmas tree. Nos. 4010, 4016, 4020, Gift. 60c, Candle. Nos. 4012, 4017, Bell. Nos. 4013, 4018, Adoration of the Shepherds.

2013, Nov. 1 Litho. *Perf. 14¾x14*

4008 A944 55c multi 1.10 1.10
4009 A945 55c multi 1.10 1.10
4010 A945 55c multi 1.10 1.10
a. Horiz. pair, #4009-4010 2.20 2.20
4011 A945 60c multi 1.25 .95
4012 A945 $1.70 multi 3.25 1.60
4013 A944 $2.55 multi 4.75 2.40
a. Souvenir sheet of 2, #4008, 4013 6.00 6.00
Nos. 4008-4013 (6) 12.55 8.25

Booklet Stamps
Self-Adhesive
Serpentine Die Cut 11¼ Syncopated

4014 A944 55c multi 1.10 .25
a. Booklet pane of 20 + 10 etiquettes 22.00
4015 A945 55c multi 1.10 .25
4016 A945 55c multi 1.10 .25
a. Booklet pane of 20, 10 each #4015-4016, + 10 etiquettes 22.00
4017 A945 $1.70 multi 3.25 1.60
a. Booklet pane of 5 16.50
4018 A944 $2.55 multi 4.75 2.40
a. Booklet pane of 5 24.00

Litho. & Embossed With Foil Application

4019 A945 55c multi 1.10 .25
a. Booklet pane of 10 11.00
4020 A945 55c multi 1.10 .25
a. Booklet pane of 10 11.00
Nos. 4014-4020 (7) 13.50 5.25

SEMI-POSTAL STAMPS

Catalogue values in this section are for Never Hinged items.

Queensland Flood Relief — SP1

Designs: No. B1, Rescuer holding baby. No. B2, Flooded buildings, ground-level view. No. B3, Rescuers taking pet from house. No. B4, Kangaroo stranded on island in flood. No. B5, Flooded buildings, aerial view.

Serpentine Die Cut 11¼ Syncopated
2011, Jan. 27 Litho.
Self-Adhesive

B1 SP1 60c+(20c) multi 1.75 1.75
B2 SP1 60c+(20c) multi 1.75 1.75
B3 SP1 60c+(20c) multi 1.75 1.75
B4 SP1 60c+(20c) multi 1.75 1.75
B5 SP1 60c+(20c) multi 1.75 1.75
a. Sheet of 10, 2 each #B1-B5 17.50
Nos. B1-B5 (5) 8.75 8.75

Surtax for Premier's Flood Relief Appeal.

Leaves in Ring and Hands — SP2

2012, June 26
Self-Adhesive

B6 SP2 60c+(20c) multi 1.75 1.75

Printed in sheets of 10. Surtax for Olivia Newton-John Cancer and Wellness Center.

AIR POST STAMPS

Airplane over Bush Lands — AP1

Unwmk.
1929, May 20 Engr. *Perf. 11*

C1 AP1 3p deep green 9.25 8.50
Never hinged 14.50
a. Booklet pane of 4 ('30) 450.00

Kingsford-Smith Type of 1931
1931, Mar. 19

C2 A8 6p gray violet 8.00 8.00
Never hinged 11.50

AP3

1931, Nov. 4

C3 AP3 6p olive brown 17.00 14.00
Never hinged 35.00

For overprint see No. CO1.

Mercury and Hemispheres AP4

1934, Dec. 1 *Perf. 11*

C4 AP4 1sh6p violet brown 40.00 8.00
Never hinged 97.50

Perf. 13½x14
1937, Oct. 22 Wmk. 228

C5 AP4 1sh6p violet brown 8.50 1.40
Never hinged 14.50

Catalogue values for unused stamps in this section, from this point to the end of the section, are for Never Hinged items.

Mercury and Globe — AP5

1949, Sept. 1 *Perf. 14½*

C6 AP5 1sh6p sepia 2.25 .60

1956, Dec. 6 Unwmk.

C7 AP5 1sh6p sepia 18.50 1.10

Super-Constellation over Globe — AP6

1958, Jan. 6 *Perf. 14½x14*
C8 AP6 2sh dark violet blue 2.75 2.25

Inauguration of Australian "Round the World" air service.

AIR POST OFFICIAL STAMP

No. C3 Overprinted

Perf. 11, 11½
1931, Nov. 17 **Unwmk.**
CO1 AP3 6p olive brown 35.00 *35.00*
Never hinged 57.50

Issued primarily for official use, but to prevent speculation, a quantity was issued for public distribution.

POSTAGE DUE STAMPS

Very fine examples of Nos. J1-J38 will have perforations touching the design on one or more sides due to the narrow spacing of the stamps on the plates. Stamps with perfs clear of the design on all four sides are scarce and will command higher prices.

D1

D2

1902 Typo. Wmk. 55 *Perf. 11½, 12*
J1 D1 ½p emerald 11.50 11.50
J2 D1 1p emerald 17.50 11.50
a. Perf. 11 *2,800.* *1,400.*
b. Perf. 11x11½ 450.00 250.00
J3 D1 2p emerald 32.00 11.50
a. Perf. 11x11½ 600.00 200.00
J4 D1 3p emerald 32.00 21.00
J5 D1 4p emerald 45.00 25.00
J6 D1 6p emerald 70.00 17.00
J7 D1 8p emerald 180.00 140.00
J8 D1 5sh emerald 400.00 125.00
Nos. J1-J8 (8) 788.00 362.50

Perf. 11½, 12, Compound with 11
1902-04
J9 D2 ½p emerald 17.50 *11.50*
a. Perf. 11 775.00 400.00
J10 D2 1p emerald, Perf 12x11 17.00 5.75
a. Perf. 11 200.00 42.50
b. Perf 11½ 400.00 200.00
c. Perf 11x11½ 37.50 11.50
J11 D2 2p emerald 23.00 5.75
a. Perf. 11 260.00 57.50
b. Perf 12 — 225.00
c. Perf 11x11½ 120.00 37.50
d. Perf 11x12 140.00 45.00
J12 D2 3p emerald 160.00 26.00
a. Perf. 11 225.00 63.00
b. Perf 12 450.00 170.00
J13 D2 4p emerald 140.00 32.00
a. Perf. 11 400.00 115.00
J14 D2 5p emerald 140.00 35.00
a. Perf. 11 500.00 86.00
b. Perf 12 100.00 23.00
J15 D2 6p emerald 160.00 29.00
a. Perf. 11 260.00 32.00
J16 D2 8p emerald 325.00 120.00
J17 D2 10p emerald 175.00 29.00
a. Perf 12x11½ 150.00 29.00
J18 D2 1sh emerald 160.00 29.00
a. Perf. 11 500.00 90.00
b. Perf 12x11½ 125.00 32.00
J19 D2 2sh emerald 200.00 32.00
a. Perf 11½, 12 200.00 40.00
J20 D2 5sh emerald 500.00 57.50
a. Perf. 11 1,700. 600.00

Perf. 11
J21 D2 10sh emerald *4,000.* *3,200.*
J22 D2 20sh emerald *8,500.* *5,500.*
Nos. J9-J20 (12) 2,017. 412.50

Perf. 11½, 12 Compound with 11
1906 **Wmk. 12**
J23 D2 ½p emerald 16.00 16.00
J24 D2 1p emerald 35.00 5.75
a. Perf. 11 *3,500.* *1,450.*
J25 D2 2p emerald 62.50 11.50
J26 D2 3p emerald 1,150. 450.00
J27 D2 4p emerald 140.00 27.50
a. Perf. 11 *4,600.* *2,900.*
J28 D2 6p emerald 490.00 35.00
Nos. J23-J28 (6) 1,893. 545.75

1907 Wmk. 13 *Perf. 11½x11*
J29 D2 ½p emerald 42.50 *85.00*
J30 D2 1p emerald 260.00 140.00
J31 D2 2p emerald 375.00 290.00
J32 D2 4p emerald 500.00 290.00
J33 D2 6p emerald 550.00 400.00
Nos. J29-J33 (5) 1,727. 1,205.

D3

D4

Perf. 11 (2sh, 10sh, 20sh), 11½x11 (1sh, 5sh)
1908-09 **Wmk. 12**
J34 D3 1sh emer ('09) 225.00 29.00
J35 D3 2sh emerald *1,800.* —
J36 D3 5sh emerald 775.00 75.00
J37 D3 10sh emerald *5,200.* —
J38 D3 20sh emerald *13,000.* —

1909-23 Wmk. 13 *Perf. 12x12½*
J39 D4 ½p green & car 32.00 *45.00*
a. Perf 11, green & rose ('14) 20.00 17.00
b. Perf 12½, green & scarlet ('13) 37.50 29.00
c. Perf 14 ('19) 20.00 17.00
J40 D4 1p green & car 23.00 9.75
a. Perf 11, yel grn & rose, thicker paper, thick yellowish gum 4,600. 1,725.
b. Perf 11, bright apple green & rose, thin paper, thin white gum ('14) 20.00 8.50
c. Perf 14 ('14) 70.00 17.00
J41 D4 2p green & car 32.00 5.75
a. Perf 11 — —
b. Perf 14 ('18) 29.00 7.50
J42 D4 3p green & car 35.00 14.50
a. Perf 14, green & rose ('16) 150.00 52.00
J43 D4 4p green & car 24.00 11.50
a. Perf 14 ('21) 200.00 70.00
J44 D4 6p green & car 35.00 14.00
a. Perf 11 — —
J45 D4 1sh green & car 33.00 9.25
a. Perf 14, yel grn & scarlet ('23) 45.00 23.00
J46 D4 2sh green & car 115.00 16.00
J47 D4 5sh green & car 175.00 17.00
J48 D4 10sh green & car 450.00 325.00
a. Perf 14, yel grn & scarlet ('21) 2,600.
J49 D4 £1 green & car 1,100. 575.00
a. Perf 14, yel grn & scarlet ('21) 1,600.
Nos. J39-J49 (11) 2,054. 1,042.

Nos. J39-J48 and J40a, J41a, J44a are from the 1909 printings and have thicker paper and thick yellowish gum. The other listings are from the 1912-23 printings on thinner paper with thin white gum.

1922-30 Wmk. 10 *Perf. 14, 11 (4p)*
J50 D4 ½p grn & car ('23) 9.25 7.50
J51 D4 1p green & car 7.50 2.25
J52 D4 1½p green & rose ('25) 4.25 7.50
J53 D4 2p green & car 9.25 4.25
J54 D4 3p green & car 17.00 3.25
J55 D4 4p green & car ('30) 17.00 8.00
a. Perf 14 52.00 23.00
J56 D4 6p green & car 37.50 18.50
Nos. J50-J56 (7) 101.75 51.25
Set, never hinged 200.00

1931-36 Wmk. 228 *Perf. 11*
J57 D4 ½p yel green & rose ('34) 23.00 23.00
J58 D4 1p yel grn & rose ('32) 9.00 2.25
a. Perf 14 14.00 11.50
J59 D4 2p yel grn & rose ('33) 10.50 2.25
a. Perf 14 11.50 11.50
J60 D4 3p yel green & rose ('36) 140.00 115.00
J61 D4 4p yel green & rose ('34) 29.00 4.50
J62 D4 6p yel green & rose ('36) 550.00 500.00
J63 D4 1sh yel green & rose ('34) 70.00 30.00
Nos. J57-J63 (7) 831.50 677.00
Set, never hinged 1,400.

D5

Engraved; Value Typo.
1938 *Perf. 14½x14*
J64 D5 ½p green & car 3.50 *3.50*
J65 D5 1p green & car 12.50 1.10
J66 D5 2p green & car 12.50 2.25
J67 D5 3p green & car 55.00 23.00
J68 D5 4p green & car 16.00 1.10
J69 D5 6p green & car 100.00 45.00
J70 D5 1sh green & car 57.50 20.00
Nos. J64-J70 (7) 257.00 95.95
Set, never hinged 400.00

Catalogue values for unused stamps in this section, from this point to the end of the section, are for Never Hinged items.

Type of 1938
Value Tablet Redrawn

Original

Redrawn

Pence denominations: "D" has melon-shaped center in redrawn tablet. The redrawn 3p differs slightly, having semi-melon-shaped "D" center, with vertical white stroke half filling it.

1sh. 1938: Numeral "1" narrow, with six background lines above.

1sh. 1947: Numeral broader, showing more white space around dotted central ornament. Three lines above.

1946-57 **Wmk. 228**
J71 D5 ½p grn & car ('56) 7.00 5.75
J72 D5 1p grn & car ('47) 4.50 1.10
J73 D5 2p green & car 8.00 1.10
J74 D5 3p green & car 10.00 1.10
J75 D5 4p grn & car ('52) 14.00 1.40
J76 D5 5p grn & car ('48) 18.50 2.25
J77 D5 6p grn & car ('47) 18.50 2.90
J78 D5 7p grn & car ('53) 8.00 7.00
J79 D5 8p grn & car ('57) 26.00 23.00
J80 D5 1sh grn & car ('47) 29.00 4.50
Nos. J71-J80 (10) 143.50 50.10

1953-54
White Tablet, Carmine Numeral
J81 D5 1sh grn & car ('54) 20.00 6.25
J82 D5 2sh green & car 26.00 14.50
J83 D5 5sh green & car 32.00 8.50
Nos. J81-J83 (3) 78.00 29.25

Issued: 2sh, 5sh, Aug. 26; 1sh, Feb. 17.

Redrawn Type of 1947-57

Two Types of Some Pence Values:

Type I — Background lines touch numeral, "D" and period.

Type II — Lines do not touch numeral, etc.

Second engraving of 1sh has sharper and thicker lines.

The ½p type II has 7 dots under the "2."

The 8p type II has distinct lines in centers of "8" and between "8" and "D."

Engr.; Value Typo.
1958-60 Unwmk. *Perf. 14½x14*
J86 D5 ½p grn & car, II 7.00 4.25
a. Six dots under the "2" 9.25 2.25
J87 D5 1p grn & car, II 5.75 1.10
a. Type I 5.75 2.25
J88 D5 3p grn & car, II 5.75 4.50
J89 D5 4p grn & car, I 11.50 10.00
a. Type II ('59) 9.25 *9.25*
J90 D5 5p grn & car, I 29.00 17.50
a. Type II ('59) 100.00 40.00
J91 D5 6p grn & car, II 10.00 5.25
J92 D5 8p grn & car, II 29.00 *29.00*
a. Indistinct lines 23.00 23.00
J93 D5 10p grn & car, II 17.00 6.25

White Tablet, Carmine Numeral
J94 D5 1sh green & car 29.00 7.00
a. 2nd redrawing ('60) 29.00 5.75
J95 D5 2sh grn & car 35.00 21.00
Nos. J86-J95 (10) 179.00 105.85

Issued: 1sh, 9/8/58; 10p, 12/9/59; 2sh, 3/8/60; 3p, 6p, 5/25/60; others, 2/27/58.

MILITARY STAMPS

Nos. 166, 191, 183A, 173, 175, 206 and 177 Overprinted in Black

a

b

c

Perf. 14½x14, 15x14, 11½, 13½x13
1946-47 **Wmk. 228**
M1 A24(a) ½p orange 3.50 3.50
Never hinged 5.75
M2 A36(b) 1p brown vio 3.50 3.50
Never hinged 5.75
a. Blue overprint 115.00 77.50
Never hinged 140.00
M3 A27(b) 3p dk vio brn 3.50 *3.50*
Never hinged 5.75
a. Double overprint 850.00
M4 A30(a) 6p brn violet 12.00 11.50
Never hinged 18.00
M5 A16(a) 1sh gray green 12.00 11.50
Never hinged 18.00
M6 A1(c) 2sh dk red brn 35.00 45.00
Never hinged 70.00
M7 A32(c) 5sh dl red brn 140.00 *200.00*
Never hinged 250.00
Nos. M1-M7 (7) 209.50 278.50

"B.C.O.F." stands for "British Commonwealth Occupation Force."

Issue dates: Nos. M1-M3, Oct. 11, 1946, Nos. M4-M7, May 8, 1947.

OFFICIAL STAMPS

Overprinted Official stamps are comparatively more difficult to find well centered than the basic issues on which they are printed. This is because poorly centered sheets that had been discarded were purposely chosen to be overprinted to save money.

Perforated Initials

In 1913-31, postage stamps were perforated "OS" for federal official use. The Scott Standard Catalogues do not list officials with perforated initials, but listings for these Australian stamps will be found in the ***Scott Classic Specialized Catalogue.***

Overprinted

On Regular Issue of 1931
1931, May 4 Unwmk. *Perf. 11, 11½*
O1 A8 2p dull red 160.00 45.00
O2 A8 3p blue 450.00 80.00

These stamps were issued primarily for official use but to prevent speculation a quantity was issued for public distribution.

Used values are for CTO examples.
Counterfeit overprints exist.

On Regular Issues of 1928-32

1932	Wmk. 203	Perf. 13½x12½		
O3	A4	2p red (II)	25.00	13.00
O4	A4	4p olive bister	40.00	26.00
		Perf. 11½, 12		
O5	A1	6p brown	97.50	90.00

1932-33	Wmk. 228	Perf. 13½x12½		
O6	A4	½p orange	9.25	6.00
a.		Inverted overprint	—	—
O7	A4	1p green (I)	6.00	2.00
O8	A4	2p red (II)	13.00	6.50
a.		Inverted overprint		—
O9	A4	3p ultra (II) ('33)	18.00	9.25
O10	A4	5p brown buff	57.50	52.50
		Perf. 11½, 12		
O11	A1	6p yellow brown	45.00	35.00
a.		Inverted overprint		—
		Nos. O6-O11 (6)	148.75	111.25
		Set, never hinged	275.00	

1932	Unwmk.	Perf. 11, 11½		
O12	A9	2p red	7.25	6.00
O13	A9	3p blue	24.00	24.00
O14	A16	1sh gray green	72.50	52.50
		Nos. O12-O14 (3)	103.75	82.50
		Set, never hinged	160.00	

AUSTRALIAN ANTARCTIC TERRITORY

Catalogue values for all unused stamps in this section are for Never Hinged items.

All stamps, except Nos. L1-L7, are also valid for postage in Australia.

Edgeworth David, Douglas Mawson and A.F. McKay (1908-09 South Pole Expedition) — A1

Australian Explorers and Map of Antarctica — A2

Designs: 8p, Loading weasel (snow truck). 1sh, Dog team and iceberg, vert. 2sh3p, Emperor penguins and map, vert.

1957-59	Engr.	*Perf. 14½, 14½x14, 14x14½* Unwmk.		
L1	A1	5p brown	.85	.30
L2	A2	8p dark blue	3.75	2.25
L3	A2	1sh dark green	3.75	2.00
L4	A2	2sh ultra ('57)	1.75	1.00
L5	A2	2sh3p green	11.50	5.75
		Nos. L1-L5 (5)	21.60	11.30
		Set, hinged	9.75	

Nos. L1 and L2 were printed as 4p and 7p stamps and surcharged typographically in black and dark blue before issuance.

Sizes of stamps: No. L2, 34x21mm; Nos. L3, L5, 21x34mm; No. L4, 43½x25½mm.

1961, July 5		*Perf. 14½*		
L6	A1	5p dark blue	1.60	.45

The denomination on No. L6 is not within a typographed circle, but is part of the engraved design.

Sir Douglas Mawson — A3

1961, Oct. 18				
L7	A3	5p dark green	.50	.40

50th anniv. of the 1911-14 Australian Antarctic Expedition.

Lookout and Iceberg — A4

Designs: 1c, Aurora australis and camera dome. 2c, Banding penguins. 5c, Branding of elephant seals. 7c, Measuring snow strata. 10c, Wind gauges. 15c, Weather balloon. 20c, Helicopter. 25c, Radio operator. 50c, Ice compression tests. $1, "Mock sun" (parahelion) and dogs. 20c, 25c, 50c and $1 horizontal.

1966-68	Photo.	*Perf. 13½x13, 13x13½* Unwmk.		
L8	A4	1c multicolored	.75	.40
L9	A4	2c multicolored	2.75	.90
L10	A4	4c multicolored	1.00	1.00
L11	A4	5c multicolored	2.25	1.10
L12	A4	7c multicolored	.75	.90
L13	A4	10c multicolored	1.00	1.00
L14	A4	15c multicolored	5.25	2.25
L15	A4	20c multicolored	8.00	2.75
L16	A4	25c multicolored	2.00	2.00
L17	A4	50c multicolored	7.50	7.50
L18	A4	$1 multicolored	25.00	15.00
		Nos. L8-L18 (11)	56.25	34.80
		Set, hinged	35.00	

Issued: 5c, 9/25/68; others, 9/28/66.

Nos. L8-L18 are on phosphorescent helecon paper. Fluorescent orange is one of the colors used in printing the 10c, 15c, 20c and 50c.

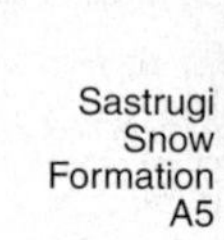
Sastrugi Snow Formation A5

1971, June 23	Photo.	*Perf. 13x13½*		
L19	A5	6c shown	1.10	1.10
L20	A5	30c Pancake ice	5.75	*6.25*

10th anniv. of the Antarctic Treaty pledging peaceful uses of and scientific cooperation in Antarctica.

Capt. Cook, Sextant, Azimuth Compass A6

Design: 35c, Chart of Cook's circumnavigation of Antarctica, and "Resolution."

1972, Sept. 13	Photo.	*Perf. 13x13½*		
L21	A6	7c bister & multi	1.40	1.40
L22	A6	35c buff & multi	5.50	5.50

Bicentenary of Capt. James Cook's circumnavigation of Antarctica.

Plankton and Krill Shrimp — A7

Mawson's D.H. Gipsy Moth, 1931 — A8

Food Chain (Essential for Survival): 7c, Adelie penguin feeding on krill shrimp. 9c, Leopard seal pursuing fish, horiz. 10c, Killer whale hunting seals, horiz. 20c, Wandering albatross, horiz. $1, Sperm whale attacking giant squid.

Explorers' Aircraft: 8c, Rymill's DH Fox Moth returning to Barry Island. 25c, Hubert Wilkins Lockheed Vega, horiz. 30c, Lincoln Ellsworth's Northrop Gamma. 35c, Lars Christensen's Avro Avian and Framnes Mountains, horiz. 50c, Richard Byrd's Ford Tri-Motor dropping US flag over South Pole.

1973, Aug. 15		*Perf. 13½x13, 13x13½*		
L23	A7	1c multicolored	.25	.25
L24	A8	5c multicolored	.25	.25
L25	A7	7c multicolored	2.00	1.10
L26	A8	8c multicolored	.35	*.60*
L27	A7	9c multicolored	.30	.30
L28	A7	10c multicolored	3.50	2.25
L29	A7	20c multicolored	1.00	.75
L30	A8	25c multicolored	.75	.75
L31	A8	30c multicolored	.75	*.85*
L32	A8	35c multicolored	.75	*.85*
L33	A8	50c multicolored	1.40	2.00
L34	A7	$1 multicolored	2.50	2.50
		Nos. L23-L34 (12)	13.80	12.45

Adm. Byrd, Plane, Mountains A9

Design: 20c, Adm. Byrd, Floyd Bennett trimotored plane, map of Antarctica.

1979, June 20	Litho.	*Perf. 15½*		
L35	A9	20c multicolored	.45	*.60*
L36	A9	55c multicolored	1.10	*1.10*

50th anniv. of first flight over South Pole by Richard Byrd (1888-1957).

"S.Y. Nimrod" A10

2c, 5c, 22c, 25c, 40c, 55c, $1 are vertical. No. L41 actually pictures the S.S. Morning.

1974-81		*Perf. 13½x13, 13x13½* Litho.		
L37	A10	1c S.Y. Aurora	.25	.25
L38	A10	2c R.Y. Penola	.25	.25
L39	A10	5c M.V. Thala Dan	.25	*.35*
L40	A10	10c H.M.S. Challenger	.40	*.60*
L41	A10	15c shown	1.60	*2.25*
L42	A10	15c S.Y. Nimrod, stern view	.35	*.85*
L43	A10	20c R.R.S. Discovery II	.40	*.85*
L44	A10	22c R.Y.S. Terra Nova	.65	*.85*
L45	A10	25c S.S. Endurance	.70	*.60*
L46	A10	30c S.S. Fram	.70	*1.10*
L47	A10	35c M.S. Nella Dan	.85	*1.10*
L48	A10	40c M.S. Kista Dan	1.10	*1.10*
L49	A10	45c L'Astrolabe	1.10	*1.10*
L50	A10	50c S.S. Norvegia	1.10	*.85*
L51	A10	55c S.Y. Discovery	1.40	*2.25*
L52	A10	$1 H.M.S. Resolution	2.75	*2.75*
		Nos. L37-L52 (16)	13.85	*17.10*

A11

1982, May 5	Litho.	*Perf. 14x13½*		
L53	A11	27c Mawson, landscape	.60	.45
L54	A11	75c Mawson, map	1.60	1.40

Sir Douglas Mawson (1882-1958), explorer.

A12

Local Wildlife: a, Light-mantled sooty albatross. b, Macquarie Isld. shags. c, Elephant seals. d, Royal penguins. e, Antarctic prions.

1983, Apr. 6	Litho.	*Perf. 14½*		
L55		Strip of 5, multi	3.50	*3.50*
a.-e.		A12 27c, any single	.70	*.70*

12th Antarctic Treaty Consultative Meeting, Canberra, Sept. 13-27 — A13

1983, Sept. 7	Litho.	*Perf. 14½*		
L56	A13	27c multicolored	.60	.50

South Magnetic Pole Expedition, 75th Anniv. A14

1984, Jan. 16				
L57	A14	30c Prismatic compass	.65	.65
L58	A14	85c Aneroid barometer	1.90	*2.00*

Dog Team, Mawson Station A15

1984-87	Litho.	*Perf. 14½x15*		
L60	A15	2c Summer afternoon	.25	.25
L61	A15	5c shown	.25	.25
L62	A15	10c Evening	.25	.25
L63	A15	15c Prince Charles Mts.	.35	.25
L64	A15	20c Morning	.40	.35
L65	A15	25c Sea ice, iceberg	.50	.45
L66	A15	30c Mt. Coates	.65	.60
L67	A15	33c Iceberg Alley, Mawson	.70	.60
L68	A15	36c Winter evening	.75	.65
L69	A15	45c Brash ice, vert.	.95	.80
L70	A15	60c Midwinter shadows	1.25	1.00
L71	A15	75c Coastline	1.60	1.40
L72	A15	85c Landing field	1.90	1.60
L73	A15	90c Pancake ice, vert.	1.90	1.60
L74	A15	$1 Emperor penguins, Auster Rookery	2.25	1.75
		Nos. L60-L74 (15)	13.95	11.80

Issued: 5, 25, 30, 75, 85c, 7/18/84; 15, 33, 45, 90c, $1, 8/7/85; 2, 10, 20, 36, 60c, 3/11/87.

Antarctic Treaty, 25th Anniv. — A16

1986, Sept. 17 Litho. *Perf. 14x13½*

L75 A16 36c multicolored	1.10	.85

Environment, Conservation and Technology A17

No. L76: a, Hour-glass dolphins and the *Nella Dan.* b, Emperor penguins and Davis Station. c, Crabeater seal and helicopters. d, Adelie penguins and snow-ice transport vehicle. e, Gray-headed albatross and photographer.

1988, July 20 Litho. *Perf. 13*

L76 Strip of 5	8.00	8.00
a.-e. A17 37c any single	1.40	1.40

Paintings by Sir Sidney Nolan (b. 1917) — A18

1989, June 14 Litho. *Perf. 14x13½*

L77 A18 39c *Antarctica*	.90	.90
L78 A18 39c *Iceberg Alley*	.90	.90
L79 A18 60c *Glacial Flow*	2.00	2.00
L80 A18 80c *Frozen Sea*	2.25	2.25
Nos. L77-L80 (4)	6.05	6.05

Aurora Australis A19

Design: $1.20, Research ship Aurora Australis.

1991, June 20 Litho. *Perf. 14½*

L81 A19 43c multicolored	.95	.95
L82 A19 $1.20 multicolored	2.50	2.50

Antarctic Treaty, 30th anniv. (No. L81).

Regional Wildlife A20

Perf. 14x14½, 14½x14

1992-93 Litho.

L83 A20 45c Adelie penguin	.95	.85
L84 A20 75c Elephant seal	1.60	1.40
L85 A20 85c Northern giant petrel	1.90	1.75
L86 A20 95c Weddell seal	2.00	1.90
L86A A20 $1 Royal penguins	2.25	2.00
L87 A20 $1.20 Emperor penguin, vert.	2.40	2.25
L88 A20 $1.40 Fur seals	3.00	2.50
L89 A20 $1.50 King penguins, vert.	3.25	2.75
Nos. L83-L89 (8)	17.35	15.40

Issued: $1, $1.40, $1.50, 1/14/93; others, 5/14/92.

The Last Huskies A21

1994, Jan. 13 Litho. *Perf. 14½*

L90 A21 45c Dog up close, vert.	1.40	1.40
L91 A21 75c Sled team	2.00	2.00
L92 A21 85c Dog seated, vert.	2.25	2.25
L93 A21 $1.05 Three dogs	2.50	2.50
Nos. L90-L93 (4)	8.15	8.15

Whales & Dolphins A22

1995, June 15 Litho. *Perf. 14½*

L94 A22 45c Humpback whale	.95	.85
L95 A22 45c Hourglass dolphin, vert.	.95	.85
L96 A22 45c Minke whale, vert.	.95	.85
a. Pair, #L95-L96	2.25	2.25
L97 A22 $1 Killer whale	2.50	2.50
a. Souvenir sheet of 4, #L94-L97	7.75	7.75
b. As "a," overprinted	*65.00*	*65.00*
c. As "a," overprinted	*40.00*	*40.00*
Nos. L94-L97 (4)	5.35	5.05

No. L97b is overprinted in gold in sheet margin with Singapore '95 emblem and: "Australia Post Exhibition Sheet No. 2," and, in both Chinese and English, with "Singapore 95 World Stamp Exhibition."

No. L97c is overprinted in gold in sheet margin with exhibition emblem, "Australian Post Exhibition Sheet No. 3" and CAPEX '96 WORLD PHILATELIC EXHIBITION / EXPOSITION PHILATELIQUE MONDIALE"

Issued: No. L97b, 9/1/95; No. L97c, 6/15/96.

Landscapes, by Christian Clare Robertson — A23

Designs: No. L98, Rafting sea ice. No. L99, Shadow on the Plateau. $1, Ice cave. $1.20, Twelve Lake.

1996, May 16 Litho. *Perf. 14½x14*

L98 A23 45c multicolored	1.25	.95
L99 A23 45c multicolored	1.25	.95
a. Pair, Nos. L98-L99	2.50	2.25
L100 A23 $1 multicolored	3.00	2.50
L101 A23 $1.20 multicolored	4.25	3.75
Nos. L98-L101 (4)	9.75	8.15

Australian Natl. Antarctic Research Expeditions, 50th Anniv. A24

Designs: No. L102, Apple field huts. No. L103, Inside an apple hut. 95c, Summer surveying. $1.05, Sea ice research. $1.20, Remote field camp.

1997, May 15 Litho. *Perf. 14x14½*

L102 A24 45c multicolored	1.10	.90
L103 A24 45c multicolored	1.10	.90
a. Pair, #L102-L103	2.25	2.25
L104 A24 95c multicolored	2.50	2.25
L105 A24 $1.05 multicolored	2.75	2.40
L106 A24 $1.20 multicolored	2.75	2.50
Nos. L102-L106 (5)	10.20	8.95

Modes of Transportion A25

Designs: No. L107, Snowmobile. No. L108, Ship, "Aurora Australis." $1, Helicopter airlifting a four-wheel drive ATV, vert. $2, Antarctic Hagglunds (rubber-tracked vehicles with fiberglass cabins), vert.

Perf. 14x14½, 14½x14

1998, Mar. 5 Litho.

L107 A25 45c multicolored	2.25	1.90
L108 A25 45c multicolored	2.25	1.90
a. Pair, #L107-L108	4.50	4.50
L109 A25 $1 multicolored	5.00	3.50
L110 A25 $2 multicolored	6.25	5.50
Nos. L107-L110 (4)	15.75	12.80

Preservation of Huts used During Mawson's Antarctic Expedition A26

Designs: No. L111, Photograph of Mawson, sailing ship Aurora. No. L112, Photograph, "Home of the Blizzard," by Frank Hurley. 90c, Photograph, "Huskie Team," by Xavier Mertz. $1.35, Huts restoration.

1999, May 13 Litho. *Perf. 14x14½*

L111 A26 45c multicolored	1.75	1.75
L112 A26 45c multicolored	1.75	1.75
a. Pair, #L111-L112	4.00	4.00
L113 A26 90c multicolored	3.75	3.25
L114 A26 $1.35 multicolored	4.25	3.75
Nos. L111-L114 (4)	11.50	10.50

Penguins A27

2000, July 24 Litho. *Perf. 13¾x14½*

L115 A27 45c Emperor penguins	3.50	3.25
L116 A27 45c Adélie penguins	3.50	3.25
a. Pair, #L115-L116	7.00	7.00

Australians in the Antarctic, Cent. — A28

No. L117: a, Penguins and icicles. b, Louis Bernacchi, physicist. c, Nimrod. d, Scientists at South Magnetic Pole. e, Griffith Taylor and Frank Debenham, geologists. f, First radio used in Antarctica. g, First flight over Antarctica. h, Sir Douglas Mawson, explorer. i, BANZARE (British, Australian and New Zealand Antarctic Research Expedition). j, Australia's claim to territory. k, Establishment of ANARE (Australian National Antarctic Research Expeditions). l, Transport. m, Aurora Australis. n, Climate research. o, Cold-weather clothing. p, Nella Dan. q, First women on Antarctica. r, Communications. s, Tourism. t, Satellite view of Antarctica.

2001, May 17 Litho. *Perf. 14¾x14*

L117 Sheet of 20	28.50	28.50
a.-e. A28 5c Any single	1.00	1.00
f.-j. A28 10c Any single	1.10	1.10
k.-o. A28 25c Any single	1.25	1.25
p.-t. A28 45c Any single	1.40	1.40

Worldwide Fund for Nature (WWF) — A29

No. L118: a, Leopard seal and pup on ice. b, Leopard seal and penguin on ice. c, Penguins, two leopard seals in water. d, Penguins, leopard seal in water.

2001, Sept. 11 Litho. *Perf. 14x14½*

L118 A29 Block of 4	9.00	8.00
a.-d. 45c Any single	2.00	1.40

Antarctic Base Stations — A30

Maps showing station locations and : a, Light Detection and Ranging Instrument, aurora australis, Davis Station. b, Diatom, Casey Station. c, Wandering albatross, Macquarie Island Station. d, Adèlie penguin, Mawson Station.

2002, July 2 Litho. *Perf. 14x14¾*

L119 A30 Block of 4, #a-d	8.00	8.00
a.-d. 45c Any single	1.75	1.75

Ships — A31

Designs: No. L120, Kista Dan, No. L121, Magga Dan. $1, Thala Dan, vert. $1.45, Nella Dan, vert.

Perf. 14x14½, 14½x14

2003, Apr. 29 Litho.

L120 A31 50c multi	1.75	1.75
L121 A31 50c multi	1.75	1.75
a. Horiz. pair, #L120-L121	3.75	3.75
L122 A31 $1 multi	3.75	3.75
L123 A31 $1.45 multi	5.50	5.50
Nos. L120-L123 (4)	12.75	12.75

Mawson Station, 50th Anniv. — A32

Designs: No. L124, Naming ceremony, 1954. No. L125, Station buildings. $1, Barge and airplane. $1.45, Auster Emperor Penguin Rookery.

2004, Feb. 13 Litho. *Perf. 14x14½*

L124 A32 50c multi	1.40	1.40
L125 A32 50c multi	1.40	1.40
a. Horiz. pair, #L124-L125	3.50	3.50
L126 A32 $1 multi	2.75	2.75
L127 A32 $1.45 multi	4.50	4.50
Nos. L124-L127 (4)	10.05	10.05

Aircraft A33

Designs: No. L128, Hughes 500 helicopter. No. L129, De Havilland DHC-2 Beaver. $1, Pilatus PC-6 Porter. $1.45, Douglas DC-3/Dakota C-47.

2005, Sept. 6 Litho. *Perf. 14x14½*

L128 A33 50c multi	1.40	1.40
L129 A33 50c multi	1.40	1.40
a. Horiz. pair, #L128-L129	3.50	3.50
L130 A33 $1 multi	2.75	2.75
L131 A33 $1.45 multi	4.50	4.50
Nos. L128-L131 (4)	10.05	10.05

AUSTRALIAN ANTARCTIC TERRITORY 50c
MACKEREL ICEFISH

Fish — A34

Designs: No. L132, Mackerel icefish. No. L133, Lanternfish. No. L134, Eaton's skate. No. L135, Patagonian toothfish.

2006, Aug. 1 Litho. *Perf. 14x14¾*

L132	A34 50c multi		1.50	1.50
L133	A34 50c multi		1.50	1.50
a.	Horiz. pair, #L132-L133		3.50	3.50
L134	A34 $1 multi		3.00	3.00
L135	A34 $1 multi		3.00	3.00
a.	Horiz. pair, #L134-L135		7.00	7.00
	Nos. L132-L135 (4)		9.00	9.00

Worldwide Fund For Nature (WWF) — A35

Royal penguins: No. L136, Four marching. No. L137, Nesting. No. L138, Two contesting territory (denomination at bottom), horiz. No. L139, Two courting (denomination at left), horiz.

2007, Aug. 7 Litho. *Perf. 14½x14*

L136	A35 50c multi	1.40	1.00
L137	A35 50c multi	1.40	1.00
a.	Horiz. pair, #L136-L137	2.75	2.00

Perf. 14x14½

L138	A35 $1 multi	2.75	2.40
L139	A35 $1 multi	2.75	2.40
a.	Vert. pair, #L138-L139	5.75	4.75
	Nos. L136-L139 (4)	8.30	6.80

International Polar Year — A36

Designs: No. L140, Astronomy. No. L141, Glaciology. No. L142, Marine biology. No. L143, Oceanography.

2008, Sept. 16 Litho. *Perf. 14x14½*

L140	A36 55c multi	.95	.70
L141	A36 55c multi	.95	.70
a.	Vert. pair, #L140-L141	2.00	1.40
L142	A36 $1.10 multi	2.00	1.60
L143	A36 $1.10 multi	2.00	1.60
a.	Vert. pair, #L142-L143	4.00	3.25
b.	Souvenir sheet, #L140-L143	6.00	4.50
	Nos. L140-L143 (4)	5.90	4.60

Discovery of South Magnetic Pole, Cent. — A37

Designs: No. L144, Crew unloading the Nimrod. No. L145, Crew depositing expedition provisions by automobile. No. L146, Men at Northern Party camp. No. L147, Alistair Mackay, Douglas Mawson,and Edgeworth David with flag at South Magnetic Pole.

2009, Jan. 8 Litho. *Perf. 14½x14*

L144	A37 55c lt bl & blk	.90	.65
L145	A37 55c lt bl & multi	.90	.65
a.	Horiz. pair, #L144-L145	1.90	1.25
L146	A37 $1.10 lt bl & blk	1.90	1.25
L147	A37 $1.10 lt bl & blk	1.90	1.25
a.	Horiz. pair, #L146-L147	3.75	2.50
b.	Souvenir sheet, #L144-L147	5.75	4.00
	Nos. L144-L147 (4)	5.60	3.80

International Polar Year — A38

Designs: 55c, Snow petrel. $2.05, Jade iceberg.

2009, Mar. 4 Litho. *Perf. 14x14¾*

L148	A38 55c multi	.80	.65
L149	A38 $2.05 multi	3.25	1.60
a.	Souvenir sheet, #L148-L149	4.00	2.25
b.	Sheet of 2, Australia #3337, Australian Antarctic Terr. #L149	5.00	5.00

Issued: No. L149b, 8/20/10. Stampex 2010, Adelaide (No. L149b).

Macquarie Island — A39

Designs: No. L150, Pleurophyllum hookeri (flower). No. L151, Southern elephant seal. No. L152, Mawson Point Stacks (green terrain). No. L153, Caroline Cove (brown terrain).

2010, Oct. 26 Litho. *Perf. 14¼*

L150	A39 60c multi	1.25	.95
L151	A39 60c multi	1.25	.95
a.	Horiz. pair, #L150-L151	2.50	1.90
L152	A39 $1.20 multi	2.50	1.90
L153	A39 $1.20 multi	2.50	1.90
a.	Horiz. pair, #L152-L153	5.00	3.80
b.	Souvenir sheet, #L150-L153	7.50	7.50
	Nos. L150-L153 (4)	7.50	5.70

A40

A41

A42

Icebergs A43

2011, June 7 Litho. *Perf. 14x14¾*

L154	Block of 4	5.00	5.00
a.	A40 60c multi	1.25	1.25
b.	A41 60c multi	1.25	1.25
c.	A42 60c multi	1.25	1.25
d.	A43 60c multi	1.25	1.25
e.	Souvenir sheet of 4, #L154a-L154d	5.00	5.00

Booklet Stamps Self-Adhesive Stamps With Grayed Frame

Serpentine Die Cut 11¼ Syncopated

L155	A40 60c multi	1.25	.25
L156	A41 60c multi	1.25	.25
L157	A42 60c multi	1.25	.25
L158	A43 60c multi	1.25	.25
a.	Booklet pane of 10, 3 each #L155-L156, 2 each #L157-L158	12.50	
	Nos. L155-L158 (4)	5.00	1.00

Australasian Antarctic Expedition, Cent. — A44

No. L159: a, Map and mast of SY Aurora. b, John King Davis (1884-1967), captain of the SY Aurora. c, SY Aurora and postmark. d, Expedition members landing at Macquarie Island. e, Birds on Macquarie Island.

2011, Aug. 2 *Perf. 14¾x14*

L159	Horiz. strip of 5	6.25	4.75
a.-e.	A44 60c Any single	1.25	.95
f.	Souvenir sheet of 5, #L159a-L159e	6.25	4.75

Dr. Philip Law (1912-2010), Polar Explorer — A45

Designs: 60c, Law. $1.20, Map of Antarctica, Law and helicopter at Arthurson Bluff. $1.80, Map of Antarctica, opening of Mawson Station.

2012, Mar. 6 Litho. *Perf. 14¾x14*

L160	A45 60c multi	1.25	.95
L161	A45 $1.20 multi	2.50	1.90
L162	A45 $1.80 multi	3.75	1.90
a.	Souvenir sheet of 3, #L160-L162	7.50	5.75
	Nos. L160-L162 (3)	7.50	4.75

Australasian Antarctic Expedition, Cent. — A46

Designs: No. L163, Main hut. No. L164, Xavier Mertz and dogs. No. L165, Belgrave Ninnis and dogs. No. L166, Bow of SY Aurora, map of Cape Denison, penguins. No. L167, Stern of SY Aurora, expedition members carrying supplies from ship.

2012, Sept. 4

L163	A46 60c multi	1.25	.95
L164	A46 60c multi	1.25	.95
L165	A46 60c multi	1.25	.95
a.	Horiz. strip of 3, #L163-L165	3.75	3.00
L166	A46 $1.20 multi	2.50	2.00
L167	A46 $1.20 multi	2.50	2.00
a.	Horiz. pair, #L166-L167	5.00	4.00
b.	Souvenir sheet of 5, #L163-L167	8.75	7.00
	Nos. L163-L167 (5)	8.75	6.85

Mountains A47

Designs: No. L168, Mt. Parsons. No. L169, Mawson Escarpment. $1.20, South Masson Range. $1.80, David Range.

2013, Mar. 12 Litho. *Perf. 14x14¾*

L168	A47 60c multi	1.25	.95
L169	A47 60c multi	1.25	.95
a.	Horiz. pair, #L168-L169	2.50	1.90
L170	A47 $1.20 multi	2.50	1.90
L171	A47 $1.80 multi	3.75	3.00
a.	Souvenir sheet of 4, #L168-L171	8.75	8.75
	Nos. L168-L171 (4)	8.75	6.80

Australasian Antarctic Expedition, Cent. — A48

Designs: No. L172, Men walking in blizzard. No. L173, Man checking wind recorder. No. L174, Weddell seal, Cape petrels. No. L175, Wireless operator Walter Hannam. No. L176, Frank Wild, leader of Western Party of Expedition.

2013, Sept. 10 *Perf. 14¾x14*

L172	A48 60c multi	1.10	.85
L173	A48 60c multi	1.10	.85
L174	A48 60c multi	1.10	.85
a.	Horiz. strip of 3, #L172-L174	3.30	2.60
L175	A48 $1.20 multi	2.25	1.75
L176	A48 $1.20 multi	2.25	1.75
a.	Horiz. pair, #L175-L176	4.50	3.50
b.	Souvenir sheet of 5, #L172-L176	8.00	8.00
	Nos. L172-L176 (5)	7.80	6.05

AUSTRIA

'os-trē-ə

LOCATION — Central Europe
GOVT. — Republic
AREA — 32,378 sq. mi.
POP. — 8,139,299 (1999 est.)
CAPITAL — Vienna

Before 1867 Austria was an absolute monarchy, which included Hungary and Lombardy-Venetia. In 1867 the Austro-Hungarian Monarchy was established, with Austria and Hungary as equal partners. After World War I, in 1918, the different nationalities established their own states and only the German-speaking parts remained, forming a republic under the name "Deutschosterreich" (German Austria), which name was shortly again changed to "Austria." In 1938 German forces occupied Austria, which became part of the German Reich. After the liberation by Allied troops in 1945, an independent republic was re-established.

60 Kreuzer = 1 Gulden
100 Neu-Kreuzer = 1 Gulden (1858)
100 Heller = 1 Krone (1899)
100 Groschen = 1 Schilling (1925)
100 Cents = 1 Euro (2002)

Catalogue values for unused stamps in this country are for Never Hinged items, beginning with Scott 432 in the regular postage section, Scott B165 in the semi-postal section, Scott C47 in the airpost section, Scott J175 in the postage due section, and Scott 4N1 in the AMG section.

Unused stamps without gum sell for about one-third or less of the values quoted.

Watermarks

Wmk. 91 — "BRIEF-MARKEN" In Double-lined Capitals Across the Middle of the Sheet

Wmk. 140 — Crown

Issues of the Austrian Monarchy (including Hungary)

Coat of Arms — A1

NINE KREUZER

Type I. One heavy line around coat of arms center. On the 9kr the top of "9" is about on a level with "Kreuzer" and not near the top of the label. Each cliche has the "9" in a different position.

Type IA. As type I, but with 1 ¼mm between "9" and "K."

Type II. One heavy line around coat of arms center. On the 9kr the top of "9" is much higher than the top of the word "Kreuzer" and nearly touches the top of the label.

Type III. As type II, but with two, thinner, lines around the center.

Wmk. K.K.H.M. in Sheet or Unwmk.
1850 Typo. *Imperf.*

The stamps of this issue were at first printed on a rough hand-made paper, varying in thickness and having a watermark in script letters K.K.H.M., the initials of Kaiserlich Königliches Handels-Ministerium (Imperial and Royal Ministry of Commerce), vertically in the gutter between the panes. Parts of these letters show on margin stamps in the sheet. From 1854 a thick, smooth machine-made paper without watermark was used.

Thin to Thick Paper

1	A1 1kr yellow	1,650.	115.00
a.	Printed on both sides	*2,000.*	150.00
b.	1kr orange	2,350.	150.00
c.	1kr brown orange	3,475.	625.00
2	A1 2kr black	1,375.	82.50
a.	Ribbed paper	—	4,550.
b.	2kr gray black	2,350.	120.00
d.	Half used as 1kr on cover		*52,500.*
3	A1 3kr red	825.00	4.00
a.	Ribbed paper	*4,000.*	160.00
b.	Laid paper	—	*19,000.*
c.	Printed on both sides		*10,000.*
4	A1 6kr brown	1,000.	6.00
a.	Ribbed paper		*2,450.*
c.	Diagonal half used as 3kr on cover		*20,000.*
5	A1 9kr blue, type II	2,350.	9.00
a.	9kr blue, type I	*2,250.*	19.00
b.	9kr blue, type IA	*15,000.*	*1,250.*
c.	Laid paper, type III		*15,000.*
d.	Printed on both sides, type II		*9,250.*

1854

Machine-made Paper, Type III

1d	A1 1kr yellow	1,450.	100.00
2c	A1 2kr black	1,750.	80.00
3e	A1 3kr red	475.00	4.25
f.	3kr red, type I	4,650.	52.50
4b	A1 6kr brown	975.00	8.25
5e	A1 9kr blue	1,025.	4.25

In 1852-54, Nos. 1-5, rouletted 14, were used in Tokay and Homonna. A 12kr blue exists, but was not issued. Value, $100,000.

The reprints are type III in brighter colors, some on paper watermarked "Briefmarken" in the sheet.

For similar design see Lombardy-Venetia A1.

A2

A3

Emperor Franz Josef — A4

A5

A6

Two Types of Each Value.

Type I. Loops of the bow at the back of the head broken, except the 2kr. In the 2kr, the "2" has a flat foot, thinning to the right. The frame line in the UR corner is thicker than the line below. In the 5kr the top frame line is unbroken.

Type II. Loops complete. Wreath projects further at top of head. In the 2kr, the "2" has a more curved foot of uniform thickness, with a shading line in the upper and lower curves. The frame line UR is thicker than the line below. In the 5kr the top frame line is broken.

1858-59 Embossed *Perf. 14½*

6	A2 2kr yellow, type II	1,225.	55.00
a.	2kr yellow, type I	3,000.	455.00
b.	2kr orange, type II	3,750.	450.00
c.	Half used as 1kr on cover		*41,500.*
7	A3 3kr black, type II	*3,150.*	240.00
a.	3kr black, type I	1,950.	300.00
8	A3 3kr green, type II ('59)	1,650.	180.00
9	A4 5kr red, type II	460.00	1.90
a.	5kr red, type I	1,850.	25.00
b.	5kr red, type II with type I frame	1,150.	37.50
10	A5 10kr brown, type II	1,050.	3.25
a.	10kr brown, type I	2,600.	50.00
b.	Half used as 5kr on cover		*18,500.*
11	A6 15kr blue, type II	1,075.	2.50
a.	Type I	2,275.	22.50
b.	Half used as 7kr on cover		—

The reprints are of type II and are perforated 10½, 11, 12, 12½ and 13. There are also imperforate reprints of Nos. 6 to 8.

For similar designs see Lombardy-Venetia A2-A6.

Franz Josef — A7

Coat of Arms — A8

1860-61 Embossed *Perf. 14*

12	A7 2kr yellow	450.00	35.00
a.	Half used as 1kr on cover		*25,000.*
13	A7 3kr green	375.00	30.00
14	A7 5kr red	290.00	1.00
15	A7 10kr brown	325.00	3.00
a.	Half used as 5kr on cover		*9,000.*
16	A7 15kr blue	475.00	3.00

The reprints are perforated 9, 9½, 10, 10½, 11, 11½, 12, 12½, 13 and 13½.

There are also imperforate reprints of the 2 and 3kr.

For similar design see Lombardy-Venetia A7. For overprints see Poland Nos. J11-J12.

1863

17	A8 2kr yellow	675.00	110.00
a.	Half used as 1kr on cover		—
18	A8 3kr green	525.00	100.00
19	A8 5kr rose	625.00	15.00
20	A8 10kr blue	1,650.	18.50
21	A8 15kr yellow brown	1,650.	18.00

For similar design see Lombardy-Venetia A1.

Wmk. 91, or, before July 1864, Unwmkd.

1863-64 *Perf. 9½*

22	A8 2kr yellow ('64)	190.00	15.00
a.	Ribbed paper		550.00
b.	Half used as 1kr on cover		*27,500.*
23	A8 3kr green ('64)	190.00	15.00
24	A8 5kr rose	55.00	.75
a.	Ribbed paper		775.00
25	A8 10kr blue	250.00	3.50
a.	Half used as 5kr on cover		*22,500.*
26	A8 15kr yellow brown	225.00	2.25
	Nos. 22-26 (5)	910.00	36.50

The reprints are perforated 10½, 11½, 13 and 13½. There are also imperforate reprints of the 2 and 3kr.

Issues of Austro-Hungarian Monarchy

From 1867 to 1871 the independent postal administrations of Austria and Hungary used the same stamps.

A9

A10

5 kr:

Type I. In arabesques in lower left corner, the small ornament at left of the curve nearest the figure "5" is short and has three points at bottom.

Type II. The ornament is prolonged within the curve and has two points at bottom. The corresponding ornament at top of the lower left corner does not touch the curve (1872).

Type III. Similar to type II but the top ornament is joined to the curve (1881). Two different printing methods were used for the 1867-74 issues. The first produced stamps on which the hair and whiskers were coarse and thick, from the second they were fine and clear.

1867-72 Wmk. 91 Typo. *Perf. 9½*

Coarse Print

27	A9 2kr yellow	120.00	3.00
a.	Half used as 1kr on cover		—
28	A9 3kr green	140.00	2.90
29	A9 5kr rose, type II	87.50	.25
a.	5kr rose, type I	95.00	.25
b.	Perf. 10½, type II	190.00	
c.	Cliché of 3kr in plate of 5kr		*37,500.*
30	A9 10kr blue	290.00	2.40
a.	Half used as 5kr on cover		—
31	A9 15kr brown	290.00	6.50
32	A9 25kr lilac	87.50	21.00
b.	25kr brown violet	325.00	65.00

Perf. 12

33	A10 50kr light brown	40.00	*130.00*
a.	50kr pale red brown	500.00	210.00
b.	50kr brownish rose	500.00	325.00
c.	Pair, imperf. btwn., vert. or horizontal	*725.00*	*1,700.*

Issues for Austria only

1874-80 *Perf. 9½*

Fine Print

34	A9 2kr yellow ('76)	14.50	.90
35	A9 3kr green ('76)	65.00	.90
36	A9 5kr rose, type III	4.50	.25
37	A9 10kr blue ('75)	160.00	.60
38	A9 15kr brown ('77)	8.75	7.75
39	A9 25kr gray lil ('78)	1.10	*190.00*
40	A10 50kr red brown	14.50	*190.00*

Perf. 9

34a	A9 2kr	250.00	65.00
35a	A9 3kr	225.00	30.00
36a	A9 5kr	87.50	3.50
37a	A9 10kr	440.00	35.00
38a	A9 15kr	625.00	130.00

Perf. 10½

34b	A9 2kr	60.00	4.50
35b	A9 3kr	100.00	2.75
36b	A9 5kr	14.50	.90
37b	A9 10kr	225.00	2.75
38b	A9 15kr	250.00	27.50

Perf. 12

No.	Type	Description	Unused	Used
34c	A9	2kr	275.00	160.00
35c	A9	3kr	250.00	27.50
36c	A9	5kr	60.00	5.00
37c	A9	10kr	525.00	130.00
38c	A9	15kr	825.00	190.00
40b	A10	50kr brown ('80)	19.00	*190.00*
c.		Perf. 10½x12	325.00	—

Perf. 13

No.	Type	Description	Unused	Used
34d	A9	2kr	325.00	*360.00*
35d	A9	3kr	225.00	36.00
36d	A9	5kr	130.00	21.00
37d	A9	10kr	275.00	100.00
38d	A9	15kr	625.00	475.00
40a	A10	50kr	30.00	*250.00*

Perf. 9x10½

No.	Type	Description	Unused	Used
34e	A9	2kr	440.00	87.50
35e	A9	3kr	360.00	77.50
36e	A9	5kr	140.00	18.00
37e	A9	10kr	410.00	105.00

Various compound perforations exist.

Values are for stamps that do not show the watermark. Stamps showing the watermark often sell for more.

For similar designs see Offices in the Turkish Empire A1-A2.

A11

Perf. 9, 9½, 10, 10½, 11½, 12, 12½

1883 Inscriptions in Black

No.	Type	Description	Unused	Used
41	A11	2kr brown	6.00	.45
42	A11	3kr green	6.00	.35
43	A11	5kr rose	75.00	.30
a.		Vert. pair, imperf. btwn.	190.00	*425.00*
44	A11	10kr blue	4.50	.35
45	A11	20kr gray	55.00	4.25
46	A11	50kr red lilac, perf 9½	375.00	80.00

The last printings of Nos. 41-46 are watermarked "ZEITUNGS-MARKEN" instead of "BRIEF-MARKEN." Values are for stamps that do not show watermark. Stamps with watermarks that are identifiable as being from "BRIEFMARKEN" sheets often sell for slightly more, while those with watermarks identifying stamps from "ZEITUNGS-MARKEN" sheets sell for significantly more. See the *Scott Classic Specialized Catalogue of Stamps and Covers* for detailed listings.

The 5kr has been reprinted in a dull red rose, perforated 10½.

For similar design see Offices in the Turkish Empire A3.

For surcharges see Offices in the Turkish Empire Nos. 15-19.

A12

A13

Perf. 9 to 13½, also Compound

1890-96 Unwmk. Granite Paper

Numerals in black, Nos. 51-61

No.	Type	Description	Unused	Used
51	A12	1kr dark gray	1.50	.30
a.		Pair, imperf. between	225.00	*540.00*
b.		Half used as ½kr on cover		*150.00*
52	A12	2kr light brown	.35	.30
53	A12	3kr gray green	.45	.30
a.		Pair, imperf. between	325.00	*650.00*
54	A12	5kr rose	.45	.30
a.		Pair, imperf. between	260.00	*450.00*
55	A12	10kr ultramarine	1.10	.30
a.		Pair, imperf. between	360.00	*650.00*
56	A12	12kr claret	2.60	.40
a.		Pair, imperf. between	—	800.00
57	A12	15kr lilac	2.60	.40
a.		Pair, imperf. between	475.00	*900.00*
58	A12	20kr olive green	37.50	2.40
59	A12	24kr gray blue	2.25	1.50
a.		Pair, imperf. between	475.00	*700.00*
60	A12	30kr dark brown	2.75	.80
61	A12	50kr violet, perf 10	6.00	*11.00*

Engr.

No.	Type	Description	Unused	Used
62	A13	1gld dark blue	3.00	3.00
63	A13	1gld pale lilac ('96)	45.00	4.50
64	A13	2gld carmine	3.25	*24.00*
65	A13	2gld gray green ('96)	15.00	*47.50*
		Nos. 51-65 (15)	123.80	97.00

Nearly all values of the 1890-1907 issues are found with numerals missing in one or more corners, some with numerals printed on the back.

For surcharges see Offices in the Turkish Empire Nos. 20-25, 28-31.

A14

Perf. 9 to 13½, also Compound

1891 Typo. Numerals in black

No.	Type	Description	Unused	Used
66	A14	20kr olive green	1.90	.30
67	A14	24kr gray blue	3.25	.95
68	A14	30kr brown	1.90	.30
a.		Pair, imperf. between	275.00	*700.00*
b.		Perf. 9	110.00	55.00
69	A14	50kr violet	1.90	.40
		Nos. 66-69 (4)	8.95	1.95

For surcharges see Offices in the Turkish Empire Nos. 26-27.

A15

A16

A17

A18

Perf. 10½ to 13½ and Compound

1899 Without Varnish Bars

Numerals in black, Nos. 70-82

No.	Type	Description	Unused	Used
70	A15	1h lilac	.75	.25
b.		Imperf.	60.00	*150.00*
c.		Perf. 10½	32.50	8.00
d.		Numerals inverted	*2,250.*	*3,400.*
71	A15	2h dark gray	2.75	.65
72	A15	3h bister brown	6.50	.25
b.		"3" in lower right corner sideways		*3,000.*
73	A15	5h blue green	7.25	.25
c.		Perf. 10½	22.50	4.75
74	A15	6h orange	.75	.25
75	A16	10h rose	16.00	.25
b.		Perf. 10½	875.00	210.00
76	A16	20h brown	5.25	.25
77	A16	25h ultramarine	60.00	.35
78	A16	30h red violet	19.00	2.75
b.		Horiz. pair, imperf. btwn.	600.00	—
80	A17	40h green	32.50	3.50
81	A17	50h gray blue	17.50	4.25
b.		All four "50's" parallel		*3,100.*
82	A17	60h brown	50.00	1.25
b.		Horiz. pair, imperf. btwn.	550.00	—
c.		Perf. 10½	105.00	5.40

Engr.

No.	Type	Description	Unused	Used
83	A18	1k carmine rose	6.00	.45
a.		1k carmine	6.00	.25
b.		Vert. pair, imperf. btwn.	250.00	*350.00*
84	A18	2k gray lilac	52.50	.45
a.		Vert. pair, imperf. btwn.	440.00	*725.00*
85	A18	4k gray green	10.50	18.00
		Nos. 70-85 (15)	287.25	33.15

For surcharges see Offices in Crete Nos. 1-7, Offices in the Turkish Empire Nos. 32-45.

1901 With Varnish Bars

No.	Type	Description	Unused	Used
70a	A15	1h lilac	1.60	.45
71a	A15	2h dark gray	6.50	.40
72a	A15	3h bister brown	.80	.25
73a	A15	5h blue green	.80	.25
74a	A15	6h orange	.80	.25
75a	A16	10h rose	.80	.25
76a	A16	20h brown	.80	.25
77a	A16	25h ultra	.80	.25
78a	A16	30h red violet	3.25	.80
79	A17	35h green	.80	.25
80a	A17	40h green	3.25	*4.75*
81a	A17	50h gray blue	4.75	*11.00*
82a	A17	60h brown	3.25	1.60
		Nos. 70a-78a,79,80a-82a (13)	28.20	20.75

The diagonal yellow bars of varnish were printed across the face to prevent cleaning.

A19

A20

A21

Perf. 12½ to 13½ and Compound

1905-07 Typo.

Without Varnish Bars

Colored Numerals

No.	Type	Description	Unused	Used
86	A19	1h lilac	.25	*.35*
87	A19	2h dark gray	.25	.25
88	A19	3h bister brown	.25	.25
89	A19	5h dk blue green	12.00	.25
90	A19	5h yellow grn ('06)	.25	.25
91	A19	6h deep orange	.25	.25
92	A20	10h carmine ('06)	.50	.25
93	A20	12h violet ('07)	1.20	.80
94	A20	20h brown ('06)	4.00	.25
95	A20	25h ultra ('06)	4.00	.40
96	A20	30h red violet ('06)	8.00	.40

Black Numerals

No.	Type	Description	Unused	Used
97	A20	10h carmine	16.00	.25
98	A20	20h brown	40.00	1.60
99	A20	25h ultra	40.00	2.40
100	A20	30h red violet	55.00	4.75

White Numerals

No.	Type	Description	Unused	Used
101	A21	35h green	2.00	.25
102	A21	40h deep violet	2.00	.80
103	A21	50h dull blue	2.00	*3.50*
104	A21	60h yellow brown	2.00	.80
105	A21	72h rose	2.00	1.75
		Nos. 86-105 (20)	191.95	19.80
		Set, never hinged	650.00	

For surcharges see Offices in Crete Nos. 8-14.

1904 *Perf. 13x13½*

With Varnish Bars

No.	Type	Description	Unused	Used
86a	A19	1h lilac	.35	*.95*
87a	A19	2h dark gray	1.40	.95
88a	A19	3h bister brown	2.00	.25
89a	A19	5h dk blue green	3.25	.25
91a	A19	6h deep orange	8.00	.30
97a	A20	10h carmine	1.75	.25
98a	A20	20h brown	29.00	1.20
99a	A20	25h ultra	29.00	.80
100a	A20	30h red violet	45.00	1.60
101a	A21	35h green	29.00	.55
102a	A21	40h deep violet	27.50	4.00
103a	A21	50h dull blue	29.00	9.50
104a	A21	60h yellow brown	40.00	1.60
105a	A21	72h rose	2.00	2.25
		Nos. 86a-105a (14)	247.25	24.45
		Set, never hinged	875.00	

Stamps of the 1901, 1904 and 1905 issues perf. 9 or 10½, also compound with 12½, were not sold at any post office, but were supplied only to some high-ranking officials. This applies also to the contemporaneous issues of Austrian Offices Abroad.

Karl VI — A22

Franz Josef — A23

Schönbrunn Palace — A24

Franz Josef — A25

Designs: 2h, Maria Theresa. 3h, Joseph II. 5h, 10h, 25h, Franz Josef. 6h, Leopold II. 12h, Franz I. 20h, Ferdinand I. 30h, Franz Josef as youth. 35h, Franz Josef in middle age. 60h, Franz Josef on horseback. 1k, Franz Josef in royal robes. 5k, Hofburg, Vienna.

1908-16 Typo. *Perf. 12½*

No.	Type	Description	Unused	Used
110a	A22	1h gray black	.25	.25
111a	A22	2h violet	.25	.25
112	A22	3h magenta	.25	.25
113	A22	5h yellow green	.25	.25
a.		Booklet pane of 6	*27.50*	
114a	A22	6h buff ('13)	.55	.80
115	A22	10h rose	.25	.25
a.		Booklet pane of 6	*82.50*	
116a	A22	12h scarlet	.80	1.20
117a	A22	20h chocolate	4.75	.45
118a	A22	25h deep blue	2.00	.45
119a	A22	30h olive green	9.50	.65
120	A22	35h slate	2.40	.25

Engr.

No.	Type	Description	Unused	Used
121	A23	50h dark green	.55	.25
a.		Vert. pair, imperf. btwn.	200.00	*400.00*
b.		Horiz. pair, imperf. btwn.	200.00	*400.00*
122	A23	60h deep carmine	.25	.25
a.		Vert. pair, imperf. btwn.	160.00	*400.00*
b.		Horiz. pair, imperf. btwn.	160.00	*400.00*
123	A23	72h dk brown	1.60	.40
124	A23	1k purple	12.00	.25
a.		Vert. pair, imperf. btwn.	200.00	*350.00*
b.		Horiz. pair, imperf. btwn.	200.00	*350.00*
125	A24	2k lake & olive grn	20.00	.40
126	A24	5k bister & dk vio	40.00	6.00
127	A25	10k blue, bis & dp brn	190.00	65.00
		Nos. 110a-127 (18)	283.20	91.70
		Set, never hinged	875.00	

Definitive set issued for the 60th year of the reign of Emperor Franz Josef.

The 1h-35h exist on both ordinary (1913) and chalk-surfaced (1908) paper. The cheaper varieties are listed above. For detailed listings, see the *Scott Classic Specialized Catalogue of Stamps and Covers.*

All values exist imperforate. They were not sold at any post office, but presented to a number of high government officials. This applies also to all imperforate stamps of later issues, including semi-postals, etc., and those of the Austrian Offices Abroad.

Litho. forgeries of No. 127 exist.

For overprint and surcharge see #J47-J48. For similar designs see Offices in Crete A5-A6, Offices in the Turkish Empire A16-A17.

Birthday Jubilee Issue

No. 144

Similar to 1908 Issue, but designs enlarged by labels at top and bottom bearing dates "1830" and "1910"

1910 Typo.

No.	Type	Description	Unused	Used
128	A22	1h gray black	4.00	*8.00*
129	A22	2h violet	4.75	*16.00*
130	A22	3h magenta	4.00	*12.00*
131	A22	5h yellow green	.25	.35
132	A22	6h buff	3.25	*12.00*
133	A22	10h rose	.25	.35
134	A22	12h scarlet	3.25	*12.00*
135	A22	20h chocolate	3.25	*12.00*
136	A22	25h deep blue	1.60	*2.40*
137	A22	30h olive green	3.25	*12.00*
138	A22	35h slate	3.25	*12.00*

Engr.

No.	Type	Description	Unused	Used
139	A23	50h dark green	5.50	*12.00*
140	A23	60h deep carmine	5.50	*12.00*
141	A23	1k purple	5.50	*16.00*
142	A24	2k lake & ol grn	140.00	*225.00*

143 A24 5k bister & dk vio 110.00 *225.00*
144 A25 10k blue, bis & dp brn 175.00 *325.00*
Nos. 128-144 (17) 472.60 *914.10*
Set, never hinged 1,050.

80th birthday of Emperor Franz Josef.
All values exist imperforate.
Litho. forgeries of Nos. 142-144 exist.

Austrian Crown — A37

Franz Josef — A38

A39

Coat of Arms — A40

1916-18 Typo.

145 A37 3h brt violet .25 .25
146 A37 5h lt green .25 .25
a. Booklet pane of 6 *15.50*
b. Booklet pane of 4 + 2 labels *30.00*
147 A37 6h deep orange .25 *.80*
148 A37 10h magenta .25 .25
a. Booklet pane of 6 *30.00*
149 A37 12h light blue .25 *.90*
150 A38 15h rose red .40 .25
a. Booklet pane of 6 *16.50*
151 A38 20h chocolate 4.00 .25
152 A38 25h blue 4.00 .80
153 A38 30h slate 6.50 .65
154 A39 40h olive green .25 .25
155 A39 50h blue green .25 .25
156 A39 60h deep blue .25 .25
157 A39 80h orange brown .25 .25
158 A39 90h red violet .25 .25
159 A39 1k car, *yel* ('18) .25 .25

Engr.

160 A40 2k dark blue 4.00 .40
161 A40 3k claret 24.00 1.20
162 A40 4k deep green 8.00 2.40
163 A40 10k deep violet 27.50 *52.50*
Nos. 145-163 (19) 81.15 62.40
Set, never hinged 240.00

Stamps of type A38 have two varieties of the frame. Stamps of type A40 have various decorations about the shield.

Nos. 145-163 exist imperf. Value set, $475 hinged, $875 never hinged.

1917 Ordinary Paper

164 A40 2k lt blue 2.00 .80
165 A40 3k car rose 47.50 .80
166 A40 4k yel grn 3.25 1.25
167 A40 10k violet 140.00 110.00
Nos. 164-167 (4) 192.75 112.85
Set, never hinged 475.00

Nos. 164-167 exist imperf. Value set, $325 unused, $650 never hinged.

See Nos. 172-175 (granite paper). For overprints and surcharges see Nos. 181-199, C1-C3, J60-J63, N1-N5, N10-N19, N33-N37, N42-N51. Western Ukraine 2, 7, 11-15, 19-28, 57-58, 85-89, 94-103, N3-N14, NJ13.

Emperor Karl I — A42

1917-18 Typo.

168 A42 15h dull red .40 .40
a. Booklet pane of 6 *16.50*
169 A42 20h dk green ('18) .40 .40
a. 20h green ('17) .80 .65
170 A42 25h blue .40 .40
171 A42 30h dull violet 2.00 .40
Nos. 168-171 (4) 3.20 1.60
Set, never hinged 13.50

Nos. 168-171 exist imperf. Value set, $160 unused, $400 never hinged.

For overprints and surcharges see Nos. N6-N9, N20, N38-N41, N52, N64. Western Ukraine 1, 8, 16-18, 90-93, N15-N18.

1918-19 Engr. Granite Paper

172 A40 2k lt blue 1.20 *.45*
a. Perf. 11½ 725.00 *1,200.*
Never hinged 1,600.
173 A40 3k car rose .40 *.80*
174 A40 4k yel grn ('19) 4.00 *20.00*
175 A40 10k lt vio ('19) 8.00 *32.50*
Nos. 172-175 (4) 13.60 *53.75*
Set, never hinged 40.00

Issues of the Republic

Austrian Stamps of 1916-18 Overprinted

1918-19 Unwmk. *Perf. 12½*

181 A37 3h bright violet .25 .25
182 A37 5h light green .25 .25
183 A37 6h deep orange .80 *3.25*
184 A37 10h magenta .25 .25
185 A37 12h light blue .40 *2.40*
186 A42 15h dull red .80 *2.00*
187 A42 20h deep green .40 .25
188 A42 25h blue .80 .25
189 A42 30h dull violet .80 .25
190 A39 40h olive green .80 .25
191 A39 50h deep green .80 *2.00*
192 A39 60h deep blue 1.20 *2.00*
193 A39 80h orange brown .40 .80
a. Inverted overprint 275.00 *325.00*
Never hinged 650.00
194 A39 90h red violet 1.20 .80
195 A39 1k carmine, *yel* 1.40 .80

Granite Paper

196 A40 2k lt blue .25 .25
a. Horiz. pair, imperf. between 240.00
Never hinged 400.00
b. Vert. pair, imperf. between 400.00
Never hinged 1,200.
c. Perf. 11½ 95.00 *110.00*
Never hinged 175.00
197 A40 3k car rose .35 *.80*
198 A40 4k yel grn 1.60 *3.25*
a. Perf. 11½ 16.00 35.00
Never hinged 32.50
199 A40 10k deep vio 9.50 *20.00*
Nos. 181-199 (19) 22.25 *40.10*
Set, never hinged 62.50

Nos. 181, 182, 184, 187-191, 194, 197 and 199 exist imperforate.

Post Horn — A43

Coat of Arms — A44

Allegory of New Republic — A45

1919-20 Typo. *Perf. 12½*
Ordinary Paper

200 A43 3h gray .25 .25
201 A44 5h yellow green .25 .25
202 A44 5h gray ('20) .25 .25
203 A43 6h orange .25 *.50*
204 A44 10h deep rose .25 .25
205 A44 10h red ('20) .25 .25
a. Thick grayish paper ('20) .25 .40
206 A43 12h grnsh blue .25 *4.00*
207 A43 15h bister ('20) .35 *.80*
a. Thick grayish paper ('20) .25 .40
208 A45 20h dark green .25 .25
a. 20h yellow green .25 .25
b. As "a," thick grysh paper ('20) 1.60 *4.00*
209 A44 25h blue .25 .25
210 A43 25h violet ('20) .25 .25
211 A45 30h dark brown .25 .25
212 A45 40h violet .25 .25
213 A45 40h lake ('20) .25 .25
214 A44 45h olive green .30 *.80*
215 A45 50h dark blue .25 .25
a. Thick grayish paper ('20) .40 *.95*
216 A43 60h olive green ('20) .25 .25
217 A44 1k carmine, *yel* .25 .25
218 A44 1k light blue ('20) .25 .25
Nos. 200-218 (19) 4.90 9.85
Set, never hinged 4.00

All values exist imperf. (For regularly issued imperfs, see Nos. 227-235.)

For overprints and surcharge see Nos. B11-B19, B30-B38, J102, N21, N27, N53, N58, N65, N71.

Parliament Building A46

1919-20 Engr. *Perf. 12½, 11½*
Granite Paper

219 A46 2k ver & blk .25 *.80*
a. Center inverted *2,750.*
Never hinged *6,500.*
b. Perf. 11½ 1.60 *3.25*
220 A46 2½k olive bis ('20) .30 *.25*
221 A46 3k blue & blk brn .25 .25
a. Perf. 11½ 5.75 *20.00*
222 A46 4k carmine & blk .25 .25
a. Center inverted *950.00* *3,250.*
Never hinged *2,400.*
b. Perf. 11½ 2.00 *6.50*
223 A46 5k black ('20) .25 .25
a. Perf. 11½x12½ 55.00 *87.50*
Never hinged 160.00
b. Perf. 11½ 2.75 *7.25*
224 A46 7½k plum .30 *.40*
a. Perf. 11½ 120.00 *240.00*
Never hinged 290.00
b. Perf. 11½x12½ 80.00 *240.00*
Never hinged 240.00
225 A46 10k olive grn & blk brn .30 *.40*
a. Perf. 11½x12½ 160.00 *300.00*
Never hinged 475.00
b. Perf. 11½ 13.50 *30.00*
Never hinged 32.50
226 A46 20k lilac & red ('20) .25 *.40*
a. Center inverted *60,000.* *40,000.*
b. Perf. 11½ 72.50 175.00
Never hinged 175.00
Nos. 219-226 (8) 2.15 *3.00*
Set, never hinged 6.75

Nos. 220-222, 225-226 exist imperforate between. Values, per pair: unused $200-$350; never hinged $400-$725.

See No. 248. For overprints and surcharge see Nos. B23-B29, B43-B49.

1920 Typo. *Imperf.*
Ordinary Paper

227 A44 5h yellow green .35 *.95*
228 A44 5h gray .25 .25
229 A44 10h deep rose .25 .25
230 A44 10h red .25 .25
231 A43 15h bister .25 .25
232 A43 25h violet .25 .25
233 A45 30h dark brown .25 .25
234 A45 40h violet .25 *.25*
235 A43 60h olive green .25 *.25*
Nos. 227-235 (9) 2.95
Set, never hinged 2.00

Arms
A47 A48

1920-21 Typo. *Perf. 12½*
White Paper

238 A47 80h rose .25 .25
239 A47 1k black brown .25 .25
241 A47 1½k green ('21) .30 .25
242 A47 2k blue .25 .30
243 A48 3k yel grn & dk grn ('21) .25 *.30*
244 A48 4k red & claret ('21) .25 .25

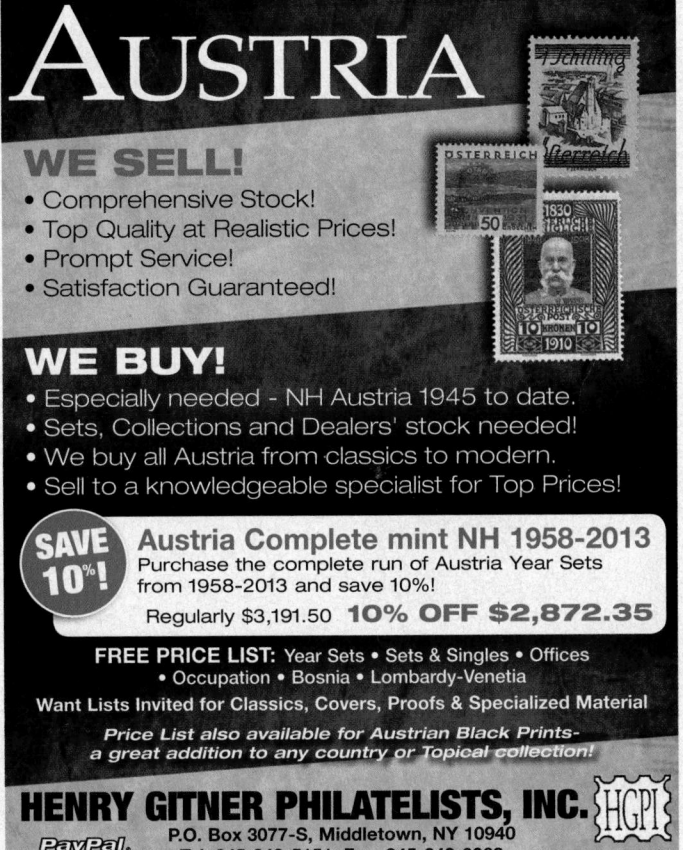

245 A48 5k vio & claret ('21) .25 .25
246 A48 7½k yellow & brown ('21) .25 *.30*
247 A48 10k ultra & blue ('21) .25 *.25*
Nos. 238-247 (9) 2.30 2.40
Set, never hinged 4.75

Nos. 238-245, 247 exist on white paper of good quality and on thick grayish paper of inferior quality; No. 246 exists only on white paper. Values are for the cheaper varieties. See the *Scott Classic Specialized Catalogue of Stamps and Covers* for detailed listings.

For overprints and surcharges see Nos. B20-B22, B39-B42.

1921 **Engr.**

248 A46 50k dk violet, *yel* .95 *1.60*
Never hinged 1.60
a. Perf. 11½ 14.50 *77.50*
Never hinged 23.00

Symbols of Agriculture A49

Symbols of Labor and Industry A50

1922-24 **Typo.** ***Perf. 12½***

250 A49 ½k olive bister .25 *.65*
251 A50 1k brown .25 .25
252 A50 2k cobalt blue .25 .25
253 A49 2½k orange brown .25 .25
254 A50 4k dull violet .25 *1.00*
255 A50 5k gray green .25 .25
256 A49 7½k gray violet .25 .25
257 A50 10k claret .25 .25
258 A49 12½k gray green .25 .25
259 A49 15k bluish green .25 .25
260 A49 20k dark blue .25 .25
261 A49 25k claret .25 .25
262 A50 30k pale gray .25 .25
263 A50 45k pale red .25 .25
264 A50 50k orange brown .25 .25
265 A50 60k yellow green .25 .25
266 A50 75k ultramarine .25 .25
267 A50 80k yellow .25 .25
268 A49 100k gray .25 .25
269 A49 120k brown .25 .25
270 A49 150k orange .25 .25
271 A49 160k light green .25 .25
272 A49 180k red .25 .25
273 A49 200k pink .25 .25
274 A49 240k dark violet .25 .25
275 A49 300k light blue .25 .25
276 A49 400k deep green 1.20 .80
a. 400k gray green .90 .40
277 A49 500k yellow .25 .25
278 A49 600k slate .25 .25
279 A49 700k brown ('24) 2.40 .25
280 A49 800k violet ('24) 1.60 *2.10*
281 A50 1000k violet ('23) 2.40 .25
282 A50 1200k car rose ('23) .80 .50
283 A50 1500k orange ('24) 2.00 .25
284 A50 1600k slate ('23) 3.25 *3.25*
285 A50 2000k dp bl ('23) 4.75 2.75
286 A50 3000k lt blue ('23) 12.00 2.40
287 A50 4000k dk bl, *bl* ('24) 6.00 2.75
Nos. 250-287 (38) 43.40 23.45
Set, never hinged 175.00

Nos. 250-287 exist imperf. Value set, $600 unused, $1,200 never hinged.

Symbols of Art and Science — A51

1922-24 **Engr.** ***Perf. 12½***

288 A51 20k dark brn .25 .25
a. Perf. 11½ 1.60 *1.60*
Never hinged 5.50
289 A51 25k blue .25 .25
a. Perf 11½ 1.25 *1.25*
Never hinged 4.00
290 A51 50k brown red .25 .25
a. Perf. 11½ 1.60 *1.60*
Never hinged 6.25
b. Vert. pair, imperf. btwn. 250.00 *350.00*
Never hinged 475.00
291 A51 100k deep grn .25 .25
a. Perf. 11½ 4.75 *4.75*
Never hinged 16.00
b. Vert. pair, imperf. btwn. — *475.00*
Never hinged —
292 A51 200k dark violet .25 .25
a. Perf. 11½ 5.50 *5.50*
Never hinged 20.00

b. Vert. pair, imperf. btwn. 250.00
Never hinged 475.00
293 A51 500k dp orange .25 *.25*
294 A51 1000k blk vio, *yel* .25 .25
a. Perf. 11½ 240.00 *240.00*
Never hinged 475.00
b. Vert. pair, imperf. btwn. 360.00
Never hinged 500.00
c. Horiz. pair, imperf. btwn. 360.00
Never hinged 500.00
295 A51 2000k olive grn, *yel* .25 .25
a. Vert. pair, imperf. btwn. 360.00
Never hinged 475.00
296 A51 3000k claret brn ('23) 10.00 .40
Never hinged 40.00
297 A51 5000k gray black ('23) 1.60 .80

Granite Paper

298 A51 10,000k red brown ('24) 4.50 *4.50*
Nos. 288-298 (11) 18.10 7.70
Set, never hinged 72.50

On Nos. 281-287, 291-298 "kronen" is abbreviated to "k" and transposed with the numerals.

Nos. 288-298 exist imperf. Value set, $410 hinged, $750 never hinged.

Numeral A52

Fields Crossed by Telegraph Wires A53

White-Shouldered Eagle — A54

Church of Minorite Friars — A55

1925-32 **Typo.** ***Perf. 12***

303 A52 1g dark gray .40 .25
304 A52 2g claret .40 .25
305 A52 3g scarlet .40 .25
306 A52 4g grnsh blue ('27) 1.20 .25
307 A52 5g brown orange 1.60 .25
308 A52 6g ultramarine 1.60 .25
309 A52 7g chocolate 1.60 .25
310 A52 8g yellow green 4.00 .25
311 A53 10g orange .80 .25
313 A53 15g red lilac .80 .25
314 A53 16g dark blue .80 .25
315 A53 18g olive green 1.20 *.80*
316 A54 20g dark violet 1.20 .25
317 A54 24g carmine 1.20 .40
318 A54 30g dark brown 1.20 .25
319 A54 40g ultramarine 1.20 .25
320 A54 45g yellow brown 1.60 .25
321 A54 50g gray 1.60 .30
322 A54 80g turquoise blue 3.50 *4.50*

Perf. 12½

Engr.

323 A55 1s deep green 20.00 1.60
a. 1s light green 375.00 24.00
Never hinged 1,750.
b. As "a," pair, imperf between 925.00
324 A55 2s brown rose 8.00 *10.50*
Nos. 303-324 (21) 54.30 *21.85*
Set, never hinged 225.00

Nos. 303-324 exist imperf. Value, set unused $475; never hinged $2,000.

For type A52 surcharged see No. B118.

Güssing — A56

National Library, Vienna — A57

15g, Hochosterwitz. 16g, 20g, Durnstein. 18g, Traunsee. 24g, Salzburg. 30g, Seewiesen. 40g, Innsbruck. 50g, Worthersee. 60g, Hohenems. 2s, St. Stephen's Cathedral, Vienna.

1929-30 **Typo.** ***Perf. 12½***

Size: 25½x21½mm

326 A56 10g brown orange .65 .25
327 A56 10g bister ('30) .65 .25
328 A56 15g violet brown .65 *1.40*
329 A56 16g dark gray .25 .25
330 A56 18g blue green .40 .50
331 A56 20g dark gray ('30) .80 .25
332 A56 24g maroon 6.50 *8.00*
333 A56 24g lake ('30) 6.50 .50
334 A56 30g dark violet 6.50 .25
335 A56 40g dark blue 8.00 .25
336 A56 50g gray violet ('30) 27.50 .25
337 A56 60g olive green 17.50 .25

Engr.

Size: 21x26mm

338 A57 1s black brown 8.00 .25
a. Horiz. pair, imperf. btwn. 260.00
Never hinged 450.00
b. Vert. pair, imperf. btwn. 260.00
Never hinged 450.00
339 A57 2s dark green 16.00 12.00
a. Horiz. pair, imperf. btwn. 325.00
Never hinged 575.00
Nos. 326-339 (14) 99.90 24.65
Set, never hinged 675.00

Nos. 326, 328-330 and 332-339 exist imperf. Values, set of 12 unused hinged $1,450, never hinged $2,000.

Type of 1929-30 Issue

Designs: 12g, Traunsee. 64g, Hohenems.

1932 ***Perf. 12***

Size: 21x16½mm

340 A56 10g olive brown .80 .25
341 A56 12g blue green 1.60 .25
342 A56 18g blue green 1.60 *3.25*
343 A56 20g dark gray .80 .25
344 A56 24g carmine rose 8.00 .25
345 A56 24g dull violet 4.75 .25
346 A56 30g dark violet 20.00 .25
347 A56 30g carmine rose 8.00 .25
a. Vert. pair, imperf. btwn. 45.00
Never hinged, #347a 60.00
348 A56 40g dark blue 24.00 1.60
349 A56 40g dark violet 8.00 .40
350 A56 50g gray violet 24.00 .40
351 A56 50g dull blue 8.00 .40
352 A56 60g gray green 65.00 4.00
353 A56 64g gray green 24.00 .40
Nos. 340-353 (14) 198.55 12.20
Set, never hinged 750.00

For overprints and surcharges see Nos. B87-B92, B119-B121.

Nos. 340-353 exist imperf. Values, set unused hinged, $575, never hinged $1,200.

Used values for Nos. 354-389 are for stamps with philatelic favor cancels. Values for postally used examples are 50%-100% more.

Burgenland A67

Tyrol A68

Costumes of various districts: 3g, Burgenland. 4g, 5g, Carinthia. 6g, 8g, Lower Austria. 12g, 20g, Upper Austria. 24g, 25g, Salzburg. 30g, 35g, Styria. 45g, Tyrol. 60g, Vorarlberg bridal couple. 64g, Vorarlberg. 1s, Viennese family. 2s, Military.

1934-35 **Typo.** ***Perf. 12***

354 A67 1g dark violet .25 .25
355 A67 3g scarlet .25 .25
356 A67 4g olive green .25 .25
357 A67 5g red violet .25 .25
358 A67 6g ultramarine .25 .25
359 A67 8g green .25 .25
360 A67 12g dark brown .25 .25
361 A67 20g yellow brown .25 .25
362 A67 24g grnsh blue .25 .25
363 A67 25g violet .25 .25
364 A67 30g maroon .25 .25
365 A67 35g rose carmine .35 *.35*

Perf. 12½

366 A68 40g slate gray .30 .25
367 A68 45g brown red .30 .25
368 A68 60g ultramarine .55 .40
369 A68 64g brown .80 .25
370 A68 1s deep violet 1.20 .65
371 A68 2s dull green 45.00 *45.00*

Designs Redrawn

Perf. 12 (6g), 12½ (2s)

372 A67 6g ultra ('35) .25 .25
373 A68 2s emerald ('35) 3.50 *3.50*
Nos. 354-373 (20) 55.00 53.65
Set, never hinged 200.00

The design of No. 358 looks as though the man's ears were on backwards, while No. 372 appears correctly.

On No. 373 there are seven feathers on each side of the eagle instead of five.

Nos. 354-373 exist imperf. Values, set unused hinged $410, never hinged $700.

For surcharges see Nos. B128-B131.

Dollfuss Mourning Issue

Engelbert Dollfuss — A85

1934-35 **Engr.** ***Perf. 12½***

374 A85 24g greenish black .35 *.35*
Never hinged 1.60
375 A85 24g indigo ('35) .80 *.80*
Never hinged 3.25

Nos. 374-375 exist imperf. Value, each unused hinged $200, never hinged $400.

"Mother and Child," by Joseph Danhauser A86

1935, May 1

376 A86 24g dark blue .80 .35
Never hinged 2.00
a. Vert. pair, imperf. btwn. 300.00
Never hinged 425.00
b. Horiz. pair, imperf. btwn. 275.00
Never hinged 400.00

Mother's Day. No. 376 exists imperf. Value, unused hinged $200, never hinged $475.

"Madonna and Child," after Painting by Dürer — A87

1936, May 5 **Photo.**

377 A87 24g violet blue .65 *.55*
Never hinged 1.75

Mother's Day. No. 377 exists imperf. Value, unused hinged $250, never hinged $400.

Farm Workers — A88

Design: 5s, Construction workers.

1936, June **Engr.** ***Perf. 12½***

378 A88 3s red orange 13.50 13.50
Never hinged 32.50
379 A88 5s brown black 32.50 *32.50*
Never hinged 52.50

Nos. 378-379 exist imperf. Values, set unused hinged $350, never hinged $800.

Engelbert Dollfuss — A90

1936, July 25

380 A90 10s dark blue 725.00 *725.00*
Never hinged 1,100.

Second anniv. of death of Engelbert Dollfuss, chancellor. Exists imperf. Value, $1,900, never hinged $3,250.

Mother and Child — A91

1937, May 5 Photo. *Perf. 12*

381 A91 24g henna brown .65 *.80*
Never hinged 1.60

Mother's Day. Exists imperf. Values, unused hinged $200, never hinged $325.

S.S. Maria Anna A92

Steamships: 24g, Uranus, 64g, Oesterreich.

1937, June 9

382 A92 12g red brown 1.10 .55
383 A92 24g deep blue 1.10 .55
384 A92 64g dark green 1.10 *.55*
Nos. 382-384 (3) 3.30 *1.65*
Set, never hinged 14.50

Centenary of steamship service on Danube River. Exist imperf. Value, set never hinged $3,500.

First Locomotive, "Austria" A95

Designs: 25g, Modern steam locomotive. 35g, Modern electric train.

1937, Nov. 22

385 A95 12g black brown .25 .25
386 A95 25g dark violet .65 *.65*
387 A95 35g brown red 2.00 *2.00*
Nos. 385-387 (3) 2.90 *2.90*
Set, never hinged 15.00

Centenary of Austrian railways. Exist imperf. Value, set never hinged $325.

Rose and Zodiac Signs — A98

1937 Engr. *Perf. 13x12½*

388 A98 12g dark green .25 *.25*
389 A98 24g dark carmine .25 .25
Set, never hinged 1.60

Nos. 388-389 exist imperf. Value, set never hinged $275.

Used values for Nos. 390-454 are for stamps with philatelic favor cancels. Postally used examples sell for substantially more.

German stamps were in use in Austria until mid-1945, when they were replaced by issues of the Russian (May) and American-British-French (June) occupation authorities.

For Use in Vienna, Lower Austria and Burgenland

Germany Nos. 509-511 and 511B Overprinted in Black

a

b

1945 Unwmk. *Perf. 14*

390 A115(a) 5pf dp yellow green .25 *.85*
391 A115(b) 6pf purple .25 *.85*
392 A115(a) 8pf red .25 *.45*
393 A115(b) 12pf carmine .25 *.45*
Nos. 390-393 (4) *2.60*
Set, never hinged 1.00

Nos. 390-393 exist with overprint inverted or double.

Germany No. 507, the 3pf, with overprint "a" was prepared, not issued, but sold to collectors after the definitive Republic issue had been placed in use. Values, $30 hinged, $65 never hinged.

German Semi-Postal Stamps, #B207, B209, B210, B283 Surcharged in Black

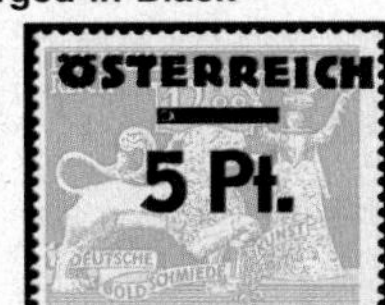

c

d

1945 *Perf. 14, 14x13½, 13½x14*

394 SP181(c) 5pf on 12pf + 88pf .25 *2.00*
395 SP184(d) 6pf on 6pf + 14pf 2.10 *17.50*
396 SP242(d) 8pf on 42pf + 108pf .25 *3.50*
397 SP183(d) 12pf on 3pf + 7pf .25 *2.00*
Nos. 394-397 (4) 2.85 *25.00*
Set, never hinged 9.75

The surcharges are spaced to fit the stamps.

Stamps of Germany, Nos. 509 to 511, 511B, 519 and 529 Overprinted

e

f

1945 Typo. *Perf. 14*

Size: 18½x22½mm

398 A115(e) 5pf dp yel grn .85 *8.00*
399 A115(f) 5pf dp yel grn 3.50 *27.50*
400 A115(e) 6pf purple .30 *3.50*
401 A115(e) 8pf red .30 *3.50*
402 A115(e) 12pf carmine .85 *4.00*

Engr.

Size: 21½x26mm

403 A115(e) 30pf olive green 6.00
a. Thin bar at bottom 15.00
Never hinged 47.50
404 A118(e) 42pf brt green 20.00
a. Thin bar at bottom 9.00
Never hinged 50.00
Nos. 398-404 (7) 31.80 *46.50*
Set, never hinged 98.00

On Nos. 403a and 404a, the bottom bar of the overprint is 2½mm wide, and, as the overprint was applied in two operations, "Osterreich" is usually not exactly centered in its diagonal slot. On Nos. 403 and 404, the bottom bar is 3mm wide, and "Osterreich" is always well centered.

Germany Nos. 524-527 (the 1m, 2m, 3m and 5m), overprinted with vertical bars and "Osterreich" similar to "e" and "f," were prepared, not issued, but sold to collectors after the definitive Republic issue had been placed in use. Value for set, $70 hinged, $150 never hinged.

Counterfeits exist of Nos. 403-404, 403a-404a and 1m-5m overprints.

For Use in Styria

Germany Nos. 506 to 511, 511A, 511B, 514 to 523 and 529 Ovptd. in Black

1945 Unwmk. Typo. *Perf. 14*

Size: 18½x22½mm

405 A115 1pf gray black 1.25 *8.00*
406 A115 3pf lt brown .75 *8.00*
407 A115 4pf slate 4.50 *27.50*
408 A115 5pf dp yel grn 1.00 *8.00*
409 A115 6pf purple .25 *1.60*
410 A115 8pf red .25 *2.50*
411 A115 10pf dark brown 1.00 *8.00*
412 A115 12pf carmine .25 *2.50*

Engr.

413 A115 15pf brown lake .40 *4.00*
414 A115 16pf pck green 10.00 *65.00*
415 A115 20pf blue 1.00 *6.50*
416 A115 24pf org brn 10.00 *65.00*

Size: 22½x26mm

417 A115 25pf brt ultra 1.25 *8.00*
418 A115 30pf olive green 1.25 *8.00*
419 A115 40pf brt red violet 1.25 *8.00*
420 A118 42pf brt green 2.00 *16.00*
421 A115 50pf myrtle green 1.75 *12.00*
422 A115 60pf dk red brown 1.75 *12.00*
423 A115 80pf indigo 1.50 *12.00*
Nos. 405-423 (19) 41.40 *282.60*
Set, never hinged 130.00

Overprinted on Nos. 524-527

Perf. 12½, 14

424 A116 1m dk slate grn 6.50 *50.00*
a. Perf. 12½ *2,000.*
Never hinged *6,500.*
425 A116 2m violet 6.50 *50.00*
a. Perf. 14 25.00 *80.00*
426 A116 3m copper red 40.00 *150.00*
427 A116 5m dark blue 150.00 *1,200.*
Nos. 424-427 (4) 203.00 *1,450.*
Set, never hinged 650.00

On the preceding four stamps the innermost vertical lines are 11.1-11.4mm apart; on the pfennig values 6½mm apart.

Counterfeits exist of Nos. 405-427 overprints.

Germany Nos. 524 to 527 Overprinted in Black

Perf. 14

428 A116 1m dk slate grn 9.00 *50.00*
429 A116 2m violet 12.50 *60.00*

Perf. 12½

430 A116 3m copper red 15.00 *90.00*
431 A116 5m dark blue 100.00 *650.00*
Nos. 428-431 (4) 136.50 *850.00*
Set, never hinged 400.00

On the preceding four stamps, "Osterreich" is thinner, measuring 16mm. On the previous set of 23 values it measures 18mm.

Counterfeits exist of Nos. 428-431 overprints.

Catalogue values for unused stamps in this section, from this point to the end of the section, are for Never Hinged items.

For Use in Vienna, Lower Austria and Burgenland

Coat of Arms
A99 A100

Typographed or Lithographed

1945, July 3 Unwmk. *Perf. 14x13½*

Size: 21x25mm

432 A99 3pf brown .25 .25
433 A99 4pf slate .25 .25
434 A99 5pf dark green .25 .25
435 A99 6pf deep violet .25 .25
436 A99 8pf orange brown .25 .25
437 A99 10pf deep brown .25 .25
438 A99 12pf rose carmine .25 .25
439 A99 15pf orange red .25 .25
440 A99 16pf dull blue green .25 .25

Perf. 14

Size: 24x28½mm

441 A99 20pf light blue .25 .25
442 A99 24pf orange .25 .25
443 A99 25pf dark blue .25 .25
444 A99 30pf deep gray grn .25 .25
445 A99 38pf ultramarine .25 .25
446 A99 40pf brt red vio .25 .25
447 A99 42pf sage green .25 .25
448 A99 50pf blue green .25 .25
449 A99 60pf maroon .25 .25
450 A99 80pf dull lilac .25 .30

Engr. *Perf. 14x13½*

451 A100 1m dark green .25 .25
452 A100 2m dark purple .25 .25
453 A100 3m dark violet .25 .25
454 A100 5m brown red .30 .30
Nos. 432-454 (23) 5.80 5.85

Nos. 432, 433, 437, 439, 440, 443, 446, 448, 449 are typographed. Nos. 434, 435, 441. 442 are lithographed; the other values exist both ways.

For overprint see No. 604.

For General Use

Lermoos, Winter Scene — A101

The Prater Woods, Vienna — A105

Wolfgang See, near Salzburg A106

Lake Constance A110

Dürnstein, Lower Austria A124

Designs: 4g, Eisenerz surface mine. 5g, Leopoldsberg, near Vienna. 6g, Hohensalzburg, Salzburg Province. 10gr, Hochosterwitz, Carinthia. 15g, Forchtenstein Castle, Burgenland. 16g, Gesäuse Valley. 24g, Höldrichs Mill, Lower Austria. 25g, Oetz Valley Outlet, Tyrol. 30g, Neusiedler Lake, Burgenland. 35g, Belvedere Palace, Vienna. 38g, Langbath Lake. 40g, Mariazell, Styria. 42g, Traunkirchen. 45g, Hartenstein Castle. 50g, Silvretta Mountains, Vorarlberg. 60g, Railroad viaducts near Semmering.

70g, Waterfall of Bad-Gastein, Salzburg. 80g, Kaiser Mountains, Tyrol. 90g, Wayside Shrine, Tragöss, Styria. 2s, St. Christof am Arlberg, Tyrol. 3s, Heiligenblut, Carinthia. 5s, Schönbrunn, Vienna.

Perf. 14x13½

1945-46 **Photo.** **Unwmk.**

455 A101 3g sapphire .25 .25
456 A101 4g dp orange ('46) .25 .25
457 A101 5g dk carmine rose .25 .25
458 A101 6g dk slate green .25 .25
459 A105 8g golden brown .25 .25
460 A106 10g dark green .25 .25
461 A106 12g dark brown .25 .25
462 A106 15g dk slate bl ('46) .25 .25
463 A106 16g chnt brn ('46) .25 .25

Perf. 13½x14

464 A110 20g dp ultra ('46) .25 .25
465 A110 24g dp yellow grn ('46) .25 .25
466 A110 25g gray black ('46) .25 .25
467 A110 30g dark red .25 .25
468 A110 35g brown red ('46) .25 .25
469 A110 38g brn olive ('46) .25 .25
470 A110 40g gray .25 .25
471 A110 42g brn org ('46) .25 .25
472 A110 45g dark blue ('46) .35 *1.60*
473 A110 50g dark blue .25 .25
474 A110 60g dark violet .25 .25
a. Imperf., pair 75.00 *85.00*
475 A110 70g Prus blue ('46) .25 *.40*
476 A110 80g brown .35 *.55*
477 A110 90g Prussian green .80 2.40
478 A124 1s dk red brn ('46) .80 .80
479 A124 2s blue gray ('46) 2.40 *4.50*
480 A124 3s dk slate grn ('46) 1.00 *5.00*
481 A124 5s dark red ('46) 1.60 *4.00*
Nos. 455-481 (27) 12.30 24.00

See Nos. 486-488, 496-515. For overprints and surcharges see Nos. 492-493, B166, B280, B287.

No. 461 Overprinted in Carmine

1946, Sept. 26

482 A106 12g dark brown .40 .40

Meeting of the Soc. for Cultural and Economic Relations with the USSR, Vienna, Sept. 26-29.

City Hall Park, Vienna A128

Hochosterwitz, Carinthia A129

Perf. 14x13½

1946-47 **Photo.** **Unwmk.**

483 A128 8g deep plum .25 .25
484 A128 8g olive brown .25 .25
a. 8g dark olive green .25 .25
485 A129 10g dk brn vio ('47) .25 .25

Perf. 13½x14

486 A110 30g blue gray ('47) .40 .40
487 A110 50g brown violet ('47) .80 .80
488 A110 60g violet blue ('47) 2.50 2.50
Nos. 483-488 (6) 4.45 4.45

See No. 502.

Franz Grillparzer A130

1947 **Engr.** *Perf. 14x13½*

489 A130 18g chocolate .40 .40

Photo.

490 A130 18g dk violet brn .65 .65

Death of Grillparzer, dramatic poet, 75th anniv.

A second printing of No. 490 on thicker paper was made in June 1947. It has a darker frame and clearer delineation of the portrait.

Issue dates: No. 489, Feb. 10; No. 490, Mar. 31.

Franz Schubert — A131

1947, Mar. 31 **Engr.**

491 A131 12g dark green .40 *.65*

150th birth anniv. of Franz Schubert, musician and composer.

Nos. 469 and 463 Surcharged in Brown

1947, Sept. 1 **Photo.** *Perf. 14*

492 A110 75g on 38g brown ol .25 *.85*
493 A106 1.40s on 16g chnt brn .25 *.45*

The surcharge on No. 493 varies from brown to black brown.

Symbols of Global Telegraphic Communication A132

1947, Nov. 5 **Engr.** *Perf. 14x13½*

495 A132 40g dark violet .40 .40

Centenary of the telegraph in Austria.

Scenic Type of 1946

1946, Aug. **Photo.** *Perf. 13½x14*

496 A124 1s dark brown 1.60 4.00
497 A124 2s dark blue 9.50 4.00
498 A124 3s dark slate green 3.25 4.25
499 A124 5s dark red 40.00 20.00
Nos. 496-499 (4) 54.35 32.25

On Nos. 478 to 481 the upper and lower panels show a screen effect. On Nos. 496 to 499 the panels appear to be solid color.

Scenic Types of 1945-46

1947-48 **Photo.** *Perf. 14x13½*

500 A101 3g bright red .25 .25
501 A101 5g bright red .25 .25
502 A129 10g bright red .25 .25
503 A106 15g brt red ('48) 2.00 1.75

Perf. 13½x14

504 A110 20g bright red .40 .25
505 A110 30g bright red .40 .25
506 A110 40g bright red .40 .25
507 A110 50g bright red .80 .25
508 A110 60g brt red ('48) 9.50 2.00
509 A110 70g brt red ('48) 4.00 .25
510 A110 80g brt red ('48) 4.00 .25
511 A110 90g brt red ('48) 4.75 .80
512 A124 1s dark violet 1.60 .25
513 A124 2s dark violet 1.20 .25
514 A124 3s dk violet ('48) 24.00 2.00
515 A124 5s dk violet ('48) 24.00 2.00
Nos. 500-515 (16) 77.80 11.30
Set, hinged 16.00

Carl Michael Ziehrer (1843-1922), Composer A133

Designs: No. 517, Adalbert Stifter (1805-68), novelist. No. 518, Anton Bruckner (1824-96), composer. 60g, Friedrich von Amerling (1803-87), painter.

1948-49 **Engr.**

516 A133 20g dull green .40 .25
517 A133 40g chocolate 8.00 4.50
518 A133 40g dark green 8.00 8.00
519 A133 60g rose brown .40 .35
Nos. 516-519 (4) 16.80 13.10

Issue dates: 20g, Jan. 21, No. 517, Sept. 6, No. 518, Sept. 3, 1949, 60g, Jan. 26.

Vorarlberg, Montafon Valley — A134

Costume of Vienna, 1850 — A135

Austrian Costumes: 3g, Tyrol, Inn Valley. 5g, Salzburg, Pinzgau. 10g, Styria, Salzkammergut. 15g, Burgenland, Lutzmannsburg. 25g, Vienna, 1850. 30g, Salzburg, Pongau. 40g, Vienna, 1840. 45g, Carinthia, Lesach Valley. 50g, Vorarlberg, Bregenzer Forest. 60g, Carinthia, Lavant Valley. 70g, Lower Austria, Wachau. 75g, Styria, Salzkammergut. 80g, Styria, Enns Valley. 90g, Central Styria. 1s, Tyrol, Puster Valley. 1.20s, Lower Austria, Vienna Woods. 1.40s, Upper Austria, Inn District. 1.45s, Wilten. 1.50s, Vienna, 1853. 1.60s, Vienna, 1830. 1.70s, East Tyrol, Kals. 2s, Upper Austria. 2.20s, Ischl, 1820. 2.40s, Kitzbuhel. 2.50s, Upper Steiermark, 1850. 2.70s, Little Walser Valley. 3s, Burgenland. 3.50s, Lower Austria, 1850. 4.50s, Gail Valley. 5s, Ziller Valley. 7s, Steiermark, Sulm Valley.

Perf. 14x13½

1948-52 **Unwmk.** **Photo.**

On Toned Paper, with Glossy Yellowish Gum

520 A134 3g gray ('50) .65 .80
521 A134 5g dk grn ('49) .25 .25
522 A134 10g deep blue .25 .25
523 A134 15g brown .40 .25
524 A134 20g yellow green .25 .25
525 A134 25g brown ('49) .25 .25
526 A134 30g dk car rose 4.00 .25
527 A134 30g dk vio ('50) .85 .25
528 A134 40g violet 3.25 .25
529 A134 40g green ('49) .65 .25
530 A134 45g violet blue 3.25 .40
531 A134 50g org brn ('49) 1.00 .25
532 A134 60g scarlet .65 .25
533 A134 70g brt bl grn ('49) .65 .25
534 A134 75g blue 5.50 .40
535 A134 80g car rose ('49) .95 .25
536 A134 90g brn vio ('49) 45.00 .35
537 A134 1s ultramarine 16.00 .25
538 A134 1s rose red ('50) 105.00 .25
539 A134 1s dk grn ('51) .65 .25
540 A134 1.20s violet ('49) .95 .25
541 A134 1.40s brown 2.40 .25
542 A134 1.45s dk car ('51) 3.25 .25
543 A134 1.50s ultra ('51) 2.00 .25
544 A134 1.60s org red ('49) .65 .25
545 A134 1.70s vio bl ('50) 3.25 .80
546 A134 2s blue green 1.25 .25
547 A134 2.20s slate ('52) 6.50 .25
548 A134 2.40s blue ('51) 2.00 .25
549 A134 2.50s brown ('52) 5.50 3.25
550 A134 2.70s dk brn ('51) .80 1.60
551 A134 3s brn car ('49) 3.25 .25
552 A134 3.50s dull grn ('51) 24.00 .25
553 A134 4.50s brn vio ('51) .80 1.60
554 A134 5s dark red vio 1.20 .25
555 A134 7s olive ('52) 4.75 2.40

Engr.

556 A135 10s gray ('50) 40.00 5.50
b. Flat white gum 275.00 17.50
Nos. 520-556 (37) 292.00 23.85
Set, hinged 62.50

1958-59

On White Paper, with Flat White Gum

521a A134 5g dk grn .25 .25
522a A134 10g deep blue .25 .25
524a A134 20g dp yel grn .25 .25
525a A134 25g dk brown ('59) .55 .55
527a A134 30g dk vio .80 .25
529a A134 40g dp bl grn .65 .25
531a A134 50g org brn .95 .25
532a A134 60g scarlet .95 .65
533a A134 70g brt bl grn .95 .25
535a A134 80g car rose .95 .25
540a A134 1.20s violet 1.60 .65
542a A134 1.45s dk car 3.25 .65
543a A134 1.50s ultramarine 4.00 .45
544a A134 1.60s brn org 4.00 3.00
547a A134 2.20s slate 6.50 .25
548a A134 2.40s blue 2.00 .90
549a A134 2.50s brown 6.50 3.25
551a A134 3s brn car 4.00 .25
552a A134 3.50s dull grn 24.00 .25
554a A134 5s dark red vio ('59) 1.60 .25
555a A134 7s olive ('59) 4.75 2.40
Nos. 521a-555a (21) 68.75 15.50
Set, hinged 15.00

Designs of the 1958-59 printing are clearer and on most values appear sharper than on the 1948-52 printings.

Pres. Karl Renner — A136

1948, Nov. 12 ***Perf. 14x13½***
557 A136 1s deep blue 2.50 2.00

Founding of the Austrian Republic, 30th anniv. See Nos. 573, 636.

Franz Gruber and Josef Mohr A137

1948, Dec. 18 ***Perf. 13½x14***
558 A137 60g red brown 6.00 4.50

130th anniv. of the hymn "Silent Night, Holy Night".

Symbolical of Child Welfare — A138

1949, May 14 Photo. ***Perf. 14x13½***
559 A138 1s bright blue 12.00 3.25

1st year of activity of UNICEF in Austria.

Johann Strauss, the Younger — A139

Designs: 30g, Johann Strauss, the elder. No. 561, Johann Strauss, the younger. No. 562, Karl Millöcker.

1949 **Engr.**

560 A139	30g	violet brown	1.60	2.00
561 A139	1s	dark blue	3.25	2.25
562 A139	1s	dark blue	16.00	12.50
		Nos. 560-562 (3)	20.85	16.75

Johann Strauss, the elder (1804-49), Johann Strauss, the younger (1825-99), and Karl Millöcker (1842-1899), composers. See No. 574.

Issue dates: No. 560, 9/24; No. 561, 6/3; No. 562, 12/31.

Esperanto Star, Olive Branches — A140

1949, June 25 **Photo.**
563 A140 20g blue green .95 .95

Austrian Esperanto Congress at Graz.

St. Gebhard — A141

1949, Aug. 6 **Engr.**
564 A141 30g dark violet 1.60 1.60

St. Gebhard (949-995), Bishop of Vorarlberg.

Letter, Roses and Post Horn A142

UPU, 75th Anniv.: 60g, Plaque. 1s, "Austria," wings and monogram.

1949, Oct. 8 ***Perf. 13½x14***

565 A142	40g	dark green	4.00	4.00
566 A142	60g	dk carmine	4.00	3.25
567 A142	1s	dk violet blue	8.00	7.25
		Nos. 565-567 (3)	16.00	14.50

Moritz Michael Daffinger — A143

Andreas Hofer — A144

Designs: 30g, Alexander Girardi. No. 569, Daffinger. No. 570, Hofer. No. 571, Josef Madersperger.

1950 **Unwmk.** ***Perf. 14x13½***

568 A144	30g	dark blue	1.60	1.20
569 A143	60g	red brown	8.00	6.50
570 A144	60g	dark violet	13.00	9.50
571 A144	60g	purple	7.25	4.00
		Nos. 568-571 (4)	29.85	21.20

Alexander Girardi (1850-1918), actor; Moritz Michael Daffinger (1790-1849), painter; Andreas Hofer (1767-1810), patriot; Josef Madersperger (1768-1850), inventor.

Issue dates: 30g, Dec. 5; No. 569, Jan. 25; No. 570, Feb. 20; No. 571, Oct. 2.

Austrian Stamp of 1850 — A146

1950, May 20 ***Perf. 14½***
572 A146 1s black, *straw* 2.00 1.60

Centenary of Austrian postage stamps.

Renner Type of 1948
Frame and Inscriptions Altered

1951, Mar. 3
573 A136 1s black, *straw* 1.20 .45

In memory of Pres. Karl Renner, 1870-1950.

Strauss Type of 1949

Portrait: 60g, Joseph Lanner.

1951, Apr. 12
574 A139 60g dk blue green 4.75 2.40

Joseph Lanner (1801-43), composer.

Martin Johann Schmidt — A147

1951, June 28 Engr. ***Perf. 14x13½***
575 A147 1sh brown red 6.50 2.40

150th death anniv. of Martin Johann Schmidt, painter.

Martin Johann Schmidt — A148

1951, Aug. 3 **Engr. and Litho.**
576 A148 1sh dk grn, ocher & pink 4.75 4.75

7th World Scout Jamboree, Bad Ischl-St. Wolfgang, Aug. 3-13, 1951.

Wilhelm Kienzl — A149

Josef Schrammel A150

Design: 1s, Karl von Ghega.

1951-52 **Engr.** **Unwmk.**

577 A149	1s	deep green ('52)	6.50	1.60
578 A149	1.50s	indigo	3.25	2.00
579 A150	1.50s	violet blue ('52)	6.50	2.00
		Nos. 577-579 (3)	16.25	5.60

Ghega (1802-60), civil engineer; Kienzl (1857-1941), composer; Schrammel (1852-95), composer. See No. 582.

Issued: 1s, 3/2; No. 578, 10/3; No. 579, 3/3.

Breakfast Pavilion, Schönbrunn A151

1952, May 24 ***Perf. 13½x14***
580 A151 1.50s dark green 6.50 2.00

Vienna Zoological Gardens, 200th anniv.

Globe as Dot Over "i" — A152

1952, July 1 ***Perf. 14x13½***
581 A152 1.50s dark blue 6.50 1.20

Formation of the Intl. Union of Socialist Youth Camp, Vienna, July 1-10, 1952.

Type Similar to A150

Portrait: 1s, Nikolaus Lenau.

1952, Aug. 13
582 A150 1s deep green 6.50 1.60

Nikolaus Lenau, pseudonym of Nikolaus Franz Niembsch von Strehlenau (1802-50), poet.

School Girl — A153

1952, Sept. 6
583 A153 2.40s dp violet blue 12.00 2.40

Issued to stimulate letter-writing between Austrian and foreign school children.

Hugo Wolf — A154

1953, Feb. 21 Engr. ***Perf. 14x13½***
587 A154 1.50s dark blue 6.50 1.60

Hugo Wolf, composer, 50th death anniv.

Pres. Theodor Körner — A155

1953, Apr. 24
588 A155 1.50s dk violet blue 6.50 1.20

80th birthday of Pres. Theodor Körner. See Nos. 591, 614.

State Theater, Linz, and Masks A156

1953, Oct. 17 ***Perf. 13½x14***
589 A156 1.50s dark gray 16.00 2.40

State Theater at Linz, 150th anniv.

Child and Christmas Tree — A157

1953, Nov. 30 *Perf. 14x13½*
590 A157 1s dark green 1.25 .65

See No. 597.

Type Similar to A155

Portrait: 1.50s, Moritz von Schwind.

1954, Jan. 21 *Perf. 14x13½*
591 A155 1.50s purple 12.00 2.40

Moritz von Schwind, painter, 150th birth anniv.

Karl von Rokitansky A158

1954, Feb. 19
592 A158 1.50s purple 14.50 2.75

Karl von Rokitansky, physician, 150th birth anniv. See No. 595.

Esperanto Star and Wreath A159

Engr. and Photo.

1954, June 5 *Perf. 13½x14*
593 A159 1s dk brown & emer 4.00 .55

Esperanto movement in Austria, 50th anniv.

A160

1954, Aug. 4 Engr. *Perf. 14x13½*
594 A160 1s dark blue green 12.00 2.75

300th birth anniv. of Johann Michael Rottmayr von Rosenbrunn, painter.

Type Similar to A158

Portrait: 1.50s, Carl Auer von Welsbach.

1954, Aug. 4
595 A158 1.50s violet blue 24.00 2.75

25th death anniv. of Carl Auer von Welsbach (1858-1929), chemist.

2nd Intl. Congress for Catholic Church Music, Vienna, Oct. 4-10 — A161

Organ, St. Florian Monastery and Cherub.

1954, Oct. 2 **Unwmk.**
596 A161 1s brown 2.40 .40

Christmas Type of 1953

1954, Nov. 30
597 A157 1s dark blue 4.00 .55

Arms of Austria and Official Publication A162

1954, Dec. 18 **Engr.**
598 A162 1s salmon & black 2.40 .40

Austria's State Printing Plant, 150th anniv., and Wiener Zeitung, government newspaper, 250th year of publication.

Parliament Building A163

Designs: 1s, Western railroad station, Vienna. 1.45s, Letters forming flag. 1.50s, Public housing, Vienna. 2.40s, Limberg dam.

1955, Apr. 27 *Perf. 13½x14*
599 A163 70g rose violet 1.60 .80
600 A163 1s deep ultra 4.75 .25
601 A163 1.45s scarlet 9.50 2.75
602 A163 1.50s brown 24.00 .40
603 A163 2.40s dk blue green 9.50 5.50
Nos. 599-603 (5) 49.35 9.70

10th anniv. of Austria's liberation.

Type of 1945 Overprinted in Blue

1955, May 15 *Perf. 14x13½*
604 A100 2s blue gray 2.40 .65

Signing of the state treaty with the US, France, Great Britain and Russia, 5/15/55.

Workers of Three Races Climbing Globe A164

1955, May 20 *Perf. 13½x14*
605 A164 1s indigo 2.40 2.00

4th congress of the Intl. Confederation of Free Trade Unions, Vienna, May.

Burgtheater, Vienna A165

Design: 2.40s, Opera House, Vienna.

1955, July 25
606 A165 1.50s light sepia 4.00 .40
607 A165 2.40s dark blue 4.75 2.40

Re-opening of the Burgtheater and Opera House in Vienna.

Symbolic of Austria's Desire to Join the UN — A166

1955, Oct. 24 **Unwmk.**
608 A166 2.40s green 13.00 3.25

Tenth anniversary of UN.

Wolfgang Amadeus Mozart, Birth Bicent. — A167

1956, Jan. 21 *Perf. 14x13½*
609 A167 2.40s slate blue 4.75 1.20

Symbolic of Austria's Joining the UN — A168

1956, Feb. 20
610 A168 2.40s chocolate 10.50 2.00

Austria's admission to the UN.

Globe Showing Energy of the Earth A169

1956, May 8 *Perf. 13½x14*
611 A169 2.40s deep blue 11.00 2.40

Fifth Intl. Power Conf., Vienna, June 17-23.

Map of Europe and City Maps — A170

Photo. and Typo.

1956, June 8 *Perf. 14x13½*
612 A170 1.45s lt grn blk & red 3.25 .80

23rd Intl. Housing and Town Planning Congress, Vienna, July 22-28.

J.B. Fischer von Erlach, Architect, 300th Birth Anniv. — A171

1956, July 20 **Engr.**
613 A171 1.50s brown .80 .80

Körner Type of 1953

1957, Jan. 11
614 A155 1.50s gray black 1.75 1.60

Death of Pres. Theodor Körner.

Dr. Julius Wagner-Jauregg, Psychiatrist, Birth Cent. — A172

1957, Mar. 7 *Perf. 14x13½*
615 A172 2.40s brn violet 4.00 2.40

Anton Wildgans, Poet, 25th Death Anniv. — A173

1957, May 3 **Unwmk.**
616 A173 1s violet blue .55 .55

Old and New Postal Motor Coach A174

1957, June 14 *Perf. 13½x14*
617 A174 1s black, *yellow* .55 .55

Austrian Postal Motor Coach Service, 50th anniv.

Gasherbrum II and Glacier A175

1957, July 27
618 A175 1.50s gray blue .55 .65

Austrian Karakorum Expedition, which climbed Mount Gasherbrum II on July 7, 1956.

A176 A177

Designs: 20g, Farmhouse at Mörbisch. 50g, Heiligenstadt, Vienna. 1s, Mariazell. 1.40s, County seat, Klagenfurt. 1.50s, Rabenhof Building, Erdberg, Vienna. 1.80s, The Mint, Hall, Tyrol. 2s, Christkindl Church. 3.40s, Steiner Gate, Krems. 4s, Vienna Gate, Hainburg. 4.50s, Schwechat Airport, Vienna. 5.50s, Chur Gate, Feldkirch. 6s, County seat, Graz. 6.40s, "Golden Roof," Innsbruck. 10s, Heidenreichstein Castle.

1957-61 **Litho.** *Perf. 14x13½*

Size: 20x25mm

618A A176 20g violet blk ('61) .25 .25
619 A176 50g bluish blk ('59) .40 .25

Engr.

620 A176 1s chocolate 1.60 .55

Typo.

621 A176 1s chocolate 1.60 .65

Litho.

622	A176	1s	choc ('59)	.40	.25
622A	A176	1.40s	brt greenish bl ('60)	.40	.25
623	A176	1.50s	rose lake ('58)	.40	.25
624	A176	1.80s	brt ultra ('60)	.40	.25
625	A176	2s	dull blue ('58)	3.00	.25
626	A176	3.40s	yel grn ('60)	1.60	1.20
627	A176	4s	brt red lil ('60)	1.75	.25
627A	A176	4.50s	dl green ('60)	2.00	1.20
628	A176	5.50s	grnsh gray ('60)	1.60	1.20
629	A176	6s	brt vio ('60)	1.60	.80
629A	A176	6.40s	brt blue ('60)	2.75	2.75

Engr.

Size: 22x28mm

630	A177	10s	dk bl grn	2.75	1.00
			Nos. 618A-630 (16)	22.50	11.35

Of the three 1s stamps above, Nos. 620 and 621 have two names in imprint (designer H. Strohofer, engraver G. Wimmer). No. 622 has only Strohofer's name.

Values for Nos. 618A-624, 626-630 are for stamps on white paper. Most denominations also come on grayish paper with yellowish gum.

See Nos. 688-702.

1960-65 Photo. *Perf. 14½x14*

Size: 17x21mm

630A A176 50g slate ('64) .25 .25

Size: 18x21½mm

630B A176 1s chocolate .25 .25

Size: 17x21mm

630C A176 1.50s dk car ('65) .35 .25
Nos. 630A-630C (3) .85 .75

Nos. 630A-630C issued in sheets and coils.

Graukogel, Badgastein
A180

1958, Feb. 1 Engr. *Perf. 14x13½*

631 A180 1.50s dark blue .45 .45

Intl. Ski Federation Alpine championships, Badgastein, Feb. 2-7.

Plane over Map of Austria
A181

1958, Mar. 27 *Perf. 13½x14*

632 A181 4s red .80 .80

Re-opening of Austrian Airlines.

Mother and Daughter — A182

1958, May 8 Unwmk. *Perf. 14x13½*

633 A182 1.50s dark blue .45 .45

Issued for Mother's Day.

Walther von der Vogelweide
A183

1958, July 17 Litho. and Engr.

634 A183 1.50s multicolored .45 .45

3rd Austrian Song Festival, Vienna, 7/17-20.

Oswald Redlich (1858-1944), Historian — A184

1958, Sept. 17 Engr.

635 A184 2.40s ultramarine .65 .45

Renner Type of 1948

1958, Nov. 12

636 A136 1.50s deep green .65 .65

Austrian Republic, 40th anniv.

Giant "E" on Map — A185

1959, Mar. 9

637 A185 2.40s emerald 1.20 .55

Idea of a United Europe.

Cigarette Machine and Trademark of Tobacco Monopoly — A186

1959, May 8 Unwmk. *Perf. 13½*

638 A186 2.40s dark olive bister .45 .40

Austrian tobacco monopoly, 175th anniv.

Archduke Johann — A187

1959, May 11 *Perf. 14x13½*

639 A187 1.50s deep green .45 .45

Archduke Johann of Austria, military leader and humanitarian, death cent.

Capercaillie
A188

Animals: 1.50s, Roe buck. 2.40s, Wild boar. 3.50s, Red deer, doe and fawn.

1959, May 20 Engr.

640	A188	1s	rose violet	.25	.25
641	A188	1.50s	blue violet	.45	.45
642	A188	2.40s	dk bl green	.65	.65
643	A188	3.50s	dark brown	.65	.65
			Nos. 640-643 (4)	2.00	2.00

Congress of the Intl. Hunting Council, Vienna, May 20-24.

Joseph Haydn (1732-1809), Composer
A189

1959, May 30 Unwmk.

644 A189 1.50s violet brown .45 .45

Coat of Arms, Tyrol — A190

1959, June 13 *Perf. 14x13½*

645 A190 1.50s rose red .45 .45

Fight for liberation of Tyrol, 150th anniv.

Antenna, Zugspitze — A191

1959, June 19 *Perf. 13½*

646 A191 2.40s dk bl grn .45 .45

Inauguration of Austria's relay system.

Field Ball Player — A192

1s, Runner. 1.80s, Gymnast on vaulting horse. 2s, Woman hurdler. 2.20s, Hammer thrower.

1959-70 Engr. *Perf. 14x13½*

647	A192	1s	lilac	.35	.25
648	A192	1.50s	blue green	.55	.45
648A	A192	1.80s	carmine ('62)	.35	.35
648B	A192	2s	rose lake ('70)	.25	.25
648C	A192	2.20s	bluish blk ('67)	.35	.35
			Nos. 647-648C (5)	1.85	1.65

Orchestral Instruments
A193

Litho. and Engr.

1959, Aug. 19 *Perf. 14x13½*

649 A193 2.40s dull bl & blk .45 .45

World tour of the Vienna Philharmonic Orchestra.

Family Fleeing over Mountains
A194

1960, Apr. 7 Engr. *Perf. 13½x14*

650 A194 3s Prussian green .55 .80

WRY, July 1, 1959-June 30, 1960.

President Adolf Schärf — A195

1960, Apr. 20 *Perf. 14x13½*

651 A195 1.50s gray olive .45 .45

Pres. Adolf Scharf, 70th birthday.

Young Hikers and Hostel
A196

1960, May 20 *Perf. 13½x14*

652 A196 1s carmine rose .40 .40

Youth hiking; youth hostel movement.

Anton Eiselsberg, Surgeon, Birth Cent. — A197

Litho. and Engr.

1960, June 20 *Perf. 14x13½*

653 A197 1.50s buff & dk brn .65 .40

Gustav Mahler (1860-1911), Composer
A198

1960, July 7 Engr.

654 A198 1.50s chocolate .65 .40

Jakob Prandtauer, Architect, 300th Birth Anniv. — A199

1960, July 16 **Unwmk.**
655 A199 1.50s Melk Abbey .65 .40

Gross Glockner Mountain Road, 25th Anniv. — A200

1960, Aug. 3
656 A200 1.80s dark blue 1.25 .40

Ionic Capital — A201

1960, Aug. 29 ***Perf. 14x13½***
657 A201 3s black *1.25 1.25*

Europa: Idea of a United Europe.

Griffen, Carinthia A202

1960, Oct. 10 **Engr.** ***Perf. 13½x14***
658 A202 1.50s slate green .40 .40

40th anniv. of the plebiscite which kept Carinthia with Austria.

Flame and Broken Chain — A203

1961, May 8 **Unwmk.** ***Perf. 14x13½***
659 A203 1.50s scarlet .35 .25

Victims in Austria's fight for freedom.

First Austrian Mail Plane, 1918 A204

1961, May 15 ***Perf. 13½x14***
660 A204 5s violet blue .95 .55

Airmail Phil. Exhib., LUPOSTA 1961, Vienna, May.

Transportation by Road, Rail and Waterway A205

Engraved and Typographed

1961, May 29 ***Perf. 13½***
661 A205 3s rose red & olive .80 .55

13th European Conference of Transportation ministers, Vienna, May 29-31.

Society of Creative Artists, Künstlerhaus, Vienna, Cent. — A206

Designs: 1s, Mountain Mower, by Albin Egger-Lienz. 1.50s, The Kiss, by August von Pettenkofen. 3s, Girl, by Anton Romako. 5s, Ariadne's Triumph, by Hans Makart.

1961, June 12 **Engr.** ***Perf. 13½x14***
Inscriptions in Red Brown
662 A206 1s rose lake .25 .25
663 A206 1.50s dull violet .40 .25
664 A206 3s olive green .80 .95
665 A206 5s blue violet 1.40 .65
Nos. 662-665 (4) 2.85 2.10

Sonnblick Mountain and Observatory A207

1961, Sept. 1 ***Perf. 14x13½***
666 A207 1.80s violet blue .40 .35

Sonnblick meteorological observatory, 75th anniv.

Mercury and Globe — A208

1961, Sept. 18
667 A208 3s black .55 .45

Intl. Banking Congress, Vienna, Sept. 1961. English inscription listing UN financial groups.

Coal Mine Shaft — A209

Designs: 1.50s, Generator. 1.80s, Iron blast furnace. 3s, Pouring steel. 5s, Oil refinery.

1961, Sept. 15 **Engr.** ***Perf. 14x13½***
668 A209 1s black .25 .25
669 A209 1.50s green .25 .25
670 A209 1.80s dark car rose .55 .45
671 A209 3s bright lilac .65 .55
672 A209 5s blue .80 .75
Nos. 668-672 (5) 2.50 2.25

15th anniversary of nationalized industry.

Arms of Burgenland A210

1961, Oct. 9 **Engr. and Litho.**
673 A210 1.50s blk, yel & dk red .35 .25

Burgenland as part of the Austrian Republic, 40th anniv.

Franz Liszt (1811-86), Composer A211

1961, Oct. 20 **Engr.**
674 A211 3s dark brown .80 .45

Parliament A212

1961, Dec. 18 ***Perf. 13½x14***
675 A212 1s brown .25 .25

Austrian Bureau of Budget, 200th anniv.

Kaprun-Mooserboden Reservoir — A213

Hydroelectric Power Plants: 1.50s, Ybbs-Persenbeug dam and locks. 1.80s, Lünersee dam and reservoir. 3s, Grossraming dam. 4s, Bisamberg transformer plant. 6.40s, St. Andrä power plant.

1962, Mar. 26 **Unwmk.**
676 A213 1s violet blue .25 .25
677 A213 1.50s red lilac .30 .25
678 A213 1.80s green .55 .55
679 A213 3s brown .55 .40
680 A213 4s rose red .65 .40
681 A213 6.40s gray 1.20 1.20
Nos. 676-681 (6) 3.50 3.05

Nationalization of the electric power industry, 15th anniv.

Johann Nestroy — A214

1962, May 25 ***Perf. 14x13½***
682 A214 1s violet .35 .35

Johann Nepomuk Nestroy, Viennese playwright, author and actor, death cent.

Friedrich Gauermann (1807-1862), Landscape Painter — A215

1962, July 6 **Engr.**
683 A215 1.50s intense blue .35 .35

Scout Emblem and Handshake A216

1962, Oct. 5
684 A216 1.50s dark green .40 .35

Austria's Boy Scouts, 50th anniv.

Lowlands Forest A217

1.50s, Deciduous forest. 3s, Fir & larch forest.

1962, Oct. 12 ***Perf. 13½x14***
685 A217 1s greenish gray .40 .40
686 A217 1.50s reddish brown .45 .45
687 A217 3s dk slate green 1.10 1.10
Nos. 685-687 (3) 1.95 1.95

Buildings Types of 1957-61

Designs: 30g, City Hall, Vienna. 40g, Porcia Castle, Spittal on the Drau. 60g, Tanners' Tower, Wels. 70g, Residenz Fountain, Salzburg. 80g, Old farmhouse, Pinzgau. 1s, Romanesque columns, Millstatt Abbey. 1.20s, Kornmesser House, Bruck on the Mur. 1.30s, Schatten Castle, Feldkirch, Vorarlberg. 2s, Dragon Fountain, Klagenfurt. 2.20s, Beethoven House, Vienna. 2.50s, Danube Bridge, Linz. 3s, Swiss Gate, Vienna. 3.50s, Esterhazy Palace, Eisenstadt. 8s, City Hall, Steyr. 20s, Melk Abbey.

1962-70 **Litho.** ***Perf. 14x13½***
Size: 20x25mm
688 A176 30g greenish gray .40 .25
689 A176 40g rose red .25 .25
690 A176 60g violet brown .40 .25
691 A176 70g dark blue .40 .25
692 A176 80g yellow brown .25 .25
693 A176 1s brown ('70) .35 .25
694 A176 1.20s red lilac .40 .25
695 A176 1.30s green ('67) .40 .40
696 A176 2s dk blue ('68) .40 .30
697 A176 2.20s green .80 .30
698 A176 2.50s violet .80 .30
699 A176 3s bright blue .90 .25
700 A176 3.50s rose carmine 1.20 .25
701 A176 8s claret ('65) 1.60 .55

Perf. 13½

Engr.

Size: 28x36½mm

702 A177 20s rose claret ('63) 3.50 2.00
Nos. 688-702 (15) 12.05 6.10

Values for Nos. 688-702 are for stamps on white paper. Some denominations also come on grayish paper with yellowish gum.

Electric Locomotive and Train of 1837 — A218

Lithographed and Engraved

1962, Nov. 9 ***Perf. 13½x14***
703 A218 3s buff & black 1.20 1.20

125th anniversary of Austrian railroads.

Postilions and Postal Clerk, 1863 — A219

1963, May 7 Photo. ***Perf. 14x13½***
704 A219 3s dk brn & citron .75 .55

First Intl. Postal Conference, Paris, cent.

Hermann Bahr, Writer, Birth Cent. — A220

Lithographed and Envraved

1963, July 19 ***Perf. 14x13½***
705 A220 1.50s blue & black .35 .35

St. Florian Statue, Kefermarkt, Contemporary and Old Fire Engines — A221

1963, Aug. 30 **Unwmk.**
706 A221 1.50s brt rose & blk .45 .45

Austrian volunteer fire brigades, cent.

Factory, Flag and "ÖGB" on Map of Austria A222

1963, Sept. 23 Litho. ***Perf. 13½x14***
707 A222 1.50s gray, red & dk brn .35 .35

5th Congress of the Austrian Trade Union Federation (ÖGB), Sept. 23-28.

Arms of Austria and Tyrol A223

1963, Sept. 27 **Unwmk.**
708 A223 1.50s tan, blk, red & yel .35 .35

Tyrol's union with Austria, 600th anniv.

Prince Eugene of Savoy (1663-1736), Austrian General — A224

1963, Oct. 18 Engr. ***Perf. 14x13½***
709 A224 1.50s violet .35 .35

Intl. Red Cross, Cent. — A225

1963, Oct. 25 **Engr. and Photo.**
710 A225 3s blk, sil & red .55 .55

Slalom A226

Sports: 1.20s, Biathlon (skier with rifle). 1.50s, Ski jump. 1.80s, Women's figure skating. 2.20s, Ice hockey. 3s, Tobogganing. 4s, Bobsledding.

Photo. and Engr.

1963, Nov. 11 ***Perf. 13½x14***

711	A226	1s	multi	.25	.25
712	A226	1.20s	multi	.25	.25
713	A226	1.50s	multi	.35	.35
714	A226	1.80s	multi	.35	.35
715	A226	2.20s	multi	.45	.45
716	A226	3s	multi	.55	.55
717	A226	4s	multi	.65	.65
	Nos. 711-717 (7)			2.85	2.85

9th Winter Olympic Games, Innsbruck, Jan. 29-Feb. 9, 1964.

Baroque Creche by Josef Thaddäus Stammel — A227

1963, Nov. 29 Engr. ***Perf. 14x13½***
718 A227 2s dark Prus green .40 .40

Flowers A228

1964, Apr. 17 Litho. ***Perf. 14***

719	A228	1s	Nasturtium	.25	.25
720	A228	1.50s	Peony	.35	.35
721	A228	1.80s	Clematis	.25	.25
722	A228	2.20s	Dahlia	.40	.40
723	A228	3s	Morning glory	.65	.65
724	A228	4s	Hollyhock	.95	.95
	Nos. 719-724 (6)			2.85	2.85

Vienna Intl. Garden Show, Apr. 16-Oct. 11.

St. Mary Magdalene and Apostle — A229

1964, May 21 Engr. ***Perf. 13½***
725 A229 1.50s bluish black .35 .35

Romanesque art in Austria. The 12th century stained-glass window is from the Weitensfeld Church, the bust of the Apostle from the portal of St. Stephen's Cathedral, Vienna.

Pallas Athena and National Council Chamber — A230

Engr. and Litho.

1964, May 25 ***Perf. 14x13½***
726 A230 1.80s black & emer .35 .35

2nd Parliamentary and Scientific Conf., Vienna.

The Kiss, by Gustav Klimt A231

1964, June 5 Litho. ***Perf. 13½***
727 A231 3s multicolored .55 .55

Re-opening of the Vienna Secession, a museum devoted to early 20th century art (art nouveau).

Brother of Mercy and Patient — A232

1964, June 11 Engr. ***Perf. 14x13½***
728 A232 1.50s dark blue .35 .35

Brothers of Mercy in Austria, 350th anniv.

"Bringing the News of Victory at Kunersdorf" by Bernardo Bellotto — A233

"The Post in Art": 1.20s, Changing Horses at Relay Station, by Julius Hörmann. 1.50s, The Honeymoon Trip, by Moritz von Schwind. 1.80s, After the Rain, by Ignaz Raffalt. 2.20s, Mailcoach in the Mountains, by Adam Klein. 3s, Changing Horses at Bavarian Border, by Friedrich Gauermann. 4s, Postal Sleigh (Truck) in the Mountains, by Adalbert Pilch. 6.40s, Saalbach Post Office, by Adalbert Pilch.

1964, June 15 ***Perf. 13½x14***

729	A233	1s	rose claret	.25	.25
730	A233	1.20s	sepia	.25	.25
731	A233	1.50s	violet blue	.35	.35
732	A233	1.80s	brt violet	.35	.35
733	A233	2.20s	black	.40	.40
734	A233	3s	dl car rose	.55	.55
735	A233	4s	slate green	.65	.65
736	A233	6.40s	dull claret	1.40	1.40
	Nos. 729-736 (8)			4.20	4.20

15th UPU Cong., Vienna, May-June 1964.

Workers — A234

1964, Sept. 4 ***Perf. 14x13½***
737 A234 1s black .25 .25

Centenary of Austrian Labor Movement.

Common Design Types pictured following the introduction.

Europa Issue, 1964

Common Design Type

1964, Sept. 14 Litho. ***Perf. 12***

Size: 21x36mm

738 CD7 3s dark blue *1.20 .80*

Emblem of Radio Austria and Transistor Radio Panel A235

1964, Oct. 1 Photo. ***Perf. 13½***
739 A235 1s black brn & red .25 .25

Forty years of Radio Austria.

6th Congress of the Intl. Graphic Federation, Vienna, Oct. 12-17 — A236

Litho. and Engr.

1964, Oct. 12 ***Perf. 14x13½***
740 A236 1.50s Old printing press .35 .35

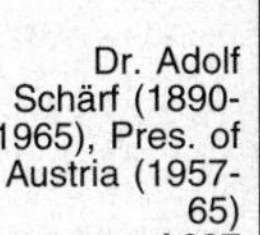

Dr. Adolf Schärf (1890-1965), Pres. of Austria (1957-65) A237

Pres. Adolf Schärf, Schärf Student Center.

Typo. and Engr.

1965, Apr. 20 ***Perf. 12***
741 A237 1.50s bluish black .35 .25

Ruins and New Buildings — A238

1965, Apr. 27 Engr. *Perf. 14x13½*

742 A238 1.80s carmine lake .35 .35

Twenty years of reconstruction.

Oldest Seal of Vienna University — A239

Photo. and Engr.

1965, May 10 *Perf. 14x13½*

743 A239 3s gold & red .55 .55

University of Vienna, 600th anniv.

St. George, 16th Century Wood Sculpture A240

1965, May 17 Engr.

744 A240 1.80s bluish black .35 .35

Art of the Danube Art School, 1490-1540, exhibition, May-Oct. 1965. The stamp background shows an engraving by Albrecht Altdorfer.

ITU Emblem, Telegraph Key and TV Antenna — A241

1965, May 17 Unwmk.

745 A241 3s violet blue .55 .55

ITU, cent.

Ferdinand Raimund — A242

Portraits: No. 746, Dr. Ignaz Philipp Semmelweis. No. 747, Bertha von Suttner. No. 749, Ferdinand Georg Waldmüller.

1965 Engr. *Perf. 14x13½*

746 A242 1.50s violet .35 .25
747 A242 1.50s bluish black .35 .35
748 A242 3s dark brown .55 .55
749 A242 3s greenish blk .55 .55
Nos. 746-749 (4) 1.80 1.70

Semmelweis (1818-65), who discovered the cause of puerperal fever and introduced antisepsis into obstetrics (No. 746). 60th anniv. of the awarding of the Nobel Prize for Peace to von Suttner (1843-1914), pacifist and author (No. 747). Raimund (1790-1836), actor and playwright (No. 748). Waldmüller (1793-1865), painter (No. 749).

Issued: No. 746, Aug. 13; No. 747, Dec. 1; No. 748, June 1; No. 749, Aug. 23.

4th Gymnaestrada, Intl. Athletic Meet, Vienna, July 20-24 — A243

1.50s, Male gymnasts with practice bars. 3s, Dancers with tambourines.

1965, July 20 Photo. and Engr.

750 A243 1.50s gray & black .35 .35
751 A243 3s bister & blk .55 .55

Red Cross and Strip of Gauze — A244

1965, Oct. 1 Litho. *Perf. 14x13½*

752 A244 3s black & red .55 .40

20th Intl. Red Cross Conference, Vienna.

Austrian Flag and Eagle with Mural Crown — A245

1965, Oct. 7 Photo. and Engr.

753 A245 1.50s gold, red & blk .35 .35

50th anniv. of the Union of Austrian Towns.

Austrian Flag, UN Headquarters and Emblem A246

Lithographed and Engraved

1965, Oct. 25 Unwmk. *Perf. 12*

754 A246 3s blk, brt bl & red .55 .40

Austria's admission to the UN, 10th anniv.

University of Technology, Vienna A247

1965, Nov. 8 Engr. *Perf. 13½x14*

755 A247 1.50s violet .35 .35

Vienna University of Technology, 150th anniv.

Map of Austria with Postal Zone Numbers — A248

1966, Jan. 14 Photo. *Perf. 12*

756 A248 1.50s yel, red & blk .35 .35

Introduction of postal zone numbers, 1/1/66.

PTT Building, Emblem and Churches of Sts. Maria Rotunda and Barbara — A249

Lithographed and Engraved

1966, Mar. 4 *Perf. 14x13½*

757 A249 1.50s blk, *dull yellow* .35 .35

Headquarters of the Post and Telegraph Administration, cent.

Maria von Ebner Eschenbach (1830-1916), Novelist, Poet — A250

1966, Mar. 11 Engr.

758 A250 3s plum .55 .40

Ferris Wheel, Prater — A251

1966, Apr. 19 Engr. *Perf. 14x13½*

759 A251 1.50s slate green .35 .35

Opening of the Prater (park), Vienna, to the public by Emperor Joseph II, 200th anniv.

Josef Hoffmann (1870-1956), Architect A252

1966, May 6 Unwmk. *Perf. 12*

760 A252 3s dark brown .55 .40

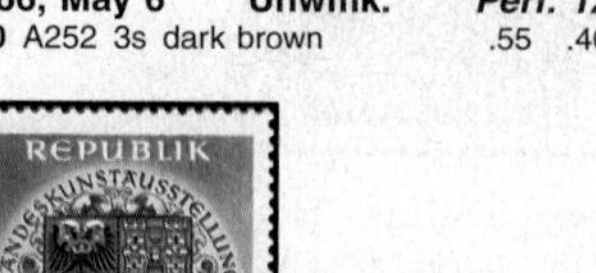

Wiener Neustadt Arms — A253

Photo. and Engr.

1966, May 27 *Perf. 14*

761 A253 1.50s multicolored .35 .35

Wiener Neustadt Art Exhib., centered around the time and person of Frederick III (1440-93).

Austrian Eagle and Emblem of National Bank A254

1966, May 27 *Perf. 14*

762 A254 3s gray grn, dk brn & dk green .55 .55

Austrian National Bank, 150th anniv.

Puppy — A255

Litho. and Engr.

1966, June 16 *Perf. 12*

763 A255 1.80s yellow & black .35 .35

120th anniv. of the Vienna Humane Society.

Alpine Flowers — A256

1.50s, Columbine. 1.80s, Turk's cap. 2.20s, Wulfenia carinthiaca. 3s, Globeflowers. 4s, Fire lily. 5s, Pasqueflower.

1966, Aug. 17 Litho. *Perf. 13½*

Flowers in Natural Colors

764 A256 1.50s dark blue .35 .35
765 A256 1.80s dark blue .35 .35
766 A256 2.20s dark blue .40 .40
767 A256 3s dark blue .55 .50
768 A256 4s dark blue .55 .50
769 A256 5s dark blue 1.00 1.00
Nos. 764-769 (6) 3.20 3.10

Fair Building A257

1966, Aug. 26 Engr. *Perf. 13½x13*

770 A257 3s violet blue .55 .40

First International Fair at Wels.

Peter Anich (1723-1766), Tirolean Cartographer and Books — A258

1966, Sept. 1 *Perf. 14x13½*

771 A258 1.80s black .35 .35

Sick Worker and Health Emblem — A259

1966, Sept. 19 Engr. and Litho.

772 A259 3s black & vermilion .55 .40

15th Occupational Medicine Congress, Vienna, Sept. 19-24.

Theater Collection: "Eunuchus" by Terence from a 1496 Edition A260

Designs: 1.80s, Map Collection: Title page of Geographia Blavania (Cronus, Hercules and celestial sphere). 2.20s, Picture Archive and Portrait Collection: View of Old Vienna after a watercolor by Anton Stutzinger. 3s, Manuscript Collection: Illustration from the 15th century "Livre du Cuer d'Amours Espris" of the Duke René d'Anjou.

Photogravure and Engraved

1966, Sept. 28 ***Perf. 13½x14***

773 A260 1.50s multicolored .35 .40
774 A260 1.80s multicolored .35 .40
775 A260 2.20s multicolored .35 .40
776 A260 3s multicolored .55 .80
Nos. 773-776 (4) 1.60 2.00

Austrian National Library.

Young Girl A261

Strawberries A262

Litho. and Engr.

1966, Oct. 3 ***Perf. 14x13½***

777 A261 3s light blue & black .55 .40

"Save the Child" society, 10th anniv.

1966, Nov. 25 Photo. ***Perf. 13½x13***

778 A262 50g shown .25 .25
779 A262 1s Grapes .25 .25
780 A262 1.50s Apple .35 .25
781 A262 1.80s Blackberries .40 .40
782 A262 2.20s Apricots .50 .50
783 A262 3s Cherries .55 .55
Nos. 778-783 (6) 2.30 2.20

Coat of Arms of University of Linz — A263

Photo. and Engr.

1966, Dec. 9 ***Perf. 14x13½***

784 A263 3s multi .55 .40

Inauguration of the Universary of Linz, Oct. 8, 1966.

Vienna Ice Skating Club, Cent. — A264

Photo. and Engr.

1967, Feb. 3 ***Perf. 14x13½***

785 A264 3s Skater, 1866 .55 .40

Ballet Dancer — A265

1967, Feb. 15 Engr. ***Perf. 11½x12***

786 A265 3s deep claret .75 .75
a. Perf. 12 2.40 2.40

"Blue Danube" waltz by Johann Strauss, cent.

Dr. Karl Schönherr (1867-1943), Poet, Playwright and Physician — A266

1967, Feb. 24 Engr. ***Perf. 14x13½***

787 A266 3s gray brown .55 .40

Ice Hockey Goalkeeper A267

Photogravure and Engraved

1967, Mar. 17 ***Perf. 13½x14***

788 A267 3s pale grn & dk bl .55 .65

Ice Hockey Championships, Vienna, Mar. 18-29.

Violin, Organ and Laurel — A268

1967, Mar. 28 Engr. ***Perf. 13½***

789 A268 3.50s indigo .55 .40

Vienna Philharmonic Orchestra, 125th anniv.

Motherhood, Watercolor by Peter Fendi — A269

1967, Apr. 28 Litho. ***Perf. 14***

790 A269 2s multicolored .40 .40

Mother's Day.

Gothic Mantle Madonna A270

1967, May 19 Engr. ***Perf. 13½x14***

791 A270 3s slate .55 .40

"Austrian Gothic," art exhibition, Krems, 1967. The Gothic wood carving is from Frauenstein in Upper Austria.

Medieval Gold Cross A271

Swan, Tapestry by Oscar Kokoschka A272

Litho. and Engr.

1967, June 9 ***Perf. 13½***

792 A271 3.50s Prus grn & multi .55 .40

Salzburg Treasure Chamber; exhibition at Salzburg Cathedral, June 12-Sept. 15.

1967, June 9 Photo.

793 A272 2s multicolored .40 .40

Nibelungen District Art Exhibition, Pöchlarn, celebrating the 700th anniversary of Pöchlarn as a city. The design is from the border of the Amor and Psyche tapestry at the Salzburg Festival Theater.

View and Arms of Vienna A273

Engraved and Photogravure

1967, June 12 ***Perf. 14x13½***

794 A273 3s black & red .55 .40

10th Europa Talks, "Science and Society in Europe," Vienna, June 13-17.

Prize Bull "Mucki" A274

1967, Aug. 28 Engr. ***Perf. 13½***

795 A274 2s deep claret .35 .35

Centenary of the Ried Festival and the Agricultural Fair.

Potato Beetle A275

Engraved and Photogravure

1967, Aug. 29 ***Perf. 13½x14***

796 A275 3s black & multi .55 .40

6th Intl. Congress for Plant Protection, Vienna.

First Locomotive Used on Brenner Pass A276

1967, Sept. 23 Photo. ***Perf. 12***

797 A276 3.50s tan & slate grn .55 .40

Centenary of railroad over Brenner Pass.

Christ in Glory — A277

1967, Oct. 9 ***Perf. 13½***

798 A277 2s multicolored .35 .35

Restoration of the Romanesque (11th century) frescoes in the Lambach monastery church.

Main Gate to Fair, Prater, Vienna A278

1967, Oct. 24 Photo. ***Perf. 13½x14***

799 A278 2s choc & buff .25 .35

Congress of Intl. Trade Fairs, Vienna, Oct., 1967.

Medal Showing Minerva and Art Symbols — A279

Litho. & Engr.

1967, Oct. 25 ***Perf. 13½***
800 A279 2s dk brn, dk bl & yel .25 .35

Vienna Academy of Fine Arts, 275th anniv. The medal was designed by Georg Raphael Donner (1693-1741) and is awarded as an artist's prize.

Frankfurt Medal for Reformation, 1717 — A280

1967, Oct. 31 **Engr.** ***Perf. 14x13½***
801 A280 3.50s blue black .55 .35

450th anniversary of the Reformation.

Mountain Range and Stone Pines A281

1967, Nov. 7 ***Perf. 13½***
802 A281 3.50s green .55 .40

Centenary of academic study of forestry.

Land Survey Monument, 1770 — A282

1967, Nov. 7 **Photo.**
803 A282 2s olive black .25 .35

150th anniversary of official land records.

St. Leopold, Window, Heiligenkreuz Abbey — A283

1967, Nov. 15 **Engr. & Photo.**
804 A283 1.80s multicolored .25 .35

Margrave Leopold III (1075-1136), patron saint of Austria.

Tragic Mask and Violin — A284

1967, Nov. 17 ***Perf. 13½***
805 A284 3.50s bluish lil & blk .55 .55

Academy of Music and Dramatic Art, 150th anniv.

Nativity from 15th Century Altar — A285

1967, Nov. 27 **Engr.** ***Perf. 14x13½***
806 A285 2s green .35 .35

Christmas.
The design shows the late Gothic carved center panel of the altar in St. John's Chapel in Nonnberg Convent, Salzburg.

Innsbruck Stadium, Alps and FISU Emblem — A286

1968, Jan. 22 **Engr.** ***Perf. 13½***
807 A286 2s dark blue .40 .35

Winter University Games under the auspices of FISU (Fédération Internationale du Sport Universitaire), Innsbruck, Jan. 21-28.

Camillo Sitte (1843-1903), Architect, City Planner — A287

1968, Apr. 17 ***Perf. 13½***
808 A287 2s black brown .25 .35

Mother and Child — A288

1968, May 7
809 A288 2s slate green .25 .35

Mother's Day.

Cup and Serpent Emblem — A289

1968, May 7 **Photo.**
810 A289 3.50s dp plum, gray & gold .55 .35

Bicentenary of the Veterinary College.

Bride with Lace Veil — A290

1968, May 24 **Engr.** ***Perf. 12***
811 A290 3.50s blue black .55 .35

Embroidery industry of Vorarlberg, cent.

Horse Race A291

1968, June 4 ***Perf. 13½***
812 A291 3.50s sepia .55 .40

Centenary of horse racing at Freudenau, Vienna.

Dr. Karl Landsteiner A292

1968, June 14 ***Perf. 14x13½***
813 A292 3.50s dark blue .55 .35

Birth cent. of Dr. Karl Landsteiner (1868-1943), pathologist, discoverer of the four main human blood types.

Peter Rosegger (1843-1918), Poet and Writer — A293

1968, June 26
814 A293 2s slate green .25 .35

Angelica Kauffmann, Self-portrait A294

1968, July 15 **Engr.** ***Perf. 14x13½***
815 A294 2s intense black .35 .35

"Angelica Kauffmann and her Contemporaries," art exhibitions, Bregenz, July 28-Oct. 13, and Vienna, Oct. 22, 1968-Jan. 6, 1969.

Bronze Statue of Young Man, 1st Century B.C. — A295

1968, July 15 **Litho. & Engr.**
816 A295 2s grnsh gray & blk .25 .35

20 years of excavations on Magdalene Mountain, Carinthia.

Bishop, Romanesque Bas-relief — A296

1968, Sept. 20 **Engr.** ***Perf. 14x13½***
817 A296 2s blue gray .35 .35

Graz-Seckau Bishopric, 750th anniv.

Koloman Moser (1868-1918), Stamp Designer, Painter — A297

Engr. & Photo.

1968, Oct. 18 ***Perf. 12***
818 A297 2s black brn & ver .35 .35

Intl. Human Rights Year — A298

1968, Oct. 18 **Photo.** ***Perf. 14x13½***
819 A298 1.50s gray, dp car & dk green .55 .35

Republic of Austria, 50th Anniv. — A299

Designs: No. 820, Pres. Karl Renner and States' arms. No. 821, Coats of arms of Austria and Austrian states. No. 822, Article I of Austrian Constitution and States' coats of arms.

Engr. & Photo.

1968, Nov. 11 ***Perf. 13½***
820 A299 2s black & multi .40 .45
821 A299 2s black & multi .40 .45
822 A299 2s black & multi .40 .45
Nos. 820-822 (3) 1.20 1.35

Hymn "Silent Night, Holy Night," 150th Anniv. — A300

Crèche, Memorial Chapel, Oberndorf-Salzburg.

1968, Nov. 29 **Engr.** ***Perf. 14x13½***
823 A300 2s slate green .35 .35

Christmas.

Angels, from Last Judgment by Troger (Röhrenbach-Greillenstein Chapel) — A301

Baroque Frescoes: No. 825, Vanquished Demons, by Paul Troger, Altenburg Abbey. No. 826, Sts. Peter and Paul, by Troger, Melk Abbey. No. 827, The Glorification of Mary, by Franz Anton Maulbertsch, Maria Treu Church, Vienna. No. 828, St. Leopold Carried into Heaven, by Maulbertsch, Ebenfurth Castle Chapel. No. 829, Symbolic figures from The Triumph of Apollo, by Maulbertsch, Halbthurn Castle.

Engr. & Photo.

1968, Dec. 11 *Perf. 13½x14*

824 A301 2s multicolored .40 .40
825 A301 2s multicolored .40 .40
826 A301 2s multicolored .40 .40
827 A301 2s multicolored .40 .40
828 A301 2s multicolored .40 .40
829 A301 2s multicolored .40 .40
Nos. 824-829 (6) 2.40 2.40

St. Stephen — A302

Statues in St. Stephen's Cathedral, Vienna: No. 831, St. Paul. No. 832, Mantle Madonna. No. 833, St. Christopher. No. 834, St. George and the Dragon. No. 835, St. Sebastian.

1969, Jan. 28 Engr. *Perf. 13½*

830 A302 2s black .40 .40
831 A302 2s rose claret .40 .40
832 A302 2s gray violet .40 .40
833 A302 2s slate blue .40 .40
834 A302 2s slate green .40 .40
835 A302 2s dk red brn .40 .40
Nos. 830-835 (6) 2.40 2.40

500th anniversary of Diocese of Vienna.

Parliament and Pallas Athena Fountain, Vienna A303

1969, Apr. 8 Engr. *Perf. 13½*

836 A303 2s greenish black .25 .30

Interparliamentary Union Conf., Vienna, 4/7-13.

Europa Issue, 1969

Common Design Type

1969, Apr. 28 Photo. *Perf. 12*

837 CD12 2s gray grn, brick red & blue *.65* .30

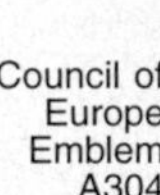

Council of Europe Emblem A304

1969, May 5

838 A304 3.50s gray, ultra, blk & yel .55 .30

20th anniversary of Council of Europe.

Frontier Guards — A305

Engr. & Photo.

1969, May 14 *Perf. 12*

839 A305 2s sepia & red .35 .35

Austrian Federal Army.

Don Giovanni, by Mozart A306

Cent. of Vienna Opera House: a, Don Giovanni, Mozart. b, Magic Flute, Mozart. c, Fidelio, Beethoven. d, Lohengrin, Wagner. e, Don Carlos, Verdi. f, Carmen, Bizet. g, Rosencavalier, Richard Strauss. h, Swan Lake, Ballet by Tchaikovsky.

1969, May 23 *Perf. 13½*

840 A306 Sheet of 8 4.75 4.75
a.-h. 2s, any single .50 .50

Centenary of Vienna Opera House.

No. 840 contains 8 stamps arranged around gold and red center label showing Opera House. Printed in sheets containing 4 Nos. 840 with wide gutters between.

Emperor Maximilian I Exhibition, Innsbruck, May 30-Oct. 5 — A307

Gothic armor of Maximilian I.

1969, June 4 **Engr.**

841 A307 2s bluish black .35 .35

19th Cong. of the Intl. Org. of Municipalities, Vienna — A308

Oldest Municipal Seal of Vienna.

1969, June 16 Photo. *Perf. 13½*

842 A308 2s tan, red & black .25 .35

SOS Children's Villages in Austria, 20th Anniv. — A309

Girl's head and village house.

Engraved and Photogravure

1969, June 16 *Perf. 13½x14*

843 A309 2s yel grn & sepia .25 .35

ILO, 50th Anniv. — A310

Hands holding wrench, and UN emblem.

1969, Aug. 22 Photo. *Perf. 13x13½*

844 A310 2s deep green .25 .35

Year of Austrians Living Abroad, 1969 — A311

Austria's flag and shield circling the world.

Engraved and Lithographed

1969, Aug. 22 *Perf. 14x13½*

845 A311 3.50s slate & red .55 .35

Etching Collection in the Albertina, Vienna, Bicent. — A312

Etchings: No. 846, Young Hare, by Dürer. No. 847, El Cid Killing a Bull, by Francisco de Goya. No. 848, Madonna with the Pomegranate, by Raphael. No. 849, The Painter, by Peter Brueghel. No. 850, Rubens' Son Nicolas, by Rubens. No. 851, Self-portrait, by Rembrandt. No. 852, Lady Reading, by Francois Guerin. No. 853, Wife of the Artist, by Egon Schiele.

Engraved and Photogravure

1969, Sept. 26 *Perf. 13½*

Gray Frame, Buff Background

846 A312 2s black & brown .40 .45
847 A312 2s black .40 .45
848 A312 2s black .40 .45
849 A312 2s black .40 .45
850 A312 2s black & salmon .40 .45
851 A312 2s black .40 .45
852 A312 2s black & salmon .40 .45
853 A312 2s black .40 .45
Nos. 846-853 (8) 3.20 3.60

President Franz Jonas — A313

1969, Oct. 3

854 A313 2s gray & vio blue .25 .35

70th birthday of Franz Jonas, Austrian Pres.

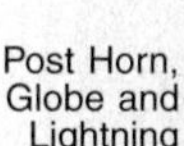

Post Horn, Globe and Lightning A314

1969, Oct. 17 *Perf. 13½x14*

855 A314 2s multicolored .25 .35

Union of Postal and Telegraph employees, 50th anniv.

Savings Box, about 1450 — A315

1969, Oct. 31 Photo. *Perf. 13x13½*

856 A315 2s silver & slate green .25 .35

The importance of savings.

Madonna, by Albin Egger-Lienz A316

Engr. & Photo.

1969, Nov. 24 *Perf. 12*

857 A316 2s dp claret & pale yel .25 .35

Christmas.

Josef Schöffel — A317

1970, Feb. 6 Engr. *Perf. 14x13½*

858 A317 2s dull purple .25 .25

60th death anniv. of Josef Schöffel, (1832-1910), who saved the Vienna Woods.

St. Klemens M. Hofbauer — A318

Engraved and Photogravure

1970, Mar. 13 *Perf. 14x13½*

859 A318 2s dk brn & lt tan .25 .25

150th death anniv. St. Klemens Maria Hofbauer (1751-1820); Redemptorist preacher in Poland and Austria, canonized in 1909.

Chancellor Leopold Figl — A319

Belvedere Palace, Vienna — A320

1970, Apr. 27 Engr. ***Perf. 13½***
860 A319 2s dark olive gray .35 .25
861 A320 2s dark rose brown .35 .25

25th anniversary of Second Republic.

European Nature Conservation Year, 1970 — A321

1970, May 19 Engr. ***Perf. 13½***
862 A321 2s Krimml waterfalls .40 .25

Leopold Franzens University, Innsbruck, 300th Anniv. — A322

St. Leopold on oldest seal of Innsbruck University.

Litho. & Engr.
1970, June 5 ***Perf. 13½***
863 A322 2s red & black .25 .25

Organ, Great Hall, Music Academy — A323

Photo. & Engr.
1970, June 5 ***Perf. 14***
864 A323 2s gold & deep claret .25 .25

Vienna Music Academy Building, cent.

Tower Clock, 1450-1550 A324

Old Clocks from Vienna Horological Museum: No. 866, Lyre clock, 1790-1815. No. 867, Pendant clock 1600-50. No. 868, Pendant watch, 1800-30. No. 869, Bracket clock, 1720-60. No. 870, French column clock, 1820-50.

1970
865 A324 1.50s buff & sepia .35 .35
866 A324 1.50s greenish & grn .25 .35
867 A324 2s pale bl & dk bl .40 .40
868 A324 2s pale rose & lake .35 .45
869 A324 3.50s buff & brown .70 .70
870 A324 3.50s pale lil & brn vio .55 .80
Nos. 865-870 (6) 2.60 3.05

Issued: Nos. 865, 867, 869, 6/22; others, 10/23.

The Beggar Student, by Carl Millöcker — A325

Operettas: No. 872, Fledermaus, by Johann Strauss. No. 873, The Dream Waltz, by Oscar Straus. No. 874, The Bird Seller, by Carl Zeller. No. 875, The Merry Widow, by Franz Lehar. No. 876, Two Hearts in Three-quarter Time, by Robert Stolz.

1970 Photo & Engr. ***Perf. 13½***
871 A325 1.50s pale grn & grn .35 .35
872 A325 1.50s yel & vio blue .25 .25
873 A325 2s pale rose & vio brn .40 .40
874 A325 2s pale grn & sep .35 .35
875 A325 3.50s pale bl & ind .70 .70
876 A325 3.50s beige & slate .55 .45
Nos. 871-876 (6) 2.60 2.50

Issued: Nos. 871, 873, 875, 7/3; others 9/11.

Bregenz Festival Stage — A326

1970, July 23 **Photo.**
877 A326 3.50s dark blue & buff .55 .40

25th anniversary of Bregenz Festival.

Salzburg Festival Emblem — A327

1970, July 27 ***Perf. 14***
878 A327 3.50s blk, red, gold & gray .55 .40

50th anniversary of Salzburg Festival.

A328

1970, Aug. 31 **Engr.**
879 A328 3.50s dark gray .55 .35

13th General Assembly of the World Veterans Federation, Aug. 28-Sept. 4. The head of St. John is from a sculpture showing the Agony in the Garden in the chapel of the Parish Church in Ried. It is attributed to Thomas Schwanthaler (1634-1702).

Thomas Koschat (1845-1914), Carinthian Song Composer A329

1970, Sept. 16 ***Perf. 14x13½***
880 A329 2s chocolate .25 .25

Mountain Scene A330

1970, Sept. 16 Photo. ***Perf. 14x13½***
881 A330 2s vio bl & pink .25 .25

Hiking and mountaineering in Austria.

Alfred Cossmann (1870-1951), Engraver — A331

1970, Oct. 2 Engr. ***Perf. 14x13½***
882 A331 2s dark brown .25 .25

Arms of Carinthia — A332

Photo. & Engr.
1970, Oct. 2 ***Perf. 14***
883 A332 2s ol, red, gold, blk & sil .25 .25

Carinthian plebiscite, 50th anniversary.

UN Emblem A333

1970, Oct. 23 Litho. ***Perf. 14x13½***
884 A333 3.50s lt blue & blk .55 .35

25th anniversary of the United Nations.

Adoration of the Shepherds, Carving from Garsten Vicarage A334

1970, Nov. 27 Engr. ***Perf. 13½x14***
885 A334 2s dk violet blue .25 .25

Christmas.

Karl Renner (1870-1950), Austrian Pres. — A335

1970, Dec. 14 Engr. ***Perf. 14x13½***
886 A335 2s deep claret .25 .25

Beethoven, by Georg Waldmüller A336

Photo. & Engr.
1970, Dec. 16 ***Perf. 13½***
887 A336 3.50s black & buff .55 .40

Ludwig van Beethoven (1770-1827), composer, birth bicentenary.

Enrica Handel-Mazzetti (1871-1955), Novelist, Poet — A337

1971, Jan. 11 Engr. ***Perf. 14x13½***
888 A337 2s sepia .25 .25

"Watch Out for Children!" A338

1971, Feb. 18 Photo. ***Perf. 13½***
889 A338 2s blk, red brn & brt grn .35 .25

Traffic safety.

Saltcellar, by Benvenuto Cellini A339

Art Treasures: 1.50s, Covered vessel, made of prase, gold and precious stones, Florentine, 1580. 2s, Emperor Joseph I, ivory statue by Matthias Steinle, 1693.

Photo. & Engr.
1971, Mar. 22 ***Perf. 14***
890 A339 1.50s gray & slate grn .40 .40
891 A339 2s gray & dp plum .50 .50
892 A339 3.50s gray, blk & bister .70 .70
Nos. 890-892 (3) 1.60 1.60

Emblem of Austrian Wholesalers' Organization A340

1971, Apr. 16 Photo. *Perf. 13½*

893 A340 3.50s multicolored .55 .35

Intl. Chamber of Commerce, 23rd Congress, Vienna, Apr. 17-23.

Jacopo de Strada, by Titian — A341

Paintings in Vienna Museum: 2s, Village Feast, by Peter Brueghel, the Elder. 3.50s, Young Venetian Woman, by Albrecht Dürer.

1971, May 6 Engr. *Perf. 13½*

894 A341 1.50s rose lake .25 .40
895 A341 2s greenish black .35 .45
896 A341 3.50s deep brown .55 .70
Nos. 894-896 (3) 1.15 1.55

Seal of Paulus of Franchenfordia, 1380 — A342

Photo. & Engr.

1971, May 6 *Perf. 13½x14*

897 A342 3.50s dk brn & bister .55 .35

Congress commemorating the centenary of the Austrian Notaries' Statute, May 5-8.

St. Matthew — A343

August Neilreich — A344

1971, May 27 *Perf. 12½x13½*

898 A343 2s brt rose lil & brn .25 .25

Exhibition of "1000 Years of Art in Krems." The statue of St. Matthew is from the Lentl Altar, created about 1520 by the Master of the Pulkau Altar.

1971, June 1 Engr. *Perf. 14x13½*

899 A344 2s brown .25 .25

August Neilreich (1803-71), botanist.

Singer with Lyre — A345

Photo. & Engr.

1971, July 1 *Perf. 13½x14*

900 A345 4s lt bl, vio bl & gold .55 .50

Intl. Choir Festival, Vienna, July 1-4.

Coat of Arms of Kitzbuhel — A346

1971, Aug. 23 *Perf. 14*

901 A346 2.50s gold & multi .35 .25

700th anniversary of the town of Kitzbuhel.

Vienna Stock Exchange — A347

1971, Sept. 1 Engr. *Perf. 13½x14*

902 A347 4s reddish brown .55 .35

Bicentenary of the Vienna Stock Exchange.

First and Latest Exhibition Halls A348

1971, Sept. 6 Photo. *Perf. 13½x13*

903 A348 2.50s dp rose lilac .35 .25

Vienna Intl. Fair, 50th anniv.

Trade Union Emblem — A349

1971, Sept. 20 *Perf. 14x13½*

904 A349 2s gray, buff & red .25 .25

Austrian Trade Union Assoc., 25th anniv.

Arms of Burgenland A350

1971, Oct. 1

905 A350 2s dk bl, gold, red & blk .25 .25

50th anniv. of Burgenland joining Austria.

Marcus Car — A351

Photo. & Engr.

1971, Oct. 1 *Perf. 14*

906 A351 4s pale green & blk .55 .40

Austrian Automobile, Motorcycle and Touring Club, 75th anniv.

Europa Bridge — A352

1971, Oct. 8 Engr. *Perf. 14x13½*

907 A352 4s violet blue .55 .40

Opening of highway over Brenner Pass.

Styria's Iron Mountain A353

Designs: 2s, Austrian Nitrogen Products, Ltd., Linz. 4s, United Austrian Iron and Steel Works, Ltd. (VÖEST), Linz Harbor.

1971, Oct. 15 *Perf. 13½*

908 A353 1.50s reddish brown .35 .40
909 A353 2s bluish black .35 .40
910 A353 4s dk slate grn .65 .80
Nos. 908-910 (3) 1.35 1.60

25 years of nationalized industry.

High-speed Train on Semmering A354

1971, Oct. 21 *Perf. 14*

911 A354 2s claret .35 .25

Inter-city rapid train service.

Trout Fisherman A355

1971, Nov. 15 *Perf. 13½*

912 A355 2s dark red brn .25 .25

Dr. Erich Tschermak-Seysenegg (1871-1962), Botanist — A356

Photo. & Engr.

1971, Nov. 15 *Perf. 14x13½*

913 A356 2s pale ol & dk pur .25 .25

Infant Jesus as Savior, by Dürer — A357

1971, Nov. 26 *Perf. 13½*

914 A357 2s gold & multi .25 .25

Christmas.

Franz Grillparzer, by Moritz Daffinger — A358

Litho. & Engr.

1972, Jan. 21 *Perf. 14x13½*

915 A358 2s buff, gold & blk .35 .25

Death cent. of Franz Grillparzer (1791-1872), dramatic poet.

Fountain, Main Square, Friesach — A359

Designs: 2s, Fountain, Heiligenkreuz Abbey. 2.50s, Leopold Fountain, Innsbruck.

1972, Feb. 23 Engr. *Perf. 14x13½*

916 A359 1.50s rose lilac .35 .25
917 A359 2s brown .35 .25
918 A359 2.50s olive .45 .65
Nos. 916-918 (3) 1.15 1.15

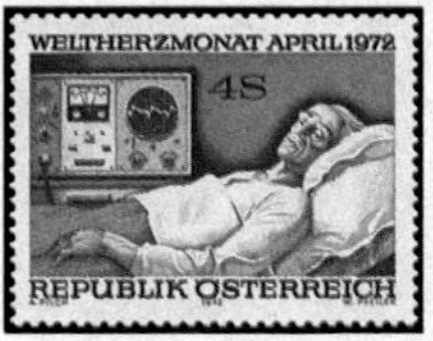

Cardiac Patient and Monitor A360

1972, Apr. 11 *Perf. 13½x14*

919 A360 4s violet brown .65 .40

World Health Day.

Conference of European Post and Telecommunications Ministers, Vienna, Apr. 11-14 — A361

St. Michael's Gate, Royal Palace, Vienna.

1972, Apr. 11 *Perf. 14x13½*

920 A361 4s violet blue .65 .40

Gurk (Carinthia) Diocese, 900th Anniv. — A362

Photo. & Engr.

1972, May 5 ***Perf. 14***

921 A362 2s Sculpture, Gurk Cathedral .35 .25

The design is after the central column supporting the sarcophagus of St. Hemma in Gurk Cathedral.

City Hall, Congress Emblem A363

1972, May 23 **Litho. & Engr.**

922 A363 4s red, blk & yel .65 .40

9th Intl. Congress of Public and Cooperative Economy, Vienna, May 23-25.

Power Line in Carnic Alps — A364

2.50s, Power Station, Semmering. 4s, Zemm Power Station (lake in Zillertaler Alps).

1972, June 28 ***Perf. 13½x14***

923 A364 70g gray & violet .25 .35
924 A364 2.50s gray & red brn .40 .45
925 A364 4s gray & slate .65 .80
Nos. 923-925 (3) 1.30 1.60

Nationalization of the power industry, 25th anniv.

Runner with Olympic Torch — A365

Engr. & Photo.

1972, Aug. 21 ***Perf. 14x13½***

926 A365 2s sepia & red .35 .25

Olympic torch relay from Olympia, Greece, to Munich, Germany, passing through Austria.

St. Hermes, by Conrad Laib — A366

1972, Aug. 21 **Engr.**

927 A366 2s violet brown .35 .25

Exhibition of Late Gothic Art, Salzburg.

Pears A367

1972, Sept. ***Perf. 14***

928 A367 2.50s dk blue & multi .40 .25

World Congress of small plot Gardeners, Vienna, Sept. 7-10.

Souvenir Sheet

Spanish Riding School, Vienna, 400th Anniv. — A368

1972, Sept. 12 ***Perf. 13½***

929 Sheet of 6 2.75 4.00
a. A368 2s Spanish walk .35 .25
b. A368 2s Piaffe .35 .25
c. A368 2.50s Levade .40 .25
d. A368 2.50s On long rein .40 .25
e. A368 4s Capriole .65 .55
f. A368 4s Courbette .65 .55

Arms of University of Agriculture A369

Photo. & Engr.

1972, Oct. 17 ***Perf. 14x13½***

930 A369 2s black & multi .35 .25

University of Agriculture, Vienna, cent.

Church and Old University — A370

1972, Nov. 7 **Engr.**

931 A370 4s red brown .65 .40

Paris Lodron University, Salzburg, 350th anniv.

Carl Michael Ziehrer — A371

1972, Nov. 14

932 A371 2s rose claret .35 .25

50th death anniv. of Carl Michael Ziehrer (1843-1922), composer.

Virgin and Child, Wood, 1420-30 A372

Photo. & Engr.

1972, Dec. 1 ***Perf. 13½***

933 A372 2s olive & chocolate .35 .25

Christmas.

Racing Sleigh, 1750 A373

Designs: 2s, Coronation landau, 1824. 2.50s, Imperial state coach, 1763.

1972, Dec. 12

934 A373 1.50s pale gray & brn .25 .25
935 A373 2s pale gray & sl grn .40 .45
936 A373 2.50s pale gray & plum .50 .65
Nos. 934-936 (3) 1.15 1.35

Collection of historic state coaches and carriages in Schönbrunn Palace.

Map of Austrian Telephone System A374

1972, Dec. 14 **Photo.** ***Perf. 14***

937 A374 2s yellow & blk .35 .25

Completion of automation of Austrian telephone system.

"Drugs are Death" A375

1973, Jan. 26 **Photo.** ***Perf. 13½x14***

938 A375 2s scarlet & multi .35 .25

Fight against drug abuse.

Alfons Petzold (1882-1923), Poet — A376

1973, Jan. 26 **Engr.** ***Perf. 14x13½***

939 A376 2s reddish brn .35 .25

Theodor Körner (1873-1957), Austrian Pres. — A377

Photo. & Engr.

1973, Apr. 24 ***Perf. 14x13½***

940 A377 2s gray & deep claret .35 .25

Douglas DC-9 A378

1973, May 14 ***Perf. 13½x14***

941 A378 2s vio bl & rose red .35 .25

First intl. airmail service, Vienna to Kiev, Mar. 31, 1918, 55th anniv.; Austrian Aviation Corporation, 50th anniv.; Austrian Airlines, 15th anniv.

Otto Loewi (1873-1961), Pharmacologist, Nobel Laureate — A379

1973, June 4 **Engr.** ***Perf. 14x13½***

942 A379 4s deep violet .65 .40

"Support" — A380

1973, June 25

943 A380 2s dark blue .35 .25

Federation of Austrian Social Insurance Institutes, 25th anniv.

Europa Issue 1973

Post Horn and Telephone A381

1973, July 9 **Photo.** ***Perf. 14***

944 A381 2.50s ocher, blk & yel *.80* .40

Dornbirn Fair Emblem A382

1973, July 27 ***Perf. 13½x14***
945 A382 2s multicolored .35 .25

Dornbirn Trade Fair, 25th anniversary.

23rd Intl. Military Pentathlon Championships, Wiener Neustadt, Aug. 13-18 — A383

1973, Aug. 13 **Engr.** ***Perf. 14x13½***
946 A383 4s Hurdles .65 .40

Leo Slezak (1873-1946), Operatic Tenor — A384

1973, Aug. 17 ***Perf. 14***
947 A384 4s dark brown .65 .40

Gate, Vienna Hofburg, and ISI Emblem — A385

Photogravure and Engraved

1973, Aug. 20 ***Perf. 14x13½***
948 A385 2s gray, dk brn & ver .35 .25

39th Congress of Intl. Statistical Institute, Vienna, Aug. 20-30.

Tegetthoff off Franz Josef Land, by Julius Payer A386

1973, Aug. 30 **Engr.** ***Perf. 13½x14***
949 A386 2.50s Prussian grn .40 .25

Discovery of Franz Josef Land by an Austrian North Pole expedition, cent.

Academy of Science, by Canaletto A387

1973, Sept. 4
950 A387 2.50s violet .40 .25

World Meteorological Organization, cent.

Arms of Viennese Tanners — A388

Photo. & Engr.

1973, Sept. 4 ***Perf. 14***
951 A388 4s red & multi .65 .40

13th Congress of the Intl. Union of Leather Chemists' Societies, Vienna, Sept. 1-7.

Max Reinhardt (1873-1943), Theatrical Director — A389

1973, Sept. 7 **Engr.** ***Perf. 13x13½***
952 A389 2s rose magenta .35 .25

Trotter A390

1973, Sept. 28 ***Perf. 13½***
953 A390 2s green .35 .25

Centenary of Vienna Trotting Association.

Ferdinand Hanusch (1866-1923), Secretary of State — A391

1973, Sept. 28 ***Perf. 14x13½***
954 A391 2s rose brown .35 .25

Police Radio Operator A392

1973, Oct. 2 ***Perf. 13½x14***
955 A392 4s violet blue .65 .40

50th anniv. of Intl. Criminal Police Org. (INTERPOL).

Josef Petzval's Photographic Lens — A393

Litho. & Engr.

1973, Oct. 8 ***Perf. 14***
956 A393 2.50s blue & multi .40 .25

EUROPHOT Photographic Cong., Vienna.

Emperor's Spring, Hell Valley A394

Photo. & Engr.

1973, Oct. 23 ***Perf. 13½x14***
957 A394 2s sepia, blue & red .35 .25

Vienna's first mountain spring water supply system, cent.

Almsee, Upper Austria — A395

Hofburg and Prince Eugene Statue, Vienna — A395a

Designs: 50g, Farmhouses, Zillertal, Tirol. 1s, Kahlenbergerdorf. 1.50s, Bludenz, Vorarlberg. 2s, Inn Bridge, Alt Finstermunz. 2.50s, Murau, Styria. 3s, Bischofsmütze, Salzburg. 3.50s, Easter Church, Oberwart. 4.50s, Windmill, Retz. 5s, Aggstein Castle, Lower Austria. 6s, Lindauer Hut, Vorarlberg. 6.50s, Holy Cross Church, Villach, Carinthia. 7s, Falkenstein Castle, Carinthia. 7.50s, Hohensalzburg. 8s, Votive column, Reiteregg, Styria. 10s, Lake Neusiedl, Burgenland. 11s, Old Town, Enns. 16s, Openair Museum, Bad Tatzmannsdorf. 20s, Myra waterfalls.

Photo. & Engr.

1973-78 ***Perf. 13½x14***

Size: 23x29mm

958	A395	50g	gray & slate green	.25	.25
959	A395	1s	brn & dk brown	.30	.25
960	A395	1.50s	rose & brown	.40	.25
961	A395	2s	gray bl & dk blue	.50	.25
962	A395	2.50s	vio & dp violet	.55	.25
963	A395	3s	lt ultra & vio blue	.65	.25
963A	A395	3.50s	dl org & brown	.75	.25
964	A395	4s	brt lil & pur	.65	.25
965	A395	4.50s	brt grn & bl green	.80	.25
966	A395	5s	lilac & vio	.80	.25
967	A395	6s	dp rose & dk violet	1.40	.25
968	A395	6.50s	bl grn & indigo	1.20	.30
969	A395	7s	sage grn & sl green	1.60	.25
970	A395	7.50s	lil rose & claret	2.00	.25
971	A395	8s	dl red & dp brown	1.75	.25
972	A395	10s	gray grn & dk green	2.10	.25
973	A395	11s	ver & dk carmine	2.00	.25
974	A395	16s	bister & brown	3.25	.35
975	A395	20s	ol bis & ol grn	4.00	.40
976	A395a	50s	gray vio & vio bl	12.00	2.40
			Nos. 958-976 (20)	36.95	7.45

Issued: Nos. 960-963, 1974; Nos. 958-959, 967, 976, 1975; Nos. 965, 971, 973, 1976; Nos. 968, 970, 974-975, 1977; No. 963A, 1978. See Nos. 1100-1109.

Nativity — A396

1973, Nov. 30 ***Perf. 14***
977 A396 2s multicolored .35 .25

Christmas. Design from 14th century stained-glass window.

Pregl — A397

1973, Dec. 12 **Engr.** ***Perf. 14x13½***
978 A397 4s deep blue .65 .40

50th anniv. of the awarding of the Nobel prize for chemistry to Fritz Pregl (1869-1930).

Radio Austria, 50th Anniv. — A398

1974, Jan. 14 **Photo.** ***Perf. 14x13½***
979 A398 2.50s Telex Machine .40 .25

Hugo Hofmannsthal (1874-1929), Poet and Playwright A399

1974, Feb. 1 **Engr.** ***Perf. 14***
980 A399 4s violet blue .65 .45

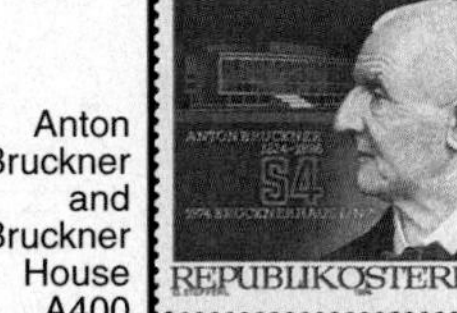

Anton Bruckner and Bruckner House A400

1974, Mar. 22 **Engr.** ***Perf. 14***
981 A400 4s brown .65 .40

Founding of Anton Bruckner House (concert hall), Linz, and birth of Anton Bruckner (1824-1896), composer, 150th anniv.

Vegetables A401

Photo. & Engr.

1974, Apr. 18 *Perf. 14*

982 A401 2s shown .35 .25
983 A401 2.50s Fruits .40 .40
984 A401 4s Flowers .80 .95
Nos. 982-984 (3) 1.55 1.60

Intl. Garden Show, Vienna, Apr. 18-Oct. 14.

Seal of Judenburg A402

1974, Apr. 24 Photo. *Perf. 14x13½*

985 A402 2s plum & multi .35 .25

750th anniversary of Judenburg.

Karl Kraus (1874-1936), Poet and Satirist — A403

1974, Apr. 6 **Engr.**

986 A403 4s dark red .65 .40

St. Michael, by Thomas Schwanthaler A404

1974, May 3

987 A404 2.50s slate green .40 .25

Exhibition of the works by the Schwanthaler Family of sculptors, (1633-1848), Reichersberg am Inn, May 3-Oct. 13.

A405

Europa: King Arthur, from tomb of Maximilian I

1974, May 8 *Perf. 13½*

988 A405 2.50s ocher & slate blue *.65 .40*

Austrian Automobile Assoc., 75th Anniv. — A406

De Dion Bouton motor tricycle.

Photo. & Engr.

1974, May 17 *Perf. 14x13½*

989 A406 2s gray & vio brn .35 .25

Satyr's Head, Terracotta A407

1974, May 22 *Perf. 13½x14*

990 A407 2s org brn, gold & blk .35 .25

Exhibition, "Renaissance in Austria," Schallaburg Castle, May 22-Nov. 14.

Road Transport Union Emblem — A408

1974, May 24 Photo. *Perf. 14x13½*

991 A408 4s deep orange & blk .65 .40

14th Congress of the Intl. Road Transport Union, Innsbruck.

Franz Anton Maulbertsch (1724-96), Painter — A409

1974, June 7 Engr. *Perf. 14x13½*

992 A409 2s Self-portrait .35 .25

Gendarmes, 1824 and 1974 A410

1974, June 7 Photo. *Perf. 13½x14*

993 A410 2s red & multi .35 .25

125th anniversary of Austrian gendarmery.

Fencing A411

Photo. & Engr.

1974, June 14 *Perf. 13½*

994 A411 2.50s red org & blk .40 .25

Transportation Symbols — A412

1974, June 18 Photo. *Perf. 14x13½*

995 A412 4s lt ultra & multi .65 .40

European Conference of Transportation Ministers, Vienna, June 18-21.

St. Virgil, Sculpture from Nonntal Church — A413

1974, June 28 Engr. *Perf. 13½x14*

996 A413 2s violet blue .35 .25

Consecration of the Cathedral of Salzburg by Scotch-Irish Bishop Feirgil (St. Virgil), 1200th anniv. Salzburg was a center of Christianization in the 8th century.

Franz Jonas and Austrian Eagle — A414

1974, June 28

997 A414 2s black .35 .25

Jonas (1899-1974), Austrian Pres., 1965-1974.

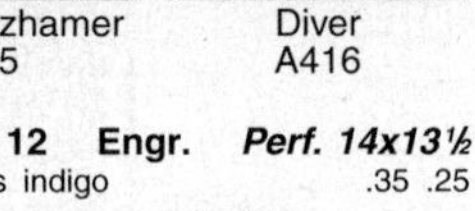

Franz Stelzhamer A415

Diver A416

1974, July 12 Engr. *Perf. 14x13½*

998 A415 2s indigo .35 .25

Franz Stelzhamer (1802-1874), poet who wrote in Upper Austrian vernacular, death cent.

Photo. & Engr.

1974, Aug. 16 *Perf. 13x13½*

999 A416 4s blue & sepia .65 .40

13th European Swimming, Diving and Water Polo Championships, Vienna, Aug. 18-25.

Ferdinand Ritter von Hebra — A417

1974, Sept. 10 Engr. *Perf. 14x13½*

1000 A417 4s brown .65 .40

30th Meeting of the Assoc. of German-speaking Dermatologists, Graz, Sept. 10-14. Dr. von Hebra (1816-1880) was a founder of modern dermatology.

Arnold Schonberg A418

1974, Sept. 13 *Perf. 13½x14*

1001 A418 2.50s purple .40 .25

Schönberg (1874-1951), composer.

Radio Station, Salzburg A419

1974, Oct. 1 Photo. *Perf. 13½x14*

1002 A419 2s multicolored .35 .25

50th anniversary of Austrian broadcasting.

Edmund Eysler (1874-1949), Composer A420

1974, Oct. 4 Engr. *Perf. 14x13½*

1003 A420 2s dark olive .25 .25

Mailman, Mail Coach and Train, UPU Emblem A421

4s, Mailman, jet, truck, 1974, & UPU emblem.

1974, Oct. 9 Photo. *Perf. 13½*

1004 A421 2s deep claret & lil .35 .25
1005 A421 4s dark blue & gray .65 .40

Centenary of Universal Postal Union.

Gauntlet Protecting Rose A422

1974, Oct. 23 Photo. *Perf. 13½x14*

1006 A422 2s multicolored .35 .25

Environment protection.

Austrian Sports Pool Emblem A423

1974, Oct. 23 Photo. *Perf. 13½x14*

1007 A423 70g multicolored .35 .25

Austrian Sports Pool (lottery), 25th anniv.

Carl Ditters von Dittersdorf (1739-1799), Composer A424

1974, Oct. 24 Engr. *Perf. 14x13½*

1008 A424 2s Prussian green .35 .25

Virgin and Child, Wood, c. 1600 — A425

1974, Nov. 29 Photo. & Engr.

1009 A425 2s brown & gold .35 .25

Christmas.

Franz Schmidt (1874-1939), Composer A426

1974, Dec. 18

1010 A426 4s gray & black .65 .40

European Architectural Heritage Year — A427

Photo. & Engr.

1975, Jan. 24 ***Perf. 13½***

1011 A427 2.50s St. Christopher .40 .25

The design shows part of a wooden figure from central panel of the retable in the Kefermarkt Church, 1490-1497.

Safety Belt and Skeleton Arms — A428

1975, Apr. 1 Photo. ***Perf. 14x13½***

1012 A428 70g violet & multi .25 .25

Introduction of obligatory use of automobile safety belts.

Stained Glass Window, Vienna City Hall — A429

1975, Apr. 2 ***Perf. 14***

1013 A429 2.50s multicolored .40 .25

11th meeting of the Council of European Municipalities, Vienna, Apr. 2-5.

Austria as Mediator A430

1975, May 2 Litho. ***Perf. 14***

1014 A430 2s blk & bister .35 .25

2nd Republic of Austria, 30th anniv.

National Forests, 50th Anniv. — A431

1975, May 6 Engr.

1015 A431 2s green .35 .25

Europa Issue 1975

High Priest, by Michael Pacher — A432

Photo. & Engr.

1975, May 27 ***Perf. 14x13½***

1016 A432 2.50s black & multi *.40 .25*

Design is detail from painting "The Marriage of Joseph and Mary," by Michael Pacher (c. 1450-1500).

Gosaukamm Funicular — A433

1975, June 23 ***Perf. 14x13½***

1017 A433 2s slate & red .35 .25

4th Intl. Funicular Cong., Vienna, 6/23-27.

Josef Misson and Mühlbach am Manhartsberg — A434

1975, June 27 ***Perf. 13½x14***

1018 A434 2s choc & redsh brn .35 .25

Josef Misson (1803-1875), poet who wrote in Lower Austrian vernacular, death cent.

Setting Sun and "P" — A435

1975, Aug. 27 Litho. ***Perf. 14x13½***

1019 A435 1.50s org, blk & bl .25 .25

Austrian Assoc. of Pensioners 25th anniv. meeting, Vienna, Aug. 1975.

Ferdinand Porsche (1875-1951), Engineer, Auto Maker A436

Photo. & Engr.

1975, Sept. 3 ***Perf. 13½x14***

1020 A436 1.50s gray & purple .25 .25

Leo Fall (1873-1925), Composer A437

1975, Sept. 16 Engr. ***Perf. 14x13½***

1021 A437 2s violet .35 .25

10th World Judo Championships, Vienna — A438

1975, Oct. 20 Photo. ***Perf. 14x13½***

1022 A438 2.50s Judo Throw .40 .25

Heinrich Angeli (1840-1925), Painter — A439

1975, Oct. 21 Engr. ***Perf. 14x13½***

1023 A439 2s rose lake .35 .25

Johann Strauss and Dancers A440

Photo. & Engr.

1975, Oct. 24 ***Perf. 13½x14***

1024 A440 4s ocher & sepia .65 .40

Johann Strauss (1825-1899), composer.

Stylized Musician Playing a Viol — A441

1975, Oct. 30 ***Perf. 14x13½***

1025 A441 2.50s silver & vio bl .40 .25

Vienna Symphony Orchestra, 75th anniv.

Symbolic House — A442

1975, Oct. 31 Photo.

1026 A442 2s multicolored .35 .25

Austrian building savings societies, 50th anniv.

Fan with "Hanswurst" Scene, 18th Century A443

1975, Nov. 14 Photo. ***Perf. 13½x14***

1027 A443 1.50s green & multi .25 .25

Salzburg Theater bicentenary.

Virgin and Child, from 15th Century Altar — A444

Photo. & Engr.

1975, Nov. 28 ***Perf. 13x13½***

1028 A444 2s gold & dull purple .35 .25

Christmas.

"The Spiral Tree," by Hundertwasser A445

Photo., Engr. & Typo.

1975, Dec. 11 ***Perf. 13½x14***

1029 A445 4s multicolored .80 .35

Austrian modern art. Friedenstreich Hundertwasser is the pseudonym of Friedrich Stowasser (1928-2000).

Old Burgtheater A446

No. 1030b, Grand staircase, new Burgtheater.

Perf. 14 (pane), 13½x14 (stamps)

1976, Apr. 8 **Engr.**

1030 Pane of 2 + label 1.20 1.40
a. A446 3s violet blue .65 .25
b. A446 3s deep brown .65 .25

Bicentenary of Vienna Burgtheater. Label (head of Pan) and inscription in vermilion.

Dr. Robert Barany (1876-1936), Winner of Nobel Prize for Medicine, 1914 — A447

Photo. & Engr.

1976, Apr. 22 ***Perf. 14x13½***

1031 A447 3s blue & brown .55 .25

Ammonite A448

1976, Apr. 30 **Photo.** ***Perf. 13½x14***

1032 A448 3s red & multi .55 .25

Vienna Museum of Natural History, Centenary Exhibition.

Carinthian Dukes' Coronation Chair — A449

Photo. & Engr.

1976, May 6 ***Perf. 14x13½***

1033 A449 3s grnsh blk & org .55 .25

Millennium of Carinthia.

Siege of Linz, 17th Century Etching — A450

1976, May 14

1034 A450 4s blk & gray grn .65 .40

Upper Austrian Peasants' War, 350th anniv.

Skittles A451

1976, May 14 ***Perf. 13½x14***

1035 A451 4s black & org .65 .40

11th World Skittles Championships, Vienna.

Duke Heinrich II, Stained-glass Window — A452

1976, May 14 ***Perf. 14***

1036 A452 3s multicolored .55 .25

Babenberg Exhibition, Lilienfeld.

St. Wolfgang, from Pacher Altar — A453

1976, May 26 **Engr.** ***Perf. 13½***

1037 A453 6s bright violet 1.10 .55

Intl. Art Exhibition at St. Wolfgang.

Europa Issue 1976

Tassilo Cup, Kremsmunster, 777 — A454

Photo. & Engr.

1976, Aug. 13 ***Perf. 14x13½***

1038 A454 4s ultra & multi *.65 .40*

Timber Fair Emblem — A455

1976, Aug. 13 **Photo.**

1039 A455 3s green & multi .55 .25

Austrian Timber Fair, Klagenfurt, 25th anniv.

Constantin Economo, M.D. (1876-1931), Neurologist A456

1976, Aug. 23 **Engr.**

1040 A456 3s dark red brown .55 .25

Administrative Court, by Salomon Klein — A457

1976, Oct. 25 **Engr.** ***Perf. 13½x14***

1041 A457 6s deep brown 1.10 .55

Austrian Central Administrative Court, cent.

Souvenir Sheet

Coats of Arms of Austrian Provinces — A458

Millennium of Austria: a, Lower Austria. b, Upper Austria. c, Styria. d, Carinthia. e, Tyrol. f, Voralberg. g, Salzburg. h, Burgenland. i, Vienna.

Photo. & Engr.

1976, Oct. 25 ***Perf. 14***

1042 Sheet of 9 3.25 3.50
a.-i. A458 2s any single .35 .40

"Cancer" A459

1976, Nov. 17 **Photo.** ***Perf. 14x13½***

1043 A459 2.50s multicolored .40 .25

Fight against cancer.

UN Emblem and Bridge — A460

1976, Nov. 17

1044 A460 3s blue & gold .55 .25

UN Industrial Development Org. (UNIDO), 10th anniv.

Punched Tape, Map of Europe A461

1976, Nov. 17 ***Perf. 14***

1045 A461 1.50s multicolored .25 .25

Austrian Press Agency (APA), 30th anniv.

Viktor Kaplan, Kaplan Turbine A462

Photo. & Engr.

1976, Nov. 26 ***Perf. 13½x14***

1046 A462 2.50s multicolored .40 .25

Viktor Kaplan (1876-1934), inventor of Kaplan turbine, birth centenary.

Nativity, by Konrad von Friesach, c. 1450 A463

1976, Nov. 26 ***Perf. 13½***

1047 A463 3s multicolored .55 .25

Christmas.

Augustin, the Piper — A464

Photo. & Engr.

1976, Dec. 29 ***Perf. 13½***

1048 A464 6s multicolored 1.10 .55

Modern Austrian art.

Rainer Maria Rilke (1875-1926), Poet — A465

1976, Dec. 29 **Engr.** ***Perf. 14x13½***

1049 A465 3s deep violet .55 .25

Vienna City Synagogue — A466

1976, Dec. 29 **Photo.** ***Perf. 13½***

1050 A466 1.50s multicolored .25 .25

Sesquicentennial of Vienna City Synagogue.

Nikolaus Joseph von Jacquin (1727-1817), Botanist — A467

1977, Feb. 16 **Engr.** ***Perf. 14x13½***

1051 A467 4s chocolate .65 .40

Oswald von Wolkenstein (1377-1445), Poet — A468

Photo. & Engr.

1977, Feb. 16 ***Perf. 14***
1052 A468 3s multicolored .55 .25

Handball A469

1977, Feb. 25 **Photo.** ***Perf. 13½x14***
1053 A469 1.50s multicolored .25 .25

World Indoor Handball Championships, Austria, Feb. 5-Mar. 6.

Alfred Kubin (1877-1959), Illustrator and Writer — A470

1977, Apr. 12 **Engr.** ***Perf. 14x13½***
1054 A470 6s dk violet blue 1.10 .55

Great Spire, St. Stephen's Cathedral A471

Designs: 3s, Heathen Tower and Frederick's Gable. 4s, Interior view with Albertinian Choir.

1977, Apr. 22 **Engr.** ***Perf. 13½***
1055 A471 2.50s dark brown .55 .30
1056 A471 3s dark blue .65 .40
1057 A471 4s rose lake .80 .55
Nos. 1055-1057 (3) 2.00 1.25

Restoration and re-opening of St. Stephen's Cathedral, Vienna, 25th anniversary.

Fritz Hermanovsky-Orlando (1877-1954), Poet and Artist — A472

Photo. & Engr.

1977, Apr. 29 ***Perf. 13½x14***
1058 A472 6s Prus green & gold 1.10 .55

Intl. Atomic Energy Agency (IAEA), 20th Anniv. — A473

1977, May 2 **Photo.** ***Perf. 14***
1059 A473 3s IAEA Emblem .55 .25

Schwanenstadt, 350th Anniv. — A474

1977, June 10 **Photo.** ***Perf. 14x13½***
1060 A474 3s Town arms .55 .25

Europa Issue 1977

Attersee, Upper Austria — A475

1977, June 10 **Engr.** ***Perf. 14***
1061 A475 6s olive green *1.20 .55*

Globe, by Vincenzo Coronelli, 1688 — A476

Photo. & Engr.

1977, June 29 ***Perf. 14***
1062 A476 3s black & buff .55 .25

5th Intl. Symposium of the Coronelli World Fed. of Friends of the Globe, Austria, June 29-July 3.

Kayak Race A477

1977, July 15 **Photo.** ***Perf. 13½x14***
1063 A477 4s multicolored .65 .40

3rd Kayak Slalom White Water Race on Lieser River, Spittal.

The Good Samaritan, by Francesco Bassano A478

1977, Sept. 16 **Photo. & Engr.**
1064 A478 1.50s brown & red .25 .25

Workers' Good Samaritan Org., 50th anniv.

Papermakers' Coat of Arms — A479

1977, Oct. 10 ***Perf. 14x13½***
1065 A479 3s multicolored .55 .25

17th Conf. of the European Committee of Pulp and Paper Technology (EUCEPA), Vienna.

Man with Austrian Flag Lifting Barbed Wire — A480

1977, Nov. 3 ***Perf. 14***
1066 A480 2.50s slate & red .40 .25

Honoring the martyrs for Austria's freedom.

"Austria," First Steam Locomotive in Austria — A481

Designs: 2.50s, Steam locomotive 214. 3s, Electric locomotive 1044.

Photo. & Engr.

1977, Nov. 17 ***Perf. 13½***
1067 A481 1.50s multicolored .40 .25
1068 A481 2.50s multicolored .65 .25
1069 A481 3s multicolored .95 .40
Nos. 1067-1069 (3) 2.00 .90

140th anniversary of Austrian railroads.

Christmas — A482

Virgin and Child, wood statue, Mariastein, Tyrol.

1977, Nov. 25 ***Perf. 14x13½***
1070 A482 3s multicolored .55 .25

Modern Austrian Art — A483

The Danube Maiden, by Wolfgang Hutter.

1977, Dec. 2 ***Perf. 13½x14***
1071 A483 6s multicolored 1.10 .55

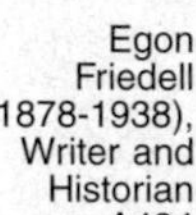

Egon Friedell (1878-1938), Writer and Historian A484

1978, Jan. 23 **Photo. & Engr.**
1072 A484 3s lt blue & blk .55 .25

Subway Train A485

1978, Feb. 24 **Photo.** ***Perf. 13½x14***
1073 A485 3s multicolored .65 .25

New Vienna subway system.

Biathlon Competition A486

1978, Feb. 28 **Photo. & Engr.**
1074 A486 4s multicolored .65 .40

Biathlon World Championships, Hochfilzen, Tyrol, Feb. 28-Mar. 5.

Leopold Kunschak (1871-1953), Political Leader — A487

1978, Mar. 13 **Engr.** ***Perf. 14x13½***
1075 A487 3s violet blue .55 .25

Coyote, Aztec Feather Shield A488

1978, Mar. 13 **Photo.** ***Perf. 13½x14***
1076 A488 3s multicolored .55 .25

Ethnographical Museum, 50th anniv. exhibition.

Alpine Farm, Woodcut by Suitbert Lobisser — A489

1978, Mar. 23 **Engr.** ***Perf. 13½***
1077 A489 3s dark brown, *buff* .55 .25

Lobisser (1878-1943), graphic artist.

Capercaillie, Hunting Bag, 1730, and Rifle, 1655 — A490

Photo. & Engr.

1978, Apr. 28 ***Perf. 13½***
1078 A490 6s multicolored 1.10 .55

Intl. Hunting Exhibition, Marchegg.

Europa Issue 1978

Riegersburg, Styria — A491

1978, May 3 **Engr.**
1079 A491 6s deep rose lilac *1.60* *.55*

Parliament, Vienna, and Map of Europe — A492

1978, May 3 **Photo.** ***Perf. 14x13½***
1080 A492 4s multicolored .65 .40

3rd Interparliamentary Conference for European Cooperation and Security, Vienna.

Admont Pietà, c. 1410 — A493

1978, May 26 **Photo. & Engr.**
1081 A493 2.50s ocher & black .40 .25

Gothic Art in Styria Exhibition, St. Lambrecht, 1978.

Ort Castle, Gmunden — A494

1978, June 9
1082 A494 3s multicolored .55 .25

700th anniversary of Gmunden City.

Child with Flowers and Fruit — A495

Photo. & Engr.

1978, June 30 ***Perf. 14x13½***
1083 A495 6s gold & multi 1.10 .55

25 years of Social Tourism.

Lehar and his Home, Bad Ischl — A496

1978, July 14 **Engr.** ***Perf. 14x13½***
1084 A496 6s slate 1.10 .55

International Lehar Congress, Bad Ischl. Franz Lehar (1870-1948), operetta composer.

Congress Emblem A497

1978, Aug. 21 **Photo.** ***Perf. 13½x14***
1085 A497 1.50s black, red & yel .25 .25

Cong. of Intl. Fed. of Building Construction and Wood Workers, Vienna, Aug. 20-24.

Ottokar of Bohemia and Rudolf of Hapsburg A498

1978, Aug. 25 **Photo. & Engr.**
1086 A498 3s multicolored .55 .25

Battle of Durnkrut and Jedenspeigen (Marchfeld), which established Hapsburg rule in Austria, 700th anniversary.

First Documentary Reference to Villach, "ad pontem uillah" — A499

1978, Sept. 8 **Litho.** ***Perf. 13½x14***
1087 A499 3s multicolored .55 .25

1100th anniversary of Villach, Carinthia.

Seal of Graz, 1440 — A500

Photo. & Engr.

1978, Sept. 13 ***Perf. 14x13½***
1088 A500 4s multicolored .65 .40

850th anniversary of Graz.

Emperor Maximilian Fishing — A501

1978, Sept. 15 ***Perf. 14x13½***
1089 A501 4s multicolored .65 .40

World Fishing Championships, Vienna, Sept. 1978.

"Aid to the Handicapped" — A502

1978, Oct. 2 **Photo.** ***Perf. 13½x14***
1090 A502 6s orange brn & blk 1.10 .55

Symbolic Column — A503

1978, Oct. 9 **Photo.** ***Perf. 13½***
1091 A503 2.50s orange, blk & gray .40 .25

9th Intl. Congress of Concrete and Prefabrication Industries, Vienna, Oct. 8-13.

Grace, by Albin Egger-Lienz A504

1978, Oct. 27 ***Perf. 13½x14***
1092 A504 6s multicolored 1.10 .55

European Family Congress, Vienna, Oct. 26-29.

Lise Meitner (1878-1968), Physicist, and Atom Symbol — A505

1978, Nov. 7 **Engr.** ***Perf. 14x13½***
1093 A505 6s dark violet 1.10 .55

Viktor Adler, by Anton Hanak A506

Photo. & Engr.

1978, Nov. 10 ***Perf. 13½x14***
1094 A506 3s vermilion & black .55 .25

Viktor Adler (1852-1918), leader of Social Democratic Party, 60th death anniversary.

Franz Schubert, by Josef Kriehuber A507

1978, Nov. 17 **Engr.** ***Perf. 14***
1095 A507 6s reddish brown 1.25 .55

Franz Schubert (1797-1828), composer.

Virgin and Child, Wilhering Church — A508

Photo. & Engr.

1978, Dec. 1 ***Perf. 12½x13½***
1096 A508 3s multicolored .55 .25

Christmas.

Archduke Johann Shelter, Grossglockner — A509

1978, Dec. 6 ***Perf. 13½x14***
1097 A509 1.50s gold & dk vio bl .25 .25

Austrian Alpine Club, centenary.

Modern Austrian Art — A510

Adam, by Rudolf Hausner.

1978, Dec. 6 **Photo.** ***Perf. 13½x14***
1098 A510 6s multicolored 1.10 .55

Universal Declaration of Human Rights, 30th Anniv. — A511

1978, Dec. 6 ***Perf. 14x13½***
1099 A511 6s Bound Hands 1.10 .55

Type of 1973

Designs: 20g, Freistadt, Upper Austria. 3s, Bishofsmutze, Salzburg. 4.20s, Hirschegg, Kleinwalsertal. 5.50s, Peace Chapel, Stoderzinken. 5.60s, Riezlern, Kleinwalsertal. 9s, Asten Carinthia. 12s, Kufstein Fortress. 14s, Weiszsee, Salzburg.

Photo. & Engr.

1978-83 ***Perf. 13½x14***

Size: 23x29mm

1100 A395 20g vio bl & dk bl .50 .25

Size: 17x21mm

1102 A395 3s lt ultra & vio bl .40 .25

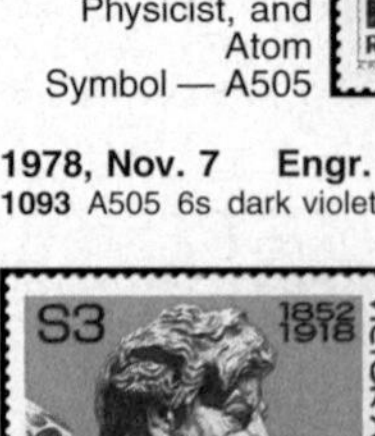

Size: 23x29mm

1104 A395 4.20s blk & grysh bl .95 .40
1105 A395 5.50s lilac & pur 1.50 .50
1106 A395 5.60s yel grn & ol grn 1.50 .70
1107 A395 9s rose & car 2.10 .40
1108 A395 12s ocher & vio brn 2.40 .35
1109 A395 14s lt green & green 3.25 .25
Nos. 1100-1109 (8) 12.60 3.10

Issued: 3s, 12/7/78; 4.20s, 6/22/79; 20g, 6/27/80; 12s, 10/3/80; 14s, 1/27/82; 5.50s, 5.60s, 7/1/82; 9s, 2/9/83.

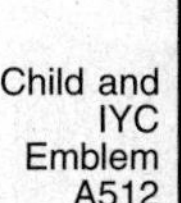
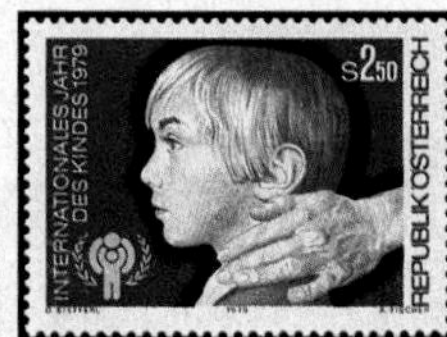

Child and IYC Emblem A512

Photo. & Engr.

1979, Jan. 16 ***Perf. 14***
1110 A512 2.50s dk blue, blk & brn .40 .25

International Year of the Child.

CCIR Emblem A513

1979, Jan. 16 Photo. ***Perf. 13½x14***
1111 A513 6s multicolored .80 .50

Intl. Radio Consultative Committee (CCIR) of the ITU, 50th anniv.

Air Rifle, Air Pistol and Club Emblem A514

Photo. & Engr.

1979, Mar. 7 ***Perf. 13½***
1112 A514 6s multicolored 1.10 .55

Austrian Shooting Club, cent., and European Air Rifle and Air Pistol Championships, Graz.

Figure Skater — A515

1979, Mar. 7 Photo. ***Perf. 14x13½***
1113 A515 4s multicolored .65 .40

World Ice Skating Championships, Vienna.

Steamer Franz I A516

Designs: 2.50s, Tugboat Linz. 3s, Passenger ship Theodor Körner.

1979, Mar. 13 Engr. ***Perf. 13½***
1114 A516 1.50s violet blue .35 .25
1115 A516 2.50s sepia .50 .35
1116 A516 3s magenta .80 .25
Nos. 1114-1116 (3) 1.65 .85

1st Danube Steamship Company, 150th anniv.

Fashion Design, by Theo Zasche, 1900 — A517

Photo. & Engr.

1979, Mar. 26 ***Perf. 13x13½***
1117 A517 2.50s multicolored .40 .25

50th Intl. Fashion Week, Vienna.

Wiener Neustadt Cathedral, 700th Anniv. — A518

1979, Mar. 27 Engr. ***Perf. 13½***
1118 A518 4s violet blue .65 .40

Teacher and Pupils, by Franz A. Zauner — A519

Photo. & Engr.

1979, Mar. 30 ***Perf. 14x13½***
1119 A519 2.50s multicolored .40 .25

Education of the deaf in Austria, 200th anniv.

Population Chart and Baroque Angel — A520

1979, Apr. 6
1120 A520 2.50s multicolored .40 .25

Austrian Central Statistical Bureau, 150th anniv.

Europa Issue, 1979

Laurenz Koschier — A521

1979, May 4
1121 A521 6s ocher & purple *1.20 .55*

Diesel Motor — A522

1979, May 4 Photo.
1122 A522 4s multicolored .65 .40

13th CIMAC Congress (Intl. Org. for Internal Combustion Machines).

Arms of Ried, Schärding and Braunau — A523

Photo. & Engr.

1979, June 1 ***Perf. 14x13½***
1123 A523 3s multicolored .55 .25

200th anniversary of Innviertel District.

Stream and City — A524

1979, June 1 ***Perf. 13½x14***
1124 A524 2.50s multicolored .40 .25

Control and eliminate water pollution.

Arms of Rottenmann A525

Photo. & Engr.

1979, June 22 ***Perf. 14x13½***
1125 A525 3s multicolored .95 .25

700th anniversary of Rottenmann.

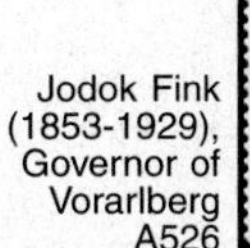

Jodok Fink (1853-1929), Governor of Vorarlberg A526

1979, June 29 Engr. ***Perf. 14***
1126 A526 3s brown carmine .55 .25

Arms of Wels, Returnees' Emblem, "Europa Sail" — A527

1979, July 6 Photo. ***Perf. 14x13½***
1127 A527 4s yellow grn & blk .65 .40

5th European Meeting of the Intl. Confederation of Former Prisoners of War, Wels, July 6-8.

Symbolic Flower, Conference Emblem — A528

1979, Aug. 20 Litho. ***Perf. 14x13½***
1128 A528 4s turq blue .65 .40

UN Conf. for Science and Technology, Vienna, Aug. 20-31.

Donaupark, UNIDO and IAEA Emblems A529

1979, Aug. 24 Engr. ***Perf. 13½x14***
1129 A529 6s grayish blue 1.10 .55

Opening of the Donaupark Intl. Center in Vienna, seat of the UN Industrial Development Org. (UNIDO) and the Intl. Atomic Energy Agency (IAEA).

Diseased Eye and Blood Vessels A530

1979, Sept. 10 Photo. ***Perf. 14***
1130 A530 2.50s multicolored .40 .25

10th World Congress of Intl. Diabetes Federation, Vienna, Sept. 9-14.

View of Stanz Valley through East Portal of Arlberg Tunnel A531

1979, Sept. 14 Photo. & Engr.
1131 A531 4s multicolored .65 .40

16th World Road Cong., Vienna, 9/16-21.

Steam Printing Press A532

Photo. & Engr.

1979, Sept. 18 ***Perf. 13½x14***
1132 A532 3s multicolored .40 .25

Austrian Government Printing Office, 175th anniv.

Richard Zsigmondy (1865-1929), Chemist — A533

1979, Sept. 21 Engr. ***Perf. 14x13½***
1133 A533 6s multicolored 1.10 .55

"Save Energy" A534

1979, Oct. 1 Photo. ***Perf. 14x13½***
1134 A534 2.50s multicolored .40 .25

Festival and Convention Center, Bregenz (Model) — A535

1979, Oct. 1 Engr. ***Perf. 14***
1135 A535 2.50s purple .40 .25

Lions International Emblem A536

1979, Oct. 11 Photo. & Engr.
1136 A536 4s multicolored .65 .40

25th Lions Europa Forum, Vienna, 10/11-13.

A537

Photo. & Engr.
1979, Oct. 19 ***Perf. 13½x14***
1137 A537 2.50s Wilhelm Exner .40 .25

Centenary of Technological Handicraft Museum, founded by Wilhelm Exner.

Modern Austrian Art — A538

The Compassionate Christ, by Hans Fronius.

1979, Oct. 23 Litho. ***Perf. 13½x14***
1138 A538 4s olive & ol blk .65 .40

Locomotive and Arms — A539

1979, Oct. 24 Photo. ***Perf. 13½x14***
1139 A539 2.50s multicolored .55 .25

Raab-Odenburg-Ebenfurt railroad, cent.

August Musger — A540

Photo. & Engr.
1979, Oct. 30 ***Perf. 14x13½***
1140 A540 2.50s bl gray & blk .40 .25

August Musger (1868-1929), developer of slow-motion film technique.

Nativity, St. Barbara's Church A541

1979, Nov. 30 ***Perf. 13½x14***
1141 A541 4s multicolored .65 .40

Christmas.

Arms of Baden — A542

1980, Jan. 25 ***Perf. 14***
1142 A542 4s multicolored .65 .40

Baden, 500th anniversary.

Fight Rheumatism A543

1980, Feb. 21 ***Perf. 13½***
1143 A543 2.50s red & aqua .40 .25

Austrian Exports — A544

1980, Feb. 21 Photo. ***Perf. 14x13½***
1144 A544 4s dark blue & red .65 .40

Austrian Red Cross Centenary A545

1980, Mar. 14 Photo. ***Perf. 13½x14***
1145 A545 2.50s multicolored .40 .25

Rudolph Kirchschlager A546

Photo. & Engr.
1980, Mar. 20 ***Perf. 14x13½***
1146 A546 4s sepia & red .65 .40

Robert Hamerling (1830-1889), Poet — A547

1980, Mar. 24 Engr. ***Perf. 13½x14***
1147 A547 2.50s olive green .40 .25

Seal of Hallein — A548

Photo. & Engr.
1980, Apr. 30 ***Perf. 14x13½***
1148 A548 4s red & black .65 .40

Hallein, 750th anniversary.

Empress Maria Theresa (1717-80) A549

Paintings by: 2.50s, Andreas Moller. 4s, Martin van Meytens. 6s, Josef Ducreux.

1980, May 13 Engr. ***Perf. 13½***
1149 A549 2.50s violet brown .65 .25
1150 A549 4s dark blue .90 .40
1151 A549 6s rose lake 1.50 .80
Nos. 1149-1151 (3) 3.05 1.45

Flags of Austria and Four Powers A550

1980, May 14 Photo. ***Perf. 13½x14***
1152 A550 4s multicolored .65 .40

State Treaty, 25th anniversary.

St. Benedict, by Meinrad Guggenbichler A551

1980, May 16 Engr. ***Perf. 14½***
1153 A551 2.50s olive green .40 .25

Congress of Benedictine Order of Austria.

Hygeia by Gustav Klimt — A552

1980, May 20 Photo. ***Perf. 14***
1154 A552 4s multicolored .65 .40

Academic teaching of hygiene, 175th anniv.

Aflenz Ground Satellite Receiving Station Inauguration A553

1980, May 30 Photo. ***Perf. 14***
1155 A553 6s multicolored 1.10 .55

Steyr, Etching, 1693 A554

Photo. & Engr.
1980, June 4 ***Perf. 13½***
1156 A554 4s multicolored .65 .40

Millennium of Steyr.

Worker, Oil Drill Head — A555

1980, June 12
1157 A555 2.50s multicolored .40 .25

Austrian oil production, 25th anniversary.

Seal of Innsbruck, 1267 A556

1980, June 23 ***Perf. 13½x14½***
1158 A556 2.50s multicolored .40 .25

Innsbruck, 800th anniversary.

Duchy of Styria, 800th Anniv. — A557

Perf. 14½x13½

1980, June 23 **Photo.**

1159 A557 4s Duke's hat .65 .40

Leo Ascher (1880-1942), Composer A558

1980, Aug. 18 **Engr.** ***Perf. 14***

1160 A558 3s dark purple .40 .25

Bible Illustration, Book of Genesis — A559

1980, Aug. 25 ***Perf. 13½***

1161 A559 4s multicolored .65 .40

10th Intl. Cong. of the Org. for Old Testament Studies.

Europa Issue 1980

Robert Stolz (1880-1975), Composer A560

1980, Aug. 25 **Engr.** ***Perf. 14x13½***

1162 A560 6s red brown *1.20* .55

Old and Modern Bridges A561

1980, Sept. 1 **Photo.** ***Perf. 13½***

1163 A561 4s multicolored .65 .40

11th Congress of the Intl. Assoc. for Bridge and Structural Engineering, Vienna.

Moon Figure, by Karl Brandstätter A562

Photo. & Engr.

1980, Oct. 10 ***Perf. 14x13½***

1164 A562 4s multicolored .65 .40

Customs Service, Sesquicentennial A563

1980, Oct. 13 **Photo.**

1165 A563 2.50s multicolored .40 .25

Gazette Masthead, 1810 A564

1980, Oct. 23 **Photo.** ***Perf. 13½***

1166 A564 2.50s multicolored .40 .25

Official Gazette of Linz, 350th anniversary.

Waidhofen Town Book Title Page, 14th Century — A565

Photo. & Engr.

1980, Oct. 24 ***Perf. 14***

1167 A565 2.50s multicolored .40 .25

Waidhofen on Thaya, 750th anniversary.

Federal Austrian Army, 25th Anniversary A566

1980, Oct. 24 **Photo.** ***Perf. 13½x14***

1168 A566 2.50s grnsh black & red .40 .25

Alfred Wegener A567

1980, Oct. 31 **Engr.**

1169 A567 4s violet blue .65 .40

Alfred Wegener (1880-1930), scientist, formulated theory of continental drift.

Robert Musil (1880-1942), Writer — A568

1980, Nov. 6 ***Perf. 14x13½***

1170 A568 4s dark red brown .65 .40

Christmas — A569

Nativity, stained glass window, Klagenfurt.

Photo. & Engr.

1980, Nov. 28 ***Perf. 13½***

1171 A569 4s multicolored .65 .40

25th Anniversary of Social Security A570

1981, Jan. 19 **Litho.** ***Perf. 13½x14***

1172 A570 2.50s multicolored .35 .25

Niebelungen Saga, 1926, by Dachauer — A571

1981, Apr. 6 **Engr.** ***Perf. 14x13½***

1173 A571 3s sepia .40 .25

Wilhelm Dachauer (1881-1951), artist and engraver.

Machinist in Wheelchair A572

1981, Apr. 6 **Photo. & Engr.**

1174 A572 6s multicolored .80 .55

Rehabilitation Intl., 3rd European Regional Conf.

Sigmund Freud (1856-1939), Psychoanalyst A573

1981, May 6 **Engr.**

1175 A573 3s rose violet .40 .25

Heating Engineers Union Congress, Vienna — A574

1981, May 11 **Photo.**

1176 A574 4s multicolored .55 .40

Kuenringer Exhibition, Zwettl Monastery A575

Azzo (founder of House of Kuenringer) and his followers, bear-skin manuscript.

1981, May 15 **Photo. & Engr.**

1177 A575 3s multicolored .40 .25

Europa — A576

1981, May 22 **Photo.**

1178 A576 6s Maypole *1.20* *.55*

Telephone Service Centenary A577

Photo. and Engr.

1981 May 29 ***Perf. 13½x14***

1179 A577 4s multicolored .55 .40

Seibersdorf Research Center, 25th Anniv. — A578

1981, June 29 **Photo.** ***Perf. 13½***

1180 A578 4s multicolored .55 .40

The Frog King (Child's Drawing) A579

1981, June 29 ***Perf. 13½x14***

1181 A579 3s multicolored .40 .25

Town Hall and Town Seal of 1250 A580

Photo. & Engr.

1981, July 17 ***Perf. 13½x14***

1182 A580 4s multicolored .55 .40

St. Veit an der Glan, 800th anniv.

Johann Florian Heller (1813-1871), Pioneer of Urinalysis — A581

1981, Aug. 31 ***Perf. 14x13½***
1183 A581 6s red brown .80 .55

11th Intl. Clinical Chemistry Congress.

Ludwig Boltzmann (1844-1906), Physicist — A582

1981, Sept. 4 Engr. ***Perf. 14x13½***
1184 A582 3s dark green .40 .25

Intl. Pharmaceutical Federation World Congress, Vienna — A583

Photo. & Engr.

1981, Sept. 7 ***Perf. 14***
1185 A583 6s Scale .80 .55

Otto Bauer, Politician, Birth Centenary A584

1981, Sept. 7 Photo. ***Perf. 14x13½***
1186 A584 4s multicolored .55 .40

Escher's Impossible Cube — A585

1981, Sept. 14
1187 A585 4s dk blue & brt blue .55 .40

10th Intl. Mathematicians' Cong., Innsbruck.

Kneeling Virgin, Detail of Coronation of Mary Altarpiece, St. Wolfgang, 500th Anniv. — A586

1981, Sept. 25 Engr. ***Perf. 14x13½***
1188 A586 3s dark blue .40 .25

South-East Fair, Graz, 75th Anniv. A587

1981, Sept. 25 Photo. ***Perf. 13½x14***
1189 A587 4s multicolored .55 .40

Holy Trinity, 12th Cent. Byzantine Miniature A588

1981, Oct. 5
1190 A588 6s multicolored .80 .55

16th Intl. Byzantine Congress.

Hans Kelsen (1881-1973), Co-author of Federal Constitution A589

1981, Oct. 9 **Engr.**
1191 A589 3s dark carmine .40 .25

Edict of Tolerance Bicen. — A590

Photo. & Engr.

1981, Oct. 9 ***Perf. 14***
1192 A590 4s Joseph II .55 .40

World Food Day A591

1981, Oct. 16 Photo. ***Perf. 13½***
1193 A591 6s multicolored .80 .55

Between the Times, by Oscar Asboth A592

1981, Oct. 22 Litho. ***Perf. 13½x14***
1194 A592 4s multicolored .55 .40

Intl. Catholic Workers' Day — A593

Photo. & Engr.

1981, Oct. 23 ***Perf. 14x13½***
1195 A593 3s multicolored .40 .25

Baron Josef Hammer-Purgstall, Founder of Oriental Studies, 125th Death Anniv. — A594

Photo. & Engr.

1981, Nov. 23 ***Perf. 14***
1196 A594 3s multicolored .40 .25

Julius Raab (1891-1964), Politician A595

1981, Nov. 27 Engr. ***Perf. 13½***
1197 A595 6s rose lake .75 .55

Nativity, Corn Straw Figures A596

1981, Nov. 27 **Photo. & Engr.**
1198 A596 4s multicolored .50 .40

Christmas.

Stefan Zweig (1881-1942), Writer — A597

1981, Nov. 27 Engr. ***Perf. 14x13½***
1199 A597 4s dull violet .50 .40

800th Anniv. of St. Nikola on the Danube A598

1981, Dec. 4 **Photo. & Engr.**
1200 A598 4s multicolored .50 .40

Vienna Emergency Medical Service Centenary A599

1981, Dec. 9 Photo. ***Perf. 13½x14***
1201 A599 3s multicolored .40 .25

Schladming-Haus Alpine World Skiing Championship — A600

1982, Jan. 27 ***Perf. 14***
1202 A600 4s multicolored .50 .35

Dorotheum (State Auction Gallery), 275th Anniv. — A601

Photo. & Engr.

1982, Mar. 12 ***Perf. 14***
1203 A601 4s multicolored .50 .35

Water Rescue Service, 25th Anniv. — A602

1982, Mar. 19 Photo. ***Perf. 14x13½***
1204 A602 5s multicolored .65 .50

St. Severin and the End of the Roman Era Exhibition — A603

Photo. & Engr.

1982, Apr. 23 ***Perf. 14x13½***
1205 A603 3s St. Severin .40 .25

Intl. Kneipp Hydropathy Congress, Vienna — A604

1982, May 4 ***Perf. 14***
1206 A604 4s multicolored .50 .40

Printing in Austria, 500th Anniv. — A605

1982, May 7
1207 A605 4s Printers' guild arms .50 .40

5th European Urology Soc. Cong., Vienna — A606

Design: Urine analysis, Canone di Avicenna manuscript.

1982, May 12 **Photo.**
1208 A606 6s multicolored .75 .55

St. Francis of Assisi, 800th Birth Anniv. — A607

1982, May 14 **Photo. & Engr.**
1209 A607 3s multicolored .40 .25

Haydn and His Time Exhibition, Rohrau — A608

1982, May 19 **Engr.** ***Perf. 13½***
1210 A608 3s olive green .50 .25

25th World Milk Day — A609

1982, May 25 **Photo.** ***Perf. 14x13½***
1211 A609 7s multicolored .95 .65

800th Anniv of Gfohl (Market Town) — A610

Photo. & Engr.

1982, May 28 ***Perf. 14***
1212 A610 4s multicolored .50 .40

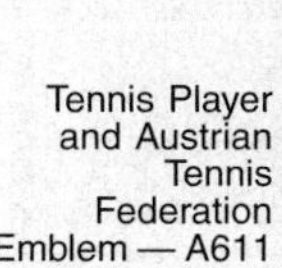

Tennis Player and Austrian Tennis Federation Emblem — A611

1982, June 11
1213 A611 3s multicolored .40 .25

900th Anniv. of City of Langenlois A612

Photo. & Engr.

1982, June 11 ***Perf. 13½x14***
1214 A612 4s multicolored .50 .35

800th Anniv. of City of Weiz — A613

1982, June 18 **Photo.** ***Perf. 14x13½***
1215 A613 4s Arms 1.10 .35

Ignaz Seipel (1876-1932), Statesman A614

1982, July 30 **Engr.** ***Perf. 14x13½***
1216 A614 3s brown violet .40 .25

Europa Issue 1982

Sesquicentennial of Linz-Freistadt-Budweis Horse-drawn Railroad — A615

1982, July 30 ***Perf. 13½***
1217 A615 6s brown *1.60 .55*

Mail Bus Service, 75th Anniv. — A616

1982, Aug. 6 **Photo.** ***Perf. 14x13½***
1218 A616 4s multicolored .50 .40

Rocket Lift-off — A617

1982, Aug. 9 ***Perf. 14***
1219 A617 4s multicolored .50 .40

2nd UN Conference on Peaceful Uses of Outer Space, Vienna, Aug. 9-21.

Geodesists' Day — A618

Photo. & Engr.

1982, Sept. 1 ***Perf. 13½x14***
1220 A618 3s Tower, Office of Standards .40 .25

Protection of Endangered Species — A619

1982, Sept. 9 ***Perf. 14***
1221 A619 3s Bustard .40 .40
1222 A619 4s Beaver .55 .55
1223 A619 6s Capercaillie .80 .80
Nos. 1221-1223 (3) 1.75 1.75

10th Anniv. of Intl. Institute for Applied Systems Analysis, Vienna A620

1982, Oct. 4 **Photo.**
1224 A620 3s Laxenburg Castle .35 .25

St. Apollonia (Patron Saint of Dentists) A621

1982, Oct. 11 **Photo. & Engr.**
1225 A621 4s multicolored .50 .40

70th Annual World Congress of Dentists.

Emmerich Kalman (1882-1953), Composer A622

1982, Oct. 22 **Engr.** ***Perf. 13½***
1226 A622 3s dark blue .40 .25

Max Mell (1882-1971), Poet — A623

1982, Nov. 10 **Photo.** ***Perf. 14x13½***
1227 A623 3s multicolored .40 .25

Christmas A624

Design: Christmas crib, Damuls Church, Vorarlberg, 1630.

Photo. & Engr.

1982, Nov. 25 ***Perf. 13½***
1228 A624 4s multicolored .50 .40

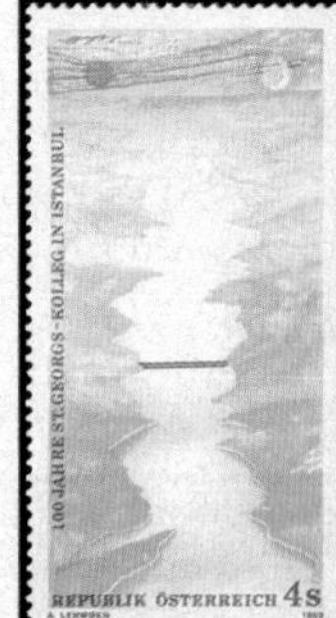

Centenary of St. George's College, Istanbul — A625

1982, Nov. 26 **Litho.** ***Perf. 14***
1229 A625 4s Bosporus .50 .40

Portrait of a Girl, by Ernst Fuchs — A626

1982, Dec. 10 **Photo. & Engr.**
1230 A626 4s multicolored .50 .40

Postal Savings Bank Centenary A627

Photo. & Engr.

1983, Jan. 12 ***Perf. 14***
1231 A627 4s Bank .50 .40

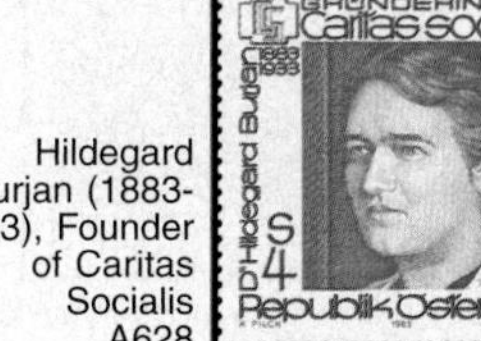

Hildegard Burjan (1883-1933), Founder of Caritas Socialis A628

1983, Jan. 28 **Engr.**
1232 A628 4s rose lake .50 .40

World Communications Year — A629

1983, Feb. 18 Photo. ***Perf. 13½x14***
1233 A629 7s multicolored .90 .55

75th Anniv. Children's Friends Org. — A630

Photo. & Engr.

1983, Feb. 23 ***Perf. 14x13½***
1234 A630 4s multicolored .50 .40

Josef Matthias Hauer (1883-1959), Composer A631

1983, Mar. 18 Engr. ***Perf. 14***
1235 A631 3s deep lilac rose .35 .25

25th Anniv. of Austrian Airlines A632

1983, Mar. 31 Photo. ***Perf. 13½x14***
1236 A632 6s multicolored .75 .55

Work Inspection Centenary A633

1983, Apr. 8 Photo. ***Perf. 13½***
1237 A633 4s multicolored .50 .40

Upper Austria Millennium Provincial Exhibition — A634

1983, Apr. 28 Photo. ***Perf. 13½***
1238 A634 3s Wels Castle, by Matthaus Merian .35 .25

Gottweig Monastery, 900th Anniv. — A635

Photo. & Engr.

1983, Apr. 29 ***Perf. 13½***
1239 A635 3s multicolored .40 .25

7th World Pacemakers Symposium A636

1983, Apr. 29 Photo. ***Perf. 14x13½***
1240 A636 4s multicolored .50 .40

Catholic Students' Org. A637

1983, May 20 Photo. ***Perf. 14***
1241 A637 4s multicolored .50 .40

Weitra, 800th Anniv. A638

Photo. & Engr.

1983, May 20 ***Perf. 13½***
1242 A638 4s multicolored .50 .40

Granting of Town Rights to Hohenems, 650th Anniv. — A639

1983, May 27 Photo. ***Perf. 14***
1243 A639 4s multicolored .50 .40

25th Anniv. of Stadthall, Vienna A640

1983, June 24 Photo. ***Perf. 14***
1244 A640 4s multicolored .50 .40

Viktor Franz Hess (1883-1964), 1936 Nobel Prize Winner in Physics — A641

1983, June 24 Engr. ***Perf. 14x13½***
1245 A641 6s dark green 1.20 .55

Europa.

Kiwanis Intl. Convention, Vienna — A642

1983, July 1 Photo. ***Perf. 13½***
1246 A642 5s multicolored .65 .50

7th World Congress of Psychiatry, Vienna — A643

1983, July 11 Photo. ***Perf. 14***
1247 A643 4s Emblem, St. Stephen's Cathedral .50 .35

Baron Carl von Hasenauer (1833-1894), Architect A644

1983, July 20 Engr. ***Perf. 13½x14***
1248 A644 3s Natural History Museum, Vienna .40 .25

27th Intl. Chamber of Commerce Professional Competition, Linz — A645

1983, Aug. 16 Photo.
1249 A645 4s Chamber building .55 .40

13th Intl. Chemotherapy Congress, Vienna, Aug. 28-Sept. 2 — A646

1983, Aug. 26
1250 A646 5s Penicillin test on cancer .55 .50

Catholics' Day — A647

1983, Sept. 9 Photo. ***Perf. 14x13½***
1251 A647 3s multicolored .40 .25

Visit of Pope John Paul II — A648

Photo. & Engr.

1983, Sept. 9 ***Perf. 13½***
1252 A648 6s multicolored .95 .55

Souvenir Sheet

Battle of 1683 to Relieve Vienna, by Frans Geffel — A649

1983, Sept. 9 ***Perf. 14***
1253 A649 6s multicolored .95 1.20

300th anniv. of Vienna's relief from Turkish siege.

Vienna Rathaus Centenary A650

1983, Sept. 23 ***Perf. 13½x14***
1254 A650 4s multicolored .55 .35

Karl von Terzaghi (1883-1963), Founder of Soil Mechanics A651

1983, Oct. 3 Engr.
1255 A651 3s dark blue .40 .25

10th Trade Unions Federal Congress, Oct. 3-8 A652

1983, Oct. 3 Photo. ***Perf. 13½***
1256 A652 3s black & red .40 .25

Evening Sun in Burgenland, by Gottfried Kumpf — A653

Photo. & Engr.

1983, Oct. 7 ***Perf. 13½x14***
1257 A653 4s multicolored .50 .40

Modling-Hinterbruhl Electric Railroad Centenary — A654

1983, Oct. 21 **Photo.**
1258 A654 3s multicolored .50 .25

Provincial Museum of Upper Austria Sesquicentennial — A655

1983, Nov. 4 **Photo. & Engr.**
1259 A655 4s Francisco-Carolinum Museum .55 .40

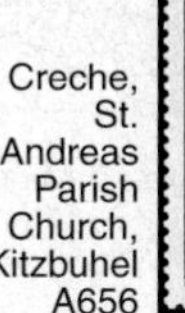

Creche, St. Andreas Parish Church, Kitzbuhel A656

1983, Nov. 25 ***Perf. 14***
1260 A656 4s multicolored .50 .40

Christmas.

Parliament Bldg. Vienna, 100th Anniv. — A657

1983, Dec. 2 **Engr.**
1261 A657 4s slate blue .55 .40

Altar Picture, St. Nikola/Pram Church — A658

1983, Dec. 6 **Photo.** ***Perf. 14x13½***
1262 A658 3s multicolored .40 .25

Wolfgang Pauli (1900-58), Physicist, Nobel Laureate — A659

1983, Dec. 15 **Engr.** ***Perf. 14½x13½***
1263 A659 6s dark red brn .80 .55

Gregor Mendel (1822-1884), Genetics Founder — A660

Photo. & Engr.

1984, Jan. 5 ***Perf. 13½***
1264 A660 4s multicolored .50 .40

Anton Hanak (1875-1934), Sculptor — A661

1984, Jan. 5
1265 A661 3s red brown & blk .40 .25

50th Anniv. of 1934 Uprising — A662

1984, Feb. 10 **Photo.** ***Perf. 14***
1266 A662 4.50s Memorial, Woellersdorf .55 .40

Wernher von Reichersberg Family, Bas-relief, 15th Cent. — A663

Photo. & Engr.

1984, Apr. 25 ***Perf. 14x13½***
1267 A663 3.50s brown & blue .40 .35

900th anniv. of Reichersberg Monastery.

Tobacco Monopoly Bicentenary A665

1984, May 4 ***Perf. 13½***
1269 A665 4.50s Cigar wrapper, tobacco plant .55 .40

1200th Anniv. of Kostendorf Municipality A666

1984, May 4
1270 A666 4.50s View, arms .55 .40

Automobile Engineers World Congress A667

1984, May 4 **Photo.** ***Perf. 13½x14***
1271 A667 5s Wheel bearing cross-section .65 .40

Europa (1959-1984) A668

1984, May 4 ***Perf. 13½***
1272 A668 6s multicolored *1.60* *.65*

Archduke Johann (1782-1859), by S. von Carolsfeld A669

Photo. & Engr.

1984, May 11 ***Perf. 14***
1273 A669 4.50s multicolored .55 .40

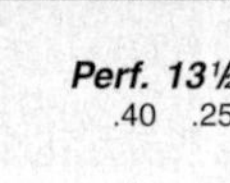

Ore and Iron Provincial Exhibition A670

1984, May 11 ***Perf. 13½***
1274 A670 3.50s Aragonite .40 .25

Era of Emperor Francis Joseph Exhibition A671

Design: Cover of Viribus Unitis, publ. by Max Herzig, 1898.

1984, May 18
1275 A671 3.50s red & gold .50 .35

City of Vocklabruck, 850th Anniv. — A672

Photo. & Engr.

1984, May 30 ***Perf. 14x13½***
1276 A672 4.50s Tower, arms .55 .40

Museum of Carinthia, Cent. — A673

Dionysius, Virinum mosaic.

1984, June 1 ***Perf. 13½***
1277 A673 3.50s multicolored .40 .25

Erosion Prevention Systems Centenary A674

1984, June 5 **Engr.** ***Perf. 14***
1278 A674 4.50s Stone reinforcement wall .55 .40

Tyrol Provincial Celebration, 1809-1984 A675

Art Exhibition: Meeting of Imperial Troops with South Tyrolean Reserves under Andreas Hofer near Sterzing in April 1809, by Ludwig Schnorr von Carolsfeld, 1830.

Photo. & Engr.

1984, June 5 ***Perf. 14x13½***
1279 A675 3.50s multicolored .40 .25

Ralph Benatzky (1884-1957), Composer A676

1984, June 5 **Engr.**
1280 A676 4s violet brown .50 .40

Christian von Ehrenfels (1859-1932), Philosopher A677

1984, June 22 Photo. *Perf. 14*
1281 A677 3.50s multicolored .40 .25

25th Anniv. of Minimundus (Model City) A678

1984, June 22 *Perf. 13½x14*
1282 A678 4s Eiffel Tower, Tower of Pisa, ferris wheel .50 .40

Blockheide Eibenstein Nature Park A679

1984 Photo. & Engr.
1283 A679 4s shown .50 .40
1284 A679 4s Lake Neusiedl .50 .40

Issued: No. 1283, June 29; No. 1284, Aug. 13.

See Nos. 1349-1354, 1492-1499, 1744, 1777, 1813, 1843.

Monasteries and Abbeys — A679a

Designs: 3.50s, Geras Monastery, Lower Austria. 4s, Stams. 4.50s, Schlagl. 5s, Benedictine Abbey of St. Paul, Levanttal. 6s, Rein-Hohenfurth.

1984-85 *Perf. 14*

1285	A679a	3.50s multi	.80	.25
1286	A679a	4s multi	.80	.25
1287	A679a	4.50s multi	.80	.25
1288	A679a	5s multi	.80	.25
1288A	A679a	6s multi	1.10	.25
	Nos. 1285-1288A (5)		4.30	1.25

Issued: 3.50s, 4/27/84; 4s, 9/28/84; 4.50s, 5/18/84; 5s, 9/27/85; 6s, 10/4/84.

See Nos. 1361-1365, 1465-1472.

Schanatobel Railroad Bridge — A680

Railroad Anniversaries: 3.50s, Arlberg centenary. 4.50s, Tauern, 75th.

1984, July 6 *Perf. 14*
1289 A680 3.50s shown .65 .40
1290 A680 4.50s Falkenstein Bridge .80 .50

Balloon Flight in Austria Bicent. — A681

1984, July 6 Photo.
1291 A681 6s Johan Stuwer's balloon .75 .55

Intl. Lawyers' Congress, Vienna — A682

1984, Aug. 31 Photo. & Engr.
1292 A682 7s Vienna Palace of Justice, emblem .95 .75

7th European Anatomy Congress, Innsbruck — A683

1984, Sept. 3 Photo.
1293 A683 6s Josef Hyrtl, anatomist .80 .50

A684

1984, Oct. 12
1294 A684 4s Window, by Karl Korab .50 .35

Johannes of Gmunden, Mathematician, 600th Birth Anniv. — A685

1984, Oct. 18
1295 A685 3.50s Clock (Immset Uhr), 1555 .40 .35

Concordia Press Club, 125th Anniv. — A686

1984, Nov. 9 Photo. *Perf. 13½*
1296 A686 4.50s Quill .55 .40

Fanny Eissler, Dancer, Death Centenary — A687

1984, Nov. 23 Photo. & Engr.
1297 A687 4s multicolored .55 .35

Christmas A688

Design: Christ is Born, Aggsbacher Altar, Herzogenburg Monastery.

1984, Nov. 30 *Perf. 14*
1298 A688 4.50s multicolored .55 .40

Karl Franzens University, Graz, 400th Anniv. — A689

1985, Jan. 4 *Perf. 14x13½*
1299 A689 3.50s Seal .40 .35

Dr. Lorenz Bohler, Surgeon, Birth Cent. — A690

1985, Jan. 15 Engr.
1300 A690 4.50s dk rose lake .55 .40

Nordic Events, Ski Championships, Seefeld — A691

1985, Jan. 17 Photo. *Perf. 13½*
1301 A691 4s Ski jumper, cross country racer .55 .40

Linz Diocese Bicentenary A692

1985, Jan. 25
1302 A692 4.50s Linz Cathedral interior .55 .40

Alban Berg (1885-1935), Composer A693

1985, Feb. 8 Engr.
1303 A693 6s bluish black .80 .55

Vocational Training Inst., 25th Anniv. A694

1985, Feb. 15 Photo. *Perf. 13½x14*
1304 A694 4.50s multicolored .55 .40

City of Bregenz, Bimillennium A695

1985, Feb. 22 *Perf. 14x13½*
1305 A695 4s multicolored .50 .35

Austrian Registration Labels Cent. A696

1985, Mar. 15 *Perf. 13½x14*
1306 A696 4.50s Label, 1885 .55 .40

Josef Stefan (1835-1893), Physicist — A697

Photo. & Engr.
1985, Mar. 22 *Perf. 14x13½*
1307 A697 6s buff, dl red brn & dk brn .80 .55

St. Leopold Exhibition, Klosterneuberg A698

St. Leopold 16th-17th cent. embroidery.

1985, Mar. 29
1308 A698 3.50s multicolored .40 .35

Liberation From German Occupation, 40th Anniv. — A699

1985, Apr. 26 **Photo.**
1309 A699 4.50s multicolored .55 .40

Painter Franz von Defregger (1835-1921) A700

1985, Apr. 26
1310 A700 3.50s Fairy tale teller .40 .35

Europa Issue 1985

Johann Joseph Fux (1660-1741), Composer, Violin and Trombone A701

Photo. & Engr.

1985, May 3 ***Perf. 13½***
1311 A701 6s lil gray & dk brn *1.60 .65*

Boheimkirchen (Market Town) Millennium — A702

1985, May 10 ***Perf. 14***
1312 A702 4.50s View, coat of arms .55 .40

European Free Trade Assoc., 25th Anniv. — A703

Mercury staff, flags of member and affiliate nations.

1985, May 10 **Photo.** ***Perf. 13½***
1313 A703 4s multicolored .50 .40

St. Polten Diocese, Bicent. — A704

Episcopal residence gate, St. Polten diocese arms.

1985, May 15 **Photo. & Engr.**
1314 A704 4.50s multicolored .55 .40

The Gumpp Family of Builders, Innsbruck — A705

Perf. 14½x13½

1985, May 17 **Photo.**
1315 A705 3.50s multicolored .40 .35

Garsten Market Town Millennium A706

Design: 17th century engraving by George Matthaus Fischer (1628-1696).

Photo. & Engr.

1985, June 7 ***Perf. 13½x14***
1316 A706 4.50s multicolored .55 .40

UN, 40th Anniv. A707

Perf. 13½x14½

1985, June 26 **Photo.**
1317 A707 4s multicolored .55 .40

Austrian membership, 30th anniv.

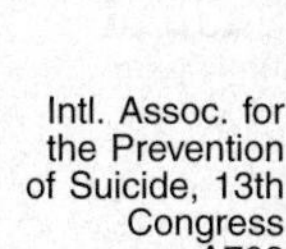

Intl. Assoc. for the Prevention of Suicide, 13th Congress A708

Photo. & Engr.

1985, June 28 ***Perf. 14***
1318 A708 5s brn, lt ap grn & yel .65 .50

Souvenir Sheet

Year of the Forest — A709

1985, June 28 ***Perf. 13½***
1319 A709 6s Healthy and damaged woodland 1.10 1.10

Kurhaus, Bad Ischl Operetta Activities Emblem A710

1985, July 5 ***Perf. 14***
1320 A710 3.50s multicolored .50 .40

Bad Ischl Festival, 25th anniv.

Intl. Competition of Fire Brigades, Vocklabruck A711

1985, July 18 **Photo.** ***Perf. 14x13½***
1321 A711 4.50s Fireman, emblem .80 .40

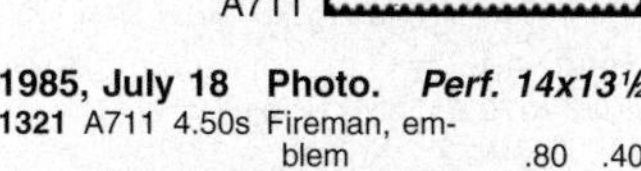

Grossglockner Alpine Motorway, 50th Anniv. — A712

Photo. & Engr.

1985, Aug. 2 ***Perf. 13½***
1322 A712 4s View of Fuschertorl .50 .40

World Chess Federation Congress, Graz — A713

1985, Aug. 28 **Photo.** ***Perf. 13½***
1323 A713 4s Checkered globe, emblem .50 .40

The Legendary Foundation of Konigstetten by Charlemagne, by Auguste Stephan, c. 1870 — A714

Photo. & Engr.

1985, Aug. 30 ***Perf. 14***
1324 A714 4.50s multicolored .55 .40

Konigstetten millennium.

Hofkirchen-Taufkirchen-Weibern Municipalities, 1200th Anniv. — A715

1985, Aug. 30 ***Perf. 13½x14***
1325 A715 4.50s View of Weiburn, municipal arms .55 .40

Dr. Adam Politzer (1835-1923), Physician A716

1985, Sept. 12 **Engr.** ***Perf. 14***
1326 A716 3.50s blue violet .50 .35

Politzer pioneered aural therapy for auditory disorders.

Intl. Assoc. of Forwarding Agents, World Congress, Vienna — A717

1985, Oct. 7 **Photo.** ***Perf. 13½***
1327 A717 6s multicolored .80 .55

Carnival Figures Riding High Bicycles, By Paul Flora A718

Photo. & Engr.

1985, Oct. 25 ***Perf. 14***
1328 A718 4s multicolored .55 .40

St. Martin on Horseback A719

1985, Nov. 8 **Photo.**
1329 A719 4.50s multicolored .55 .40

Eisenstadt Diocese, 25th anniv.

Creche, Marble Bas-relief, Salzburg — A720

Photo. & Engr.

1985, Nov. 29 ***Perf. 13½***
1330 A720 4.50s gold, dl vio & buff .55 .35

Christmas.

Hanns Horbiger (1860-1931), Inventor A721

1985, Nov. 29 ***Perf. 14***
1331 A721 3.50s gold & sepia .40 .35

Aqueduct, Hundsau Brook, Near Gostling A722

1985, Nov. 29 ***Perf. 13½x14½***
1332 A722 3.50s red, bluish blk & brt ultra .40 .35

Vienna Aqueduct, 75th anniv.

Chateau de la Muette, Paris Headquarters — A723

1985, Dec. 13
1333 A723 4s sep, rose lil & gold .50 .40

Org. for Economic Cooperation and Development, 25th anniv.

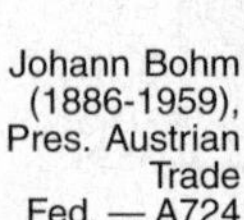

Johann Bohm (1886-1959), Pres. Austrian Trade Fed. — A724

1986, Jan. 24 **Photo.** ***Perf. 14***
1334 A724 4.50s blk, ver & grayish black .55 .45

Intl. Peace Year — A725

Perf. 13½x14½

1986, Jan. 24 **Photo.**
1335 A725 6s multicolored .75 .50

Digital Telephone Service Introduction A726

1986, Jan. 29 **Photo.**
1336 A726 5s Push-button keyboard .55 .40

Johann Georg Albrechtsberger (b. 1736), Composer — A727

Photo. & Engr.

1986, Jan. 31 ***Perf. 13½x14½***
1337 A727 3.50s Klosterneuberg organ .40 .35

Korneuburg, 850th Anniv. — A728

1986, Feb. 7 **Photo.** ***Perf. 14***
1338 A728 5s multicolored .65 .40

Self-portrait, by Oskar Kokoschka (b.1886) — A729

Perf. 14½x13½

1986, Feb. 28 **Photo.**
1339 A729 4s multicolored .55 .35

Admission to Council of Europe, 30th Anniv. — A730

1986, Feb. 28 **Photo.** ***Perf. 13x13½***
1340 A730 6s multicolored .80 .55

Clemens Holzmeister (b. 1886), Architect, Salzburg Festival Theater, 1926 — A731

Photo. & Engr.

1986, Mar. 27 ***Perf. 13½***
1341 A731 4s sepia & redsh brn .50 .40

3rd Intl. Geotextile Congress, Vienna A732

1986, Apr. 7 **Photo.** ***Perf. 13½x14½***
1342 A732 5s multicolored .65 .40

Prince Eugen and Schlosshof Castle A733

Photo. & Engr.

1986, Apr. 21 ***Perf. 14***
1343 A733 4s multicolored .50 .40

Prince Eugen Exhibition, Schlosshof and Niederweiden.

St. Florian Monastery, Upper Austria A734

1986, Apr. 24
1344 A734 4s multicolored .50 .40

The World of Baroque provincial exhibition, St. Florian.

Herberstein Castle, Arms of Styria A735

1986, May 2 ***Perf. 13½x14½***
1345 A735 4s multicolored .50 .40

Europa 1986 — A736

1986, May 2 ***Perf. 13½***
1346 A736 6s Pasque flower *1.60* *.55*

Wagner, Scene from Opera Lohengrin — A737

1986, May 21
1347 A737 4s multicolored .50 .40

Intl. Richard Wagner Congress, Vienna.

Antimonite A738

1986, May 23 ***Perf. 13½x14½***
1348 A738 4s multicolored .50 .40

Burgenland Provincial Minerals Exhibition.

Scenery Type of 1984

1986-89 **Photo. & Engr.** ***Perf. 14***
1349 A679 5s Martinswall, Tyrol .75 .50
1350 A679 5s Tschauko Falls, Carinthia .65 .50
1351 A679 5s Dachstein Ice Caves .65 .40
1352 A679 5s Gauertal, Montafon .65 .40
1353 A679 5s Krimmler Waterfalls .65 .50
1354 A679 5s Lusthauswasser .65 .40
Nos. 1349-1354 (6) 4.00 2.70

Issued: No. 1349, 6/13/86; No. 1350, 7/4/86; No. 1351, 6/11/87; No. 1352, 8/21/87; No. 1353, 8/19/88; No. 1354, 9/1/89.

Waidhofen on Ybbs Township, 800th Anniv. — A739

1986, June 20 **Photo.** ***Perf. 13½***
1355 A739 4s multicolored .55 .40

Salzburg Local Railway, Cent. A740

1986, Aug. 8 **Photo.** ***Perf. 14***
1356 A740 4s multicolored .55 .40

Seals of Dukes Leopold Of Austria, Otakar of Styria, and Georgenberg Church — A741

1986, Aug. 14 **Photo. & Engr.**
1357 A741 5s multicolored .65 .50

Georgenberg Treaty, 800th anniv.

Julius Tandler (1869-1936), Social Reformer A742

1986, Aug. 22
1358 A742 4s multicolored .50 .40

Sonnblick Observatory, Cent. A743

Photo. & Engr.

1986, Sept. 5 ***Perf. 13½x14½***
1359 A743 4s Observatory, 1886 .50 .40

Discovery of Mandrake Root — A744

1986, Sept. 8 ***Perf. 14½x13½***
1360 A744 5s multicolored .65 .40

European Assoc. for Anesthesiology, 7th cong.

Monasteries and Abbeys Type of 1984

Designs: 5.50s, St. Gerold's Provostry, Vorarlberg. 7s, Loretto Monastery, Burgenland. 7.50s, Dominican Convent, Vienna. 8s, Zwettl Monastery. 10s, Wilten Monastery.

1986-88 **Photo. & Engr.** ***Perf. 14***
1361 A679a 5.50s multicolored 1.10 .25
1362 A679a 7s multicolored 1.60 .25
1363 A679a 7.50s multicolored 1.60 .25
1364 A679a 8s multicolored 1.60 .25
1365 A679a 10s multicolored 1.90 .25
Nos. 1361-1365 (5) 7.80 1.25

Issued: 5.50s, 9/12/86; 7.50s, 10/3; 7s, 8/14/87; 8s, 5/27/88; 10s, 3/18/88.

Otto Stoessl (d. 1936), Writer — A745

Photo. & Engr.
1986, Sept. 19 ***Perf. 14***
1366 A745 4s multicolored .50 .40

Vienna Fire Brigade, 300th Anniv. — A746

1986, Sept. 19 **Photo.**
1367 A746 4s Fireman, 1686 .80 .40

Silk Viennese Hunting Tapestry A747

Photo. & Engr.
1986, Sept. 19 ***Perf. 14***
1368 A747 5s multicolored .65 .50

Intl. conf. on Oriental Carpets, Vienna, Budapest.

A748

Photo. & Engr.
1986, Oct. 10 ***Perf. 14***
1369 A748 5s Minister at pulpit .65 .50

Protestant Act, 25th anniv., and Protestant Patent of Franz Josef I ensuring religious equality, 125th anniv.

Disintegration, by Walter Schmogner A749

1986, Oct. 17 ***Perf. 13½x14***
1370 A749 4s multicolored .55 .40

Franz Liszt, Composer, and Birthplace, Burgenland A750

1986, Oct. 17 ***Perf. 13½***
1371 A750 5s green & sepia .65 .40

Souvenir Sheet

European Security Conference, Vienna — A751

1986, Nov. 4 ***Perf. 13½x14***
1372 A751 6s Vienna .90 1.20

Strettweg Cart, 7th Cent. B.C. A752

Photo. & Engr.
1986, Nov. 26 ***Perf. 14***
1373 A752 4s multicolored .50 .40

Joanneum Styrian Land Museum, 175th anniv.

Christmas A753

Design: The Little Crib, bas-relief by Schwanthaler (1740-1810), Schlierbach Monastery.

1986, Nov. 28
1374 A753 5s gold & rose lake .65 .50

Federal Chamber of Commerce, 40th Anniv. — A754

1986, Dec. 2 **Photo.**
1375 A754 5s multicolored .65 .50

Industry A755

1986-91 ***Perf. 14x13½***
1376 A755 4s Steel workers .50 .40
1377 A755 4s Office worker, computer .55 .40
1378 A755 4s Lab assistant .55 .35
1379 A755 4.50s Textile worker .55 .40
1380 A755 5s Bricklayer .65 .50
Nos. 1376-1380 (5) 2.80 2.05

Issued: No. 1376, 12/4/86; No. 1377, 10/5/87; No. 1378, 10/21/88; 5s, 10/10/89; 4.50s, 10/11/91.

The Educated Eye, by Arnulf Rainer — A756

1987, Jan. 22 **Photo.** ***Perf. 13½x14***
1386 A756 5s multicolored .80 .60

Adult education in Vienna, cent.

The Large Blue Madonna, by Anton Faistauer (1887-1970) — A757

Paintings: 6s, Self-portrait, 1922, by A. Paris Gutersloh (1887-1973).

1987, Feb. 13 ***Perf. 14***
1387 A757 4s multicolored .60 .40
1388 A757 6s multicolored 1.00 .70

Europa 1987 — A758

Photo. & Engr.
1987, Apr. 6 ***Perf. 13½x14***
1389 A758 6s Hundertwasser House *2.00 1.00*

World Ice Hockey Championships, Vienna — A759

Perf. 13½x14½
1987, Apr. 17 **Photo.**
1390 A759 5s multicolored 1.00 .60

Opening of the Austria Center, Vienna A760

1987, Apr. 22
1391 A760 5s multicolored 1.00 .60

Salzburg City Charter, 700th Anniv. A761

1987, Apr. 24
1392 A761 5s multicolored 1.10 .70

Work-Men-Machines, Provincial Exhibition, Upper Austria — A762

Photo. & Engr.
1987, Apr. 29 ***Perf. 14***
1393 A762 4s Factory, 1920 .70 .40

Equal Rights for Men and Women — A763

1987, Apr. 29 **Photo.** ***Perf. 13½***
1394 A763 5s multicolored .80 .60

Adele Block-Bauer I, Abstract by Gustav Klimt — A764

Photo. & Engr.
1987, May 8 ***Perf. 13½***
1395 A764 4s multicolored .70 .40

The Era of Emperor Franz Joseph, provincial exhibition, Lower Austria.

Arthur Schnitzler (1862-1931), Poet — A765

1987, May 15 ***Perf. 14½x13½***

1396 A765 6s multicolored .90 .70

Von Raitenau, View of Salzburg A766

1987, May 15 ***Perf. 14***

1397 A766 4s multicolored .60 .50

Prince Archbishop Wolf Dietrich von Raitenau, patron of baroque architecture in Salzburg, provincial exhibition.

Lace, Lustenau Municipal Arms A767

1987, May 22

1398 A767 5s multicolored .80 .60

Lustenau, 1100th anniv.

Souvenir Sheet

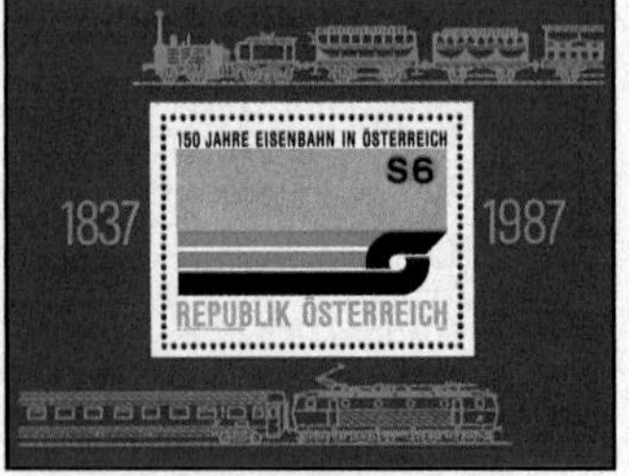

Austrian Railways Sesquicentenary — A768

1987, June 5 **Photo.** ***Perf. 13½***

1399 A768 6s multicolored 1.10 1.10

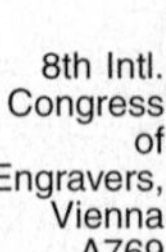

8th Intl. Congress of Engravers, Vienna A769

Photo. & Engr.

1987, June 17 ***Perf. 14***

1400 A769 5s gray, gray brn & dull rose .80 .50

Dr. Karl Josef Bayer (1847-1904), Chemist — A770

1987, June 22 ***Perf. 14x13½***

1401 A770 5s multicolored .80 .60

Eighth Intl. Light Metals Congress, June 22-26, Leoben and Vienna; Bayer Technique for producing aluminum oxide from bauxite, cent.

Shipping on Achensee, Cent. — A771

1987, June 26 **Photo.**

1402 A771 4s multicolored .60 .50

Ombudsmen's Office, 10th Anniv. — A772

1987, July 1

1403 A772 5s Palais Rottal, Vienna .80 .60

Dr. Erwin Schrodinger (1887-1961), 1933 Nobel Laureate in Physics — A773

1987, Aug. 11 **Photo. & Engr.**

1404 A773 5s dull olive bister, choc & buff .80 .60

Freistadt Exhibitions, 125th Anniv. A774

1987, Aug. 11 ***Perf. 14x14½***

1405 A774 5s multicolored .80 .60

Arbing, 850th Anniv. — A775

1987, Aug. 21 ***Perf. 13½***

1406 A775 5s multicolored .80 .60

1987 World Cycling Championships, Villach to Vienna — A776

1987, Aug. 25 ***Perf. 14***

1407 A776 5s multicolored .80 .60

World Congress of Savings Banks, Vienna A777

Perf. 13½x14½

1987, Sept. 9 **Photo.**

1408 A777 5s multicolored .80 .60

Johann Michael Haydn (1737-1806), Composer A778

Perf. 13½x14½

1987, Sept. 14 **Engr.**

1409 A778 4s dull violet .60 .50

Paul Hofhaymer (1459-1537), Composer A779

Photo. & Engr.

1987, Sept. 11 ***Perf. 14***

1410 A779 4s gold, blk & ultra .60 .50

Bearded Vulture — A780

1987, Sept. 25

1411 A780 4s multicolored .60 .50

Innsbruck Zoo, 25th anniv.

Baumgottinnen, by Arnulf Neuwirth — A781

1987, Oct. 9 ***Perf. 14x13½***

1412 A781 5s multicolored .80 .50

Modern Art.

Gambling Monopoly, 200th Anniv. — A782

Perf. 14½x13½

1987, Oct. 30 **Photo.**

1413 A782 5s Lottery drum .80 .60

Christoph Willibald Gluck (1714-1787), Composer A784

Photo. & Engr.

1987, Nov. 13 ***Perf. 14***

1415 A784 5s cream & blk .80 .60

Oskar Helmer (b. 1887), Politician — A785

1987, Nov. 13

1416 A785 4s multicolored .60 .50

Joseph Mohr (1792-1848) and Franz Gruber (1787-1863), Opening Bars of "Silent Night, Holy Night" — A786

1987, Nov. 27

1417 A786 5s multicolored 1.20 .60

Christmas.

Intl. Education Congress of Salesian Fathers — A787

Photo. & Engr.

1988, Jan. 12 ***Perf. 13½***

1418 A787 5s St. John Bosco, children .80 .60

Ernst Mach (1838-1916), Physicist — A788

Photo. & Engr.

1988, Feb. 19 ***Perf. 14½x13½***

1419 A788 6s multicolored .90 .60

Village with Bridge (1904), by Franz von Zulow (1883-1963), Painter — A789

1988, Feb. 25 **Photo.** ***Perf. 14½x14***

1420 A789 4s multicolored .70 .50

Biedermeier Provincial Exhibition, Vormarz in Vienna — A790

Painting: Confiscation, by Ferdinand Georg Waldmuller (1793-1865).

Photo. & Engr.

1988, Mar. 11 ***Perf. 14***

1421 A790 4s multicolored .70 .50

Anschluss of March 11, 1938 — A791

1988, Mar. 11 **Photo.** ***Perf. 13½***

1422 A791 5s gray olive, brn blk & ver .80 .50

No. 2 Aigen Steam Locomotive, 1887 A792

1988, Mar. 22 ***Perf. 13½x14½***

1423 A792 4s shown .80 .50

1424 A792 5s Electric train, Josepsplatz 1.00 .60

Muhlkreis Railway, cent. (4s); Vienna Local Railway, cent. (5s).

World Wildlife Fund — A793

Photo. & Engr.

1988, Apr. 15 ***Perf. 13½x14***

1425 A793 5s Bee eater .90 .60

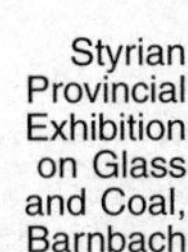

Styrian Provincial Exhibition on Glass and Coal, Barnbach A794

1988, Apr. 29 ***Perf. 13½***

1426 A794 4s Frosted glass .70 .50

Intl. Red Cross, 125th Anniv. — A795

1988, May 6 **Photo.** ***Perf. 14***

1427 A795 12s grn, brt red & blk 1.90 1.25

Gothic Silver Censer — A796

1988, May 6 **Photo. & Engr.**

1428 A796 4s multicolored .60 .50

Art and Monasticism at the Birth of Austria, lower Austrian provincial exhibition, Seitenstetten.

Europa 1988 A797

Communication and transportation.

1988, May 13 **Photo.**

1429 A797 6s multicolored *1.50 .60*

Mattsee Monastery and Lion of Alz — A798

1988, May 18 **Photo. & Engr.**

1430 A798 4s multicolored .70 .50

Provincial exhibition at Mattsee Monastery: Bavarian Tribes in Salzburg.

Weinberg Castle A799

Perf. 13½x14½

1988, May 20 **Photo.**

1431 A799 4s multicolored .70 .50

Upper Austrian provincial exhibition: Weinberg Castle.

Odon von Horwath (1901-1938), Dramatist — A800

Photo. & Engr.

1988, June 1 ***Perf. 14½x13½***

1432 A800 6s olive bis & slate grn .90 .60

Stockerau Festival, 25th Anniv. — A801

1988, June 17 ***Perf. 14***

1433 A801 5s Stockerau Town Hall .80 .50

Tauern Motorway Opening — A802

1988, June 24 **Photo.** ***Perf. 13½x14***

1434 A802 4s multicolored .70 .50

Brixlegg, 1200th Anniv. A803

Photo. & Engr.

1988, July 1 ***Perf. 13½x14½***

1435 A803 5s multicolored .90 .50

View of Klagenfurt, Engraving by Matthaus Merian (1593-1650) — A804

Photo. & Engr.

1988, Aug. 12 ***Perf. 14***

1436 A804 5s multicolored .80 .60

Carinthian Postal Service, 400th Anniv.

Brixen-im-Thale, 1200th Anniv. — A805

1988, Aug. 12

1437 A805 5s multicolored .80 .50

Feldkirchen, 1100th Anniv. — A806

1988, Sept. 2 ***Perf. 13½***

1438 A806 5s multicolored .80 .50

Feldbach, 800th Anniv. A807

1988, Sept. 15 **Photo. & Engr.**

1439 A807 5s multicolored .80 .60

Ansfelden, 1200th Anniv. — A808

1988, Sept. 23 ***Perf. 14***

1440 A808 5s multicolored .80 .50

Exports A809

1988, Oct. 18 **Photo.** ***Perf. 14x13½***

1441 A809 8s multicolored 2.25 2.00

No. 1441 has a holographic image. Soaking in water may affect the hologram.

Vienna Concert Hall, 75th Anniv. A810

Photo. & Engr.

1988, Oct. 19 ***Perf. 13½***

1442 A810 5s multicolored .80 .60

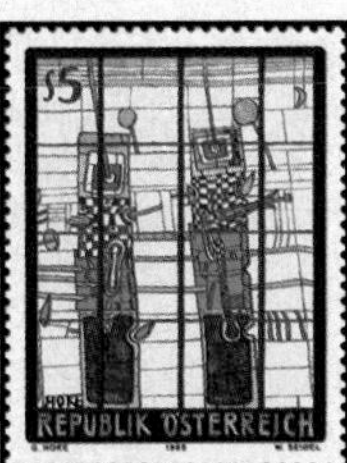

The Watchmen, by Giselbert Hoke — A811

1988, Oct. 21 ***Perf. 14***

1443 A811 5s multicolored .80 .60

Social Democrats Unification Party Congress, Cent. — A812

1988, Nov. 11 Photo. ***Perf. 14½x14***
1444 A812 4s multicolored .70 .60

Leopold Schonbauer (1888-1963), Physician — A813

Photo. & Engr.
1988, Nov. 11 ***Perf. 14½x13½***
1445 A813 4s multicolored .65 .50

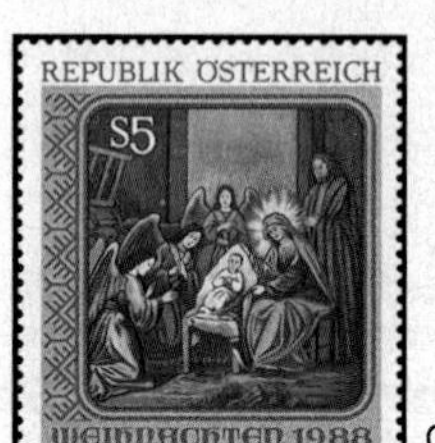

Christmas A814

Nativity painting from St. Barbara's Church.

1988, Nov. 25 ***Perf. 14***
1446 A814 5s multicolored .80 .60

Benedictine Monastery, Melk, 900th Anniv. — A815

Design: Fresco by Paul Troger.

1989, Mar. 17 Photo. & Engr.
1447 A815 5s multicolored .80 .50

Madonna and Child, by Lucas Cranach (1472-1553) A816

1989, Mar. 17 ***Perf. 14½x13½***
1448 A816 4s multicolored .60 .50

Diocese of Innsbruck, 25th anniv.

Marianne Hainisch (1839-1936), Women's Rights Activist — A817

1989, Mar. 24 ***Perf. 14x13½***
1449 A817 6s multicolored 1.00 .70

Glider Plane and Parachutist A818

1989, Mar. 31 Photo. ***Perf. 14***
1450 A818 6s multicolored 1.00 .70

World Gliding Championships, Wiener Neustadt, and World Parachuting Championships, Damuls.

Bruck an der Leitha Commune, 750th Anniv. — A819

Painting by Georg Matthaus Vischer (1628-1696).

1989, Apr. 21
1451 A819 5s multicolored .80 .50

Die Malerei, 1904, by Rudolf Jettmar (1869-1939) A820

Perf. 14½x13½
1989, Apr. 21 Photo.
1452 A820 5s multicolored .80 .50

Holy Trinity Church, Stadl-Paura A821

1989, Apr. 26 Photo. & Engr.
1453 A821 5s multicolored .80 .50

Michael Prunner (1669-1739), baroque architect.

Eduard Suess (1831-1914), Structural Geologist and Map — A822

Portrait by J. Krieher (1800-1876).

1989, Apr. 26
1454 A822 6s multicolored .90 .80

Ludwig Wittgenstein (1889-1951), Philosopher A823

1989, Apr. 26
1455 A823 5s multicolored .80 .50

Styrian Provincial Exhibition, Judenburg A824

Design: Judenburg, 17th cent., an engraving by Georg Matthaus Vischer.

1989, Apr. 28 ***Perf. 14x13½***
1456 A824 4s multicolored .70 .50

Industrial Technology Exhibition, Pottenstein — A825

1989, Apr. 28 Photo. ***Perf. 13½***
1457 A825 4s Steam engine .70 .50

Radstadt Township, 700th Anniv. A826

1989, May 3 Photo. ***Perf. 13½x14½***
1458 A826 5s multicolored .80 .50

Europa 1989 A827

1989, May 5
1459 A827 6s Toy boat *1.50 .60*

Monastery Church at Lambach, 900th Anniv. — A828

Photo. & Engr.
1989, May 19 ***Perf. 14***
1460 A828 4s multicolored .70 .50

Paddle Steamer *Gisela* A829

1989, May 19 Photo. ***Perf. 13½***
1461 A829 5s multicolored 1.25 .60

Shipping on the Traunsee, 150th anniv.

St. Andra im Lavanttal, 650th Anniv. A830

Period cityscape by Matthaus Merian.

1989, May 26 Photo. & Engr.
1462 A830 5s multicolored .80 .60

Richard Strauss (1864-1949), Composer A831

Photo. & Engr.
1989, June 1 ***Perf. 14½x13½***
1463 A831 6s dark brn, gold & red brn 1.00 .70

Achensee Railway, Cent. A832

1989, June 8 Photo. ***Perf. 13½***
1464 A832 5s multicolored 1.00 .50

Monastery Type of 1984

Design: 50g, Vorau Abbey, Styria. 1s, Monastery of Mehrerau, Vorarlberg. 1.50s, Monastery of the German Order in Vienna. 2s, Bendictine Monastery, Michaelbeuern. 11s, Engelszell Abbey. 12s, Monastery of the Hospitalers, Eisenstadt. 17s, St. Peter, Salzburg. 20s, Wernberg Monastery.

1989-92 Photo. & Engr. ***Perf. 14***

1465	A679a	50g multi	.25	.25
1466	A679a	1s multi	.25	.25
1467	A679a	1.50s multi	.25	.25
1468	A679a	2s multi	.50	.25
1469	A679a	11s multi	2.50	.50
1470	A679a	12s multi	4.00	.90
1471	A679a	17s multi	4.50	.90
1472	A679a	20s multi	6.00	.60
		Nos. 1465-1472 (8)	18.25	3.90

Issued: 1s, 9/1/89; 17s, 6/29/89; 11s, 3/9/90; 50g, 10/12/90; 20s, 5/3/91; 2s, 9/27/91; 1.50s, 10/23/92; 12s, 6/17/92.

Interparliamentary Union, Cent. — A833

Photo. & Engr.
1989, June 30 ***Perf. 14***
1475 A833 6s Parliament, Vienna 1.00 .70

Social Security in Austria, Cent. — A834

1989, Aug. 1 **Photo.**
1476 A834 5s multicolored .80 .50

UN Offices in Vienna, 10th Anniv. A835

1989, Aug. 23
1477 A835 8s multicolored 1.50 .80

Wildalpen, 850th Anniv. A836

Photo. & Engr.
1989, Sept. 15 ***Perf. 13½x14***
1478 A836 5s Foundry, coat of arms .80 .60

33rd Congress of the Association for Quality Assurance (EOQC) — A837

1989, Sept. 18 **Photo.** ***Perf. 14x13½***
1479 A837 6s multicolored .90 .70

14th World Congress of the Soc. for Criminal Law (AIDP) A838

Photo. & Engr.
1989, Oct. 2 ***Perf. 13½***
1480 A838 6s Justice Palace, Vienna .90 .70

Lebensbaum, by Ernst Steiner — A839

1989, Oct. 10 ***Perf. 13½x14***
1481 A839 5s multicolored .80 .60

Georg Trakl (1887-1914), Expressionist Poet — A840

1989, Nov. 6 **Photo.** ***Perf. 14½x13½***
1482 A840 4s Trakl .70 .50
1483 A840 4s Anzengruber .70 .50

Ludwig Anzengruber (1839-1889), playwright and novelist.

Alfred Fried (1864-1921), Pacifist, Publisher and 1911 Nobel Laureate — A841

1989, Nov. 10 **Photo. & Engr.**
1484 A841 6s multicolored 1.00 .70

Parish Church Christ Child, by Johann Carl Reslfeld A842

1989, Dec. 1 ***Perf. 13½x14½***
1485 A842 5s multicolored .80 .60

Christmas.

Postal Communications in Europe, 500th Anniv. — A843

The Young Post Rider, an Engraving by Albrecht Durer

Photo. & Engr.
1990, Jan. 12 ***Perf. 14***
1486 A843 5s multicolored 1.00 .60

See Belgium No. 1332, Germany No. 1592, Berlin No. 9N584 and German Democratic Republic No. 2791.

Hahnenkamm Alpine Competition, Kitzbuhel, 50th Anniv. — A844

Perf. 13½x14½
1990, Jan. 12 **Photo.**
1487 A844 5s multicolored .90 .65

Salomon Sulzer (1804-90), Cantor and Composer A845

Perf. 14½x13½
1990, Jan. 17 **Photo.**
1488 A845 4.50s multicolored .75 .55

Friedrich Emich (1860-1940), Chemist — A846

1990, Jan. 22 **Photo. & Engr.**
1489 A846 6s claret & pale green 1.00 .75

Miniature from the *Market Book of Grein,* by Ulrich Schreier, c. 1490 A847

1990, Mar. 9 ***Perf. 14***
1490 A847 5s multicolored .90 .65

City of Linz, 500th anniv.

University Seals — A848

1990, Apr. 6
1491 A848 5s multicolored .90 .65

625th Anniv. of Vienna University and 175th anniv. of Vienna Technical University.

Scenery Type of 1984

1990-97 ***Perf. 14***
1492 A679 5s Styrian Vineyards .90 .65
1493 A679 5s Obir Caverns .90 .65
1494 A679 5s Natural Bridge, Vorarlberg .90 .65
1495 A679 6s Wilder Kaiser Mountain, Tyrol 1.10 .80
1496 A679 6s Peggau Cave, Styria .90 .75
1497 A679 6s Moorland, swamp, Heidenreichstein .90 .55
1498 A679 6s Hohe Tauern Natl. Park 1.00 .60
1499 A679 6s Nussberg Vineyards 1.10 1.10
Nos. 1492-1499 (8) 7.70 5.75

Issued: No. 1492, 4/27; No. 1493, 3/26/91; No. 1494, 2/5/92; No. 1495, 2/19/93; No. 1496, 4/29/94; No. 1497, 5/19/95; No. 1498, 3/29/96; No. 1499, 2/21/97.

Anthering, 1200th Anniv. — A849

Church and municipal arms.

1990, Apr. 27 **Photo.** ***Perf. 14x13½***
1500 A849 7s multicolored 1.10 .70

Labor Day, Cent. — A850

1990, Apr. 30 **Photo.** ***Perf. 13½***
1501 A850 4.50s multicolored .80 .65

Seckau Abbey, 850th Anniv. — A851

1990, May 4 **Engr.** ***Perf. 14x13½***
1502 A851 4.50s bluish black .80 .60

Ebene Reichenau Post Office A852

1990, May 4 **Photo.** ***Perf. 13½x14***
1503 A852 7s multicolored *2.25 1.10*

Europa.

Hans Makart (1840-84), Self-Portrait A853

Self Portrait: 5s, Egon Schiele (1890-1918).

Photo. & Engr.
1990, May 29 ***Perf. 14***
1504 A853 4.50s multicolored .80 .70
1505 A853 5s multicolored 1.00 1.00

Ferdinand Raimund (1790-1836), Actor — A854

1990, June 1 **Photo.** ***Perf. 14x13½***
1506 A854 4.50s multicolored .80 .65

Christ Healing the Sick by Rembrandt A855

Photo. & Engr.
1990, June 5 ***Perf. 14***
1507 A855 7s multicolored 1.25 1.00

2nd Intl. Christus Medicus Cong., Bad Ischl.

Hardegg, 700th Anniv. — A856

Photo. & Engr.

1990, June 8 ***Perf. 13½x14***
1508 A856 4.50s multicolored .80 .65

Oberdrauburg, 750th Anniv. — A857

1990, June 8 **Photo.**
1509 A857 5s multicolored 1.00 .65

Gumpoldskirchen, 850th Anniv. — A858

Photo. & Engr.

1990, June 15 ***Perf. 13½***
1510 A858 5s multicolored 1.00 .65

Mathias Zdarsky (1856-1940), Alpine Skier — A859

1990, June 20 ***Perf. 14x13½***
1511 A859 5s multicolored .90 .65

Telegraph, 1880, Anton Tschechow, 1978 — A860

1990, June 28 **Photo.** ***Perf. 14***
1512 A860 9s multicolored 1.50 1.10

Modern shipbuilding in Austria, 150th anniv.

Joseph Friedrich Perkonig (1890-1959), Novelist — A861

Photo. & Engr.

1990, Aug. 3 ***Perf. 14x13½***
1513 A861 5s gold & brown .85 .65

Herr des Regenbogens, by Robert Zeppel-Sperl A862

Photo. & Engr.

1990, Aug. 30 ***Perf. 13½x14***
1514 A862 5s multicolored .85 .65

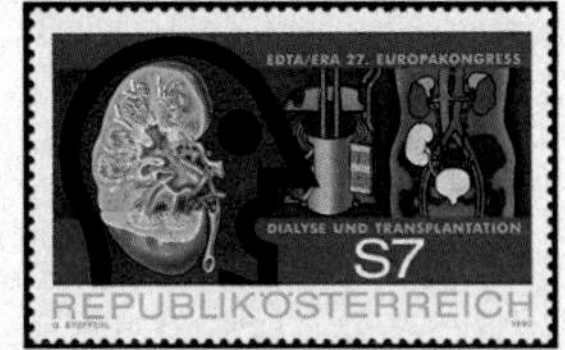

European Dialysis and Transplantation Society, 27th Congress — A863

1990, Sept. 4 **Photo.** ***Perf. 14***
1515 A863 7s multicolored 1.25 .80

Franz Werfel (1890-1945), Writer — A864

Photo. & Engr.

1990, Sept. 11 ***Perf. 14x13½***
1516 A864 5s multicolored .90 .65

Austrian Forces in UN Peace Keeping Forces, 30th Anniv. A865

1990, Sept. 20 **Photo.** ***Perf. 13½***
1517 A865 7s multicolored 1.25 .80

Federal and State Arms A866

1990, Sept. 24 **Photo. & Engr.**
1518 A866 5s multicolored .90 .55

Federalism in Austria.

Mining Univ., Leoben, 150th Anniv. — A867

Photo & Engr.

1990, Oct. 22 ***Perf. 14***
1519 A867 4.50s blk, bl grn & red .80 .45

Karl Freiherr von Vogelsang (1818-90), Politician — A868

Photo. & Engr.

1990, Nov. 8 ***Perf. 14x13½***
1520 A868 4.50s multicolored .80 .45

Metalworkers and Miners Trade Union, Cent. — A869

1990, Nov. 16 ***Perf. 14***
1521 A869 5s multicolored .90 .65

3rd World Curling Championships A870

1990, Nov. 23 **Photo.** ***Perf. 14x13½***
1522 A870 7s multicolored 1.25 .80

Palmhouse at Schonbrunn — A871

1990, Nov. 30 ***Perf. 14***
1523 A871 5s multicolored .90 .65

Christmas A872

Altar in Klosterneuburg Abbey by the Master from Verdun.

Photo. & Engr.

1990, Nov. 23 ***Perf. 13½***
1524 A872 5s multicolored .90 .55

Franz Grillparzer (1791-1872), Dramatic Poet — A873

Photo. & Engr.

1991, Jan. 15 ***Perf. 14x13½***
1525 A873 4.50s multicolored .80 .55

Alpine Skiing World Championship, Saalbach-Hinterglemm — A874

1991, Jan. 21 ***Perf. 13½***
1526 A874 5s multicolored .90 .65

Bruno Kreisky (1911-90), Chancellor A875

1991, Jan. 21 **Photo.** ***Perf. 14x13½***
1527 A875 5s multicolored .95 .70

Friedrich Freiherr von Schmidt (1825-1891), Architect — A876

1991, Jan. 21 ***Perf. 14***
1528 A876 7s multicolored 1.40 1.10

Visual Arts A877

Designs: 4.50s, Donner Fountain, Vienna, by Raphael Donner (1693-1741), sculptor. 5s, Kitzbuhel in Winter, by Alfons Walde (1891-1958), painter. 7s, Vienna Stock Exchange, Theophil Hansen (1813-1891), architect.

1991, Feb. 8
1529 A877 4.50s multicolored .75 .75
1530 A877 5s multicolored .85 .85
1531 A877 7s multicolored 1.10 1.10
Nos. 1529-1531 (3) 2.70 2.70

See No. 1543.

Marie von Ebner Eschenbach (1830-1916), Novelist A878

1991, Mar. 12 **Engr.** ***Perf. 13½x14½***
1532 A878 4.50s rose violet .80 .55

Miniature Sheet

A879

Design: a, Wolfgang Amadeus Mozart (1756-1791), Composer. b, Magic Flute Fountain, Vienna.

Photo. & Engr.

1991, Mar. 22 ***Perf. 13½***
1533 Sheet of 2 + label 2.40 3.25
a.-b. A879 5s any single .80 .80

Spittal an der Drau, 800th Anniv. A880

1991, Apr. 11 ***Perf. 14***
1534 A880 4.50s multicolored .75 .60

Europa A881

1991, May 3 Photo. ***Perf. 14***
1535 A881 7s ERS-1 satellite *2.75 1.00*

Garden Banquet by Anthony Bays A882

1991, May 10 Photo. ***Perf. 13½***
1536 A882 5s multicolored .90 .65

Vorarlberg Provincial Exhibition, Hohenems.

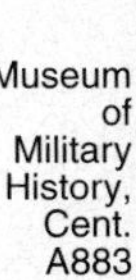

Museum of Military History, Cent. A883

7s, Interior of Museum of Art History.

Photo. & Engr.

1991, May 24 ***Perf. 13½***
1537 A883 5s multicolored .95 .95
1538 A883 7s multicolored 1.40 1.40

Museum of Art History, Cent. (No. 1538).

Grein, 500th Anniv. A884

1991, May 24 Photo. ***Perf. 14***
1539 A884 4.50s multicolored .80 .65

Tulln, 1200th Anniv. A885

1991, May 24 ***Perf. 13½x14***
1540 A885 5s multicolored .95 .65

Completion of Karawanken Tunnels — A886

1991, May 31 ***Perf. 14x13½***
1541 A886 7s multicolored 1.25 1.00

5th Anniv. of St. Polten as Provincial Capital of Lower Austria A887

1991, July 5 Photo. ***Perf. 14***
1542 A887 5s multicolored 1.00 .65

Visual Arts Type of 1991

Design: 4.50s, Karlsplatz Station of Vienna Subway by Otto Wagner (1841-1918), Architect.

1991, July 12 Photo. & Engr.
1543 A877 4.50s multicolored .75 .60

Rowing and Junior Canoeing World Championships, Vienna — A888

1991, Aug. 20 Photo. ***Perf. 13½x14***
1544 A888 5s multicolored .85 .70

European Congress of Radiologists — A889

1991, Sept. 13 ***Perf. 14***
1545 A889 7s multicolored 1.20 1.00

Paracelsus (1493-1541), Physician — A890

1991, Sept. 27 ***Perf. 14x13½***
1546 A890 4.50s multicolored .75 .60

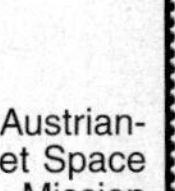

Joint Austrian-Soviet Space Mission A891

1991, Oct. 2 ***Perf. 14***
1547 A891 9s multicolored 1.50 1.25

Austrian Folk Festivals A892

4.50s, Almabtrieb, Tyrol. 5s, Winzerkrone, Vienna. 7s, Ernte-Monstranz, Styria.

1991, Oct. 4 Photo. & Engr.
1548 A892 4.50s multicolored .75 .60
1549 A892 5s multicolored .90 .75
1550 A892 7s multicolored 1.20 1.00
Nos. 1548-1550 (3) 2.85 2.35

See Nos. 1577-1579, 1619-1621, 1633-1635, 1671-1673, 1694, 1705-1706, 1714, 1730, 1741, 1752-1753, 1762, 1778, 1799-1800, 1805-1806, 1824, 1836-1838, 1954, 2020, 2050.

The General by Rudolph Pointner A893

Photo. & Engr.

1991, Oct. 11 ***Perf. 13½x14***
1551 A893 5s multicolored .85 .70

Birth of Christ, Baumgartenberg Church — A894

1991, Nov. 29
1552 A894 5s multicolored .85 .85

Christmas.

Julius Raab, Politician, Birth Cent. — A895

1991, Nov. 29 ***Perf. 14x13½***
1553 A895 4.50s red brn & brn .75 .60

1992 Winter and Summer Olympic Games A897

1992, Jan. 14 Photo. ***Perf. 14***
1555 A897 7s multicolored 1.25 1.00

Trade Union of Clerks in Private Enterprises, Cent. — A898

1992, Jan. 14
1556 A898 5.50s multicolored .95 .80

8th Natural Run Toboggan World Championships A899

1992, Jan. 29 ***Perf. 14x13½***
1557 A899 5s multicolored .90 .75

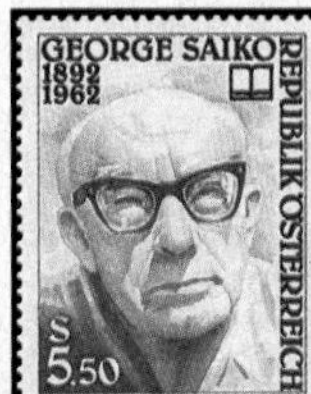

George Saiko, Writer, Birth Cent. — A900

1992, Feb. 5 Engr. ***Perf. 14x13½***
1558 A900 5.50s brown .95 .80

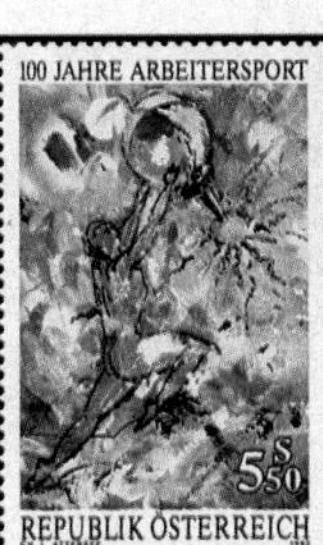

Worker's Sports, Cent. — A901

1992, Feb. 5 Photo. ***Perf. 14***
1559 A901 5.50s multicolored .95 .80

Souvenir Sheet

Vienna Philharmonic Orchestra, 150th Anniv. — A902

Photo. & Engr.

1992, Mar. 27 *Perf. 14*
1560 A902 5.50s multicolored 1.25 1.60

Scientists A903

Designs: 5s, Franz Joseph Muller von Reichenstein (1742-1825), discoverer of tellurium. 5.50s, Dr. Paul Kitaibel (1757-1817), botanist. 6s, Christian Johann Doppler (1803-1853), physicist. 7s, Richard Kuhn (1900-1967), chemist.

1992, Mar. 27 **Photo.**
1561 A903 5s multicolored .90 .75
1562 A903 5.50s multicolored .90 .75
1563 A903 6s multicolored 1.10 .85
1564 A903 7s multicolored 1.25 1.10
Nos. 1561-1564 (4) 4.15 3.45

Railway Workers Union, Cent. A904

1992, Apr. 2 *Perf. 14x13½*
1565 A904 5.50s black & red 1.00 .65

Norbert Hanrieder (1842-1913), Poet — A905

Photo. & Engr.

1992, Apr. 30 *Perf. 14x13½*
1566 A905 5.50s purple & buff 1.10 .90

Carl Zeller (1842-1898) and Karl Millocker (1842-1899), Operetta Composers A906

Photo. & Engr.

1992, Apr. 30 *Perf. 14*
1567 A906 6s multicolored 1.10 .85

LD Steel Mill, 40th Anniv. A907

1992, May 8 **Photo.** *Perf. 14x13½*
1568 A907 5s multicolored .95 .70

Discovery of America, 500th Anniv. A908

Photo. & Engr.

1992, May 8 *Perf. 14*
1569 A908 7s multicolored *2.25 1.10*

Europa.

Austro-Swiss Treaty on Regulation of Rhine River, Cent. — A909

1992, May 8 **Photo.** *Perf. 13½x14*
1570 A909 7s multicolored 1.25 1.10

Protection of the Alps — A910

1992, May 22 *Perf. 14x13½*
1571 A910 5.50s multicolored 1.00 .85

See Switzerland No. 916.

Dr. Anna Dengel (1892-1980), Physician — A911

1992, May 22 **Photo. & Engr.**
1572 A911 5.50s multicolored 1.00 .65

Sebastian Rieger (1867-1953), Poet — A912

1992, May 22 **Engr.**
1573 A912 5s red brown .85 .70

Lienz, 750th Anniv. A913

1992, June 17 **Photo.** *Perf. 14x13½*
1574 A913 5s Town Hall .90 .70

Intl. Congress of Austrian Society of Surgeons A914

Photo. & Engr.

1992, June 17 *Perf. 14*
1575 A914 6s multicolored 1.10 .90

Dr. Kurt Waldheim, President of Austria, 1986-92 — A915

1992, June 22 *Perf. 14x13½*
1576 A915 5.50s multicolored 1.00 .85

Folk Festivals Type of 1991

Designs: 5s, Marksman's target, Lower Austria. 5.50s, Peasant's chest, Carinthia. 7s, Votive icon, Vorarlberg.

Photo. & Engr.

1992, Sept. 18 *Perf. 14*
1577 A892 5s multicolored .90 .90
1578 A892 5.50s multicolored 1.10 1.10
1579 A892 7s multicolored 1.25 1.25
Nos. 1577-1579 (3) 3.25 3.25

Marchfeld Canal — A917

1992, Oct. 9 **Photo.** *Perf. 13½x14*
1580 A917 5s multicolored .90 .70

5th Intl. Ombudsman Conference, Vienna — A918

Photo & Engr.

1992, Oct. 9 *Perf. 14*
1581 A918 5.50s multicolored .95 .65

The Clearance of Seawater, by Peter Pongratz A919

1992, Oct. 9
1582 A919 5.50s multicolored .95 .75

Academy of Fine Arts, 300th Anniv. — A920

Photo. & Engr.

1992, Oct. 23 *Perf. 14*
1583 A920 5s red & blue .90 .75

Birth of Christ, by Johann Georg Schmidt A921

1992, Nov. 27 *Perf. 14x13½*
1584 A921 5.50s multicolored 1.10 .65

Christmas.

Veit Koniger, Sculptor, Death Bicent. A922

Photo. & Engr.

1992, Nov. 27 *Perf. 14*
1585 A922 5s multicolored .90 .80

Herman Potocnik, Theoretician of Geosynchronous Satellite Orbit, Birth Cent. — A923

1992, Nov. 27 **Photo.**
1586 A923 10s multicolored 2.00 1.60

Famous Buildings A924

5s, Statues & dome of Imperial Palace, Vienna, designed by Joseph Emanuel Fischer von Erlach. 5.50s, Kinsky Palace, designed by Lukas von Hildebrandt. 7s, Vienna State Opera, designed by Eduard van der Null & August Siccard von Siccardsburg.

1993, Jan. 22 **Photo. & Engr.**
1587 A924 5s multicolored 1.00 .80
1588 A924 5.50s multicolored 1.10 .90
1589 A924 7s multicolored 1.40 1.10
Nos. 1587-1589 (3) 3.50 2.80

Joseph Emanuel Fischer von Erlach, 300th birth anniv. (No. 1587). Johann Lukas von Hildebrandt, 325th birth anniv. (No. 1588). Eduard van der Null, August Siccard von Siccardsburg, 125th death anniv. (No. 1589).

Radio Dispatched Medical Service, 25th Anniv. — A925

1993, Feb. 19 **Photo.**
1590 A925 5s multicolored 1.00 .80

Typewriter Made by Peter Mitterhofer (1822-1893) A926

1993, Feb. 19 ***Perf. 13½x14***
1591 A926 17s multicolored 3.50 2.75

Popular Entertainers — A927

Strada del Sole, by Rainhard Fendrich.

1993, Mar. 19 **Photo.** ***Perf. 14***
1592 A927 5.50s multicolored 1.00 .80

See Nos. 1626, 1639.

Charles Sealsfield (1793-1864), Writer A928

Photo. & Engr.

1993, Mar. 19 ***Perf. 13½x14***
1593 A928 10s multicolored 1.75 1.40

Rights of the Child — A930

1993, Apr. 16 **Photo.** ***Perf. 13½x14***
1595 A930 7s multicolored 1.25 1.00

Flying Harlequin, by Paul Flora A931

1993, Apr. 16 **Photo. & Engr.**
1596 A931 7s multicolored *3.75 1.00*

Europa.

Monastery of Admont — A932

Designs: 1s, Detail of abbesse's crosier, St. Gabriel Abbey, Styria. 5.50s, Death, wooden statue by Josef Stammel (1695-1765). 6s, Stained glass, Mariastern-Gwiggen Monastery. 7s, Marble lion, Franciscan Monastery, Salzburg. 7.50s, Cupola fresco, by Paul Troger, Monastery of Altenburg. 8s, Gothic entry, Wilhering Monastery, Upper Austria. 10s, Altarpiece, St. Peregrinus praying, Maria Luggau Monastery. 20s, Crosier, Fiecht Monastery. 26s, Sculpture of Mater Dolorosa, Franciscan Monastery, Schwaz, Tirol. 30s, Madonna of Scottish Order, Schottenstift Monastery, Vienna.

Photo. & Engr.

1993-95 ***Perf. 13¾x14***

1599	A932	1s multicolored	.25	.25
1600	A932	5.50s multicolored	2.00	.25
1601	A932	6s multicolored	1.25	.25
1602	A932	7s multicolored	1.75	.25
1603	A932	7.50s multicolored	2.00	.55
1604	A932	8s multicolored	2.25	.65
1605	A932	10s multicolored	2.50	.50
1606	A932	20s multicolored	5.00	.55
1607	A932	26s multicolored	6.00	.75
1608	A932	30s multicolored	8.00	1.25
		Nos. 1599-1608 (10)	31.00	5.25

Issued: 5.50s, 4/16; 6s, 9/17; 20s, 10/8; 7.50s, 4/4/94; 10s, 8/26/94; 30s, 10/7/94; 7s, 11/18/94; 8s, 9/15/95; 26s, 10/6/95; 1s, 4/28/95.

Peter Rosegger (1843-1918), Poet — A933

1993, May 5 **Photo.** ***Perf. 14x13½***
1617 A933 5.50s green & black 1.00 .80

Lake Constance Steamer Hohentwiel A934

1993, May 5 **Photo.** ***Perf. 14***
1618 A934 6s multicolored 1.50 .85

See Germany No. 1786, Switzerland No. 931.

Folk Festivals Type of 1991

Designs: 5s, Corpus Christi Day Procession, Upper Austria. 5.50s, Blockdrawing, Burgenland. 7s, Cracking whip when snow is melting, Salzburg.

Photo. & Engr.

1993, June 11 ***Perf. 14***

1619	A892	5s multicolored	.90	.70
1620	A892	5.50s multicolored	1.00	.80
1621	A892	7s multicolored	1.10	1.00
		Nos. 1619-1621 (3)	3.00	2.50

UN Conference on Human Rights, Vienna A935

1993, June 11 **Photo.**
1622 A935 10s multicolored 1.75 1.40

Franz Jagerstatter (1907-1943), Conscientious Objector — A936

1993, Aug. 6 **Photo.** ***Perf. 14x13½***
1623 A936 5.50s multicolored 1.00 .80

Schafberg Railway, Cent. A937

1993, Aug. 6 ***Perf. 13½x14***
1624 A937 6s multicolored 1.10 .90

Self-portrait with Puppet, by Rudolf Wacker (1893-1939) A938

Photo. & Engr.

1993, Aug. 6 ***Perf. 14***
1625 A938 6s multicolored 1.10 .90

Popular Entertainers Type of 1993

Design: 5.50s, Granny, by Ludwig Hirsch.

1993, Sept. 3 **Photo.** ***Perf. 14***
1626 A927 5.50s multicolored 1.00 .80

Vienna Mens' Choral Society, 150th Anniv. A940

1993, Sept. 17 **Photo.** ***Perf. 14***
1627 A940 5s multicolored .90 .75

Easter, by Max Weiler — A941

Photo. & Engr.

1993, Oct. 8 ***Perf. 13½x14***
1628 A941 5.50s multicolored 1.00 .80

99 Heads, by Hundertwasser A942

1993, Oct. 8
1629 A942 7s multicolored 2.00 1.00

Council of Europe Conference, Vienna.

Austrian Republic, 75th Anniv. — A943

Design: 5.50s, Statue of Pallas Athena.

Photo. & Engr.

1993, Nov. 12 ***Perf. 13½x14***
1630 A943 5.50s multicolored 1.00 .80

Trade Unions in Austria, Cent. A944

1993, Nov. 12 **Photo.** ***Perf. 14***
1631 A944 5.50s multicolored 1.00 .80

Birth of Christ, by Master of the Krainburger Altar — A945

Photo. & Engr.

1993, Nov. 26 ***Perf. 13½x14***
1632 A945 5.50s multicolored 1.00 .80

Christmas.

Folklore and Customs Type of 1991

Antiques: 5.50s, Dolls, cradle, Vorarlberg. 6s, Sled, Steiermark. 7s, Godparent's bowl, Upper Austria.

Photo. & Engr.

1994, Jan. 28 ***Perf. 14***

1633	A892	5.50s multicolored	.90	.70
1634	A892	6s multicolored	1.10	.80
1635	A892	7s multicolored	1.25	.90
		Nos. 1633-1635 (3)	3.25	2.40

1994 Winter Olympics, Lillehammer, Norway — A946

1994, Feb. 9
1636 A946 7s multicolored 1.25 1.00

Vienna Mint, 800th Anniv. A947

1994, Feb. 18
1637 A947 6s multicolored 1.10 .90

Lying Lady, by Herbert Boeckl (1894-1966) — A948

1994, Mar. 18 Photo. *Perf. 14x13½*
1638 A948 5.50s multicolored 1.00 .70

Popular Entertainers Type of 1993

Design: 6s, Rock Me Amadeus, by Falco.

1994, Mar. 18 ***Perf. 14***
1639 A927 6s multicolored 1.00 .80

Wiener Neustadt, 800th Anniv. — A949

1994, Mar. 18
1640 A949 6s multicolored 1.00 .80

Lake Rudolph, Teleki-Hohnel Expedition — A950

Photo. & Engr.

1994, May 27 ***Perf. 14x13½***
1641 A950 7s multicolored *1.40 1.00*

Europa.

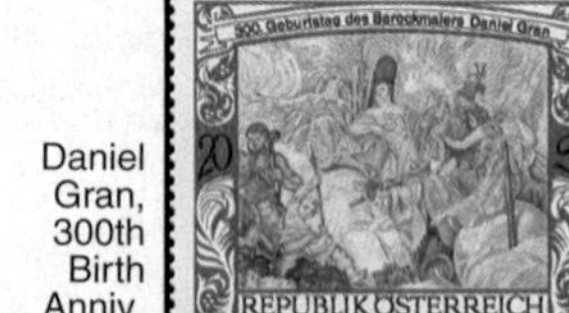

Daniel Gran, 300th Birth Anniv. A951

Fresco: 20s, Allegory of Theology, Jurisprudence and Medicine.

1994, May 27
1642 A951 20s multicolored 3.75 2.00

Carinthian Summer Festival, 25th Anniv. — A952

Design: 5.50s, Scene from The Prodigal Son.

Photo. & Engr.

1994, June 17 ***Perf. 14***
1643 A952 5.50s lake & gold 1.00 .75

Railway Centennials — A953

1994 Photo. & Engr. *Perf. 14*
1647 A953 5.50s Gailtal 1.00 .80
1648 A953 6s Murtal 1.25 .80

Issued: 5.50s, 6s, 6/17/94.

Hermann Gmeiner, 75th Birth Anniv. — A954

1994, June 17 ***Perf. 14x13½***
1656 A954 7s multicolored 1.25 1.00

Karl Seitz (1869-1950) Politician A955

1994, Aug. 12 Photo. *Perf. 14*
1657 A955 5.50s multicolored 1.00 .80

Karl Bohm (1894-1981), Conductor A956

Photo. & Engr.

1994, Aug. 26 ***Perf. 14x13½***
1658 A956 7s gold & dk blue 1.25 1.00

Ethnic Minorities in Austria A957

1994, Sept. 9 Photo. *Perf. 13½*
1659 A957 5.50s multicolored 1.00 .80

Franz Theodor Csokor (1885-1969), Writer — A958

7s, Joseph Roth (1894-1939), writer.

1994, Sept. 9 ***Perf. 14x13½***
1660 A958 6s multicolored 1.00 .80
1661 A958 7s multicolored 1.25 1.00

Savings Banks in Austria, 175th Anniv. — A959

Photo. & Engr.

1994, Oct. 7 ***Perf. 14x13½***
1662 A959 7s Coin bank 1.25 1.00

Modern Art — A960

Design: 6s, "Head," by Franz Ringel.

1994, Oct. 7 ***Perf. 13½x14***
1663 A960 6s multicolored 1.10 .90

Austrian Working Environment — A961

1994, Nov. 18 Photo. *Perf. 14*
1664 A961 6s Stewardess, child 1.10 .90

See Nos. 1690, 1703, 1736, 1773, 1828, 1859.

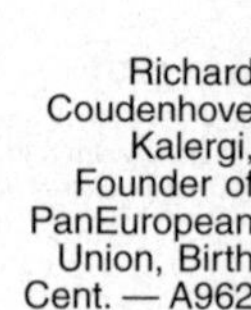

Richard Coudenhove Kalergi, Founder of PanEuropean Union, Birth Cent. — A962

Photo. & Engr.

1994, Nov. 18 ***Perf. 13½***
1665 A962 10s multicolored 1.90 1.50

Birth of Christ, by Anton Wollenek A963

1994, Nov. 25 ***Perf. 14***
1666 A963 6s multicolored 1.10 .90

Christmas.

Membership in European Union — A964

1995, Jan. 13 Photo. *Perf. 14*
1667 A964 7s multicolored 1.25 1.00

Adolf Loos (1870-1933), Architect A965

1995, Jan. 13
1668 A965 10s House, Vienna 1.90 1.50

Official Representation for Workers, 75th Anniv. — A966

1995, Feb. 24 ***Perf. 14x13½***
1669 A966 6s multicolored 1.10 .90

Austrian Gymnastics and Sports Assoc., 50th Anniv. — A967

1995, Feb. 24
1670 A967 6s multicolored 1.10 .90

Folklore and Customs Type of 1991

Designs: 5.50s, Belt, Gailtal, Carinthia. 6s, Vineyard watchman's costume, Vienna. 7s, Bonnet, Wachau, Lower Austria.

Photo. & Engr.

1995, Mar. 24 ***Perf. 14***
1671 A892 5.50s multicolored 1.00 .60
1672 A892 6s multicolored 1.00 .70
1673 A892 7s multicolored 1.25 .80
Nos. 1671-1673 (3) 3.25 2.10

Second Republic, 50th Anniv. — A968

1995, Apr. 27
1674 A968 6s State seal 1.25 1.00

History of Mining & Industry A969

Design: Blast furnaces, old Heft ironworks.

1995, Apr. 28 *Perf. 13½x14*
1675 A969 5.50s multicolored 1.10 .90

Carinthian Provincial Exhibition.

Nature Lovers Club, Cent. — A970

1995, Apr. 28 *Perf. 14*
1676 A970 5.50s multicolored 1.10 .90

Europa — A971

1995, May 19 *Perf. 14*
1677 A971 7s multicolored *1.50 1.25*

1995 Conference of Ministers of Transportation, Vienna — A972

1995, May 26 Photo. *Perf. 14*
1678 A972 7s multicolored 1.40 1.25

Bregenz Festival, 50th Anniv. A973

1995, June 9
1679 A973 6s multicolored 1.25 1.00

St. Gebhard (949-995) A974

Stained glass window, by Martin Hausle.

1995, June 9
1680 A974 7.50s multicolored 1.50 1.25

UN, 50th Anniv. — A975

1995, June 26 Photo. *Perf. 14*
1681 A975 10s multicolored 2.00 .70

Josef Loschmidt (1821-95), Chemist — A976

Photo. & Engr.
1995, June 26 *Perf. 14x13½*
1682 A976 20s multicolored 4.50 1.50

Salzburg Festival, 75th Anniv. — A977

Photo. & Engr.
1995, Aug. 18 *Perf. 13½x14*
1683 A977 6s multicolored 1.25 1.00

Kathe Leichter, Resistance Member, Birth Cent. — A978

1995, Aug. 18 *Perf. 14x13½*
1684 A978 6s buff, black & red 1.25 1.00

Europaisches Landschaftsbild, by Adolf Frohner — A979

1995, Aug. 18
1685 A979 6s multicolored 1.25 1.00

Operetta Composers A980

Designs: 6s, Franz von Suppe (1819-95), scene from "The Beautiful Galathea." 7s, Nico Dostal (b. 1895), scene from "The Hungarian Wedding."

1995, Sept. 15 *Perf. 14*
1686 A980 6s multicolored 1.00 .60
1687 A980 7s multicolored 1.25 .70

See Croatia No. 253.

University of Klagenfurt, 25th Anniv. — A981

1995, Oct. 6 Photo. *Perf. 14*
1688 A981 5.50s multicolored 1.10 .90

Carinthian Referendum, 75th Anniv. — A982

1995, Oct. 6 Photo. & Engr.
1689 A982 6s multicolored 1.25 1.00

Austria Working Environment Type of 1994

1995, Oct. 20
1690 A961 6s Post office official 1.25 1.00

Composers A983

6s, Anton von Webern (1883-1945). 7s, Ludwig van Beethoven (1770-1827).

1995, Oct. 20 *Perf. 13½x14*
1691 A983 6s orange & blue 1.00 .60
1692 A983 7s orange & red 1.25 .70

Christmas A984

Photo. & Engr.
1995, Dec. 1 *Perf. 13½*
1693 A984 6s Christ Child 1.25 1.00

Folklore and Customs Type of 1991

Design: Roller and Scheller in "Procession of Masked Groups in Imst," Tyrol.

Photo. & Engr.
1996, Feb. 9 *Perf. 14*
1694 A892 6s multicolored 1.25 1.00

Maria Theresa Academy, 250th Anniv. — A985

1996, Feb. 9
1695 A985 6s multicolored 1.25 1.00

1996 World Ski Jumping Championships A986

1996, Feb. 9 Photo.
1696 A986 7s multicolored 1.40 1.10

New Western Pier, Vienna Intl. Airport A987

1996, Mar. 28 Photo. *Perf. 14*
1697 A987 7s multicolored 1.40 1.10

A988

6s, Mother with Child, by Peter Fendi (1796-1842). 7s, Self-portrait, by Leopold Kupelwieser (1795-1862).

1996, Mar. 29
1698 A988 6s multicolored 1.25 1.00
1699 A988 7s multicolored 1.40 1.10

Anton Bruckner (1824-96), Composer, Organist A989

Photo. & Engr.
1996, Apr. 26 *Perf. 14*
1700 A989 5.50s Organ, music 1.10 .90

Georg Matthäus Vischer, 300th Death Anniv. A990

1996, Apr. 26
1701 A990 10s Kollmitz Castle 2.00 1.50

City of Klagenfurt, 800th Anniv. — A991

1996, May 3
1702 A991 6s Ancient square 1.25 1.00

Austrian Working Environment Type of 1994

1996, May 17
1703 A961 6s Chef, waitress 1.25 1.00

Paula von Preradovic, Author A992

1996, May 17 ***Perf. 13½x14***
1704 A992 7s black, gray & buff *1.50 1.10*

Europa.

Folklore and Customs Type of 1991

Designs: 5.50s, Corpus Christi poles, Salzburg. 7s, Tyrolian riflemen.

Photo. & Engr.

1996, June 21 ***Perf. 14***
1705 A892 5.50s multicolored 1.00 .80
1706 A892 7s multicolored 1.25 1.00

1996 Summer Olympic Games, Atlanta — A993

1996, June 21
1707 A993 10s multicolored 1.90 1.50

Burgenland Province, 75th Anniv. — A994

1996, Sept. 20
1708 A994 6s multicolored 1.10 .90

Austrian Mountain Rescue Service, Cent. — A995

1996, Sept. 27
1709 A995 6s multicolored 1.10 .90

Austria Millennium A996

Designs: a, Deed by Otto III. b, Empress Maria Theresa, Josef II. c, Duke Henry II. d, 1848 Revolution. e, Rudolf IV. f, Dr. Karl Renner, 1st Republic. g, Emperor Maximilian I. h, State Treaty of 1955, 2nd Republic. i, Imperial Crown of Rudolf II. j, Austria, Europe.

Photo. & Engr.

1996, Oct. 25 ***Perf. 14***
1710 Sheet of 10 19.00 20.00
a.-b. A996 6s any single .90 .90
c.-f. A996 7s any single 1.10 1.10
g.-h. A996 10s any single 1.50 1.50
i.-j. A996 20s any single 3.00 3.00

Power Station, by Reinhard Artberg A997

1996, Nov. 22
1711 A997 7s multicolored 1.25 1.25

UNICEF, 50th Anniv. — A998

1996, Nov. 22 **Photo.**
1712 A998 10s multicolored 1.90 1.90

Christmas A999

1996, Nov. 29 **Photo. & Engr.**
1713 A999 6s multicolored 1.25 1.00

Folklore and Customs Type of 1991

Epiphany Carol Singers, Burgenland.

Photo. & Engr.

1997, Jan. 17 ***Perf. 14***
1714 A892 7s multicolored 1.25 1.00

Theodor Kramer, Poet, Birth Cent. — A1000

1997, Jan. 17 **Engr.**
1715 A1000 5.50s deep blue 1.00 .80

Austrian Academy of Sciences, 150th Anniv. — A1001

1997, Feb. 21 **Photo.** ***Perf. 14***
1716 A1001 10s multicolored 1.75 1.40

Austrian Electricity Board, 50th Anniv. A1002

1997, Mar. 21
1717 A1002 6s multicolored 1.00 .80

The Cruel Lady of Forchtenstein Castle, Burgenland A1003

Photo. & Engr.

1997, Mar. 21 ***Perf. 14***
1718 A1003 7s multicolored 1.10 .95

See Nos. 1731, 1733, 1745-1746, 1763, 1775, 1794, 1802, 1804, 1810-1811.

Erich Wolfgang Korngold (1897-1957), Composer A1004

Design: Scene from opera, "The Dead City."

1997, Mar. 21
1719 A1004 20s bl, blk & gold 4.50 2.00

Vienna Rapid, Austrian Soccer Champions — A1005

1997, Apr. 25 **Photo.** ***Perf. 14***
1720 A1005 7s multicolored 1.25 1.00

See Nos. 1754, 1779, 1807, 1839.

Deer Feeding in Wintertime A1006

1997, Apr. 25
1721 A1006 7s multicolored 1.25 1.00

See Nos. 1747, 1782, 1808, 1835.

St. Peter Canisius (1521-97) A1007

1997, Apr. 25 ***Photo. & Engr.***
1722 A1007 7.50s Canisius Altar, Innsbruck 1.25 1.10

Composers — A1008

Designs: 6s, Johannes Brahms (1833-1897). 10s, Franz Schubert (1797-1828).

1997, May 9
1723 A1008 6s gold & vio bl 1.00 .80
1724 A1008 10s purple & gold 1.75 1.40

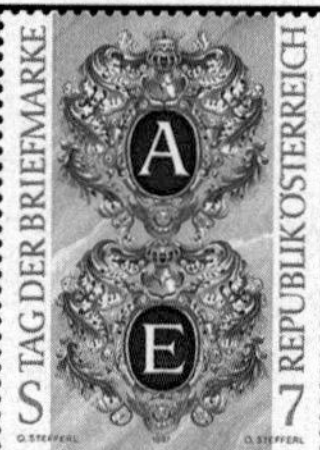
Stamp Day — A1009

1997, May 9 ***Perf. 13½***
1725 A1009 7s "A" and "E" 1.25 1.00

See Nos. B357-B362, 1765, 1791, 1818. The 1st letters spell "Briefmarke," the 2nd "Philatelie."

Child's View of "Town Band of Bremen" A1010

1997, May 23 **Photo.**
1726 A1010 7s multicolored *1.50 1.00*

Europa.

Technical Surveyance Assoc., 125th Anniv. A1011

1997, June 13 **Photo.** ***Perf. 14***
1727 A1011 7s multicolored 1.40 1.10

Railways A1012

Designs: 6s, Hochschneeberg Cog Railway. 7.50s, Wiener Neustadt-Odenburg Railway.

1997, June 13 **Photo. & Engr.**
1728 A1012 6s multicolored 1.25 .95
1729 A1012 7.50s multicolored 1.50 1.25

Folklore and Customs Type of 1991

Photo. & Engr.

1997, July 11 ***Perf. 14***
1730 A892 6.50s Marching band, Tyrol 1.25 1.00

Stories and Legends Type of 1997

Design: Dragon of Klagenfurt.

1997, July 11
1731 A1003 6.50s multicolored 1.60 1.00

Karl Heinrich Waggerl, Birth Cent. — A1013

1997, July 11
1732 A1013 7s multicolored 1.40 1.00

Stories and Legends Type of 1997

Design: Danube water nymph rescuing ferryman, Upper Austria.

Photo. & Engr.

1997, Sept. 19 ***Perf. 14***
1733 A1003 14s multicolored 3.25 2.10

1997 Orthopedics Congress, Vienna — A1014

1997, Sept. 19 **Photo.** ***Perf. 14***
1734 A1014 8s Adolph Lorenz 1.60 1.25

Vienna Agricultural University, 125th Anniv. A1015

1997, Sept. 19
1735 A1015 9s multicolored 1.75 1.40

Austrian Working Environment Type of 1994

Photo. & Engr.

1997, Oct. 17 ***Perf. 14***
1736 A961 6.50s Nurse, patient 1.25 1.00

"House in Wind," by Helmut Schickhofer — A1016

1997, Oct. 17
1737 A1016 7s multicolored 1.40 1.00

Blind Persons Assocs. in Austria, Cent. — A1017

Photo. & Embossed

1997, Oct. 17
1738 A1017 7s multicolored 1.40 1.00

No. 1738 has embossed Braille inscription.

Dr. Thomas Klestil, Pres. of Austria, 65th birthday — A1018

Photo. & Engr.

1997, Oct. 31 ***Perf. 14x13½***
1739 A1018 7s multicolored 1.40 1.00

Oskar Werner (1922-84), Actor — A1019

1997, Oct. 31 ***Perf. 14***
1740 A1019 7s multicolored 1.40 1.00

Folklore and Customs Type of 1991

Upper Austria tower wind players, Steyr.

Photo. & Engr.

1997, Nov. 21 ***Perf. 14***
1741 A892 6.50s multicolored 1.25 1.00

Light Into Darkness Relief Organization, 25th Anniv. — A1020

1997, Nov. 28 **Photo.** ***Perf. 14***
1742 A1020 7s multicolored 1.40 1.00

Christmas A1021

Photo. & Engr.

1997, Nov. 28 ***Perf. 14***
1743 A1021 7s Mariazell Madonna 1.40 1.00

Scenery Type of 1984

Kalkalpen Natl. Park, Upper Austria.

Photo. & Engr.

1998, Jan. 23 ***Perf. 14***
1744 A679 7s multicolored 1.10 .85

Stories and Legends Type of 1997

Designs: 9s, The Charming Augustin. 13s, Pied Piper from Korneuburg.

1998, Jan. 23
1745 A1003 9s multicolored 2.25 1.00
1746 A1003 13s multicolored 3.25 1.50

Hunting and Environment Type

1998, Feb. 6 **Photo.**
1747 A1006 9s Black cocks 1.50 1.00

1998 Winter Olympic Games, Nagano — A1022

1998, Feb. 6 **Photo. & Engr.**
1748 A1022 14s multicolored 2.50 1.60

Lithographic Printing, Bicent. A1023

Portrait of Aloys Senefelder (1771-1834), inventor of lithography, on printing stone.

1998, Mar. 13 **Litho.** ***Perf. 13½***
1749 A1023 7s multicolored 1.25 1.00

Joseph Binder (1898-1972), Graphic Artist — A1024

1998, Mar. 13 **Photo.** ***Perf. 14***
1750 A1024 7s Poster 1.40 1.00

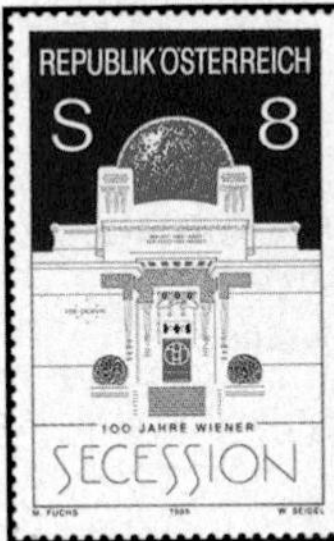

Wiener Secession, Cent. (Assoc. of Artists in Austria-Viennese Secession) A1025

1998, Mar. 13 **Photo. & Engr.**
1751 A1025 8s multicolored 1.40 1.25

Folklore and Customs Type of 1991

6.50s, Fiacre, Vienna. 7s, Christ figure, Palm Sunday Donkey Procession, Tyrol.

1998, Apr. 3
1752 A892 6.50s multicolored 1.25 .95
1753 A892 7s multicolored 1.40 1.00

Soccer Champions Type of 1997

1998, Apr. 17 **Photo.**
1754 A1005 7s Austria-Memphis Club 1.40 1.00

Salzburg Archdiocese, 1200th Anniv. A1026

1998, Apr. 17 **Photo. & Engr.**
1755 A1026 7s multicolored 1.40 1.00

St. Florian, Patron Saint of Fire Brigades A1027

1998, Apr. 17 **Photo.**
1756 A1027 7s multicolored 1.40 1.00

Railway Centennials A1028

No. 1757, Ybbs Railway. No. 1758, Pöstlingberg Railway. No. 1759, Pinzgau Railway.

1998 **Photo. & Engr.** ***Perf. 14***
1757 A1028 6.50s multicolored 1.25 1.00
1758 A1028 6.50s multicolored 1.25 1.00
1759 A1028 6.50s multicolored 1.25 1.00
Nos. 1757-1759 (3) 3.75 3.00

Issued: No. 1757, 5/15; No. 1758, 6/12; No. 1759, 7/17.

Ferdinandeum, Federal Museum of Tyrol, 175th Anniv. A1029

1998, May 15
1760 A1029 7s multicolored 1.40 1.00

Vienna Festival Weeks — A1030

1998, May 15
1761 A1030 7s Townhall *1.60 1.00*

Europa.

Folklore and Customs Type of 1991

Samson figure & the Zwergin, Lungau district, Salzburg.

1998, June 5
1762 A892 6.50s multicolored 1.25 1.00

Stories and Legends Type of 1997

Design: 25s, Saint Konrad collecting spring water in his handkerchief, Ems Castle.

1998, June 5
1763 A1003 25s multicolored 6.00 2.50

Christine Lavant, Poet, 25th Death Anniv. A1031

1998, June 5 **Photo.**
1764 A1031 7s multicolored 1.40 1.00

Stamp Day Type of 1997

Photo. & Engr.

1998, June 12 ***Perf. 13½***

1765 A1009 7s "R" and "L" 1.40 1.00

See Nos. 1725, 1791,1818, B357-B362. The 1st letters spell "Briefmarke," the 2nd "Philatelie."

Austrian Presidency of the European Union — A1032

1998, July 1 **Photo.** ***Perf. 13½x14***

1766 A1032 7s multicolored 1.40 1.00

The People's Opera, Vienna, Centennial & Franz Lehar (1870-1948), Composer — A1033

1998, Sept. 10 **Photo.** ***Perf. 14***

1767 A1033 6.50s multicolored 1.25 .85

Elizabeth, Empress of Austria (1837-98) A1034

1998, Sept. 10 **Photo. & Engr.**

1768 A1034 7s multicolored 1.40 .90

Vienna University for Commercial Sudies, Cent. — A1035

1998, Sept. 10 **Photo.**

1769 A1035 7s multicolored 1.40 .90

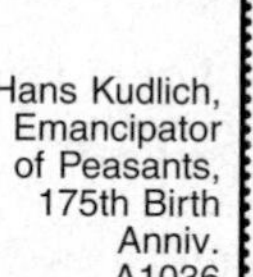

Hans Kudlich, Emancipator of Peasants, 175th Birth Anniv. A1036

Photo. & Engr.

1998, Oct. 23 ***Perf. 14***

1770 A1036 6.50s multicolored 1.25 .90

"My Garden," by Hans Staudacher A1037

1998, Oct. 23

1771 A1037 7s multicolored 1.25 .90

City of Eisenstadt, 350th Anniv. — A1038

1998, Oct. 23

1772 A1038 7s multicolored 1.25 .90

Austrian Working Environment Type of 1994

Photo. & Engr.

1998, Nov. 6 ***Perf. 14***

1773 A961 6.50s Reporter, photographer 1.10 .85

Christmas A1039

1423 Fresco from Tainach/Tinje Church, Carinthia.

1998, Nov. 27

1774 A1039 7s multicolored 1.25 .85

Stories and Legends Type of 1997

The Dark Maiden of Hardegg Castle.

Photo. & Engr.

1999, Feb. 19 ***Perf. 14***

1775 A1003 8s multicolored 1.25 .85

1999 Nordic Skiing World Championships, Mt. Dachstein, Ramsau A1040

1999, Feb. 19

1776 A1040 7s multicolored 1.10 .85

Scenery Type of 1984

Bohemian Forest, Upper Austria.

Photo. & Engr.

1999, Mar. 19 ***Perf. 14***

1777 A679 7s multicolored 1.10 .85

Folklore and Customs Type of 1991

Traditional walking pilgrimage to Mariazell.

1999, Mar. 19

1778 A892 6.50s multicolored 1.00 .75

Soccer Champions Type of 1997

Design: Soccer Club SK Puntigamer Sturm Graz.

1999, Apr. 16 **Photo.** ***Perf. 14***

1779 A1005 7s multicolored 1.10 .85

Schönnbrun Palace, UNESCO World Heritage Site — A1041

Photo. & Engr.

1999, Apr. 16 ***Perf. 14***

1780 A1041 13s multicolored 2.25 1.50

See Nos. 1826, 1845, 1928.

Austrian Patent Office, Cent. — A1042

1999, Apr. 16

1781 A1042 7s multicolored 1.10 .85

Hunting and Environment Type of 1997

1999, May 7 **Litho.** ***Perf. 14***

1782 A1006 6.50s Partridges 1.00 .75

Austrian General Sport Federation, 50th Anniv. — A1043

1999, May 7 **Engr.** ***Perf. 14***

1783 A1043 7s multicolored 1.10 .80

Council of Europe, 50th Anniv. A1044

1999, May 7 **Photo.** ***Perf. 13½x14***

1784 A1044 14s multicolored 2.50 2.00

Karl Jenschke (1899-1969), Automobile Designer A1045

1999, May 28

1785 A1045 7s Steyr automobile 1.10 .80

Marble Relief of St. Martin A1046

Design: 9s, St. Anne, Mary and Jesus.

1999 **Photo. & Engr.** ***Perf. 14***

1786 A1046 8s multicolored 1.40 .95

Perf. 13¾

1787 A1046 9s multicolored 1.75 1.10

Issued: 8s, 5/28; 9s, 9/17.

See Nos. 1817, 1830, 1851-1852.

Austrian Social Welfare Service, 125th Anniv. A1047

1999, June 4 **Litho.** ***Perf. 13¾***

1788 A1047 7s multicolored 1.25 .80

Johann Strauss, the Younger (1825-99), Composer A1048

8s, Johann Strauss, the Elder (1804-49).

1999, June 4 **Photo. & Engr.**

1789 A1048 7s multicolored 1.25 .80

1790 A1048 8s multicolored 1.30 .95

Stamp Day Type of 1997

1999, June 18 ***Perf. 13½***

1791 A1009 7s "K" and "I" 1.25 .80

See Nos. 1725, 1765, 1818, B357-B362. The 1st letters spell "Briefmarke," the 2nd "Philatelie."

Donau-Auen Natl. Park — A1049

1999, June 18 ***Perf. 13¾***

1792 A1049 7s multicolored *1.60 1.00*

Europa.

Natl. Gendarmery, 150th Anniv. — A1050

1999, June 18

1793 A1050 7s multicolored 1.25 .80

Stories and Legends Type of 1997

Design: The Holy Notburga.

Photo. & Engr.

1999, Aug. 27 *Perf. 13¾x14*
1794 A1003 20s multicolored 5.00 2.50

Graz Opera House, 100th Anniv. — A1051

Photo. & Engr.

1999, Sept. 17 *Perf. 13¾*
1795 A1051 6.50s multicolored 1.25 .75

International Year of Older Persons — A1052

1999, Sept. 17 **Photo.** *Perf. 13¾*
1796 A1052 7s multicolored 1.25 .85

Federation of Austrian Trade Unions, 14th Congress A1053

1999, Oct. 15 **Litho.** *Perf. 13¾*
1797 A1053 6.50s multicolored 1.25 .75

"Caffee Girardi," by Wolfgang Herzig — A1054

Photo. & Engr.

1999, Oct. 22 *Perf. 13¾x14*
1798 A1054 7s multicolored 1.25 .85

Folklore & Customs Type of 1991

7s, The Pummerin, Bell in St. Stephen's Cathedral, Vienna. 8s, Pumpkin Festival, Lower Austria.

1999 **Photo. & Engr.** *Perf. 13¾*
1799 A892 7s multicolored 1.25 .85
1800 A892 8s multicolored 1.40 .95

Issued: 8s, 10/22; 7s, 11/12.

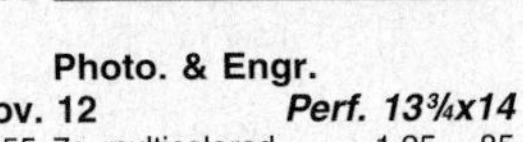

National Institute of Geology, 150th Anniv. A1055

Photo. & Engr.

1999, Nov. 12 *Perf. 13¾x14*
1801 A1055 7s multicolored 1.25 .85

Stories & Legends Type of 1997

Design: 32s, Discovery of Erzberg.

Photo. & Engr.

1999, Nov. 12 *Perf. 13¾x14*
1802 A1003 32s multicolored 9.00 4.00

Christmas A1056

Photo. & Engr.

1999, Nov. 26 *Perf. 13¾*
1803 A1056 7s Pinkafeld creche 1.25 .85

Stories & Legends Type of 1997

Design: 10s, House of the Basilisk, Vienna.

Photo. & Engr.

2000, Jan. 21 *Perf. 13¾x14*
1804 A1003 10s multi 2.50 1.50
a. Souvenir sheet of 1 35.00 35.00

No. 1804a was sold only with the purchase of an 80s ticket to the Vienna Intl. Philatelic Exhibition.

Folklore & Customs Type of 1991

Designs: 6.50s, Schleicherlaufen Festival, Telfs. 7s, Carrying miniature churches, Bad Eisenkappel.

2000 **Photo. & Engr.** *Perf. 13¾*
1805 A892 6.50s multi 1.25 1.25
1806 A892 7s multi 1.25 1.25

Issued: 6.50s, 2/11; 7s, 1/21.

Soccer Champions Type of 1997

Design: Tirol Soccer Club.

2000, Mar. 3 **Photo.** *Perf. 13¾*
1807 A1005 7s multi 1.25 1.00

Hunting and Environment Type of 1997

2000, Mar. 3 *Perf. 14x14¼*
1808 A1006 7s Ibex 1.25 1.00

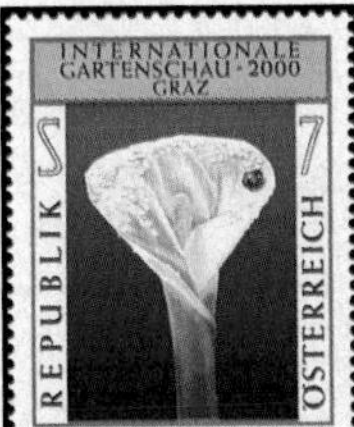

Intl. Gardening Exhibition, Graz — A1057

Photo. & Embossed

2000, Mar. 3 *Perf. 13½x13¾*
1809 A1057 7s multi 1.25 1.25

Stories & Legends Type of 1997

Designs: 22s, The Witch's Ride. 23s, The Bread Loaf Monument.

2000 **Photo. & Engr.** *Perf. 13¾x14*
1810 A1003 22s multi 4.50 4.50
1811 A1003 23s multi 4.50 6.00

Issued: 22s, 4/28. 23s, 6/16.

First Ascent of Grossglockner, Bicent. A1058

2000, Apr. 28 *Perf. 13¾*
1812 A1058 7s multi 1.25 1.00

Scenery Type of 1984

Design: Sonnblick Glacier, Granatspitze, Weisssee, Salzburg.

2000, May 9 *Perf. 13¾x14*
1813 A679 7s multi 1.25 1.25

Europa, 2000

Common Design Type

2000, May 9 **Photo.** *Perf. 14¼x13½*
1814 CD17 7s multi *1.40 1.40*

Klagenfurt Airport, 75th Anniv. A1059

2000, May 19 *Perf. 13¾*
1815 A1059 7s multi 1.25 1.25

Protection of Historical Monuments, 150th Anniv. — A1060

Photo. & Engr.

2000, May 19 *Perf. 14x13¼*
1816 A1060 8s multi 1.40 1.10

Religious Art Type of 1999

Design: 9s, Illustration of St. Malachy from book, *The Life of Bishop Malachy.*

2000, May 19 *Perf. 13¾*
1817 A1046 9s multi 1.65 1.25

Stamp Day Type of 1997

2000, May 30 *Perf. 13½*
1818 A1009 7s "E" and "E" 1.25 1.25

See Nos. 1725, 1765, 1791, B357-B362. The 1st letters spell "Briefmarke," the 2nd "Philatelie."

Austrian Postage Stamps, 150th Anniv. A1061

2000, May 30 *Perf. 13¾*
1819 A1061 7s Nos. 5, 1818 1.25 1.25

Children's Television Character, Confetti A1062

2000, May 31
1820 A1062 7s multi 1.25 1.25

See Nos. 1841, 1914.

Blue Blues, by Friedensreich Hundertwasser (1928-2000), Artist — A1063

Colors of seven solid vertical panels at top: a, Silver. b, Red. c, Red violet. d, Black.

2000, June 2
1821 Sheet of 4 8.00 10.00
a.-d. A1063 7s Any single 1.50 1.25

Discovery of Human Blood Types, Cent. A1064

Perf. 13¾x13½

2000, June 16 **Photo.**
1822 A1064 8s multi 1.40 1.40

Scheduled Motorized Vehicle Passenger Transportation, Cent. — A1065

Photo. & Engr.

2000, June 16 *Perf. 14*
1823 A1065 9s multi 1.75 1.75

Folklore & Customs Type of 1991

7s, Intl. meeting of rafters, Carinthia.

Photo. & Engr.

2000, Aug. 25 *Perf. 13¾*
1824 A892 7s multi 1.25 1.25

Vienna Philharmonic Orchestra, Cent. — A1066

2000, Sept. 15
1825 A1066 7s multi 1.25 1.25

World Heritage Site Type of 1999

Hallstatt-Dachstein and Salzkammergut

2000, Sept. 15
1826 A1041 7s multi 1.25 1.25

2000 Summer Olympics, Sydney — A1068

2000, Sept. 15 *Perf. 14x13¾*
1827 A1068 9s multi 1.60 1.60

Working Environment Type of 1994

2000, Sept. 29

1828 A961 6.50s Papermaker, printer 1.25 1.25

Turf Turkey, by Ida Szigethy A1069

2000, Oct. 13 ***Perf. 13¾***

1829 A1069 7s multi 1.25 1.25

Religious Art Type of 1999

Design: 8s, Illuminated text, Codex 965.

2000, Oct. 13

1830 A1046 8s multi 1.50 1.50

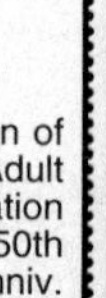

Association of Austrian Adult Education Centers, 50th Anniv. A1070

Photo. & Engr.

2000, Nov. 24 ***Perf. 13¾***

1831 A1070 7s multi 1.25 1.25

Vaccinations in Austria, Bicent. — A1071

2000, Nov. 24 ***Perf. 14¼x13½***

1832 A1071 7s multi 1.25 1.25

Christmas A1072

Altar sidewing, St. Martin's Church, Ludesch.

2000, Dec. 1 ***Perf. 13¾***

1833 A1072 7s multi 1.25 1.25

2001 Alpine Skiing World Championships, St. Anton am Arlberg — A1073

2000, Dec. 15 ***Perf. 14x13¾***

1834 A1073 7s multi 1.25 1.25

Hunting & Environment Type of 1997

2001, Feb. 16 Photo. ***Perf. 14x14¼***

1835 A1006 7s Ducks 1.25 1.25

Folklore & Customs Type of 1991

Designs: No. 1836, Lenten altar cloths, Eastern Tyrol. No. 1837, Water disk shooting, Prebersee. No. 1838, Boat Mill, Mureck.

2001 Photo. & Engr. ***Perf. 13¾***

1836 A892 7s multi 1.25 1.25
1837 A892 7s multi 1.25 1.25
1838 A892 8s multi 1.40 1.40
Nos. 1836-1838 (3) 3.90 3.90

Issued: No. 1836, 5/4/01. No. 1838, 3/30/01. No. 1837, 8/24/01.

Soccer Champions Type of 1997

2001, Mar. 30 Photo. ***Perf. 13¾***

1839 A1005 7s Wustenrot Salzburg 1.25 1.25

Zillertal Railway, Cent. A1074

Photo. & Engr.

2001, Mar. 30 ***Perf. 13¾***

1840 A1074 7s multi 1.25 1.25

Children's Television Character Type of 2000

2001, Apr. 20 Photo. ***Perf. 13¾***

1841 A1062 7s Rolf Rüdiger 1.25 1.25

Salzburg Airport, 75th Anniv. A1075

Photo. & Engr.

2001, Apr. 20 ***Perf. 13½x14¼***

1842 A1075 14s multi 2.75 2.75

Scenery Type of 1984

Design: Bärenschützkamm, Styria.

Photo. & Engr.

2001, May 4 ***Perf. 13¾***

1843 A679 7s multi 1.40 1.40

Europa A1076

2001, May 18 Photo. ***Perf. 13¾***

1844 A1076 15s multi *2.50 2.50*

UNESCO World Heritage Type of 1999

Design: Semmering Railway.

Photo. & Engr.

2001, June 8 ***Perf. 13¾***

1845 A1041 35s multi 8.50 8.50

Austrian Aero Club, Cent. — A1077

2001, June 8 ***Perf. 13¾x14***

1846 A1077 7s multi 1.40 1.40

UN High Commissioner for Refugees, 50th Anniv. — A1078

2001, June 8 ***Perf. 14x13¾***

1847 A1078 21s multi 4.25 4.25

7th IVV Hiking Olympics A1079

2001, June 22 Photo. ***Perf. 13¾***

1848 A1079 7s multi 1.40 1.40

Military Post Offices Abroad A1080

2001, June 22

1849 A1080 7s multi 1.40 1.40

Conversion of East-West Railway to Four Tracks A1081

Photo. & Engr.

2001, Aug. 31 ***Perf. 13¾***

1850 A1081 7s multi 1.40 1.40

Religious Art Type of 1999

Designs: 7s, Church vestment cut from Turkish tent, 1683. 10s, Pluvial.

2001 Photo. & Engr. ***Perf. 13¾***

1851 A1046 7s multi 1.40 1.40
1852 A1046 10s multi 1.90 1.90

Issued: 7s, 10/5; 10s, 9/14.

Johann Nestroy (1801-62), Playwright A1082

2001, Sept. 14

1853 A1082 7s multi 1.40 1.40

The Continents (Detail), by Helmut Leherb — A1083

2001, Sept. 14

1854 A1083 7s multi 1.40 1.40

Joseph Ritter von Führich (1800-76), Painter — A1084

2001, Sept. 14 ***Perf. 14***

1855 A1084 8s multi 1.60 1.60

Leopold Ludwig Döbler (1801-64), Magician A1085

2001, Oct. 5

1856 A1085 7s multi 1.40 1.40

Meteorology and Geodynamics Institute, 150th Anniv. — A1086

2001, Oct. 5

1857 A1086 12s multi 2.50 2.50

Cat King, by Manfred Deix — A1087

2001, Oct. 5 ***Perf. 13¾***

1858 A1087 19s multi 4.25 4.25

See No. 1903.

Working Environment Type of 1994

2001, Oct. 16 *Perf. 14*

1859 A961 7s Public servants 1.40 1.40

Christmas A1088

Photo. & Engr.

2001, Nov. 30 *Perf. 14*

1860 A1088 7s multi 1.40 1.40

100 Cents = 1 Euro (€)

Introduction of the Euro — A1089

Photo. & Embossed with Foil Application

2002, Jan. 1 *Perf. 13½x13¾*

1861 A1089 €3.27 multi 8.50 8.50

Austrian Scenes — A1090

Designs: 4c, Schönlaterngasse, Vienna. 7c, Stations of the Cross, Lower Austria Province. 13c, Cow in pasture, Tyrol Province. 17c, Street, Hadres. 20c, Sailboats on Wörther See, Carinthia. 25c, Rock with crosses, Mondsee, Upper Austria. 27c, Farmhouse, Salzburg Province. 45c, St. Martin's Chapel, Kleinwalser Valley, Vorarlberg. 51c, Schönlaterngasse, Vienna. 55c, Houses, Steyr. 58c, Street, Hadres. 73c, Farmhouse, Salzburg Province. 75c, Ship in Lake Constance (Bodensee), Vorarlberg Province. 87c, Cow in pasture, Tyrol Province. €1, Farmhouse, Rossegg. €1.25, Wine press house, Eisenberg. €2.03, Stations of the Cross, Lower Austria Province. €3.75, Roadside shrine, Carinthia Province.

2002-03 Photo. *Perf. 13¾x14*

No.	Type	Value			
1862	A1090	4c	multi	.25	.25
1863	A1090	7c	multi	.25	.25
1863A	A1090	13c	multi	.35	.35
1864	A1090	17c	multi	.45	.45
1865	A1090	20c	multi	.55	.50
1865A	A1090	25c	multi	.65	.50
1866	A1090	27c	multi	.70	.50
1866A	A1090	45c	multi	1.25	1.25
1867	A1090	51c	multi	1.40	.70
1868	A1090	55c	multi	1.50	1.40
1869	A1090	58c	multi	1.50	.70
1872	A1090	73c	multi	1.90	.90
1873	A1090	75c	multi	2.00	1.40
1875	A1090	87c	multi	2.25	1.10
1876	A1090	€1	multi	2.75	2.10
1877	A1090	€1.25	multi	3.25	2.50
1879	A1090	€2.03	multi	5.25	2.50
1880	A1090	€3.75	multi	9.75	8.50
	Nos. 1862-1880 (18)			36.00	25.85

Issued: 51c, 58c, 73c, 87c, €2.03, 1/1/02. 4c, 7c, 13c, 17c, 27c, 6/2/03; 55c, 75c, €1, €1.25, €3.75, 5/30/03. 20c, 25c, 7/18/03. 45c, 12/5/03.

For surcharges see Nos. 1969, 1979-1986, 2047, B376.

2002 Winter Olympics, Salt Lake City — A1091

Photo. & Engr.

2002, Feb. 8 *Perf. 14x13¾*

1882 A1091 73c multi 1.90 1.90

Love — A1092

2002, Feb. 14 Photo. *Perf. 14¼x14*

1883 A1092 87c multi 2.25 2.25

Intl. Women's Day — A1093

2002, Mar. 8 *Perf. 13¾*

1884 A1093 51c multi 1.40 1.40

Promotion of Youth Philately — A1094

Cartoon characters: No. 1885, Girls Mel and Lucy. No. 1886, Sisco and Mauritius (boy and dog). No. 1887, Edison and Gogo (girl and boy).

2002 Photo. *Perf. 14x13¾*

No.	Type	Value			
1885	A1094	58c	multi	1.75	1.75
1886	A1094	58c	multi	1.75	1.75
1887	A1094	58c	multi	1.75	1.75
	Nos. 1885-1887 (3)			5.25	5.25

Issued: No. 1885, 4/5. No. 1886, 5/10. No. 1887, 11/22.

Roses — A1095

2002, Apr. 5 Photo. *Perf. 14x13¾*

1888 A1095 58c multi 1.75 1.75

80th Anniversary of Marianneum, by Alfred Kubin — A1096

2002, Apr. 10 *Perf. 13½x13¾*

1889 A1096 87c black & buff 2.25 2.25

Caritas — A1097

2002, Apr. 26

1890 A1097 51c multi 1.40 1.40

Europa A1098

2002, May 3 *Perf. 13¾*

1891 A1098 87c multi *2.25 2.25*

Lilienfeld Monastery, 800th Anniv. A1099

Photo. & Engr.

2002, May 17 *Perf. 13¾*

1892 A1099 €2.03 multi 5.25 5.25

Children's Television Character Type of 2000

2002, May 23 Photo. *Perf. 13¾*

1893 A1062 51c Mimi 1.40 1.40

Souvenir Sheet

Schönnbrunn Zoo, 250th Anniv. — A1100

No. 1894: a, Orangutan, leopard, lioness, zebras. b, Various birds. c, Lion, antelope, turtle, crocodile, jellyfish. d, Antelope, elephant, birds, jellyfish, fish, ray.

Photo. & Engr.

2002, June 3 *Perf. 13½x14¼*

No.	Type	Value			
1894	A1100	Sheet of 4		11.50	11.50
a.		51c multi		1.50	1.50
b.		58c multi		1.75	1.75
c.		87c multi		2.50	2.50
d.		€1.38 multi		4.00	4.00

Teddy Bears, Cent. — A1101

2002, June 4 Photo. *Perf. 14¼x14*

1895 A1101 51c multi 1.40 1.40

Crystal Cup from Innsbruck Glassworks A1102

Photo. & Engr.

2002, June 21 *Perf. 13¾*

1896 A1102 €1.60 multi 4.25 4.25

Traditional arts and crafts.

Chair by Michael Thonet, 1860 — A1103

2002, June 21 **Photo.**

1897 A1103 €1.38 multi 3.75 3.75

Austrian design.

Museum of Contemporary Art, Vienna — A1104

2002, Sept. 4 Photo. *Perf. 14x13¾*

1898 A1104 58c multi 1.50 1.50

Austrians Living Abroad — A1105

Photo. & Engr.

2002, Sept. 5 *Perf. 13¾x14*

1899 A1105 €2.47 multi 6.50 6.50

Clown Doctor
A1106

2002, Sept. 10 Photo. *Perf. 13¾*
1900 A1106 51c multi 1.40 1.40

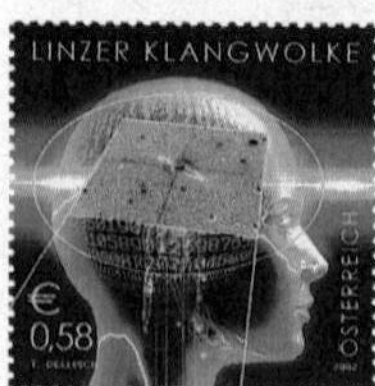

Linz "Sound Cloud" A1107

2002, Sept. 13
1901 A1107 58c multi 1.50 1.50

OAF Gräf & Stift Type 40/45 Automobile A1108

2002, Sept. 27
1902 A1108 51c multi 1.40 1.40

See No. 1925.

Pet Type of 2001

Design: Dog King, by Manfred Deix.

2002, Oct. 4 Photo. *Perf. 13¾*
1903 A1087 51c multi 1.40 1.40

Train at Vienna South Railway Station A1109

2002, Oct. 4 Photo. & Engr.
1904 A1109 51c multi 1.40 1.40

See Nos. 1921, 1958, 2023, 2059, 2105, 2114, 2166, 2171, 2215, 2249, 2279, 2330, 2337.

Schützenhaus, by Karl Goldammer A1110

2002, Oct. 11
1905 A1110 51c multi 1.40 1.40

Souvenir Sheet

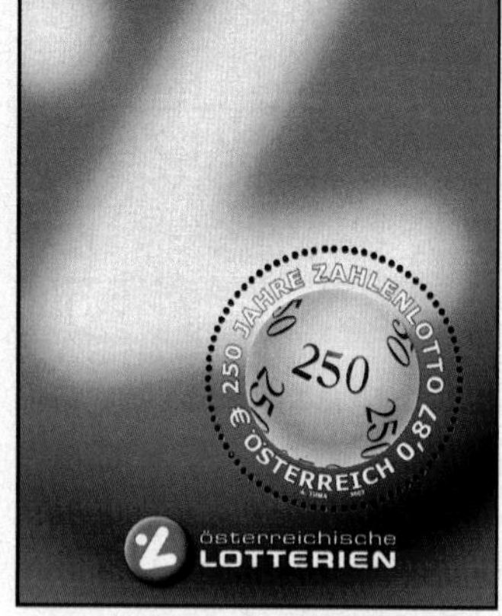

National Lottery, 250th Anniv. — A1111

2002, Oct. 17 Photo. *Perf.*
1906 A1111 87c multi 2.50 2.50

Thayatal Natl. Park A1112

Photo. & Engr.

2002, Oct. 25 *Perf. 13¾*
1907 A1112 58c multi 1.60 1.60

Puch 175 SV Motorcycle A1113

2002, Nov. 8 Photo. *Perf. 14x13¾*
1908 A1113 58c multi 1.60 1.60

One Eye, by Wolfgang Homola A1114

2002, Nov. 15 *Perf. 13¾*
1909 A1114 €1.38 multi 3.75 3.75

Austrian design.

Christmas — A1115

Photo. & Engr.

2002, Nov. 29 *Perf. 14x14¼*
1910 A1115 51c multi 1.40 1.40

A1115a

2003, Jan. 22 Litho. *Perf. 13¾x14*
1910A A1115a 45c multi 8.00 8.00

Graz, 2003 European Cultural Capital A1116

Perf. 13½x14¼

2003, Mar. 14 Photo.
1911 A1116 58c multi 1.60 1.60

Heart, Wedding Rings and Pigeons — A1117

2003, Mar. 21 *Perf. 14¼x13½*
1912 A1117 58c multi 1.60 1.60

Billy Wilder (1906-2002), Movie Director — A1118

2003, Mar. 21
1913 A1118 58c gray black 1.50 1.50

Children's Television Character Type of 2000

2003, Apr. 11 Photo. *Perf. 13¾*
1914 A1062 51c Kasperl 1.40 1.40

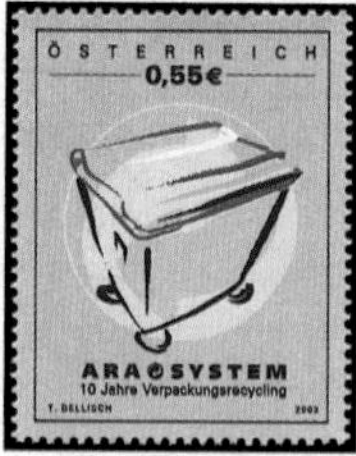

Implementation of Waste Recycling System, 10th Anniv. — A1119

2003, Apr. 11
1915 A1119 55c multi 1.40 1.40

Bar Service No. 248, Glassware by Adolf Loos — A1120

2003, Apr. 11
1916 A1120 €1.38 multi 3.50 3.50

Austrian design.

Souvenir Sheet

Panda Research in Austria — A1121

2003, Apr. 14 *Perf. 14x14¼*
1917 A1121 Sheet of 2 5.25 5.25
a. 75c Two pandas 2.25 2.25
b. €1 Two pandas, diff. 3.00 3.00

No. 1917b is 38mm in diameter.

St. Georgen am Längsee Convent, 1000th Anniv. A1122

2003, Apr. 25 *Perf. 13¾*
1918 A1122 87c multi 2.25 2.25

Souvenir Sheet

Marcel Prawy (1911-2003), Musical Impresario — A1123

2003, Apr. 25
1919 A1123 €1.75 multi 5.25 5.25

Europa A1124

2003, May 9
1920 A1124 €1.02 multi 2.75 2.75

Railways Type of 2002

Photo. & Engr.

2003, June 6 *Perf. 13¾*
1921 A1109 75c OEBB Series 5045 2.00 2.00

Salzach River Bridge, Laufen, Germany — Oberndorf, Austria A1125

Photo. & Engr.

2003, June 12 *Perf. 13½*
1922 A1125 55c multi 1.50 1.50

See Germany No. 2245.

Souvenir Sheet

Ford Motor Company, Cent. — A1126

No. 1923: a, Model T. b, Henry Ford (1863-1947). c, 2003 Ford Streetka.

Perf. 13½x14¼

2003, June 16 **Photo.**

1923 A1126 Sheet of 3 + label 5.00 5.00
a.-c. 55c Any single 1.50 1.50

Souvenir Sheet

Rolling Stones — A1127

No. 1924: a, Guitarist Keith Richards. b, Singer Mick Jagger. c, Drummer Charlie Watts. d, Guitarist Ron Wood smoking cigarette.

2003, June 18 ***Perf. 14x13½***

1924 A1127 Sheet of 4 6.50 6.50
a.-d. 55c Any single 1.60 1.60

Vehicle Type of 2002

Design: Rosenbauer Panther 8x8 airport fire engine.

2003, June 20 ***Perf. 13¾***

1925 A1108 55c multi 1.50 1.50

Bible Year — A1128

2003, June 20

1926 A1128 55c multi 1.50 1.50

Prenez le Temps d'Aimer, by Kiki Kogelnik (1935-97) A1129

2003, July 3 **Photo. & Engr.**

1927 A1129 55c multi 1.50 1.50

UNESCO World Heritage Type of 1999

Design: Neusiedler See.

Photo. & Engr.

2003, July 11 ***Perf. 13¾***

1928 A1041 €1 multi 2.75 2.75

Samurai and Geisha A1130

2003, July 19 **Photo.** ***Perf. 13¾***

1929 A1130 55c multi 1.50 1.50

Exhibition of Japanese Shogun Era Culture, Leoben Kunsthalle, Vienna.

Performance of Turandot at St. Margarethen Opera Festival — A1131

2003, July 24 ***Perf. 14x13¾***

1930 A1131 55c multi 1.50 1.50

Children's Welfare — A1132

2003, Sept. 12 **Photo.** ***Perf. 13x13½***

1931 A1132 55c multi 1.50 1.50

Water Tower, Wiener Neustadt A1133

2003, Sept. 18 ***Perf. 13¾***

1932 A1133 55c multi 1.40 1.40

50th Austrian Local Government Conference.

Thank You A1134

2003, Sept. 19

1933 A1134 55c multi 1.40 1.40

Mail Order Business A1135

2003, Sept. 24 ***Perf. 13¾x14***

1934 A1135 55c multi 1.40 1.40

Werner Schlager, 2003 Table Tennis World Champion — A1136

2003, Sept. 25 ***Perf. 14x13¾***

1935 A1136 55c multi 1.40 1.40

Jugend-Phila Graz '03 Youth Philatelic Exhibition — A1137

2003, Sept. 26

1936 A1137 55c multi 1.40 1.40

Performance of Musical "Elisabeth," Theater an der Wien, Vienna — A1138

2003, Oct. 1

1937 A1138 55c multi 1.40 1.40

Souvenir Sheet

Judith I, by Gustav Klimt — A1139

Photo. & Engr.

2003, Oct. 10 ***Perf. 13½x13¾***

1938 A1139 €2.10 multi 6.25 6.25

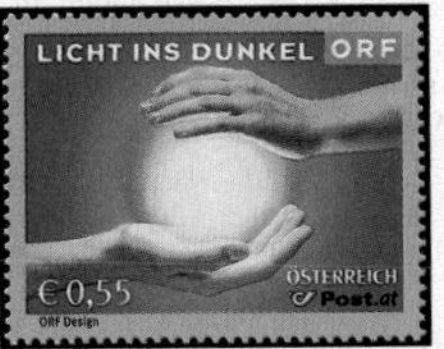

Licht Ins Dunkel Fund-Raising Campaign for the Handicapped, 30th Anniv. — A1140

Perf. 13¾x13½

2003, Nov. 11 **Photo.**

1939 A1140 55c multi 1.40 1.40

Bösendorfer Piano — A1141

Jazz Pianist Oscar Peterson and Bösendorfer Piano A1142

Photo. & Engr.

2003, Nov. 19 ***Perf. 13¾***

1940 A1141 75c multi 2.00 2.00

Photo.

Perf. 13½x12¾

1941 A1142 €1.25 multi 3.25 3.25

Bösendorfer pianos, 175th anniv.

Christmas A1143

Photo. & Engr.

2003, Nov. 28 ***Perf. 13¾x14***

1942 A1143 55c multi 1.40 1.40

A1144

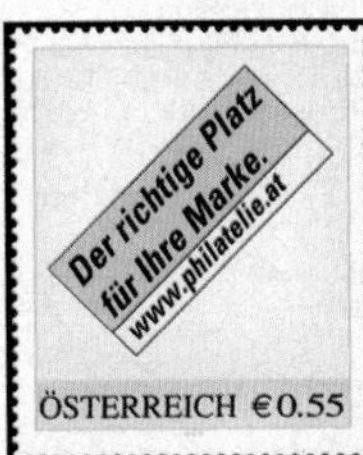

Personalized Stamps A1145

2003, Dec. 5 **Photo.** ***Perf. 13¾***

1943 A1144 55c multi 1.40 1.40
1944 A1145 55c multi 1.40 1.40

Stamp vignettes could be personalized by customers, presumably for an extra fee.

A quantity of Nos. 1943 and 1944 were later imprinted with various commercial themes and offered by Austria Post in full panes at a premium over face value. Only examples as illustrated, bearing generic vignettes, were sold at the face value shown on the stamp. In 2006, Nos. 1943 and 1944 were offered with other denominations that lacked the euro sign. Stamps with similar frames in colors other than yellow and blue, as seen on No. 2036, and stamps with country names and denominations in white were created starting in 2013.

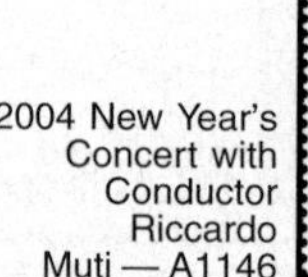

2004 New Year's Concert with Conductor Riccardo Muti — A1146

2004, Jan. 1 **Photo.** ***Perf. 13¾***
1945 A1146 €1 multi 2.50 2.50

Seiji Ozawa, Conductor of Vienna State Opera A1147

2004, Jan. 16 **Photo.** ***Perf. 13¾***
1946 A1147 €1 multi 2.75 2.75

José Carreras, 30th Anniv. at Vienna State Opera A1148

2004, Feb. 23 **Photo.** ***Perf. 13¾***
1947 A1148 €1 multi 2.50 2.50

Austrian Soccer Association, Cent. — A1149

No. 1948: a, Gerhard Hanappi. b, Mathias Sindelar. c, Soccer ball, centenary emblem. d, Bruno Pezzey. e, Ernst Ocwirk. f, Walter Zeman. g, Herbert Prohaska. h, Hans Krankl. i, Andreas Herzog. j, Anton Polster.

2004, Mar. 18
1948 A1149 Sheet of 10 15.00 15.00
a.-j. 55c Any single 1.40 1.40

Easter — A1150

2004, Mar. 26
1949 A1150 55c multi 1.40 1.40

Life Ball, Charity Ball for AIDS Research — A1151

2004, Mar. 29 ***Perf. 14x13¾***
1950 A1151 55c multi 1.40 1.40

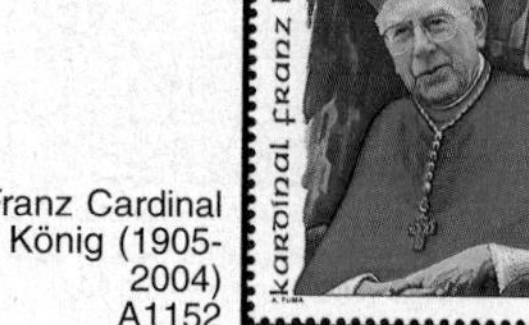

Franz Cardinal König (1905-2004) A1152

Photo. & Engr.
2004, Mar. 30 ***Perf. 14¼***
1951 A1152 €1 multi 2.75 2.75

Souvenir Sheet

Wedding of Emperor Franz Joseph and Empress Elizabeth von Wittelsbach, 150th Anniv. — A1153

No. 1952: a, Emperor and Empress on honeymoon in Laxenburg (29x36mm). b, Wedding procession (29x36mm). c, Emperor and Empress (31x38mm).

2004, Apr. 23 ***Perf. 14¼x14***
1952 A1153 Sheet of 3 12.50 12.50
a. €1.25 multi 3.25 3.25
b. €1.50 multi 4.00 4.00
c. €1.75 multi 4.50 4.50

Souvenir Sheet

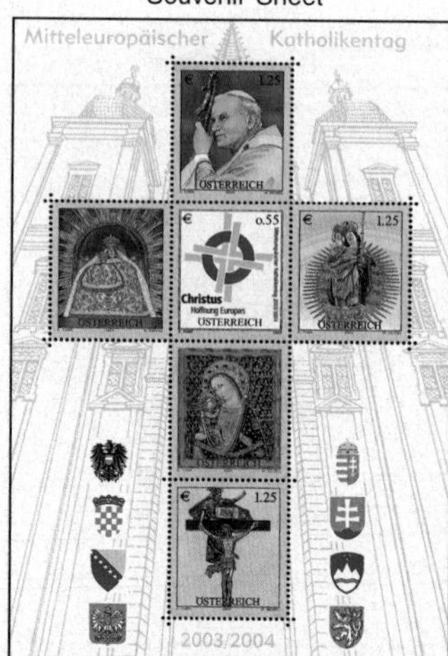

Central European Catholics' Day — A1154

No. 1953: a, Catholics' Day emblem. b, Pope John Paul II. c, Madonna and Child, Mariazell Basilica (silver panel at bottom). d, Mother of God on the Column of the Blessed Virgin, Mariazell Basilica. e, Virgin Mary and Child, Mariazell Basilica (gold frame). f, Altar crucifix, Mariazell Basilica.

Photo. (55c), Photo. & Engr.
2004, Apr. 28 ***Perf. 14***
1953 A1154 Sheet of 6 17.50 17.50
a. 55c multi 1.50 1.50
b.-f. €1.25 Any single 3.25 3.25

Folklore & Customs Type of 1991

Design: Barrel sliding, Klosterneuburg.

Photo. & Engr.
2004, May 8 ***Perf. 13¾***
1954 A892 55c multi 1.40 1.40

Joe Zawinul, Jazz Musician A1155

2004, May 24 **Photo.** ***Perf. 13¾***
1955 A1155 55c multi 1.40 1.40

Europa A1156

2004, June 4 ***Perf. 13¾x14***
1956 A1156 75c multi 2.00 2.00

Papal Order of the Holy Sepulchre of Jerusalem — A1157

Photo. & Engr.
2004, June 4 ***Perf. 13¾***
1957 A1157 125c multi 3.50 3.50

Railways Type of 2002
Photo. & Engr.
2004, June 19 ***Perf. 13¾***
1958 A1109 55c Engerth locomotive 1.40 1.40

21st Danube Island Festival, Vienna A1158

2004, June 25 **Photo.** ***Perf. 13¾x14***
1959 A1158 55c multi 1.40 1.40

Theodor Herzl (1860-1904), Zionist Leader A1159

2004, July 6 ***Perf. 13¾***
1960 A1159 55c multi 1.40 1.40

See Hungary No. 3903, Israel No. 1566.

Arnold Schwarzenegger, Governor of California, Actor — A1160

Perf. 13½x14¼
2004, July 30 **Photo.**
1961 A1160 100c multi 2.75 2.75

Ernst Happel (1925-92), Soccer Coach — A1161

2004, Aug. 17 ***Perf. 14x13½***
1962 A1161 100c red & black 2.50 2.50

Winning Entry in Tom Turbo Television Show Children's Stamp Design Contest A1162

2004, Sept. 9 **Photo.** ***Perf. 13¾***
1963 A1162 55c multi 1.40 1.40

Tom Tom, Tom Tomette and Schneckodemus, Cartoon by Thomas Kostron — A1163

2004, Sept. 10 ***Perf. 14¼x14***
1964 A1163 55c multi 1.40 1.40

Incorporation of Floridsdorf into Vienna, Cent. — A1164

Photo. & Engr.
2004, Sept. 17 ***Perf. 14x13¾***
1965 A1164 55c multi 1.40 1.40

Souvenir Sheet

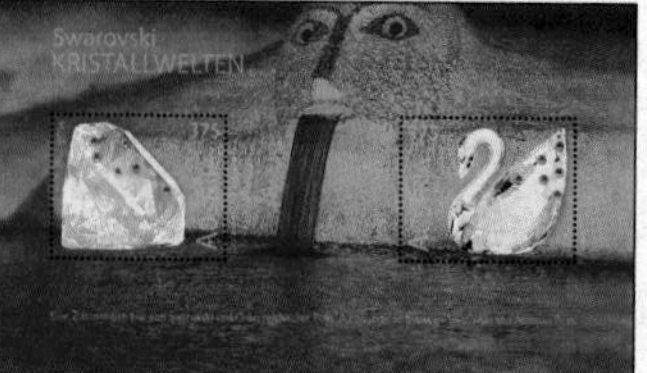

Swarovski Crystal — A1165

No. 1966: a, Crystal. b, Swan.

Photo. With Glass Crystals Affixed

2004, Sept. 20 ***Perf. 14x14¼***

1966 A1165 Sheet of 2 20.00 20.00
a.-b. 375c Either single 10.00 10.00

Six crystals are affixed to each stamp. Sheet was sold with a protective sleeve.

Hermann Maier, Skier — A1166

2004, Sept. 25 Photo. ***Perf. 14x13¾***

1967 A1166 55c multi 1.40 1.40

Kaspar's Winter Scene, by Josef Bramer A1167

Photo. & Engr.

2004, Oct. 8 ***Perf. 13½x13¾***

1968 A1167 55c multi 1.50 1.50

No. 1867 Surcharged

2004, Oct. 13 Photo. ***Perf. 13¾x14***

1969 A1090 55c on 51c #1867 1.50 1.50

Woman Waiting, by Silvia Gredenberg A1168

2004, Oct. 15 Photo. ***Perf. 13¾x14***

1970 A1168 55c multi 1.50 1.50

Souvenir Sheet

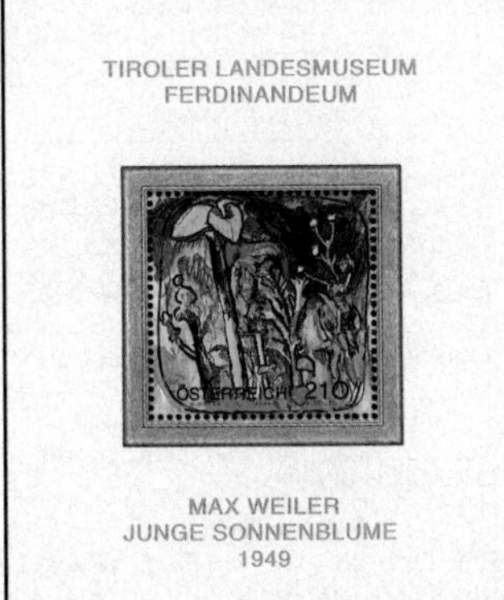

Young Sunflower, by Max Weiler — A1169

Photo. & Engr.

2004, Oct. 18 ***Perf. 13¾***

1971 A1169 210c multi 6.00 6.00

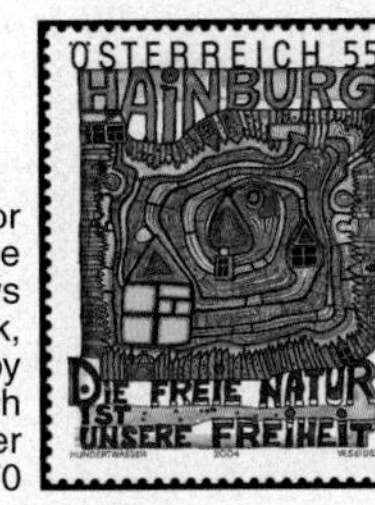

Poster for Danube Meadows National Park, by Friedensreich Hundertwasser A1170

Photo. & Engr.

2004, Oct. 22 ***Perf. 13½x13¾***

1972 A1170 55c multi 1.50 1.50

Federal Army, 50th Anniv. — A1171

2004, Oct. 26 Photo. ***Perf. 13¾***

1973 A1171 55c multi 1.50 1.50

Nikolaus Harnoncourt, Conductor, 75th Birthday — A1172

2004, Oct. 29

1974 A1172 100c multi 2.75 2.75

Christmas A1173

Photo. & Engr.

2004, Nov. 26 ***Perf. 13½x13¾***

1975 A1173 55c multi 1.50 1.50

2005 New Year's Concert With Conductor Lorin Maazel — A1174

2005, Jan. 1 Photo. ***Perf. 13¾***

1976 A1174 €1 multi 2.75 2.75

Herbert von Karajan Center, 10th Anniv. A1175

2005, Jan. 14 ***Perf. 14x14¼***

1977 A1175 55c multi 1.50 1.50

Stephan Eberharter, Skier — A1176

2005, Jan. 20 ***Perf. 14x13¾***

1978 A1176 55c multi 1.50 1.50

Nos. 1863A, 1864, 1866, 1867, 1869, 1872, 1875 and 1879 Surcharged

g

h

i

j

k

l

m

n

2005 Photo. ***Perf. 13¾x14***

1979	A1090(g)	55c on 13c multi	1.50	1.50
1980	A1090(h)	55c on 17c multi	1.50	1.50
1981	A1090(i)	55c on 27c multi	1.50	1.50
1982	A1090(j)	55c on 51c multi	1.50	1.50
1983	A1090(k)	55c on 58c multi	1.50	1.50
1984	A1090(l)	55c on 73c multi	1.50	1.50
1985	A1090(m)	55c on 87c multi	1.50	1.50
1986	A1090(n)	55c on €2.03 multi	1.50	1.50
		Nos. 1979-1986 (8)	12.00	12.00

Issued: Nos. 1979, 1980, 2/11; Nos. 1981, 1986, 2/18; Nos. 1982, 1983, 2/4; Nos. 1984, 1985, 1/25.

Rotary International, Cent. — A1177

2005, Feb. 23 Photo. ***Perf. 14x14¼***

1987 A1177 55c multi 1.50 1.50

Max Schmeling (1905-2005), Boxer A1178

Photo. & Engr.

2005, Mar. 1 ***Perf. 13¾x14***

1988 A1178 100c multi 2.75 2.75

Venus at a Mirror, by Peter Paul Rubens A1179

2005, Mar. 7 ***Perf. 13¾***

1989 A1179 125c multi 3.00 3.00

See Liechtenstein No. 1314.

Souvenir Sheet

Carl Djerassi, Chemist and Novelist — A1180

2005, Mar. 8 Photo. ***Perf. 14***

1990 A1180 100c multi 2.75 2.75

Pope John Paul II (1920-2005) A1181

Photo. & Engr.

2005, Apr. 14 ***Perf. 13½x14¼***

1991 A1181 €1 multi 2.75 2.75

Zodiac A1182

New Year 2005 (Year of the Rooster) A1183

Die Cut Perf. 14 Syncopated

2005-06 **Photo.**

Self-Adhesive
Booklet Stamps

1992 A1182 55c Taurus 4.00 4.00
1993 A1182 55c Gemini 4.00 4.00
1994 A1182 55c Cancer 4.00 4.00
1995 A1183 55c Red rooster 4.00 4.00
a. Booklet pane, 2 each #1992-1995 35.00
1996 A1182 55c Leo 4.00 4.00
1997 A1182 55c Virgo 4.00 4.00
1998 A1182 55c Libra 4.00 4.00
1999 A1183 55c Yellow rooster 4.00 4.00
a. Booklet pane, 2 each #1996-1999 35.00
2000 A1182 55c Scorpio 4.00 4.00
2001 A1182 55c Sagittarius 4.00 4.00
2002 A1182 55c Capricorn 4.00 4.00
2003 A1183 55c Orange rooster 4.00 4.00
a. Booklet pane, 2 each #2000-2003 35.00
2004 A1182 55c Aquarius 4.00 4.00
2005 A1182 55c Pisces 4.00 4.00
2006 A1182 55c Aries 4.00 4.00
2007 A1183 55c Red dog 4.00 4.00
a. Booklet pane, 2 each #2004-2007 35.00

Issued: Nos. 1992-1995, 4/21. Nos. 1996-1999, 7/22; 2000-2003, 10/24; Nos. 2004-2007, 1/20/06.

Austrian Imperial Post Office, Jerusalem — A1184

Photo. & Engr.

2005, Apr. 22 ***Perf. 13¾***
2008 A1184 100c multi 2.75 2.75

Patron Saints of Austrian Regions A1185

Designs: No. 2009, St. Florian, patron saint of Upper Austria. No. 2010, St. Joseph, patron saint of Styria.

2005 **Photo. & Engr.** ***Perf. 13¼***
2009 A1185 55c multi 1.50 1.50
2010 A1185 55c multi 1.50 1.50

Issued: No. 2009, 5/4; No. 2010, 6/10.
See Nos. 2053, 2062, 2089, 2120, 2162, 2187, 2232.

Liberation of Mauthausen Concentration Camp, 60th Anniv. — A1186

2005, May 6
2011 A1186 55c multi 1.50 1.50

Souvenir Sheet

Second Republic, 60th Anniv. — A1187

No. 2012: a, Heraldic eagle and "60" (35x35mm). b, Signatures on State Treaty (42x35mm).

2005, May 15
2012 A1187 Sheet of 2 3.00 3.00
a.-b. 55c Either single 1.50 1.50

Heidi Klum, 2005 Life Ball Attendee — A1188

2005, May 20 ***Perf. 14x13¾***
2013 A1188 75c multi 2.00 2.00

Europa A1189

2005, May 28 ***Perf. 13¾***
2014 A1189 75c multi 1.50 1.50

Jochen Rindt, Formula I Race Car Driver — A1190

2005, June 11 **Photo.** ***Perf. 14x13¾***
2015 A1190 55c multi 1.50 1.50

Niki Lauda, Formula I Race Car Driver — A1191

2005, Sept. 13 **Photo.** ***Perf. 14x13¾***
2016 A1191 55c multi 1.50 1.50

A €1.25 stamp picturing the Dalai Lama exists. Advance complimentary examples were sent out before the issue was canceled. It is believed approximately 30 examples are extant. An auction sale in 2008 realized €5,683 for the first public sale of the stamp.

Premiere of Animated Movie "Madagascar" A1192

2005, July 7 **Photo.** ***Perf. 14***
2017 A1192 55c multi 1.50 1.50

Inachis Io — A1193

Photo. & Engr.

2005, July 15 ***Perf. 13½x14¼***
2018 A1193 55c multi 1.50 1.50

Edelweiss A1194

2005, July 19 **Embroidered** ***Imperf.***

Self-Adhesive

2019 A1194 375c green & white 11.00 11.00

Folklore & Customs Type of 1991

Design: Frankenburger Dice Game, Upper Austria.

Photo. & Engr.

2005, July 29 ***Perf. 13¾***
2020 A892 55c multi 1.50 1.50

Halloween A1195

2005, Sept. 16 **Photo.** ***Perf. 13¾***
2021 A1195 55c multi 1.50 1.50

Souvenir Sheet

Row of Houses, by Egon Schiele (1890-1918) — A1196

Photo. & Engr.

2005, Sept. 21 ***Perf. 13¾***
2022 A1196 210c multi 6.25 6.25

Railways Type of 2002

2005, Sept. 30
2023 A1109 55c Montafon Railway ET 10.103 1.50 1.50

Montafon Railway, cent.

Landhaus, Klagenfurt A1197

Photo. & Engr.

2005, Oct. 7 ***Perf. 13¾x13½***
2024 A1197 75c multi 2.00 2.00

Master of Woods, by Karl Hodina A1198

2005, Oct. 14 ***Perf. 13½x13¾***
2025 A1198 55c multi 1.50 1.50

Adalbert Stifter (1805-68), Writer — A1199

2005, Oct. 21 **Photo.** ***Perf. 13¾***
2026 A1199 55c multi 1.50 1.50

Souvenir Sheet

Reopening of National Theater and State Opera House, 50th Anniv. — A1200

No. 2027: a, National Theater. b, State Opera House.

2005, Oct. 25 **Engr.** ***Perf. 13½x14¼***
2027 A1200 Sheet of 2 + central label 3.25 3.25
a.-b. 55c Either single 1.60 1.60

Souvenir Sheet

Cyclorama of Salzburg, by Johann Sattler — A1201

No. 2028: a, Denomination at left. b, Denomination at right.

Photo. & Engr.

2005, Oct. 26 ***Perf. 13¾x13½***
2028 A1201 Sheet of 2 8.00 8.00
a.-b. 125c Either single 3.75 3.75

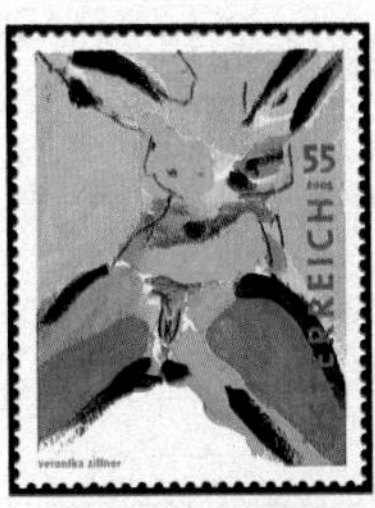

Expectation, by Veronika Zillner — A1202

Perf. 13½x13¾

2005, Oct. 28 **Photo.**
2029 A1202 55c multi 1.50 1.50

Opening of Film, *The Chronicles of Narnia: The Lion, the Witch and the Wardrobe* A1203

2005, Nov. 8 ***Perf. 13¾***
2030 A1203 55c multi 1.50 1.50

Visitation of Mary Chapel, by Reinhold Stecher A1204

2005, Nov. 14 ***Perf. 13¾x14***
2031 A1204 55c multi 1.50 1.50

Advent and Christmas.

Teutonic Order in Austria, 800th Anniv. A1205

Photo. & Engr.

2005, Nov. 18 ***Perf. 14***
2032 A1205 55c multi 1.50 1.50

Christmas A1206

2005, Nov. 25 **Photo.** ***Perf. 14x14¼***
2033 A1206 55c multi 1.50 1.50

2006 New Year's Concert With Conductor Mariss Jansons A1207

2006, Jan. 1 **Photo.** ***Perf. 13¾x14***
2034 A1207 75c multi 1.75 1.75

Austrian Presidency of European Union A1208

Photo. & Engr.

2006, Jan. 1 ***Perf. 14x14¼***
2035 A1208 75c multi 2.25 2.25

Personalized Stamp — A1209

2006, Jan. 1 **Photo.** ***Perf. 14x13¾***
2036 A1209 55c multi 1.50 1.50

Stamp vignettes could be personalized by customers, presumably for an extra fee.

A quantity of No. 2036 was later imprinted with various commercial themes and offered by Austria Post in full panes at a substantial premium over face value.

Other denominations could be ordered, as well as stamps with vertically oriented frames, but the example of No. 2036 shown is the only stamp with a "generic" vignette that sold for the face value shown on the stamp.

See note after No. 1944.

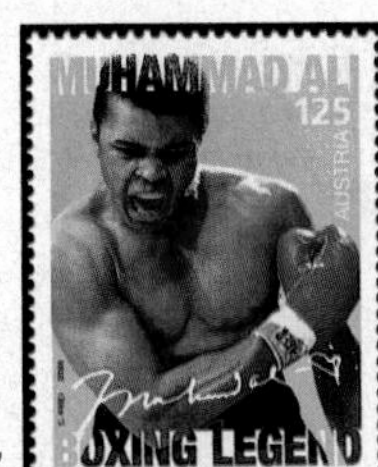

Muhammad Ali, Boxer — A1211

2006, Jan. 14 **Photo.** ***Perf. 13¾x14***
2038 A1211 125c multi 3.00 3.00

Wolfgang Amadeus Mozart (1756-91), Composer A1212

Photo. & Embossed

2006, Jan. 27 ***Perf. 13½x13¾***
2039 A1212 55c multi 1.50 1.50

Europa Stamps, 50th Anniv. — A1213

2006, Mar. 3 **Photo.** ***Perf. 14***
2040 A1213 125c multi 3.75 3.75

Lost in Her Dreams, by Friedrich von Amerling A1214

Photo. & Engr.

2006, Mar. 6 ***Perf. 13¾***
2041 A1214 125c multi 3.75 3.75

See Liechtenstein No. 1342.

Souvenir Sheet

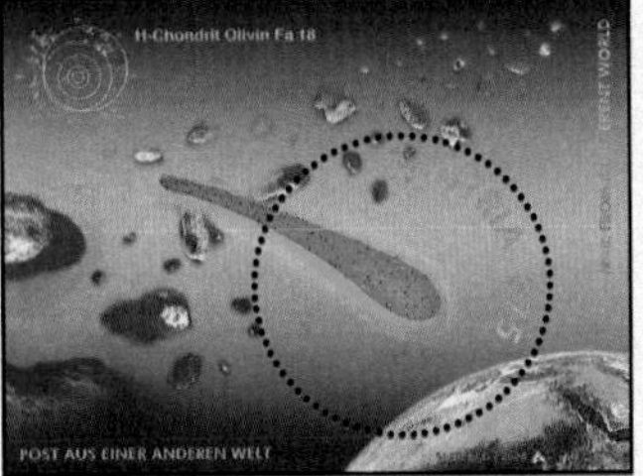

Meteor — A1215

2006, Mar. 24 **Photo.** ***Perf.***
2042 A1215 375c multi 11.00 11.00

Meteorite particles are embedded in the ink used on the meteor.

Karlheinz Böhm, Founder of Menschen für Menschen Foundation, and His Wife, Almaz — A1216

2006, Mar. 30 ***Perf. 14***
2043 A1216 100c multi 3.00 3.00

Menschen für Menschen Foundation, 25th anniv.

Souvenir Sheet

Freemasonry in Austria — A1217

2006, Apr. 6 **Photo. & Engr.**
2044 A1217 100c multi 3.00 3.00

Couch of Sigmund Freud (1856-1939), Psychoanalyst A1218

2006, Apr. 10 **Photo.**
2045 A1218 55c multi 1.60 1.60

Franz Beckenbauer, by Andy Warhol A1219

2006, Apr. 12 ***Perf. 13¾***
2046 A1219 75c multi 2.25 2.25

No. 1863 Surcharged

2006, May 15 **Photo.** ***Perf. 13¾x14***
2047 A1090 55c on 7c #1863 1.60 1.60

Falco (Hans Hölzl, 1957-98), Rock Musician — A1220

Photo. & Engr.

2006, May 18 ***Perf. 14¼x13½***
2048 A1220 55c multi 1.60 1.60

Naomi Campbell, 2006 Life Ball Attendee — A1221

2006, May 20 **Photo.** ***Perf. 14x13¾***
2049 A1221 75c multi 2.25 2.25

Folklore & Customs Type of 1991

Design: Kranzelreiten, Weitensfeld.

Photo. & Engr.

2006, June 4 ***Perf. 13¾***
2050 A892 55c multi 1.60 1.60

Miniature Sheet

Formula I Race Car Drivers — A1222

No. 2051: a, Jim Clark (1936-68). b, Jacky Ickx. c, Jackie Stewart. d, Alain Prost. e, Stirling Moss. f, Mario Andretti. g, Bruce McLaren (1937-70). h, Jack Brabham.

2006, June 7 Photo. ***Perf. 14x13¾***

2051 A1222 Sheet of 8 25.00 25.00
a.-d. 55c Any single 1.60 1.60
e.-f. 75c Either single 2.25 2.25
g. 100c multi 3.00 3.00
h. 125c multi 3.75 3.75

Compare with types A1190-A1191.

Initial Stock Offering of Austria Post — A1223

2006, June 8 ***Perf. 13¾***
2052 A1223 55c multi 1.60 1.60

Patron Saints Type of 2005

Design: St. Hemma, patron saint of Carinthia.

Photo. & Engr.

2006, June 27 ***Perf. 13¾***
2053 A1185 55c multi 1.60 1.60

Federal Chamber of Industry and Commerce, 60th Anniv. — A1224

2006, June 28 Photo. ***Perf. 14***
2054 A1224 55c sil, blk & red 1.60 1.60

Wolfgang Amadeus Mozart and Salzburg — A1225

2006, June 30
2055 A1225 55c multi 1.60 1.60

Activities in Salzburg commemorating 250th anniv. of the birth of Mozart.

Ottfried Fischer, Television Actor — A1226

2006, July 1 ***Perf. 13¾x14***
2056 A1226 55c multi 1.60 1.60

Europa A1227

2006, July 1 ***Perf. 14***
2057 A1227 75c multi 1.75 1.75

St. Anne's Column, Innsbruck, 300th Anniv. — A1228

Photo. & Engr.

2006, July 26 ***Perf. 14***
2058 A1228 55c multi 1.60 1.60

Railways Type of 2002

2006, Aug. 19 ***Perf. 13¾***
2059 A1109 55c Pyhrn Railway locomotive 1.60 1.60

Pyhrn Railway, cent.

Souvenir Sheet

Fireworks — A1229

No. 2060: a, Fireworks over Hong Kong Harbor. b, Fireworks over Prater Ferris wheel, Vienna.

Photo. With Glass Beads Affixed

2006, Aug. 22 ***Perf. 14***
2060 A1229 Sheet of 2 22.50 22.50
a.-b. 375c Either single 11.00 11.00
c. Sheet, Austria #2060b, Hong Kong #1208a 32.50 32.50

See Hong Kong Nos. 1206-1208. No. 2060c, sold for €12.40 in Austria and for $120 in Hong Kong and is identical to Hong Kong No. 1208c.

Lynx Lynx A1230

Photo. & Engr.

2006, Aug. 25 ***Perf. 13½x14¼***
2061 A1230 55c multi 1.60 1.60

Patron Saints Type of 2005

Design: St. Gebhard, patron saint of Vorarlberg.

Photo. & Engr.

2006, Sept. 1 ***Perf. 13¾***
2062 A1185 55c multi 1.60 1.60

Steyr 220 Automobile — A1231

2006, Sept. 9 **Photo.**
2063 A1231 55c multi 1.60 1.60

KTM R 125 Tarzan Motorcycle A1232

2006, Sept. 10 ***Perf. 14¼***
2064 A1232 55c multi 1.60 1.60

Benjamin Raich, Skier — A1233

2006, Sept. 23 ***Perf. 14***
2065 A1233 55c multi 1.60 1.60

Musical Instruments A1234

Designs: No. 2066, Seven-stringed qin, China. No. 2067, Bösendorfer piano, Austria.

2006, Sept. 26 ***Perf. 13½x14¼***
2066 A1234 55c multi 1.60 1.60
2067 A1234 55c multi 1.60 1.60

See People's Republic of China Nos. 3531-3532.

Youngboy Vienna Austria 2005, by Cornelia Schlesinger — A1235

2006, Sept. 29 ***Perf. 14x14¼***
2068 A1235 55c multi 1.60 1.60

Homo Sapiens, by Valentin Oman — A1236

Photo. & Engr.

2006, Oct. 9 ***Perf. 13¾x14***
2069 A1236 55c multi 1.60 1.60

Wildlife — A1237

Designs: No. 2070, Emys orbicularis. No. 2071, Geronticus eremita. No. 2072, Ursus arctos.

Die Cut Perf. 13¾x13½

2006, Nov. 6 **Photo.**

Self-Adhesive

Coil Stamp

2070 A1237 55c multi 1.60 1.60

Booklet Stamps

Size: 32x27mm

Die Cut Perf. 14 Syncopated

2071 A1237 55c multi 1.60 1.60
2072 A1237 55c multi 1.60 1.60
a. Booklet pane, 5 each #2071-2072 16.00
Nos. 2070-2072 (3) 4.80 4.80

See Nos. 2092-2094, 2122, 2140-2141, 2154-2155, 2164-2165, 2216-2217, 2235-2237, 2259-2260.

Holy Family at Rest, by Franz Weiss — A1238

Christkindl Pilgrimage Church, by Bishop Reinhold Stecher — A1239

2006 ***Perf. 14x14¼***
2073 A1238 55c multi 1.60 1.60

Perf. 14¼x13½

2074 A1239 55c multi 1.60 1.60

Christmas. Issued: No. 2073, 11/10; No. 2074, 11/24.

1,000 imperf examples of No. 2074 were sold to benefit a charity.

Lviv, Ukraine, 750th Anniv. — A1240

Photo. & Engr.

2006, Dec. 1 ***Perf. 14x13¾***
2075 A1240 55c multi 1.60 1.60

No. 2075 was printed in sheets of 10 stamps and 5 labels. See Ukraine No. 651.

Michael Schumacher, Formula I Race Car Driver — A1241

2006, Dec. 4 Photo. ***Perf. 13½x14***
2076 A1241 75c multi 2.25 2.25

Compare with No. 2103A.

Austrian Stamp and Coin Dealers Association, Cent. A1242

Photo. & Engr.

2006, Dec. 8 *Perf. 13¾*
2077 A1242 55c Type N1 1.60 1.60

2007 New Year's Concert With Conductor Zubin Mehta A1243

2007, Jan. 1 **Photo.** *Perf. 13¾*
2078 A1243 75c multi 2.25 2.25

Flowers — A1244

Designs: 55c, Alpine rose, edelweiss, and blue gentian. 75c, Christmas rose. 125c, Liverwort, tall cowslip, and daphne.

2007, Jan. 26 *Perf. 13¾x14*
2079 A1244 55c multi 1.60 1.60
2080 A1244 75c multi 2.25 2.25
2081 A1244 125c multi 3.75 3.75
Nos. 2079-2081 (3) 7.60 7.60

See Nos. 2096-2101, 2130, 2169.

"Mankind and Technology" A1245

Serpentine Die Cut 13¾x14
2007, Feb. 15 **Litho.**
Coil Stamp
Self-Adhesive
2082 A1245 55c multi 1.60 1.60

Lower Austria Fire and Earth Exhibition — A1246

2007, Feb. 16 **Litho.** *Perf. 13¾*
2083 A1246 55c multi 1.60 1.60

Miniature Sheet

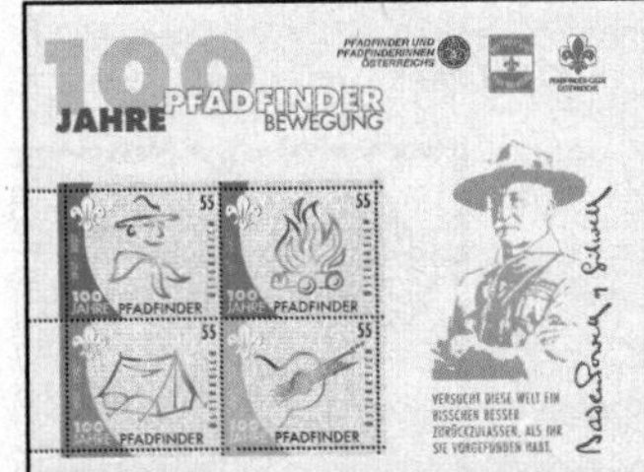
Scouting, Cent. — A1247

No. 2084: a, Scout. b, Campfire. c, Tent. d, Guitar.

2007, Feb. 22
2084 A1247 Sheet of 4 6.50 6.50
a.-d. 55c Any single 1.60 1.60

Roe Deer — A1248

2007, Feb. 23 **Photo.** *Perf. 14¼x14*
2085 A1248 75c multi 2.25 2.25

Portrait of a Lady, by Bernardino Zaganelli da Cotignola A1249

Photo. & Engr.
2007, Mar. 5 *Perf. 13¾x13½*
2086 A1249 125c multi 3.75 3.75

Printed in sheets of 8. See Liechtenstein No. 1370.

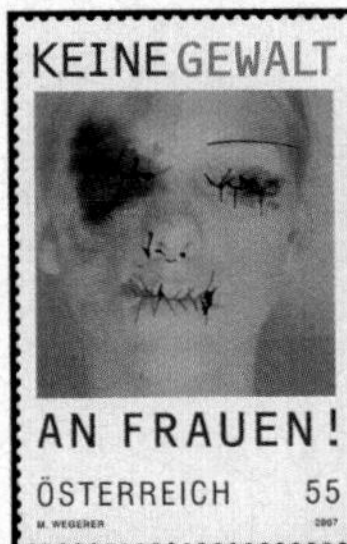
Campaign to End Violence Against Women A1250

2007, Mar. 8 **Litho.** *Perf. 13¾x14*
2087 A1250 55c multi 1.60 1.60

Easter Rattles A1251

2007, Mar. 9 *Perf. 13¾*
2088 A1251 55c multi 1.60 1.60

Patron Saints Type of 2005

Design: St. Klemens Maria Hofbauer, patron saint of Vienna.

Photo. & Engr.
2007, Mar. 15 *Perf. 13¾x14*
2089 A1185 55c multi 1.60 1.60

Roses — A1252

2007, Mar. 17 **Litho.** *Perf. 14*
2090 A1252 (55c) multi 1.60 1.60

Congratulations — A1253

2007, Mar. 30 *Perf. 13¾*
2091 A1253 (55c) multi 1.60 1.60

Wildlife Type of 2006

Designs: No. 2092, Myotis brandtii. No. 2093, Salamandra salamandra. No. 2094, Astacus astacus.

Serpentine Die Cut 13½
2007 **Photo.**
Self-Adhesive
Coil Stamp
2092 A1237 55c multi 1.60 1.60

Booklet Stamps
Size: 32x27mm
Die Cut Perf. 14 Syncopated
2093 A1237 55c multi 1.60 1.60
2094 A1237 55c multi 1.60 1.60
a. Booklet pane, 5 each #2093-2094 16.00

Issued: No. 2092, 4/20; Nos. 2093-2094, 3/31.

Pope Benedict XVI, 80th Birthday — A1254

2007, Apr. 12 **Photo.** *Perf. 14*
2095 A1254 100c multi 3.00 3.00

Flowers Type of 2004

Designs: 4c, Dandelions (Löwenzahn). 10c, Scotch laburnum (Alpen-goldregen). 65c, Guelder rose (Gewöhnlicher schneeball). 100c, Violets (velichen). 115c, Gentian (Fransenzian). 140c, Clematis (Waldrebe).

2007 *Perf. 13¾x14*
2096 A1244 4c multi .25 .25
2097 A1244 10c multi .30 .25
2098 A1244 65c multi 1.90 1.90
2099 A1244 100c multi 3.00 3.00
2100 A1244 115c multi 3.50 3.50
2101 A1244 140c multi 4.25 4.25
Nos. 2096-2101 (6) 13.20 13.15

Issued: 100c, 4/27. 4c, 10c, 65c, 115c, 140c, 8/25.

Austrian Workers' Samaritan Federation, 80th Anniv. A1255

Photo. & Engr.
2007, May 18 *Perf. 13¾*
2102 A1255 55c multi 1.60 1.60

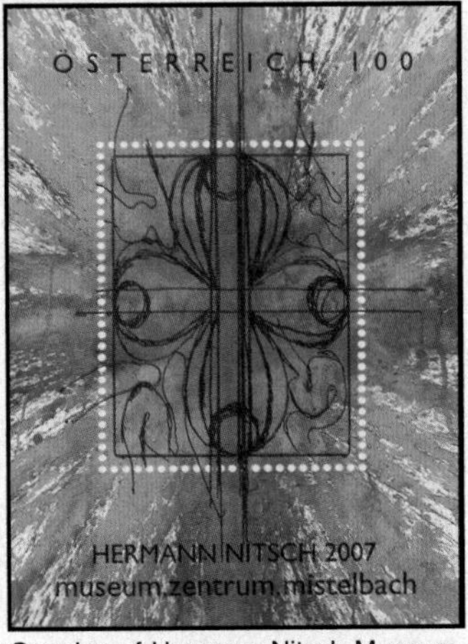
Opening of Hermann Nitsch Museum, Mistelbach — A1256

2007, May 25 *Imperf.*
2103 A1256 100c multi 3.00 3.00

Michael Schumacher Type of 2006 Redrawn

2007, May 29 **Photo.** *Perf. 13¾x14*
2103A A1241 75c multi 3.00 3.00

No. 2076 is inscribed "Weltmeister 1994 1995." No. 2103A is inscribed "Weltmeister 1995 1996," and has a thicker signature and grayer hair.

Miniature Sheet

Formula I Race Car Drivers — A1257

No. 2104: a, Phil Hill. b, Clay Regazzoni (1939-2006). c, Gerhard Berger. d, Juan Manuel Fangio (1911-95). e, John Surtees. f, Mika Häkkinen. g, Graham Hill (1929-75). h, Emerson Fittipaldi.

2007, May 29 **Litho.** *Perf. 14*
2104 A1257 Sheet of 8 13.00 13.00
a.-h. 55c Any single 1.60 1.60

Railroads Type of 2002
Photo. & Engr.
2007, May 31 *Perf. 13¾*
2105 A1109 55c Mariazell Railway locomotive 1.60 1.60

Mariazell Railway, cent.

Mariazell Basilica, 850th Anniv. A1258

2007, June 1 **Litho.**
2106 A1258 55c multi 1.60 1.60

Souvenir Sheet

UEFA European Soccer Championships, Austria and Switzerland — A1259

No. 2107 — Mascots Trix and Flix: a, Chasing ball. b, Holding trophy. c, Running toward each other. d, Celebrating.

2007, June 5 ***Perf. 13¼x12¾***

2107	A1259	Sheet of 4	3.50	3.50
a.		20c multi	.60	.60
b.		25c multi	.75	.75
c.		30c multi	.90	.90
d.		35c multi	1.00	1.00

Souvenir Sheet

Self-Portrait of Angelika Kauffmann — A1260

Photo. & Engr.

2007, June 15 ***Perf. 13½***

2108 A1260 210c multi 6.25 6.25

Europa A1261

2007, June 16 Litho. ***Perf. 14¼x14***

2109 A1261 55c multi 1.60 1.60

Ignaz Joseph Pleyel (1757-1831), Composer A1262

Photo. & Engr.

2007, June 17 ***Perf. 14***

2110 A1262 €1 multi 3.00 3.00

Premiere of Animated Movie, "Shrek the Third" — A1263

Perf. 13½x13¾

2007, June 21 **Litho.**

2111 A1263 55c multi 1.60 1.60

Essl Museum, Klosterneuberg A1264

Serpentine Die Cut 13½

2007, July 2 **Photo.**

Self-Adhesive

Coil Stamp

2112 A1264 55c multi 1.60 1.60

Wilhelm Kienzl (1857-1941), Composer — A1265

2007, July 13 Photo. ***Perf. 13¾***

2113 A1265 75c multi 2.25 2.25

Railways Type of 2002

Photo. & Engr.

2007, Aug. 4 ***Perf. 13¾***

2114 A1109 75c Bregenz Forest Railway 2.25 2.25

Man, by Astrid Bernhart A1266

2007, Aug. 24 Photo. ***Perf. 13¾***

2115 A1266 55c multi 1.60 1.60

Haliaeetus Albicilla A1267

2007, Sept. 7

2116 A1267 55c multi 1.60 1.60

Printed in sheets of 8 + central label. See Serbia No. 399.

Necklace by Josef Hoffmann (1870-1956) — A1268

Litho. & Embossed With Foil Application

2007, Sept. 14 ***Imperf.***

2117 A1268 265c multi 7.50 5.25

Oil Production in Austria, 75th Anniv. A1269

2007, Sept. 17 Litho. ***Perf. 14x13¾***

2118 A1269 75c multi 1.80 1.80

Portions of the design were applied by a thermographic process producing a shiny, raised effect.

Deer, by Friedrich Gauermann (1807-62) — A1270

2007, Sept. 20 **Photo. & Engr.**

2119 A1270 55c multi 1.60 1.50

Patron Saints Type of 2005

Design: St. Rupert, patron saint of Salzburg.

2007, Sept. 24 ***Perf. 13¾x14***

2120 A1185 55c multi 1.60 1.50

Niki Hosp, Skier — A1271

2007, Sept. 29 Litho. ***Perf. 14x13¾***

2121 A1271 55c multi 1.60 1.50

Wildlife Type of 2006

Serpentine Die Cut 13½

2007, Oct. 10 **Photo.**

Coil Stamp

Self-Adhesive

2122 A1237 75c Lucanus cervus 2.25 2.25

Linz Cathedral Key, Carved by Michael Blümelhuber (1865-1936) A1272

Photo. & Engr.

2007, Oct. 12 ***Perf. 13¾x14***

2123 A1272 75c multi 2.10 1.75

Christiane Hörbiger, Actress — A1273

2007, Oct. 13 Litho. ***Perf. 14x13¾***

2124 A1273 55c multi 1.60 1.50

Vienna State Opera's Performance of Queen of Spades, by P. I. Tchaikovsky — A1274

2007, Oct. 28 ***Perf. 13¾***

2125 A1274 55c multi 1.60 .60

Nativity Scene, Chapel of Sts. Peter and Paul, Oberwöllan A1275

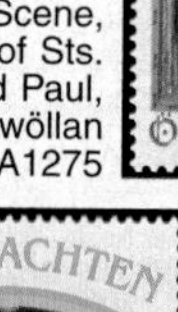

Nativity Scene, St. Barbara's Church, Vienna A1276

2007 **Photo.** ***Perf. 13¾***

2126 A1275 55c multi 1.60 1.60

Perf. 14¼x14

2127 A1276 65c multi 1.90 1.90

Christmas. Issued: 55c, 11/23; 65c, 11/9.

House of the Sea Aquarium, Vienna A1277

Perf. 13½x13¼

2007, Nov. 29 **Litho.**

2128 A1277 55c multi 1.60 1.60

Portions of the design were applied by a thermographic process, producing a shiny, raised effect.

Thomas Gottschalk, Television Personality — A1278

2007, Dec. 8 ***Perf. 13½x13¾***
2129 A1278 65c multi 1.90 1.90

Flowers Type of 2004

Design: 15c, Lady's slippers (Frauenschuh).

2008, Jan. 15 Photo. ***Perf. 13¾x14***
2130 A1244 15c multi .45 .45

Miniature Sheet

Venues of UEFA Euro 2008 Soccer Championships — A1279

No. 2131: a, Vienna. b, Salzburg. c, Klagenfurt. d, Innsbruck-Tirol. e, Zurich. f, Basel. g, Bern. h, Geneva.

2008, Jan. 17 Litho. ***Perf. 14***
2131 A1279 Sheet of 8 14.00 14.00
a.-d. 55c Any single 1.60 1.60
e.-h. 65c Any single 1.90 1.90

Mascots Trix and Flix A1280

Emblem A1281

Serpentine Die Cut 13¾
2008, Jan. 22 **Photo.**
Coil Stamps
Self-Adhesive
2132 A1280 55c multi 1.75 1.75
2133 A1281 65c multi 2.00 2.00

UEFA Euro 2008 Soccer Championships, Austria and Switzerland.

Martina, by Hans Robert Pippal (1915-98) A1282

2008, Jan. 31 Photo. ***Perf. 13¾x14***
2134 A1282 65c multi 2.00 2.00

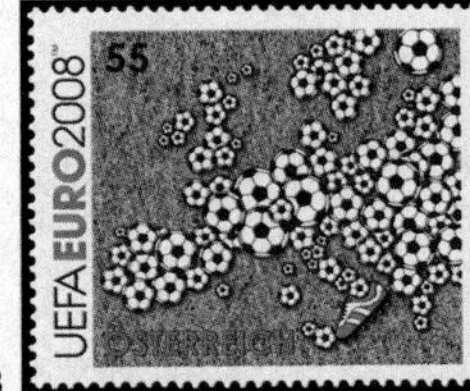

A1283

Children's Art A1284

2008, Feb. 4 Litho. ***Perf. 13¾***
2135 A1283 55c multi 1.75 1.75
2136 A1284 55c multi 1.75 1.75

UEFA Euro 2008 Soccer Championships, Austria and Switzerland.

Vienna Landmarks Type of Semi-Postals
Souvenir Sheet

2008, Feb. 15 Photo. ***Perf. 13¾***
2137 Sheet of 3 + 2 labels 5.50 5.50
a. SP209 55c multi 1.75 1.75
b. SP211 55c multi 1.75 1.75
c. SP213 65c multi 2.00 2.00

2008 Vienna Intl. Stamp Exhibition (WIPA).

Children's Art A1285

2008, Feb. 19 Litho. ***Perf. 13¾***
2138 A1285 65c multi 2.00 2.00

UEFA Euro 2008 Soccer Championships, Austria and Switzerland.

Defense, by Maria Lassnig A1286

2008, Feb. 21
2139 A1286 55c multi 1.75 1.75

UEFA Euro 2008 Soccer Championships, Austria and Switzerland.

Wildlife Type of 2006

Designs: No. 2140, Hyla arborea. No. 2141, Alcedo atthis.

Die Cut Perf. 14 Syncopated
2008, Feb. 25 **Photo.**
Booklet Stamps
Self-Adhesive
Size: 32x27mm
2140 A1237 65c multi 2.00 2.00
2141 A1237 65c multi 2.00 2.00
a. Booklet pane of 10, 5 each #2140-2141, + 10 etiquettes 20.00

Austrian Airlines, 50th Anniv. — A1287

Litho. With Foil Application
2008, Feb. 28 ***Perf. 14***
2142 A1287 140c multi 4.25 4.25

Vienna State Opera Production of "The Force of Destiny," by Giuseppe Verdi — A1288

2008, Mar. 1 Litho. ***Perf. 13¾***
2143 A1288 55c multi 1.75 1.75

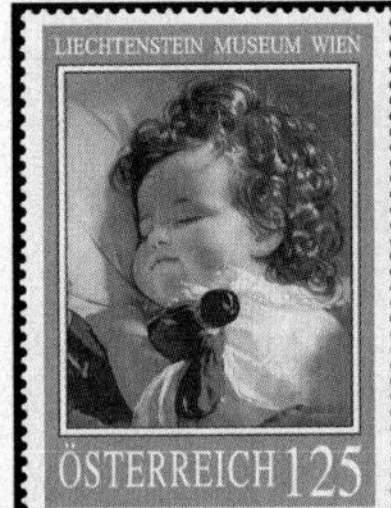

Sleeping Princess Maria Franziska, by Friedrich von Amerling A1289

Photo. & Engr.
2008, Mar. 3 ***Perf. 13¾x13½***
2144 A1289 125c multi 4.00 4.00

See Liechtenstein No. 1407.

Painting by Soshana A1290

2008, Mar. 7 Photo. ***Perf. 13½x13¾***
2145 A1290 55c multi 1.75 1.75

Soccer Ball — A1291

Silk-screened
2008, Mar. 12 ***Die Cut***
Self-Adhesive
2146 A1291 375c multi 11.50 11.50

No. 2146 is printed on the same polyurethane foam material used to make soccer balls for the UEFA Euro 2008 Soccer Championships.

Soccer Player, Ball and Field — A1292

2008, Mar. 20 Litho. ***Perf. 14***
2147 A1292 55c multi 1.75 1.75

UEFA Euro 2008 Soccer Championships, Austria and Switzerland.

Children's Art A1293

2008, Apr. 2 Litho. ***Perf. 13¾***
2148 A1293 125c multi 4.00 4.00

UEFA Euro 2008 Soccer Championships, Austria and Switzerland.

Wachau UNESCO World Heritage Site A1294

2008, Apr. 9 **Photo. & Engr.**
2149 A1294 100c multi 3.25 3.25

A1295

Children's Art — A1296

2008 **Litho.**
2150 A1295 55c multi 1.75 1.75
2151 A1296 100c multi 3.25 3.25

Issued: 55c, 4/18; 100c, 4/19. UEFA 2008 Soccer Championships, Austria and Switzerland.

Tyrolean Federation of Traditional Provincial Costumes, Cent. — A1297

2008, Apr. 26 ***Perf. 14x13¾***
2152 A1297 75c multi 2.40 2.40

Miniature Sheet

Goal by Andreas Herzog Against Sweden In 1997 World Cup Qualifying Match — A1298

Litho. With Three-Dimensional Plastic Affixed

2008, May 5 ***Serpentine Die Cut 9***

Self-Adhesive

2153 A1298 545c multi 17.00 17.00

UEFA 2008 Soccer Championships, Austria and Switzerland.

Wildlife Type of 2006

Designs: No. 2154, Erinaceus concolor. No. 2155, Lepus europaeus.

Die Cut Perf. 14 Syncopated

2008, May 5 **Photo.**

Booklet Stamps

Self-Adhesive

Size: 32x27mm

2154 A1237 55c multi 1.75 1.75
2155 A1237 55c multi 1.75 1.75
a. Booklet pane of 10, 5 each #2154-2155 17.50

Federal Stud Farm, Piber — A1299

2008, May 9 **Litho.** ***Perf. 14***

2156 A1299 55c multi 1.75 1.75

Grass of Soccer Field — A1300

2008, May 10 ***Perf. 13¾***

2157 A1300 75c multi 2.40 2.40

UEFA 2008 Soccer Championships, Austria and Switzerland.

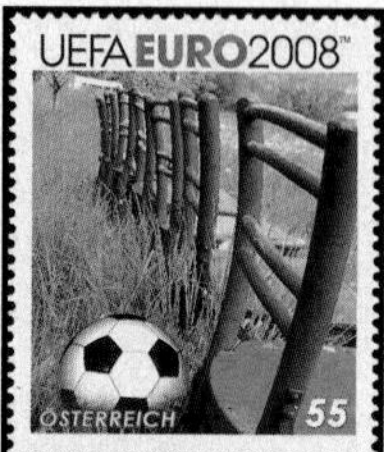

Soccer Ball and Chairs A1301

2008, May 16

2158 A1301 55c multi 1.75 1.75

UEFA 2008 Soccer Championships, Austria and Switzerland.

Miniature Sheets

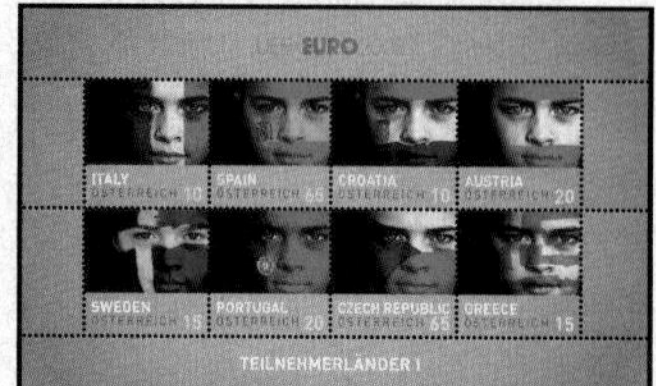

Face Painted with Flags of Countries — A1302

No. 2159: a, Italy. b, Croatia. c, Sweden. d, Greece. e, Austria. f, Portugal. g, Spain. h, Czech Republic.

No. 2160: a, Switzerland. b, Germany. c, Romania. d, Turkey. e, Netherlands. f, Poland. g, Russia. h, France.

2008, May 16 ***Perf. 14***

2159 A1302 Sheet of 8 7.00 7.00
a.-b. 10c Either single .30 .30
c.-d. 15c Either single .45 .45
e.-f. 20c Either single .65 .65
g.-h. 65c Either single 2.10 2.10
2160 A1302 Sheet of 8 9.25 9.25
a.-b. 25c Either single .80 .80
c.-d. 30c Either single .95 .95
e.-f. 35c Either single 1.10 1.10
g.-h. 55c Either single 1.75 1.75

UEFA 2008 Soccer Championships, Austria and Switzerland.

Souvenir Sheet

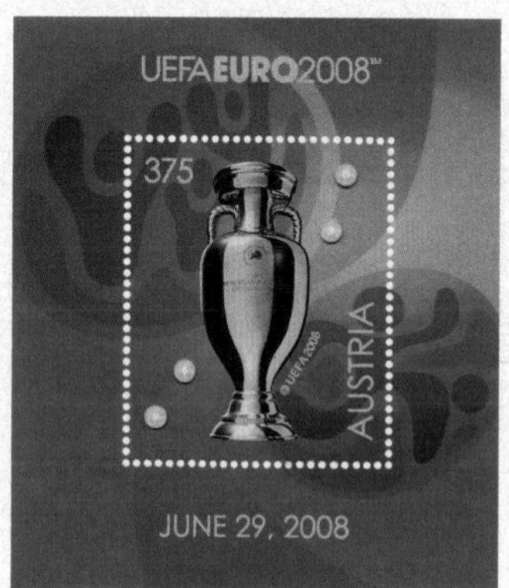

Henri Delaunay Cup — A1303

Photo. With Synthetic Crystals Affixed

2008, June 5 ***Perf. 13¾***

2161 A1303 375c multi 12.00 12.00

UEFA 2008 Soccer Championships, Austria and Switzerland.

Patron Saints Type of 2005

Design: St. Notburga, patron saint of Tyrol.

2008, June 6 **Photo. & Engr.**

2162 A1185 55c multi 1.75 1.75

Europa A1304

2008, June 6 **Photo.**

2163 A1304 65c multi 1.60 1.60

Wildlife Type of 2006

Designs: No. 2164, Upupa epops. No. 2165, Hemaris fuciformis.

Booklet Stamps

Self-Adhesive

Die Cut Perf. 14 Syncopated

2008, June 13 **Size: 32x27mm**

2164 A1237 75c multi 2.40 2.40
2165 A1237 75c multi 2.40 2.40
a. Booklet pane of 10, 5 each #2164-2165 24.00

Railways Type of 2002

Photo. & Engr.

2008, June 20 ***Perf. 13¾***

2166 A1109 75c Vienna Urban Railway locomotive 2.40 2.40

Vienna Urban Railway, 110th anniv.

Letterbox, by Josef Maria Olbrich (1867-1908) — A1305

2008, Aug. 5 **Litho.** ***Perf. 14***

2167 A1305 65c multi 2.00 2.00

Souvenir Sheet

Willendorf Venus — A1306

Litho. with Three-Dimensional Plastic Affixed

2008, Aug. 8 ***Serpentine Die Cut 9¼***

2168 A1306 375c multi 11.50 11.50

This stamp was a gift for standing order customers. It was not made available for sale.

Flowers Type of 2004

Design: 50c, Columbine (Akelei).

2008, Sept. 1 **Photo.** ***Perf. 13¾***

2169 A1244 50c multi 1.50 1.50

Vienna Skyline — A1307

Coil Stamp

Photo. With Foil Application

Serpentine Die Cut 13½x14

2008, Sept. 2 **Self-Adhesive**

2170 A1307 55c multi 1.60 1.60

2008 Vienna Intl. Stamp Exhibition (WIPA).

Railways Type of 2002

Photo. & Engr.

2008, Sept. 10 ***Perf. 13¾***

2171 A1109 100c Princess Elizabeth Western Railway train 3.00 3.00

Princess Elizabeth Western Railway, 150th anniv.

Souvenir Sheet

Mail Coach — A1308

2008, Sept. 12

2172 A1308 265c multi 7.75 7.75

Praga 2008 Intl. Stamp Exhibition, Prague, and 2008 Vienna Intl. Stamp Exhibition. See Czech Republic No. 3398.

Miniature Sheet

Art by Friedensreich Hundertwasser (1928-2000) — A1309

Various unnamed works of art.

2008, Sept. 18 ***Perf. 13¾x14***

2173 A1309 Sheet of 4 10.50 10.50
a. 55c multi 1.60 1.60
b. 75c multi 2.25 2.25
c. €1 multi 3.00 3.00
d. €1.25 multi 3.50 3.50

Nude Woman, by Dina Larot — A1310

2008, Sept. 19 **Litho.** ***Perf. 13¾x14***

2174 A1310 55c multi 1.60 1.60

Gentian Flower A1311

Embroidered

2008, Sept. 19 ***Imperf.***

Self-Adhesive

2175 A1311 375c tan & dark blue 11.00 11.00

Maximilian Schell, Actor — A1312

2008, Sept. 20 Litho. ***Perf. 13¾***

2176 A1312 100c multi 3.00 3.00

Romy Schneider (1938-82), Actress A1313

2008, Sept. 21 **Photo.**

2177 A1313 100c multi 3.00 3.00

Spain, UEFA Euro 2008 Soccer Champions — A1314

2008, Sept. 27 **Litho.**

2178 A1314 65c multi 1.90 1.90

Markus Rogan, Swimmer A1315

2008. Sept. 27

2179 A1315 100c multi 3.00 3.00

Thomas Morgenstern, Skier — A1316

2008, Sept. 27 ***Perf. 14x13¾***

2180 A1316 100c multi 3.00 3.00

70th Birthday of Pres. Heinz Fischer — A1317

2008, Oct. 7 Litho. ***Perf. 14¼x13½***

2181 A1317 55c multi 1.50 1.50

Advertising Art for Manner Neapolitan Wafers A1318

2008, Oct. 16 ***Perf. 13¾***

2182 A1318 55c multi 1.40 1.40

Koloman Moser (1868-1918), Artist — A1319

2008, Oct. 31 ***Perf. 14¼x13½***

2183 A1319 130c multi 3.50 3.50

Lobby of Imperial Post Office, Trieste A1320

2008, Nov. 3 ***Perf. 13¾***

2184 A1320 65c multi 1.75 1.75

Adoration of the Magi, by Unknown Artist A1321

The First Christmas Tree in Ried, by Felix Ignaz Pollinger A1322

2008 **Photo.**

2185 A1321 55c multi 1.40 1.40

2186 A1322 65c multi 1.75 1.75

Issued: 55c, 11/21; 65c, 11/5.

Patron Saints Type of 2005

Design: St. Martin, patron saint of Burgenland.

2008, Nov. 7 **Photo. & Engr.**

2187 A1185 55c multi 1.40 1.40

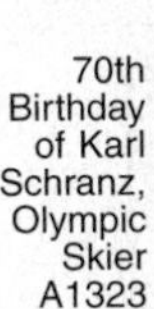

70th Birthday of Karl Schranz, Olympic Skier A1323

2008, Nov. 11 **Litho.**

2188 A1323 65c multi 1.75 1.75

Souvenir Sheet

Salt and Pepper Shaker by Benvenulto Cellini — A1324

No. 2189: a, Female figure. b, Male figure.

Litho. & Embossed

2009, Jan. 24 ***Perf. 14***

2189 A1324 Sheet of 2 11.00 11.00

a.-b. 210c Either single 5.50 5.50

Landskron Castle — A1325

Serpentine Die Cut 13¾x13½

2009, Jan. 30 **Photo.**

Self-Adhesive

Coil Stamp

2190 A1325 55c multi 1.40 1.40

Advertising Art for Pez Candy A1326

2009, Feb. 6 Litho. ***Perf. 13¾***

2191 A1326 55c multi 1.40 1.40

Imperial Post Office, Cracow A1327

2009, Feb. 13

2192 A1327 100c multi 2.60 2.60

Raimondo Montecucculi (1609-80), Military Leader A1328

2009, Feb. 20

2193 A1328 130c multi 3.50 3.50

SOS Children's Villages, 60th Anniv. — A1329

2009, Mar. 6 Litho. ***Perf. 14x13¾***

2194 A1329 55c multi 1.40 1.40

Lewis Hamilton, 2008 Formula 1 Racing Champion — A1330

2009, Mar. 17

2195 A1330 100c multi 2.60 2.60

Mercedes Silver Arrow at Vienna Technical Museum — A1331

Litho. With Three-Dimensional Plastic Affixed

Serpentine Die Cut 9¼

2009, Mar. 17 **Self-Adhesive**

2196 A1331 265c multi 6.75 6.75

Schönbrunn Palace, Vienna — A1332

2009, Mar. 20 Litho. ***Perf. 13½x13***

2197 A1332 65c multi 1.75 1.75

Preservation of Polar Regions and Glaciers A1333

2009, Mar. 26 ***Perf. 14¼***

2198 A1333 65c multi 1.75 1.75

Steyr-Daimler-Puch Haflinger, 50th Anniv. — A1334

2009, Mar. 27 ***Perf. 13¾***

2199 A1334 55c multi 1.40 1.40

Joseph Haydn (1732-1809), Composer A1335

2009, Mar. 31

2200 A1335 65c multi 1.75 1.75

Tyto Alba — A1336

Serpentine Die Cut 13½

2009, Apr. 5 **Litho.**

Self-Adhesive

Coil Stamp

2201 A1336 55c multi 1.50 1.50

Souvenir Sheet

Art By Christo — A1337

No. 2202: a, Drawing of wrapped Flak Tower. b, Model of building with tower.

2009, Apr. 15 ***Perf. 14***

2202 A1337 Sheet of 2 3.00 3.00

a.-b. 55c Either single 1.50 1.50

Fred Zinnemann (1907-97), Film Director A1338

2009, Apr. 29 ***Perf. 13¾***

2203 A1338 55c multi 1.50 1.50

St. Pölten, 850th Anniv. A1339

2009, May 2 **Litho.** ***Perf. 13¼x13¾***

2204 A1339 55c multi 1.50 1.50

Vienna State Opera Production of *The Ring of the Nibelungen* A1340

2009, May 2 ***Perf. 13½x13¾***

2205 A1340 100c multi 2.75 2.75

Propeller Steamer Thalia, Cent. — A1341

2009, May 7 ***Perf. 14x13¼***

2206 A1341 55c multi 1.50 1.50

Baptismal Font, Old Cathedral, Linz — A1342

Litho. & Engr.

2009, May 8 ***Perf. 13¾***

2207 A1342 55c multi 1.50 1.50

Vienna State Opera House, 140th Anniv. — A1343

2009, May 25 **Litho.** ***Perf. 14x13¼***

2208 A1343 100c multi 2.75 2.75

Miniature Sheet

Formula 1 Personalities — A1344

No. 2209: a, Wolfgang Graf Berghe von Trips (1928-61), race car driver. b, Gilles Villeneuve (1950-82), race car driver. c, James Hunt (1947-93), race car driver. d, Bernie Ecclestone, president of Formula One Management.

2009, May 27 ***Perf. 14x13¾***

2209 A1344 Sheet of 4 6.00 6.00

a.-d. 55c Any single 1.50 1.50

Souvenir Sheet

Battle of Aspern and Essling, Bicent. — A1345

2009, June 4 **Litho.** ***Perf. 14***

2210 A1345 110c multi 3.25 3.25

Europa A1346

2009, June 5 ***Perf. 13¾***

2211 A1346 65c multi 1.90 1.90

Intl. Year of Astronomy.

Graz Historic Center UNESCO World Heritage Site A1347

2009, June 12 **Photo. & Engr.**

2212 A1347 100c multi 3.00 3.00

Wiener Neustadt Airfield, Cent. — A1348

2009, June 12 **Litho.** ***Perf. 14***

2213 A1348 140c multi 4.00 4.00

Rosalia Alpina — A1349

Serpentine Die Cut 13½x14

2009, June 19 **Photo.**

Coil Stamp

Self-Adhesive

2214 A1349 75c multi 2.10 2.10

Railways Type of 2002

Photo & Engr.

2009, June 20 ***Perf. 13¾***

2215 A1109 75c Wachau Railway train 2.10 2.10

Wachau Railway, cent.

Wildlife Type of 2006

Designs: No. 2216, Apis mellifera. No. 2217, Merops apiaster.

Die Cut Perf. 14 Syncopated

2009, Aug. 28 **Photo.**

Booklet Stamps

Self-Adhesive

Size: 32x27mm

2216 A1237 55c multi 1.60 1.60

2217 A1237 55c multi 1.60 1.60

a. Booklet pane of 10, 5 each #2216-2217 16.00

This stamp, released Sept. 1, 2009, was a gift for standing order customers. It was not made available for sale.

Premiere of Movie, *The Third Man*, 60th Anniv. — A1350

2009, Sept. 2 **Litho.** ***Perf. 14***

2218 A1350 65c multi 1.90 1.90

Opening of Border Between Austria and Hungary, 20th Anniv. A1351

2009, Sept. 10 ***Perf. 12***

2219 A1351 65c multi 1.90 1.90

See Germany No. 2548, Hungary No. 4136.

Souvenir Sheet

Archaeological Excavations of Roman Military Camps — A1352

Litho. & Engr.

2009, Sept. 11 ***Perf. 13¾x14***

2220 A1352 Sheet of 2 3.50 3.50

a. 55c Carnuntum 1.60 1.60

b. 65c Gerulata 1.90 1.90

See Slovakia No. 579.

Bertha von Suttner (1843-1914), Novelist, 1905 Nobel Peace Laureate A1353

2009, Sept. 12 **Litho.** ***Perf. 14¼x14***

2221 A1353 55c multi 1.60 1.60

Souvenir Sheet

Rosary Triptych, by Ernst Fuchs — A1354

No. 2222: a, Glorious Rosary. b, Joyful Rosary. c, Sorrowful Rosary.

Litho. & Engr.

2009, Sept. 18 ***Perf. 14x13¾***

2222 A1354 Sheet of 3 7.00 7.00

a. 55c multi 1.60 1.60

b. 75c multi 2.25 2.25

c. 100c multi 3.00 3.00

Gregor Schlierenzauer, Ski Jumper — A1355

Wolfgang Loitzl, Ski Jumper — A1356

2009, Sept. 26 Litho. ***Perf. 14x13¼***
2223 A1355 100c multi 3.00 3.00
2224 A1356 100c multi 3.00 3.00

Drösing-Zistersdorf Local Railway, 120th Anniv. — A1357

2009, Oct. 4 Litho. ***Perf. 13¼x13¾***
2225 A1357 100c multi 3.00 3.00

Woman Rocking on a Chair, by Leander Kaiser — A1358

2009, Oct. 9 ***Perf. 13¾***
2226 A1358 55c multi 1.75 1.75

Souvenir Sheet

Austria - Japan Year — A1359

No. 2227 — Paintings: a, Portrait of Emilie Flöge, by Gustav Klimt. b, Autumn Clothing, by Shoen Uemura.

2009, Oct. 16 ***Perf. 13½***
2227 A1359 Sheet of 2 8.50 8.50
a.-b. 140c Either single 4.25 4.25

See Japan No. 3166.

Souvenir Sheet

Paintings by Diego Velázquez — A1360

No. 2228: a, The Royal Family of Felipe IV. b, The Infanta Margarita Teresa in a Blue Dress.

2009, Oct. 22 Photo. ***Perf. 14x13¾***
2228 A1360 Sheet of 2 3.75 3.75
a. 55c multi 1.75 1.75
b. 65c multi 2.00 2.00

A1361

Christmas A1362

2009 Litho. ***Perf. 14x13¾***
2229 A1361 55c multi 1.75 1.75

Perf. 14

2230 A1362 65c multi 2.00 2.00

Issued: No. 2229, 11/20; No. 2230, 11/6.

Advertising Art for Palmers Underwear A1363

2009, Nov. 12 ***Perf. 13¾***
2231 A1363 55c multi 1.75 1.75

Patron Saint Type of 2005

Design: St. Leopold, patron saint of Lower Austria.

Photo. & Engr.

2009, Nov. 13 ***Perf. 13½x14***
2232 A1185 55c multi 1.75 1.75

Essl Museum, 10th Anniv. A1364

2009, Nov. 21 Litho. ***Perf. 14***
2233 A1364 55c multi 1.75 1.75

Souvenir Sheet

Charles Darwin (1809-82), Naturalist — A1365

No. 2234: a, Monkey with book. b, Boy and mirror held by monkey. c, Monkey with arm extended.

Photo. & Engr.

2009, Nov. 24 ***Perf. 14¼x13½***
2234 A1365 Sheet of 3 5.25 5.25
a.-c. 55c Any single 1.75 1.75

Wildlife Type of 2006

Designs: 65c, Felis silvestris. No. 2236, Lutra lutra. No. 2237, Salmo trutta fario.

Coil Stamp

Serpentine Die Cut 13½x14

2010 Litho. Self-Adhesive
2235 A1237 65c multi 1.90 1.90

Booklet Stamps

Size: 32x27mm

Die Cut Perf. 14 Syncopated

2236 A1237 75c multi 2.10 2.10
2237 A1237 75c multi 2.10 2.10
a. Booklet pane of 10, 5 each #2236-2237 21.00

Issued: Nos. 2236-2237, 1/8; No. 2235, 1/13.

Salzburg Old Town Center UNESCO World Heritage Site A1366

Photo. & Engr.

2010, Jan. 29 ***Perf. 13¾***
2238 A1366 100c multi 2.75 2.75

Otto Preminger (1905-86), Film Director A1367

2010, Feb. 5 Litho. ***Perf. 13¾***
2239 A1367 55c multi 1.50 1.50

Roger Federer, Tennis Player A1368

2010, Feb. 8 ***Perf. 14x13¾***
2240 A1368 65c multi 1.75 1.75

Annual Rings of Scent and Bliss, by Helmut Kand — A1369

2010, Feb. 10 ***Perf. 13¾***
2241 A1369 55c multi 1.50 1.50

Prince Eugene of Savoy (1663-1736) A1370

2010, Feb. 12
2242 A1370 65c multi 1.75 1.75

Advertising Art for Kleinbahn A1371

2010, Feb. 16
2243 A1371 55c multi 1.50 1.50

Souvenir Sheet

The Tyrolean Land Army - Year Nine, by Joseph Anton Koch — A1372

2010, Feb. 19 ***Perf. 14***
2244 A1372 175c multi 4.75 4.75

Andreas Hofer (1767-1810), leader of 1809 Tyrolean Uprising.

Vienna State Opera Production of "Medea," by Aribert Reimann A1373

2010, Feb. 24 ***Perf. 14x13¾***
2245 A1373 100c multi 2.75 2.75

Soon the Sun Will Rise, by Max Weiler (1910-2001) A1374

2010, Mar. 18 Litho. *Perf. 14*

2246 A1374 75c multi 2.10 2.10

Lady in Yellow, by Max Kurzweil (1867-1916) A1375

2010, Mar. 19 *Perf. 14x13½*

2247 A1375 65c multi 1.75 1.75

Belvedere Castle, Vienna A1376

2010, Mar. 24 *Perf. 13½x12¾*

2248 A1376 65c multi 1.75 1.75

Railways Type of 2002

Photo. & Engr.

2010, Apr. 10 *Perf. 13¾*

2249 A1109 100c Graz-Köflacher Railway train 2.75 2.75

Graz-Köflacher Railway, 150th anniv.

Hradcany Castle, Prague A1377

2010, Apr. 16 Litho.

2250 A1377 65c multi 1.75 1.75

Souvenir Sheet

Empress Elizabeth, by F. X. Winterhalter — A1378

2010, Apr. 30 *Perf. 13¼x14*

2251 A1378 55c multi 1.50 1.50

Expo 2010, Shanghai.

Mendel Funicular Railway A1379

2010, May 8 *Perf. 13¾*

2252 A1379 65c multi 1.75 1.75

Austria Post Collection Box on Postman's Legs A1380

2010, May 10 Litho. *Perf. 13¾*

2253 A1380 55c multi 1.40 1.40

Hof Palace — A1381

2010, May 13 Litho. *Perf. 14x13¼*

2254 A1381 55c multi 1.40 1.40

Maria Taferl, 350th Anniv. A1382

2010, May 16 *Perf. 13¾*

2255 A1382 55c multi 1.40 1.40

Gustav Mahler (1860-1911), Composer — A1383

2010, May 18 *Perf. 14x13¾*

2256 A1383 100c multi 2.60 2.60

Salzburg Festival, 90th Anniv. A1384

2010, May 20 *Perf. 13¾*

2257 A1384 55c multi 1.40 1.40

Crozier of Archbishop Gebhard of Salzburg A1385

2010, May 28 Photo. & Engr.

2258 A1385 75c multi 1.90 1.90

Wildlife Type of 2006

Designs: 55c, Coracias garrulus. 75c, Aquila chrysaetos.

Coil Stamps

Serpentine Die Cut 13½x14

2010, May 28 Litho.

Self-Adhesive

2259 A1237 55c multi 1.40 1.40
2260 A1237 75c multi 1.90 1.90

Europa A1386

2010, June 11 Litho. *Perf. 13¾*

2261 A1386 65c multi 1.60 1.60

Self-portrait, by Egon Schiele (1890-1918) — A1387

2010, June 12 Photo. & Engr.

2262 A1387 140c multi 3.50 3.50

Second Viennese Mountain Spring Pipeline, Cent. — A1388

2010, June 14 Litho. *Perf. 14x13½*

2263 A1388 55c multi 1.40 1.40

Simon Wiesenthal (1908-2005), Hunter of Nazi War Criminals — A1389

2010, June 14 *Perf. 12½x12¾*

2264 A1389 75c multi 1.90 1.90

The Star of David is made up of tiny holes made by a laser. See Israel No. 1820.

Ioan Holender, Vienna State Opera Director, 75th Birthday — A1390

2010, June 20 *Perf. 14x13¾*

2265 A1390 100c multi 2.50 2.50

Palatinate Church, Karnburg A1391

2010, June 25 Litho. *Perf. 13¾*

2266 A1391 100c multi 2.50 2.50

Johann Joseph Fux (1660-1741), Composer — A1392

2010, June 26 *Perf. 14*

2267 A1392 100c multi 2.50 2.50

Grete Rehor (1910-87), Politician — A1393

2010, June 29 *Perf. 13¾*

2268 A1393 55c multi 1.40 1.40

REGENBOGEN PARADE 15 JAHRE Österreich 55

Vienna Rainbow Parade, 15th Anniv. A1394

2010, July 3 *Perf. 14x14¼*

2269 A1394 55c multi 1.40 1.40

Spielfeld Strass - Bad Radkersburg Railway, 125th Anniv. — A1395

2010, July 10 *Perf. 13¾*

2270 A1395 65c multi 1.75 1.75

Grafenegg Castle — A1396

Coil Stamp

Serpentine Die Cut 13¾

2010, July 17 **Self-Adhesive**
2271 A1396 55c multi 1.50 1.50

La Plume, by Alphonse Mucha (1860-1939), Illustrator A1397

2010, July 23 ***Perf. 13¾***
2272 A1397 115c multi 3.00 3.00

Diocese of Eisenstadt, 50th Anniv. — A1398

2010, Aug. 12 **Litho.** ***Perf. 13¾***
2273 A1398 55c multi 1.50 1.50

Mother Teresa (1910-97), Humanitarian — A1399

2010, Aug. 26 ***Perf. 14***
2274 A1399 130c multi 3.50 3.50

This stamp, released Sept. 3, 2010, was a gift for standing order customers. It was not made available for sale.

Souvenir Sheet

Orient Express — A1400

No. 2275 — Locomotives and views of: a, Sinaia, Romania. b, Salzburg, Austria.

2010, Sept. 6 **Litho.** ***Perf. 14x14¼***
2275 A1400 Sheet of 2 3.50 3.50
a.-b. 65c Either single 1.75 1.75

See Romania Nos. 5205-5206.

Crucifix by Jakob Adlhart, St. Peter's Archabbey, Salzburg A1401

Photo. & Engr.

2010, Sept. 14 ***Perf. 13¾***
2276 A1401 100c multi 2.75 2.75

Organization of Petroleum Exporting Countries, 50th Anniv. A1402

2010, Sept. 14 **Litho.** ***Perf. 13¾***
2277 A1402 140c multi 4.00 4.00

Petit Point Embroidery — A1403

Litho. With Embroidery Affixed

2010, Sept. 17 ***Imperf.***
2278 A1403 265c multi 7.50 7.50

Railways Type of 2002

Photo. & Engr.

2010, Sept. 19 ***Perf. 13¾***
2279 A1109 100c Wechsel Railway train 2.75 2.75

Wechsel Railway, cent.

Andreas and Wolfgang Linger, Lugers — A1404

2010, Sept. 25 **Litho.** ***Perf. 14x13¾***
2280 A1404 100c multi 2.75 2.75

Modern Furniture by Peter Zuchi A1405

2010, Oct. 1 **Litho.** ***Perf. 13¾***
2281 A1405 65c multi 1.90 1.90

Archduchess Maria Theresa (1717-80) A1406

2010, Oct. 8
2282 A1406 65c multi 1.90 1.90

Souvenir Sheet

Weather Stations in Austria and Argentina — A1407

No. 2283 — Weather station in: a, Stadtpark, Vienna. b, Buenos Aires Botanical Garden.

2010, Oct. 13
2283 A1407 Sheet of 2 5.75 5.75
a. 65c multi 1.90 1.90
b. 140c multi 3.75 3.75

See Argentina No. 2596.

Ornithopter of Jakob Degen (1760-1848), Inventor A1408

2010, Oct. 15
2284 A1408 125c multi 3.50 3.50

Missions Abroad for Austrian Armed Forces, 50th Anniv. — A1409

2010, Oct. 26 ***Perf. 14x13½***
2285 A1409 65c multi 1.90 1.90

Historic Center of Vienna UNESCO World Heritage Site A1410

Photo. & Engr.

2010, Nov. 5 ***Perf. 13¾***
2286 A1410 100c multi 3.00 3.00

Nativity A1411

Innsbruck Buildings, Christmas Tree — A1412

Adoration of the Magi — A1413

2010 **Litho.** ***Perf. 14¼***
2287 A1411 55c multi 1.50 1.50

Perf. 13¾x14

2288 A1412 65c multi 1.75 1.75

Coil Stamp

Self-Adhesive

Serpentine Die Cut 13¾x13½

2289 A1413 (55c) multi 1.50 1.50

Christmas. Issued: No. 2287, 11/19; No. 2288, 11/11; No. 2289, 11/12.

Emperor Franz Josef and Dr. Anton Freiherr von Eiselsberg A1414

2011, Jan. 21 ***Perf. 13¾x14***
2290 A1414 55c multi 1.50 1.50

Austria Cancer Aid, cent.

Imperial Post Office, Maribor A1415

2011, Jan. 21 ***Perf. 13¾***
2291 A1415 65c multi 1.75 1.75

Violin and Bow A1416

2011, Jan. 21 ***Perf. 13½x14¼***

2292 A1416 75c multi 2.10 2.10

Chancellor Bruno Kreisky (1911-90) A1417

2011, Jan. 22 ***Perf. 13¾***

2293 A1417 55c multi 1.50 1.50

Miniature Sheet

Joanneum, Graz, Bicent. — A1418

2011, Jan. 26 ***Perf.***

2294 A1418 100c multi 2.75 2.75

Franz Liszt (1811-86), Composer A1419

2011, Jan. 29 ***Perf. 13½x14***

2295 A1419 65c multi 1.75 1.75

Hedy Lamarr (1914-2000), Actress A1420

2011, Feb. 4 ***Perf. 13¾***

2296 A1420 55c multi 1.50 1.50

Advertising Art for Schweden-Bomben Confections — A1421

2011, Feb. 15 ***Perf. 13¾***

2297 A1421 55c multi 1.50 1.50

Austria Wien Soccer Team, Cent. A1422

2011, Mar. 15 ***Perf. 13¾x14***

2298 A1422 65c multi 1.90 1.90

KTM 125 D.O.H.C. Apfelbeck Motorcycle — A1423

2011, Mar. 15 ***Perf. 14x13¾***

2299 A1423 75c multi 2.25 2.25

Puch 500 Automobile — A1424

2011, Mar. 17

2300 A1424 65c multi 1.90 1.90

Karl Gölsdorf (1861-1916), Locomotive Designer — A1425

2011, Mar. 22 ***Perf. 13¼x13¾***

2301 A1425 65c multi 1.90 1.90

Vienna Kunsthaus, 20th Anniv. — A1426

Photo. & Engr.

2011, Apr. 8 ***Perf. 13¾***

2302 A1426 175c multi 5.25 5.25

Café Hewelka, Vienna A1427

2011, Apr. 11 **Litho.**

2303 A1427 62c multi 1.90 1.90

Manned Space Flight, 50th Anniv. A1428

2011, Apr. 12 ***Perf. 13¼x13¾***

2304 A1428 65c multi 1.90 1.90

2011 Lower Austrian Regional Exhibition A1429

2011, Apr. 16 ***Perf. 13¾x14***

2305 A1429 62c multi 1.75 1.75

Architecture A1430

Designs: 7c, Ars Electronica Center, Linz. No. 2307, Kunsthaus and Universal Museum Joanneum, Graz. No. 2308, Lentos Kunstmuseum, Linz. No. 2309, Forum Stadtpark, Graz. No. 2310, Museum Moderner Kunst Stiftung Ludwig (Ludwig Foundation Museum of Modern Art), Vienna. No. 2311, Kunsthaus, Bregenz, vert. No. 2312, Kunsthalle, Krems, vert. No. 2313, Museum der Moderne Mönchsberg (Mönchsberg Museum of Modern Art), Salzburg. No. 2314, Essl Museum Klosterneuburg. 145c, Project Space Karlsplatz, Kunsthalle, Vienna. 170c, MAK Center Schindler Chase House, Los Angeles. 340c, Austrian Cultural Forum, New York City, vert.

Die Cut Perf. 13¼

2011, May 1 **Litho.**

Coil Stamps
Self-Adhesive
Background Color
Without Name of Architect

2306 A1430 7c gray .25 .25
2307 A1430 62c light blue 1.75 1.75
2308 A1430 70c yel org 2.00 2.00
2309 A1430 90c lilac 2.60 2.60
Nos. 2306-2309 (4) 6.60 6.60

Booklet Stamps

2310 A1430 62c light blue 1.75 1.75
a. Booklet pane of 4 7.00
2311 A1430 62c light blue 1.75 1.75
2312 A1430 62c light blue 1.75 1.75
a. Booklet pane of 10, 5 each #2311-2312 17.50
2313 A1430 70c yel org 2.00 2.00
a. Booklet pane of 4 + 4 etiquettes 8.00
2314 A1430 90c lilac 2.60 2.60
a. Booklet pane of 4 10.50
2315 A1430 145c blue green 4.25 4.25
a. Booklet pane of 4 17.00
2316 A1430 170c pale orange 5.00 5.00
a. Booklet pane of 4 + 4 etiquettes 20.00
2317 A1430 340c yellow 9.75 9.75
a. Booklet pane of 4 39.00
Nos. 2310-2317 (8) 28.85 28.85

See Nos. 2325, 2357-2364, 2393-2394.

Budweis-Linz-Gmunden Horse-Drawn Railway, 175th Anniv. — A1431

2011, May 1 **Litho.** ***Perf. 14x13¾***

2318 A1431 62c multi 1.75 1.75

CARE Austria, 25th Anniv. — A1432

2011, May 1

2319 A1432 70c multi 2.00 2.00

Mekhitarists In Vienna, 200th Anniv. A1433

2011, May 1 ***Perf. 14¼x14***

2320 A1433 90c multi 2.60 2.60

Pöllauberg Pilgrimage Church — A1434

2011, May 20 ***Perf. 14x13¾***

2321 A1434 62c multi 1.75 1.75

The Tower of Babel, by Pieter Brueghel the Elder A1435

Photo. & Engr.

2011, June 11 ***Perf. 13¾***

2322 A1435 145c multi 4.25 2.10

Souvenir Sheet

HANS MAKART

1840 - 1884

Paintings by Hans Makart (1840-84) — A1436

No. 2323: a, Portrait of Dora Fournier-Gabillon. b, The Triumph of Ariadne.

2011, June 9 **Litho.** ***Perf. 14***

2323 A1436 Sheet of 2 7.00 7.00

a. 70c multi 2.00 1.00

b. 170c multi 5.00 2.50

Miniature Sheet

Austria, Country of Forests A1437

2011, June 15 ***Perf.***

2324 A1437 90c multi 2.60 1.25

Values are for stamp with surrounding selvage.

Architecture Type of 2011

Design: Liaunig Museum, Neuhaus.

2011, June 20 **Litho.** ***Perf. 14x13¾***

2325 A1430 5c black .25 .25

Austrian Military Aviation, Cent. A1438

2011, July 1 **Litho.** ***Perf. 14***

2326 A1438 62c multi 1.75 1.75

Tassilo Chalice, Kremsmünster Monastery A1439

Litho. & Engr.

2011, July 1 ***Perf. 13¾***

2327 A1439 145c multi 4.25 4.25

St. Christopher Brotherhood, 625th Anniv. — A1440

2011, July 9 **Litho.** ***Perf. 14***

2328 A1440 62c multi 1.75 1.75

Organization for Economic Cooperation and Development, 50th Anniv. A1441

2011, July 11 ***Perf. 13¾***

2329 A1441 70c multi 2.00 2.00

Railways Type of 2002

2011, July 15 **Photo. & Engr.**

2330 A1109 90c Stammersdorf Railway train 2.60 2.60

Stammersdorf Local Railway, cent.

Bronze Relief by Ulrich Henn, Rankweil Basilica A1442

2011, Sept. 2 ***Perf. 13¾***

2331 A1442 90c multi 2.50 2.50

Ferdinand Raimund (1790-1836), Playwright — A1443

2011, Sept. 4 **Litho.** ***Perf. 14x13¾***

2332 A1443 62c multi 1.75 1.75

Austrian Soccer Championships, Cent. — A1444

2011, Sept. 6 ***Perf. 13¼x13¾***

2333 A1444 62c multi 1.75 1.75

Künstlerhaus, Vienna, Cent. — A1445

2011, Sept. 7 ***Perf. 14x13¾***

2334 A1445 62c multi 1.75 1.75

Souvenir Sheet

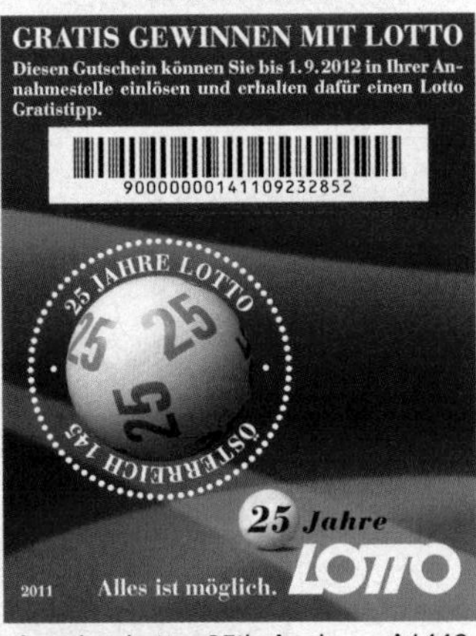

Austrian Lotto, 25th Anniv. — A1446

2011, Sept. 7 ***Perf.***

2335 A1446 145c multi 4.00 4.00

The top of No. 2335, separated by a row of rouletting, serves as a voucher for a free bet in the Austrian Lotto.

Souvenir Sheet

Europa — A1447

2011, Sept. 8 ***Perf. 13¾***

2336 A1447 170c multi 4.75 4.75

Intl. Year of Forests. No. 2336 is an envelope containing spruce seeds. Rouletting around the souvenir sheet allows it to be removed from the rest of the envelope. Unused values are for the complete envelope with seeds.

Railways Type of 2002

Photo. & Engr.

2011, Sept. 10 ***Perf. 13¾***

2337 A1109 90c Erzberg Railway train 2.50 2.50

Erzberg Railway, 120th anniv.

Carbon Dioxide Neutral Delivery of Mail — A1448

2011, Sept. 10 **Litho.**

2338 A1448 62c multi 1.75 1.75

Portrait of Walburga Neuzil, by Egon Schiele A1449

2011. Sept. 23 ***Perf. 13¾***

2339 A1449 62c multi 1.75 1.75

Leopold Museum, Vienna, 10th anniv.

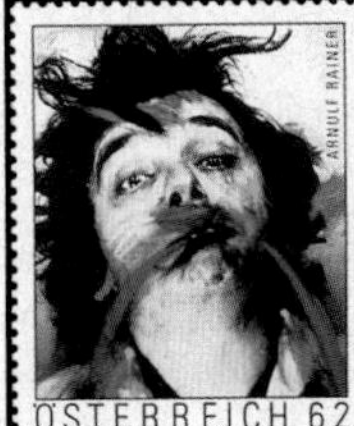

Elisabeth Görgl, 2011 Women's Super-G Skiing World Champion — A1450

2011, Sept. 24 ***Perf. 14x13¾***

2340 A1450 62c multi 1.75 1.75

Angst, Painting by Arnulf Rainer A1451

O.T. 014, 2003, Photograph by Eva Schlegel A1452

2011, Oct. 1 ***Perf. 13¾***

2341 A1451 62c multi 1.75 1.75

2342 A1452 70c multi 1.90 1.90

Trademark Austria — A1453

2011, Oct. 4 ***Perf. 14***

2343 A1453 62c multi 1.75 1.75

Loisium Wine Center, Langenlois — A1454

2011, Oct. 7 ***Perf. 14x13¾***

2344 A1454 62c multi 1.75 1.75

The Song of Songs, Painting by Arik Brauer — A1455

Photo. & Engr.

2011, Oct. 14 ***Perf. 13½***

2345 A1455 170c multi 4.75 4.75

Burgenland Statehood, 90th Anniv. — A1456

2011, Oct. 21 **Litho.** ***Perf. 13¾***

2346 A1456 90c multi 2.50 2.50

Nativity, by Unknown Artist — A1457

Chapel of St. Quirinus A1458

Madonna and Child — A1459

2011 ***Perf. 13¾x14***

2347 A1457 62c multi 1.75 1.75
2348 A1458 70c multi 1.90 1.90

Coil Stamp
Self-Adhesive
Die Cut Perf. 13½x13¼

2349 A1459 62c multi 1.75 1.75

Christmas. Issued: No. 2347, 11/25; No. 2348, 11/11; No. 2349, 11/18.

Reopening of Vienna Western Railway Station — A1460

2011, Nov. 23 ***Perf. 14x13¾***

2350 A1460 70c multi 1.90 1.90

Wolfgang Amadeus Mozart (1756-91), Composer A1461

2011, Dec. 5 ***Perf. 13½x14***

2351 A1461 70c multi 1.90 1.90

Miniature Sheet

Vienna Music Association, Bicent. — A1462

2012, Jan. 1 **Litho.** ***Perf.***

2352 A1462 90c multi 2.40 2.40

1959 Lohner L 125 Scooter A1463

2012, Jan. 2 ***Perf. 13¾***

2353 A1463 145c multi 3.75 3.75

Carl Ritter von Ghega (1802-60), Railway Builder, and Kalte Rinne Viaduct — A1464

2012, Jan. 10 ***Perf. 13½x13¾***

2354 A1464 70c multi 1.90 1.90

Kalte Rinne Viaduct, 160th anniv.

Alpine Association, 150th Anniv. — A1465

2012, Jan. 12 ***Perf. 14x13¾***

2355 A1465 62c multi 1.75 1.75

Vienna Rapid Transit Railway, 50th Anniv. A1466

2012, Jan. 17 ***Perf. 14x14¼***

2356 A1466 62c multi 1.75 1.75

Architecture Type of 2011 With Names of Architects Added

Designs: No. 2357, Like #2307, Spacelab Cook-Fournier architect. No. 2358, Like #2308, Weber Hofer Partner AG architect. No. 2359, Like #2309, Giselbrecht & Zinganel architect. No. 2360, Frauenmuseum (Women's Museum), Hittisau, Cukrowicz Nachbaur Architekten architect. No. 2361, Like #2311, Peter Zumthor architect, vert. No. 2362, Like #2310, Ortner & Ortner architect. No. 2363, Like #2313, Friedrich Hoff Zwink architect. No. 2364, Like #2316, Rudolph M. Schindler architect.

2012 **Litho.** ***Die Cut Perf. 13¼***

Self-Adhesive
Coil Stamps
Background Color

2357 A1430 62c light blue 1.75 1.75
2358 A1430 70c yel org 1.90 1.90
2359 A1430 90c lilac 2.40 2.40
2360 A1430 145c blue green 3.75 3.75
a. Booklet pane of 4 15.00
Nos. 2357-2360 (4) 9.80 9.80

Booklet Stamps

2361 A1430 62c light blue 1.75 1.75
a. Booklet pane of 10 17.50
2362 A1430 62c light blue 1.60 1.60
a. Booklet pane of 4 6.50
2363 A1430 70c yel org 1.90 1.90
a. Booklet pane of 4 + 4 etiquettes 7.75
2364 A1430 170c pale orange 4.50 4.50
a. Booklet pane of 4 + 4 etiquettes 18.00
Nos. 2361-2364 (4) 9.75 9.75

Issued: Nos. 2357, 2361, 2/3; No. 2358, 1/30; Nos. 2359, 2360, 2363, 4/27; Nos. 2360a, 2364, 1/18; No. 2362, 5/18.

This stamp, released Feb. 15, 2012, was a gift for standing order customers. It was not made available for sale.

2012 Vienna Opera Ball — A1467

2012, Feb. 16 **Litho.** ***Perf. 13¾***

2365 A1467 70c multi 1.90 1.90

Stöckl, Photograph by Elfie Semotan — A1468

2012, Feb. 24 ***Perf. 14x13¾***

2366 A1468 70c multi 1.90 1.90

Steyr XII Taxi-Landaulet — A1469

2012, Mar. 26 ***Perf. 13¾***

2367 A1469 70c multi 1.90 1.90

Viennese Oboe A1470

2012, Mar. 26 ***Perf. 13½x14¼***

2368 A1470 90c multi 2.40 2.40

Character From Children's Book "I Am Me," by Mira Lobe A1471

2012, Mar. 27 ***Perf. 13¾***

2369 A1471 62c multi 1.75 1.75

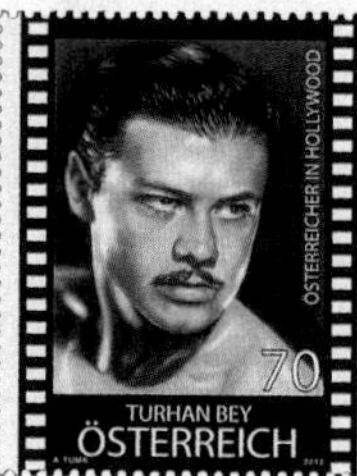

Turhan Bey, Actor A1472

2012, Mar. 30 **Litho.**

2370 A1472 70c multi 1.90 1.90

Enns, 800th Anniv. — A1473

Litho. & Engr.

2012, Apr. 22 ***Perf. 13¾x14***

2371 A1473 145c multi 3.75 3.75

Bavaria-Upper Austria Provincial Exhibition — A1474

2012, Apr. 26 **Litho.** ***Perf. 13½x14¼***

2372 A1474 70c multi 1.90 1.90

Herzogenburg Priory, 900th Anniv. — A1475

2012, May 5 ***Perf. 13¾***

2373 A1475 90c multi 2.25 2.25

Discovery of Cosmic Radiation by Victor F. Hess (1883-1964) — A1476

Litho. With Foil Application

2012, May 5 ***Perf. 14x13¾***

2374 A1476 145c multi 3.75 3.75

SV Ried Soccer Team, Cent. — A1477

2012, May 6 **Litho.** ***Perf. 13¾***
2375 A1477 62c multi 1.60 1.60

Souvenir Sheet

Prater Ferris Wheel, Vienna — A1478

2012, May 11 ***Perf. 13½x14¼***
2376 A1478 70c multi 1.75 1.75

Europa.

Paddlewheel Steamship Schönbrunn, Cent. A1479

2012, May 12 ***Perf. 13¾***
2377 A1479 90c multi 2.25 2.25

Johann Nepomuk Nestroy (1801-62), Playwright and Actor — A1480

2012, May 24 **Litho. & Engr.**
2378 A1480 145c multi 3.75 3.75

Self-portrait, by Anton Faistauer (1887-1930) A1481

2012, June 2 **Litho.**
2379 A1481 70c multi 1.75 1.75

Stockerau, 1000th Anniv. A1482

2012, June 3
2380 A1482 62c multi 1.60 1.60

Stained-Glass Window, Lilienfeld Monastery A1483

2012, June 8 **Litho. & Engr.**
2381 A1483 145c multi 3.75 3.75

Johann Puch (1862-1914), Bicycle Manufacturer A1484

2012, June 27 **Litho.** ***Perf. 13¾x14***
2382 A1484 145c multi 3.75 3.75

Caritas Austria Charity Anti-Hunger Campaign — A1485

2012, July 2 ***Perf. 14x14¼***
2383 A1485 62c multi 1.60 1.60

A1486

A1487

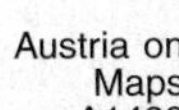
Austria on Maps A1488

2012, June 6 ***Die Cut Perf. 13¼***

Coil Stamps
Self-Adhesive

2384	A1486	(62c) multi	1.60	1.60
2385	A1487	(70c) multi	1.75	1.75
2386	A1488	(€1.70) multi	4.25	4.25
		Nos. 2384-2386 (3)	7.60	7.60

Wolkenturm Open-air Stage, Grafenegg A1489

2012, July 14 ***Perf. 13¾***
2387 A1489 70c multi 1.75 1.75

Portrait of Fritza Riedler, by Gustav Klimt (1862-1918) A1490

2012, July 14
2388 A1490 170c multi 4.25 4.25

Imperial Post Office, Zagreb A1491

2012, July 17
2389 A1491 70c multi 1.75 1.75

Votive Church, Vienna, Painting by Rudolf von Alt (1812-1905) A1492

Litho. & Engr.
2012, Aug. 23 ***Perf. 13¾***
2390 A1492 170c multi 4.50 4.50

Gmundner Ceramics A1493

2012, Aug. 24 **Litho.**
2391 A1493 62c multi 1.60 1.60

Steigl Brewery, Salzburg, Horse-drawn Barrel Cart and Beer Stein — A1494

2012, Aug. 26
2392 A1494 62c multi 1.60 1.60

Architecture Type of 2011 With Names of Architects Added

Designs: No. 2393, Like #2314, Heinz Tesar architect. No. 2394, Like #2317, Raimund Abraham architect.

Die Cut Perf. 13¼

2012, Sept. 14 **Litho.**

Self-Adhesive
Booklet Stamps
Background Color

2393	A1430	90c lilac	2.40	2.40
a.		Booklet pane of 4	9.75	
2394	A1430	340c yellow	8.75	8.75
a.		Booklet pane of 4	35.00	

Vulpes Vulpes A1495

2012, Sept. 14 **Litho.** ***Perf. 14x14¼***
2395 A1495 90c multi 2.40 2.40

St. Stephan's Church, Baden, 700th Anniv. A1496

2012, Sept. 16 ***Perf. 13¾x14***
2396 A1496 90c multi 2.40 2.40

Alpenzoo, Innsbruck, 50th Anniv. — A1497

2012, Sept. 22 ***Perf. 13¼x14***
2397 A1497 70c multi 1.90 1.90

Gerlinde Kaltenbrunner, Mountaineer — A1498

2012, Sept. 29 ***Perf. 14x13¾***
2398 A1498 62c multi 1.60 1.60

St. Michael From Mondsee Basilica Altarpiece
A1499

Litho. & Engr.

2012, Sept. 29 *Perf. 13¾*
2399 A1499 145c multi 3.75 3.75

Mittenwald Railway, Cent. — A1500

2012, Sept. 29 *Perf. 14x13¾*
2400 A1500 145c multi 3.75 3.75

Miniature Sheet

Characters From Movie *Madagascar 3: Europe's Most Wanted* — A1501

No. 2401: a, Penguin lighting fuse of cannon, mouth of Alex the Lion. b, Marty the Zebra, and Gloria the Hippo, in cannon. c, Penguins, part of head of Alex the Lion. d, Part of head of Alex the Lion, Melman the Giraffe.

Serpentine Die Cut 14

2012, Oct. 5 Litho. Self-Adhesive
2401 A1501 Sheet of 4 7.50
a.-b. 62c Either single 1.60 1.60
c. 70c multi 1.90 1.90
d. 90c multi 2.40 2.40

Sleeping Child, by Bernardo Strozzi
A1502

Litho. & Engr.

2012, Oct. 6 *Perf. 13¾*
2402 A1502 170c multi 4.50 4.50

Souvenir Sheet

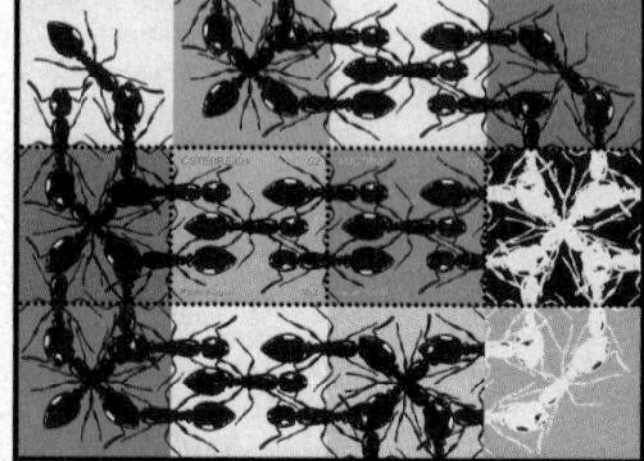

Ants, Painting by Peter Kogler — A1503

2012, Oct. 6 Litho. *Perf. 14*
2403 A1503 Sheet of 2 3.50 3.50
a. 62c gray, brt org red & blk 1.60 1.60
b. 70c brt org red, gray & blk 1.90 1.90

Self-Portrait With Red Hat, by Marie-Louise von Motesiczky
A1504

2012, Oct. 10 *Perf. 13¾x14*
2404 A1504 62c multi 1.60 1.60

Carl Auer von Welsbach (1858-1929), Inventor, and Gas Lamp — A1505

2012, Oct. 13 *Perf. 13¼x14*
2405 A1505 62c multi 1.60 1.60

Concession for Raab-Oedenberg-Ebenfurth Railroad, 140th Anniv. — A1506

2012, Oct. 15 *Perf. 14x13¼*
2406 A1506 62c multi 1.60 1.60

Wine Glass, Wine, Grapes and Windmill
A1507

2012, Oct. 19 *Perf. 13¼x14*
2407 A1507 62c multi 1.60 1.60

Vienna International Film Festival, 50th Anniv. — A1508

2012, Oct. 25 *Perf. 14x13¾*
2408 A1508 70c multi 1.90 1.90

Souvenir Sheet

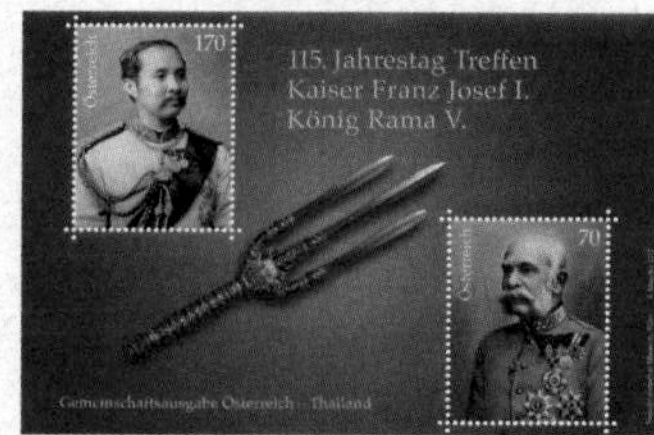

Meeting of Emperor Franz Josef and King Chulalongkorn of Thailand, 115th Anniv. — A1509

No. 2409: a, Emperor Franz Josef. b, King Chulalongkorn.

2012, Nov. 10 *Perf. 14¼x13½*
2409 A1509 Sheet of 2 6.50 6.50
a. 70c multi 1.90 1.90
b. 170c multi 4.50 4.50

See Thailand No. 2714.

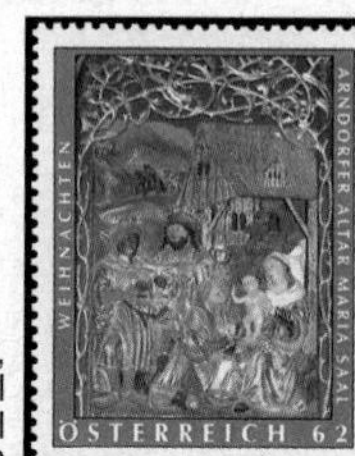

Arndorfer Altar, Maria Saal Cathedral
A1510

Church of St. George, Kals am Grossglockner
A1511

Hunters in Snow, by Pieter Breughel, the Elder
A1512

Adoration of the Magi, by Jacopo Bassano
A1513

2012 *Perf. 13¾*
2410 A1510 62c multi 1.60 1.60

Perf. 13¾x14
2411 A1511 70c multi 1.90 1.90

Coil Stamps
Self-Adhesive
Die Cut Perf. 13
2412 A1512 62c multi 1.60 1.60
2413 A1513 70c multi 1.90 1.90

Christmas. Issued: Nos. 2410, 2412, 11/30; Nos. 2411, 2413, 11/16.

Lenz Moser Wines
A1514

2012, Nov. 17 *Perf. 13¾x14*
2414 A1514 62c multi 1.60 1.60

Railways in Austria, 175th Anniv. — A1515

2012, Nov. 23 *Perf. 14x13¾*
2415 A1515 90c multi 2.40 2.40

2013 World Alpine Skiing Championships, Schladming
A1516

Paintings by Christian Ludwig Attersee: 62c, Freedom in the Snow. 70c, Styrian Heart. 90c, Slalom Dance.

2013, Jan. 2 *Perf. 13¾x14*

Panel Color
2416 A1516 62c orange 1.75 1.75
2417 A1516 70c dark red 1.90 1.90
2418 A1516 90c yel green 2.40 2.40
Nos. 2416-2418 (3) 6.05 6.05

Bergisel Ski Jump, Innsbruck
A1517

2013, Jan. 4 *Perf. 13¾*
2419 A1517 62c multi 1.75 1.75

Diversity in Unity
A1518

2013, Jan. 21
2420 A1518 70c multi 1.90 1.90

1953 Halleiner Motor Works 250 BJ Motorbike
A1519

2013, Jan. 21

2421 A1519 220c multi 6.00 6.00

This stamp, released Feb. 13, 2013, was a gift for standing order customers. It was not made available for sale.

Best Wishes
A1520

2013, Feb. 20 Litho. *Perf. 14*

2422 A1520 (62c) multi 1.60 1.60

Salzburg Marionette Theater, Cent. — A1521

2013, Feb. 27 *Perf. 13¾x14*

2423 A1521 62c multi 1.60 1.60

1948 Porsche 356 No. 1 Roadster
A1522

2013, Feb. 28 *Perf. 13¾*

2424 A1522 70c multi 1.90 1.90

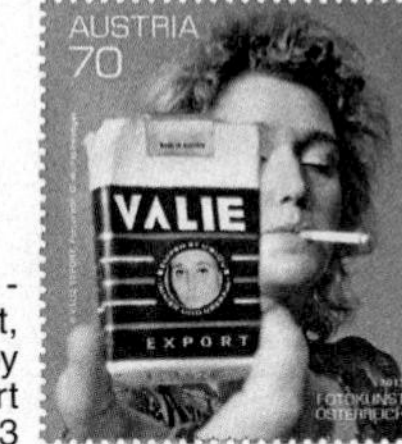

Valie Export - Smart Export, Photograph by Valie Export
A1523

2013, Mar. 13

2425 A1523 70c black 1.90 1.90

Bruck Locomotive at Baden Station, c. 1846 — A1524

2013, Mar. 13 *Perf. 14x13¾*

2426 A1524 145c multi 4.50 4.50

Rupicapra Rupicapra
A1525

Litho. & Engr.

2013, Mar. 14 *Perf. 14x14¼*

2427 A1525 90c multi 2.40 2.40

Page Illumination, St. Florian Monastery
A1526

2013, Mar. 15 *Perf. 13¾*

2428 A1526 90c multi 2.40 2.40

Senta Berger, Actress
A1527

2013, Mar. 22 Litho.

2429 A1527 70c multi 1.90 1.90

Preseren Square, Ljubljana, Slovenia
A1528

2013, Apr. 6

2430 A1528 62c multi 1.60 1.60

Souvenir Sheet

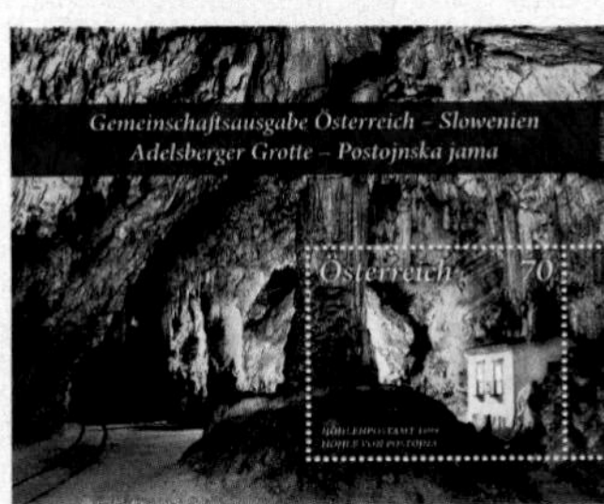

Underground Post Office in Postojna Cave, Slovenia — A1529

2013, Apr. 6 *Perf. 13¾*

2431 A1529 70c multi 1.90 1.90

See Slovenia No. 982.

Music Theater at Landestheater, Linz — A1530

2013, Apr. 11

2432 A1530 62c multi 1.60 1.60

Landhaus Bacher Restaurant, Mautern — A1531

2013, Apr. 11

2433 A1531 62c multi 1.60 1.60

30th Vienna City Marathon — A1532

2013, Apr. 14 *Perf. 14*

2434 A1532 62c multi 1.60 1.60

Vienna Horn
A1533

2013, Apr. 15 *Perf. 13½x14¼*

2435 A1533 90c multi 2.40 2.40

Julius Lott (1836-83), Builder of Arlberg Railroad
A1534

2013, Apr. 17 *Perf. 13¼x13¾*

2436 A1534 70c multi 1.90 1.90

Toboggan Ride, Wurstelprater Amusement Park, Vienna, Cent. — A1535

2013, Apr. 19 *Perf. 13¾*

2437 A1535 62c multi 1.60 1.60

Souvenir Sheet

Attersee Area Transportation Centenaries — A1536

No. 2438: a, Shipping on Attersee, cent. b, Attergau Railway, cent.

2013, Apr. 19 *Perf. 14x13¾*

2438 A1536 Sheet of 2 3.50 3.50

a. 62c multi 1.60 1.60

b. 70c multi 1.90 1.90

Hohentwiel Paddle-wheeled Steamer, Cent. — A1537

2013, May 4 *Perf. 13¾*

2439 A1537 62c multi 1.75 1.75

Austrian Open-Air Museum, Stübing, 50th Anniv.
A1538

2013, May 5 *Perf. 14x14¼*

2440 A1538 70c multi 1.90 1.90

Souvenir Sheet

Europa — A1539

2013, May 6 *Die Cut*

Self-Adhesive

2441 A1539 70c multi 1.90 1.90

International Red Cross, 150th Anniv. — A1540

2013, May 8 *Perf. 14*

2442 A1540 62c multi 1.75 1.75

Vienna Concert House, Cent. — A1541

2013, May 11 Litho.

2443 A1541 90c multi 2.40 2.40

Robert Jungk (1913-94), Journalist A1542

2013, May 13 *Perf. 13¾*
2444 A1542 90c multi 2.40 2.40

Franz West (1947-2012), Artist — A1543

2013, May 14
2445 A1543 70c black 1.90 1.90

South Styrian Wine Region — A1544

2013, May 24 *Perf. 13¼x14*
2446 A1544 62c multi 1.75 1.75

St. Theodul, Patron Saint of the Walsers A1545

Litho. & Engr.

2013, May 29 *Perf. 13¾*
2447 A1545 145c multi 4.00 4.00

Walser settlements in Vorarlberg, 700th anniv.

Souvenir Sheet

Pilgrimage to Maria Luggau, 500th Anniv. — A1546

2013, May 31 **Litho.** *Perf. 13x13¼*
2448 A1546 170c multi 4.75 4.75

St. Anna's Children's Cancer Research Institute, 25th Anniv. — A1547

2013, June 6 *Perf. 14*
2449 A1547 62c multi 1.75 1.75

Austrian Nature Protection League, Cent. — A1548

2013, June 7
2450 A1548 90c multi 2.40 2.40

Fairtrade Austria, 20th Anniv. — A1549

2013, June 21 *Perf. 13¾*
2451 A1549 62c multi 1.60 1.60

Lorenz I. Bordogna von Taxis (1510-59), Tyrolean Postmaster A1550

2013, June 25 **Litho. & Engr.**
2452 A1550 145c multi 3.75 3.75

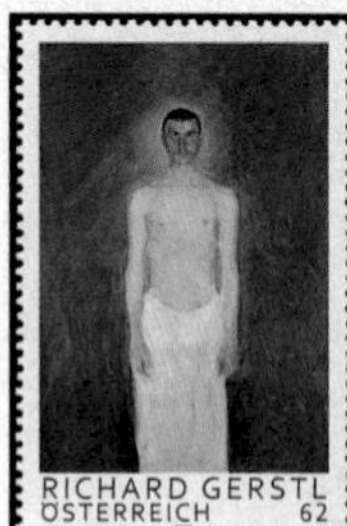

Self-portrait, by Richard Gerstl (1883-1908) A1551

2013, June 27 **Litho.** *Perf. 14*
2453 A1551 62c multi 1.60 1.60

Vorau Monastery, 850th Anniv. — A1552

Perf. 13¾x13½

2013, June 28 **Litho. & Engr.**
2454 A1552 145c brown & blk 3.75 3.75

Wacker Soccer Team, Innsbruck, Cent. — A1553

2013, July 5 **Litho.** *Perf. 13¾*
2455 A1553 62c multi 1.60 1.60

Ausserfern Railway, Cent. A1554

2013, July 6 *Perf. 13½x14¼*
2456 A1554 70c multi 1.90 1.90

Traditional Women's Clothing From Gmunden A1555

2013, Aug. 23 *Perf. 13¼x14*
2457 A1555 62c multi 1.75 1.75

Volunteer Fire Departments in Austria, 150th Anniv. A1556

Perf. 13½x14¼

2013, Sept. 7 **Litho. & Engr.**
2458 A1556 90c multi 2.40 2.40

Stylized Landmarks A1557

Austrian flag and: No. 2459, Lindwurm Fountain, Brunnen. No. 2460, Hohensalzburg Fortress, Salzburg. No. 2461, Pöstlingberg Church, Linz. No. 2462, Goldenes Dachl (Golden Roof), Innsbruck, vert. No. 2463, St. Martin's Tower, Bregenz, vert. No. 2464, Bergkirche, Eisenstadt, vert. No. 2465, Landhaus, St. Pölten, vert.

Die Cut Perf. 14

2013, Sept. 12 **Litho.**

Coil Stamps Self-Adhesive

2459 A1557 62c multi 1.75 1.75
2460 A1557 90c multi 2.40 2.40
2461 A1557 145c multi 4.00 4.00
Nos. 2459-2461 (3) 8.15 8.15

Booklet Stamps

2462 A1557 62c multi 1.75 1.75
a. Booklet pane of 4 7.00
2463 A1557 62c multi 1.75 1.75
a. Booklet pane of 10 17.50
2464 A1557 90c multi 2.40 2.40
a. Booklet pane of 4 9.75
2465 A1557 145c multi 4.00 4.00
a. Booklet pane of 4 16.00
Nos. 2462-2465 (4) 9.90 9.90

Souvenir Sheet

Holiday Travel with the Express Mail, Painting by Karl Schnorpfeil (1875-1937) — A1558

2013, Sept. 12 *Perf. 14*
2466 A1558 70c multi 1.90 1.90

Helene Winterstein-Kamberesky (1900-66), Inventor of Waterproof Mascara — A1559

2013, Sept. 13 *Perf. 13¼x14*
2467 A1559 70c multi 1.90 1.90

Advertising Art for Engelhofer Bonbons A1560

2013, Sept. 13 *Perf. 13¾x14*
2468 A1560 70c multi 1.90 1.90

Icon of St. Nicholas of Myra, Russian Orthodox Cathedral, Vienna A1561

Litho. & Engr.

2013, Sept. 20 *Perf. 13¾*
2469 A1561 145c multi 4.00 4.00

Madonna and Child, Painting by Lorenzo Lotto (1480-1557) — A1562

2013, Sept. 26
2470 A1562 170c multi 4.75 4.75

Tyrolean Ski Federation, Cent. — A1563

2013, Oct. 11 Litho. ***Perf. 14***
2471 A1563 62c multi 1.75 1.75

St. Martin's Church, Linz — A1564

2013, Oct. 11 Litho. ***Perf. 14***
2472 A1564 62c multi 1.75 1.75

Burgtheater, Vienna, 125th Anniv. — A1565

2013, Oct. 11 Litho. ***Perf. 13¾***
2473 A1565 70c multi 1.90 1.90

Scene From "Orient, 1st Part," Video Art by Markus Schinwald A1566

2013, Oct. 14 Litho. ***Perf. 14***
2474 A1566 145c multi 4.00 4.00

Miniature Sheet

Halloween — A1567

No. 2475 — Haunted house and: a, Ghost, witch on broom, spider. b, Bats, vampire. c, Skeleton, graveyard. d, Jack o'lanterns.

Serpentine Die Cut 14¼
2013, Oct. 14 Litho.

Self-Adhesive

2475 A1567 Sheet of 4 7.00
a.-d. 62c Any single 1.75 1.75

Adoration of the Shepherds from Altarpiece of St. Michael's Church, Lungau A1568

St. Georgenberg-Fiecht Abbey — A1569

Franz Xaver Gruber (1787-1863), Composer of "Silent Night," and Silent Night Chapel, Oberndorf — A1570

The Nativity, Painting by Joos van Cleve — A1571

2013 Litho. ***Perf. 13¾x14***
2476 A1568 62c multi 1.75 1.75
2477 A1569 70c multi 2.00 2.00

Coil Stamps
Self-Adhesive

Die Cut Perf. 14x14¼
2478 A1570 62c multi 1.75 1.75

Die Cut Perf. 13x13½
2479 A1571 70c multi 2.00 2.00

Christmas. No. 2479 lacks country name. Issued: Nos. 2476, 2478, 11/29; Nos. 2477, 2479, 11/15.

E.V.A., by Franz Graf — A1572

2013, Dec. 5 Litho. ***Perf. 13¾x14***
2480 A1572 145c black 4.00 4.00

SEMI-POSTAL STAMPS

Issues of the Monarchy

Emperor Franz Josef — SP1

Perf. 12½
1914, Oct. 4 Typo. Unwmk.
B1 SP1 5h green .40 *.80*
B2 SP1 10h rose .80 *1.60*
Set, never hinged 2.75

Nos. B1-B2 were sold at an advance of 2h each over face value. Exist imperf.; value, set $120.

The Firing Step — SP2

Designs: 5h+2h, Cavalry. 10h+2h, Siege gun. 20h+3h, Battleship. 35h+3h, Airplane.

1915, May 1
B3 SP2 3h + 1h violet brn 1.20 *.40*
B4 SP2 5h + 2h green .25 .25
B5 SP2 10h + 2h deep rose .25 .25
B6 SP2 20h + 3h Prus blue 4.00 *2.40*
B7 SP2 35h + 3h ultra 6.50 *5.50*
Nos. B3-B7 (5) 12.20 *8.80*
Set, never hinged 35.00

Exist imperf. Value, set $325 hinged and $525 never hinged.

Issues of the Republic

Types of Austria, 1919-20, Overprinted in Black

1920, Sept. 16 ***Perf. 12½***
B11 A44 5h gray, *yellow* .55 *1.60*
B12 A44 10h red, *pink* .55 *1.25*
B13 A43 15h bister, *yel* .25 *.80*
B14 A45 20h dark grn, *bl* .25 *.65*
B15 A43 25h violet, *pink* .25 *.75*
B16 A45 30h brown, *buff* 1.40 *2.90*
B17 A45 40h carmine, *yel* .25 *.80*
B18 A45 50h dark bl, *blue* .25 *.65*
B19 A43 60h ol grn, *azure* 1.40 *2.75*
B20 A47 80h red .35 *.75*
B21 A47 1k orange brown .35 *.80*
B22 A47 2k pale blue .35 *.80*

Granite Paper

Imperf

B23 A46 2½k brown red .40 *1.00*
B24 A46 3k dk blue & green .50 *1.25*
B25 A46 4k carmine & violet .65 *1.50*
B26 A46 5k blue .55 *1.25*
B27 A46 7½k yellow green .55 *1.25*
B28 A46 10k gray grn & red .55 *1.40*
B29 A46 20k lilac & orange .75 *1.75*
Nos. B11-B29 (19) 10.15 *23.90*
Set, never hinged 26.00

Carinthia Plebiscite. Sold at three times face value for the benefit of the Plebiscite Propaganda Fund.

Nos. B11-B19 exist imperf. Values, set unused hinged $290, never hinged $400.

Types of Regular Issues of 1919-21 Overprinted

1921, Mar. 1 ***Perf. 12½***
B30 A44 5h gray, *yellow* .25 *.80*
B31 A44 10h orange brown .25 *.80*
B32 A43 15h gray .25 *.80*
B33 A45 20h green, *yellow* .25 *.80*
B34 A43 25h blue, *yellow* .25 *.80*
B35 A45 30h violet, *bl* .50 *1.60*
B36 A45 40h org brn, *pink* .55 *2.00*
B37 A45 50h green, *blue* 1.25 *3.25*
B38 A43 60h lilac, *yellow* .50 *1.60*
B39 A47 80h pale blue .50 *1.60*
B40 A47 1k red org, *blue* .40 *1.60*
B41 A47 1½k green, *yellow* .25 *.80*
B42 A47 2k lilac brown .25 *.80*

Overprinted

B43 A46 2½k light blue .25 *.80*
B44 A46 3k ol grn & brn red .25 *.80*
B45 A46 4k lilac & orange .80 *2.75*
B46 A46 5k olive green .25 *1.60*
B47 A46 7½k brown red .30 *1.60*
B48 A46 10k blue & olive grn .30 *1.60*
B49 A46 20k car rose & vio .50 *2.40*
Nos. B30-B49 (20) 8.10 *28.80*
Set, never hinged 18.00

Nos. B30-B49 were sold at three times face value, the excess going to help flood victims. Exists imperf. Values, set unused hinged $300, never hinged $525.

Nos. B50-B76, B93-B98, B112-B117, B122-B127, B132-B137 and B146-B164 exist imperf, on handmade paper, printed in black or in colors other than those of the issued stamps. These are proofs.

Franz Joseph Haydn — SP9

Musicians: 5k, Mozart. 7½k, Beethoven. 10k, Schubert. 25k, Anton Bruckner. 50k, Johann Strauss (son). 100k, Hugo Wolf.

1922, Apr. 24 Engr. ***Perf. 12½***
B50 SP9 2½k brown, perf. 11½ 7.25 7.25
a. Perf. 12½ 11.00 *12.00*
Never hinged 30.00
B51 SP9 5k dark blue 1.25 1.25
B52 SP9 7½k black 2.00 2.00
a. Perf. 11½ 110.00 110.00
Never hinged 240.00
B53 SP9 10k dark violet 2.75 2.40
a. Perf. 11½ 3.25 3.25
Never hinged 16.00
B54 SP9 25k dark green 4.75 *4.75*
a. Perf. 11½ 4.75 4.75
Never hinged 16.00
B55 SP9 50k claret 2.40 2.40
B56 SP9 100k brown olive 8.00 *8.00*
a. Perf. 11½ 10.50 10.50
Never hinged 47.50
Nos. B50-B56 (7) 28.40 *28.05*
Set, never hinged 72.50

These stamps were sold at 10 times face value, the excess being given to needy musicians.

Used values are for examples with philatelic favor cancels. Postally used stamps are worth 50%-100% more.

All values exist imperf. Values, set unused hinged $900, never hinged $1,750.

A 1969 souvenir sheet without postal validity contains reprints of the 5k in black, 7½k in claret and 50k in dark blue, each overprinted "NEUDRUCK" in black at top. It was issued for the Vienna State Opera Centenary Exhibition.

View of Bregenz — SP16

Designs: 120k, Mirabelle Gardens, Salzburg. 160k, Church at Eisenstadt. 180k, Assembly House, Klagenfurt. 200k, "Golden Roof," Innsbruck. 240k, Main Square, Linz.

400k, Castle Hill, Graz. 600k, Abbey at Melk. 1000k, Upper Belvedere, Vienna.

Various Frames

1923, May 22 *Perf. 12½*

B57	SP16	100k dk green	4.00	*4.00*
B58	SP16	120k deep blue	4.00	*4.00*
B59	SP16	160k dk violet	4.00	*4.00*
B60	SP16	180k red violet	4.00	*4.00*
B61	SP16	200k lake	4.00	*4.00*
B62	SP16	240k red brown	4.00	*4.00*
B63	SP16	400k dark brown	4.00	*4.00*
B64	SP16	600k olive brn	4.00	*4.00*
B65	SP16	1000k black	4.00	*4.00*
		Nos. B57-B65 (9)	36.00	*36.00*
		Set, never hinged	100.00	

Nos. B57-B65 were sold at five times face value, the excess going to needy artists.

Used values are for examples with philatelic favor cancels. Values for postally used: Nos. B57-B64, each $8; No. B65 $14.

All values exist imperf. on both regular and handmade papers. Values, set hinged $700, never hinged $1,000.

Feebleness — SP25

Designs: 300k+900k, Aid to industry. 500k+1500k, Orphans and widow. 600k+1800k, Indigent old man. 1000k+3000k, Alleviation of hunger.

1924, Sept. 6 **Photo.**

B66	SP25	100k + 300k yel grn	4.00	*4.00*
B67	SP25	300k + 900k red brn	4.00	*4.00*
B68	SP25	500k + 1500k brn vio	4.00	*4.00*
B69	SP25	600k + 1800k pck bl	8.00	*6.50*
B70	SP25	1000k + 3000k brn org	9.50	*8.00*
		Nos. B66-B70 (5)	29.50	*26.50*
		Set, never hinged	67.50	

The surtax was for child welfare and anti-tuberculosis work.

Used values are for examples with philatelic favor cancels. Values for postally used are 2-2.5 times values shown.

Set exists imperf. Values, set unused hinged $350, never hinged $525.

Siegfried Slays the Dragon — SP30

Designs: 8g+2g, Gunther's voyage to Iceland. 15g+5g, Brunhild accusing Kriemhild. 20g+5g, Nymphs telling Hagen the future. 24g+6g, Rudiger von Bechelaren welcomes the Nibelungen. 40g+10g, Dietrich von Bern vanquishes Hagen.

1926, Mar. 8 **Engr.**

B71	SP30	3g + 2g olive blk	.95	.80
B72	SP30	8g + 2g indigo	.40	.40
B73	SP30	15g + 5g dk claret	.35	.35
B74	SP30	20g + 5g olive grn	.50	.50
B75	SP30	24g + 6g dk violet	.50	.50
B76	SP30	40g + 10g red brn	2.40	2.40
		Nos. B71-B76 (6)	5.10	4.95
		Set, never hinged	15.00	

Nibelungen issue. The surtax was for child welfare.

Nos. B71-B76 were printed in two sizes: 27 ½x28 ½mm and 28 ½x27 ½mm.

Used values are for examples with philatelic favor cancels. Values for postally used are 1.5 times values shown.

Nos. B71-B76 exist imperf. Values, set unused hinged $350, never hinged $500.

Pres. Michael Hainisch — SP36

1928, Nov. 5

B77	SP36	10g dark brown	5.50	4.75
B78	SP36	15g red brown	5.50	4.75
B79	SP36	30g black	5.50	4.75
B80	SP36	40g indigo	5.50	4.75
		Nos. B77-B80 (4)	22.00	*19.00*
		Set, never hinged	37.50	

Tenth anniversary of Austrian Republic. Sold at double face value, the premium aiding war orphans and children of war invalids.

Used values are for examples with philatelic favor cancels. Values for postally used are 2.5 times values shown.

Set exists imperf, without gum. Value, set $625.

Pres. Wilhelm Miklas — SP37

1930, Oct. 4

B81	SP37	10g light brown	7.25	*7.25*
B82	SP37	20g red	7.25	*7.25*
B83	SP37	30g brown violet	7.25	*7.25*
B84	SP37	40g indigo	7.25	*7.25*
B85	SP37	50g dark green	7.25	*7.25*
B86	SP37	1s black brown	7.25	*7.25*
		Nos. B81-B86 (6)	43.50	*43.50*
		Set, never hinged	125.00	

Nos. B81-B86 were sold at double face value. The excess aided the anti-tuberculosis campaign and the building of sanatoria in Carinthia.

Used values are for examples with philatelic favor cancels. Values for postally used are 3 times values shown.

Set exists imperf, without gum. Value, set $950.

Regular Issue of 1929-30 Overprinted in Various Colors

1931, June 20

B87	A56	10g bister (Bl)	27.50	*27.50*
B88	A56	20g dk gray (R)	27.50	*27.50*
B89	A56	30g dk violet (Gl)	27.50	*27.50*
B90	A56	40g dk blue (Gl)	27.50	*27.50*
B91	A56	50g gray vio (O)	27.50	*27.50*
B92	A57	1s black brn (Bk)	27.50	*27.50*
		Nos. B87-B92 (6)	165.00	*165.00*
		Set, never hinged	550.00	

Rotary convention, Vienna.

Nos. B87 to B92 were sold at double their face values. The excess was added to the beneficent funds of Rotary International.

Used values are for examples with philatelic favor cancels. Values for postally used are 2 times values shown.

Ferdinand Raimund — SP38

Poets: 20g, Franz Grillparzer. 30g, Johann Nestroy. 40g, Adalbert Stifter. 50g, Ludwig Anzengruber. 1s, Peter Rosegger.

1931, Sept. 12

B93	SP38	10g dark violet	13.50	*11.00*
B94	SP38	20g gray black	13.50	*11.00*
B95	SP38	30g orange red	13.50	*11.00*
B96	SP38	40g dull blue	13.50	*11.00*
B97	SP38	50g gray green	13.50	*11.00*
B98	SP38	1s yellow brown	13.50	*11.00*
		Nos. B93-B98 (6)	81.00	*66.00*
		Set, never hinged	160.00	

Nos. B93-B98 were sold at double face value. The surtax aided unemployed young people.

Used values are for examples with philatelic favor cancels. Values for postally used are 3 times values shown.

Set exists imperf, without gum. Value, set $950.

Chancellor Ignaz Seipel — SP44

1932, Oct. 12 *Perf. 13*

B99	SP44	50g ultra	12.00	*9.50*
		Never hinged	27.50	

Msgr. Ignaz Seipel, Chancellor of Austria, 1922-29. Sold at double face value, the excess aiding wounded veterans of World War I.

Used value is for a cancelled-to-order example. Value for postally used $27.50.

Exists imperf, without gum. Value $800.

Ferdinand Georg Waldmüller SP45

Artists: 24g, Moritz von Schwind. 30g, Rudolf von Alt. 40g, Hans Makart. 64g, Gustav Klimt. 1s, Albin Egger-Lienz.

1932, Nov. 21

B100	SP45	12g slate green	20.00	*16.00*
B101	SP45	24g dp violet	20.00	*16.00*
B102	SP45	30g dark red	20.00	*16.00*
B103	SP45	40g dark gray	20.00	*16.00*
B104	SP45	64g dark brown	20.00	*16.00*
B105	SP45	1s claret	20.00	*16.00*
		Nos. B100-B105 (6)	120.00	*96.00*
		Set, never hinged	260.00	

Nos. B100 to B105 were sold at double their face values. The surtax was for the assistance of charitable institutions.

Used values are for examples with philatelic favor cancels. Values for postally used, each $60.

Set exists imperf, without gum. Value, set $1,200.

Mountain Climbing SP51

Designs: 24g, Ski gliding. 30g, Walking on skis. 50g, Ski jumping.

1933, Jan. 9 **Photo.** *Perf. 12½*

B106	SP51	12g dark green	6.50	*6.50*
B107	SP51	24g dark violet	95.00	*75.00*
B108	SP51	30g brown red	12.00	*12.00*
B109	SP51	50g dark blue	95.00	*75.00*
		Nos. B106-B109 (4)	208.50	*168.50*
		Set, never hinged	525.00	

Meeting of the Intl. Ski Federation, Innsbruck, Feb. 8-13.

These stamps were sold at double their face value. The surtax was for the benefit of "Youth in Distress."

Used values are for examples with philatelic favor cancels. Values for postally used, 25%-80% higher.

Set exists imperf, without gum. Value, set $4,000.

Stagecoach, after Painting by Moritz von Schwind — SP55

1933, June 23 **Engr.** *Perf. 12½*

Ordinary Paper

B110	SP55	50g deep ultra	150.00	150.00
		Never hinged	260.00	
	a.	Granite paper	325.00	325.00
		Never hinged	600.00	

Sheets of 25.

Used values are for examples with philatelic favor cancels. Values for postally used, 50% higher.

Nos. B110 and B110a exist imperf. Value, No. B110 unused hinged, $2,400.

Souvenir Sheet

Perf. 12

Granite Paper

B111		Sheet of 4	2,500.	2,400.
		Never hinged	3,050.	
	a.	SP55 50g deep ultra	475.00	475.00
		Never hinged	650.00	

Intl. Phil. Exhib., Vienna, 1933. In addition to the postal value of 50g the stamp was sold at a premium of 50g for charity and of 1.60s for the admission fee to the exhibition.

Size of No. B111: 126x103mm.

Used values are for examples with philatelic favor cancels. Values for postally used, 35% higher.

A 50g dark red in souvenir sheet, with dark blue overprint ("NEUDRUCK WIPA 1965"), had no postal validity.

Even though the margins No. B111 have no gum, the sheet sells for a premium when definitely never hinged.

No. B111 exists imperf.

St. Stephen's Cathedral in 1683 — SP56

Marco d'Aviano, Papal Legate — SP57

Designs: 30g, Count Ernst Rudiger von Starhemberg. 40g, John III Sobieski, King of Poland. 50g, Karl V, Duke of Lorraine. 64g, Burgomaster Johann Andreas von Liebenberg.

1933, Sept. 6 **Photo.** *Perf. 12½*

B112	SP56	12g dark green	24.00	*20.00*
B113	SP57	24g dark violet	20.00	*16.00*
B114	SP57	30g brown red	20.00	*16.00*
B115	SP57	40g blue black	32.50	*20.00*
B116	SP57	50g dark blue	20.00	*16.00*
B117	SP57	64g olive brown	27.50	*16.00*
		Nos. B112-B117 (6)	144.00	*104.00*
		Set, never hinged	350.00	

Deliverance of Vienna from the Turks, 250th anniv., and Pan-German Catholic Congress, Sept. 6, 1933.

The stamps were sold at double their face value, the excess being for the aid of Catholic works of charity.

Used values are for examples with philatelic favor cancels. Values for postally used, 2-3 times values shown.

Types of Regular Issue of 1925-30 Surcharged

a

b

c

1933, Dec. 15

B118	A52(a)	5g + 2g ol grn	.25	*.25*
B119	A56(b)	12g + 3g lt blue	.25	*.25*
B120	A56(b)	24g + 6g brn org	.25	*.25*

			Unused	Used
B121	A57(c)	1s + 50g org red	35.00	*32.50*
		Nos. B118-B121 (4)	35.75	*33.25*
		Set, never hinged	75.00	

Winterhelp.

Used values are for examples with philatelic favor cancels. Values for postally used, 2-3 times values shown.

Anton Pilgram — SP62

Architects: 24g, J. B. Fischer von Erlach. 30g, Jakob Prandtauer. 40g, A. von Siccardsburg & E. van der Null. 60g, Heinrich von Ferstel. 64g, Otto Wagner.

1934, Dec. 2 Engr. *Perf. 12½*

Thick Yellowish Paper

B122	SP62	12g black	9.50	8.00
B123	SP62	24g dull violet	9.50	8.00
B124	SP62	30g carmine	9.50	8.00
B125	SP62	40g brown	9.50	8.00
B126	SP62	60g blue	9.50	8.00
B127	SP62	64g dull green	9.50	8.00
		Nos. B122-B127 (6)	57.00	*48.00*
		Set, never hinged	120.00	

Used values are for examples with philatelic favor cancels. Values for postally used, each $20.

Exist imperf. Values, set unused hinged $650, never hinged $850.

Nos. B124-B127 exist in horiz. pairs imperf. between. Value, each $250-$325.

These stamps were sold at double their face value. The surtax on this and the following issues was devoted to general charity.

Types of Regular Issue of 1934 Surcharged in Black

c

d

1935, Nov. 11 *Perf. 12, 12½*

B128	A67(d)	5g + 2g emerald	.50	*.80*
B129	A67(d)	12g + 3g blue	.95	.95
B130	A67(d)	24g + 6g lt brown	.50	*.80*
B131	A68(c)	1s + 50g ver	32.50	32.50
		Nos. B128-B131 (4)	34.45	35.05
		Set, never hinged	80.00	

Winterhelp. Set exists imperf. Values, set unused hinged $175, never hinged $260.

Set without surcharge unused hinged $250, never hinged $325.

Prince Eugene of Savoy — SP68

Military Leaders: 24g, Field Marshal Laudon. 30g, Archduke Karl. 40g, Field Marshal Josef Radetzky. 60g, Admiral Wilhelm Tegetthoff. 64g, Field Marshal Franz Conrad Hotzendorff.

1935, Dec. 1 *Perf. 12½*

B132	SP68	12g brown	10.50	9.50
B133	SP68	24g dark green	10.50	9.50
B134	SP68	30g claret	10.50	9.50
B135	SP68	40g slate	10.50	9.50
B136	SP68	60g deep ultra	10.50	9.50
B137	SP68	64g dark violet	10.50	9.50
		Nos. B132-B137 (6)	63.00	57.00
		Set, never hinged	125.00	

These stamps were sold at double their face value.

Used values are for examples with philatelic favor cancels. Values for postally used, each $20.

Set exists imperf. Values, set unused hinged $650, never hinged $850.

Slalom Turn — SP74

Designs: 24g, Jumper taking off. 35g, Slalom turn. 60g, Innsbruck view.

1936, Feb. 20 Photo.

B138	SP74	12g Prus green	1.60	1.60
B139	SP74	24g dp violet	2.40	2.40
B140	SP74	35g rose car	24.00	24.00
B141	SP74	60g sapphire	24.00	24.00
		Nos. B138-B141 (4)	52.00	52.00
		Set, never hinged	130.00	

Ski concourse issue. These stamps were sold at twice face value.

Used values are for examples with philatelic favor cancels. Value for postally used set, $110.

Set exists imperf. Values, set unused hinged $600, never hinged $750.

St. Martin of Tours — SP78

Designs: 12g+3g, Medical clinic. 24g+6g, St. Elizabeth of Hungary. 1s+1s, "Flame of Charity."

1936, Nov. 2 Unwmk.

B142	SP78	5g + 2g dp green	.25	.25
B143	SP78	12g + 3g dp violet	.25	.25
B144	SP78	24g + 6g dp blue	.35	.35
B145	SP78	1s + 1s dk car	7.50	7.50
		Nos. B142-B145 (4)	8.35	8.35
		Set, never hinged	14.00	

Winterhelp.

Used values are for examples with philatelic favor cancels. Values for postally used: Nos. B142-B144, each 80¢; No. B145, $19.

Set exists imperf. Values, set unused hinged $400, never hinged $500.

Josef Ressel — SP82

Inventors: 24g, Karl von Ghega. 30g, Josef Werndl. 40g, Carl Auer von Welsbach. 60g, Robert von Lieben. 64g, Viktor Kaplan.

1936, Dec. 6 Engr.

B146	SP82	12g dk brown	2.75	2.75
B147	SP82	24g dk violet	2.75	2.75
B148	SP82	30g dp claret	2.75	2.75
B149	SP82	40g gray violet	2.75	2.75
B150	SP82	60g vio blue	2.75	2.75
B151	SP82	64g dk slate green	2.75	2.75
		Nos. B146-B151 (6)	16.50	16.50
		Set, never hinged	47.50	

These stamps were sold at double their face value.

Used values are for examples with philatelic favor cancels. Values for postally used: each $6.75.

Exists imperf, without gum. Value, set unused hinged $800, never hinged $1,000.

Nurse and Infant — SP88

12g+3g, Mother and child. 24g+6g, Nursing the aged. 1s+1s, Sister of Mercy with patient.

1937, Oct. 18 Photo.

B152	SP88	5g + 2g dk green	.30	.25
B153	SP88	12g + 3g dk brown	.30	.25
B154	SP88	24g + 6g dk blue	.30	.25
B155	SP88	1s + 1s dk carmine	4.00	3.50
		Nos. B152-B155 (4)	4.90	4.25
		Set, never hinged	11.00	

Winterhelp.

Used values are for examples with philatelic favor cancels. Values for postally used: Nos. B152-B154, each 40c; No. B155, $13.50.

Set exists imperf. Values, set unused hinged $125, never hinged $160.

Gerhard van Swieten — SP92

Physicians: 8g, Leopold Auenbrugger von Auenbrugg. 12g, Karl von Rokitansky. 20g, Joseph Skoda. 24g, Ferdinand von Hebra. 30g, Ferdinand von Arlt. 40g, Joseph Hyrtl. 60g, Theodor Billroth. 64g, Theodor Meynert.

1937, Dec. 5 Engr. *Perf. 12½*

B156	SP92	5g choc	2.40	2.00
B157	SP92	8g dk red	2.40	2.00
B158	SP92	12g brown blk	2.40	2.00
B159	SP92	20g dk green	2.40	2.00
B160	SP92	24g dk violet	2.40	2.00
B161	SP92	30g brown car	2.40	2.00
B162	SP92	40g dp olive grn	2.40	2.00
B163	SP92	60g indigo	2.40	2.00
B164	SP92	64g brown vio	2.40	2.00
		Nos. B156-B164 (9)	21.60	18.00
		Set, never hinged	52.50	

These stamps were sold at double their face value.

Used values are for examples with philatelic favor cancels. Values for postally used: each $5.25.

Set exists imperf, without gum. Value, set $2,250.

Catalogue values for unused stamps in this section, from this point to the end of the section, are for Never Hinged items.

The Dawn of Peace — SP101

1945, Sept. 10 Photo. *Perf. 14*

B165	SP101	1s + 10s dk green	1.25	.80

Used value is for examples with philatelic favor cancels. Postally used value $2.40.

No. 467 Surcharged in Black

1946, June 25

B166	A110	30g + 20g dk red	2.50	2.50

First anniversary of United Nations.

Used value is for examples with philatelic favor cancels. Postally used value $4.75.

Pres. Karl Renner SP102

1946 Engr. *Perf. 13½x14*

B167	SP102	1s + 1s dk slate grn	4.75	.80
B168	SP102	2s + 2s dk blue vio	4.75	.80
B169	SP102	3s + 3s dk purple	4.75	.80
B170	SP102	5s + 5s dk vio brn	4.75	.80
		Nos. B167-B170 (4)	19.00	3.20

Used values are for examples with philatelic favor cancels. Postally used values, each $8.

See Nos. B185-B188.

Nazi Sword Piercing Austria — SP103

Sweeping Away Fascist Symbols — SP104

Designs: 8g+6g, St. Stephen's Cathedral in Flames. 12g+12g, Pleading hand in concentration camp. 30g+30g, Hand choking Nazi serpent. 42g+42g, Hammer breaking Nazi pillar. 1s+1s, Oath of allegiance. 2s+2s, Austrian eagle and burning swastika.

Unwmk.

1946, Sept. 16 Photo. *Perf. 14*

B171	SP103	5g + (3g) dk brown	.40	.40
B172	SP104	6g + (4g) dk slate grn	.25	.25
B173	SP104	8g + (6g) orange red	.25	.25
B174	SP104	12g + (12g) slate blk	.25	.25
B175	SP104	30g + (30g) violet	.25	.25
B176	SP104	42g + (42g) dull brn	.25	.25
B177	SP104	1s + 1s dk red	.40	.40
B178	SP104	2s + 2s dk car rose	.80	.80
		Nos. B171-B178 (8)	2.85	2.85

Anti-fascist propaganda.

Used values are for examples with philatelic favor cancels. Postally used values approx. 2-3 times values shown.

A 5g + 3g black olive brown stamp showing SS lightning bolt striking map of Austria and 12g + 12g black gray blue depicting skull with Hitler mask were prepared but not issued. Value, each $1,050.

Race Horse with Foal SP111

Various Race Horses.

1946, Oct. 20 Engr. *Perf. 13½x14*

B179	SP111	16g + 16g rose brown	1.60	1.60
B180	SP111	24g + 24g dk purple	1.60	1.60
B181	SP111	60g + 60g dk green	1.60	1.60
B182	SP111	1s + 1s dk blue gray	1.60	1.60
B183	SP111	2s + 2s yel brown	5.75	4.00
		Nos. B179-B183 (5)	12.15	10.40

Austria Prize race, Vienna.

Used values are for examples with philatelic favor cancels. Postally used values 2-2.5 times values shown.

St. Ruprecht's Church, Vienna — SP116

1946, Oct. 30 ***Perf. 14x13½***

B184 SP116 30g + 70g dark red .40 .40

Founding of Austria, 950th anniv. The surtax aided the Stamp Day celebration.

Used value is for examples with philatelic favor cancels. Postally used value $2.

Renner Type of 1946

Souvenir Sheets

1946, Sept. 5 ***Imperf.***

B185 Sheet of 8 500.00 450.00
a. SP102 1s+1s dk slate grn 62.50 32.50
B186 Sheet of 8 500.00 450.00
a. SP102 2s+2s dk blue vio 62.50 32.50
B187 Sheet of 8 500.00 450.00
a. SP102 3s+3s dark purple 62.50 32.50
B188 Sheet of 8 500.00 450.00
a. SP102 5s+5s dk vio brown 62.50 32.50

First anniv. of Austria's liberation. Sheets of 8 plus center label showing arms.

Values for used examples are for those with philatelic favor cancels. Postally used values: singles, each $275; sheets, each $3,250.

Statue of Rudolf IV the Founder — SP118

Designs: 5g+20g, Tomb of Frederick III. 6g+24g, Main pulpit. 8g+32g, Statue of St. Stephen. 10g+40g, Madonna of the Domestics statue. 12g+48g, High altar. 30g+1.20s, Organ, destroyed in 1945. 50g+1.80s, Anton Pilgram statue. 1s+5s, Cathedral from northeast. 2s+10s, Southwest corner of cathedral.

1946, Dec. 12 **Engr.** ***Perf. 14x13½***

B189 SP118 3g + 12g brown .25 .25
B190 SP118 5g + 20g dk vio brown .25 .25
B191 SP118 6g + 24g dk blue .25 .25
B192 SP118 8g + 32g dk grn .25 .25
B193 SP118 10g + 40g dp blue .25 .25
B194 SP118 12g + 48g dk vio .25 .25
B195 SP118 30g + 1.20s car 1.25 1.25
B196 SP118 50g + 1.80s dk bl 1.60 1.60
B197 SP118 1s + 5s brn vio 2.00 2.00
B198 SP118 2s + 10s vio brn 4.00 4.00
Nos. B189-B198 (10) 10.35 10.35

The surtax aided reconstruction of St. Stephen's Cathedral, Vienna.

Values for used examples are for those with philatelic favor cancels. Postally used value, set $24.

Reaping Wheat — SP128

Designs: 8g+2g, Log raft. 10g+5g, Cement factory. 12g+8g, Coal mine. 18g+12g, Oil derricks. 30g+10g, Textile machinery. 35g+15g, Iron furnace. 60g+20g, Electric power lines.

1947, Mar. 23 ***Perf. 14x13½***

B199 SP128 3g + 2g yel brown .40 .30
B200 SP128 8g + 2g dk bl grn .40 .30
B201 SP128 10g + 5g slate blk .40 .30
B202 SP128 12g + 8g dark pur .40 .30
B203 SP128 18g + 12g ol green .40 .30
B204 SP128 30g + 10g deep cl .40 .30
B205 SP128 35g + 15g crimson .40 .30
B206 SP128 60g + 20g dk blue .40 .30
Nos. B199-B206 (8) 3.20 *2.40*

Vienna International Sample Fair, 1947.

Values for used examples are for those with philatelic favor cancels. Postally used value, set $8.

Race Horse and Jockey SP136

1947, June 29 ***Perf. 13½x14***

B207 SP136 60g + 20g deep blue, *pale pink* .40 .40

Value for used is for examples with philatelic favor cancels. Postally used value $1.25.

Cup of Corvinus SP137

Designs: 8g+2g, Statue of Providence, Vienna. 10g+5g, Abbey at Melk. 12g+8g, Picture of a Woman, by Kriehuber. 18g+12g, Children at the Window, by Waldmuller. 20g+10g, Entrance, Upper Belvedere Palace. 30g+10g, Nymph Egeria, Schönbrunn Castle. 35g+15g, National Library, Vienna. 48g+12g, "Workshop of a Printer of Engravings," by Schmutzer. 60g+20g, Girl with Straw Hat, by Amerling.

1947, June 20 ***Perf. 14x13½***

B208 SP137 3g + 2g brown .40 .30
B209 SP137 8g + 2g dk blue grn .40 .30
B210 SP137 10g + 5g dp claret .40 .30
B211 SP137 12g + 8g dk purple .40 .30
B212 SP137 18g + 12g golden brn .40 .30
B213 SP137 20g + 10g sepia .40 .30
B214 SP137 30g + 10g dk yel grn .40 .30
B215 SP137 35g + 15g deep car .40 .30
B216 SP137 48g + 12g dk brn vio .65 .50
B217 SP137 60g + 20g dp blue .65 .50
Nos. B208-B217 (10) 4.50 3.40

Values for used examples are for those with philatelic favor cancels. Postally used value, double values shown.

Prisoner of War — SP147

12g+8g, Prisoners' Mail, 18g+12g, Prison camp visitor. 35g+15g, Family reunion. 60g+20g, "Industry" beckoning. 1s+40g, Sower.

1947, Aug. 30

B218 SP147 8g + 2g dk green .25 .25
B219 SP147 12g + 8g dk vio brn .25 .25
B220 SP147 18g + 12g black brn .25 .25
B221 SP147 35g + 15g rose brn .25 .25
B222 SP147 60g + 20g dp blue .25 .25
B223 SP147 1s + 40g redsh brn .25 .25
Nos. B218-B223 (6) 1.50 1.50

Values for used examples are for those with philatelic favor cancels. Postally used value, set $5.50.

Olympic Flame and Emblem — SP153

1948, Jan. 16 **Engr.**

B224 SP153 1s + 50g dark blue .55 .55

The surtax was used to help defray expenses of Austria's 1948 Olympics team.

Laabenbach Bridge Neulengbach SP154

Designs: 20g+10g, Dam, Vermunt Lake. 30g+10g, Danube Port, Vienna. 40g+20g, Mining, Erzberg. 45g+20g, Tracks, Southern Railway Station, Vienna. 60g+30g, Communal housing project, Vienna. 75g+35g, Gas Works, Vienna. 80g+40g, Oil refinery. 1s+50g, Gesäuse Highway, Styria. 1.40s+70g, Parliament Building, Vienna.

1948, Feb. 18 ***Perf. 14x13½***

B225 SP154 10g + 5g slate blk .25 .25
B226 SP154 20g + 10g lilac .25 .25
B227 SP154 30g + 10g dull grn .50 .50
B228 SP154 40g + 20g ol brn .25 .25
B229 SP154 45g + 20g dk blue .25 .25
B230 SP154 60g + 30g dk red .25 .25
B231 SP154 75g + 35g dk vio brn .25 .25
B232 SP154 80g + 40g vio brn .25 .25
B233 SP154 1s + 50g dp blue .25 .25
B234 SP154 1.40s + 70g dp car .50 .50
Nos. B225-B234 (10) 3.00 3.00

The surtax was for the Reconstruction Fund.

Violet — SP155

Designs: 20g+10g, Anemone. 30g+10g, Crocus. 40g+20g, Yellow primrose. 45g+20g, Pasqueflower. 60g+30g, Rhododendron. 75g+35g, Dogrose. 80g+40g, Cyclamen. 1s+50g, Alpine Gentian. 1.40s+70g, Edelweiss.

1948, May 14 **Engr. & Typo.**

B235 SP155 10g + 5g multi .35 .35
B236 SP155 20g + 10g multi .25 .25
B237 SP155 30g + 10g multi 3.25 3.00
B238 SP155 40g + 20g multi .65 .40
B239 SP155 45g + 20g multi .25 .25
B240 SP155 60g + 30g multi .25 .25
B241 SP155 75g + 35g multi .25 .25
B242 SP155 80g + 40g multi .25 .25
B243 SP155 1s + 50g multi .35 .35
B244 SP155 1.40s + 70g multi 1.60 1.60
Nos. B235-B244 (10) 7.45 6.95

Hans Makart — SP156

Designs: 20g+10g, Künstlerhaus, Vienna. 40g+20g, Carl Kundmann. 50g+25g, A. S. von Siccardsburg. 60g+30g, Hans Canon. 1s+50g, William Unger. 1.40s+70g, Friedrich von Schmidt.

1948, June 15 **Unwmk.** **Engr.**

B245 SP156 20g + 10g dp yel green 8.00 6.50
B246 SP156 30g + 15g dark brown 2.50 2.50
B247 SP156 40g + 20g ind 4.00 *5.50*
B248 SP156 50g + 25g dk vio 4.75 3.25
B249 SP156 60g + 30g dk red 5.50 3.25
B250 SP156 1s + 50g dk blue 5.50 5.50
B251 SP156 1.40s + 70g red brown 12.50 16.00
Nos. B245-B251 (7) 42.75 42.50

Kunstlerhaus, home of the leading Austrian Artists Association, 80th anniv.

St. Rupert — SP157

Designs: 30g+15g, Cathedral and Fountain. 40g+20g, Facade of Cathedral. 50g+25g, Cathedral from South. 60g+30g, Abbey of St. Peter. 80g+40g, Inside Cathedral. 1s+50g, Salzburg Cathedral and Castle. 1.40s+70g, Madonna by Michael Pacher.

1948, Aug. 6 ***Perf. 14x13½***

B252 SP157 20g + 10g dp grn 8.00 8.00
B253 SP157 30g + 15g red brn 2.50 *3.25*
B254 SP157 40g + 20g sl blk 2.75 *3.25*
B255 SP157 50g + 25g choc .40 .80
B256 SP157 60g + 30g dk red .40 .80
B257 SP157 80g + 40g dk brn vio .40 .80
B258 SP157 1s + 50g dp blue .80 .80
B259 SP157 1.40s + 70g dk grn 2.50 3.25
Nos. B252-B259 (8) 17.75 20.95

The surtax was to aid in the reconstruction of Salzburg Cathedral.

Easter — SP158

Designs: 60g+20g, St. Nicholas Day. 1s+25g, Birthday. 1.40s+35g, Christmas.

Inscribed: "Gluckliche Kindheit"

1949, Apr. 13 **Unwmk.**

B260 SP158 40g + 10g brn vio 16.00 18.00
B261 SP158 60g + 20g brn red 16.00 18.00
B262 SP158 1s + 25g dp ultra 16.00 18.00
B263 SP158 1.40s + 35g dk grn 16.00 18.00
Nos. B260-B263 (4) 64.00 72.00

The surtax was for Child Welfare.

Arms of Austria, 1230 — SP159

1949, Aug. 17 **Engr. & Photo.**

B264 SP159 40g + 10g 1230 9.50 9.50

Engraved and Typographed

B265 SP159 60g + 15g 1450 8.00 8.00
B266 SP159 1s + 25g 1600 8.00 8.00
B267 SP159 1.60s + 40g 1945 12.00 12.00
Nos. B264-B267 (4) 37.50 37.50

Surtax was for returned prisoners of war.

SP160

Laurel Branch, Stamps and Magnifier

1949, Dec. 3 **Engr.**
B268 SP160 60g + 15g dark red 3.25 2.75

Stamp Day, Dec. 3-4.

Arms of Austria and Carinthia SP161

Carinthian with Austrian Flag — SP162

Design: 1.70s+40g, Casting ballot.

1950, Oct. 10 **Photo.** ***Perf. 14x13½***
B269 SP161 60g + 15g 32.50 27.50
B270 SP162 1s + 25g 40.00 32.50
B271 SP162 1.70s + 40g 47.50 35.00
Nos. B269-B271 (3) 120.00 95.00

Plebiscite in Carinthia, 30th anniv.

Collector Examining Cover — SP163

1950, Dec. 2 **Engr.**
B272 SP163 60g + 15g blue grn 9.50 8.00

Stamp Day.

Miner and Mine — SP164

60g+15g, Mason holding brick and trowel. 1s+25g, Bridge builder with hook and chain. 1.70s+40g, Electrician, pole and insulators.

1951, Mar. 10 **Unwmk.**
B273 SP164 40g + 10g dark brown 16.00 14.50
B274 SP164 60g + 15g dk grn 12.00 14.50
B275 SP164 1s + 25g red brown 12.00 14.50
B276 SP164 1.70s + 40g vio bl 16.00 14.50
Nos. B273-B276 (4) 56.00 58.00

Issued to publicize Austrian reconstruction.

Laurel Branch and Olympic Circles SP165

1952, Jan. 26 ***Perf. 13½x14***
B277 SP165 2.40s + 60g grnsh black 20.00 20.00

The surtax was used to help defray expenses of Austria's athletes in the 1952 Olympic Games.

Cupid as Postman SP166

1952, Mar. 10 ***Perf. 14x13½***
B278 SP166 1.50s + 35g dark brn car 20.00 20.00

Stamp Day.

Sculpture, "Christ, The Almighty" SP167

1952, Sept. 6 ***Perf. 13½x14***
B279 SP167 1s + 25g grnsh gray 11.50 12.00

Austrian Catholic Conv., Vienna, 9/11-14.

Type of 1945-46 Ovptd. in Gold

1953, Aug. 29 **Unwmk.**
B280 A124 1s + 25g on 5s dl bl 2.50 2.50

60th anniv. of labor unions in Austria.

Bummerlhaus Steyr — SP168

Designs: 1s+25g, Johannes Kepler. 1.50s+40g, Lutheran Bible, 1st edition. 2.40s+60g, Theophil von Hansen. 3s+75g, Reconstructed Lutheran School, Vienna.

1953, Nov. 5 **Engr.** ***Perf. 14x13½***
B281 SP168 70g + 15g vio brn .25 .25
B282 SP168 1s + 25g dk gray blue .25 .25
B283 SP168 1.50s + 40g choc .80 .80
B284 SP168 2.40s + 60g dk grn 3.25 3.25
B285 SP168 3s + 75g dk pur 6.50 6.50
Nos. B281-B285 (5) 11.05 11.05

The surtax was used toward reconstruction of the Lutheran School, Vienna.

Globe and Philatelic Accessories SP169

1953, Dec. 5
B286 SP169 1s + 25g chocolate 6.50 6.50

Stamp Day.

Type of 1945-46 with Denomination Replaced by Asterisks

Overprinted in Brown

1954, Feb. 19 ***Perf. 13½x14***
B287 A124 1s + 20g blue gray .40 .50

Surtax for aid to avalanche victims.

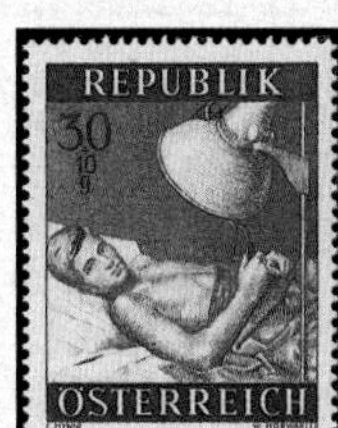

Patient Under Sun Lamp — SP170

Designs: 70g+15g, Physician using microscope. 1s+25g, Mother and children. 1.45s+35g, Operating room. 1.50s+35g, Baby on scale. 2.40s+60g, Nurse.

1954 **Engr.** ***Perf. 14x13½***
B288 SP170 30g + 10g pur 1.25 1.60
B289 SP170 70g + 15g dk brn .25 .25
B290 SP170 1s + 25g dk bl .25 .25
B291 SP170 1.45s + 35g dk bl green .55 .35
B292 SP170 1.50s + 35g dk red 5.50 5.50
B293 SP170 2.40s + 60g dk red brown 6.50 8.00
Nos. B288-B293 (6) 14.30 15.95

The surtax was for social welfare.

Early Vienna-Ulm Ferryboat SP171

1954, Dec. 4 ***Perf. 13½x14***
B294 SP171 1s + 25g dk gray grn 6.50 6.50

Stamp Day.

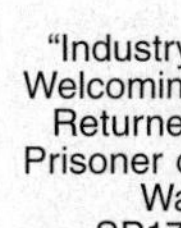

"Industry" Welcoming Returned Prisoner of War SP172

1955, June 29
B295 SP172 1s + 25g red brn 2.50 2.50

Surtax for returned prisoners of war and relatives of prisoners not yet released.

Collector Looking at Album — SP173

1955, Dec. 3 ***Perf. 14x13½***
B296 SP173 1s + 25g vio brn 4.00 4.00

Stamp Day. The surtax was for the promotion of Austrian philately.

Ornamental Shield and Letter — SP174

1956, Dec. 1 **Engr.**
B297 SP174 1s + 25g scarlet 3.25 3.25

Stamp Day. See note after No. B296.

Arms of Austria, 1945 — SP175

Engr. & Typo.

1956, Dec. 21 ***Perf. 14x13½***
B298 SP175 1.50s + 50g on 1.60s + 40g gray & red .65 .65

The surtax was for Hungarian refugees.

New Post Office, Linz 2 SP176

Design: 2.40s+60g, Post office, Kitzbuhel.

1957-58 **Engr.** ***Perf. 13½x14***
B299 SP176 1s + 25g dk sl grn 2.40 3.25
B300 SP176 2.40s + 60g blue .95 .95

Stamp Day. See note after B296. Issue dates: 1s, Nov. 30, 1957. 2.40s, Dec. 6, 1958. See No. B303.

Roman Carriage from Tomb at Maria Saal SP177

Litho. & Engr.

1959, Dec. 5 ***Perf. 13½x14***
B301 SP177 2.40s + 60g pale lil & blk .80 1.00

Stamp Day.

Progressive Die Proof under Magnifying Glass
SP178

1960, Dec. 2 Engr. *Perf. 13½x14*
B302 SP178 3s + 70g vio brn .95 .95

Stamp Day.

Post Office Type of 1957

Design: 3s+70g, Post Office, Rust.

1961, Dec. 1 Unwmk. *Perf. 13½*
B303 SP176 3s + 70g dk bl grn .95 .95

Stamp Day. See note after No. B296.

Hands of Stamp Engraver at Work
SP179

1962, Nov. 30 *Perf. 13½x14*
B304 SP179 3s + 70g dull pur 1.25 1.25

Stamp Day.

Railroad Exit, Post Office Vienna 101
SP180

1963, Nov. 29 Litho. & Engr.
B305 SP180 3s + 70g tan & blk .65 .65

Stamp Day.

View of Vienna, North
SP181

Designs: Various view of Vienna with compass indicating direction.

1964, July 20 Litho. *Perf. 13½x14*

B306	SP181 1.50s + 30g ("N")	.35	.40
B307	SP181 1.50s + 30g ("NO")	.35	.40
B308	SP181 1.50s + 30g ("O")	.35	.40
B309	SP181 1.50s + 30g ("SO")	.35	.40
B310	SP181 1.50s + 30g ("S")	.35	.40
B311	SP181 1.50s + 30g ("SW")	.35	.40
B312	SP181 1.50s + 30g ("W")	.35	.40
B313	SP181 1.50s + 30g ("NW")	.35	.40
	Nos. B306-B313 (8)	2.80	3.20

Vienna Intl. Phil. Exhib. (WIPA 1965).

Post Bus Terminal, St. Gilgen, Wolfgangsee — SP182

1964, Dec. 4 Unwmk. *Perf. 13½*
B314 SP182 3s + 70g multi .55 .55

Stamp Day.

Wall Painting, Tomb at Thebes — SP183

Development of Writing: 1.80s+50g, Cuneiform writing on stone tablet and man's head from Assyrian palace. 2.20s+60g, Wax tablet with Latin writing, Corinthian column. 3s+80g, Gothic writing on sealed letter, Gothic window from Munster Cathedral. 4s+1s, Letter with seal and postmark and upright desk. 5s+1.20s, Typewriter.

Litho. & Engr.

1965, June 4 *Perf. 14x13½*

B315	SP183 1.50s + 40g multi	.35	.35
B316	SP183 1.80s + 50g multi	.35	.35
B317	SP183 2.20s + 60g multi	.50	.50
B318	SP183 3s + 80g multi	.55	.55
B319	SP183 4s + 1s multi	.65	.65
B320	SP183 5s + 1.20s multi	.95	.95
	Nos. B315-B320 (6)	3.35	3.35

Vienna Intl. Phil. Exhib., WIPA, June 4-13.

Mailman Distributing Mail
SP184

1965, Dec. 3 Engr. *Perf. 13½x14*
B321 SP184 3s + 70g blue grn .50 .80

Stamp Day.

Letter Carrier, 16th Century — SP185

Litho. & Engr.

1966, Dec. 2 *Perf. 13½*
B322 SP185 3s + 70g multi .55 .55

Stamp Day. Design is from Ambras Heroes' Book, Austrian National Library.

Letter Carrier, 16th Century Playing Card — SP186

Engr. & Photo.

1967, Dec. 1 *Perf. 13x13½*
B323 SP186 3.50s + 80g multi .55 .80

Stamp Day.

Mercury, Bas-relief from Purkersdorf
SP187

1968, Nov. 29 Engr. *Perf. 13½*
B324 SP187 3.50s + 80g slate green .55 .80

Stamp Day.

Unken Post Station Sign, 1710 — SP188

Engr. & Photo.

1969, Dec. 5 *Perf. 12*
B325 SP188 3.50s + 80g tan, red & blk .55 1.20

Stamp Day. Design is from a watercolor by Friedrich Zeller.

Saddle, Bag, Harness and Post Horn — SP189

Engr. & Litho.

1970, Dec. 4 *Perf. 13½x14*
B326 SP189 3.50s + 80g gray blk & yel .55 1.20

Stamp Day.

"50 Years"
SP190

Engr. & Photo.

1971, Dec. 3 *Perf. 13½*
B327 SP190 4s + 1.50s gold & red brn .75 1.20

50th anniversary of the Federation of Austrian Philatelic Societies.

Local Post Carrier — SP191

1972, Dec. 1 Engr. *Perf. 14x13½*
B328 SP191 4s + 1s olive green .75 .65

Stamp Day.

Gabriel, by Lorenz Luchsperger, 15th Century — SP192

1973, Nov. 30
B329 SP192 4s + 1s maroon .65 1.10

Stamp Day.

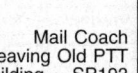

Mail Coach Leaving Old PTT Building — SP193

1974, Nov. 29 Engr. *Perf. 14x13½*
B330 SP193 4s + 2s violet blue .75 .75

Stamp Day.

Alpine Skiing, Women's
SP194

Designs: 1.50s+70g, Ice hockey. 2s+90g, Ski jump. 4s+1.90s, Bobsledding.

1975, Mar. 14 Photo. *Perf. 13½x14*

B331	SP194 1s + 50g multi	.25	.25
B332	SP194 1.50s + 70g multi	.25	.25
B333	SP194 2s + 90g multi	.40	.40
B334	SP194 4s + 1.90s multi	.80	.80
	Nos. B331-B334 (4)	1.70	1.70

1975, Nov. 14

Designs: 70g+30g, Figure skating, pair. 2s+1s, Cross-country skiing. 2.50s+1s, Luge. 4s+2s, Biathlon.

B335	SP194 70g + 30g multi	.25	.40
B336	SP194 2s + 1s multi	.40	.65
B337	SP194 2.50s + 1s multi	.40	.65
B338	SP194 4s + 2s multi	.75	1.20
	Nos. B335-B338 (4)	1.80	2.90

12th Winter Olympic Games, Innsbruck, Feb. 4-15, 1976.

Austria Nos. 5, 250, 455 — SP195

Photo. & Engr.

1975, Nov. 28 *Perf. 14*
B339 SP195 4s + 2s multi .75 1.20

Stamp Day; 125th anniv. of Austrian stamps.

Postilion's Gala Hat and Horn
SP196

1976, Dec. 3 *Perf. 13½x14*
B340 SP196 6s + 2s blk & lt vio 1.10 1.00

Stamp Day.

Emanuel Herrmann
SP197

1977, Dec. 2 *Perf. 14x13½*
B341 SP197 6s + 2s multi 1.25 1.10

Stamp Day. Emanuel Herrmann (1839-1902), economist, invented postal card. Austria issued first postal card in 1869.

Post Bus, 1913
SP198

1978, Dec. 1 Photo. *Perf. 13½x14*
B342 SP198 10s + 5s multi 2.00 1.20

Stamp Day.

Heroes' Square, Vienna
SP199

Photo. & Engr.

1979, Nov. 30 *Perf. 13½*
B343 SP199 16s + 8s multi 3.00 2.40

No. B343 Inscribed "2. Phase"

1980, Nov. 21
B344 SP199 16s + 8s multi 3.25 2.40

Souvenir Sheet

1981, Feb. 20
B345 SP199 16s + 8s multi 2.75 2.75

WIPA 1981 Phil. Exhib., Vienna, May 22-31. No. B345 contains one stamp without inscription.

Mainz-Weber Mailbox, 1870 — SP200

1982, Nov. 26 Photo. & Engr.
B346 SP200 6s + 3s multi 1.40 1.25

Stamp Day.

Boy Examining Cover
SP201

Photo. & Engr.

1983, Oct. 21 *Perf. 14*
B347 SP201 6s + 3s multi 1.25 1.00

Stamp Day. See Nos. B349-B352, B354-B355.

World Winter Games for the Handicapped — SP202

1984, Jan. 5 Photo. *Perf. 13½x13*
B348 SP202 4s + 2s Downhill skier .75 .75

Stamp Day Type of 1983

Designs: No. B349, Seschemnofer III burial chamber detail, pyramid of Cheops, Gizeh. No. B350, Roman messenger on horseback. No. B351, Nuremberg messenger, 16th cent. No. B352, *The Postmaster* (detail), 1841, lithograph by Carl Schuster.

1984-87 Photo. & Engr. *Perf. 14*
B349 SP201 6s + 3s multi 1.25 1.10
B350 SP201 6s + 3s multi 1.25 1.00
B351 SP201 6s + 3s multi 1.25 1.00
B352 SP201 6s + 3s multi 1.25 1.10
Nos. B349-B352 (4) 5.00 4.20

Issued: No. B349, 11/30/84; No. B350, 11/28/85; No. B351, 11/28/86; No. B352, 11/19/87.

4th World Winter Sports Championships for the Disabled, Innsbruck — SP203

1988, Jan. 15 Photo. *Perf. 13½*
B353 SP203 5s + 2.50s multi 1.40 1.10

Stamp Day Type of 1983

Designs: No. B354, Railway mail car. No. B355, Hansa-Brandenburg CI mail plane.

1988-89 Photo. & Engr. *Perf. 14*
B354 SP201 6s +3s multi 1.75 1.40
B355 SP201 6s +3s multi 1.75 1.40

Issued: No. B354, Nov. 17; No. B355, May 24, 1989.

Stamp Day — SP204

1990, May 25 Photo. *Perf. 13½*
B356 SP204 7s +3s multi 1.75 1.40

SP205

1991, May 29 Photo. & Engr.
B357 SP205 7s +3s B & P 1.75 1.75

1992, May 22
B358 SP205 7s +3s R & H 1.75 1.75

1993, May 5
B359 SP205 7s +3s I & I 1.75 1.75

1994, May 27
B360 SP205 7s +3s E & L 1.90 1.90

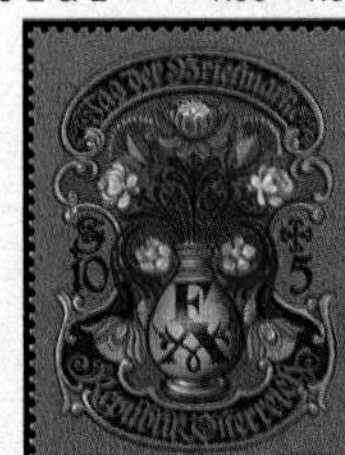
SP205a

1995, May 26
B361 SP205a 10s +5s F & A 2.40 2.40

1996, May 17
B362 SP205a 10s +5s M & T 2.60 2.60
Nos. B357-B362,1725,1765,1791 (9) 16.05 14.95

Stamp Day. The 1st letters spell "Briefmarke," the 2nd "Philatelie."
For "A" & "E," see No. 1725; "R" & "L," No. 1765; "K" & "I," No. 1791; "E" & "E," No. 1818.

Special Olympics Winter Games
SP206

1993, Mar. 19 Photo. *Perf. 13½x14*
B367 SP206 6s +3s multi 1.90 1.90

Vienna Intl. Postage Stamp Exhibition (WIPA), 2000 — SP207

Designs: No. B368, #5, postman on bicycle. No. B369, #339, early mail truck. No. B370, #525, airplane, service vehicles.

1997-2000 Photo. & Engr. *Perf. 14*
B368 SP207 27s +13s multi 7.00 7.00
B369 SP207 32s +13s multi 8.00 8.00
B370 SP207 32s +16s multi 9.00 9.00
a. Souvenir sheet, #B368-B370 + label 30.00 30.00
Nos. B368-B370 (3) 24.00 24.00

Stamps from No. B370a are dated "2000."
Issued: No. B368, 5/23; No. B369, 11/6/98; No. B370, 9/17/99. No. B370a, 2000.

Stamp Day — SP208

Designs: No. B372, 1919 Mail car. No. B373, Siemens M 320 mail wagon, 1987. No B374, Oeffag C II mail plane. No. B375, Junkers F13 airplane.

Photo. & Engr.

2001, May 18 *Perf. 13¾*
B371 SP208 20s +10s multi + label 8.50 8.50

2002, May 24
B372 SP208 €1.60 +80c multi + label 7.25 7.25

2003, May 23
B373 SP208 €2.54 +€1.26 multi + label 11.50 11.50

2004, May 7
B374 SP208 €2.65 +€1.30 multi + label 12.00 12.00

2005, May 27
B375 SP208 265c +130c multi + label 12.00 12.00

See No. B377.

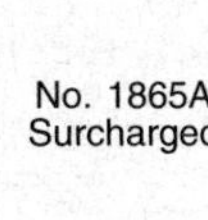

No. 1865A Surcharged

2006, Apr. 21 Photo. *Perf. 13¾x14*
B376 A1090 75c +425c on 25c #1865A 11.00 11.00

Surtax was for flood relief. Standing order customers were able to purchase this stamp for the 75c franking value.

Stamp Day Type of 2001

Design: Airbus A310-300.

Photo. & Engr.

2006, July 2 *Perf. 13¾*
B377 SP208 265c +130c multi + label 10.00 10.00

Printed in sheets of 5 stamps + 5 labels.

Ferris Wheel, Vienna
SP209

2006, Aug. 26 Photo. *Perf. 13¾*
B378 SP209 55c +20c multi 2.25 2.25
a. Inscribed "OSTERREICH" (from #B382a) 2.25 2.25

2008 Vienna Intl. Stamp Exhibition (WIPA), Vienna. See No. 2137a.
No. B378 is inscribed "Osterrreich."

German and Austrian Philatelic Exhibition, Bad Reichenhall
SP210

2006, Oct. 6 Photo. *Perf. 14¼x14*
B379 SP210 55c +20c multi 2.25 2.25

Gloriette, Schönbrunn Palace — SP211

2007, Mar. 16 Photo. *Perf. 13¾*
B380 SP211 55c +20c multi 2.25 2.25

2008 Vienna Intl. Stamp Exhibition (WIPA). See No. 2137b.

Steamer Wien
SP212

2007, June 15
B381 SP212 265c +130c multi 11.50 11.50

Stamp Day.

St. Stephen's Cathedral, Vienna — SP213

2008, Jan. 18 Photo. *Perf. 13¾*
B382 SP213 55c +20c multi 2.25 2.25
a. Souvenir sheet, #B378, B380, B382 7.25 7.25

2008 Vienna Intl. Stamp Exhibition (WIPA). See No. 2137c.
No. B382a issued 9/18.

Paddle-wheel Steamer Schönbrunn — SP214

2008, Sept. 18	**Photo.**	***Perf. 13¾***		
B383 SP214	265c +130c multi		11.50	11.50

Stamp Day.

MS Osterreich SP215

2009, Sept. 11	**Litho.**	***Perf. 13¾***		
B384 SP215	265c +130c multi		11.50	11.50

Stamp Day.

Gmunden SP216

2010, Aug. 27	**Litho.**	***Perf. 13¾***		
B385 SP216	265c +130c multi		10.50	10.50

Stamp Day.

Graz SP217

2011, May 13		***Perf. 13¾***		
B386 SP217	272c+136c multi		11.50	11.50

Stamp Day.

Federation of Austrian Philatelist Societies, 90th Anniv. — SP218

2011, Sept. 10		***Perf. 14¼x14***		
B387 SP218	62c+20c multi		2.25	2.25

Breast Cancer Research SP219

2011, Sept. 28		***Perf. 13¾***		
B388 SP219	90c+10c multi		2.75	2.75

Surtax for Austrian Cancer Aid Society.

Karlsplatz SP220

2012, May 11				
B389 SP220	272c +136c multi		10.50	10.50

Stamp Day.

Winning Drawing in "Children for Integration" Stamp Design Contest SP221

2012, Aug. 31				
B390 SP221	62c +20c multi		2.10	2.10

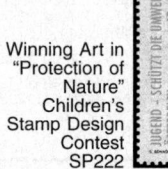

Winning Art in "Protection of Nature" Children's Stamp Design Contest SP222

2013, June 13				
B391 SP222	62c +20c multi		2.25	2.25

Salzburg SP223

2013, Aug. 22				
B392 SP223	282c+141c multi		11.50	11.50

Stamp Day.

AIR POST STAMPS

Issues of the Monarchy

Types of Regular Issue of 1916 Surcharged

1918, Mar. 30	**Unwmk.**	***Perf. 12½***		
C1	A40	1.50k on 2k lilac	1.60	*7.50*
C2	A40	2.50k on 3k ocher	10.50	*32.50*
a.		Inverted surcharge	*1,200.*	
		Never hinged	2,400.	
b.		Perf. 11½	725.00	*1,100.*
		Never hinged	1,600.	
c.		Perf. 12½x11½	65.00	*140.00*
		Never hinged	160.00	

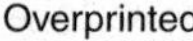
Overprinted

C3	A40	4k gray	4.75	*20.00*
		Nos. C1-C3 (3)	16.85	*60.00*
		Set, never hinged	40.00	

Exist imperf, without gum. Value, set $450.

Nos. C1-C3 also exist without surcharge or overprint. Values, set perf unused hinged $475, never hinged $1,050. Values, set imperf, unused hinged $425, never hinged $850.

Nos. C1-C3 were printed on grayish and on white paper. See the *Scott Classic Specialized Catalogue of Stamps and Covers* for detailed listing.

A 7k on 10k red brown was prepared but not regularly issued. Values: perf, $650 unused hinged, $1,600 never hinged; imperf, without gum, $1,050.

Issues of the Republic

Hawk — AP1

Wilhelm Kress — AP2

1922-24		**Typo.**	***Perf. 12½***	
C4	AP1	300k claret	.35	.35
C5	AP1	400k green ('24)	5.00	4.75
C6	AP1	600k bister	.25	.25
C7	AP1	900k brn orange	.25	.25
		Engr.		
C8	AP2	1200k brn violet	.25	.25
C9	AP2	2400k slate	.25	.25
C10	AP2	3000k dp brn ('23)	3.25	2.75
C11	AP2	4800k dark bl ('23)	2.75	2.75
		Nos. C4-C11 (8)	12.35	11.60
		Set, never hinged	29.00	

Values for used are for stamps with philatelic favor cancels. Postally used value, set $45.

Set exists imperf. Values, set unused hinged $350, never hinged $500.

Plane and Pilot's Head — AP3

Airplane Passing Crane — AP4

1925-30		**Typo.**	***Perf. 12½***	
C12	AP3	2g gray brown	.40	.40
C13	AP3	5g red	.40	.40
a.		Horiz. pair, imperf. btwn.	800.00	
		Never hinged	1,250.	
C14	AP3	6g dark blue	.80	.80
C15	AP3	8g yel green	.80	.80
C16	AP3	10g dp org ('26)	.80	.80
a.		Horiz. pair, imperf. btwn.	800.00	
		Never hinged	1,250.	
C17	AP3	15g red vio ('26)	.40	.40
a.		Horiz. pair, imperf. btwn.	800.00	
		Never hinged	1,250.	
C18	AP3	20g org brn ('30)	11.00	11.00
C19	AP3	25g blk vio ('30)	4.75	4.75
C20	AP3	30g bister ('26)	8.00	8.00
C21	AP3	50g bl gray ('26)	13.50	13.50
C22	AP3	80g dk grn ('30)	2.40	2.40
		Photo.		
C23	AP4	10g orange red	.80	.80
a.		Horiz. pair, imperf. btwn.	800.00	
		Never hinged	1,250.	
C24	AP4	15g claret	.80	.80
C25	AP4	30g brn violet	.80	.80
C26	AP4	50g gray black	.80	.80
C27	AP4	1s deep blue	8.00	8.00
C28	AP4	2s dark green	1.60	1.60
a.		Vertical pair, imperf. btwn.	800.00	
		Never hinged	1,250.	
C29	AP4	3s red brn ('26)	52.50	52.50
C30	AP4	5s indigo ('26)	13.50	13.50
		Size: 25½x32mm		
C31	AP4	10s blk brown, *gray* ('26)	8.00	8.00
		Nos. C12-C31 (20)	130.05	130.05
		Set, never hinged	325.00	

Values for used are for stamps with philatelic favor cancels. Postally used value, set $200.

Exists imperf. Values, set unused hinged $850, never hinged $1,100.

Airplane over Güssing Castle — AP5

Airplane over the Danube — AP6

Designs (each includes plane): 10g, Maria-Worth. 15g, Durnstein. 20g, Hallstatt. 25g, Salzburg. 30g, Upper Dachstein and Schladminger Glacier. 40g, Lake Wetter. 50g, Arlberg. 60g, St. Stephen's Cathedral. 80g, Church of the Minorites. 2s, Railroad viaduct, Carinthia. 3s, Gross Glockner mountain. 5s, Aerial railway. 10s, Seaplane and yachts.

1935, Aug. 16		**Engr.**	***Perf. 12½***	
C32	AP5	5g rose violet	.25	.25
C33	AP5	10g red orange	.25	.25
C34	AP5	15g yel green	.80	.80
C35	AP5	20g gray blue	.25	.25
C36	AP5	25g violet brn	.25	.25
C37	AP5	30g brn orange	.25	.25
C38	AP5	40g gray green	.25	.25
C39	AP5	50g light sl bl	.25	.25
C40	AP5	60g black brn	.35	.35
C41	AP5	80g light brown	.40	.40
C42	AP6	1s rose red	.35	.35
C43	AP6	2s olive green	2.40	2.00
C44	AP6	3s yellow brn	12.00	8.00
C45	AP6	5s dark green	4.00	2.75
C46	AP6	10s slate blue	52.50	52.50
		Nos. C32-C46 (15)	74.55	68.90
		Set, never hinged	150.00	

Values for used are for stamps with philatelic favor cancels. Postally used value, set $175.

Set exists imperf. Values, set unused hinged $375, never hinged $475.

Catalogue values for unused stamps in this section, from this point to the end of the section, are for Never Hinged items.

Windmill, Neusiedler Lake Shore — AP20

1s, Roman arch, Carnuntum. 2s, Town Hall, Gmund. 3s, Schieder Lake, Hinterstoder. 4s, Praegraten, Eastern Tyrol. 5s, Torsäule, Salzburg. 10s, St. Charles Church, Vienna.

1947		**Unwmk.**	***Perf. 14x13½***	
C47	AP20	50g black brown	.40	.40
C48	AP20	1s dark brn vio	.40	.40
C49	AP20	2s dark green	.40	.40
C50	AP20	3s chocolate	2.40	2.40
C51	AP20	4s dark green	2.00	2.00
C52	AP20	5s dark blue	2.00	2.00
C53	AP20	10s dark blue	.80	.80
		Nos. C47-C53 (7)	8.40	8.40

Used values for examples with philatelic favor cancels. Postally used value, set $27.50.

Rooks
AP27

Birds: 1s, Barn swallows. 2s, Blackheaded gulls. 3s, Great cormorants. 5s, Buzzard. 10s, Gray heron. 20s, Golden eagle.

1950-53 *Perf. 13½x14*
C54 AP27 60g dark bl vio 1.60 1.60
C55 AP27 1s dark vio blue ('53) 16.00 16.00
C56 AP27 2s dark blue 12.50 9.50
C57 AP27 3s dk slate green ('53) 120.00 95.00
C58 AP27 5s red brn ('53) 120.00 95.00
C59 AP27 10s gray vio ('53) 52.50 47.50
C60 AP27 20s brn blk ('52) 10.00 8.50
Nos. C54-C60 (7) 332.60 273.10
Set, hinged 190.00

Value at lower left on Nos. C59 and C60.
No. C60 exists imperf.

Etrich "Dove" AP28

Designs: 3.50s, Twin-engine jet airliner. 5s, Four-engine jet airliner.

1968, May 31 **Engr.** *Perf. 13½x14*
C61 AP28 2s olive bister .35 .35
C62 AP28 3.50s slate green .55 .65
C63 AP28 5s dark blue 1.10 1.40
Nos. C61-C63 (3) 2.00 2.40

IFA WIEN 1968 (International Air Post Exhibition), Vienna, May 30-June 4.

POSTAGE DUE STAMPS

Issues of the Monarchy

D1

D2

Perf. 10 to 13½
1894-95 **Typo.** **Wmk. 91**
J1 D1 1kr brown 2.00 1.25
a. Perf. 13½ 45.00 62.50
b. Half used as ½kr on cover 80.00
J2 D1 2kr brown ('95) 2.75 2.40
a. Pair, imperf. btwn. 200.00 300.00
b. Half used as 1kr on cover 200.00
J3 D1 3kr brown 3.25 1.25
a. Half used as 1½kr on cover 160.00
J4 D1 5kr brown 3.25 .80
a. Perf. 13½ 25.00 25.00
b. Pair, imperf. btwn. 160.00 *250.00*
J5 D1 6kr brown ('95) 2.75 *6.50*
a. Half used as 3kr on cover 200.00
J6 D1 7kr brown ('95) .80 *6.00*
a. Vert. pair, imperf. btwn. 275.00 *550.00*
b. Horiz. pair, imperf. btwn. 275.00 *550.00*
J7 D1 10kr brown 4.75 .95
a. Half used as 5kr on cover 140.00
J8 D1 20kr brown .80 *6.00*
J9 D1 50kr brown 35.00 72.50
Nos. J1-J9 (9) 55.35 97.65

Values for Nos. J1-J9 are for stamps that do not show the watermark. Stamps showing the watermark often sell for more.
See Nos. J204-J231.

1899-1900 *Imperf.*
J10 D2 1h brown .25 *.40*
J11 D2 2h brown .25 *.55*
J12 D2 3h brown ('00) .25 *.40*
J13 D2 4h brown 2.00 2.00
J14 D2 5h brown ('00) 1.60 *1.25*
J15 D2 6h brown .25 *.50*
J16 D2 10h brown .25 *.50*
J17 D2 12h brown .35 *2.40*
J18 D2 15h brown .35 *1.60*
J19 D2 20h brown 24.00 4.75
J20 D2 40h brown 2.40 *2.60*
J21 D2 100h brown 4.75 3.25
Nos. J10-J21 (12) 36.70 20.20

Perf. 10½, 12½, 13½ and Compound
J22 D2 1h brown .55 .25
J23 D2 2h brown .40 .25
J24 D2 3h brown ('00) .40 .25
J25 D2 4h brown .65 .25
J26 D2 5h brown ('00) .55 .25
J27 D2 6h brown .40 .25
J28 D2 10h brown .55 .25
J29 D2 12h brown .55 .75
J30 D2 15h brown .80 .80
J31 D2 20h brown .95 .25
J32 D2 40h brown 1.25 .75
J33 D2 100h brown 24.00 2.00
Nos. J22-J33 (12) 31.05 6.30

Nos. J10-J33 exist on unwmkd. paper.
For surcharges see Offices in the Turkish Empire Nos. J1-J5.

D3

Ordinary Thin Paper
1910-13 **Unwmk.** *Perf. 12½*
J34 D3 1h carmine .80 *1.60*
J35 D3 2h carmine .50 .35
d. Half used as 1h on cover 95.00
J36 D3 4h carmine .50 .25
c. Half used as 2h on cover 95.00
J37 D3 6h carmine .50 .25
J38 D3 10h carmine .50 .25
c. Half used as 5h on cover 47.50
J39 D3 14h carmine ('13) 4.00 2.75
J40 D3 20h carmine 8.00 .25
c. Half used as 10h on cover 95.00
J41 D3 25h carmine ('10) 8.00 6.50
J42 D3 30h carmine 8.00 .35
J43 D3 50h carmine 12.00 .40
J44 D3 100h carmine 16.00 .80
Never hinged 65.00
Nos. J34-J44 (11) 62.60 17.90

All values exist on ordinary paper, Nos. J34-J38, J40, J42-J44 on chalky paper and Nos. J34-J38, J40, J44 on thin ordinary paper. In most cases, values are for the least expensive stamp of the types. Some of the expensive types sell for considerably more.
All values exist imperf.
See Offices in the Turkish Empire type D3.

1911, July 16
J45 D3 5k violet 80.00 12.50
J46 D3 10k violet 240.00 4.00

Nos. J45-J46 exist imperf. Value set: unused hinged $900; never hinged $1,200.

Regular Issue of 1908 Overprinted or Surcharged in Carmine or Black

a

b

1916, Oct. 21
J47 A22 1h gray (C) .25 .25
a. Pair, one without overprint 210.00
Never hinged 300.00
J48 A22 15h on 2h vio (Bk) .25 *.55*
a. Inverted surcharge 400.00
Never hinged 750.00
Set, never hinged 1.60

D4

D5

Perf. 12½, 12½x13 (#J57-J59)
1916, Oct. 1
J49 D4 5h rose red .25 .25
J50 D4 10h rose red .25 .25
a. Half used as 5h on cover 65.00
J51 D4 15h rose red .25 .25
J52 D4 20h rose red .25 .25
J53 D4 25h rose red .25 *.95*
J54 D4 30h rose red .25 *.40*
a. Half used as 15h on cover 160.00
J55 D4 40h rose red .25 *.40*
a. Half used as 20h on cover 140.00
J56 D4 50h rose red .95 *3.25*
J57 D5 1k ultramarine .25 *.40*
a. Horiz. pair, imperf. btwn. 250.00 *550.00*
Never hinged 550.00
J58 D5 5k ultramarine 2.75 *3.25*
J59 D5 10k ultramarine 3.50 1.60
Nos. J49-J59 (11) 9.20 *11.25*
Set, never hinged 32.50

Exists imperf. Value set: unused hinged $150, never hinged $400.
For overprints see J64-J74, Western Ukraine Nos. 54-55, NJ1-NJ6, Poland Nos. J1-J10.

Type of Regular Issue of 1916 Surcharged

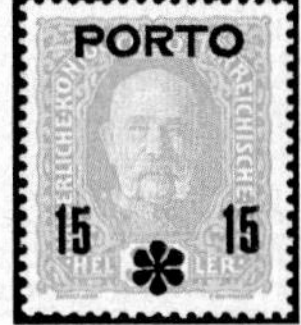

1917
J60 A38 10h on 24h blue 1.60 .55
J61 A38 15h on 36h violet .50 .25
J62 A38 20h on 54h orange .25 *.40*
J63 A38 50h on 42h chocolate .35 .35
Nos. J60-J63 (4) 2.70 1.55
Set, never hinged 14.00

All values of this issue are known imperforate, also without surcharge, perforated and imperforate. Values, set imperf unused hinged $160, never hinged $250. Value of set without surcharge imperf unused hinged $200, never hinged $350. Same values for set without surcharge, perf 12½.
For overprints see Western Ukraine Nos. 57-58.

Issues of the Republic

Postage Due Stamps of 1916 Overprinted

1919
J64 D4 5h rose red .25 .25
a. Inverted overprint 250.00 325.00
Never hinged 325.00
J65 D4 10h rose red .25 .25
J66 D4 15h rose red .25 *.40*
J67 D4 20h rose red .25 *.40*
J68 D4 25h rose red 8.00 *27.50*
J69 D4 30h rose red .25 *.40*
J70 D4 40h rose red .25 *.80*
J71 D4 50h rose red .30 *1.25*
J72 D5 1k ultramarine 4.50 *16.00*
J73 D5 5k ultramarine 8.75 *16.00*
J74 D5 10k ultramarine 10.50 4.00
Nos. J64-J74 (11) 33.55 *67.25*
Set, never hinged 100.00

Nos. J64, J65, J67, J70 exist imperf. Value, 4 values hinged $325.

D6

D7

1920-21 *Perf. 12½*
J75 D6 5h bright red .25 *.35*
J76 D6 10h bright red .25 .25
J77 D6 15h bright red .25 *1.60*
J78 D6 20h bright red .25 .25
J79 D6 25h bright red .25 *1.60*
J80 D6 30h bright red .25 *.35*
J81 D6 40h bright red .25 *.35*
J82 D6 50h bright red .25 *.35*
J83 D6 80h bright red .25 *.45*
J84 D7 1k ultramarine .25 .35
J85 D7 1½k ultra ('21) .25 .35
J86 D7 2k ultra ('21) .25 .35
J87 D7 3k ultra ('21) .25 *.95*
J88 D7 4k ultra ('21) .25 *.95*
J89 D7 5k ultramarine .25 .35
J90 D7 8k ultra ('21) .25 *.95*
J91 D7 10k ultramarine .25 *.45*
J92 D7 20k ultra ('21) .30 *2.00*
Nos. J75-J92 (18) *12.25*
Set, never hinged 4.75

Nos. J84-J92 exist on white paper and on grayish white paper. Values are for the cheaper varieties. See the *Scott Classic Specialized Catalogue* for detailed listings.
Nos. J84 to J92 exist imperf. Values, set unused hinged $150, never hinged $250.

Imperf
J93 D6 5h bright red .25 *.65*
J94 D6 10h bright red .25 *.40*
J95 D6 15h bright red .25 *1.60*
J96 D6 20h bright red .25 *.40*
J97 D6 25h bright red .25 *1.60*
J98 D6 30h bright red .25 *1.25*
J99 D6 40h bright red .25 *.65*
J100 D6 50h bright red .25 *1.10*
J101 D6 80h bright red .25 *.85*
Nos. J93-J101 (9) *8.50*
Set, never hinged 3.25

No. 207a Surcharged in Dark Blue

1921, Dec. *Perf. 12½*
J102 A43 7½k on 15h bister .25 *.25*
Never hinged .25
a. Inverted surcharge 450.00 *500.00*

D8

1922
J103 D8 1k reddish buff .25 *.35*
J104 D8 2k reddish buff .25 *.40*
J105 D8 4k reddish buff .25 *.65*
J106 D8 5k reddish buff .25 *.35*
J107 D8 7½k reddish buff .25 *1.20*
J108 D8 10k blue green .25 *.50*
J109 D8 15k blue green .25 *.75*
J110 D8 20k blue green .25 *.55*
J111 D8 25k blue green .25 *1.25*
J112 D8 40k blue green .25 *.40*
J113 D8 50k blue green .25 *1.25*
Nos. J103-J113 (11) *7.65*
Set, never hinged 5.25

Issue date: Nos. J108-J113, June 2.

D9

D10

1922-24
J114 D9 10k cobalt blue .25 *.40*
J115 D9 15k cobalt blue .25 *.55*
J116 D9 20k cobalt blue .25 *.55*
J117 D9 50k cobalt blue .25 *.55*
J118 D10 100k plum .25 .25
J119 D10 150k plum .25 .25
J120 D10 200k plum .25 .25
J121 D10 400k plum .25 .25
J122 D10 600k plum ('23) .25 *.40*
J123 D10 800k plum .25 .25
J124 D10 1,000k plum ('23) .25 .25
J125 D10 1,200k plum ('23) 1.00 *4.75*
J126 D10 1,500k plum ('24) .25 *.80*
J127 D10 1,800k plum ('24) 3.25 *12.00*
J128 D10 2,000k plum ('23) .40 *1.60*
J129 D10 3,000k plum ('24) 5.50 *24.00*
J130 D10 4,000k plum ('24) 3.25 *20.00*
J131 D10 6,000k plum ('24) 3.25 *27.50*
Nos. J114-J131 (18) 19.65 *94.60*
Set, never hinged 70.00

J103-J131 sets exist imperf. Values, both sets unused hinged $450, never hinged $650.

D11

D12

1925-34 ***Perf. 12½***

J132 D11 1g red .25 .25
J133 D11 2g red .25 .25
J134 D11 3g red .25 .25
J135 D11 4g red .25 .25
J136 D11 5g red ('27) .25 .25
J137 D11 6g red .25 *.25*
J138 D11 8g red .25 .25
J139 D11 10g dark blue .25 .25
J140 D11 12g dark blue .25 .25
J141 D11 14g dark blue ('27) .25 .25
J142 D11 15g dark blue .25 .25
J143 D11 16g dark blue ('29) .25 .25
J144 D11 18g dark blue ('34) 1.25 *2.75*
J145 D11 20g dark blue .25 .25
J146 D11 23g dark blue .40 .25
J147 D11 24g dark blue ('32) 1.60 .25
J148 D11 28g dark blue ('27) 1.60 .25
J149 D11 30g dark blue .25 .25
J150 D11 31g dark blue ('29) 1.25 .25
J151 D11 35g dark blue ('30) 1.25 .25
J152 D11 39g dark blue ('32) 1.60 .25
J153 D11 40g dark blue 2.00 *2.50*
J154 D11 60g dark blue 2.00 2.00
J155 D12 1s dark green 2.75 1.25
J156 D12 2s dark green 25.00 4.00
J157 D12 5s dark green 87.50 45.00
J158 D12 10s dark green 35.00 8.00
Nos. J132-J158 (27) 166.70 70.50
Set, never hinged 575.00

Issues of 1925-27 exist imperf. Values, set of 18 unused hinged $600, never hinged $800.

Issued: 3g, 2s-10s, Dec; 5g, 28g, 1/1; 14g, June; 31g, 2/1; 35g, Jan; 24g, 39g, Sept; 16g, May; 18g, 6/25; others, 6/1.

Coat of Arms
D13 D14

1935, June 1

J159 D13 1g red .25 .25
J160 D13 2g red .25 .25
J161 D13 3g red .25 .25
J162 D13 5g red .25 .25
J163 D13 10g blue .25 .25
J164 D13 12g blue .25 .25
J165 D13 15g blue .25 *.50*
J166 D13 20g blue .25 .25
J167 D13 24g blue .25 .25
J168 D13 30g blue .25 .25
J169 D13 39g blue .35 .25
J170 D13 60g blue .50 *1.25*
J171 D14 1s green .80 .35
J172 D14 2s green 1.50 1.00
J173 D14 5s green 3.00 *4.00*
J174 D14 10s green 4.75 .65
Nos. J159-J174 (16) 13.40 10.25
Set, never hinged 55.00

On Nos. J163-J170, background lines are horiz.

Nos. J159-J174 exist imperf. Values, set unused hinged $160, never hinged $350.

Catalogue values for unused stamps in this section, from this point to the end of the section, are for Never Hinged items.

D15

1945 Unwmk. Typo. ***Perf. 10½***

J175 D15 1g vermilion .25 *.25*
J176 D15 2g vermilion .25 *.25*
J177 D15 3g vermilion .25 .25
J178 D15 5g vermilion .25 .25
J179 D15 10g vermilion .25 .25
J180 D15 12g vermilion .25 .25
J181 D15 20g vermilion .25 .25
J182 D15 24g vermilion .25 *.40*
J183 D15 30g vermilion .25 *.40*
J184 D15 60g vermilion .25 *.40*
J185 D15 1s violet .25 *.40*
J186 D15 2s violet .25 *.80*
J187 D15 5s violet .25 *.80*
J188 D15 10s violet .25 *.80*
Nos. J175-J188 (14) 3.50 *5.75*

Issued: 1g-60g, Sept. 10; 1s-10s, Sept. 24.

Occupation Stamps of the Allied Military Government Overprinted in Black

1946 ***Perf. 11***

J189 OS1 3g deep orange .25 .25
J190 OS1 5g bright green .25 .25
J191 OS1 6g red violet .25 .25
J192 OS1 8g rose pink .25 .25
J193 OS1 10g light gray .25 .25
J194 OS1 12g pale buff brown .25 .25
J195 OS1 15g rose red .25 .25
J196 OS1 20g copper brown .25 .25
J197 OS1 25g deep blue .25 .25
J198 OS1 30g bright violet .25 .25
J199 OS1 40g light ultra .25 .25
J200 OS1 60g light olive grn .25 .25
J201 OS1 1s dark violet .25 .25
J202 OS1 2s yellow .50 *.80*
J203 OS1 5s deep ultra .50 *.80*
Nos. J189-J203 (15) 4.25 4.85

Nos. J189-J203 were issued by the Renner Government. Inverted overprints exist on about half of the denominations.

Issued: 3g-60g, Apr. 23; 1s-5s, May 20.

Type of 1894-95
Inscribed "Republik Osterreich"

1947 Typo. ***Perf. 14***

J204 D1 1g chocolate .25 .40
J205 D1 2g chocolate .25 .40
J206 D1 3g chocolate .25 .40
J207 D1 5g chocolate .25 .25
J208 D1 8g chocolate .25 .25
J209 D1 10g chocolate .25 .40
J210 D1 12g chocolate .25 .25
J211 D1 15g chocolate .25 .25
J212 D1 16g chocolate .30 *.95*
J213 D1 17g chocolate .30 *.95*
J214 D1 18g chocolate .30 *.95*
J215 D1 20g chocolate .75 .25
J216 D1 24g chocolate .35 *.95*
J217 D1 30g chocolate .25 *.25*
J218 D1 36g chocolate .75 *1.40*
J219 D1 40g chocolate .25 .25
J220 D1 42g chocolate .80 *1.40*
J221 D1 48g chocolate .80 *1.40*
J222 D1 50g chocolate .75 .35
J223 D1 60g chocolate .25 *.35*
J224 D1 70g chocolate .25 .35
J225 D1 80g chocolate 4.50 1.60
J226 D1 1s blue .25 .35
J227 D1 1.15s blue 3.25 .50
J228 D1 1.20s blue 3.25 1.25
J229 D1 2s blue .35 .35
J230 D1 5s blue .35 .35
J231 D1 10s blue .40 .40
Nos. J204-J231 (28) 20.45 17.20

Issue dates: 1g, 20g, 50g, 80g, 1.15s, 1.20s, Sept. 25, others, Aug. 14.

D16

1949-57

J232 D16 1g carmine .35 .25
J233 D16 2g carmine .35 .25
J234 D16 4g carmine ('51) .50 .35
J235 D16 5g carmine 1.90 .40
J236 D16 8g carmine ('51) 1.90 1.60
J237 D16 10g carmine .35 .25
J238 D16 20g carmine .35 .25
J239 D16 30g carmine .35 .25
J240 D16 40g carmine .35 .25
J241 D16 50g carmine .35 .25
J242 D16 60g carmine ('50) 10.50 .40
J243 D16 63g carmine ('57) 4.75 3.50
J244 D16 70g carmine .40 .25
J245 D16 80g carmine .35 .25
J246 D16 90g carmine ('50) .55 .25
J247 D16 1s purple .40 .25
J248 D16 1.20s purple .55 .40
J249 D16 1.35s purple .40 .35
J250 D16 1.40s purple ('51) .40 .40
J251 D16 1.50s purple ('53) .40 .25
J252 D16 1.65s purple ('50) .40 .40
J253 D16 1.70s purple .40 .40
J254 D16 2s purple 1.40 .25
J255 D16 2.50s purple ('51) .75 .25
J256 D16 3s purple ('51) .80 .25
J257 D16 4s purple ('51) 1.00 1.00
J258 D16 5s purple 1.25 .25
J259 D16 10s purple 2.40 .25
Nos. J232-J259 (28) 33.85 13.45

Issued: 60g, 90g, 1.65s, 8/7; 4g, 8g, 1.40s, 2.50s-4s, 12/4; 1.50s, 2/18; 63g, 4/30; others, 11/17.

D17

1985-89 Photo. ***Perf. 14***
Background Color

J260 D17 10g brt yel ('86) .25 .25
J261 D17 20g pink ('86) .25 .25
J262 D17 50g orange ('86) .25 *.25*
J263 D17 1s lt blue ('86) .25 *.35*
J264 D17 2s pale brn ('86) .25 *.50*
J265 D17 3s violet ('86) .40 *.55*
J266 D17 5s ocher .85 .65
J267 D17 10s pale grn ('89) 1.75 1.75
Nos. J260-J267 (8) 4.25 4.55

Issue dates: 5s, Dec. 12. 20g, 1s, 3s, Mar. 19. 10g, 50g, 2s, Oct. 3. 10s, June 30.

MILITARY STAMPS

Issues of the Austro-Hungarian Military Authorities for the Occupied Territories in World War I

See Bosnia and Herzegovina for similar designs inscribed "MILITARPOST" instead of "FELDPOST."

Stamps of Bosnia of 1912-14 Overprinted

1915 Unwmk. ***Perf. 12½***

M1 A23 1h olive green .25 *.40*
M2 A23 2h bright blue .25 *.40*
M3 A23 3h claret .25 *.40*
M4 A23 5h green .25 *.25*
M5 A23 6h dark gray .25 *.40*
M6 A23 10h rose carmine .25 *.25*
M7 A23 12h deep ol grn .25 *.80*
M8 A23 20h orange brn .35 *.80*
M9 A23 25h ultramarine .25 *.80*
M10 A23 30h orange red 3.25 *6.50*
M11 A24 35h myrtle grn 2.50 *4.75*
M12 A24 40h dark violet 2.50 *4.75*
M13 A24 45h olive brown 2.50 *4.75*
M14 A24 50h slate blue 2.50 *4.75*
M15 A24 60h brn violet .40 *.80*
M16 A24 72h dark blue 2.50 *4.75*
M17 A25 1k brn vio, *straw* 2.50 *4.75*
M18 A25 2k dk gray, *blue* 2.50 *4.75*
M19 A26 3k car, *green* 20.00 *47.50*
M20 A26 5k dk vio, *gray* 20.00 *40.00*
M21 A25 10k dk ultra, *gray* 150.00 *300.00*
Nos. M1-M21 (21) 213.50 *432.55*
Set, never hinged 420.00

Exists imperf. Values, set unused hinged $450, never hinged $875.

Nos. M1-M21 also exist with overprint double, inverted and in red. These varieties were made by order of an official but were not regularly issued. Values, each set: unused $325; never hinged $650.

M1

M2

Emperor Franz Josef

Perf. 11½, 12½ and Compound

1915-17 Engr.

M22 M1 1h olive green .25 *.25*
M23 M1 2h dull blue .25 *.35*
M24 M1 3h claret .25 *.25*
M25 M1 5h green .25 *.25*
a. Perf. 11½ 100.00 *150.00*
Never hinged 200.00
b. Perf. 11½x12½ 150.00 *240.00*
Never hinged 325.00
c. Perf. 12½x11½ 200.00 *325.00*
Never hinged 400.00
M26 M1 6h dark gray .25 *.35*
M27 M1 10h rose carmine .25 *.25*
M28 M1 10h gray bl ('17) .25 *.35*
M29 M1 12h deep olive grn .25 *.40*
M30 M1 15h car rose ('17) .25 *.40*
a. Perf. 11½ 8.00 *27.50*
Never hinged 27.50
M31 M1 20h orange brn .35 *.40*
M32 M1 20h ol green ('17) .25 *.50*
M33 M1 25h ultramarine .25 *.35*
M34 M1 30h vermilion .35 *.50*
M35 M1 35h dark green .35 *.65*
M36 M1 40h dark violet .35 *.65*
M37 M1 45h olive brown .35 *.65*
M38 M1 50h myrtle green .35 *.65*
M39 M1 60h brown violet .35 *.65*
M40 M1 72h dark blue .35 *.65*
M41 M1 80h org brn ('17) .35 .35
M42 M1 90h magenta ('17) .80 *1.25*
M43 M2 1k brn vio, *straw* 1.60 *2.50*
M44 M2 2k dk gray, *blue* .80 1.60
M45 M2 3k car, *green* .80 *6.50*
M46 M2 4k dark violet, *gray* ('17) .80 *8.00*
M47 M2 5k dk vio, *gray* 20.00 *37.50*
M48 M2 10k dk ultra, *gray* 4.00 *16.00*
Nos. M22-M48 (27) 34.70 *82.20*
Set, never hinged 125.00

Nos. M22-M48 exist imperf. Values, set unused hinged $250, never hinged $475.

Emperor Karl I
M3 M4

1917-18 ***Perf. 12½***

M49 M3 1h grnsh blue ('18) .25 .25
a. Perf. 11½ 5.50 *16.00*
Never hinged 16.00
M50 M3 2h red org ('18) .25 *.25*
M51 M3 3h olive gray .25 *.25*
a. Perf. 11½ 20.00 *47.50*
Never hinged 47.50
b. Perf. 11½x12½ 32.50 *80.00*
Never hinged 80.00
M52 M3 5h olive green .25 *.25*
M53 M3 6h violet .25 *.25*
M54 M3 10h orange brn .25 *.25*
M55 M3 12h blue .25 *.25*
a. Perf. 11½ 4.00 *12.00*
Never hinged 12.00
M56 M3 15h bright rose .25 *.25*
M57 M3 20h red brown .25 *.25*
M58 M3 25h ultramarine .25 *.55*
M59 M3 30h slate .25 .25
M60 M3 40h olive bister .25 *.25*
a. Perf. 11½ 2.50 *6.50*
Never hinged 6.50
M61 M3 50h deep green .25 *.25*
a. Perf. 11½ 8.00 *32.50*
Never hinged 32.50
M62 M3 60h car rose .25 *.40*
M63 M3 80h dull blue .25 *.25*
M64 M3 90h dk violet .35 *.80*
M65 M4 2k rose, *straw* .25 *.25*
a. Perf. 11½ 4.00 *12.00*
Never hinged 12.00
M66 M4 3k green, *blue* 1.25 *2.75*
M67 M4 4k rose, *green* 16.00 *24.00*
a. Perf. 11½ 40.00 *80.00*
Never hinged 80.00
M68 M4 10k dl vio, *gray* 1.25 *8.00*
a. Perf. 11½ 16.00 *47.50*
Never hinged 47.50
Nos. M49-M68 (20) 22.85 *40.00*
Set, never hinged 87.50

Nos. M49-M68 exist imperf. Values, set unused hinged $160, never hinged $325. Also exist in pairs, imperf between. Values, each: unused $60, never hinged $120.

See No. M82. For surcharges and overprints see Italy Nos. N1-N19, Western Ukraine Nos. 34-53, 75-81.

Emperor Karl I — M5

1918 Typo. ***Perf. 12½***

M69 M5 1h grnsh blue 24.00
M70 M5 2h orange 9.50
M71 M5 3h olive gray 9.50
M72 M5 5h yellow green .40
M73 M5 10h dark brown .40
M74 M5 20h red .80
M75 M5 25h blue .80
M76 M5 30h bister 95.00
M77 M5 45h dark slate 95.00

M78 M5 50h deep green 47.50
M79 M5 60h violet 95.00
M80 M5 80h rose 65.00
M81 M5 90h brown violet 1.60

Engr.

M82 M4 1k ol bister, *blue* .40
Nos. M69-M82 (14) 444.90
Set, never hinged 1,050.

Nos. M69-M82 were on sale at the Vienna post office for a few days before the Armistice signing. They were never issued at the Army Post Offices. They exist imperf. Values, set unused hinged $800, never hinged $1,600.

For surcharges see Italy Nos. N20-N33, Romania 1N35-1N47.

MILITARY SEMI-POSTAL STAMPS

Emperor Karl I — MSP7

Empress Zita — MSP8

Perf. 12½x13

1918, July 20 Unwmk. Typo.

MB1 MSP7 10h gray green .40 *.80*
MB2 MSP8 20h magenta .40 *.80*
MB3 MSP7 45h blue .40 *.80*
Nos. MB1-MB3 (3) 1.20 *2.40*
Set, never hinged 3.00

These stamps were sold at a premium of 10h each over face value. The surtax was for "Karl's Fund."

For overprints see Western Ukraine Nos. 31-33.

Exist imperf. Values, set hinged unused $95, never hinged $240.

MILITARY NEWSPAPER STAMPS

Mercury — MN1

1916 Unwmk. Typo. ***Perf. 12½***

MP1 MN1 2h blue .25 *.35*
a. Perf. 11½ 1.25 *2.00*
Never hinged 3.25
b. Perf. 12½x11½ 240.00 240.00
Never hinged 450.00
MP2 MN1 6h orange .50 *1.50*
MP3 MN1 10h carmine .55 *1.50*
MP4 MN1 20h brown 1.25 *1.50*
a. Perf. 11½ 4.00 *8.00*
Never hinged 8.00
Nos. MP1-MP4 (4) 2.55 *4.85*
Set, never hinged 8.00

Exist imperf. Values, Nos. MP2-MP3, unused hinged each $1.60, never hinged $6.50; Nos. MP1, MP4, unused hinged each $40, never hinged $120.

For surcharges see Italy Nos. NP1-NP4.

NEWSPAPER STAMPS

From 1851 to 1866, the Austrian Newspaper Stamps were also used in Lombardy-Venetia.

Values for unused stamps 1851-67 are for fine examples with original gum. Examples without gum sell for about a third or less of the figures quoted.

Issues of the Monarchy

Mercury — N1

Three Types

Type I — The "G" has no crossbar.

Type II — The "G" has a crossbar.

Type IIa — as type II but the rosette is deformed. Two spots of color in the "G."

1851-56 Unwmk. Typo. ***Imperf.***

Machine-made Paper

P1 N1 (0.6kr) bl, type IIa 175.00 110.00
a. Blue, type I 250.00 130.00
b. Ribbed paper 625.00 240.00
c. Blue, type II 600.00 250.00
P2 N1 (6kr) yel, type I *31,000. 10,000.*
P3 N1 (30kr) rose, type I — *13,000.*
P4 N1 (6kr) scar, type II ('56) *85,000. 13,500.*

From 1852 No. P3 and from 1856 No. P2 were used as 0.6 kreuzer values.

Values for Nos. P2-P3 unused are for stamps without gum. Pale shades sell at considerably lower values.

Originals of Nos. P2 and P3 are usually in pale colors and poorly printed. Values are for stamps clearly printed and in bright colors. Numerous reprints of Nos. P1 to P4 were made between 1866 and 1904. Those of Nos. P2 and P3 are always well printed and in much deeper colors. All reprints are in type I, but occasionally show faint traces of a crossbar on "G" of "ZEITUNGS."

N2

N3

Two Types of the 1858-59 Issue

Type I — Loops of the bow at the back of the head broken.

Type II — Loops complete. Wreath projects further at top of head.

1858-59 Embossed

P5 N2 (1kr) blue, type I 650.00 625.00
P6 N2 (1kr) lilac, type II ('59) 875.00 300.00

1861

P7 N3 (1kr) gray 175.00 175.00
a. (1kr) gray lilac 625.00 240.00
b. (1kr) deep lilac 2,500. 800.00

The embossing on the reprints of the 1858-59 and 1861 issues is not as sharp as on the originals.

N4

Wmk. 91, or, before July 1864, Unwmkd.

1863

P8 N4 (1.05kr) gray 45.00 16.50
a. Tete beche pair *125,000.*
b. (1.05kr) gray lilac 100.00 20.00

Values are for stamps that do not show the watermark. Stamps showing the watermark often sell for more.

The embossing of the reprints is not as sharp as on the originals.

Mercury
N5 N6

Three Types

Type I — Helmet not defined at back, more or less blurred. Two thick short lines in front of wing of helmet. Shadow on front of face not separated from hair.

Type II — Helmet distinctly defined. Four thin short lines in front of wing. Shadow on front of face clearly defined from hair.

Type III — Outer white circle around head is open at top (closed on types I and II). Greek border at top and bottom is wider than on types I and II.

Coarse Print

1867-73 Typo. Wmk. 91

P9 N5 (1kr) vio, type I 75.00 8.50
a. (1kr) violet, type II ('73) 225.00 25.00

1874-76 Fine Print

P9B N5 (1kr) violet, type III ('76) .55 .40
c. (1kr) gray lilac, type I ('76) 225.00 32.50
d. (1kr) violet, type II 65.00 8.50
e. Double impression, type III 175.00

Stamps of this issue, except No. P9Bc, exist in many shades, from gray to lilac brown and deep violet. Stamps in type III exist also privately perforated or rouletted.

1880

P10 N6 ½kr blue green 8.50 1.25

Nos. P9B and P10 also exist on thicker paper without sheet watermark and No. P10 exists with unofficial perforation.

N7

Without Varnish Bars

1899 Unwmk. ***Imperf.***

P11 N7 2h dark blue .25 .25
P12 N7 6h orange 1.60 *2.00*
P13 N7 10h brown 1.60 .95
P14 N7 20h rose 1.60 2.00
Nos. P11-P14 (4) 5.05 5.20

1901 With Varnish Bars

P11a N7 2h dark blue 2.40 .25
P12a N7 6h orange 16.00 24.00
P13a N7 10h brown 16.00 8.00
P14a N7 20h rose 20.00 *65.00*
Nos. P11a-P14a (4) 54.40 97.25

Nos. P11-P14 were re-issued in 1905. They exist privately perforated.

Mercury
N8 N9

1908 ***Imperf.***

P15 N8 2h dark blue .80 .25
a. Tete beche pair 200.00 *325.00*
P16 N8 6h orange 3.25 .50
P17 N8 10h carmine 3.25 .40
P18 N8 20h brown 3.25 .40
Nos. P15-P18 (4) 10.55 1.55

All values are found on chalky, regular and thin ordinary paper. They exist privately perforated.

1916 ***Imperf.***

P19 N9 2h brown .25 *.40*
P20 N9 4h green .35 *1.25*
P21 N9 6h dark blue .55 *1.25*
P22 N9 10h orange .60 *1.25*
P23 N9 30h claret .55 *1.60*
Nos. P19-P23 (5) 2.30 5.75
Set, never hinged 9.50

Nos. P19-P23 exist privately perforated.

Issues of the Republic

Newspaper Stamps of 1916 Overprinted

1919

P24 N9 2h brown .25 *.80*
P25 N9 4h green .40 *6.50*
P26 N9 6h dark blue .25 *8.00*
P27 N9 10h orange .40 *9.50*
P28 N9 30h claret .25 *16.00*
Nos. P24-P28 (5) 1.55 *40.80*
Set, never hinged 3.25

Nos. P24-P28 exist privately perforated.

Mercury
N10 N11

1920-21 ***Imperf.***

P29 N10 2h violet .25 .25
P30 N10 4h brown .25 *.25*
P31 N10 5h slate .25 .25
P32 N10 6h turq blue .25 .25
P33 N10 8h green .25 *.40*
P34 N10 9h yellow ('21) .25 .25
P35 N10 10h red .25 .25
P36 N10 12h blue .25 *.40*
P37 N10 15h lilac ('21) .25 .25
P38 N10 18h blue grn ('21) .25 *.25*
P39 N10 20h orange .25 *.25*
P40 N10 30h yellow brn ('21) .25 .25
P41 N10 45h green ('21) .25 *.40*
P42 N10 60h claret .25 .25
P43 N10 72h chocolate ('21) .25 *.40*
P44 N10 90h violet ('21) .25 *.80*
P45 N10 1.20k red ('21) .25 *.80*
P46 N10 2.40k yellow grn ('21) .25 *.80*
P47 N10 3k gray ('21) .25 *.80*
Nos. P29-P47 (19) 7.55
Set, never hinged 4.00

Nos. P37-P40, P42, P44 and P47 exist also on thick grayish paper. Values are for the cheaper varieties. See the *Scott Classic Specialized Catalogue* for detailed listings.

Nos. P29-P47 exist privately perforated.

1921-22

P48 N11 45h gray .25 .25
P49 N11 75h brown org ('22) .25 .25
P50 N11 1.50k ol bister ('22) .25 .25
P51 N11 1.80k gray blue ('22) .25 .25
P52 N11 2.25k light brown .25 .25
P53 N11 3k dull green ('22) .25 .25
P54 N11 6k claret ('22) .25 *.25*
P55 N11 7.50k bister .25 *.40*
Nos. P48-P55 (8) *2.15*
Set, never hinged 4.75

Used values are for cancelled-to-order stamps. Postally used examples are worth much more.

Nos. P48-P55 exist privately perforated.

NEWSPAPER TAX STAMPS

Values for unused stamps 1853-59 are for examples in fine condition with gum. Examples without gum sell for about one-third or less of the figures quoted.

Issues of the Monarchy

NT1

Unwmk.

1853, Mar. 1 Typo. ***Imperf.***

PR1 NT1 2kr green 1,800. 57.50

The reprints are in finer print than the more coarsely printed originals, and on a smooth toned paper.

Values for Nos. PR2-PR9 are for stamps that do not show the watermark. Stamps showing the watermark often sell for more.

NT2

Two Types.

Type I — The banderol on the Crown of the left eagle touches the beak of the eagle.

Type II — The banderol does not touch the beak.

Wmk. 91, or, before July 1864, Unwmkd.

1858-59

PR2	NT2 1kr blue, type II ('59)	50.00	5.50
a.	1kr blue, type I	1,225.	190.00
b.	Printed on both sides, type II		—
PR3	NT2 2kr brown, type II ('59)	47.50	6.75
a.	2kr red brown, type II	600.00	240.00
PR4	NT2 4kr brn, type I	425.00	*1,100.*

Nos. PR2a, PR3a, and PR4 were printed only on unwatermarked paper. Nos. PR2 and PR3 exist on unwatermarked and watermarked paper.

Nos. PR2 and PR3 exist in coarse and (after 1874) in fine print, like the contemporary postage stamps.

The reprints of the 4kr brown are of type II and on a smooth toned paper.

Issue date: 4kr, Nov. 1.

See Lombardy-Venetia for the 1kr in black and the 2kr, 4fk in red.

NT3

1877 **Redrawn**

PR5	NT3 1kr blue	12.50	1.40
a.	1kr pale ultramarine		*2,900.*
PR6	NT3 2kr brown	14.00	6.75

In the redrawn stamps the shield is larger and the vertical bar has eight lines above the white square and nine below, instead of five.

Nos. PR5 and PR6 exist also watermarked "WECHSEL" instead of "ZEITUNGS-MARKEN."

NT4

1890, June 1

PR7	NT4 1kr brown	9.00	1.00
PR8	NT4 2kr green	10.00	1.50

#PR5-PR8 exist with private perforation.

NT5

1890, June 1 **Wmk. 91** ***Perf. 12½***

PR9	NT5 25kr carmine	95.00	*200.00*

Nos. PR1-PR9 did not pay postage, but were a fiscal tax, collected by the postal authorities on newspapers.

SPECIAL HANDLING STAMPS

(For Printed Matter Only) Issues of the Monarchy

Mercury SH1

1916 **Unwmk.** ***Perf. 12½***

QE1	SH1 2h claret, *yellow*	1.20	*4.00*
QE2	SH1 5h dp green, *yellow*	1.20	*4.00*
	Set, never hinged	6.50	

SH2

1917 ***Perf. 12½***

QE3	SH2 2h claret, *yellow*	.25	*.40*
a.	Pair, imperf. between	325.00	*650.00*
	Never hinged	650.00	
b.	Perf. 11½x12½	150.00	*260.00*
	Never hinged	800.00	
c.	Perf. 12½x11½	225.00	*325.00*
	Never hinged	950.00	
d.	Perf. 11½	1.60	*4.00*
	Never hinged	4.00	
QE4	SH2 5h dp green, *yellow*	.25	*.40*
a.	Pair, imperf. between	325.00	*650.00*
	Never hinged	650.00	
b.	Perf. 11½x12½	120.00	*150.00*
	Never hinged	800.00	
c.	Perf. 12½x11½	190.00	*260.00*
	Never hinged	950.00	
d.	Perf. 11½	1.60	*4.00*
	Never hinged	4.00	
	Set, never hinged	1.60	

Nos. QE1-QE4 exist imperforate.

Issues of the Republic

Nos. QE3 and QE4 Overprinted

1919

QE5	SH2 2h claret, *yellow*	.35	.25
a.	Inverted overprint	325.00	
	Never hinged	650.00	
b.	Perf. 11½x12½	6.00	*12.00*
	Never hinged	10.50	
c.	Perf. 12½x11½	110.00	*290.00*
	Never hinged	325.00	
d.	Perf. 11½	.40	*1.25*
	Never hinged	1.25	
QE6	SH2 5h deep green, *yellow*	.35	*.25*
a.	Perf. 11½x12½	1.60	*4.50*
	Never hinged	4.00	
b.	Perf. 12½x11½	40.00	*95.00*
	Never hinged	87.50	
c.	Perf. 11½	.35	*.80*
	Never hinged	.80	
	Set, never hinged	1.60	

Nos. QE5 and QE6 exist imperforate. Value, set unused hinged $175; never hinged $360.

Dark Blue Surcharge — SH3

1921

QE7	SH3 50h on 2h claret, *yel*	.25	*.80*
	Never hinged	.80	

SH4

1922 ***Perf. 12½***

QE8	SH4 50h lilac, *yellow*	.25	*.25*
	Never hinged	.40	

Nos. QE5-QE8 exist in vertical pairs, imperf between. No. QE8 exists imperf. Value: unused hinged $125; never hinged $250.

OCCUPATION STAMPS

Issued under Italian Occupation

Issued in Trieste

Austrian Stamps of 1916-18 Overprinted

1918 **Unwmk.** ***Perf. 12½***

N1	A37 3h bright vio	1.60	1.60
a.	Double overprint	57.50	57.50
b.	Inverted overprint	57.50	57.50
N2	A37 5h light grn	1.60	1.60
a.	Inverted overprint	57.50	57.50
c.	Double overprint	—	57.50
N3	A37 6h dp orange	2.50	2.50
N4	A37 10h magenta	25.00	4.00
a.	Inverted overprint	57.50	57.50
N5	A37 12h light bl	3.25	3.25
a.	Double overprint	57.50	57.50
N6	A42 15h dull red	1.60	1.60
a.	Inverted overprint	57.50	57.50
b.	Double overprint	57.50	57.50
N7	A42 20h dark green	1.60	1.60
a.	Inverted overprint	57.50	57.50
c.	Double overprint	140.00	
N8	A42 25h deep blue	12.50	12.50
a.	Inverted overprint	225.00	225.00
N9	A42 30h dl violet	3.25	3.25
N10	A39 40h olive grn	275.00	*290.00*
N11	A39 50h dark green	12.50	12.50
N12	A39 60h deep blue	29.00	29.00
N13	A39 80h orange brn	20.00	20.00
a.	Inverted overprint	—	
N14	A39 1k car, *yel*	20.00	20.00
a.	Double overprint	130.00	
N15	A40 2k light bl	450.00	*500.00*
	Never hinged	900.00	
N16	A40 4k yellow grn	1,050.	*1,250.*
	Never hinged	2,600.	

Handstamped

N17	A40 10k dp violet	*30,000.*	*52,000.*
	Never hinged	*45,000.*	

Granite Paper

N18	A40 2k light blue	675.00	
	Never hinged	1,350.	
N19	A40 3k car rose	650.00	*700.00*
	Never hinged	1,300.	
	Nos. N1-N14 (14)	409.40	403.40
	Set, never hinged	975.00	

Some authorities question the authenticity of No. N18.

Counterfeits of Nos. N10, N15-N19 are plentiful.

A variety of N19 exists on ordinary paper. Only 50 examples are known. Values, $8,250 unused, $12,250 never hinged.

A 90h stamp was printed but not issued because the Austrian stamps were replaced by Italian stamps. Only 50 90h were printed. Values, $4,100 unused, $8,000 never hinged.

Italian Stamps of 1901-18 Overprinted

Wmk. 140 ***Perf. 14***

N20	A42 1c brown	3.25	*8.25*
a.	Inverted overprint	32.50	32.50
N21	A43 2c orange brn	3.25	*8.25*
a.	Inverted overprint	29.00	29.00
N22	A48 5c green	2.50	2.50
a.	Inverted overprint	57.50	57.50
b.	Double overprint	140.00	
N23	A48 10c claret	2.50	2.50
a.	Inverted overprint	85.00	*85.00*
b.	Double overprint	140.00	
N24	A50 20c brn orange	2.50	*3.25*
a.	Inverted overprint	110.00	110.00
b.	Double overprint	130.00	130.00
N25	A49 25c blue	2.50	*4.00*
a.	Double overprint	—	
b.	Inverted overprint	130.00	130.00
N26	A49 40c brown	16.00	*29.00*
a.	Inverted overprint	—	
N27	A45 45c olive grn	6.50	*10.00*
a.	Inverted overprint	160.00	160.00
N28	A49 50c violet	12.50	12.50
N29	A49 60c brown car	85.00	*160.00*
a.	Inverted overprint	—	
b.	Double overprint	375.00	
N30	A46 1 l brn & green	40.00	*57.50*
a.	Inverted overprint	—	
	Nos. N20-N30 (11)	176.50	*297.75*
	Set, never hinged	525.00	

Italian Stamps of 1901-18 Surcharged

N31	A48 5h on 5c green	1.60	*3.25*
	Never hinged	4.00	
a.	"5" omitted	125.00	125.00
b.	Inverted surcharge	125.00	125.00
N32	A50 20h on 20c brn org	1.60	3.25
	Never hinged	4.00	
a.	Double surcharge	125.00	125.00

Issued in the Trentino

Austrian Stamps of 1916-18 Overprinted

1918 **Unwmk.** ***Perf. 12½***

N33	A37 3h bright vio	12.50	12.50
a.	Double overprint	130.00	130.00
b.	Inverted overprint	125.00	125.00
N34	A37 5h light grn	10.00	5.00
a.	"8 nov. 1918"	*3,400.*	
b.	Inverted overprint	125.00	125.00
N35	A37 6h dp orange	125.00	110.00
N36	A37 10h magenta	10.00	8.25
a.	"8 nov. 1918"	250.00	250.00
N37	A37 12h light blue	325.00	290.00
N38	A42 15h dull red	12.50	10.00
N39	A42 20h dark green	8.25	8.25
a.	"8 nov. 1918"	325.00	325.00
b.	Double overprint	130.00	130.00
c.	Inverted overprint	57.50	57.50
	Never hinged	*1,900.*	
N40	A42 25h deep blue	75.00	65.00
N41	A42 30h dl violet	29.00	25.00
	Never hinged	42.50	
N42	A39 40h olive grn	100.00	90.00
N43	A39 50h dark green	65.00	50.00
a.	Inverted overprint	325.00	325.00
N44	A39 60h deep blue	110.00	90.00
a.	Double overprint	325.00	325.00
N45	A39 80h orange brn	160.00	130.00
N46	A39 90h red violet	2,250.	3,100.
N47	A39 1k car, *yel*	150.00	125.00
N48	A40 2k light blue	750.00	*900.00*
N49	A40 4k yel green	*3,400.*	*4,100.*
N50a	A40 10k dp violet, gray ovpt.	*25,000.*	*25,000.*

Granite Paper

N51	A40 2k light blue	*1,650.*	*2,250.*
	Never hinged	*3,300.*	

Counterfeits of Nos. N33-N51 are plentiful.

Italian Stamps of 1901-18 Overprinted

Wmk. 140 ***Perf. 14***

N52	A42 1c brown	4.00	*11.50*
a.	Inverted overprint	110.00	110.00
b.	Double overprint	125.00	
N53	A43 2c orange brn	4.00	*11.50*
a.	Inverted overprint	110.00	110.00
N54	A48 5c green	4.00	*11.50*
a.	Inverted overprint	110.00	110.00
b.	Double overprint	125.00	125.00
N55	A48 10c claret	4.00	*11.50*
a.	Inverted overprint	160.00	160.00
b.	Double overprint	125.00	125.00
N56	A50 20c brn orange	4.00	*11.50*
a.	Inverted overprint	160.00	160.00
N57	A49 40c brown	130.00	85.00
N58	A45 45c olive grn	65.00	85.00
a.	Double overprint	375.00	*375.00*
N59	A49 50c violet	65.00	*85.00*
N60	A46 1 l brn & green	65.00	*85.00*
a.	Double overprint	375.00	*375.00*
	Nos. N52-N60 (9)	345.00	397.50

Italian Stamps of 1906-18 Surcharged

N61	A48 5h on 5c green	2.50	*4.00*
N62	A48 10h on 10c claret	2.50	*4.00*
a.	Inverted overprint	110.00	*110.00*
N63	A50 20h on 20c brn org	2.50	*4.00*
a.	Double surcharge	110.00	*110.00*
	Nos. N61-N63 (3)	7.50	*12.00*

General Issue

Italian Stamps of 1901-18 Surcharged

1919

N64	A42 1c on 1c brown	1.60	*4.00*
a.	Inverted surcharge	25.00	25.00
N65	A43 2c on 2c org brn	1.60	*4.00*
a.	Double surcharge	375.00	
b.	Inverted surcharge	20.00	20.00
N66	A48 5c on 5c green	1.60	1.60
a.	Inverted surcharge	65.00	65.00
b.	Double surcharge	125.00	
N67	A48 10c on 10c claret	1.60	1.60
a.	Inverted surcharge	65.00	65.00
b.	Double surcharge	125.00	125.00
N68	A50 20c on 20c brn org	1.60	1.60
a.	Double surcharge	160.00	*160.00*
b.	Half used as 10c on cover		400.00
N69	A49 25c on 25c blue	1.60	*2.50*
a.	Double surcharge	160.00	
N70	A49 40c on 40c brown	1.60	*4.00*
a.	"ccrona"	150.00	150.00
N71	A45 45c on 45c ol grn	1.60	*4.00*
a.	Inverted surcharge	180.00	180.00
N72	A49 50c on 50c violet	1.60	*4.00*
N73	A49 60c on 60c brn car	1.60	*4.00*
a.	"00" for "60"	180.00	*180.00*

Italian No. 87 Surcharged

N74	A46	1cor on 1 l brn & green	5.00	10.00
		Nos. N64-N74 (11)	21.00	41.30

Surcharges similar to these but differing in style or arrangement of type were used in Dalmatia.

OCCUPATION SPECIAL DELIVERY STAMPS

Issued in Trieste

Special Delivery Stamp of Italy of 1903 Overprinted

1918 Wmk. 140 Perf. 14

NE1	SD1	25c rose red	75.00	130.00
a.		Inverted overprint	400.00	400.00

General Issue

Special Delivery Stamps of Italy of 1903-09 Surcharged

1919

NE2	SD1	25c on 25c rose	2.50	3.25
a.		Double surcharge	130.00	130.00
NE3	SD2	30c on 30c bl & rose	4.00	6.50
a.		Pair, one stamp without surcharge		1,500.

OCCUPATION POSTAGE DUE STAMPS

Issued in Trieste

Postage Due Stamps of Italy, 1870-94, Overprinted

1918 Wmk. 140 Perf. 14

NJ1	D3	5c buff & mag	1.60	1.60
a.		Inverted overprint	29.00	29.00
b.		Double overprint	260.00	
NJ2	D3	10c buff & mag	1.60	1.60
a.		Inverted overprint	110.00	110.00
NJ3	D3	20c buff & mag	3.25	3.25
a.		Double overprint	260.00	
b.		Inverted overprint	110.00	110.00
NJ4	D3	30c buff & mag	6.50	6.50
NJ5	D3	40c buff & mag	50.00	60.00
a.		Inverted overprint	375.00	375.00
NJ6	D3	50c buff & mag	110.00	160.00
a.		Inverted overprint	450.00	450.00
NJ7	D3	1 l bl & mag	250.00	500.00
		Nos. NJ1-NJ7 (7)	422.95	732.95

General Issue

Postage Due Stamps of Italy, 1870-1903 Surcharged

1919

Buff & Magenta

NJ8	D3	5c on 5c	2.50	2.50
a.		Inverted overprint	37.50	37.50
NJ9	D3	10c on 10c	2.50	2.50
a.		Center and surcharge invtd.	260.00	260.00
NJ10	D3	20c on 20c	4.00	2.50
a.		Double overprint	260.00	260.00
NJ11	D3	30c on 30c	4.00	5.00
NJ12	D3	40c on 40c	4.00	5.00
NJ13	D3	50c on 50c	6.50	8.25

Surcharged

NJ14	D3	1cor on 1 l bl & mag	6.50	12.50
NJ15	D3	2cor on 2 l bl & mag	75.00	160.00
NJ16	D3	5cor on 5 l bl & mag	75.00	160.00
		Nos. NJ8-NJ16 (9)	180.00	358.25

A. M. G. ISSUE FOR AUSTRIA

Catalogue values for unused stamps in this section are for Never Hinged items.

Issued jointly by the Allied Military Government of the US and Great Britain, for civilian use in areas under American, British and French occupation. (Upper Austria, Salzburg, Tyrol, Vorarlberg, Styria and Carinthia).

OS1

1945 Unwmk. Litho. Perf. 11

4N1	OS1	1g aquamarine	.25	.25
4N2	OS1	3g deep orange	.25	.25
4N3	OS1	4g buff	.25	.25
4N4	OS1	5g bright green	.25	.25
4N5	OS1	6g red violet	.25	.25
4N6	OS1	8g rose pink	.25	.25
4N7	OS1	10g light gray	.25	.25
4N8	OS1	12g pale buff brown	.25	.25
4N9	OS1	15g rose red	.25	.25
4N10	OS1	20g copper brown	.25	.25
4N11	OS1	25g deep blue	.30	.30
4N12	OS1	30g bright violet	.30	.30
4N13	OS1	40g light ultra	.30	.30
4N14	OS1	60g light olive grn	.40	.40
4N15	OS1	1s dark violet	.40	.40
4N16	OS1	2s yellow	.95	.95
4N17	OS1	5s deep ultra	.95	.95
		Nos. 4N1-4N17 (17)	6.10	6.10

Used values are for examples with philatelic favor cancels. Postally used are worth much more.

For Nos. 4N2, 4N4-4N17 overprinted "PORTO" see Nos. J189-J203.

AUSTRIAN OFFICES ABROAD

These stamps were on sale and usable at all Austrian post-offices in Crete and in the Turkish Empire.

100 Centimes = 1 Franc

OFFICES IN CRETE

Used values are italicized for stamps often found with false cancellations.

Stamps of Austria of 1899-1901 Issue, Surcharged in Black

a

b

c

d

On Nos. 73a, 75a, 77a, 81a
Granite Paper
With Varnish Bars

1903-04 Unwmk. Perf. 12½, 13½

1	A15(a)	5c on 5h blue green	1.20	4.75
2	A16(b)	10c on 10h rose	.80	4.75
3	A16(b)	25c on 25h ultra	40.00	32.50
4	A17(c)	50c on 50h gray blue	10.50	160.00

On Nos. 83, 83a, 84, 85
Without Varnish Bars

5	A18(d)	1fr on 1k car rose	1.20	140.00
a.		1fr on 1k carmine	9.50	—
b.		Horiz. or vert. pair, imperf. between	225.00	—
6	A18(d)	2fr on 2k ('04)	8.00	400.00
7	A18(d)	4fr on 4k ('04)	12.00	650.00
		Nos. 1-7 (7)	73.70	1,392.

Surcharged on Austrian Stamps of 1904-05

On Nos. 89, 97

1905 Without Varnish Bars

8a	A19(a)	5c on 5h blue green	55.00	55.00
9	A20(b)	10c on 10h car	.55	16.00

On Nos. 89a, 97a, 99a, 103a
With Varnish Bars

8	A19(a)	5c on 5h bl grn	2.40	5.50
9a	A20(b)	10c on 10h carmine	32.50	65.00
10	A20(b)	25c on 25h ultra	.55	140.00
11	A21(b)	50c on 50h dl bl	.80	650.00

Surcharged on Austrian Stamps and Type of 1906-07
Without Varnish Bars

1907 Perf. 12½, 13½

12	A19(a)	5c on 5h yel green (#90)	.80	4.00
13	A20(b)	10c on 10h car (#92)	1.00	40.00
14	A20(b)	15c on 15h vio	.80	40.00
		Nos. 12-14 (3)	2.60	84.00

A5

A6

1908 Typo. Perf. 12½

15	A5	5c green, *yellow*	.25	1.00
16	A5	10c scarlet, *rose*	.35	1.20
17	A5	15c brown, *buff*	.45	8.00
18	A5	25c dp blue, *blue*	16.00	6.50

Engr.

19	A6	50c lake, *yellow*	4.00	32.50
20	A6	1fr brown, *gray*	8.00	60.00
a.		Vert pair, imperf. btwn.	200.00	
		Nos. 15-20 (6)	29.05	109.20

Nos. 15-18 are on paper colored on the surface only. All values exist imperforate.

60th year of the reign of Emperor Franz Josef, for permanent use.

Paper Colored Through

1914 Typo.

21	A5	10c rose, *rose*	1.25	2,300.
22	A5	25c ultra, *blue*	.80	190.00

Nos. 21 and 22 exist imperforate.

OFFICES IN THE TURKISH EMPIRE

From 1863 to 1867 the stamps of Lombardy-Venetia (Nos. 15 to 24) were used at the Austrian Offices in the Turkish Empire.

100 Soldi = 1 Florin
40 Paras = 1 Piaster

Values for unused stamps are for examples with gum. Examples without gum sell for about one-third or less of the figures quoted. Used values are italicized for stamps often found with false cancellations.

For similar designs in Kreuzers, see early Austria.

A1

A2

Two different printing methods were used, as in the 1867-74 issues of Austria. They may be distinguished by the coarse or fine lines of the hair and whiskers and by the paper, which is more transparent on the later issue.

1867 Typo. Wmk. 91 Perf. 9½

Coarse Print

1	A1	2sld orange	2.40	27.50
a.		2sld yellow	65.00	80.00
2	A1	3sld green	150.00	67.50
a.		3sld dark green	325.00	200.00
3	A1	5sld red	240.00	14.00
a.		5sld carmine	325.00	40.00
b.		5sld red lilac	275.00	24.00
4	A1	10sld blue	200.00	2.40
a.		10sld light blue	275.00	3.25
b.		10sld dark blue	240.00	3.25
5	A1	15sld brown	24.00	8.00
a.		15sld dark brown	95.00	65.00
b.		15sld reddish brown	40.00	16.00
c.		15sld gray brown	80.00	16.00
6	A1	25sld violet	24.00	40.00
a.		25sld brown violet	40.00	60.00
b.		25sld gray lilac	120.00	47.50
7	A2	50sld brn, perf. 10½	1.25	65.00
a.		Perf. 12	100.00	110.00
b.		Perf. 13	325.00	—
k.		Perf. 9	27.50	140.00
l.		50sld pale red brn, perf. 12	160.00	160.00
m.		Vert. pair, imperf. btwn.	300.00	550.00
n.		Horiz. pair, imperf. btwn.	300.00	550.00
o.		Perf. 10½x9	85.00	160.00

Perf. 9, 9½, 10½ and Compound

1876-83 Fine Print

7C	A1	2sld yellow ('83)	.40	3,000.
7D	A1	3sld green ('78)	1.20	27.50
7E	A1	5sld red ('78)	.40	24.00
7F	A1	10sld blue	100.00	1.25
7I	A1	15sld org brn ('81)	12.00	160.00
7J	A1	25sld gray lilac ('83)	.80	360.00
		Nos. 7C-7J (6)	114.80	3,572.

The 10 soldi was reprinted in deep dull blue, perforated 10½. Value, $6.50.

A3

1883 Perf. 9½

8	A3	2sld brown	.25	190.00
9	A3	3sld green	1.20	35.00
10	A3	5sld rose	.25	20.00
11	A3	10sld blue	.80	.80
12	A3	20sld gray, perf. 10	6.50	600.00
a.		Perf. 9½	1.60	9.50
13	A3	50sld red lilac	1.25	20.00
		Nos. 8-13 (6)	10.25	865.80

No. 9 Surcharged

10 PARAS ON 3 SOLDI:
Type I — Surcharge 16½mm across. "PARA" about ½mm above bottom of "10." 2mm space between "10" and "P"; 1½mm between "A" and "10." Perf. 9½ only.
Type II — Surcharge 15¼ to 16mm across. "PARA" on same line with figures or slightly higher or lower. 1½mm space between "10" and "P"; 1mm between "A" and "10." Perf. 9½ and 10.

1886 *Perf. 9½, 10*

14 A4 10pa on 3sld green, type II, perf. 10 .35 *8.00*
a. 10pa on 3sld green, type I 200.00 500.00
b. Inverted surcharge, type I *2,000.*

Same surcharge on Austria Nos. 42-46

1888

15 A5 10pa on 3kr grn 4.00 12.00
a. "01 PARA 10" *1,200.*
16 A5 20pa on 5kr rose .40 *12.00*
a. Double surcharge 400.00
Never hinged 1,200.
17 A5 1pi on 10kr blue 65.00 1.60
a. Perf. 13½ 800.00
b. Double surcharge —
18 A5 2pi on 20kr gray 1.60 *6.50*
19 A5 5pi on 50kr vio 2.00 *20.00*
Nos. 15-19 (5) 73.00 52.10

Austria Nos. 52-55, 58, 61 Surcharged

1890-92 Unwmk. *Perf. 9 to 13½*
Granite Paper

20 A6 8pa on 2kr brn ('92) .25 .65
a. Perf. 9½ 12.00 16.00
21 A6 10pa on 3kr green .55 .65
a. Pair, imperf. between *550.00*
22 A6 20pa on 5kr rose .35 *.65*
23 A6 1pi on 10kr ultra .40 .25
a. Pair, imperf. between *550.00*
24 A6 2pi on 20kr ol grn 8.00 *32.50*
25 A6 5pi on 50kr violet 12.00 *72.50*
Nos. 20-25 (6) 21.55 *107.20*

See note after Austria No. 65 on missing numerals, etc.

Austria Nos. 66, 69 Surcharged

1891 *Perf. 10 to 13½*

26 A14 2pi on 20kr green 6.50 1.60
a. Perf. 9¼ 200.00 160.00
27 A14 5pi on 50kr violet 3.25 3.25

Two types of the surcharge on No. 26 exist.

Austria Nos. 62-65 Surcharged

1892 *Perf. 10½, 11½*

28 A8 10pi on 1gld blue 12.00 *32.50*
29 A8 20pi on 2gld car 16.00 *60.00*
a. Double surcharge —

1896 *Perf. 10½, 11½, 12½*

30 A8 10pi on 1gld pale lilac 18.50 *22.50*
31 A8 20pi on 2gld gray grn 37.50 *75.00*

Austria Nos. 73, 75, 77, 81, 83-85 Surcharged

#32-35

#36-38

Perf. 12½, 13½ and Compound

1900 Without Varnish Bars

32 A9 10pa on 5h bl grn 4.75 .80
33 A10 20pa on 10h rose 5.50 .80
b. Perf. 12½x10½ 400.00 350.00
34 A10 1pi on 25h ultra 3.25 .40
35 A11 2pi on 50h gray bl 8.00 4.00
36 A12 5pi on 1k car rose .55 .40
a. 5pi on 1k carmine .80 *1.20*
b. Horiz. or vert. pair, imperf. btwn. 160.00
37 A12 10pi on 2k gray lil 2.00 *3.50*
38 A12 20pi on 4k gray grn 1.60 *8.00*
Nos. 32-38 (7) 25.65 *17.90*

In the surcharge on Nos. 37 and 38 "piaster" is printed "PIAST."

1901 With Varnish Bars

32a A9 10pa on 5h blue green 1.60 2.75
33a A10 20pa on 10h rose 2.40 *400.00*
34a A10 1pi on 25h ultra 1.20 .80
35b A11 2pi on 50h gray blue 2.75 8.00
Nos. 32a-35b (4) 7.95 411.55

A4

A5

A6

1906 *Perf. 12½ to 13½*
Without Varnish Bars

39 A4 10pa dark green 12.00 4.00
40 A5 20pa rose .80 *1.20*
41 A5 1pi ultra .80 .40
42 A6 2pi gray blue .80 *1.20*
Nos. 39-42 (4) 14.40 6.80

1903 With Varnish Bars

39a A4 10pa dark green 4.75 2.00
40a A5 20pa rose 3.25 .80
41a A5 1pi ultra 2.40 .40
42a A6 2pi gray blue 160.00 3.25
Nos. 39a-42a (4) 170.40 6.45

1907 Without Varnish Bars

43 A4 10pa yellow green .55 *2.00*
45 A5 30pa violet .55 *4.00*

A7

A8

1908 Typo. *Perf. 12½*

46 A7 10pa green, *yellow* .25 *.40*
47 A7 20pa scarlet, *rose* .25 *.40*
48 A7 30pa brown, *buff* .40 *2.00*
49 A7 1pi deep bl, *blue* 14.50 .25
50 A7 60pa vio, *bluish* .65 *5.50*

Engr.

51 A8 2pi lake, *yellow* .65 .25
52 A8 5pi brown, *gray* .65 *.95*
53 A8 10pi green, *yellow* .95 *2.40*
54 A8 20pi blue, *gray* 2.40 *4.75*
Nos. 46-54 (9) 20.70 *16.90*

Nos. 46-50 are on paper colored on the surface only. 60th year of the reign of Emperor Franz Josef I, for permanent use.

Nos. 46-50 exist imperforate. Values, set: unused $275, never hinged $650.

Paper Colored Through

1913-14 Typo.

57 A7 20pa rose, *rose* ('14) .55 *650.00*
58 A7 1pi ultra, *blue* .35 *.55*

Nos. 57 and 58 exist imperforate.

POSTAGE DUE STAMPS

Type of Austria D2 Surcharged in Black

1902 Unwmk. *Perf. 12½, 13½*

J1 D2 10pa on 5h gray green 1.60 *8.00*
J2 D2 20pa on 10h gray green 1.60 *12.00*
J3 D2 1pi on 20h gray green 1.60 *12.00*
J4 D2 2pi on 40h gray green 1.60 *12.00*
J5 D2 5pi on 100h gray green 1.60 *8.00*
Nos. J1-J5 (5) 8.00 *52.00*

Shades of Nos. J1-J5 exist, varying from yellowish to dark green.

D3

1908 Typo. *Perf. 12½*
Chalky Paper

J6 D3 ¼pi pale green 3.25 *13.50*
J7 D3 ½pi pale green 2.00 *11.00*
J8 D3 1pi pale green 2.40 *8.00*
J9 D3 1½pi pale green 1.20 *24.00*
J10 D3 2pi pale green 1.60 *20.00*
J11 D3 5pi pale green 2.40 *14.50*
J12 D3 10pi pale green 16.00 *150.00*
J13 D3 20pi pale green 11.00 *160.00*
J14 D3 30pi pale green 16.00 14.50
Nos. J6-J14 (9) 55.85 *415.50*

Nos. J6-J14 exist in distinct shades of green and on thick chalky, regular and thin ordinary paper. Values are for the least expensive variety. For comprehensive listings, see Scott Classic Specialized Catalogue.
No. J6-J14 exist imperforate.
Forgeries exist.

LOMBARDY-VENETIA

Formerly a kingdom in the north of Italy forming part of the Austrian Empire. Milan and Venice were the two principal cities. Lombardy was annexed to Sardinia in 1859, and Venetia to the kingdom of Italy in 1866.

100 Centesimi = 1 Lira
100 Soldi = 1 Florin (1858)

Unused examples without gum of Nos. 1-24 are worth approximately 20% of the values given, which are for stamps with original gum as defined in the catalogue introduction.

For similar designs in Kreuzers, see early Austria.

Coat of Arms — A1

15 CENTESIMI:
Type I — "5" is on a level with the "1." One heavy line around coat of arms center.
Type II — As type I, but "5" is a trifle sideways and is higher than the "1."
Type III — As type II, but two, thinner, lines around center.
45 CENTESIMI:
Type I — Lower part of "45" is lower than "Centes." One heavy line around coat of arms center. "45" varies in height and distance from "Centes."
Type II — One heavy line around coat of arms center. Lower part of "45" is on a level with lower part of "Centes."
Type III — As type II, but two, thinner, lines around center.

Wmk. K.K.H.M. in Sheet or Unwmkd.

1850 Typo. ***Imperf.***
Thick to Thin Paper

1 A1 5c buff 6,000. 200.00
On cover, single franking 625.00
a. Printed on both sides *21,500.* 675.00
b. 5c yellow *11,250.* 650.00
c. 5c orange 6,500. 225.00
d. 5c lemon yellow — *2,500.*
3 A1 10c black 6,000. 200.00
a. 10c gray black 6,000. 175.00
4 A1 15c red, type III 1,900. 7.50
b. 15c red, type I *4,500.* 29.00
c. Ribbed paper, type II — 900.00
d. Ribbed paper, type I *27,500.* 275.00
f. 15c red, type II *2,400.* 30.00
5 A1 30c brown 6,750. 26.50
a. Ribbed paper 13,500. 175.00
6 A1 45c blue, type III *20,000.* 60.00
a. 45c blue, type I *21,250.* 60.00
b. Ribbed paper, type I — 750.00
c. 45c blue, type II *190,000.* 75.00

1854
Machine-made Paper, Type III

3c A1 10c black *12,250.* 500.00
4g A1 15c pale red *2,100.* 6.00
5b A1 30c brown ('55) *7,500.* 26.50
6d A1 45c blue *18,000.* 75.00

See note about the paper of the 1850 issue of Austria. *The reprints are type III, in brighter colors.*

A2

A3

A4

A5

A6

Two Types of Each Value.
Type I — Loops of the bow at the back of the head broken.
Type II — Loops complete. Wreath projects further at top of head.

1858-62 Embossed *Perf. 14½*

7 A2 2s yel, type II 2,400. 150.00
a. 2s yellow, type I 12,000. 900.00
8 A3 3s black, type II 18,000. 190.00
a. 3s black, type I 6,750. 375.00
b. Perf. 16, type I — 2,250.
c. Perf. 15x16 or 16x15, type I *12,500.* 750.00
9 A3 3s grn, type II ('62) 1,325. 140.00
10 A4 5s red, type II 750.00 12.00
a. 5s red, type I 2,400. 45.00
b. Printed on both sides, type II *6,750.*
11 A5 10s brown, type II 5,250. 24.00
a. 10s brown, type I 1,500. 140.00
12 A6 15s blue, type II 6,000. 125.00
No gum 1,500.
a. 15s blue, type I 12,000. 225.00
b. Printed on both sides, type II *18,750.*

The reprints are of type II and are perforated 10½, 11, 11½, 12, 12½ and 13. There are also imperforate reprints of Nos. 7-9.

A7

1861-62 ***Perf. 14***

No.	Type	Description	Unused	Used
13	A7	5s red	7,125.	7.00
14	A7	10s brown ('62)	13,000.	75.00

The reprints are perforated 9, 9 ½, 10½, 11, 12, 12½ and 13. There are also imperforate reprints of the 2 and 3s.

The 2, 3 and 15s of this type exist only as reprints.

A8

1863

No.	Type	Description	Unused	Used
15	A8	2s yellow	425.00	225.00
16	A8	3s green	5,250.	125.00
17	A8	5s rose	6,750.	37.50
18	A8	10s blue	14,000.	90.00
19	A8	15s yellow brown	12,000.	340.00

1864-65 **Wmk. 91** ***Perf. 9½***

No.	Type	Description	Unused	Used
20	A8	2s yellow ('65)	640.00	*900.00*
21	A8	3s green	55.00	52.50
22	A8	5s rose	9.00	11.50
23	A8	10s blue	110.00	22.50
24	A8	15s yellow brown	1,250.	210.00

Nos. 15-24 reprints are perforated 10½ and 13. There are also imperforate reprints of the 2s and 3s.

NEWSPAPER TAX STAMPS

From 1853 to 1858 the Austrian Newspaper Tax Stamp 2kr green (No. PR1) was also used in Lombardy-Venetia, at the value of 10 centesimi.

NT1

Type I — The banderol of the left eagle touches the beak of the eagle.

Type II — The banderol does not touch the beak.

1858-59 **Unwmk.** **Typo.** ***Imperf.***

No.	Type	Description	Unused	Used
PR1	NT1	1kr black, type I ('59)	3,750.	*4,750.*
PR2	NT1	2kr red, type II ('59)	500.00	75.00
a.		Watermark 91	1,650.	115.00
PR3	NT1	4kr red, type I	*150,000.*	*5,500.*

The reprints are on a smooth toned paper and are all of type II.

AZERBAIJAN

ˌa-zər-ˌbī-ˈjän

(Azerbaidjan)

LOCATION — Southernmost part of Russia in Eastern Europe, bounded by Georgia, Dagestan, Caspian Sea, Iran and Armenia

GOVT. — A Soviet Socialist Republic

AREA — 33,430 sq. mi.

POP. — 7,908,224 (1999 est)

CAPITAL — Baku

With Armenia and Georgia, Azerbaijan made up the Transcaucasian Federation of Soviet Republics.

Stamps of Azerbaijan were replaced in 1923 by those of Transcaucasian Federated Republics.

With the breakup of the Soviet Union on Dec. 26, 1991, Azerbaijan and ten former Soviet republics established the Commonwealth of Independent States.

100 Kopecks = 1 Ruble

100 Giapiks = 1 Manat (1992)

Catalogue values for unused stamps in this country are for Never Hinged items, beginning with Scott 350 in the regular postage section, and Scott C1 in the air post section.

National Republic

Standard Bearer — A1

Farmer at Sunset — A2

Baku — A3

Temple of Eternal Fires — A4

1919 **Unwmk.** **Litho.** ***Imperf.***

No.	Type	Description	Unused	Used
1	A1	10k multicolored	.25	*.30*
2	A1	20k multicolored	.25	*.30*
3	A2	40k green, yellow & blk	.25	*.30*
4	A2	60k red, yellow & blk	.25	*.35*
5	A2	1r blue, yellow & blk	.45	*.50*
6	A3	2r red, bister & blk	.45	*.50*
7	A3	5r blue, bister & blk	1.90	*1.75*
8	A3	10r olive grn, bis & blk	1.90	*1.75*
9	A4	25r blue, red & black	3.25	*40.00*
10	A4	50r ol grn, red & black	4.50	*4.75*
		Nos. 1-10 (10)	13.45	*50.50*

The two printings of Nos. 1-10 are distinguished by the grayish or thin white paper. Both have yellowish gum. White paper examples are worth five times the above values.

For surcharges see Nos. 57-64, 75-80.

Soviet Socialist Republic

Symbols of Labor — A5

Oil Well — A6

Bibi Eibatt Oil Field — A7

Khan's Palace, Baku — A8

Globe and Workers — A9

Maiden's Tower, Baku — A10

Goukasoff House A11

Blacksmiths — A12

Hall of Judgment, Baku — A13

1922

No.	Type	Description	Unused	Used
15	A5	1r gray green	.25	*.35*
16	A6	2r olive black	.60	*.60*
17	A7	5r gray brown	.25	*.35*
18	A8	10r gray	.60	*.70*
19	A9	25r orange brown	.25	*.40*
20	A10	50r violet	.25	*.40*
21	A11	100r dull red	.35	*.50*
22	A12	150r blue	.35	*.50*
23	A9	250r violet & buff	.35	*.50*
24	A13	400r dark blue	.40	*.50*
25	A12	500r gray vio & blk	.40	*.50*
26	A13	1000r dk blue & rose	.40	*.60*
27	A8	2000r blue & black	.40	*.50*
28	A7	3000r brown & blue	.45	*.50*
a.		Tete beche pair	18.00	18.00
29	A11	5000r black, *ol grn*	.75	*.90*
		Nos. 15-29 (15)	6.05	*7.80*

Counterfeits exist of Nos. 1-29. They generally sell for more than genuine examples.

For overprints and surcharges see Nos. 32-41, 43, 45-55, 65-72, 300-304, 307-333.

Nos. 15, 17, 23, 28, 27 Handstamped from Metal Dies in a Numbering Machine

1922

No.	Type	Description	Unused	Used
32	A5	10,000r on 1r	19.50	17.50
33	A7	15,000r on 5r	19.50	*27.50*
34	A9	33,000r on 250r	6.25	6.25
35	A7	50,000r on 3000r	32.50	10.00
36	A8	66,000r on 2000r	19.50	12.00
		Nos. 32-36 (5)	97.25	73.25

Same Surcharges on Regular Issue and Semi-Postal Stamps of 1922

1922-23

No.	Type	Description	Unused	Used
36A	A7	500r on 5r	180.00	*190.00*
37	A6	1000r on 2r	30.00	*36.00*
38	A8	2000r on 10r	18.00	9.00
39	A8	5000r on 2000r	9.00	3.75
40	A11	15,000r on 5000r	15.00	12.00
41	A5	20,000r on 1r	24.00	14.50
42	SP1	25,000r on 500r	*60.00*	—
43	A7	50,000r on 5r	60.00	60.00
44	SP2	50,000r on 1000r	*60.00*	—
45	A11	50,000r on 5000r	18.00	18.00
45A	A8	60,000r on 2000r	120.00	*225.00*
46	A11	70,000r on 5000r	150.00	47.50
47	A6	100,000r on 2r	18.00	18.00
48	A8	200,000r on 10r	12.00	12.00
49	A9	200,000r on 25r	18.00	19.00
50	A7	300,000r on 3000r	50.00	50.00
51	A8	500,000r on 2000r	30.00	30.00

Regular Issue Stamps of 1922-23 Surcharged

No.	Type	Description	Unused	Used
52	A7	500r on #33	*650.00*	*700.00*
53	A11	15,000r on #46	*650.00*	*700.00*
54	A7	300,000r on #35	*750.00*	*800.00*
55	A8	500,000r on #36	*650.00*	*700.00*

The surcharged semi-postal stamps were used for regular postage.

Same Surcharges on Stamps of 1919

No.	Type	Description	Unused	Used
57	A1	25,000r on 10k	.85	*1.50*
58	A1	50,000r on 20k	.85	*1.50*
59	A2	75,000r on 40k	2.00	*4.00*
60	A2	100,000r on 60k	.85	*1.50*
61	A2	200,000r on 1r	.85	*1.50*
62	A3	300,000r on 2r	1.10	*1.50*
63	A3	500,000r on 5r	1.10	*1.50*
64	A2	750,000r on 40k	4.25	*5.50*
		Nos. 57-64 (8)	11.85	*18.50*

Handstamped from Settings of Rubber Type in Black or Violet

Nos. 65-66, 72-80

Nos. 67-70

On Stamps of 1922

No.	Type	Description	Unused	Used
65	A6	100,000r on 2r	27.50	27.50
66	A8	200,000r on 10r	80.00	*80.00*
67	A8	200,000r on 10r (V)	80.00	80.00
68	A9	200,000r on 25r (V)	80.00	80.00
a.		Black surcharge	80.00	*80.00*
69	A7	300,000r on 3000r (V)	40.00	40.00
70	A8	500,000r on 2000r (V)	72.50	72.50
a.		Black surcharge	90.00	*90.00*
72	A11	1,500,000r on 5000r (V)	140.00	140.00
a.		Black surcharge	120.00	120.00

On Stamps of 1919

No.	Type	Description	Unused	Used
75	A1	50,000r on 20k	4.00	
76	A2	75,000r on 40k	4.00	
77	A2	100,000r on 60k	4.00	
78	A2	200,000r on 1r	4.00	
79	A3	300,000r on 2r	4.00	
80	A3	500,000r on 5r	4.00	

Inverted and double surcharges of Nos. 32-80 sell for twice the normal price.

Counterfeits exist of Nos. 32-80.

Baku Province

Regular and Semi-Postal Stamps of 1922 Handstamped in Violet or Black

The overprint reads "Bakinskoi P(ochtovoy) K(ontory)," meaning Baku Post Office.

1922 Unwmk. *Imperf.*

300	A5	1r gray green	100.00	
301	A7	5r gray brown	100.00	200.00
302	A12	150r blue	100.00	100.00
303	A9	250r violet & buff	100.00	200.00
304	A13	400r dark blue	75.00	75.00
305	SP1	500r bl & pale bl	100.00	150.00
306	SP2	1000r brown & bis	100.00	
307	A8	2000r blue & black	120.00	150.00
308	A7	3000r brown & blue	100.00	
309	A11	5000r black, *ol grn*	120.00	
		Nos. 300-309 (10)	1,015.	

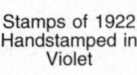

Stamps of 1922 Handstamped in Violet

БАКИНСКАГО Г-П-Т.О. №1

Ovpt. reads: Baku Post, Telegraph Office No. 1.

1924 Overprint 24x2mm

312	A12	150r blue	65.00	
313	A9	250r violet & buff	65.00	
314	A13	400r dark blue	65.00	
317	A8	2000r blue & black	65.00	
318	A7	3000r brn & blue	65.00	
319	A11	5000r black, *ol grn*	200.00	

Overprint 30x3½mm

323	A12	150r blue	100.00	125.00
324	A9	250r violet & buff	100.00	
325	A13	400r dark blue	100.00	100.00
328	A8	2000r blue & black	100.00	100.00
329	A7	3000r brn & blue	100.00	150.00
330	A11	5000r black, *ol grn*	100.00	

Overprinted on Nos. 32-33, 35

331	A5	10,000r on 1r	500.00
332	A7	15,000r on 5r	500.00
333	A7	50,000r on 3000r	500.00
		Nos. 312-333 (15)	2,625.

The overprinted semipostal stamps were used for regular postage.

A 24x2mm handstamp on #17, B1-B2, and 30x3½mm on Nos. 15, 17, B1-B2, was of private origin.

Catalogue values for unused stamps in this section, from this point to the end of the section, are for Never Hinged items.

Flag, Map — A20

Unwmk.

1992, Mar. 26 Litho. *Perf. 14*

350 A20 35k multicolored 1.50 1.50

For surcharge, see No. 733.

Caspian Sea — A21

1992, May 7 *Perf. 12*

351	A21	25g on 15k multi	.40	.40
a.		Booklet pane of 12	5.00	
		Complete booklet, #351a	6.00	
352	A21	35g on 15k multi	.50	.50
353	A21	50g on 15k multi	.65	.65
354	A21	1.50m on 15k multi	2.25	2.25
355	A21	2.50m on 15k multi	3.50	3.50
		Nos. 351-355 (5)	7.30	7.30

Nos. 351-355 are sucharged on the Azerbaijan value of a National Park series featuring one stamp for each republic, prepared by the Soviet Union but not issued. Value for the unoverprinted Azerbaijan stamp, $1.25.

For additional surcharges see Nos. 435, 501-504.

Iran-Azerbaijan Telecommunications — A21a

1993 Photo. *Perf. 13x13½*

355A A21a 15g multicolored *1.25 1.25*

See Iran No. 2544.

For surcharges see Nos. 403-406.

Horses A22

1993, Feb. 1 Litho. *Perf. 13*

356	A22	20g shown	.25	.25
357	A22	30g Kabarda	.25	.25
358	A22	50g Qarabair	.25	.25
359	A22	1m Don	.25	.25
360	A22	2.50m Yakut	.40	.40
361	A22	5m Orlov	.80	.80
362	A22	10m Diliboz	1.75	1.75
		Nos. 356-362 (7)	3.95	3.95

Perf. 12½

Souvenir Sheet

362A A22 8m Qarabag 1.50 1.50

For overprints see Nos. 629-636.

Maiden's Tower — A23

1992-93 Litho. *Perf. 12½x12*

363	A23	10g blk & blue grn	.25	.25
365	A23	20g black & red	.25	.25
367	A23	50g black & blue grn	.25	.25
368	A23	50g black & yellow	.50	.50
370	A23	1m black & rose lilac	.25	.25
372	A23	1.50m black & blue	1.25	1.25
373	A23	2.50m black & yellow	.50	.50
374	A23	5m black & green	.75	.75
		Nos. 363-374 (8)	4.00	4.00

Issued: 10g, 20g, 1.50m, No. 367, Dec. 20; No. 368, 1m, 2.50m, 5m, June 20, 1993.

For surcharges see Nos. 550-557, 757.

Government Building — A24

1993, Oct. 12 Litho. *Perf. 12½*

375	A24	25g yellow & black	.30	.30
376	A24	30g green & black	.30	.30
377	A24	50g blue & black	.60	.60
378	A24	1m red & black	1.00	1.00
		Nos. 375-378 (4)	2.20	2.20

For surcharges see No. 407-414.

Flowers — A25

1993, Aug. 12 Litho. *Perf. 12½*

379	A25	25g Tulipa eichleri	.25	.25
380	A25	50g Puschkinia scilloides	.25	.25
381	A25	1m Iris elegantissima	.25	.25
382	A25	1.50m Iris acutiloba	.35	.35
383	A25	5m Tulipa florenskyii	.85	.85
384	A25	10m Iris reticulata	1.60	1.60
		Nos. 379-384 (6)	3.55	3.55

Souvenir Sheet

Perf. 13

385 A25 10m Muscari elecostomum 1.75 1.75

No. 385 contains one 32x40mm stamp.

For surcharge, see No. 809.

Fish A26

25g, Acipenser guldenstadti. 50g, Acipenser stellatus. 1m, Rutilus frisii kutum. 1.50m, Rutilus rutilus caspicus. 5m, Salmo trutta caspius. No. 391, Alosa kessleri. No. 392, Huso huso.

1993, Aug. 27 *Perf. 12½*

386	A26	25g multicolored	.25	.25
387	A26	50g multicolored	.25	.25
388	A26	1m multicolored	.25	.25
389	A26	1.50m multicolored	.35	.35
390	A26	5m multicolored	.85	.85
391	A26	10m multicolored	1.60	1.60
		Nos. 386-391 (6)	3.55	3.55

Souvenir Sheet

Perf. 13

392 A26 10m multicolored 1.75 1.75

No. 392 contains one 40x32mm stamp.

For surcharges, see Nos. 810, 813.

Pres. Heydar A. Aliyev — A27

Design: No. 394, Map of Nakhichevan.

1993, Sept. 12 Litho. *Perf. 12½x13*

393	A27	25m multicolored	2.00	1.60
394	A27	25m multicolored	2.00	1.60
a.		Pair, #393-394	4.25	4.25
b.		Souv. sheet, #393-394, perf. 12	*90.00*	
c.		Souv. sheet, #393-394, perf. 12	15.00	

Name on map spelled "Naxcivan" on No. 394c. It is spelled "Haxcivan" on Nos. 394-394b.

No. 394c issued Sept. 20, 1993.

Shirvanshah's Palace, UNESCO World Heritage Site, Baku — A28

Style of tombs: 2m, Shirvanshah's Palace, 13th-14th cent. 4m, Turbe mausoleum, 15th cent. 8m, Divan-Khana, 15th cent.

1994, Jan. 17 Litho. *Perf. 11*

395	A28	2m red, silver & black	.25	.25
396	A28	4m green, silver & black	.35	.35
397	A28	8m blue, silver & black	.75	.75
		Nos. 395-397 (3)	1.35	1.35

For surcharges, see Nos. 753, 758-759, 808.

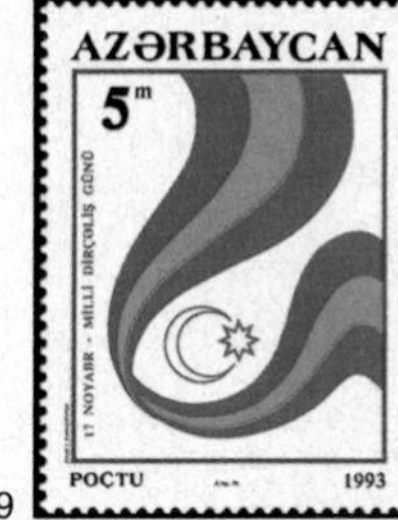

A29

1994, Jan. 17 *Perf. 12½*

398	A29	5m Natl. Colors, Star, Crescent	.45	.45
399	A29	8m Natl. coat of arms	.80	.80

For surcharges, see Nos. 816, 817.

A30

1994, Jan. 17 *Perf. 12½*

400 A30 10m multi + label .75 .75

Mohammed Fizuli (1494-1556), poet.

Mammed Amin Rasulzade (1884-1955), 1st President — A31

Jalil Mamedkulizade, Writer, 125th Birth Anniv. — A32

1994, May 21 ***Perf. 12½, 13 (#402)***
401 A31 15m blk, yel & brown 1.25 1.25
402 A32 20m black, blue & gold 1.00 1.00

No. 402 printed se-tenant with label.
For surcharges, see Nos. 814, 867.

No. 355A Surcharged

1994, Jan. 18 **Photo.** ***Perf. 13x13½***
403 A21a 2m on 15g .25 .25
404 A21a 20m on 15g .65 .65
405 A21a 25m on 15g .85 .85
406 A21a 50m on 15g 2.25 2.25
a. Vert. strip of 4, #403-406 *5.00 5.00*
Nos. 403-406 (4) 4.00 4.00

Nos. 375-378 Surcharged

1994, Feb. 22 **Litho.** ***Perf. 12½***
407 A24 5m on 1m #375 .50 .50
408 A24 10m on 30g #377 .50 .50
409 A24 15m on 30g #377 .50 .50
a. Pair, #408-409 1.25 1.25
410 A24 20m on 50g #378 .50 .50
411 A24 25m on 1m #375 .60 .60
a. Pair, #407, 411 1.40 1.40
412 A24 40m on 50g #378 1.10 1.10
a. Pair, #410, 412 1.75 1.75
413 A24 50m on 25g #376 1.50 1.50
414 A24 100m on 25g #376 2.25 2.25
a. Pair, #413-414 4.00 4.00
Nos. 407-414 (8) 7.45 7.45

Baku Oil Fields — A33

Designs: 15m, Temple of Eternal Fires. 20m, Oil derricks. 25m, Early tanker. 50m, Ludwig Nobel, Robert Nobel, Petr Bilderling, Alfred Nobel.

1994, June 10 **Photo.** ***Perf. 13***
415 A33 15m multicolored .30 .30
416 A33 20m multicolored .40 .40
417 A33 25m multicolored .45 .45
418 A33 50m multicolored 1.10 1.10
a. Souvenir sheet of 1 1.50 1.50
Nos. 415-418 (4) 2.25 2.25

See Turkmenistan Nos. 39-43.

Minerals — A34

1994, June 15 **Litho.** ***Perf. 13***
419 A34 5m Laumontite .30 .30
420 A34 10m Epidot calcite .50 .50
421 A34 15m Andradite .75 .75
422 A34 20m Amethyst 1.00 1.00
a. Souvenir sheet, #419-422 + 2 labels, perf. 12 2.50 2.50
Nos. 419-422 (4) 2.55 2.55

For surcharges, see Nos. 760, 762-764.

Posthorn — A35

1994, June 28 **Litho.** ***Perf. 12½***
426 A35 5m black & red .25 .25
427 A35 10m black & green .25 .25
428 A35 20m black & blue .40 .40
429 A35 25m black & yellow .40 .40
431 A35 40m black & brown .75 .75
Nos. 426-431 (5) 2.05 2.05

For surcharges see Nos. 487-489A, 752, 761, 765, 811.

No. 351 Surcharged

Unwmk.

1994, Oct. 17 **Litho.** ***Perf. 12***
435 A21 400m on 25g multi 3.00 3.00

Souvenir Sheet

Pres. Heydar A. Aliyev — A36

1994, Oct. 28 **Litho.** ***Perf. 14***
436 A36 150m multicolored 4.00 4.00

Ships of the Caspian Sea A37

Designs: a, Tugboat, "Captain Racebov." b, "Azerbaijan." c, Balt Ro Ro line, "Merkuri I." d, Tanker, "Tovuz." e, Tanker.

1994, Oct. 28
437 A37 50m Strip of 5, #a.-e. 2.00 2.00

Issued in sheets of 15 stamps. The background of the sheet shows a nautical chart, giving each stamp a different background. Value $6.50.

1994 World Cup Soccer Championships, U.S. — A38

Various soccer plays. Denominations: 5m, 10m, 20m, 25m, 30m, 50m, 80m.

1994, June 17 **Litho.** ***Perf. 13***
438-444 A38 Set of 7 3.25 3.25

Souvenir Sheet

445 A38 100m multicolored 1.75 1.75

No. 445 contains one 32x40mm stamp and is a continuous design.

Dinosaurs — A39

Designs: 5m, Coelophysis, segisaurus. 10m, Pentaceratops, tyrannosaurids. 20m, Segnosaurus, oviraptor. 25m, Albertosaurus, corythosaurus. 30m, Iguanodons. 50m, Stegosaurus, allosaurus. 80m, Tyrannosaurus, saurolophus.
100m, Phobetor.

1994, Sept. 15
446-452 A39 Set of 7 3.25 3.25

Souvenir Sheet
Perf. 12½

453 A39 100m multicolored 1.75 1.75

No. 453 contains one 40x32mm stamp and is a continuous design.

Lyrurus Mlokosiewiczki — A40

a, 50m, Female on nest. b, 80m, Female on mountain cliff. c, 100m, 2 males. d, 120m, Male.

1994, Dec. 15 **Litho.** ***Perf. 12½***
454 A40 Block of 4, #a.-d. 6.00 6.00

World Wildlife Fund.

Raptors A41

10m, Haliaeetus albicilla. 15m, Aguila heliaca. 20m, Aguila rapax. 25m, Gypaetus barbatus, vert. 50m, Falco cherrug, vert.
100m, Aguila chrysaetos.

1994, Nov. 15 **Litho.** ***Perf. 13***
458-462 A41 Set of 5 3.25 3.25

Souvenir Sheet
Perf. 12½

463 A41 100m multicolored 1.75 1.75

No. 463 contains one 40x32mm stamp and is a continuous design.

Cats A42

Designs: 10m, Felis libica, vert. 15m, Felis otocolobus, vert. 20m, Felis lyns, vert. 25m, Felis pardus. 50m, Panthera tigrus.
100m, Panthera tigrus adult and cub, vert.

1994, Dec. 14 ***Perf. 13***
464-468 A42 Set of 5 3.25 3.25

Souvenir Sheet

469 A42 100m multicolored 1.75 1.75

No. 469 contains one 32x40mm stamp and is a continuous design.
For overprints see Nos. 637-642.

Butterflies A43

Designs: 10m, Parnassius apollo. 25m, Zegris menestho. 50m, Manduca atropos. 60m, Pararge adrastoides.

1995, Jan. 23 **Litho.** ***Perf. 14***
470 A43 10m multicolored .30 .30
471 A43 25m multicolored .65 .65
472 A43 50m multicolored 1.15 1.15
473 A43 60m multicolored 1.50 1.50
a. Souvenir sheet of 4, #470-473 3.50 3.50
Nos. 470-473 (4) 3.60 3.60

For surcharges, see Nos. 783-786, 786a.

Intl. Olympic Committee, Cent. — A44

Designs: No. 474, Pierre de Coubertin. No. 475, Discus. No. 476, Javelin.

1994, Dec. 15 **Litho.** ***Perf. 12***
474-476 A44 100m Set of 3 3.00 3.00

A45

1994 Winter Olympic medalists, Lillehammer: 10m, Aleksei Urmanov, Russia, figure skating, 25, Nancy Kerrigan, US, figure skating. 40m Bonnie Blair, US, speed skating, horiz. 50m, Takanori Kano, Japan, ski jumping, horiz. 80m, Philip LaRouche, Canada, freestyle skiing. 100m, Four-man bobsled, Germany.
200m, Katja Seizinger, skiing, Germany, vert.

1995, Feb. 10 **Litho.** ***Perf. 14***
478-483 A45 Set of 6 3.50 3.50

Souvenir Sheet

484 A45 200m multicolored 3.25 3.25

Miniature Sheet

A46

No. 485, 100m: a, Mary Cleave, U.S. b, Valentina Tereshkova, Russia. c, Tamara Jernigan, U.S. d, Wendy Lawrence, U.S.
No. 486, 100m: a, Mae Jemison, U.S. b, Catherine Coleman, U.S. c, Ellen Shulman, U.S. d, M.E. Weber, U.S.

1995, Feb. 21
485-486 A46 Set of 2, #a-d 6.00 6.00

First manned moon landing, 25th anniv. (in 1994).

Nos. 426-428 Surcharged

1995 Litho. *Perf. 12½*

487 A35 100m on 5m #426 .25 .25
488 A35 250m on 10m #427 .40 .40
488A A35 400m on 25m No. 429 .50 .50
489 A35 500m on 20m #428 .65 .65
489A A35 900m on 40m No. 431 1.25 1.25
Nos. 487-489A (5) 3.05 3.05

Issued: No. 488A, 7/7; Nos. 487-488, 489, 2/28.

Mushrooms — A47

Designs: 100m, Gymnopilus spectabilis. 250m, Fly agaris. 300m, Lepiota procera. 400m, Hygrophorus spectosus.
500m, Fly agaris, diff.

1995, Sept. 1 Litho. *Perf. 14*

490-493 A47 Set of 4 3.75 3.75

Souvenir Sheet

494 A47 500m multicolored 2.25 2.25

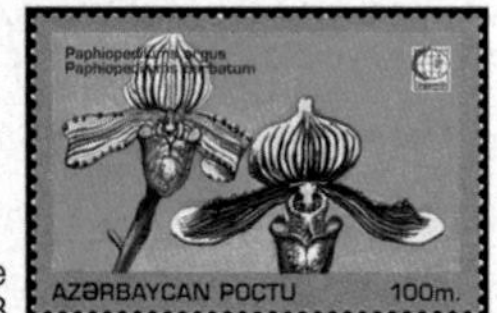

Singapore '95 — A48

Orchids: 100m, Paphiopedilum argus, paphiopedilum barbatum. 250m, Maxillaria picta. 300m, Laeliocattleya. 400m, Dendrobium nobile.
500m, Cattleya gloriette.

1995, Sept. 1

495-498 A48 Set of 4 3.75 3.75

Souvenir Sheet

499 A48 500m multicolored 2.25 2.25

UN, 50th Anniv. A49

Design: 250m, Azerbaijan Pres. Heydar A. Aliyev, UN Sec. Gen. Boutros Boutros-Ghali.

1995, Sept. 15

500 A49 250m multicolored 2.50 2.50

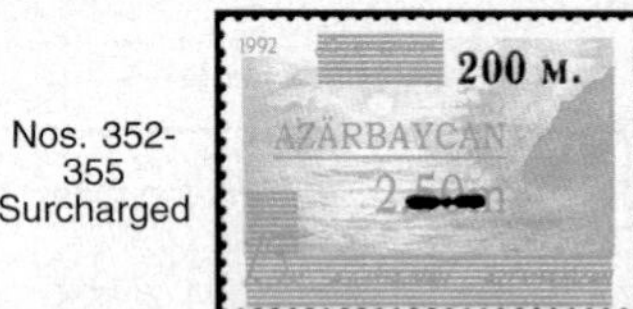

Nos. 352-355 Surcharged

1995 Litho. *Perf. 12*

501 A21 200m on 2.50m #355 .50 .50
502 A21 600m on 35g #352 1.50 1.50
503 A21 800m on 50q #353 2.00 2.00
504 A21 1000m on 1.50m #354 2.50 2.50
Nos. 501-504 (4) 6.50 6.50

Uzeyir Hacibeyov (1885-1948) A50

400m, Ali Aga Iskenderov (1895-1965).

1995, June 30 Litho. *Perf. 12x12½*

505 A50 250m silver gray & black .40 .40
506 A50 400m gold bister & brn .85 .85

Balloons and Airships A51

100m, First hydrogen balloon, 1784. 150m, 1st motorized balloon, 1883. 250m, First elliptical balloon, 1784. 300m, 1st Scott Baldwin dirigible, 1904. 400m, US Marine balloon, 1917. 500m, Pedal-powered dirigible, 1909.
800m, 1st rigid dirigible designed by Hugo Eckener, 1924.

1995, July 20 Litho. *Perf. 13*

507 A51 100m multi, vert. .25 .25
508 A51 150m multi, vert. .35 .35
509 A51 250m multi .50 .50
510 A51 300m multi .60 .60
511 A51 400m multi .90 .90
512 A51 500m multi 1.25 1.25
Nos. 507-512 (6) 3.85 3.85

Souvenir Sheet

513 A51 800m multicolored 2.75 2.75

Marine Life A52

50m, Loligo vulgaris. 100m, Orchistoma pileus. 150m, Pegea confoederata. 250m, Polyorchis karafutoensis. 300m, Agalma okeni.
500m, Corolla spectabillis.

1995, June 2 Litho. *Perf. 13*

514 A52 50m multi .25 .25
515 A52 100m multi .45 .45
516 A52 150m multi .60 .60
517 A52 250m multi, vert. 1.10 1.10
518 A52 300m multi, vert. 1.25 1.25
Nos. 514-518 (5) 3.65 3.65

Souvenir Sheet

519 A52 500m multicolored 2.50 2.50

Turtles A53

Designs: 50m, Chelus fimbriatus. 100m, Caretta caretta. 150m, Geochelone pardalis. 250m, Geochelone elegans. 300m, Testudo hermanni.
500m, Macroclemys temmincki.

1995, June 12 Litho. *Perf. 13*

520 A53 50m multicolored .25 .25
521 A53 100m multicolored .45 .45
522 A53 150m multicolored .60 .60
523 A53 250m multicolored 1.10 1.10
524 A53 300m multicolored 1.25 1.25
Nos. 520-524 (5) 3.65 3.65

Souvenir Sheet

525 A53 500m multicolored 2.50 2.50

1998 World Cup Soccer Championships, France — A54

Various soccer plays.

1995, Sept. 30 Litho. *Perf. 12½*

526 A54 100m orange & multi .40 .40
527 A54 150m green & multi .55 .55
528 A54 250m yel org & multi .80 .80
529 A54 300m yellow & multi 1.00 1.00
530 A54 400m blue & multi 1.40 1.40
Nos. 526-530 (5) 4.15 4.15

Souvenir Sheet

Perf. 13

531 A54 600m multicolored 2.25 2.25

Domestic Cats — A55

1995, Oct. 30 *Perf. 12½*

532 A55 100m Persian .35 .35
533 A55 150m Chartreux .50 .50
534 A55 250m Somali .65 .65
535 A55 300m Longhair Scottish fold .80 .80
536 A55 400m Cumric 1.00 1.00
537 A55 500m Turkish angora 1.25 1.25
Nos. 532-537 (6) 4.55 4.55

Souvenir Sheet

538 A55 800m Birman 2.00 2.00

No. 538 contains one 32x40mm stamp.

Fauna and Flora — A56

Designs: 100m, Horse. 200m, Muscari elecostomum, vert. 250m, Huso huso. 300m, Aquila chrysaetos. 400m, Panthera tigrus. 500m, Lyrurus miokosiewickzi, facing right. 1000m, Lyrurus miokosiewickzi, facing left.

1995, Nov. 30

539 A56 100m multicolored .25 .25
540 A56 200m multicolored .50 .50
541 A56 250m multicolored .60 .60
542 A56 300m multicolored .75 .75
543 A56 400m multicolored 1.00 1.00
544 A56 500m multicolored 1.50 1.50
545 A56 1000m multicolored 2.50 2.50
Nos. 539-545 (7) 7.10 7.10

John Lennon (1940-80) A57

1995, Dec. 8 *Perf. 14½*

546 A57 500m multicolored 1.75 1.75

Issued in sheet of 16 plus label.

Miniature Sheet

Locomotives — A58

Designs: No. 547a, 4-4-0, America. b, J3 Hudson, US. c, 2-8-2. d, 2-6-2, Germany. e, 2-8-2, Germany. f, 2-6-2, Italy. g, G-C5, Japan. h, 2-10-2 QJ, China. i, 0-10-0, China.
500m, Electric passenger train, vert.

1996, Feb. 1 *Perf. 14*

547 A58 100m Sheet of 9, #a.-i. 6.50 6.50

Souvenir Sheet

548 A58 500m multicolored 3.25 3.25

Dr. M. Topchibashev, Surgeon — A59

1996, Feb. 1

549 A59 300m multicolored 1.25 1.25

Nos. 363, 365, 367-368, 370, 372-374 Surcharged

1995, Jan. 4 Litho. *Perf. 12½x12*

550 A23 250m on 10g #363 .75 .75
551 A23 250m on 20g #365 .75 .75
552 A23 250m on 50g #368 .75 .75
553 A23 250m on 1.50m #372 .75 .75
554 A23 500m on 50g #367 1.50 1.50
555 A23 500m on 1m #370 1.50 1.50
556 A23 500m on 2.50m #373 1.50 1.50
557 A23 500m on 5m #374 1.50 1.50
Nos. 550-557 (8) 9.00 9.00

1996 Olympic Games, Atlanta A60

1996, Apr. 9 Litho. *Perf. 14*

568 A60 50m Carl Lewis .25 .25
569 A60 100m Muhammed Ali .40 .40
570 A60 150m Li Ning .40 .40
571 A60 200m Said Aouita .55 .55
572 A60 250m Olga Korbut .70 .70
573 A60 300m Nadia Comaneci .90 .90
574 A60 400m Greg Louganis 1.00 1.00
Nos. 568-574 (7) 4.20 4.20

Souvenir Sheet

575 A60 500m Nazim Hüseynov, vert. 1.90 1.90

Husein Aliyev (1911-91), Artist A61

Paintings: 100m, Water bird, swamp. 200m, Landscape.

1996, Apr. 16 Litho. *Perf. 14*

576 A61 100m multicolored 1.00 1.00
577 A61 200m multicolored 1.50 1.50
a. Pair, #576-577 + label 2.50 2.50

No. 577a issued in sheets of 6 stamps.

Resid Behbudov (1915-89), Singer — A62

1996, Apr. 22 *Perf. 12½*

578 A62 100m multicolored 1.30 1.30

A63

1996, Mar. 20
579 A63 250m multicolored 1.25 1.25

Novruz Bayrami, natl. holiday.

A64

1996, May 28 **Litho.** ***Perf. 14***
580 A64 250m multicolored 1.25 1.25

Independence, 5th anniv.

A65

1996, Apr. 22 **Litho.** ***Perf. 12½***
581 A65 100m multicolored 1.25 1.25

Yusif Memmedeliyev (1905-95), chemist.

A66

Jerusalem, 3000th Anniv.: a, 100m, Wailing Wall. b, 250m, Inside cathedral. c, 300m, Dome of the Rock.
500m, Windmill.

1996, June 7 ***Perf. 14***
582 A66 Sheet of 3, #a.-c. 3.50 3.50

Souvenir Sheet

583 A66 500m multicolored 4.00 4.00

For overprints see Nos. 643-644.

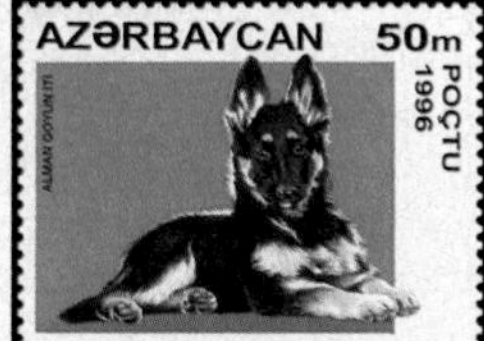

Dogs A67

Designs: 50m, German shepherd. 100m, Basset hound. 150m, Collie. 200m, Bull terrier. 300m, Boxer. 400m, Cocker spaniel.
500m, Sharpei.

1996, June 18 ***Perf. 13***
584-589 A67 Set of 6 3.75 3.75

Souvenir Sheet

590 A67 500m multicolored 2.25 2.25

Birds — A68

Designs: 50m, Tetraenura regia. 100m, Coliuspasser macrourus. 150m, Oriolus xanthornus. 200m, Oriolus oriolus. 300m, Sturnus vulgaris. 400m, Serinus mozambicus.
500m, Merops apiaster.

1996, June 19 ***Perf. 13***
591-596 A68 Set of 6 3.75 3.75

Souvenir Sheet

597 A68 500m multicolored 2.25 2.25

Roses — A69

Designs: 50m, Burgundy. 100m, Virgo. 150m, Rose gaujard. 200m, Luna. 300m, Lady rose. 400m, Landora.
500m, Lougsor, horiz.

1996, June 19
598-603 A69 Set of 6 3.75 3.75

Souvenir Sheet

604 A69 500m multicolored 2.25 2.25

A70

1996, July 8 **Litho.** ***Perf. 14***
605 A70 500m multicolored 1.25 1.25

UNICEF, 50th anniv.

A71

Competing teams: 100m, Spain, Bulgaria. 150m, Romania, France. 200m, Czech Republic, Germany. 250m, England, Israel. 300m, Croatia, Turkey. 400m, Italy, Russia.
500m, Trophy cup.

1996, July 22
606-611 A71 Set of 6 5.00 5.00

Souvenir Sheet

612 A71 500m multicolored 2.50 2.50

Euro '96, European Soccer Championships, Great Britain.

Ships A72

Ship, home country: 100m, Chinese junk. 150m, Danmark, Denmark. 200m, Nippon Maru, Japan. 250m, Mircea, Romania. 300m, Kruzenshtern, Russia. 400m, Ariadne, Germany.
500m, Tovarishch, Russia, vert.

1996, Aug. 26 **Litho.** ***Perf. 14***
613-618 A72 Set of 6 5.00 5.00

Souvenir Sheet

619 A72 500m multicolored 3.75 3.75

For overprints see Nos. 645-651.

Baxram Gur Kills a Dragon, Sculpture — A73

1997, Mar. 6 **Litho.** ***Perf. 13½x13***
620 A73 250m black & yellow .50 .50
621 A73 400m black & vermilion .65 .65
622 A73 500m black & green .85 .85
623 A73 1000m black & purple 1.75 1.75
Nos. 620-623 (4) 3.75 3.75

See No. 671.

Famous Personalities — A74

No. 624, Aziz Mamed-Kerim Ogli Aliyev (1897-1962), politician. No. 625, Illyas Efendiyev (1914-96), writer. No. 626, Fatali Khan-Khoyski (1875-1920), politician. No. 627, Nariman Narimanov (1870-1925), politician, writer.

1997, Mar. 25 **Litho.** ***Perf. 14***

Background Color

624 A74 250m tan 1.10 1.10
625 A74 250m gray blue 1.10 1.10
626 A74 250m pale red 1.10 1.10
627 A74 250m pale olive 1.10 1.10
Nos. 624-627 (4) 4.40 4.40

Qobustan Prehistoric Art — A75

Rock carvings: a, Oxen. b, Large horned animals. c, Six figures.

1997, May 19 **Litho.** ***Perf. 14***
628 A75 500m Sheet of 3, #a.-c. 5.25 5.25

For overprint see No. 674.

#356-362A, 464-469 Ovptd. in Red

1997, June 2 **Litho.** ***Perf. 13***

Denominations as Before

629-635 A22 Set of 7 11.00 11.00

Souvenir Sheet

636 A22 8m multicolored 6.00 6.00

Location of overprint varies. No. 636 is ovptd. both on stamp and in sheet margin.

1997, June 2

Denominations as Before

637-641 A42 Set of 5 8.00 8.00

Souvenir Sheet

642 A42 100m multicolored 6.50 6.50

Location of overprint varies. No. 642 is ovptd. both on stamp and in sheet margin.

Nos. 582-583, 613-619 Ovptd.

1997, June 2 ***Perf. 14***
643 A66 Sheet of 3, #a.-c. 7.25 7.25

Souvenir Sheet

644 A66 500m multicolored 7.25 7.25

Size and location of overprint varies. Overprint appears both on stamp and in sheet margin.

1997, June 2 ***Perf. 14***

Denominations as Before

645-650 A72 Set of 6 7.25 7.25

Souvenir Sheet

651 A72 500m multicolored 7.25 7.25

Location of overprint varies. No. 651 is ovptd. both on stamp and in sheet margin.

Grimm's Fairy Tales — A76

The Town Musicians of Bremen: No. 652: a, Dog. b, Dancing donkey, cat. c, Rooster.
500m, Animals looking through window at treaure chest, man.

1997, July 1 ***Perf. 13½x14***
652 A76 250m Sheet of 3, #a.-c. 6.00 6.00

Souvenir Sheet

653 A76 500m multicolored 5.00 5.00

Caspian Seals A77

Designs: a, Seal looking right. b, Mountain top, seal looking forward. c, Seal, seagull. d, Seal looking left. e, Seal looking forward. f, Small seal.
500m, Mother nursing pup.

1997, July 1
654 A77 250m Sheet of 6, #a.-f. 5.75 5.75

Souvenir Sheet

655 A77 500m multicolored 4.00 4.00

Traditional Musical Instruments — A77a

1997, Aug. 4 Litho. *Perf. 14*

656 A77a 250m Qaval 1.00 1.00
657 A77a 250m Tanbur 1.00 1.00
658 A77a 500m Cenq 2.00 2.00
Nos. 656-658 (3) 4.00 4.00

A78 A79

Azerbaijan Oil Industry: a, Early oil derricks, building. b, Off-shore oil drilling platform.

1997, Aug. 18 *Perf. 14½*

Souvenir Sheet

659 A78 500m Sheet of 2, #a.-b. 4.00 4.00

1997, Sept. 12 *Perf. 14x13½*

660 A79 250m Hagani Shirvany, poet 1.25 1.25

Issued in sheets of 4 + 5 labels. Value $6.50.

Mosques A80

No. 661, Ashaqi Qovgar-agi, Shusha, 1874-75. No. 662, Momuna-Zatun, Naxcivan, 1187. No. 663, Taza-pir, Baku (1905-14).

1997, Sept. 18 Litho. *Perf. 14*

661 A80 250m multicolored 1.00 1.00
662 A80 250m multicolored 1.00 1.00
663 A80 250m multicolored 1.00 1.00
Nos. 661-663 (3) 3.00 3.00

H.C. Rasulbekov (1917-1984), Communications Official — A81

1997, Oct. 6 Litho. *Perf. 14*

664 A81 250m multicolored 1.10 1.10

1998 World Cup Soccer Championships, France — A82

Winning team photos: No. 665: a, Italy, 1938. b, Argentina, 1986. c, Uruguay, 1980. d, Brazil, 1994. e, England, 1966. f, Germany, 1990.

1500m, Tofiq Bahramov, "Golden Whistle" prize winner, 1966, vert.

1997, Oct. 15

665 A82 250m Sheet of 6, #a.-f. 5.00 5.00

Souvenir Sheet

666 A82 1500m multicolored 4.00 4.00

A83 A84

Figure skaters: No. 667: a, Katarina Witt, Germany. b, Elvis Stojko, Canada. c, Midori Ito, Japan. d, Silhouettes of various winter sports against natl. flag. e, Hand holding Olympic torch. f, Kristi Yamaguchi, US. g, John Curry, England. h, Lu Chen, China.

No. 668, Gordeyeva and Grinkov, Russia.

1998, Jan. 13 Litho. *Perf. 14*

667 A83 250m Sheet of 8, #a.-h. 5.50 5.50

Souvenir Sheet

668 A83 500m multicolored 4.00 4.00

1998 Winter Olympic Games, Nagano.

1998, Feb. 4 *Perf. 13½*

Diana, Princess of Wales (1961-97): No. 669, Wearing black turtleneck. No. 670, Wearing violet dress.

669 A84 400m multicolored .85 .85
670 A84 400m multicolored .85 .85

Nos. 669-670 were each issued in sheets of 6. Value, set of 2 sheets $10.

Sculpture Type of 1997

1998, Mar. 23 Litho. *Perf. 13½x13*

671 A73 100m blk & bright pink 1.25 1.25

Hasan Aliyev, Ecologist, 90th Birth Anniv. A85

1998, Apr. 3 *Perf. 14*

672 A85 500m multicolored 1.25 1.25

Souvenir Sheet

Pres. Heydar Aliyev, 75th Birthday — A86

1998, May 10 *Perf. 13½*

673 A86 500m multicolored 3.50 3.50

No. 628 Ovptd.

1998, May 13 *Perf. 14*

674 A75 500m Sheet of 3, #a.-c. 10.00 10.00

Additional inscription in sheet margin reads "ISRAEL 98 — WORLD STAMP EXHIBITION / TEL-AVIV 13-21 MAY 1998."

Artists A87

No. 675, Gara Garayev, composer. No. 676, Ashug Alesker, folk musician, poet. No. 677, Mohammad-Hossein Shahriar, poet.

1998, June 7 Litho. *Perf. 14*

675 A87 250m multicolored 1.00 1.00
676 A87 250m multicolored 1.00 1.00
677 A87 250m multicolored 1.00 1.00
Nos. 675-677 (3) 3.00 3.00

Bul-Bul, Singer, Birth Cent. — A88

1998, July 7

678 A88 500m multicolored 1.25 1.25

Disney Characters at World Rapid Chess Championship — A89

Designs: 250m, Minnie, Mickey.

No. 679: a, Minnie, Mickey. b, Goofy. c, Donald. d, Pluto. e, Minnie. f, Daisy. g, Goofy, Donald. h, Mickey.

No. 680, 4000m, Donald, Mickey. No. 681, 4000m, Minnie, Mickey.

1998 *Perf. 13½*

678A A89 250m multicolored *4.50 4.50*

Perf. 13½x14

679 A89 500m Sheet of 8, #a.-h. *32.50 32.50*

Souvenir Sheets

680-681 A89 Set of 2 *50.00 50.00*

Issued: 250m, 12/28; others, 11/13.

New Year Holiday A90

Europa: 1000m, Woman rolling dough. 3000m, Men performing at holiday festival.

1998, Dec. 29 Litho. *Perf. 13x12½*

682 A90 1000m multicolored *1.75 1.75*
683 A90 3000m multicolored *3.75 3.75*

Nos. 682-683 Ovptd.

1999, Apr. 27 Litho. *Perf. 13x12½*

684 A90 1000m on #682 *1.75 1.75*
685 A90 3000m on #683 *3.50 3.50*

A91 A92

Europa: 1000m, Rose flamingo, Gizilagach Natl. Park. 3000m, Deer, Girkan Natl. Park.

1999, Apr. 28 *Perf. 12½x12¾*

686 A91 1000m multicolored *1.75 1.75*
687 A91 3000m multicolored *3.75 3.75*

1999, Aug. 3 Litho. *Perf. 11¼x11¾*

Towers: 1000m, Dord Kundge, 14th cent. 3000m, Danravy, 13th cent.

688 A92 1000m black & blue 1.00 1.00
689 A92 3000m black & red 3.00 3.00

See Nos. 701-702, 717-718, 731-732, 744, 754.

For surcharge, see No. 815.

A93

Naxçivan Autonomous Republic, 75th anniv.: a, Pres. Heydar Aliyev, flag. b, Map of Naxçivan.

1999, Oct. 9 *Perf. 12*

690 A93 1000m Pair, #a.-b. 4.00 4.00
c. Souvenir sheet, pair, #a.-b. 4.00 4.00

A94

1999, Oct. 20 *Perf. 12½x12*

691 A94 250m multicolored 1.40 1.40

Jafar Jabbarly (1899-1934), playwright.

Souvenir Sheet

A95

80th anniv. of Azerbaijan postage stamps: a, #1. b, #3. c, #7. d, #10. b-d horiz.

Perf. 14¾x14½ (a), 14½x13¾ (b-d)
1999, Oct. 30
692 A95 500m Sheet of 4, #a.-d. 4.50 4.50
Exists imperf. Value, $20.

A96

Baku Caravansary: No. 693, Inner courtyard. No. 694, Facade, camels.

1999, Dec. 29 Litho. *Perf. 13*
693-694 A96 500m Set of 2 4.00 4.00

A97

1999, Dec. 29 *Perf. 12*
695 A97 1000m multi 2.00 2.00
Council of Europe, 50th anniv.

A98

Azerbaijan flag, UPU emblem and: a, 250m, Dove. b, 3000m, Computer, satellite.

1999, Dec. 29
696 A98 Pair, #a.-b. 4.00 4.00
UPU, 125th anniv.

Souvenir Sheet

Epic Legend Kitabi Dede Gorgud, 1300th Anniv. — A99

Designs: a, Beyrek fights with camel. b, Wounded Tural on horseback. c, Gazan Khan sleeping, horse.

1999, Dec. 29 *Perf. 12¼x11¾*
697 A99 1000m Sheet of 3, #a.-c. 4.00 4.00

Europa, 2000
Common Design Type

2000, Feb. 7 Litho. *Perf. 12¾x13*
698 CD17 1000m multi *1.00 1.00*
699 CD17 3000m multi *7.00 7.00*

Souvenir Sheet

Baku Transportation — A100

Designs: a, Phaeton. b, Horse-drawn tram. c, Electric tram. d, Trolleybus.

2000, Feb. 15 Litho. *Perf. 12½x12*
700 A100 500m Sheet of 4, #a-d 5.00 5.00

Tower Type of 1999

100m, Ramany Castle, 14th cent, horiz. 250m, Nardaran Castle, 14th cent., horiz.

2000, May 5 Litho. *Perf. 11¾x11¼*
701 A92 100m black & orange .40 .40
702 A92 250m black & green 1.00 1.00

World Meteorological Organization, 50th Anniv. — A101

2000, May 5 *Perf. 12*
703 A101 1000m multi 1.25 1.25

Worldwide Fund for Nature — A102

Aythya nyroca: a, One in flight. b, Two on rocks, three in water. c, One on rocks, three in water. d, One in water, three in flight.

2000, May 5 *Perf. 12½x12*
704 A102 500m Block of 4, #a-d 4.50 4.50

2000 Summer Olympics, Sydney — A103

Designs: a, Wrestling. b, Weight lifting. c, Boxing. d, Running.

2000, May 5 *Perf. 12x12½*
705 A103 500m Block of 4, #a-d 5.00 5.00

Souvenir Sheet

Phasianus Colchicus — A104

2000, June 21 Litho. *Perf. 13½x13*
706 A104 2000m multi 5.00 5.00

Fruit A105

No. 707: a, Cydonia oblonga. b, Punica granatum. c, Persica L. d, Ficus carica.

2000, June 21 *Perf. 13x13¼*
707 Sheet of 4 5.25 5.25
a.-d. A105 500m Any single 1.25 1.25

Rasul Rza (1911-81), Poet A106

2000, Sept. 28 Litho. *Perf. 13x13¼*
708 A106 250m multi 1.25 1.25

Reptiles A107

No. 709: a, Vipera lebetina. b, Laserta saxcola. c, Vipera xanthina. d, Phrynocephalus mystaceus.

No. 710, Natrix tessellata, Phrynocephalus helioscopus, vert.

2000, Sept. 28 *Perf. 13½x13*
709 Sheet of 4 6.50 6.50
a.-d. A107 500m Any single 1.50 1.50

Souvenir Sheet
Perf. 13x13½
710 A107 500m multi 3.00 3.00

Sabit Rahman (1910-70), Writer A108

2000, Nov. 17 *Perf. 13x13¼*
711 A108 1000m multi 1.60 1.60

Intl. Year for the Culture of Peace — A109

2000, Nov. 17 *Perf. 13¼x13*
712 A109 3000m multi 3.50 3.50

Souvenir Sheet

2000 Olympic Medalists — A110

No. 713: a, Namig Abdullaev, 54kg freestyle wrestling gold medalist. b, Zemfira Meftahaddinova, women's skeet shooting gold medalist. c, Vugar Alakbarov, middleweight boxing bronze medalist.

2001, Jan. 26 Litho. *Perf. 13½x13¾*
713 A110 1000m Sheet of 3, #a-c 5.00 5.00
Dated 2000.

Europa — A111

Caspian Sea and: 1000m, Seal. 3000m, Sturgeon, crab, jellyfish.

Perf. 13½x13¼
2001, Mar. 28 Litho.
714-715 A111 Set of 2 *8.50 8.50*
715a Pane, 4 each #714-715 *32.50*

Stamps in the middle two columns of No. 715a are tete beche. No. 715a was sold with booklet cover, but unattached to it.

Admission of Azerbaijan to Council of Europe A112

2001, Apr. 25 *Perf. 13¼x13½*
716 A112 1000m multi 1.90 1.90

Tower Type of 1999

Designs: 100m, Sheki, 18th cent., horiz. 250m, Sheki, 12th-13th cent., horiz.

2001, July 27 *Perf. 14x13¾*
717 A92 100m black & lilac .50 .50
718 A92 250m black & yellow 1.25 1.25

Souvenir Sheet

UN High Commissioner for Refugees, 50th Anniv. — A113

2001, Aug. 22 *Perf. 13¼x13½*
719 A113 3000m multi 4.00 4.00

Souvenir Sheet

Nasir ad-Din at-Tusi (1201-74), Scientist — A114

2001, Sept. 7 ***Perf. 13¼***
720 A114 3000m multi 4.00 4.00

Commonwealth of Independent States, 10th Anniv. — A115

2001, Oct. 8 Litho. ***Perf. 13½x13¼***
721 A115 1000m multi 2.00 2.00

Souvenir Sheet

First Manned Space Flight, 40th Anniv. — A116

2001, Nov. 6 ***Perf. 13¼x13½***
722 A116 3000m multi 4.00 4.00

Independence, 10th Anniv. — A117

Litho. & Embossed with Foil Application

2001, Dec. 1 ***Perf. 13¼***
723 A117 5000m gold & multi 11.50 11.50

Owls — A118

No. 724: a, Asio flammeus. b, Strix aluco. c, Otus scops. d, Asio otus. e, Bubo bubo, wings at side. f, Athene noctua.

No. 725, Bubo bubo, wings extended.

2001, Dec. 1 Litho. ***Perf. 13¼x13***
724 A118 1000m Sheet of 6, #a-f 6.75 6.75

Souvenir Sheet

725 A118 1000m shown 3.50 3.50

Visit of Russian Pres. Vladimir Putin A119

2001, Dec. 20 ***Perf. 13***
726 A119 1000m multi 2.00 2.00

Natl. Olympic Committee, 10th Anniv. — A120

2002, Mar. 6 ***Perf. 13¼x13½***
727 A120 3000m multi 3.00 3.00

Europa — A121

Designs: 1000m, Tight rope walker, musicians, strong man, acrobat. 3000m, Trapeze artist, juggler, horse trainer.

2002, Mar. 11 ***Perf. 13½x13¼***
728-729 A121 Set of 2 *6.50 6.50*
729a Booklet pane, 2 each #728-729, perf. 13½x13¼ on 3 sides *13.50* —
Complete booklet, #729a *13.50*

Azerbaijan — People's Republic of China Diplomatic Relations, 10th Anniv. A122

2002, Mar. 28 Litho. ***Perf. 12***
730 A122 1000m multi 1.60 1.60

Tower Type of 1999

Designs: 100m, Molla Panah Vagif Mausoleum, Shusha. 250m, Mosque, Agdam.

2002, Apr. 23 ***Perf. 13½x14***
731 A92 100m blk & ol grn .50 .50
732 A92 250m blk & tan .90 .90

For surcharge, see No. 812.

No. 350 Surcharged in Red

Method & Perf. As Before

2002, May 8
733 A20 1000m on 35k multi 1.60 1.60

New Azerbaijan Party, 10th Anniv. — A123

2002, June 1 ***Perf. 13½***
734 A123 3000m multi 3.00 3.00

Butterflies — A124

No. 735: a, Danaus chrysippus. b, Papilio orientalis. c, Thaleropis jonia. d, Vanessa atalanta. e, Argynnis alexandra. f, Brahmaea christophi.

2002, June 19 ***Perf. 13***
735 A124 1000m Sheet of 6, #a-f 9.00 9.00

In Remembrance of Sept. 11, 2001 Terrorist Attacks — A125

2002, Sept. 18 ***Perf. 13½x13¼***
736 A125 1500m multi 1.75 1.75

Printed in sheets of 3. Value $5.50.

Baku Telegraph Office, 70th Anniv. — A126

2002, Sept. 18 ***Perf. 14¼x14***
737 A126 3000m multi 3.50 3.50

Rauf Gadjiev, Composer, 80th Anniv. of Birth A127

2002, Sept. 18 ***Perf. 14x14¼***
738 A127 5000m multi 4.00 4.00

Souvenir Sheet

Visit of Pope John Paul II — A128

2002, Sept. 18 ***Perf. 13¼x13½***
739 A128 1500m multi 3.50 3.50

Souvenir Sheet

European Junior Chess Championships — A129

Baku skyline and stylized chess pieces: a, King, queen, pawns. b, Knights, pawn. c, Two elephants, rook, pawn. d, King, queen, rook, pawn.

2002, Sept. 18 ***Perf. 12¾x13¼***
740 A129 1500m Sheet of 4, #a-d 8.50 8.50

Souvenir Sheet

Turkey's Third Place Finish in 2002 World Cup Soccer Championships — A130

2002, Oct. 16 ***Perf. 13¼x13***
741 A130 5000m multi 5.50 5.50

Women for Peace — A131

2002, Nov. 1 ***Perf. 14¼x14***
742 A131 3000m multi 3.50 3.50

Souvenir Sheet

Aquarium Fish — A132

No. 743: a, Betta splendens. b, Symphysodon aequifasciatus. c, Pterophylium scalare. d, Carassius auratus auratus. e, Melanotaenia boesemani. f, Cichlasoma meeki.

2002, Dec. 27 Litho. *Perf. 13½*
743 A132 1000m Sheet of 6, #a-f 8.00 8.00

Tower Type of 1999

Design: Askeran Towers, 18th cent., horiz.

2003, Jan. 8 *Perf. 14x13½*
744 A92 250m black & lt blue .75 .75

Europa A133

Posters: 1000m, Stop Terrorism. 3000m, Sport is the Health of the Nation

2003, Mar. 12 *Perf. 13½*
745-746 A133 Set of 2 7.00 7.00
746a Booklet pane, 2 each #745-746, perf. 13½ on 3 sides 14.00 14.00

No. 746a was sold with booklet cover, but unattached to it.

Admission to UPU, 10th Anniv. — A134

2003, Apr. 8 *Perf. 14¼x14*
747 A134 3000m multi 3.50 3.50

Nakhichevan — A135

2003, Apr. 8 *Perf. 14x14¼*
748 A135 3000m multi 3.25 3.25

For surcharge see No. 851.

Baku — Tbilisi — Ceyhan Oil Pipeline — A136

2003, Apr. 8 *Perf. 13¾x14¼*
749 A136 3000m multi 3.50 3.50

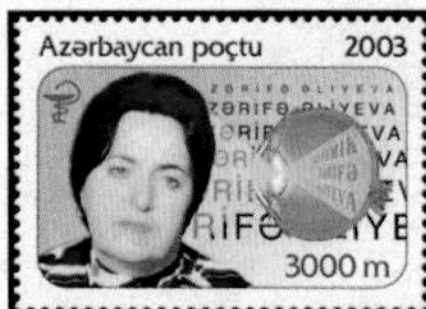

Zarifa Aliyeva (1923-85), Ophthalmologist — A137

2003, Apr. 28 *Perf. 14x14¼*
750 A137 3000m multi 3.25 3.25

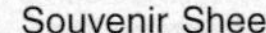

Souvenir Sheet

Pres. Heydar Aliyev, 80th Birthday — A138

Litho. With Foil Application

2003, May 2 *Perf. 11½*
751 A138 10,000m multi 11.50 11.50

Nos. 397, 429 Surcharged

Methods and Perfs As Before

2003, May 27
752 A35 500m on 25m #429 .90 .90
753 A28 1000m on 8m #397 2.00 2.00

Towers Type of 1999

Design: 1000m, Ganja Doors on tower walls, Shusha.

2003, Aug. 13 Litho. *Perf. 13¾*
754 A92 1000m black 1.25 1.25

Souvenir Sheet

Automobiles — A139

No. 755: a, QAZ-11-73. b, QAZ-M-20 Pobeda. c, QAZ-12 Zim. d, QAZ-21 Volqa.

2003, Aug. 13 *Perf. 11½*
755 A139 500m Sheet of 4, #a-d 4.00 4.00

Arshin Mal Alan, Musical Comedy by Uzeyir Hadjibekov, 90th Anniv. — A140

2003, Nov. 21 Litho. *Perf. 14¼x14*
756 A140 10,000m multi 8.00 8.00

Nos. 757-759, 761, 765 Surcharged

Nos. 760, 762-764 Surcharged

Methods and Perfs as Before

2003, Dec. 11

757	A23	500m on 50g #367	1.25	1.25
758	A28	500m on 2m #395	1.25	1.25
759	A28	500m on 4m #396	1.25	1.25
760	A34	500m on 5m #419	1.25	1.25
761	A35	500m on 5m #426	1.25	1.25
762	A34	500m on 10m #420	1.25	1.25
763	A34	500m on 15m #421	1.25	1.25
764	A34	500m on 20m #422	1.25	1.25
a.		On #422a	4.75	4.75
765	A35	500m on 40m #431	1.25	1.25
		Nos. 757-765 (9)	11.25	11.25

Souvenir Sheet

Sheki National Park — A141

No. 766: a, Bear. b, Raccoon. c, Boar. d, Fox.

2003, Dec. 30 Litho. *Perf. 11½*
766 A141 3000m Sheet of 4, #a-d 10.50 10.50

Nakhichevan Autonomous Republic, 80th Anniv. — A142

2004, Jan. 3 *Perf. 14¼x14*
767 A142 3000m multi 2.75 2.75

For surcharge see No. 852.

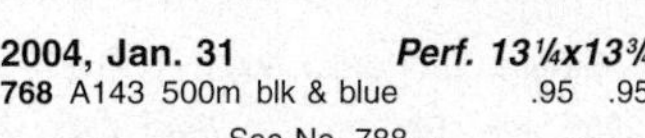
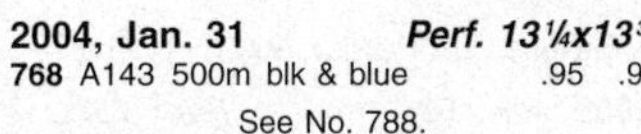

Dove of Peace Monument, Sumgayit — A143

2004, Jan. 31 *Perf. 13¼x13¾*
768 A143 500m blk & blue .95 .95

See No. 788.

Europa A144

Designs: 1000m, Geygel Lake. 3000m, Baku.

2004, Mar. 16 *Perf. 13¼x13½*
769-770 A144 Set of 2 6.25 6.25
770a Booklet pane, 2 each #769-770, perf. 13¼x13½ on 3 sides 14.00 —

No. 770a was sold with booklet cover, but unattached to it.

Molla Juma, Poet, 150th Anniv. of Birth A145

2004, Mar. 25 *Perf. 14x14¼*
771 A145 500m multi 1.25 1.25

2004 Summer Olympics, Athens — A146

No. 772: a, Pole vault. b, Wrestling. c, Running. d, Greek amphora.

2004, Apr. 15 *Perf. 14¼x14*
772 A146 500m Block of 4, #a-d 4.50 4.50

FIFA (Fédération Internationale de Football Association), Cent. — A147

No. 773 — Soccer stadium, FIFA emblem and: a, World Cup. b, Player wearing jersey #11. b, Player wearing jersey #9. c, Goalie.

2004, Apr. 15 *Perf. 14x14¼*
773 A147 500m Block of 4, #a-d 5.25 5.25

Pres. Heydar Aliyev (1923-2003) A148

2004, May 10 Litho. *Perf. 14¼x14*
774 A148 500m multi .95 .95

See Nos. 794, 818.

Great Silk Way — A149

2004, June 7
775 A149 3000m multi 3.25 3.25

Costumes of the 19th Century — A150

Man and woman from: No. 776, 500m, Baku (Baki). No. 777, 500m, Karabakh (Qarabag). No. 778, 500m, Nakhichevan (Naxçivan). No. 779, 500m, Shemakha (Samaxi).

2004, July 8

776-779 A150 Set of 4 5.00 5.00
779a Miniature sheet, 2 each #776-779 11.00 11.00

Internet, 35th Anniv. A151

2004, Sept. 29 Litho. ***Perf. 14x14¼***

780 A151 3000m multi 3.25 3.25

Souvenir Sheet

Pres. Heydar Aliyev (1923-2003) — A152

2004, Dec. 10 ***Perf. 11½***

781 A152 10,000m multi 7.00 7.00

Worldwide Fund for Nature (WWF) — A153

No. 782 — Panthera pardus ciscaucasica: a, Adult on tree branch. b, Two cubs behind branch. c, Adult with mouth open. d, Adult and cub.

2005, Jan. 7 ***Perf. 14x14¼***

782 A153 1000m Block of 4, #a-d 3.25 3.25

Nos. 470-473, 473a Surcharged in Red

2005, Feb. 1 Litho. ***Perf. 14***

783 A43 1000m on 10m #470 .90 .90
784 A43 1000m on 25m #471 .90 .90
785 A43 1000m on 50m #472 .90 .90
786 A43 1000m on 60m #473 .90 .90
a. Souvenir sheet, #783-786 3.50 3.50
Nos. 783-786 (4) 3.60 3.60

Taxation Ministry, 5th Anniv. — A154

2005, Feb. 5 ***Perf. 14¼x14***

787 A154 3000m multi 2.75 2.75

Local Monuments Type of 2004

Design: Observatory, Samaxi.

2005, Mar. 10 ***Perf. 13¼x13¾***

788 A143 500m blk & red vio .85 .85

Orchids — A155

Designs: 500m, Cephalanthera rubra. 1000m, Orchis papilionacea. 1500m, Epipactis atrorubens. 3000m, Orchis purpurea.

2005, Mar. 10 ***Perf. 13¼x13***

789-792 A155 Set of 4 6.50 6.50
a. Souvenir sheet, #789-792 6.50 6.50

End of World War II, 60th Anniv. A156

2005, Apr. 6 ***Perf. 14x14¼***

793 A156 1000m multi 1.50 1.50

Pres. Aliyev Type of 2004

2005, Apr. 18 ***Perf. 14¼x14***

794 A148 1000m bl grn & multi 1.50 1.50

Europa A157

Designs: 1000m, Plov. 3000m, Dolma.

2005, Apr. 18 ***Perf. 13¾x14***

795-796 A157 Set of 2 *7.00 7.00*

Booklet Stamps

797 A157 1000m Like #795 *1.90 1.90*
798 A157 3000m Like #796 *6.00 6.00*
a. Booklet pane of 4, 2 each #797-798 *16.00* —
b. Booklet pane of 6, 3 each #797-798 *24.50* —
Complete booklet, #798a-798b *40.00*

For surcharges see Nos. 838-839.

National Academy of Sciences, 60th Anniv. A158

2005, May 5 Litho. ***Perf. 14x14¼***

799 A158 1000m multi 1.50 1.50

Souvenir Sheet

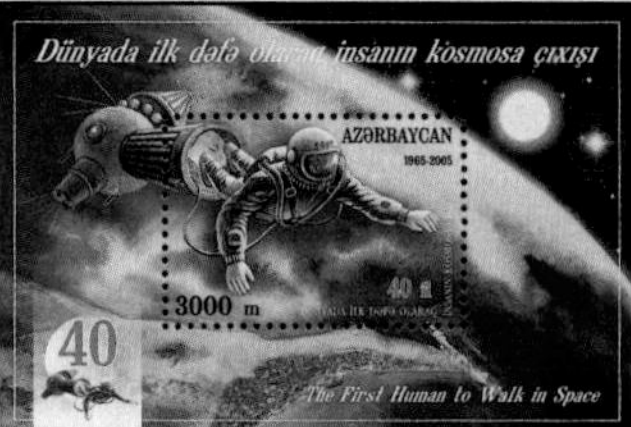

First Spacewalk, 40th Anniv. — A159

2005, June 1 ***Perf. 11½***

800 A159 3000m multi 4.25 4.25

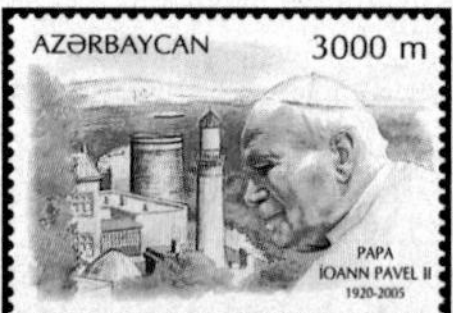

World Summit on the Information Society, Tunis A160

2005, June 24 ***Perf. 14x14¼***

801 A160 1000m multi 1.75 1.75

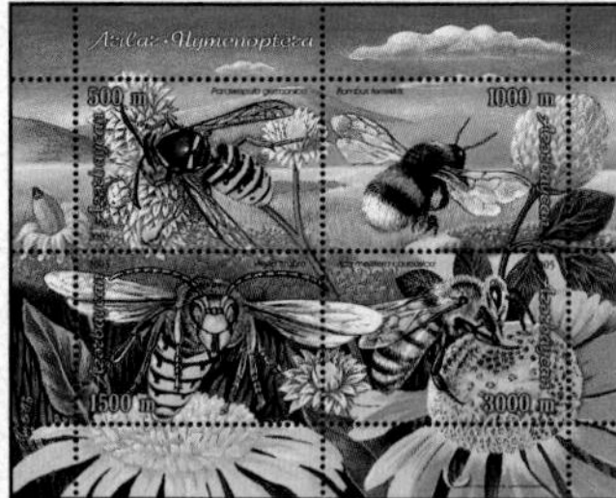

Pope John Paul II (1920-2005) — A161

2005, June 24

802 A161 3000m multi 3.25 3.25

For surcharge see No. 853.

Souvenir Sheet

Bees — A162

No. 803: a, 500m, Paravespula germanica. b, 1000m, Bombus terrestris. c, 1500m, Vespa crabro. d, 3000m, Apis mellifera caucasica.

2005, July 27

803 A162 Sheet of 4, #a-d 6.50 6.50

European Philatelic Cooperation, 50th Anniv. (in 2006) — A163

Emblem and vignettes of Europa stamps: No. 804, France #805, Germany #748. No. 805, Azerbaijan #682-683. No. 806, Azerbaijan #698-699. No. 807, Stamps similar to Azerbaijan #745-746.

2005, Oct. 25 ***Perf. 12¾x13***

Background Color

804 A163 3000m gray green *2.25 2.25*
a. Souvenir sheet of 1 *2.25 2.25*
b. Pair, imperf. *5.00 5.00*
805 A163 3000m tan *2.25 2.25*
a. Souvenir sheet of 1 *2.25 2.25*
b. Pair, imperf. *5.00 5.00*
806 A163 3000m yel green *2.25 2.25*
a. Souvenir sheet of 1 *2.25 2.25*
b. Pair, imperf. *5.00 5.00*
807 A163 3000m red orange *2.25 2.25*
a. Souvenir sheet of 1 *2.25 2.25*
b. Pair, imperf. *5.00 5.00*
Nos. 804-807 (4) *9.00 9.00*

For surcharges see Nos. 854-857.

Nos. 381, 387-388, 395, 398-399, 402, 429, 689, and 731 Srchd. in Black, Blue or Red

Methods and Perfs As Before

2006, Jan. 1

808 A28 5g on 8m #395 .40 .40
809 A25 10g on 1m #381 .50 .50
810 A26 10g on 1m #388 .50 .50
811 A35 10g on 25m #429 .65 .65
812 A92 10g on 100m #731 .65 .65
813 A26 20g on 50g #387 .75 .75
814 A32 20g on 20m #402 (Bl) .75 .75
815 A92 20g on 3000m #689 .85 .85
816 A29 60g on 5m #398 (R) 3.75 3.75
817 A29 60g on 8m #399 (R) 3.75 3.75
Nos. 808-817 (10) 12.55 12.55

Pres. Aliyev Type of 2004

2006, Jan. 1 Litho. ***Perf. 14¼x14***

818 A148 60g multi 3.00 3.00

Mosque, Länkäran — A164

2006, Jan. 1 Litho. ***Perf. 13½x14***

819 A164 10g blk & blue .45 .45

Fortress, Lachin — A165

2006, Jan. 1 Litho. ***Perf. 13½x14***

820 A165 20g blk & bister 1.00 1.00

OPEC Intl. Development Fund, 30th Anniv. — A166

2006, Jan. 30 Litho. ***Perf. 14¼x14***

821 A166 5g multi 1.00 1.00

Europa — A167

Monuments and: 20g, Hands, circle of stars. 60g, Dancers, man at computer, oil well, globes.

2006, Mar. 1 ***Perf. 13½x13¼***

822-823 A167 Set of 2 7.00 7.00

823a Booklet pane, 2 each #822-823, perf. 13½x13¾ on 3 sides 17.00 17.00

No. 823a was sold with booklet cover, but unattached to it. The middle columns of the booklet are tete-beche.

2006 World Cup Soccer Championships, Germany — A168

No. 824 — Soccer players and: a, 20g, 2006 World Cup emblem. b, 60g, Emblem, map of Germany.

2006, Mar. 14 ***Perf. 13½***

824 A168 Horiz. pair, #a-b 4.25 4.25

Poets A169

Designs: 10g, Samed Vurgun. 20g, Suleyman Rustam.

2006, Mar. 16 ***Perf. 14x14¼***

825-826 A169 Set of 2 1.60 1.60

Russia Year in Azerbaijan — A170

No. 827: a, 10g, St. Basil's Cathedral, Moscow, Russian flag and arms. b, 20g, Taza Pir Mosque, Azerbaijani flag and arms. c, 30g, Maiden Tower, Azerbaijani flag and arms. d, 60g, Kremlin, Moscow, Russian flag and arms.

2006, Apr. 17 ***Perf. 14x14¼***

827 A170 Block of 4, #a-d 4.00 4.00

Printed in sheets containing two each of Nos. 827a-827d, and 2 labels.

Gulistan Mausoleum, Nakhichevan A171

2006, May 22 Litho. ***Perf. 14¼x14***

828 A171 20g multi 1.00 1.00

World Information Organization Day — A172

2006, June 12

829 A172 1m multi 3.25 3.25

Karabakh Horses A173

Designs: Nos. 830, 834a, 20g, Khan, 1867. Nos. 831, 834b, 20g, Zaman, 1952. Nos. 832, 834c, 20g, Sarvan, 1987. Nos. 833, 834d, 20g, Qar-qar, 2001.
60g, Aliyetmaz, 1867, vert.

2006, June 27 ***Perf. 14x14¼***

Size: 40x28mm

830-833 A173 Set of 4 4.00 4.00

Miniature Sheet

Stamp Size: 52x37mm

Perf. 13½

834 A173 20g Sheet of 4, #a-d 4.00 4.00

Souvenir Sheet

Stamp Size: 28x40mm

Perf. 14¼x14

835 A173 60g multi 3.00 3.00

Summuqqala Tower, Qax — A174

Mausoleum of Nezami, Gäncä — A175

2006, Aug. 3 ***Perf. 13½x14***

836 A174 10g blk & lilac .60 .60

837 A175 20g blk & rose 1.10 1.10

Nos. 797-798 Surcharged

Methods and Perfs As Before

2006, Sept. 28 **Size: 45x35mm**

838 A157 20g on 1000m #797 *1.75 1.75*

839 A157 60g on 3000m #798 *5.50 5.50*

a. Sheet of 4, 2 each #838-839 *14.50 14.50*

b. Sheet of 6, 3 each #838-839 *21.00 21.00*

Nos. 839a-839b were not sold in a booklet, like the unsurcharged stamps. The margins of Nos. 839a-839b, have an overprint commemorating the 50th anniversary of Europa stamps.

Regional Communications Commonwealth, 15th Anniv. — A176

2006, Oct. 9 Litho. ***Perf. 14x14¼***

840 A176 20g multi 1.60 1.60

Independence, 15th Anniv. — A177

2006, Oct. 18

841 A177 20g multi 1.60 1.60

Miniature Sheet

Fire Trucks — A178

No. 842: a, 10g, AMO-F15, 1926. b, 20g, PMQ-1, 1932. c, 60g, PMQ-9, 1950. d, 1m, ATS 2, 5-40, 1998.

2006, Dec. 28

842 A178 Sheet of 4, #a-d 6.50 6.50

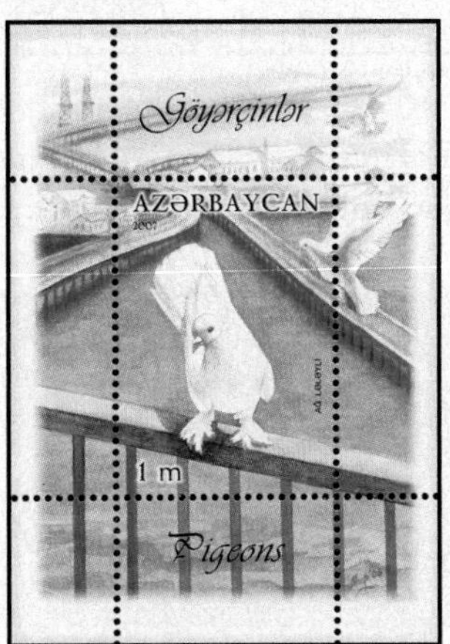

Pigeons — A179

No. 843, horiz.: a, Three pigeons. b, Sogani and Qara Ebres pigeons. c, Qirmizi and Qirmizi Cep pigeons. d, Ag Dugus and Qarabas pigeons. e, Two Qara pigeons. f, Qara and Qirmizi Cil pigeons.
1m, Ag Leleyli pigeon.

2007, Jan. 24 ***Perf. 14x14¼***

843 A179 20g Sheet of 6, #a-f 6.00 6.00

Souvenir Sheet

Perf. 14¼x14

844 A179 1m multi 4.00 4.00

Customs Service Buidings — A180

No. 845 — Building for: a, 20g, Baku Customs. b, 60g, Azerbaijan Customs.

2007, Jan. 30 ***Perf. 14¼x14***

845 A180 Horiz. pair, #a-b, + central label 4.25 4.25

Souvenir Sheet

Fall of Khojali, 15th Anniv. — A181

2007, Feb. 26 Litho. ***Perf. 14¼x14***

846 A181 1m multi + 2 labels 4.00 4.00

Europa — A182

Scouting emblem and: 20g, Dove, tents. 60g, Scout, kite.

2007, Apr. 2 ***Perf. 13½x13¼***

847-848 A182 Set of 2 *6.50 6.50*

848a Booklet pane, 4 each #847-848, perf. 13½x13¼ on 3 sides *14.00 14.00*

Scouting, cent. No. 848a was sold with booklet cover, but unattached to it. The middle columns of the booklet are tete-beche.

Friendship Between Azerbaijan and Japan A183

2007, Apr. 5 ***Perf. 14x14¼***

849 A183 1m multi 4.00 4.00

Mosque, Göyçay — A184

2007, Apr. 20 ***Perf. 14x13½***

850 A184 10g blk & yellow .50 .50

Nos. 748, 767, 802, 804-807 Surcharged in Black or Red

Methods and Perfs As Before

2007, Apr. 20

851 A135 60g on 3000m #748 *2.75 2.75*

852 A142 60g on 3000m #767 (R) *2.75 2.75*

853 A161 60g on 3000m #802 *2.75 2.75*

854 A163 60g on 3000m #804 (R) *2.75 2.75*

a. Pair, imperf. *5.50 5.50*

855 A163 60g on 3000m #805 (R) *2.75 2.75*

a. Pair, imperf. *5.50 5.50*

856 A163 60g on 3000m #806 (R) *2.75 2.75*

a. Pair, imperf. *5.50 5.50*

857 A163 60g on 3000m #807 (R) *2.75 2.75*

a. Pair, imperf. *5.50 5.50*

Nos. 851-857 (7) *19.25 19.25*

Dog Fight, by Azim Azimade A185

Wedding, by Azim Azimade A186

2007, June 5 Litho. *Perf. 14x14¼*

858	Horiz. pair with central label	*2.50 2.50*
a.	A185 20g multi	*1.25 1.25*
b.	A186 20g multi	*1.25 1.25*

Azermarka, 15th Anniv. — A187

2007, July 14 ***Perf. 14¼x14***

859 A187 50g multi *3.25 3.25*

Knut, Polar Bear Cub Born in Berlin Zoo A188

2007, Aug. 15 ***Perf. 13x13¼***

860	A188 60g shown	*3.75 3.75*
a.	Souvenir sheet of 4	*15.00 15.00*

Souvenir Sheet

861 A188 1m Knut, vert. *6.00 6.00*

No. 861 contains one 30x38mm stamp.

Flowers — A189

No. 862: a, 10g, Gagea alexeenkoana. b, 20g, Centaurea ficher. c, 40g, Galanthus caucasicus. d, 60g, Ophrys caucasica.
1m, Ophrys caucasica, diff.

2007, Aug. 20 ***Perf. 14x14¼***

862 A189 Sheet of 4, #a-d *4.50 4.50*

Souvenir Sheet

863 A189 1m multi *3.50 3.50*

Hüseyn Cavid (1882-1941), Writer — A190

2007, Sept. 19

864 A190 20g multi *1.40 1.40*

Bridges — A191

No. 865: a, 10g, Xudaferin Bridge. b, 20g, Qazançi Bridge. c, 30g, Qudyalçay Bridge. d, 50g, Gancaçay Bridge.
60g, Xudaferin Bridge, diff.

2007, Nov. 1 Litho. *Perf. 14x14¼*

865 A191 Sheet of 4, #a-d *5.50 5.50*

Souvenir Sheet

866 A191 60g multi *3.00 3.00*

No. 401 Surcharged

Methods and Perfs As Before

2007, Nov. 28

867 A31 10g on 15m #401 .50 .50

Xudaferin Bridge, Jabrayil — A192

Fortress, Kalbacar — A193

2007, Nov. 28 Litho. *Perf. 14x13½*

868	A192	10g blk & pale org	.60 .60
869	A193	20g blk & green	1.00 1.00

Souvenir Sheet

Launch of Sputnik 1, 50th Anniv. — A194

2007, Nov. 28 ***Perf. 14¼x14***

870 A194 1m multi 5.25 5.25

Souvenir Sheet

Lt. Gen. Karim Karimov (1917-2003), USSR Space Flight Commission Chairman — A195

2007, Dec. 30

871 A195 1m multi 5.25 5.25

2008 Summer Olympics, Beijing — A196

No. 872: a, 20g, Judo. b, 30g, Weight lifting. c, 40g, Wrestling. d, 60g, Boxing.

2008, Feb. 25 ***Perf. 14x14¼***

872 A196 Block of 4, #a-d *6.50 6.50*

Europa — A197

Designs: 20g, Open envelope. 60g, Computer monitor.
1m, Dove.

2008, Mar. 13 Litho. *Perf. 13½*

873-874	A197	Set of 2	6.50 6.50
874a		Booklet pane, 4 each #873-874, perf. 13½ on 3 sides	26.00 26.00

Souvenir Sheet

Perf. 13¼x13¾

875 A197 1m multi 6.50 6.50

No. 874a was sold with booklet cover, but unattached to it. The middle columns of the booklet are tete-beche.
No. 875 contains one 18x25mm stamp.

Tower, Qazak — A198

2008, Apr. 8 ***Perf. 13½x14***

876 A198 10g blk & sal pink .50 .50

Nakhichevan Drama Theater, 125th Anniv. — A199

2008, Apr. 9 ***Perf. 14x14¼***

877 A199 20g multi *1.75 1.75*

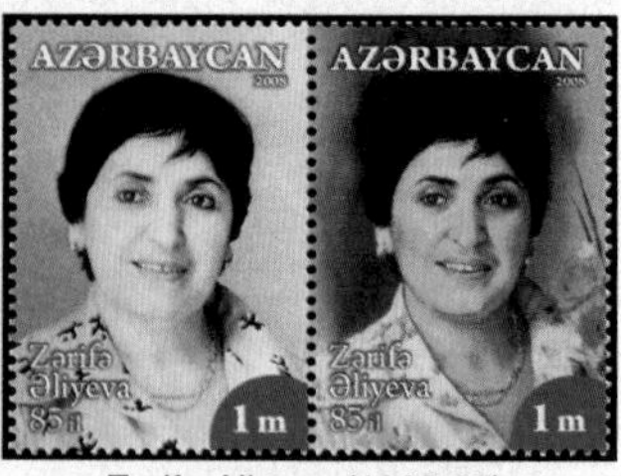

Zarifa Aliyeva (1923-85), Ophthalmologist, Wife of Pres. Heydar Aliyev — A200

Pres. Heydar Aliyev (1923-2003) — A201

No. 878 — Mrs. Aliyeva: a, Plain background. b, Flower in background.
No. 879 — Pres. Aliyev: a, And Azerbaijan flag. b, Blue and green background.

2008 Litho. *Perf. 14¼x14*

878	A200	1m Pair, #a-b	9.00 9.00
879	A201	1m Pair, #a-b	9.00 9.00

Issued: No. 878, 4/28; No. 879, 5/2. Nos. 878 and 879 were each printed in sheets containing four of each stamp of that particular pair and a central label.

Azerbaijan Republic, 90th Anniv. A202

2008, May 28 ***Perf. 14x14¼***

880 A202 20g multi *1.75 1.75*

Mikayil Müsfiq (1908-39), Poet A203

2008, June 6

881 A203 20g multi *1.75 1.75*

Physicists A204

Designs: No. 882, 20g, Lev Landau (1908-68). No. 883, 20g, Hasan Abdullayev (1918-93).

2008, July 21 Litho. *Perf. 14x14¼*

882-883 A204 Set of 2 *3.25 3.25*

Miniature Sheet

Caspian Shipping Company, 150th Anniv. — A205

No. 884: a, 20g, Tanker Heydar Aliyev. b, 30g, Ferry Azerbaijan. c, 50g, Cargo ship Bestekar Qara Qarayev. d, 60g, Cargo ship Maestro Niyaz. e, 1m, Tanker Vandal.

2008, Sept. 21 ***Perf. 13½***
884 A205 Sheet of 5, #a-e, + 4 labels *11.00 11.00*

Jewelry — A206

No. 885: a, Earring 12th-13th cent. b, Pendant, 19th cent.

2008, Sept. 18 ***Perf. 11½***
885 A206 60g Horiz. pair, #a-b, + central label *6.25 6.25*

See Ukraine No. 742.

Khanagah Mausoleum, Culfa A207

Garabaghla Mausoleum, Sarur A208

2008, Oct. 3 Litho. ***Perf. 14x13½***
886 A207 10g blk & brown .50 .50

Perf. 13½x14
887 A208 20g blk & gray 1.00 1.00

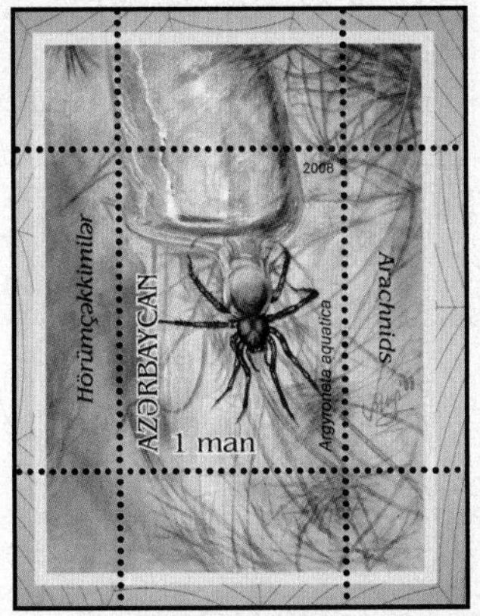

Arachnids — A209

No. 888: a, 5g, Galeodes araneoides. b, 10g, Buthus occitanus. c, 20g, Pisaura mirabilis. d, 30g, Latrodectus tredecimguttatus. e, 40g, Araneus diadematus. f, 60g, Tegenaria domestica.
1m, Argyroneta aquatica.

2008, Dec. 2 ***Perf. 14¼x14***
888 A209 Sheet of 6, #a-f *6.50 6.50*

Souvenir Sheet

889 A209 1m multi *5.00 5.00*

Mir Jalal (1908-78), Writer — A210

2008, Dec. 17
890 A210 60g multi 2.75 2.75

Azerbaijan postal authorities declared as illegal miniature sheets dated 2008 depicting the Pope and Princess Diana, Mushrooms, Dinosaurs, Horses, Dogs, Animals and Cats.

Miniature Sheet

Nakhichevan Autonomous Republic, 85th Anniv. — A211

No. 891 — Buildings: a, H. Javid Mausoleum (white building with steps at left). b, Heydar Aliyev School (with curved front, flowers at right). c, Nakhichevan Ministry of Economy building (with island gardens). d, Library, Nakhichevan State University (with red roof and striped curbs). e, Conservatory, Nakhichevan State University (with striped curbs). f, Physiotherapy Center (with curved front and circular garden). g, Tebriz Hotel (with dome at right). h, Medical Center of Nakhichevan (with curved front with brown vertical lines on wings).

2009, Feb. 7
891 A211 20g Sheet of 8, #a-h, + central label *8.25 8.25*

Baku, Center of Islamic Culture — A212

Designs: 10g, Emblem. 20g, Emblem and Maiden Tower, Baku.

2009, Feb. 18 ***Perf. 13½x14***
892-893 A212 Set of 2 1.75 1.75

Souvenir Sheet

Preservation of Polar Regions and Glaciers — A213

No. 894 — Emblem and map of: a, Antarctica. b, Greenland and Arctic region.

2009, Mar. 3 ***Perf. 13¾x13½***
894 A213 1m Sheet of 2, #a-b *8.50 8.50*

10th Economic Cooperation Organization Summit, Tehran — A214

2009, Apr. 2 ***Perf. 14¼x14***
895 A214 1m multi *4.50 4.50*

See Iran 2981, compare with Pakistan 1111.

Europa — A215

Designs: 20g, Nasir ad-Din at-Tusi (1201-74), scientist. 60g, Samaxi Observatory and Moon.
1m, Earth, Moon, telescope of Galileo.

2009, Apr. 13 ***Perf. 13½x13¼***
896-897 A215 Set of 2 *6.50 6.50*
897a Booklet pane of 8, 4 each #896-897, perf. 13½x13¼ on 3 sides *26.00* —

Souvenir Sheet

898 A215 1m multi *6.50 6.50*

Intl. Year of Astronomy. No. 897a was sold with booklet cover, but unattached to it. The middle columns of the booklet pane are tete-beche.

Azerbaijan's Cooperation With NATO, 15th Anniv. — A216

2009, May 4 Litho. ***Perf. 14x14¼***
899 A216 20g multi 1.25 1.25

Printed in sheets of 8 + 2 labels.

European Council, 60th Anniv. A217

2009, May 5
900 A217 60g multi *3.25 3.25*

European Court of Human Rights, 50th Anniv. A218

2009, May 5
901 A218 60g multi *3.25 3.25*

Sumqayit, 60th Anniv. — A219

2009, June 1 ***Perf. 13½x14***
902 A219 10g multi .90 .90

Butterflies — A220

Designs: 10g, Vanessa atalanta. 20g, Papilio alexanor orientalis.

2009, June 1
903-904 A220 Set of 2 *1.75 1.75*

See Nos.913-914, 928-929, 939.

Diplomatic Service, 90th Anniv. — A221

2009, July 9 Litho. ***Perf. 14¼x14***
905 A221 60g multi *3.25 3.25*

Printed in sheets of 8 + central label.

Jalil Mammadguluzadeh (1869-1932), Writer — A222

2009, July 10
906 A222 20g multi 1.50 1.50

Leyla Mammadbeyova (1909-89), Test Pilot — A223

2009, Sept. 19 Litho. ***Perf. 14x14¼***
907 A223 20g multi 1.50 1.50

State Oil Fund, 10th Anniv. — A224

2009, Oct. 8 ***Perf. 14¼x14***
908 A224 60g multi *2.75 2.75*

Printed in sheets of 8 + central label.

Universal Postal Union, 135th Anniv. A225

No. 909 — Background color: a, 20g, Pale orange. b, 60g, Rose pink.

2009, Oct. 9 ***Perf. 14x14¼***
909 A225 Pair, #a-b 4.00 4.00

Miniature Sheet

Birds — A226

No. 910: a, 10g, Platalea leucorodia. b, 20g, Phalacrocorax pygmaeus. c, 60g, Numenius tenuirostris. d, 1m, Porphyrio porphyrio.

2009, Oct. 19 **Litho.**
910 A226 Sheet of 4, #a-d 7.50 7.50

Souvenir Sheet

Azerbaijan, 2009 European Chess Champions — A227

No. 911 — Chess pieces and map of: a, 50g, Europe. b, 1m, Azerbaijan.

2009, Oct. 8 ***Perf. 14¼x14***
911 A227 Sheet of 2, #a-b 7.00 7.00

Miniature Sheet

Paintings by Sattar Bahlulzadeh (1909-74) — A228

No. 912: a, Qedim Samaxi (Ancient Shamakhi). b, Zeferanla Narlar (Saffron with Pomegranates). c, Buzovna Sahil (Buzovna Shore). d, Menzere (View). e, Laleler (Poppies). f, Qirmizi Menzere (Red View).

2009, Dec. 15 ***Perf. 14x14¼***
912 A228 20g Sheet of 6, #a-f, + 3 central labels 7.25 7.25

Butterflies Type of 2009

Designs: 10g, Thaleropis jonia. 20g, Danaus chrysippus.

2010, Jan. 11 ***Perf. 13½x14***
913-914 A220 Set of 2 1.50 1.50

Souvenir Sheet

January 20, 1990 Baku Massacre — A229

2010, Jan. 20 ***Perf. 14¼x14***
915 A229 1m multi + 2 labels 4.50 4.50

Ministry of Taxation, 10th Anniv. A230

2010, Feb. 11 ***Perf. 14x14¼***
916 A230 60g multi 3.25 3.25

New Year 2010 (Year of the Tiger) — A231

Litho. With Foil Application

2010, Mar. 1 ***Perf. 14¼x14***
917 A231 60g multi 3.25 3.25

Azerbaijan Red Crescent Society, 90th Anniv. A232

2010, Mar. 10 Litho. ***Perf. 14x14¼***
918 A232 60g multi 3.25 3.25

Europa — A233

Characters from children's stories: 20g, Boy, dog and bear. 60g, Lion, wolf, duck, fox. 1m, Ogre and children.

2010, Mar. 16 ***Perf. 13x13¼***
919-920 A233 Set of 2 6.00 6.00
920a Booklet pane of 8, 4 each #919-920, perf. 13 on 3 sides 25.00 —

Souvenir Sheet

Perf. 13

921 A233 1m multi 7.25 7.25

No. 920a was sold with booklet cover, but unattached to it. The middle columns of the booklet pane are tete-beche.

Peonies — A234

No. 922 — Flower color: a, Yellow. b, Pink. c, White. d, Red.
20g, Peonies in vase.

2010, Apr. 10 ***Perf. 13¼***
922 A234 10g Sheet of 4, #a-d 2.50 2.50

Souvenir Sheet

923 A234 20g multi 2.50 2.50

Victory in World War II, 65th Anniv. — A235

No. 924 — 65th anniversary emblem and: a, 10g, Soviet soldiers in front of statue in Berlin. b, 20g, Soviet soldiers raising Soviet flag over Reichstag building, Berlin. c, 60g, Soviet airplane, rail tanker.

2010, Apr. 20 Litho. ***Perf. 14¼x14***
924 A235 Horiz. strip of 3 4.50 4.50

Printed in sheets containing two strips separated by a horizontal strip of three labels.

2010 World Cup Soccer Championships, South Africa — A236

No. 925 — Soccer player and 2010 World Cup: a, 20g, Emblem. b, 60g, Mascot.

2010, May 18 ***Perf. 14x14¼***
925 A236 Pair, #a-b 4.50 4.50

Souvenir Sheet

Azerbaijan Pavilion, Expo 2010, Shanghai — A237

2010, May 18 ***Perf. 13¼***
926 A237 60g multi 3.00 3.00

Alesker Alekberov (1910-63), Actor A238

2010, June 18 ***Perf. 14x14¼***
927 A238 20g multi 1.50 1.50

Butterflies Type of 2009

Designs: 10g, Argynnis alexandra. 20g, Brahmaea christophi.

2010, July 15 ***Perf. 13½x14***
928-929 A220 Set of 2 1.60 1.60

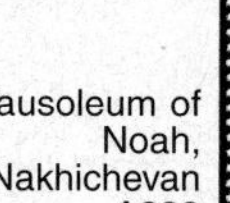
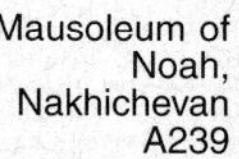

Mausoleum of Noah, Nakhichevan A239

2010, July 19 ***Perf. 14¼x14***
930 A239 60g multi 3.00 3.00

Buildings in Baku's Old City — A240

No. 931: a, 10g, Shirvanshah Palace, 12th-15th cent. b, 20g, Bazaar Square, 15th cent. c, 30g, Fortress archways, 19th cent. d, 40g, Came Mosque, 14th cent. e, 50g, Qasim Bey Bathhouse, 15th cent. f, 60g, Multam and Bukhara Caravansaries, 15th cent.

No. 932, vert.: a, 10g, Maiden Tower, 6th cent. b, 20g, Muhammad Mosque, 11th cent. c, 30g, Fortress walls, 12th cent. d, 40g, Palace Mosque, 15th cent. e, 50g, Shirvanshah Tomb, 15th cent. f, 60g, Divankhana, 15th cent.

1m, Shirvanshah Palace complex, 12th-15th cent.

2010, July 26 ***Perf. 13½***

Sheets of 6, #a-f

931-932 A240 Set of 2 17.00 17.00

Souvenir Sheet

Perf. 14¼x14

933 A240 1m multi 4.00 4.00

No. 933 contains one 56x40mm stamp.

Souvenir Sheet

Temples — A241

No. 934: a, Ateshgah, Baku, Azerbaijan. b, Pyramid of the Sun, Teotihuacan, Mexico.

2010, Oct. 12 Litho. ***Perf. 14x14¼***
934 A241 60g Sheet of 2 5.50 5.50

See Mexico No. 2699.

Shafaat Mehdiyev (1910-93), Geologist A242

2010, Nov. 5 ***Perf. 14x14¼***
935 A242 60g multi 3.00 3.00

Cats — A243

No. 936: a, 10g, Scottish fold cat. b, 2g, Persian cat. c, 30g, Somali cat. d, 40g, British shorthaired cat. e, 50g, Burmese cat. f, 60g, Maine Coon cat.
1m, Angora cat.

2010, Nov. 8 ***Perf. 14¼x14***
936 A243 Sheet of 6, #a-f *8.25 8.25*

Souvenir Sheet

937 A243 1m multi *4.25 4.25*

Birds of the Caspian Sea — A244

No. 938: a, Ardeola ralloides. b, Phoenicopterus roseus.

2010, Nov. 24 ***Perf. 14¼x14***
938 A244 60g Pair, #a-b *5.00 5.00*

See Kazakhstan No. 632.

Butterflies Type of 2009

2010, Dec. 15 ***Perf. 13½x14***
939 A220 10g Parnassius apollo *1.00 1.00*

Flowers — A245

Designs: 20g, Centaurea fischeri. 50g, Gagea alexeenkoana.

2011, Mar. 10 ***Perf. 13½x14***
940-941 A245 Set of 2 *3.00 3.00*

See Nos. 951-952.

Novruz Festival — A246

2011, Mar. 18 Litho. ***Perf. 14¼x14***
942 A246 30g multi *1.50 1.50*

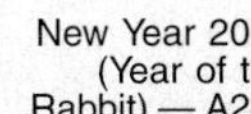

New Year 2011 (Year of the Rabbit) — A247

Litho. With Foil Application

2011, Mar. 18
943 A247 1m multi *4.00 4.00*

Admission of Azerbaijan to European Council, 10th Anniv. — A248

2011, Mar. 18 Litho. ***Perf. 14x14¼***
944 A248 1m multi *4.00 4.00*

Europa A249

Designs: 20g, Ulmus densa. 60g, Platanus orientalis.
1m, Parrotia persica.

2011, Apr. 8 ***Perf. 13¼x13***
945 A249 20g multi *1.50 1.50*
a. Perf. 13 on 3 sides *1.50 1.50*
946 A249 60g multi *4.50 4.50*
a. Perf. 13 on 3 sides *4.50 4.50*
b. Booklet pane of 8, 4 each #945a-946a *24.00 —*

Souvenir Sheet

947 A249 1m multi *6.00 6.00*

Intl. Year of Forests. No. 946b was sold with booklet cover, but unattached to it. The middle columns of the booklet pane are tete-beche.

Souvenir Sheet

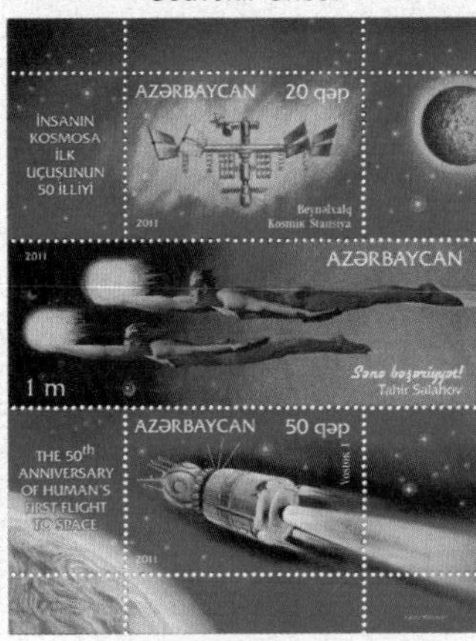

First Manned Space Flight, 50th Anniv. — A250

No. 948: a, 20g, International Space Station (40x28mm). b, 50g, Vostok 1 (40x28mm). c, 1m, To You Mankind, painting by Tahir Salakhov (79x28mm).

Perf. 14x14¼, 14 Horiz. (1m)

2011, Apr. 12
948 A250 Sheet of 3, #a-c *7.50 7.50*

Huseyn Aliyev (1911-91), Painter — A251

2011, Apr. 22 ***Perf. 14¼x14***
949 A251 60g multi *2.75 2.75*

Musical Instruments — A252

No. 950: a, Hurdy-gurdy (tekerli lira), Belarus. b, Tar, Azerbaijan.

2011, May 25 Litho. ***Perf. 14x14¼***
950 A252 50g Pair, #a-b *4.25 4.25*

See Belarus No. 770.

Flowers Type of 2011

Designs: 10g, Ophrys caucasica. 30g, Galanthus caucasicus.

2011, June 20 ***Perf. 13½x14***
951-952 A245 Set of 2 *2.00 2.00*

Souvenir Sheet

Victory of Eldar Qasimov and Nigar Camal in 2011 Eurovision Song Contest — A253

2011, July 5 ***Perf. 14¼x14***
953 A253 1m multi *4.50 4.50*

Heydar Aliyev Palace, Nakhchivan — A254

2011, July 15 ***Perf. 14x14¼***
954 A254 60g multi *2.50 2.50*

A255

No. 955: a, Behbud Aga Sahtaxtinski (1881-1924), Minister of State Control. b, Map of Azerbaijan at 1921 signing of Treaty of Kars.

2011, July 15
955 A255 60g Horiz. pair, #a-b *5.25 5.25*

Chrysanthemums — A256

No. 956 — Chrysanthemums at: a, 10g, Right. b, 20g, Left.

2011, Aug. 3 ***Perf. 12¾x13***
956 A256 Horiz. pair, #a-b *1.50 1.50*

Printed in sheets containing 3 pairs.

Miniature Sheet

Medals and Orders of Azerbaijan — A257

No. 957: a, Order of Heydar Aliyev. b, Gold Star medal. c, Order of Independence (Istiqlal). d, Order of Shah Ismail (Sah Ismayil). e, Order of the Azerbaijani Flag (Azerbaycan Bayragi). f, Order of Honor (Seref). g, Order of Glory (Söhret). h, Order of Friendship (Dostluq). i, Order of Service to the Motherland (Vetene Xidmete Göre).

2011, Sept. 5 ***Perf. 13½***
957 A257 60g Sheet of 9, #a-i *20.00 20.00*

Miniature Sheets

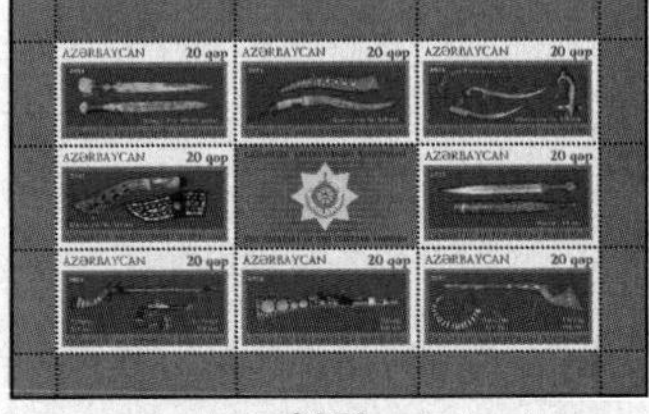

A258

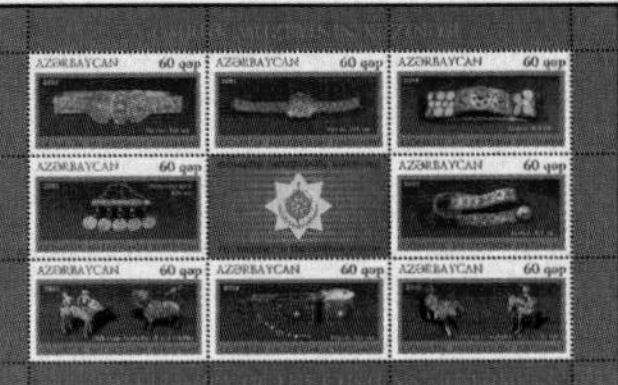

Items in Customs Museum — A259

No. 958: a, Two daggers, 12th-7th cent. B.C. b, Curved dagger with thin blade and scabbard, 19th cent. c, Curved sword, scabbard, sword handle, 19th cent. d, Dagger with wide blade and scabbard, 19th cent. e, Straight dagger and scabbard, 20th cent. f, Rifle and pistol, 19th cent. g, Rifle, 19th cent. h, Rifle and powder horn, 19th cent.

No. 959: a, Belt with oval and rectanuglar panels, 19th cent. b, Belt with loops at bottom and oval buckle, 19th cent. c, Belt with round buttons, 19th cent. d, Cylindrical case with chain and pendants, 19th cent. e, Belt with loops at bottom and round buckle, 19th cent. f, Decorative statues depicting people on amimals, 1st cent. B.C. g, Rübab, 19th cent. h, Decorative statues depicting two-headed animal and horseman, 1st cent. B.C.

2011, Sept. 5
958 A258 20g Sheet of 8, #a-h, + central label *6.00 6.00*
959 A259 60g Sheet of 8, #a-h, + central label *18.00 18.00*

Nizami Ganjavi (1141-1209), Poet — A260

No. 960 — Ganjavi facing: a, Right. b, Left.

2011, Sept. 21 **Litho.**
960 A260 30g Horiz. pair, #a-b, + central label *3.00 3.00*

Regional Communications Commonwealth, 20th Anniv. — A261

2011, Sept. 23 ***Perf. 14x14¼***
961 A261 50g multi *2.50 2.50*

Commonwealth of Independent States, 20th Anniv. — A262

2011, Sept. 23
962 A262 60g multi *3.00 3.00*

Independence, 20th Anniv. — A263

No. 963: a, Azerbaijan coat of arms. b, Azerbaijan flag. c, Azerbaijan national anthem. d, Azerbaijan map.
No. 964, 2m, Flag and map of Azerbaijan. No. 965, 2m, Pres. Heydar Aliyev and flag.

Litho. & Embossed With Foil Application

2011, Oct. 11 ***Perf. 13½x13***
963 A263 1m Sheet of 4, #a-d *12.50 12.50*

Souvenir Sheets

964-965 A263 Set of 2 *12.50 12.50*

Azerbaijan's Candidacy for Seat on United Nations Security Council — A264

2011, Oct. 21 **Litho.** ***Perf. 14x14¼***
966 A264 60g multi *2.75 2.75*

Worldwide Fund for Nature (WWF) — A265

No. 967 — Circaetus gallicus: a, 20g, Two birds in flight. b, 30g, Two adults and chick. c, 50g, Two adults. d, 60g, One adult attacking prey.

2011, Oct. 28
967 A265 Block of 4, #a-d *6.00 6.00*
e. Souvenir sheet of 4, #967a-967d *6.00 6.00*
f. Souvenir sheet of 8, 2 separated vertical rows of #967a-967d *12.00 12.00*

Flag Day — A266

2011, Nov. 9 ***Perf. 14¼x14***
968 A266 30g multi *1.60 1.60*

Karabakh Horses — A267

Various horses: 10g, 20g, 30g, 50g.

2011, Nov. 16 ***Perf. 14x13½***
969-972 A267 Set of 4 *4.50 4.50*

Abbas Zamanov (1911-93), Literary Critic — A268

2011, Dec. 1 ***Perf. 14¼x14***
973 A268 60g multi *3.00 3.00*

First Use of Telephone in Azerbaijan, 130th Anniv. A269

2011, Dec. 6 ***Perf. 14x14¼***
974 A269 1m multi *3.50 3.50*

Dogs — A270

No. 975: a, 10g, Shar Pei. b, 20g, Dalmatian. c, 30g, Labrador retriever. d, 40g, Doberman Pinscher. e, 50g, Chow Chow. f, 60g, German Shepherd.
1m, Caucasian Shepherds, horiz.

2011, Dec. 10 ***Perf. 14¼x14***
975 A270 Sheet of 6, #a-f *8.00 8.00*

Souvenir Sheet

Perf. 14x14¼

976 A270 1m multi *4.00 4.00*

Souvenir Sheet

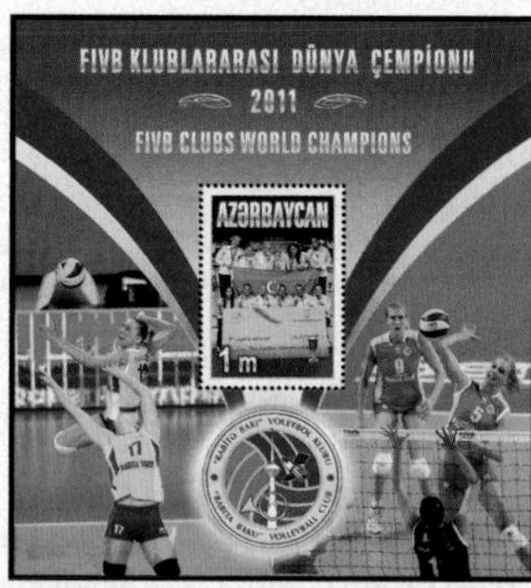

World Championship of Rabita Baku Women's Volleyball Team — A271

2011, Dec. 26 ***Perf. 14¼x14***
977 A271 1m multi *4.50 4.50*

New Year 2012 (Year of the Dragon) A272

2012, Jan. 5 **Litho.** ***Perf. 13¼***
978 A272 20g multi *1.00 1.00*

Central Bank of Azerbaijan, 20th Anniv. A273

2012, Feb. 12 ***Perf. 14x14¼***
979 A273 50g multi *2.50 2.50*

Bahruz Kengerli (1892-1922), Painter — A274

2012, Mar. 15 ***Perf. 14¼x14***
980 A274 20g multi *1.25 1.25*

Europa A275

Designs: 20g, Beach on Caspian Sea, airplane, sailboat. 60g, Skier and chairlift.
1m, Baku International Airport, vert.

2012, Mar. 15 ***Perf. 13¼x13***
981-982 A275 Set of 2 *6.50 6.50*
982a Booklet pane of 8, 4 each #981-982, perf. 13 on 3 sides *26.00 —*

Souvenir Sheet

Perf. 13x13¼

983 A275 1m multi *7.00 7.00*

No. 982a was sold with, but unattached to, a booklet cover.

A276

A277

2012 Eurovision Song Contest, Baku — A278

No. 984: a, 10g, Flame Towers. b, 20g, Heydar Aliyev Center. c, 30g, SOCAR (State Oil Company of Azerbaijan) Tower. d, 40g, Baku Hilton Hotel. e, 50g, Port Baku Residences. f, 60g, Absheron Marriott Hotel.
No. 985: a, 10g, Heydar Aliyev Palace. b, 20g, Opera and Ballet Theater. c, 30g, Philharmonic Hall. d, 40g, Green Theater. e, 50g, Mugam Center. f, 60g, Rashid Behbudov State Song Theater.
No. 986: a, 10g, Shirvansahlar Palace. b, 20g, Government House. c, 30g, Baku City Hall. d, 40g, Nizami Museum of Azerbaijani Literature. e, 50g, Heydar Aliyev Foundation Building. f, 60g, Presidium of Azerbaijan National Academy of Sciences.
No. 987, Eurovision Song Contest emblem, Shirvansahlar Palace. No. 988, Flame, Eurovision Song Contest emblem.

Litho. & Embossed With Foil Application

2012, May 14

984 A276 Sheet of 6, #a-f *6.50 6.50*
985 A277 Sheet of 6, #a-f *6.50 6.50*
986 A278 Sheet of 6, #a-f *6.50 6.50*
Nos. 984-986 (3) 16.50 16.50

Souvenir Sheets

987 A278 60g multi *2.50 2.50*
988 A278 60g multi *2.50 2.50*

Diplomatic Relations Between Azerbaijan and People's Republic of China, 20th Anniv. A279

2012, June 13 Litho. ***Perf. 14x14¼***
989 A279 50g multi *2.50 2.50*

Mirza Fatali Axundzade (1812-78), Writer — A280

2012, June 30 ***Perf. 14¼x14***
990 A280 20g multi *1.50 1.50*

Mirza Alakbar Sabir (1862-1911), Philosopher A281

2012, July 10
991 A281 20g multi *1.50 1.50*

Souvenir Sheet

Azermarka, 20th Anniv. — A282

2012, July 14 ***Perf. 14x14¼***
992 A282 1m multi *4.50 4.50*

Mammed Said Ordubadi (1872-1950), Writer — A283

2012, Aug. 17 ***Perf. 14¼x14***
993 A283 50g multi *2.25 2.25*

Müslüm Magomayev (1942-2008), Singer — A284

2012, Aug. 17
994 A284 50g multi *2.25 2.25*

Aythya Nyroca — A285

Various depictions of Aythya nyroca.

2012, Sept. 12 ***Perf. 14x13½***

Frame Color

995 A285 10g yellow *.40 .40*
996 A285 20g rose lilac *.75 .75*
997 A285 50g light blue *1.75 1.75*
Nos. 995-997 (3) 2.90 2.90

Baku and Arms — A286

National Flag and Symbol — A287

2012, Apr. 6 ***Perf. 14xx14¼***
998 A286 60g multi + label *3.00 3.00*

Perf. 14¼x14

999 A287 60g multi + label *3.00 3.00*

Souvenir Sheet

Diplomatic Relations Between Azerbaijan and Egypt, 20th Anniv. — A288

No. 1000: a, Maiden's Tower, Azerbaijan. b, Sphinx and Pyramids, Egypt.

2012, June 13 ***Perf. 14x14¼***
1000 A288 60g Sheet of 2, #a-b *5.00 5.00*

Huseyn Javid (1882-1941), Poet — A289

2012, Oct. 24 ***Perf. 14¼x14***
1001 A289 20g multi *1.25 1.25*

Souvenir Sheet

Karabakh Costumes of the 19th Century — A290

No. 1002 — Emblem of Regional Communications Commonwealth and: a, Woman and girl. b, Man and boy.

2012, Oct. 29
1002 A290 50g Sheet of 2, #a-b *4.50 4.50*

Souvenir Sheet

Diplomatic Relations Between Azerbaijan and Poland, 540th Anniv. — A291

No. 1003: a, Sultan Uzun Hasan (1423-78). b, King Casimir IV of Poland (1427-92).

2012, Oct. 29
1003 A291 60g Sheet of 2, #a-b *5.00 5.00*

Birds — A292

No. 1004: a, 10g, Goose. b, 20g, Turkey. c, 30g, Chicken. d, 40g, Guinea fowl. e, 50g, Duck. f, 60g, Quail.
1m, Rooster, hen and chick.

2012, Nov. 5
1004 A292 Sheet of 6, #a-f *8.00 8.00*

Souvenir Sheet

1005 A292 1m multi *4.00 4.00*

Azerbaijan Olympic Committee, 20th Anniv. A293

2012, Nov. 7 ***Perf. 14x14¼***
1006 A293 20g multi *1.25 1.25*

Souvenir Sheet

Baku-Tbilisi-Kars Railway — A294

No. 1007 — Map of: a, Western Azerbaijan showing Kars and Tbilisi. b, Eastern Azerbaijan showing Baku.

2012, Nov. 12
1007 A294 60g Sheet of 2, #a-b *5.50 5.50*

Developmental Partnership With World Bank, 20th Anniv. — A295

2012, Dec. 14
1008 A295 50g multi *2.25 2.25*

Souvenir Sheet

First Azerbaijan Telecommunications Satellite — A296

2013, Jan. 15 ***Perf. 12x12¼***
1009 A296 1m multi *4.25 4.25*

Miniature Sheet

New Year 2013 (Year of the Snake) — A297

No. 1010: a, Fish on Chinese character. b, Deer on Chinese character. c, Cranes on Chinese character. d, Bird on Chinese character. e, Snake.

2013, Jan. 23 ***Perf. 13¼***
1010 A297 20g Sheet of 20, #1010a-1010d, 16 #1010e *14.50 14.50*

Europa
A298

Postal vehicles: 20g, Truck. 60g, Van. 1m, Horse-drawn carriage.

2013, Feb. 25 ***Perf. 13¼x13***

1011-1012 A298 Set of 2 *6.00 6.00*
1012a Booklet pane of 8, 4 each #1011-1012, perf. 13 on 3 sides *24.00 24.00*

Souvenir Sheet

1013 A298 1m multi *6.00 6.00*

No. 1012a was sold with, but unattached to, a booklet cover. The two different stamps are found tete-beche within the booklet.

Intl. Association of Academies of Science, 20th Anniv. — A299

2013, Apr. 10 ***Perf. 14¼x14***

1014 A299 20g multi *1.10 1.10*

Miniature Sheet

Lighthouses — A300

No. 1015: a, Süvelan Lighthouse. b, Amburan Lighthouse. c, Böyük Zire Lighthouse. d, Abşeron Lighthouse. e, Cilov Lighthouse.

2013, Apr. 11 ***Perf. 12***

1015 A300 50g Sheet of 5, #a-e, + label *7.75 7.75*

Islam Safarli (1923-74), Poet — A301

Alimardan Topchubashov (1863-1934), Politician — A302

Hokuma Gurbanova (1913-88), Actress A303

Nigar Rafibeyli (1913-81), Writer A304

2013, Apr. 19 ***Perf. 14¼x14***

1016 A301 20g multi *1.10 1.10*

Perf. 14x14¼

1017 A302 20g multi *1.10 1.10*
1018 A303 20g multi *1.10 1.10*
1019 A304 20g multi *1.10 1.10*
Nos. 1016-1019 (4) 4.40 4.40

Souvenir Sheet

Dancers — A305

No. 1020: a, Terekeme dancers, Azerbaijan. b, Kryzhachok dancers, Belarus.

2013, Apr. 24 ***Perf. 13½x13***

1020 A305 50g Sheet of 2, #a-b *3.25 3.25*

See Belarus No. 855.

Souvenir Sheet

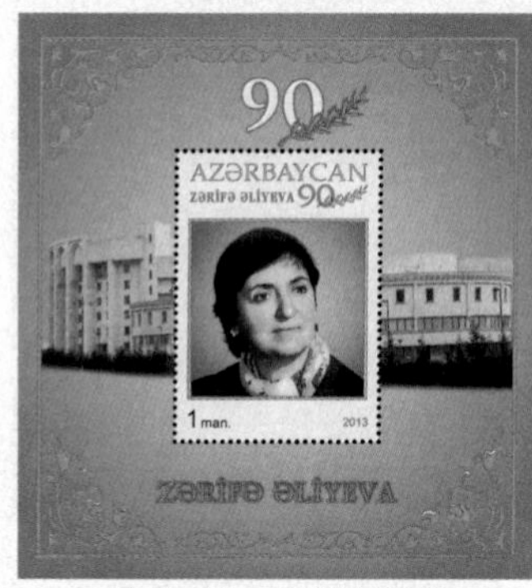

Zarifa Aliyeva (1923-85), Ophthalmologist, Wife of Pres. Heydar Aliyev — A306

Litho. & Embossed With Foil Application

2013, Apr. 28

1021 A306 1m multi *3.25 3.25*

Pres. Heydar Aliyev (1923-2003), Order of St. Andrew the Apostle — A307

2013, May 6 **Litho.** ***Perf. 13½***

1022 A307 50g multi *2.25 2.25*

See Russia No. 7442.

A308

A309

Pres. Heydar Aliyev (1923-2003) — A310

No. 1023 — Pres. Aliyev: a, As young man in suit and tie. b, As young man in army uniform. c, As older man, wearing medals. d, Waving. e, Behind microphone, with hand on book. f, With soldiers, holding binoculars.

No. 1024 — Pres. Aliyev with: a, Turkish Pres. Süleyman Demirel, seated on red chairs. b, U.S. Pres. Bill Clinton. c, German Chancellor Helmut Kohl, paneled wall in background. d, Russian Pres. Vladimir Putin, picture frame behind Putin's head. e, French Pres. Jacques Chirac, seated on sofa. f, People's Republic of China Pres. Jiang Zemin.

1m, Pres. Aliyev and flag of Azerbaijan.

Litho. & Embossed With Foil Application

Perf. 13½x13, 13x13½ (#1024)

2013, May 10

1023 A308 50g Sheet of 6, #a-f *9.50 9.50*
1024 A309 50g Sheet of 6, #a-f *9.50 9.50*

Souvenir Sheet

1025 A310 1m multi *3.25 3.25*

Mahsati Ganjavi (c. 1089-1159), Poet — A311

2013, May 14 **Litho.** ***Perf. 14¼x14***

1026 A311 60g multi *2.25 2.25*

Souvenir Sheet

Diplomatic Relations Between Belarus and Azerbaijan, 20th Anniv. — A312

Litho. (Sheet Margin Litho. With Foil Application)

2013, June 11 ***Perf. 12***

1027 A312 1m multi *3.25 3.25*

See Belarus No. 862.

Souvenir Sheet

Fabric Designs Depicting Peacocks — A313

No. 1028 — Peacock from: a, Hungarian embroidered pillow cover (white background). b, Azeri woven horse blanket (tan background).

2013, June 15 **Litho.** ***Perf. 14x14¼***

1028 A313 60g Sheet of 2, #a-b *4.50 4.50*

See Hungary No. 4287.

Souvenir Sheet

Space Flight of Valentina Tereshkova, First Woman in Space, 50th Anniv. — A314

2013, June 16

1029 A314 1m multi *3.75 3.75*

Souvenir Sheet

Armed Forces of Azerbaijan, 95th Anniv. — A315

2013, June 26 ***Perf. 14¼x14***

1030 A315 1m multi *3.25 3.25*

Birds — A316

Designs: 10g, Merops persicus. 20g, Coracias garrulus. 30g, Alcedo atthis. 50g, Upupa epops. 60g, Garrulus glandarius.

2013, July 16 **Litho.** ***Perf. 13x13¼***

1031 A316 10g multi *.35 .35*
1032 A316 20g multi *.70 .70*
1033 A316 30g multi *1.10 1.10*

1034 A316 50g multi *1.75 1.75*
1035 A316 60g multi *2.10 2.10*
Nos. 1031-1035 (5) 6.00 6.00

State Management of Radio Frequencies, 45th Anniv. — A317

2013, Sept. 3 Litho. ***Perf. 13***
1036 A317 60g multi *2.40 2.40*

State Committee for Securities, 15th Anniv. A318

2013, Sept. 6 Litho. ***Perf. 14x14¼***
1037 A318 60g multi *2.40 2.40*

Memmed Araz (1933-2004), Poet — A319

2013, Sept. 10 Litho. ***Perf. 14¼x14***
1038 A319 20g multi *1.25 1.25*

Souvenir Sheet

Communications — A320

No. 1039: a, Building, people in office, wagon. b, Transmission tower, satellite, satellite dish, women at computers.

2013, Sept. 17 Litho. ***Perf. 14¼x14***
1039 A320 50g Sheet of 2, #a-b *4.75 4.75*

SEMI-POSTAL STAMPS

Carrying Food to Sufferers SP1

1922 Unwmk. ***Imperf.***
B1 SP1 500r blue & pale blue .40 *.75*

For overprint and surcharge see Nos. 42, 305.

Widow and Orphans — SP2

1922
B2 SP2 1000r brown & bister .75 *1.25*

Counterfeits exist.
For overprint and surcharge see Nos. 44, 306.

Russian stamps of 1909-18 were privately overprinted as above in red, blue or black by a group of Entente officers working with Russian soldiers returning from Persia. Azerbaijan was not occupied by the Allies. There is evidence that existing covers (some seemingly postmarked at Baku, dated Oct. 19, 1917, and at Tabriz, Russian Consulate, Apr. 25, 1917) are fakes.

AIR POST STAMP

Catalogue values for all stamps in this section are for never hinged items.

Eagle — AP1

1995, Oct. 16 Litho. ***Perf. 14***
C1 AP1 2200m multicolored 4.00 4.00

AZORES

'ā-ˌzōrz

LOCATION — Group of islands in the North Atlantic Ocean, due west of Portugal
AREA — 922 sq. mi.
POP. — 253,935 (1930)
CAPITAL — Ponta Delgada

Azores stamps were supplanted by those of Portugal in 1931.

In 1934-45, #RA5-RA11, RAJ1-RAJ4, and many stamps between #155-223 were used for regular postage in Portugal.

The Azores were declared an autonomous, or self-governing, region of Portugal in 1976. See Portugal for issues since 1980.

1000 Reis = 1 Milreis
100 Centavos = 1 Escudo (1912)

Stamps of Portugal Overprinted in Black or Carmine — a

A second type of this overprint has a broad "O" and open "S."

1868 Unwmk. ***Imperf.***
1 A14 5r black *3,500. 2,400.*
2 A14 10r yellow *13,750. 10,000.*
3 A14 20r bister 200.00 140.00
4 A14 50r green 200.00 140.00
5 A14 80r orange 200.00 150.00
6 A14 100r lilac 200.00 150.00

The reprints are on thick chalky white wove paper, ungummed, and on thin ivory paper with shiny white gum. Value $35-42.50 each.

1868-70 ***Perf. 12½***

5 REIS:
Type I — The "5" at the right is 1mm from end of label.
Type II — The "5" is 1½mm from end of label.

7 A14 5r black, type I (C) 60.00 30.00
a. Type II 70.00 70.00
8 A14 10r yellow 100.00 40.00
a. Inverted overprint *250.00 150.00*
9 A14 20r bister 50.00 65.00
10 A14 25r rose 50.00 11.00
a. Inverted overprint — —
11 A14 50r green 160.00 150.00
12 A14 80r orange 160.00 150.00
13 A14 100r lilac ('69) 160.00 150.00
14 A14 120r blue 150.00 130.00
15 A14 240r violet 700.00 400.00

The reprints are on thick chalky white paper ungummed, perf 13½, and on thin ivory paper with shiny white gum, perf 13½. Value $30 each.

Overprint Type B

1871-75 ***Perf. 12½***
21 A15 5r black (C) 13.50 8.75
a. Inverted overprint *47.50 42.50*
23 A15 10r yellow 30.00 25.00
a. Inverted overprint — —
b. Double overprint 60.00 47.50
24 A15 20r bister 30.00 26.00
25 A15 25r rose 17.00 4.25
a. Inverted overprint — —
b. Double overprint *40.00*
c. Perf. 14 190.00 85.00
d. Dbl. impression of stamp — —
26 A15 50r green 85.00 42.50
27 A15 80r orange 90.00 50.00
28 A15 100r lilac 90.00 60.00
a. Perf. 14 195.00 150.00
29 A15 120r blue 175.00 125.00
a. Inverted overprint — —
30 A15 240r violet 850.00 675.00

Nos. 21-29 exist with overprint "b."

The reprints are of type "b." All values exist are on thick chalky white paper ungummed, perf 13½ (value, each $29) and also on thin white paper with shiny white gum and perforated 13½ (value, each $30). The 5r, 10r, 15r, 50r and 120r also exist on thick chalky white paper ungummed, perf 12½. Value, each $80.

Overprinted in Black — c

15 REIS:
Type I — The figures of value, 1 and 5, at the right in upper label are close together.
Type II — The figures of value at the right in upper label are spaced.

1875-80 ***Perf. 13½***
31 A15 10r blue green 150.00 125.00
32 A15 10r yellow green 150.00 125.00
33b A15 15r lilac brown 20.00 18.00
a. Inverted overprint *150.00*
34 A15 50r blue 140.00 60.00
35 A15 150r blue 200.00 175.00
36 A15 150r yellow 300.00 175.00
37 A15 300r violet 95.00 65.00

The reprints have the same papers, gum and perforations as those of the preceding issue.

Black Overprint

1880 ***Perf. 12½***
38 A17 25r gray 150.00 95.00
39 A18 25r red lilac 60.00 9.50
b. 25r gray — —
d. As "c," double overprint

Overprint in Carmine or Black

1881-82
40 A16 5r black (C) 29.00 12.00
41 A23 25r brown ('82) 55.00 8.00
a. Double overprint
42 A19 50r blue 190.00 47.50
Nos. 40-42 (3) 274.00 67.50

Reprints of Nos. 38, 39, 39a, 40 and 42 have the same papers, gum and perforations as those of preceding issues.

Overprinted in Red or Black — d

15, 20 REIS

Type I — The figures of value are some distance apart and close to the end of the label.
Type II — The figures are closer together and farther from the end of the label. On the 15 reis this is particularly apparent in the upper right figures.

1882-85 ***Perf. 12½***
43 A16 5r black (R) 20.00 10.00
44 A21 5r slate 19.00 4.50
a. Double overprint —
c. Inverted overprint —
45 A15 10r green 90.00 50.00
a. Inverted overprint — —
46 A22 10r green ('84) 32.50 14.00
a. Double overprint —
47 A15 15r lilac brn 35.00 20.00
b. Inverted overprint — —
48 A15 20r bister 70.00 40.00
a. Inverted overprint — —
49 A15 20r carmine ('85) 150.00 125.00
a. Double overprint 190.00 —
50 A23 25r brown 30.00 4.50
51 A15 50r blue *2,000. 1,250.*
52 A24 50r blue 24.00 3.50
a. Double overprint — —
53 A15 80r yellow 80.00 62.50
a. 80r orange 125.00 110.00
b. Double overprint — —
54 A15 100r lilac 125.00 95.00
55 A15 150r blue *1,800. 900.00*
56b A15 150r yellow 65.00 57.50
57b A15 300r violet 87.50 77.50
58 A21 5r slate (R) 25.00 6.00
59 A24a 500r black 195.00 175.00
60 A15 1000r black (R) 150.00 125.00

This set was issued on both ordinary and enamel surfaced papers. Nos. 51 and 55 exist only on ordinary paper, Nos. 44, 46, 49 and 53 only on surfaced paper, and the other values on both types of paper. Values for Nos. 56b and 57b are for stamps printed on surfaced paper. Stamps on ordinary paper are worth more.

For specialized listings of this issue and other early Azore stamps, see the *Scott Classic Specialized Catalogue.*

Reprints of the 1882-85 issues have the same papers, gum and perforations as those of preceding issues.

1887 **Black Overprint**
61 A25 20r pink 50.00 19.00
a. Inverted overprint — —
b. Double overprint — —
62 A26 25r lilac rose 60.00 3.00
a. Inverted overprint — —
b. Double ovpt., one invtd. — —
63 A26 25r red violet 60.00 3.00
a. Double overprint — —
64 A24a 500r red violet 200.00 110.00
a. Perf. 13½ 400.00 240.00
Nos. 61-64 (4) 370.00 135.00

Nos. 58-64 inclusive have been reprinted on thin white paper with shiny white gum and perforated 13½. Value: Nos. 58, 61-64, each $22.50; No. 59, $85; No. 60, $50.

Prince Henry the Navigator Issue

Portugal Nos. 97-109 Overprinted

1894, Mar. 4 *Perf. 14*

65	A46	5r orange yel	3.50	3.00
a.		Inverted overprint	*60.00*	*60.00*
66	A46	10r violet rose	3.50	3.00
a.		Double overprint	—	—
b.		Inverted overprint	—	—
67	A46	15r brown	4.25	4.00
68	A46	20r violet	4.50	4.25
a.		Double overprint		—
69	A47	25r green	5.00	4.50
a.		Double overprint	*75.00*	*75.00*
b.		Inverted overprint	*75.00*	*75.00*
70	A47	50r blue	12.50	6.75
71	A47	75r dp carmine	22.50	9.50
72	A47	80r yellow grn	27.50	10.00
73	A47	100r lt brn, *pale buff*	27.50	8.00
a.		Double overprint		—
74	A48	150r lt car, *pale rose*	40.00	19.00
75	A48	300r dk bl, *sal buff*	60.00	30.00
76	A48	500r brn vio, *pale lil*	90.00	45.00
77	A48	1000r gray blk, *yelsh*	200.00	70.00
a.		Double overprint	700.00	500.00
		Nos. 65-77 (13)	500.75	217.00

St. Anthony of Padua Issue

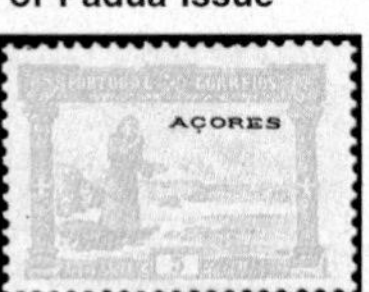

Portugal Nos. 132-146 Overprinted in Red or Black

1895, June 13 *Perf. 12*

78	A50	2½r black (R)	3.00	1.25
79	A51	5r brown yel	9.50	3.00
80	A51	10r red lilac	9.50	4.50
81	A51	15r red brown	14.50	7.00
82	A51	20r gray lilac	16.00	9.50
83	A51	25r green & vio	10.00	3.00
84	A52	50r blue & brn	32.50	15.00
85	A52	75r rose & brn	47.50	40.00
86	A52	80r lt green & brn	55.00	47.50
87	A52	100r choc & blk	55.00	42.50
88	A53	150r vio rose & bis	125.00	100.00
89	A53	200r blue & bis	150.00	100.00
90	A53	300r slate & bis	200.00	110.00
91	A53	500r vio brn & grn	350.00	150.00
92	A53	1000r violet & grn	600.00	225.00
		Nos. 78-92 (15)	1,677.	858.25

7th cent. of the birth of Saint Anthony of Padua.

Common Design Types pictured following the introduction.

Vasco da Gama Issue

Common Design Types

1898, Apr. 1 *Perf. 14, 15*

93	CD20	2½r blue green	3.50	1.25
94	CD21	5r red	3.50	1.50
95	CD22	10r gray lilac	7.00	3.00
96	CD23	25r yellow green	7.00	3.00
97	CD24	50r dark blue	10.00	9.50
98	CD25	75r violet brown	21.00	14.00
99	CD26	100r bister brown	27.50	14.00
100	CD27	150r bister	42.50	30.00
		Nos. 93-100 (8)	122.00	76.25

For overprints and surcharges see Nos. 141-148.

King Carlos — A28

1906 **Typo.** *Perf. 11½x12*

101	A28	2½r gray	.45	.40
a.		Inverted overprint	*35.00*	*35.00*
102	A28	5r orange yel	.45	.40
a.		Inverted overprint	*35.00*	*35.00*
103	A28	10r yellow grn	.45	.40
104	A28	20r gray vio	.70	.50
105	A28	25r carmine	.70	.40
106	A28	50r ultra	6.00	4.75
107	A28	75r brown, *straw*	2.10	*1.25*
108	A28	100r dk blue, *bl*	2.10	*1.40*
109	A28	200r red lilac, *pnksh*	2.25	*1.40*
110	A28	300r dk blue, *rose*	6.75	*5.75*
111	A28	500r black, *blue*	16.00	14.00
		Nos. 101-111 (11)	37.95	30.65

"Acores" and letters and figures in the corners are in red on the 2½, 10, 20, 75 and 500r and in black on the other values.

King Manuel II — A29

1910, Apr. 1 *Perf. 14x15*

112	A29	2½r violet	.50	.40
113	A29	5r black	.50	.40
114	A29	10r dk green	.50	.40
115	A29	15r lilac brn	.90	.65
116	A29	20r carmine	1.25	1.00
117	A29	25r violet brn	.50	.50
a.		Perf. 11½	3.00	1.60
118	A29	50r blue	3.00	1.60
119	A29	75r bister brn	3.00	1.60
120	A29	80r slate	3.00	1.60
121	A29	100r brown, *lt grn*	5.00	3.75
122	A29	200r green, *sal*	5.00	3.75
123	A29	300r black, *blue*	3.00	2.75
124	A29	500r olive & brown	9.50	10.00
125	A29	1000r blue & black	21.00	19.00
		Nos. 112-125 (14)	56.65	47.40

The errors of color 10r black, 15r dark green, 25r black and 50r carmine are considered to be proofs.

Stamps of 1910 Overprinted in Carmine or Green

1910

126	A29	2½r violet	.40	.35
a.		Inverted overprint	12.50	12.50
127	A29	5r black	.40	.35
a.		Inverted overprint	12.50	12.50
128	A29	10r dk green	.40	.35
a.		Inverted overprint	12.50	12.50
129	A29	15r lilac brn	1.90	1.40
a.		Inverted overprint	12.50	12.50
130	A29	20r carmine (G)	1.90	1.40
a.		Inverted overprint	22.50	22.50
b.		Double overprint	22.50	22.50
131	A29	25r violet brn	.40	.30
a.		Perf. 11½	65.00	57.50
132	A29	50r blue	1.40	1.25
133	A29	75r bister brn	1.40	.95
a.		Double overprint	12.50	12.50
134	A29	80r slate	1.40	.95
135	A29	100r brown, *grn*	1.10	.90
136	A29	200r green, *sal*	1.10	*.95*
137	A29	300r black, *blue*	3.50	2.25
138	A29	500r olive & brn	4.50	*3.25*
139	A29	1000r blue & blk	11.00	*7.00*
		Nos. 126-139 (14)	30.80	*21.65*

Vasco da Gama Issue Overprinted or Surcharged in Black

e 

f 

g 

1911 *Perf. 14, 15*

141	CD20(e)	2½r blue green	.65	.50
142	CD21(f)	15r on 5r red	.65	.50
143	CD23(e)	25r yellow grn	.65	.50
144	CD24(e)	50r dk blue	2.25	1.40
145	CD25(e)	75r violet brn	1.90	1.75
146	CD27(f)	80r on 150r bister	2.00	1.90
147	CD26(e)	100r yellow brn	2.10	1.90
a.		Double surcharge	40.00	40.00
148	CD22(g)	1000r on 10r lilac	20.00	15.00
		Nos. 141-148 (8)	30.20	23.45

Postage Due Stamps of Portugal Overprinted or Surcharged in Black

1911 *Perf. 12*

149	D1	5r black	1.25	1.10
150	D1	10r magenta	2.75	1.10
a.		"Acores" double	20.00	15.00
151	D1	20r orange	5.25	3.75
152	D1	200r brn, *buff*	30.00	20.00
a.		"Acores" inverted	75.00	
153	D1	300r on 50r slate	30.00	19.00
154	D1	500r on 100r car, *pink*	30.00	18.00
		Nos. 149-154 (6)	99.25	62.95

Ceres Issue of Portugal Overprinted in Black or Carmine

With Imprint
Chalky Paper

1912-19 *Perf. 15x14*

155	A64	¼c olive brown	3.00	1.25
156	A64	½c black (C)	3.00	1.25
157	A64	1c deep green ('13)	3.00	1.25
158	A64	1½c choc ('13)	4.00	3.00
159	A64	2c carmine	6.00	3.00
160	A64	2½c violet	5.00	1.10
161	A64	5c dp blue	5.00	1.10
162	A64	7½c yel brn	12.00	7.00
163	A64	8c slate ('13)	12.00	7.00
164	A64	10c org brn ('13)	13.00	7.50
165	A64	15c plum ('13)	17.00	7.50
166	A64	20c vio brn, *grn* ('13)	15.00	7.00
167	A64	30c brn, *pink* ('13)	80.00	60.00
168	A64	30c brn, *yel* ('19)	2.25	1.90
169	A64	50c org, *sal* ('13)	6.50	2.75
170	A64	50c org, *yellow* ('13)	6.50	2.75
171	A64	1e dp grn, *bl*	7.00	6.00

Nos. 155 and 160 also exist on glazed non-chalky paper.

Perf. 12x11½

172	A64	14c dk bl, *yel* ('20)	3.00	*1.90*
		Nos. 155-172 (18)	203.25	123.25

Ordinary Paper

1917-21 *Perf. 15x14*

173	A64	¼c olive brown	.55	.40
a.		Inverted overprint	12.50	9.50
174	A64	½c black (C)	.55	.40
175	A64	1c deep green ('17)	1.10	.80
a.		Inverted overprint	12.50	
176	A64	1c deep brown ('18)	.55	.40
a.		Inverted overprint	17.50	
177	A64	1½c choc	1.10	.80
a.		Inverted overprint	13.00	
178	A64	1½c deep green ('18)	.55	.50
a.		Inverted overprint	17.50	
179	A64	2c carmine	.80	.65
a.		Inverted overprint	20.00	
180	A64	2c orange	.55	.50
a.		Inverted overprint	25.00	
181	A64	2½c violet	.80	.65
182	A64	3c rose ('18)	.80	.65
183	A64	3½c lt grn ('18)	.55	.50
184	A64	4c lt grn ('19)	.55	.50
185	A64	5c deep blue	.80	.65
186	A64	5c yellow brown ('21)	.75	.65
187	A64	6c dull rose ('20)	.55	.50
188	A64	7½c yellow brown	6.75	3.75
189	A64	7½c dp bl ('18)	1.90	1.75
190	A64	8c slate	.80	.70
191	A64	10c orange brown	8.00	4.00
192	A64	15c plum	.85	.65
193	A64	30c gray brn ('21)	1.90	1.60
194	A64	60c blue ('21)	1.90	1.50
		Never hinged	2.75	
		Nos. 173-194 (22)	32.65	22.50

Examples of thick carton paper varieties exist. See *Scott Classic Specialized Catalogue of Stamps & Covers 1840-1940* for listings.

1918-26 *Perf. 12x11½*

195	A64	¼c olive brown	.55	.55
196	A64	½c black (C) ('17)	.55	.40
197	A64	1c deep brown	.55	.40
198	A64	1½c deep green	.90	.70
199	A64	2c orange	.55	.50
a.		Inverted overprint	24.00	
200	A64	3c rose	.90	.65
201	A64	3c dull ultra ('25)	.40	.30
202	A64	4c lt grn ('19)	.55	.50
a.		Inverted overprint	21.00	
203	A64	5c olive brown ('21)	.55	.50
204A	A64	6c dull rose ('20)	.55	.50
204	A64	6c choc ('25)	.55	.50
205	A64	7½c dp bl ('19)	75.00	50.00
206	A64	8c bl grn ('22)	.80	.55
207	A64	8c orange ('25)	1.00	.95
208	A64	10c orange brown	.55	.50
209	A64	12c bl gray ('20)	2.75	1.75
210	A64	12c dp grn ('22)	.90	.75
a.		Inverted overprint	20.00	
211	A64	13½c chlky bl ('20)	2.75	1.90
212	A64	15c blk (R) ('23)	.55	.50
213	A64	16c brt ultra ('24)	.95	.90
214	A64	20c choc	.90	.75
215	A64	20c deep green ('23)	1.25	.95
a.		Double overprint	22.50	22.50
216	A64	20c gray ('24)	.80	.60
217	A64	24c grnsh bl ('21)	.90	.55
218	A64	25c salmon ('23)	.70	.50
219	A64	30c gray brn ('21)	1.90	1.60
220	A64	32c dp grn ('25)	2.75	2.40
221	A64	36c red ('21)	.85	.65
222	A64	40c dp blue ('23)	1.00	.70
223	A64	40c blk brn ('24)	1.90	1.00
224	A64	48c brt rose ('24)	5.00	3.00
225	A64	50c yellow ('23)	1.90	1.50
226	A64	60c blue ('21)	1.90	1.50
227	A64	64c pale ultra ('24)	5.00	2.25
228	A64	75c dull rose ('23)	5.00	4.00
229	A64	80c dull rose ('21)	2.50	2.10
230	A64	80c violet ('24)	2.50	1.90
231	A64	90c chlky bl ('21)	2.50	2.10
232	A64	96c dp rose ('26)	7.50	3.50
233	A64	1e violet ('21)	2.50	2.10
234	A64	1.10e yel brn ('21)	2.75	2.10
235	A64	1.20e yel grn ('21)	3.25	2.10
236	A64	2e slate grn ('21)	10.00	6.50
		Nos. 195-236 (34)	149.75	101.65

Examples of thick carton paper and other varieties exist. See *Scott Classic Specialized Catalogue of Stamps & Covers 1840-1940* for listings.

1924-30 *Perf. 12x11½*

Glazed Paper

237	A64	1e gray vio	3.75	3.25
237A	A64	1.20e buff	8.25	6.00
237B	A64	1.50e blk vio	9.75	6.75
237C	A64	1.50e lilac ('25)	8.50	6.75
237D	A64	1.60e dp bl ('25)	8.50	7.00
237E	A64	2.40e apple grn ('26)	100.00	60.00
237F	A64	3e lil pink ('26)	120.00	60.00
237G	A64	3.20e gray grn ('25)	9.75	9.50
237H	A64	5e emer ('24)	19.00	10.00
237I	A64	10e pink ('24)	90.00	27.50
237J	A64	20e pale turq ('25)	175.00	82.50
		Nos. 237-237J (11)	492.50	259.25

For same overprint on surcharged stamps see Nos. 300-306. For same design without imprint see Nos. 307-313.

Castello-Branco Issue

Stamps of Portugal, 1925, Overprinted in Black or Red

1925, Mar. 29 *Perf. 12½*

238	A73	2c orange	.25	.25
239	A73	3c green	.25	.25
240	A73	4c ultra (R)	.25	.25
241	A73	5c scarlet	.25	.25
242	A74	10c pale blue	.25	.25
243	A74	16c red orange	.40	.30
244	A75	25c car rose	.40	.30
245	A74	32c green	.50	.50
246	A75	40c grn & blk (R)	.50	.50
247	A74	48c red brn	1.10	1.10
248	A76	50c blue green	1.10	1.00
249	A76	64c orange brn	1.10	1.00
250	A76	75c gray blk (R)	1.10	1.00
251	A75	80c brown	1.10	1.00
252	A76	96c car rose	1.40	1.10
253	A77	1.50e dk bl, *bl* (R)	1.40	1.10
254	A75	1.60e indigo (R)	1.50	1.40
255	A77	2e dk grn, *grn* (R)	2.50	2.10
256	A77	2.40e red, *org*	3.25	2.40
257	A77	3.20e blk, *grn* (R)	6.00	5.25
		Nos. 238-257 (20)	24.60	21.30

First Independence Issue

Stamps of Portugal, 1926, Overprinted in Red

1926, Aug. 13 *Perf. 14, 14½*

Center in Black

258	A79	2c orange	.35	.35
259	A80	3c ultra	.35	.35
260	A79	4c yellow grn	.35	.35
261	A80	5c black brn	.35	.35
262	A79	6c ocher	.35	.35
263	A80	15c dk green	.75	.70
264	A81	20c dull violet	.75	.70
265	A82	25c scarlet	.75	.70
266	A81	32c deep green	.75	.70
267	A82	40c yellow brn	.75	.70
268	A82	50c olive bis	2.00	2.00
269	A82	75c red brown	2.10	2.10
270	A83	1e black violet	3.00	3.00
271	A84	4.50e olive green	10.00	10.00
		Nos. 258-271 (14)	22.60	22.35

The use of these stamps instead of those of the regular issue was obligatory on Aug. 13th and 14th, Nov. 30th and Dec. 1st, 1926.

Second Independence Issue

Same Overprint on Stamps of Portugal, 1927, in Red

1927, Nov. 29 **Center in Black**

272	A86	2c lt brown	.30	.30
273	A87	3c ultra	.30	.30
274	A86	4c orange	.30	.30
275	A88	5c dk brown	.30	.30
276	A89	6c orange brn	.30	.30
277	A87	15c black brn	.30	.30
278	A86	25c gray	1.25	1.25
279	A89	32c blue grn	1.25	1.25
280	A90	40c yellow grn	1.00	.75
281	A90	96c red	4.00	3.25
282	A88	1.60e myrtle grn	4.00	3.25
283	A91	4.50e bister	10.00	8.75
		Nos. 272-283 (12)	23.30	20.30

Third Independence Issue

Same Overprint on Stamps of Portugal, 1928, in Red

1928, Nov. 27 **Center in Black**

284	A93	2c lt blue	.30	.30
285	A94	3c lt green	.30	.30
286	A95	4c lake	.30	.30
287	A96	5c olive grn	.30	.30
288	A97	6c orange brn	.30	.30
289	A94	15c slate	.65	.60
290	A95	16c dk violet	.75	.75
291	A93	25c ultra	.75	.75
292	A97	32c dk green	.80	.80
293	A96	40c olive brn	.80	.80
294	A95	50c red orange	1.75	1.75
295	A94	80c lt gray	1.75	1.75
296	A97	96c carmine	3.00	3.00
297	A96	1e claret	3.00	3.00
298	A93	1.60e dk blue	3.00	3.00
299	A98	4.50e yellow	8.75	8.50
		Nos. 284-299 (16)	26.50	26.20

A31

A32

Black Overprint

1929-30 *Perf. 12x11½, 15x14*

300	A31	4c on 25c pink ('30)	.75	.75
301	A31	4c on 60c dp blue	1.40	1.40
a.		Perf. 15x14	4.75	4.75
302	A31	10c on 25c pink	1.50	1.50
303	A31	12c on 25c pink	1.40	1.40
304	A31	15c on 25c pink	1.40	1.40
305	A31	20c on 25c pink	2.50	2.40
306	A31	40c on 1.10e yel brn	5.00	4.75
		Nos. 300-306 (7)	13.95	13.60

Black or Red Overprint

1930 *Perf. 14*

Without Imprint at Foot

307	A32	4c orange	.90	.70
308	A32	5c dp brown	3.00	2.75
309	A32	10c vermilion	1.50	1.10
310	A32	15c black (R)	1.50	1.10
311	A32	40c brt green	1.40	.90
312	A32	80c violet	15.00	12.00
313	A32	1.60e dk blue	4.00	1.75
		Nos. 307-313 (7)	27.30	20.30

Black or Red Overprint

1930-31 *Perf. 12x11½*

With Imprint at Foot

313A	A64	4c orange	.55	.50
313B	A64	5c black brown	4.00	3.25
313C	A64	6c red brown ('31)	.40	.30
313D	A64	15c black (C)	.95	.70
313E	A64	16c deep blue	2.75	1.90
313F	A64	32c deep green	3.25	2.25
313G	A64	40c bright green	1.50	.75
313H	A64	48c dull pink ('31)	3.50	3.00
313I	A64	50c bister	4.75	3.50
313J	A64	50c red brown ('31)	4.75	3.50
313K	A64	64c brown rose ('31)	9.00	5.00
313L	A64	75c carmine rose	4.75	3.50
313M	A64	80c dk grn ('31)	4.75	3.00
313N	A64	1e brn lake ('30)	40.00	27.50
313O	A64	1.25e dk blue	2.75	2.25

POSTAGE DUE STAMPS

Portugal Nos. J7-J13 Overprinted in Black — D2

1904 **Unwmk.** *Perf. 12*

J1	D2	5r brown	1.25	1.10
J2	D2	10r orange	1.40	1.10
J3	D2	20r lilac	2.25	1.10
J4	D2	30r gray green	2.25	1.75
a.		Double overprint		
J5	D2	40r gray violet	4.00	2.40
J6	D2	50r carmine	6.75	4.50
J7	D2	100r dull blue	8.50	8.25
		Nos. J1-J7 (7)	26.40	20.20

Same Overprinted in Carmine or Green (Portugal Nos. J14-J20)

1911

J8	D2	5r brown	.75	.65
J9	D2	10r orange	.75	.65
J10	D2	20r lilac	.95	.85
J11	D2	30r gray green	.95	.85
J12	D2	40r gray violet	1.50	1.10
J13	D2	50r carmine (G)	7.75	7.50
J14	D2	100r dull blue	2.75	2.75
		Nos. J8-J14 (7)	15.40	14.35

Portugal Nos. J21-J27 Overprinted in Black — D3

1918

J15	D3	½c brown	.75	.75
a.		Inverted overprint	6.00	
b.		Double overprint	6.00	
J16	D3	1c orange	.75	.75
a.		Inverted overprint	6.00	
b.		Double overprint	6.00	
J17	D3	2c red lilac	.95	.85
a.		Inverted overprint	4.00	
b.		Double overprint	6.00	
J18	D3	3c green	.75	.75
a.		Inverted overprint	6.00	
b.		Double overprint	6.00	
J19	D3	4c gray	.75	.75
a.		Inverted overprint	6.00	
b.		Double overprint	6.00	
J20	D3	5c rose	.75	.75
b.		Double overprint	6.00	
J21	D3	10c dark blue	.75	.75
		Nos. J15-J21 (7)	5.45	5.35

Stamps and Type of Portugal Postage Dues, 1921-27, Overprinted in Black

1922-24 *Perf. 11½x12*

J30	D3	½c gray green ('23)	.35	.35
J31	D3	1c gray green ('23)	.55	.45
J32	D3	2c gray green ('23)	.55	.45
J33	D3	3c gray green ('24)	.90	.45
J34	D3	8c gray green ('24)	.90	.45
J35	D3	10c gray green ('24)	.90	.45
J36	D3	12c gray green ('24)	.90	.45
J37	D3	16c gray green ('24)	.95	.45
J38	D3	20c gray green	.95	.45
J39	D3	24c gray green	.95	.45
J40	D3	32c gray green ('24)	.95	.45
J41	D3	36c gray green	.95	.60
J42	D3	40c gray green ('24)	.95	.60
J43	D3	48c gray green ('24)	.95	.60
J44	D3	50c gray green	.95	.60
J45	D3	60c gray green	1.50	.70
J46	D3	72c gray green	1.50	.70
J47	D3	80c gray green ('24)	5.00	4.25
J48	D3	1.20e gray green	5.75	4.75
		Nos. J30-J48 (19)	26.40	17.65

NEWSPAPER STAMPS

Newspaper Stamps of Portugal, Nos. P1, P1a, Overprinted Types c & d in Black or Red and

N3

Perf. 12½, 13½ (#P4)

1876-88 **Unwmk.**

P1	N1	2½r (c) olive	13.00	5.50
a.		Inverted overprint		
P2	N1	2½r (d) olive ('82)	5.75	1.90
a.		Inverted overprint	—	—
b.		Double overprint	—	—
P3	N3	2r black ('85)	6.00	3.00
a.		Inverted overprint	—	
b.		Double overprint, one inverted	—	
P4	N1	2½r (d) bister ('82)	5.75	1.90
a.		Double overprint	9.00	
P5	N3	2r black (R) ('88)	19.00	16.00
		Nos. P1-P5 (5)	49.50	28.30

Reprints of the newspaper stamps have the same papers, gum and perforations as reprints of the regular issues. Value $2 each.

PARCEL POST STAMPS

Portugal Nos. Q1-Q17 Ovptd. in Black or Red

1921-22 **Unwmk.** *Perf. 12*

Q1	PP1	1c lilac brown	.50	.45
a.		Inverted overprint	6.00	
Q2	PP1	2c orange	.50	.45
a.		Inverted overprint	6.00	
Q3	PP1	5c light brown	.50	.45
a.		Inverted overprint	6.00	
b.		Double overprint	6.00	
Q4	PP1	10c red brown	.75	.45
a.		Inverted overprint	6.00	
b.		Double overprint	6.00	
Q5	PP1	20c gray blue	.75	.45
a.		Inverted overprint	6.00	
b.		Double overprint	6.00	
Q6	PP1	40c carmine	.75	.45
a.		Double overprint	8.00	
Q7	PP1	50c black (R)	1.00	*1.90*
Q8	PP1	60c dark blue (R)	1.00	*1.90*
Q9	PP1	70c gray brown	2.50	1.25
a.		Double overprint	6.00	
Q10	PP1	80c ultra	2.50	1.25
Q11	PP1	90c light violet	2.50	1.25
Q12	PP1	1e light green	2.50	1.25
Q13	PP1	2e pale lilac	5.00	3.50
Q14	PP1	3e olive	10.00	3.75
Q15	PP1	4e ultra	12.00	3.75
Q16	PP1	5e gray	12.00	7.25
Q17	PP1	10e chocolate	50.00	25.00
		Nos. Q1-Q17 (17)	104.75	54.75

POSTAL TAX STAMPS

These stamps represent a special fee for the delivery of postal matter on certain days in the year. The money derived from their sale is applied to works of public charity.

Nos. 128 and 157 Overprinted in Carmine

1911-13 **Unwmk.** *Perf. 14x15*

RA1	A29	10r dark green	1.50	1.10

The 20r of this type was for use on telegrams. Value $2.25 unused, $1.90 used.

Perf. 15x14

RA2	A64	1c deep green	5.00	3.75

The 2c of this type was for use on telegrams. Value $7.00 unused, $5.00 used.

Portugal No. RA4 Overprinted in Black

1915 *Perf. 12*

RA3	PT2	1c carmine	.65	.35

The 2c of this type was for use on telegrams. Value $1.10 unused, 85c used.

Postal Tax Stamp of 1915 Surcharged

1924

RA4	PT2	15c on 1c rose	1.10	*.90*

The 30c on 2c of this type was for use on telegrams. Value $3.00 unused, $1.90 used.

Comrades of the Great War Issue

Postal Tax Stamps of Portugal, 1925, Overprinted

1925, Apr. 8 *Perf. 11*

RA5 PT3 10c brown 1.10 1.10
RA6 PT3 10c green 1.10 1.10
RA7 PT3 10c rose 1.10 1.10
RA8 PT3 10c ultra 1.10 1.10
Nos. RA5-RA8 (4) 4.40 4.40

The use of Nos. RA5-RA11 in addition to the regular postage was compulsory on certain days. If the tax represented by these stamps was not prepaid, it was collected by means of Postal Tax Due Stamps.

Pombal Issue

Common Design Types

1925 *Perf. 12½*

RA9 CD28 20c dp grn & blk 1.10 1.10
RA10 CD29 20c dp grn & blk 1.10 1.10
RA11 CD30 20c dp grn & blk 1.10 1.10
Nos. RA9-RA11 (3) 3.30 3.30

POSTAL TAX DUE STAMPS

Portugal No. RAJ1 Ovptd. in Black

1925, Apr. 8 Unwmk. *Perf. 11x11½*

RAJ1 PTD1 20c brown orange 1.10 .95

See note after No. RA8.

Pombal Issue

Common Design Types

1925, May 8 *Perf. 12½*

RAJ2 CD28 40c dp grn & blk 1.10 *2.00*
RAJ3 CD29 40c dp grn & blk 1.10 *2.00*
RAJ4 CD30 40c dp grn & blk 1.10 *2.00*
Nos. RAJ2-RAJ4 (3) 3.30 *6.00*

See note after No. RA8.

BAHAMAS

bə-'hä-məs

LOCATION — A group of about 700 islands and 2,000 rocks in the West Indies, off the coast of Florida. Only 30 islands are inhabited.
GOVT. — Independent state in British Commonwealth
AREA — 5,382 sq. mi.
POP. — 283,705 (1999 est.)
CAPITAL — Nassau

The principal island, on which the capital is located, is New Providence. The Bahamas obtained internal self-government on January 7, 1964, and independence on July 10, 1973.

12 Pence = 1 Shilling
20 Shillings = 1 Pound
100 Cents = 1 Dollar (1966)

Catalogue values for unused stamps in this country are for Never Hinged items, beginning with Scott 130, and Scott C1 in the air post section.

Values for unused stamps are for examples with original gum as defined in the catalogue introduction. Very fine examples of Nos. 2-26 will have perforations touching the design or frameline on at least one side due to the narrow spacing of the stamps on the plates. Stamps with perfs clear of the design or framelines on all four sides are extremely scarce and will command higher prices.

Pen cancellations usually indicate revenue use. Such stamps sell for much less than postally canceled examples. Beware of stamps with revenue or pen cancellations removed and forged postal cancellations added.

Queen Victoria
A1 A2

1859-60 Unwmk. Engr. *Imperf.*

1 A1 1p dull lake, thin paper ('60) 75.00 *1,900.*
a. 1p reddish lake, thick paper *6,000.* *2,850.*
b. 1p brownish lake, thick paper *6,000.* *2,850.*

Most unused examples of No. 1 are remainders, and false cancellations are plentiful.

1861 *Rough Perf. 14 to 16*

2 A1 1p lake 925. 425.
a. Clean-cut perf. ('60) 7,250. 950.
3 A2 4p dull rose 1,800. 500.
a. Imperf. between, pair *37,500.*
4 A2 6p gray lilac 5,500. 750.
a. Pale lilac 4,250. 650.

No. 2 exists perf 11 to 12½. This is a trial perforation by Perkins, Bacon and was not sent to the colony. Value, $2,850.

1862 *Perf. 11½, 12*

5 A1 1p lake 1,250. 225.
a. Pair, imperf. between *6,250.*
6 A2 4p dull rose 4,500. 500.
7 A2 6p gray violet 13,500. 625.

No.5a was not issued in the Bahamas. It is unique and faulty.

Nos. 5-7 exist with perf. 11½ or 12 compound with 11. See the *Scott Classic Specialized Catalogue.*

Perf. 13

8 A1 1p brown lake 950. 160.
a. 1p carmine lake 1,150. 200.
9 A2 4p rose 3,500. 475.
10 A2 6p gray violet 4,250. 600.
a. 6p dull violet 3,500. 575.

Queen Victoria — A3

Engr., Typo. (A3)

1863-65 Wmk. 1 *Perf. 12½*

11 A1 1p lake 140.00 90.00
a. 1p brown lake 120.00 85.00
b. 1p rose lake 160.00 95.00
c. 1p rose red 70.00 55.00
d. 1p red 75.00 55.00
12 A1 1p vermilion 90.00 57.50
13 A2 4p rose 375.00 75.00
a. 4p rose lake 575.00 100.00
b. 4p bright rose 375.00 75.00
14 A2 6p dk violet 200.00 85.00
a. 6p violet 325.00 115.00
b. 6p rose lilac *8,500.* *3,500.*
c. 6p lilac 475.00 90.00
15 A3 1sh green ('65) 3,250. 375.00

For surcharge see No. 26.

1863-81 Engr., Typo. (A3) *Perf. 14*

16 A1 1p vermilion 70.00 20.00
17 A1 1p car lake (anil.) 1,500.
18 A2 4p rose 475.00 50.00
a. 4p deep rose ('76) 550.00 50.00
b. 4p dull rose 1,900. 50.00
19 A3 1sh green ('80) 10.00 10.00
a. 1sh dark green 350.00 50.00

Some examples of No. 16 show a light aniline appearance and care should be taken not to confuse these with No. 17. All known used examples of No. 17 bear fiscal cancels.

Engr., Typo. (A3)

1882-98 **Wmk. 2**

20 A1 1p vermilion 575.00 75.00
21 A2 4p rose 1,500. 75.00
22 A3 1sh green 50.00 18.00
23 A3 1sh blue grn ('98) 45.00 37.50

Perf. 12

24 A1 1p vermilion 60.00 22.50
25 A2 4p rose 700.00 60.00

No. 14a Surcharged in Black

1883 Engr. Wmk. 1 *Perf. 12½*

26 A2 4p on 6p violet 725. 500.
a. Inverted surcharge *25,000.* *12,000.*

The surcharge, being handstamped, is found in various positions. Counterfeit overprints exist.

Queen Victoria — A5 Queen's Staircase — A6

1884-90 Typo. Wmk. 2 *Perf. 14*

27 A5 1p carmine rose 9.00 3.25
a. 1p pale rose 95.00 16.00
b. 1p car (aniline) 4.00 *8.50*
28 A5 2½p ultra 12.50 3.00
a. 2½p dull blue 95.00 22.50
29 A5 4p yellow 12.50 5.00
30 A5 6p violet 7.50 *37.50*
31 A5 5sh olive green 85.00 *95.00*
32 A5 £1 brown 350.00 *275.00*
Revenue cancellation *55.00*
Nos. 27-32 (6) 476.50 *418.75*

Cleaned fiscally used examples of No. 32 are often found with forged postmarks of small post offices added, especially dated "AU 29 94."

1901-03 Engr. Wmk. 1

33 A6 1p carmine & blk 15.00 *4.00*
34 A6 5p org & blk ('03) 11.00 *66.00*
35 A6 2sh ultra & blk ('03) 35.00 *65.00*
36 A6 3sh green & blk ('03) 50.00 *75.00*
Nos. 33-36 (4) 111.00 *210.00*

See Nos. 48, 58-62, 71, 78, 81-82.

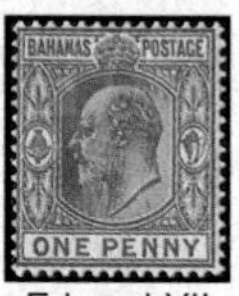

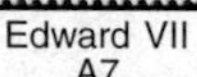

Edward VII A7 George V A8

1902 Wmk. 2 Typo.

37 A7 1p carmine rose 2.00 3.25
38 A7 2½p ultra 8.50 1.75
39 A7 4p orange 20.00 *77.50*
40 A7 6p bister brn 5.00 *30.00*
41 A7 1sh gray blk & car 26.00 *65.00*
42 A7 5sh violet & ultra 85.00 *110.00*
43 A7 £1 green & blk 325.00 *425.00*
Nos. 37-43 (7) 471.50 *712.50*

Beware of forged postmarks, especially dated "2 MAR 10."

1906-11 Wmk. 3

44 A7 ½p green 6.25 4.00
45 A7 1p car rose 32.50 1.75
46 A7 2½p ultra ('07) 32.50 32.50
47 A7 6p bister brn ('11) 30.00 *60.00*
Nos. 44-47 (4) 101.25 *98.25*

1911-19 Engr.

48 A6 1p red & gray blk ('16) 6.00 3.25
a. 1p carmine & black ('11) 23.00 3.50

For overprints see Nos. B1-B2.

1912-19 Typo.

49 A8 ½p green 1.00 *12.50*
50 A8 1p car rose (aniline) 4.50 .45
50A A8 2p gray ('19) 3.00 *3.75*
51 A8 2½p ultra 6.00 *35.00*
52 A8 4p orange 3.25 *20.00*
53 A8 6p bister brown 2.25 *7.00*

Chalky Paper

54 A8 1sh black & car 2.25 *11.50*
55 A8 5sh violet & ultra 50.00 *90.00*
56 A8 £1 dull grn & blk 250.00 *425.00*
Nos. 49-56 (9) 322.25 *605.20*

1917-19 Engr.

58 A6 3p reddish pur, *buff* 7.00 6.25
59 A6 3p brown & blk ('19) 2.75 *5.00*
60 A6 5p violet & blk 3.50 *9.00*
61 A6 2sh ultra & black 37.50 *70.00*
62 A6 3sh green & black 82.50 70.00
Nos. 58-62 (5) 133.25 *160.25*

Peace Commemorative Issue

King George V and Seal of Bahamas — A9

1920, Mar. 1 Engr. *Perf. 14*

65 A9 ½p gray green 1.25 *7.00*
66 A9 1p deep red 3.50 1.25
67 A9 2p gray 3.50 *9.50*
68 A9 3p brown 3.50 *11.50*
69 A9 1sh dark green 22.50 *45.00*
Nos. 65-69 (5) 34.25 *74.25*

Types of 1901-12
Typo., Engr. (A6)

1921-34 Wmk. 4

70 A8 ½p green ('24) .65 .50
71 A6 1p car & black 3.50 *2.75*
72 A8 1p car rose 1.25 .25
73 A8 1½p fawn ('34) 13.00 1.25
74 A8 2p gray ('27) 1.90 *3.00*
75 A8 2½p ultra ('22) 1.25 *3.00*
76 A8 3p violet, *yel* ('31) 8.25 *20.00*
77 A8 4p yellow ('24) 1.90 *5.25*
78 A6 5p red vio & gray blk ('29) 5.50 *57.50*
79 A8 6p bister brn ('22) 1.25 *3.00*
80 A8 1sh blk & red ('26) 6.00 *7.25*
81 A6 2sh ultra & blk ('22) 30.00 27.50
82 A6 3sh grn & blk ('24) 60.00 *82.50*
83 A8 5sh vio & ultra ('24) 45.00 *85.00*
84 A8 £1 grn & blk ('26) 215.00 *425.00*
Nos. 70-84 (15) 394.45 *723.75*

The 3p, 1sh, 5sh and £1 are on chalky paper.

Seal of Bahamas — A10

1930, Jan. 2 Engr. *Perf. 12*

85 A10 1p red & black 3.50 *3.50*
86 A10 3p dp brown & blk 5.50 *19.00*
87 A10 5p dk vio & blk 5.50 *19.00*
88 A10 2sh ultra & black 22.50 *62.50*
89 A10 3sh dp green & blk 52.50 *110.00*
Nos. 85-89 (5) 89.50 *214.00*

The dates on the stamps commemorate important events in the history of the colony. The 1st British occupation was in 1629. The Bahamas were ceded to Great Britain in 1729 and a treaty of peace was signed by that country, France and Spain.

Type of 1930 Issue
Without Dates at Top

1931-46

90 A10 2sh ultra & black 15.00 9.00
a. 2sh ultra & slate purple 30.00 *37.50*
91 A10 3sh dp green & blk 10.00 7.00
a. 3sh deep grn & slate purple 37.50 35.00

Nos. 90a-91a are on thicker paper with yellowish gum. Later printings are on thinner white paper with colorless gum.

For overprints see Nos. 126-127.

Common Design Types pictured following the introduction.

Silver Jubilee Issue
Common Design Type

1935, May 6 *Perf. 13½x14*
92 CD301 1½p car & blue 1.25 *4.00*
93 CD301 2½p blue & brn 6.25 *10.00*
94 CD301 6p ol grn & lt bl 8.75 *15.00*
95 CD301 1sh brt vio & ind 8.75 *14.00*
Nos. 92-95 (4) 25.00 *43.00*
Set, never hinged 35.00

Flamingos in Flight A11

1935, May 22 *Perf. 12½*
96 A11 8p car & ultra 7.25 4.25
Never hinged 10.00

Coronation Issue
Common Design Type

1937, May 12 *Perf. 13½x14*
97 CD302 ½p dp green .25 .25
98 CD302 1½p brown .35 1.40
99 CD302 2½p brt ultra .55 1.40
Nos. 97-99 (3) 1.15 3.05
Set, never hinged 1.75

George VI — A12

Sea Gardens, Nassau A13

Fort Charlotte A14

Flamingos in Flight A15

1938-46 **Typo.** **Wmk. 4** *Perf. 14*
100 A12 ½p green 1.00 *1.60*
101 A12 1p carmine 7.00 4.50
Complete booklet, 12 #101 in blocks of 6 and 8 #102 in folded block —
101A A12 1p pale gray ('41) .50 *.90*
102 A12 1½pred brown 1.25 1.60
103 A12 2p gray 14.00 5.75
103B A12 2p carmine ('41) .85 .85
c. "TWO PENCE" double *15,000.*
104 A12 2½pultra 2.75 *1.90*
104A A12 2½plt violet ('43) 1.10 1.60
b. "2½ PENNY" double 3,250. —
105 A12 3p lt violet 13.00 5.00
105A A12 3p ultra ('43) .50 *1.60*

Engr.
Perf. 12½
106 A13 4p red org & blue .80 *1.25*
107 A14 6p blue & ol grn .65 *1.25*
108 A15 8p car & ultra 7.25 3.25

Typo.
Perf. 14
109 A12 10p yel org ('46) 2.25 .55
110 A12 1sh black & bright red 11.50 1.00
112 A12 5sh pur & ultra 17.50 17.50
113 A12 £1 bl grn & blk 45.00 *60.00*
Nos. 100-113 (17) 126.90 *110.10*
Set, never hinged 190.00

Nos. 110-113 printed on chalky and ordinary paper.

See the *Scott Classic Specialized Catalogue of Stamps & Covers* for listings of shades.

See Nos. 154-156. For overprints see Nos. 116-125, 128-129.

No. 104 Surcharged in Black

1940, Nov. 28 *Perf. 14*
115 A12 3p on 2½p ultra 1.25 *2.75*
Never hinged 1.90

Stamps of 1931-42 Overprinted in Black

1492
LANDFALL
OF
COLUMBUS
1942

1942, Oct. 12 *Perf. 14, 12½, 12*
116 A12 ½p green .25 .75
117 A12 1p gray .25 .75
118 A12 1½p red brn .35 .75
119 A12 2p carmine .40 .80
120 A12 2½p ultra .40 .80
121 A12 3p ultra .25 .80
122 A13 4p red org & blue .35 1.10
123 A14 6p blue & ol grn .35 2.10
124 A15 8p car & ultra 1.10 .85
125 A12 1sh blk & car (#110c) 6.50 11.00
126 A10 2sh dk ultra & blk 6.75 *11.50*
127 A10 3sh dp grn & sl pur(#91a) 6.50 *8.00*
128 A12 5sh lilac & ultra (#112a) 17.50 *16.00*
129 A12 £1 green & black 22.50 *27.50*
Nos. 116-129 (14) 63.45 *82.70*
Set, never hinged 95.00

450th anniv. of the discovery of America by Columbus.

Nos. 125, 128-129 printed on chalky and original paper.

Two printings of the basic stamps were overprinted, the first withdark gum, the second with white gum.

For shades, see the *Scott Classic Catalogue.*

Catalogue values for unused stamps in this section, from this point to the end of the section, are for Never Hinged items.

Peace Issue
Common Design Type
Perf. 13½x14

1946, Nov. 11 **Engr.** **Wmk. 4**
130 CD303 1½p brown .25 .70
131 CD303 3p deep blue .25 .70

Infant Welfare Clinic A16

Designs: 1p, Modern agriculture. 1½p, Sisal. 2p, Native straw work. 2½p, Modern dairying. 3p, Fishing fleet. 4p, Out island settlement. 6p, Tuna fishing. 8p, Paradise Beach. 10p, Modern hotel. 1sh, Yacht racing. 2sh, Water skiing. 3sh, Shipbuilding. 5sh, Modern transportation. 10sh, Modern salt production. £1, Parliament Building.

1948, Oct. 11 **Unwmk.** *Perf. 12*
132 A16 ½p orange .40 *1.60*
133 A16 1p olive green .40 .45
134 A16 1½p olive bister .40 *1.00*
135 A16 2p vermilion .40 .50
136 A16 2½p red brown .85 *1.00*
137 A16 3p brt ultra 3.25 1.10
138 A16 4p gray black .75 .90
139 A16 6p emerald 2.75 1.00
140 A16 8p violet 1.25 .90
141 A16 10p rose car 1.25 .75
142 A16 1sh olive brn 3.00 1.25
143 A16 2sh claret 6.25 *11.00*
144 A16 3sh brt blue 12.50 *11.00*
145 A16 5sh purple 20.00 6.50
146 A16 10sh dk gray 15.00 13.00
147 A16 £1 red orange 16.50 *18.00*
Nos. 132-147 (16) 84.95 *69.95*

300th anniv., in 1947, of the settlement of the colony.

Silver Wedding Issue
Common Design Type
Perf. 14x14½

1948, Dec. 1 **Wmk. 4** **Photo.**
148 CD304 1½p red brown .25 .30

Engr.; Name Typo.
Perf. 11½x11
149 CD305 £1 gray green 45.00 40.00

UPU Issue
Common Design Types
Engr.; Name Typo. on #151 & 152

1949, Oct. 10 *Perf. 13½, 11x11½*
150 CD306 2½p violet .45 *.80*
151 CD307 3p indigo 2.75 *3.75*
152 CD308 6p blue gray .90 *3.50*
153 CD309 1sh rose car 1.50 1.50
Nos. 150-153 (4) 5.60 9.55

George VI Type of 1938
Perf. 13½x14

1951-52 **Wmk. 4** **Typo.**
154 A12 ½p claret ('52) 1.25 *3.25*
a. Wmk. 4a (error) *4,750.*
Lightly hinged 3,250.
155 A12 2p green 1.60 1.00
156 A12 3p rose red ('52) .75 *4.00*
Nos. 154-156 (3) 3.60 *8.25*

Coronation Issue
Common Design Type

1953, June 3 **Engr.** *Perf. 13½x13*
157 CD312 6p blue & black 1.25 .75

Infant Welfare Clinic A17

Designs: 1p, Modern Agriculture. 1½p, Out island settlement. 2p, Native strawwork. 3p, Fishing fleet. 4p, Water skiing. 5p, Modern dairying. 6p, Modern transportation. 8p, Paradise Beach. 10p, Modern hotels. 1sh, Yacht racing. 2sh, Sisal. 2sh6p, Shipbuilding. 5sh, Tuna fishing. 10sh, Modern salt production. £1, Parliament Building.

1954, Jan. 1 *Perf. 11x11½*
158 A17 ½p red org & blk .25 *1.90*
159 A17 1p org brn & ol grn .25 *.35*
160 A17 1½p black & blue .25 *.60*
161 A17 2p dk grn & brn org .25 *.35*
Complete booklet, 8 each #159, 160, 161, in blocks of 4 30.00
162 A17 3p dp car & blk .60 *.75*
163 A17 4p lil rose & bl green .30 .30
164 A17 5p dp ultra & brn 1.60 *2.40*
165 A17 6p blk & aqua 2.00 .25
166 A17 8p rose vio & blk .75 .40
Complete booklet, 4 each #163, 165, 166, in blocks of 4 40.00
167 A17 10p ultra & blk .35 .25
168 A17 1sh ol brn & ultra 1.35 .25
169 A17 2sh blk & brn org 2.25 .60
170 A17 2sh6p dp bl & blk 4.00 2.40
171 A17 5sh dp org & emer 20.00 .75
172 A17 10sh grnsh blk & black 27.00 3.50
173 A17 £1 vio & grnsh black 25.00 8.00
Nos. 158-173 (16) 86.20 23.05

See No. 203. For types overprinted or surcharged see Nos. 181-182, 185-200, 202.

Queen Elizabeth II — A18

Wmk. 314

1959, June 10 **Engr.** *Perf. 13*
174 A18 1p dk red & black .25 .25
175 A18 2p green & black .25 .25
176 A18 6p blue & black .50 .50
177 A18 10p brown & black .80 .80
Nos. 174-177 (4) 1.80 1.80

Cent. of the 1st postage stamp of Bahamas.

Christ Church Cathedral, Nassau — A19

Perf. 14x13

1962, Jan. 30 **Photo.** **Unwmk.**
178 A19 8p shown .55 .55
179 A19 10p Public library .60 .60

Centenary of the city of Nassau.

Freedom from Hunger Issue
Common Design Type
Perf. 14x14½

1963, June 4 **Wmk. 314**
180 CD314 8p sepia .65 .65
a. "8d," "BAHAMAS" omitted 1,100. *2,000.*

Nos. 166-167 Overprinted: "BAHAMAS TALKS/ 1962"
Perf. 11x11½

1963, July 15 **Engr.** **Wmk. 4**
181 A17 8p rose vio & black .35 .35
182 A17 10p ultra & black .65 .65

Meeting of Pres. Kennedy and Prime Minister Harold Macmillan, Dec. 1962.

Red Cross Centenary Issue
Common Design Type
Wmk. 314

1963, Sept. 2 **Litho.** *Perf. 13*
183 CD315 1p black & red .30 .30
184 CD315 10p ultra & red 2.00 2.25

Type of 1954 Overprinted: "NEW CONSTITUTION/ 1964"
Designs as Before
Perf. 11x11½

1964, Jan. 7 **Engr.** **Wmk. 314**
185 A17 ½p red org & blk .30 *1.10*
186 A17 1p org brn & ol green .30 .30
187 A17 1½p black & blue .90 *1.10*
188 A17 2p dk grn & brn org .30 .30
189 A17 3p dp car & blk 1.75 1.75
190 A17 4p lil rose & bl green .50 *.70*
191 A17 5p dp ultra & brn .50 *1.90*
192 A17 6p blk & aqua 2.40 .40
193 A17 8p rose vio & blk .90 .40
194 A17 10p ultra & black .40 .30
195 A17 1sh ol brn & ultra 1.40 .30
196 A17 2sh blk & brn org 1.75 1.75
197 A17 2sh6p dp bl & blk 3.00 3.00
198 A17 5sh dp org & emer 7.00 3.25
199 A17 10sh grnsh blk & black 7.25 5.50
200 A17 £1 vio & grnsh black 8.50 *20.00*
Nos. 185-200 (16) 37.15 42.05

Shakespeare Issue
Common Design Type
Perf. 14x14½

1964, Apr. 23 **Photo.** **Wmk. 314**
201 CD316 6p greenish blue .60 .35

Type of 1954 Surcharged with Olympic Rings, New Value and Bars
Perf. 11x11½

1964, Oct. 1 **Engr.** **Wmk. 314**
202 A17 8p on 1sh ol brn & ultra .90 .90

18th Olympic Games, Tokyo, Oct. 10-25.

Queen Type of 1954

1964, Oct. 6 **Wmk. 314**
203 A17 2p dk grn & brn org 1.10 .50

Colony Badge A21

Designs: 1p, Out Island Regatta. 1½p, Princess Margaret Hospital. 2p, High School. 3p, Flamingo. 4p, Liner "Queen Elizabeth." 6p, Island development. 8p, Yachting. 10p, Public Square, Nassau. 1sh, Sea Garden, Nassau. 2sh, Cannons at Fort Charlotte. 2sh6p, Sea plane and jetliner. 5sh, 1914 Williamson film project and 1939 underwater post office. 10sh, Conch shell. £1, Columbus' flagship.

Engr. and Litho.

1965, Jan. 7 ***Perf. 13½x13***

204 A21 ½p multi, *bluish* .25 *1.40*
205 A21 1p multi .25 *.95*
206 A21 1½p multi .25 *2.00*
207 A21 2p multi .25 .25
Complete booklet, 8 each #205, 206, 207, in blocks of 4 22.50
208 A21 3p multi 2.00 .25
209 A21 4p multi 2.50 2.10
210 A21 6p multi .30 .25
211 A21 8p multi .40 .40
Complete booklet, 4 each #209, 210, 211, in blocks of 4 22.50
212 A21 10p multi .30 .25
213 A21 1sh multi, *grnsh* .40 .25
214 A21 2sh multi, *grnsh* .90 *1.40*
215 A21 2sh6p multi 2.25 *3.75*
216 A21 5sh multi 2.25 1.10
217 A21 10sh multi 14.00 4.00
218 A21 £1 multi 15.00 10.50
Nos. 204-218 (15) 41.30 28.85

Booklet panes were issued Mar. 23, 1965.
See Nos. 252-266. For surcharges see Nos. 221, 230-244.

ITU Issue
Common Design Type
Perf. 11x11½

1965, May 17 **Litho.** **Wmk. 314**

219 CD317 1p emerald & org .25 .25
220 CD317 2sh lilac & olive 1.10 1.10

No. 211 Surcharged

Engr. & Litho.

1965, July 12 ***Perf. 13½x13***

221 A21 9p on 8p multi .45 .30

Intl. Cooperation Year Issue
Common Design Type
Wmk. 314

1965, Oct. 25 **Litho.** ***Perf. 14½***

222 CD318 ½p blue grn & claret .25 *.75*
223 CD318 1sh lt violet & grn .40 .65

Churchill Memorial Issue
Common Design Type

1966, Jan. 24 **Photo.** ***Perf. 14***

224 CD319 ½p multicolored .25 .25
225 CD319 2p multicolored .45 .25
226 CD319 10p multicolored .80 *1.10*
227 CD319 1sh multicolored .80 *1.60*
Nos. 224-227 (4) 2.30 *3.20*

Royal Visit Issue
Common Design Type Inscribed "Royal Visit / 1966"

1966, Feb. 4 **Litho.** ***Perf. 11x12***

228 CD320 6p violet blue .80 .80
229 CD320 1sh dk car rose 2.25 2.25

Nos. 204-218 Surcharged

Engr. & Litho.
Perf. 13½x13

1966, May 25 **Wmk. 314**

230 A21 1c on ½p multi .25 .25
231 A21 2c on 1p multi .25 .25
232 A21 3c on 2p multi .25 .25
233 A21 4c on 3p multi .25 .25
234 A21 5c on 4p multi .25 .25
a. Surch. omitted, vert. strip of 7-10 *3,250.*
235 A21 8c on 6p multi .25 .25
236 A21 10c on 8p multi .25 .25
237 A21 11c on 1½p multi .45 .25
238 A21 12c on 10p multi .50 .30
239 A21 15c on 1sh multi .60 .35
240 A21 22c on 2sh multi .75 .40
241 A21 50c on 2sh6p multi 1.60 1.35
242 A21 $1 on 5sh multi 3.00 2.75
243 A21 $2 on 10sh multi 6.50 5.50
244 A21 $3 on £1 multi 9.50 8.00
Nos. 230-244 (15) 24.65 20.65

The denominations are next to the bars instead of below on Nos. 232, 235-240; the length of the bars varies to cover old denomination.

No. 234a, if single, is identical with No. 209, but distinguishable if in vertical strip of 7 to 10. No. 234 was printed in sheets of 100 (10x10); No. 209 in sheets of 60 (10x6).

World Cup Soccer Issue
Common Design Type

1966, July 1 **Litho.** ***Perf. 14***

245 CD321 8c multicolored .25 .25
246 CD321 15c multicolored .40 .40

WHO Headquarters Issue
Common Design Type

1966, Sept. 20 **Litho.** ***Perf. 14***

247 CD322 11c multicolored .30 .30
248 CD322 15c multicolored .50 .50

UNESCO Anniversary Issue
Common Design Type

1966, Dec. 1 **Litho.** ***Perf. 14***

249 CD323 3c "Education" .25 .25
250 CD323 15c "Science" .35 .35
251 CD323 $1 "Culture" 1.75 1.75
Nos. 249-251 (3) 2.35 2.35

Type of 1965
Values in Cents and Dollars

1c, Colony badge. 2c, Out Island Regatta. 3c, High School. 4c, Flamingo. 5c, Liner "Oceanic." 8c, Island development. 10c, Yachting. 11c, Princess Margaret Hospital. 12c, Public Square, Nassau. 15c, Sea Garden, Nassau. 22c, Cannon at Fort Charlotte. 50c, Sea plane, jetliner. $1, 1914 Williamson film project, 1939 underwater post office. $2, Conch shell. $3, Columbus' flagship.

Engr. & Litho.

1967, May 25 ***Perf. 13½x13***
Toned Paper

252 A21 1c brown & multi .30 *4.00*
253 A21 2c grn, slate & bl .30 *1.00*
254 A21 3c grn, indigo & vio .30 .35
255 A21 4c ultra, blue & red 4.25 .80
256 A21 5c pur, bl & indigo 1.10 *4.50*
257 A21 8c dk brn, bl & dl grn .30 .35
258 A21 10c car rose, bl & pur .35 *1.10*
259 A21 11c bl, grn & rose red .30 *1.40*
260 A21 12c ol grn, bl & lt brn .30 .35
261 A21 15c rose & multi .65 .35
262 A21 22c rose red, brn & bl .75 *1.10*
263 A21 50c emer, ol & bl 2.25 1.25
264 A21 $1 sep, brn org & dk blue 2.25 1.10
265 A21 $2 green & multi 14.00 5.00
266 A21 $3 pur, bl & brn org 4.25 3.00
Nos. 252-266 (15) 31.65 25.65

1970-71 **White Paper**

252a A21 1c brown & multi .50 *4.00*
253a A21 2c grn, slate & bl 1.60 *8.00*
254a A21 3c grn, indigo & vio 55.00 6.00
255a A21 4c ultra, blue & red 14.00 *22.50*
256a A21 5c pur, bl & indigo 1.60 *8.00*
257a A21 8c dk brn, bl & dl grn 190.00 20.00
258a A21 10c car rose, bl & pur 1.10 *5.00*
259a A21 11c bl, grn & rose red .95 *3.00*
260a A21 12c ol grn, bl & lt brn ('71) 14.00 *30.00*
261a A21 15c rose & multi 220.00 25.00
262a A21 22c rose red, brn & bl 1.60 *7.50*
263a A21 50c emer, ol & bl 2.50 *5.00*
264a A21 $1 sep, brn org & dk blue ('71) 22.00 *70.00*
265a A21 $2 green & multi ('71) 32.50 *85.00*
266a A21 $3 pur, bl & brn org ('71) 32.50 *85.00*
Nos. 252a-266a (15) 589.85 *384.00*

Nos. 252-266 are on toned paper. Nos. 252a-266a are on very white, untinted paper. Because of the difference in papers and the use of some new plates, there are sharp differences in shade on most values.

Seal of Bahamas, Queen Elizabeth II and Lord Baden-Powell — A22

60th anniv. of world Scouting: 15c, Scout emblem and portraits as on 3c.

Perf. 14x13½

1967, Sept. 1 **Photo.** **Wmk. 314**

267 A22 3c multicolored .25 .25
268 A22 15c multicolored .60 .25

Human Rights Flame and Globe A23

Intl. Human Rights Year: 12c, Human rights flame and scales of justice. $1, Human rights flame and Seal of Bahamas.

1968, May 13 **Litho.** ***Perf. 14***

269 A23 3c multicolored .25 .25
270 A23 12c multicolored .30 .30
271 A23 $1 multicolored 1.10 1.10
Nos. 269-271 (3) 1.65 1.65

Golf — A24

Tourist Publicity: 11c, Yachting. 15c, Horse racing. 50c, Water skiing.

1968, Aug. 20 **Unwmk.** ***Perf. 13½***

272 A24 5c multicolored 2.00 2.00
273 A24 11c multicolored 2.00 2.00
274 A24 15c multicolored 2.50 2.50
275 A24 50c multicolored 3.50 3.50
Nos. 272-275 (4) 10.00 10.00

Olympic Monument and Sailboat — A25

Olympic Monument, San Salvador Island, Bahamas, and: 11c, Long jump. 50c, Running. $1, Sailing.

1968, Sept. 30 **Photo.** ***Perf. 14½x14***

276 A25 5c multicolored .45 .45
277 A25 11c multicolored .75 .75
278 A25 50c multicolored 1.00 1.00
279 A25 $1 multicolored 2.75 2.75
Nos. 276-279 (4) 4.95 4.95

19th Olympic Games, Mexico City, 10/12-27.

Legislative Building — A26

Designs: 10c, Bahamas mace and Big Ben, London, vert. 12c, Local straw market, vert. 15c, Horse-drawn surrey.

Perf. 14½

1968, Nov. 1 **Unwmk.** **Litho.**

280 A26 3c brt blue & multi .25 .25
281 A26 10c yel, blk & blue .25 .25
282 A26 12c brt rose & multi .25 .25
283 A26 15c green & multi .25 .25
Nos. 280-283 (4) 1.00 1.00

14th Commonwealth Parliamentary Conf., Nassau, Nov. 1-8.

$100 Coin with Queen Elizabeth II and Landing of Columbus — A27

Gold Coins with Elizabeth II on Obverse: 12c, $50 coin and Santa Maria flagship. 15c, $20 coin and Nassau Harbor Lighthouse. $1, $10 coin and Fort.

Engr. on Gold Paper

1968, Dec. 2 **Unwmk.** ***Perf. 13½***

284 A27 3c dark red .55 .55
285 A27 12c dark green .90 .90
286 A27 15c lilac 1.10 1.10
287 A27 $1 black 2.75 2.75
Nos. 284-287 (4) 5.30 5.30

First gold coinage in the Bahamas.

Bahamas Postal Card and Airplane Wing — A28

Design: 15c, Seaplane, 1929.

Perf. 14½x14

1969, Jan. 30 **Litho.** **Unwmk.**

288 A28 12c multicolored .75 .75
289 A28 15c multicolored .90 .90

50th anniv. of the 1st flight from Nassau, Bahamas, to Miami, Fla., Jan. 30, 1919.

Game Fishing Boats A29

Designs: 11c, Paradise Beach. 12c, Sunfish sailboats. 15c, Parade on Rawson Square.

1969, Aug. 26 **Litho.** **Wmk. 314**

290 A29 3c multicolored .25 .25
291 A29 11c multicolored .55 .55
292 A29 12c multicolored .60 .60
293 A29 15c multicolored .75 .75
a. Souvenir sheet of 4, #290-293 4.00 4.00
Nos. 290-293 (4) 2.15 2.15

Tourist publicity.

Holy Family, by Nicolas Poussin — A30

Paintings: 3c, Adoration of the Shepherds, by Louis Le Nain. 12c, Adoration of the Kings, by Gerard David. 15c, Adoration of the Kings, by Vincenzo Foppa.

1969, Oct. 15 Photo. *Perf. 12*

294 A30 3c red & multi .25 .25
295 A30 11c emerald & multi .25 .25
296 A30 12c ultra & multi .30 .30
297 A30 15c multicolored .40 .40
Nos. 294-297 (4) 1.20 1.20

Christmas.

Girl Guides, Globe and Flags A31

Designs: 12c, Yellow elder and Brownie emblem. 15c, Ranger emblem.

1970, Feb. 23 Wmk. 314 *Perf. 14½*

298 A31 3c vio blue, yel & red .25 .25
299 A31 12c dk brn, grn & yel .50 .50
300 A31 15c vio bl, bluish grn & yel .70 .70
Nos. 298-300 (3) 1.45 1.45

60th anniversary of the Girl Guides.

Opening of UPU Headquarters, Bern — A32

1970, May 20 Litho. *Perf. 14½*

301 A32 3c vermilion & multi .25 .25
302 A32 15c orange & multi .35 .35

Bus and Globe A33

Globe and: 11c, Train. 12c, Sailboat and ship. 15c, Plane.

1970, July 14 *Perf. 13½x13*

303 A33 3c orange & multi .85 .85
304 A33 11c emerald & multi 1.75 1.75
305 A33 12c multicolored 1.75 1.75
306 A33 15c blue & multi 1.75 1.75
a. Souvenir sheet of 4, #303-306 11.50 11.50
Nos. 303-306 (4) 6.10 6.10

Issued to promote good will through world-wide travel and tourism.

People, Palms and Flamingo — A34

15c, Red Cross Headquarters, Nassau & marlin.

1970, Aug. 18 *Perf. 14x14½*

307 A34 3c multicolored 1.00 .65
308 A34 15c multicolored 1.00 *1.60*

Centenary of British Red Cross Society.

Nativity by G. B. Pittoni — A35

Christmas: 11c, Holy Family, by Anton Raphael Mengs. 12c, Adoration of the Shepherds, by Giorgione. 15c, Adoration of the Shepherds, School of Seville.

Perf. 12½x13

1970, Nov. 3 Litho. Wmk. 314

309 A35 3c multicolored .25 .25
310 A35 11c red org & multi .30 .30
311 A35 12c emerald & multi .30 .30
312 A35 15c blue & multi .45 .45
a. Souv. sheet of 4, #309-312 + 3 labels 2.25 2.25
Nos. 309-312 (4) 1.30 1.30

International Airport A36

2c, Breadfruit. 3c, Straw market. 4c, 6c, Hawksbill turtle. 5c, Grouper. 7c, 12c, Hibiscus. 8c, Yellow elder. 10c, Bahamian sponge boat. 11c, Flamingos. 15c, Bonefish. 18c, 22c, Royal poinciana. 50c, Post office, Nassau. $1, Pineapple, vert. $2, Crayfish, vert. $3, "Junkanoo" (costumed drummer), vert.

Wmk. 314 Upright (Sideways on $1, $2, $3)

1971 *Perf. 14½x14, 14x14½*

313 A36 1c blue & multi .25 .30
314 A36 2c red & multi .25 .35
315 A36 3c lilac & multi .25 .30
316 A36 4c brown & multi 1.75 *8.50*
317 A36 5c dp org & multi .70 .55
318 A36 6c brown & multi .45 1.10
319 A36 7c green & multi 1.90 *3.75*
320 A36 8c yel & multi .65 *1.40*
321 A36 10c red & multi .60 .30
322 A36 11c red & multi 2.40 2.75
323 A36 12c green & multi 1.90 *2.75*
324 A36 15c gray & multi .60 .35
325 A36 18c multicolored .70 .55
326 A36 22c green & multi 2.90 *12.00*
327 A36 50c multicolored 1.40 *1.50*
328 A36 $1 red & multi 6.50 2.25
329 A36 $2 blue & multi 4.75 5.25
330 A36 $3 vio bl & multi 3.75 *8.00*
Nos. 313-330 (18) 31.70 *51.95*

See Nos. 398-401, 426-443.

Wmk. 314 Sideways (Upright on $1, $2, $3)

1973

317a A36 5c 17.50 *24.00*
320a A36 8c 4.25 *6.75*
327a A36 50c 3.25 *5.00*
328a A36 $1 3.25 *5.00*
329a A36 $2 3.25 *5.00*
330a A36 $3 4.50 *7.25*
Nos. 317a-330a (6) 36.00 53.00

1976 Wmk. 373

313a A36 1c .25 .25
314a A36 2c .25 .25
315a A36 3c .25 .25
317b A36 5c .25 .25
320b A36 8c .25 .25
321a A36 10c .25 .25
327b A36 50c 3.25 *4.25*
328b A36 $1 6.75 *8.75*
329b A36 $2 13.50 *16.00*
330b A36 $3 20.00 *26.00*
Nos. 313a-330b (10) 45.00 56.50

Snowflake with Peace Signs A37

Christmas: 11c, "Peace on Earth" with doves. 15c, Christmas wreath around old Bahamas coat of arms. 18c, Star of Bethlehem over palms.

Perf. 14x14½

1971 Photo. Wmk. 314

331 A37 3c dp lil rose, gold & org .25 .25
332 A37 11c violet & gold .30 .30
333 A37 15c gold embossed & multi .30 .30
334 A37 18c brt bl, gold & vio bl .35 .35
a. Souv. sheet, #331-334, perf 15 2.25 2.25
Nos. 331-334 (4) 1.20 1.20

High Jump, Arms of Bahamas — A38

Olympic Rings, Compass, Arms of Bahamas and: 11c, Bicycling. 15c, Running. 18c, Sailing.

1972, June 27 Litho. *Perf. 13x13½*

335 A38 10c lt violet & multi .50 .50
336 A38 11c ocher & multi .65 .65
337 A38 15c yel green & multi .90 .90
338 A38 18c blue & multi 1.30 1.30
a. Souvenir sheet of 4, #335-338 5.50 5.50
Nos. 335-338 (4) 3.35 3.35

20th Olympic Games, Munich, 8/26-9/10.

Shepherd and Star of Bethlehem — A39

Designs: 6c, Bells. 15c, Holly and monstrance. 20c, Poinsettia.

1972, Oct. 3 Wmk. 314 *Perf. 14*

339 A39 3c gold & multi .25 .25
340 A39 6c black & multi .25 .25
341 A39 15c black & multi .30 .30
342 A39 20c gold & multi .50 .50
a. Souvenir sheet of 4, #339-342 2.50 2.50
Nos. 339-342 (4) 1.30 1.30

Christmas. Gold on 15c is embossed.

Souvenir Sheet

Map of Bahama Islands — A40

1972, Nov. 1 Litho. *Perf. 15*

343 A40 Sheet of 4 6.75 6.75
a. 11c blue & multi .50 .50
b. 15c blue & multi .75 .75
c. 18c blue & multi .90 .90
d. 50c blue & multi 2.75 2.75

Tourism Year of the Americas.

Silver Wedding Issue, 1972

Common Design Type

Design: Queen Elizabeth II, Prince Philip, mace and galleon.

Perf. 14x14½

1972, Nov. 13 Photo. Wmk. 314

344 CD324 11c car rose & multi .25 .25
345 CD324 18c violet & multi .35 .35

Weather Satellite, WMO Emblem A41

1973, Apr. 3 Litho. *Perf. 14*

346 A41 15c shown .55 .45
347 A41 18c Weather radar .75 .65

Intl. meteorological cooperation, cent.

Clarence A. Bain — A42

Independence: 11c, New Bahamian coat of arms. 15c, New flag and Government House. $1, Milo B. Butler, Sr.

1973 Wmk. 314 *Perf. 14½x14*

348 A42 3c lilac & multi .25 .25
349 A42 11c lt blue & multi .35 .35
350 A42 15c lt green & multi .60 .60
351 A42 $1 yel & multi 1.25 1.25
a. Souvenir sheet of 4, #348-351 3.00 3.00
Nos. 348-351 (4) 2.45 2.45

Issued: Nos. 348-350, 7/10; Nos. 351, 351a, 8/1.

Virgin in Prayer, by Sassoferrato A43

Christmas: 11c, Virgin and Child with St. John, by Filippino Lippi. 15c, Choir of Angels, by Marmion. 18c, The Two Trinities, by Murillo.

1973, Oct. 16 Litho. *Perf. 14*

352 A43 3c blue & multi .25 .25
353 A43 11c multicolored .30 .30
354 A43 15c gray grn & multi .30 .30
355 A43 18c lil rose & multi .40 .40
a. Souvenir sheet of 4, #352-355 1.50 *2.00*
Nos. 352-355 (4) 1.25 1.25

Agriculture, Science and Medicine — A44

18c, Symbols of engineering, art, and law.

1974, Feb. 5 Litho. *Perf. 13½x14*

356 A44 15c dull grn & multi .35 .35
357 A44 18c multicolored .50 .50

University of the West Indies, 25th anniv.

UPU Emblem A45

Designs: 13c, UPU emblem, vert. 14c, UPU emblem. 18c, UPU monument, Bern, vert.

1974, Apr. 23 *Perf. 14*

358 A45 3c multicolored .25 .25
359 A45 13c multicolored .30 .30
360 A45 14c olive bis & multi .30 .30
361 A45 18c multicolored .35 .35
a. Souvenir sheet of 4, #358-361 1.30 *2.00*
Nos. 358-361 (4) 1.20 1.20

Centenary of Universal Postal Union.

Roseate Spoonbills, Trust Emblem — A46

Protected Birds (National Trust Emblem and): 14c, White-crowned pigeons. 21c, White-tailed tropic birds. 36c, Bahamian parrot.

1974, Sept. 10 **Litho.** *Perf. 14*

362 A46 13c multicolored 1.50 .65
363 A46 14c multicolored 1.50 .55
364 A46 21c multicolored 2.00 1.00
365 A46 36c multicolored 2.50 *4.25*
a. Souvenir sheet of 4, #362-365 11.00 11.00
Nos. 362-365 (4) 7.50 6.45

Bahamas National Trust, 15th anniv.

Holy Family, by Jacques de Stella A47

Christmas: 10c, Virgin and Child, by Girolamo Romanino. 12c, Virgin and Child with St. John and St. Catherine, by Andrea Previtali. 21c, Virgin and Child with Angels, by Previtali.

1974, Oct. 29 **Wmk. 314** *Perf. 13*

366 A47 8c black & multi .25 .25
367 A47 10c green & multi .30 .30
368 A47 12c red & multi .30 .30
369 A47 21c ultra & multi .40 .40
a. Souvenir sheet of 4, #366-369 1.75 *2.25*
Nos. 366-369 (4) 1.25 1.25

Anteos Maerula A48

1975, Feb. 4 **Litho.** *Perf. 14x13½*

370 A48 3c shown .50 .30
371 A48 14c Eurema nicippe 1.40 .75
372 A48 18c Papilio andraemon 1.50 .95
373 A48 21c Euptoieta hegesia 1.75 1.40
a. Souvenir sheet of 4, #370-373 11.00 11.00
Nos. 370-373 (4) 5.15 3.40

Sheep Raising A49

Designs: 14c, Electric reel fishing, vert. 18c, Growing food. 21c, Crude oil refinery, vert.

Unwmk.

1975, May 27 **Litho.** *Perf. 14*

374 A49 3c dull grn & multi .25 .25
375 A49 14c green & multi .25 .25
376 A49 18c brown & multi .25 .25
377 A49 21c vio bl & multi .80 .45
a. Souvenir sheet of 4, #374-377 1.40 1.40
Nos. 374-377 (4) 1.55 1.20

Economic diversification.

Rowena Rand, Staff and Chrismon — A50

Plant and IWY Emblem — A51

Wmk. 373

1975, July 22 **Litho.** *Perf. 14*

378 A50 14c multicolored .30 *.40*
379 A51 18c multicolored .35 *.60*

International Women's Year.

Adoration of the Shepherds, by Perugino — A52

Christmas: 8c, 18c, Adoration of the Kings, by Ghirlandaio. 21c, like 3c.

1975, Dec. 2 **Litho.** *Perf. 13½*

380 A52 3c dk green & multi .25 .25
381 A52 8c dk violet & multi .25 .25
382 A52 18c purple & multi .65 .65
383 A52 21c maroon & multi .70 .70
a. Souvenir sheet of 4, #380-383 2.50 *3.00*
Nos. 380-383 (4) 1.85 1.85

Telephones, 1876 and 1976 — A53

Designs: 16c, Radio-telephone link, Deleporte, Nassau (radar). 21c, Alexander Graham Bell. 25c, Communications satellite.

1976, Mar. 23 **Litho.** *Perf. 14*

384 A53 3c multicolored .25 .25
385 A53 16c multicolored .35 .35
386 A53 21c multicolored .50 .50
387 A53 25c multicolored .60 .60
Nos. 384-387 (4) 1.70 1.70

Centenary of first telephone call by Alexander Graham Bell, Mar. 10, 1876.

Bicycling and Olympic Rings — A54

Olympic Rings and: 16c, Long jump. 25c, Sailing. 40c, Boxing.

1976, July 13 **Litho.** *Perf. 14*

388 A54 8c magenta & blue 1.75 .30
389 A54 16c orange & brn .50 .40
390 A54 25c magenta & blue .65 .65
391 A54 40c orange & brn .80 1.00
a. Souvenir sheet of 4, #388-391 4.00 4.00
Nos. 388-391 (4) 3.70 2.35

21st Olympic Games, Montreal, Canada, July 17-Aug. 1.

John Murray, Earl of Dunmore A55

Design: 16c, Map of US and Bahamas.

1976, June 1 **Wmk. 373** *Perf. 14*

392 A55 16c multicolored .45 .45
393 A55 $1 multicolored 1.75 1.75
a. Souvenir sheet of 4, #393 8.25 *9.25*

American Bicentennial.

Virgin and Child, Filippo Lippi — A56

Christmas: 21c, Adoration of the Shepherds, School of Seville. 25c, Adoration of the Kings, by Vincenzo Foppa. 40c, Virgin and Child, by Vivarini.

1976, Oct. 19 **Litho.** *Perf. 14½x14*

394 A56 3c brt blue & multi .25 .25
395 A56 21c dp org & multi .25 .25
396 A56 25c emerald & multi .25 .25
397 A56 40c red lilac & multi .40 .40
a. Souvenir sheet of 4, #394-397 1.75 1.75
Nos. 394-397 (4) 1.15 1.15

Type of 1971

16c, Hibiscus. 21c, Breadfruit. 25c, Hawksbill turtle. 40c, Bahamian sponge boat.

1976, Nov. 2 **Litho.** **Wmk. 373**

398 A36 16c emerald & multi 1.40 *1.75*
399 A36 21c vermilion & multi 1.75 *4.25*
400 A36 25c brown & multi 2.00 *2.10*
401 A36 40c vermilion & multi 6.00 3.25
Nos. 398-401 (4) 11.15 11.35

Elizabeth II Seated under Gold Canopy — A57

16c, Coronation. 21c, Taking and signing of oath. 40c, Queen holding orb and scepter.

1977, Feb. 7 *Perf. 12*

402 A57 8c silver & multi .25 .25
403 A57 16c silver & multi .25 .25
404 A57 21c silver & multi .25 .25
405 A57 40c silver & multi .30 .30
a. Souvenir sheet of 4, #402-405 1.25 *2.00*
Nos. 402-405 (4) 1.05 1.05

Reign of Queen Elizabeth II, 25th anniv. For surcharges see Nos. 412-415.

Featherduster — A58

Marine Life: 8c, Porkfish. 16c, Elkhorn coral. 21c, Soft coral and sponge.

1977, May 24 **Litho.** *Perf. 13½*

406 A58 3c multicolored .65 .40
407 A58 8c multicolored 1.10 .55
408 A58 16c multicolored 1.25 .85
409 A58 21c multicolored 1.40 1.10
a. Souv. sheet, #406-409, perf 14½ 5.50 5.50
Nos. 406-409 (4) 4.40 2.90

Campfire and Shower A59

1977, Sept. 27 **Litho.** **Wmk. 373**

410 A59 16c shown .65 .55
411 A59 21c Boating 1.00 .70

6th Caribbean Jamboree, Kingston, Jamaica, Aug. 5-14.

Nos. 402-405a Overprinted: "Royal Visit / October 1977"

1977, Oct. 19 **Litho.** *Perf. 12*

412 A57 8c silver & multi .25 .25
413 A57 16c silver & multi .25 .25
414 A57 21c silver & multi .25 .25
415 A57 40c silver & multi .35 .35
a. Souvenir sheet of 4 1.50 *2.00*
Nos. 412-415 (4) 1.10 1.10

Caribbean visit of Queen Elizabeth II, Oct. 19-20.

Virgin and Child — A60

Crèche Figurines: 16c, Three Kings. 21c, Adoration of the Kings. 25c, Three Kings.

1977, Oct. 25 **Litho.** *Perf. 13½*

416 A60 3c gold & multi .25 .25
417 A60 16c gold & multi .25 .25
418 A60 21c gold & multi .25 .25
419 A60 25c gold & multi .30 .30
a. Souv. sheet, #416-419, perf 14½ 1.60 *3.25*
Nos. 416-419 (4) 1.05 1.05

Christmas.

Nassau Public Library — A61

Architectural Heritage: 8c, St. Matthew's Church. 16c, Government House. 18c, The Hermitage, Cat Island.

1978, Mar. 28 **Litho.** *Perf. 14½x14*

420 A61 3c black & yel green .25 .25
421 A61 8c black & lt blue .25 .25
422 A61 16c black & lilac rose .25 .25
423 A61 18c black & salmon .25 .25
a. Souvenir sheet of 4, #420-423 1.00 *1.60*
Nos. 420-423 (4) 1.00 1.00

Scepter, St. Edward's Crown, Orb — A62

Perf. 14x13½

1978, June 27 **Litho.** **Wmk. 373**

424 A62 16c shown .25 .25
425 A62 $1 Elizabeth II 1.00 .55
a. Souvenir sheet of 2, #424-425 1.75 1.75

Coronation of Queen Elizabeth II, 25th anniv.

Type of 1971

Designs as before and: 16c, Hibiscus. 25c, Hawksbill turtle.

Perf. 14½x14, 14x14½

1978, June **Unwmk.**

426	A36	1c blue & multi	1.25	1.40
430	A36	5c dp org & multi	1.90	2.10
436	A36	16c brt grn & multi	2.50	3.00
439	A36	25c brown & multi	10.50	13.50
440	A36	50c lemon & multi	4.50	5.75
441	A36	$1 lemon & multi	4.50	5.75
442	A36	$2 blue & multi	7.50	10.00
443	A36	$3 vio bl & multi	7.50	10.00
		Nos. 426-443 (8)	40.15	51.50

Angels and Palms A63

Christmas: 5c, Coat of arms within wreath, and sailing ships.

Perf. 14x14½

1978, Nov. 14 **Litho.** **Wmk. 373**

444	A63	5c car, pink & gold	.25	.25
445	A63	21c ultra, dk bl & gold	.30	.30
a.		Souvenir sheet of 2, #444-445	4.00	4.00

Baby Walking, IYC Emblem — A64

IYC Emblem and: 16c, Children playing leapfrog. 21c, Girl skipping rope. 25c, Building blocks with "IYC" and emblem.

Perf. 13½x13

1979, May 15 **Litho.** **Wmk. 373**

446	A64	5c multicolored	.25	.25
447	A64	16c multicolored	.30	.30
448	A64	21c multicolored	.50	.50
449	A64	25c multicolored	.60	.60
a.		Souv. sheet, #446-449, perf 14	2.00	2.00
		Nos. 446-449 (4)	1.65	1.65

International Year of the Child.

Rowland Hill and Penny Black — A65

21c, Stamp printing press, 1840, Bahamas #7. 25c, Great Britain #27 with 1850's Nassau cancellation, Great Britain #29. 40c, Early mailboat, Bahamas #1.

1979, Aug. 14 *Perf. 13½x14*

450	A65	10c multicolored	.50	.30
451	A65	21c multicolored	.65	.50
452	A65	25c multicolored	.65	.65
453	A65	40c multicolored	.70	.70
a.		Souvenir sheet of 4, #450-453	2.75	2.75
		Nos. 450-453 (4)	2.50	2.15

Sir Rowland Hill (1795-1879), originator of penny postage.

Commonwealth Plaque over Map of Bahamas — A66

Designs: 21c, Parliament buildings. 25c, Legislative chamber. $1, Senate chamber.

1979, Sept. 27 **Litho.** *Perf. 13½*

454	A66	16c multicolored	.30	.30
455	A66	21c multicolored	.35	.35
456	A66	25c multicolored	.35	.35
457	A66	$1 multicolored	1.40	1.40
a.		Souvenir sheet of 4, #454-457	3.50	3.50
		Nos. 454-457 (4)	2.40	2.40

Parliament of Bahamas, 250th anniv.

Headdress A67

Christmas: Goombay Carnival costumes.

1979, Nov. 6 **Litho.** *Perf. 13*

458	A67	5c multicolored	.25	.25
459	A67	10c multicolored	.25	.25
460	A67	16c multicolored	.25	.25
461	A67	21c multicolored	.25	.25
462	A67	25c multicolored	.30	.25
463	A67	40c multicolored	.45	.40
a.		Souv. sheet, 458-463, perf 13½	2.50	*3.75*
		Nos. 458-463 (6)	1.75	1.65

Columbus' Landing, 1492 A68

1980, July 9 **Litho.** *Perf. 15*

464	A68	1c shown	.60	2.40
465	A68	3c Blackbeard	.25	2.40
466	A68	5c Articles, 1647, Eleuthera map	.25	1.25
467	A68	10c Ceremonial mace	.25	.40
468	A68	12c Col. Andrew Deveaux	.25	1.90
469	A68	15c Slave trading, Vendue House	1.75	1.25
470	A68	16c Shipwreck salvage, 19th cent.	.30	1.25
471	A68	18c Blockade runner, 1860s	.35	2.40
472	A68	21c Bootlegging, 1919-1929	.40	2.40
473	A68	25c Pineapple cultivation	.45	2.40
474	A68	40c Sponge clipping	.70	1.90
475	A68	50c Victoria & Colonial Hotels	.95	1.40
476	A68	$1 Modern agriculture	1.75	4.00
477	A68	$2 Ship, jet	3.50	5.50
478	A68	$3 Central Bank, Arms	5.50	3.75
479	A68	$5 Prince Charles, Prime Minister Pindling	9.00	5.75
		Nos. 464-479 (16)	26.25	*40.35*

For overprints and surcharges see Nos. 496-499, 532-535.

1985, Nov. 6 **Wmk. 384**

464a	A68	1c	3.75	2.50
465a	A68	3c	5.00	3.50
467a	A68	10c	5.50	4.00
473a	A68	25c	11.00	9.00
		Nos. 464a-473a (4)	25.25	19.00

Virgin and Child, Straw Figures — A69

1980, Oct. 28 **Litho.** *Perf. 14½*

480	A69	5c shown	.25	.25
481	A69	21c Three kings	.25	.35
482	A69	25c Angel	.30	.25
483	A69	$1 Christmas tree	1.00	.90
a.		Souvenir sheet of 4, #480-483	1.75	*2.50*
		Nos. 480-483 (4)	1.80	1.75

Christmas.

Man with Crutch, Sun Rays A70

1981, Feb. 10 **Litho.** *Perf. 14½*

484	A70	5c shown	.25	.25
485	A70	$1 Man in wheelchair	1.25	1.25
a.		Souvenir sheet of 2, #484-485	1.75	*2.50*

International Year of the Disabled.

Grand Bahama Tracking Station A71

Satellite Views: 20c, Bahamas. 25c, Eleuthera. 50c, Andros and New Providence.

Wmk. 373

1981, Apr. 21 **Litho.** *Perf. 13½*

486	A71	10c multi	.25	.25
487	A71	20c multi, vert.	.40	.40
488	A71	25c multi	.60	.60
489	A71	50c multi, vert.	1.25	1.25
a.		Souvenir sheet of 4, #486-489	2.75	2.75
		Nos. 486-489 (4)	2.50	2.50

Prince Charles and Lady Diana — A72

Wmk. 373

1981, July 22 **Litho.** *Perf. 14½*

490	A72	30c shown	.40	.25
491	A72	$2 Charles, Prime Minister	3.75	1.75
a.		Souvenir sheet of 2, #490-491	7.25	3.25

Royal wedding.

Bahama Ducks A73

Wmk. 373

1981, Aug. 25 **Litho.** *Perf. 14*

492	A73	5c shown	1.40	.75
493	A73	20c Reddish egrets	2.50	1.00
494	A73	25c Brown boobies	2.50	1.25
495	A73	$1 West Indian tree ducks	4.50	4.50
a.		Souvenir sheet of 4, #492-495	11.00	11.00
		Nos. 492-495 (4)	10.90	7.50

See Nos. 514-517.

Nos. 466-467, 473, 475 Overprinted: "COMMONWEALTH FINANCE MINISTERS' MEETING 21-23 SEPTEMBER 1981"

1981, Sept. **Litho.** *Perf. 15*

496	A68	5c multicolored	.35	.35
497	A68	10c multicolored	.35	.35
498	A68	25c multicolored	.60	.60
499	A68	50c multicolored	1.25	1.25
		Nos. 496-499 (4)	2.55	2.55

World Food Day A74

Perf. 13x13½

1981, Oct. 16 **Wmk. 373**

500	A74	5c Chickens	.25	.25
501	A74	20c Sheep	.30	.30
502	A74	30c Lobster	.50	.50
503	A74	50c Pigs	1.00	1.00
a.		Souvenir sheet of 4, #500-503	3.25	3.25
		Nos. 500-503 (4)	2.05	2.05

Christmas — A75

Wmk. 373

1981, Nov. 23 **Litho.** *Perf. 14*

504	Sheet of 9	7.50	7.50
a.	A75 5c Father Christmas	.50	.50
b.	A75 5c shown	.50	.50
c.	A75 5c St. Nicholas, Holland	.50	.50
d.	A75 25c Lussibruden, Sweden	.75	.75
e.	A75 25c Mother and child	.75	.75
f.	A75 25c King Wenceslas, Czechoslovakia	.75	.75
g.	A75 30c Mother and child	.75	.75
h.	A75 30c Mother and child standing	.75	.75
i.	A75 $1 Christkindl angel, Germany	1.60	1.60

TB Bacillus Centenary A76

1982, Feb. 3 **Litho.** *Perf. 14*

505	A76	5c Koch	.70	.70
506	A76	16c X-ray	1.40	1.40
507	A76	21c Microscopes	1.60	1.60
508	A76	$1 Mantoux test	3.25	3.25
a.		Souv. sheet, #505-508, perf 14½	7.50	7.50
		Nos. 505-508 (4)	6.95	6.95

Flamingoes A77

Designs: a, Females. b, Males. c, Nesting. d, Juvenile birds. e, Immature birds. No. 509 in continuous design.

Wmk. 373

1982, Apr. 28 **Litho.** *Perf. 14*

509	Strip of 5, multicolored	12.50	12.50
a.-e.	A77 25c any single	2.40	2.40

Princess Diana Issue

Common Design Type

1982, July 1 **Litho.** *Perf. 14*

510	CD333	16c Arms	.55	.25
511	CD333	25c Diana	1.10	.60
512	CD333	40c Wedding	1.60	1.00
513	CD333	$1 Portrait	2.75	2.00
		Nos. 510-513 (4)	6.00	3.85

Bird Type of 1981

Wmk. 373

1982, Aug. 18 **Litho.** *Perf. 14*

514	A73	10c Bat	1.00	.35
515	A73	16c Hutia	1.40	.45
516	A73	21c Racoon	1.60	.90
517	A73	$1 Dolphins	4.25	2.40
a.		Souvenir sheet of 4, #514-517	8.50	8.50
		Nos. 514-517 (4)	8.25	4.10

28th Commonwealth Parliamentary Conference A78

Perf. 14x13½

1982, Oct. 16 Litho. Wmk. 373

518 A78 5c Plaque .25 .25
519 A78 25c Assoc. arms .65 .65
520 A78 40c Natl. arms 1.00 1.00
521 A78 50c House of Assembly 1.25 1.25
Nos. 518-521 (4) 3.15 3.15

Christmas A79

Designs: 5c, Wesley Methodist Church, Baillou Hill Road. 12c, Centerville Seventh Day Adventist Church. 15c, Church of God of Prophecy, East Street. 21c, Bethel Baptist Church, Meeting Street. 25c, St. Francis Xavier Catholic Church, West Hill Street. $1, Holy Cross Anglican Church, Highbury Park.

1982, Nov. 3 *Perf. 14*

522 A79 5c multicolored .25 .25
523 A79 12c multicolored .25 .25
524 A79 15c multicolored .30 .30
525 A79 21c multicolored .40 .40
526 A79 25c multicolored .40 .40
527 A79 $1 multicolored 1.40 1.40
Nos. 522-527 (6) 3.00 3.00

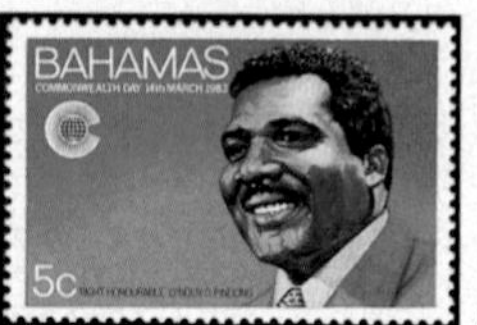

A80

1983, Mar. 14 Litho.

528 A80 5c Lynden O. Pindling .25 .25
529 A80 25c Flags .50 .50
530 A80 35c Map .50 .50
531 A80 $1 Ocean liner 1.35 1.35
Nos. 528-531 (4) 2.60 2.60

Commonwealth Day.

Nos. 469-472 Surcharged

1983, Apr. 5 Litho. *Perf. 15*

532 A68 20c on 15c multi .60 .60
533 A68 31c on 21c multi .70 .70
534 A68 35c on 16c multi 1.50 1.50
535 A68 80c on 18c multi 2.10 2.10
Nos. 532-535 (4) 4.90 4.90

30th Anniv. of Customs Cooperation Council — A81

Perf. 14x13½

1983, May 31 Wmk. 373

536 A81 31c Officers, ship 1.75 .55
537 A81 $1 Officers, jet 3.50 2.40

10th Anniv. of Independence A82

1983, July 6 Litho. *Perf. 14*

538 A82 $1 Flag raising 1.50 1.50
a. Souvenir sheet, perf. 12 2.25 2.25

Local Butterflies A83

1983, Aug. 24 *Perf. 14½x14*

539 A83 5c Carters skipper 1.50 .30
540 A83 25c Giant southern white 2.75 .55
541 A83 31c Large orange sulphur 2.75 .85
542 A83 50c Flambeau 3.00 1.40
a. Souvenir sheet of 4 10.50 10.50
Nos. 539-542 (4) 10.00 3.10

No. 542a contains Nos. 539-542, perf. 14 and perf. 14½x14.

American Loyalists Arrival Bicentenary — A84

Paintings by Alton Lowe.

1983, Sept. 28 *Perf. 14*

543 A84 5c Loyalist Dreams .25 .25
544 A84 31c New Plymouth, Abaco .55 .55
545 A84 35c New Plymouth Hotel .65 .65
546 A84 50c Island Hope .90 .90
a. Souvenir sheet of 4, #543-546 2.25 2.25
Nos. 543-546 (4) 2.35 2.35

Christmas — A85 125th Anniv. of Bahamas Stamps — A86

Children's designs: 5c, Christmas Bells, by Monica Pinder. 20c, The Flamingo by Cory Bullard. 25c, The Yellow Hibiscus with Christmas Candle by Monique A. Bailey. 31c, Santa goes a Sailing by Sabrina Seiler, horiz. 35c, Silhouette scene with palm trees by James Blake. 50c, Silhouette scene with Pelicans, by Erik Russell, horiz.

1983, Nov. 1 *Perf. 14*

547 A85 5c multicolored .25 .25
548 A85 20c multicolored .40 .40
549 A85 25c multicolored .50 .50
550 A85 31c multicolored .65 .65
551 A85 35c multicolored .75 .75
552 A85 50c multicolored .90 .90
Nos. 547-552 (6) 3.45 3.45

1984, Feb. 22 Litho. *Perf. 14*

553 A86 5c No. 3 .25 .25
554 A86 $1 No. 1 2.25 2.25

Lloyd's List Issue

Common Design Type

Wmk. 373

1984, Apr. 25 Litho. *Perf. 14½*

555 CD335 5c Trent .55 .25
556 CD335 31c Orinoco 1.00 .60
557 CD335 35c Nassau Harbor 1.25 .70
558 CD335 50c Container ship Oropesa 1.75 1.40
Nos. 555-558 (4) 4.55 2.95

1984 Summer Olympics A87

1984, June 20 Litho. *Perf. 14x14½*

559 A87 5c Running .30 .30
560 A87 25c Discus .60 .60
561 A87 31c Boxing .60 .60
562 A87 $1 Basketball 4.50 4.50
a. Souvenir sheet of 4, #559-562 7.00 7.00
Nos. 559-562 (4) 6.00 6.00

Flags of Bahamas and Caribbean Community — A88

Wmk. 373

1984, July 4 Litho. *Perf. 14*

563 A88 50c multicolored 1.25 1.25

Conference of Heads of Government of Caribbean Community, 5th Meeting.

Allen's Cay Iguana A89

1984, Aug. 15 *Perf. 14*

564 A89 5c shown .45 .25
565 A89 25c Curly-tailed lizard 2.10 .75
566 A89 35c Greenhouse frog 2.60 1.10
567 A89 50c Atlantic green turtle 2.75 2.75
a. Souvenir sheet of 4, #564-567 9.25 9.25
Nos. 564-567 (4) 7.90 4.85

25th Anniv. of Natl. Trust — A90 Christmas — A91

Wildlife: a, Calliphlox evelynae. b, Megaceryle alcyon, Eleutherodactylus planirostris. c, Phoebis sennae, Phoenicopterus ruber, Himantopus himantopus, Phoebus sennae. d, Urbanus proteus, Chelonia mydas. e, Pandion haliaetus.

Continuous design.

1984, Aug. 15 Litho. *Perf. 14*

568 Strip of 5 19.00 19.00
a.-e. A90 31c any single 3.75 3.75

1984, Nov. 7 Litho. *Perf. 13½x13*

Madonna and Child Paintings.

569 A91 5c Titian .50 .40
570 A91 31c Anais Colin 1.40 1.25
571 A91 35c Elena Caula 1.60 1.40
a. Souvenir sheet of 3, #569-571 2.75 2.75
Nos. 569-571 (3) 3.50 3.05

Girl Guides, 75th Anniv., Intl. Youth Year A92

1985, Feb. 22 Litho. *Perf. 14*

572 A92 5c Brownies .75 .40
573 A92 25c Camping 1.50 .85
574 A92 31c Girl Guides 1.90 1.10
575 A92 35c Rangers 2.50 1.60
a. Souvenir sheet of 4, #572-575 7.25 7.25
Nos. 572-575 (4) 6.65 3.95

Audubon Birth Bicentenary — A93

Wmk. 373

1985, Apr. 24 Litho. *Perf. 14*

576 A93 5c Killdeer 1.10 .85
577 A93 31c Mourning dove, vert. 2.50 .85
578 A93 35c Mourning doves, diff., vert. 2.50 1.00
579 A93 $1 Killdeers, diff. 4.75 4.75
Nos. 576-579 (4) 10.85 7.45

Queen Mother 85th Birthday

Common Design Type

Perf. 14½x14

1985, June 7 Litho. Wmk. 384

580 CD336 5c Portrait, 1927 .40 .25
581 CD336 25c At christening of Peter Phillips .80 .45
582 CD336 35c Portrait, 1985 .90 .65
583 CD336 50c Holding Prince Henry 1.60 1.60
Nos. 580-583 (4) 3.70 2.95

Souvenir Sheet

584 CD336 $1.25 In a pony and trap 4.25 3.50

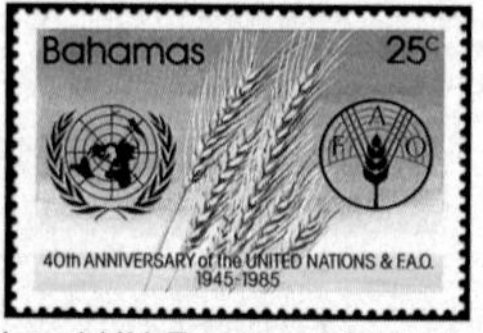

UN and UN Food and Agriculture Org., 40th Annivs. — A94

Wmk. 373

1985, Aug. 26 Litho. *Perf. 14*

585 A94 25c Wheat, emblems 1.10 1.10

Commonwealth Heads of Government Meeting, 1985 — A95

1985, Oct. 16 Wmk. 373 *Perf. 14½*

586 A95 31c Queen Elizabeth II 3.00 3.00
587 A95 35c Flag, Commonwealth emblem 3.00 3.00

Christmas A96

Paintings by Alton Roland Lowe: 5c, Grandma's Christmas Bouquet. 25c, Junkanoo Romeo and Juliet, vert. 31c, Bunce Girl, vert. 35c, Home for Christmas.

1985, Nov. 5 *Perf. 13*
588 A96 5c multicolored .70 .40
589 A96 25c multicolored 1.75 1.10
590 A96 31c multicolored 1.90 1.40
591 A96 35c multicolored 1.90 1.90
a. Souv. sheet, #588-591, perf 14 6.00 6.00
Nos. 588-591 (4) 6.25 4.80

Queen Elizabeth II 60th Birthday
Common Design Type

Designs: 10c, Age 1, 1927. 25c, Coronation, Westminster Abbey, 1953. 35c, Giving speech, royal visit, Bahamas. 40c, At Djakova, Yugoslavia, state visit, 1972. $1, Visiting Crown Agents, 1983.

1986, Apr. 21 Wmk. 384 *Perf. 14½*
592 CD337 10c scar, blk & sil .25 *.30*
593 CD337 25c ultra & multi .30 *.40*
594 CD337 35c green & multi .45 *.60*
595 CD337 40c violet & multi .50 *.65*
596 CD337 $1 rose vio & multi 1.25 *1.75*
Nos. 592-596 (5) 2.75 *3.70*

AMERIPEX '86 — A97

1986, May 19 *Perf. 14*
597 A97 5c Nos. 464, 471 1.10 .45
598 A97 25c Nos. 288-289 2.40 .45
599 A97 31c No. 392 2.60 .60
600 A97 50c No. 489a 3.50 3.00
601 A97 $1 Statue of Liberty, vert. 4.25 *4.75*
a. Souvenir sheet of one 8.50 8.50
Nos. 597-601 (5) 13.85 9.25

Statue of Liberty, cent.

Royal Wedding Issue, 1986
Common Design Type

Designs: 10c, Formal engagement. $1, Andrew in dress uniform.

1986, July 23 *Perf. 14½x14*
602 CD338 10c multicolored .25 .25
603 CD338 $1 multicolored 2.50 2.50

Fish
A98

1986-87 Wmk. 384 *Perf. 14*
604 A98 5c Rock beauty 1.10 .60
605 A98 10c Stoplight parrotfish 1.10 .65
606 A98 15c Jacknife fish 1.90 1.40
607 A98 20c Flamefish 1.75 1.40
608 A98 25c Swissguard basslet 2.10 1.40
609 A98 30c Spotfin butterflyfish 1.50 1.40
610 A98 35c Queen triggerfish 1.75 *2.10*
611 A98 40c Four-eyed butterflyfish 1.75 1.50
612 A98 45c Fairy basslet 1.90 1.25
613 A98 50c Queen angelfish 2.75 *2.75*
614 A98 60c Blue chromis 3.00 *4.25*
615 A98 $1 Spanish hogfish 3.75 3.00
616 A98 $2 Harlequin bass 4.00 *6.75*
617 A98 $3 Blackbar soldierfish 7.75 6.00
618 A98 $5 Pygmy angelfish 8.75 7.75
618A A99 $10 Red hind ('87) 21.00 19.00
Nos. 604-618A (16) 65.85 61.20

Issue dates: $10, Jan. 2, others, Aug. 5.

1988, Aug. 15
Inscribed "1988"
611a A98 40c Four-eyed butterflyfish 2.50 2.50
615a A98 $1 Spanish hogfish 5.50 5.50
616a A98 $2 Harlequin bass 25.00 *20.00*
Nos. 611a-616a (3) 33.00 28.00

1990, Aug.
Inscribed "1990"
605b A98 10c Stoplight parrotfish 2.00 *2.50*
608b A98 25c Swissguard basslet 2.25 *2.50*
611b A98 40c Four-eyed butterflyfish — —
612b A98 45c Fairy basslet 2.75 *3.00*
613b A98 50c Queen angelfish 3.50 *3.00*
615b A98 $1 Spanish hogfish — —
617b A98 $3 Blackbar soldierfish 8.00 *15.00*
618b A98 $5 Pygmy angelfish 11.00 *16.00*
Nos. 605b-618b (6) 29.50 *42.00*

1987, June 25 Wmk. 373
Inscribed "1987"
604c 5c .80 1.00
d. Inscribed"1989" —
605c 10c .90 .45
d. Inscribed"1988" —
606c 15c 1.00 .60
611c 40c 2.50 1.25
612c 45c 3.00 1.75
613c 50c 3.25 2.00
614c 60c 3.75 2.25
615c $1 6.50 4.25
616c $2 12.00 8.00
Nos. 604c-616c (9) 33.70 21.55

Christ Church Cathedral — A99

Wmk. 373
1986, Sept. 16 Litho. *Perf. 14½*
619 A99 10c View, 19th cent. .45 .40
620 A99 40c View, 1986 1.00 .90
a. Souvenir sheet of 2, #619-620 5.00 5.00

City of Nassau, Diocese of Nassau and the Bahamas and Christ Church, 125th anniv.

Christmas, Intl. Peace Year
A100

Wmk. 384
1986, Nov. 4 Litho. *Perf. 14*
621 A100 10c Nativity .45 .25
622 A100 40c Flight to Egypt 1.30 1.00
623 A100 45c Children praying 1.50 1.40
624 A100 50c Exchanging gifts 1.90 *2.25*
a. Souvenir sheet of 4, #621-624 10.00 10.00
Nos. 621-624 (4) 5.15 4.90

Pirates of the Caribbean — A101

A102

Wmk. 373
1987, June 2 Litho. *Perf. 14½*
625 A101 10c Anne Bonney 3.50 1.60
626 A101 40c Blackbeard (d. 1718) 7.75 7.75
627 A101 45c Capt. Edward England 7.75 5.00
628 A101 50c Capt. Woodes Rogers (c. 1679-1732) 8.25 8.25
Nos. 625-628 (4) 27.25 22.60

Souvenir Sheet
629 A102 $1.25 Map of the Bahamas 16.00 16.00

Paintings of Lighthouses by Alton Roland Lowe
A103

1987, Mar. 31 Wmk. 384
630 A103 10c Great Isaac 4.25 1.25
631 A103 40c Bird Rock 7.50 1.75
632 A103 45c Castle Is. 8.25 1.90
633 A103 $1 Hole in the Wall 12.50 12.50
Nos. 630-633 (4) 32.50 17.40

Tourist Transportation
A104

Ships: No. 634a, Cruise ship, sailboat. b, Cruise ships, tugboat, speedboat. c, Pleasure boat leaving harbor, sailboat. d, Pleasure boat docked, sailboats. e, Sailboats.
Aircraft: No. 635a, Bahamasair plane. b, Bahamasair and Pan Am aircraft. c, Aircraft, radar tower. d, Control tower, aircraft. e, Helicopter, planes.

1987, Aug. 26 Wmk. 373 *Perf. 14*
634 Strip of 5 13.50 13.50
a.-e. A104 40c any single 2.50 2.50
635 Strip of 5 13.50 13.50
a.-e. A104 40c any single 2.50 2.50

Orchids Painted by Alton Roland Lowe
A105

1987, Oct. 20 Wmk. 384 *Perf. 14½*
636 A105 10c Cattleyopis lindenii 2.40 .85
637 A105 40c Encyclia lucayana 4.50 1.40
638 A105 45c Encyclia hodgeana 4.50 1.40
639 A105 50c Encyclia lleidae 4.50 4.50
a. Souvenir sheet of 4, #636-639 16.00 16.00
Nos. 636-639 (4) 15.90 8.15

Christmas.

Discovery of America, 500th Anniv. (in 1992) — A106

10c, Ferdinand & Isabella. 40c, Columbus before the Talavera Committee. 45c, Lucayan village. 50c, Lucayan potters. $1.50, Map, c. 1500.

Perf. 14x14½
1988, Feb. 23 Litho. Wmk. 373
640 A106 10c multicolored 1.40 1.00
641 A106 40c multicolored 2.50 2.50
642 A106 45c multicolored 3.00 3.00
643 A106 50c multicolored 3.25 3.25
Nos. 640-643 (4) 10.15 9.75

Souvenir Sheet
644 A106 $1.50 multicolored 11.00 11.00

See Nos. 663-667, 688-692, 725-729, 749-753, 762.

World Wildlife Fund
A107

Whistling ducks, Dendrocygna arborea.

1988, Apr. 29 *Perf. 14½*
645 A107 5c Ducks in flight 3.50 1.25
646 A107 10c Among marine plants 4.00 1.25
647 A107 20c Adults, ducklings 6.50 1.50
648 A107 45c Wading 10.00 2.75
Nos. 645-648 (4) 24.00 6.75

Abolition of Slavery, 150th Anniv.
A108

1988, Aug. 9 *Perf. 14*
649 A108 10c African hut .75 .50
650 A108 40c Basket weavers in hut, Grantstown 2.00 1.40

1988 Summer Olympics, Seoul
A109

Games emblem and details of painting by James Martin: 10c, Olympic flame, high jump, hammer throw, basketball and gymnastics. 40c, Swimming, boxing, weight lifting, archery and running. 45c, Gymnastics, shot put and javelin. $1, Running, cycling and gymnastics.

Wmk. 384
1988, Aug. 30 Litho. *Perf. 14*
651 A109 10c multicolored .90 .40
652 A109 40c multicolored 1.25 .55
653 A109 45c multicolored 1.25 .55
654 A109 $1 multicolored 4.50 4.50
a. Souvenir sheet of 4, #651-654 8.75 8.75
Nos. 651-654 (4) 7.90 6.00

Lloyds of London, 300th Anniv.
Common Design Type

Designs: 10c, Lloyds List No. 560, 1740. 40c, Freeport Harbor, horiz. 45c, Space shuttle over the Bahamas, horiz. $1, Supply ship Yarmouth Castle on fire.

1988, Oct. 4 Wmk. 373
655 CD341 10c multicolored .65 .45
656 CD341 40c multicolored 2.25 .75
657 CD341 45c multicolored 2.25 .75
658 CD341 $1 multicolored 3.75 3.00
Nos. 655-658 (4) 8.90 4.95

Christmas Carols — A110

Designs: 10c, O' Little Town of Bethlehem. 40c, Little Donkey. 45c, Silent Night. 50c, Hark! The Herald Angels Sing.

1988, Nov. 21 Wmk. 384 Perf. 14½

659 A110 10c multicolored .80 .30
660 A110 40c multicolored 2.10 .75
661 A110 45c multicolored 2.25 .90
662 A110 50c multicolored 2.50 2.50
a. Souvenir sheet of 4, #659-662 5.75 5.75
Nos. 659-662 (4) 7.65 4.45

Discovery of America Type

Design: 10c, Columbus as chartmaker. 40c, Development of the caravel. 45c, Navigational tools. 50c, Arawak artifacts. $1.50, Caravel under construction, an illumination from the Nuremburg Chronicles, 15th cent.

Perf. 14½x14

1989, Jan. 25 Litho. Wmk. 373

663 A106 10c multicolored 2.40 .65
664 A106 40c multicolored 3.75 1.25
665 A106 45c multicolored 3.75 1.25
666 A106 50c multicolored 3.75 3.50
Nos. 663-666 (4) 13.65 6.65

Souvenir Sheet

667 A106 $1.50 multicolored 7.00 7.00

Hummingbirds A111

Wmk. 384

1989, Mar. 29 Litho. Perf. 14½

668 A111 10c Cuban emerald 3.25 1.60
669 A111 40c Ruby-throated 4.75 2.50
670 A111 45c Bahama wood-star 5.50 2.50
671 A111 50c Rufous 6.50 6.50
Nos. 668-671 (4) 20.00 13.10

Intl. Red Cross and Red Crescent Organizations, 125th Annivs. — A112

1989, May 31 Perf. 14x14½

672 A112 10c Water safety 2.50 .85
673 A112 $1 Dunant, Battle of Solferino 5.75 3.50

Moon Landing, 20th Anniv.

Common Design Type

Apollo 8: 10c, Apollo Communications System, Grand Bahama Is. 40c, James Lovell Jr., William Anders and Frank Borman. 45c, Mission emblem. $1, The Rising Earth (photograph). $2, Astronaut practicing lunar surface activities at Manned Spacecraft Center, Houston, in training for Apollo 11 mission.

1989, July 20 Perf. 14x13½

Size of Nos. 674-675: 29x29mm

674 CD342 10c multicolored 1.60 .65
675 CD342 40c multicolored 2.40 1.40
676 CD342 45c multicolored 2.75 1.40
677 CD342 $1 multicolored 4.25 4.25
Nos. 674-677 (4) 11.00 7.70

Souvenir Sheet

678 CD342 $2 multicolored 12.00 12.00

Christmas A113

Designs: 10c, Church of the Nativity, Bethlehem. 40c, Basilica of the Annunciation, Nazareth. 45c, By the Sea of Galilee, Tabgha. $1, Church of the Holy Sepulcher, Jerusalem.

Perf. 14½x14

1989, Oct. 16 Wmk. 373

679 A113 10c multicolored 1.25 .35
680 A113 40c multicolored 2.10 .65
681 A113 45c multicolored 2.10 .65
682 A113 $1 multicolored 5.25 5.25
a. Souvenir sheet of 4, #679-682 12.00 12.00
Nos. 679-682 (4) 10.70 6.90

World Stamp Expo '89 A114

Expo emblem and: 10c, Earth, #359. 40c, UPU Headquarters, #301. 45c, US Capitol, #601. $1, Passenger jet, #150. $2, Washington, DC, on map.

1989, Nov. 17 Wmk. 384 Perf. 14

683 A114 10c multicolored 1.00 .40
684 A114 40c multicolored 2.25 .70
685 A114 45c multicolored 2.25 .75
686 A114 $1 multicolored 7.25 7.25
Nos. 683-686 (4) 12.75 9.10

Souvenir Sheet

Perf. 14½x14

687 A114 $2 multicolored 13.00 13.00

No. 687 contains one 31x38mm stamp.

Discovery of America Type of 1988

10c, Caravel launch. 40c, Provisioning ships. 45c, Shortening sails. 50c, Lucayan fishermen. $1.50, Columbus's fleet departing from Cadiz.

Perf. 14½x14

1990, Jan. 24 Litho. Wmk. 373

688 A106 10c multicolored 2.25 .85
689 A106 40c multicolored 2.25 1.60
690 A106 45c multicolored 2.75 1.60
691 A106 50c multicolored 2.75 *3.50*
Nos. 688-691 (4) 10.00 *7.55*

Souvenir Sheet

692 A106 $1.50 multicolored 9.25 9.25

Organization of American States, Cent. — A115

1990, Mar. 14 Wmk. 384 Perf. 14

693 A115 40c multicolored 3.25 3.25

Souvenir Sheet

Stamp World London '90 — A116

Aircraft: a, Spitfire I. b, Hurricane IIc.

1990, May 3 Wmk. 384

694 A116 Sheet of 2 14.00 14.00
a.-b. $1 any single 4.75 4.75

For surcharge see No. B3.

Intl. Literacy Year A117

10c, Teacher helping student. 40c, Children reading to each other. 50c, Children reading aloud.

1990, June 27 Wmk. 384 Perf. 14

695 A117 10c multicolored 2.10 .45
696 A117 40c multicolored 2.75 1.40
697 A117 50c multicolored 2.75 *4.50*
Nos. 695-697 (3) 7.60 6.35

Queen Mother, 90th Birthday

Common Design Types

1990, Aug. 4 Perf. 14x15

698 CD343 40c Portrait, c. 1938 1.40 1.40

Perf. 14½

699 CD344 $1.50 At garden party, 1938 4.25 4.25

Bahamian Parrot — A118

1990, Sept. 26 Wmk. 373 Perf. 14

700 A118 10c shown 1.75 .60
701 A118 40c In flight 3.25 1.25
702 A118 45c Head 3.50 1.25
703 A118 50c On branch 4.00 4.00
Nos. 700-703 (4) 12.50 7.10

Souvenir Sheet

704 A118 $1.50 On branch, diff. 13.00 13.00

Christmas A119

Wmk. 373

1990, Nov. 5 Litho. Perf. 13½

705 A119 10c Angel appears to Mary 1.00 .55
706 A119 40c Nativity 1.60 .65
707 A119 45c Angel appears to shepherds 1.60 .65
708 A119 $1 Three kings 4.50 4.50
a. Souvenir sheet of 4, #705-708 16.50 16.50
Nos. 705-708 (4) 8.70 6.35

Birds — A120

Wmk. 384

1991, Feb. 4 Litho. Perf. 14

709 A120 5c Green heron 1.90 1.90
710 A120 10c Turkey vulture 2.25 2.25
711 A120 15c Osprey 1.75 .70
712 A120 20c Clapper rail 2.25 .80
713 A120 25c Royal tern 1.40 .70
714 A120 30c Key West quail dove 3.75 .80
715 A120 40c Smooth-billed ani 4.00 .70
716 A120 45c Burrowing owl 6.00 .80
717 A120 50c Hairy woodpecker 4.75 .80
718 A120 55c Mangrove cuckoo 4.00 .80
719 A120 60c Bahama mockingbird 4.50 .80
720 A120 70c Red-winged blackbird 4.50 1.75
721 A120 $1 Thick-billed vireo 5.25 1.50
722 A120 $2 Bahama yellowthroat 11.50 8.25
723 A120 $5 Stripe-headed tanager 14.50 10.50
724 A120 $10 Greater Antillean bullfinch 27.50 17.00
Nos. 709-724 (16) 99.80 50.05

Issued: $10, 7/1/91; others, 2/4/91.

1993 Dated "1993" Wmk. 373

710a 10c multicolored .45 .45
713a 25c multicolored 1.10 1.10
714a 30c multicolored 1.40 1.40
715a 40c multicolored 1.75 1.75
718a 55c multicolored 2.50 2.50
723a $5 multicolored 22.50 22.50
Nos. 710a-723a (6) 29.70 29.70

Issued: 40c, 12/31/93; others, 9/23/93.

1995 Dated "1995"

711b 15c multicolored 1.75 .75
713b 25c multicolored 1.10 1.10
715b 40c multicolored 2.50 2.50
718b 55c multicolored 2.50 2.50
723b $5 multicolored 14.50 14.50
Nos. 711b-723b (5) 22.35 21.35

Discovery of America Type

Designs: 15c, Columbus practices celestial navigation. 40c, The fleet in rough seas. 55c, Natives on the beach. 60c, Map of voyage. $1.50, Pinta's crew sights land.

Perf. 14½x14

1991, Apr. 9 Litho. Wmk. 384

725 A106 15c multicolored 1.90 .80
726 A106 40c multicolored 3.25 2.00
727 A106 55c multicolored 3.50 2.40
728 A106 60c multicolored 4.25 4.25
Nos. 725-728 (4) 12.90 9.45

Souvenir Sheet

729 A106 $1.50 multicolored 13.00 13.00

Elizabeth & Philip, Birthdays

Common Design Types

Wmk. 384

1991, June 17 Litho. Perf. 14½

730 CD346 15c multicolored 1.25 1.25
731 CD345 $1 multicolored 2.75 2.75
a. Pair, #730-731 + label 4.00 4.00

Hurricane Awareness — A121

Designs: 15c, Weather radar image of Hurricane Hugo. 40c, Anatomy of hurricane rotating around eye. 55c, Flooding caused by Hurricane David. 60c, Lockheed WP-3D Orion.

1991, Aug. 28 Perf. 14

732 A121 15c multicolored 1.90 .55
733 A121 40c multicolored 2.75 1.50
734 A121 55c multicolored 3.50 2.40
735 A121 60c multicolored 4.25 4.25
Nos. 732-735 (4) 12.40 8.70

Christmas A122

Designs: 15c, The Annunciation. 55c, Mary and Joseph traveling to Bethlehem. 60c, Angel appearing to shepherds. $1, Adoration of the Magi.

1991, Oct. 28 Wmk. 373 Perf. 14

736 A122 15c multicolored .85 .30
737 A122 55c multicolored 2.25 .90
738 A122 60c multicolored 2.40 1.25
739 A122 $1 multicolored 3.75 3.75
a. Souvenir sheet of 4, #736-739 11.50 11.50
Nos. 736-739 (4) 9.25 6.20

Majority Rule, 25th Anniv. A123

Designs: 15c, First Progressive Liberal Party cabinet. 40c, Signing of Independence Constitution. 55c, Handing over constitutional instrument, vert. 60c, First Bahamian Governor-General, Sir Milo Butler, vert.

Wmk. 373

1992, Jan. 10 Litho. *Perf. 14*

740 A123 15c multicolored 1.10 .55
741 A123 40c multicolored 2.10 1.60
742 A123 55c multicolored 2.25 2.10
743 A123 60c multicolored 2.75 *3.00*
Nos. 740-743 (4) 8.20 7.25

Queen Elizabeth II's Accession to the Throne, 40th Anniv.
Common Design Type

Wmk. 373

1992, Feb. 6 Litho. *Perf. 14*

744 CD349 15c multicolored .75 .30
745 CD349 40c multicolored 1.25 .55
746 CD349 55c multicolored 1.25 .70
747 CD349 60c multicolored 1.75 1.25
748 CD349 $1 multicolored 1.90 1.90
Nos. 744-748 (5) 6.90 4.70

Discovery of America Type

Designs: 15c, Lucayans first sight of fleet. 40c, Approaching Bahamas coastline. 55c, Lucayans about to meet Columbus. 60c, Columbus gives thanks for safe arrival. $1.50, Monument to Columbus' landing.

Perf. 14½x14

1992, Mar. 17 Litho. Wmk. 384

749 A106 15c multicolored 1.50 .80
750 A106 40c multicolored 2.10 1.60
751 A106 55c multicolored 2.25 2.10
752 A106 60c multicolored 2.50 3.25
Nos. 749-752 (4) 8.35 7.75

Souvenir Sheet

753 A106 $1.50 multicolored 6.00 6.00

Templeton, Galbraith and Hansberger Ltd. Building — A124

Wmk. 384

1992, Apr. 22 Litho. *Perf. 14½*

754 A124 55c multicolored 2.25 2.25

Templeton Prize for Progress in Religion, 20th Anniv.

1992 Summer Olympics, Barcelona A125

Perf. 14½x14

1992, June 2 Wmk. 373

755 A125 15c Pole vault .80 .35
756 A125 40c Javelin 1.25 .90
757 A125 55c Hurdling 1.50 1.50
758 A125 60c Basketball 7.00 6.00
Nos. 755-758 (4) 10.55 8.75

Souvenir Sheet

759 A125 $2 Sailing 10.00 10.00

Intl. Conference on Nutrition — A126

15c, Drought-affected earth, starving child. 55c, Hand holding plant, stalks of grain.

Perf. 14½x13

1992, Aug. 11 Litho. Wmk. 373

760 A126 15c multicolored 1.50 1.10
761 A126 55c multicolored 3.25 2.75

Discovery of America Type
Souvenir Sheet

Perf. 14x13½

1992, Oct. 12 Litho. Wmk. 384

762 A106 $2 Coming ashore 7.50 7.50

Christmas A127

1992, Nov. 2 Wmk. 373 *Perf. 14*

763 A127 15c The Annunciation .80 .30
764 A127 55c Nativity Scene 2.00 .90
765 A127 60c Angel, shepherds 2.25 1.25
766 A127 70c The Magi 2.50 2.50
a. Souvenir sheet of 4, #763-766 9.00 9.00
Nos. 763-766 (4) 7.55 4.95

The Contract, Farm Labor Program, 50th Anniv. A128

Bahamian, American flags and: 15c, Silhouette of worker's head. 55c, Onions. 60c, Citrus fruits. 70c, Apples.

Perf. 14x14½

1993, Mar. 16 Litho. Wmk. 384

767 A128 15c multicolored 1.90 .75
768 A128 55c multicolored 2.75 1.50
769 A128 60c multicolored 2.75 2.50
770 A128 70c multicolored 3.50 3.50
Nos. 767-770 (4) 10.90 8.25

Royal Air Force, 75th Anniv.
Common Design Type

Designs: 15c, Westland Wapiti. 40c, Gloster Gladiator. 55c, DeHavilland Vampire. 70c, English Electric Lightning.

No. 775a, Avro Shackleton. b, Fairey Battle. c, Douglas Boston. d, DeHavilland DH9a.

Wmk. 373

1993, Apr. 1 Litho. *Perf. 14*

771 CD350 15c multicolored 2.00 .85
772 CD350 40c multicolored 3.00 1.60
773 CD350 55c multicolored 3.50 2.25
774 CD350 70c multicolored 4.50 4.50
Nos. 771-774 (4) 13.00 9.20

Souvenir Sheet of 4

775 CD350 60c #a.-d. 13.00 13.00

Coronation of Queen Elizabeth II, 40th Anniv. A129

Wmk. 373

1993, June 2 Litho. *Perf. 13½*

776 A129 15c Nos. 424-425 .90 .65
777 A129 55c No. 157 2.25 2.25
778 A129 60c Nos. 402-403 2.40 2.40
779 A129 70c Nos. 404-405 2.75 2.75
Nos. 776-779 (4) 8.30 8.05

A130

Natl. symbols: 15c, Lignum vitae. 55c, Yellow elder. 60c, Blue marlin. 70c, Flamingo.

1993, July 8 Litho. *Perf. 14*

780 A130 15c multicolored .60 .35
781 A130 55c multicolored 1.75 1.75
782 A130 60c multicolored 2.10 2.10
783 A130 70c multicolored 3.00 3.00
Nos. 780-783 (4) 7.45 7.20

Independence, 20th anniv.

A131

Wildflowers.

1993, Sept. 8 Litho. *Perf. 14*

784 A131 15c Cordia 1.60 .55
785 A131 55c Seaside morning glory 3.75 1.60
786 A131 60c Poinciana 4.00 2.50
787 A131 70c Spider lily 4.25 4.25
Nos. 784-787 (4) 13.60 8.90

Christmas A132

1993, Nov. 1 Litho. *Perf. 14*

788 A132 15c Angel, Mary 1.25 .55
789 A132 55c Shepherds, angel 3.00 1.90
790 A132 60c Holy family 3.75 3.25
791 A132 70c Three wise men 4.25 4.25
Nos. 788-791 (4) 12.25 9.95

Souvenir Sheet

792 A132 $1 Madonna and Child 8.50 8.50

Intl. Year of the Family A133

Wmk. 384

1994, Feb. 18 Litho. *Perf. 13½*

793 A133 15c shown 1.25 .45
794 A133 55c Children studying 2.50 1.40
795 A133 60c Son, father fishing 3.50 2.10
796 A133 70c Children, grandmother 4.25 *4.50*
Nos. 793-796 (4) 11.50 8.45

Hong Kong '94.

Royal Visit — A134

Designs: 15c, Bahamas, United Kingdom flags. 55c, Royal Yacht Britannia. 60c, Queen Elizabeth II. 70c, Prince Philip, Queen.

Perf. 14x13½

1994, Mar. 7 Wmk. 373

797 A134 15c multicolored 1.10 .35
798 A134 55c multicolored 3.25 1.60
799 A134 60c multicolored 3.25 1.90
800 A134 70c multicolored 3.25 3.25
Nos. 797-800 (4) 10.85 7.10

Natl. Family Island Regatta, 40th Anniv. A135

Designs: 15c, 55c, 60c, 70c, Various sailing boats at sea. $2, Beached yacht, vert.

Wmk. 373

1994, Apr. 27 Litho. *Perf. 14*

801 A135 15c multicolored 1.00 .35
802 A135 55c multicolored 2.25 1.10
803 A135 60c multicolored 2.25 2.25
804 A135 70c multicolored 4.00 4.00
Nos. 801-804 (4) 9.50 7.70

Souvenir Sheet

805 A135 $2 multicolored 11.00 11.00

Intl. Olympic Committee, Cent. — A136

Flag, Olympic rings, and: 15c, Nos. 276-279, horiz. 55c, Nos. 388-391. 60c, Nos. 559-562, horiz. 70c, Nos. 755-758.

Wmk. 373

1994, May 31 Litho. *Perf. 14*

806 A136 15c multicolored 2.10 .60
807 A136 55c multicolored 3.50 1.40
808 A136 60c multicolored 3.50 3.50
809 A136 70c multicolored 4.00 4.00
Nos. 806-809 (4) 13.10 9.50

Souvenir Sheet

First Recipients of the Order of the Caribbean Community — A137

Perf. 13x14

1994, July 5 Litho. Wmk. 373

810 A137 $2 multicolored 8.50 8.50

A138

Butterfly, flower: 15c, Canna skipper, canna. 55c, Cloudless sulphur, cassia. 60c, White peacock, passion flower. 70c, Devillier's swallowtail, calico flower.

1994, Aug. 16 Litho. *Perf. 14*

811 A138 15c multicolored 1.75 .40
812 A138 55c multicolored 3.25 1.25
813 A138 60c multicolored 3.25 3.25
814 A138 70c multicolored 3.75 3.75
Nos. 811-814 (4) 12.00 8.65

A139

Marine Life: a, Cuban hogfish, Spanish hogfish. b, Tomate, squirrelfish. c, French angelfish. d, Queen angelfish. e, Rock beauty.
$2, Rock beauty, queen angelfish.

1994, Sept. 13 ***Perf. 13½x14***

815	A139	40c Strip of 5, #a.-e.	8.75	8.75

Souvenir Sheet

816	A139	$2 multicolored	10.00	10.00

Christmas — A140

Wmk. 384

1994, Oct. 31 **Litho.** ***Perf. 14***

817	A140	15c Angel	.50	.30
818	A140	55c Holy family	1.50	1.50
819	A140	60c Shepherds	1.75	1.75
820	A140	70c Magi	2.25	2.25
		Nos. 817-820 (4)	6.00	5.80

Souvenir Sheet

821	A140	$2 Christ Child, vert.	6.50	6.50

College of the Bahamas, 20th Anniv. — A141

Designs: 15c, Lion. 70c, Queen Elizabeth II, college facade.

Wmk. 373

1995, Feb. 8 **Litho.** ***Perf. 14***

822	A141	15c multicolored	.40	.40
823	A141	70c multicolored	2.25	2.25

End of World War II, 50th Anniv.

Common Design Types

Designs: 15c, Bahamian soldiers on parade. 55c, Neutrality patrols flown by PBY-5A flying boats. 60c, Bahamian women in all three services. 70c, B-24 Liberator, Bahamians in RAF.
$2, Reverse of War Medal 1939-45.

Wmk. 373

1995, May 8 **Litho.** ***Perf. 13½***

824	CD351	15c multicolored	1.25	.45
825	CD351	55c multicolored	3.75	1.25
826	CD351	60c multicolored	3.75	3.75
827	CD351	70c multicolored	4.75	4.75
		Nos. 824-827 (4)	13.50	10.20

Souvenir Sheet

Perf. 14

828	CD352	$2 multicolored	8.50	8.50

Kirtland's Warbler — A142

No. 829, 15c, Female at nest. No. 829A, 15c Singing male. No. 829B, 25c, Female feeding young. No. 829C, 25c, Immature bird feeding, prior to migration.
$2, Female on branch overlooking lake.

Wmk. 373

1995, June 7 **Litho.** ***Perf. 13½***

829	A142	15c multi	1.25	1.25
829A	A142	15c multi	1.25	1.25
829B	A142	25c multi	1.25	1.25
829C	A142	25c multi	1.25	1.25
d.		Strip of 4, as #829-829C, wmk. inverted	5.25	5.25

Souvenir Sheet

Perf. 13

830	A142	$2 multicolored	11.00	11.00

World Wildlife Fund (No. 829).

Nos. 829-829C were printed both in individual sheets of 50, with watermark upright, and in sheets of 16, containing four No. 829d.

No. 830 contains one 42x28mm stamp and has continuous design.

Tourism A143

Designs: 15c, Eleuthera Cliffs. 55c, Clarence Town, Long Island. 60c, Albert Lowe Museum. 70c, Yachting.

Wmk. 384

1995, July 18 **Litho.** ***Perf. 14½***

831	A143	15c multicolored	1.10	.60
832	A143	55c multicolored	2.75	1.25
833	A143	60c multicolored	3.25	3.25
834	A143	70c multicolored	4.00	4.00
		Nos. 831-834 (4)	11.10	9.10

FAO, 50th Anniv. A144

Designs: 15c, Pig, poultry farming. 55c, Horticultural methods. 60c, Healthy eating. 70c, Sustainable fishing.

Perf. 13½x13

1995, Sept. 5 **Litho.** **Wmk. 373**

835	A144	15c multicolored	1.05	.35
836	A144	55c multicolored	2.10	1.00
837	A144	60c multicolored	2.60	2.60
838	A144	70c multicolored	3.75	3.75
		Nos. 835-838 (4)	9.50	7.70

UN, 50th Anniv.

Common Design Type

Designs: 15c, Sikorsky S-55, UNEF, Sinai, 1957. 55c, Ferret armored car, UNEF, Sinai, 1957. 60c, Fokker F-27, UNAMIC/UNTAC, Cambodia, 1991-93. 70c, Lockheed Hercules.

Wmk. 373

1995, Oct. 25 **Litho.** ***Perf. 14***

839	CD353	15c multicolored	1.00	.40
840	CD353	55c multicolored	2.25	1.90
841	CD353	60c multicolored	2.25	2.25
842	CD353	70c multicolored	2.50	2.50
		Nos. 839-842 (4)	8.00	7.05

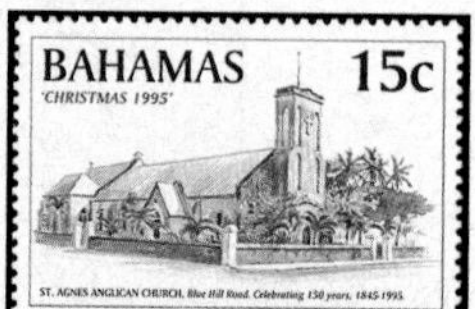

Christmas — A145

Designs: 15c, St. Agnes Anglican Church. 55c, Church of God. 60c, Sacred Heart Roman Catholic Church. 70c, Salem Union Baptist Church.

1995, Nov. 17

843	A145	15c multicolored	.50	.40
844	A145	55c multicolored	1.75	1.75
845	A145	60c multicolored	1.75	1.75
846	A145	70c multicolored	2.10	*2.40*
		Nos. 843-846 (4)	6.10	6.30

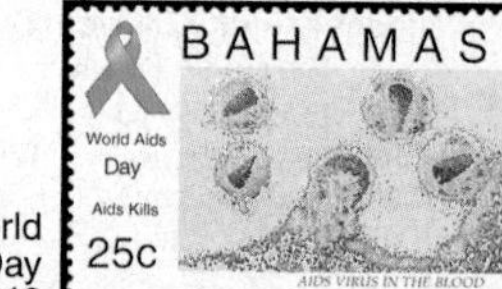

World AIDS Day A146

1995, Dec. 1

847	A146	25c Virus in blood	1.00	1.00
848	A146	70c Scientific research	2.25	2.25

Shells A147

Designs: 5c, Sunrise tellin. 10c, Queen conch. 15c, Angular triton. 20c, True tulip. 25c, Reticulated cowrie-helmet. 30c, Sand dollar. 40c, Lace short-frond murex. 45c, Inflated sea biscuit. 50c, West Indian top shell (magpie). 55c, Spiny oyster. 60c, King helmet. 70c, Lion's paw. $1, Crown cone. $2, Atlantic partridge tun. $5, Wide-mouthed purpura. $10, Triton's trumpet.

Wmk. 373 sideways

1996 **Litho.** ***Perf. 14***

849	A147	5c multicolored	.25	.25
850	A147	10c multicolored	.30	.25
851	A147	15c multicolored	.40	.35
852	A147	20c multicolored	.65	.45
853	A147	25c multicolored	.70	.50
854	A147	30c multicolored	2.10	.55
855	A147	40c multicolored	1.25	.55
856	A147	45c multicolored	2.75	.60
857	A147	50c multicolored	1.40	.60
858	A147	55c multicolored	3.25	.75
859	A147	60c multicolored	1.75	.75
860	A147	70c multicolored	2.10	.95
a.		Souvenir sheet of 1	4.00	4.00
861	A147	$1 multicolored	3.50	1.00
a.		Souvenir sheet of 1	4.00	4.00
862	A147	$2 multicolored	7.25	1.90
863	A147	$5 multicolored	14.50	4.00
864	A147	$10 multicolored	27.50	9.50
		Nos. 849-864 (16)	69.65	22.95

Issued: $10, 7/1; others, 1/2.

No. 860a issued 6/20/97 for return of Hong Kong to China.

No. 861a issued 2/3/97 for Hong Kong '97.

See Nos. 962-964.

1997 **Wmk. 373 upright**

Inscribed "1997"

849b	A147	5c multicolored	1.50	*1.20*
850b	A147	10c multicolored	.90	*.80*
851b	A147	15c multicolored	1.50	.30
852b	A147	20c multicolored	1.50	.55
853b	A147	25c multicolored	1.75	.50
854b	A147	30c multicolored	1.75	.65
855b	A147	40c multicolored	2.75	.85
856b	A147	45c multicolored	2.50	1.25
857b	A147	50c multicolored	2.75	1.00
858b	A147	55c multicolored	2.75	1.25
859b	A147	60c multicolored	3.75	1.25
860b	A147	70c multicolored	3.75	1.90
861b	A147	$1 multicolored	5.00	2.50
862b	A147	$2 multicolored	9.00	6.25
863b	A147	$5 multicolored	16.00	*13.00*
864b	A147	$10 multicolored	30.00	*24.00*
		Nos. 849b-864b (16)	87.15	*57.25*

Issued: Nos. 861b-864b, 7/1; Nos. 849b-860b, 9/22.

1999 **Inscribed "1999"**

849c	A147	5c multicolored	1.50	*1.20*
850c	A147	10c multicolored	.90	*.80*
851c	A147	15c multicolored	1.50	.30
852c	A147	20c multicolored	1.50	.55
853c	A147	25c multicolored	1.75	.50
855c	A147	40c multicolored	2.75	.85
857c	A147	50c multicolored	2.75	1.00
859c	A147	60c multicolored	3.75	1.25
860c	A147	70c multicolored	3.75	1.90
861c	A147	$1 multicolored	5.00	2.50
862c	A147	$2 multicolored	9.00	6.25
863c	A147	$5 multicolored	16.00	*13.00*
864c	A147	$10 multicolored	30.00	*24.00*
		Nos. 849c-864c (13)	80.15	*54.10*

2000 **Inscribed "2000"**

849d	A147	5c multicolored	1.10	*1.20*
851d	A147	15c multicolored	1.10	.30
853d	A147	25c multicolored	1.35	.50
857d	A147	50c multicolored	2.25	1.00
860d	A147	70c multicolored	3.00	1.90
862d	A147	$2 multicolored	7.00	6.25
		Nos. 849d-862d (6)	15.80	*11.15*

2001 **Inscribed "2001"**

851e	A147	15c multicolored	1.50	.30
853e	A147	25c multicolored	1.75	.50
857e	A147	50c multicolored	2.75	1.00
861e	A147	$1 multicolored	5.00	2.50
862e	A147	$2 multicolored	9.00	6.25
		Nos. 851e-862e (5)	20.00	10.55

Radio, Cent. A148

Designs: 15c, East Goodwin Lightship, Marconi apparatus suspended from masthead. 55c, Arrest of Dr. Crippen, newspaper headline telling of wireless message from SS Montrose. 60c, SS Philadelphia, first readable transatlantic messages. 70c, Yacht Elettra, Guglielmo Marconi.
$2, SS Titantic, SS Carpathia.

1996, Feb. 4 **Litho.** ***Perf. 13½***

865	A148	15c multicolored	2.00	.50
866	A148	55c multicolored	2.75	1.50
867	A148	60c multicolored	3.00	2.75
868	A148	70c multicolored	3.25	3.75
		Nos. 865-868 (4)	11.00	8.50

Souvenir Sheet

869	A148	$2 multicolored	10.00	10.00

A149

A150

Wmk. 384

1996, June 25 **Litho.** ***Perf. 13½***

870	A149	15c Swimming	.60	.40
871	A149	55c Track	1.25	1.00
872	A149	60c Basketball	2.50	1.75
873	A149	70c Long jump	1.90	*2.40*
		Nos. 870-873 (4)	6.25	5.55

Souvenir Sheet

874	A149	$2 Javelin, 1896	6.00	6.00

Modern Olympic Games, cent.

Wmk. 384

1996, Sept. 3 **Litho.** ***Perf. 14***

Reptiles: 15c, Green anole. 55c, Fowl snake. 60c, Inagua freshwater turtle. 70c, Acklins rock iguana.

875	A150	15c multicolored	.90	.90
876	A150	55c multicolored	1.75	1.75
877	A150	60c multicolored	2.50	2.50
878	A150	70c multicolored	3.00	3.00
a.		Souvenir sheet, #875-878	8.75	8.75
		Nos. 875-878 (4)	8.15	8.15

Environmental protection.

Christmas A151

Designs: 15c, Angel Gabriel and Mary. 55c, Mary and Joseph. 60c, Shepherds. 70c, Magi.
$2, Presentation at the Temple.

Wmk. 373

1996, Nov. 4 **Litho.** ***Perf. 14***

879	A151	15c multicolored	1.10	.40
880	A151	55c multicolored	2.75	.90
881	A151	60c multicolored	3.00	1.40
882	A151	70c multicolored	3.25	3.25
		Nos. 879-882 (4)	10.10	5.95

Souvenir Sheet

883	A151	$2 multicolored	5.50	5.50

Archives Dept., 25th Anniv. — A152

Perf. 14½x14

1996, Dec. 9 Litho. Wmk. 384

884 A152 55c shown 2.25 2.25

Souvenir Sheet

Perf. 14x13½

885 A152 $2 Building, horiz. 6.50 6.50

Queen Elizabeth II and Prince Philip, 50th Wedding Anniv. — A153

Designs: No. 886, Queen. No. 887, Grenadier Guards. No. 888, Prince Philip. No. 889, Queen reviewing Grenadier Guards. No. 890, Prince holding trophy, Queen opening jewel box. No. 891, Prince on polo pony.

$2, Queen, Prince riding in open carriage, horiz.

Wmk. 373

1997, July 9 Litho. *Perf. 13*

886 A153 50c multicolored 2.00 2.00
887 A153 50c multicolored 2.00 2.00
a. Pair, #886-887 4.25 4.25
888 A153 60c multicolored 2.40 2.40
889 A153 60c multicolored 2.40 2.40
a. Pair, #888-889 5.00 5.00
890 A153 70c multicolored 2.50 2.50
891 A153 70c multicolored 2.50 2.50
a. Pair, #890-891 5.25 5.25
Nos. 886-891 (6) 13.80 13.80

Souvenir Sheet

892 A153 $2 multicolored 8.25 8.25

Intl. Year of the Reefs A154

Various pictures of marine life and coral.

Perf. 14x14½

1997, Sept. 3 Litho. Wmk. 384

893 A154 15c multicolored 1.25 .55
894 A154 55c multicolored 2.75 1.25
895 A154 60c multicolored 2.75 1.75
896 A154 70c multicolored 3.25 3.25
Nos. 893-896 (4) 10.00 6.80

Christmas — A155

Perf. 13x13½

1997, Oct. 6 Litho. Wmk. 373

897 A155 15c Angel 1.25 .30
898 A155 55c Madonna & Child 2.50 .95
899 A155 60c Shepherd 2.75 1.60
900 A155 70c Magi 3.50 3.50
Nos. 897-900 (4) 10.00 6.35

Souvenir Sheet

901 A155 $2 Christ Child 10.00 10.00

Diana, Princess of Wales (1961-97)

Common Design Type

Various portraits: 902: a, 55c. b, 60c. c, 70c.

Perf. 14½x14

1998, Mar. 31 Litho. Wmk. 373

901A CD355 15c multicolored .80 .80

Sheet of 4

902 CD355 #a.-c., 901A 4.50 4.50

Organization of American States, 50th Anniv. — A156

Map of North and South America, national flags, and: 15c, "New Vision" paper. 55c, Building.

1998, Apr. 14 *Perf. 13½x14*

903 A156 15c multicolored .40 .40
904 A156 55c multicolored 2.00 2.00

University of the West Indies, 50th Anniv. — A157

1998, Apr. 14

905 A157 55c multicolored 2.25 2.25

Universal Declaration of Human Rights, 50th Anniv. — A158

1998, Apr. 14

906 A158 55c multicolored 2.50 2.50

Royal Air Force, 80th Anniv.

Common Design Type of 1993 Re-Inscribed

Designs: 15c, Handley Page Hyderabad. 55c, Hawker Demon. 60c, Gloster Meteor F.8. 70c, Lockheed Neptune MR.1.

No. 911: a, Sopwith Camel. b, Short 184. c, Supermarine Spitfire PR.19. d, North American Mitchell III.

1998, Apr. 1

907 CD350 15c multicolored .85 .55
908 CD350 55c multicolored 1.50 1.10
909 CD350 60c multicolored 1.90 1.90
910 CD350 70c multicolored 2.50 2.50
Nos. 907-910 (4) 6.75 6.05

Souvenir Sheet

911 CD350 50c Sheet of 4, #a.-d. 7.50 7.50

Independence, 25th Anniv. — A159

15c, Supreme Court Building. 55c, Nassau Library. 60c, Government House. 70c, Gregory Arch.

$2, Exuma-Family Island Regatta, George Town.

Wmk. 373

1998, July 10 Litho. *Perf. 13½*

912 A159 15c multicolored 1.10 .75
913 A159 55c multicolored 2.25 1.50
914 A159 60c multicolored 2.50 2.50
915 A159 70c multicolored 3.00 3.00
Nos. 912-915 (4) 8.85 7.75

Souvenir Sheet

916 A159 $2 multicolored 7.50 7.50

Castaway Cay, Disney Cruise Lines A160

1998, Aug. 1 *Perf. 14*

917 A160 55c Daytime 2.25 2.25
918 A160 55c Nighttime 2.25 2.25
a. Pair, #917-918 4.50 4.50
b. Bklt. pane, 5 each #917-918 22.50
Complete booklet, #918b 25.00

MS Ryndam, Half Moon Cay — A161

1998, Aug. 19 *Perf. 13½x13*

919 A161 55c multicolored 5.25 2.50

Roses A162

Wmk. 373

1998, Sept. 8 Litho. *Perf. 14*

920 A162 55c Yellow cream 1.90 1.90
921 A162 55c Big red 1.90 1.90
922 A162 55c Seven sisters 1.90 1.90
923 A162 55c Barrel pink 1.90 1.90
924 A162 55c Island beauty 1.90 1.90
a. Bklt. pane, 2 each #920-924 19.00
Complete booklet, #924a 19.00
Nos. 920-924 (5) 9.50 9.50

Souvenir Sheet

925 A162 55c like #924 3.00 3.00

No. 925 has parts of other roses extending into center left and upper left area of stamp.

Intl. Year of the Ocean — A163

Wmk. 373

1998, Nov. 24 Litho. *Perf. 14*

926 A163 15c Killer whale 1.25 .75
927 A163 55c Tropical fish 2.00 2.00

Christmas A164

1998, Dec. 11

928 A164 15c The Annunciation .75 .40
929 A164 55c Shepherds, star 1.60 .70
930 A164 60c Magi 1.90 1.60
931 A164 70c Flight into Egypt 2.25 2.25
Nos. 928-931 (4) 6.50 4.95

Souvenir Sheet

932 A164 $2 Nativity scene 6.25 6.25

Timothy Gibson, Composer of Natl. Anthem A165

1998 Litho. Wmk. 373 *Perf. 13½*

933 A165 60c multicolored 1.75 1.75

Independence, 25th anniv.

National Trust, 40th Anniv. — A166

Flamingos on the beach: a, One chick, adults. b, Two chicks, adults. c, One chick spreading wings, adults. d, Six in flight over others. e, Three ascending into flight.

Wmk. 384

1999, Feb. 9 Litho. *Perf. 14*

934 A166 55c Strip of 5, #a.-e. 9.75 9.75

No. 934 is a continuous design.

See Nos. 940, 961, 969.

Australia '99, World Stamp Expo A167

Maritime history: 15c, Arawak Indians. 55c, Santa Maria. 60c, Blackbeard's ship, Queen Anne's Revenge. 70c, Banshee running Union blockade, US Civil War.

$2, American invasion of Fort Nassau, 1776.

Perf. 14x14½

1999, Mar. 9 Wmk. 373

935 A167 15c multicolored .50 .45
936 A167 55c multicolored 1.90 1.60
937 A167 60c multicolored 2.50 1.90
938 A167 70c multicolored 2.75 2.75
Nos. 935-938 (4) 7.65 6.70

Souvenir Sheet

939 A167 $2 multicolored 7.00 7.00

National Trust, 40th Anniv. Type

Marine life: a, Dolphin. b, Large fish, four in background. c, Several fish, coral. d, Turtle, fish, coral. e, Lobster, coral.

Wmk. 384

1999, Apr. 6 Litho. *Perf. 14*

940 A166 55c Strip of 5, #a.-e. 9.75 9.75

No. 940 is a continuous design.

Bahamas Historical Society, 40th Anniv. A168

1999, June 9 Litho. *Perf. 13*

941 A168 $1 multicolored 2.00 2.00

1st Manned Moon Landing, 30th Anniv.

Common Design Type

15c, Ascent module in assembly area. 65c, Apollo command & service module. 70c, Descent stage. 80c, Module turns to dock with service module.

$2, Looking at earth from moon.

Perf. 14x13¾

1999, July 20 Litho. Wmk. 384

942	CD357	15c multicolored	.80	.80
943	CD357	65c multicolored	2.10	2.10
944	CD357	70c multicolored	2.10	2.10
945	CD357	80c multicolored	2.10	2.10
		Nos. 942-945 (4)	7.10	7.10

Souvenir Sheet

Perf. 14

946	CD357	$2 multicolored	7.00	7.00

No. 946 contains one 40mm circular stamp 40mm.

UPU, 125th Anniv. A170

Wmk. 384

1999, Aug. 17 Litho. *Perf. 13½*

947	A170	15c Mail Packet Delaware	1.10	.65
948	A170	65c S.S. Atlantis	2.50	1.75
949	A170	70c M.V. Queen of Bermuda	3.00	2.00
950	A170	80c USS Saufley	3.25	3.25
		Nos. 947-950 (4)	9.85	7.65

Queen Mother's Century

Common Design Type

Queen Mother: 15c, At Hertfordshire Hospital. 65c, With Princess Elizabeth. 70c, With Prince Andrew. 80c, With Irish Guards.

$2, With brother David and 1966 British World Cup team members.

Wmk. 373

1999, Aug. Litho. *Perf. 13½*

951	CD358	15c multicolored	.75	.50
952	CD358	65c multicolored	2.25	1.40
953	CD358	70c multicolored	2.25	2.25
954	CD358	80c multicolored	2.25	2.25
		Nos. 951-954 (4)	7.50	6.40

Souvenir Sheet

955	CD358	$2 multicolored	6.50	6.50

Environmental Protection — A171

15c, Turtle pond. 65c, Green turtles, limestone cliffs. 70c, Barracudas. 80c, Sea fans on reef.

$2, Atlantic bottlenose dolphin.

Wmk. 373

1999, Sept. 21 Litho. *Perf. 13¾*

956	A171	15c multicolored	.75	.50
957	A171	65c multicolored	1.75	1.50
958	A171	70c multicolored	2.25	2.25
959	A171	80c multicolored	2.50	2.50
		Nos. 956-959 (4)	7.25	6.75

Souvenir Sheet

960	A171	$2 multicolored	7.00	7.00

National Trust Type of 1999

Designs: a, Tern. b, Heron, c, Hummingbird, orange flower. d, Duck. e, Parrot.

Wmk. 384

1999, Oct. 8 Litho. *Perf. 14¼*

961	A166	65c Strip of 5, #a.-e.	11.00	11.00

Shell Type of 1996

1999 Litho. Wmk. 373 *Perf. 14*

962	A147	35c Like #854	1.50	1.50
963	A147	65c Like #856	6.00	2.75
964	A147	80c Like #858	3.75	3.75
		Nos. 962-964 (3)	11.25	8.00

Christmas A172

People in various Junkanoo costumes.

Perf. 14½x14¼

1999, Oct. 25 Litho. Wmk. 373

965	A172	15c multicolored	.55	.55
966	A172	65c multicolored	1.40	1.40
967	A172	70c multicolored	2.50	2.50
968	A172	80c multicolored	2.75	2.75
		Nos. 965-968 (4)	7.20	7.20

National Trust Type of 1999

Designs: a, Orchid. b, Rodent. c, Hummingbird, red flowers. d, Lizard. e, Hibiscus.

Wmk. 384

1999, Oct. 8 Litho. *Perf. 14¼*

969	A166	65c Strip of 5, #a.-e.	13.50	13.50

Historic Fishing Villages A173

15c, New Plymouth. 65c, Cherokee Sound. 70c, Hope Town. 80c, Spanish Wells.

Perf. 13¼x13

2000, Jan. 25 Litho. Wmk. 373

970	A173	15c multi	1.00	.65
971	A173	65c multi	2.40	1.50
972	A173	70c multi	3.25	3.25
973	A173	80c multi	3.75	3.75
		Nos. 970-973 (4)	10.40	9.15

Souvenir Sheet

1999 World Champions in Women's 4x100-Meter Relay Race — A174

Wmk. 373

2000, Feb. 22 Litho. *Perf. 14½*

974	A174	$2 multi	4.50	4.50

Bush Medicine Plants A175

Perf. 14¼x14½

2000, May 2 Litho. Wmk. 373

975	A175	15c Prickly pear	.65	.65
976	A175	65c Buttercup	1.50	1.50
977	A175	70c Shepherd's needle	1.90	1.90
978	A175	80c Five fingers	2.25	2.25
		Nos. 975-978 (4)	6.30	6.30

See Nos. 1040-1043, 1076-1079, 1131-1134.

The Stamp Show 2000, London A176

Battle of Britain, 60th anniv.: 15c, Quick turnaround, rearm and refuel. 65c, Squadron leader R. Stanford-Tuck in Hurricane 1. 70c, Melee. 80c, Tally ho.

$2, Airplanes in flight.

2000, May 22 *Perf. 13¼x13½*

979	A176	15c multi	1.10	.75
980	A176	65c multi	2.25	2.25
981	A176	70c multi	2.40	2.40
982	A176	80c multi	2.40	2.40
		Nos. 979-982 (4)	8.15	7.80

Souvenir Sheet

983	A176	$2 multi	7.00	7.00

Souvenir Sheet

Bahamas Cooperatives — A177

2000, June 27 Litho. *Perf. 14*

984	A177	$2 multi	6.00	6.00

2000 Summer Olympics, Sydney A178

15c, Swimming. 65c, Triple jump. 70c, Women's 4x100 meter relay. 80c, Yachting.

2000, July 17 *Perf. 14¼x14½*

985-988	A178	Set of 4	6.00	6.00

Christmas A179

Orchids: 15c, Cockle-shell orchid. 65c, Pleated encyclia. 70c, Pine pink. 80c, Graceful encyclia.

2000, Nov. 7 *Perf. 14½x14¼*

989-992	A179	Set of 4	7.75	7.75

Bahamas Humane Society, 76th Anniv. A180

Designs: 15c, Education. 65c, Fund raising. 70c, Veterinary care. 80c, Animal rescue.

Wmk. 373

2000, Dec. 12 Litho. *Perf. 14*

993-996	A180	Set of 4	10.00	10.00

Early Settlements A181

Designs: 15c, Meadow St., Inagua. 65c, Bain Town. 70c, Hope Town, Abaco. 80c, The Blue Hills.

Wmk. 373

2001, Feb. 6 Litho. *Perf. 14¼*

997-1000	A181	Set of 4	7.00	7.00

Sir Lynden Pindling (1930-2000), Prime Minister — A182

Pindling and: 15c, Microphone. 65c, Flag.

2001, Mar. 22 *Perf. 14½x14¼*

1001-1002	A182	Set of 2	2.25	2.25
1001a		Inscribed "10th July, 1973"	1.25	1.25

No. 1001 is inscribed "10th July, 1972." Issued: No. 1001a, 8/6/01.

Edible Wild Fruits A183

Designs: 15c, Cocoplum. 65c, Guana berry. 70c, Mastic. 80c, Seagrape.

2001, May 15 *Perf. 14¼x14½*

1003-1006	A183	Set of 4	6.50	6.50

Birds and Eggs A184

Designs: 5c, Reddish egret. 10c, Purple gallinule. 15c, Antillean nighthawk. 20c, Wilson's plover. 25c, Killdeer. 30c, Bahama woodstar. 40c, Bahama swallow. 50c, Bahama mockingbird. 60c, Black-cowled oriole. 65c, Great lizard cuckoo. 70c, Audubon's shearwater. 80c, Gray kingbird. $1, Bananaquit. $2, Yellow warbler. $5, Antillean bullfinch. $10, Roseate spoonbill.

Wmk. 373

2001, July 1 Litho. *Perf. 14*

Inscribed "2001"

1007	A184	5c multi	.25	.25
1008	A184	10c multi	.25	.25
1009	A184	15c multi	.50	.50
1010	A184	20c multi	.65	.65
1011	A184	25c multi	.80	.80
1012	A184	30c multi	1.00	1.00
1013	A184	40c multi	1.25	1.25
1014	A184	50c multi	1.60	1.60
1015	A184	60c multi	2.00	2.00
1016	A184	65c multi	2.00	2.00
1017	A184	70c multi	2.25	2.25
1018	A184	80c multi	2.50	2.50
1019	A184	$1 multi	3.25	3.25
1020	A184	$2 multi	6.50	6.50
1021	A184	$5 multi	16.00	16.00
1022	A184	$10 multi	32.50	32.50
		Nos. 1007-1022 (16)	73.30	73.30

Name of Bird in Black

Inscribed "2004"

1022A	A184	25c multi	*7.50*	*7.50*

Issued: Nos. 1007-1022 7/1/01; No. 1022A, 9/04.

Name of bird on No. 1011 is in brown.

2002 Inscribed "2002"

1010a	A184	20c multi	.65	.65
1011a	A184	25c multi	.80	.80
1013a	A184	40c multi	1.25	1.25
1022b	A184	$10 multi	32.50	32.50
		Nos. 1010a-1022b (4)	35.20	35.20

2005 Inscribed "2005"

1022Aa	A184	25c multi	*8.50*	*8.50*

Visits of Royal Navy Ships A185

HMS: 15c, Norfolk, 1933. 25c, Scarborough, 1930s. 50c, Bahamas, 1944. 65c, Battleaxe,

1979. 70c, Invincible, 1997. 80c, Norfolk, 2000.

Wmk. 373

2001, Aug. 21 Litho. *Perf. 14*
1023-1028 A185 Set of 6 12.00 12.00

Christmas — A186

Paintings: 15c, The Adoration of the Shepherds, by Peter Paul Rubens. 65c, Adoration of the Magi, by Rubens and Anthony Van Dyck. 70c, The Holy Virgin in the Wreath of Flowers, by Rubens and Jan Breughel. 80c, The Holy Virgin Adored by Angels, by Rubens.

2001, Nov. 6
1029-1032 A186 Set of 4 7.00 7.00

Reign Of Queen Elizabeth II, 50th Anniv. Issue

Common Design Type

Designs: Nos. 1033, 1037a, 15c, Princess Elizabeth, 1946. Nos. 1034, 1037b, 65c, In 1992. Nos. 1035, 1037c, 70c, With Prince Edward, 1965. Nos. 1036, 1037d, 80c, In 1996. No. 1037e, $2, 1955 portrait by Annigoni (38x50mm).

Perf. 14¼x14½, 13¾ (#1037e)

2002, Feb. 6 Litho. Wmk. 373

With Gold Frames

1033 CD360 15c multicolored .50 .50
1034 CD360 65c multicolored 1.00 1.00
1035 CD360 70c multicolored 1.75 1.75
1036 CD360 80c multicolored 2.00 2.00
Nos. 1033-1036 (4) 5.25 5.25

Souvenir Sheet

Without Gold Frames

1037 CD360 Sheet of 5, #a-e 10.50 10.50

Souvenir Sheet

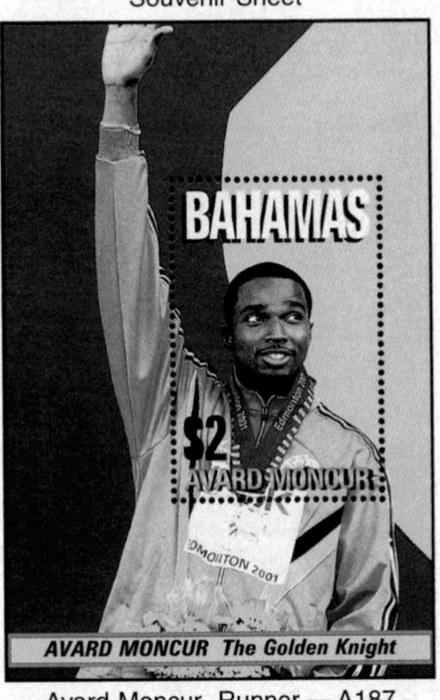

Avard Moncur, Runner — A187

Perf. 14x13¾

2002, Apr. 16 Litho. Wmk. 373
1038 A187 $2 multi 5.50 5.50

In Remembrance of Sept. 11, 2001 Terrorist Attacks — A188

Wmk. 373

2002, May 14 Litho. *Perf. 13¾*
1039 A188 $1 multi 4.75 4.75

Printed in sheets of four.

Bush Medicine Plants Type of 2000

Designs: 15c, Wild sage (lantana). 65c, Seaside maho. 70c, Sea ox-eye. 80c, Mexican poppy thistle.

Perf. 14¼x14½

2002, July 2 Litho. Wmk. 373
1040-1043 A175 Set of 4 8.00 8.00

Queen Mother Elizabeth (1900-2002)

Common Design Type

Designs: 15c, Wearing hat and maple leaf brooch. 65c, Wearing black hat.
No. 1046: a, 70c, Wearing flowered hat. b, 80c, Wearing blue hat.

Wmk. 373

2002, Aug. 5 Litho. *Perf. 14¼*

With Purple Frames

1044 CD361 15c multicolored .60 .60
1045 CD361 65c multicolored 2.75 2.75

Souvenir Sheet

Without Purple Frames

Perf. 14½x14¼

1046 CD361 Sheet of 2, #a-b 6.00 6.00

Flora and Fauna — A189

Plates from *The Natural History of Carolina, Florida and the Bahama Islands,* by Mark Catesby: 15c, Rice birds and rice. 25c, Alligator and red mangrove. 50c, Parrotfish. 65c, Ilatehera duck and sea oxeye. 70c, Flamingo and gorgonian coral. 80c, Crested bittern and inkberry.

Wmk. 373

2002, Oct. 1 Litho. *Perf. 14¼*
1047-1052 A189 Set of 6 11.50 11.50

Christmas A190

Carols: 15c, While Shepherds Watched Their Flocks. 65c, We Three Kings of Orient Are. 70c, Once in Royal David's City. 80c, I Saw Three Ships.

2002, Oct. 29 *Perf. 14¼x14½*
1053-1056 A190 Set of 4 8.00 8.00

Inagua National Park A191

Photos of various birds by: 15c, Alexander Sprunt IV. 25c, Mrs. Lynn Holowesko. 50c, Bahamas National Trust. 65c, Terra Aqua. 70c, Terra Aqua, diff. 80c, Henry Nixon.

Wmk. 373

2003, Feb. 18 Litho. *Perf. 14*
1057-1062 A191 Set of 6 8.50 8.50

Pirates — A192

Designs: 15c, Capt. Edward Teach ("Blackbeard"). 25c, Capt. John Rackham ("Calico Jack"). 50c, Anne Bonney. 65c, Capt. Woodes Rogers. 70c, Sir John Hawkins. 80c, Capt. Bartholomew Roberts ("Black Bart").

2003, Mar. 18
1063-1068 A192 Set of 6 12.00 12.00

50th Natl. Family Island Regatta — A193

Arms, birds and various sailors and sailboats: 15c, 65c, 70c, 80c.

2003, Apr. 30 *Perf. 13¾*
1069-1072 A193 Set of 4 8.25 8.25

Coronation of Queen Elizabeth II, 50th Anniv.

Common Design Type

Designs: Nos. 1073, 65c, 1075a, 15c, Queen with crown, orb and scepter. Nos. 1074, 80c, 1075b, 70c, Queen and family on Buckingham Palace balcony.

Perf. 14¼x14½

2003, June 2 Litho. Wmk. 373

Vignettes Framed, Red Background

1073 CD363 65c multicolored 2.75 2.75
1074 CD363 80c multicolored 3.75 3.75

Souvenir Sheet

Vignettes Without Frame, Purple Panel

1075 CD363 Sheet of 2, #a-b 6.50 6.50

Bush Medicine Plants Type of 2000

Designs: 15c, Asystasia. 65c, Cassia. 70c, Lignum vitae. 80c, Snowberry.

Wmk. 373

2003, July 8 Litho. *Perf. 13¾*
1076-1079 A175 Set of 4 7.50 7.50

Powered Flight, Cent. — A194

Designs: 15c, Piper Cub. 25c, DH Tiger Moth. 50c, Lockheed SR-71A Blackbird. 65c, Supermarine S6B. 70c, North American "Miss America" P-51D Mustang. 80c, Douglas DC3 Dakota.

Perf. 13¼x13¾

2003, Sept. 16 Litho.

Stamps + Label

1080-1085 A194 Set of 6 11.00 11.00

Christmas — A195

St. Matthew's Anglican Church, Nassau: 15c, Altar, vert. 65c, Altar. 70c, Exterior. 80c, Exterior, vert.

Perf. 14¾x14, 14x14¾

2003, Oct. 28 Litho. Wmk. 373
1086-1089 A195 Set of 4 7.25 7.25

Waters of Life — A196

Paintings by Alton Roland Lowe: 15c, Crawfishin'. 65c, Summer. 70c, The Whelkers. 80c, Annual Visit.

2003, Nov. 24 *Perf. 13¾*
1090-1093 A196 Set of 4 7.50 7.50

Harrold and Wilson Ponds A197

Designs: 15c, Birds on and near dead tree. 25c, Bird in water, bird on branch. 50c, Kayakers. 65c, Birds in water. 70c, Birds in water, diff. 80c, Bird watchers.

Wmk. 373

2004, Feb. 24 Litho. *Perf. 13¾*
1094-1099 A197 Set of 6 10.00 10.00

John Wesley (1703-91), Religious Leader A198

Designs: 15c, Methodist Church, Cupid's Bay, Governor's Harbor. 25c, Methodist Church, Grants Town, Nassau. 50c, Chapel, Marsh Harbor, vert. 65c, Ebeneezer Methodist Church. 70c, Trinity Methodist Church. 80c, Portrait of Wesley, by Antonius Roberts.

Wmk. 373

2004, Apr. 27 Litho. *Perf. 13¾*
1100-1105 A198 Set of 6 9.25 9.25

Royal Horticultural Society, Bicent. — A199

Flowers: 15c, Cattleya orchid. 65c, Hibiscus. 70c, Canna lily. 80c, Thunbergia.

Wmk. 373

2004, May 25 Litho. *Perf. 14*
1106-1109 A199 Set of 4 9.25 9.25
1109a Sheet, 5 each #1106-1109, + 5 labels 47.50 47.50

Lighthouses A200

Designs: 15c, Elbow Reef. 50c, Great Stirrup. 65c, Great Isaac. 70c, Hole in the Wall. 80c, Hog Island.

Wmk. 373

2004, July 7 Litho. *Perf. 14*
1110-1114 A200 Set of 5 11.00 11.00

See Nos. 1154-1158.

2004 Summer Olympics, Athens — A201

Designs: 15c, Boxing. 50c, Swimming. 65c, Tennis. 70c, Track.

Perf. 13½x13¼

2004, Aug. 24 Litho. Wmk. 373
1115-1118 A201 Set of 4 9.25 9.25

Children's Junkanoo and Christmas — A202

Designs: 15c, Anticipation. 25c, First time. 50c, On the move, vert. 65c, I'm ready, vert. 70c, Trumpet player, vert. 80c, Drummer boy, vert.

Wmk. 373

2004, Oct. 26 Litho. *Perf. 14*
1119-1124 A202 Set of 6 8.00 8.00

Merchant Ships A203

Designs: 15c, RMS Mauretania. 25c, MV Adonia. 50c, MS Royal Princess. 65c, SS Queen of Nassau. 70c, RMS Transvaal Castle. 80c, SS Norway.

Wmk. 373

2004, Dec. 7 Litho. *Perf. 13¼*
1125-1130 A203 Set of 6 12.50 12.50

Bush Medicine Plants Type of 2000

Designs: 15c, Aloe. 25c, Red stopper. 50c, Blue flower. 65c, Bay lavender.

2005, Feb. 8 *Perf. 13¾*
1131-1134 A175 Set of 4 4.25 4.25

Royal Bahamas Defense Force, 25th Anniv. A204

Designs: 15c, Soliders training in camouflage uniforms. 25c, HMBS Abaco. 50c, HMDS Bahamas. 65c, Six defense force members in various uniforms.

2005, Mar. 29 *Perf. 14*
1135-1138 A204 Set of 4 5.50 5.50

Connections Between Bahamas and Key West, Florida — A205

Paintings by Alton Roland Lowe: 15c, William Curry. 25c, Captain John Bartlum's House, horiz. 50c, Captain John Bartlum. 65c, Captain Tuggy Roberts' House, horiz.

2005, Apr. 26
1139-1142 A205 Set of 4 5.50 5.50

Battle of Trafalgar, Bicent. — A206

Designs: 15c, 1801 RN Pattern Tower Sea Service pistols. 25c, Royal Marine, 1805. 50c, HMS Boreas off Bahamas, 1787, horiz. 65c, The death of Nelson, horiz. 70c, HMS Victory, horiz. 80c, The Achille surrendering to HMS Polyphemus, horiz.

No. 1149: a, Admiral Cuthbert Collingwood. b, HMS Polyphemus.

Wmk. 373, Unwmkd. (70c)

2005, Apr. 29 *Perf. 13¼*
1143-1148 A206 Set of 6 12.50 12.50

Souvenir Sheet

1149 A206 $1 Sheet of 2, #a-b 8.50 8.50

No. 1147 has particles of wood from the HMS Victory embedded in areas covered by a thermographic process that produces a raised, shiny effect.

European Philatelic Cooperation, 50th Anniv. (in 2006) — A207

Flags of Bahamas and European Union, seascape, map of Europe in: 15c, Blue violet. 25c, Dull blue green. 50c, Yellow bister. $5, Green.

Unwmk.

2005, June 1 Litho. *Perf. 14*
1150-1153 A207 Set of 4 18.00 18.00
1153a Souvenir sheet, #1150-1153 18.00 18.00

Europa stamps, 50th anniv. (in 2006).

Lighthouses Type of 2004

Designs: 15c, Bird Rock. 50c, Castle Island. 65c, San Salvador. 70c, Great Inagua. 80c, Cay Lobos.

Wmk. 373

2005, July 6 Litho. *Perf. 14*
1154-1158 A200 Set of 5 10.50 10.50

Pope John Paul II (1920-2005) A208

Wmk. 373

2005, Aug. 18 Litho. *Perf. 14*
1159 A208 $1 multi 3.75 3.75

Souvenir Sheet

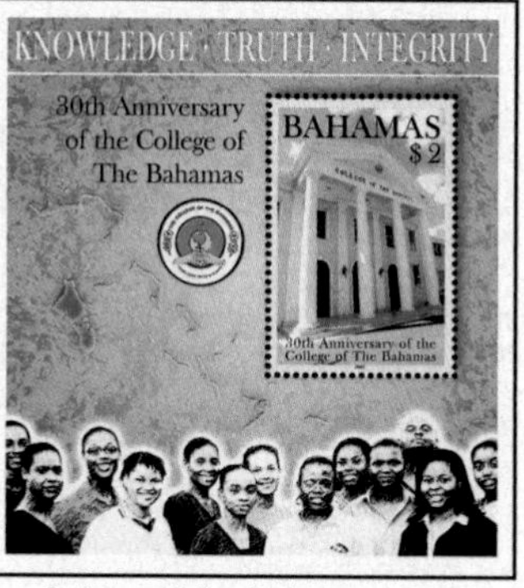

College of the Bahamas, 30th Anniv. — A209

Wmk. 373

2005, Oct. 18 Litho. *Perf. 14*
1160 A209 $2 multi 7.00 7.00

Christmas — A210

Stories by Hans Christian Andersen (1805-75): 15c, The Little Fir Tree. 25c, The Princess and the Pea. 50c, The Tin Soldier. 65c, Thumbelina.

2005, Nov. 8
1161-1164 A210 Set of 4 5.00 5.00

BirdLife International A211

Various depictions of Bahama nuthatch: 15c, 25c, 50c, 65c, 70c, 80c.

Wmk. 373

2006, Mar. 28 Litho. *Perf. 13¾*
1165-1170 A211 Set of 6 9.00 9.00
1170a Souvenir sheet, #1165-1170 14.00 14.00

Queen Elizabeth II, 80th Birthday A212

Queen Elizabeth II: 15c, As child. 25c, Wearing tiara. 50c, Wearing blue hat. 65c, Wearing white hat.

No. 1175: a, Like 25c. b, Like 50c.

2006, Apr. 21 *Perf. 14*
1171-1174 A212 Set of 4 5.00 5.00

Souvenir Sheet

1175 A212 $1.50 Sheet of 2, #a-b 8.00 8.00

ZNS Broadcasting Network, 70th Anniv. — A213

Designs: 15c, Map of Bahamas, Harcourt R. Bethel, ZNS General Manager. 25c, Map of Bahamas, ZNS Network emblem. 50c, ZNS building. 65c, ZNS building and tower. 70c, Map of Bahamas and radio antenna. 80c, Map of Bahamas, ZNS Radio emblem and microphone.

2006, May 26
1176-1181 A213 Set of 6 8.25 8.25

Flowers A214

Designs: 5c, Amaryllis. 10c, Barleria. 15c, Yesterday, today and tomorrow. 25c, Desert rose. 35c, Poor man's orchid. 40c, Frangipani. 55c, Herald's trumpet. 65c, Oleander. 75c, Bird of paradise. 80c, Plumbago. 90c, Rose. $1, Rubber vine. $2, Star of Bethlehem. $5, Angel's trumpet. $10, Wine lily.

Wmk. 373

2006, July 3 Litho. *Perf. 14*

Inscribed "2006"

1182 A214 5c multi .25 .25
1183 A214 10c multi .25 .25
1184 A214 25c multi .60 .60
1185 A214 35c multi .80 .80
1186 A214 40c multi .90 .90
1187 A214 55c multi 1.25 1.25
1188 A214 65c multi 1.50 1.50
1189 A214 75c multi 1.60 1.60
1190 A214 80c multi 1.25 1.25
1191 A214 90c multi 2.10 2.10
1192 A214 $1 multi 2.25 2.25
1193 A214 $2 multi 4.50 4.50
1194 A214 $5 multi 11.00 11.00
1195 A214 $10 multi 22.50 22.50
Nos. 1182-1195 (14) 50.75 50.75

Wmk. 406

1195B A214 15c multi .30 .30

2007 Wmk. 373 Inscribed "2007"
1182a A214 5c multi — —
1183a A214 10c multi — —

2008 Wmk. 373 Inscribed "2008"
1192b A214 $1 multi 2.00 2.00
1193b A214 $2 multi 4.00 4.00
1194b A214 $5 multi 10.00 10.00
1195c A214 $10 multi 20.00 20.00
Nos. 1192b-1195c (4) 36.00 36.00

2008, Aug. Wmk. 406
1182b 5c .25 .25
1183b 10c .25 .25
1186a 40c .80 .80
1187a 55c 1.10 1.10
1188a 65c 1.40 1.40
1189a 75c 1.50 1.50
1190a 80c 1.60 1.60
1191a 90c 1.90 1.90
1192a $1 2.00 2.00
1193a $2 4.00 4.00
1194a $5 10.00 10.00
1195a $10 20.00 20.00
Nos. 1182b-1195a (12) 44.80 44.80

Dated "2009"

Wmk. 406

1182c 5c multi .60 .60
1183c 10c multi .60 .60

Flowering Vines A215

Designs: 15c, Blue pea. 50c, Allamanda. 65c, Morning glory. 70c, Sky vine.

Perf. 12½x13

2006, Oct. 31 Litho. Wmk. 373
1196-1199 A215 Set of 4 5.25 5.25

Christmas A216

Designs: 15c, Christmas Sunday. 25c, Christmas dinner. 50c, Bay Street shopping. 65c, Boxing Day Junkanoo. 70c, Watch Night service. 80c, New Year's Day Junkanoo.

2006, Nov. 28 ***Perf. 13x13¼***
1200-1205 A216 Set of 6 7.75 7.75

Worldwide Fund for Nature (WWF) — A217

Blaineville's beaked whales: 15c, Whale breaching surface of water. 25c, Three whales. 50c, One whale underwater. 60c, Three whales, diff.

Wmk. 373
2007, Jan. 23 **Litho.** ***Perf. 14***
1206-1209 A217 Set of 4 4.50 4.50
1209a Miniature sheet, 4 each #1206-1209 19.00 19.00

Wedding of Queen Elizabeth II and Prince Philip, 60th Anniv. — A218

Designs: 15c, Portrait of couple. 25c, Couple in coach. 50c, Couple on balcony. 65c, Couple passing line of people.
$5, Color portrait of couple.

Wmk. 373
2007, June 1 **Litho.** ***Perf. 13¾***
1210-1213 A218 Set of 4 4.25 4.25

Souvenir Sheet
Perf. 14
1214 A218 $5 multi 13.00 13.00

No. 1214 contains one 43x57mm stamp.

Scouting, Cent. A219

Designs: 15c, Two Scouts at church service, hands of bugler. 25c, Scout on rope, hands tying knot. 50c, Scouts at campfire, hand holding compass. 65c, Scouts at attention, hand giving salute.
No. 1219, vert.: a, 70c, Scouts playing baseball. b, 80c, Lord Robert Baden-Powell.

2007, July 9 ***Perf. 13¾***
1215-1218 A219 Set of 4 5.00 5.00

Souvenir Sheet
1219 A219 Sheet of 2, #a-b 3.50 3.50

Governor General's Youth Award, 20th Anniv. — A220

Designs: 15c, Youths building walkway. 25c, Youths painting. 50c, Youths in kayak. 65c, Youths on hike. 70c, Award emblem.

Perf. 12½x13
2007, Sept. 18 **Litho.** **Wmk. 373**
1220-1224 A220 Set of 5 6.00 6.00

Christmas — A221

Various Christmas ornaments made of seashells with background colors of: 15c, Purple. 25c, Red violet. 50c, Orange. 65c, Red brown. 70c, Lemon. 80c, Green.

2007, Nov. 13 ***Perf. 14***
1225-1230 A221 Set of 6 8.00 8.00

Rev. Charles Wesley (1707-88), Hymn Writer A222

Designs: 15c, Church choir, cross. 50c, Stained glass window showing Charles Wesley and brother, John, vert. 65c, Charles Wesley and frontispiece of *Hymns and Sacred Poems in Two Volumes*, vert. 70c, Harbour Island Methodist Church.

Perf. 12½x13¼, 13¼x12½
2007, Dec. 13
1231-1234 A222 Set of 4 5.25 5.25

Butterflies A223

Designs: 15c, Zebra longwing. 25c, Julia. 50c, Cloudless sulphur. 65c, Queen. 70c, Long-tailed skipper. 80c, Gulf fritillary.

Wmk. 373
2008, Feb. 18 **Litho.** ***Perf. 14***
1235-1240 A223 Set of 6 7.50 7.50
1240a Miniature sheet, #1235-1240 7.50 7.50

Military Uniforms — A224

Designs: 15c, His Majesty's Independent Company. 25c, 47th Regiment of Foot. 50c, 99th Regiment of Foot. 65c, Royal Artillery. 70c Black Garrison Companies.

2008, Mar. 20
1241-1245 A224 Set of 5 5.25 5.25

2008 Summer Olympics, Beijing A225

Designs: 15c, Bamboo, runner. 50c, Dragon, high jump. 65c, Lanterns, javelin. 70c, Fish, runner.

Wmk. 373
2008, Apr. 30 **Litho.** ***Perf. 13½***
1246-1249 A225 Set of 4 4.75 4.75

Royal Bank of Canada in the Bahamas, Cent. A226

Designs: 15c, Anniversary emblem. 25c, Regional head office. 50c, Main branch office, Nassau, early 1900s. 65c, New Carmichael Road office. 70c, Bankers Ross McDonald and Nathaniel Beneby Jr.

Perf. 12½x13¼
2008, Sept. 22 **Litho.** **Wmk. 406**
1250-1254 A226 Set of 5 6.00 6.00

National Aeronautics and Space Administration, 50th Anniv. — A227

Designs: 15c, Launch of Space Shuttle Discovery. 25c, Apollo 16 over Moon. 50c, Skylab 3. 65c, Hubble Space Telescope. 70c, Swan Nebula. 80c, Carina Nebula.

Wmk. 373
2008, Oct. 1 **Litho.** ***Perf. 13¾***
1255-1260 A227 Set of 6 7.50 7.50

Christmas A228

Paintings by Leonhard Diefenbach: 15c, Adoration of the Magi. 50c, Magi at the Court of King Herod. 65c, Shepherds. 70c, Adoration of the Shepherds.

Perf. 12½x13
2008, Nov. 11 **Litho.** **Wmk. 406**
1261-1264 A228 Set of 4 6.00 6.00

University of the West Indies, 60th Anniv. A229

Anniversary emblem and: 15c, Men and women in doctor's jackets. 25c, Plaque honoring renaming of Clinical Training Program. 65c, Arms and diploma.

2008, Nov. 25
1265-1267 A229 Set of 3 3.75 3.75

Treaty of Paris, 225th Anniv. A230

Designs: 15c, Battle of Lexington. 50c, Washington Crossing the Delaware. 65c, Signatories of the Treaty of Paris, by Benjamin West. 70c, Signed treaty.

2008, Dec. 9
1268-1271 A230 Set of 4 5.00 5.00

Rare Birds — A231

Designs: 15c, Bahamas oriole. 50c, Rose-throated parrot. 65c, Great lizard cuckoo. 70c, Audubon's shearwater.

Wmk. 373
2009, Jan. 6 **Litho.** ***Perf. 13¾***
1272-1275 A231 Set of 4 6.50 6.50

Potcake Dogs A232

Dogs named: 15c, Tripod. 50c, Amigo. 65c, Turtle. 70c, Oreo.

Perf. 12½x13¼
2009, May 1 **Wmk. 406**
1276-1279 A232 Set of 4 6.50 6.50

Miniature Sheet

Peonies — A233

No. 1280 — Panel color: a, Pale yellow. b, White. c, Pink. d, Pale blue. e, Pale orange. f, Light green. g, Light yellow. h, Bluish gray.

Perf. 13¼
2009, Apr. 10 **Litho.** **Unwmk.**
1280 A233 50c Sheet of 8, #a-h 9.00 9.00

First Bahamas Postage Stamp, 150th Anniv. — A234

No. 1281 — Bahamas #1b with background color of: a, Pink. b, Light blue. c, Light green. d, Lilac.

2009, May 26 Wmk. 406 *Perf. 13*

1281 A234 15c Block of 4, #a-d 1.50 1.50
e. Souvenir sheet, #1281 1.50 1.50

Naval Aviation, Cent. A235

Royal Navy airplanes: 15c, Hawker Sea Hurricane. 65c, Hawker Sea Fury. 70c, Fairey Gannet. 80c, De Havilland Sea Vampire.
$2, Airplane on Merchant Aircraft Carrier MV Empire MacKendrick.

2009, June 16 Wmk. 406 *Perf. 14*

1282-1285 A235 Set of 4 5.00 5.00

Souvenir Sheet

1286 A235 $2 multi 4.50 4.50

Nos. 1282-1285 each were printed in sheets of 8 + central label.

Christmas A236

Designs: 15c, Church of God of Prophecy. 25c, Mission Baptist Church. 50c, Grant's Town Seventh-Day Adventist Church. 65c, Wesley Methodist Church. 70c, St. Francis Xavier Cathedral. 80c, St. Ambrose Anglican Church.

Wmk. 406

2009, Nov. 18 Litho. *Perf. 13¾*

1287-1292 A236 Set of 6 6.75 6.75

Souvenir Sheet

British Commonwealth, 60th Anniv. — A237

2009, Nov. 24

1293 A237 $2 multi 4.50 4.50

Friends of the Environment — A238

Designs: 15c, Whale, dolphin. 50c, Parrot, conch. 65c, Lizard, turtle. 70c, Stork, tree.

2010, Mar. 3 *Perf. 12¾x13*

1294-1297 A238 Set of 4 4.25 4.25

Battle of Britain, 70th Anniv. — A239

Various photographs of Sir Winston Churchill and words from his speeches: 15c, "We shall never surrender." 25c, "The Battle of Britain is about to begin." 50c, "Never in the field of human conflict was so much owed by so many to so few." 65c, "This was their finest hour." 70c, "Upon this battle depends the survival of Christian civilization." 80c, "We shall fight on the beaches."
$2, Sir Douglas Bader.

2010, June 18 *Perf. 12¾*

1298-1303 A239 Set of 6 6.75 6.75

Souvenir Sheet

1303A A239 $2 black & gray 4.50 4.50

Hurricane Awareness A240

Designs: 15c, Palm trees in hurricane. 50c, Map of hurricane track. 65c, Hurricane, reconnaissance airplane. 70c, National Emergency Management Agency emblem as eye of hurricane.

Perf. 12½x13

2010, Sept. 28 Wmk. 406

1304-1307 A240 Set of 4 7.00 7.00

Christmas — A241

Fireworks and: 15c, Palm tree, cruise ship. 50c, Atlantis Hotel. 65c, Tail of jet airplane. 70c, Fort Fincastle, Water Tower.

Unwmk.

2010, Nov. 10 Litho. *Perf. 14*

1308-1311 A241 Set of 4 7.00 7.00

Sir Victor Sassoon Heart Foundation — A242

Designs: 15c, Heart Ball. 50c, Doctor examining child. 65c, Doctor examining child, diff. 70c, Sir Victor Sassoon (1881-1961), businessman.

Unwmk.

2011, Feb. 12 Litho. *Perf. 14*

1312-1315 A242 Set of 4 4.00 4.00

Service of Queen Elizabeth II and Prince Philip — A243

Designs: 15c, Queen Elizabeth II. 50c, Queen and Prince Philip. 65c, Queen and Prince Philip, diff. 70c, Queen and Prince Philip, diff. $1, Queen and Prince Philip, diff. $2, Prince Philip.
$2.50, Queen and Prince Philip, diff.

2011, Mar. 23 Litho. *Perf. 13¼*

1316-1321 A243 Set of 6 10.00 10.00
1321a Sheet of 6, #1316-1321, + 3 labels 10.00 10.00

Souvenir Sheet

1322 A243 $2.50 multi 5.00 5.00

Wedding of Prince William and Catherine Middleton — A244

Couple: 15c, In 2008. 50c, At St. James's Palace. 65c, Kissing on Buckingham Palace balcony after wedding.
$5, After wedding at Westninster Abbey, vert.

2011, June 21 *Perf. 14*

1323-1325 A244 Set of 3 2.60 2.60

Souvenir Sheet

Perf. 14¾x14¼

1326 A244 $5 multi 10.00 10.00

No. 1326 contains one 29x46mm stamp.

Establishment of City of Nassau and Anglican Diocese, 150th Anniv. — A245

Designs: 15c, Christ Church Cathedral. 50c, Rawson Square. 65c, Government House. 70c, Bay Street. $1, Bishop Charles Caulfield. $2, Royal Governor Charles Bayley.

2011, Sept. 12 *Perf. 12½x13*

1327-1332 A245 Set of 6 10.00 10.00

Christmas A246

Angel and: 15c, Virgin Mary. 25c, Mary and Joseph. 50c, Magi. 65c, Infant Jesus and lambs. 70c, Shepherds. 80c, Mary and Jesus.

2011, Nov. 17 *Perf. 13½x13¼*

1333-1338 A246 Set of 6 6.25 6.25

Marine Life A247

Designs: 5c, Sea fan. 10c, Christmas tree worm. 15c, Elkhorn coral. 20c, Cushion sea star. 25c, Queen conch. 30c, Hawksbill turtle. 40c, Green moray eel. 50c, Bonefish. 60c, Spidder crab. 65c, Spiny lobster. 70c, Nassau grouper. 80c, Yellowtail snapper. $1, Great barracuda. $2, Spotted eagle ray. $5, Caribbean reef shark. $10, Bottlenose dolphin.

2012, Jan. 3 *Perf. 13¼x13½*

1339 A247 5c multi .25 .25
1340 A247 10c multi .25 .25
1341 A247 15c multi .30 .30
1342 A247 20c multi .40 .40
1343 A247 25c multi .50 .50
1344 A247 30c multi .60 .60
1345 A247 40c multi .80 .80
1346 A247 50c multi 1.00 1.00
1347 A247 60c multi 1.25 1.25
1348 A247 65c multi 1.40 1.40
1349 A247 70c multi 1.40 1.40
1350 A247 80c multi 1.60 1.60
1351 A247 $1 multi 2.00 2.00
1352 A247 $2 multi 4.00 4.00
1353 A247 $5 multi 10.00 10.00
1354 A247 $10 multi 20.00 20.00
Nos. 1339-1354 (16) 45.75 45.75

Worldwide Fund for Nature (WWF) — A248

Caribbean flamingo: Nos. 1355, 1359a, 15c, Head. Nos. 1356, 1359b, 50c, Chick and egg. Nos. 1357, 1359c, 65c, Adults feeding. Nos. 1358, 1359d, 70c, Adults standing, facing right.
$5, Adults standing, facing left.

2012, Mar. 21 *Perf. 14*

Stamps With White Frames

1355-1358 A248 Set of 4 4.00 4.00

Stamps Without White Frames

1359 A248 Horiz. strip of 4, #a-d 4.00 4.00

Souvenir Sheet

1360 A248 $5 multi 10.00 10.00

Royal Visit of Prince Harry — A250

Diamond and: 15c, Prince Harry in uniform. 50c, Prince Harry holding Bahamian flags. 65c, Prince Harry and young girl. 70c, Queen Elizabeth II.

2012, Aug. 16 Litho. *Perf. 14*

1365-1368 A250 Set of 4 4.00 4.00

Reign of Queen Elizabeth II, 60th anniv.

Woman Suffragists — A251

Designs: 15c, Mary Ingraham (1901-82). 25c, Georgianna Symonette (1902-65). 50c, Mabel Walker (1902-87). 65c, Eugenia Lockhart (1908-89). 70c, Dame Albertha Isaacs (1900-97). 80c, Dr. Doris Johnson (1921-83).

2012, Oct. 10
1369-1374 A251 Set of 6 6.25 6.25

Christmas A252

Designs: 15c, Annunciation. 25c, Mary and Joseph arrive in Bethlehem. 50c, Holy Family. 65c, Shepherds. 70c, Magi. 80c, Flight into Egypt.

2012, Nov. 1 ***Perf. 13½***
1375-1380 A252 Set of 6 6.25 6.25

2012 Summer Olympics, London — A249

Emblem of 2012 Summer Olympics and: 15c, Boxing, Houses of Parliament. 50c, High jump, Nelson's Column. 65c, Swimming, Tower Bridge. 70c, Runner, Olympic Stadium.

2012, July 11 ***Perf. 13½***
1361-1364 A249 Set of 4 4.00 4.00

Items Produced for Coronations — A253

Coronation of Queen Elizabeth II, 60th Anniv. — A254

Items produced for coronation of: 65c, Queen Victoria. 70c, King Edward VII. 80c, King George V. $1, King George VI. $2, Queen Elizabeth II.

2013, Feb. 6 ***Perf. 14***
1381-1385 A253 Set of 5 10.50 10.50

Souvenir Sheet
Perf. 14¾x14

1386 A254 $3 multi 6.00 6.00

Nos. 1381-1385 each were printed in sheets of 8 + label.

Royal Bahamas Police Force Band, 120th Anniv. A255

Designs: 15c, Sir William Murphy presenting gallantry medal to Constable Fred Neville Seymour (first conductor of band), 1948. 25c, Band greeting Royal Yacht Britannia, 1975. 50c, Band, building in background. 65c, Band, water and buildings in background. 70c, Drummer. 80c, Band passing under arch.

2013, May 15
1387-1392 A255 Set of 6 6.25 6.25

Independence, 40th Anniv. — A256

Designs: 15c, Bahamas Independence Conference. 25c, Sir Milo Butler (1906-79), Governor-General, Butler inspecting troops. 50c, Sir Lynden Pindling (1930-2000), Prime Minister, arms of Bahamas. 65c, HMBS Flamingo and four crewmen killed in 1980 sinking of ship by Cuban Air Force. 70c, Rhodes Scholars Christian Campbell, Desiree Cox and Myron Rolle.

2013, July 8
1393-1397 A256 Set of 5 4.50 4.50

SEMI-POSTAL STAMPS

No. 48 Overprinted in Red

1917, May 18 **Wmk. 3** ***Perf. 14***
B1 A6 1p car & black .50 *2.50*

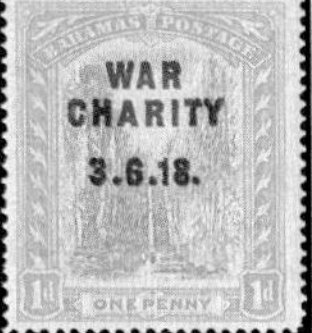
Type of 1911 Overprinted in Red

1919, Jan. 1
B2 A6 1p red & black .40 *3.25*
a. Double overprint *2,750.*

This stamp was originally scheduled for release in 1918.

No. 694 Surcharged
Souvenir Sheet

Wmk. 384
1992, Nov. 16 **Litho.** ***Perf. 14***
B3 A116 Sheet of 2, #a.-b. 20.00 20.00

AIR POST STAMPS

Catalogue values for all unused stamps in this section are for Never Hinged items.

Manned Flight Bicentenary — AP1

Airplanes.

Wmk. 373
1983, Oct. 13 **Litho.** ***Perf. 14***

C1	AP1 10c Consolidated Catalina	.65	.25
a.	Without emblem ('85)	3.00	.50
b.	Without emblem, wmk. 384 ('86)	2.50	1.00
C2	AP1 25c Avro Tudor IV	.85	.40
a.	Without emblem ('85)	6.00	1.00
b.	Without emblem, wmk. 384 ('86)	5.00	2.00
C3	AP1 31c Avro Lancastrian	1.00	.55
a.	Without emblem ('85)	1.75	.55
C4	AP1 35c Consolidated Commodore	.80	.60
a.	Without emblem ('85)	3.25	.65
	Nos. C1-C4 (4)	3.30	1.80

Aircraft AP2

1987, July 7

C5	AP2 15c Bahamasair Boeing 737	3.50	2.50
C6	AP2 40c Eastern Boeing 757	4.50	3.00
C7	AP2 45c Pan Am Airbus A300 B4	4.50	3.00
C8	AP2 50c British Airways Boeing 747	4.50	4.50
	Nos. C5-C8 (4)	17.00	13.00

SPECIAL DELIVERY STAMPS

No. 34 Overprinted

1916 **Wmk. 1** ***Perf. 14***

E1	A6 5p orange & black	7.50	*47.50*
a.	Double overprint	*1,000.*	*1,500.*
b.	Inverted overprint	*1,750.*	*1,800.*
c.	Double ovpt., one invtd.	*1,550.*	*1,750.*
d.	Pair, one without overprint	*35,000.*	*50,000.*

The No. E1 overprint exists in two types. Type I (illustrated) is much scarcer. Type II shows "SPECIAL" farther right, so that the letter "I" is slightly right of the vertical line of the "E" below it.

Type of Regular Issue of 1903 Overprinted

1917, July 2 **Wmk. 3**
E2 A6 5p orange & black .80 *11.00*

No. 60 Overprinted in Red

1918
E3 A6 5p violet & black .60 *4.00*

WAR TAX STAMPS

Stamps of 1912-18 Overprinted

1918, Feb. 21 **Wmk. 3** ***Perf. 14***

MR1	A8 ½p green	11.50	*55.00*
a.	Double overprint	—	—
b.	Inverted overprint	—	—
MR2	A8 1p car rose	1.25	*1.00*
a.	Double overprint	—	—
b.	Inverted overprint	—	—
MR3	A6 3p brown, *yel*	3.75	*3.50*
a.	Inverted overprint	*1,400.*	*1,500.*
b.	Double overprint	*2,000.*	*2,150.*
MR4	A8 1sh black & red	125.00	*175.00*
a.	Double overprint	—	—
	Nos. MR1-MR4 (4)	141.50	*234.50*

Same Overprint on No. 48a

1918, July 10

MR5	A6 1p car & black	4.50	*6.50*
a.	Double overprint	*2,150.*	*2,400.*
b.	Double ovpt., one invtd.	*1,100.*	—
c.	Inverted overprint	*1,900.*	*2,000.*

Nos. 49-50, 54 Overprinted in Black or Red

MR6	A8 ½p green	2.25	2.25
MR7	A8 1p car rose	2.25	.45
a.	Watermarked sideways	600.00	
MR8	A8 1sh black & red (R)	11.50	3.50
	Nos. MR6-MR8 (3)	16.00	6.20

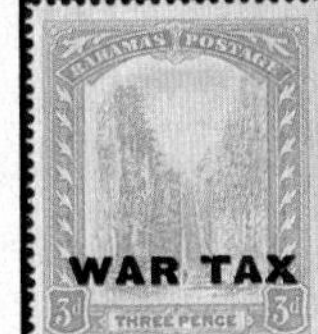
Nos. 58-59 Overprinted

1918-19

MR9	A6 3p brown, *yel*	.90	*3.25*
MR10	A6 3p brown & blk ('19)	.90	*3.75*

Nos. 49-50, 54 Overprinted in Red or Black

1919, July 14

MR11	A8 ½p green (R)	.40	*1.60*
MR12	A8 1p car rose	1.90	*1.90*
MR13	A8 1sh black & red (R)	27.50	*55.00*
	Nos. MR11-MR13 (3)	29.80	*58.50*

No. 59 Overprinted

MR14 A6 3p brown & black 1.00 *10.00*

BAHRAIN

bä-'rān

LOCATION — An archipelago in the Persian Gulf, including the islands of Bahrain, Muharraq, Sitra, Nebi Saleh, Kasasifeh and Arad.
GOVT. — Independent sheikdom
AREA — 255 sq. mi.
POP. — 629,090 (1999 est.)
CAPITAL — Manama

Bahrain was a British-protected territory until it became an independent state on August 15, 1971.

12 Pies = 1 Anna
16 Annas = 1 Rupee
100 Naye Paise = 1 Rupee (1957)
1000 Fils = 1 Dinar (1966)

Catalogue values for unused stamps in this country are for Never Hinged items, beginning with Scott 62 in the regular postage section and Scott MR2 in the postal tax section.

Indian Postal Administration

Stamps of India, 1926-32, Overprinted in Black — a

Wmk. Multiple Stars (196)

1933, Aug. 10 *Perf. 14*

1 A46 3p gray 7.50 .75
2 A47 ½a green 12.00 4.00
3 A68 9p dark green 8.00 3.50
4 A48 1a dark brown 11.00 3.00
5 A69 1a3p violet 12.00 2.75
6 A60 2a vermilion 15.00 20.00
7 A51 3a blue 29.00 *67.50*
8 A70 3a6p deep blue 7.00 .50
9 A61 4a olive green 27.50 *65.00*
10 A54 8a red violet 10.00 .50
11 A55 12a claret 12.50 1.75

Overprinted in Black — b

12 A56 1r green & brown 25.00 11.00
13 A56 2r brn org & car rose 40.00 42.50
14 A56 5r dk violet & ultra 190.00 165.00
Nos. 1-14 (14) 406.50 387.75

Stamps of India, 1926-32, Overprinted Type "a" in Black

1934

15 A72 1a dark brown 15.00 .60
a. Complete booklet, containing 16 #15, wmk inverted, in four blocks of 4 *1,500.*
16 A51 3a carmine rose 8.50 .75
17 A52 4a olive green 9.75 .70
Nos. 15-17 (3) 33.25 2.05

The cover of No. 15a is red and black on tan, with Mysore Sandal Soup advertisement on front.

India Nos. 138, 111, 111a Overprinted Type "a" in Black

1935-37 *Perf. 13½x14, 14*

18 A71 ½a green 8.50 2.25
19 A49 2a vermilion 65.00 10.00
a. Small die ('37) 100.00 .30

India Stamps of 1937 Overprinted Type "a" in Black

1938-41 Wmk. 196 *Perf. 13½x14*

20 A80 3p slate 12.00 8.00
21 A80 ½a brown 7.00 .30
22 A80 9p green 9.00 *14.00*
23 A80 1a carmine 8.00 .30
24 A81 2a scarlet 4.00 6.00
26 A81 3a yel grn ('41) 8.00 12.00
27 A81 3a6p ultra 4.00 *10.00*
28 A81 4a dk brn ('41) 125.00 90.00
30 A81 8a bl vio ('40) 180.00 42.50
31 A81 12a car lake ('40) 105.00 55.00

Overprinted Type "b" in Black

32 A82 1r brn & slate 4.75 2.50
33 A82 2r dk brn & dk vio 12.00 11.00
34 A82 5r dp ultra & dk grn 10.00 *16.00*
35 A82 10r rose car & dk vio ('41) 60.00 60.00
36 A82 15r dk grn & dk brn ('41) 60.00 90.00
37 A82 25r dk vio & bl vio ('41) 95.00 *110.00*
Nos. 20-37 (16) 703.75 527.60
Set, never hinged 1,000.

India Stamps of 1941-43 Overprinted Type "a" in Black

1942-44 Wmk. 196 *Perf. 13½x14*

38 A83 3p slate 2.00 2.50
39 A83 ½a rose vio ('44) 3.00 *4.50*
40 A83 9p lt green ('43) 11.00 *24.00*
41 A83 1a car rose ('44) 5.00 1.00
42 A84 1a3p bister ('43) 6.50 *22.50*
43 A84 1½a dk pur ('43) 4.25 *8.50*
45 A84 2a scarlet ('43) 4.25 2.00
46 A84 3a violet ('43) 14.00 8.00
47 A84 3½a ultra 4.50 *27.50*
48 A85 4a chocolate 3.00 2.50
49 A85 6a peacock blue 14.00 *13.00*
50 A85 8a blue vio ('43) 7.00 4.50
51 A85 12a car lake 10.00 6.50
Nos. 38-51 (13) 88.50 *127.00*
Set, never hinged 135.00

British Postal Administration

See Oman (Muscat) for similar stamps with surcharge of new value only.

Great Britain Nos. 258 to 263, 243 and 248 Surcharged in Black — c

1948-49 Wmk. 251 *Perf. 14½x14*

52 A101 ½a on ½p green .50 *1.75*
53 A101 1a on 1p vermilion .50 *3.50*
54 A101 1½a on 1½p lt red brn .50 *4.75*
55 A101 2a on 2p lt orange .50 .30
56 A101 2½a on 2½p ultra .75 *7.00*
57 A101 3a on 3p violet .50 .30
58 A102 6a on 6p rose lilac .50 .30
59 A103 1r on 1sh brown 1.25 .35

Great Britain Nos. 249A, 250 and 251A Surcharged in Black

Wmk. 259 *Perf. 14*

60 A104 2r on 2sh6p yel grn 4.50 *8.00*
61 A104 5r on 5sh dull red 4.75 *8.50*
61A A105 10r on 10sh ultra 65.00 *70.00*
Nos. 52-61A (11) 79.25 *104.75*
Set, never hinged 115.00

Surcharge bars at bottom on No. 61A.
Issued: 10r, 7/4/49; others, 4/1/48.

Catalogue values for unused stamps in this section, from this point to the end of the section, are for Never Hinged items.

Silver Wedding Issue

Great Britain Nos. 267 and 268 Surcharged in Black

Perf. 14½x14, 14x14½

1948, Apr. 26 Wmk. 251

62 A109 2½a on 2½p .95 *2.50*
63 A110 15r on £1 37.50 *70.00*

Three bars obliterate the original denomination on No. 63.

Olympic Issue

Great Britain Nos. 271 to 274 Surcharged "BAHRAIN" and New Value in Black

1948, July 29 *Perf. 14½x14*

64 A113 2½a on 2½p brt ultra 1.40 *4.75*
a. Double surcharge 3,250. *4,000.*
65 A114 3a on 3p dp vio 1.10 *4.25*
66 A115 6a on 6p red vio 1.75 *4.25*
67 A116 1r on 1sh dk brn 2.75 *4.25*
Nos. 64-67 (4) 7.00 *17.50*

A square of dots obliterates the original denomination on No. 67.

UPU Issue

Great Britain Nos. 276 to 279 Surcharged "BAHRAIN," New Value and Square of Dots in Black

1949, Oct. 10 Photo. *Perf. 14½x14*

68 A117 2½a on 2½p brt ultra .90 *3.50*
69 A118 3a on 3p brt vio 1.10 *5.25*
70 A119 6a on 6p red vio 1.00 *4.25*
71 A120 1r on 1sh brown 2.00 *3.75*
Nos. 68-71 (4) 5.00 *16.75*

Great Britain Nos. 280-285 Surcharged Type "c" in Black

1950-51 Wmk. 251

72 A101 ½a on ½p lt org 3.00 3.00
73 A101 1a on 1p ultra 3.50 .35
74 A101 1½a on 1½p green 3.50 *17.50*
75 A101 2a on 2p lt red brn 2.00 .35
76 A101 2½a on 2½p ver 3.75 *16.00*
77 A102 4a on 4p ultra 3.75 1.90

Great Britain Nos. 286-288 Surcharged in Black

Three types of surcharge on No. 78: Type I, "2" level with "RUPEES;" Type II, "2" raised higher than "RUPEES," 15mm between "BAHRAIN" and "2 RUPEES;" Type III, as type II, but 16mm between "BAHRAIN" and "2 RUPEES."

Perf. 11x12

Wmk. 259

78 A121 2r on 2sh6p green, type I ('51) 40.00 15.00
a. 2r on 2sh6p, type II ('53) 140.00 55.00
b. 2r on 2sh6p, type III ('55) 1,350. 140.00
79 A121 5r on 5sh dl red 17.50 6.50
80 A122 10r on 10sh ultra 40.00 10.50
Nos. 72-80 (9) 117.00 *71.10*

Longer bars, at lower right, on No. 80.
Issued: 4a, Nov. 2, 1950; others, May 3, 1951.

Stamps of Great Britain, 1952-54, Surcharged "BAHRAIN" and New Value in Black or Dark Blue

1952-54 Wmk. 298 *Perf. 14½x14*

81 A126 ½a on ½p red org ('53) .30 .25
a. "½" omitted 200.00 *375.00*
82 A126 1a on 1p ultra .30 .25
83 A126 1½a on 1½p grn .30 .25
84 A126 2a on 2p red brn .30 .25
85 A127 2½a on 2½p scar .60 *1.75*
86 A127 3a on 3p dk pur (Dk Bl) 1.10 .25
87 A128 4a on 4p ultra 12.00 .50
88 A129 6a on 6p lil rose 4.00 .45
89 A132 12a on 1sh3p dk grn 4.00 .75
90 A131 1r on 1sh6p dk bl 4.00 1.00
Nos. 81-90 (10) 26.90 5.70

Issued: Nos. 83, 85, 12/5; Nos. 81-82, 84, 8/31/53; Nos. 87, 89-90, 11/2/53; Nos. 86, 88, 1/18/54.

Six stamps of this design picturing Sheik Sulman bin Hamad Al Kalifah were for local use in 1953-57. Value, mint set $30.

Six stamps of similar design (same sheik, "Bahrain" vertical at left) were issued in 1961 for local use. Value, mint set, $12.50.

Coronation Issue

Great Britain Nos. 313-316 Surcharged "BAHRAIN" and New Value in Black

Perf. 14½x14

1953, June 3 Wmk. 298

92 A134 2½a on 2½p scar 1.25 1.00
93 A135 4a on 4p brt ultra 2.00 5.00
94 A136 12a on 1sh3p dk grn 5.75 4.50
95 A137 1r on 1sh6p dk bl 6.25 2.25
Nos. 92-95 (4) 15.25 12.75

Squares of dots obliterate the original denominations on Nos. 94-95.

Great Britain Nos. 309-311 Surcharged "BAHRAIN" and New Value in Black

1955 Wmk. 308 Engr. *Perf. 11x12*

96 A133 2r on 2sh6p dk brn 5.50 2.00
97 A133 5r on 5sh crimson 9.50 3.50
98 A133 10r on 10sh brt ultra 25.00 5.00
Nos. 96-98 (3) 40.00 10.50

Three slightly different types of surcharge are found on the 2r; two on 5r and 10r.

Great Britain Nos. 317, 323, 325, 332-333 Surcharged "BAHRAIN" and New Value

Perf. 14½x14

1956-57 Wmk. 308 Photo.

99 A126 ½a on ½p red org .55 .25
100 A128 4a on 4p ultra 6.50 *22.50*
101 A129 6a on 6p lil rose 1.00 .80
102 A132 12a on 1sh3p dk green 7.75 *12.00*
103 A131 1r on 1sh6p dk bl ('57) 11.50 .25
Nos. 99-103 (5) 27.30 *35.80*

Great Britain Nos. 317-325, 328, 332 Surcharged "BAHRAIN" and New Value

1957, Apr. 1

104 A129 1np on 5p lt brown .25 .25
105 A126 3np on ½p red org .50 *3.00*
106 A126 6np on 1p ultra .50 *3.00*
107 A126 9np on 1½p green .50 *3.00*
108 A126 12np on 2p red brn .35 *.70*
109 A127 15np on 2½p scar, type I .40 .25
a. Type II 1.10 *5.00*
110 A127 20np on 3p dk pur .25 .25
111 A128 25np on 4p ultra 1.00 *2.50*
112 A129 40np on 6p lil rose .75 .25
113 A130 50np on 9p dp ol grn 3.75 *4.50*
114 A132 75np on 1sh3p dk grn 2.50 .60
Nos. 104-114 (11) 10.75 *18.30*

The arrangement of the surcharge varies on different values: there are three bars through value on No. 113.

Jubilee Jamboree Issue

Great Britain Nos. 334-336 Surcharged "BAHRAIN," New Value and Square of Dots in Black

Perf. 14½x14

1957, Aug. 1 Photo. Wmk. 308

115 A138 15np on 2½p scar .35 *.40*
116 A138 25np on 4p ultra .50 .50
117 A138 75np on 1sh3p dk grn .75 *1.10*
Nos. 115-117 (3) 1.60 *2.00*

Great Britain No. 357 Surcharged "BAHRAIN/ NP 15 NP" in Black

1960 Wmk. 322 *Perf. 14½x14*

118 A127 15np on 2½p scar, type II 5.00 *12.00*

A1

Sheik Sulman bin Hamad Al Khalifah — A2

Perf. 14½x14

1960, July 1 Photo. Unwmk.

No.	Type	Value	Color	Unused	Used
119	A1	5np	lt ultra	.25	.25
120	A1	15np	orange	.25	.25
121	A1	20np	lt violet	.25	.25
122	A1	30np	olive bister	.25	.25
123	A1	40np	gray	.25	.25
124	A1	50np	emerald	.25	.25
125	A1	75np	red brown	.60	.25

Engr.

Perf. 13x13½

No.	Type	Value	Color	Unused	Used
126	A2	1r	gray	2.50	.60
127	A2	2r	carmine	3.75	2.00
128	A2	5r	ultra	5.50	3.25
129	A2	10r	olive green	15.00	6.00
			Nos. 119-129 (11)	28.85	13.60

Sheik Isa bin Sulman Al Khalifah A3

Bahrain Airport A4

Designs: 5r, 10r, Deep water jetty.

1964, Feb. 22 Photo. *Perf. 14½x14*

No.	Type	Value	Color	Unused	Used
130	A3	5np	ultra	.25	.25
131	A3	15np	orange	.25	.25
132	A3	20np	brt purple	.25	.25
133	A3	30np	brown olive	.25	.25
134	A3	40np	slate	.25	.25
135	A3	50np	emerald	.70	.90
136	A3	75np	chestnut	1.00	.35

Engr.

Perf. 13½x13

No.	Type	Value	Color	Unused	Used
137	A4	1r	black	9.00	2.40
138	A4	2r	rose red	11.00	3.00
139	A4	5r	violet blue	15.00	15.00
140	A4	10r	dull green	20.00	20.00
			Nos. 130-140 (11)	57.95	42.90

Bahrain Postal Administration

Sheik Isa bin Sulman Al Khalifah — A5

Sheik and Bahrain International Airport — A6

Pearl Divers — A7

Bab al Bahrain, Suq Al-Khamis Mosque, Sheik, Emblem, etc. — A8

Designs: 50f, 75f, Pier, Mina Sulman harbor. 200f, Falcon and horse race. 500f, "Hospitality," pouring coffee and Sheik's Palace.

Perf. 14½x14

1966, Jan. 1 Photo. Unwmk.

No.	Type	Value	Color	Unused	Used
141	A5	5f	green	.50	.35
142	A5	10f	dark red	.50	.35
143	A5	15f	ultra	.50	.35
144	A5	20f	magenta	.50	.35

Perf. 13½x14

No.	Type	Value	Color	Unused	Used
145	A6	30f	green & black	.60	.35
146	A6	40f	blue & black	.70	.35
147	A6	50f	dp car rose & blk	.80	.55
148	A6	75f	violet & black	1.00	.70

Perf. 14½x14

No.	Type	Value	Color	Unused	Used
149	A7	100f	dk blue & yel	3.25	1.25
150	A7	200f	dk green & org	14.00	2.75
151	A7	500f	red brown & yel	12.00	5.00
152	A8	1d	multicolored	21.00	10.00
			Nos. 141-152 (12)	55.35	22.35

Produce, Date Palm, Ship, Truck and Plane — A9

1966, Mar. 28 Litho. *Perf. 13x13½*

No.	Type	Value	Color	Unused	Used
153	A9	10f	red & blue green	1.10	.45
154	A9	20f	green & vio	1.60	.95
155	A9	40f	olive bis & lt bl	3.25	1.75
156	A9	200f	vio blue & pink	11.00	9.00
			Nos. 153-156 (4)	16.95	12.15

6th Bahrain Trade Fair & Agricultural Show.

Map of Bahrain and WHO Emblem — A10

1968, June Unwmk. *Perf. 13½x14*

No.	Type	Value	Color	Unused	Used
157	A10	20f	gray & black	1.75	.65
158	A10	40f	blue grn & black	4.25	1.75
159	A10	150f	dp rose & black	14.00	6.50
			Nos. 157-159 (3)	20.00	8.90

20th anniv. of the WHO.

Isa Town A11

1968, Nov. 18 Litho. *Perf. 14½*

No.	Type	Value	Color	Unused	Used
160	A11	50f	shown	6.00	2.50
161	A11	80f	Market	9.00	3.50
162	A11	120f	Stadium	14.50	6.25
163	A11	150f	Mosque	17.50	9.75
			Nos. 160-163 (4)	47.00	22.00

Education Symbol — A12

1969, Apr. Litho. *Perf. 13*

No.	Type	Value	Color	Unused	Used
164	A12	40f	multicolored	1.90	1.40
165	A12	60f	multicolored	4.00	2.25
166	A12	150f	multicolored	9.25	4.75
			Nos. 164-166 (3)	15.15	8.40

50th anniversary of education in Bahrain.

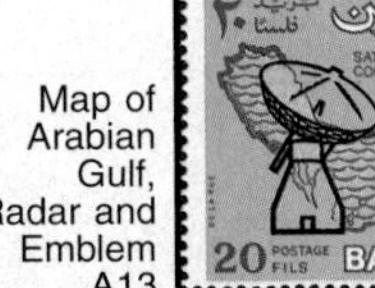

Map of Arabian Gulf, Radar and Emblem A13

Designs: 40f, 150f, Radar installation and emblem of Cable & Wireless Ltd., vert.

Perf. 14x13½, 13½x14

1969, July 14 Litho.

No.	Type	Value	Color	Unused	Used
167	A13	20f	lt green & multi	4.00	1.10
168	A13	40f	vio blue & multi	6.25	2.75
169	A13	100f	ocher & multi	12.50	6.25
170	A13	150f	rose lilac & multi	20.00	10.50
			Nos. 167-170 (4)	42.75	20.60

Opening of the satellite earth station (connected through the Indian Ocean satellite Intelsat III) at Ras Abu Jarjur, July 14.

Municipal Building, Arms and Map of Bahrain A14

1970, Feb. 23 Litho. *Perf. 12x12½*

No.	Type	Value	Color	Unused	Used
171	A14	30f	blue & multi	4.25	3.00
172	A14	150f	multicolored	14.50	11.50

2nd Conf. of the Arab Cities' Org.

Copper Bull's Head A15

Conf. Emblem and: 80f, Gateway to Qalat al Bahrain, 7th cent. B.C. 120f, Aerial view of grave mounds, Bahrain. 150f, Dilmun seal, 2000 B.C.

1970, Mar. 1 Photo. *Perf. 14½*

No.	Type	Value	Color	Unused	Used
173	A15	60f	multicolored	7.00	2.25
174	A15	80f	multicolored	9.00	2.50
175	A15	120f	multicolored	11.00	4.00
176	A15	150f	multicolored	14.00	4.75
			Nos. 173-176 (4)	41.00	13.50

3rd Intl. Asian Archaeological Conf., Bahrain.

Vickers VC 10, Big Ben and Minaret A16

1970, Apr. 5 Litho. *Perf. 14½x14*

No.	Type	Value	Color	Unused	Used
177	A16	30f	multicolored	6.00	1.00
178	A16	60f	multicolored	10.00	2.25
179	A16	120f	multicolored	16.00	7.25
			Nos. 177-179 (3)	32.00	10.50

1st flight to London from the Arabian Gulf Area by Gulf Aviation Company.

Intl. Education Year Emblem A17

120f, Education Year emblem & students.

1970, Nov. 1 Litho. *Perf. 14½x14*

No.	Type	Value	Color	Unused	Used
180	A17	60f	blk, blue & org	6.25	3.50
181	A17	120f	multicolored	11.50	7.00

Independent State

Declaration of Bahrain Independence, Aug. 15, 1971 — A18

Designs: 30f, "Freedom" with dove and torch, and globe. 60f, Government House, Manama. 120f, 150f, Bahrain coat of arms.

1971, Oct. 2 Photo. *Perf. 14½x14*

No.	Type	Value	Color	Unused	Used
182	A18	30f	gold & multi	4.00	1.75
183	A18	60f	gold & multi	7.00	3.75
184	A18	120f	gold & multi	13.00	7.50
185	A18	150f	gold & multi	17.50	9.50
			Nos. 182-185 (4)	41.50	22.50

UN Emblem and Sails — A19

30f, 60f, Dhow with sails showing UN and Arab League emblems, horiz. 150f, as 120f.

Perf. 14x14½, 14½x14

1972, Feb. 1 Litho.

No.	Type	Value	Color	Unused	Used
186	A19	30f	multicolored	6.25	5.00
187	A19	60f	red, gray & multi	10.00	8.50
188	A19	120f	dull blue & multi	13.00	11.00
189	A19	150f	multicolored	24.00	21.00
			Nos. 186-189 (4)	53.25	45.50

Bahrain's admission to the Arab League and the United Nations.

"Your Heart is your Health" — A20

1972, Apr. 7 Litho. *Perf. 14½x14*

No.	Type	Value	Color	Unused	Used
190	A20	30f	black & multi	7.00	6.75
191	A20	60f	gray & multi	12.00	11.50

World Health Day.

UN and FAO Emblems A21

1973, May 12 Litho. *Perf. 12½x13*

192 A21 30f org red, pur & grn 6.00 5.25
193 A21 60f ocher, brn & grn 9.75 9.50

World Food Programs, 10th anniversary.

People of Various Races, Human Rights Flame — A22

1973, Nov. Litho. *Perf. 14x14½*

194 A22 30f blue, blk & brn 6.00 5.75
195 A22 60f lake, blk & brn 13.00 12.50

25th anniversary of the Universal Declaration of Human Rights.

Flour Mill A23

60f, Intl. Airport. 120f, Sulmaniya Medical Center. 150f, ALBA aluminum smelting plant.

1973, Dec. 16 Photo. *Perf. 14½*

196 A23 30f multicolored 2.25 1.75
197 A23 60f multicolored 3.50 3.00
198 A23 120f multicolored 6.25 5.75
199 A23 150f multicolored 7.00 7.00
Nos. 196-199 (4) 19.00 17.50

National Day.

Letters and UPU Emblem — A24

Carrier Pigeon and UPU Emblem A25

60f, UPU emblem & letters. 150f, Like 120f.

1974, Feb. 4 Litho. *Perf. 13½*

200 A24 30f blue & multi 2.00 1.60
201 A24 60f emerald & multi 3.50 2.75

Perf. 12½x13½

202 A25 120f ultra & multi 4.25 4.50
203 A25 150f yellow & multi 6.00 6.50
Nos. 200-203 (4) 15.75 15.35

Bahrain's admission to UPU.

Traffic Signals — A26

1974, May 4 Litho. *Perf. 14½*

204 A26 30f org brown & multi 4.50 4.50
205 A26 60f brt blue & multi 9.50 9.50

International Traffic Day.

Jet, Globe, Mail Coach and UPU Emblem — A27

1974, Sept. 1 Photo. *Perf. 14x14½*

206 A27 30f multicolored 1.00 1.00
207 A27 60f multicolored 2.00 2.00
208 A27 120f multicolored 4.75 4.75
209 A27 150f multicolored 5.50 5.50
Nos. 206-209 (4) 13.25 13.25

Centenary of Universal Postal Union.

National Day Emblem, Sitra Power Station — A28

National Day: 120f, 150f, Bahrain dry dock.

1974, Dec. 16 Litho. *Perf. 14½*

210 A28 30f blue & multi 1.10 1.10
211 A28 60f green & multi 2.25 1.75
212 A28 120f lil rose & multi 4.75 4.75
213 A28 150f ver & multi 5.75 5.75
Nos. 210-213 (4) 13.85 13.35

Woman's Silk Gown — A29

Various women's costumes.

Photo.; Gold Embossed

1975, Feb. 1 *Perf. 14½x14*

214 A29 30f blue grn & multi 1.25 1.25
215 A29 60f vio blue & multi 2.00 2.00
216 A29 120f rose red & multi 4.25 4.25
217 A29 150f multicolored 5.00 5.00
Nos. 214-217 (4) 12.50 12.50

Pendant — A30

Designs: Various jewelry.

1975, Apr. 1 Photo. *Perf. 14½x14*

218 A30 30f olive & multi 1.60 1.60
219 A30 60f dp pur & multi 3.00 3.00
220 A30 120f dp car & multi 5.25 5.25
221 A30 150f dp blue & multi 6.75 6.75
Nos. 218-221 (4) 16.60 16.60

Woman Planting Flower, IWY Emblem — A31

60f, Educated woman holding IWY emblem.

1975, July 28 Litho. *Perf. 14½*

222 A31 30f multicolored 2.40 2.40
223 A31 60f multicolored 5.50 5.50

International Women's Year.

Miniature Sheet

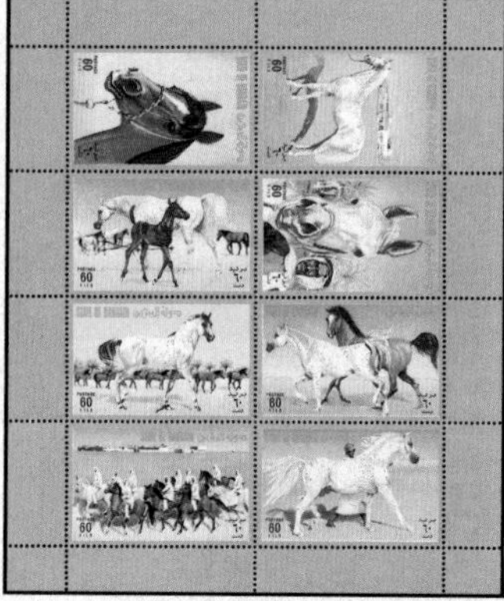

Arabian Stallion — A32

No. 224 — Arabian horses: a, Brown head. b, White mare. c, Mare and foal. d, White head. e, White mare. f, Mare and stallion. g, Bedouins on horseback. Nos. 224a, 224b, 224d are vert.

Perf. 14x14½, 14½x14

1975, Sept. 1 Photo.

224 Sheet of 8 70.00 37.50
a.-h. A32 60f any single 8.25 4.00

Flag of Bahrain — A33

Map of Bahrain — A34

Sheik Isa — A35

1976-80 Litho. *Perf. 14½*

225 A33 5f red & ultra .40 .25
226 A33 10f red & green .40 .25
227 A33 15f red & black .40 .25
228 A33 20f red & brown .55 .25
228A A34 25f gray & blk ('79) .80 .25
229 A34 40f blue & black .80 .30
229A A34 50f yel grn & blk ('79) .80 .45
230 A34 60f dl grn & blk ('77) 1.10 .55
231 A34 80f rose lil & blk 1.90 .80
232 A34 100f lt red brn & blk ('77) 1.90 1.00
233 A34 150f org & black 3.25 1.40
234 A34 200f yel & black 4.25 1.90

Engr.

Perf. 12x12½

235 A35 300f lt grn & grn 6.25 3.00
236 A35 400f pink & red brn 8.25 4.50
237 A35 500f lt bl & dk bl 10.50 5.25
238 A35 1d gray & sepia 17.50 8.00
239 A35 2d rose & vio ('80) 27.50 12.50
240 A35 3d buff & brn ('80) 57.50 24.00
Nos. 225-240 (18) 144.05 64.90

A later printing of the 100f-200f, and possibly others, has a larger printer's imprint at bottom.

Concorde at London Airport — A36

Designs: No. 245, Concorde at Bahrain Airport. No. 246, Concorde over London to Bahrain map. No. 247, Concorde on runway at night.

1976, Jan. 22 Photo. *Perf. 13x14*

244 A36 80f gold & multi 3.75 2.75
245 A36 80f gold & multi 3.75 2.75
246 A36 80f gold & multi 3.75 2.75
247 A36 80f gold & multi 3.75 2.75
a. Souvenir sheet of 4 18.00 18.00
b. Block of 4, #244-247 17.00 16.00

1st commercial flight of supersonic jet Concorde, London to Bahrain, Jan. 21. No. 247a contains 4 stamps with simulated perfs.

Soldier, Flag and Arms of Bahrain — A37

1976, Feb. 5 Litho. *Perf. 14½*

248 A37 40f yellow & multi 3.50 3.50
249 A37 80f lt blue & multi 6.50 6.50

Defense Force Day.

Sheik Isa, King Khalid, Bahrain and Saudi Flags A38

1976, Mar. 23 Litho. *Perf. 14½*

250 A38 40f gold & multi 4.50 2.25
251 A38 80f silver & multi 8.00 4.00

Visit of King Khalid of Saudi Arabia.

New Housing, Housing Ministry's Seal — A39

1976, Dec. 16 Litho. *Perf. 14½*

252 A39 40f rose & multi 3.00 2.00
253 A39 80f blue & multi 6.00 4.00

National Day.

APU Emblem A40

1977, Apr. 12 Litho. *Perf. 14½*

254	A40 40f silver & multi	2.00	1.90
255	A40 80f rose & multi	5.00	4.25

Arab Postal Union, 25th anniversary.

Miniature Sheet

Saluki dogs — A41

No. 256 — Saluki dogs: a, Dogs on Beach and Dhow. b, Dog and camels. c, Dog and gazelles. d, Dog and Ruler's Palace. e, Dog's head. f, Heads of two dogs. g, Dog in dunes. h, Playing dogs.

1977, July Photo. *Perf. 14x14½*

256	Sheet of 8	42.50	42.50
a.-h.	A41 80f any single	5.00	4.50

Students and Candle A42

1977, Sept. 8 Litho. *Perf. 14½*

257	A42 40f multicolored	2.50	2.50
258	A42 80f multicolored	4.75	4.75

International Literacy Day.

Shipyard and Flags A43

1977, Dec. 16 Litho. *Perf. 14½*

259	A43 40f multicolored	2.50	1.75
260	A43 80f multicolored	5.00	3.50

Inauguration of Arab Shipbuilding and Repair Yard Co.

Antenna, ITU Emblem A44

1978, May 17 Litho. *Perf. 14½*

261	A44 40f yellow & multi	2.00	1.75
262	A44 80f silver & multi	4.25	3.50

10th World Telecommunications Day.

Ghanja Dhow — A45

Dhows of the Arabian Gulf. Nos. 267-270 vertical.

Perf. 14x14½, 14½x14

1979, June 16 Photo.

263	A45 100f shown	6.00	6.00
264	A45 100f Zarook	6.00	6.00
265	A45 100f Shu'ai	6.00	6.00
266	A45 100f Jaliboot	6.00	6.00
267	A45 100f Baghla	6.00	6.00
268	A45 100f Sambuk	6.00	6.00
269	A45 100f Boom	6.00	6.00
270	A45 100f Kotia	6.00	6.00
a.	Block of 8, #263-270	70.00	70.00

Learning to Walk — A46

IYC Emblem and: 100f, Hands surrounding girl, UN emblem.

1979 Litho. *Perf. 14½*

271	A46 50f multicolored	3.00	2.25
272	A46 100f multicolored	5.50	4.50

International Year of the Child.

Hegira, 1,500th Anniv. — A47

1980 Photo. *Perf. 13x13½*

273	A47 50f multicolored	.75	.75
274	A47 100f multicolored	1.50	1.50
a.	Miniature sheet of 1	12.00	12.00
275	A47 150f multicolored	2.75	2.75
276	A47 200f multicolored	4.00	4.00
	Nos. 273-276 (4)	9.00	9.00

Falcon A48

Various falcons.

Perf. 13½x14, 14x13½

1980, Nov. 1 Photo.

277	Block of 8	37.50	22.50
a.-h.	A48 100f any single	4.50	2.75

IYD Emblem, Sheik Isa A49

1981, Mar. 21 Litho. *Perf. 14½*

278	A49 50f multicolored	3.50	2.50
279	A49 100f multicolored	6.50	5.25

International Year of the Disabled.

50th Anniversary of Electricity in Bahrain — A50

1981, Apr. 26 Litho. *Perf. 14½*

280	A50 50f multicolored	3.50	2.25
281	A50 100f multicolored	6.50	4.00

Stone Cutting — A51

1981, July 1 Photo. *Perf. 14x13½*

282	A51 50f shown	1.10	.95
283	A51 100f Pottery	2.00	1.60
284	A51 150f Weaving	4.00	3.75
285	A51 200f Basket making	4.50	4.00
	Nos. 282-285 (4)	11.60	10.30

Hegira (Pilgrimage Year) — A52

Various mosques.

1981, Oct. 1 Photo. *Perf. 14x13½*

286	A52 50f multicolored	1.25	1.00
287	A52 100f multicolored	2.25	1.90
288	A52 150f multicolored	3.00	2.75
289	A52 200f multicolored	4.75	4.00
	Nos. 286-289 (4)	11.25	9.65

Sheik Isa, 20th Anniv. of Coronation A53

1981, Dec. 16 Photo. *Perf. 14x13½*

290	A53 15f multicolored	.90	.55
291	A53 50f multicolored	1.50	1.25
292	A53 100f multicolored	2.50	2.00
293	A53 150f multicolored	4.00	3.25
294	A53 200f multicolored	5.50	3.75
	Nos. 290-294 (5)	14.40	10.80

Wildlife in al Areen Park — A54

No. 295: a, Gazelle. b, Oryx. c, Dhub lizard. d, Arabian hares. e, Oryxes. f, Reems.

1982, Mar. 1 Photo. *Perf. 13½x14*

295	Sheet of 6	18.00	18.00
a.-f.	A54 100f any single	2.75	2.75

3rd Session of Gulf Supreme Council, Nov. — A55

1982, Nov. 9 Litho. *Perf. 14½*

296	A55 50f blue & multi	1.50	1.50
297	A55 100f green & multi	3.75	3.75

Opening of Madinat Hamad Housing Development — A56

1983, Dec. 1 Litho. *Perf. 14½*

298	A56 50f multicolored	2.00	1.40
299	A56 100f multicolored	5.00	4.00

Al Khalifa Dynasty Bicentenary — A57

No. 300 — Sheiks or emblems: a, 500fr, Isa bin Sulman. b, Emblem (tan & multi). c, Isa bin Ali, 1869-1932. d, Hamad bin Isa, 1932-42. e, Sulman bin Hamad, 1942-61. f, Emblem (pale green & multi). g, Emblem (lemon & multi). h, Emblem (light blue & multi). i, Emblem (gray & multi).

1983, Dec. 16 Litho. *Perf. 14½*

300	Sheet of 9	14.50	14.50
a.-i.	A57 100f any single	1.40	1.40

Souvenir Sheet

301	A57 500f multicolored	12.50	12.50

No. 301 contains one stamp 60x38mm.

Gulf Co-operation Council Traffic Week — A58

1984, Apr. 30 Litho. *Perf. 14½*

302	A58 15f multicolored	.75	.75
303	A58 50f multicolored	1.75	1.75
304	A58 100f multicolored	3.50	3.50
	Nos. 302-304 (3)	6.00	6.00

1984 Summer Olympics A59

1984, Sept. 15 *Perf. 14½*

305	A59 15f Hurdles	.30	.30
306	A59 50f Equestrian	1.10	1.10
307	A59 100f Diving	2.25	2.25
308	A59 150f Fencing	2.75	2.75
309	A59 200f Shooting	5.00	5.00
	Nos. 305-309 (5)	11.40	11.40

Postal Service Cent. A60

1984, Dec. 8 Photo. *Perf. 12x11½*

310	A60	15f multicolored	.65	.65
311	A60	50f multicolored	2.00	2.00
312	A60	100f multicolored	3.75	3.75
		Nos. 310-312 (3)	6.40	6.40

Miniature Sheet

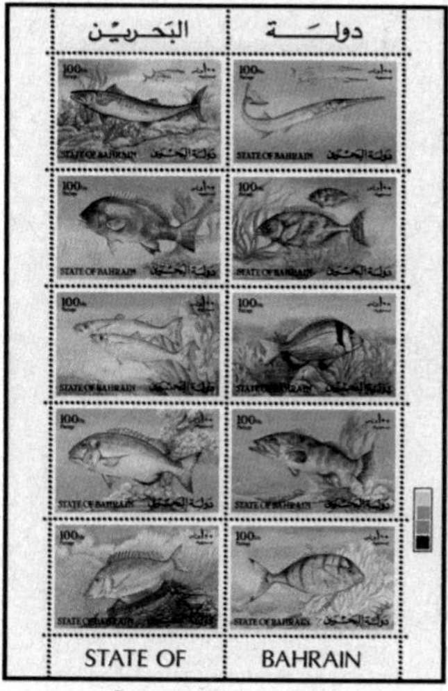

Coastal Fish — A61

Various fish.

1985, Feb. 10 Photo. *Perf. 13½x14*

313		Sheet of 10	30.00	30.00
a.-j.	A61	100f any single	3.00	3.00

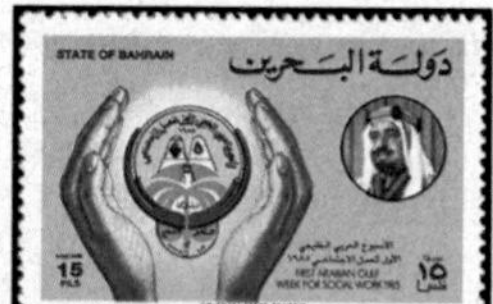

1st Arab Gulf States Week for Social Work A62

1985, Oct. 15 Litho. *Perf. 14½*

314	A62	15f multicolored	.65	.35
315	A62	50f multicolored	1.50	1.50
316	A62	100f multicolored	4.25	3.50
		Nos. 314-316 (3)	6.40	5.35

Intl. Youth Year A63

1985, Nov. 16

317	A63	15f multicolored	.65	.35
318	A63	50f multicolored	1.60	1.50
319	A63	100f multicolored	4.75	3.25
		Nos. 317-319 (3)	7.00	5.10

Bahrain-Saudi Arabia Causeway Opening — A64

1986, Nov. Litho. *Perf. 14½*

320	A64	15f Causeway, aerial view	.80	.80
321	A64	50f Island	2.00	2.00
322	A64	100f Causeway	3.50	3.50
		Nos. 320-322 (3)	6.30	6.30

Sheik Isa, 25th Anniv. as the Emir — A65

1986, Dec. 16

323	A65	15f multicolored	.65	.65
324	A65	50f multicolored	1.60	1.60
325	A65	100f multicolored	2.50	2.50
a.		Souvenir sheet of 3, #323-325	9.00	6.00
		Nos. 323-325 (3)	4.75	4.75

WHO, 40th Anniv. A66

1988, Apr. 30 Litho. *Perf. 14½*

326	A66	50f multicolored	1.00	1.00
327	A66	150f multicolored	2.50	2.50

Opening of Ahmed Al Fateh Islamic Center A67

1988, June 2 Litho. *Perf. 14½*

328	A67	50f multicolored	1.00	1.00
329	A67	150f multicolored	2.50	2.50

1988 Summer Olympics, Seoul — A68

1988, Sept. 17 Litho. *Perf. 14½*

330	A68	50f Running	.65	.65
331	A68	80f Equestrian	1.10	1.10
332	A68	150f Fencing	2.00	2.00
333	A68	200f Soccer	3.75	3.75
		Nos. 330-333 (4)	7.50	7.50

Gulf Cooperation Council Supreme Council 9th Regular Session, Bahrain — A69

1988, Dec. 19 Litho. *Perf. 14½*

334	A69	50f multicolored	1.00	1.00
335	A69	150f multicolored	2.50	2.00

Miniature Sheets

Camels — A70

No. 336: a, Close-up of head, rider in background. b, Camel kneeling at rest. c, Two adults, calf. d, Three adults. e, Camel facing right. f, Mount and rider (facing left).

No. 337, vert.: a, Man walking in front of camel, oil well. b, Man walking in front of camel. c, Oil well, camel's head. d, Mount and rider (facing forward). e, Mount and rider (facing right). f, Two dromedaries at a run.

Perf. 13½x14, 14x13½

1989, June 15

336		Sheet of 6	11.00	11.00
a.-f.		A70 150f any single	1.75	1.75
337		Sheet of 6	11.00	11.00
a.-f.		A70 150f any single	1.75	1.75

Sheik Isa — A71

1989, Dec. 16 Litho. *Perf. 13½x14*

338	A71	25f multicolored	.65	.25
339	A71	40f multicolored	.75	.30
340	A71	50f multicolored	.80	.35
341	A71	60f multicolored	.85	.40
342	A71	75f multicolored	.90	.50
343	A71	80f multicolored	.80	.55
344	A71	100f multicolored	.95	.65
345	A71	120f multicolored	1.25	.85
346	A71	150f multicolored	1.75	.95
347	A71	200f multicolored	2.00	1.40
a.		Souv. sheet of 10, #338-347	11.50	11.50
		Nos. 338-347 (10)	10.70	6.20

Houbara (Bustard) — A72

No. 348: a, Two birds facing right. b, Two birds facing each other. c, Chicks. d, Adult, chick. e, Adult, facing right, vert. f, In flight. g, Adult facing right. h, Chick, facing left, vert. i, Adult facing left. j, Adult male, close-up. k, Courtship display. l, Two birds facing left.

1990, Feb. 17 Photo. *Perf. 14*

348		Sheet of 12	23.00	23.00
a.-l.		A72 150f any single	1.40	1.40

Gulf Air, 40th Anniv. A73

1990, Mar. 24 Litho. *Perf. 14½*

360	A73	50f multicolored	.60	.60
361	A73	80f multicolored	1.00	1.00
362	A73	150f multicolored	2.00	2.00
363	A73	200f multicolored	3.00	3.00
		Nos. 360-363 (4)	6.60	6.60

Chamber of Commerce, 50th Anniv. — A74

1990, May 26

364	A74	50f multicolored	.60	.60
365	A74	80f multicolored	1.10	1.10
366	A74	150f multicolored	1.90	1.90
367	A74	200f multicolored	2.75	2.75
		Nos. 364-367 (4)	6.35	6.35

Intl. Literacy Year A75

1990, Sept. 8 Litho. *Perf. 14½*

368	A75	50f multicolored	.55	.55
369	A75	80f multicolored	.90	.90
370	A75	150f multicolored	1.75	1.75
371	A75	200f multicolored	2.25	2.25
		Nos. 368-371 (4)	5.45	5.45

Miniature Sheet

Indigenous Birds — A76

No. 372: a, Galerida cristata. b, Upupa epops. c, Pycnonotus leucogenys. d, Streptopelia turtur. e, Streptopelia decaocto. f, Falco tinnunculus. g, Passer domesticus, horiz. h, Lanius excubitor, horiz. i, Psittacula krameri.

1991, Sept. 15 Litho. *Perf. 14½*

372		Sheet of 9	22.50	22.50
a.-i.		A76 150f any single	2.10	2.10

See Nos. 382, 407.

Coronation of Sheik Isa, 30th Anniv. — A77

Design: Nos. 374, 376, 378, 380, 381a, Portrait at left, leaves.

Litho. & Embossed

1991, Dec. 16 *Perf. 14½*

373	A77	50f multicolored	.60	.60
374	A77	50f multicolored	.60	.60
375	A77	80f multicolored	1.00	1.00
376	A77	80f multicolored	1.00	1.00
377	A77	150f multicolored	2.00	2.00
378	A77	150f multicolored	2.00	2.00
379	A77	200f multicolored	2.75	2.75
380	A77	200f multicolored	2.75	2.75
		Nos. 373-380 (8)	12.70	12.70

Souvenir Sheet

Perf. 14x14½

381		Sheet of 2	12.50	12.50
a.-b.		A77 500f any single	5.75	5.75

No. 381 contains 41x31mm stamps.

Indigenous Birds Type of 1991

Miniature Sheet

No. 382: a, Ciconia ciconia. b, Merops apiaster. c, Sturnus vulgaris. d, Hypocolius ampelinus. e, Cuculus canorus. f, Turdus viscivorus. g, Coracias garrulus. h, Carduelis carduelis. i, Lanius collurio. j, Turdus iliacus, horiz. k, Motacilla alba, horiz. l, Oriolus oriolus, horiz. m, Erithacus rubecula. n, Luscinia luscinia. o, Muscicapa striata. p, Hirundo rustica.

1992, Mar. 21 Litho. *Perf. 14½*

382		Sheet of 16	30.00	30.00
a.-p.		A76 150f any single	1.50	1.50

Miniature Sheet

Horse Racing — A78

No. 383: a, Horses leaving starting gate. b, Trainers leading horses. c, Horses racing around turn. d, Horses in stretch racing by flags. e, Two horses racing by grandstand. f, Five horses galloping. g, Two brown horses racing. h, Black horse, gray horse racing.

1992, May 22

383 Sheet of 8 14.50 14.50
a.-h. A78 150f any single 1.40 1.40

1992 Summer Olympics, Barcelona — A79

1992, July 25 Litho. *Perf. 14½*

384 A79 50f Equestrian .65 .65
385 A79 80f Running 1.00 1.00
386 A79 150f Judo 2.00 2.00
387 A79 200f Cycling 2.75 2.75
Nos. 384-387 (4) 6.40 6.40

Bahrain Intl. Airport, 60th Anniv. A80

1992, Oct. 27 Litho. *Perf. 14½*

388 A80 50f multicolored .50 .50
389 A80 80f multicolored .90 .90
390 A80 150f multicolored 1.75 1.75
391 A80 200f multicolored 2.50 2.50
Nos. 388-391 (4) 5.65 5.65

Children's Art — A81

Designs: 50f, Girl jumping rope, vert. 80f, Women in traditional dress, vert. 150f, Women stirring kettle. 200f, Fishermen.

1992, Nov. 28 Litho. *Perf. 14½*

392 A81 50f multicolored .45 .45
393 A81 80f multicolored .80 .80
394 A81 150f multicolored 1.60 1.60
395 A81 200f multicolored 2.40 2.40
Nos. 392-395 (4) 5.25 5.25

Inauguration of Expansion of Aluminum Bahrain — A82

50f, Ore funicular. 80f, Smelting pot. 150f, Mill. 200f, Cylindrical aluminum ingots.

1992, Dec. 16

396 A82 50f multicolored .45 .45
397 A82 80f multicolored .80 .80
398 A82 150f multicolored 1.60 1.60
399 A82 200f multicolored 2.40 2.40
Nos. 396-399 (4) 5.25 5.25

Bahrain Defense Force, 25th Anniv. A83

Designs: 50f, Artillery forces, vert. 80f, Fighters, tanks, and ship, vert. 150f, Frigate. 200f, Jet fighter.

Perf. 13½x13, 13x13½

1993, Feb. 5 Litho.

400 A83 50f multicolored .55 .55
401 A83 80f multicolored .85 .85
402 A83 150f multicolored 1.60 1.60
403 A83 200f multicolored 2.25 2.25
Nos. 400-403 (4) 5.25 5.25

World Meteorology Day — A84

Designs: 50f, Satellite image of Bahrain, vert. 150f, Infrared satellite map of world. 200f, Earth, seen from space, vert.

1993, Mar. 23 Litho. *Perf. 14½*

404 A84 50f multicolored .85 .85
405 A84 150f multicolored 2.00 2.00
406 A84 200f multicolored 3.50 3.50
Nos. 404-406 (3) 6.35 6.35

Bird Type of 1991

Miniature Sheet

No. 407: a, Ardea purpurea. b, Gallinula chloropus. c, Phalacrocorax nigrogularis. d, Dromas ardeola. e, Alcedo atthis. f, Vanellus vanellus. g, Haematopus ostralegus, horiz. h, Nycticorax nycticorax. i, Sterna caspia, horiz. j, Arenaria interpres, horiz. k, Rallus aquaticus, horiz. l, Anas platyrhychos, horia. m, Larus fuscus, horiz.

1993, May 22 Litho. *Perf. 14½*

407 Sheet of 13 + 2 labels 27.50 27.50
a.-m. A76 150f any single 2.10 2.10

Gazella Subgutturosa Marica — A85

1993, July 24 Litho. *Perf. 14½*

408 A85 25f Calf 1.40 1.40
409 A85 50f Female standing 2.75 2.75
410 A85 50f Female walking 2.75 2.75
411 A85 150f Male 6.75 6.75
Nos. 408-411 (4) 13.65 13.65

World Wildlife Federation.

Wild Flowers — A86

Designs: a, Lycium shawii. b, Alhagi maurorum. c, Caparis spinosa. d, Cistanche phelypae. e, Asphodelus tenuifolius. f, Limonium axillare. g, Cynomorium coccineum. h, Calligonum polygonoides.

1993, Oct. 16 Litho. *Perf. 13½x13*

412 A86 150f Sheet of 8, #a.-h. 11.50 11.50

A87

1994, Jan. 22 Litho. *Perf. 14½*

Background Color

413 A87 50f yellow .75 .75
414 A87 80f blue green 1.10 1.10
415 A87 150f purple 1.75 1.75
416 A87 200f blue 2.75 2.75
Nos. 413-416 (4) 6.35 6.35

Intl. Year of the Family.

Butterflies — A88

No. 417: a, Lepidochrysops arabicus. b, Ypthima bolanica. c, Eurema brigitta. d, Precis limnoria. e, Aglais urticae. f, Colotis protomedia. g, Salamis anacardii. h, Byblia ilithyia.

No. 418: a, Papilio machaon. b, Agrodiaetus loewii. c, Vanessa cardui. d, Papilio demoleus. e, Hamanumida daedalus. f, Funonia orithya. g, Funonia chorimine. h, Colias croceus.

Perf. 13½x13, 13x13½

1994, Mar. 21 Litho.

417 A88 50f Sheet of 8, #a.-h. 4.00 4.00
418 A88 150f Sheet of 8, #a.-h. 12.00 12.00

No. 418 is horiz.

A89

1994, May 8 Litho. *Perf. 14½*

419 A89 50f lilac & multi .80 .80
420 A89 80f yellow & multi 1.10 1.10
421 A89 150f salmon & multi 2.10 2.10
422 A89 200f green blue & multi 3.00 3.00
Nos. 419-422 (4) 7.00 7.00

Intl. Red Cross & Red Crescent Societies, 75th anniv.

1994 World Cup Soccer Championships, US — A90

Designs: 50f, Goalkeeper. 80f, Heading ball. 150f, Dribbling ball. 200f, Slide tackle.

1994, June 17 Litho. *Perf. 14*

423 A90 50f multicolored .75 .75
424 A90 80f multicolored 1.00 1.00
425 A90 150f multicolored 1.75 1.75
426 A90 200f multicolored 2.75 2.75
Nos. 423-426 (4) 6.25 6.25

Bahrain's First Satellite Earth Station, 25th Anniv. — A91

1994, July 14

427 A91 50f blue & multi .75 .75
428 A91 80f yellow & multi 1.10 1.10
429 A91 150f violet & multi 2.10 2.10
430 A91 200f pink, yellow & multi 3.25 3.25
Nos. 427-430 (4) 7.20 7.20

Education in Bahrain, 75th Anniv. — A92

1994, Nov. 19 Litho. *Perf. 14½*

431 A92 50f yellow & multi .75 .75
432 A92 80f buff & multi 1.00 1.00
433 A92 150f salmon & multi 1.90 1.90
434 A92 200f pink & multi 2.75 2.75
Nos. 431-434 (4) 6.40 6.40

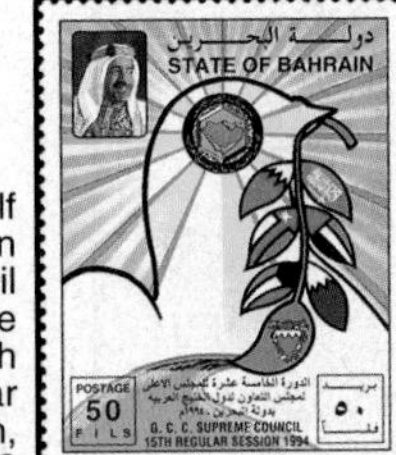

Gulf Cooperation Council Supreme Council, 15th Regular Session, Bahrain — A93

1994, Dec. 19 *Perf. 14*

435 A93 50f blue green & multi .75 .75
436 A93 80f brown & multi 1.00 1.00
437 A93 150f lilac rose & multi 1.75 1.75
438 A93 200f blue & multi 2.75 2.75
Nos. 435-438 (4) 6.25 6.25

Date Palm A94

Designs: 80f, Flowering stage. 100f, Dates beginning to ripen. 200f, Dates up close. 250f, Trees from distance.

500f, Pitcher, basket of dates.

1995, Mar. 21 Litho. *Perf. 14*

439	A94	80f multicolored	.55	.55
440	A94	100f multicolored	.70	.70
441	A94	200f multicolored	1.50	1.50
442	A94	250f multicolored	1.75	1.75
		Nos. 439-442 (4)	4.50	4.50

Souvenir Sheet

443	A94	500f multicolored	4.25	4.25

No. 443 contains one 65x48mm stamp.

Fight Against Polio A95

1995, Apr. 22 Litho. *Perf. 13x13½*

444	A95	80f pink & multi	.65	.65
445	A95	200f blue & multi	1.60	1.60
446	A95	250f lt brown & multi	2.50	2.50
		Nos. 444-446 (3)	4.75	4.75

World Health Day.

1st Natl. Industries Exhibition A96

1995, May 15

447	A96	80f blue green & multi	.60	.60
448	A96	200f lilac & multi	1.50	1.50
449	A96	250f lt brown & multi	2.25	2.25
		Nos. 447-449 (3)	4.35	4.35

FAO, 50th Anniv. A97

Fields of various crops.

1995, June 17 Litho. *Perf. 14*

450	A97	80f lilac & multi	.60	.60
451	A97	200f blue & multi	1.90	1.90
452	A97	250f lt pink & multi	2.75	2.75
		Nos. 450-452 (3)	5.25	5.25

Arab League, 50th Anniv. — A98

1995, Sept. 14 Litho. *Perf. 14½*

453	A98	80f pink & multi	.65	.65
454	A98	200f blue & multi	1.60	1.60
455	A98	250f yellow & multi	2.50	2.50
		Nos. 453-455 (3)	4.75	4.75

UN, 50th Anniv. A99

1995, Oct. 24 Litho. *Perf. 14½*

456	A99	80f yellow & multi	.60	.60
457	A99	100f green & multi	1.00	1.00
458	A99	200f pink & multi	2.00	2.00
459	A99	250f blue & multi	2.75	2.75
		Nos. 456-459 (4)	6.35	6.35

Miniature Sheet

Traditional Architecture — A100

No. 460 — Example of architecture, detail: a, Tower with balcony. b, Arched windows behind balcony. c, Double doors under arch. d, Four rows of square windows above row of arched windows. e, Door flanked by two windows. f, Three windows.

1995, Nov. 20 Litho. *Perf. 14½*

460	A100	200f Sheet of 6, #a.-f.	10.00	10.00

National Day — A101

1995, Dec. 16 Litho. *Perf. 14½*

461	A101	80f blue & multi	.85	.85
462	A101	100f green & multi	1.10	1.10
463	A101	200f violet & multi	2.40	2.40
464	A101	250f blue grn & multi	2.75	2.75
		Nos. 461-464 (4)	7.10	7.10

Public Library, 50th Anniv. — A102

1996, Mar. 23 Litho. *Perf. 14*

465	A102	80f pink & multi	.75	.75
466	A102	200f green & multi	2.00	2.00
467	A102	250f blue & multi	2.50	2.50
		Nos. 465-467 (3)	5.25	5.25

Pearl Diving — A103

Designs: 80f, Group of divers on ship, three in water. 100f, Five divers in water, ship. 200f, Diver underneath water. 250f, Diver being pulled up, underwater scene.

500f, Lantern, weight, scales, pearls, knife.

1996, May 8 Litho. *Perf. 14*

468	A103	80f multicolored	.90	.90
469	A103	100f multicolored	1.25	1.25
470	A103	200f multicolored	2.50	2.50
471	A103	250f multicolored	3.00	3.00
		Nos. 468-471 (4)	7.65	7.65

Souvenir Sheet

Perf. 14½

472	A103	500f multicolored	6.50	6.50

No. 472 contains one 70x70mm stamp.

1996 Summer Olympics, Atlanta — A104

1996, July 19 Litho. *Perf. 14*

473	A104	80f olive & multi	.85	.85
474	A104	100f pink & multi	1.10	1.10
475	A104	200f blue grn & multi	2.40	2.40
476	A104	250f orange & multi	2.75	2.75
		Nos. 473-476 (4)	7.10	7.10

Interpol, Intl. Criminal Police Organization — A105

1996, Sept. 25 Litho. *Perf. 14*

477	A105	80f blue & multi	1.00	1.00
478	A105	100f yellow & multi	1.25	1.25
479	A105	200f pink & multi	2.75	2.75
480	A105	250f green & multi	3.50	3.50
		Nos. 477-480 (4)	8.50	8.50

Aluminum Production in Bahrain, 25th Anniv. — A106

1996, Nov. 20 Litho. *Perf. 14*

481	A106	80f bister & multi	1.00	1.00
482	A106	100f orange & multi	1.25	1.25
483	A106	200f blue & multi	2.75	2.75
484	A106	250f green & multi	3.50	3.50
		Nos. 481-484 (4)	8.50	8.50

Accession to the Throne by Sheik Isa Bin Salman Al Khalifa, 35th Anniv. — A107

1996, Dec. 16

485	A107	80f gray & multi	.80	.45
486	A107	100f green & multi	1.10	.60
487	A107	200f pink & multi	2.25	1.25
488	A107	250f blue & multi	2.75	1.60
		Nos. 485-488 (4)	6.90	3.90

Bahrain Refinery, 60th Anniv. — A108

1997, Jan. 15 Litho. *Perf. 14*

489	A108	80f red & multi	1.25	1.25
490	A108	200f blue & multi	3.00	3.00
491	A108	250f yellow & multi	3.25	3.25
		Nos. 489-491 (3)	7.50	7.50

Pure Strains of Arabian Horses, Amiri Stud A109

No. 492: a, Musannaan, Al-Jellabieh, Rabdaan. b, Kuheilaan weld umm zorayr. c, Al-Jellaby. d, Musannaan. e, Kuheilaan aladiyat. f, Kuheilaan aafas. g, Al-Dhahma. h, Mlolshaan. i, Al-Kray. j, Krush. k, Al Hamdaany. l, Hadhfaan. m, Rabda. n, Al-Suwaitieh. o, Al-Obeyah. p, Al-Shuwaimeh. q, Al-Ma'anaghieh. r, Al-Tuwaisah. s, Wadhna. t, Al-Saqlawieh. u, Al-Shawafah.

1997, Apr. 23 Litho. *Perf. 14x14½*

492	A109	200f Sheet of 21, #a.-u.	40.00	40.00

9th Men's Junior World Volleyball Championship — A110

1997, Aug. 21 Litho. *Perf. 14x14½*

493	A110	80f brown & multi	1.00	1.00
494	A110	100f green & multi	1.25	1.25
495	A110	200f gray brn & multi	2.40	2.40
496	A110	250f blue & multi	2.75	2.75
		Nos. 493-496 (4)	7.40	7.40

Montreal Protocol on Substances that Deplete Ozone Layer, 10th Anniv. — A111

1997, Sept. 16 Litho. *Perf. 14½*

497	A111	80f yellow & multi	.75	.75
498	A111	100f purple & multi	1.00	1.00
499	A111	200f red & multi	2.00	2.00
500	A111	250f green & multi	2.75	2.75
		Nos. 497-500 (4)	6.50	6.50

Sheikh Isa Bin Salman Bridge A112

Designs: 80f, Pylon, supports. 200f, Center of bridge. 250f, 500f, Entire span.

1997, Dec. 28 Litho. *Perf. 13x13½*

501	A112	80f multicolored	1.10	1.10
502	A112	200f multicolored	2.50	2.50

Size: 76x26mm

503	A112	250f multicolored	2.75	2.75
		Nos. 501-503 (3)	6.35	6.35

Souvenir Sheet

504	A112	500f multicolored	5.00	5.00

Inuaguration of Urea Plant, GPIC (Refinery) Complex — A113

Designs: 80f, View of plant from Persian Gulf. 200f, Plant facilities. 250f, Aerial view.

1998, Mar. 3 Litho. *Perf. 13x13½*
505 A113 80f multicolored .80 .80
506 A113 200f multicolored 2.25 2.25
507 A113 250f multicolored 3.25 3.25
Nos. 505-507 (3) 6.30 6.30

World Health Organization, 50th Anniv. — A114

1998, May 11 Litho. *Perf. 14*
508 A114 80f orange & multi 1.00 1.00
509 A114 200f green & multi 2.25 2.25
510 A114 250f gray & multi 2.75 2.75
Nos. 508-510 (3) 6.00 6.00

1998 World Cup Soccer Championships, France — A115

Designs: 200f, Soccer balls, world maps, vert. 250f, Players, globe, vert.

1998, June 10
511 A115 80f multicolored 1.10 1.10
512 A115 200f multicolored 2.75 2.75
513 A115 250f multicolored 3.25 3.25
Nos. 511-513 (3) 7.10 7.10

14th Arabian Gulf Soccer Cup, Bahrain A116

Design: 200f, 250f, Soccer ball.

1998, Oct. 30 Litho. *Perf. 14*
514 A116 80f shown 1.10 1.10
515 A116 200f pale violet & multi 2.75 2.75
516 A116 250f bister & multi 3.25 3.25
Nos. 514-516 (3) 7.10 7.10

Grand Competition for Holy Koran Recitation A117

1999, Jan. 9 Litho. *Perf. 14*
517 A117 100f gray olive & multi 1.25 1.25
518 A117 200f yellow & multi 2.75 2.75
519 A117 250f green & multi 3.00 3.00
Nos. 517-519 (3) 7.00 7.00

Isa Bin Salman Al-Khalifa (1933-99), Emir of Bahrain — A118

Natl. flag, map and: 100f, 500f, Emir holding sword, vert. 250f, Portrait up close, vert.

Perf. 13¼ (#520, 522), 14¼ (#521)
1999, June 5 Litho.
520 A118 100f multicolored 1.10 1.10
521 A118 200f multicolored 2.50 2.50
522 A118 250f multicolored 3.75 3.75
Nos. 520-522 (3) 7.35 7.35

Souvenir Sheet
Perf. 14½x13
523 A118 500f multicolored 6.50 6.50

Nos. 520, 522 are 31x50mm. No. 523 contains one 67x102mm stamp.

Intl. Year of Older Persons A119

1999, Oct. 9 Litho. *Perf. 13x13½*
524 A119 100f multi 1.10 1.10
525 A119 200f multi, diff. 2.40 2.40
526 A119 250f multi, diff. 2.75 2.75
Nos. 524-526 (3) 6.25 6.25

Bahrain Stock Exchange, 10th Anniv. — A120

1999, Nov. 24 Litho. *Perf. 14¼*
527 A120 100f shown .60 .60
528 A120 200f Pearl Monument, bridge 1.40 1.40
529 A120 250f Globe 1.60 1.60
Nos. 527-529 (3) 3.60 3.60

Hamad Bin Isa Al-Khalifa, Emir of Bahrain — A121

Emir Hamad: 100f, 500f, Receiving flag from late Emir. 200f, And flag. 250f, And map.

1999, Dec. 16 Litho. *Perf. 14½*
531 A121 100f multi 1.25 1.25
532 A121 200f multi 2.40 2.40
533 A121 250f multi 2.75 2.75
Nos. 531-533 (3) 6.40 6.40

Souvenir Sheet
Perf. 13¼x12¾
534 A121 500f multi 5.00 5.00

Dilmun Culture Exhibition A122

Map of Bahrain and: 100f, Bull's head, seal. 200f, Bull's head. 250f, Seal.

2000, Feb. 26 Litho. *Perf. 14¼*
535 A122 100f multi 1.10 1.10
536 A122 200f multi 1.90 1.90
537 A122 250f multi 2.25 2.25
Nos. 535-537 (3) 5.25 5.25

Gulf Air, 50th Anniv. A123

Map of Bahrain and: 100f, Emblem, world map. 200f, Emblem. 250f, Birds.

2000, Mar. 24
538 A123 100f multi 1.25 1.25
539 A123 200f multi 2.40 2.40
540 A123 250f multi 2.75 2.75
Nos. 538-540 (3) 6.40 6.40

Made in Bahrain Exhibition — A124

2000, May 9 *Perf. 14½*
541 A124 100f shown 1.40 1.40
542 A124 200f Emblem, diff. 3.50 3.50
543 A124 250f Oil refinery 4.50 4.50
Nos. 541-543 (3) 9.40 9.40

Souvenir Sheet

Passage Through Time — A125

No. 544: a, Minarets, fort, flag on dhow's stern. b, Dhows, oil refinery. c, Minaret, date picker. d, Satellite dishes, fort, flag. e, Bridge, pool. f, Woman, jar, dhows. g, Dhows, coffee pot. h, Man with falcon, horse and rider. i, Pearl divers. j, Oyster shuckers. k, Men casting nets. l, Men repairing nets.

Litho. with Foil Application
2000, Oct. 9 *Perf. 14¼*
544 Sheet of 12 23.00 23.00
a.-d. A125 100f Any single 1.00 1.00
e.-h. A125 200f Any single 2.00 2.00
i.-l. A125 250f Any single 2.50 2.50

21st Supreme Council Session of the Gulf Co-operation Council — A126

Designs: 100f, Emblem. 200f, Flags.

2000, Dec. 30 Litho. *Perf. 14¼*
545-546 A126 Set of 2 4.50 4.50

Beit al-Quran, Manama — A127

Designs: 100f, Stained-glass window. 200f, Building illuminated at dusk. 250f, Building during day.
500f, Building during day, stained-glass window, building illuminated at dusk.

2001, Feb. 18 Litho. *Perf. 14¼*
547-549 A127 Set of 3 5.00 5.00

Size: 170x80mm
Imperf
550 A127 500f multi 5.00 5.00

Housing and Agriculture Ministry, 25th Anniv. — A128

Various buildings: 100f, 150f, 200f, 250f.

2001, Apr. 28 *Perf. 14¼*
551-554 A128 Set of 4 5.00 5.00

Intl. Volunteers Year — A129

Emblem and: 100f, Stylized people with arms raised, vert. 150f, Clasped hands. 200f, Stars. 250f, Stylized people holding hands.

2001, Sept. 29 Litho. *Perf. 14¼*
555-558 A129 Set of 4 7.25 7.25

Day of the Arab Woman A130

Designs: 100f, Emblem. 200f, Emblem and rings. 250f, Women, horiz.

2002, Feb. 1 Litho. *Perf. 14¼*
559-561 A130 Set of 3 5.75 5.75

Souvenir Sheet

2002 World Cup Soccer Championships, Japan and Korea — A131

No. 562: a, 100f. b, 200f, c, 250f.

2002, May 31
562 A131 Sheet of 3, #a-c 6.50 6.50

King Hamad — A132

2002, July 15 Litho. *Perf. 13½x13¾*
Background Color

563	A132	25f gray	.25	.25
564	A132	40f brt purple	.25	.25
565	A132	50f dark gray	.30	.30
566	A132	60f dk bl green	.50	.50
567	A132	80f blue	.60	.60
568	A132	100f orange brown	.85	.85
569	A132	125f cerise	.95	.95
570	A132	150f pinkish orange	1.25	1.25
571	A132	200f olive green	1.75	1.75
572	A132	250f rose pink	2.10	2.10
573	A132	300f tan	2.40	2.40
574	A132	400f dull green	3.00	3.00

Size: 26x36mm
Perf. 13¼x13

575	A132	500f rose violet	4.00	4.00
a.		Perf. 13¼x13x13¼x14	4.00	4.00
576	A132	1d dull orange	7.75	7.75
577	A132	2d gray blue	16.00	16.00
578	A132	3d brown violet	24.00	24.00
a.		Souvenir sheet, #563-574, 575a, 576-578	67.50	67.50
		Nos. 563-578 (16)	65.95	65.95

World Teachers' Day — A133

Background color: 100f, Gray green. 200f, Gray.

2002, Oct. 5 Litho. *Perf. 13¼x13*
579-580 A133 Set of 2 3.00 3.00

Parliamentary Elections — A134

Designs: 100f, Flag. 200f, Hand placing ballot in box, vert.

2002, Oct. 24 *Perf. 13x13¼, 13¼x13*
581-582 A134 Set of 2 2.75 2.75

National Day — A135

King Hamad, flag and background color of: 100f, Gray. 200f, Brown violet, vert. 250f, Dark red, vert.

Perf. 13x13¼, 13¼x13
2002, Dec. 16 Litho.
583-585 A135 Set of 3 5.75 5.75

Arab Summit Conference 2003 A136

No. 586: a, Bahrain. b, Sudan. c, Saudi Arabia. d, Djibouti. e, Algeria. f, Tunisia. g, United Arab Emirates. h, Jordan. i, Comoro Islands. j, Qatar. k, Palestine. l, Oman. m, Iraq. n, Somalia. o, Syria. p, Yemen. q, Mauritania. r, Morocco. s, Egypt. t, Libya. u, Lebanon. v, Kuwait.

500f, Montage of scenes.

Litho. With Foil Application
2003, Mar. 1 *Perf. 13*

586		Sheet of 22	40.00	40.00
a.-h.	A136	100f Any single	.95	.95
i.-o.	A136	200f Any single	2.00	2.00
p.-v.	A136	250f Any single	2.25	2.25

Size: 120x103mm
Imperf

587 A136 500f multi 4.50 4.50

World Health Day A137

UN and Healthy Environments for Children Emblems and: 100f, Children, flowers. 200f, Stylized children.

2003, Apr. 7 Litho. *Perf. 14¼*
588-589 A137 Set of 2 3.25 3.25

World Environment Day — A138

No. 590: a, Swan. b, Peacock. c, Flamingo. d, Ostrich. e, Rumex vesicarius. f, Arnebia hispidissima. g, Capparis spinosa. h, Cassia italica. i, Crab. j, Turtle. k, Sting ray. l, Shark.

2003, June 5 *Perf. 13*

590		Sheet of 12	24.00	24.00
a.-d.	A138	100f Any single	1.00	1.00
e.-h.	A138	200f Any single	2.00	2.00
i.-l.	A138	250f Any single	3.00	3.00

Intl. Children's Day — A139

No. 591, vert.: a, 100f, Child reading book. b, 150f, Child looking at flowers.

No. 592: a, 200f, Children in field. b, 250f, Children in classroom.

2003, Nov. 20 Litho. *Perf. 14¼*
Vert. Pairs, #a-b
591-592 A139 Set of 2 7.25 7.25

Printed in sheets containing four of each pair.

National Day — A140

King Hamad on horse with panel color of: 100f, Bronze. 200f, Gold. 250f, Silver.

500f, No panel.

Litho. with Foil Application
2003, Dec. 16 *Perf. 14½*
593-595 A140 Set of 3 4.75 4.75

Souvenir Sheet

596 A140 500f multi 4.25 4.25

No. 596 contains one 55x95mm stamp.

Mother's Day A141

Designs: 100f, Mother and infant. 200f, Mother reading to child.

2004, Mar. 21 Litho. *Perf. 13x13¼*
597-598 A141 Set of 2 2.50 2.50

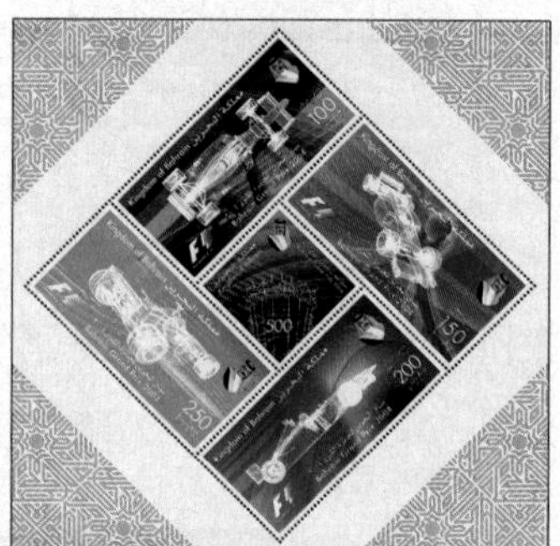
Bahrain Formula 1 Grand Prix — A142

No. 599: a, 100f, Race car, red background (76x36mm). b, 150f, Race car, green background (76x36mm). c, 200f, Race car, blue background (76x36mm). d, 250f, Race car, orange background (76x36mm). e, 500f, Race tower (51x51mm).

2004, Apr. 4 Litho. *Perf. 13*
599 A142 Sheet of 5, #a-e 10.00 10.00

Intl. Day Against Drugs A143

UN emblem and: 100f, People reaching out to addict. 150f, Addict's arm. 200f, Addict and snake-like needles. 250f, Arms reaching out.

2004, June 24 *Perf. 14¼*
600-603 A143 Set of 4 6.25 6.25

2004 Summer Olympics, Athens — A144

No. 604: a, 100f, Track. b, 150f, Swimming. c, 200f, Sailboarding. d, 250f, Shooting.

2004, Aug. 13
604 A144 Sheet of 4, #a-d 5.25 5.25

Gulf Cooperation Council, 25th Regular Session A145

Emblem and: 100f, Hands. 200f, Draped flags. 250f, Circle of flags.

500f, Bridge, boats and buildings.

2004, Dec. 20 Litho. *Perf. 14¼*
605-607 A145 Set of 3 3.00 3.00

Souvenir Sheet
Perf. 13¼

608 A145 500f multi 2.75 2.75

No. 608 contains one 175x54mm stamp.

Bahrain Garden Fair A146

Emblem and various flowers: 100f, 200f, 250f.

2005, Mar. 3 *Perf. 13x13¼*
609-611 A146 Set of 3 3.75 3.75

Inauguration of Constitutional Court — A147

Background colors: 100f, Brown black. 200f, Orange brown. 250f, Blue.

2005, Apr. 18 *Perf. 14½*
612-614 A147 Set of 3 4.00 4.00

Discovery of Artifacts of Dilmon Civilization, 50th Anniv. — A148

Designs: No. 615, 100f, Figurine of human. No. 616, 100f, Sculpted discs. No. 617, 100f, Equestrian statue. No. 618, 200f, Overturned jar and artifacts. No. 619, 200f, Two jars. No. 620, 200f, Jar and lidded jar. No. 621, 250f, Wall, horiz. No. 622, 250f, Steps, horiz. No. 623, 250f, Aerial view of archaeological site, horiz.

500f, Wall, Arab and Western men, horiz.

2005, Apr. 27 Litho. *Perf. 14¼*
615-623 A148 Set of 9 7.75 7.75
623a Minaiture sheet, #615-623 7.75 7.75

Souvenir Sheet

Perf. 14½

624 A148 500f multi 3.75 3.75

No. 624 contains one 88x58mm stamp.

National Day A149

King Hamad and various buildings: 100f, 200f, 250f. 200f is vert.

2005, Dec. 16 Litho. *Perf. 14¼*
625-627 A149 Set of 3 3.00 3.00

A150

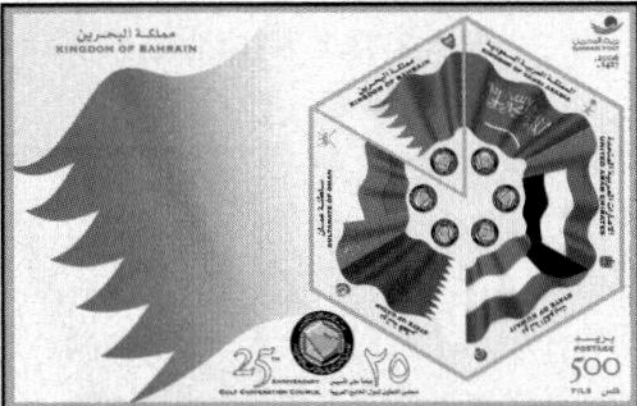

Gulf Cooperation Council, 25th Anniv. — A151

Litho. With Foil Application

2006, May 25 *Perf. 14*
628 A150 100f multi 1.75 1.75

Imperf

Size: 165x105mm

629 A151 500f multi 4.00 4.00

See Kuwait Nos. 1646-1647, Oman Nos. 477-478, Qatar Nos. 1107-1108, Saudi Arabia No. 1378, and United Arab Emirates Nos. 831-832.

2006 World Cup Soccer Championships, Germany — A152

Emir Hamad and: 100f, Emblem. 200f, Emblem, globe, soccer ball, spheres. 250f, Emblem, globe.

2006, June 9 Litho. *Perf. 14¼*
630-632 A152 Set of 3 3.25 3.25

National Day — A153

King Hamad: 100f, Holding flag and book. 200f, With crown above head. 250f, With crown above head, profile portrait. 500f, Like 100f (36x50mm).

Perf. 14¼, 14 (500f)

2006, Dec. 16 Litho.
633-636 A153 Set of 4 5.75 5.75

Gulf Cooperation Council Consumer Protection Day — A154

Designs: 100d, Gulf Cooperation Council emblem, people under umbrella. 200d, People under umbrella of Gulf Cooperation Council flags.

2007, Mar. 1 *Perf. 13x13¼*
637-638 A154 Set of 2 1.60 1.60

Each stamp printed in sheet of 20 + 5 labels.

National Day — A155

King Hamad: 100f, And crown. 200f, Waving, horiz. 250f, With men, boats, horsemen, horiz.

2007, Dec. 16 Litho. *Perf. 14¼*
639-641 A155 Set of 3 3.00 3.00
640a Souvenir sheet, 2 each #639-640, perf. 13¼ 3.25 3.25

Arab Productive Families Day — A156

Hands of: 100f, Wood carver and basket weaver. 200f, Decoration nailer and seamstress.

2008, Mar. 15 *Perf. 13¼*
642-643 A156 Set of 2 1.60 1.60

Intl. Nurses Day A157

Designs: 100f, Operating room. 200f, Nurses and child.

2008, May 12 *Perf. 14¼*
644-645 A157 Set of 2 1.60 1.60

Third Session of Ministerial Meeting of Arab-Chinese Cooperation Forum, Manama — A158

Emblem, Great Wall of China and: 100f, Arch. 200f, Building.

2008, May 21 *Perf. 13*
646-647 A158 Set of 2 1.60 1.60

"Business Friendly" Advertising Campaign — A159

Text "Business Friendly" in various styles: 100f, 200f.

2008, Aug. 1 Litho. *Perf. 13¼x13*
648-649 A159 Set of 2 2.00 2.00

Souvenir Sheet

2008 Summer Olympics, Beijing — A160

No. 650: a, 100f, Runner crossing finish line. b, 200f, Equestrian.

2008, Aug. 8 *Perf. 14x13*
650 A160 Sheet of 2, #a-b 2.00 2.00

Miniature Sheets

A161

Bahraini Ardha — A162

No. 651 — Color of sky: a, Purple. b, Red brown. c, Blue gray. d, Red violet. e, Gray. f, Yellow orange. g, Blue green. h, Dull brown.

No. 652 — Man in foreground: a, Carrying flag. b, In white robes. c, In red orange robes holding sword.

2008, Dec. 16 *Perf. 13¼x13*
651 A161 100f Sheet of 8, #a-h 5.00 5.00

Perf. 14

652 A162 200f Sheet of 3, #a-c 3.25 3.25

First Gulf Cooperation Council and Association of South East Asian Nations Ministerial Meeting, Manama A163

Emblems and: 100f, Dhow. 200f, Dhow, diff.

2009, June 29 Litho. *Perf. 14¼*
653-654 A163 Set of 2 1.75 1.75

Souvenir Sheet

Arab Postal Day — A164

No. 655 — Emblem and: a, World map, pigeon. b, Camel caravan.

Litho. With Foil Application

2009, Aug. 3 *Perf. 13¼*
655 A164 500f Sheet of 2, #a-b 5.75 5.75

Palm Tree Symposium — A165

2009, Nov. 10 Litho. *Perf. 14¼*
656 A165 100f multi .65 .65

A166

Bahraini Women's Day A167

2009, Dec. 1 *Perf. 13x13¼*
657 A166 100f multi .65 .65
658 A167 200f multi 1.10 1.10

Miniature Sheet

Education in Bahrain, 90th Anniv. — A168

No. 659: a, 100f, Boys outside of school building. b, 100f, Students in math class. c, 200f, Student holding soldering iron. d, 200f, Graduates. e, 250f, Teacher pointing to diagram. f, 250f, Students seated in class.

2009, Dec. 14 *Perf. 13¼x14¼*
659 A168 Sheet of 6, #a-f 6.75 6.75

National Day A169

Designs: 100f, Flag, map, King Hamad with crown above head, brown background at UL. 200f, As 100f, with blue background at UL. 250f, King Hamad with other sheikhs, buildings, map, horsemen, and flag.
500f, As 250f.

Litho. With Foil Application

2009, Dec. 16 ***Perf. 14¼***
660-662 A169 Set of 3 3.50 3.50

Size: 126x101mm

Imperf

663 A169 500f multi 5.75 5.75

Bahrain Intl. Airshow A170

Airshow emblem and: 100f, King Hamad, airplanes. 200f, Curved red lines.

2010, Jan. 21 Litho. ***Perf. 13¼x13***
664-665 A170 Set of 2 1.90 1.90

2010 World Cup Soccer Championships, South Africa — A171

2010 World Cup: 100f, Emblem. 200f, Mascot. 250f, Soccer ball, globe, horiz. (36x26mm).

Perf. 13, 13x13¼ (250f)

2010, June 11 **Litho.**
666-668 A171 Set of 3 3.00 3.00

World Post Day — A172

2010, Oct. 9 ***Perf. 13***
669 A172 250f multi 1.40 1.40

National Day — A173

King Hamad and stylized dove: 100f, Holding ballot above ballot box. 200f, Holding scales of justice. 250f, Writing, vert.

2010, Dec. 16 ***Perf. 14¼***
670-672 A173 Set of 3 3.00 3.00

Bahraini Women's Day — A174

King Hamad and: 100f, Round Supreme Council for Women 10th anniversary emblem. 200f, Rectangular emblem with circles.
500f, King Hamad and buildings.

2011, Dec. 1 ***Perf. 14¼***
673-674 A174 Set of 2 1.60 1.60

Souvenir Sheet

Perf. 13¼x13

675 A174 500f multi 2.75 2.75

No. 675 contains one 90x35mm stamp.

National Day — A175

King Hamad and: 100f, People, heart with Arabic inscription. 200f, Stylized bird over map of Bahrain. 250f, Stylized boat on water, vert.

2011, Dec. 16 ***Perf. 14¼***
676-678 A175 Set of 3 3.00 3.00

Discovery of Oil in Bahrain, 80th Anniv. — A176

Designs: 100f, Airplane over Bahrain Petroleum Company building. 150f, Bahrain Petroleum Company Center of Excellence. 200f, Bridge, man, boy, dhow. 250f, Oil tanks, solar energy facility.

2012, June 17
679-682 A176 Set of 4 3.75 3.75

Royal Charity Organization, 10th Anniv. — A177

2012, July 31
683 A177 250f multi 1.40 1.40

Arab Postal Day — A178

2012, Aug. 3 ***Perf. 12¾x13¼***
684 A178 250f multi 1.40 1.40

6th World Urban Forum, Naples, Italy A179

Emblem and: No. 685, 200f, United Nations Secretary-General Ban Ki-Moon giving award to King Hamad. No. 686, 200f, Bridge, city skyline. No. 687, 200f, Building with wind turbines.

2012, Sept. 1
685-687 A179 Set of 3 3.25 3.25
687a Souvenir sheet of 3, #685-687, perf. 13½x13 4.75 4.75

No. 687a sold for 900f.

Manama, 2012 Capital of Arab Culture A180

2012, Sept. 27 ***Perf. 14¼***
688 A180 200f multi 1.10 1.10

World Habitat Day A181

Designs: No. 689, 100f, Building, denomination in black. No. 690, 100f, Building, diff., denomination in white. No. 691, 100f, Buildings around pond.

2012, Oct. 1 ***Perf. 14¼***
689-691 A181 Set of 3 1.60 1.60

A souvenir sheet containing perf. 13½x13 examples of Nos. 689-691 sold for 900f.

Opening of National Theater, Manama A182

2012, Nov. 12
692 A182 250f multi 1.40 1.40

A183

33rd Supreme Council Summit of the Gulf Cooperation Council A184

Litho. With Foil Application

2012, Dec. 24
693 A183 200f multi 1.10 1.10
694 A184 200f multi 1.10 1.10

Insurance Day — A187

Bahrain Insurance Association emblem and: 100f, Dhows and stylized city skyline. 200f, House, automobile, airplane, medical bag, stethoscope. 250f, Insurance Day emblem.

2013, Mar. 26 Litho. ***Perf. 14¼***
698-700 A187 Set of 3 3.00 3.00

WAR TAX STAMPS

WT1

1973, Oct. 21 Litho. ***Perf. 14½***
MR1 WT1 5f sky blue *200.00 125.00*

Catalogue values for all unused stamps in this section, from this point to the end of the section, are for Never Hinged items.

WT2

1974 Litho. ***Perf. 14½***
MR2 WT2 5f light blue 7.00 .70
a. Perf. 14½x13½ 7.00

No. MR2a was issued around 1988.

BANGKOK

'baŋ,käk

LOCATION — Capital of Siam (Thailand)

Stamps were issued by Great Britain under rights obtained in the treaty of 1855. These were in use until July 1, 1885, when the stamps of Siam were designated as the only official postage stamps to be used in the kingdom.

100 Cents = 1 Dollar

Excellent counterfeits of Nos. 1-22 are plentiful.

Stamps of Straits Settlements Overprinted in Black

1882 Wmk. 1 *Perf. 14*

No.	Type	Value	Color	Unused	Used
1	A2	2c	brown	*4,500.*	*1,950.*
2	A2	4c	rose	*4,250.*	*1,650.*
b.			Double overprint		*9,750.*
3	A6	5c	brown violet	*475.*	*500.*
4	A2	6c	violet	*325.*	*150.*
5	A3	8c	yel orange	*3,250.*	290.
6	A7	10c	slate	*575.*	*190.*
7	A3	12c	blue	*1,200.*	*600.*
8	A3	24c	green	*900.*	*190.*
9	A4	30c	claret	*57,500.*	*39,000.*
10	A5	96c	olive gray	*9,750.*	*4,000.*

See note after No. 20.

1882-83 Wmk. 2

No.	Type	Value	Color	Unused	Used
11	A2	2c	brown	*600.00*	*450.00*
12	A2	2c	rose ('83)	*75.00*	*57.50*
a.			Inverted overprint	*19,000.*	*14,000.*
b.			Double overprint	*3,500.*	*3,500.*
c.			Triple overprint	*13,000.*	
13	A2	4c	rose	*800.00*	*400.00*
14	A2	4c	brown ('83)	*100.00*	*90.00*
a.			Double overprint	4,500.	
15	A6	5c	ultra ('83)	*325.00*	*210.00*
16	A2	6c	violet ('83)	*250.00*	*140.00*
a.			Double overprint	*9,000.*	
17	A3	8c	yel orange	*200.00*	*82.50*
a.			Inverted overprint	*27,000.*	*15,000.*
18	A7	10c	slate	*225.00*	*110.00*
19	A3	12c	violet brn ('83)	*375.00*	*190.00*
20	A3	24c	green	*7,500.*	*3,750.*

Double overprints must have two clear impressions. Partial double overprints exist on a number of values of these issues. They sell for a modest premium over catalogue value depending on how much of the impression is present.

1883 Wmk. 1

No.	Type	Value	Color	Unused	Used
21	A5	2c on 32c	pale red	*3,500.*	*3,500.*

On Straits Settlements No. 9

1885 Wmk. 38

No.	Type	Value	Color	Unused	Used
22	A7	32c on 2a	yel (B+B)	*45,000.*	—

BANGLADESH

,bäŋ-glə-'desh

LOCATION — In southern, central Asia, touching India, Burma, and the Bay of Bengal

GOVT. — Republic in the British Commonwealth

AREA — 55,598 sq. mi.

POP. — 127,117,967 (1999 est.)

CAPITAL — Dhaka (Dacca)

Bangladesh, formerly East Pakistan, broke away from Pakistan in April 1971, proclaiming its independence. It consists of 14 former eastern districts of Bengal and the former Sylhet district of Assam province of India.

100 Paisas = 1 Rupee

100 Paisas (Poishas) = 1 Taka (1972)

Catalogue values for all unused stamps in this country are for Never Hinged items.

Various stamps of Pakistan were handstamped locally for use in Bangladesh from March 26, 1971 until April 30, 1973. Thousands of varieties exist.

Map of Bangladesh A1

Sheik Mujibur Rahman A2

Designs: 20p, "Dacca University Massacre." 50p, "A Nation of 75 Million People." 1r, Flag of Independence (showing map). 2r, Ballot box. 3r, Broken chain. 10r, "Support Bangladesh" and map.

Perf. 14x14½

1971, July 29 Litho. Unwmk.

No.	Type	Value	Color	Unused	Used
1	A1	10p	red, dk pur & lt bl	.25	.25
2	A1	20p	bl, grn, red & yel	.25	.25
3	A1	50p	dp org, gray & brn	.25	.25
4	A1	1r	red, emer & yel	.30	.30
5	A1	2r	lil rose, lt & dk bl	.50	.50
6	A1	3r	blue, emer & grn	.60	.60
7	A2	5r	dp org, tan & blk	1.25	1.25
8	A1	10r	gold, dk bl & lil rose	2.00	2.00
			Nos. 1-8 (8)	5.40	5.40

A set of 15 stamps of types A1 and A2 in new paisa-taka values and colors was rejected by Bangladesh officials and not issued. Bangladesh representatives in England released these stamps, which were not valid, on Feb. 1, 1972. Value, set $8.

Imperfs of Nos. 1-8 were in the Format International liquidation. They are not errors.

Nos. 1-8 Overprinted in Black or Red

1971, Dec. 20

No.	Type	Value	Color	Unused	Used
9	A1	10p	multicolored	.25	.25
10	A1	20p	multicolored	.20	
11	A1	50p	multicolored	.35	
12	A1	1r	multicolored	.75	
13	A1	2r	multicolored	1.10	
14	A1	3r	multicolored	1.50	
15	A2	5r	multicolored (R)	4.00	4.00
16	A1	10r	multicolored	5.00	*5.00*
			Nos. 9-16 (8)	13.15	

Liberation of Bangladesh.

The 10p, 5r and 10r were issued in Dacca, but Nos. 10-14 were not put on sale in Bangladesh.

Monument — A3

1972, Feb. 21 Litho. *Perf. 13*

No.	Type	Value	Color	Unused	Used
32	A3	20p	green & rose	.70	.70

Language Movement Martyrs.

"Independence" A4

1972, Mar. 26 Photo. *Perf. 13*

No.	Type	Value	Color	Unused	Used
33	A4	20p	maroon & red	.35	.35
34	A4	60p	dark blue & red	.45	.45
35	A4	75p	purple & red	.60	.60
			Nos. 33-35 (3)	1.40	1.40

First anniversary of independence.

Doves of Peace — A5

Flower Growing from Ruin — A6

1972, Dec. 16 Litho. *Perf. 13*

No.	Type	Value	Color	Unused	Used
36	A5	20p	ocher & multi	.25	.25
37	A5	60p	lilac & multi	.30	.30
38	A5	75p	yellow green & multi	.40	.40
			Nos. 36-38 (3)	.95	.95

Victory Day, Dec. 16.

1973, Mar. 25 Litho. *Perf. 13*

No.	Type	Value	Color	Unused	Used
39	A6	20p	ocher & multi	.40	.40
40	A6	60p	brown & multi	.65	.65
41	A6	1.35t	violet blue & multi	1.00	1.00
			Nos. 39-41 (3)	2.05	2.05

Martyrs of the war of liberation.

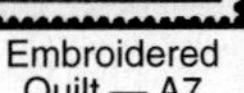

Embroidered Quilt — A7

Hilsa — A8

Court of Justice — A9

Designs: 3p, Jute field. 5p, Jack fruit. 10p, Farmer plowing with ox team. 20p, Hibiscus rosenensis. 25p, Tiger. 60p, Bamboo and water lilies. 75p, Women picking tea. 90p, Handicrafts. 2t, Collecting date palm juice, vert. 5t, Net fishing. 10t, Sixty-dome Mosque.

Perf. 14x14½, 14½x14

1973, Apr. 30 Litho.

Size: 21x28mm, 28x21mm

No.	Type	Value	Color	Unused	Used
42	A7	2p	black	.25	.25
43	A7	3p	bright green	.35	.35
44	A7	5p	light brown	.35	.35
45	A7	10p	black	.35	.35
46	A7	20p	olive	1.00	1.00
47	A7	25p	red lilac	4.50	4.50
48	A8	50p	rose lilac	4.00	4.00
49	A7	60p	gray	2.00	2.00
50	A7	75p	orange	2.00	2.00
51	A7	90p	red brown	2.25	2.25

Taka Expressed as "TA"

Size: 35x22mm

No.	Type	Value	Color	Unused	Used
52	A9	1t	violet	10.00	10.00
53	A9	2t	greenish gray	10.00	10.00
54	A9	5t	grayish blue	10.00	10.00
55	A9	10t	rose	10.00	10.00
			Nos. 42-55 (14)	57.05	57.05

See Nos. 82-85, 95-106, 165-176, 356. For overprints see Nos. O1-O10, O13.

Human Rights Flame A10

Family, Chart, Map of Bangladesh A11

1973, Dec. 10 Litho. *Perf. 13x13½*

No.	Type	Value	Color	Unused	Used
56	A10	10p	blue & multi	.25	.25
57	A10	1.25t	violet & multi	.40	.40

25th anniversary of the Universal Declaration of Human Rights.

1974, Feb. 10 Litho. *Perf. 13½*

No.	Type	Value	Color	Unused	Used
58	A11	20p	blue grn & multi	.25	.25
59	A11	25p	brt blue & multi	.25	.25
60	A11	75p	red & multi	.25	.25
			Nos. 58-60 (3)	.75	.75

First census in Bangladesh.

For overprints see Nos. 194-196.

Copernicus, Heliocentric System — A12

1974, July 22 Litho. *Perf. 13½*

No.	Type	Value	Color	Unused	Used
61	A12	25p	violet, blk & org	.25	.25
62	A12	75p	emerald, blk & org	.75	.75

Nicolaus Copernicus (1473-1543), Polish astronomer.

Flag and UN Headquarters A13

1974, Sept. 25 Litho. *Perf. 13½*

No.	Type	Value	Color	Unused	Used
63	A13	25p	lilac & multi	.25	.25
64	A13	1t	blue & multi	.60	.60

Admission of Bangladesh to the UN.

A14

A15

Designs: 25p, 1.75t, UPU emblem. 1.25t, 5t, Mail runner. 25p, 1.25t, country and denomination appear on a yellow background, 1.75t, 5t, blue background.

1974, Oct. 9 *Perf. 13½*

No.	Type	Value	Color	Unused	Used
65	A14	25p	multicolored	.25	.25
66	A14	1.25t	multicolored	.35	.35
67	A14	1.75t	multicolored	.50	.50
68	A14	5t	multicolored	1.25	1.25
a.			Souv. sheet of 4, #65-68, imperf.	*100.00*	
			Nos. 65-68 (4)	2.35	2.35

1974, Nov. 4 Litho.

69 A15 25p Royal bengal tiger 1.00 1.00
70 A15 50p Tiger cub 1.10 1.10
71 A15 2t Swimming tiger 3.00 3.00
Nos. 69-71 (3) 5.10 5.10

"Save the Tiger," World Wildlife Fund.

Type of 1973
Taka Expressed in Bengali

1974-75 ***Perf. 14½x14, 14x14½***
Size: 35x22mm

82 A9 1t violet 5.00 5.00
83 A9 2t grayish green 7.00 7.00
84 A9 5t grayish blue ('75) 12.00 12.00
85 A9 10t rose ('75) 25.00 25.00
Nos. 82-85 (4) 49.00 49.00

See Nos. 350-356. For overprints see Nos. O11-O12, O14.

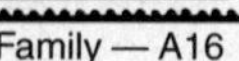

Family — A16

Children — A17

Family A18

1974, Dec. 30 Litho. ***Perf. 14***

86 A16 25p ocher & multi .25 .25
87 A17 70p claret & multi .35 .35
88 A18 1.25t multicolored .60 .60
Nos. 86-88 (3) 1.20 1.20

Family planning. The numerals on No. 87 look like "90" but mean "70."

Betbunia Satellite Earth Station — A19

1975, June 14 Litho. ***Perf. 14***

89 A19 25p red, black & silver .25 .25
90 A19 1t vio blue, blk & silver .60 .60

Opening of Betbunia Satellite Earth Station.

Allegory, IWY Emblem A20

1975, Dec. 31 Litho. ***Perf. 15***

91 A20 50p rose & multi .25 .25
92 A20 2t lt lilac & multi .70 .70

International Women's Year.

Types of 1973 Redrawn

1976-77 Litho. ***Perf. 15x14½***
Size: 18x23mm, 23x18mm

95 A7 5p green .30 .30
96 A7 10p black .40 .40
97 A7 20p olive green 1.75 1.75
98 A7 25p rose lilac 7.00 7.00
99 A8 50p rose lilac 6.00 6.00
100 A7 60p gray 1.00 1.00
101 A7 75p olive 3.50 3.50
102 A7 90p red brown 1.00 1.00

Taka Expressed in Bengali
Size: 32x20mm, 20x32mm

103 A9 1t violet 3.50 3.50
104 A9 2t greenish gray 12.00 12.00
105 A9 5t grayish blue 6.00 6.00
106 A9 10t rose ('77) 10.00 10.00
Nos. 95-106 (12) 52.45 52.45

For overprints see Nos. O16-O25.

Telephones, 1876 and 1976 — A21

Alexander Graham Bell — A22

1976, Mar. 10 Litho. ***Perf. 15***

107 A21 2.25t multicolored .25 .25
108 A22 5t multicolored 1.00 1.00

Centenary of first telephone call by Alexander Graham Bell, Mar. 10, 1876.

Eye and Healthful Food A23

1976, Apr. 7 Litho. ***Perf. 15***

109 A23 30p yellow & multi .40 .40
110 A23 2.25t orange & multi 1.90 1.90

World Health Day: Foresight prevents blindness.

Liberty Bell A24

Designs: 2.25t, Statue of Liberty, New York Skyline. 5t, Mayflower. 10t, Mt. Rushmore, presidents' heads.

1976, May 29 Photo. ***Perf. 13½x14***

111 A24 30p multicolored .30 .30
112 A24 2.25t multicolored .50 .50
113 A24 5t multicolored 1.25 1.25
114 A24 10t multicolored 1.25 1.25
a. Souv. sheet, #111-114, perf 13 6.00 6.00
Nos. 111-114 (4) 3.30 3.30

American Bicentennial. Sheet exists imperf. Value, $100.

Weaver, Chemist, Farmer, Student and Emblem — A25

1976, July 29 Litho. ***Perf. 15***

115 A25 30p multicolored .25 .25
116 A25 2.25t multicolored .85 .85

25th anniversary of Colombo Plan. For overprint see No. 252.

Hurdles — A26

Montreal Olympic Emblem and: 30p, Running, horiz. 1t, High jump. 2.25t, Swimming, horiz. 3.50t, Gymnastics. 5t, Soccer.

1976, Nov. 29 Litho. ***Perf. 15***

117 A26 25p multicolored 1.00 1.00
118 A26 30p multicolored .30 .30
119 A26 1t multicolored .30 .30
120 A26 2.25t multicolored .45 .45
121 A26 3.50t multicolored .50 .50
122 A26 5t multicolored .75 .75
Nos. 117-122 (6) 3.30 3.30

21st Olympic Games, Montreal, Canada, July 17-Aug. 1.

Coronation Ceremony — A27

Designs: 2.25t, Queen Elizabeth II. 10t, Queen and Prince Philip.

1977, Feb. 7 ***Perf. 14x15***

123 A27 30p multicolored .25 .25
124 A27 2.25t multicolored .65 .65
125 A27 10t multicolored 1.10 1.10
a. Souv. sheet, #123-125, perf 14½ 2.50 3.50
Nos. 123-125 (3) 2.00 2.00

25th anniv. of the reign of Elizabeth II. For overprint see No. 228B.

Qazi Nazrul Islam — A28

Nazrul A29

1977, Aug. 29 Litho. ***Perf. 14***

126 A28 40p lt green & black .25 .25
127 A29 2.25t multicolored .45 .45

Qazi Nazrul Islam (1899-1976), natl. poet.

Pigeon Carrying Letter A30

1977, Sept. 29 Litho. ***Perf. 14***

128 A30 30p multicolored .25 .25
129 A30 2.25t multicolored .40 .40

Asian-Oceanic Postal Union (AOPU), 15th anniversary.

Leopard A31

40p and 1t are vert.

1977, Nov. 9 Litho. ***Perf. 13***

130 A31 40p Asiatic black bear .25 .25
131 A31 1t Axis deer .35 .35
132 A31 2.25t shown .80 .80
133 A31 3.50t Gayal 1.25 1.25
134 A31 4t Elephant 1.75 1.75
135 A31 5t Bengal tiger 2.50 2.50
Nos. 130-135 (6) 6.90 6.90

Campfire, Tent, Scout Emblem — A32

Designs: 3.50t, Emblem, first aid, signaling, horiz. 5t, Scout emblem and oath.

1978, Jan. 22 Litho. ***Perf. 13***

136 A32 40p multicolored .30 .30
137 A32 3.50t multicolored 1.45 1.45
138 A32 5t multicolored 3.25 3.25
Nos. 136-138 (3) 5.00 5.00

1st National Boy Scout Jamboree, Jan. 22. For overprint see No. 269.

Champac — A33

Flowers and Flowering Trees: 1t, Pudding pipe tree. 2.25t, Flamboyant tree. 3.50t, Water lilies. 4t, Butea. 5t, Anthocephalus indicus.

1978, Mar. 31 Litho. ***Perf. 13***

139 A33 40p multicolored .25 .25
140 A33 1t multicolored .60 .60
141 A33 2.25t multicolored .80 .80
142 A33 3.50t multicolored 1.00 1.00
143 A33 4t multicolored 1.10 1.10
144 A33 5t multicolored 1.30 1.30
Nos. 139-144 (6) 5.05 5.05

For overprints see Nos. 259A-259F.

Crown, Scepter and Staff of State — A34

Designs: 3.50t, Royal family on balcony. 5t, Queen Elizabeth II and Prince Philip. 10t, Queen in coronation regalia, Westminster Abbey.

1978, May 20 ***Perf. 14***

145 A34 40p multicolored .25 .25
146 A34 3.50t multicolored .30 .30
147 A34 5t multicolored .60 .60

148 A34 10t multicolored .80 .80
a. Souv. sheet, #145-148, perf 14½ 3.00 3.00
Nos. 145-148 (4) 1.95 1.95

Coronation of Queen Elizabeth II, 25th anniv.

Alan Cobham's DH50, 1926 — A35

Planes: 2.25t, Capt. Hans Bertram's Junkers W33 Atlantis, 1932-33. 3.50t, Wright brothers' plane. 5t, Concorde.

1978, June 15 Litho. *Perf. 13*
149 A35 40p multicolored .25 .25
150 A35 2.25t multicolored .60 .60
151 A35 3.50t multicolored 1.00 1.00
152 A35 5t multicolored 4.75 4.75
Nos. 149-152 (4) 6.60 6.60

75th anniversary of powered flight.

Holy Kaaba, Mecca — A37

Design: 3.50t, Pilgrims at Mt. Arafat, horiz.

1978, Nov. 9 Litho. *Perf. 13*
154 A37 40p multicolored .35 .35
155 A37 3.50t multicolored 1.25 1.25

Pilgrimage to Mecca.

Jasim Uddin, Poet A38

1979, Mar. 14 Litho. *Perf. 14*
156 A38 40p multicolored .50 .50

Rowland Hill — A39

Hill and Stamps of Bangladesh: 3.50t, No. 1, horiz. 10t, No. 66, horiz.

1979, Nov. 26 Litho. *Perf. 14*
157 A39 40p multicolored .25 .25
158 A39 3.50t multicolored .60 .60
159 A39 10t multicolored 1.35 1.35
a. Souvenir sheet of 3, #157-159 5.00 5.00
Nos. 157-159 (3) 2.20 2.20

Sir Rowland Hill (1795-1879), originator of penny postage.

Moulana Bhashani — A40

1979, Nov. 17 *Perf. 12½*
160 A40 40p multicolored .60 .60

Moulana Abdul Hamid Khan Bhashani (1880-1976), philosopher and statesman.

A41

IYC Emblem and: 40p, Boys and Hoops. 3.50t, Boys flying kites. 5t, Children jumping.

1979, Dec. 17 Litho. *Perf. 14x14½*
161 A41 40p multicolored .30 .30
162 A41 3.50t multicolored .50 .50
163 A41 5t multicolored .75 .75
a. Souv. sheet, #161-163, perf 14½ 3.00 3.00
Nos. 161-163 (3) 1.55 1.55

International Year of the Child.

Type of 1973

Designs: 5p, Lalbag Fort. 10p, Fenchungan Fertilizer Factory, vert. 15p, Pineapple. 20p, Gas well. 25p, Jute on boat. 30p, Banana tree. 40p, Baitul Mukarram Mosque. 50p, Baitul Mukarram Mosque. 80p, Garh excavations. 1ta, Dotara (musical instrument.) 2t, Karnaphuli Dam.

1979-82 Photo. *Perf. 14½*
Size: 18x23mm, 23x18mm
165 A7 5p brown ('79) .25 .25
166 A7 10p Prus blue .25 .25
167 A7 15p yellow org ('81) .25 .25
168 A7 20p dk carmine ('79) .25 .25
169 A7 25p dk blue ('82) .30 .30
170 A7 30p lt olive grn ('80) 3.50 3.50
171 A9 40p rose magenta ('79) .65 .65
172 A9 50p black & gray ('81) 6.50 6.50
173 A7 80p dk brown ('80) .50 .50
174 A7 1t red lilac ('81) 8.50 8.50
175 A7 2t brt ultra ('81) 4.25 4.25
Nos. 165-175 (11) 25.20 25.20

For overprints see Nos. O27-O36.

A42

Rotary Intl., 75th Anniv.: 40p, Rotary emblem, diff.

1980, Feb. 23 Litho. *Perf. 14*
179 A42 40p multicolored .30 .30
180 A42 5t ultra & gold 1.00 1.00

For overprints see Nos. 285-286.

Canal Digging A43

1980, Mar. 27 Litho. *Perf. 14*
181 A43 40p multicolored .75 .60

Sher-e-Bangla A.K. Fazlul Huq (1873-1962), Natl. Leader — A44

1980, Apr. 27 Litho. *Perf. 14*
182 A44 40p multicolored .60 .40

Early Mail Transport, London 1980 Emblem — A45

1980, May 5
183 A45 1t shown .25 .25
184 A45 10t Modern mail transport 1.75 1.25
a. Souvenir sheet of 2, #183-184 2.75 *2.75*

London 80 Intl. Stamp Exhib., May 6-14.

Dome of the Rock — A46

Adult Education — A47

1980, Aug. 21 Litho. *Perf. 14½*
185 A46 50p violet rose 1.75 .60

For the families of Palestinians.

A 50p stamp for the Palestinian liberation struggle was prepared for issue on the same day as No. 185, but was not issued because of errors in the Arabic inscription in the design. Value, $3.

1980, Aug. 23 *Perf. 13½*
186 A47 50p multicolored .75 .50

Beach Scene A48

1980, Sept. 27 Litho. *Perf. 14*
187 A48 50p shown .75 .75
188 A48 5t Beach scene, diff. 1.25 *1.50*
a. Souvenir sheet of 2, #187-188 2.25 *2.25*
b. Pair, #187-188 2.00 *2.25*

World Tourism Conference, Manila, Sept. 27. No. 188b has continuous design.

For overprints see Nos. 243-244.

Hegira (Pilgrimage Year) — A49

1980, Nov. 11 Photo. *Perf. 14*
189 A49 50p multicolored 1.00 .50

A50

Design: Deer and Boy Scout emblem.

1981, Jan. 1 Litho. *Perf. 14*
190 A50 50p multicolored .75 .30
191 A50 5t multicolored 1.25 *3.00*

5th Asia-Pacific and 2nd Bangladesh Scout Jamboree, 1980-1981.

For overprint, see No. 321.

A51

1980, Dec. 9 Litho. *Perf. 14*
192 A51 50p multicolored .25 .25
193 A51 2t multicolored .50 .50

Begum Roquiah (1880-1932), educator.

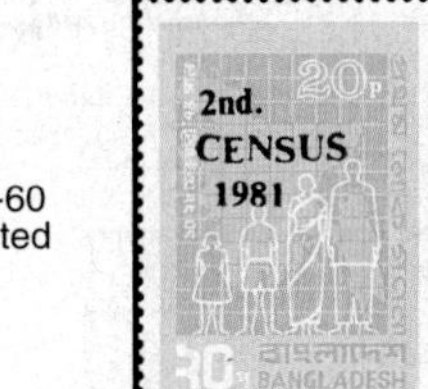

Nos. 58-60 Overprinted

1981, Mar. 6 *Perf. 13½*
194 A11 20p multicolored .25 .25
195 A11 25p multicolored .25 .25
196 A11 75p multicolored .25 .25
Nos. 194-196 (3) .75 .75

A52

1981, Mar. 16 Litho. *Perf. 14*
197 A52 1t multicolored .55 .40
198 A52 15t multicolored 3.00 *3.25*
a. Souvenir sheet of 2, #197-198 5.00 5.00

Queen Mother Elizabeth, 80th birthday (1980).

A53

1981, Mar. 26
199 A53 50p Citizen Holding Rifle & Flag .25 .25
200 A53 2t People, map .75 .75

10th anniversary of independence.

For overprint on 199, see No. 210A.

UN Conference on Least-developed Countries, Paris — A54

1981, Sept. 1 Litho. *Perf. 14x13½*

201 A54 50p multicolored .75 .25

Birth Centenary of Kemal Ataturk (First President of Turkey) — A55

1981, Nov. 10 Litho. *Perf. 14*

202 A55 50p Portrait .60 .60
203 A55 1t Portrait, diff. 1.25 1.25

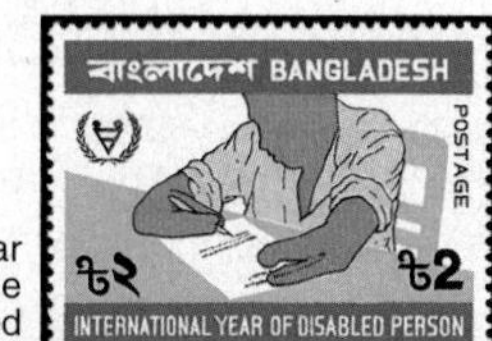

Intl. Year of the Disabled A56

1981, Dec. 26 Litho. *Perf. 14*

204 A56 50p Sign language, vert. .60 .35
205 A56 2t Amputee 1.60 1.60

World Food Day, Oct. 16 — A57

1981, Dec. 31 Litho. *Perf. 13½x14*

206 A57 50p multicolored 1.00 *1.25*

A58

1982, May 22 Litho. *Perf. 13½x14*

207 A58 50p Boat hauling rice straw 1.00 *1.40*

10th Anniv. of UN Conf. on Human Environment.

For overprint see No. 281.

A59

1982, Oct. 9

208 A59 50p multicolored .70 *1.00*

Dr. Kazi Motahar Hossain, educator and statistician.

Scouting Year A60

1982, Oct. 21 Litho. *Perf. 14*

209 A60 50p Emblem, knots 1.00 .50
210 A60 2t Baden-Powell, vert. 3.75 3.75

No. 199 Overprinted

1982, Nov. 21 Litho. *Perf. 14*

210A A53 50p multi 5.00 5.00

Armed Forces Day.

Capt. Mohiuddin Jahangir A61

No. 211 — Liberation heroes (tablet color): b, Sepoy Hamidur Rahman (pale green). c, Sepoy Mohammed Mustafa Kamal (rose claret). d, Mohammad Ruhul Amin (yellow). e, M. Matiur Rahman (olive bister). f, Lance-Naik Munshi Abdur Rouf (brown orange). g, Lance-Naik Nur Mouhammad (bright yellow green).

1982, Dec. 16 Litho. *Perf. 14*

211 Strip of 7 4.00 *4.50*
a.-g. A61 50p multicolored .50 .50

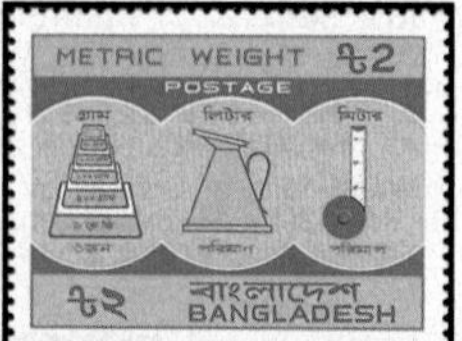

Metric System A62

1983, Jan. 10 Litho. *Perf. 14*

212 A62 50p Mail scale, vert. .60 .60
213 A62 2t Weights, measures 2.40 2.40

TB Bacillus Centenary A63

1983, Feb. 20 Litho. *Perf. 14*

214 A63 50p Koch 1.75 1.75
215 A63 1t Slides, microscope 3.00 3.00

A64

1983, Mar. 14 Litho. *Perf. 14*

216 A64 1t Open stage theater .25 .25
217 A64 3t Boat race .25 .25
218 A64 10t Snake dance .55 .55
219 A64 15t Tea garden .90 .90
Nos. 216-219 (4) 1.95 1.95

Commonwealth Day.

Jnantapash Shahidullah (1885-1969), Educator and Linguist — A65

1983, July 10 Litho. *Perf. 14*

220 A65 50p multicolored 1.25 1.25

Birds A66

Designs: 50p, Copsychus saularis. 2t, Halcyon smyrnensis, vert. 3.75t, Dinopium benghalense, vert. 5t, Carina scutulota.

1983, Aug. 17 Litho. *Perf. 14*

221 A66 50p multi 1.75 .65
222 A66 2t multi 2.25 2.25
223 A66 3.75t multi 2.50 2.25
224 A66 5t multi 3.00 3.00
a. Souvenir sheet of 4, #221-224 18.00 18.00
Nos. 221-224 (4) 9.50 8.15

No. 224a sold for 13t.

Local Fish A67

1983, Oct. 31 Litho. *Perf. 14*

225 A67 50p Macrobrachium rosengergii 1.75 .85
226 A67 2t Stromateus cinereus 2.00 2.00
227 A67 3.75t Labeo rohita 2.50 2.25
228 A67 5t Anabas testudineus 3.00 *3.25*
a. Souv. sheet of 4, #225-228, imperf. 18.00 18.00
Nos. 225-228 (4) 9.25 8.35

No. 228a sold for 13t.

No. 125 Overprinted in Red

1983, Nov. 14 Litho. *Perf. 14*

228B A27 10t multicolored 8.25 8.25

No. 228B also exists with the overprint reading "Nov. '33" instead of "Nov. '83." Value, $15.

World Communications Year — A68

1983, Dec. 21 Litho. *Perf. 14*

229 A68 50p Messenger, vert. .50 .50
230 A68 5t Jet, train, ship, vert. 3.00 3.00
231 A68 10t Dish antenna, messenger 4.00 4.00
Nos. 229-231 (3) 7.50 7.50

Hall A69

1983, Dec. 5 Litho. *Perf. 14*

232 A69 50p Sangsad Bhaban .25 .25
233 A69 5t Shait Gumbaz 3.00 3.00

14th Islamic Foreign Ministers Conference.

A70

Perf. 11½x12½, 12½x11½

1983, Dec. 21

234 A70 5p Mailboat .40 .40
235 A70 10p Dacca P.O. counter .40 .30
236 A70 15p IWTA Terminal .50 .30
237 A70 20p Sorting mail 1.50 .30
238 A70 25p Mail delivery .75 .30
239 A70 30p Postman at mailbox .75 .30
240 A70 50p Mobile post office 1.50 .30

Size: 30½x18½mm

Perf. 12x11½

241 A70 1t Kamalapur Railway Station 1.50 .40
242 A70 2t Zia Intl. Airport 2.25 1.75
242A A70 5t Khulna P.O. 4.00 4.00
Nos. 234-242A (10) 13.55 8.35

Nos. 235-237, 239-242A horiz.

Nos. 234-240 reprinted on cream paper.

See Nos. 270-271. For overprints see Nos. O37-O46, O48, O51-O52.

No. 188b Overprinted in Red in English

or Bengali

1984, Feb. 1 Litho. *Perf. 14*

243 A48 50p Beach Scene 1.25 1.25
244 A48 5t Beach Scene, diff. 4.00 4.00
a. Pair, #243-244 5.75 5.75

1st Bangladesh Natl. Philatelic Exhibition, 1984. No. 244a has continuous design.

A71

1984, May 17 *Perf. 14½*

245 50p Girl examining stamp album 1.00 1.00
246 7.50t Boy updating collection 3.50 3.50
a. Souvenir sheet of 2, #245-246 7.00 7.00
b. A71 Pair, #245-246 5.00 5.00
c. As "a," overprinted 10.00 10.00

No. 246a sold for 10t.
Overprint in sheet margin of No. 246c reads: "SILVER JUBILEE / BANGLADESH POSTAGE STAMPS 1971-96."

Dacca Zoo — A72

1984, July 17 Litho. *Perf. 14*

247 A72 1t Sarus crane, gavial 2.10 1.25
248 A72 2t Peafowl, royal Bengal tiger 3.75 3.75

Postal Life Insurance, Cent. — A73

1984, Dec. 3

249 A73 1t Chicken hawk, hen .90 .40
250 A73 5t Beneficiaries 3.50 3.50

Abbasudin Ahmad, Bengali Singer — A74

1984, Dec. 24

251 A74 3t multicolored 1.25 1.00

No. 116 Ovptd. for KHULNAPEX '84 Stamp Exhibition

1984, Dec. 29 Litho. *Perf. 15*

252 A25 2.25t multicolored 2.25 2.25

1984 Summer Olympics, Los Angeles A75

1984, Dec. 31 *Perf. 14*

253 A75 1t Bicycling 2.10 2.10
254 A75 5t Field hockey 3.75 3.75
255 A75 10t Volleyball 4.25 4.25
Nos. 253-255 (3) 10.10 10.10

Islamic Development Bank, 9th Annual Congress, Dacca — A76

1985, Feb. 2

256 A76 1t Farmer .75 .30
257 A76 5t Four Asian races 2.00 2.00

UN Child Survival Campaign A77

1985, Mar. 14

258 A77 1t Breastfeeding .40 .25
259 A77 10t Growth monitoring 3.00 3.00

Nos. 139-144 Ovptd. in Bengali for Local Elections

1985, May 16 Litho. *Perf. 13*

259A A33 40p multicolored .75 *1.00*
259B A33 1t multicolored .85 .50
259C A33 2.25t multicolored 1.10 *1.40*
259D A33 3.50t multicolored 1.25 *2.00*
259E A33 4t multicolored 1.25 *2.00*
259F A33 5t multicolored 1.25 *2.25*
Nos. 259A-259F (6) 6.45 *9.15*

UN Decade for Women — A78

1985, July 18 *Perf. 14*

260 A78 1t shown .40 .25
261 A78 10t Technology 2.10 2.10

UN, 40th Anniv. A79

1985, Sept. 15

262 A79 1t UN building .25 .25
263 A79 10t World map, natl. flag 1.75 1.75

11th anniv. of UN admission.

Intl. Youth Year — A80

1985, Nov. 2 Litho. *Perf. 14*

264 A80 1t Scissors, pencil .30 .30
265 A80 5t Hammer, wrenches .65 .65

Seven Doves, Council Emblem — A81

1985, Dec. 8 Litho. *Perf. 14*

266 A81 1t shown .40 .40
267 A81 5t Flags, lotus blossom 1.00 1.00

1st South Asian Regional Council Summit, SARC, Dacca.

Shilpacharya Zainul Abedin (1914-1976), Founder, Dacca College of Art — A82

1985, Dec. 28

268 A82 3t multicolored 1.50 .75

No. 138 Overprinted Reading Up

1985, Dec. 29 *Perf. 13*

269 A32 5t multicolored 5.00 5.00

3rd Natl. Scout Jamboree.
The overprint comes in two types.

Postal Services Type of 1983-84

1986-93 Litho. *Perf. 12x11½*
Size: 30½x19mm

270 A70 3t Sorting machine 3.50 1.25

Perf. 12x12½
Size: 33½x22½mm

271 A70 4t Chittagong Port 1.25 .75

Issued: 3t, Jan. 11, 1986; 4t, Apr. 22, 1993.
For overprint see No. O46.

Fishing Net, by Safiuddin Ahmed A83

Paintings by Bengali artists: 5t, Happy Return, by Quamrul Hassan. 10t, Levelling the Plowed Field, by Zainul Abedin.

1986, Apr. 6 Litho. *Perf. 14*

275 A83 1t multicolored .35 .35
276 A83 5t multicolored .75 .75
277 A83 10t multicolored 1.25 1.25
Nos. 275-277 (3) 2.35 2.35

For overprint see No. 322.

1986 World Cup Soccer Championships, Mexico — A84

1986, June 29 *Perf. 15x14*

278 A84 1t Stealing the ball .85 .35
279 A84 10t Goal 5.00 5.00

Souvenir Sheet
Imperf

279A A84 20t multicolored 15.00 15.00

No. 279A contains one stamp 62x45mm with simulated perfs.

Gen. M.A.G. Osmani (1918-1984), Liberation Forces Commander-in-Chief — A85

1986, Sept. 10 Litho. *Perf. 14*

280 A85 3t multicolored 3.00 3.00

No. 207 Ovptd.

1986, Dec. 3 Litho. *Perf. 13½x14*

281 A58 50p on #207 4.00 4.00

Intl. Peace Year — A86

A87

1986, Dec. 25 Litho. ***Perf. 12x12½***

282 A86	1t shown	.85	.50
283 A86	10t City ruins, flower	3.50	3.50

Souvenir Sheet

284 A87	20t shown	3.00	3.00

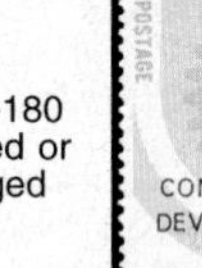

Nos. 179-180 Overprinted or Surcharged

1987, Jan. 12 ***Perf. 14***

285 A42	1t on 40p multicolored	.35	.35
286 A42	5t multicolored	.85	.85

Language Movement, 35th Anniv. — A88

1987, Feb. 21 ***Perf. 12½x12***

287	3t Protestors	1.50	1.50
288	3t Memorial	1.50	1.50
a.	A88 Pair, Nos. 287-288	3.50	3.50

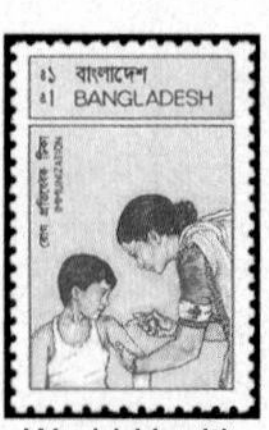

World Health Day — A89

Bengali New Year — A90

1987, Apr. 7 ***Perf. 11½x12***

289 A89	1t Child immunization	3.50	3.50

See No. 318.

1987, Apr. 16 ***Perf. 12x12½***

290 A90	1t Bengali script, embroidery	.25	.25
291 A90	10t shown	1.00	1.00

Jute Carpet A91

Exports: 1t, Jute shika (wall hanging, bowl-holder and mats), vert. 10t, Table lamp and shade, vert.

Perf. 12x12½, 12½x12

1987, May 18 **Litho.**

292 A91	1t multicolored	.25	.25
293 A91	5t shown	.35	.35
294 A91	10t multicolored	.75	.75
	Nos. 292-294 (3)	1.35	1.35

Ustad Ayet Ali Khan (1884-1967), Composer, and Surbahar A92

1987, Sept. 8 ***Perf. 12x12½***

295 A92	5t multicolored	2.00	1.00

Transportation — A93

1987, Oct. 24 Litho. ***Perf. 12½x12***

296 A93	2t Palanquin	.50	.50
297 A93	3t Bicycle rickshaw	1.00	1.00
298 A93	5t Paddle steamer	1.50	1.50
299 A93	7t Train	5.00	5.00
300 A93	10t Ox cart	2.00	2.00
	Nos. 296-300 (5)	10.00	10.00

For overprint see No. 424.

Hossain Shahid Suhrawardy (1893-1963), Politician — A94

1987, Dec. 5 Litho. ***Perf. 12x12½***

301 A94	3t multicolored	.75	.75

Intl. Year of Shelter for the Homeless — A95

1987, Dec. 15 ***Perf. 12½x12***

302	5t Homeless people	.60	.60
303	5t Prosperous community	.60	.60
a.	A95 Pair, Nos. 302-303	1.25	1.25

Natl. Democracy, 1st Anniv. — A96

Design: Pres. Hossain Mohammed Ershad addressing parliament.

1987, Dec. 31

304 A96	10t multicolored	2.25	2.25

Woman Tending Crop A97

1988, Jan. 26

305 A97	3t shown	.50	.50
306 A97	5t Milking cow, village	.75	.75

Intl. Fund for Agricultural Development (IFAD) Seminar on Loans for Women in Rural Areas.

1988 Summer Olympics, Seoul — A98

No. 307 — Seoul Olympics emblem and: a, Basketball. b, Weight lifting. c, Women's tennis. d, Shooting. e, Boxing.

1988, Sept. 29 Litho. ***Perf. 11½***

307	Strip of 5	9.00	9.00
a.-e.	A98 5t any single	1.75	1.75

Historical Sites A99

Designs: 1t, Shait Gumbaz Mosque (interior), Bagerhat. 4t, Paharpur Monastery. 5t, Kantanagar Temple, Dinajpur. 10t, Lalbag Fort, Dacca.

1988, Oct. 9 ***Perf. 12½x12***

308 A99	1t multicolored	1.00	1.00
309 A99	4t multicolored	1.25	1.25
310 A99	5t multicolored	1.25	1.25
311 A99	10t multicolored	2.50	2.50
	Nos. 308-311 (4)	6.00	6.00

Qudrat-i-Khuda (1900-1977), Scientist — A100

1988, Nov. 3 ***Perf. 12x12½***

312 A100	5t multicolored	.75	.60

Asia Cup Cricket — A101

1988, Nov. 27

313	Strip of 3	6.00	6.00
a.	A101 1t Wicketkeeper	.35	.35
b.	A101 5t Batsman	1.50	1.50
c.	A101 10t Bowler	4.00	4.00

Intl. Red Cross and Red Crescent Organizations, 125th Annivs. — A102

1988, Oct. 26 Litho. ***Perf. 12x12½***

314 A102	5t Emblems, Dunant	2.25	.75
315 A102	10t Blood donation	3.75	2.25

Dacca G.P.O., 25th Anniv. — A103

1988, Dec. 6 ***Perf. 12***

316 A103	1t Exterior	.30	.25
317 A103	5t Sales counter	.85	.50

World Health Day Type of 1987

1988, Jan. 16 Litho. ***Perf. 11½x12***

318 A89	25p Oral rehydration	.85	.85

32nd Meeting of the Colombo Plan Consultative Committee, Dacca — A104

1988, Nov. 29 ***Perf. 12x12½***

319 A104	3t multicolored	.50	.50
320 A104	10t multicolored	.75	.75

No. 191 Ovptd.

1988, Dec. 29 Litho. ***Perf. 14***

321 A50	5t multicolored	6.00	5.00

5th Natl. Rover Moot (Scouting).

No. 277 Overprinted

1989, Mar. 1

322 A83	10t multicolored	2.00	2.00

4th Asiatic Exposition.

A106

1989, Mar. 13 Litho. *Perf. 12x12½*
324 A106 10t multicolored 1.25 1.25

Police academy, Sardah, 75th anniv.

A107

Modernizing water supply services.

1989, Mar. 7 Litho. *Perf. 12x12½*
325 A107 10t multicolored 1.25 1.25

12th Natl. Science & Technology Week.

A108

French Revolution, Bicent. — A109

Scenes from the revolution: 5t, Close-up of revolutionaries destroying the Bastille, vert. No. 326b, Liberty guiding the people. No. 326c, Women's march on Versailles, vert. No. 327a, Celebration of the Federation on the Champ de Mars. No. 327b, Storming of the Bastille. 25t, Montage of scenes, #326a-326c.

1989, July 12 *Perf. 14*
326 Sheet of 3 + label 3.50 3.50
a. A108 5t multicolored .70 .70
b.-c. A108 10t any single 1.10 1.10

Perf. 14x15
327 Strip of 2 + label 4.00 4.00
a.-b. A109 17t any single 1.75 1.75

Size: 152x88mm

Imperf
328 A108 25t multicolored 4.00 4.00
Nos. 326-328 (3) 11.50 11.50

Labels picture the revolution anniv. emblem.

Rural Development in Asia and the Pacific (CIRDAP), 10th Anniv. — A110

1989, Aug. 10 Litho. *Perf. 12½x12*
329 5t multi .75 .75
330 10t multi 1.25 1.25
a. Pair, Nos. 329-330 3.50 3.50

Child Survival A111

1989, Aug. 22
331 A111 1t shown .40 .40
332 A111 10t Women and children, diff. 1.25 1.25

SOS Children's Village, 40th anniv.

Involvement of the Bangladesh Army in UN Peace-keeping Operations, 1st Anniv. — A112

1989, Sept. 12 *Perf. 12x12½*
333 A112 4t shown 1.00 1.00
334 A112 10t Camp, two soldiers 2.50 2.50

2nd Asian Poetry Festival, Dacca — A113

1989, Nov. 17 Litho. *Perf. 12x12½*
335 A113 2t multicolored .25 .25
336 A113 10t multicolored 1.50 1.50

State Printing Office A114

1989, Dec. 7 *Perf. 13½*
337 A114 10t multicolored 1.50 1.50

Bangladesh Television, 25th Anniv. — A115

1989, Dec. 25 Litho. *Perf. 12½x12*
338 A115 5t shown .75 .75
339 A115 10t Emblem, flowers, diff. 2.00 2.00

World Wildlife Fund A116

Gavialis gangeticus: 50p, In water. 2p, Gavial's jaws. 4t, Four gavials. 10t, Two gavials resting.

1990, Jan. 31 Litho. *Perf. 14*
340 A116 50p multi 1.00 .80
341 A116 2t multi 1.15 1.05
342 A116 4t multi 1.75 1.75
343 A116 10t multi 3.50 3.50
a. Block of 4, #340-343 8.00 8.00
Nos. 340-343 (4) 7.40 7.10

A117

1990, Feb. 2 *Perf. 14*
344 A117 6t multicolored 1.25 1.25

Natl. Population Day.

A118

1990, May 6 *Perf. 14*
345 A118 7t shown 2.75 2.75
346 A118 10t Penny Black, No. 230 4.00 4.00

Penny Black, 150th anniv.

Justice Syed Mahbub Murshed, (1911-1979) — A119

1990, Apr. 3 Litho. *Perf. 12½x12*
347 A119 5t multicolored 3.50 3.50

Intl. Literacy Year — A120

Design: 10t, Boy teaching girl to write.

1990, Apr. 10 *Perf. 12x12½*
348 A120 6t multicolored 1.75 1.75
349 A120 10t multicolored 3.25 3.25

Type of 1973 Redrawn and

Loading Cargo Plane — A121

Curzon Hall — A122

Fertilizer Plant — A123

Postal Academy, Rajshahi A124

Salimullah Hall — A125

Bangla Academy — A126

Designs: No. 356, Sixty-dome Mosque (English inscription at LR).

1989-99 *Perf. 12x11½, 12, 12x12½*
350 A121 3t multicolored .50 .50
a. Perf. 14¼x14 .75 .25
351 A122 5t gray blk & red brn .75 .25
a. Perf. 14¼ .75 .25
352 A123 10t carmine 1.25 1.25
353 A124 20t multicolored 3.25 3.25

Perf. 14½x14
354 A125 6t blue gray & yel 1.50 1.50

Perf. 14x14½
355 A126 2t brown & green 1.00 .50

Perf. 14¼
Size: 35x22 mm
Taka Expressed in Bengali
356 A9 10t rose 1.40 1.10
Nos. 350-356 (7) 9.65 8.35

Issued: 5t, 3/31; 3t, 4/30; 10t, 20t, 7/8; 6t, 1/30/91; 2t, 12/3/93; No. 356, 3/18/99; No. 351a, 8/31/99.

No. 356 is very similar to No. 85 but differs in several ways: the inscription "Sixty-Dome Mosque" has been enlarged and moved from the upper left of the vignette to the lower right; a Bengali inscription has been added in its place at upper left; and the entire design has been lightened condiderably, especially in the skyline of the mosque.

For overprints see Nos. O47A-O47B, O50.

World Cup Soccer Championships, Italy — A133

1990, June 12 Litho. *Perf. 14*
362 A133 8t shown 4.00 4.00
363 A133 10t Soccer player, diff. 4.50 4.50

Size: 115x79mm

Imperf
364 A133 25t Colosseum, soccer ball 25.00 25.00
Nos. 362-364 (3) 33.50 33.50

Fruits — A134

1990, July 16 *Perf. 12x12½*
365 A134 1t Mangifera indica .50 .50
366 A134 2t Psidium guayava .65 .65
367 A134 3t Citrullus vulgaris .80 .80
368 A134 4t Carica papaya 1.25 1.25
369 A134 5t Artocarpus heterophyllus 1.75 1.75
370 A134 10t Averrhoa carambola 3.50 3.50
Nos. 365-370 (6) 8.45 8.45

UN Conference on Least Developed Nations, Paris — A135

1990, Sept. 3 Litho. ***Perf. 14***
371 A135 10t multicolored 2.50 2.50

Asia-Pacific Postal Training Center, 20th Anniv. — A136

1990, Sept. 10 ***Perf. 13½x14***
372 2t multicolored 1.00 1.00
373 6t multicolored 2.50 2.50
a. A136 Pair, #372-373 4.00 4.00

No. 373a has continuous design.

11th Asian Games, Beijing A137

1990, Sept. 22 ***Perf. 14***
374 A137 2t Rowing 1.50 .50
375 A137 4t Kabaddi 1.75 .40
376 A137 8t Wrestling 2.75 2.00
377 A137 10t Badminton 4.50 2.75
Nos. 374-377 (4) 10.50 5.65

Lalon Shah, Poet — A138

1990, Oct. 17 Litho. ***Perf. 14***
378 A138 6t multicolored 2.10 1.75

UN Development Program, 40th Anniv. — A139

1990, Oct. 24 Litho. ***Perf. 14***
379 A139 6t multicolored 2.00 1.75

A139a

A140

1990, Nov. 29 Litho. ***Perf. 14½x14***
379A A139a 2t brown .30 .30

Immunization program. See No. 560. For surcharge see O47.

1990, Dec. 24 Litho. ***Perf. 13½x12***

Butterflies.

380 A140 6t Danaus chrysippus 3.00 3.00
381 A140 6t Precis almana 3.00 3.00
382 A140 10t Ixias pyrene 5.00 5.00
383 A140 10t Danaus plexippus 5.00 5.00
a. Block of 4, #380-383 18.00 18.00
Nos. 380-383 (4) 16.00 16.00

UN Decade Against Drugs A141

1991, Jan 1 Litho. ***Perf. 14x13½***
384 A141 2t Drugs, map 1.75 .75
385 A141 4t shown 3.50 3.50

Third National Census — A142

1991, Mar. 12 Litho. ***Perf. 14***
386 A142 4t multicolored 1.75 1.75

Independence, 20th Anniv. — A143

No. 387: a, Invincible Bangla statue. b, Freedom Fighter statue. c, Mujibnagar Memorial. d, Eternal flame. e, National Martyrs' Memorial.

1991, Mar. 26 ***Perf. 13½***
387 A143 4t Strip of 5, #a.-e. 8.00 8.00
a.-e. Any single 1.25 1.25

No. 387 printed in continuous design.

A144

Pres. Ziaur Rahman, 10th Death Anniv. — A145

1991, May 30 ***Perf. 14***
388 A144 50p multicolored .30 .30
389 A145 2t multicolored 1.50 1.50
a. Souvenir sheet of 2, #388-389 2.75 2.75

No. 389a sold for 10t.

Endangered Animals — A146

1991, June 16 ***Perf. 12***
390 A146 2t Petaurista petaurista 2.50 2.50
391 A146 4t Presbytis entellus, vert. 2.50 2.50
392 A146 6t Buceros bicornis, vert. 2.50 2.50
a. Pair, #391-392 6.00 6.00
393 A146 10t Manis crassicaudata 4.50 4.50
a. Pair, #390, 393 8.00 8.00
Nos. 390-393 (4) 12.00 12.00

Kaikobad (1857-1951), Poet — A147

1991, July 21 Litho. ***Perf. 14***
394 A147 6t multicolored 1.75 1.75

Rabindranath Tagore, Poet, 50th Anniv. of Death — A148

1991, Aug. 7
395 A148 4t multicolored 1.50 1.50

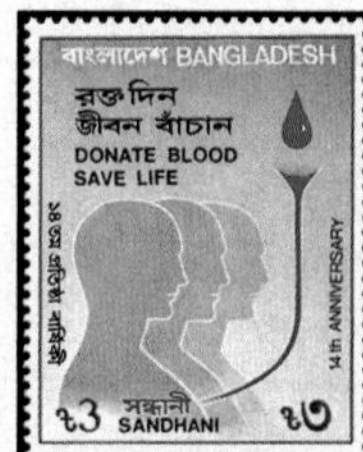

Blood and Eye Donations A149

1991, Sept. 19
396 A149 3t shown 1.50 1.50
397 A149 5t Blind man and eye 2.25 2.25

Sandhani, Medical Students Association, 14th anniversary.

Shahid Naziruddin, Leader of Democratic Movement, 1st Anniv. of Death — A150

1991, Oct. 10
398 A150 2t multicolored 1.75 .75

Shaheed Noor Hossain, 4th Death Anniv. — A151

1991, Nov. 10 Litho. ***Perf. 14***
399 A151 2t multicolored 1.50 1.40

Archaeological Treasures of Mainamati — A152

No. 400: a, Bronze Stupa with images of Buddha. b, Bowl and pitcher. c, Ruins of Salban Vihara Monastery. d, Gold coins. e, Terra-cotta plaque.

1991, Nov. 26 Litho. ***Perf. 13½***
400 A152 4t Strip of 5, #a.-e. 12.00 12.00
a.-e. Any single 2.00 2.00

Mass Uprising, First Anniv. A153

1991, Dec. 6 ***Perf. 14***
401 A153 4t multicolored 1.50 1.25

Miniature Sheets

Martyred Intellectuals Who Died in 1971 — A154

No. 402: a, A.N.M. Munier Chowdhury. b, Ghyasuddin Ahmad. c, S.M.A. Rashidul Hasan. d, Muhammad Anwar Pasha. e, Dr. Md. Mortaza. f, Shahid Saber. g, Fazlur Rahman Khan. h, Ranada Prasad Saha. i, Adhyaksha Joges Chandra Ghose. j, Santosh Chandra Bhattacharyya.

No. 403: a, Dr. Gobinda Chandra Deb. b, A.N.M. Muniruzzaman. c, Mufazzal Haider Chaudhury. d, Dr. Abdul Alim Choudhury. e, Sirajuddin Hossain. f, Shahidulla Kaiser. g, Altaf Mahmud. h, Dr. Jyotirmay Guha Thakurta. i, Dr. Md. Abul Khair. j, Dr. Serajul Haque Khan.

No. 404: a, Dr. Mohammad Fazle Rabbi. b, Mir Abdul Quyyum. c, A.N.M. Golam Mostafa.

d, Dhirendranath Dutta. e, S.A. Mannan (Ladu Bhai). f, Nizamuddin Ahmad. g, Abul Bashar Chowdhury. h, Selina Parveen. i, Dr. Abul Kalam Azad. j, Saidul Hassan.

No. 404K: l, LCDR. Moazzam Hussain. m, Muhammad Habibur Rahman. n, Khandoker Abu Taleb. o, Moshiur Rahman. p, Md. Abdul Muktadir. q, Nutan Chandra Sinha. r, Syed Nazmul Haque. s, Dr. Mohammed Amin Uddin. t, Dr. N.A.M. Faizul Mohee. u, Sukha Ranjan Somaddar.

1991-93 Litho. *Perf. 13½*

402 A154 2t Sheet of 10, #a-j + 5 labels 15.00 15.00
a.-j. Any single .50 .50
403 A154 2t Sheet of 10, #a-j + 5 labels 15.00 15.00
a.-j. Any single .50 .50
404 A154 2t Sheet of 10, #a-j + 5 labels 15.00 15.00
a.-j. Any single .50 .50

Perf. 14½

404K A154 2t Sheet of 10, #l-u + 5 labels 6.00 6.00
l.-u. Any single .50 .50

Independence, 20th anniv. Issued: Nos. 402-404, 12/14/91; No. 404K, 12/14/93.

See Nos. 470-471, 499-500, 534-535, 558-559, 568-569, 595-596, 627-628.

Shrimp — A155

1991, Dec. 31 *Perf. 14*

405 6t Penaeus monodon 3.00 3.00
406 6t Metapenaeus monoceros 3.00 3.00
a. A155 Pair, #405-406 6.50 6.50

Shaheed Mirze Abu Raihan Jaglu, 5th Death Anniv. A156

1992, Feb. 8 Litho. *Perf. 14x13½*

407 A156 2t multicolored 1.75 1.50

World Environment Day — A157

Design: 4t, Scenes of environmental protection and pollution control, vert.

1992, June 5 Litho. *Perf. 14*

408 A157 4t multicolored 1.25 1.25
409 A157 10t multicolored 2.50 2.50

Nawab Sirajuddaulah of Bengal (1733-1757) A158

1992, July 2 Litho. *Perf. 14*

410 A158 10t multicolored 1.75 1.25

Syed Ismail Hossain Sirajee (1880-1931), Writer & Poet — A159

1992, July 17

411 A159 4t multicolored 1.50 1.50

Tree Week — A160

1992, July 17 Litho. *Perf. 14*

412 A160 2t Couple planting tree, horiz. 1.75 1.75
413 A160 4t Birds, trees 2.50 2.50

1992 Summer Olympics, Barcelona — A161

No. 414 — Olympic rings and: a, 4t, Rowing. b, 6t, Hands holding Olympic torch. c, 10t, Peace doves. d, 10t, Clasped hands.

1992, July 25 Litho. *Perf. 14*

414 A161 Block of 4, #a.-d. 9.00 9.00
a.-d. Any single 2.00 2.00

The Star Mosque, 18th Cent. A162

1992, Oct. 29 Litho. *Perf. 14½x14*

415 A162 10t multicolored 3.00 3.00

Masnad-E-Ala Isa Khan, 393rd Anniv. of Death — A163

1992, Sept. 15 *Perf. 14x14½*

416 A163 4t multicolored 1.75 1.25

7th SAARC Summit, Dacca — A164

1992, Dec. 5

417 A164 6t Flags of members 1.75 1.75
418 A164 10t Emblem 2.25 2.25

1992 Bangladesh Natl. Philatelic Exhibition — A165

No. 419: a, Elephant and mahout, ivory work, 19th cent. b, Post rider, mail box and postman delivering mail to villager.

1992, Sept. 26 *Perf. 14½x14*

419 A165 10t Pair, #a.-b. + label 5.50 5.50
a.-b. Either single 2.50 2.50
c. Souv. sheet, imperf. *6.00 6.00*

No. 419c contains one strip of No. 419 with simulated perforations and sold for 25t.

1992 Intl. Conference on Nutrition, Rome — A166

1992, Dec. 5

420 A166 4t multicolored 1.50 1.00

Meer Nisar Ali Titumeer (1782-1831) — A167

1992, Nov. 19 Litho. *Perf. 14½x14*

421 A167 10t multicolored 2.25 2.25

Archaeological Relics, Mahasthan — A168

No. 422 — Relics from 3rd century B.C.-15th century A.D.: a, Terracotta seal and head. b, Terracotta hamsa. c, Terracotta Surya image. d, Gupta stone columns.

1992, Nov. 30 Litho. *Perf. 14½x14*

422 A168 10t Strip of 4, #a.-d. 10.50 10.50
a.-d. Any single 2.50 2.50

Canal Digging — A169

No. 423: a, Workers digging canal. b, Completed project.

1993, Mar. 31 Litho. *Perf. 14½x14*

423 A169 2t Pair, #a.-b. 2.50 2.50
a.-b. Either single .80 .80

No. 300 Overprinted

1992, Aug. 18 Litho. *Perf. 12½x12*

424 A93 10t multicolored 3.00 3.00

Syed Abdus Samad (1895-1964), Soccer Player — A170

1993, Feb. 2 *Perf. 14x14½*

425 A170 2t multicolored 2.00 1.00

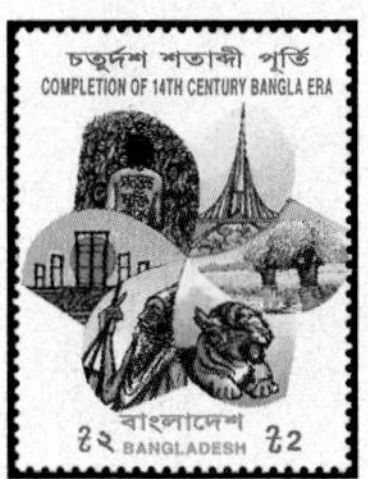

A171

1993, Apr. 14

426 A171 2t multicolored 1.25 .85

Completion of 14th cent. Bengali era.

Haji Shariat Ullah (1770-1839), Social Reformer, Religious and Political Leader — A172

1993, Mar. 10 Litho. *Perf. 14x14½*

427 A172 2t multicolored 2.00 1.25

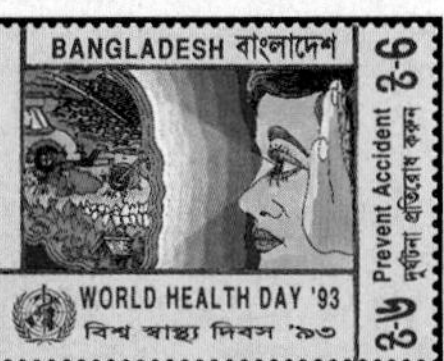

World Health Day A173

1993, Apr. 7 *Perf. 14½x14, 14x14½*

428 A173 6t Prevent accidents 2.50 2.50
429 A173 10t Prevent violence, vert. 3.00 3.00

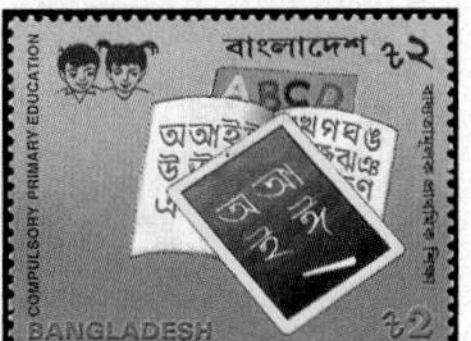

Compulsory Primary Education — A174

1993, May 26

430	A174	2t Slate, chalk, books	1.25	1.25
431	A174	2t Hand writing, children, vert.	1.25	1.25

Nawab Sir Salimullah (1871-1915), Social Reformer — A175

1993, June 7 Litho. ***Perf. 14½x14***

432	A175	4t multicolored	1.40	1.00

Fishing Industry A176

1993, Aug. 15 Litho. ***Perf. 14½x14***

433	A176	2t multicolored	1.00	.75

Tomb of Sultan Ghiyasuddin Azam Shah — A177

1993, Dec. 30 Litho. ***Perf. 14½x14***

434	A177	10t multicolored	1.50	1.50

Scenic Views A178

Designs: No. 435, Sunderban. No. 436, Madhabkunda Waterfall, vert. No. 437, River, mountains, vert. No. 438, Beach, Kuakata.

1993, Oct. 30 ***Perf. 14½x14, 14x14½***

435	A178	10t multicolored	2.50	2.50
436	A178	10t multicolored	2.50	2.50
437	A178	10t multicolored	2.50	2.50
438	A178	10t multicolored	2.50	2.50
a.		Souv. sheet, #435-438, imperf	12.00	12.00
		Nos. 435-438 (4)	10.00	10.00

No. 438a sold for 50t and has simulated perfs.

6th Asian Art Biennial, Bangladesh A179

1993, Nov. 7 Litho. ***Perf. 14x14½***

439	A179	10t multicolored	1.50	1.50

Foy's Lake A180

1993, Nov. 6 ***Perf. 14½x14***

440	A180	10t multicolored	2.00	2.00

Tourism month.

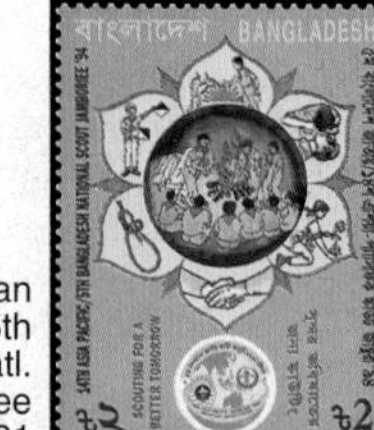

14th Asian Pacific, 5th Bangladesh Natl. Scout Jamboree A181

1994, Jan. 5 ***Perf. 14x14½***

441	A181	2t multicolored	.50	.30

Oral Rehydration Solution, 25th Anniv. — A182

1994, Feb. 5 Litho. ***Perf. 13½x14***

442	A182	2t multicolored	.75	.75

6th SAF Games, Dhaka A183

1993, Dec. 6 ***Perf. 14x13½, 13½x14***

443	A183	2t Shot put	.60	.75
444	A183	4t Runners, vert.	.60	.75

Mosques A184

Mosques: 4t, Interior, Chhota Sona, Nawabgonj. No. 446, Exterior, Chhota Sona. No. 447, Exterior, Baba Adam's, Munshigonj.

1994, Mar. 30 Litho. ***Perf. 14x13½***

445	A184	4t multicolored	.75	.75
446	A184	6t multicolored	.75	.75
447	A184	6t multicolored	.75	.75
		Nos. 445-447 (3)	2.25	2.25

For overprint see No. 509.

ILO, 75th Anniv. A185

Designs: 4t, People, oxen working in fields. 10t, Man rotating gearwheel, vert.

Perf. 14x13½, 13½x14

1994, Apr. 11 Litho.

448	A185	4t multicolored	.65	.50
449	A185	10t multicolored	1.50	1.50

Bangla Era, 15th Cent. — A186

1994, Apr. 14 ***Perf. 13½x14***

450	A186	2t multicolored	.75	.50

Traditional Festivals A187

1994, May 12 ***Perf. 14x13½***

451	A187	4t Folk Festival	.75	.50
452	A187	4t Baishakhi Festival	.75	.50

Intl. Year of the Family — A188

1994, May 15 ***Perf. 13½x14***

453	A188	10t multicolored	2.10	2.10

Tree Planting Campaign A189

1994, June 15 Litho. ***Perf. 13½x14***

454	A189	4t Family planting trees	1.00	1.00
455	A189	6t Hands, seedlings	1.25	1.25

1994 World Cup Soccer Championships, US — A190

Soccer player's uniform colors: a, Red, yellow & blue. b, Yellow, green, & red.

1994, June 17 Litho. ***Perf. 14½***

456	A190	20t Pair, #a.-b. + label	8.50	8.50
a.-b.		Either single	4.00	4.00
		Complete booklet, #456	40.00	

No. 456 was printed in panes of 15 (3x5), with each horizontal row containing Nos. 456a and 456b with a connecting label depicting the championship mascot. The booklet contains two No. 456, attached to the booklet cover by sheet selvage.

Jamuna Multi-Purpose Bridge — A191

1994, July 24 ***Perf. 14½x14***

457	A191	4t multicolored	3.00	1.00

Birds — A192

Designs: 4t, Oriolus xanthornus. No. 459, Gallus gallus. No. 460, Dicrurus paradiseus. No. 461, Dendrocitta vagabunda.

1994, Aug. 31 ***Perf. 14x14½***

458	A192	4t multicolored	.75	.75
459	A192	6t multicolored	1.25	1.25
460	A192	6t multicolored	1.25	1.25
461	A192	6t multicolored	1.25	1.25
a.		Souvenir sheet, #458-461	5.00	5.00
		Nos. 458-461 (4)	4.50	4.50

No. 461a sold for 25t.

Dr. Mohammad Ibrahim (1911-89), Pioneer in Treatment of Diabetes — A193

1994, Sept. 6 Litho. ***Perf. 14½x14***

462	A193	2t multicolored	.75	.50

Nawab Faizunnessa Chowdhurani (1834-1903), Social Reformer A194

1994, Sept. 23 ***Perf. 14x14½***

463	A194	2t multicolored	.75	.50

12th Asian Games, Hiroshima, Japan A195

1994, Oct. 2 ***Perf. 14½x14***

464	A195	4t multicolored	1.75	1.00

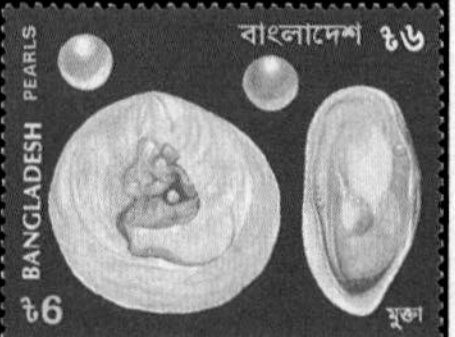

Shells A196

Designs: No. 465, White, pink pearls, oysters. No. 466, Snail, three other shells. No.

467, Scallop, other shells. No. 468, Spiral shaped shells, vert.

Perf. 14½x14, 14x14½

1994, Oct. 30 **Litho.**

465 A196 6t multicolored 2.25 2.25
466 A196 6t multicolored 2.25 2.25
467 A196 6t multicolored 2.25 2.25
468 A196 6t multicolored 2.25 2.25
Nos. 465-468 (4) 9.00 9.00

Democracy Demonstration, Death of Dr. Shamsul Alam Khan Milon, 4th Anniv. — A197

1994, Nov. 27 ***Perf. 14½x14***
469 A197 2t multicolored .75 .45

Martyred Intellectual Type of 1991

No. 470: a, Dr. Harinath Dey. b, Dr. Lt. Col. A.F. Ziaur Rahman. c, Mamum Mahmud. d, Mohsin Ali Dewan. e, Dr. Lt. Col. N.A.M. Jahangir. f, Shah Abdul Majid. g, Muhammad Akhter. h, Meherunnesa.

No. 471: a, Dr. Kasiruddin Talukder. b, Fazlul Haque Choudhury. c, Md. Shamsuzzaman. d, A.K.M. Shamsuddin. e, Lt. Mohammad Anwarul Azim. f, Nurul Amin Khan. g, Mohammad Sadeque. h, Md. Araz Ali.

1994, Dec. 14 ***Perf. 14½***
470 A154 2t Sheet of 8, #a-h + 4 labels 3.50 3.50
a.-h. Any single .35 .35
471 A154 2t Sheet of 8, #a-h + 4 lables 3.50 3.50
a.-h. Any single .35 .35

Vegetables A199

1994, Dec. 24 ***Perf. 14x14½, 14½x14***
472 A199 4t Diplazium esculentum 1.10 1.10
473 A199 4t Momordica charantia 1.10 1.10
474 A199 6t Lagenaria siceraria 1.50 1.50
475 A199 6t Trichosanthes dioica 1.50 1.50
476 A199 10t Solanum melongena 2.10 2.10
477 A199 10t Cucurbita maxima 2.10 2.10
Nos. 472-477 (6) 9.40 9.40

Nos. 472-476 are vert.

World Tourism Organization, 20th Anniv. — A200

1995, Jan. 2 ***Perf. 14½x14***
478 A200 10t multicolored 2.50 2.50

Intl. Trade Fair, Dhaka A201

Designs: 4t, Trade products. 6t, Factories, emblems of industry.

1995, Jan. 7 **Litho.** ***Perf. 14x14½***
479 A201 4t multicolored .65 .65
480 A201 6t multicolored 1.25 1.25

Bangladesh Rifles, Bicent. — A202

1995, Jan. 10 **Litho.** ***Perf. 14½x14***
481 A202 2t shown .85 .85
482 A202 4t Building, battalion 2.25 2.25

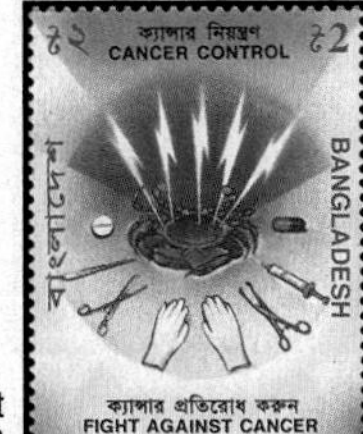

Fight Against Cancer — A203

1995, Apr. 7 **Litho.** ***Perf. 14x14½***
483 A203 2t multicolored .75 .75

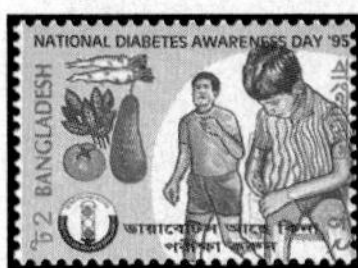

Natl. Diabetes Awareness Day — A204

1995, Feb. 28 ***Perf. 14***
484 A204 2t multicolored 1.50 .80

For overprint see No. O49.

Munshi Mohammad Meherullah (1861-1907), Educator A205

1995, June 7 **Litho.** ***Perf. 14x14½***
485 A205 2t multicolored .75 .45

FAO, 50th Anniv. — A206

1995, Oct. 16 **Litho.** ***Perf. 14***
486 A206 10t multicolored 1.25 1.25

UN, 50th Anniv. A207

UN emblem, "50," and: 2t, Dove of peace, UN headquarters. No. 488, "1945," earth from space, "1995." No. 489, Hands of different nationalities clasping, UN headquarters.

1995, Oct. 24 ***Perf. 14½x14***
487 A207 2t multicolored .75 .75
488 A207 10t multicolored .75 .75
489 A207 10t multicolored 1.75 1.75
Nos. 487-489 (3) 3.25 3.25

Flowers — A208

Designs: No. 490, Bombax ceiba. No. 491, Lagerstroemia speciosa. No. 492, Gloriosa superba. No. 493, Canna indica. No. 494, Bauhinia purpurea. No. 495, Passiflora incarnata.

1995, Oct. 9 ***Perf. 14½x14, 14x14½***
490 A208 6t multicolored 2.00 2.00
491 A208 6t multi, vert. 2.00 2.00
492 A208 10t multi, vert. 2.25 2.25
493 A208 10t multi, vert. 2.25 2.25
494 A208 10t multi, vert. 2.25 2.25
495 A208 10t multi, vert. 2.25 2.25
Nos. 490-495 (6) 13.00 13.00

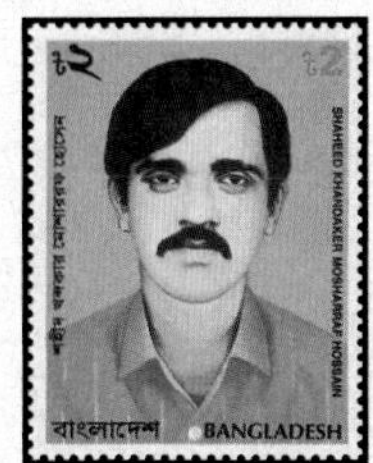

Shaheed Khandaker Mosharraf Hossain A208a

1995, Oct. 16 **Litho.** ***Perf. 13¾x14¼***
496 A208a 2t multi — —

No. 496 was removed from sale shortly after release.

18th Eastern Regional Conference on Tuberculosis and Respiratory Diseases, Dhaka — A209

1995, Oct. 29 **Litho.** ***Perf. 14½x14***
497 A209 6t multicolored 2.25 .75

South Asian Assoc. for Regional Cooperation (SAARC), 10th Anniv. — A210

1995, Dec. 8 **Litho.** ***Perf. 14x14½***
498 A210 2t multicolored 1.75 .75

Martyred Intellectual Type of 1991

No. 499: a, Shaikh Habibur Rahman. b, Dr. Major Naimul Islam. c, Md. Shahidullah. d, Ataur Rahman Khan Khadim. e, A.B.M. Ashraful Islam Bhuiyan. f, Dr. Md. Sadat Ali. g, Sarafat Ali. h, M.A. Sayeed.

No. 500: a, Abdul Ahad. b, Lt. Col. Mohammad Abdul Qadir. c, Mozammel Hoque Chowdhury. d, Rafiqul Haider Chowdhury. e, Dr. Azharul Haque. f, A.K. Shamsuddin. g, Anudwaipayan Bhattacharjee. h, Lutfunnahar Helena.

1995, Dec. 14 **Litho.** ***Perf. 14½x14***
499 A154 2t Sheet of 8, #a-h + 4 labels 6.00 6.00
a.-h. Any single .60 .60
500 A154 2t Sheet of 8, #a-h + 4 labels 6.00 6.00
a.-h. Any single .60 .60

Second Asian Pacific Community Development Scout Camp — A211

1995, Dec. 18 **Litho.** ***Perf. 14x14½***
501 A211 2t multicolored 1.25 .75

Volleyball, Cent. — A212

1995, Dec. 25
502 A212 6t multicolored 1.00 .75

Traditional Costumes — A213

Designs: No. 503, Man in punjabi and lungi, vert. No. 504, Woman in sari, vert. No. 505, Christian bride and groom, vert. No. 506, Muslim bridal couple, vert. No. 507, Hindu bridal couple. No. 508, Buddhist bridal couple.

1995, Dec. 25 ***Perf. 14x14½, 14½x14***
503 A213 6t multicolored 1.75 1.75
504 A213 6t multicolored 1.75 1.75
505 A213 10t multicolored 2.25 2.25
506 A213 10t multicolored 2.25 2.25
507 A213 10t multicolored 2.25 2.25
508 A213 10t multicolored 2.25 2.25
Nos. 503-508 (6) 12.50 12.50

No. 446 Ovptd. in Red

1995 **Litho.** ***Perf. 14x13½***
509 A184 6t multicolored 2.75 2.75

Shaheed Amanullah Mohammad Asaduzzaman (1942-69) A214

1996, Jan. 20 ***Perf. 14x14½***
510 A214 2t multicolored .55 .30

1996 World Cup Cricket Championships — A215

1996, Feb. 14 ***Perf. 14x14½, 14½x14***

511 A215 4t Pitching, vert. 1.40 .60
512 A215 6t At bat, vert. 1.75 .90
513 A215 10t shown 2.50 2.50
Nos. 511-513 (3) 5.65 4.00

Independence, 25th Anniv. — A216

Designs: No. 514, Natl. Martrys' Memorial. No. 515, Industrial development. No. 516, 1971 Destruction of war. No. 517, Educational development. No. 518, Development in communication. No. 519, Development in health.

1996, Mar. 26 **Litho.** ***Perf. 14x14½***

514 A216 4t multicolored .85 .85
515 A216 4t multicolored .85 .85
516 A216 4t multicolored .85 .85
517 A216 4t multicolored .85 .85
518 A216 4t multicolored .85 .85
519 A216 4t multicolored .85 .85
Nos. 514-519 (6) 5.10 5.10

Michael Madhusudan Dutt (1824-73), Writer — A217

1996, June 29 **Litho.** ***Perf. 14x14½***

520 A217 4t multicolored .85 .35

1996 Summer Olympic Games, Atlanta A218

1996, July 19 **Litho.** ***Perf. 14***

521 A218 4t Gymnast, vert. .40 .25
522 A218 6t Judo, vert. .60 .35
523 A218 10t High jumper .75 .75
524 A218 10t Runners .75 .75
a. Souvenir sheet, #521-524 4.00 4.00
Nos. 521-524 (4) 2.50 2.10

No. 524a sold for 50t. Exists imperf.

Sheikh Mujibur Rahman (1920-75), Prime Minister — A219

Design: No. 527, Maulana Mohammad Akrum Khan (1868-1968).

1996 **Litho.** ***Perf. 14x14½***

526 A219 4t multicolored .75 .30
527 A219 4t multicolored .65 .25

Issued: No. 526, 8/15/96, No. 527, 8/18/96.

Ustad Alauddin Khan (1862-1972), Musician A220

1996, Sept. 6 **Litho.** ***Perf. 14x14½***

528 A220 4t multicolored .75 .25

Children's Paintings A221

Perf. 14x14½, 14½x14

1996, Oct. 9 **Litho.**

529 A221 2t Kingfisher, vert. .60 .45
530 A221 4t River Crossing .80 .45

Jailed, 21st Death Anniv. — A222

No. 531: a, Syed Nazrul Islam. b, Tajuddin Ahmad. c, M. Monsoor Ali. d, A.H.M. Quamaruzzaman.

1996, Nov. 3 **Litho.** ***Perf. 14x14½***

531 A222 4t Block of 4, #a.-d. 1.75 1.75

UNICEF, 50th Anniv. — A223

Designs: 4t, Children receiving food, medicine, aid. 10t, Mother holding infant.

1996, Dec. 11

532 A223 4t multicolored .60 .40
533 A223 10t multicolored 1.40 1.40

Martyred Intellectual Type of 1991

No. 534: a, Dr. Jekrul Haque. b, Munshi Kabiruddin Ahmed. c, Md. Abdul Jabbar. d, Mohammad Amir. e, A.K.M. Shamsul Huq Khan. f, Dr. Siddique Ahmed. g, Dr. Soleman Khan. h, S.B.M. Mizanur Rahman.

No. 535: a, Aminuddin. b, Md. Nazrul Islam. c, Zahirul Islam. d, A.K. Lutfor Rahman. e, Afsar Hossain. f, Abul Hashem Mian. g, A.T.M. Alamgir. h, Baser Ali.

1996, Dec. 14 **Litho.** ***Perf. 14½x14***

534 A154 2t Sheet of 8, #a-h + 4 labels 4.75 4.75
535 A154 2t Sheet of 8, #a-h + 4 labels 4.75 4.75

Victory Day, 25th Anniv. A224

Designs: 4t, People celebrating, natl. flag. 6t, Soldiers, monument, vert.

1996, Dec. 16 ***Perf. 14½x14, 14x14½***

536 A224 4t multicolored .35 .35
537 A224 6t multicolored 1.00 1.00

Paul Harris (1868-1947), Founder of Rotary Intl. — A225

1997, Feb. 18 **Litho.** ***Perf. 14x14½***

538 A225 4t multicolored .75 .45

Sheikh Mujibur Rahman's Mar. 7 Speech, 26th Anniv. — A226

1997, Mar. 7 ***Perf. 12½***

539 A226 4t multicolored .75 .45

Sheikh Mujibur Rahman (1920-75) A227

1997, Mar. 17 ***Perf. 14x14½***

540 A227 4t multicolored .75 .45

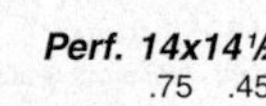

Independence, 25th Anniv. (in 1996) — A228

1997, Mar. 26 **Litho.** ***Perf. 12½***

541 A228 4t multi .75 .45

Heinrich von Stephan (1831-97) A229

1997, Apr. 8 **Litho.** ***Perf. 14x14½***

542 A229 4t multicolored .75 .45

Livestock A230

1997, Apr. 10 **Litho.** ***Perf. 14½x14***

543 A230 4t Goat 1.00 .90
544 A230 4t Sheep 1.00 .90
545 A230 6t Cow 1.25 1.00
546 A230 6t Buffalo 1.25 1.00
Nos. 543-546 (4) 4.50 3.80

Paintings — A231

Designs: 6t, "Tilling the Field-2," by S.M. Sultan (1923-94). 10t, "Three Women," by Quamrul Hassan (1921-88).

1997, June 26 **Litho.** ***Perf. 12½***

547 A231 6t multicolored .65 .65
548 A231 10t multicolored 1.25 1.25

6th Intl. Cricket Council Trophy Championship, Malaysia — A232

1997, Sept. 4

549 A232 10t multicolored 4.25 4.25

Ancient Mosques A233

Designs: 4t, Kusumba Mosque, Naogaon, 1558. 6t, Atiya Mosque, Tangail, 1609. 10t, Bagha Mosque, Rajshahi, 1523.

1997, Sept. 4 **Litho.** ***Perf. 14½x14***

550 A233 4t multicolored .75 .40
551 A233 6t multicolored 1.00 .55
552 A233 10t multicolored 1.50 *2.00*
Nos. 550-552 (3) 3.25 2.95

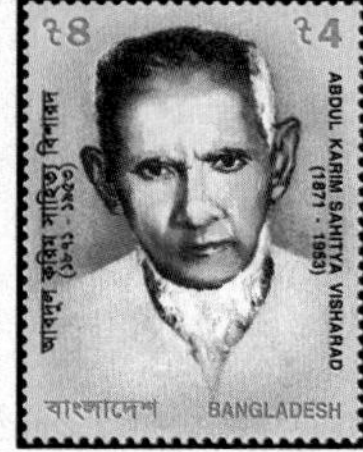

Abdul Karim Sahitya Visharad (1871-1953), Scholar — A234

1997, Oct. 11 ***Perf. 14x14½***

553 A234 4t multicolored .75 .30

9th Asia-Pacific, 7th Bangladesh Rover Moot '97 — A235

1997, Oct. 25 *Perf. 14x14½*
554 A235 2t multicolored .75 .30

Armed Forces, 25th Anniv. A236

1997, Nov. 11 *Perf. 14½x14*
555 A236 2t multicolored 1.10 .55

East Bengal Regiment, 50th Anniv. A237

1998, Feb. 15
556 A237 2t multicolored 1.10 .60

Mohammad Mansooruddin (1904-87) A238

1998, Feb. 4 *Perf. 14x14½*
557 A238 4t multicolored 1.75 1.00

Martyred Intellectual Type of 1991

No. 558: a, Dr. Shamsuddin Ahmed. b, Mohammad Salimullah. c, Mohiuddin Haider. d, A.B.M. Abdur Rahim. e, Nitya Nanda Paul. f, Abdul Jabber. g, Dr. A.B.M. Humayun Kabir. h, Khaja Nizamuddin Bhuiyan.

No. 559: a, Gulam Hossain. b, Ali Karim. c, Md. Moazzem Hossain. d, Rafiqul Islam. e, M. Nur Hussain. f, Captain Mahmood Hossain Akonda. g, Abdul Wahab Talukder. h, Dr. Hasimoy Hazra.

1997, Dec. 14
558 A154 2t Sheet of 8, #a-h, + 4 labels 6.00 6.00
559 A154 2t Sheet of 8, #a-h, + 4 labels 6.00 6.00

Immunization Type of 1990

1998, Jan. 22 *Perf. 14½x14*
560 A139a 1t green .25 .25

For overprint see No. O53.

Bulbul Chowdhury (1919-54), Dancer — A239

1998, May 17 *Perf. 14x14½*
561 A239 4t multicolored .75 .25

Opening of the Bangabandhu Bridge — A240

Designs: 4t, East approach road. 6t, West approach road. 8t, River training works. 10t, Bangabandhu Bridge.

1998, June 23 *Perf. 14*
562 A240 4t multicolored .80 .80
563 A240 6t multicolored .95 .95
564 A240 8t multicolored 1.25 1.25
565 A240 10t multicolored 1.60 1.60
Nos. 562-565 (4) 4.60 4.60

1998 World Cup Soccer Championships, France — A241

1998, June 10
566 A241 6t Trophy 1.10 .45
567 A241 18t Player, trophy 2.75 2.75

Martyred Intellectural Type of 1991

No. 568: a, Md. Khorshed Ali Sarker. b, Abu Yakub Mahfuz. c, S.M. Nurul Huda. d, Nazmul Hoque Sarker. e, Md. Taslim Uddin. f, Gulam Mostafa. g, A. H. Nurul Alam. h, Timir Kanti Dev.

No. 569: a, Altaf Hossain. b, Aminul Hoque. c, S.M. Fazlul Hoque. d, Mozammel Ali. e, Syed Akbar Hossain. f, Sk. Abdus Salam. g, Abdur Rahman. h, Dr. Shyamal Kanti Lala.

1998, Dec. 14 Litho. *Perf. 14½x14*
Sheets of 8, #a-h, + 4 labels
568-569 A154 2t Set of 2 11.50 11.50

Princess Diana (1961-97) — A242

No. 570 — Diana in: a, 8t, Hat. b, 18t, Black dress. c, 22t, Blue dress.

1998, June 6 Litho. *Perf. 14¼*
570 A242 Horiz. strip of 3, #a-c 6.50 6.50

World Solar Program, 1996-2005 A243

Perf. 13¾x14¼
1998, Sept. 24 **Litho.**
571 A243 10t multi 1.50 1.50

World Habitat Day — A244

1998, Oct. 5
572 A244 4t multi 1.50 .75

Intl. Fund for Agricultural Development, 20th Anniv. — A245

Sunflower and: 6t, Farmers, "20." 10t, Vegetables, pickers.

1998, Oct. 17
573 A245 6t multi .75 .45
574 A245 10t multi 1.25 1.25

For overprint see No. 668.

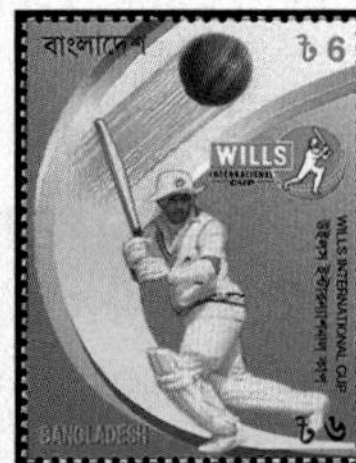
Wills Intl. Cup Cricket Matches A246

1998, Oct. 28
575 A246 6t multi 2.25 1.50

Begum Rokeya (1880-1932), Author, Educator — A247

1998, Dec. 9 Litho. *Perf. 14¼x13¾*
576 A247 4t multi 1.25 .75

Universal Declaration of Human Rights, 50th Anniv. — A248

1998, Dec. 10 *Perf. 13¾x14¼*
577 A248 10t multi 1.25 1.25

UN Peacekeeping, 50th Anniv. — A249

1998, Dec. 30 *Perf. 13¾x14¼*
578 A249 10t multi 1.25 1.25

Qazi Nazrul Islam (1899-1976), Poet — A250

1998, Dec. 31 *Perf. 14¼*
579 A250 6t multi 1.25 .90

Sixth National Scout Jamboree A251

1999, Feb. 6 *Perf. 13¾x14¼*
580 A251 2t multi 1.10 .50

Surjya Sen (1894-1934), Anti-Colonial Leader — A252

1999, Mar. 22 *Perf. 14¼x13¾*
581 A252 4t multi 1.25 .55

Dr. Fazlur Rahman Khan (1929-82), Architect of Sears Tower, Chicago — A253

1999, Apr. 13 *Perf. 13¾x14¼*
582 A253 4t multi 1.10 .65

ICC Cricket World Cup, England — A254

Designs: 8t, Emblems. 10t, Bangladesh flag, cricket ball, tiger.

1999, May 11 *Perf. 13¾x14¼*

583 A254 8t multi 2.75 2.75
584 A254 10t multi 3.00 3.00
a. Souv. sheet, #583-584, perf 14¼ *6.25 6.25*

No. 584a sold for 30t.

Mother Teresa (1910-97) A255

1999, Sept. 5 *Perf. 13¾x14¼*

585 A255 4t multi 1.50 .90

Admission to UN, 25th Anniv. — A256

1999, Sept. 13

586 A256 8t multi .95 .60

Shaheed Mohammad Maizuddin (1930-84) A257

1999, Sept. 27

587 A257 2t multi .85 .50

Intl. Year of Older Persons — A258

1999, Oct. 1

588 A258 6t multi 1.25 .70

World Habitat Day A259

1999, Oct. 4 *Perf. 14¼x13¾*

589 A259 4t multi 1.25 .55

UPU, 125th Anniv. A260

1999, Oct. 9 *Perf. 14¼x13¾*

590 A260 4t Truck .85 .60
591 A260 4t Motorcycle .85 .60
592 A260 6t Boat 1.25 1.25
593 A260 6t Airplanes 1.25 1.25
a. Souv. sheet, #590-593, perf 14¼ *6.00 6.00*
Nos. 590-593 (4) 4.20 3.70

No. 593a sold for 25t. No. 593a exists imperf. Value, $15.

Sir Jagadis Chandra Bose (1858-1937), Physicist A261

1999, Nov. 5 *Perf. 13¾x14¼*

594 A261 4t multi 1.10 .50

Martyred Intellectuals Type of 1991

No. 595: a, Dr. Mohammad Shafi. b, Maulana Kasimuddin Ahmed. c, Quazi Ali Imam. d, Sultanuddin Ahmed. e, A.S.M. Ershadullah. f, Mohammad Fazlur Rahman. g, Dr. Capt. A. K. M. Farooq. h, Md. Latafot Hossain Joarder.

No. 596 — Martyred intellectuals who died in 1971: a, Ram Ranjan Bhattacharjya. b, Abani Mohan Dutta. c, Sunawar Ali. d, Abdul Kader Miah. e, Dr. Major Rezaur Rahman. f, Md. Shafiqul Anowar. g, A.A.M. Mozammel Hoque. h, Khandkar Abul Kashem.

1999, Dec. 14 **Litho.** *Perf. 14¼*

595 A154 2t Sheet of 8, #a-h, + 4 labels 7.00 7.00
596 A154 2r Sheet of 8, #a-h, + 4 labels 5.50 5.50

Millennium — A262

Designs: 4t, Natl. Martyr's Memorial, flag. 6t, Satellite, computer, satellite dish, Bangabandhu Bridge, vert.

Perf. 14¼x13¾, 13¾x14¼

2000, Jan. 1 **Litho.**

597-598 A262 Set of 2 2.50 2.50

Fifth Cub Camporee A263

2000, Feb. 13 *Perf. 13¾x14¼*

599 A263 2t multi .95 .95

Jibanananda Das (1899-1954), Poet — A264

1999, Nov. 22

600 A264 4t multi .95 .95

Dr. Muhammad Shamsuzzoha (1934-69), Educator A265

2000, Feb. 18

601 A265 4t multi .95 .50

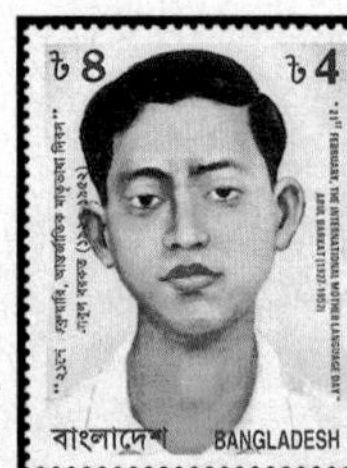

Intl. Mother Language Day — A266

Martyrs: No. 602, 4t, Abul Barkat (1927-52). No. 603, 4t, Abdul Jabbar (1919-52). No. 604, 4t, Shafiur Rahman (1918-52). No. 605, 4t, Rafiq Uddin Ahmad (1926-52).

2000, Feb. 21

602-605 A266 Set of 4 2.40 2.40

World Meteorological Organization, 50th Anniv. — A267

2000, Mar. 23

606 A267 10t multi 1.50 1.50

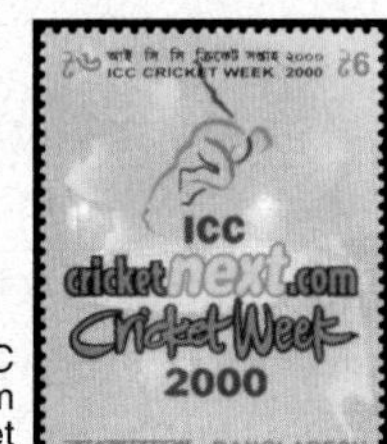

ICC Cricketnext.com Cricket Week — A268

2000, Apr. 8

607 A268 6t multi 1.50 1.00

Insects — A269

Designs: 2t, Wasp. 4t, Grasshopper. 6t, Apis indica. 10t, Bombyx mori.

2000, May 18 *Perf. 14¼*

608-611 A269 Set of 4 4.25 4.25

Fauna A270

Designs: No. 612, 4t, Gekko gecko. No. 613, 4t, Hystrix indica. No. 614, 6t, Python molurus. No. 615, 6t, Varanus bengalensis.

2000, May 18 *Perf. 14¼x13¾*

612-615 A270 Set of 4 4.00 4.00

7th Pepsi Asia Cricket Cup — A271

2000, May 28 *Perf. 13¾x14¼*

616 A271 6t multi 1.90 1.10

Birds A272

Designs: No. 617, 4t, Amaurornis phoenicurus. No. 618, 4t, Gallicrex cinerea. No. 619, 6t, Phalacrocorax niger, vert. No. 620, 6t, Ardeola grayii, vert.

Perf. 14¼x13¾, 13¾x14¼

2000, July 15

617-620 A272 Set of 4 4.25 4.25

For overprint, see No. 723.

2000 Summer Olympics, Sydney — A273

Shot putters: 6t, Woman. 10t, Man.

2000, Sept. 18 *Perf. 13¾x14¼*

621-622 A273 Set of 2 2.50 2.50

Bangladesh — People's Republic of China Diplomatic Relations, 25th Anniv. — A274

2000, Oct. 4 **Litho.** *Perf. 12½*

623 A274 6t multi 1.10 .75

Idrakpur Fort, Munshigonj — A275

Vajrasattva Bhojavihara Mainamati, Comilla — A276

Perf. 14¼x13¾, 13¾x14¼

2000, Nov. 5 Litho.

624 A275 4t multi	.65	.50
625 A276 6t multi	1.10	.85

Intl. Volunteers Year (in 2001) — A277

2000, Dec. 5 Litho. *Perf. 13¾x14¼*

626 A277 6t multi	1.25	.75

Martyred Intellectuals Type of 1991

No. 627, 2t: a, M. A. Gofur. b, Faizur Rahman Ahmed. c, Muslimuddin Miah. d, Sgt. Shamsul Karim Khan. e, Bhikku Zinananda. f, Abdul Jabber. g, Sekander Hayat Chowdhury. h, Chishty Shah Helalur Rahman.

No. 628, 2t: a, Birendra Nath Sarker. b, A. K. M. Nurul Haque. c, Sibendra Nath Mukherjee. d, Zahir Raihan. e, Ferdous Dowla Bablu. f, Capt. A. K. M. Nurul Absur. g, Mizanur Rahman Miju. h, Dr. Shamshad Ali.

2000 Litho. *Perf. 12½*

Sheets of 8, #a-h, + 4 labels

627-628 A154 Set of 2	8.00	8.00

Hason Raza (1854-1922) A278

2000 ? *Perf. 13¾x14¼*

629 A278 6t multi	1.50	.75

2001 Census — A279

2001, Jan. 23 Litho. *Perf. 13¾x14¼*

630 A279 4t multi	1.50	.75

UN High Commissioner for Refugees, 50th Anniv. (in 2001) — A280

Perf. 13¾x14¼

2000, Dec. 14 Litho.

631 A280 10t multi	1.50	1.50

Hunger-Free Bangladesh — A281

Perf. 14¼x13¾

2001, Mar. 17 Litho.

632 A281 6t multi	1.50	1.00

Peasant Women, by Rashid Chowdhury A282

2001, Apr. 1 Litho. *Perf. 13¾x14¼*

633 A282 10t multi	2.25	2.25

Houses of Worship — A283

No. 634: a, Lalbagh Kella Mosque. b, Uttara Ganabhavan, Natore. c, Armenian Church, Armanitola. d, Panam Nagar, Sonargaon.

2001, Apr. 30 *Perf. 14¼x13¾*

634 A283 6t Block of 4, #a-d	4.50	4.50

World No Tobacco Day A284

2001, May 31 Litho. *Perf. 14¼x13¾*

635 A284 10t multi	2.25	2.25

Artists — A285

No. 636: a, Ustad Gul Mohammad Khan (1876-1979). b, Ustad Khadem Hossain Khan (1923-91). c, Gouhar Jamil (1928-80). d, Abdul Alim (1931-74).

2001, May 31 *Perf. 13¾x14¼*

636 A285 6t Block of 4, #a-d	4.00	4.00

Begum Sufia Kamal (1911-99), Poet — A286

2001, June 20

637 A286 4t multi	.95	.30

Fish — A287

No. 638: a, Hilsa. b, Tengra. c, Punti. d, Khalisa.

2001, July 9 *Perf. 14¼x13¾*

638 A287 10t Block of 4, #a-d	4.50	4.50

First Completion of Parliamentary Term — A288

2001, July 13

639 A288 10t multi	3.25	2.40

8th Parliamentary Elections — A289

2001, Sept. 30

640 A289 2t multi	.95	.45

Year of Dialogue Among Civilizations A290

2001, Oct. 24 *Perf. 14¼*

641 A290 10t multi	2.50	2.50
a. Souvenir sheet of 1	5.25	5.25

No. 641a sold for 30t.

Meer Mosharraf Hossain (1847-1912) A291

2001, Nov. 13 *Perf. 13¾x14¼*

642 A291 4t multi	1.25	.40

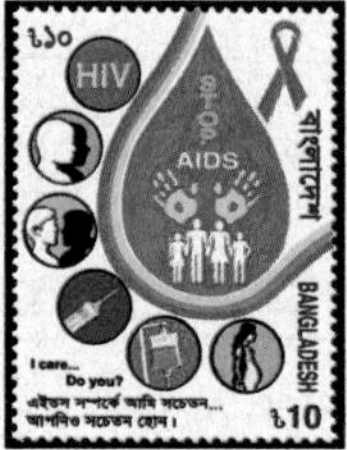
World AIDS Day — A292

2001, Dec. 1

643 A292 10t multi	1.75	1.75

Victory in War of Independence, 30th Anniv. — A293

Medals: a, Bir Bikram. b, Bir Protik. c, Bir Sreshto. d, Bir Uttom.

2001, Dec. 16

644 Horiz. strip of 4	8.50	8.50
a.-d. A293 10t Any single	1.75	1.75

10th Asian Art Biennale — A294

2002, Jan. 9 Litho. *Perf. 13¾x14¼*

645 A294 10t multi	*1.50*	*1.50*

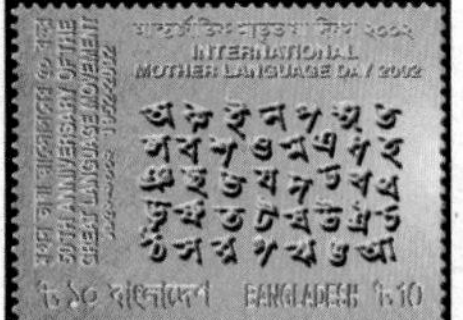
Great Language Movement, 50th Anniv. A295

No. 646: a, 38 symbols. b, Monument. c, 30 symbols.

30t, Emblem, vert.

2002, Feb. 21 *Perf. 14¼x13¾*

646 Horiz. strip of 3	4.25	4.25
a.-c. A295 10t Any single	1.40	1.40

Souvenir Sheet

Perf. 14¼

647 A295 30t multi	4.25	4.25

Rokuon-ji Temple, Japan — A296

2002, Apr. 11 Litho. *Perf. 13¾x14¼*

648 A296 10t multi	1.40	1.25

Bangladesh-Japan diplomatic relations, 30th anniv.

Poverty Alleviation Through Goat Production
A297

2002, Apr. 27 *Perf. 14¼x13¾*
649 A297 2t multi .55 .25

United Nations Special Session on Children — A298

2002, Apr. 28 *Perf. 13¾x14¼*
650 A298 10t multi 1.50 1.50

Mohammad Nasiruddin (1888-1994), Journalist
A299

2002, May 21
651 A299 4t multi 1.10 .35

A300

Tree Planting Campaign
A301

Perf. 14¼x13¾, 13¾x14¼
2002, June 15
652 A300 10t shown 1.40 1.40
653 A300 10t Tree, vert. 1.40 1.40
654 A301 10t shown 1.40 1.40
Nos. 652-654 (3) 4.20 4.20

2002 World Cup Soccer Championships, Japan and Korea — A303

No. 656: a, Flags of participants, trophy in UR. b, World map, soccer field, trophy. c, Flags, trophy in UL.

2002, May 31 Litho. *Perf. 14¼x13¾*
656 Horiz. strip of 3 4.25 4.25
a.-c. A303 10t Any single 1.25 1.25

SOS Children's Village, 30th Anniv. — A304

2002, July 9 Litho. *Perf. 13¾x14¼*
657 A304 6t multi 1.40 .40

World Population Day — A305

2002, July 11
658 A305 6t multi 1.40 .40

Fish
A306

Designs: No. 659, 4t, Labeo gonius. No. 660, 4t, Ompook pabda.

2002, Aug. 10 *Perf. 14¼x13¾*
659-660 A306 Set of 2 1.60 1.60

Bangladesh - United Kingdom Friendship Bridge — A307

2002, Sept. 10
661 A307 4t multi 1.40 .35

World Habitat Day — A308

2002, Oct. 7 *Perf. 13¾x14¼*
662 A308 4t multi 1.40 .35

Children's Games
A309

Designs: No. 663, 4t, Dariabandha. No. 664, 4t, Kanamachee.

2002, Nov. 10 *Perf. 14¼x13¾*
663-664 A309 Set of 2 2.00 2.00

For overprint see No. 686.

National Book Year (in 2002) — A310

2003, Jan. 1 Litho. *Perf. 13¾x14¼*
665 A310 6t multi .65 .35

Jasimuddin (1903-76), Poet — A311

2003, Jan. 1
666 A311 5t multi .65 .35

South Asian Soccer Federation Championships
A312

2003, Jan. 10
667 A312 10t multi 1.90 1.50

No. 574 Overprinted

Perf. 13¾x14¼
2003, Feb. 19 **Litho.**
668 A245 10t multi 1.90 1.90

Shefa-ul-mulk Hakim Habib-ur-Rahman — A313

Perf. 13¾x14¼
2003, Feb. 23 **Litho.**
669 A313 8t multi .75 .75

Pres. Ziaur Rahman (1936-81)
A314

2003, May 29
670 A314 4t multi .75 .35

Tree Planting Campaigns
A315

Designs: 6t, Fruit, woman and child planting tree. 8t, Family, hands with seedling, vert. 12t, Tree, fruit, family, vert.

2003 *Perf. 14¼x13¾, 13¾x14¼*
671-673 A315 Set of 3 5.50 5.50

Issued: 6t, 6/12; 8t, 12t, 6/1.

Fruit tree planting fortnight (No. 671); National tree plantation campaign (Nos. 672-673).

Labeo Calbasu
A316

Perf. 14¼x13¾
2003, Aug. 12 **Litho.**
674 A316 2t multi .65 .65

Inauguration of Rajshahi - Dhaka Rail Link — A317

2003, Aug. 14 *Perf. 13¾x14¼*
675 A317 10t multi 1.90 1.90

49th Commonwealth Parliamentary Conference — A318

2003, Oct. 7 *Perf. 14¼x13¾*
676 A318 10t multi 1.50 .80

Eid Mubarak A319

2003, Nov. 25 ***Perf. 13¾x14¼***
677 A319 4t multi 1.50 1.50

Intl. Center for Diarrheal Disease Research, Bangladesh, 25th Anniv. — A320

2003, Dec. 7
678 A320 10t multi 1.50 1.50

Rajshahi University, 50th Anniv. — A321

2003, Dec. 21 ***Perf. 14¼x13¾***
679 A321 4t multi 1.50 1.00

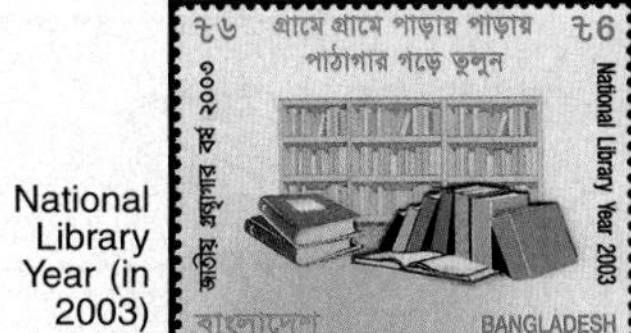

National Library Year (in 2003) A322

2004, Jan. 1 Litho. ***Perf. 14¼x13¾***
680 A322 6t multi .75 .75

Seventh Bangladesh and Eighth SAARC Scout Jamboree — A323

2004, Jan. 6
681 A323 2t multi .75 .75

Sport and the Environment — A324

2004, Jan. 10
682 A324 10t multi 1.50 1.50

11th Asian Art Biennale A325

2004, Jan. 15
683 A325 5t multi .65 .65

National Day A326

2004, Mar. 24
684 A326 5t multi .60 .60

World Health Day A327

2004, Apr. 7
685 A327 6t multi .60 .60

No. 663 Overprinted

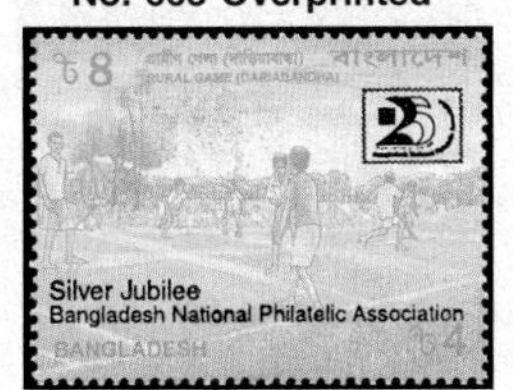

2004, May 31
686 A309 4t multi .60 .60

National Tree Plantation Campaign — A328

No. 687: a, Fruit, stylized tree. b, Trees and other plants.

2004, June 1 Litho. ***Perf. 13¾x14¼***
687 A328 10t Horiz. pair, #a-b .70 .70

Bangladesh - Iran Friendship — A329

No. 688: a, Tower, Iranian flag, poet Hafez Shirazi. b, Tower, Bangladesh flag, poet Nazrul Islam.

2004, June 3 Litho. ***Perf. 14¼x13¾***
688 A329 10t Horiz. pair, #a-b 2.75 2.75

Fruit Tree Planting Fortnight A330

2004, June 6 ***Perf. 13¾x14¼***
689 A330 10t multi 1.20 .75

Intl. Year of Rice A331

2004, June 21 ***Perf. 14¼x13¾***
690 A331 5t multi .60 .60

World Population Day — A332

2004, July 11 Litho. ***Perf. 13¾x14¼***
691 A332 6t multi .50 .50

Bangladesh Partnership With United Nations, 30th Anniv. — A333

2004, Sept. 16 ***Perf. 14¼x13¾***
692 A333 4t multi .50 .50

Bhasani Novo Theater, Dhaka A334

2004, Sept. 25
693 A334 4t multi .50 .50

Rotary International, Cent. (in 2005) — A335

2004, Oct. 22 Litho. ***Perf. 13¾x14¼***
694 A335 4t multi .25 .25

Miniature Sheet

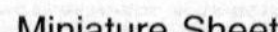

Flowers — A336

No. 695: a, Argemone mexicana. b, Cyanotis axillaris. c, Thevetia peruvians. d, Pentapetes phoenicea. e, Aegle marmelos. f, Datura stramonium.

2004, Dec. 1 Litho. ***Perf. 14¼x12½***
695 A336 5t Sheet of 6, #a-f 3.25 3.25

13th South Asian Association for Regional Cooperation Summit, Dhaka — A337

2004, Dec. 8 ***Perf. 13¾x14¼***
696 A337 6t multi .50 .50

Fish — A338

No. 697: a, Sperata aor. b, Notopterus notepterus.

Perf. 14¼x13¾
2004, Dec. 20 **Litho.**
697 A338 10t Horiz. pair, #a-b .70 .70

6th National Cub Scout Camporee A339

Perf. 13¾x14¼
2004, Dec. 26 **Litho.**
698 A339 6t multi .75 .75

Intl. Year of Microcredit — A340

No. 699: a, 4t, Woman with bowl, globe on cart with coin wheels. b, 10t, Woman pushing handle on coin and globe pulley system.

2005, Jan. 15 ***Perf. 14¼x13¾***
699 A340 Horiz. pair, #a-b 1.75 1.75

South Asia Tourism Year A341

2005, Feb. 1
700 A341 4t multi .75 .75

Independence Day — A342

2005, Mar. 24
701 A342 10t multi 1.25 1.25

Cooperative Movement, Cent. — A343

2005, Mar. 31 ***Perf. 13¾x14¼***
702 A343 5t multi .75 .75

National Tree Planting Campaign — A344

No. 703: a, Family planting tree. b, Three trees.

2005, June 1 ***Perf. 14¼x13¾***
703 A344 6t Horiz. pair, #a-b 1.50 1.50

Famous Men — A345

No. 704: a, G. A. Mannan (1933-92), choreographer. b, Ustad Phuljhuri Khan (1920-82), musician. c, Usted Abed Hossain Khan (1928-96), musician. d, Ustad Munshi Raisuddin (1901-73), musician.

2005, June 5 ***Perf. 13¾x14¼***
704 A345 6t Block of 4, #a-d 2.25 2.25

Nandus Nandus A346

2005, Aug. 7 ***Perf. 14¼x13¾***
705 A346 10t multi 1.25 1.25

Dr. Nawab Ali (1902-77), Physician A347

2005, Dec. 4 Litho. ***Perf. 13¾x14¼***
706 A347 8t multi .25 .25

Science Book Year (in 2005) A348

2006, Jan. 1 ***Perf. 14¼x13¾***
707 A348 10t multi .30 .30

World Summit on the Information Society, Tunis (in 2005) — A349

2006, Jan. 22
708 A349 10t multi .30 .30

OPEC Intl. Development Fund, 30th Anniv. — A350

2006, Jan. 28
709 A350 10t multi .30 .30

Diplomatic Relations Between Bangladesh and People's Republic of China, 30th Anniv. — A351

No. 710: a, Tienanmen Square, Beijing. b, National Assembly Building, Dhaka. c, Gabkhan River Bridge, Bangladesh. d, Great Wall of China.

2006, Mar. 6 ***Perf. 12***
710 Horiz. strip of 4 2.75 2.75
a.-d. A351 10t Any single .50 .40
e. Souvenir sheet, #710a-710d 3.25 3.25

National Day A352

2006, Mar. 26 ***Perf. 14¼x13¾***
711 A352 10t multi .50 .50

World Health Day — A353

2006, July 19 Litho. ***Perf. 13¾x14¼***
712 A353 6t multi .25 .25

ICC Under 19 World Cricket Cup (in 2004) — A354

2006, July 19
713 A354 10t multi .30 .30

Tree Planting Campaign and Tree Fair — A355

2006, June 5 ***Perf. 14¼x13¾***
714 A355 10t multi .30 .30

Five Years of Peace and Development A356

2006, Oct. 25 Litho. ***Perf. 13¾x14¼***
715 A356 10t multi .30 .30

World AIDS Day — A357

2006, Dec. 6
716 A357 10t multi .30 .30

Mohamed Habibullah Bahar Choudhury (1906-66), Writer — A358

2007, June 25
717 A358 10t multi .30 .30

Intl. Women's Day — A359

2007, Mar. 8
718 A359 10t multi .30 .30

World Health Day — A360

2007, Apr. 7
719 A360 6t multi .25 .25

Natl. Tree Planting Campaign A361

2007, June 3
720 A361 10t multi .30 .30

Scouting, Cent. — A362

No. 721 — Scouting Centenary emblem and: a, Scouts. b, Lord Robert Baden-Powell.

2007, July 9 ***Perf. 14¼x13¾***
721 A362 10t Horiz. pair, #a-b .60 .60

2007 ICC Cricket World Cup, West Indies — A363

No. 722: a, Cricket World Cup, bowler, tiger, horiz. b, Batsman, Cricket World cup, horiz. c, Cricket players, bails, wickets, glove and balls. d, Players, Cricket World Cup.

Perf. 14¼x13¾ (horiz. stamps), 13¾x14¼
2007, Apr. 19
722 A363 10t Block of 4, #a-d 1.25 1.25

No. 617 Overprinted

Methods and Perfs. As Before

2007, July 29
723 A272 4t multicolored .25 .25

Dr. Muhammad Yunus, 2006 Nobel Peace Prize Winner — A364

Perf. 13¾x14¼

2007, Aug. 29 **Litho.**
724 A364 10t multi 20.00 20.00

On Sept. 2, 2007 No. 724 was withdrawn from sale because "Muhammad" was abbreviated rather than spelled out, and the Nobel medal shown was for Medicine and not Peace,

Dr. Muhammad Yunus, 2006 Nobel Peace Prize Winner — A365

2007, Sept. 7 **Litho.** ***Perf. 13¾x14¼***
725 A365 10t multi .30 .30

Bangladesh Flood Relief — A366

No. 726: a, Three children standing in flood water. b, People and goats in flood water. c, People on corrugated metal roof. d, Line of people standing in flood water. e, People with food bowls, inundated buildings.

2007, Sept. 13 ***Perf. 13½x12½***
726 Sheet of 5 1.00 1.00
a.-e. A366 2t Any single .25 .25

No. 726 was printed as a sheet of six stamps. The upper left stamp, showing Prime Minister Fakhruddin Ahmed, was removed from all sheets prior to sale, because he did not give permission for his image to be used on the stamp.

2007 ICC World Twenty20 Cricket Tournament, South Africa — A367

No. 727: a, Batsman, map of South Africa. b, Cricket match.

2007, Sept. 24 ***Perf. 14¼x13¾***
727 A367 4t Horiz. pair, #a-b .75 .75

Intl. Migrants Day A368

2007, Dec. 18
728 A368 10t multi .30 .30

Independence Day — A369

2008, Mar. 25 ***Perf. 13¾x14¼***
729 A369 10t multi .30 .30

World Health Day A370

2008, Apr. 7 **Litho.** ***Perf. 14½x13¾***
730 A370 10t multi .30 .30

Sundarbans UNESCO World Heritage Site — A371

No. 731: a, Deer. b, River. c, Man in jungle. d, Tiger.

2008, Apr. 18 ***Perf. 14½x13¾***
731 A371 10t Block of 4, #a-d 2.00 2.00
e. Souvenir sheet, #731a-731d, perf. 13¾ 3.00 3.00
f. As "e," imperf. 5.00 5.00

Nos. 731e and 731f each sold for 50t.

Reign of Aga Khan, 50th Anniv. — A372

Text "Celebrating 50 Years": No. 732, 3t, Against green background. No. 733, 3t, Against red background. No. 734, 6t, In circle, denomination in white. No. 735, 6t, In circle, denomination in gold.

2008, May 19 ***Perf. 13¾x14½***
732-735 A372 Set of 4 .55 .55

2008 Summer Olympics, Beijing — A373

No. 736: a, 10t, Runners. b, 15t, Shooting. c, 20t, Mascots of 2008 Summer Olympics. d, 25t, Greece #117, Bangladesh #122, Pierre de Coubertin.

2008, July 6 ***Perf. 14½x13¾***
736 A373 Block of 4, #a-d 2.10 2.10

Stamp Day — A374

2008, July 29 ***Imperf.***
737 A374 50t multi 1.50 1.50

Miniature Sheet

Japan International Cooperation Agency — A375

No. 738: a, 3t, Khepupara Radar Station, Patuakhali. b, 7t, Vocational training program. c, 10t, Jamuna Multi-purpose Bridge. d, 10t, Polio vaccination program.

2008, Sept. 23 ***Perf. 12½x12***
738 A375 Sheet of 4, #a-d .90 .90

Dhaka Chamber of Commerce and Industry, 50th Anniv. — A376

2008, Oct. 23 **Litho.** ***Perf. 13¾x14½***
739 A376 10t multi .30 .30

Agriculture Day — A377

2008, Nov. 15
740 A377 4t multi .25 .25

Nimtali Deuri, Dhaka A378

2008, Nov. 28 ***Perf. 14½x13¾***
741 A378 6t multi .25 .25

Dhaka as capital city, 400th anniv.

Beach, Cox's Bazar — A379

2008, Nov. 30 ***Perf. 12½***
742 A379 10t multi .30 .30

Intl. Day of Persons with Disabilities A380

2008, Dec. 3 ***Perf. 14½x13¾***
743 A380 3t multi .25 .25

Intl. Year of Sanitation A381

2008, Dec. 24 ***Perf. 13¾x14½***
744 A381 3t multi .25 .25

Souvenir Sheet

Bangladesh No. 32 — A382

2009, Feb. 20 ***Perf. 12½x14½***
745 A382 50t multi 1.50 1.50

Intl. Mother Language Day.

Sheikh Mujibur Rahman (1920-75), President, and Children — A383

2009, Mar. 16 ***Perf. 12½***
746 A383 10t multi .30 .30

Children's Day.

National Day — A384

2009, Mar. 25
747 A384 3t multi .25 .25

World Health Day — A385

2009, Apr. 7 Litho. ***Perf. 13¾x14½***
748 A385 3t multi .25 .25

Souvenir Sheet

China 2009 World Stamp Exhibition, Luoyang — A386

No. 749: a, 10t, Exhibition emblem. b, 10t, Exhibition mascot. c, 20t, Ox.

2009, Apr. 10 ***Perf. 14½x12½***
749 A386 Sheet of 3, #a-c, + label 1.25 1.25

No. 749 also was issued in a quantity of 750 with serial numbers. Value, $35.

Shamsun Nahar Mahmud (1908-64), Educator A387

2009, May 26 ***Perf. 13¾x14½***
750 A387 4t multi .25 .25

Natl. Tree Plantation Campaign and Tree Fair — A388

2009, May 31
751 A388 3t multi .25 .25

Daylight Savings Time — A389

2009, June 19 ***Perf. 12x13¾***
752 A389 5t multi .25 .25

World Population Day A390

2009, July 11 ***Perf. 14½x13¾***
753 A390 6t multi .25 .25

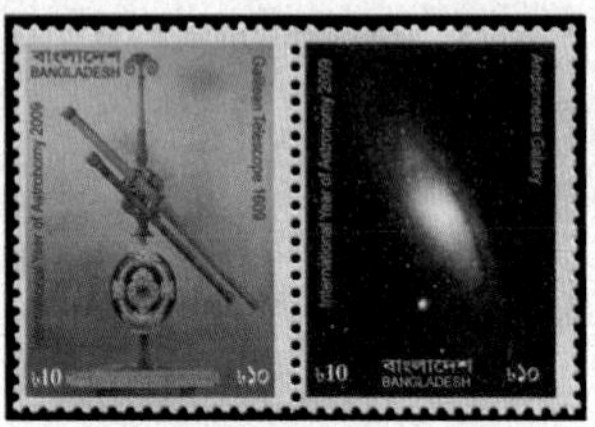

Intl. Year of Astronomy — A391

No. 754: a, Telescope of Galileo Galilei, 1609. b, Andromeda Galaxy.

2009, July 19 ***Perf. 12***
754 A391 10t Pair, #a-b .60 .60

Miniature Sheet

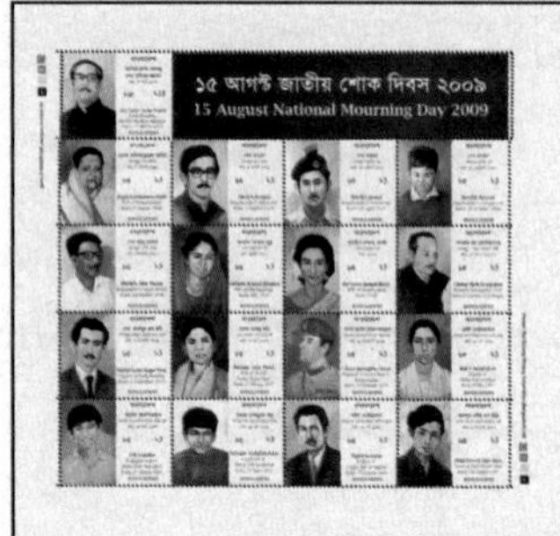

National Mourning Day — A392

No. 755: a, 3t, Begum Fazilatunnessa Mujib. b, 3t, Sheikh Kamal. c, 3t, Sheikh Jamal. d, 3t, Sheikh Russel. e, 3t, Sheikh Abu Naser. f, 3t, Sultana Kamal Khuku. g, 3t, Parveen Jamal Rosy. h, 3t, Abdur Rab Serniabat. i, 3t, Sheikh Fazlul Haque Moni. j, 3t, Begum Arju Moni. k, 3t, Colonel Jamiluddin Ahmed. l, 3t, Baby Serniabat. m, 3t, Arif Serniabat. n, 3t, Sukanto Abullah Babu. o, 3t, Shahid Serniabat. p, 3t, Abdul Nayeem Khan Rintu. q, 15t, Sheikh Mujibur Rahman, President of Bangladesh.

2009, Aug. 12
755 A392 Sheet of 17, #a-q, + label 1.90 1.90

Stamps depict members of family of Sheikh Mujibur Rahman killed in Aug. 15, 1975, army coup.

World Food Day — A393

No. 756: a, Medal. b, Various foods. c, Boat carrying crops. d, Fishing boat, net full of fish.

2009, Oct. 16 Litho. ***Perf. 14¼x13¾***
756 A393 3t Block of 4, #a-d .35 .35

Center for the Rehabilitation of the Paralyzed, 30th Anniv. — A394

No. 757: a, Entrance to Center, two women. b, Patients and staff.

2009, Nov. 12 ***Perf. 12¼x12½***
757 A394 7t Horiz. pair, #a-b .40 .40

Prof. Abdul Moktader (1909-93), Educator A395

2009, Dec. 27 ***Perf. 14¼x13¾***
758 A395 4t multi .25 .25

Eighth National Scout Jamboree A396

2010, Jan. 16
759 A396 10t multi .30 .30

Miniature Sheet

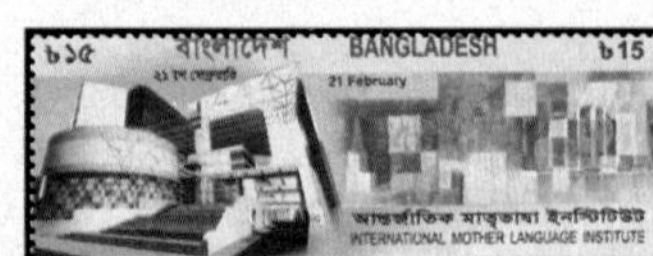

Rose Varieties Cultivated in Bangladesh — A397

No. 760: a, Alec's Red. b, Royal Highness. c, Queen Elizabeth. d, Ballerina. e, Alexander. f, Blue Moon. g, Papa Meilland. h, Double Delight. i, Iceberg. j, Sonia. k, Sunblest. l, Picadilly. m, Pascali.

2010, Feb. 11 ***Perf. 12***
760 A397 10t Sheet of 13, #a-m, + label 3.75 3.75

Opening of Intl. Mother Language Institute, Dhaka — A398

2010. Feb. 21
761 A398 15t multi .45 .45

Intl. Women's Day A399

2010, Mar. 3 ***Perf. 14¼x13¾***
762 A399 5t multi .25 .25

A souvenir sheet containing one 10t stamp commemorating National Children's Day sold for 25t.

Miniature Sheet

National Day — A400

No. 763 — Liberation War Monuments at: a, Public Library Campus, Brahman Baria. b, Shafipur, Gazipur. c, Jagannath Hall, Dhaka University. d, Vocational Training Institute, Rangpur.

2010, Mar. 26 ***Perf. 14¾x14¼***
763 A400 5t Sheet of 4, #a-d .60 .60

2010 Intl. Cricket Council World Twenty 20 Tournament, West Indies A401

2010, Apr. 22 Litho. ***Perf. 13¼***
764 A401 15t multi .45 .45

Souvenir Sheet

Bangabandhu Sheikh Mujib Medical University, 12th Anniv. — A402

2010, May 2 ***Perf. 13¾x12***
765 A402 20t multi .60 .60

Natl. Tree Planting Campaign and Tree Fair A403

2010, June 1 ***Perf. 14¼x14***
766 A403 6t multi .25 .25

Dhaka as Capital City, 400th Anniv. — A404

No. 767: a, The Great Katra, Mughal era. b, Buckland Bund on Buriganga River, British era. c, Kamlapur Railway Station, Pakistan era. d, Dhaka in 2008.

2010, June 16 ***Perf. 12x14¼***
767 A404 10t Block of 4, #a-d 1.25 1.25

Intl. Center for Diarrheal Disease Research in Bangladesh, 50th Anniv. A405

2010, June 20 ***Perf. 13½***
768 A405 5t gold & black .25 .25

2010 World Cup Soccer Championships, South Africa — A406

No. 769: a, Two players. b, Three players. c, Mascot.

2010, July 11 ***Perf. 14¼x13¾***
769 Horiz. strip of 3 1.25 1.25
a.-b. A406 10t Either single .30 .30
c. A406 20t multi .60 .60

Souvenir Sheet

Bangkok 2010 Intl. Stamp Exhibition — A407

No. 770: a, Raj Banbihar (Buddhist Monastery), Rangamati, Bangladesh. b, Buddha Dhatu Jadi (Buddhist temple), Bandarban, Bangladesh.

2010, Aug. 2 ***Perf. 12***
770 A407 20t Sheet of 2, #a-b 1.25 1.25

No. 770 also was issued in a quantity of 2,000 with serial numbers. Value, $25.

Miniature Sheet

Indigenous People — A408

No. 771: a, Chakma woman with blue and red clothes. b, Chakma woman with sash. c, Chakma woman weaving. d, Two Chakma women. e, Marma woman with flower above ear. f, Marma woman holding bouquet of flowers. g, Marma women picking crops. h, Marma women dancing. i, Mru woman with red blouse. j, Mru woman with bracelets on arms. k, Mru women pounding grain. l, Mru man spearing animal in pen. m, Tripura woman with red clothes. n, Tripura woman with pale pink clothes. o, Tripura women carrying wood. p, Tripura woman dancing. q, Pangkhua woman. r, Pangkhua woman and man. s, Pangkhua man with basket. t, Pangkhua man with bull's skull.

2010, Aug. 2 **Litho.** ***Perf. 12***
771 A408 5t Sheet of 20, #a-t 3.00 3.00

No. 771 also was issued in a quantity of 1,000 inscribed "Bangkok 2010 - 25th Asian International Stamp Exhibition Bangladesh Participation" in the left and right margins. Value, $45.

Birds — A409

No. 772: a, House sparrow. b, Red munia. c, Spotted dove. d, Common myna.

2010, Sept. 27
772 A409 10t Block of 4, #a-d 1.25 1.25

A souvenir sheet containing No. 772 sold for 100t; value, $4. An imperf. souvenir sheet of No. 772 inscribed "Portugal 2010 World Philatelic Exhibition Bangladesh Participation" exists; value, $20. A pane of four No. 772 (16 stamps) inscribed "Portugal 2010 World Philatelic Exhibition Bangladesh Participation" exists; value, $35.

Year of the Tiger — A410

2010, Sept. 28 ***Perf. 13¼x13***
773 A410 50t multi 1.50 1.50

A souvenir sheet containing No. 773 exists. Value, $15.

Abu Nayem Mohammed Nazibudding Khan (1954-71), Fredom Fighter — A411

2010, Dec. 14 ***Perf. 13½***
774 A411 3t multi .30 .30

Population and Housing Census — A412

2011, Jan. 27 ***Perf. 13¾x14¼***
775 A412 3t multi .60 .60

Seventh National Cub Scout Camporee — A413

2011, Feb. 9 ***Perf. 14¼x13¾***
776 A413 10t multi .60 .60

1972 Return to Bangladesh of Sheikh Mujibur Rahman (1920-75) A414

No. 777: a, Rahman and followers. b, Rahman waving to crowd. c, Rahman.

2011, Feb. 10 ***Perf. 13½***
777 Horiz. strip of 3 1.25 1.25
a.-b. A414 5t Either single .35 .35
c. A414 10t multi .45 .45

Mahatma Gandhi (1869-1948) — A415

No. 778 — Gandhi: a, At Laksham Railway Station on way to Noakhali. b, With others at Noakhali. c, Alone at Noakhali.

2011, Feb. 10 **Litho.**
778 Horiz. strip of 3 1.50 1.50
a. A415 10t multi .35 .35
b. A415 15t multi .50 .30
c. A415 20t multi .65 .65
d. Sheet of 6, 2 each #778a-778c 3.00 3.00

Indipex 2011 World Philatelic Exhibition, New Delhi

2011 ICC Cricket World Cup Championships, Bangladesh A416

No. 779: a, Bowler. b, Batsman. c, Wicket-keeper. d, Fielder.
50t, Players and umpire, horiz.

2011, Feb. 23 ***Perf. 12½***
779 Horiz. strip of 4 2.40 2.40
a.-d. A416 20t Any single .60 .60

Size: 127x91mm

Imperf

780 A416 50t multi 1.50 1.50

Intl. Anti-Corruption Day (in 2010) — A417

2011, Feb. 24 ***Perf. 12½***
781 A417 5t multi .50 .50

Miniature Sheet

Independence, 40th Anniv. — A418

No. 782: a, 10t, Bangabandhu Square Fountain, Dhaka (32x41mm). b, 10t, Victory of Bangla Monument, Chittagong (32x41mm). c, 10t, Memorial of Liberation War, Rajarbagh Police Line, Dhaka (32x43mm). d, 10t, Invincible Bhoirab, Kishoreganj (32x43mm). e, 20t, Sheikh Mujibur Rahman (1920-75), First President of Bangladesh (32x84mm).

Perf. 12x12x14¼x12 (#782a-782b), 14¼x12x12x12 (#782c-782d), 12
2011, Mar. 26
782 A418 Sheet of 5, #a-e 1.75 1.75

Probashi Kallyan Bank — A419

2011, Apr. 20 ***Perf. 12½***
783 A419 10t multi .60 .60

Sir Rabindranath Tagore (1861-1941), Poet — A420

No. 784 — Tagore and: a, Shilaidaha, Kushtia. b, Shahjadpur, Siraganj. c, Dakkhindihi, Khulna. d, Patishar, Naogaon.

2011, May 6 ***Perf. 13½***
784 A420 10t Block of 4, #a-d 1.60 1.60

A souvenir sheet containing a perf. 14¼x13½ example of No. 784 sold for 100t. Value, $1.75

National Tree Planting Campaign — A421

2011, June 1 ***Perf. 14¼x13¾***
785 A421 10t multi .60 .60

Qazi Nazrul Islam (1899-1976), National Poet — A422

No. 786 — Nazrul Islam and: a, House with red roof. b, House, pond and sign. c, Building with arches. d, Sculpture, Nazrul Museum.

Perf. 13¾x14¼

2011, June 24 **Litho.**
786 A422 10t Block of 4, #a-d 1.60 1.60

Imperforate and Perf. 14¼x13¾ examples of souvenir sheets containing Nos. 786a-786d each sold for 100t. Value, $1.75

Rare Turtles — A423

No. 787: a, Hardella thurjii. b, Geoclemys hamiltonii.

2011, July 17 ***Perf. 14¼x13¼***
787 A423 10t Horiz. pair, #a-b 1.20 1.20

A miniature sheet containing four 10t stamps depicting rare animals of Bangladesh sold for 100t. Value, $4.

Miniature Sheet

Birds of the Sundarbans World Heritage Site — A424

No. 788: a, Heliopais personata. b, Leptoptilos javanicus. c, Haliaeetus leucogaster. d, Bubo coromandus. e, Pelargopsis amauroptera. f, Halcyon coromanda. g, Alcedo meninting. h, Halcyon pileata. i, Todiramphus chloris. j, Treron bicincta. k, Gorsachius melanolophus. l, Pitta megarhyncha.

2011, July 17 Litho. ***Perf. 13¾x12***
788 A424 10t Sheet of 12, #a-l 3.25 3.25

No. 788 exists in a quantity of 3,600 with serial number and inscription for Phila Nippon '11 exhibition; value, $20.

Stringed Instruments — A425

No. 789: a, Dotara (orange background). b, Ektara (green background). c, Sarinda (pale lilac background). d, Sarangi (blue background).

2011, July 21 ***Perf. 14¼x13¾***
789 A425 5t Block of 4, #a-d 2.00 2.00

Miniature Sheet

Silver Coins — A426

No. 790 — Silver coins from reign of: a, Sultan Fakhr al-Din Mubarak Shah, 1334-49. b, Sultan Shams al-Din Ilyas Shah, 1342-57. c, Sultan Ghiyath al-Din A'zam Shah, 1389-1410. d, Sultan Jalal al-Din Muhammad Shah, 1415-32.

2011, July 21 ***Perf. 13¾x12***
790 A426 10t Sheet of 4, #a-d 2.00 2.00

Miniature Sheet

PhilaNippon '11 Intl. Philatelic Exhibition, Yokohama — A427

No. 791: a, Imperial Palace, Tokyo. b, Cherry blossoms. c, Mt. Fuji. d, Kiyomizu Temple, Kyoto. e, Sumo wrestling.

2011, July 21 ***Perf. 12x13¾***
791 A427 10t Sheet of 5, #a-d 3.00 3.00

No. 791 sold for 100t.

Dhaka Club, Cent. A428

2011, Aug. 19 ***Perf. 14¼x13¾***
792 A428 3t multi .25 .25

E-Asia 2011 Conference, Dhaka — A429

2011, Dec. 1 **Litho.**
793 A429 10t multi .25 .25

Victory in War of Independence, 40th Anniv. — A430

2011, Dec. 16
794 A430 10t multi .25 .25

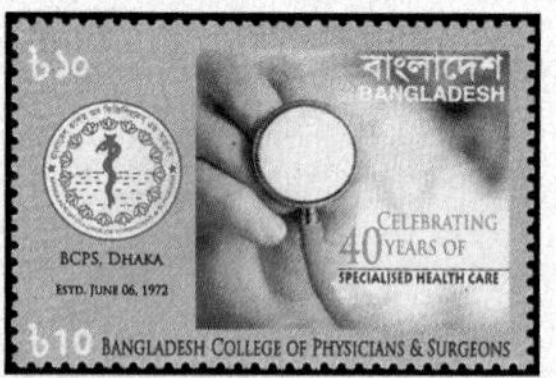

Bangladesh College of Physicians and Surgeons, 40th Anniv. — A431

2011, Dec. 28 ***Perf. 12½***
795 A431 10t multi .25 .25

Language Movement, 60th Anniv. — A432

2012, Feb. 28 ***Perf. 13¼x13½***
796 A432 21t multi .55 .55

National Day — A433

2012, Mar. 26 ***Perf. 13¾x14¼***
797 A433 26t multi .65 .65

National Plantation Day A434

2012, June 5 ***Perf. 14¼x13¾***
798 A434 10t multi .25 .25

Endangered Animals — A435

No. 799: a, 15t, Gyps bengalensis. b, 25t, Semnopithecus entellus.

2012, June 14
799 A435 Horiz. pair, #a-b 1.00 1.00

A souvenir sheet containing imperforate examples of Nos. 799a and 799b sold for 100t.

Birds A436

No. 800: a, Ichthyophaga ichthyaetus. b, Centropus bengalensis.

2012, June 14 ***Perf. 13¼***
800 Horiz. pair + central label 1.00 1.00
a.-b. A436 20t Either single .50 .50

Indonesia 2012 World Stamp Championship, Jakarta. Perf. 12x13½ and imperforate sheets containing four 10t stamps depicting different birds each sold for 100t.

Butterflies — A437

No. 801: a, Leopard lacewing. b, Striped tiger. c, Lemon pansy. d, Knight.

2012, June 14 ***Perf. 12x13¼***
801 A437 10t Block of 4, #a-d 1.00 1.00
e. Block of 4, #801a-801d, perf. 12¾ 1.00 1.00

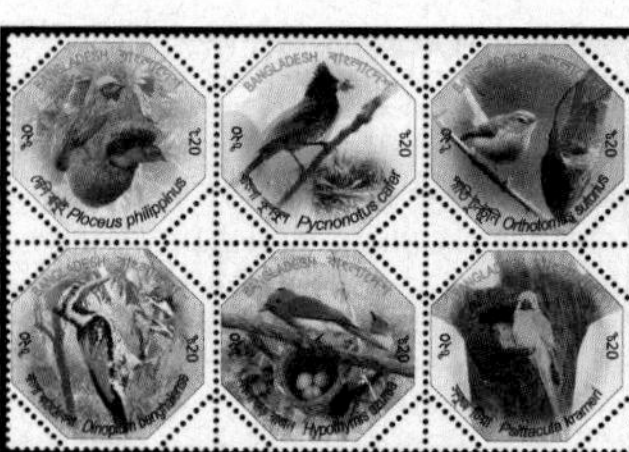

Birds and Their Nests — A438

No. 802: a, Ploceus philippinus. b, Pycnonotus cafer. c, Orthotomus sutorius. d, Dinopium benghalense. e, Hypothymis azurea. f, Psittacula krameri.

2012, June 14 ***Perf. 13***
802 A438 20t Block of 6, #a-f 3.00 3.00
g. Souvenir sheet of 6, #802a-802f, imperf. 3.75 3.75

No. 802g sold for 150t.

Rotary International in Bangladesh, 75th Anniv. — A439

2012, July 1 *Perf. 14¼x13¾*
803 A439 10t multi .25 .25

Open Heart Surgery in Bangladesh, 30th Anniv. (in 2011) — A440

2012, Sept. 12 *Perf. 13½*
804 A440 10t multi .25 .25

Intl. Ozone Day A441

2012, Sept. 16 *Perf. 14¼x13¾*
805 A441 10t multi .25 .25

Montreal Protocol, 25th anniv.

24th Asia Pacific Regional Scout Conference A442

2012, Nov. 24 *Perf. 13¾x14¼*
806 A442 20t multi .50 .50

Bangladesh Police Academy, Cent. — A443

2012, Dec. 6 *Perf. 14¼x13¾*
807 A443 12t multi .30 .30

Asia-Pacific Postal Union, 50th Anniv. (in 2012) — A444

2013, Jan. 13
808 A444 3t multi .25 .25

SOS Children's Villages in Bangladesh, 40th Anniv. — A446

2013, Jan. 30 Litho. *Perf. 13¾x14¼*
810 A446 10t multi .25 .25

Audit Day A447

2013, Feb. 7 *Perf. 14¼x13¾*
811 A447 5t multi .25 .25

Sheikh Mujibur Rahman (1920-75), Prime Minister — A448

2013, Mar. 26 *Perf. 13¾x14¼*
812 A448 10t multi .25 .25

Independence, 42nd anniv.

National Tree Planting Campaign A449

2013, June 5 *Perf. 14¼x13¾*
813 A449 10t multi .25 .25

Bangladesh National Museum, Cent. — A450

2013, July 8 *Perf. 12¾*
814 A450 10t multi .25 .25

Statue of Buddha, Dharmarajika Maha Vihara, Dhaka — A451

2013, July 30 *Perf. 13¾x14¼*
815 A451 10t multi .25 .25

A souvenir sheet with one perf. 13¼ example of No. 815 sold for 40t.

Flowers — A452

No. 816: a, Mimosa pudica. b, Mesua nagassarium. c, Dillenia indica. d, Wrightia coccinea.

2013, July 30 *Perf. 12x13½*
816 A452 10t Block of 4, #a-d 1.10 1.10

Tiger Protection — A453

No. 817: a, Tiger with grass showing above head, Bengali text on top line. b, Two tigers, English text on top line. c, Tiger, English text on top line. d, Tiger with trees and sky above head, Bengali text on top line.

2013, July 30 *Perf. 13¼*
817 A453 10t Block of 4, #a-d 1.10 1.10
e. Souvenir sheet of 4, #817a-817d, perf. 12x13½ 2.10 2.10

No. 817e sold for 80t. An imperforate sheet similar to No. 817e, but with the Bangladesh flag and Thailand 2013 World Stamp Exhibition emblem in the sheet margin, sold for 100t.

Miniature Sheet

Endangered Animals — A454

No. 818: a, 6t, Lutra lutra. b, 8t, Naja naja. c, 10t, Nycticebus bengalensis. d, 12t, Hoolock hoolock.

2013, July 30 *Perf. 13½x13¼*
818 A454 Sheet of 4, #a-d 1.60 1.60
e. Like No. 818, imperf. 1.90 1.90

No. 818 sold for 60t. No. 818e sold for 70t, and has the emblem for the Thailand 2013 World Stamp Exhibition in sheet margin.

OFFICIAL STAMPS

Nos. 42-47, 49-50, 52, 82-84 and 54 Overprinted in Black or Red

Perf. 14x14½, 14½x14

1973-75 **Litho.**

O1	A7	2p black (R)	.25	*2.10*
O2	A7	3p brt green	.25	*2.10*
O3	A7	5p lt brown	.30	.25
O4	A7	10p black (R)	.30	.25
O5	A7	20p olive	2.75	.25
O6	A7	25p red lilac	6.00	.25
O8	A7	60p gray (R)	6.00	3.25
O9	A7	75p orange ('74)	2.25	.40
O10	A9	1t violet (#52)	19.00	8.25
O11	A9	1t violet (#82)	7.50	.70
O12	A9	2t grayish grn ('74)	10.50	3.25
O13	A9	5t gray blue (#54)	7.50	*13.50*
O14	A9	5t grysh bl (#84) ('75)	17.50	17.50
		Nos. O1-O14 (13)	80.10	52.05

Issue date: Apr. 30, 1973.

Nos. 95-101, 103-105 Overprinted "SERVICE" in Black or Red

1976 Litho. *Perf. 15x14½, 14½x15*

O16	A7	5p green	2.50	1.50
O17	A7	10p black (R)	3.50	1.50
O18	A7	20p olive	4.00	1.50
O19	A7	25p rose	5.50	1.50
O20	A8	50p rose lilac	6.25	.90
O21	A7	60p gray (R)	.65	*3.75*
O22	A7	75p olive	.65	*5.00*

Perf. 15

O23	A9	1t violet	5.00	.70
O24	A9	2t greenish gray	.80	*3.25*
O25	A9	5t grayish blue	.65	*3.25*
		Nos. O16-O25 (10)	29.50	22.85

Nos. 165-175 Ovptd. "SERVICE"

1979-82 Photo. *Perf. 14½*

O27	A7	5p brown	2.40	*3.25*
O28	A7	10p Prussian blue	2.40	*3.50*
O29	A7	15p yellow orange	2.40	*3.25*
O30	A7	20p dk carmine	2.10	*3.25*
O31	A7	25p dk blue ('82)	1.25	*3.25*
O31A	A7	30p lt ol grn ('80)	4.50	3.75
O32	A9	40p rose magenta	3.75	3.25
O33	A9	50p gray ('81)	.60	.25
O34	A7	80p dark brown	3.25	.65
O35	A7	1t red lilac ('81)	.60	.25
O36	A7	2t brt ultra ('81)	.70	*3.50*
		Nos. O27-O36 (11)	23.95	28.15

#234-242, 271 Ovptd. "Service" in Red, Diagonally Up on #O43A, 1t, 2t, 4t

1983-93 *Perf. 11½x12½, 12½x11½*

O37	A70	5p bluish green	.25	.25
O38	A70	10p deep magenta	.25	.25
O39	A70	15p blue	.25	.25
O40	A70	20p dark gray	.25	.25
O41	A70	25p slate	.25	.25
O42	A70	30p gray brown	.25	.25
O43	A70	50p yellow brown	.25	.25
O43A	A70	50p yellow brown	.25	.25

Size: 30½x28½mm

Perf. 12x11½

O44	A70	1t ultramarine	1.50	.25
O45	A70	2t Prussian blue	.25	.25

Perf. 12

O46	A70	4t blue	2.50	1.00
		Nos. O37-O46 (11)	6.25	3.50

Issued: 4t, 7/27/92; No. O43A, 1993(?); others, 12/21/83.

No. 379A Ovptd. in Red

1990 Litho. *Perf. 14½x14*
O47 A139a 2t brown 1.00 1.00

No. 350 Ovptd. "Service" Diagonally in Red

1994, July 16 Litho. *Perf. 12x11½*
O47A A122 3t multicolored *11.50 11.50*

No. 354 Ovptd. in Red

1992, Nov. 22 Litho. *Perf. 14½x14*
O47B A125 6t blue gray & yel *1.00 1.00*

No. 241 Ovptd. in Red

1992, Sept. 16 Litho. *Perf. 12x11½*
O48 A70 1t ultramarine 1.00 1.00

No. 484 Ovptd. in Red

1996 Litho. *Perf. 14*
O49 A204 2t multicolored *2.75 2.75*

No. 351 Ovptd. in Blue

1997? Litho. *Perf. 12*
O50 A122 5t multicolored *.30 .30*

Bengali overprint reads from top to bottom.

Nos. 235, 237 Ovptd. in Black or Red

1997? *Perf. 12½x11½*
O51 A70 10p on #235 *.75 .75*
O52 A70 20p on #237 (R) *1.50 1.50*

No. 560 Ovptd. in Red

1998 Litho. *Perf. 14½x14*
O53 A139a 1t green *.25 .25*

BARBADOS

bär-ˈbā-ˌdōs

LOCATION — A West Indies island east of the Windwards
GOVT. — Independent state in the British Commonwealth
AREA — 166 sq. mi.
POP. — 266,100 (1997 est.)
CAPITAL — Bridgetown

The British colony of Barbados became an independent state on November 30, 1966.

4 Farthings = 1 Penny
12 Pence = 1 Shilling
20 Shillings = 1 Pound
100 Cents = 1 Dollar (1950)

Catalogue values for unused stamps in this country are for Never Hinged items, beginning with Scott 207 in the regular postage section, Scott B2 in the semi-postal section and Scott J1 in the postage due section.

Watermarks

Wmk. 5 — Small Star

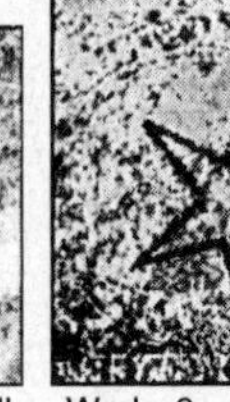
Wmk. 6 — Large Star

Values for unused stamps are for examples with original gum as defined in the catalogue introduction. Very fine examples of Nos. 10-42a, 44-59a will have perforations touching the design on at least one side due to the narrow spacing of the stamps on the plates and imperfect perforation methods. Stamps with perfs clear of the design on all four sides are extremely scarce and will command higher prices.

Britannia
A1 A2

1852-55 Unwmk. Engr. *Imperf.*
Blued Paper
1 A1 (½p) deep green 150.00 *375.00*
a. (½p) yellow green 9,000. 800.00
2 A1 (1p) dark blue 40.00 *80.00*
Pair, on cover 500.00
a. (1p) blue 65.00 *225.00*
3 A1 (2p) slate blue 30.00
a. (2p) grayish slate 315.00 *1,375.*
b. As "a," vert. half used as 1p on cover *9,000.*
4 A1 (4p) brown red ('55) 125.00 *325.00*
Nos. 1-4 (4) 345.00

No. 3 was not placed in use. Beware of color changelings of Nos. 2-3 that may resemble No. 3a. Certificates of authenticity are required for Nos. 3a and 3b.

Use of No. 3b was authorized from Aug. 4 to Sept. 21, 1854.

1855-58 White Paper
5 A1 (½p) deep green ('58) 190.00 *230.00*
a. (½p) yellow green ('57) 600.00 125.00
6 A1 (1p) blue 90.00 70.00
a. (1p) pale blue 170.00 *80.00*

It is believed that the (4p) brownish red on white paper exists only as No. 17b.

1859
8 A2 6p rose red 850.00 140.00
9 A2 1sh black 260.00 85.00

Pin-perf. 14
10 A1 (½p) pale yel grn 2,900. 500.00
11 A1 (1p) blue 2,400. 175.00

Pin-perf. 12½
12 A1 (½p) pale yel grn *9,500.* 800.00
12A A1 (1p) blue — 1,725.

Pin-perf. 14x12½
12B A1 (½p) pale yel grn — *8,500.*

1861 *Clean-Cut Perf. 14 to 16*
13 A1 (½p) dark blue grn 190.00 21.00
14 A1 (1p) pale blue 800.00 85.00
a. (1p) blue 925.00 90.00
b. Half used as ½p on cover —

Rough Perf. 14 to 16
15 A1 (½p) green 30.00 47.50
a. (½p) blue green 62.50 *85.00*
b. Imperf., pair 800.00
16 A1 (1p) blue 75.00 4.25
a. Diagonal half used as ½p on cover —
b. Imperf., pair 850.00 *650.00*
c. (1p) deep blue 75.00 4.25
17 A1 (4p) rose red 160.00 75.00
a. (4p) brown red 190.00 80.00
b. As "a," imperf., pair 1,700.
c. (4p) rose red, imperf., pair 1,150.
18 A1 (4p) vermilion 350.00 105.00
a. Imperf., pair 1,575.
19 A2 6p rose red 400.00 24.00
20 A2 6p orange ver 160.00 34.00
a. 6p vermilion 180.00 30.00
b. Imperf., pair 800.00 *1,100.*
21 A2 1sh brownish black 77.50 10.50
b. Horiz. pair, imperf. btwn. 9,500.
c. 1sh blue (error) *20,000.*

No. 21c was never placed in use. All examples are pen-marked (some have been removed) and have clipped perfs on one or more sides.

Use of No. 14b, 16a was authorized from 4/63-11/66. Only two full covers are known with bisected 1p stamps. The bisected stamps (Nos. 14b, 16a, 33a, 51b) are typically found on fragments or partial covers.

Perf. 11 to 13
22 A1 (½p) deep green *16,000.*
23 A1 (1p) blue *2,500.*

Nos. 22 and 23 were never placed in use.

1870 Wmk. 6 *Rough Perf. 14 to 16*
24 A1 (½p) green 180.00 10.00
a. Imperf., pair (#24) 1,200.
b. (½p) yellow green 240.00 52.50
25 A1 (1p) blue 2,600. 67.50
a. Imperf., pair *3,000.*
26 A1 (4p) dull red 1,675. 125.00
27 A2 6p vermilion 1,050. 90.00
28 A2 1sh black 475.00 21.00

1871 Wmk. 5
29 A1 (1p) blue 190.00 4.25
30 A1 (4p) rose red 1,375. 67.50
31 A2 6p vermilion 750.00 26.00
32 A2 1sh black 275.00 16.75

1872 *Clean-Cut Perf. 14½ to 16*
33 A1 (1p) blue 350.00 3.25
a. Diagonal half used as ½p on cover —
34 A2 6p vermilion 1,000. 90.00
35 A2 1sh black 200.00 17.00

Perf. 11 to 13x14½ to 16
36 A1 (½p) blue green 400.00 67.50
37 A1 (4p) vermilion 850.00 125.00

1873 *Perf. 14*
38 A2 3p claret 375.00 140.00

Wmk. 6
Clean-Cut Perf. 14½ to 16
39 A1 (½p) blue green 475.00 27.50
40 A1 (4p) rose red 1,475. 265.00
41 A2 6p vermilion 950.00 95.00
a. Imperf., pair 105.00 *1,750.*
b. Horiz. pair, imperf. btwn. 10,500.
42 A2 1sh black 170.00 22.50
a. Horiz. pair, imperf. btwn. 9,500.

Britannia — A3

1873 Wmk. 5 *Perf. 15½x15*
43 A3 5sh dull rose 1,200. 375.00

For surcharged bisects see Nos. 57-59.

1874 Wmk. 6 *Perf. 14*
44 A2 ½p blue green 57.50 16.00
45 A2 1p blue 137.50 5.00

Clean-Cut Perf. 14½ to 16
45A A2 1p blue *20,000.*

1875 Wmk. 1 *Perf. 12½*
46 A2 ½p yellow green 90.00 8.50
47 A2 4p scarlet 350.00 27.50
48 A2 6p orange 750.00 80.00
49 A2 1sh purple 575.00 5.00
Nos. 46-49 (4) 1,765. 121.00

1875-78 *Perf. 14*
50 A2 ½p yel green ('76) 24.00 1.00
51 A2 1p ultramarine 135.00 2.25
a. Half used as ½p on cover *1,350.*
b. 1p gray blue 135.00 1.60
c. Watermarked sideways *1,000.*
52 A2 3p violet ('78) 170.00 15.00
53 A2 4p rose red 160.00 15.00
a. 4p scarlet 240.00 4.50
b. As "a," perf. 14x12½ *9,000.* —
54 A2 4p lake 575.00 4.50
55 A2 6p chrome yel 160.00 2.40
a. 6p yellow, wmkd. sideways 400.00 11.00
56 A2 1sh purple ('76) 170.00 8.50
a. 1sh violet *7,750.* 45.00
b. 1sh dull mauve 575.00 5.75
c. Half used as 6p on cover —

Nos. 48, 49, 55, 56 have the watermark sideways.

No. 53b was never placed in use.

A4

A5

Large Surcharge, ("1" 7mm High, "D" 2¾mm High)

1878 Wmk. 5 *Perf. 15½x15*
Slanting Serif
57 A4 1p on half of 5sh *6,250.* 850.00
a. Unsevered pair *27,500.* *2,750.*
b. Unsevered horiz. pair, #57 + 58 *5,500.*
d. Unsevered horiz. pair, #57 + 58, imperf. between *42,500.*
e. Unsevered horiz. pair, #57 + 59 42,500. 9,000.

Straight Serif
58 A4 1p on half of 5sh 7,500. 1,050.
a. Unsevered pair 4,750.

Small Surcharge, ("1" 6mm, "D" 2½mm High)
59 A5 1p on half of 5sh *9,500.* *1,175.*
a. Unsevered pair *37,500.* *5,250.*

On Nos. 57, 58 and 59 the surcharge is found reading upwards or downwards.

The perforation, which divides the stamp into halves, measures 11½ to 13.

The old denomination has been cut off the bottom of the stamps.

Queen Victoria — A6

1882-85 Typo. Wmk. 2 *Perf. 14*
60 A6 ½p green 31.50 2.25
61 A6 1p carmine rose 52.50 1.35
a. 1p rose 90.00 2.75
b. Half used as ½p on cover 1,800.
62 A6 2½p dull blue 145.00 1.70
a. 2½p ultramarine 125.00 1.70
63 A6 3p magenta 8.50 *30.00*
a. 3p lilac 125.00 50.00
64 A6 4p slate 375.00 4.75
65 A6 4p brown ('85) 16.00 2.25
66 A6 6p olive gray 85.00 52.50
67 A6 1sh orange brown 32.50 24.00
68 A6 5sh bister 180.00 *215.00*
Nos. 60-68 (9) 926.00 *333.80*

No. 65 Surcharged in Black

1892
69 A6 ½p on 4p brown 2.75 *6.50*
a. Without hyphen 21.00 *40.00*
b. Double surcharge, one albino —
c. Double surch., red & black 950.00 *1,275.*
d. As "c," without hyphen 3,750. *4,250.*

A8

Badge of Colony — A9

1892-1903 Wmk. 2

70 A8 1f sl & car ('96) 2.75 .25
71 A8 ½p green 2.75 .25
72 A8 1p carmine rose 5.50 .25
73 A8 2p sl & org ('99) 10.50 1.25
74 A8 2½p ultramarine 20.00 .25
75 A8 5p olive brn 8.00 5.25
76 A8 6p vio & car 18.50 3.00
77 A8 8p org & ultra 4.50 *32.50*
78 A8 10p bl grn & car 9.50 10.00
79 A8 2sh6p slate & org 55.00 70.00
80 A8 2sh6p pur & grn ('03) 160.00 *325.00*
Nos. 70-80 (11) 297.00 *448.00*

See Nos. 90-101. For surcharge see No B1.

Victoria Jubilee Issue

1897 Wmk. 1

81 A9 1f gray & car 9.50 .75
82 A9 ½p gray green 9.50 .75
83 A9 1p carmine rose 10.50 .75
84 A9 2½p ultra 15.00 1.00
85 A9 5p dk olive brn 34.00 21.50
86 A9 6p vio & car 45.00 27.50
87 A9 8p org & ultra 24.00 *28.50*
88 A9 10p bl grn & car 70.00 *62.50*
89 A9 2sh6p slate & org 100.00 65.00
Nos. 81-89 (9) 317.50 *208.25*

Bluish Paper

81a A9 1f gray & car 32.50 *35.00*
82a A9 ½p gray green 32.50 *35.00*
83a A9 1p carmine rose 44.00 *47.50*
84a A9 2½p ultra 45.00 *52.50*
85a A9 5p dk olive brn 260.00 *300.00*
86a A9 6p vio & car 150.00 165.00
87a A9 8p org & ultra 160.00 *175.00*
88a A9 10p bl grn & car 215.00 *275.00*
89a A9 2sh6p slate & org *150.00* *150.00*
Nos. 81a-89a (9) 1,089. *1,235.*

Badge Type of 1892-1903

1904-10 Wmk. 3

90 A8 1f gray & car 13.75 3.25
91 A8 1f brown ('09) 10.75 .35
92 A8 ½p green 27.50 .25
93 A8 1p carmine rose 27.50 .25
94 A8 1p carmine ('09) 27.50 .25
95 A8 2p gray ('09) 10.00 *21.00*
96 A8 2½p ultramarine 28.50 .35
97 A8 6p vio & car 32.50 *32.50*
98 A8 6p dl vio & vio ('10) 22.50 *35.00*
99 A8 8p org & ultra 70.00 *135.00*
100 A8 1sh blk, *grn* ('10) 17.00 *18.00*
101 A8 2sh6p pur & green 70.00 *160.00*
Nos. 90-101 (12) 357.50 *406.20*

Nelson Centenary Issue

Lord Nelson Monument — A10

1906 Engr. Wmk. 1

102 A10 1f gray & black 17.00 2.50
103 A10 ½p green & black 12.00 .40
104 A10 1p car & black 15.00 .25
105 A10 2p org & black 2.75 *5.50*
106 A10 2½p ultra & black 4.50 1.50
107 A10 6p lilac & black 22.50 *30.00*
108 A10 1sh rose & black 26.00 *62.50*
Nos. 102-108 (7) 99.75 *102.65*

See Nos. 110-112.

The "Olive Blossom" A11

1906, Aug. 15 Wmk. 3

109 A11 1p blk, green & blue 18.00 .30

Tercentenary of the 1st British landing.

Nelson Type of 1906

1907, July 6 Wmk. 3

110 A10 1f gray & black 6.25 *10.00*
111 A10 2p org & black 32.50 *47.50*
112 A10 2½p ultra & black 10.00 *50.00*
a. 2½p indigo & black 825.00 *1,000.*
Nos. 110-112 (3) 48.75 *107.50*

A12

A13

King George V — A14

1912 Typo.

116 A12 ¼p brown 1.90 1.90
117 A12 ½p green 4.75 .25
a. Booklet pane of 6
118 A12 1p carmine 12.00 .25
a. 1p scarlet 45.00 4.25
b. Booklet pane of 6
119 A12 2p gray 7.00 *21.00*
120 A12 2½p ultramarine 1.90 .75
121 A13 3p violet, *yel* 2.25 *17.50*
122 A13 4p blk & scar, *yel* 4.50 *25.00*
123 A13 6p vio & red vio 15.00 15.00
124 A14 1sh black, *green* 14.00 *25.00*
125 A14 2sh vio & ultra, *bl* 65.00 *70.00*
126 A14 3sh grn & violet 115.00 *130.00*
Nos. 116-126 (11) 243.30 *306.65*

Seal of the Colony — A15

1916-18 Engr.

127 A15 ¼p brown .90 .50
128 A15 ½p green 3.00 .25
129 A15 1p red 3.00 .25
130 A15 2p gray 12.75 *37.50*
131 A15 2½p ultramarine 6.50 3.75
132 A15 3p violet, *yel* 9.50 *14.75*
133 A15 4p red, *yel* 1.35 *17.50*
134 A15 4p red & black ('18) 1.00 *4.50*
135 A15 6p claret 10.50 8.00
136 A15 1sh black, *green* 12.75 *13.50*
137 A15 2sh violet, *blue* 20.00 9.25
138 A15 3sh dark violet 75.00 *180.00*
139 A15 3sh dk vio & grn ('18) 30.00 *115.00*
a. 3sh bright violet & green ('18) 300.00 *450.00*
Nos. 127-139 (13) 186.25 *404.75*

Nos. 134 and 139 are from a re-engraved die. The central medallion is not surrounded by a line and there are various other small alterations.

Victory Issue

Victory
A16 A17

1920, Sept. 9 Wmk. 3

140 A16 ¼p bister & black .35 .85
141 A16 ½p yel green & blk 1.85 .25
a. Booklet pane of 2
142 A16 1p org red & blk 5.00 .25
a. Booklet pane of 2
143 A16 2p gray & black 3.25 *17.00*
144 A16 2½p ultra & dk bl 3.50 *28.50*
145 A16 3p red lilac & blk 3.75 *8.00*
146 A16 4p gray grn & blk 4.00 *8.75*
147 A16 6p orange & blk 5.00 *24.00*
148 A17 1sh yel green & blk 20.00 *52.50*
149 A17 2sh brown & blk 52.50 *80.00*
150 A17 3sh orange & blk 57.50 *100.00*

1921, Aug. 22 Wmk. 4

151 A16 1p orange red & blk 21.00 .35
Nos. 140-151 (12) 177.70 *320.45*

A18

A19

1921-24 Wmk. 4

152 A18 ¼p brown .30 .25
153 A18 ½p green 1.90 1.00
154 A18 1p carmine 1.00 .25
155 A18 2p gray 2.00 .25
156 A18 2½p ultramarine 1.90 *10.00*
158 A18 6p claret 4.35 *7.50*
159 A18 1sh blk, *emer* ('24) 60.00 *160.00*
160 A18 2sh dk vio, *blue* 12.50 *24.00*
161 A18 3sh dark violet 25.00 *90.00*

Wmk. 3

162 A18 3p violet, *yel* 2.50 *10.00*
163 A18 4p red, *yel* 2.25 *25.00*
164 A18 1sh black, *green* 7.00 *24.00*
Nos. 152-164 (12) 120.70 *352.25*

1925-35 Wmk. 4 *Perf. 14*

165 A19 ¼p brown .30 .25
166 A19 ½p green .65 .25
a. Perf. 13½x12½ ('32) 9.50 .25
b. Booklet pane of 10
167 A19 1p carmine .65 .25
a. Perf. 13½x12½ ('32) 10.50 .60
b. Booklet pane of 10
168 A19 1½p org, perf. 13½x12½ ('32) 6.50 1.25
a. Booklet pane of 6
b. Perf. 14 17.50 4.00
169 A19 2p gray .80 *4.00*
170 A19 2½p ultramarine .60 *1.00*
a. Perf. 13½x12½ ('32) 19.00 8.50
171 A19 3p vio brn, *yel* 1.25 .55
172 A19 3p red brn, *yel* ('35) 7.50 7.50
173 A19 4p red, *yel* .95 *1.25*
174 A19 6p claret 1.25 1.10
175 A19 1sh blk, *emerald* 2.50 *8.50*
a. Perf. 13½x12½ ('32) 75.00 50.00
176 A19 1sh brn blk, *yel grn* ('32) 6.00 *12.50*
177 A19 2sh violet, *bl* 8.75 9.00
178 A19 2sh6p car, *blue* ('32) 32.50 *45.00*
179 A19 3sh dark violet 14.00 *21.00*
Nos. 165-179 (15) 84.20 *113.40*

Charles I and George V — A20

1927, Feb. 17 *Perf. 12½*

180 A20 1p carmine lake 1.25 .90

Tercentenary of the settlement of Barbados.

Common Design Types pictured following the introduction.

Silver Jubilee Issue

Common Design Type

1935, May 6 *Perf. 11x12*

186 CD301 1p car & dk bl 2.25 .35
187 CD301 1½p blk & ultra 5.50 *9.75*
188 CD301 2½p ultra & brn 3.00 *7.00*
189 CD301 1sh brn vio & ind 25.00 *37.50*
Nos. 186-189 (4) 35.75 54.60
Set, never hinged 45.00

Coronation Issue

Common Design Type

1937, May 14 *Perf. 13½x14*

190 CD302 1p carmine .25 .25
191 CD302 1½p brown .40 *.80*
192 CD302 2½p bright ultra .45 *.90*
Nos. 190-192 (3) 1.10 1.95
Set, never hinged 2.50

A21

1938-47 *Perf. 13-14 & Compound*

193 A21 ½p green 5.00 .25
b. Perf. 14 55.00 1.50
c. Booklet pane of 10
193A A21 ½p bister ('42) .25 *.45*
194 A21 1p carmine 14.00 .25
b. Perf. 13½x13 195.00 5.00
c. Booklet pane of 10
194A A21 1p green ('42) .25 .25
d. Perf. 13½x13 3.50 1.00
195 A21 1½p red orange .25 *.65*
c. Perf. 14 4.75 .80
d. Booklet pane of 6
195A A21 2p rose lake ('41) .90 *3.75*
195B A21 2p bright rose red ('43) .50 *1.00*
e. Perf. 14 .50 *2.10*
196 A21 2½p ultramarine .65 *.95*
197 A21 3p brown .65 *3.50*
b. Perf. 14 .25 .75
197A A21 3p deep bl ('47) .65 *2.50*
198 A21 4p black .25 .25
a. Perf. 14 .65 *6.50*
199 A21 6p violet .65 .65
199A A21 8p red vio ('46) .45 *3.25*
200 A21 1sh brn olive 1.40 .25
a. 1sh olive green 12.50 3.00
201 A21 2sh6p brown vio 7.00 2.25
201A A21 5sh indigo ('41) 6.50 *11.00*
Nos. 193-201A (16) 39.35 31.20
Set, never hinged 57.50

For surcharge see No. 209.

Kings Charles I, George VI Assembly Chamber and Mace A22

Perf. 13½x14

1939, June 27 Engr. Wmk. 4

202 A22 ½p deep green 2.15 2.00
203 A22 1p scarlet 2.15 1.35
204 A22 1½p deep orange 2.25 .65
205 A22 2½p ultramarine 3.25 *9.00*
206 A22 3p yellow brown 3.25 *6.00*
Nos. 202-206 (5) 13.05 *19.00*
Set, never hinged 21.00

Tercentenary of the General Assembly.

Catalogue values for unused stamps in this section, from this point to the end of the section, are for Never Hinged items.

Peace Issue

Common Design Type

1946, Sept. 18

207 CD303 1½p deep orange .25 .55
208 CD303 3p brown .25 .55

Nos. 195e, 195B, Surcharged in Black

1947, Apr. 21 *Perf. 14*

209 A21 1p on 2p brt rose red 2.40 5.25
b. Perf. 13½x13 3.25 *6.50*
c. As "b.," double surcharge *3,250.*

Silver Wedding Issue

Common Design Types

Perf. 14x14½

1948, Nov. 24 Photo. Wmk. 4

210 CD304 1½p orange .35 .55

Engraved; Name Typographed

Perf. 11½x11

211 CD305 5sh dark blue 18.00 12.50

UPU Issue
Common Design Types

1949, Oct. 10 ***Perf. 13½, 11x11½***

212 CD306 1½p red orange .55 2.15
213 CD307 3p indigo 2.75 7.50
214 CD308 4p gray .55 3.50
215 CD309 1sh olive .55 1.00
Nos. 212-215 (4) 4.40 14.15

Dover Fort — A23

Admiral Nelson Statue — A24

Designs: 2c, Sugar cane breeding. 3c, Public buildings. 6c, Casting net. 8c, Intercolonial schooner. 12c, Flying Fish. 24c, Old Main Guard Garrison. 48c, Cathedral. 60c, Careenage. $1.20, Map. $2.40, Great Seal, 1660.

Perf. 11x11½ (A23), 13x13½ (A24)

1950, May 1 **Engr.** **Wmk. 4**

216 A23 1c slate .35 *4.75*
217 A23 2c emerald .25 *3.25*
218 A23 3c slate & brown 1.25 *4.25*
219 A24 4c carmine .30 .40
220 A23 6c blue .35 *2.50*
221 A23 8c choc & blue 1.60 *4.00*
222 A23 12c olive & aqua 1.25 1.85
223 A23 24c gray & red 1.25 .55
224 A24 48c violet 11.00 9.00
225 A23 60c brn car & bl grn 14.00 13.75
226 A24 $1.20 olive & car 14.00 5.50
227 A23 $2.40 gray 27.50 45.00
Nos. 216-227 (12) 73.10 94.80

University Issue
Common Design Types

1951, Feb. 16 ***Perf. 14x14½***

228 CD310 3c turq bl & choc .60 .30
229 CD311 12c ol brn & turq bl 1.25 1.25

Stamp of 1852 A25

Perf. 13½

1952, Apr. 15 **Wmk. 4** **Engr.**

230 A25 3c slate bl & dp grn .40 .30
231 A25 4c rose pink & bl .50 *1.00*
232 A25 12c emer & slate bl .50 *1.00*
233 A25 24c gray blk & red brn 1.00 .80
Nos. 230-233 (4) 2.40 *3.10*

Centenary of Barbados postage stamps.

Coronation Issue
Common Design Type

1953, June 4 ***Perf. 13½x13***

234 CD312 4c red orange & black 1.00 .25

Harbor Police A26

Designs as in 1950 with portrait of Queen Elizabeth II. $2.40, Great Seal, 1660 ("E II R").

Perf. 11x11½ (horiz.), 13x13½ (vert.)

1953-57 **Engr.**

235 A23 1c slate ('53) .25 *1.00*
236 A23 2c grnsh blue & deep org .25 *.75*
237 A23 3c emerald & blk 1.60 1.10
238 A24 4c orange & gray .25 .25
239 A26 5c dp car & dp bl 1.60 .75
240 A23 6c red brown .70 .75
241 A23 8c brt blue & blk .95 .40
242 A23 12c brn ol & aqua 1.60 .25
243 A23 24c gray & red ('56) .95 .25
244 A24 48c violet ('56) 10.00 1.25
245 A23 60c brown car & blue grn ('56) 16.00 5.25
246 A24 $1.20 ol & car ('56) 30.00 4.50
247 A23 $2.40 gray ('57) 2.10 *2.25*
Nos. 235-247 (13) 66.25 18.75

See Nos. 257-264.

West Indies Federation
Common Design Type

Perf. 11½x11

1958, Apr. 23 **Wmk. 314**

248 CD313 3c green .40 .25
249 CD313 6c blue .65 *2.25*
250 CD313 12c carmine rose .65 .40
Nos. 248-250 (3) 1.70 *2.90*

Deep Water Harbor, Bridgetown A27

1961, May 6 **Engr.** ***Perf. 11x11½***

251 A27 4c orange & black .25 *.50*
252 A27 8c ultra & black .30 *.60*
253 A27 24c black & pink .45 *.60*
Nos. 251-253 (3) 1.00 1.70

Deep Water Harbor at Bridgetown opening.

Scout Emblem and Map of Barbados — A28

Perf. 11½x11

1962, Mar. 9 **Wmk. 314**

254 A28 4c orange & black .60 .25
255 A28 12c gray & blue 1.75 .25
256 A28 $1.20 greenish gray & carmine rose 1.75 *3.75*
Nos. 254-256 (3) 4.10 *4.25*

50th anniv. of the founding of the Boy Scouts of Barbados.

Queen Types of 1953-57

Perf. 11x11½, 13x13½

1964-65 **Engr.** **Wmk. 314**

257 A23 1c slate .70 *4.50*
258 A24 4c orange & gray .40 *.60*
259 A23 8c brt bl & blk ('65) .60 .40
260 A23 12c brn ol & aqua ('65) .75
261 A23 24c gray & red .75 *.85*
262 A24 48c violet 3.75 1.50
263 A23 60c brn car & bl grn 13.00 4.00
264 A23 $2.40 gray ('65) 1.75 1.75
Nos. 257-264 (8) 21.70
Nos. 257-259,261-264 (7) 15.50

The 12c was never put on sale in Barbados.

ITU Issue
Common Design Type

Perf. 11x11½

1965, May 17 **Litho.** **Wmk. 314**

265 CD317 2c lilac & ver .25 .25
266 CD317 48c yellow & gray 1.25 1.00

Sea Horse A29

Designs: 1c, Deep sea coral. 2c, Lobster. 4c, Sea urchin. 5c, Staghorn coral. 6c, Butterflyfish. 8c, File shell. 12c, Balloonfish. 15c, Angelfish. 25c, Brain coral. 35c, Brittle star. 50c, Flyingfish. $1, Queen conch shell. $2.50, Fiddler crab.

Wmk. 314 Upright

1965, July 15 **Photo.** ***Perf. 14x13½***

267 A29 1c dk blue, pink & black .35 .35
268 A29 2c car rose, sepia & orange .30 .25
269 A29 3c org, brn & sep *("Hippocanpus")* .60 *.60*
270 A29 4c ol grn & dk bl .30 .35
a. Imperf., pair *325.00* 250.00
271 A29 5c lil, brn & pink .45 .60
272 A29 6c greenish bl, yel & blk .55 .50
273 A29 8c ultra, orange, red & black .45 .35
274 A29 12c rose lil, yel & blk .50 .35
275 A29 15c red, yel & blk 1.10 .80
276 A29 25c yel brn & ultra 1.40 1.10
277 A29 35c grn, rose brn & blk 2.00 .35
278 A29 50c yel grn & ultra 2.75 .95
279 A29 $1 gray & multi 3.75 2.00
280 A29 $2.50 lt bl & multi 4.00 5.25
Nos. 267-280 (14) 18.50 13.80

1966-69 **Wmk. 314 Sideways**

Design: $5, "Dolphin" (coryphaena hippurus).

267a A29 1c .25 .25
268a A29 2c ('67) .30 *1.40*
269A A29 3c *("Hippocampus")* ('67) .30 *2.75*
270b A29 4c .55 .25
271a A29 5c .45 .25
272a A29 6c ('67) .70 .25
273a A29 8c ('67) .70 .25
274a A29 12c ('67) .50 .25
275a A29 15c 2.10 .25
276a A29 25c 2.10 .40
277a A29 35c 2.40 .65
278a A29 50c 2.10 *4.25*
279a A29 $1 6.00 1.00
280a A29 $2.50 7.50 3.00
280B A29 $5 dk ol & multi ('69) 17.50 12.00
Nos. 267a-280B (15) 43.45 27.20

For surcharge see No. 327.

Churchill Memorial Issue
Common Design Type

1966, Jan. 24 **Wmk. 314** ***Perf. 14***

281 CD319 1c multicolored .30 *3.00*
282 CD319 4c multicolored .45 .25
283 CD319 25c multicolored 1.00 .50
284 CD319 35c multicolored 1.25 .70
Nos. 281-284 (4) 3.00 4.45

Royal Visit Issue
Common Design Type

1966, Feb. 4 **Litho.** ***Perf. 11x12***

285 CD320 3c violet blue .50 .25
286 CD320 35c dark car rose 2.50 1.75

UNESCO Anniversary Issue
Common Design Type

1967, Jan. 6 **Litho.** ***Perf. 14***

287 CD323 4c "Education" .25 .25
288 CD323 12c "Science" .90 .55
289 CD323 25c "Culture" 1.35 1.35
Nos. 287-289 (3) 2.50 2.15

Arms of Barbados — A30

Designs: 25c, Hilton Hotel, horiz. 35c, Garfield Sobers, captain of Barbados and West Indies Cricket Team. 50c, Pine Hill Dairy, horiz.

1966, Dec. 2 **Unwmk.** **Photo.**

290 A30 4c multicolored .25 .25
291 A30 25c multicolored .25 .25
292 A30 35c multicolored 2.00 .80
293 A30 50c multicolored .85 .85
Nos. 290-293 (4) 3.35 2.15

Barbados' independence, Nov. 30, 1966.

Policeman and Anchor Monument — A31

Designs: 25c, Policeman with telescope. 35c, Police motor launch, horiz. 50c, Policemen at Harbor Gate.

1967, Oct. 16 **Litho.** ***Perf. 13½x14***

294 A31 4c multicolored .25 .25
295 A31 25c multicolored .40 .25
296 A31 35c multicolored .45 .25
297 A31 50c multicolored .70 .70
Nos. 294-297 (4) 1.80 1.45

Centenary of Bridgetown Harbor Police.
For surcharge see No. 322.

Independence Arch — A32

1st Anniv. of Independence: 4c, Sir Winston Scott, Governor-General, vert. 35c, Treasury Building. 50c, Parliament Building.

Perf. 14½x14, 14x14½

1967, Dec. 4 **Photo.** **Unwmk.**

298 A32 4c multicolored .25 .25
299 A32 25c multicolored .25 .25
300 A32 35c multicolored .30 .30
301 A32 50c multicolored .40 .40
Nos. 298-301 (4) 1.20 1.20

UN Building, — A33

1968, Feb. 27 ***Perf. 14½x14***

302 A33 15c multicolored .40 .40

20th anniv. of the UN Economic Commission for Latin America.

Radar Antenna on Top of Old — A34

Designs: 25c, Caribbean Meteorological Institute, Barbados, horiz. 50c, HARP gun used in High Altitude Research Program, at Paragon in Christ Church, Barbados.

Perf. 14x14½, 14½x14

1968, June 4 **Photo.** **Unwmk.**

303 A34 3c violet & multi .25 .25
304 A34 25c vermilion & multi .25 .25
305 A34 50c orange & multi .40 .40
Nos. 303-305 (3) .90 .90

World Meteorological Day.

Girl Scout at Campfire, — A35

Lady Baden-Powell, Queen Elizabeth II and: 25c, Pax Hill Headquarters. 35c, Girl Scout badge.

Perf. 14x14½

1968, Aug. 29 Photo. Unwmk.

306 A35 3c dp ultra, blk & gold .25 .25
307 A35 25c bluish green, black & gold .35 .35
308 A35 35c org yel, blk & gold .65 .65
Nos. 306-308 (3) 1.25 1.25

Barbados Girl Scouts' 50th anniv.

Human Rights Flame and Escape A36

Designs: 4c, Human Rights flame, hands, and broken chain. 25c, Human Rights flame, family and broken chain.

Perf. 11x11½

1968, Dec. 10 Litho. Unwmk.

309 A36 4c violet, gray grn & red brown .25 .25
310 A36 25c org, blk & blue .25 .25
311 A36 35c greenish blue, blue, blk & org .25 .25
Nos. 309-311 (3) .75 .75

International Human Rights Year.

In the Paddock A37

Horse Racing: 25c, "They're off!" 35c, On the flat. 50c, The Finish.

1969, Mar. 15 Litho. *Perf. 14½*

312 A37 4c multicolored .25 .25
313 A37 25c multicolored .25 .25
314 A37 35c multicolored .30 .30
315 A37 50c multicolored .40 .40
a. Souvenir sheet of 4, #312-315 3.50 3.50
Nos. 312-315 (4) 1.20 1.20

Map of Caribbean — A38

Design: 12c, 50c, "Strength in Unity," horiz.

Perf. 14x14½, 14½x14

1969, May 6 Photo. Wmk. 314

316 A38 5c brown & multi .25 .25
317 A38 12c ultra & multi .25 .25
318 A38 25c green & multi .25 .25
319 A38 50c magenta & multi .25 .25
Nos. 316-319 (4) 1.00 1.00

1st anniv. of CARIFTA (Caribbean Free Trade Area).

ILO Emblem A39

Perf. 14x13

1969, Aug. 5 Litho. Unwmk.

320 A39 4c bl grn, brt grn & blk .25 .25
321 A39 25c red brn, brt mag & red .25 .25

50th anniv. of the ILO.

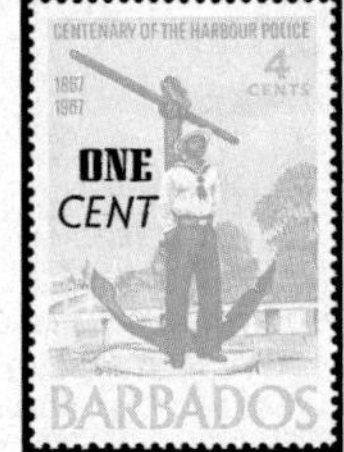

No. 294 Surcharged

1969, Aug. 30 *Perf. 13½x14*

322 A31 1c on 4c multicolored .45 .45

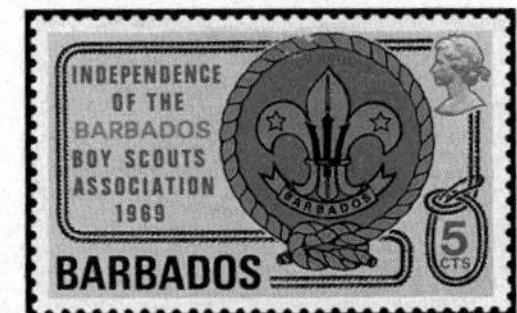

Barbados Boy Scout Emblem — A40

Designs: 25c, Sea Scouts rowing in Bridgetown harbor. 35c, Campfire. 50c, Various Scouts in front of National Headquarters and Training Center, Hazelwood.

Perf. 13½x13

1969, Dec. 16 Litho. Unwmk.

323 A40 5c multicolored .25 .25
324 A40 25c multicolored .65 .25
325 A40 35c multicolored .85 .25
326 A40 50c multicolored 1.25 1.25
a. Souvenir sheet of 4, #323-326 15.00 15.00
Nos. 323-326 (4) 3.00 2.00

Attainment of independence by the Barbados Boy Scout Assoc.

No. 271a Surcharged

Wmk. 314 Sideways

1970, Mar. 11 Photo. *Perf. 14x13½*

327 A29 4c on 5c multicolored .50 .50

This locally applied surcharge exists in several variations: double, triple, on back, in pair with one missing, etc.

Lion at Gun Hill — A41

Barbados Museum A42

2c, Trafalgar Fountain. 3c, Montefiore Drinking Fountain. 4c, St. James' Monument. 5c, St. Ann's Fort. 6c, Old Sugar Mill, Morgan Lewis. 8c, Cenotaph. 10c, South Point Lighthouse. 15c, Sharon Moravian Church. 25c, George Washington House. 35c, St. Nicholas Abbey. 50c, Bowmanston Pumping Station. $1, Queen Elizabeth Hospital. $2.50, Modern sugar factory. $5, Seawell Intl. Airport.

Wmk. 314 Upright (A41), Sideways (A42)

Perf. 12½x13, 13x12½

1970, May 4 Photo.

328 A41 1c bl grn & multi .25 *.80*
329 A41 2c crimson & multi .25 *.80*
330 A41 3c blue & multi .25 *.80*
331 A41 4c yellow & multi .85 .25
332 A41 5c dp org & multi .25 .25
333 A41 6c dull yel & multi .30 .30
334 A41 8c dp blue & multi .25 .25
335 A41 10c red & multi 2.75 .50
336 A42 12c ultra & multi 1.25 .25
337 A42 15c yellow & multi .25 *.70*
338 A42 25c orange & multi .25 .25
339 A42 35c pink & multi .25 *.70*
340 A42 50c bl grn & multi .40 *1.00*
341 A42 $1 emerald & multi .55 *2.50*
342 A42 $2.50 ver & multi 1.75 *4.00*
343 A42 $5 yellow & multi 6.00 *11.00*
Nos. 328-343 (16) 15.85 24.35

Nos. 328-332, 334-343 were reissued in 1971 on glazed paper.

Wmk. 314 Sideways (A41), Upright (A42)

1972-74

331a A41 4c 2.10 1.75
332a A41 5c 1.90 1.75
333a A41 6c 5.50 *11.50*
334a A41 8c 2.10 1.50
335a A41 10c ('74) 4.25 *6.75*
336a A42 12c 2.10 *4.00*
337a A42 15c 1.10 1.50
338a A42 25c 3.50 3.00
339a A42 35c 3.00 .80
340a A42 50c 4.25 1.75
341a A42 $1 7.75 *3.25*
342a A42 $2.50 ('73) 5.50 *8.25*
343a A42 $5 ('73) 5.75 *5.25*
Nos. 331a-343a (13) 48.80 51.05

For surcharge, see No. 391.

Primary Education, UN and — A43

UN and Education Year Emblems and: 5c, Secondary education (student with microscope). 25c, Technical education (men working with power drill). 50c, University building.

1970, June 26 Litho. *Perf. 14*

344 A43 4c multicolored .25 .25
345 A43 5c multicolored .25 .25
346 A43 25c multicolored .30 .30
347 A43 50c multicolored .40 .40
Nos. 344-347 (4) 1.20 1.20

UN, 25th anniv., and Intl. Education Year.

Minnie Root A44

Flowers: 1c, Barbados Easter lily, vert. 10c, Eyelash orchid. 25c, Pride of Barbados, vert. 35c, Christmas hope.

1970, Aug. 24 Litho. Wmk. 314

348 A44 1c green .25 .25
349 A44 5c deep magenta .60 .25
350 A44 10c dark blue 2.10 .40
351 A44 25c brt orange brown 1.60 .95
352 A44 35c blue 1.60 1.10
a. Souvenir sheet of 5 4.00 4.00
Nos. 348-352 (5) 6.15 2.95

No. 352a contains 5 imperf. stamps similar to Nos. 348-352 with simulated perforations.

Christ Carrying Cross — A45

Easter: 10c, 50c, Resurrection, by Benjamin West, St. George's Anglican Church. 35c like 4c, Window from St. Margaret's Anglican Church, St. John.

1971, Apr. 7 Wmk. 314 *Perf. 14*

353 A45 4c purple & multi .25 .25
354 A45 10c silver & multi .25 .25
355 A45 35c brt blue & multi .25 .25
356 A45 50c gold & multi .25 .25
Nos. 353-356 (4) 1.00 1.00

Sailfish Craft A46

Tourism: 5c, Tennis. 12c, Horseback riding. 25c, Water-skiing. 50c, Scuba diving.

1971, Aug. 17 *Perf. 14x14½*

357 A46 1c multicolored .25 .25
358 A46 5c multicolored .40 .25
359 A46 12c multicolored .65 .25
360 A46 25c multicolored .40 .25
361 A46 50c multicolored .55 .55
Nos. 357-361 (5) 2.25 1.55

Samuel Jackman Prescod — A47

1971, Sept. 26 *Perf. 14*

362 A47 3c orange & multi .25 .25
363 A47 35c ultra & multi .35 .25

Samuel Jackman Prescod (1806-1871), 1st black member of Barbados Assembly.

Coat of Arms A48

15c, 50c, Flag and map of Barbados.

1971, Nov. 23

364 A48 4c light blue & multi .30 .25
365 A48 15c multicolored .60 .25
366 A48 25c yel green & multi .60 .25
367 A48 50c blue & multi 1.25 1.25
Nos. 364-367 (4) 2.75 2.00

5th anniv. of independence.

Telegraphy, 1872 and 1972 — A49

Designs: 10c, "Stanley Angwin" off St. Lawrence Coast. 35c, Earth station and Intelsat 4. 50c, Mt. Misery tropospheric scatter station.

1972, Mar. 28 Litho. *Perf. 14*

368 A49 4c purple & multi .25 .25
369 A49 10c emerald & multi .25 .25
370 A49 35c red & multi .45 .25
371 A49 50c orange & multi .70 .70
Nos. 368-371 (4) 1.65 1.45

Centenary of telecommunications to and from Barbados.

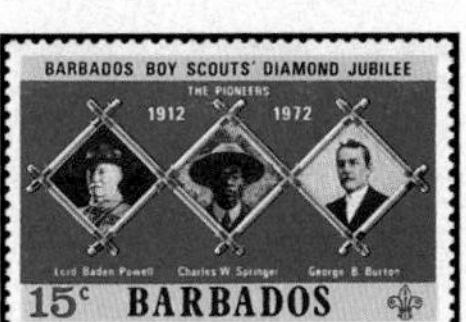

Lord Baden-Powell, Charles — A50

5c, Map of Barbados and Combermere School, vert. 25c, Photograph of 1922 troop. 50c, Flags of various Boy Scout troops.

1972, Aug. 1

372 A50 5c ultra & multi .25 .25
373 A50 15c ultra & multi .25 .25
374 A50 25c ultra & multi .55 .25
375 A50 50c ultra & multi 1.00 1.00
Nos. 372-375 (4) 2.05 1.75

60th anniv. of Barbados Boy Scouts and 4th Caribbean Jamboree.

Bookmobile, Open Book — A51

Intl. Book Year: 15c, Visual aids truck. 25c, Central Library, Bridgetown. $1, Codrington College.

1972, Oct. 31 Litho. Wmk. 314

376 A51 4c brt pink & multi .30 .25
377 A51 15c dull org & multi .35 .25
378 A51 25c buff & multi .35 .25
379 A51 $1 lt violet & multi 1.50 1.50
Nos. 376-379 (4) 2.50 2.25

Pottery Wheels A52

Barbados pottery industry: 15c, Kiln. 25c, Finished pottery, Chalky Mount. $1, Pottery on sale at market.

1973, Mar. 1 Wmk. 314 *Perf. 14*

380 A52 5c dull red & multi .25 .25
381 A52 15c olive grn & multi .25 .25
382 A52 25c gray & multi .40 .25
383 A52 $1 yellow & multi 1.50 1.50
Nos. 380-383 (4) 2.40 2.25

First Flight in Barbados, — A53

Aircraft: 15c, First flight to Barbados, De Havilland biplane, 1928. 25c, Passenger plane, 1939. 50c, Vickers VC-10 over control tower, 1973.

1973, July 25 *Perf. 12½x12*

384 A53 5c blue & multi .40 .25
385 A53 15c vio blue & multi 1.35 .25
386 A53 25c multicolored 1.60 .30
387 A53 50c blue & multi 2.75 2.50
Nos. 384-387 (4) 6.10 3.30

Chancellor Sir Hugh Wooding — A54

Designs: 25c, Sherlock Hall, Cave Hill Campus. 35c, Cave Hill Campus.

1973, Dec. 11 *Perf. 13x14*

388 A54 5c dp orange & multi .25 .25
389 A54 25c red brown & multi .25 .25
390 A54 35c multicolored .30 .30
Nos. 388-390 (3) .80 .80

25th anniv. of the Univ. of the West Indies.

No. 338a Surcharged

1974, Apr. 30 Photo. *Perf. 13x12½*

391 A42 4c on 25c multi .45 .45
a. "4c." omitted 17.00

Old Sailboat A55

Designs: 35c, Rowboat. 50c, Motor-powered fishing boat. $1, Trawler "Calamar."

1974, June 11 Wmk. 314 *Perf. 14*

392 A55 15c blue & multi .25 .25
393 A55 35c multicolored .30 .25
394 A55 50c vio blue & multi .35 .35
395 A55 $1 blue & multi 2.75 2.75
a. Souvenir sheet of 4, #392-395 6.25 6.25
Nos. 392-395 (4) 3.65 3.60

Fishing boats of Barbados.

Fire Orchid — A56

Orchids. 1c, 20c, 25c, $2.50, $5 horizontal.

Wmk. 314 Sideways; Upright (1c, 20c, 25c, $1, $10)

1974-77 Photo. *Perf. 14*

396 A56 1c Cattleya gaskelliana alba .25 *1.25*
397 A56 2c shown .25 *1.25*
398 A56 3c Rose Marie .45 *1.00*
399 A56 4c Fiery red orchid 1.75 .90
400 A56 5c Schomburgkia humboltii .50 .25
401 A56 8c Dancing dolls 1.50 .90
402 A56 10c Spider orchids .80 .25
403 A56 12c Dendrobium aggregatum .65 *2.75*
404 A56 15c Lady slippers .65 .65
404C A56 20c Spathoglottis 5.00 4.75
405 A56 25c Eyelash .80 .70
406 A56 35c Bletia patula 2.00 1.75
406B A56 45c Sunset Glow 6.75 4.50
407 A56 50c Sunset Glow 6.75 4.25

Perf. 14½x14, 14x14½

408 A56 $1 Ascocenda red gem 10.00 3.25
409 A56 $2.50 Brassolaeliocattleya nugget 2.50 *2.10*
410 A56 $5 Caularthron bicornutum 2.50 *6.00*
411 A56 $10 Moon orchid 2.75 *13.00*
Nos. 396-411 (18) 45.85 *49.50*

Issued: 20c, 45c, 5/3/77; others, 9/16/74.
For surcharge see No. B2.

Wmk. 314 Upright; Sideways (1c, 25c, $1)

1976 *Perf. 14*

396a A56 1c multicolored .90 *4.00*
397a A56 2c multicolored 1.10 *4.00*
398a A56 3c multicolored 1.25 *4.50*
399a A56 4c multicolored .90 *4.50*
402a A56 10c multicolored 1.75 *4.50*
404a A56 15c multicolored 1.50 *1.50*
405a A56 25c multicolored 3.00 1.50
406a A56 35c multicolored 3.25 2.00

Perf. 14½x14

408a A56 $1 multicolored 9.50 7.00
Nos. 396a-408a (9) 23.15 33.50

1975 Wmk. 373 *Perf. 14*

396b A56 1c multicolored .25 *1.60*
397b A56 2c multicolored .25 *1.60*
398b A56 3c multicolored .25 *1.60*
399b A56 4c multicolored .70 *3.50*
400b A56 5c multicolored .45 .25
402b A56 10c multicolored .45 .25
403b A56 12c multicolored 10.00 .25
404b A56 15c multicolored .95 .25
405b A56 25c multicolored .95 .25
406c A56 45c multicolored .80 .25
407b A56 50c multicolored 8.00 7.25

Perf. 14½x14, 14x14½

408b A56 $1 multicolored 12.50 *16.00*
409b A56 $2.50 multicolored 12.50 5.75
410b A56 $5 multicolored 12.50 9.25
411b A56 $10 multicolored 15.00 16.00
Nos. 396b-411b (15) 75.55 *64.05*

UPU Emblem, Barbados No. 64 — A57

Cent. of the UPU: 35c, Letters encircling globe. 50c, Barbados coat of arms. $1, Map of Barbados, sailing ship and jet.

1974, Oct. 9 Litho. *Perf. 14½*

412 A57 8c brt rose, org & gray .25 .25
413 A57 35c red, blk, & ocher .25 .25
414 A57 50c vio blue, bl & sil .25 .25
415 A57 $1 ultra, blk & brn .60 .60
a. Souvenir sheet of 4, #412-415 2.25 2.25
Nos. 412-415 (4) 1.35 1.35

Yacht Britannia off Barbados — A58

Royal Visit, Feb. 1975: 35c, $1, Palms and sunset.

1975, Feb. 18

416 A58 8c brown & multi .95 .35
417 A58 25c blue & multi 1.50 .35
418 A58 35c purple & multi .75 .40
419 A58 $1 violet & multi 1.80 *4.75*
Nos. 416-419 (4) 5.00 *5.85*

St. Michael's Cathedral — A59

Designs: 15c, Bishop Coleridge. 50c, All Saint's Church. $1, St. Michael, stained glass window, St. Michael's Cathedral.

Wmk. 314

1975, July 29 Litho. *Perf. 14*

420 A59 5c blue & multi .25 .25
421 A59 15c lilac & multi .25 .25
422 A59 50c green & multi .50 .50
423 A59 $1 multicolored .80 .80
a. Souvenir sheet of 4, #420-423 1.80 *2.00*
Nos. 420-423 (4) 1.80 1.80

Anglican Diocese in Barbados, sesquicentennial.

Pony Float A60

Designs: 25c, Stiltsman (band and masqueraders). 35c, Maypole dancing. 50c, Cuban dancers.

1975, Nov. 18 Litho. Wmk. 373

424 A60 8c yellow & multi .25 .25
425 A60 25c buff & multi .25 .25
426 A60 35c ultra & multi .25 .25
427 A60 50c orange & multi .30 .30
a. Souvenir sheet of 4, #424-427 1.25 1.25
Nos. 424-427 (4) 1.05 1.05

Crop-over (harvest) festival.

Sailing Ship, 17th Cent. — A61

350th Anniv. of 1st Settlement: 10c, Bearded fig tree and fruit. 25c, Ogilvy's 17th cent. map. $1, Capt. John Powell.

1975, Dec. 17 Wmk. 373 *Perf. 13½*

428 A61 4c lt blue & multi .55 .25
429 A61 10c lt blue & multi .35 .25
430 A61 25c yellow & multi 1.05 .40
431 A61 $1 dk red & multi 1.05 1.05
a. Souvenir sheet of 4, #428-431 3.50 3.50
Nos. 428-431 (4) 3.00 1.95

Coat of Arms — A62

Coil Stamps

1975, Dec. Unwmk. *Perf. 15x14*

432 A62 5c light blue .30 *.75*
433 A62 25c violet .40 *1.00*

Map of West Indies, Bats, A63

Prudential Cup — A64

1976, July 7 Litho. *Perf. 14*

438 A63 25c lt blue & multi 1.35 1.35
439 A64 45c lilac rose & black 1.35 1.35

World Cricket Cup, won by West Indies Team, 1975.

Map of South Carolina settled — A65

American Bicentennial: 25c, George Washington and map of Bridge Town area. 50c, Declaration of Independence. $1, Masonic emblem and Prince Hall, founder and Grand Master of African Grand Lodge, Boston, 1790-1807.

1976, Aug. 17 Wmk. 373 *Perf. 13½*

440 A65 15c multicolored .65 .25
441 A65 25c multicolored .65 .25
442 A65 50c multicolored 1.00 1.00
443 A65 $1 multicolored 1.40 1.40
Nos. 440-443 (4) 3.70 2.90

Mailman with Bicycle A66

PO Act, 125th anniv.: 35c, Mailman on motor scooter. 50c, Cover with Barbados No. 2. $1, Mail truck.

1976, Oct. 19 Litho. *Perf. 14*
444 A66 8c rose red, blk & bis .25 .25
445 A66 35c multicolored .25 .25
446 A66 50c vio blue & multi .35 .35
447 A66 $1 red & multi .60 *1.00*
Nos. 444-447 (4) 1.45 *1.85*

Coast Guard Vessels A67

Designs: 15c, Bank note, reverse, showing Barbados Parliament. 25c, National anthem by Van Roland Edwards (music) and Irvine Burgie (lyrics). $1, Independence Day parade.

1976, Nov. 30 *Perf. 13x13½*
448 A67 5c multicolored .30 .25
449 A67 15c multicolored .30 .25
450 A67 25c yel, brown & blk .30 .25
451 A67 $1 multicolored 1.25 1.25
a. Souvenir sheet of 4, #448-451 2.75 2.75
Nos. 448-451 (4) 2.15 2.00

10th anniv. of independence.

Queen Knighting Garfield — A68

Designs: 50c, Queen arriving at Westminster Abbey. $1, Queen leaving coach.

1977, Feb. 7 *Perf. 14x13½*
452 A68 15c silver & multi .25 .25
453 A68 50c silver & multi .45 .45
454 A68 $1 silver & multi .85 .85
Nos. 452-454 (3) 1.55 1.55

25th anniv. of the reign of Queen Elizabeth II. See Nos. 467-469.

Underwater Park — A69

Beauty of Barbados: 35c, Royal palms, vert. 50c, Underwater caves. $1, Stalagmite in Harrison's Cave, vert.

1977, May 3 Wmk. 373 *Perf. 14*
455 A69 5c multicolored .25 .25
456 A69 35c multicolored .50 .25
457 A69 50c multicolored .65 .75
458 A69 $1 multicolored 1.25 1.25
a. Souvenir sheet of 4, #455-458 4.00 4.00
Nos. 455-458 (4) 2.65 2.50

House of Commons Maces — A70

Charles I Handing Charter — A71

Designs: 25c, Speaker's chair. 50c, Senate Chamber. $1, Sam Lord's Castle, horiz.

1977, Aug. 2 Litho. *Perf. 13½*
459 A70 10c red brown & yel .25 .25
460 A70 25c slate grn & org .25 .25
461 A70 50c dk green, grn & yel .25 .25
462 A70 $1 dk & lt blue & org .55 .55
Nos. 459-462 (4) 1.30 1.30

13th Regional Conference of Commonwealth Parliamentary Association.

Perf. 13½x13, 13x13½
1977, Oct. 11 Litho. Wmk. 373

Designs: 12c, Charter scroll. 45c, Charles I and Earl of Carlisle, horiz. $1, Map of Barbados, by Richard Ligon, 1657, horiz.

463 A71 12c buff & multi .25 .25
464 A71 25c buff & multi .25 .25
465 A71 45c buff & multi .25 .25
466 A71 $1 buff & multi .55 .55
Nos. 463-466 (4) 1.30 1.30

350th anniv. of charter granting Barbados to the Earl of Carlisle.

Silver Jubilee Type, 1977, Inscribed: "ROYAL VISIT"

1977, Oct. 31 Unwmk. *Roulette 5*
467 A68 15c silver & multi .40 .40
468 A68 50c silver & multi .25 .25
469 A68 $1 silver & multi .55 .55
Nos. 467-469 (3) 1.20 1.20

Caribbean visit of Queen Elizabeth II. Printed on peelable paper backing inscribed in ultramarine multiple rows: "SILVER JUBILEE ROYAL VISIT BARBADOS." Printed with die-cut label inscribed in black "BEND & PEEL" attached at left of stamp. Sheets of 50 stamps and 50 labels.

Gibson's Map of Bridgetown, — A72

25c, Bridgetown, engraving by S. Copens, 1695. 45c, Trafalgar Square, Bridgetown, drawing by J. M. Carter, 1835. $1, The Bridges, 1978.

Wmk. 373
1978, Mar. 1 Litho. *Perf. 14½*
470 A72 12c gold & multi .25 .25
471 A72 25c gold & multi .25 .25
472 A72 45c gold & multi .25 .25
473 A72 $1 gold & multi .25 .25
Nos. 470-473 (4) 1.00 1.00

350th anniv. of founding of Bridgetown.

Elizabeth II Coronation Anniv. Issue
Souvenir Sheet
Common Design Types

1978, Apr. 21 Unwmk. *Perf. 15*
474 Sheet of 6 1.35 1.35
a. CD326 50c Griffin of Edward III .25 .25
b. CD327 50c Elizabeth II .25 .25
c. CD328 50c Pelican .25 .25

No. 474 contains 2 se-tenant strips of Nos. 474a-474c, separated by horizontal gutter with commemorative and descriptive inscriptions and showing central part of coronation with coach.

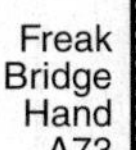

Freak Bridge Hand A73

10c, World Bridge Fed. emblem. 45c, Central American and Caribbean Bridge Fed. emblem. $1, Map of Caribbean, cards.

Wmk. 373
1978, June 6 Litho. *Perf. 14½*
475 A73 5c multicolored .25 .25
476 A73 10c multicolored .25 .25
477 A73 45c multicolored .25 .25
478 A73 $1 multicolored .60 .60
a. Souvenir sheet of 4, #475-478 2.10 2.10
Nos. 475-478 (4) 1.35 1.35

7th Regional Bridge Tournament, Dover Centre, Barbados, June 5-14.

Girl Guides' Camp — A74

Designs: 28c, Girl Guides helping children and handicapped. 50c, Badge with "60," vert. $1, Badge with initials, vert.

1978, Aug. 1 Litho. *Perf. 13½*
479 A74 12c multicolored .25 .25
480 A74 28c multicolored .45 .25
481 A74 50c multicolored .65 .35
482 A74 $1 multicolored .90 .90
Nos. 479-482 (4) 2.25 1.75

Girl Guides of Barbados, 60th anniv.

Garment Industry A75

Industries of Barbados: 28c, Cooper, vert. 45c, Blacksmith, vert. 50c, Wrought iron industry.

1978, Nov. 14 Litho. *Perf. 14*
483 A75 12c multicolored .25 .25
484 A75 28c multicolored .25 .25
485 A75 45c multicolored .35 .35
486 A75 50c multicolored .40 .40
Nos. 483-486 (4) 1.25 1.25

Early Mail Steamer A76

Ships: 25c, Q.E.II in Deep Water Harbour. 50c, Ra II (raft) nearing Barbados. $1, Early mail steamer.

1979, Feb. 8 Litho. *Perf. 13x13½*
487 A76 12c multicolored .45 .25
488 A76 25c multicolored .65 .25
489 A76 50c multicolored 1.00 1.00
490 A76 $1 multicolored 1.35 1.35
Nos. 487-490 (4) 3.45 2.85

Barbados No. 235 A77

28c, Barbados #430, vert. 45c, Penny Black and Maltese postmark, vert. 50c, Barbados #21b.

Wmk. 373
1979, May 8 Litho. *Perf. 14*
491 A77 12c multicolored .25 .25
492 A77 28c multicolored .25 .25
493 A77 45c multicolored .35 .35
Nos. 491-493 (3) .85 .85

Souvenir Sheet
494 A77 50c multicolored 1.00 1.00

Sir Rowland Hill (1795-1879), originator of penny postage.

Birds — A78

Launcher Transported through — A79

1979-81 Photo. Wmk. 373 *Perf. 14*
495 A78 1c Grass canaries .25 *1.25*
496 A78 2c Rain birds .25 *1.25*
497 A78 5c Sparrows .25 *.70*
498 A78 8c Frigate birds 1.25 *2.25*
499 A78 10c Cattle egrets .25 *.40*
500 A78 12c Green gaulins .75 *1.50*
501 A78 20c Hummingbirds .30 *.55*
502 A78 25c Ground doves .30 *.60*
503 A78 28c Blackbirds 3.00 2.00
504 A78 35c Green-throated caribs 1.10 *.70*
505 A78 45c Wood doves 2.25 1.50
506 A78 50c Ramiers 2.25 2.00
506A A78 55c Black-breasted plover ('81) 6.00 3.50
507 A78 70c Yellow breasts 3.25 *3.50*
508 A78 $1 Pee whistlers 3.25 1.50
509 A78 $2.50 Christmas birds 3.25 *6.00*
510 A78 $5 Kingfishers 4.75 *9.00*
511 A78 $10 Red-seal coot 7.00 *14.00*
Nos. 495-511 (18) 39.70 *52.20*

Issue dates: 55c, Sept. 1; others, Aug. 7.
See Nos. 570-572. For surcharges see No. 563-565

1979, Oct. 9 Photo.

Designs: 10c, Gun on landing craft, Foul Bay, horiz. 20c, Firing of 16-inch launcher by day. 28c, Bath Earth Station and Intelsat IV-A, horiz. 45c, ITOS/NOAA over Caribbean, horiz. 50c, Intelsat IV-A over Atlantic, and globe. $1, Lunar landing module, horiz.

512 A79 10c multicolored .30 .25
513 A79 12c multicolored .30 .25
514 A79 20c multicolored .35 .25
515 A79 28c multicolored .35 .30
516 A79 45c multicolored .60 .55
517 A79 50c multicolored .60 .60
Nos. 512-517 (6) 2.50 2.20

Souvenir Sheet
518 A79 $1 multicolored 1.75 1.75

Space exploration. No. 518 commemorates 10th anniversary of first moon landing.
No. 516 is incorrectly inscribed "Intelsat."

Family, IYC Emblem — A80

IYC Emblem and: 28c, Children holding hands and map of Barbados. 45c, Boy and teacher. 50c, Children playing. $1, Boy and girl flying kite.

1979, Nov. 27 Litho. *Perf. 14*
519 A80 12c multicolored .25 .25
520 A80 28c multicolored .25 .25
521 A80 45c multicolored .25 .25
522 A80 50c multicolored .25 .25
523 A80 $1 multicolored .25 .25
Nos. 519-523 (5) 1.25 1.25

Map of Barbados, Anniversary — A81

Rotary Intl., 75th Anniv.: 28c, Map of district 404. 50c, 75th anniv. emblem. $1, Paul P. Harris, founder.

1980, Feb. 19 Litho. *Perf. 13½*

524 A81 12c multicolored .25 .25
525 A81 28c multicolored .25 .25
526 A81 50c multicolored .25 .25
527 A81 $1 multicolored .30 .30
Nos. 524-527 (4) 1.05 1.05

A82

12c, Regiment volunteer, artillery company, 1909. 35c, Drum major. 50c, Sovereign's, regimental flags. $1, e, Women's corps.

Wmk. 373

1980, Apr. 8 Litho. *Perf. 14½*

528 A82 12c multicolored .35 .25
529 A82 35c multicolored .45 .35
530 A82 50c multicolored .55 .45
531 A82 $1 multicolored .65 .65
Nos. 528-531 (4) 2.00 1.70

Barbados Regiment, 75th anniv.

Souvenir Sheets

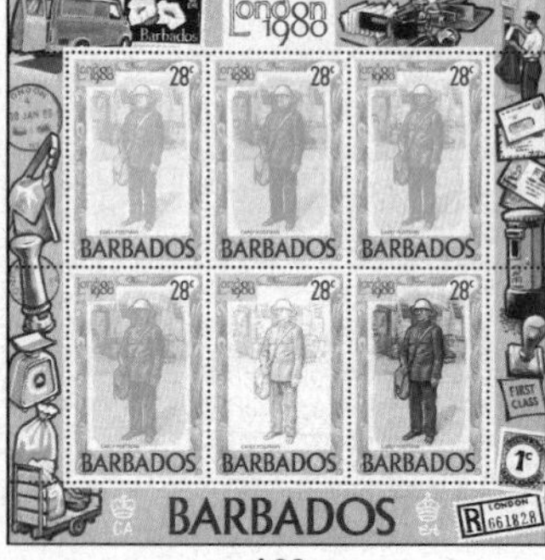

A83

Early mailman, London 1980 emblem. The vignette is a different color for each stamp.

Wmk. 373

1980, May 6 Litho. *Perf. 14*

532 Sheet of 6 .90 .90
a.-f. A83 28c any single .25 .25
533 Sheet of 6 1.00 1.00
a.-f. A83 50c any single .25 .25

London 80 Intl. Stamp Exhib., May 6-14.

Underwater Scenes — A84

1980, Sept. 30 Litho. *Perf. 13½*

534 A84 12c multicolored .25 .25
535 A84 28c multicolored .50 .30
536 A84 50c multicolored .70 .40
537 A84 $1 multicolored 1.10 1.10
a. Souvenir sheet of 4, #534-537 3.75 3.75
Nos. 534-537 (4) 2.55 2.05

Bathsheba Railroad Station — A85

1981, Jan. 13 Litho. *Perf. 14½*

538 A85 12c shown .25 .25
539 A85 28c Cab stand, The Green .25 .25
540 A85 45c Mule-drawn tram .30 .30
541 A85 70c Horse-drawn bus .50 .50
542 A85 $1 Fairchild St. railroad station .75 .75
Nos. 538-542 (5) 2.05 2.05

See Nos. 577-580.

Visually Handicapped Girl — A86

1981, May 19 Litho. *Perf. 14*

543 A86 10c shown .25 .25
544 A86 25c Sign language alphabet, vert. .25 .25
545 A86 45c Blind people crossing street, vert. .45 .35
546 A86 $2.50 Baseball game .90 .90
Nos. 543-546 (4) 1.85 1.75

International Year of the Disabled.

Royal Wedding Issue
Common Design Type
Wmk. 373

1981, July 22 Litho. *Perf. 13½*

547 CD331 28c Bouquet .25 .25
548 CD331 50c Charles .25 .25
549 CD331 $2.50 Couple .40 .40
Nos. 547-549 (3) .90 .90

4th Caribbean Arts Festival (CARIFESTA), A87

1981, Aug. 11 Litho. *Perf. 14½*

550 A87 15c Landship maneuver .25 .25
551 A87 20c Yoruba dancer .25 .25
552 A87 40c Tuk band .30 .30
553 A87 55c Frank Collymore (sculpture) .45 .45
554 A87 $1 Barbados Harbor (painting) .70 .70
Nos. 550-554 (5) 1.95 1.95

Hurricane Gladys, View from A88

1981, Sept. 29 Litho. *Perf. 14*

555 A88 35c Satellite view over Barbados .50 .25
556 A88 50c shown .65 .45
557 A88 60c Police watch 1.00 .65
558 A88 $1 Spotter plane 1.35 1.35
Nos. 555-558 (4) 3.50 2.70

Harrison's Cave — A89

Perf. 14x14½

1981, Dec. 1 Litho. Wmk. 373

559 A89 10c Twin Falls .25 .25
560 A89 20c Rotunda Room Stream .25 .25
561 A89 55c Rotunda Room formation .40 .40
562 A89 $2.50 Cascade Pool 1.60 1.60
Nos. 559-562 (4) 2.50 2.50

Nos. 503, 505, 507 Surcharged

1981, Sept. 1 Photo. *Perf. 14*

563 A78 15c on 28c multi .25 .25
564 A78 40c on 45c multi .30 .30
565 A78 60c on 70c multi .50 .50
Nos. 563-565 (3) 1.05 1.05

Black Belly Sheep A90

1982, Feb. 9 Litho.

566 A90 40c Ram .30 .30
567 A90 50c Ewe .40 .40
568 A90 60c Ewe, lambs .50 .50
569 A90 $1 Pair, map .80 .80
Nos. 566-569 (4) 2.00 2.00

Bird Type of 1979
Wmk. 373

1982, Mar. 1 Photo. *Perf. 14*

570 A78 15c like #503 6.00 5.00
571 A78 40c like #506 6.00 5.50
572 A78 60c like #507 6.00 *6.00*
Nos. 570-572 (3) 18.00 *16.50*

Transportation Type

1982, Apr. 6 Litho. *Perf. 14½*

577 A85 20c Lighter .25 .25
578 A85 35c Rowboat .40 .40
579 A85 55c Speightstown schooner .60 .60
580 A85 $2.50 Inter-colonial schooner 2.50 2.50
Nos. 577-580 (4) 3.75 3.75

Early marine transport.

Visit of Pres. Ronald Reagan — A92

1982, Apr. 8 Litho. *Perf. 14*

581 A92 20c Barbados Flag, arms .55 .55
582 A92 20c US Flag, arms .55 .55
a. Pair, Nos. 581-582 1.10 1.10
583 A92 55c like #581 .70 .70
584 A92 55c like #582 .70 .70
a. Pair, Nos. 583-584 1.40 1.40
Nos. 581-584 (4) 2.50 2.50

Printed in sheets of 8 with gutter showing Pres. Reagan and Prime Minister Tom Adams.

Princess Diana Issue
Common Design Type

1982, July 1 Litho. *Perf. 14½*

585 CD333 20c Arms .25 .25
586 CD333 60c Diana .55 .40
587 CD333 $1.20 Wedding 1.00 1.00
588 CD333 $2.50 Portrait 1.60 1.60
Nos. 585-588 (4) 3.40 3.25

Scouting Year — A93

Washington's 250th Birth — A94

1982, Sept. 7 Wmk. 373 *Perf. 14*

589 A93 15c Helping woman .60 .25
590 A93 40c Sign, emblem, flag, horiz. 1.90 .40
591 A93 55c Religious service, horiz. 1.10 .75
592 A93 $1 Flags 1.70 1.70
Nos. 589-592 (4) 5.30 3.10

Souvenir Sheet

593 A93 $1.50 Laws 5.00 5.00

1982, Nov. 2 *Perf. 13½x13*

594 A94 10c Arms .25 .25
595 A94 55c Washington's house, Barbados .40 .40
596 A94 60c Taking command .40 .40
597 A94 $2.50 Taking oath 1.20 1.20
Nos. 594-597 (4) 2.25 2.25

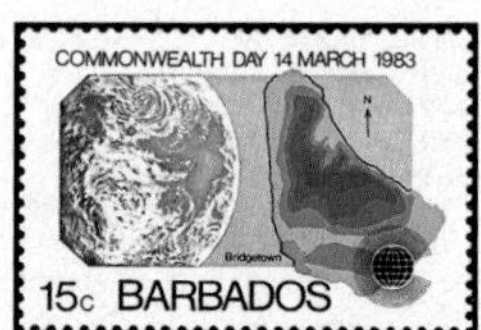

A95

1983, Mar. 14 Litho. *Perf. 14*

598 A95 15c Map, globe .25 .25
599 A95 40c Beach .35 .25
600 A95 60c Sugar cane harvest .45 .45
601 A95 $1 Cricket game 1.70 1.70
Nos. 598-601 (4) 2.75 2.65

Commonwealth Day.

Gulf Fritillary A96

Perf. 13½x13

1983, Feb. 8 Litho. Wmk. 373

602 A96 20c shown 1.60 .55
603 A96 40c Monarch 2.50 .55
604 A96 55c Mimic 2.50 .65
605 A96 $2.50 Hanno Blue 5.25 5.00
Nos. 602-605 (4) 11.85 6.75

Manned Flight Bicentenary — A97

1983, June 14 Litho. *Perf. 14*

606 A97 20c US Navy dirigible .45 .25
607 A97 40c Douglas DC-3 1.20 .55
608 A97 55c Vickers Viscount 1.30 .70
609 A97 $1 Lockheed TriStar 1.75 1.75
Nos. 606-609 (4) 4.70 3.25

Nash 600, 1941 A98

1983, Aug. 9 Litho. *Perf. 14*
610 A98 25c shown .70 .30
611 A98 45c Dodge, 1938 .80 .45
612 A98 75c Ford Model AA, 1930 1.25 1.25
613 A98 $2.50 Dodge Four, 1918 2.60 2.60
Nos. 610-613 (4) 5.35 4.60

A99

A100

1983, Aug. 30 Litho. *Perf. 14*
614 A99 20c Players .45 .30
615 A99 65c Emblem, map .85 .55
616 A99 $1 Cup 1.20 1.20
Nos. 614-616 (3) 2.50 2.05

World Cup Table Tennis Championship.

1983, Nov. 1 *Perf. 14*

Christmas: 10c, 25c, Angel with lute, painting details. $2, The Virgin and Child, by Masaccio.

617 A100 10c multicolored .30 .25
618 A100 25c multicolored .70 .25

Souvenir Sheet

619 A100 $2 multicolored 3.00 3.00

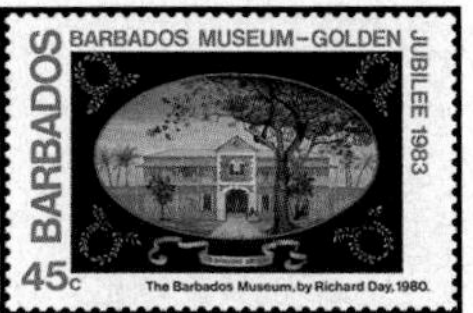

Barbados Museum, Golden A101

Museum Paintings: 45c, by Richard Day. 75c, St. Ann's Garrison in Barbados by W.S. Hedges. $2.50, Needham's Point, Carlisle Bay.

1983, Nov. 1 *Perf. 14*
620 A101 45c multicolored 1.10 .50
621 A101 75c multicolored 1.70 1.70
622 A101 $2.50 multicolored 5.50 5.50
Nos. 620-622 (3) 8.30 7.70

1984 Olympics, Los Angeles A102

1984, Apr. 3 Litho. *Perf. 14*
623 A102 50c Track & field .80 .60
624 A102 65c Shooting 1.00 .75
625 A102 75c Sailing 1.10 1.10
626 A102 $1 Bicycling 3.50 3.50
a. Souvenir sheet of 4, #623-626 8.75 8.75
Nos. 623-626 (4) 6.40 5.95

Lloyd's List Issue

Common Design Type

1984, Apr. 25 Litho. *Perf. 14½*
627 CD335 45c World map 1.05 .60
628 CD335 50c Bridgetown Harbor 1.25 .75
629 CD335 75c Philosopher 1.90 1.90
630 CD335 $1 Sea Princess 1.90 1.90
Nos. 627-630 (4) 6.10 5.15

Souvenir Sheet

1984 UPU Congress — A103

1984, June 6 Litho. *Perf. 13½*
631 A103 $2 #213, UPU emblem 4.50 4.50

World Chess Fed., 60th Anniv. A104

1984, Aug. 8 *Perf. 14x14½*
632 A104 25c Junior match 1.60 .40
633 A104 45c Knights 1.75 .65
634 A104 65c Queens 2.00 1.75
635 A104 $2 Rooks 4.75 4.75
Nos. 632-635 (4) 10.10 7.55

Christmas — A105

1984, Oct. 24 Litho. *Perf. 14*
636 A105 50c Poinsettia 1.80 1.00
637 A105 65c Snow-on-the-mountain 2.00 1.80
638 A105 75c Christmas candle 2.25 2.25
639 A105 $1 Christmas hope 2.50 2.50
Nos. 636-639 (4) 8.55 7.55

Marine Life A106

1985 Litho. Wmk. 373 *Perf. 14*
640 A106 1c Bristle worm .90 .90
641 A106 2c Spotted trunk fish .90 .90
642 A106 5c Coney fish 3.00 3.00
643 A106 10c Pink-tipped anemone 1.00 1.00
645 A106 20c Christmas tree worm 2.75 2.75
646 A106 25c Hermit crab 1.90 1.90
648 A106 35c Animal flower 4.50 4.50
649 A106 40c Vase sponge 4.50 4.50
650 A106 45c Spotted moray 1.90 1.90
651 A106 50c Ghost crab 3.25 3.25
653 A106 65c Flamingo tongue snail 3.25 3.25
654 A106 75c Sergeant major fish 3.25 3.25
656 A106 $1 Caribbean warty anemone 3.50 3.50
657 A106 $2.50 Green turtle 9.00 9.00
658 A106 $5 Rock beauty 10.50 10.50
659 A106 $10 Elkhorn coral 11.50 11.50
Nos. 640-659 (16) 65.60 65.60

Issued: 10c, 20c, 25c, 50c, $2.50, $5, 2/26; 5c, 35c, 40c, 65c, $10, 4/9; 1c, 2c, 45c, 75c, $1, 5/7.

1987, Sep. 15 Inscribed "1987"
640a A106 1c 4.00 4.00
641a A106 2c 4.00 4.00
645a A106 20c 7.00 7.00
651a A106 50c 9.00 9.00
654a A106 75c 15.00 15.00
658a A106 $5 20.00 20.00
Nos. 640a-658a (6) 59.00 59.00

Without Imprint

1986, Jan. 6 Wmk. 384
642b A106 5c 1.25 1.25
643b A106 10c 1.25 1.25
645b A106 20c 1.25 1.25
646b A106 25c 3.00 1.75
648b A106 35c 1.75 1.75
651b A106 50c 2.50 2.50
657b A106 $2.50 4.75 4.75
658b A106 $5 8.25 8.25
659b A106 $10 10.50 10.50
Nos. 642b-659b (9) 34.50 33.25

1986 Inscribed "1986"
640c A106 1c .40 *3.00*
641c A106 2c .40 *3.00*
643c A106 10c .40 .40
645c A106 20c .40 .40
646c A106 25c .50 .50
649c A106 40c .60 .60
650c A106 45c .80 .60
651c A106 50c .80 .80
653c A106 65c .85 .85
654c A106 75c .90 .90
656c A106 $1 1.10 1.10
657c A106 $2.50 2.50 *7.50*
658c A106 $5 5.00 *10.00*
659c A106 $10 10.00 *10.00*
Nos. 640c-659c (14) 24.65 *39.65*

Issued: 1c, 2c, 40c, 45c, 7/23. 10c, 25c, 50c-$10, 8/18.

1987 Inscribed "1987"
642d A106 5c 20.00 10.00
643d A106 10c .40 .40
646d A106 25c .50 .50
648d A106 35c 20.00 10.00
649d A106 40c .60 .60
650d A106 45c .80 .60
653d A106 65c .85 .85
654d A106 75c .90 .90
656d A106 $1 1.10 1.10
659d A106 $10 10.00 *10.00*
Nos. 642d-659d (10) 55.15 34.95

1988 Inscribed "1988"
643e A106 10c .40 .40

Queen Mother 85th Birthday

Common Design Type

Perf. 14½x14

1985, June 7 Litho. Wmk. 384
660 CD336 25c At Buckingham Palace, 1930 .35 .30
661 CD336 65c With Lady Diana, 1981 2.50 1.25
662 CD336 75c At the docks .80 .80
663 CD336 $1 Holding Prince Henry .85 .85
Nos. 660-663 (4) 4.50 3.20

Souvenir Sheet

664 CD336 $2 Opening the Garden Center, Syon House 3.50 3.50

Audubon Birth Bicentenary — A107

Illustrations of North American bird species. Nos. 666-668 vert.

Wmk. 373

1985, Aug. 6 Litho. *Perf. 14*
665 A107 45c Falco peregrinus 2.25 1.00
666 A107 65c Dendroica discolor 2.40 2.25
667 A107 75c Ardea herodias 2.75 2.60
668 A107 $1 Dendroica petechia 3.00 3.00
Nos. 665-668 (4) 10.40 8.85

Satellite Orbiting Earth A108

1985, Sept. 10
669 A108 75c multicolored 1.00 1.00

INTELSAT, Intl. Telecommunications Satellite Consortium, 20th anniv.

Royal Barbados Police, 150th Anniv. — A109

1985, Nov. 19
670 A109 25c Traffic Dept. 2.25 .75
671 A109 50c Police Band 1.60 1.10
672 A109 65c Dog Force 1.80 1.60
673 A109 $1 Mounted Police 2.00 2.00
Nos. 670-673 (4) 7.65 5.45

Souvenir Sheet

674 A109 $2 Band on parade, horiz. 3.50 3.50

Queen Elizabeth II 60th Birthday

Common Design Type

Designs: 25c, Age 2. 50c, Senate House opening, University College of the West Indies, Jamaica, 1953. 65c, With Prince Philip, Caribbean Tour, 1985. 75c, Banquet, state visit to Sao Paulo, Brazil, 1968. $2, Visiting Crown Agents, 1983.

Perf. 14x14½

1986, Apr. 21 Litho. Wmk. 384
675 CD337 25c scar, blk & sil .30 .25
676 CD337 50c ultra & multi .50 .45
677 CD337 65c green & multi .60 .55
678 CD337 75c violet & multi .60 .60
679 CD337 $2 rose vio & multi 1.35 1.35
Nos. 675-679 (5) 3.35 3.20

EXPO '86, Vancouver — A110

1986, May 2 *Perf. 14*
680 A110 50c Trans-Canada North Star 1.00 .70
681 A110 $2.50 Lady Nelson 2.40 2.40

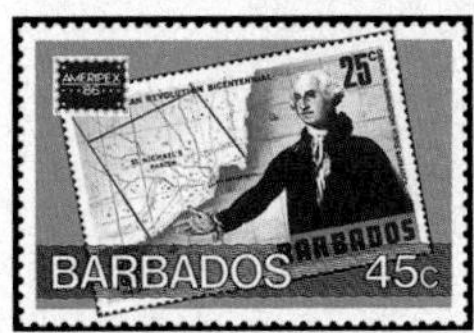

AMERIPEX '86 — A111

1986, May 22 Wmk. 373
682 A111 45c No. 441 .95 .50
683 A111 50c No. 442 1.05 .65
684 A111 65c No. 558 1.20 1.20
685 A111 $1 Nos. 583-584 1.50 1.50
Nos. 682-685 (4) 4.70 3.85

Souvenir Sheet

686 A111 $2 Statue of Liberty, NY Harbor 11.00 11.00

Statue of Liberty, cent.

Royal Wedding Issue, 1986

Common Design Type

Designs: 45c, Informal portrait. $1, Andrew in navy uniform.

Perf. 14½x14

1986, July 23 Litho. Wmk. 384
687 CD338 45c multicolored .75 .50
688 CD338 $1 multicolored 1.25 .75

Electrification of Barbados, A112

10c, Transporting utility poles, 1923. 25c, Heathfield ladder, 1935. 65c, Transport fleet, 1941. $2, Bucket truck, 1986.

Wmk. 384

1986, Sept. 16 Litho. *Perf. 14*

689 A112 10c multi .25 .25
690 A112 25c multi, vert. .35 .30
691 A112 65c multi .85 .75
692 A112 $2 multi, vert. 2.10 2.10
Nos. 689-692 (4) 3.55 3.40

Christmas — A113

Church windows and flowers.

1986, Oct. 28 Wmk. 373

693 A113 25c Alpinia purpurata .30 .25
694 A113 50c Anthurium andraeanum .50 .50
695 A113 75c Heliconia rostrata .90 .90
696 A113 $2 Heliconia psittacorum 1.75 1.75
Nos. 693-696 (4) 3.45 3.40

Natl. Special Olympics, 10th Anniv. A114

1987, Mar. 27 Wmk. 373 *Perf. 14*

697 A114 15c Shot put .25 .25
698 A114 45c Wheelchair race .50 .50
699 A114 65c Girl's long jump .75 .75
700 A114 $2 Emblem, creed 2.25 2.25
Nos. 697-700 (4) 3.75 3.75

CAPEX '87 — A115

1987, June 12

701 A115 25c Barn swallow 2.75 .65
702 A115 50c Yellow warbler 3.25 1.75
703 A115 65c Audubon's shearwater 3.25 1.75
704 A115 75c Black-whiskered vireo 3.50 3.50
705 A115 $1 Scarlet tanager 3.75 3.75
Nos. 701-705 (5) 16.50 11.40

Natl. Scouting Movement, 75th Anniv. — A116

1987, July 24 *Perf. 14x14½*

706 A116 10c Scout sign .25 .25
707 A116 25c Campfire .65 .30
708 A116 65c Merit badges, etc. 1.40 .70
709 A116 $2 Marching band 3.50 3.50
Nos. 706-709 (4) 5.80 4.75

Bridgetown Synagogue Restoration A117

1987, Oct. 6 Wmk. 384 *Perf. 14½*

710 A117 50c Exterior 3.25 2.40
711 A117 65c Interior 3.50 3.50
712 A117 75c Ten Commandments, vert. 3.75 3.75
713 A117 $1 Marble laver, vert. 4.50 4.50
Nos. 710-713 (4) 15.00 14.15

Natl. Independence, 21st Anniv. — A118

E.W. Barrow (1920-87), Father of Independence — A119

25c, Coat of arms, seal of the colony. 45c, Natl. flag, Union Jack. 65c, Silver dollar, penny. $2, Old and new regimental flags, Queen Elizabeth's colors.

1987, Nov. 24 Litho. *Perf. 14½*

714 A118 25c multicolored .55 .25
715 A118 45c multicolored 1.35 .45
716 A118 65c multicolored 1.35 .65
717 A118 $2 multicolored 4.50 3.25
Nos. 714-717 (4) 7.75 4.60

Souvenir Sheet

718 A119 $1.50 multicolored 2.40 2.40

Cricket A120

Bat, wicket posts, ball, 18th cent. belt buckle and batters: 15c, E.A. "Manny" Martindale. 45c, George Challenor. 50c, Herman C. Griffith. 75c, Harold Austin. $2, Frank Worrell.

1988 Litho. Wmk. 373 *Perf. 14*

719 A120 15c multicolored 3.25 1.10
720 A120 45c multicolored 4.00 1.10
720A A120 50c multicolored 4.75 2.75
721 A120 75c multicolored 5.00 4.00
722 A120 $2 multicolored 5.75 5.75
Nos. 719-722 (5) 22.75 14.70

The 50c was originally printed with the wrong photograph but was not issued. Copies of the error have appeared on the market.

Issued: No. 720A, July 11; others, June 6.

Lizards — A121

1988, June 13

723 A121 10c Kentropyx borckianus 2.25 .65
724 A121 50c Hemidactylus mabouia 3.25 1.10
725 A121 65c Anolis extremus 3.75 1.60
726 A121 $2 Gymnophthalmus underwoodii 8.00 7.50
Nos. 723-726 (4) 17.25 10.85

1988 Summer Olympics, Seoul — A122

Wmk. 373

1988, Aug. 2 Litho. *Perf. 14½*

727 A122 25c Cycling 2.00 .55
728 A122 45c Running .85 .45
729 A122 75c Swimming 1.00 .85
730 A122 $2 Yachting 2.25 2.10
a. Souvenir sheet of 4, #727-730 7.50 7.50
Nos. 727-730 (4) 6.10 3.95

Lloyds of London, 300th Anniv.

Common Design Type

40c, Royal Exchange, 1774. 50c, Sugar mill (windmill), horiz. 65c, Container ship Author, horiz. $2, Sinking of the Titanic, 1912.

1988, Oct. 18 Litho. *Perf. 14*

731 CD341 40c multicolored 1.00 .45
732 CD341 50c multicolored 1.25 .55
733 CD341 65c multicolored 2.50 .70
734 CD341 $2 multicolored 6.75 6.00
Nos. 731-734 (4) 11.50 7.70

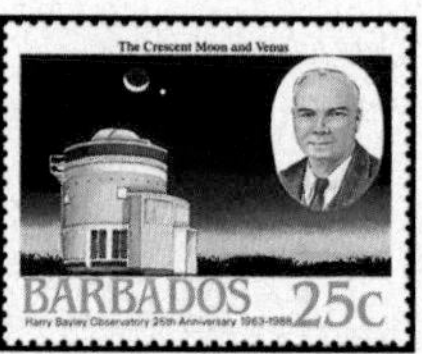

Harry Bayley Observatory, 25th Anniv. A123

Designs: 25c, Observatory, crescent Moon, Venus and Harry Bayley. 65c, Observatory and constellations. 75c, Andromeda Galaxy and telescope. $2, Orion Constellation.

1988, Nov. 28 Wmk. 384 *Perf. 14½*

735 A123 25c multicolored .90 .35
736 A123 65c multicolored 2.00 .95
737 A123 75c multicolored 2.25 1.25
738 A123 $2 multicolored 4.25 4.25
Nos. 735-738 (4) 9.40 6.80

Commercial Aviation, 50th Anniv. — A124

Designs: 25c, Caribbean Airline Liat BAe748. 65c, Pan American DC-8. 75c, Two British Airways Concordes, Grantley Adams Intl. Airport. $2, Two Caribbean Air Cargo Boeing 707-351c.

1989, Mar. 20 Litho. *Perf. 14*

739 A124 25c multicolored 3.00 .65
740 A124 65c multicolored 4.25 1.60
741 A124 75c multicolored 4.25 1.60
742 A124 $2 multicolored 6.75 6.00
Nos. 739-742 (4) 18.25 9.85

Parliament, 350th Anniv. A125

1989, July 19 Litho. *Perf. 13½*

743 A125 25c Assembly chamber .55 .30
744 A125 50c The Speaker .85 .55
745 A125 75c Parliament, c. 1882 1.50 .80
746 A125 $2.50 Queen in Parliament 3.50 3.00
Nos. 743-746 (4) 6.40 4.65

See No. 752.

Wildlife Preservation — A126

1989, Aug. 1 *Perf. 14x13½*

747 A126 10c Wild hare, vert. 1.00 .50
748 A126 50c Red-footed tortoise 2.00 1.00
749 A126 65c Green monkey, vert. 2.75 1.60
750 A126 $2 Toad 4.50 4.50
Nos. 747-750 (4) 10.25 7.60

Souvenir Sheet

751 A126 $1 Mongoose, vert. 2.40 2.40

Parliament Anniv. Type of 1989

Souvenir Sheet

1989, Oct. 9 Wmk. 373 *Perf. 13½*

752 A125 $1 The Mace 2.00 2.00

35th Commonwealth Parliamentary Conf.

Wild Plants — A127

Inscribed "1989"

1989, Nov. 1 Wmk. 373 *Perf. 14½*

753 A127 2c Bread'n cheese .75 1.10
754 A127 5c Scarlet cordia 1.20 1.40
755 A127 10c Columnar cactus 1.20 .70
756 A127 20c Spiderlily 1.20 .70
757 A127 25c Rock balsam 1.20 .40
758 A127 30c Hollyhock 1.75 .55
759 A127 45c Yellow shak-shak 1.50 .80
760 A127 50c Whitewood 1.75 .85
761 A127 55c Bluebell 2.40 1.40
762 A127 65c Prickly sage 1.80 1.40
763 A127 70c Seaside samphire 3.00 3.50
764 A127 80c Flat-hand dildo 4.00 3.75
765 A127 $1.10 Lent tree 3.50 4.00
766 A127 $2.50 Rodwood 4.75 4.75
767 A127 $5 Cowitch 7.75 9.00
768 A127 $10 Maypole 15.00 17.00
Nos. 753-768 (16) 52.75 51.30

1991-92 Inscribed "1991"

754a A127 5c Scarlet cordia .50 .50
755a A127 10c Columnar cactus .50 .40
756a A127 20c Spiderlily .50 .40
758A A127 35c Red sage 1.25 1.00
763a A127 70c Seaside samphire 1.25 1.25
764A A127 90c Herring-bone 1.75 1.75
765a A127 $1.10 Lent tree 1.75 1.75
Nos. 754a-765a (7) 7.50 7.05

Nos. 758A and 764A issued June 9, 1992 (inscribed 1991)

For overprints see Nos. 788-790.

Inscribed "1990"

1990 Litho. Wmk. 384

753b A127 2c .40 .35
754b A127 5c .40 .35
755b A127 10c .40 .35
756b A127 20c .40 .35
757b A127 25c .55 .45
759b A127 45c .85 .75
760b A127 50c 1.00 1.00
762b A127 65c 1.25 1.25
766b A127 $2.50 4.50 4.50
767b A127 $5 9.00 8.75
768b A127 $10 18.00 17.50
Nos. 753b-768b (11) 36.75 35.60

World Stamp Expo '89, Washington, DC — A128

Water sports.

1989, Nov. 17 Wmk. 384 *Perf. 14*

769 A128 25c Water skiing 1.60 .55
770 A128 50c Yachting 2.75 1.40
771 A128 65c Scuba diving 2.75 2.00
772 A128 $2.50 Surfing 7.25 7.25
Nos. 769-772 (4) 14.35 11.20

Horse Racing A129

Wmk. 373

1990, May 3 Litho. *Perf. 14*

773 A129 25c Bugler, jockeys .70 .40
774 A129 45c Parade ring 1.05 .65
775 A129 75c In the straight 1.50 1.05
776 A129 $2 Winner, vert. 3.75 3.75
Nos. 773-776 (4) 7.00 5.85

Barbados No. 2 — A130

Stamps on stamps: No. 778, Barbados #61. 65c, Barbados #73. $2.50, Barbados #121. No. 781a, Great Britain #1. No. 781b, Barbados #108.

1990, May 3

777 A130 25c shown 1.60 .55
778 A130 50c multicolored 2.40 1.25
779 A130 65c multicolored 2.50 1.75
780 A130 $2.50 multicolored 5.50 5.50
Nos. 777-780 (4) 12.00 9.05

Souvenir Sheet

781 Sheet of 2 4.25 4.25
a.-b. A130 50c any single 1.50 1.50

Stamp World London '90.

Queen Mother, 90th Birthday

Common Design Types

1990, Aug. 8 Wmk. 384 *Perf. 14x15*

782 CD343 75c At age 23 1.00 .70

Perf. 14½

783 CD344 $2.50 Engagement portrait, 1923 3.00 3.00

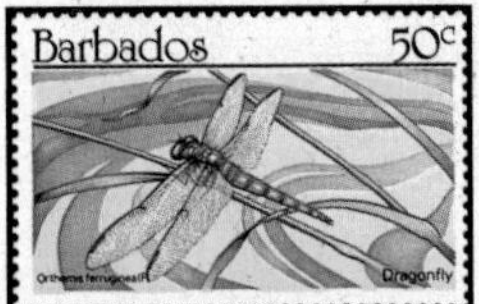

Insects A131

Wmk. 373

1990, Oct. 16 Litho. *Perf. 14*

784 A131 50c Dragonfly 2.00 1.10
785 A131 65c Black hardback beetle 2.40 1.25
786 A131 75c Green grasshopper 2.75 1.75
787 A131 $2 God-horse 5.00 5.00
Nos. 784-787 (4) 12.15 9.10

Nos. 757, 764 and 766 Overprinted

1990, Nov. 21 *Perf. 14½*

788 A127 25c on No. 757 2.10 .65
789 A127 80c on No. 764 3.75 2.75
790 A127 $2.50 on No. 766 9.00 9.00
Nos. 788-790 (3) 14.85 12.40

Christmas — A132

1990, Dec. 4 *Perf. 14*

791 A132 20c Christmas star 1.05 .30
792 A132 50c Nativity scene 1.50 .65
793 A132 $1 Stained glass window 2.75 1.90
794 A132 $2 Angel 4.50 4.50
Nos. 791-794 (4) 9.80 7.35

Yellow Warbler A133

1991, Mar. 4

795 A133 10c shown 1.50 1.00
796 A133 20c Male, female, nest 3.00 1.00
797 A133 45c Female, chicks 3.75 1.00
798 A133 $1 Male, fledgling 5.75 5.50
Nos. 795-798 (4) 14.00 8.50

World Wildlife Fund.

Fishing A134

Perf. 13½x14, 14x13½

1991, June 18 Litho. Wmk. 373

799 A134 5c Daily catch, vert. .65 .55
800 A134 50c Line fishing 2.10 1.00
801 A134 75c Cleaning fish 2.75 1.40
802 A134 $2.50 Game fishing, vert. 5.50 5.50
Nos. 799-802 (4) 11.00 8.45

Freemasonry in Barbados, 250th Anniv. — A135

Designs: 25c, Masonic Building, Bridgetown. 65c, Compass and square. 75c, Royal arch jewel. $2.50, Columns, apron and centenary badge.

1991, Sept. 17 *Perf. 14*

803 A135 25c multicolored 1.80 .65
804 A135 65c multicolored 2.75 1.30
805 A135 75c multicolored 2.75 1.30
806 A135 $2.50 multicolored 6.50 6.50
Nos. 803-806 (4) 13.80 9.75

Butterflies A136

1991, Nov. 15 Wmk. 384

807 A136 20c Polydamus swallowtail 1.50 .55
808 A136 50c Long-tailed skipper, vert. 2.00 .85
809 A136 65c Cloudless sulphur 2.40 1.25
810 A136 $2.50 Caribbean buckeye, vert. 5.50 5.50
Nos. 807-810 (4) 11.40 8.15

Souvenir Sheet

811 A136 $4 Painted lady 12.50 12.50

Phila Nippon '91.

Independence, 25th Anniv. — A137

Governor-General Dame Nita Barrow and: 10c, Students in classrom. 25c, Barbados Workers Union headquarters. 65c, Building industry. 75c, Agriculture. $1, Inoculations given at health clinic. $2.50, Gordon Greenidge, Desmond Haynes, cricket players (no portrait).

1991, Nov. 20 Wmk. 373

812 A137 10c multicolored .30 .30
813 A137 25c multicolored .45 .45
814 A137 65c multicolored 1.05 1.05
815 A137 75c multicolored 1.30 1.30
816 A137 $1 multicolored 1.50 1.50
Nos. 812-816 (5) 4.60 4.60

Souvenir Sheet

817 A137 $2.50 multi, vert. 14.50 14.50

Easter — A138

Wmk. 384

1992, Apr. 7 Litho. *Perf. 14*

818 A138 35c Christ carrying cross .80 .40
819 A138 70c Christ on cross 1.50 1.00
820 A138 90c Christ taken down from cross 1.75 1.50
821 A138 $3 Christ risen 4.50 4.50
Nos. 818-821 (4) 8.55 7.40

Flowering Trees — A139

Perf. 14x13½

1992, June 9 Litho. Wmk. 373

822 A139 10c Cannon ball .85 .55
823 A139 30c Golden shower 1.50 .65
824 A139 80c Frangipani 3.00 3.00
825 A139 $1.10 Flamboyant 3.75 3.75
Nos. 822-825 (4) 9.10 7.95

Orchids A140

Designs: 55c, Epidendrum "Costa Rica." 65c, Cattleya guttaca. 70c, Laeliacattleya "Splashing Around." $1.40, Phalaenopsis "Kathy Saegert."

1992, Sept. 8 *Perf. 13½x14*

826 A140 55c multicolored 1.10 .65
827 A140 65c multicolored 1.50 1.10
828 A140 70c multicolored 1.50 1.10
829 A140 $1.40 multicolored 2.40 2.40
Nos. 826-829 (4) 6.50 5.25

For overprints see Nos. 838-841.

Transport and Tourism A141

Designs: 5c, Mini Moke, Gun Hill Signal Station, St. George. 35c, Tour bus, Bathsheba Beach, St. Joseph. 90c, BWIA McDonnell Douglas MD 83, Grantley Adams Airport. $2, Cruise ship Festivale, deep water harbor, Bridgetown.

Wmk. 373

1992, Dec. 15 Litho. *Perf. 14½*

830 A141 5c multicolored .65 .60
831 A141 35c multicolored 1.40 .40
832 A141 90c multicolored 3.00 2.75
833 A141 $2 multicolored 4.75 4.75
Nos. 830-833 (4) 9.80 8.50

Cacti and Succulents A142

Wmk. 373

1993, Feb. 9 Litho. *Perf. 14*

834 A142 10c Barbados gooseberry .75 .40
835 A142 35c Night-blooming cereus 1.80 .50
836 A142 $1.40 Aloe 4.25 4.25
837 A142 $2 Scrunchineel 4.75 4.75
Nos. 834-837 (4) 11.55 9.90

Nos. 826-829 Ovptd. "WORLD ORCHID CONFERENCE 1993" on 2 or 4 lines

Perf. 13½x14

1993, Apr. 1 Litho. Wmk. 373

838 A140 55c on #826 multi 1.75 1.75
839 A140 65c on #827 multi 2.00 2.00
840 A140 70c on #828 multi 2.00 2.00
841 A140 $1.40 on #829 multi 3.00 3.00
Nos. 838-841 (4) 8.75 8.75

Royal Air Force, 75th Anniv.

Common Design Type

Designs: 10c, Hawker Hunter. 30c, Handley Page Victor. 70c, Hawker Typhoon. $3, Hawker Hurricane.

No. 846a, Armstrong Whitworth Siskin 3a. b, Supermarine S.6B. c, Supermarine Walrus. d, Hawker Hart.

1993, Apr. 1 *Perf. 14*

842 CD350 10c multicolored 1.00 .55
843 CD350 30c multicolored 1.40 .55
844 CD350 70c multicolored 2.00 2.00
845 CD350 $3 multicolored 4.50 4.50
Nos. 842-845 (4) 8.90 7.60

Souvenir Sheet

846 CD350 50c Sheet of 4, #a.-d. 4.00 4.00

Cannon
A143

Designs: 5c, 18-pounder Culverin, 1625, Denmark Fort. 45c, 6-pounder Commonwealth gun, 1649-1660, St. Ann's Fort. $1, 9-pounder Demi-culverin, 1691, The Main Guard. $2.50, 32-pounder Demi-cannon, 1693-94, Charles Fort.

Wmk. 373

1993, June 8 Litho. *Perf. 13*

847 A143 5c multicolored .40 .40
848 A143 45c multicolored 1.20 .60
849 A143 $1 multicolored 2.40 2.40
850 A143 $2.50 multicolored 3.75 3.75
Nos. 847-850 (4) 7.75 7.15

Barbados Museum, 60th Anniv. — A144

Designs: 10c, Shell box, carved figure. 75c, Map, print of three people. 90c, Silver cup, print of soldier. $1.10, Map.

Wmk. 373

1993, Sept. 14 Litho. *Perf. 14*

851 A144 10c multicolored .55 .55
852 A144 75c multicolored 1.80 1.80
853 A144 90c multicolored 2.40 2.40
854 A144 $1.10 multicolored 2.75 2.75
Nos. 851-854 (4) 7.50 7.50

A145

Prehistoric Aquatic Reptiles: a, Plesiosaurus. b, Ichthyosaurus. c, Elasmosaurus. d, Mosasaurus. e, Archelon. Continuous design.

Wmk. 373

1993, Oct. 28 Litho. *Perf. 13*

855 A145 90c Strip of 5, #a.-e. 13.00 13.00

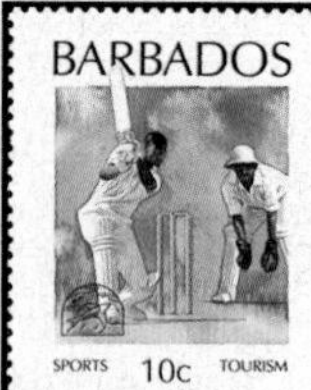

A146

Wmk. 384

1994, Jan. 11 Litho. *Perf. 14*

856 A146 10c Cricket 1.40 .75
857 A146 35c Motor racing 1.50 .55
858 A146 50c Golf 2.60 1.80
859 A146 70c Run Barbados 10k 2.00 2.00
860 A146 $1.40 Swimming 2.40 2.40
Nos. 856-860 (5) 9.90 7.50

Sports & tourism.

Migratory Birds
A147

Wmk. 373

1994, Feb. 18 Litho. *Perf. 14*

861 A147 10c Whimbrel .70 .70
862 A147 35c American golden plover 1.40 .70
863 A147 70c Ruddy turnstone 2.25 2.25
864 A147 $3 Tricolored heron 5.25 5.25
Nos. 861-864 (4) 9.60 8.90

Hong Kong '94.

1st UN Conference of Small Island Developing States — A148

1994, Apr. 25 *Perf. 14x14½*

865 A148 10c Bathsheba .45 .25
866 A148 65c Pico Tenneriffe 1.50 .90
867 A148 90c Ragged Point Lighthouse 4.00 2.00
868 A148 $2.50 Consett Bay 3.75 3.75
Nos. 865-868 (4) 9.70 6.90

Order of the Caribbean Community
A149

First award recipients: No. 869, Sir Shridath Ramphal, statesman, Guyana. No. 870, Derek Walcott, writer, Nobel Laureate, St. Lucia. No. 871, William Demas, economist, Trinidad and Tobago.

Wmk. 373

1994, July 4 Litho. *Perf. 14*

869 A149 70c multicolored 1.00 1.00
870 A149 70c multicolored 1.00 1.00
871 A149 70c multicolored 1.00 1.00
Nos. 869-871 (3) 3.00 3.00

Ships
A150

Designs: 5c, Dutch Flyut, 1695. 10c, Geestport, 1994. 25c, HMS Victory, 1805. 30c, Royal Viking Queen, 1994. 35c, HMS Barbados, 1945. 45c, Faraday, 1924. 50c, USCG Hamilton, 1974. 65c, HMCS Saguenay, 1939. 70c, Inanda, 1928. 80c, HMS Rodney, 1944. 90c, USS John F. Kennedy, 1982. $1.10, William & John, 1627. $5, USCG Champlain, 1931. $10, Artist, 1877.

Wmk. 373

1994, Aug. 16 Litho. *Perf. 14*

872 A150 5c multicolored .50 .50
873 A150 10c multicolored .50 .50
874 A150 25c multicolored .50 .50
875 A150 30c multicolored .80 .80
876 A150 35c multicolored .95 .95
877 A150 45c multicolored 1.05 1.05
878 A150 50c multicolored 1.20 1.20
879 A150 65c multicolored 1.60 1.60
880 A150 70c multicolored 1.80 1.80
881 A150 80c multicolored 2.40 2.40
882 A150 90c multicolored 2.60 2.60
883 A150 $1.10 multicolored 3.00 3.00
884 A150 $5 multicolored 11.50 11.50
885 A150 $10 multicolored 23.00 23.00
Nos. 872-885 (14) 51.40 51.40

1997 Inscribed "1997"

872a A150 5c multicolored .95 .95
873a A150 10c multicolored .95 .95
874a A150 25c multicolored 1.15 .70
875a A150 30c multicolored 1.90 .70
876a A150 35c multicolored 1.90 .95
877a A150 45c multicolored 1.90 .95
880a A150 70c multicolored 3.50 .70
882a A150 90c multicolored 4.00 2.75
885a A150 $10 multicolored 13.50 13.50
Nos. 872a-885a (9) 29.75 22.15

1998 Inscribed "1998"

872b A150 5c multicolored .50 .50
873b A150 10c multicolored .50 .50
877b A150 45c multicolored 1.10 .75
880b A150 70c multicolored 2.60 2.60
Nos. 872b-880b (4) 4.70 4.35

1999 Inscribed "1999"

873c A150 10c multicolored 1.80 .85
877c A150 45c multicolored 2.60 .65
885c A150 $10 multicolored 20.00 20.00
Nos. 873c-885c (3) 24.40 21.50

1996 Wmk. 384

872d A150 5c .45 .45
873d A150 10c .45 .45
875d A150 30c .55 .55
876d A150 35c .70 .70
877d A150 45c 1.00 1.00
878d A150 50c 1.15 1.15
879d A150 65c 1.30 1.30
880d A150 70c 1.60 1.60
881d A150 80c 1.80 1.80
882d A150 90c 2.25 2.25
883d A150 $1.10 2.50 2.50
884d A150 $5 10.50 10.50
Nos. 872d-884d (12) 24.25 24.25

Inscribed "1996."

Issued: Nos. 875d-877d, 879d-882d, 9/1; others, May 1.

West India Regiment, Bicent. — A151

Designs: 30c, 2nd Regiment, 1860. 50c, 4th Regiment, Light Company, 1795. 70c, 3rd Regiment, drum major, 1860. $1, 5th Regiment, undress, working dress, 1815. $1.10, 1st, 2nd Regiments, Review Order, 1874.

Perf. 15x14

1995, Feb. 21 Litho. Wmk. 373

886 A151 30c multicolored .70 .40
887 A151 50c multicolored 1.00 .65
888 A151 70c multicolored 1.35 1.35
889 A151 $1 multicolored 1.60 1.60
890 A151 $1.10 multicolored 1.90 1.90
Nos. 886-890 (5) 6.55 5.90

End of World War II

Common Design Type

10c, Barbadians serving in the Middle East. 35c, Lancaster bomber. 55c, Spitfire fighter. $2.50, SS Davisian sunk off Barbados, July 10, 1940.

$2, Reverse of War Medal 1939-45.

Wmk. 373

1995, May 8 Litho. *Perf. 14*

891 CD351 10c multicolored 1.00 .65
892 CD351 35c multicolored 1.45 .65
893 CD351 55c multicolored 1.90 .95
894 CD351 $2.50 multicolored 5.00 5.00
Nos. 891-894 (4) 9.35 7.25

Souvenir Sheet

895 CD352 $2 multicolored 3.50 3.50

Combermere School, 300th Anniv. — A152

Designs: 5c, Scouting, Combermere 1st Barbados, 1912. 20c, Violin, sheet music. 35c, Cricket, Sir Frank Worrell, vert. 90c, Frank Collymore, #553. $3, Landscape.

Wmk. 373

1995, July 25 Litho. *Perf. 14*

896 A152 5c multicolored .45 .45
897 A152 20c multicolored .65 .65
898 A152 35c multicolored 1.90 .65
899 A152 $3 multicolored 2.75 2.75
Nos. 896-899 (4) 5.75 4.50

Souvenir Sheet

900 Sheet of 5, #896-899, 900a 6.75 6.75
a. A152 90c multicolored 1.00 1.00

UN, 50th Anniv.

Common Design Type

Designs: 30c, Douglas C-124 Globemaster, Korea 1950-53. 45c, Royal Navy Sea King helicopter. $1.40, Wessex helicopter, UNFICYP, Cyprus 1964. $2, Gazelle helicopter, UNFICYP, Cyprus 1964.

Wmk. 373

1995, Oct. 24 Litho. *Perf. 14*

901 CD353 30c multicolored .95 .55
902 CD353 45c multicolored 1.40 .70
903 CD353 $1.40 multicolored 2.10 2.10
904 CD353 $2 multicolored 2.10 2.10
Nos. 901-904 (4) 6.55 5.45

Water Lilies — A153

Wmk. 373

1995, Dec. 19 Litho. *Perf. 14*

905 A153 10c Blue beauty .60 .45
906 A153 65c White water lily 1.45 1.45
907 A153 70c Sacred lotus 1.45 1.45
908 A153 $3 Water hyacinth 4.00 4.00
Nos. 905-908 (4) 7.50 7.35

Barbados Philatelic Society, Cent.
A154

Magnifiying glass, tongs, and: 10c, #70. 55c, #109. $1.10, #148. $1.40, #192.

Wmk. 373

1996, Jan. 30 Litho. *Perf. 14*

909 A154 10c multicolored .40 .35
910 A154 55c multicolored .75 .55
911 A154 $1.10 multicolored 1.75 1.75
912 A154 $1.40 multicolored 1.90 1.90
Nos. 909-912 (4) 4.80 4.55

A155

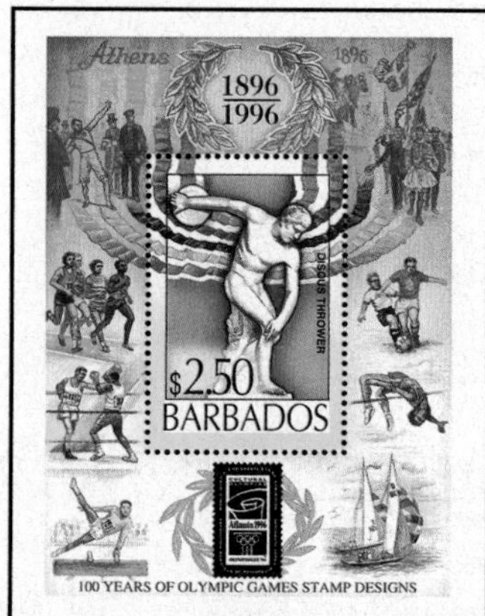

Modern Olympic Games, Cent. — A156

1996, Apr. 2 Litho. *Perf. 14*

913 A155 20c Soccer .60 .40
914 A155 30c Relay race .65 .40
915 A155 55c Basketball 2.25 .85

916	A155	$3 Rhythmic gymnastics	3.25	3.25
		Nos. 913-916 (4)	6.75	4.90

Souvenir Sheet

917	A156	$2.50 Discus thrower	3.00	3.00

Olymphilex '96 (No. 917).

CAPEX '96 A157

Transportation links with Canada: 10c, Canadian Airlines DC10. 90c, Air Canada Boeing 767. $1, Air Canada 320 Airbus. $1.40, Canadian Airlines Boeing 767.

Wmk. 373

1996, June 7 Litho. *Perf. 14*

918	A157	10c multicolored	.50	.45
919	A157	90c multicolored	1.75	1.25
920	A157	$1 multicolored	1.75	1.75
921	A157	$1.40 multicolored	2.25	2.25
		Nos. 918-921 (4)	6.25	5.70

Chattel Houses A158

House features: 35c, Shed roof, lattice work. 70c, Pedimented porch, carved wooden trim. $1.10, Decorative, elegant porch. $2, Hip roof, bell pelmet window hoods.

1996, June 7

922	A158	35c multicolored	.55	.35
923	A158	70c multicolored	1.05	.75
924	A158	$1.10 multicolored	1.30	1.30
925	A158	$2 multicolored	2.10	2.10
		Nos. 922-925 (4)	5.00	4.50

Christmas A159

Children's paintings: 10c, Going to Church on Christmas morning. 30c, The Tuk Band. 55c, Caroling on Christmas. $2.50, Decorated houses.

Wmk. 373

1996, Nov. 12 Litho. *Perf. 14½*

926	A159	10c multicolored	.50	.25
927	A159	30c multicolored	.75	.45
928	A159	55c multicolored	1.05	.70
929	A159	$2.50 multicolored	2.50	2.50
		Nos. 926-929 (4)	4.80	3.90

UNICEF, 50th anniv.

Hong Kong '97 — A160

Dogs: 10c, Doberman pinscher. 30c, German shepherd. 90c, Japanese akita. $3, Irish red setter.

Perf. 14x14½

1997, Feb. 12 Litho. Wmk. 373

930	A160	10c multicolored	.90	.50
931	A160	30c multicolored	1.70	.50
932	A160	90c multicolored	2.50	1.45
933	A160	$3 multicolored	5.25	5.25
		Nos. 930-933 (4)	10.35	7.70

Visit of US Pres. Clinton to Barbados, May 1997 A161

35c, Barbados flag, arms. 90c, US flag, arms.

1997, May 9 Litho. *Perf. 14*

934	A161	35c multicolored	1.00	1.00
935	A161	90c multicolored	1.50	1.50
a.		Pair, #934-935	2.75	2.75

Issued in sheets of 8 stamps + 2 labels.

Shells — A162

5c, Measled cowry. 35c, Trumpet triton. 90c, Scotch bonnet. $2, West Indian murex.

$2.50, Sea bottom with miscellaneous shells.

1997, July 29 Litho. *Perf. 14*

936	A162	5c multicolored	.40	.40
937	A162	35c multicolored	.95	.35
938	A162	90c multicolored	1.80	.95
939	A162	$2 multicolored	2.50	2.50
		Nos. 936-939 (4)	5.65	4.20

Souvenir Sheet

940	A162	$2.50 multicolored	4.00	4.00

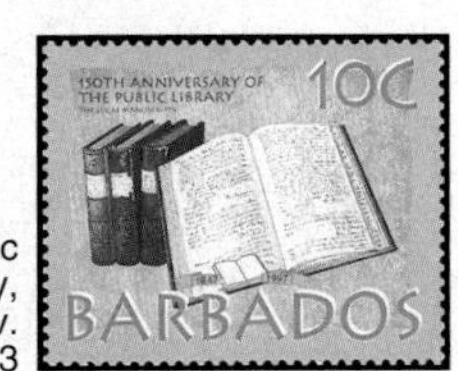

Public Library, 150th Anniv. A163

Designs: 10c, Lucas manuscripts. 30c, Storytelling to children. 70c, Bookmobile. $3, Information technology.

1997, Oct. 1 Litho. *Perf. 14*

941	A163	10c multicolored	.30	.25
942	A163	30c multicolored	.65	.35
943	A163	70c multicolored	1.50	.70
944	A163	$3 multicolored	3.25	3.25
		Nos. 941-944 (4)	5.70	4.55

Fruit — A164

1997, Dec. 16 Litho. *Perf. 14½*

945	A164	35c Barbados cherry	.65	.40
946	A164	40c Sugar apple	.75	.40
947	A164	$1.15 Soursop	1.75	1.75
948	A164	$1.70 Papaya	2.40	2.40
		Nos. 945-948 (4)	5.55	4.95

Souvenir Sheet

Sir Grantley Adams, Birth Cent. — A165

a, Natl. Arms. b, Grantley Adams. c, Natl. flag.

1998, Apr. 27 Litho. *Perf. 13*

949	A165	$1 Sheet of 3, #a.-c.	8.25	8.25

Diana, Princess of Wales (1961-97)

Common Design Type of 1998

Portraits wearing: a, Blue hat. b, Red suit jacket. c, Tiara. d, Black and white.

1998, May *Perf. 14½x14*

950	CD355	$1.15 Sheet of 4, #a.-d.	5.00	5.00

Organization of American States, 50th Anniv. — A166

Designs: 15c, Beach during storm, beach during sunny day. $1, Dancers in native costumes. $2.50, Judge reading at podium, statue of justice.

1998, June 30 Litho. *Perf. 14*

951	A166	15c multicolored	.25	.25
952	A166	$1 multicolored	.90	.90
953	A166	$2.50 multicolored	2.40	2.40
		Nos. 951-953 (3)	3.55	3.55

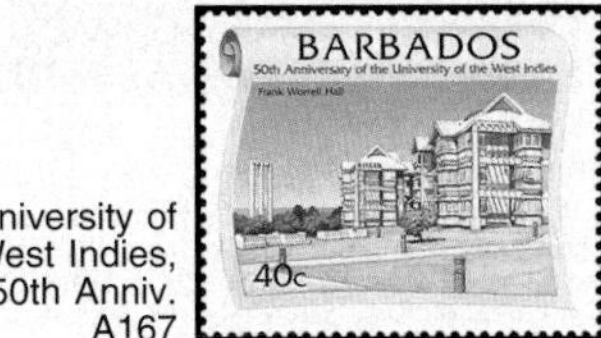

University of West Indies, 50th Anniv. A167

1998, July 20 *Perf. 14½*

954	A167	40c Frank Worrell Hall	.55	.35
955	A167	$1.15 Graduation	1.40	1.40
956	A167	$1.40 Plaque, hummingbird	1.80	1.80
957	A167	$1.75 Quadrangle	3.00	3.00
		Nos. 954-957 (4)	6.75	6.55

Tourism A168

1998, Dec. 1 Litho. *Perf. 14*

958	A168	10c Catamaran, vert.	.35	.35
959	A168	45c Jolly Roger	1.15	.45
960	A168	70c Atlantis submarine	1.75	1.25
961	A168	$2 MV Harbor Master, vert.	3.75	3.75
		Nos. 958-961 (4)	7.00	5.80

Australia '99, World Stamp Expo — A169

1999, Mar. 19 Litho. *Perf. 14*

962	A169	$4 Sailboat	5.00	5.00

Piping Plover A170

World Wildlife Fund: 10c, Juvenile in shallow water. 45c, Female with eggs. 50c, Fledglings in nest, male, female. 70c, Male.

1999, Apr. 27 Litho. *Perf. 14*

963	A170	10c multicolored	.25	.25
964	A170	45c multicolored	1.00	.75
965	A170	50c multicolored	1.00	1.00
966	A170	70c multicolored	1.30	1.30
		Nos. 963-966 (4)	3.55	3.30

1st Manned Moon Landing, 30th Anniv.

Common Design Type

Designs: 40c, Astronaut training. 45c, First stage separation. $1.15, Lunar module. $1.40, Docking with service module.

$2.50, Looking at earth from moon.

Perf. 14x13¾

1999, July 20 Litho. Wmk. 384

967	CD357	40c multicolored	.75	.50
968	CD357	45c multicolored	.75	.50
969	CD357	$1.15 multicolored	1.90	1.50
970	CD357	$1.40 multicolored	2.00	2.00
		Nos. 967-970 (4)	5.40	4.50

Souvenir Sheet

Perf. 14

971	CD357	$2.50 multicolored	3.00	3.00

No. 971 contains one 40mm circular stamp.

Rabbits A171

Designs: a, Rabbit running. b, Rabbit profile. c, Rabbit nursing young. d, Two rabbits leaping. e, Two rabbits at rest.

Perf. 14x14½

1999, Aug. 21 Litho. Wmk. 373

972	A171	70c Strip of 5, #a.-e.	9.00	9.00

China 1999 World Philatelic Exhibition.

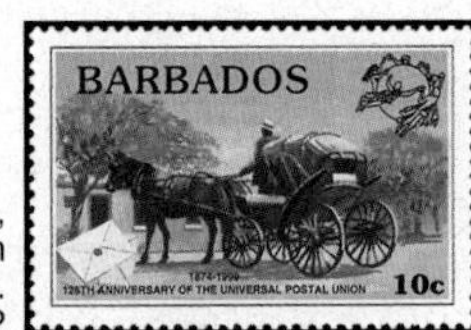

UPU, 125th Anniv. A172

1999, Oct. 11 Litho. *Perf. 14*

973	A172	10c Mail coach	1.10	.45
974	A172	45c Mail van	1.60	.55
975	A172	$1.75 Airplane	2.25	2.25
976	A172	$2 Computers	2.50	2.50
		Nos. 973-976 (4)	7.45	5.75

Souvenir Sheet

Millennium — A173

Wmk. 373

2000, Feb. 8 Litho. *Perf. 14*

977	A173	$3 multi	5.00	5.00

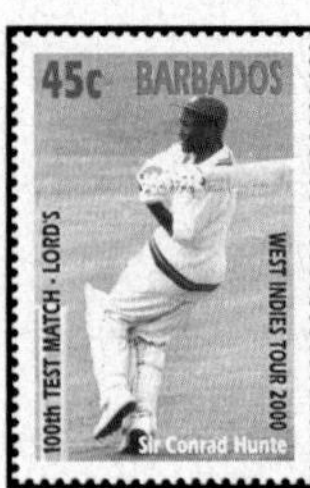

100th Test Cricket Match at Lord's Ground — A174

Designs: 45c, Sir Conrad Hunte. 90c, Malcolm Marshall. $2, Sir Garfield St. A. Sobers. $2.50, Lord's Ground, horiz.

Wmk. 373

2000, May 22 Litho. *Perf. 14*

978	A174	45c multi	1.00	.45
979	A174	90c multi	2.00	.90
980	A174	$2 multi	3.50	3.50
		Nos. 978-980 (3)	6.50	4.85

Souvenir Sheet

981 A174 $2.50 multi 4.50 4.50

The Stamp Show 2000, London (No. 981).

Sites in Barbados A175

5c, Drax Hall House. 10c, Reaping sugar cane. 40c, Needham's Point Lighthouse. 45c, Port St. Charles. 65c, Synagogue. 70c, Bridgetown port (boats point right). No. 987A, 70c, Bridgetown port (boats point left). 90c, Harrison's Cave. $1.15, Villa Nova. $1.40, Cricket at Kensington Oval. $1.75, Sunbury House. $2, Bethel Methodist Church. $3, Barbados Wildlife Reserve. $5, Royal Westmoreland golf course. $10, Grantley Adams Intl. Airport.

Wmk. 373

2000, May 22 Litho. *Perf. 14*

982	A175	5c multi	.25	.25
983	A175	10c multi, vert.	.25	.25
a.		Inscribed "2002"	1.25	1.25
b.		Inscribed "2004"	1.60	1.60
984	A175	40c multi, vert.	.50	.50
985	A175	45c multi	.60	.60
986	A175	65c multi	.90	.90
987	A175	70c multi	1.10	1.10
987A	A175	70c multi	1.10	1.10
988	A175	90c multi	1.35	1.35
989	A175	$1.15 multi	1.75	1.75
990	A175	$1.40 multi	1.90	1.90
991	A175	$1.75 multi	2.50	2.50
992	A175	$2 multi	3.00	3.00
993	A175	$3 multi, vert.	4.25	4.25
994	A175	$5 multi, vert.	7.75	7.75
995	A175	$10 multi	14.50	14.50
		Nos. 982-995 (15)	41.70	41.70

Nos. 982-987, 988-995 issued 5/22.

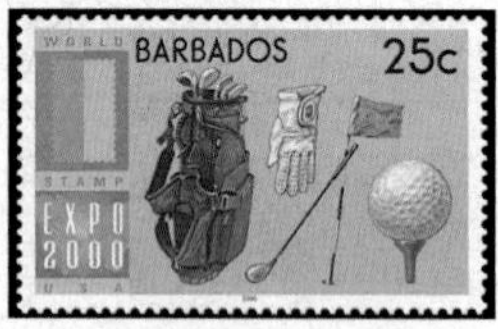

World Stamp Expo 2000, Anaheim — A176

25c, Golf equipment. 40c, Golfer on golf ball. $1.40, Golfer at tee. $2, Golfer putting.

Perf. 14½x14¼

2000, July 7 Litho. Wmk. 373

996-999 A176 Set of 4 7.00 7.00

Vintage Cars A177

Designs: 10c, 1947 Bentley Mk VI. 30c, Vanden Plas Princess. 90c, 1952 Austin Atlantic. $3, 1950 Bentley Special.

Perf. 14¼x14½

2000, Nov. 7 Wmk. 373

1000-1003 A177 Set of 4 6.50 6.50

Souvenir Sheet

Hong Kong 2001 Stamp Exhibition — A178

Wmk. 373

2001, Feb. 1 Litho. *Perf. 13¼*

1004 A178 $3 Thread snake 4.75 4.75

Deep Sea Creatures — A179

No. 1005: a, Lizard fish. b, Goldentail moray. c, Blackbar soldierfish. d, Golden zoanthid. e, Sponge brittle star. f, Magnificent feather duster. g, Bearded fireworm. h, Lima shell. i, Yellow tube sponge.

Wmk. 373

2001, May 31 Litho. *Perf. 13½*

1005 A179 45c Sheet of 9, #a-i 5.75 5.75

Phila Nippon '01, Japan A180

Various kites: 10c, 65c, $1.40, $1.75.

2001, Aug. 1 *Perf. 14*

1006-1009 A180 Set of 4 4.75 4.75

George Washington's Visit to Barbados, 250th Anniv. — A181

Designs: 45c, Washington, ship, trunk, dockworker. 50c, Washington, ship, palm trees. $1.15, Washington, Declaration of Independence. $2.50, Fort at Needham's Point. $3, Portrait of Washington.

Wmk. 373

2001, Nov. 2 Litho. *Perf. 13¼*

1010-1013 A181 Set of 4 6.50 6.50

Souvenir Sheet

1014 A181 $3 multi 3.75 3.75

Independence, 35th Anniv. — A182

Designs: 25c, Bank Holiday Bear. 45c, Tuk band. $1, Landship Movement Maypole dance. $2, National anthem, saxophone and guitar.

2001, Nov. 29 Litho. *Perf. 14*

1015-1018 A182 Set of 4 6.25 6.25

Reign Of Queen Elizabeth II, 50th Anniv. Issue

Common Design Type

Designs: Nos. 1019, 1023a, 10c, Princess Elizabeth. Nos. 1020, 1023b, 70c, Wearing red hat. Nos. 1021, 1023c, $1, Wearing crown. Nos. 1022, 1023d, $1.40, Wearing purple hat. No. 1023e, $3, 1955 portrait by Annigoni (38x50mm).

Perf. 14¼x14½, 13¾ (#1023e)

2002, Feb. 6 Wmk. 373

With Gold Frames

1019	CD360	10c multicolored	.35	.35
1020	CD360	70c multicolored	1.25	1.25
1021	CD360	$1 multicolored	1.40	1.40
1022	CD360	$1.40 multicolored	2.00	2.00
		Nos. 1019-1022 (4)	5.00	5.00

Souvenir Sheet

Without Gold Frames

1023 CD360 Sheet of 5, #a-e 7.25 7.25

Inland Post, 150th Anniv. A183

Map of Barbados and: 10c, #1. 45c, Early postman. $1.15, Steam packet R.M.S. Esk. $2, BWIA Tristar.

2002, Apr. 15 *Perf. 14*

1024-1027 A183 Set of 4 5.25 5.25

Flowers — A184

Designs: 10c, Red ginger, vert. 40c, Heliconia caribaea, vert. $1.40, Tube rose. $2.50, Anthurium.

Perf. 14¾x14, 14x14¾

2002, May 30 Litho.

1028-1031 A184 Set of 4 5.00 5.00

First Settlement, 375th Anniv. — A185

Designs: 10c, Drax Hall, St. George. 45c, Donkey cart truck. $1.15, Remains of cattle mill, Gibbons. $3, Morgan Lewis, St. Andrew.

Wmk. 373

2002, Sept. 6 Litho. *Perf. 14*

1032-1035 A185 Set of 4 8.00 8.00

Christmas A186

Designs: 45c, Traditional Christmas fare. $1.15, Christmas morning in the park. $1.40, Nativity scene.

2002, Nov. 11

1036-1038 A186 Set of 3 4.00 4.00

Pan-American Health Organization, Cent. — A187

Designs: 10c, AIDS awareness. 70c, Health and longevity. $1.15, Director General Sir George Alleyne. $2, Women's health.

Wmk. 373

2002, Dec. 2 Litho. *Perf. 14*

1039-1042 A187 Set of 4 5.75 5.25

Royal Navy Ships A188

Designs: 10c, HMS Tartar, 1764. 70c, HMS Barbadoes, 1803. $1.15, HMS Valerian, 1926. $2.50, HMS Victorious, 1941.

Wmk. 373

2003, May 26 Litho. *Perf. 14*

1043-1046 A188 Set of 4 7.25 7.25

Settlement Of Bridgetown, 375th Anniv. — A189

Designs: 10c, Broad Street, c. 1900. $1.15, Swan Street, 1900. $1.40, Roebuck Street, c. 1880. $2, Chamberlain Bridge.

Wmk. 373

2003, July 7 Litho. *Perf. 14*

1047-1050 A189 Set of 4 7.25 7.25

1050a Souvenir sheet, #1047-1050 7.50 7.50

Powered Flight, Cent. — A190

Designs: 10c, McDonnell F2H-2 Banshee. 45c, Vickers Viscount 700. 50c, Douglas DC-9-30. $1.15, Short Sunderland MK II. $1.40, North American P-51D Mustang. $2.50, Concorde.

Stamps + Labels

Perf. 13¼x13¾

2003, Sept. 22 Litho. Wmk. 373

1051-1056 A190 Set of 6 7.75 7.75

Festivals — A191

No. 1057: a, Fishermen hauling in catch, Oistins Fish Festival. b, Saxophonist, Barbados Jazz Festival. c, Costumed man and woman, Crop Over Festival. d, Dancers, National Independence Festival of Creative

Arts. e, Choir, National Independence Festival of Creative Arts. f, Three people in costume, Crop Over Festival. g, Bassist, Barbados Jazz Festival. h, Fish boning, Oistins Fish Festival.

Wmk. 373

2003, Nov. 24 Litho. *Perf. 13¾*
1057 A191 45c Sheet of 8, #a-h, + central label 9.75 9.75

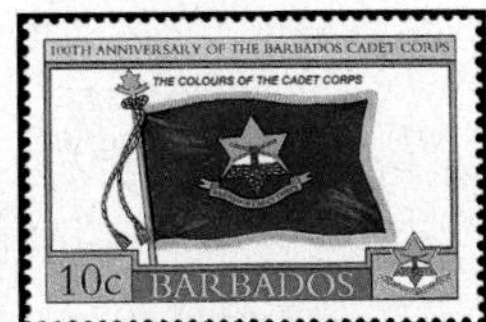

Cadet Corps, Cent. A192

Designs: 10c, Cadet Corps Flag. 25c, Regular Band marching. 50c, Toy Soldier Band. $1, Sea Cadets. $3, Map reading.

Wmk. 373

2004, July 19 Litho. *Perf. 14*
1058-1062 A192 Set of 5 8.00 8.00

2004 Summer Olympics, Athens — A193

Designs: 10, Swimming. 70c, Shooting. $1.15, Running. $2, Judo.

Wmk. 373

2004, Aug. 16 Litho. *Perf. 14*
1063-1066 A193 Set of 4 7.00 7.00

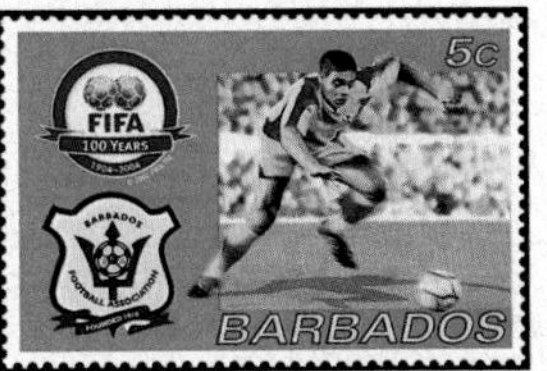

FIFA (Fédération Internationale de Football Association), Cent. — A194

Various soccer players: 5c, 90c, $1.40, $2.50.

Perf. 14x14¾

2004, Oct. 20 Litho. Wmk. 373
1067-1070 A194 Set of 4 6.50 6.50

Corals — A195

No. 1071: a, Brain coral. b, Pillar coral (yellow). c, Pillar coral (tan). d, Fan coral. e, Yellow pencil coral.
$3.50, Maze coral.

2004, Nov. 15 *Perf. 14x14¼*
1071 Horiz. strip of 5 11.00 11.00
a.-e. A195 $1 Any single 2.10 2.10

Souvenir Sheet
Perf. 13¼

1072 A195 $3.50 multi 5.75 5.75

No. 1072 contains one 36x36mm stamp.

Butterflies A196

Designs: 50c, White peacock. $1, Great southern white. $1.40, Orion. $2.50, Mimic. $8, Monarch.

Wmk. 373

2005, Apr. 21 Litho. *Perf. 14*
1073-1076 A196 Set of 4 11.50 11.50

Souvenir Sheet

1077 A196 $8 multi 10.00 10.00

Pacific Explorer 2005 World Stamp Expo, Sydney.

Trees A197

Designs: 5c, Baobab, 10c, African tulip tree. 25c, Rose of Sharon. 45c, Black willow. 50c, Black pearl tree. 75c, Seaside mahoe. 90c, Quickstick. $1, Jerusalem thorn. $1.15, Pink cassia. $1.40, Orchid tree. $1.75, Yellow poui. $2.10, Lignum vitae. $3, Wild cinnamon. $5, Pride of India. $10, Immortelle.

Wmk. 373

2005, July 20 Litho. *Perf. 13¾*

1078	A197	5c	multi	.25	.25
1079	A197	10c	multi	.25	.25
1080	A197	25c	multi	.35	.35
1081	A197	45c	multi	.60	.60
1082	A197	50c	multi	.65	.65
1083	A197	75c	multi	.85	.85
1084	A197	90c	multi	1.00	1.00
1085	A197	$1	multi	1.10	1.10
1086	A197	$1.15	multi	1.60	1.60
1087	A197	$1.40	multi	1.75	1.75
1088	A197	$1.75	multi	2.25	2.25
1089	A197	$2.10	multi	2.75	2.75
1090	A197	$3	multi	3.75	3.75
1091	A197	$5	multi	6.00	6.00
1092	A197	$10	multi	11.50	11.50
	Nos. 1078-1092 (15)			34.65	34.65

Dated "2010"

2010 Wmk. 406 Litho. *Perf. 13¾*

1078a	5c multi	.25	.25
1079a	10c multi	.25	.25
1082a	50c multi	.50	.50
1086a	$1.15 multi	1.25	1.25
1087a	$1.40 multi	1.40	1.40
1088a	$1.75 multi	1.75	1.75
	Nos. 1078a-1088a (6)	5.40	5.40

Barbados Fire Service, 50th Anniv. A198

Designs: 5c, Three firefighters. 10c, Parade at firehouse. 90c, Yellow fire truck. $1.15, Old fire trucks. $2.50, Red fire truck.

Wmk. 373

2005, Sept. 26 Litho. *Perf. 14*
1093-1097 A198 Set of 5 9.50 9.50

Extreme Anoles A199

Designs: 10c, Three anoles. 50c, Two anoles. $1.75, One anole. $2, Hatchling and eggs.

Wmk. 373

2005, Nov. 28 Litho. *Perf. 14*
1098-1101 A199 Set of 4 8.00 8.00

Worldwide Fund for Nature (WWF) A200

Queen angelfish and: 10c, Diver. $1.15, Coral. $1.40, Sea floor. $2.10, Coral, diff.

Wmk. 373

2006, Jan. 30 Litho. *Perf. 14*
1102-1105 A200 Set of 4 6.50 6.50
1105a Sheet, 2 each #1102-1105 13.00 13.00

Washington 2006 World Philatelic Exhibition — A201

Children: 10c, Reading. 50c, Playing wheelchair basketball. $2, At computer. $2.50, Playing violins.

Perf. 13¼x13½

2006, May 26 Litho. Wmk. 373
1106-1109 A201 Set of 4 6.50 6.50

Cave Shepherd Store, Cent. A202

Store facades from around: 10c, 1911. 50c, 2000. $1.75, 1975. $2, 1920.

Wmk. 373

2006, Nov. 1 Litho. *Perf. 13¾*
1110-1113 A202 Set of 4 6.00 6.00

Enfranchisement of Free Colored and Black Barbadians, 175th Anniv. — A203

Designs: 10c, Old Town Hall, Coleridge Street. 50c, Samuel Jackman Prescod (1806-71). $1.40, Introduction of ballot box, 1885. $2.50, Sir James Lyon, Governor from 1829-33.

2006, Nov. 27
1114-1117 A203 Set of 4 5.25 5.25

2007 ICC Cricket World Cup — A204

Designs: $1.75, Joel "Big Bird" Garner. $2.10, Old Kensington Oval, horiz. $3, New Kensington Oval, horiz.
$10, ICC Cricket World Cup.

Wmk. 373

2007, Mar. 19 Litho. *Perf. 14*
1118-1120 A204 Set of 3 7.00 7.00

Souvenir Sheet
Litho. & Embossed

1121 A204 $10 multi 10.00 10.00

Abolition of Slavery, Bicent. — A205

Designs: 10c, Sculpture of Bussa, slave revolt leader. $1, William Wilberforce, British abolitionist. $1.75, Slave hut, horiz. $2, Freedom celebration, 1838, horiz.
$3, Slave ship.

Perf. 14¾x14¼, 14¼x14¾

2007, Mar. 26 Litho. Wmk. 373
1122-1125 A205 Set of 4 5.00 5.00

Souvenir Sheet

1126 A205 $3 multi 3.00 3.00

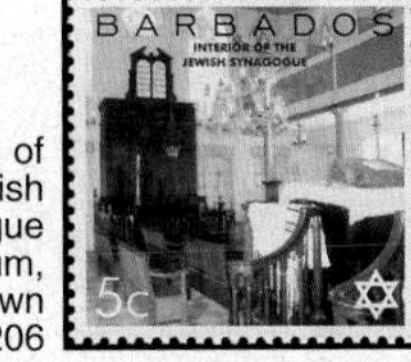

Opening of Jewish Synagogue Museum, Bridgetown A206

Designs: 5c, Interior of synagogue. 10c, Museum building. $1.40, Hanukiah. $2.50, Stained-glass window.

2007, May 15 *Perf. 12½x13*
1127-1130 A206 Set of 4 4.25 4.25

Turtles A207

Turtles: 10c, Green. 50c, Loggerhead. $1, Hawksbill. $2.50, Leatherback.

Perf. 12½x13

2007, Oct. 29 Litho. Unwmk.
1131-1134 A207 Set of 4 4.25 4.25

Algae — A208

Designs: 10c, Padina gymnospora. 50c, Ulva lactuta. $1.75, Sargassum platycarpum. $2, Udotea conglutinata.

Wmk. 373

2008, July 14 Litho. *Perf. 13¾*
1135-1138 A208 Set of 4 4.50 4.50

Barbadians and Aircraft — A209

Designs: 10c, Second Barbados Contingent. 50c, Warren Alleyne, Supermarine Spitfire Mk IX. $1.75, Wing Commander Aubrey Inniss, Bristol Beaufighter Mk VIC. $2, Flying Officer Errol Barrow, Avro Lancaster B Mk 1.
$6, Concorde over Barbados.

Wmk. 373

2008, July 30 Litho. *Perf. 14*
1139-1142 A209 Set of 4 4.50 4.50

Souvenir Sheet

1143 A209 $6 multi 6.00 6.00

Christmas A210

Paintings: 10c, Christmas Moon, by Alison Chapman-Andrews. 50c, Preparing for Christmas, bu Virgil Broodhagen. $1.40, Christmas Candles, by Darla Trotman. $3, Poinsettia and Snow on the Mountain, by Trotman.

2008, Nov. 11 Wmk. 406 *Perf. 13½*
1144-1147 A210 Set of 4 5.00 5.00

Louis Braille (1809-52), Educator of the Blind — A211

Braille and: 50c, Hands of worker using pliers. $1.40, Worker caning chair. $1.75, Student reading Braille text at Braille typewriter. $2, "Louis Braille" in Braille text.

2009, July 6 *Perf. 14*
1148-1151 A211 Set of 4 5.75 5.75

Restructured Criminal Court, 300th Anniv. — A212

Designs: 10c, New Court House. 50c, Handcuffs, seal of the court. $1.40, Judge's robe, wig and gavel. $2.50, Old Court House.

Wmk. 406

2009, Nov. 10 Litho. *Perf. 12½*
1152-1155 A212 Set of 4 4.50 4.50

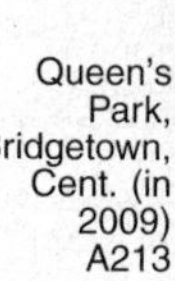

Queen's Park, Bridgetown, Cent. (in 2009) A213

Designs: 90c, Queen's Park Fountain. $1, Baobab tree. $1.40, Queen's Park House. $2, Band stand.

$4, Band stand at park's opening.

Perf. 12½x13

2010, Jan. 11 Unwmk.
1156-1159 A213 Set of 4 5.50 5.50

Souvenir Sheet

1160 A213 $4 multi 4.00 4.00

Fireball World Championships Regatta — A214

Various racing sailboats: 10c, 50c, 90c, $1.75, $2.

2010, Apr. 23 Wmk. 406 *Perf. 14*
1161-1165 A214 Set of 5 5.25 5.25

Girl Guides, Cent. A215

Girl Guides: 10c, At camp. 50c, Giving salute. $1, In various uniforms. $2.50, On parade.

$3.50, Centenary emblem, emblems of Girl Guides and Barbados Girl Guides.

Perf. 14¼x14

2010, Sept. 22 Litho. Wmk. 406
1166-1169 A215 Set of 4 4.25 4.25

Souvenir Sheet

1170 A215 $3.50 multi 3.50 3.50

Fruits — A216

Designs: 5c, Golden apples. 10c Coconuts. 35c, Cashews. 40c, Mammy apples. 60c, Barbados cherries. 65c, Sugar apples. 80c, Sea grapes. $1, Tamarinds. $1.25, Carambolas. $1.50, Mangos. $1.80, Bananas. $2.20, Guavas. $2.75, Avocados. $3, Gooseberries. $5, Soursops. $10, Pomegranates.

Unwmk.

2011, Feb. 7 Litho. *Perf. 13*

1171	A216	5c multi	.25	.25
1172	A216	10c multi	.25	.25
1173	A216	35c multi	.35	.35
1174	A216	40c multi	.40	.40
1175	A216	60c multi	.60	.60
1176	A216	65c multi	.65	.65
1177	A216	80c multi	.80	.80
1178	A216	$1 multi	1.00	1.00
1179	A216	$1.25 multi	1.25	1.25
1180	A216	$1.50 multi	1.50	1.50
1181	A216	$1.80 multi	1.90	1.90
1182	A216	$2.20 multi	2.25	2.25
1183	A216	$2.75 multi	2.75	2.75
1184	A216	$3 multi	3.00	3.00
1185	A216	$5 multi	5.00	5.00
1186	A216	$10 multi	10.00	10.00
		Nos. 1171-1186 (16)	31.95	31.95

Sailor's Valentines (Shell Art) — A217

Designs: 10c, Valentine from 1800s. 65c, "With My Love." $2.20, "Live Today, Hope Tomorrow." $2.75, "Evermore."

Perf. 12½x13

2011, Feb. 14 Wmk. 406
1187-1190 A217 Set of 4 5.75 5.75

Wedding of Prince William and Catherine Middleton — A218

Designs: 15c, Middleton in wedding dress with attendant. 65c, Couple in carriage. $1.80, Couple holding hands, vert. $2.20, Couple waving, vert.

Wmk. 406

2011, Aug. 3 Litho. *Perf. 14*
1191-1194 A218 Set of 4 5.00 5.00

Reign of Queen Elizabeth II, 60th Anniv. A219

Queen Elizabeth II: 10c, Exiting Barbados Parliament, 1989. $1.40, Wearing tiara, 1952. $2.10, Inspecting Barbados soldiers, 1977. $2.50, At Goddard Space Flight Center, Maryland, 2007.

$4, Queen Elizabeth II and Prince Philip at opening of Barbados Parliament, 1987.

2012, Mar. 12 Wmk. 406 *Perf. 13*
1195-1198 A219 Set of 4 6.25 6.25

Souvenir Sheet

Perf. 13½x13

1199 A219 $4 multi 4.00 4.00

No. 1199 contains one 60x40mm stamp.

Bridgetown Landmarks A220

Designs: 10c, Gun Hill Signal Station. 65c, Clock tower, Main Guardhouse, Bridgetown Garrison. $2, St. Mary's Church, horiz. $2.75, Public Library, horiz.

2012, July 18 *Perf. 14*
1200-1203 A220 Set of 4 5.50 5.50

National Trust, 50th anniv.

Bridgetown Port, 50th Anniv. (in 2011) — A221

Designs: 10c, Pelican Island. 65c, Lightermen delivering cargo. $1.75, Tugboat Barbados II. $2.80, Aerial view of Bridgetown Port.

2012, Oct. 1
1204-1207 A221 Set of 4 5.50 5.50

Lighthouses A222

Designs: 65c, Harrison Point Lighthouse. $1.50, South Point Lighthouse. $1.80, Needham's Point Lighthouse. $2.20, East Point Lighthouse.

2013, June 13
1208-1211 A222 Set of 4 6.25 6.25

SEMI-POSTAL STAMPS

No. 73 Surcharged in Red

Perf. 14

1907, Jan. 25 Typo. Wmk. 2

B1	A8 1p on 2p sl & org		3.75	*10.00*
a.	No period after 1d		55.00	*92.50*
b.	Inverted surcharge		2.00	*7.50*
c.	Inverted surcharge, no period after 1d		47.50	*105.00*
d.	Double surcharge		925.00	*1,000.*
e.	Dbl. surch., both invtd.		925.00	
f.	Dbl. surch., one invtd.		*1,200.*	
g.	Vert. pair, one normal, one surcharge double			*1,200.*
h.	Pair with surcharges tête-bêche		1,500.	

Catalogue values for unused stamps in this section, from this point to the end of the section, are for Never Hinged items.

No. 406 Surcharged

1979, May 29 Photo. Wmk. 314
B2 A56 28c + 4c on 35c multi .70 .70

The surtax was for victims of the eruption of Mt. Soufrière.

POSTAGE DUE STAMPS

Catalogue values for unused stamps in this section are for Never Hinged items.

D1

1934-47 Typo. Wmk. 4 *Perf. 14*

J1	D1	½p green ('35)	1.60	8.50
J2	D1	1p black	1.60	1.75
a.		Half used as ½p on cover		*2,500.*
J3	D1	3p dk car rose ('47)	26.00	23.00
		Nos. J1-J3 (3)	29.20	33.25

A 2nd die of the 1p was introduced in 1947.

Use of #J2a was authorized from Mar. 1934 through Feb. 1935. Some examples have "½d" written on the bisect in black or red ink.

1950

J4	D1	1c green	3.75	*32.50*
J5	D1	2c black	7.00	*17.00*
J6	D1	6c carmine rose	16.00	*17.50*
		Nos. J4-J6 (3)	26.75	*67.00*

Values are for 1953 chalky paper printing. Values on ordinary paper, unused $30, used $65.

Wmk. 4a (error)

J4a	D1	1c green	425.00
J5a	D1	2c black	800.00
J6a	D1	6c carmine rose	175.00
		Nos. J4a-J6a (3)	1,400.

1965, Aug. 3 Wmk. 314 *Perf. 14*

J7	D1	1c green	.50	*4.50*
J8	D1	2c black	.60	*5.50*
J9	D1	6c carmine rose	1.50	*13.00*
a.		Wmk. sideways, perf 14x13½	10.50	*20.00*
		Nos. J7-J9 (3)	2.60	*23.00*

Issued: No. J9a, 2/4/74.

Wmk. 314 Sideways

1974, Dec. 4			*Perf. 13x13½*	
J8b	D1	2c	8.00	*20.00*
J9b	D1	6c	8.00	*20.00*

D2

Designs: Each stamp shows different stylized flower in background.

Perf. 13½x14

1976, May 12	Litho.	Wmk. 373	
J10 D2	1c brt pink & mag	.35	.80
J11 D2	2c lt & dk vio blue	.35	.80
J12 D2	5c yellow & brown	.35	.80
J13 D2	10c lilac & purple	.45	1.05
J14 D2	25c yel green & dk grn	1.10	3.00
J15 D2	$1 rose & red	1.10	3.00
	Nos. J10-J15 (6)	3.70	9.45

1985, July			*Perf. 15x14*	
J10a	D2	1c	.50	.50
J11a	D2	2c	.50	.50
J12a	D2	5c	.50	.50
J13a	D2	10c	.50	.50
J14a	D2	25c	.50	.50
	Nos. J10a-J14a (5)		2.50	2.50

WAR TAX STAMP

No. 118 Overprinted

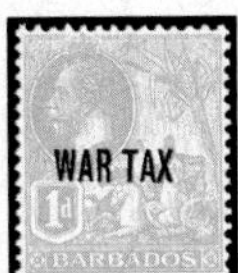

1917	Wmk. 3	*Perf. 14*	
MR1 A12 1p carmine		.55	.25
a. Imperf., pair		*2,500.*	

BARBUDA

bär-'büd-ə

LOCATION — In northern Leeward Islands, West Indies
GOVT. — Dependency of Antigua
AREA — 63 sq. mi.
POP. — 1,500 (1995 est.)
See Antigua.

12 Pence = 1 Shilling
100 Cents = 1 Dollar (1951)

Catalogue values for unused stamps in this country are for Never Hinged items, beginning with Scott 12 in the regular postage section, and Scott B1 in the semi-postal section.

Watermark

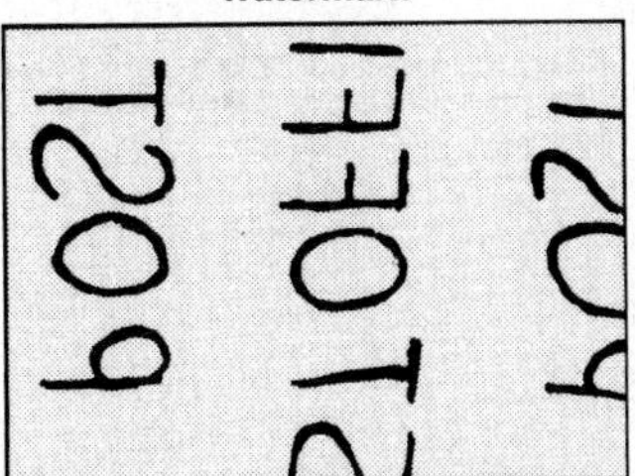

Wmk. 380 — "POST OFFICE"

Leeward Islands Stamps of 1912-22 Ovptd. in Black or Red

Die II

For description of dies I and II, see Dies of British Colonial Stamps in the catalogue introduction.

1922, July 13		Wmk. 4	*Perf. 14*	
1	A5	½p green	1.75	*13.00*
2	A5	1p rose red	1.75	*13.00*
3	A5	2p gray	1.75	*10.50*
4	A5	2½p ultramarine	1.75	*11.00*
5	A5	6p vio & red vio	2.40	*23.00*
6	A5	2sh vio & ultra, *bl*	16.00	*62.50*
7	A5	3sh green & violet	35.00	*100.00*
8	A5	4sh blk & scar (R)	42.50	*100.00*
		Wmk. 3		
9	A5	3p violet, *yel*	2.10	*17.00*
10	A5	1sh blk, *emer* (R)	1.90	*12.00*
11	A5	5sh grn & red, *yel*	87.50	*200.00*
		Nos. 1-11 (11)	194.40	*562.00*
		Set, never hinged	400.00	

Beware of forgeries, especially used examples dated June 1, 1923.

Catalogue values for unused stamps in this section, from this point to the end of the section, are for Never Hinged items.

Map — B1

Fish — B2

1968-70	Litho.	Unwmk.	*Perf. 14*	
12 B1	½c blk, salmon pink & red brn		.25	*2.75*
13 B1	1c blk, org & brt org		.50	.25
14 B1	2c blk, brt pink & brt rose		1.50	.70
15 B1	3c blk, yel & org yel		.50	.40
16 B1	4c blk, lt grn & brt grn		1.75	*2.75*
17 B1	5c blk, bl grn & brt bl grn		1.50	.25
18 B1	6c blk, lt lil & red lil		.75	*3.00*
19 B1	10c blk, lt bl & dk bl		.75	*1.40*
20 B1	15c blk, dl grn & grn		.60	*3.00*
21 B2	20c Great barracuda		2.00	*2.40*
22 B2	25c Great amberjack		.60	.40
23 B2	35c French angelfish		2.25	.45
24 B2	50c Porkfish		1.00	.75
25 B2	75c Striped parrotfish		1.00	1.00
26 B2	$1 Longspine squirrelfish		1.25	*3.00*
27 B2	$2.50 Catalufa		3.00	*6.25*
28 B2	$5 Blue chromis		6.00	*8.50*
	Nos. 12-28 (17)		25.20	37.25

Issued: ½c-15c, 11/19/68; 20c, 7/22/70; 25c-75c, 2/5/69; others, 3/6/69.
For surcharge see No. 80.

1968 Summer Olympics, Mexico City — B3

Designs: 25c, Running, Aztec calendar stone. 35c, High jumping, Aztec statue. 75c, Yachting, Aztec lion mask. $1, Soccer, Aztec carved stone.

1968, Dec. 20			
29 B3	25c multicolored	.45	.25
30 B3	35c multicolored	.55	.30
31 B3	75c multicolored	.95	.45
	Nos. 29-31 (3)	1.95	1.00

Souvenir Sheet

32 B3	$1 multicolored	3.00	*3.75*

The Ascension, by Orcagna — B4

1969, Mar. 24			
33 B4	25c blue & black	.25	*.45*
34 B4	35c dp carmine & blk	.25	*.50*
35 B4	75c violet & black	.25	*.55*
	Nos. 33-35 (3)	.75	1.50

Easter.

3rd Caribbean Boy Scout Jamboree — B5

1969, Aug. 7			
36 B5	35c Flag ceremony	.50	*.55*
37 B5	35c Campfire	.60	*.70*
38 B5	75c Rowing	.80	*.95*
	Nos. 36-38 (3)	1.90	2.20

The Sistine Madonna, by Raphael — B6

1969, Oct. 20			
39 B6	½c multicolored	.25	*.30*
40 B6	25c multicolored	.25	.25
41 B6	35c multicolored	.25	.25
42 B6	75c multicolored	.25	*.40*
	Nos. 39-42 (4)	1.00	1.20

Christmas.

English Monarchs — B7

No. 43, William I. No. 44, William II. No. 45, Henry I. No. 46, Stephen. No. 47, Henry II. No. 48, Richard I. No. 49, John. No. 50, Henry III. No. 51, Edward I. No. 52, Edward II. No. 53, Edward III. No. 54, Richard II. No. 55, Henry IV. No. 56, Henry V. No. 57, Henry VI. No. 58, Edward IV. No. 59, Edward V. No. 60, Richard III. No. 61, Henry VII. No. 62, Henry VIII. No. 63, Edward VI. No. 64, Lady Jane Grey. No. 65, Mary I. No. 66, Elizabeth I. No. 67, James I. No. 68, Charles I. No. 69, Charles II. No. 70, James II. No. 71, William III. No. 72, Mary II. No. 73, Anne. No. 74, George I. No. 75, George II. No. 76, George III. No. 77, George IV. No. 78, William IV. No. 79, Victoria.

1970-71		*Perf. 14½x14*	
43-79 B7	35c Set of 37	12.00	*17.50*

Issued: 1970, No. 43, 2/16; No. 44, 3/2; No. 45, 3/16; No. 46, 4/4; No. 47, 4/15; No. 48, 5/1; No. 49, 5/15; No. 50, 6/1; No. 51, 6/15; No. 52, 7/1; No. 53, 7/15; No. 54, 8/1; No. 55, 8/15; No. 56, 9/1; No. 57, 9/15; No. 58, 10/1; No. 59, 10/15; No. 60, 11/2; No. 61, 11/16; No. 62, 12/1; No. 63, 12/15.

1971; No. 64, 1/2; No. 65, 1/15; No. 66, 2/1; No. 67, 2/15; No. 68, 3/1; No. 69, 3/15; No. 70, 4/1; No. 71, 4/15; No. 72, 5/1; No. 73, 5/15; No. 74, 6/1; No. 75, 6/15; No. 76, 7/1; No. 77, 7/15; No. 78, 8/2; No. 79, 8/16.

See Nos. 622-627 for other Monarchs.

No. 12 Surcharged

1970, Feb. 26		*Perf. 14*	
80 B1	20c on 1/2c multicolored	.40	.40

Easter — B8

1970, Mar. 16			
81 B8	25c Carrying Cross	.25	.30
82 B8	35c Descent from cross	.25	.30
83 B8	75c Crucifixion	.25	.35
a.	Strip of 3, #81-83	.70	.70

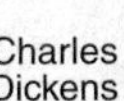

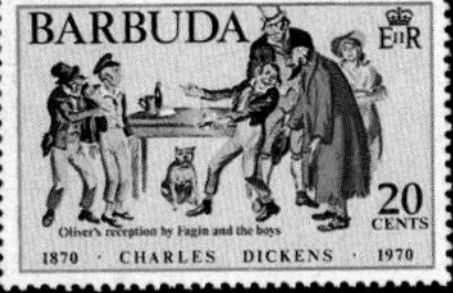

Charles Dickens B9

1970, July 10			
84 B9	20c Oliver Twist	.30	.30
85 B9	75c Old Curiosity Shop	.65	.65

Christmas — B10

Designs: 20c, Madonna of the Meadow, by Giovanni Bellini. 50c, Madonna, Child and Angels from Wilton Diptych. 75c, Nativity, by Piero della Francesca.

1970, Oct. 15			
86 B10	20c multicolored	.25	.25
87 B10	50c multicolored	.25	.30
88 B10	75c multicolored	.25	.35
	Nos. 86-88 (3)	.75	.90

British Red Cross, Cent. B11

1970, Dec. 21			
89 B11	20c Patient in wheelchair, vert.	.25	*.40*
90 B11	35c shown	.25	*.50*
91 B11	75c Child care	.40	*.85*
	Nos. 89-91 (3)	.90	*1.75*

Easter — B12

Details from the Mond Crucifixion, by Raphael.

1971, Apr. 7

No.	Type	Description	Unused	Used
92	B12	35c Angel	.25	.95
93	B12	50c Crucifixion	.25	1.10
94	B12	75c Angel, diff.	.30	1.25
a.		Strip of 3, #92-94	.85	3.50

Martello Tower B13

1971, May 10

No.	Type	Description	Unused	Used
95	B13	20c shown	.25	.40
96	B13	25c Sailboats	.25	.45
97	B13	50c Hotel bungalows	.25	.50
98	B13	75c Government House, mystery stone	.40	.70
		Nos. 95-98 (4)	1.15	2.05

Christmas — B14

Paintings: ½c, The Granduca Madonna, by Raphael. 35c, The Ansidei Madonna, by Raphael. 50c, The Virgin and Child, by Botticelli. 75c, The Madonna of the Trees, by Bellini.

1971, Oct. 4

No.	Type	Description	Unused	Used
99	B14	½c multicolored	.25	.25
100	B14	35c multicolored	.25	.25
101	B14	50c multicolored	.25	.25
102	B14	75c multicolored	.25	.30
		Nos. 99-102 (4)	1.00	1.05

A set of four stamps for Durer (20c, 35c, 50c, 75c) was not authorized. Value $12.

All stamps are types of Antigua or overprinted on stamps of Antigua unless otherwise specified. Many of the "BARBUDA" overprints are vertical.

Antigua Nos. 321-322 (Wedding of Princess Anne and Mark Phillips) Ovptd. "BARBUDA"

1973, Nov. 14 *Perf. 13½*

No.	Type	Description	Unused	Used
103	A65	35c multicolored	7.50	5.75
104	A65	$2 multicolored	2.50	3.00

Antigua Nos. 313-315a (Butterfly costumes) Ovptd. in Red "BARBUDA"

1973, Nov. 26 *Perf. 13½x14*

No.	Type	Description	Unused	Used
105	A63	20c multicolored	.25	.25
106	A63	35c multicolored	.50	.60
107	A63	75c multicolored	.85	.85
		Nos. 105-107 (3)	1.60	1.70

Souvenir Sheet

No.	Type	Description	Unused	Used
108		Sheet of 4, #105-107, 108a	1.75	2.50
a.	A63	5c multicolored		

Carnival, 1973.

Antigua Nos. 307, 309, 311, 311a (Uniforms) Ovptd. "BARBUDA"

Perf. 14x13½

1973, Nov. 26 **Wmk. 314**

No.	Type	Description	Unused	Used
109	A53	½c multicolored	.25	.25
110	A53	20c multicolored	.25	.25
111	A53	75c multicolored	.55	.35
		Nos. 109-111 (3)	1.05	.85

Souvenir Sheet

No.	Type	Description	Unused	Used
112		Sheet of 5, #109-111, 112a-112b + label	3.50	3.50
a.	A53	10c multicolored		
b.	A53	35c multicolored		

Antigua Nos. 241a, 242-243, 244a, 245-248, 249a, 250-254, 255a, 256, 256a, 257 Ovptd. "BARBUDA"

Wmk. 314 Sideways, Upright

1973-74 *Perf. 14*

No.	Type	Description	Unused	Used
113	A51	½c multicolored	.35	.50
114	A51	1c multicolored	.35	.50
115	A51	2c multicolored	.55	.60
116	A51	3c multicolored	.55	.50
117	A51	4c multicolored	.75	.65
118	A51	5c multicolored	1.00	1.00
119	A51	6c multicolored	1.00	1.00
120	A51	10c multicolored	1.25	1.25
121	A51	15c multicolored	1.25	1.25
122	A51	20c multicolored	1.25	1.40
123	A51	25c multicolored	1.25	1.40
124	A51	35c multicolored	1.25	1.40
125	A51	50c multicolored	1.25	1.40
126	A51	75c multicolored	1.25	1.40
127	A51	$1 multicolored	1.25	1.40
128	A51	$2.50 multicolored	3.00	5.25
a.		Wmk. upright	10.50	11.50
129	A51	$5 multicolored	3.75	7.00
		Nos. 113-129 (17)	21.30	27.90

Issue dates: ½c, 3c, 15c, $1, $2.50, Feb. 18, 1974. Others, Nov. 26.

Antigua Nos. 316-320a (Christmas) Ovptd. in Silver or Red "BARBUDA"

Perf. 14½

1973, Dec. 11 **Photo.** **Unwmk.**

No.	Type	Description	Unused	Used
130	A64	3c multicolored	.25	.25
131	A64	5c multicolored	.25	.25
132	A64	20c multicolored	.25	.25
133	A64	35c multicolored (R)	.25	.25
134	A64	$1 multicolored (R)	.25	.25
		Nos. 130-134 (5)	1.25	1.25

Souvenir Sheet

No.	Type	Description	Unused	Used
135		Sheet of 5 + label	6.00	9.00
a.	A64	35c multicolored (S)		
b.	A64	$1 multicolored (S)		

No. 135 contains Nos. 130-132, 135a-135b.

Antigua Nos. 323-324a (Visit of Princess Anne and Mark Phillips to Antigua) Ovptd. "BARBUDA"

1973, Dec. 16 **Litho.** *Perf. 13½*

No.	Type	Description	Unused	Used
136	A65	35c multicolored	.25	.25
137	A65	$2 multicolored	1.25	1.25
a.		Souvenir sheet of 2, #136-137	6.00	7.00

Antigua Nos. 325-328 (University of West Indies) Ovptd. "BARBUDA"

1974, Feb. 18 **Wmk. 314**

No.	Type	Description	Unused	Used
138	A66	5c multicolored	.25	.25
139	A66	20c multicolored	.25	.25
140	A66	35c multicolored	.25	.25
141	A66	75c multicolored	.25	.25
		Nos. 138-141 (4)	1.00	1.00

Antigua Nos. 329-333 (Uniforms) Ovptd. "BARBUDA"

1974, May 1 *Perf. 14x13½*

No.	Type	Description	Unused	Used
142	A53	½c multicolored	.25	.25
143	A53	10c multicolored	.25	.25
144	A53	20c multicolored	.25	.25
145	A53	35c multicolored	.35	.25
146	A53	75c multicolored	.50	.40
		Nos. 142-146 (5)	1.60	1.40

No. 333a exists with overprint.

Antigua Nos. 334-340 Ovptd. Type "a" or "b" in Red

a & b

1974, July 15 **Unwmk.** *Perf. 14½*

Se-tenant Pairs Overprinted Type "a" on Left Stamp, Type "b" on Right Stamp

No.	Type	Description	Unused	Used
148	A67	½c multicolored	.25	.25
149	A67	1c multicolored	.25	.25
150	A67	2c multicolored	.40	.25
151	A67	5c multicolored	1.00	.50
152	A67	20c multicolored	.95	1.50
153	A67	35c multicolored	3.00	4.50
154	A67	$1 multicolored	6.50	12.00
		Nos. 148-154 (7)	12.35	19.25

Souvenir Sheet

Perf. 13

No.	Type	Description	Unused	Used
155		Sheet of 7 + label	7.50	11.50
a.	A67	½c multicolored	.25	.35
b.	A67	1c multicolored	.25	.35
c.	A67	2c multicolored	.25	.35
d.	A67	5c multicolored	.25	.35
e.	A67	20c multicolored	1.00	1.60
f.	A67	35c multicolored	1.25	3.25
g.	A67	$1 multicolored	4.00	4.75

UPU, cent.

Antigua Nos. 341-344a (Steel bands - Carnival 1974) Ovptd. "BARBUDA"

1974, Aug. 14 **Wmk. 314** *Perf. 14*

No.	Type	Description	Unused	Used
156	A68	5c multicolored	.25	.25
157	A68	20c multicolored	.25	.25
158	A68	35c multicolored	.25	.25
159	A68	75c multicolored	.25	.25
a.		Souvenir sheet of 4, #156-159	1.00	1.00
		Nos. 156-159 (4)	1.00	1.00

Antigua Nos. 345-348a Overprinted

and

World Cup Soccer Championships — B16

Various soccer plays.

1974, Sept. 2 **Unwmk.** *Perf. 15, 14*

No.	Type	Description	Unused	Used
160	A69	5c multicolored	.25	.25
161	A69	35c multicolored	.25	.25
162	B16	35c multicolored	.25	.25
163	A69	75c multicolored	.25	.25
164	A69	$1 multicolored	.25	.25
a.		Souv. sheet of 4, #160-161, 163-164 + 2 labels, perf. 13½	1.25	1.25
165	B16	$1.20 multicolored	.40	.40
166	B16	$2.50 multicolored	.60	.70
a.		Souv. sheet of 3, #162, 165-166	1.40	1.40
		Nos. 160-166 (7)	2.25	2.35

UPU, Cent. — B17

1974, Sept. 30 *Perf. 14x13½*

No.	Type	Description	Unused	Used
167	B17	35c Ship letter, 1833	.25	.25
168	B17	$1.20 #1, 2 on FDC	.25	.30
169	B17	$2.50 Airplane, map	.40	.50
a.		Souvenir sheet of 3, #167-169	1.90	1.90
		Nos. 167-169 (3)	.90	1.05

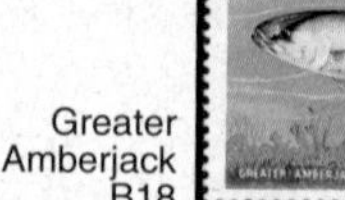

Greater Amberjack B18

1974-75 *Perf. 14x14½, 14½x14*

No.	Type	Description	Unused	Used
170	B18	½c Oleander, rose bay	.25	.65
171	B18	1c Blue petrea	.40	.65
172	B18	2c Poinsettia	.40	.65
173	B18	3c Cassia tree	.40	.65
174	B18	4c shown	3.50	.65
175	B18	5c Holy Trinity School	.45	.25
176	B18	6c Snorkeling	.45	.60
177	B18	10c Pilgrim Holiness Church	.45	.40
178	B18	15c New Cottage Hospital	.45	.40
179	B18	20c Post Office & Treasury	.45	.40
180	B18	25c Island jetty & boats	.90	.70
181	B18	35c Martello Tower	.90	.70

Size: 39x25mm

Perf. 14

No.	Type	Description	Unused	Used
182	B18	50c Warden's House	.90	.70
183	B18	75c Inter-island air service	3.00	2.25
184	B18	$1 Tortoise	2.00	1.75

Size: 45x29mm

Perf. 13½x14

No.	Type	Description	Unused	Used
185	B18	$2.50 Spiny lobster	2.25	4.50
186	B18	$5 Frigate birds	8.00	7.00
a.		Perf. 14x15	17.50	22.50

Size: 34x47mm

No.	Type	Description	Unused	Used
187	B18	$10 Hibiscus	5.00	8.75
		Nos. 170-187 (18)	30.15	31.65

Nos. 170-173, 180, 187 vert.

Issued: 4c, 5c, 6c, 10c, 15c, 20c, 25c, 35c, 75c, 10/15/74; ½c, 1c, 2c, 3c, 50c, $1, $2.50, No. 186, 1/6/75; No. 186a, 7/24/75; $10, 9/19/75.

For overprints see Nos. 213-214.

Antigua Nos. 349-352a Ovptd. in Red

and

Winston Churchill, Birth Cent. — B19

1974 *Perf. 14½, 13½x14*

No.	Type	Description	Unused	Used
188	A70	5c multicolored	.25	.25
189	B19	5c Making broadcast	.25	.25
190	A70	35c multicolored	.30	.25
191	B19	35c Portrait	.25	.25
192	A70	75c multicolored	.50	.50
193	B19	75c Painting	.25	.25
194	A70	$1 multicolored	.85	.80
a.		Souv. sheet of 4, #188, 190, 192, 194	10.50	20.00
195	B19	$1 Victory sign	.35	.30
a.		Souv. sheet of 4, #189, 191, 193, 195	1.50	2.00
		Nos. 188-195 (8)	3.00	2.85

Issue dates: Nos. 188, 190, 192, 194, Oct. 15, others, Nov. 20. For overprints see Nos. 213-214.

Antigua Nos. 353-360a (Christmas paintings) Ovptd. "BARBUDA"

1974, Nov. 25 *Perf. 14½*

No.	Type	Description	Unused	Used
196	A71	½c multicolored	.25	.25
197	A71	1c multicolored	.25	.25
198	A71	2c multicolored	.25	.25
199	A71	3c multicolored	.25	.25
200	A71	5c multicolored	.25	.25
201	A71	20c multicolored	.25	.25
202	A71	35c multicolored	.25	.25
203	A71	75c multicolored	.25	.25
a.		Souv. sheet, #200-203, perf 13½	1.10	1.40
		Nos. 196-203 (8)	2.00	2.00

Antigua Nos. 369-373a (Nelson's Dockyard) Ovptd. "BARBUDA"

1975, Mar. 17

No.	Type	Description	Unused	Used
204	A72	5c multicolored	.25	.25
205	A72	15c multicolored	.45	.35
206	A72	35c multicolored	.55	.45
207	A72	50c multicolored	.65	.65
208	A72	$1 multicolored	.75	.75
a.		Souv. sheet of 5, #204-208 + label, perf. 13½x14	3.00	4.25
		Nos. 204-208 (5)	2.65	2.45

Stamps from No. 208a are 43x28mm.

Battle of the Saints
B20

1975, May 30 *Perf. 13½x14*

209 B20 35c shown .75 .75
210 B20 50c Two ships 1.00 1.00
211 B20 75c Ships firing 1.25 1.25
212 B20 95c Sailors abandoning ship 1.50 1.50
Nos. 209-212 (4) 4.50 4.50

Barbuda No. 186a Ovptd.

a

b

1975, July 2 *Perf. 14x15*

213 B18 (a) $5 multicolored 6.00 *7.50*
214 B18 (b) $5 multicolored 6.00 *7.50*

Overprint "a" is in 1st and 3rd vertical rows, "b" 2nd and 4th. The 5th row has no overprint. This can be collected se-tenant either as Nos. 213, 214 or 213, 214 and 186a. Value, strip of three, $22.50.

Military Uniforms — B21

Designs: 35c, Officer of 65th Foot, 1763. 50c, Grenadier, 27th Foot, 1701-1710. 75c, Officer of 21st Foot, 1793-1796. 95c, Officer, Royal Regiment of Artillery, 1800.

1975, Sept. 17 *Perf. 14*

215 B21 35c multicolored .50 .50
216 B21 50c multicolored .75 .75
217 B21 75c multicolored 1.25 1.25
218 B21 95c multicolored 1.50 1.50
Nos. 215-218 (4) 4.00 4.00

Barbuda Nos. 189, 191, 193, 195 Ovptd.

1975, Oct. 24 *Perf. 13½x14*

219 B19 5c multicolored .25 .25
220 B19 35c multicolored .25 .25
221 B19 75c multicolored .25 .25
222 B19 $1 multicolored .30 .25
Nos. 219-222 (4) 1.05 1.00

Antigua Nos. 394-401a (Christmas) Ovptd. "BARBUDA"

1975, Nov. 17 *Perf. 14*

223 A77 ½c multicolored .25 .25
224 A77 1c multicolored .25 .25
225 A77 2c multicolored .25 .25
226 A77 3c multicolored .25 .25
227 A77 5c multicolored .25 .25
228 A77 10c multicolored .25 .25
229 A77 35c multicolored .25 .25
230 A77 $2 multicolored .25 .25
a. Souvenir sheet of 4, #227-230 2.00 2.25
Nos. 223-230 (8) 2.00 2.00

Antigua Nos. 402-404 (World Cup Cricket) Ovptd. "BARBUDA"

1975, Dec. 15 *Perf. 14*

231 A78 5c multicolored 1.40 1.40
232 A78 35c multicolored 2.75 2.75
233 A78 $2 multicolored 5.00 5.00
Nos. 231-233 (3) 9.15 9.15

American Revolution, Bicent.
B22

Details from Surrender of Cornwallis at Yorktown, by Trumbull: No. 234a, British officers. b, Gen. Benjamin Lincoln. c, Washington, Allied officers.

The Battle of Princeton: No. 235a, Infantry. b, Battle. c, Cannon fire.

Surrender of Burgoyne at Saratoga by Trumbull: No. 236a, Mounted officer. b, Washington, Burgoyne. c, American officers.

Signing the Declaration of Independence, by Trumbull: No. 237a, Delegates to Continental Congress. b, Adams, Sherman, Livingston, Jefferson and Franklin. c, Hancock, Thomson, Read, Dickinson, and Rutledge. Strips of 3 have continuous designs.

1976, Mar. 8 *Perf. 13½x13*

234 B22 15c Strip of 3, #a.-c. .30 .30
235 B22 35c Strip of 3, #a.-c. 1.00 1.00
d. Souvenir sheet, #234-235 1.50 1.50
236 B22 $1 Strip of 3, #a.-c. 1.25 1.25
237 B22 $2 Strip of 3, #a.-c. 2.25 2.25
d. Souvenir sheet, #236-237 3.75 3.75

See Nos. 244-247.

Birds
B23

1976, June 30 *Perf. 13½x14*

238 B23 35c Bananaquits 1.25 .65
239 B23 50c Blue-hooded euphonia 1.25 .75
240 B23 75c Royal tern 1.60 1.00
241 B23 95c Killdeer 1.90 1.10
242 B23 $1.25 Glossy cowbird 1.90 1.10
243 B23 $2 Purple gallinule 1.90 1.40
Nos. 238-243 (6) 9.80 6.00

Barbuda #234-237 With Inscription Added at Top Across the Three Stamps in Blue

1976, Aug. 12 *Perf. 13½x14*

Size: 38x31mm

244 B22 15c Strip of 3, #a.-c. .30 .30
245 B22 35c Strip of 3, #a.-c. .50 .50
d. Souvenir sheet of 2, #244-245 1.25 1.25
246 B22 $1 Strip of 3, #a.-c. .75 .75
247 B22 $2 Strip of 3, #a.-c. 1.25 1.25
d. Souvenir sheet, #246-247 3.00 3.00

Nos. 244-247 are perforated on outside edges; imperf. vertically within.

Antigua Nos. 448-452 (Christmas) Ovptd. "BARBUDA"

1976, Dec. 2 *Perf. 14*

248 A85 8c multicolored .25 .25
249 A85 10c multicolored .25 .25
250 A85 15c multicolored .25 .25
251 A85 50c multicolored .25 .25
252 A85 $1 multicolored .25 .25
Nos. 248-252 (5) 1.25 1.25

Antigua Nos. 431-437 (Olympic Games) Ovptd. "BARBUDA"

1976, Dec. 28 *Perf. 15*

253 A82 ½c yellow & multi .25 .25
254 A82 1c purple & multi .25 .25
255 A82 2c emerald & multi .25 .25
256 A82 15c brt blue & multi .25 .25
257 A82 30c olive & multi .25 .25
258 A82 $1 orange & multi .25 .25
259 A82 $2 red & multi .25 .25
a. Souv. sheet, #256-259, perf 13½ 3.00 3.00
Nos. 253-259 (7) 1.75 1.75

Telephone, Cent. — B24

1977, Jan. 31 *Perf. 14*

260 B24 75c shown .25 *.25*
261 B24 $1.25 Satellite dish, television .25 *.35*
262 B24 $2 Satellites in earth orbit .50 *.60*
a. Souv. sheet, #260-262, perf 15 2.00 *2.25*
Nos. 260-262 (3) 1.00 *1.20*

Coronation of Queen Elizabeth II, 25th Anniv. — B25

Designs: Nos. 263a, St. Margaret's Church, Westminster. b, Westminster Abbey entrance. c, Westminster Abbey.

Nos. 264a, Riders on horseback. b, Coronation coach. c, Team of horses. Strips of 3 have continuous designs.

1977, Feb. 7 *Perf. 13½x13*

263 B25 75c Strip of 3, #a.-c. .45 .45
264 B25 $1.25 Strip of 3, #a.-c. .60 .60

Souvenir Sheet

265 B25 Sheet of 6 1.25 1.25

Nos. 263a-264c se-tenant with labels. No. 265 contains Nos. 263a-264c with silver borders.

Antigua Nos. 405-422 (1976 Definitives) Ovptd. "BARBUDA"

1977, Apr. 4 *Perf. 15*

266 A79 ½c multicolored .25 .25
267 A79 1c multicolored .30 .25
268 A79 2c multicolored .30 .25
269 A79 3c multicolored .30 .25
270 A79 4c multicolored .30 .25
271 A79 5c multicolored .30 .25
272 A79 6c multicolored .30 .25
273 A79 10c multicolored .30 .25
274 A79 15c multicolored .30 .25
275 A79 20c multicolored .30 .25
276 A79 25c multicolored .30 .25
277 A79 35c multicolored .35 .30
278 A79 50c multicolored .40 .40
279 A79 75c multicolored .40 .40
280 A79 $1 multicolored .75 .75

Perf. 13½x14

281 A80 $2.50 multicolored 2.10 2.40
282 A80 $5 multicolored 4.00 4.50
283 A80 $10 multicolored 8.00 9.00
Nos. 266-283 (18) 19.25 20.50

For overprints see Nos. 506-516.

Antigua Nos. 459-464 (Royal Family) Ovptd. "BARBUDA"

1977, Apr. 4 *Perf. 13½x14, 12*

284 A87 10c multicolored .25 .25
285 A87 30c multicolored .25 .25
286 A87 50c multicolored .25 .25
287 A87 90c multicolored .25 .35
288 A87 $2.50 multicolored .50 1.00
Nos. 284-288 (5) 1.50 2.10

Souvenir Sheet

289 A87 $5 multicolored 1.50 1.50

A booklet of self-adhesive stamps contains one pane of six rouletted and die cut 50c stamps in design of 90c (silver overprint), and one pane of one die cut $5 (gold overprint) in changed colors. Panes have marginal inscriptions.

For overprints see Nos. 312-317.

Antigua Nos. 465-471a (Boy Scouts) Ovptd. "BARBUDA"

1977, June 13 *Perf. 14*

290 A88 ½c multicolored .25 .25
291 A88 1c multicolored .25 .25
292 A88 2c multicolored .25 .25
293 A88 10c multicolored .25 .25
294 A88 30c multicolroed .55 .55
295 A88 50c multicolored .75 .75
296 A88 $2 multicolored 1.50 1.50
a. Souvenir sheet of 3, #294-296 4.00 4.00
Nos. 290-296 (7) 3.80 3.80

Overprint is slightly smaller on No. 296a.

Antigua Nos. 472-476a (Carnival) Ovptd. "BARBUDA"

1977, Aug. 12

297 A89 10c multicolored .25 .25
298 A89 30c multicolored .25 .25
299 A89 50c multicolored .25 .25
300 A89 90c multicolored .25 .25
301 A89 $1 multicolored .25 .30
a. Souvenir sheet of 4, #298-301 1.90 1.90
Nos. 297-301 (5) 1.25 1.30

Royal Visit
B26

1977, Oct. 27 *Perf. 14½*

302 B26 50c Royal yacht Britannia .25 .25
303 B26 $1.50 Jubliee emblem .25 .25
304 B26 $2.50 Flags .40 .50
a. Souvenir sheet of 3, #302-304 1.50 1.50
Nos. 302-304 (3) .90 1.00

Antigua Nos. 483-489 (Christmas) Ovptd. "BARBUDA"

1977, Nov. 15 *Perf. 14*

305 A90 ½c multicolored .25 .25
306 A90 1c multicolored .25 .25
307 A90 2c multicolored .25 .25
308 A90 8c multicolored .25 .25
309 A90 10c multicolored .25 .25
310 A90 25c multicolored .25 .25
311 A90 $2 multicolored .25 .25
a. Souvenir sheet of 4, #308-311 1.60 1.60
Nos. 305-311 (7) 1.75 1.75

Antigua Nos. 477-482 (Royal Visit overprints) Ovptd. "BARBUDA" in Black

1977, Dec. 20 *Perf. 12*

312 A87 10c multicolored .25 .25
313 A87 30c multicolored .25 .25
314 A87 50c multicolored .25 .25
315 A87 90c multicolored .25 .25
316 A87 $2.50 multicolored .40 .40
Nos. 312-316 (5) 1.40 1.40

Nos. 312-316 exist with blue overprint.

1977, Nov. 28 *Perf. 13½x14*

312a A87 10c multicolored .25 .25
313a A87 30c multicolored .25 .25
314a A87 50c multicolored .25 .25
315a A87 90c multicolored .25 .25
316a A87 $2.50 multicolored .40 .40
Nos. 312a-316a (5) 1.40 1.40

Souvenir Sheet

317 A87 $5 multicolored 1.75 1.75

Overprint of Nos. 312a-316a differs from that on Nos. 312-316.

Anniversaries — B27

First navigable airships, 75th anniv: No. 318a, Zeppelin LZ1. b, German Naval airship L31. c, Graf Zeppelin. d, Gondola on military airship.

Soviet space program, 20th anniv: No. 319a, Sputnik, 1957. b, Vostok rocket, 1961. c, Voskhod rocket, 1964. d, Space walk, 1965.

Lindbergh's Atlantic crossing, 50th anniv: No. 320a, Fueling for flight. b, New York take-off. c, Spirit of St. Louis. d, Welcome in England.

Coronation of Queen Elizabeth II, 25th anniv: No. 321a, Lion of England. b, Unicorn of Scotland. c, Yale of Beaufort. d, Falcon of Plantagenets.

Rubens, 400th birth anniv: No. 322a, Two lions. b, Daniel in the Lion's Den. c, Two lions lying down. d, Lion at Daniel's feet. Block of 4 has continuous design.

1977, Dec. 29 *Perf. 14½x14*

Blocks of 4

318 B27 75c #a.-d. 1.75 1.75
319 B27 95c #a.-d. 2.10 2.10
320 B27 $1.25 #a.-d. 2.40 2.40
321 B27 $2 #a.-d. 3.00 3.00
322 B27 $5 #a.-d. 3.00 *4.00*
e. Min. sheet, #318-322 + 4 labels 11.00 *18.00*
Nos. 318-322 (5) 12.25 *13.25*

Antigua Nos. 490-494a (10th Anniversary of Statehood) Ovptd. "BARBUDA"

1978, Feb. 15 *Perf. 13x13½*

323 A91 10c multicolored .25 .25
324 A91 15c multicolored .25 .25
325 A91 50c multicolored 1.25 .80
326 A91 90c multicolored .40 .40
327 A91 $2 multicolored .55 *.90*
a. Souv. sheet, #324-327, perf 14 6.25 5.00
Nos. 323-327 (5) 2.70 2.60

Pieta, by Michelangelo — B28

Works by Michelangelo: 95c, Holy Family. $1.25, Libyan Sibyl. $2, The Flood.

1978, Mar. 23 *Perf. 13½x14*

328 B28 75c multicolored .25 .25
329 B28 95c multicolored .25 .25
330 B28 $1.25 multicolored .25 .25
331 B28 $2 multicolored .25 .25
a. Souvenir sheet of 4, #328-331 2.50 2.50
Nos. 328-331 (4) 1.00 1.00

Antigua Nos. 495-502 (Wright Brothers) Ovptd. "BARBUDA"

1978, Mar. 23 *Perf. 14*

332 A92 ½c multicolored .25 .25
333 A92 1c multicolored .25 .25
334 A92 2c multicolored .25 .25
335 A92 10c multicolored .25 .25
336 A92 50c multicolored .40 .40
337 A92 90c multicolored .55 .45
338 A92 $2 multicolored 1.25 1.10
Nos. 332-338 (7) 3.20 2.95

Souvenir Sheet

339 A92 $2.50 multicolored 2.25 *3.25*

Antigua Nos. 503-507 (Sailing Week) Ovptd. "BARBUDA"

1978, May 22 *Perf. 14½*

340 A93 10c multicolored .25 .25
341 A93 50c multicolored .45 .45
342 A93 90c multicolored .75 .75
343 A93 $2 multicolored 1.40 1.40
Nos. 340-343 (4) 2.85 2.85

Souvenir Sheet

344 A93 $2.50 multicolored 2.25 *3.00*

Coronation of Queen Elizabeth II, 25th Anniv. — B29

Crowns: No. 345a, St. Edward's. b, Imperial State. No. 346a, Queen Mary's. b, Queen Mother's. No. 347a, Queen Consort's. b, Queen Victoria's.

1978, June 2 *Perf. 15*

Miniature Sheets of Two Each Plus Two Labels

345 B29 75c Sheet of 4 .75 .75
346 B29 $1.50 Sheet of 4 1.25 1.25
347 B29 $2.50 Sheet of 4 2.00 2.00

Souvenir Sheet

Perf. 14½

348 B29 Sheet of 6, #345a-347b 1.50 *2.50*

Antigua Nos. 508-514 (QEII Coronation Anniversary) Ovptd. in Black or Deep Rose Lilac "BARBUDA"

1978 *Perf. 14*

349 A94 10c multicolored .25 .25
350 A94 30c multicolored .25 .25
351 A94 50c multicolored .25 .25
352 A94 90c multicolored .40 .40
353 A94 $2.50 multicolored .75 .75
Nos. 349-353 (5) 1.90 1.90

Souvenir Sheet

354 A94 $5 multicolored 1.60 1.60

Self-adhesive

355 Souvenir booklet 6.50 6.50
a. A95 Bklt. pane, 3 each 25c and 50c, die cut, rouletted (DRL) 1.50 1.50
b. A95 $5 Bklt. pane of 1, die cut 5.00 5.00

Issued: Nos. 349-354, June 2; #355, Oct. 12.

Antigua Nos. 515-518 (World Cup Soccer) Ovptd. "BARBUDA"

1978, Sept. 12 *Perf. 15*

356 A96 10c multicolored .25 .25
357 A96 15c multicolored .25 .25
358 A96 $3 multicolored 1.00 1.00
Nos. 356-358 (3) 1.50 1.50

Souvenir Sheet

359 Sheet of 4 1.50 1.50
a. A96 25c multicolored .25 .25
b. A96 30c multicolored .25 .25
c. A96 50c multicolored .25 .25
d. A96 $2 multicolored .75 .75

Antigua Nos. 519-523 (Flowers) Ovptd. "BARBUDA"

1978, Nov. 20 *Perf. 14*

360 A97 25c multicolored .45 .45
361 A97 50c multicolored .65 .65
362 A97 90c multicolored .90 *1.00*
363 A97 $2 multicolored 2.00 *2.50*
Nos. 360-363 (4) 4.00 *4.60*

Souvenir Sheet

364 A97 $2.50 multicolored 4.00 4.00

Flora and Fauna B30

1978, Nov. 20 *Perf. 15*

365 B30 25c Blackbar soldierfish 3.00 3.00
366 B30 50c Painted lady 4.75 4.75
367 B30 75c Dwarf poinciana 3.50 *4.75*
368 B30 95c Zebra butterfly 4.75 *5.00*
369 B30 $1.25 Bougainvillea 3.25 *5.00*
Nos. 365-369 (5) 19.25 *22.50*

Antigua Nos. 524-527 (Christmas) Ovptd. in Silver "BARBUDA"

1978, Nov. 20 *Perf. 14*

370 A98 8c multicolored .25 .25
371 A98 25c multicolored .25 .25
372 A98 $2 multicolored .85 .85
Nos. 370-372 (3) 1.35 1.35

Souvenir Sheet

373 A98 $4 multicolored 2.25 2.25

Events and Annivs. B31

Designs: 75c, 1978 World Cup Soccer Championships, vert. 95c, Wright Brothers 1st powered flight, 75th anniv. $1.25, First Trans-Atlantic balloon flight, Aug. 1978. $2, Coronation of Elizabeth II, 25th anniv., vert.

1978, Dec. 20 *Perf. 14*

374 B31 75c multicolored .55 .55
375 B31 95c multicolored .65 .65
376 B31 $1.25 multicolored .95 .95
377 B31 $2 multicolored 1.10 1.10
a. Souv. sheet, #374-377, imperf 7.50 *8.00*
Nos. 374-377 (4) 3.25 3.25

No. 377a has simulated perfs.

Nos. 528-532 Overprinted in Bright Blue

and

Sir Rowland Hill, Death Cent. — B32

1979, Apr. 4

378 A99 25c multicolored .25 .25
379 A99 50c multicolored .35 .35
380 B32 75c Sir Rowland Hill, vert. .40 .40
381 B32 95c Mail coach, 1840 .50 .50
382 A99 $1 multicolored .65 .65
383 B32 $1.25 London's first pillar box, 1855 .70 .70
384 B32 $2 St. Martin's Post Office, London, vert. 1.10 1.10
a. Souvenir sheet of 4, #380-381, 383-384, imperf. 2.75 2.75
385 A99 $2 multicolored 1.40 1.40
Nos. 378-385 (8) 5.35 5.35

Souvenir Sheet

386 A99 $2.50 multicolored 2.00 2.00

No. 384a has simulated perfs.
For overprints see Nos. 423-426.

Antigua Nos. 533-536 (Easter) Ovptd. "BARBUDA"

1979, Apr. 16

387 A100 10c multicolored .40 .40
388 A100 50c multicolored .60 .60
389 A100 $4 multicolored 1.50 1.50
Nos. 387-389 (3) 2.50 2.50

Souvenir Sheet

390 A100 $2.50 multicolored 1.25 *1.50*

Intl. Civil Aviation Organization, 30th Anniv. — B33

1979, May 24 *Perf. 13½x14*

391 B33 75c Passengers leaving 747 .30 .40
392 B33 95c Air traffic controllers .40 .50
393 B33 $1.25 Plane on runway .50 .60
a. Block of 3, #391-393 + label 1.50 1.50

Antigua Nos. 537-541 (Int'l Year of the Child) Ovptd. "BARBUDA"

1979, May 24 *Perf. 14*

394 A101 25c multicolored .30 .30
395 A101 50c multicolored .45 .45
396 A101 90c multicolored 1.00 1.00
397 A101 $2 multicolored 1.25 1.25
Nos. 394-397 (4) 3.00 3.00

Souvenir Sheet

398 A101 $5 multicolored 2.25 2.25

Antigua Nos. 542-546 (Sport Fish) Ovptd. "BARBUDA"

1979, Aug. 1 *Perf. 14½*

399 A102 30c multicolored .40 .30
400 A102 50c multicolored .55 .50
401 A102 90c multicolored .70 .70
402 A102 $3 multicolored 1.50 *2.00*
Nos. 399-402 (4) 3.15 *3.50*

Souvenir Sheet

403 A102 $2.50 multicolored 1.90 *2.25*

Antigua Nos. 547-551 (Capt. Cook) Ovptd. "BARBUDA"

1979, Aug. 1 *Perf. 14*

404 A103 25c multicolored .55 .45
405 A103 50c multicolored 1.40 .60
406 A103 90c multicolored 1.40 .75
407 A103 $3 multicolored 2.75 2.10
Nos. 404-407 (4) 6.10 3.90

Souvenir Sheet

408 A103 $2.50 multicolored 2.75 2.75

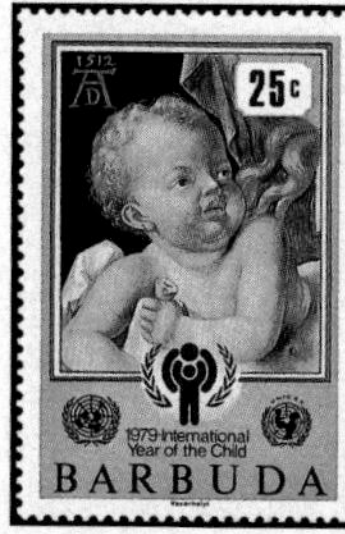

Intl. Year of the Child — B34

Details of the Christ Child from various paintings by Durer: 25c, 1512. 50c, 1516. 75c, 1526. $1.25, 1502.

1979, Sept. 24 *Perf. 14x13½*

409 B34 25c multicolored .25 .25
410 B34 50c multicolored .25 .25
411 B34 75c multicolored .25 .25
412 B34 $1.25 multicolored .35 .35
a. Souvenir sheet of 4, #409-412 1.25 1.25
Nos. 409-412 (4) 1.10 1.10

Antigua Nos. 552-556 (Christmas) Ovptd. "BARBUDA"

1979, Nov. 21 *Perf. 14*

413 A104 8c multicolored .25 .25
414 A104 25c multicolored .25 .25
415 A104 50c multicolored .40 .25
416 A104 $4 multicolored 1.25 1.25
Nos. 413-416 (4) 2.15 2.00

Souvenir Sheet

Perf. 12x12½

417 A104 $3 multicolored 1.50 1.50

Antigua Nos. 557-561 (Moscow Olympics) Ovptd. "BARBUDA"

1980, Mar. 18

418 A105 10c multicolored .25 .25
419 A105 25c multicolroed .25 .25
420 A105 $1 multicolored .35 .35
421 A105 $2 multicolored .50 .50
Nos. 418-421 (4) 1.35 1.35

Souvenir Sheet

422 A105 $3 multicolored 1.75 2.25

Antigua Nos. 571A-571D (London '80 Ovpts.) Overprinted "BARBUDA" in Dark Blue

1980, May 6 *Perf. 12*

423 A99 25c multicolored .35 .25
424 A99 50c multicolored .45 .50
425 A99 $1 multicolored .75 .85
426 A99 $2 multicolored 2.50 1.90
Nos. 423-426 (4) 4.05 3.50

Nos. 423-426 exist without the "London 1980" overprint.

First Moon Landing, 10th Anniv. — B35

1980, May 21 *Perf. 13½x14*

427 B35 75c Crew badge .45 .45
428 B35 95c Plaque left on moon .50 .50
429 B35 $1.25 Lunar, command modules .60 .60
430 B35 $2 Lunar module .95 .95
a. Souvenir sheet of 4, #427-430 2.50 2.50
Nos. 427-430 (4) 2.50 2.50

American Widgeon B36

1980, June 16 *Perf. 14½x14*

431 B36 1c shown .70 .45
432 B36 2c Snowy plover .70 .45
433 B36 4c Rose-breasted grosbeak .80 .45
434 B36 6c Mangrove cuckoo .80 .45
435 B36 10c Adelaide's warbler .80 .45
436 B36 15c Scaly-breasted thrasher .80 .45
437 B36 20c Yellow-crowned night heron 1.00 .45
438 B36 25c Bridled quail dove 1.00 .45
439 B36 35c Carib grackle 1.00 *1.60*
440 B36 50c Northern pintail 1.10 .45
441 B36 75c Black-whiskered vireo 1.25 .50
442 B36 $1 Blue-winged teal 1.40 .85

Perf. 14x14½

443 B36 $1.50 Green-throated carib 2.00 1.10
444 B36 $2 Red-necked pigeon 3.25 1.60
445 B36 $2.50 Stolid flycatcher 4.00 1.90
446 B36 $5 Yellow-bellied sapsucker 4.50 3.75
447 B36 $7.50 Caribbean elaenia 6.25 *6.50*
448 B36 $10 Great egret 8.50 7.75
Nos. 431-448 (18) 39.85 29.60

Nos. 443-448 vert.

Antigua Nos. 572-578 (Paintings) Ovptd. "BARBUDA"

1980, July 29 *Perf. 13½x14, 14x13½*

449 A106a 10c multicolored .25 .25
450 A106a 30c multicolored .25 .25
451 A106a 50c multicolored .40 .40
452 A106a 90c multicolored .50 .50
453 A106a $1 multicolored .50 .50
454 A106a $4 multicolored 2.25 2.25
Nos. 449-454 (6) 4.15 4.15

Souvenir Sheet

Perf. 14

455 A106a $5 multicolored 3.50 3.50

Antigua Nos. 579-583 (Rotary Int'l) Ovptd. "BARBUDA"

1980, Sept. 8 *Perf. 14*

456 A107 30c multicolored .25 .25
457 A107 50c multicolored .25 .25
458 A107 90c multicolored .35 .35
459 A107 $3 multicolored 1.10 1.10
Nos. 456-459 (4) 1.95 1.95

Souvenir Sheet

460 A107 $5 multicolored 3.00 *3.50*

Antigua Nos. 584-586 (Queen Mother) Optd. "BARBUDA"

1980, Oct. 6

461 A108 10c multicolored .50 .30
462 A108 $2.50 multicolored 2.50 2.50

Souvenir Sheet

Perf. 12

463 A108 $3 multicolored 3.00 3.00

Antigua Nos. 587-591 (Birds) Ovptd. "BARBUDA"

1980, Dec. 8 *Perf. 14*

464 A109 10c multicolored 3.50 1.25
465 A109 30c multicolored 4.50 1.60
466 A109 $1 multicolored 5.50 3.50
467 A109 $2 multicolored 6.50 6.25
Nos. 464-467 (4) 20.00 12.60

Souvenir Sheet

468 A109 $2.50 multicolored 10.00 7.75

Antigua Nos. 602-606 (Locomotives) Ovptd. "BARBUDA"

1981, Jan. 26

469 A111 25c multicolored 1.75 .45
470 A111 50c multicolored 2.00 .55
471 A111 90c multicolored 2.75 .80
472 A111 $3 multicolored 4.00 1.90
Nos. 469-472 (4) 10.50 3.70

Souvenir Sheet

473 A111 $2.50 multicolored 3.00 3.00

Famous Women — B37

1981, Mar. 9 *Perf. 14x13½*

474 B37 50c Florence Nightingale .25 .25
475 B37 90c Marie Curie .55 .55
476 B37 $1 Amy Johnson .50 .50
477 B37 $4 Eleanor Roosevelt .70 .70
Nos. 474-477 (4) 2.00 2.00

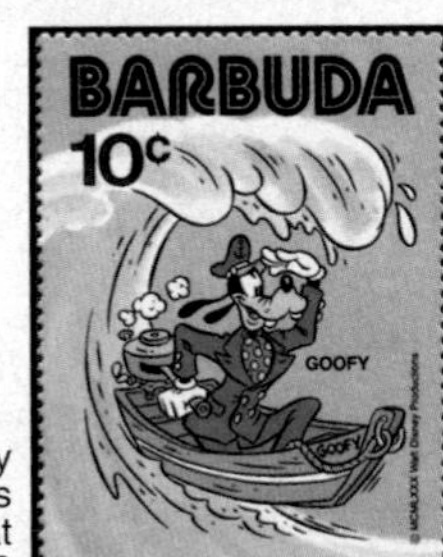

Walt Disney Characters at Sea — B38

1981, May 15 *Perf. 13½x14*

478 B38 10c Goofy 1.60 .40
479 B38 20c Donald Duck 1.75 .50
480 B38 25c Mickey Mouse 2.40 .75
481 B38 30c Goofy fishing 2.40 1.00
482 B38 35c Goofy sailing 2.40 1.00
483 B38 40c Mickey fishing 2.75 1.40
484 B38 75c Donald Duck boating 3.00 1.75
485 B38 $1 Minnie Mouse 3.75 2.25
486 B38 $2 Chip 'n Dale 4.75 3.50
Nos. 478-486 (9) 24.80 12.55

Souvenir Sheet

487 B38 $2.50 Donald Duck, diff. 14.00 14.00

Antigua Nos. 618-622 (Picasso) Ovptd. "BARBUDA"

1981, June 9 *Perf. 14*

488 A112 10c multicolored .25 .25
489 A112 50c multicolored .50 .50
490 A112 90c multicolored 1.00 1.00
491 A112 $4 multicolored 2.50 2.50
Nos. 488-491 (4) 4.25 4.25

Souvenir Sheet

Perf. 14x14½

492 A112 $5 multicolored 4.50 4.50

Miniature Sheets

Royal Wedding — B39

a-b, $1, L & R sides of Buckingham Palace. c-d, $1.50, L & R sides of Caernarvon Castle. e-f, $4, L & R sides of Highgrove House.

1981, July 27 *Perf. 11x11½*

Sheets of 6, #a-f

493 B39 blk & salmon 3.00 3.00
494 B39 blk & purple 3.00 3.00
495 B39 blk & gray grn 3.00 3.00

Souvenir Sheet

Perf. 11½x11

496 B39 $5 St. Paul's Cathedral, vert. 1.25 1.25

Stamps of same denomination have continuous design. For surcharges see Nos. 592-594.

Common Design Types pictured following the introduction.

Antigua Nos. 623-627 (Royal Wedding) Ovptd. in Black or Silver "BARBUDA"

1981, Aug. 14 *Perf. 14*

497 CD331a 25c multicolored .25 .25
498 CD331a 50c multicolored .25 .25
499 CD331a $4 multicolored .70 .70
Nos. 497-499 (3) 1.20 1.20

Souvenir Sheet

500 CD331 $5 multicolored 1.25 1.25

Self-adhesive

501 CD331 Booklet 8.50 8.50
a. Pane of 6 (2x25c, 2x$1, 2x$2), Charles, die cut, rouletted (S) 4.00 4.00
b. Pane of 1, $5 Couple, die cut (S) 4.00 4.00

Issued: Nos. 497-500, Aug. 24; No. 501, Oct. 12.

For surcharge see No. B1.

Intl. Year of the Disabled B40

1981, Sept. 14 *Perf. 14*

502 B40 50c Travel .50 .50
503 B40 90c Braille, sign language .50 .50
504 B40 $1 Helping hands .50 .50
505 B40 $4 Mobility aids .75 .75
Nos. 502-505 (4) 2.25 2.25

Antigua Nos. 607-617 (Independence Ovpts.) Ovptd. "BARBUDA"

1981, Nov. 1 *Perf. 15*

506 A79 6c multicolored .25 .25
507 A79 10c multicolored .25 .25
508 A79 20c multicolored .25 .25
509 A79 25c multicolored .30 .25
510 A79 35c multicolored .45 .30
511 A79 50c multicolored .60 .40
512 A79 75c multicolored .85 .60
513 A79 $1 multicolored 1.25 .75

Perf. 13½x14

514 A80 $2.50 multicolored 3.00 1.90
515 A80 $5 multicolored 5.75 3.75
516 A80 $10 multicolored 11.50 7.50
Nos. 506-516 (11) 24.45 16.20

Antigua Nos. 628-632 (Girl Guides) Ovptd. "BARBUDA"

1981, Dec. 14 *Perf. 15*

517 A113 10c multicolored 1.10 .25
518 A113 50c multicolored 1.90 .55
519 A113 90c multicolored 2.75 1.00
520 A113 $2.50 multicolored 4.25 2.75
Nos. 517-520 (4) 10.00 4.55

Souvenir Sheet

521 A113 $5 multicolored 6.50 6.50

Antigua Nos. 643-647 (Int'l Year of the Diabled) Ovptd. "BARBUDA"

1981, Dec. 14

522 A116 10c multicolored .25 .25
523 A116 50c multicolored .50 .50
524 A116 90c multicolored 1.00 1.00
525 A116 $2 multicolored 2.00 2.00
Nos. 522-525 (4) 3.75 3.75

Souvenir Sheet

526 A116 $4 multicolored 3.00 3.00

Antigua Nos. 638-642 (Christmas) Ovptd. in Black or Silver "BARBUDA"

1981, Dec. 22

527 A115 8c multi .25 .25
528 A115 30c multi .40 .40
529 A115 $1 multi (S) .50 .50
530 A115 $3 multi 1.75 1.75
Nos. 527-530 (4) 2.90 2.90

Souvenir Sheet

531 A115 $5 multi 2.25 *2.50*

Birth of Prince William — B41

Various portraits.

1982, June 21 **Wmk. 380** *Perf. 14*

532 B41 $1 buff & multi .65 .65
533 B41 $2.50 lt pink & multi 1.25 1.25
534 B41 $5 lt lilac & multi 2.75 2.75
Nos. 532-534 (3) 4.65 4.65

Souvenir Sheet

535 B41 $4 Couple 4.75 4.75

See Nos. 540-543.

The overprint on stamps of Antigua, from here on, read "BARBUDA MAIL" in one or two lines.

Antigua Nos. 672-675 (Royal Baby) Ovptd. in Black or Silver

Perf. 14½x14

1982, Oct. 12 **Unwmk.**

536 CD332 90c multi .60 .60
537 CD332 $1 multi (S) .65 .65
538 CD332 $4 multi (S) 2.75 2.75
Nos. 536-538 (3) 4.00 4.00

Souvenir Sheet

539 CD332 $5 multi 4.00 4.00

Barbuda Nos. 532-535 Inscribed at Top

Various portraits.

Perf. 14x14½

1982, July 1 **Wmk. 380**

540 B41 $1 lt grn & multi 1.40 .60
541 B41 $2.50 pale sal & multi 2.25 1.50
542 B41 $5 lt bl & multi 3.25 3.00
Nos. 540-542 (3) 6.90 5.10

Souvenir Sheet

543 B41 $4 Couple 5.00 5.00

Antigua Nos. 663-666 (Diana) Ovptd. in Black or Silver

Perf. 14½x14

1982, Aug. 30 **Unwmk.**

544 CD332 90c multi .70 .50
545 CD332 $1 multi (S) .80 .60
546 CD332 $4 multi 3.25 1.60
Nos. 544-546 (3) 4.75 2.70

Souvenir Sheet

547 CD332 $5 multi 5.00 5.00

Antigua Nos. 676-683 (Washington/FDR) Overprinted

1982, Dec. 6 *Perf. 15*

551 A121 10c multicolored .25 .25
552 A121 25c multicolored .40 .25
553 A121 45c multicolored 1.75 .50
554 A121 60c multicolored .50 .50
555 A121 $1 multicolored 2.25 .75
556 A121 $3 multicolored 1.75 1.25
Nos. 551-556 (6) 6.90 3.50

Souvenir Sheets

557 A121 $4 on #682 3.50 *5.00*
558 A121 $4 on #683 3.50 *5.00*

Antigua Nos. 684-688 (Christmas) Overprinted

1982, Dec. 6 *Perf. 14*

559 A122 10c multicolored .25 .25
560 A122 30c multicolored .35 .35
561 A122 $1 multicolored .75 .75
562 A122 $4 multicolored 2.00 2.00
Nos. 559-562 (4) 3.35 3.35

Souvenir Sheet

563 A122 $5 multicolored 3.00 *4.00*

Antigua Nos. 689-693 (Raphael) Overprinted

1983, Mar. 14 *Perf. 14½*
564 A123 45c multicolored .25 .25
565 A123 50c multicolored .35 .35
566 A123 60c multicolored .35 .35
567 A123 $4 multicolored 2.25 2.25
Nos. 564-567 (4) 3.20 3.20

Souvenir Sheet

568 A123 $5 multicolored 2.50 2.50

Antigua Nos. 694-697 (Commonwealth Day) Overprinted

1983, Mar. 14 *Perf. 14*
569 A124 25c multicolored .60 .60
570 A124 45c multicolored .85 .85
571 A124 60c multicolored 1.40 *1.50*
572 A124 $3 multicolored 3.50 *4.00*
Nos. 569-572 (4) 6.35 *6.95*

Antigua Nos. 698-702 (WCY) Overprinted

1983, Apr. 12
573 A125 15c multicolored 2.50 .30
574 A125 50c multicolored 4.50 1.40
575 A125 60c multicolored 4.00 1.40
576 A125 $3 multicolored 6.25 4.00
Nos. 573-576 (4) 17.25 7.10

Souvenir Sheet

577 A125 $5 multicolored 5.00 *5.75*

First Manned Balloon Flight, Bicent. — B43

1983, June 13
578 B43 $1 Vincenzo Lunardi, 1785 .50 .50
579 B43 $1.50 Montgolfier brothers, 1783 .75 .75
580 B43 $2.50 Blanchard & Jeffries, 1785 1.25 1.25
Nos. 578-580 (3) 2.50 2.50

Souvenir Sheet

581 B43 $5 Graf Zeppelin, 1928 4.50 4.75

Antigua Nos. 703-707 (Marine Mammals) Overprinted

1983, July 4 *Perf. 15*
582 A126 15c multicolored 2.75 .75
583 A126 50c multicolored 10.00 3.75
584 A126 60c multicolored 11.50 4.00
585 A126 $3 multicolored 16.00 7.00
Nos. 582-585 (4) 40.25 15.50

Souvenir Sheet

586 A126 $5 multicolored 15.00 12.50

Antigua Nos. 726-730 (Flight) Overprinted

1983, Sept. 12
587 A128 30c multicolored 2.00 1.10
588 A128 50c multicolored 2.25 1.40
589 A128 60c multicolored 2.75 1.75
590 A128 $4 multicolored 8.00 7.25
Nos. 587-590 (4) 15.00 11.50

Souvenir Sheet

591 A128 $5 multicolored 7.50 *7.75*

Barbuda Nos. 493-495 Surcharged 45c on $1, 50c on $1.50 & 60c on $4

1983, Oct. 21 *Perf. 11½x11*
592 B39 Sheet of 6, #493 3.50 3.50
593 B39 Sheet of 6, #494 3.50 3.50
594 B39 Sheet of 6, #495 3.50 3.50

Antigua Nos. 708-725 (Definitives) Overprinted

1983, Oct. 28 *Perf. 14*
595 A127 1c multicolored .25 .25
596 A127 2c multicolored .25 .25
597 A127 3c multicolored .25 .25
598 A127 5c multicolored .25 .25
599 A127 10c multicolored .50 .30
600 A127 15c multicolored .85 .30
601 A127 20c multicolored .90 .30
602 A127 25c multicolored .95 .30
603 A127 30c multicolored 1.25 .50
604 A127 40c multicolored 1.50 .70
605 A127 45c multicolored 1.60 .70
606 A127 50c multicolored 1.75 .70
607 A127 60c multicolored 2.10 .90
608 A127 $1 multicolored 2.75 1.75
609 A127 $2 multicolored 3.50 3.50
610 A127 $2.50 multicolored 5.75 5.75
611 A127 $5 multicolored 6.25 6.25
612 A127 $10 multicolored 9.50 *16.00*
Nos. 595-612 (18) 40.15 *38.95*

Antigua Nos. 731-735 (Christmas) Overprinted

1983, Oct. 28 *Perf. 14*
613 A129 10c multicolored .25 .25
614 A129 30c multicolored .25 .25
615 A129 $1 multicolored .85 *.90*
616 A129 $4 multicolored 3.75 *4.00*
Nos. 613-616 (4) 5.10 *5.40*

Souvenir Sheet

617 A129 $5 multicolored 6.00 6.00

Antigua Nos. 736-739 (Methodists) Ovptd. in Black or Silver

1983, Dec. 14 *Perf. 14*
618 A130 15c multicolored (S) .45 .25
619 A130 50c multicolored (S) .75 .50
620 A130 60c multicolored .75 .60
621 A130 $3 multicolored 3.25 3.25
Nos. 618-621 (4) 5.20 4.60

Members of Royal Family — B44

1984, Feb. 14 *Perf. 14½x14*
622 B44 $1 Edward VII .75 *1.50*
623 B44 $1 George V .75 *1.50*
624 B44 $1 George VI .75 *1.50*
625 B44 $1 Elizabeth II .75 *1.50*
626 B44 $1 Prince Charles .75 *1.50*
627 B44 $1 Prince William .75 *1.50*
Nos. 622-627 (6) 4.50 *9.00*

Nos. 740-744 Overprinted

and

1984 Summer Olympics, Los Angeles — B45

1984 *Perf. 15, 13½ (B45)*
628 A131 25c multicolored .35 .25
629 A131 50c multicolored .50 .40
630 A131 90c multicolored .60 .45
631 B45 $1.50 Olympic Stadium, Athens .75 .75
632 B45 $2.50 Olympic Stadium, Los Angeles 1.50 1.50
633 A131 $3 multicolored 3.00 *2.50*
634 B45 $5 Torch bearer 3.00 *4.00*
a. Souv. sheet of 1, perf. 15 3.25 *4.00*
Nos. 628-634 (7) 9.70 9.85

Souvenir Sheet

635 A131 $5 multicolored 6.50 *7.25*

Issue dates: A131, Apr. 26, B45, July 27.

Antigua Nos. 755-759 (Flowers) Overprinted

1984, July 12 *Perf. 15*
636 A133 15c multicolored 1.25 .90
637 A133 50c multicolored 1.60 1.60
638 A133 60c multicolored 1.90 1.90
639 A133 $3 multicolored 3.25 *4.00*
Nos. 636-639 (4) 8.00 *8.40*

Souvenir Sheet

640 A133 $5 multicolored 6.00 6.00

Antigua Nos. 745-749 (Ships) Overprinted

1984, July 12
641 A132 45c multicolored 3.75 .85
642 A132 50c multicolored 3.75 1.00
643 A132 60c multicolored 4.75 1.25
644 A132 $4 multicolored 11.50 9.25
Nos. 641-644 (4) 23.75 12.35

Souvenir Sheet

645 A132 $5 multicolored 11.50 10.75

Antigua Nos. 760-767 (U.S. Presidents) Ovptd. in Black or Silver

1984, Oct. 1 *Perf. 14*
646 A134 10c multicolored (S) .25 .25
647 A134 20c multicolored .35 .35
648 A134 30c multicolored .45 .45
649 A134 40c multicolored .70 .70
650 A134 90c multicolored (S) 1.25 1.25
651 A134 $1.10 multicolored (S) 1.25 *1.50*
652 A134 $1.50 multicolored (S) 1.75 *2.40*
653 A134 $2 multicolored 2.25 *3.00*
Nos. 646-653 (8) 8.25 *9.90*

Antigua Nos. 768-772 (Slavery) Overprinted

1984, Oct. 1
654 A135 40c multicolored .70 .70
655 A135 50c multicolored .90 .90
656 A135 60c multicolored 1.25 1.25
657 A135 $3 multicolored 3.50 3.50
Nos. 654-657 (4) 6.35 6.35

Souvenir Sheet

658 A135 $5 multicolored 6.75 6.75

Antigua Nos. 773-778 (Birds) Overprinted

1984, Nov. 21 *Perf. 15*
659 A136 40c multicolored 4.25 1.00
660 A136 50c multicolored 4.75 1.10
661 A136 60c multicolored 5.00 1.25
662 A136 $2 multicolored 6.75 3.00
663 A136 $3 multicolored 7.00 5.00
Nos. 659-663 (5) 27.75 11.35

Souvenir Sheet

664 A136 $5 multicolored 24.00 24.00

Antigua Nos. 782-791 (Paintings) Overprinted in Silver

1984 *Perf. 15*
665 A137a 15c multicolored .25 .25
666 A137a 25c multicolored .40 .40
667 A137a 50c multicolored .80 .50
668 A137a 60c multicolored 1.00 1.00
669 A137a 70c multicolored 1.25 1.25
670 A137a 90c multiclored 1.40 1.40
671 A137a $3 multicolored 2.50 2.50
672 A137a $4 multicolored 3.50 3.50
Nos. 665-672 (8) 11.10 10.80

Souvenir Sheets

673 A137a $5 #790 4.00 *5.00*
674 A137a $5 #791, horiz. 4.00 *5.00*

Issued: Correggio, 11/21; Degas, 11/30.

Antigua Nos. 779-781 (AUSIPEX '84) Overprinted

1984, Nov. 30
675 A137 $1 multicolored 1.00 1.00
676 A137 $5 multicolored 4.00 *5.00*

Souvenir Sheet

677 A137 $5 multicolored 5.00 *6.00*

Antigua Nos. 819-827 (20th Century Leaders) Overprinted

1985, Feb. 18
678 A139 60c multicolored 6.50 6.00
679 A139 60c multicolored 6.50 6.00
680 A139 60c multicolored 6.50 6.00
681 A139 60c multicolored 6.50 6.00
682 A139 $1 multicolored 7.50 6.75
683 A139 $1 multicolored 7.50 6.75
684 A139 $1 multicolored 7.50 6.75
685 A139 $1 multicolored 7.50 6.75
Nos. 678-685 (8) 56.00 51.00

Souvenir Sheet

686 A139 $5 multicolored 13.00 13.00

Queen Mother (Lady Elizabeth Bowes-Lyon), 1907 — B46

1985, Feb. 26 *Perf. 14x14½*
687 B46 15c shown .40 .40
688 B46 45c Duchess of York, 1926 .50 .50
689 B46 50c Coronation, 1937 .50 .50
690 B46 60c Queen Mother .50 .50
691 B46 90c Wearing tiara .60 .60
692 B46 $2 Wearing blue hat 1.00 1.00
693 B46 $3 With children 1.50 1.50
Nos. 687-693 (7) 5.00 5.00

For overprints see Nos. 724-728, 733, 735.

Antigua Nos. 828-834 (Statue of Liberty) Overprinted

1985, May 10 *Perf. 15*
694 A140 25c multicolored .45 .45
695 A140 30c multicolored .60 .60
696 A140 50c multicolored .60 .60
697 A140 90c multicolored 1.10 1.10
698 A140 $1 multicolored 1.25 1.25
699 A140 $3 multicolored 3.25 3.25
Nos. 694-699 (6) 7.25 7.25

Souvenir Sheet

700 A140 $5 multicolored 6.00 6.00

Audubon, Birth Bicentenary — B47

1985, Apr. 4 *Perf. 14*
701 B47 45c Roseate tern .45 .45
702 B47 50c Mangrove cuckoo .50 .50
703 B47 60c Yellow-crowned night heron .60 .60
704 B47 $5 Brown pelican 5.00 5.00
Nos. 701-704 (4) 6.55 6.55

Antigua Nos. 845-849, 910-913 (Audubon) Ovptd. in Black or Silver

1985-86 *Perf. 15, 12½x12*

705 A143 60c on #910 (S) 9.75 7.00
706 A143 90c on #845 12.00 8.25
707 A143 90c on #911 (S) 12.00 8.25
708 A143 $1 on #846 12.00 8.25
709 A143 $1.50 on #847 13.00 11.00
710 A143 $1.50 on #912 15.00 13.00
711 A143 $3 on #848 25.00 22.50
712 A143 $3 on #913 27.50 25.00
Nos. 705-712 (8) 126.25 103.25

Souvenir Sheet

713 A143 $5 on #849 45.00 4.50

Issue dates: Nos. 706, 708-709, 711, 713, July 18, 1985. Others, Dec. 1986.

Antigua Nos. 850-854 (Butterflies) Overprinted

1985, July 18 *Perf. 14*

714 A144 25c multicolored 9.50 9.00
715 A144 60c multicolored 11.00 10.00
716 A144 95c multicolored 14.00 13.50
717 A144 $4 multicolored 25.00 25.00
Nos. 714-717 (4) 59.50 57.50

Souvenir Sheet

718 A144 $5 multicolored 42.50 42.50

Antigua Nos. 840-844 (Motorcycles) Overprinted

1985, Aug. 2

719 A142 10c multicolored 1.75 1.50
720 A142 30c multicolored 2.75 2.25
721 A142 60c multicolored 3.75 3.50
722 A142 $4 multicolored 12.00 12.00
Nos. 719-722 (4) 20.25 19.25

Souvenir Sheet

723 A142 $5 multicolored 15.00 15.00

Barbuda Nos. 687-693 Overprinted in Silver or Black

Antigua Nos. 866A-870 (Queen Mother) Ovptd. in Silver or Black

Perf. 14, 12x12½ (#729, 731, 736)

1985-86

724 B46 15c multi .50 .50
725 B46 45c multi .70 .70
726 B46 50c multi .85 .85
727 B46 60c multi 1.10 1.10
728 B46 90c multi 1.50 1.50
729 A148 90c multi 1.50 1.50
730 A148 $1 multi (S) 1.75 1.75
731 A148 $1 like #730 1.75 1.75
732 A148 $1.50 multi (S) 2.75 2.75
733 B46 $2 multi 3.25 3.25
734 A148 $2.50 multi 4.25 4.25
735 B46 $3 multi 5.50 5.50
736 A148 $3 multi 5.50 5.50
Nos. 724-736 (13) 30.90 30.90

Souvenir Sheet

737 A148 $5 multi 18.00 18.00

Queen Mother's 85th birthday.

Issue dates: 15c, 45c, 50c, 60c, No. 728, $2, No. 735, Aug. 2. No. 730, $1.50, $2.50, Nov. 8. Others, Dec. 1986. Nos. 729, 731, 736 issued in sheets of 5 plus label.

Antigua Nos. 835-839 (Scenes) Overprinted

1985, Aug. 30 *Perf. 15*

738 A141 15c multicolored .45 .45
739 A141 50c multicolored .75 .75
740 A141 60c multicolored .80 .80
741 A141 $3 multicolored 4.50 4.50
Nos. 738-741 (4) 6.50 6.50

Souvenir Sheet

742 A141 $5 multicolored 7.50 7.50

Antigua Nos. 855-859 (Airplanes) Overprinted

1985, Aug. 30 *Perf. 14*

743 A145 30c multicolored 2.10 2.10
744 A145 90c multicolored 3.50 3.50
745 A145 $1.50 multicolored 4.50 4.50
746 A145 $3 multicolored 6.00 6.00
Nos. 743-746 (4) 16.10 16.10

Souvenir Sheet

747 A145 $5 multicolored 9.25 9.25

Antigua Nos. 860-861 (Maimonides) Overprinted

1985, Nov. 25 *Perf. 14*

748 A146 $2 yellow green 13.00 13.00

Souvenir Sheet

749 A146 $5 deep brown 12.50 12.50

Antigua Nos. 871-875 (Marine Life) Ovptd. in Black or Silver

1985, Nov. 25

750 A149 15c multi (S) 9.50 2.25
751 A149 45c multi 9.50 1.10
752 A149 60c multi 9.50 2.25
753 A149 $3 multi (S) 21.00 8.75
Nos. 750-753 (4) 49.50 14.35

Souvenir Sheet

754 A149 $5 multi 26.00 26.00

Antigua Nos. 862-866 (Youth Year) Overprinted

1986, Feb. 17

755 A147 25c multicolored .35 .35
756 A147 50c multicolored .65 .65
757 A147 60c multicolored .75 .75
758 A147 $3 multicolored 3.50 3.50
Nos. 755-758 (4) 5.25 5.25

Souvenir Sheet

759 A147 $5 multicolored 7.25 7.25

Antigua Nos. 886-889 (Royal Visit) Overprinted

1986, Feb. 17 *Perf. 14½*

760 A152 60c multicolored 3.75 1.10
761 A152 $1 multicolored 3.75 2.40
762 A152 $4 multicolored 10.50 9.75
Nos. 760-762 (3) 18.00 13.25

Souvenir Sheet

763 A152 $5 multicolored 17.50 17.50

Antigua Nos. 876-880 (Bach) Overprinted

1986, Mar. 10 *Perf. 14*

764 A150 25c multicolored 4.50 1.10
765 A150 50c multicolored 4.50 3.00
766 A150 $1 multicolored 6.00 5.75
767 A140 $3 multicolored 11.00 10.50
Nos. 764-767 (4) 26.00 20.35

Souvenir Sheet

768 A150 $5 multicolored 40.00 40.00

Antigua Nos. 881-885 (Girl Guides) Overprinted

1986, Mar. 10 *Perf. 14*

769 A151 15c multicolored 3.00 2.25
770 A151 45c multicolored 5.25 5.25
771 A151 60c multicolored 5.25 5.25
772 A151 $3 multicolored 14.50 14.00
Nos. 769-772 (4) 28.00 26.75

Souvenir Sheet

773 A151 $5 multicolored 47.50 42.50

Antigua Nos. 905-909 (Christmas) Overprinted

1986, Apr. 4 *Perf. 15*

774 A156 10c multicolored .65 .65
775 A156 25c multicolored 1.40 1.40
776 A156 60c multicolored 2.40 2.40
777 A156 $4 multicolored 7.00 7.00
Nos. 774-777 (4) 11.45 11.45

Souvenir Sheet

778 A156 $5 multicolored 8.00 8.00

Queen Elizabeth II, 60th Birthday B48

1986, Apr. 21

779 B48 $1 Shaking hands 1.00 1.00
780 B48 $2 Talking with woman 1.00 1.00
781 B48 $2.50 With officer 1.00 1.00
Nos. 779-781 (3) 3.00 3.00

Souvenir Sheet

Perf. 13½x14

782 B48 $5 Portraits 7.50 7.50

No. 782 contains one 34x27mm stamp.

Antigua Nos. 925-928 (Queen's Birthday) Overprinted in Silver or Black

1986, Aug. 12

783 CD339 60c multi 1.60 1.60
784 CD339 $1 multi 2.50 2.50
785 CD339 $4 multi 10.00 10.00
Nos. 783-785 (3) 14.10 14.10

Souvenir Sheet

786 CD339 $5 multi (Bk) 11.50 11.50

Nos. 920-924 Overprinted and

Halley's Comet B49

1986 *Perf. 14, 15 (B49)*

787 A158 5c multicolored 2.25 2.25
788 A158 10c multicolored 2.25 2.25
789 A158 60c multicolored 6.25 5.50
790 B49 $1 shown 1.10 1.10
791 B49 $2.50 Early telescope, dish antenna, vert. 1.60 1.60
792 A158 $4 multicolored 17.00 15.00
793 B49 $5 World map, comet 2.75 2.75
Nos. 787-793 (7) 33.20 30.45

Souvenir Sheet

794 A159 $5 multicolored 11.50 11.50

Issued: Nos. 790-791, 793, 7/10; others, 9/22.

Antigua Nos. 901-904 (UN) Overprinted

1986, Aug. 12 *Perf. 13½x14*

795 A155 40c multicolored 3.50 3.50
796 A155 $1 multicolored 5.25 5.25
797 A155 $3 multicolored 9.00 9.00
Nos. 795-797 (3) 17.75 17.75

Souvenir Sheet

Perf. 14x13½

798 A155 $5 multicolored 27.50 27.50

Antigua Nos. 915-919 (World Cup Soccer) Overprinted

1986, Aug. 28 *Perf. 14*

799 A157 30c multicolored 4.25 1.10
800 A157 60c multicolored 6.25 6.00
801 A157 $1 multicolored 6.75 6.50
802 A157 $4 multicolored 12.50 12.50
Nos. 799-802 (4) 29.75 26.10

Souvenir Sheet

803 A157 $5 multicolored 30.00 30.00

See Nos. 848-851.

Antigua Nos. 934-938 (AMERIPEX '86) Overprinted

1986, Aug. 28 **Litho.** *Perf. 15*

804 A161 25c multicolored 5.50 5.25
805 A161 50c multicolored 6.75 6.50
806 A161 $1 multicolored 9.50 9.25
807 A161 $3 multicolored 16.00 16.00
Nos. 804-807 (4) 37.75 37.00

Souvenir Sheet

808 A161 $5 multicolored 22.50 22.50

Antigua Nos. 939-942 (Royal Wedding) Ovptd. in Silver

1986, Sept. 22 *Perf. 14*

809 CD340 45c multicolored .60 .55
810 CD340 60c multicolored .80 .75
811 CD340 $4 multicolored 5.75 5.75
Nos. 809-811 (3) 7.15 7.05

Souvenir Sheet

812 CD340 $5 multicolored 8.75 8.75

Antigua Nos. 943-947 (Conch Shells) Overprinted in Silver or Black

1986, Nov. 10 *Perf. 15*

813 A162 15c multicolored 6.25 6.25
814 A162 45c multicolored 6.50 6.50
815 A162 60c multicolored 9.50 9.50
816 A162 $3 multicolored 20.00 *24.00*
Nos. 813-816 (4) 42.25 *46.25*

Souvenir Sheet

817 A162 $5 multi (Bk) 35.00 35.00

Antigua Nos. 948-957 (Flowers) Overprinted

1986, Nov. 10

818 A163 10c multicolored .50 .50
819 A163 15c multicolored .50 .50
820 A163 50c multicolored 1.00 1.00
821 A163 60c multicolored 1.25 1.25
822 A163 70c multicolored 1.40 1.40
823 A163 $1 multicolored 2.00 2.00
824 A163 $3 multicolored 6.00 6.00
825 A163 $4 multicolored 7.00 7.00
Nos. 818-825 (8) 19.65 19.65

Souvenir Sheets

826 A163 $4 multicolored 25.00 25.00
827 A163 $5 multicolored 25.00 25.00

Antigua Nos. 958-962 (Fungi) Overprinted

1986, Nov. 28

828 A164 10c multicolored 2.25 2.25
829 A164 50c multicolored 8.50 8.50
830 A164 $1 multicolored 13.00 13.00
831 A164 $4 multicolored 24.00 24.00
Nos. 828-831 (4) 47.75 47.75

Souvenir Sheet

832 A164 $5 multicolored 47.50 47.50

Antigua Nos. 929-933 (Boats) Overprinted

1987, Jan. 12 *Perf. 14*

833 A160 30c multicolored 2.40 1.10
834 A160 60c multicolored 4.25 1.90
835 A160 $1 multicolored 5.50 3.25
836 A160 $3 multicolored 10.50 10.50
Nos. 833-836 (4) 22.65 16.75

Souvenir Sheet

837 A160 $5 multicolored 45.00 45.00

Antigua Nos. 968-972A (Classic Cars) Overprinted

1987, Jan. 12

838 A165 10c multicolored .90 .70
839 A165 15c multicolored 1.40 .65
840 A165 50c multicolored 1.60 1.50
841 A165 60c multicolored 1.90 1.75
842 A165 70c multicolored 2.10 1.90
843 A165 $1 multicolored 3.00 3.00
844 A165 $3 multicolored 8.00 8.00
845 A165 $4 multicolored 10.00 10.00
Nos. 838-845 (8) 28.90 27.50

Souvenir Sheets

846 A165 $5 multi (#972) 22.50 22.50
847 A165 $5 multi (#972A) 22.50 22.50

Automobile, cent.

Antigua Nos. 963-966 (World Cup Winners Ovpts.) Overprinted

1987, Mar. 10

848 A157 30c multicolored 3.50 1.75
849 A157 60c multicolored 4.75 3.25
850 A157 $1 multicolored 6.00 5.25
851 A157 $4 multicolored 21.00 21.00
Nos. 848-851 (4) 35.25 31.25

See Nos. 799-802.

Antigua Nos. 1000-1004 (America's Cup) Overprinted

1987, Apr. 23 *Perf. 15*

852 A170 30c multicolored 1.40 .70
853 A170 60c multicolored 1.90 .80
854 A170 $1 multicolored 3.00 1.40
855 A170 $3 multicolored 4.25 3.25
Nos. 852-855 (4) 10.55 6.15

Souvenir Sheet

856 A171 $5 multicolored 9.00 9.00

Antigua Nos. 1005-1014 (WWF) Overprinted

1987, July 1 *Perf. 14*

857 A172 15c multicolored *50.00 25.00*
858 A173 30c multicolored *6.75 5.00*
859 A172 40c multicolored *65.00 27.50*
860 A173 50c multicolored *9.00 7.50*
861 A172 60c multicolored *90.00 45.00*
862 A172 $1 multicolored *95.00 45.00*
863 A173 $2 multicolored *17.50 17.50*
864 A173 $3 multicolored *17.50 17.50*
Nos. 857-864 (8) 350.75 190.00

Souvenir Sheets

865	A172	$5 multicolored	*125.00*	*85.00*
866	A173	$5 multicolored	*125.00*	*85.00*

Antigua Nos. 1025-1034 (Transportation) Overprinted

1987, July 28 ***Perf. 15***

867	A175	10c multicolored	3.75	3.75
868	A175	15c multicolored	4.00	2.75
869	A175	30c multicolored	4.25	1.75
870	A175	50c multicolored	4.75	1.75
871	A175	60c multicolored	5.50	2.40
872	A175	70c multicolored	5.75	5.50
873	A175	90c multicolored	7.25	7.00
874	A175	$1.50 multicolored	12.00	12.50
875	A175	$2 multicolored	14.50	16.00
876	A175	$3 multicolored	24.00	24.00
		Nos. 867-876 (10)	85.75	77.40

Marine Life B50

1987, July 28

877	B50	5c Shore crab	.25	.25
878	B50	10c Sea cucumber	.25	.25
879	B50	15c Stop light parrotfish	.25	.25
880	B50	25c Banded coral shrimp	.25	*.30*
881	B50	35c Spotted drum	.30	*.40*
882	B50	60c Thorny star-fish	.35	*.45*
883	B50	75c Atlantic trumpet triton	.40	*.90*
884	B50	90c Feather-star, yellow beaker sponge	.50	1.10
885	B50	$1 Blue gorgonian, vert.	.60	1.10
886	B50	$1.25 Slender filefish, vert.	.70	1.25
887	B50	$5 Barred hamlet, vert.	1.50	8.00
888	B50	$7.50 Fairy basslet, vert.	2.75	9.25
889	B50	$10 Fire coral, butterfly fish, vert.	5.00	11.50
		Nos. 877-889 (13)	13.10	*35.00*

For surcharges see Nos. 1133-1134.

Antigua Nos. 1048-1052 (Seoul Olympics) Ovptd. in Silver or Black

1987, Oct. 12 ***Perf. 14***

890	A178	10c multicolored	.85	.85
891	A178	60c multicolored	2.10	2.10
892	A178	$1 multicolored	3.25	3.25
893	A178	$3 multicolored	9.75	9.75
		Nos. 890-893 (4)	15.95	15.95

Souvenir Sheet

894	A178	$5 multi (Bk)	17.50	17.50

1988 Summer Olympics, Seoul.

Antigua Nos. 990-999 (Chagall) Ovptd. in Black or Silver

1987, Oct. 12 ***Perf. 13½x14***

895	A169	10c multicolored	1.00	1.25
896	A169	30c multicolored	1.25	1.00
897	A169	40c multicolored	1.60	1.25
898	A169	60c multicolored	2.25	2.00
899	A169	90c multicolored	3.50	3.00
900	A169	$1 multicolored (S)	4.00	3.50
901	A169	$3 multicolored	9.25	9.25
902	A169	$4 multicolored	12.50	12.50
		Nos. 895-902 (8)	35.35	33.75

Size: 110x95mm

Imperf

903	A169	$5 multicolored	17.50	17.50
904	A169	$5 multicolored (S)	17.50	17.50

Antigua Nos. 1015-1024 (Statue of Liberty) Ovptd. in Silver or Black

1987, Nov. 5 ***Perf. 14***

905	A174	15c multicolored	.70	.70
906	A174	30c multicolored	.90	.90
907	A174	45c multicolored	1.25	1.25
908	A174	50c multicolored (Bk)	1.40	1.40
909	A174	60c multicolored	1.75	1.75
910	A174	90c multicolored	2.50	2.50
911	A174	$1 multicolored	3.00	3.00
912	A174	$2 multicolored	6.00	6.00
913	A174	$3 multicolored (Bk)	8.25	8.25
914	A174	$5 multicolored	14.00	14.00
		Nos. 905-914 (10)	39.75	39.75

Antigua Nos. 1040-1047 (Entertainers) Ovptd. in Black or Silver

1987, Nov. 5

915	A177	15c multicolored	*4.75*	*1.90*
916	A177	30c multicolored	*10.00*	*3.50*
917	A177	45c multicolored	*4.75*	*2.00*
918	A177	50c multicolored	*4.75*	*2.25*
919	A177	60c multicolored	*16.00*	*4.00*
920	A177	$1 multicolored	*7.50*	*3.75*
921	A177	$2 multicolored	*10.50*	*7.00*
922	A177	$3 multicolored (S)	*32.50*	*14.00*
		Nos. 915-922 (8)	90.75	38.40

Antigua Nos. 1035-1039 (Reptiles & Amphibians) Overprinted

1987, Dec. 8

923	A176	30c multicolored	4.25	2.75
924	A176	60c multicolored	8.50	5.25
925	A176	$1 multicolored	13.50	8.25
926	A176	$3 multicolored	40.00	40.00
		Nos. 923-926 (4)	66.25	56.25

Souvenir Sheet

927	A176	$5 multicolored	45.00	40.00

Antigua Nos. 1063-1067 (Christmas) Overprinted

1988, Jan. 12

928	A181	45c multicolored	1.00	1.00
929	A181	60c multicolored	1.50	1.50
930	A181	$1 multicolored	2.50	2.50
931	A181	$4 multicolored	9.50	9.50
		Nos. 928-931 (4)	14.50	14.50

Souvenir Sheet

932	A181	$5 multicolored	14.50	14.50

Antigua Nos. 1083-1091 (Salvation Army) Overprinted

1988, Mar. 25

933	A184	25c multicolored	1.50	1.25
934	A184	30c multicolored	1.75	1.25
935	A184	40c multicolored	1.90	1.50
936	A184	45c multicolored	2.00	1.75
937	A184	50c multicolored	2.10	2.00
938	A184	60c multicolored	2.75	2.50
939	A184	$1 multicolored	4.00	4.00
940	A184	$2 multicolored	8.00	8.00
		Nos. 933-940 (8)	24.00	22.25

Souvenir Sheet

941	A184	$5 multicolored	42.50	42.50

Antigua Nos. 1058-1062 (U.S. Constitution) Ovptd. in Silver

1988, May 6

942	A180	15c multicolored	.40	.40
943	A180	45c multicolored	.70	.70
944	A180	60c multicolored	1.00	1.00
945	A180	$4 multicolored	6.00	6.00
		Nos. 942-945 (4)	8.10	8.10

Souvenir Sheet

946	A180	$5 multicolored	7.50	7.50

Antigua Nos. 1068-1072 (Royal Wedding Anniv.) Overprinted

1988, July 4

947	A182	25c multicolored	3.25	1.50
948	A182	60c multicolored	4.75	2.00
949	A182	$2 multicolored	6.75	6.50
950	A182	$3 multicolored	9.25	9.25
		Nos. 947-950 (4)	24.00	19.25

Souvenir Sheet

951	A182	$5 multicolored	22.50	17.00

Antigua Nos. 1073-1082 (Birds) Overprinted

1988, July 4

952	A183	10c multicolored	3.50	2.40
953	A183	15c multicolored	4.50	2.40
954	A183	50c multicolored	4.75	3.75
955	A183	60c multicolored	5.50	5.00
956	A183	70c multicolored	7.00	5.25
957	A183	$1 multicolored	8.75	7.25
958	A183	$3 multicolored	20.00	20.00
959	A183	$4 multicolored	30.00	30.00
		Nos. 952-959 (8)	84.00	76.05

Souvenir Sheets

960	A183	$5 multi (#1081)	30.00	26.00
961	A183	$5 multi (#1082)	30.00	26.00

Antigua Nos. 1092-1101 (Columbus) Overprinted

1988, July 25

962	A185	10c multicolored	3.50	1.25
963	A185	30c multicolored	3.75	1.50
964	A185	45c multicolored	4.75	2.25
965	A185	60c multicolored	4.50	3.25
966	A185	90c multicolored	5.00	4.25
967	A185	$1 multicolored	6.25	5.00
968	A185	$3 multicolored	14.00	14.00
969	A185	$4 multicolored	18.00	18.00
		Nos. 962-969 (8)	59.75	49.50

Souvenir Sheets

970	A185	$5 multi (#1100)	21.50	21.50
971	A185	$5 multi (#1101)	21.50	21.50

Antigua Nos. 1102-1111 (Titian Paintings) Overprinted

1988, July 25 ***Perf. 13½x14***

972	A187	30c multicolored	1.00	.75
973	A187	40c multicolored	1.10	.90
974	A187	45c multicolored	1.25	1.00
975	A187	50c multicolored	1.40	1.25
976	A187	$1 multicolored	2.25	2.25
977	A187	$2 multicolored	5.25	5.25
978	A187	$3 multicolored	6.75	6.75
979	A187	$4 multicolored	10.00	10.00
		Nos. 972-979 (8)	29.00	28.15

Souvenir Sheets

980	A187	$5 multi (#1110)	15.00	15.00
981	A187	$5 multi (#1111)	15.00	15.00

Antigua Nos. 1053-1057 (Scout Jamboree) Overprinted

1988, Aug. 25 ***Perf. 15***

982	A179	10c multicolored	4.00	2.25
983	A179	60c multicolored	10.00	4.00
984	A179	$1 multicolored	5.00	4.25
985	A179	$3 multicolored	10.00	10.00
		Nos. 982-985 (4)	29.00	20.50

Souvenir Sheet

986	A179	$5 multicolored	26.00	26.00

Antigua Nos. 1112-1116 (Sailboats) Overprinted

1988, Aug. 25

987	A188	30c multicolored	1.60	1.25
988	A188	60c multicolored	2.25	2.25
989	A188	$1 multicolored	3.00	3.00
990	A188	$3 multicolored	8.50	8.50
		Nos. 987-990 (4)	15.35	15.00

Souvenir Sheet

991	A188	$5 multicolored	20.00	17.50

Antigua Nos. 1127-1136 (Flowering Trees) Overprinted

1988, Sept. 16 ***Perf. 14***

992	A190	10c multicolored	.45	.50
993	A190	30c multicolored	.60	.60
994	A190	50c multicolored	.75	.75
995	A190	90c multicolored	1.10	1.10
996	A190	$1 multicolored	1.60	1.60
997	A190	$2 multicolored	3.00	3.00
998	A190	$3 multicolored	4.25	4.25
999	A190	$4 multicolored	5.25	5.25
		Nos. 992-999 (8)	17.00	17.05

Souvenir Sheets

1000	A191	$5 multi (#1135)	9.00	9.00
1001	A191	$5 multi (#1136)	9.00	9.00

Antigua Nos. 1140-1144 (Seoul Olympics) Overprinted

1988, Sept. 16

1002	A192	40c multicolored	2.00	1.10
1003	A192	60c multicolored	2.75	1.75
1004	A192	$1 multicolored	4.00	3.00
1005	A192	$3 multicolored	6.50	6.50
		Nos. 1002-1005 (4)	15.25	12.35

Souvenir Sheet

1006	A192	$5 multicolored	15.00	15.00

Antigua Nos. 1145-1162 (Butterflies) Overprinted

1988-90

1007	A193	1c multicolored	.60	.60
1008	A193	2c multicolored	.60	.60
1009	A193	3c multicolored	.60	.60
1010	A193	5c multicolored	.60	.60
1011	A193	10c multicolored	.60	.60
1012	A193	15c multicolored	.60	.60
1013	A193	20c multicolored	.60	.60
1014	A193	25c multicolored	.60	.60
1015	A193	30c multicolored	.70	.70
1016	A193	40c multicolored	.80	.80
1017	A193	45c multicolored	1.00	1.00
1018	A193	50c multicolored	1.10	1.10
1019	A193	60c multicolored	1.40	1.40
1020	A193	$1 multicolored	2.10	2.10
1021	A193	$2 multicolored	4.50	4.50
1022	A193	$2.50 multicolored	5.25	5.25
1023	A193	$5 multicolored	11.00	11.00
1024	A193	$10 multicolored	22.50	22.50
1025	A193	$20 multi ('90)	30.00	30.00
		Nos. 1007-1025 (19)	85.15	85.15

Issue dates: $20, May 4, others Dec. 8.

The overprint on No. 1025 is in a thin sans-serif typeface, while Nos. 1007-1024 are overprinted with a thick serif typeface.

Antigua Nos. 1162A-1167 (Kennedy) Overprinted

1989, Apr. 28

1026	A194	1c multicolored	.70	*1.25*
1027	A194	2c multicolored	.70	*1.25*
1028	A194	3c multicolored	.70	*1.25*
1029	A194	4c multicolored	.70	*1.25*
1030	A194	30c multicolored	1.50	.90
1031	A194	60c multicolored	3.75	1.75
1032	A194	$1 multicolored	4.50	3.00
1033	A194	$4 multicolored	11.50	11.50
		Nos. 1026-1033 (8)	24.05	22.15

Souvenir Sheet

1034	A194	$5 multicolored	16.00	16.00

Antigua Nos. 1175-1176 (Arawaks) Overprinted

1989, May 24

1035	A196	$1.50 Strip of 4, #a.-d.	27.50	27.50

Souvenir Sheet

1036	A196	$6 multicolored	15.00	*18.00*

Antigua Nos. 1177-1186 (Jets) Overprinted

1989, May 29

1037	A197	10c multicolored	2.25	1.90
1038	A197	30c multicolored	2.60	1.90
1039	A197	40c multicolored	3.25	2.75
1040	A197	60c multicolored	3.75	3.75
1041	A197	$1 multicolored	5.25	5.25
1042	A197	$2 multicolored	8.50	8.50
1043	A197	$3 multicolored	13.50	13.50
1044	A197	$4 multicolored	20.00	20.00
		Nos. 1037-1044 (8)	59.10	57.55

Souvenir Sheets

1045	A197	$7 multi (#1185)	37.50	30.00
1046	A197	$7 multi (#1186)	37.50	30.00

Antigua Nos. 1187-1196 (Cruise Ships) Overprinted

1989, Sept. 18

1047	A198	25c multicolored	3.50	1.60
1048	A198	45c multicolored	4.25	2.10
1049	A198	50c multicolored	4.25	3.00
1050	A198	60c multicolored	5.50	3.25
1051	A198	75c multicolored	5.50	4.50
1052	A198	90c multicolored	7.25	6.25
1053	A198	$3 multicolored	13.00	13.00
1054	A198	$4 multicolored	17.00	17.00
		Nos. 1047-1054 (8)	60.25	50.70

Souvenir Sheets

1055	A198	$6 multi (#1195)	40.00	35.00
1056	A198	$6 multi (#1196)	40.00	35.00

Antigua Nos. 1197-1206 (Hiroshige Paintings) Overprinted

1989, Dec. 14 ***Perf. 14x13½***

1057	A199	25c multicolored	2.75	1.25
1058	A199	45c multicolored	3.25	1.90
1059	A199	50c multicolored	3.75	2.75
1060	A199	60c multicolored	4.00	3.25
1061	A199	$1 multicolored	4.75	5.00
1062	A199	$2 multicolored	8.00	8.00
1063	A199	$3 multicolored	11.50	11.50
1064	A199	$4 multicolored	16.00	16.00
		Nos. 1057-1064 (8)	54.00	49.65

Souvenir Sheets

1065	A199	$5 multi (#1205)	30.00	27.50
1066	A199	$5 multi (#1206)	30.00	27.50

Antigua Nos. 1217-1222 (World Cup Soccer) Overprinted

1989, Dec. 20 ***Perf. 14***

1067	A201	15c multicolored	1.90	.90
1068	A201	25c multicolored	1.90	.90
1069	A201	$1 multicolored	3.00	3.00
1070	A201	$4 multicolored	11.00	11.00
		Nos. 1067-1070 (4)	17.80	15.80

Souvenir Sheets

1071	A201	$5 multi (#1221)	22.50	22.50
1072	A201	$5 multi (#1222)	22.50	22.50

Antigua Nos. 1264-1273 (Christmas) Overprinted

1989, Dec. 20

1073	A208	10c multicolored	.60	.60
1074	A208	25c multicolored	.60	.60
1075	A208	30c multicolored	.70	.60
1076	A208	50c multicolored	.90	.90
1077	A208	60c multicolored	1.10	1.10
1078	A208	70c multicolored	1.50	1.25
1079	A208	$4 multicolored	5.50	5.50
1080	A208	$5 multicolored	7.00	7.00
		Nos. 1073-1080 (8)	17.90	17.55

Souvenir Sheets

1081	A208	$5 multi (#1272)	15.00	15.00
1082	A208	$5 multi (#1273)	15.00	15.00

Antigua Nos. 1223-1232 (Mushrooms) Overprinted

1990, Feb. 21

1083	A202	10c multicolored	2.75	1.75
1084	A202	25c multicolored	2.75	1.75
1085	A202	50c multicolored	4.50	3.50
1086	A202	60c multicolored	4.75	4.00
1087	A202	75c multicolored	6.00	5.00
1088	A202	$1 multicolored	7.25	6.50
1089	A202	$3 multicolored	20.00	20.00
1090	A202	$4 multicolored	27.50	27.50
		Nos. 1083-1090 (8)	75.50	70.00

Souvenir Sheets

1091 A202 $6 multi (#1231) 45.00 37.50
1092 A202 $6 multi (#1232) 45.00 37.50

Antigua Nos. 1233-1237 (Wildlife) Overprinted

1990, Mar. 30

1093 A203 25c multicolored 1.40 .90
1094 A203 45c multicolored 3.50 1.40
1095 A203 60c multicolored 3.50 2.10
1096 A203 $4 multicolored 14.00 14.00
Nos. 1093-1096 (4) 22.40 18.40

Souvenir Sheet

1097 A203 $5 multicolored 32.50 32.50

Antigua Nos. 1258-1262 (Moon Landing) Overprinted

1990, Mar. 30

1098 A206 10c multicolored 1.40 1.40
1099 A206 45c multicolored 2.00 2.00
1100 A206 $1 multicolored 5.25 5.25
1101 A206 $4 multicolored 21.00 21.00
Nos. 1098-1101 (4) 29.65 29.65

Souvenir Sheet

1102 A206 $5 multicolored 32.50 32.50

Antigua Nos. 1275-1284 (America) Overprinted

1990, June 6

1103 A210 10c multicolored 1.90 .75
1104 A210 20c multicolored 1.90 .75
1105 A210 25c multicolored 2.25 .75
1106 A210 45c multicolored 2.50 1.10
1107 A210 60c multicolored 2.75 1.60
1108 A210 $2 multicolored 5.75 5.75
1109 A210 $3 multicolored 8.50 8.50
1110 A210 $4 multicolored 11.50 11.50
Nos. 1103-1110 (8) 37.05 30.70

Souvenir Sheets

1111 A210 $5 multi (#1283) 21.00 21.00
1112 A210 $5 multi (#1284) 21.00 21.00

Antigua Nos. 1285-1294 (Orchids) Overprinted

1990, July 12

1113 A211 15c multicolored 3.50 1.50
1114 A211 45c multicolored 2.75 2.25
1115 A211 50c multicolored 3.00 3.00
1116 A211 60c multicolored 3.25 3.25
1117 A211 $1 multicolored 5.75 5.75
1118 A211 $2 multicolored 11.50 11.50
1119 A211 $3 multicolored 17.00 17.00
1120 A211 $5 multicolored 30.00 30.00
Nos. 1113-1120 (8) 76.75 74.25

Souvenir Sheets

1121 A211 $6 multi (#1293) 30.00 26.00
1122 A211 $6 multi (#1294) 30.00 26.00

Antigua Nos. 1295-1304 (Fish) Overprinted

1990, Aug. 14

1123 A212 10c multicolored 3.00 1.75
1124 A212 15c multicolored 3.00 1.75
1125 A212 50c multicolored 3.25 2.40
1126 A212 60c multicolored 4.25 3.00
1127 A212 $1 multicolored 5.50 5.00
1128 A212 $2 multicolored 9.25 9.25
1129 A212 $3 multicolored 14.00 14.00
1130 A212 $4 multicolored 19.00 19.00
Nos. 1123-1130 (8) 61.25 56.15

Souvenir Sheets

1131 A212 $5 multi (#1303) 30.00 26.00
1132 A212 $5 multi (#1304) 30.00 26.00

Barbuda Nos. 888-889 Surcharged "1st Anniversary / Hurricane Hugo / 16th September, 1989-1990"

1990, Sept. 17 *Perf. 15*

1133 B50 $5 on $7.50 16.00 16.00
1134 B50 $7.50 on $10 24.00 24.00

Antigua Nos. 1324-1328 (Queen Mother) Overprinted

1990, Oct. 12 *Perf. 14*

1135 A217 15c multicolored 13.00 3.00
1136 A217 35c multicolored 17.00 2.50
1137 A217 75c multicolored 26.00 5.50
1138 A217 $3 multicolored 45.00 26.00
Nos. 1135-1138 (4) 101.00 37.00

Souvenir Sheet

1139 A217 $6 multicolored 95.00 47.50

Antigua No. 1313 Ovptd. in Silver

Miniature Sheet

1990, Dec. 14

1140 A215 45c Sheet of 20, #a.-t. 100.00 100.00

Antigua Nos. 1360-1369 (Christmas) Overprinted

1990, Dec. 14 *Perf. 14x13½, 13½x14*

1141 A221 25c multicolored .85 .85
1142 A221 30c multicolored 1.10 1.10
1143 A221 40c multicolored 1.25 1.25
1144 A221 60c multicolored 1.75 1.75
1145 A221 $1 multicolored 3.25 3.25
1146 A221 $2 multicolored 6.25 6.25
1147 A221 $4 multicolored 15.00 15.00
1148 A221 $5 multicolored 15.00 15.00
Nos. 1141-1148 (8) 44.45 44.45

Souvenir Sheets

1149 A221 $6 multi (#1368) 22.50 22.50
1150 A221 $6 multi (#1369) 22.50 22.50

Antigua Nos. 1305-1308 (Penny Black) Overprinted

1991, Feb. 4 *Perf. 15x14*

1151 A213 45c green 6.00 2.10
1152 A213 60c bright rose 7.00 3.00
1153 A213 $5 bright ultra 27.50 25.00
Nos. 1151-1153 (3) 40.50 30.10

Souvenir Sheet

1154 A213 $6 black 40.00 40.00

Antigua Nos. 1309-1312 (Stamp World London '90) Overprinted

1991, Feb. 4 *Perf. 13½*

1155 A214 50c red & deep grn 6.25 3.25
1156 A214 75c red & vio brn 7.50 4.75
1157 A214 $4 red & brt ultra 24.00 24.00
Nos. 1155-1157 (3) 37.75 32.00

Souvenir Sheet

1158 A214 $6 red & black 40.00 40.00

Birds — B52

1991, Mar. 25 **Litho.** *Perf. 14*

1164 B52 60c Troupial 2.75 1.10
1168 B52 $2 Christmas bird 4.50 3.75
1169 B52 $4 Rose-breasted grosbeak 7.50 7.50
1171 B52 $7 Stolid flycatcher 12.50 *14.50*
Nos. 1164-1171 (4) 27.25 *26.85*

Antigua Nos. 1329-1333 (Barcelona '92) Overprinted

1991, Apr. 23 **Litho.** *Perf. 14*

1173 A218 50c multicolored 3.50 1.60
1174 A218 75c multicolored 4.25 2.25
1175 A218 $1 multicolored 5.25 3.00
1176 A218 $5 multicolored 16.00 16.00
Nos. 1173-1176 (4) 29.00 22.85

Souvenir Sheet

1177 A218 $6 multicolored 29.00 29.00

Antigua Nos. 1350-1359 (Birds) Overprinted

1991, Apr. 23

1178 A220 10c multicolored 3.00 2.00
1179 A220 25c multicolored 3.75 1.25
1180 A220 50c multicolored 4.25 2.40
1181 A220 60c multicolored 4.50 2.75
1182 A220 $1 multicolored 5.25 5.00
1183 A220 $2 multicolored 9.25 9.25
1184 A220 $3 multicolored 14.00 14.00
1185 A220 $4 multicolored 16.00 *18.00*
Nos. 1178-1185 (8) 60.00 54.65

Souvenir Sheets

1186 A220 $6 multi (#1358) 30.00 26.00
1187 A220 $6 multi (#1359) 30.00 26.00

Antigua Nos. 1370-1379 (Rubens Paintings) Overprinted

1991, June 21 *Perf. 14x13½*

1188 A222 25c multicolored 1.10 1.10
1189 A222 45c multicolored 1.90 1.90
1190 A222 50c multicolored 2.10 2.10
1191 A222 60c multicolored 2.40 2.40
1192 A222 $1 multicolored 4.00 4.00
1193 A222 $2 multicolored 8.00 8.00
1194 A222 $3 multicolored 12.00 12.00
1195 A222 $4 multicolored 16.00 16.00
Nos. 1188-1195 (8) 47.50 47.50

Souvenir Sheets

1196 A222 $6 multi (#1378) 24.00 24.00
1197 A222 $6 multi (#1379) 24.00 24.00

Antigua Nos. 1380-1390 (World War II) Overprinted

1991, July 25 **Litho.** *Perf. 14*

1198 A223 10c multicolored 5.75 2.10
1199 A223 15c multicolored 7.00 2.10
1200 A223 25c multicolored 8.00 2.10
1201 A223 45c multicolored 14.00 3.75
1202 A223 50c multicolored 8.00 4.25
1203 A223 $1 multicolored 18.00 8.00
1204 A223 $2 multicolored 17.50 16.00
1205 A223 $4 multicolored 22.50 22.50
1206 A223 $5 multicolored 22.50 22.50
Nos. 1198-1206 (9) 123.25 83.30

Souvenir Sheets

1207 A223 $6 multi (#1389) 55.00 42.50
1208 A223 $6 multi (#1390) 55.00 42.50

Antigua Nos. 1411-1420 (Voyages) Overprinted

1991, Aug. 26 **Litho.** *Perf. 14*

1209 A226 10c multicolored 2.10 1.40
1210 A226 15c multicolored 2.40 1.40
1211 A226 45c multicolored 2.75 .95
1212 A226 60c multicolored 3.00 2.10
1213 A226 $1 multicolored 3.75 3.25
1214 A226 $2 multicolored 7.00 6.75
1215 A226 $4 multicolored 18.00 18.00
1216 A226 $5 multicolored 20.00 20.00
Nos. 1209-1216 (8) 59.00 53.85

Souvenir Sheets

1217 A226 $6 multi (#1419) 27.50 25.00
1218 A226 $6 multi (#1420) 27.50 25.00

Antigua Nos. 1401-1410 (Butterflies) Overprinted

1991, Oct. 18

1219 A225 10c multicolored 4.50 2.10
1220 A225 35c multicolored 4.75 2.75
1221 A225 50c multicolored 5.75 3.00
1222 A225 75c multicolored 6.75 3.25
1223 A225 $1 multicolored 7.00 4.25
1224 A225 $2 multicolored 9.00 9.00
1225 A225 $4 multicolored 14.00 14.00
1226 A225 $5 multicolored 16.00 16.00
Nos. 1219-1226 (8) 67.75 54.35

Souvenir Sheets

1227 A225 $6 multi (#1409) 37.50 30.00
1228 A225 $6 multi (#1410) 37.50 30.00

Antigua Nos. 1446-1455 (Royal Family) Overprinted

1991, Nov. 18

1229 CD347 10c multicolored 4.50 2.40
1230 CD347 15c multicolored 5.75 1.75
1231 CD347 20c multicolored 5.75 1.75
1232 CD347 40c multicolored 6.75 1.75
1233 CD347 $1 multicolored 7.00 5.50
1234 CD347 $2 multicolored 9.00 9.75
1235 CD347 $4 multicolored 15.00 21.00
1236 CD347 $5 multicolored 17.50 21.00
Nos. 1229-1236 (8) 71.25 64.90

Souvenir Sheets

1237 CD347 $4 multi (#1454) 37.50 37.50
1238 CD347 $4 multi (#1455) 37.50 37.50

Antigua Nos. 1503-1510 (Christmas) Overprinted

1991, Dec. 24 *Perf. 12*

1239 A238 10c multicolored 3.00 1.75
1240 A238 30c multicolored 3.25 .95
1241 A238 40c multicolored 3.50 1.10
1242 A238 60c multicolored 3.75 1.75
1243 A238 $1 multicolored 4.00 2.75
1244 A238 $3 multicolored 7.00 7.00
1245 A238 $4 multicolored 10.50 10.50
1246 A238 $5 multicolored 13.00 13.00
Nos. 1239-1246 (8) 48.00 38.80

Antigua Nos. 1421-1435 (Van Gogh Paintings) Overprinted

1992, Feb. 20 *Perf. 13½*

1249 A227 5c multicolored 2.00 2.00
1250 A227 10c multicolored 2.25 2.00
1251 A227 15c multicolored 2.25 1.10
1252 A227 25c multicolored 2.25 1.10
1253 A227 30c multicolored 2.40 1.10
1254 A227 40c multicolored 2.50 1.10
1255 A227 50c multicolored 2.50 1.75
1256 A227 75c multicolored 4.25 2.40
1257 A227 $2 multicolored 7.00 3.25
1258 A227 $3 multicolored 8.50 8.50
1259 A227 $4 multicolored 10.50 10.50
1260 A227 $5 multicolored 13.00 13.00
Nos. 1249-1260 (12) 59.40 47.80

Size: 102x76mm

Imperf

1261 A227 $5 multi (#1433) 19.00 19.00
1262 A227 $5 multi (#1434) 19.00 19.00
1263 A227 $6 multi 22.50 22.50

Antigua Nos. 1476-1485 (De Gaulle) Overprinted

1992, Apr. 7 **Litho.** *Perf. 14*

1264 A231 10c multi 3.25 2.10
1265 A231 15c multi, vert. 3.50 2.10
1266 A231 45c multi, vert. 4.75 1.25
1267 A231 60c multi, vert. 5.25 1.75
1268 A231 $1 multi 6.00 3.25
1269 A231 $2 multi 9.00 9.00
1270 A231 $4 multi 16.00 16.00
1271 A231 $5 multi, vert. 17.00 17.00
Nos. 1264-1271 (8) 64.75 52.45

Souvenir Sheets

1272 A231 $6 multi (#1484) 32.50 30.00
1273 A231 $6 multi (#1485) 32.50 30.00

Antigua Nos. 1551-1560 (Easter) Overprinted

1992, Apr. 16 **Litho.** *Perf. 14x13½*

1274 A242 10c multicolored 2.25 1.40
1275 A242 15c multicolored 2.50 1.40
1276 A242 30c multicolored 2.75 1.00
1277 A242 40c multicolored 3.00 1.40
1278 A242 $1 multicolored 4.75 3.25
1279 A242 $2 multicolored 8.75 8.75
1280 A242 $4 multicolored 12.50 12.50
1281 A242 $5 multicolored 16.00 16.00
Nos. 1274-1281 (8) 52.50 45.70

Souvenir Sheets

1282 A242 $6 multi (#1559) 26.00 26.00
1283 A242 $6 multi (#1560) 26.00 26.00

Antigua Nos. 1489-1492 (Scouts) Overprinted

1992, June 19 **Litho.** *Perf. 14*

1284 A234 75c multi 4.00 2.50
1285 A234 $2 multi, vert. 4.25 4.25
1286 A234 $3.50 multi 6.00 6.00
Nos. 1284-1286 (3) 14.25 12.75

Souvenir Sheet

1287 A234 $5 multi, vert. 30.00 30.00

Antigua Nos. 1493-1494 (Mozart) Overprinted

1992, June 19

1288 A235 $1.50 multi 12.50 6.75
1289 A235 $4 multi 15.00 15.00

Antigua Nos. 1495-1496 (Glider, Locomotive) Overprinted

1992, June 19

1290 A236 $2 multi 4.25 4.25
1291 A236 $2.50 multi, vert. 12.50 6.75

Antigua Nos. 1499-1502 (Brandenburg Gate) Overprinted

1992, June 19

1292 A237 25c multicolored 1.40 1.00
1293 A237 $2 multicolored 4.25 4.25
1294 A237 $3 multicolored 4.75 4.75

Souvenir Sheet

1295 A237 $4 multicolored 32.50 32.50
Nos. 1292-1295 (4) 42.90 42.50

Antigua No. 1488 (Pearl Harbor) Overprinted

1992, Aug. 12 **Litho.** *Perf. 14½x15*

1295A A233 $1 Sheet of 10, #b-k 125.00 95.00

Antigua Nos. 1571-1578 (America) Overprinted

1992, Oct. 12 **Litho.** *Perf. 14*

1296 A244 15c multicolored 2.75 1.25
1297 A244 30c multicolored 3.00 1.75
1298 A244 40c multicolored 3.50 1.90
1299 A244 $1 multicolored 5.50 5.00
1300 A244 $2 multicolored 13.00 9.75
1301 A244 $4 multicolored 20.00 20.00
Nos. 1296-1301 (6) 47.75 39.65

Souvenir Sheets

1302 A244 $6 multicolored 25.00 22.50
1303 A244 $6 multicolored 25.00 22.50

Antigua Nos. 1599-1600 (America) Overprinted

1992, Oct. 12 *Perf. 14½*

1304 A247 $1 multicolored 6.25 5.50
1305 A247 $2 multicolored 11.50 10.50

Antigua Nos. 1513-1518 (QEII Accession) Overprinted

1992, Nov. 3 *Perf. 14*

1306 CD348 10c multicolored 9.50 3.25
1307 CD348 30c multicolored 11.50 2.25
1308 CD348 $1 multicolored 16.00 5.75
1309 CD348 $5 multicolored 27.50 22.50
Nos. 1306-1309 (4) 64.50 33.75

Souvenir Sheets

1310 CD348 $6 multi (#1517) 40.00 32.50
1311 CD348 $6 multi (#1518) 40.00 32.50

Antigua Nos. 1541-1550 (Dinosaurs) Ovptd. "BARBUDA / MAIL"

1992, Dec. 8

1312 A241 10c multicolored 4.75 3.00
1313 A241 15c multicolored 5.50 2.75
1314 A241 30c multicolored 6.75 1.75
1315 A241 50c multicolored 6.75 3.25
1316 A241 $1 multicolored 8.25 5.50
1317 A241 $2 multicolored 13.00 11.50
1318 A241 $4 multicolored 16.00 16.00
1319 A241 $5 multicolored 19.00 19.00
Nos. 1312-1319 (8) 80.00 62.75

Souvenir Sheets

1320 A241 $6 multi (#1549) 40.00 30.00
1321 A241 $6 multi (#1550) 40.00 30.00

Antigua Nos. 1609-1618 (Christmas) Ovptd. "BARBUDA MAIL"

1992, Dec. 8 Litho. *Perf. 13½x14*

1322 A251 10c multicolored 4.00 1.25
1323 A251 25c multicolored 4.00 1.25
1324 A251 30c multicolored 4.00 1.60
1325 A251 40c multicolored 4.50 1.90
1326 A251 60c multicolored 5.75 2.75
1327 A251 $1 multicolored 7.00 3.25
1328 A251 $4 multicolored 17.00 18.00
1329 A251 $5 multicolored 21.00 21.00
Nos. 1322-1329 (8) 67.25 51.00

Souvenir Sheets

1330 A251 $6 multi (#1616) 35.00 35.00
1331 A251 $6 multi (#1617) 35.00 35.00

Antigua No. 1601 (Mega-Event Stamp Show) Ovptd. "BARBUDA MAIL"

1992 Litho. *Perf. 14*

Souvenir Sheet

1332 A248 $6 multicolored 29.00 29.00

Antigua Nos. 1519-1528 (Mushrooms) Ovptd.

1993, Jan. 25 Litho. *Perf. 14*

1333 A239 10c multicolored 2.50 1.10
1334 A239 15c multicolored 3.25 1.10
1335 A239 30c multicolored 4.25 1.75
1336 A239 40c multicolored 5.75 3.25
1337 A239 $1 multicolored 8.00 5.25
1338 A239 $2 multicolored 14.00 14.00
1339 A239 $4 multicolored 18.00 18.00
1340 A239 $5 multicolored 22.50 22.50
Nos. 1332-1339 (8) 84.75 73.45

Souvenir Sheets

1341 A239 $6 multi (#1527) 40.00 37.50
1342 A239 $6 multi (#1528) 40.00 37.50

Antigua Nos. 1561-1570 (Spanish Art) Ovptd.

1993, Mar. 22 Litho. *Perf. 13*

1343 A243 10c multicolored 3.25 2.00
1344 A243 15c multicolored 3.75 2.00
1345 A243 30c multicolored 4.50 2.00
1346 A243 40c multicolored 5.25 2.00
1347 A243 $1 multicolored 7.00 4.50
1348 A243 $2 multicolored 9.25 9.25
1349 A243 $4 multicolored 15.00 15.00
1350 A243 $5 multicolored 17.00 17.00
Nos. 1343-1350 (8) 65.00 53.75

Imperf

Size: 120x95mm

1351 A243 $6 multi (#1569) 32.50 32.50
1352 A243 $6 multi (#1570) 32.50 32.50

Antigua Nos. 1589-1598 (Nature) Ovptd.

1993, May 10 Litho. *Perf. 14*

1353 A246 10c multicolored 3.75 2.00
1354 A246 25c multicolored 4.25 2.00
1355 A246 45c multicolored 4.75 2.00
1356 A246 60c multicolored 5.00 2.25
1357 A246 $1 multicolored 6.50 3.75
1358 A246 $2 multicolored 9.00 9.00
1359 A246 $4 multicolored 14.50 14.50
1360 A246 $5 multicolored 17.00 17.00
Nos. 1353-1360 (8) 64.75 52.50

Souvenir Sheets

1361 A246 $6 multi (#1597) 30.00 27.50
1362 A246 $6 multi (#1598) 30.00 27.50

Antigua Nos. 1603-1608 (Inventors/Pioneers) Ovptd.

1993, June 29 Litho. *Perf. 14*

1363 A250 10c multicolored 1.25 *1.50*
1364 A250 25c multicolored 4.50 1.40
1365 A250 30c multicolored 2.75 1.40
1366 A250 40c multicolored 4.50 1.40
1367 A250 60c multicolored 8.00 2.75
1368 A250 $1 multicolored 5.75 4.25
1369 A250 $4 multicolored 12.50 12.50
1370 A250 $5 multicolored 15.00 15.00
Nos. 1363-1370 (8) 54.25 40.20

Souvenir Sheets

1371 A250 $6 multi (#1607) 26.00 26.00
1372 A250 $6 multi (#1608) 26.00 26.00

Antigua Nos. 1619-1632 (Anniversaries/Events) Ovptd.

1993, Aug. 16 Litho. *Perf. 14*

1373 A252 10c multi 3.75 2.00
1374 A252 40c multi 6.50 1.75
1375 A253 45c multi 1.40 1.00
1376 A252 75c multi 2.00 1.75
1377 A252 $1 multi 4.50 3.00
1378 A252 $1.50 multi 5.75 4.50
1379 A252 $2 multi 20.00 9.25
1380 A253 $2 multi (#1626) 11.50 8.00
1381 A253 $2 multi (#1627) 5.75 5.75
1382 A252 $2.25 multi 5.75 5.75
1383 A252 $3 multi 8.25 8.25
1384 A252 $4 multi (#1630) 10.50 10.50
1385 A252 $4 multi (#1631) 10.50 10.50
1386 A252 $6 multi 12.50 12.50
Nos. 1373-1386 (14) 108.65 84.50

Souvenir Sheets

1387 A252 $6 multi (#1633) *22.50 22.50*
1388 A252 $6 multi (#1634) *22.50 22.50*
1389 A252 $6 multi (#1635) *22.50 22.50*
1390 A252 $6 multi (#1636) *22.50 22.50*
Nos. 1387-1390 (4) 90.00 90.00

Antigua Nos. 1650-1659 (Flowers) Ovptd.

1993, Sept. 21 Litho. *Perf. 14*

1391 A256 15c multicolored 3.00 2.00
1392 A256 25c multicolored 3.75 1.40
1393 A256 30c multicolored 4.25 1.75
1394 A256 40c multicolored 4.75 2.00
1395 A256 $1 multicolored 5.25 4.25
1396 A256 $2 multicolored 6.50 6.50
1397 A256 $4 multicolored 12.50 12.50
1398 A256 $5 multicolored 14.50 14.50
Nos. 1391-1398 (8) 54.50 44.90

Souvenir Sheets

1399 A256 $6 multi (#1658) 25.00 25.00
1400 A256 $6 multi (#1659) 25.00 25.00

Barbuda Nos. 1164-1171 Overprinted

1993, Oct. 9 Litho. *Perf. 14*

1400A B52 60c multi (#1164) *2.75 2.75*
1400B B52 $2 multi (#1168) *8.75 8.75*
1400C B52 $4 multi (#1169) *17.50 17.50*
1400D B52 $7 multi (#1171) *30.00 30.00*
Nos. 1400A-1400D (4) 59.00 59.00

Antigua No. 1660-1662 (Endangered Species) Ovptd.

1993, Nov. 11 Litho. *Perf. 14*

1401 A257 $1 Sheet of 12, #a.-l. 100.00 100.00

Souvenir Sheets

1401M A257 $6 multi (#1661) 20.00 20.00
1401N A257 $6 multi (#1662) 20.00 20.00

Antigua Nos. 1647, 1649 (Louvre) Overprinted

1994, Jan. 6 Litho. *Perf. 12*

1401O A255 $1 Sheet of 8, #p-w, + label *55.00 55.00*

Souvenir Sheet

1994, Jan. 6 Litho. *Perf. 14½*

1401X A255 $6 multi (#1649) *45.00 45.00*

Antigua Nos. 1697-1710 (Soccer) Ovptd.

1994, Mar. 3 Litho. *Perf. 14*

1404-1415 A267 $2 Set of 12 75.00 75.00

Souvenir Sheets

1416 A267 $6 multi (#1709) 27.50 27.50
1417 A267 $6 multi (#1710) 27.50 27.50

Antigua Nos. 1676-1678 (Japanese Royal Wedding) Ovptd.

1994, Apr. 21 Litho. *Perf. 14*

1418 A260 40c multicolored 2.50 1.25
1419 A260 $3 multicolored 5.75 5.75

Souvenir Sheet

1420 A260 $6 multicolored 20.00 20.00

Antigua Nos. 1679-1682 (Picasso) Ovptd.

1994, Apr. 21

1421-1423 A261 Set of 3 12.00 10.00

Souvenir Sheet

1424 A261 $6 multicolored 20.00 20.00

Antigua Nos. 1683-1685 (Copernicus) Ovptd.

1994, Apr. 21

1425 A262 40c multicolored 2.50 1.25
1426 A262 $4 multicolored 7.50 7.50

Souvenir Sheet

1427 A262 $5 multicolored 20.00 20.00

Antigua Nos. 1686-1688 (Willy Brandt) Ovptd.

1994, Apr. 21

1428 A263 30c multicolored 2.50 1.25
1429 A263 $4 multicolored 7.50 7.50

Souvenir Sheet

1430 A263 $6 multicolored 17.50 17.50

Antigua Nos. 1692-1693 (Clinton) Ovptd.

1994, Apr. 21

1431 A265 $5 multicolored 7.75 7.75

Souvenir Sheet

1432 A265 $6 multicolored 20.00 20.00

Antigua Nos. 1694-1696 (Lillehammer Olympics) Ovptd.

1994, Apr. 21

1433 A266 15c multicolored 2.75 2.00
1434 A266 $5 multicolored 7.75 7.75

Souvenir Sheet

1435 A266 $6 multicolored 17.50 17.50

Antigua Nos. 1732-1735 (Masons) Ovptd.

1994, Apr. 21

1436-1439 A270 Set of 4 30.00 9.50

Antigua Nos. 1711-1720 (Aviation) Ovptd.

1994, June 15

1440-1446 A268 Set of 7 55.00 52.50

Souvenir Sheets

1447 A268 $6 multi (#1718) 24.00 24.00
1448 A268 $6 multi (#1719) 24.00 24.00
1449 A268 $6 multi (#1720) 24.00 24.00

Antigua Nos. 1736-1741 (Cars) Ovptd.

1994, June 15

1450-1453 A271 30c Set of 4 42.50 42.50

Souvenir Sheets

1454 A271 $6 multi (#1740) 22.50 22.50
1455 A271 $6 multi (#1741) 22.50 22.50

Antigua Nos. 1753-1762 (Fine Art) Overprinted

1994, Aug. 18 Litho. *Perf. 13½x14*

1455A-1455H A273 Set of 8 47.50 47.50

Souvenir Sheets

1455I A273 $6 multi (#1761) *22.50 22.50*
1455J A273 $6 multi (#1762) *22.50 22.50*

Antigua Nos. 1689-1691 (Polska '93) Ovptd.

1994, Sept. 21 Litho. *Perf. 14*

1456 A264 $1 multicolored 8.50 5.75
1457 A264 $3 multicolored 17.50 17.50

Souvenir Sheet

1458 A264 $6 multicolored 26.00 26.00

Antigua Nos. 1786-1795 (Orchids) Ovptd.

1994, Sept. 21 Litho. *Perf. 14*

1459-1466 A279 Set of 8 65.00 52.50

Souvenir Sheets

1467 A279 $6 multi (#1794) 32.50 32.50
1468 A279 $6 multi (#1795) 32.50 32.50

Antigua Nos. 1776-1781 (Sierra Club) Ovptd.

1994, Nov. 3 Litho. *Perf. 14*

1469 A277 $1.50 multi (#1776) 47.50 40.00
1470 A277 $1.50 multi (#1777) 47.50 40.00

Souvenir Sheets

1471 A277 $1.50 multi (#1778) 9.00 9.00
1472 A277 $1.50 multi (#1779) 9.00 9.00
1472A A277 $1.50 multi (#1780) 9.00 9.00
1472B A277 $1.50 multi (#1781) 9.00 9.00

Antigua Nos. 1835-1842 (Soccer) Ovptd.

1995, Jan. 12 Litho. *Perf. 14*

1473-1478 A291 Set of 6 35.00 35.00

Souvenir Sheets

1479 A291 $6 multi (#1841) 17.50 16.00
1480 A291 $6 multi (#1842) 17.50 16.00

Antigua Nos. 1857-1866 (Christmas) Ovptd.

1995, Jan. 12 Litho. *Perf. 14*

1481-1488 A295 Set of 8 35.00 30.00

Souvenir Sheets

Perf. 13½x14

1489 A295 $6 multi (#1865) 17.50 17.50
1490 A295 $6 multi (#1866) 17.50 17.50

Antigua Nos. 1829-1834 (Country Music) Ovptd.

1996, Feb. 14 Litho. *Perf. 14*

1491 A290 75c multi (#1829) 15.00 14.00
1492 A290 75c multi (#1830) 15.00 14.00
1493 A290 75c multi (#1831) 15.00 14.00

Souvenir Sheets

1494 A290 $6 multi (#1832) 17.00 17.00
1495 A290 $6 multi (#1833) 17.00 17.00
1496 A290 $6 multi (#1834) 17.00 17.00

Antigua Nos. 1867-1881 (Birds) Ovptd.

1996 Litho. *Perf. 14½x14*

1497 A296 15c multi (#1867) 1.10 .90
1498 A296 25c multi (#1868) 1.25 1.00
1499 A296 35c multi (#1869) 1.40 1.00
1500 A296 40c multi (#1870) 1.50 1.00
1501 A296 45c multi (#1871) 1.75 1.00
1502 A296 60c multi (#1872) 1.75 1.40
1503 A296 65c multi (#1873) 1.75 1.40
1504 A296 70c multi (#1873) 2.00 1.60
1505 A296 75c multi (#1874) 2.10 1.75
1506 A296 90c multi (#1875) 2.25 *3.50*
1507 A296 $1.20 multi (#1876) 2.50 *5.75*
1508 A296 $2 multi (#1877) 3.25 *8.00*
1509 A296 $5 multi (#1878) 7.00 *10.00*
1510 A296 $10 multi (#1879) 14.00 *13.50*
1511 A296 $20 multi (#1880) 21.00 *29.00*
Nos. 1497-1511 (15) 64.60 *80.80*

Antigua Nos. 1806-1808 (Marine Life) Ovptd.

1996, Jan. 22 Litho. *Perf. 14*

1512 A281 50c Sheet of 9, #a.-i. 16.00 16.00

Souvenir Sheets

1513 A281 $6 multi (#1807) 15.00 15.00
1514 A281 $6 multi (#1808) 15.00 15.00

Antigua Nos. 1949-1956 (Christmas) Ovptd.

1996, Jan. 22 *Perf. 13½x14*

1515-1520 A314 Set of 6 22.50 22.50

Souvenir Sheets

1521 A314 $5 multi (#1955) 14.00 14.00
1522 A314 $6 multi (#1956) 16.00 16.00

Antigua Nos. 1763-1765 (Hong Kong '94) Overprinted

1995, Feb. 24 Litho. *Perf. 14*

1523 A274 40c multi (#1763) *9.00 6.75*
1524 A274 40c multi (#1764) *9.00 6.75*
a. Horiz. pair, #1523-1524 *19.00 19.00*

Miniature Sheet

1525 A274 40c Sheet of 6, #a-f (#1765) *19.00 19.00*

Antigua Nos. 1814-1815 (Olympics) Overprinted

1995, Feb. 24 Litho. *Perf. 14*

1526-1527 A284 Set of 2 *15.00 15.00*

An additional item was released in this set. The editors would like to examine it.

Antigua Nos. 1782-1785 (Year of the Dog) Overprinted

1995, Apr. 4 Litho. *Perf. 14*

1529 A278 50c Sheet of 12, #a-l *22.50 20.00*
1530 A278 75c Sheet of 12, #a-l *27.50 22.00*

Souvenir Sheets

1531 A278 $6 multi (#1784) *26.00 21.00*
1532 A278 $6 multi (#1785) *26.00 21.00*

Antigua Nos. 1817-1820 (Cricket) Overprinted

1995, May 18 Litho. *Perf. 14*
1533-1535 A286 Set of 3 *22.50 20.00*

Souvenir Sheet

1535A A286 $3 multi (#1820) *19.00 16.00*

Antigua Nos. 1824-1828 (Philakorea '94) Overprinted

Perf. 14, 13½ (#1494H)

1995, July 12 Litho.
1536-1538 A288 Set of 3 *40.00 40.00*

Miniature Sheet

1539 A289 75c Sheet of 8, #a-h (#1827) *20.00 20.00*

Souvenir Sheet

1540 A288 $4 multi (#1828) *55.00 55.00*

Antigua Nos. 1843-1845 (Caribbean) Overprinted

1995, May 18 Litho. *Perf. 14*
1541-1543 A292 Set of 3 *10.50 10.50*

Antigua No. 1809 (Year Family) Overprinted

1995, July 12 Litho. *Perf. 14*
1543A A282 90c multi *6.25 6.25*

Antigua Nos. 1821-1823 (Moon Landing) Overprinted

1995, July 12 Litho. *Perf. 14*
1544 A287 $1.50 Sheet of 6, #a-f (#1821) *27.50 20.00*
1545 A287 $1.50 Sheet of 6, #a-f (#1822) *27.50 20.00*

Souvenir Sheet

1545G A287 $6 multi (#1823) *35.00 30.00*

Antigua Nos. 1810-1813 (D-Day) Ovptd.

1995, Sept. 29 Litho. *Perf. 14*
1546-1548 A283 Set of 3 *42.50 32.50*

Souvenir Sheet

1549 A283 $6 multi (#1813) *35.00 35.00*

End of World War II, 50th Anniv. — B53

Design: German bombers over St. Paul's Cathedral, London.

1995, Nov. 13 Litho. *Perf. 13*
1550 B53 $8 multicolored 42.50 37.50

For overprints and surcharges see Nos. 1639, B3.

Queen Elizabeth, the Queen Mother, 95th Birthday B54

1995, Nov. 20
1551 B54 $7.50 multicolored 32.50 32.50

For overprints and surcharges see Nos. 1638, B2.

United Nations, 50th Anniv. — B55

1995, Nov. 27
1552 B55 $8 New York City 22.50 22.50

For surcharge see No. B4.

Antigua Nos. 1955-1956 (Christmas) Overprinted

1996, Jan. 22 Litho. *Perf. 13½x14*

Souvenir Sheets

1552G A314 $5 multi (#1955) *13.00 12.00*
1552H A314 $6 multi (#1956) *14.50 13.00*

Six additional items were issued in this set. The editors would like to examine any examples.

Antigua Nos. 1848, 1850-1851, 1854-1856 (Birds) Ovptd.

1996, Feb. 14 Litho. *Perf. 14*
1553 A294 15c multi (#1848) .85 .85
1553A A294 40c multi (#1850) 2.40 2.40
1554 A294 $1 multi (#1851) 3.25 3.25
1555 A294 $4 multi (#1854) 12.50 12.50
Nos. 1553-1555 (4) 19.00 19.00

Souvenir Sheets

1556 A294 $6 multi (#1855) 17.50 17.50
1557 A294 $6 multi (#1856) 17.50 17.50

Antigua Nos. 1882-1890 (Prehistoric Animals) Ovptd.

1996, June 13 Litho. *Perf. 14*
1558-1563 A297 Set of 6 29.00 29.00
1564 A297 75c Sheet of 12, #a-l 32.50 32.50

Souvenir Sheets

1565 A297 $6 multi (#1889) 22.50 22.50
1566 A297 $6 multi (#1890) 22.50 22.50

Antigua Nos. 1891-1898 (Atlanta Olympics) Ovptd.

1996, July 16 Litho. *Perf. 14*
1567-1572 A298 Set of 6 24.00 24.00

Souvenir Sheets

1573 A298 $6 multi (#1897) 16.00 16.00
1574 A298 $6 multi (#1898) 16.00 16.00

Antigua Nos. 1930-1933 (Boy Scouts) Ovptd.

1996, Sept. 10
1575 A310 $1.20 Strip of 3, #a.-c. (#1930) 14.50 14.50
1576 A310 $1.20 Strip of 3, #a.-c. (#1931) 14.50 14.50

Souvenir Sheets

1577 A310 $6 multi (#1932) 11.00 11.00
1578 A310 $6 multi (#1933) 11.00 11.00

Antigua Nos. 1945-1948 (Nobel Prize) Ovptd.

1996, Oct. 25 Litho. *Perf. 14*
1579 A313 $1 Sheet of 9, #a.-i. (#1945) 16.00 16.00
1580 A313 $1 Sheet of 9, #a.-i. (#1946) 16.00 16.00

Souvenir Sheets

1581 A313 $6 multi (#1947) 15.00 15.00
1582 A313 $6 multi (#1948) 15.00 15.00

Antigua Nos. 2001-2002 (QEII Birthday) Ovptd.

1996, Nov. 14 *Perf. 13½x14*
1583 A323 $2 Strip of 3, #a.-c. 16.00 16.00

Souvenir Sheet

1584 A323 $6 multicolored 18.00 18.00

Antigua Nos. 2018-2025 (Christmas) Ovptd.

1997, Jan. 28 Litho. *Perf. 13½x14*
1585-1590 A328 Set of 6 15.00 15.00

Souvenir Sheets

1591 A328 $6 multi (#2024) 15.00 15.00
1592 A328 $6 multi (#2025) 15.00 15.00

Antigua Nos. 1905-1906 (FAO) Ovptd.

1997, Feb. 24 *Perf. 14*
1593 A301 Strip of 3, #a.-c. 12.50 12.50

Souvenir Sheet

1594 A301 $6 multicolored 16.00 16.00

Antigua Nos. 1907-1908 (Rotary) Ovptd.

1997, Feb. 24
1595 A302 $5 multicolored 16.00 16.00

Souvenir Sheet

1596 A302 $6 multicolored 18.00 18.00

Antigua Nos. 1899-1902 (World War II) Ovptd.

1997, Apr. 4 Litho. *Perf. 14*
1597 A299 $1.20 Sheet of 6, #a.-f. 32.50 32.50
1598 A299 $1.20 Sheet of 8, #a.-h. 24.00 24.00

Souvenir Sheets

1599 A299 $3 multi (#1901) 22.50 22.50
1600 A299 $6 multi (#1902) 24.00 24.00

Antigua Nos. 1903-1904 (UN) Ovptd.

1997 Litho. *Perf. 14*
1601 A300 Strip of 3, #a.-c. 10.50 10.50

Souvenir Sheet

1602 A300 $6 multicolored 14.50 14.50

Antigua Nos. 1909-1910 (Queen Mother) Ovptd.

1997 *Perf. 13½x14*
1603 A303 $1.50 Strip or block of 4, #a.-d. 21.00 21.00

Souvenir Sheet

1604 A303 $6 multicolored 22.50 22.50

Antigua Nos. 1913-1917 (Bees) Ovptd.

1997 Litho. *Perf. 14*
1605-1608 A305 Set of 4 17.50 17.50

Souvenir Sheet

1609 A305 $6 multicolored 18.00 17.00

Antigua Nos. 1918-1919 (Cats) Ovptd.

1997
1610 A306 45c Sheet of 12, #a-l 24.00 24.00

Souvenir Sheet

1611 A306 $6 multicolored 18.00 18.00

Antigua Nos. 1928-1929 (Flowers) Ovptd.

1997
1612 A309 75c Sheet of 12, #a-l 20.00 20.00

Souvenir Sheet

1613 A309 $6 multicolored 18.00 18.00

Antigua Nos. 1934-1942 (Trains) Ovptd.

1997, May 30 Litho. *Perf. 14*
1614-1619 A311 Set of 6 14.00 14.00
1620 A311 $1.20 Sheet of 9, #a.-i. 16.00 16.00

Souvenir Sheets

1621 A311 $6 multi (#1941) 16.00 16.00
1621A A311 $6 multi (#1942) 16.00 16.00

Antigua Nos. 1911-1912 (Ducks) Ovptd.

1997 Litho. *Perf. 14*
1622 A304 75c Sheet of 12, #a-l 25.00 25.00

Souvenir Sheet

1623 A304 $6 multicolored 21.00 21.00

Antigua Nos. 1943-1944 (Birds) Ovptd.

1997
1624 A312 75c Sheet of 12, #a-l 8.75 8.75

Souvenir Sheet

1625 A312 $6 multicolored 10.00 10.00

Antigua Nos. 1967-1970 (Mushrooms) Ovptd.

1997
1626 A317 75c Strips of 4, #a.-d. (#1967) 10.00 10.00
1627 A317 75c Strips of 4, #a.-d. (#1968) 10.00 10.00

Souvenir Sheets

1628 A317 $6 multi (#1969) 15.00 15.00
1629 A317 $6 multi (#1970) 15.00 15.00

Antigua Nos. 1970A-1974 (Ships) Ovptd.

1997, Nov. 3 Litho. *Perf. 14*
1629A-1629F A318 Set of 6 7.00 7.00
1629G A318 $1.20 Sheet of 6, #k-p (#1971) 15.00 15.00
1629H A318 $1.50 Sheet of 6, #q-v (#1972) 15.00 15.00

Souvenir Sheets

1629I A318 $6 multi (#1973) 12.50 12.50
1629J A318 $6 multi (#1974) 12.50 12.50

Antigua Nos. 2111-2118 (Christmas) Ovptd.

1997 Litho. *Perf. 14*
1630-1635 A345 Set of 6 13.50 13.50

Souvenir Sheets

1636 A345 $6 multi (#2117) 11.00 11.00
1637 A345 $6 multi (#2118) 11.00 11.00

Antigua Nos. 2069-2070 (Royal Anniv.) Ovptd.

1997, Nov. 3 Litho. *Perf. 14*
1637A A337 $1 Sheet of 6, #c-h (#2069) 18.00 18.00

Souvenir Sheet

1637B A337 $6 multi (#2070) 24.00 24.00

Nos. 1550-1551 Ovptd. in Gold

1997, July 25 Litho. *Perf. 13*
1638 B54 $7.50 on #1551 17.50 17.50
1639 B53 $8 on #1550 17.50 17.50

Antigua Nos. 1983-1986 (Sea Birds) Ovptd.

1998 Litho. *Perf. 14*
1640 A320 75c Vert. strip, #a.-d. (#1983) 8.50 8.50
1641 A320 75c Vert. strip, #a.-d. (#1984) 8.50 8.50

Souvenir Sheets

1643 A320 $5 multi (#1985) 10.50 10.50
1644 A320 $6 multi (#1986) 11.50 11.50

Antigua Nos. 1975-1982 (Atlanta Olympics) Overprinted

1998, Mar. 25 Litho. *Perf. 14*
1644A-1644D A319 Set of 4 *12.50 12.50*
1644E A319 90c Sheet of 9, #f-n (#1979) *14.50 14.50*
1644O A319 90c Sheet of 9, #p-x (#1980) *14.50 14.50*

Souvenir Sheets

1644Y A319 $5 multi (#1981) *11.00 11.00*
1644Z A319 $6 multi (#1982) *11.00 11.00*

Antigua Nos. 2003-2004 (Cavalry) Ovptd.

1998 Litho. *Perf. 14*
1645 A324 60c Block of 4, #a.-d. 13.50 13.50

Souvenir Sheet

1646 A324 $6 multi 14.50 14.50

Antigua Nos. 2013-2017 (Radio) Overprinted

1998, Mar. 25 Litho. *Perf. 14*
1646A-1646D A327 Set of 4 *15.00 15.00*

Souvenir Sheet

1646E A327 $6 multi *19.00 19.00*

Antigua Nos. 2094-2102 (Soccer) Ovptd.

1998

1647-1652 A342 Set of 6 13.50 13.50
1653 A342 $1 Sheet of 8 + label 22.50 22.50

Souvenir Sheets

1654 A342 $6 multi (#2101) 12.00 12.00
1655 A342 $6 multi (#2102) 12.00 12.00

Antigua Nos. 2005-2008 (UNICEF) Ovptd.

1998 Litho. *Perf. 14*

1656-1658 A325 Set of 3 12.50 12.50

Souvenir Sheet

1659 A325 $6 multicolored 15.00 15.00

Antigua Nos. 2009-2012 (Jerusalem) Ovptd.

1998

1660-1662 A326 Set of 3 13.50 13.50

Souvenir Sheet

1663 A326 $6 multicolored 14.50 14.50

Antigua Nos. 2119-2122 (Diana) Ovptd.

1998 Litho. *Perf. 14*

1664 A346 $1.65 Sheet of 6, #a-f (#2119) 15.00 15.00
1665 A346 $1.65 Sheet of 6, #a-f (#2120) 15.00 15.00

Souvenir Sheets

1666 A346 $6 multi (#2121) 10.00 10.00
1667 A346 $6 multi (#2122) 10.00 10.00

Antigua Nos. 2037-2038 (Broadway) Ovptd.

1998 Litho. *Perf. 14*

1668 A330 $1 Sheet of 9, #a.-i. (#2037) 26.00 26.00

Souvenir Sheet

1669 A330 $6 multi (#2038) 22.50 22.50

Antigua Nos. 2063-2064 (Chaplin) Ovtpd.

1998

1670 A334 $1 Sheet of 9, #a.-i. (#2063) 26.00 26.00

Souvenir Sheet

1671 A334 $6 multi (#2064) 22.50 22.50

Antigua Nos. 2039-2047 (Butterflies) Ovptd.

1998 Litho. *Perf. 14*

1672-1675 A331 Set of 4 15.00 15.00
1676 A331 $1.10 Sheet of 9, #a.-i. (#2043) 21.00 21.00
1677 A331 $1.10 Sheet of 9, #a.-i. (#2044) 21.00 21.00

Souvenir Sheets

1678 A331 $6 multi (#2045) 14.50 14.50
1679 A331 $6 multi (#2046) 14.50 14.50
1680 A331 $6 multi (#2047) 14.50 14.50

Antigua Nos. 2140-2148 (Lighthouses) Ovptd.

1998

1681-1688 A349 Set of 8 27.50 27.50

Souvenir Sheet

1689 A349 $6 multi (#2148) 27.50 27.50

Antigua Nos. 2211-2219 (Christmas) Ovptd.

1998

1690-1696 A366 Set of 7 17.50 17.50

Souvenir Sheets

1697 A366 $6 multi (#2218) 12.00 12.00
1698 A366 $6 multi (#2219) 12.00 12.00

Antigua Nos. 2058-2062 (Animals) Ovptd.

1998 Litho. *Perf. 14*

1699 A333 $1.20 Sheet of 6, #a.-f. (#2058) 16.00 16.00
1700 A333 $1.65 Sheet of 6, #a.-f. (#2059) 19.00 19.00

Souvenir Sheets

1701 A333 $6 multi (#2060) 13.00 13.00
1702 A333 $6 multi (#2061) 13.00 13.00
1703 A333 $6 multi (#2062) 13.00 13.00

Antigua Nos. 2067-2068 (Von Stephan) Ovptd.

1999 Litho. *Perf. 14*

1704 A336 $1.75 Sheet of 3, #a.-c. 18.00 18.00

Souvenir Sheet

1705 A336 $6 multi (#2068) 15.00 15.00

Antigua Nos. 2071-2072 (Fairy Tales) Ovptd.

1999 *Perf. 13½x14*

1706 A338 $1.75 Sheet of 3, #a.-c. 18.00 18.00

Souvenir Sheet

1707 A338 $6 multi (#2072) 14.50 14.50

Antigua Nos. 2084-2093 (Orchids) Ovptd.

1999 Litho. *Perf. 14*

1708-1713 A341 Set of 6 18.00 18.00
1714 A341 $1.65 Sheet of 8, #a.-h. (#2090) 27.50 27.50
1715 A341 $1.65 Sheet of 8, #a.-h. (#2091) 27.50 27.50

Souvenir Sheets

1716 A341 $6 multi (#2092) 17.00 17.00
1717 A341 $6 multi (#2093) 17.00 17.00

Antigua Nos. 2065-2066 (Rotary) Ovptd.

1999 Litho. *Perf. 14*

1718 A335 $1.75 multicolored 13.50 13.50

Souvenir Sheet

1719 A335 $6 multicolored 14.50 14.50

Antigua Nos. 2075-2083 (Mushrooms) Ovptd.

1999

1720-1725 A340 Set of 6 22.50 22.50
1726 A340 $1.75 Sheet of 6, #a.-f. 26.00 26.00

Souvenir Sheets

1727 A340 $6 multi (#2082) 17.00 17.00
1728 A340 $6 multi (#2083) 17.00 17.00

Antigua No. 2184 (Diana) Ovptd.

1999

1729 A358 $1.20 multicolored 6.50 6.50

Antigua Nos. 2268, 2269 (Royal Wedding) Overprinted "BARBOUDA MAIL"

1999, Aug. 12 Litho. *Perf. 13½*

1729A A378 $3 Sheet of 3, #b-d — —
1729E A378 $6 multi *15.00 15.00*

An additional sheet was released in this set. The editors would like to examine it.

Antigua Nos. 2107-2110 (Trains) Ovptd.

1999 Litho. *Perf. 14*

1730 A344 $1.65 Sheet of 6, #a.-f. (#2107) 13.50 13.50
1731 A344 $1.65 Sheet of 6, #a.-f. (#2108) 13.50 13.50

Souvenir Sheets

1732 A344 $6 brown (#2109) 10.00 10.00
1733 A344 $6 brown (#2110) 10.00 10.00

Antigua Nos. 2133-2139 (Church) Ovptd.

1999

1734-1739 A348 Set of 6 9.25 9.25

Souvenir Sheet

1740 A348 $6 multi (#2139) 10.50 10.50

Antigua Nos. 2155-2161 (High School) Ovptd.

1999

1741-1746 A351 Set of 6 13.00 13.00

Souvenir Sheet

1747 A351 $6 multi (#2161) 12.00 12.00

Antigua Nos. 2295-2301 (Christmas) Ovptd.

1999 *Perf. 13¾*

1748-1753 A383 Set of 6 16.00 16.00

Souvenir Sheet

1754 A383 $6 multi (#2301) 13.50 13.50

Antigua Nos. 2103-2106 (Animals) Ovptd.

2000 Litho. *Perf. 14*

1755 A343 $1.65 Sheet of 6, #a-f (#2103) 22.50 22.50
1756 A343 $1.65 Sheet of 6, #a-f (#2104) 22.50 22.50

Souvenir Sheets

1757 A343 $6 multi (#2105) 19.00 19.00
1758 A343 $6 multi (#2106) 19.00 19.00

Antigua Nos. 2123-2132 (Fish) Ovptd.

2000

1759-1764 A347 Set of 6 16.00 16.00
1765 A347 $1.65 Sheet of 6, #a-f (#2129) 21.00 21.00
1766 A347 $1.65 Sheet of 6, #a-f (#2130) 21.00 21.00

Souvenir Sheets

1767 A347 $6 multi (#2131) 20.00 20.00
1768 A347 $6 multi (#2132) 20.00 20.00

Antigua Nos. 2166-2170 (Ships) Ovptd.

2000 Litho. *Perf. 14x14½*

1769 A353 $1.75 Sheet of 3, #a-c (#2166) 15.00 15.00
1770 A353 $1.75 Sheet of 3, #a-c (#2167) 15.00 15.00

Souvenir Sheets

1771 A353 $6 multi (#2168) 10.00 10.00
1772 A353 $6 multi (#2169) 10.00 10.00
1773 A353 $6 multi (#2170) 10.00 10.00

Antigua Nos. 2172-2175 (Antique Autos) Ovptd.

2000 *Perf. 14*

1774 A355 $1.65 Sheet of 6, #a-f (#2172) 17.50 17.50
1775 A355 $1.65 Sheet of 6, #a-f (#2173) 17.50 17.50

Souvenir Sheets

1776 A355 $6 multi (#2174) 12.00 12.00
1777 A355 $6 multi (#2175) 12.00 12.00

Antigua Nos. 2194-2197 (Scouts) Ovptd.

2000

1778-1780 A361 Set of 3 12.50 12.50

Souvenir Sheet

1781 A361 $6 multi 16.00 16.00

Antigua No. 2198 (OAS) Ovptd.

2000 *Perf. 13½*

1782 A362 $1 multi 7.25 7.25

Antigua Nos. 2176-2179 (Aircraft) Overprinted

2000, Apr. 4 Litho. *Perf. 14*

1783 A356 $1.65 Sheet of 6, #a-f (#2176) *20.00 20.00*
1784 A356 $1.65 Sheet of 6, #a-f (#2177) *20.00 20.00*

Souvenir Sheets

1785 A356 $6 multi (#2178) *15.00 15.00*
1786 A356 $6 multi (#2179) *15.00 15.00*

Antigua Nos. 2373-2374 (Queen Mother) Overprinted

Litho., Margin Embossed

2000, Aug. 4 *Perf. 14*

1787 A404 $2 Sheet of 4, #a-d + label *22.50 22.50*

Souvenir Sheet

Perf. 13¾

1788 A404 $6 multi *18.00 18.00*

Antigua No. 2242 (John Glenn) Overprinted

2000, Nov. 30 Litho. *Perf. 14*

1789 A371 $1.75 Sheet of 4, #a-d *29.00 29.00*

Antigua Nos. 2243-2246 (Space) Overprinted

2000, Nov. 30 Litho. *Perf. 14*

1790 A372 $1.65 Sheet of 6, #a-f (#2243) *15.00 15.00*
1791 A372 $1.65 Sheet of 6, #a-f (#2244) *15.00 15.00*

Souvenir Sheets

1792 A372 $6 multi (#2245) *15.00 15.00*
1793 A372 $6 multi (#2246) *15.00 15.00*

Antigua Nos. 2386-2389 (Battle of Britain) Overprinted

2000, Nov. 30 Litho. *Perf. 14*

1794 A409 $1.20 Sheet of 8, #a-h (#2386) *30.00 30.00*
1795 A409 $1.20 Sheet of 8, #a-h (#2387) *30.00 30.00*

Souvenir Sheets

1796 A409 $6 multi (#2388) *20.00 20.00*
1797 A409 $6 multi (#2389) *20.00 20.00*

Antigua No. 2186 (Gandhi) Overprinted

2000, Oct. Litho. *Perf. 14*

1810 A359 $1 multi (#2186) — —

Four additional stamps exist in this set. The editors would like to examine any examples.

SEMI-POSTAL STAMPS

Catalogue values for unused stamps in this section are for Never Hinged items.

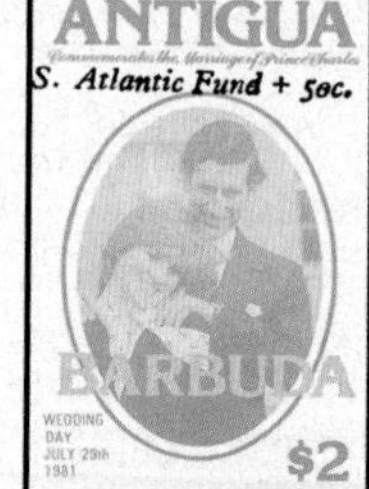

Barbuda No. 501 Crudely Surcharged

1982, June 28 Self-Adhesive

B1 CD331 Booklet 16.00

Nos. 1550-1552 Surcharged in Silver

1995, Nov. Litho. *Perf. 13*

B2 B54 $7.50 +$1 on #1551 8.00 *11.00*
B3 B53 $8 +$1 on #1550 18.00 16.00
B4 B55 $8 +$1 on #1552 8.00 *11.00*
Nos. B2-B4 (3) 34.00 38.00

BASUTOLAND

bə-ˈsü-tə-ˌland

LOCATION — An enclave in the state of South Africa
GOVT. — British Crown Colony
AREA — 11,716 sq. mi.
POP. — 733,000 (est. 1964)
CAPITAL — Maseru

The Colony, a former independent native state, was annexed to the Cape Colony in 1871. In 1883 control was transferred directly to the British Crown. Stamps of the Cape of Good Hope were used from 1871 to 1910 and those of the Union of South Africa from 1910 to 1933. Basutoland became the independent state of Lesotho on Oct. 4, 1966.

12 Pence = 1 Shilling
100 Cents = 1 Rand (1961)

Catalogue values for unused stamps in this country are for Never Hinged items, beginning with Scott 29 in the regular postage section and Scott J1 in the postage due section.

George V — A1

Crocodile and River Scene

Perf. 12½

1933, Dec. 1 Engr. Wmk. 4

1 A1 ½p emerald 1.50 *2.40*
2 A1 1p carmine 1.25 *1.75*
3 A1 2p red violet 1.50 *1.10*
4 A1 3p ultra 1.25 *1.40*
5 A1 4p slate 2.75 *9.50*
6 A1 6p yellow 3.00 *2.40*
7 A1 1sh red orange 3.50 *5.00*
8 A1 2sh6p dk brown 35.00 *57.50*
9 A1 5sh violet 67.50 *87.50*
10 A1 10sh olive green 200.00 *200.00*
Nos. 1-10 (10) 317.25 *368.55*
Set, never hinged 700.00

Common Design Types pictured following the introduction.

Silver Jubilee Issue
Common Design Type

1935, May 4 ***Perf. 13½x14***

11 CD301 1p car & blue .85 *3.00*
12 CD301 2p gray blk & ultra 1.25 *3.00*
13 CD301 3p blue & brown 5.50 *7.00*
14 CD301 6p brt vio & indigo 5.75 *7.00*
Nos. 11-14 (4) 13.35 *20.00*
Set, never hinged 20.00

Coronation Issue
Common Design Type

1937, May 12 ***Perf. 13½x14***

15 CD302 1p carmine .25 *1.00*
16 CD302 2p rose violet .45 *1.00*
17 CD302 3p bright ultra .55 *1.00*
Nos. 15-17 (3) 1.25 *3.00*
Set, never hinged 1.75

George VI — A2

1938, Apr. 1 ***Perf. 12½***

18 A2 ½p emerald .25 *1.25*
19 A2 1p rose car .75 *.85*
20 A2 1½p light blue .40 *.65*
21 A2 2p rose lilac .30 *.80*
22 A2 3p ultra .30 *1.50*
23 A2 4p gray 1.50 *4.25*
24 A2 6p yel ocher 2.00 *1.75*
25 A2 1sh red orange 2.00 *1.40*
26 A2 2sh6p black brown 11.50 *9.00*
27 A2 5sh violet 25.00 *10.00*
28 A2 10sh olive green 25.00 *22.50*
Nos. 18-28 (11) 69.00 *53.95*
Set, never hinged 110.00

Catalogue values for unused stamps in this section, from this point to the end of the section, are for Never Hinged items.

Peace Issue

South Africa Nos. 100-102 Overprinted

Basic stamps inscribed alternately in English and Afrikaans.

1945, Dec. 3 Wmk. 201 ***Perf. 14***

29 A42 1p rose pink & choc, pair .70 .90
a. Single, English .25 .25
b. Single, Afrikaans .25 .25
30 A43 2p vio & slate blue, pair .70 .75
a. Single, English .25 .25
b. Single, Afrikaans .25 .25
31 A43 3p ultra & dp ultra, pair .70 .95
a. Single, English .25 .25
b. Single, Afrikaans .25 .25
Nos. 29-31 (3) 2.10 2.60

King George VI — A3

King George VI and Queen Elizabeth A4

Princess Margaret Rose and Princess Elizabeth A5

Royal British Family A6

Perf. 12½

1947, Feb. 17 Wmk. 4 Engr.

35 A3 1p red .25 .25
36 A4 2p green .25 .25
37 A5 3p ultra .25 .25
38 A6 1sh dark violet .25 .25
Nos. 35-38 (4) 1.00 1.00

Visit of the British Royal Family, Mar. 11-12, 1947.

Silver Wedding Issue
Common Design Types

1948, Dec. 1 Photo. ***Perf. 14x14½***

39 CD304 1½p brt ultra .30 .25

Engr.; Name Typo.
Perf. 11½

40 CD305 10sh dk brown olive 50.00 *50.00*

UPU Issue
Common Design Types
Engr.; Name Typo. on 3p, 6p
Perf. 13½, 11x11½

1949, Oct. 10 Wmk. 4

41 CD306 1½p blue .50 *1.50*
42 CD307 3p indigo 2.25 *2.00*
43 CD308 6p orange yel 1.25 *5.00*
44 CD309 1sh red brown .75 *1.50*
Nos. 41-44 (4) 4.75 *10.00*

Coronation Issue
Common Design Type

1953, June 3 Engr. ***Perf. 13½x13***

45 CD312 2p red violet & black .50 *.60*

Qiloane Hill — A7

Shearing Angora Goats — A8

Designs: 1p, Orange River. 2p, Mosotho horseman. 3p, Basuto household. 4½p, Maletsunyane falls. 6p, Herdboy with lesiba. 1sh, Pastoral scene. 1sh3p, Plane at Lancers Gap. 2sh6p, Old Fort Leribe. 5sh, Mission cave house.

Perf. 13½, 11½ (#56)

1954, Oct. 18 Wmk. 4

46 A7 ½p dk brown & gray .50 .25
47 A7 1p dp grn & gray blk .40 .25
48 A7 2p org & dp blue 1.00 .25
49 A7 3p car & ol green 2.00 .40
50 A7 4½p dp blue & ind 1.50 .25
51 A7 6p dk grn & org brn 2.00 .25
52 A7 1sh rose vio & dk ol green 2.00 .40
53 A7 1sh3p aqua & brown 27.50 9.00
54 A7 2sh6p lilac rose & dp ultra 27.50 11.00
55 A7 5sh dp car & black 11.00 *12.00*
56 A8 10sh dp cl & black 35.00 27.50
Nos. 46-56 (11) 110.40 *61.55*

See Nos. 72-82, 87-91. For surcharges see Nos. 57, 61-71.

No. 48 Surcharged

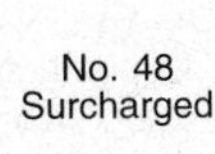

1959, Aug. 1

57 A7 ½p on 2p org & dp blue .30 .25

Chief Moshoeshoe (Moshesh) — A9

Designs: 1sh, Council chamber. 1sh3p, Mosotho on horseback.

Perf. 13x13½

1959, Dec. 15 Wmk. 314

58 A9 3p lt yel, grn & blk .60 .25
59 A9 1sh green & pink .60 .25
60 A9 1sh3p orange & ultra .80 .50
Nos. 58-60 (3) 2.00 1.00

Institution of the Basutoland National Council.

Nos. 46-56 Surcharged with New Value

2½c I — 2½c II — 3½c I — 3½c II
5c I — 5c II — 10c I — 10c II
12½c I — 12½c II
25c I — 25c II — 25c III
50c I — 50c II — R1 I — R1 II — R1 III

Perf. 13½, 11½ (#71)

1961, Feb. 14 Wmk. 4

61 A7 ½c on ½p .25 .25
a. Double surcharge 550.00
62 A7 1c on 1p .25 .25
63 A7 2c on 2p .90 *1.00*
a. Inverted surcharge 170.00
64 A7 2½c on 3p (II) .25 .25
a. Type I .25 .25
b. Inverted surcharge (II) 8,000. 8,000.
65 A7 3½c on 4½p (I) .35 .25
a. Type II 3.00 *7.50*
66 A7 5c on 6p (II) .50 .25
a. Type I .40 .25
67 A7 10c on 1sh (I) .50 .25
a. Type II 140.00 *160.00*
68 A7 12½c on 1sh3p (II) 10.00 3.25
a. Type I 6.00 2.25
69 A7 25c on 2sh6p (I) 1.50 .75
a. Type II 47.50 12.50
b. Type III 1.25 *2.00*
70 A7 50c on 5sh (II) 4.50 4.00
a. Type I 6.50 4.25
71 A8 1r on 10sh (III) 27.50 25.00
a. Type I 55.00 25.00
b. Type II 27.50 *60.00*
Nos. 61-71 (11) 46.50 35.50

Surcharge types on Nos. 64-71 are numbered chronologically.

Types of 1954
Value in Cents and Rands

Designs: ½c, Qiloane Hill. 1c, Orange River. 2c, Mosotho horseman. 2½c, Basuto household. 3½c, Maletsunyane Falls. 5c, Herdboy with lesiba. 10c, Pastoral scene. 12½c, Plane at Lancers Gap. 25c, Old Fort Leribe. 50c, Mission cave house. 1r, Shearing Angora goats.

1961-63 Wmk. 4 Engr. ***Perf. 13½***

72 A7 ½c dk brn & gray ('62) .25 *.30*
73 A7 1c dp grn & gray blk ('62) .25 *.50*
74 A7 2c org & dp bl ('62) 3.00 1.50
75 A7 2½c car & ol grn 2.00 .60
76 A7 3½c dp bl & ind ('62) .45 *1.50*
77 A7 5c dk grn & org brn ('62) .65 *.85*
78 A7 10c rose vio & dk ol ('62) .40 *.50*
79 A7 12½c aqua & brn ('62) 24.00 11.00
80 A7 25c lilac rose & dp ultra ('62) 6.50 6.50
81 A7 50c dp car & blk ('62) 19.00 *19.00*

Perf. 11½

82 A8 1r dp cl & blk ('63) 55.00 *25.00*
Nos. 72-82 (11) 111.50 *67.25*

See Nos. 87-91. For overprints on stamps and types see Lesotho Nos. 5-14, 20a.

Freedom from Hunger Issue
Common Design Type
Perf. 14x14½

1963, June 4 Photo. Wmk. 314

83 CD314 12½c lilac .50 .25

Red Cross Centenary Issue
Common Design Type

1963, Sept. 2 Litho. ***Perf. 13***

84 CD315 2½c black & red .30 .25
85 CD315 12½c ultra & red .90 .65

Queen Type of 1961-63

1964 Engr. ***Perf. 13½***

87 A7 1c grn & gray blk .25 *.35*
88 A7 2½c car & ol green .25 *.30*
89 A7 5c dk green & org brn .45 *.75*

90 A7 12½c aqua & brown 7.00 1.75
91 A7 50c dp car & black 8.00 *11.00*
Nos. 87-91 (5) 15.95 *14.15*

Mosotho Woman and Child — A10

Designs: 3½c, Maseru border post. 5c, Mountains. 12½c, Legislative Building.

Perf. 14x13½

1965, May 10 Photo. Wmk. 314

97 A10 2½c ultra & multi .25 .25
98 A10 3½c blue & bister .40 .30
99 A10 5c blue & ocher .40 .30
100 A10 12½c lt blue, blk & buff .65 .70
Nos. 97-100 (4) 1.70 1.55

Attainment of self-government.

ITU Issue
Common Design Type

1965, May 17 Litho. *Perf. 11x11½*

101 CD317 1c ver & red lilac .25 .25
102 CD317 20c grnsh bl & org brn .60 .40

Intl. Cooperation Year Issue
Common Design Type

1965, Oct. 25 Wmk. 314 *Perf. 14½*

103 CD318 ½c blue grn & cl .25 *.50*
104 CD318 12½c lt vio & green .50 .35

Churchill Memorial Issue
Common Design Type

1966, Jan. 24 Photo. *Perf. 14*

Design in Black, Gold and Carmine Rose

105 CD319 1c bright blue .25 *1.00*
106 CD319 2½c green .55 .25
107 CD319 10c brown .75 .50
108 CD319 22½c violet 1.25 1.00
Nos. 105-108 (4) 2.80 2.75

POSTAGE DUE STAMPS

Catalogue values for all unused stamps in this section are for Never Hinged items.

D1

1933-52 Wmk. 4 Typo. *Perf. 14*
Chalky Paper

J1 D1 1p dark red ('51) 2.00 *8.00*
a. 1p carmine, ordinary paper 3.00 *13.00*
b. 1p dk car, ordinary paper ('38) 50.00 *60.00*
c. Wmk. 4a (error) 140.00
d. Wmk. 4, crown missing (error) 350.00
J2 D1 2p lt violet ('52) .40 *25.00*
a. 2p lt violet, ordinary paper 9.50 *24.00*
b. Wmk. 4a (error) 150.00
c. Wmk. 4, crown missing (error) 375.00

For surcharge see No. J7.

Coat of Arms — D2

1956, Dec. 1

J3 D2 1p carmine .50 *3.00*
J4 D2 2p dark purple .50 *6.00*

Nos. J2-J4 Surcharged

1961

J5 D2 1c on 1p carmine .25 *.40*
J6 D2 1c on 2p dk purple .25 *1.25*
J7 D1 5c on 2p lt violet 1.50 *7.00*
a. Wmk. 4a (error) 350.00
b. Wmk. 4, crown missing (error) 1,800.
J8 D2 5c on 2p dark pur ("5" 7½mm high) .25 .45
a. "5" 3½mm high 15.00 *50.00*
Nos. J5-J8 (4) 2.25 9.10

Value in Cents

1964 Wmk. 314 *Perf. 14*

J9 D2 1c carmine *4.25 25.00*
J10 D2 5c dark purple *4.25 25.00*

For overprints see Lesotho Nos. J1-J2.

OFFICIAL STAMPS

Nos. 1-3 and 6 Overprinted "OFFICIAL"

1934 Wmk. 4 Engr. *Perf. 12½*

O1 A1 ½p emerald *14,000. 7,500.*
O2 A1 1p carmine *5,000. 3,750.*
O3 A1 2p red violet *5,500. 1,250.*
O4 A1 6p yellow *14,000. 5,000.*

Counterfeits exist.

BATUM

bä-ˈtüm

LOCATION — A seaport on the Black Sea

Batum is the capital of Adzhar, a territory which, in 1921, became an autonomous republic of the Georgian Soviet Socialist Republic.

Stamps of Batum were issued under the administration of British forces which occupied Batum and environs between December, 1918, and July, 1920, following the Treaty of Versailles.

100 Kopecks = 1 Ruble

Counterfeits of Nos. 1-65 abound.

A1

1919 Unwmk. Litho. *Imperf.*

1 A1 5k green 8.00 *24.00*
2 A1 10k ultramarine 8.00 *24.00*
3 A1 50k yellow 4.75 *9.00*
4 A1 1r red brown 6.50 *8.50*
5 A1 3r violet 11.50 *20.00*
6 A1 5r brown 12.00 *35.00*
Nos. 1-6 (6) 50.75 *120.50*

For overprints and surcharges see Nos. 13-20, 51-65.

Nos. 7-12, 21-50: numbers in parentheses are those of the basic Russian stamps.

Russian Stamps of 1909-17 Surcharged

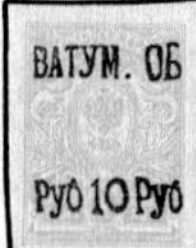

1919 On Stamps of 1917

7 10r on 1k orange (#119) 75.00 *75.00*
8 10r on 3k red (#121) 26.50 *32.50*

On Stamp of 1909-12
Perf. 14x14½

9 10r on 5k claret (#77) 950.00 950.00

On Stamp of 1917

10 10r on 10k on 7k light blue (#117) 975.00 725.00
Nos. 7-10 (4) 2,026. 1,782.

Russian Stamps of 1909-13 Surcharged

1919

11 35k on 4k carmine (#76) *1,950. 6,000.*
12 35k on 4k dull red (#91) *6,500. 13,000.*

This surcharge was intended for postal cards. A few cards which bore adhesive stamps were also surcharged.

Values are for stamps off card and without gum.

Type of 1919 Issue Overprinted

1919 Unwmk. *Imperf.*

13 A1 5k green 22.50 *15.00*
14 A1 10k dark blue 15.00 *17.50*
15 A1 25k orange 22.50 *17.50*
16 A1 1r pale blue 5.50 *17.50*
17 A1 2r salmon pink 1.25 *7.00*
18 A1 3r violet 1.25 *7.00*
19 A1 5r brown 1.50 *7.00*
a. "CCUPATION" *475.00 475.00*
20 A1 7r dull red 5.00 *9.50*
Nos. 13-20 (8) 74.50 *98.00*

Russian Stamps of 1909-17 Surcharged in Various Colors

10r & 50r

15r

On Stamps of 1917

1919-20 *Imperf.*

21 10r on 3k red (#121) 25.00 *27.50*
a. Inverted overprint 500.00
22 15r on 1k org (R) (#119) 60.00 *100.00*
23 15r on 1k org (Bk) (#119) 100.00 *150.00*
a. Inverted overprint 750.00 750.00
24 15r on 1k org (V) (#119) 75.00 *95.00*
25 50r on 1k org (#119) 975.00 *675.00*
26 50r on 2k green (#120) 975.00 *1,100.*

On Stamps of 1909-17
Perf. 14x14½

27 50r on 2k green (#74) 975.00 850.00
28 50r on 3k red (#75) 1,700. *2,500.*
29 50r on 4k car (#76) 1,500. *1,500.*
30 50r on 5k claret (#77) 975.00 *975.00*
31 50r on 10k dk blue (R) (#79) 2,250. *3,500.*
32 50r on 15k red brn & blue (#81) 700.00 *850.00*

Surcharged

On Stamps of 1909-17

33 25r on 5k cl (Bk) (#77) 100.00 *150.00*
34 25r on 5k cl (Bl) (#77) 100.00 *150.00*
a. Inverted overprint 250.00
35 25r on 10k on 7k lt blue (Bk) (#117) 150.00 *175.00*
36 25r on 10k on 7k lt blue (Bl) (#117) 100.00 *87.50*
37 25r on 20k on 14k bl & rose (Bk) (#118) 95.00 *150.00*
38 25r on 20k on 14k bl & rose (Bl) (#118) 200.00 *110.00*
39 25r on 25k grn & gray vio (Bk) (#83) 160.00 *175.00*
a. Inverted overprint 250.00
40 25r on 25k grn & gray vio (Bl) (#83) 100.00 135.00
41 25r on 50k vio & green (Bk) (#85a) 100.00 *110.00*
a. Inverted overprint 250.00
42 25r on 50k vio & green (Bl) (#85a) 100.00 *105.00*
43 50r on 2k green (#74) 200.00 145.00
44 50r on 3k red (#75) 200.00 145.00
45 50r on 4k car (#76) 200.00 *250.00*
46 50r on 5k claret (#77) 200.00 100.00

On Stamps of 1917
Imperf

47 50r on 2k green (#120) 975.00 *650.00*
48 50r on 3k red (#121) 975.00 *675.00*
49 50r on 5k claret (#123) *1,500. 1,650.*

On Stamp of 1913
Perf. 13½

50 50r on 4k dull red (Bl) (#91) 100.00 *95.00*

Nos. 3, 13 and 15 Surcharged in Black or Blue

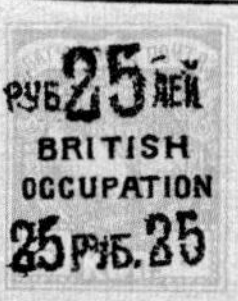

1920 *Imperf.*

51 A1 25r on 5k green 75.00 *100.00*
52 A1 25r on 5k grn (Bl) 250.00 70.00
53 A1 25r on 25k orange 35.00 *45.00*
54 A1 25r on 25k org (Bl) *125.00 140.00*
55 A1 50r on 50k yellow 30.00 *30.00*
56 A1 50r on 50k yel (Bl) 100.00 125.00
Nos. 51-56 (6) *615.00 510.00*

The surcharges on Nos. 21-56 inclusive are handstamped and are known double, inverted, etc.

Tree Type of 1919 Overprinted Like Nos. 13-20

1920

57 A1 1r orange brown 2.25 *12.00*
58 A1 2r gray blue 2.25 *12.00*
59 A1 3r rose 2.25 *12.00*
60 A1 5r black brown 2.25 *12.00*
61 A1 7r yellow 2.25 *12.00*
62 A1 10r dark green 2.25 *12.00*
63 A1 15r violet 2.75 *17.50*
64 A1 25r vermilion 2.50 *16.00*
65 A1 50r dark blue 2.75 *20.00*
Nos. 57-65 (9) 21.50 *125.50*

The variety "BPITISH" occurs on Nos. 57-65. Value, about $150 each.

BECHUANALAND

ˌbech-ˈwä-nə-ˌland

(British Bechuanaland)

LOCATION — Southern Africa
GOVT. — A British Crown Colony, which included the area of the former Stellaland, annexed in 1895 to the Cape of Good Hope Colony.
AREA — 51,424 sq. mi.
POP. — 72,700 (1891)
CAPITAL — Vryburg

British Bechuanaland stamps were also used in Bechuanaland Protectorate until 1897.

12 Pence = 1 Shilling
20 Shillings = 1 Pound

Watermarks

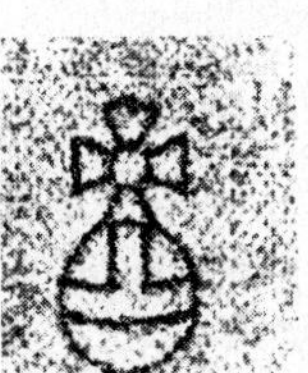
Wmk. 29 — Orb

Wmk. 14 — VR in Italics

Cape of Good Hope Stamps of 1871-85 Overprinted

1885-87 Wmk. 1 *Perf. 14*

Black Overprint

1 A6 4p blue ('86) 85.00 *85.00*

Wmk. 2

Black Overprint

3 A6 3p claret 50.00 *60.00*

Red Overprint

4 A6 ½p black 30.00 35.00
a. Overprint in lake 5,500. *10,000.*
b. Double overprint in lake & blk 900.00 *1,100.*

Wmk. Anchor (16)

Black Overprint

5 A6 ½p black ('87) 12.00 *25.00*
a. "ritish" 2,500. *2,600.*
b. Double overprint 4,250.
6 A6 1p rose 25.00 11.00
a. "ritish" *7,500.* *4,250.*
b. Double overprint *2,200.*
7 A6 2p bister 45.00 11.00
a. "ritish" 9,000. *5,500.*
b. Double overprint 2,500.
8 A3 6p violet 175.00 47.50
9 A3 1sh green ('86) 325.00 190.00
a. "ritish" *22,500.* *18,000.*

There is no period after Bechuanaland on the genuine stamps.

Black Ovpt. on Great Britain #111

1887 Wmk. 30

10 A54 ½p vermilion 1.50 *1.50*
a. Double overprint 2,700.

For overprints see Bechuanaland Protectorate Nos. 51-53.

A1

A2

A3

1887 Typo. Wmk. 29

Country Name in Black

11 A1 1p lilac 22.50 3.50
12 A1 2p lilac 100.00 2.75
13 A1 3p lilac 8.00 *7.00*
14 A1 4p lilac 60.00 2.75
15 A1 6p lilac 72.50 3.00

Wmk. 14

16 A2 1sh green 37.50 8.50
17 A2 2sh green 60.00 47.50
18 A2 2sh6p green 72.50 72.50
19 A2 5sh green 110.00 *180.00*
Pen cancellation 4.50
20 A2 10sh green 225.00 *400.00*
Pen cancellation 30.00

Wmk. 29

21 A3 £1 lilac 1,100. *900.00*
Pen cancellation 47.50
22 A3 £5 lilac 4,000. *1,900.*
Pen cancellation 200.00

The corner designs and central oval differs on No. 22.

For overprints see Bechuanaland Protectorate Nos. 54-58, 60-66. For surcharges see Nos. 23-28, 30, AR2, Cape of Good Hope No. 171.

Beware of cleaned pen (fiscal) cancellations and forged postmarks on Nos. 21-22.

Nos. 11-12, 14-16 Surcharged

1888

Country Name in Black

Black Surcharge

23 A1 1p on 1p lilac 9.25 8.00
a. Double surcharge
24 A1 6p on 6p lilac 145.00 20.00

Red Surcharge

25 A1 2p on 2p lilac 55.00 3.75
a. "2" with curved tail 325.00 180.00
26 A1 4p on 4p lilac 425.00 *550.00*

Green Surcharge

27 A1 2p on 2p lilac *4,000.*
a. "2" with curved tail —

Blue Surcharge

27A A1 6p on 6p lilac *25,000.*

Wmk. 14

Black Surcharge

28 A2 1sh on 1sh green 220.00 100.00

Cape of Good Hope No.41 Overprinted in Green

1889 Wmk. 16

29 A4 ½p black 4.75 *35.00*
a. Double ovpt., one inverted 3,500.
b. Double ovpt., one vertical 1,200.
c. Pair, one stamp without ovpt. 10,000.

Exists with "British" missing from shifted overprint.

No. 13 Surcharged in Black

1888 Wmk. 29

30 A1 ½p on 3p lilac & blk 250.00 *300.00*

Stamps with errors of spelling in the surcharge are fakes.

Cape of Good Hope Nos. 43-44 Overprinted in Black, Reading Up

1891 Wmk. 16

31 A4 1p rose 12.00 *15.00*
a. Horiz. pair, one without overprint *25,000.*
b. "British" omitted — —
c. "Bechuanaland" omitted 3,000.
32 A4 2p bister 5.50 2.75
a. Without period 325.00 *390.00*

See Nos. 38-39.

Stamps of Great Britain Overprinted in Black

1891-94 Wmk. 30

33 A40 1p lilac 7.25 1.90
34 A56 2p green & car 21.00 5.00
35 A59 4p brown & green 3.75 .80
a. Half used as 2p on cover *3,000.*
36 A62 6p violet, *rose* 7.50 2.50
37 A65 1sh green ('94) 16.00 *19.50*
a. Half used as 6p on cover —
Nos. 33-37 (5) 55.50 *29.70*

For surcharges, see Cape of Good Hope Nos. 172, 176-177.

Cape of Good Hope Nos. 43-44 Overprinted, Reading Down

1893-95 Wmk. 16

38 A6 1p rose 3.50 3.00
a. No dots over the "i's" of "British" 150.00 *155.00*
c. As "a," reading up *4,000.*
d. Pair, one without overprint
39 A6 2p bister ('95) 10.00 3.00
a. Double overprint 1,700. 850.00
b. No dots over the "i's" of "British" 275.00 160.00
d. As "b," reading up 4,500.

The missing dot-over-i variety exists only on this issue. Nos. 38c and 39d resulted from the sheets being fed into the press upside down.

Nos. 38-39 exist with "British" missing (from shifted overprint).

Cape of Good Hope No. 42 Overprinted

"BECHUANALAND" 16mm Long Overprint Lines 13mm Apart

1897

40 A6 ½p light green 3.25 *17.00*

"BECHUANALAND" 15mm Long Overprint Lines 10½mm Apart

41 A6 ½p light green 17.00 *65.00*

"BECHUANALAND" 15mm Long Overprint Lines 13½mm Apart

42 A6 ½p light green 35.00 *95.00*
Nos. 40-42 (3) 55.25 *177.00*

Nos. 40-42 actually are issues of Bechuanaland Protectorate.

BECHUANALAND PROTECTORATE

ˌbech-ˈwä-nə-ˌland prə-ˈtek-t̩ə-ˌrət

LOCATION — In central South Africa, north of the Republic of South Africa, east of South West Africa and bounded on the north by the Caprivi Strip of South West Africa and on the east by Southern Rhodesia
GOVT. — British Protectorate
AREA — 222,000 sq. mi.
POP. — 540,400 (1964)
CAPITAL — Vryburg (to 1895), Mafeking (to 1965), Gaberones

Bechuanaland Protectorate became self-governing in 1965 and achieved indepencence as the republic of Botswana, Sept. 30, 1966.

12 Pence = 1 Shilling
20 Shillings = 1 Pound
100 Cents = 1 Rand (1961)

Catalogue values for unused stamps in this country are for Never Hinged items, beginning with Scott 137 in the regular postage section and Scott J7 in the postage due section.

Additional Overprint in Black on Bechuanaland No. 10

a

b

c

1888-90 Wmk. 30 *Perf. 14*

51 A54(a) ½p vermilion ('90) 225.00 *425.00*
a. Double overprint 1,800. *2,200.*
b. "Protectorrte"
c. As "b," double overprint *20,000.*
52 A54(b) ½p vermilion ('88) 12.00 *50.00*
a. Double overprint *375.00*
53 A54(c) ½p vermilion ('90) 200.00 *225.00*
a. Inverted overprint 87.50 *110.00*
b. Double overprint 125.00 *190.00*
c. As "a," double 700.00 *850.00*
d. "Portectorate" — —
e. As "a," "Portectorate" *20,000.* —

For surcharge see No. 68.

Bechuanaland Nos. 16-20 Overprinted Type "b" in Black

Wmk. 14

Country Name in Black

54 A2 1sh green 120.00 60.00
a. First "o" omitted *6,750.* 3,750.
55 A2 2sh green 700.00 *1,200.*
a. First "o" omitted *20,000.* —
56 A2 2sh6p green 650.00 *1,100.*
a. First "o" omitted *18,000.* —
57 A2 5sh green 1,400. *2,750.*
a. First "o" omitted *25,000.* —
58 A2 10sh green 5,250. *6,500.*
a. First "o" omitted *25,000.* —

Bechuanaland Nos. 11-15 Ovptd. Type "b" and Srchd. in Black

1888 **Wmk. 29**

Country Name in Black

60 A1 1p on 1p lilac 17.50 *16.00*
a. Short "1" 475.00 *550.00*
61 A1 2p on 2p lilac 37.50 20.00
a. "2" with curved tail 900.00 550.00
63 A1 3p on 3p reddish lilac 180.00 *225.00*
64 A1 4p on 4p lilac 450.00 475.00
a. Small "4" *5,500.* *5,500.*
65 A1 6p on 6p lilac 100.00 50.00

In #60 the "1" is 2½mm high; in #60a, 2mm.

Value Surcharged in Red

66 A1 4p on 4p lilac 120.00 50.00

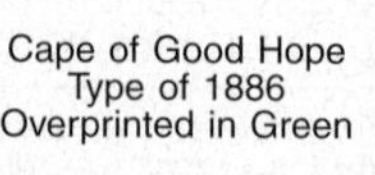

Cape of Good Hope Type of 1886 Overprinted in Green

1889 **Wmk. 16**

67 A6 ½p black 6.00 *55.00*
a. Double overprint 600.00 *800.00*

No. 67 exists with "Bechuanaland" missing and with ovpt. words reversed (from shifted overprint).

Bechuanaland Protectorate No. 52 Surcharged in Black

Wmk. 30

68 A54 4p on ½p ver 40.00 6.00
a. Inverted surcharge *4,500.*
b. "rpence" omitted *7,000.*

Stamps of Great Britain 1881-87, Overprinted in Black

1897, Oct.

69 A54 ½p vermilion 1.75 *2.50*
70 A40 1p lilac 4.50 .85
71 A56 2p green & car 9.50 *4.00*
72 A58 3p violet, *yel* 6.25 *10.00*
73 A59 4p brown & green 24.00 22.50
74 A62 6p violet, *rose* 25.00 12.50
Nos. 69-74 (6) 71.00 52.35

For surcharges see Cape of Good Hope Nos. 167-170, 173-175.

Same on Great Britain No. 125

1902, Feb. 25

75 A54 ½p blue green 1.75 *4.00*

Stamps of Great Britain, 1902, Overprinted in Black

1904-12

76 A66 ½p gray green ('06) 2.75 *3.25*
77 A66 1p car ('05) 10.00 .65
78 A66 2½p ultra 12.00 7.50
79 A74 1sh scar & grn ('12) 55.00 *170.00*
Nos. 76-79 (4) 79.75 *181.40*

Same on Great Britain No. 143

1908

80 A66 ½p pale yel green 4.25 4.00

Transvaal No. 274 overprinted "Bechuanaland Protectorate," formerly listed as No. 81, now appears as No. AR1 in the Postal-Fiscal Stamps section.

Great Britain No. 154 Overprinted Like Nos. 76-79

1912, Sept. **Wmk. 30** ***Perf. 15x14***

82 A81 1p scarlet 3.50 .90

Great Britain Stamps of 1912-13 Overprinted Like Nos. 76-79

Wmk. Crown and GvR (33)

1913-24

83 A82 ½p green 1.40 *2.00*
84 A83 1p scarlet ('15) 3.25 .85
85 A84 1½p red brn ('20) 7.00 *3.50*
86 A85 2p reddish orange (I) 13.00 *4.25*
b. 2p orange (II) ('24) 47.50 4.00
87 A86 2½p ultra 4.00 *27.50*
88 A87 3p bluish violet 6.75 *13.50*
89 A88 4p slate green 7.25 *32.50*
90 A89 6p dull violet 9.00 *24.00*
91 A90 1sh bister 20.00 *37.50*
Nos. 83-91 (9) 71.65 *145.60*

The dies of No. 86 are the same as in Great Britain 1912-13 issue.

Wmk. 34 ***Perf. 11x12***

92 A91 2sh6p dark brown ('15) 150.00 *300.00*
a. 2sh6p light brown ('16) 125.00 *300.00*
93 A91 5sh rose carmine ('14) 180.00 *450.00*
a. 5sh carmine ('19) 350.00 *500.00*

Nos. 92, 93 were printed by Waterlow Bros. & Layton; Nos. 92a, 93a were printed by Thomas De La Rue & Co.

Same Overprint On Retouched Seahorses Stamps of 1919 (Great Britain Nos. 179, 180)

1920-23

94 A91 2sh6p gray brown 100.00 *200.00*
95 A91 5sh car rose 140.00 *325.00*

Nos. 94-95 measure 22.5-23mm vertically. Most examples have a small dot of color at top center, outside of frameline. Perforation holes are larger and usually are evenly spaced.

Great Britain Stamps of 1924 Overprinted like Nos. 76-79

Wmk. Crown and Block GvR Multiple (35)

1925-27 ***Perf. 15x14***

96 A82 ½p green ('27) 1.65 *2.00*
97 A83 1p scarlet 2.25 1.00
99 A85 2p deep org (II) 2.50 1.25
101 A87 3p violet ('26) 5.50 *25.00*
102 A88 4p slate green ('26) 8.00 *55.00*
103 A89 6p dull violet, chalky paper 70.00 *100.00*
104 A90 1sh bister ('26) 11.00 *30.00*
Nos. 96-104 (7) 100.90 *214.25*

George V — A11

Perf. 12½

1932, Dec. 12 **Engr.** **Wmk. 4**

105 A11 ½p green 2.75 .35
a. Horiz. pair, imperf between *27,000.*
106 A11 1p carmine 1.75 .40
107 A11 2p red brown 1.75 .45
108 A11 3p ultra 4.00 *4.00*
109 A11 4p orange 4.00 *9.00*
110 A11 6p red violet 5.50 *7.00*
111 A11 1sh blk & ol grn 4.00 *8.00*
112 A11 2sh black & org 27.50 *70.00*
113 A11 2sh6p black & car 26.00 *50.00*
114 A11 3sh black & red vio 47.50 *60.00*
115 A11 5sh black & ultra 100.00 *125.00*
116 A11 10sh blk & red brown 250.00 *275.00*
Nos. 105-116 (12) 474.75 *609.20*

Common Design Types pictured following the introduction.

Silver Jubilee Issue

Common Design Type

1935, May 4 ***Perf. 11x12***

117 CD301 1p car & blue 1.25 *5.50*
118 CD301 2p black & ultra 1.50 5.50
119 CD301 3p ultra & brown 3.25 6.00
120 CD301 6p brown vio & ind 7.75 *6.00*
Nos. 117-120 (4) 13.75 23.00
Set, never hinged 21.00

Coronation Issue

Common Design Type

1937, May 12 ***Perf. 13½x14***

121 CD302 1p carmine .25 *.50*
122 CD302 2p brown .30 *1.25*
123 CD302 3p bright ultra .40 *1.60*
Nos. 121-123 (3) .95 3.35
Set, never hinged 1.75

George VI, Cattle and Baobab Tree — A12

1938, Apr. 1 ***Perf. 12½***

124 A12 ½p green 2.00 *3.50*
125 A12 1p rose car .70 .65
126 A12 1½p light blue 1.25 *1.25*
127 A12 2p brown .60 *.75*
128 A12 3p ultra .75 *3.00*
129 A12 4p orange 1.75 *4.50*
130 A12 6p rose violet 3.00 3.50
131 A12 1sh blk & ol grn 3.25 *8.50*
133 A12 2sh6p black & car 9.00 *18.00*
135 A12 5sh black & ultra 22.50 *27.50*
136 A12 10sh black & brn 17.50 *32.50*
Nos. 124-136 (11) 62.30 *103.65*
Set, never hinged 95.00

Catalogue values for unused stamps in this section, from this point to the end of the section, are for Never Hinged items.

Peace Issue

South Africa Nos. 100-102 Overprinted

Basic stamps inscribed alternately in English and Afrikaans.

1945, Dec. 3 **Wmk. 201** ***Perf. 14***

137 A42 1p rose pink & choc, pair .75 *1.50*
a. Single, English .25 .25
b. Single, Afrikaans .25 .25
138 A43 2p vio & slate blue, pair .55 *1.50*
a. Single, English .25 .25
b. Single, Afrikaans .25 .25
139 A43 3p ultra & dp ultra, pair .75 *1.75*
a. Single, English .25 .25
b. Single, Afrikaans .25 .25
Nos. 137-139 (3) 2.05 *4.75*

World War II victory of the Allies.

Royal Visit Issue

Types of Basutoland, 1947

Perf. 12½

1947, Feb. 17 **Wmk. 4** **Engr.**

143 A3 1p red .25 .25
144 A4 2p green .25 .25
145 A5 3p ultra .25 .25
146 A6 1sh dark violet .25 .25
Nos. 143-146 (4) 1.00 1.00

Visit of the British Royal Family, 4/17/47.

Silver Wedding Issue

Common Design Types

1948, Dec. 1 **Photo.** ***Perf. 14x14½***

147 CD304 1½p brt ultra .35 .25

Engr.; Name Typo.

Perf. 11½x11

148 CD305 10sh gray black 42.50 *47.50*

UPU Issue

Common Design Types

Engr.; Name Typo. on 3p and 6p

1949, Oct. 10 ***Perf. 13½, 11x11½***

149 CD306 1½p blue .30 *1.00*
150 CD307 3p indigo 1.50 1.50
151 CD308 6p red lilac .80 *2.75*
152 CD309 1sh olive .75 *2.00*
Nos. 149-152 (4) 3.35 *7.25*

Coronation Issue

Common Design Type

1953, June 3 **Engr.** ***Perf. 13½x13***

153 CD312 2p brown & black .75 .35

Elizabeth II — A13

1955-58 ***Perf. 13x13½***

154 A13 ½p green .60 .35
155 A13 1p rose car 1.00 .25
156 A13 2p brown 1.50 .35
157 A13 3p ultra 3.75 1.75
158 A13 4p orange ('58) *10.00* *10.00*
159 A13 4½p indigo 1.75 1.25
160 A13 6p rose violet 1.50 .90
161 A13 1sh blk & ol grn 1.50 *1.50*
162 A13 1sh3p blk & rose vio 15.00 8.00
163 A13 2sh6p black & car 13.50 10.50
164 A13 5sh black & ultra 18.00 15.00
165 A13 10sh black & brn 40.00 19.00
Nos. 154-165 (12) 108.10 *68.85*

For surcharges see Nos. 169-179.

Victoria, Elizabeth II and Water Hole — A14

Perf. 14½x14

1960, Jan. 21 **Photo.** **Wmk. 314**

166 A14 1p brown & black .50 *.60*
167 A14 3p car rose & black .50 *.60*
168 A14 6p ultra & black .50 *.60*
Nos. 166-168 (3) 1.50 1.80

Proclamation of the Protectorate, 75th anniv.

Nos. 155-165 Surcharged

Elizabeth II, Type III

1c I — 1c II

3½c I — 3½c II — 3½c III

5c I — 5c II — R1 I — R1 II

Perf. 13x13½

1961, Feb. 14 **Wmk. 4** **Engr.**

169 1c on 1p (I) .35 .25
a. Type II .45 .25
170 2c on 2p .25 .25
171 2½c on 2p .35 .25
a. Pair, one without surcharge *12,000.*
172 2½c on 3p 4.50 *8.00*
173 3½c on 4p (III) .25 .25
a. Type I .60 .60
b. Type II 2.25 *4.00*

174 5c on 6p (II) .25 .25
a. Type I .80 *1.25*
175 10c on 1sh .30 .30
a. Pair, one without surcharge *20,000.*
176 12½c on 1sh3p ("12½c" 11¼mm wide) .65 .55
a. "12½c" 12½mm wide .85 .75
177 25c on 2sh6p 1.75 .80
178 50c on 5sh 2.25 *3.00*
179 1r on 10sh (II, "R1" at lower center) 17.50 *17.50*
a. Type II, "R1" at lower left 17.50 10.00
b. Type I 425.00 140.00
Nos. 169-179 (11) 28.40 31.40

Nos. 173a and 173b are found in the same sheet; each comes with "3½c" in both wide and narrow settings.

Surch. types are numbered chronologically.

African Golden Oriole — A15

Baobab Tree — A16

Designs: 2c, African hoopoe. 2½c, Scarlet-chested sunbird. 3½c, Cape widow bird (Yellow bishop). 5c, Swallow-tailed bee-eater. 7½c, Gray hornbill. 10c, Red-headed weaver. 12½c, Brown-hooded kingfisher. 20c, Woman musician. 35c, Woman grinding corn. 50c, Bechuana ox. 1r, Lion. 2r, Police camel patrol.

Perf. 14x14½, 14½x14

1961, Oct. 2 Photo. Wmk. 314

180 A15 1c lilac, blk & yel 1.75 .55
181 A15 2c pale ol, blk & org 2.25 *4.25*
182 A15 2½c bis, blk, grn & dp car 1.75 .25
183 A15 3½c pink, blk & yel 2.75 *4.00*
184 A15 5c dl org, blk, grn & bl 3.50 1.25
185 A15 7½c yel grn, blk, red & brn 2.25 *2.75*
186 A15 10c aqua & multi 2.25 .75
187 A15 12½c gray, yel, red & blue 19.00 6.00
188 A15 20c gray & brn 3.75 3.75
189 A16 25c yel & dk brn 4.50 2.00
190 A15 35c dp org & ultra 4.00 *4.00*
191 A16 50c lt ol grn & sep 2.75 *2.75*
192 A15 1r ocher & black 9.00 3.00
193 A15 2r blue & brn 30.00 12.50
Nos. 180-193 (14) 89.50 47.80

For overprints see Botswana Nos. 5-18.

Freedom from Hunger Issue
Common Design Type

1963, June 4 *Perf. 14x14½*

194 CD314 12½c green .50 .50

Red Cross Centenary Issue
Common Design Type

1963, Sept. 2 Litho. *Perf. 13*

195 CD315 2½c black & red .25 .25
196 CD315 12½c ultra & red .80 .80

Shakespeare Issue
Common Design Type

1964, Apr. 23 Photo. *Perf. 14x14½*

197 CD316 12½c red brown .35 .35

Notwani River Dam, Gaberones Water Supply — A17

Wmk. 314

1965, Mar. 1 Photo. *Perf. 14½*

198 A17 2½c dark red & gold .25 .25
199 A17 5c deep ultra & gold .30 .25
200 A17 12½c brown & gold .40 .40
201 A17 25c emerald & gold .60 .60
Nos. 198-201 (4) 1.55 1.50

Internal self-government, Mar. 1, 1965.

ITU Issue
Common Design Type

Perf. 11x11½

1965, May 17 Litho. Wmk. 314

202 CD317 2½c ver & dl yel .35 .25
203 CD317 12½c red lil & pale brn .85 .50

Intl. Cooperation Year Issue
Common Design Type

1965, Oct. 25 *Perf. 14½*

204 CD318 1c bl grn & claret .25 *.40*
205 CD318 12½c lt vio & grn .75 .75

Churchill Memorial Issue
Common Design Type

1966, Jan. 24 Photo. *Perf. 14*

Design in Black, Gold and Carmine Rose

206 CD319 1c bright blue .25 *.75*
207 CD319 2½c green .45 .25
208 CD319 12½c brown 1.00 .50
209 CD319 20c violet 1.10 .80
Nos. 206-209 (4) 2.80 2.30

Haslar Smoke Generator — A18

Wmk. 314

1966, June 1 Photo. *Perf. 14½*

210 A18 2½c shown .35 .25
211 A18 5c Bugler .35 .25
212 A18 15c Gun site .40 .40
213 A18 35c Regimental cap badge 1.00 .85
Nos. 210-213 (4) 2.10 1.75

25th anniv. of the Bechuanaland Pioneers and Gunners of World War II.

POSTAL-FISCAL STAMPS

Transvaal No. 274 Overprinted

1910, July Wmk. 3

AR1 A27 12sh6p brn org & blk 190.00 *375.00*

This stamp was issued for fiscal use in January 1907, but the "POSTAGE" inscription was not obliterated, and examples were accepted for postal use during 1910-11.

Bechuanaland No. 16 surcharged "£5"

1918 Wmk. 29

AR2 A1 £5 on 1sh green *18,000.* —

The known used examples of AR2 are all fiscally used.

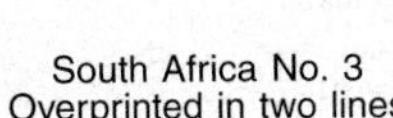

South Africa No. 3 Overprinted in two lines

1922 Wmk. 177

AR3 A2 1p rose red 50.00 *155.00*

POSTAGE DUE STAMPS

Postage Due Stamps of Great Britain Overprinted

On Stamp of 1914-22

1926 Wmk. 33 *Perf. 14x14½*

J1 D1 1p carmine 11.00 *125.00*

On Stamps of 1924-30
Wmk. 35

J2 D1 ½p emerald 11.00 *75.00*

Overprinted

J3 D1 2p black brown 11.00 *100.00*
Nos. J1-J3 (3) 33.00 *300.00*
Set, never hinged 52.50

D2

1932 Wmk. 4 Typo. *Perf. 14½*

J4 D2 ½p olive green 6.75 *60.00*
J5 D2 1p carmine rose 8.00 *10.00*
a. 1p carmine ('58) 1.50 27.50
J6 D2 2p dull violet 10.00 *55.00*
a. 2p violet ('58) 1.75 22.00
c. As "a," thick "d" 42.50
Nos. J4-J6 (3) 24.75 *125.00*
Set, never hinged 40.00

Nos. J5a, J6a and J6b are on chalky paper. For detailed listings, see the Scott Classic Specialized catalogue.

Catalogue values for unused stamps in this section, from this point to the end of the section, are for Never Hinged items.

Nos. J4-J6 Surcharged

Type I

Type II

1961, Feb. 14 Chalky Paper

J7 D2 1c on 1p car rose, II .25 *1.75*
a. Type I .30 .60
b. Double surcharge, II 325.00
c. Ordinary paper, II 17.50 *55.00*
J8 D2 2c on 2p dull vio, II .25 *2.00*
a. Thick "d," II 4.75
b. Ordinary paper, II 160.00 *140.00*
c. As "b," thick "d" *700.00*
d. Type I .35 *1.75*
e. As "d," thick "d" 7.50

Ordinary Paper

J9 D2 5c on ½p ol green, I .50 *.75*
Nos. J7-J9 (3) 1.00 *4.50*

Denominations in Cents

1961 Wmk. 4 *Perf. 14*

J10 D2 1c carmine rose .30 *2.25*
J11 D2 2c dull violet .30 *2.00*
J12 D2 5c olive green .50 *2.00*
Nos. J10-J12 (3) 1.10 *6.25*

BELARUS

ˌbē-lə-ˈrüs

(Byelorussia)

(White Russia)

LOCATION — Eastern Europe, bounded by Russia, Latvia, Lithuania and Poland

GOVT. — Independent republic, member of the Commonwealth of Independent States

AREA — 80,134 sq. mi.

POP. — 10,401,784 (1999 est.)

CAPITAL — Minsk

With the breakup of the Soviet Union on Dec. 26, 1991, Belarus and ten former Soviet republics established the Commonwealth of Independent States.

100 Kopecks = 1 Ruble

Catalogue values for all unused stamps in this country are for Never Hinged items.

Five denominations, perf and imperf, of this design produced in 1920 were not put in use. Value $5. Forgeries abound.

Cross of Ephrosinia of Polotsk — A1

1992, Mar. 20 Litho. *Perf. 12x12½*

1 A1 1r multicolored .35 .35

For overprint and surcharge see Nos. 17, 230.

R.R. Schurma (1892-1978), Composer A2

1992, Apr. 10 Photo. *Perf. 12x11½*

2 A2 20k blue & black .35 .35

For surcharge see No. 203.

Arms of Polotsk — A3

Designs: No. 13, Stag jumping fence. No. 14, Man's head, sword.

1992-94 Photo. *Perf. 12x11½*

11 A3 2r shown .35 .35

Perf. 12x12½

12 A3 25r Minsk .35 .35
13 A3 700r Grodno .45 .45
14 A3 700r Vitebsk .45 .45
Nos. 11-14 (4) 1.60 1.60

Issued: 2r, 6/9/92; 25r, 11/11/93; Nos. 13, 14, 10/17/94.

National Symbols A4

Designs: No. 15, Natl. arms. No. 16, Map, flag.

1992, Aug. 31 Litho. *Perf. 12x12½*

15 A4 5r black, red & yellow .50 .50
16 A4 5r multicolored .50 .50

For surcharges see Nos. 55-58, 61-64.

No. 1 Overprinted

Cross of Ephrosinia of Polotsk — A5

1992, Sept. 25 Litho. *Perf. 12x12½*

17 A1 1r on #1 multi .35 .35

Souvenir Sheet

Perf. 12

18 A5 5r multicolored .60 .60

Orthodox Church in Belarus, 1000th anniv.

No. 18, imperf, was issued Feb. 15, 1993. Value $1.25.

For surcharges see Nos. 59-60, 65-66.

Buildings A6

Designs: No. 19, Church of Boris Gleb, Grodno, 12th cent. No. 20, World Castle, 16th cent. No. 21, Nyasvizh Castle, 16th-19th cent. No. 22, Kamyanets Tower, 12th-13th cent, vert. No. 23, Church of Ephrosinia of Polotsk, 12th cent., vert. No. 24, Calvinist Church, Zaslaw, 16th cent., vert.

1992, Oct. 15 Litho. *Perf. 12*

19 A6 2r multicolored .25 .25
20 A6 2r multicolored .25 .25
21 A6 2r multicolored .25 .25
22 A6 2r multicolored .25 .25
23 A6 2r multicolored .25 .25
24 A6 2r multicolored .25 .25
Nos. 19-24 (6) 1.50 1.50

Centuries of construction are in Roman numerals.

Natl. Arms — A7

1992-94 Litho. *Perf. 12x12½*

25 A7 30k light blue .25 .25
26 A7 45k olive green .25 .25
27 A7 50k green .25 .25
28 A7 1r brown .25 .25
29 A7 2r red brown .25 .25
30 A7 3r org yellow .25 .25
31 A7 5r blue .25 .25
32 A7 10r red .50 .35
33 A7 15r violet .35 .25
34 A7 25r yellow green .50 .40
35 A7 50r bright pink .25 .25
36 A7 100r henna brown .50 .30
37 A7 150r plum .75 .40
38 A7 200r blue green .25 .25
39 A7 300r salmon pink .25 .25
40 A7 600r light lilac .40 .25
40A A7 1000r rose carmine .65 .25
40B A7 3000r gray blue 1.50 .50
Nos. 25-40B (18) 7.65 5.20

Issued: 30k, 45k, 50k, 11/10; 1r-3r, 10r, 1/4/93; 5r, 15r, 25r, 2/9/93; 50r, 100r, 150r, 6/16/93; 200r-3,000r, 12/28/94; others, 1992.

For surcharges see Nos. 72-74, 141-142, 211A-212.

Ceramics A8

Designs: No. 41, Pitcher and bowl. No. 42, Four pieces on tree branches. No. 43, Two large pitchers. No. 44, One large pitcher.

1992, Dec. 24 Litho. *Perf. 11½*

41 A8 1r multicolored .25 .25
42 A8 1r multicolored .25 .25
43 A8 1r multicolored .25 .25
44 A8 1r multicolored .25 .25
Nos. 41-44 (4) 1.00 1.00

M. I. Garetzky (1893-1938), Writer — A9

1993, June 22 Photo. *Perf. 12x11½*

45 A9 50r magenta .40 .40

Straw Figures A10

Designs: 5r, Chickens. 10r, Child, mother, vert. 15r, Woman, vert. 25r, Man with scythe, woman with rake, vert.

Perf. 12x11½, 11½x12

1993, Apr. 22 Litho.

47 A10 5r multicolored .25 .25
48 A10 10r multicolored .25 .25
49 A10 15r multicolored .25 .25
50 A10 25r multicolored .40 .40
Nos. 47-50 (4) 1.15 1.15

First World Congress of White Russians — A11

1993, July 8 Litho. *Perf. 12*

51 A11 50r multicolored .60 .60

Europa — A12

Paintings by Chagall: No. 52, Promenade, vert. No. 53, Man Over Vitebsk. 2500r, Allegory.

1993, Oct. 12 Litho. *Perf. 14*

52 A12 1500r multicolored *6.00 6.00*
53 A12 1500r multicolored *6.00 6.00*
a. Pair, #52-53 *12.00 12.00*

Souvenir Sheet

54 A12 2500r multicolored *40.00 40.00*

Nos. 15-16, 18 Surcharged

Size and location of surcharge varies.

1993, Oct. 15 Litho. *Perf. 12x12½*

55 A4(a) 1500r on 5r #15 *4.50 4.50*
56 A4(b) 1500r on 5r #15 *4.50 4.50*
a. Pair, #55-56 *11.50 11.50*
57 A4(c) 1500r on 5r #16 *4.50 4.50*
58 A4(d) 1500r on 5r #16 *4.50 4.50*
a. Pair, #57-58 *11.50 11.50*
Nos. 55-58 (4) *18.00 18.00*

Souvenir Sheets

Perf. 12

Overprints "e" & "f" on No. 18 are slightly different and have the wording at right reading down and Olympic Rings in upper left corner. No. 59 in Belarusian and No. 60 in English.

59 A5(e) 1500r on 5r #18 *10.00 10.00*
60 A5(f) 1500r on 5r #18 *10.00 10.00*

Nos. 59 and 60 exist imperf. Value, each $15. The status of No. 60 is in question.

Nos. 15-16, 18 Surcharged

Size and location of surcharge varies.

1993, Oct. 15 Litho. *Perf. 12x12½*

61 A4(g) 1500r on 5r #15 *4.50 4.50*
62 A4(h) 1500r on 5r #15 *4.50 4.50*
a. Pair, #61-62 *11.50 11.50*
63 A4(i) 1500r on 5r #16 *4.50 4.50*
64 A4(j) 1500r on 5r #16 *4.50 4.50*
a. Pair, #63-64 *11.50 11.50*
Nos. 61-64 (4) *18.00 18.00*

Souvenir Sheets

Perf. 12

Overprints "k" & "l" on No. 18 are slightly different and have the wording at right reading down. No. 65 in Belarusian and No. 66 in English.

65 A5(k) 1500r on 5r #18 *10.00 10.00*
66 A5(l) 1500r on 5r #18 *10.00 10.00*

The status of Nos. 65-66 are in question. They exist imperf. Value, each $15.

Stansilavski Church A13

1993, Nov. 24 Litho. *Perf. 12*

67 A13 150r multicolored .50 .50

For surcharge see No. 242.

Famous People A14

Designs: 50r, Kastus Kalinovsky, led 1863 independence movement. No. 69, Prince Rogvold of Polotsk, map of Polotsk. No. 70, Princess Rogneda, daughter of Rogvold, fortress. 100r, Statue of Simon Budny (1530-93), writer and printer, vert.

1993 *Perf. 12x12½, 12½x12*

68 A14 50r multicolored .30 .30
69 A14 75r multicolored .30 .30
70 A14 75r multicolored .30 .30
71 A14 100r multicolored .30 .30
Nos. 68-71 (4) 1.20 1.20

Issued: 50r, 12/29; 75r, 12/30; 100r, 12/31.

Nos. 27, 29, 30 Surcharged

1994, Feb. 1 Photo. ***Perf. 12x12½***

No.	Type	Description	Unused	Used
72	A7	15r on 30k light green	.30	.30
73	A7	25r on 45k olive green	.30	.30
74	A7	50r on 50k green	.30	.30
		Nos. 72-74 (3)	.90	.90

Birds — A15

1994, Jan. 19 Litho. ***Perf. 11½***

No.	Type	Description	Unused	Used
75	A15	20r Aguila chrysaetos	.25	.25
76	A15	40r Cygnus olor	.25	.25
77	A15	40r Alcedo atthis	.25	.25
a.		Block of 3, #75-77 + label	.60	.60

See Nos. 87-89. For surcharge see No. 303.

Six World Wildlife Fund labels with 1000r denominations depicting 3 different animals and 3 different birds exist. They were not valid for postage.

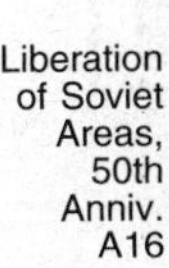

Liberation of Soviet Areas, 50th Anniv. A16

No. 78 — Battle maps and: a, Katyusha rockets, liberation of Russia. b, Fighter planes, liberation of Ukraine. c, Combined offensive, liberation of Belarus.

1994, July 3 Litho. ***Perf. 12***

No.	Type	Description	Unused	Used
78	A16	500r Block of 3 #a.-c. + label	.55	.55

See Russia No. 6213, Ukraine No. 195.

1994 Winter Olympics, Lillehammer A17

1994, Aug. 30 Litho. ***Perf. 12x12½***

No.	Type	Description	Unused	Used
79	A17	1000r Speed skating	.30	.30
80	A17	1000r Women's figure skating	.30	.30
81	A17	1000r Hockey	.30	.30
82	A17	1000r Cross-country skiing	.30	.30
83	A17	1000r Biathlon	.30	.30
		Nos. 79-83 (5)	1.50	1.50

Painters — A18

Designs: No. 84, Farmer, oxen in field, by Ferdinand Rushchyts. No. 85, Knight on horseback, by Jasev Drazdovich. No. 86, Couple walking up path, by Petra Sergievich.

1994, July 18 Litho. ***Perf. 12***

No.	Type	Description	Unused	Used
84	A18	300r multicolored	.25	.25
85	A18	300r multicolored	.25	.25
86	A18	300r multicolored	.25	.25
		Nos. 84-86 (3)	.75	.75

For overprint see No. 127.

Bird Type of 1994

1994, Sept. 30 ***Perf. 11½***

No.	Type	Description	Unused	Used
87	A15	300r like #75	.25	.25
88	A15	400r like #76	.25	.25
89	A15	400r like #77	.25	.25
		Nos. 87-89 (3)	.75	.75

Ilya Yefimovich Repin (1844-1930), Ukrainian Painter — A19

Designs: No. 90, Self-portrait. No. 91, Repin Museum.

1994, Oct. 31 Litho. ***Perf. 12x12½***

No.	Type	Description	Unused	Used
90		1000r multicolored	.30	.30
91		1000r multicolored	.30	.30
a.		A19 Pair, #90-91	.60	.60

Churches A20

Designs: No. 92, Sacred Consolidated Church, Sinkavitsch, 16th cent. No. 93, Sts. Peter and Paul Cathedral, Gomel, 19th cent.

1994, Oct. 20 Litho. ***Perf. 12***

No.	Type	Description	Unused	Used
92	A20	700r multicolored	.25	.25
93	A20	700r multicolored	.25	.25

Kosciuszko Uprising, Bicent. (in 1994) — A21

Battle scene and: No. 94, Tomasz Vaishetcki (1754-1816). No. 95, Jakov Jasinski (1761-94). No. 96, Tadeusz Kosziuszko (1746-1817). No. 97, Mikhail K. Aginski (1765-1833).

1995, Jan. 11 ***Perf. 12½x12***

No.	Type	Description	Unused	Used
94	A21	600r multicolored	.30	.30
95	A21	600r multicolored	.30	.30
96	A21	1000r multicolored	.30	.30
97	A21	1000r multicolored	.30	.30
		Nos. 94-97 (4)	1.20	1.20

End of World War II, 50th Anniv. — A22

1995, May 4 Litho. ***Perf. 13½***

No.	Type	Description	Unused	Used
98	A22	180r multicolored	.25	.25
99	A22	600r multicolored	.25	.25

Nos. 98-99 exist imperf. Value, set $125.

A23

1995, May 7 ***Perf. 14***

No.	Type	Description	Unused	Used
100	A23	600r A Popov	.35	.35

Radio, cent. Exists imperf. Value, $35.

A24

1995-96 Litho. ***Perf. 13x14***

No.	Type	Description	Unused	Used
102	A24	180r olive brown & red	.25	.25
103	A24	200r gray green & bister	.25	.25
105	A24	280r green & blue	.25	.25
109	A24	600r plum & bister	.35	.35
		Nos. 102-109 (4)	1.10	1.10

No. 102 exists imperf. Value, $30.
Issued: 180r, 5/10/95; 280r, 5/18/95; 600r, 8/29/95; 200r, 1/30/96.
For surcharges see Nos. 401-402.

Ivan Chersky (1845-92), Geographer A25

1995, May 15 Litho. ***Perf. 13½x14***

No.	Type	Description	Unused	Used
113	A25	600r multicolored	.35	.35

Exists imperf. Value, $45.

Traditional Costumes — A26

Designs: 600r, Woman wearing shawl, coat, ankle length skirt, man with long coat. 1200r, Woman wearing shawl & apron holding child, man wearing vest, knickers.

1995, July 13 Litho. ***Perf. 14½x14***

No.	Type	Description	Unused	Used
114	A26	180r multicolored	.25	.25
115	A26	600r multicolored	.25	.25
116	A26	1200r multicolored	.35	.35
		Nos. 114-116 (3)	.85	.85

See Nos. 164-167, 214-216.

World Wildlife Fund — A27

Various depictions of beaver.

1995, July 20 ***Perf. 12***

No.	Type	Description	Unused	Used
117	A27	300r multi	.30	.30
118	A27	450r multi	.30	.30
119	A27	450r multi, horiz.	.30	.30
120	A27	800r multi, horiz.	.30	.30
		Nos. 117-120 (4)	1.20	1.20

A28

A29

1995, Aug. 29 Litho. ***Perf. 14***

No.	Type	Description	Unused	Used
121	A28	600r Book Fair	.30	.30

Exists imperf. Value, $50.

1995, Oct. 3 Litho. ***Perf. 14***

No.	Type	Description	Unused	Used
122	A29	600r Natl. arms	.25	.25
123	A29	600r Flag	.25	.25

New national symbols. Nos. 122-123 exist imperf. Value, set $100.

UN, 50th Anniv. — A30

1995, Oct. 24 Litho. ***Perf. 13½x14***

No.	Type	Description	Unused	Used
124	A30	600r bister, black & blue	.30	.30

Exists imperf. Value, $40.

Churches A31

Designs: No. 125, Mstislav, 17th-19th cent. No. 126, Kamai, 17th cent.

1995, Nov. 21 ***Perf. 14***

No.	Type	Description	Unused	Used
125	A31	600r multicolored	.25	.25
126	A31	600r multicolored	.25	.25

No. 84 Overprinted

1995, Dec. 27 Litho. ***Perf. 12***

No.	Type	Description	Unused	Used
127	A18	300r multicolored	.25	.25

P. V. Sukhi (1895-1975), Airplane Designer A32

1995, Dec. 27 ***Perf. 13½***

No.	Type	Description	Unused	Used
128	A32	600r multicolored	.25	.25

Exists imperf. Value, $45.

Wildlife A33

Designs: 1000r, Lynx lynx. No. 130, Capreolus capreolus. No. 131, Ursus arctos. 3000r, Alces alces. 5000r, Bison bonasus. 10,000r, Cervus elaphus, vert.

1995-96 Litho. *Perf. 14*

129	A33	1000r multi	.30	.30
130	A33	2000r multi, vert.	.35	.35
131	A33	2000r multi	.35	.35
132	A33	3000r multi, vert.	.40	.40
133	A33	5000r multi	.55	.55
		Nos. 129-133 (5)	1.95	1.95

Souvenir Sheet

Imperf

134	A33	10,000r multicolored	2.50	2.50

Issued: Nos. 129-133, 2/6/96; No. 134, 12/29/95.

For surcharge, see No. 607.

Famous People — A34

Designs: 600r, L. Sapega (1557-1633), statesman. 1200r, K. Semyanovitch (1600-51), military scholar. 1800r, S. Polotzki (1629-80), writer.

1995, Dec. 30 Litho. *Perf. 12*

135	A34	600r multicolored	.30	.30
136	A34	1200r multicolored	.30	.30
137	A34	1800r multicolored	.30	.30
		Nos. 135-137 (3)	.90	.90

Miniature Sheet

Butterflies — A35

No. 138: a, Apatura iris. b, Lopinga achine. c, Callimorpha dominula. d, Catocala fraxini. e, Papilio machaon. f, Parnassius apollo. g, Ammobiota hebe. h, Colias palaeno.

No. 139, Proserpinus proserpina. No. 140, Vacciniina optilete.

1996, Mar. 29 Litho. *Perf. 14*

138	A35	300r Sheet of 8, #a.-h.	4.00	4.00

Souvenir Sheets

139-140	A35	1000r Set of 2	9.50	9.50

Inscribed 1995.

Nos. 28, 34 Surcharged in Green or Red

1996 Litho. *Perf. 12x12½*

141	A7	(B) on 1r #28 (G)	.25	.25
142	A7	(A) on 25r #34 (R)	.25	.25

Nos. 141-142 were valued at 200r and 400r, respectively, on day of issue.

Issued: No. 141, 2/28; No. 142, 3/13.

Souvenir Sheet

Beaver — A36

1996, Mar. 26 Litho. *Perf. 12½x12*

143	A36	1200r multicolored	.35	.35

Kondrat Krapiva (1896-1991), Writer — A37

1996, Mar. 5 Litho. *Perf. 14x14½*

144	A37	1000r multicolored	.25	.25

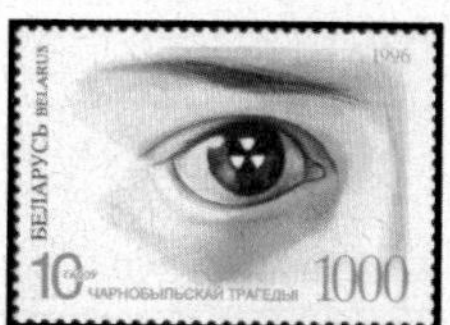

Chernobyl Disaster, 10th Anniv. A38

No. 145 — Radiation symbol and: a, Eye. b, Leaf showing contamination. c, Boarded-up window.

1996, Apr. 10 Litho. *Perf. 14*

145	A38	1000r Block of 3, #a.-c. + label	.50	.50

Coat of Arms — A39

1996, May 6 Litho. *Perf. 13½*

146	A39	100r blue & black	.25	.25
147	A39	500r green & black	.25	.25
148	A39	600r ver & black	.25	.25
149	A39	1000r org & black	.25	.25
150	A39	1500r dp lil rose & blk	.25	.25
151	A39	1800r violet & black	.25	.25
152	A39	2200r rose vio & blk	.25	.25
153	A39	3300r yellow & blk	.30	.30
154	A39	5000r grn bl & blk	.40	.55
155	A39	10,000r ap grn & blk	.90	1.10
156	A39	30,000r brn & black	2.75	3.00
157	A39	50,000r red brn & blk	4.50	5.25
		Nos. 146-157 (12)	10.60	11.95

See Nos. 182, 196-201. For surcharges see Nos. 395-399.

Agreement with Russia A40

1996, June 14 *Perf. 13½x14*

158	A40	1500r multicolored	.40	.40

Exists imperf. Value, $40.

1996 Summer Olympic Games, Atlanta A41

1996, July 15 Litho. *Perf. 14*

159	A41	3000r Rhythmic gymnastics	.55	.55
160	A41	3000r Discus	.55	.55
161	A41	3000r Wrestling	.55	.55
162	A41	3000r Weight lifting	.55	.55
		Nos. 159-162 (4)	2.20	2.20

Nos. 159-162 exist imperf. Value, set $300.

Souvenir Sheet

Imperf

163	A41	5000r Shooting, vert.	1.00	1.00

No. 163 has simulated perforations.

Regional Costume Type of 1995

Couples in traditional 19th cent. costumes: 1800r, Kapilska-Kletzky region. 2200r, David-Gorodok-Turai region. 3300r, Kobrin region. 5000r, Naralyan region.

1996, Aug. 13 Litho. *Perf. 14*

164	A26	1800r multicolored	.30	.30
165	A26	2200r multicolored	.35	.35
166	A26	3300r multicolored	.40	.40
		Nos. 164-166 (3)	1.05	1.05

Souvenir Sheet

Imperf

167	A26	5000r multicolored	1.00	1.00

Medicinal Plants — A42

No. 168, Sanguisorba officinaus. No. 169, Acorus calamus. 2200r, Potentilla erecta. 3300r, Frangula alnus. 5000r, Menyanthes trifoliata.

1996, Aug. 15 *Perf. 14x13½*

168	A42	1500r multicolored	.25	.25
169	A42	1500r multicolored	.25	.25
170	A42	2200r multicolored	.25	.25
171	A42	3300r multicolored	.35	.35
		Nos. 168-171 (4)	1.10	1.10

Souvenir Sheet

Imperf

172	A42	5000r multicolored	.90	.90

Birds A44

No. 173: a, Ardea cinerea. b, Ciconia nigra. c, Phalacrocorax caroo. d, Ciconia ciconia. e, Larus ridibundus. f, Gallinago gallinago. g, Chlidonias leucopterus. h, Remiz pendulinus. i, Botaurus stellaris. j, Fulica atra. k, Ixobrychus minutus. l, Alcedo atthts.

No. 174: a, Anas crecca. b, Anas strepera. c, Anas acuta. d, Anas platyrhynchos. e, Aythya marila. f, Clangula hyemalis. g, Anas clypeata. h, Anas querquedula. i, Anas penelope. j, Arthya nyroca. k, Bucephala clangula. l, Mergus merganser. m, Mergus albellus. n, Aythya fuligula. o, Mergus serrator. p, Aythya ferina.

Each 1000r: No. 175, Aythya ferina, diff. No. 176, Gallinago gallinago, diff.

1996, Sept. 10 Litho. *Perf. 14*

173	A44	400r Sheet of 12, #a.-l.	6.00	6.00
174	A44	400r Sheet of 16, #a.-p.	6.00	6.00

Souvenir Sheets

175-176	A44	Set of 2	8.00	8.00

Grammar Book, 1596 — A45

1996, Sept. 19 Litho. *Perf. 14x13½*

177	A45	1500r multicolored	.35	.35

Exists imperf. Value, $30.

Churches A46

1996, Sept. 24 *Perf. 14x14½*

178	A46	3300r Pinsk	.35	.35
179	A46	3300r Mogilev, 17th cent.	.35	.35

Nos. 178-179 exist imperf.

Mikola Shchakatskin (1896-1940), Art Critic — A47

1996, Oct. 16

180	A47	2000r multicolored	.40	.40

Minsk Telephone Station, Cent. A48

1996, Nov. 14

181	A48	2000r multicolored	.40	.40

Natl. Arms Type of 1996

1996, Nov. 21 Litho. *Perf. 13½x14*

182	A39	200r gray green & black	.35	.35

Pres. Aleksandr G. Lukashenka, Natl. Flag — A49

1996, Dec. 6 Litho. *Perf. 13½*

183	A49	2500r multicolored	.40	.40

Famous Men — A50

Designs: No. 184, Kyril Turovski (1130-81), Bishop of Turov. No. 185, Mikola Gusovski

(1470-1533), writer. No. 186, Mikolaj Radziwil (1515-65), chancellor of Lithuania.

1996, Dec. 17 *Perf. 13½*

184 A50 3000r multicolored .40 .40
185 A50 3000r multicolored .40 .40
186 A50 3000r multicolored .40 .40
Nos. 184-186 (3) 1.20 1.20

New Year — A51

Designs: 1500r, Christmas tree, buildings in Minsk.

1996, Dec. 21 *Perf. 14*

187 A51 1500r multicolored .25 .25
188 A51 2000r multicolored, vert. .30 .30

Nos. 187-188 exist imperf. Value, set $50.

Natl. Museum of Art, Minsk — A52

Icons: No. 189, Madonna and Child, Smolensk, 16th cent. No. 190, Paraskeva, 16th cent. No. 191, Ilya, 17th cent. No. 192, Three saints, 18th cent.
5000r, Birth of Christ, by Peter Yacijevitsch, 1649.

1996, Dec. 26 *Perf. 13½*

189 A52 3500r multicolored .35 .35
190 A52 3500r multicolored .35 .35
191 A52 3500r multicolored .35 .35
192 A52 3500r multicolored .35 .35
Nos. 189-192 (4) 1.40 1.40

Souvenir Sheet

Imperf

193 A46 5000r multicolored .90 .90

Georgi K. Zhukov (1896-1974), Soviet Marshal A53

1997, Jan. 3 *Perf. 13½*

194 A53 2000r multicolored .35 .35

Kupala Natl. Theater, Minsk — A54

1997, Jan. 3 *Perf. 13½x14*

195 A54 3500r multicolored .45 .45

Exists imperf.

Coat of Arms Type of 1996

1997 **Litho.** *Perf. 13½x14*

196 A39 400r lt brown & black .30 .30
197 A39 800r dull blue & black .30 .30
198 A39 1500r brt blue & black .55 .55
199 A39 2000r apple green & black .70 .70
200 A39 2500r dk blue & black .60 .60
201 A39 3000r brown & black .55 .55
Nos. 196-201 (6) 3.00 3.00

Issued: 400r, 2000r, 1/9; 1500r, 1/16; 800r, 2500r, 3000r, 9/22.
For surcharge see No. 398.

V.K. Byalynitsky-Birulya (1872-1957), Painter — A55

1997, Feb. 26 *Perf. 14*

202 A55 2000r multicolored .40 .40

No. 2 Surcharged in Gray

1997, Mar. 10 **Photo.** *Perf. 12x11½*

203 A2 3500r on 20k bl & blk .60 .60

Fish — A56

Designs: 2000r, Salmo trutta. 3000r, Vimba vimba. No. 206, Thymallus thymallus. No. 207, Barbus barbus.
5000r, Acipenser ruthenus.

1997, Apr. 10 **Litho.** *Perf. 13½x14*

204 A56 2000r multicolored .30 .30
205 A56 3000r multicolored .40 .40
206 A56 4500r multicolored .50 .50
207 A56 4500r multicolored .50 .50
Nos. 204-207 (4) 1.70 1.70

Souvenir Sheet

208 A56 5000r multicolored 1.00 1.00

Intl. Conference on Sustainable Development of Countries with Economies in Transition — A57

Designs: 3000r, Earth with "SOS" formed in atmosphere. 4500r, Hand above flora and fauna.

1997, Apr. 16 *Perf. 14x14½*

209 A57 3000r multicolored .50 .50
210 A57 4500r multicolored .75 .75
a. Pair, #209-210 + label 1.25 1.25

Entry into UPU, 50th Anniv. — A58

1997, May 13 *Perf. 14½x14*

211 A58 3000r multicolored .55 .55

Nos. 28-29 Surcharged in Violet Blue

1997 **Litho.** *Perf. 12x12½*

211A A7 100r on 1r brown *8.00 8.00*
212 A7 100r on 2r red brown .25 .25

Issued: 2r, 5/22. No. 211A, surcharged in error, was not regularly issued.

World War II Liberation Day, July 3 — A59

1997, June 26 *Perf. 14½x14*

213 A59 3000r multicolored .50 .50

Traditional Costume Type

Men and women in 19th cent. costumes, regions: 2000r, Dzisna. 3000r, Navagrudak. 4500r, Byhau.

1997, July 10

214 A26 2000r multicolored .30 .30
215 A26 3000r multicolored .50 .50
216 A26 4500r multicolored .75 .75
Nos. 214-216 (3) 1.55 1.55

Book Printing in Belarus, 480th Anniv. — A60

Designs: No. 217, Text, Vilnius period. No. 218, Text, Prague period. 4000r, F. Skorina (1488-1535), Polatsk period. 7500r, F. Skorina, Krakow period.

1997, Sept. 7 *Perf. 13½*

217 A60 3000r shown .30 .30
218 A60 3000r gray, black & red .30 .30
219 A60 4000r gray, black & red .40 .40
220 A60 7500r gray, black & red .75 .75
Nos. 217-220 (4) 1.75 1.75

Pinsk Jesuit College A61

1997, Sept. 13 *Perf. 14x14½*

221 A61 3000r multicolored .50 .50

National Library, 75th Anniv. A62

1997, Sept. 15

222 A62 3000r multicolored .50 .50

Belarus School for the Blind, Cent. A63

1997, Sept. 28 **Litho.** *Perf. 14x14¼*

223 A63 3000r multicolored .50 .50

Intl. Children's Day — A64

1997, Sept. 28 **Litho.** *Perf. 14x14½*

224 A64 3000r multicolored .50 .50

Fight Against AIDS — A65

1997, Oct. 14 *Perf. 14½x14*

225 A65 4000r multicolored .50 .50

Farm Tractors A66

Designs: 3300r, Belarus "1221." 4400r, First wheel tractor, 1953. No. 228, Belarus "952." No. 229, Belarus "680."

1997, Oct. 16 *Perf. 14x14½*

226 A66 3300r multicolored .35 .35
227 A66 4400r multicolored .50 .50
228 A66 7500r multicolored .70 .70
229 A66 7500r multicolored .70 .70
a. Sheet, 2 ea #226-229 + label 5.25 5.25
Nos. 226-229 (4) 2.25 2.25

No. 1 Surcharged

1997, Dec. 8 **Litho.** *Perf. 12x12½*

230 A1 3000r on 1r multi .50 .50

Holiday Greetings A68

1997, Dec. 23 **Litho.** *Perf. 14x14¼*

231 A68 1400r New Year .25 .25
232 A68 4400r Christmas .50 .50

1998 Winter Olympic Games, Nagano — A69

Designs: a, 2000r, Cross country skiing. b, 3300r, Ice hockey. c, 4400r, Biathlon. d, 7500r, Freestyle skiing.

1998, Feb. 3 **Litho.** *Perf. 13½*

233 A69 Block of 4, #a.-d. 1.50 1.50

P.M. Mascherov (1918-80), Author — A70

1998, Feb. 12 Litho. *Perf. 13½*

234 A70 2500r multicolored .45 .45

Minsk Automobile Plant — A71

Dump trucks: 1400r, 1947 MAZ-205. 2000r, 1968 MAZ-503B. 3000r, 1977 MAZ-5549. 4400r, 1985 MAZ-5551. 7500r, 1994 MAZ-5516.

1998, Apr. 23 Litho. *Perf. 13½*

235 A71 1400r multicolored .40 .40
236 A71 2000r multicolored .40 .40
237 A71 3000r multicolored .50 .50
238 A71 4400r multicolored .70 .70
239 A71 7500r multicolored 1.10 1.10
a. Souvenir sheet, #235-239 + label 2.00 2.00
Nos. 235-239 (5) 3.10 3.10

A72 A73

1998, May 5 Litho. *Perf. 14*

240 A72 15,000r multicolored *1.00 1.00*

Europa. Town of Nesvizh, 775th Anniv.

1998, May 20 Litho. *Perf. 14*

241 A73 8600r multicolored 1.60 1.60

Adam Mickiewicz (1798-1855), poet.

No. 67 Surcharged in Silver with Post Horn, New Value and Cyrillic Text

1998, May 22 *Perf. 12*

242 A13 8600r on 150r multi .50 .50

St. Petersburt-Mahilyou Post Route, 225th anniv.

A74

Songbirds from Red Book of Belarus: 1500r, Luscinia svecica. 3200r, Remiz pendulinus. 3800r, Acrocephalus paludicola. 5300r, Locustella luscinioides. 8600r, Parus cyanus.

1998, May 29 *Perf. 14*

243 A74 1500r multicolored .30 .30
244 A74 3200r multicolored .40 .40
245 A74 3800r multicolored .40 .40
246 A74 5300r multicolored .60 .60
247 A74 8600r multicolored .80 .80
a. Sheet, 2 each #243-247 5.00 5.00
Nos. 243-247 (5) 2.50 2.50

A75

Designs: 100r, Water-powered mill. 200r, Windmill. 500r, Stork. 1000r, Bison. 2000r, Christmas Star. 3200r, Dulcimer. 5000r, Church, Synkovichy. 5300r, Hurdy-gurdy. 10,000r, Flaming wheel.

1998 *Perf. 13½x14*

248 A75 100r green & black .25 .25
249 A75 200r brown & black .25 .25
250 A75 500r bl, lt blu & blk .25 .25
251 A75 1000r grn, lt grn & blk .25 .25
252 A75 2000r bl, lt bl & blk .25 .25
253 A75 3200r ap grn & blk .50 .50
254 A75 5000r bl, lt bl & blk .25 .25
255 A75 5300r bis, blk & buff .75 .75
256 A75 10,000r org, lt org & blk .30 .30
Nos. 248-256 (9) 3.05 3.05

Issued: 100r, 200r, 7/1; 3200r, 5300r, 6/23; 2000r, 10,000r, 8/5;

See Nos. 282-288, 331-335, 338-339, 361, 363, 409-413. For surcharge see No. 400.

Belarussian Auto Works (BelAZ), 50th Anniv. — A76

Designs: 1500r, Front end loader.

Large quarry truck models: 3200r, #75131. 3800r, #75303. 5300r, #75483. 8600r, #755.

1998, Aug. 12 *Perf. 14x14½*

259 A76 1500r multicolored .25 .25
260 A76 3200r multicolored .25 .25
261 A76 3800r multicolored .25 .25
262 A76 5300r multicolored .25 .25
263 A76 8600r multicolored .25 .25
a. Sheet of 5, #259-263 + label 1.50 1.50

A77

Mushrooms: 2500r, Morchella esculenta. 3800r, Morchella conica. 4600r, Macrolepiota rhacodes. 5800r, Marcrolepiota procera. 9400r, Coprinus comatus.

1998, Sept. 10 Litho. *Perf. 14¼x14*

264 A77 2500r multicolored .25 .25
265 A77 3800r multicolored .25 .25
266 A77 4600r multicolored .25 .25
267 A77 5800r multicolored .25 .25
268 A77 9400r multicolored .25 .25
Nos. 264-268 (5) 1.25 1.25

Tête-bêche pair

264a A77 2500r .50 .50
265a A77 3800r .50 .50
266a A77 4600r .60 .60
267a A77 5800r .70 .70
268a A77 9400r 1.00 1.00

See Nos. 316-320.

Wooden Sculptures — A78

Designs: 3400r, Naversha, 12-13th cent. 3800r, Archangel Michael, 1470-1480. 5800r, Prophet Zacharias, 1642-1646. 9400r, Madonna and Child, 16th cent.

1998, Oct. 6 *Perf. 13½*

269 A78 3400r multicolored .25 .25
270 A78 3800r multicolored .25 .25
271 A78 5800r multicolored .25 .25
272 A78 9400r multicolored .25 .25
Nos. 269-272 (4) 1.00 1.00

World Stamp Day — A79

1998, Oct. 9 *Perf. 14x14½*

273 A79 5500r multicolored .30 .30

Paintings from Natl. Art Museum — A80

3000r, "Kalozha" (church), by V.K. Tsvirko (1913-93). 3500r, "Corner Living Room," by S.U. Zhukovsky (1875-1944). 5000r, "Winter Dream," by V.K. Byalynitsky-Birulya (1872-1957). 5500r, "Portrait of a Girl," by I.I. Alyashkevich (1777-1830). 10,000r, "Woman with a Bowl of Fruit," by I.F. Hrutski (1810-85).

1998, Oct. 20 *Perf. 13½*

274 A80 3000r multi .30 .30
275 A80 3500r multi .30 .30
276 A80 5000r multi .30 .30
277 A80 5500r multi, vert. .30 .30
278 A80 10,000r multi, vert. .30 .30
Nos. 274-278 (5) 1.50 1.50

A81 A82

1998, Nov. 25 *Perf. 14½x14*

279 A81 7100r multicolored .30 .30

Universal Declaration of Human Rights, 50th anniv.

1998, Nov. 30

Christmas and New Year: No. 280, Girl wearing short yellow coat, rabbit, log cabin. No. 281, Rabbit, girl wearing long fur-trimmed pink coat, hat.

280 A82 5500r multicolored .25 .25
281 A82 5500r multicolored .25 .25
a. Pair, #280-281 .40 .40

Type of 1998

Designs: 800r, Church. 1500r, Dulcimer. 3000r, Hurdy-gurdy. 30,000r, Water-powered mill. 50,000r, Windmill. 100,000r, Exhibition center, Minsk, horiz. 500,000r, Dancers.

Perf. 13½x14, 14x13½

1998-99 Litho.

282 A75 800r red lil, pale lil & blk .25 .25
283 A75 1500r golden brn, buff & blk .25 .25
284 A75 3000r yel, pale yel & blk .25 .25
285 A75 30,000r Prus bl, lt bl & blk .25 .25
286 A75 50,000r org, pale org & blk .40 .40
287 A75 100,000r brt pink & blk .60 .60
288 A75 500,000r brn & blk 2.00 2.00
Nos. 282-288 (7) 4.00 4.00

Issued: 800r, 2/5/99; 1500r, 3000r, 12/22/98; 30,000r, 50,000r, 4/14/99; 100,000r, 4/22/99; 500,000r, 6/25/99.

Statues of Aleksander Pushkin and Adam Mickiewicz, St. Petersburg — A95

1999, Jan. 20 Litho. *Perf. 13½*

294 A95 15,300r multi .30 .30

Trucks Made In Minsk — A96

10,000r, Model 8007. 15,000r, Model 543M rocket launcher. No. 297, Model 7907. No. 298, Model 543m with radar.

No. 299: a, 50,000r, Model 7917. b, 150,000r, Model 74135.

1999, Feb. 23

295 A96 10,000r multi .30 .30
296 A96 15,000r multi .30 .30
297 A96 30,000r multi .40 .40
298 A96 30,000r multi .40 .40
Nos. 295-298 (4) 1.40 1.40

Souvenir Sheet

299 A96 Sheet of 6, #295-298, 299a, 299b + 3 labels 2.25 2.25

No. 295 printed in sheets of 8.

See Nos. 322-323.

Glassware in National History and Culture Museum A97

1999, Mar. 4

300 A97 30,000r Goblet .25 .25
301 A97 30,000r Three pieces .25 .25
302 A97 100,000r Lamp .60 .60
Nos. 300-302 (3) 1.10 1.10

No. 77a Surcharged in Red

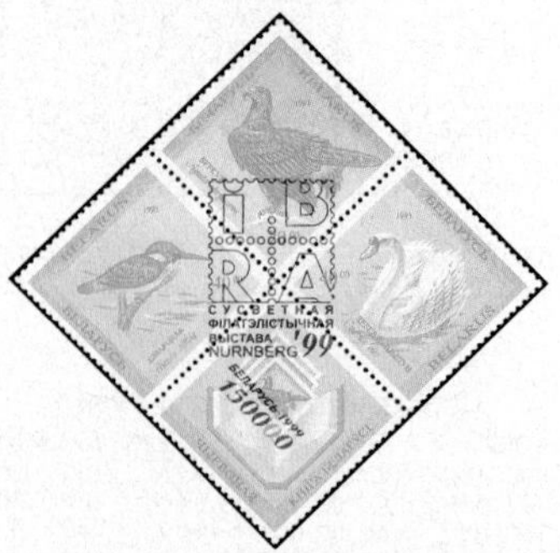

1999, Apr. 26 Litho. *Perf. 11½*

303 A15 150,000r on No. 77a 1.10 1.10

Europa — A98

Nature Reserves: No. 304, Berezina, 1925. No. 305, Belovezhskaya Forest, 1939.

1999, Apr. 27 Litho. *Perf. 13½*
304 A98 150,000r multicolored *1.00 1.00*
305 A98 150,000r multicolored *1.00 1.00*

Regional Architecture — A99

1999, June 10 Litho. *Perf. 13½*
306 A99 50,000r Well .35 .35
307 A99 50,000r House .35 .35
308 A99 100,000r Windmill .80 .80
Nos. 306-308 (3) 1.50 1.50

No. 306 printed in sheets of 8.

Paintings A100

Designs; 30,000r, Portrait of Y. M. Pen, by A. M. Brazer. 60,000r, St. Anthony's Church, Vitebsk, by S. B. Yudovin. No. 311, Street in Vitebsk, by Y. M. Pen. No. 312, House in Vitebsk, by M. P. Michalap, horiz.
200,000r, Etching by Marc Chagall.

1999, July 2
309 A100 30,000r multi .25 .25
310 A100 60,000r multi .35 .35
311 A100 100,000r multi .50 .50
312 A100 100,000r multi .50 .50
Nos. 309-312 (4) 1.60 1.60

Souvenir Sheet

313 A100 200,000r multi 2.00 2.00

V. M. Karvat (1958-96), Hero — A101

1999, Aug. 12
314 A101 25,000r multi .30 .30

UPU, 125th Anniv. — A102

No. 315: a, Minsk post office, 1954. b, First Minsk post office, 1800.

1999, Aug. 20
315 A102 150,000r Pair, #a.-b. 1.25 1.25

Mushroom Type of 1998

Designs: 30,000r, Flammulina velutipes. 50,000r, Kuehneromyces mutabilis. 75,000r, Lyophyllum connatum. 100,000r, Lyophyllum decastes.
150,000r, Armillariella mellea.

1999, Aug. 21 *Perf. 14¼x14*
316 A77 30,000r multi .25 .25
a. Tete beche pair .50 .50
317 A77 50,000r multi .45 .45
a. Tete beche pair .90 .90
318 A77 75,000r multi .70 .70
a. Tete beche pair 1.40 1.40
319 A77 100,000r multi 1.00 1.00
a. Tete beche pair 2.00 2.00
Nos. 316-319 (4) 2.40 2.40

Souvenir Sheet

320 A77 150,000r multi 1.10 1.10
a. Tete beche pair 2.25 2.25

Left margin of No. 320 is perforated, and sheet contains two labels.

Re-annexation of Western Belarus from Poland, 60th Anniv. — A103

1999, Sept. 17 Litho. *Perf. 13½x14*
321 A103 29,000r multi .30 .30

Truck Type of 1999

51,000r, MAZ-6430. 86,000r, MAZ-4370.

1999, Nov. 15 Litho. *Perf. 13½*
322 A96 51,000r multi .25 .25
323 A96 86,000r multi .35 .35

Children's Art — A104

1999, Nov. 25
324 A104 32,000r shown .25 .25
325 A104 59,000r Girl, vert. .25 .25

New Year A105

No. 326: a, Bear, snow-covered trees. b, People, snowman.

1999, Nov. 30 *Perf. 14x14¼*
326 A105 30,000r Pair, #a-b, + central label .30 .30

Christianity, 2000th Anniv. — A106

Designs: 50r, Spaso-Preobrazhenskaya Church, Polotsk. 75r, St. Atistratig Cathedral, Slutsk. 100r, Rev, Serafim Sorovsky Church, Beloozersk.

2000, Jan. 1 *Perf. 14¼x14*
327 A106 50r multi .35 .35
328 A106 75r multi .60 .60
329 A106 100r multi .90 .90
Nos. 327-329 (3) 1.85 1.85

Souvenir Sheet

Christianity, 2000th Anniversary — A107

No. 330: a, Mother of God mosaic, St. Sofia, Cathedral, Kiev, 11th cent. b, Christ Pantocrator fresco, Church of the Savoior's Transfiguration, Polotsk, 12th cent. c, Volodymyr Madonna, Tretiakov Gallery, Moscow, 12th cent.

2000, Jan. 5 *Perf. 12x12¼*
330 A107 100r Sheet of 3, #a-c 1.25 1.25

See Ukraine No. 370, Russia No. 6568.

Type of 1998 and

Kryzhachok Dancers — A108

2000-02 Litho. *Perf. 13¼x13¾*
Inscribed "2000"
331 A75 1r Bison .25 .25
332 A75 2r Christmas star .25 .25
333 A75 3r Hurdy-gurdy .25 .25
334 A75 5r Church, Synkovichy .25 .25
335 A75 10r Flaming wheel .25 .25
336 A108 A Kupala folk holiday .25 .25
337 A108 20r Kryzhachok dancers .25 .25
338 A75 30r Water-powered mill .25 .25
339 A75 50r Windmill, orange frame .40 .40
Nos. 331-339 (9) 2.40 2.40

Inscribed "2002"
333a A75 3r Hurdy-gurdy .25 .25
336a A108 A Kupala folk holiday .25 .25
337a A108 20r Kryzhachok dancers .25 .25
339a A75 50r Windmill, bister brn frame .30 .30
Nos. 333a-339a (4) 1.05 1.05

Booklet Stamp
Self-Adhesive
Serpentine Die Cut 5¾
340 A108 20r red & black .30 .30
a. Booklet pane of 18 3.00
Booklet, #340a 3.00

No. 336 sold for 19r on day of issue.
No. 340 has a line below the country name. Nos. 337 and 364 have lines of microprinting below the country name.
Issued: 1r, 5r, 10r, 1/6; No. 340, 1/14; 2r, 30r, 1/29; 3r, A, No. 337, 3/10; 50r, 4/6; Nos. 333a, 337a, 2/12/02; No. 336a, 4/24/02; No. 339a, 8/8/02.
See Nos. 362, 364-370, 414.

Sukhoi Fighter Aircraft A109

Designs: Nos. 341, 344a, Su-24. Nos. 342, 344b, Su-25. Nos. 343, 344c, Su-27.

2000, Feb. 23 Litho. *Perf. 14x14¼*
341 A109 50r multicolored .35 .35
342 A109 50r multicolored .35 .35
343 A109 50r multicolored .35 .35
Nos. 341-343 (3) 1.05 1.05

Souvenir Sheet

344 Sheet of 3 + label 1.50 1.50
a.-c. A109 150r Any single .50 .50

See Nos. 383-384.

Birds — A110

Designs: No. 345, Mergellus albelius. No. 346, Burhinus oedicnemus. 75r, Lagopus lagopus. 100r, Aquila pomarina, vert.

Perf. 13½x13¾, 13¾x13½
2000, Mar. 22
345 A110 50r multi .45 .45
346 A110 50r multi .45 .45
347 A110 75r multi .60 .60
348 A110 100r multi .90 .90
Nos. 345-348 (4) 2.40 2.40

Partisan Madonna of Minsk, by M. Savitsky — A111

2000, Apr. 27 *Perf. 13½*
349 A111 100r multi .50 .50

End of World War II, 55th anniv.

Europa, 2000
Common Design Type

2000, May 9 *Perf. 14x13½*
350 CD17 250r multi *2.00 2.00*
a. Tete beche pair *5.00 5.00*

Ballet — A112

Designs: 100r, Male dancer lifting female dancer. 150r, Dancer with crown.

2000, May 25 Litho. *Perf. 13¾x13½*
351 A112 100r multi .50 .50

Souvenir Sheet

352 A112 150r multi + label .80 .80

UN High Commissioner for Refugees, 50th Anniv. — A113

2000, Aug. 23 Litho. *Perf. 13½x14*
353 A113 50r multi .30 .30

Worldwide Fund for Nature (WWF) — A114

Lynx lynx: No. 354, 100r, Close-up of head. No. 355, 100r, On tree. No. 356, 150r, On snow. No. 357, 150r, Adult and young.

2000, Aug. 25 *Perf. 14x13½*
354-357 A114 Block of 4 2.75 2.75
357a Sheet, 2 each #354-357 6.00 6.00

Intl. Year of Culture of Peace A115

2000, Sept. 5 Litho. ***Perf. 13½x14***

358 A115 100r multi .50 .50

2000 Summer Olympics, Sydney — A116

No. 359: a, Gymnast on rings. b, Kayak. c, Rhythmic gymnastics.

2000, Sept. 10 Litho. ***Perf. 14x13½***

359 A116 100r Strip of 3, #a-c 1.25 1.25

Souvenir Sheet

360 A116 400r Runner + label 1.60 1.60

Compare Nos. 360 and 382.

Types of 1998 and 2000

Designs: 20r, Kryzhachok dancers. 30r, Water-powered mill. B, Dazhynki Crop Festival. A, Kupala folk holiday. 50r, Windmill. 100r, Exhibition center, Minsk, horiz. 200r, Vitebsk Town Hall. 500r, Dancers.

13¼x14, 14x13¼ (#361), Serpentine Die Cut 5¾ (#364-370)

2000-01 Litho.

361 A75 100r brt pink & blk .45 .45
a. Inscribed "2002" .30 .30
362 A108 200r yel grn & blk ('01) .60 .60
a. Inscribed "2003" .60 .60
363 A75 500r brn & blk ('01) 1.25 1.25
a. Inscribed "2003" 1.50 1.50

Self-Adhesive

364 A108 20r red & black .25 .25
365 A108 30r green & black .25 .25
366 A108 B yel & black .25 .25
367 A108 A blue & black .25 .25
368 A108 50r brown & black .25 .25
369 A108 100r brt pink & blk ('01) .25 .25
370 A108 200r yel grn & blk ('01) .50 .50
Nos. 361-370 (10) 4.30 4.30

Issued: 20r, 30r, B, A, 50r, 11/8/00. No. 362, 500r, 3/19/01; No. 361, 10/18/00; No. 370, 3/29/01.

No. 364 has a line of microprinting below country name, No. 340 has hairline. Nos. 366-367 sold for 34r and 39r respectively on day of issue. Nos. 364-368 each issued in sheets of 24.

Amber — A117

Halite — A118

Flint — A119

Sylvite — A120

2000, Nov. 22 Litho. ***Perf. 14x14¼***

371 A117 200r multi .65 .65
372 A118 200r multi .65 .65
373 A119 200r multi .65 .65
374 A120 200r multi .65 .65
Nos. 371-374 (4) 2.60 2.60

New Year 2001 — A121

2000, Nov. 28 Litho. ***Perf. 14x13½***

375 A121 200r multi .65 .65

Christmas — A122

2000, Dec. 5

376 A122 100r multi .35 .35

A123

Children's Art Contest Winners A124

2000, Dec. 26 ***Perf. 13½***

377 A123 100r multi .30 .30
378 A124 100r multi .30 .30

St. Euphrosyne of Polotsk, 900th Anniv. of Birth — A125

2001, Jan. 5 Litho. ***Imperf.***

379 A125 500r multi 1.50 1.50

Brest Arms — A126 Gomel Arms — A127

2001, Jan. 10 ***Perf. 14¼x14***

380 A126 200r multi .55 .55
381 A127 200r multi .55 .55

Souvenir Sheet

Medal Count From 2000 Summer Olympics, Sydney — A128

Perf. 13¾x13½

2001, Feb. 22 Litho.

382 A128 1000r multi + label 3.25 3.25

Sukhoi Airplane Type of 2000

Designs: No. 383, 250r, RD (ANT-25), 1933. No. 384, 250r, Rodina (ANT-37), 1936.

2001, Feb. 23 Litho. ***Perf. 14x14¼***

383-384 A109 Set of 2 2.00 2.00

Beetles — A130

No. 385: a, Lucanus cervus. b, Oryctes nasicornis.

Perf. 13½x13¾

2001, Mar. 22 Litho.

385 A130 300r Pair, #a-b 2.00 2.00

Flowers — A131

Designs: 200r, Nymphaea alba. 400r, Cypripedium calceolus.

2001, Apr. 25 Litho. ***Perf. 14x14¼***

386-387 A131 Set of 2 2.00 2.00
a. Booklet pane of 12, 6 each #386-387 22.50 —
Booklet, #387a 22.50

The two center vertical pairs in No. 387a are Tête-bêche.

Europa — A132

Chernobyl Nuclear Disaster, 15th Anniv. — A133

National Parks: 400r, Prypyatski. 1000r, Narachanski.

2001, May 4 ***Perf. 13¾x13½***

388-389 A132 Set of 2 *7.50 7.50*

2001, June 9

390 A133 50r multi .40 .40

Native Costumes — A134

Designs: 200r, Woman and children, Slutsk, 19th cent. 1000r, Man, woman and child, Pinsk, 19th cent.

2001, June 15 ***Perf. 14¼x14***

391-392 A134 Set of 2 3.00 3.00
a. Booklet pane of 6, 3 each #391-392 10.00 —
Booklet, #392a 10.00

Independence, 10th Anniv. — A135

Litho. with Hologram Affixed

2001, July 3 ***Perf. 14¼x14***

393 A135 500r multi 1.25 1.25

Commonwealth of Independent States, 10th Anniv. — A136

2001, July 12 Litho. ***Perf. 14x13½***

394 A136 195r multi .50 .50

Nos. 102, 105, 146, 148, 150, 153, 198 and 248 Surcharged in Black, Red or Blue

Methods and Perfs as Before

2001

395 A39 400r on 100r #146 .60 .60
396 A39 400r on 600r #148 .60 .60
397 A39 400r on 1500r #150 .60 .60
398 A39 400r on 1500r #198 .60 .60
399 A39 400r on 3300r #153 .60 .60
400 A75 1000r on 100r #248 (R) 2.00 2.00
401 A24 1000r on 180r #102 (Bl) 2.00 2.00
402 A24 1000r on 280r #105 2.00 2.00
Nos. 395-402 (8) 9.00 9.00

Issued: No. 397, 8/10; others 10/8.

Folktales — A137

Designs: 100r, The Blue Suit Made Inside Out. 200r, Okh and the Golden Snuffbox.

2001, Aug. 24 Litho. ***Perf. 13½***

403-404 A137 Set of 2 1.00 1.00

Year of Dialogue Among Civilizations A138

2001, Sept. 5 ***Perf. 14¼x14***
405 A138 400r multi 1.00 1.00
a. Tête-bêche pair 2.75 2.75

Souvenir Sheet

Otto Y. Shmidt (1891-1956), Arctic Explorer — A139

2001, Sept. 30 ***Perf. 14x13½***
406 A139 3000r multi 7.00 7.00

Water Sports — A140

Designs: 200r, Sailboarding. 1000r, Waterskiing.

2001, Oct. 25 ***Perf. 13¾x13½***
407 A140 200r multi .65 .65
408 A140 1000r multi 3.25 3.25
a. Booklet pane, 2 each #407-408 6.25 6.25
Booklet, #408a 6.25
b. Souvenir sheet, #408 + 2 labels 2.25 2.25

Types of 1998-2000 Redrawn, Type of 2000 and

A141

Designs: 1r, Bison, with microprinting added in tree branch. 2r, Christmas star, with microprinting replacing line below country name. 5r, Church, Synkovichy, with microprinting replacing lower line in church window. 10r, Flaming wheel, with microprinting replacing line in fire. 30r, Water-powered mill, with microprinting in vertical posts to right of water wheel. B, Dazhynki Crop Festival. H, Church, Polotsk. C, Railway station, Brest. 1000r, Arms of Francis Skaryna, first Belarussian printer. 2000r, City Hall, Minsk. 3000r, City Hall, Nesvizh. 5000r, City Hall, Chechersk.

2001-02 **Litho.** ***Perf. 13¼x14***
409 A75 1r grn, lt grn & blk .25 .25
410 A75 2r bl, lt bl & blk .25 .25
411 A75 5r dk bl, lt bl & blk .25 .25
412 A75 10r org, lt org & blk .25 .25
413 A75 30r bl grn, lt bl & blk .25 .25
414 A108 B bister & blk .25 .25
415 A141 H lt yel, bis & blk .50 .50
416 A141 C lt yel, ol grn & blk .60 .60
417 A141 1000r pink, rose & blk 2.00 2.00
418 A141 2000r lt bl, bl & blk 3.25 3.25
a. Inscribed "2007" 1.60 1.60
419 A141 3000r lt org, org & blk 4.75 4.75
420 A141 5000r lt grn, grn & blk 8.00 8.00
Nos. 409-420 (12) 20.60 20.60

Nos. 414-416 sold for 55r, 236r and 314r respectively on day of issue. Issued: 1r, 2r, 1/28/02; 5r, 2/1/02; 10r, 2/12/02; 30r, 7/10/02; B, 3/22/02; H, C, 7/16/02, 1000r, 2000r, 3000r, 5000r, 11/16.
See No. 612.

House of Mercy, Minsk A142

2001, Nov. 30 ***Perf. 13¾x14¼***
421 A142 200r multi .50 .50

Christmas A143 — New Year's Day A144

2001, Dec. 3 ***Perf. 14¼x14***
422 A143 100r multi .40 .40
423 A144 100r multi .40 .40

Yevgeniy V. Klumov (1876-1944), Surgeon A145

2001, Dec. 16 ***Perf. 13½x14***
424 A145 100r multi .40 .40

Arms of Borisov — A146

2002, Jan. 25 ***Perf. 14¼x14***
425 A146 200r multi .50 .50

2002 Winter Olympics, Salt Lake City — A147

Designs: No. 426, 300r, Slalom. No. 427, 300r, Figure skating. No. 428, 500r, Biathlon. No. 429, 500r, Ski jumping.

2002, Feb. 1 ***Perf. 13½x14***
426-429 A147 Set of 4 4.25 4.25

Formica Rufa — A148

2002, Mar. 20
430 A148 200r shown .50 .50
431 A148 1000r Colony, vert. 2.25 2.25
a. Booklet pane, 2 #430-431 + 2 labels 8.00 —
Complete booklet, #431a 8.00
b. Souvenir sheet, #431 + 2 labels 2.50 2.50

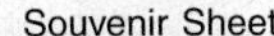
Souvenir Sheet

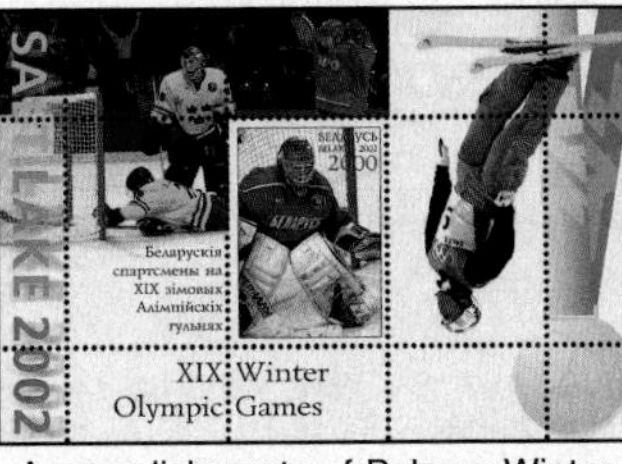

Accomplishments of Belarus Winter Olympics Athletes — A149

2002, Apr. 10 ***Perf. 14x13½***
432 A149 2000r multi + 2 labels 2.75 2.75

Europa — A150

Designs: 400r, Clown. 500r, Horse.

2002, Apr. 30
433-434 A150 Set of 2 2.75 2.75

Janka Kupala (1882-1942), Poet — A151 — Jakub Kolas (1882-1956), Poet — A152

2002
435 A151 100r multi .50 .50
436 A152 100r multi .50 .50

Souvenir Sheet

437 Sheet of 2 + central label 2.25 2.25
a. A151 500r red & multi 1.00 1.00
b. A152 500r red & multi 1.00 1.00

Issued: No. 435, 7/6; No. 436, 9/21; No. 437, 6/27.

Flowers — A153

Designs: 30r, Trifolium. 50r, Matricaria. 100r, Pulsatilla patens. 200r, Nuphar lutea. 500r, Chamaenerion angustifolium.
B, Linum. A, Centaurea cyanus. H, Campanula. C, Rhododendron.

2002 **Litho.** ***Serpentine Die Cut 9***
Self-Adhesive
438 A153 30r multi .25 .25
439 A153 50r multi .25 .25
440 A153 100r multi .25 .25
441 A153 200r multi .35 .35
442 A153 500r multi .90 .90

Booklet Stamps

443 A153 B multi .25 .25
a. Booklet pane of 6 1.75
Complete booklet, 4 #443a 10.00
444 A153 A multi .30 .30
a. Booklet pane of 6 2.50
Complete booklet, 4 #444a 14.00
445 A153 H multi .50 .50
a. Booklet pane of 6 2.50
Complete booklet, 4 #445a 10.00
446 A153 C multi .60 .60
a. Booklet pane of 6 3.50
Complete booklet, 4 #446a 14.00
Nos. 438-446 (9) 3.65 3.65

Nos. 443-446 sold for 75r, 90r, 236r and 314r respectively on day of issue.
Issued: 200r, 500r, 9/12; B, H, 7/24; A, C, 8/6. 30r, 50r, 100r, 8/28.

Children's Activities A154

Designs: 90r, Go-carting. 230r, Model airplane flying.

2002, July 25 **Litho.** ***Perf. 13½x14***
447-448 A154 Set of 2 1.00 1.00

Souvenir Sheet

Bird Life International — A155

No. 449: a, Ciconia ciconia. b, Oriolus oriolus. c, Motacilla alba.

2002, July 30
449 A155 200r Sheet of 3, #a-c, + label 1.75 1.75

Bridges — A156

Designs: 200r, Svisloch River Bridge, Minsk. 300r, Sozh River Bridge, Gomel. 500r, Western Dvina River Bridge, Vitebsk.

2002, Aug. 20 ***Perf. 13½***
450-452 A156 Set of 3 2.50 2.50

Intl. Year of Ecotourism A157

2002, Sept. 10 ***Perf. 13½x14***
453 A157 300r multi 1.00 1.00
a. Booklet pane of 4 + 4 labels 14.00 —
Complete booklet, #453a 14.00

No. 453 printed in sheets of 12 + 8 labels.

Souvenir Sheet

Space Exploration, 45th Anniv. — A158

2002, Nov. 28 **Litho.** ***Perf. 13½***
454 A158 3000r multi 4.50 4.50

Paintings in National Art Museum — A159

Designs: No. 455, 300r, Battle of Nyemize, by M. Filipovich, 1922. No. 456, 300r, By the Church, by F. Rushchits, 1899, vert.

2002, Nov. 28 Litho. *Perf. 13½*
455-456 A159 Set of 2 1.60 1.60

Christmas and New Year's Day — A160

Designs: No. 457, 300r, Santa Claus. No. 458, 300r, Angel with bell.

2002, Dec. 5 Litho. *Perf. 14x13½*
457-458 A160 Set of 2 1.75 1.75

Arms — A161

Designs: No. 459, 300r, Minsk (shown). No. 460, 300r, David-Gorodok.

2003, Jan. 24 *Perf. 14¼x14*
459-460 A161 Set of 2 1.00 1.00

See Nos. 490-491, 543-545

Souvenir Sheet

Kasimir S. Malevich (1878-1935), Artist — A162

2003, Feb. 21
461 A162 3000r multi + label 3.75 3.75

Reptiles A163

Designs: 300r, Coronella austriaca. 600r, Emys orbicularis.

2003, Mar. 12 *Perf. 13½x14*
462-463 A163 Set of 2 1.00 1.00
463a Miniature sheet, 4 each #462-463 5.00 5.00

Intl. Year of Fresh Water A164

Passer Domesticus A165

2003, Mar. 25 *Perf. 14¼x14*
464 A164 370r multi .60 .60

2003, Mar. 31 *Perf. 14x13½*
465 A165 630r multi .90 .90

Printed in sheets of 7 + label.
See No. 520.

Children's Activities A166

Designs: No. 466, 300r, Rollerblading. No. 467, 300r, Scooter riding, vert.

2003, Apr. 22 *Perf. 13½x14, 14x13½*
466-467 A166 Set of 2 .90 .90

A167

Europa — A168

2003, Apr. 24
468 A167 400r multi *.50 .50*
a. Booklet pane of 8 *5.00 —*
Complete booklet, #468a *7.00*
469 A168 700r multi *1.25 1.25*
a. Booklet pane of 8 *10.00 —*
Complete booklet, #469a *12.00*

Endangered Flowers — A169

Designs: 270r, Trollius europaeus. 740r, Iris sibirica.

2003, June 30 *Perf. 14x13½*
470-471 A169 Set of 2 1.60 1.60
471a Miniature sheet, 4 each #470-471 6.50 6.50

Traditional Clothing — A170

Clothing of: 380r, West Polesye region. 430r, Mogilyov region.

2003, July 10 Litho. *Perf. 14¼x14*
472-473 A170 Set of 2 1.50 1.50
473a Sheet, 4 each #472-473 + central label 4.50 —

See Nos. 564-565.

Souvenir Sheet

Yachting — A171

No. 474: a, Boat with blue sails. b, Boat with red and white sail, vert.

2003, July 22 Litho. *Perf. 13½*
474 A171 1000r Sheet of 2, #a-b 2.50 2.50

Souvenir Sheets

A172

Exhibits at Natl. Museum of History and Culture — A173

Designs: 1000r, Stone ax head, early Bronze Age. No. 476, Ceramic bowl, early Bronze Age. No. 477, Weapon, 14th cent.

2003, Aug. 20
475 A172 1000r multi 1.00 1.00
476 A173 1500r multi + label 2.00 2.00
477 A173 1500r multi + label 2.00 2.00

Wooden Buildings — A174

Designs: 270r, Horse stable, Povitie, 19th cent. 430r, St. George's Church, Sinkevichi, 1724. 740r, Water mill, Volma, 19th-20th cent.

2003, Sept. 18
478-480 A174 Set of 3 1.50 1.50
480a Souvenir sheet, #478-480 1.50 1.50

Dogs — A175

Designs: 270r, Golden retriever. 380r, Mastiff. 430r, German shepherd.

2003, Oct. 14 *Perf. 14x13½*
481-483 A175 Set of 3 1.50 1.50
483a Souvenir sheet, 2 each #481-483, + 2 labels 3.00 3.00

FIFA (Fédération Internationale de Football Association), Cent. (in 2004) — A176

Designs: No. 484, 380r, Player dribbling ball. No. 485, 380r, Goalie holding ball, vert. 460r, Players, diff. 780r, Goalie holding ball, diff., vert.

Perf. 14x14¼, 14¼x14
2003, Nov. 14 Litho.
484-487 A176 Set of 4 2.50 2.50

Christmas and New Year's Day — A177

2003, Nov. 15 *Perf. 14x13½*
488 A177 380r Angel .45 .45
a. Miniature sheet of 6 2.75 2.75
489 A177 780r Santa Claus 1.00 1.00
a. Miniature sheet of 6 6.00 6.00
b. Booklet pane, 4 each #488-489 5.75 —
Complete booklet, #489b 5.75

Arms Type of 2003

Designs: 460r, Slonim. 780r, Zaslavl.

2004, Jan. 20 *Perf. 14¼x14*
490-491 A161 Set of 2 1.50 1.50

There Came Spring, by Pavel Maslennikov — A178

2004, Feb. 1 *Perf. 13½*
492 A178 290r multi .60 .60

Fruit — A179

Designs: 5r, Prunus spinosa. 10r, Vaccinium vitis-idaea. 20r, Vaccinium myrtillus. 30r, Oxycoccus palustris. 50r, Vaccinium uliginosum. 100r, Rubus idaeus. B, Fragaria ananassa. A, Ribes rubrum. 200r, Rubus caesius. H, Ribes nigrum. 300r, Rubus saxatilis. C, Grossularia reclinata. 500r, Fragaria. P, Hippophae rhamnoides. 1000r, Cerasus vulgaris.

2004 *Perf. 13¼x13¾*
493 A179 5r multi .25 .25
494 A179 10r multi .25 .25
495 A179 20r multi .25 .25
496 A179 30r multi .25 .25
497 A179 50r multi .25 .25
498 A179 100r multi .25 .25
499 A179 B multi .25 .25
500 A179 A multi .25 .25
501 A179 200r multi .25 .25
502 A179 H multi .40 .40
503 A179 300r multi .40 .40
504 A179 C multi .50 .50
505 A179 500r multi .50 .50
506 A179 P multi .80 .80
507 A179 1000r multi 1.00 1.00
a. Miniature sheet, #493-507 5.00 5.00
Nos. 493-507 (15) 5.85 5.85

Issued: 5r, 10r, 20r, 30r, A, P, 2/9; 50r, 100r, B, 200r, H, 300r, C, 500r, 1000r, 2/13. Nos. 499, 500, 502, 504 and 506 each sold for 100r, 120r, 290r, 420r and 780r respectively on day of issue.

St. Valentine's Day — A180

2004, Feb. 14 *Perf. 13½x13¾*
508 A180 H multi .50 .50
a. Miniature sheet of 7 + label 4.00 4.00

No. 508 sold for 290r on day of issue.

Trees — A181

Designs: 100r, Alnus incana. B, Betula pendula. A, Pinus sylvsetris. 200r, Viburnum opulus. H, Fraxinus excelsior. 300r, Tilia cordata. 400r, Corylus avellana. C, Sorbus aucuparia. 500r, Quercus robur. P, Carpinus betulus. 1000r, Ulmus laevis.

2004, Mar. 23 ***Serpentine Die Cut 9***
Self-Adhesive

509 A181	100r multi		.25	.25
510 A181	B multi		.25	.25
511 A181	A multi		.25	.25
512 A181	200r multi		.25	.25
513 A181	H multi		.40	.40
514 A181	300r multi		.40	.40
515 A181	400r multi		.60	.60
516 A181	C multi		.65	.65
517 A181	500r multi		.75	.75
518 A181	P multi		1.20	1.20
519 A181	1000r multi		1.50	1.50
a.	Miniature sheet, #509-519, + label		6.50	6.50
	Nos. 509-519 (11)		6.50	6.50

Nos. 510, 511, 513, 516 and 518 each sold for 100r, 120r, 290r, 420r and 780r respectively on day of issue.

Bird Type of 2003

2004, Mar. 31 ***Perf. 13¾x13½***
520 A165 870r Delichon urbica 1.25 1.25

Printed in sheets of 7 + label.

World Under-18 Ice Hockey Championships, Minsk — A182

2004, Apr. 16 **Litho.**
521 A182 320r multi .75 .75

Printed in sheets of 18 + 2 labels.

Europa A183

Designs: 320r, Mushroom picker. 870r, Fisherman.

2004, May 4 ***Perf. 13½x13¾***

522 A183 320r multi		.40	.40
a.	Booklet pane of 7 + label	*2.75*	—
	Complete booklet, #522a	*4.00*	
523 A183 870r multi		*1.10*	*1.10*
a.	Booklet pane of 7 + label	*7.50*	—
	Complete booklet, #523a	*8.75*	

Souvenir Sheet

Liberation of Belarus, 60th Anniv. — A184

No. 524: a, 500r, Monument to Soviet Army (30x40mm). b, 1000r, The Parade of Partisans in Minsk, by Y. Zaitsev.

2004, May 4 ***Perf. 13½***
524 A184 Sheet of 2, #a-b 2.00 2.00

Locomotives and Railroad Stations — A185

Designs: 320r, Series D 1-3-0, Mosty Station. 870r, Series A 2-3-0, Vitebsk Station.

2004, May 31 **Litho.** ***Perf. 14x14¼***
525-526 A185 Set of 2 1.75 1.75
526a Sheet of 12, 6 each #525-526 20.00 20.00

Insects A186

Designs: 320r, Polistes gallicus. 505r, Bombus lucorum.
2000r, Apis mellifera.

2004, June 3 ***Perf. 13½x13¾***
527-528 A186 Set of 2 1.00 1.00

Souvenir Sheet
Perf. 13½x13¼

529 A186 2000r multi 2.25 2.25

No. 529 contains one 40x30mm stamp.

Souvenir Sheet

Paintings by Yehuda Pen (1854-1937) — A187

No. 530: a, Self-portrait. b, Watchmaker, horiz.

Perf. 13¼x13½, 13½x13¼ (#530b)
2004, June 5
530 A187 1000r Sheet of 2, #a-b 2.25 2.25

2004 Summer Olympics, Athens A188

Designs: 320r, Cycling. 505r, Hammer throw. 870r, Tennis.

2004, July 13 ***Perf. 14x14¼***
531-533 A188 Set of 3 2.25 2.25

Butterflies — A189

Designs: 300r, Euphydryas maturna. 500r, Pericallia matronula. 800r, Zerynthia polyxena. 1200r, Eudia pavonia.

2004, Sept. 10 ***Perf. 14¼x14***
534-537 A189 Set of 4 4.25 4.25
a. Miniature sheet, 3 each #534-537 + 4 labels *17.00 17.00*

Souvenir Sheet

Gold Medalists at 2004 Summer Olympics — A190

No. 538: a, Yuliya Nesterenko. b, Igor Makarov.

2004, Oct. 7 **Litho.** ***Perf. 14x13½***
538 A190 500r Sheet of 2, #a-b, + central label 1.75 1.75

Horses — A191

No. 539: a, Byelorussian harness horse (UL stamp). b, Andalusian horse (UR stamp). c, Head of Byelorussian harness horse (LL stamp). d, Head of Andalusian horse (LR stamp).

2004, Oct. 27 ***Perf. 12½x12***
539 A191 500r Sheet of 4, #a-d 2.25 2.25

Cats — A192

No. 540: a, 300r, Persian. b, 500r, Thai (denomination at UL). c, 500r, Red Persian (denomination at LR). d, 800r, Mixed breed (denomination at UL). e, 800r, British Shorthair (denomination at LL).

2004, Oct. 29 ***Perf. 13½x14***
540 A192 Sheet of 5, #a-e, + label 3.00 3.00

Happy New Year — A193

2004, Dec. 8 **Litho.** ***Perf. 13¾x13½***
541 A193 320r multi .50 .50

Minsk Metro Stations — A194

No. 542: a, Victory Square Station (gray panel). b, Yakub Kolas Square Station (yellow orange panel).

2004, Dec. 22 ***Perf. 13½***
542 Horiz. pair *2.50 2.50*
a.-b. A194 560r Either single *1.25 1.25*

Arms Type of 2003

Designs: 160r, Dubrovno. 350r, Kamenets. 900r, Mogilyov.

2005, Jan. 25 ***Perf. 14¼x14***
543-545 A161 Set of 3 1.60 1.60

Gerasim Bogomolov (1905-81), Hydrologist — A195

2005, Feb. 18 ***Perf. 13¾x13½***
546 A195 350r multi .50 .50

Souvenir Sheet

Icons — A196

No. 547: a, Virgin of Vladimir, by Fyodor Povny. b, Nativity, by Georgi Sutulin and Olga Belaya. c, Archangel Michael, by Andrei Kosikov.

Litho. with Foil Application

2005, Mar. 22 ***Perf. 11½***
547 A196 1500r Sheet of 3, #a-c *4.50 4.50*

Strix Nebulosa A197

Perf. 13½x13¾

2005, Mar. 31 **Litho.**
548 A197 900r multi 1.00 1.00

A198

A199

A200

End of World War II, 60th Anniv. A201

No. 553: a, Signing of surrender documents. b, Victory parade (52x30mm).

2005, Apr. 12 ***Perf. 13½x13¾***

549 A198 A multi .30 .30
550 A199 H multi .45 .45
551 A200 H multi .45 .45
552 A201 P multi 1.25 1.25
Nos. 549-552 (4) 2.45 2.45

Souvenir Sheet

Perf. 13½x13¼, 13½ (#553b)

553 A201 1000r Sheet of 2, #a-b *2.50 2.50*

No. 549 sold for 160r, Nos. 550 and 551 each sold for 360r, and No. 552 sold for 930r on day of issue.

Souvenir Sheet

Fauna — A202

No. 554: a, 500r, Aquila danga. b, 500r, Catocala sponsa. c, 1000r, Castor fiber. d, 1000r, Meles meles.

2005, Apr. 15 ***Perf. 12***

554 A202 Sheet of 4, #a-d, + label *3.00 3.00*

See Russia No. 6906.

Europa A203

Designs: 500r, Scallions, carrot, onion, peppers and tomato. 1000r, Bread and hat.

2005, May 4 ***Perf. 13½x13¾***

555-556 A203 Set of 2 *1.50 1.50*
555a Booklet pane of 7 + label *3.50* —
Complete booklet, #555a *3.50*
556a Booklet pane of 7 + label *8.50* —
Complete booklet, #556a *8.50*

Stefaniya Stanyuta (1905-2000), Actress — A204

2005, May 13 Litho. ***Perf. 13¾x13½***

557 A204 160r multi *.50 .50*

Printed in sheets of 16 + 4 labels.

Souvenir Sheet

Hans Christian Andersen (1805-75), Author — A205

2005, May 20 ***Perf. 13¼x13½***

558 A205 2000r multi 2.00 2.00

Worldwide Fund for Nature (WWF) A206

Ciconia nigra: No. 559, In flight. No. 560, Standing on one leg.
No. 561: a, Head. b, Legs and chicks.

2005, June 2 ***Perf. 13½x13¾***

559 A206 500r multi .50 .50
560 A206 500r multi .50 .50
561 A206 1000r Vert. pair, #a-b 2.00 2.00
c. Block of 4, #559, 560, 561a, 561b 3.25 3.25

Harvesting, by Mikhail Sevruk — A207

2005, July 14 ***Perf. 13½***

562 A207 170r multi .30 .30

World Summit on the Information Society, Tunis — A208

2005, July 20

563 A208 360r multi .40 .40

Traditional Clothing Type of 2003

Women wearing clothing of: 360r, Mosty region. 570r, Lepel region.

2005, Aug. 18 ***Perf. 14¼x14***

564-565 A170 Set of 2 1.00 1.00
565a Sheet of 8, 4 each #564-565, + central label 4.00 4.00

Intl. Year of Sport and Physical Education A209

2005, Aug. 30 ***Perf. 13½x13¾***

566 A209 570r multi .60 .60

Volkovysk, 1000th Anniv. — A210

2005, Sept. 2 ***Perf. 13½***

567 A210 360r multi .40 .40

Turov Eparchy, 1000th Anniv. — A211

2005, Sept. 17 ***Perf. 13¾x13½***

568 A211 360r multi .40 .40

Chess — A212

No. 569 — Background color: a, Dark red. b, Orange brown.

2005, Sept. 23 ***Perf. 14x14¼***

569 A212 500r Pair, #a-b 1.00 1.00
c. Booklet pane, 3 #569a, 4 #569b + label 6.00 —
Complete booklet, #569c 6.00
d. Booklet pane, 3 #569a, 4 #569b + label, imperf. 6.00 —
Complete booklet, #569d 6.00

Souvenir Sheet

Castles — A213

No. 570: a, 500r, Vytautas Castle, Grodno. b, 1000r, Lida Castle, Lida.

2005, Nov. 15 ***Perf. 13½x14***

570 A213 Sheet of 2, #a-b 2.00 2.00

New Year's Day & Christmas A214

2005, Dec. 5 Litho. ***Perf. 14x14¼***

571 A214 360r multi 1.00 1.00

Printed in sheets of 9 and in sheets of 8 + label.

2006 Winter Olympics, Turin A215

2006, Jan. 16 ***Perf. 13½x14***

572 A215 500r Snowboarding 1.75 1.75

Souvenir Sheet

Perf. 14x13½

573 A215 2000r Freestyle skiing, vert. 4.00 4.00

No. 573 contains one 30x40mm stamp.

Arms of Turov — A216

Arms of Novogrudok A217

2006, Jan. 30 ***Perf. 14¼x14***

574 A216 500r multi .95 .95
575 A217 500r multi .95 .95

Vanellus Vanellus A218

2006, Apr. 18 ***Perf. 13½x14***

576 A218 930r multi 1.25 1.25

Printed in sheets of 7 + label.

Chernobyl Nuclear Accident, 20th Anniv. A219

2006, Apr. 19

577 A219 360r multi .80 .80

Europa — A220

Children's drawings: 500r, Penguins, by Lina Filippoch. 1000r, Pegasus, by Daria Buneeva, horiz.

2006, May 4 ***Perf. 14x13½, 13½x14***

578-579 A220 Set of 2 1.75 1.75
578a Booklet pane of 7 + label 4.25 —
Complete booklet, #578a 4.25
579a Booklet pane of 7 + label 8.50 —
Complete booklet, #579a 8.50

Ivan Shamyakin (1921-2004), Writer — A221

2006, June 2 *Perf. 14x14¼*
580 A221 360r multi .45 .45

Birds — A222

Designs: 10r, Oenanthe oenanthe. 20r, Parus caeruleus. 30r, Ficedula hypoleuca. 50r, Carduelis cannabina. 100r, Sylvia curruca. (160r), Erithacus rubecula. (190r), Phoenicurus ochruros. 200r, Fringilla coelebs. 300r, Passer montanus. (360r), Parus major. 500r, Carduelis chloris. 1000r, Coccothraustes coccothraustes.

2006, June 16 *Perf. 13½x14*

581 A222	10r multi		.25	.25
582 A222	20r multi		.25	.25
583 A222	30r multi		.25	.25
584 A222	50r multi		.25	.25
585 A222	100r multi		.25	.25
586 A222	(160r) multi		.25	.25
587 A222	(190r) multi		.25	.25
588 A222	200r multi		.25	.25
589 A222	300r multi		.30	.30
590 A222	(360r) multi		.40	.40
591 A222	500r multi		.60	.60
592 A222	1000r multi		1.00	1.00
a.	Souvenir sheet, #581-592		4.50	4.50
	Nos. 581-592 (12)		4.30	4.30

Bats A223

Designs: No. 593, 500r, No. 596a, 1000r, Myotis dascyneme. No. 594, 500r, No. 596b, 1000r, Vespertilio murinus. No. 595, 500r, No. 596c, 1000r, Barbastella barbastellus.

2006, June 19 *Perf. 14x14¼*
593-595 A223 Set of 3 1.60 1.60

Souvenir Sheet

Perf. 13½x13¼

596 A223 1000r Sheet of 3, #a-c 4.00 4.00

Souvenir Sheet

Belarus Medals at 2006 Winter Olympics — A224

Perf. 13¾x13½

2006, June 22 **Litho.**
597 A224 2000r multi + 2 labels 2.50 2.50

Souvenir Sheet

Augustow Canal — A225

2006, Aug. 11 *Perf. 14x14¼*
598 A225 2000r multi 2.50 2.50

Locomotives and Railroad Stations — A226

Designs: No. 599, 1000r, Ov class locomotive, Brest Station (shown). No. 600, 1000r, E class locomotive, Molodechno Station.

2006, Sept. 8
599-600 A226 Set of 2 2.00 2.00
600a Miniature sheet, 4 each #599-600, + central label 7.50 7.50

Orchids A227

Designs: No. 601, 1000r, Dachylorhiza majalis and insect. No. 602, 1000r, Cephalanthera rubra and dragonfly facing right. No. 603, 1000r, Cephalanthera rubra and dragonfly facing left.

Perf. 13½x13¾

2006, Sept. 16 **Litho.**
601-603 A227 Set of 3 3.25 3.25
602a Miniature sheet, 4 each #601-602 9.00 9.00

Renewable Energy A228

Designs: 210r, Wind turbines. 970d, Hydroelectric power station.

2006, Oct. 10 **Litho.** *Perf. 14x14¼*
604-605 A228 Set of 2 1.25 1.25
605a Miniature sheet, 3 each #604-605 3.75 3.75

Regional Communications Commonwealth, 15th Anniv. — A229

2006, Oct. 13 *Perf. 13½x13¾*
606 A229 410r multi 1.75 1.75

No. 134 Surcharged in Silver and Black

2006, Nov. 10 **Litho.** *Imperf.*
607 A33 3500r on 10,000r #134 4.25 4.25

Belfila 2006 National Philatelic Exhibition.

Discus Fish — A230

Various discus fish with denominations in: No. 608, 500r, White (shown). No. 609, 500r, White, diff. No. 610, 500r, Blue. No. 611, 500r, Yellow.

2006, Nov. 16 *Perf. 13½x14*
608-611 A230 Set of 4 2.00 2.00
611a Sheet of 8, 2 each #608-611 6.00 6.00

Buildings Type of 2001-02

Perf. 13½x13¾

2006, Dec. 20 **Litho.**
612 A141 3000r Shklov City Hall 2.50 2.50

New Year 2007 — A231

No. 613 — Tree and stars in: a, Dark blue. b, White.

2006, Dec. 22 *Perf. 13¾x13½*
613 A231 500r Pair, #a-b 1.25 1.25

Printed in sheets containing three of each stamp.

Arms of Krugloe — A232

Arms of Pinsk — A233

2007, Jan. 22 *Perf. 14¼x14*
614 A232 600r multi 1.00 1.00
615 A233 600r multi 1.00 1.00

Napoleon Orda (1807-83), Artist and Musician — A234

Perf. 13¾x13½

2007, Feb. 14 **Litho.**
616 A234 2000r multi + label 7.50 7.50

Printed in sheets of 2 stamps + 2 labels.

Luscinia Luscinia A235

2007, Mar. 26 *Perf. 13½x13¾*
617 A235 1000r multi 3.75 3.75

Printed in sheets of 7 stamps + label.

Europa — A236

Scouting emblem, "100," and: 500r, Knot. 1000r, Emblem of Natl. Scout Association.

2007, May 4 **Litho.** *Perf. 14¼x14*
618-619 A236 Set of 2 3.00 3.00
619a Booklet pane, 4 #618, 3 #619, + label 11.00 11.00
Complete booklet, #619a 11.00

Scouting, cent.

Wildlife A237

Designs: No. 620, Vulpes vulpes. No. 621, Mustela putorius. No. 622, Dryomys nitedula. No. 623, Sciurus vulgaris.

Serpentine Die Cut 9¼

2007, June 19 **Self-Adhesive**

620 A237	B multi	.30	.30
621 A237	B multi	.30	.30
622 A237	A multi	.30	.30
623 A237	A multi	.30	.30
a.	Miniature sheet, 2 each #620-623, + central label	2.50	2.50
	Nos. 620-623 (4)	1.20	1.20

On day of issue, Nos. 620 and 621 each sold for 190r, and Nos. 622 and 623 each sold for 220r.

Souvenir Sheet

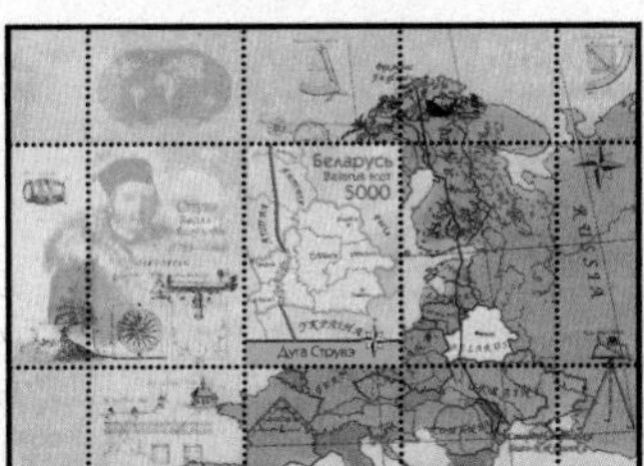

Struve Geodetic Arc — A238

2007, Sept. 20 *Perf. 14¼x14*
624 A238 5000r multi + 2 labels 5.00 5.00

Birds A239

No. 625 — Birds of the Cepkeliai Nature Reserve, Lithuania, and Katra Sanctuary, Belarus: a, Gallinago media. b, Crex crex.

2007, Oct. 3 Litho. ***Perf. 13½x13¾***

625 Horiz. pair + central label 2.00 2.00
a.-b. A239 1000r Either single 1.00 1.00

Printed in sheets of 3 pairs. See Lithuania No. 848.

BirdLife International A240

Birds: No. 626, 500r, Surnia ululu. No. 627, 500r, Nyctea scandiaca. No. 628, 1000r, Glaucidium passerinum. No. 629, 1000r, Asio flammeus.

2007, Nov. 23 ***Perf. 13¾x13½***

626-629 A240 Set of 4 4.50 4.50
629a Miniature sheet, 2 each #626-629 9.00 9.00

Nos. 626-629 each printed in sheets of 7 + label.

Portraits by Unknown Artists in National Museum A241

Designs: Nos. 630a, 631a, Kshishtof Veselovsky, 1636. Nos. 630b, 631b, Griesel Sapega, 1632. Nos. 630c, 631c, Alexandra Marianna Veselovskaya, 1640.

2007, Nov. 28 ***Perf. 13½***

630 Horiz. strip of 3 7.50 7.50
a.-c. A241 1050r Any single 2.40 2.40

Souvenir Sheet

631 Sheet of 3 9.00 9.00
a.-c. A241 1500r Any single 3.00 3.00

No. 630 printed in sheets of 2 strips.

Christmas and New Year's Day — A242

Designs: No. 632, 240r, Children making snowman. No. 633, 240r, Child giving present to another child.

No. 634: a, Boy holding sack. b, Girl holding snowflake.

2007, Dec. 7 ***Perf. 13¾x13½***

632-633 A242 Set of 2 2.00 2.00

Souvenir Sheet

634 Sheet, #632-633, 634a-634b + 2 labels 7.00 7.00
a.-b. A242 1500r Either single 3.00 3.00

Nos. 632-633 were each printed in sheets of 7 + label.

Christmas and New Year's Day — A243

No. 635: a, Christmas tree. b, Candle.

2007, Dec. 7

635 A243 1050r Pair, #a-b 3.75 3.75
c. Souvenir sheet, #635a-635b 4.50 4.50

No. 635 was printed in sheets containing 4 each Nos. 635a-635b.

Church Bells — A244

Various bells from: 600r, 1937. 1000r, 19th cent. 1200r, 1928.
2500r, 18th cent.

2007, Dec. 7 ***Perf. 13½***

636-638 A244 Set of 3 3.50 3.50

Souvenir Sheet

Perf. 14x14¼

639 A244 2500r multi 3.50 3.50

No. 639 contains one 40x28mm stamp.

Weaver — A245

Blacksmith — A246

2007, Dec. 21 ***Perf. 13½***

640 A245 600r multi .80 .80
641 A246 600r multi .80 .80

Nos. 640-641 each printed in sheets of 6.

Farm Animals — A247

Designs: 240r, Sheep. 440r, Ram. 500r, Pig. 1050r, Cows. 1500r, Goats.

2007, Dec. 29 **Litho.**

642-646 A247 Set of 5 5.00 5.00

Nos. 642-646 each printed in sheets of 6.

Hunting — A248

Designs: 440r, Falconry. 1050r, Deer hunt, horiz.

Perf. 13¾x13½, 13½x13¾

2008, Jan. 30

647-648 A248 Set of 2 1.60 1.60

Nos. 647-648 each printed in sheets of 8.

Vincent Dunin-Marcinkevich (1808-84), Writer — A249

2008, Feb. 4 ***Perf. 14¼x14***

649 A249 440r multi 1.10 1.10

Printed in sheets of 8.

Souvenir Sheet

Prince Konstantin Ostrozhsky (1526-1608) — A250

2008, Feb. 17

650 A250 2500r multi + label 3.25 3.25

Egretta Alba — A251

2008, Mar. 13 ***Perf. 13¾x13½***

651 A251 1050r multi 2.50 2.50

Printed in sheets of 7 + label.

Intl. Telecommunications, Information and Bank Technologies Exhibition — A252

2008, Apr. 4 ***Perf. 14x14¼***

652 A252 (440r) multi 1.90 1.90

Printed in sheets of 8.

Europa A253

Designs: No. 653, 1000r, Letter on birch bark. No. 654, 1000r, Computer keyboard, envelopes, "@" symbol.

2008, May 28 Litho. ***Perf. 13½x14***

653-654 A253 Set of 2 2.25 2.25
654a Booklet pane, 3 each #653-654 + 2 labels 7.50 —
Complete booklet, #654a 7.50

Mammals — A254

Designs: 10r, Nyctereutes procyonoides. 200r, Mustela lutreola. 300r, Lepus europaeus. 400r, Canis lupus. 1000r, Martes martes.

2008, June 10 ***Perf. 13½x14***

655 A254 10r multi .25 .25
656 A254 200r multi .25 .25
657 A254 300r multi .40 .40
658 A254 400r multi .50 .50
659 A254 1000r multi 1.00 1.00
a. Miniature sheet, 3 each #655-659 7.50 7.50
Nos. 655-659 (5) 2.40 2.40

See No. 681.

Flowers — A255

Designs: 20r, Paeonia lactiflora. 30r, Petunia hybrida. 50r, Narcissus hybridus. 100r, Tulipa gesneriana. (200r), Dahlia cultorum. (240r), Rosa hybrida. (440r), Zinnia elegans. 500r, Lilium hybrida.

2008, June 10

660 A255 20r multi .25 .25
661 A255 30r multi .25 .25
662 A255 50r multi .25 .25
663 A255 100r multi .25 .25
664 A255 (200r) multi .25 .25
665 A255 (240r) multi .35 .35
666 A255 (440r) multi .45 .45
667 A255 500r multi .55 .55
a. Miniature sheet, 3 each #660-667 6.50 6.50
Nos. 660-667 (8) 2.60 2.60

Mushrooms — A256

Designs: 1000r, Cantharellus cibarius. 1500r, Boletus edulis.

2008, July 8 Litho. ***Perf. 14x13½***

668-669 A256 Set of 2 4.50 4.50

2008 Summer Olympics, Beijing A257

2008, Aug. 15 ***Perf. 14x14¼***

670 A257 1000r multi 2.75 2.75

Miniature Sheets

Orders of Belarus — A258

Medals of Belarus — A259

No. 671: a, Order of Exceptional Courage (star in white circle). b, Order of Military Glory (two soldiers in blue laureated circle). c, First, second and third class Orders of the Motherland (three orders with ribbons). d, First, second and third class Orders for Service to the Motherland (three orders without ribbons). e, Order of Friendship of Peoples (Blue violet ribbon). f, Order of Honor (two people in circle within a diamond). g, Order of Francysk Skaryna (red ribbon). h, Order of Mother (light and dark blue ribbon).

No. 672: a, Medal of Note for Military Service (round medal with star, torch, red and green banner). b, Medal of Hero of Belarus (star-shaped medal). c, Medal for Bravery (round medal with airplanes, tank and text). d, Medal for Labor Achievements (round medal with gray and red ribbon). e, First, second and third class medals for Perfect Service (three round medals with green and red ribbons). f, Medal of Note in Guarding the Civil Order (round medal with blue ribbon with red stripes). g, Medal of Note for Guarding the State Border (round medal with border guard and boundary marker). h, Medal of Francysk Skaryna (green and white ribbon).

2008, Aug. 28 *Perf. 13½*

671 A258 1000r Sheet of 8, #a-h, + 2 labels 8.00 8.00
672 A259 1000r Sheet of 8, #a-h, + 2 labels 8.00 8.00

Arms of Orsha — A260

Arms of Vitsebsk — A261

Arms of Nesvizh — A262

2008 *Perf. 14¼x14*

673 A260 500r multi .75 .75
674 A261 600r multi .90 .90
675 A262 1000r multi 1.40 1.40
Nos. 673-675 (3) 3.05 3.05

Issued: 600r, 9/15; 500r, 1000r, 9/19.

Remembrance of the Holocaust — A263

2008, Oct. 21 *Perf. 13½x13¾*

676 A263 500r multi 1.90 1.90

Printed in sheets of 8 + label.

Souvenir Sheet

Baptism of Vladimir I (Christianization of Kievan Rus), 1020th Anniv. — A264

No. 677: a, Holy Virgin of Iljinsk and Chernigov. b, Christ Pantocrator. c, Grand Prince Vladimir.

2008, Oct. 25 *Perf. 13½*

677 A264 1500r Sheet of 3, #a-c 5.00 5.00

Souvenir Sheet

Nesvizh Castle, 425th Anniv. — A265

2008, Dec. 8 Litho. *Perf. 13½x14*

678 A265 3000r multi + label 3.25 3.25

Christmas and New Year's Day — A266

New Year's Day — A267

2008, Dec. 9 *Perf. 14x13½*

679 A266 500r multi .50 .50

Perf. 13½

680 A267 1000r multi 1.00 1.00

Mammals Type of 2008

2008, Dec. 10 *Perf. 13½x14*

681 A254 5000r Bison bonasus 4.00 4.00

BirdLife International A268

Owls: No. 682, 500r, Bubo bubo. No. 683, 500r, Athene noctua. No. 684, 1000r, Otus scops. No. 685, 1000r, Strix uralensis.

2008, Dec. 22 *Perf. 14x13½*

682-685 A268 Set of 4 3.00 3.00
685a Sheet of 8, 2 each #682-685 7.00 7.00

Nos. 682-685 each were printed in sheets of 7 + label.

Louis Braille (1809-52), Educator of the Blind — A269

2009, Jan. 4 *Perf. 13½x14*

686 A269 700r multi .70 .70

Vladimir Muliavin (1941-2003), Folk Singer — A270

2009, Jan. 12 **Litho.**

687 A270 1000r multi + label .80 .80

Withdrawal of Soviet Troops From Afghanistan, 20th Anniv. A271

2009, Jan. 20

688 A271 400r multi .40 .40

Printed in sheets of 8 + central label.

Commonwealth of Independent States Executive Committee Building, Minsk — A272

2009, Feb. 18 *Perf. 14x14¼*

689 A272 500r multi .50 .50

Miniature Sheet

Folk Holidays — A273

No. 690: a, Kaliady (people walking in snow carrying torches). b, Spring greetings (child in white robe). c, Dazhynki (woman in field of rye). d, Kupalle (woman holding flower).

2009, Mar. 1 *Perf. 14x13½*

690 A273 500r Sheet of 4, #a-d, + 4 labels 1.75 1.75

Anser Anser A274

2009, Mar. 31 *Perf. 13½x14*

691 A274 1000r multi .80 .80

Printed in sheets of 7 + label.

Europa A275

Designs: No. 692, 1000r, Armillary sphere, telescope of Galileo. No. 693, 1000r, Moon, dish antenna, satellite.

2009, Apr. 15 *Perf. 13½x14*

692-693 A275 Set of 2 2.00 2.00
693a Booklet pane of 6, 3 each #692-693, + 2 labels 6.00 —
Complete booklet, #693a 6.00

Intl. Year of Astronomy. Nos. 692-693 each were printed in sheets of 7 + label.

Souvenir Sheet

Year of Native Land — A276

2009, Apr. 21 Litho. *Perf. 13½x14*

694 A276 2500r multi 2.00 2.00

Poultry — A277

Designs: No. 695, 1000r, Geese. No. 696, 1000r, Ducks.
3000r, Rooster and hen, horiz.

2009, May 5 *Perf. 14¼x14*

695-696 A277 Set of 2 1.75 1.75

Souvenir Sheet

Perf. 13½x13¾

697 A277 3000r multi + 2 labels 2.75 2.75

Endangered Flora — A278

Designs: No. 698, 1500r, Anemone sylvestris. No. 699, 1500r, Scorzonera glabra.

2009, June 8 *Perf. 14¼x14*

698-699 A278 Set of 2 2.50 2.50

Nos. 698-699 each were printed in sheets of 5 + label.

Souvenir Sheet

Liberation From Nazi Control, 65th Anniv. — A279

No. 700: a, Victory Square, Minsk. b, Women in Minsk, 1944.

2009, June 26 ***Perf. 14x13½***
700 A279 500r Sheet of 2, #a-b .80 .80

Air Sports A280

Designs: No. 701, 1500r, Two Yak-52 airplanes. No. 702, 1500r, An-2 airplane and skydiver.

2009, July 4 ***Perf. 13½x14***
701-702 A280 Set of 2 2.50 2.50

Nos. 701-702 each were printed in sheets of 5 + label.

Andrei A. Gromyko (1909-89), Foreign Affairs Minister of Soviet Union — A281

2009, July 18 ***Perf. 14x13½***
703 A281 800r multi .60 .60

Holy Virgin of Borkolabovo, 350th Anniv. — A282

2009, July 24 ***Perf. 14¼x14***
704 A282 1380r multi 1.50 1.50

Arms of Smorgon — A283

Arms of Kobrin — A284

2009 **Litho.**
705 A283 1000r multi .80 .80
706 A284 1000r multi .80 .80

Issued: No. 705, 9/6; No. 706, 9/19. Nos. 705-706 each were printed in sheets of 8 + label.

Souvenir Sheet

Belovezhskaya Puscha National Park — A285

No. 707: a, Deer. b, Aurochs. c, Wild boars.

2009, Oct. 3 ***Perf. 14x14¼***
707 A285 1500r Sheet of 3, #a-c 4.00 4.00

First Telegraph Line Between Minsk and Bobruisk, 150th Anniv. A286

2009, Oct. 16 ***Perf. 13½x14***
708 A286 1380r multi 1.00 1.00

Printed in sheets of 7 + 2 labels.

Galina K. Makarova (1919-93), Actress A287

2009, Oct. 23
709 A287 800r multi .60 .60

Printed in sheets of 5 + label.

Paintings in Natl. Art Museum — A288

Designs: No. 710, 1000r, Sky Blue Day, by Vitaly K. Tsvirko, 1980. No. 711, 1000r, Evening in Minsk Province, by Apollinary G. Goravsky, 1870s.

2009, Nov. 5 **Litho.** ***Perf. 13½***
710-711 A288 Set of 2 1.60 1.60

Souvenir Sheet

Christmas and New Year's Day — A289

No. 712: a, Decorated tree. b, Angel.

2009, Nov. 12 ***Perf. 13¼x13½***
712 A289 1500r Sheet of 2, #a-b, + central label 2.50 2.50

Souvenir Sheet

Russian Blue Cats — A290

No. 713: a, Head of adult cat. b, Two kittens. c, Three kittens.

2009, Nov. 23 ***Perf. 13½***
713 A290 2500r Sheet of 3, #a-c, + label 4.50 4.50

Sports Facilities in Minsk — A291

No. 714: a, Soccer Stadium (with arched roof). b, Minsk Arena (circular building).

2009, Nov. 30
714 A291 1500r Vert. pair, #a-b 2.25 2.25

Printed in sheets containing 2 pairs and 2 labels.

Souvenir Sheet

Foundation Treaty of the Union State (Economic and Political Confederation With Russia), 10th Anniv. — A292

Litho. With Foil Application

2009, Dec. 8 ***Perf. 14¼x14***
715 A292 4500r multi + 2 labels 4.00 4.00

Souvenir Sheet

2010 Winter Olympics, Vancouver — A293

2010, Jan. 25 **Litho.** ***Perf. 13½x14***
716 A293 3000r multi + 5 labels 2.50 2.50

Souvenir Sheet

Paintings by Ivan Khrutski (1810-85) — A294

No. 717: a, Self-portrait, 1884. b, Still Life with Dead Game, Vegetables and Mushrooms, 1854.

2010, Feb. 8 ***Perf. 14x14¼***
717 A294 1500r Sheet of 2, #a-b 2.50 2.50

Ivan Naumenko (1925-2006), Writer — A295

2010, Feb. 16 ***Perf. 13½***
718 A295 800r multi .50 .50

Printed in sheets of 5 + label.

Falco Tinnunculus A296

2010, Mar. 19 ***Perf. 13½x13¾***
719 A296 1000r multi .75 .75

Printed in sheets of 7 + label.

Souvenir Sheet

Slutsk Sashes — A297

No. 720: a, Iosif Zhagel wearing sash. b, Slutsk Gate, Nesvizh. c, Detail of Slutsk sash.

2010, Mar. 26 ***Perf. 14x14¼***
720 A297 1000r Sheet of 3, #a-c 2.50 2.50

Europa A298

Designs: No. 721, 1000r, Boy reading book, book characters. No. 722, 1000r, Girl reading book, butterfly.

2010, Mar. 30 ***Perf. 13½x14***
721-722 A298 Set of 2 1.50 1.50
722a Booklet pane of 6, 3 each #721-722, + 2 labels 4.50 —
Complete booklet, #722a 4.50

A299

End of World War II, 65th Anniv. — A300

No. 724: a, 500r, Soldiers at liberation of Minsk. b, 1500r, Berlin Liberation Monument.

2010, Apr. 16 *Perf. 14x13½*

723 A299 500r multi .35 .35

Souvenir Sheet

724 A300 Sheet of 2, #a-b, + label 1.50 1.50

No. 723 was printed in sheets of 5 + label.

Souvenir Sheet

Intl. Year of Biodiversity — A301

No. 725: a, 300r, Bears. b, 300r, Fish. c, 2400r, Birds, "2010," waves, man, child, tree.

2010, Apr. 23 *Perf. 13½x14*

725 A301 Sheet of 3, #a-c 2.25 2.25

Expo 2010, Shanghai — A302

2010, May 1 *Perf. 14x13½*

726 A302 500r multi .35 .35

Postal Agreement With Sovereign Military Order of Malta — A303

2010, June 21 **Litho.** *Perf. 13½*

727 A303 (920r) multi 1.25 1.25

Sailboats — A304

Designs: 920r, Optimist class. 1420r, Luch class.

2010, June 28 *Perf. 14¼x14*

728-729 A304 Set of 2 2.00 2.00

Nos. 728-729 each were printed in sheets of 7 + label.

Battle of Grunwald, 600th Anniv. A305

2010, July 15 *Perf. 14x14¼*

730 A305 1500r multi 1.10 1.10

Printed in sheets of 4.

Darya Domracheva, Bronze Medalist in Biathlon — A306

Sergei Novikov, Silver Medalist in Biathlon — A307

Aleksei Grishin, Gold Medalist in Freestyle Skiing — A308

2010, July 23 *Perf. 14x13½*

731 A306 (290r) multi .40 .40

732 A307 (920r) multi 1.00 1.00

733 A308 (1420r) multi 1.60 1.60

a. Sheet of 6, 2 each #731-733 + 3 labels 6.25 6.25

Nos. 731-733 (3) 3.00 3.00

Belarussian medalists at 2010 Winter Olympics, Vancouver. Nos. 731-732 each were printed in sheets of 8 + label.

Miniature Sheet

Belarussian Gold Medalists at 2008 Summer Olympics, Beijing — A309

No. 734: a, Men's canoe doubles team. b, Aksana Miankova, women's hammer throw. c, Andrei Aramnau, weightlifting. d, Men's kayak fours team.

2010, July 24 *Perf. 14¼x14*

734 A309 1000r Sheet of 4, #a-d 3.00 3.00

S Class Locomotive, Vilenski Railroad Station, Minsk — A310

Shch Class Locomotive, Mogilyov Railroad Station — A311

2010, Aug. 2 *Perf. 12x12¼*

735 A310 1000r multi 1.25 1.25

736 A311 1000r multi 1.25 1.25

a. Sheet of 10, 5 each #735-736, + 2 labels 12.50 12.50

Nos. 735-736 each were printed in sheets of 11 + label.

Worldwide Fund for Nature (WWF) A312

Various depictions of Ophiogomphus cecilia: 900r, 1000r, 1400r, 1500r.

2010, Aug. 10 *Perf. 13½x14*

737-740 A312 Set of 4 3.75 3.75

740a Sheet of 8, 2 each #737-740 7.50 7.50

Mushrooms — A313

Designs: No. 741, 500r, Clavaridelphus pistillaris and bird. No. 742, 500r, Langermannia gigantea and bird. No. 743, 500r, Hericium coralloides and bird. No. 744, 1000r, Sparassis laminosa and butterfly. No. 745, 1000r, Polyporus umbellatus and rodent.

2010, Aug. 18 *Perf. 14x13½*

741-745 A313 Set of 5 4.75 4.75

Nos. 741-745 each were printed in sheets of 9 + label.

Arms of Khoiniki — A314

Arms of Lida — A315

2010 **Litho.** *Perf. 14¼x14*

746 A314 900r multi .60 .60

747 A315 1400r multi 1.00 1.00

Issued: 900r, 9/5; 1400r, 9/24.

Souvenir Sheet

Republican Trade Union Palace of Culture — A316

2010, Sept. 15 *Perf. 13½*

748 A316 2000r multi + label 1.50 1.50

United Nations, 65th Anniv. A317

2010, Oct. 24 **Litho.** *Perf. 13½x13*

749 A317 1000r multi .75 .75

Printed in sheets of 5 + label.

Russian Spaniel — A318

Irish Setter — A319

Russo-European Laika — A320

2010, Nov. 10 *Perf. 13x13½*

750 A318 1000r multi .75 .75

751 A319 1000r multi .75 .75

752 A320 1000r multi .75 .75

a. Souvenir sheet of 6, 2 each #750-752, + 3 labels 4.50 4.50

Nos. 750-752 (3) 2.25 2.25

New Year 2011 — A321

Christmas — A322

2010, Nov. 12 *Perf. 13½*

753 A321 1000r multi .75 .75

754 A322 1000r multi .75 .75

a. Souvenir sheet of 4, 2 each #753-754, + 4 labels 3.00 3.00

Nos. 753-754 each were printed in sheets of 7 + label.

2010 Junior Eurovision Song Contest, Minsk A323

2010, Nov. 20 *Perf. 13½x14*

755 A323 (1010r) multi 1.60 1.60

Printed in sheets of 10 + 2 labels.

Arms of Gantsevichi A324

2010, Nov. 20 ***Perf. 14¼x14***

756 A324 900r multi .60 .60

Souvenir Sheet

Mir Castle — A325

Litho. & Embossed

2010, Dec. 16 ***Perf. 13x13½***

757 A325 5000r multi 3.50 3.50

Primula Elatior — A326

Orchis Ustulata — A327

2011, Jan. 10 Litho. ***Perf. 12¼x12***

758 A326 (1160r) multi 1.25 1.25

759 A327 (1790r) multi 1.90 1.90

a. Souvenir sheet of 4, 2 each #758-759, + 2 labels 13.00 13.00

Endangered flowers.

Preservation of Polar Regions and Glaciers — A328

Designs: 1500r, Map of Antarctica, penguins. 2500r, Map of Arctic region, polar bear.

2011, Feb. 11

760-761 A328 Set of 2 5.25 5.25

761a Tête-bêche pair, #760-761 5.25 5.25

761b Souvenir sheet, 3 #761a 12.00 12.00

Nos. 760-761 each were printed in sheets of 5 + label.

Numenius Arquata A329

Perf. 13½x13¾

2011, Mar. 14 **Litho.**

762 A329 1500r multi .60 .60

Printed in sheets of 7 + label.

Souvenir Sheets

Cross of St. Euphrosyne of Polotsk, 850th Anniv. — A330

Cross with denomination in: 5000r, Red. 10,000r, Gold.

Litho. & Embossed

2011, Mar. 21 ***Perf. 13x13½***

763 A330 5000r multi 4.50 4.50

Litho. & Embossed With Foil Application

764 A330 10,000r multi 8.50 8.50

First Man in Space, 50th Anniv. — A331

2011, Apr. 12 Litho. ***Perf. 13x13½***

765 A331 (1160r) multi 1.25 1.25

Europa — A332

Forest and: 2000r, Buck. 2500r, Bison.

2011, Apr. 14 ***Perf. 12½x12***

766-767 A332 Set of 2 3.00 3.00

767a Sheet of 6, 3 each #766-767 13.00 13.00

Intl. Year of Forests.

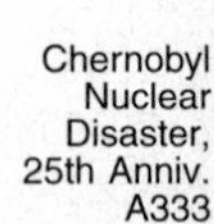

Chernobyl Nuclear Disaster, 25th Anniv. A333

2011, Apr. 26 ***Perf. 13½x13***

768 A333 (1330r) multi 1.25 1.25

AIDS Prevention, 30th Anniv. — A334

2011, May 12 ***Perf. 13¾x13½***

769 A334 (1330r) multi 1.25 1.25

Printed in sheets of 8 + central label.

Musical Instruments — A335

No. 770: a, Tar, Azerbaijan. b, Hurdy-gurdy, Belarus.

2011, May 25 ***Perf. 14x14¼***

770 A335 (1330r) Pair, #a-b 2.50 2.50

See Azerbaijan No. 950.

Capitals of Belarus and Armenia — A336

No. 771 — Buildings and arms of: a, Minsk, Belarus ("Belarus" at left). b, Yerevan, Armenia ("Belarus" at right).

2011, June 1 ***Perf. 13½***

771 A336 (1330r) Horiz. pair, #a-b 2.50 2.50

See Armenia No. 875.

Commonweath of Independent States, 20th Anniv. — A337

2011, June 28 ***Perf. 13½x13¾***

772 A337 (1330r) multi 1.25 1.25

Souvenir Sheet

Diplomatic Relations Between Belarus and Venezuela, 15th Anniv. — A338

2011, July 5 ***Perf. 12¼x12***

773 A338 3000r multi 1.25 1.25

Slavianski Bazaar Intl. Arts Festival, Vitebsk — A339

No. 774: a, (360r), Stage, Vitebsk coat of arms. b, (1400r), Slavianski Bazaar emblem, Vitebsk Town Hall.

2011, July 8 ***Perf. 13½x13***

774 A339 Horiz. pair, #a-b 1.50 1.50

A340

Equestrian Sports — A341

Designs: No. 775, (1400r), Horse racing. No. 776, (1400r), Dressage. No. 777, (1400r), Jumping.

No. 778, Dressage half-pass, vert.

2011, July 12 ***Perf. 12x12¼***

775-777 A340 Set of 3 3.50 3.50

Souvenir Sheet

Perf. 12¼x12

778 A341 (2160r) multi 1.60 1.60

Non-Aligned Movement, 50th Anniv. — A342

2011, Aug. 2 ***Perf. 14x13½***

779 A342 (1400r) multi 1.25 1.25

Lota Lota A343

Esox Lucius A344

2011, Aug. 18 ***Perf. 14x14¼***

780 A343 (1400r) multi 1.10 1.10

781 A344 (2160r) multi 1.75 1.75

a. Souvenir sheet of 6, 3 each #780-781 8.75 8.75

Regional Communications Commonwealth, 20th Anniv. — A345

2011, Sept. 20 ***Perf. 13½x13***

782 A345 (1540r) multi 1.25 1.25

Souvenir Sheet

Buildings in Belarus and Iran — A346

No. 783: a, Mir Castle (building with steeples), Mir, Belarus. b, Arg of Karim Khan (building with round turrets), Shiraz, Iran.

2011, Sept. 28 *Perf. 12x12¼*

783 A346 (2380r) Sheet of 2, #a-b 3.00 3.00

See Iran No. 3046.

Arms of Molodechno A347

2011, Sept. 30 *Perf. 12*

784 A347 (1620r) multi 1.25 1.25

Costumes of Malorita Region — A348

Costumes of Kalinkovichi Region — A349

2011, Oct. 11 *Perf. 14x13½*

785 A348 (1620r) multi 1.10 1.10
786 A349 (2500r) multi 1.75 1.75
a. Souvenir sheet of 8, 4 each #785-786 11.00 11.00

New Year 2012 — A350

Christmas — A351

Litho. & Embossed With Foil Application

2011, Nov. 11 *Perf. 12*

787 A350 (2450r) multi 1.10 1.10
788 A351 (3750r) multi 1.75 1.75

Poster Pigeons A352

Starominsk Stately Piegons A353

Strasser Pigeons A354

2011, Nov. 28 Litho. *Perf. 12x12¼*

789 A352 5000r multi 2.00 2.00
790 A353 5000r multi 2.00 2.00
791 A354 5000r multi 2.00 2.00
a. Souvenir sheet of 6, 2 each #789-791 12.00 12.00
Nos. 789-791 (3) 6.00 6.00

Souvenir Sheet

Diplomatic Relations Between Belarus and People's Republic of China, 20th Anniv. — A355

Litho. & Embossed

2012, Jan. 20 *Perf. 12¼x12*

792 A355 15,000r multi 5.50 5.50

Geometric Designs
A356 A357

2012, Jan. 27 Litho. *Perf. 13½x13*

793 A356 (1100r) gray & red .55 .55
794 A357 (1650r) multi .80 .80

Souvenir Sheet

Orthodox Churches — A358

No. 795: a, St. Sophia Cathedral, Polotsk, and trees. b, All Saints Monument Church, Minsk, and lamp post.

2012, Feb. 22 *Perf. 12¼x12*

795 A358 10,000r Sheet of 2, #a-b 7.00 7.00

A359 A360

Architecture
A361 A362

Designs: 50r, Mahiliou Town Hall. 100r, Kamianets Tower. 200r, Nesvizh Castle, Nesvizh. 500r, Epiphany Church, Polatsk. (500r), Kosava Palace, Kosava. 1000r, Rumyantsev-Paskevich Palace, Homel. 2000r, Mir Castle, Mir. (2450r), Red Church, Minsk. (3750r), Church-fortress, Murovanka. 5000r, Main Post Office, Minsk. 10,000r, Lida Castle, Lida. 20,000r, Bernardine Monastery, Budslau.

2012, Mar. 2 Litho. *Perf. 13½x13*

796 A359 50r multi .25 .25
797 A359 100r multi .25 .25
798 A359 200r multi .25 .25
799 A359 500r multi .25 .25
800 A360 (500r) multi .25 .25
801 A359 1000r multi .40 .40
802 A359 2000r multi .75 .75
803 A361 (2450r) multi .95 .95
804 A362 (3750r) multi 1.50 1.50
805 A359 5000r multi 1.90 1.90
806 A359 10,000r multi 3.75 3.75
807 A359 20,000r multi 7.75 7.75
Nos. 796-807 (12) 18.25 18.25

Self-Adhesive

Die Cut

808 A359 50r multi .25 .25
809 A359 100r multi .25 .25
810 A359 200r multi .25 .25
811 A359 500r multi .25 .25
812 A360 (500r) multi .25 .25
813 A359 1000r multi .40 .40
814 A359 2000r multi .75 .75
815 A361 (2450r) multi .95 .95
816 A362 (3750r) multi 1.50 1.50
817 A359 5000r multi 1.90 1.90
818 A359 10,000r multi 3.75 3.75
819 A359 20,000r multi 7.75 7.75
Nos. 808-819 (12) 18.25 18.25

Europa — A363

No. 820 — People facing: a, Right. b, Left.

2012, Mar. 12 *Perf. 13x13½*

820 A363 5000r Horiz. pair, #a-b 4.50 4.50
c. Souvenir sheet of 6, 3 each #820a-820b 13.50 13.50

Apus Apus — A364

2012, Mar. 22 *Perf. 14x13½*

821 A364 (3750r) multi 2.50 2.50

Printed in sheets of 7 + label.

Costumes From Turov and Mozyr Regions — A365

Costumes From Liahovichi Region — A366

2012, Apr. 12 *Perf. 14¼x14*

822 A365 (2750r) multi 1.75 1.75
823 A366 (4250r) multi 2.75 2.75
a. Souvenir sheet of 8, 2 each #822-823 + label 13.50 13.50

Polypodium Vulgare and Silhouette of Butterfly — A367

Salvinia Natans and Silhouette of Fish A368

Litho. & Embossed

2012, May 3 *Perf. 12x12¼*

824 A367 (2750r) multi 1.75 1.75
825 A368 (4250r) multi 2.75 2.75
a. Souvenir sheet of 8, 4 each #824-825 13.50 13.50

Endangered plants.

Souvenir Sheet

Diplomatic Relations Between Belarus and Cuba, 20th Anniv. — A369

Litho. (Margin Litho. & Embossed)

2012, May 25 *Perf. 12¼x12*

826 A369 15,000r multi 6.75 6.75

Hemiechinus Auritus — A370

Erinaceus Concolor A371

2012, June 20 Litho. *Perf. 12x12¼*

827 A370 (3300r) multi 1.75 1.75
828 A371 (5100r) multi 2.75 2.75
a. Souvenir sheet of 4, 2 each #827-828 9.00 9.00

See Kazakhstan No.

Triturus Cristatus A372

Lissotriton Vulgaris A373

2012, June 25 *Perf. 13*

829 A372 (3300r) multi 1.75 1.75
830 A373 (5100r) multi 2.75 2.75
a. Souvenir sheet of 4, 2 each #829-830 9.00 9.00

See Russia No. 7367.

Souvenir Sheet

Portrait of Marc Chagall, by Yuri Pen — A374

2012, July 7 ***Perf. 13½x13***
831 A374 15,000r multi 6.75 6.75

Marc Chagall (1887-1985), painter.

French Invasion, Bicent. A375

2012, July 10 ***Perf. 13½x14***
832 A375 (5100r) multi 2.50 2.50

Printed in sheets of 8 + central label.

Eurasian Economic Community — A376

Litho. & Embossed

2012, July 26 ***Perf. 13x13½***
833 A376 (3300r) multi 2.00 2.00

Printed in sheets of 10 + 5 labels.

Belarussian Railway, 150th Anniv. — A377

2012, Aug. 1 **Litho.**
834 A377 (5100r) multi 2.50 2.50

Arms of Glubokoe — A378

Arms of Gorki — A379

2012, Aug. 21 ***Perf. 12***
835 A378 (4800r) multi 2.00 2.00
836 A379 (5800r) multi 2.50 2.50

Fire and Rescue Sports in Belarus, 75th Anniv. A380

2012, Sept. 8 ***Perf. 13½x14***
837 A380 5000r multi 2.10 2.10

Maxim Tank (1912-95), Poet — A381

2012, Sept. 15 ***Perf. 13x13½***
838 A381 (4800r) multi 2.00 2.00

Christmas — A382 New Year's Day — A383

Litho. & Embossed With Foil Application

2012, Nov. 20 ***Perf. 12¼x12***
839 A382 (3000r) blue & gold 1.25 1.25
840 A383 (4500r) sil & grn 1.90 1.90

Souvenir Sheet

Diplomatic Relations Between Belarus and Israel, 20th Anniv. — A384

2012, Dec. 18 **Litho.**
841 A384 15,000r multi 6.50 6.50

A385

A386

2012 Summer Olympics, London A387

2012, Dec. 21 ***Perf. 12x12¼***
842 A385 (4500r) bronze & blk 1.90 1.90
843 A386 (5500r) sil & blk 2.40 2.40
844 A387 (5800r) gold & blk 2.50 2.50
Nos. 842-844 (3) 6.80 6.80

2013 World Track Cycling Championships, Minsk — A388

2013, Jan. 28 ***Perf. 12***
845 A388 (5500r) multi 2.40 2.40

Botrychium Matricariifolium A389

Coracias Garrulus A390

2013, Jan. 31 ***Perf. 12¼x12, 12x12¼***
846 A389 (5500r) multi 2.40 2.40
847 A390 (5800r) multi 2.50 2.50
a. Souvenir sheet of 2, #846-847 5.00 5.00

Endangered flora and fauna.

A391 A392

Embroidery A393

2013, Feb. 12 ***Perf. 12***
848 A391 (3000r) multi 1.25 1.25
849 A392 (4500r) multi 1.90 1.90
850 A393 (5500r) multi 2.40 2.40
Nos. 848-850 (3) 5.55 5.55

Upupa Epops A394

2013, Mar. 12 ***Perf. 13½x13***
851 A394 (5800r) multi 2.75 2.75

Khatyn Massacre, 70th Anniv. — A395

2013, Mar. 22
852 A395 (4500r) multi 2.25 2.25

Souvenir Sheet

Belarussian Landscape - Drecheluki Country Estate, by Yuliy Klever — A396

2013, Apr. 10 ***Perf. 13x13½***
853 A396 15,000r multi 6.00 6.00

20th Intl. Telecommunications, Information and Banking Technologies Exhibition, Minsk — A397

2013, Apr. 23 ***Perf. 12x12¼***
854 A397 (3000r) multi 1.60 1.60

Souvenir Sheet

Dancers — A398

No. 855: a, Kryzhachok dancers, Belarus (man without hat). b, Terekeme dancers, Azerbaijan (man with hat).

2013, Apr. 24 ***Perf. 13½x13¼***
855 A398 5000r Sheet of 2, #a-b 4.00 4.00

See Azerbaijan No. 1020.

Peugeot Partner Mail Van A399

MAZ 437143-340 Mail Truck A400

2013, Apr. 29 ***Perf. 12x12¼***
856 A399 (5500r) multi 2.60 2.60
857 A400 (5800r) multi 2.75 2.75
a. Souvenir sheet of 4, 2 each #856-857, + label 11.00 11.00

Europa.

Souvenir Sheet

St. Cyril of Turov (1130-82) — A401

Litho. With Foil Application

2013, May 11

858 A401 15,000r multi 6.00 6.00

National Academic Bolshoi Opera and Ballet Theater — A402

2013, May 22 Litho. ***Perf. 13x13½***

859 A402 (5500r) multi 2.75 2.75

Souvenir Sheet

Slavonic Alphabet of Saints Cyril and Methodius, 1150th Anniv. — A403

Litho. With Foil Application

2013, May 24 ***Perf. 13½x13***

860 A403 15,000r multi 6.25 6.25

2013 Belarussian Presidency of the Commonwealth of Independent States — A404

2013, May 30 Litho.

861 A404 (4500r) multi 2.25 2.25

Souvenir Sheet

Diplomatic Relations Between Azerbaijan and Belarus, 20th Anniv. — A405

Litho. (Sheet Margin Litho. With Foil Application)

2013, June 11 ***Perf. 12¼x12***

862 A405 15,000r multi 6.25 6.25

See Azerbaijan No. 1027.

Defense of Brest Fortress, 1941 — A406

2013, June 21 Litho. ***Perf. 13x13½***

863 A406 (5500r) multi 2.25 2.25

Souvenir Sheet

Madonna and Child Icon, National Sanctuary, Budslau, 400th Anniv. — A407

Litho. & Embossed (Sheet Margin Litho. With Foil Application)

2013, July 6 ***Perf. 12x12¼***

864 A407 15,000r multi 6.25 6.25

Panthera Pardis Orientalis A408

Ovis Musimon A409

Haliaeetus Pelagicus A410

Panthera Tigris Altaica A411

2013, July 9 Litho. ***Perf. 12x12¼***

865 A408 (4000r) multi 1.75 1.75
866 A409 (5500r) multi 2.25 2.25
867 A410 (6500r) multi 2.75 2.75
868 A411 (7000r) multi 3.00 3.00
a. Souvenir sheet of 4, #865-868, + 2 labels 9.75 9.75
Nos. 865-868 (4) 9.75 9.75

Animals in Belarusian zoos.

Belarussian State Puppet Theater, Minsk, 75th Anniv. A412

2013, July 10

869 A412 (5500r) multi 2.25 2.25

Souvenir Sheet

Christianization of Russia, 1025th Anniv. — A413

No. 870 — Icons depicting: a, The Lamentation of Christ, 19th cent. b, Old Testament Trinity, 18th cent. c, Christ Pantocrator, 18th cent.

Litho., Margin Litho. With Foil Application

2013, July 28 ***Perf. 13½x13***

870 A413 5000r Sheet of 3, #a-c 5.75 5.75

See Russia No. 7466, Ukraine No.

Tennis Players — A414

No. 871: a, Victoria Azarenka serving. b, Maxim Mirnyi chasing ball.

2013, Aug. 14 Litho. ***Perf. 13½x13***

871 A414 (7000r) Pair, #a-b 5.75 5.75

Arms of Bykhov — A415

Arms of Zhlobin — A416

2013 Litho. ***Perf. 14¼x14***

872 A415 (6500r) multi 2.60 2.60
873 A416 (6500r) multi 2.60 2.60

Issued: No. 872, 8/20; No. 873, 9/4.

BELGIAN CONGO

'bel-jən 'käŋ-ˌgō

LOCATION — Central Africa
GOVT. — Belgian colony
AREA — 902,082 sq. mi. (estimated)
POP. — 12,660,000 (1956)
CAPITAL — Léopoldville

Congo was an independent state, founded by Leopold II of Belgium, until 1908 when it was annexed to Belgium as a colony. In 1960 it became the independent Republic of the Congo. See Congo Democratic Republic and Zaire.

100 Centimes = 1 Franc

Catalogue values for unused stamps in this country are for Never Hinged items, beginning with Scott 187 in the regular postage section, Scott B32 in the semi-postal section, Scott C17 in the airpost section, and Scott J8 in the postage due section.

Independent State

A1

A2

King Leopold II — A3

1886 Unwmk. Typo. ***Perf. 15***

1	A1	5c green	14.00	*25.00*
2	A1	10c rose	5.50	*6.00*
3	A2	25c blue	55.00	45.00
4	A3	50c olive green	9.00	9.00
5	A1	5fr lilac	400.00	325.00
a.		Perf. 14	1,100.	650.00
b.		5fr deep lilac	850.00	525.00

Counterfeits exist.
For surcharge see No. Q1.

King Leopold II — A4

1887-94

6	A4	5c grn ('89)	1.00	*1.25*
7	A4	10c rose ('89)	1.75	1.75
8	A4	25c blue ('89)	1.75	1.75
9	A4	50c reddish brown	65.00	30.00
10	A4	50c gray ('94)	4.00	*22.50*
11	A4	5fr violet	1,300.	550.00
12	A4	5fr gray ('92)	165.00	140.00
		On portion of parcel wrapper		*1,250.*
13	A4	10fr buff ('91)	625.00	425.00

The 25fr amd 50fr in gray were not issued. Values, each $35.

Counterfeits exist of Nos. 10-13, 25fr and 50fr unused, use, genuine stamps with faked cancels and counterfeit stamps with genuine cancels.

For surcharges, see Nos. Q3-Q6.

Port Matadi — A5

River Scene on the Congo, Stanley Falls — A6

Inkissi Falls — A7

Railroad Bridge on M'pozo River — A8

Hunting Elephants A9

Bangala Chief and Wife — A10

1894-1901 Engr. *Perf. 12½ to 15*

No.	Type	Description	Unused	Used
14	A5	5c pale bl & blk	19.00	19.00
15	A5	5c red brn & blk ('95)	4.25	1.75
16	A5	5c grn & blk ('00)	2.25	.60
17	A6	10c red brn & blk	19.00	*19.00*
18	A6	10c grnsh bl & blk ('95)	3.50	1.90
a.		Center inverted	*3,000.*	*2,750.*
19	A6	10c car & blk ('00)	4.50	1.10
20	A7	25c yel org & blk	5.00	3.50
21	A7	25c lt bl & blk ('00)	5.25	2.50
22	A8	50c grn & blk	2.00	2.00
23	A8	50c ol & blk ('00)	5.00	1.25
24	A9	1fr lilac & blk	32.50	19.00
a.		1fr rose lilac & black	475.00	37.50
25	A9	1fr car & blk ('01)	400.00	9.50
26	A10	5fr lake & blk	55.00	40.00
a.		5fr carmine rose & black	125.00	62.50
		Nos. 14-26 (13)	557.25	121.10

For overprintes see Nos. 31-32, 34, 36-37, 39.

Climbing Oil Palms — A11

Congo Canoe A12

1896

No.	Type	Description	Unused	Used
27	A11	15c ocher & blk	5.00	1.25
28	A12	40c bluish grn & blk	5.00	4.00

For overprints see Nos. 33, 35.

Congo Village A13

River Steamer on the Congo A14

1898

No.	Type	Description	Unused	Used
29	A13	3.50fr red & blk	200.00	140.00
a.		Perf. 14x12	550.00	350.00
30	A14	10fr yel grn & blk	190.00	50.00
a.		Center inverted	*25,000.*	
b.		Perf. 12	725.00	52.50
c.		Perf. 12x14	475.00	—
		As "c," pen canceled		21.00

Nos. 29-30 exist imperf. Value, set $850.
For overprints see Nos. 38, 40.

Belgian Congo

Overprinted

1908

No.	Type	Description	Unused	Used
31	A5	5c green & blk	8.75	8.75
a.		Handstamped	5.50	3.25
32	A6	10c car & blk	16.00	16.00
a.		Handstamped	5.50	3.25
33	A11	15c ocher & blk	8.75	8.75
a.		Handstamped	8.50	5.50
34	A7	25c lt blue & blk	5.75	3.25
a.		Handstamped	12.50	5.00
c.		Double overprint (#34)	300.00	
35	A12	40c bluish grn & blk	3.25	3.25
a.		Handstamped	16.00	9.25
36	A8	50c olive & blk	6.25	3.25
a.		Handstamped	8.00	5.50
b.		As #36, inverted overprint	775.00	
37	A9	1fr car & blk	27.50	8.75
a.		Handstamped	75.00	17.50
38	A13	3.50fr red & blk	40.00	32.50
a.		Handstamped	450.00	200.00
b.		As #38, inverted overprint	750.00	—
39	A10	5fr car & blk	72.50	37.50
a.		Handstamped	150.00	80.00
40	A14	10fr yel grn & blk	140.00	35.00
a.		Perf. 14½	375.00	—
b.		Handstamped	275.00	92.50
c.		Handstamped, perf. 14½	575.00	325.00
		Nos. 31-40 (10)	328.75	157.00

Most of the above handstamps are also found inverted and double.

There are two types of handstamped overprints, those applied in Brussels and those applied locally. There are eight types of each overprint. Values listed are the lowest for each stamp.

Counterfeits of the handstamped overprints exist.

Port Matadi A15

River Scene on the Congo, Stanley Falls — A16

Climbing Oil Palms — A17

Railroad Bridge on M'pozo River — A18

1909 ***Perf. 14***

No.	Type	Description	Unused	Used
41	A15	5c green & blk	1.00	1.00
42	A16	10c carmine & blk	1.00	.65
43	A17	15c ocher & blk	37.50	20.00
44	A18	50c olive & blk	4.25	2.75
		Nos. 41-44 (4)	43.75	24.40

Port Matadi A19

River Scene on the Congo, Stanley Falls — A20

Climbing Oil Palms — A21

Inkissi Falls — A22

Congo Canoe A23

Railroad Bridge on M'pozo River — A24

Hunting Elephants A25

Congo Village A26

Bangala Chief and Wife — A27

River Steamer on the Congo A28

1910-15 Engr. *Perf. 14, 15*

No.	Type	Description	Unused	Used
45	A19	5c green & blk	.75	.30
46	A20	10c carmine & blk	.75	.30
47	A21	15c ocher & blk	.70	.30
48	A21	15c grn & blk ('15)	.60	.25
a.		Booklet pane of 10	25.00	
49	A22	25c blue & blk	2.25	.60
50	A23	40c bluish grn & blk	3.25	3.00
51	A23	40c brn red & blk ('15)	5.50	3.25
52	A24	50c olive & blk	5.00	2.75
53	A24	50c brn lake & blk ('15)	9.50	3.00
54	A25	1fr carmine & blk	4.50	4.00
55	A25	1fr ol bis & blk ('15)	3.50	1.25
56	A26	3fr red & blk	22.50	14.50
57	A27	5fr carmine & blk	32.50	32.50
58	A27	5fr ocher & blk ('15)	2.50	1.25
59	A28	10fr green & blk	27.50	27.50
		Nos. 45-59 (15)	121.30	94.75

Nos. 48, 51, 53, 55 and 58 exist imperforate. Value, set $150.

For overprints and surcharges see Nos. 64-76, 81-86, B5-B9.

Port Matadi A29

Stanley Falls, Congo River — A30

Inkissi Falls — A31

TEN CENTIMES.

Type I — Large white space at top of picture and two small white spots at lower edge. Vignette does not fill frame.

Type II — Vignette completely fills frame.

1915

No.	Type	Description	Unused	Used
60	A29	5c green & blk	.30	.25
a.		Booklet pane of 10	19.00	
61	A30	10c car & blk (II)	.30	.25
a.		10c carmine & black (I)	.30	.25
d.		Booklet pane of 10 (II)	25.00	
62	A31	25c blue & blk	1.50	.50
a.		Booklet pane of 10	125.00	
		Nos. 60-62 (3)	2.10	1.00
		Set, never hinged	8.00	

Nos. 60-62 exist imperforate. Value, set $15.

For surcharges see Nos. 77-80, 87, B1-B4.

Stamps of 1910 Issue Surcharged in Red or Black

1921

No.	Type	Description	Unused	Used
64	A23	5c on 40c bluish grn & blk (R)	.40	.40
65	A19	10c on 5c grn & blk (R)	.40	.40
66	A24	15c on 50c ol & blk (R)	.40	.40
a.		Inverted surcharge		275.00
67	A21	25c on 15c ocher & blk (R)	2.75	1.60
68	A20	30c on 10c car & blk	.75	.75
69	A22	50c on 25c bl & blk (R)	2.75	1.60
		Nos. 64-69 (6)	7.45	5.15
		Set, never hinged	13.00	

The position of the new value and the bars varies on Nos. 64 to 69.

No. 54 Overprinted

1921

No.	Type	Description	Unused	Used
70	A25	1fr carmine & blk	1.60	1.60
a.		Double overprint	125.00	
71	A26	3fr red & blk	4.00	4.00
72	A27	5fr carmine & blk	11.00	11.00
73	A28	10fr green & blk (R)	8.75	6.25
		Nos. 70-73 (4)	25.35	22.85
		Set, never hinged	67.50	

Belgian Surcharges

Nos. 51, 53, 60-62 Surcharged in Black or Red

1922

No.	Type	Description	Unused	Used
74	A24	5c on 50c	.65	.65
75	A29	10c on 5c (R)	.65	.50
76	A23	25c on 40c (R)	3.75	.60
77	A30	30c on 10c (II)	.40	.40
a.		30c on 10c (I)	.65	.35
b.		Double surcharge	6.00	6.00
78	A31	50c on 25c (R)	1.25	.45
		Nos. 74-78 (5)	6.70	2.60
		Set, never hinged	16.00	

No. 74 has the surcharge at each side.

Congo Surcharges

Nos. 60, 51 Surcharged in Red or Black

a

b

1922

80 A29 10c on 5c (R) .70 .70
Never hinged 2.25
a. Inverted surcharge 25.00 25.00
b. Double surcharge 6.00
c. Double surch., one invtd. 50.00
d. Pair, one without surcharge 52.50
e. On No. 45 325.00 325.00
81 A23 25c on 40c 1.25 .65
Never hinged 4.00
a. Inverted surcharge 25.00 25.00
b. Double surcharge 6.75
c. "25c" double
d. 25c on 5c, No. 60 225.00 225.00

Nos. 55, 58 Surcharged in Red

1922

84 A25 10c on 1fr (R) .75 .75
Never hinged 2.25
a. Double surcharge 17.50
b. Inverted surcharge 25.00 25.00
85 A27 25c on 5fr 2.50 2.50
Never hinged 7.00

Nos. 68, 77 Handstamped

86 A20 25c on 30c on 10c 30.00 20.00
Never hinged 42.50
87 A30 25c on 30c on 10c (II) 20.00 20.00
Never hinged 42.50

Nos. 86-87 exist with handstamp surcharge inverted.

Counterfeit handstamped surcharges exist.

Ubangi Woman — A32

Watusi Cattle — A44

Designs: 10c, Baluba woman. 15c, Babuende woman. No. 91, 40c, 1.25fr, 1.50fr, 1.75fr, Ubangi man. 25c, Basketmaking. 30c, 35c, No. 101, Weaving. No. 102, Carving wood. 50c, Archer. Nos. 92, 100, Weaving. 1fr, Making pottery. 3fr, Working rubber. 5fr, Making palm oil. 10fr, African elephant.

1923-27 Engr. *Perf. 12*

88 A32 5c yellow .35 .25
89 A32 10c green .25 .25
90 A32 15c olive brown .25 .25
91 A32 20c olive grn ('24) .25 .25
92 A44 20c green ('26) .50 .25
93 A44 25c red brown .30 .25
94 A44 30c rose red ('24) .65 .65
95 A44 30c olive grn ('25) .30 .25
96 A44 35c green ('27) .75 .45
97 A32 40c violet ('25) .30 .25
98 A44 50c gray blue .30 .25
99 A44 50c buff ('25) .65 .25
100 A44 75c red orange .30 .25
101 A44 75c gray bl ('25) .65 .35
102 A44 75c salmon red ('26) .30 .25
103 A44 1fr bister brown 1.00 .40
104 A44 1fr dl blue ('25) .65 .25
105 A44 1fr rose red ('27) 1.25 .25
106 A32 1.25fr dl blue ('26) .95 .40
107 A32 1.50fr dl blue ('26) .95 .30
108 A32 1.75fr dl blue ('27) 8.00 6.25
109 A44 3fr gray brn ('24) 8.00 4.00
110 A44 5fr gray ('24) 15.00 8.00
111 A44 10fr gray blk ('24) 30.00 15.00

1925-26

112 A44 45c dk vio ('26) .70 .40
113 A44 60c carmine rose .70 .30
Nos. 88-113 (26) 73.30 40.00
Set, never hinged 250.00

For surcharges see Nos. 114, 136-138, 157.

No. 107 Surcharged

1927, June 14

114 A32 1.75fr on 1.50fr dl bl 1.00 1.00
Never hinged 2.00

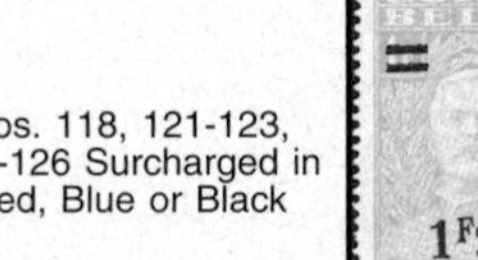

Sir Henry Morton Stanley — A45

1928, June 30 *Perf. 14*

115 A45 5c gray blk .25 .25
116 A45 10c dp violet .25 .25
117 A45 20c orange red .50 .30
118 A45 35c green 1.25 .75
119 A45 40c red brown .60 .25
120 A45 60c black brn 1.00 .50
121 A45 1fr carmine .40 .25
122 A45 1.60fr dk gray 10.50 8.75
123 A45 1.75fr dp blue 2.25 1.00
124 A45 2fr dk brown 1.60 .95
125 A45 2.75fr red violet 10.50 .45
126 A45 3.50fr rose lake 1.75 1.25
127 A45 5fr slate grn 1.50 1.25
128 A45 10fr violet blue 2.25 1.25
129 A45 20fr claret 10.50 7.50
Nos. 115-129 (15) 45.10 24.95
Set, never hinged 140.00

Sir Henry M. Stanley (1841-1904), explorer.

Nos. 118, 121-123, 125-126 Surcharged in Red, Blue or Black

1931, Jan. 15

130 A45 40c on 35c 1.60 .75
131 A45 1.25fr on 1fr (Bl) 1.00 .25
132 A45 2fr on 1.60fr 1.60 .50
133 A45 2fr on 1.75fr 1.60 .45
134 A45 3.25fr on 2.75fr (Bk) 4.50 3.25
135 A45 3.25fr on 3.50fr (Bk) 8.75 7.50

Nos. 96, 108, 112 Surcharged in Red

Perf. 12½, 12

136 A44 40c on 35c grn 6.50 5.75
137 A44 50c on 45c dk vio 3.75 2.50

No. 108 Surcharged

138 A32 2(fr) on 1.75fr dl bl 17.50 15.00
Nos. 130-138 (9) 46.80 35.95
Set, never hinged 160.00

View of Sankuru River — A46

Flute Players — A50

Designs: 15c, Kivu Kraal. 20c, Sankuru River rapids. 25c, Uele hut. 50c, Musicians of Lake Leopold II. 60c, Batetelas drummers. 75c, Mangbetu woman. 1fr, Domesticated elephant of Api. 1.25fr, Mangbetu chief. 1.50fr, 2fr, Village of Mondimbi. 2.50fr, 3.25fr, Okapi. 4fr, Canoes at Stanleyville. 5fr, Woman preparing cassava. 10fr, Baluba chief. 20fr, Young woman of Irumu.

1931-37 Engr. *Perf. 11½*

139 A46 10c gray brn ('32) .25 .25
140 A46 15c gray ('32) .25 .25
141 A46 20c brn lil ('32) .25 .25
142 A46 25c dp blue ('32) .25 .25
143 A50 40c dp grn ('32) .30 .30
144 A46 50c violet ('32) .25 .25
b. Booklet pane of 8 6.25
145 A50 60c vio brn ('32) .30 .30
146 A50 75c rose ('32) .30 .30
b. Booklet pane of 8 5.50
147 A50 1fr rose red ('32) .30 .30
148 A50 1.25fr red brown .30 .30
b. Booklet pane of 8 5.50
149 A46 1.50fr dk ol gray ('37) .30 .30
b. Booklet pane of 8 11.00
150 A46 2fr ultra ('32) .35 .30
151 A46 2.50fr dp blue ('37) .50 .30
b. Booklet pane of 8 15.00
152 A46 3.25fr gray blk ('32) .80 .50
153 A46 4fr dl vio ('32) .50 .30
154 A50 5fr dp vio ('32) 1.00 .40
155 A50 10fr red ('32) 1.25 1.00
156 A50 20fr blk brn ('32) 2.50 1.50
Nos. 139-156 (18) 9.95 7.35
Set, never hinged 27.50

No. 109 Surcharged in Red

1932, Mar. 15 *Perf. 12*

157 A44 3.25fr on 3fr gray brn 8.75 5.75
Never hinged 25.00

King Albert Memorial Issue

King Albert — A62

1934, May 7 Photo. *Perf. 11½*

158 A62 1.50fr black 1.25 .90
Never hinged 3.25

No. 158 exists imperf. Value, $67.50.

Leopold I, Leopold II, Albert I, Leopold III — A63

1935, Aug. 15 Engr. *Perf. 12½x12*

159 A63 50c green 2.00 1.25
160 A63 1.25fr dk carmine 2.00 .40
161 A63 1.50fr brown vio 2.00 .40
162 A63 2.40fr brown org 6.25 6.25
163 A63 2.50fr lt blue 6.25 2.25
164 A63 4fr brt violet 6.25 3.25
165 A63 5fr black brn 6.25 3.25
Nos. 159-165 (7) 31.00 17.05
Set, never hinged 87.50

Founding of Congo Free State, 50th anniv.

Nos. 159-165 exist imperf. Value set, $3,500.

For surcharges see Nos. B21-B22.

Molindi River — A64

Bamboos — A65

Suza River — A66

Rutshuru River — A67

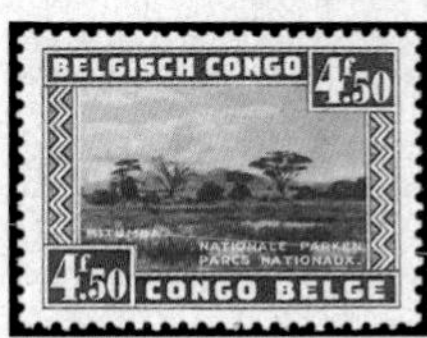

Karisimbi A68

Mitumba Forest A69

1937-38 Photo. *Perf. 11½*

166 A64 5c purple & blk .30 .25
167 A65 90c car & brn .70 .35
168 A66 1.50fr dp red brn & blk .50 .40
169 A67 2.40fr ol blk & brn .40 .30
170 A68 2.50fr dp ultra & blk .65 .30
171 A69 4.50fr dk grn & brn .85 .70
172 A69 4.50fr car & sep .40 .30
Nos. 166-172 (7) 3.80 2.60
Set, never hinged 7.50

National Parks.

Nos. 166-171 were issued Mar. 1, 1938. Exist imperf. Value, set $100.

No. 172 was issued in sheets of four measuring 140x111mm. It was sold by subscription, the subscription closing Dec. 31, 1938. Value: unused $3.75. Exists imperf. Value, $1,250.

See No. B26. For surcharges see Nos. 184, 186.

King Albert Memorial, Leopoldville — A70

1941, Feb. 7 Litho. *Perf. 11*

No.	Type	Value	Color	Unused	Used
173	A70	10c	lt gray	.50	.30
174	A70	15c	brown vio	.55	.30
175	A70	25c	lt blue	.65	.45
176	A70	50c	lt violet	.65	.30
177	A70	75c	rose pink	2.25	.65
178	A70	1.25fr	gray	.65	.50
179	A70	1.75fr	orange	1.60	.70
180	A70	2.50fr	carmine	1.25	.35
181	A70	2.75fr	vio blue	1.75	1.25
182	A70	5fr	lt olive grn	8.75	8.75
183	A70	10fr	rose red	6.75	5.25
			Nos. 173-183 (11)	25.35	18.80
			Set, never hinged	92.50	

Exist imperforate. Value, set $62.50.
For surcharge see No. 185.

Nos. 168, 179, 169 Surcharged in Blue or Black

Nos. 184, 186

No. 185

1941-42 *Perf. 11½, 11*

No.	Type	Value	Color	Unused	Used
184	A66	5c on 1.50fr	(Bl)	.25	.25
a.			Inverted surcharge	27.50	27.50
185	A70	75c on 1.75fr	('42)	.50	.40
a.			Inverted surcharge	27.50	27.50
186	A67	2.50(fr) on 2.40fr	('42)	1.50	1.00
a.			Double surcharge	27.50	27.50
b.			Inverted surcharge	27.50	27.50
			Nos. 184-186 (3)	2.25	1.65
			Set, never hinged	5.00	

Catalogue values for unused stamps in this section, from this point to the end of the section, are for Never Hinged items.

A71

Oil Palms — A72

Congo Woman — A73

Leopard A74

Askari — A75

Okapi A76

Inscribed "Congo Belge Belgisch Congo"

1942, May 23 Engr. *Perf. 12½*

No.	Type	Value	Color	Unused	Used
187	A71	5c	red	.25	.25
188	A72	10c	olive grn	.25	.25
189	A72	15c	brown car	.25	.25
190	A72	20c	dp ultra	.25	.25
191	A72	25c	brown vio	.25	.25
192	A72	30c	blue	.25	.25
193	A72	50c	dp green	.25	.25
194	A72	60c	chestnut	.25	.25
195	A73	75c	dl lil & blk	.35	.25
196	A73	1fr	dk brn & blk	.35	.25
197	A73	1.25fr	rose red & blk	.35	.25
198	A74	1.75fr	dk gray brn	1.50	.90
199	A74	2fr	ocher	1.50	.25
200	A74	2.50fr	carmine	1.50	.25
201	A75	3.50fr	dk ol grn	.75	.25
202	A75	5fr	orange	1.50	.25
203	A75	6fr	brt ultra	1.50	.25
204	A75	7fr	black	1.50	.25
205	A75	10fr	dp brown	1.50	.25
206	A76	20fr	plum & blk	16.00	1.25
			Nos. 187-206 (20)	30.30	6.65

Same Inscribed "Belgisch Congo Congo Belge"

No.	Type	Value	Color	Unused	Used
207	A72	10c	olive grn	.25	.25
208	A72	15c	brown car	.25	.25
209	A72	20c	dp ultra	.25	.25
210	A72	25c	brown vio	.25	.25
211	A72	30c	blue	.25	.25
212	A72	50c	dp green	.25	.25
213	A72	60c	chestnut	.25	.25
214	A73	75c	dl lil & blk	.25	.25
215	A73	1fr	dk brn & blk	.35	.25
216	A73	1.25fr	rose red & blk	.35	.25
217	A74	1.75fr	dk gray brn	1.25	.35
218	A74	2fr	ocher	1.25	.25
219	A74	2.50fr	carmine	1.25	.25
220	A75	3.50fr	dk ol grn	.90	.25
221	A75	5fr	orange	1.25	.25
222	A75	6fr	brt ultra	1.25	.25
223	A75	7fr	black	1.25	.25
224	A75	10fr	dp brown	1.25	.25
225	A76	20fr	plum & blk	15.00	1.25
			Nos. 207-225 (19)	27.35	5.85

Miniature sheets of Nos. 193, 194, 197, 200, 211, 214, 217 and 219 were printed in 1944 by the Belgian Government in London and given to the Belgian political review, Message, which distributed them to its subscribers, one a month. Value per sheet, about $100.

Remainders of these eight miniature sheets received marginal overprints in various colors in 1950, specifying a surtax of 100fr per sheet and paying tribute to the UPU. These sheets, together with four of Ruanda-Urundi, were sold by the Committee of Cultural Works (and not at post offices) in sets of 12 for 1,217.15 francs. Set value, $1,750.

Nos. 187-227 imperforate had no franking value. Value, set $275.

For surcharges see Nos. B34-B37.

Congo Woman — A77

Askari — A78

1943, Jan. 1

No.	Type	Value	Color	Unused	Used
226	A77	50fr	ultra & blk	11.00	1.60
227	A78	100fr	car & blk	16.00	2.75

Slaves and Arab Guards A79

Auguste Lambermont A80

Design: 10fr, Leopold II.

Perf. 13x11½, 12½x12

1947 Engr. Unwmk.

No.	Type	Value	Color	Unused	Used
228	A79	1.25fr	black brown	.40	.25
229	A80	3.50fr	dark blue	.60	.25
230	A80	10fr	red orange	1.60	.25
			Nos. 228-230 (3)	2.60	.75

50th anniv. of the abolition of slavery in Belgian Congo. See Nos. 261-262.

Baluba Carving of Former King — A82

Carved figures and masks of Baluba tribe: 10c, 50c, 2fr, "Ndoha," figure of tribal king. 15c, 70c, 1.20fr, 2.50fr, "Tshimanyi," an idol. 20c, 75c, 1.60fr, 3.50fr, "Buangakokoma," statue of kneeling beggar. 25c, 1fr, 2.40fr, 5fr, "Mbuta," sacred double cup, carved with two faces, Man and Woman. 40c, 1.25fr, 6fr, 8fr, "Ngadimuashi," female mask. 1.50fr, 3fr, 10fr, 50fr, "Buadi-Muadi," mask with squared features. 6.50fr, 20fr, 100fr, "Mbowa," executioner's mask with buffalo horns.

1947-50 *Perf. 12½*

No.	Type	Value	Color	Unused	Used
231	A82	10c	dp org ('48)	.30	.25
232	A82	15c	ultra ('48)	.30	.25
233	A82	20c	brt bl ('48)	.30	.25
234	A82	25c	rose car ('48)	.30	.25
235	A82	40c	violet ('48)	.30	.25
236	A82	50c	olive brn	.30	.25
237	A82	70c	yel grn ('48)	.30	.25
238	A82	75c	magenta ('48)	.30	.25
239	A82	1fr	yel org & dk vio	2.75	.25
240	A82	1.20fr	gray & brn ('50)	.30	.25
241	A82	1.25fr	lt bl grn & mag ('48)	.40	.25
242	A82	1.50fr	ol & mag ('50)	20.00	5.00
243	A82	1.60fr	bl gray & brt bl ('50)	.75	.25
244	A82	2fr	org & mag ('48)	.30	.25
245	A82	2.40fr	bl grn & dk grn ('50)	.50	.25
246	A82	2.50fr	brn red & bl grn	.60	.25
247	A82	3fr	lt ultra & ind ('49)	8.50	.25
248	A82	3.50fr	lt bl & blk ('48)	6.75	.30
249	A82	5fr	bis & mag ('48)	2.50	.25
250	A82	6fr	brn org & ind ('48)	3.00	.25
251	A82	6.50fr	red org & red brn ('49)	4.00	.40
252	A82	8fr	gray bl & dk grn ('50)	3.25	.35
253	A82	10fr	pale vio & red brn ('48)	50.00	.30
254	A82	20fr	red org & vio brn ('48)	5.50	.40
255	A82	50fr	dp org & blk ('48)	9.50	.40
256	A82	100fr	crim & blk brn ('48)	12.00	.75
			Nos. 231-256 (26)	133.00	12.40

Railroad Train and Map — A83

1948, July 1 Unwmk. *Perf. 13½*

No.	Type	Value	Color	Unused	Used
257	A83	2.50fr	dp bl & grn	1.40	.55

50th anniv. of railway service in the Congo.

Globe and Ship A84

1949, Nov. 21 *Perf. 11½*

Granite Paper

No.	Type	Value	Color	Unused	Used
258	A84	4fr	violet blue	1.25	.65

75th anniv. of the UPU.

Allegorical Figure and Map — A85

1950, Aug. 12 *Perf. 12x12½*

No.	Type	Value	Color	Unused	Used
259	A85	3fr	blue & indigo	3.75	.35
260	A85	6.50fr	car rose & blk brn	3.75	.35

Establishment of Katanga Province, 50th anniv.

Portrait Type of 1947

Designs: 1.50fr, Cardinal Lavigerie. 3fr, Baron Dhanis.

Perf. 12½x12

1951, June 25 Unwmk.

No.	Type	Value	Color	Unused	Used
261	A80	1.50fr	purple	3.25	.35
262	A80	3fr	black brown	3.25	.35

Littonia — A86

1952-53 Photo. *Perf. 11½*

Granite Paper

Flowers in Natural Colors

Size: 21x25½mm

No.	Type	Value	Name	Unused	Used
263	A86	10c	Dissotis	.35	.25
264	A86	15c	Protea	.25	.25
265	A86	20c	Vellozia	.30	.25
266	A86	25c	shown	.35	.25
267	A86	40c	Ipomoea	.35	.25
268	A86	50c	Angraecum	.70	.25
269	A86	60c	Euphorbia	.60	.25
270	A86	75c	Ochna	.80	.25
271	A86	1fr	Hibiscus	.80	.25
272	A86	1.25fr	Protea ('53)	2.00	.60
273	A86	1.50fr	Schrizoglossum	1.50	.25
274	A86	2fr	Ansellia	2.00	.25
275	A86	3fr	Costus	1.75	.25
276	A86	4fr	Nymphaea	2.50	.25
277	A86	5fr	Thunbergia	2.75	.25
278	A86	6.50fr	Thonningia	2.75	.25
279	A86	7fr	Gerbera	3.50	.25
280	A86	8fr	Gloriosa ('53)	5.00	.35
281	A86	10fr	Silene ('53)	6.75	.50
282	A86	20fr	Aristolochia	11.00	.50

Size: 22x32mm

No.	Type	Value	Name	Unused	Used
283	A86	50fr	Eulophia ('53)	22.50	1.75
284	A86	100fr	Crytosepalum ('53)	32.50	2.25
			Nos. 263-284 (22)	101.00	9.95

Nos. 264, 269 and 270 with additional surcharges are varieties of Congo Democratic Republic Nos. 324, 327 and 328.

St. Francis Xavier — A86a

1953, Jan. 5 Engr. *Perf. 12½x13*

285 A86a 1.50fr ultra & gray blk 1.00 .50

400th death anniv. of St. Francis Xavier.

Canoe on Lake Kivu — A87

1953, Jan. 5 *Perf. 14*

286 A87 3fr car & blk 3.75 .45
287 A87 7fr dp bl & brn org 3.75 .50

Issued to publicize the Kivu Festival, 1953.

Royal Colonial Institute Jubilee Medal A88

Design: 6.50fr, Same with altered background and transposed inscriptions.

1954, Dec. 27 Photo. *Perf. 13½*

288 A88 4.50fr indigo & gray 2.50 .75
289 A88 6.50fr dk grn & brn 2.00 .30

25th anniv. of the founding of the Belgian Royal Colonial Institute. Exist imperf. Value, set $30.

King Baudouin and Tropical Scene A89

Designs: King and various views.

Inscribed "Congo Belge-Belgisch Congo"

Engr.; Portrait Photo.

1955, Feb. 15 Unwmk. *Perf. 11½*

Portrait in Black

290 A89 1.50fr rose car 19.00 2.50
291 A89 3fr green 11.00 2.00
292 A89 4.50fr ultra 11.00 1.25
293 A89 6.50fr dp claret 15.00 .60

Inscribed "Belgisch Congo-Congo Belge"

294 A89 1.50fr rose car 19.00 2.50
295 A89 3fr green 11.00 2.00
296 A89 4.50fr ultra 11.00 1.25
297 A89 6.50fr deep claret 15.00 .60
Nos. 290-297 (8) 112.00 12.70

Exist imperf. Value, set $225.

Map of Africa and Emblem of Royal Touring Club — A90

1955, July 26 Engr. *Perf. 11½*

Inscription in French

298 A90 6.50fr vio blue 4.00 .60

Inscription in Flemish

299 A90 6.50fr vio blue 4.00 .60

5th International Congress of African Tourism, Elisabethville, July 26-Aug. 4. Nos. 298-299 printed in alternate rows.
Exist imperf. Value, set $30.

Kings of Belgium A91

1958, July 1 Unwmk. *Perf. 12½*

300 A91 1fr rose vio 1.10 .25
301 A91 1.50fr ultra 1.10 .25
302 A91 3fr rose car 1.10 .25
303 A91 5fr green 2.00 .55
304 A91 6.50fr brn red 1.60 .25
305 A91 10fr dl vio 1.90 .25
Nos. 300-305 (6) 8.80 1.80

Belgium's annexation of Congo, 50th anniv. Exist imperf. Value, set $30.

Roan Antelope — A92

Black Buffaloes A93

Designs: 20c, White rhinoceros. 40c, Giraffe. 50c, Thick-tailed bushbaby. 1fr, Gorilla. 2fr, Black-and-white colobus (monkey). 3fr, Elephants. 5fr, Okapis. 6.50fr, Impala. 8fr, Giant pangolin. 10fr, Eland and zebras.

1959, Oct. 15 Photo. *Perf. 11½*

Granite Paper

306 A92 10c bl & brn .30 .25
307 A93 20c red org & slate .30 .25
308 A92 40c brn & bl .30 .25
309 A93 50c brt ultra, red & sep .30 .25
310 A92 1fr brn, grn & blk .30 .25
311 A93 1.50fr blk & org yel .30 .25
312 A92 2fr crim, blk & brn .40 .25
313 A93 3fr blk, gray & lil rose 1.00 .25
314 A92 5fr brn, dk brn & brt grn 1.25 .25
315 A93 6.50fr bl, brn & org yel 1.50 .25
316 A92 8fr org brn, ol bis & lil 1.50 .40
317 A93 10fr multi 2.00 .25
Nos. 306-317 (12) 9.45 3.15

Exist imperf. Value, set $77.50.

Madonna and Child — A94

1959, Dec. 1 Unwmk. *Perf. 11½*

318 A94 50c golden brn, ocher & red brn .25 .25
319 A94 1fr dk bl, pur & red brn .25 .25
320 A94 2fr gray, brt bl & red brn .50 .25
Nos. 318-320 (3) 1.00 .75

Exist imperf. Value, set $30.

Map of Africa and Symbolic Honeycomb A95

1960, Feb. 19 Unwmk. *Perf. 11½*

Inscription in French

321 A95 3fr gray & red .40 .25

Inscription in Flemish

322 A95 3fr gray & red .40 .25

Commission for Technical Co-operation in Africa South of the Sahara (C. C. T. A.), 10th anniv. Exists imperf. Value, set $15.

SEMI-POSTAL STAMPS

Types of 1910-15 Issues Surcharged in Red

1918, May 15 Unwmk. *Perf. 14, 15*

B1 A29 5c + 10c grn & bl .50 .50
B2 A30 10c + 15c car & bl (I) .50 .50
B3 A21 15c + 20c bl grn & bl .50 .50
B4 A31 25c + 25c dp bl & pale bl .50 .50
B5 A23 40c + 40c brn red & bl .75 .75
B6 A24 50c + 50c brn lake & bl .75 .75
B7 A25 1fr + 1fr ol bis & bl 3.00 3.00
B8 A27 5fr + 5fr ocher & bl 15.00 15.00
B9 A28 10fr + 10fr grn & bl 160.00 160.00
Nos. B1-B9 (9) 181.50 *181.50*
Set, never hinged 500.00

The position of the cross and the added value varies on the different stamps.
Nos. B1-B9 exist imperforate without gum. Value, set $525.
Perf 15 examples of Nos. B1-B6 are worth approximately twice the values shown.

SP1

Design: No. B11, Inscribed "Belgisch Congo."

1925, July 8 *Perf. 12½*

B10 SP1 25c + 25c carmine & blk .40 .40
B11 SP1 25c + 25c carmine & blk .40 .40
  a. Pair, Nos. B10-B11 1.00 1.00
  Never hinged 1.60

Colonial campaigns in 1914-1918.
The surtax helped erect at Kinshasa a monument to those who died in World War I.

Nurse Weighing Child — SP3

First Aid Station SP5

Designs: 20c+10c, Missionary & Child. 60c+30c, Congo hospital. 1fr+50c, Dispensary service. 1.75fr+75c, Convalescent area. 3.50fr+1.50fr, Instruction on bathing infant. 5fr+2.50fr, Operating room. 10fr+5fr, Students.

1930, Jan. 16 Engr. *Perf. 11½*

B12 SP3 10c + 5c ver 1.00 1.00
B13 SP3 20c + 10c dp brn 1.25 1.25
B14 SP5 35c + 15c dp grn 1.90 1.90
B15 SP5 60c + 30c dl vio 2.25 2.25
B16 SP3 1fr + 50c dk car 3.75 3.75
B17 SP5 1.75fr + 75c dp bl 8.75 8.75
B18 SP5 3.50fr + 1.50fr rose lake 11.00 11.00
B19 SP5 5fr + 2.50fr red brn 15.00 15.00
B20 SP5 10fr + 5fr gray blk 17.50 17.50
Nos. B12-B20 (9) 62.40 62.40
Set, never hinged 160.00

The surtax was intended to aid welfare work among the natives, especially the children.

Nos. 161, 163 Surcharged "+50c" in Blue or Red

1936, May 15 *Perf. 12½x12*

B21 A63 1.50fr + 50c (Bl) 8.75 6.25
B22 A63 2.50fr + 50c (R) 4.50 3.00
Set, never hinged 25.00

Surtax was for the King Albert Memorial Fund.

Queen Astrid with Congolese Children — SP12

1936, Aug. 29 Photo. *Perf. 12½*

B23 SP12 1.25fr + 5c dark brown .65 .65
B24 SP12 1.50fr + 10c dull rose .65 .65
B25 SP12 2.50fr + 25c dark blue 1.25 1.25
Nos. B23-B25 (3) 2.55 2.55
Set, never hinged 7.00

Issued in memory of Queen Astrid. The surtax was for the aid of the National League for Protection of Native Children.

National Park Type of 1937-38

Souvenir Sheet

1938, Oct. 3 *Perf. 11½*

Star in Yellow

B26 Sheet of 6 67.50 67.50
  Never hinged 125.00
  On first day cover 75.00
  a. A64 5c ultra & light brown 6.50 6.50
  b. A65 90c ultra & light brown 6.50 6.50
  c. A66 1.50fr ultra & light brown 6.50 6.50
  d. A67 2.40fr ultra & light brown 6.50 6.50
  e. A68 2.50fr ultra & light brown 6.50 6.50
  f. A69 4.50fr ultra & light brown 6.50 6.50

Intl. Tourist Cong. A surtax of 3.15fr was for the benefit of the Congo Tourist Service. Exists imperf. Value $1,350.

Marabou Storks and Vultures — SP14

Buffon's Kob — SP15

Designs: 1.50fr+1.50fr, Pygmy chimpanzees. 4.50fr+4.50fr, Dwarf crocodiles. 5fr+5fr, Lioness.

1939, June 6 Photo. *Perf. 14*

B27 SP14 1fr + 1fr dp claret 8.75 8.75
B28 SP15 1.25fr + 1.25fr car 8.75 8.75
B29 SP15 1.50fr + 1.50fr brt pur 8.75 8.75

B30 SP14 4.50fr + 4.50fr sl grn 8.75 8.75
B31 SP15 5fr + 5fr brown 8.75 8.75
Nos. B27-B31 (5) 43.75 43.75
Set, never hinged 95.00

Surtax for the Leopoldville Zoological Gardens. Exists imperf. Value $225.
Sold in full sets by subscription.

Catalogue values for unused stamps in this section, from this point to the end of the section, are for Never Hinged items.

Lion of Belgium and Inscription "Belgium Shall Rise Again" — SP19

1942, Feb. 17 Engr. *Perf. 12½*
B32 SP19 10fr + 40fr brt grn 3.00 2.50
B33 SP19 10fr + 40fr vio bl 3.00 2.50

Nos. 193, 216, 198 and 220 Surcharged in Red

a

Ten voordeele van het Roode Kruis + 100 Fr. Au profit de la Croix Rouge

b

c

1945
B34 A72 (a) 50c + 50fr 6.75 4.00
B35 A73 (b) 1.25fr + 100fr 6.75 4.00
B36 A74 (c) 1.75fr + 100fr 6.75 4.00
B37 A75 (b) 3.50fr + 100fr 6.75 4.00
Nos. B34-B37 (4) 27.00 *16.00*

The surtax was for the Red Cross.
Sold in full sets by subscription.

Mozart at Age 7 — SP20

Queen Elisabeth and Sonata by Mozart — SP21

Perf. 11½
1956, Oct. 10 Unwmk. Engr.
B38 SP20 4.50fr + 1.50fr brt lil 7.00 3.25
B39 SP21 6.50fr + 2.50fr ultra 9.50 4.50

200th anniv. of the birth of Wolfgang Amadeus Mozart. Exist imperf.
The surtax was for the Pro-Mozart Committee.
Exist imperf. Value, set $35.

Nurse and Children SP22

Designs: 4.50fr+50c, Patient receiving injection. 6.50fr+40c, Patient being bandaged.

1957, Dec. 10 Photo. *Perf. 13x10½*
Cross in Carmine
B40 SP22 3fr + 50c dk bl 1.60 .60
B41 SP22 4.50fr + 50c dk grn 1.75 .60
B42 SP22 6.50fr + 50c red brn 2.00 1.40
Nos. B40-B42 (3) 5.35 2.60

The surtax was for the Red Cross.
Exist imperf. Value, set $92.50.

High Jump SP23

1960, May 2 Unwmk. *Perf. 13½*
B43 SP23 50c + 25c shown .35 .40
B44 SP23 1.50fr + 50c Hurdles 1.00 .40
B45 SP23 2fr + 1fr Soccer 1.10 .40
B46 SP23 3fr + 1.25fr Javelin 1.25 *1.10*
B47 SP23 6.50fr + 3.50fr Discus 2.75 *1.25*
Nos. B43-B47 (5) 6.45 *3.55*

17th Olympic Games, Rome, Aug. 25-Sept. 11. The surtax was for the youth of Congo.
Exist imperf. Value, set $125.

AIR POST STAMPS

Wharf on Congo River AP1

Congo "Country Store" AP2

View of Congo River AP3

Stronghold in the Interior — AP4

Unwmk.
1920, July 1 Engr. *Perf. 12*
C1 AP1 50c orange & blk .75 .25
C2 AP2 1fr dull vio & blk .80 .25
C3 AP3 2fr blue & blk 1.25 .60
C4 AP4 5fr green & blk 2.25 1.00
Nos. C1-C4 (4) 5.05 2.10
Set, never hinged 14.00

Kraal AP5

Porters on Safari AP6

1930, Apr. 2
C5 AP5 15fr dk brn & blk 3.50 1.25
C6 AP6 30fr brn vio & blk 4.00 2.00
Set, never hinged 25.00

Fokker F VII over Congo AP7

1934, Jan. 22 *Perf. 13½x14*
C7 AP7 50c gray black .35 .25
C8 AP7 1fr dk carmine .60 .25
a. Booklet pane of 8 8.00
C9 AP7 1.50fr green .60 .25
C10 AP7 3fr brown .35 .25
C11 AP7 4.50fr brt ultra .60 .25
a. Booklet pane of 8 14.00
C12 AP7 5fr red brown 1.00 .35
C13 AP7 15fr brown vio 1.25 .60
C14 AP7 30fr red orange 2.25 1.90
C15 AP7 50fr violet 6.50 3.50
Nos. C7-C15 (9) 13.50 7.60
Set, never hinged 32.50

The 1fr, 3fr, 4.50fr, 5fr, 15fr exist imperf. Values: 3fr, $37.50; 5fr, $60; 15fr, $32.50.

No. C10 Surcharged in Blue with New Value and Bars

1936, Mar. 25
C16 AP7 3.50fr on 3fr brown .60 .25
Never hinged 1.25

Catalogue values for unused stamps in this section, from this point to the end of the section, are for Never Hinged items.

No. C9 Surcharged in Black

1942, Apr. 27
C17 AP7 50c on 1.50fr green 1.25 .40
a. Inverted surcharge 50.00 19.00

POSTAGE DUE STAMPS

In 1908-23 regular postage stamps handstamped "TAXES" or "TAXE," usually boxed, were used in lieu of postage due stamps.

D1

1923 Typo. Unwmk. *Perf. 14*
J1 D1 5c black brown .25 .25
J2 D1 10c rose red .25 .25
J3 D1 15c violet .25 .25
J4 D1 30c green .30 .25
J5 D1 50c ultramarine .40 .35
J6 D1 50c blue ('29) .45 .35
J7 D1 1fr gray .55 .40
Nos. J1-J7 (7) 2.45 2.10
Set, never hinged 6.00

Nos. J1-J7 exist imperf. Value, set $37.50.

Catalogue values for unused stamps in this section, from this point to the end of the section, are for Never Hinged items.

D2

D3

1943 *Perf. 14x14½*
J8 D2 10c olive green .30 .25
J9 D2 20c dark ultramarine .30 .25
J10 D2 50c green .30 .25
J11 D2 1fr dark brown .30 .25
J12 D2 2fr yellow orange .30 .25
Nos. J8-J12 (5) 1.50 1.25

1943 *Perf. 12½*
J8a D2 10c olive green .90 .30
J9a D2 20c dark ultramarine .90 .30
J10a D2 50c green .90 .30
J11a D2 1fr dark brown .95 .50
J12a D2 2fr yellow orange 1.60 .50
Nos. J8a-J12a (5) 5.25 1.90

1957 Engr. *Perf. 11½*
J13 D3 10c olive brown .35 .25
J14 D3 20c claret .55 .25
J15 D3 50c green .55 .25
J16 D3 1fr light blue .55 .30
J17 D3 2fr vermilion .65 .45
J18 D3 4fr .80 .60
J19 D3 6fr violet blue 1.10 .60
Nos. J13-J19 (7) 4.55 2.70

Exist imperf. Value, set $20.

PARCEL POST STAMPS

Handstamped Surcharges in Black or Blue on Nos. 5, 11-12

PP1

PP2

PP3

1887-93 Unwmk. *Perf. 15*
Q1 PP1 3.50fr on 5fr lilac 1,400. 1,000.
Q3 PP2 3.50fr on 5fr vio 1,200. 675.00
Q4 PP3 3.50fr on 5fr vio ('88) 950.00 550.00
Q6 PP3 3.50fr on 5fr gray ('93) 190.00 190.00
Never hinged 250.00

Nos. Q1, Q3-Q4, and Q6 are known with inverted surcharge and double surcharge, and No. Q6 in pair with unsurcharged stamp. These varieties sell for somewhat more than the normal surcharges.

Genuine stamps with counterfeit surcharges, counterfeit stamps with counterfeit surcharges, and both with counterfeit cancels exist.

BELGIUM

'bel-jəm

LOCATION — Western Europe, bordering the North Sea
GOVT. — Constitutional Monarchy
AREA — 11,778 sq. mi.
POP. — 10,396,421 (2004)
CAPITAL — Brussels

100 Centimes = 1 Franc
100 Cents = 1 Euro (2002)

Catalogue values for unused stamps in this country are for Never Hinged items, beginning with Scott 322 in the regular postage section, Scott B370 in the semi-postal section, Scott C8 in the airpost section, Scott CB1 in the airpost semi-postal section, Scott F1 in the registration stamp section, Scott J40 in the postage due section, Scott M1 in the military stamp section, Scott O36 in the officials section, and Scott Q267 in the parcel post section.

Watermarks

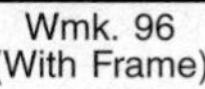
Wmk. 96 (With Frame)

Wmk. 96a (No Frame)

King Leopold I
A1 A2

Wmk. Two "L's" Framed (96)

Engr.			Imperf.
1	A1 10c brown	*2,600.*	100.00
a.	10c red brown	*4,300.*	425.00
b.	10c bister brown	*2,900.*	140.00
c.	10c dark brown	*2,650.*	85.00
2	A1 20c blue	*2,650.*	57.50
a.	20c milky blue	*3,700.*	160.00
b.	20c greenish blue	*3,900.*	290.00

The reprints are on thick and thin wove and thick laid paper unwatermarked.

A pale blue shade exists that is often confused with the milky blue.

A souvenir sheet containing reproductions of the 10c, 20c and 40c of 1849-51 with black burelage on back was issued Oct. 17, 1949, for the cent. of the 1st Belgian stamps. It was sold at BEPITEC 1949, an intl. stamp exhib. at Brussels, and was not valid. Value, $15.

1849-50		Thin Paper	
3	A2 10c brown ('50)	*2,500.*	100.00
4	A2 20c blue ('50)	*2,200.*	62.50
5	A2 40c carmine rose	*2,000.*	525.00

Nos. 3-5 were printed on both thick and thin paper. See *Scott Classic Specialized Catalog of Stamps & Covers* for detailed listings.

Wmk. Two "L's" Without Frame (96a)

1851-54			
6	A2 10c brown	625.00	8.50
a.	Ribbed paper ('54)	1,000.	62.50
7	A2 20c blue	800.00	8.00
a.	Ribbed paper ('54)	1,000.	62.50
8	A2 40c car rose	*4,250.*	110.00
a.	Ribbed paper ('54)	*5,000.*	260.00

Nos. 6-8 were printed on both thin and thick paper. See *Scott Classic Specialized Catalogue of Stamps & Covers* for detailed listings.

Nos. 6a, 7a, 8a must have regular and parallel ribs covering the whole stamp.

1858-61			Unwmk.
9	A2 1c green ('61)	*225.00*	125.00
10	A2 10c brown	475.00	9.00
11	A2 20c blue	500.00	9.00
12	A2 40c vermilion	*3,750.*	150.00

Nos. 9 and 13 were valid for postage on newspapers and printed matter only.

Nos. 10-12 were printed in two sizes: 21mm high (with a 16½mm high oval) and 22mm high (with a 17¼mm high oval). The 22mm high stamps were issued in 1861. See *Scott Classic Specialized Catalogue of Stamps & Covers* for detailed listings.

Reprints of Nos. 9 to 12 are on thin wove paper. The colors are brighter than those of the originals. They were made from the dies and show lines outside the stamps.

Values for Nos. 13-16 are for stamps with perfs cutting into the design. Values for perforated stamps from Nos. 17 through 107 are for examples with perforations touching the design on one or two sides. Stamps with all perforations clear are exceptional and command substantial premiums.

1863-65			Perf. 14½
13	A2 1c green	62.50	26.00
14	A2 10c brown	80.00	3.75
15	A2 20c blue	80.00	3.50
16	A2 40c carmine rose	450.00	25.00
	Nos. 13-16 (4)	672.50	58.25

Nos. 13-16 also come perf 12½ and 12½x13½, which were issued in 1863. Values differ. See the *Scott Classic Specialized Catalogue* for detailed listings.

King Leopold I — A3a
A3

A4

A4a

A5

London Print

1865	Typo.		Perf. 14
17	A5 1fr pale violet	1,750.	110.00

Brussels Print
Thick or Thin Paper

1865-67			Perf. 15, 14½x14
18	A3 10c slate ('67)	185.00	2.25
b.	Pair, imperf. between		—
19	A3a 20c blue ('67)	290.00	2.00
20	A4 30c brown ('67)	625.00	11.00
b.	Pair, imperf. between	*2,000.*	
21	A4a 40c rose ('67)	775.00	20.00
22	A5 1fr violet	2,000.	97.50

Nos. 18-22 are valued as perf. 15. Nos. 18-22 also come perf. 14½x14, issued in 1865-66. Values differ. See the *Scott Classic Specialized Catalogue.* Nos. 18b and 20b are from the earlier printings.

The reprints are on thin paper, imperforate and ungummed.

Coat of Arms — A6

1866-67			Imperf.
23	A6 1c gray	250.00	150.00

			Perf. 15, 14½x14
24a	A6 1c gray	45.00	16.00
25b	A6 2c blue ('67)	140.00	90.00
26b	A6 5c brown	175.00	90.00
	Nos. 23-26b (4)	610.00	346.00

Nos. 23-26b were valid for postage on newspapers and printed matter only.

Values are for perf. 15 stamps. Values for 14½x14 differ. See the *Scott Classic Specialized Catalogue* for detailed listings.

Counterfeits exist.

Reprints of Nos. 24-26 are on thin paper, imperforate and without gum.

Imperf. varieties of 1869-1912 (between Nos. 28-105) are without gum.

A7 A8

A9 A10

A11 A12

A13 A14

King Leopold II — A15

1869-70			Perf. 15
28	A7 1c green	8.25	.40
29	A7 2c ultra ('70)	25.00	1.65
30	A7 5c buff ('70)	62.50	.75
31	A7 8c lilac ('70)	67.50	50.00
32	A8 10c green	27.50	.40
33	A9 20c lt ultra ('70)	125.00	.90
34	A10 30c buff ('70)	80.00	4.00
35	A11 40c brt rose ('70)	135.00	6.50
36	A12 1fr dull lilac ('70)	400.00	17.00
a.	1fr rose lilac	500.00	20.00
	Never hinged	850.00	
	Nos. 28-36 (9)	930.75	81.60

The frames and inscriptions of Nos. 30, 31 and 42 differ slightly from the illustration.

Minor "broken letter" varieties exist on several values.

Nos. 28-30, 32-33, 35-38 also were printed in aniline colors. These are not valued separately.

Nos. 28-36 exist imperforate, without gum. The 1c and 2c are valued from $55 to $85. The 40c and 1fr stamps are scarcer, valued from $500 to $675. Some denominations exist with gum. Pairs command premiums. Large multiples are scarce.

See Nos. 40-43, 49-51, 55.

1875-78			
37	A13 25c olive bister	165.00	1.45
a.	25c ocher	185.00	1.55
38	A14 50c gray	275.00	11.00
	Roller cancel		12.50
a.	50c gray black	325.00	50.00
b.	50c deep black	1,750.	250.00
39	A15 5fr dp red brown	*1,700.*	1,450.
	Roller cancel		700.00
a.	5fr pale brown ('78)	*3,750.*	1,450.
	Roller cancel		700.00

No. 37 exists imperforate, without gum. Value, $250.

Dangerous counterfeits of No. 39 exist.

Printed in Aniline Colors

1881			Perf. 14
40	A7 1c gray green	18.00	.85
41	A7 2c lt ultra	19.00	3.00
42	A7 5c orange buff	55.00	1.25
a.	5c red orange	55.00	1.25
43	A8 10c gray green	27.50	1.10
44	A13 25c olive bister	95.00	3.00
	Nos. 40-44 (5)	214.50	9.20

See note following No. 36.

A16

A17

A18

A19

1883			
45	A16 10c carmine	27.50	2.50
46	A17 20c gray	175.00	10.00
47	A18 25c blue	360.00	35.00
	Roller cancel		15.00
48	A19 50c violet	325.00	35.00
	Roller cancel		15.00
	Nos. 45-48 (4)	887.50	82.50

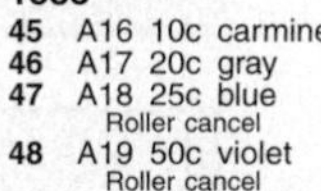

A20

A21

A22

1884-85 *Perf. 14*

No.	Type	Description	Unused	Used
49	A7	1c olive green	16.00	.75
50	A7	1c gray	4.25	.40
51	A7	5c green	37.50	.40
52	A20	10c rose, *bluish*	12.50	.40
a.		Grayish paper	13.50	.50
c.		Yellowish paper	*225.00*	22.50
53	A21	25c blue, *pink* ('85)	15.00	.75
54	A22	1fr brown, *grnsh*	*750.00*	17.50

The frame and inscription of No. 51 differ slightly from the illustration.

See note after No. 36.

Nos. 50-54 exist imperforate, without gum. The 1c and 10c stamps are valued from $32.50 to $55. The 5c, 25c and 1fr stamps are valued from $160 to $375.

A23

A24

A25 A26

1886-91

No.	Type	Description	Unused	Used
55	A7	2c purple brn ('88)	13.50	1.65
56	A23	20c olive, *grnsh*	200.00	1.65
b.		20c deep olive, *grnsh*	210.00	1.90
57	A24	35c vio brn, *brnsh* ('91)	18.00	3.00
58	A25	50c bister, *yelsh*	12.50	2.25
59	A26	2fr violet, *pale lil*	72.50	35.00
		Roller cancel		7.50
		Nos. 55-59 (5)	316.50	43.55

Nos. 56 and 57 exist imperforate, without gum. No. 56 is valued at $275. No. 57 is valued at $55.

Values quoted for Nos. 60-107 are for stamps with label attached. Stamps without label sell for much less.

Coat of Arms
A27

King Leopold
A28

1893-1900

No.	Type	Description	Unused	Used
60	A27	1c gray	1.00	.25
61	A27	2c yellow	1.00	1.10
a.		Wmkd. coat of arms in sheet ('95)	—	—
62	A27	2c violet brn ('94)	1.65	.40
63	A27	2c red brown ('98)	3.00	.90
64	A27	5c yellow grn	9.00	.30
65	A28	10c orange brn	4.00	.30
66	A28	10c brt rose ('00)	3.25	.40
67	A28	20c olive green	15.00	.60
68	A28	25c ultra	10.00	.50
a.		No ball to "5" in upper left corner	32.50	12.50
69	A28	35c violet brn	22.50	1.50
a.		35c red brown	35.00	2.40
70	A28	50c bister	57.50	20.00
71	A28	50c gray ('97)	62.50	2.50
72	A28	1fr car, *lt grn*	80.00	20.00
73	A28	1fr orange ('00)	100.00	5.00
74	A28	2fr lilac, *rose*	80.00	70.00
75	A28	2fr lilac ('00)	160.00	13.50
		Nos. 60-75 (16)	610.40	137.25

Antwerp Exhibition Issue

Arms of Antwerp — A29

1894

No.	Type	Description	Unused	Used
76	A29	5c green, *rose*	4.75	3.25
77	A29	10c carmine, *bluish*	3.75	2.50
78	A29	25c blue, *rose*	1.00	1.00
		Nos. 76-78 (3)	9.50	6.75

Brussels Exhibition Issue

St. Michael and Satan
A30 A31

1896-97 *Perf. 14x14*

No.	Type	Description	Unused	Used
79	A30	5c dp violet	1.00	.60
80	A31	10c orange brown	8.50	3.50
81	A31	10c lilac brown	.50	.35
		Nos. 79-81 (3)	10.00	4.45

A32

A33

A34

A35

A36

A37

A38

A39

Two types of 1c:

I — Periods after "Dimanche" and "Zondag" in label.

II — No period after "Dimanche." Period often missing after "Zondag."

1905-11 *Perf. 14*

No.	Type	Description	Unused	Used
82	A32	1c gray (I) ('07)	1.50	.25
a.		Type II ('08)	2.00	.60
83	A32	2c red brown ('07)	14.50	5.75
84	A32	5c green ('07)	11.50	.60
85	A33	10c dull rose	1.75	.60
86	A34	20c olive grn	26.00	1.00
87	A35	25c ultra	12.00	.85
a.		25c deep blue ('11)	13.50	2.00
88	A36	35c red brn	27.50	2.40
89	A37	50c bluish gray	95.00	4.00
90	A38	1fr yellow orange	110.00	8.00

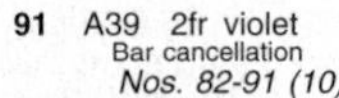

No.	Type	Description	Unused	Used
91	A39	2fr violet	75.00	22.50
		Bar cancellation		5.00
		Nos. 82-91 (10)	374.75	45.95

A40

A41

Lion of Belgium — A42

A43

King
Albert I — A44

1912

No.	Type	Description	Unused	Used
92	A40	1c orange	.25	.25
93	A41	2c orange brn	.25	.45
94	A42	5c green	.25	.25
95	A43	10c red	.75	.40
96	A43	20c olive grn	16.00	4.00
97	A43	35c bister brn	1.00	.70
98	A43	40c green	16.00	14.50
99	A43	50c gray	1.00	.80
100	A43	1fr orange	4.00	3.00
101	A43	2fr violet	17.50	17.50
102	A44	5fr plum	80.00	25.00
		Nos. 92-102 (11)	137.00	66.85

Counterfeits exist of Nos. 97-102. Those of No. 102 are common.

For overprints see Nos. Q49-Q50, Q52, Q55-Q55A, Q57-Q60.

A45

1912-13 **Larger Head**

No.	Type	Description	Unused	Used
103	A45	10c red	.40	.25
a.		Without engraver's name	.25	*.25*
104	A45	20c olive green ('13)	.40	.40
a.		Without engraver's name	2.00	2.00
105	A45	25c ultramarine	.25	*.30*
a.		With engraver's name	4.25	*.30*
107	A45	40c green ('13)	.50	*.60*
		Nos. 103-107 (3)	1.30	1.25

For overprints see Nos. Q51, Q53-Q54, Q56.

Albert I
A46

Cloth Hall of Ypres
A47

Bridge of
Dinant — A48

Library of
Louvain — A49

Scheldt River
at Antwerp
A50

Anti-slavery
Campaign in
the Congo
A51

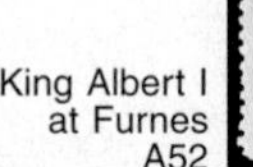

King Albert I
at Furnes
A52

Kings of
Belgium
Leopold I,
Albert I,
Leopold II
A53

1915-20 **Typo.** *Perf. 14*

No.	Type	Description	Unused	Used
108	A46	1c orange	.25	.25
109	A46	2c chocolate	.25	.25
110	A46	3c gray blk ('20)	.30	.25
111	A46	5c green	1.00	.25
112	A46	10c carmine	.90	.25
113	A46	15c purple	1.50	.25
114	A46	20c red violet	3.00	.25
115	A46	25c blue	.50	.40
		Engr.		
116	A47	35c brown org & blk	.50	.30
117	A48	40c green & black	1.00	.30
a.		Vert. pair, imperf. btwn.		
118	A49	50c car rose & blk	4.50	.30
119	A50	1fr violet	32.50	1.00
120	A51	2fr slate	21.00	2.00
121	A52	5fr dp blue	275.00	125.00
		Telegraph or railroad cancel		55.00
122	A53	10fr brown	20.00	20.00
		Nos. 108-122 (15)	362.20	151.05

Two types each of the 1c, 10c and 20c; three of the 2c and 15c; four of the 5c, differing in the top left corner.

See No. 138. For surcharges see Nos. B34-B47.

Perron of Liege
(Fountain) — A54

Size: 18¼x28½mm

1919, July 25 *Perf. 11½*

No.	Type	Description	Unused	Used
123	A54	25c blue	2.40	.35
a.		25c deep blue	3.00	.45

1919, July 19

No.	Type	Description	Unused	Used
123B	A54	25c blue	400.00	400.00
c.		Sheet of 10	6,000.	*6,000.*

No. 123B is the first printing, which was issued in sheets of 10. Nos. 123 and 123a were later printings, issued in sheets of 100.

King Albert in Trench
Helmet — A55

Perf. 11, 11½, 11½x11, 11x11½

1919 **Size: 18½x22mm**

124 A55 1c lilac brn .25 .25
125 A55 2c olive .25 .25

Size: 22x26

126 A55 5c green .25 .25
127 A55 10c carmine, 22x26¾mm .25 .25
a. Size: 22½x26mm 1.00 .60
128 A55 15c gray vio, 22x26¾mm .30 .30
a. Size: 22½x26mm 2.40 .60
129 A55 20c olive blk 1.10 1.10
130 A55 25c deep blue 1.60 1.60
131 A55 35c bister brn 3.00 3.00
132 A55 40c red 5.00 5.00
133 A55 50c red brn 9.50 10.00
134 A55 1fr lt orange 40.00 40.00
135 A55 2fr violet 375.00 375.00

Size: 28x33½mm

136 A55 5fr car lake 100.00 100.00
137 A55 10fr claret 110.00 110.00
Nos. 124-137 (14) 646.50 647.00
Set, never hinged 1,150.

Type of 1915 Inscribed: "FRANK" instead of "FRANKEN"

1919, Dec. *Perf. 14, 15*

138 A52 5fr deep blue 1.75 1.25
Never hinged 3.00

Town Hall at Termonde — A56

1920 *Perf. 11½*

139 A56 65c claret & black, 27x22mm .75 .25
Never hinged 1.50
a. Center inverted *67,500.*
b. Size: 26¼x22½mm 5.75 2.40
Never hinged 13.50

For surcharge see No. 143.

Nos. B48-B50 Surcharged in Red or Black

1921 *Perf. 12*

140 SP6 20c on 5c + 5c (R) .60 .25
a. Inverted surcharge 625.00 625.00
Never hinged 1,100.
141 SP7 20c on 10c + 5c .40 .25
142 SP8 20c on 15c + 15c (R) .60 .25
a. Inverted surcharge 625.00 625.00
Never hinged 1,100.

No. 139 Surcharged in Red

143 A56 55c on 65c claret & blk 1.50 .35
a. Pair, one without surcharge 2.25 .85
Nos. 140-143 (4) 3.10 1.10
Set, never hinged 8.50

A58

1922-27 **Typo.** *Perf. 14*

144 A58 1c orange .25 .25
145 A58 2c olive ('26) .25 .25
146 A58 3c fawn .25 .25
147 A58 5c gray .25 .25
148 A58 10c blue grn .25 .25
149 A58 15c plum ('23) .25 .25
150 A58 20c black brn .25 .25
151 A58 25c magenta .25 .25
a. 25c dull violet ('23) .50 .25
152 A58 30c vermilion .50 .25
153 A58 30c rose ('25) .35 .25
154 A58 35c red brown .35 .30
155 A58 35c blue grn ('27) .80 .35
156 A58 40c rose .50 .25
157 A58 50c bister ('25) .50 .25
158 A58 60c olive brn ('27) 3.00 .25
159 A58 1.25fr dp blue ('26) 1.10 1.10
160 A58 1.50fr brt blue ('26) 1.60 .45
b. 1.50fr intense bright blue ('30) 11.50 3.00
161 A58 1.75fr ultra ('27) 1.40 .25
a. Tete beche pair 5.00 5.00
c. Bklt. pane of 4 + 2 labels 40.00
Nos. 144-161 (18) 12.10 5.70
Set, never hinged 27.50

See Nos. 185-190. For overprints and surcharges see Nos. 191-195, 197, B56, O1-O6.

A59

1921-25 **Engr.**

Perf. 11, 11x11½, 11½, 11½x11, 11½x12, 11½x12½, 12½

162 A59 50c dull blue .30 .25
163 A59 75c scarlet ('22) .25 .25
164 A59 75c ultra ('24) .45 .25
165 A59 1fr black brn ('22) .80 .25
166 A59 1fr dk blue ('25) .60 .25
167 A59 2fr dk green ('22) .90 .25
168 A59 5fr brown vio ('23) 13.50 *15.00*
169 A59 10fr magenta ('22) 9.00 6.50
Nos. 162-169 (8) 25.80 *23.00*
Set, never hinged 52.50

No. 162 measures 18x20¾mm and was printed in sheets of 100.

Philatelic Exhibition Issues

1921, May 26 *Perf. 11½*

170 A59 50c dark blue 3.50 3.50
Never hinged 4.75
a. Sheet of 25 200.00 175.00
Never hinged 225.00

No. 170 measures 17½x21¼mm, was printed in sheets of 25 and sold at the Philatelic Exhibition at Brussels.

The sheet normally has pin holes and a cancellation-like marking in the margin. These are considered unused and the condition valued here.

Souvenir Sheet

1924, May 24 *Perf. 11½*

171 Sheet of 4 140.00 140.00
Never hinged 260.00
a. A59 5fr red brown 10.00 10.00
Never hinged 12.00

Sold only at the Intl. Phil. Exhib., Brussels. Sheet size: 130x145mm.

The sheet normally has pin holes and a cancellation-like marking in the margin. These are considered unused and the condition valued here.

Kings Leopold I and Albert I — A60

1925 *Perf. 14*

172 A60 10c dp green 7.25 7.25
173 A60 15c dull vio 3.75 4.50
174 A60 20c red brown 3.75 4.50
175 A60 25c grnsh black 3.75 4.50
176 A60 30c vermilion 3.75 4.50
177 A60 35c lt blue 3.75 4.50
178 A60 40c brnsh blk 3.75 4.50
179 A60 50c yellow brn 3.75 4.50
180 A60 75c dk blue 3.75 4.50
181 A60 1fr dk violet 6.50 6.50
182 A60 2fr ultra 4.00 4.00
183 A60 5fr blue blk 3.75 4.50
184 A60 10fr dp rose 6.50 8.00
Nos. 172-184 (13) 58.00 66.25
Set, never hinged 126.00

75th anniv. of Belgian postage stamps.

Nos. 172-184 were sold only in sets and only by The Administration of Posts, not at post offices.

A61

1926-27 **Typo.**

185 A61 75c dk violet .75 .70
186 A61 1fr pale yellow .60 .35
187 A61 1fr rose red ('27) 1.00 .25
a. Tete beche pair 7.50 4.50
c. Bklt. pane 4 + 2 labels 25.00
188 A61 2fr Prus blue 2.50 .45
189 A61 5fr emerald ('27) 27.50 1.60
190 A61 10fr dk brown ('27) 60.00 7.75
Nos. 185-190 (6) 92.35 11.10
Set, never hinged 249.00

For overprints and surcharge see Nos. 196, Q174-Q175.

Stamps of 1921-27 Surcharged in Carmine, Red or Blue

1927

191 A58 3c on 2c olive (C) .25 .25
192 A58 10c on 15c plum (R) .25 .25
193 A58 35c on 40c rose (Bl) .45 .25
194 A58 1.75fr on 1.50fr brt bl (C) 2.25 .80
Nos. 191-194 (4) 3.20 1.55
Set, never hinged 3.75

Nos. 153, 185 and 159 Surcharged in Black

1929, Jan. 1

195 A58 5c on 30c rose .25 .25
196 A61 5c on 75c dk violet .25 .25
197 A58 5c on 1.25fr dp blue .25 .25
Nos. 195-197 (3) .75 .75
Set, never hinged .65

The surcharge on Nos. 195-197 is a precancelation which alters the value of the stamp to which it is applied.

Values for precanceled stamps in unused column are for those which have not been through the post and have original gum. Values in second column are for postally used, gumless stamps.

A63

1929-32 **Typo.** *Perf. 14*

198 A63 1c orange .25 .25
199 A63 2c emerald ('31) .45 .45
200 A63 3c red brown .25 .25
201 A63 5c slate .25 .25
c. Bklt. pane of 4 + 2 labels 8.25
202 A63 10c olive grn .25 .25
c. Bklt. pane of 4 + 2 labels 4.50
203 A63 20c brt violet 1.00 .25
204 A63 25c rose red .45 .25
c. Bklt. pane of 4 + 2 labels 8.25
205 A63 35c green .60 .25
c. Bklt. pane of 4 + 2 labels 9.75
206 A63 40c red vio ('30) .30 .25
c. Bklt. pane of 4 + 2 labels 9.75
207 A63 50c dp blue .45 .25
c. Bklt. pane of 4 + 2 labels 8.25
208 A63 60c rose ('30) 2.00 .25
c. Bklt. pane of 4 + 2 labels 30.00
209 A63 70c org brn ('30) 1.10 .25
c. Bklt. pane of 4 + 2 labels 22.50
210 A63 75c dk blue ('30) 2.00 .25
b. 75c blue violet 2.40 .25
211 A63 75c dp brown ('32) 6.00 .25
b. Bklt. pane of 4 + 2 labels 100.00
Nos. 198-211 (14) 15.35 3.70
Set, never hinged 55.00

For overprints and surcharges see Nos. 225-226, 240-241, 254-256, 309, O7-O15.

Tete Beche Pairs

201a	A63	5c	.60	.60
202a	A63	10c	.30	.30
204a	A63	25c	1.75	1.75
205a	A63	35c	2.75	2.75
206a	A63	40c	2.75	2.75
207a	A63	50c	2.25	2.25
208a	A63	60c	8.00	7.50
209a	A63	70c	6.00	5.00
210a	A63	75c	9.00	8.50
211a	A63	75c	27.50	25.00
Nos. 201a-211a (10)			60.90	56.40
Set, never hinged			110.00	

Tete-beche gutter pairs also exist.

A64

1929, Jan. 25 **Engr.** *Perf. 14½, 14*

212 A64 10fr dk brown 15.00 4.00
213 A64 20fr dk green 85.00 20.00
214 A64 50fr red violet 13.50 13.50
a. Perf. 14½ 37.50 40.00
215 A64 100fr brownish lake 13.50 13.50
a. Perf. 14½ 37.50 40.00
Nos. 212-215 (4) 127.00 51.00
Set, never hinged 276.50

Peter Paul Rubens — A65

Zenobe Gramme — A66

1930, Apr. 26 **Photo.** *Perf. 12½x12*

216 A65 35c blue green .40 .25
217 A66 35c blue green .40 .25
Set, never hinged 2.10

No. 216 issued for the Antwerp Exhibition, No. 217 the Liege Exhibition.

Leopold I, by Lievin de Winne — A67

Leopold II, by Joseph Leempoels — A68

Design: 1.75fr, Albert I.

1930, July 1 **Engr.** *Perf. 11½*

218 A67 60c brown violet .25 .25
219 A68 1fr carmine 1.10 1.10
220 A68 1.75fr dk blue 2.75 1.25
Nos. 218-220 (3) 4.10 2.60
Set, never hinged 9.60

Centenary of Belgian independence.

For overprints see Nos. 222-224.

Antwerp Exhibition Issue

Souvenir Sheet

Arms of Antwerp A70

1930, Aug. 9 *Perf. 11½*

221 A70 4fr Sheet of 1 275.00 240.00
Never hinged 600.00
a. Single stamp 100.00 80.00

Size: 142x141mm. Inscription in lower margin "ATELIER DU TIMBRE-1930-ZEGELFABRIEK." Each purchaser of a ticket to the Antwerp Phil. Exhib., Aug. 9-15, was allowed to purchase one stamp. The ticket cost 6 francs.

The sheet normally has pin holes and a cancellation-like marking in the margin. These are considered unused and the condition valued here.

Nos. 218-220 Overprinted in Blue or Red

1930, Oct.
222 A67 60c brown vio (Bl) 2.00 2.00
223 A68 1fr carmine (Bl) 8.25 7.75
224 A68 1.75fr dk blue (R) 14.50 14.50
Nos. 222-224 (3) 24.75 24.25
Set, never hinged 55.00

50th meeting of the administrative council of the Intl. Labor Bureau at Brussels.

The names of the painters and the initials of the engraver have been added at the foot of these stamps.

Stamps of 1929-30 Surcharged in Blue or Black

1931, Feb. 20 ***Perf. 14***
225 A63 2c on 3c red brown (Bl) .25 .25
226 A63 10c on 60c rose (Bk) .50 .25
Set, never hinged 3.75

The surcharge on No. 226 is a precancelation which alters the denomination. See note after No. 197.

King Albert — A71a
A71

1931, June 15 **Photo.**
227 A71 1fr brown carmine .50 .25
Never hinged 1.00

1932, June 1
228 A71a 75c bister brown 1.25 .25
Never hinged 5.00
a. Tete beche pair 6.75 6.75
Never hinged 17.50
c. Bklt. pane 4 + 2 labels 18.00

See No. 257. For overprint see No. O18.

A72

1931-32 **Engr.**
229 A72 1.25fr gray black .75 .50
230 A72 1.50fr brown vio 1.25 .50
231 A72 1.75fr dp blue .80 .25
232 A72 2fr red brown 1.10 .25
233 A72 2.45fr dp violet 1.90 .40
234 A72 2.50fr black brn ('32) 10.00 .50
235 A72 5fr dp green 18.00 1.10
236 A72 10fr claret 45.00 12.50
Nos. 229-236 (8) 78.80 16.00
Set, never hinged 249.00

Nos. 206 and 209 Surcharged as No. 226, but dated "1932"

1932, Jan. 1
240 A63 10c on 40c red vio 2.50 .30
241 A63 10c on 70c org brn 2.00 .25
Set, never hinged 22.50

See note after No. 197.

Gleaner
A73

Mercury
A74

1932, June 1 **Typo.** ***Perf. 13½x14***
245 A73 2c pale green .35 .35
246 A74 5c dp orange .25 .25
247 A73 10c olive grn .25 .25
a. Tete beche pair 4.00 4.00
Never hinged 5.75
c. Bklt. pane 4 + 2 labels 15.00
248 A74 20c brt violet 1.00 .25
249 A73 25c deep red .60 .25
a. Tete beche pair 3.50 3.50
Never hinged 5.00
c. Bklt. pane 4 + 2 labels 15.00
250 A74 35c dp green 2.40 .25
Nos. 245-250 (6) 4.85 1.60
Set, never hinged 14.50

For overprints see Nos. O16-O17.

Auguste Piccard's Balloon — A75

1932, Nov. 26 **Engr.** ***Perf. 11½***
251 A75 75c red brown 3.50 .30
252 A75 1.75fr dk blue 13.50 2.10
253 A75 2.50fr dk violet 17.00 11.50
Nos. 251-253 (3) 34.00 13.90
Set, never hinged 110.00

Issued in commemoration of Prof. Auguste Piccard's two ascents to the stratosphere.

Nos. 206 and 209 Surcharged as No. 226, but dated "1933"

1933, Nov. ***Perf. 14***
254 A63 10c on 40c red vio 14.00 4.00
255 A63 10c on 70c org brn 12.50 1.50
Set, never hinged 80.00

No. 206 Surcharged as No. 226, but dated "1934"

1934, Feb.
256 A63 10c on 40c red vio 12.50 1.50
Never hinged 50.00

For Nos. 254 to 256 see note after No. 197.

Regummed examples of Nos. 254-256 are plentiful.

King Albert Memorial Issue

Type of 1932 with Black Margins

1934, Mar. 10 **Photo.**
257 A71a 75c black .30 .25
Never hinged .60

Congo Pavilion — A76

Designs: 1fr, Brussels pavilion. 1.50fr, "Old Brussels." 1.75fr, Belgian pavilion.

1934, July 1 ***Perf. 14x13½***
258 A76 35c green .75 .30
259 A76 1fr dk carmine 1.25 .40
260 A76 1.50fr brown 5.00 .80
261 A76 1.75fr blue 5.00 .30
Nos. 258-261 (4) 12.00 1.80
Set, never hinged 45.00

Brussels Intl. Exhib. of 1935.

King Leopold III
A80 A81

1934-35 ***Perf. 13½x14***
262 A80 70c olive blk ('35) .35 .25
a. Tete beche pair 1.50 1.00
c. Bklt. pane 4 + 2 labels 6.25
263 A80 75c brown .65 .25

Perf. 14x13½
264 A81 1fr rose car ('35) 3.25 .35
Nos. 262-264 (3) 4.25 .85
Set, never hinged 10.00

For overprint see No. O19.

Coat of Arms — A82

1935-48 **Typo.** ***Perf. 14***
265 A82 2c green ('37) .25 .25
266 A82 5c orange .25 .25
267 A82 10c olive bister .25 .25
a. Tete beche pair .30 .25
Never hinged .50
b. Bklt. pane 4 + 2 labels 4.50
268 A82 15c dk violet .25 .25
269 A82 20c lilac .25 .25
270 A82 25c carmine rose .25 .25
a. Tete beche pair .30 .40
Never hinged .55
c. Bklt. pane 4 + 2 labels 4.50
271 A82 25c yel org ('46) .25 .25
272 A82 30c brown .25 .25
273 A82 35c green .25 .25
a. Tete beche pair .30 .30
Never hinged .50
c. Bklt. pane 4 + 2 labels 3.00
274 A82 40c red vio ('38) .25 .25
275 A82 50c blue .40 .25
276 A82 60c slate ('41) .25 .25
277 A82 65c red lilac ('46) .25 .25
278 A82 70c lt blue grn ('45) .25 .25
279 A82 75c lilac rose ('45) .25 .25
280 A82 80c green ('48) 3.50 .40
281 A82 90c dull vio ('46) .25 .25
282 A82 1fr red brown ('45) .25 .25
Nos. 265-282 (18) 7.90 4.65
Set, never hinged 17.00

Several stamps of type A82 exist in various shades.

Nos. 265, 361 were privately overprinted and surcharged "+10FR." by the Association Belgo-Americaine for the dedication of the Bastogne Memorial, July 16, 1950. The overprint is in six types. Value $1.50 per set.

See design O1. For overprints and surcharges see Nos. 312-313, 361-364, 390-394, O20-O22, O24, O26-O28, O33.

A83

A83a

Perf. 14, 14x13½, 11½
1936-56 **Photo.**

Size: 17½x21¾mm
283 A83 70c brown .30 .25
a. Tete beche pair .80 .80
Never hinged 1.40
c. Bklt. pane 4 + 2 labels 7.50

Size: 20¾x24mm
284 A83a 1fr rose car .30 .25
285 A83a 1.20fr dk brown ('51) .80 .25
a. Perf. 11½ ('56) 1.20 .25
Never hinged 2.75
286 A83a 1.50fr brt red vio ('43) .40 .30
287 A83a 1.75fr dp ultra ('43) .25 .25
288 A83a 1.75fr dk car ('50) .25 .25
289 A83a 2fr dk pur ('43) 1.00 1.00
290 A83a 2.25fr grnsh blk ('43) .25 .25
291 A83a 2.50fr org red ('51) 1.75 .30
a. Perf. 11½ ('56) 20.00 .25
Never hinged 60.00
292 A83a 3.25fr chestnut ('43) .25 .25
293 A83a 5fr dp green ('43) 1.00 .40
Nos. 283-293 (11) 6.55 3.75
Set, never hinged 17.00

Nos. 287-288, 290-291, 293 inscribed "Belgie-Belgique."

See designs A85, A91. For overprints and surcharges see Nos. 314, O23, O25, O29, O31, O34.

A84

1936-51 **Engr.** ***Perf. 14x13½***
294 A84 1.50fr rose lilac ('41) .60 .35
295 A84 1.75fr dull blue .25 .25
296 A84 2fr dull vio .40 .30
297 A84 2.25fr gray vio ('41) .25 .25
298 A84 2.45fr black 32.50 .70
299 A84 2.50fr ol blk ('40) 2.00 .25
300 A84 3.25fr org brn ('41) .30 .25
301 A84 5fr dull green 2.40 .50
302 A84 10fr vio brn .60 .25
a. 10fr light brown 10.00 .25
Never hinged 30.00
303 A84 20fr vermilion 1.00 .30
a. 20fr rose orange ('36) 1.15 .40
Never hinged 4.00

Perf. 11½
304 A84 3fr yel brn ('51) .55 .25
305 A84 4fr bl, *bluish* ('50) 4.75 .25
a. White paper 9.00 .25
Never hinged 14.50
306 A84 6fr brt rose car ('51) 2.75 .25
307 A84 10fr brn vio ('51) .55 .25
308 A84 20fr red ('51) 1.10 .25
Nos. 294-308 (15) 50.00 4.65
Set, never hinged 150.00

See No. 1159. For overprint and surcharges see Nos. 316-317, O32.

No. 206 Surcharged as No. 226, but dated "1937"

1937 **Unwmk.** ***Perf. 14***
309 A63 10c on 40c red vio .25 .25
Never hinged .30

See note after No. 197.

A85

1938-41 **Photo.** ***Perf. 13½x14***
310 A85 75c olive gray .25 .25
a. Tete beche pair .75 .80
Never hinged 1.50
c. Bklt. pane 4 + 2 labels 6.75
311 A85 1fr rose pink ('41) .25 .25
a. Tete beche pair .25 .25
Never hinged .40
b. Booklet pane of 6 2.25
c. Bklt. pane 4 + 2 labels 2.25
Set, never hinged .80

For overprints and surcharges see Nos. 315, O25, O30, O35.

Nos. 272, 274, 283, 310, 299, 298 Srchd. in Blue, Black, Carmine or Red

a

b

c

1938-42
312 A82 (a) 10c on 30c (Bl) .25 .25
313 A82 (a) 10c on 40c (Bl) .25 .25
314 A83 (b) 10c on 70c (Bk) .25 .25
315 A85 (b) 50c on 75c (C) .25 .25
316 A84 (c) 2.25fr on 2.50fr (C) .45 .45

No.	Type	Description	Unused	Used
317	A84 (c)	2.50fr on 2.45fr (R)	11.00	.25
		Nos. 312-317 (6)	12.45	1.70
		Set, never hinged	26.00	

Issue date: No. 317, Oct. 31, 1938.

Basilica and Bell Tower — A86

Water Exhibition Buildings — A87

Designs: 1.50fr, Albert Canal and Park. 1.75fr, Eygenbilsen Cut in Albert Canal.

1938, Oct. 31 ***Perf. 14x13½, 13½x14***

No.	Type	Description	Unused	Used
318	A86	35c dk blue grn	.25	.25
319	A87	1fr rose red	.45	.30
320	A87	1.50fr vio brn	1.10	.60
321	A87	1.75fr ultra	1.25	.25
		Nos. 318-321 (4)	3.05	1.40
		Set, never hinged	11.00	

Intl. Water Exhibition, Liège, 1939.

Catalogue values for unused stamps in this section, from this point to the end of the section, are for Never Hinged items.

Lion Rampant — A90

1944 Unwmk. Photo. ***Perf. 12½***

Inscribed: "Belgique-Belgie"

No.	Type	Description	Unused	Used
322	A90	5c chocolate	.25	.25
323	A90	10c green	.25	.25
324	A90	25c lt blue	.25	.25
325	A90	35c brown	.25	.25
326	A90	50c lt bl grn	.25	.25
327	A90	75c purple	.25	.25
328	A90	1fr vermilion	.25	.25
329	A90	1.25fr chestnut	.25	.25
330	A90	1.50fr orange	1.10	.40
331	A90	1.75fr brt ultra	.25	.25
332	A90	2fr aqua	6.50	2.10
333	A90	2.75fr dp mag	.25	.25
334	A90	3fr claret	.75	.60
335	A90	3.50fr sl blk	.75	.60
336	A90	5fr dk olive	14.00	5.00
337	A90	10fr black	1.25	1.10
		Nos. 322-337 (16)	26.85	12.30

Inscribed: "Belgie-Belgique"

No.	Type	Description	Unused	Used
338	A90	5c chocolate	.25	.25
339	A90	10c green	.25	.25
340	A90	25c lt bl	.25	.25
341	A90	35c brown	.25	.25
342	A90	50c lt bl grn	.25	.25
343	A90	75c purple	.25	.25
344	A90	1fr vermilion	.25	.25
345	A90	1.25fr chestnut	.25	.25
346	A90	1.50fr orange	.30	*.45*
347	A90	1.75fr brt ultra	.25	.25
348	A90	2fr aqua	2.00	2.00
349	A90	2.75fr dp magenta	.25	.25
350	A90	3fr claret	.65	*.75*
351	A90	3.50fr slate blk	.65	*.75*
352	A90	5fr dark olive	5.75	5.00
353	A90	10fr black	1.00	*1.25*
		Nos. 338-353 (16)	12.85	12.70

Leopold III, Crown and V — A91

1944-57 ***Perf. 14x13½***

No.	Type	Description	Unused	Used
354	A91	1fr brt rose red	.60	.25
355	A91	1.50fr magenta	.80	.25
356	A91	1.75fr dp ultra	.80	.85
357	A91	2fr dp vio	2.40	.25
358	A91	2.25fr grnsh blk	.90	1.00
359	A91	3.25fr chnt brn	1.25	.25
360	A91	5fr dk bl grn	4.75	.25
a.		Perf. 11½ ('57)	200.00	.25
		Nos. 354-360 (7)	11.50	3.10

Nos. 355, 357, 359 inscribed "Belgique-Belgie."

For surcharges see Nos. 365-367 and footnote following No. 367.

Stamps of 1935-41 Overprinted in Red

1944 ***Perf. 14***

No.	Type	Description	Unused	Used
361	A82	2c pale green	.25	.25
362	A82	15c indigo	.25	.25
363	A82	20c brt violet	.25	.25
364	A82	60c slate	.25	.25
		Nos. 361-364 (4)	1.00	1.00

See note following No. 282.

Nos. 355, 357, and 360 Srchd. Typographically in Black or Carmine

1946 ***Perf. 14x13½***

No.	Type	Description	Unused	Used
365	A91	On 1.50fr magenta	.70	.25
366	A91	On 2fr dp vio (C)	1.90	.70
367	A91	On 5fr dk bl grn (C)	2.00	.30
		Nos. 365-367 (3)	4.60	1.25

To provide denominations created by a reduction in postal rates, the Government produced Nos. 365-367 by typographed surcharge. Also, each post office was authorized on May 20, 1946, to surcharge its stock of 1.50fr, 2fr and 5fr stamps "-10 percent." Hundreds of types and sizes of this surcharge exist, both hand-stamped and typographed. These include the "1,35," "1,80" and "4,50" applied at Ghislenghien.

M. S. Prince Baudouin — A92

2.25fr, S.S. Marie Henriette. 3.15fr, S.S. Diamant.

Perf. 14x13½, 13½x14

1946, June 15 Photo. Unwmk.

No.	Type	Description	Unused	Used
368	A92	1.35fr brt bluish grn	.25	.25
369	A92	2.25fr slate green	.45	.25
370	A92	3.15fr slate black	.50	.25
		Nos. 368-370 (3)	1.20	.75

Centenary of the steamship line between Ostend and Dover.

No. 368 exists in two sizes: 21¼x18¼mm and 21x17mm. Nos. 369-370 are 24½x20mm.

Capt. Adrien de Gerlache — A95

Belgica and Explorers A96

1947, June ***Perf. 14x13½, 11½***

No.	Type	Description	Unused	Used
371	A95	1.35fr crimson rose	.45	.25
372	A96	2.25fr gray black	3.50	2.00

50th anniv. of Capt. Adrien de Gerlache's Antarctic Expedition.

Joseph A. F. Plateau — A97

1947, June ***Perf. 14x13½***

No.	Type	Description	Unused	Used
373	A97	3.15fr deep blue	1.10	.25

Issued to mark the World Film and Fine Arts Festival, Brussels, June, 1947.

Chemical Industry — A98

Industrial Arts — A99

Agriculture A100

Textile Industry A102

Communications Center — A101

Iron Manufacture A103

Photogravure (#374-376, 378), Typographed (#377, 380), Engraved

1948 Unwmk. ***Perf. 11½***

No.	Type	Description	Unused	Used
374	A98	60c blue grn	1.00	.25
375	A98	1.20fr brown	2.75	.25
376	A99	1.35fr red brown	1.00	.25
377	A100	1.75fr brt red	1.90	.25
378	A99	1.75fr dk gray grn	1.40	.25
379	A101	2.25fr gray blue	2.40	.50
380	A100	2.50fr dk car rose	7.00	.60
381	A101	3fr brt red vio	10.50	.55
382	A102	3.15fr deep blue	2.40	.65
383	A102	4fr brt ultra	9.00	.40
384	A103	6fr blue green	20.00	.60
385	A103	6.30fr brt red vio	2.50	2.00
		Nos. 374-385 (12)	61.85	6.55

See Nos. O42-O46.

Leopold I — A104

1949, July 1 Engr. ***Perf. 14x13½***

No.	Type	Description	Unused	Used
386	A104	90c dk green	1.10	.55
387	A104	1.75fr brown	.90	.25
388	A104	3fr red	9.25	3.25
389	A104	4fr deep blue	7.75	1.40
		Nos. 386-389 (4)	19.00	5.45

Cent. of Belgium's 1st postage stamps. See note on souvenir sheet below No. 2.

Stamps of 1935-45 Precanceled and Surcharged in Black

1949 ***Perf. 14***

No.	Type	Description	Unused	Used
390	A82	5c on 15c dk vio	.25	.25
391	A82	5c on 30c brown	.25	.25
392	A82	5c on 40c red vio	.25	.25
393	A82	20c on 70c lt bl grn	.30	.35
394	A82	20c on 75c lil rose	.25	.25

Similar Surcharge and Precancellation in Black on Nos. B455-B458

Perf. 14x13½

No.	Type	Description	Unused	Used
395	SP251	10c on #B455	3.50	3.00
396	SP251	40c on #B456	1.10	.85
397	SP251	80c on #B457	.65	.50
398	SP251	1.20fr on #B458	2.25	1.50
		Nos. 390-398 (9)	8.80	7.20

See note after No. 197.

St. Mary Magdalene, from Painting by Gerard David — A105

1949, July 15 Photo. ***Perf. 11***

No.	Type	Description	Unused	Used
399	A105	1.75fr dark brown	.70	.35

Gerard David Exhibition at Bruges, 1949.

Allegory of UPU A106

1949, Oct. 1 Engr. ***Perf. 11½***

No.	Type	Description	Unused	Used
400	A106	4fr deep blue	4.50	2.50

75th anniv. of the UPU.

Symbolical of Pension Fund A107

Lion Rampant A108

Perf. 11½

1950, May 1 Unwmk. Photo.

No.	Type	Description	Unused	Used
401	A107	1.75fr dark brown	.50	.25

General Pension Fund founding, cent.

1951, Feb. 15 Engr. ***Perf. 11½***

No.	Type	Description	Unused	Used
402	A108	20c blue	.25	.25

1951-75 Typo. ***Perf. 13½x14***

Size: 17½x21mm

No.	Type	Description	Unused	Used
403	A108	2c org brn ('60)	.25	.25
404	A108	3c brt lil ('60)	.25	.25
405	A108	5c pale violet	.25	.25
406	A108	5c brt pink ('74)	.25	.25
407	A108	10c red orange	.25	.25
408	A108	15c brt pink ('59)	.25	.25
409	A108	20c claret	.25	.25
410	A108	25c green	1.75	.25
411	A108	25c lt bl grn ('66)	.25	.25
412	A108	30c gray grn ('57)	.25	.25
413	A108	40c brown olive	.25	.25
414	A108	50c ultra	.25	.25
a.		50c light blue	.25	.25
415	A108	60c lilac rose	.25	.25
416	A108	65c violet brn	12.50	.55
417	A108	75c bluish lilac	.25	.25
418	A108	80c emerald	.75	.25

419 A108 90c deep blue .75 .25
420 A108 1fr rose .25 .25
421 A108 2fr emerald ('73) .25 .25
422 A108 2.50fr brown ('70) .25 .25
423 A108 3fr brt pink ('70) .25 .25
424 A108 4fr brt rose lil ('74) .25 .25
425 A108 4.50fr blue ('74) .30 .25
426 A108 5fr brt lilac ('75) .30 .25

Size: 17x20½mm

427 A108 1.50fr dk sl grn ('69) .25 .25

Perf. 13½x13

428 A108 2fr emerald ('68) .25 .25

Photo. ***Perf. 11½***

Size: 20½x24mm

429 A108 50c light blue ('61) .45 .25
430 A108 60c lilac rose ('66) 1.10 .70
431 A108 1fr carmine rose ('59) .25 .25

Perf. 13½x12½

Size: 17½x22mm

432 A108 50c lt blue ('75) .25 .25
a. Booklet pane of 4 (#432, 784 and 2 #785) + labels 1.00
b. Booklet pane of 4 (#432 and 3 #787) + labels 1.50
433 A108 1fr rose ('69) 2.00 .90
434 A108 2fr emerald ('72) .50 .30
e. Booklet pane of 6 (4 #434 + 2 #475) 5.50
f. Booklet pane of 5 (#434, 4 #476 + label) 8.00
Nos. 403-434 (32) 25.90 9.45

Counterfeits exist of No. 416. Nos. 429, 431 also issued in coils with black control number on back of every fifth stamp. Nos. 432-434 issued in booklet panes only. No. 432 has one straightedge, and stamps in the pane are tete-beche. Each pane has 2 labels showing Belgian postal emblem and a large selvage with postal code instructions.

Nos. 433-434 have 1 or 2 straight-edges. Panes have a large selvage with inscription or map of Belgium showing postal zones.

See designs A386, O5. For surcharges see Nos. 477-478, 563-567.

Francois de Tassis (Franz von Taxis) — A109

Portraits: 1.75fr, Jean-Baptiste of Thurn & Taxis. 2fr, Baron Leonard I. 2.50fr, Count Lamoral I. 3fr, Count Leonard II. 4fr, Count Lamoral II. 5fr, Prince Eugene Alexander. 5.75fr, Prince Anselme Francois. 8fr, Prince Alexander Ferdinand. 10fr, Prince Charles Anselme. 20fr, Prince Charles Alexander.

1952, May 14 **Engr.** ***Perf. 11½***

Laid Paper

435 A109 80c olive grn .85 .35
436 A109 1.75fr red org .85 .35
437 A109 2fr violet brn 1.75 .45
438 A109 2.50fr carmine 2.50 1.75
439 A109 3fr olive bis 2.25 1.10
440 A109 4fr ultra 3.25 .90
441 A109 5fr red brn 4.50 1.90
442 A109 5.75fr blue vio 7.50 2.40
443 A109 8fr gray 14.00 3.00
444 A109 10fr rose vio 18.00 4.50
445 A109 20fr brown 80.00 24.50
Nos. 435-445,B514 (12) 275.45 141.20

13th UPU Cong., Brussels, 1952.

King Baudouin
A110 A111

1952-58 **Engr.** ***Perf. 11½***

Size: 21x24mm

446 A110 1.50fr gray green 1.25 .25
447 A110 2fr crimson .45 .25
448 A110 4fr ultra 6.75 .25

Size: 24½x35mm

449 A110 50fr gray brn 24.00 .25
a. 50fr violet brown 100.00 .60
450 A110 100fr rose red ('58) 16.00 .25

1953-72 **Photo.** ***Perf. 11½***

451 A111 1.50fr gray .25 .25
452 A111 2fr rose carmine 7.25 .25
453 A111 2fr green .25 .25
454 A111 2.50fr red brn ('57) .60 .25
a. 2.50fr orange brown ('70) .25 .25
455 A111 3fr rose lil ('58) .40 .25
456 A111 3.50fr brt yel grn ('58) .75 .25
457 A111 4fr brt ultra .50 .25
458 A111 4.50fr dk red brn ('62) 3.00 .25
459 A111 5fr violet ('57) 1.25 .25
460 A111 6fr dp pink ('58) .75 .25
461 A111 6.50fr gray ('60) 95.00 15.00
462 A111 7fr blue ('60) .90 .25
463 A111 7.50fr grysh brn ('58) 87.50 16.00
464 A111 8fr bluish gray ('58) 1.25 .25
465 A111 8.50fr claret ('58) 20.00 .45
466 A111 9fr gray ('58) 95.00 1.90
467 A111 12fr lt bl grn ('66) 13.50 .45
468 A111 30fr red org ('58) 11.50 .25

Redrawn

469 A111 2.50fr org brn ('71) .35 .25
470 A111 4.50fr brown ('72) 2.25 .60
471 A111 7fr blue ('71) .60 .25

Perf. 13½x12½

Size: 17½x22mm

472 A111 1.50fr gray ('70) .60 .30
b. Bklt. pane of 10 6.50
c. Bklt. pane, 3 #472, 3 #475 15.00
473 A111 2.50fr org brn ('70) 6.00 5.00
h. Bklt. pane, 1 #473, 5 #475 16.00
474 A111 3fr lilac rose ('69) .60 .25
a. Bklt. pane of 5 + label 25.00
b. Bklt. pane, 2 #433, 6 #474 18.00
475 A111 3.50fr brt yel grn ('70) .60 .25
476 A111 4.50fr dull red brn ('72) .60 .35
Nos. 446-476 (31) 399.70 45.55

Nos. 451, 453, 454a, 455, 456, 458 also issued in coils with black control number on back of every fifth stamp. These coils, except for No. 451, are on luminescent paper.

On Nos. 469-471, the 2, 4 and 7 are 3mm high. The background around the head is white. On Nos. 454, 458, 462 the 2, 4 and 7 are 2½mm high and the background is tinted.

Nos. 472-476 issued in booklets only and have 1 or 2 straight-edges. All panes have a large selvage with inscription or map.

See designs M1, O3.

Luminescent Paper

Stamps issued on both ordinary and luminescent paper include: Nos. 307-308, 430-431, 449-451, 453-460, 462, 464, 467-468, 472, 643-644, 650-651, 837, Q385, Q410.

Stamps issued only on luminescent paper include: Nos. 433, 454a, 472b, 473-474, 649, 652-658, 664-670, 679-682, 688-690, 694-696, 698-703, 705-711, 713-726, 729-747, 751-754, 756-757, 759, 761-762, 764, 766, 769, 772, 774, 778, 789, 791-793, 795, 797-799, 801-807, 809-811, 814-818, 820-834, 836, 838-848.

See note after No. 857.

Nos. 416 and 419 Surcharged and Precanceled in Black

1954, Jan. 1 **Unwmk.** ***Perf. 13½x14***

477 A108 20c on 65c vio brn 1.75 .30
478 A108 20c on 90c dp blue 1.75 .25

See note after No. 197.

Map and Rotary Emblem
A112

80c, Mermaid and Mercury holding emblem. 4fr, Rotary emblem and two globes.

1954, Sept. 10 **Engr.** ***Perf. 11½***

479 A112 20c red .25 .25
480 A112 80c dark green .65 .30
481 A112 4fr ultra 1.40 .50
Nos. 479-481 (3) 2.30 1.05

5th regional conf. of Rotary Intl. at Ostend. No. 481 for Rotary 50th Anniv. (in 1955).

A souv. sheet containing one each, imperf., was sold for 500 francs. It was not valid for postage. Value, $200.

The Rabot and Begonia — A113

Designs: 2.50fr, The Oudeburg and azalea. 4fr, "Three Towers" and orchid.

1955, Feb. 15 **Photo.**

482 A113 80c brt carmine 1.00 .40
483 A113 2.50fr black brn 8.50 3.00
484 A113 4fr dk rose brn 5.50 1.00
Nos. 482-484 (3) 15.00 4.40

Ghent Intl. Flower Exhibition, 1955.

Homage to Charles V as a Child, by Albrecht de Vriendt
A114

Charles V, by Titian — A115

4fr, Abdication of Charles V, by Louis Gallait.

1955, Mar. 25 **Unwmk.** ***Perf. 11½***

485 A114 20c rose red .25 .25
486 A115 2fr dk gray green 1.90 .25
487 A114 4fr blue 5.00 1.25
Nos. 485-487 (3) 7.15 1.75

Charles V Exhibition, Ghent, 1955.

Emile Verhaeren, by Montald Constant — A116

1955, May 11 **Engr.**

488 A116 20c dark gray .25 .25

Birth cent. of Verhaeren, poet.

Allegory of Textile Manufacture
A117

1955, May 11

489 A117 2fr violet brown 1.00 .25

2nd Intl. Textile Exhibition, Brussels, June 1955.

"The Foolish Virgin" by Rik Wouters — A118

1955, June 10

490 A118 1.20fr olive green 1.10 1.10
491 A118 2fr violet 1.60 .25

3rd biennial exhibition of sculpture, Antwerp, June 11-Sept. 10, 1955.

"Departure of Volunteers from Liege, 1830" by Charles Soubre — A119

1955, Sept. 10 **Photo.**

492 A119 20c grnsh slate .25 .25
493 A119 2fr chocolate .90 .25

Exhibition "The Romantic Movement in Liege Province," Sept. 10-Oct. 31, 1955; and 125th anniv. of Belgium's independence from the Netherlands.

Pelican Giving Blood to Young — A120

1956, Jan. 14 **Engr.**

494 A120 2fr brt carmine .35 .25

Blood donor service of the Belgian Red Cross.

Buildings of Tournai, Ghent and Antwerp — A121

1956, July 14 **Photo.**

495 A121 2fr brt ultra .30 .25

The Scheldt exhibition (Scaldis) at Tournai, Ghent and Antwerp, July-Sept. 1956.

Europa Issue

"Rebuilding Europe" — A122

1956, Sept. 15 **Engr.**

496 A122 2fr lt green *1.25* .25
497 A122 4fr purple *7.75* *.45*

Issued to symbolize the cooperation among the six countries comprising the Coal and Steel Community.

Train on Map of Belgium and Luxembourg A123

1956, Sept. 29
498 A123 2fr dark blue .45 .25

Issued to mark the electrification of the Brussels-Luxembourg railroad.

Edouard Anseele — A124

1956, Oct. 27
499 A124 20c violet brown .25 .25

Cent. of the birth of Edouard Anseele, statesman, and in connection with an exhibition held in his honor at Ghent.

"The Atom" and Exposition Emblem — A125

1957-58 **Unwmk.**

500	A125	2fr	carmine rose	.25	.25
501	A125	2.50fr	green ('58)	.40	.25
502	A125	4fr	brt violet blue	.55	.25
503	A125	5fr	claret ('58)	1.25	.55
	Nos. 500-503 (4)			2.45	1.30

1958 World's Fair at Brussels.

Emperor Maximilian I Receiving Letter — A126

1957, May 19
504 A126 2fr claret .40 .25

Day of the Stamp, May 19, 1957.

Sikorsky S-58 Helicopter A127

1957, June 15
505 A127 4fr gray grn & brt bl .80 .45

100,000th passenger carried by Sabena helicopter service, June 15, 1957.

Zeebrugge Harbor A128

1957, July 6
506 A128 2fr dark blue .40 .25

50th anniv. of the completion of the port of Zeebrugge-Bruges.

Leopold I Entering Brussels, 1831 — A129

Leopold I Arriving at Belgian Border A130

1957, July 17 **Photo.**
507 A129 20c dk gray grn .25 .25
508 A130 2fr lilac .55 .25

126th anniv. of the arrival in Belgium of King Leopold I.

Boy Scout and Girl Scout Emblems A131

Design: 4fr, Robert Lord Baden-Powell, painted by David Jaggers, vert.

Perf. 11½
1957, July 29 **Unwmk.** **Engr.**
509 A131 80c gray .25 .25
510 A131 4fr light green 1.10 .45

Cent. of the birth of Lord Baden-Powell, founder of the Boy Scout movement.

"Kneeling Woman" by Lehmbruck — A132

1957, Aug. 20 **Photo.**
511 A132 2.50fr dk blue grn 1.10 .85

4th Biennial Exposition of Sculpture, Antwerp, May 25-Sept. 15.

"United Europe" — A133

1957, Sept. 16 **Engr.** ***Perf. 11½***
512 A133 2fr dk violet brn *.50* .25
513 A133 4fr dark blue *1.50* .35

Europa: United Europe for peace and prosperity.

Queen Elisabeth Assisting at Operation, by Allard L'Olivier A134

Perf. 11½
1957, Nov. 23 **Unwmk.** **Engr.**
514 A134 30c rose lilac .25 .25

50th anniv. of the founding of the Edith Cavell-Marie Depage and St. Camille schools of nursing.

Post Horn and Historic Postal Insignia A135

1958, Mar. 16 **Photo.** ***Perf. 11½***
515 A135 2.50fr gray .25 .25

Postal Museum Day.

United Nations Issue

International Labor Organization A136

Allegory of UN — A137

Designs: 1fr, FAO. 2fr, World Bank. 2.50fr, UNESCO. 3fr, UN Pavilion. 5fr, ITU. 8fr, Intl. Monetary Fund. 11fr, WHO. 20fr, UPU.

Perf. 11½
1958, Apr. 17 **Unwmk.** **Engr.**

516	A136	50c	gray	.90	*1.40*
517	A136	1fr	claret	.30	*.45*
518	A137	1.50fr	dp ultra	.30	*.45*
519	A137	2fr	gray brown	.85	*1.25*
520	A136	2.50fr	olive grn	.30	*.45*
521	A136	3fr	grnsh blue	.85	*1.25*
522	A137	5fr	rose lilac	.55	*.90*
523	A136	8fr	red brown	1.00	*1.60*
524	A136	11fr	dull lilac	1.25	*2.00*
525	A136	20fr	car rose	1.60	*2.50*
	Nos. 516-525,C15-C20 (16)			10.40	*14.70*

World's Fair, Brussels, Apr. 17-Oct. 19.
Postally valid only from the UN pavilion at the Brussels Fair. Proceeds went toward financing the UN exhibits.

Eugène Ysaye A138

1958, Sept. 1
526 A138 30c dk blue & plum .25 .25

Ysaye (1858-1931), violinist, composer.

Common Design Types pictured in section at front of book.

Europa Issue, 1958
Common Design Type
1958, Sept. 13 **Photo.**
Size: 24½x35mm
527 CD1 2.50fr brt red & blue *1.00* .25
528 CD1 5fr brt blue & red *3.25* .35

Issued to show the European Postal Union at the service of European integration.

Universal Declaration of Human Rights, 10th Anniv. — A140

Infant and UN Emblem.

1958, Dec. 10 **Engr.**
529 A140 2.50fr blue gray .30 .25

Charles V, Jean-Baptiste of Thurn and Taxis — A141

1959, Mar. 15 **Unwmk.**
530 A141 2.50fr green .40 .25

Issued for the Day of the Stamp. Design from painting by J.-E. van den Bussche.

NATO Emblem — A142

1959, Apr. 3 **Photo.** ***Perf. 11½***
531 A142 2.50fr dp red & dk bl .45 .25
532 A142 5fr emerald & dk bl 1.25 *.80*

10th anniv. of NATO. See No. 720.

City Hall, Audenarde — A143

1959, Aug. 17 **Engr.**
533 A143 2.50fr deep claret .30 .25

Pope Adrian VI, by Jan van Scorel — A144

1959, Aug. 31 ***Perf. 11½***
534 A144 2.50fr dark red .25 .25
535 A144 5fr Prus blue .55 .55

500th anniv. of the birth of Pope Adrian VI.

Europa Issue, 1959
Common Design Type
1959, Sept. 19 **Photo.**
Size: 24x35½mm
536 CD2 2.50fr dark red *.30* .25
537 CD2 5fr brt grnsh blue *1.25* .35

Boeing 707 A146

Engraved and Photogravure
1959, Dec. 1 ***Perf. 11½***
538 A146 6fr dk bl gray & car 1.90 .80

Inauguration of jet flights by Sabena Airlines.

Countess of Taxis — A147

1960, Mar. 21 Engr. *Perf. 11½*

539 A147 3fr dark blue		.85	.25

Alexandrine de Rye, Countess of Taxis, Grand Mistress of the Netherlands Posts, 1628-1645, and day of the stamp, Mar. 21, 1960. The painting of the Countess is by Nicholas van der Eggermans.

24th Ghent Intl. Flower Exhibition — A148

1960, Mar. 28 Unwmk.

540 A148	40c Indian azalea	.25	.25
541 A148	3fr Begonia	.90	.25
542 A148	6fr Anthurium, bromelia	1.00	.90
	Nos. 540-542 (3)	2.15	1.40

Steel Workers, by Constantin Meunier — A149

Design: 3fr, The sower, field and dock workers, from "Monument to Labor," Brussels, by Constantin Meunier, horiz.

Engraved and Photogravure

1960, Apr. 30 *Perf. 11½*

543 A149	40c claret & brt red	.25	.25
544 A149	3fr brown & brt red	.85	.25

Socialist Party of Belgium, 75th anniv.

Congo River Boat Pilot — A150

Designs: 40c, Medical team. 1fr, Planting tree. 2fr, Sculptors. 2.50fr, Shot put. 3fr, Congolese officials. 6fr, Congolese and Belgian girls playing with doll. 8fr, Boy pointing on globe to independent Congo.

1960, June 30 Photo. *Perf. 11½*

Size: 35x24mm

545 A150	10c	bright red	.30	.25
546 A150	40c	rose claret	.45	.25
547 A150	1fr	brt lilac	.85	.75
548 A150	2fr	gray green	.95	.85
549 A150	2.50fr	blue	1.00	.75
550 A150	3fr	dk bl gray	1.00	.45

Size: 51x35mm

551 A150	6fr	violet bl	3.00	1.90
552 A150	8fr	dk brown	8.00	4.00
		Nos. 545-552 (8)	15.55	9.20

Independence of Congo.

Europa Issue, 1960

Common Design Type

1960, Sept. 17

Size: 35x24½mm

553 CD3	3fr claret	*.40*	.25
554 CD3	6fr gray	*.85*	*.30*
	Nos. 553-554 (2)	1.25	.55

Children Examining Stamp and Globe — A152

1960, Oct. 1 Photo. *Perf. 11½*

555 A152	40c bis & blk + label	.25	.25

Promoting stamp collecting among children.

H. J. W. Frère-Orban A153

Engraved and Photogravure

1960, Oct. 17 Unwmk.

Portrait in Brown

556 A153	10c	orange yel	.25	.25
557 A153	40c	blue grn	.25	.25
558 A153	1.50fr	brt violet	.70	.70
559 A153	3fr	red	1.10	.25
		Nos. 556-559 (4)	2.30	1.45

Centenary of Communal Credit Society.

King Baudouin and Queen Fabiola A154

1960, Dec. 13 Photo. *Perf. 11½*

Portraits in Dark Brown

560 A154	40c green	.35	.25
561 A154	3fr red lilac	.90	.25
562 A154	6fr dull blue	2.25	.65
	Nos. 560-562 (3)	3.50	1.15

Wedding of King Baudouin and Dona Fabiola de Mora y Aragon, Dec. 15, 1960.

Nos. 412, 414 Surcharged

1961-68 Typo. *Perf. 13½x14*

563 A108	15c on 30c gray grn	.25	.25
564 A108	15c on 50c blue ('68)	.25	.25
565 A108	20c on 30c gray grn	.25	.25
	Nos. 563-565 (3)	.75	.75

No. 412 Surcharged and Precanceled

1961

566 A108	15c on 30c gray grn	.90	.25
567 A108	20c on 30c gray grn	1.90	1.40

See note after No. 197.

Nicolaus Rockox, by Anthony Van Dyck — A155

Engraved and Photogravure

1961, Mar. 18 *Perf. 11½*

568 A155	3fr bister, blk & brn	.35	.25

400th anniv. of the birth of Nicolaus Rockox, mayor of Antwerp.

Seal of Jan Bode, Alderman of Antwerp, 1264 — A156

1961, Apr. 16 Photo.

569 A156	3fr buff & brown	.35	.25

Issued for Stamp Day, April 16.

Senate Building, Brussels, Laurel and Sword A157

Engraved and Photogravure

1961, Sept. 14 Unwmk. *Perf. 11½*

570 A157	3fr brn & Prus grn	.55	.25
571 A157	6fr dk brn & dk car	1.10	.45

50th Conference of the Interparliamentary Union, Brussels, Sept. 14-22.

Europa Issue, 1961

Common Design Type

1961, Sept. 16 Photo.

572 CD4	3fr yel grn & dk grn	.25	.25
573 CD4	6fr org brn & blk	*.50*	.25

Atomic Reactor Plant, BR2, Mol — A159

Designs: 3fr, Atomic Reactor BR3, vert. 6fr, Atomic Reactor plant BR3.

1961, Nov. 8 Unwmk. *Perf. 11½*

574 A159	40c dk blue grn	.25	.25
575 A159	3fr red lilac	.25	.25
576 A159	6fr bright blue	.50	.35
	Nos. 574-576 (3)	1.00	.85

Atomic nuclear research center at Mol.

Horta Museum — A160

1962, Feb. 15 Engr.

577 A160	3fr red brown	.30	.25

Baron Victor Horta (1861-1947), architect.

Postrider, 16th Century A161

Engraved and Photogravure

1962, Mar. 25 *Perf. 11½*

Chalky Paper

578 A161	3fr brn & slate grn	.30	.25

Stamp Day. See No. 677.

Gerard Mercator (Gerhard Kremer, 1512-1594), Cartographer A162

Engraved and Photogravure

1962, Apr. 14 Unwmk.

579 A162	3fr sepia & gray	.30	.25

Bro. Alexis-Marie Gochet (1835-1910), Geographer, Educator — A163

Portrait: 3fr, Canon Pierre-Joseph Triest (1760-1836), educator and founder of hospitals and orphanages.

1962, May 19 Engr. *Perf. 11½*

580 A163	2fr dark blue	.30	.25
581 A163	3fr golden brown	.30	.25

Europa Issue, 1962

Common Design Type

1962, Sept. 15 Photo.

582 CD5	3fr dp car, citron & blk	.25	.25
583 CD5	6fr olive, citron & blk	*.40*	*.40*

Hand with Barbed Wire and Freed Hand — A165

1962, Sept. 16 Engr. & Photo.

584 A165	40c lt blue & blk	.25	.25

Issued in memory of concentration camp victims.

Adam, by Michelangelo, Broken Chain and UN Emblem — A166

1962, Nov. 24 *Perf. 11½*

585 A166	3fr gray & blk	.25	.25
586 A166	6fr lt redsh brn & dk brn	.45	.30

UN Declaration of Human Rights.

Henri Pirenne (1862-1935), Historian — A167

1963, Jan. 15 Engr.

587 A167	3fr ultramarine	.35	.25

Swordsmen and Ghent Belfry A168

3fr, Modern fencers. 6fr, Arms of the Royal and Knightly Guild of St. Michael, vert.

Engraved and Photogravure

1963, Mar. 23 Unwmk. *Perf. 11½*

588 A168 1fr brn red & pale bl .25 .25
589 A168 3fr dk vio & yel grn .25 .25
590 A168 6fr gray, blk, red, bl & gold .65 .35
Nos. 588-590 (3) 1.15 .85

350th anniv. of the granting of a charter to the Ghent guild of fencers.

Stagecoach A169

1963, Apr. 7

591 A169 3fr gray & ocher .25 .25

Stamp Day. See No. 678.

Hotel des Postes, Paris, Stagecoach and Stamp, 1863 A170

Perf. 11½

1963, May 7 Unwmk. Engr.

592 A170 6fr dk brn, gray & yel grn .55 .35

Cent. of the 1st Intl. Postal Conf., Paris, 1863.

"Peace," Child in Rye Field — A171

1963, May 8 Engr. & Photo.

593 A171 3fr grn, blk, yel & brn .30 .25
594 A171 6fr buff, blk, brn & org .75 .30

May 8th Movement for Peace. (On May 8, 1945, World War II ended in Europe).

Allegory and Shields of 17 Member Nations A172

1963, June 13 Unwmk. *Perf. 11½*

595 A172 6fr blue & black .55 .30

10th anniversary of the Conference of European Transport Ministers.

Seal of Union of Belgian Towns — A173

1963, June 17

596 A173 6fr grn, red, blk & gold .55 .35

Intl. Union of Municipalities, 50th anniv.

Caravelle over Brussels National Airport A174

Photogravure and Engraved

1963, Sept. 1 Unwmk. *Perf. 11½*

597 A174 3fr green & gray .30 .25

40th anniversary of SABENA airline.

Europa Issue, 1963

Common Design Type

1963, Sept. 14 Photo.

Size: 35x24mm

598 CD6 3fr blk, dl red & lt brn *.70* .25
599 CD6 6fr blk, lt bl & lt brn *.90* *.30*
Nos. 598-599 (2) 1.60 .55

Jules Destrée A176

Design: No. 601, Henry Van de Velde.

Perf. 11½

1963, Nov. 16 Unwmk. Engr.

600 A176 1fr rose lilac .25 .25
601 A176 1fr green .25 .25

Jules Destrée (1863-1936), statesman and founder of the Royal Academy of French Language and Literature, and of Henry Van de Velde (1863-1957), architect.

No. 600 incorrectly inscribed "1864."

Development of the Mail, Bas-relief — A177

1963, Nov. 23 Engr. & Photo.

602 A177 50c dl red, slate & blk .25 .25

Postal checking service, 50th anniv.

Dr. Armauer G. Hansen A178

Fight Against Leprosy: 2fr, Leprosarium. 5fr, Father Joseph Damien.

1964, Jan. 25 Unwmk. *Perf. 11½*

603 A178 1fr brown org & blk .25 .25
604 A178 2fr brown org & blk .25 .25
605 A178 5fr brown org & blk .45 .35
a. Souvenir sheet of 3, #603-605 2.75 2.75
Nos. 603-605 (3) .95 .85

No. 605a sold for 12fr.

Andreas Vesalius (1514-64), Anatomist — A179

Jules Boulvin (1855-1920), Mechanical Engineer A180

Design: 2fr, Henri Jaspar (1870-1939), statesman and lawyer.

Engraved and Photogravure

1964, Mar. 2 Unwmk. *Perf. 11½*

606 A179 50c pale grn & blk .25 .25
607 A180 1fr pale grn & blk .25 .25
608 A180 2fr pale grn & blk .25 .25
Nos. 606-608 (3) .75 .75

Postilion of Liege, 1830-40 — A181

1964, Apr. 5 Engr. *Perf. 11½*

609 A181 3fr black .25 .25

Issued for Stamp Day 1964.

Arms of Ostend A182

1964, May 16 Photo.

610 A182 3fr ultra, ver, gold & blk .25 .25

Millennium of Ostend.

Flame, Hammer and Globe — A183

1fr, "SI" and globe. 2fr, Flame over wavy lines.

1964, July 18 Unwmk. *Perf. 11½*

611 A183 50c dark blue & red .25 .25
612 A183 1fr dark blue & red .25 .25
613 A183 2fr dark blue & red .25 .25
Nos. 611-613 (3) .75 .75

Centenary of the First Socialist International, founded in London, Sept. 28, 1864.

Europa Issue, 1964

Common Design Type

1964, Sept. 12 Photo. *Perf. 11½*

Size: 24x35½mm

614 CD7 3fr yel grn, dk car & gray *.50* .25
615 CD7 6fr car rose, yel grn & bl *.90* *.35*

Benelux Issue

King Baudouin, Queen Juliana and Grand Duchess Charlotte — A185

1964, Oct. 12

616 A185 3fr olive, lt grn & mar .40 .25

20th anniv. of the customs union of Belgium, Netherlands and Luxembourg.

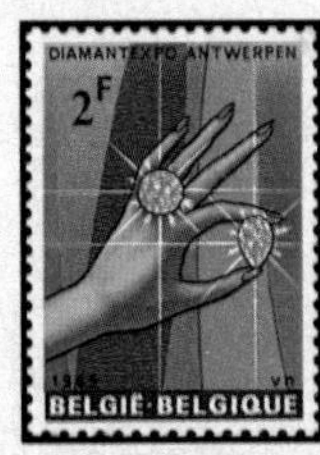

Hand, Round & Pear-shaped Diamonds — A186

1965, Jan. 23 Unwmk. *Perf. 11½*

617 A186 2fr ultra, dp car & blk .25 .25

Diamond Exhibition "Diamantexpo," Antwerp, July 10-28, 1965.

Symbols of Textile Industry — A187

1965, Jan. 25 Photo.

618 A187 1fr blue, red & blk .25 .25

Eighth textile industry exhibition "Textirama," Ghent, Jan. 29-Feb. 2, 1965.

Vriesia — A188

Designs: 2fr, Echinocactus. 3fr, Stapelia.

1965, Feb. 13 Engr. & Photo.

619 A188 1fr multicolored .25 .25
620 A188 2fr multicolored .25 .25
621 A188 3fr multicolored .25 .25
a. Souvenir sheet of 3, #619-621 2.00 2.00
Nos. 619-621 (3) .75 .75

25th Ghent International Flower Exhibition, Apr. 24-May 3, 1965.

No. 621a was issued Apr. 26 and sold for 20fr.

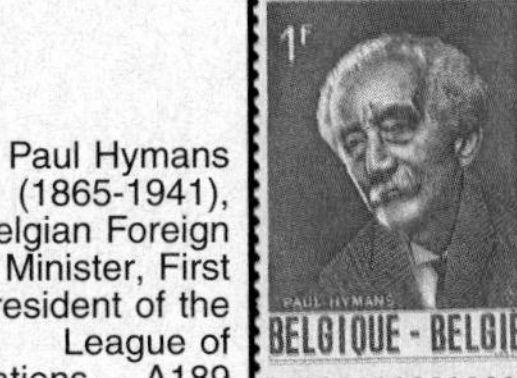

Paul Hymans (1865-1941), Belgian Foreign Minister, First President of the League of Nations — A189

1965, Feb. 24 Engr. *Perf. 11½*

622 A189 1fr dull purple .25 .25

Peter Paul Rubens — A190

2fr, Frans Snyders. 3fr, Adam van Noort. 6fr, Anthony Van Dyck. 8fr, Jacob Jordaens.

1965, Mar. 15 Photo. & Engr.
Portraits in Sepia

623 A190 1fr carmine rose .25 .25
624 A190 2fr blue green .25 .25
625 A190 3fr plum .25 .25
626 A190 6fr deep carmine .50 .25
627 A190 8fr dark blue .80 .40
Nos. 623-627 (5) 2.05 1.40

Issued to commemorate the founding of the General Savings and Pensions Bank.

Sir Rowland Hill as Philatelist — A191

1965, Mar. 27 Engr. *Perf. 11½*
628 A191 50c blue green .25 .25

Issued to publicize youth philately. The design is from a mural by J. E. Van den Bussche in the General Post Office, Brussels.

Postmaster, c. 1833 — A192

1965, Apr. 26 Unwmk. *Perf. 11½*
629 A192 3fr emerald .25 .25

Issued for Stamp Day.

Telephone, Globe and Teletype Paper — A193

1965, May 8 Photo.
630 A193 2fr dull purple & blk .25 .25

Cent. of the ITU.

Staircase, Affligem Abbey — A194

1965, May 27 Engr.
631 A194 1fr gray blue .25 .25

St. Jean Berchmans and his Birthplace A195

1965, May 27 Engr. & Photo.
632 A195 2fr dk brn & red brn .25 .25

Issued to honor St. Jean Berchmans (1599-1621), Jesuit "Saint of the Daily Life."

TOC H Lamp and Arms of Poperinge — A196

1965, June 19 Photo. *Perf. 11½*
633 A196 3fr ol bis, blk & car .25 .25

50th anniv. of the founding of Talbot House in Poperinge, which served British soldiers in World War I, and where the TOC H Movement began (Christian Social Service; TOC H is army code for Poperinge Center).

Belgian Farmers' Association (Boerenbond), 75th Anniv. — A197

50c, Farmer with tractor. 3fr, Farmer with horse-drawn roller.

Engraved and Photogravure
1965, July 17 Unwmk. *Perf. 11½*
634 A197 50c bl, ol, bis brn & blk .25 .25
635 A197 3fr bl, ol grn, ol & blk .25 .25

Europa Issue, 1965
Common Design Type

1965, Sept. 25 *Perf. 11½*
Size: 35½x24mm

636 CD8 1fr dl rose & blk .25 .25
637 CD8 3fr grnsh gray & blk .25 .25

Leopold I (1790-1865) A199

1965, Nov. 13 Engr.
638 A199 3fr sepia .25 .25
639 A199 6fr bright violet .55 .40

The designs of the vignettes are similar to A4 and A5.

Joseph Lebeau(1794-1865), Foreign Minister — A200

1965, Nov. 13 Photo.
640 A200 1fr multicolored .25 .25

Tourist Issue

Grapes and Houses, Hoeilaart A201

Bridge and Castle, Huy A202

No. 643, British War Memorial, Ypres. No. 644, Castle Spontin. No. 645, City Hall, Louvain. No. 646, Ourthe Valley. No. 647, Romanesque Cathedral, gothic fountain, Nivalles. No. 648, Water mill, Kasterlee. No. 649, City Hall, Cloth Guild and Statue of Margarethe of Austria, Malines. No. 650, Town Hall, Lier. No. 651, Castle Bouillon. No. 652, Fountain and Kursaal Spa. No. 653, Windmill, Bokrijk. No. 654, Mountain road, Vielsalm. No. 655, View of Furnes. No. 656, City Hall and Belfry, Mons. No. 657, St. Martin's Church, Aalst. No. 658, Abbey and fountain, St. Hubert.

1965-71 Engr. *Perf. 11½*
641 A201 50c vio bl, lt bl & yel grn .25 .25
642 A202 50c sl grn, lt bl & red brn .25 .25
643 A202 1fr grn, lt bl, sal & brn .25 .25
644 A202 1fr ind, lt bl & ol .25 .25
645 A201 1fr brt rose lil, lt bl & blk .25 .25
646 A202 1fr blk, grnsh bl & ol .25 .25
647 A201 1.50fr sl, sky bl & bis .25 .25
648 A202 1.50fr blk, bl & ol .25 .25
649 A202 1.50fr dk bl & buff .25 .25
650 A201 2fr brn, lt bl & ind .25 .25
651 A202 2fr dk brn, grn & ocher .25 .25
652 A202 2fr bl, brt grn & blk .25 .25
653 A202 2fr blk, lt bl & yel .25 .25
654 A202 2fr blk, lt bl & yel grn .25 .25
655 A202 2fr car, lt bl & dk brn .25 .25
656 A201 2.50fr vio, buff & blk .25 .25
657 A201 2.50fr vio, lt bl, blk & ol .25 .25
658 A201 2.50fr vio bl & yel .25 .25
Nos. 641-658 (18) 4.50 4.50

Issued: Nos. 641-642, 11/13/65; Nos. 643-644, 7/15/67; Nos. 645-646, 12/16/68; Nos. 647-648, 7/6/70; Nos. 649, 656, 12/11/71; Nos. 650-651, 11/11/66; Nos. 652-653, 6/24/68; Nos. 654-655, 9/6/69; Nos. 657-658, 9/11/71.

Queen Elisabeth Type of Semi-Postal Issue, 1956

1965, Dec. 23 Photo. *Perf. 11½*
659 SP305 3fr dark gray .25 .25

Queen Elisabeth (1876-1965).

A dark frame has been added in design of No. 659; 1956 date has been changed to 1965; inscription in bottom panel is Koningin Elisabeth Reine Elisabeth 3F.

"Peace on Earth" A203

Arms of Pope Paul VI — A204

1fr, "Looking toward a Better Future" (family, new buildings, sun & landscape).

1966, Feb. 12 Photo. *Perf. 11½*
660 A203 50c multicolored .25 .25
661 A203 1fr ocher, blk & bl .25 .25
662 A204 3fr gray, gold, car & blk .25 .25
Nos. 660-662 (3) .75 .75

75th anniv. of the encyclical by Pope Leo XIII "Rerum Novarum," which proclaimed the general principles for the organization of modern industrial society.

Rural Mailman, 19th Century — A205

1966, Apr. 17 Photo. Unwmk.
663 A205 3fr blk, dl yel & pale lil .25 .25

Stamp Day. For overprint see No. 673.

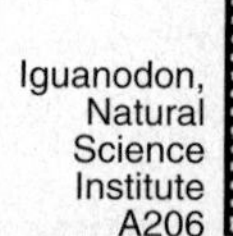

Iguanodon, Natural Science Institute A206

Arend-Roland Comet, Observatory A207

Designs: No. 665, Ancestral head and spiral pattern, Kasai; Central Africa Museum. No. 666, Snowflakes, Meteorological Institute. No. 667, Seal of Charles V, Royal Archives. No. 668, Medieval scholar, Royal Library. 8fr, Satellite and rocket, Space Aeronautics Institute.

1966, May 28 Engr. & Photo.
664 A206 1fr green & blk .25 .25
665 A206 2fr gray, blk & brn org .25 .25
666 A206 2fr blue, blk & yel .25 .25
667 A207 3fr dp rose, blk & gold .25 .25
668 A207 3fr multicolored .25 .25
669 A207 6fr ultra, yel & blk .40 .25
670 A207 8fr multicolored .55 .40
Nos. 664-670 (7) 2.20 1.90

National scientific heritage.

Atom Symbol and Retort — A208

Engraved and Photogravure

1966, July 9 Unwmk. *Perf. 11½*

671 A208 6fr gray, blk & red .50 .25

Issued to publicize the European chemical plant, EUROCHEMIC, at Mol.

August Kekulé, Benzene Ring — A209

1966, July 9

672 A209 3fr brt blue & blk .25 .25

August Friedrich Kekule (1829-96), chemistry professor at University of Ghent (1858-67).

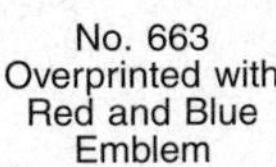

No. 663 Overprinted with Red and Blue Emblem

1966, July 11 Photo.

673 A205 3fr multicolored .25 .25

19th Intl. P.T.T. Cong., Brussels, July 11-15.

Rik Wouters (1882-1916), Self-portrait A210

1966, Sept. 6 Photo. *Perf. 11½*

674 A210 60c multicolored .25 .25

Europa Issue, 1966

Common Design Type

1966, Sept. 24 Engr. *Perf. 11½*

Size: 24x34mm

675 CD9 3fr brt green .25 .25
676 CD9 6fr brt rose lilac *.55 .25*

Types of 1962-1963 Overprinted in Black and Red

1966, Nov. 11 Engr. & Photo.

677 A161 60c sepia & grnsh gray .25 .25
678 A169 3fr sepia & pale bister .25 .25

75th anniv., Royal Fed. of Phil. Circles of Belgium. Overprint shows emblem of F.I.P.

Lions Emblem — A214

1967, Jan. 14 *Perf. 11½*

679 A214 3fr gray, blk & bl .25 .25
680 A214 6fr lt green, blk & vio .40 .25

Lions Club Intl., 50th anniv.

Pistol by Leonhard Cleuter A215

1967, Feb. 11 Photo.

681 A215 2fr dp car, blk & cream .25 .25

Fire Arms Museum in Liege.

International Tourist Year Emblem A216

1967, Feb. 11

682 A216 6fr ver, ultra & blk .50 .25

International Tourist Year, 1967.

Birches and Trientalis A217

Design: No. 684, Dunes, beach grass, privet and blue thistles.

1967, Mar. 11 Photo. *Perf. 11½*

683 A217 1fr multicolored .25 .25
684 A217 1fr multicolored .25 .25

Issued to publicize the nature preserves at Hautes Fagnes and Westhoek.

Paul Emile Janson(1872-1944), Lawyer, Statesman — A218

1967, Apr. 15 Engr. *Perf. 11½*

685 A218 10fr blue .80 .25

Postilion A219

1967, Apr. 16 Photo. & Engr.

686 A219 3fr rose red & claret .25 .25

Issued for Stamp Day, 1967.

Inscribed: "FITCE"

1967, June 24 *Perf. 11½*

687 A219 10fr ultra, sep & emer .80 .45

Issued to commemorate the meeting of the Federation of Common Market Telecommunications Engineers, Brussels, July 3-8.

Europa Issue, 1967

Common Design Type

1967, May 2 Photo.

Size: 24x35mm

688 CD10 3fr blk, lt bl & red *.25* .25
689 CD10 6fr blk, grnsh gray & yel *.80 .30*

Flax, Shuttle and Mills — A221

1967, June 3 Photo. *Perf. 11½*

690 A221 6fr tan & multi .50 .25

Belgian linen industry.

Old Kursaal, Ostend — A222

1967, June 3 Engr. & Photo.

691 A222 2fr dk brn, lt bl & yel .25 .25

700th anniversary of Ostend as a city.

Charles Plisnier and Lodewijk de Raet Foundations A223

Designs: No. 692, Caesar Crossing Rubicon, 15th Century Tapestry. No. 693, Emperor Maximilian Killing a Boar, 16th cent. tapestry.

1967, Sept. 2 Photo. *Perf. 11½*

692 A223 1fr multicolored .25 .25
693 A223 1fr multicolored .25 .25

Universities of Ghent and Liège, 150th Anniv. — A224

Arms of Universities: No. 694, Ghent. No. 695, Liege.

Engraved and Photogravure

1967, Sept. 30 *Perf. 11½*

694 A224 3fr gray & multi .25 .25
695 A224 3fr gray & multi .25 .25

Princess Margaret of York — A225

1967, Sept. 30 Photo.

696 A225 6fr multicolored .50 .30

British Week, Sept. 28-Oct. 2.

"Virga Jesse," Hasselt — A226

1967, Nov. 11 Engr. *Perf. 11½*

697 A226 1fr slate blue .25 .25

Christmas, 1967.

Hand Guarding Worker — A227

1968, Feb. 3 Photo. *Perf. 11½*

698 A227 3fr multicolored .25 .25

Issued to publicize industrial safety.

Military Mailman, 1916, by James Thiriar — A228

Engraved and Photogravure

1968, Mar. 17 *Perf. 11½*

699 A228 3fr sepia, lt bl & brn .25 .25

Issued for Stamp Day, 1968.

View of Grammont and Seal of Baudouin VI — A229

Historic Sites: 3fr, Theux-Franchimont fortress, sword and seal. 6fr, Neolithic cave and artifacts, Spiennes. 10fr, Roman oil lamp and St. Medard's Church, Wervik.

1968, Apr. 13 Photo. *Perf. 11½*

700 A229 2fr bl, blk, lil & rose .25 .25
701 A229 3fr orange, blk & car .25 .25
702 A229 6fr ultra, ind & bis .50 .25
703 A229 10fr tan, blk, yel & gray .80 .30
Nos. 700-703 (4) 1.80 1.05

Stamp of 1866, No. 23 — A230

1968, Apr. 13 Engr. *Perf. 13*

704 A230 1fr black .25 .25

Centenary of the Malines Stamp Printery.

Europa Issue, 1968
Common Design Type

1968, Apr. 27 Photo. *Perf. 11½*
Size: 35x24mm

705	CD11	3fr dl grn, gold & blk	*.30*	*.25*
706	CD11	6fr carmine, sil & blk	*.95*	*.25*

St. Laurent Abbey, Liège — A232

Designs: 3fr, Gothic Church, Lissweghe. No. 709. Barges in Zandvliet locks. No. 710, Ship in Neuzen lock, Ghent Canal. 10fr, Ronquieres canal ship lift.

Engraved and Photogravure

1968, Sept. 7 ***Perf. 11½***

707	A232	2fr ultra, gray ol & sep	.25	.25
708	A232	3fr ol bis, gray & sep	.25	.25
709	A232	6fr ind, brt bl & sep	.55	.25
710	A232	6fr black, grnsh bl & ol	.55	.25
711	A232	10fr bister, brt bl & sep	.80	.30
		Nos. 707-711 (5)	2.40	1.30

No. 710 issued Dec. 14 for opening of lock at Neuzen, Netherlands.

Christmas Candle — A233

1968, Dec. 7 ***Perf. 11½***

712	A233	1fr multicolored	.25	.25

Christmas, 1968.

St. Albertus Magnus — A234

1969, Feb. 15 Engr. *Perf. 11½*

713	A234	2fr sepia	.25	.25

The Church of St. Paul in Antwerp (16th century) was destroyed by fire in Apr. 1968.

Ruins of Aulne Abbey, Gozee — A235

1969, Feb. 15 Engr. & Photo.

714	A235	3fr brt pink & blk	.25	.25

Aulne Abbey was destroyed in 1794 during the French Revolution.

The Travelers, Roman Sculpture — A236

1969, Mar. 15 Engr. *Perf. 11½*

715	A236	2fr violet brown	.25	.25

2,000th anniversary of city of Arlon.

Broodjes Chapel, Antwerp — A237

1969, Mar. 15 Engr. & Photo.

716	A237	3fr gray & blk	.25	.25

150th anniv. of public education in Antwerp.

Post Office Train — A238

1969, Apr. 13 Photo. *Perf. 11½*

717	A238	3fr multicolored	.25	.25

Issued for Stamp Day.

Europa Issue, 1969
Common Design Type

1969, Apr. 26 Size: 35x24mm

718	CD12	3fr lt grn, brn & blk	*.25*	.25
719	CD12	6fr sal, rose car & blk	*.50*	*.25*

NATO Type of 1959 Redrawn and Dated "1949-1969"

1969, May 31 Photo. *Perf. 11½*

720	A142	6fr org brn & ultra	.50	.30

20th anniv. of NATO. No. 720 inscribed Belgique-Belgie and OTAN-NAVO.

Construction Workers, by F. Leger — A240

1969, May 31

721	A240	3fr multicolored	.25	.25

50th anniversary of the ILO.

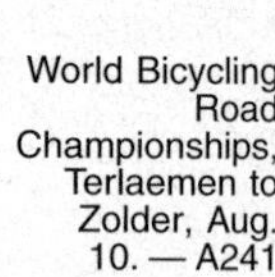

World Bicycling Road Championships, Terlaemen to Zolder, Aug. 10. — A241

1969, July 5 Photo. *Perf. 11½*

722	A241	6fr Bicyclist	.50	.30

Ribbon in Benelux Colors — A242

1969, Sept. 6 Photo. *Perf. 11½*

723	A242	3fr blk, red, ultra & yel	.25	.25

Signing of the customs union of Belgium, Netherlands & Luxembourg, 25th anniv.

Annevoie Garden and Pascali Rose A243

No. 725, Lochristi Garden and begonia.

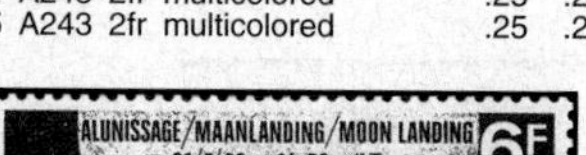

1969, Sept. 6

724	A243	2fr multicolored	.25	.25
725	A243	2fr multicolored	.25	.25

Armstrong, Collins, Aldrin and Map Showing Tranquillity Base — A245

1969, Sept. 20 Photo.

726	A245	6fr black	.50	.25

See note after Algeria No. 427. See No. B846.

Wounded Veteran — A246

1969, Oct. 11 Engr. *Perf. 11½*

727	A246	1fr blue gray	.25	.25

Natl. war veterans' aid organization (O.N.I.G.). The design is similar to type SP10.

Mailman — A247

1969, Oct. 18 Photo.

728	A247	1fr deep rose & multi	.25	.25

Issued to publicize youth philately. Design by Danielle Saintenoy, 14.

Kennedy Tunnel Under the Schelde, Antwerp A248

6fr, Three highways crossing near Loncin.

1969, Nov. 8 Engr. *Perf. 11½*

729	A248	3fr multicolored	.25	.25
730	A248	6fr multicolored	.40	.35

Issued to publicize the John F. Kennedy Tunnel under the Schelde and the Walloon auto route and interchange near Loncin.

Henry Carton de Wiart, by Gaston Geleyn — A249

1969, Nov. 8

731	A249	6fr sepia	.50	.35

Count de Wiart (1869-1951), statesman.

The Census at Bethlehem (detail), by Peter Brueghel A250

1969, Dec. 13 Photo.

732	A250	1.50fr multicolored	.25	.25

Christmas, 1969.

Symbols of Bank's Activity, 100fr Coin A251

1969, Dec. 13 Engr. & Photo.

733	A251	3.50fr lt ultra, blk & sil	.25	.25

50th anniv. of the Industrial Credit Bank (Societe nationale de credit a l'industrie).

Camellia — A252

1970, Jan. 31 Photo. *Perf. 11½*

734	A252	1.50fr shown	.25	.25
735	A252	2.50fr Water lily	.25	.25
736	A252	3.50fr Azalea	.30	.25
a.		Souvenir sheet of 3, #734-736	2.00	2.00
		Nos. 734-736 (3)	.80	.75

Ghent Int'l Flower Exhibition. No. 736a was issued Apr. 25 and sold for 25fr.

Beeches in Botanical Garden — A253

1970, Mar. 7 Engr. & Photo.

737	A253	3.50fr shown	.30	.25
738	A253	7fr Birches	.55	.45

European Nature Conservation Year.

Youth Stamp Day — A254

1970, Apr. 4 Photo.

739	A254	1.50fr Mailman	.25	.25

New UPU Headquarters and Monument, Bern — A255

1970, Apr. 12 **Engr. & Photo.**
740 A255 3.50fr grn & lt grn .30 .25

Opening of the new UPU Headquarters, Bern.

Europa Issue, 1970
Common Design Type

1970, May 1 **Photo.** ***Perf. 11½***
Size: 35x24mm

741 CD13 3.50fr rose cl, yel & blk *.30* .25
742 CD13 7fr ultra, pink & blk *.80* *.30*

Cooperative Alliance Emblem — A257

1970, June 27 **Photo.** ***Perf. 11½***
743 A257 7fr black & org .55 .25

Intl. Cooperative Alliance, 75th anniv.

Ship in Ghent Terneuzen Lock, Zelzate A258

Design: No. 745, Clock Tower, Virton, vert.

1970, June 27 **Engr. & Photo.**
744 A258 2.50fr indigo & lt bl .25 .25
745 A258 2.50fr dk pur & ocher .25 .25

King Baudouin — A259

1970-80 **Engr.** ***Perf. 11½***

746 A259 1.75fr green ('71) .25 .25
747 A259 2.25fr gray grn ('72) .35 .25
748 A259 2.50fr gray grn ('74) .25 .25
749 A259 3fr emerald ('73) .25 .25
750 A259 3.25fr violet brn ('75) .25 .25
751 A259 3.50fr orange brn .25 .25
752 A259 3.50fr brown ('71) .35 .25
753 A259 4fr blue ('72) .35 .25
754 A259 4.50fr brown ('72) .30 .25
755 A259 4.50fr grnsh bl ('74) .30 .25
756 A259 5fr lilac ('72) .70 .25
757 A259 6fr rose car ('72) .40 .25
758 A259 6.50fr vio blk ('74) .45 .25
759 A259 7fr ver ('71) .50 .25
760 A259 7.50fr brt pink ('75) .50 .25
761 A259 8fr black ('72) .55 .25
762 A259 9fr ol bis ('71) .70 .25
763 A259 9fr red brn ('80) .70 .25
764 A259 10fr rose car ('71) .70 .25
765 A259 11fr gray ('76) .80 .25
766 A259 12fr Prus bl ('72) 2.25 .25
767 A259 13fr slate ('75) .90 .25
768 A259 14fr gray grn ('76) 1.00 .25
769 A259 15fr lt vio ('71) 1.00 .25
770 A259 16fr green ('77) 1.60 .25
771 A259 17fr dull mag ('75) 1.10 .25
772 A259 18fr steel bl ('71) 1.25 .25
773 A259 18fr grnsh bl ('80) 1.60 .25
774 A259 20fr vio bl ('71) 1.25 .25
775 A259 22fr black ('74) 1.60 1.40
776 A259 22fr lt grn ('79) 1.50 .25
777 A259 25fr lilac ('75) 1.60 .25
778 A259 30fr ocher ('72) 2.00 .25
779 A259 35fr emer ('80) 3.00 .25
780 A259 40fr dk blue ('77) 3.50 .30
781 A259 45fr brown ('80) 4.25 .40

Perf. 12½x13½
Photo.
Size: 22x17mm

782 A259 3fr emerald ('73) 1.00 .75
a. Booklet pane of 4 (#782 and 3 #783) + labels 10.00
783 A259 4fr blue ('73) .60 .50
784 A259 4.50fr grnsh bl ('75) .40 .30
785 A259 5fr lilac ('73) .35 .25
a. Booklet pane of 4 + labels 2.75
786 A259 6fr carmine ('78) .40 .25
787 A259 6.50fr dull pur ('75) .45 .25
788 A259 8fr gray ('78) .55 .25
Nos. 746-788 (43) 42.05 12.90

No. 751 issued Sept. 7, 1970, King Baudouin's 40th birthday, and is inscribed "1930-1970." Dates are omitted on other stamps of type A259.

Nos. 754, 756 also issued in coils in 1973 and Nos. 757, 761 in 1978, with black control number on back of every fifth stamp.

Nos. 782-788 issued in booklets only. Nos. 782, 784 have one straight-edge, Nos. 786, 788 have two. The rest have one or two. Stamps in the panes are tete-beche. Each pane has two labels showing Belgian Postal emblem with a large selvage with postal code instructions. Nos. 786, 788 not luminescent.

See designs M2, O4. See Nos. 432a, 432b, 977a, 977b.

UN Headquarters, NY — A260

1970, Sept. 12 **Engr. & Photo.**
789 A260 7fr dk brn & Prus bl .55 .25

25th anniversary of the United Nations.

25th International Fair at Ghent, Sept. 12-27 — A261

1970, Sept. 19
790 A261 1.50fr Fair emblem .25 .25

Queen Fabiola — A262

1970, Sept. 19
791 A262 3.50fr lt blue & blk .30 .25

Issued to publicize the Queen Fabiola Foundation for Mental Health.

The Mason, by Georges Minne — A263

1970, Oct. 17 ***Perf. 11½***
792 A263 3.50fr dull yel & sep .30 .25

50th anniv. of the National Housing Society.

Man, Woman and City — A264

1970, Oct. 17 **Photo.**
793 A264 2.50fr black & multi .25 .25

Social Security System, 25th anniv.

Madonna with the Grapes, by Jean Gossaert — A265

1970, Nov. 14 **Engr.** ***Perf. 11½***
794 A265 1.50fr dark brown .25 .25

Christmas 1970.

Arms of Eupen, Malmédy and Saint-Vith A266

Engraved and Photogravure

1970, Dec. 12 ***Perf. 11½***
795 A266 7fr sepia & dk brn .55 .25

The 50th anniversary of the return of the districts of Eupen, Malmédy and Saint-Vith.

Automatic Telephone — A267

1971, Jan. 16 **Photo.** ***Perf. 11½***
796 A267 1.50fr multicolored .25 .25

Automatization of Belgian telephone system.

50th Automobile Show, Brussels, Jan. 19-31 A268

1971, Jan. 16
797 A268 2.50fr "Auto" .25 .25

Belgian Touring Club, 75th Anniv. — A269

1971, Feb. 13
798 A269 3.50fr Club emblem .30 .25

Tournai Cathedral A270

1971, Feb. 13 **Engr.**
799 A270 7fr bright blue .55 .25

Cathedral of Tournal, 8th centenary.

"The Letter Box," by T. Lobrichon — A271

1971, Mar. 13 **Engr.** ***Perf. 11½***
800 A271 1.50fr dark brown .25 .25

Youth philately.

Albert I, Jules Destrée and Academy — A272

Engraved and Photogravure

1971, Apr. 17 ***Perf. 11½***
801 A272 7fr gray & blk .55 .35

Founding of the Royal Academy of Language and French Literature, 50th anniv.

Stamp Day — A273

1971, Apr. 25
802 A273 3.50fr Mailman .30 .25

Europa Issue, 1971
Common Design Type

1971, May 1 **Photo.**
Size: 35x24mm

803 CD14 3.50fr olive & blk *.55* .25
804 CD14 7fr dk ol grn & blk *.75* *.30*

Radar Ground Station A275

1971, May 15 **Photo.** ***Perf. 11½***
805 A275 7fr multicolored .55 .35

3rd World Telecommunications Day.

Antarctic Explorer, Ship and Penguins — A276

1971, June 19 Photo. *Perf. 11½*

806 A276 10fr multicolored .80 .45

Tenth anniversary of the Antarctic Treaty pledging peaceful uses of and scientific cooperation in Antarctica.

Abbey of Notre Dame, Orval, 900th Anniv. — A277

1971, June 26 Engr. *Perf. 11½*

807 A277 2.50fr Orval Abbey .25 .25

Georges Hubin (1863-1947), Socialist Leader, Minister of State — A278

1971, June 26 Engr. & Photo.

808 A278 1.50fr vio bl & blk .25 .25

Mr. and Mrs. Goliath, the Giants of Ath — A279

View of Ghent A280

1971, Aug. 7 Photo.

809 A279 2.50fr multicolored .25 .25

Engr.

810 A280 2.50fr gray brown .25 .25

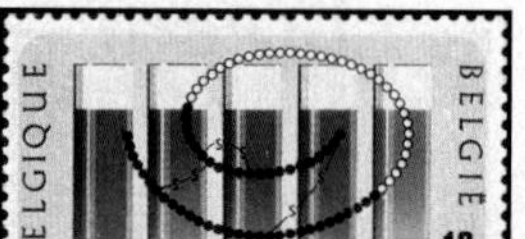

Test Tubes and Insulin Molecular Diagram — A281

1971, Aug. 7 Photo.

811 A281 10fr lt gray & multi .80 .45

50th anniversary of the discovery of insulin.

Family and "50" — A283

1971, Sept. 11 Photo.

812 A283 1.50fr green & multi .25 .25

Belgian Large Families League, 50th anniv.

Achaemenidaen Tomb, Buzpar, and Persian Coat of Arms — A284

Engraved and Photogravure

1971, Oct. 2 *Perf. 11½*

813 A284 7fr multicolored .55 .35

2500th anniversary of the founding of the Persian empire by Cyrus the Great.

Dr. Jules Bordet (1870-1945), Serologist, Immunologist A285

Portrait: No. 815, Stijn Streuvels(1871-1945), Novelist (pen name Frank Lateur).

1971, Oct. 2 Engr.

814 A285 3.50fr slate green .25 .25

815 A285 3.50fr dark brown .25 .25

Flight into Egypt, Anonymous A286

1971, Nov. 13 Photo.

816 A286 1.50fr multicolored .25 .25

Christmas 1971.

Federation of Belgian Industries (FIB), 25th Anniv. — A287

1971, Nov. 13

817 A287 3.50fr black, ultra & gold .30 .25

International Book Year 1972 — A288

1972, Feb. 19

818 A288 7fr bister, blk & bl .55 .30

Coins of Belgium and Luxembourg A289

1972, Feb. 19 Engr. & Photo.

819 A289 1.50fr orange, blk & sil .25 .25

Economic Union of Belgium and Luxembourg, 50th anniversary.

Traffic Signal and Road Signs — A290

1972, Feb. 19 Photo.

820 A290 3.50fr blue & multi .30 .25

Via Secura (road safety), 25th anniversary.

Belgica '72 Emblem A291

1972, Mar. 27

821 A291 3.50fr choc, bl & lil .30 .25

International Philatelic Exhibition, Brussels, June 24-July 9.

"Your Heart is your Health" — A292

1972, Mar. 27

822 A292 7fr blk, gray, red & bl .55 .30

World Health Day.

Auguste Vermeylen (1872-1945), Flemish Writer, Educator — A293

Portrait, by Isidore Opsomer.

1972, Mar. 27

823 A293 2.50fr multicolored .25 .25

Stamp Day 1972 — A294

1972, Apr. 23

824 A294 3.50fr Astronaut on Moon .30 .25

Europa Issue 1972

Common Design Type

1972, Apr. 29 Size: 24x35mm

825 CD15 3.50fr lt blue & multi *.35* .25

826 CD15 7fr rose & multi *.60* *.30*

"Freedom of the Press" — A296

1972, May 13 Photo. *Perf. 11½*

827 A296 2.50fr multicolored .25 .25

50th anniv. of the BELGA news information agency and 25th Congress of the Intl. Federation of Newspaper Editors (F.I.E.J.), Brussels, May 15-19.

Freight Cars with Automatic Coupling A297

1972, June 3

828 A297 7fr blue & multi .55 .30

Intl. Railroad Union, 50th anniv.

View of Couvin — A298

No. 830, Aldeneik Church, Maaseik, vert.

1972, June 24 Engr. *Perf. 13½x14*

829 A298 2.50fr bl, vio brn & sl grn .25 .25

830 A298 2.50fr dk brown & bl .25 .25

Beatrice, by Gustave de Smet — A299

1972, Sept. 9 Photo. *Perf. 11½*

831 A299 3fr multicolored .30 .25

Youth philately.

Radar Station, Intelsat 4 — A300

1972, Sept. 16
832 A300 3.50fr lt bl, sil & blk .30 .25

Opening of the Lessive satellite earth station.

Frans Masereel(1889-1972), Wood Engraver — A301

1972, Oct. 21
833 A301 4.50fr Self-portrait .35 .25

Adoration of the Kings, by Felix Timmermans A302

1972, Nov. 11 Photo. *Perf. 11½*
834 A302 3.50fr black & multi .30 .25

Christmas 1972.

Maria Theresa, Anonymous A303

1972, Dec. 16 Photo. *Perf. 11½*
835 A303 2fr multicolored .25 .25

200th anniversary of the Belgian Academy of Science, Literature and Art, founded by Empress Maria Theresa.

WMO Emblem, Meteorological Institute, Ukkel — A304

1973, Mar. 24 Photo. *Perf. 11½*
836 A304 9fr blue & multi .65 .35

Cent. of intl. meteorological cooperation.

Natl. Industrial Fire Prevention Campaign — A305

1973, Mar. 24
837 A305 2fr "Fire" .25 .25

Man and WHO Emblem — A306

1973, Apr. 7
838 A306 8fr dk red, ocher & blk .65 .35

25th anniv. of WHO.

Europa Issue 1973
Common Design Type

1973, Apr. 28 Size: 35x24mm
839 CD16 4.50fr org brn, vio bl & yel *.35* .25
840 CD16 8fr olive, dk bl & yel *.65* *.40*

Thurn and Taxis Courier — A308

Engraved and Photogravure
1973, Apr. 28 *Perf. 11½*
841 A308 4.50fr black & red brn .35 .25

Stamp Day.

Arrows Circling Globe — A309

1973, May 12 Photo.
842 A309 3.50fr dp ocher & multi .30 .25

5th International Telecommunications Day.

Workers' Sports Exhibition Poster, Ghent, 1913 A310

1973, May 12
843 A310 4.50fr multicolored .35 .25

60th anniversary of the International Workers' Sports Movement.

Fair Emblem A311

1973, May 12 Photo. *Perf. 11½*
844 A311 4.50fr multicolored .35 .25

25th International Fair, Liege, May 12-27.

DC-10 and 1923 Biplane over Brussels Airport — A312

Design: 10fr, Tips biplane, 1908.

1973, May 19 Engr. & Photo.
845 A312 8fr gray bl, blk & ultra .65 .35
846 A312 10fr grn, lt bl & blk .80 .40

50th anniv. of SABENA, Belgian airline (8fr) and 25th anniv. of the "Vieilles Tiges" Belgian flying pioneers' society (10fr).

Adolphe Sax and Tenor Saxophone A313

1973, Sept. 15 Photo.
847 A313 9fr green, blk & bl .70 .30

Adolphe Sax (1814-1894), inventor of saxophone.

Fresco from Bathhouse, Ostend — A314

1973, Sept. 15
848 A314 4.50fr multicolored .35 .25

Year of the Spa.

St. Nicholas Church, Eupen — A315

No. 850, Town Hall, Leau. No. 851, Aarshot Church. No. 852, Chimay Castle. No. 853, Gemmenich Border: Belgium, Germany, Netherlands. No. 854, St. Monan and church, Nassogne. No. 855, Church tower, Dottignes. No. 856, Grand-Place, Sint-Truiden.

1973-75 Engr. *Perf. 13*
849 A315 2fr plum, sep & lt vio .25 .25
850 A315 3fr black, lt bl & mar .50 .25
851 A315 3fr brn blk & yel .30 .25
852 A315 4fr grnsh blk & grnsh bl .35 .25
853 A315 4fr grnsh blk & bl .40 .25
854 A315 4fr grnsh blk & bl .40 .25
855 A315 4.50fr multicolored .50 .25
856 A315 5fr multicolored .50 .25
Nos. 849-856 (8) 3.20 2.00

Nos. 851, 855 not luminescent. Nos. 850, 852-854, 856 horiz.

Charley, by Henri Evenepoel — A316

1973, Oct. 13 Photo. *Perf. 11½*
857 A316 3fr multicolored .25 .25

Youth philately.

Luminescent Paper
Starting with No. 858, all stamps are on luminescent paper unless otherwise noted.

Jean-Baptiste Moens — A317

1973, Oct. 13 Engr. & Photo.
858 A317 10fr multi + label .80 .45

50th anniversary of the Belgian Stamp Dealers' Association. Printed in sheets of 12 stamps and 12 labels showing association emblem.

Adoration of the Shepherds, by Hugo van der Goes — A318

1973, Nov. 17 Engr. *Perf. 11½*
859 A318 4fr blue .30 .25

Christmas 1973.

Louis Pierard, by M. I. Ianchelevici A319

1973, Nov. 17 Engr. & Photo.
860 A319 4fr vermilion & buff .30 .25

Louis Pierard (1886-1952), journalist, member of Parliament.

Highway, Automobile Club Emblem A320

1973, Nov. 17 **Photo.**

861 A320 5fr yellow & multi .40 .25

Flemish Automobile Club, 50th anniv.

Early Microphone, Emblem of Radio Belgium — A321

1973, Nov. 24 **Engr. & Photo.**

862 A321 4fr blue & black .30 .25

50th anniversary of Radio Belgium.

Felicien Rops (1833-1898), Painter, Engraver A323

Engraved and Photogravure

1973, Dec. 8 ***Perf. 11½***

863 A323 7fr Self-portrait .55 .25

King Albert, (1875-1934) A324

1974, Feb. 16 **Photo.** ***Perf. 11½***

864 A324 4fr Prus green & blk .30 .25

Sun, Bird, Flowers and Girl — A325

1974, Mar. 25 **Photo.** ***Perf. 11½***

865 A325 3fr violet & multi .25 .25

Protection of the environment.

NATO Emblem A326

1974, Apr. 20 **Photo.** ***Perf. 11½***

866 A326 10fr dp to lt blue .80 .40

25th anniversary of the signing of the North Atlantic Treaty.

Hubert Krains — A327

1974, Apr. 27 **Engr. & Photo.**

867 A327 5fr black & gray .40 .25

Stamp Day.

Europa Issue 1974

"Destroyed City," by Ossip Zadkine — A328

Design: 10fr, Solidarity, by Georges Minne.

1974, May 4

868 A328 5fr black & red *.65* *.25*

869 A328 10fr black & ultra *.80* *.40*

Children A329

1974, May 18 **Photo.** ***Perf. 11½***

870 A329 4fr lt blue & multi .30 .25

10th Lay Youth Festival.

Planetarium, Brussels A330

Soleilmont Abbey Ruins — A331

4fr, Pillory, Braine-le-Chateau. 7fr, Fountain, Ghent (procession symbolic of Chamber of Rhetoric). 10fr, Belfry, Bruges, vert.

Engr. and Photo.

1974, June 22 ***Perf. 11½***

871 A330 3fr sky blue & blk .25 .25

872 A330 4fr lilac rose & blk .35 .25

873 A331 5fr lt green & blk .40 .25

874 A331 7fr dull yellow & blk .55 .25

875 A330 10fr black, blue & brn .80 .45

Nos. 871-875 (5) 2.35 1.45

Historic buildings and monuments.

"BENELUX" A332

1974, Sept. 7 **Photo.** ***Perf. 11½***

876 A332 5fr bl grn, dk grn & lt bl .40 .25

30th anniversary of the signing of the customs union of Belgium, Netherlands and Luxembourg.

Jan Vekemans, by Cornelis de Vos — A333

1974, Sept. 14

877 A333 3fr multicolored .25 .25

Youth philately.

Leon Tresignies, Willebroek Canal Bridge A334

1974, Sept. 28 **Engr. & Photo.**

878 A334 4fr brn & ol grn .30 .25

60th death anniversary of Corporal Leon Tresignies (1886-1914), hero of World War I.

Montgomery Blair, UPU Emblem A335

10fr, Heinrich von Stephan, UPU emblem.

1974, Oct. 5 ***Perf. 11½***

879 A335 5fr green & blk .40 .25

880 A335 10fr brick red & blk .80 .40

Centenary of Universal Postal Union.

Symbolic Chart — A336

1974, Oct. 12 **Photo.** ***Perf. 11½***

881 A336 7fr multicolored .55 .30

Central Economic Council, 25th anniv.

Rotary Emblem A337

1974, Oct. 19

882 A337 10fr multicolored .80 .35

Rotary International of Belgium.

Wild Boar (Regimental Emblem) — A338

1974, Oct. 26

883 A338 3fr multicolored .25 .25

Granting of the colors to the Ardennes Chasseurs Regiment, 40th anniversary.

Angel, by Van Eyck Brothers — A341

1974, Nov. 16 ***Perf. 11½***

884 A341 4fr rose lilac .30 .25

Christmas 1974. The Angel shown is from the triptyque "The Mystical Lamb" in the Saint-Bavon Cathedral, Ghent.

Adolphe Quetelet, by J. Odevaere — A342

1974, Dec. 14 **Engr. & Photo.**

885 A342 10fr black & buff .80 .40

Death centenary of Adolphe Quetelet (1796-1874), statistician, astronomer and Secretary of Royal Academy of Brussels.

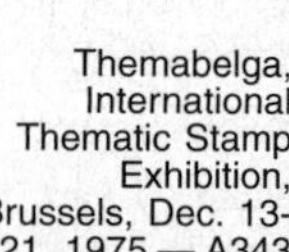

Themabelga, International Thematic Stamp Exhibition, Brussels, Dec. 13-21, 1975 — A343

1975, Feb. 15 **Photo.** ***Perf. 11½***

912 A343 6.50fr Themabelga emblem .50 .25

Ghent Intl. Flower Exhib., Apr. 26-May 5 — A344

1975, Feb. 22

913 A344 4.50fr Neoregelia carolinae .35 .25

Photogravure and Engraved

914 A344 5fr Coltsfoot .40 .25

915 A344 6.50fr Azalea .50 .25

Nos. 913-915 (3) 1.25 .75

Charles Buls Normal School for Boys, Brussels, Cent. — A345

School emblem, man Leading boy.

1975, Mar. 15 ***Perf. 11½***

916 A345 4.50fr black & multi .35 .25

Davids Foundation Emblem A346

1975, Mar. 22 **Photo.**
917 A346 5fr yellow & multi .40 .25

Centenary of the Davids Foundation, a Catholic organization for the promotion of Flemish through education and books.

King Albert (1875-1934) A347

1975, Apr. 5 **Engr. & Photo.**
918 A347 10fr black & maroon .80 .35

Mailman, 1840, by James Thiriar — A348

1975, Apr. 19 **Engr.** ***Perf. 11½***
919 A348 6.50fr dull magenta .50 .25

Stamp Day 1975.

St. John, from Last Supper, by Bouts — A349

Europa: 10fr, Woman's Head, detail from "Trial by Fire," by Dirk Bouts.

1975, Apr. 26 **Engr. & Photo.**
920 A349 6.50fr black, grn & blue *.65* .25
921 A349 10fr black, ocher & red *.90* *.45*

Liberation of Concentration Camps, 30th Anniv. — A350

Concentration Camp Symbols: "B" denoted political prisoners, "KG" prisoners of war.

1975, May 3 **Photo.**
922 A350 4.50fr multicolored .35 .25

Hospice of St. John, Bruges A351

Church of St. Loup, Namur — A352

Design: 10fr, Martyrs' Square, Brussels.

1975, May 12 **Engr.** ***Perf. 11½***
926 A351 4.50fr deep rose lilac .35 .25
927 A352 5fr slate green .40 .25
928 A351 10fr bright blue .80 .35
Nos. 926-928 (3) 1.55 .85

European Architectural Heritage Year.

Library, Louvain University, Ryckmans and Cerfaux A355

1975, June 7 **Photo.** ***Perf. 11½***
931 A355 10fr dull blue & sepia .80 .25

25th anniversary of Louvain Bible Colloquium, founded by Professors Gonzague Ryckmans (1887-1969) and Lucien Cerfaux (1883-1968).

"Metamorphose" by Pol Mara — A356

1975, June 14
932 A356 7fr multicolored .55 .25

Queen Fabiola Mental Health Foundation.

Marie Popelin, Palace of Justice, Brussels — A357

1975, June 21 **Engr. & Photo.**
933 A357 6.50fr green & claret .50 .25

International Women's Year 1975. Marie Popelin (1846-1913), first Belgian woman doctor of law.

Assia, by Charles Despiau — A358

1975, Sept. 6 ***Perf. 11½***
934 A358 5fr yellow grn & blk .40 .25

Middelheim Outdoor Museum, 25th anniv.

Cornelia Vekemans, by Cornelis de Vos — A359

1975, Sept. 20 **Photo.**
935 A359 4.50fr multicolored .35 .25

Youth philately.

Map of Schelde-Rhine Canal — A360

1975, Sept. 20
936 A360 10fr multicolored .80 .30

Opening of connection between the Schelde and Rhine, Sept. 23, 1975.

National Bank, W. F. Orban, Founder A361

Photogravure and Engraved

1975, Oct. 11 ***Perf. 12½x13***
937 A361 25fr multicolored 2.00 .40

Natl. Bank of Belgium, 125th anniv.

Edmond Thieffry and Plane, 1925 A362

1975, Oct. 18 ***Perf. 11½***
938 A362 7fr black & lilac .55 .30

First flight Brussels to Kinshasa, Congo, 50th anniversary.

"Seat of Wisdom" St. Peter's, Louvain — A363

1975, Nov. 8 ***Perf. 11½***
939 A363 6.50fr blue, blk & grn .50 .25

University of Louvain, 550th anniversary.

Angels, by Rogier van der Weyden A364

1975, Nov. 15
940 A364 5fr multicolored .40 .25

Christmas 1975.

Willemsfonds Emblem — A365

1976, Feb. 21 **Photo.** ***Perf. 11½***
941 A365 5fr multicolored .40 .25

Willems Foundation, which supports Flemish language and literature, 125th anniv.

American Bicentennial Emblem — A366

1976, Mar. 13 **Photo.** ***Perf. 11½***
942 A366 14fr multi + label 1.10 .45

American Bicentennial. Black engraved inscription on labels commemorates arrival of first Walloon settlers in Nieu Nederland.

Cardinal Mercier — A367

1976, Mar. 20 **Engr.**
943 A367 4.50fr brt rose lilac .35 .25

Desire Joseph Cardinal Mercier (1851-1926), professor at Louvain University, spiritual and patriotic leader during World War I.

Flemish Economic Organization (Vlaams Ekonomisch Verbond), 50th Anniv. — A368

1976, Apr. 3 **Photo.** ***Perf. 11½***
944 A368 6.50fr multicolored .50 .25

General Post Office, Brussels A369

1976, Apr. 24 **Engr.** ***Perf. 11½***
945 A369 6.50fr sepia .50 .25

Stamp Day.

Potter's Hands A370

Europa: 6.50fr, Basket maker, vert.

1976, May 8 **Photo.**
946 A370 6.50fr multicolored *.70* .25
947 A370 14fr multicolored *1.60* *.40*

Truck on Road A371

1976, May 8
948 A371 14fr black, yel & red 1.10 .40

15th Intl. Road Union Cong., Brussels, May 9-13.

Queen Elisabeth (1876-1965) A372

1976, May 24 ***Perf. 11½***
949 A372 14fr green 1.10 .40

Ardennes Draft Horses A373

1976, June 19
950 A373 5fr multicolored .40 .25

Ardennes Draft Horses Assoc., 50th anniv.

Souvenir Sheets

King Baudouin — A374

1976, June 26
951 A374 Sheet of 3 2.75 2.75
a. 4.50fr gray .70 .70
b. 6.50fr ocher .70 .70
c. 10fr brick red .80 .80
952 A374 Sheet of 2 4.25 4.25
a. 20fr yellow green 1.60 1.60
b. 30fr Prussian blue 2.40 2.40

25th anniv. of the reign of King Baudouin. No. 951 sold for 30fr, No. 952 for 70fr. The surtax went to a new foundation for the improvement of living conditions in honor of the King.

Electric Train and Society Emblem — A375

1976, Sept. 11 **Photo.** ***Perf. 11½***
953 A375 6.50fr multi .50 .25

Natl. Belgian Railroad Soc., 50th anniv.

William of Nassau, Prince of Orange — A376

1976, Sept. 11 **Engr.**
954 A376 10fr slate green .80 .35

400th anniv. of the pacification of Ghent.

New Subway Train A377

1976, Sept. 18 **Photo.**
955 A377 6.50fr multi .50 .25

Opening of first line of Brussels subway.

Young Musician, by W. C. Duyster — A378

1976, Oct. 2 **Photo.** ***Perf. 11½***
956 A378 4.50fr multi .35 .25

Young musicians and youth philately.

Charles Bernard — A379

St. Jerome in the Mountains, by Le Patinier — A380

Blind Leading the Blind, by Breughel the Elder A381

No. 958, Fernand Victor Toussaint van Boelaere. No. 959, St. Jerome in the Mountains, by Le Patinier, vert.

1976, Oct. 16 **Engr.**
957 A379 5fr violet .40 .25
958 A379 5fr red brn & sepia .40 .25
959 A380 6.50fr dark brown .50 .25
960 A381 6.50fr slate green .50 .25
Nos. 957-960 (4) 1.80 1.00

Charles Bernard (1875-1961), French-speaking journalist; Toussaint van Boelaere (1875-1947), Flemish journalist; No. 959, Charles Plisnier Belgian-French Cultural Society. No. 960, Assoc. for Language Promotion.

Remouchamps Caves — A382

Hunnegem Priory, Gramont, and Madonna A383

Designs: No. 963, River Lys and St. Martin's Church. No. 964, Ham-sur-Heure Castle.

1976, Oct. 23 **Engr.** ***Perf. 13***
961 A382 4.50fr multi .35 .25
962 A383 4.50fr multi .35 .25
963 A383 5fr multi .40 .25
964 A383 5fr multi .40 .25
Nos. 961-964 (4) 1.50 1.00

Tourism. Nos. 961-962 are not luminescent.

Nativity, by Master of Flemalle — A384

1976, Nov. 20 ***Perf. 11½***
965 A384 5fr violet .40 .25

Christmas 1976.

Rubens' Monogram — A385

1977, Feb. 12 **Photo. & Engr.**
966 A385 6.50fr lilac & blk .50 .25

Peter Paul Rubens (1577-1640), painter.

Heraldic Lion — A386

1977-85 **Typo.** ***Perf. 13½x14***
Size: 17x20mm
967 A386 50c brn ('80) .25 .25
a. 50c orange brown ('85) .25 .25
968 A386 1fr brt lil .25 .25
a. 1fr bright rose lilac ('84) .25 .25
969 A386 1.50fr gray ('78) .25 .25
970 A386 2fr orange ('78) .25 .25
970A A386 2.50fr yel grn ('81) .25 .25
971 A386 2.75fr Prus bl ('80) .30 .25
972 A386 3fr vio ('78) .30 .25
a. 3fr dull violet ('84) .25 .25
973 A386 4fr red brn ('80) .30 .25
a. 4fr rose brown ('85) .30 .25
974 A386 4.50fr lt ultra .35 .25
975 A386 5fr grn ('80) .40 .25
a. 5fr emerald green ('84) .40 .25
976 A386 6fr dl red brn .50 .25
a. 6fr light red brown ('85) .50 .25
Nos. 967-976 (11) 3.40 2.75

Nos. 967-976 were printed on various papers.

1978, Aug. **Photo.** ***Perf. 13½x12½***
Size: 17x22mm
Booklet Stamps
977 A386 1fr brt lilac .25 .25
a. Bklt. pane, #977-978, 2 #786 1.50
b. Bklt. pane, #977, 979, 2 #788 2.00
978 A386 2fr yellow .30 .30
979 A386 3fr violet .50 .50
Nos. 977-979 (3) 1.05 1.05

Each pane has 2 labels showing Belgian Postal emblem, also a large selvage with zip code instructions. No. 977-979 not luminescent.

See Nos. 1084-1088, design O5.

Anniversary Emblem A387

1977, Mar. 14 **Photo.** ***Perf. 11½***
982 A387 6.50fr sil & multi .50 .25

Royal Belgian Association of Civil and Agricultural Engineers, 50th anniversary.

Birds and Lions Emblem A388

1977, Mar. 28
983 A388 14fr multi 1.10 .30

Belgian District #112 of Lions Intl., 25th anniv.

Pillar Box, 1852 — A389

1977, Apr. 23 **Engr.**
984 A389 6.50fr slate green .50 .25

Stamp Day 1977.

Gileppe Dam, Jalhay A390

Europa: 14fr, War Memorial, Yser at Nieuport.

1977, May 7 **Photo.** ***Perf. 11½***
985 A390 6.50fr multi *.60* .25
986 A390 14fr multi *.80* *.40*

Mars and Mercury Association Emblem — A391

1977, May 14
987 A391 5fr multi .40 .25

Mars and Mercury Association of Reserve and Retired Officers, 50th anniversary.

Prince de Hornes Coat of Arms — A392

Conversion of St. Hubertus — A394

Battle of the Golden Spur, from Oxford Chest — A393

Designs: 6.50fr, Froissart writing book, vert.

1977, June 11 Engr. *Perf. 11½*
988 A392 4.50fr violet .35 .25
989 A393 5fr red .40 .25
990 A393 6.50fr dark brown .50 .25
991 A394 14fr slate green 1.10 .40
Nos. 988-991 (4) 2.35 1.15

300th anniv. of the Principality of Overijse (4.50fr); 675th anniv. of the Battle of the Golden Spur (5f); 600th anniv. of publication of 1st volume of the Chronicles of Jehan Froissart (6.50fr); 1250th anniv. of the death of St. Hubertus (14fr).

Rubens, Self-portrait A395

1977, June 25 Photo.
992 A395 5fr multi .40 .25
a. Souvenir sheet of 3 1.40 1.00

Peter Paul Rubens (1577-1640), painter. Stamps in No. 992a are 37¼mm high, No. 992, 35¼mm. No. 992a sold for 20fr.

Open Book, from The Lamb of God, by Van Eyck Brothers — A396

1977, Sept. 3 Photo. *Perf. 11½*
993 A396 10fr multi .80 .35

Intl. Federation of Library Associations (IFLA), 50th Anniv. Cong., Brussels, Sept. 5-10.

Gymnast and Soccer Player — A397

6.50fr, Fencers in wheelchairs, horiz. 10fr, Basketball players. 14fr, Hockey players.

1977, Sept. 10
994 A397 4.50fr multi .35 .25
995 A397 6.50fr multi .50 .25
996 A397 10fr multi .80 .35
997 A397 14fr multi 1.10 .40
Nos. 994-997 (4) 2.75 1.25

Workers' Gymnastics and Sports Center, 50th anniversary (4.50fr); sport for the Handicapped (6.50fr); 20th European Basketball Championships (10fr); First World Hockey Cup (14fr).

Europalia 77 Emblem — A398

1977, Sept. 17
998 A398 5fr gray & multi .40 .25

5th Europalia Arts Festival, featuring German Federal Republic, Belgium, Oct.-Nov. 1977.

The Egg Farmer, by Gustave De Smet — A399

1977, Oct. 8 Engr. & Photo.
999 A399 4.50fr bister & blk .35 .25

Publicity for Belgian eggs.

Mother and Daughter with Album, by Constant Cap A400

1977, Oct. 15 Engr.
1000 A400 4.50fr dark brown .35 .25

Youth Philately.

Bailiff's House, Gembloux — A401

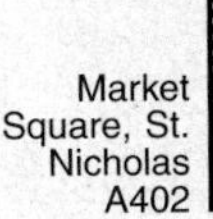

Market Square, St. Nicholas A402

No. 1002, St. Aldegonde Church & Cultural Center. No. 1004, Statue and bridge, Liège.

1977, Oct. 22
1001 A401 4.50fr multi .35 .25
1002 A401 4.50fr multi .35 .25
1003 A402 5fr multi .40 .25
1004 A402 5fr multi .40 .25
Nos. 1001-1004 (4) 1.50 1.00

Tourism. Nos. 1001-1004 not luminescent. See Nos. 1017-1018, 1037-1040.

Nativity, by Rogier van der Weyden — A403

1977, Nov. 11 Engr.
1005 A403 5fr rose red .40 .25

Christmas 1977.

Symbols of Transportation and Map — A404

Campidoglio Palace, Rome, and Map — A406

Designs: No. 1007, European Parliament, Strasbourg, Emblem, vert. No. 1009, Paul-Henri Spaak and map of 19 European member countries.

1978, Mar. 18 Photo. *Perf. 11½*
1006 A404 10fr blue & multi 1.10 .25
1007 A404 10fr blue & multi 1.10 .25
1008 A406 14fr blue & multi 1.25 .55
1009 A406 14fr blue & multi 1.25 .55
Nos. 1006-1009 (4) 4.70 1.60

European Action: 25th anniversary of the European Transport Ministers' Conference; 1st general elections for European Parliament; 20th anniversary of the signing of the Treaty of Rome; Paul Henri Spaak (1899-1972), Belgian statesman who worked for the establishment of European Community.

Grimbergen Abbey — A407

1978, Apr. 1 Engr.
1010 A407 4.50fr red brown .35 .25

850th anniversary of the Premonstratensian Abbey at Grimbergen.

Ostend Chamber of Commerce and Industry, 175th Anniv. — A408

1978, Apr. 8 Photo.
1011 A408 8fr Emblem .65 .25

No. 39 with First Day Cancel — A409

1978, Apr. 15
1012 A409 8fr multicolored .65 .25

Stamp Day.

Europa Issue

Pont des Trous, Tournai A410

8fr, Antwerp Cathedral, by Vaclav Hollar.

Photogravure and Engraved

1978, May 6 *Perf. 11½*
1013 A410 8fr multi, vert. *.85* .25
1014 A410 14fr multi *1.10* *.40*

Virgin of Ghent, Porcelain Plaque — A411

Paul Pastur Workers' University, Charleroi — A412

1978, Sept. 16 Photo. *Perf. 11½*
1015 A411 6fr multicolored .50 .25
1016 A412 8fr multicolored .65 .25

Municipal education in Ghent, 150th anniversary; Paul Pastur Workers' University, Charleroi, 75th anniv. Nos. 1015-1016 are not luminescent.

Types of 1977 and

Tourist Guide, Brussels A413

No. 1017, Jonathas House, Enghien. No. 1018, View of Wetteren and couple in local costume. No. 1020, Prince Carnival, Eupen-St. Vith.

1978, Sept. 25 Photo. & Engr.
1017 A401 4.50fr multi .35 .25
1018 A402 4.50fr multi .35 .25
1019 A413 6fr multi .50 .25
1020 A413 6fr multi .50 .25
Nos. 1017-1020 (4) 1.70 1.00

Tourism. Nos. 1017-1020 are not luminescent.

Royal Flemish Engineer's Organization, 50th Anniv. — A414

1978, Oct. 7 Photo.
1021 A414 8fr Emblem .65 .25

Young Philatelist A415

1978, Oct. 14 Engr. *Perf. 11½*
1022 A415 4.50fr dk violet .35 .25

Youth philately.

Nativity, Notre Dame, Huy — A416

1978, Nov. 18 Engr. *Perf. 11½*
1023 A416 6fr black .50 .25

Christmas 1978.

Tyll Eulenspiegel, Lay Action Emblem — A417

1979, Mar. 3 Photo. *Perf. 11½*
1024 A417 4.50fr multi .35 .25

10th anniversary of Lay Action Centers.

European Parliament Emblem — A418

1979, Mar. 3
1025 A418 8fr multicolored .65 .25

European Parliament, first direct elections, June 7-10.

St. Michael Banishing Lucifer — A419

1979, Mar. 17 Photo. & Engr.
1026 A419 4.50fr rose red & blk .35 .25
1027 A419 8fr brt green & blk .65 .25

Millennium of Brussels.

NATO Emblem and Monument A420

1979, Mar. 31 Photo.
1028 A420 3fr multicolored 1.90 .45

NATO, 30th anniv.

Prisoner's Head — A421

1979, Apr. 7 Photo. & Engr.
1029 A421 6fr orange & blk .50 .25

25th anniversary of the National Political Prisoners' Monument at Breendonk.

Belgium No. Q2 — A422

1979, Apr. 21 Photo. *Perf. 11½*
1030 A422 8fr multicolored .65 .25

Stamp Day 1979.

Mail Coach and Truck A423

Europa: 14fr, Chappe's heliograph, Intelsat satellite and dish antenna.

1979, Apr. 28 Photo. & Engr.
1031 A423 8fr multicolored *.85* .25
1032 A423 14fr multicolored *1.60* *.35*

Chamber of Commerce Emblem — A424

1979, May 19 Photo. *Perf. 11½*
1033 A424 8fr multicolored .65 .25

Verviers Chamber of Commerce and Industry, 175th anniversary.

"50" Emblem A425

1979, June 9 Photo. *Perf. 11½*
1034 A425 4.50fr gold & ultra .35 .25

Natl. Fund for Professional Credit, 50th anniv.

Merchants, Roman Bas-relief A426

1979, June 9
1035 A426 10fr multicolored .80 .30

Belgian Chamber of Trade and Commerce, 50th anniversary.

"Tintin" as Philatelist A427

1979, Sept. 29 Photo. *Perf. 11½*
1036 A427 8fr multicolored 2.00 .65

Youth philately.

Tourism Types of 1977

Designs: No. 1037, Belfry, Thuin. No. 1038, Royal Museum of Central Africa, Tervuren. No. 1039, St. Nicholas Church and cattle, Ciney. No. 1040, St. John's Church and statue of Our Lady, Poperinge.

Perf. 11½ (A401), 13 (A402)
1979, Oct. 22 Photo. & Engr.
1037 A401 5fr multicolored .40 .25
1038 A402 5fr multicolored .40 .25
1039 A401 6fr multicolored .50 .25
1040 A402 6fr multicolored .50 .25
Nos. 1037-1040 (4) 1.80 1.00

Francois Auguste Gevaert A429

Piano, String Instruments A430

Design: 6fr, Emmanuel Durlet.

1979, Nov. 3 *Perf. 11½*
1041 A429 5fr brown .40 .25
1042 A429 6fr brown .50 .25
1043 A430 14fr brown 1.10 .40
Nos. 1041-1043 (3) 2.00 .90

Francois Auguste Gevaert (1828-1908), musicologist and composer; Emmanuel Durlet (1893-1977), pianist; Queen Elisabeth Musical Chapel Foundation, 40th anniv.

Virgin and Child, Notre Dame, Foy — A431

1979, Nov. 24 Photo. & Engr.
1044 A431 6fr lt grnsh blue .50 .25

Christmas 1979.

Independence, 150th Anniversary — A432

1980, Jan. 26 Photo. *Perf. 11½*
1045 A432 9fr purple .70 .25

Frans van Cauwelaert (1880-1961), Minister of State — A433

1980, Feb. 25 Engr.
1046 A433 5fr gray .40 .25

Ghent Flower Show, Apr. 19-27 — A434

1980, Mar. 10 Photo.
1047 A434 5fr Spring flowers .40 .25
1048 A434 6.50fr Summer flowers .50 .25
1049 A434 9fr Autumn flowers .70 .25
Nos. 1047-1049 (3) 1.60 .75

P.T.T., 50th Anniv. A435

1980, Apr. 14 Photo. *Perf. 11½*
1050 A435 10fr multicolored .80 .25

Belgium No. C4 — A436

1980, Apr. 21
1051 A436 9fr multicolored .70 .25

Stamp Day.

Europa — A437

9fr, St. Benedict, by Hans Memling. 14fr, Margaret of Austria (1480-1530).

1980, Apr. 28
1052 A437 9fr multicolored *.70* .25
1053 A437 14fr multicolored *1.10* *.35*

4th Interparliamentary Conf. for European Cooperation & Security, Brussels, May 12-18 — A438

1980, May 10 Photo. *Perf. 11½*
1054 A438 5fr Palais des Nations, Brussels .40 .25

Golden Carriage, 1780, Mons A439

Tourism: No. 1056, Canal landscape, Damme.

1980, May 17
1055 A439 6.50fr multi .50 .25
1056 A439 6.50fr multi .50 .25

Souvenir Sheet

Royal Mint Theater, Brussels — A440

Photo. & Engr.

1980, May 31 *Perf. 11½*

1057 A440 50fr black 4.50 4.50

150th anniv. of independence. Sold for 75fr.

King Baudouin, 50th Birthday — A441

1980, Sept. 6 Photo. *Perf. 11½*

1058 A441 9fr rose claret .70 .25

View of Chiny A442

Portal and Court, Diest — A443

1980 Engr. *Perf. 13*

1059 A442 5fr multicolored .40 .25

1060 A443 5fr multicolored .40 .25

Tourism. Nos. 1059-1060 are not luminescent.

Issued: No. 1059, 9/27; No. 1060, 12/13.

See Nos. 1072-1075, 1120-1125.

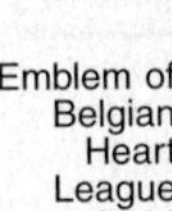

Emblem of Belgian Heart League A444

1980, Oct. 4 Photo. *Perf. 11½*

1061 A444 14fr blue & magenta 1.10 .50

Heart Week, Oct. 20-25.

Rodenbach Statue, Roulers — A445

1980, Oct. 11

1062 A445 9fr multicolored .70 .25

Albrecht Rodenbach (1856-1880), poet.

Youth Philately — A446

1980, Oct. 27 Photo. *Perf. 11½*

1063 A446 5fr multicolored .40 .25

National Broadcasting Service, 50th Anniversary A447

1980, Nov. 10

1064 A447 10fr gray & blk .80 .35

Garland and Nativity, by Daniel Seghers, 17th Century A448

1980, Nov. 17

1065 A448 6.50fr multicolored .50 .25

Christmas 1980.

Baron de Gerlache, by F.J. Navez — A449

Leopold I, By Geefs A450

9fr, Baron de Stassart, by F.J. Navez.

1981, Mar. 16 Photo. *Perf. 11½*

1066 A449 6fr multicolored .50 .25

1067 A449 9fr multicolored .70 .25

Photogravure and Engraved

1068 A450 50fr multicolored 4.00 .55

Sesquicentennial of Chamber of Deputies, Senate and Dynasty.

Tchantchès and Op-Signoorke, Puppets — A451

Photogravure and Engraved

1981, May 4 *Perf. 11½*

1069 A451 9fr shown *.80* .25

1070 A451 14fr d'Artagnan and Woltje *1.10* *.45*

Europa.

Impression of M.A. de Cock (Founder of Post Museum) — A452

1981, May 18 Photo.

1071 A452 9fr multicolored .70 .25

Stamp Day.

Tourism Types of 1980

No. 1072, Virgin and Child statue, Our Lady's Church, Tongre-Notre Dame. No. 1073, Egmont Castle, Zottegem. No. 1074, Eau d'Heure River. No. 1075, Tongerlo Abbey, Antwerp.

1981, June 15 Engr. *Perf. 11½*

1072 A442 6fr multi .50 .25

1073 A442 6fr multi .50 .25

1074 A443 6.50fr multi .55 .25

1075 A443 6.50fr multi .55 .25

Nos. 1072-1075 (4) 2.10 1.00

Soccer Player — A453

1981, Sept. 5 Photo. *Perf. 11½*

1076 A453 6fr multicolored .50 .25

Soccer in Belgium centenary; Royal Antwerp Soccer Club.

E. Remouchamps, Founder — A454

1981, Sept. 5 Photo. & Engr.

1077 A454 6.50fr multi .50 .25

Walloon Language and Literature Club 125th anniv.

Audit Office Sesquicentennial — A455

1981, Sept. 12 Engr.

1078 A455 10fr tan & dk brn .80 .25

French Horn A456

1981, Sept. 12 Photo.

1079 A456 6.50fr multi .50 .25

Vredekring (Peace Circle) Band of Antwerp centenary.

Souvenir Sheet

Pieta, by Ben Genaux — A457

1981, Sept. 19 Photo. *Perf. 11½*

1080 A457 20fr multicolored 1.75 1.40

Mining disaster at Marcinelle, 25th anniv. Sold for 30fr.

Mausoleum of Marie of Burgundy and Charles the Bold, Bruges — A458

1981, Oct. 10 Photo. & Engr.

1081 A458 50fr multi 4.00 .70

Youth Philately — A459

1981, Oct. 24 Photo.

1082 A459 6fr multi .50 .25

Type of 1977 and

A459a

A460

King Baudouin — A460a

Photo. and Engr.; Photo.

1980-86 ***Perf. 13½x14, 11½***

1084 A386	65c brt rose	.25	.25
1085 A386	1fr on 5fr grn	.25	.25
1086 A386	7fr brt rose	.55	.25
1087 A386	8fr grnsh bl	.65	.25
1088 A386	9fr dl org	.70	.25
1089 A459a	10fr blue	.80	.25
1090 A459a	11fr dl red	.90	.25
1091 A459a	12fr grn	.95	.25
1092 A459a	13fr scar	1.00	.25
1093 A459a	15fr red org	1.75	.25
1094 A459a	20fr dk bl	1.75	.25
1095 A459a	22fr lilac	2.50	.60
1096 A459a	23fr gray grn	2.75	.30
1097 A459a	30fr brown	2.10	.25
1098 A459a	40fr red org	3.50	.25
1099 A460	50fr lt grnsh bl & bl	4.75	.25
1100 A460a	50fr tan & dk brn	5.00	.25
1101 A460	65fr pale lil & blk	6.00	.70
1102 A460	100fr lt bis brn & dk bl	9.75	.40
1103 A460a	100fr lt bl & dk bl	13.50	.25
	Nos. 1084-1103 (20)	59.40	6.00

Issued: 65c, 4/14/80; 1fr, 5/3/82; 7fr, 5/17/82; 8fr, 5/9/83; 9fr, 2/11/85; 65fr, No. 1099, 1102, 11/5/81; 10fr, 11/15/82; 11fr, 4/5/83; 12fr, 1/23/84; 15fr, 22fr, 30fr, No. 1100, 3/26/84; 20fr, 40fr, No. 1103, 6/12/84; 23fr, 2/25/85; 13fr, 3/10/86. See Nos. 1231-1234.

Printed on various papers.

Max Waller, Movement Founder — A461

Designs: 6.50fr, The Spirit Drinkers, by Gustave van de Woestyne. 9fr, Fernand Severin, poet, 50th death anniv. 10fr, Jan van Ruusbroec, Flemish mystic, 500th birth anniv. 14fr, Thought and Man TV series, 25th anniv.

1981, Nov. 7

1104 A461	6fr multi	.50	.25
1105 A461	6.50fr multi	.55	.25
1106 A461	9fr multi	.70	.25
1107 A461	10fr multi	.80	.30
1108 A461	14fr multi	1.10	.40
	Nos. 1104-1108 (5)	3.65	1.45

La Jeune Belgique cultural movement cent. (6fr).

Nativity, 16th Cent. Engraving — A466

1981, Nov. 21

1109 A466 6.50fr multi .50 .25

Christmas 1981.

Royal Conservatory of Music Sesquicentennial — A467

Design: 9fr, Judiciary sesquicentennial.

1982, Jan. 25 **Photo.** ***Perf. 11½***

1110 A467	6.50fr multi	.50	.25
1111 A467	9fr multi	.70	.25

A468

1982, Mar. 1

1112 A468	6fr Cyclotron	.50	.25
1113 A468	14fr Galaxy, telescope	1.10	.35
1114 A468	50fr Koch	4.00	.65
	Nos. 1112-1114 (3)	5.60	1.25

Radio-isotope production, Natl. Radio-elements Institute, Fleurus (6fr); Royal Belgian Observatory (14fr); centenary of TB bacillus discovery (50fr).

Joseph Lemaire (1882-1966), Minister of State — A469

1982, Apr. 17 **Photo.** ***Perf. 11½***

1115 A469 6.50fr multi .50 .25

Europa 1982 A470

1982, May 1

1116 A470	10fr Universal suffrage	*1.00*	.25
1117 A470	17fr Edict of Tolerance, 1781	*1.75*	*.35*

Stamp Day — A471

1982, May 22 **Photo. & Engr.**

1118 A471 10fr multi .80 .25

67th World Esperanto Congress, Anvers A472

1982, June 7 **Photo.** ***Perf. 11½***

1119 A472 12fr Tower of Babel .95 .35

Tourism Type of 1980

Designs: No. 1120, Tower of Gosselies. No. 1121, Zwijveke Abbey, Dendermonde. No. 1122, Stavelot Abbey. No. 1123, Villers-la-Ville Abbey ruins. No. 1124, Geraardsbergen Abbey entrance. No. 1125, Beveren Pillory.

1982, June 21 **Photo. & Engr.**

1120 A443	7fr lt bl & blk	.55	.25
1121 A443	7fr lt grn & blk	.55	.25
1122 A442	7.50fr tan & dk brn	.60	.25
1123 A442	7.50fr lt vio & pur	.60	.25
1124 A443	7.50fr slate & blk	.60	.25
1125 A443	7.50fr beige & blk	.60	.25
	Nos. 1120-1125 (6)	3.50	1.50

Self Portrait, by L.P. Boon (b. 1912) — A473

Designs: 10fr, Adoration of the Shepherds, by Hugo van der Goes (1440-1482). 12fr, The King on His Throne, carving by M. de Ghelderode (1898-1962). 17fr, Madonna and Child, by Pieter Paulus (1881-1959).

1982, Sept. 13 **Photo.** ***Perf. 11½***

1126 A473	7fr multicolored	.55	.25
1127 A473	10fr multicolored	.80	.25
1128 A473	12fr multicolored	.95	.35
1129 A473	17fr multicolored	1.40	.35
	Nos. 1126-1129 (4)	3.70	1.20

Abraham Hans, Writer (1882-1932) A474

1982, Sept. 27

1130 A474 17fr multicolored 1.40 .35

Youth Philately and Scouting A475

1982, Oct. 2 **Photo.** ***Perf. 11½***

1131 A475 7fr multicolored .55 .25

Grand Orient Lodge of Belgium Sesquicentennial A476

1982, Oct. 16 **Photo. & Engr.**

1132 A476 10fr Man taking oath .80 .25

Cardinal Joseph Cardijn (1882-1967) A477

1982, Nov. 13 **Photo.**

1133 A477 10fr multicolored .80 .25

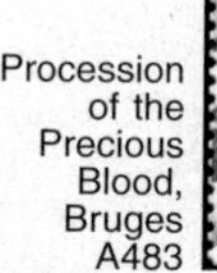

St. Francis of Assisi (1182-1226) A478

1982, Nov. 27

1134 A478 20fr multicolored 1.60 .40

Horse-drawn Trolley A479

1983, Feb. 12 **Photo.** ***Perf. 11½***

1135 A479	7.50fr shown	.70	.25
1136 A479	10fr Electric trolley	1.00	.25
1137 A479	50fr Trolley, diff.	4.00	.50
	Nos. 1135-1137 (3)	5.70	1.00

Intl. Fed. for Periodical Press, 24th World Congress, Brussels, May 11-13 A480

1983, Mar. 19 **Photo.** ***Perf. 11½***

1138 A480 20fr multicolored 1.60 .40

Homage to Women A481

1983, Apr. 16

1139 A481	8fr Operator	.70	.25
1140 A481	11fr Homemaker	.90	.25
1141 A481	20fr Executive	1.60	.40
	Nos. 1139-1141 (3)	3.20	.90

Stamp Day — A482

1983, Apr. 23

1142 A482 11fr multicolored .90 .25

Procession of the Precious Blood, Bruges A483

1983, Apr. 30 **Photo.** ***Perf. 11½***

1143 A483 8fr multi .65 .25

The design of No. 1143 is continuous, and collectors often prefer pairs to demonstrate this feature. Value, unused or used, $2.

Europa 1983 — A484

Paintings by P. Delvaux. 11fr vert.

1983, May 14

1144 A484	11fr Common Man	*.90*	.25
1145 A484	20fr Night Train	*1.60*	*.45*

Manned Flight Bicentenary A485

1983, June 11 **Photo.** ***Perf. 11½***

1146 A485	11fr Balloon over city	.90	.25
1147 A485	22fr Country	1.75	.50

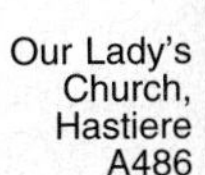

Our Lady's Church, Hastiere
A486

1983, June 25

1148 A486 8fr shown			.65	.25
1149 A486 8fr Landen			.65	.25
1150 A486 8fr Park, Mouscron			.65	.25
1151 A486 8fr Wijnendale Castle, Torhout			.65	.25
Nos. 1148-1151 (4)			2.60	1.00

Tineke Festival, Heule — A487

1983, Sept. 10 **Photo.**

1152 A487 8fr multi .65 .25

Enterprise Year Emblem
A488

1983, Sept. 24

1153 A488 11fr multicolored .90 .25

European year for small and medium-sized enterprises and craft industry.

Youth Philately — A489

1983, Oct. 10 **Photo.** ***Perf. 11½***

1154 A489 8fr multicolored .65 .25

Belgian Exports
A490

1983, Oct. 24 ***Perf. 11½***

1155 A490 10fr Diamond industry	.80	.25
1156 A490 10fr Metallurgy	.80	.25
1157 A490 10fr Textile industry	.80	.25
Nos. 1155-1157 (3)	2.40	.75

See Nos. 1161-1164.

Hendrik Conscience (1812-1883), Novelist — A491

1983, Nov. 7

1158 A491 20fr multicolored 1.60 .35

Leopold III Type of 1936

1983, Dec. 12 **Engr.** ***Perf. 12x11½***

1159 A84 11fr black .90 .25

Leopold III memorial (1901-1983), King 1934-1951.

Free University of Brussels, Sesqui. — A492

Photogravure and Engraved

1984, Jan. 14 ***Perf. 11½***

1160 A492 11fr multicolored .90 .25

Exports Type of 1983

1984, Jan. 28 **Photo.**

1161 A490 11fr Chemicals	.90	.25
1162 A490 11fr Food	.90	.25
1163 A490 11fr Transportation equipment	.90	.25
1164 A490 11fr Technology	.90	.25
Nos. 1161-1164 (4)	3.60	1.00

King Albert I, 50th Death Anniv. — A494

1984, Feb. 11 **Photo. & Engr.**

1165 A494 8fr tan & dk brn .65 .25

1984 Summer Olympic Games — A495

1984, Mar. 3 **Photo.**

Souvenir Sheet

1166 Sheet of 2	2.75	2.75
a. A495 10fr Archery	.80	.55
b. A495 24fr Dressage	1.90	1.40

See Nos. B1029-B1030.

Family, Globe, Birds — A496

1984, Mar. 24 **Photo.** ***Perf. 11½***

1167 A496 12fr multicolored .95 .25

"Movement without a Name" peace org.

St. John Bosco Canonization
A497

1984, Apr. 7

1168 A497 8fr multicolored .65 .25

Europa (1959-84)
A498

1984, May 5 **Photo.** ***Perf. 11½***

1169 A498 12fr black & red	*.95*	.25
1170 A498 22fr black & ultra	*1.75*	*.30*

Stamp Day — A499

1984, May 19

1171 A499 12fr No. 52 .95 .25

2nd European Parliament Elections
A500

1984, May 26

1172 A500 12fr multicolored .95 .25

Royal Military School, 150th Anniv. — A501

1984, June 9 **Photo.** ***Perf. 11½***

1173 A501 22fr Hat 1.75 .40

Notre-Dame de la Chappelle, Brussels
A502

Churches: No. 1175, St. Martin's, Montignyle-Tilleul. No. 1176, Tielt, vert.

Perf. 11½x12, 12x11½

1984, June 23 **Photo. & Engr.**

1174 A502 10fr multicolored	.80	.30
1175 A502 10fr multicolored	.80	.30
1176 A502 10fr multicolored	.80	.30
Nos. 1174-1176 (3)	2.40	.90

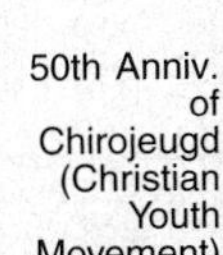

50th Anniv. of Chirojeugd (Christian Youth Movement)
A503

1984, Sept. 15 **Photo.** ***Perf. 11½***

1177 A503 10fr Emblem .80 .30

Affligem Abbey
A504

1984, Oct. 6 **Photo. & Engr.**

1178 A504 8fr Averbode, vert.	.65	.30
1179 A504 22fr Chimay, vert.	1.75	.50
1180 A504 24fr Rochefort, vert.	1.90	.50
1181 A504 50fr shown	4.00	.70
Nos. 1178-1181 (4)	8.30	2.00

Youth Philately
A505

1984, Oct. 20 **Photo.**

1182 A505 8fr Postman smurf 1.25 .35

Arthur Meulemans (1884-1966), Composer — A506

1984, Nov. 17 **Photo. & Engr.**

1183 A506 12fr multi .95 .25

St. Norbert, 850th Death Anniv. — A507

1985, Jan. 14 **Photo. & Engr.**

1184 A507 22fr sepia & beige 1.75 .40

Europalia '85 — A508

1985, Jan. 21 **Photo.**

1185 A508 12fr Virgin of Louvain .95 .25

Belgian Assoc. of Professional Journalists, Cent.
A509

1985, Feb. 11 **Photo.**

1186 A509 9fr multicolored .70 .25

Ghent Flower Festival, Orchids — A510

Photogravure and Engraved

1985, Mar. 18 ***Perf. 11½***

1187 A510 12fr Vanda coerules	.95	.25
1188 A510 12fr Phalaenopsis	.95	.25
1189 A510 12fr Suphrolaelio cattlea riffe	.95	.25
Nos. 1187-1189 (3)	2.85	.75

Visit of Pope John Paul II A511

1985, Apr. 1 **Photo.**
1190 A511 12fr multicolored .95 .25

Belgian Worker's Party Cent. A512

1985, Apr. 15 **Photo.**
1191 A512 9fr Chained factory gate .70 .25
1192 A512 12fr Broken wall, red flag .95 .25

Jean de Bast (1883-1975), Engraver A513

1985, Apr. 22 **Engr.**
1193 A513 12fr blue black .95 .25

Stamp Day.

Public Transportation Year — A514

Design: 9fr, Steam tram locomotive Type 18, 1896. 12fr, Locomotive Elephant and tender, 1835. 23fr, Type 23 tank engine, 1904. 24fr, Type I Pacific locomotive, 1935. 50fr, Type 27 electric locomotive, 1975.

1985, May 6 **Photo.**
1194 A514 9fr multicolored .70 .25
1195 A514 12fr multicolored .95 .25
1196 A514 23fr multicolored 1.90 .50
1197 A514 24fr multicolored 2.00 .50
Nos. 1194-1197 (4) 5.55 1.50

Souvenir Sheet

1198 A514 50fr multicolored 4.00 4.00

Europa 1985 A515

1985, May 13 **Photo.**
1199 A515 12fr Cesar Franck at organ, 1887 *.95 .25*
1200 A515 23fr Folk figures *1.90 .40*

26th Navigation Congress, Brussels A516

1985, June 10 **Photo.** ***Perf. 11½***
1201 A516 23fr Zeebruge Harbor 1.90 .50
1202 A516 23fr Projected lock at Strepy-Thieu 1.90 .50

St. Martin's Church, Marcinelle A517

Tourism: No. 1203, Church of the Assumption of Our Lady, Avernas-le-Baudouin, vert. No. 1204, Church of the Old Beguinage, Tongres, vert. No. 1206, Private residence, Puyenbroeck.

1985, June 24 ***Perf. 11½***
1203 A517 12fr multicolored .95 .25
1204 A517 12fr multicolored .95 .25
1205 A517 12fr multicolored .95 .25
1206 A517 12fr multicolored .95 .25
Nos. 1203-1206 (4) 3.80 1.00

Queen Astrid (1905-1935) A518

1985, Sept. 2 ***Perf. 11½***
1207 A518 12fr brown .95 .25

Baking Pies for the Mattetart of Geraardsbergen A519

Folk events: 24fr, Children dancing, centenary of the St. Lambert de Hermalle-Argenteau Les Rouges youth organization.

1985, Sept. 16
1208 A519 12fr multicolored .95 .25
1209 A519 24fr multicolored 2.00 .40

Liberation from German Occupation, 40th Anniv. — A520

Allegories: 9fr, Dove, liberation of concentration camps. 23fr, Battle of Ardennes. 24fr, Destroyer, liberation of the River Scheldt estuary.

1985, Sept. 30 **Photo.** ***Perf. 11½***
1210 A520 9fr multicolored .70 .25
1211 A520 23fr multicolored 1.90 .65
1212 A520 24fr multicolored 2.00 .70
Nos. 1210-1212 (3) 4.60 1.60

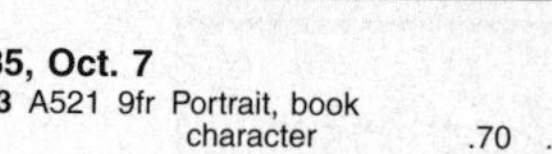

Ernest Claes (1885-1968), Author A521

1985, Oct. 7
1213 A521 9fr Portrait, book character .70 .25

Intl. Youth Year — A522

1985, Oct. 21
1214 A522 9fr Nude in repose, angel .70 .25

King Baudouin & Queen Fabiola, 25th Wedding Anniv. — A523

1985, Dec. 9
1215 A523 12fr multicolored 1.00 .40

Birds — A524

Photo. (50c-2fr, No. 1220, 4.50fr-6fr, No. 1229, 10fr), Typo. (Others)

1985-91 ***Perf. 11½***
1216 A524 50c Roitelet huppe .25 .25
1217 A524 1fr Pic epeichette .30 .25
1218 A524 2fr Moineau friquet .25 .25
1219 A524 3fr Gros bec .50 .25
1220 A524 3fr Bruant des roseaux .35 .25
1221 A524 3.50fr Rouge gorge .30 .25
1222 A524 4fr Gorge bleue .40 .25
1223 A524 4.50fr Traquet Patre .45 .25
1224 A524 5fr Sittele torche-pot .40 .25
1225 A524 6fr Bouvreuil .60 .25
1226 A524 7fr Mesange bleue .60 .25
1227 A524 8fr Martin-pecheur .70 .25
1228 A524 9fr Chardonneret 1.00 .25
1229 A524 9fr Grive musicienne .70 .25
1230 A524 10fr Pinson .80 .25
Nos. 1216-1230 (15) 7.60 3.75

Issued: 7fr, 9/7/87; 5fr, 6fr, 9/12/88; 4fr, 4/17/89; 2fr, 12/4/89; 1fr, 1/8/90; 10fr, 1/15/90; 50c, Nos. 1220, 1229, 9/30/91; others, 9/30/85.

Printed on various papers.

See Nos. 1432-1447, 1627, 1641, 1645, 1651, 1660, 1676, 1696, 1700, 1702-1703, 1714-1715. For stamps denominated in francs and euros, see Nos. 1785-1790A, 1836-1840. For stamps denominated in euros only, see Nos. 1912-1916, 1970-1979, 2071-2076, 2123-2127, 2218-2222, 2278-2280, 2346-2347, 2402-2403, 2409-2411, 2481.

King Type of 1981

1986-90 **Photo.** ***Perf. 11½***
1231 A459a 14fr dark gray 1.10 .25
1232 A459a 24fr dk grysh green 2.00 .30
1233 A459a 25fr blue black 2.10 .25
1234 A460a 200fr sage grn & dl gray grn 22.50 .75
Nos. 1231-1234 (4) 27.70 1.55

Issued: 24fr, 4/7/86; 200fr, 11/3/86; 14fr, 1/15/90; 25fr, 2/19/90.

Printed on various papers.

Congo Stamp Cent. — A525

1986, Jan. 27 **Photo.** ***Perf. 11½***
1236 A525 10fr Belgian Congo #3 1.40 .25

See Zaire No. 1230.

Carnival Cities of Aalst and Binche A526

Folklore: masks, giants.

1986, Feb. 3
1237 A526 9fr Aalst Belfry .70 .25
1238 A526 12fr Binche Gilles .95 .25

Intl. Peace Year — A527

1986, Mar. 10
1239 A527 23fr Emblem, dove 1.90 .40

Stamp Day — A528

1986, Apr. 21 **Photo.** ***Perf. 11½***
1240 A528 13fr Artifacts 1.00 .40

Europa 1986 A529

1986, May 5
1241 A529 13fr Fish *1.00* .25
1242 A529 24fr Flora *2.25 .45*

Dogs — A530

1986, May 26 **Photo.** ***Perf. 11½***
1243 A530 9fr Malines sheep-dog .70 .30
1244 A530 13fr Tervueren sheep-dog 1.00 .45
1245 A530 24fr Groenendael sheepdog 2.00 .80
1246 A530 26fr Flemish cattle dog 2.10 .85
Nos. 1243-1246 (4) 5.80 2.40

St. Ludger's Church, Zele — A531

No. 1248, Waver Town Hall. No. 1249, Nederzwalm Canal. No. 1250, Chapel of Our Lady of the Dunes, Bredene. No. 1251, Licot

Castle, Viroinval. No. 1252, Eynenbourg Castle, La Calamine.

1986, June 30 Photo. & Engr.

1247	A531	9fr multi	.70	.30
1248	A531	9fr multi	.70	.30
1249	A531	13fr multi, horiz.	1.00	.45
1250	A531	13fr multi	1.00	.45
1251	A531	13fr multi, horiz.	1.00	.45
1252	A531	13fr multi, horiz.	1.00	.45
		Nos. 1247-1252 (6)	5.40	2.40

Youth Philately A532

1986, Sept. 1 Photo. *Perf. 11½*

1253 A532 9fr dl ol grn, blk & dk red .70 .35

Cartoon Exhibition, Knokke.

Famous Men — A533

Designs: 9fr, Constant Permeke, painter, sculptor. 13fr, Baron Michel-Edmond de Selys Longchamps, scientist. 24fr, Felix Timmermans, writer. 26fr, Maurice Careme, poet.

1986, Sept. 29

1254	A533	9fr multicolored	.70	.30
1255	A533	13fr multicolored	1.00	.45
1256	A533	24fr multicolored	1.90	.80
1257	A533	26fr multicolored	2.10	.90
		Nos. 1254-1257 (4)	5.70	2.45

Royal Academy for Dutch Language and Literature, Cent. A534

1986, Oct. 6 Engr.

1258 A534 9fr dark blue .70 .30

Natl. Beer Industry A535

Perf. 12½x11½

1986, Oct. 13 Photo.

1259 A535 13fr Glass, barley, hops 1.00 .50

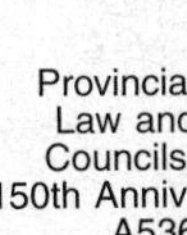

Provincial Law and Councils, 150th Anniv. A536

1986, Oct. 27 *Perf. 11½*

1260 A536 13fr Stylized map 1.00 .50

Christian Trade Union, Cent. A537

1986, Dec. 13 Photo. *Perf. 11½*

1261	A537	9fr shown	.70	.35
1262	A537	13fr design reversed	1.00	.50

Flanders Technology Intl. — A538

1987, Mar. 2 Photo.

1263 A538 13fr multi 1.00 .50

EUROPALIA '87, Austrian Cultural Events — A539

Design: Woman, detail of a fresco by Gustav Klimt, Palais Stoclet, Brussels.

1987, Apr. 4 Photo. *Perf. 11½*

1264 A539 13fr multicolored 1.00 .50

Stamp Day 1987 — A540

Portrait: Jakob Wiener (1815-1899), 1st engraver of Belgian stamps.

1987, Apr. 11 Photo. & Engr.

1265 A540 13fr lt greenish blue & sage grn 1.00 .50

Folklore A541

1987, Apr. 25 Photo.

1266	A541	9fr Penitents procession, Veurne	.70	.35
1267	A541	13fr Play of John and Alice, Wavre	1.00	.50

Europa 1987 — A542

Modern architecture: 13fr, Louvain-la-Neuve Church. 24fr, Regional Housing Assoc. Tower, St. Maartensdal at Louvain.

1987, May 9 Photo.

1268	A542	13fr multicolored	*1.00*	.25
1269	A542	24fr multicolored	*2.10*	*.40*

Statue of Andre-Ernest Gretry (1741-1813), French Composer A543

1987, May 23

1270 A543 24fr multicolored 1.90 1.00

Wallonie Royal Opera, Liege, 20th anniv.

Tourism — A544

No. 1271, Statues of Jan Breydel and Pieter de Conin, Bruges. No. 1272, Boondael Chapel, Brussels. No. 1273, Windmill, Keerbergen. No. 1274, St. Christopher's Church, Racour. No. 1275, Virelles Lake, Chimay.

1987, June 13

1271	A544	13fr multicolored	1.00	.55
1272	A544	13fr multicolored	1.00	.55
1273	A544	13fr multicolored	1.00	.55
1274	A544	13fr multicolored	1.00	.55
1275	A544	13fr multicolored	1.00	.55
		Nos. 1271-1275 (5)	5.00	2.75

Royal Belgian Rowing Assoc., Cent. — A545

European Volleyball Championships A546

1987, Sept. 5

1276	A545	9fr multicolored	.70	.40
1277	A546	13fr multicolored	1.00	.55

Foreign Trade Year — A547

1987, Sept. 12

1278 A547 13fr multi 1.00 .55

Belgian Social Reform, Cent. A548

1987, Sept. 19

1279 A548 26fr Leisure, by P. Paulus 2.10 1.10

Youth Philately A549

1987, Oct. 3

1280 A549 9fr multi 1.75 .50

Newspaper Centennials A550

1987, Dec. 12

1281	A550	9fr Le Soir	.70	.40
1282	A550	9fr Hett Lattste Nieuws, vert.	.70	.40

The Sea — A551

Designs: a, Lighthouse, trawler, rider and mount. b, Trawler, youths playing volleyball on beach. c, Cruise ship, sailboat, beach and cabana. d, Shore, birds.

1988, Feb. 6 Photo. *Perf. 11½*

1283		Strip of 4 + label	3.25	3.25
a.-d.		A551 10fr any single	.80	.55

No. 1283 has a continuous design.

Dynamism of the Regions A552

1988, Mar. 5 Photo. *Perf. 11½*

1284	A552	13fr Operation Athena	1.00	.60
1285	A552	13fr Flanders Alive Campaign	1.00	.60

Stamp Day — A553

Painting: 19th Cent. Postman, by James Thiriar.

1988, Apr. 16 Photo. & Engr.

1286 A553 13fr buff & sepia 1.00 .60

Europa 1988 — A554

Transport and communication.

1988, May 9 Photo. *Perf. 11½*

1287	A554	13fr Satellite dish	*1.10*	.25
1288	A554	24fr Non-polluting combustion engine	*1.90*	*1.00*

Tourism A555

Designs: No. 1289, Romanesque watch-tower, ca. 12th-13th cent., Amay, vert. No. 1290, Our Lady of Hanswijk Basilica, 988, Mechelen, vert. No. 1291, St. Sernin's Church, 16th cent., Waimes. No. 1292, Old Town Hall, 1637, and village water pump, 1761, Peer, vert. No. 1293, Our Lady of Bon-Secours Basilica, 1892, Peruwelz.

Photo. & Engr.

1988, June 20 *Perf. 11½*

1289 A555	9fr beige & blk	.70	.40
1290 A555	9fr lt blue & blk	.70	.40
1291 A555	9fr pale blue grn & blk	.70	.40
1292 A555	13fr pale pink & blk	1.00	.55
1293 A555	13fr pale gray & blk	1.00	.55
	Nos. 1289-1293 (5)	4.10	2.30

Our Lady of Hanswijk Basilica millennium (No. 1290); Waimes village, 1100th anniv. (No. 1291).

Jean Monnet (1888-1979), French Economist — A556

1988, Sept. 12 *Perf. 11½*
1294 A556 13fr black 1.00 .50

Tapestry in the Hall of the Royal Academy of Medicine — A557

Academies building and: No. 1296, Lyre, quill pen, open book and atomic symbols.

1988, Sept. 17 **Photo.**
1295 A557 9fr shown .70 .40
1296 A557 9fr multi .70 .40

Royal Academy of Medicine (No. 1295); Royal Academy of Science, Literature and Fine Arts (No. 1296).

Cultural Heritage A558

Artifacts: 9fr, Statue and mask in the Antwerp Ethnographical Museum. 13fr, Sarcophagus, St. Martin's Church, Trazegnies. 24fr, Church organ, Geraardsbergen. 26fr, Shrine, St. Hadelin's Church, Vise.

1988, Sept. 24

1297 A558 9fr multi	.70	.40
1298 A558 13fr multi	1.00	.50
1299 A558 24fr multi	1.90	1.00
1300 A558 26fr multi	2.10	1.00
Nos. 1297-1300 (4)	5.70	2.90

Youth Philately A559

1988, Oct. 10
1301 A559 9fr multi 1.60 .50

Natl. Postal Savings Bank, 75th Anniv. A560

1988, Nov. 7
1302 A560 13fr multi 1.00 .50

Christmas 1988 and New Year 1989 A561

1988, Nov. 21
1303 A561 9fr Winter landscape .70 .40

Royal Mounted Guard, 50th Anniv. A562

1988, Dec. 12
1304 A562 13fr multi 1.00 .55

Printing Presses A563

9fr, J. Moretus I, Antwerp Museum, vert. 24fr, Stanhope, Printing Museum, Brussels, vert. 26fr, Litho Krause, Royal Museum, Mariemont.

1988, Dec. 19 **Engr.**

1305 A563 9fr bl blk & blk	.70	.40
1306 A563 24fr dark red brn	1.90	1.10
1307 A563 26fr grn & slate grn	2.10	1.25
Nos. 1305-1307 (3)	4.70	2.75

Lace A564

1989, Mar. 20 **Photo.**

1308 A564 9fr Marche-en-Famenne	.70	.40
1309 A564 13fr Brussels	1.00	.50
1310 A564 13fr Brugge	1.00	.50
Nos. 1308-1310 (3)	2.70	1.40

Stamp Day A565

1989, Apr. 24 **Photo. & Engr.**
1311 A565 13fr Mail coach, post chaise 1.00 .55

Europa 1989 — A566

Children's toys.

1989, May 8 **Photo.**
1312 A566 13fr Marbles, horiz. *1.25* .30
1313 A566 24fr Jumping-jack *1.90* *.90*

Royal Academy of Fine Arts, Antwerp, 325th Anniv. — A567

1989, May 22 *Perf. 11½*
1314 A567 13fr multi 1.00 .50

European Parliament 3rd Elections — A568

1989, June 5 **Photo.**
1315 A568 13fr Brussels 1.00 .50

Declaration of Rights of Man and the Citizen, Bicent. — A569

1989, June 12 *Perf. 11½*
1316 A569 13fr multi + label 1.00 .50

Tourism A570

No. 1317, St. Tillo's Church, Izegem. No. 1318, Logne Castle, Ferrieres. No. 1319, St. Laurentius's Church, Lokeren. No. 1320, Antoing Castle, Antoing.

1989, June 26 **Photo. & Engr.**

1317 A570 9fr multi	.70	.40
1318 A570 9fr multi, vert.	.70	.40
1319 A570 13fr multi, vert.	1.00	.50
1320 A570 13fr multi, vert.	1.00	.50
Nos. 1317-1320 (4)	3.40	1.80

Ducks — A571

1989, Sept. 4 **Photo.** *Perf. 12*

Booklet Stamps

1321 A571 13fr Mallard (8a)	1.25	.50
1322 A571 13fr Winter teal (8b)	1.25	.50
1323 A571 13fr Shoveller (8c)	1.25	.50
1324 A571 13fr Pintail (8d)	1.25	.50
a. Bklt. pane of 4, #1321-1324	5.00	
Complete booklet, #1324a	5.00	

Shigefusa Uesugi, a Seated Japanese Warrior, 13th Cent. A572

1989, Sept. 18 *Perf. 11½*
1325 A572 24fr multicolored 1.60 .50

Europalia.

Education League, 125th Anniv. — A573

1989, Sept. 25
1326 A573 13fr multicolored 1.00 .25

Treaty of London, 150th Anniv. — A574

1989, Oct. 2 **Photo.**
1327 A574 13fr Map of Limburg Provinces 1.00 .25

See Netherlands No. 750.

Mr. Nibbs — A575

1989, Oct. 9 *Perf. 11½*
1328 A575 9fr multicolored 1.25 .35

Youth philately promotion.

Christmas, New Year 1990 A576

1989, Nov. 20 **Photo.**
1329 A576 9fr Salvation Army band .70 .25

Fr. Damien (1840-89), Missionary, Molokai Is. Leper Colony, Hawaii A577

1989, Nov. 27 **Photo.**
1330 A577 24fr multicolored 1.90 .50

Father Adolf Daens — A578

1989, Dec. 11 **Photo. & Engr.**
1331 A578 9fr pale & dk grn .70 .25

The Young Post Rider, an Engraving by Albrecht Durer A579

Ghent Flower Festival A580

1990, Jan. 12 **Photo. & Engr.**
1332 A579 14fr buff & red blk 1.10 .55

Postal communications in Europe, 500th anniv.

See Austria No. 1486, Germany No. 1592, Berlin No. 9N584 and German Democratic Republic No. 2791.

1990, Mar. 3 **Photo.**
1333 A580 10fr *Iris florentina* .80 .40
1334 A580 14fr *Cattleya harrisoniana* 1.10 .55
1335 A580 14fr *Lilium bulbiferum* 1.10 .55
Nos. 1333-1335 (3) 3.00 1.50

Intl. Women's Day — A581

1990, Mar. 12 **Photo.** ***Perf. 11½***
1336 A581 25fr Emilienne Brunfaut 2.00 1.00

Wheelchair Basketball — A582

Sports.

1990, Mar. 19
1337 A582 10fr multicolored .80 .40
1338 A582 14fr multicolored 1.10 .60
1339 A582 25fr shown 2.00 1.60
Nos. 1337-1339 (3) 3.90 2.60

Special Olympics (10fr); and 1990 World Cup Soccer Championships, Italy (14fr).

Natl. Water Supply Soc., 75th Anniv. A583

1990, Apr. 2
1340 A583 14fr Water means life 1.10 .60

Postman Roulin, by Van Gogh — A584

1990, Apr. 9
1341 A584 14fr multicolored 1.10 .60

Stamp Day.

Labor Day, Cent. A585

1990, Apr. 30
1342 A585 25fr multicolored 2.00 1.00

Europa 1990 A586

Post offices.

1990, May 7 **Photo. & Engr.**
1343 A586 14fr Ostend 1 *1.10* .25
1344 A586 25fr Liege 1, vert. *2.50* *.85*

18-Day Campaign, 1940 — A587

1990, May 14 **Photo.** ***Perf. 11½***
1345 A587 14fr Lys Monument, Courtrai 1.10 .60

Resistance of German occupation.

Stamp Collecting Promotion Type of 1988

Souvenir Sheet

Various flowers from *Sixty Roses for a Queen,* by P.J. Redoute (1759-1769): a, Rose tricolore. b, Belle Rubaree. c, Mycrophylla. d, Amelie rose. e, Adelaide rose. f, Helene rose.

1990, June 2 **Photo. & Engr.**
1346 Sheet of 6 36.00 36.00
a.-c. SP487 14fr any single 2.50 2.50
d.-f. SP487 25fr any single 3.00 3.00

BELGICA '90, Brussels, June 2-10. sold for 220fr.

Battle of Waterloo, 1815 — A588

Design: Marshal Ney leading the French cavalry.

1990, June 18 **Photo.**
1352 A588 25fr multi + label 2.00 1.40

Tourism A589

1990, July 9
1353 A589 10fr Antwerp .80 .45
1354 A589 10fr Dendermonde .80 .45
1355 A589 14fr Gerpinnes, vert. 1.10 .60
1356 A589 14fr Lommel 1.10 .60
1357 A589 14fr Watermael 1.10 .60
Nos. 1353-1357 (5) 4.90 2.70

A590

A590a

King Baudouin A590b

1990-92 **Photo.** ***Perf. 11½***
1364 A590 14fr multicolored 1.10 .25
1365 A590a 15fr rose car 1.25 .25
1366 A590a 28fr blue green 2.25 .45
1367 A590b 100fr slate green 8.00 .50
Nos. 1364-1367 (4) 12.60 1.45

Issue dates: 14fr, Sept. 7; 15fr, Apr. 1; 28fr, Aug. 3, 1992; 100fr, Sept. 14, 1992.

Fish A591

Designs: No. 1383, Perch (Perche). No. 1384, Minnow (Vairon). No. 1385, Bitterling (Bouviere). No. 1386, Stickleback (Epinoche).

1990, Sept. 8 ***Perf. 12***
1383 A591 14fr multicolored 1.75 .65
1384 A591 14fr multicolored 1.75 .65
1385 A591 14fr multicolored 1.75 .65
1386 A591 14fr multicolored 1.75 .65
a. Bklt. pane of 4, #1383-1386 7.00
Complete booklet, #1386a 7.25

Youth Philately A592

1990, Oct. 13 ***Perf. 11½***
1387 A592 10fr multicolored 1.50 .50

St. Bernard, 900th Birth Anniv. — A593

1990, Nov. 5 **Photo & Engr.**
1388 A593 25fr black & buff 2.00 1.10

Winter Scene by Jozef Lucas A594

1990, Nov. 12 **Photo.**
1389 A594 10fr .80 .40

Christmas.

Self-Portrait A595

Paintings by David Teniers (1610-1690).

1990, Dec. 3
1390 A595 10fr shown .80 .40
1391 A595 14fr Dancers 1.10 .60
1392 A595 25fr Bowlers 2.00 1.10
Nos. 1390-1392 (3) 3.90 2.10

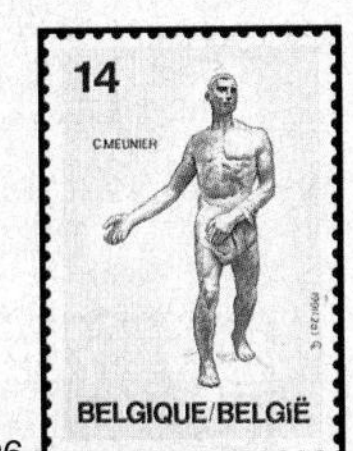

A596

Designs: 14fr, The Sower by Constantin Meunier (1831-1905). 25fr, Brabo Fountain by Jef Lambeaux (1852-1908).

Photo. & Engr.

1991, Mar. 18 ***Perf. 11½***
1393 A596 14fr buff & blk 1.10 .60
1394 A596 25fr lt bl & dk bl 2.00 1.10

A597

1991, Apr. 8 **Photo.** ***Perf. 11½***
1395 A597 10fr Rhythmic gymnastics .80 .50
1396 A597 10fr Korfball .80 .50

No. 1395, European Youth Olympics. No. 1396, Korfball World Championships.

Stamp Printing Office, Mechlin — A598

1991, Apr. 22
1397 A598 14fr multicolored 1.10 .65

Stamp Day.

Liberal Trade Union, Cent. A599

1991, Apr. 29
1398 A599 25fr blue & lt blue 2.00 1.10

Europa A600

1991, May 6
1399 A600 14fr Olympus-1 satellite *1.25* .25
1400 A600 25fr Hermes space shuttle *2.50* *1.00*

Rerum Novarum Encyclical, Cent. A601

1991, May 13 **Photo.** ***Perf. 11½***
1401 A601 14fr multicolored 1.10 .65

Princess Isabel & Philip le Bon — A602

1991, May 27 **Photo.** ***Perf. 11½***
1402 A602 14fr multicolored 1.10 .65

Europalia '91. See Portugal No. 1861.

Tourism A603

Designs: No. 1403, Neptune's Grotto, Couvin. No. 1404, Dieleghem Abbey, Jette. No. 1405, Town Hall, Niel, vert. No. 1406, Nature Reserve, Hautes Fagnes. No. 1407, Legend of giant Rolarius, Roeselare, vert.

1991, June 17 **Photo. & Engr.**
1403 A603 14fr multicolored 1.10 .65
1404 A603 14fr multicolored 1.10 .65
1405 A603 14fr multicolored 1.10 .65
1406 A603 14fr multicolored 1.10 .65
1407 A603 14fr multicolored 1.10 .65
Nos. 1403-1407 (5) 5.50 3.25

King Baudouin, Coronation, 40th Anniv. and 60th Birthday A604

1991, June 24 **Photo.**
1408 A604 14fr multicolored 1.90 .65

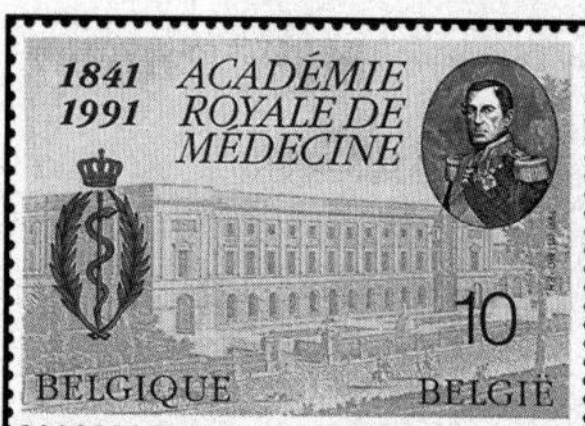

Royal Academy of Medicine, 150th Anniv. — A605

Photo. & Engr.
1991, Sept. 2 ***Perf. 11½***
1409 A605 10fr multicolored .80 .50

The English Coast at Dover by Alfred W. Finch (1854-1930) A606

1991, Sept. 9 **Photo.**
1410 A606 25fr multicolored 2.00 1.10

See Finland Nos. 868-869.

Mushrooms — A607

No. 1411, Amanita phalloides (13A). No. 1412, Amanita rubescens (13B). No. 1413, Boletus erythropus (13C). No. 1414, Hygrocybe persistens (13D).

1991, Sept. 16 **Photo.** ***Perf. 12***
Booklet Stamps
1411 A607 14fr multicolored 1.75 .90
1412 A607 14fr multicolored 1.75 .90
1413 A607 14fr multicolored 1.75 .90
1414 A607 14fr multicolored 1.75 .90
a. Bklt. pane of 4, #1411-1414 7.00
Complete booklet, #1414a 7.25

Doctors Without Borders A608

Design: No. 1415, Amnesty Intl.

1991, Sept. 23 ***Perf. 11½***
1415 A608 25fr multicolored 2.00 1.10
1416 A608 25fr multicolored 2.00 1.10

Telecom '91 — A609

1991, Oct. 7 **Photo.** ***Perf. 11½***
1417 A609 14fr multicolored 1.10 .70

6th World Forum and Exposition on Telecommunications, Geneva, Switzerland.

Youth Philately — A610

Cartoon characters: No. 1418, Blake and Mortimer, by Edgar P. Jacobs (16a). No. 1419, Cori the ship boy, by Bob De Moor (16b). No. 1420, Cities of the Fantastic, by Francois Schuiten (16c). No. 1421, Boule and Bill, by Jean Roba (16d).

1991, Oct. 14 ***Perf. 12***
Booklet Stamps
1418 A610 14fr multicolored 1.75 1.00
1419 A610 14fr multicolored 1.75 1.00
1420 A610 14fr multicolored 1.75 1.00
1421 A610 14fr multicolored 1.75 1.00
a. Bklt. pane of 4, #1418-1421 7.00
Complete booklet, #1421a 7.25

Belgian Newspapers, Cent. — A611

1991, Nov. 4 **Photo.** ***Perf. 11½***
1422 A611 10fr Gazet Van Antwerpen .80 .50
1423 A611 10fr Het Volk .80 .50

Icon of Madonna and Child, Chevetogne Abbey A612

1991, Nov. 25 **Photo.** ***Perf. 11½***
1424 A612 10fr multicolored .80 .50

Christmas.

Wolfgang Amadeus Mozart, Death Bicent. — A613

1991, Dec. 2 **Photo.** ***Perf. 11½***
1425 A613 25fr multicolored 2.00 1.25

A614

1992, Feb. 10 **Photo.** ***Perf. 11½***
1426 A614 14fr Fire fighting 1.10 .60

Belgian Resistance in WWII — A615

1992, Feb. 24
1427 A615 14fr multicolored 1.10 .60

Belgian Carpet Industry — A616

Antwerp Diamond Club, Cent. A617

Design: 14fr, Chef's hat, cutlery.

1992, Mar. 9
1428 A616 10fr multicolored .80 .40
1429 A616 14fr multicolored 1.10 .60
1430 A617 27fr multicolored 2.25 1.10
Nos. 1428-1430 (3) 4.15 2.10

Belgian Association of Master Chefs.

Expo '92, Seville A618

1992, Mar. 23
1431 A618 14fr multicolored 1.10 .60

Bird Type of 1985

1992-96 **Photo.** ***Perf. 11½***
1432 A524 1fr Sizerin flamme .25 .25
1433 A524 2fr Merle noir .25 .25
1434 A524 2fr Grive mauvis .25 .25
1435 A524 4fr Gobe mouche noir .30 .25
1436 A524 4fr Bergeronette grise .30 .25
1437 A524 5fr Etourneau sansonnet .40 .25
1438 A524 5fr Hirondelle de cheminee .40 .25
1439 A524 5.50fr Geai des chenes .45 .25
1440 A524 6fr Cincle plongeur .50 .25
1441 A524 6.50fr Phragmite des joncs .55 .30
1442 A524 7fr Loriot .60 .25
1443 A524 8fr Mesange charbonniere .65 .25
1444 A524 10fr Verdier .80 .25
1445 A524 11fr Troglodyte mignon .90 .25
1446 A524 13fr Moineau domestique 1.00 .25

1446A	A524	14fr Pouillot fitis	1.10	.25
1447	A524	16fr Jaseur boreal	1.25	.25
		Nos. 1432-1447 (17)	9.95	4.30

Issued: 11fr, 4/1/92; 1fr, 2fr, 6fr, 8fr, 10fr, 6/92; 4fr, 5fr, 7fr, 9/7/92; 5.50fr, 9/27/93; 13fr, 16fr, 1/3/94; 6.50fr, 10/3/94; 14fr, 12/18/95; No. 1435A, 5/6/96; No. 1433A, 1434, 7/1/96.

Printed on various papers.

See No. 1838 for similar stamp with additional Euro denomination.

Jean Van Noten (1903-1982), Stamp Designer — A619

Photo. & Engr.

1992, Apr. 13 ***Perf. 11½***

1448 A619 15fr ver & black 1.25 .70

Stamp Day.

Abstract Painting by Jo Delahaut — A620

No. 1449, Witte Magie No. 6, by Roger Raveel.

1992, Apr. 27 **Photo.** ***Perf. 11½***

1449	A620	15fr multi, vert.	1.25	.65
1450	A620	15fr multi	1.25	.65

European Discovery of America, 500th Anniv. — A621

1992, May 2

1451	A621	15fr shown	*1.25*	*.30*
1452	A621	28fr 500, globe, astrolabe	*2.25*	*1.10*

Europa.

Fight Racism — A622

1992, May 18 **Photo.** ***Perf. 11½***

1453 A622 15fr black, gray & pink 1.25 .70

Paintings from Orsay Museum, Paris — A623

Paintings by Belgian artists: 11fr, The Hamlet, by Jacob Smits. 15fr, The Bath, by Alfred Stevens. 30fr, The Man at the Helm, by Theo Van Rysselberghe.

1992, June 15 **Photo.** ***Perf. 11½***

1454	A623	11fr multicolored	.90	.50
1455	A623	15fr multicolored	1.25	.70
1456	A623	30fr multicolored	2.40	1.40
		Nos. 1454-1456 (3)	4.55	2.60

Tourism — A624

Designs: No. 1457, Manneken Pis Fountain, Brussels. No. 1458, Landcommander Castle Alden Biesen, Bilzen, horiz. No. 1459, Building facade, Andenne. No. 1460, Fools' Monday Carnival, Renaix, horiz. No. 1461, Great Procession, Tournai, horiz.

Photo. & Engr.

1992, July 6 ***Perf. 11½***

1457	A624	15fr multicolored	1.25	.70
1458	A624	15fr multicolored	1.25	.70
1459	A624	15fr multicolored	1.25	.70
1460	A624	15fr multicolored	1.25	.70
1461	A624	15fr multicolored	1.25	.70
		Nos. 1457-1461 (5)	6.25	3.50

Village of Andenne, 1300th anniv. (No. 1459). Grand Procession of Tournai, 900th anniv. (No. 1461).

Animals — A625

1992, Sept. 7 **Photo.** ***Perf. 12***

Booklet Stamps

1462	A625	15fr Polecat (13a)	1.50	.80
1463	A625	15fr Squirrel (13b)	1.50	.80
1464	A625	15fr Hedgehog (13c)	1.50	.80
1465	A625	15fr Dormouse (13d)	1.50	.80
a.		Bklt. pane of 4, #1462-1465	6.00	
		Complete booklet, #1465a	6.00	

Brabant Revolution — A626

Design: 15fr, Troops fighting and Henri Van der Noot, Jean Andre Van der Meersch, and Jean Francois Vonck, rebel leaders.

Photo. & Engr.

1992, Sept. 21 ***Perf. 11½***

1466 A626 15fr multicolored 1.25 .70

Arms of Thurn and Taxis — A627

1992, Oct. 5 **Photo.** ***Perf. 11½***

1467 A627 15fr multicolored 1.25 .70

Gaston Lagaffe, by Andre Franquin A628

1992, Oct. 12

1468 A628 15fr multicolored 1.25 .70

Youth philately.

Single European Market — A629

1992, Oct. 26

1469 A629 15fr multicolored 1.25 .70

Antwerp Zoo, 150th Anniv. — A630

1992, Nov. 16

1470	A630	15fr Okapi	1.25	.70
1471	A630	30fr Tamarin	2.40	1.75

The Brussels Place Royale in Winter, by Luc De Decker A631

1992, Nov. 23

1472 A631 11fr multicolored .90 .50

Christmas.

History A632

Designs: 11fr, Council of Leptines, 1250th anniv. 15fr, 28fr, Missale Romanum of Matthias Corvinus (Matyas Hunyadi, King of Hungary) (diff. details). 30fr, Battles of Neerwinden (1693, 1793).

1993, Mar. 15 **Photo.** ***Perf. 11½***

1473	A632	11fr multicolored	.90	.50
1474	A632	15fr multicolored	1.25	.70
1475	A632	30fr multicolored	2.40	1.40
		Nos. 1473-1475 (3)	4.55	2.60

Souvenir Sheet

1476 A632 28fr multicolored 2.25 1.40

Size of No. 1474, 80x28mm. No. 1476 contains one 55x40mm stamp.

See Hungary No. 3385-3386.

A633

A634

Antwerp, Cultural City of Europe A635

Designs: No. 1477, Panoramic view of Antwerp. No. 1478, Antwerp Town Hall, designed by Cornelis Floris. No. 1479, Woman's Head and Warrior's Torso, by Jacob Jordaens. No. 1480, St. Job's Altar (detail), Schoonbroek. No. 1481, Angels on stained glass window, Mater Dei Chapel of Institut Marie-Josee, by Eugeen Yoors, vert.

1993, Mar. 22

1477	A633	15fr multicolored	1.25	.70
1478	A634	15fr multicolored	1.25	.70
1479	A635	15fr gray & multi	1.25	.70
1480	A635	15fr green & multi	1.25	.70
1481	A635	15fr blue & multi	1.25	.70
		Nos. 1477-1481 (5)	6.25	3.50

Antwerp '93.

Stamp Day — A636

1993, Apr. 5

1482 A636 15fr No. 74 1.25 .70

Contemporary Paintings — A637

Europa: 15fr, Florence 1960, by Gaston Bertrand. 28fr, De Sjees, by Constant Permeke.

1993, Apr. 26 **Photo.** ***Perf. 11½***

1483	A637	15fr multicolored	*1.25*	*.25*
1484	A637	28fr multicolored	*2.25*	*1.00*

Butterflies — A638

1993, May 10

1485 A638 15fr Vanessa atalanta 1.25 .70
1486 A638 15fr Apatura iris 1.25 .70
1487 A638 15fr Inachis io 1.25 .70
1488 A638 15fr Aglais urticae 1.25 .70
Nos. 1485-1488 (4) 5.00 2.80

Alumni Assoc. (UAE), Free University of Brussels, 150th Anniv. A639

1993, May 17

1489 A639 15fr blue & black 1.25 .70

Europalia '93 — A640

1993, May 24

1490 A640 15fr Mayan statuette 1.25 .70

Folklore A641

Designs: 11fr, Ommegang Procession, Brussels. 15fr, Royal Moncrabeau Folk Group, Namur. 28fr, Stilt walkers of Merchtem, vert.

1993, June 7 Photo. *Perf. 11½*

1491 A641 11fr multicolored .90 .50
1492 A641 15fr multicolored 1.25 .70
1493 A641 28fr multicolored 2.25 1.25
Nos. 1491-1493 (3) 4.40 2.45

Tourism A642

Castles: No. 1494, La Hulpe. No. 1495, Cortewalle (Beveren). No. 1496, Jehay. No. 1497, Arenberg (Heverlee), vert. No. 1498, Raeren.

Photo. & Engr.

1993, June 21 *Perf. 11½*

1494 A642 15fr pale green & blk 1.25 .70
1495 A642 15fr pale lilac & black 1.25 .70
1496 A642 15fr pale blue & black 1.25 .70
1497 A642 15fr pale brn & black 1.25 .70
1498 A642 15fr pale olive & blk 1.25 .70
Nos. 1494-1498 (5) 6.25 3.50

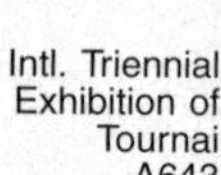

Intl. Triennial Exhibition of Tournai A643

1993, July 5 Photo. *Perf. 11½*

1499 A643 15fr black, blue & red 1.25 .70

Belgian Presidency of European Community Council A644

1993, Aug. 9 Photo. *Perf. 11½*

1500 A644 15fr multicolored 1.25 .70

Rene Magritte (1898-1967), Artist — A645

1993, Aug. 9

1501 A645 30fr multicolored 2.40 1.40

King Baudouin (1930-1993) — A646

1993, Aug. 17 Photo. *Perf. 11½*

1502 A646 15fr black & gray 1.25 .70

European House Cats — A647

1993, Sept. 6 Photo. *Perf. 12*

Booklet Stamps

1503 A647 15fr Brown & white (10a) 1.25 .70
1504 A647 15fr Black & white (10b) 1.25 .70
1505 A647 15fr Gray tabby (10c) 1.25 .70
1506 A647 15fr Calico (10d) 1.25 .70
a. Booklet pane of 4, #1503-1506 5.00
Complete booklet, #1506a 5.00

Publication of De Humani Corporis Fabrica, by Andreas Vesalius, 1543 — A648

1993, Oct. 4 Photo. *Perf. 11½*

1507 A648 15fr multicolored 1.25 .70

Air Hostess Natacha, by Francois Walthery — A649

1993, Oct. 18

1508 A649 15fr multicolored 1.25 .65

Youth philately.

Publication of "Faux Soir," 50th Anniv. — A650

1993, Nov. 8 Photo. *Perf. 11½*

1509 A650 11fr multicolored .90 .45

Notre-Dame de la Chapelle, Brussels A651

1993, Nov. 22 Photo. *Perf. 11½*

1510 A651 11fr multicolored .90 .50

Christmas, New Year.

Children, Future Decisionmakers — A652

1993, Dec. 13 Photo. *Perf. 11½*

1511 A652 15fr multicolored 1.25 .70

A653

A654

A655

A655a

King Albert II

1993-98 Photo. *Perf. 11½*

1512 A653 16fr lt gray & multi 1.25 .25
1513 A653 16fr lt & dk bl grn 1.25 .25
1514 A655 16fr multi 1.25 .25
1515 A655 16fr blue 1.25 .25
1516 A655 17fr blue 1.40 .25
1517 A655 18fr olive black 1.40 .25
1518 A655 19fr dp gray vio 1.50 .30
1519 A653 20fr cream & brn 1.60 .40
1520 A655 20fr brown 1.60 .30
1521 A655 25fr sepia 2.00 .25
1522 A655 28fr claret 2.25 .30
1523 A653 30fr red lilac 2.40 .25
1524 A655 32fr violet blue 2.50 .25
1525 A653 32fr cream & org brn 2.50 .25
1526 A655 34fr dk bl gray 2.75 .40
1527 A655 36fr dk sl bl 3.00 .30
1528 A653 40fr pink & car 3.25 .30
1529 A653 50fr green 4.00 .35
1530 A655 50fr green 4.00 .40
1531 A654 100fr multi 8.00 .50
1532 A654 200fr multi 16.00 2.50
Nos. 1512-1532 (21) 65.15 8.55

Coil Stamp

1536 A655a 19fr deep gray vio 1.50 .30

Issued: No. 1512, 12/15/93; No. 1513, 1/17/94; 30fr, 2/4/94; No. 1525, 3/7/94; 50fr, 4/18/94; No. 1519, 6/6/94; 40fr, 6/20/94; 100fr, 10/3/94; 200fr, 5/2/95; No. 1514, 6/6/96; No. 1515, 1530, 28fr, 9/2/96; 17fr, 12/16/96; 34fr, 36fr, 2/10/97; 18fr, 4/7/97; No. 1518, 7/7/97; 25fr, 4/20/98; No. 1536, 8/10/98; No. 1520, 10/19/98; No. 1524, 11/9/98.

Paintings A656

Designs: No. 1537, The Malleable Darkness, by Octave Landuyt. No. 1538, Ma Toute Belle, by Serge Vandercam, vert.

1994, Jan. 31 Photo. *Perf. 11½*

1537 A656 16fr multicolored 1.25 .70
1538 A656 16fr multicolored 1.25 .70

Airplanes A657

13fr, Hanriot-Dupont HD-1. 15fr, Spad XIII. 30fr, Schreck FBA-H. 32fr, Stampe-Vertongen SV-4B.

1994, Feb. 28

1539 A657 13fr multicolored 1.00 .50
1540 A657 15fr multicolored 1.25 .65
1541 A657 30fr multicolored 2.40 1.25
1542 A657 32fr multicolored 2.50 1.40
Nos. 1539-1542 (4) 7.15 3.80

Daily Newspapers — A658

No. 1543, "Le Jour-Le Courier," cent., vert. No. 1544, "La Wallonie," 75th anniv.

1994, Mar. 21 Photo. *Perf. 11½*

1543 A658 16fr multicolored 1.25 .70
1544 A658 16fr multicolored 1.25 .70

Fall of the Golden Calf (Detail), by Fernand Allard l'Olivier — A659

1994, Mar. 28

1545 A659 16fr multicolored 1.25 .70

Charter of Quaregnon, cent.

Stamp Day — A660

1994, Apr. 11 Photo. *Perf. 11½*

1546 A660 16fr No. 102 1.25 .70

History A661

Scenes from Brabantse Yeesten, 15th cent. illuminated manuscript: 13fr, Reconciliation between John I and Arnold, squire of Wezemaal. 16fr, Tournament at wedding of Charles the Bold and Margaret of York. 30fr, Battle of Woeringen.

1994, Apr. 25
1547 A661 13fr multicolored 1.00 .55
1548 A661 16fr multicolored 1.25 .70
1549 A661 30fr multicolored 2.40 1.25
Nos. 1547-1549 (3) 4.65 2.50

No. 1549 is 81x28mm.

Europa — A662

Designs: 16fr, Abbe Georges Lemaitre (1894-1966), proposed "big-bang" theory of origins of universe. 30fr, Gerardus Mercator (1512-94), cartographer, astronomer.

1994, May 9 Photo. *Perf. 11½*
1550 A662 16fr multicolored *1.25* .25
1551 A662 30fr multicolored *2.40* *1.00*

Papal Visit A663

No. 1552, Father Damien (1840-89). No. 1553, St. Mutien-Marie (1841-1917), Christian educator.

1994, May 16 *Perf. 11½x12*
1552 A663 16fr multicolored 1.25 .70
1553 A663 16fr multicolored 1.25 .70

Tourism A664

Churches: No. 1554, St. Peter's, Bertem. No. 1555, St. Bavo's, Kanegem, vert. No. 1556, Royal St. Mary's, Schaarbeek. No. 1557, St. Gery's, Aubechies. No. 1558, Sts. Peter and Paul, Saint-Severin, Condroz, vert.

1994, June 13 Photo. *Perf. 11½*
1554 A664 16fr multicolored 1.25 .70
1555 A664 16fr multicolored 1.25 .70
1556 A664 16fr multicolored 1.25 .70
1557 A664 16fr multicolored 1.25 .70
1558 A664 16fr multicolored 1.25 .70
Nos. 1554-1558 (5) 6.25 3.50

Guillaume Lekeu (1870-94), Composer A665

Design: No. 1560, Detail of painting by Hans Memling (c.1430-94).

1994, Aug. 16 Photo. *Perf. 11½*
1559 A665 16fr multicolored 1.25 .75
1560 A665 16fr multicolored 1.25 .75

Liberation of Belgium, 50th Anniv. — A666

Design: 16fr, General Crerar, Field Marshal Montgomery, Gen. Bradley, Belgium landscape.

1994, Sept. 5 Photo. *Perf. 11x11½*
1561 A666 16fr multicolored 1.25 .70

Wildflowers — A667

Designs: No. 1562, Caltha palustris. No. 1563, Cephalanthera damasonium. No. 1564, Calystegia soldanella. No. 1565, Epipactis helleborine.

1994, Sept. 26 Photo. *Perf. 12*
Booklet Stamps
1562 A667 16fr multi (14a) 1.25 .75
1563 A667 16fr multi (14b) 1.25 .75
1564 A667 16fr multi (14c) 1.25 .75
1565 A667 16fr multi (14d) 1.25 .75
a. Booklet pane of 4, #1562-1565 5.00
Complete booklet, #1565a 5.00
Nos. 1562-1565 (4) 5.00 3.00

Cubitus the Dog, by Luc Dupanloup — A668

1994, Oct. 10 *Perf. 11½*
1566 A668 16fr multicolored 1.25 .75

Youth philately.

Georges Simenon (1903-89), Writer A669

Photo. & Engr.
1994, Oct. 17 *Perf. 11½*
1567 A669 16fr multicolored 1.25 .75

See France No. 2443, Switzerland No. 948.

Christmas A670

1994, Dec. 5 Photo. *Perf. 11½*
1568 A670 13fr multicolored 1.00 .65

Anniversaries and Events — A671

No. 1569, August Vermeylen Fund, 50th anniv. No. 1570, Belgian Touring Club, cent. No. 1571, Assoc. of Belgian Enterprises, cent. No. 1572, Dept. of Social Security, 50th anniv.

1995, Feb. 13 Photo. *Perf. 11½*
1569 A671 16fr multicolored 1.25 .75
1570 A671 16fr multicolored 1.25 .75
1571 A671 16fr multicolored 1.25 .75
1572 A671 16fr multicolored 1.25 .75
Nos. 1569-1572 (4) 5.00 3.00

Flowers of Ghent A672

1995, Mar. 6
1573 A672 13fr Hibiscus rosa-sinensis 1.00 .65
1574 A672 16fr Rhododendron simsii 1.25 .75
1575 A672 30fr Fuchsia hybrida 2.40 1.60
Nos. 1573-1575 (3) 4.65 3.00

Games — A673

1995, Mar. 20
1576 A673 13fr Crossword puzzles 1.00 .70
1577 A673 16fr Chess 1.25 .75
1578 A673 30fr Scrabble 2.40 1.60
1579 A673 34fr Cards 2.75 1.75
Nos. 1576-1579 (4) 7.40 4.80

Stamp Day — A674

1995, Apr. 10 Photo. & Engr.
1580 A674 16fr Frans de Troyer 1.25 .75

Peace & Freedom A675

Europa: 16fr, Broken barbed wire, prison guard tower. 30fr, Mushroom cloud, "Never again."

1995, Apr. 24 Photo. *Perf. 11½*
1581 A675 16fr multicolored *1.25* .25
1582 A675 30fr multicolored *2.40* *1.10*

Liberation of concentration camps, 50th anniv. (No. 1581). Nuclear Non-Proliferation Treaty, 25th anniv. (No. 1582).

Battle of Fontenoy, 250th Anniv. — A676

16fr, Irish soldiers, Cross of Fontenoy.

1995, May 15 Photo. *Perf. 11½*
1583 A676 16fr multicolored 1.25 .75

See Ireland No. 967.

UN, 50th Anniv. A677

1995, May 22 Photo. *Perf. 11½*
1584 A677 16fr multicolored 1.25 .75

"Sauvagemont, Maransart," by Pierre Alechinsky — A678

No. 1586: "Telegram-style," by Pol Mara.

1995, June 6
1585 A678 16fr multicolored 1.25 .75
1586 A678 16fr multicolored 1.25 .75

Tourism A679

Architectural designs: No. 1587, Cauchie house, Brussels, by Paul Cauchie (1875-1952). No. 1588, De Viif Werelddelen, corner building, Antwerp, by Frans Smet-Verhas (1851-1925). No. 1589, House, Liege, by Paul Jaspar (1859-1945).

1995, June 26
1587 A679 16fr multicolored 1.25 .75
1588 A679 16fr multicolored 1.25 .75
1589 A679 16fr multicolored 1.25 .75
Nos. 1587-1589 (3) 3.75 2.25

Sailing Ships — A680

1995, Aug. 21 Photo. *Perf. 12*
Booklet Stamps
1590 A680 16fr Mercator 1.25 .70
1591 A680 16fr Kruzenstern 1.25 .70
1592 A680 16fr Sagres II 1.25 .70
1593 A680 16fr Amerigo Vespucci 1.25 .70
a. Booklet pane of 4, #1590-1593 5.00
Complete booklet, #1593a 5.00
Nos. 1590-1593 (4) 5.00 2.80

België Belgique 13

MINERVA 1908

Classic Motorcycles A681

1995, Sept. 25 Photo. *Perf. 11½*

1594 A681 13fr 1908 Minerva 1.00 .65
1595 A681 16fr 1913 FN, vert. 1.25 .80
1596 A681 30fr 1929 La Mondiale 2.40 1.50
1597 A681 32fr 1937 Gillet, vert. 2.50 1.60
Nos. 1594-1597 (4) 7.15 4.55

Comic Character, Sammy, by Arthur Berckmans A682

1995, Oct. 9 Photo. *Perf. 11½*

1598 A682 16fr multicolored 1.25 .80

Youth philately.

King's Day A683

16fr, King Albert II and Queen Paola.

1995, Nov. 15 Photo. *Perf. 11½*

1599 A683 16fr multicolored 1.25 .80

Christmas — A684

13fr, Nativity scene from "Breviary," book of devotions, c. 1500.

1995, Nov. 20

1600 A684 13fr multicolored 1.00 .70

Liberal Party, 150th Anniv. — A685

1996, Mar. 4 Photo. *Perf. 11½*

1601 A685 16fr multicolored 1.25 .80

Portrait of Emile Mayrisch (1862-1928), by Théo Van Rysselberghe (1862-1926) — A686

1996, Mar. 2

1602 A686 (A) multicolored 2.00 .80

No. 1602 was valued at 16fr on day of issue.

See Luxembourg No. 939.

Oscar Bonnevalle, Stamp Designer — A687

1996, Apr. 1

1603 A687 16fr multicolored 1.25 .80

Stamp Day.

Insects A688

No. 1604, Sympetrum sanguineum. No. 1605, Bombus terrestris. No. 1606, Lucanus cervus. No. 1607, Melolontha melolontha. No. 1608, Gryllus campestris. No. 1609, Coccinella septempunctata.

1996, Apr. 1 Photo. *Perf. 12*

Booklet Stamps

1604 A688 16fr multicolored 1.25 .80
1605 A688 16fr multicolored 1.25 .80
1606 A688 16fr multicolored 1.25 .80
1607 A688 16fr multicolored 1.25 .80
1608 A688 16fr multicolored 1.25 .80
1609 A688 16fr multicolored 1.25 .80
a. Booklet pane, #1604-1609 7.50
Complete booklet, #1609a 7.50
Nos. 1604-1609 (6) 7.50 4.80

Famous Women A689

Europa: 16fr, Yvonne Nevejean (1900-87), saved Jewish children during World War II. 30fr, Marie Gevers (1883-1975), poet.

1996, May 6 Photo. *Perf. 11½*

1610 A689 16fr multicolored *1.25* .25
1611 A689 30fr multicolored *2.40* *1.10*

Tourism — A690

Designs: No. 1612, Grotto of Han-Sur-Lesse, horiz. No. 1613, Village of Begijnendijk as separate community, bicent.

1996, June 10 Photo. *Perf. 11½*

1612 A690 16fr multicolored 1.25 .80
1613 A690 16fr multicolored 1.25 .80

Architecture in Brussels — A691

No. 1614, La Maison du Roi (Grand Place). No. 1615, Galeries Royales Saint-Hubert. No. 1616, Le Palais d'Egmont, Le Petit Sablon, horiz. No. 1617, Le Cinquantenaire, horiz.

1996, June 10

1614 A691 16fr multi (7a) 1.25 .80
1615 A691 16fr multi (7b) 1.25 .80
1616 A691 16fr multi (7c) 1.25 .80
1617 A691 16fr multi (7d) 1.25 .80
Nos. 1614-1617 (4) 5.00 3.20

Auto Races at Spa, Cent. A692

1996, July 1

1618 A692 16fr 1900 German 6CV 1.25 .80
1619 A692 16fr 1925 Alfa Romeo P2 1.25 .80
1620 A692 16fr 1939 Mercedes Benz W154 1.25 .80
1621 A692 16fr 1967 Ferrari 330P 1.25 .80
Nos. 1618-1621 (4) 5.00 3.20

Paintings of Historical Figures — A693

Portraits from town hall triptych, Zierikzee, Netherlands: No. 1622, Philip I, the Handsome (1478-1506). No. 1623, Juana of Castile, the Mad (1479-1555).

1996, Sept. 2 Photo. *Perf. 11½*

1622 A693 16fr multicolored 1.25 .80
1623 A693 16fr multicolored 1.25 .80

Paintings from National Gallery, London — A694

14fr, Reading Man, by Rogier Van Der Weyden (1399-1464). 16fr, Susanna Fourment, by Peter Paul Rubens (1577-1640). 30fr, A Man in a Turban, by Jan Van Eyck (1390-1441).

1996, Sept. 2

1624 A694 14fr multicolored 1.10 .70
1625 A694 16fr multicolored 1.25 .80
1626 A694 30fr multicolored 2.40 1.50
Nos. 1624-1626 (3) 4.75 3.00

Bird Type of 1985

1996, Oct. 7 Photo. *Perf. 11½*

1627 A524 6fr Tarin des aulnes .50 .25

Comic Character, Cloro, by Raymond Macherot — A695

1996, Oct. 7

1628 A695 16fr multicolored 1.25 .80

Youth Philately.

Almanac of Mons, by Fr. Charles Letellier, 150th Anniv. A696

1996, Oct. 7

1629 A696 16fr multicolored 1.25 .80

Music and Literature A697

No. 1630, Arthur Grumiaux (1921-86), violinist. No. 1631, Flor Peeters (1903-86), organist. No. 1632, Christian Dotremont (1922-79), poet, artist. No. 1633, Paul Van Ostaijen (1896-1928), writer.

Photo. & Engr.

1996, Oct. 28 *Perf. 11½*

1630 A697 16fr multicolored 1.25 .80
1631 A697 16fr multicolored 1.25 .80
1632 A697 16fr multicolored 1.25 .80
1633 A697 16fr multicolored 1.25 .80
Nos. 1630-1633 (4) 5.00 3.20

Christmas and New Year — A698

Scenes from Christmas Market: a, Decorated trees, rooftops. b, Lighted greeting signs. c, Church. d, Selling desert items. e, Selling Nativity scenes. f, Selling meat. g, Santa ringing bell. h, Man smoking pipe, people with presents. i, People shopping.

1996, Nov. 18 Photo. *Perf. 11½*

1634 A698 Sheet of 9, #a.-i. 7.50 7.50
a.-i. 14fr Any single .70 .70

Catholic Faculty University, Mons, Cent. A699

1997, Jan. 20 Photo. *Perf. 11½*

1635 A699 17fr multicolored 1.40 .80

Opera at Theatre Royal de la Monnaie, Brussels — A700

No. 1636, Marie Sasse (1834-1907), soprano. No. 1637, Ernest Van Dijck (1861-1923), tenor. No. 1638, Hector Dufranne (1870-1951), baritone. No. 1639, Clara Clairbert (1899-1970), soprano.

1997, Feb. 10

1636 A700 17fr multicolored 1.40 .75
1637 A700 17fr multicolored 1.40 .75
1638 A700 17fr multicolored 1.40 .75
1639 A700 17fr multicolored 1.40 .75
Nos. 1636-1639 (4) 5.60 3.00

Eastern Cantons — A701

1997, Feb. 10 Photo. *Perf. 11½*

1640 A701 17fr multicolored 1.40 .75

Bird Type of 1985

1997, Mar. 10

1641 A524 15fr Mesange boreale 1.25 .25

UN Peace-Keeping Forces — A702

1997, Mar. 10

1642 A702 17fr multicolored 1.40 .75

Stories and Legends A703

Europa: 17fr, "De Bokkenrijders" (The Goat Riders). 30fr, Jean de Berneau.

1997, Mar. 10 Photo. *Perf. 11½*

1643 A703 17fr multicolored *1.40 .25*
1644 A703 30fr multicolored *2.40 1.00*

Bird Type of 1985

1997, Apr. 7 Size: 35x25mm

1645 A524 150fr Pie bavarde, horiz. 7.50 2.50

See No. 1840 for similar stamp with additional Euro denomination.

Constant Spinoy (1924-93), Stamp Engraver — A704

1997, Apr. 7 Photo. & Engr.

1646 A704 17fr multicolored 1.40 .75

Stamp Day.

Intl. Flower Show, Liege — A705

1997, Apr. 21 Photo.

1647 A705 17fr multicolored 1.40 .75

Paintings by Paul Delvaux (1897-1994) A706

Details or entire paintings: 15fr, Woman with garland of leaves in hair. 17fr, Nude, horiz. 32fr, Woman wearing hat, trolley.

1997, Apr. 21

1648 A706 15fr multicolored 1.25 .65
1649 A706 17fr multicolored 1.40 .75
1650 A706 32fr multicolored 2.50 1.40
Nos. 1648-1650 (3) 5.15 2.80

Bird Type of 1985

1997, May 7 Photo. *Perf. 11½*

1651 A524 3fr Alouette des champs .25 .25

Queen Paola, 60th Birthday A707

1997, May 26

1652 A707 17fr Belvedere Castle 1.25 .75

See Italy No. 2147.

Cartoon Character, "Jommeke," by Jef Nys — A708

1997, May 26

1653 A708 17fr multicolored 1.25 .75

World Congress of Rose Societies — A709

Roses: No. 1654, Rosa damascena coccinea. No. 1655, Rosa sulfurea. No. 1656, Rosa centifolia.

1997, July 7 Photo. *Perf. 11½*

1654 A709 17fr multicolored 1.25 .90
1655 A709 17fr multicolored 1.25 .90
1656 A709 17fr multicolored 1.25 .90
Nos. 1654-1656 (3) 3.75 2.70

Churches — A710

No. 1657, Basilica of St. Martin, Halle. No. 1658, Notre Dame Church, Laeken, horiz. No. 1659, Basilica of St. Martin, Liège.

1997, July 7 Photo. & Engr.

1657 A710 17fr multicolored 1.25 .90
1658 A710 17fr multicolored 1.25 .90
1659 A710 17fr multicolored 1.25 .90
Nos. 1657-1659 (3) 3.75 2.70

Bird Type of 1985

1997, Sept. 1 Photo. *Perf. 11½*

1660 A524 7fr Bergeronnette printaniere .55 .30

Bees and Apiculture — A711

No. 1661, Queen, workers. No. 1662, Development of the larvae. No. 1663, Bee exiting cell. No. 1664, Bee collecting nectar. No. 1665, Two bees. No. 1666, Two bees on honeycomb.

1997, Sept. 1 Photo. *Perf. 12*

Booklet Stamps

1661 A711 17fr multi (15a) 1.40 .75
1662 A711 17fr multi (15b) 1.40 .75
1663 A711 17fr multi (15c) 1.40 .75
1664 A711 17fr multi (15d) 1.40 .75
1665 A711 17fr multi (15e) 1.40 .75
1666 A711 17fr multi (15f) 1.40 .75
a. Booklet pane of 6, #1661-1666 8.50
Complete booklet, #1666a 8.50
Nos. 1661-1666 (6) 8.40 4.50

Craftsmen A712

1997, Sept. 1 *Perf. 11½*

1667 A712 17fr Stone cutter 1.40 .60
1668 A712 17fr Mason 1.40 .60
1669 A712 17fr Carpenter 1.40 .60
1670 A712 17fr Blacksmith 1.40 .60
Nos. 1667-1670 (4) 5.60 2.40

Antarctic Expedition by the Belgica, Cent. — A713

1997, Sept. 22 Photo. *Perf. 11½*

1671 A713 17fr multicolored 1.40 .75

Royal Museum of Central Africa, Cent. — A714

No. 1672, Mask, Shaba, Congo. No. 1673, Outside view of museum, horiz. 34fr, Dish Bearer sculpture, Buli area, Congo.

1997, Sept. 22 Photo. *Perf. 11½*

1672 A714 17fr multicolored 1.40 .75
1673 A714 17fr multicolored 1.40 .75
1674 A714 34fr multicolored 2.75 1.50
Nos. 1672-1674 (3) 5.55 3.00

No. 1673 is 25x73mm.

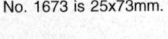

"Fairon," by Pierre Grahame — A715

Christmas.

1997, Oct. 25 Photo. *Perf. 11½*

1675 A715 15fr multicolored 1.25 .70

Bird Type of 1985

1997, Dec. 1 Photo. *Perf. 11½*

1676 A524 15fr Mesange boreale, horiz. 1.25 .75

No. 1676 issued in coil rolls with every fifth stamp numbered on reverse.

Rhododendron A716

Booklet Stamp

Serpentine Die Cut 13½ on 2 or 3 Sides

1997, Dec. 1 Self-Adhesive

1677 A716 (17fr) multicolored 1.40 .25
a. Booklet pane of 10 14.50

By its nature, No. 1677a is a complete booklet. The peelable backing serves as a booklet cover.

Compare with design A757.

"Thalys" High Speed Train — A717

1998, Jan. 19 Photo. *Perf. 11½*

1678 A717 17fr multicolored 1.40 .75

Woman Suffrage in Belgium, 50th Anniv. — A718

1998, Jan. 19

1679 A718 17fr multicolored 1.40 .75

Gerard Walschap (1898-1989), Poet, Playwright — A719

No. 1681, Norge (1898-1990), writer

1998, Feb. 16 Photo. *Perf. 11½*

1680 A719 17fr multicolored 1.40 .70
1681 A719 17fr multicolored 1.40 .70

Paintings, by René Magritte (1898-1967) — A720

No. 1682, "La Magie Noire (Black Magic)," nude woman. No. 1683, "La Corde Sensible (Heartstring)," cloud over champagne glass. No. 1684, "Le Chateau des Pyrenees (Castle of the Pyranees)," castle atop floating rock.

1998, Mar. 9 Photo. *Perf. 11½*

1682 A720 17fr multi, vert. 1.40 .70
1683 A720 17fr multi 1.40 .70
1684 A720 17fr multi, vert. 1.40 .70
Nos. 1682-1684 (3) 4.20 2.10

Belgian Artists — A721

Details or entire paintings: No. 1685, "La Foire aux Amours," by Félicien Rops (1833-98). No. 1686, "Hospitality for the Strangers," by Gustave van de Woestijne (1881-1947). No. 1687, Self-portrait, "The Man with the Beard," by Felix de Boeck (1898-1995). No. 1688, "Black Writing Mixed with Colors," by Karel Appel & Christian Cotremont of COBRA.

1998, Mar. 9 *Perf. 12*

Booklet Stamps

1685 A721 17fr multicolored 1.40 .70
1686 A721 17fr multicolored 1.40 .70
1687 A721 17fr multicolored 1.40 .70
1688 A721 17fr multicolored 1.40 .70
a. Booklet pane, #1685-1688 5.75
Complete booklet, #1688a 5.75
Nos. 1685-1688 (4) 5.60 2.80

Museum of Fine Arts, Ghent, bicent. (No. 1686). COBRA art movement of painters and poets, 50th anniv. (No. 1688).

Sabena Airlines, 75th Anniv. — A722

1998, Apr. 20 Photo. *Perf. 11½*

1689 A722 17fr multicolored 1.40 .70

Belgian Stamp Dealers' Assoc., 75th Anniv. A723

1998, Apr. 20

1690 A723 17fr multicolored 1.40 .70

"The Return," by René Magritte (1898-1967) — A724

1998, Apr. 20

1691 A724 17fr multicolored 1.40 .70

See France No. 2637.

Wildlife A725

1998, Apr. 20

1692 A725 17fr Vulpes vulpes 1.40 .70
1693 A725 17fr Cervus elaphus 1.40 .70
1694 A725 17fr Sus scrofa 1.40 .70
1695 A725 17fr Capreolus capreolus 1.40 .70
Nos. 1692-1695 (4) 5.60 2.80

"Souvenir Sheets"

Starting in 1998, items looking like souvenir sheets have appeared in the market. The 1998 item is similar to No. 1695. The 1999 item is similar to No. 1725. The 2000 item is similar to No. 1811. These have no postal value.

Bird Type of 1985

1998, May 4 Photo. *Perf. 11½*

1696 A524 1fr Mesange huppee .25 .25

Edmund Struyf (1911-96), Founder of Pro-Post, Assoc. for Promotion of Philately — A726

1998, May 4 Photo. & Engr.

1697 A726 17fr multicolored 1.40 .70

Stamp Day.

Natl. Festivals A727

1998, May 4 Photo. *Perf. 11½*

1698 A727 17fr Torhout & Werchter Rock Festival *1.40 .70*
1699 A727 17fr Wallonia Festival *1.40 .70*

Europa.

Bird Type of 1985

1998, July 6 Photo. *Perf. 11½*

1700 A524 7.50fr Pie-grieche grise .60 .25

See No. 1837 for similar stamp with additional Euro denomination.

European Heritage Days — A728

a, Logo. b, Bourla Theatre, Antwerp. c, La Halle, Durbuy. d, Halletoren, Kortrijk. e, Louvain Town Hall. f, Perron, Liège. g, Royal Theatre, Namur. h, Aspremont-Lynden Castle, Rekem. i, Neo-Gothic kiosk, Sint-Niklaas. j, Chapelle Saint Vincent, Tournai. k, Villers-la-Ville Abbey. l, Saint Gilles Town Hall, Brussels.

1998, July 6

1701 A728 Sheet of 12 17.00 9.00
a.-l. 17fr Any single 1.40 .75

Bird Type of 1985

1998 Photo. *Perf. 11½*

1702 A524 9fr Pic vert .70 .25
1703 A524 10fr Turtle dove .80 .25

Issued: 9fr, 8/10; 10fr, 9/28/98.

Free Thinking A729

1998, Aug. 10 Photo. *Perf. 11½*

1704 A729 17fr multicolored 1.40 .75

Philips van Marnix van Sint-Aldegonde (1540-98), Author — A730

1998, Aug. 10

1705 A730 17fr multicolored 1.40 .75

Mniszech Palace (Belgian Embassy), Warsaw, Bicent. A731

Photo. & Engr.

1998, Sept. 28 *Perf. 11½*

1706 A731 17fr multicolored 1.40 .75

See Poland No. 3420.

Contemporary Belgium Films — A732

1998, Sept. 28 Photo.

1707 A732 17fr "Le Huitieme Jour" 1.40 .75
1708 A732 17fr "Daens" 1.40 .75

Cartoon Characters, "Chick Bill" and "Ric Hochet" — A733

1998, Oct. 19 Photo. *Perf. 11½*

1709 A733 17fr multicolored 1.40 .75

Youth philately.

Assoc. of Space Explorers, 14th World Congress, Brussels — A734

1998, Oct. 19

1710 A734 17fr multicolored 1.40 .75

World Post Day A735

1998, Oct. 19 Photo. *Perf. 11½*

1711 A735 34fr blue & dark blue 2.75 1.50

World Assoc. for the Development of Philately.

FGTB-ABVV Trade Union, Cent. — A736

Center panel of triptych by Constant Draz (1875-)

1998, Nov. 9 Photo. *Perf. 11½*

1712 A736 17fr multicolored 1.40 .75

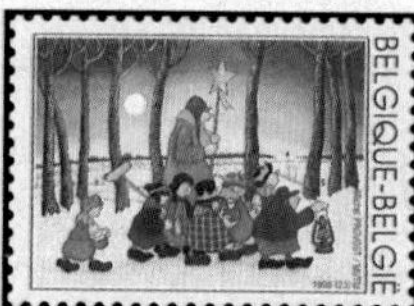

Christmas and New Year — A737

1998, Nov. 9

1713 A737 (17fr) multicolored 1.40 .75

Bird Type of 1985

1998-99 Photo. *Perf. 11½*

1714 A524 16fr Mesange noire 1.25 .65
1715 A524 21fr Grive litorne, horiz. 1.75 .85

No. 1715 also issued in coils with number on reverse of every 5th stamp.

Issued: 16fr, 1/25/99; 21fr, 12/14/98.

See No. 1839 for similar stamp with additional Euro denomination.

A738

A739

Greetings Stamps: No. 1716, Burning candle. No. 1717, Stork carrying a heart. No. 1718, Wristwatch. No. 1719, Four leaf clover with one leaf a heart. No. 1720, Two doves. No. 1721, Heart with arrow through it. No. 1722, Heart-shaped head on woman. No. 1723, Heart-shaped head on man.

1999, Jan. 25 Photo. *Perf. 12*

Booklet Stamps

1716 A738 (17fr) multicolored 1.40 .75
1717 A738 (17fr) multicolored 1.40 .75
1718 A738 (17fr) multicolored 1.40 .75
1719 A738 (17fr) multicolored 1.40 .75
1720 A738 (17fr) multicolored 1.40 .75
1721 A738 (17fr) multicolored 1.40 .75
1722 A738 (17fr) multicolored 1.40 .75
1723 A738 (17fr) multicolored 1.40 .75
a. Booklet pane, #1716-1723 12.00
Complete booklet, #1723a 12.00
Nos. 1716-1723 (8) 11.20 6.00

Nos. 1716-1717, 1719-1720 each also issued in sheets of 20 on July 1. Value, each sheet, $30.

1999, Feb. 22 Photo. *Perf. 11½*

Owls.

1724	A739	17fr	Tyto alba	1.40	.70
1725	A739	17fr	Athene noctua	1.40	.70
1726	A739	17fr	Strix aluco	1.40	.70
1727	A739	17fr	Asio otus	1.40	.70
			Nos. 1724-1727 (4)	5.60	2.80

NATO, 50th Anniv. A740

1999, Mar. 15

1728	A740	17fr	Leopard tank	1.40	.70
1729	A740	17fr	F16 fighter	1.40	.70
1730	A740	17fr	Frigate Wandelaar	1.40	.70
1731	A740	17fr	Hospital tent	1.40	.70
1732	A740	17fr	General staff	1.40	.70
			Nos. 1728-1732 (5)	7.00	3.50

UPU, 125th Anniv. A741

1999, Mar. 15

1733 A741 34fr multicolored 2.75 1.40

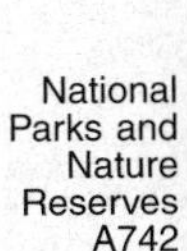

National Parks and Nature Reserves A742

Europa: No. 1734, De Bunt, near town of Hamme. No. 1735, Harchies-Hensies-Pommeroeul.

1999, Apr. 12

1734	A742	17fr	multicolored	*1.40*	*.65*
1735	A742	17fr	multicolored	*1.40*	*.65*

First Belgian Postage Stamps, 150th Anniv. A743

Photo. & Engr.

1999, Apr. 26 *Perf. 11½*

1736	A743	17fr	No. 1	1.40	.70
1737	A743	17fr	No. 2	1.40	.70
a.			Pair, #1736-1737	3.00	1.40

Painting, "My Favorite Room," by James Ensor (1860-1949) — A744

Designs: No. 1739, Woman Eating Oysters, vert. 30fr, Triumph Over Death, vert. 32fr, Old Lady With Masks, vert.

1999, May 17 Photo. *Perf. 11½*

1738	A744	17fr	multicolored	1.40	.70
1739	A744	17fr	multicolored	1.40	.70
1740	A744	30fr	multicolored	2.40	1.40
1741	A744	32fr	multicolored	2.50	1.50
			Nos. 1738-1741 (4)	7.70	4.30

See Israel No. 1365A.

Issued: No. 1738, 5/17; Nos. 1739-1741, 9/11.

Tourism — A745

No. 1742, Giants at Geraardsbergen Fair, vert. No. 1743, Cart d'Or procession of the Confrérie de la Miséracordie, Mons.

1999, June 7 Photo. *Perf. 11½*

1742	A745	17fr	multi (10a)	1.40	.70
1743	A745	17fr	multi (10b)	1.40	.70

Belgian Chocolate A746

1999, June 7

1744	A746	17fr	Bean picker	1.40	.70
1745	A746	17fr	Candy maker	1.40	.70
1746	A746	17fr	Consumer	1.40	.70
			Nos. 1744-1746 (3)	4.20	2.10

King Albert and Queen Paola, 40th Wedding Anniv. — A747

1999, July 2 Photo. *Perf. 11½*

1747 A747 17fr multicolored 1.40 .70

Royalty Type of Semi-Postal Stamps

Souvenir Sheet

Kings: a, 50fr, Leopold I. b, 32fr, Leopold II. c, 17fr, Albert I. d, 17fr, Leopold III. e, 32fr, Baudouin. f, 50fr, Albert II.

Photo. & Engr.

1999, Sept. 29 *Perf. 11½*

1748 SP514 Sheet of 6, #a.-f. 20.00 20.00

Bruphila '99. No. 1748 sold for 300fr.

Nobel Laureates in Peace — A750

Designs: 17fr, Henri La Fontaine (1854-1943). 21fr, Auguste Beernaert (1829-1912).

Photo. & Engr.

1999, Sept. 30 *Perf. 11½*

1749	A750	17fr	red & gold	1.40	.70
1750	A750	21fr	blue & gold	1.75	.85

See Sweden Nos. 2357-2358.

A751

A752

A753

A754

King Albert II

1999-2001 Photo. *Perf. 11¾x11½*

1752	A751	17fr	multicolored	1.40	.25
1753	A751	17fr	prus blue	1.40	.25
1754	A751	19fr	blue	1.50	.25
1755	A751	20fr	yel brown	1.60	.25
1756	A752	23fr	violet	1.90	.25
1757	A751	25fr	brown	2.00	.30
1758	A751	30fr	vio black	2.40	.35
1759	A751	32fr	green	2.50	.30
1760	A751	34fr	gray blue	2.75	.35
1761	A751	36fr	brown	3.00	.40
			Nos. 1752-1761 (10)	20.45	2.95

Engr.

Perf. 11½

1766 A753 50fr blue 4.00 .55

Photo. *Perf. 11½*

1768 A754 100fr multi 8.00 1.10

Engr.

1769	A753	200fr	claret	16.00	2.25
			Nos. 1752-1769 (13)	48.45	6.85

No. 1756 issued in coils.

Issued: 17fr, 10/4; 19fr, 1/24/00; 30fr, 4/3/00; 32fr, 6/19/00; 23fr, 9/4/00; 50fr, 9/11/00; No. 1753, 11/18/00; 36fr, 12/4/00; 20fr, 25fr, 34fr, 100fr, 200fr, 3/26/01.

Youth Philately — A756

Comic strips: a, Corentin, by Paul Cuvelier (16a). b, Jerry Spring, by Jijé (16b). c, Gil Jourdan, by Maurice Tillieux (16c). d, La Patrouille des Castors, by Mitacq (16d). e, Entrance hall of Belgian Comic Strip Museum (16e). f, Hassan & Kadour, by Jacques Laudy (16f). g, Buck Danny, by Victor Hubinon (16g). h, Tif et Tondu, by Fernand Dineur (16h). i, Les Timour, by Sirius (16i).

1999, Oct. 2 Photo. *Perf. 11½*

1771	A756		Sheet of 9, #a.-i.	13.50	6.00
a.-i		17fr	Any single	1.40	.60

Geranium — A757

Tulip — A758

Die Cut 10x9¾ on 2 or 3 sides

1999-2000 Photo.

Self-Adhesive

Booklet Stamps

1772	A757 (17fr) multi		1.40	.25
a.	Complete booklet, 10 #1772		14.00	
1773	A758 (21fr) multi		1.75	.25
a.	Booklet, 10 #1773		17.50	

Die Cut Perf. 11¼

Coil Stamps

Litho.

1774 A757 (17fr) multi 2.00 .25

Photo.

Serpentine Die Cut 13¾

1774A	A757 (17fr) multi		1.40	.25
1775	A758 (21fr) multi		1.75	.25

Nos. 1774-1775 are on a waxed backing paper larger than the stamp.

Issued: No. 1773, 4/17/00; No. 1774A, 2/01. others, 11/22/99.

No. 1774A is dated 2000.

Christmas — A762

1999, Nov. 8 Photo. *Perf. 11½*

1776 A762 17fr multi 1.40 .65

Wedding of Prince Philippe and Mathilde d'Udekem d'Acoz, Dec. 4 — A763

1999, Nov. 29

1777 A763 17fr shown 1.40 .65

Souvenir Sheet

1778 A763 21fr Couple, diff. 1.75 .80

The 20th Century

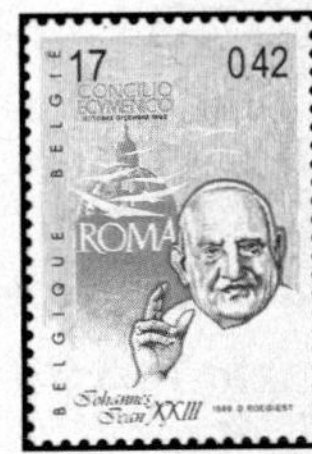

A764

A764a

A764b

A764c

No. 1779: a, Pope John XXIII. b, King Baudouin. c, Willy Brandt. d, John F. Kennedy. e, Mahatma Gandhi. f, Dr. Martin Luther King, Jr. g, Lenin. h, Che Guevara. i, Golda Meir. j, Nelson Mandela. k, Jesse Owens, Modern Olympic Games. l, Soccer. m, Tour de France. n, Edith Piaf. o, The Beatles. p, Charlie Chaplin. q, Tourism. r, Youth movements. s, Tinitin comic strips. t, Philately.

No. 1780: a, Yser front, World War I. b, Concentration camps. c, First atomic bomb. d, Yalta Conference. e, United Nations. f, Decolonization. g, Vietnam War. h, Collapse of the Berlin Wall. i, Peace movements. j, Middle East conflict. k, Rene Magritte, artist. l, Le Corbusier, architect. m, Bertolt Brecht, dramatist. n, James Joyce, novelist. o, Anne Teresa de Keersmaeker, choreographer. p, Bela Bartók, composer. q, Andy Warhol, artist. r, Maria Callas, opera singer. s, Henry Moore, sculptor. t, Toots Thielemans, Charlie Parker, jazz musicians.

No. 1781: a, Ovide Decroly, pedagogue. b, Alternative energy. c, Aviation. d, Sigmund Freud, psychologist. e, Space travel. f, Claude Lévi-Strauss, anthropologist. g, Genetics. h, Pierre Teilhard de Chardin, theologist. i, Max Weber, sociologist, j, Albert Einstein, physicist. k, Penicillin. l, Ilya Prigogine, chemist. m, Roland Barthes, semiotician. n, Simone de Beauvoir, feminist. o, Information. p, John Maynard Keynes, economist. q, Marc Bloch, historian. r, Atomic energy, J. Robert Oppenheimer, physicist. s, Pierre and Marie Curie, physicists. t, Ludwig Josef Wittgenstein, philosopher.

No. 1782: a, Social housing policy. b, May 1968 student protests. c, Telecommunications. d, Wealth and poverty. e, Secularization (laicisation). f, Urbanization. g, Universal suffrage. h, Social security. i, Education (enseignement). j, Aging of the population (vieillissement de la population). k, European Union. l, Universal Declaration of Human Rights. m, Consumer society. n, Women's liberation. o, Deindustrialization. p, Oil crises. q, Mobility. r, Contraception. s, Radio and television. t, Home appliances (appareils menagers).

1999-2002 Photo. *Perf. 11½*

1779 Sheet of 20 25.00 25.00
a.-t. A764 17fr Any single 1.25 1.25
1780 Sheet of 20 25.00 25.00
a.-t. A764a 17fr Any single 1.25 1.25
1781 Sheet of 20 25.00 25.00
a.-t. A764b 17fr Any single 1.25 1.25
1782 Sheet of 20 25.00 25.00
a.-t. A764c 41c Any single 1.25 1.25
Nos. 1779-1782 (4) 100.00 100.00

Issued: No. 1779, 12/6/99. No. 1780, 11/20/00. No. 1781, 10/22/01. No. 1782, 10/28/02.

Denominations on No. 1782 are in euros.

Year 2000 A765

2000, Jan. 3 Photo. *Perf. 11¾x11½*

1783 A765 17fr multi 1.40 .65

Brussels, 2000 European City of Culture — A766

Brussels skyline and: a, Seven people. b, Harmonica player, dancer. c, Airplane, train, ships.

2000, Jan. 24 Photo. *Perf. 11½*

1784 Strip of 3 + 2 labels 4.25 2.00
a.-c. A766 17fr any single 1.40 .65

Bird Type of 1985 Without "F" and With Euro Denomination

2000 Photo. *Perf. 11¾*

1785 A524 1fr Beccroisé des sapins .25 .25
1786 A524 2fr Grimpereau des jardins .25 .25
1787 A524 3fr Pipit parlouse .25 .25
1788 A524 5fr Pinson du nord .40 .25
1789 A524 10fr Pouillot siffleur .80 .25
1790 A524 16fr Pie grièche écorcheur 1.25 .25
1790A A524 16fr Pie grièche écoucheur, horiz. 1.25 .25
Nos. 1785-1790A (7) 4.45 1.75

No. 1790A issued in coils.

Issued: No. 1790, 1/24; 1fr, 2fr, 3fr, 5fr, 5/8; 10fr, 9/11; No. 1790A, 9/4.

Holy Roman Emperor Charles V (1500-58) A767

2000, Feb. 21 Photo. *Perf. 11½*

1791 A767 17fr shown 1.40 .60
1792 A767 21fr At age 40 1.75 .75

Souvenir Sheet

1793 A767 34fr In armor 2.75 1.25
a. Ovptd. in margin 2.75 1.25

No. 1793a was issued 10/6/00 and overprint in margin reads "ESPANA 2000 / Exposición Mundial de Filatelia / Madrid 6-14/X/2000."

See Spain Nos. 3026-3028.

World Mathematics Year — A768

2000, Feb. 21

1794 A768 17fr multi 1.40 .60

Stampin' The Future Children's Stamp Design Contest Winner — A769

2000, Feb. 21

1795 A769 17fr multi 1.40 .60

European Soccer Championships, Belgium and Netherlands — A770

2000, Mar. 27

1796 A770 Pair + label 3.25 1.25
a. 17fr Players 1.40 .60
b. 21fr Ball 1.75 .65

Serpentine Die Cut 10x9¾ on 3 sides

Booklet Stamp

Self-Adhesive

Size: 21x27mm

1797 A770 (17fr) Players, diff. 1.40 .60
a. Booklet, 10 #1797 14.50

See Netherlands Nos. 1045-1046.

Worldwide Fund for Nature — A771

Endangered amphibians and reptiles: No. 1798, Vipera berus. No. 1799, Lacerta agilis, vert. No. 1800, Hyla arborea, vert. No. 1801, Salamandra salamandra.

Perf. 11¾x11½, 11½x11¾

2000, Mar. 27 Photo.

1798 A771 17fr multi 1.40 .65
1799 A771 17fr multi 1.40 .65
1800 A771 17fr multi 1.40 .65
1801 A771 17fr multi 1.40 .65
Nos. 1798-1801 (4) 5.60 2.60

Stamp Day — A772

2000, Apr. 3 Photo. *Perf. 11½*

1802 A772 17fr multi 1.40 .60

Franz von Taxis — A773

2000, Apr. 3

1803 A773 17fr multi + label 1.40 .60

Postal system in Europe, 500th anniv., Belgica 2001 Stamp Exhibition.

Ghent Flower Show A774

Designs: 16fr, Iris spuria. 17fr, Rhododendron, horiz. 21fr, Begonia.

2000, Apr. 17

1804 A774 16fr multi 1.25 .55
1805 A774 17fr multi 1.40 .60
1806 A774 21fr multi 1.75 .70
Nos. 1804-1806 (3) 4.40 1.85

Prince Philippe's Fund A775

2000, Apr. 17

1807 A775 17fr multi 1.40 .60

2000 Summer Olympics and Paralympics, Sydney A776

Designs: 17fr, Belgian Olympic team emblem. No. 1809, Taekwondo. No. 1810, Wheelchair racer, horiz.

30fr+7fr, Swimmer in triathlon, horiz.

2000, May 8

1808 A776 17fr multi 1.40 .60
1809 A776 17fr +4fr multi 1.75 .95
1810 A776 17fr +4fr multi 1.75 .95
Nos. 1808-1810 (3) 4.90 2.50

Souvenir Sheet

1811 A776 30fr +7fr multi 3.00 1.60

Olymphilex 2000 (No. 1811).

Opening of Musical Instrument Museum, Brussels — A777

No. 1812, Harpsichord (15a). No. 1813, Violin (15b). No. 1814, Lutes (15c). No. 1815, Treble viol (15d). No. 1816, Trumpets (15e). No. 1817, Johann Sebastian Bach (15f).

2000, May 8 Photo. *Perf. 11¾*

Booklet Stamps

1812 A777 (17fr) multi 1.40 .60
1813 A777 (17fr) multi 1.40 .60
1814 A777 (17fr) multi 1.40 .60
1815 A777 (17fr) multi 1.40 .60
1816 A777 (17fr) multi 1.40 .60
1817 A777 (17fr) multi 1.40 .60
a. Booklet pane, #1812-1817 8.50
Booklet, #1817a 8.50
Nos. 1812-1817 (6) 8.40 3.60

Europa, 2000

Common Design Type

2000, May 9 *Perf. 11½*

1818 CD17 (21fr) multi *1.75 .75*

UNESCO World Heritage Sites A778

Designs: No. 1819, Flemish Béguinages. No. 1820, Grand-Place, Brussels. No. 1821, Boat lifts, Canal du Centre.

2000, June 19 *Perf. 11½x11¾*

1819 A778 17fr multi 1.40 .60
1820 A778 17fr multi 1.40 .60
1821 A778 17fr multi 1.40 .60
Nos. 1819-1821 (3) 4.20 1.80

Tourism A779

Churches and their organs: No. 1822, Norbertine Abbey Church, Grimbergen. No. 1823, Collégiale Sainte Waudru, Mons. No. 1824, O.-L.-V. Hemelvaartkerk, Ninove. No. 1825, St. Peter's Church, Bastogne.

2000, June 19 *Perf. 11½*

1822 A779 17fr multi 1.40 .60
1823 A779 17fr multi 1.40 .60
1824 A779 17fr multi 1.40 .60
1825 A779 17fr multi 1.40 .60
Nos. 1822-1825 (4) 5.60 2.40

A780

2000, Sept. 4 Photo. *Perf. 11¾*

1826 A780 17fr multi 4.50 1.60

European Postal Services, 500th Anniv., Belgica 2001 Stamp Exhibition. No. 1826 issued in coils.

Youth Philately — A781

2000, Sept. 11 ***Perf. 11¾x11½***
1827 A781 17fr multi 1.40 .50

Hainault Flower Show A782

2000, Sept. 11 ***Perf. 11½x11¾***
1828 A782 17fr multi 1.40 .50

Violets — A783

Die Cut Perf. 10x9¾ on 2 or 3 Sides
2000, Sept. 11 **Photo.**
Booklet Stamp
Self-Adhesive
1829 A783 (17fr) multi 1.40 .25
a. Booklet, 10 #1829 14.50

Contemporary Art — A784

No. 1831, Bing of the Ferro Lusto X, by Panamarenko. No. 1832, Construction, by Anne-Mie Van Kerckhoven. No. 1833, Belgique Eternelle, by J. & L. Charlier. No. 1834, Roses from series "Les Belles de Nuit," by Marie-Jo Lafontaine.

Perf. 11½x11¾, 11¾x11½
2000, Oct. 16 **Photo.**
1831 A784 17fr multi (21a) 1.40 .50
1832 A784 17fr multi (21b), vert. 1.40 .50
1833 A784 17fr multi (21c) 1.40 .50
1834 A784 17fr multi (21d) 1.40 .50
Nos. 1831-1834 (4) 5.60 2.00

Christmas — A785

2000, Nov. 20 **Photo.** ***Perf. 11½***
1835 A785 17fr multi 1.40 .50

Bird Type of 1985
Without F and With Euro Denomination

2000-01 **Photo.** ***Perf. 11¾***
1836 A524 50c Roitelet huppe .25 .25
1837 A524 7.50fr Pie-grieche grise .60 .25
1838 A524 8fr Mesange charbonniere .65 .25
1838A A524 16fr Sterne pierregarin 1.25 .25
1839 A524 21fr Grive litorne, horiz. 1.75 .25

Perf. 11½x11¾
Size: 35x25mm
1840 A524 150fr Pie bavarde, horiz. 12.00 1.75
Nos. 1836-1840 (6) 16.50 3.00

Issued: 8fr, 12/4/00. 50c, 7.50fr, 21fr, 150fr, 3/26/01; 16fr, 6/9/01. Numbers have been reserved for additional stamps in this set.

Holy Year 2000 — A786

Photo. & Engr.
2000, Dec. 27 ***Perf. 11½***
1841 A786 17fr 1.40 .50

Royalty Type of Semi-Postal Stamps
Souvenir Sheet

Queens: a, 50fr, Louise-Marie. b, 32fr, Marie-Henriette. c, 17fr, Elisabeth. d, 17fr, Astrid. e, 32fr, Fabiola. f, 50fr, Paola.

Photo. & Engr.
2001, Feb. 12 ***Perf. 11½***
1842 SP514 Sheet of 6, #a-f 18.00 18.00

No. 1842 sold for 300fr.

Zénobe Gramme (1826-1901), Electrical Engineer — A787

2001, Mar. 19 **Photo.**
1843 A787 17fr multi 1.40 .50

Catholic University of Louvain, 575th Anniv. — A788

2001, Mar. 19
1844 A788 17fr multi 1.40 .50

Europa — A789

2001, Apr. 23 **Photo.** ***Perf. 11½***
1845 A789 21fr multi *1.75 .65*

Musical and Literary Personalities — A790

Designs: No. 1846, Willem Elsschot (1882-1960), writer. No. 1847, Albert Ayguesparse (1900-96), writer.
21fr, Queen Elisabeth (1876-1965), patron of Queen Elisabeth Intl. Music Competition, horiz.

2001, Apr. 23 **Photo.** ***Perf. 11½***
1846 A790 17fr multi 1.40 .50
1847 A790 17fr multi 1.40 .50

Souvenir Sheet
1848 A790 21fr multi 1.75 .70

Queen Elisabeth Intl. Music Competition, 50th anniv. (No. 1848).

Belgian Natl. Railway Company, 75th Anniv. — A790A

No. 1848A: b, 1938 Type 12 locomotive No. 12004. c, 1971 Series 06 dual engine No. 671. d, 1991 Series 03 threefold engine No. 328.

2001, May 7 **Photo.** ***Perf. 11¾x11½***
1848A Horiz. strip of 3 + 2 labels 4.50 1.50
b.-d. A790A 17fr Any single 1.40 .50

A791

European Posts, 500th Anniv. — A792

Designs: No. 1849, Franz von Taxis, 16th cent. postrider. No. 1850, 17th cent. postman on road near Brussels. No. 1851, 18th cent. postman, quill pen, postal notice. No. 1852, 19th cent. postman, train, Belgium #2 on cover. No. 1853, 20th cent. postman, motorcycle, airplanes, mailboxes.
No. 1854: 150fr, 21st cent. postwoman, Belgica 2001 emblem.

Perf. 11¾x11½
2001, June 9 **Photo.**
Stamp + label
1849 A791 17fr multi 1.40 .50
1850 A792 17fr multi 1.40 .50
1851 A792 17fr multi 1.40 .50
1852 A792 17fr multi 1.40 .50
1853 A792 17fr multi 1.40 .50
Nos. 1849-1853 (5) 7.00 2.50

Souvenir Sheet
1854 A792 150fr multi 16.00 16.00

Nos. 1849 printed in sheets of 10 stamps + 10 labels. For Nos. 1850-1853, each is printed in sheets of 12 stamps + 12 labels.
No. 1854 contains one 38x48mm stamp without an attached label, and sold for 300fr, with the surtax going to Pro Post for the promotion of philately.

Houses of Worship — A793

Designs: 17fr, Hassan II Mosque, Casablanca, Morocco. 34fr, Koekelberg Basilica.

2001, June 10 **Photo.** ***Perf. 11½***
1855 A793 17fr multi 1.40 .50
1856 A793 34fr multi 2.75 1.10

See Morocco Nos. 897-898.

Musées Royaux des Beaux Arts, Brussels, 200th Anniv. — A794

No. 1857: a, Winter Landscape With Skaters, by Pieter Breughel the Elder. b, Study of a Negro's Head, by Peter Paul Rubens. c, Sunday, by Frits Van den Berghe. d, Mussel Triumph II, by Marcel Broodthaers.

2001, June 11 **Photo.** ***Perf. 12***
1857 Booklet pane of 4 5.75
a.-d. A794 17fr Any single 1.40 .50
Booklet, #1857 5.75

Ancient Chinese Receptacles A795

Designs: 17fr, Earthenware vase. 34fr, Porcelain coffee pot.

2001, June 12 **Photo.** ***Perf. 11½***
1858 A795 17fr multi 1.40 .50
1859 A795 34fr multi 2.75 1.10

See People's Republic of China Nos. 3108-3109.

Youth Philately — A796

2001, June 13
1860 A796 17fr multi 1.40 .50

Belgian Chairmanship of European Union A797

2001, June 15
1861 A797 17fr multi 1.40 .50

Tourism — A798

Town hall belfries: No. 1862, Binche. No. 1863, Dixmude.

2001, Aug. 6 ***Perf. 11½x11¾***

1862 A798 17fr multi 1.40 .50
1863 A798 17fr multi 1.40 .50

Farmsteads — A799

2001, Aug. 6 ***Perf. 11¾x11½***

1864 A799 17fr Damme 1.40 .50
1865 A799 17fr Beauvechain 1.40 .50
1866 A799 17fr Leuven 1.40 .50
1867 A799 17fr Honnelles 1.40 .50
1868 A799 17fr Hasselt 1.40 .50
Nos. 1864-1868 (5) 7.00 2.50

Stam and Pilou, Mascots of Stampilou Youth Philatelic Club — A800

2001, Oct. 8 **Photo.** ***Die Cut***

Self-Adhesive

Booklet Stamp

1869 A800 (17fr) multi 1.40 .50
a. Booklet of 5 + 5 labels 7.25

Stamp Day.

Christmas A801

2001, Nov. 12 **Photo.** ***Perf. 11½***

1870 A801 15fr multi 1.25 .50

Violets A802

Belgian Post Emblem A802a

Narcissus — A803 Tulips — A804

2001, Dec. 10 **Photo.** ***Perf. 11½***

1871 A802 (17fr) multi 1.90 1.90
1871A A802a (17fr) red 1.90 1.90

Self-Adhesive
Booklet Stamps

Die Cut Perf. 10 on 2 or 3 Sides

1872 A803 (17fr) multi 1.40 .25
a. Booklet pane of 10 14.00

Die Cut Perf. 9¾ on 3 Sides

1873 A804 (21fr) multi 1.75 .25
a. Booklet pane of 10 17.50
Nos. 1871-1873 (4) 6.95 4.30

Issued: No. 1871, 10/17; No. 1871A, 12/1. Nos. 1872, 1873, 12/10.

Nos. 1871 and 1871A were each issued in sheets of 15 stamps + 15 labels that could be personalized. The sheets sold for 605fr.

Death Announcement Stamp — A805

2001, Dec. 10 **Photo.** ***Perf. 11½***

1874 A805 (17fr) multi 1.40 .55

See Nos. 1936 and 2035.

Tintin in Africa — A806

Tintin: 17fr, In jungle. 34fr, In automobile.

2001, Dec. 31

1875 A806 17fr multi 1.40 .55

Souvenir Sheet

1876 A806 34fr multi 3.00 1.50

No. 1876 contains one 48x37mm stamp. See Democratic Republic of Congo (Zaire) Nos. 1613-1614.

100 Cents = 1 Euro (€)

King Albert II — A807

King Albert II — A808

King Albert II — A809

King Albert II — A810

2002-06 **Photo.** ***Perf. 11½***

1877 A808 7c red & gray bl .25 .25
1879 A807 42c red 1.25 .25
1881 A807 47c dark green 1.40 .25
1882 A808 49c red 1.40 .25
1882A A809 49c red 1.40 .25
1882B A809 50c red 1.50 .30
1882C A810 50c multi 1.50 .30
1883 A807 52c blue 1.50 .25
1884 A810 52c red & carmine 1.50 .35
1885 A807 59c dk blue 1.75 .30
1886 A807 60c blue 1.75 .35
1887 A807 60c brt blue + etiquette 1.75 .40
1888 A807 70c brt blue + etiquette 2.00 .45
1888A A810 70c blue 2.00 .45
1889 A808 79c red & ultra 2.25 .40
1890 A809 79c red & ultra 2.25 .50
1891 A809 80c red & ultra 2.25 .45
1892 A807 80c ultra + etiquette 2.25 .50
1893 A810 83c red & bl vio 2.40 .50
1895 A808 €4.21 red & purple 12.50 2.40
Nos. 1877-1895 (20) 44.85 9.15

Issued: 42c, 52c, 1/1/02. 47c, 5/6/02. 7c, 49c, 59c, No. 1889, 11/4/02. €4.21, 8/11/03. No. 1890, 10/6/03. No. 1882A, 10/27/03; 50c, 60c, 80c, 4/19/04. Nos. 1887, 1892, 9/27/04. 70c, 3/21/05. Nos. 1882C, 1888A, 7/21/05. No. 1884, 1/23/06. No. 1893, 3/20/06.

No. 1888A is inscribed "A Prior" at left.

World Cyclo-Cross and Road Bicycling Championships A811

Royal Belgian Tennis Federation, Cent. — A812

No. 1897: a, Rider looking back. b, Rider with fist in air.

No. 1898: a, Women's tennis. b, Men's tennis.

2002, Jan. 21 **Photo.** ***Perf. 11½***

1897 A811 Vert. pair 2.50 1.10
a.-b. 42c Any single 1.25 .55
1898 A812 Horiz. pair 2.50 1.10
a.-b. 42c Any single 1.25 .55

University of Antwerp, 150th Anniv. A813

2002, Feb. 11 **Photo. & Engr.**

1899 A813 42c multi 1.25 .55

Bruges, 2002 European Capital of Culture A814

Designs: No. 1900, Restorations and new architecture (4a). No. 1901, Classical and contemporary music (4b). No. 1902, Classical exhibitions and contemporary art (4c).

2002, Mar. 4 **Photo.**

1900 A814 42c multi 1.25 .55
1901 A814 42c multi 1.25 .55
1902 A814 42c multi 1.25 .55
Nos. 1900-1902 (3) 3.75 1.65

Anna Bijns (1494-1575), Poet — A815

Anna Boch (1848-1936), Painter — A816

2002, Mar. 4

1903 A815 42c multi 1.25 .55
1904 A816 84c multi 2.50 1.10

Stamp Day — A817

2002, Apr. 22 **Photo.** ***Perf. 11½***

1905 A817 47c multi 1.40 .60

Belgian Dog Breeds — A818

Designs: No. 1906, Schipperke. No. 1907, Bouvier des Ardennes. No. 1908, Saint-Hubert. No. 1909, Brussels griffon. No. 1910, Papillon.

2002, Apr. 22 **Photo.** ***Perf. 11½***

Stamp + Label

1906 A818 42c multi 1.25 .60
1907 A818 42c multi 1.25 .60
1908 A818 42c multi 1.25 .60
1909 A818 42c multi 1.25 .60
1910 A818 42c multi 1.25 .60
a. Vert. strip of 5, #1906-1910, + 5 labels 6.50 3.00
Nos. 1906-1910 (5) 6.25 3.00

Europa A819

2002, May 6

1911 A819 52c multi *1.50 .70*

Bird Type of 1985 With Euro Denominations Only

2002-03 **Photo.** ***Perf. 11½***

1912 A524 7c Pigeon colombin .25 .25
1913 A524 25c Huitrier pie .75 .25
1913A A524 35c Pic epeiche 1.00 .25
1913B A524 41c Tourterelle Turque 1.25 .25
1913C A524 57c Guifette noire 1.60 .30
1913D A524 70c Chevalier gambette 2.00 .35

Size:38x27mm

1914 A524 €1 Traquet motteux, horiz. 3.00 .50
1915 A524 €2 Grand gravelot, horiz. 6.00 1.00
1916 A524 €5 Combattant varie, horiz. 14.50 2.50
Nos. 1912-1916 (9) 30.35 5.65

Issued: 7c, 5/6. 25c, 7/15. 35c, 3/31/03. 41c, 57c, 70c, €1, €2, €5, 11/4/02. This is an expanding set.

Leffe Abbey, 850th Anniv. — A820

2002, June 10 Photo. *Perf. 11½*
1917 A820 42c multi + label 1.25 .60

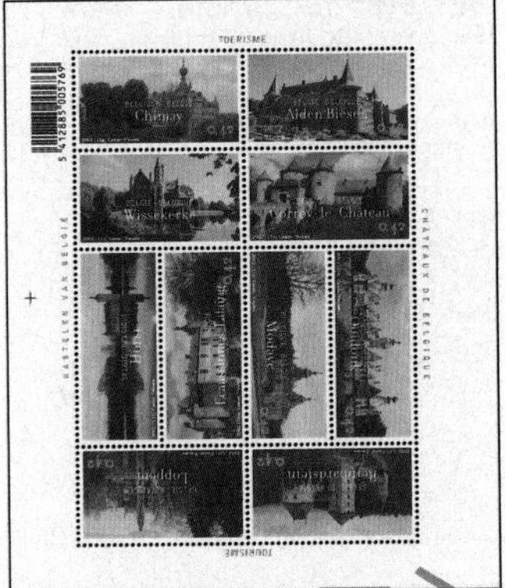
Castles — A821

No. 1918: a, Chimay. b, Alden Biesen. c, Wissekerke. d, Corroy-le-Château. e, Reinhardstein. f, Loppem. g, Horst. h, Ecaussinnes-Lalaing. i, Ooidonk. j, Modave. Nos. 1918a-1918f are 45x24mm; Nos. 1918g-1918j are 52x21mm.

2002, June 10
1918 A821 Sheet of 10 13.00 6.00
a.-j. 42c Any single 1.25 .60

Belgian Post Emblem — A821a

2002, June 15 Photo. *Perf. 11½*
1918K A821a (42c) red 2.10 2.10

Issued in sheets of 15 stamps + 15 labels that could be personalized. The sheets sold for €16.

Horses A822

Designs: 40c, Jumping. 42c, Driving, vert. 52c, St. Paul's Horse Procession, Opwijk, cent., vert.

2002, July 1 Photo. *Perf. 11½*
1919 A822 40c multi 1.25 .60
1920 A822 42c multi 1.25 .65

Souvenir Sheet

1921 A822 52c multi 1.50 1.50

No. 1921 contains one 38x49mm stamp.

Battle of the Courtrai, 700th Anniv. — A823

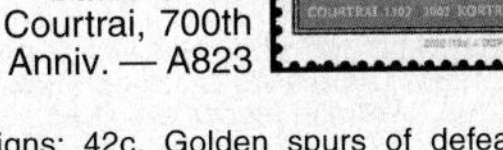

Designs: 42c, Golden spurs of defeated French knights. 52c, Castle.
57c, Battle scene, horiz.

2002, July 15
1922 A823 42c multi 1.25 .65
1923 A823 52c multi 1.50 .75

Souvenir Sheet

1924 A823 57c multi 1.60 1.60

No. 1924 contains one 49x38mm stamp.

Windmills — A824

Designs: 42c, Onze-Lieve-Vrouw-Lombeek windmill, Belgium. 52c, Ilha do Faial windmill, Azores.

2002, July 15 Photo. *Perf. 11½*
1925 A824 42c multi 1.25 .65
1926 A824 52c multi 1.50 .75

See Portugal Azores Nos. 471-472.

Lace — A825

Lace from: 42c, Liedekerke, Belgium. 74c, Pag Island, Croatia.

2002, July 15
1927 A825 42c multi 1.25 .65
1928 A825 74c multi 2.25 1.10

See Croatia Nos. 497-498.

Youth Philately A826

2002, July 15 Photo. *Perf. 11½*
1929 A826 42c multi 1.25 .75

Rights of the Child — A827

2002, Sept. 30 Photo. *Perf. 11½*
1930 A827 42c multi 1.25 .60

Jean Rey (1902-83), Politician — A828

2002, Sept. 30 Photo. & Engr.
1931 A828 52c dk bl & lt bl 1.50 .75

Christmas — A829

No. 1932: a, Family at ice cream truck. b, Ski jumper in Christmas tree. c, Sledder in air, skier in snow. d, Skier on hillside. e, Skiers with torches. f, Boy with ice cream cone. g, Children in snowball fight. h, Children, man and snowman. i, People at snack stand. j, Cow, policeman and burglars.

2002, Oct. 28 Photo.
1932 A829 Sheet of 10 12.50 6.25
a.-j. 41c Any single 1.25 .60

Princess Elizabeth, 1st Birthday A830

Designs: 49c, Princess Elizabeth, vert. 59c, Princesses Elizabeth and Mathilde, Prince Philippe.
84c, Princess Elizabeth, diff.

2002, Nov. 4 Photo. *Perf. 11½*
1933 A830 49c multi 1.40 .75
1934 A830 59c multi 1.75 .95

Souvenir Sheet

1935 A830 84c multi 2.50 2.50

No. 1935 contains one 48x37mm stamp. Margins on sheets of No. 1933, inscribed "Prior," served as etiquettes.

Death Announcement Stamp — A831

2002, Nov. 4
1936 A831 (49c) multi 1.40 .25

Compare with type A882.

Crocuses — A832

Booklet Stamp
Die Cut Perf. 10 on 2 or 3 Sides
2002, Nov. 4 Self-Adhesive
1937 A832 (49c) multi 1.40 .25
a. Booklet pane of 10 14.00

Coil Stamp
Serpentine Die Cut 13¼x13½x13¾x14
1938 A832 (49c) multi 1.40 .25

Compare illustration A832 with A859.

80th Birthday of Cartoonist Marc Sleen — A833

Designs: 49c, Nero and Adhemar. 82c, Sleen with cartoon characters.

2002, Dec. 30 *Perf. 11½*
1939 A833 49c multi 1.40 .75

Souvenir Sheet

1940 A833 82c multi 2.40 2.40

No. 1940 contains one 48x37mm stamp. Margins on sheets of No. 1939, inscribed "Prior," served as etiquettes.

Henry van de Velde (1863-1957), Architect — A834

Designs: 49c, New House, Tervuren, 1927-28 (1a). No. 1942, Paris World's Fair Pavilion, 1937 (1b), vert. No. 1943, Book Tower, Ghent (1c), vert.
84c, Marie Sèthe, wife of van de Velde, on Art Nouveau staircase, vert.

2003, Jan. 27
1941 A834 49c multi 1.40 .80
1942 A834 59c multi 1.75 .95
1943 A834 59c multi 1.75 .95
Nos. 1941-1943 (3) 4.90 2.70

Souvenir Sheet

1944 A834 84c multi 2.50 2.50

No. 1944 contains one 37x48mm stamp. Margins on sheets of No. 1941, inscribed "Prior," served as etiquettes.

Love for Service Occupations A835

No. 1945: a, Firefighters. b, Police. c, Civil defense workers. d, Nurses. e, Postal workers. f, Birdcage and hearts.

2003, Jan. 27
1945 Sheet of 10, #1945e-1945f, 2 each #1945a-1945d 15.00 15.00
a.-f. A835 49c Any single 1.40 .80

Margins on sheets, inscribed "Prior," served as etiquettes.

Hector Berlioz (1803-69), Composer A836

2003, Feb. 24
1946 A836 59c multi 1.75 .95

Traditional Sports A837

Designs: No. 1947, Lawn bowling (4a). No. 1948, Archery (4b).
82c, Pigeon racing, vert.

2003, Feb. 24
1947 A837 49c multi 1.40 .80
1948 A837 49c multi 1.40 .80

Souvenir Sheet

1949 A837 82c multi 2.40 1.75

No. 1949 contains one 37x48mm stamp. Margins on sheets of Nos. 1947-1948, inscribed "Prior," served as etiquettes.

Organization Anniversaries
A838

Designs: No. 1950, Association of Engineers of Mons sesquicentennial (5a). No. 1951, Solvay Business School centennial (5b).

2003, Mar. 17

1950	A838 49c multi		1.40	.80
1951	A838 49c multi		1.40	.80

Margins on sheets of Nos. 1950-1951, inscribed "Prior," served as etiquettes.

Liège International Flower Show — A839

2003, Apr. 28 Photo. *Perf. 11½*

1952	A839 49c multi	1.40	.80

Margins on sheets, inscribed "Prior," served as etiquettes.

Georges Simenon (1903-89), Writer — A840

Designs: 49c, Poster for "Maigret Sets a Trap." 59c, Poster for "The Cat." 84c, Simenon at typewriter.

2003, Apr. 28

1953	A840 49c multi	1.40	.80
1954	A840 59c multi	1.75	1.10

Souvenir Sheet

1955	A840 84c multi	2.50	2.00

No. 1955 contains one 38x48mm stamp. Margins on sheets of No. 1953, inscribed "Prior," served as etiquettes.

Carillons — A841

No. 1956: a, St. Rombout's Cathedral, Mechelen (denomination at left). b, Sts. Peter and Paul Cathedral, St. Petersburg, Russia (denomination at right).

Photo. & Engr.

2003, May 12 *Perf. 11½*

1956	A841 Horiz. pair	4.00	2.25
a.-b.	59c Either single	1.75	1.10

See Russia No. 6767.

Stamp Day — A842

2003, May 19 Photo. *Perf. 11½*

1957	A842 49c multi	1.40	.95

Margins on sheets, inscribed "Prior," served as etiquettes.

Youth Philately — A843

2003, May 19

1958	A843 49c multi	1.40	.95

Margins on sheets, inscribed "Prior," served as etiquettes.

Belgian Post Emblem — A844

2003 Photo. *Perf. 11½*

1959	A844 49c red	2.50	2.50

Issued in sheets of 15 stamps + 15 labels that could be personalized. The sheets sold for €16.

Minerals
A845

No. 1960: a, Calcite (11a). b, Quartz (11b). c, Barite (11c). d, Galena (11d). e, Turquoise (11e).

2003, June 30 Photo. *Perf. 11½*

1960	Vert. strip of 5	7.00	7.00
a.-e.	A845 49c Any single	1.40	.80

Issued in sheets of 2 strips. Margins on sheets, inscribed "Prior," served as etiquettes.

Europa — A846

2003, June 30

1961	A846 59c multi	*1.75*	*1.00*

Tourism — A847

No. 1962: a, La Robe de Mariée, by Paul Delvaux (Koksijde, 13a). b, Tapestry (Oudenaarde, 13b). c, Fist sculpture by Rik Poot, City Hall (Vilvoorde, 13c). d, Royal Castle, playing card suits (Turnhout, 13d). e, Statue of Ambiorix, Gallo-Roman Museum (Tongeren, 13e). f, Fountain by Pol Bury, mineshaft frame (La Louvière, 13f), g, City Hall, lion statue (Braine l'Alleud, 13g). h, Forest, Mardasson Memorial (Bastogne, 13i). i, Büchtelturm, snow-covered tree (Sankt Vith, 13j). j, Saxophone, Citadel (Dinant, 13h).

2003, July 7

1962	A847 Sheet of 10	13.00	13.00
a.-g.	41c Any single	1.25	.65
h.-i.	52c Either single	1.50	.85
j.	57c multi	1.60	.95

Statues and Fountains — A848

Designs: No. 1963, Monument to the Seasonal Worker, Rillaar (14a). No. 1964, La Toinade, Treignes (14b). No. 1965, Hamont Textile Teut, Hamont-Achel (14c). No. 1966, Vaartkapoen, Brussels (14d). No. 1967, Maca, Wavre (14e).

2003, July 7

1963	A848 49c multi	1.40	.85
1964	A848 49c multi	1.40	.85
1965	A848 49c multi	1.40	.85
1966	A848 49c multi	1.40	.85
1967	A848 49c multi	1.40	.85
	Nos. 1963-1967 (5)	7.00	4.25

Margins on sheets, inscribed "Prior," served as etiquettes.

A849

Kings Baudouin and Albert II — A850

2003, Aug. 11

1968	A849 49c multi	1.40	.85

Souvenir Sheet

1969	A850 Sheet of 2	4.50	4.50
a.	59c King Baudouin	1.75	.95
b.	84c King Albert II	2.50	1.40

Reign of King Albert II, 10th anniv.

Bird Type of 1985 with Euro Denominations Only

2003-04 Photo. *Perf. 11½*

1970	A524	1c Rossignol philomèle	.25	.25
1971	A524	2c Becassine des Marais	.25	.25
1972	A524	40c Gobemouche gris	1.10	.25
1973	A524	44c Hirondelle de fenetre	1.25	.25
1974	A524	52c Huppe fasciée	1.50	.30
1975	A524	55c Petit gravelot	1.60	.30
1976	A524	65c Mouette rieuse	1.90	.40
1977	A524	75c Pluvier doré	2.25	.45

Size: 38x27mm

1978	A524	€3.72 Poule d'Eau	11.00	2.25
1979	A524	€4 Hibou grand-duc	12.00	2.40
		Nos. 1970-1979 (10)	33.10	7.10

Issued: 2c, 52c, 8/11. 1c, 40c, 44c, 55c, 65c, 75c, €4, 4/19/04. €3.72, 10/27. This is an expanding set. Numbers may change.

Europalia Italia Festival, Belgium
A851

Designs: 49c, Still Life, by Giorgio Morandi. 59c, 1947 Cisitalia 202, designed by Battista Pininfarina.

2003, Sept. 15 Photo. *Perf. 11½*

1980	A851 49c multi	1.40	.55
1981	A851 59c multi	1.75	.70

See Italy Nos. 2568-2569. Margins on sheets of No. 1980, inscribed "Prior," served as etiquettes.

Saint Nicholas — A852

2003, Oct. 27

1982	A852 49c multi	1.40	.55

Margins on sheets, inscribed "Prior," served as etiquettes.

Social Cohesion
A853

2003, Oct. 27

1983	A853 49c multi	1.40	.55

Margins on sheets, inscribed "Prior," served as etiquettes.

Miniature Sheet

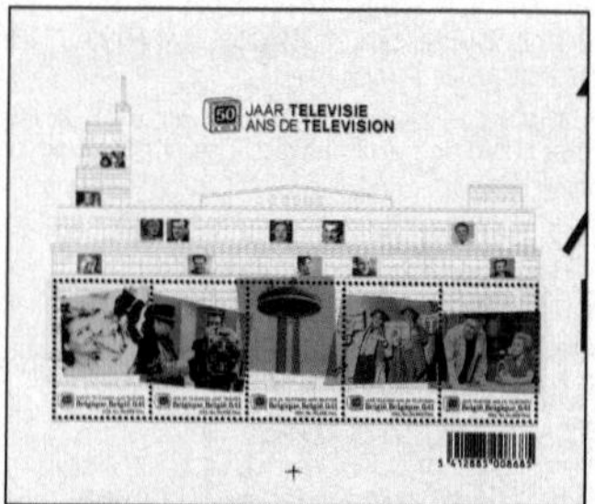

Belgian Television, 50th Anniv. — A854

No. 1984: a, Jardin Extraordinaire (yellow panel, 18a). b, Old camera (blue panel, 18b). c, Broadcasting tower (green panel, 18c). d, Cassiers and Jef Burm (red violet panel, 18d). e, Schipper Naast Mathilde (red panel, 18e).

2003, Nov. 3

1984	A854 Sheet of 5	6.25	6.25
a.-e.	41c Any single	1.25	.50

Books — A855

Authors — A856

Books and: No. 1985, Man with apple (19a). No. 1986, Duplicating machine (19b), horiz. No. 1987, Woman reader, cat (19c).

2003, Nov. 12

1985 A855 49c multi 1.40 .60
1986 A855 49c multi 1.40 .60
1987 A855 49c multi 1.40 .60
Nos. 1985-1987 (3) 4.20 1.80

Margins on sheets, inscribed "Prior," served as etiquettes.

2003, Nov. 12

Designs: 49c, Maurice Gilliams (1900-82). 59c, Marguerite Yourcenar (1903-87).

1988 A856 49c brown 1.40 .60
1989 A856 59c org brn & org 1.75 .70

Margins on sheets of No. 1988, inscribed "Prior," served as etiquettes.

Christmas — A857

2003, Nov. 17

1990 A857 41c multi + label 1.25 .50

Yellow Tulips — A858 Crocuses — A859

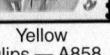

Booklet Stamp

Die Cut Perf. 9¾ on 2 or 3 Sides

2003 Photo. Self-Adhesive

1991 A858 (59c) multi 1.75 .35
a. Booklet pane of 10 17.50

Coil Stamp

Serpentine Die Cut 13¾x14x13¼x13½

1992 A859 (49c) multi 1.40 .30

Issued: No. 1991, 11/12. Compare illustration A859 with A832.

Tennis Players — A860

Designs: No. 1993, Justine Henin-Hardenne. No. 1994, Kim Clijsters, horiz.

2003, Nov. 24 ***Perf. 11½***

1993 A860 49c multi 1.40 .60
1994 A860 49c multi 1.40 .60

Margins on sheets, inscribed "Prior," served as etiquettes.

Red Carnations A861

Booklet Stamp

Die Cut Perf. 9¾ on 2 or 3 Sides

2004, Jan. 19 Self-Adhesive

1995 A861 (49c) multi 1.40 .30
a. Booklet pane of 10 14.00

Miniature Sheet

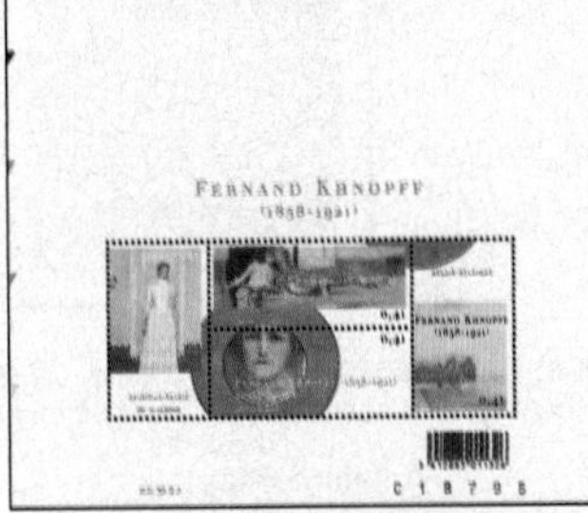

Art by Fernand Khnopff (1858-1921) — A862

No. 1996: a, Portrait of Marguerite Khnopff (1a, 27x48mm). b, Caresses (1b, 55x24mm). c, Brown Eyes and a Blue Flower (1c, 55x24mm). d, An Abandoned City (1d, 27x48mm).

2004, Jan. 19 ***Perf. 11½***

1996 A862 Sheet of 4 5.00 5.00
a.-d. 41c Any single 1.25 .50

Youth Philately A863

2004, Jan. 19

1997 A863 41c multi 1.25 .50

Miniature Sheet

Famous Belgians — A864

No. 1998: a, Peter Piot, director of UN Program on AIDS (3a). b, Nicole Van Goethem, film director (3b). c, Dirk Frimout and Frank de Winne, astronauts (3c). d, Jacques Rogge, Intl. Olympic Committee President (3d). e, Christian de Duve, 1974 Nobel laureate in Physiology or Medicine (3e). f, Gabrielle Petit, World War II heroine (3f). g, Catherine Verfaille and Christine Van Broeckhoven, medical researchers (3g). h, Jacques Stibbe, philatelist (3h). i, Queen Fabiola (3i). j, Adrien van der Burch, patron of 1935 Brussels Intl. Exhibition (3j).

2004, Feb. 16

1998 A864 Sheet of 10 16.00 16.00
a.-j. 57c Any single 1.60 .70

Stamp Day A865

2004, Feb. 16

1999 A865 41c multi 1.25 .50

Sugar Industry A866

Designs: No. 2000, Sugar beet (5a). No. 2001, Refinery (5b). No. 2002, Street in Tienen (5c).

2004, Mar. 15

2000 A866 49c multi 1.40 .60
2001 A866 49c multi 1.40 .60
2002 A866 49c multi 1.40 .60
Nos. 2000-2002 (3) 4.20 1.80

Miniature Sheet

Tintin and the Moon — A867

No. 2003: a, Model of Tintin and rocket (6a). b, Technical sketch of rockets for "Destination Moon" (6b). c, Tintin on spacecraft mattress, from "Destination Moon" (6c). d, Tintin on spacecraft ladder, from "Explorers on the Moon" (6d). e, Tintin on Moon, from "Explorers on the Moon" (6e).

2004, Mar. 15

2003 A867 Sheet of 5 6.25 6.25
a.-e. 41c Any single 1.25 .50

European Parliament Elections A868

2004, Apr. 19

2004 A868 22c multi .65 .25

Miniature Sheet

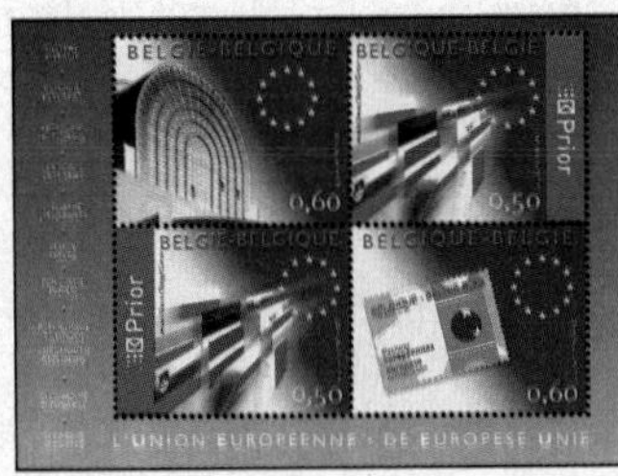

Expansion of the European Union — A869

No. 2005: a, Flags of newly-added countries, "Prior" at right (8bis b). b, As "a," "Prior" at left (8bis c). c, European Parliament, Brussels (8bis a). d, #2004 (8bis d).

2004, Apr. 19 ***Perf. 11½***

2005 A869 Sheet of 4, #a-d 6.50 6.50
a.-b. 50c Either single 1.50 .60
c.-d. 60c Either single 1.75 .70

Religious Buildings — A870

Designs: No. 2006, Chapel in the Woods, Buggenhout (9a). No. 2007, Sanctuary, Banneaux. (9b). No. 2008, Scherpenheuvel Basilica, Montaigu (9c). No. 2009, Sanctuary, Beauraing, horiz. (9d).

2004, Apr. 19 **Engr.**

2006 A870 49c green 1.40 .60
2007 A870 49c brown 1.40 .60
2008 A870 49c purple 1.40 .60
2009 A870 49c blue 1.40 .60
Nos. 2006-2009 (4) 5.60 2.40

Margins on sheets, inscribed "Prior," served as etiquettes.

A871

Belgian Post Emblem — A872

2004, Apr. 19 **Photo.**

2010 A871 49c red 1.40 .60
2011 A872 (49c) red 1.40 .60

Compare illustration A871 with A844.

Liège A873

Designs: No. 2012, Museum of Modern and Contemporary Art, sculpture, by Jef Lambeaux (10a). No. 2013, Bridge designed by Santiago Calatrava (10b).

75c, Steel foundry equipment, vert. (10c).

2004, May 17 Photo. ***Perf. 11½***

2012 A873 44c multi 1.25 .55
2013 A873 44c multi 1.25 .55

Souvenir Sheet

2014 A873 75c multi 2.25 2.25

No. 2014 contains one 38x49mm stamp.

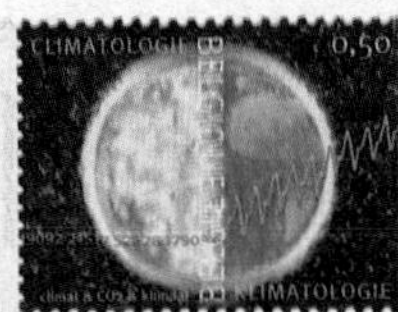

Climatology A874

Designs: 50c, Climate and cabon dioxide (11a). 65c, Relations between Sun and Earth (11b). No. 2017, Earth (11c). No. 2018, Sun (11d).

2004, May 17

2015 A874 50c multi 1.50 .60
2016 A874 65c multi 1.90 .80
2017 A874 80c multi 2.40 .95
2018 A874 80c multi 2.40 .95
Nos. 2015-2018 (4) 8.20 3.30

Margins on sheets of Nos. 2015 and 2017, inscribed "Prior," served as etiquettes.

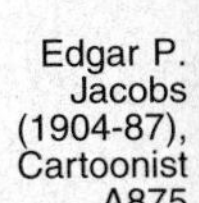

Edgar P. Jacobs (1904-87), Cartoonist A875

Blake and Mortimer, by Jacobs — A876

2004, May 24

2019 A875 60c multi 1.75 .75

Souvenir Sheet

2020 A876 €1.20 multi 3.50 3.00

See France No. 3027.

Jazz Musicians A877

Designs: No. 2021, Django Reinhardt (1910-53), guitarist (13a). No. 2022, Fud Candrix (1908-74), saxophonist (13b). No. 2023, René Thomas (1927-75), guitarist (13c). No. 2024, Jack Sels (1922-70), saxophonist (13d). No. 2025, Bobby Jaspar (1926-63), saxophonist (13e).

2004, May 24

2021 A877 50c multi 1.50 .60
2022 A877 50c multi 1.50 .60
2023 A877 50c multi 1.50 .60
2024 A877 50c multi 1.50 .60
2025 A877 50c multi 1.50 .60
Nos. 2021-2025 (5) 7.50 3.00

Expansion of European Union — A878

No. 2026 — Flags of newly-admitted countries: a, Cyprus. b, Estonia. c, Hungary. d, Latvia. e, Lithuania. f, Malta. g, Poland. h, Czech Republic. i, Slovakia. j, Slovenia.

Die Cut Perf. 10 on 2 or 3 Sides

2004, June 7 **Photo.**

Self-Adhesive

2026 Booklet pane of 10 12.50
a.-j. A878 44c Any single 1.25 .55

King Albert II, 70th Birthday A879

2004, June 7 ***Perf. 11½***

2027 A879 50c shown 1.50 .60

Souvenir Sheet

2028 A879 80c Close-up 2.40 2.40

Margins on sheets of No. 2027, inscribed "Prior," served as etiquettes. No. 2028 contains one 38x49mm stamp.

Europa A880

Photography contest winners: No. 2029, The Belgian Coast, by Muriel Vekemans (15a). No. 2030, The Belgian Ardennes, by Freddy Deburghgraeve (15b).

2004, June 7

2029 A880 55c multi *1.60 .60*
2030 A880 55c multi *1.60 .60*

2004 Summer Olympics, Athens A881

Designs: 50c, Women's basketball, vert. 55c, Mountain biking. 60c, Pole vault. 80c, Olympic torch.

2004, July 12

2031 A881 50c multi 1.50 .60
2032 A881 55c multi 1.60 .70
2033 A881 60c multi 1.75 .75
Nos. 2031-2033 (3) 4.85 2.05

Souvenir Sheet

2034 A881 80c multi 2.00 2.00

Margins on sheets of No. 2031, inscribed "Prior," served as etiquettes. No. 2034 contains one 49x38mm stamp.

Death Announcement Stamp — A882

2004, Sept. 20

2035 A882 (50c) multi 1.50 .60

Compare with type A831.

Sculptures by Idel Ianchelevici (1909-94) — A883

Designs: 50c, L'appel (18a). 55c, Perennis Perdurat Poeta (18b).

2004, Sept. 20

2036 A883 50c multi 1.50 .60
2037 A883 55c multi 1.60 .70

Margins on sheets of No. 2036, inscribed "Prior," served as etiquettes.
See Romania Nos. 4666-4667.

Impatiens — A884

Booklet Stamp

Die Cut Perf. 10x9¾ on 2 or 3 Sides

2004 **Photo.** **Self-Adhesive**

2038 A884 (50c) multi 1.50 .30
a. Booklet pane of 10 15.00

Coil Stamp

Serpentine Die Cut 13¾x14

2039 A884 (50c) multi 1.50 .30

Issued: No. 2038, 9/27; No. 2039, 12/15.

Belgian World War II Volunteers Medal A885

2004, Sept. 27 **Photo.** ***Perf. 11½***

2040 A885 50c multi 1.50 .60

Miniature Sheet

Forest Week — A886

No. 2041: a, Squirrel and blackcap. b, Nightingale, robin and red admiral butterfly. c, Bumblebee, vole, flowers, mushrooms, head of weasel. d, Jay, flowers, rear of weasel, left wing of peacock butterfly.

2004, Sept. 27

2041 A886 Sheet of 4 5.00 5.00
a.-d. 44c Any single 1.25 .55

Miniature Sheet

Belgica 2006 World Youth Philatelic Exhibition — A887

No. 2042: a, Pony. b, Robin. c, Kitten. d, Puppy. e, Fish.

2004, Oct. 18

2042 A887 Sheet of 5 13.00 13.00
a.-e. 44c Any single 2.60 2.60

No. 2042 sold for €5, with €2.80 of this going to fund the exhibition.

Halloween — A888

Designs: No. 2043, Witch, bats and black cat. No. 2044, Jack o'lantern and bats.

Booklet Stamp

Die Cut Perf. 10x9¾ on 2 or 3 Sides

2004, Oct. 18 **Self-Adhesive**

2043 A888 44c multi 1.25 .30
2044 A888 44c multi 1.25 .30
a. Booklet pane, 5 each #2043-2044 12.50

Writers A889

Designs: 50c, Raymond Jean de Kremer (pen names Jean Ray and John Flanders) (1887-1964). 75c, Johan Daisne (1912-78). 80c, Gérald Bertot (pen name Thomas Owen) (1910-2002), vert.

2004, Nov. 3 ***Perf. 11½***

2045 A889 50c multi 1.50 .70
2046 A889 75c multi 2.25 .95
2047 A889 80c multi 2.40 1.10
Nos. 2045-2047 (3) 6.15 2.75

Margins on sheets of Nos. 2045 and 2047, inscribed "Prior," served as etiquettes.

Battle of the Bulge, 60th Anniv. A890

Designs: 44c, Urban warfare. 55c, Tank, war victims, vert. 65c, Soldiers in forest.

2004, Nov. 3

2048 A890 44c multi 1.25 .60
2049 A890 55c multi 1.60 .70
2050 A890 65c multi 1.90 .85
Nos. 2048-2050 (3) 4.75 2.15

Christmas A891

Paintings by Peter Paul Rubens: No. 2051, The Flight Into Egypt. Nos. 2052, 2053, Adoration of the Magi.

2004, Nov. 22 ***Perf. 11½***

2051 A891 44c tan & multi 1.25 .60
2052 A891 44c blue & multi 1.25 .60

Self-Adhesive

Booklet Stamp

Size: 22x22mm

Die Cut Perf. 10x9¾ on 2 or 3 Sides

2053 A891 44c blue & multi 1.25 .60
a. Booklet pane of 10 12.50

See Germany Nos. B946-B947.

Miniature Sheet

Champion Motocross Riders — A892

No. 2054: a, René Baeten. b, Jacky Martens. c, Georges Jobe. d, Joel Robert. e, Eric Geboers. f, Roger De Coster. g, Stefan Everts. h, Gaston Rahier. i, Joel Smets. j, Harry Everts. k, André Malherbe. l, Steve Ramon.

2004, Nov. 22 ***Perf. 11½***

2054 A892 Sheet of 12 + central label and 12 etiquettes 16.00 16.00
a.-l. 50c Any single 1.25 .65

Belgian Post Emblem — A893

2005, Jan. 17
2055 A893 6c red .25 .25

Women's Council, Cent. — A894

2005, Jan. 17 Photo. *Perf. 11½*
2056 A894 50c multi 1.50 .65

Margins on sheets, inscribed "Prior," served as etiquettes.

Michel Vaillant, Comic Strip by Jean Graton A895

2005, Jan. 17 Photo. *Perf. 11½*
2057 A895 50c multi 1.50 .65

Website for Belgium's 175th Anniversary Celebrations A896

Die Cut Perf. 10 on 3 Sides
2005, Feb. 14 Photo.
Self-Adhesive
Booklet Stamp
2058 A896 (50c) multi 1.50 .30
a. Booklet pane of 10 15.00

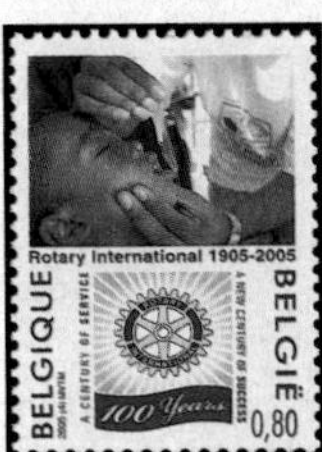

Rotary International, Cent. — A897

2005, Feb. 14 *Perf. 11½*
2059 A897 80c multi 2.40 1.10

Linguists A898

Designs: No. 2060, Maurice Grevisse (1895-1980), French language grammarian (5a). No. 2061, Johan Hendrik van Dale (1828-72), Dutch language lexicographer (5b).

2004, Feb. 12
2060 A898 55c multi 1.60 .75
2061 A898 55c multi 1.60 .75

Souvenir Sheet

King Albert II and Queen Paola — A899

2005, Feb. 28
2062 A899 75c multi 2.25 2.25

Belgian Independence, 175th anniv.
No. 2062 was later sold in a presentation folder that additionally contained a €4 silver stamp depicting Kings Leopold I and Albert I. This folder sold for €10.

Miniature Sheet

Belgian Independence, 175th Anniv. — A900

No. 2063 — History of Belgium: a, First train (6bis a). b, Bakuba dancer, Belgian Congo (6bis b). c, Teacher in classroom (6bis c). d, Industrialization (6bis d). e, Family (Social progress) (6bis e). f, War (6bis f). g, 1958 World's Fair (6bis g). h, Street sign (Federalism) (6bis h). i, Berlaymont Building (Europe) (6bis i). j, L'Ombre et son Ombre, by René Magritte (Art) (6bis j).

2005, Feb. 28
2063 A900 Sheet of 10 12.50 12.50
a.-j. 44c Any single 1.25 .60

A901

Belgica 2006 World Youth Philatelic Exhibition — A902

Designs: Nos. 2064a, 2065, Space Shuttle (8a). Nos. 2064b, 2067, Airplane (8b). Nos. 2064c, 2066, Train (8c). Nos. 2064d, 2068 Race car (8d). Nos. 2064e, 2069, Motorboat (8e).

2005, Mar. 21 *Perf. 11½*
2064 A901 Sheet of 5 13.00 13.00
a.-e. 44c Any single 2.60 2.60

Booklet Stamps
Self-Adhesive
Die Cut Perf. 10 on 3 Sides
2065 A902 44c multi 1.25 .30
2066 A902 44c multi 1.25 .30
2067 A902 44c multi 1.25 .30
2068 A902 44c multi 1.25 .30
2069 A902 44c multi 1.25 .30
a. Booklet pane, 2 each #2065-2069 12.50

No. 2064 sold for €5, with €2.80 of this going to fund the exhibition.

Belgian Post Emblem — A903

2005, Mar. 21 *Perf. 11½*
2070 A903 10c bright blue .50 .25

Bird Type of 1985 With Euro Denominations Only
2005 Photo. *Perf. 11½*
2071 A524 3c Mesange nonnette .25 .25
2072 A524 5c Bruant zizi .25 .25
2073 A524 20c Mouette melanocephale .60 .25
2074 A524 44c Pigeon ramier 1.25 .30
2075 A524 60c Perdrix grise 1.75 .40
2076 A524 75c Roitelet triple-bandeau 2.25 .50
Nos. 2072-2076 (5) 6.10 1.70

Issued: 5c, 20c, 60c, 3/21. 3c, 44c, 75c, 4/4.

Rose Varieties A904

Designs: 44c, Belinda (9a). 70c, Pink Iceberg, vert. (9b). 80c, Old Master (9c).

2005, Apr. 4 Photo. *Perf. 11½*
2077 A904 44c multi 1.25 .55
2078 A904 70c multi 2.00 .95
2079 A904 80c multi 2.40 1.10
Nos. 2077-2079 (3) 5.65 2.60

2005 Ghent Flower Show. Nos. 2077-2079 are impregnated with a rose scent. Margins on sheets of No. 2079, inscribed "Prior," served as etiquettes.

Europa — A905

No. 2080: a, The Children's Table, by Gustave van de Woestijne (10a). b, Still Life With Oysters, Fruit and Pastry, by Clara Peeters (10b).

2005, Apr. 4
2080 A905 Horiz. pair *3.75 1.50*
a.-b. 60c Either single *1.75 .70*

Black Stork A906

2005, Apr. 4 Photo. & Engr.
2081 A906 €4 multi 12.00 5.25

Stamp Day.

End of World War II, 60th Anniv. A907

Designs: No. 2082, Soldiers and civilians celebrating (12a). No. 2083, Drawing of concentration camp internee, by Wilchar (12b). No. 2084, Photograph of liberated concentration camp internees (12c).

2005, May 9 Photo.
2082 A907 44c multi 1.25 .55
2083 A907 44c multi 1.25 .55
2084 A907 44c multi 1.25 .55
Nos. 2082-2084 (3) 3.75 1.65

Return of Last Belgian Battalion from Korean War, 50th Anniv. — A908

2005, May 9 *Perf. 11½*
2085 A908 44c multi 1.25 .55

Clocks — A909

Designs: No. 2086, Zimmer Tower clock, Lier (14a). No. 2087, Belfry of Mons clock (14b). No. 2088, Mont des Arts clock, Brussels (14c).

2005, May 9 Engr.
2086 A909 44c deep blue 1.25 .55
2087 A909 44c dark brown 1.25 .55
2088 A909 44c brown 1.25 .55
Nos. 2086-2088 (3) 3.75 1.65

Vacations A910

Designs: No. 2089, Woman on beach, bird (14bis a). No. 2090, Man in Ardennes Forest, deer (14bis b).

2005, May 9 Photo.
2089 A910 50c multi + etiquette 1.50 .60
2090 A910 50c multi + etiquette 1.50 .60

Hearts — A911

Darwinhybrid Tulips — A912

Baby Boy — A913

Baby Girl — A914

Doves and Wedding Rings — A915

Wedding Rings — A916

Die Cut Perf. 9¾ on 2 or 3 Sides

2005, May 9 **Photo.**

Booklet Stamps

Self-Adhesive

2091	A911	(50c) multi	1.50	.30
a.		Booklet pane of 10	15.00	
2092	A912	A multi	2.00	.45
a.		Booklet pane of 10	20.00	
2093	A913	80c multi	2.40	.50
a.		Booklet pane of 10	24.00	
2094	A914	80c multi	2.40	.50
a.		Booklet pane of 10	24.00	
2095	A915	80c multi	2.40	.50
2096	A916	80c multi	2.40	.50
a.		Booklet pane of 10, 5 each #2095-2096	24.00	
		Nos. 2091-2096 (6)	13.10	2.75

No. 2092 sold for 70c on day of issue.

Miniature Sheet

International Judo Champions From Belgium — A917

No. 2097: a, Robert Van de Walle (15a). b, Ingrid Berghmans (15b). c, Ulla Werbrouck (15c). d, Gella Vandecaveye (15d). e, Christel Deliège (15e). f, Johan Laats (15f).

2005, June 20 **Photo.** ***Perf. 11½***

2097	A917	Sheet of 6	9.00	9.00
a.-f.		50c Any single	1.50	.60

Tapestries and Carpets — A918

Designs: 44c, L'humanité Assaillie par les Sept Péchés Capitaux tapestry, Belgium (16a). 60c, Carpet from Hereke region, Turkey (16b).

2005, June 20

2098	A918	44c multi	1.25	.55
2099	A918	60c multi	1.75	.70

See Turkey Nos. 2943-2944.

National Radio Broadcasting Institute, 75th Anniv. — A919

2005, June 20

2100	A919	50c multi	1.50	.60

Margins on sheets, inscribed "Prior," served as etiquettes.

Souvenir Sheet

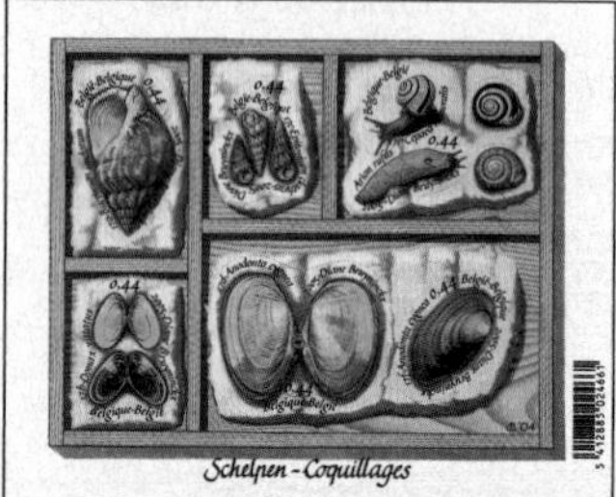

Shells and Snails — A920

No. 2101: a, Buccinum undatum (31x46mm, 17a). b, Donax vittatus (29x38mm, 17b). c, Epitonium clathrus (25x33mm, 17c). d, Interior of Anodonta cygnea (42x48mm, 17d). e, Cepaea nemoralis, Arion rufus (33x40mm, 17e). f, Exterior of Anodonta cygnea (32x34mm, 17f).

2005, July 25 **Photo.** ***Die Cut***

Self-Adhesive

2101	A920	Sheet of 6	7.50	
a.-f.		44c Any single	1.25	.55

Chrysanthemums A921

Die Cut Perf. 10 on 2 or 3 Sides

2005, Sept. 12 **Photo.**

Self-Adhesive

Booklet Stamp

2102	A921	(50c) multi	1.50	.35
a.		Booklet pane of 10	15.00	

Shrine of Our Lady, by Nicolas of Verdun, 800th Anniv. A922

2005, Sept. 12 **Photo.** ***Perf. 11½***

2103	A922	75c multi	2.25	.95

Buildings in Belgium and Singapore — A923

Designs: No. 2104, Belgian Center for Comic Strip Art, Brussels (19a). No. 2105, Museum of Musical Instruments, Brussels (19b). No. 2106, Shops on Bukit Pasoh Road, Singapore (19c). No. 2107, Shop on Kandahar Street, Singapore (19d).

2005, Sept. 12

2104	A923	44c multi	1.25	.55
2105	A923	44c multi	1.25	.55
2106	A923	65c multi	1.90	.80
2107	A923	65c multi	1.90	.80
		Nos. 2104-2107 (4)	6.30	2.70

See Singapore Nos. 1160-1163.

Europalia Festival A924

Paintings by Russian artists: 50c, The Reaper, by Kasimir Malevitch (19bis a). 70c, Allegorical Scene, by Sergei Sudeikin (19bis b).

2005, Sept. 12

2108	A924	50c multi	1.50	.60
2109	A924	70c multi	2.00	.85

Margins on sheets of No. 2108, inscribed "Prior," served as etiquettes.

Miniature Sheet

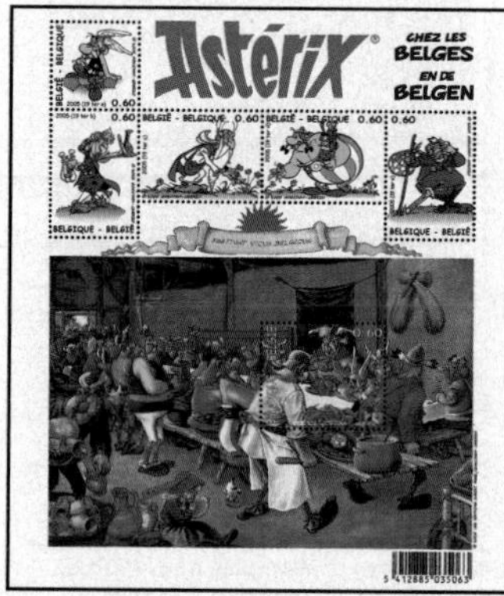

Asterix in Belgium — A925

No. 2110: a, Asterix (27x27mm, 19 ter a). b, Cacofonix (27x40mm, 19 ter b). c, Getafix (38x28mm, 19 ter c) d, Obelix (38x28mm, 19 ter d). e, Vitalstatistix (27x40mm, 19 ter e). f, Asterix at banquet (38x32mm, 19 ter f).

2005, Sept. 24 **Photo.** ***Perf. 11½***

2110	A925	Sheet of 6	10.50	10.50
a.-f.		60c Any single	1.75	.70

Miniature Sheet

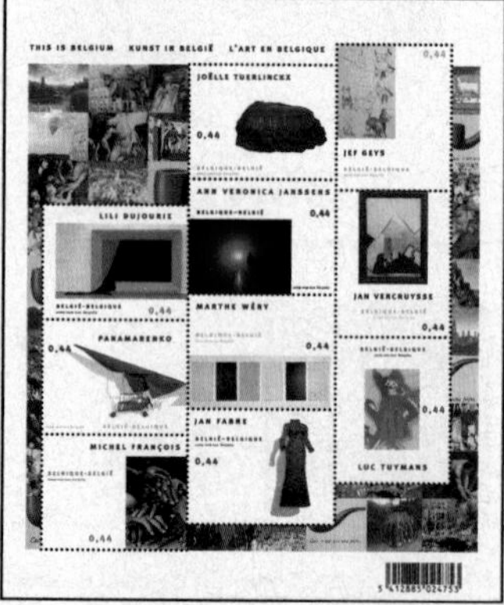

Contemporary Art — A926

No. 2111: a, La Traviata, by Lili Dujourie (20b). b, Donderwalk, by Panamarenko (20h). c, Jeu de Mains, by Michel François (20a). d, OBJET Noir, by Joelle Tuerlinckx (20c). e, Représentation d'un Corps Rond, by Ann Veronica Janssens (20g). f, Tournus, by Marthe Wéry (20e). g, Mur de Montée des Anges, by Jan Fabre (20d). h, ABC Ecole d Paris, by Jef Geys, vert. (20f). i, Portrait of an Artist by Himself (XII), by Jan Vercruysse, vert. (20i). j, Figuur op de Rug Gezien, by Luc Tuymans, vert. (20j).

2005, Oct. 10

2111	A926	Sheet of 10	12.50	12.50
a.-j.		44c multi	1.25	.55

Miniature Sheet

Hans Christian Andersen (1805-75), Author — A927

No. 2112 — Stories by Andersen: a, The Princess and the Pea (21a). b, The Ugly Duckling (21b). c, Thumbelina (21c). d, The Little Mermaid (21d). e, The Emperor's New Clothes (21e).

2005, Oct. 10 **Photo.** ***Perf. 11½***

2112	A927	Sheet of 5	7.50	7.50
a.-e.		50c Any single	1.50	.60

Left margins on No. 2112, inscribed "Prior" served as etiquettes.

Hans Christian Andersen (1805-75), Author — A927a

Nos. 2113: a, The Princess and the Pea, "Prior" at L (21a). b, As "a," "Prior" at R. c, The Ugly Duckling, "Prior" at L (21b). d, As "c," "Prior" at R. e, Thumbelina, "Prior" at L (21c). f, As "e," "Prior" at R. g, The Little Mermaid, "Prior" at L (21d). h, As "g," "Prior" at R. i, The Emperor's New Clothes, "Prior" at L (21d). j, As "i," "Prior" at R.

Die Cut 9¾ on 2 or 3 Sides

2005, Oct. 10 **Photo.**

Self-Adhesive

2113		Booklet pane of 10	15.00	
a.-j.		A927a 50c Any single	1.50	.60

Brass Band Musicians — A928

No. 2114: a, Bass drum (22a). b, Trumpet (22b). c, Sousaphone (22c). d, Clarinet (22d). e, Tuba (22e).

2005, Oct. 31 ***Perf. 11½***

2114		Booklet pane of 5+5 etiquettes	7.50	—
a.-e.		A928 50c Any single	1.50	.60
		Complete booklet, #2114	7.50	

Writers — A929

No. 2118: a, Maurits Sabbe (1873-1938) (23a). b, Arthur Masson (1896-1970) (23b).

2005, Oct. 31 Photo. *Perf. 11½*

2118 A929 Horiz. pair 2.50 2.50
a.-b. 44c Either single 1.25 .55

Christmas — A930

2005, Oct. 31 Photo. *Perf. 11½*

2119 A930 44c multi 1.25 .55

Christmas Type of 2005

Die Cut Perf. 9¾ on 2 or 3 Sides

2005, Oct. 31 Photo.

Booklet Stamp

Self-Adhesive

Size: 18x26mm

2120 A930 44c multi 1.25 .55
a. Booklet pane of 10 12.50

Queen Astrid (1905-35) — A931

Queen Astrid: 44c, Wearing tiara (25a). 80c, Holding son (25b).

2005, Oct. 31 Photo. *Perf. 11½*

2121 A931 44c multi 1.25 .55

Souvenir Sheet

2122 A931 80c multi 2.40 .95

No. 2122 contains one 38x49mm stamp.

Bird Type of 1985 With Euro Denominations Only

2006 Photo. *Perf. 11½*

2123 A524 23c Grebe à cou noir .65 .25
2124 A524 30c Râle des genêts .90 .25
2125 A524 46c Avocette 1.40 .30
2126 A524 78c Barge à queue noire 2.25 .45

Size: 38x27mm

2127 A524 €4.30 Grebe huppé 12.50 3.00
Nos. 2123-2127 (5) 17.70 4.25

Issued: 30c, 46c, 1/23; 78c, 3/20; €4.30, 5/15. 23c, 6/6.

Wolfgang Amadeus Mozart (1756-91), Composer — A932

2006, Jan. 23 Photo. *Perf. 11½*

2128 A932 70c multi 2.00 .85

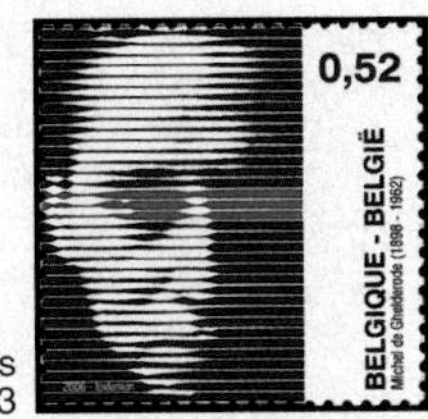

Playwrights A933

Designs: 52c, Michel de Ghelderode (1898-1962). 78c, Herman Teirlinck (1879-1967).

2006, Jan. 23

2129 A933 52c blk & blue 1.50 .65
2130 A933 78c blk & red vio 2.25 .95

Margins on sheets of No. 2129, inscribed "Prior," served as etiquettes.

Composers of Polyphonic Music — A934

No. 2131: a, Guillaume Dufay (c. 1400-74) and Gilles Binchois (c. 1400-60). b, Johannes Ockeghem (c. 1410-97). c, Jacob Obrecht (c. 1457-1505). d, Adriaan Willaert (c. 1490-1562). e, Orlandus Lassus (1532-94).

2006, Jan. 23

2131 Booklet pane of 5 8.75 —
a.-e. A934 60c Any single 1.75 .70
Complete booklet, #2131 8.75

Farm Animals — A935

No. 2132: a, Donkey. b, Chicken and rooster. c, Two ducks. d, Pig and piglets. e, Cow. f, Goat. g, Two rabbits. h, Two horses. i, Sheep. j, Three geese.

2006, Jan. 23 *Die Cut Perf. 10x9¾*

Self-Adhesive

2132 Booklet pane of 10 14.00
a.-j. A935 46c Any single 1.40 .55

Crossbowmen

A936 A937

2006, Feb. 20 *Perf. 11½*

2133 A936 46c multi 1.40 .55

Booklet Stamp

Self-Adhesive

2134 A937 (52c) multi 1.50 .60
a. Booklet pane of 10 15.00

Souvenir Sheet

Democracy in Belgium, 175th Anniv. — A938

No. 938: a, Senate chambers (red brown floor). b, King Leopold I, vert. c, Chamber of Representatives (green floor).

2006, Feb. 20

2135 A938 Sheet of 3 + 2 labels 4.25 2.50
a.-c. 46c Any single 1.40 .50

Souvenir Sheet

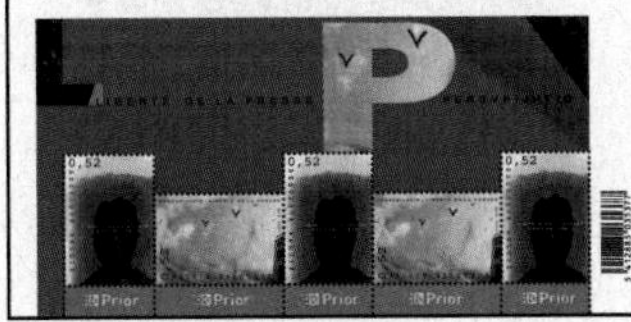

Freedom of the Press — A939

No. 2136: a, Face with open mouth. b, Stylized birds and building, horiz.

2006, Feb. 20

2136 A939 Sheet, 3 #2136a, 2 #2136b + 5 etiquettes 7.50 4.50
a.-b. 52c Either single 1.50 .65

Stamp Festival

A940

A941

2006, Mar. 20 Photo. *Perf. 11½*

2137 A940 46c multi 1.40 .55

Booklet Stamps

Self-Adhesive

2138 A941 (52c) "Prior" at L 1.50 .60
2139 A941 (52c) "Prior" at R 1.50 .60
a. Booklet pane, 5 each #2138-2139 15.00

Justus Lipsius (1547-1606), Philologist — A942

Photo. & Engr.

2006, Mar. 20 *Perf. 11½*

2140 A942 70c buff & brown 2.00 .85

Start of Giro d'Italia Cycling Race in Wallonia — A943

2006, Apr. 24 Photo.

2141 A943 52c multi 1.40 .65

Printed in sheets of 5. Margins on sheets, inscribed "Prior," served as etiquettes.

Painting Details — A944

No. 2142 — Paintings by Lambert Lombard (1506-66): a, L'Offrande de Joachim Refusée (six men). b, Auguste et la Sybile de Tibur (four men).

No. 2143 — Paintings by Léon Spilliaert (1881-1946): a, Duizeling (figure on staircase). b, De Dame met de Hoed (woman in hat).

2006, Apr. 24

2142 A944 Vert. pair 4.00 1.60
a.-b. 65c Either single 1.90 .80
2143 A944 Vert. pair 4.00 1.60
a.-b. 65c Either single 1.90 .80

Souvenir Sheet

Memorial Van Damme Track and Field Competition — A945

No. 2144 — Runners of the 1970s and 1980s: a, John Walker. b, Alberto Juantorena. c, Ivo Van Damme. d, Sebastian Coe. e, Steve Ovett.

2006, Apr. 24 *Perf. 11½*

2144 A945 Sheet of 5 + 5 etiquettes 7.50 3.25
a.-e. 52c Any single 1.50 .65

Miniature Sheet

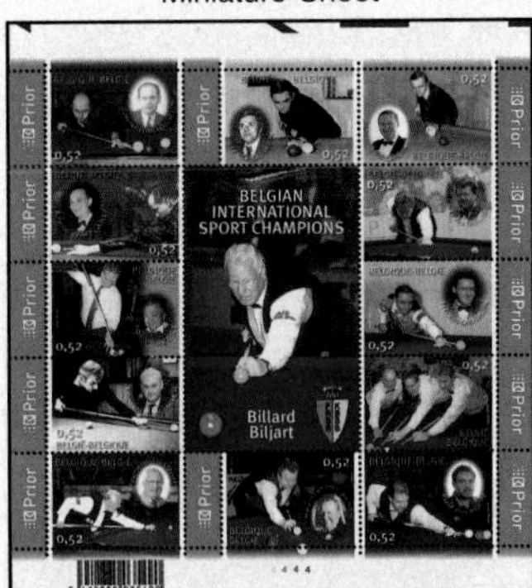

International Billiards Champions From Belgium — A946

No. 2145: a, Clément Van Hassel. b, Tony Schrauwen. c, Léo Corin. d, Emile Wafflard. e, Ludo Dielis. f, Jos Vervest. g, Frédéric Caudron. h, Laurent Boulanger. i, Paul Stroobants, Eddy Leppens, and Peter De Backer. j, Raymond Ceulemans. k, Raymond Steylaerts. l, Jozef Philipoom.

2006, Apr. 26

2145 A946 Sheet of 12 + label + 12 etiquettes 18.00 7.50
a.-l. 52c Any single 1.50 .60

Belgica 2006 Intl. Philatelic Exhibition, Brussels
A947 A948

2006, May 15 ***Perf. 11½***

Size:21x25mm

2146 A947 46c multi 1.40 .60

Size:22x26mm

2146A A947 46c multi 12.00 9.50

Booklet Stamp
Self-Adhesive

Die Cut Perf. 9¾x10 on 2 or 3 Sides

2147 A948 (52c) multi 1.50 .70
a. Booklet pane of 10 15.00

No. 2146A was available in sheets with personalizable labels in November and December 2006, and afterwards available without labels.

Red Cross — A949

Booklet Stamp

Die Cut Perf. 10x9¾ on 2 or 3 Sides

2006, May 15 **Self-Adhesive**

Location of "Prior"

2148 A949 (52c) At left 1.50 .70
2149 A949 (52c) At right 1.50 .70
a. Booklet pane, 5 each #2148-2149 15.00

See No. B1172.

Lighthouses A950

Photo. & Engr.

2006, May 15 ***Perf. 11½***

2150 A950 46c Blankenberge 1.40 .60
2151 A950 46c Heist 1.40 .60
2152 A950 46c Nieuwpoort 1.40 .60
2153 A950 46c Ostend 1.40 .60
Nos. 2150-2153 (4) 5.60 2.40

Souvenir Sheet

Fish of the North Sea — A951

No. 2154: a, Petite roussette (dogfish, 50x26mm). b, Cabillaud (cod, 47x26mm). c, Raie bouclée (thornback ray, 50x26mm). d, Hareng (herring, 33x25mm). e, Plie (flounder, 33x25mm).

2006, May 15 **Photo.**

2154 A951 Sheet of 5 7.00 3.25
a.-e. 46c Any single 1.40 .65

Belgian Olympic and Interfederal Committee, Cent. — A952

2006, June 6 **Photo.** ***Perf. 11½***

2155 A952 52c multi 1.50 .70

Souvenir Sheet

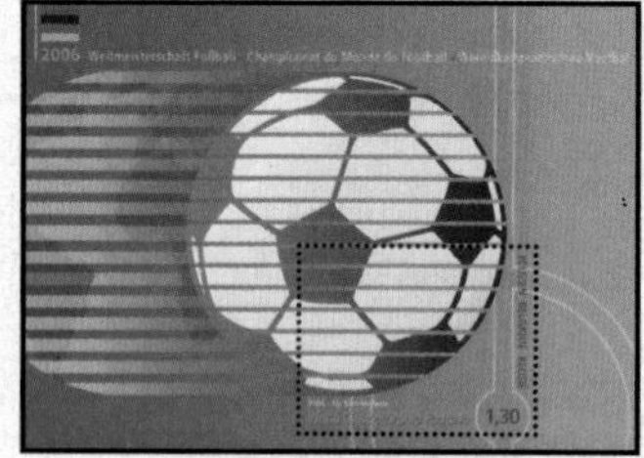

2006 World Cup Soccer Championships, Germany — A953

2006, June 6

2156 A953 €1.30 multi 3.75 2.10

Miniature Sheet

Scenes of Wallonian Villages — A954

No. 2157: a, House and flowers, Deigné. b, Arch, Mélin. c, Statue, Saint-Hadelin Church, Celles. d, Bridge, Lompret. e, Fountain, Ny.

2006, June 6

2157 A954 Sheet of 5 7.50 3.50
a.-e. 52c Any single 1.50 .70

Centaurea — A955

Booklet Stamp

Die Cut Perf. 9¾ on 2 or 3 Sides

2006, Aug. 7 **Self-Adhesive**

2158 A955 (52c) multi 1.50 .35
a. Booklet pane of 10 15.00

Marcinelle Coal Mine Disaster, 50th Anniv. A956

2006, Aug. 7 ***Perf. 11½***

2159 A956 70c multi 2.00 .95

Rembrandt Tulips — A957

Die Cut Perf. 9¾ on 2 or 3 Sides

2006, Sept. 25 **Photo.**

Self-Adhesive
Booklet Stamp

2160 A957 A multi 2.00 .45
a. Booklet pane of 10 20.00

No. 2160 sold for 70c on day of issue.

Institute of Tropical Medicine, Antwerp, Cent. — A958

2006, Sept. 25 ***Perf. 11½***

2161 A958 80c multi 2.40 1.00

Oosterlingenhuis, Bruges — A959

Oosters Huis, Antwerp — A960

2006, Sept. 25

2162 A959 70c multi 2.00 .90
2163 A960 80c multi 2.40 1.00

Hanseatic League, 650th anniv.

Belgian Philatelic Academy — A961

2006, Oct. 23 **Photo.** ***Perf. 11½***

2164 A961 52c multi 1.40 .70

Printed in sheets of 10. Margins on sheets, inscribed "Prior," served as etiquettes.

Souvenir Sheet

Belgica 2006 Intl. Philatelic Exhibition, Brussels — A962

No. 2165: a, Tennis ball. b, Tulips as stemware. c, Butterflies as four-leaf clover. d, Illuminated tent. e, Vignettes of Nos. 2165a-2165d with speech balloons.

2006, Nov. 16

2165 A962 Sheet of 5 13.50 13.50
a.-e. 46c Any single 2.60 2.60

No. 2165 sold for €5.

Souvenir Sheet

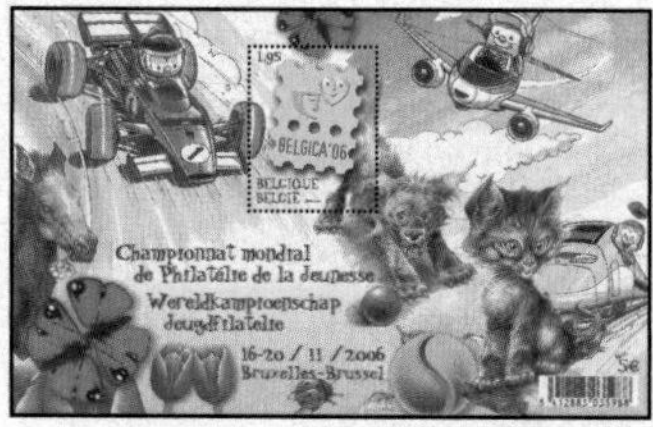

Belgica 2006 Emblem — A963

2006, Nov. 16

2166 A963 €1.95 multi 13.50 13.50

No. 2166 sold for €5.

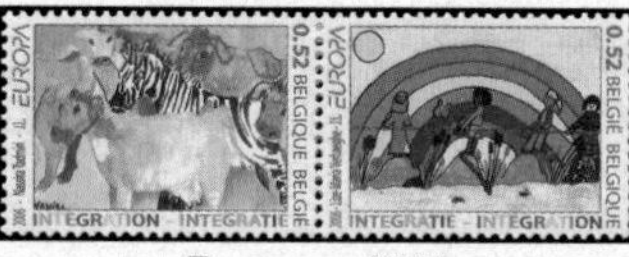

Europa — A964

No. 2167 — Children's drawings: a, Zebra and cows, by Nassira Tadmiri. b, People and rainbow, by Lize-Maria Verhaeghe.

2006, Nov. 17

2167 A964 Horiz. pair 2.80 2.80
a.-b. 52c Either single 1.40 .70

Printed in sheets of 5 pairs. Margins on sheets, inscibed "Prior," served as etiquettes.

A965

Paintings by COBRA Group Artists — A966

No. 2168: a, New Skin, by Pierre Alechinsky. b, Untitled by Asger Jorn.

2006, Nov. 17 ***Perf. 11½***

Souvenir Sheet

2168 A965 Sheet of 2 3.25 3.25
a. 46c multi 1.25 1.25
b. 70c multi 2.00 2.00

Booklet Stamp
Self-Adhesive

Die Cut Perf. 9¾ on 2 or 3 Sides

2169 A966 (52c) Like #2168a 1.40 .70
a. Booklet pane of 10 14.00

See Denmark Nos. 1367-1370.

A967

Dance — A968

Designs: Nos. 2170a, 2173, Rock and roll. Nos. 2170b, 2172, Waltz. Nos. 2170c, 2171, Tango. Nos. 2170d, 2174, Cha cha cha. Nos. 2170e, 2175, Samba.

2006, Nov. 18 ***Perf. 11½***

2170	A967	Sheet of 5	8.00	8.00
a.-e.		60c Any single	1.60	.80

Booklet Stamps
Self-Adhesive
Die Cut Perf. 9¾ on 2 or 3 Sides

2171	A968	(52c) multi	1.40	.70
2172	A968	(52c) multi	1.40	.70
2173	A968	(52c) multi	1.40	.70
2174	A968	(52c) multi	1.40	.70
2175	A968	(52c) multi	1.40	.70
a.		Booklet pane of 10, 2 each #2171-2175	14.00	

Kramikske, Comic Strip by Jean-Pol Vandenbroeck A969

2006, Nov. 19 ***Perf. 11½***

2176	A969	46c multi	1.25	.60

Youth philately.

Miniature Sheet

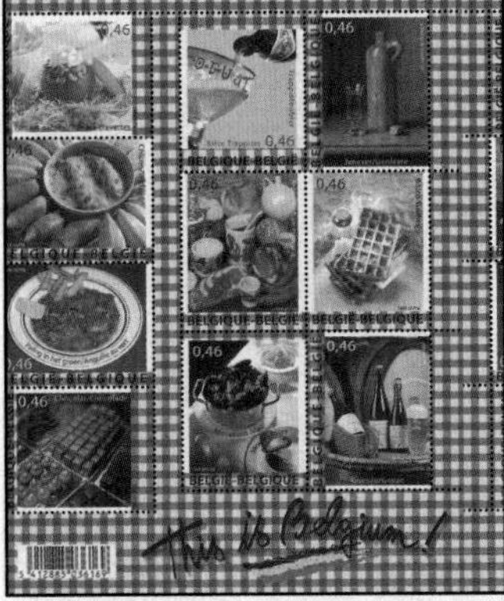

Belgian Foods and Beverages — A970

No. 2177: a, Shrimps and tomato. b, Witloof chicory (Belgian endive). c, Eel in green sauce. d, Chocolate. e, Orval beer, vert. f, Gin, vert. g, Ham, sausages, bread and condiments, vert. h, Waffles, vert. i, Mussels, vert. j, Geuze (doubly-fermented beer), vert.

2006, Nov. 19 ***Perf. 11½***

2177	A970	Sheet of 10	12.50	12.50
a.-j.		46c Any single	1.25	.60

Angel Playing Psaltery — A971

Angel Playing Trumpet Marine — A972

Angel Playing Lute — A973

Angel Playing Trumpet — A974

Angel Playing Shawm — A975

Head of Angel — A976

Angels painted by Hans Memling: No. 2179, Head of angel on #2178a. No. 2180, Head of angel on #2178b. No. 2181, Head of angel on #2178c. No. 2182, Head of angel on #2178d. No. 2183, Head of angel on #2178e.

2006, Nov. 20 ***Perf. 12x11¾***

2178		Horiz. strip of 5	6.25	6.25
a.		A971 46c multi	1.25	.60
b.		A972 46c multi	1.25	.60
c.		A973 46c multi	1.25	.60
d.		A974 46c multi	1.25	.60
e.		A975 46c multi	1.25	.60

Booklet Stamps
Self-Adhesive
Die Cut Perf. 9¾ on 2 or 3 Sides

2179	A976	46c multi	1.25	.60
2180	A976	46c multi	1.25	.60
2181	A976	46c multi	1.25	.60
2182	A976	46c multi	1.25	.60
2183	A976	46c multi	1.25	.60
a.		Booklet pane of 10, 2 each #2179-2183	12.50	
		Nos. 2179-2183 (5)	6.25	3.00

Christmas.

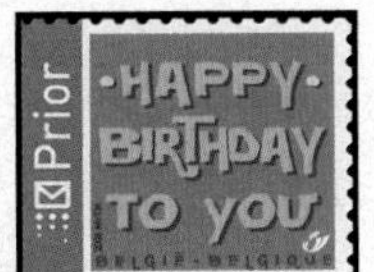

"Happy Birthday to You" — A977

Birthday Cake — A978

Booklet Stamp
Die Cut Perf. 9¾ on 2 or 3 Sides
2006, Nov. 20 **Self-Adhesive**

2184	A977	(52c) "Prior" at left	1.40	.70
2185	A978	(52c) "Prior" at right	1.40	.70
2186	A978	(52c) "Prior" at left	1.40	.70
2187	A977	(52c) "Prior" at right	1.40	.70
a.		Booklet pane of 10, 3 each #2184-2185, 2 each #2186-2187	14.00	
		Nos. 2184-2187 (4)	5.60	2.80

Christmas — A979

2006, Nov. 20 **Photo.** ***Perf. 11½***

2188	A979	46c multi	12.00	9.50

No. 2188 was available in sheets with personalizable labels in November and December 2006, and afterwards available without labels. Compare types A979 and A930.

Bicycle — A980

Bowling Ball and Pins — A981

Golf Club and Ball — A982

Bicycle — A983

Bowling Ball and Pins — A984

Golf Club and Ball — A985

2007, Jan. 8 **Photo.** ***Perf. 11½***

2189	A980	46c multi	1.25	.60
2190	A981	60c multi	1.60	.80
2191	A982	65c multi	1.75	.85
		Nos. 2189-2191 (3)	4.60	2.25

Booklet Stamps
Self-Adhesive
Die Cut Perf. 9¾ on 2 or 3 Sides

2192	A983	(52c) "Prior" at left	1.40	1.40
2193	A983	(52c) "Prior" at right	1.40	1.40
a.		Booklet pane, 5 each #2192-2193	14.00	
2194	A984	(52c) "Prior" at left	1.40	1.40
2195	A984	(52c) "Prior" at right	1.40	1.40
a.		Booklet pane, 5 each #2194-2195	14.00	
2196	A985	(52c) "Prior" at left	1.40	1.40
2197	A985	(52c) "Prior" at right	1.40	1.40
a.		Booklet pane, 5 each #2196-2197	14.00	
		Nos. 2192-2197 (6)	8.40	8.40

World Cross-country Cycling Championships, Hooglede-Gits.

King Albert II Type of 2005 and

King Albert II — A986

King Albert II, Numeral on European Union Flag — A987

King Albert II, Numeral on Globe — A988

2007-09 **Photo.** ***Perf. 11½***

2200	A986	1	red & gray	1.50	.40
2202	A810	80c	bl, bl gray & blk	2.10	.55
2203	A987	1	blue & multi	2.25	1.10
2204	A810	90c	bl, brn gray & blk	2.40	.60
2205	A988	1	brn org & multi	2.50	1.25
2206	A986	2	grn & gray	3.00	.75
2210	A986	3	dk bl & gray	4.50	1.10
2211	A987	3	bl grn & multi	6.75	3.50
2213	A986	5	vio & gray	7.50	1.90
2214	A988	3	red vio & multi	7.50	3.75
2216	A986	7	brn & gray	10.50	2.60
			Nos. 2200-2216 (11)	50.50	17.50

Issued: Nos. 2202, 2204, 1/29; Nos. 2200, 2206, 2210, 2213, 2216, 10/1, Nos. 2203, 2205, 2211, 2214, 1/2/09.

Nos. 2202 and 2204 are inscribed "A Prior" at left.

Stamps of type A987 were intended for usee to destinations within Europe, and type A988 for use to destinations outside of Europe.

On day of issue, No. 2200 sold for 52c, No. 2203, for 80c, No. 2205, for 90c, No. 2206, for €1.04, No. 2210, for €1.56, No. 2211, for €2.40, No. 2213, for €2.60, No. 2214, for €2.70, and No. 2216, for €3.64.

Bird Type of 1985 With Euro Denominations Only

2007 **Photo.** ***Perf. 11½***

2218	A524	5c	Sarcelle d'hiver	.25	.25
2218A	A524	6c	Chouette cheveche	.25	.25
2219	A524	10c	Chouette de Tengmalm	.25	.25
2220	A524	23c	Choucas des Tours	.60	.25
2220A	A524	40c	Hibou moyen-duc	1.25	.30
2221	A524	70c	Martinet noir	1.90	.50
2222	A524	75c	Faucon crecerelle	2.00	.50
			Nos. 2218-2222 (7)	6.50	2.30

Issued: 5c, 10c, 2/26; 23c, 3/26; 70c, 75c, 1/29; 6c, 7/9; 40c, 11/12.

Alix, Comic Strip by Jacques Martin A990

2007, Jan. 29

2223	A990	52c multi	1.40	.70

Youth philately. Printed in sheets of 5. Margins on sheets, inscribed "Prior," served as etiquettes.

Miniature Sheet

Accordions — A991

No. 2224: a, Accordion with piano-like keyboard at left. b, Concertina with hexagonal ends. c, Bohemians accordion. d, Accordion with brown and black trim. e, Accordion with red trim.

2007, Jan. 29

2224	A991	Sheet of 5 + 5 etiquettes	7.00	7.00
a.-e.		52c Any single	1.40	.70

Red Cross Mobile Library for Hospitals — A992

Booklet Stamps
Die Cut Perf. 9¾ on 2 or 3 Sides
2007, Feb. 26 **Self-Adhesive**

2225	A992	(52c) "Prior" at left	1.40	.70
2226	A992	(52c) "Prior" ar right	1.40	.70
a.		Booklet pane, 5 each #2225-2226	14.00	

See No. B1175.

Miniature Sheet

Female Writers — A993

No. 2227: a, Julia Tulkens (1902-95), poet. b, Madeleine Bourdouxhe (1906-96), novelist. c, Christine D'haen, poet. d, Jacqueline Harpman, novelist. e, Maria Rosseels (1916-2005), novelist.

2007, Feb. 26 *Perf. 11½*

2227 A993 Sheet of 5 + 5 etiquettes 7.00 7.00
a.-e. 52c Any single 1.40 .70

Stoclet House, Brussels, Designed by Josef Hoffmann — A994

Designs: 52c, Building interior. 80c, Building exterior.

2007, Mar. 26

2228 A994 52c multi 1.40 .70
2229 A994 80c multi 2.25 1.10

Margins of sheets of No. 2228, inscribed "Prior," served as etiquettes. See Czech Republic Nos. 3338-3339.

Souvenir Sheet

Popular Theater — A995

No. 2230: a, Scene from "Tati l'Pèriki." b, Romain Deconinck, actor and impresario, vert. c, Scene from "Le Mariage de Mademoiselle Beulemans."

2007, Mar. 26 **Photo.** *Perf. 11¾*

2230 A995 Sheet of 3 + 2 labels 3.75 3.75
a.-c. 46c Any single 1.25 .60

European Union, 50th Anniv. — A996

2007, Apr. 30 *Perf. 11¼x11½*

2231 A996 80c multi 2.25 1.10

Europa — A997

Designs: 46c, Lord Robert Baden-Powell, founder of Scouting movement. 75c, Scouts.

2007, Apr. 30 *Perf. 11½x11¼*

2232 A997 46c multi 1.25 .65

Souvenir Sheet

Perf. 11½

2233 A997 75c multi 2.10 2.10

Scouting, cent. No. 2233 contains one 38x49mm stamp.

The Adventures of Tintin A998

No. 2234 — Tintin book covers translated in: a, French (Tintin au Pays des Soviets). b, Danish (Tintin i Congo). c, English (Tintin in America). d, Luxemburgian (Dem Pharao seng Zigaren). e, Chinese (dragon on cover). f, Portuguese (O Idolo Roubado). g, Bengali (Tintin in boat on cover). h, Slovak (Zezlo Král'a Otakara). i, Russian (Tintin and camels on cover). j, Icelandic (Dularfulla Stjarnan). k, Polish (Tajemnica Jednorozca). l, Afrikaans (Die Skat van Rackham die Rooie). m, Tintin author, Hergé. n, Arabic (Tintin and men with man in chair above table on cover). o, Spanish (El Templo del Sol). p, German (Im Reiche des Schwarzend Goldes). q, Finnish (Päämääränä Kuu). r, Swedish (Manen Tur Och Retur). s, Japanese (Tintin and men behind rocks on cover). t, Turkish (Ambardaki Kömür). u, Tibetan (Tintin on snowy mountain). v, Italian (I Gioielli della Castafiore). w, Indonesian (Penerbangan 714). x, Greek (Tintin and Mayan temple on cover). y, Dutch (Kuifje en de Alfa-Kunst).

2007, May 22 *Perf. 11½*

2234 Sheet of 25 32.00 32.00
a.-y. A998 46c Any single 1.25 .65

Museums — A999

Designs: 46c, Museum of Fashion, Hasselt. 75c, Notre Dame à la Rose Hospital Museum, Lessines. 92c, Jewish Museum of Belgium, Brussels.

2007, June 18 **Photo.** *Perf. 11½*

2235 A999 46c multi 1.25 .60
2236 A999 75c multi 2.10 1.10
2237 A999 92c multi 2.50 1.25
Nos. 2235-2237 (3) 5.85 2.95

Souvenir Sheet

Opening of Princess Elisabeth Base, Antarctica — A1000

2007, June 18

2238 A1000 75c multi 2.10 2.10

A1001

Vacations A1002

Designs: Nos. 2239, 2241, 2242, Woman, man with kite. Nos. 2240, 2243, 2244, People carrying canoe and woman.

2007 **Photo.** *Perf. 11½*

2239 A1001 52c multi 1.50 .75
2240 A1001 52c multi 1.50 .75

Booklet Stamps
Self-Adhesive
Die Cut Perf. 9¾ on 2 or 3 Sides

2241 A1002 (52c) "Prior" at left 1.50 .75
2242 A1002 (52c) "Prior" at right 1.50 .75
a. Booklet pane of 10, 5 each #2241-2242 15.00
2243 A1002 (52c) "Prior" at left 1.50 .75
2244 A1002 (52c) "Prior" at right 1.50 .75
a. Booklet pane of 10, 5 each #2243-2244 15.00
Nos. 2239-2244 (6) 9.00 4.50

Issued: Nos. 2239-2240, 7/9; Nos. 2241-2244, 6/18. Margins on sheets of Nos. 2239-2240, inscribed "Prior," served as etiquettes.

Tour de France in Belgium — A1003

2007, July 9 *Perf. 11½*

2245 A1003 52c multi 1.50 .75

Printed in sheets of 5. Margins on sheets, inscribed "Prior," served as etiquettes.

A1004

Port of Zeebrugge, Cent. — A1005

2007, July 9 *Perf. 11½*

2246 A1004 €1.04 multi 3.00 1.50

Booklet Stamps
Self-Adhesive
Die Cut Perf. 9¾ on 2 or 3 Sides

2247 A1005 (52c) "Prior" at left 1.50 .75
2248 A1005 (52c) "Prior" at right 1.50 .75
a. Booklet pane of 10, 5 each #2247-2248 15.00
Nos. 2246-2248 (3) 6.00 3.00

Margins on sheets of No. 2246, inscribed "Prior," served as etiquettes.

Tourism — A1006

Designs: No. 2249, Athénée François Bovesse, Namur. No. 2250, Collège Saint-Michel, Brussels. No. 2251, Heilig Hart College, Maasmechelen.

Photo. & Engr.

2007, Sept. 3 *Perf. 11½*

2249 A1006 52c multi 1.50 .75
2250 A1006 52c multi 1.50 .75
2251 A1006 52c multi 1.50 .75
Nos. 2249-2251 (3) 4.50 2.25

Tombeau du Géant, Botassart A1007

2007, Sept. 3 **Photo.**

2252 A1007 52c multi 1.50 .75

Rotunda of Luxembourg Train Station, Luxembourg A1008

2007, Sept. 3 **Photo. & Engr.**

2253 A1008 80c multi 2.25 1.10

See Luxembourg No. 1221.

Miniature Sheet

Scenes From Films By Belgian Directors — A1009

No. 2254: a, Misère au Borinage, by Henri Storck. b, Le Fils, by Jean-Pierre and Luc Dardenne. c, The Man Who Had His Hair Cut Short, by André Delvaux. d, Malpertuis, by Harry Kümel. e, Dust, by Marion Hansel.

2007, Sept. 3 **Photo.**

2254 A1009 Sheet of 5 7.50 7.50
a.-e. 52c Any single 1.50 .75

Souvenir Sheet

Queen Paola, 70th Birthday — A1010

2007, Sept. 3

2255 A1010 €1.04 multi 3.00 1.50

Belgian Post Emblem — A1011

2007, Oct. 1 Photo. *Perf. 11½*

2256 A1011 1 red & black 1.50 .40

Sold for 52c on day of issue.

Fruit — A1012

No. 2257: a, Pears. b, Strawberries. c, Red currants. d, Apples. e, Grapes. f, Cherries. g, Raspberries. h, Peaches. i, Plums. j, Blackberries.

Die Cut Perf. 9¾ on 2 or 3 Sides

2007, Oct. 1 Photo.

Self-Adhesive

2257 Booklet pane of 10 15.00
a.-j. A1012 1 Any single 1.50 .40

Nos. 2257a-2257j each sold for 52c on day of issue.

Mourning Stamp A1013

2007, Oct. 15 *Perf. 11½*

2258 A1013 1 multi 1.50 .75

Sold for 52c on day of issue.

Miniature Sheet

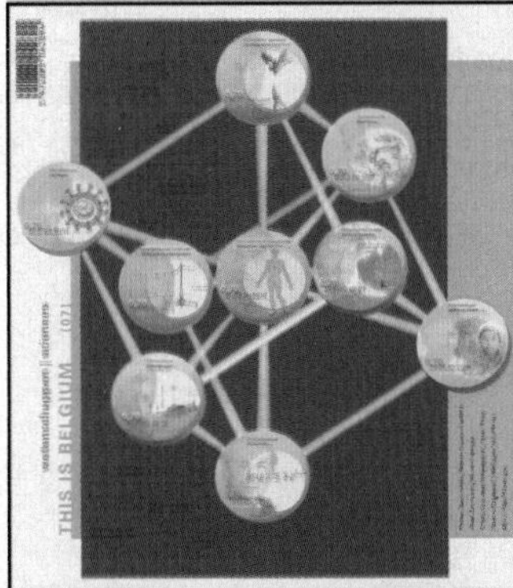

Scientists — A1014

No. 2259 — Scientist and field: a, Marc Van Montagu, molecular genetics. b, Paul Janssen, pharmaceutical entrepreneur. c, Lise Thiry, microbiology. d, Chris Van den Wyngaert, international criminal law. e, Peter Carmeliet, molecular medicine. f, Philippe Van Parijs, social philosophy. g, Marie-Claire Foblets, anthropology. h, André Berger, climatology. i, Pierre Deligne, mathematics.

2007, Oct. 15 *Die Cut*

Self-Adhesive

2259 A1014 Sheet of 9 18.00 18.00
a.-i. 70c Any single 2.00 1.00

Postage Stamp Festival A1015

Designs: Nos. 2260a, 2261, Man with pipe, book, typewriter. Nos. 2260b, 2262, Woman, hearts, vase, picture frame, typewriter. Nos. 2260c, 2263, Man, musical symbols, typewriter. Nos. 2260d, 2264, Woman in cat costume, typewriter. Nos. 2260e, 2265, Boy at computer.

2007, Oct. 15 *Perf. 11½*

2260 A1015 Sheet of 5 7.50 7.50
a.-e. 1 Any single 1.50 .75

Booklet Stamps

Self-Adhesive

Size: 28x20mm

Die Cut Perf. 9¾ on 2 or 3 Sides

2261 A1015 1 multi 1.50 .40
2262 A1015 1 multi 1.50 .40
2263 A1015 1 multi 1.50 .40
2264 A1015 1 multi 1.50 .40
2265 A1015 1 multi 1.50 .40
a. Booklet pane of 10, 2 each #2261-2265 15.00
Nos. 2261-2265 (5) 7.50 2.00

On day of issue, Nos. 2260a-2260e, 2261-2265 each sold for 52c.

Dahlias — A1016

Tulips — A1017

Petunias A1018

2007, Oct. 15 Self-Adhesive

Coil Stamp

Serpentine Die Cut 13¾x14

2266 A1016 1 multi 1.50 .40

Booklet Stamps

Die Cut Perf. 9¾ on 2 or 3 Sides

2267 A1016 1 multi 1.50 .40
a. Booklet pane of 10 15.00
2268 A1017 A multi 2.40 .60
a. Booklet pane of 10 24.00
2269 A1018 2 multi 3.00 .75
a. Booklet pane of 10 30.00
Nos. 2266-2269 (4) 8.40 2.15

On day of issue, Nos. 2266-2267 each sold for 52c; No. 2268, for 80c; No. 2269, for €1.04.

Les Chemins de la Liberté (Le Voyage), by Thierry Merget A1019

2007, Nov. 12 Photo. *Perf. 11½*

2270 A1019 1 multi 1.60 .80

Miniature Sheet

International Billiards Champions From Belgium — A1020

No. 2271: a, Piet J. Van Duppen. b, Albert Collette. c, Gustaaf Van Belle. d, Piet Sels. e, Gaston De Doncker. f, Théo Moons. g, René Gabriels. h, Victor Luypaerts. i, René Vingerhoedt.

2007, Nov. 12

2271 A1020 Sheet of 9 14.50 14.50
a.-i. 1 Any single 1.60 .80

On day of issue, Nos. 2271a-2271i each sold for 52c.

Bride and Groom A1021

Father and Infant Son A1022

Mother and Infant Daughter — A1023

Booklet Stamps

Die Cut 9¾ on 2 or 3 Sides

2007, Nov. 12 Self-Adhesive

2272 A1021 1 multi 1.60 .40
a. Booklet pane of 10 16.00
2273 A1022 1 multi 1.60 .40
a. Booklet pane of 10 16.00
2274 A1023 1 multi 1.60 .40
a. Booklet pane of 10 16.00
Nos. 2272-2274 (3) 4.80 1.20

On day of issue, Nos. 2272-2274 each sold for 52c.

Christmas

A1024 A1025

2007, Nov. 12 *Perf. 11½*

2275 A1024 1 multi 1.60 .80

Booklet Stamps

Self-Adhesive

Size: 24x29mm

Die Cut Perf. 9¾ on 2 or 3 Sides

2276 A1024 1 multi 1.40 .40
a. Booklet pane of 10 14.00
2277 A1025 A multi 2.10 1.10
a. Booklet pane of 10 21.00

On day of issue, Nos. 2275 and 2276 each had a franking value of 52c, and No. 2277 had a franking value of 80c. On day of issue, No. 2276a sold for €4.68, and No. 2277a sold for €7.20.

Bird Type of 1985 With Euro Denominations Only

2008, Jan. 21 Photo. *Perf. 11½*

2278 A524 10c Accenteur mouchet + etiquette .30 .25
2279 A524 15c Cassenoix moucheté + etiquette .45 .25

Size: 38x27mm

2280 A524 €4.40 Faucon pélerin 13.00 3.25
Nos. 2278-2280 (3) 13.75 3.75

Red Cross Blood Donation A1026

Die Cut Perf. 9¾ on 2 or 3 Sides

2008, Jan. 21 Photo.

Booklet Stamp

Self-Adhesive

2281 A1026 1 multi 1.60 .80
a. Booklet pane of 10 16.00

See No. B1176. No. 2281 sold for 52c on day of issue.

Miniature Sheet

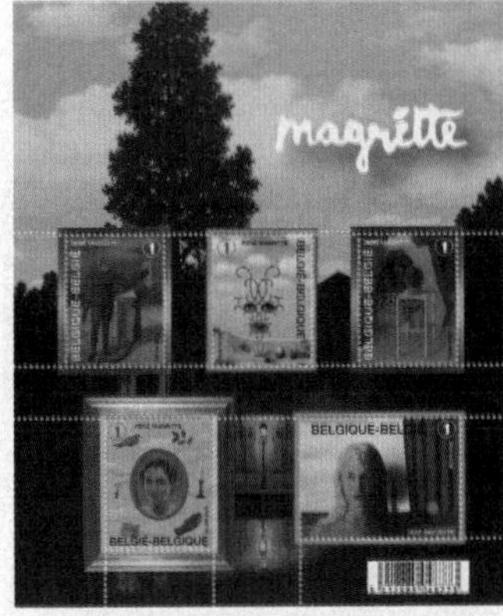

Paintings by René Magritte (1898-1967) — A1027

No. 2282: a, The Man from the Sea, 1927 (30x40mm). b, Scheherazade, 1950 (30x40mm). c, Midnight Marriage, 1926 (30x40mm). d, Georgette, 1935 (33x40mm). e, The Ignorant Fairy, 1956 (49x37mm).

Perf. 11½, 11¼x11½ (#2282b)

2008, Jan. 21

2282 A1027 Sheet of 5 + 2 labels 8.00 8.00
a.-e. 1 Any single 1.60 .80

Nos. 2282a-2282e each sold for 52c on day of issue. Ungummed imperforate examples of No. 2282 were given as gifts to some standing order subscribers, and were not sold.

Toys — A1028

No. 2283: a, Automobile. b, Baby carriage. c, Doll. d, Airplane. e, Horse. f, Tram. g, Diabolo. h, Teddy bear. i, Top. j, Scooter.

Die Cut Perf. 9¾ on 2 or 3 Sides

2008, Feb. 11 **Self-Adhesive**

2283 Booklet pane of 10 16.50
a.-j. A1028 1 Any single 1.60 .80

Nos. 2283a-2283j each sold for 54c on day of issue.

Jeremiah, Comic Book Character by Hermann Huppen A1029

2008, Feb. 11 ***Perf. 11½***

2284 A1029 1 multi 1.60 .80

No. 2284 sold for 54c on day of issue.

Souvenir Sheet

Floralies of Ghent Flower Show, Bicent. — A1030

2008, Feb. 11

2285 A1030 80c multi 2.50 1.25

Jewish Community in Belgium, Bicent. A1031

2008, Mar. 17 **Photo. & Engr.**

2286 A1031 90c multi 3.00 1.50

Detective Novels — A1032

No. 2287: a, L'Assassin Habite au 21, by Stanislas-André Steeman. b, De Zaak Alzheimer, by Jef Geeraerts.

2008, Mar. 17 **Photo.**

2287 A1032 Horiz. pair, #a-b 3.50 1.75
a.-b. 1 Either single 1.75 .85

Nos. 2287a-2287b each sold for 54c on day of issue.

Trams A1033

Designs: 1, Coastal tram. 80c, Charleroi tram. 90c, Brussels tram.

2008, Apr. 14

2288 A1033 1 multi 1.75 .85
2289 A1033 80c multi 2.50 1.25
2290 A1033 90c multi 2.75 1.40
Nos. 2288-2290 (3) 7.00 3.50

No. 2289 sold for 54c on day of issue.

Miniature Sheet

Antverpia 2010 Intl. Philatelic Exhibition — A1034

No. 2291: a, Train, building. b, Buildings, statue. c, Port, cargo containers. d, Models, Flanders Fashion Institute Building. e, Woman wearing necklace, diamonds.

2008, Apr. 14 ***Perf. 11½***

2291 A1034 Sheet of 5 15.50 15.50
a.-e. 1 Any single 3.00 3.00

On day of issue, No. 2291 sold for €5 but Nos. 2291a-2291e each had a 54c franking value.

Miniature Sheet

Spirou, Comic Strip by André Franquin — A1035

No. 2292: a, Count of Champignac (with magnifying glass). b, Fantasio. c, Spirou. d, Seccotine (girl). e, Zorglub (bearded man).

2008, Apr. 14

2292 A1035 Sheet of 5 8.75 8.75
a.-e. 1 Any single 1.75 .85

Nos. 2292a-2292e each sold for 54c on day of issue.

Mickey Mouse, 80th Anniv. — A1036

2008, May 19 **Photo.** ***Perf. 11½***

2293 A1036 1 multi 1.75 .85

Sold for 54c on day of issue. Printed in sheets of 5.

Diversity at Work — A1037

2008, May 19

2294 A1037 2 multi 3.50 1.75

Sold for €1.08 on day of issue.

Souvenir Sheet

La Constance and Les Elèves de Thémis Masonic Lodges, Bicent. — A1038

2008, May 19 **Litho.**

2295 A1038 3 multi 5.25 5.25

Sold for €1.62 on day of issue.

Europa A1039

2008, May 19 **Photo.** ***Perf. 11½***

2296 A1039 80c multi 2.60 1.25

Booklet Stamp

Self-Adhesive

Size: 30x24mm

Die Cut Perf. 9¾ on 2 or 3 Sides

2297 A1039 1 multi 1.75 .85
a. Booklet pane of 10 17.50

No. 2297 sold for 54c on day of issue.

Tagetes Patula — A1040

Orange Favorite Tulips — A1041

Booklet Stamps

Die Cut Perf. 9¾ on 2 or 3 Sides

2008, May 19 **Self-Adhesive**

2298 A1040 1 multi 1.75 .85
a. Booklet pane of 10 17.50
2299 A1041 A multi 2.60 1.25
a. Booklet pane of 10 26.00

On day of issue, No. 2298 sold for 54c, and No. 2299 sold for 80c. See No. 2316.

Souvenir Sheet

Queen Fabiola, 80th Birthday — A1042

No. 2300: a, Queen Fabiola and King Baudouin, black and white photo. b, Drawing of Queen Fabiola. c, Queen Fabiola and King Baudouin, color photo.

2008, June 11 ***Perf. 11½***

2300 A1042 Sheet of 3 5.25 5.25
a.-c. 1 Any single 1.75 .85

Nos. 2300a-2300c each sold for 54c on day of issue.

Sculptures A1043

Designs: 1, La Mer, by George Grard. 80c, Sculpture from Imago series, by Emile Desmedt. 90c, Autoportrait, by Gérald Dederen.

2008, June 11 **Litho.**

2301 A1043 1 multi 1.75 .85
2302 A1043 80c multi 2.50 1.25
2303 A1043 90c multi 2.75 1.40
Nos. 2301-2303 (3) 7.00 3.50

No. 2301 sold for 54c on day of issue.

A1044

Outdoor Activities A1045

Family: Nos. 2304, 2306, Cycling. Nos. 2305, 2307, Walking.

2008, June 11 ***Perf. 11½***

2304 A1044 1 multi 1.75 .85
2305 A1044 1 multi 1.75 .85

Booklet Stamps

Self-Adhesive

Die Cut Perf. 9¾ on 2 or 3 Sides

2306 A1045 1 multi 1.75 .85
a. Booklet pane of 10 17.50
2307 A1045 1 multi 1.75 .85
a. Booklet pane of 10 17.50

On day of issue, Nos. 2304-2307 each sold for 54c.

Folklore and Traditions A1046

Designs: No. 2308, Hopduvelfeesten, Asse. No. 2309, Planting of the Meyboom, Brussels, 700th anniv., vert. No. 2310, Eupen Carnival, vert. No. 2311, Royal Walloon Cabaret Company, Tournai, cent., vert.

Photo. & Engr.

2008 July 14 ***Perf. 11½***

2308 A1046 1 multi 1.75 .85
2309 A1046 1 multi 1.75 .85
2310 A1046 1 multi 1.75 .85
2311 A1046 1 multi 1.75 .85
Nos. 2308-2311 (4) 7.00 3.40

On day of issue Nos. 2308-2311 each sold for 54c.

2008 Summer Olympics, Beijing — A1047

Designs: 1, BMX racer. 90c, Women's relay race, horiz.
2, Tennis, horiz.

2008, July 14 **Photo.**

2312 A1047 1 multi 1.75 .85

2313 A1047 90c multi 3.00 1.50

Souvenir Sheet

2314 A1047 2 multi 3.50 1.75

No. 2314 contains one 48x38mm stamp. On day of issue, Nos. 2312 and 2314 sold for 54c and €1.08, respectively.

Miniature Sheet

Brussels World's Fair, 50th Anniv. — A1048

No. 2315: a, Soviet Union Pavilion and plaza (red panel). b, Thailand Pavilion (yellow panel). c, Hostesses carrying flags (green panel). d, Fair's star emblems (blue panel). e, Atomium (red violet panel).

Perf. 11½ on 3 or 4 Sides

2008, July 14

2315 A1048 Sheet of 5 + 4 labels 8.75 8.75
a.-e. 1 Any single 1.75 .85

On day of issue, Nos. 2315a-2315e each sold for 54c.

Tagetes Patula Type of 2008

Serpentine Die Cut 13¼x13½

2008, Sept. 29 **Photo.**

Coil Stamp

Self-Adhesive

2316 A1040 1 multi 1.50 .40

On day of issue No. 2316 sold for 54c.

St. Gabriel Guild (Religion on Stamps Society), 50th Anniv. A1049

Photo. & Engr.

2008, Sept. 29 ***Perf. 11½***

2317 A1049 1 multi 1.50 .75

Sold for 54c on day of issue.

Miniature Sheet

Photography — A1050

No. 2318 — Photography by: a, Tim Dirven. b, Paul Ausloos. c, Léonard Missone. d, Harry Gruyaert. e, Stephan Vanfleteren.

2008, Sept. 29 **Photo.**

2318 A1050 Sheet of 5 7.50 7.50
a.-e. 80c Any single 1.50 .75

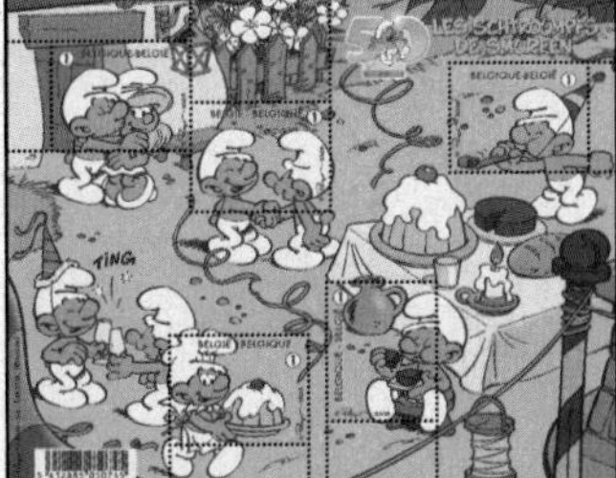

A1051

Smurfs — A1052

No. 2319: a, Smurf and Smurfette kissing. b, Smurfs shaking hands. c, Smurf blowing noisemaker. d, Smurf carrying dessert. e, Smurf eating cake, vert.

No. 2320, Smurf waving, orange background. No. 2321, Smurfette. No. 2322, Papa Smurf. No. 2323, Smurf with drum, horiz. No. 2324, Smurf writing letter. No. 2325, Smurf giggling. No. 2326, Smurf carrying mail bag and letter. No. 2327, Brainy Smurf (with glasses). No. 2328, Gargamel. No. 2329, Smurf with mail bag, letter and posthorn, horiz.

Perf. 11¾x11¼, 11¼(#2319e)

2008, Sept. 29

2319 A1051 Sheet of 5 7.50 7.50
a.-e. 1 Any single 1.50 .75

Booklet Stamps

Self-Adhesive

Die Cut Per. 10 on 2 or 3 Sides

2320 A1052 1 multi 1.50 .75
2321 A1052 1 multi 1.50 .75
2322 A1052 1 multi 1.50 .75
2323 A1052 1 multi 1.50 .75
2324 A1052 1 multi 1.50 .75
2325 A1052 1 multi 1.50 .75
2326 A1052 1 multi 1.50 .75
2327 A1052 1 multi 1.50 .75
2328 A1052 1 multi 1.50 .75
2329 A1052 1 multi 1.50 .75
a. Booklet pane of 10, #2320-2329 15.00
Nos. 2320-2329 (10) 15.00 7.50

On day of issue, Nos. 2319a-2319e and 2320-2329 each sold for 54c.

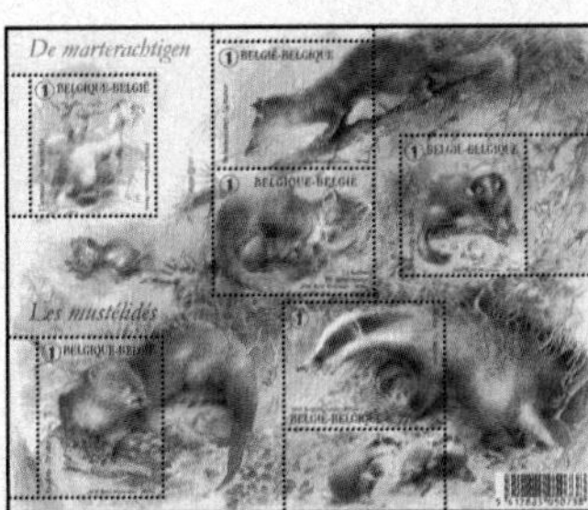

A1053

Mustelids A1054

No. 2330: a, Ermine, vert. (hermine, 38x42mm). b, Sable (martre, 48x38mm). c, Marten (fouine, 48x38mm). d, Polecat, vert. (putois, 38x42mm). e, Otter, vert. (38x48mm). f, Badger (blaireau, 48x38mm).

No. 2331, Marten (martre). No. 2332, Marten (fouine). No. 2333, Polecat. No. 2334, Otter. No. 2335, Badger.

Perf. 11½x11¼, 11½ (#2330e, 2330f)

2008, Sept. 29

2330 A1053 Sheet of 6 9.00 9.00
a.-f. 1 Any single 1.50 .75

Booklet Stamps

Self-Adhesive

Die Cut Perf. 10 on 2 or 3 Sides

2331 A1054 1 multi 1.50 .75
2332 A1054 1 multi 1.50 .75
2333 A1054 1 multi 1.50 .75
2334 A1054 1 multi 1.50 .75
2335 A1054 1 multi 1.50 .75
a. Booklet pane of 10, 2 each #2331-2335 15.00
Nos. 2331-2335 (5) 7.50 3.75

On day of issue, Nos. 2330a-2330f and 2331-2335 each sold for 54c.

Belgian Congo, Cent. A1055

Photo. & Engr.

2008, Oct. 20 ***Perf. 11½***

2336 A1055 1 Belgian Congo #37 1.40 .70

On day of issue, No. 2336 sold for 54c.

Museums A1056

Designs: 1, National Footwear Museum, Izegem. No. 2338, Musée en Piconrue, Bastogne. No. 2339, David and Alice van Buuren Museum, Brussels.

2008, Oct. 20 **Litho.**

2337 A1056 1 multi 1.40 .70
2338 A1056 80c multi 2.10 1.10
2339 A1056 80c multi 2.10 1.10
Nos. 2337-2339 (3) 5.60 2.90

On day of issue, No. 2337 sold for 54c.

Souvenir Sheet

End of World War I, 90th Anniv. — A1057

No. 2340: a, Soldiers at Menin Gate, Ypres. b, Statue of King Albert I, Nieuwpoort. c, Poppies.

Perf. 11½x11¼

2008, Oct. 20 **Photo.**

2340 A1057 Sheet of 3 7.00 7.00
a.-c. 90c Any single 2.25 1.10

Universal Declaration of Human Rights, 60th Anniv. — A1058

2008, Nov. 12 ***Perf. 11½***

2341 A1058 90c multi 2.25 1.10

Miniature Sheet

Belgian Music — A1059

No. 2342: a, Queen Elisabeth Competition. b, José Van Dam. c, Rock Werchter. d, Philippe Herreweghe and Collegium Vocale Gent. e, dEUS. f, Conductor Robert Groslot and orchestra. g, Philip Catherine. h, Vaya Con Dios. i, Salvatore Adamo and Will Tura. j, Jacques Brel.

2008, Nov. 12 ***Perf. 11¾x11¼***

2342 A1059 Sheet of 10 + label 21.00 21.00
a.-j. 80c Any single 2.10 1.10

A1060

Christmas

A1061 A1062

No. 2343 — Stained-glass window: a, Désiré Cardinal Mercier. b, St. Francis holding Cross. c, Mary, Joseph and Holy Spirit. d, Franciscan monk. e, Infant Jesus.

2008, Nov. 12 ***Perf. 11¼***

2343 A1060 Sheet of 5 7.00 7.00
a.-e. 1 Any single 1.40 .70

Booklet Stamps

Self-Adhesive

Die Cut Perf. 9¾ on 2 or 3 Sides

2344 A1061 1 multi 1.40 .70
a. Booklet pane of 10 14.00
2345 A1062 (80c) multi 2.10 1.10
a. Booklet pane of 10 21.00

On day of issue, Nos. 2343a-2343e and 2344 each sold for 54c.

Bird Type of 1985 With Euro Denominations Only

2009 **Photo.** ***Perf. 11½***

2346 A524 27c Bécasse des bois .75 .35

Size: 31x27mm

2347 A524 €4.60 Pygargue a queue blanche 13.00 6.50

Issued: 27c, 4/6; €4.60, 1/2.

Tulipa Bakeri — A1063

Booklet Stamps

Die Cut Perf. 9¾ on 2 or 3 Sides

2009, Jan. 2 **Self-Adhesive**

2348 A1063 1 multi	2.25	1.10
a. Booklet pane of 10	22.50	

On day of issue, No. 2348 sold for 80c.

Miniature Sheet

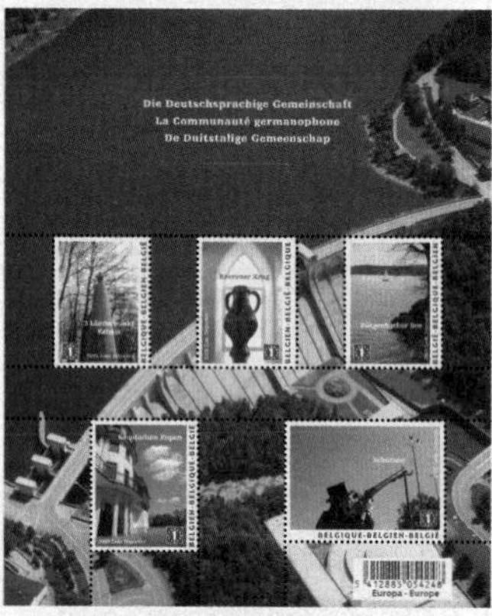

German-speaking Community in Belgium — A1064

No. 2349: a, Marker at border of Belgium, Germany and Netherlands, near Kelmis (30x40mm). b, Jug from Raeren (30x40mm). c, Bütgenbach Lake (30x40mm). d, Eupen Sanitorium (33x40mm). e, Marksman, horiz. (49x37mm).

2009, Jan. 19 ***Perf. 11½***

2349 A1064 Sheet of 5	10.50	10.50
a.-e. 1 Any single	2.10	2.10

On day of issue, Nos. 2349a-2349e each sold for 80c.

Introduction of the Euro, 10th Anniv. — A1065

Booklet Stamps

Die Cut Perf. 9¾ on 2 or 3 Sides

2009, Jan. 19 **Self-Adhesive**

2350 A1065 1 dk blue & blue	1.40	.70
a. Booklet pane of 10	14.00	

No. 2350 sold for 54c on day of issue.

Louis Braille (1809-52), Educator of the Blind — A1066

Photo., Engr. & Embossed

2009, Feb. 23 ***Perf. 11½***

2351 A1066 1 multi	1.50	.75

Sold for 59c on day of issue.

River and Canal Barge A1067

2009, Feb. 23 **Photo.**

2352 A1067 2 multi	3.00	1.50

Sold for €1.18 on day of issue.

Postage Stamp Festival — A1068

2009, Mar. 9

2353 A1068 1 multi	1.60	.80

Sold for 59c on day of issue.

Famous Women — A1069

No. 2354: a, Marthe Boel (1877-1956), President of Intl. Council of Women. b, Lily Boeykens (1930-2005), Belgian representative to U.N. Commission on the Status of Women.

2009, Mar. 9 **Litho.**

2354 A1069 Horiz. pair	3.25	1.60
a.-b. 1 Either single	1.60	.80

On day of issue, Nos. 2354a-2354b each sold for 59c.

Souvenir Sheet

Preservation of Polar Regions and Glaciers — A1070

No. 2355: a, Penguins. b, Polar bear.

2009, Mar. 9 ***Perf. 11½***

2355 A1070 Sheet of 2	5.75	5.75
a.-b. 1 Either single	2.75	1.40

On day of issue, Nos. 2355a-2355b each sold for €1.05.

Souvenir Sheet

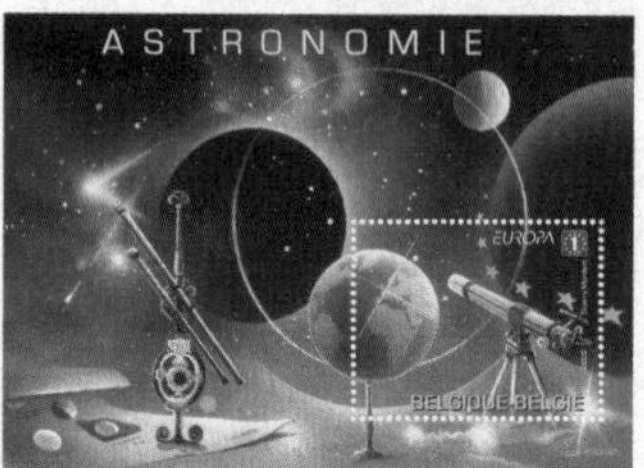

Europa — A1071

2009, Apr. 6

2356 A1071 1 multi	2.40	1.25

Intl. Year of Astronomy. Sold for 90c on day of issue.

Miniature Sheet

UNESCO World Heritage Sites — A1072

No. 2357: a, Neolithic Flint Mines, Spiennes. b, Notre-Dame Cathedral, Tournai. c, Plantin-Moretus Museum, Antwerp. d, Historic Center of Bruges. e, Town Houses of Architect Victor Horta, Brussels.

2009, Apr. 6 **Photo. & Engr.**

2357 A1072 Sheet of 5	14.00	14.00
a.-e. 1 Any single	2.75	1.40

On day of issue, Nos. 2357a-2357e each sold for €1.05.

A1073

A1074

A1075

A1076

Characters From Animated Movie "Suske en Wiske - De Texas Rakkers" — A1077

Die Cut Perf. 9¾ on 2 or 3 Sides

2009, Apr. 6 **Photo.**

Booklet Stamps

Self-Adhesive

2358 A1073 1 multi	1.60	.80
2359 A1074 1 multi	1.60	.80
2360 A1075 1 multi	1.60	.80
2361 A1076 1 multi	1.60	.80
2362 A1077 1 multi	1.60	.80
a. Booklet pane of 10, 2 each #2358-2362	16.00	
Nos. 2358-2362 (5)	8.00	4.00

On day of issue, Nos. 2358-2362 each sold for 59c.

Miniature Sheet

Antverpia 2010 European Philatelic Championships, Antwerp — A1078

No. 2363: a, Antwerp Museum of Contemporary Art, Flemish Village, by Luc Tuymans. b, Orbino, sculpture by Luc Deleu, Middelheim Museum. c, Actors, Toneelhuis Theater. d, Poster for movie, "Hollywood on the Scheldt," Roma Cinema. e, Writings of Willem Elsschot, sculpture of Elsschot by Wilfried Pas.

2009, May 11 **Photo.** ***Perf. 11½***

2363 A1078 Sheet of 5	15.50	15.50
a.-e. 1 Any single	3.00	3.00

No. 2363 sold for €5.50. Nos. 2363a-2363e each had a franking value of 59c on day of issue.

Composers A1079

Designs: No. 2364, Henry Purcell (1659-95). No. 2365, Georg Friedrich Handel (1685-1759). No. 2366, Joseph Haydn (1732-1809). No. 2367, Felix Mendelssohn-Bartholdy (1809-47). No. 2368, Clara Schumann (1819-96).

2009, May 11 ***Perf. 11¾x11½***

Booklet Stamps

2364 A1079 1 multi	2.50	1.25
2365 A1079 1 multi	2.50	1.25
2366 A1079 1 multi	2.50	1.25
2367 A1079 1 multi	2.50	1.25
2368 A1079 1 multi	2.50	1.25
a. Booklet pane of 5, #2364-2368	12.50	—
Complete booklet, #2368a	12.50	
Nos. 2364-2368 (5)	12.50	6.25

On day of issue Nos. 2364-2368 each sold for 90c.

Vacations — A1080

Designs: No. 2369, Man with camera. No. 2370, Woman with camera.

Booklet Stamps

Die Cut Perf. 9¾ on 2 or 3 Sides

2009, May 11 **Self-Adhesive**

2369 A1080 1 multi	1.75	.45
2370 A1080 1 multi	1.75	.45
a. Booklet pane of 10, 5 each #2369-2370	17.50	

On day of issue Nos. 2369-2370 each sold for 59c.

Aviation and Space Exploration Milestones A1081

No. 2371: a, First command of International Space Station by European, 2009. b, Apollo 11 moon landing, 1969. c, First flight of Concorde, 1969. d, Circumnavigational flight of Graf Zeppelin, 1929. e, Flight by Louis Blériot across English Channel, 1909.

Photo. (#2371a), Photo. & Engr.

2009, June 8 ***Perf. 11½***

2371 Vert. strip of 5	8.75	8.75
a.-e. A1081 1 Any single	1.75	.85

Nos. 2371a-2371e each sold for 59c on day of issue. No. 2371 was printed in sheets containing two strips.

Energy Conservation A1082

Designs: No. 2372, Fluorescent light bulb. No. 2373, Windmill. No. 2374, Bus. No. 2375, Solar energy. No. 2376, Insulated house.

Booklet Stamps

Die Cut Perf. 9¾ on 2 or 3 Sides

2009, June 8 **Self-Adhesive**

2372 A1082 1 multi	1.75	.45
2373 A1082 1 multi	1.75	.45
2374 A1082 1 multi	1.75	.45
2375 A1082 1 multi	1.75	.45

2376 A1082 1 multi 1.75 .45
a. Booklet pane of 10, 2 each #2372-2376 17.50
Nos. 2372-2376 (5) 8.75 2.25

On day of issue Nos. 2372-2376 each sold for 59c.

Yoko Tsuno, Comic Strip by Roger Leloup — A1083

2009, June 29 Photo. *Perf. 11½*
2377 A1083 1 multi 1.75 .85

Sold for 59c on day of issue.

Souvenir Sheet

50th Wedding Anniv. of King Albert II and Queen Paola — A1084

2009, June 29 Litho.
2378 A1084 3 multi 5.00 2.50

Sold for €1.77 on day of issue.

Maurice Béjart (1927-2007), Choreographer A1085

2009, Aug. 31 Litho.
2379 A1085 1 multi 2.60 1.40

Sold for 90c on day of issue.

1950s Citroen Mail Van A1086

1960s Bedford Mail Van A1087

1970s Renault Mail Van A1088

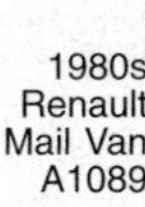

1980s Renault Mail Van A1089

2009 Citroen Mail Van A1090

2009, Aug. 31 Photo. & Engr.
2380 A1086 1 multi 1.75 .85
2381 A1087 1 multi 1.75 .85
2382 A1088 1 multi 1.75 .85
2383 A1089 1 multi 1.75 .85
2384 A1090 1 multi 1.75 .85
a. Vert. strip of 5, #2380-2384 8.75 4.25
Nos. 2380-2384 (5) 8.75 4.25

On day of issue, Nos. 2380-2384 each sold for 59c.

Circus Performers — A1091

Designs: No. 2385, Musicians. No. 2386, Bicyclist on tightrope. No. 2387, Magician levitating woman. No. 2388, Human pyramid. No. 2389, Trapeze artists. No. 2390, Clown on ball and acrobat. No. 2391, Acrobats with ball. No. 2392, Magician with doves and rabbit. No. 2393, Acrobat on horseback. No. 2394, Juggler on unicycle.

Die Cut Perf. 10 on 2 or 3 Sides
2009, Aug. 31 Photo.
Booklet Stamps
Self-Adhesive

2385 A1091 1 multi 1.75 .45
2386 A1091 1 multi 1.75 .45
2387 A1091 1 multi 1.75 .45
2388 A1091 1 multi 1.75 .45
2389 A1091 1 multi 1.75 .45
2390 A1091 1 multi 1.75 .45
2391 A1091 1 multi 1.75 .45
2392 A1091 1 multi 1.75 .45
2393 A1091 1 multi 1.75 .45
2394 A1091 1 multi 1.75 .45
a. Booklet pane of 10, #2385-2394 17.50
Nos. 2385-2394 (10) 17.50 4.50

On day of issue, Nos. 2385-2394 each sold for 59c.

The Triptych of the Seven Sacraments, Detail of Painting by Rogier van der Weyden — A1092

2009, Sept. 21 Litho. *Perf. 11½*
2395 A1092 2 multi 3.50 1.75

Opening of Leuven Museum exhibition of works by Rogier van der Weyden. Sold for €1.18 on day of issue.

Miniature Sheet

Mont des Arts District, Brussels — A1093

No. 2396: a, General State Archives (40x33mm). b, Royal Museum of Fine Arts of Belgium (40x33mm). c, Royal Library of Belgium (40x33mm). d, Brussels Meeting Center (40x33mm). e, Old Palace of Brussels (38x49mm). f, Saint Jacques-sur-Coudenberg Church, Protestant Chapel (49x38mm). g, Palace of Fine Arts (40x33mm). h, Royal Belgian Film Archive (40x33mm). i, Belvue Museum (40x33mm). j, Musical Instruments Museum (40x33mm).

Perf. 11½ on 2, 3 or 4 Sides
2009, Sept. 21 Photo.
2396 A1093 Sheet of 10 17.50 8.75
a.-j. 1 Any single 1.75 .85

Nos. 2396a-2396j each sold for 59c on day of issue.

Chinese Dragon — A1094

Booklet Stamps
Die Cut Perf. 10 on 2 or 3 Sides
2009, Oct. 5 Self-Adhesive
2397 A1094 1 multi 1.75 .85
a. Booklet pane of 10 17.50

Europalia China Cultural Festival. No. 2397 sold for 59c on day of issue.

Canonization of Father Damien (1840-89) — A1095

2009, Oct. 5 *Perf. 11½*
2398 A1095 1 multi 2.75 1.40

Sold for 90c on day of issue.

Souvenir Sheet

Comic Strip Museum Festival — A1096

2009, Oct. 5 Photo.
2399 A1096 1 multi 3.25 1.60

Sold for €1.05 on day of issue. Imperforate examples were gifts to standing order customers.

Miniature Sheet

Toy Trains — A1097

No. 2400: a, Streamline Mettoy train (blue locomotive and cars). b, Märklin Bavarian locomotive "Aloisus" (locomotive with gold-trimmed window and smokestack). c, Märklin SNCB locomotive tender (locomotive facing left with red trim). d, Märklin Haine-St. Pierre SNCB Diesel locomotive (locomotive with green and yellow trim). e, Märklin Storchenbein locomotive tender replica (locomotive with front wheel in red). f, Märklin Type 16 SNCB locomotives (gray locomotives with yellow and red trim). g, French tin toy train and cars (red locomotive and cars). h, Märklin ICE Deutsches Bahn locomotives (white locomotives with red trim). i, Unpainted French wooden toy train and cars. j, Blue and red Belgian wooden locomotive with pull string.

2009, Oct. 5 *Perf. 11¾x11¼*
2400 A1097 Sheet of 10 17.50 8.75
a.-j. 1 Any single 1.75 .85

Nos. 2400a-2400j each sold for 59c on day of issue.

Miniature Sheet

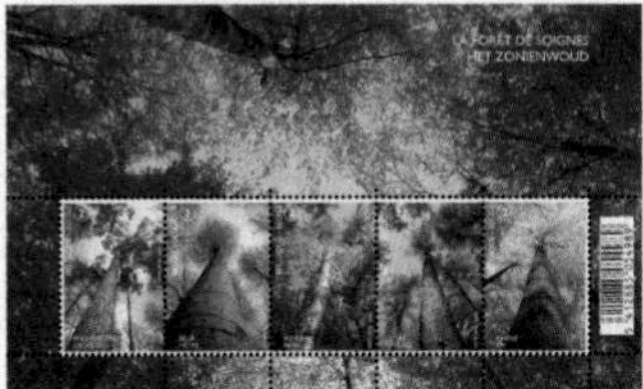

Trees — A1098

No. 2401: a, Scotch pine (pin sylvestre). b, Beech (hêtre). c, Birch (bouleau). d, Larch (mélèze). e, Oak (chêne).

2009, Oct. 5 Litho. *Perf. 11½*
2401 A1098 Sheet of 5 17.50 8.75
a.-e. 2 Any single 3.50 1.75

Nos. 2401a-2401e each sold for €1.18 on day of issue.

Bird Type of 1985 With Euro Denominations Only

2009, Sept. 21 Litho. *Perf. 11½*
2402 A524 1c Pic noir .25 .25
2403 A524 10c Chouette hulotte .30 .25

Miniature Sheet

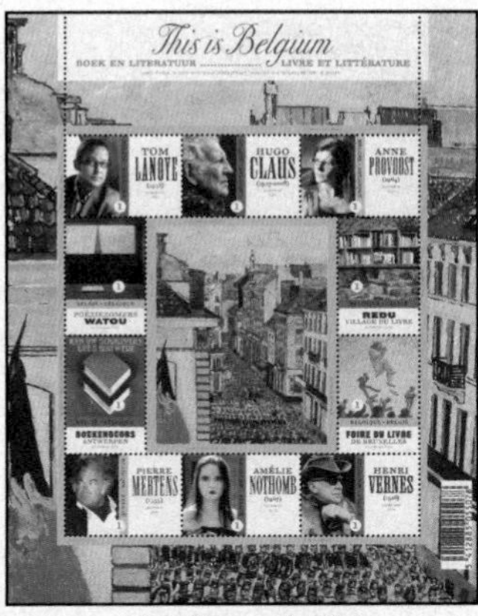

Literature — A1099

No. 2404: a, Tom Lanoye, writer. b, Hugo Claus (1929-2008), writer. c, Anne Provoost, writer. d, Poetry Summers, Watou, vert. e, Redu, town with 22 book stores, vert. f, Boekenbeurs Antwerpen, vert. g, Brussels Book Fair, vert. h, Pierre Mertens, writer. i, Amélie Nothomb, writer. j, Henri Vernes, writer.

2009, Nov. 3 Photo. *Perf. 11½*

2404 A1099 Sheet of 10 17.50 17.50
a.-j. 1 Any single 1.75 .85

Nos. 2404a-2404j each sold for 59c on day of issue.

A1100

Christmas
A1101

Yellow panel at: No. 2406, Left. No. 2407, Right.

Booklet Stamps

Die Cut Perf. 9¾ on 2, 3 or 4 Sides

2009, Nov. 3 Self-Adhesive

2405 A1100 1 multi 1.75 .45
a. Booklet pane of 10 17.50
2406 A1101 1 multi 2.75 1.40
2407 A1101 1 multi 2.75 1.40
a. Booklet pane of 10, 5 each #2406-2407 27.50
Nos. 2405-2407 (3) 7.25 3.25

On day of issue, No. 2405 sold for 59c and Nos. 2406-2407 each sold for 90c.

Mourning
Stamp — A1102

Die Cut Perf. 10 on 2 or 3 Sides

2010, Jan. 4 Photo.

Booklet Stamp

Self-Adhesive

2408 A1102 1 multi 1.75 .85
a. Booklet pane of 10 17.50

No. 2408 sold for 59c on day of issue.

Bird Type of 1985 With Euro Denominations Only

2010 Photo. *Perf. 11½*

2409 A524 5c Grèbe castagneux .25 .25

Size: 32x23mm

2410 A524 €4.09 Faisan de colchide 10.50 5.25

Size: 27x32mm

2411 A524 €4.60 Chouette effraie 13.00 6.50
Nos. 2409-2411 (3) 23.75 12.00

Issued: 5c, 1/18; €4.09, 6/14; €4.60, 1/4.

Organ Donation
A1103

Booklet Stamps

Die Cut Perf. 10 on 2 or 3 Sides

2010, Jan. 18 Self-Adhesive

2412 A1103 1 multi 1.75 .85
a. Booklet pane of 10 17.50

No. 2412 sold for 59c on day of issue.

Souvenir Sheet

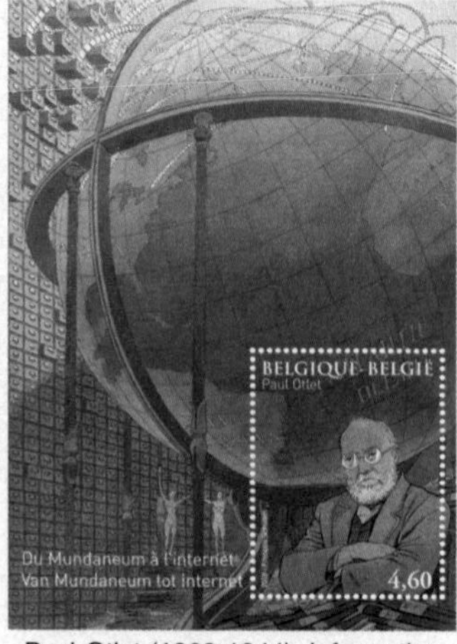

Paul Otlet (1868-1944), Information Scientist — A1104

2010, Jan. 18 Litho. *Perf. 11½*

2413 A1104 €4.60 multi 13.00 6.50

Miniature Sheet

Antverpia 2010 European Philatelic Championship, Antwerp — A1105

No. 2414: a, Magnifying glass, #2414e, 2414f, emblem of Royal National Association of Belgian Postage Stamp Circles. b, Shopping center, Antwerp. c, Antwerp Zoo. d, Museum aan de Stroom, Antwerp. e, House and self-portrait of Peter Paul Rubens, Antwerp. f, Antwerp City Hall and Cathedral.

2010, Jan. 18

2414 A1105 Sheet of 6 18.00 18.00
a.-f. 1 Any single 3.00 3.00

Royal National Association of Belgian Postage Stamp Circles, 120th anniv. Nos. 2414a-2414f each had a franking value of 59c on the day of issue. No. 2414 sold for €6.50, with the remaining €2.96 going to Antverpia 2010.

Largo Winch, Comic Strip by Philippe Francq A1106

2010, Feb. 22 *Perf. 11½*

2415 A1106 1 multi 1.60 .80

Sold for 59c on day of issue.

Authors Who Lived in Brussels — A1107

Designs: No. 2416, Paul Verlaine, Arthur Rimbaud. No. 2417, Charles Baudelaire. No. 2418, Multatuli. No. 2419, Charlotte & Emily Bronte. No. 2420, Victor Hugo.

2010, Feb. 22 *Perf. 11½*

Booklet Stamps

2416 A1107 2 multi 3.25 1.60
2417 A1107 2 multi 3.25 1.60
2418 A1107 2 multi 3.25 1.60
2419 A1107 2 multi 3.25 1.60
2420 A1107 2 multi 3.25 1.60
a. Booklet pane of 5, #2416-2420 16.50 —
Complete booklet, #2420a 16.50
Nos. 2416-2420 (5) 16.25 8.00

On day of issue, Nos. 2416-2420 each sold for €1.18.

Ghent Floralies — A1108

No. 2421: a, Nicotiana alata. b, Lychnis coronaria.

2010, Mar. 15 Photo. & Engr.

2421 A1108 Vert. pair 3.25 1.60
a.-b. 1 Either single 1.60 .80

On day of issue, Nos. 2421a-2421b each sold for 59c.

Souvenir Sheet

Europa — A1109

No. 2422: a, Boy on books, dog reading book. b, Girl on mushroom, cat reading book.

2010, Mar. 15 Litho.

2422 A1109 Sheet of 2 14.50 7.25
a.-b. 3 Either single 7.25 3.50

On day of issue, Nos. 2422a-2422b each sold for €2.70.

Baby Animals
A1110

Die Cut Perf. 10 on 2 or 3 Sides

2010, Mar. 15 Photo.

Booklet Stamps

Self-Adhesive

2423 A1110 1 Two chicks 1.60 .80
2424 A1110 1 Two rabbits 1.60 .80
2425 A1110 1 Kitten 1.60 .80
2426 A1110 1 Two ducklings 1.60 .80
2427 A1110 1 Colt 1.60 .80
2428 A1110 1 Puppy sitting 1.60 .80
2429 A1110 1 Puppy lying 1.60 .80
2430 A1110 1 Two kittens 1.60 .80
2431 A1110 1 Head of colt 1.60 .80
2432 A1110 1 Two lambs 1.60 .80
a. Booklet pane of 10, #2423-2432 16.00
Nos. 2423-2432 (10) 16.00 8.00

On day of issue, Nos. 2423-2432 each sold for 59c.

Prince Philippe, 50th Birthday A1111

2010, Apr. 15 Litho. *Perf. 11½*

2433 A1111 2 multi 3.25 1.60

Sold for €1.18 on day of issue.

Winning Designs in "Save the Earth" Children's Stamp Design Contest A1112

No. 2434 — Category and artist: a, Oceans and Seas, by Igor Volt. b, Forests, by Lander Keyaerts. c, Endangered Species, by Eva Sterkens. d, Climate, by Lucie Octave. e, Energy, by Louise Van Goylen.

2010, Apr. 15

2434 Vert. strip of 5 8.00 4.00
a.-e. A1112 1 Any single 1.60 .80

Nos. 2434a-2434e each sold for 59c on day of issue.

Souvenir Sheet

Antverpia 2010 European Philatelic Championship, Antwerp — A1113

2010, Apr. 15

2435 A1113 3 multi 13.50 13.50

No. 2435 sold for €5. The stamp had a franking value of €1.77 on the day of issue, with the remaining €3.23 of the sale price going to Antverpia 2010.

Miniature Sheet

Bird Paintings by André Buzin — A1114

No. 2436: a, Buse variable. b, Faucon hobereau. c, Epervier d'Europe. d, Milan royal. e, Autour des palombes.

2010, Apr. 15

2436	A1114	Sheet of 5	12.00	12.00
a.-e.		1 Any single	2.40	1.25

Use of Buzin's bird paintings on Belgium's definitive stamps, 25th anniv. Nos. 2436a-2436e each sold for 90c on day of issue.

Miniature Sheet

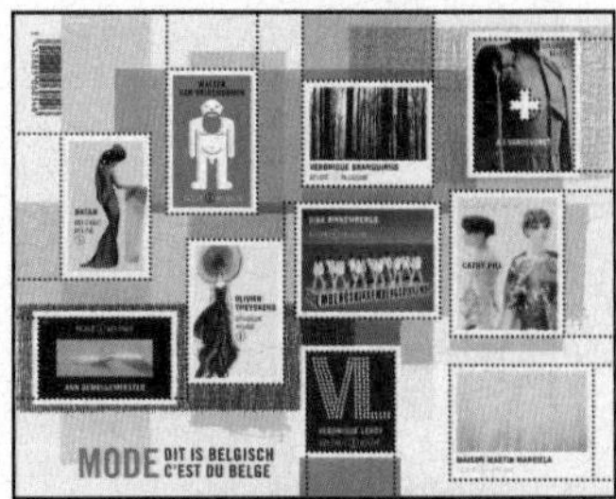

Fashion Houses — A1115

No. 2437: a, Natan (30x48mm). b, Walter Van Beirendonck (30x48mm). c, Veronique Branquinho, horiz. (43x35mm). d, A. F. Vandevorst (33x44mm). e, Olivier Theyskens (32x48mm). f, Dirk Bikkembergs, horiz. (48x38mm). g, Cathy Pill (38x48mm). h, Ann Demeulemeester, horiz. (44x27mm). i, Veronique Leroy (29x33mm). j, Maison Martin Margiela, horiz. (48x38mm).

2010, Apr. 15 **Photo.**

2437	A1115	Sheet of 10	16.00	16.00
a.-j.		1 Any single	1.60	.80

Nos. 2437a-2437j each sold for 59c on day of issue. No. 2437d has a perforated cross in the vignette.

Belgian Railways, 175th Anniv. A1116

Photo. & Engr.

2010, May 10 ***Perf. 11½***

2438	A1116	2 multi	3.00	1.50

Sold for €1.18 on day of issue.

Parties — A1117

Designs: No. 2439, Man and woman with noisemakers. No. 2440, Hands holding gift and bouquet of roses. No. 2441, Man's hand holding Chinese lantern, woman wearing mask. No. 2442, Hands of servers holding trays with birthday cake and drinks. No. 2443, Girl sipping drink, boy holding balloon.

Die Cut Perf. 10 on 2 or 3 Sides

2010, May 10 **Photo.**

Booklet Stamps

Self-Adhesive

Background Color

2439	A1117	1 green	1.50	.75
2440	A1117	1 red	1.50	.75
2441	A1117	1 violet	1.50	.75
2442	A1117	1 blue	1.50	.75
2443	A1117	1 orange	1.50	.75
a.		Booklet pane of 10, 2 each #2439-2443	15.00	
		Nos. 2439-2443 (5)	7.50	3.75

Nos. 2439-2443 each sold for 59c on day of issue.

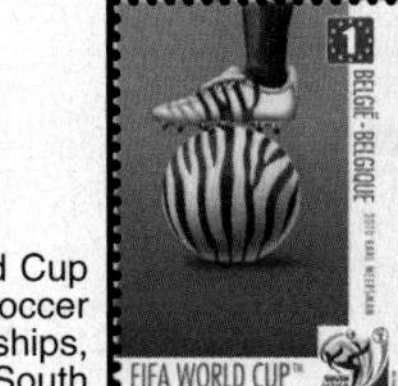

2010 World Cup Soccer Championships, South Africa — A1118

2010 Youth Olympics, Singapore A1119

Eddy Merckx, Professional Cyclist — A1120

2010, June 14 **Litho.** ***Perf. 11½***

2444	A1118	1 multi	2.25	1.10
2445	A1119	1 multi	2.75	1.40
2446	A1120	2 multi	3.00	1.50
		Nos. 2444-2446 (3)	8.00	4.00

On day of issue, No. 2444 sold for 90c, No. 2445 sold for €1.05, and No. 2446 sold for €1.18.

Independence of Belgian Congo, 50th Anniv. — A1121

2010, June 14

2447	A1121	1 multi	2.75	1.40

Sold for €1.05 on day of issue.

National Elections — A1122

2010, May 12 **Photo.** ***Perf. 11½***

2448	A1122	1 multi	.70	.35

Sold for 28c on day of issue.

Belgian Presidency of the European Union Council A1123

2010, July 1 **Litho.** ***Perf. 11½***

2449	A1123	1 multi	2.25	1.10

Sold for 90c on day of issue.

Miniature Sheet

High-rise Buildings — A1124

No. 2450: a, Le Tonneau, Brussels. b, Sint-Maartensdal, Louvain. c, Le Fer à Cheval, Brussels. d, Boerentoren, Antwerp. e, La Cité de Droixhe, Liège.

2010, Aug. 30

2450	A1124	Sheet of 5	12.00	6.25
a.-e.		1 Any single	2.40	1.25

Nos. 2450a-2450e each sold for 90c on day of issue. Imperforate sheets were gifts to standing order customers.

Fletsknooppunten A1125

Le Ravel — A1126

Die Cut Perf. 10 on 2 or 3 Sides

2010, Aug. 30 **Photo.**

Booklet Stamps

Self-Adhesive

2451	A1125	1 multi	1.60	.80
2452	A1126	1 multi	1.60	.80
a.		Booklet pane of 10, 5 each #2451-2452	16.00	

Bicycle paths. Nos. 2451-2452 each sold for 59c on day of issue.

1953 Ford Mail Bus A1127

1931 Mail Train Car A1128

1979 Bedford Mail Truck A1129

1968 Mail Train Car A1130

2009 Volvo Mail Truck A1131

Photo. & Engr.

2010, Aug. 30 ***Perf. 11½***

2453	A1127	1 multi	1.60	.80
2454	A1128	1 multi	1.60	.80
2455	A1129	1 multi	1.60	.80
2456	A1130	1 multi	1.60	.80
2457	A1131	1 multi	1.60	.80
a.		Vert. strip of 5, #2453-2457	8.00	4.00
		Nos. 2453-2457 (5)	8.00	4.00

On day of issue, Nos. 2453-2457 each sold for 59c.

De Mena Recreation Center, Rotselaar A1132

Telematics Center, Marche-en-Famenne — A1133

Wiels Center for Contemporary Art, Brussels — A1134

2010, Sept. 20 **Litho.**

2458	A1132	1 multi	2.50	1.25
2459	A1133	1 multi	3.00	1.50
2460	A1134	2 multi	3.25	1.60
		Nos. 2458-2460 (3)	8.75	4.35

Repurposed brewery buildings. On day of issue, No. 2458 sold for 90c; No. 2459, for €1.05; No. 2460, for €1.18.

Miniature Sheet

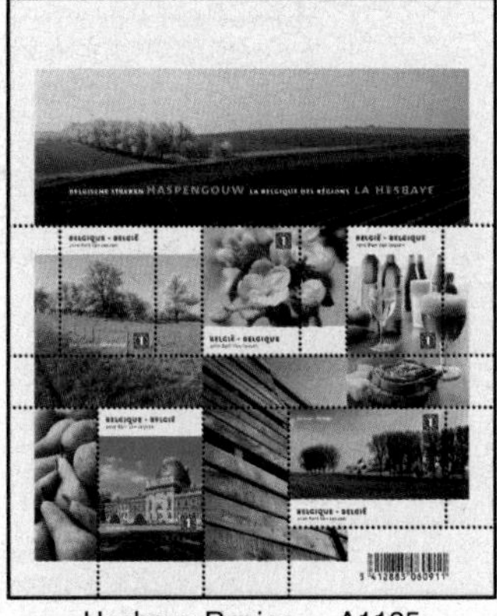

Hesbaye Region — A1135

No. 2461: a, Blossoming orchard, Sint-Truiden (30x40mm). b, Fruit blossoms (30x40mm). c, Fruit, wine and beer (30x40mm). d, Hélécine (33x40mm). e, Farm, Perwez (49x37mm).

Perf. 11¼x11½ (#a-c), 11½ (#d-e)

2010, Sept. 20 **Photo.**

2461	A1135	Sheet of 5 + 2 labels	12.50	6.25
a.-e.		1 Any single	2.50	1.25

On day of issue, Nos. 2461a-2461e each sold for 90c.

Bpost Emblem — A1136

2010, Oct. 18 **Photo.** ***Perf. 11½***

2462 A1136 1 multi 1.75 .85

Sold for 59c on day of issue.

Tools A1137

Tools of: No. 2463, Cordonnier (shoemaker). No. 2464, Sabotier (clog maker). No. 2465, Maréchal-ferrant (farrier). No. 2466, Blanchisseuse (washerwoman). No. 2467, Fileuse (spinner).

2010, Oct. 18 **Litho.**

2463 A1137 1 multi 1.75 .85
2464 A1137 1 multi 1.75 .85
2465 A1137 1 multi 1.75 .85
2466 A1137 1 multi 1.75 .85
2467 A1137 1 multi 1.75 .85
a. Vert. strip of 5, #2463-2467 8.75 4.25
Nos. 2463-2467 (5) 8.75 4.25

Nos. 2463-2467 each sold for 59c on day of issue.

Pays de Connaisance A1138 — Voyage Dans la Lune A1139

Un Cri — A1140

L'Etranger A1141

La Mer ce Grand Sculpteur A1142

Oiseau A1143

Waha Church Window — A1144 — Pluie — A1145

Un Monde — A1146 — L'Aube — A1147

Serpentine Die Cut 8

2010, Oct. 18 **Litho.**

Booklet Stamps Self-Adhesive

2468 A1138 1 multi 1.75 .85
2469 A1139 1 multi 1.75 .85
2470 A1140 1 multi 1.75 .85
2471 A1141 1 multi 1.75 .85
2472 A1142 1 multi 1.75 .85
2473 A1143 1 multi 1.75 .85
2474 A1144 1 multi 1.75 .85
2475 A1145 1 multi 1.75 .85
2476 A1146 1 multi 1.75 .85
2477 A1147 1 multi 1.75 .85
a. Booklet pane of 10, #2468-2477 17.50
Nos. 2468-2477 (10) 17.50 8.50

Art of Jean-Michel Folon (1934-2005). Nos. 2468-2477 each sold for 59c on day of issue.

Souvenir Sheet

Primitive Flemish Paintings — A1148

No. 2478: a, Madonna and Child, by Roger de la Pasture. b, Portrait of Laurent Froimont, by Rogier van der Weyden.

2010, Nov. 8 ***Perf. 11½***

2478 A1148 Sheet of 2 15.00 15.00
a.-b. 3 Either single 7.50 3.75

Nos. 2478a-2478b each sold for €2.70 on day of issue. See France No. 3924.

Christmas A1149

Santa Claus, reindeer and sleigh facing: No. 2479, Left. No. 2480, Right.

Die Cut Perf. 9¾ on 2 or 3 Sides

2010, Nov. 8 **Photo.**

Booklet Stamps Self-Adhesive

2479 A1149 1 multi 1.60 .80
a. Booklet pane of 10 16.00
2480 A1149 1 multi 2.50 1.25
a. Booklet pane of 10 25.00

On day of issue, No. 2479 sold for 59c and No. 2480 sold for 90c.

Bird Type of 1985 With Euro Denominations Only

2011, Jan. 3 **Litho.** ***Perf. 11½***

2481 A524 8c Canard pilet .25 .25

Liberaliztion of Postal Market — A1150

2011, Jan. 3 **Litho.** ***Perf. 11½***

2482 A1150 1 multi 1.75 .85

Sold for 61c on day of issue.

Intl. Year of Chemistry A1151

2011, Jan. 17

2483 A1151 1 multi 1.75 .85

Sold for 61c on day of issue.

Signs of the Zodiac — A1152

Serpentine Die Cut 7½

2011, Jan. 17 **Self-Adhesive**

2484 A1152 1 multi 1.75 .85

Sold for 61c on day of issue. Printed in sheets of 10 + 12 stickers depicting the Zodiac signs, which could be placed on the stamp.

Homes of Authors A1153

Designs: No. 2485, La Maison Blanche, home of Maurice Carême, Anderlecht. No. 2486, Domus Erasmi, home of Desiderius Erasmus, Anderlecht. No. 2487, Het Lijsternest, home of Stijn Streuvels, Ingooigem.

2011, Jan. 17

2485 A1153 1 multi 2.60 1.25
2486 A1153 1 multi 3.00 1.50
2487 A1153 2 multi 3.50 1.75
Nos. 2485-2487 (3) 9.10 4.50

On day of issue, No. 2485 sold for 93c; No. 2486, for €1.10; and No. 2487, for €1.22.

G. Dam, Painting by Luc Tuymans A1154

2011, Feb. 14

2488 A1154 1 multi 1.75 .85

Sold for 61c on day of issue.

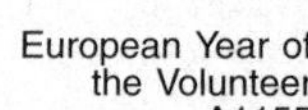

European Year of the Volunteer A1155

Die Cut Perf. 9¾ on 2 or 3 Sides

2011, Feb. 14 **Photo.**

Booklet Stamp Self-Adhesive

2489 A1155 1 multi 1.75 .85
a. Booklet pane of 10 17.50

No. 2489 sold for 61c on day of issue.

Belgian Art Masterpieces — A1156

Belgian Architecture A1157

Atomium and Manneken Pis, Brussels A1158

Tank and Mardasson Memorial, Bastogne A1159

Lion's Mound, Waterloo A1160

Serpentine Die Cut 8

2011, Feb. 14 **Litho.**

Booklet Stamps Self-Adhesive

2490 A1156 1 multi 3.25 1.60
2491 A1157 1 multi 3.25 1.60
2492 A1158 1 multi 3.25 1.60
2493 A1159 1 multi 3.25 1.60
2494 A1160 1 multi 3.25 1.60
a. Booklet pane of 5, #2490-2494 16.50
Nos. 2490-2494 (5) 16.25 8.00

On day of issue, Nos. 2490-2494 each sold for €1.10.

Bal du Rat Mort, Drawing by James Ensor — A1161

2011, Mar. 7 ***Perf. 11½***

2495 A1161 1 multi 1.75 .85

Cercle Coecilia, 150th anniv. Sold for 61c on day of issue.

Miniature Sheet

Vegetables — A1162

No. 2496: a, Vitellote (purple potato) and topinambour (Jerusalem artichoke). b, Pâtisson (patty pan squash). c, Carotte violette (purple carrot) and panais (parsnip). d, Bette (chard). e, Cardon (cardoon).

2011, Mar. 7 **Photo.**

2496	A1162	Sheet of 5	15.00	15.00
a.-e.		1 Any single	3.00	1.50

On day of issue, Nos. 2496a-2496e each sold for €1.10.

Miniature Sheet

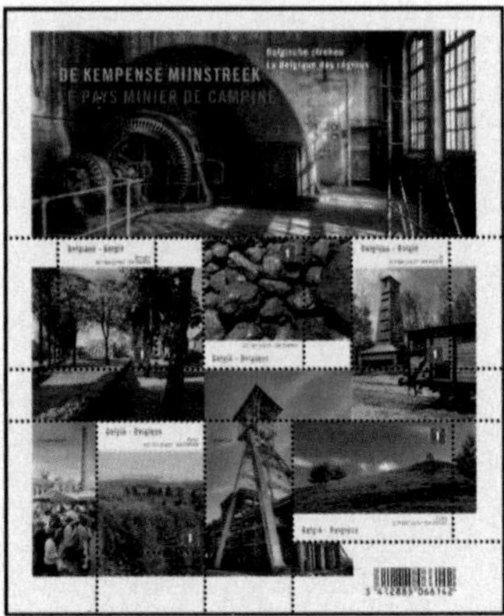

Mining Heritage of the Campine Region — A1163

No. 2497: a, Miner's housing, Beringen (31x40mm). b, Coal (31x40mm). c, Shaft tower, railway car, As (31x40mm). d, Slagheap and countryside, Zolder (33x40mm). e, People on slagheap, Eisden (49x37mm).

2011, Apr. 4 **Photo.**

2497	A1163	Sheet of 5	14.00	14.00
a.-e.		1 Any single	2.75	1.40

On day of issue, Nos. 2497a-2497e each sold for 93c.

Fair Scenes — A1164

Designs: No. 2498, Flying swings. No. 2499, Fortune-teller. No. 2500, Man and woman on carousel horses. No. 2501, Roller coaster. No. 2502, Ferris wheel. No. 2503, Shooting gallery. No. 2504, Cotton candy vendor. No. 2505, Bumper cars. No. 2506, Boy and carousel. No. 2507, Haunted house.

Die Cut Perf. 9¾ on 2 or 3 Sides

2011, Apr. 4 **Photo.**

Booklet Stamps
Self-Adhesive

2498	A1164	1 multi	1.75	.90
2499	A1164	1 multi	1.75	.90
2500	A1164	1 multi	1.75	.90
2501	A1164	1 multi	1.75	.90
2502	A1164	1 multi	1.75	.90
2503	A1164	1 multi	1.75	.90
2504	A1164	1 multi	1.75	.90
2505	A1164	1 multi	1.75	.90
2506	A1164	1 multi	1.75	.90
2507	A1164	1 multi	1.75	.90
a.		Booklet pane of 10, #2498-2507	17.50	
		Nos. 2498-2507 (10)	17.50	9.00

On day of issue Nos. 2498-2507 each sold for 61c.

A1165

A1166

A1167

A1168

Mailboxes A1169

Photo. & Engr.

2011, May 16 ***Perf. 11½***

2508	A1165	1 multi	1.75	.90
2509	A1166	1 multi	1.75	.90
2510	A1167	1 multi	1.75	.90
2511	A1168	1 multi	1.75	.90
2512	A1169	1 multi	1.75	.90
a.		Horiz. strip of 5, #2508-2512	8.75	4.50
		Nos. 2508-2512 (5)	8.75	4.50

On day of issue, Nos. 2518-2512 each sold for 61c.

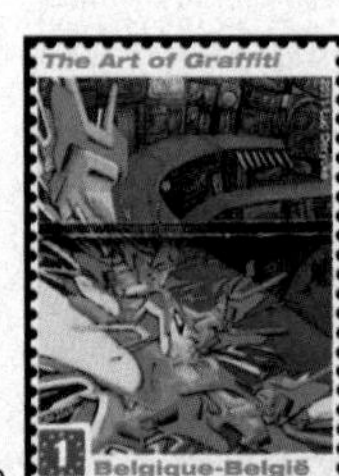

A1170

A1171

A1172

A1173

The Art of Graffiti
Belgique-België

Graffiti on De Wand Tram Station Walls, Laeken — A1174

2011, May 16 **Litho.**

2513		Sheet of 5	14.00	7.00
a.	A1170	1 multi	2.75	1.40
b.	A1171	1 multi	2.75	1.40
c.	A1172	1 multi	2.75	1.40
d.	A1173	1 multi	2.75	1.40
e.	A1174	1 multi	2.75	1.40

On day of issue, Nos. 2513a-2513e each sold for 93c.

Miniature Sheet

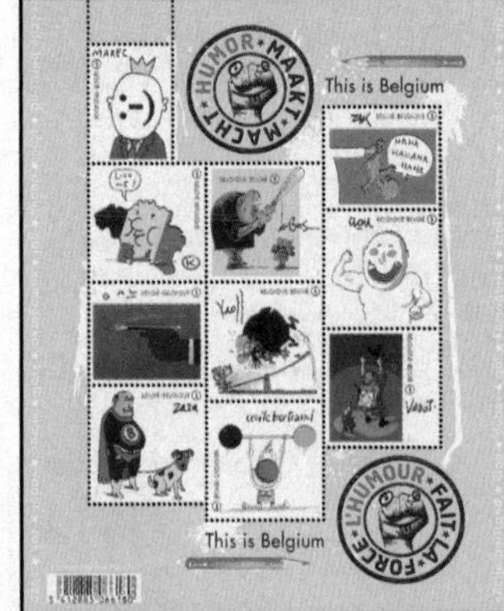

Cartoon Art — A1175

No. 2514: a, Head with crown and emoticon face, by Marec (Marc de Cloedt) (27x38mm). b, Laughing baby being held by ankles, by Zak (Jacques Moeraert) (38x33mm). c, Map of Belgium with face and arms, by Kamagurka (Luc Zeebroek) (38x38mm). d, Large man with club and small man sticking out tongue, by Frédéric du Bus (38x38mm). e, Man with pencil for mouth flexing muscles by Clou (Christian Louis) (38x38mm). f, Pencil as gun, by Gal (Gerard Alsteens) (38x33mm). g, Small jester flipping large man off see-saw, by Pierre Kroll (38x38mm). h, Green creature drawing happy face on paper on soldier's back, by Nicolas Vadot (38x38mm). i, Man in superhero costume with dog on leash, by Zaza (Klaas Storme) (38x38mm). j, Clown lifting barbell, by Cécile Bertrand (38x38mm).

2011, June 27 **Photo.**

2514	A1175	Sheet of 10	17.50	8.50
a.-j.		1 Any single	1.75	.85

On day of issue, Nos. 2514a-2514j each sold for 61c.

Miniature Sheet

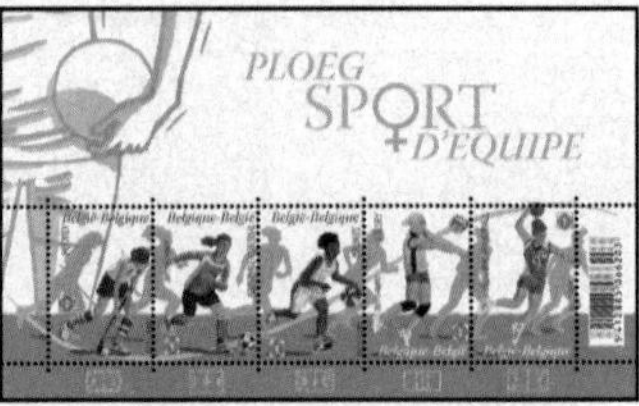

Women's Sports — A1176

No. 2515: a, Field hockey. b, Soccer. c, Basketball. d, Volleyball. e, Handball.

2011, June 27 **Litho.**

2515	A1176	Sheet of 5	16.50	8.00
a.-e.		1 Any single	3.25	1.60

On day of issue, Nos. 2515a-2515e each sold for €1.10.

Posters by Henri de Toulouse-Lautrec (1864-1901) A1177

Designs: No. 2516, Confetti. No. 2517, Aristide Bruant Dans son Cabaret. No. 2518, May Milton. No. 2519, Divan Japonais. No. 2520, Reine de Joie. No. 2521, Le Salon des Cent (La Passagère du 54). No. 2522, Caudieux. No. 2523, Jane Avril. No. 2524, Eldorado-Aristide Bruant Dans son Cabaret. No. 2525, Moulin Rouge, La Goulue.

2011, June 27 ***Serpentine Die Cut 8***

Booklet Stamps
Self-Adhesive

2516	A1177	1 multi	1.75	.85
2517	A1177	1 multi	1.75	.85
2518	A1177	1 multi	1.75	.85
2519	A1177	1 multi	1.75	.85
2520	A1177	1 multi	1.75	.85
2521	A1177	1 multi	1.75	.85
2522	A1177	1 multi	1.75	.85
2523	A1177	1 multi	1.75	.85
2524	A1177	1 multi	1.75	.85
2525	A1177	1 multi	1.75	.85
a.		Booklet pane of 10, #2516-2525	17.50	
		Nos. 2516-2525 (10)	17.50	8.50

On day of issue, Nos. 2516-2525 each sold for 61c.

Miniature Sheet

Courthouses — A1178

No. 2526 — Courthouse in: a, Arlon. b, Ghent. c, Mons. d, Antwerp. e, Charleroi.

2011, Aug. 29 **Litho.** ***Perf. 11½***

2526	A1178	Sheet of 5	17.50	8.75
a.-e.		2 Any single	3.50	1.75

On day of issue, Nos. 2526a-2526e each sold for €1.22.

Miniature Sheet

Tintin — A1179

No. 2527, Scenes from Tintin cartoons, animated and live-action films: a, Tintin and the Crab with the Golden Claws, 1947. b, Tintin and the Crab with the Golden Claws, 1941. c, Black Island (animated), 1961. d, Black Island, 1938. e, Tintin and the Golden Fleece (live-action), 1961. f, Tintin and the Blue Oranges, 1964. g, Tintin and the Sun Temple, 1969. h, Tintin and the Sun Temple, 1949. i, Tintin and the Blue Lotus, 1991. j, Tintin and the Blue Lotus, 1936.

2011, Aug. 29

2527 A1179 Sheet of 10 17.50 8.75
a.-j. 1 Any single 1.75 .85

On day of issue, Nos. 2527a-2527j each sold for 61c. Imperforate sheets were gifts to standing order customers.

Souvenir Sheet

Europa — A1180

No. 2528: a, Eurasian jay. b, Fawn.

2011, Sept. 19

2528 A1180 Sheet of 2 15.50 7.50
a.-b. 3 Either single 7.75 3.75

Intl. Year of Forests. On day of issue, Nos. 2528a-2528b each sold for €2.79.

Bpost Emblem — A1181

2011-12 Photo. ***Perf. 11¾x11½***

2529 A1181 1 multi 1.75 .85
2530 A1181 2 multi 3.50 1.75

Self-Adhesive

Die Cut Perf. 11¾x11½

2531 A1181 1 multi 1.75 .85
2532 A1181 2 multi 3.50 1.75

Issued: Nos. 2529, 2531, 9/19. Nos. 2530, 2532, 3/12/12. On day of issue, Nos. 2529 and 2531 each sold for 61c, and Nos. 2530 and 2532 each sold for €1.30.

Queen Paola and Child — A1182

2011, Oct. 17 Litho. ***Perf. 11½***

2533 A1182 1 multi 1.75 .85

No. 2533 sold for 61c on day of issue.

Miniature Sheet

Candies — A1183

No. 2534: a, Babeluttes (wrapped caramel pieces) (25x33mm). b, Cuberdons (chocolate-covered jellies) (26x47mm). c, Caramels (25x33mm). d, Guimauves (marshmallows) (26x50mm). e, Gommes (gummy bears) (26x50mm).

2011, Oct. 17 Photo.

2534 A1183 Sheet of 5 13.00 13.00
a.-e. 1 Any single 2.60 1.25

Nos. 2534a-2534e each sold for 93c on day of issue.

Souvenir Sheet

Europalia Intl. Arts Festival, Brazil — A1184

No. 2535 — Brazilian Indians wearing: a, Headdress of feathers. b, Earrings.

2011, Nov. 2 Litho.

2535 A1184 Sheet of 2 10.00 10.00
a.-b. 3 Either single 5.00 2.50

Nos. 2535a-2535b each sold for €1.83 on day of issue. See Brazil No.

Snowman A1185

Angel — A1186

Die Cut Perf. 9¾ on 2 or 3 Sides

2011, Nov. 2 Photo.

Booklet Stamps

Self-Adhesive

2536 A1185 1 multi 1.75 .85
a. Booklet pane of 10 17.50
2537 A1186 1 multi 2.60 1.25
a. Booklet pane of 10 26.00

Christmas. On day of issue, Nos. 2536 and 2537 sold for 61c and 93c, respectively.

Detail From Mayan Calendar A1187

2012, Jan. 16 Litho. ***Perf. 11½***

2538 A1187 1 multi 3.25 1.60

No. 2538 sold for €1.19 on day of issue.

Miniature Sheet

Trappist Beer Brands — A1188

No. 2539 — Bottle, cap and goblet of: a, Achel. b, Chimay. c, Orval. d, Rochefort. e, Westmalle. f, Westvleteren.

Perf. 11½ on 3 or 4 Sides

2012, Jan. 16

2539 A1188 Sheet of 6 16.00 16.00
a.-f. 1 Any single 2.60 1.25

Nos. 2539a-2539f each sold for 99c on day of issue.

Mythical Creatures A1189

Designs: No. 2540, Mermaid (sirène). No. 2541, Werewolf (loup-garou). No. 2542, Unicorn (licorne). No. 2543, Dragon. No. 2544, Winged serpent (amphiptère). No. 2545, Pegasus. No. 2546, Griffin (griffon). No. 2547, Centaur. No. 2548, Sphinx. No. 2549, Harpy (harpie).

Die Cut Perf. 9¾ on 2 or 3 Sides

2012, Jan. 16 Photo.

Booklet Stamps

Self-Adhesive

2540 A1189 1 multi 1.75 .85
2541 A1189 1 multi 1.75 .85
2542 A1189 1 multi 1.75 .85
2543 A1189 1 multi 1.75 .85
2544 A1189 1 multi 1.75 .85
2545 A1189 1 multi 1.75 .85
2546 A1189 1 multi 1.75 .85
2547 A1189 1 multi 1.75 .85
2548 A1189 1 multi 1.75 .85
2549 A1189 1 multi 1.75 .85
a. Booklet pane of 10, #2540-2549 17.50
Nos. 2540-2549 (10) 17.50 8.50

Nos. 2540-2549 each sold for 65c on day of issue. See Nos. 2608-2617.

Souvenir Sheet

Europa — A1190

No. 2550 — Various Belgian tourist attractions with country name at: a, LL. b, UR.

2012, Feb. 13 Litho. ***Perf. 11½***

2550 A1190 Sheet of 2 16.00 16.00
a.-b. 3 Either single 8.00 4.00

Nos. 2550a-2550b each sold for €2.97 on day of issue.

Calligraphy — A1191

Designs: No. 2551, Latin calligraphy. No. 2552, Arabic calligraphy. No. 2553, Chinese calligraphy. No. 2554, Hindi calligraphy. No. 2555, Greek calligraphy.

Perf. 11¼x11¾

2012, Feb. 13 Photo.

Booklet Stamps

2551 A1191 1 multi 3.25 1.60
2552 A1191 1 multi 3.25 1.60
2553 A1191 1 multi 3.25 1.60
2554 A1191 1 multi 3.25 1.60
2555 A1191 1 multi 3.25 1.60
a. Booklet pane of 5, #2551-2555 16.50 —
Complete booklet, #2555a 16.50
Nos. 2551-2555 (5) 16.25 8.00

Nos. 2551-2555 each sold for €1.19 on day of issue.

Souvenir Sheet

Cartographers — A1192

No. 2556: a, Gerardus Mercator (1512-94). b, Jodocus Hondius (1563-1612).

Photo. & Engr.

2012, Mar. 12 ***Perf. 11½***

2556 A1192 Sheet of 2 19.00 19.00
a.-b. 3 Either single 9.50 4.75

Nos. 2556a-2556b each sold for €3.57 on day of issue.

Cirque du Soleil Performers A1193

Décrocher La Lune A1194

A New Day — A1195

La Rêve A1196

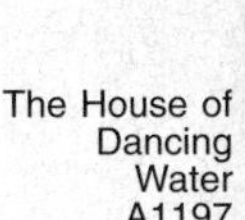

The House of Dancing Water A1197

Serpentine Die Cut 8

2012, Mar. 12 Litho.

Booklet Stamps
Self-Adhesive

2557	A1193	1 multi	2.60	1.25
2558	A1194	1 multi	2.60	1.25
2559	A1195	1 multi	2.60	1.25
2560	A1196	1 multi	2.60	1.25
2561	A1197	1 multi	2.60	1.25
a.		Booklet pane of 5, #2557-2561	13.00	
		Nos. 2557-2561 (5)	13.00	6.25

Scenes from theater productions of director Franco Dragone. Nos. 2557-2561 each sold for 99c on day of issue.

Souvenir Sheet

Sinking of the Titanic, Cent. — A1198

No. 2562 — Stereoptic images of the sinking of the Titanic with top line of smoke from smokestack touching white square around "3": a, At LL corner of square. b, Directly below "3."

2012, Apr. 16 ***Perf. 11½***

2562	A1198	Sheet of 2	19.00	19.00
a.-b.		3 Either single	9.50	4.75

Nos. 2562a-2562b each sold for €3.57 on day of issue. See Finland (Aland Islands) No. 328.

Pets — A1199

Designs: No. 2563, Canaries. No. 2564, Guinea pig. No. 2565, Cat. No. 2566, Goldfish. No. 2567, Parakeets. No. 2568, Shetland pony. No. 2569, Chihuahua. No. 2570, Hamsters. No. 2571, Rabbits. No. 2572, Dog with tongue visible.

Die Cut Perf. 9¾ on 2 or 3 Sides

2012, Apr. 16 Photo.

Booklet Stamps
Self-Adhesive

2563	A1199	1 multi	1.75	.85
2564	A1199	1 multi	1.75	.85
2565	A1199	1 multi	1.75	.85
2566	A1199	1 multi	1.75	.85
2567	A1199	1 multi	1.75	.85
2568	A1199	1 multi	1.75	.85
2569	A1199	1 multi	1.75	.85
2570	A1199	1 multi	1.75	.85
2571	A1199	1 multi	1.75	.85
2572	A1199	1 multi	1.75	.85
a.		Booklet pane of 10, #2563-2572	17.50	
		Nos. 2563-2572 (10)	17.50	8.50

Nos. 2563-2572 each sold for 65c on day of issue.

Floristan Sunflower, by Jef Geys — A1200

2012, May 21 Litho. ***Perf. 11½***

2573	A1200	1 multi	1.75	.85

Exhibition of art by Jef Geys, Royal Museum of Fine Arts, Brussels. No. 2573 sold for 65c on day of issue.

2012 Summer Olympics, London A1201

2012, May 21

2574	A1201	1 multi	3.00	1.50

No. 2574 sold for €1.19 on day of issue.

Independence of Rwanda and Burundi, 50th Anniv. — A1202

Designs: No. 2575, Rwandan basket with lid. No. 2576, Burundian drum.

2012, May 21

2575	A1202	1 yel & multi	3.00	1.50
2576	A1202	1 red & multi	3.00	1.50

Nos. 2575-2576 each sold for €1.19 on day of issue.

Cabaret on the Banks of the River, by Jan Breughel — A1203

2012, June 25

2577	A1203	1 multi	1.60	.80

Exhibition of philatelic collection of Prince Albert II of Monaco, Bruges. No. 2577 sold for 65c on day of issue. See Monaco No. 2681.

Pieris Brassicae A1204

Papilion Machaon A1205

Die Cut Perf. 10 on 2 or 3 Sides

2012, June 25 Photo.

Booklet Stamps
Self-Adhesive

2578	A1204	1 multi	1.60	.40
a.		Booklet pane of 10	16.00	

Die Cut Perf. 10 on 3 Sides

2579	A1205	1 multi	2.50	.65
a.		Booklet pane of 5	12.50	

On day of issue No. 2578 sold for 65c and No. 2579 sold for 99c.

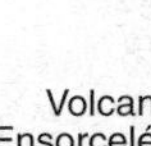

Volcan Ensorcelé A1206

A Propos de Binche A1207

Sans Espoir de Bâtiment Pour Anvers ni Même Pour l'Escault A1208

Parfois, C'est l'Inverse A1209

A la Ligne A1210

Aquarelle Estampillée A1211

Labyrinthe d'Apparat A1212

Encreur A1213

Nuages en Pantalon A1214

Le Dernier Jour A1215

2012, June 25 ***Sawtooth Die Cut 8¼***

Booklet Stamps
Self-Adhesive

2580	A1206	1 multi	1.60	.80
2581	A1207	1 multi	1.60	.80
2582	A1208	1 multi	1.60	.80
2583	A1209	1 multi	1.60	.80
2584	A1210	1 multi	1.60	.80
2585	A1211	1 multi	1.60	.80
2586	A1212	1 multi	1.60	.80
2587	A1213	1 multi	1.60	.80
2588	A1214	1 multi	1.60	.80
2589	A1215	1 multi	1.60	.80
a.		Booklet pane of 10, #2580-2589	16.00	
		Nos. 2580-2589 (10)	16.00	8.00

Paintings by Pierre Alechinsky. Nos. 2580-2589 each sold for 65c on day of issue.

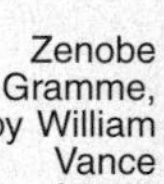

Zenobe Gramme, by William Vance A1216

2012, Sept. 17 Litho. ***Perf. 11½***

2590	A1216	1 multi	1.75	.85

No. 2590 sold for 65c on day of issue.

Miniature Sheet

Comic Strip Characters — A1217

No. 2591: a, Gil and Jo (boy and parrot, yellow green background), by Jef Nys (36x24mm). b, Gaston Lagaffe (light blue background), by André Franquin (27x40mm). c, Bob and Bobette (country name in red), by Willy Vandersteen (38x24mm). d, Jerry Spring (cowboy holding hat), by Jijé (40x27mm). e, Cori le Moussaillon (boy climbing rope ladder on ship's mast), by Bob de Moor (27x40mm). f, Tintin (with dog Snowy), by Hergé (32x36mm). g, Blake and Mortimer (two men, yellow green background), by Edgar P. Jacobs (40x27mm). h, Néro (man walking), by Marc Sleen (27x40mm). i, Lucky Luke (cowboy wearing hat), by Morris (27x40mm). j, The Smurfs, by Peyo (40x27mm).

Perf. 11½, 11¾ (#2591f)

2012, Sept. 17 Photo.

2591	A1217	Sheet of 10	17.50	17.50
a.-j.		1 Any single	1.75	.85

Nos. 2591a-2591j each sold for 65c on day of issue. Imperforate examples of No. 2591 were gifts to standing order customers.

Tree Leaves — A1218

Designs: No. 2592, Acer macrophyllum. No. 2593, Acer palmatum. No. 2594, Morus nigra. No. 2595, Sorbus alnifolia. No. 2596, Ginkgo biloba. No. 2597, Betula pendula. No. 2598, Fagus sylvatica. No. 2599, Aesculus hippocastanum. No. 2600, Euonymus europaeus. No. 2601, Quercus pondaim.

Die Cut Perf. 9¾ on 2 or 3 Sides

2012, Sept. 17

Booklet Stamps
Self-Adhesive

2592	A1218	1 multi	1.75	.85
2593	A1218	1 multi	1.75	.85
2594	A1218	1 multi	1.75	.85
2595	A1218	1 multi	1.75	.85
2596	A1218	1 multi	1.75	.85
2597	A1218	1 multi	1.75	.85
2598	A1218	1 multi	1.75	.85
2599	A1218	1 multi	1.75	.85
2600	A1218	1 multi	1.75	.85
2601	A1218	1 multi	1.75	.85
a.		Booklet pane of 10, #2592-2601	17.50	
		Nos. 2592-2601 (10)	17.50	8.50

Nos. 2592-2601 each sold for 65c on day of issue.

An Offering to Ceres, by Jacob Jordaens — A1219

2012, Oct. 8 Litho. ***Perf. 11½***

2602 A1219 1 multi 1.75 .85

No. 2602 sold for 65c on day of issue.

St. Martin Festival — A1220

2012, Oct. 8

2603 A1220 1 multi 1.75 .85

No. 2603 sold for 65c on day of issue.

Miniature Sheet

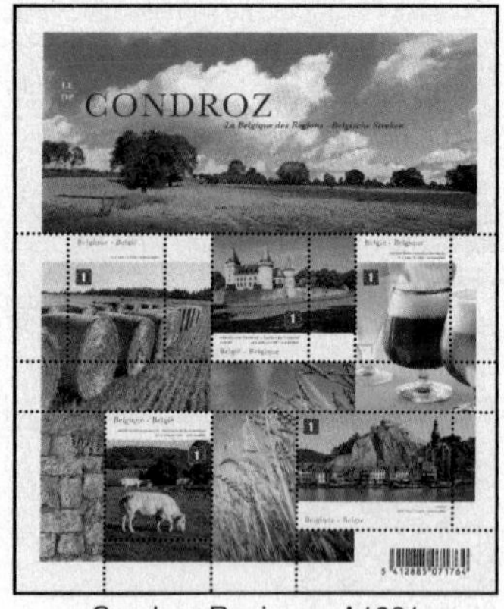

Condroz Region — A1221

No. 2604: a, Hay rolls in field (30x40mm). b, Fontaine Castle (30x40mm). c, Glasses of regional beers (30x40mm). d, Belgian blue-white cattle grazing (33x40mm). e, Dinant (49x37mm).

Perf. 11¼x11½, 11½ (#2604d, 2604e)
2012, Oct. 8 Photo.

2604 A1221 Sheet of 5 +2 labels 13.00 13.00
a.-e. 1 Any single 2.60 1.25

Nos. 2604a-2604e each sold for 99c on day of issue.

Apatura Ilia — A1222

Serpentine Die Cut 13¼x14
2012, Oct. 29
Coil Stamp
Self-Adhesive

2605 A1222 1 multi 1.75 .85

No. 2605 sold for 65c on day of sale.

Christmas
A1223 A1224

Die Cut Perf. 9¾ on 2 or 3 Sides
2012, Oct. 29
Booklet Stamps
Self-Adhesive

2606 A1223 1 multi 1.75 .85
a. Booklet pane of 10 17.50
2607 A1224 1 multi 2.60 1.25
a. Booklet pane of 10 26.00

On day of issue, No. 2606 sold for 65c; No. 2607, for 99c.

Mythical Creatures Type of 2012

Designs: No. 2608, Devil (diable). No. 2609, Troll. No. 2610, Ghost (fantôme). No. 2611, Magician (magicien). No. 2612, Witch (sorcière). No. 2613, Dwarf (nain). No. 2614, Fairy (fée). No. 2615, Giant (géant). No. 2616, Prince. No. 2617, Elf.

2013, Jan. 21
Booklet Stamps
Self-Adhesive

2608 A1189 1 multi 1.90 .95
2609 A1189 1 multi 1.90 .95
2610 A1189 1 multi 1.90 .95
2611 A1189 1 multi 1.90 .95
2612 A1189 1 multi 1.90 .95
2613 A1189 1 multi 1.90 .95
2614 A1189 1 multi 1.90 .95
2615 A1189 1 multi 1.90 .95
2616 A1189 1 multi 1.90 .95
2617 A1189 1 multi 1.90 .95
a. Booklet pane of 10, #2608-2617 19.00
Nos. 2608-2617 (10) 19.00 9.50

Nos. 2608-2617 each sold for 67c on day of issue.

Black Grouse A1225

2013, Jan. 21 Litho. ***Perf. 11¾x11½***

2618 A1225 (40c) multi 1.10 .55

Princess Mathilde, 40th Birthday — A1226

2013, Jan. 21 ***Perf. 11½***

2619 A1226 1 multi 1.90 .95

No. 2619 sold for 67c on day of issue.

Kid Paddle, Animated Cartoon by Midam A1227

2013, Jan. 21

2620 A1227 1 multi 1.90 .95

No. 2620 sold for 67c on day of issue.

Miniature Sheet

Road Safety — A1228

No. 2621 — Winning designs in stamp design contest: a, Road and sign with smile, by Jean-Louis Rondia. b, Automobile, traffic light, cyclist, flowers, by Ellen Labey. c, Child and woman in crosswalk, by Kiattisak Nulong. d, Snail on road at night, by Jean-Louis Verbaert. e, Cyclist and traffic light, by Antoine Buscemi.

Litho. & Silk-screened
2013, Feb. 11 ***Perf. 13¼x13½***

2621 A1228 Sheet of 5 17.50 8.75
a.-e. 2 Any single 3.50 1.75

Nos. 2621a-2621e each sold for €1.34 on day of issue.

Souvenir Sheet

Europa — A1229

No. 2622 — Postal van facing: a, Right. b, Left.

2013, Feb. 11 Litho. ***Perf. 11½***

2622 A1229 Sheet of 2 16.00 8.00
a.-b. 3 Either single 8.00 4.00

Nos. 2622a-2622b each sold for €3.09 on day of issue.

Tour des Flandres Bicycle Race, Cent. — A1230

2013, Mar. 25

2623 A1230 1 multi 1.75 .85

No. 2623 sold for 67c on day of issue.

Miniature Sheet

Chocolates — A1231

No. 2624: a, Spiral in chocolate granules. b, Stack of chocolate pieces. c, Heart-shaped candy. d, Cookie with chocolate frosting, horiz. e, Squares of chocolate and piece of candy, horiz.

2013, Mar. 25 ***Perf. 12***

2624 A1231 Sheet of 5 16.50 8.00
a.-e. 1 Any single 3.25 1.60

Nos. 2624a-2624e each sold for €1.24 on day of issue. No. 2624 is impregnated with a chocolate scent.

Bpost Emblem — A1232

Perf. 11¾x11½
2013, Mar. 25 Photo.
Self-Adhesive

2625 A1232 1 multi + label 2.75 1.40

No. 2625 sold for €1.03. The label shown is generic, and labels could be personalized for an additional charge. Compare with Type A1181.

Vanessa Atalanta — A1233 Aglais Urticae — A1234

Die Cut Perf. 10 on 3 Sides
2013, Mar. 25 Self-Adhesive
Booklet Stamps

2626 A1233 1 multi 3.25 1.60
a. Booklet pane of 5 16.50
2627 A1234 2 multi 3.50 1.75
a. Booklet pane of 5 17.50

On day of issue No. 2626 sold for €1.24, and No. 2627 sold for €1.34.

Souvenir Sheet

First Airmail Flight in Deperdussin Monoplane, Cent. — A1235

No. 2628 — Monoplane: a, On ground at Saint-Denis-Westrem. b, In air at Berchem-Sainte-Agathe.

Photo. & Engr.

2013, Apr. 15 *Perf. 11½*

2628 A1235 Sheet of 2 16.50 8.25
a.-b. 3 Either single 8.25 4.00

On day of issue, Nos. 2628a-2628b each sold for €3.09.

The Valley of the Sambre A1236

The Promenade A1237

Summer Afternoon (Tea in the Garden) A1238

Arab Fantasy A1239

Portrait of Marguerite Van Mons A1240

Marie Sèthe at the Harmonium A1241

Bathing Woman A1242

Sisters of the Painter Schlobach A1243

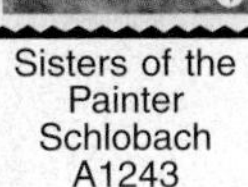

A Reading by Emile Verhaeren A1244

The Artist's Wife and Daughter A1245

Sawtooth Die Cut 8¼

2013, Apr. 15 **Litho.**

Booklet Stamps
Self-Adhesive

2629	A1236	1 multi	1.75	.85
2630	A1237	1 multi	1.75	.85
2631	A1238	1 multi	1.75	.85
2632	A1239	1 multi	1.75	.85
2633	A1240	1 multi	1.75	.85
2634	A1241	1 multi	1.75	.85
2635	A1242	1 multi	1.75	.85
2636	A1243	1 multi	1.75	.85
2637	A1244	1 multi	1.75	.85
2638	A1245	1 multi	1.75	.85
a.	Booklet pane of 10, #2629-2638		17.50	
	Nos. 2629-2638 (10)		17.50	8.50

Paintings by Théo van Rysselberghe (1862-1926). On day of issue, Nos. 2629-2638 each sold for 67c.

Opera Houses and Scenes from Operas by Richard Wagner (1813-83) and Giuseppe Verdi (1813-1901) A1246

Designs: No. 2639, Ghent Opera House, scene from *Das Rheingold,* by Wagner. No. 2640, Antwerp Opera House, scene from *Don Carlos,* by Verdi. No. 2641, Brussels Opera House (at UR), scene from *Macbeth,* by Verdi. No. 2642, Brussels Opera House (at UL), scene from *Parsifal,* by Wagner. No. 2643, Liège Opera House, scene from *Otello,* by Verdi

Photo. & Engr.

2013, May 13 *Perf. 11½*

Booklet Stamps

2639	A1246	1 multi	2.75	1.40
2640	A1246	1 multi	2.75	1.40
2641	A1246	1 multi	2.75	1.40
2642	A1246	1 multi	2.75	1.40
2643	A1246	1 multi	2.75	1.40
a.	Booklet pane of 5, #2639-2643		14.00	—
	Complete booklet, #2643a		14.00	
	Nos. 2639-2643 (5)		13.75	7.00

On day of issue, Nos. 2639-2643 each sold for €1.03.

Animals in Antwerp Zoo — A1247

Designs: No. 2644, Eyes of owl. No. 2645, Trunk of elephant. No. 2646, Nose and mouth of lion. No. 2647, Heads of two penguins. No. 2648, Head of seal. No. 2649, Head of zebra. No. 2650, Eye of tiger. No. 2651, Eyes of lion tamarin. No. 2652, Head and hindquarters of okapi. No. 2653, Necks of giraffes.

Die Cut Perf. 10 on 2 or 3 Sides

2013, May 13 **Photo.**

Booklet Stamps
Self-Adhesive

2644	A1247	1 multi	1.90	.95
2645	A1247	1 multi	1.90	.95
2646	A1247	1 multi	1.90	.95
2647	A1247	1 multi	1.90	.95
2648	A1247	1 multi	1.90	.95
2649	A1247	1 multi	1.90	.95
2650	A1247	1 multi	1.90	.95
2651	A1247	1 multi	1.90	.95
2652	A1247	1 multi	1.90	.95
2653	A1247	1 multi	1.90	.95
a.	Booklet pane of 10, #2644-2653		19.00	
	Nos. 2644-2653 (10)		19.00	9.50

On day of issue, Nos. 2644-2653 each sold for 67c.

Music Festivals A1248

2013, June 24 **Litho.** *Perf. 11½*

2654 A1248 1 multi 1.75 .85

No. 2654 sold for 67c on day of issue.

Miniature Sheet

Royal Meteorological Institue, Cent. — A1249

No. 2655: a, Royal Meteorological Institute Building (60x30mm). b, Cloud over Sun, tree in spring (40x30mm). c, Sun over tree in summer (40x30mm). d, Rain cloud over tree in sutumn (40x30mm). e, Snow cloud over tree in winter (40x30mm).

Perf. 13¼ (#2655a), 13x13¼

2013, June 24

2655 A1249 Sheet of 5 14.00 7.00
a.-e. 1 Any single 2.75 1.40

On day of issue, Nos. 2655a-2655e each sold for €1.03. The leaves on the trees on Nos. 2655b-2655e are printed in thermochromic ink and change colors when the stamp is warmed.

Souvenir Sheet

Twenty Year Reign of King Albert II — A1250

No. 2656 — King Albert II wearing: a, Uniform and sash. b, Overcoat and scarf.

2013, June 24 *Perf. 11½*

2656 A1250 Sheet of 2 16.50 8.25
a.-b. 3 Either single 8.25 4.00

On day of issue, Nos. 2656a-2656b each sold for €3.09.

Souvenir Sheet

Belgian Kings — A1251

No. 2657: a, King Philippe (crown at UL). b, King Albert II (crown at UR).

2013, Sept. 2 **Litho.** *Perf. 11½*

2657 A1251 Sheet of 2 16.50 8.50
a.-b. 3 Either single 8.25 4.25

Abdication of King Albert II and ascension to throne of King Philippe. Nos. 2657a-2657b eachs old for €3.09 on day of issue.

Lily — A1252

Die Cut Perf. 9¾ on 2 or 3 Sides

2013, Sept. 13 **Photo.**

Booklet Stamp
Self-Adhesive

2658 A1252 1 multi 1.90 .95
a. Booklet pane of 10 19.00

No. 2658 sold for 67c on day of issue.

Good Luck Symbols — A1253

Designs: No. 2659, Hand with crossed fingers. No. 2660, Numeral "7." No. 2661, Horseshoe. No. 2662, Four-leaf clover. No. 2663, Ladybug.

Die Cut Perf. 9¾ on 2 or 3 Sides

2013, Sept. 13 **Litho.**

Booklet Stamps
Self-Adhesive

2659	A1253	1 multi	1.90	.95
2660	A1253	1 multi	1.90	.95
2661	A1253	1 multi	1.90	.95
2662	A1253	1 multi	1.90	.95
2663	A1253	1 multi	1.90	.95
a.	Booklet pane of 10, 2 each #2659-2663		19.00	
	Nos. 2659-2663 (5)		9.50	4.75

Nos. 2659-2663 each sold for 67c on day of issue.

Souvenir Sheet

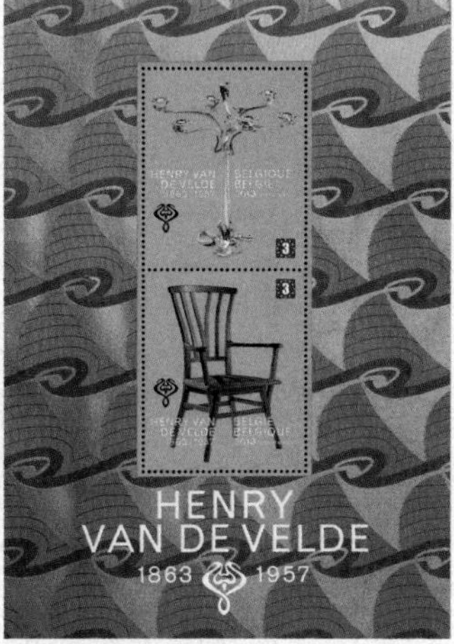

Household Items Created by Henry Van de Velde (1863-1957), Interior Designer — A1254

No. 2664: a, Candelabra. b, Chair.

2013, Sept. 13 **Litho.** *Perf. 13½x14*

2664 A1254 Sheet of 2 16.50 8.50
a.-b. 3 Either single 8.25 4.25

Nos. 2664a-2664b each sold for €3.09 on day of issue.

International Red Cross, 150th Anniv. — A1255

2013, Oct. 28 **Litho.** *Perf. 11½*

2665 A1255 1 multi 3.50 1.75

No. 2665 sold for €1.24 on day of issue.

Photograph From Red Star Line Museum, Antwerp A1256

Photograph From War Museum, Bastogne A1257

Photographs From Dossin Barracks Museum of Deportation and Resistance, Mechlin — A1258

2013, Oct. 28 Litho. *Perf. 11½*

2666	A1256	1 multi	1.90	.95
2667	A1257	1 multi	1.90	.95
2668	A1258	1 multi	1.90	.95
		Nos. 2666-2668 (3)	5.70	2.85

Nos. 2666-2668 each sold for 67c on day of issue.

Christmas
A1259 A1260

Die Cut Perf. 9¾ on 2 or 3 Sides
2013, Oct. 28 Photo.
Booklet Stamps
Self-Adhesive

2669	A1259	1 multi	1.90	.95
a.		Booklet pane of 10	19.00	
2670	A1260	1 multi	2.75	1.40
a.		Booklet pane of 10	27.50	

On day of issue No. 2669 sold for 67c and No. 2670 sold for €1.03.

A1261

A1262

King Philippe
A1263

Perf. 11¾x11½
2013, Oct. 28 Photo.

2671	A1261	1 multi	2.10	.55
2672	A1262	1 multi	3.00	.75
2673	A1263	1 multi	3.75	.95
		Nos. 2671-2673 (3)	8.85	2.25

On day of issue, Nos. 2671-2673 sold for 77c, €1.13, and €1.34, respectively, but each stamp sold for 10c less if purchased in quantities of 10.

SEMI-POSTAL STAMPS

Values quoted for Nos. B1-B24 are for stamps with label attached. Copies without label sell for one-tenth or less.

St. Martin of Tours Dividing His Cloak with a Beggar
SP1 SP2

Unwmk.
1910, June 1 Typo. *Perf. 14*

B1	SP1	1c gray	.75	.75
B2	SP1	2c purple brn	8.00	8.00
B3	SP1	5c peacock blue	1.90	1.90
B4	SP1	10c brown red	1.90	1.90
B5	SP2	1c gray green	1.90	1.90
B6	SP2	2c violet brn	5.00	5.00
B7	SP2	5c peacock blue	2.25	2.25
B8	SP2	10c carmine	2.25	2.25
		Nos. B1-B8 (8)	23.95	23.95
		Set, never hinged	65.00	

Overprinted "1911" in Black

1911, Apr. 1

B9	SP1	1c gray	27.50	16.00
a.		Inverted overprint		
B10	SP1	2c purple brn	125.00	72.50
B11	SP1	5c peacock blue	8.00	5.25
B12	SP1	10c brown red	8.00	5.25
B13	SP2	1c gray green	42.50	27.50
B14	SP2	2c violet brn	60.00	32.50
B15	SP2	5c peacock blue	8.00	5.25
B16	SP2	10c carmine	8.00	5.25
		Nos. B9-B16 (8)	287.00	169.50
		Set, never hinged	600.00	

Overprinted "CHARLEROI-1911"

1911, June

B17	SP1	1c gray	4.00	2.50
B18	SP1	2c purple brn	16.00	10.00
B19	SP1	5c peacock blue	9.00	6.50
B20	SP1	10c brown red	9.00	6.50
B21	SP2	1c gray green	4.00	2.50
B22	SP2	2c violet brn	11.00	9.00
B23	SP2	5c peacock blue	9.00	6.50
B24	SP2	10c carmine	9.00	6.50
		Nos. B17-B24 (8)	71.00	50.00
		Set, never hinged	175.00	

Nos. B1-B24 were sold at double face value, except the 10c denominations which were sold for 15c. The surtax benefited the national anti-tuberculosis organization.

King Albert I — SP3

1914, Oct. 3 Litho.

B25	SP3	5c green & red	*5.00*	*5.00*
B26	SP3	10c red	*1.00*	*1.00*
B27	SP3	20c violet & red	*15.00*	*15.00*
		Nos. B25-B27 (3)	*21.00*	*21.00*
		Set, never hinged	*90.00*	

Counterfeits of Nos. B25-B27 abound. Probably as many as 90% of the stamps on the market are counterfeits. Values are for genuine examples.

Merode Monument — SP4

1914, Oct. 3

B28	SP4	5c green & red	*4.50*	*3.00*
B29	SP4	10c red	*7.50*	*7.50*
B30	SP4	20c violet & red	*75.00*	*75.00*
		Nos. B28-B30 (3)	*87.00*	*85.50*
		Set, never hinged	*175.00*	

Counterfeits of Nos. B28-B30 abound. Probably as many as 90% of the stamps on the market are counterfeits. Genuine stamps have a tail on the "Q" of "BELGIQUE" at the top of the stamp, counterfeits don't have a tail. Values are for genuine examples.

King Albert I — SP5

1915, Jan. 1 *Perf. 12, 14*

B31	SP5	5c green & red	5.00	3.00
a.		Perf. 12x14	16.00	12.00
B32	SP5	10c rose & red	20.00	6.00
B33	SP5	20c violet & red	25.00	14.00
a.		Perf. 14x12	500.00	250.00
b.		Perf. 12	50.00	32.50
		Nos. B31-B33 (3)	50.00	23.00
		Set, never hinged	150.00	

Nos. B25-B33 were sold at double face value. The surtax benefited the Red Cross.

Types of Regular Issue of 1915 Surcharged in Red

Nos. B34-B40

Nos. B41-B43

Nos. B44-B47

1918, Jan. 15 Typo. *Perf. 14*

B34	A46	1c + 1c dp orange	.50	.50
B35	A46	2c + 2c brown	.60	.60
B36	A46	5c + 5c blue grn	1.40	1.40
B37	A46	10c + 10c red	2.25	2.25
B38	A46	15c + 15c brt violet	3.25	3.25
B39	A46	20c + 20c plum	7.50	7.50
B40	A46	25c + 25c ultra	7.50	7.50

Engr.

B41	A47	35c + 35c lt vio & blk	10.00	10.00
B42	A48	40c + 40c dull red & blk	10.00	10.00
B43	A49	50c + 50c turq blue & blk	12.00	12.00
B44	A50	1fr + 1fr bluish slate	35.00	35.00
B45	A51	2fr + 2fr dp gray grn	100.00	100.00
B46	A52	5fr + 5fr brown	250.00	250.00
B47	A53	10fr + 10fr dp blue	550.00	500.00
		Nos. B34-B47 (14)	990.00	940.00
		Set, never hinged	2,000.	

Discus Thrower — SP6

Racing Chariot — SP7

Runner — SP8

1920, May 20 Engr. *Perf. 12*

B48	SP6	5c + 5c dp green	1.40	1.40
B49	SP7	10c + 5c carmine	1.40	1.40
B50	SP8	15c + 15c dk brown	3.00	3.00
		Nos. B48-B50 (3)	5.80	5.80
		Set, never hinged	17.00	

7th Olympic Games, 1920. Surtax benefited wounded soldiers. Exists imperf.

For surcharges see Nos. 140-142.

Allegory: Asking Alms from the Crown
SP9

Wounded Veteran
SP10

1922, May 20

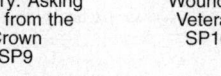

B51	SP9	20c + 20c brown	1.40	1.40
		Never hinged	2.75	

1923, July 5

B52	SP10	20c + 20c slate gray	2.50	2.50
		Never hinged	7.50	

Surtax on Nos. B51-B52 was to aid wounded veterans.

SP11

1925, Dec. 15 Typo. *Perf. 14*

B53	SP11	15c + 5c dull vio & red	.50	.25
B54	SP11	30c + 5c gray & red	.25	.25
B55	SP11	1fr + 10c chalky blue & red	1.25	1.40
		Nos. B53-B55 (3)	2.00	1.90
		Set, never hinged	3.00	

Surtax for the Natl. Anti-Tuberculosis League.

SP12

St. Martin, by Van Dyck
SP13 SP14

1926, Feb. 10

B56	SP12	30c + 30c bluish grn (red surch.)	.50	.50
B57	SP13	1fr + 1fr lt blue	7.25	7.25
B58	SP14	1fr + 1fr lt blue	1.10	1.25
		Nos. B56-B58 (3)	8.85	9.00
		Set, never hinged	20.00	

The surtax aided victims of the Meuse flood.

Lion and Cross of Lorraine — SP15

Queen Elisabeth and King Albert
SP16

1926, Dec. 6 Typo. *Perf. 14*

B59	SP15	5c + 5c dk brown	.25	.25
B60	SP15	20c + 5c red brown	.45	.40
B61	SP15	50c + 5c dull violet	.30	.25

Engr. *Perf. 11½*

B62	SP16	1.50fr + 25c dk blue	.75	.70
B63	SP16	5fr + 1fr rose red	6.50	6.00
		Nos. B59-B63 (5)	8.25	7.60
		Set, never hinged	16.00	

Surtax was used to benefit tubercular war veterans.

Boat Adrift
SP17

1927, Dec. 15 Engr. *Perf. 11½, 14*

B64	SP17	25c + 10c dk brn	.70	.70
B65	SP17	35c + 10c yel grn	.70	.70
B66	SP17	60c + 10c dp violet	.60	.40

No.	Type	Description	Unused	Used
B67	SP17	1.75fr + 25c dk blue	1.50	*2.00*
B68	SP17	5fr + 1fr plum	4.50	*4.75*
		Nos. B64-B68 (5)	8.00	*8.55*
		Set, never hinged	16.00	

The surtax on these stamps was divided among several charitable associations.

Ogives of Orval Abbey — SP18

Monk Carving Capital of Column — SP19

Ruins of Orval Abbey SP20

Design: 60c+15c, 1.75fr+25c, 3fr+1fr, Countess Matilda recovering her ring.

1928, Sept. 15 Photo. *Perf. 11½*

No.	Type	Description	Unused	Used
B69	SP18	5c + 5c red & gold	.25	.25
B70	SP18	25c + 5c dk vio & gold	.45	.45
		Engr.		
B71	SP19	35c + 10c dp grn	1.25	1.25
B72	SP19	60c + 15c red brn	.75	.25
B73	SP19	1.75fr + 25c dk blue	3.25	2.10
B74	SP19	2fr + 40c dp vio	25.00	21.00
B75	SP19	3fr + 1fr red	22.50	20.00
		Perf. 14		
B76	SP20	5fr + 5fr rose lake	15.50	15.50
B77	SP20	10fr + 10fr ol green	15.50	15.50
		Nos. B69-B77 (9)	84.45	76.30
		Set, never hinged	150.00	

Surtax for the restoration of the ruined Orval Abbey.

St. Waudru, Mons — SP22

St. Rombaut, Malines — SP23

Designs: 25c + 15c, Cathedral of Tournai. 60c + 15c, St. Bavon, Ghent. 1.75fr + 25c, St. Gudule, Brussels. 5fr + 5fr, Louvain Library.

1928, Dec. 1 Photo. *Perf. 14, 11½*

No.	Type	Description	Unused	Used
B78	SP22	5c + 5c carmine	.25	.25
B79	SP22	25c + 15c ol brn	.25	.25
		Engr.		
B80	SP23	35c + 10c dp grn	1.50	1.50
B81	SP23	60c + 15c red brn	.45	.45
B82	SP23	1.75fr + 25c vio bl	10.50	10.50
B83	SP23	5fr + 5fr red vio	21.00	21.00
		Nos. B78-B83 (6)	33.95	33.95
		Set, never hinged	65.00	

The surtax was for anti-tuberculosis work.

Nos. B69-B77 with this overprint in blue or red were privately produced. They were for the laying of the 1st stone toward the restoration of the ruined Abbey of Orval. Value, set, $650.

Forgeries of the overprint exist.

Waterfall at Coo — SP28

Bayard Rock, Dinant — SP29

Designs: 35c+10c, Menin Gate, Ypres. 60c+15c, Promenade d'Orleans, Spa. 1.75fr+25c, Antwerp Harbor. 5fr+5fr, Quai Vert, Bruges.

1929, Dec. 2 Engr. *Perf. 11½*

No.	Type	Description	Unused	Used
B93	SP28	5c + 5c red brn	.25	.25
B94	SP29	25c + 15c gray blk	.95	.90
B95	SP28	35c + 10c green	1.25	1.40
B96	SP28	60c + 15c rose lake	.85	.75
B97	SP28	1.75fr + 25c dp blue	6.75	6.75
		Perf. 14		
B98	SP29	5fr + 5fr dl vio	40.00	40.00
		Nos. B93-B98 (6)	50.05	50.05
		Set, never hinged	70.00	

Bornhem — SP34

Beloeil — SP35

Gaesbeek SP36

25c + 15c, Wynendaele. 70c + 15c, Oydonck. 1fr + 25c, Ghent. 1.75fr + 25c, Bouillon.

1930, Dec. 1 Photo. *Perf. 14*

No.	Type	Description	Unused	Used
B99	SP34	10c + 5c violet	.25	*.30*
B100	SP34	25c + 15c olive brn	.60	.60
		Engr.		
B101	SP35	40c + 10c brn vio	.80	*1.00*
B102	SP35	70c + 15c gray blk	.55	.55
B103	SP35	1fr + 25c rose lake	5.50	5.50
B104	SP35	1.75fr + 25c dp bl	7.25	4.50
B105	SP36	5fr + 5fr gray grn	45.00	*52.50*
		Nos. B99-B105 (7)	59.95	*64.95*
		Set, never hinged	80.00	

Philatelic Exhibition Issue

Souvenir Sheet

Prince Leopold — SP41

1931, July 18 Photo. *Perf. 14*

No.	Type	Description	Unused	Used
B106	SP41	2.45fr + 55c car brn	225.00	225.00
		Never hinged	650.00	
a.		Single stamp	100.00	

Sold exclusively at the Brussels Phil. Exhib., July 18-21, 1931. Size: 122x159mm. Surtax for the Veterans' Relief Fund.

The sheet normally has pin holes and a cancellation-like marking in the margin. These are considered unused and the condition valued here.

Queen Elisabeth — SP42

1931, Dec. 1 Engr.

No.	Type	Description	Unused	Used
B107	SP42	10c + 5c red brn	.30	*.50*
B108	SP42	25c + 15c dk vio	1.40	*1.50*
B109	SP42	50c + 10c dk grn	1.10	*1.25*
B110	SP42	75c + 15c blk brn	.95	.85
B111	SP42	1fr + 25c rose lake	8.00	7.25
B112	SP42	1.75fr + 25c ultra	5.75	4.75
B113	SP42	5fr + 5fr brn vio	65.00	65.00
		Nos. B107-B113 (7)	82.50	81.10
		Set, never hinged	150.00	

The surtax was for the National Anti-Tuberculosis League.

Désiré Cardinal Mercier — SP43

Mercier Protecting Children and Aged at Malines — SP44

Mercier as Professor at Louvain University — SP45

Mercier in Full Canonicals, Giving His Blessing SP46

1932, June 10 Photo. *Perf. 14½x14*

No.	Type	Description	Unused	Used
B114	SP43	10c + 10c dk violet	1.10	*.70*
B115	SP43	50c + 30c brt violet	2.75	*3.00*
B116	SP43	75c + 25c olive brn	2.75	2.75
B117	SP43	1fr + 2fr brown red	7.25	7.25
		Engr. *Perf. 11½*		
B118	SP44	1.75fr + 75c dp blue	85.00	*100.00*
B119	SP45	2.50fr + 2.50fr dk brn	85.00	85.00
B120	SP44	3fr + 4.50fr dull grn	85.00	85.00
B121	SP45	5fr + 20fr vio brn	95.00	*100.00*
B122	SP46	10fr + 40fr brn lake	210.00	*250.00*
		Nos. B114-B122 (9)	573.85	*633.70*
		Set, never hinged	950.00	

Honoring Cardinal Mercier and to obtain funds to erect a monument to his memory.

Belgian Infantryman SP47

Sanatorium at Waterloo SP48

1932, Aug. 4 *Perf. 14½x14*

No.	Type	Description	Unused	Used
B123	SP47	75c + 3.25fr red brn	80.00	80.00
		Never hinged	125.00	
B124	SP47	1.75fr + 4.25fr dk blue	80.00	80.00
		Never hinged	125.00	

Honoring Belgian soldiers who fought in WWI and to obtain funds to erect a natl. monument to their glory.

1932, Dec. 1 Photo. *Perf. 13½x14*

No.	Type	Description	Unused	Used
B125	SP48	10c + 5c dk vio	.30	*.90*
B126	SP48	25c + 15c red vio	1.00	*1.25*
B127	SP48	50c + 10c red brn	1.00	*1.25*
B128	SP48	75c + 15c ol brn	1.00	.80
B129	SP48	1fr + 25c dp red	15.00	12.50
B130	SP48	1.75fr + 25c dp blue	12.00	11.00
B131	SP48	5fr + 5fr gray grn	100.00	*110.00*
		Nos. B125-B131 (7)	130.30	*137.70*
		Set, never hinged	250.00	

Surtax for the assistance of the Natl. Anti-Tuberculosis Society at Waterloo.

View of Old Abbey SP49

Ruins of Old Abbey — SP50

Count de Chiny Presenting First Abbey to Countess Matilda SP56

Restoration of Abbey in XVI and XVII Centuries SP57

Abbey in XVIII Century, Maria Theresa and Charles V — SP58

Madonna and Arms of Seven Abbeys SP60

Designs: 25c+15c, Guests, courtyard, 50c+25c, Transept. 75c+50c, Bell Tower. 1fr+1.25fr, Fountain. 1.25fr+1.75fr, Cloisters. 5fr+20fr, Duke of Brabant placing 1st stone of new abbey.

1933, Oct. 15 ***Perf. 14***

No.	Type	Description	Unused	Used
B132	SP49	5c + 5c dull grn	57.50	*65.00*
B133	SP50	10c + 15c ol grn	52.50	*57.50*
B134	SP49	25c + 15c dk brn	52.50	*57.50*
B135	SP50	50c + 25c red brn	52.50	*57.50*
B136	SP50	75c + 50c dp grn	52.50	*57.50*
B137	SP50	1fr + 1.25fr cop red	52.50	*57.50*
B138	SP49	1.25fr + 1.75fr gray blk	52.50	*57.50*
B139	SP56	1.75fr + 2.75fr blue	60.00	*65.00*
B140	SP57	2fr + 3fr mag	60.00	*65.00*
B141	SP58	2.50fr + 5fr dull brn	60.00	*65.00*
B142	SP56	5fr + 20fr vio	65.00	*65.00*
		Perf. 11½		
B143	SP60	10fr + 40fr bl	375.00	*375.00*
		Nos. B132-B143 (12)	992.50	*1,045.*
		Set, never hinged	1,500.	

The surtax was for a fund to aid in the restoration of Orval Abbey. Counterfeits exist.

"Tuberculosis Society" SP61

Peter Benoit SP62

1933, Dec. 1 **Engr.** ***Perf. 14x13½***

No.	Type	Description	Unused	Used
B144	SP61	10c + 5c blk	1.50	1.50
B145	SP61	25c + 15c vio	5.00	5.00
B146	SP61	50c + 10c red brn	3.75	3.75
B147	SP61	75c + 15c blk brn	16.00	15.00
B148	SP61	1fr + 25c cl	18.00	18.00
B149	SP61	1.75fr + 25c vio bl	21.00	21.00
B150	SP61	5fr + 5fr lilac	175.00	140.00
		Nos. B144-B150 (7)	240.25	204.25
		Set, never hinged	350.00	

The surtax was for anti-tuberculosis work.

1934, June 1 **Photo.**

No.	Type	Description	Unused	Used
B151	SP62	75c + 25c olive brn	6.00	6.00
		Never hinged	12.50	

The surtax was to raise funds for the Peter Benoit Memorial.

SP63

King Leopold III — SP64

1934, Sept. 15

No.	Type	Description	Unused	Used
B152	SP63	75c + 25c ol blk	18.00	17.00
		Never hinged	37.50	
a.		Sheet of 20	925.00	925.00
		Never hinged	1,100.	
B153	SP64	1fr + 25c red vio	17.00	16.00
		Never hinged	37.50	
a.		Sheet of 20	925.00	925.00
		Never hinged	1,100.	

The surtax aided the National War Veterans' Fund. Sold for 4.50fr a set at the Exhibition of War Postmarks 1914-18, held at Brussels by the Royal Philatelic Club of Veterans. The price included an exhibition ticket. Sold at Brussels post office Sept. 18-22. No. B152 printed in sheets of 20 (4x5) and 100 (10x10). No. B153 printed in sheets of 20 (4x5) and 150 (10x15).

1934, Sept. 24

No.	Type	Description	Unused	Used
B154	SP63	75c + 25c violet	1.50	1.50
		Never hinged	2.50	
B155	SP64	1fr + 25c red brn	10.50	10.50
		Never hinged	20.00	

The surtax aided the National War Veterans' Fund. No. B154 printed in sheets of 100 (10x10); No. B155 in sheets of 150 (10x15). These stamps remained in use one year.

Crusader SP65

1934, Nov. 17 **Engr.** ***Perf. 13½x14***

Cross in Red

No.	Type	Description	Unused	Used
B156	SP65	10c + 5c blk	1.50	1.50
B157	SP65	25c + 15c brn	2.10	2.00
B158	SP65	50c + 10c dull grn	2.10	2.10
B159	SP65	75c + 15c vio brn	1.00	1.00
B160	SP65	1fr + 25c rose	10.50	10.50
B161	SP65	1.75fr + 25c ultra	9.00	9.00
B162	SP65	5fr + 5fr brn vio	125.00	125.00
		Nos. B156-B162 (7)	151.20	151.10
		Set, never hinged	550.00	

The surtax was for anti-tuberculosis work.

Prince Baudouin, Princess Josephine and Prince Albert SP66

1935, Apr. 10 **Photo.**

No.	Type	Description	Unused	Used
B163	SP66	35c + 15c dk grn	1.25	1.10
B164	SP66	70c + 30c red brn	1.25	.90
B165	SP66	1.75fr + 50c dk blue	4.50	*5.25*
		Nos. B163-B165 (3)	7.00	*7.25*
		Set, never hinged	20.00	

Surtax was for Child Welfare Society.

Stagecoach — SP67

1935, Apr. 27

No.	Type	Description	Unused	Used
B166	SP67	10c + 10c ol blk	.75	.80
B167	SP67	25c + 25c bis brn	2.25	2.10
B168	SP67	35c + 25c dk green	3.00	2.75
		Nos. B166-B168 (3)	6.00	5.65
		Set, never hinged	15.00	

Printed in sheets of 10. Value, set of 3, $175.

Souvenir Sheet

Franz von Taxis — SP68

1935, May 25 **Engr.** ***Perf. 14***

No.	Type	Description	Unused	Used
B169	SP68	5fr + 5fr grnsh blk	150.00	150.00
		Never hinged	450.00	
a.		Single stamp	115.00	
		Never hinged	140.00	

Sheets measure 91½x117mm.

Nos. B166-B169 were issued for the Brussels Philatelic Exhibition (SITEB).

The sheet normally has pin holes and a cancellation-like marking in the margin. These are considered unused and the condition valued here.

Queen Astrid — SP69

1935 **Photo.** ***Perf. 11½***

Borders in Black

No.	Type	Description	Unused	Used
B170	SP69	10c + 5c ol blk	.25	.25
B171	SP69	25c + 15c brown	.25	*.30*
B172	SP69	35c + 5c dk green	.25	*.25*
B173	SP69	50c + 10c rose lil	.80	.65
B174	SP69	70c + 5c gray blk	.25	.25
B175	SP69	1fr + 25c red	1.00	.85
B176	SP69	1.75fr + 25c blue	2.40	1.75
B177	SP69	2.45fr + 55c dk vio	3.00	*3.25*
		Nos. B170-B177 (8)	8.20	7.55
		Set, never hinged	25.00	

Queen Astrid Memorial issue. The surtax was divided among several charitable organizations.

Issued: No. B174, 10/31; others, 12/1.

Borgerhout Philatelic Exhibition Issue

Souvenir Sheet

Town Hall, Borgerhout SP70

1936, Oct. 3

No.	Type	Description	Unused	Used
B178	SP70	70c + 30c pur brn	90.00	62.50
		Never hinged	275.00	
a.		Single stamp	45.00	
		Never hinged	60.00	

Sheet measures 115x126mm.

The sheet normally has pin holes and a cancellation-like marking in the margin. These are considered unused and the condition valued here.

Town Hall and Belfry of Charleroi SP71

Prince Baudouin SP72

Charleroi Youth Exhibition

Souvenir Sheet

1936, Oct. 18 **Engr.**

No.	Type	Description	Unused	Used
B179	SP71	2.45fr + 55c gray blue	65.00	60.00
		Never hinged	150.00	
a.		Single stamp	45.00	
		Never hinged	60.00	

Sheet measures 95x120mm.

The sheet normally has pin holes and a cancellation-like marking in the margin. These are considered unused and the condition valued here.

1936, Dec. 1 **Photo.** ***Perf. 14x13½***

No.	Type	Description	Unused	Used
B180	SP72	10c + 5c dk brown	.25	.25
B181	SP72	25c + 5c violet	.25	*.25*
B182	SP72	35c + 5c dk green	.25	*.25*
B183	SP72	50c + 5c vio brn	.50	*.60*
B184	SP72	70c + 5c ol grn	.25	.25
B185	SP72	1fr + 25c cerise	1.10	.45
B186	SP72	1.75fr + 25c ultra	1.90	1.10
B187	SP72	2.45fr + 2.55fr vio rose	5.25	*6.75*
		Nos. B180-B187 (8)	9.75	*9.90*
		Set, never hinged	30.00	

The surtax was for the assistance of the National Anti-Tuberculosis Society.

1937, Jan. 10

No.	Type	Description	Unused	Used
B188	SP72	2.45fr + 2.55fr slate	2.50	2.50
		Never hinged	6.50	

Intl. Stamp Day. Surtax for the benefit of the Brussels Postal Museum, the Royal Belgian Phil. Fed. and the Anti-Tuberculosis Soc.

Queen Astrid and Prince Baudouin SP73

Queen Mother Elisabeth SP74

1937, Apr. 15 ***Perf. 11½***

No.	Type	Description	Unused	Used
B189	SP73	10c + 5c magenta	.25	.25
B190	SP73	25c + 5c ol blk	.25	*.25*
B191	SP73	35c + 5c dk grn	.25	*.25*
B192	SP73	50c + 5c violet	1.25	*1.25*
B193	SP73	70c + 5c slate	.25	*.30*
B194	SP73	1fr + 25c dk car	1.60	1.40
B195	SP73	1.75fr + 25c dp ultra	2.75	2.75
B196	SP73	2.45fr + 1.55fr dk brn	6.75	6.50
		Nos. B189-B196 (8)	13.35	12.95
		Set, never hinged	45.00	

The surtax was to raise funds for Public Utility Works.

1937, Sept. 15 ***Perf. 14x13½***

No.	Type	Description	Unused	Used
B197	SP74	70c + 5c int black	.30	.30
B198	SP74	1.75fr + 25c brt ultra	.70	.70
		Set, never hinged	2.00	

Souvenir Sheet

Perf. 11½

No.	Type	Description	Unused	Used
B199		Sheet of 4	45.00	25.00
		Never hinged	125.00	
a.		SP74 1.50fr+2.50fr red brn	4.25	3.75
b.		SP74 2.45fr+3.55fr red vio	3.75	2.25

Issued for the benefit of the Queen Elisabeth Music Foundation in connection with the Eugene Ysaye intl. competition.

No. B199 contains two se-tenant pairs of Nos. B199a and B199b. Size: 111x145mm. On sale one day, Sept. 15, at Brussels.

The sheet normally has pin holes and a cancellation-like marking in the margin. These are considered unused and the condition valued here.

Princess Josephine-Charlotte
SP75

1937, Dec. 1 ***Perf. 14x13½***

B200 SP75 10c + 5c sl grn .25 .25
B201 SP75 25c + 5c lt brn .25 .25
B202 SP75 35c + 5c yel grn .25 .25
B203 SP75 50c + 5c ol gray .70 .60
B204 SP75 70c + 5c brn red .25 .25
B205 SP75 1fr + 25c red 1.25 .90
B206 SP75 1.75fr + 25c vio bl 1.50 1.25
B207 SP75 2.45fr + 2.55fr mag 5.75 *6.00*
Nos. B200-B207 (8) 10.20 *9.75*
Set, never hinged 30.00

King Albert Memorial Issue
Souvenir Sheet

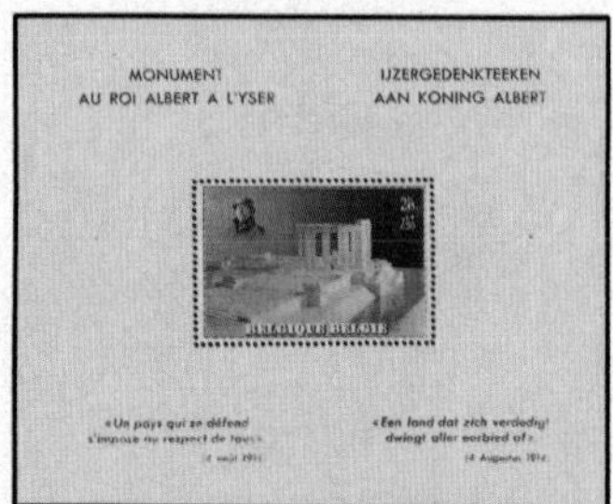

King Albert Memorial — SP76

1938, Feb. 17 ***Perf. 11½***

B208 SP76 2.45fr + 7.55fr brn vio 20.00 16.50
Never hinged 62.50

Dedication of the monument to King Albert.
The sheet normally has pin holes and a cancellation-like marking in the margin. These are considered unused and the condition valued here. Sheets without the "cancellation" are extremely scarce. Values: unused, $525; never hinged, $1,000.

King Leopold III in Military Plane
SP77

1938, Mar. 15

B209 SP77 10c + 5c car brn .25 *.30*
B210 SP77 35c + 5c dp grn .35 *.90*
B211 SP77 70c + 5c gray blk .95 .75
B212 SP77 1.75fr + 25c ultra 2.25 2.10
B213 SP77 2.45fr + 2.55fr pur 5.25 4.50
Nos. B209-B213 (5) 9.05 8.55
Set, never hinged 22.50

The surtax was for the benefit of the National Fund for Aeronautical Propaganda.

Basilica of Koekelberg
SP78

Interior View of the Basilica of Koekelberg
SP79

1938, June 1 **Photo.**

B214 SP78 10c + 5c lt brn .25 .25
B215 SP78 35c + 5c grn .25 .25
B216 SP78 70c + 5c gray grn .25 .25
B217 SP78 1fr + 25c car .70 .60
B218 SP78 1.75fr + 25c ultra .70 .70
B219 SP78 2.45fr + 2.55fr brn vio 3.25 *3.75*

Engr.

B220 SP79 5fr + 5fr dl grn 12.25 11.50
Nos. B214-B220 (7) 17.65 17.30
Set, never hinged 35.00

Souvenir Sheet

1938, July 21 **Engr.** ***Perf. 14***

B221 SP79 5fr + 5fr lt vio 16.00 16.00
Never hinged 25.00

The surtax was for a fund to aid in completing the National Basilica of the Sacred Heart at Koekelberg.
Nos. B214, B216 and B218 are different views of the exterior of the Basilica.
The sheet normally has pin holes and a cancellation-like marking in the margin. These are considered unused and the condition valued here.

Stamps of 1938 Surcharged in Black

Nos. B222-B223

No. B224

1938, Nov. 10 ***Perf. 11½***

B222 SP78 40c on 35c+5c grn .50 *.60*
B223 SP78 75c on 70c+5c gray grn .75 *.90*
B224 SP78 2.50 + 2.50fr on 2.45+2.55fr 6.75 *7.50*
Nos. B222-B224 (3) 8.00 *9.00*
Set, never hinged 19.00

Prince Albert of Liege — SP81

1938, Dec. 10 **Photo.** ***Perf. 14x13½***

B225 SP81 10c + 5c brown .25 .25
B226 SP81 30c + 5c mag .25 *.30*
B227 SP81 40c + 5c olive gray .25 *.30*
B228 SP81 75c + 5c slate grn .25 .25
B229 SP81 1fr + 25c dk car .75 *1.10*
B230 SP81 1.75fr + 25c ultra .75 *1.10*
B231 SP81 2.50fr + 2.50fr dp grn 5.25 *8.25*
B232 SP81 5fr + 5fr brn lake 16.00 12.50
Nos. B225-B232 (8) 23.75 24.05
Set, never hinged 70.00

Henri Dunant
SP82

Florence Nightingale
SP83

Queen Mother Elisabeth and Royal Children — SP84

Queen Astrid — SP86

King Leopold and Royal Children
SP85

Queen Mother Elisabeth and Wounded Soldier — SP87

1939, Apr. 1 **Photo.** ***Perf. 11½***

Cross in Carmine

B233 SP82 10c + 5c brn .25 .25
B234 SP83 30c + 5c brn car .45 .45
B235 SP84 40c + 5c ol gray .25 *.30*
B236 SP85 75c + 5c slate blk .60 .25
B237 SP84 1fr + 25c brt rose 3.00 1.60
B238 SP85 1.75fr + 25c brt ultra .90 *1.25*
B239 SP86 2.50fr + 2.50fr dl vio 1.90 *2.40*
B240 SP87 5fr + 5fr gray grn 6.50 *8.25*
Nos. B233-B240 (8) 13.85 *14.75*
Set, never hinged 42.50

75th anniversary of the founding of the International Red Cross Society.
In 1941, No. B240 was privately overprinted with a circular red cross overprint and 1941 date. Value, $105.

Rubens' House, Antwerp
SP88

"Albert and Nicolas Rubens" — SP89

Arcade, Rubens' House
SP90

"Helena Fourment and Her Children" — SP91

Rubens and Isabelle Brandt — SP92

Peter Paul Rubens — SP93

"The Velvet Hat" — SP94

"Descent from the Cross"
SP95

1939, July 1

B241 SP88 10c + 5c brn .25 .25
B242 SP89 40c + 5c brn car .25 .25
B243 SP90 75c + 5c ol blk .65 .65
B244 SP91 1fr + 25c rose 2.50 2.50
B245 SP92 1.50fr + 25c sep 2.75 2.75
B246 SP93 1.75fr + 25c dp ultra 4.50 4.50
B247 SP94 2.50fr + 2.50fr brt red vio 15.00 *15.00*
B248 SP95 5fr + 5fr slate gray 19.00 19.00
Nos. B241-B248 (8) 44.90 44.90
Set, never hinged 140.00

Issued to honor Peter Paul Rubens. The surtax was used to restore Rubens' home in Antwerp.

"Martin van Nieuwenhove" by Hans Memling (1430?-1495), Flemish Painter — SP96

1939, July 1

B249 SP96 75c + 75c olive blk 2.75 2.75
Never hinged 4.50

Twelfth Century Monks at Work — SP97

Reconstructed Tower Seen through Cloister — SP98

Monks Laboring in the Fields
SP99

Orval Abbey, Aerial View
SP100

Bishop Heylen of Namur, Madonna and Abbot General Smets of the Trappists — SP101

King Albert I and King Leopold III and Shrine — SP102

1939, July 20

B250	SP97	75c + 75c ol blk	3.50	3.75
B251	SP98	1fr + 1fr rose red	2.25	2.25
B252	SP99	1.50fr + 1.50fr dl brn	2.25	2.25
B253	SP100	1.75fr + 1.75fr saph	2.25	2.25
B254	SP101	2.50fr + 2.50fr brt red vio	10.00	9.00
B255	SP102	5fr + 5fr brn car	10.00	10.00
		Nos. B250-B255 (6)	30.25	29.50
		Set, never hinged	82.50	

The surtax was used for the restoration of the Abbey of Orval.

Bruges
SP103

Furnes
SP104

Belfries: 30c+5c, Thuin. 40c+5c, Lierre. 75c+5c, Mons. 1.75fr+25c, Namur. 2.50fr+2.50fr, Alost. 5fr+5fr, Tournai.

1939, Dec. 1 Photo. *Perf. 14x13½*

B256	SP103	10c + 5c ol gray	.25	*.25*
B257	SP103	30c + 5c brn org	.30	*.40*
B258	SP103	40c + 5c brt red vio	.50	*.50*
B259	SP103	75c + 5c olive blk	.25	*.25*

Engr.

B260	SP104	1fr + 25c rose car	1.25	*1.50*
B261	SP104	1.75fr + 25c dk blue	1.25	*1.50*
B262	SP104	2.50fr + 2.50fr dp red brn	8.75	*9.50*
B263	SP104	5fr + 5fr pur	12.00	*13.25*
		Nos. B256-B263 (8)	24.55	*27.15*
		Set, never hinged	65.00	

Mons
SP111

Ghent
SP112

Coats of Arms: 40c+10c, Arel. 50c+10c, Bruges. 75c+15c, Namur. 1fr+25c, Hasselt. 1.75fr+50c, Brussels. 2.50fr+2.50fr, Antwerp. 5fr+5fr, Liege.

1940-41 Typo. *Perf. 14x13½*

B264	SP111	10c + 5c multi	.25	.25
B265	SP112	30c + 5c multi	.25	.25
B266	SP111	40c + 10c multi	.25	.25
B267	SP112	50c + 10c multi	.25	.25
B268	SP111	75c + 15c multi	.25	.25
B269	SP112	1fr + 25c multi	.30	.30
B270	SP111	1.75fr + 50c multi	.45	.40
B271	SP112	2.50fr + 2.50fr multi	1.25	1.25
B272	SP111	5fr + 5fr multi	1.50	1.50
		Nos. B264-B272 (9)	4.75	4.70
		Set, never hinged	8.50	

Nos. B264, B269-B272 issued in 1941. Surtax for winter relief. See No. B279.

Queen Elisabeth Music Chapel
SP120

Bust of Prince Albert of Liege — SP121

1940, Nov. Photo. *Perf. 11½*

B273	SP120	75c + 75c slate	3.50	3.50
B274	SP120	1fr + 1fr rose red	1.25	1.25
B275	SP121	1.50fr + 1.50fr Prus grn	1.25	1.25
B276	SP121	1.75fr + 1.75fr ultra	1.25	1.25
B277	SP120	2.50fr + 2.50fr brn org	3.50	3.50
B278	SP121	5fr + 5fr red vio	3.50	3.50
		Nos. B273-B278 (6)	14.25	14.25
		Set, never hinged	55.00	

The surtax was for the Queen Elisabeth Music Foundation. Nos. B273-B278 were not authorized for postal use, but were sold to advance subscribers either mint or canceled to order. See Nos. B317-B318.

Arms Types of 1940-41
Souvenir Sheets
Cross and City Name in Carmine
Arms in Color of Stamp
Perf. 14x13½, Imperf.

1941, May Typo.

B279		Sheet of 9	16.00	16.00
		Never hinged	18.00	
a.	SP111	10c + 5c slate	1.10	*1.25*
b.	SP112	30c + 5c emerald	1.10	*1.25*
c.	SP111	40c + 10c chocolate	1.10	*1.25*
d.	SP112	50c + 10c light violet	1.10	*1.25*
e.	SP111	75c + 15c dull purple	1.10	*1.25*
f.	SP112	1fr + 25c carmine	1.10	*1.25*
g.	SP111	1.75fr + 50c dull blue	1.10	*1.25*
h.	SP112	2.50fr + 2.50fr ol gray	1.10	*1.25*
i.	SP111	5fr + 5fr dull violet	4.00	*4.25*

The sheets measure 106x148mm. The surtax was used for relief work.

Painting
SP123

Sculpture
SP124

Monks Studying Plans of Orval Abbey — SP128

Designs: 40c+60c, 2fr+3.50fr, Monk carrying candle. 50c+65c, 1.75fr+2.50fr, Monk praying. 75c+1fr, 3fr+5fr, Two monks singing.

1941, June Photo. *Perf. 11½*

B281	SP123	10c + 15c brn org	.40	.40
B282	SP124	30c + 30c ol gray	.40	.40
B283	SP124	40c + 60c dp brn	.40	.40
B284	SP124	50c + 65c vio	.40	.40
B285	SP124	75c + 1fr brt red vio	.40	.40
B286	SP124	1fr + 1.50fr rose red	.40	.40
B287	SP123	1.25fr + 1.75fr dp yel grn	.40	.40
B288	SP123	1.75fr + 2.50fr dp ultra	.40	.40
B289	SP123	2fr + 3.50fr red vio	.40	.40
B290	SP124	2.50fr + 4.50fr dl red brn	.40	.40
B291	SP124	3fr + 5fr dk ol grn	.40	.40
B292	SP128	5fr + 10fr grnsh blk	1.40	1.40
		Nos. B281-B292 (12)	5.80	5.80
		Set, never hinged	11.50	

The surtax was used for the restoration of the Abbey of Orval.

Maria Theresa
SP129

Charles the Bold
SP130

Portraits (in various frames): 35c+5c, Charles of Lorraine. 50c+10c, Margaret of Parma. 60c+10c, Charles V. 1fr+15c, Johanna of Castile. 1.50fr+1fr, Philip the Good. 1.75fr+1.75fr, Margaret of Austria. 3.25fr+3.25fr, Archduke Albert. 5fr+5fr, Archduchess Isabella.

1941-42 Photo.

B293	SP129	10c + 5c ol blk	.25	.25
B294	SP129	35c + 5c dl grn	.25	.25
B295	SP129	50c + 10c brn	.25	.25
B296	SP129	60c + 10c pur	.25	.25
B297	SP129	1fr + 15c brt car rose	.25	.25
B298	SP129	1.50fr + 1fr red vio	.25	.25
B299	SP129	1.75fr + 1.75fr ryl bl	.25	.25
B300	SP130	2.25fr + 2.25fr dl red brn	.30	.30
B301	SP129	3.25fr + 3.25fr lt brn	.40	.40
B302	SP129	5fr + 5fr sl grn	.80	.80
		Nos. B293-B302 (10)	3.25	3.25
		Set, never hinged	5.00	

Souvenir Sheet

Archduke Albert and Archduchess Isabella — SP139

B302A	SP139	Sheet of 2 ('42)	11.00	11.00
		Never hinged	14.50	
b.		3.25fr+6.75fr turquoise blue	4.50	4.50
c.		5fr+10fr dark carmine	4.50	4.50

The surtax was for the benefit of National Social Service Work among soldiers' families.

Souvenir Sheets

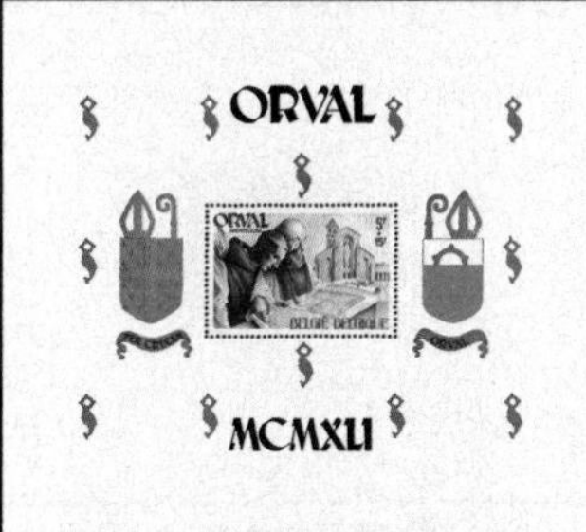

Monks Studying Plans of Orval Abbey — SP140

1941, Oct. Photo. *Perf. 11½*
Inscribed "Belgie-Belgique"

B303	SP140	5fr + 15fr ultra	10.00	10.00
		Never hinged	22.50	

Inscribed "Belgique-Belgie"
Imperf

B304	SP140	5fr + 15fr ultra	10.00	10.00
		Never hinged	22.50	

Surtax for the restoration of Orval Abbey.
No. B304 exists perforated.
In 1942 these sheets were privately trimmed and overprinted "1142 1942" and ornament.

St. Martin Statue, Church of Dinant
SP141

Lennik, Saint-Quentin
SP142

St. Martin's Church, Saint-Trond
SP146

Statues of St. Martin: 50c+10c, 3.25fr+3.25fr, Beck, Limburg. 60c+10c, 2.25fr+2.25fr, Dave on the Meuse. 1.75fr+50c, Hal, Brabant.

1941-42 Photo. *Perf. 11½*

B305	SP141	10c + 5c chest	.25	.25
B306	SP142	35c + 5c dk bl grn	.25	.25
B307	SP142	50c + 10c vio	.25	.25

B308 SP142 60c + 10c dp brn .25 .25
B309 SP142 1fr + 15c car .25 .25
B310 SP141 1.50fr + 25c sl grn .25 .25
B311 SP142 1.75fr + 50c dk ultra .30 .30
B312 SP142 2.25fr + 2.25fr red vio .30 .30
B313 SP142 3.25fr + 3.25fr brn vio .35 .35
B314 SP146 5fr + 5fr dk ol grn .70 .70
Nos. B305-B314 (10) 3.15 3.15
Set, never hinged 5.00

Souvenir Sheets

Inscribed "Belgie-Belgique"

B315 SP146 5fr + 20fr vio brn ('42) 22.50 22.50
Never hinged 32.50

Inscribed "Belgique-Belgie"

Imperf

B316 SP146 5fr + 20fr vio brn ('42) 22.50 22.50
Never hinged 32.50

In 1956, the Bureau Europeen de la Jeunesse et de l'Enfance privately overprinted Nos. B315-B316: "Congres Europeen de l'education 7-12 Mai 1956," in dark red and dark green respectively. A black bar obliterates "Winterhulp-Secours d'Hiver."

Souvenir Sheets

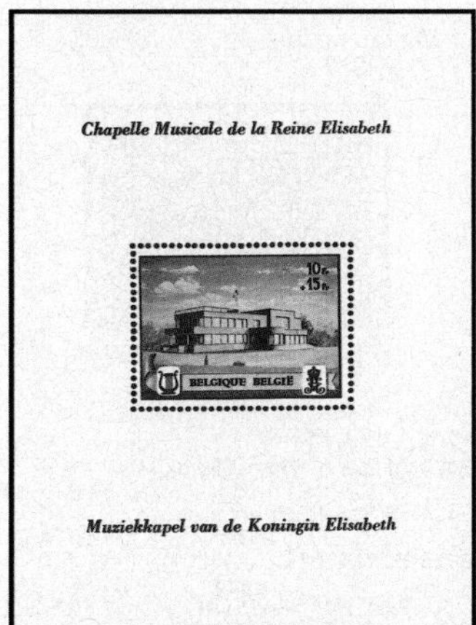

Queen Elisabeth Music Chapel — SP147

1941, Dec. 1 Photo. *Perf. 11½*

Inscribed "Belgique-Belgie"

B317 SP147 10fr + 15fr ol blk 6.50 6.00
Never hinged 9.50

Inscribed "Belgie-Belgique"

Imperf

B318 SP147 10fr + 15fr ol blk 6.50 6.00
Never hinged 9.50

The surtax was for the Queen Elisabeth Music Foundation. These sheets were perforated with the monogram of Queen Elisabeth in 1942. Value, $3 each.

In 1954 Nos. B317-B318 were overprinted for the birth cent. of Edgar Tinel, composer. These overprinted sheets were not postally valid. Value, $4 each.

Jean Bollandus SP148

Christophe Plantin SP156

Designs: 35c+5c, Andreas Vesalius. 50c+10c, Simon Stevinus. 60c+10c, Jean Van Helmont. 1fr+15c, Rembert Dodoens. 1.75fr+50c, Gerardus Mercator. 3.25fr+3.25fr, Abraham Ortelius. 5fr+5fr, Justus Lipsius.

1942, May 15 Photo. *Perf. 14x13½*

B319 SP148 10c + 5c dl brn .25 .25
B320 SP148 35c + 5c gray grn .25 .25
B321 SP148 50c + 10c fawn .25 .25
B322 SP148 60c + 10c grnsh blk .25 .25

Engr.

B323 SP148 1fr + 15c brt rose .25 .25
B324 SP148 1.75fr + 50c dl bl .25 .25
B325 SP148 3.25fr + 3.25fr lil rose .25 .25
B326 SP148 5fr + 5fr vio .25 .25

Perf. 13½x14

B327 SP156 10fr + 30fr red org 1.40 1.40
Nos. B319-B327 (9) 3.40 3.40
Set, never hinged 3.50

The surtax was used to help fight tuberculosis.

No. B327 was sold by subscription at the Brussels Post Office, July 1-10, 1942.

Belgian Prisoner — SP158

1942, Oct. 1 *Perf. 11½*

B331 SP158 5fr + 45fr olive gray 7.00 7.00
Never hinged 16.00

The surtax was for prisoners of war. Value includes a brown inscribed label which alternates with the stamps in the sheet.

SP159

SP164

SP162

SP168

Various Statues of St. Martin.

1942-43

B332 SP159 10c + 5c org .25 .25
B333 SP159 35c + 5c dk bl grn .25 .25
B334 SP159 50c + 10c dp brn .25 .25
B335 SP162 60c + 10c blk .25 .25
B336 SP159 1fr + 15c brt rose .25 .25
B337 SP164 1.50fr + 25c grnsh blk .25 .25
B338 SP164 1.75fr + 50c dk bl .25 .25
B339 SP162 2.25fr + 2.25fr brn .30 .30
B340 SP162 3.25fr + 3.25fr brt red vio .45 .45
B341 SP168 5fr + 10fr hn brn 1.25 1.25
B342 SP168 10fr + 20fr rose brn & vio brn ('43) 1.10 1.10

Inscribed "Belgique-Belgie"

B343 SP168 10fr + 20fr gldn brn & vio brn ('43) 1.40 1.40
Nos. B332-B343 (12) 6.25 6.25
Set, never hinged 12.50

The surtax was for winter relief.

Issue dates: Nos. B332-B341, Nov. 12, 1942; Nos. B342-B343, Apr. 3, 1943.

Prisoners of War — SP170

No. B345, 2 prisoners with package from home.

1943, May Photo. *Perf. 11½*

B344 SP170 1fr + 30fr ver 2.75 2.75
B345 SP170 1fr + 30fr brn rose 2.50 2.50
Set, never hinged 9.50

The surtax was used for prisoners of war.

Roof Tiler SP172

Coppersmith SP173

Statues in Petit Sablon Park, Brussels: 35c+5c, Blacksmith. 60c+10c, Gunsmith. 1fr+15c, Armsmith. 1.75fr+75c, Goldsmith. 3.25fr+3.25fr, Fishdealer. 5fr+25fr, Watchmaker.

1943, June 1

B346 SP172 10c + 5c chnt brn .25 .25
B347 SP172 35c + 5c grn .25 .25
B348 SP173 50c + 10c dk brn .25 .25
B349 SP173 60c + 10c slate .25 .25
B350 SP173 1fr + 15c dl rose brn .25 .25
B351 SP173 1.75fr + 75c ultra .25 .25
B352 SP173 3.25fr + 3.25fr brt red vio .40 .40
B353 SP173 5fr + 25fr dk pur .90 .90
Nos. B346-B353 (8) 2.80 2.80
Set, never hinged 3.75

Surtax for the control of tuberculosis.

"O" SP180

"ORVAL" — SP185

1943, Oct. 9

B354 SP180 50c + 1fr "O" .50 .50
B355 SP180 60c + 1.90fr "R" .30 .25
B356 SP180 1fr + 3fr "V" .30 .25
B357 SP180 1.75fr + 5.25fr "A" .30 .25
B358 SP180 3.25fr + 16.75fr "L" .40 .40
B359 SP185 5fr + 30fr dp brn .85 .85
Nos. B354-B359 (6) 2.65 2.50
Set, never hinged 4.50

Surtax aided restoration of Orval Abbey.

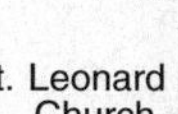

St. Leonard Church, Leau SP186

St. Martin Church, Courtrai — SP190

Basilica of St. Martin, Angre — SP191

Notre Dame, Hal — SP193

St. Martin SP194

35c+5c, St. Martin Church, Dion-le-Val. 50c+15c, St. Martin Church, Alost. 60c+20c, St. Martin Church, Liege. 3.25fr+11.75fr, St. Martin Church, Loppem. No. B369, St. Martin, beggar & Meuse landscape.

1943-44

B360 SP186 10c + 5c dp brn .25 .25
B361 SP186 35c + 5c dk bl grn .25 .25
B362 SP186 50c + 15c ol blk .30 .30
B363 SP186 60c + 20c brt red vio .30 .40
B364 SP190 1fr + 1fr rose brn .40 .40
B365 SP191 1.75fr + 4.25fr dp ultra .90 .60
B366 SP186 3.25fr + 11.75fr red lil 1.25 1.25
B367 SP193 5fr + 25fr dk bl 1.90 1.90
B368 SP194 10fr + 30fr gray grn ('44) 1.50 1.50
B369 SP194 10fr + 30fr blk brn ('44) 1.50 1.50
Nos. B360-B369 (10) 8.55 8.35
Set, never hinged 18.00

Surtax for winter relief.

Catalogue values for unused stamps in this section, from this point to the end of the section, are for Never Hinged items.

"Daedalus and Icarus" SP196

Sir Anthony Van Dyck, Self-portrait SP200

Paintings by Van Dyck: 50c+2.50fr. "The Good Samaritan." 60c+3.40fr, Detail of "Christ Healing the Paralytic." 1fr+5fr, "Madonna and Child." 5fr+30fr, "St. Sebastian."

1944, Apr. 16 Photo. *Perf. 11½*
Crosses in Carmine

B370 SP196 35c + 1.65fr dk sl grn .45 .30
B371 SP196 50c + 2.50fr grnsh blk .45 .30
B372 SP196 60c + 3.40fr blk brn .45 .30
B373 SP196 1fr + 5fr dk car .70 .45
B374 SP200 1.75fr + 8.25fr int bl .75 .60
B375 SP196 5fr + 30fr cop brn 1.10 .70
Nos. B370-B375 (6) 3.90 2.65

The surtax was for the Belgian Red Cross.

Jan van Eyck — SP202

Godfrey of Bouillon — SP203

Designs: 50c+25c, Jacob van Maerlant. 60c+40c, Jean Joses de Dinant. 1fr+50c, Jacob van Artevelde. 1.75fr+4.25fr, Charles Joseph de Ligne. 2.25fr+8.25fr, Andre Gretry. 3.25fr+11.25fr, Jan Moretus-Plantin. 5fr+35fr, Jan van Ruysbroeck.

1944, May 31

B376 SP202 10c + 15c dk pur .75 .25
B377 SP203 35c + 15c green .50 .25
B378 SP203 50c + 25c chnt brn .50 .25
B379 SP203 60c + 40c ol blk .50 .25
B380 SP203 1fr + 50c rose brn .50 .25
B381 SP203 1.75fr + 4.25fr ultra .50 .25
B382 SP203 2.25fr + 8.25fr grnsh blk 1.10 .55
B383 SP203 3.25fr + 11.25fr dk brn .50 .25
B384 SP203 5fr + 35fr sl bl 1.60 .70
Nos. B376-B384 (9) 6.45 3.00

The surtax was for prisoners of war.

Sons of Aymon Astride Bayard SP211

Brabo Slaying the Giant Antigoon SP212

Till Eulenspiegel Singing to Nele SP214

50c+10c, St. Hubert converted by stag with crucifix. 1fr+15fr, St. George slaying the dragon. 1.75fr+5.25fr, Genevieve of Brabant with son & roe-deer. 3.25fr+11.75fr, Tchantches wrestling with the Saracen. 5fr+25fr, St. Gertrude rescuing the knight with the cards.

1944, June 25

B385 SP211 10c + 5c choc .25 .25
B386 SP212 35c + 5c dk bl grn .25 .25
B387 SP211 50c + 10c dl vio .25 .25
B388 SP214 60c + 10c blk brn .25 .25
B389 SP214 1fr + 15c rose brn .25 .25
B390 SP214 1.75fr + 5.25fr ultra .25 *.30*
B391 SP211 3.25fr + 11.75fr grnsh blk .35 *.50*
B392 SP211 5fr + 25fr dk bl .45 *.70*
Nos. B385-B392 (8) 2.30 *2.75*

The surtax was for the control of tuberculosis.

Nos. B385-B389 were overprinted "Breendonk+10fr." in 1946 by the Union Royale Philatelique for an exhibition at Brussels. They had no postal validity. Value same as unused set without overprint.

Union of the Flemish and Walloon Peoples in their Sorrow — SP219

Union in Reconstruction — SP220

Perf. 11½

1945, May 1 Unwmk. Photo.

B395 SP219 1fr + 30fr carmine 1.60 .90
B396 SP220 1¾fr + 30fr brt ultra 1.60 .90

1945, July 21
Size: 34½x23½mm

B397 SP219 1fr + 9fr scarlet .40 .25
B398 SP220 1fr + 9fr car rose .40 .25
Nos. B395-B398 (4) 4.00 2.30

Surtax for the postal employees' relief fund.

Prisoner of War SP221

Reunion SP222

Awaiting Execution SP223

Symbolical Figures "Recovery of Freedom" SP225

Design: 70c+30c, 3.50fr+3.50fr, Member of Resistance Movement.

1945, Sept. 10

B399 SP221 10c + 15c orange .25 .25
B400 SP222 20c + 20c dp pur .25 .25
B401 SP223 60c + 25c sepia .25 .25
B402 SP221 70c + 30c dp yel grn .25 .25
B403 SP221 75c + 50c org brn .25 .25
B404 SP222 1fr + 75c brt bl grn .25 .25
B405 SP223 1.50fr + 1fr brt red .25 .25
B406 SP221 3.50fr + 3.50fr brt bl 1.60 1.10
B407 SP225 5fr + 40fr brown 2.25 1.25
Nos. B399-B407 (9) 5.60 4.10

The surtax was for the benefit of prisoners of war, displaced persons, families of executed victims and members of the Resistance Movement.

Arms of West Flanders — SP226

Arms of Provinces: 20c+20c, Luxembourg. 60c+25c, East Flanders. 70c+30c, Namur. 75c+50c, Limburg. 1fr+75c, Hainaut. 1.50fr+1fr, Antwerp. 3.50fr+1.50fr, Liege. 5fr+45fr, Brabant.

1945, Dec. 1

B408 SP226 10c + 15c sl blk & sl gray .25 .25
B409 SP226 20c + 20c rose car & rose .25 .25
B410 SP226 60c + 25c dk brn & pale brn .25 .25
B411 SP226 70c + 30c dk grn & lt grn .25 .25
B412 SP226 75c + 50c org brn & pale org brn .25 .25
B413 SP226 1fr + 75c pur & lt pur .25 .25
B414 SP226 1.50fr + 1fr car & rose .25 .25
B415 SP226 3.50fr + 1.50fr dp bl & gray bl .60 .50
B416 SP226 5fr + 45fr dp mag & cer 3.75 2.00
Nos. B408-B416 (9) 6.10 4.25

The surtax was for tuberculosis prevention.

Father Joseph Damien — SP227

Father Damien Comforting Leper — SP229

Leper Colony, Molokai Island, Hawaii SP228

Perf. 11½

1946, July 15 Unwmk. Photo.

B417 SP227 65c + 75c dk blue 1.90 .65
B418 SP228 1.35fr + 2fr brown 1.90 .65
B419 SP229 1.75fr + 18fr rose brn 1.90 1.10

The surtax was for the erection of a museum in Louvain.

Symbols of Wisdom and Patriotism SP230

"In Memoriam" SP232

François Bovesse SP231

1946, July 15

B420 SP230 65c + 75c violet 1.90 .65
B421 SP231 1.35fr + 2fr dk org brn 1.90 .80
B422 SP232 1.75fr + 18fr car rose 1.90 1.10

The surtax was for the erection of a "House of the Fine Arts" at Namur.

Emile Vandervelde SP233

Sower SP235

Vandervelde, Laborer and Family — SP234

1946, July 15

B423 SP233 65c + 75c dk sl grn 1.90 .65
B424 SP234 1.35fr + 2fr dk vio bl 1.90 .80
B425 SP235 1.75fr + 18fr dp car 1.90 1.10
Nos. B417-B425 (9) 17.10 7.50

The surtax was for the Emile Vanderveide Institute, to promote social, economic and cultural activities.

For surcharges see Nos. CB4-CB12.

Pepin of Herstal — SP236

Malines — SP241

1fr+50c, Charlemagne. 1.50fr+1fr, Godfrey of Bouillon. 3.50fr+1.50fr, Robert of Jerusalem. Nos. B430-B431, Baldwin of Constantinople.

1946, Sept. 15 Engr. *Perf. 11½x11*

B426 SP236 75c + 25c grn .60 .35
B427 SP236 1fr + 50c vio .90 .50
B428 SP236 1.50fr + 1fr plum 1.25 .65
B429 SP236 3.50fr + 1.50fr brt bl 1.50 .75
B430 SP236 5fr + 45fr red vio 12.00 7.00
B431 SP236 5fr + 45fr red org 15.00 7.75
Nos. B426-B431 (6) 31.25 17.00

The surtax on Nos. B426-B429 was for the benefit of former prisoners of war, displaced persons, the families of executed patriots, and former members of the Resistance Movement.

The surtax on Nos. B430-B431 was divided among several welfare, national celebration and educational organizations.

Issue dates: Nos. B426-B429, Apr. 15; No. B430, Sept. 15; No. B431, Nov. 15.

See Nos. B437-B441, B465-B466, B472-B476.

1946, Dec. 2 ***Perf. 11½***

Coats of Arms: 90c+60c, Dinant. 1.35fr+1.15fr, Ostend. 3.15fr+1.85fr, Verviers. 4.50fr+45.50fr, Louvain.

B432 SP241 65c + 35c rose car .55 .50
B433 SP241 90c + 60c lem .65 .50
B434 SP241 1.35fr + 1.15fr dp grn .65 .50
B435 SP241 3.15fr + 1.85fr bl 1.50 1.25
B436 SP241 4.50fr + 45.50fr dk vio brn 16.00 14.00
Nos. B432-B436 (5) 19.35 16.75

The surtax was for anti-tuberculosis work. See Nos. B442-B446.

Type of 1946

Designs: 65c+35c, John II, Duke of Brabant. 90c+60c, Count Philip of Alsace. 1.35fr+1.15fr, William the Good. 3.15fr+1.85fr, Bishop Notger of Liege. 20fr+20fr, Philip the Noble.

1947, Sept. 25 **Engr.** ***Perf. 11½x11***

B437 SP236 65c + 35c Prus grn 1.10 .50
B438 SP236 90c + 60c yel grn 1.60 .75
B439 SP236 1.35fr + 1.15fr car 3.00 1.10
B440 SP236 3.15fr + 1.85fr ultra 3.75 1.60
B441 SP236 20fr + 20fr red vio 52.50 42.50
Nos. B437-B441 (5) 61.95 46.45

The surtax was for victims of World War II.

Arms Type of 1946 Dated "1947"

Coats of Arms: 65c+35c, Nivelles. 90c+60c, St. Trond. 1.35fr+1.15fr, Charleroi. 3.15fr+1.85fr, St. Nicolas. 20fr+20fr, Bouillon.

1947, Dec. 15 ***Perf. 11½***

B442 SP241 65c + 35c org .80 .65
B443 SP241 90c + 60c dp cl .70 .65
B444 SP241 1.35fr + 1.15fr dk brn 1.00 .70
B445 SP241 3.15fr + 1.85fr dp bl 2.60 1.75
B446 SP241 20fr + 20fr dk grn 24.00 15.00
Nos. B442-B446 (5) 29.10 18.75

The surtax was for anti-tuberculosis work.

St. Benedict and King Totila — SP247

Achel Abbey SP248

3.15fr+2.85fr, St. Benedict, legislator & builder. 10fr+10fr, Death of St. Benedict.

1948, Apr. 5 **Photo.**

B447 SP247 65c + 65c red brn 1.25 .55
B448 SP248 1.35fr + 1.35fr grnsh black 1.75 .55
B449 SP247 3.15fr + 2.85fr dp ultra 2.50 1.90
B450 SP247 10fr + 10fr brt red vio 12.50 10.00
Nos. B447-B450 (4) 18.00 13.00

The surtax was to aid the Abbey of the Trappist Fathers at Achel.

St. Begga and Chevremont Castle — SP249

Chevremont Basilica and Convent SP250

3.15fr+2.85fr, Madonna of Chevremont & Chapel. 10fr+10fr, Madonna of Mt. Carmel.

1948, Apr. 5 **Unwmk.**

B451 SP249 65c + 65c bl grn 1.00 .55
B452 SP250 1.35fr + 1.35fr dk car rose 1.60 .55
B453 SP249 3.15fr + 2.85fr dp bl 2.75 1.90
B454 SP249 10fr + 10fr dp brn 12.00 10.00
Nos. B451-B454 (4) 17.35 13.00

The surtax was to aid the Basilica of the Carmelite Fathers of Chèvremont.

Anseele Monument Showing French Inscription — SP251

90c+60c, View of Ghent. 1.35fr+1.15fr, Van Artevelde monument, Ghent. 3.15fr+1.85fr. Anseele Monument, Flemish inscription.

1948, June 21 ***Perf. 14x13½***

B455 SP251 65c + 35c rose red 2.75 1.10
B456 SP251 90c + 60c gray 3.50 1.90
B457 SP251 1.35fr + 1.15fr hn brn 2.25 1.50
B458 SP251 3.15fr + 1.85fr brt bl 8.50 5.00
a. Souv. sheet, #B455-B458 200.00 85.00
Nos. B455-B458 (4) 17.00 9.50

Issued to honor Edouard Anseele, statesman, founder of the Belgian Socialist Party.
No. B458a sold for 50fr.
For surcharges see Nos. 395-398.

Statue "The Unloader" SP252

Underground Fighter SP253

1948, Sept. 4 ***Perf. 11½x11***

B460 SP252 10fr + 10fr gray grn 52.50 24.50
B461 SP253 10fr + 10fr red brn 22.50 12.50

The surtax was used toward erection of monuments at Antwerp and Liege.

Portrait Type of 1946 and

Double Barred Cross — SP254

Designs: 4fr+3.25fr, Isabella of Austria. 20fr+20fr, Archduke Albert of Austria.

1948, Dec. 15 **Photo.** ***Perf. 13½x14***

B462 SP254 20c + 5c dk sl grn .50 .25
B463 SP254 1.20fr + 30c mag 1.25 .70
B464 SP254 1.75fr + 25c red 1.75 .60

Engr. ***Perf. 11½x11***

B465 SP236 4fr + 3.25fr ultra 9.50 6.50
B466 SP236 20fr + 20fr Prus grn 42.50 30.00
Nos. B462-B466 (5) 55.50 38.05

The surtax was divided among several charities.

Souvenir Sheets

Rogier van der Weyden Paintings — SP255

Paintings by van der Weyden (No. B466A): 90c, Virgin and Child. 1.75fr, Christ on the Cross. 4fr, Mary Magdalene.
Paintings by Jordaens (No. B466B): 90c, Woman Reading. 1.75fr, The Flutist. 4fr, Old Woman Reading Letter.

1949, Apr. 1 **Photo.** ***Perf. 11½***

B466A SP255 Sheet of 3 200.00 175.00
c. 90c deep brown 55.00 50.00
d. 1.75fr deep rose lilac 55.00 50.00
e. 4fr dark violet blue 55.00 50.00
B466B SP255 Sheet of 3 200.00 175.00
f. 90c dark violet 55.00 50.00
g. 1.75fr red 55.00 50.00
h. 4fr blue 55.00 50.00

The surtax went to various cultural and philanthropic organizations. Sheets sold for 50fr each.
Gum on Nos. B466A-B466B is irregularly applied.

Guido Gezelle — SP256

1949, Nov. 15 **Photo.** ***Perf. 14x13½***

B467 SP256 1.75fr + 75c dk Prus grn 2.50 1.75

50th anniversary of the death of Guido Gezelle, poet. The surtax was for the Guido Gezelle Museum, Bruges.

Portrait Type of 1946 and

Arnica — SP257

Designs: 65c+10c, Sand grass. 90c+10c, Wood myrtle. 1.20fr+30c, Field poppy. 1.75fr+25c, Philip the Good. 3fr+1.50fr, Charles V. 4fr+2fr, Maria-Christina. 6fr+3fr, Charles of Lorraine. 8fr+4fr, Maria-Theresa.

1949, Dec. 20 **Typo.** ***Perf. 13½x14***

B468 SP257 20c + 5c multi .55 .55
B469 SP257 65c + 10c multi 1.40 1.25
B470 SP257 90c + 10c multi 2.25 1.60
B471 SP257 1.20fr + 30c multi 2.75 1.90

Engr. ***Perf. 11½x11***

B472 SP236 1.75fr + 25c red org 1.50 .90
B473 SP236 3fr + 1.50fr dp claret 11.00 7.50
B474 SP236 4fr + 2fr ultra 11.00 8.75
B475 SP236 6fr + 3fr choc 20.00 12.00
B476 SP236 8fr + 4fr dl grn 21.00 12.50
Nos. B468-B476 (9) 71.45 46.95

The surtax was apportioned among several welfare organizations.

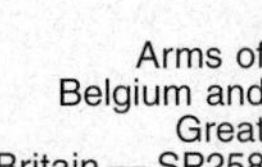

Arms of Belgium and Great Britain — SP258

British Memorial — SP260

Design: 2.50fr+50c, British tanks at Hertain.

Perf. 13½x14, 11½

1950, Mar. 15 **Engr.**

B477 SP258 80c + 20c grn 1.50 1.00
B478 SP258 2.50fr + 50c red 5.00 3.75
B479 SP260 4fr + 2fr dp bl 9.25 6.25
Nos. B477-B479 (3) 15.75 11.00

6th anniv. of the liberation of Belgian territory by the British army.

Hurdling SP261

Relay Race SP262

Designs: 90c+10c, Javelin throwing. 4fr+2fr, Pole vault. 8fr+4fr, Foot race.

Perf. 14x13½, 13½x14

1950, July 1 **Engr.** **Unwmk.**

B480 SP261 20c + 5c brt grn .45 .25
B481 SP261 90c + 10c vio brn 3.75 1.50
B482 SP262 1.75fr + 25c car 7.25 1.75
a. Souvenir sheet of 1 80.00 50.00
B483 SP261 4fr + 2fr lt bl 35.00 17.00
B484 SP261 8fr + 4fr dp grn 37.50 24.00
Nos. B480-B484 (5) 83.95 44.50

Issued to publicize the European Athletic Games, Brussels, August 1950.
The margins of No. B482a were trimmed in April, 1951, and an overprint ("25 Francs pour le Fonds Sportif-25e Foire Internationale Bruxelles") was added in red in French and in black in Flemish by a private committee. These pairs of altered sheets were sold at the Brussels Fair. Value, set of 2 altered sheets, $25.

Gentian — SP263

Sijsele Sanatorium SP264

Tombeek Sanatorium SP265

Designs: 65c+10c, Cotton Grass. 90c+10c, Foxglove. 1.20fr+30c, Limonia. 4fr+2fr, Jauche Sanatorium.

1950, Dec. 20 **Typo.** ***Perf. 14x13½***

B485 SP263 20c + 5c multi .80 .40
B486 SP263 65c + 10c multi 1.50 .85
B487 SP263 90c + 10c multi 1.60 1.10
B488 SP263 1.20fr + 30c multi 2.75 2.25

Perf. 11½

Engr.

Cross in Red

B489 SP264 1.75fr + 25c car 2.50 1.40
B490 SP264 4fr + 2fr blue 18.00 8.25
B491 SP265 8fr + 4fr bl grn 25.00 17.50
Nos. B485-B491 (7) 52.15 31.75

The surtax was for tuberculosis prevention and other charitable purposes.

Chemist
SP266

Allegory of Peace
SP268

Colonial Instructor and Class
SP267

1951, Mar. 27 **Unwmk.**

B492 SP266 80c + 20c grn 1.40 1.00
B493 SP267 2.50fr + 50c vio brn 10.00 5.50
B494 SP268 4fr + 2fr dp bl 12.00 6.75
Nos. B492-B494 (3) 23.40 13.25

Surtax for the reconstruction fund of the UNESCO.

Monument to Political Prisoners — SP269

Fort of Breendonk
SP270

8fr+4fr, Monument: profile of figure on pedestal.

1951, Aug. 20 **Photo.** ***Perf. 11½***

B495 SP269 1.75fr + 25c blk brn 3.00 1.90
B496 SP270 4fr + 2fr bl & sl gray 32.50 17.50
B497 SP269 8fr + 4fr dk bl grn 32.50 20.00
Nos. B495-B497 (3) 68.00 39.40

The surtax was for the erection of a national monument.

Queen Elisabeth — SP271

1951, Sept. 22

B498 SP271 90c + 10c grnsh gray 4.00 .90
B499 SP271 1.75fr + 25c plum 9.00 2.00
B500 SP271 3fr + 1fr green 32.50 15.00
B501 SP271 4fr + 2fr gray bl 35.00 16.00
B502 SP271 8fr + 4fr sepia 45.00 20.00
Nos. B498-B502 (5) 125.50 53.90

The surtax was for the Queen Elisabeth Medical Foundation.

Cross, Sun Rays and Dragon — SP272

Beersel Castle
SP273

Horst Castle — SP274

Castles: 4fr+2fr, Lavaux St. Anne. 8fr+4fr, Veves.

1951, Dec. 17 **Engr.** **Unwmk.**

B503 SP272 20c + 5c red .35 .25
B504 SP272 65c + 10c dp ultra .85 .60
B505 SP272 90c + 10c sep .90 .80
B506 SP272 1.20fr + 30c rose vio 1.40 .90
B507 SP273 1.75fr + 75c red brn 4.00 1.50
B508 SP274 3fr + 1fr yel grn 14.00 8.25
B509 SP273 4fr + 2fr blue 17.00 9.25
B510 SP274 8fr + 4fr gray 26.50 14.50
Nos. B503-B510 (8) 65.00 36.05

The surtax was for anti-tuberculosis work. See Nos. B523-B526, B547-B550.

Main Altar
SP275

Basilica of the Sacred Heart Koekelberg
SP276

Procession Bearing Relics of St. Albert of Louvain — SP277

1952, Mar. 1 **Photo.** ***Perf. 11½***

B511 SP275 1.75fr + 25c blk brn 1.50 1.25
B512 SP276 4fr + 2fr indigo 16.00 8.25

Engr.

B513 SP277 8fr + 4fr vio brn 25.00 11.50
a. Souv. sheet, #B511-B513 425.00 175.00
Nos. B511-B513 (3) 42.50 21.00

25th anniv. of the Cardinalate of J. E. Van Roey, Primate of Belgium. The surtax was for the Basilica. No. B513a sold for 30fr.

Beaulieu Castle, Malines
SP278

August Vermeylen
SP279

1952, May 14 **Engr.**

Laid Paper

B514 SP278 40fr + 10fr lt grnsh bl 140.00 100.00

Issued on the occasion of the 13th Universal Postal Union Congress, Brussels, 1952.

Perf. 11½

1952, Oct. 24 **Unwmk.** **Photo.**

Portraits: 80c+40c, Karel Van de Woestijne. 90c+45c, Charles de Coster. 1.75fr+75c, M. Maeterlinck. 4fr+2fr, Emile Verhaeren. 8fr+4fr, Hendrik Conscience.

B515 SP279 65c + 30c pur 5.75 2.25
B516 SP279 80c + 40c dk grn 6.00 2.75
B517 SP279 90c + 45c sepia 6.25 3.00
B518 SP279 1.75fr + 75c cer 14.50 5.00
B519 SP279 4fr + 2fr bl vio 37.50 17.50
B520 SP279 8fr + 4fr dk brn 45.00 22.50
Nos. B515-B520 (6) 115.00 53.00

1952, Nov. 15

4fr, Emile Verhaeren. 8fr, Hendrik Conscience.

B521 SP279 4fr (+ 9fr) blue 160.00 80.00
B522 SP279 8fr (+ 9fr) dk car rose 160.00 80.00

On Nos. B521-B522, the denomination is repeated at either side of the stamp. The surtax is expressed on se-tenant labels bearing quotations of Verhaeren (in French) and Conscience (in Flemish). Value is for stamp with label.

A 9-line black overprint was privately applied to these labels: "Conference Internationale de la Musique Bruxelles UNESCO International Music Conference Brussels 1953*" Value, $125.

Type of 1951 Dated "1952," and

Arms of Malmédy — SP281

Castle Ruins, Burgreuland
SP282

Designs: 4fr+2fr, Vesdre Dam, Eupen. 8fr+4fr, St. Vitus, patron saint of Saint-Vith.

1952, Dec. 15 **Engr.**

B523 SP272 20c + 5c red brn .50 .50
B524 SP272 80c + 20c grn .95 .70
B525 SP272 1.20fr + 30c lil rose 2.00 1.10
B526 SP272 1.50fr + 50c ol brn 2.00 1.10
B527 SP281 2fr + 75c car 3.50 3.50
B528 SP282 3fr + 1.50fr choc 22.50 13.50
B529 SP281 4fr + 2fr blue 21.00 12.00
B530 SP281 8fr + 4fr vio brn 22.50 16.00
Nos. B523-B530 (8) 74.95 48.40

The surtax on Nos. B523-B530 was for anti-tuberculosis and other charitable works.

Walthère Dewé
SP283

Princess Josephine-Charlotte
SP284

1953, Feb. 16 **Photo.**

B531 SP283 2fr + 1fr brn car 3.25 1.75

The surtax was for the construction of a memorial to Walthère Dewé, Underground leader in World War II.

1953, Mar. 14 **Cross in Red**

B532 SP284 80c + 20c ol grn 3.50 1.50
B533 SP284 1.20fr + 30c brn 3.25 1.25
B534 SP284 2fr + 50c rose lake 2.75 1.25
a. Booklet pane of 8 80.00 65.00
B535 SP284 2.50fr + 50c crim 17.50 10.00
B536 SP284 4fr + 1fr brt blue 19.00 8.75
B537 SP284 5fr + 2fr sl grn 19.00 8.75
Nos. B532-B537 (6) 65.00 31.50

The surtax was for the Belgian Red Cross.

The selvage of No. B534a is inscribed in French. Value for selvage inscribed in Dutch, $220.

Boats at Dock
SP285

Bridge and Citadel, Namur — SP286

Allegory — SP287

Designs: 1.20fr+30c, Bridge at Bouillon. 2fr+50c, Antwerp waterfront. 4fr+2fr, Wharf at Ghent. 8fr+4fr, Meuse River at Freyr.

1953, June 22 **Unwmk.** ***Perf. 11½***

B538 SP285 80c + 20c grn 2.25 1.00
B539 SP285 1.20fr + 30c redsh brn 6.00 2.75
B540 SP285 2fr + 50c sep 6.75 2.75
B541 SP286 2.50fr + 50c dp mag 16.00 8.00
B542 SP286 4fr + 2fr vio bl 26.50 13.00
B543 SP286 8fr + 4fr gray blk 32.50 15.00
Nos. B538-B543 (6) 90.00 42.50

The surtax was used to promote tourism in the Ardenne-Meuse region and for various cultural works.

1953, Oct. 26 **Engr.**

B544 SP287 80c + 20c grn 3.50 2.50
B545 SP287 2.50fr + 1fr rose car 32.50 24.00
B546 SP287 4fr + 1.50fr blue 37.50 30.00
Nos. B544-B546 (3) 73.50 56.50

The surtax was for the European Bureau of Childhood and Youth.

Type of 1951 Dated "1953," and

Ernest Malvoz — SP288

Robert Koch SP289

Portraits: 3fr+1.50fr, Carlo Forlanini. 4fr+2fr, Leon Charles Albert Calmette.

1953, Dec. 15

B547	SP272	20c + 5c blue	.60	.55
B548	SP272	80c + 20c rose vio	1.60	.70
B549	SP272	1.20fr + 30c choc	2.50	1.00
B550	SP272	1.50fr + 50c dk gray	3.00	1.25
B551	SP288	2fr + 75c dk grn	4.00	1.75
B552	SP288	3fr + 1.50fr dk red	17.50	9.25
B553	SP288	4fr + 2fr ultra	20.00	11.00
B554	SP289	8fr + 4fr choc	25.00	13.50
		Nos. B547-B554 (8)	74.20	39.00

The surtax was for anti-tuberculosis and other charitable works.

King Albert I Statue — SP290

Albert I Monument, Namur SP291

9fr+4.50fr, Cliffs of Marche-les-Dames.

1954, Feb. 17 **Photo.**

B555	SP290	2fr + 50c chnt brn	10.00	3.75
B556	SP291	4fr + 2fr blue	32.50	14.50
B557	SP290	9fr + 4.50fr ol blk	27.50	15.00
		Nos. B555-B557 (3)	70.00	33.25

20th anniv. of the death of King Albert I. The surtax aided in the erection of the monument pictured on No. B556.

Political Prisoners' Monument SP292

Camp and Fort, Breendonk SP293

Design: 9fr+4.50fr, Political prisoners' monument (profile).

1954, Apr. 1 **Unwmk.** ***Perf. 11½***

B558	SP292	2fr + 1fr red	22.50	11.00
B559	SP293	4fr + 2fr dk brn	50.00	22.50
B560	SP292	9fr + 4.50fr ol grn	52.50	26.50
		Nos. B558-B560 (3)	125.00	60.00

The surtax was used toward the creation of a monument to political prisoners.

Gatehouse and Gateway SP294

Nuns in Courtyard SP295

Our Lady of the Vine SP296

2fr+1fr, Swans in stream. 7fr+3.50fr Nuns at well. 8fr+4fr, Statue above door.

1954, May 15

B561	SP294	80c + 20c dk bl grn	1.00	.75
B562	SP294	2fr + 1fr crim	12.00	1.60
B563	SP295	4fr + 2fr violet	17.00	10.00
B564	SP295	7fr + 3.50fr lil rose	40.00	21.00
B565	SP295	8fr + 4fr brown	40.00	21.00
B566	SP296	9fr + 4.50fr gray bl	65.00	32.50
		Nos. B561-B566 (6)	175.00	86.85

The surtax was for the Friends of the Beguinage of Bruges.

Child's Head — SP297

"The Blind Man and the Paralytic," by Antoine Carte SP298

1954, Dec. 1 **Engr.**

B567	SP297	20c + 5c dk grn	.50	.50
B568	SP297	80c + 20c dk gray	1.00	.90
B569	SP297	1.20fr + 30c org brn	2.00	1.00
B570	SP297	1.50fr + 50c pur	3.50	2.00
B571	SP298	2fr + 75c rose car	8.00	3.75
B572	SP298	4fr + 1fr brt blue	20.00	12.50
		Nos. B567-B572 (6)	35.00	20.65

The surtax was for anti-tuberculosis work.

Ernest Solvay SP299

Jean-Jacques Dony — SP300

Portraits: 1.20fr+30c, Egide Walschaerts. 2fr+50c, Leo H. Baekeland. 3fr+1fr, Jean-Etienne Lenoir. 4fr+2fr, Emile Fourcault and Emile Gobbe.

Perf. 11½

1955, Oct. 22 **Unwmk.** **Photo.**

B573	SP299	20c + 5c brn & dk brn	.40	.35
B574	SP300	80c + 20c vio	1.00	.50
B575	SP299	1.20fr + 30c ind	6.25	3.25
B576	SP300	2fr + 50c dp car	5.50	3.00
B577	SP300	3fr + 1fr dk grn	14.50	8.50
B578	SP299	4fr + 2fr brown	14.50	8.50
		Nos. B573-B578 (6)	42.15	24.10

Issued in honor of Belgian scientists.
The surtax was for the benefit of various cultural organizations.

"The Joys of Spring" by E. Canneel SP301

Einar Holböll SP302

Portraits: 4fr+2fr, John D. Rockefeller. 8fr+4fr, Sir Robert W. Philip.

1955, Dec. 5 **Unwmk.** ***Perf. 11½***

B579	SP301	20c + 5c red lil	.70	.30
B580	SP301	80c + 20c green	1.00	.65
B581	SP301	1.20fr + 30c redsh brn	2.50	.90
B582	SP301	1.50fr + 50c vio bl	3.00	1.10
B583	SP302	2fr + 50c car	9.50	4.75
B584	SP302	4fr + 2fr ultra	26.00	12.00
B585	SP302	8fr + 4fr ol gray	27.50	15.00
		Nos. B579-B585 (7)	70.20	34.70

The surtax was for anti-tuberculosis work.

Palace of Charles of Lorraine — SP303

Queen Elisabeth and Sonata by Mozart — SP304

Design: 2fr+1fr, Mozart at age 7.

1956, Mar. 19 **Engr.**

B586	SP303	80c + 20c steel bl	1.00	1.00
B587	SP303	2fr + 1fr rose lake	4.25	3.00
B588	SP304	4fr + 2fr dull pur	8.00	4.25
		Nos. B586-B588 (3)	13.25	8.25

200th anniversary of the birth of Wolfgang Amadeus Mozart, composer.
The surtax was for the benefit of the Pro-Mozart Committee in Belgium.

Queen Elisabeth — SP305

1956, Aug. 16 **Photo.**

B589	SP305	80c + 20c slate grn	1.00	1.00
B590	SP305	2fr + 1fr deep plum	3.50	1.90
B591	SP305	4fr + 2fr brown	5.00	2.75
		Nos. B589-B591 (3)	9.50	5.65

Issued in honor of the 80th birthday of Queen Elisabeth. The surtax went to the Queen Elisabeth Foundation. See No. 659.

Ship with Cross — SP306

Infant on Scales SP307

Rehabilitation SP308

Design: 4fr+2fr, X-Ray examination.

1956, Dec. 17 **Engr.**

B592	SP306	20c + 5c redsh brn	.35	.30
B593	SP306	80c + 20c grn	.75	.60
B594	SP306	1.20fr + 30c dl lil	.90	.60
B595	SP306	1.5fr + 50c lt sl bl	1.10	.90
B596	SP307	2fr + 50c ol grn	3.50	2.10
B597	SP307	4fr + 2fr dl pur	14.50	8.75
B598	SP308	8fr + 4fr dp car	16.00	10.50
		Nos. B592-B598 (7)	37.10	23.75

The surtax was for anti-tuberculosis work.

Charles Plisnier and Albrecht Rodenbach SP309

80c+20c, Emiel Vliebergh & Maurice Wilmotte. 1.20fr+30c, Paul Pastur & Julius Hoste. 2fr+50c, Lodewijk de Raet & Jules Destree. 3fr+1fr, Constantin Meunier & Constant Permeke. 4fr+2fr, Lieven Gevaert & Edouard Empain.

Perf. 11½

1957, June 8 **Unwmk.** **Photo.**

B599	SP309	20c + 5c brt vio	.40	.35
B600	SP309	80c + 20c lt red brn	.55	.35
B601	SP309	1.20f + 30c blk brn	.70	.60

B602 SP309 2fr + 50c claret 1.90 1.25
B603 SP309 3fr + 1fr dk ol grn 2.75 1.90
B604 SP309 4fr + 2fr vio bl 3.25 2.50
Nos. B599-B604 (6) 9.55 6.95

The surtax was for the benefit of various cultural organizations.

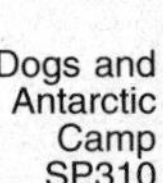

Dogs and Antarctic Camp SP310

1957, Oct. 18 Engr. *Perf. 11½*
B605 SP310 5fr + 2.50fr gray, org & vio brn 3.25 2.25
a. Sheet of 4, #B605b 175.00 140.00
b. Blue, slate & red brown 35.00 29.00

Surtax for Belgian Antarctic Expedition, 1957-58.

Gen. Patton's Grave and Flag SP311

Gen. George S. Patton, Jr. — SP312

Designs: 2.50fr+50c, Memorial, Bastogne. 3fr+1fr, Gen. Patton decorating Brig. Gen. Anthony C. McAuliffe. 6fr+3fr, Tanks of 1918 and 1944.

1957, Oct. 28 Photo.
Size: 36x25mm, 25x36mm

B606 SP311 1fr + 50c dk gray 2.00 1.00
B607 SP311 2.50fr + 50c ol grn 3.00 1.60
B608 SP311 3fr + 1fr red brn 3.75 2.10
B609 SP312 5fr + 2.50fr grysh bl 8.75 5.50

Size: 53x35mm

B610 SP311 6fr + 3fr pale brn car 12.00 8.00
Nos. B606-B610 (5) 29.50 18.20

The surtax was for the General Patton Memorial Committee and Patriotic Societies.

Adolphe Max — SP313

1957, Nov. 10 Engr.
B611 SP313 2.50fr + 1fr ultra 1.25 .75

18th anniversary of the death of Adolphe Max, mayor of Brussels. The surtax was for the national "Adolphe Max" fund.

"Chinels," Fosses SP314

"Op Signoorken," Malines SP315

Infanta Isabella Shooting Crossbow SP316

Legends: 1.50fr+50c, St. Remacle and the wolf. 2fr+1fr, Longman and the pea soup. 5fr+2fr, The Virgin with Inkwell, vert. 6fr+2.50fr, "Gilles" (clowns), Binche.

1957, Dec. 14 Engr. & Photo.
B612 SP314 30c + 20c .25 .30
B613 SP315 1fr + 50c .40 .30
B614 SP314 1.50fr + 50c .80 .50
B615 SP315 2fr + 1fr 1.10 1.00
B616 SP316 2.50fr + 1fr 1.90 1.40
B617 SP316 5fr + 2fr 3.50 2.75
B618 SP316 6fr + 2.50fr 4.50 3.25
Nos. B612-B618 (7) 12.45 9.50

The surtax was for anti-tuberculosis work. See Nos. B631-B637.

Benelux Gate SP317

Designs: 1fr+50c, Civil Engineering Pavilion. 1.50fr+50c, Belgian Congo & Ruanda-Urundi Pavilion. 2.50fr+1fr, Belgium 1900. 3fr+1.50fr, Atomium. 5fr+3fr, Telexpo Pavilion.

Perf. 11½
1958, Apr. 15 Unwmk. Engr.
Size: 35½x24½mm

B619 SP317 30c + 20c multi .25 .25
B620 SP317 1fr + 50c multi .25 .25
B621 SP317 1.50fr + 50c multi .25 .25
B622 SP317 2.50fr + 1fr multi .45 .45
B623 SP317 3fr + 1.50fr multi .90 .50

Size: 49x33mm

B624 SP317 5fr + 3fr multi 1.50 1.00
Nos. B619-B624 (6) 3.60 2.70

World's Fair, Brussels, Apr. 17-Oct. 19.

Marguerite van Eyck by Jan van Eyck — SP318

Christ Carrying Cross, by Hieronymus Bosch SP319

Paintings: 1.50fr+50c, St. Donatien, Jan Gossart. 2.50fr+1fr, Self-portrait, Lambert Lombard. 3fr+1.50fr, The Rower, James Ensor. 5fr+3fr, Henriette, Henri Evenepoel.

1958, Oct. 30 Photo. *Perf. 11½*
Various Frames in Ocher and Brown

B625 SP318 30c + 20c dk ol grn .45 .30
B626 SP319 1fr + 50c mar .75 .70
B627 SP318 1.50fr + 50c vio bl 1.10 .75
B628 SP318 2.50fr + 1fr dk brn 2.25 1.60
B629 SP319 3fr + 1.50fr dl red 3.25 2.00
B630 SP318 5fr + 3fr brt bl 5.25 5.00
Nos. B625-B630 (6) 13.05 10.35

The surtax was for the benefit of various cultural organizations.

Type of 1957

Legends: 40c+10c, Elizabeth, Countess of Hoogstraten. 1fr+50c, Jean de Nivelles. 1.50fr+50c, St. Evermare play, Russon. 2fr+1fr, The Penitents of Furnes. 2.50fr+1fr, Manger and "Pax." 5fr+2fr, Sambre-Meuse procession. 6fr+2.50fr, Our Lady of Peace and "Pax," vert.

Engraved and Photogravure
1958, Dec. 6 Unwmk. *Perf. 11½*

B631 SP314 40c + 10c ultra & brt grn .30 .25
B632 SP315 1fr + 50c gray brn & org .40 .30
B633 SP315 1.50fr + 50c cl & brt grn .60 .35
B634 SP314 2fr + 1fr brn & red .70 .50
B635 SP316 2.50fr + 1fr vio brn & bl grn 2.50 1.90
B636 SP316 5fr + 2fr cl & bl 3.75 3.00
B637 SP316 6fr + 2.50fr bl & rose red 4.75 4.50
Nos. B631-B637 (7) 13.00 10.80

The surtax was for anti-tuberculosis work.

"Europe of the Heart" SP320

1959, Feb. 25 Photo. Unwmk.
B638 SP320 1fr + 50c red lil .55 .30
B639 SP320 2.50fr + 1fr dk grn .95 .90
B640 SP320 5fr + 2.50fr dp brn 1.25 1.10
Nos. B638-B640 (3) 2.75 2.30

The surtax was for aid for displaced persons.

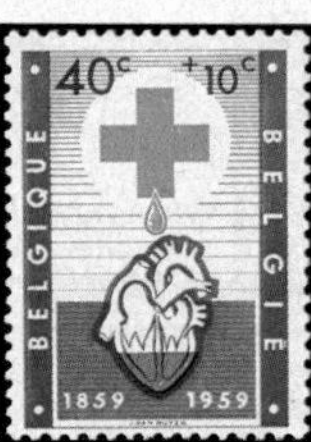

Allegory of Blood Transfusion SP321

Henri Dunant and Battlefield at Solferino — SP322

Design: 2.50fr+1fr, 3fr+1.50fr, Red Cross, broken sword and drop of blood, horiz.

1959, June 10 Photo. *Perf. 11½*
B641 SP321 40c + 10c .60 .30
B642 SP321 1fr + 50c 1.10 .45
B643 SP321 1.50fr + 50c 3.00 1.60
B644 SP321 2.50fr + 1fr 3.50 1.90
B645 SP321 3fr + 1.50fr 6.00 3.50
B646 SP322 5fr + 3fr 11.50 5.50
Nos. B641-B646 (6) 25.70 13.25

Cent. of the Intl. Red Cross idea. Surtax for the Red Cross and patriotic organizations.

Philip the Good — SP323

Arms of Philip the Good SP324

Designs: 1fr+50c, Charles the Bold. 1.50fr+50c, Emperor Maximilian of Austria. 2.50fr+1fr, Philip the Fair. 3fr+1.50fr, Charles V. Portraits from miniatures by Simon Bening (c. 1483-1561).

1959, July 4 Engr.
B647 SP323 40c + 10c multi .50 .35
B648 SP323 1fr + 50c multi .80 .50
B649 SP323 1.50fr + 50c multi 1.25 .80
B650 SP323 2.50fr + 1fr multi 2.25 1.90
B651 SP323 3fr + 1.50fr multi 4.00 3.00
B652 SP324 5fr + 3fr multi 5.50 4.00
Nos. B647-B652 (6) 14.30 10.55

The surtax was for the Royal Library, Brussels.

Portraits show Grand Masters of the Order of the Golden Fleece.

Whale, Antwerp SP325

Carnival, Stavelot SP326

Designs: 1fr+50c, Dragon, Mons. 2fr+50c, Prince Carnival, Eupen. 3fr+1fr, Jester and cats, Ypres. 6fr+2fr, Holy Family, horiz. 7fr+3fr, Madonna, Liége, horiz.

Engraved and Photogravure
1959, Dec. 5 *Perf. 11½*

B653 SP325 40c + 10c cit, Prus bl & red .45 .40
B654 SP325 1fr + 50c ol & grn .75 .60
B655 SP325 2fr + 50c lt brn, org & cl .50 .40
B656 SP326 2.50fr + 1fr gray, pur & ultra .80 .60
B657 SP326 3fr + 1fr gray, mar & yel 1.75 1.25
B658 SP326 6fr + 2fr ol, brt bl & hn brn 4.00 2.50
B659 SP326 7fr + 3fr chlky bl & org yel 5.25 4.25
Nos. B653-B659 (7) 13.50 10.00

The surtax was for anti-tuberculosis work.

Child Refugee — SP327

Designs: 3fr+1.50fr, Man. 6fr+3fr, Woman.

1960, Apr. 7 Engr.
B660 SP327 40c + 10c rose claret .25 .25
B661 SP327 3fr + 1.50fr gray brn .65 .50
B662 SP327 6fr + 3fr dk bl 1.60 1.10
a. Souvenir sheet of 3 85.00 75.00
Nos. B660-B662 (3) 2.50 1.85

World Refugee Year, 7/1/59-6/30/60.

No. B662a contains Nos. B660-B662 with colors changed: 40c+10c, dull purple; 3fr+1.50fr, red brown; 6fr+3fr, henna brown.

Parachutists and Plane SP328

Designs: 2fr+50c, 2.50fr+1fr, Parachutists coming in for landing, vert 3fr+1fr, 6fr+2fr, Parachutist walking with parachute.

Photogravure and Engraved

1960, June 13 *Perf. 11½*

Multicolored

B663 SP328 40c + 10c .25 .25
B664 SP328 1fr + 50c 1.50 .70
B665 SP328 2fr + 50c 3.25 2.10
B666 SP328 2.50fr + 1fr 6.00 3.25
B667 SP328 3fr + 1fr 6.00 3.25
B668 SP328 6fr + 2fr 7.00 4.50
Nos. B663-B668 (6) 24.00 14.05

The surtax was for various patriotic and cultural organizations.

Mother and Child, Planes and Rainbow SP329

Designs: 40c+10c, Brussels Airport, planes and rainbow. 6fr+3fr, Rainbow connecting Congo and Belgium, and planes, vert

Perf. 11½

1960, Aug. 3 Unwmk. Photo.

Size: 35x24mm

B669 SP329 40c + 10c grnsh blue .25 .25
B670 SP329 3fr + 1.50fr brt red 2.50 2.25

Size: 35x52mm

B671 SP329 6fr + 3fr violet 4.75 3.50
Nos. B669-B671 (3) 7.50 6.00

The surtax was for refugees from Congo.

Infant, Milk Bottle and Mug — SP330

UNICEF: 1fr+50c, Nurse and children of 3 races. 2fr+50c, Refugee woman carrying gift clothes. 2.50fr+1fr, Negro nurse weighing infant. 3fr+1fr, Children of various races dancing. 6fr+2fr, Refugee boys.

Photogravure and Engraved

1960, Oct. 8 *Perf. 11½*

B672 SP330 40c + 10c gldn brn, yel & bl grn .25 .25
B673 SP330 1fr + 50c ol gray, mar & slate 1.40 .75
B674 SP330 2fr + 50c vio, pale brn & brt grn 1.90 1.40
B675 SP330 2.50fr + 1fr dk red, sep & lt bl 2.00 1.40
B676 SP330 3fr + 1fr bl grn, red org & dl vio 2.50 1.60
B677 SP330 6fr + 2fr ultra, emer & brn 4.00 3.25
Nos. B672-B677 (6) 12.05 8.65

Tapestry SP331

Belgian handicrafts: 1fr+50c, Cut crystal vases, vert. 2fr+50c, Lace, vert. 2.50fr+1fr, Metal plate & jug. 3fr+1fr, Diamonds. 6fr+2fr, Ceramics.

1960, Dec. 5 *Perf. 11½*

Multicolored

B678 SP331 40c + 10c .25 .25
B679 SP331 1fr + 50c 1.00 1.00
B680 SP331 2fr + 50c 2.00 1.50
B681 SP331 2.50fr + 1fr 3.00 2.25
B682 SP331 3fr + 1fr 3.50 2.25
B683 SP331 6fr + 2fr 5.00 4.00
Nos. B678-B683 (6) 14.75 11.25

The surtax was for anti-tuberculosis work.

Jacob Kats and Abbe Nicolas Pietkin SP332

Portraits: 1fr+50c, Albert Mockel and J. F. Willems. 2fr+50c, Jan van Rijswijck and Xavier M. Neujean. 2.50fr+1fr, Joseph Demarteau and A. Van de Perre. 3fr+1fr, Canon Jan-Baptist David and Albert du Bois. 6fr+2fr, Henri Vieuxtemps and Willem de Mol.

1961, Apr. 22 Unwmk. *Perf. 11½*

Multicolored

Portraits in Gray Brown

B684 SP332 40c + 10c .50 .30
B685 SP332 1fr + 50c 2.25 1.25
B686 SP332 2fr + 50c 3.75 3.00
B687 SP332 2.50fr + 1fr 3.75 3.00
B688 SP332 3fr + 1fr 4.25 3.00
B689 SP332 6fr + 2fr 6.00 4.50
Nos. B684-B689 (6) 20.50 15.05

The surtax was for the benefit of various cultural organizations.

White Rhinoceros SP333

Animals: 1fr+50c, Przewalski horses. 2fr+50c, Okapi. 2.50fr+1fr, Giraffe, horiz. 3fr+1fr, Lesser panda, horiz. 6fr+2fr, European elk, horiz.

Perf. 11½

1961, June 5 Unwmk. Photo.

Multicolored

B690 SP333 40c + 10c .25 .25
B691 SP333 1fr + 50c 1.10 1.00
B692 SP333 2fr + 50c 1.60 1.40
B693 SP333 2.50fr + 1fr 2.00 1.50
B694 SP333 3fr + 1fr 2.25 1.50
B695 SP333 6fr + 2fr 2.75 2.10
Nos. B690-B695 (6) 9.95 7.75

The surtax was for various philanthropic organizations.

Antonius Cardinal Perrenot de Granvelle — SP334

Designs: 3fr+1.50fr, Arms of Cardinal de Granvelle. 6fr+3fr, Tower and crosier, symbolic of collaboration between Malines and the Archbishopric.

1961, July 29 Engr.

B696 SP334 40c + 10c mag, car & brn .25 .25
B697 SP334 3fr + 1.50fr multi .70 .60
B698 SP334 6fr + 3fr mag pur & bis 1.40 1.10
Nos. B696-B698 (3) 2.35 1.95

400th anniv. of Malines as an Archbishopric.

Mother and Child by Pierre Paulus — SP335

Plaintings: 1fr+50c, Mother Love, Francois-Joseph Navez. 2fr+50c, Motherhood, Constant Permeke. 2.50fr+1fr, Madonna and Child, Rogier van der Weyden. 3fr+1fr, Madonna with Apple, Hans Memling. 6fr+2fr, Madonna of the Forget-me-not, Peter Paul Rubens.

1961, Dec. 2 Photo. *Perf. 11½*

Gold Frame

B699 SP335 40c + 10c dp brn .25 .25
B700 SP335 1fr + 50c brt bl .60 .55
B701 SP335 2fr + 50c rose red 1.00 .90
B702 SP335 2.50fr + 1fr mag 1.10 .90
B703 SP335 3fr + 1fr vio bl 1.00 .90
B704 SP335 6fr + 2fr dk sl grn 1.75 1.50
Nos. B699-B704 (6) 5.70 5.00

The surtax was for anti-tuberculosis work.

Castle of the Counts of Male — SP336

Designs: 90c+10c, Royal library, horiz. 1fr+50c, Church of Our Lady, Tongres. 2fr+50c, Collegiate Church, Soignies, horiz. 2.50fr+1fr, Church of Our Lady, Malines. 3fr+1fr, St. Denis Abbey, Broqueroi. 6fr+2fr, Cloth Hall, Ypres, horiz.

1962, Mar. 12 Engr. *Perf. 11½*

B705 SP336 40c + 10c brt grn .25 .25
B706 SP336 90c + 10c lil rose .25 .25
B707 SP336 1fr + 50c dl vio .40 .45
B708 SP336 2fr + 50c violet .70 .60
B709 SP336 2.50fr + 1fr red brn 1.10 .85
B710 SP336 3fr + 1fr bl grn 1.25 .85
B711 SP336 6fr + 2fr car rose 1.90 1.40
Nos. B705-B711 (7) 5.85 4.65

The surtax was for various cultural and philanthropic organizations.

Andean Cock of the Rock — SP337

Birds: 1fr+50c, Red lory. 2fr+50c, Guinea touraco. 2.50fr+1fr, Keel-billed toucan. 3fr+1fr, Great bird of paradise. 6fr+2fr, Congolese peacock.

Engraved and Photogravure

1962, June 23 Unwmk. *Perf. 11½*

B712 SP337 40c + 10c multi .25 .25
B713 SP337 1fr + 50c multi .45 .25
B714 SP337 2fr + 50c multi .75 .70
B715 SP337 2.50fr + 1fr multi 1.00 .90
B716 SP337 3fr + 1fr multi 1.40 1.25
B717 SP337 6fr + 2fr multi 2.00 1.75
Nos. B712-B717 (6) 5.85 5.10

The surtax was for various philanthropic organizations.

Handicapped Child — SP338

Handicapped Children: 40c+10c, Reading Braille. 2fr+50c, Deaf-mute girl with earphones and electronic equipment, horiz. 2.50fr+1fr, Child with ball (cerebral palsy). 3fr+1fr, Girl with crutches (polio). 6fr+2fr, Sitting boys playing ball, horiz.

1962, Sept. 22 Photo.

B718 SP338 40c + 10c choc .25 .25
B719 SP338 1fr + 50c rose red .45 .45
B720 SP338 2fr + 50c brt lil 1.00 .90
B721 SP338 2.50fr + 1fr dl grn 1.00 .90
B722 SP338 3fr + 1fr dk blue 1.00 .90
B723 SP338 6fr + 2fr dk brn 1.50 1.25
Nos. B718-B723 (6) 5.20 4.65

The surtax was for various institutions for handicapped children.

Queen Louise-Marie SP339

Belgian Queens: No. B725, like No. B724 with "ML" initials. 1fr+50c, Marie-Henriette. 2fr+1fr, Elisabeth. 3fr+1.50fr, Astrid. 8fr+2.50fr, Fabiola.

1962, Dec. 8 Photo. & Engr.

Gray, Black & Gold

B724 SP339 40c + 10c ("L") .25 .25
B725 SP339 40c + 10c ("ML") .25 .25
B726 SP339 1fr + 50c .60 .50
B727 SP339 2fr + 1fr 1.25 1.10
B728 SP339 3fr + 1.50fr 1.60 1.40
B729 SP339 8fr + 2.50fr 1.90 1.60
Nos. B724-B729 (6) 5.85 5.10

The surtax was for anti-tuberculosis work.

British War Memorial (Porte de Menin), Ypres SP340

1962, Dec. 26 Engr. *Perf. 11½*

B730 SP340 1fr + 50c multi .50 .50

Millennium of the city of Ypres. Issued in sheets of eight.

Peace Bell Ringing over Globe — SP341

Engraved and Photogravure

1963, Feb. 18 Unwmk. *Perf. 11½*

B731 SP341 3fr +1.50fr multi 1.60 1.60
a. Sheet of 4 7.75 7.75
B732 SP341 6fr +3fr multi .80 .80

The surtax was for the installation of the Peace Bell (Bourdon de la Paix) at Koekelberg Basilica and for the benefit of various cultural organizations.

No. B731 was issued in sheets of 4, No. B732 in sheets of 30.

The Sower by Brueghel — SP342

Designs: 3fr+1fr, The Harvest, by Brueghel, horiz. 6fr+2fr, "Bread," by Anton Carte, horiz.

1963, Mar. 21 *Perf. 11½*
B733 SP342 2fr +1fr multi .25 .25
B734 SP342 3fr +1fr multi .40 .30
B735 SP342 6fr +2fr multi .55 .50
Nos. B733-B735 (3) 1.20 1.05

FAO "Freedom from Hunger" campaign.

Speed Racing — SP343

2fr+1fr, Bicyclists at check point, horiz. 3fr+1.50fr, Team racing, horiz. 6fr+3fr, Pace setters.

Perf. 11½

1963, July 13 **Unwmk.** **Engr.**
B736 SP343 1fr + 50c multi .25 .25
B737 SP343 2fr + 1fr bl, car, blk & ol gray .25 .25
B738 SP343 3fr + 1.50fr multi .35 .35
B739 SP343 6fr + 3fr multi .55 .55
Nos. B736-B739 (4) 1.40 1.40

80th anniversary of the founding of the Belgian Bicycle League. The surtax was for athletes at the 1964 Olympic Games.

Princess Paola with Princess Astrid — SP344

Prince Albert and Family — SP345

Designs: 40c+10c, Prince Philippe. 2fr+50c, Princess Astrid. 2.50fr+1fr, Princess Paola. 6fr+2fr, Prince Albert.

1963, Sept. 28 **Photo.**
B740 SP344 40c + 10c .25 .25
B741 SP344 1fr + 50c .35 .30
B742 SP344 2fr + 50c .45 .40
B743 SP344 2.50fr + 1fr .45 .40
B744 SP345 3fr + 1fr brn & multi .65 .65
B745 SP345 3fr + 1fr yel grn & multi 2.00 2.00
a. Booklet pane of 8 19.00 19.00
B746 SP344 6fr + 2fr 1.60 1.60
Nos. B740-B746 (7) 5.75 5.60

Cent. of the Intl. Red Cross. No. B745 issued in booklet panes of 8, which are in two forms: French and Flemish inscriptions in top and bottom margins transposed. Value the same.

Daughter of Balthazar Gerbier, Painted by Rubens — SP346

Jesus, St. John and Cherubs by Rubens — SP347

Portraits (Rubens' sons): 1fr+40c, Nicolas, 2 yrs. old. 2fr+50c, Franz. 2.50fr+1fr, Nicolas, 6 yrs. old. 3fr+1fr, Albert.

Photogravure and Engraved

1963, Dec. 7 **Unwmk.** *Perf. 11½*
B747 SP346 50c + 10c .25 .25
B748 SP346 1fr + 40c .25 .25
B749 SP346 2fr + 50c .30 .30
B750 SP346 2.50fr + 1fr .65 .65
B751 SP346 3fr + 1fr .55 .55
B752 SP347 6fr + 2fr .90 .90
Nos. B747-B752 (6) 2.90 2.90

The surtax was for anti-tuberculosis work. See No. B771.

John Quincy Adams and Lord Gambier Signing Treaty of Ghent, by Amédée Forestier — SP348

1964, May 16 **Photo.** *Perf. 11½*
B753 SP348 6fr + 3fr dk blue .75 .75

Signing of the Treaty of Ghent between the US and Great Britain, Dec. 24, 1814.

Philip van Marnix — SP349

Portraits: 3fr+1.50fr, Ida de Bure Calvin. 6fr+3fr, Jacob Jordaens.

1964, May 30 **Engr.**
B754 SP349 1fr + 50c blue gray .25 .25
B755 SP349 3fr + 1.50fr rose pink .25 .25
B756 SP349 6fr + 3fr redsh brn .70 .70
Nos. B754-B756 (3) 1.20 1.20

Issued to honor Protestantism in Belgium. The surtax was for the erection of a Protestant church.

Foot Soldier, 1918 — SP350

Designs: 2fr+1fr, Flag bearer, Guides Regiment, 1914. 3fr+1.50fr, Trumpeter of the Grenadiers and drummers, 1914.

1964, Aug. 1 **Photo.** *Perf. 11½*
B757 SP350 1fr + 50c multi .25 .25
B758 SP350 2fr + 1fr multi .25 .25
B759 SP350 3fr + 1.50fr multi .35 .35
Nos. B757-B759 (3) .85 .85

50th anniversary of the German aggression against Belgium in 1914. The surtax aided patriotic undertakings.

Battle of Bastogne — SP351

6fr+3fr, Liberation of the estuary of the Escaut.

1964, Aug. 1 **Unwmk.**
B760 SP351 3fr + 1fr multi .25 .25
B761 SP351 6fr + 3fr multi .70 .70

Belgium's Resistance and liberation of World War II. The surtax was to help found an International Student Center at Antwerp and to aid cultural undertakings.

Souvenir Sheets

Rogier van der Weyden Paintings — SP352

Descent From the Cross — SP353

1964, Sept. 19 **Photo.** *Perf. 11½*
B762 SP352 Sheet of 3 4.25 4.25
a. 1fr Philip the Good 1.10 1.10
b. 2fr Portrait of a Lady 1.10 1.10
c. 3fr Man with Arrow 1.10 1.10

Engr.
B763 SP353 8fr red brown 4.25 4.25

Rogier van der Weyden (Roger de La Pasture, 1400-64). The surtax went to various cultural organizations. No. B762 sold for 14fr, No. B763 for 16fr.

Ancient View of the Pand — SP354

3fr+1fr, Present view of the Pand from Lys River.

1964, Oct. 10 **Photo.**
B764 SP354 2fr + 1fr blk, grnsh bl & ultra .40 .40
B765 SP354 3fr + 1fr lil rose, bl & dk brn .40 .40

The surtax was for the restoration of the Pand Dominican Abbey in Ghent.

Type of 1963 and

Child of Charles I, Painted by Van Dyck — SP355

Designs: 1fr+40c, William of Orange with his bride, by Van Dyck. 2fr+1fr, Portrait of a small boy with dogs by Erasmus Quellin and Jan Fyt. 3fr+1fr, Alexander Farnese by Antonio Moro. 4fr+2fr, William II, Prince of Orange by Van Dyck. 6fr+3fr, Artist's children by Cornelis De Vos.

1964, Dec. 5 **Engr.** *Perf. 11½*
B766 SP355 50c + 10c rose claret .25 .25
B767 SP355 1fr + 40c car rose .25 .25
B768 SP355 2fr + 1fr vio brn .25 .25
B769 SP355 3fr + 1fr gray .30 .30
B770 SP355 4fr + 2fr vio bl .50 .50
B771 SP347 6fr + 3fr brt pur .70 .70
Nos. B766-B771 (6) 2.25 2.25

The surtax was for anti-tuberculosis work.

Liberator, Shaking Prisoner's Hand, Concentration Camp — SP356

Designs: 1fr+50c, Prisoner's hand reaching for the sun. 3fr+1.50fr, Searchlights and tank breaking down barbed wire, horiz. 8fr+5fr, Rose growing amid the ruins, horiz.

Engraved and Photogravure

1965, May 8 **Unwmk.** *Perf. 11½*
B772 SP356 50c + 50c tan, blk & buff .25 .25
B773 SP356 1fr + 50c multi .25 .25
B774 SP356 3fr + 1.50fr dl lil & blk .35 .35
B775 SP356 8fr + 5fr multi .70 .70
Nos. B772-B775 (4) 1.55 1.55

20th anniv. of the liberation of the concentration camps for political prisoners and prisoners of war.

Stoclet House, Brussels SP357

Stoclet House: 6fr+3fr, Hall with marble foundation, vert. 8fr+4fr, View of house from garden.

1965, June 21
B776 SP357 3fr + 1fr slate & tan .30 .30
B777 SP357 6fr + 3fr sepia .50 .50
B778 SP357 8fr + 4fr vio brn & tan .65 .65
Nos. B776-B778 (3) 1.45 1.45

Austrian architect Josef Hoffmann (1870-1956), builder of the art nouveau residence of Adolphe Stoclet, engineer and financier.

Jackson's Chameleon SP358

Animals from Antwerp Zoo: 2fr+1fr, Common iguanas. 3fr+1.50fr, African monitor. 6fr+3fr, Komodo monitor. 8fr+4fr, Nile softshell turtle.

1965, Oct. 16 Photo. *Perf. 11½*

B779 SP358 1fr + 50c multi .25 .25
B780 SP358 2fr + 1fr multi .25 .25
B781 SP358 3fr + 1.50fr multi .35 .35
B782 SP358 6fr + 3fr multi .50 .50
Nos. B779-B782 (4) 1.35 1.35

Miniature Sheet

B783 SP358 8fr + 4fr multi 1.75 1.75

The surtax was for various cultural and philanthropic organizations. No. B783 contains one stamp, size: 52x35mm.

Boatmen's and Archers' Guild Halls SP359

Buildings on Grand-Place, Brussels: 1fr+40c, Brewers' Hall. 2fr+1fr, "King of Spain." 3fr+1.50fr, "Dukes of Brabant." 10fr+4.50fr, Tower of City Hall and St. Michael.

1965, Dec. 4 Engr. *Perf. 11½*

Size: 35x24mm

B784 SP359 50c + 10c ultra .25 .25
B785 SP359 1fr + 40c bl grn .25 .25
B786 SP359 2fr + 1fr rose cl .25 .25
B787 SP359 3fr + 1.50fr violet .35 .35

Size: 24x44mm

B788 SP359 10fr + 4.50fr sep & gray .80 .80
Nos. B784-B788 (5) 1.90 1.90

The surtax was for anti-tuberculosis work.

Souvenir Sheets

Queen Elisabeth — SP360

Design: No. B790, Types of 1931 and 1956.

1966, Apr. 16 Photo. *Perf. 11½*

B789 SP360 Sheet of 2 + label 1.50 1.50
a. SP74 3fr dk brn & gray grn .60 .60
b. SP87 3fr dk brn, yel grn & gold .60 .60
B790 SP360 Sheet of 2 + label 1.50 1.50
a. SP42 3fr dk brn & dl bl .60 .60
b. SP304 3fr dk brn & gray .60 .60

The surtax went to various cultural organizations.
Each sheet sold for 20fr.

Luminescent Paper

was used in printing Nos. B789-B790, B801-B806, B808-B809, B811-B823, B825-B831, B833-B835, B837-B840, B842-B846, B848-B850, B852-B854, B856-B863, and from B865 onward unless otherwise noted. In many cases the low value of the set is not on luminescent paper. This will not be noted.

Diver — SP361

Design: 10fr+4fr, Swimmer at start.

1966, May 9 Engr.

B791 SP361 60c + 40c Prus grn, ol & org brn .25 .25
B792 SP361 10fr + 4fr ol grn, org brn & mag .80 .80

Issued to publicize the importance of swimming instruction.

Minorites' Convent, Liège — SP362

Designs: 1fr+50c, Val-Dieu Abbey, Aubel. 2fr+1fr, View and seal of Huy. 10fr+4.50fr, Statue of Ambiorix by Jules Bertin, and tower, Tongeren.

1966, Aug. 27 Engr. *Perf. 11½*

B793 SP362 60c + 40c multi .25 .25
B794 SP362 1fr + 50c multi .25 .25
B795 SP362 2fr + 1fr multi .25 .25
B796 SP362 10fr + 4.50fr multi .80 .80
Nos. B793-B796 (4) 1.55 1.55

The surtax was for various patriotic and cultural organizations.

Surveyor and Dog Team SP363

3fr+1.50fr, Adrien de Gerlache, "Belgica." 6fr+3fr, Surveyor, weather balloon, ship. 10fr+5fr, Penguins, "Magga Dan" (ship used for 1964, 1965 & 1966 expeditions).

1966, Oct. 8 Engr. *Perf. 11½*

B797 SP363 1fr + 50c bl grn .25 .25
B798 SP363 3fr + 1.50fr pale vio .25 .25
B799 SP363 6fr + 3fr dk car .50 .50
Nos. B797-B799 (3) 1.00 1.00

Souvenir Sheet

Engraved and Photogravure

B800 SP363 10fr + 5fr dk gray, sky bl & dk red 1.00 1.00

Belgian Antarctic expeditions. No. B800 contains one 52x35mm stamp.

Boy with Ball and Dog — SP364

Designs: 2fr+1fr, Girl skipping rope. 3fr+1.50fr, Girl and boy blowing soap bubbles. 6fr+3fr, Girl and boy rolling hoops, horiz. 8fr+3.50fr, Four children at play and cat, horiz.

1966, Dec. 3 *Perf. 11½*

B801 SP364 1fr + 1fr pink & blk .25 .25
B802 SP364 2fr + 1fr lt bluish grn & blk .25 .25
B803 SP364 3fr + 1.50fr lt vio & blk .25 .25
B804 SP364 6fr + 3fr pale sal & dk brn .50 .50
B805 SP364 8fr + 3.50fr lt yel grn & dk brn .65 .65
Nos. B801-B805 (5) 1.90 1.90

The surtax was for anti-tuberculosis work.

Souvenir Sheet

Refugees — SP365

1fr, Boy receiving clothes. 2fr, Tibetan children. 3fr, African mother and children.

1967, Mar. 11 Photo. *Perf. 11½*

B806 SP365 Sheet of 3 1.25 1.25
a. 1fr black & yellow .30 .30
b. 2fr black & blue .30 .30
c. 3fr black & orange .40 .40

Issued to help refugees around the world. Sheet has black border with Belgian P.T.T. and UN Refugee emblems. Sold for 20fr.

Robert Schuman SP366

Colonial Brotherhood Emblem SP368

Kongolo Memorial, Gentinnes SP367

1967, June 24 Engr. *Perf. 11½*

B807 SP366 2fr + 1fr gray blue .25 .25

Engraved and Photogravure

B808 SP367 5fr + 2fr brn & olive .40 .40
B809 SP368 10fr + 5fr multi .85 .85
Nos. B807-B809 (3) 1.50 1.50

Robert Schuman (1886-1963), French statesman, one of the founders of European Steel and Coal Community, 1st pres. of European Parliament (2fr+1fr); Kongolo Memorial, erected in memory of missionary and civilian victims in the Congo (5fr+2fr); a memorial for African Troops, Brussels (10fr+5fr).

Preaching Fool from "Praise of Folly" by Erasmus SP369

Erasmus, by Quentin Massys SP370

Designs: 2fr+1fr, Exhorting Fool from Praise of Folly. 5fr+2fr, Thomas More's Family, by Hans Holbein, horiz. 6fr+3fr, Pierre Gilles (Aegidius), by Quentin Massys.

Photogravure and Engraved (SP369); Photogravure (SP370)

1967, Sept. 2 Unwmk. *Perf. 11*

B810 SP369 1fr + 50c tan, blk, bl & car .25 .25
B811 SP369 2fr + 1fr tan, blk & car .25 .25
B812 SP370 3fr + 1.50fr multi .25 .25
B813 SP369 5fr + 2fr tan, blk & car .45 .45
B814 SP370 6fr + 3fr multi .55 .55
Nos. B810-B814 (5) 1.75 1.75

Issued to commemorate Erasmus (1466(?)-1536), Dutch scholar and his era.

Souvenir Sheet

Pro-Post Association Emblem — SP371

Engraved and Photogravure

1967, Oct. 21 *Perf. 11½*

B815 SP371 10fr + 5fr multi 1.00 1.00

Issued to publicize the POSTPHILA Philatelic Exhibition, Brussels, Oct. 21-29.

Detail from Brueghel's "Children's Games" — SP372

Designs: Various Children's Games. Singles of Nos. B816-B821 arranged in 2 rows of 3 show complete painting by Pieter Brueghel.

1967, Dec. 9 Photo. *Perf. 11½*

B816 SP372 1fr + 50c multi .25 .25
B817 SP372 2fr + 50c multi .25 .25
B818 SP372 3fr + 1fr multi .30 .30
B819 SP372 6fr + 3fr multi .50 .50
B820 SP372 10fr + 4fr multi .85 .85
B821 SP372 13fr + 6fr multi 1.10 1.10
Nos. B816-B821 (6) 3.25 3.25

Queen Fabiola Holding Refugee Child from Congo — SP373

6fr+3fr, Queen Elisabeth & Dr. Depage.

1968, Apr. 27 Photo. *Perf. 11½*

Cross in Red

B822 SP373 6fr + 3fr sepia & gray .65 .65
B823 SP373 10fr + 5fr sepia & gray .95 .95

The surtax was for the Red Cross.

Woman Gymnast and Calendar Stone SP374

Yachting and "The Swimmer" by Andrien — SP375

Designs: 2fr+1fr, Weight lifter and Mayan motif. 3fr+1.50fr, Hurdler, colossus of Tula and animal head from Kukulkan. 6fr+2fr, Bicyclists and Chichen Itza Temple.

Engraved and Photogravure

1968, May 27 ***Perf. 11½***

B824 SP374 1fr + 50c multi .25 .25
B825 SP374 2fr + 1fr multi .25 .25
B826 SP374 3fr + 1.50fr multi .25 .25
B827 SP374 6fr + 2fr multi .55 .55

Photo.

B828 SP375 13fr + 5fr multi 1.10 1.10
Nos. B824-B828 (5) 2.40 2.40

Issued to publicize the 19th Olympic Games, Mexico City, Oct. 12-27.

"Explosion" SP376

Designs (Paintings by Pol Mara): 12fr+5fr, "Fire." 13fr+5fr, "Tornado."

1968, June 22 **Photo.**

B829 SP376 10fr + 5fr multi .80 .80
B830 SP376 12fr + 5fr multi .95 .95
B831 SP376 13fr + 5fr multi 1.25 1.25
Nos. B829-B831 (3) 3.00 3.00

The surtax was for disaster victims.

Undulate Triggerfish SP377

Tropical Fish: 3fr+1.50fr, Angelfish. 6fr+3fr, Turkeyfish (Pterois volitans). 10fr+5fr, Orange butterflyfish.

1968, Oct. 19 **Engr. & Photo.**

B832 SP377 1fr + 50c multi .25 .25
B833 SP377 3fr + 1.50fr multi .25 .25
B834 SP377 6fr + 3fr multi .55 .55
B835 SP377 10fr + 5fr multi .80 .80
Nos. B832-B835 (4) 1.85 1.85

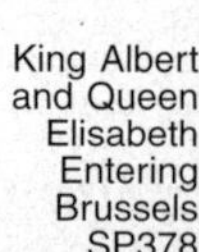

King Albert and Queen Elisabeth Entering Brussels SP378

Tomb of the Unknown Soldier and Eternal Flame, Brussels — SP379

Designs: 1fr+50c, King Albert, Queen Elisabeth and Crown Prince Leopold on balcony, Bruges, vert. 6fr+3fr, King and Queen entering Liège.

1968, Nov. 9 **Photo.** ***Perf. 11½***

B836 SP378 1fr + 50c multi .25 .25
B837 SP378 3fr + 1.50fr multi .25 .25
B838 SP378 6fr + 3fr multi .50 .50

Engraved and Photogravure

B839 SP379 10fr + 5fr multi .80 .80
Nos. B836-B839 (4) 1.80 1.80

50th anniv. of the victory in World War I.

Souvenir Sheet

The Painter and the Amateur, by Peter Brueghel — SP380

1969, May 10 **Engr.** ***Perf. 11½***

B840 SP380 10fr + 5fr sepia 1.10 1.10

Issued to publicize the POSTPHILA 1969 Philatelic Exhibition, Brussels, May 10-18.

Huts, by Ivanka D. Pancheva, Bulgaria — SP381

Children's Drawings and UNICEF Emblem: 3fr+1.50fr, "My Art" (Santa Claus), by Claes Patric, Belgium. 6fr+3fr, "In the Sun" (young boy), by Helena Rejchlova, Czechoslovakia. 10fr+5fr, "Out for a Walk" by Phillis Sporn, US, horiz.

1969, May 31 **Photo.** ***Perf. 11½***

B841 SP381 1fr + 50c multi .25 .25
B842 SP381 3fr + 1.50fr multi .25 .25
B843 SP381 6fr + 3fr multi .55 .55
B844 SP381 10fr + 5fr multi .85 .85
Nos. B841-B844 (4) 1.90 1.90

The surtax was for philanthropic purposes.

Msgr. Victor Scheppers SP382

1969, July 5 **Engr.**

B845 SP382 6fr + 3fr rose claret .70 .70

Msgr. Victor Scheppers (1802-77), prison reformer and founder of the Brothers of Mechlin (Scheppers).

Moon Landing Type of 1969

Souvenir Sheet

Design: 20fr+10fr, Armstrong, Collins and Aldrin and moon with Tranquillity Base, vert.

1969, Sept. 20 **Photo.** ***Perf. 11½***

B846 A245 20fr + 10fr indigo 3.00 3.00

See note after No. 726.

Heads from Alexander the Great Tapestry, 15th Century — SP383

Designs from Tapestries: 3fr+1.50fr, Fiddler from "The Feast," c. 1700. 10fr+4fr, Head of beggar from "The Healing of the Paralytic," 16th century.

1969, Sept. 20

B847 SP383 1fr + 50c multi .25 .25
B848 SP383 3fr + 1.50fr multi .40 .40
B849 SP383 10fr + 4fr multi 1.00 1.00
Nos. B847-B849 (3) 1.65 1.65

The surtax was for philanthropic purposes.

Bearded Antwerp Bantam SP384

1969, Nov. 8 **Engr. & Photo.**

B850 SP384 10fr + 5fr multi 1.00 1.00

Angel Playing Lute — SP385

Designs from Stained Glass Windows: 1.50fr+50c, Angel with trumpet, St. Waudru's, Mons. 7fr+3fr, Angel with viol, St. Jacques', Liège. 9fr+4fr, King with bagpipes, Royal Art Museum, Brussels.

1969, Dec. 13 **Photo.**

Size: 24x35mm

B851 SP385 1.50fr + 50c multi .25 .25
B852 SP385 3.50fr + 1.50fr multi .30 .30
B853 SP385 7fr + 3fr multi .65 .65

Size: 35x52mm

B854 SP386 9fr + 4fr multi 1.00 1.00
Nos. B851-B854 (4) 2.20 2.20

The surtax was for philanthropic purposes.

Farm and Windmill, Open-air Museum, Bokrijk SP386

Belgian Museums: 3.50fr+1.50fr, Stage Coach Inn, Courcelles. 7fr+3fr, "The Thresher of Trevires," Gallo-Roman sculpture, Gaumais Museum, Virton. 9fr+4fr, "The Sovereigns," by Henry Moore, Middelheim Museum, Antwerp.

Engraved and Photogravure

1970, May 30 ***Perf. 11½***

B855 SP386 1.50fr + 50c multi .25 .25
B856 SP386 3.50fr + 1.50fr multi .30 .30
B857 SP386 7fr + 3fr multi .60 .60
B858 SP386 9fr + 4fr multi .75 .75
Nos. B855-B858 (4) 1.90 1.90

The surtax went to various culture organizations.

"Resistance" SP387

Design: 7fr+3fr, "Liberation of Camps." The designs were originally used as book covers.

1970, July 4 **Photo.** ***Perf. 11½***

B859 SP387 3.50fr + 1.50fr blk, gray grn & dp car .35 .35
B860 SP387 7fr + 3fr blk, lil & dp car .60 .60

Honoring the Resistance Movement and 25th anniv. of the liberation of concentration camps.

Fishing Rod and Reel SP388

Design: 9fr+4fr, Hockey stick and puck, vert.

1970, Sept. 19 **Engr. & Photo.**

B861 SP388 3.50fr + 1.50fr multi .30 .30
B862 SP388 9fr + 4fr multi .70 .70

Souvenir Sheet

Belgium Nos. 31, 36, 39 — SP389

1970, Oct. 10 ***Perf. 11½***

B863 SP389 Sheet of 3 4.75 4.75
a. 1.50fr + 50c black & dull lilac 1.40 1.40
b. 3.50fr + 1.50fr black & lilac 1.40 1.40
c. 9fr + 4fr black & red brown 1.40 1.40

BELGICA 72 International Philatelic Exhibition, Brussels, June 24-July 9.

Camille Huysmans (1871-1968) SP390

3.50fr+1.50fr, Joseph Cardinal Cardijn (1882-1967). 7fr+3fr, Maria Baers (1883-1959). 9fr+4fr, Paul Pastur (1866-1938).

1970, Nov. 14 ***Perf. 11½***

Portraits in Sepia

B864 SP390 1.50fr + 50c car rose .25 .25
B865 SP390 3.50fr + 1.50fr lilac .30 .30
B866 SP390 7fr + 3fr green .55 .55
B867 SP390 9fr + 4fr blue .75 .75
Nos. B864-B867 (4) 1.85 1.85

"Anxious City" (Detail) by Paul Delvaux — SP391

7fr+3fr, "The Memory," by Rene Magritte.

1970, Dec. 12 **Photo.**

B868 SP391 3.50fr + 1.50fr multi .30 .30
B869 SP391 7fr + 3fr multi .65 .65

Notre Dame du Vivier, Marche-les-Dames — SP392

7fr+3fr, Turnhout Beguinage and Beguine.

1971, Mar. 13 ***Perf. 11½***

B870 SP392 3.50fr + 1.50fr multi .30 .30
B871 SP392 7fr + 3fr multi .65 .65

The surtax was for philanthropic purposes.

Red Cross — SP393

1971, May 22 **Photo.** ***Perf. 11½***

B872 SP393 10fr + 5fr crim & blk .80 .80

Belgian Red Cross.

Discobolus and Munich Cathedral — SP394

1971, June 19 **Engr. & Photo.**

B873 SP394 7fr + 3fr bl & blk .65 .65

Publicity for the 20th Summer Olympic Games, Munich 1972.

Festival of Flanders — SP395

Design: 7fr+3fr, Wallonia Festival.

1971, Sept. 11 **Photo.** ***Perf. 11½***

B874 SP395 3.50fr + 1.50fr multi .30 .30
B875 SP395 7fr + 3fr multi .65 .65

Attre Palace — SP396

Steen Palace, Elewijt — SP397

Design: 10fr+5fr, Royal Palace, Brussels.

1971, Oct. 23 **Engr.**

B876 SP396 3.50fr + 1.50fr sl grn .30 .30
B877 SP397 7fr + 3fr red brn .65 .65
B878 SP396 10fr + 5fr vio bl .90 .90
Nos. B876-B878 (3) 1.85 1.85

Surtax was for BELGICA 72, International Philatelic Exposition.

Ox Fly, tabanus bromius SP398

Insects: 1.50fr+50c, Luna moth, vert. 7fr+3fr, Wasp, polistes gallicus. 9fr+4fr, Tiger beetle, vert.

1971, Dec. 11 **Photo.** ***Perf. 11½***

B879 SP398 1.50fr + 50c multi .25 .25
B880 SP398 3.50fr + 1.50fr multi .30 .30
B881 SP398 7fr + 3fr multi .65 .65
B882 SP398 9fr + 4fr multi .75 .75
Nos. B879-B882 (4) 1.95 1.95

Surtax was for philanthropic purposes.

Leopold I on #1 — SP399

2fr+1fr, Leopold I on #5. 2.50fr+1fr, Leopold II on #45. 3.50fr+1.50fr, Leopold II on #48. 6fr+3fr, Albert I on #135. 7fr+3fr, Albert I on #214. 10fr+5fr, Albert I on #231. 15fr+7.50fr, Leopold III on #290. 20fr+10fr, King Baudouin on #718.

Engraved and Photogravure

1972, June 24 ***Perf. 11½***

B883 SP399 1.50fr + 50c .25 .25
B884 SP399 2fr + 1fr .25 .25
B885 SP399 2.50 + 1fr .30 .30
B886 SP399 3.50fr + 1.50fr .35 .35
B887 SP399 6fr + 3fr .50 .50
B888 SP399 7fr + 3fr .70 .70
B889 SP399 10fr + 5fr .90 .90
B890 SP399 15fr + 7fr 1.25 1.25
B891 SP399 20fr + 10fr 2.00 2.00
Nos. B883-B891 (9) 6.50 6.50

Belgica 72, Intl. Philatelic Exhibition, Brussels, June 24-July 9. Nos. B883-B891 issued in sheets of 10 and of 20 (2 tete beche sheets with gutter between). Sold in complete sets.

Epilepsy Emblem — SP400

1972, Sept. 9 **Photo.** ***Perf. 11½***

B892 SP400 10fr + 5fr multi .80 .80

The surtax was for the William Lennox Center for epilepsy research and treatment.

Gray Lag Goose — SP401

Designs: 4.50fr+2fr, Lapwing. 8fr+4fr, Stork. 9fr+4.50fr, Kestrel, horiz.

1972, Dec. 16 **Photo.** ***Perf. 11½***

B893 SP401 2fr + 1fr multi .25 .25
B894 SP401 4.50fr + 2fr multi .45 .45
B895 SP401 8fr + 4fr multi .75 .75
B896 SP401 9fr + 4.50fr multi .80 .80
Nos. B893-B896 (4) 2.25 2.25

Bijloke Abbey, Ghent — SP402

4.50fr+2fr, St. Ursmer Collegiate Church, Lobbes. 8fr+4fr, Park Abbey, Heverle. 9fr+4.50fr, Abbey, Floreffe.

1973, Mar. 24 **Engr.** ***Perf. 11½***

B897 SP402 2fr + 1fr sl grn .25 .25
B898 SP402 4.50fr + 2fr brown .40 .40
B899 SP402 8fr + 4fr rose lil .75 .75
B900 SP402 9fr + 4.50fr brt bl .90 .90
Nos. B897-B900 (4) 2.30 2.30

Basketball SP403

1973, Apr. 7 **Photo. & Engr.**

B901 SP403 10fr + 5fr multi .80 .80

First World Basketball Championships of the Handicapped, Bruges, Apr. 16-21.

Dirk Martens' Printing Press — SP404

Lady Talbot, by Petrus Christus — SP405

Hadrian and Marcus Aurelius Coins SP406

Council of Malines, by Coussaert — SP407

Designs: 3.50fr+1.50fr, Head of Amon and Tutankhamen's cartouche. 10fr+5fr, Three-master of Ostend Merchant Company.

Photogravure and Engraved; Photogravure (#B906)

1973, June 23 ***Perf. 11½***

B902 SP404 2fr + 1fr multi .25 .25
B903 SP404 3.50fr + 1.50fr multi .30 .30
B904 SP405 4.50fr + 2fr multi .35 .35
B905 SP406 8fr + 4fr multi .65 .65
B906 SP407 9fr + 4.50fr multi .85 .85
B907 SP407 10fr + 5fr multi 1.50 1.50
Nos. B902-B907 (6) 3.90 3.90

500th anniv. of 1st book printed in Belgium (No. B902); 50th anniv. of Queen Elisabeth Egyptological Foundation (No. B903); 500th anniv. of death of painter Petrus Christus (No. B904); Discovery of Roman treasure at Luttre-Liberchies (No. B905); 500th anniv. of Great Council of Malines (No. B906); 250th anniv. of the Ostend Merchant Company (No. B907).

No. B902 is not luminescent.

Queen of Hearts — SP408

Old Playing Cards: No. B909, King of Clubs. No. B910, Jack of Diamonds. No. B911, King of Spades.

1973, Dec. 8 **Photo.** ***Perf. 11½***

B908 SP408 5fr + 2.50fr multi .50 .50
B909 SP408 5fr + 2.50fr multi .50 .50
B910 SP408 5fr + 2.50fr multi .50 .50
B911 SP408 5fr + 2.50fr multi .50 .50
a. Strip of 4, #B908-B911 2.00 2.00

Surtax was for philanthropic purposes.

Symbol of Blood Donations SP409

Design: 10fr+5fr, Traffic lights, Red Cross (symbolic of road accidents).

1974, Feb. 23 **Photo.** ***Perf. 11½***

B912 SP409 4fr + 2fr multi .35 .35
B913 SP409 10fr + 5fr multi .90 .90

The Red Cross as blood collector and aid to accident victims.

Armand Jamar, Self-portrait SP410

Designs: 5fr+2.50fr, Anton Bergmann and view of Lierre. 7fr+3.50fr, Henri Vieuxtemps and view of Verviers. 10fr+5fr, James Ensor, self-portrait, and masks.

1974, Apr. 6 **Photo.** ***Perf. 11½***

Size: 24x35mm

B914 SP410 4fr + 2fr multi .35 .35
B915 SP410 5fr + 2.50fr multi .40 .40
B916 SP410 7fr + 3.50fr multi .55 .55

Size: 35x52mm

B917 SP410 10fr + 5fr multi .85 .85
Nos. B914-B917 (4) 2.15 2.15

Van Gogh, Self-portrait and House at Cuesmes — SP411

1974, Sept. 21 Photo. *Perf. 11½*

B918 SP411 10fr + 5fr multi .90 .90

Opening of Vincent van Gogh House at Cuesmes, where he worked as teacher.

Gentian — SP412

Spotted Cat's Ear — SP414

Badger SP413

Design: 7fr+3.50fr, Beetle.

1974, Dec. 8 Photo. *Perf. 11½*

B919	SP412	4fr + 2fr multi	.35	.35
B920	SP413	5fr + 2.50fr multi	.50	.50
B921	SP413	7fr + 3.50fr multi	.60	.60
B922	SP414	10fr + 5fr multi	.95	.95
		Nos. B919-B922 (4)	2.40	2.40

Pesaro Palace, Venice SP415

St. Bavon Abbey, Ghent SP416

Virgin and Child, by Michelangelo SP417

1975, Apr. 12 Engr. *Perf. 11½*

B923	SP415	6.50fr + 2.50fr brn	.55	.55
B924	SP416	10fr + 4.50 vio brn	.85	.85
B925	SP417	15fr + 6.50fr brt bl	1.25	1.25
		Nos. B923-B925 (3)	2.65	2.65

Surtax was for various cultural organizations.

Frans Hemerijckx and Leprosarium, Kasai — SP418

1975, Sept. 13 Photo. *Perf. 11½*

B926 SP418 20fr + 10fr multi 1.75 1.75

Dr. Frans Hemerijckx (1902-1969), tropical medicine and leprosy expert.

Emile Moyson — SP419

Beheading of St. Dympna — SP420a

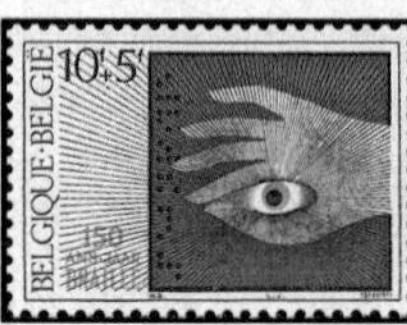

Hand Reading Braille SP420

No. B928, Dr. Ferdinand Augustin Snellaert.

1975, Nov. 22 Engr. *Perf. 11½*

B927	SP419	4.50fr + 2fr lilac	.35	.35
B928	SP419	6.50fr + 3fr green	.60	.60

Engraved and Photogravure

B929 SP420 10fr + 5fr multi .90 .90

Photo.

B930	SP420a	13fr + 6fr multi	1.10	1.10
		Nos. B927-B930 (4)	2.95	2.95

Emile Moyson (1838-1868), freedom fighter for the rights of Flemings and Walloons; Dr. Snellaert (1809-1872), physician and Flemish patriot; Louis Braille (1809-1852), sesquicentennial of invention of Braille system of writing for the blind; St. Dympna, patron saint of Geel, famous for treatment of mentally ill.

The Cheese Vendor — SP421

Designs (THEMABELGA Emblem and): No. B932, Potato vendor. No. B933, Basket carrier. No. B934, Shrimp fisherman with horse, horiz. No. B935, Knife grinder, horiz. No. B936, Milk vendor with dog cart, horiz.

1975, Dec. 13 Engr. & Photo.

B931	SP421	4.50fr + 1.50fr multi	.35	.35
B932	SP421	6.50fr + 3fr multi	.55	.55
B933	SP421	6.50fr + 3fr multi	.55	.55
B934	SP421	10fr + 5fr multi	.80	.80
B935	SP421	10fr + 5fr multi	.80	.80
B936	SP421	30fr + 15fr multi	2.40	2.40
		Nos. B931-B936 (6)	5.45	5.45

THEMABELGA Intl. Topical Philatelic Exhib., Brussels, Dec. 13-21. Issued in sheets of 10 (5x2).

Blackface Fund Collector — SP422

1976, Feb. 14 Photo. *Perf. 11½*

B937 SP422 10fr + 5fr multi .90 .90

"Conservatoire Africain" philanthropic soc., cent., and to publicize the Princess Paola creches.

Swimming and Olympic Emblem SP423

Montreal Olympic Games Emblem and: 5fr+2fr, Running, vert. 6.50fr+2.50fr, Equestrian.

1976, Apr. 10 Photo. *Perf. 11½*

B938	SP423	4.50fr + 1.50fr multi	.35	.35
B939	SP423	5fr + 2fr multi	.40	.40
B940	SP423	6.50fr + 2.50fr multi	.55	.55
		Nos. B938-B940 (3)	1.30	1.30

21st Olympic Games, Montreal, Canada, July 17-Aug. 1.

Queen Elisabeth Playing Violin SP424

and *Perf. 11½*

1976, May 1 Engr. Photo.

B941 SP424 14fr + 6fr blk & cl 1.10 1.10

Queen Elisabeth International Music Competition, 25th anniversary.

Souvenir Sheet

Jan Olieslagers, Bleriot Monoplane, Aero Club Emblem — SP425

Engraved and Photogravure

1976, June 12 *Perf. 11½*

B942 SP425 25fr + 10fr multi 2.25 2.25

Royal Belgian Aero Club, 75th anniversary, and Jan Olieslagers (1883-1942), aviation pioneer.

Adoration of the Shepherds (detail), by Rubens — SP426

Rubens Paintings (Details): 4.50fr, Descent from the Cross. No. B945, The Virgin with the Parrot. No. B946, Adoration of the Kings. No. B947, Last Communion of St. Francis. 30fr+15fr, Virgin and Child.

1976, Sept. 4 Photo. *Perf. 11½*

Size: 35x52mm

B943 SP426 4.50fr + 1.50fr multi .45 .45

Size: 24x35mm

B944	SP426	6.50fr + 3fr multi	.55	.55
B945	SP426	6.50fr + 3fr multi	.55	.55
B946	SP426	10fr + 5fr multi	.90	.90
B947	SP426	10fr + 5fr multi	.90	.90

Size: 35x52mm

B948	SP426	30fr + 15fr multi	2.40	2.40
		Nos. B943-B948 (6)	5.75	5.75

Peter Paul Rubens (1577-1640), Flemish painter, 400th birth anniversary.

Dwarf, by Velazquez SP427

1976, Nov. 6 Photo. *Perf. 11½*

B949 SP427 14fr + 6fr multi 1.25 1.25

Surtax was for the National Association for the Mentally Handicapped.

Dr. Albert Hustin SP428

Red Cross and Rheumatism Year Emblem SP429

1977, Feb. 19 Photo. *Perf. 11½*

B950	SP428	6.50fr + 2.50 multi	.60	.60
B951	SP429	14fr + 7fr multi	1.10	1.10

Belgian Red Cross.

Bordet Atheneum, Empress Maria Theresa SP430

Conductor and Orchestra, by E. Tytgat SP431

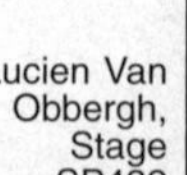

Lucien Van Obbergh, Stage SP432

Humanistic Society Emblem SP433

Camille Lemonnier SP434

Design: No. B953, Marie-Therese College, Herve, and coat of arms.

1977, Mar. 21 Photo. *Perf. 11½*

B952 SP430 4.50fr + 1fr multi .35 .35
B953 SP430 4.50fr + 1fr multi .35 .35
B954 SP431 5fr + 2fr multi .40 .40
B955 SP432 6.50fr + 2fr multi .55 .55
B956 SP433 6.50fr + 2fr blk & red .55 .55

Engr.

B957 SP434 10fr + 5fr slate bl .80 .80
Nos. B952-B957 (6) 3.00 3.00

Bicentenaries of the Jules Bordet Atheneum, Brussels, and the Marie-Therese College, Herve (Nos. B952-B953); 50th anniv. of the Brussels Philharmonic Soc., and Artists' Union (Nos. B954-B955): 25th anniv. of the Flemish Humanistic Organization (No. B956); 75th anniv. of the French-speaking Belgian writers' organization (No. B957).

Young Soccer Players — SP435

1977, Apr. 18 Photo.

B958 SP435 10fr + 5fr multi .90 .90

30th Intl. Junior Soccer Tournament.

Albert-Edouard Janssen, Financier — SP436

Famous Men: No. B960, Joseph Wauters (1875-1929), editor of Le Peuple, and newspaper. No. B961, Jean Capart (1877-1947), Egyptologist, and hieroglyph. No. B962, August de Boeck (1865-1937), composer, and score.

1977, Dec. 3 Engr. *Perf. 11½*

B959 SP436 5fr + 2.50fr brown .40 .40
B960 SP436 5fr + 2.50fr red .40 .40
B961 SP436 10fr + 5fr magenta .80 .80
B962 SP436 10fr + 5fr blue gray .80 .80
Nos. B959-B962 (4) 2.40 2.40

Abandoned Child SP437

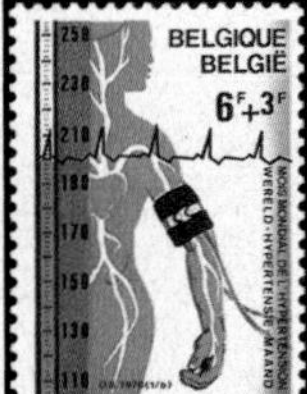

Checking Blood Pressure SP438

De Mick Sanatorium, Brasschaat — SP439

1978, Feb. 18 Photo. *Perf. 11½*

B963 SP437 4.50fr + 1.50fr multi .35 .35
B964 SP438 6fr + 3fr multi .50 .50
B965 SP439 10fr + 5fr multi .80 .80
Nos. B963-B965 (3) 1.65 1.65

Help for abandoned children (No. B963); fight against hypertension (No. B964); fight against tuberculosis (No. B965).

Actors and Theater SP440

Karel van de Woestijne SP441

Designs: No. B967, Harquebusier, Harquebusier Palace and coat of arms. 10fr+5fr, John of Austria and his signature.

Engraved and Photogravure

1978, June 17 *Perf. 11½*

B966 SP440 6fr + 3fr multi .50 .50
B967 SP440 6fr + 3fr multi .50 .50

Engr.

B968 SP441 8fr + 4fr black .65 .65
B969 SP441 10fr + 5fr black .80 .80
Nos. B966-B969 (4) 2.45 2.45

Cent. of Royal Flemish Theater, Brussels (No. B966); 400th anniv. of Harquebusiers' Guild of Vise, Liege (No. 967); Karel van de Woestijne (1878-1929), poet (No. B968); 400th anniv. of signing of Perpetual Edict by John of Austria (No. 969).

Lake Placid '80 and Belgian Olympic Emblems — SP442

Moscow '80 Emblem and: 8fr+3.50fr, Kremlin Towers, Belgian Olympic Committee emblem. 7fr+3fr, Runners from Greek vase, Lake Placid '80 emblem, Olympic rings. 14fr+6fr, Olympic flame, Lake Placid '80, Belgian emblems, Olympic rings.

1978, Nov. 4 Photo. *Perf. 11½*

B970 SP442 6fr + 2.50fr multi .50 .50
B971 SP442 8fr + 3.50fr multi .65 .65

Souvenir Sheet

B972 Sheet of 2 1.90 1.90
a. SP442 7fr + 3fr multi .65 .65
b. SP442 14fr + 6fr multi 1.25 1.25

Surtax was for 1980 Olympic Games.

Great Synagogue, Brussels — SP443

Dancers SP444

Father Pire, African Village SP445

1978, Dec. 2 Engr. *Perf. 11½*

B973 SP443 6fr + 2fr sepia .50 .50

Photo.

B974 SP444 8fr + 3fr multi .65 .65
B975 SP445 14fr + 7fr multi 1.25 1.25
Nos. B973-B975 (3) 2.40 2.40

Centenary of Great Synagogue of Brussels; Flemish Catholic Youth Action Organization, 50th anniversary; Nobel Peace Prize awarded to Father Dominique Pire for his "Heart Open to the World" movement, 20th anniversary.

Young People Giving First Aid — SP446

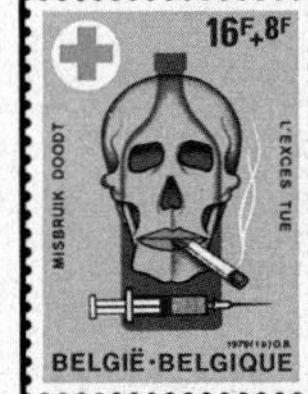

Skull with Bottle, Cigarette, Syringe — SP447

1979, Feb. 10 Photo. *Perf. 11½*

B976 SP446 8fr + 3fr multi .70 .70
B977 SP447 16fr + 8fr multi 1.40 1.40

Belgian Red Cross.

Beatrice Soetkens with Statue of Virgin Mary SP448

Details from Tapestries, 1516-1518, Showing Legend of Our Lady of Sand: 8fr+3fr, Francois de Tassis accepting letter from Emperor Frederick III (beginning of postal service). 14fr+7fr, Arrival of statue, Francois de Tassis and Philip the Fair. No. B981, Statue carried in procession by future Emperor Charles V and his brother Ferdinand. No. B982, Ship carrying Beatrice Soetkens with statue to Brussels, horiz.

1979, May 5 Photo. *Perf. 11½*

B978 SP448 6fr + 2fr multi .50 .50
B979 SP448 8fr + 3fr multi .65 .65
B980 SP448 14fr + 7fr multi 1.25 1.25
B981 SP448 20fr + 10fr multi 1.90 1.90
Nos. B978-B981 (4) 4.30 4.30

Souvenir Sheet

B982 SP448 20fr + 10fr multi 2.00 2.00

The surtax was for festivities in connection with the millennium of Brussels.

Notre Dame Abbey, Brussels — SP449

Designs: 8fr+3fr, Beauvoorde Castle. 14fr+7fr, 1st issue of "Courrier de L'Escaut" and Barthelemy Dumortier, founder. 20fr+10fr, Shrine of St. Hermes, Renaix.

Engraved and Photogravure

1979, Sept. 15 *Perf. 11½*

B983 SP449 6fr + 2fr multi .50 .50
B984 SP449 8fr + 3fr multi .65 .65
B985 SP449 14fr + 7fr multi 1.25 1.25
B986 SP449 20fr + 10fr multi 1.90 1.90
Nos. B983-B986 (4) 4.30 4.30

50th anniv. of restoration of Notre Dame de la Cambre Abbey; historic Beauvoorde Castle, 15th cent. sesquicentennial of the regional newspaper "Le Courrier de L'Escaut"; 850th anniv. of the consecration of the Collegiate Church of St. Hermes, Renaix.

Grand-Hornu Coal Mine — SP450

1979, Oct. 22 Engr. *Perf. 11½*

B987 SP450 10fr + 5fr blk .90 .90

Henry Heyman SP451

Veterans Organization Medal SP452

Boy and IYC Emblem — SP453

1979, Dec. 8 Photo. *Perf. 11½*

B988 SP451 8fr + 3fr multi .65 .65
B989 SP452 10fr + 5fr multi .80 .80
B990 SP453 16fr + 8fr multi 1.25 1.25
Nos. B988-B990 (3) 2.70 2.70

Henri Heyman (1879-1958), Minister of State; Disabled Veterans' Organization, 50th anniv.; Intl. Year of the Child.

Ivo Van Damme, Olympic Rings — SP454

1980, May 3 **Photo.** ***Perf. 11½***

B991 SP454 20fr + 10fr multi 1.75 1.75

Ivo Van Damme (1954-1976), silver medalist, 800-meter race, Montreal Olympics, 1976. Surtax was for Van Damme Memorial Foundation.

Queen Louis-Marie, King Leopold I — SP455

150th Anniversary of Independence (Queens and Kings): 9fr+3fr, Marie Henriette. Leopold II. 14fr+6fr, Elisabeth, Albert I. 17fr+8fr, Astrid, Leopold III. 25fr+10fr, Fabiola, Baudouin.

Photogravure and Engraved

1980, May 31 ***Perf. 11½***

B992 SP455 6.50 + 1.50fr multi .55 .55
B993 SP455 9 + 3fr multi .75 .75
B994 SP455 14 + 6fr multi 1.25 1.25
B995 SP455 17 + 8fr multi 1.40 1.40
B996 SP455 25 + 10fr multi 2.10 2.10
Nos. B992-B996 (5) 6.05 6.05

Miner, by Constantine Meunier SP456

Seal of Bishop Notger, First Prince-Bishop — SP457

9fr+3fr, Brewer, 16th century, from St. Lambert's reliquary, vert. 25fr+10fr, Virgin and Child, 13th century, St. John's Collegiate Church, Liege.

1980, Sept. 13 **Photo.** ***Perf. 11½***

B997 SP456 9 + 3fr multi .75 .75
B998 SP456 17 + 6fr multi 1.40 1.40
B999 SP456 25 + 10fr multi 2.10 2.10
Nos. B997-B999 (3) 4.25 4.25

Souvenir Sheet

B1000 SP457 20 + 10fr multi 2.00 2.00

Millennium of the Principality of Liege.

Visual and Oral Handicaps SP458

Intl. Year of the Disabled: 10fr+5fr, Cerebral handicap, vert.

1981, Feb. 9 **Photo.** ***Perf. 11½***

B1001 SP458 10 + 5fr multi 1.00 1.00
B1002 SP458 25 + 10fr multi 2.25 2.25

Dove with Red Cross Carrying Globe SP459

Design: 10fr+5fr, Atomic model, vert.

1981, Apr. 6 **Photo.** ***Perf. 11½***

B1003 SP459 10 + 5fr multi .90 .90
B1004 SP459 25 + 10fr multi 2.10 2.10

Red Cross and: 15th Intl. Radiology Congress, Brussels, June 24-July 1 (No. B1003); intl. disaster relief (No. B1004).

Ovide Decroly SP460

1981, June 1 **Photo.** ***Perf. 11½***

B1005 SP460 35 + 15fr multi 3.00 3.00

Ovide Decroly (1871-1932), developer of educational psychology.

Mounted Police Officer — SP461

Anniversaries: 9fr+4fr, Gendarmerie (State Police Force), 150th. 20fr+7fr, Carabineers Regiment, 150th. 40fr+20fr, Guides Regiment.

1981, Dec. 7 **Photo.** ***Perf. 11½***

B1006 SP461 9 + 4fr multi .85 .85
B1007 SP461 20 + 7fr multi 1.75 1.75
B1008 SP461 40 + 20fr multi 3.50 3.50
Nos. B1006-B1008 (3) 6.10 6.10

Billiards — SP462

1982, Mar. 29 **Photo.** ***Perf. 11½***

B1009 SP462 6 + 2fr shown .80 .80
B1010 SP462 9 + 4fr Cycling 1.10 1.10
B1011 SP462 10 + 5fr Soccer 1.25 1.25
B1012 SP462 50 + 14fr Yachting 4.00 4.00
Nos. B1009-B1012 (4) 7.15 7.15

Souvenir Sheet

B1013 Sheet of 4 7.50 7.50
a. SP462 25fr like #B1009 1.75 1.75
b. SP462 25fr like #B1010 1.75 1.75
c. SP462 25fr like #B1011 1.75 1.75
d. SP462 25fr like #B1012 1.75 1.75

No. B1013 shows designs in changed colors.

Christmas SP463

1982, Nov. 6

B1014 SP463 10 + 1fr multi .80 .80

Surtax was for tuberculosis research.

Belgica '82 Intl. Stamp Exhibition, Brussels, Dec. 11-19 SP464

Messengers (Prints). Nos. B1016-B1018 vert.

Photogravure and Engraved

1982, Dec. 11 ***Perf. 11½***

B1015 SP464 7 + 2fr multi .55 .55
B1016 SP464 7.50 + 2.50fr multi .60 .60
B1017 SP464 10 + 3fr multi .80 .80
B1018 SP464 17 + 7fr multi 1.40 1.40
B1019 SP464 20 + 9fr multi 1.60 1.60
B1020 SP464 25 + 10fr multi 2.00 2.00
Nos. B1015-B1020 (6) 6.95 6.95

Souvenir Sheet

B1021 SP464 50 + 25fr multi 6.00 6.00

No. B1021 contains one 48x37mm stamp.

50th Anniv. of Catholic Charities — SP465

1983, Jan. 22 **Photo.** ***Perf. 11½***

B1022 SP465 10 + 2fr multi .80 .80

Mountain Climbing — SP466

1983, Mar. 7 **Photo.**

B1023 SP466 12 + 3fr shown 1.00 1.00
B1024 SP466 20 + 5fr Hiking 1.75 1.75

Surtax was for Red Cross.

Madonna by Jef Wauters — SP467

1983, Nov. 21 **Photo.** ***Perf. 11½***

B1025 SP467 11 + 1fr multi .80 .80

Rifles Uniform — SP468

1983, Dec. 5 **Photo.** ***Perf. 11½***

B1026 SP468 8 + 2fr shown .75 .75
B1027 SP468 11 + 2fr Lancers uniform 1.25 1.25
B1028 SP468 50 + 12fr Grenadiers uniform 4.00 4.00
Nos. B1026-B1028 (3) 6.00 6.00

Type of 1984

1984, Mar. 3 **Photo.** ***Perf. 11½***

B1029 A495 8 + 2fr Judo, horiz. .65 .65
B1030 A495 12 + 3fr Wind surfing 1.00 1.00

50th Anniv. of Natl. Lottery SP469

1984, Mar. 31 **Photo.** ***Perf. 11½***

B1031 SP469 12 + 3fr multi 1.00 1.00

Brussels Modern Art Museum Opening SP470

Paintings: 8fr+2fr, Les Masques Singuliers, by James Ensor. 12fr+3fr, Empire des Lumieres, by Rene Magritte. 22fr+5fr, The End, by Jan Cox. 50fr+13fr, Rhythm No. 6, by Jo Delahaut.

1984, Sept. 1 **Photo.**

B1032 SP470 8 + 2fr multi .75 .75
B1033 SP470 12 + 3fr multi 1.25 1.25
B1034 SP470 22 + 5fr multi 1.75 1.75
B1035 SP470 50 + 13fr multi 4.00 4.00
Nos. B1032-B1035 (4) 7.75 7.75

Child with Parents — SP471

1984, Nov. 3 **Photo.**

B1036 SP471 10 + 2fr shown .80 .80
B1037 SP471 12 + 3fr Siblings 1.00 1.00
B1038 SP471 15 + 3fr Merry-go-round 1.25 1.25
Nos. B1036-B1038 (3) 3.05 3.05

Surtax was for children's programs.

Christmas 1984 SP472

1984, Dec. 1

B1039 SP472 12 + 1fr Three Kings 1.00 1.00

Belgian Red Cross Blood Transfusion Service, 50th Anniv. — SP473

1985, Mar. 4 **Photo.** ***Perf. 11½***

B1040 SP473 9 + 2fr Tree .80 .80
B1041 SP473 23 + 5fr Hearts 1.90 1.90

Surtax was for the Belgian Red Cross.

Solidarity SP474

Castles.

1985, Nov. 4 Photo. & Engr.

B1042 SP474 9 + 2fr Trazegnies .80 .80
B1043 SP474 12 + 3fr Laarne 1.00 1.00
B1044 SP474 23 + 5fr Turnhout 1.90 1.90
B1045 SP474 50 + 12fr Colonster 4.00 4.00
Nos. B1042-B1045 (4) 7.70 7.70

Christmas 1985, New Year 1986 — SP475

Painting: Miniature from the Book of Hours, by Jean duc de Berry.

1985, Nov. 25 Photo.

B1046 SP475 12 + 1fr multi .90 .90

King Baudouin Foundation SP476

1986, Mar. 24 Photo.

B1047 SP476 12 + 3fr Emblem 1.25 1.25

Surtax for the foundation.

Madonna SP477

Adoration of the Mystic Lamb, St. Bavon Cathedral Altarpiece, Ghent — SP478

Paintings by Hubert van Eyck (c. 1370-1426).

1986, Apr. 5 Photo. *Perf. 11½*

B1048 SP477 9 + 2fr shown .75 .75
B1049 SP477 13 + 3fr Christ in Majesty 1.10 1.10
B1050 SP477 24 + 6fr St. John the Baptist 2.00 2.00
Nos. B1048-B1050 (3) 3.85 3.85

Souvenir Sheet

B1051 SP478 50 + 12fr multi 8.00 8.00

Surtax for cultural organizations.

Antique Automobiles SP479

1986, Nov. 3 Photo.

B1052 SP479 9 + 2fr Lenoir, 1863 .75 .75
B1053 SP479 13 + 3fr Pipe de Tourisme, 1911 1.10 1.10
B1054 SP479 24 + 6fr Minerva 22 HP, 1930 2.00 2.00
B1055 SP479 26 + 6fr FN 8 Cylinder, 1931 2.10 2.10
Nos. B1052-B1055 (4) 5.95 5.95

Christmas 1986, New Year 1987 SP480

1986, Nov. 24 Photo.

B1056 SP480 13 + 1fr Village in winter 1.00 1.00

Natl. Red Cross — SP482

Nobel Prize winners for physiology (1938) and medicine (1974): No. B1058, Corneille Heymans (1892-1968). No. B1059, A. Claude (1899-1983).

Photogravure and Engraved

1987, Feb. 16 *Perf. 11½*

B1058 SP482 13 + 3fr dk brn & red 1.25 1.25
B1059 SP482 24 + 6fr dk brn & red 2.25 2.25

European Conservation Year — SP483

1987, Mar. 16 Photo.

B1060 SP483 9 + 2fr Bee orchid .90 .90
B1061 SP483 24 + 6fr Horse-shoe bat 2.00 2.00
B1062 SP483 26 + 6fr Peregrine falcon 2.50 2.50
Nos. B1060-B1062 (3) 5.40 5.40

Castles — SP484

1987, Oct. 17 Photo. & Engr.

B1063 SP484 9 + 2fr Rixensart .80 .80
B1064 SP484 13 + 3fr Westerlo 1.10 1.10
B1065 SP484 26 + 5fr Fallais 2.10 2.10
B1066 SP484 50 + 12fr Gaasbeek 4.00 4.00
Nos. B1063-B1066 (4) 8.00 8.00

Christmas 1987 — SP485

Painting: Holy Family, by Rev. Father Lens.

1987, Nov. 14 Photo.

B1067 SP485 13 + 1fr multi 1.10 1.10

White and Yellow Cross of Belgium, 50th Anniv. — SP486

1987, Dec. 5

B1068 SP486 9 + 2fr multi 1.00 1.00

Promote Philately — SP487

Various flowers from Sixty Roses for a Queen, by P. J. Redoute (1759-1840).

1988, Apr. 25 Photo. *Perf. 11½*

B1069 SP487 13 + 3fr shown 1.25 1.25
B1070 SP487 24 + 6fr multi, diff. 2.10 2.10

Souvenir Sheet

B1071 SP487 50 + 12fr multi, diff. 8.00 8.00

See Nos. B1081-B1083, B1089-B1091, 1346.

1988 Summer Olympics, Seoul — SP488

1988, June 6 Photo. *Perf. 11½*

B1072 SP488 9fr + 2fr Table tennis 1.10 1.10
B1073 SP488 13fr + 3fr Cycling 1.25 1.25

Souvenir Sheet

B1074 SP488 50fr + 12fr Marathon runners 9.00 9.00

Solidarity — SP489

1988, Oct. 24 Photo. *Perf. 12x11½*

B1075 SP489 9fr + 2fr Jacques Brel 1.25 1.25
B1076 SP489 13fr + 3fr Jef Denyn 1.40 1.40
B1077 SP489 26fr + 6fr Fr. Ferdinand Verbiest 2.10 2.10
Nos. B1075-B1077 (3) 4.75 4.75

Belgian Red Cross SP490

Paintings: No. B1078, *Crucifixion of Christ*, by Rogier van der Weyden (c. 1399-1464). No. B1079, *Virgin and Child*, by David (c. 1460-1523). B1089, *The Good Samaritan*, by Denis van Alsloot.

1989, Feb. 20 Photo. *Perf. 11½*

B1078 SP490 9fr + 2fr multi 1.00 1.00
B1079 SP490 13fr + 3fr multi 1.40 1.40
B1080 SP490 24fr + 6fr multi 2.10 2.10
Nos. B1078-B1080 (3) 4.50 4.50

Stamp Collecting Promotion Type of 1988

Various flowers from *Sixty Roses for a Queen*, by P.J. Redoute (1759-1840) and inscriptions: No. B1081, "Centfeuille unique melee de rouge." No. B1082, "Bengale a grandes feuilles." No. B1083, Aeme vibere (tea roses).

1989, Apr. 17

B1081 SP487 13fr + 5fr multi 1.40 1.40
B1082 SP487 24fr + 6fr multi 2.10 2.10

Souvenir Sheet

B1083 SP487 50fr + 17fr multi 8.00 8.00

Solidarity SP491

Royal Greenhouses of Laeken.

1989, Oct. 23

B1084 SP491 9fr + 3fr Exterior 1.00 1.00
B1085 SP491 13fr + 4fr Interior, vert. 1.40 1.40
B1086 SP491 24fr + 5fr Dome exterior, vert. 1.90 1.90
B1087 SP491 26fr + 6fr Dome interior, vert. 2.10 2.10
Nos. B1084-B1087 (4) 6.40 6.40

Queen Elisabeth Chapelle Musicale, 50th Anniv. — SP492

1989, Nov. 6

B1088 SP492 24fr + 6fr G clef 2.00 2.00

Stamp Collecting Promotion Type of 1988

Various flowers from *Sixty Roses for a Queen*, by P.J. Redoute (1759-1840): No. B1089, *Bengale desprez.* No. B1090, *Bengale philippe.* No. B1091, *Maria leonida.*

1990, Feb. 5

B1089 SP487 14fr + 7fr multi 1.50 1.50
B1090 SP487 25fr + 12fr multi 2.50 2.50

Souvenir Sheet

B1091 SP487 50fr + 20fr multi 8.00 8.00

Youth and Music — SP493

14fr+3fr, Beethoven & Lamoraal, Count of Egmont (1522-1568). 25fr+6fr, Joseph Cantre (1890-1957), drawing & sculpture.

1990, Oct. 6

B1092 SP493 10fr + 2fr multi 1.90 1.90
B1093 SP493 14fr + 3fr multi 2.40 2.40
B1094 SP493 25fr + 6fr multi 3.25 3.25
Nos. B1092-B1094 (3) 7.55 7.55

King Baudouin & Queen Fabiola, 30th Wedding Anniv. — SP494

1990, Dec. 10

B1095 SP494 50fr +15fr multi 8.00 8.00

Belgian Red Cross SP495

Details from paintings: No. B1096, The Temptation of St. Anthony by Hieronymus Bosch. No. B1097, The Annunciation by Dirk Bouts.

1991, Feb. 25, Photo. *Perf. 11½*

B1096 SP495 14fr +3fr multi 2.25 2.25
B1097 SP495 25fr +6fr multi 3.25 3.25

Belgian Film Personalities — SP496

10fr+2fr, Charles Dekeukeleire (1905-71), producer. 14fr+3fr, Jacques Ledoux (1921-88), film conservationist. 25fr+6fr, Jacques Feyder (1899-1948), director.

1991, Oct. 28 Photo. *Perf. 11½*

B1098 SP496 10fr +2fr multi 1.00 1.00
B1099 SP496 14fr +3fr multi 1.50 1.50
B1100 SP496 25fr +6fr multi 2.75 2.75
Nos. B1098-B1100 (3) 5.25 5.25

1992 Winter and Summer Olympics, Albertville and Barcelona SP497

1992, Jan. 20 Photo. *Perf. 11½*

B1101 SP497 10fr +2fr Speed skating 1.10 1.10
B1102 SP497 10fr +2fr Baseball 1.10 1.10
B1103 SP497 14fr +3fr Women's tennis, horiz. 1.60 1.60
B1104 SP497 25fr +6fr Skeet shooting 3.00 3.00
Nos. B1101-B1104 (4) 6.80 6.80

Folk Legends SP498

11fr + 2fr, Proud Margaret. 15fr + 3fr, Gustine Maca & the Witches. 28fr + 6fr, Reynard the Fox.

1992, June 22 Photo. *Perf. 11½*

B1105 SP498 11fr +2fr multi 1.25 1.25
B1106 SP498 15fr +3fr multi 1.75 1.75
B1107 SP498 28fr +6fr multi 3.00 3.00
Nos. B1105-B1107 (3) 6.00 6.00

Belgian Red Cross SP499

Paintings: 15fr + 3fr, Man with the Pointed Hat, by Adriaen Brouwer (1605-1638). 28fr + 7fr, Nereid and Triton, by Peter Paul Rubens, horiz.

1993, Feb. 15 Photo. *Perf. 11½*

B1108 SP499 15fr +3fr multi 1.90 1.90
B1109 SP499 28fr +7fr multi 4.00 4.00

Fight Against Cancer SP500

1993, Sept. 20 Photo. *Perf. 11½*

B1110 SP500 15fr +3fr multi 1.50 1.50

Intl. Olympic Committee, Cent. — SP501

No. B1112, Soccer players. No. B1113, Figure skater.

1994, Feb. 14 Photo. *Perf. 11½*

B1111 SP501 16fr +3fr multi 1.75 1.75
B1112 SP501 16fr +3fr multi 1.75 1.75
B1113 SP501 16fr +3fr multi 1.75 1.75
Nos. B1111-B1113 (3) 5.25 5.25

1994 World Cup Soccer Championships, Los Angeles (No. B1112). 1994 Winter Olympics, Lillehammer, Norway (No. B1113).

Porcelain — SP502

Designs: No. B1114, Tournai plate, Museum of Mariemont-Morlanweiz. No. B1115, Etterbeek cup, saucer, Municipal Museum, Louvain. 50fr+11fr, Delft earthenware jars, Pharmacy Museum of Maaseik.

1994, June 27 Photo. *Perf. 11½*

B1114 SP502 16fr +3fr multi 1.50 1.50
B1115 SP502 16fr +3fr multi 1.50 1.50

Souvenir Sheet

B1116 SP502 50fr +11fr multi 7.50 7.50

No. B1116 contains one 49x38mm stamp.

Solidarity SP503

Design: 16fr+3fr, Hearing-impaired person.

1994, Nov. 14 Photo. *Perf. 11½*

B1117 SP503 16fr +3fr multi 1.25 1.25

Museums — SP504

No. B1118, Natl. Flax Museum, Kortrijk. No. B1119, Natl. Water & Fountain Museum, Genval.
34fr+6fr, Intl. Carnival and Mask Museum, Binche.

1995, Jan. 30 Photo. *Perf. 11½*

B1118 SP504 16fr +3fr multi 1.25 1.25
B1119 SP504 16fr +3fr multi 1.25 1.25

Souvenir Sheet

B1120 SP504 34fr +6fr multi 3.00 3.00

Surtax for promotion of philately.

"Souvenir Sheets"

Beginning in 1995 items looking like souvenir sheets have appeared in the market. The 1995 one has the design used for No. B1120. The 1996 one has the design similar to the one used for No. B1128. The 1997 one has the design used for No. B1131. In 2000, the design of No. 1811 was used. These have no postal value.

Royal Belgian Soccer Assoc., Cent. SP505

1995, Aug. 21 Photo. *Perf. 11½*

B1121 SP505 16fr +4fr multi 1.40 1.40

Belgian Red Cross SP506

No. B1122, Princess Astrid, chairwoman of Belgian Red Cross. No. B1123, Wilhelm C. Röntgen (1845-1923), discoverer of the X-ray. No. B1124, Louis Pasteur (1822-95), scientist.

1995, Sept. 11

B1122 SP506 16fr +3fr multi 1.25 1.25
B1123 SP506 16fr +3fr multi 1.25 1.25
B1124 SP506 16fr +3fr multi 1.25 1.25
Nos. B1122-B1124 (3) 3.75 3.75

Solidarity — SP507

1995, Nov. 6 Photo. *Perf. 11½*

B1125 SP507 16fr +4fr multi 1.25 1.25

Surtax for fight against AIDS.

Museums — SP508

No. B1126, Museum of Walloon Life, Liège. No. B1127, Natl. Gin Museum, Hasselt.
34fr+6fr, Butchers' Guild Hall Museum, Antwerp.

1996, Feb. 19 Photo. *Perf. 11½*

B1126 SP508 16fr +4fr multi 1.25 1.25
B1127 SP508 16fr +4fr multi 1.25 1.25

Souvenir Sheet

B1128 SP508 34fr +6fr multi 3.00 3.00

Modern Olympic Games, Cent. SP509

1996, July 1 Photo. *Perf. 11½*

B1129 SP509 16fr +4fr Table tennis 1.25 1.25
B1130 SP509 16fr +4fr Swimming 1.25 1.25

Souvenir Sheet

B1131 SP509 34fr +6fr High jump 2.75 2.75

No. B1131 contains one 49x38mm stamp.

UNICEF, 50th Anniv. SP510

1996, Nov. 18 Photo. *Perf. 11½*

B1132 SP510 16fr +4fr multi 1.40 1.40

Museums SP511

No. B1133, Deportation and Resistance Museum, Mechlin. No. B1134, Iron Museum, Saint Hubert.
41fr+9fr, Horta Museum, Saint Gilles.

1997, Jan. 20 Photo. *Perf. 11½*

B1133 SP511 17fr +4fr multi 1.40 1.40
B1134 SP511 17fr +4fr multi 1.40 1.40

Souvenir Sheet

B1135 SP511 41fr +9fr multi 4.50 4.50

Surtax for "Pro-Post" association.

Judo — SP512

1997, May 5 Photo. *Perf. 11½*

B1136 SP512 17fr +4fr Men's (10a) 1.25 1.25
B1137 SP512 17fr +4fr Women's (10b) 1.25 1.25

Surtax for Belgian Olympic Committee.

Solidarity — SP513

1997, Oct. 25
B1138 SP513 17fr +4fr multi 1.25 1.25

Surtax for Multiple Sclerosis research.

King Leopold III — SP514

32fr+15fr, King Baudouin I. 50fr+25fr, King Albert II.

1998, Feb. 16 Engr. *Perf. 11½*
B1139 SP514 17fr +8fr dk grn 1.50 1.50
B1140 SP514 32fr +15fr dk brn blk 2.75 2.75

Souvenir Sheet

B1141 SP514 50fr +25fr dk vio brn 5.50 5.50

See Nos. B1146-B1148, 1748, B1154-B1156, 1842, B1158-B1160.

Sports SP515

1998, June 8 Photo. *Perf. 11½*
B1142 SP515 17fr +4fr Pelota 1.25 1.25
B1143 SP515 17fr +4fr Handball 1.25 1.25

Souvenir Sheet

B1144 SP515 30fr +7fr Soccer 2.50 2.50

1998 World Cup Soccer Championships, France (No. B1144).

Assist the Blind — SP516

Photo. & Embossed

1998, Nov. 9 *Perf. 11½*
B1145 SP516 17fr +4fr multi 1.40 1.40

Face value is indicated in Braille.

Royalty Type of 1998

Designs: 17fr+8fr, King Albert I. 32fr+15fr, King Leopold II. 50fr+25fr, King Leopold I.

1999, Jan. 25 Engr. *Perf. 11½*
B1146 SP514 17fr +8fr deep green 1.50 1.50
B1147 SP514 32fr +15fr black 2.75 2.75

Souvenir Sheet

B1148 SP514 50fr +25fr deep brown 4.50 4.50

Motorcycles — SP517

1999, May 17 Photo. *Perf. 11½*
B1149 SP517 17fr +4fr Speed race 1.40 1.40
B1150 SP517 17fr +4fr Trial, vert. 1.40 1.40

Souvenir Sheet

B1151 SP517 30fr +7fr Motocross, vert. 2.50 2.50

Solidarity SP518

No. 1152, First aid. No. 1153, Dental care, vert.

1999, Nov. 8 Photo. *Perf. 11½*
B1152 SP518 17fr +4fr multi 1.40 1.40
B1153 SP518 17fr +4fr multi 1.40 1.40

Royalty Type of 1998

Queens: 17fr + 8fr, Astrid (1905-35). 32fr +15fr, Fabiola (b. 1928). 50fr +25fr, Paola (b. 1937).

Photo. & Engr.

2000, Jan. 24 *Perf. 11½*
B1154 SP514 17fr +8fr green 1.50 1.50
B1155 SP514 32fr +15fr black 2.75 2.75

Souvenir Sheet

B1156 SP514 50fr +25fr claret 4.00 4.00

Red Cross/Red Crescent SP519

2000, Mar. 27 Photo. *Perf. 11½*
B1157 SP519 17fr +4fr multi 1.10 1.10

Royalty Type of 1998

Queens: 17fr+8fr, Elisabeth (1876-1965). 32fr+15fr, Marie-Henriette (1836-1902). 50fr+25fr, Louise-Marie (1812-50).

Photo. & Engr.

2001, Feb. 12 *Perf. 11½*
B1158 SP514 17fr +8fr green 1.50 1.50
B1159 SP514 32fr +15fr black 2.75 2.75

Souvenir Sheet

B1160 SP514 50fr +25fr brown 4.00 4.00

Sports SP520

World championship meets: No. B1161, Cycle track racing, Antwerp. No. B1162, Artistic gymnastics, Ghent.

2001, June 14 Photo. *Perf. 11½*
B1161 SP520 17fr +4fr multi 1.40 1.40
B1162 SP520 17fr +4fr multi 1.40 1.40

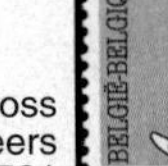

Red Cross Volunteers SP521

2001, Sept. 10
B1163 SP521 17fr +4fr multi 1.40 1.40

Winning Drawing in Belgica 2001 Children's Stamp Design Contest SP522

2002, Feb. 11 Photo. *Perf. 11½*
B1164 SP522 42c +10c multi 1.25 1.25

Red Cross Emergency Aid SP523

2002, June 5 Photo. *Perf. 11½*
B1165 SP523 84c +12c multi 2.50 2.50

Red Cross — SP524

No. B1166: a, Helicopter and rescue worker (6a). b, Rescue worker on shoulders of another (6b). c, Nurse attending to accident victim (6c).

2003, Mar. 31 Photo. *Perf. 11½*
B1166 Vert. strip of 3 + 2 labels 4.00 4.00
a.-c. SP524 41c +9c any single 1.25 1.25

Argenteuil, by Edouard Manet — SP525

2003, Sept. 15 Photo. *Perf. 11½*
B1167 SP525 49c +11c multi 1.50 1.50

Margins on sheets, inscribed "Prior," served as etiquettes.

The Temptation of Saint Anthony, by Salvador Dali SP526

2004, Apr. 19 Photo. *Perf. 11½*
B1168 SP526 49c +11c multi 1.50 1.50

Margins on sheets, inscribed "Prior," served as etiquettes.

Red Cross Workers SP527

2004, July 12 Photo. *Perf. 11½*
B1169 SP527 50c +11c multi 1.50 1.50

Margins on sheets, inscribed "Prior," served as etiquettes.

The Violinist, by Kees van Dongen — SP528

2005, Jan. 17 Photo. *Perf. 11½*
B1170 SP528 50c +12c multi 1.60 1.60

Margins on sheets, inscribed "Prior," served as etiquettes.

Dec. 26, 2004 Tsunami Victim Relief SP529

2005, Feb. 28
B1171 SP529 50c +12c multi 1.75 1.75

Margins on sheets, inscribed "Prior," served as etiquettes. Surtax for Red Cross health care infrastructure relief efforts.

Red Cross SP530

2006, May 15 Photo. *Perf. 11½*
B1172 SP530 52c +12c multi 1.75 1.75

Margins on sheets, inscribed "Prior," served as etiquettes.

The Kleptomaniac, by Théodore Gericault, and Ghent Museum of Fine Arts — SP531

2006, Oct. 23 Photo. *Perf. 11½*
B1173 SP531 52c +12c multi 1.75 1.75

Printed in sheets of 5. Margins on sheets, inscibed "Prior," served as etiquettes. Surtax for promotion of philately.

Souvenir Sheet

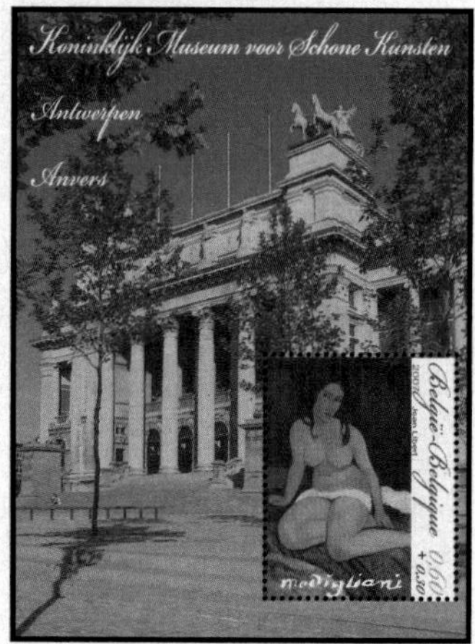

Seated Nude, by Amedeo Modigliani — SP532

2007, Jan. 8 Photo. ***Perf. 11½***
B1174 SP532 60c +30c multi 2.40 2.40

Surtax for promotion of philately.

Red Cross Mobile Library for Hospitals SP533

2007, Feb. 26
B1175 SP533 52c +25c multi 2.10 2.10

Printed in sheets of 10. Margins on sheets, inscribed "Prior," served as etiquettes.

Red Cross Blood Donation SP534

2008, Jan. 21 Photo. ***Perf. 11½***
B1176 SP534 1 +25c multi 2.25 2.25

No. B1176 sold for 77c on day of issue.

Souvenir Sheet

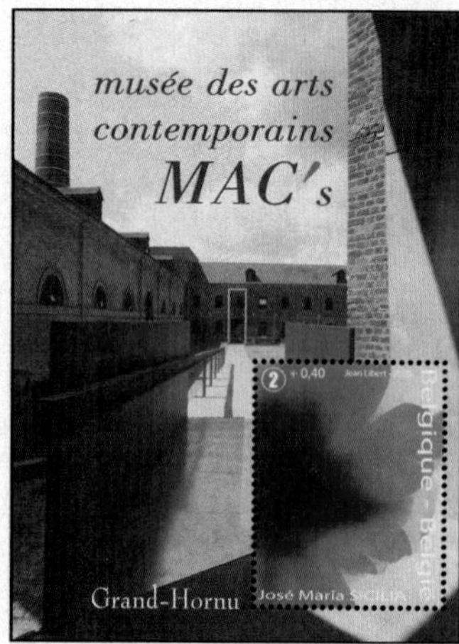

La Luz que se Apaga, by José Maria Sicilia — SP535

2008, Jan. 21
B1177 SP535 2 +40c multi 4.25 4.25

No. B1177 sold for €1.44 on day of issue.

Red Cross Drinking Water Projects — SP536

2009, Feb. 23 Litho. ***Perf. 11½***
B1178 SP536 1 +25c multi 2.25 2.25

On day of issue, No. B1178 sold for 84c.

Souvenir Sheet

Belgium No. 139a — SP537

2009, Nov. 3 Litho. ***Perf. 11½***
B1179 SP537 (90c) + 40c multi 4.00 4.00

Surtax for promotion of philately.

Miniature Sheet

Grand Place, Brussels — SP538

No. B1180: a, Statue of St. Michael, spire of City Hall. b, Star, Swan and Golden Tree Guildhouses. c, House of the Dukes of Brabant (one building), horiz. d, King of Spain, Wheelbarrow, Bag and Claw Guildhouses, horiz. e, Breadhouse (Maison du Roi).

Photo. & Engr.

2011, Sept. 19 ***Perf. 11½***
B1180 SP538 Sheet of 5 17.50 17.50
a.-e. 1 + (61c) Any single 3.50 3.50

On day of issue, Nos. B1180a-B1180e each had a franking value of 61c.

Miniature Sheet

Grand-Place, Bruges — SP539

No. B1181: a, Statue of Jan Breydel and Pieter de Coninck. b, Belfry. c Provincial House, horiz. d, Boechoute, Craenenburg, Die Maene Houses, Pathé Cinema, horiz..e, Spainge, Diephuis and Le Panier d'Or Houses.

2012, Oct. 29
B1181 SP539 Sheet of 5 17.50 17.50
a.-e. SP539 1 + (65c) Any single 3.50 3.50

On day of issue, Nos. B1181a-B1181e each had a franking value of 65c.

Statue of Marie-Christine de Lalaing — SP540

Belfry — SP541

Cloth Hall — SP542

Grange Aux Dimes — SP543

"The Oath" Statue — SP544

Photo. & Engr.

2013, Oct. 28 ***Perf. 11½***
B1182 Sheet of 5 19.00 19.00
a. SP540 1+(67c) multi 3.75 3.75
b. SP541 1+(67c) multi 3.75 3.75
c. SP542 1+(67c) multi 3.75 3.75
d. SP543 1+(67c) multi 3.75 3.75
e. SP544 1+(67c) multi 3.75 3.75

Capture of Tournai by King Henry VIII of England, 500th anniv. Nos. B1182a-B1182e each had a franking value of 67c on day of issue.

AIR POST STAMPS

Fokker FVII/3m over Ostend AP1

Designs: 1.50fr, Plane over St. Hubert. 2fr, over Namur. 5fr, over Brussels.

Perf. 11½

1930, Apr. 30 Unwmk. Photo.
C1 AP1 50c blue .45 .45
C2 AP1 1.50fr black brn 2.50 2.50
C3 AP1 2fr deep green 2.00 .90
C4 AP1 5fr brown lake 2.00 1.10
Nos. C1-C4 (4) 6.95 4.95
Set, never hinged 22.50

Nos. C1-C4 exist imperf.

1930, Dec. 5
C5 AP1 5fr dark violet 30.00 30.00
Never hinged 65.00

Issued for use on a mail carrying flight from Brussels to Leopoldville, Belgian Congo, starting Dec. 7.
Exists imperf.

Nos. C2 and C4 Surcharged in Carmine or Blue

1935, May 23
C6 AP1 1fr on 1.50fr (C) .55 .40
C7 AP1 4fr on 5fr (Bl) 8.75 8.00
Set, never hinged 42.50

Catalogue values for unused stamps in this section, from this point to the end of the section, are for Never Hinged items.

DC-4 Skymaster, Sabena Airline AP5

1946, Apr. 20 Engr. ***Perf. 11½***
C8 AP5 6fr blue .75 .25
C9 AP5 8.50fr violet brn 1.00 .45
C10 AP5 50fr yellow grn 5.00 .90
a. Perf. 12x11½ ('54) 325.00 1.40
C11 AP5 100fr gray 8.25 2.00
a. Perf. 12x11½ ('54) 100.00 1.40
Nos. C8-C11 (4) 15.00 3.60

Evolution of Postal Transportation — AP6

1949, July 1
C12 AP6 50fr dark brown 52.50 20.00

Centenary of Belgian postage stamps.

Glider — AP7

Design: 7fr, "Tipsy" plane.

1951, June 18 **Photo.** ***Perf. 13½***

C12A	Strip of 2 + label	82.50	65.00
b.	AP7 6fr dark blue	32.50	20.00
c.	AP7 7fr carmine rose	32.50	20.00

For the 50th anniv. of the Aero Club of Belgium. The strip sold for 50fr.

1951, July 25 ***Perf. 13½***

C13	AP7	6fr sepia	5.75	.25
C14	AP7	7fr Prus green	5.75	.95

UN Types of Regular Issue, 1958

Designs: 5fr, ICAO. 6fr, World Meteorological Organization. 7.50fr, Protection of Refugees. 8fr, General Agreement on Tariffs and Trade. 9fr, UNICEF. 10fr, Atomic Energy Agency.

Perf. 11½

1958, Apr. 17 **Unwmk.** **Engr.**

C15	A137	5fr dull blue	.25	.30
C16	A136	6fr yellow grn	.30	.45
C17	A137	7.50fr lilac	.35	.30
C18	A136	8fr sepia	.40	.30
C19	A137	9fr carmine	.45	.50
C20	A136	10fr redsh brown	.75	.60
		Nos. C15-C20 (6)	2.50	2.45

World's Fair, Brussels, Apr. 17-Oct. 19. See note after No. 476.

AIR POST SEMI-POSTAL STAMPS

Catalogue values for unused stamps in this section are for Never Hinged items.

American Soldier in Combat — SPAP1

Perf. 11x11½

1946, June 15 **Unwmk.** **Engr.**

CB1	SPAP1	17.50fr + 62.50fr dl brn	2.00	.90
CB2	SPAP1	17.50fr + 62.50fr dl gray grn	2.00	.90

Surtax for an American memorial at Bastogne.

An overprint, "Hommage a Roosevelt," was privately applied to Nos. CB1-CB2 in 1947 by the Association Belgo-Americaine. Value, $5.

In 1950 another private overprint was applied, in red, to Nos. CB1-CB2. It consists of "16-12-1944, 25-1-1945, Dedication July 16, 1950" and outlines of the American eagle emblem and the Bastogne Memorial. Value, $12. Similar overprints were applied to Nos. 265 and 361.

Flight Allegory SPAP2

1946, Sept. 7 ***Perf. 11½***

CB3	SPAP2	2fr + 8fr brt vio	.60	*1.00*

The surtax was for the benefit of aviation.

Nos. B417-B425 Surcharged in Various Arrangements in Red or Dark Blue

Type I

Type II

Type I — Top line "POSTE AERIENNE"
Type II — Top line "LUCHTPOST"

1947, May 18 **Photo.** ***Perf. 11½***

Type I

CB4	SP227	1fr + 2fr (R)	.75	*.50*
CB5	SP228	1.50fr + 2.50fr	.75	*.50*
CB6	SP229	2fr + 45fr	.75	*.50*
CB7	SP230	1fr + 2fr (R)	.75	*.50*
CB8	SP231	1.50fr + 2.50fr	.75	*.50*
CB9	SP232	2fr + 45fr	.75	*.50*
CB10	SP233	1fr + 2fr (R)	.75	*.50*
CB11	SP234	1.50fr + 2.50fr (R)	.75	*.50*
CB12	SP235	2fr + 45fr	.75	*.50*

Type II

CB4A	SP227	1fr + 2fr (R)	.75	*.50*
CB5A	SP228	1.50fr + 2.50fr	.75	*.50*
CB6A	SP229	2fr + 45fr	.75	*.50*
CB7A	SP230	1fr + 2fr (R)	.75	*.50*
CB8A	SP231	1.50fr + 2.50fr	.75	*.50*
CB9A	SP232	2fr + 45fr	.75	*.50*
CB10A	SP233	1fr + 2fr (R)	.75	*.50*
CB11A	SP234	1.50fr + 2.50fr (R)	.75	*.50*
CB12A	SP235	2fr + 45fr	.75	*.50*
		Nos. CB4-CB12A (18)	13.50	*9.00*

Issued for CIPEX, NYC. In 1948 Nos. CB4-CB12 and CB4A-CB12A were punched with the letters "IMABA," and the inscription "Imaba du 21 au 29 aout 1948" was applied to the backs. Value $20.

Helicopter Leaving Airport SPAP3

1950, Aug. 7

CB13	SPAP3	7fr + 3fr blue	9.00	5.25

Surtax for the Natl. Aeronautical Committee.

SPECIAL DELIVERY STAMPS

From 1874 to 1903 certain hexagonal telegraph stamps were used as special delivery stamps.

Town Hall, Brussels — SD1

2.35fr, Street in Ghent. 3.50fr, Bishop's Palace, Liege. 5.25fr, Notre Dame Cathedral, Antwerp.

1929 **Unwmk.** **Photo.** ***Perf. 11½***

E1	SD1	1.75fr dark blue	.80	.30
E2	SD1	2.35fr carmine	1.75	.45
E3	SD1	3.50fr dark violet	11.00	10.00
E4	SD1	5.25fr olive green	10.50	10.00

Eupen — SD2

1931

E5	SD2	2.45fr dark green	17.00	2.50
		Nos. E1-E5 (5)	41.05	23.25
		Set, never hinged	110.00	

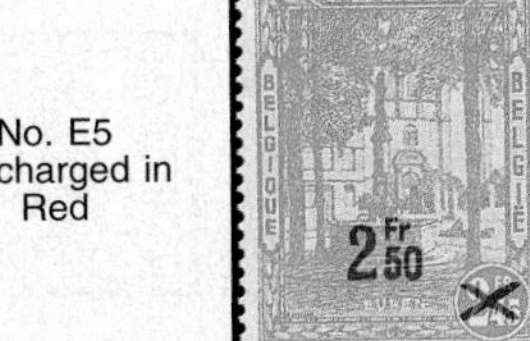

No. E5 Surcharged in Red

1932

E6	SD2	2.50fr on 2.45fr dk grn	18.00	2.00
		Never hinged	60.00	

REGISTRATION STAMPS

Catalogue values in this section are for Never Hinged items.

Osprey — R1

2011, Jan. 3 **Litho.** ***Perf. 11½x11¾***

F1	R1	(€4.70) multi	12.50	6.25

Short-eared Owl — R2

2012, Feb. 13 ***Perf. 11½***

F2	R2	(€4.35) multi	11.50	5.75

Arctic Tern — R3

2013, Jan. 21 ***Perf. 11½x11¾***

F3	R3	(€5.03) multi	14.00	7.00

Lapwing — R4

2013, Sept. 13 **Litho.** ***Perf. 11½***

F4	R4	(€1.20) multi	3.25	1.60

POSTAGE DUE STAMPS

D1

1870 **Unwmk.** **Typo.** ***Perf. 15***

J1	D1	10c green	3.75	2.00
J2	D1	20c ultra, thin paper	30.00	3.75

In 1909 many bisects of Nos. J1-J2 were created. The 10c bisect used as 5c on piece sells for $3.50.

No. J2 was also printed in aniline ink on thin paper. Value about the same.

D2

1895-09 ***Perf. 14***

J3	D2	5c yellow grn	.25	.25
J4	D2	10c orange brn	17.50	1.75
J5	D2	10c carmine ('00)	.25	.25
J6	D2	20c olive green	.25	.25
J7	D2	30c pale blue ('09)	.30	.25
J8	D2	50c yellow brn	17.50	5.00
J9	D2	50c gray ('00)	.75	.45
J10	D2	1fr carmine	20.00	11.50
J11	D2	1fr ocher ('00)	6.50	5.00
		Nos. J3-J11 (9)	63.30	24.70

1916 **Redrawn**

J12	D2	5c blue grn	25.00	7.00
J13	D2	10c carmine	42.50	11.00
J14	D2	20c dp gray grn	42.50	15.00
J15	D2	30c brt blue	6.00	5.00
J16	D2	50c gray	125.00	60.00
		Nos. J12-J16 (5)	241.00	98.00

In the redrawn stamps the lions have a heavy, colored outline. There is a thick vertical line at the outer edge of the design on each side.

D3

1919 ***Perf. 14***

J17	D3	5c green	.40	.50
J18	D3	10c carmine	.95	.35
J19	D3	20c gray green	7.25	1.25
J20	D3	30c bright blue	1.40	.40
J21	D3	50c gray	2.75	.50
		Nos. J17-J21 (5)	12.75	3.00
		Set, never hinged	40.00	

The 5c, 10c, 20c and 50c values also exist perf 14x15.

D4

1922-32

J22	D4	5c dk gray	.25	.25
J23	D4	10c green	.25	.25
J24	D4	20c deep brown	.25	.25
J25	D4	30c ver ('24)	.65	.25
a.		30c rose red	1.00	.45
J26	D4	40c red brn ('25)	.25	.25
J27	D4	50c ultra	1.90	.25
J28	D4	70c red brn ('29)	.30	.25
J29	D4	1fr violet ('25)	.45	.25
J30	D4	1fr rose lilac ('32)	.55	.25
J31	D4	1.20fr ol grn ('29)	.65	.45
J32	D4	1.50fr ol grn ('32)	.65	.45
J33	D4	2fr violet ('29)	.75	.25
J34	D4	3.50fr dp blue ('29)	1.00	.25
		Nos. J22-J34 (13)	7.90	3.65
		Set, never hinged	15.00	

1934-46 ***Perf. 14x13½***

J35	D4	35c green ('35)	.40	*.45*
J36	D4	50c slate	.25	.25
J37	D4	60c carmine ('38)	.40	.30
J38	D4	80c slate ('38)	.30	.25
J39	D4	1.40fr gray ('35)	.65	.45
J39A	D4	3fr org brn ('46)	1.50	.60
J39B	D4	7fr brt red vio ('46)	2.25	*3.25*
		Nos. J35-J39B (7)	5.75	*5.55*
		Set, never hinged	12.00	

See Nos. J54-J61.

Catalogue values for unused stamps in this section, from this point to the end of the section, are for Never Hinged items.

D5

1945 **Typo.** ***Perf. 12½***

Inscribed "TE BETALEN" at Top

J40	D5	10c gray olive	.25	.25
J41	D5	20c ultramarine	.25	.25
J42	D5	30c carmine	.25	.25
J43	D5	40c black violet	.25	.25
J44	D5	50c dl bl grn	.25	.25
J45	D5	1fr sepia	.25	.25
J46	D5	2fr red orange	.25	.25

Inscribed "A PAYER" at Top

J47	D5	10c gray olive	.25	.25
J48	D5	20c ultramarine	.25	.25
J49	D5	30c carmine	.25	.25
J50	D5	40c black vio	.25	.25
J51	D5	50c dl bl grn	.25	.25

J52 D5 1fr sepia .25 .25
J53 D5 2fr red orange .25 .25
Nos. J40-J53 (14) 3.50 3.50

Type of 1922-32

1949-53 Typo. *Perf. 14x13½*

J54 D4 65c emerald 7.00 3.75
J55 D4 1.60fr lilac rose ('53) 14.00 6.50
J56 D4 1.80fr red 15.00 6.50
J57 D4 2.40fr gray lilac ('53) 9.00 4.00
J58 D4 4fr deep blue ('53) 11.00 .50
J59 D4 5fr red brown 3.50 .40
J60 D4 8fr lilac rose 10.00 3.75
J61 D4 10fr dark violet 7.25 3.75
Nos. J54-J61 (8) 76.75 29.15

D6

Numerals 6½mm or More High

1966-70 Photo.

J62 D6 1fr brt pink .25 .25
J63 D6 2fr blue green .25 .25
J64 D6 3fr blue .25 .25
J65 D6 5fr purple .30 .25
J66 D6 6fr bister brn .45 .25
J67 D6 7fr red org ('70) .50 .30
J68 D6 20fr slate grn 1.75 1.00
Nos. J62-J68 (7) 3.75 2.55

Printed on various papers.

Numerals 4½-5½mm High

1985-87 Photo. *Perf. 14x13½*

J69 D6 1fr lilac rose .25 .25
J70 D6 2fr dull blue grn .25 .25
J71 D6 3fr greenish blue .25 .25
J72 D6 4fr green .25 .25
J73 D6 5fr lt violet .30 .25
J73A D6 6fr brown .35 .25
J74 D6 7fr brt orange .40 .30
J75 D6 8fr pale gray .45 .30
J76 D6 9fr rose lake .50 .35
J77 D6 10fr lt red brown .55 .40
J78 D6 20fr lt olive grn 1.25 1.10
Nos. J69-J78 (11) 4.80 3.95

Printed on various papers.

Issue dates: 3fr, 4fr, 8fr-10fr, Mar. 25, 1985. 6fr, 9/5/86. 20fr, 9/8/86. 2fr, 11/12/86. 6fr, 9/5/86. 1fr, 5fr, 7fr, 1987.

MILITARY STAMPS

Catalogue values for unused stamps in this section are for Never Hinged items.

King Baudouin
M1 M2

Unwmk.

1967, July 17 Photo. *Perf. 11*

M1 M1 1.50fr greenish gray .25 .25

1971-75 Engr. *Perf. 11½*

M2 M2 1.75fr green .50 .45
M3 M2 2.25fr gray green ('72) .35 .30
M4 M2 2.50fr gray green ('74) .25 .25
M5 M2 3.25fr vio brown ('75) .30 .25
Nos. M2-M5 (4) 1.40 1.25

Nos. M1-M3 are luminescent, Nos. M4-M5 are not.

MILITARY PARCEL POST STAMP

Type of Parcel Post Stamp of 1938 Srchd. in Blue

1939 Unwmk. *Perf. 13½*

MQ1 PP19 3fr on 5.50fr copper red .30 .25
Never hinged .60

OFFICIAL STAMPS

For franking the official correspondence of the Administration of the Belgian National Railways.

Most examples of Nos. O1-O25 in the marketplace are counterfeits. Values are for genuine examples.

Regular Issue of 1921-27 Overprinted in Black

1929-30 Unwmk. *Perf. 14*

O1 A58 5c gray .25 .25
O2 A58 10c blue green .30 .40
O3 A58 35c blue green .40 .30
O4 A58 60c olive green .45 .30
O5 A58 1.50fr brt blue 8.00 6.25
O6 A58 1.75fr ultra ('30) 1.75 2.00
Nos. O1-O6 (6) 11.15 9.50

Same Overprint, in Red or Black, on Regular Issues of 1929-30

1929-31

O7 A63 5c slate (R) .25 .35
O8 A63 10c olive grn (R) .50 .40
O9 A63 25c rose red (Bk) 1.50 .85
O10 A63 35c dp green (R) 1.75 .50
O11 A63 40c red vio (Bk) 1.25 .45
O12 A63 50c dp blue (R) ('31) .80 .35
O13 A63 60c rose (Bk) 10.00 6.00
O14 A63 70c orange brn (Bk) 4.25 1.25
O15 A63 75c black vio (R) ('31) 4.00 .85
Nos. O7-O15 (9) 24.30 11.00

Overprinted on Regular Issue of 1932

1932

O16 A73 10c olive grn (R) .50 .60
O17 A74 35c dp green 9.00 .75
O18 A71a 75c bister brn (R) 1.50 .30
Nos. O16-O18 (3) 11.00 1.65

Overprinted on No. 262 in Red

1935 *Perf. 13½x14*

O19 A80 70c olive black 2.75 .25

Regular Stamps of 1935-36 Overprinted in Red

1936-38 *Perf. 13½, 13½x14, 14*

O20 A82 10c olive bister .25 *.35*
O21 A82 35c green .25 *.40*
O22 A82 50c dark blue .45 .35
O23 A83 70c brown 1.50 .65

Overprinted in Black or Red on Regular Issue of 1938 *Perf. 13½x14*

O24 A82 40c red violet (Bk) .30 *.35*
O25 A85 75c olive gray (R) .65 .30
Nos. O20-O25 (6) 3.40 2.40

Regular Issues of 1935-41 Overprinted in Red or Dark Blue

1941-44 *Perf. 14, 14x13½, 13½x14*

O26 A82 10c olive bister .25 .25
a. Inverted overprint *65.00 65.00*
O27 A82 40c red violet .55 *.75*
O28 A82 50c dark blue .25 .25
a. Inverted overprint *77.50 77.50*
O29 A83a 1fr rose car (Bl) .45 .35
O30 A85 1fr rose pink (Bl) .25 .25
O31 A83a 2.25fr grnsh blk ('44) .30 *.50*
O32 A84 2.25fr gray violet .45 *.70*
Nos. O26-O32 (7) 2.50 *3.05*

Nos. O21, O23 and O25 Surcharged with New Values in Black or Red

1942

O33 A82 10c on 35c green .25 *.35*
O34 A83 50c on 70c brown .25 .25
O35 A85 50c on 75c ol gray (R) .25 .25
Nos. O33-O35 (3) .75 .85

Counterfeits exist of Nos. O26-O35.

Catalogue values for unused stamps in this section, from this point to the end of the section, are for Never Hinged items.

O1

1946-48 Unwmk. *Perf. 14*

O36 O1 10c olive bister .25 .25
O37 O1 20c brt violet 3.00 .90
O38 O1 50c dk blue .25 .25
O39 O1 65c red lilac ('48) 4.00 1.10
O40 O1 75c lilac rose .25 .25
O41 O1 90c brown violet 5.00 .35
Nos. O36-O41 (6) 12.75 3.10

Types A99, A101 and A102 with "B" Emblem Added to Design

1948 *Perf. 11½*

O42 A99 1.35fr red brown 4.25 .75
O43 A99 1.75fr dk gray green 6.00 .45
O44 A101 3fr brt red violet 27.50 8.00
O45 A102 3.15fr deep blue 11.00 7.00
O46 A102 4fr brt ultra 22.50 13.00
Nos. O42-O46 (5) 71.25 29.20

O2

1953-66 Typo. *Perf. 13½x14*

O47 O2 10c orange .65 .25
O48 O2 20c red lilac 3.50 .70
O49 O2 30c gray green ('58) 1.40 .55
O50 O2 40c olive gray .50 .25
O51 O2 50c light blue .75 .25
O51A O2 60c lilac rose ('66) 1.10 .55
O52 O2 65c red lilac 30.00 22.50
O53 O2 80c emerald 4.50 1.10
O54 O2 90c deep blue 6.75 1.10
O55 O2 1fr rose .45 .25
Nos. O47-O55 (10) 49.60 27.50

See Nos. O66, O68.

King Baudouin — O3

1954-70 Photo. *Perf. 11½*

O56 O3 1.50fr gray .30 .25
O57 O3 2fr rose red 40.00 .25
O58 O3 2fr blue grn ('59) .30 .25
O59 O3 2.50fr red brown ('58) 32.50 .75
O60 O3 3fr red lilac ('58) 1.50 .25
O61 O3 3.50fr yel green ('70) .75 .25
O62 O3 4fr brt blue 1.00 .25
O63 O3 6fr car rose ('58) 1.50 .60
Nos. O56-O63 (8) 77.85 2.85

Printed on various papers.

Type of 1953-66 Redrawn

1970-75 Typo. *Perf. 13½x14*

O66 O2 1.50fr grnsh gray ('75) .25 .25
O68 O2 2.50fr brown .25 .25

King Baudouin — O4

1971-73 Engr. *Perf. 11½*

O71 O4 3.50fr org brn ('73) .35 .25
O72 O4 4.50fr brown ('73) .35 .25
O73 O4 7fr red .40 .50
O74 O4 15fr violet .75 .30
Nos. O71-O74 (4) 1.85 1.30

Nos. O71-O74 were printed on various papers.

1974-80

O75 O4 3fr yellow grn 1.50 1.00
O76 O4 4fr blue 1.50 .50
O77 O4 4.50fr grnsh bl ('75) .30 .25
O78 O4 5fr lilac .30 .25
O79 O4 6fr carmine ('78) .35 .25
O80 O4 6.50fr black ('76) .40 .35
O81 O4 8fr bluish blk ('78) .50 .25
O82 O4 9fr lt red brn ('80) .55 .25
O83 O4 10fr rose carmine .60 .25
O84 O4 25fr lilac ('76) 1.50 .50
O85 O4 30fr org brn ('78) 1.75 .50
Nos. O75-O85 (11) 9.25 4.35

Heraldic Lion — O5

1977-82 Typo. *Perf. 13½x14*

O87 O5 50c brown ('82) .25 .25
O92 O5 1fr lilac ('82) .25 .25
O94 O5 2fr orange ('82) .25 .25
O95 O5 4fr red brown .25 .25
O96 O5 5fr green ('80) .25 .25
Nos. O87-O96 (5) 1.25 1.25

Nos. O87-O96 were printed on various papers.

NEWSPAPER STAMPS

Most examples of Nos. P1-P40 in the marketplace are counterfeits. Values are for genuine examples.

Parcel Post Stamps of 1923-27 Overprinted

Perf. 14½x14, 14x14½

1928 Unwmk.

P1 PP12 10c vermilion .25 *.40*
P2 PP12 20c turq blue .25 *.40*
P3 PP12 40c olive grn .25 *.40*
P4 PP12 60c orange .70 *.90*
P5 PP12 70c dk brown .45 .40
P6 PP12 80c violet .60 *.70*
P7 PP12 90c slate 2.25 2.00
P8 PP13 1fr brt blue .90 .60
a. 1fr ultramarine 12.00 5.00
P10 PP13 2fr olive grn 1.50 .60
P11 PP13 3fr orange red 1.60 .90
P12 PP13 4fr rose 2.25 1.10
P13 PP13 5fr violet 2.25 1.00
P14 PP13 6fr bister brn 4.50 1.75
P15 PP13 7fr orange 5.00 2.25
P16 PP13 8fr dk brown 6.00 2.75
P17 PP13 9fr red violet 10.00 3.00
P18 PP13 10fr blue green 9.00 2.75
P19 PP13 20fr magenta 15.00 7.00
Nos. P1-P8,P10-P19 (18) 62.75 28.90

Parcel Post Stamps of 1923-28 Overprinted

1929-31

P20 PP12 10c vermilion .25 .25
P21 PP12 20c turq blue .25 .25
P22 PP12 40c olive green .30 .25
a. Inverted overprint

No.	Type	Description	Unused	Used
P23	PP12	60c orange	.55	.35
P24	PP12	70c dk brown	.55	.25
P25	PP12	80c violet	.60	.25
P26	PP12	90c gray	2.00	1.00
P27	PP13	1fr ultra	.60	.25
a.		1fr bright blue	4.00	2.50
P28	PP13	1.10fr org brn ('31)	6.25	1.40
P29	PP13	1.50fr gray vio ('31)	6.25	1.90
P30	PP13	2fr olive green	2.00	.25
P31	PP13	2.10fr sl gray ('31)	17.00	12.00
P32	PP13	3fr orange red	2.25	.45
P33	PP13	4fr rose	2.25	.70
P34	PP13	5fr violet	3.00	.55
P35	PP13	6fr bister brn	3.75	1.00
P36	PP13	7fr orange	3.75	1.00
P37	PP13	8fr dk brown	3.75	1.00
P38	PP13	9fr red violet	5.25	1.50
P39	PP13	10fr blue green	3.75	1.10
P40	PP13	20fr magenta	13.00	4.50
		Nos. P20-P40 (21)	77.35	30.20

PARCEL POST AND RAILWAY STAMPS

Values for used Railway Stamps (Chemins de Fer) stamps are for copies with railway cancellations. Railway Stamps with postal cancellations sell for twice as much.

Coat of Arms — PP1

1879-82 Unwmk. Typo. *Perf. 14*

No.	Type	Description	Unused	Used
Q1	PP1	10c violet brown	110.00	5.75
Q2	PP1	20c blue	275.00	17.50
Q3	PP1	25c green ('81)	375.00	10.00
Q4	PP1	50c carmine	1,750.	10.00
Q5	PP1	80c yellow	2,000.	57.50
Q6	PP1	1fr gray ('82)	275.00	16.00

Used examples of Nos. Q1-Q6 with pinholes, a normal state, sell for approximately 40-60 percent of the values given.

Most of the stamps of 1882-1902 (Nos. Q7 to Q28) are without watermark. Twice in each sheet of 100 stamps they have one of three watermarks: (1) A winged wheel and "Chemins de Fer de l'Etat Belge," (2) Coat of Arms of Belgium and "Royaume de Belgique," (3) Larger Coat of Arms, without inscription.

PP2

1882-94 *Perf. 15½x14¼*

No.	Type	Description	Unused	Used
Q7	PP2	10c brown ('86)	20.00	1.50
Q8	PP2	15c gray ('94)	8.75	7.25
Q9	PP2	20c blue ('86)	65.00	7.00
Q10	PP2	25c yel grn ('91)	72.50	4.25
Q11	PP2	50c carmine	72.50	2.50
Q12	PP2	80c brnsh buff	72.50	.90
Q13	PP2	80c lemon	75.00	1.60
Q14	PP2	1fr lavender	350.00	3.00
Q15	PP2	2fr yel buff ('94)	210.00	67.50

Counterfeits exist.

PP3

Name of engraver below frame

1895-97

Numerals in Black, except 1fr, 2fr

No.	Type	Description	Unused	Used
Q16	PP3	10c red brown ('96)	11.00	.60
Q17	PP3	15c gray	11.00	7.00
Q18	PP3	20c blue	17.50	1.00
Q19	PP3	25c green	17.50	1.25
Q20	PP3	50c carmine	25.00	.80
Q21	PP3	60c violet ('96)	50.00	1.00
Q22	PP3	80c ol yel ('96)	50.00	1.40
Q23	PP3	1fr lilac brown	175.00	3.00
Q24	PP3	2fr yel buff ('97)	200.00	15.00

Counterfeits exist.

1901-02 Numerals in Black

No.	Type	Description	Unused	Used
Q25	PP3	30c orange	21.00	2.00
Q26	PP3	40c green	26.00	1.75
Q27	PP3	70c blue	50.00	1.40
a.		Numerals omitted	*750.00*	
b.		Numerals printed on reverse	*750.00*	
Q28	PP3	90c red	65.00	2.00
		Nos. Q25-Q28 (4)	162.00	7.15

Winged Wheel PP4

Without engraver's name

1902-14 *Perf. 15*

No.	Type	Description	Unused	Used
Q29	PP3	10c yel brn & slate	.25	.25
Q30	PP3	15c slate & vio	.25	.25
Q31	PP3	20c ultra & yel brn	.25	.25
Q32	PP3	25c yel grn & red	.25	.25
Q33	PP3	30c orange & bl grn	.25	.25
Q34	PP3	35c bister & bl grn ('12)	.35	.25
Q35	PP3	40c blue grn & vio	.25	.25
Q36	PP3	50c pale rose & vio	.25	.25
Q37	PP3	55c lilac brn & ultra ('14)	.35	.25
Q38	PP3	60c violet & red	.25	.25
Q39	PP3	70c blue & red	.25	.25
Q40	PP3	80c lemon & vio brn	.25	.25
Q41	PP3	90c red & yel grn	.25	.25
Q42	PP4	1fr vio brn & org	.25	.25
Q43	PP4	1.10fr rose & blk ('06)	.25	.25
Q44	PP4	2fr ocher & bl grn	.25	.25
Q45	PP4	3fr black & ultra	.35	.25
Q46	PP4	4fr yel grn & red ('13)	1.25	.70
Q47	PP4	5fr org & bl grn ('13)	.55	.55
Q48	PP4	10fr ol yel & brn vio ('13)	.90	.55
		Nos. Q29-Q48 (20)	7.25	6.05

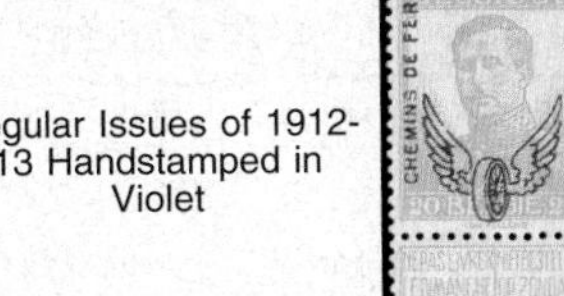

Regular Issues of 1912-13 Handstamped in Violet

1915 *Perf. 14*

No.	Type	Description	Unused	Used
Q49	A42	5c green	190.00	160.00
Q50	A43	10c red	1,400.	1,400.
Q51	A45	10c red	230.00	200.00
a.		With engraver's name	775.00	775.00
Q52	A43	20c olive grn	*1,600.*	*1,600.*
Q53	A45	20c olive grn	260.00	225.00
a.		With engraver's name	775.00	775.00
Q54	A45	25c ultra	260.00	225.00
a.		With engraver's name	775.00	775.00
Q55	A43	35c bister brn	350.00	300.00
Q55A	A43	40c green	*2,500.*	*2,500.*
Q56	A45	40c green	325.00	275.00
Q57	A45	50c gray	325.00	275.00
Q58	A43	1fr orange	325.00	275.00
Q59	A43	2fr violet	*1,900.*	*1,650.*
Q60	A44	5fr plum	*4,000.*	*3,500.*

Excellent forgeries of this overprint exist.

PP5

PP6

1916 Litho. *Perf. 13½*

No.	Type	Description	Unused	Used
Q61	PP5	10c pale blue	1.10	.25
Q62	PP5	15c olive grn	1.40	.50
Q63	PP5	20c red	2.25	.50
Q64	PP5	25c lt brown	2.25	.50
Q65	PP5	30c lilac	1.40	.50
Q66	PP5	35c gray	1.40	.45
Q67	PP5	40c orange yel	3.00	1.50
Q68	PP5	50c bister	2.25	.45
Q69	PP5	55c brown	3.00	2.25
Q70	PP5	60c gray vio	2.25	.45
Q71	PP5	70c green	2.25	.45
Q72	PP5	80c red brown	2.25	.45
Q73	PP5	90c blue	2.25	.45
Q74	PP6	1fr gray	2.25	.45
Q75	PP6	1.10fr ultra *(Franken)*	27.50	21.00
Q76	PP6	2fr red	25.00	.45
Q77	PP6	3fr violet	25.00	.45
Q78	PP6	4fr emerald	45.00	1.50
Q79	PP6	5fr brown	45.00	3.00
Q80	PP6	10fr orange	45.00	1.50
		Nos. Q61-Q80 (20)	241.80	37.05

Type of 1916 Inscribed "FRANK" instead of "FRANKEN"

1920

No.	Type	Description	Unused	Used
Q81	PP6	1.10fr ultra	2.00	.45

PP7

PP8

1920 *Perf. 14*

No.	Type	Description	Unused	Used
Q82	PP7	10c blue grn	1.75	.75
Q83	PP7	15c olive grn	1.75	1.10
Q84	PP7	20c red	1.75	.75
Q85	PP7	25c gray brn	2.50	.75
Q86	PP7	30c red vio	27.00	22.50
Q87	PP7	40c pale org	11.00	.75
Q88	PP7	50c bister	9.00	.75
Q89	PP7	55c pale brown	5.50	4.50
Q90	PP7	60c dk violet	10.00	.75
Q91	PP7	70c green	18.00	1.10
Q92	PP7	80c red brown	40.00	1.50
Q93	PP7	90c dull blue	10.00	.75
Q94	PP8	1fr gray	85.00	1.50
Q95	PP8	1.10fr ultra	26.00	2.00
Q96	PP8	1.20fr dk green	11.00	.75
Q97	PP8	1.40fr black brn	11.00	.75
Q98	PP8	2fr vermilion	110.00	1.25
Q99	PP8	3fr red vio	125.00	.85
Q100	PP8	4fr yel grn	125.00	.75
Q101	PP8	5fr bister brn	125.00	.75
Q102	PP8	10fr brown org	125.00	.75
		Nos. Q82-Q102 (21)	881.25	45.30

PP9

PP10

Types PP7 and PP9 differ in the position of the wheel and the tablet above it.

Types PP8 and PP10 differ in the bars below "FR".

There are many other variations in the designs.

1920-21 Typo.

No.	Type	Description	Unused	Used
Q103	PP9	10c carmine	.30	.25
Q104	PP9	15c yel grn	.30	.25
Q105	PP9	20c blue grn	.70	.25
Q106	PP9	25c ultra	.65	.25
Q107	PP9	30c chocolate	.85	.25
Q108	PP9	35c orange brn	.90	.30
Q109	PP9	40c orange	1.10	.25
Q110	PP9	50c rose	1.10	.25
Q111	PP9	55c yel ('21)	4.50	3.25
Q112	PP9	60c dull rose	1.10	.25
Q113	PP9	70c emerald	3.00	.40
Q114	PP9	80c violet	2.25	.25
Q115	PP9	90c lemon	37.50	21.00
Q116	PP9	90c claret	4.50	.40
Q117	PP10	1fr buff	4.50	.35
Q118	PP10	1fr red brown	4.00	.30
Q119	PP10	1.10fr ultra	1.60	.45
Q120	PP10	1.20fr orange	6.25	.30
Q121	PP10	1.40fr yellow	10.00	1.75
Q122	PP10	1.60fr turq blue	18.00	.70
Q123	PP10	1.60fr emerald	40.00	.70
Q124	PP10	2fr pale rose	26.00	.30
Q125	PP10	3fr dp rose	24.00	.30
Q126	PP10	4fr emerald	24.00	.30
Q127	PP10	5fr lt violet	17.50	.30
Q128	PP10	10fr lemon	110.00	9.00
Q129	PP10	10fr dk brown	22.50	.30
Q130	PP10	15fr dp rose ('21)	22.50	.30
Q131	PP10	20fr dk blue ('21)	325.00	3.00
		Nos. Q103-Q131 (29)	714.60	45.95

PP11

1922 Engr. *Perf. 11½*

No.	Type	Description	Unused	Used
Q132	PP11	2fr black	4.00	.25
Q133	PP11	3fr brown	37.50	.25
Q134	PP11	4fr green	9.00	.25
Q135	PP11	5r claret	9.00	.25
Q136	PP11	10fr yel brown	10.00	.25
Q137	PP11	15fr rose red	10.00	.25
Q138	PP11	20fr blue	67.50	.25
		Nos. Q132-Q138 (7)	147.00	1.75

PP12

PP13

Perf. 14x13½, 13½x14

1923-40 Typo.

No.	Type	Description	Unused	Used
Q139	PP12	5c red brn	.25	.25
Q140	PP12	10c vermilion	.25	.25
Q141	PP12	15c ultra	.25	.30
Q142	PP12	20c turq blue	.25	.25
Q143	PP12	30c brn vio ('27)	.25	.25
Q144	PP12	40c olive grn	.25	.25
Q145	PP12	50c mag ('27)	.25	.25
Q146	PP12	60c orange	.25	.25
Q147	PP12	70c dk brn ('24)	.25	.25
Q148	PP12	80c violet	.25	.25
Q149	PP12	90c sl ('27)	1.25	.25
Q150	PP13	1fr ultra	.35	.25
Q151	PP13	1fr brt blue ('28)	.55	.25
Q152	PP13	1.10fr orange	3.00	.30
Q153	PP13	1.50fr turq blue	3.25	.30
Q154	PP13	1.70fr dp brown ('31)	.75	.60
Q155	PP13	1.80fr claret	4.25	.60
Q156	PP13	2fr olive grn ('24)	.35	.25
Q157	PP13	2.10fr gray grn	7.50	.85
Q158	PP13	2.40fr dp violet	4.00	.85
Q159	PP13	2.70fr gray ('24)	35.00	1.40
Q160	PP13	3fr org red	.45	.25
Q161	PP13	3.30fr brn ('24)	55.00	1.40
Q162	PP13	4fr rose ('24)	.55	.25
Q163	PP13	5fr vio ('24)	.90	.25
Q163A	PP13	5fr brn vio ('40)	.45	.30
Q164	PP13	6fr bis brn ('27)	.50	.25
Q165	PP13	7fr org ('27)	.90	.25
Q166	PP13	8fr dp brown ('27)	.75	.25
Q167	PP13	9fr red vio ('27)	2.50	.25
Q168	PP13	10fr blue grn ('27)	1.10	.25
Q168A	PP13	10fr blk ('40)	5.75	5.00
Q169	PP13	20fr mag ('27)	1.90	.25
Q170	PP13	30fr turq grn ('31)	6.00	.40
Q171	PP13	40fr gray ('31)	55.00	.75
Q172	PP13	50fr bis ('27)	9.00	.30
		Nos. Q139-Q172 (36)	203.50	18.85

See Nos. Q239-Q262. For overprints see Nos. Q216-Q238. Stamps overprinted "Bagages Reisgoed" are revenues.

No. Q158 Srchd.

1924 **Green Surcharge**
Q173 PP13 2.30fr on 2.40fr violet 5.00 .85
Never hinged 30.00
a. Inverted surcharge 57.50

Type of Regular Issue of 1926-27 Overprinted

1928 ***Perf. 14***
Q174 A61 4fr buff 7.50 1.10
Q175 A61 5fr bister 7.50 1.25
Set, never hinged 55.00

Central P.O., Brussels PP15

1929-30 **Engr.** ***Perf. 11½***
Q176 PP15 3fr black brn 2.00 .25
Q177 PP15 4fr gray 2.00 .25
Q178 PP15 5fr carmine 2.00 .25
Q179 PP15 6fr vio brn ('30) 29.00 32.50
Nos. Q176-Q179 (4) 35.00 33.25
Set, never hinged 115.00

No. Q179 Surcharged in Blue

1933
Q180 PP15 4(fr) on 6fr vio brn 25.00 .25
Never hinged 105.00

Modern Locomotive PP16

1934 **Photo.** ***Perf. 13½x14***
Q181 PP16 3fr dk green 40.00 9.00
Q182 PP16 4fr red violet 9.50 .25
Q183 PP16 5fr dp rose 37.50 .25
Nos. Q181-Q183 (3) 87.00 9.50
Set, never hinged 275.00

Modern Railroad Train — PP17

Old Railroad Train — PP18

1935 **Engr.** ***Perf. 14x13½, 13½x14***
Q184 PP17 10c rose car .45 .25
Q185 PP17 20c violet .50 .25
Q186 PP17 30c black brn .65 .45
Q187 PP17 40c dk blue .80 .25
Q188 PP17 50c orange red .80 .25
Q189 PP17 60c green .90 .25
Q190 PP17 70c ultra 1.00 .25
Q191 PP17 80c olive blk .90 .25
Q192 PP17 90c rose lake 1.25 .65
Q193 PP18 1fr brown vio 1.25 .25
Q194 PP18 2fr gray blk 2.75 .25
Q195 PP18 3fr red org 3.50 .25
Q196 PP18 4fr violet brn 4.25 .25
Q197 PP18 5fr plum 4.50 .25
Q198 PP18 6fr dp green 5.00 .25
Q199 PP18 7fr dp violet 24.00 .25
Q200 PP18 8fr olive blk 24.00 .25
Q201 PP18 9fr dk blue 24.00 .25
Q202 PP18 10fr car lake 24.00 .25
Q203 PP18 20fr green 125.00 .25
Q204 PP18 30fr violet 125.00 2.75
Q205 PP18 40fr black brn 125.00 3.50
Q206 PP18 50fr rose car 140.00 2.75
Q207 PP18 100fr ultra 350.00 62.50
Nos. Q184-Q207 (24) 989.50 77.10
Set, never hinged 3,375.

Centenary of Belgian State Railway.

Winged Wheel PP19

Surcharged in Red or Blue

1938 **Photo.** ***Perf. 13½***
Q208 PP19 5fr on 3.50fr dk grn 22.50 1.50
Q209 PP19 5fr on 4.50fr rose vio (Bl) .25 .25
Q210 PP19 6fr on 5.50fr cop red (Bl) .50 .25
a. Half used as 3fr on piece 8.00
Nos. Q208-Q210 (3) 23.25 2.00
Set, never hinged 75.00

Nos. Q208-Q210 exist without surcharge. Value, set, $750.

See Nos. MQ1, Q297-Q299.

Symbolizing Unity Achieved Through Railroads PP20

1939 **Engr.** ***Perf. 13½x14***
Q211 PP20 20c redsh brn 5.00 *5.25*
Q212 PP20 50c vio bl 5.00 *5.25*
Q213 PP20 2fr rose red 5.00 *5.25*
Q214 PP20 9fr slate grn 5.00 *5.25*
Q215 PP20 10fr dk vio 5.00 *5.25*
Nos. Q211-Q215 (5) 25.00 *26.25*
Set, never hinged 30.00

Railroad Exposition and Cong. held at Brussels.

Parcel Post Stamps of 1925-27 Overprinted in Blue or Carmine

Perf. 14½x14, 14x14½
1940 **Unwmk.**
Q216 PP12 10c vermilion .25 .25
Q217 PP12 20c turq bl (C) .25 .25
Q218 PP12 30c brn vio .25 .25
Q219 PP12 40c ol grn (C) .25 .25
Q220 PP12 50c magenta .25 .25
Q221 PP12 60c orange .60 *.55*
Q222 PP12 70c dk brn .25 .25
Q223 PP12 80c vio (C) .25 .25
Q224 PP12 90c slate (C) .25 .25
Q225 PP13 1fr ultra (C) .25 .25
Q226 PP13 2fr ol grn (C) .25 .25
a. Ovpt. inverted 140.00 75.00
Q227 PP13 3fr org red .25 .25
Q228 PP13 4fr rose .25 .25
Q229 PP13 5fr vio (C) .25 .25
Q230 PP13 6fr bis brn .35 .25
Q231 PP13 7fr orange .35 .25
Q232 PP13 8fr dp brn .35 .25
Q233 PP13 9fr red vio .35 .25
Q234 PP13 10fr bl grn (C) .35 .25
Q235 PP13 20fr magenta .60 .25
Q236 PP13 30fr turq grn (C) 1.10 .75
Q237 PP13 40fr gray (C) 2.25 *2.10*
Q238 PP13 50fr bister 1.60 1.10
Nos. Q216-Q238 (23) 11.15 9.25
Set, never hinged 18.00

Types of 1923-40

1941
Q239 PP12 10c dl olive .25 .25
Q240 PP12 20c lt vio .25 .25
Q241 PP12 30c fawn .25 .25
Q242 PP12 40c dull blue .25 .25
Q243 PP12 50c lt grn .25 .25
Q244 PP12 60c gray .25 .25
Q245 PP12 70c chalky grn .25 .25
Q246 PP12 80c orange .25 .25
Q247 PP12 90c rose lilac .25 .25
Q248 PP13 1fr lt yel grn .25 .25
Q249 PP13 2fr vio brn .40 .25
Q250 PP13 3fr slate .45 .25
Q251 PP13 4fr dl olive .50 .25
Q252 PP13 5fr rose lilac .50 .25
Q253 PP13 5fr black .85 .30
Q254 PP13 6fr org ver .75 .30
Q255 PP13 7fr lilac .75 .25
Q256 PP13 8fr chalky grn .75 .25
Q257 PP13 9fr blue .90 .25
Q258 PP13 10fr rose lilac .90 .25
Q259 PP13 20fr milky blue 2.75 .40
Q260 PP13 30fr orange 5.00 .80
Q261 PP13 40fr rose 6.25 .80
Q262 PP13 50fr brt red vio 10.00 .70
Nos. Q239-Q262 (24) 33.25 7.80
Set, never hinged 90.00

Adjusting Tie Plates — PP21

Engineer at Throttle — PP22

Freight Station Interior — PP23

Signal and Electric Train — PP24

1942 **Engr.** ***Perf. 14x13½***
Q263 PP21 9.20fr red org .60 *.85*
Q264 PP22 12.30fr dp grn .60 *.90*
Q265 PP23 14.30fr dk car .80 *1.25*

Perf. 11½
Q266 PP24 100fr ultra 20.00 17.00
Nos. Q263-Q266 (4) 22.00 20.00
Set, never hinged 25.00

Catalogue values for unused stamps in this section, from this point to the end of the section, are for Never Hinged items.

PP25

PP26

PP27

1945-46 **Photo.** **Unwmk.**
Q267 PP25 10c ol blk ('46) .35 .30
Q268 PP25 20c dp vio .35 .30
Q269 PP25 30c chnt brn ('46) .35 .30
Q270 PP25 40c dp bl ('46) .35 .30
Q271 PP25 50c peacock grn .35 .30
Q272 PP25 60c blk ('46) .35 .30
Q273 PP25 70c emer ('46) .45 .30
Q274 PP25 80c orange .75 .30
Q275 PP25 90c brn vio ('46) .35 .30
Q276 PP26 1fr bl grn ('46) .35 .30
Q277 PP26 2fr blk brn .35 .30
Q278 PP26 3fr grnsh blk ('46) 2.00 .30
Q279 PP26 4fr dark blue .45 .30
Q280 PP26 5fr sepia .50 .30
Q281 PP26 6fr dk ol grn ('46) 2.25 .30
Q282 PP26 7fr dk vio ('46) .75 .30
Q283 PP26 8fr red org .75 .30
Q284 PP26 9fr dp bl ('46) .90 .30
Q285 PP27 10fr dk red ('46) 3.25 .30
Q286 PP27 10fr sepia ('46) 1.90 .30
Q287 PP27 20fr dk yel grn ('46) 1.00 .30
Q288 PP27 30fr dp vio 1.00 .30
Q289 PP27 40fr rose pink 1.00 .30
Q290 PP27 50fr brt bl ('46) 16.00 .70
Nos. Q267-Q290 (24) 36.10 7.60

Mercury — PP28

1945-46 ***Perf. 13½x13***
Q291 PP28 3fr emer ('46) .25 .25
Q292 PP28 5fr ultra .25 .25
Q293 PP28 6fr red .25 .25

Inscribed "Belgique-Belgie"
Q294 PP28 3fr emer ('46) .25 .25
Q295 PP28 5fr ultra .25 .25
Q296 PP28 6fr red .25 .25
Nos. Q291-Q296 (6) 1.50 1.50

Winged Wheel Type of 1938
Carmine Surcharge

1946 ***Perf. 13½x14***
Q297 PP19 8fr on 5.50fr brn .65 .25
Q298 PP19 10fr on 5.50fr dk bl .75 .25
Q299 PP19 12fr on 5.50fr vio 1.10 .25
Nos. Q297-Q299 (3) 2.50 .75

Railway Crossing PP29

1947 **Engr.** ***Perf. 12½***
Q300 PP29 100fr dark green 7.00 .25

Crossbowman with Train — PP30

1947 **Photo.** ***Perf. 11½***
Q301 PP30 8fr dark olive brn 1.00 .25
Q302 PP30 10fr gray & blue 1.10 .25
Q303 PP30 12fr dark violet 1.60 .45
Nos. Q301-Q303 (3) 3.70 .95

Nos. Q301-3 Srchd.

1948
Q304 PP30 9fr on 8fr 1.25 .25
Q305 PP30 11fr on 10fr 1.25 .25
Q306 PP30 13.50fr on 12fr 2.00 .25
Nos. Q304-Q306 (3) 4.50 .75

Delivery of Parcel PP31

1948

Q307 PP31 9fr chocolate 6.50 .25
Q308 PP31 11fr brown car 7.00 .25
Q309 PP31 13.50fr gray 10.50 .25
Nos. Q307-Q309 (3) 24.00 .75

Locomotive of 1835 PP32

Various Locomotives.

Lathe Work in Frame Differs

1949 Engr. *Perf. 12½*

Q310 PP32 ½fr dark brown .65 .25
Q311 PP32 1fr carmine rose .80 .25
Q312 PP32 2fr deep ultra 1.10 .25
Q313 PP32 3fr dp magenta 2.25 .25
Q314 PP32 4fr blue green 3.00 .25
Q315 PP32 5fr orange red 3.00 .25
Q316 PP32 6fr brown vio 3.25 .30
Q317 PP32 7fr yellow grn 4.50 .25
Q318 PP32 8fr grnsh blue 5.50 .25
Q319 PP32 9fr yellow brn 6.50 .30
Q320 PP32 10fr citron 8.00 .25
Q321 PP32 20fr orange 12.00 .25
Q322 PP32 30fr blue 20.00 .25
Q323 PP32 40fr lilac rose 35.00 .30
Q324 PP32 50fr violet 60.00 .35
Q325 PP32 100fr red 100.00 .25

Engraved; Center Typographed

Q326 PP32 10fr car rose & blk 12.00 1.75
Nos. Q310-Q326 (17) 277.55 6.00

See No. Q337.

1949 Engr.

Design: Electric locomotive.

Q327 PP32 60fr black brown 25.00 .25

Opening of Charleroi-Brussels electric railway line, Oct. 15, 1949.

Mailing Parcel Post PP33

Sorting PP34

Loading PP35

1950-52 *Perf. 12x12½, 12½*

Q328 PP33 11fr red orange 6.00 .25
Q329 PP33 12fr red vio ('51) 20.00 1.50
Q330 PP34 13fr dk blue grn 6.00 .25
Q331 PP34 15fr ultra ('51) 15.00 .30
Q332 PP35 16fr gray 6.00 .25
Q333 PP33 17fr brown ('52) 8.00 .25
Q334 PP35 18fr brt car ('51) 16.00 .45
Q335 PP35 20fr brn org ('52) 8.00 .25
Nos. Q328-Q335 (8) 85.00 3.50

For surcharges see Nos. Q338-Q340.

Mercury and Winged Wheel — PP36

1951

Q336 PP36 25fr dark blue 15.00 11.50

25th anniv. of the founding of the Natl. Soc. of Belgian Railroads.

Type of 1949

Design: Electric locomotive.

1952 Unwmk. *Perf. 11½*

Q337 PP32 300fr red violet 150.00 .50

Nos. Q331, Q328 and Q334 Surcharged with New Value and "X" in Red, Blue or Green

1953 *Perf. 12x12½*

Q338 PP34 13fr on 15fr (R) 60.00 3.00
Q339 PP33 17fr on 11fr (Bl) 35.00 2.25
Q340 PP35 20fr on 18fr (G) 30.00 2.50
Nos. Q338-Q340 (3) 125.00 7.75

Electric Train, 1952 PP37

1953 Engr.

Q341 PP37 200fr dk yel grn & vio brn 250.00 4.00
Q342 PP37 200fr dk green 225.00 1.00

No. Q341 was issued to commemorate the opening of the railway link connecting Brussels North and South Stations, Oct. 4, 1952.

New North Station, Brussels — PP38

Chapelle Station, Brussels PP39

Designs: No. Q348, 15fr, Congress Station. 10fr, 20fr, 30fr, 40fr, 50fr, South Station. 100fr, 200fr, 300fr, Central Station.

1953-57 Unwmk. *Perf. 11½*

Q343 PP38 1fr bister .30 .25
Q344 PP38 2fr slate .45 .25
Q345 PP38 3fr blue grn .60 .25
Q346 PP38 4fr orange .90 .25
Q347 PP38 5fr red brn 2.75 .25
Q348 PP38 5fr dk red brn 10.00 .25
Q349 PP38 6fr rose vio 1.10 .25
Q350 PP38 7fr brt green 1.10 .25
Q351 PP38 8fr rose red 1.40 .25
Q352 PP38 9fr brt grnsh bl 2.00 .25
Q353 PP38 10fr lt grn 2.25 .25
Q354 PP38 15fr dl red 13.00 .25
Q355 PP38 20fr blue 4.00 .25
Q356 PP38 30fr purple 6.25 .25
Q357 PP38 40fr brt purple 8.00 .25
Q358 PP38 50fr lilac rose 10.00 .25
Q359 PP39 60fr brt purple 20.00 .25
Q360 PP39 80fr brown vio 35.00 .25
Q361 PP39 100fr emerald 18.00 .25
Q361A PP39 200fr brt vio bl 95.00 1.60
Q361B PP39 300fr lilac rose 175.00 2.25
Nos. Q343-Q361B (21) 407.10 8.60

Issued: #Q347, 20fr, 30fr, 1953; 80fr, 1955; 200fr, 1956; 300fr, 1957; others, 1954.

See Nos. Q407, Q431-Q432.

Electric Train — PP40

1954

Q362 PP40 13fr chocolate 22.50 .25
Q363 PP40 18fr dark blue 22.50 .25
Q364 PP40 21fr lilac rose 22.50 .50
Nos. Q362-Q364 (3) 67.50 1.00

Nos. Q362-Q364 Surcharged with New Value and "X" in Blue, Red or Green

1956

Q365 PP40 14fr on 13fr (B) 8.00 .25
Q366 PP40 19fr on 18fr (R) 8.25 .25
Q367 PP40 22fr on 21fr (G) 8.75 .45
Nos. Q365-Q367 (3) 25.00 .95

Mercury and Winged Wheel — PP41

1957 Engr. *Perf. 11½*

Q368 PP41 14fr brt green 7.75 .25
Q369 PP41 19fr olive gray 8.00 .25
Q370 PP41 22fr carmine rose 8.75 .30
Nos. Q368-Q370 (3) 24.50 .80

Nos. Q369-Q370 Surcharged with New Value and "X" in Pink or Green

1959

Q371 PP41 20fr on 19fr (P) 22.50 .35
Q372 PP41 20fr on 22fr (G) 27.50 .55

Old North Station, Brussels PP42

1959 Engr. *Perf. 11½*

Q373 PP42 20fr olive green 12.50 .25

See Nos. Q381, Q383. For surcharges see Nos. Q378, Q382, Q384.

Diesel and Electric Locomotives and Association Emblem PP43

1960 Unwmk. *Perf. 11½*

Q374 PP43 20fr red 45.00 30.00
Q375 PP43 50fr dark blue 45.00 30.00
Q376 PP43 60fr red lilac 45.00 30.00
Q377 PP43 70fr emerald 45.00 30.00
Nos. Q374-Q377 (4) 180.00 120.00

Intl. Assoc. of Railway Congresses, 75th anniv.

No. Q373 Surcharged with New Value and "X" in Red

1961

Q378 PP42 24fr on 20fr ol grn 60.00 .25

South Station, Brussels — PP44

1962 Unwmk. *Perf. 11½*

Q379 PP44 24fr dull red 6.25 .25

No. Q379 Surcharged with New Value and "X" in Light Green

1963

Q380 PP44 26fr on 24fr dl red 6.50 .25

Type of 1959

Design: 26fr, Central Station, Antwerp.

1963 Engr. *Perf. 11½*

Q381 PP42 26fr blue 6.25 1.75

No. Q381 Surcharged in Red

1964, Apr. 20

Q382 PP42 28fr on 26fr blue 6.25 .25

Type of 1959

Design: 28fr, St. Peter's Station, Ghent.

1965 Engr. *Perf. 11½*

Q383 PP42 28fr red lilac 6.25 1.40

Nos. Q383 Surcharged in Green

1966

Q384 PP42 35fr on 28fr red lil 6.25 .25

Arlon Railroad Station PP45

Perf. 11½

1967, Aug. Unwmk. Engr.

Q385 PP45 25fr bister 10.00 .25
Q386 PP45 30fr blue green 5.00 .25
Q387 PP45 35fr deep blue 7.00 .35
Nos. Q385-Q387 (3) 22.00 .85

No. Q385 exists on luminescent paper. Value, $500.

See #Q408. For surcharges see #Q410-Q412.

Electric Train PP46

Designs: 2fr, 3fr, 4fr, 5fr, 6fr, 7fr, 8fr, 9fr, like 1fr. 10fr, 20fr, 30fr, 40fr, Train going right. 50fr, 60fr, 70fr, 80fr, 90fr, Train going left. 100fr, 200fr, 300fr, Diesel train.

1968-73 Engr. *Perf. 11½*

Q388 PP46 1fr olive bis .25 .25
Q389 PP46 2fr slate .25 .25
Q390 PP46 3fr blue green .55 .25
Q391 PP46 4fr orange .55 .25
Q392 PP46 5fr brown .65 .25
Q393 PP46 6fr plum .55 .25
Q394 PP46 7fr brt green .65 .25
Q395 PP46 8fr carmine .85 .25
Q396 PP46 9fr blue 1.40 .25
Q397 PP46 10fr green 2.75 .25
Q398 PP46 20fr dk blue 1.60 .25
Q399 PP46 30fr dk purple 4.00 .25
Q400 PP46 40fr brt lilac 5.50 .25
Q401 PP46 50fr brt pink 6.75 .25
Q402 PP46 60fr brt violet 8.25 .30
Q402A PP46 70fr dp bister ('73) 10.00 .30
Q403 PP46 80fr dk brown 6.75 .25
Q403A PP46 90fr yel grn ('73) 5.50 .30
Q404 PP46 100fr emerald 11.00 .25
Q405 PP46 200fr violet blue 13.00 .50
Q406 PP46 300fr lilac rose 22.50 1.25
Nos. Q388-Q406 (21) 103.30 6.65

Printed on various papers.

See No. Q409.

Types of 1953-68

10fr, Congress Station, Brussels. 40fr, Arlon Station. 500fr, Electric train going left.

1968, June Engr. *Perf. 11½*

Q407 PP38 10fr gray 1.50 .25
Q408 PP45 40fr vermilion 22.50 .25
Q409 PP46 500fr yellow 32.50 1.90
Nos. Q407-Q409 (3) 56.50 2.40

Nos. Q385, Q387 and Q408 Surcharged with New Value and "X"

1970, Dec.

Q410 PP45 37fr on 25fr bister 45.00 6.00
Q411 PP45 48fr on 35fr dp bl 13.00 5.00
Q412 PP45 53fr on 40fr ver 15.00 6.00
Nos. Q410-Q412 (3) 73.00 17.00

No. Q410 was also issued on non-luminescent paper. Value $175.

Ostend Station PP47

1971, Mar. Engr. *Perf. 11½*

Q413	PP47	32fr bis & blk	2.50	2.25
Q414	PP47	37fr gray & blk	5.00	4.00
Q415	PP47	42fr bl & blk	4.00	3.00
Q416	PP47	44fr brt rose & blk	4.50	3.00
Q417	PP47	46fr vio & blk	4.50	3.00
Q418	PP47	50fr brick red & blk	5.25	3.25
Q419	PP47	52fr sep & blk	7.00	4.75
Q420	PP47	54fr yel grn & blk	5.75	3.25
Q421	PP47	61fr grnsh bl & blk	5.75	4.00
		Nos. Q413-Q421 (9)	44.25	30.50

Nos. Q413-Q416, Q419-Q421 Surcharged with New Value and "X"

1971, Dec. 15

Denomination in Black

Q422	PP47	34fr on 32fr bister	2.00	.65
Q423	PP47	40fr on 37fr gray	2.50	.75
Q424	PP47	47fr on 44fr brt rose	2.75	.85
Q425	PP47	53fr on 42fr blue	3.25	.90
Q426	PP47	56fr on 52fr sepia	3.25	1.10
Q427	PP47	59fr on 54fr yel grn	3.25	1.10
Q428	PP47	66fr on 61fr grnsh blue	4.00	1.25
		Nos. Q422-Q428 (7)	21.00	6.60

Track, Underpinning of Railroad Car and Emblems — PP48

1972, Mar. Photo.

Q429	PP48	100fr emer, red & blk	10.00	1.90

Centenary of International Railroad Union.

Congress Emblem PP49

1974, Apr. Photo. *Perf. 11½*

Q430	PP49	100fr yel, blk & red	8.00	2.25

4th International Symposium on Railroad Cybernetics, Washington, DC, Apr. 1974.

Type of 1953-1957

1975, June 1 Engr. *Perf. 11½*

Q431	PP38	20fr emerald	1.75	.40
Q432	PP38	50fr blue	3.75	.60

Railroad Tracks PP50

1976, June 10 Photo. *Perf. 11½*

Q433	PP50	20fr ultra & multi	3.00	.70
Q434	PP50	50fr brt grn & multi	1.75	1.00
Q435	PP50	100fr dp org & multi	4.00	1.50
Q436	PP50	150fr brt lil & multi	6.25	2.25
		Nos. Q433-Q436 (4)	15.00	5.45

Railroad Station — PP51

1977 Photo. *Perf. 11½*

Q437	PP51	1000fr multi	55.00	22.50

Also issued on luminescent paper. See note following No. Q465.

Freight Car — PP52

Designs: 1fr-9fr, Freight car. 10fr-40fr, Hopper car. 50fr-90fr, Maintenance car. 100fr-500fr, Liquid fuel car.

1980, Dec. 16 Engr. *Perf. 11½*

Q438	PP52	1fr bis brn & blk	.30	.30
Q439	PP52	2fr claret & blk	.30	.30
Q440	PP52	3fr brt bl & blk	.30	.30
Q441	PP52	4fr grnsh blk & blk	.30	.30
Q442	PP52	5fr sepia & blk	.30	.30
Q443	PP52	6fr dp org & blk	.40	.40
Q444	PP52	7fr purple & blk	.50	.50
Q445	PP52	8fr black	.50	.50
Q446	PP52	9fr green & blk	.50	.50
Q447	PP52	10fr yel bis & blk	.50	.50
Q448	PP52	20fr grnsh bl & blk	1.25	.50
Q449	PP52	30fr bister & blk	2.25	.50
Q450	PP52	40fr lt lil & blk	2.50	.50
Q451	PP52	50fr dk brn & blk	2.75	.70
Q452	PP52	60fr olive & blk	3.25	.70
Q453	PP52	70fr vio bl & blk	5.00	5.00
Q454	PP52	80fr vio brn & blk	5.25	1.00
Q455	PP52	90fr lil rose & blk	7.00	7.00
Q456	PP52	100fr crim rose & blk	6.25	1.50
Q457	PP52	200fr brn & blk	12.50	1.75
Q458	PP52	300fr ol gray & blk	18.00	2.50
Q459	PP52	500fr dl pur & blk	32.50	5.25
		Nos. Q438-Q459 (22)	102.40	30.80

Train in Station — PP53

1982 Engr. *Perf. 11½*

Q460	PP53	10fr red & blk	1.75	.25
Q461	PP53	20fr green & blk	1.25	.50
Q462	PP53	50fr sepia & blk	4.25	.75
Q463	PP53	100fr blue & blk	7.25	2.75
		Nos. Q460-Q463 (4)	14.50	4.25

Electric Locomotives PP54

1985, May 3 Photo. *Perf. 11½*

Q464	PP54	250fr BB-150	15.00	12.00
Q465	PP54	500fr BB-120	35.00	17.50

Seven limited edition souvenir sheets exist. These include souvenir sheets of 4 of #Q437, Q464-Q465 with French or Flemish inscriptions, value $2,500, and a bilingual sheet with one each of #Q437, Q464-Q465, value $150.

Stylized Castle, Gabled Station and Electric Rail Car — PP55

1987, Oct. 12 Engr. *Perf. 11½*

Q466	PP55	10fr dk red & blk	1.00	.75
Q467	PP55	20fr dk grn & blk	1.50	1.50
Q468	PP55	50fr dk brn & blk	4.50	2.50
Q469	PP55	100fr dk lil & blk	8.00	4.00
Q470	PP55	150fr dark olive bister & blk	12.50	6.25
		Nos. Q466-Q470 (5)	27.50	15.00

Beginning in 1996, items looking like Parcel Post and Railway stamps have appeared in the market. Though sold by the Philatelic Bureau of the Belgian Post Office, these stamps are part of an ongoing series of Charity items that lack postal validity.

Kilopost — PP56

Maximum package weights: Nos. Q471, Q480, 0.5kg. Nos. Q472, Q481, 1kg. Nos. Q473, Q482, 2kg. Nos. Q474, Q483, 3kg. No. Q475, Q484, 4kg. No. Q476, Q485, 5kg. Nos. Q477, Q486, 10kg. Nos. Q478, Q487, 20kg. No. Q479, Q488, 30kg.

2003-04 Litho. *Perf. 11½*

Color of Box

Q471	PP56	(€2.48) org	18.00	2.00
Q472	PP56	(€3.10) red	18.00	2.00
Q473	PP56	(€3.72) blue	18.00	3.00
Q474	PP56	(€5.21) yel	24.00	3.00
Q475	PP56	(€5.95) pur	30.00	4.00
Q476	PP56	(€6.69) grn	25.00	6.00
Q477	PP56	(€7.44) mar	30.00	9.00
Q478	PP56	(€8.68) brn	42.00	16.00
Q479	PP56	(€11.16) aqua	55.00	35.00

Self-Adhesive

Booklet Stamps

Serpentine Die Cut 8 Horiz.

Q480	PP56	(€2.48) org	12.00	2.00
a.		Booklet pane of 5	60.00	
Q481	PP56	(€3.10) red	13.00	2.50
a.		Booklet pane of 5	65.00	
Q482	PP56	(€3.72) blue	15.00	3.00
a.		Booklet pane of 5	75.00	
Q483	PP56	(€5.21) yel	20.00	1.50
a.		Booklet pane of 5	125.00	
Q484	PP56	(€5.95) pur	24.00	2.00
a.		Booklet pane of 5	150.00	
Q485	PP56	(€6.69) grn	26.00	3.00
a.		Booklet pane of 5	175.00	
Q486	PP56	(€7.44) mar	30.00	6.00
a.		Booklet pane of 5	190.00	
Q487	PP56	(€8.68) brn	35.00	10.00
a.		Booklet pane of 5	225.00	
Q488	PP56	(€11.16) aqua	45.00	20.00
a.		Booklet pane of 5	275.00	
		Nos. Q471-Q488 (18)	480.00	130.00

Issued: Nos. Q471-Q482, 11/17. Nos. Q486-Q487, 2004. Nos. Q483-Q485, Q488, 2004.

Kilopost — PP57

Booklet Stamps

Die Cut Perf. 9¾ on 3 Sides

2005-07 Photo. Self-Adhesive

Color of Box

Q489	PP57	(€3.10) red	9.00	.50
a.		Booklet pane of 5	45.00	
Q490	PP57	(€13) blue	32.50	2.00
a.		Booklet pane of 5	165.00	
Q491	PP57	(€2.60) green ('07)	7.00	.40
a.		Booklet pane of 5	35.00	

Kilopost — PP58

Die Cut Perf. 10 on 3 Sides

2007, Aug. 1 Litho.

Booklet Stamps

Self-Adhesive

Q492	PP58	(€3) "Prior" at left	10.00	5.00
Q493	PP58	(€3) "Prior" at right	10.00	5.00
a.		Booklet pane of 5, 3 #Q492, 2 #Q493	50.00	

ISSUED UNDER GERMAN OCCUPATION

German Stamps of 1906-11 Surcharged

Nos. N1-N6

Nos. N7-N9

Wmk. Lozenges (125)

1914-15 *Perf. 14, 14½*

N1	A16	3c on 3pf brown	.45	.25
N2	A16	5c on 5pf green	.40	.25
N3	A16	10c on 10pf car	.50	.25
N4	A16	25c on 20pf ultra	.50	.25
N5	A16	50c on 40pf lake & blk	2.50	1.25
N6	A16	75c on 60pf mag	.90	*1.25*
N7	A16	1fr on 80pf lake & blk, *rose*	2.50	1.75
N8	A17	1fr25c on 1m car	20.00	12.50
N9	A21	2fr50c on 2m gray bl	18.00	15.00
		Nos. N1-N9 (9)	45.75	32.75
		Set, never hinged	160.00	

German Stamps of 1906-18 Surcharged

Nos. N10-N21

No. N22

Nos. N23-N25

1916-18

N10	A22	2c on 2pf drab	.25	.25
N11	A16	3c on 3pf brn	.35	.25
N12	A16	5c on 5pf grn	.35	.25
N13	A22	8c on 7½pf org	.65	.35
N14	A16	10c on 10pf car	.25	.25
N15	A22	15c on 15pf yel brn	.65	.25
N16	A22	15c on 15pf dk vio	.65	.45
N17	A16	20c on 25pf org & blk, *yel*	.35	.35
N18	A16	25c on 20pf ultra	.35	.25
a.		25c on 20pf blue	.40	.25
N19	A16	40c on 30pf org & blk, *buff*	.40	.30
N20	A16	50c on 40pf lake & blk	.35	.30
N21	A16	75c on 60pf mag	1.00	*12.50*

N22	A16	1fr on 80pf lake & blk, *rose*	2.00	*2.50*
N23	A17	1fr25c on 1m car	2.00	2.00
N24	A21	2fr50c on 2m gray bl	27.50	25.00
a.		2fr50c on 1m car (error)		*3,500.*
N25	A20	6fr25c on 5m sl & car	40.00	37.50
		Nos. N10-N25 (16)	77.10	82.75
		Set, never hinged	145.00	

A similar series of stamps without "Belgien" was used in parts of Belgium and France while occupied by German forces. See France Nos. N15-N26.

BELIZE

bə-ˈlēz

LOCATION — Central America bordering on Caribbean Sea to east, Mexico to north, Guatemala to west
GOVT. — Independent state
AREA — 8,867 sq. mi.
POP. — 219,296 (1996 est.)
CAPITAL — Belmopan

Belize was known as British Honduras until 1973. The former British colony achieved independence in September 1981.

100 Cents = 1 Dollar

Catalogue values for all unused stamps in this country are for Never Hinged items.

British Honduras Regular Issue 1968-72 Ovptd. in Black on Silver Panel

Wmk. 314 (½c, 5c, $5), Unwmkd.

1973, June 1 Litho. *Perf. 13x12½*

No.	Type	Denom.	Description	Unused	Used
312	A37	½c	multi (#235)	.25	.25
313	A37	1c	multi (#214)	.25	.25
314	A37	2c	multi (#215)	.25	.25
315	A37	3c	multi (#216)	.25	.25
316	A37	4c	multi (#217)	.25	.25
317	A37	5c	multi (#238)	.25	.25
318	A37	10c	multi (#219)	.25	.25
319	A37	15c	multi (#220)	.25	.25
320	A37	25c	multi (#221)	.30	.35
321	A37	50c	multi (#222)	.60	*.70*
322	A37	$1	multi (#223)	.80	*1.25*
323	A37	$2	multi (#224)	1.75	*2.50*
324	A37	$5	multi (#240)	3.25	*5.00*
			Nos. 312-324 (13)	8.70	*11.80*

No. 315 with silver panel omitted exists canceled. Nos. 313 and 319 exist with silver panel double.

Common Design Types pictured following the introduction.

Princess Anne's Wedding Issue
Common Design Type

1973, Nov. 14 Wmk. 314 *Perf. 14*

No.	Type	Denom.	Description	Unused	Used
325	CD325	26c	blue grn & multi	.25	.25
326	CD325	50c	ocher & multi	.25	.25

Crana A50

1974, Jan. 1 Litho. *Perf. 13½*

No.	Type	Denom.	Description	Unused	Used
327	A50	½c	shown	.25	*.70*
328	A50	1c	Jewfish	.25	*.40*
329	A50	2c	White-lipped peccary	.30	*.40*
330	A50	3c	Grouper	.25	*.25*
331	A50	4c	Collared anteater	.25	*.40*
332	A50	5c	Bonefish	.25	*.25*
333	A50	10c	Paca	.25	*.25*
334	A50	15c	Dolphinfish	.25	*.25*
335	A50	25c	Kinkajou	.30	*.50*
336	A50	50c	Muttonfish	.50	*.90*
337	A50	$1	Tayra	.95	*1.75*
338	A50	$2	Great barracudas	1.75	*3.25*
339	A50	$5	Mountain lion	3.25	*5.50*
			Nos. 327-339 (13)	8.80	*14.80*

Stag, Mayan Pottery A51

Designs: Mayan pottery decorations.

1974, May 1 *Perf. 14½*

No.	Type	Denom.	Description	Unused	Used
340	A51	3c	shown	.25	.25
341	A51	6c	Fire snake	.25	.25
342	A51	16c	Mouse	.25	.25
343	A51	26c	Eagle	.45	.45
344	A51	50c	Parrot	1.00	1.00
			Nos. 340-344 (5)	2.20	2.20

Parides Arcas A52

Designs: Butterflies of Belize.

Wmk. 314 Sideways

1974-77 *Perf. 14*

No.	Type	Denom.	Description	Unused	Used
345	A52	½c	shown	1.10	*5.00*
346	A52	1c	Thecla regalis	1.25	*1.75*
347	A52	2c	Colobura dirce	1.00	*1.25*
348	A52	3c	Catonephele numilia	1.75	.80
349	A52	4c	Battus belus	3.00	.70
350	A52	5c	Callicore patelina	3.25	.70
351	A52	10c	Callicore astala	1.75	.80

Perf. 14x15; 14 (26, 35c)

No.	Type	Denom.	Description	Unused	Used
352	A52	15c	Nessaea aglaura	4.00	.80
a.			Watermark upright ('75)	1.50	1.40
353	A52	16c	Prepona pseudojoiceyi	6.50	*9.00*
354	A52	25c	Papilio thoas	6.00	.50
a.			Watermark upright ('77)	7.00	2.50
355	A52	26c	Hamadryas arethusa	4.00	*4.25*
356	A52	50c	Thecla bathildis	3.50	.80
a.			Watermark upright ('77)	7.00	2.50
357	A52	$1	Caligo uranus	7.50	7.25
358	A52	$2	Heliconius sapho	5.00	1.60
359	A52	$5	Eurytides philolaus	7.00	7.50
a.			Watermark upright ('75)	7.00	8.25
360	A52	$10	Philaethria dido	12.00	5.00
			Nos. 345-360 (16)	68.60	47.70

Issue dates: No. 355A, July 25, 1977; No. 360, Jan. 2, 1975; others Sept. 2, 1974.

For surcharges & overprint see Nos. 380, 386, 395.

1975-78 Wmk. 373

No.	Type	Denom.	Description	Unused	Used
345a	A52	½c	multicolored	3.00	*7.50*
347a	A52	2c	multi ('77)	.80	*.85*
348a	A52	3c	multi ('77)	1.75	.85
349a	A52	4c	multi ('77)	4.25	.75
350a	A52	5c	multi ('77)	4.25	.75
351a	A52	10c	multicolored	4.50	.75
352b	A52	15c	multi ('77)	1.00	1.50
354b	A52	25c	multi ('78)	6.50	.90
355A	A52	35c	Parides arcas ('77)	14.00	6.50
			Nos. 345a-355A (9)	40.05	20.35

For overprints and surcharges see Nos. 395-396, 424, 426-427.

Churchill and Coronation Coach of Queen Elizabeth II — A53

$1, Churchill & Williamsburg, VA Liberty Bell.

Wmk. 373

1974, Nov. 30 Litho. *Perf. 14*

No.	Type	Denom.	Description	Unused	Used
363	A53	50c	multicolored	.25	.25
364	A53	$1	multicolored	.40	.40

Sir Winston Churchill (1874-1965).

Mayan Urn — A54

Designs: Various Mayan vessels.

1975, June 2 Wmk. 314 *Perf. 14*

No.	Type	Denom.	Description	Unused	Used
365	A54	3c	lt green & multi	.25	.25
366	A54	6c	lt blue & multi	.25	.25
367	A54	16c	dull yel & multi	.35	.30
368	A54	26c	lilac & multi	.50	.35
369	A54	50c	lt brown & multi	.65	*1.75*
			Nos. 365-369 (5)	2.00	2.90

Musicians A55

Christmas: 26c, Nativity (Thatched hut and children). 50c, Drummers, vert. $1, Map of Belize, star, fleeing family, vert.

Perf. 14x14½, 14½x14

1975, Nov. 17 Litho. Wmk. 314

No.	Type	Denom.	Description	Unused	Used
370	A55	6c	multicolored	.25	.25
371	A55	26c	multicolored	.35	.25
372	A55	50c	multicolored	.45	*.55*
373	A55	$1	multicolored	1.00	*1.60*
			Nos. 370-373 (4)	2.05	*2.65*

William Wrigley, Jr., Sapodilla Tree — A56

Bicentennial Emblem and: 35c, Charles Lindbergh and "Spirit of St. Louis." $1, John Lloyd Stephens and Mayan temple.

1976, Mar. 29 Wmk. 373 *Perf. 14½*

No.	Type	Denom.	Description	Unused	Used
374	A56	10c	multicolored	.25	.25
375	A56	35c	multicolored	.25	*.40*
376	A56	$1	multicolored	.60	*1.50*
			Nos. 374-376 (3)	1.10	*2.15*

American Bicentennial.

Bicycling A57

Wmk. 373

1976, July 17 Litho. *Perf. 14½*

No.	Type	Denom.	Description	Unused	Used
377	A57	35c	shown	.25	.25
378	A57	45c	Running	.25	.25
379	A57	$1	Shooting	.75	*1.40*
			Nos. 377-379 (3)	1.25	1.90

21st Olympic Games, Montreal, Canada, July 17-Aug. 1.

No. 355 Surcharged

Wmk. 314

1976, Aug. 30 Litho. *Perf. 14*

No.	Type	Denom.	Description	Unused	Used
380	A52	20c	on 26c multi	*2.50*	*2.75*

Map of West Indies, Bats, Wicket and Ball — A57a

Prudential Cup — A57b

Unwmk.

1976, Oct. 18 Litho. *Perf. 14*

No.	Type	Denom.	Description	Unused	Used
381	A57a	35c	lt blue & multi	.50	.60
382	A57b	$1	lilac rose & blk	1.25	*1.75*

World Cricket Cup, won by West Indies Team, 1975.

Royal Visit, 1975 A58

Designs: 35c, Rose window and Queen's head. $2, Queen surrounded by bishops.

1977, Feb. 7 Litho. *Perf. 13½x14*

No.	Type	Denom.	Description	Unused	Used
383	A58	10c	multicolored	.25	.25
384	A58	35c	multicolored	.25	.25
385	A58	$2	multicolored	.55	*.90*
			Nos. 383-385 (3)	1.05	1.40

25th anniv. of the reign of Elizabeth II.

No. 352 Surcharged

1977 Wmk. 314 *Perf. 14x15*

No.	Type	Denom.	Description	Unused	Used
386	A52	5c	on 15c multi	2.50	2.50

The first setting has the "5c" close to the the right edge of the block (varies). The second, and more common, setting has about 7mm from the right edge to the "5c."

Red-capped Manakin — A59

Designs: Birds of Belize.

Wmk. 373

1977, Sept. 3 Litho. *Perf. 14½*

No.	Type	Denom.	Description	Unused	Used
387	A59	8c	shown	.85	.60
388	A59	10c	Hooded oriole	1.00	.35
389	A59	25c	Blue-crowned motmot	1.50	.65
390	A59	35c	Slaty-breasted tinamou	1.75	.85
391	A59	45c	Ocellated turkey	2.00	1.50
392	A59	$1	White hawk	4.00	*6.00*
a.			Souvenir sheet of 6, #387-392	12.50	*12.50*
			Nos. 387-392 (6)	11.10	9.95

See Nos. 398-403, 416-421, 500-501. For overprints and surcharges see No. 502.

Medical Laboratory
A60

Design: $1, Mobile medical unit and children receiving treatment.

1977, Dec. 2 *Perf. 13½*
393 A60 35c multicolored .25 .25
394 A60 $1 multicolored .75 .75
a. Souvenir sheet of 2, #393-394 1.25 *1.60*

Pan American Health Org., 75th anniv.

Nos. 351 and 355A Overprinted in Gold: "BELIZE DEFENCE FORCE / 1ST JANUARY 1978"

Wmk. 314, 373

1978, Feb. 15 Litho. *Perf. 14*
395 A52 10c multicolored 1.00 1.00
396 A52 35c multicolored 2.50 2.50

Elizabeth II Coronation Anniversary Issue

Common Design Types
Souvenir Sheet

1978, Apr. 21 Unwmk. *Perf. 15*
397 Sheet of 6 1.75 1.75
a. CD326 75c White lion of Mortimer .30 .30
b. CD327 75c Elizabeth II .30 .30
c. CD328 75c Jaguar (Maya god) .30 .30
Nos. 397 (1) 1.75 1.75

No. 397 contains 2 se-tenant strips of Nos. 397a-397c, separated by horizontal gutter with commemorative and descriptive inscriptions and showing central part of coronation procession with coach.

Bird Type of 1977

Wmk. 373

1978, July 31 Litho. *Perf. 14½*
398 A59 10c White-crowned parrot .80 .40
399 A59 25c Crimson-collared tanager 1.00 .50
400 A59 35c Citreoline trogon 1.50 .75
401 A59 45c Sungrebe 1.75 1.75
402 A59 50c Muscovy duck 2.00 *2.00*
403 A59 $1 King vulture 3.00 *6.00*
a. Souvenir sheet of 6, #398-403 11.50 *11.50*
Nos. 398-403 (6) 10.05 *11.40*

Russelia Sarmentosa
A61

Wild Flowers and Ferns: 15c, Lygodium polymorphum. 35c, Heliconia aurantiaca. 45c, Adiantum tetraphyllum. 50c, Angelonia ciliaris. $1, Thelypteris obliterata.

1978, Oct. 16 Litho. *Perf. 14x13½*
404 A61 10c multicolored .25 .25
405 A61 15c multicolored .35 .35
406 A61 35c multicolored .35 .35
407 A61 45c multicolored .35 .35
408 A61 50c multicolored .50 .45
409 A61 $1 multicolored 1.00 .95
Nos. 404-409 (6) 2.80 2.70

Christmas.

Internal Airmail Service, 1937 — A62

Mail Service: 10c, MV Heron, 1949. 35c, Dugout canoe on river, 1920. 45c, Stann Creek railroad, 1910. 50c, Mounted courier, 1882. $2, RMS Eagle, 1856, and "paid" cancel.

Perf. 13½x14

1979, Jan. 15 Litho. Wmk. 373
410 A62 5c multicolored .45 .45
411 A62 10c multicolored .45 .25
412 A62 35c multicolored .45 .30
413 A62 45c multicolored .80 .80
414 A62 50c multicolored .80 .80
415 A62 $2 multicolored 2.75 2.75
Nos. 410-415 (6) 5.70 5.35

Centenary of membership in UPU.

Bird Type of 1977

1979, Apr. 16 Unwmk. *Perf. 14½*
416 A59 10c Boat-billed heron .70 .35
417 A59 25c Gray-necked wood rail 1.00 .35
418 A59 35c Lineated woodpecker 1.10 .60
419 A59 45c Blue gray tanager 1.25 .75
420 A59 50c Laughing falcon 1.25 1.25
421 A59 $1 Long-tailed hermit 1.75 *4.00*
a. Souvenir sheet of 6, #416-421 8.50 8.50
Nos. 416-421 (6) 7.05 7.30

Nos. 477, 354b, 595, 355A, 599, 651 Surcharged

No. 422

No. 428

1979-83 Litho. *Perf. 14*
422 A67 10c on 15c multi 6.75 5.00
423 A67 10c on 15c multi *17.50* —
424 A52 10c on 25c multi 3.00 2.25
424A A67 10c on 35c multi —
b. Round obliterator —
425 A76 10c on 35c multi *60.00*
426 A52 15c on 35c multi *100.00*
427 A52 15c on 35c multi 4.00 2.25
428 A76 $1.25 on $2 multi 30.00 16.00
429 A81 $1.25 on $2 multi 10.00 *12.00*

No. 422 has a square the width of the "10c" obliterating the old value. No. 423 has a rectangle that is wider than the "10c."

No. 424A has a square obliterator.

No. 426 has "15c" at top of stamp, No. 427 has "15c" at right of rectangle. Type differs.

No. 429 has rectangular obliterator with new value at top of stamp.

Many errors exist from printer's waste.

Issued: No. 426, 3/79; No. 427, 6/79; No. 424, 3/31/80; No. 422, 8/22/81; No. 423, 1/28/83; No. 425, 4/15/83; Nos. 428-429, 6/9/83.

Used Stamps

Postally used stamps are valued the same as unused. Canceled-to-order stamps are of minimal value. Most used stamps from No. 430-679 exist CTO. Most of these appeared on the market after the contract was canceled and were not authorized. The cancellations are printed and the paper differs from the issued stamps.

Imperforate Stamps

Stamps from No. 430-679 exist imperforate in small quantities.

Queen Elizabeth II, 25th Anniv. of Coronation — A63

Designs: 25c, No. 439, Paslow Bldg., #397c. 50c, Parliament, London, #397a. 75c, Coronation coach. $1, Queen on horseback, vert. $2, Prince of Wales, vert. $3, Queen and Prince Philip, vert. $4, Queen Elizabeth II, portrait, vert. No. 437, St. Edward's Crown, vert. No. 438a, $5, Princess Anne on horseback, Montreal Olympics, vert. No. 438b, $10, Queen, Montreal Olympics, vert.

Unwmk.

1979, May 31 Litho. *Perf. 14*
430 A63 25c multicolored 2.25
431 A63 50c multicolored 2.75
432 A63 75c multicolored 3.75
433 A63 $1 multicolored 4.75
434 A63 $2 multicolored 4.75
435 A63 $3 multicolored 4.75
436 A63 $4 multicolored 4.75
437 A63 $5 multicolored 5.50
Nos. 430-437 (8) 33.25

Souvenir Sheets

438 A63 Sheet of 2, #a.-b. 22.50
439 A63 $15 multicolored 22.50

Powered Flight, 75th Anniv. — A64

1979, July 30
440 A64 4c Safety, 1909 .85
441 A64 25c Boeing 707 2.50
442 A64 50c Concorde 6.00
443 A64 75c Handley Page W8b, 1922 3.50
444 A64 $1 AVRO F, 1912 3.50
445 A64 $1.50 Cody, 1910 5.00
446 A64 $2 Triplane Roe II, 1909 5.00
447 A64 $3 Santos-Dumont, 1906 5.00
448 A64 $4 Wright Brothers Flyer, 1903 6.00
Nos. 440-448 (9) 37.35

Souvenir Sheets

Perf. 14½

449 Sheet of 2 19.00
a. A64 $5 Dunne D.5, 1910 9.50
b. A64 $5 Great Britain #581 9.50
450 A64 $10 Belize Airways Jet 19.00

Sir Rowland Hill, death cent., "75th anniv." of ICAO.

1980 Summer Olympics, Moscow — A65

1979, Oct. 10 *Perf. 14*
451 A65 25c Handball 1.00
452 A65 50c Weight lifting 1.40
453 A65 75c Track 2.00
454 A65 $1 Soccer 2.50
455 A65 $2 Sailing 3.75
456 A65 $3 Swimming 4.00
457 A65 $4 Boxing 5.25
458 A65 $5 Cycling 10.50
Nos. 451-458 (8) 30.40

Souvenir Sheets

Perf. 14½

459 Sheet of 2 20.00
a. A65 $5 Track, diff. 6.25
b. A65 $10 Boxing, diff. 11.50
460 A65 $15 Cycling, diff. 20.00

1980 Winter Olympics, Lake Placid — A66

1979, Dec. 4 *Perf. 14*
461 A66 25c Torch .25
462 A66 50c Slalom skiing .60
463 A66 75c Figure skating .95
464 A66 $1 Downhill skiing 1.25
465 A66 $2 Speed skating 2.50
466 A66 $3 Cross country skiing 3.50
467 A66 $4 Biathlon 4.75
468 A66 $5 Olympic medals 6.00
Nos. 461-468 (8) 19.80

Souvenir Sheets

Perf. 14½

469 Sheet of 2 14.00
a. A66 $5 Torch bearers 4.25
b. A66 $10 Medals, diff. 7.75
470 A66 $15 Torch, diff. 14.00

See Nos. 503-512.

Cypraea Zebra
A67

1980, Jan. 7 Litho. *Perf. 14*

Inscribed "1980"

471 A67 1c shown 1.00
472 A67 2c Macrocallista maculata 1.25
473 A67 3c Arca zebra, vert. 1.40
474 A67 4c Chama macerophylla, vert. 1.40
475 A67 5c Latirus cariniferus 1.40
476 A67 10c Conus spurius, vert. 1.60
477 A67 15c Murex cabritii, vert. 2.50
478 A67 20c Atrina rigida 2.75
479 A67 25c Chlamys imbricata, vert. 3.00
480 A67 35c Conus granulatus 3.25
481 A67 45c Tellina radiata, vert. 3.75
482 A67 50c Leucozonia nassa 4.25
483 A67 85c Tripterotyphis triangularis 5.50
484 A67 $1 Strombus gigas, vert. 6.50
485 A67 $2 Strombus gallus, vert. 11.00
486 A67 $5 Fasciolaria tulipa 16.00
487 A67 $10 Arene cruentata 19.00
Nos. 471-487 (17) 85.55

1981

Inscribed "1981"

476a A67 10c 12.50
482a A67 50c 12.50
483a A67 85c 12.50
484a A67 $1 17.50
Nos. 476a-484a (4) 55.00

Souvenir Sheets

488 A67 Sheet of 2, 85c, $5 30.00 12.00
489 A67 Sheet of 2, $2, $10 45.00 22.50

Stamps in Nos. 488-489 have different color border and are of a slightly different size than the sheet stamps.

For overprints and surcharges see Nos. 422-423, 424A, 572-589, 592-593.

Intl. Year of the Child — A68

Various children. No. 498a, Three children. No. 498b, Madonna and Child by Durer. No. 499, Children before Christmas tree.

1980, Mar. 15 Litho. *Perf. 14*

No.	Type	Description	Value
490	A68	25c multicolored	.95
491	A68	50c multicolored	1.40
492	A68	75c multicolored	2.00
493	A68	$1 multicolored	2.10
494	A68	$1.50 multicolored	3.00
495	A68	$2 multicolored	3.25
496	A68	$3 multicolored	5.25
497	A68	$4 multicolored	6.00
		Nos. 490-497 (8)	23.95

Souvenir Sheets

Perf. 13½

No.	Type	Description	Value
498	A68	$5 Sheet of 2, #a.-b.	15.00
499	A68	$10 multicolored	15.00

No. 498 contains two 35x54mm stamps. No. 499 contains one 73x110mm stamp.

Bird Type of 1977

Souvenir Sheets

1980, June 16 Unwmk. *Perf. 13½*

No.	Description	Unused	Used
500	Sheet of 6	65.00	65.00
a.	A59 10c Jabiru	8.25	8.25
b.	A59 25c Barred antshrike	9.00	9.00
c.	A59 35c Royal flycatcher	9.75	9.75
d.	A59 45c White-necked puffbird	9.75	9.75
e.	A59 50c Ornate hawk-eagle	10.00	10.00
f.	A59 $1 Golden-masked tanager	10.50	10.50
g.	Sheet of 12	160.00	160.00
501	Sheet of 2	42.50	42.50
a.	A59 $2 Jabiru	17.00	17.00
b.	A59 $3 Golden-masked tanager	23.00	23.00

No. 500g contains 2 each Nos. 500a-500f with gutter between; inscribed "Protection of Environment" and "Wildlife Protection."

No. 392 Surcharged

1980, Oct. 3 Litho. *Perf. 13½*

No.	Description	Unused	Used
502	Sheet of 6	80.00	80.00
a.	A59 10c multicolored	10.00	10.00
b.	A59 25c multicolored	11.00	11.00
c.	A59 35c multicolored	11.00	11.00
d.	A59 40c on 45c multi	12.00	12.00
e.	A59 40c on 50c multi	12.00	12.00
f.	A59 40c on $1 multi	12.00	12.00

ESPAMER '80 Stamp Exhibition, Madrid, Spain, Oct. 3-12.

1980 Winter Olympics, Lake Placid — A69

Events and winning country: 25c, Men's speed skating, US. 50c, Ice hockey, US. 75c, No. 512, Men's figure skating, Great Britain. $1, Alpine skiing, Austria. $1.50, Women's giant slalom, Germany. $2, Women's speed skating, Netherlands. $3, Cross country skiing, Sweden. $5, Men's giant slalom, Sweden. Nos. 511a ($5), 511b ($10), Speed skating, US.

1980, Aug. 20 Litho. *Perf. 14*

No.	Type	Description	Value
503	A69	25c multicolored	.40
504	A69	50c multicolored	.70
505	A69	75c multicolored	1.00
506	A69	$1 multicolored	1.25
507	A69	$1.50 multicolored	2.25
508	A69	$2 multicolored	2.75
509	A69	$3 multicolored	4.25
510	A69	$5 multicolored	6.50
		Nos. 503-510 (8)	19.10

Souvenir Sheets

Perf. 14½

No.	Type	Description	Value
511	A69	Sheet of 2, #a.-b.	16.00
512	A69	$10 multicolored	16.00

Nos. 503-510 issued with se-tenant label. Values of stamps with labels are the same.

Intl. Year of the Child — A70

Nos. 513-521: Scenes from Sleeping Beauty. $8, Detail from Paumgartner Family Altarpiece by Albrecht Durer.

1980, Nov. 24 *Perf. 14*

No.	Type	Description	Value
513	A70	35c multicolored	3.25
514	A70	40c multicolored	3.75
515	A70	50c multicolored	4.25
516	A70	75c multicolored	4.50
517	A70	$1 multicolored	5.00
518	A70	$1.50 multicolored	7.00
519	A70	$3 multicolored	9.00
520	A70	$4 multicolored	9.00
		Nos. 513-520 (8)	45.75

Souvenir Sheets

Perf. 14½

No.	Type	Description	Value
521		Sheet of 2	27.50
a.		A70 $5 Marriage	9.00
b.		A70 $5 Couple on horseback	9.00
522	A70	$8 multicolored	22.50

Nos. 513-520 issued with se-tenent label.

Queen Mother Elizabeth, 80th Birthday — A71

1980, Dec. 12

No.	Type	Description	Value
523	A71	$1 multicolored	6.00

Souvenir Sheet

Perf. 14½

No.	Type	Description	Value
524	A71	$5 multicolored	22.50

No. 524 contains one 46x31mm stamp. No. 523 issued in sheet of 6.

Christmas — A72

1980, Dec. 30 Litho. *Perf. 14*

No.	Type	Description	Value
525	A72	25c Annunciation	.85
526	A72	50c Bethlehem	1.50
527	A72	75c Holy Family	1.75
528	A72	$1 Nativity	2.10
529	A72	$1.50 Flight into Egypt	2.75
530	A72	$2 Shepherds	3.25
531	A72	$3 With angel	3.75
532	A72	$4 Adoration	4.25
		Nos. 525-532 (8)	20.20

Souvenir Sheets

Perf. 14½

No.	Type	Description	Value
533	A72	$5 Nativity	11.50
534	A72	$10 Madonna & Child	24.00

Nos. 525-532 each issued in sheets of 20 + 10 labels. The 2nd and 5th vertical rows consist of labels.

Nos. 529, 532, 534 Surcharged

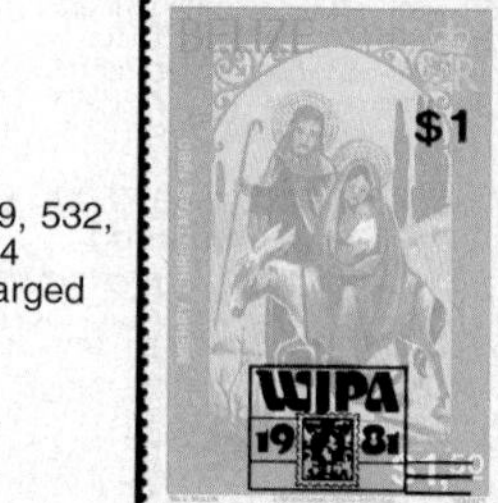

1981, May 22

No.	Type	Description	Value
535	A72	$1 on $1.50 multi	17.00
536	A72	$2 on $4 multi	19.00

Souvenir Sheet

Perf. 14½

No.	Type	Description	Value
537	A72	$2 on $10 multi	37.50

Location of overprint and surcharge varies.

Intl. Rotary Club — A73

Designs: 25c, Paul P. Harris, founder. 50c, No. 546, Rotary, project emblem. $1, No. 545b, 75th anniv. emblem. $1.50 Diploma, horiz. $2, No. 545a, Project Hippocrates. $3, 75th anniv. project emblems, horiz. No. 544, Hands reach out, horiz.

1981, May 26 *Perf. 14*

No.	Type	Description	Value
538	A73	25c multicolored	2.40
539	A73	50c multicolored	3.75
540	A73	$1 multicolored	5.50
541	A73	$1.50 multicolored	7.75
542	A73	$2 multicolored	9.00
543	A73	$3 multicolored	10.50
544	A73	$5 multicolored	13.50
		Nos. 538-544 (7)	52.40

Souvenir Sheets

Perf. 14½

No.	Type	Description	Value
545		Sheet of 2	45.00
a.		A73 $5 multicolored	15.00
b.		A73 $10 multicolored	30.00
546	A73	$10 multicolored	30.00

Originally scheduled to be issued Mar. 30, the set was postponed and issued without a 75c stamp. Supposedly some of the 75c were sold to the public. Value $2500.

For overprints and surcharges see Nos. 563-571, 590-591.

Royal Wedding of Prince Charles and Lady Diana — A74

1981, July 16 *Perf. 13½x14*

No.	Type	Description	Value
548	A74	50c Coat of Arms	.50
549	A74	$1 Prince Charles	1.25
550	A74	$1.50 Couple	1.75

Size: 25x43mm

Perf. 13½

No.	Type	Description	Value
551	A74	50c like No. 548	.50
552	A74	$1 like No. 549	1.25
553	A74	$1.50 like No. 550	1.75
		Nos. 548-553 (6)	7.00

Miniature Sheet

Perf. 14½

No.	Type	Description	Value
554		Sheet of 3, #554a-554c	3.00
a.		A74 $3 like No. 550	1.00
b.		A74 $3 like No. 548	1.00
c.		A74 $3 like No. 549	1.00

Nos. 551-553 issued in sheets of 6 + 3 labels. No. 554 contains three 35x50mm stamps.

For overprints see Nos. 659-665.

1984 Olympics A75

1981, Sept. 14 *Perf. 14*

No.	Type	Description	Value
555	A75	85c Track	3.50
556	A75	$1 Cycling	9.00
557	A75	$1.50 Boxing	6.25
558	A75	$2 Emblems	6.75
559	A75	$3 Baron Coubertin	8.50
560	A75	$5 Torch, emblems	10.00
		Nos. 555-560 (6)	44.00

Souvenir Sheets

Perf. 13½

No.	Type	Description	Value
561		Sheet of 2	50.00
a.		A75 $5 like No. 559	15.00
b.		A75 $10 like No. 560	35.00

Perf. 14½

No.	Type	Description	Value
562	A75	$15 like No. 558	50.00

No. 561 contains two 35x54mm stamps. No. 562 contains one 46x68mm stamp.

Nos. 561-562 exist with gold background.

Nos. 538-546 Overprinted in Black or Gold

1981, Sept. 21 *Perf. 14*

No.	Type	Description	Value
563	A73	25c multicolored (G)	3.00
564	A73	50c multicolored	4.00
565	A73	$1 multicolored	5.00
566	A73	$1.50 multicolored	6.25
567	A73	$2 multicolored (G)	7.00
568	A73	$3 multicolored	8.25
569	A73	$5 multicolored	11.00
		Nos. 563-569 (7)	44.50

Souvenir Sheets

Perf. 14½

No.	Type	Description	Value
570	A73	Sheet of 2, #a.-b. (G)	35.00
571	A73	$10 multicolored	30.00

Size of overprint varies.

Nos. 471-483, 485-489 Ovptd.

Belize

Independence 21 Sept.,1981

1981, Sept. 21
572 A67 1c multicolored 1.75
573 A67 2c multicolored 1.75
574 A67 3c multicolored 2.00
575 A67 4c multicolored 2.00
576 A67 5c multicolored 2.00
577 A67 10c multicolored 2.75
a. Inscribed "1980" —
578 A67 15c multicolored 4.00
579 A67 20c multicolored 4.00
580 A67 25c multicolored 5.00
581 A67 35c multicolored 5.00
582 A67 45c multicolored 5.75
583 A67 50c multicolored 5.75
584 A67 85c multicolored 7.50
585 A67 $2 multicolored 15.00
586 A67 $5 multicolored 17.50
587 A67 $10 multicolored 24.00
Nos. 572-587 (16) 105.75

Souvenir Sheets

588 A67 Sheet of 2, #488 35.00
589 A67 Sheet of 2, #489 40.00

Size and style of overprint varies, italic on horiz. stamps, upright on vert. stamps and upright capitals on souvenir sheets.

The 10c is dated 1981. Less than 16 sheets dated 1980 were also overprinted.

Nos. 541, 545 Surcharged

1981, Nov. 13 ***Perf. 14***
590 A73 $1 on $1.50 multi 24.00

Souvenir Sheet

Perf. 14½

591 Sheet of 2 35.00
a. A73 $1 on $5 multicolored 17.50
b. A73 $1 on $10 multicolored 17.50

Espamer '81.

Nos. 488, 489 Surcharged in Red

1981, Nov. 14 ***Perf. 14½***

Souvenir Sheets

592 Sheet of 2 60.00
a. A67 $1 on 85c 27.50
b. A67 $1 on $5 27.50
593 Sheet of 2 60.00
a. A67 $1 on $2 27.50
b. A67 $1 on $10 27.50

Independence — A76

1981-82 ***Perf. 14***
594 A76 10c Flag 3.00
595 A76 35c Map, vert. 5.50
596 A76 50c Black orchid, vert. 15.00
597 A76 85c Tapir 5.00
598 A76 $1 Mahogany tree, vert. 5.00
599 A76 $2 Keel-billed toucan 22.50
Nos. 594-599 (6) 56.00

Souvenir Sheet

Perf. 14½

600 A76 $5 like 10c 45.00

Issued: 50c-$2, 12/18; 10c, 35c, $5, 2/10/82.

For surcharges see Nos. 425, 428, 616.

1982 World Cup Soccer Championships, Spain — A77

1981, Dec. 28 ***Perf. 14***
601 A77 10c Uruguay '30, '50 3.00
602 A77 25c Italy '34, '38 4.50
603 A77 50c Germany '54, '74 6.75
604 A77 $1 Brazil '58, '62, '70 7.50
605 A77 $1.50 Argentina '78 8.75
606 A77 $2 England '66 9.75
Nos. 601-606 (6) 40.25

Souvenir Sheets

Perf. 14½

607 A77 $2 Emblem 21.00
608 A77 $3 Player 27.50

No. 608 contains one 46x78mm stamp.

For surcharge see No. 617.

Sailing Ships — A78

1982, Mar. 15 ***Perf. 14***
609 A78 10c Man of war, 19th cent. 4.25
610 A78 25c Madagascar, 1837 6.25
611 A78 35c Whitby, 1838 6.75
612 A78 50c China, 1838 8.00
613 A78 85c Swiftsure, 1850 9.75
614 A78 $2 Windsor Castle, 1857 14.50
Nos. 609-614 (6) 49.50

Souvenir Sheet

Perf. 14½

615 A78 $5 19th cent. ships 60.00

Nos. 599 and 606 Surcharged

1982, Apr. 28
616 A76 $1 on $2 multi 19.00
617 A77 $1 on $2 multi 19.00

Essen '82 Philatelic Exhibition.

Princess of Wales, 21st Birthday — A79

Various portraits.

1982, May 20 ***Perf. 13½x14***
618 A79 50c multicolored 2.40
619 A79 $1 multicolored 3.00
620 A79 $1.50 multicolored 3.00

Size: 25x42mm

Perf. 13½

621 A79 50c like No. 618 2.40
622 A79 $1 like No. 619 3.00
623 A79 $1.50 like No. 620 3.00
Nos. 618-623 (6) 16.80

Souvenir Sheet

Stamp Size: 31x47mm

Perf. 14½

624 A79 $3 Sheet of 3, #a.-c. like #618-620 10.50

Nos. 618-620 also exist with gold borders, size: 30x45mm. Value, set $16.

Overprinted in Silver

1982, Oct. 21 ***Perf. 13½x14***
628 A79 50c multicolored .55
629 A79 $1 multicolored .70
630 A79 $1.50 multicolored .95

Size: 25x42mm

Perf. 13½

631 A79 50c multicolored .55
632 A79 $1 multicolored .70
633 A79 $1.50 multicolored .95
Nos. 628-633 (6) 4.40

Souvenir Sheet

Perf. 14½

634 A79 $3 Sheet of 3, #a.-c. 13.00

Size of overprint varies. The overprint exists on the gold bordered stamps. Value, set $25.

No. 634 exists with a second type of overprint.

Boy Scouts — A80

1982, Aug. 31 ***Perf. 14***
638 A80 10c Building camp fire 2.50
639 A80 25c Bird watching 5.00
640 A80 35c Playing guitar 3.75
641 A80 50c Hiking 4.00
642 A80 85c Flag, scouts 5.50
643 A80 $2 Salute 6.50
Nos. 638-643 (6) 27.25

Souvenir Sheets

Perf. 14½

644 A80 $2 Scout holding flag, vert. 27.50
645 A80 $3 Lord Baden Powell, vert. 27.50

Scouting, 75th anniv. and Lord Baden Powell, 125th birth anniv.

For overprints see Nos. 653-658.

Marine Life — A81

1982, Sept. 20 ***Perf. 14***
646 A81 10c Gorgonia ventalina 4.00
647 A81 35c Carpilius corallinus 7.00
648 A81 50c Plexaura flexuosa 7.75
649 A81 85c Condylactis gigantea 8.00
650 A81 $1 Stenopus hispidus 10.00
651 A81 $2 Abudefduf saxatilis 12.50
Nos. 646-651 (6) 49.25

Souvenir Sheet

Perf. 14½

652 A81 $5 Scyllarides aequinoctialis 67.50

For surcharge see No. 429.

Nos. 638-643 Overprinted in Gold

1982, Oct. 1 ***Perf. 14***
653 A80 10c Building camp fire 4.25
654 A80 25c Bird watching 7.50
655 A80 35c Playing guitar 6.50
656 A80 50c Hiking 7.50
657 A80 85c Flag, scouts 12.00
658 A80 $2 Salute 19.00
Nos. 653-658 (6) 56.75

Overprint is different on Nos. 654-655.

Sheets include labels with native Christmas themes.

Nos. 548-554 Overprinted in Gold Similar to Nos. 628-634

1982, Oct. 25 ***Perf. 13½x14***
659 A74 50c Coat of Arms 4.00
660 A74 $1 Prince Charles 7.50
661 A74 $1.50 Couple 10.00

Size: 25x43mm

Perf. 13½

662 A74 50c like No. 659 .65
663 A74 $1 like No. 660 .90
664 A74 $1.50 like No. 661 1.40
Nos. 659-664 (6) 24.45

Miniature Sheet

Perf. 14½

665 Sheet of 3, #665a-665c 11.50
a. A74 $3 like No. 661 3.25
b. A74 $3 like No. 659 3.25
c. A74 $3 like No. 660 3.25

Nos. 662-664 issued in sheets of 6 plus 3 labels. No. 665 contains three 35x50mm stamps. Size and style of overprint varies.

Visit by Pope John Paul II A82

1983, Mar. 7 ***Perf. 13½***
666 A82 50c Belize Cathedral 6.25

Souvenir Sheet

Perf. 14½

667 A82 $2.50 Pope John Paul II 37.50

No. 667 contains one 30x47mm stamp.

No. 666 issued in sheet of 6.

Commonwealth Day — A83

1983, Mar. 14 ***Perf. 13½***
668 A83 35c Map, vert. .40
669 A83 50c Maya Stella .55
670 A83 85c Supreme Court Bldg. 1.00
671 A83 $2 University Center 2.50
Nos. 668-671 (4) 4.45

Issued in miniature sheets of 4. Other formats are suspect.

First Manned Flight, Bicent. — A84

1983, May 16 ***Perf. 14***

672 A84 10c Flying boat, 1670 4.25
673 A84 25c Flying machine, 1709 5.75
674 A84 50c Airship Guyton de Morveau 6.00
675 A84 85c Dirigible 7.50
676 A84 $1 Clement Bayard 8.00
677 A84 $1.50 Great Britain R-34 8.75
Nos. 672-677 (6) 40.25

Souvenir Sheets

Perf. 14½

678 A84 $3 Nassau Balloon 25.00
679 A84 $3 Montgolfier Brothers balloon, vert. 25.00

"Errors"

Many "errors," including imperforates, exist of Nos. 680-898. These unauthorized varieties were printed without the knowledge of the Belize postal service. There may be large quantities of them.

Mayan Monuments — A85

1983, Nov. 14 Litho. ***Perf. 13½x14***

680 A85 10c Altun Ha .25 .25
681 A85 15c Xunantunich .25 .25
682 A85 75c Cerros .60 .60
683 A85 $2 Lamanai 1.40 *1.75*
Nos. 680-683 (4) 2.50 2.85

Souvenir Sheet

684 A85 $3 Xunantunich, diff. 2.75 2.75

World Communications Year — A86

1983, Nov. 28 ***Perf. 14***

685 A86 10c Belmopan Earth Station .45 .30
686 A86 15c Telstar 2 .70 .30
687 A86 75c UPU monument 1.10 1.10
688 A86 $2 Mail boat 3.00 *4.50*
Nos. 685-688 (4) 5.25 6.20

Jaguar, World Wildlife Fund Emblem A87

1983, Dec. 9

689 A87 5c Sitting .60 *.90*
690 A87 10c Standing .75 .75
691 A87 85c Swimming 3.00 *3.75*
692 A87 $1 Walking 3.75 *4.25*
Nos. 689-692 (4) 8.10 9.65

Souvenir Sheet

693 A87 $3 Sitting in tree 5.00 5.00

No. 693 contains one stamp 45x28mm.

Christmas — A88

Scenes from mass celebrated by Pope John Paul II during visit, Mar.

1983, Dec. 22

694 A88 10c multicolored .60 .60
695 A88 15c multicolored .60 .60
696 A88 75c multicolored 1.25 1.25
697 A88 $2 multicolored 2.25 2.25
Nos. 694-697 (4) 4.70 4.70

Souvenir Sheet

698 A88 $3 multicolored 4.25 4.25

Foureye Butterflyfish — A89

1984, Feb. 27 ***Perf. 15***

699 A89 1c shown .35 .35
700 A89 2c Cushion star .50 .50
701 A89 3c Flower coral .35 .35
702 A89 4c Fairy basslets .50 .50
703 A89 5c Spanish hogfish .60 .60
704 A89 6c Star-eyed hermit crab .60 .60
705 A89 10c Sea fans, fire sponge .75 .75
706 A89 15c Blueheads .95 .95
707 A89 25c Blue-striped grunt 1.25 1.25
708 A89 50c Coral crab 1.75 1.75
709 A89 60c Tube sponge 1.75 1.75
710 A89 75c Brain coral 3.00 3.00
711 A89 $1 Yellow-tail snapper 1.75 1.75
712 A89 $2 Common lettuce slug 2.40 2.40
713 A89 $5 Yellow damselfish 2.75 2.75
714 A89 $10 Rock beauty 3.75 3.75
Nos. 699-714 (16) 23.00 23.00

For overprints and surcharge see Nos. 715-716, 762A-762C, 922.

The 50c, 60c, 75c, $1 exist inscribed "1986" in selvage.

1988, July ***Perf. 13½***

705a A89 10c .75 .75
706a A89 15c 1.00 1.00
707a A89 25c 1.40 1.40
708a A89 50c 2.10 2.10
709a A89 60c 2.10 2.10
711a A89 $1 2.75 2.75
Nos. 705a-711a (6) 10.10 10.10

Nos. 705, 708 Overprinted: "VISIT OF THE LORD / ARCHBISHOP OF CANTERBURY / 8th-11th MARCH 1984"

1984, Mar. 8

715 A89 10c multicolored 1.75 1.60
716 A89 50c multicolored 3.00 *3.25*

1984 Summer Olympics — A90

1984, Apr. 30 ***Perf. 13½x14***

717 A90 25c Shooting .35 .35
718 A90 75c Boxing 1.10 1.10
719 A90 $1 Running 1.50 1.50
720 A90 $2 Bicycling 2.75 2.75
Nos. 717-720 (4) 5.70 5.70

Souvenir Sheet

721 A90 $3 Discus 3.50 3.50

1984 Summer Olympics — A91

1984, Apr. 30 Litho. ***Perf. 14½***

Booklet Stamps

722 A91 5c Running .25 .25
a. Booklet pane of 4 1.10
723 A91 20c Javelin .30 .30
a. Booklet pane of 4 1.35
724 A91 25c Shot put .40 .40
a. Booklet pane of 4 1.75
725 A91 $2 Torch 2.75 2.75
a. Booklet pane of 4 11.50
Complete booklet, #722a-725a 16.00
Nos. 722-725 (4) 3.70 3.70

Ausipex '84 — A92

1984, Sept. 26 Litho. ***Perf. 15***

726 A92 15c Br. Honduras #3 .25 .25
727 A92 30c Bath-Bristol mail coach, 1784 .40 .40
728 A92 65c Penny Black, Rowland Hill .80 .80
729 A92 75c Railroad Pier, Commerce Bight .95 .95

Perf. 14

730 A92 $2 Royal Exhibition Bldgs. 2.00 2.00
Nos. 726-730 (5) 4.40 4.40

Souvenir Sheet

731 A92 $3 Australia #132, Br. Hond. #3 1.50 1.50

House of Tudor, 500th Anniv. — A93

White-fronted Parrot — A94

1984, Oct. 15 ***Perf. 14***

732 A93 50c Queen Victoria .35 .35
733 A93 50c Prince Albert .35 .35
a. Sheet of 4, 2 each, #732-733 1.50
734 A93 75c King George VI .55 .55
735 A93 75c Queen Elizabeth .55 .55
a. Sheet of 4, 2 each, #734-735 2.25
736 A93 $1 Prince Charles .75 .75
737 A93 $1 Princess Diana .75 .75
a. Sheet of 4, 2 each, #736-737 3.00
Nos. 732-737 (6) 3.30 3.30

Souvenir Sheet

738 Sheet of 2 2.25 2.25
a. A93 $1.50 Prince Philip 1.10 1.10
b. A93 $1.50 Queen Elizabeth II 1.10 1.10

1984, Nov. 1 ***Perf. 11***

Parrots: b, White-capped. c, Red-lored. d, Mealy. b, d, horiz.

739 Block of 4 12.50 12.50
a.-d. A94 $1 any single 2.75 2.75

Miniature Sheet

Perf. 14

740 A94 $3 Scarlet macaw 6.00 6.00

No. 740 contains one 48x32mm stamp.

Mayan Artifacts — A95

1984, Nov. 30 ***Perf. 15***

741 A95 25c Incense holder, 1450 .25 .25
742 A95 75c Cylindrical vase, 675 .75 .75
743 A95 $1 Tripod vase, 500 1.00 1.00
744 A95 $2 Kinich Ahau (sun god) 2.00 2.00
Nos. 741-744 (4) 4.00 4.00

Girl Guides 75th Anniv., Intl. Youth Year A96

1985, Mar. 15 Litho. ***Perf. 15***

745 A96 25c Gov.-Gen. Gordon .50 .50
746 A96 50c Camping .70 .70
747 A96 90c Map reading .95 .95
748 A96 $1.25 Students in laboratory 1.10 1.10
749 A96 $2 Lady Baden-Powell 1.50 1.50
Nos. 745-749 (5) 4.75 4.75

Each stamp shows the scouting and IYY emblems.

For overprints see Nos. 777-781.

Audubon Birth Bicentenary — A97

Illustrations by Audubon. 10c, 25c, 75c, $1, $5 vert.

Perf. 14, 15 ($1)

1985, May 30 Litho.

750 A97 10c White-tailed kite 1.00 1.00
751 A97 15c Cuvier's kinglet 1.40 1.40
752 A97 25c Painted bunting 1.40 1.40
753 A97 75c Belted kingfisher 1.40 1.40
754 A97 $1 Northern cardinal 1.40 1.40
755 A97 $3 Long-billed curlew 2.25 2.25
Nos. 750-755 (6) 8.85 8.85

Souvenir Sheet

Perf. 13½x14

756 A97 $5 Portrait of Audubon, 1826, by John Syme 7.00 7.00

No. 756 contains one 38x51mm stamp. See No. 909A.

Queen Mother, 85th Birthday — A98

Designs: 10c, The Queen Consort and Princess Elizabeth, 1928. 15c, Queen Mother, Elizabeth. 75c, Queen Mother waving a greeting. No. 760, Royal family photograph, christening of Prince Henry. $2, Holding the infant Prince Henry. No. 762, Queen Mother, diff.

1985, June 20

757 A98 10c shown .25 .25
758 A98 15c multicolored .25 .25
759 A98 75c multicolored 1.25 1.25
760 A98 $5 multicolored 3.75 3.75
Nos. 757-760 (4) 5.50 5.50

Souvenir Sheets

761	A98	$2 multicolored	2.50	2.50
762	A98	$5 multicolored	5.00	5.00

Nos. 761-762 contain one 38x51mm stamp. For overprints see Nos. 771-776.

Nos. 705-706, 708 Ovptd.

1985, June 24 *Perf. 15*

762A	A89	10c multicolored	2.00	1.00
762B	A89	15c multicolored	2.00	1.00
762C	A89	50c multicolored	3.25	*4.50*
		Nos. 762A-762C (3)	7.25	6.50

Miniature Sheet

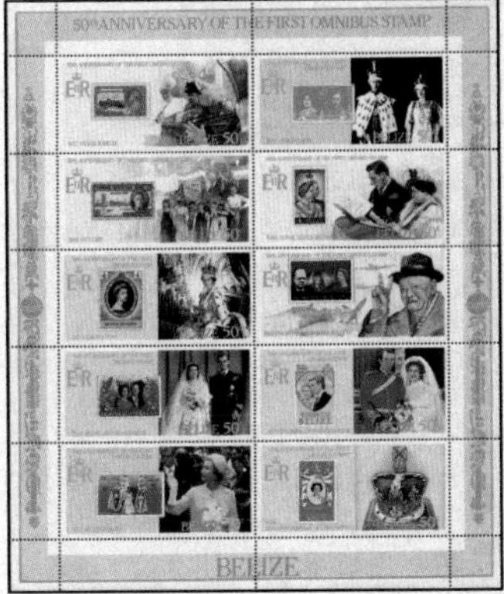

Commonwealth Stamp Omnibus, 50th Anniv. — A99

British Honduras Nos. 111-112, 127, 129, 143, 194, 307 and Belize Nos. 326, 385 and 397b on: a, George V and Queen Mary in an open carriage. b, George VI and Queen Consort Elizabeth crowned. c, Civilians celebrating the end of WWII. d, George VI and Queen Consort at mass service. e, Elizabeth II wearing robes of state and the imperial crown. f, Winston Churchill, WWII fighter planes. g, Bridal photograph of Elizabeth II and Prince Philip. h, Bridal photograph of Princess Anne and Capt. Mark Phillips. i, Elizabeth II. j, Imperial crown.

1985, July 25 *Perf. 14½x14*

763		Sheet of 10	7.00	7.00
a.-j.		A99 50c any single	.55	.55

Souvenir Sheet

Perf. 14

764	A99	$5 Elizabeth II coronation photograph	5.25	5.25

No. 764 contains one 38x51mm stamp. For overprints see Nos. 796-797.

British Post Office, 350th Anniv. A100

1985, Aug. 1 *Perf. 15*

765	A100	10c Postboy, letters	.55	.55
766	A100	15c Packet, privateer	.70	.70
767	A100	25c Duke of Marlborough	.85	.85
768	A100	75c Diana	1.50	1.50
769	A100	$1 Falmouth P.O. packet	1.50	1.50
770	A100	$3 S. S. Conway	2.75	2.75
		Nos. 765-770 (6)	7.85	7.85

Nos. 757-762 Overprinted

1985, Sept. 5 **Litho.** *Perf. 15*

771	A98	10c multicolored	.60	.60
772	A98	15c multicolored	.80	.80
773	A98	75c multicolored	1.75	1.75
774	A98	$5 multicolored	4.00	4.00
		Nos. 771-774 (4)	7.15	7.15

Souvenir Sheets

775	A98	$2 multicolored	2.25	2.25
776	A98	$5 multicolored	6.00	6.00

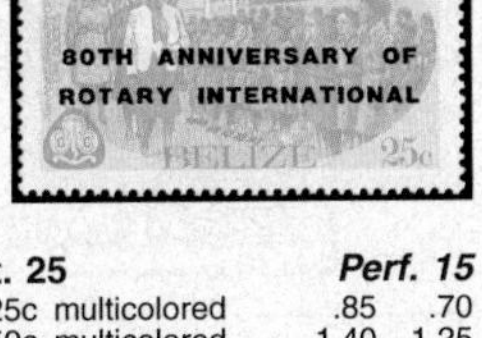

Nos. 745-749 Ovptd.

1985, Sept. 25 *Perf. 15*

777	A96	25c multicolored	.85	.70
778	A96	50c multicolored	1.40	1.25
779	A96	90c multicolored	1.75	1.60
780	A96	$1.25 multicolored	2.75	*3.00*
781	A96	$2 multicolored	3.50	*3.75*
		Nos. 777-781 (5)	10.25	10.30

Royal Visit — A101

1985, Oct. 9 *Perf. 15x14½*

782	A101	25c Royal and natl. flags	.40	.40
783	A101	75c Elizabeth II	1.20	1.20

Size: 81x38mm

784	A101	$4 Britannia	6.25	6.25
a.		Strip of 3, #782-784	8.00	8.00
		Nos. 782-784 (3)	7.85	7.85

Souvenir Sheet

Perf. 13½x14

785	A101	$5 Elizabeth II, diff.	6.00	6.00

No. 785 contains one 38x51mm stamp.

Disneyland, 30th Anniv. A102

Characters from "It's a Small World."

1985, Nov. 1 *Perf. 11*

786	A102	1c Royal Canadian Mounted Police	.25	.25
787	A102	2c American Indian	.25	.25
788	A102	3c Inca of the Andes	.25	.25
789	A102	4c Africa	.25	.25
790	A102	5c Far East	.25	.25
791	A102	6c Belize	.25	.25
792	A102	50c Balkans	2.25	2.25
793	A102	$1.50 Saudi Arabia	3.75	3.75
794	A102	$3 Japan	5.00	5.00
		Nos. 786-794 (9)	12.50	12.50

Souvenir Sheet

Perf. 14

795	A102	$4 Montage	9.50	9.50

Christmas.

Nos. 763-764 Overprinted

1985, Dec. 20 *Perf. 14½x14*

796		Sheet of 10	9.00	9.00
a.-j.		A99 50c, any single	.90	.90

Souvenir Sheet

797	A99	$5 multicolored	6.50	6.50

Women in Folk Costumes — A103

1986, Jan. 15 *Perf. 15*

798	A103	5c India	1.00	.45
799	A103	10c Maya	1.10	.45
800	A103	15c Garifuna	1.40	.50
801	A103	25c Creole	1.75	.50
802	A103	50c China	2.50	1.75
803	A103	75c Lebanon	3.00	3.00
804	A103	$1 Europe	3.00	3.00
805	A103	$2 South America	4.00	4.00
		Nos. 798-805 (8)	17.75	13.65

Souvenir Sheet

Perf. 14

806	A103	$5 Maya, So. America	10.50	10.50

No. 806 contains one 38x51mm stamp.

Miniature Sheet

A104

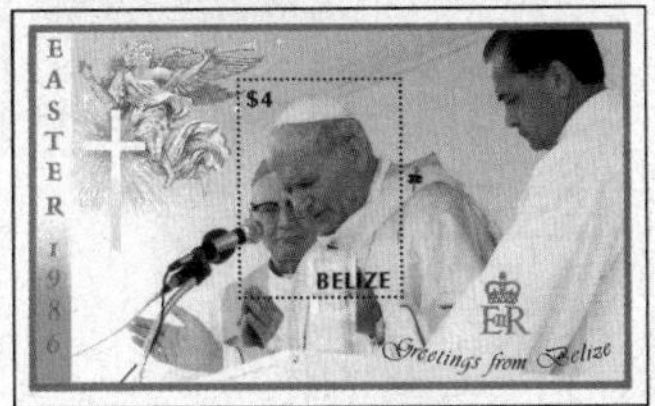

Easter — A105

Papal arms, crucifix and: a, Pius X. b, Benedict XV. c, Pius XI. d, Pius XII. e, John XXIII. f, Paul VI. g, John Paul I. h, John Paul II. No. 573, John Paul II saying mass in Belize.

1986, Apr. 15 **Litho.** *Perf. 11*

807		Sheet of 8 + label	13.00	13.00
a.-h.		A104 50c, any single	1.50	1.50

Souvenir Sheet

Perf. 14

808	A105	$4 multi	15.00	15.00

No. 807 contains center label picturing the Vatican, and papal crest.

Queen Elizabeth II, 60th Birthday — A106

A107

1986, Apr. 21 *Perf. 14*

809		Strip of 3	1.50	1.50
a.		A106 25c Age 2	.25	.25
b.		A106 50c Coronation	.50	.50
c.		A106 75c Riding horse	.75	.75
810	A106	$3 Wearing crown jewels	3.00	3.00

Souvenir Sheet

811	A107	$4 Portrait	4.00	4.00

A108

Halley's Comet — A109

1986, Apr. 30

812		Strip of 3	2.00	*3.00*
a.		A108 10c Planet-A probe	.40	*.80*
b.		A108 15c Sighting, 1910	.50	*.95*
c.		A108 50c Giotto probe	1.10	1.25
813		Strip of 3	5.00	*5.50*
a.		A108 75c Weather bureau	1.00	*1.10*
b.		A108 $1 US space telescope, shuttle	1.25	*1.40*
c.		A108 $2 Edmond Halley	2.75	*3.00*

Souvenir Sheet

814	A109	$4 Computer graphics	9.00	9.00

Miniature Sheet

A110

US Presidents — A111

1986, May *Perf. 11*

815 Sheet of 6 + 3 labels 5.25 5.25
a. A110 10c George Washington .30 .30
b. A110 20c John Adams .30 .30
c. A110 30c Thomas Jefferson .35 .35
d. A110 50c James Madison .50 .50
e. A110 $1.50 James Monroe 1.40 1.40
f. A110 $2 John Quincy Adams 1.90 1.90

Souvenir Sheet

Perf. 14

816 A111 $4 Washington 6.00 6.00

No. 815 contains 3 center labels picturing the great seal of the US.

Issue dates: No. 815, May 5; No. 816, May 7.

A112

Statue of Liberty, Cent. — A113

Designs: 25c, Bartholdi, statue. 50c, Statue, US centennial celebration, Philadelphia, 1876. 75c, Statue close-up, flags, 1886 unveiling. $3, Flags, statue close-up. $4, Statue, New York City skyline.

1986, May 15 *Perf. 14*

817 Strip of 3 4.50 4.50
a. A112 25c multicolored .35 .35
b. A112 75c multicolored .90 .90
c. A112 $3 multicolored 3.25 3.25
818 A112 50c multicolored .75 .75

Souvenir Sheet

819 A113 $4 multicolored 6.00 6.00

A114

AMERIPEX '86, Chicago, May 22-June 1 — A115

1986, May 22

820 Strip of 3 1.75 *2.25*
a. A114 10c British Honduras No. 3 .30 *.50*
b. A114 15c Stamp of 1981 .45 *.60*
c. A114 50c US No. C3a 1.00 *1.10*
821 Strip of 3 7.50 *8.50*
a. A114 75c USS Constitution 1.60 *2.10*
b. A114 $1 Liberty Bell 1.90 *2.40*
c. A114 $2 White House 4.00 4.00

Souvenir Sheet

822 A115 $4 Capitol Building 5.50 5.50

For overprints see Nos. 835-837.

1986 World Cup Soccer Championships, Mexico — A116

Designs: 25c, England vs. Brazil. 50c, Mexican player, Mayan statues. 75c, Belize players. $3, Aztec calendar stone, Mexico. $4, Flags composing soccer balls.

1986, June 16 **Litho.** *Perf. 11*

823 A116 25c multicolored 1.90 1.90
824 A116 50c multicolored 2.10 2.10
825 A116 75c multicolored 2.40 2.40
826 A116 $3 multicolored 2.75 2.75
Nos. 823-826 (4) 9.15 9.15

Souvenir Sheet

Perf. 14

827 A116 $4 multicolored 8.50 8.50

Nos. 823-826 printed in sheets of 8 plus label picturing Azteca Stadium, 2 each value per sheet.

Nos. 823-827 Overprinted

1986, Aug. 15

828 A116 25c multicolored .50 .50
829 A116 50c multicolored 1.10 1.10
830 A116 75c multicolored 1.50 1.50
831 A116 $3 multicolored 7.25 7.25
Nos. 828-831 (4) 10.35 10.35

Souvenir Sheet

832 A116 $4 multicolored 10.00 10.00

A117

Wedding of Prince Andrew and Sarah Ferguson A118

1986, July 23 *Perf. 14x14½*

833 Strip of 3 3.75 3.75
a. A117 25c Sarah .25 .25
b. A117 75c Andrew .70 .70
c. A117 $3 Couple 2.25 2.25

Souvenir Sheet

Perf. 14½

834 Sheet of 2 5.75 5.75
a. A118 $1 Sarah, diff. 1.50 1.50
b. A118 $3 Andrew, diff. 3.75 3.75

Size of No. 833c: 92x41mm.

Nos. 820-822 Overprinted

1986, Aug. 28 **Litho.** *Perf. 14*

835 Strip of 3 1.75 1.75
a. A114 10c multicolored .30 .30
b. A114 15c multicolored .30 .30
c. A114 50c multicolored .90 .90
836 Strip of 3 6.50 6.50
a. A114 75c multicolored 1.25 1.25
b. A114 $1 multicolored 1.75 1.75
c. A114 $2 multicolored 3.50 3.50

Souvenir Sheet

837 A115 $4 multicolored 8.00 8.00

A119

Intl. Peace Year — A120

Children.

1986, Oct. 3 **Litho.** *Perf. 14*

838 A119 25c Infant .40 .40
839 A119 50c Caucasians .70 .70
840 A119 75c Oriental 1.10 1.10
841 A119 $3 Indian, caucasian 4.00 4.00
Nos. 838-841 (4) 6.20 6.20

Souvenir Sheet

842 A120 $4 shown 6.00 6.00

Nos. 838-841 printed se-tenant in sheets of 8 (2 each) plus center label.

Fungi — A121

Toucans — A122

1986, Oct. 30 *Perf. 14*

843 A121 5c Amanita lilloi .45 .45
844 A122 10c Keel-billed toucan .45 .45
845 A121 20c Boletellus cubensis .60 .60
846 A122 25c Collared aracari .75 .75
847 A121 75c Psilocybe caerulescens 2.40 2.40
848 A122 $1 Emerald toucanet 3.00 3.00
849 A122 $1.25 Crimson-rumped toucan 3.50 3.50
850 A121 $2 Russula puiggarii 6.00 6.00
Nos. 843-850 (8) 17.15 17.15

Stamps of the same design printed in sheets of 8 plus center label picturing Audubon Society emblem. Value $18 each.

Christmas A123

Disney characters.

1986, Nov. 14 *Perf. 11*

851 Sheet of 9 13.50 13.50
a. A123 2c Jose Carioca .25 .25
b. A123 3c Carioca, Panchito, Donald .25 .25
c. A123 4c Daisy .25 .25
d. A123 5c Mickey, Minnie .25 .25
e. A123 6c Carioca playing music .25 .25
f. A123 50c Panchito, Donald 1.50 1.50
g. A123 65c Donald, Carioca 1.75 1.75
h. A123 $1.35 Donald 3.25 3.25
i. A123 $2 Goofy 5.00 5.00

Souvenir Sheet

Perf. 14

852 A123 $4 Donald 12.50 12.50

Marriage of Queen Elizabeth II and the Duke of Edinburgh, 40th Anniv. — A124

A125

1987, Oct. 7 **Litho.** *Perf. 15*

853 A124 25c Elizabeth, 1947 .30 .30
854 A124 75c Couple, c. 1980 .55 .55
855 A124 $1 Elizabeth, 1986 .65 .65
856 A124 $4 Wearing robes of Order of the Garter 1.25 1.25
Nos. 853-856 (4) 2.75 2.75

Souvenir Sheet

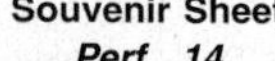

Perf. 14

857 A125 $6 shown 7.75 7.75

A126

America's Cup 1986-87 — A127

Yachts that competed in the 1987 finals.

1987, Oct. 21 *Perf. 15*

858 A126 25c America II .50 .50
859 A126 75c Stars and Stripes .65 .65
860 A126 $1 Australia II .80 .80
861 A126 $4 White Crusader 1.75 1.75
Nos. 858-861 (4) 3.70 3.70

Souvenir Sheet

Perf. 14

862 A127 $6 Australia II sails 8.25 8.25

Woodcarvings by Sir George Gabb (b. 1928) — A128

A129

1987, Nov. 4 *Perf. 15*

863 A128 25c Mother and Child .50 .50
864 A128 75c Standing Form .65 .65
865 A128 $1 Love-Doves .80 .80
866 A128 $4 Depiction of Music 1.75 1.75
Nos. 863-866 (4) 3.70 3.70

Souvenir Sheet

Perf. 14

867 A129 $6 African Heritage 6.75 6.75

A130

Indigenous Primates — A131

1987, Nov. 11 *Perf. 15*

868 A130 25c Black spider monkey .40 .40
869 A130 75c Male black howler .70 .70
870 A130 $1 Spider monkeys 1.00 1.00
871 A130 $4 Howler monkeys 2.50 2.50
Nos. 868-871 (4) 4.60 4.60

Souvenir Sheet

Perf. 14

872 A131 $6 Black spider, diff. 8.00 8.00

Natl. Girl Guides Movement, 50th Anniv. — A132

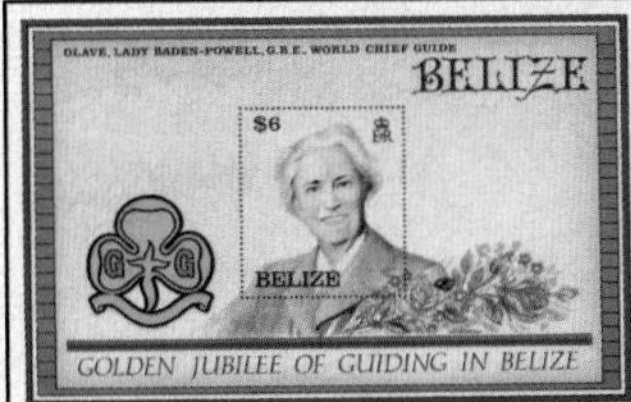

Lady Olave Baden-Powell, Founder — A133

1987, Nov. 25 *Perf. 15*

873 A132 25c Flag-bearers .70 .70
874 A132 75c Camping 1.25 1.25
875 A132 $1 On parade, camp 1.60 1.60
876 A132 $4 Olave Baden-Powell 4.75 4.75
Nos. 873-876 (4) 8.30 8.30

Souvenir Sheet

Perf. 14

877 A133 $6 Lady Olave, diff. 6.75 6.75

Intl. Year of Shelter for the Homeless A134

1987, Dec. 3 *Perf. 15*

878 A134 25c Tent dwellings .75 .75
879 A134 75c Urban slum 1.40 1.40
880 A134 $1 Tents, diff. 1.60 1.60
881 A134 $4 Construction 3.25 3.25
Nos. 878-881 (4) 7.00 7.00

Orchids A135

Illustrations from Reichenbachia, published by Henry F. Sander in 1886: 1c, Laelia euspatha. 2c, Cattleya citrina. 3c, Masdevallia bachousiana. 4c, Cypripedium tautzianum. 5c, Trichopilia suavis alba. 6c, Odontoglossum hebraicum. 7c, Cattleya trianaei schroederiana. 10c, Saccolabium giganteum. 30c, Cattleya warscewiczii. 50c, Chysis bractescens. 70c, Cattleya rochellensis. $1, Laelia elegans schilleriana. $1.50, Laelia anceps percivaliana. #895, $3, Laelia gouldiana. #896, $3, Odontoglossum roezlii. $5, Cattleya dowiana aurea.

1987, Dec. 16 **Litho.** *Perf. 14*

882-895 A135 Set of 14 20.00 20.00

Miniature Sheets

896-897 A135 Set of 2 17.50 17.50

Nos. 882-887 and 889-894 printed in blocks of six. Sheets of 14 contain 2 blocks of Nos. 882-887 plus 2 No. 888 and center label or 2 blocks of Nos. 889-894 plus center strip containing 2 No. 895 and center label. Center labels picture various illustrations from Reichenbachia.

Nos. 896-897 contain one 44x51mm stamp.

Miniature Sheet

Easter — A136

Stations of the Cross (in sequential order): a, Jesus condemned to death. b, Carries the cross. c, Falls the first time. d, Meets his mother, Mary. e, Cyrenean takes up the cross. f, Veronica wipes Jesus's face. g, Falls the second time. h, Consoles the women of Jerusalem. i, Falls the third time. j, Stripped of his robes. k, Nailed to the cross. l, Dies. m, Taken down from the cross. n, Laid in the sepulcher.

1988, Mar. 21 *Perf. 14*

898 Sheet of 14 + label 8.00 8.00
a.-n. A136 40c, any single .50 .50

A $6 souvenir sheet was prepared but not issued.

1988 Summer Olympics, Seoul — A137

1988, Aug. 15 **Litho.** *Perf. 14*

899 A137 10c Basketball 2.75 1.00
900 A137 25c Volleyball 1.40 .40
901 A137 60c Table tennis 1.40 .75
902 A137 75c Diving 1.40 .95
903 A137 $1 Judo 1.60 1.40
904 A137 $2 Field hockey 7.25 5.75
Nos. 899-904 (6) 15.80 10.25

Souvenir Sheet

905 A137 $3 Women's gymnastics 9.75 9.75

Intl. Red Cross, 125th Anniv. A138

1988, Nov. 18 **Litho.** *Perf. 14*

906 A138 60c Travelling nurse, 1912 4.50 1.90
907 A138 75c Hospital ship, ambulance boat, 1937 5.00 2.40
908 A138 $1 Ambulance, 1956 5.50 3.00
909 A138 $2 Ambulance plane, 1940 7.00 *8.00*
Nos. 906-909 (4) 22.00 15.30

Audubon Type of 1985

1988

909A A97 60c Painted bunting — —

Indigenous Small Animals — A139

1989 **Litho.** **Wmk. 384** *Perf. 14*

910 A139 10c Gibnut (agouti) 3.75 3.75

Unwmk.

911 A139 25c Four-eyed opossum, vert. 3.75 3.75
a. Wmk. 384 5.00 5.00
912 A139 50c Ant bear 4.50 3.50
913 A139 60c like 10c 4.50 3.75
914 A139 75c Antelope 4.50 3.75
915 A139 $2 Peccary 7.00 7.00
Nos. 910-915 (6) 28.00 25.50

Issued: 10c, 7/23; No. 911a, 12/6; others, 2/24.

Moon Landing, 20th Anniv.

Common Design Type

Apollo 9: 25c, Command service and lunar modules docked in space. 50c, Command service module. 75c, Mission emblem. $1, First manned lunar module in space. $5, Apollo 11 command service module.

Perf. 14x13½

1989, July 20 **Wmk. 384**

Size of Nos. 680-681: 29x29mm

916 CD342 25c multicolored 1.90 .60
917 CD342 50c multicolored 3.00 1.50
918 CD342 75c multicolored 3.50 2.40
919 CD342 $1 multicolored 4.00 4.00
Nos. 916-919 (4) 12.40 8.50

Souvenir Sheet

920 CD342 $5 multi 15.00 15.00

No. 920 Overprinted

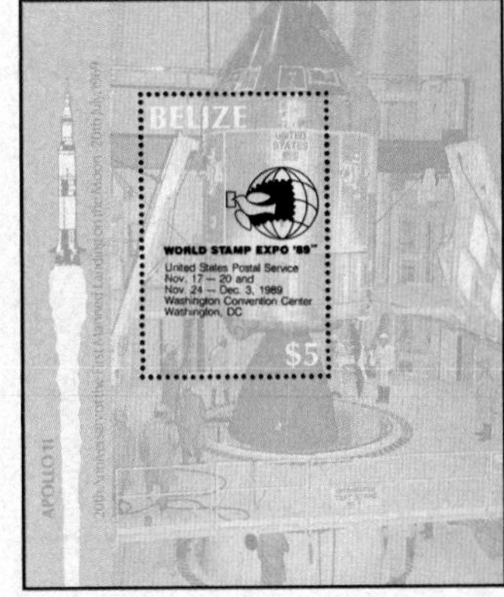

1989, Nov. 17 *Perf. 14x13½*

921 CD342 $5 multicolored 13.00 13.00

World Stamp Expo '89.

No. 704 Surcharged

1989, Nov. 15 *Perf. 15*

922 A89 5c on 6c multi *30.00*

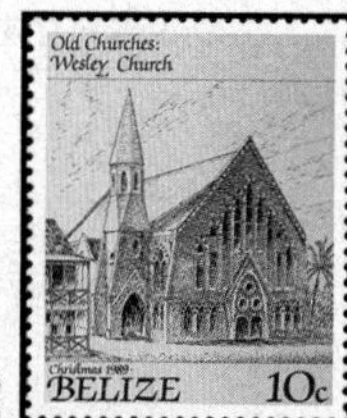

Christmas A140

Old churches.

Wmk. 384

1989, Dec. 13 Litho. *Perf. 14*

927 A140 10c Wesley .45 .25
928 A140 25c Baptist .55 .25
929 A140 60c St. John's Cathedral 1.25 .90
930 A140 75c St. Andrew's Presbyterian 1.75 1.25
931 A140 $1 Holy Redeemer Cathedral 2.00 2.00
Nos. 927-931 (5) 6.00 4.65

A141

Birds and Butterflies: 5c, Piranga leucoptera, Catonephele numilia female. 10c, Ramphastos sulfuratus, Nessaea aglaura. 15c, Fregata magnificens, Eurytides philolaus. 25c, Jabiru mycteria, Heliconius sapho. 30c, Ardea herodias, Colobura dirce. 50c, Icterus galbula, Hamadryas arethusia. 60c, Ara macao, Thecla regalis. 75c, Cyanerpes cyaneus, Callicore patelina. $1, Pulsatrix perspicillata, Caligo uranus. $2, Cyanocorax yncas, Philaethria dido. $5, Cathartes aura, Battus belus. $10, Pandion haliaetus, Papilio thoas.

Wmk. 373

1990, Mar. 1 Litho. *Perf. 14*

932 A141 5c multicolored .95 *1.10*
933 A141 10c multicolored 1.40 1.25
a. Inscribed "1993" 2.25 2.00
934 A141 15c multicolored 1.40 .65
935 A141 25c multicolored 1.40 .65
936 A141 30c multicolored 1.75 .85
937 A141 50c multicolored 2.00 1.00
938 A141 60c multicolored 2.25 1.10
939 A141 75c multicolored 2.50 1.40
940 A141 $1 multicolored 4.00 2.50
941 A141 $2 multicolored 4.50 4.50
942 A141 $5 multicolored 8.00 *8.50*
943 A141 $10 multicolored 13.50 *15.00*
Nos. 932-943 (12) 43.65 38.50

For overprints and surcharge see Nos. 944, 1021, 1030.

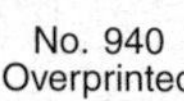

No. 940 Overprinted

1990, Mar. 1

944 A141 $1 multicolored 8.00 8.00

Turtles A142

Wmk. 373

1990, Aug. 8 Litho. *Perf. 14*

945 A142 10c Green 1.50 .70
946 A142 25c Hawksbill 2.40 .70
947 A142 60c Loggerhead 3.75 2.40
948 A142 75c Loggerhead, diff. 4.00 4.00
949 A142 $1 Bocatora 4.75 4.75
950 A142 $2 Hicatee 6.75 *8.75*
Nos. 945-950 (6) 23.15 21.30

Battle of Britain, 50th Anniv. A143

Aircraft.

1990, Sept. 15 Wmk. 384 *Perf. 13½*

951 A143 10c Fairey Battle 2.40 .90
952 A143 25c Bristol Beaufort 4.00 4.00
953 A143 60c Bristol Blenheim 4.75 4.75
954 A143 75c Armstrong-Whitworth Whitley 4.75 4.75
955 A143 $1 Vickers-Armstrong Wellington 4.75 4.75
956 A143 $2 Handley-Page Hampden 6.00 6.00
Nos. 951-956 (6) 26.65 25.15

Orchids — A144

1990, Nov. 1 Wmk. 384 *Perf. 14*

957 A144 25c Cattleya bowringiana 1.50 .30
958 A144 50c Rhyncholaelia digbyana 2.40 .70
959 A144 60c Sobralia macrantha 2.50 1.60
960 A144 75c Chysis bractescens 2.50 1.60
961 A144 $1 Vanilla planifolia 3.50 3.50
962 A144 $2 Epidendrum polyanthum 5.00 5.00
Nos. 957-962 (6) 17.40 12.70

Christmas.

Indigenous Fauna — A145

1991, Apr. 10

963 A145 25c Iguana 1.60 .50
964 A145 50c Crocodile 2.50 1.25
965 A145 60c Manatee 3.00 3.00
966 A145 75c Boa constrictor 3.25 3.25
967 A145 $1 Tapir 4.00 4.00
968 A145 $2 Jaguar 5.50 5.50
Nos. 963-968 (6) 19.85 17.50

Elizabeth & Philip, Birthdays
Common Design Types

1991, June 17 *Perf. 14½*

969 CD345 $1 multicolored 1.75 1.75
970 CD346 $1 multicolored 1.75 1.75
a. Pair, #969-970 + label 3.75 3.75

Hurricanes — A146

1991, July 31 Wmk. 373 *Perf. 14*

971 A146 60c Weather radar 2.50 1.75
972 A146 75c Weather observation station 2.75 2.00
973 A146 $1 Scene after hurricane 2.75 2.75
974 A146 $2 Hurricane Gilbert 4.25 4.25
Nos. 971-974 (4) 12.25 10.75

Independence, 10th Anniv. — A147

Famous Men: 25c, Thomas V. Ramos (1887-1955). 60c, Sir Isaiah Morter (1860-1924). 75c, Antonio Soberanis (1897-1975). $1, Santiago Ricalde (1920-1975).

1991, Sept. 4 Wmk. 384

975 A147 25c multicolored 1.00 .40
976 A147 60c multicolored 2.10 2.10
977 A147 75c multicolored 2.10 2.10
978 A147 $1 multicolored 2.50 2.50
Nos. 975-978 (4) 7.70 7.10

Folktales A148

Christmas.

Wmk. 373

1991, Nov. 6 Litho. *Perf. 14*

979 A148 25c Anansi 2.00 .45
980 A148 50c Jack-O-Lantern 2.75 1.00
981 A148 60c Tata Duende, vert. 3.25 2.40
982 A148 75c Xtabai 3.25 2.40
983 A148 $1 Warrie Massa, vert. 3.75 3.75
984 A148 $2 Old Heg 5.75 5.75
Nos. 979-984 (6) 20.75 15.75

See Nos. 999-1002.

Orchids — A149

Easter: 25c, Gongora quinquenervis. 50c, Oncidium sphacelatum. 60c, Encyclia bractescens. 75c, Epidendrum ciliare. $1, Psygmorchis pusilla. $2, Galeandra batemanii.

1992, Apr. 1

985 A149 25c multicolored 1.75 .50
986 A149 50c multicolored 3.00 1.10
987 A149 60c multicolored 3.25 3.25
988 A149 75c multicolored 3.25 3.25
989 A149 $1 multicolored 3.75 *3.75*
990 A149 $2 multicolored 5.50 *7.50*
Nos. 985-990 (6) 20.50 19.35

Famous Belizeans A150

Designs: 25c, Gwendolyn Lizarraga, MBE (1901-75). 60c, Rafael Fonseca, CMG, OBE (1921-78). 75c, Vivian Seay, MBE (1881-1971). $1, Samuel A. Haynes (1898-1971).

1992, Aug. 26 *Perf. 13x12½*

991 A150 25c multicolored 1.00 .40
992 A150 60c multicolored 2.10 2.10
993 A150 75c multicolored 2.40 2.40
994 A150 $1 multicolored 2.75 2.75
Nos. 991-994 (4) 8.25 7.65

See Nos. 1013-1016.

Discovery of America, 500th Anniv. — A151

Mayan ruins, modern buildings: 25c, Xunantunich, National Assembly. 60c, Altun Ha, Supreme Court Building. 75c, Santa Rita, Tower Hill Sugar Factory. $5, Lamanai, The Citrus Company.

Perf. 13½x14

1992, Oct. 1 Litho. Wmk. 384

995 A151 25c multicolored 1.60 .40
996 A151 60c multicolored 2.50 1.60
997 A151 75c multicolored 2.50 2.00
998 A151 $5 multicolored 13.50 13.50
Nos. 995-998 (4) 20.10 17.50

Folklore Type of 1991

Christmas.

Perf. 13x12½

1992, Nov. 16 Litho. Wmk. 373

999 A148 25c Hashishi Pampi .55 .30
1000 A148 60c Cadejo 1.10 1.10
1001 A148 $1 La Sucia, vert. 1.75 1.75
1002 A148 $5 Sisimito 7.50 7.50
Nos. 999-1002 (4) 10.90 10.65

Royal Air Force, 75th Anniv.
Common Design Type

Designs: 25c, Aerospatiale Puma. 50c, British Aerospace Harrier. 60c, DeHavilland Mosquito. 75c, Avro Lancaster. $1, Consolidated Liberator. $3, Short Stirling.

Wmk. 373

1993, Apr. 1 Litho. *Perf. 14*

1003 CD350 25c multicolored 2.00 1.25
1004 CD350 50c multicolored 2.40 1.75
1005 CD350 60c multicolored 2.75 2.10
1006 CD350 75c multicolored 2.75 2.10
1007 CD350 $1 multicolored 3.25 *3.75*
1008 CD350 $3 multicolored 6.25 *7.75*
Nos. 1003-1008 (6) 19.40 18.70

1993 World Orchid Conference, Glasgow — A152

Perf. 14½x14

1993, Apr. 24 Litho. Wmk. 384

1009 A152 25c Lycaste aromatica .75 .35
1010 A152 60c Sobralia decora 1.50 1.10
1011 A152 $1 Maxillaria alba 2.00 1.90
1012 A152 $2 Brassavola nodosa 3.50 3.50
Nos. 1009-1012 (4) 7.75 6.85

Famous Belizeans Type of 1992

Designs: 25c, Herbert Watkin Beaumont (1880-1978). 60c, Dr. Selvyn Walford Young (1899-1977). 75c, Cleopatra White (1898-1987). $1, Dr. Karl Heusner (1872-1960).

Wmk. 384

1993, Aug. 11 Litho. *Perf. 14*

1013 A150 25c multicolored .60 .35
1014 A150 60c multicolored 1.25 1.25
1015 A150 75c multicolored 1.40 1.40
1016 A150 $1 multicolored 1.75 1.75
Nos. 1013-1016 (4) 5.00 4.75

Christmas — A153

Wmk. 373

1993, Nov. 3 Litho. *Perf. 14*

1017 A153 25c Boom and chime band 1.25 .50
1018 A153 60c John Canoe dance 2.40 1.50
1019 A153 75c Cortez dance 2.40 1.50
1020 A153 $2 Maya Musical Group 6.00 6.00
Nos. 1017-1020 (4) 12.05 9.50

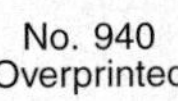

No. 940 Overprinted

Wmk. 373

1994, Feb. 18 Litho. *Perf. 14*

1021 A141 $1 multicolored 4.75 4.25

Royal Visit — A154

Designs: 25c, Belize, United Kingdom Flags. 60c, Queen Elizabeth II wearing hat. 75c, Queen. $1, Queen, Prince Philip.

Perf. 14½x14

1994, Feb. 24 Litho. Wmk. 373

1022 A154 25c multicolored 1.90 .90
1023 A154 60c multicolored 2.50 1.90
1024 A154 75c multicolored 3.25 2.25
1025 A154 $1 multicolored 3.75 3.75
Nos. 1022-1025 (4) 11.40 8.80

Bats A155

Wmk. 384

1994, May 30 Litho. *Perf. 14*

1026 A155 25c Insect feeder .95 .30
1027 A155 60c Fruit feeder 1.60 .90
1028 A155 75c Fish feeder 2.00 1.10
1029 A155 $2 Common vampire 4.50 4.50
Nos. 1026-1029 (4) 9.05 6.80

No. 939 Surcharged

Wmk. 373

1994, Aug. 18 Litho. *Perf. 14*

1030 A141 10c on 75c multi 2.75 2.75

Christmas A156

Orchids: 25c, Cycnoches chlorochilon. 60c, Brassavolas cucullata. 75c, Sobralia mucronata. $1, Nidema Boothii.

1994, Nov. 7 Wmk. 384

1031 A156 25c multicolored 1.25 .60
1032 A156 60c multicolored 1.75 1.25
1033 A156 75c multicolored 2.10 2.10
1034 A156 $1 multicolored 2.40 *3.00*
Nos. 1031-1034 (4) 7.50 6.95

For overprints see Nos. 1051-1054.

Insects A157

Wmk. 373

1995, Jan. 11 Litho. *Perf. 14*

Without date imprint

1035 A157 5c Ground beetle .75 *.90*
1036 A157 10c Harlequin beetle .85 *.90*
1037 A157 15c Giant water bug .90 .85
1038 A157 25c Peanut-head bug 1.25 .25
1039 A157 30c Coconut weevil 1.00 .30
1040 A157 50c Mantis 1.60 1.75
1041 A157 60c Tarantula wasp 1.75 1.60
1042 A157 75c Rhinoceros beetle 2.25 1.90
1043 A157 $1 Metallic wood borer 2.50 2.25
1044 A157 $2 Dobson fly 6.00 6.00
1045 A157 $5 Click beetle 9.75 9.75
1046 A157 $10 Long-horned beetle 17.00 17.00
Nos. 1035-1046 (12) 45.60 43.45

For overprints see Nos. 1063-1066.

1996, Oct. 14

Inscribed "1996"

1035a	A157	5c	.75	*.90*
1036a	A157	10c	.85	*.90*
1037a	A157	15c	.90	.85
1038a	A157	25c	1.25	.25
1039a	A157	30c	1.00	.30
1040a	A157	50c	1.60	1.75
1041a	A157	60c	1.75	1.60
1042a	A157	75c	2.25	1.90
1043a	A157	$1	2.50	2.25
1044a	A157	$2	6.00	6.00
1045a	A157	$5	9.75	9.75
1046a	A157	$10	17.00	17.00
Nos. 1035a-1046a (12)			45.60	43.45

End of World War II, 50th Anniv.

Common Design Type

Designs: 25c, War Memorial Cenotaph. 60c, Remembrance Sunday. 75c, British Honduras Forestry Unit. $1, Wellington Bomber.

Wmk. 373

1995, May 8 Litho. *Perf. 13½*

1047 CD351 25c multicolored .60 .35
1048 CD351 60c multicolored 1.75 1.40
1049 CD351 75c multicolored 1.75 1.75
1050 CD351 $1 multicolored 2.40 2.40
Nos. 1047-1050 (4) 6.50 5.90

Nos. 1031-1034 Ovptd. in Blue

1995, Sept. 1 Wmk. 384 *Perf. 14*

1051 A156 25c on No. 1031 1.25 .65
1052 A156 60c on No. 1032 2.25 2.25
1053 A156 75c on No. 1033 2.50 2.50
1054 A156 $1 on No. 1034 3.25 3.25
Nos. 1051-1054 (4) 9.25 8.65

UN, 50th Anniv.

Common Design Type

Designs: 25c, M113 Light reconnaissance vehicle. 60c, Sultan, armored command vehicle. 75c, Leyland/DAF 8x4 "Drops" vehicle. $2, Warrior infantry combat vehicle.

Wmk. 384

1995, Oct. 24 Litho. *Perf. 14*

1055 CD353 25c multicolored .45 .35
1056 CD353 60c multicolored 1.10 1.10
1057 CD353 75c multicolored 1.40 1.40
1058 CD353 $2 multicolored 2.75 2.75
Nos. 1055-1058 (4) 5.70 5.60

Christmas A158

Doves: 25c, Blue ground. 60c, White-fronted. 75c, Ruddy ground. $1, White-winged.

1995, Nov. 6 Wmk. 373

1059 A158 25c multicolored .70 .30
1060 A158 60c multicolored 1.40 1.40
1061 A158 75c multicolored 1.75 1.75
1062 A158 $1 multicolored 2.50 2.50
Nos. 1059-1062 (4) 6.35 5.95

Nos. 1037, 1039-1040, 1044 Ovptd.

Wmk. 373

1996, May 17 Litho. *Perf. 14*

1063 A157 15c on #1037 .40 .25
1064 A157 30c on #1039 .90 .50
1065 A157 50c on #1040 1.10 .80
1066 A157 $2 on #1044 3.75 3.75
Nos. 1063-1066 (4) 6.15 5.30

CAPEX '96 A159

Trains: 25c, Unloading banana train onto freighter, Commerce Bight Pier. 60c, Engine No. 1, Stann Creek Station. 75c, Mahogany log train, Hunslet 0-6-0 Side Tank Engine No. 4. $3, LMS Jubilee Class 4-6-0 Locomotive No. 5602 "British Honduras."

Perf. 13½x13

1996, June 6 Litho. Wmk. 373

1067 A159 25c multicolored 1.40 .65
1068 A159 60c multicolored 2.10 1.75
1069 A159 75c multicolored 2.10 1.75
1070 A159 $3 multicolored 5.00 5.00
Nos. 1067-1070 (4) 10.60 9.15

Christmas — A160

Orchids: 25c, Epidendrum stamfordianum. 60c, Oncidium carthagenense. 75c, Oerstedella verrucosa. $1, Coryanthes speciosa.

Wmk. 373

1996, Nov. 6 Litho. *Perf. 14*

1071 A160 25c multicolored 1.00 .35
1072 A160 60c multicolored 1.50 1.10
1073 A160 75c multicolored 1.75 1.75
1074 A160 $1 multicolored 2.50 2.50
Nos. 1071-1074 (4) 6.75 5.70

Hong Kong '97 A161

Cattle: 25c, Red poll. 60c, Brahman. 75c, Longhorn. $1, Charbray.

Wmk. 373

1997, Feb. 12 Litho. *Perf. 14*

1075 A161 25c multicolored .90 .40
1076 A161 60c multicolored 1.40 1.40
1077 A161 75c multicolored 1.90 1.60
1078 A161 $1 multicolored 2.00 2.00
Nos. 1075-1078 (4) 6.20 5.40

Snakes — A162 Howler Monkeys — A163

25c, Coral snake. 60c, Green vine snake. 75c, Yellow-jawed tommygoff. $1, Speckled racer.

Wmk. 373

1997, May 28 Litho. *Perf. 14*

1079 A162 25c multicolored .95 .35
1080 A162 60c multicolored 1.40 1.10
1081 A162 75c multicolored 1.60 1.60
1082 A162 $1 multicolored 2.00 2.00
Nos. 1079-1082 (4) 5.95 5.05

Wmk. 373

1997, Aug. 13 Litho. *Perf. 14*

World Wildlife Fund: 10c, Adult male. 25c, Female feeding. 60c, Female with infant. 75c, Juvenile feeding.

1083 A163 10c multicolored .55 .50
1084 A163 25c multicolored .75 .75
1085 A163 60c multicolored 1.25 1.25
1086 A163 75c multicolored 1.50 *2.25*
Nos. 1083-1086 (4) 4.05 4.75

Christmas A164

Orchids: 25c, Maxillaria elatior. 60c, Dimerandra emarginata. 75c, Macradenia brassavolae. $1, Ornithocephalus gladiatus.

Wmk. 373

1997, Nov. 21 Litho. *Perf. 14*

1087 A164 25c multicolored .75 .40
1088 A164 60c multicolored 1.40 .75
1089 A164 75c multicolored 1.90 1.90
1090 A164 $1 multicolored 2.50 2.50
Nos. 1087-1090 (4) 6.55 5.55

Diana, Princess of Wales (1961-97)

Common Design Type

Designs: a, Up close portrait, smiling. b, Wearing evening dress. c, Up close portrait, serious. d, Holding bouquet of flowers.

Perf. 14½x14

1998, Mar. 31 Litho. Wmk. 373

1091 CD355 $1 Sheet of 4, #a.-d. 5.50 5.50

University of West Indies, 50th Anniv. A165

Wmk. 373

1998, July 22 Litho. *Perf. 13*

1092 A165 $1 multicolored 1.75 1.75

Organization of American States, 50th Anniv. A166

Designs: 25c, Children working computers, connecting high schools to the internet. $1, Map of Central America, Inter American Drug Abuse Control Commission.

1998, July 22

1093 A166 25c multicolored .50 .50
1094 A166 $1 multicolored 2.00 2.00

Battle of St. George's Cay, Bicent. A167

Views of Old Belize from St. George, vert: No. 1095, Woman, child beside small boat. No. 1096, Soldiers at dock, cannon. No. 1097, Cannon balls, cannon, boats in water.

25c, Bayman gun flats. 60c, Bayman sloops. 75c, Schooners. $1, HMS Merlin. $2, Spanish flagship.

1998, Aug. 5 *Perf. 13½*

1095 A167 10c multicolored .55 *.90*
1096 A167 10c multicolored .55 *.90*
1097 A167 10c multicolored .55 *.90*
a. Strip of 3, #1095-1097 1.75 *3.00*
1098 A167 25c multicolored 1.25 .55
1099 A167 60c multicolored 1.40 1.40
1100 A167 75c multicolored 1.60 1.60
1101 A167 $1 multicolored 2.00 2.00
1102 A167 $2 multicolored 3.50 *4.50*
Nos. 1095-1102 (8) 11.40 12.75

A168

Christmas — Flowers: 25c, Brassia maculata. 60c, Encyclia radiata. 75c, Stanhopea ecornuta. $1, Isochilius carnosiflorus.

1998, Nov. 4 *Perf. 14*

1103 A168 25c multicolored .30 .25
1104 A168 60c multicolored .75 .65
1105 A168 75c multicolored .85 .85
1106 A168 $1 multicolored 1.25 1.25
Nos. 1103-1106 (4) 3.15 3.00

A169

Easter — Orchids: 10c, Eucharis grandiflora. 25c, Hippeastrum puniceum. 60c, Zephyranthes citrina. $1, Hymenocallis littoralis.

1999, Mar. 17 *Perf. 13*

1107 A169 10c multicolored .30 .25
1108 A169 25c multicolored .90 .70
1109 A169 60c multicolored 1.10 .95
1110 A169 $1 multicolored 1.40 1.40
Nos. 1107-1110 (4) 3.70 3.30

UPU, 125th Anniv. A170

1999, Oct. 18 *Perf. 13¼*

1111 A170 25c Bicycle .75 .60
1112 A170 60c Truck 1.00 .80
1113 A170 75c Mailship "Dee" 1.25 1.10
1114 A170 $1 Airplane 1.60 *2.00*
Nos. 1111-1114 (4) 4.60 4.50

Christmas — A171

Designs: 25c, Holy Family with Jesus and St. John, by school of Peter Paul Rubens. 60c, The Holy Family with St. John, by unknown artist. 75c, Madonna with Child, St. John and Angel, by unknown artist. $1, Madonna with Child and St. John by Andrea da Salerno.

1999, Dec. 6 *Perf. 14*

1115 A171 25c multicolored .55 .55
1116 A171 60c multicolored .85 .75
1117 A171 75c multicolored 1.10 1.10
1118 A171 $1 multicolored 1.50 *1.75*
Nos. 1115-1118 (4) 4.00 4.15

Fauna A172

Wmk. 373

2000, Feb. 15 Litho. *Perf. 14*

Without date imprint

1119 A172 5c Iguana .35 .30
1120 A172 10c Gibnut .35 .30
1121 A172 15c Howler monkey .40 .30
1122 A172 25c Ant bear .45 .35
1123 A172 30c Hawksbill turtle .55 .55
1124 A172 50c Antelope .85 .85
1125 A172 60c Jaguar 1.10 1.10
1126 A172 75c Manatee 1.40 1.40
1127 A172 $1 Crocodile 1.75 1.75
1128 A172 $2 Tapir 2.50 2.50
1129 A172 $5 Collared peccary 7.25 7.25
1130 A172 $10 Boa constrictor 13.00 13.00
Nos. 1119-1130 (12) 29.95 29.65

For surcharges see Nos. 1181-1183.

2003, Sept. Inscribed "2003"

1120a A172 10c .35 .30
1121a A172 15c .40 .30
1122a A172 25c .45 .35
1123a A172 30c .55 .35
1124a A172 50c .90 .85
1125a A172 60c 1.20 1.10
1126a A172 75c 1.50 1.40
1127a A172 $1 1.90 1.75
1128a A172 $2 3.00 2.50
1129a A172 $5 8.00 8.00
1130a A172 $10 15.00 15.00
Nos. 1120a-1130a (11) 33.25 31.90

Fruits A173

Wmk. 373

2000, Apr. 19 Litho. *Perf. 14*

1131 A173 25c Mango .65 .40
1132 A173 60c Cashew 1.10 1.10
1133 A173 75c Papaya 1.40 1.40
1134 A173 $1 Banana 1.75 *2.00*
Nos. 1131-1134 (4) 4.90 4.90

People's United Party, 50th Anniv. A174

10c, Birth of party politics, 9/29/50. 25c, People gain voting rights, 4/28/54. 60c, Self-government, 1/1/64. 75c, Building the new capital Belmopan, 1967-70. $1, Independence, 9/21/81.

Perf. 13¼x13¾

2000, Sept. 18 Litho. Wmk. 373

1135-1139 A174 Set of 5 5.25 5.25

Christmas A175

Orchids: 25c, Bletia purpurea. 60c, Cyrtopodium punctata. 75c, Cycnoches egertonianum. $1, Catasetum integerrimum.

Perf. 14½x14¼

2000 Litho. Wmk. 373

1140-1143 A175 Set of 4 6.00 6.00

Independence, 20th Anniv. — A176

Designs: 25c, Education. 60c, Shrimp farming. 75c, Privassion Cascade, vert. $2, Map, vert.

Wmk. 373

2001, Oct. 3 Litho. *Perf. 14*

1144-1147 A176 Set of 4 7.50 7.50

Christmas A177

Orchids: 25c, Sobralia fragrans. 60c, Encyclia cordigera. 75c, Maxillaria fulgens. $1, Epidendrum nocturnum.

Wmk. 373

2001, Dec. 28 Litho. *Perf. 14*

1148-1151 A177 Set of 4 5.75 5.75

Reign Of Queen Elizabeth II, 50th Anniv. Issue

Common Design Type

Designs: Nos. 1152, 1156a, 25c, Princess Elizabeth, 1943. Nos. 1153, 1156b, 60c, In 1952. Nos. 1154, 1156c, 75c, With Prince Charles and Princess Anne. Nos. 1155, 1156d, $1, In 1995. No. 1156e, $5, 1955 portrait by Annigoni (38x50mm).

Perf. 14¼x14½, 13¾ (#1156e)

2002, Feb. 6 Litho. Wmk. 373

With Gold Frames

1152 CD360 25c multicolored .25 .25
1153 CD360 60c multicolored 1.00 .90
1154 CD360 75c multicolored 1.25 1.10
1155 CD360 $1 multicolored 1.50 1.40
Nos. 1152-1155 (4) 4.00 3.65

Souvenir Sheet

Without Gold Frames

1156 CD360 Sheet of 5, #a-e 11.50 11.50

Christmas — A178

Orchids: 25c, Dichaea neglecta. 50c, Epidendrum hawkesii. 60c, Encyclia belizensis. 75c, Eriopsis biloba. $1, Harbenaria monorrhiza. $2, Mormodes buccinator.

Wmk. 373

2002, Dec. 12 Litho. *Perf. 14*

1157-1162 A178 Set of 6 12.00 11.50

Belize Defense Force, 25th Anniv. A179

Wmk. 373

2003, Jan. 29 Litho. *Perf. 14*

1163 A179 25c multi .65 .40

Powered Flight, Cent. — A180

Designs: 25c, Avro Shackleton Mk 3. 60c, Lockheed L-749 Constellation. 75c, SEPECAT Jaguar GR 1. $3, British Aerospace Harrier GR 3.

$5, Spirit of St. Louis lands in Belize, Dec. 30, 1927.

Wmk. 373

2003, Sept. 17 Litho. *Perf. 14*

Stamps + Label

1164-1167 A180 Set of 4 8.50 8.50

Souvenir Sheet

1168 A180 $5 multi 9.00 9.00

For surcharge see No. 1185.

Christmas A181

Scarlet macaw: 25c, Close-up of head. 60c, Pair on tree. 75c, Three eating clay. $5, Pair in flight.

2003, Nov. 5 *Perf. 13¾*

1169-1172 A181 Set of 4 15.00 15.00

For surcharge see No. 1184.

Whale Shark A182

Various depictions of whale shark: 25c, 60c, 75c, $5.

Wmk. 373

2004, Aug. 16 Litho. *Perf. 13½*

1173-1176 A182 Set of 4 12.00 12.00

Worldwide Fund for Nature (WWF) — A183

Various depictions of Central American wooly opossum with denominations in: 25c, Green, vert. 60c, Blue, vert. 75c, Orange. $5, Red violet.

Perf. 14¼x14, 14x14¼

2004, Nov. 8 Litho. Wmk. 373
1177-1180 A183 Set of 4 11.00 11.00

Nos. 1124-1126 Surcharged

Wmk. 373

2004-2005 Litho. *Perf. 14*
1181 A172 10c on 50c #1124 .25 .25
1182 A172 10c on 60c #1125 ('05) .25 .25
1183 A172 15c on 75c #1126 .25 .25
Nos. 1181-1183 (3) .75 .75

Issued: Nos. 1181, 1183, 10/4/04. No. 1182, 1/31/05.
Nos. 1181 and 1182 exist dated "2003."

No. 1170 Surcharged

Wmk. 373

2005, July 15 Litho. *Perf. 13¾*
1184 A181 10c on 60c #1170 — —

No. 1165 Surcharged

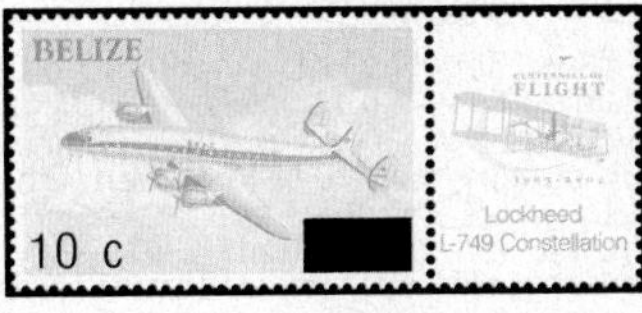

Wmk. 373

2005, July Litho. *Perf. 14*
1185 A180 10c on 60c #1165 — —

Pope John Paul II (1920-2005) A184

Wmk. 373

2005, Aug. 18 Litho. *Perf. 14*
1186 A184 $1 multi 1.50 1.50

Ecological and Heritage Sites — A185

Designs: 5c, Guanacaste National Park. 10c, Government House of Culture. 15c, Lubaantun Archaeological Reserve. 25c, Altun Ha Archaeological Reserve. 30c, Nohoch Che'n Archaeological Reserve. 50c, Goff's Caye. 60c, Nlue Hole Natural Monument. 75c, Lamanai Archaeological Reserve. $1, Half Moon Caye and Lighthouse. $2, Placencia Peninsula. $5, Museum of Belize. $10, Cerros Archaeological Reserve.

2005, Aug. 31 Wmk. 373 *Perf. 14*
1187 A185 5c multi .25 .25
1188 A185 10c multi .25 .25
1189 A185 15c multi .25 .25
1190 A185 25c multi .30 .30
a. Wmk. 406 .30 .30
1191 A185 30c multi .35 .35
1192 A185 50c multi .60 .60
1193 A185 60c multi .70 .70
1194 A185 75c multi .85 .85
1195 A185 $1 multi 1.10 1.10
1196 A185 $2 multi 2.50 2.50
1197 A185 $5 multi 5.50 5.50
1198 A185 $10 multi 11.00 11.00
Nos. 1187-1198 (12) 23.65 23.65

Issued: No. 1190a, Feb. 2009.

Europa Stamps, 50th Anniv. A186

Stamps commemorating 125th anniv. of the UPU: 25c, #1111. 75c, #1112. $3, #1113. $5, #1114.

Perf. 13x13¼

2006, Mar. 22 Litho. Unwmk.
1199-1202 A186 Set of 4 12.00 12.00
1202a Souvenir sheet, #1199-1202 12.00 12.00

Independence, 25th Anniv. — A187

Designs: 25c, Prime Minister George Price. 30c, National symbols, horiz. 60c, Map of Belize. $1, 1981 Independence logo. $5, Constitution, horiz.

Perf. 13¼x12½, 12½x13¼

2006, July 3 Litho. Wmk. 373
1203-1207 A187 Set of 5 9.00 9.00

Breast Cancer Research — A188

2006, Oct. 26 Litho. *Perf. 13½x13¼*
1208 A188 $1 multi 2.50 2.50

Art by Belizean Artists — A189

Designs: 25c, Sleeping Giant, sculpture, by George Gabb. 30c, Market Scene, by Louis Belisle, horiz. 60c, The Original Turtle Shell Band, by Pen Cayetano, horiz. 75c, Have Some Coconut Water, by Benjamin Nicholas. $2, Untitled sculpture by Reuben Miguel. $3, Mural at Corozal Town Hall, by Manuel Villamor.

Wmk. 373

2007, May 9 Litho. *Perf. 14*
1209-1214 A189 Set of 6 7.00 7.00

Abolition of the Slave Trade Act, Bicent. — A190

Perf. 12½x13

2007, Sept. 26 Litho. Wmk. 373
1215 A190 $2 multi 2.40 2.40

University of the West Indies, 60th Anniv. A191

Wmk. 373

2008, Nov. 14 Litho. *Perf. 13*
1216 A191 $1 multi 1.50 1.50

Endangered Birds — A192

Designs: 25c, Yellow-headed parrot. 60c, Harpy eagle. $1, Slate-colored seedeater. $2, Green honeycreeper. $5, Great curassow.

Wmk. 406

2009, July 8 Litho. *Perf. 12½*
1217-1221 A192 Set of 5 10.00 10.00

Christmas — A193

Orchids: 25c, Encyclia polybulbon. 60c, Oncidium ensatum. $2, Encyclia livida. $5, Epidendrum difforme.

Wmk. 406

2010, Dec. 8 Litho. *Perf. 12½*
1222-1225 A193 Set of 4 8.00 8.00

Reign of Queen Elizabeth II, 60th Anniv. — A194

Various photographs of Queen Elizabeth II: 25c, 60c, 75c, $1, $2, $5.
$10, Queen Elizabeth II, diff.

Perf. 13¼

2012, Feb. 6 Litho. Unwmk.
1226-1231 A194 Set of 6 10.00 10.00
1231a Sheet of 6, #1226-1231, + 3 labels 10.00 10.00

Souvenir Sheet

1232 A194 $10 multi 10.50 10.50

No. 1188 Surcharged in Black and Silver

Method, Perf. and Watermark As Before

2012 ?
1233 A185 25c on 10c #1188 —

A195

Coronation of Queen Elizabeth II, 60th Anniv. — A196

Various photographs of Queen Elizabeth II: 25c, 60c, 75c, $5.

Perf. 13½x13¼

2013, Apr. 19 Litho. Wmk. 406
1234-1237 A195 Set of 4 6.50 6.50

Souvenir Sheet

Perf. 14¾x14¼

1238 A196 $10 multi 10.00 10.00

SEMI-POSTAL STAMPS

World Cup Soccer Championship — SP1

Designs: 20c+10c, 30c+15c, Scotland vs. New Zealand (diff.). 40c+20c, Kuwait vs. France. 60c+30c, Italy vs. Brazil. No. B5, France vs. Northern Ireland. $1.50+75c, Austria vs. Chile. No. B7, Italy vs. Germany, vert. $2+$1, England vs. France, vert.

1982, Dec. 10 Litho. *Perf. 14*

B1	SP1	20c +10c multi	3.25	1.50
B2	SP1	30c +15c multi	3.25	1.50
B3	SP1	40c +20c multi	3.25	1.50
B4	SP1	60c +30c multi	4.25	1.90
B5	SP1	$1 +50c multi	5.00	2.25
B6	SP1	$1.50 +75c multi	6.00	3.00
		Nos. B1-B6 (6)	25.00	11.65

Souvenir Sheets

Perf. 14½

B7	SP1	$1 +50c multi	15.00	7.25
B8	SP1	$2 +$1 multi	15.00	7.25

Nos. B7-B8 each contain one 50x70mm stamp.

POSTAGE DUE STAMPS

Numeral — D2

Each denomination has different border.

1976, July 1 Litho. Wmk. 373

J6	D2	1c green & red	.25	*1.50*
J7	D2	2c violet & rose lil	.25	*1.50*
J8	D2	5c ocher & brt grn	.30	*1.90*
J9	D2	15c brown org & yel grn	.40	*2.40*
J10	D2	25c slate grn & org	.60	*2.75*
		Nos. J6-J10 (5)	1.80	*10.05*

CAYES OF BELIZE

Catalogue values for all unused stamps in this country are for Never Hinged items.

Spiny Lobster A1

Perf. 14½x14, 14x14½

1984, May 30 Litho. Unwmk.

1	A1	1c shown	.45	.45
2	A1	2c Blue crab	.45	.45
3	A1	5c Red-footed booby	.45	.45
4	A1	10c Brown pelican	.45	.45
5	A1	15c White-tailed deer	.45	.45
6	A1	25c Lighthouse, English Caye	.45	.45
7	A1	75c Spanish galleon, Santa Yaga, c. 1750	1.25	1.25
8	A1	$3 Map of Ambergris Caye, vert.	5.00	5.00
a.		Souvenir booklet	25.00	
9	A1	$5 Jetty, windsurfers	8.75	8.75
		Nos. 1-9 (9)	17.70	17.70

No. 8a contains four panes. One has one $3 stamp, one has a block of four 25c stamps, two have blocks of four 75c stamps but different text. The stamps are larger than Nos. 6-8, have slightly different colors and are perf. 14½.

The $1 stamp was not issued. Eighteen sheets of 40 were sold for postage by accident.

Lloyd's List Issue

Common Design Type

1984, June 6 *Perf. 14½x14*

10	CD335	25c Queen Elizabeth 2	.25	.25
11	CD335	75c Lutine Bell	.55	.55
12	CD335	$1 Loss of the Fishburn	.75	.75
13	CD335	$2 Trafalgar Sword	1.50	1.50
		Nos. 10-13 (4)	3.05	3.05

1984 Summer Olympics, Los Angeles — A2

1984, Oct. 5 *Perf. 15*

14	A2	10c Yachting	.25	.25
15	A2	15c Windsurfing	.25	.25
16	A2	75c Swimming	.85	.85
17	A2	$2 Kayaking	2.40	2.40
		Nos. 14-17 (4)	3.75	3.75

No. 17 inscribed Canoeing.

First Cayes Stamps, 90th Anniv. A3

1984, Nov. 5

18	A3	10c 1895 cover	.25	.25
19	A3	15c Sydney Cuthbert	.25	.25
20	A3	75c Cuthbert's steam yacht	.75	.75
21	A3	$2 British Honduras #133	2.10	2.10
		Nos. 18-21 (4)	3.35	3.35

Audubon Birth Bicentenary — A4

Illustrations by Audubon.

1985, May 20 *Perf. 14*

22	A4	25c Blue-winged teal	.35	.35
23	A4	75c Semipalmated sandpiper	.90	.90
24	A4	$1 Yellow-crowned night heron, vert.	1.30	1.30
25	A4	$3 Common gallinule	3.50	3.50
		Nos. 22-25 (4)	6.05	6.05

Shipwrecks — A5

a, Oxford, c. 1675. b, Santa Yaga, 1780. c, No. 27, Comet, 1822. d, Yeldham, 1800.

1985, June 5 *Perf. 15*

26	A5	$1 Strip of 4+label, #a.-d.	4.50	4.50

Souvenir Sheet

Perf. 13½x14

27	A5	$5 multicolored	5.50	5.50

No. 27 contains one 38x51mm stamp. No. 26 has continuous design.

BENIN

bə-'nin

French Colony

LOCATION — West Coast of Africa
GOVT. — French Possession
AREA — 8,627 sq. mi.
POP. — 493,000 (approx.)
CAPITAL — Benin

In 1895 the French possessions known as Benin were incorporated into the colony of Dahomey and postage stamps of Dahomey superseded those of Benin. Dahomey took the name Benin when it became a republic in 1975.

100 Centimes = 1 Franc

Catalogue values for unused stamps in this country are for Never Hinged items, beginning with Scott 342 in the regular postage section, Scott C240 in the airpost section, Scott J44 in the postage due section, and Scott Q8 in the parcel post section.

Watermark

Wmk. 385

Handstamped on Stamps of French Colonies

1892 Unwmk. *Perf. 14x13½*

Black Overprint

1	A9	1c blk, *bluish*	200.00	170.00
2	A9	2c brn, *buff*	180.00	150.00
3	A9	4c claret, *lav*	80.00	72.50
4	A9	5c grn, *grnsh*	36.00	28.00
5	A9	10c blk, *lavender*	100.00	72.50
6	A9	15c blue	40.00	28.00
7	A9	20c red, *grn*	250.00	220.00
8	A9	25c blk, *rose*	125.00	72.50
9	A9	30c brn, *yelsh*	210.00	190.00
10	A9	35c blk, *orange*	210.00	190.00
11	A9	40c red, *straw*	180.00	170.00
12	A9	75c car, *rose*	500.00	350.00
13	A9	1fr brnz grn, *straw*	450.00	375.00

Red Overprint

14	A9	15c blue	120.00	100.00

Blue Overprint

15	A9	5c grn, *grnsh*	2,600.	1,200.
15A	A9	15c blue	2,600.	1,200.

For inverted overprints and double overprints and pairs, one without overprint, see the *Scott Classic Specialized Catalogue.*

The overprints of Nos. 1-15A are of four types, three without accent on "E." They exist diagonal.

Counterfeits exist of Nos. 1-19.

Additional Surcharge in Red or Black

1892

16	A9	01c on 5c grn, *grnsh*	360.00	250.00
a.		Double surcharge	1,000.	1,000.
17	A9	40c on 15c blue	225.00	120.00
a.		Double surcharge		*3,800.*
18	A9	75c on 15c blue	1,000.	600.00
19	A9	75c on 15c bl (Bk)	3,500.	2,800.

Counterfeits exist.

Navigation and Commerce
A3 A4

1893 Typo. *Perf. 14x13½*

Name of Colony in Blue or Carmine

20	A3	1c blk, *bluish*	5.25	3.25
21	A3	2c brn, *buff*	6.75	4.75
22	A3	4c claret, *lav*	6.25	4.75
23	A3	5c grn, *grnsh*	9.00	6.50
24	A3	10c blk, *lavender*	9.75	6.50
a.		Name of country omitted		*6,500.*
25	A3	15c blue, quadrille paper	45.00	30.00
26	A3	20c red, *grn*	25.00	21.00
27	A3	25c blk, *rose*	60.00	37.50
28	A3	30c brn, *bis*	27.50	21.00
29	A3	40c red, *straw*	6.25	6.25
30	A3	50c car, *rose*	6.75	7.25
31	A3	75c vio, *org*	14.00	12.50
32	A3	1fr brnz grn, *straw*	77.50	77.50
		Nos. 20-32 (13)	299.00	238.75

Perf. 13½x14 stamps are counterfeits.

1894 *Perf. 14x13½*

33	A4	1c blk, *bluish*	3.00	3.25
34	A4	2c brn, *buff*	4.00	3.25
35	A4	4c claret, *lav*	4.50	3.75
36	A4	5c grn, *grnsh*	6.50	4.00
37	A4	10c blk, *lavender*	6.75	6.00
38	A4	15c bl, quadrille paper	13.50	6.00
39	A4	20c red, *grn*	13.00	9.50
40	A4	25c blk, *rose*	15.00	7.50
41	A4	30c brn, *bis*	10.50	10.50
42	A4	40c red, *straw*	26.00	17.00
43	A4	50c car, *rose*	32.50	16.00
44	A4	75c vio, *org*	26.00	15.00
45	A4	1fr brnz grn, *straw*	7.50	6.50
		Nos. 33-45 (13)	168.75	108.25

Perf. 13½x14 stamps are counterfeits.

PEOPLE'S REPUBLIC OF BENIN

LOCATION — West Coast of Africa
GOVT. — Republic.
AREA — 43,483 sq. mi.
POP. — 6,305,567 (1999 est.)
CAPITAL — Porto Novo (Cotonou is the seat of government)

The Republic of Dahomey proclaimed itself the People's Republic of Benin on Nov. 30, 1975. See Dahomey for stamps issued before then. The country became the Republic of Benin in 1990.

Catalogue values for unused stamps in this section are for Never Hinged items.

Allamanda Cathartica — A83

Flowers: 35fr, Ixora coccinea. 45fr, Hibiscus, 60fr, Phaemeria magnifica.

Unwmk.

1975, Dec. 8 Photo. *Perf. 13*

342 A83 10fr lilac & multi .45 .35
343 A83 35fr gray & multi 1.10 .50
344 A83 45fr multi 1.25 .70
345 A83 60fr blue & multi 1.90 1.10
Nos. 342-345 (4) 4.70 2.65

For surcharges see Nos. 612, 618, 690B, 719, 723, 788, 1364, 1413, 1416, 1418, 1463, Q18A.

Flag Bearers, Arms of Benin — A84

Design: 60fr, Speaker, wall with "PRPB," flag and arms of Benin. 100fr, Flag and arms of Benin.

1976, Apr. 30 Litho. *Perf. 12*

346 A84 50fr ocher & multi .85 .55
347 A84 60fr ocher & multi 1.10 .55
348 A84 100fr multi 2.10 .85
Nos. 346-348 (3) 4.05 1.95

Proclamation of the People's Republic of Benin. Nov. 30, 1975.
For surcharge, see No. Q16A.

A.G. Bell, Satellite and 1876 Telephone — A85

1976, July 9 Litho. *Perf. 13*

349 A85 200fr lilac, red & brn 3.75 2.25

Centenary of first telephone call by Alexander Graham Bell, Mar. 10, 1876.
For overprints, see Nos. Q16, Q16A and Q16B.

Dahomey Nos. 277-278 Surcharged

1976, July 19 Photo. *Perf. 12½x13*

350 A57 50fr on 1fr multi .90 .35
351 A57 60fr on 2fr multi 1.00 .45

For overprint & surcharge see Nos. 654A, 711.

African Jamboree, Nigeria 1976 — A86

1976, Aug. 16 Litho. *Perf. 12½x13*

352 A86 50fr Scouts Cooking .85 .60
353 A86 70fr Three scouts 1.25 .70

Blood Bank, Cotonou — A87

Designs: 50fr, Accident and first aid station. 60fr, Blood donation.

1976, Sept. 24 Litho. *Perf. 13*

354 A87 5fr multicolored .25 .25
355 A87 50fr multicolored .70 .45
356 A87 60fr multicolored 1.25 .70
Nos. 354-356 (3) 2.20 1.40

National Blood Donors Day.
For overprint, see No. Q12.

A88

1976, Oct. 4 Litho. *Perf. 13x12½*

357 A88 20fr Manioc .55 .25
358 A88 50fr Corn 1.00 .45
359 A88 60fr Cacao 1.40 .55
360 A88 150fr Cotton 3.00 1.25
Nos. 357-360 (4) 5.95 2.50

Natl. agricultural production campaign.
For opverprint and surcharge see Nos. 565, Q10C.

A89

1976, Oct. 25

361 A89 50fr Classroom 1.10 .55

Third anniversary of KPARO newspaper, used in local language studies.

Roan Antelope — A90

Penhari National Park: 30fr, Buffalo. 50fr, Hippopotamus, horiz. 70fr, Lion.

1976, Nov. 8 Photo.

362 A90 10fr multicolored .45 .30
363 A90 30fr multicolored .90 .75
364 A90 50fr multicolored 1.90 1.25
365 A90 70fr multicolored 2.25 1.40
Nos. 362-365 (4) 5.50 3.70

Flags, Wall, Broken Chains — A91

150fr, Corn, raised hands with weapons.

1976, Nov. 30 Litho. *Perf. 12½*

366 A91 40fr multicolored .65 .30
367 A91 150fr multicolored 2.25 .95

First anniversary of proclamation of the People's Republic of Benin.
For surcharge, see No. Q14.

Table Tennis, Map of Africa (Games' Emblem) — A92

Design: 50fr, Stadium, Cotonou.

1976, Dec. 26 Litho. *Perf. 13*

368 A92 10fr multi .40 .25
369 A92 50fr multi 1.25 .40

West African University Games, Cotonou, Dec. 26-31.
For overprint, see No. Q25.

Europafrica Issue

Planes over Africa and Europe — A93

1977, May 13 Litho. *Perf. 13*

370 A93 200fr multi 3.50 2.75

For surcharge see No. 590.

Snake A94

1977, June 13 Litho. *Perf. 13x13½*

371 A94 2fr shown .50 .25
372 A94 3fr Tortoise .60 .25
373 A94 5fr Zebus .75 .25
374 A94 10fr Cats 1.25 .25
Nos. 371-374 (4) 3.10 1.00

For surcharge, see No. 446A.

Patients at Clinic A95

1977, Aug. 2 Litho. *Perf. 12½*

375 A95 100fr multi 1.75 .80

World Rheumatism Year.
For overprint, see No. Q21.

Karate, Map of Africa — A96

Designs: 100fr, Javelin, map of Africa, Benin Flag, horiz. 150fr, Hurdles.

1977, Aug. 30 Litho. *Perf. 12½*

376 A96 90fr multi 1.50 .90
377 A96 100fr multi 1.75 1.00
378 A96 150fr multi 2.50 1.60
a. Souvenir sheet of 3, #376-378 7.75 7.50
Nos. 376-378 (3) 5.75 3.50

2nd West African Games, Lagos, Nigeria.
For surcharges, see Nos. 925, Q20, Q33.

Chairman Mao — A97

Lister and Vaporizer — A98

1977, Sept. 9 Litho. *Perf. 13x12½*

379 A97 100fr multicolored 3.50 2.00

Mao Tse-tung (1893-1976), Chinese communist leader.

1977, Sept. 20 Engr. *Perf. 13*

Designs: 150fr, Scalpels and flames, symbols of antisepsis, and Red Cross.

380 A98 150fr multi 2.25 1.10
381 A98 210fr multi 2.75 1.90

Joseph Lister (1827-1912), surgeon, founder of antiseptic surgery.
For surcharges see Nos. 560, 566, 919.

Guelege Mask, Ethnographic Museum, Porto Novo — A99

Designs: 50fr, Jar, symbol of unity, emblem of King Ghezo, Historical Museum, Abomey, vert. 210fr, Abomey Museum.

1977, Oct. 17 *Perf. 13*

382 A99 50fr red & multi .75 .55
383 A99 60fr blk, bl & bister 1.25 .70
384 A99 210fr multi 3.50 1.75
Nos. 382-384 (3) 5.50 3.00

For surcharge see Nos. 562, 920.

Atacora Falls — A100

Tourist Publicity: 60fr, Pile houses, Ganvie, horiz. 150fr, Round huts, Savalou.

1977, Oct. 24 Litho. *Perf. 12½*

385	A100	50fr multi	.70	.45
386	A100	60fr multi	1.25	.70
387	A100	150fr multi	2.50	1.50
a.		Souvenir sheet of 3, #385-387	5.00	5.00
		Nos. 385-387 (3)	4.45	2.65

Mother and Child, Owl of Wisdom — A101

150fr, Chopping down magical tree, horiz.

Perf. 12½x13, 13x12½

1977, Dec. 3 Photo.

388	A101	60fr multi	1.25	.75
389	A101	150fr multi	3.00	1.50

Campaign against witchcraft.
For surcharge see No. 576.

Battle Scene — A102

1978, Jan. 16 Litho. *Perf. 12½*

390	A102	50fr multi	1.40	.70

Victory of people of Benin over imperialist forces.

Map, People and Houses of Benin — A103

1978, Feb. 1

391	A103	50fr multi	.90	.50

General population and dwelling census.

Alexander Fleming, Microscope and Penicillin — A104

1978, Mar. 12 Litho. *Perf. 13*

392	A104	300fr multi	5.50	2.25

Alexnader Fleming (1881-1955), 50th anniversary of discovery of penicillin.

Abdoulaye Issa, Weapons and Fighters A105

1978, Apr. 1 *Perf. 12½x13*

393	A105	100fr red, blk & gold	1.25	.60

First anniversary of death of Abdoulaye Issa and National Day of Benin's Youth.

Ed Hadj Omar and Horseback Rider — A106

Design: 90fr, L'Almamy Samory Toure (1830-1900) and horseback riders.

1976, Apr. 10 *Perf. 13x12½*

394	A106	90fr red & multi	1.40	.50
395	A106	100fr multi	1.40	.60

African heroes of resistance against colonialism.

ITU Emblem, Satellite, Landscape — A107

1978, May 17 Litho. *Perf. 13*

396	A107	100fr multi	1.75	.80

10th World Telecommunications Day.

Soccer Player, Stadium, Argentina '78 Emblem — A108

Designs (Argentina '78 Emblem and): 300fr, Soccer players and ball, vert. 500fr, Soccer player, globe with ball on map.

1978, June 1 Litho. *Perf. 12½*

397	A108	200fr multi	2.25	1.25
398	A108	300fr multi	3.50	2.00
399	A108	500fr multi	5.75	3.50
a.		Souvenir sheet of 3, perf. 12	15.00	15.00
		Nos. 397-399 (3)	11.50	6.75

11th World Cup Soccer Championship, Argentina, June 1-25. No. 399a contains 3 stamps similar to Nos. 397-399 in changed colors.

For surcharges and overprints see Nos. 591, 593, 595, 1477.

Nos. 397-399a Overprinted in Red Brown

a

b

c

1978, June 25 Litho. *Perf. 12½*

400	A108 (a)	200fr multi	2.25	1.40
401	A108 (b)	300fr multi	3.50	2.50
402	A108 (c)	500fr multi	5.75	4.00
a.		Souvenir sheet of 3	15.00	15.00
		Nos. 400-402 (3)	11.50	7.90

Argentina's victory in 1978 Soccer Championship.

For surcharges and overprints, see Nos. 596, 591A, 1478.

Games' Flag over Africa, Basketball Players — A109

Designs: 60fr, Map of Africa, volleyball players. 80fr, Map of Benin, bicyclists.

1978, July 13 *Perf. 13x12½*

403	A109	50fr lt bl & multi	.65	.25
404	A109	60fr ultra & multi	.90	.50
405	A109	80fr multi	1.25	.65
a.		Souvenir sheet of 3	4.50	4.50
		Nos. 403-405 (3)	2.80	1.40

3rd African Games, Algiers, July 13-28. No. 405a contains 3 stamps in changed colors similar to Nos. 403-405.

Martin Luther King, Jr. — A110

1978, July 30 *Perf. 12½*

406	A110	300fr multi	4.00	2.25

Martin Luther King, Jr. (1929-1968), American civil rights leader.

For surcharge see No. 592.

Kanna Taxi, Oueme A111

60fr Leatherworker & goods. 70fr, Drummer & tom-toms. 100fr, Metalworker & calabashes.

1978, Aug. 26

407	A111	50fr multi	1.00	.45
408	A111	60fr multi	1.10	.45
409	A111	70fr multi	1.50	.50
410	A111	100fr multi	1.90	.60
		Nos. 407-410 (4)	5.50	2.00

Getting to know Benin through its provinces.

Map of Italy and Exhibition Poster — A112

1978, Aug. 26 Litho. *Perf. 13*

411	A112	200fr multi	2.50	1.50

Riccione 1978 Philatelic Exhibition.

For overprint see No. 537.

Poultry Breeding — A113

1978 Oct. 5 Photo. *Perf. 12½x13*

412	A113	10fr Turkeys	.35	.25
413	A113	20fr Ducks	.80	.30
414	A113	50fr Chicken	2.25	.70
415	A113	60fr Guinea fowl	2.50	.90
		Nos. 412-415 (4)	5.90	2.15

Royal Messenger, UPU Emblem — A114

UPU Emblem and: 60fr, Boatsman, ship & car. 90fr, Special messenger & plane.

1978, Oct. 16 ***Perf. 13x12½, 12½x13***

416 A114 50fr multi 1.10 .45
417 A114 60fr multi, vert. 1.25 .60
418 A114 90fr multi, vert. 1.50 .80
Nos. 416-418 (3) 3.85 1.85

Centenary of change of "General Postal Union" to "Universal Postal Union."
For surcharge see No. 1009.

Raoul Follereau A115

1978, Dec. 17 **Litho.** ***Perf. 12½***

419 A115 200fr multi 2.25 1.00

Raoul Follereau (1903-1977), apostle to the lepers and educator of the blind.

IYC Emblem A116

Intl. Year of the Child: 20fr, Globe as balloon carrying childern. 50fr, Children of various races surrounding globe.

1979, Feb. 20 **Litho.** ***Perf. 12x13***

420 A116 10fr multi .25 .25
421 A116 20fr multi .30 .25
422 A116 50fr multi .50 .35
Nos. 420-422 (3) 1.05 .85

Hydrangea — A117

Flowers: 25fr, Assangokan. 30fr, Geranium. 40fr, Water lilies, horiz.

Perf. 13x12½, 12½x13

1979, Feb. 28 **Litho.**

423 A117 20fr multi .25 .25
424 A117 25fr multi .55 .25
425 A117 30fr multi .90 .35
426 A117 40fr mutli 1.00 .35
Nos. 423-426 (4) 2.70 1.20

Emblem: Map of Africa and Members' Flags A118

60fr, Map of Benin & flags. 80fr, OCAM flag & map of Africa showing member states.

1979, Mar. 20 **Litho.** ***Perf. 12x13***

427 A118 50fr multi .65 .35
428 A118 60fr multi 1.00 .50
429 A118 80fr multi 1.25 .65
Nos. 427-429 (3) 2.90 1.50

OCAM Summit Conf., Cotonou, Mar. 20-28.
For overprints see Nos. 434-436.

Tower, Waves, Satellite, ITU Emblem A119

1979, May 17 **Litho.** ***Perf. 12½***

430 A119 50fr multi .85 .50

World Telecommunications Day.

Bank Building and Sculpture A120

1979, May 26 **Litho.**

431 A120 50fr multi 1.75 .50

Opening of Headquarters of West African Savings Bank in Dakar.

Guelede Mask, Abomey Tapestry, Malaconotus Bird — A121

Design: 50fr, Jet, canoe, satellite, UPU and exhibition emblems.

1979, June 8 **Litho.** ***Perf. 13***

432 A121 15fr multi 2.00 .80

Engr.

433 A121 50fr multi 2.50 1.10

Philexafrique II, Libreville, Gabon, June 8-17. Nos. 432, 433 each printed in sheets of 10 with 5 labels showing exhibition emblem.
For surcharges, see Nos. 1061A-1061C.

Nos. 427-429 Overprinted: "26 au 28 juin 1979" and Dots

1979, June 26

434 A118 50fr multi .90 .35
435 A118 60fr multi 1.00 .65
436 A118 80fr multi 1.25 .65
Nos. 434-436 (3) 3.15 1.65

2nd OCAM Summit Conf., June 26-28.

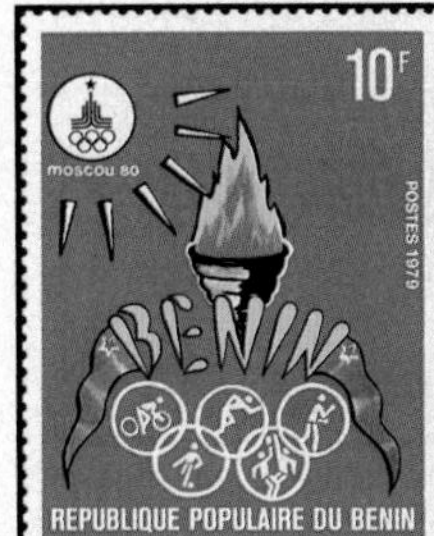

Olympic Flame, and Emblems A122

Pre-Olympic Year: 50fr, High jump.

1979, July 1 **Litho.**

437 A122 10fr multi .25 .25
438 A122 50fr multi 1.10 .80

Antelope A123

Animals: 10fr, Giraffes, map of Benin, vert 20fr, Chimpanzee. 50fr, Elephants, map of Benin, vert.

1979, Oct. 1 **Litho.** ***Perf. 13***

439 A123 5fr multi .50 .30
440 A123 10fr multi .65 .50
441 A123 20fr multi .95 .65
442 A123 50fr multi 2.25 .80
Nos. 439-442 (4) 4.35 2.25

Map of Africa, Emblem and Jet — A124

1979, Dec. 12 **Litho.** ***Perf. 12½***

443 A124 50fr multi .65 .30
444 A124 60fr multi .65 .30

ASECNA (Air Safety Board), 20th anniv.

Mail Services A125

50fr, Post Office and headquarters, vert.

1979, Dec. 19 **Litho.** ***Perf. 13***

445 A125 50fr multi .60 .30
446 A125 60fr multi .60 .30

Office of Posts and Telecommunications, 20th anniversary.

No. 371 Surcharged

Methods and Perfs As Before

1979

446A A94 50fr on 2fr #371 *160.00 40.00*

Lenin and Globe — A126

1980, Apr. 22 **Litho.** ***Perf. 12½***

447 A126 50fr shown .85 .30
448 A126 150fr Lenin in library 2.25 .90

Lenin, 110th birth anniversary.
For surcharge, see No. Q8.

Monument to King Behanzin A126a

Litho. & Embossed

1980, May 31 ***Perf. 12½***

448A A126a 1000fr gold & multi 15.00 10.00

For overprint see No. Q10A.

Cotonou Club Emlem — A127

1980, Feb. 23 **Litho.** ***Perf. 12½***

449 A127 90fr shown 1.10 .50
450 A127 200fr Rotary emblem on globe, horiz. 2.10 .95

Rotary International, 75th anniversary.
For surcharge see No. 915.

Galileo, Astrolabe — A128

1980, Apr. 2

451 A128 70fr shown .90 .55
452 A128 100fr Copernicus, solar system 1.50 .70

Discovery of Pluto, 50th anniversary.

Abu Simbel, UNESCO Emblem — A129

1980, Apr. 15 ***Perf. 13***

453 A129 50fr Column, vert. .65 .30
454 A129 60fr Ramses II, vert. .75 .50
455 A129 150fr shown 1.75 1.00
Nos. 453-455 (3) 3.15 1.80

UNESCO campaign to save Nubian monuments, 20h anniversary.

Monument, Martyrs' Square, Cotonou
A130

Designs: Various monuments in Martyrs' Square. Cotonou. 60fr, 70fr, 100fr, horiz.

1980, May 2 *Perf. 12½x13, 13x12½*

456 A130 50fr multi .50 .25
457 A130 60fr multi .65 .25
458 A130 70fr multi .75 .35
459 A130 100fr multi 1.25 .50
Nos. 456-459 (4) 3.15 1.35

For overprint, see No. Q9. For surcharge see No. 539.

Musical Instruments — A131

1980, May 20 *Perf. 12½*

460 A131 5fr Assan, vert. .35 .25
461 A131 10fr Tinbo .35 .25
462 A131 15fr Tam-tam sato, vert. .50 .25
463 A131 20fr Kora .50 .25
464 A131 30fr Gangan 1.10 .60
465 A131 50fr Sinhoun 1.75 .90
Nos. 460-465 (6) 4.55 2.50

First Non-stop Flight, Paris-New York — A132

1980, June 2 **Litho.** *Perf. 12½*

466 A132 90fr shown 1.10 .60
467 A132 100fr Dieudonne Coste, Maurice Bellonte 1.10 .60

For surcharges see Nos. 564, 926.

Lunokhod I on the Moon — A133

1980, June 15 **Engr.** *Perf. 13*

468 A133 90fr multi 1.00 .60

Lunokhod I Soviet unmanned moon mission, 10th anniv. See No. C290.

Olympic Flame and Mischa, Moscow '80 Emblem — A134

1980, July 16 **Litho.** *Perf. 12½*

469 A134 50fr shown .65 .30
470 A134 60fr Equestrian, vert. .65 .40
471 A134 70fr Judo .90 .45
472 A134 200fr Flag, sports, globe, vert. 2.10 .95
473 A134 300fr Weight lifting, vert. 3.25 1.75
Nos. 469-473 (5) 7.55 3.85

22nd Summer Olympic Games, Moscow, July 19-Aug. 3.
For overprint, see No. Q10. For surcharges see Nos. 559, 561.

Telephone and Rising Sun
A135

World Telecommunications Day: 50fr, Farmer on telephone, vert.

1980, May 17 **Litho.** *Perf. 12½*

474 A135 50fr multi .60 .30
475 A135 60fr multi .60 .30

Cotonou West African Community Village
A136

Designs: View of Cotonou.

1980, July 26 *Perf. 13x13½*

476 A136 50fr multi .70 .30
477 A136 60fr multi .70 .35
478 A136 70fr multi 1.10 .80
Nos. 476-478 (3) 2.50 1.45

For surcharge see No. 540.

Agbadja Dancers — A137

Designs: Dancers and muscians.

1980, Aug. 1 *Perf. 12½*

479 A137 30fr multi .60 .35
480 A137 50fr multi .95 .60
481 A137 60fr multi 1.10 .70
Nos. 479-481 (3) 2.65 1.65

Fisherman
A138

Philippines under Magnifier
A139

Designs: 5fr, Throwing net. 15fr, Canoe and shore fishing. 20fr, Basket traps. 50fr, Hauling net. 60fr, River fishing. All horiz.

1980, Sept. 1

482 A138 5fr multi .25 .25
483 A138 10fr multi .30 .25
484 A138 15fr multi .40 .25
485 A138 20fr multi .45 .25
486 A138 50fr multi 1.00 .45
487 A138 60fr multi 1.10 .45
Nos. 482-487 (6) 3.50 1.90

For surcharge see No. 535.

Perf. 13x13½, 13x½x13

1980, Sept. 27

World Tourism Conference, Manila, Sept. 27: 60fr, Emblem on flag, hand pointing to Manila on globe, horiz.

488 A139 50fr multi .75 .35
489 A139 60fr multi .95 .45

For surcharge see No. 557.

A140

1980, Oct. 1 *Perf. 12½*

490 A140 40fr Othreis materna 1.00 .40
491 A140 50fr Othreis fullonia 1.25 .50
492 A140 200fr Oryctes sp. 4.00 1.50
Nos. 490-492 (3) 6.25 2.40

A141

Photo.

Perf. 13½

1980, Oct. 24

493 A141 75fr multi .90 .35

African Postal Union, 5th Anniv.

A142

1980, Nov. 4 *Perf. 12½x13*

494 A142 30fr shown .30 .25
495 A142 50fr Freed prisoner .70 .25
496 A142 60fr Man holding torch .75 .30
Nos. 494-496 (3) 1.75 .80

Declaration of human rights, 30th anniv.
For surcharge, see No. Q15.

A143

Self-portrait, by Vincent van Gogh, 1888.

1980, Dec. 1 **Litho.** *Perf. 13*

497 A143 100fr shown 2.10 .90
498 A143 300fr Facteur Roulin 5.75 2.75

Vincent van Gogh (1853-1890), artist.
For surcharge see No. 579.

Offenbach and Scene from Orpheus in the Underworld — A144

1980, Dec. 15 **Engr.**

499 A144 50fr shown 1.40 .80
500 A144 60fr Paris Life 2.25 1.10

Jacques Offenbach (1819-1880), composer.
For surcharge, see No. Q13.

Kepler and Satellites — A145

1980, Dec. 20

501 A145 50fr Kepler, diagram, vert. .80 .35
502 A145 60fr shown 1.10 .55

Johannes Kepler (1571-1630), astronomer.

Intl. Year of the Disabled — A146

1981, Apr. 10 **Litho.** *Perf. 12½*

503 A146 115fr multi 1.50 .70

For surcharge see No. 582.

20th Anniv. of Manned Space Flight — A147

1981, May 30 *Perf. 13*

504 A147 500fr multi 6.00 3.00

For surcharges see Nos. 580, 790.

13th World Telecommunications Day — A148

1981, May 30 Litho. *Perf. 12½*
505 A148 115fr multi 1.25 .50

For surcharge see No. 583.

Amaryllis A149

1981, June 20 *Perf. 12½*
506 A149 10fr shown .30 .25
507 A149 20fr Eischornia crassipes, vert. .65 .35
508 A149 80fr Parkia biglobosa, vert. 1.50 .50
Nos. 506-508 (3) 2.45 1.10

For surcharge see No. 542.

Benin Sheraton Hotel A150

1981, July
509 A150 100fr multi 1.25 .50

For surcharge see No. 541.

Guinea Pig — A151

1981, July 31 *Perf. 13x13½*
510 A151 5fr shown .50 .35
511 A151 60fr Cat 1.25 .60
512 A151 80fr Dogs 1.60 1.10
Nos. 510-512 (3) 3.35 2.05

For surcharges see Nos. 536, 543, 563.

World UPU Day — A152

1981, Oct. 9 Engr. *Perf. 13*
513 A152 100fr red brn & blk 1.10 .55

25th Intl. Letter Writing Week, Oct. 6-12 — A153

1981, Oct. 15
514 A153 100fr dk bl & pur 1.00 .50

For surcharge see No. 558.

West African Economic Community A154

1981, Nov. 20 Litho. *Perf. 12½*
515 A154 60fr multi .80 .30

West African Rice Development Assoc. 10th Anniv. — A155

1981, Dec. 10 *Perf. 13x13½*
516 A155 60fr multi .80 .30

TB Bacillus Centenary A156

1982, Mar. 1 Litho. *Perf. 13*
517 A156 115fr multi 1.90 .75

For surcharge see No. 584.

West African Economic Community, 5th Summit Conference A157

1982, May 27 *Perf. 12½*
518 A157 60fr multi .70 .30

1982 World Cup — A158

1982, June 1 *Perf. 13*
519 A158 90fr Players 1.00 .45
520 A158 300fr Flags on leg 3.25 1.25

For overprints and surcharges see Nos. 523-524, 594, 789.

France No. B349 Magnified, Map of France — A159

1982, June 11
521 A159 90fr multi 1.10 .50

For surcharge see No. 916.

PHILEXFRANCE '82 Stamp Exhibition, Paris, June 11-21.

George Washington — A160

1982, Mar. 10 Litho. *Perf. 14*
522 A160 200fr Washington, flag, map 2.50 1.00

For surcharge see No. 577.

Nos. 519-520 Overprinted

1982, Aug. 16 *Perf. 12½*
523 A158 90fr multi 1.25 .55
524 A158 300fr multi 3.75 1.50

Italy's victory in 1982 World Cup.
For surcharge see No. 811.

Bluethroat A161

1982, Sept. 1 *Perf. 14x14½, 14½x14*
525 A161 5fr Daoelo gigas, vert. 1.10 .45
526 A161 10fr shown 1.60 .45
527 A161 15fr Swallow, vert. 1.60 .45
528 A161 20fr Kingfisher, weaver bird, vert. 2.50 .60
529 A161 30fr Great sedge warbler 3.75 .80
530 A161 60fr Common warbler 5.25 1.10
531 A161 80fr Owl, vert. 9.50 2.50
532 A161 100fr Cockatoo, vert. 12.00 3.25
Nos. 525-532 (8) 37.30 9.60

ITU Plenipotentiaries Conference, Nairobi, Sept. — A162

1982, Sept. 26 *Perf. 13*
533 A162 200fr Map 2.00 1.00

For surcharge see No. 585.

13th World UPU Day — A163

1982, Oct. 9 Engr. *Perf. 13*
534 A163 100fr Monument 1.10 .45

Nos. 482, 510, 411 Overprinted in Red or Blue

No. 535

No. 536 — "UAPT 1982" 3mm tall

No. 537

Perf. 13, 12½, 13x13½

1982, Nov. Litho.
535 A138 60fr on 5fr multi 4.00 .35
536 A151 60fr on 5fr multi .95 .35
a. "UAPT 1982" 2mm tall 8.00 —
537 A112 200fr multi (Bl) 2.40 1.00
Nos. 535-537 (3) 7.35 1.70

Visit of French Pres. Francois Mitterrand A164

1983, Jan. 15 Litho. *Perf. 12½x13*
538 A164 90fr multi 1.60 .75

For surcharge see No. 917.

Nos. 458, 476, 508-509, 512 Surcharged

No. 539

No. 540

No. 541

No. 542

No. 543

Perf. 13x12½, 13x13½, 12½

1983 **Litho.**

539	A130	60fr on 70fr multi	2.10	.70
540	A136	60fr on 50fr multi	2.10	.70
541	A150	60fr on 100fr multi	2.10	.95
542	A149	75fr on 80fr multi	2.10	1.40
543	A151	75fr on 80fr multi	2.10	1.40
		Nos. 539-543 (5)	10.50	5.15

Seme Oil Rig — A165

1983, Apr. 28 **Litho.** ***Perf. 13x12½***

544	A165	125fr multi	1.60	.70

World Communications Year — A166

1983, May 17 **Litho.** ***Perf. 13***

545	A166	185fr multi	2.00	.75

For surcharge see No. 898.

Riccione '83, Stamp Show — A167

1983, Aug. 27 **Litho.** ***Perf. 13***

546	A167	500fr multi	5.00	2.00

For surcharge see No. 922.

Benin Red Cross, 20th Anniv. A168

1983, Sept. 5 **Photo.** ***Perf. 13***

547	A168	105fr multi	1.40	.60

For surcharge see No. 581.

Handicrafts A169

Designs: 75fr, Handcarved lion chairs and table. 90fr, Natural tree table and stools. 200fr, Monkeys holding jar.

1983, Sept. 18 **Litho.** ***Perf. 13***

548	A169	75fr multi	.95	.35
549	A169	90fr multi	1.25	.45
550	A169	200fr multi	2.00	.85
		Nos. 548-550 (3)	4.20	1.65

For surcharge see No. 578.

14th UPU Day — A170

1983, Oct. 9 **Engr.** ***Perf. 13***

551	A170	125fr multi	1.40	.70

For surcharge see No. 575.

Religious Movements A171

1983, Oct. 31 **Litho.** ***Perf. 14x15***

552	A171	75fr Zangbeto	1.10	.55
553	A171	75fr Egoun	1.10	.55

Plaited Hair Styles — A172

1983, Nov. 14

554	A172	30fr Rockcoco	.35	.25
555	A172	75fr Serpent	.95	.55
556	A172	90fr Songas	1.40	.70
		Nos. 554-556 (3)	2.70	1.50

Stamps of 1976-81 Surcharged

No. 557

No. 558

No. 559

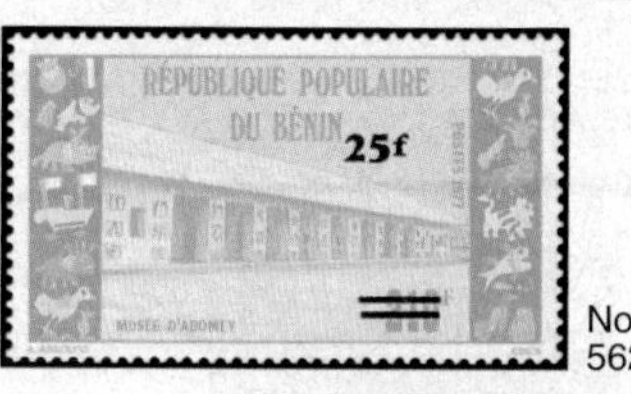
No. 560

No. 561

No. 562

No. 563

No. 564

No. 565

No. 566

1983, Nov.

557	A139	5fr on 50fr #488	6.50	1.25
558	A153	10fr on 100fr #514	6.50	1.25
559	A134	15fr on 200fr #472	6.50	1.25
560	A98	15fr on 210fr #381	6.50	1.25
561	A134	25fr on 70fr #471	6.50	1.25
562	A99	25fr on 210fr #384	6.50	1.25
563	A151	75fr on 5fr #510	6.50	1.25
564	A132	75fr on 100fr #467	6.50	1.25
565	A88	75fr on 150fr #360	6.50	1.25
566	A98	75fr on 150fr #380	6.50	1.25
		Nos. 557-566 (10)	65.00	12.50

Alfred Nobel (1833-96) A173

1983, Dec. 19 **Litho.** ***Perf. 15x14***

567	A173	300fr multi	3.00	1.40

For surcharge see No. 923.

Council of Unity — A174

1984, May 29 **Litho.** ***Perf. 12***

568	A174	75fr multi	.80	.30
569	A174	90fr multi	1.10	.35

For surcharge see No. 918.

1984 UPU Congress A175

1984, June 18 **Litho.** ***Perf. 13***

570	A175	90fr multi	1.00	.50

Abomey Calavi Earth Station A176

1984, June 29 **Litho.** ***Perf. 12½x13***

571	A176	75fr Satellite dish	.80	.45

Traditional Costumes A177

1984, July 2 **Litho.** ***Perf. 13½x13***

572	A177	5fr Koumboro	.25	.25
573	A177	10fr Taka	.30	.25
574	A177	20fr Toko	.40	.30
		Nos. 572-574 (3)	.95	.80

Nos. 389, 498, 503-505, 517, 522, 533, 547, 550 and 551 Surcharged

No. 575

No. 576

No. 577

No. 578

No. 579

No. 580

No. 581

No. 582

No. 583

No. 584

No. 585

1984, Sept.

575	A170	5fr on 125fr #551	7.25	1.40
576	A101	5fr on 150fr #389	7.25	1.40
577	A160	10fr on 200fr #522	7.25	1.40
578	A169	10fr on 200fr #550	7.25	1.40
579	A143	15fr on 300fr #498	7.25	1.40
580	A147	40fr on 500fr #504	7.25	1.40
581	A168	75fr on 105fr #547	7.25	1.40
582	A146	75fr on 115fr #503	7.25	1.40
583	A148	75fr on 115fr #505	7.25	1.40
584	A156	75fr on 115fr #517	7.25	1.40
585	A162	75fr on 200fr #533	7.25	1.40
		Nos. 575-585 (11)	79.75	15.40

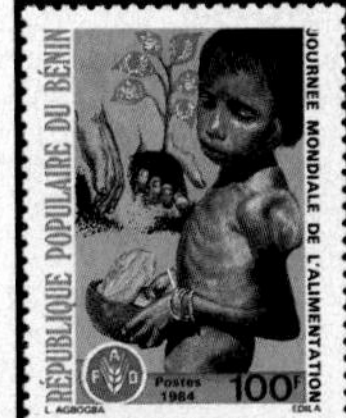

World Food Day — A178

1984, Oct. 16 Litho. *Perf. 12½*

586	A178	100fr Malnourished child	1.00	.50

Dinosaurs A179

1984, Dec. 14 Litho. *Perf. 13½*

587	A179	75fr Anatosaurus	6.00	1.00
588	A179	90fr Brontosaurus	6.00	1.00

Cultural & Technical Cooperation Agency, 15th Anniv. — A180

1985, Mar 20 Litho. *Perf. 13*

589	A180	300fr Emblem, globe, hands, book	3.00	1.25

Stamps of 1977-82 Surcharged

No. 590

No. 591

No. 591A

No. 592

No. 593

No. 594

No. 595

No. 596

1985, Mar.

590	A93	75fr on 200fr #370	13.00	2.50
591	A108	75fr on 200fr #397	13.00	2.50
591A	A108(a)	75fr on 200fr #400	50.00	3.00
592	A110	75fr on 300fr #406	13.00	2.50
593	A108	75fr on 300fr #398	13.00	2.50
594	A158	90fr on 300fr #520	13.00	2.50
595	A108	90fr on 500fr #399	13.00	2.50
596	A108	90fr on 500fr #402	13.00	2.50
		Nos. 590-591,592-596 (7)	91.00	17.50

End of World War II, 40th Anniv. — A180a

1985, May Litho. *Perf. 12*

596A	A180a	100fr multicolored	*70.00*	*17.50*

Traditional Dances A181

1985, June 1 Litho. *Perf. 15x14½*

597	A181	75fr Teke, Borgou Tribe	1.00	.50
598	A181	100fr Tipen'ti, L'Atacora Tribe	1.25	.65

Intl. Youth Year — A182

1985, July 16 *Perf. 13½*

599	A182	150fr multi	1.50	.75

1986 World Cup Soccer Championships, Mexico — A183

1985, July 22 *Perf. 13x12½*

600	A183	200fr multi	2.00	1.00

Beginning with Scott 601, Benin again surcharged stamps of Dahomey with a variety of surcharges. While the listings that follow contain hundreds surcharged stamps, the Scott editors still need to examine many more other stamps, in order to list all of those that are currently known to exist.

The size and location of the surcharge varies from stamp to stamp. The type face used in the surcharge may also vary from issue to issue.

a

b

c

55 f

République
Populaire
du Bénin

d

e

f

g

h

i

j

Dahomey No. 336 Surcharged with Black Bars and New Value

1985, Aug. *Perf. 12½*

601 A78(a) 15fr on 40fr multi 6.00 1.10

ASECNA Airlines, 25th Anniv. — A184

1985, Sept. 16 *Perf. 13*

602 A184 150fr multi 2.00 .75

UN 40th Anniv. A185

1985, Oct. 24 *Perf. 12½*

603 A185 250fr multi 2.50 1.25

Benin UN membership, 25th anniv.

ITALIA'85, Rome A186

1985, Oct. 25 *Perf. 13½*

604 A186 200fr multi 2.00 1.25

PHILEXAFRICA '85, Lome — A187

1985, Nov. 16 *Perf. 13*

605 A187 250fr #569, labor emblem 5.00 3.00

606 A187 250fr #C252, Gabon #366, magnified stamp 4.00 2.75

a. Pair, Nos. 605-606 + label 11.00 11.00

For surcharges, see Nos. 653B-653C.

Audubon Birth Bicent. — A188

1985, Oct. 17 Litho. *Perf. 14x15*

607 A188 150fr Skua gull 4.00 1.50

608 A188 300fr Oyster catcher 9.25 2.50

Mushrooms and Toadstools A189

1985, Oct. 17

609 A189 35fr Boletus edible 1.50 .60

610 A189 40fr Amanite phalloide 2.25 1.10

611 A189 100fr Brown chanterelle 5.50 2.50

Nos. 609-611 (3) 9.25 4.20

Dahomey #282, 292, Benin #343 Surcharged

1986, Mar. **Photo.**

612 A83(b) 75fr on 35fr #343 5.00 1.10

613 A57(c) 90fr on 70fr #282 5.00 1.10

614 A60(b) 90fr on 140fr #292 5.00 1.10

Nos. 612-614 (3) 15.00 3.30

African Parliamentary Union, 10th Anniv. — A190

1986, May 8 Litho. *Perf. 13x12½*

615 A190 100fr multi 1.00 .50

9th Conference, Cotonou, May 8-10.

Halley's Comet — A191

1986, May 30 *Perf. 12½x12*

616 A191 205fr multi 3.25 1.50

For surcharge see No. 809.

Dahomey No. 283, Benin No. 344 Surcharged

Engraved, Photogravure

1986, June *Perf. 13*

617 A58(b) 100fr on 40fr #283 4.00 1.25

618 A83(b) 150fr on 45fr #344 4.00 1.25

1986 World Cup Soccer Championships, Mexico — A192

1986, June 29 **Litho.**

619 A192 500fr multi 5.00 2.50

For surcharge see No. 792.

Fight against Desert Encroachment — A193

1986, July 16 *Perf. 13½*

620 A193 150fr multi 1.75 .95

King Behanzin — A194

Amazon — A194a

1986-88 Engr. *Perf. 13*

621 A194 40fr black .30 .25
622 A194a 100fr brt blue .80 .50
623 A194 125fr maroon 1.10 .75
624 A194a 150fr violet 1.60 .80
625 A194 190fr dark ultra 1.75 1.10
627 A194 220fr dark grn 2.00 1.25
Nos. 621-627 (6) 7.55 4.65

Issued: 100fr, 150fr, 8/1/; others, 10/1/88.
See No. 636. For surcharge see No. 787.

Flowers — A195

Perf. 13x12½, 12½x13

1986, Sept. 1 Litho.

631 A195 100fr Haemanthus 1.10 .70
632 A195 205fr Hemerocalle, horiz. 3.00 1.10

For surcharge see No. 1061F.

Butterflies A196

No. 633, Day peacock, little tortoiseshell, morio. No. 634, Aurora, machaon and fair lady.

1986, Sept. 15

633 A196 150fr shown 3.50 1.50
634 A196 150fr multi 3.50 1.50

Dahomey Nos. 290, 307 Overprinted Perfs. & Printing Methods as Before

1985, Oct. 15

634A A67(b) 50fr on #307 *55.00 25.00*
634B A60(d) 150fr on 100fr #290 *55.00 25.00*

Statue of Liberty, Cent. — A197

1986, Oct. 28 Litho. *Perf. 12½*

635 A197 250fr multi 3.25 1.25

King Behanzin — A198

1986, Oct. 30 *Perf. 13½*

636 A198 440fr multi 5.50 2.50

Behanzin, leader of resistance movement against French occupation (1886-1894).
For surcharge see No. 921.

Brazilian Cultural Week, Cotonou — A200

1987, Jan. 17 *Perf. 12½*

638 A200 150fr multi 1.50 .75

Rotary Intl. District 910 Conference, Cotonou, Apr. 23-25 — A201

1987, Apr. 23 Litho. *Perf. 13½*

639 A201 300fr Center for the Blind, Cotonou 3.50 1.50

Automobile Cent. — A202

Modern car and: 150fr, Steam tricycle, by De Dion-Bouton and Trepardoux, 1887. 300fr, Gas-driven Victoria, by Daimler, 1886.

1987, July 1 *Perf. 12½*

640 A202 150fr multi 1.50 .75
641 A202 300fr multi 3.50 1.50

For surcharge see No. 679B.

Snake Temple Baptism — A203

1987, July 20 *Perf. 13½*

642 A203 100fr multi 1.75 .75

Shellfish A204

1987, July 24 *Perf. 12½*

643 A204 100fr crayfish 1.40 .80
644 A204 150fr crab 2.10 1.00

G. Hansen, R. Follerau — A205

1987, Sept. 4 *Perf. 13*

645 A205 200fr Cure Leprosy 2.75 1.25

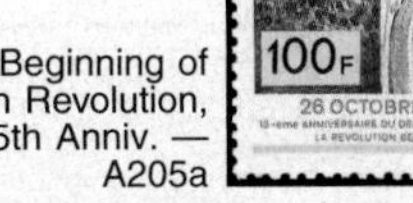
Beginning of Benin Revolution, 15th Anniv. — A205a

1987, Oct. 28 Litho. *Perf. 12x12½*

645A A205a 100fr multi 115.00 3.00

October Revolution, 70th Anniv. — A205b

1987, Nov. 7 Litho. *Perf. 12x12½*

645B A205b 150fr multi 115.00 3.00

Locust Control A206

1987, Dec. 7 Litho. *Perf. 12½x13*

646 A206 100fr multi 1.40 .75

Christmas 1987 A207

1987, Dec. 21 *Perf. 13*

647 A207 150fr multi 1.60 1.00

Dahomey No. 268 overprinted and No. 284 Surcharged

1987 Engr. *Perf. 13*

647A A58(b) 15fr on 100fr #284 50.00 25.00
647B A53(b) 40fr on #268 65.00 25.00

See Nos. C362, C369.

Intl. Red Cross and Red Crescent Organizations, 125th Anniv. — A208

1988, May 25 Litho. *Perf. 13½*

648 A208 200fr multi 2.00 1.00

A209

1988, July 11 *Perf. 12½*

649 A209 200fr multi 2.10 1.25

Martin Luther King, Jr. (1929-68), American civil rights leader.

A210

1988, May 25 Litho. *Perf. 13½*

650 A210 125fr multi 1.40 .65

Organization of African Unity, 25th anniv.

WHO, 40th Anniv. — A211

1988, Sept. 1 Litho. *Perf. 13x12½*

651 A211 175fr multi 1.60 .90

Alma Ata Declaration, 10th anniv.; Health Care for All on Earth by the Year 2000.
For surcharge see No. 786.

Ganvie Lake Village — A212

1988, Sept. 4 *Perf. 13½*

652 A212 125fr shown 1.25 .65
653 A212 190fr Boatman, village, diff. 2.00 1.00

Benin Nos. 605, 606 Surcharged

1988 Method and Perf. as Before

653B A187 190fr on 250fr #605 35.00 17.50
653C A187 190F on 250fr #606 35.00 17.50

A213

1988, Aug. 14 ***Perf. 12½***

654 A213 125fr multi 1.75 1.75

1st Benin Scout Jamboree, Aug. 12-19.

Benin No. 351, Dahomey Nos. 296, 328 Surcharged

1988

Printing Method & Perfs as Before

654A A57(d) 10fr on 60fr on 2fr #351 *50.00 25.00*
654B A62(d) 10fr on 65fr #296 *50.00 25.00*
654E A74(d) 150fr on 200fr #328 *50.00 25.00*

A214

Ritual Offering to Hebiesso, God of Thunder and Lightning.

1988, Dec. 30 Litho. ***Perf. 13***

655 A214 125fr multicolored 1.40 .60

Dahomey Nos. 161, 247, 302, 309, 333, 339, 341 Surcharged

1988 Photo. ***Perf. 12½x13***

655A A19(d) 5fr on 3fr #161 *50.00 25.00*
655B A68(d) 20fr on 100fr #309 *50.00 25.00*
655C A82(d) 30fr on 150fr #341 *50.00 25.00*
655D A76(d) 25fr on 100fr #333 *50.00 25.00*
655E A45(b) 50fr on 45fr #247 *60.00 35.00*
655F A81(d) 55fr on 200fr #339 *80.00 40.00*
655G A65(b) 65fr on 85fr #302 *80.00 40.00*

These are part of a set of 10. Another set of 19 surcharges also is known to exist. The editors need to see the rest of these stamps before listings can be created.

No. 380 Overprinted

1989 Engr. ***Perf. 13***

655H A98 150fr multi *240.00* —

Rural Development Council, 30th Anniv. — A214a

1989, May 29 Litho. ***Perf. 15x14***

655K A214a 75fr multicolored *95.00*

World Wildlife Fund — A216

Roseate terns, *Sterna dougalli.*

1989, Jan. 30 Litho. ***Perf. 13***

657 A216 10fr Three terns 1.75 .50
658 A216 15fr Feeding on fish 2.00 .50
659 A216 50fr Perched 3.75 1.75
660 A216 125fr In flight 6.50 3.25
Nos. 657-660 (4) 14.00 6.00

Eiffel Tower Cent. — A217

1989, Apr. 24 Litho. ***Perf. 13x12½***

661 A217 190fr multi 2.75 1.25

PHILEXFRANCE '89, French Revolution Bicent. — A218

Design: Bastille, emblems, Declaration of Human Rights and Citizenship, France No. B252-B253.

1989, July 7 ***Perf. 13***

662 A218 190fr multicolored 2.75 1.50

Electric Corp. of Benin, 20th Anniv. A219

1989, Oct. Litho. ***Perf. 12½x13***

663 A219 125fr multicolored 1.50 .70

Fish A220

1989, Sept. 22 ***Perf. 13½***

664 A220 125fr Lote 1.50 .70
665 A220 190fr Pike, salmon 2.40 1.10

Death of King Glele, Cent. — A221

1989, Dec. 16 Litho. ***Perf. 13½***

666 A221 190fr multicolored 2.00 1.00

Christmas A222

1989, Dec. 25 ***Perf. 13***

667 A222 200fr Holy family 2.00 1.00

Benin Posts & Telecommunications, Cent. — A223

1990, Jan. 1 ***Perf. 13½***

668 A223 125fr multicolored 1.40 .70

Fruits and Flora A224

1990, Jan. 23 Litho. ***Perf. 11½***

669 A224 60fr Oranges .65 .45
670 A224 190fr Kaufmann Tulips, vert. 2.50 1.25
671 A224 250fr Cashews, vert. 2.75 1.40
Nos. 669-671 (3) 5.90 3.10

Dated 1989.

No. 669 exists with "Populaire" obliterated by black marker.

Moon Landing, 20th Anniv. A225

1990, Jan. 23

672 A225 190fr multicolored 2.00 .90

Dated 1989.

World Cup Soccer Championships, Italy — A226

1990, June 8 Litho. ***Perf. 12½***

673 A226 125fr shown 1.25 .60
674 A226 190fr Character trademark, vert. 2.00 .90

For overprint see No. 676.

Post, Telephone & Telegraph Administration in Benin, Cent. — A227

1990, July 1 ***Perf. 13***

675 A227 150fr multicolored 1.75 .70

No. 673 Overprinted

1990 Litho. ***Perf. 12½***

676 A226 125fr multicolored 1.40 .70

Charles de Gaulle (1890-1970) — A228

1990, Nov. 22 Litho. ***Perf. 13***

677 A228 190fr multicolored 2.25 1.50

See No. 689.

Galileo Probe and Jupiter A229

1990, Dec. 1
678 A229 100fr multicolored 1.10 .65

For overprint see No. 681.

A230

1990, Dec. 25 Litho. *Perf. 12½x13*
679 A230 200fr multicolored 2.00 1.25

Christmas.

Benin No. 641 Surcharged

1990
Perf. & Printing Method as Before
679B A202(e) 190fr on 300fr #641 65.00 24.00

A230a

A231

1990 Litho. *Perf. 11½x12*
679C A230a 125fr multi 125.00 —

National People's Congress.

1991, Sept. 3 Litho. *Perf. 13½*
680 A231 125fr multicolored 1.50 .70

Independence, 31st anniv.

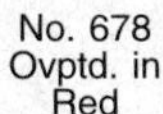

No. 678 Ovptd. in Red

1991 *Perf. 13*
681 A229 100fr multicolored 1.10 .75

French Open Tennis Championships, Cent. — A232

1991 *Perf. 13½*
682 A232 125fr multicolored 1.60 1.00

African Tourism Year — A233

1991
683 A233 190fr multicolored 2.25 1.50

Christmas A234

1991, Dec. 2 Litho. *Perf. 13½*
684 A234 125fr multicolored 1.40 .70

Dancer of Guelede — A235

1991, Dec. 2
685 A235 190fr multicolored 2.25 1.00

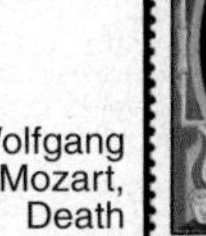

Wolfgang Amadeus Mozart, Death Bicent. — A236

1991, Dec. 2
686 A236 1000fr multicolored 12.00 7.75

For surcharge see No. 793.

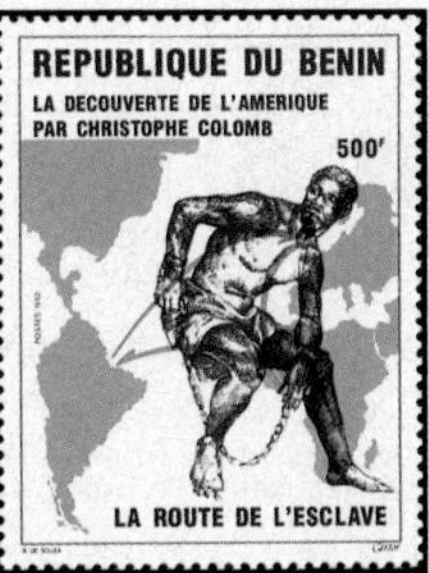

Discovery of America, 500th Anniv. A237

1000fr, Columbus coming ashore, horiz.

1992, Apr. 24 Litho. *Perf. 13*
687 A237 500fr blk, blue & brn 5.25 3.50
688 A237 1000fr multicolored 10.50 7.00
a. Souvenir sheet, #687-688 17.50 16.00

De Gaulle Type of 1990

1992 Litho. *Perf. 13*
689 A228 300fr like #677 3.25 2.00

Intl. Conference on Nutrition, Rome — A238

1992, Dec. 5 Litho. *Perf. 13*
690 A238 190fr multicolored 2.00 1.40

For surcharge see 928.

Dahomey Nos. 160, 266, 303, 311, 327, 334, 338, C161 Surcharged or Overprinted (No. 690A), Benin No. 342 Overprinted (No. 690B)

1992
Perfs. & Printing Methods as Before
690A A66(e) 5fr on #303 *67.50 32.50*
690B A83(e) 10fr on #342 *55.00 32.50*
690E A80(f) 35fr on #338 *50.00 25.00*
690F A19(e) 125fr on 2fr #160 *55.00 32.50*
690G AP54(f) 125fr on 65fr #C161 *80.00 40.00*
690H A77(f) 125fr on 65fr #334 (G) *80.00 40.00*
690I CD137(e) 125fr on 100fr #311 *125.00 72.50*
690J A52(f) 190fr on 45fr #266 *60.00 35.00*
690K A74(f) 125fr on 100fr #327 *125.00 65.00*

Visit of Pope John Paul II, Feb. 3-5 — A239

Ouidah 92, First Festival of Voodoo Culture — A240

1993, Feb. 3 Litho. *Perf. 13x12½*
691 A239 190fr multicolored 2.25 1.25

1993, Feb. 8 *Perf. 13½*
692 A240 125fr multicolored 1.40 .80

Well of Possotome, Eurystome A241

1993, May 25 Litho. *Perf. 12½*
693 A241 125fr multicolored 3.25 1.25

OAU, 30th Anniv. A242

1993, June 7 Litho. *Perf. 13½*
694 A242 125fr multicolored 1.25 .75

John F. Kennedy — A243

1993, June 24 *Perf. 13*
695 A243 190fr shown 2.25 1.25
696 A243 190fr Martin Luther King, vert. 2.25 1.25

Assassinations of Kennedy, 30th anniv. (No. 695), and King, 25th anniv. (No. 696).

Dahomey Nos. 161, 173, 175, 277, 312, 335 Overprinted or Surcharged

1993
Perfs. & Printing Methods as Before
697 A21(e) 5fr on #175 60.00 32.50
698 A69(f) 5fr on #312 80.00 40.00
700 A19(f) 10fr on 3fr #161 50.00 24.00
701 A77(f) 10fr on 100fr #335 45.00 24.00
703 A57(f) 20fr on 1fr #277 40.00 25.00
704 A21(f) 25fr on 1fr #173 140.00 70.00

Benin Nos. 343, 345, 350, Dahomey Nos. 169, 226-227, 249, 256, 273, 276, 295, 283, 286, 319, 328, 333 Surcharged or Overprinted (Nos. 711, 713)

No. 727

1994-95
707 A38(f) 5fr on 1fr #226 60.00 32.50
708 A47(e) 10fr on 90fr #256 40.00 25.00
709 A71(f) 25fr on #319 40.00 25.00

710 A59(e) 40fr on #286 60.00 35.00
711 A57(e) 50fr on 1fr #350 50.00 25.00
712 A58(e) 80fr on 40fr #283 40.00 20.00
713 A76(g) 100fr on #333 50.00 25.00
715 A38(f) 135fr on 3fr #227 75.00 —
718 A62(e) 135fr on 30fr #295 75.00 —
719 A83(g) 135fr on 35fr #343 75.00 35.00
720 A56(h) 135fr on 40fr #276 35.00 —
722 A20(e) 135fr on 60fr #169 50.00 25.00
723 A83(g) 135fr on 60fr #345 75.00 40.00
724 A55(e) 135fr on 70fr #273 65.00 35.00
725 A45(e) 200fr on 100fr #249 60.00 30.00
727 A74(f) 200fr on Dahomey #328 250.00 125.00

UNESCO Conference on The Slave Route — A244

1994 **Litho.** ***Perf. 13x13½***
728 A244 135fr multi 55.00 17.50
729 A244 200fr multicolored 85.00 25.00
730 A244 300fr multicolored 55.00 17.50

Natitingou Scout Encampment A245

1994 ***Perf. 12¾x12½***
731 A245 135fr multi 65.00 1.25

Intl. Year of the Family A246

1994 **Litho.** ***Perf. 12½***
732 A246 200fr multicolored 65.00 1.25

1994 World Cup Soccer Championships, US — A247

1994 **Litho.** ***Perf. 13x13½***
733 A247 300fr multicolored 160.00 6.25

1996 Summer Olympics, Atlanta — A248

Perf. 12½x13, 13x12½
1995, Apr. 30 **Litho.**
734 A248 45fr Water polo .30 .30
735 A248 50fr Javelin .35 .35
736 A248 75fr Weight lifting .55 .55
737 A248 100fr Tennis .75 .75
738 A248 135fr Baseball .95 .95
739 A248 200fr Synchronized swimming 1.40 1.40
Nos. 734-739 (6) 4.30 4.30

Souvenir Sheet
740 A248 300fr Diving *3.00 3.00*

Nos. 735-740 are vert. No. 740 contains one 32x40mm stamp.
For surcharges, see Nos. 1241, 1257.

Dogs A249

1995, Aug. 23 **Litho.** ***Perf. 12½***
741 A249 40fr German shepherd .30 .30
742 A249 50fr Beagle .40 .40
743 A249 75fr Great dane .55 .55
744 A249 100fr Boxer .75 .75
745 A249 135fr Pointer .95 .95
746 A249 200fr Fox terrier 1.40 1.40
Nos. 741-746 (6) 4.35 4.35

Souvenir Sheet
747 A249 300fr Schnauzer *3.75 3.75*

For surcharges, see Nos. 1222, 1258.

Ships A250

Designs: 40fr, Steam driven paddle boat, 1788. 50fr, Paddle steamer Charlotte, 1802. 75fr, Transatlantic steamship, Citta de Catania. 100fr, Hovercraft Mountbatten SR-N4. 135fr, QE II. 200fr, Japanese experimental atomic energy ship, Mutsu-NEF.
300fr, Paddle-steamer Savannah, 1819.

1995, May 20
748 A250 40fr multicolored .30 .30
749 A250 50fr multicolored .40 .40
750 A250 75fr multicolored .55 .55
751 A250 100fr multicolored .75 .75
752 A250 135fr multicolored .95 .95
753 A250 200fr multicolored 1.40 1.40
Nos. 748-753 (6) 4.35 4.35

Souvenir Sheet
754 A250 300fr multicolored *3.00 3.00*

No. 754 contains one 40x32mm stamp.
For surcharges, see Nos. 1223, 1259.

Primates A251

1995, June 30
755 A251 50fr Pan troglodytes .30 .30
756 A251 75fr Mandrillus sphinx .35 .35
757 A251 100fr Colobus .60 .60
758 A251 135fr Macaca sylvanus .80 .80
759 A251 200fr Comopithecus hamadryas 1.10 1.10
Nos. 755-759 (5) 3.15 3.15

Souvenir Sheet
760 A251 300fr Papio cynocephalus *3.50 3.50*

No. 760 contains one 32x40mm stamp.
For surcharges, see Nos. 1242, 1260.

Domestic Cats A252

1995, July 30 **Litho.** ***Perf. 12½x13***
761 A252 40fr Shorthair tabby .30 .30
762 A252 50fr Ruddy red .40 .40
763 A252 75fr White longhair .60 .60
764 A252 100fr Seal color point .80 .80
765 A252 135fr Tabby point 1.00 1.00
766 A252 200fr Black shorthair 1.50 1.50
Nos. 761-766 (6) 4.60 4.60

Souvenir Sheet
767 A252 300fr Cat in basket *3.75 3.75*

No. 767 contains one 40x32mm stamp.
For surcharges, see Nos. 1224, 1261.

Flowers — A253

Designs: 40fr, Dracunculus vulgaris. 50fr, Narcissus watieri. 75fr, Amaryllis belladonna. 100fr, Nymphaea capensis. 135fr, Chrysanthemum carinatum. 200fr, Iris tingitana.

1995, Oct. 15 **Litho.** ***Perf. 12½***
768 A253 40fr multicolored .25 .25
769 A253 50fr multicolored .35 .35
770 A253 75fr multicolored .50 .50
771 A253 100fr multicolored .65 .65
772 A253 135fr multicolored .75 .75
773 A253 200fr multicolored 1.10 1.10
Nos. 768-773 (6) 3.60 3.60

For surcharges, see Nos. 1225, 1262.

Wild Animals A254

50fr, Panthera leo. 75fr, Syncerus caffer. 100fr, Pan troglodytes. 135fr, Aepyceros melampus. 200fr, Geosciurus inaurus.
300fr, Loxodonta, vert.

Perf. 13x12½, 12½x13
1995, Sept. 20
774 A254 50fr multicolored .35 .35
775 A254 75fr multicolored .45 .45
776 A254 100fr multicolored .65 .65
777 A254 135fr multicolored .95 .95
778 A254 200fr multicolored 1.25 1.25
Nos. 774-778 (5) 3.65 3.65

Souvenir Sheet
779 A254 300fr multicolored *3.50 3.50*

Nos. 774-777 are vert. No. 779 contains one 32x40mm stamp.
For surcharge, see No. 1263.

Birds Feeding Their Chicks — A255

Designs: 40fr, Cocothraustes cocothraustes. 50fr, Streptopelia chinensis. 75fr, Falco peregrinus. 100fr, Dendroica fusca. 135fr, Larus ridibundus. 200fr, Pelecanus onocrotalus.

1995, Aug. 28 ***Perf. 12½x13***
780 A255 40fr multicolored .25 .25
781 A255 50fr multicolored .35 .35
782 A255 75fr multicolored .50 .50
783 A255 100fr multicolored .70 .70
784 A255 135fr multicolored .75 .75
785 A255 200fr multicolored 1.20 1.20
Nos. 780-785 (6) 3.75 3.75

For surcharges, see Nos. 1226, 1243.

Benin Nos. 344, 504, 519, 619, 627, 651, 686 and Dahomey No. 291 Surcharged

1994-95
Printing Method and Perfs as Before
786 A211 25fr on 175fr #651 50.00 25.00
787 A194 50fr on 220fr #627 27.50 —
788 A83(h) 150fr on 45fr #344 40.00
789 A158 150fr on 90fr #519 60.00 30.00
790 A147 150fr on 500fr #504 60.00 15.00
791 A60(f) 200fr on 135fr #291 60.00 30.00
792 A192 200fr on 500fr #619 75.00 35.00
793 A236 250fr on 1000fr #686 60.00 30.00

Natl. Arms — A256

1995 **Litho.** ***Perf. 12½***
793A A256 135fr yellow & multi 1.00 1.00
793B A256 150fr yel grn & multi 1.10 1.10
794 A256 200fr multicolored 1.25 1.10

See Nos. 948-951. For surcharge see No. 1021A

Orchids — A257

Designs: 40fr, Angraecum sesquipedale. 50fr, Polystachya virginea. 75fr, Disa uniflora. 100fr, Ansellia africana. 135fr, Angraecum eichlerianum. 200fr, Jumellea confusa.

1995, Nov. 10 **Litho.** ***Perf. 12½***
795 A257 40fr multicolored .25 .25
796 A257 50fr multicolored .35 .35
797 A257 75fr multicolored .50 .50
798 A257 100fr multicolored .70 .70
799 A257 135fr multicolored .75 .75
800 A257 200fr multicolored 1.20 1.20
Nos. 795-800 (6) 3.75 3.75

For surcharges, see Nos. 1227, 1244.

Butterflies A258

Designs: 40fr, Graphium policenes. 50fr, Vanessa atalanta. 75fr, Polymmatus icarus. 100fr, Danaus chrysipus. 135fr, Cynthia cardui. 200fr, Argus celbulina.
1000fr, Charaxes jasius.

1996, Mar. 10
801 A258 40fr multicolored .40 .40
802 A258 50fr multicolored .40 .40
803 A258 75fr multicolored .80 .80
804 A258 100fr multicolored .90 .90

805	A258	135fr multicolored	1.25	1.25
806	A258	200fr multicolored	2.00	2.00
		Nos. 801-806 (6)	5.75	5.75

Souvenir Sheet

807	A258	1000fr multicolored	*7.00*	*7.00*

For surcharge, see No. 1228.

CHINA '96, Beijing A259

Designs: a, 40fr, Dancer in traditional Chinese costume. b, 50fr, Exhibition emblem. c, 75fr, Water lily. d, 100fr, Temple of Heaven.

1996, Apr. 8

808	A259	Block of 4, #a.-d.	*4.50*	*4.50*

Benin Nos. 523, 616 and Dahomey No. 306 Surcharged or Overprinted (No. 810)

1996?

Perfs. & Printing Methods as Before

809	A191	5fr on 205fr #616	60.00	35.00
810	A67(g)	35fr on #306	60.00	35.00
811	A158	150fr on 90fr #523	140.00	65.00

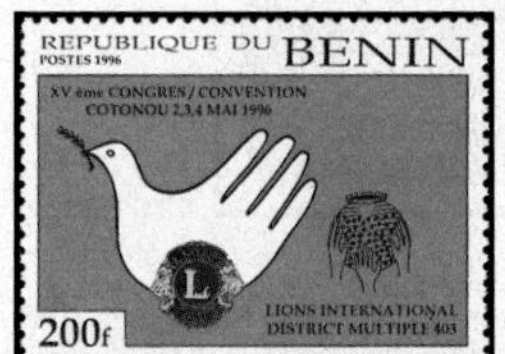

15th Lions Intl. District Convention — A260

1996 Litho. *Perf. 12½*

811A	A260	100fr multicolored	.40	.40
811B	A260	135fr green & multi	1.25	1.25
812	A260	150fr yellow & multi	1.25	1.25
813	A260	200fr red & multi	1.60	1.60
		Nos. 811A-813 (4)	4.50	4.50

For surcharge see No. 1021B.
Issued: No. 811A, 12/27; others, 5/2.

La Francoponie Conference A261

1995, Dec. 2 Litho. *Perf. 12½*

814	A261	150fr pink & multi	1.00	.80
815	A261	200fr blue & multi	1.50	1.00

Cats — A262

1995, Nov. 2 Litho. *Perf. 13*

816	A262	40fr Lynx lynx	.35	.35
817	A262	50fr Felis concolor	.45	.45
818	A262	75fr Acinonyx jubatus	.55	.55
819	A262	100fr Panthera pardus	.75	.75
820	A262	135fr Panthera tigris	1.00	1.00
821	A262	200fr Panthera leo	1.50	1.50
		Nos. 816-821 (6)	4.60	4.60

For surcharges, see Nos. 1229, 1245, 1264.

1998 World Cup Soccer Championships, France — A263

Various soccer players.

1996, Feb. 10 Litho. *Perf. 13*

822	A263	40fr multicolored	.35	.35
823	A263	50fr multicolored	.45	.45
824	A263	75fr multicolored	.60	.60
825	A263	100fr multicolored	.90	.90
826	A263	135fr multicolored	1.00	1.00
827	A263	200fr multicolored	1.60	1.60
		Nos. 822-827 (6)	4.90	4.90

Souvenir Sheet

Perf. 12½

828	A263	1000fr multicolored	*5.00*	*5.00*

No. 828 contains one 32x40mm stamp.
For surcharges, see Nos. 1246, 1265

1996 Summer Olympic Games, Atlanta — A264

1996, Jan. 28 Litho. *Perf. 13*

829	A264	40fr Diving	.30	.30
830	A264	50fr Tennis	.30	.30
831	A264	75fr Running	.70	.70
832	A264	100fr Gymnastics	.80	.80
833	A264	135fr Weight lifting	1.10	1.10
834	A264	200fr Shooting	1.40	1.40
		Nos. 829-834 (6)	4.60	4.60

Souvenir Sheet

835	A264	1000fr Water polo	*5.50*	*5.50*

No. 835 contains one 32x40mm stamp.
For surcharges, see Nos. 1230, 1247, 1266.

Christmas Paintings — A265

Entire paintings or details: 40fr, Holy Family Under the Oak Tree, by Raphael. 50fr, The Holy Family, by Raphael. 75fr, St. John the Baptist as a Child, by Murillo. 100fr, The Virgin of Balances, by Leonardo da Vinci. 135fr, The Virgin and the Infant, by Gerard David. 200fr, Adoration of the Magi, by Juan Batista Mayno.
1000fr, Rest on the Flight into Egypt, by Murillo.

1996, May 5 Litho. *Perf. 13*

836	A265	40fr multicolored	.30	.30
837	A265	50fr multicolored	.30	.30
838	A265	75fr multicolored	.75	.75
839	A265	100fr multicolored	.95	.95
840	A265	135fr multicolored	1.10	1.10
841	A265	200fr multicolored	1.75	1.75
		Nos. 836-841 (6)	5.15	5.15

Souvenir Sheet

842	A265	1000fr multicolored	*6.50*	*6.50*

No. 842 contains one 40x32mm stamp.
For surcharges, see Nos. 1231, 1248, 1267.

Wild Cats — A266

Designs: 40fr, Leptailurus serval. 50fr, Profelis temmincki. 75fr, Leopardus pardalis. 100fr, Lynx rufus. 135fr, Prionailurus bengalensis. 200fr, Felis euphtilura.
1000fr, Neofelis nebulosa.

1996, June 10 Litho. *Perf. 12x12½*

843	A266	40fr multicolored	.25	.25
844	A266	50fr multicolored	.25	.25
845	A266	75fr multicolored	.45	.45
846	A266	100fr multicolored	.55	.55
847	A266	135fr multicolored	.80	.80
848	A266	200fr multicolored	1.25	1.25
		Nos. 843-848 (6)	3.55	3.55

Souvenir Sheet

Perf. 12½

849	A266	1000fr multicolored	*5.50*	*5.50*

No. 849 contains one 32x40mm stamp.
For surcharges, see Nos. 1232, 1268.

Sailing Ships A267

1996, May 27 *Perf. 13x12½*

850	A267	40fr Thermopylae	.25	.25
851	A267	50fr 5-masted bark	.30	.30
852	A267	75fr Nightingale	.55	.55
853	A267	100fr Opium clipper	.65	.65
854	A267	135fr The Torrens	1.00	1.00
855	A267	200fr English clipper	1.40	1.40
		Nos. 850-855 (6)	4.15	4.15

Souvenir Sheet

Perf. 13

856	A267	1000fr Opium clipper, diff.	*5.50*	*5.50*

No. 856 contains one 32x40mm stamp.
For surcharges, see Nos. 1209, 1249, 1269.

Olymphilex '96 — A268

1996, July 2 *Perf. 13*

857	A268	40fr Running	.30	.30
858	A268	50fr Kayaking	.30	.30
859	A268	75fr Gymnastics	.75	.75
860	A268	100fr Soccer	.80	.80
861	A268	135fr Tennis	1.10	1.10
862	A268	200fr Baseball	1.75	1.75
		Nos. 857-862 (6)	5.00	5.00

Souvenir Sheet

863	A268	1000fr Basketball	*5.50*	*5.50*

No. 863 contains one 32x40mm stamp.
For surcharges, see Nos. 1233, 1250, 1270.

Modern Olympic Games, Cent. — A269

a, 40fr, Gold medal, woman hurdler. b, 50fr, Runner, Olympic flame. c, 75fr, Pierre de Coubertin, map of US. d, 100fr, Map of US, "1996."

1996, June 20

864	A269	Block of 4, #a.-d.	*5.00*	*5.00*

No. 864 is a continuous design.
For surcharge, see No. 1236.

Horses A270

Various horses.

1996, Aug. 10 Litho. *Perf. 13*

865	A270	40fr multi, vert.	.30	.30
866	A270	50fr multi, vert.	.30	.30
867	A270	75fr multi, vert.	.60	.60
868	A270	100fr multi, vert.	.70	.70
869	A270	135fr multi, vert.	1.00	1.00
870	A270	200fr multicolored	1.50	1.50
		Nos. 865-870 (6)	4.40	4.40

For surcharges, see Nos. 1251, 1271.

Flowering Cacti — A271

40fr, Parodia subterranea. 50fr, Astrophytum senile. 75fr, Echinocereus melanocentrus. 100fr, Turbinicarpus kinkerianus. 135fr, Astrophytum capricorne. 200fr, Nelloydia grandiflora.

1996, July 25

871	A271	40fr multicolored	.30	.30
872	A271	50fr multicolored	.30	.30
873	A271	75fr multicolored	.70	.70
874	A271	100fr multicolored	.80	.80
875	A271	135fr multicolored	1.10	1.10
876	A271	200fr multicolored	1.75	1.75
		Nos. 871-876 (6)	4.95	4.95

For surcharges, see Nos. 1210, 1234, 1272.

Mushrooms A272

Designs: 40fr, Stropharia cubensis. 50fr, Psilocybe zapotecorum. 75fr, Psilocybe mexicana. 100fr, Conocybe siligineoides. 135fr, Psilocybe caerulescens mazatecorum. 200fr, Psilocybe caerulescens nigripes.
1000fr, Psilocybe aztecorum, horiz.

1996, Sept. 30

877 A272 40fr multicolored .30 .30
878 A272 50fr multicolored .30 .30
879 A272 75fr multicolored .70 .70
880 A272 100fr multicolored .80 .80
881 A272 135fr multicolored 1.10 1.10
882 A272 200fr multicolored 1.60 1.60
Nos. 877-882 (6) 4.80 4.80

Souvenir Sheet

Perf. 12½

883 A272 1000fr multicolored *5.50 5.50*

No. 883 contains one 40x32mm stamp.
For surcharge on No. 877, see No. 1235.

Prehistoric Animals — A273

1996, Aug. 30 ***Perf. 12½***

884 A273 40fr Longisquama, vert. .30 .30
885 A273 50fr Dimophodon, vert. .30 .30
886 A273 75fr Dunkleosteus .60 .60
887 A273 100fr Eryops .70 .70
888 A273 135fr Peloneustes 1.00 1.00
889 A273 200fr Deinonychus 1.60 1.60
Nos. 884-889 (6) 4.50 4.50

For surcharges on No. 886, see Nos. 1236 and 1252.

Birds — A274

Designs: 40fr, Campephilus principalis. 50fr, Picathartes oreas. 75fr, Strigops habroptilus. 100fr, Amazona vittata. 135fr, Nipponia nippon. 200fr, Gymnogyps californianus.
1000fr, Paradisea rudolphi.

1996, Sept. 10

890 A274 40fr multicolored .25 .25
891 A274 50fr multicolored .25 .25
892 A274 75fr multicolored .50 .50
893 A274 100fr multicolored .60 .60
894 A274 135fr multicolored .85 .85
895 A274 200fr multicolored 1.40 1.40
Nos. 890-895 (6) 3.85 3.85

Souvenir Sheet

896 A274 1000fr multicolored *4.50 4.50*

No. 896 contains one 32x40mm stamp.
For surcharges, see Nos. 1253, 1315.

Dahomey No. 235 Overprinted, Benin No. 545 Surcharged

199?

Perfs. & Printing Methods as Before

897 A40(e) 30fr on #235 37.50 20.00
898 A166 75fr on 185fr #545 60.00 30.00

Dahomey Nos. 208, 239-241, 257-258, 261, 269, 274, 283, 320, 326, 334-336, 337 Surcharged or Overprinted (No. 899)

1996?

Perfs. & Printing Methods as Before

899 A77(f) 100fr on #335 60.00 30.00
900 A79(e) 125fr on 150fr #337 35.00 20.00
901 A77(h) 135fr on 65fr #334 120.00 60.00
902 A42(e) 150fr on 30fr #239 *32.50* 20.00
903 A43(h) 150fr on 30fr #241 *35.00*
904 A48(h) 150fr on 30fr #257 *32.50*
905 A50(h) 150fr on 30fr #261 *32.50*
906 CD132(h) 150fr on 40fr #269 *28.00*
907 A58(h) 150fr on 40fr #283 *32.50*
908 A71(e) 150fr on 40fr #320 *72.50*
909 A74(e) 150fr on 40fr #326 *240.00*
910 A78(e) 150fr on 40fr #336 *32.50*
911 A32(e) 150fr on 50fr #208 *72.50*
912 A42(e) 150fr on 70fr #240 *32.50*
913 A48(h) 150fr on 70fr #258 *28.00*
914 A55(h) 150fr on 200fr #274

Benin Nos. 381, 384, 449, 521, 538, 546, 567, 569, 636, Surcharged

1996?

Perfs. & Printing Methods as Before

915 A127 10fr on 90fr #449 50.00 —
916 A159 10fr on 90fr #521 50.00 25.00
917 A164 10fr on 90fr #538 50.00 25.00
918 A174 10fr on 90fr #569 40.00 25.00
919 A98 40fr on 210fr #381 65.00 —
920 A99 40fr on 210fr #384 70.00 —
921 A198 75fr on 440fr #636 60.00 30.00
922 A167 100fr on 500fr #546 60.00 30.00
923 A173 125fr on 300fr #567 45.00 25.00

Obliterator on No. 922 has either one or two bars. Pairs of No. 922 exist with each stamp having a different obliterator.

Nos. 376, 466, 690 Surcharged

No. 926

1995 **Method and Perf. as Before**

925 A96 10fr on 90fr #376 45.00 25.00
926 A132 10fr on 90fr #466 45.00 —
928 A238 150fr on 190fr #690 25.00 15.00

Ungulates — A275

Designs: 40fr, Aepyceros melampus. 50fr, Kobus ellipsiprymnus. 75fr, Caffer caffer. 100fr, Connochaetes taurinus. 135fr, Okapia johnstoni. 200fr, Tragelaphus strepsiceros.

1996, Oct. 15 **Litho.** ***Perf. 12½x12***

930 A275 40fr multicolored .30 .30
931 A275 50fr multicolored .30 .30
932 A275 75fr multicolored .60 .60
933 A275 100fr multicolored .75 .75
934 A275 135fr multicolored .90 .90
935 A275 200fr multicolored 1.40 1.40
Nos. 930-935 (6) 4.25 4.25

For surcharges, see Nos. 1237, 1254.

Marine Mammals — A276

Designs: 40fr, Delphinapterus leucas. 50fr, Tursiops truncatus. 75fr, Belaenoptera musculus. 100fr, Eubalaena australis. 135fr, Gramphidelphis griseus. 200fr, Orcinus orca.

1996, Nov. 5 ***Perf. 13***

936 A276 40fr multicolored .30 .30
937 A276 50fr multicolored .30 .30
938 A276 75fr multicolored .60 .60
939 A276 100fr multicolored .70 .70
940 A276 135fr multicolored 1.00 1.00
941 A276 200fr multicolored 1.60 1.60
Nos. 936-941 (6) 4.50 4.50

For surcharges, see Nos. 1238, 1255, 1273.

Fish A277

1996, Dec. 4 **Litho.** ***Perf. 12½***

942 A277 50fr Pomacanthidae, vert. .35 .35
943 A277 75fr Acanthuridae .50 .50
944 A277 100fr Carangidae .70 .70
945 A277 135fr Chaetodontidae .85 .85
946 A277 200fr Chaetodontidae, diff. 1.40 1.40
Nos. 942-946 (5) 3.80 3.80

Souvenir Sheet

947 A277 1000fr Scaridae *5.50 5.50*

No. 947 contains one 40x32mm stamp.
For surcharges, see Nos. 1256, 1274.

Coat of Arms Type of 1995

1996-97 ***Perf. 12½***

948 A256 100fr multicolored .50 .50
949 A256 135fr lt yellow & multi .70 .35
950 A256 150fr lt bl grn & multi 1.10 .70
951 A256 200fr lt orange & multi 1.20 .70
Nos. 948-951 (4) 3.50 2.25

Nos. 949-951 have "Republique du Benin" at bottom.
Issued: 100fr, 12/27/96; 135fr, 150fr, 200fr, 5/15/97.
For surcharge see No. 1021A.

Military Uniforms — A278

Regiments of European infantry: 135fr, Grenadier, Glassenapp. 150fr, Officer, Von Groben. 200fr, Musketeer, Comte Dohna. 270fr, Bombardier. 300fr, Gendarme. 400fr, Dragoon, Mollendorf.
1000fr, Soldiers, flag, horses, vert.

1997, Feb. 20

952 A278 135fr multicolored .70 .70
953 A278 150fr multicolored 1.10 1.10
954 A278 200fr multicolored 1.20 .95
955 A278 270fr multicolored 1.40 1.10
956 A278 300fr multicolored 1.75 1.75
957 A278 400fr multicolored 2.10 2.10
Nos. 952-957 (6) 8.25 7.70

Souvenir Sheet

Perf. 13

958 A278 1000fr multicolored 5.50 5.50

No. 958 contains one 32x40mm stamp.
For surcharge on No. 955, see No. 1275.

Trains A279

135fr, Steam turbine, Reid Maclead, 1920. 150fr, Experimental high speed, 1935. 200fr, Renard Argent, 1935. 270fr, Class No. 21-C-6, 1941. 300fr, Diesel, 1960. 400fr, Diesel, 1960, diff.
1000fr, Coronation Scot, 1937.

1997, Mar. 26 **Litho.** ***Perf. 13***

959 A279 135fr multicolored .65 .65
960 A279 150fr multicolored 1.00 .55
961 A279 200fr multicolored 1.10 .75
962 A279 270fr multicolored 1.25 1.10
963 A279 300fr multicolored 1.60 1.10
964 A279 400fr multicolored 1.90 1.60
Nos. 959-964 (6) 7.50 5.75

Souvenir Sheet

965 A279 1000fr multicolored 5.25 5.25

No. 965 contains one 40x32mm stamp.
For surcharge on No. 962, see No. 1276.

1998 World Cup Soccer Championship, France — A280

Various soccer plays.

1997, Apr. 9 ***Perf. 12½x13***

966 A280 135fr multicolored .60 .40
967 A280 150fr multicolored .70 .40
968 A280 200fr multicolored 1.00 .80
969 A280 270fr multicolored 1.20 .90
970 A280 300fr multi, horiz. 1.50 1.25
971 A280 400fr multi, horiz. 2.00 1.90
Nos. 966-971 (6) 7.00 5.65

Souvenir Sheet

972 A280 1000fr multicolored 5.00 5.00

No. 972 contains one 40x32mm stamp.
For surcharge on No. 969, see No. 1277.

Orchids — A281

Phalaenopsis: 135fr, Penetrate. 150fr, Golden sands. 200fr, Sun spots. 270fr, Fuscata. 300fr, Christi floyd. 400fr, Cayanne.
1000fr, Janet kuhn.

1997, June 9 **Litho.** ***Perf. 12½x13***

973 A281 135fr multicolored 1.00 1.00
974 A281 150fr multicolored 1.25 1.25
975 A281 200fr multicolored 1.75 1.75
976 A281 270fr multicolored 2.00 2.00
977 A281 300fr multicolored 2.50 2.50
978 A281 400fr multicolored 3.25 3.25
Nos. 973-978 (6) 11.75 11.75

Souvenir Sheet

Perf. 12½

979 A281 1000fr multicolored 9.00 9.00

No. 979 contains one 32x40mm stamp.
For surcharge on No. 976, see No. 1278.

Dogs — A282

Designs: 135fr, Irish setter. 150fr, Saluki. 200fr, Doberman pinscher. 270fr, Siberian husky. 300fr, Basenji. 400fr, Boxer.
1000fr, Rhodesian ridgeback.

1997, May 30 ***Perf. 13***

980 A282 135fr multicolored .70 .70
981 A282 150fr multicolored 1.25 1.25
982 A282 200fr multicolored 1.60 1.60
983 A282 270fr multicolored 1.75 1.75
984 A282 300fr multicolored 2.10 2.10
985 A282 400fr multicolored 2.10 2.10
Nos. 980-985 (6) 9.50 9.50

Souvenir Sheet

Perf. 12½

986 A282 1000fr multicolored 5.50 5.50

No. 986 contains one 32x40mm stamp.
For surcharge on No. 983, see No. 1279.

Antique Automobiles — A283

1997, July 5 Litho. *Perf. 13x12½*

987 A283 135fr 1905 Buick .75 .75
988 A283 150fr 1903 Ford .85 .85
989 A283 200fr 1913 Stanley 1.10 .90
990 A283 270fr 1911 Stoddar-Dayton 1.25 1.00
991 A283 300fr 1934 Cadillac 1.60 1.25
992 A283 400fr 1931 Cadillac 2.25 1.60
Nos. 987-992 (6) 7.80 6.35

Souvenir Sheet

Perf. 13

993 A283 1000fr 1928 Ford 5.50 5.50

No. 993 contains one 40x32mm stamp.
For surcharge on No. 990, see No. 1280.

Songbirds — A284

Designs: 135fr, Pyrrhula pyrrhula. 150fr, Carduelis spinus. 200fr, Turdus torquatus. 270fr, Parus cristatus. 300fr, Nucifraga caryocatactes. 400fr, Luscinia megarhynchos.
1000fr, Motacilla flava.

1997, July 30 *Perf. 13x12½*

994 A284 135fr multicolored .75 .75
995 A284 150fr multicolored .95 .95
996 A284 200fr multicolored 1.25 1.25
997 A284 270fr multicolored 1.75 1.75
998 A284 300fr multicolored 1.75 1.75
999 A284 400fr multicolored 2.75 2.75
Nos. 994-999 (6) 9.20 9.20

Souvenir Sheet

Perf. 12½

1000 A284 1000fr multicolored 5.75 5.75

No. 1000 contains one 32x40mm stamp.
For surcharge on No. 997, see No. 1281.

Flowering Cactus — A285

Designs: 135fr, Faucaria lupina. 150fr, Conophytum bilobun. 200fr, Lithops aucampiae. 270fr, Lithops helmutii. 300fr, Stapelia grandiflora. 400fr, Lithops fulviceps.
1000fr, Pleiospilos willowmorensis.

1997, Aug. 30 Litho. *Perf. 13x12½*

1001 A285 135fr multicolored .85 .50
1002 A285 150fr multicolored 1.00 .75
1003 A285 200fr multicolored 1.20 1.00
1004 A285 270fr multicolored 1.50 1.20
1005 A285 300fr multicolored 1.75 1.40
1006 A285 400fr multicolored 2.40 2.00
Nos. 1001-1006 (6) 8.70 6.85

Souvenir Sheet

Perf. 12½

1007 A285 1000fr multicolored 5.50 5.50

No. 1007 contains one 32x40mm stamp.
For surcharge on No. 1004, see No. 1282.

Benin No. 418 Surcharged

1995

Perfs. & Printing Methods as Before

1009 A114 10fr on 90fr #418 50.00 25.00

Benin Nos. 813, 948 Surcharged

Printing Methods and Perfs as before

1997-99 (?)

1021A A256 135fr on 100fr #948 45.00 25.00
1021B A260 135fr on 200fr #813 45.00 25.00

Early Locomotives — A286

Designs: 135fr, Puffing Billy, 1813. 150fr, La Fusée, 1829. 200fr, Royal George, 1827. 270fr, Nouveauté, 1829. 300fr, Locomotion, 1825, vert. 400fr, Sans Pareil, 1829, vert.
1000fr, Trevithick locomotive.

1997, Dec. 3 Litho. *Perf. 13*

1022 A286 135fr multicolored .85 .85
1023 A286 150fr multicolored .95 .95
1024 A286 200fr multicolored 1.20 1.20
1025 A286 270fr multicolored 1.50 1.50
1026 A286 300fr multicolored 1.60 1.60
1027 A286 400fr multicolored 2.40 2.40
Nos. 1022-1027 (6) 8.50 8.50

Souvenir Sheet

1028 A286 1000fr multicolored 6.00 6.00

No. 1028 contains one 40x32mm stamp.
For surcharge on No. 1025, see No. 1283.

Mushrooms A287

Designs: 135fr, Amanita caesarea. 150fr, Cortinarius collinitus. 200fr, Amanita bisporigera. 270fr, Amanita rubescens. 300fr, Russula virescens. 400fr, Amanita inaurata.
1000fr, Amanita muscaria.

1997, Nov. 5 Litho. *Perf. 13*

1029 A287 135fr multicolored .85 .85
1030 A287 150fr multicolored .95 .95
1031 A287 200fr multicolored 1.20 1.20
1032 A287 270fr multicolored 1.40 1.40
1033 A287 300fr multicolored 1.75 1.75
1034 A287 400fr multicolored 2.40 2.40
Nos. 1029-1034 (6) 8.55 8.55

Souvenir Sheet

1035 A287 1000fr multicolored 5.75 5.75

No. 1035 contains one 32x40mm stamp.
For surcharge on No. 1032, see No. 1284.

Assoc. of African Petroleum Producers, 10th Anniv. — A288

1997, Oct. 20 Litho. *Perf. 13*

1036 A288 135fr green & multi .70 .70
1037 A288 200fr orange & multi 1.10 1.10
1038 A288 300fr blue & multi 1.75 1.75
1039 A288 500fr yellow & multi 3.50 3.50

For surcharge, see No. 1061E.

Old Sailing Vessels — A289

Designs: 135fr, Egyptian. 150fr, Greek. 200fr, Assyrian-Phoenician. 270fr, Roman. 300fr, Norman. 400fr, Mediterranean.
1000fr, English.

1997, Sept. 10 Litho. *Perf. 12½*

1040 A289 135fr multicolored .75 .75
1041 A289 150fr multicolored .95 .95
1042 A289 200fr multicolored 1.20 1.20
1043 A289 270fr multicolored 1.40 1.40
1044 A289 300fr multicolored 1.60 1.60
1045 A289 400fr multicolored 2.40 2.40
Nos. 1040-1045 (6) 8.30 8.30

Souvenir Sheet

1046 A289 1000fr multicolored 6.00 6.00

No. 1046 contains one 32x40mm stamp.
For surcharge on No. 1043, see No. 1285.

Fish A290

Designs: 135fr, Epinephelus fasciatus. 150fr, Apogon victoriae. 200fr, Scarus gibbus. 270fr, Pygoplites diacanthus. 300fr, Cirrhilabrus punctatus. 400fr, Cirrhitichthys oxycephalus.
1000fr, Bodianus bilunulatus.

1997, Sept. 15 Litho. *Perf. 12½*

1047 A290 135fr multicolored .75 .75
1048 A290 150fr multicolored .95 .95
1049 A290 200fr multicolored 1.20 1.20
1050 A290 270fr multicolored 1.40 1.40
1051 A290 300fr multicolored 1.60 1.60
1052 A290 400fr multicolored 2.25 2.25
Nos. 1047-1052 (6) 8.15 8.15

Souvenir Sheet

Perf. 13

1053 A290 1000fr multicolored 6.00 6.00

No. 1053 contains one 40x32mm stamp.
For surcharge, see Nos. 1286, 1408.

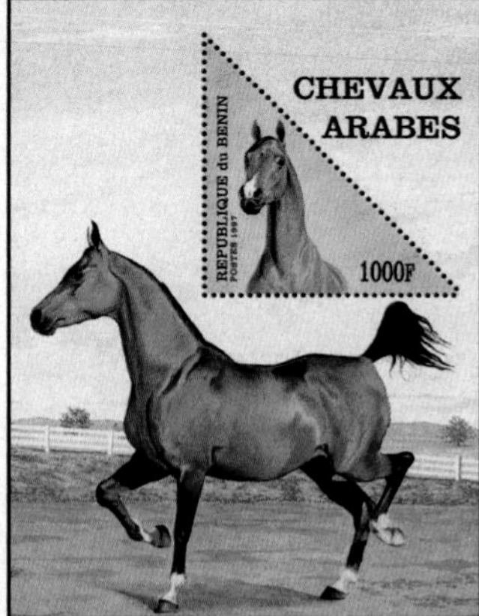

Arabian Horse — A291

Various horses. Denominations and background colors: d, 135fr, green. e, 150fr, red brown. f, 200fr, yellow. g, 270fr, orange brown. h, 300fr, tan. i, 400fr, olive green.

1997, May 25 Litho. *Perf. 12½*

1053A A291 Pair, #d.-e. 1.50 1.50
1053B A291 Pair, #f.-g. 2.75 2.75
1053C A291 Pair, #h.-i. 4.00 4.00
Nos. 1053A-1053C (3) 8.25 8.25

Souvenir Sheet

1054 A291 1000fr multicolored 5.75 5.75

Dahomey No. 266 Surcharged

Methods and Perfs As Before

1997

1054B A52(h) 35fr on 45fr #266 75.00 40.00

Mushrooms A292

135fr, Tephrocybe carbonaria. 150fr, Suillus luteus. 200fr, Pleurotus ostreatus. 270fr, Hohenbuehelia geogenia. 300fr, Tylopilus felleus. 400fr, Lepiota leucothites.
1000fr, Gymnopilus junonius.

1998, Apr. 28 Litho. *Perf. 12½*

1055 A292 135fr multicolored .75 .75
1056 A292 150fr multicolored .85 .85
1057 A292 200fr multicolored 1.10 1.10
1058 A292 270fr multicolored 1.25 1.25
1059 A292 300fr multicolored 1.60 1.60
1060 A292 400fr multicolored 2.25 2.25
Nos. 1055-1060 (6) 7.80 7.80

Souvenir Sheet

1061 A292 1000fr multicolored 5.00 5.00

For surcharge on No. 1058, see No. 1287.

Nos. 432, 433, 632, 1037 Surcharged or Overprinted

No. 1061F

1998 Method and Perf. as Before

1061A A121(h) 15fr on #432 *87.50 47.50*
1061B A121(h) 35fr on 50fr #433 *47.50 24.00*
1061C A121(h) 50fr on #433 *47.50 24.00*
1061E A288 135fr on 200fr #1037 *47.50 24.00*
1061F A195(h) 150fr on 205fr #632 *47.50 24.00*

Fire Fighting Apparatus — A293

135fr, Philadelphia Double Deck, 1885. 150fr, Veteran, 1850. 200fr, Merry Weather, 1894. 270fr, Horse-drawn wagon, 19th cent. 300fr, 1948 Jeep. 400fr, Chevrolet 6400.
1000fr, 1952 American-La France-Foamite Corp.

1998, Apr. 30 Litho. *Perf. 12¾*

1062 A293 135fr multicolored .65 .65
1063 A293 150fr multicolored .85 .85
1064 A293 200fr multicolored 1.10 1.10
1065 A293 270fr multicolored 1.50 1.50
1066 A293 300fr multicolored 1.60 1.60
1067 A293 400fr multicolored 2.00 2.00
Nos. 1062-1067 (6) 7.70 7.70

Souvenir Sheet

1068 A293 1000fr multicolored 5.50 5.50

No. 1068 contains one 40x32mm stamp.
For surcharge on No. 1065, see No. 1288.

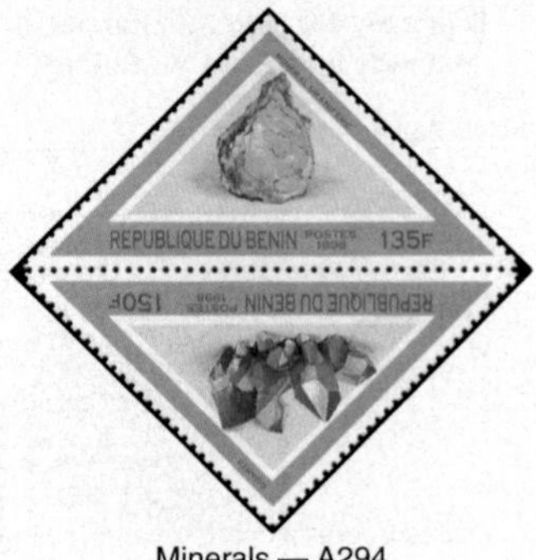

Minerals — A294

No. 1069a, 135fr, Uranifere. No. 1069b, 150fr, Quartz. No. 1070a, 200fr, Aragonite. No. 1070b, 270fr, Malachite. No. 1071a, 300fr, Turquoise. No. 1071b, 400fr, Corundum.
1000fr, Marble.

1998, June 5 Litho. *Perf. 12½*

1069 A294 Pair, #a.-b. 1.50 1.50
1070 A294 Pair, #a.-b. 2.50 2.50
1071 A294 Pair, #a.-b. 3.75 3.75
Nos. 1069-1071 (3) 7.75 7.75

Souvenir Sheet

1072 A294 1000fr multicolored 5.00 5.00

Locomotives — A295

Designs: 135fr, Red 0-6-0. 150fr, 0-4-4. 200fr, Brown 0-6-0. 270fr, Purple 0-6-0. 300fr, Blue 0-6-0. 400fr, "Helvetia" 0-6-0.
1000fr, "Shelby Steel" 0-6-0.

1998, June 30 Litho. *Perf. 12¾*

1073 A295 135fr multicolored .65 .65
1074 A295 150fr multicolored .80 .80
1075 A295 200fr multicolored 1.00 1.00
1076 A295 270fr multicolored 1.20 1.20
1077 A295 300fr multicolored 1.40 1.40
1078 A295 400fr multicolored 2.00 2.00
Nos. 1073-1078 (6) 7.05 7.05

Souvenir Sheet

Perf. 13

1079 A295 1000fr multicolored 5.00 5.00

No. 1079 contains one 40x32mm stamp.
For surcharge on No. 1076, see No. 1289.

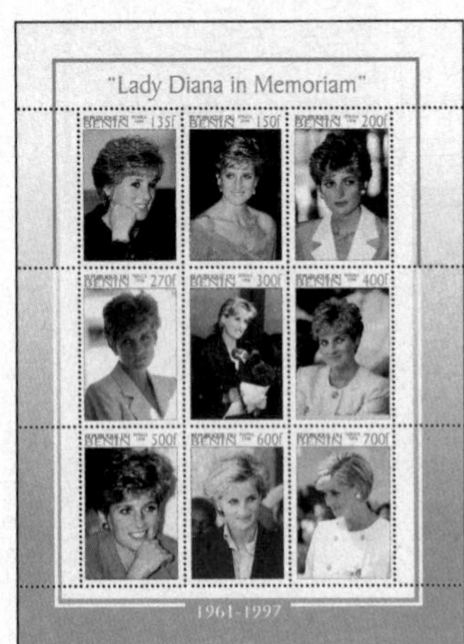

Diana, Princess of Wales (1961-97) — A296

Portraits: a, 135fr. b, 150fr. c, 200fr. d, 270fr. e, 300fr. f, 400fr. g, 500fr. h, 600fr. i, 700fr.

1998, July 10 Litho. *Perf. 12½*

1083 A296 Sheet of 9, #a.-i. 19.00 19.00

Dahomey No. 302 Surcharged

1997?

Perfs. & Printing Method as Before

1084 A65(h) 35fr on 85fr #302 75.00 40.00

Dinosaurs — A297

No. 1085: a, 135fr, Sordes. b, 150fr, Scaphognatus. c, 200fr, Dsungaripterus. d, 270fr, Brontosaurus. e, 300fr, Diplodocus. f, 400fr, Coelurus, Baryonyx. g, 500fr, Kronosaurus, Ichthyosaurus. h, 600fr, Ceratosaurus. i, 700fr, Yangchuansaurus.

1998, July 25 Litho. *Perf. 12¾*

1085 A297 Sheet of 9, #a-i 15.00 15.00

Python Regius A298

Various views of python: a, 135fr. b, 150fr. c, 200fr. d, 2000fr.

1999, Apr. 27 Litho. *Perf. 13*

1086 A298 Strip of 4, #a.-d. 10.00 10.00

World Wildlife Fund.

Dogs — A299

1998, July 31 Litho. *Perf. 12¾*

1087 A299 135fr Beagle .60 .60
1088 A299 150fr Dalmatian .65 .65
1089 A299 200fr Dachshund .80 .80
1090 A299 270fr Cairn terrier 1.00 1.00
1091 A299 300fr Shih Tzu 1.20 1.20
1092 A299 400fr Pug 1.60 1.60
Nos. 1087-1092 (6) 5.85 5.85

Souvenir Sheet

Perf. 13

1093 A299 1000fr Springer spaniel, horiz. 4.50 4.50

No. 1093 contains one 40x32mm stamp.
For surcharge on No. 1090, see No. 1290.

Cats A300

135fr, Abyssinian. 150fr, Striped shorthair. 200fr, Siamese. 270fr, Red striped cat. 300fr, Gray cat with black stripes. 400fr, Manx.
1000fr, Cat with orange, black and white fur.

Perf. 12¼x12½, 12½x12¼

1998, Aug. 10 Litho.

1094 A300 135fr multi, vert. .55 .55
1095 A300 150fr multi, vert. .75 .75
1096 A300 200fr multi, vert. 1.10 1.10
1097 A300 270fr multi 1.25 1.25
1098 A300 300fr multi 1.40 1.40
1099 A300 400fr multi 1.75 1.75
Nos. 1094-1099 (6) 6.80 6.80

Souvenir Sheet

Perf. 13

1100 A300 1000fr multicolored 4.50 4.50

No. 1100 contains one 40x32mm stamp.
For surcharge on No. 1097, see No. 1291.

Antique Automobiles — A301

Designs: 135fr, 1910 Bugatti 13. 150fr, 1903 Clément. 200fr, 1914 Stutz Bearcat. 270fr, 1907 Darracq. 300fr, 1913 Napier. 400fr, 1911 Pierce-Arrow.
1000fr, 1904 Piccolo, vert.

1998, Oct. 12 Litho. *Perf. 12¾*

1101 A301 135fr multi .60 .60
1102 A301 150fr multi .65 .65
1103 A301 200fr multi .85 .85
1104 A301 270fr multi 1.00 1.00
1105 A301 300fr multi 1.20 1.20
1106 A301 400fr multi 1.60 1.60
Nos. 1101-1106 (6) 5.90 5.90

Souvenir Sheet

Perf. 12¾x12½

1107 A301 1000fr multi 4.50 4.50

No. 1107 contains one 32x40mm stamp.
For surcharge on No. 1104, see No. 1292.

Butterflies — A301a

Designs: 135fr, Parnassius apollo. 150fr, Anthocharis cardamines. 200fr, Nymphalis antiopa. 250fr, Parage aegeria. 300fr, Palaeochrysophanus hippothoe. 400fr, Carterocephalus palaemon.
1000fr, Aglais urticae.

1998, Dec. 10 Litho. *Perf. 12¾*

1107A-1107F A301a Set of 6 7.00 7.00

Souvenir Sheet

Perf. 13

1107G A301a 1000fr multi 4.00 4.00

No. 1107G contains one 40x32mm stamp.

African Wildlife — A302

Designs: 50fr, Ceratotherium simun. 100fr, Hipotragus niger. No. 1110, Phacochoerus aethiopicus. No. 1111, Hyaena brunnea. No. 1112, Colobus guereza. No. 1113, Hippopotamus amphibius. No. 1114, Cyncerus caffer caffer. No. 1115, Equus zebra. No. 1116, Acinonyx jubatus. No. 1117, Panthera leo leo. 400fr, Lycaon pictus. 500fr, Perodicticus potto.

Perf. 12¼x12½

1999, Mar. 10 Litho.

1108 A302 50fr gray .25 .25
1109 A302 100fr brt violet .45 .45
1110 A302 135fr gray green .60 .60
1111 A302 135fr black .60 .60
1112 A302 150fr gray blue .70 .70
1113 A302 150fr emerald .70 .70
1114 A302 200fr dull brown .90 .90
1115 A302 200fr blue .90 .90
1116 A302 300fr henna brown 1.40 1.40
1117 A302 300fr brown 1.40 1.40
1118 A302 400fr red brown 1.90 1.90
1119 A302 500fr deep bister 2.10 2.10
Nos. 1108-1119 (12) 11.90 11.90

Birds — A303

Designs: 135fr, Chloebia gouldiae. 150fr, Sicalis flaveola. 200fr, Quelea quelea. 270fr, Euplectes afer. 300fr, Paroaria coronata. 400fr, Emberiza flaviventris.
1000fr, Mandingoa nitidula.

1999, Jan. 30 Litho. *Perf. 12¾*

1120-1125 A303 Set of 6 6.00 6.00

Souvenir Sheet

Perf. 12½

1126 A303 1000fr multi 4.00 4.00

No. 1126 contains one 32x40mm stamp.
For No. 1123 surcharge, see No. 1293.

Orchids A304

Designs: 50fr, Brassocattleya cliftonii. 100fr, Wilsonara. 150fr, Cypripedium paeony. 300fr, Cymbidium babylon. 400fr, Cattleya. 500fr, Miltonia minx.

1999, Apr. 25 Litho. *Perf. 12¾*

1127 A304 50fr multi .25 .25
1128 A304 100fr multi .45 .45
1129 A304 150fr multi .70 .70
1130 A304 300fr multi 1.40 1.40
1131 A304 400fr multi 1.90 1.90
1132 A304 500fr multi 2.10 2.10
Nos. 1127-1132 (6) 6.80 6.80

Souvenir Sheet

Perf. 13

1133 A304 1000fr Miltonia (isis) 4.50 4.50

No. 1133 contains one 28x36mm stamp.
For surcharge, see No. 1239.

Chess Players A305

Designs: 135fr, Mikhail Tal. 150fr, Emanuel Lasker. 200fr, José Raul Capablanca. 270fr, Alexander Alekhine. 300fr, Max Euwe. 400fr, Mikhail Botvinnik.
1000fr, Wilhelm Steinitz.

1999, Mar. 28 Litho. *Perf. 12¾*

1134-1139 A305 Set of 6 5.50 5.50

Souvenir Sheet

Perf. 13

1140 A305 1000fr multi 5.00 5.00

No. 1140 contains one 32x40mm stamp.
For surcharge on No. 1137, see No. 1294.

Ancient Sailing Ships A306

Designs: 135fr, Ceylonese canot. 150fr, Tanka-tim. 200fr, Sampan. 270fr, Polynesian canot. 300fr, Japanese junk. 400fr, Dacca-pulwar.

1000fr, Chinese junk.

1999, Feb. 15 Litho. *Perf. 12¾*

1141-1146	A306	Set of 6	5.50	5.50

Souvenir Sheet

Perf. 12½

1147	A306	1000fr multi	3.75	3.75

No. 1147 contains one 40x32mm stamp.

For surcharge on No. 1144, see No. 1295.

Fish — A307

Designs: 135fr, Notopterus chitala. 150fr, Puntius filamentosus. 200fr, Epaizeorhynchos bicolor. 270fr, Rasbora maculata. 300fr, Pristolepis fasciatus. 400fr, Betta splendens.

1000fr, Trichogaster trichopterus.

1999, May 10 Litho. *Perf. 12½x12¼*

1148	A307	135fr multi	.55	.55
1149	A307	150fr multi	.65	.65
1150	A307	200fr multi	.80	.80
1151	A307	270fr multi	.95	.95
1152	A307	300fr multi	1.10	1.10
1153	A307	400fr multi	1.60	1.60
		Nos. 1148-1153 (6)	5.65	5.65

Souvenir Sheet

Perf. 13x13¼

1154	A307	1000fr multi	4.00	4.00

No. 1154 contains one 40x32mm stamp. For surcharge, see No. 1347.

Grand Prix de l'Amitie — A308

1999 Litho. *Perf. 13½x13*

1154A	A308	135fr multi	—	—
1155	A308	150fr multi	—	—
1156	A308	200fr multi	—	—
1157	A308	300fr multi	—	—
1157A	A308	500fr multi	—	—
1158	A308	1000fr multi	—	—
		Nos. 1154A-1158 (6)	400.00	—

No. 1157A exists as a souvenir sheet of 1. Value, unused $200.

Early Steam Vehicles A309

Designs: 135fr, 1786 tricycle made by A. Murdock. 150fr, 1800 locomotive made by Richard Trevithick. 200fr, 1803 locomotive made by Trevithick. 270fr, 1811 locomotive made by John Blenkinsop. 300fr, 1829 locomotive, Stourbridge Lion. 400fr, 1830 locomotive, Tom Thumb.

1000fr, 1760 locomotive made by Isaac Newton, horiz.

1999, June 18 Litho. *Perf. 12¾*

1159-1164	A309	Set of 6	6.00	6.00

Souvenir Sheet

Perf. 13

1165	A309	1000fr multi	4.00	4.00

No. 1165 contains one 40x32 mm stamp.

Council of the Entente, 40th Anniv. A310

1999-2001 Litho. *Perf. 13x13¼*

1166 A310 135fr multi, dated "1999"		—	—
a.	Perf. 13½x13¼, dated "2000"	—	—
b.	Perf. 13½x13¼, dated "2001"	—	—
c.	Perf. 13, dated "2001"	—	—
d.	Perf. 13x13¼, dated "2000"		—
e.	Perf. 13x13¼, dated "2001"		—
1167 A310 150fr multi, dated "1999"			—
a.	Perf. 13½x13¼, dated "2001"	—	—
b.	Perf. 13x13¼, dated "2001"	—	—
c.	Perf. 13x13¼, dated "2000"		—
d.	Perf. 13½x13¼, dated "2000"		—
1168 A310 200fr multi, dated "1999"			—
a.	Perf. 13x13¼, dated "2000"	—	—
b.	Perf. 13½x13¼, dated "2001"	—	—
c.	Perf. 13x13¼, dated "2001"		—
d.	Perf. 13½x13¼, dated "2000"		—

The editors suspect other stamps in this set have been issued and would like to examine them.

For surcharges, see Nos. 1316-1322.

Snakes A311

Designs: 135fr, Elaphe longissima. 150fr, Pituophis melanoleucus. 200fr, Natrix natrix. 270fr, Oxybelis fulgidus. 300fr, Epicrates subflavus. 400fr, Crotalus atrox.

1000fr, Vipera berus.

1999, July 18 Litho. *Perf. 12¾*

1170-1175	A311	Set of 6	5.50	5.50

Souvenir Sheet

Perf. 13

1176	A311	1000fr multi	4.00	4.00

No. 1176 contains one 40x32mm stamp.

China 1999 World Philatelic Exhibition — A312

No. 1177: a, 50fr, Rocket testing, 14th cent. b, 100fr, Jiuquan space launch center. c, 135fr, DFH-3 communications satellite. d, 150fr, Launch of a foreign satellite. e, 200fr, Long March rocket CZ-2C. f, 300fr, Ship Yuan Wang. g, 400fr, Satellite dish. h, 500fr, Cacheted stamped covers.

1999, Aug. 22 *Perf. 12½*

1177	A312	Sheet of 8, #a-h	10.00	10.00

SOS Children's Villages, 50th Anniv. — A313

Denominations and panel colors: 135fr, Light green. 200fr, Pink. 300fr, Light blue. 500fr, Yellow.

1999, Oct. 15 Litho. *Perf. 12¾*

1178-1181	A313	Set of 4	5.25	5.25

For surcharges, see Nos. 1208, 1240, 1296.

Souvenir Sheet

Manchester United, 1999 English Soccer Champions — A314

No. 1182: a, 135fr, Players celebrating on platform. b, 200fr, Players in action. c, 300fr, Players celebrating. d, 400fr, Stadium. e, 500fr, Trophies. f, 1000fr, Player with trophy.

1999, Oct. 15 *Perf. 13¼*

1182	A314	Sheet of 6, #a-f	13.00	13.00

The sets formerly listed as Nos. 1183-1189 (New Year 2000 - Year of the Dragon) and 1211-1217 (Dogs) were apparently prepared but not issued. These and two other sets, depicting insects (5 stamps and a souvenir sheet) and songbirds (12 stamps) were not sold in Benin, and they were not valid for postage.

Wild Cats A316

Designs: 135fr, Acinonyx jubatus. 150fr, Panthera onca. 200fr, Panthera uncia. 270fr, Panthera pardus. 300fr, Felis concolor. 400fr, Panthera tigris.

1000fr, Panthera leo.

Perf. 12½x12¼

1999, Sept. 28 Litho.

1190-1195	A316	Set of 6	6.50	6.50

Souvenir Sheet

1196	A316	1000fr multi	4.50	4.50

For surcharge, see No. 1350.

Cacti — A317

Designs: 135fr, Mammillaria lenta. 150fr, Oehmea nelsonii. 200fr, Neobesseya rosiflora. 270fr, Opuntia gosseliniana. 300fr, Parodia nivosa. 400fr, Rebutia senilis.

1000fr, Opuntia retrorsa, vert.

1999, Oct. 10 Litho. *Perf. 12¼*

1197-1202	A317	Set of 6	6.50	6.50

Souvenir Sheet

Perf. 12½

1203	A317	1000fr multi	4.50	4.50

No. 1203 contains one 32x40mm rectangular stamp.

Birds A318

No. 1204: a, 135fr, Estrilda locustella. b, 150fr, Estrilda melanotis.

No. 1205: a, 200fr, Pytelia melba. b, 270fr, Uraeginthus bengalensis.

No. 1206: a, 300fr, Pyromelana orix. b, 400fr, Ploceus cucullatus.

1000fr, Steganura paradisea.

1999, Dec. 7 Litho. *Perf. 12¼*

Pairs, #a-b

1204-1206	A318	Set of 3	5.50	5.50

Souvenir Sheet

1207	A318	1000fr multi	3.75	3.75

No. 1180 Surcharged

Method and Perf. as Before

2000 ?

1208	A313	135fr on 300fr #1180		

Nos. 850, 873 Surcharged

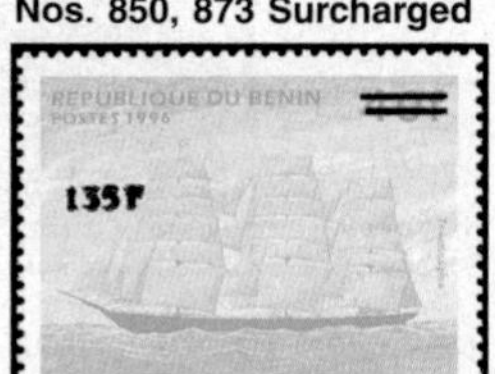

Methods and Perfs. as Before

2000 ?

1209	A267	135fr on 40fr #850	150.00	75.00
1210	A271	150fr on 75fr #873	75.00	40.00

Lions A319

Designs: 135fr, Lion lying on side. 150fr, Lion walking. 200fr, Lions hunting zebras.

2001 Litho. *Perf. 12*

1211	A319	135fr multi	1.40	1.40
1212	A319	150fr multi	1.50	1.50

Size: 65x22mm

1213	A319	200fr multi	2.10	2.10

Three 750fr stamps and a 1500fr souvenir sheet depicting lions and their prey were not authorized by Benin postal officials.

Fire Vehicles — A319a

Designs: 135fr, 1890 hose wagon. 150fr, 1900 fire truck. 200fr, 1903 fire truck. No. 1214C, 750fr, 1913 ladder truck. No. 1214D, 750fr, 1923 ladder truck.

2001 Litho. *Perf. 12*

1214	A319a	135fr multi	—	—
1214A	A319a	150fr multi	—	—
1214B	A319a	200fr multi	—	—
1214C	A319a	750fr multi	—	—
1214D	A319a	750fr multi	—	—

Benin postal authorities declared a 750fr stamp depiciting a 1940 ladder truck and a 1500fr souvenir sheet depicting an 1877 pumper as "not authorized."

A319b

A319c

Primates — A319d

Designs: 150fr, Head of gorilla. 200fr, Gorilla.

2001 Litho. *Perf. 12*

1215	A319b	135fr shown	—	—
1215A	A319b	150fr multi	—	—
1215B	A319b	200fr multi	—	—
1215C	A319c	750fr shown	—	—
1215D	A319d	750fr shown	—	—

Benin postal authorities declared another 750fr stamp depiciting a primate and a 1500fr souvenir sheet depicting a gorilla as "not authorized."

Abdus Salam, 1979 Nobel Physics Laureate — A320

Abdus Salam and Building A321

2001 Litho. *Perf. 13¼x13*

1218	A320	135fr multi	—	—
1219	A321	150fr multi	—	—
1220	A321	200fr multi	—	—

Edward Bouchet Abdus Salam Institute Intl. Conference on Physics and High Technology for the Development of Africa, Cotonou. The editors suspect there may be additional stamps in this set and would like to examine any examples. Numbers may change.

Nos. 1218-1220 exist dated 2002.

For surcharge on No. 1219, see No. 1323.

Various Stamps of 1995-99 Surcharged Like No. 1209

No. 1222

No. 1296

Methods and Perfs As Before

2000

1222	A249	135fr on 40fr #741	*160.00*	*80.00*
1223	A250	135fr on 40fr #748	*160.00*	*80.00*
1224	A252	135fr on 40fr #761	*160.00*	*80.00*
1225	A253	135fr on 40fr #768	*160.00*	*80.00*
1226	A255	135fr on 40fr #780	*160.00*	*80.00*
1227	A257	135fr on 40fr #795	*160.00*	*80.00*
1228	A258	135fr on 40fr #801	*160.00*	*80.00*
1229	A262	135fr on 40fr #816	*160.00*	*80.00*
1230	A264	135fr on 40fr #829	*160.00*	*80.00*
1231	A265	135fr on 40fr #836	*160.00*	*80.00*
1232	A266	135fr on 40fr #843	*160.00*	*80.00*
1233	A268	135fr on 40fr #857	*160.00*	*80.00*
1234	A271	135fr on 40fr #871	*160.00*	*80.00*
1235	A272	135fr on 40fr #877	*160.00*	*80.00*
1236	A273	135fr on 40fr #884	*160.00*	*80.00*
1237	A275	135fr on 40fr #930	*160.00*	*80.00*
1238	A276	135fr on 40fr #936	*160.00*	*80.00*
1239	A304	135fr on 400fr #1131	*160.00*	*80.00*
1240	A313	135fr on 500fr #1181	*400.00*	*200.00*
1241	A248	150fr on 75fr #736	*80.00*	*40.00*
1242	A251	150fr on 75fr #756	*80.00*	*40.00*
1243	A255	150fr on 75fr #782	*80.00*	*40.00*
1244	A257	150fr on 75fr #797	*80.00*	*40.00*
1245	A262	150fr on 75fr #818	*80.00*	*40.00*
1246	A263	150fr on 75fr #824	*80.00*	*40.00*
1247	A264	150fr on 75fr #831	*80.00*	*40.00*
1248	A265	150fr on 75fr #838	*80.00*	*40.00*
1249	A267	150fr on 75fr #852	*80.00*	*40.00*
1250	A268	150fr on 75fr #859	*80.00*	*40.00*
1251	A270	150fr on 75fr #867	*80.00*	*40.00*
1252	A273	150fr on 75fr #886	*80.00*	*40.00*
1253	A274	150fr on 75fr #892	*80.00*	*40.00*
1254	A275	150fr on 75fr #932	*80.00*	*40.00*
1255	A276	150fr on 75fr #938	*80.00*	*40.00*
1256	A277	150fr on 75fr #943	*80.00*	*40.00*
1257	A248	150fr on 100fr #737	*80.00*	*40.00*
1258	A249	150fr on 100fr #744	*80.00*	*40.00*
1259	A250	150fr on 100fr #751	*80.00*	*40.00*
1260	A251	150fr on 100fr #757	*80.00*	*40.00*
1261	A252	150fr on 100fr #764	*80.00*	*40.00*
1262	A253	150fr on 100fr #771	*80.00*	*40.00*
1263	A254	150fr on 100fr #776	*80.00*	*40.00*
1264	A262	150fr on 100fr #819	*80.00*	*40.00*
1265	A263	150fr on 100fr #825	*80.00*	*40.00*
1266	A264	150fr on 100fr #832	*80.00*	*40.00*
1267	A265	150fr on 100fr #839	*80.00*	*40.00*
1268	A266	150fr on 100fr #846	*80.00*	*40.00*
1269	A267	150fr on 100fr #853	*80.00*	*40.00*
1270	A268	150fr on 100fr #860	*80.00*	*40.00*
1271	A270	150fr on 100fr #868	*80.00*	*40.00*
1272	A271	150fr on 100fr #874	*80.00*	*40.00*
1273	A276	150fr on 100fr #939	*80.00*	*40.00*
1274	A277	150fr on 100fr #944	*80.00*	*40.00*
1275	A278	150fr on 270fr #955	*80.00*	*40.00*
1276	A279	150fr on 270fr #962	*80.00*	*40.00*
1277	A280	150fr on 270fr #969	*80.00*	*40.00*
1278	A281	150fr on 270fr #976	*80.00*	*40.00*
1279	A282	150fr on 270fr #983	*80.00*	*40.00*
1280	A283	150fr on 270fr #990	*80.00*	*40.00*
1281	A284	150fr on 270fr #997	*80.00*	*40.00*
1282	A285	150fr on 270fr #1004	*80.00*	*40.00*
1283	A286	150fr on 270fr #1025	*80.00*	*40.00*
1284	A287	150fr on 270fr #1032	*80.00*	*40.00*
1285	A289	150fr on 270fr #1043	*80.00*	*40.00*
1286	A290	150fr on 270fr #1050	*80.00*	*40.00*
1287	A292	150fr on 270fr #1058	*80.00*	*40.00*
1288	A293	150fr on 270fr #1065	*80.00*	*40.00*
1289	A295	150fr on 270fr #1076	*80.00*	*40.00*
1290	A299	150fr on 270fr #1090	*80.00*	*40.00*
1291	A300	150fr on 270fr #1097	*80.00*	*40.00*
1292	A301	150fr on 270fr #1104	*80.00*	*40.00*
1293	A303	150fr on 270fr #1123	*80.00*	*40.00*
1294	A305	150fr on 270fr #1137	*80.00*	*40.00*
1295	A306	150fr on 270fr #1144	*80.00*	*40.00*
1296	A313	150fr on 500fr #1181	*80.00*	*40.00*

Items inscribed "Republique du Benin" that were not authorized by Benin postal officials but which have appeared on the philatelic market include:

Sheet of 15 stamps with various denominations depicting dogs.

Sheet of 9 stamps with various denominations depicting American movie stars, Isabella Rosselini.

Sheets of 6 stamps of various denominations depicting Pope John Paul II, bats, deer, dolphins, frogs, geckos, hares, hummingbirds, kangaroos, lemurs, owls (2 different), pandas, penguins, pigeons, porcupines, rodents, sea gulls, snakes, squirrels, thrushes, toads, turtles.

Souvenir sheets with one 1000fr stamp depicting Isabella Rosselini (2 different), bats, deer, dolphins, frogs, geckos, hares, hummingbirds, kangaroos, lemurs, pigeons, porcupines, rodents, sea gulls, snakes, squirrels, thrushes, toads, turtles.

Sheet of 9 stamps with various denominations depicting Polar bears, Dogs, Wild cats.

Sheet of 8 stamps with various denominations depicting Spiderman, Vin Diesel.

Sheet of 6 stamps with various denominations depicting Lighthouses (2 different), Tigers (2 different), Turtles, Military aircraft.

Sheet of 12 stamps with various denominations depicting Marilyn Monroe (2 different), French firefighters, Carlos Cartagena, Sean Gallimore, Land of the Rising Fun.

Sheets of 10 stamps with various denominations depicting Wolves, Bears, Birds, Elvis Presley.

Sheet of 9 stamps with 100fr denominations depicting Pope John Paul II with Princess Diana.

Sheets of 9 stamps with various denominations depicting Lighthouses (4 different), Windmills (3 different), Looney Tunes characters (3 different), English soccer players and teams (3 different), Paintings of nudes (2 different), Harry Potter (2 different), The Lord of the Rings: The Two Towers (2 different), Terminator 3, Britney Spears, Elvis Presley, Marilyn Monroe, Red Cross, Endangered Animals, Nature Conservancy, Orchids, Gorillas, Cheetahs, Elephants, Lions, Tigers, Horses, Dinosaurs (with Scout emblem), Dinosaurs (without emblems), Trains, Al Buell, Billy DeVorss, Boris Lopez, Edward D'Ancona, Luis Royo Nude Miyazawa, Pearl Frush, Sexy Models, Top Models.

Sheet of 8 stamps with various denominations depicting Horses, Robbie Williams.

Sheet of 6 stamps with 500fr denominations depicting Marilyn Monroe (2 different), Lighthouses, Motorcycles, Trains, Ferrari racing cars, Actresses, Partially nude models.

Sheet of 6 stamps with 300fr denominations depicting Shunga.

Sheets of 6 stamps with 200fr denominations depicting Scenes from Lighthouses, French tales, Wild cats (with scout emblem), Trains.

Sheets of 6 stamps with 100fr denominations depicting Dinosaurs (2 different), Dinosaurs (with Rotary emblem) (2 different), Fire Engines (2 different), Arctic Animals, Lions, Wolves, Prehistoric Elephants, Domestic Cats (with Scout and Rotary emblem), Domestic Cats (without emblems), Dogs, Owls (with Scout emblem), Owls (without emblems), Sparrowhawks, Falcons, Trains, Elvis Presley, Marilyn Monroe, The Beatles.

Sheets of 6 stamps with various denominations depicting Paintings in the Prado (11 differerent), Impressionist Paintings (5 different), Classic Movies (3 different), Marilyn Monroe (3 different), Elvis Presley (perf. and imperf.) (3 different), 75th Academy Awards (2 different), Turtles (2 different), Parrots (with Scout emblem) (2 different), Owl paintings of Pollyanna Pickering (2 different), Trains (2 different), Motorcycles (2 different), Ferrari racing cars, Classic automobiles, Scenes from Japanese tale "Spirited Away," Dogs, Butterflies on Orchids, Dinosaurs, Audubon paintings of animals, Nature Conservancy, James Bond films, Vincent van Gogh, paintings of Nudes, Military aircraft, Pope John Paul II, Elvis Presley, Japanese women, Jazz musicians, Anton Corbijo, Baron Jerry von Lind, Dorian Cleavenger, Drew Posada, Helmut Newton, Matt Hughes, Edvard Runci, Top Models.

Sheet of 4 stamps with 1000fr denominations depicting Winnie the Pooh.

Sheet of 4 stamps with various denominations depicting Madonna, AC/DC, Backstreet Boys, The Beatles, Bee Gees, The Doors, Freddy Mercury, Kiss, Led Zeppelin, Metallica, Mick Jagger, Queen, Bob Hope.

Sheet of 3 stamps with 1000fr denominations depicting Scenes from children's stories.

Sheets of 3 stamps with various denominations depicting Nature Conservancy (2 different), Fighter Airplanes, Trains, Automobiles, Pope John Paul II with Mother Teresa and Princess Diana (perf. and imperf.).

Sheets of 2 stamps with 1000fr denominations depicting Nature Conservancy, Pope John Paul II.

Sheets of 2 stamps with 500fr denominations depicting Dinosaurs, Pandas, Chess, Trains, Elvis Presley.

Souvenir sheets of 1 stamp with 3000fr denomination depicting Gullivera Part I, Gullivera Part II.

Souvenir sheets of 1 stamp with 1000fr denomination depicting Disney Characters, Elvis Presley and various scenes from children's stories (15 different), Marilyn Monroe (11 different), Birds (10 different), Elvis Presley (6 different), Windmills (4 different), Aircraft

(4 different), Pope John Paul II with Princess Diana (4 different), Lighthouses (3 different); Ricky Carralero (3 different), Pope John Paul II (2 different), Automobiles (2 different), Trains (2 different), Endangered Animals (2 different), Dinosaurs (with Scout emblem) (2 different), Dinosaurs (without emblems) (2 different), Baron Jerry von Lind (2 different), Dorian Cleavenger (2 different), Drew Posada (2 different), Dogs, Penguins, Water Birds, Sea Creatures, Audubon painting of a fox, Nature Conservancy, Madonna, Nadja Auermann, Vincent van Gogh, Painting of a Nude, Japanese Women, Manchester United soccer team, Firefighters, Matt Hughes, Carlos Cartagena, Pope John Paul II with Mother Teresa.

Souvenir sheets of 1 stamp with 500fr denomination depicting James Bond films (3 different), The Beatles (2 different), Owls, Al Buell, Freeman Elliot, Peter Driben, Land of the Rising Fun, Pope John Paul II.

Gate of No Return Slave Route Monument, Ouidah — A322

2003, June 23 Litho. *Perf. 12¾*

1297 A322 135fr multi — —
1298 A322 150fr multi — —
1299 A322 200fr multi — —
1300 A322 300fr multi — —
1301 A322 1000fr multi — —

Souvenir Sheet

1301A A322 1000fr Gate, vert. — —

Two additional stamps were released in this set. The editors would like to examine any examples.

Da Silva Museum of Afro-Brazilian Arts and Culture, Porto-Novo — A323

2003, Nov. 10 Litho. *Perf. 13x13¼*

Panel Color

1302 A323 25fr blue — —
1303 A323 175fr red violet — —
1304 A323 250fr green — —
1305 A323 300fr olive green — —
1306 A323 500fr blue — —
1307 A323 1000fr black — —

For surcharges, see Nos. 1355, 1406.

Cercopithecus Erythrogaster Erythrogaster A324

2003, Dec. 19 Litho. *Perf. 13¼x13*

Panel Color

1308 A324 50fr gray blue —
1309 A324 175fr blue — —
1310 A324 250fr bister — —
1311 A324 300fr green — —
1312 A324 400fr brown —
1313 A324 500fr orange — —
1314 A324 600fr dk blue gray —
a. Souvenir sheet of 2, #1313-1314 — —

For surcharges, see Nos. 1334, 1356-1361, 1411, 1448.

Nos. 890 and 1167b Surcharged

1000fr surcharges : Type 1, Top serif on "1." Type 2, Top and bottom serif on "1." Type 3, No serifs on "1."

Methods and Perfs. As Before

2003-04 ?

1315 A274 135fr on 40fr #890 75.00 40.00
1316 A310 135fr on 150fr #1167b 60.00 30.00
1317 A310 300fr on 150fr #1167b 12.00 8.00
1318 A310 500fr on 150fr #1167b 12.00 8.00
1319 A310 500fr on 150fr #1167b, large "5" — —
1320 A310 1000fr on 150fr #1167b, type 1 — —
1321 A310 1000fr on 150fr #1167b, type 2 — —
1322 A310 1000fr on 150fr #1167b, type 3 — —

No. 1319 has a large "5" with a top line that curves. No. 1318 has a smaller "5" with a top line that is straight but has an upward-pointing serif.

No. 1219 Surcharged

Methods and Perfs As Before

2003 ?

1323 A321 135fr on 150fr multi 15.00 8.00

Fight Against Child Trafficking A325

Denomination color: 175fr, Yellow. 250fr, Dark blue. 300fr, White. 400fr, Light blue.

2004, Aug. 31 Litho. *Perf. 13x13¼*

1324-1327 A325 Set of 4 — —

For surcharges, see Nos. 1365, 1446.

Rotary International, Cent — A326

Denomination color: 50fr, Purple. 175fr, Red. 250fr, Black. 300fr, Brown. 400fr, Green. 500fr, Orange. Inscription on 175fr, 250fr, 300fr reads "ACD / Cotonou du 13 au 16 Avril 2005."

2005, Feb. 1 *Perf. 13¼x13*

1328-1333 A326 Set of 6 — —
1333a Souvenir sheet of 1 — —

Benin postal officials have declared as "not authorized" the following items:

Sheet of 9 stamps with various denominations depicting Harry Potter and the Prisoner of Azkaban, The Lord of the Rings: The Return of the King, Prince William, Princess Diana, Asian lighthouses.

Sheet of 8 stamps with various denominations depicting Marilyn Monroe.

Strip of 8 stamps with various denominations depicting Cats.

Sheet of 6 stamps with various denominations depicting Shells.

Souvenir sheets of one stamp with 1000fr denomination depicting Asian lighthouses (2), Cats.

Benin Nos. 1151, 1193, 1305, 1308, 1310-1311 Surcharged

No. 1310

Methods and Perfs As Before

2005-08 ?

1334 A324 175fr on 50fr #1308 4.50 3.00
1347 A307 175fr on 270fr #1151 30.00 20.00
1350 A316 175fr on 270fr #1193 30.00 20.00
1355 A323 175fr on 300fr #1305 4.50 4.50
1356 A324 175fr on 300fr #1311 4.50 4.50
1357 A324 175fr on 250fr #1310 4.00 2.50
1358 A324 200fr on 250fr #1310, thin numerals and "F" — —
1359 A324 200fr on 250fr #1310, thick numerals, "F" with short arms — —
1360 A324 200fr on 250fr #1310, thick numerals and "F" — —
1361 A324 200fr on 250fr #1310, thick numerals and thin "F" — —

Dahomey Nos. 317, 338, C169 and Benin Nos. 342, 1325 Srchd. or Ovptd.

No. 1364

Methods and Perfs As Before

2008 ?

1362 A80(f) 175fr on 35fr Dahomey #338 35.00 25.00
1363 A71(f) 175fr on 5fr Dahomey #317 *35.00 25.00*
1364 A83(f) 175fr on 10fr #342 *30.00 20.00*
1365 A325 175fr on 250fr #1325 *4.00 2.50*
1366 AP59(f) 250fr on Dahomey #C169 *20.00 10.00*

Benin postal officials have declared as "illegal" various items commemorating the 50th anniversary of Europa stamps.

Dahomey Nos. 179, 195, 287, 319 and 331 Overprinted Type "g"

Methods and Perfs As Before

2005-09 (?)

1367 A23(g) 25fr multi (#179) *110.00 60.00*
1368 A27(g) 25fr multi (#195) *30.00 15.00*
1369 A60(g) 25fr multi (#287) *50.00 25.00*
1370 A71(g) 25fr multi (#319) *110.00 60.00*
1371 A76(g) 25fr multi (#331) *20.00 10.00*
Nos. 1367-1371 (5) 320.00 170.00

Various Dahomey and Benin Stamps Surcharged With Various Surcharge Types and

k

Methods and Perfs As Before

2005-09 (?)

1372 A21(k) 25fr on 1fr Dah. #173 *20.00 10.00*
1373 A57(k) 25fr on 1fr Dah. #277 *40.00 20.00*
a. With obliterator over "Dahomey" omitted —
1374 A15(k) 25fr on 3fr Dah. #143 *70.00 35.00*
1375 A19(k) 25fr on 3fr Dah. #161 *20.00 10.00*
1376 A38(k) 25fr on 3fr Dah. #227 *150.00 75.00*
1377 A24(k) 25fr on 4fr Dah. #182 *30.00 15.00*
1378 A69(k) 25fr on 5fr Dah. #312 *175.00 85.00*
1379 A71(k) 25fr on 5fr Dah. #317 *150.00 75.00*
1380 A63(k) 25fr on 10fr Dah. #297 *150.00 75.00*
1381 A71(k) 25fr on 10fr Dah. #318 *125.00 70.00*
1382 A21(k) 25fr on 15fr Dah. #176 *40.00 20.00*
1383 A69(k) 25fr on 15fr Dah. #313 *200.00 100.00*
1384 A21(k) 25fr on 20fr Dah. #177 *30.00 15.00*
1385 A33(k) 25fr on 30fr Dah. #210 *20.00 10.00*
1386 A41(k) 25fr on 30fr Dah. #237 *50.00 25.00*
1387 A46(k) 25fr on 30fr Dah. #250 *40.00 20.00*
1388 A52(k) 25fr on 30fr Dah. #265 *50.00 25.00*
1389 A62(k) 25fr on 30fr Dah. #295 *40.00 20.00*
1390 A38(k) 50fr on 30fr Dah. #231 *60.00 30.00*
1391 A42(k) 50fr on 30fr Dah. #239 *40.00 20.00*
1392 A43(k) 50fr on 30fr Dah. #241 *30.00 15.00*
1393 A63(k) 50fr on 35fr Dah. #298 *75.00 35.00*

1394 A69(k) 50fr on 35fr Dah. #314 *75.00 35.00*
1395 A74(k) 50fr on 35fr Dah. #325 *75.00 35.00*
1396 CD132(k) 50fr on 40fr Dah. #269 *75.00 35.00*
1397 A63(k) 50fr on 40fr Dah. #299 *100.00 50.00*
1398 A72(k) 50fr on 40fr Dah. #321 *50.00 25.00*
1399 A74(k) 50fr on 40fr Dah. #326 *100.00 50.00*
1400 A78(k) 50fr on 40fr Dah. #336 *20.00 10.00*
1401 A57(f) 175fr on 1fr Dah. #277 *15.00 10.00*
1402 A38(k) 175fr on 3fr Dah. #227 *45.00 30.00*
1403 A66(f) 175fr on 5fr Dah. #303 *15.00 7.50*
1406 A323 175fr on 250fr Ben. #1304 *4.50 4.50*
1408 A290 175fr on 270fr Ben. #1050 *200.00* —
1411 A324 175fr on 400fr #1312 *4.00 2.50*
1413 A63(k) 200fr on 35fr Ben. #343 *90.00 45.00*
1414 A76(k) 200fr on 40fr Dah. #332 *30.00 15.00*
1415 A45(k) 200fr on 45fr Dah. #247 *75.00 35.00*
1416 A83(k) 200fr on 45fr Ben. #344 *150.00 75.00*
1417 A19(k) 200fr on 50fr Dah. #168 *120.00 60.00*
1418 A83(k) 200fr on 60fr Ben. #345 *90.00 45.00*
1419 A77(k) 200fr on 65fr Dah. #334 *30.00 15.00*
1420 A45(k) 200fr on 70fr Dah. #248 *75.00 35.00*
1421 A45(k) 200fr on 100fr Dah. #249 *50.00 25.00*
1422 A60(k) 200fr on 100fr Dah. #290 *25.00 12.50*
1423 A77(k) 200fr on 100fr Dah. #335 *25.00 12.50*
1429 A58(k) 300fr on 40fr Dah. #283 *40.00 20.00*
1430 A59(k) 300fr on 40fr Dah. #286 *50.00 25.00*
1431 A60(k) 300fr on 40fr Dah. #289 *20.00 10.00*
1432 A71(k) 300fr on 40fr Dah. #320 *75.00 35.00*
1433 A52(k) 300fr on 45fr Dah. #266 *40.00 20.00*
1434 A67(k) 300fr on 50fr Dah. #307 *40.00 20.00*
1435 A72(k) 300fr on 50fr Dah. #322 *85.00 45.00*
1436 A82(k) 300fr on 50fr Dah. #340 *40.00 20.00*
1437 A65(k) 300fr on 85fr Dah. #302 *40.00 20.00*
1438 A47(k) 300fr on 90fr Dah. #256 *90.00 45.00*
1439 A68(k) 300fr on 100fr Dah. #309 *45.00 20.00*
1440 CD137(k) 300fr on 100fr Dah. #311 *35.00 20.00*
1441 A72(k) 300fr on 100fr Dah. #323 *90.00 45.00*
1442 A74(k) 300fr on 100fr Dah. #327 *90.00 45.00*
1443 A76(k) 300fr on 100fr Dah. #333 *40.00 20.00*
1444 A74(f) 300fr on 200fr Dah. #328 *50.00 30.00*
1445 A81(f) 300fr on 200fr Dah. #339 *35.00 25.00*
1446 A325 500fr on 300fr Ben. #1326 *7.50 4.50*
1448 A324 1000fr on 300fr Ben. #1311 *11.50 11.50*

Léopold Sédar Senghor (1906-2001), First President of Senegal — A327

Denomination color: 175fr, Red. 300fr, Blue green.

2006 Litho. *Perf. 13x13¼*
1451-1452 A327 Set of 2 4.00 4.00

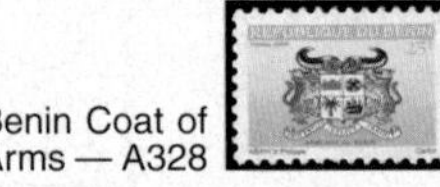

Benin Coat of Arms — A328

2008, Jan. 1 Litho. *Perf. 13¼x13½*
Denomination Color

1453 A328 25fr blue green .25 .25
1454 A328 50fr org brown .40 .40
1455 A328 75fr brown .60 .60
1456 A328 100fr red .80 .80

Size: 36x27mm
Perf. 13x13¼

1457 A328 200fr purple 1.60 1.60
1458 A328 250fr green 1.90 1.90
1459 A328 500fr blue gray 4.00 4.00
1460 A328 5000fr red brown 40.00 40.00
Nos. 1453-1460 (8) 49.55 49.55

For surcharges see Nos. 1461, 1473-1476.

No. 1458 Surcharged

2008 ? Litho. *Perf. 13x13¼*
1461 A328 200fr on 250fr #1458 *60.00 35.00*

Miniature Sheet

2008 Summer Olympics, Beijing — A329

No. 1462: a, Running. b, Taekwondo. c, Swimming. d, Taekwondo, swimming and running.

2008, Oct. 1 Litho. *Perf. 12¾x13½*
1462 A329 200fr Sheet of 4, #a-d *10.00 10.00*

Dahomey Nos. 181, 251, 276, 292, 329, 341 and Benin No. 342 Srchd.

No. 1463

Methods and Perfs As Before
2009

1463 A83(k) 25fr on 10fr Ben. #342 *125.00 65.00*
1464 A56(k) 50fr on 20fr Dah. #276 *25.00 10.00*
1465 A46(k) 300fr on 70fr Dah. #251 *70.00 35.00*
1466 A23(k) 300fr on 100fr Dah. #181 *25.00 10.00*
1467 A60(k) 400fr on 140fr Dah. #292 *25.00 15.00*
1468 A75(k) 1000fr on 35fr Dah. #329 *75.00 35.00*
1469 A82(k) 1000fr on 150fr Dah. #341 *25.00 16.50*
Nos. 1463-1469 (7) *370.00 186.50*

Dahomey Nos. 291 and 306 Surcharged
Methods and Perfs As Before
2009

1470 A60(k) 400fr on 135fr Dahomey #291 *60.00 30.00*
1471 A67(k) 1000fr on 35fr Dahomey #306 *45.00 25.00*

Dahomey No. C35 Surcharged With "Poste Aerienne" Obliterated
Method and Perf. As Before
2009 ?

1472 AP15(f) 500fr on 200fr Dah. #C35 *75.00 45.00*

No. 1457 Surcharged

2009 Method and Perf. As Before

1473 A328 250fr on 200fr #1457 *6.00 6.00*
1474 A328 300fr on 200fr #1457 *6.00 6.00*
1475 A328 500fr on 200fr #1457 *6.00 6.00*
1476 A328 600fr on 200fr #1457 *6.00 6.00*
Nos. 1473-1476 (4) *24.00 24.00*

Benin Nos. 399a, 402a With "POPULAIRE" Obliterated
Methods and Perfs As Before
2009

1477 A108 On sheet of 3, #a-c (#399a) *27.50 27.50*
1478 A108 On sheet of 3, #a-c (#402a) *32.50 32.50*

Independence, 50th Anniv. — A330

50th anniversary emblem and: 250fr, Dancer. 300fr, Tractor, flags of Benin since 1960. 500fr, Godomey highway interchange.

2010, Aug. 1 Litho. *Perf. 12¾x13*
1479-1481 A330 Set of 3 10.50 10.50

Bernardin Cardinal Gantin (1922-2008) A331

Country name and outline of denomination in: 250fr, Green. 300fr, Red. 600fr, Black.

2011 *Perf. 13¼x13*
1482-1484 A331 Set of 3 *8.00 8.00*

Visit of Pope Benedict XVI to Benin A332

Color of top panel: 250fr, Blue. 300fr, Red violet. 400fr, Purple. 500fr, Red. 1000fr, Bister.

2011, Sept. 22 *Perf. 13x13¼*
1485-1489 A332 Set of 5 *24.00 24.00*

AIR POST STAMPS

PEOPLE'S REPUBLIC

Catalogue values for unused stamps in this section are for Never Hinged items.

Nativity, by Aert van Leyden — AP84

Christmas: 85fr, Adoration of the Kings, by Rubens, vert. 140fr, Adoration of the Shepherds, by Charles Lebrun. 300fr, The Virgin with the Blue Diadem, by Raphael, vert.

1975, Dec. 19 Litho. *Perf. 13*

C240 AP84 40fr gold & multi .90 .45
C241 AP84 85fr gold & multi 1.25 .80
C242 AP84 140fr gold & multi 2.50 1.10
C243 AP84 300fr gold & multi 5.40 2.75
Nos. C240-C243 (4) 10.05 5.10

For surcharges see Nos. C357C, C362, C367, C407, C407A, C424, C432, C583, C589.

Slalom, Innsbruck Olympic Emblem — AP85

Innsbruck Olympic Games Emblem and: 150fr, Bobsledding, vert. 300fr, Figure skating, pairs.

1976, June 28 Litho. *Perf. 12½*

C244	AP85 60fr multi	1.50	.65
C245	AP85 150fr multi	2.50	1.60
C246	AP85 300fr multi	5.25	3.25
	Nos. C244-C246 (3)	9.25	5.50

12th Winter Olympic Games, Innsbruck, Austria, Feb. 4-15.

For overprint on No. C246, see No. Q22.

Dahomey Nos. C263-C265 Overprinted or Surcharged

No. C247

1976, July 4 Engr. *Perf. 13*

C247	AP86 135fr multi	1.90	1.25
C248	AP86 210fr on 300fr multi	2.75	1.60
C249	AP86 380fr on 500fr multi	5.75	2.75
	Nos. C247-C249 (3)	10.40	5.60

The overprint includes a bar covering "DU DAHOMEY" in shades of brown; "POPULAIRE DU BENIN" is blue on Nos. C247-C248, red on No. C249. The surcharge and bars over old value are blue on No. C248, red, brown on No. C249.

Long Jump AP86

Designs (Olympic Rings and): 150fr, Basketball, vert. 200fr, Hurdles.

1976, July 16 Photo. *Perf. 13*

C250	AP86 60fr multi	1.00	.55
C251	AP86 150fr multi	2.25	1.25
C252	AP86 200fr multi	3.00	1.75
a.	Souv. sheet of 3, #C250-C252	8.75	8.75
	Nos. C250-C252 (3)	6.25	3.55

21st Olympic Games, Montreal, Canada, July 17-Aug 1.

Konrad Adenauer and Cologne Cathedral — AP87

Design: 90fr, Konrad Adenauer, vert.

1976, Aug. 27 Engr. *Perf. 13*

C253	AP87 90fr multi	1.60	.90
C254	AP87 250fr multi	4.75	1.90

Konrad Adenauer (1876-1967), German Chancellor, birth centenary.

For surcharges, see Nos. C289B, Q17, Q17A, Q26, Q27.

Children's Heads and Flying Fish (Dahomey Type A32) — AP88

210fr, Lion cub's head, Benin design A3, vert.

1976, Sept. 13

C255	AP88 60fr Prus bl & vio bl	1.25	.60
C256	AP88 210fr multi	3.50	1.60

JUVAROUEN 76, Intl. Youth Phil. Exhib., Rouen, France, Apr. 25-May 2.

For surcharges see Nos. C300, C494, C542, C543.

Apollo 14 Emblem and Blast-off — AP89

270fr, Landing craft and man on moon.

1976, Oct. 18 Engr. *Perf. 13*

C257	AP89 130fr multi	1.75	.75
C258	AP89 270fr multi	3.50	1.50

Apollo 14 Moon Mission, 5th anniversary.

For surcharges see Nos. C312, C454.

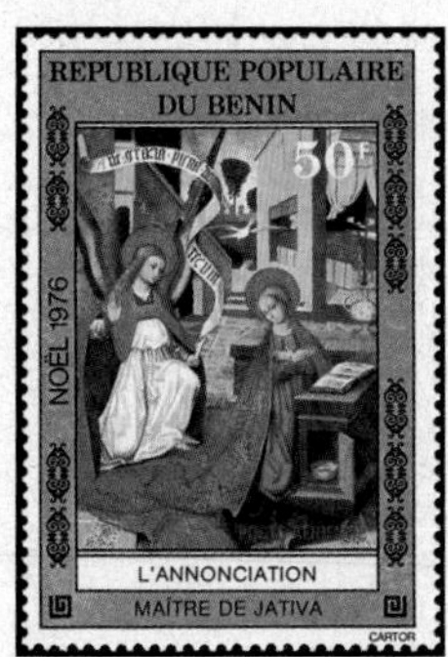

Annunciation, by Master of Jativa — AP90

Christmas: 60fr, Nativity, by Gerard David. 270fr, Adoration of the Kings, Dutch School. 300fr, Flight into Egypt, by Gentile Fabriano, horiz.

1976, Dec. 20 Litho. *Perf. 12½*

C259	AP90 50fr gold & multi	.95	.50
C260	AP90 60fr gold & multi	1.00	.65
C261	AP90 270fr gold & multi	4.00	2.10
C262	AP90 300fr gold & multi	4.50	2.50
	Nos. C259-C262 (4)	10.45	5.75

For surcharges see Nos. C310, C321, C484.

Gamblers and Lottery Emblem — AP91

1977, Mar. 13 Litho. *Perf. 13*

C263	AP91 50fr multi	.90	.50

National lottery, 10th anniversary.

Sassenage Castle, Grenoble — AP92

1977, May 16 *Perf. 12½*

C264	AP92 200fr multi	2.75	1.25

10th anniv. of Intl. French Language Council.

For surcharge see No. C334.

Concorde, Supersonic Plane — AP93

Designs: 150fr, Zeppelin. 300fr, Charles A. Lindbergh and Spirit of St. Louis. 500fr, Charles Nungesser and François Coli, French aviators lost over Atlantic, 1927.

1977, July 25 Engr. *Perf. 13*

C265	AP93 80fr ultra & red	1.00	.50
C266	AP93 150fr multi	2.10	1.00
C267	AP93 300fr multi	3.25	2.10
C268	AP93 500fr multi	6.50	4.00
	Nos. C265-C268 (4)	12.85	7.60

Aviation history.

For overprint and surcharges see Nos. C274, C316, C336, C496.

Soccer Player — AP94

200fr, Soccer players and Games' emblem.

1977, July 28 Litho. *Perf. 12½x12*

C269	AP94 60fr multi	.95	.55
C270	AP94 200fr multi	2.75	1.90

World Soccer Cup elimination games.

For surcharges see Nos. C289A, C308.

Miss Haverfield, by Gainsborough — AP95

Designs: 150fr, Self-portrait, by Rubens. 200fr, Anguish, man's head by Da Vinci.

1977, Oct. 3 Engr. *Perf. 13*

C271	AP95 100fr sl grn & mar	2.75	.80
C272	AP95 150fr red brn & dk brn	4.00	1.90
C273	AP95 200fr brn & red	6.00	2.50
	Nos. C271-C273 (3)	12.75	5.20

For surcharges see Nos. C309, C317.

No. C265 Overprinted

1977, Nov. 22 Engr. *Perf. 13*

C274	AP93 80fr ultra & red	2.00	.90

Concorde, 1st commercial flight, Paris to NY.

Viking on Mars — AP96

150fr, Isaac Newton, apple globe, stars. 200fr, Vladimir M. Komarov, spacecraft and earth. 500fr, Dog Laika, rocket and space.

1977, Nov. 28 Engr. *Perf. 13*

C275	AP96 100fr multi	1.25	.75
C276	AP96 150fr multi	1.90	1.10
C277	AP96 200fr multi	3.25	1.40
C278	AP96 500fr multi	8.00	3.75
	Nos. C275-C278 (4)	14.40	7.00

Operation Viking on Mars; Isaac Newton (1642-1727); 10th death anniv. of Russian cosmonaut Vladimir M. Komarov; 20th anniv. of 1st living creature in space.

For surcharges see Nos. C301, C314, C497, Q18.

Monument, Red Star Place, Cotonou AP97

Lithographed; Gold Embossed

1977 Nov. 30 *Perf. 12½*

C279	AP97 500fr multi	7.25	3.50

Suzanne Fourment, by Rubens AP98

380fr, Nicholas Rubens, by Rubens.

1977, Dec. 12 Engr. *Perf. 13*

C280	AP98 200fr multi	3.75	1.75
C281	AP98 380fr claret & ocher	6.00	2.75

For surcharges see Nos. C311, C313, C483.

Parthenon and UNESCO Emblem — AP99

Designs: 70fr, Acropolis and frieze showing Pan-Athenaic procession, vert. 250fr, Parthenon and frieze showing horsemen, vert.

1978, Sept. 22 Litho. *Perf. 12½x12*

C282 AP99 70fr multi	.75	.25
C283 AP99 250fr multi	2.75	1.60
C284 AP99 500fr multi	5.50	2.50
Nos. C282-C284 (3)	9.00	4.35

Save the Parthenon in Athens campaign.
For surcharge see No. C338.

Philexafrique II — Essen Issue
Common Design Types

Designs: No. C285, Buffalo and Dahomey #C33. No. C286, Wild ducks and Baden #1.

1978, Nov. 1 Litho. *Perf. 12½*

C285 CD138 100fr multi	4.50	2.25
C286 CD139 100fr multi	4.50	2.25
a. Pair, #C285-C286	10.00	10.00

For surcharges, see Nos, C535-C536.

Wilbur and Orville Wright and Flyer — AP100

1978, Dec. 28 Engr. *Perf. 13*
C287 AP100 500fr multi 6.50 3.00

75th anniversary of 1st powered flight.
For surcharge see No. C339.

Cook's Ships, Hawaii, World Map — AP101

Design: 50fr, Battle at Kowrowa.

1979, June 1 Engr. *Perf. 13*

C288 AP101 20fr multi	.90	.30
C289 AP101 50fr multi	1.10	.50

Capt. James Cook (1728-1779), explorer.

No. C253, C269 Surcharged

1979
Perfs. & Printing Method as Before

C289A AP94 50fr on 60fr #C269	80.00	40.00
C289B AP87 50fr on 90fr #C253	80.00	40.00

Lunokhod Type of 1980

1980, June 15 Engr. *Perf. 13*
Size: 27x48mm
C290 A133 210fr multi 3.00 1.40

For surcharges see Nos. C305, C450.

Soccer Players — AP102

1981, Mar. 31 Litho. *Perf. 13*

C291 AP102 200fr Ball, globe	2.10	.80
C292 AP102 500fr shown	5.25	2.40

ESPANA '82 World Soccer Cup eliminations.
For surcharges see Nos. C335, C455, Q10B.

Prince Charles and Lady Diana, London Bridge — AP103

1981, July 29 Litho. *Perf. 12½*
C293 AP103 500fr multi 5.00 2.25

Royal wedding.
For surcharges see Nos. C323, C500.

Three Musicians, by Pablo Picasso (1881-1973) — AP104

Perf. 12½x13, 13x12½
1981, Nov. 2 Litho.

C294 AP104 300fr Dance, vert.	3.50	1.25
C295 AP104 500fr shown	6.50	2.00

For surcharges see Nos. C320, C340.

1300th Anniv. of Bulgaria AP105

1981, Dec. 2 Litho. *Perf. 13*
C296 AP105 100fr multi 1.00 .45

Visit of Pope John Paul II — AP106

1982, Feb. 17 Litho. *Perf. 13*
C297 AP106 80fr multi 2.25 1.00

20th Anniv. of John Glenn's Flight — AP107

1982, Feb. 21 Litho. *Perf. 13*
C298 AP107 500fr multi 6.00 2.50

For surcharge see No. C315.

Scouting Year AP108

1982, June 1 *Perf. 12½*
C299 AP108 105fr multi 1.25 .80

For surcharge see No. C324.

Nos. C256, C275 Surcharged

No. C300

No. C301

1982, Nov. Engr. *Perf. 13*

C300 AP88 50fr on 210fr multi	2.50	2.50
C301 AP96 50fr on 100fr multi	2.50	2.50

Monet in Boat, by Claude Monet (1832-1883) — AP109

1982, Dec. 6 Litho. *Perf. 13x12½*
C302 AP109 300fr multi 7.75 2.50

For surcharge see No. C326.

Christmas 1982 AP110

Virgin and Child Paintings.

1982, Dec. 20 *Perf. 12½x13*

C303 AP110 200fr Matthias Grunewald	2.50	1.25
C304 AP110 300fr Correggio	3.50	1.60

For surcharges see Nos. C325, C337.

No. C290 Surcharged

1983 Engr. *Perf. 13*
C305 A133 75fr on 210fr multi 2.25 1.25

Bangkok '83 Stamp Exhibition AP111

1983, Aug. 4 Photo. *Perf. 13*
C306 AP111 300fr multi 3.25 1.50

For surcharge see No. C322.

Christmas 1983 AP112

1983, Dec. 26 Litho. *Perf. 12½x13*
C307 AP112 200fr Loretto Madonna, by Raphael 3.00 1.20

For surcharge see No. C319.

Types of 1976-82 Surcharged

No. C308

No. C309

No. C310

No. C311

No. C312

No. C313

No. C314

No. C315

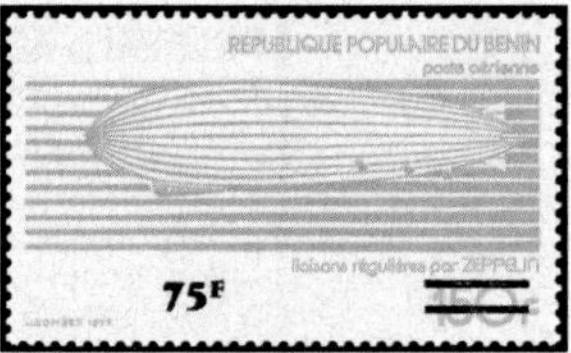

No. C316

No. C317

1983, Nov.

C308 AP94 10fr on 200fr C270 6.50 1.10
C309 AP95 15fr on 200fr C273 6.50 1.10
C310 AP90 15fr on 270fr C261 6.50 1.10
C311 AP98 20fr on 200fr C280 6.50 1.10
C312 AP89 25fr on 270fr C258 6.50 1.10
C313 AP98 25fr on 380fr C281 6.50 1.10
C314 AP96 30fr on 200fr C277 6.50 1.10
C315 AP107 40fr on 500fr C298 6.50 1.10
C316 AP93 75fr on 150fr C266 6.50 1.10
C317 AP95 75fr on 150fr C272 6.50 1.10
Nos. C308-C317 (10) 65.00 11.00

Summer Olympics — AP113

1984, July 16 Litho. ***Perf. 13x13½***

C318 AP113 300fr Sam the Eagle, mascot 3.25 1.50

Nos. C262, C293-C294, C299, C302, C304, C306-C307 Surcharged

No. C319

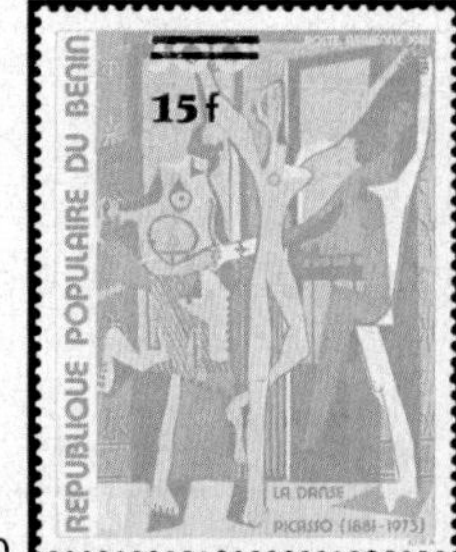

No. C320

No. C321

No. C322

No. C323

No. C324

No. C325

No. C326

1984, Sept.

C319 AP112 15fr on 200fr #C307 7.25 2.00
C320 AP104 15fr on 300fr #C294 7.25 2.00
C321 AP90 25fr on 300fr #C262 7.25 2.00
C322 AP111 25fr on 300fr #C306 7.25 2.00
C323 AP103 40fr on 500fr #C293 7.25 2.00
C324 AP108 75fr on 105fr #C299 7.25 2.00
C325 AP110 90fr on 200fr #C304 7.25 2.00
C326 AP109 90fr on 300fr #C302 7.25 2.00
Nos. C319-C326 (8) 58.00 16.00

Christmas 1984 AP114

1984, Dec. 17 Litho. ***Perf. 12½x13***

C327 AP114 500fr Virgin and Child, by Murillo 6.00 2.50

For surcharge see No. C486

Ships — AP115

1984, Dec. 28 Litho. ***Perf. 13***

C328 AP115 90fr Sidon merchant ship 1.40 .65
C329 AP115 125fr Wavertree, vert. 2.25 .90

Benin-S.O.M. Postal Convention AP116

Wmk. 385

1985, Apr. 15 Litho. ***Perf. 13½***

C330 AP116 75fr Benin arms .90 .30
C331 AP116 75fr Sovereign Order of Malta .90 .30
a. Pair, #C330-C331 2.40 2.40

PHILEXAFRICA III, Lome — AP117

1985, June 24 ***Perf. 13***

C332 AP117 200fr Oil platform 2.50 1.50
C333 AP117 200fr Soccer players 2.50 1.50
a. Pair, #C332-C333 + label 6.00 4.50

For surcharges see Nos. C485-C485A.

Stamps of 1977-82 Surcharged

No. C334

No. C335

No. C336

No. C337

No. C338

No. C339

No. C340

1985, Mar.

C334	AP92	75fr on 200fr #C264	10.00	2.50
C335	AP102	75fr on 200fr #C291	10.00	2.50
C336	AP93	75fr on 300fr #C267	10.00	2.50
C337	AP110	75fr on 300fr #C304	10.00	2.50
C338	AP99	90fr on 500fr #C284	10.00	2.50
C339	AP100	90fr on 500fr #C287	10.00	2.50
C340	AP104	90fr on 500fr #C295	10.00	2.50
		Nos. C334-C340 (7)	70.00	17.50

Dahomey Stamps of 1971-75 Surcharged

No. C341

No. C342

No. C343

No. C343A

No. C344

No. C345

No. C346

No. C347

No. C348

No. C349

No. C350

1985, Aug.

C341	AP87(i)	25fr on 40fr #C266	6.00	1.10
C342	AP49(a)	40fr #C142	6.00	1.10
C343	AP56(i)	75fr on 85fr #C164	6.00	1.10
C343A	AP56(b)(i)	75fr on 85fr Dahomey #C171	*75.00*	*2.50*
C344	AP60(a)	75fr on 100fr #C173	6.00	1.10
C345	AP64(i)	75fr on 125fr #C186	6.00	1.10
C346	AP56(i)	90fr on 20fr #C163	6.00	1.10
C347	A61(i)	90fr on 150fr #C153	6.00	1.10
C348	AP49(a)	90fr on 200fr #C143	6.00	1.10
C349	AP78(j)	90fr on 200fr #C237	6.00	1.10
C350	AP78(j)	150fr #C236	6.00	1.10
		Nos. C341-C350 (11)	135.00	13.50

Christmas — AP118

1985, Dec. 20 Litho. ***Perf. 13x12½***

C351 AP118 500fr multi 5.50 3.00

For surcharge see No. C449.

Dahomey Nos. C34-C37, C84, C131 Surcharged or Overprinted

No. C352

No. C353

No. C354

No. C355

No. C356

No. C357

1986 Photo. Perfs. as before

C352 AP33(b) 75fr on 70fr #C84 4.75 1.00
C353 AP14(b) 75fr on 100fr #C34 4.75 1.00
C354 AP15(b) 75fr on 200fr #C35 4.75 1.00
C355 AP15(b) 90fr on 250fr #C36 4.75 1.00
C356 AP45(b) 100fr #C131 4.50 1.00
C357 AP14(b) 150fr on 500fr #C37 4.50 1.00
Nos. C352-C357 (6) 28.00 6.00

Issued: 75fr, 90fr, Mar; 100fr, 150fr, June.

Dahomey Nos. C82, C139, C141, C146, Benin No. C243 Surcharged

1986
Perfs. & Printing Methods as Before

C357A AP33(d) 15fr on 45fr #C82 50.00 25.00
C357B AP48(d) 25fr on 200fr #C141 (S) 50.00 25.00
C357C AP84(d) 30fr on 300fr Benin #C243 40.00 25.00
C357D AP48(d) 100fr on #C139 50.00 25.00
C357E CD135(d) 100fr on #C146 60.00 25.00

Christmas — AP119

1986, Dec. 24 Litho. *Perf. 13x12½*

C358 AP119 300fr multi 3.50 1.50

Air Africa, 25th Anniv. AP120

1986, Dec. 30 *Perf. 12½*

C359 AP120 100fr multi 1.10 .55

Intl. Agricultural Development Fund (FIDA), 10th Anniv. — AP121

1987, Dec. 14 Litho. *Perf. 13½*

C360 AP121 500fr multi 5.00 2.50

Christmas — AP122

1988, Dec. 23 Litho. *Perf. 13x12½*

C361 AP122 500fr Adoration of the Magi, storyteller 5.00 2.40

No. C241 Surcharged

1989, Apr. 24 Litho. *Perf. 13*

C362 AP84(b) 15fr on 85fr multi 30.00 15.00

Dahomey Nos. C37, C53, C152, C156, C165, C175, C182, C234, Benin No. C242 Surcharged or Overprinted

1987
Perfs. & Printing Methods as Before

C363 AP77 20fr on 250fr #C234 50.00 20.00
C364 AP48(b) 25fr on 150fr #C175 (S&B) 50.00 20.00
C365 AP63(b) 40fr on 15fr #C182 42.50 20.00
C366 AP48(b) 40fr on 100fr #C152 40.00 20.00
C367 AP84(b) 50fr on 140fr #C242 50.00 25.00
C368 AP14(b) 50fr on 500fr #C37 50.00 25.00
C369 AP22(b) 80fr on #C53 50.00 25.00
C370 AP56(b) 80fr on 150fr #C165 50.00 25.00
C373 AP52(b) 100fr on #C156 50.00 20.00

Dahomey Nos. C140, C144, C158, C166, C177, C185, C188 C191, C195, C207, C233, C260, C262 Surcharged

No. C376

No. C382

1988
Perfs. & Printing Methods as Before

C374 AP50(d) 10fr on 50fr #C144 50.00 25.00
C375 AP64(d) 10fr on 65fr #C185 50.00 25.00
C376 AP72(d) 15fr on 150fr #C207 50.00 25.00
C377 AP67(d) 25fr on 200fr #C191 50.00 25.00
C378 AP61(d) 40fr on 35fr #C195 50.00 25.00
C380 AP53(d) 70fr on 250fr #C158 50.00 25.00
C381 AP48(d) 100fr on #C140 30.00 15.00
C382 AP65(d) 100fr on #C188 40.00 20.00
C383 AP84(d) 100fr on #C260 45.00 20.00
C384 AP61(f) 125fr on #C177 40.00 20.00
C385 AP86(d) 125fr on 75fr #C262 45.00 20.00
C386 AP57(d) 150fr on 100fr #C166 50.00 25.00
C387 AP77(d) 190fr on 100fr #C233 45.00 20.00

Dahomey Nos. C179, C181, C196, C203, C208 Surcharged in Black or Violet

1988-89
Perfs. & Printing Methods as Before

C388 AP61(d) 25fr on 100fr #C196 60.00 30.00
C390 AP62 40fr on 100fr #C181 60.00 30.00
C391 AP73(d) 40fr on 150fr #C208 45.00 25.00
C391A AP70(j) 125fr on 150fr #C203 (V) 45.00 25.00
C392 AP61(d) 125fr on 250fr #C179 45.00 25.00
C393 AP87(d) 190fr on 250fr Dah. #C267 75.00 40.00

Issued: No. C391A, 1989.

Dahomey Nos. C108, C147-C148, C162, C167, C178, C187, C194 Surcharged or Overprinted

No. C394A

1992
Perfs. & Printing Methods as Before

C394 AP51(f) 70fr on #C148 60.00 30.00
C394A AP51(e) 70fr on #C148 60.00 30.00
C395 AP55(e) 100fr on #C162 45.00 25.00
C396 AP68(g) 100fr on #C194 120.00 60.00
C397 AP51(e) 125fr on 40fr #C147 20.00 12.50
C398 A52(f) 125fr on 70fr #C108 60.00 30.00
C400 AP64a(e) 125fr on 100fr #C187 45.00 25.00
C401 AP61(f) 190fr on 140fr #C178 45.00 25.00
C402 AP58(f) 190fr on 150fr #C167 60.00 30.00

Dahomey Nos. C145, C149-C150, C163, C182, C189, C198, C257, C264 Surcharged, Benin No. C241 Surcharged

No. C407A

1993
Perfs. & Printing Methods as Before

C403 AP51(e) 5fr on 100fr #C149 45.00 25.00
C404 AP50(f) 10fr on 100fr #C145 45.00 25.00
C404A AP56(f) 20fr on #C163 30.00 15.00
C405 AP51(f) 20fr on 200fr #C150 50.00 35.00
C406 AP83(f) 20fr on 500fr #C257 50.00 35.00
C407 AP84(e) 25fr on 85fr #C241 45.00 25.00
C407A AP84(f) 25fr on 85fr #C241 25.00
C409 AP63(f) 30fr on 15fr #C182 32.50 15.00
C410 AP61(f) 30fr on 200fr #C198 21.00 12.50
C411 AP66(b) 35fr on #C189 45.00 25.00
C412 AP86(g) 300fr on #C264 50.00 25.00

Dahomey Nos. C14, C31, C33, C34, C54, C101, C110, C128, C144, C151, C152, C153, C155, C179, C191, C197, C198, C203, C222, C234, C236, C250, C253, C254-C256, C261, Benin C240, C242 Surcharged or Overprinted

No. C420

1994-95?
Perfs. & Printing Methods as Before

C413 AP61(g) 10fr on 100fr #C253 85.00 40.00
C414 AP52(e) 15fr on 40fr #C155 45.00 25.00
C415 AP83(f) 25fr on 200fr #C256 50.00 25.00
C416 AP83(f) 35fr on #C255 45.00 25.00
C417 AP49(g) 50fr on #C101 62.50 35.00
C418 AP48(g) 75fr on 40fr #C151 40.00 20.00
C419 AP4(g) 100fr on #C14 40.00 20.00
C420 AP22(h) 100fr on #C54 50.00 25.00
C421 AP50(g) 125fr on 50fr #C144 40.00 20.00
C422 AP75(e) 125fr on 65fr #C222 40.00 20.00
C424 AP84(g) 135fr on 40fr #C240 50.00 —
C425 AP21(f) 135fr on 45fr #C110 62.50 —
C426 AP14(e) 135fr on 50fr #C33 62.50 —
C429 AP43(e) 135fr on 70fr #C128 90.00 —
C430 AP81(f) 135fr on 250fr #C250 50.00 —
C431 AP61(g) 135fr on 250fr #C254 50.00 25.00
C432 AP84(f) 150fr on 140fr #C242 25.00 15.00
C433 A61(b) 150fr on #C153 75.00 —
C434 AP61(f) 150fr on #C197 50.00 25.00
C435 AP13(e) 200fr on 100fr #C31 125.00 65.00
C436 AP14(e) 200fr on 100fr #C34 50.00 25.00
C437 AP48(e) 200fr on 100fr #C152 45.00 20.00
C439 AP61(e) 200fr on 100fr #C253 45.00 25.00
C440 AP78(f) 200fr on 150fr #C236 80.00 40.00
C441 AP67(f) 200fr on #C191 60.00 35.00
C442 AP61(g) 200fr on #C198 45.00 20.00

C444 AP61(e) 200fr on 250fr #C179 45.00 —
C445 AP61(e) 200fr on 250fr #C234 75.00
C446 AP61(e) 200fr on 250fr #C254 50.00
C447 AP85(f) 300fr on #C261 65.00 35.00

Benin No. C351 Surcharged

1994-95

Printing Method and Perfs as Before

C449 AP118 200fr on 500fr #C351 60.00 30.00

Benin No. C290 Surcharged, Dahomey Nos. C206, C257 Surcharged

1996?

Perfs. & Printing Methods as Before

C450 A133 40fr on 210fr #C290 60.00 30.00
C451 AP83(f) 200fr on 500fr #C257 65.00 35.00
C452 AP72(f) 1000fr on 150fr #C206 50.00 25.00

Dahomey No. C265 Surcharged, Benin Nos. C258, C292 Surcharged

1996?

Perfs. & Printing Methods as Before

C453 AP86(g) 25fr on 500fr #C265 42.50 25.00
C454 AP89 35fr on 270fr #C258 62.50 —
C455 AP102 100fr on 500fr #C292 62.50 30.00

Dahomey Nos. C61, C74, C85, C88, C94, C106, C109, C111, C113, C115, C120, C124-C125, C130, C135-C136, C138, C142-C143, C150, C157, C204-C205, C207-C208, C260, C263 Surcharged

No. C458

No. C461

No. C464

No. C465

No. C467

No. C469

No. C471

No. C474

No. C475

No. C476

No. C478

No. C479

No. C480

No. C482

1996?

Perfs. & Printing Methods as Before

C456 AP48(e) 70fr on 100fr #C138 75.00 40.00
C457 AP34(h) 150fr on #C88 35.00 —
C458 AP21(e) 150fr on #C115 45.00 —
C459 AP72(e) 150fr on #C207 35.00 —
C460 AP73(h) 150fr on #C208 35.00 —
C461 AP34(e) 150fr on 30fr #C85 40.00 —
C462 AP31(h) 150fr on 30fr #C74 35.00 —
C463 AP21(e) 150fr on 30fr #C109 35.00 —
C464 AP40(e) 150fr on 40fr on 30fr #C120 35.00 —
C465 AP47(e) 150fr on 40fr #C136 35.00 —
C466 AP49(e) 150fr on 40fr #C142 35.00 —
C467 CD128(h) 150fr on 50fr #C94 40.00 —
C468 AP38(h) 150fr on 50fr #C106 27.50 —
C469 AP71(e) 150fr on 50fr #C204 35.00 —
C470 AP54(h) 150fr on 70fr #C124 35.00 —
C471 CD124(h) 150fr on 100fr #C61 35.00 —
C472 AP21(e) 150fr on 100fr #C113 35.00 —
C473 AP53(h) 150fr on 100fr #C157 29.00 —
C474 AP84(h) 150fr on 100fr #C260 12.50 —
C475 AP21(h) 150fr on 110fr #C111 35.00 —
C476 AP44(h) 150fr on 110fr #C130 40.00 —
C477 AP54(h) 150fr on 120fr #C125 35.00 —
C478 AP86(g) 150fr on 135fr #C263 62.50 —
C479 AP46(h) 150fr on 200fr #C135 35.00 —
C480 AP49(e) 150fr on 200fr #C143 35.00 —
C481 AP51(h) 150fr on 200fr #C150 35.00 —
C482 AP71(e) 150fr on 200fr #C205 29.00 —

Benin Nos. C261, C281, C327, C332-C333 Surcharged, Dahomey Nos. C201, C127, C175 Surcharged

No. C483

No. C488

1996-97?

Perfs. & Printing Methods as Before

C483 AP98 30fr on 380fr #C281 42.50 20.00
C484 AP90 35fr on 270fr #C261 60.00 35.00
C485 AP117 125fr on 200fr #C332 35.00 15.00
C485A AP117 125fr on 200fr #C333 35.00 15.00
C486 AP114 200fr on 500fr #C327 60.00 30.00
C488 AP43(h) 150fr on 40fr #C127 22.50 —
C489 AP70(f) 150fr on 50fr #C201 35.00 15.00
C490 AP48(e) 200fr on 150fr #C175 62.50 35.00

No. C256, C268, C278 Surcharged

No. C494

No. C497

Method and Perf. as Before

1995-96 ?

C494 AP88 40fr on 210fr #C256 ('96) 50.00 25.00
C496 AP93 150fr on 500fr #C268 30.00 15.00
C497 AP96 150fr on 500fr #C278 22.50 12.00

Benin No. C293 Surcharged, Dahomey Nos. C147, C250 Surcharged Type e or f

No. C503

1995-97?

Perf. & Printing Methods as Before

C500 AP103 150fr on 500fr #C293 22.50 —
C503 AP51(e) 135fr on 40fr #C147 70.00 35.00
C509 AP81(f) 150fr on 250fr #C250 80.00 40.00

Dahomey Nos. #C86, C126, C70 Surcharged

No. C513

1995-99?

Perfs. & Printing Methods as Before

C513 AP34(h) 35fr on 45fr #C86 80.00 40.00
C515 AP42(h) 35fr on 100fr on 200fr #C126 80.00 40.00
C516 AP29(h) 35fr on 100fr #C70 50.00 25.00

Dahomey Nos. C72, C93, C105, C112, C139, C168, C223, Benin Nos. C285-C286 Surcharged or Overprinted

No. C523

No. C537

Method and Perf. as Before

1997 ?

C517 AP30(h) 35fr on 55fr Dahomey #C72 80.00 40.00
C522 AP35(h) 35fr on 100fr Dahomey #C93 50.00 25.00
C523 A51(h) 35fr on 100fr Dahomey #C105 50.00 25.00
C526 AP48(h) 35fr on 100fr #C139 80.00 40.00
C530 AP75(h) 35fr on 125fr Dahomey #C223 80.00 40.00
C532 AP21(h) 35fr on 200fr Dahomey #C112 80.00 40.00
C535 CD138(h) 100fr on #C285 50.00 25.00
C536 CD139(h) 100fr on #C286 50.00 25.00
C537 AP58 300fr on 200fr Dahomey #C168 *30.00 20.00*

Dahomey Nos. C15, C172, C206, C224, C256, C257 Surcharged or Overprinted

No. C538

No. C539

No. C540

No. C541

No. C542

No. C543

Method and Perf. as Before

1997 ?

C538 AP56(f) 175fr on 150fr Dahomey #C172 *50.00 35.00*
C539 AP72(f) 175fr on 150fr Dahomey #C206 *50.00 35.00*
C540 AP75(f) 300fr on 200fr Dahomey #C224 *55.00 30.00*
C541 AP4(f) 500fr on Dahomey #C15 *40.00 25.00*
C542 AP63(f) 500fr on 200fr Dahomey #C256 *30.00 20.00*
C543 AP63(f) 500fr on Dahomey #C257 *40.00 25.00*

Dahomey Nos. C36, C48, C141, C150, C191, C237, C256, C261, C264, C265 Overprinted Types "f" or "g"

Methods and Perfs As Before

2005-09 (?)

C544 AP21(g) 200fr multi (#C48) *50.00 25.00*
C545 AP48(g) 200fr multi (#C141) *35.00 15.00*
C546 AP51(g) 200fr multi (#C150) *40.00 20.00*
C547 AP67(g) 200fr multi (#C191) *40.00 20.00*
C548 AP78(g) 200fr multi (#C237) *100.00 50.00*
C549 AP83(g) 200fr multi (#C256) *125.00 65.00*
C550 AP15(f) 250fr multi (#C36) 80.00 40.00
C554 AP35(f) 300fr multi (#C261) *55.00 30.00*
C555 AP86(f) 300fr multi (#C264) *30.00 20.00*
C557 AP86(f) 500fr multi (#C265) *35.00 20.00*

Various Stamps of Dahomey and Benin Surcharged Type "f" or "k"

Methods and Perfs As Before

2005-09 (?)

C558 AP63(k) 25fr on 15fr Dah. #C182 *125.00 70.00*
C559 AP56(k) 25fr on 20fr Dah. #C163 *40.00 20.00*
C560 AP63(k) 25fr on 20fr Dah. #C183 *110.00 60.00*
C561 AP30(k) 50fr on 30fr Dah. #C71 *25.00 12.00*
C562 AP31(k) 50fr on 30fr Dah. #C74 *25.00 12.00*
C563 AP35(k) 50fr on 30fr Dah. #C89 *30.00 15.00*
C564 AP66(k) 50fr on 35fr Dah. #C189 *40.00 20.00*
C565 AP61(k) 50fr on 35fr Dah. #C195 *25.00 12.00*
C566 AP43(k) 50fr on 40fr Dah. #C127 *25.00 12.00*
C567 AP47(k) 50fr on 40fr Dah. #C136 *150.00 75.00*
C568 AP49(k) 50fr on 40fr Dah. #C142 *40.00 20.00*
C569 AP52(k) 50fr on 40fr Dah. #C155 *40.00 20.00*
C570 AP62(k) 50fr on 40fr Dah. #C180 *60.00 30.00*
C571 AP63(k) 50fr on 40fr Dah. #C184 *75.00 40.00*
C572 AP24(f) 175fr on 70fr Dah. #C58 *40.00 20.00*
C574 AP32(f) 175fr on 70fr Dah. #C79 *35.00 20.00*
C576 AP86(f) 175fr on 135fr Dah. #C263 *17.50 10.00*
C578 AP48(f) 175fr on 150fr Dah. #C175 *30.00 20.00*
C579 AP72(f) 175fr on 150fr Dah. #C207 *40.00 25.00*
C580 AP83(k) 200fr on 35fr Dah. #C255 *100.00 50.00*
C581 AP51(k) 200fr on 40fr Dah. #C147 *35.00 17.50*
C582 AP87(k) 200fr on 40fr Dah. #C266 *40.00 20.00*
C583 AP84(k) 200fr on 40fr Ben. #C240 *40.00 20.00*
C584 AP33(k) 200fr on 45fr Dah. #C82 *60.00 30.00*
C585 AP50(k) 200fr on 50fr Dah. #C144 *35.00 17.50*
C586 AP75(k) 200fr on 65fr Dah. #C222 *125.00 70.00*
C587 AP28(k) 200fr on 70fr Dah. #C68 *40.00 20.00*
C588 AP86(k) 200fr on 75fr Dah. #C262 *35.00 17.50*
C589 AP84(k) 200fr on 85fr Ben. #C241 *100.00 50.00*
C590 AP14(k) 200fr on 100fr Dah. #C34 *110.00 60.00*
C591 AP68(k) 200fr on 100fr Dah. #C194 *50.00 25.00*
C592 AP48(k) 300fr on 40fr Dah. #C151 *60.00 30.00*
C593 AP66(k) 300fr on 40fr Dah. #C190 *35.00 17.50*
C594 AP32(k) 300fr on 45fr Dah. #C78 *75.00 40.00*
C595 AP21(k) 300fr on 45fr Dah. #C110 *35.00 17.50*
C596 A49(k) 300fr on 50fr Dah. #C101 *20.00 10.00*
C597 AP70(k) 300fr on 50fr Dah. #C201 *35.00 17.50*
C598 AP71(k) 300fr on 50fr Dah. #C204 *100.00 50.00*
C599 AP36(k) 300fr on 60fr Dah. #C98 *70.00 35.00*
C600 AP54(k) 300fr on 65fr Dah. #C161 *35.00 17.50*
C601 AP64(k) 300fr on 65fr Dah. #C185 *50.00 25.00*
C602 AP24(k) 300fr on 70fr Dah. #C58 *40.00 20.00*
C603 AP31(k) 300fr on 70fr Dah. #C76 *40.00 20.00*
C604 AP51(k) 300fr on 70fr Dah. #C148 *35.00 17.50*
C605 AP36(k) 300fr on 75fr Dah. #C99 *70.00 35.00*
C606 AP22(k) 300fr on 80fr Dah. #C53 *85.00 42.50*
C607 AP56(b)(k) 300fr on 85fr Dah. #C171 *40.00 20.00*
C608 AP44(k) 300fr on 90fr Dah. #C129 *40.00 20.00*
C609 AP4(k) 300fr on 100fr Dah. #C14 *25.00 12.50*
C610 AP6(k) 300fr on 100fr Dah. #C20 *25.00 12.50*
C611 AP10(k) 300fr on 100fr Dah. #C28 *40.00 20.00*
C612 AP22(k) 300fr on 100fr Dah. #C54 *60.00 30.00*
C613 AP30(k) 300fr on 100fr Dah. #C73 *35.00 17.50*
C614 AP32(k) 300fr on 100fr Dah. #C80 *80.00 40.00*
C615 AP35(k) 300fr on 100fr Dah. #C91 *35.00 17.50*
C616 AP45(k) 300fr on 100fr Dah. #C131 *35.00 17.50*
C617 AP48(k) 300fr on 100fr Dah. #C139 *35.00 17.50*
C618 AP48(k) 300fr on 100fr Dah. #C140 *35.00 17.50*

C619 CD135(k) 300fr on 100fr Dah. #C146 *60.00 30.00*
C620 AP55(k) 300fr on 100fr Dah. #C162 *40.00 20.00*
C621 AP57(k) 300fr on 100fr Dah. #C166 *40.00 20.00*
C622 AP60(k) 300fr on 100fr Dah. #C173 *40.00 20.00*
C623 AP62(k) 300fr on 100fr Dah. #C181 *40.00 20.00*
C624 AP65(k) 300fr on 100fr Dah. #C188 *40.00 20.00*
C625 AP69(k) 300fr on 100fr Dah. #C200 *35.00 17.50*
C626 AP77(k) 300fr on 100fr Dah. #C233 *40.00 20.00*
C628 AP61(k) 400fr on 35fr Dah. #C176 *40.00 20.00*
C629 AP35(k) 400fr on 100fr Dah. #C93 *40.00 20.00*
C630 AP50(k) 400fr on 100fr Dah. #C145 *35.00 17.50*
C631 AP51(k) 400fr on 100fr Dah. #C149 *40.00 20.00*
C632 AP70(k) 400fr on 125fr Dah. #C202 *40.00 20.00*
C634 AP70(k) 1000fr on 150fr Dah. #C203 *30.00 15.00*
C635 AP73(k) 1000fr on 150fr Dah. #C208 *70.00 35.00*
C636 AP78(k) 1000fr on 150fr Dah. #C236 *90.00 45.00*

There are three surcharge types on No. C560. Values are for the least expensive type.

Dahomey Nos. C92, C116, C138, C152, C153, C157, C158, C167, C186, C192, C197, C207, C250 and C253 Surcharged

Methods and Perfs As Before

2009

C637 AP39(k) 400fr on 100fr #C116 *30.00 15.00*
C638 AP48(k) 400fr on 100fr #C138 *40.00 20.00*
C639 AP48(k) 400fr on 100fr #C152 *30.00 15.00*
C640 AP53(k) 400fr on 100fr #C157 *25.00 15.00*
C641 AP61(k) 400fr on 100fr #C253 *40.00 20.00*
C642 AP64(k) 400fr on 125fr #C186 *50.00 25.00*
C643 AP58(k) 400fr on 150fr #C167 *25.00 15.00*
C644 AP68(k) 1000fr on 35fr #C192 *60.00 30.00*
C645 A61(k) 1000fr on 150fr #C153 *40.00 20.00*
C646 AP61(k) 1000fr on 150fr #C197 *40.00 20.00*
C647 AP72(k) 1000fr on 150fr #C207 *90.00 45.00*
C648 AP35(k) 1000fr on 200fr #C92 *25.00 15.00*
C649 AP53(k) 1000fr on 250fr #C158 *25.00 15.00*
C650 AP81(k) 1000fr on 250fr #C250 *40.00 20.00*
Nos. C637-C650 (14) 560.00 290.00

Dahomey No. C164 Surcharged

2009 Method and Perf. As Before

C651A AP56(k) 300fr on 85fr Dah. #C164 *40.00 20.00*

Dahomey No. C177 Surcharged

2009 Method and Perf. As Before

C652 AP61(k) 400fr on 125fr Dahomey #C177 *40.00 20.00*

Dahomey No. C223 Surcharged

2009 Method and Perf. As Before

C653 AP75(k) 400fr on 125fr #C223 *50.00 25.00*

POSTAGE DUE STAMPS

French Colony

Handstamped in Black on Postage Due Stamps of French Colonies

1894	**Unwmk.**		*Imperf.*
J1 D1	5c black	175.00	70.00
J2 D1	10c black	175.00	70.00
J3 D1	20c black	175.00	70.00
J4 D1	30c black	175.00	70.00
	Nos. J1-J4 (4)	700.00	280.00

Nos. J1-J4 exist with overprint in various positions.

Catalogue values for unused stamps in this section are for Never Hinged items.

People's Republic

Pineapples D6

Mail Delivery D7

Designs: 20fr, Cashew, vert. 40fr, Oranges. 50fr, Akee. 80fr, Mail delivery by boat.

1978, Sept. 5	**Photo.**		*Perf. 13*
J44 D6	10fr multicolored	.30	.25
J45 D6	20fr multicolored	.55	.45
J46 D6	40fr multicolored	1.00	.65
J47 D6	50fr multicolored	1.40	.90

Engr.

J48 D7	60fr multi	1.10	.65
J49 D7	80fr multi	1.40	.90
	Nos. J44-J49 (6)	5.75	3.80

PARCEL POST STAMPS

Catalogue values for unused stamps in this section are for Never Hinged items.

Nos. 448-448A, 459, 473, C292 Overprinted or Surcharged "Colis Postaux"

No. Q8

No. Q9

No. Q10

No. Q10A

No. Q10B

Perfs. and Printing Methods as Before

1982, Nov.				
Q8	A126	100fr on 150fr	20.00	12.50
Q9	A130	100fr multi	70.00	35.00
Q10	A134	300fr multi	20.00	12.50
Q10A	A126a	1000fr multi	25.00	12.50
Q10B	AP102	5000fr on 500fr	70.00	35.00
		Nos. Q8-Q10B (5)	205.00	107.50

No. 358 Overprinted "COLIS / POSTAUX" Vertically Reading Down

Method and Perf as Before

1984 ?

Q10C A88 50fr multi 170.00 85.00

Dahomey No. C205 Surcharged

1989 Photo. *Perf. 12½x13*

Q11 AP71 500fr on 200fr multi 25.00 12.50

Dahomey No. C224, Benin Nos. 344, 349, 354, 367, 495, 499, C254, C278 Overprinted or Surcharged

No. Q14

Methods and Perfs as Before

1989-90				
Q12	A87	5fr multi (#354)	70.00	35.00
Q13	A144	15fr on 50fr multi (#499)	35.00	17.50
Q14	A91	60fr on 150fr multi (#367)	50.00	25.00
Q15	A142	75fr on 50fr multi (#495)	35.00	17.50
Q16	A85	200fr multi (#349)	50.00	25.00
Q16A	A85	200fr multi (#349)	50.00	25.00
Q16B	A85	200fr multi (#349)	—	—
Q17	AP87	250fr multi (#C254)	50.00	25.00
Q17A	AP87	250fr multi (#C254)	50.00	25.00
Q17B	AP75	300fr on 200fr multi (Dahomey #C224)	50.00	25.00
Q18	AP96	500fr multi (#C278)	70.00	35.00
Q18A	A83	500fr on 45fr multi (#344)	90.00	45.00

Nos. Q14, Q15 have "Republique de Benin" overprint.

Nos. Q16 and Q17 have overprint in sans-serif type. Nos. Q16A and Q17A have overprint in serifed type.

Nos. Q16A, Q16B, Q17, Q17A have obliterator over "POPULAIRE." No. Q16B has overprint in sans-serif type.

Nos. 375, 378, C246 Surcharged or Overprinted "Colis Postaux"

Methods and Perfs as Before

1998				
Q20	A96	60fr on 150fr multi (#378)	50.00	25.00
Q21	A95	100fr multi (#375)	50.00	25.00
Q22	AP85	300fr multi (#C246)	90.00	45.00

Dahomey No. C157, Benin Nos. 368, C254 Overprinted "COLIS / POSTAUX"

1998 ? Method and Perf as Before

Q25	A92	10fr on #368	350.00	225.00
Q25A	AP53	10fr on 100fr (Dahomey #C157)	175.00	100.00
Q26	AP87	5000fr on 250fr (#C254)	50.00	25.00
Q27	AP87	5000fr on 250fr (#C254)	50.00	25.00

No. Q25A has the overprinted word "Populaire" obliterated. No. Q26 has "Colis Postaux" in sans-serif type. Nos. Q27 has "Colis Postaux" in serifed type.

No. 378 Surcharged With "Colis Postaux" in Serifed Type

Method and Perf. As Before

2009 (?)

Q33 A96 60fr on 150fr #378 *50.00 25.00*

No. Q20 has "Colis Postaux" in sans-serif type.

BERMUDA

„bər-'myü-də

LOCATION — A group of about 150 small islands of which only 20 are inhabited, lying in the Atlantic Ocean about 580 miles southeast of Cape Hatteras.
GOVT. — British Crown Colony
AREA — 20.5 sq. mi.
POP. — 62,471 (1999 est.)
CAPITAL — Hamilton

Bermuda achieved internal self-government in 1968.

4 Farthings = 1 Penny
12 Pence = 1 Shilling
20 Shillings = 1 Pound
100 Cents = 1 Dollar (1970)

Catalogue values for unused stamps in this country are for Never Hinged items, beginning with Scott 131.

POSTMASTER STAMPS

PM1

1848-56 — Unwmk. — *Imperf.*

No.	Description	Unused	Used
X1	PM1 1p blk, *bluish* (1848)		*170,000.*
a.	Dated 1849		*200,000.*
X2	PM1 1p red, *bluish* (1856)		*225,000.*
a.	Dated 1854		*375,000.*
X3	PM1 1p red (1853)		*175,000.*

PM2

Same inscribed "ST GEORGES"

1860

No.	Description	Unused	Used
X4	PM2 (1p) red, *yellowish*		*100,000.*

Same inscribed "HAMILTON"

1861

No.	Description	Unused	Used
X5	PM2 (1p) red, *bluish*		*130,000.*
X6	PM2 (1p) red		*38,500.*

Nos. X1-X3 were produced and used by Postmaster William B. Perot of Hamilton. No. X4 is attributed to Postmaster James H. Thies of St. George's.

Only a few of each stamp exist. Values reflect actual sales figures for stamps in the condition in which they are found.

GENERAL ISSUES

Values for unused stamps are for examples with original gum as defined in the catalogue introduction. Very fine examples of Nos. 1-1a, 2-15b will have perforations touching the design (or framelines where applicable) on at least one side due to the narrow spacing of the stamps on the plates. Stamps with perfs clear of the design on all four sides are scarce and will command higher prices.

Queen Victoria
A1 A2

A3

A4

A5

1865-74 — Typo. — Wmk. 1 — *Perf. 14*

No.	Description	Unused	Used
1	A1 1p rose red	110.00	1.75
b.	Imperf.	*85,000.*	*27,000.*
2	A2 2p blue ('66)	450.00	32.00
3	A3 3p buff ('73)	600.00	80.00
4	A4 6p brown lilac	2,300.	90.00
5	A4 6p lilac ('74)	30.00	17.00
6	A5 1sh green	450.00	70.00
	Nos. 1-6 (6)	3,940.	290.75

See Nos. 7-9, 19-21, 23, 25. For surcharges see Nos. 10-15.
No. 1b is a proof.

1882-1903 — *Perf. 14x12½*

No.	Description	Unused	Used
7	A3 3p buff	210.00	75.00
8	A4 6p violet ('03)	17.00	*27.50*
9	A5 1sh green ('94)	20.00	*150.00*
a.	Vert. strip of 3, perf. all around & imperf. btwn.	*13,750.*	
	Nos. 7-9 (3)	247.00	*252.50*

Handstamped Diagonally

1874 — *Perf. 14*

No.	Description	Unused	Used
10	A5 3p on 1sh green	1,700.	950.

Handstamped Diagonally

No.	Description	Unused	Used
11	A1 3p on 1p rose	*19,000.*	*20,000.*
12	A5 3p on 1sh green	2,850.	975.
a.	"P" with top like "R"	2,300.	1,100.

No. 11 is stated to be an essay, but a few examples are known used. Nos. 10-12 are found with double or partly double surcharges.

Surcharged in Black

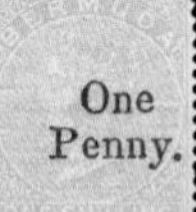

1875

No.	Description	Unused	Used
13	A2 1p on 2p blue	875.00	475.00
a.	Without period	*27,500.*	*13,250.*
14	A3 1p on 3p buff	550.00	425.00
15	A5 1p on 1sh green	675.00	310.00
a.	Inverted surcharge	—	*50,000.*
b.	Without period	*40,000.*	*20,000.*

A6

A7

1880 — Wmk. 1

No.	Description	Unused	Used
16	A6 ½p brown	7.50	*5.25*
17	A7 4p orange	21.00	2.50

See Nos. 18, 24.

A8

A9

1883-1904 — Wmk. 2

No.	Description	Unused	Used
18	A6 ½p deep gray grn ('93)	4.50	1.00
a.	½p green ('92)	7.50	4.50
19	A1 1p aniline car ('89)	17.00	.30
a.	1p dull rose	200.00	5.25
b.	1p rose red	100.00	4.00
c.	1p carmine rose ('86)	75.00	1.00
20	A2 2p blue ('86)	70.00	7.00
21	A2 2p brn pur ('98)	4.75	2.00
a.	2p aniline pur ('93)	17.50	5.00
22	A8 2½p ultra ('84)	16.00	.50
a.	2½p deep ultra	24.00	3.75
23	A3 3p gray ('86)	27.50	9.50
24	A7 4p brown org ('04)	37.50	*62.50*
25	A5 1sh ol bis ('93)	19.00	21.00
a.	1sh yellow brown	22.00	21.00
	Nos. 18-25 (8)	196.25	*103.80*

Black Surcharge

1901

No.	Description	Unused	Used
26	A9 1f on 1sh gray	5.00	1.25

Dry Dock — A10

1902-03

No.	Description	Unused	Used
28	A10 ½p gray grn & blk ('03)	15.00	3.75
29	A10 1p car rose & brown	10.00	.35
30	A10 3p ol grn & violet	5.00	*3.50*
	Nos. 28-30 (3)	30.00	7.60

1906-10 — Wmk. 3

No.	Description	Unused	Used
31	A10 ¼p pur & brn ('08)	2.10	1.90
32	A10 ½p gray grn & blk	24.00	1.25
33	A10 ½p green ('09)	17.50	4.25
34	A10 1p car rose & brn	37.50	.25
35	A10 1p carmine ('08)	22.00	.50
36	A10 2p orange & gray	9.25	*13.50*
37	A10 2½p blue & brown	28.00	9.50
38	A10 2½p ultra ('10)	24.00	9.50
39	A10 4p vio brn & blue ('09)	3.75	*20.00*
	Nos. 31-39 (9)	168.10	*60.65*

Caravel
A11

King George V
A12

1910-24 — Engr. — *Perf. 14*

No.	Description	Unused	Used
40	A11 ¼p brown ('12)	2.10	*3.00*
a.	¼p pale brown	2.00	*1.75*
41	A11 ½p yel green	3.25	.30
a.	½p dark green ('18)	15.00	1.50
42	A11 1p red (I)	20.00	.35
a.	1p carmine (I) ('19)	67.50	10.00
43	A11 2p gray ('13)	5.00	*19.00*
44	A11 2½p ultra (I) ('12)	4.25	.75
45	A11 3p violet, *yel* ('13)	3.00	*7.50*
46	A11 4p red, *yellow* ('19)	14.00	*15.00*
47	A11 6p claret ('24)	12.50	*9.00*
48	A11 1sh blk, *green* ('12)	6.00	*5.00*
a.	1sh black, *olive* ('25)	6.00	*21.00*

Typographed

Chalky Paper

49	A12	2sh ultra & dl vio, *bl* ('20)	22.50	*62.50*
50	A12	2sh6p red & blk, *bl*	35.00	*100.00*
51	A12	4sh car & black ('20)	75.00	*200.00*
52	A12	5sh red & grn, *yellow*	75.00	*150.00*
53	A12	10sh red & grn, *green*	225.00	*425.00*
54	A12	£1 black & vio, *red*	400.00	*700.00*
		Nos. 40-54 (15)	902.60	*1,697.*

Types I of 1p and 2½p are illustrated above Nos. 81-97.

The 1p was printed from two plates, the 2nd of which, No. 42a, exists only in carmine on opaque paper with a bluish tinge. Compare No. MR1 (as No. 42) and MR2 (as No. 42a).

Revenue cancellations are found on Nos. 52-54.

See Nos. 81-97.

Seal of the Colony and King George V A13

1920-21 Wmk. 3 Ordinary Paper

55	A13	¼p brown	4.00	*27.00*
56	A13	½p green	9.50	*18.00*
57	A13	2p gray	17.00	*55.00*

Chalky Paper

58	A13	3p vio & dl vio, *yel*	15.00	*55.00*
59	A13	4p red & blk, *yellow*	15.00	*42.50*
60	A13	1sh blk, *gray grn*	20.00	*60.00*

Ordinary Paper

Wmk. 4

67	A13	1p rose red	4.50	.35
68	A13	2½p ultra	19.00	20.00

Chalky Paper

69	A13	6p red vio & dl vio	32.50	*95.00*
		Nos. 55-60,67-69 (9)	136.50	*372.85*

Issued: 6p, 1/19/21; others, 11/11/20.

King George V A14

1921, May 12 Engr.

71	A14	¼p brown	4.25	*4.50*
72	A14	½p green	3.50	*8.50*
73	A14	1p carmine	9.00	.45

Wmk. 3

74	A14	2p gray	11.50	*50.00*
75	A14	2½p ultra	14.00	6.00
76	A14	3p vio, *orange*	6.90	*20.00*
77	A14	4p scarlet, *org*	20.00	*32.00*
78	A14	6p claret	19.00	*65.00*
79	A14	1sh blk, *green*	29.00	*65.00*
		Nos. 71-79 (9)	117.15	*251.45*

Tercentenary of "Local Representative Institutions" (Nos. 55-79).

Types of 1910-20 Issue

Type I

Types of 1p

Type II

Type III

Type I, figure "1" has pointed serifs, scroll at top left very weak.

Type II, thick "1" with square serifs, scroll weak.

Type III, thinner "1" with long square serifs, scroll complete with strong line.

Types of 2½p

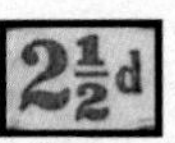

Type I

Type II

Type I, small "d," short, thick figures of value.

Type II, larger "d," taller, thinner figures of value.

1922-34 Wmk. 4

81	A11	¼p brown ('28)	1.90	*3.75*
82	A11	½p green	1.90	.25
83	A11	1p car, III ('28)	15.00	.35
a.		1p carmine, II ('26)	55.00	7.50
b.		1p carmine, I	21.00	.75
84	A11	1½p red brown ('34)	11.00	.45
85	A11	2p gray ('23)	1.90	1.90
86	A11	2½p ap grn ('23)	3.25	1.90
87	A11	2½p ultra, II ('32)	2.10	.90
a.		2½p ultra, I ('26)	5.00	.60
88	A11	3p ultra ('24)	20.00	*32.50*
89	A11	3p vio, *yellow* ('26)	5.00	1.25
90	A11	4p red, *yellow* ('24)	2.50	1.25
91	A11	6p claret ('24)	1.25	1.00
92	A11	1sh blk, *emer* ('27)	8.00	*11.00*
93	A11	1sh brn blk, *yel grn* ('34)	42.50	*62.50*

Chalky Paper

94	A12	2sh ultra & vio, *bl* ('27)	55.00	*87.50*
a.		2sh bl & dp vio, *dp bl* ('31)	67.50	*100.00*
95	A12	2sh 6p red & blk, *bl* ('27)	75.00	125.00
a.		2sh6p pale org ver & blk, *gray bl* ('30)	3,500.	3,250.
b.		2sh6p ver & blk, *deep blue* ('31)	100.00	*150.00*
96	A12	10sh red & grn, *emer* ('24)	160.00	*300.00*
a.		10sh dp red & pale grn, *dp emer* ('31)	175.00	*350.00*
97	A12	12sh 6p ocher & gray blk ('32)	300.00	*425.00*
		Nos. 81-97 (17)	706.30	*1,056.*

Revenue cancellations are found on Nos. 94-97.

For the 12sh6p with "Revenue" on both sides, see No. AR1.

Common Design Types pictured following the introduction.

Silver Jubilee Issue

Common Design Type

1935, May 6 Perf. 11x12

100	CD301	1p car & dk bl	.60	*2.25*
101	CD301	1½p blk & ultra	.90	*3.50*
102	CD301	2½p ultra & brn	1.50	2.50
103	CD301	1sh brn vio & ind	15.00	*50.00*
		Nos. 100-103 (4)	18.00	*58.25*
		Set, never hinged	35.00	

Hamilton Harbor — A15

South Shore — A16

Yacht "Lucie" — A17

Grape Bay — A18

Typical Cottage — A19

Scene at Par-la-Ville — A20

1936-40 Perf. 12

105	A15	½p blue green	.25	.25
106	A16	1p car & black	.55	.35
107	A16	1½p choc & black	1.25	.60
108	A17	2p lt bl & blk	6.00	2.00
109	A17	2p brn blk & turq bl ('38)	55.00	16.00
109A	A17	2p red & ultra ('40)	1.25	1.25
110	A18	2½p dk bl & lt bl	1.25	.30
111	A19	3p car & black	3.25	2.75
112	A20	6p vio & rose lake	1.00	.25
113	A18	1sh deep green	4.00	*19.00*
114	A15	1sh6p brown	.60	.25
		Nos. 105-114 (11)	74.40	43.00
		Set, never hinged	100.00	

No. 108, blue border and black center. No. 109, black border, blue center.

Coronation Issue

Common Design Type

1937, May 14 Perf. 13½x14

115	CD302	1p carmine	.25	*1.50*
116	CD302	1½p brown	.35	*1.75*
117	CD302	2½p bright ultra	.65	*1.75*
		Nos. 115-117 (3)	1.25	5.00
		Set, never hinged	1.75	

Hamilton Harbor — A21

Grape Bay — A22

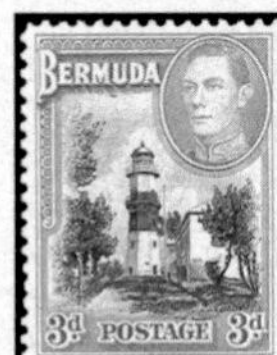

St. David's Lighthouse A23

King George VI A25

Bermudian Water Scene and Yellow-billed Tropic Bird — A24

1938-51 Wmk. 4 Perf. 12

118	A21	1p red & blk	.60	.25
a.		1p rose red & black	16.00	1.40
119	A21	1½p vio brn & blue	4.75	1.40
a.		1½p dl vio brn & bl ('43)	4.00	.25
120	A22	2½p blue & lt bl	8.50	1.00
120A	A22	2½p ol brn & lt bl ('41)	2.50	1.25
b.		2½p dk ol blk & pale blue ('43)	2.50	1.40
121	A23	3p car & blk	16.00	2.25
121A	A23	3p dp ultra & blk ('42)	1.40	.25
c.		3p brt ultra & blk ('41)	1.40	.25
		Complete booklet, 6 each #118, 119, 109A, 120Ab, 121Ac	160.00	
		Complete booklet, 6 #121Ac and 18 #112, in blocks of 6, and 12 air mail labels	180.00	
121D	A24	7½p yel grn, bl & blk ('41)	5.00	2.00
122	A22	1sh green	1.60	.55

Typo.

Perf. 13

123	A25	2sh ultra & red vio, *bl* ('50)	13.50	12.00
a.		2sh ultra & vio, *bl*, perf. 14	9.25	3.50
b.		2sh ultra & dl vio, *bl* (mottled paper), perf. 14 ('42)	9.25	3.50
124	A25	2sh 6p red & blk, *bl*	14.50	8.75
a.		Perf. 14	26.00	8.75
125	A25	5sh red & grn, *yel*	17.00	15.00
a.		Perf. 14	60.00	20.00
126	A25	10sh red & grn, *grn* ('51)	40.00	*32.50*
a.		10sh brn lake & grn, *grn*, perf. 14	140.00	100.00
b.		10sh red & grn, *grn*, perf. 14 ('39)	225.00	200.00
127	A25	12sh 6p org & gray blk	87.50	72.50
a.		12sh 6p org & gray, perf. 14	110.00	60.00
b.		12sh 6p yel & gray, perf. 14 ('47)	725.00	600.00
c.		12sh 6p brn org & gray, perf. 14	275.00	100.00

Wmk. 3

128	A25	£1 blk & vio, *red* ('51)	52.50	*62.50*
a.		£1 blk & pur, *red*, perf. 14	300.00	140.00
b.		£1 blk & dk vio, *salmon*, perf. 14 ('42)	87.50	67.50
		Nos. 118-128 (14)	265.35	212.20
		Set, never hinged	450.00	

No. 127b is the so-called "lemon yellow" shade.

Revenue cancellations are found on Nos. 123-128. Stamps with removed revenue cancellations and forged postmarks are abundant.

No. 118a Surcharged in Black

1940, Dec. 20 Wmk. 4 Perf. 12

129	A21	½p on 1p rose red & blk	.30	2.40
		Never hinged	1.00	

Catalogue values for unused stamps in this section, from this point to the end of the section, are for Never Hinged items.

Peace Issue
Common Design Type
Perf. 13½x14

1946, Nov. 6 Engr. Wmk. 4
131 CD303 1½p brown .25 .25
132 CD303 3p deep blue .30 .30

Silver Wedding Issue
Common Design Types

1948, Dec. 1 Photo. *Perf. 14x14½*
133 CD304 1½p red brown .25 .25

Engr.; Name Typo.
Perf. 11½x11
134 CD305 £1 rose carmine 47.50 *55.00*

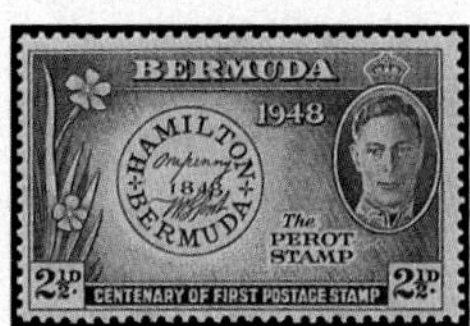

Postmaster Stamp of 1848 — A26

1949, Apr. 11 Engr. *Perf. 13x13½*
135 A26 2½p dk brown & dp bl .25 .25
136 A26 3p dp blue & black .25 .25
137 A26 6p green & rose vio .45 .45
Nos. 135-137 (3) .95 .95

No. 137 shows a different floral arrangement.
Bermuda's first postage stamp, cent.

UPU Issue
Common Design Types
Engr.; Name Typo.

1949, Oct. 10 *Perf. 13½, 11x11½*
138 CD306 2½p slate .50 *1.75*
139 CD307 3p indigo 1.25 1.00
140 CD308 6p rose violet 1.00 .80
141 CD309 1sh blue green 2.00 2.00
Nos. 138-141 (4) 4.75 5.55

Coronation Issue
Common Design Type

1953, June 4 Engr. *Perf. 13½x13*
142 CD312 1½p dk blue & blk .85 .40

A27

Easter Lilies — A28

Designs: 1p, 4p, Perot stamp. 2p, Racing dinghy. 2½p, Sir George Somers and "Sea Venture." 3p, 1sh3p, Map. 4½p, 9p, "Sea Venture," boat, hog coin and Perot stamp. 6p, 8p, Yellow-billed tropic bird. 1sh, Hog coins. 2sh, Arms of St. George. 2sh6p, Warwick Fort. 5sh, Hog coin. 10sh, Earliest hog coin. £1, Arms of Bermuda.

1953-58 *Perf. 13½x13, 13x13½*
143 A27 ½p olive green .50 *1.50*
144 A27 1p rose red & blk 1.25 .55
145 A28 1½p dull green .30 .25
146 A27 2p red & ultra .55 .55
147 A27 2½p carmine rose 2.10 .60
148 A27 3p vio *(Sandy's)* .35 .25
149 A27 3p violet *(Sandys)* ('57) 1.10 .25
150 A27 4p dp ultra & blk .30 *1.25*
151 A27 4½p green .55 *1.25*
152 A27 6p dk bluish grn & blk 5.00 .75
153 A27 8p red & blk ('55) 2.50 .45
154 A27 9p violet ('58) 7.25 3.00
155 A27 1sh orange .55 .25
156 A27 1sh3p blue *(Sandy's)* 3.75 .45
157 A27 1sh3p blue *(Sandys)* ('57) 7.25 .60
158 A27 2sh yellow brown 4.00 1.10
159 A28 2sh6p scarlet 4.75 .70
160 A27 5sh dp car rose 19.50 1.10
161 A27 10sh deep ultra 13.50 8.00

Engr. and Typo.
162 A27 £1 dp ol grn & multi 25.00 24.00
Nos. 143-162 (20) 100.05 46.85

For overprints, see Nos. 164-167.

Type of 1953 Inscribed "ROYAL VISIT 1953"

Design: 6p, Yellow-billed tropic bird.

1953, Nov. 26 Engr.
163 A27 6p dk bluish grn & blk .50 .25

Visit of Queen Elizabeth II and the Duke of Edinburgh, 1953.

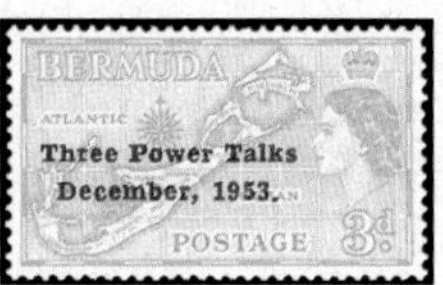

Nos. 148 and 156 Overprinted in Violet Blue or Red

1953, Dec. 8 *Perf. 13½x13*
164 A27 3p violet .25 .25
165 A27 1sh3p blue (R) .25 .25

Three Power Conference, Tucker's Town, December 1953.

Nos. 153 and 156 Overprinted in Black or Red

1956, June 22
166 A27 8p red & black .35 .60
167 A27 1sh3p blue (R) .35 .60

Newport-Bermuda Yacht Race, 50th anniv.

Perot Post Office, Hamilton A29

Perf. 13½x13
1959, Jan. 1 Engr. Wmk. 4
168 A29 6p lilac & black .70 .25

Restoration and reopening of the post office operated at Hamilton by W. B. Perot in the mid-nineteenth century.

Arms of James I and Elizabeth II — A30

Engr. and Litho.
1959, July 29 Wmk. 314 *Perf. 13*
Coats of Arms in Blue, Yellow & Red
169 A30 1½p dark blue .35 .35
170 A30 3p gray .40 .40
171 A30 4p rose violet .50 .50
172 A30 8p violet gray .50 .50
173 A30 9p olive green .50 .50
174 A30 1sh3p orange brown .50 .50
Nos. 169-174 (6) 2.75 2.75

350th anniv. of the shipwreck of the "Sea Venture" which resulted in the first permanent settlement of Bermuda.

The Old Rectory, St. George's, 1730 A31

Designs: 2p, Church of St. Peter. 3p, Government House. 4p, Cathedral, Hamilton. 5p, No. 185A, H.M. Dockyard. 6p, Perot's Post Office, 1848. 8p, General Post Office, 1869. 9p, Library and Historical Society. 1sh, Christ Church, Warwick, 1719. 1sh3p, City Hall, Hamilton. 10p, No. 185, Bermuda Cottage, 1705. 2sh, Town of St. George. 2sh3p, Bermuda House, 1710. 2sh6p, Bermuda House, 18th century. 5sh, Colonial Secretariat, 1833. 10sh, Old Post Office, Somerset, 1890. £1, House of Assembly, 1815.

Wmk. 314 Upright
1962-65 Photo. *Perf. 12½*
175 A31 1p org, lil & blk .25 *.60*
176 A31 2p sl, lt vio, grn & yel .25 .25
a. Light vio omitted *1,000.* 1,000.
b. Green omitted 7,500.
d. Imperf., pair *2,250.*
177 A31 3p lt bl & yel brn .25 .25
178 A31 4p car rose & red brn .25 *.40*
179 A31 5p dk bl & pink 1.50 *2.50*
180 A31 6p emer, lt & dk bl .25 *.30*
181 A31 8p grn, dp org & ultra .30 *.40*
182 A31 9p org brn & grnsh bl .25 *.30*
182A A31 10p brt vio & bis ('65) 8.75 1.25
183 A31 1sh multi .25 .25
184 A31 1sh3p sl, lem & rose car .90 .25
185 A31 1sh6p brt vio & bis 2.50 2.50
186 A31 2sh brn & org 2.75 1.40
187 A31 2sh3p brn & brt yel grn 2.10 *6.75*
188 A31 2sh6p grn, yel & sep .65 .40
189 A31 5sh choc & brt grn 1.10 *1.25*
190 A31 10sh dl grn, buff & rose car 4.50 *5.50*
191 A31 £1 cit, bis, blk & org 14.00 14.00
Nos. 175-191 (18) 40.80 38.55

See No. 252a. For surcharges see Nos. 238-254.

No. 177a, yellow-brown omitted, is no longer listed. All reported examples show traces of the yellow-brown.

1966-69 Wmk. 314 Sideways
Unnamed Colors as in 1962-65 Issue
176c A31 2p ('69) 5.50 *6.50*
181a A31 8p ('67) .65 *1.60*
182b A31 10p 1.90 .90
183a A31 1sh ('67) .95 *1.40*
185A A31 1sh6p indigo & rose 4.50 *2.75*
186a A31 2sh ('67) 4.50 *5.00*
Nos. 176c-186a (6) 18.00 18.15

For surcharges see Nos. 239, 245-246, 248-249.

Freedom from Hunger Issue
Common Design Type

1963, June 4 *Perf. 14x14½*
192 CD314 1sh3p sepia 1.00 .50

Red Cross Centenary Issue
Common Design Type
Wmk. 314

1963, Sept. 2 Litho. *Perf. 13*
193 CD315 3p black & red .50 .30
194 CD315 1sh3p ultra & red 2.25 2.25

Finn Boat — A32

Wmk. 314
1964, Sept. 28 Photo. *Perf. 13½*
195 A32 3p blue, vio & red .40 .40

18th Olympic Games, Tokyo, Oct. 10-25.

ITU Issue
Common Design Type
Perf. 11x11½

1965, May 17 Litho. Wmk. 314
196 CD317 3p blue & emerald .65 .50
197 CD317 2sh yel & vio blue 1.50 *1.75*

Scout Badge and Royal Cipher A33

1965, July 24 Photo. *Perf. 12½*
198 A33 2sh multicolored .55 .55

50th anniversary of Scouting in Bermuda.

Intl. Cooperation Year Issue
Common Design Type

1965, Oct. 25 Litho. *Perf. 14½*
199 CD318 4p blue grn & cl .50 .25
200 CD318 2sh6p lt violet & grn 1.75 1.00

Churchill Memorial Issue
Common Design Type

1966, Jan. 24 Photo. *Perf. 14*
Design in Black, Gold and Carmine Rose
201 CD319 3p bright blue .55 .55
202 CD319 6p green .85 .85
203 CD319 10p brown 1.10 1.10
204 CD319 1sh3p violet 1.50 1.50
Nos. 201-204 (4) 4.00 4.00

World Cup Soccer Issue
Common Design Type

1966, July 1 Litho. *Perf. 14*
205 CD321 10p multicolored .50 .50
206 CD321 2sh6p multicolored 1.25 1.25

UNESCO Anniversary Issue
Common Design Type

1966, Dec. 1 Litho. *Perf. 14*
207 CD323 4p "Education" .50 .40
208 CD323 1sh3p "Science" 1.40 1.25
209 CD323 2sh "Culture" 2.40 2.25
Nos. 207-209 (3) 4.30 3.90

Post Office, Hamilton A34

Wmk. 314
1967, June 23 Photo. *Perf. 14½*
210 A34 3p vio blue & multi .25 .25
211 A34 1sh orange & multi .25 .25
212 A34 1sh6p green & multi .30 .25
213 A34 2sh6p red & multi .30 .25
Nos. 210-213 (4) 1.10 1.00

Opening of the new GPO, Hamilton.

Cable Ship Mercury A35

Designs: 1sh, Map of Bermuda and Virgin Islands, telephone and microphone. 1sh6p, Radio tower, television set, telephone and cable. 2sh6p, Cable at sea bottom and ship.

1967, Sept. 14 Photo. Wmk. 314
214 A35 3p multicolored .25 .25
215 A35 1sh multicolored .30 .30
216 A35 1sh6p multicolored .30 .30
217 A35 2sh6p multicolored .50 .50
Nos. 214-217 (4) 1.35 1.35

Completion of the Bermuda-Tortola, Virgin Islands, telephone link.

Human Rights Flame, Globe and Doves A36

1968, Feb. 1 Litho. *Perf. 14x14½*

218 A36 3p indigo, lt grn & bl .30 .25
219 A36 1sh brown, lt bl & bl .30 .25
220 A36 1sh6p black, pink & blue .30 .25
221 A36 2sh6p green, yellow & bl .30 .25
Nos. 218-221 (4) 1.20 1.00

International Human Rights Year.

Mace A37

Nos. 224-225, House of Assembly, Bermuda, Parliament, London & royal cipher.

1968, July 1 Photo. *Perf. 14½*

222 A37 3p rose red & multi .30 .25
223 A37 1sh ultra & multi .30 .25
224 A37 1sh6p yellow & multi .30 .25
225 A37 2sh6p multicolored .30 .25
Nos. 222-225 (4) 1.20 1.00

New constitution.

Olympic Sports and Rings A38

1968, Sept. 24 Wmk. 314 *Perf. 12½*

226 A38 3p lilac & multi .25 .25
a. Rose brown omitted ("3d BERMUDA") *4,750. 5,000.*
227 A38 1sh multicolored .35 .35
228 A38 1sh6p multicolored .60 .60
229 A38 2sh6p multicolored .90 .90
Nos. 226-229 (4) 2.10 2.10

19th Olympic Games, Mexico City, 10/12-27.

Girl Guides A39

Designs: 1sh, Like 3p. 1sh6p, 2sh6p, Girl Guides and arms of Bermuda.

1969, Feb. 17 Litho. *Perf. 14*

230 A39 3p lilac & multi .25 .25
231 A39 1sh green & multi .35 .25
232 A39 1sh6p gray & multi .40 .40
233 A39 2sh6p red & multi .60 *1.25*
Nos. 230-233 (4) 1.60 2.15

Bermuda Girl Guides, 50th anniv.

Gold and Emerald Cross — A40

Design: 4p, 2sh, Different background.

1969, Sept. 29 Photo. *Perf. 14½x14*

Cross in Yellow, Brown and Emerald

234 A40 4p violet .30 .25
235 A40 1sh3p green .45 .25
236 A40 2sh black .55 *.90*
237 A40 2sh6p carmine rose .60 *1.75*
Nos. 234-237 (4) 1.90 3.15

Treasures salvaged off the coast of Bermuda. The cross shown is from the Tucker treasure from the 16th century Spanish galleon San Pedro.

Buildings Issue and Type of 1962-69 Surcharged with New Value and Bar in Black or Brown

1970, Feb. 6 Wmk. 314 *Perf. 12½*

238 A31 1c on 1p multi .25 *1.75*
239 A31 2c on 2p multi .25 .25
a. Watermark upright 2.50 *4.50*
b. Light violet omitted *1,000.*
c. Pair, one without surch. *7,500.*
240 A31 3c on 3p multi .25 .25
241 A31 4c on 4p multi (Br) .25 .25
242 A31 5c on 8p multi .25 *2.25*
243 A31 6c on 6p multi .25 *1.75*
244 A31 9c on 9p multi (Br) .40 *2.75*
245 A31 10c on 10p multi .40 .25
246 A31 12c on 1sh multi .40 *1.25*
247 A31 15c on 1sh3p multi 2.00 1.75
248 A31 18c on 1sh6p multi 1.00 .70
249 A31 24c on 2sh multi 1.10 *3.25*
250 A31 30c on 2sh6p multi 1.25 *3.00*
251 A31 36c on 2sh3p multi 2.25 *8.00*
252 A31 60c on 5sh multi 2.90 *4.00*
a. Surcharge omitted *1,500.*
253 A31 $1.20 on 10sh multi 5.25 *14.00*
254 A31 $2.40 on £1 multi 8.00 *19.00*
Nos. 238-254 (17) 26.45 *64.45*

Watermark upright on 1c, 3c to 9c and 36c; sideways on others. Watermark is sideways on No. 252a, upright on No. 189.

Spathiphyllum — A41

Flowers: 2c, Bottlebrush. 3c, Oleander, vert. 4c, Bermudiana. 5c, Poinsettia. 6c, Hibiscus. 9c, Cereus. 10c, Bougainvillea, vert. 12c, Jacaranda. 15c, Passion flower. 18c, Coralita. 24c, Morning glory. 30c, Tecoma. 36c, Angel's trumpet. 60c, Plumbago. $1.20, Bird of paradise. $2.40, Chalice cup.

Wmk. 314, Sideways on Horiz. Stamps

1970, July 6 *Perf. 14*

255 A41 1c lt grn & multi .35 *.50*
256 A41 2c pale bl & multi .60 .50
257 A41 3c yellow & multi .35 *.50*
258 A41 4c buff & multi .35 *.50*
259 A41 5c pink & multi .85 .50
a. Imperf., pair 1,500.
260 A41 6c org & multi .85 .60
261 A41 9c lt grn & multi .60 .50
262 A41 10c pale sal & multi .60 .50
263 A41 12c pale yel & multi 2.10 1.75
264 A41 15c buff & multi 2.50 1.50
265 A41 18c pale sal & multi 6.50 2.50
266 A41 24c pink & multi 4.25 4.25
267 A41 30c plum & multi 2.90 1.60
268 A41 36c dk gray & multi 3.50 2.40
269 A41 60c gray & multi 4.75 4.00
270 A41 $1.20 blue & multi 7.75 7.25
271 A41 $2.40 multicolored 15.00 15.00
Nos. 255-271 (17) 53.80 44.35

See Nos. 322-328. For overprints see Nos. 288-291.

1974-76 Wmk. 314 Upright

259b A41 5c multicolored 3.25 *3.75*
260a A41 6c multicolored 7.25 *8.25*
263a A41 12c multicolored 6.00 *7.00*
267a A41 30c multicolored ('76) 9.75 *11.00*
Nos. 259b-267a (4) 26.25 *30.00*

Issued: 30c, June 11; others, June 13.

1975-76 Wmk. 373

256a A41 2c multicolored 1.75 1.25
260b A41 6c multicolored 8.00 7.00

Issued: 2c, Dec. 8; 6c, June 11, 1976.

State House, St. George's, 1622-1815 — A42

Designs: 15c, The Sessions House, Hamilton, 1893. 18c, First Assembly House, St. Peter's Church, St. George's. 24c, Temporary Assembly House, Hamilton, 1815-26.

1970, Oct. 12 Litho. *Perf. 14*

272 A42 4c multicolored .25 .25
273 A42 15c multicolored .25 .25
274 A42 18c multicolored .30 .30
275 A42 24c multicolored .50 *.90*
a. Souvenir sheet of 4, #272-275 2.25 2.25
Nos. 272-275 (4) 1.30 1.70

350th anniv. of Bermuda's Parliament.

Street in St. George's A43

"Keep Bermuda Beautiful": 15c, Horseshoe Bay. 18c, Gibb's Hill Lighthouse. 24c, View of Hamilton Harbor.

1971, Feb. 8 Wmk. 314 *Perf. 14*

276 A43 4c multicolored .25 .25
277 A43 15c multicolored .80 .80
278 A43 18c multicolored 2.10 2.10
279 A43 24c multicolored 1.75 1.75
Nos. 276-279 (4) 4.90 4.90

Building of "Deliverance" — A44

Designs: 15c, "Deliverance" and "Patience" arriving in Jamestown, Va., 1610, vert. 18c, Wreck of "Sea Venture," vert. 24c, "Deliverance" and "Patience" under sail, 1610.

1971, May 10 Litho. Wmk. 314

280 A44 4c multicolored .90 .30
281 A44 15c brown & multi 2.40 2.40
282 A44 18c purple & multi 2.40 2.40
283 A44 24c blue & multi 2.75 2.75
Nos. 280-283 (4) 8.45 7.85

Voyage of Sir George Somers to Jamestown, Va., from Bermuda, 1610.

Ocean View Golf Course A45

Golf Courses: 15c, Port Royal. 18c, Castle Harbour. 24c, Belmont.

1971, Nov. 1 *Perf. 13*

284 A45 4c multicolored 1.10 .25
285 A45 15c multicolored 2.10 .90
286 A45 18c multicolored 2.25 1.40
287 A45 24c multicolored 2.75 2.75
Nos. 284-287 (4) 8.20 5.30

Golfing in Bermuda.

Nos. 258, 264-266 Overprinted: "HEATH-NIXON / DECEMBER 1971"

1971, Dec. 20 Photo. *Perf. 14*

288 A41 4c buff & multi .25 .25
289 A41 15c buff & multi .25 .25
290 A41 18c pale sal & multi .40 .40
291 A41 24c pink & multi .50 .50
Nos. 288-291 (4) 1.40 1.40

Meeting of President Richard M. Nixon and Prime Minister Edward Heath of Great Britain, at Hamilton, Dec. 20-21, 1971.

Bonefish A46

1972, Aug. 7 Litho. *Perf. 13½x14*

292 A46 4c shown .50 .25
293 A46 15c Wahoo .50 .50
294 A46 18c Yellowfin tuna .60 .60
295 A46 24c Greater amberjack .65 .65
Nos. 292-295 (4) 2.25 2.00

World fishing records.

Silver Wedding Issue, 1972

Common Design Type

Design: Queen Elizabeth II, Prince Philip, Admiralty oar and mace.

1972, Nov. 20 Photo. *Perf. 14x14½*

296 CD324 4c violet & multi .25 .25
297 CD324 15c car rose & multi .25 .25

Palmettos — A47

1973, Sept. 3 Wmk. 314 *Perf. 14*

298 A47 4c shown .40 .25
299 A47 15c Olivewood 1.10 1.10
a. Brown (Queen's head, "15c") omitted 2,250.
300 A47 18c Bermuda cedar 1.25 1.25
301 A47 24c Mahogany 1.25 1.25
Nos. 298-301 (4) 4.00 3.85

Bermuda National Trust, and "Plant a Tree" campaign.

Princess Anne's Wedding Issue

Common Design Type

1973, Nov. 21 Litho.

302 CD325 15c lilac & multi .25 .25
303 CD325 18c slate & multi .25 .25

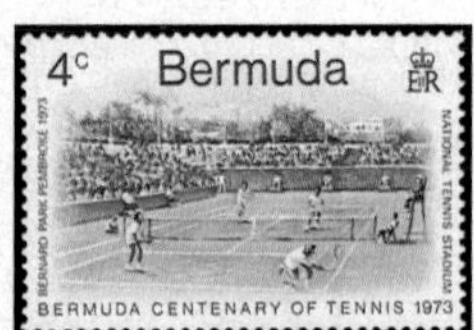

National Tennis Stadium, Pembroke, 1973 — A48

15c, Bermuda's 1st tennis court, Pembroke, 1873. 18c, Britain's 1st tennis court, Leamington Spa, 1872. 24c, 1t US tennis club, Staten Island, 1874.

1973, Dec. 17 Wmk. 314

304 A48 4c black & multi .35 .25
305 A48 15c black & multi .70 .70
306 A48 18c black & multi .85 .85
307 A48 24c black & multi 1.00 1.00
Nos. 304-307 (4) 2.90 2.80

Centenary of tennis in Bermuda.

Rotary Emblem, Weather Vane, City Hall, Hamilton A49

Rotary Emblem and: 17c, St. Peter's Church, St. George's. 20c, Somerset Drawbridge, Somerset. 25c, Map of Bermuda on globe, 1626.

1974, June 24 *Perf. 14*

308 A49 5c emerald & multi .25 .25
309 A49 17c blue & multi .60 .45
310 A49 20c yel org & multi .65 .65
311 A49 25c lt violet & multi .80 .80
Nos. 308-311 (4) 2.30 2.15

50th anniv. of Rotary Intl. in Bermuda.

Jack of Clubs and a Good Bridge Hand — A50

Bermuda Bowl and: 17c, Queen of diamonds. 20c, King of hearts. 25c, Ace of spades.

1975, Jan. 27 Litho. Wmk. 314

No.	Description	Unused	Used
312	A50 5c blue & multi	.35	.25
313	A50 17c dull yel & multi	.65	.65
314	A50 20c ver & multi	.75	*1.50*
315	A50 25c lilac & multi	.75	*2.25*
	Nos. 312-315 (4)	2.50	4.65

World Bridge Championship, Bermuda, Jan. 1975.

Queen Elizabeth II and Prince Philip — A51

Perf. 14x14½

1975, Feb. 17 Photo. Wmk. 373

No.	Description	Unused	Used
316	A51 17c multicolored	.85	.85
317	A51 20c dk blue & multi	.95	.95

Royal Visit, Feb. 16-18, 1975.

British Cavalier Flying Boat, 1937 A52

17c, U.S. Navy airship "Los Angeles," 1925, flying from Lakehurst, NJ to Hamilton, Bermuda. 20c, Constellation over Kindley Field, 1946. 25c, Boeing 747 on tarmac, 1970.

1975, Apr. 28 Litho. *Perf. 14*

No.	Description	Unused	Used
318	A52 5c lt green & multi	.45	.25
319	A52 17c lt ultra & multi	1.75	1.40
320	A52 20c multicolored	1.90	1.90
321	A52 25c rose lil & multi	2.25	2.25
a.	Souvenir sheet of 4, #318-321	14.00	14.00
	Nos. 318-321 (4)	6.35	5.80

Airmail service to Bermuda, 50th anniv.

Flower Type of 1970

1975, June 2 Photo. Wmk. 314

No.	Description	Unused	Used
322	A41 17c Passion flower	3.25	*4.00*
323	A41 20c Coralita	3.25	*4.00*
324	A41 25c Morning glory	3.25	*4.00*
325	A41 40c Angel's trumpet	3.25	*4.00*
326	A41 $1 Plumbago	3.75	*4.50*
327	A41 $2 Bird-of-paradise flower	6.25	*7.50*
328	A41 $3 Chalice cup	12.50	*15.00*
	Nos. 322-328 (7)	35.50	*43.00*

Royal Magazine Break-in A54

17c, Sympathizers rowing towards magazine. 20c, Loading gun powder barrels onto ships. 25c, Gun powder barrels on beach.

Perf. 13x13½

1975, Oct. 27 Litho. Wmk. 373

No.	Description	Unused	Used
329	A54 5c multicolored	.25	.25
330	A54 17c multicolored	.50	.55
331	A54 20c multicolored	.60	*1.25*
332	A54 25c multicolored	.65	*1.40*
a.	Souv. sheet, #329-332, perf 14	4.50	6.00
	Nos. 329-332 (4)	2.00	3.45

Gunpowder Plot, 1775, American War of Independence.

Bermuda Biological Station A55

Designs: 5c, Launching of bathysphere from "Ready," vert. 20c, Sailing ship Challenger, 1873. 25c, Descent of Beebe's bathysphere, 1934, and marine life, vert.

1976, Mar. 29 Litho. *Perf. 14*

No.	Description	Unused	Used
333	A55 5c multicolored	.40	.25
334	A55 17c multicolored	.80	.80
335	A55 20c multicolored	.95	.95
336	A55 25c multicolored	1.10	1.10
	Nos. 333-336 (4)	3.25	3.10

Bermuda Biological Station, 50th anniv.

Christian Radich, Norway A56

Tall Ships: 12c, Juan Sebastian de Elcano, Spain. 17c, Eagle, US. 20c, Sir Winston Churchill, Great Britain. 40c, Kruzenshtern, USSR. $1, Cutty Sark (silver trophy).

1976, June 15 Litho. *Perf. 13*

No.	Description	Unused	Used
337	A56 5c lt green & multi	1.05	.25
338	A56 12c violet & multi	1.15	*2.00*
339	A56 17c ultra & multi	1.15	*1.50*
340	A56 20c blue & multi	1.15	*1.50*
341	A56 40c yellow & multi	1.40	*2.25*
342	A56 $1 sl grn & multi	1.75	*5.00*
	Nos. 337-342 (6)	7.65	*12.50*

Trans-Atlantic Cutty Sark International Tall Ships Race, Plymouth, England-New York City (Operation Sail '76).

Silver Cup Trophy and Crossed Club Flags A57

Designs: 17c, St. George's Cricket Club and emblem. 20c, Somerset Cricket Club and emblem. 25c, Cricket match.

1976, Aug. 16 Wmk. 373 *Perf. 14½*

No.	Description	Unused	Used
343	A57 5c multicolored	.45	.25
344	A57 17c multicolored	.85	.85
345	A57 20c multicolored	1.10	1.10
346	A57 25c multicolored	1.75	1.75
	Nos. 343-346 (4)	4.15	3.95

St. George's and Somerset Cricket Club matches, 75th anniversary.

Queen's Visit to Bermuda, 1975 — A58

Designs: 20c, St. Edward's Crown. $1, Queen seated in Chair of Estate.

1977, Feb. 7 Litho. *Perf. 14x13½*

No.	Description	Unused	Used
347	A58 5c silver & multi	.30	.30
348	A58 20c silver & multi	.30	.30
349	A58 $1 silver & multi	.60	.60
	Nos. 347-349 (3)	1.20	1.20

Reign of Queen Elizabeth II, 25th anniv.

Stockdale House, St. George's A59

UPU Emblem and: 15c, Perot Post Office and Perot Stamp. 17c, St. George's Post Office, c. 1860. 20c, Old GPO, Hamilton, c. 1935. 40c, New GPO, Hamilton, 1967.

1977, June 20 Litho. *Perf. 13x13½*

No.	Description	Unused	Used
350	A59 5c multicolored	.25	.25
351	A59 15c multicolored	.45	.45
352	A59 17c multicolored	.45	.45
353	A59 20c multicolored	.50	.50
354	A59 40c multicolored	.80	.80
	Nos. 350-354 (5)	2.45	2.45

Bermuda's UPU membership, cent.

Sailing Ship, 17th Century, Approaching Castle Island — A60

Designs: 15c, King's pilot leaving 18th century naval ship at Murray's Anchorage. 17c, Pilot gigs racing to meet steamship, early 19th century. 20c, Harvest Queen, late 19th century. 40c, Pilot cutter and Queen Elizabeth II off St. David's Lighthouse.

Perf. 13½x14

1977, Sept. 26 Wmk. 373

No.	Description	Unused	Used
355	A60 5c multicolored	.65	.25
356	A60 15c multicolored	1.00	.90
357	A60 17c multicolored	1.10	.90
358	A60 20c multicolored	1.25	1.25
359	A60 40c multicolored	2.25	2.25
	Nos. 355-359 (5)	6.25	5.55

Piloting in Bermuda waters.

Elizabeth II A61

Designs: 8c, Great Seal of Elizabeth I. 50c, Great Seal of Elizabeth II.

1978, Aug. 28 Litho. *Perf. 14x13½*

No.	Description	Unused	Used
360	A61 8c gold & multi	.25	.25
361	A61 50c gold & multi	.40	.40
362	A61 $1 gold & multi	.80	.80
	Nos. 360-362 (3)	1.45	1.45

25th anniv. of coronation of Elizabeth II.

White-tailed Tropicbird — A62

Perf. 14; 14x14½ (4c, 5c, $2, $3, $5)

1978-79 Photo. Wmk. 373

No.	Description	Unused	Used
363	A62 3c shown	2.25	2.25
364	A62 4c White-eyed vireo	2.60	2.60
365	A62 5c Eastern bluebird	1.15	1.15
366	A62 7c Whistling tree frog	.45	.45
367	A62 8c Cardinal	1.15	.45
368	A62 10c Spiny lobster	.25	.25
369	A62 12c Land crab	.30	.30
370	A62 15c Skink	.30	.30
371	A62 20c Four-eyed butterflyfish	.35	.35
372	A62 25c Red hind	.45	.45
a.	Greenish blue (background) omitted	4,750.	
373	A62 30c Monarch butterfly	1.90	1.90
374	A62 40c Rock beauty	.60	.60
375	A62 50c Banded butterflyfish	.75	.75
376	A62 $1 Blue angelfish	2.10	2.10
377	A62 $2 Humpback whale	3.00	3.00
378	A62 $3 Green turtle	4.50	4.50
379	A62 $5 Bermuda Petrel	7.75	7.75
	Nos. 363-379 (17)	29.85	29.15

Issued: 3c, 4c, 5c, 8c, $5, 1978; others, 1979.

For surcharge see No. 509.

Map of Bermuda, by George Somers, 1609 — A63

Old Maps of Bermuda: 15c, by John Seller, 1685. 20c, by Herman Moll, 1729, vert. 25c, by Desbruslins, 1740. 50c, by John Speed, 1626.

1979, May 14 Litho. *Perf. 13½*

No.	Description	Unused	Used
380	A63 8c multicolored	.25	.25
381	A63 15c multicolored	.30	.25
382	A63 20c multicolored	.35	.30
383	A63 25c multicolored	.40	.40
384	A63 50c multicolored	.55	*.80*
	Nos. 380-384 (5)	1.85	2.00

Bermuda Police Centenary — A64

20c, Traffic direction, horiz. 25c, Water patrol, horiz. 50c, Motorbike and patrol car.

1979, Nov. 26 Wmk. 373 *Perf. 14*

No.	Description	Unused	Used
385	A64 8c multicolored	.45	.25
386	A64 20c multicolored	.75	.75
387	A64 25c multicolored	.90	.90
388	A64 50c multicolored	1.15	1.15
	Nos. 385-388 (4)	3.25	3.05

Bermuda No. X1, Penny Black — A65

Bermuda #X1 and: 20c, Hill. 25c, "Paid 1" marking on cover. 50c, "Paid 1" marking.

1980, Feb. 25 Litho. *Perf. 13½x14*

No.	Description	Unused	Used
389	A65 8c multicolored	.25	.25
390	A65 20c multicolored	.50	.40
391	A65 25c multicolored	.50	.50
392	A65 50c multicolored	.55	.55
	Nos. 389-392 (4)	1.80	1.70

Sir Rowland Hill (1795-1879), originator of penny postage.

Tristar-500, London 1980 Emblem — A66

1980, May 6 Litho. *Perf. 13x14*
393 A66 25c shown .45 .25
394 A66 50c "Orduna," 1926 .70 .50
395 A66 $1 "Delta," 1856 1.40 1.40
396 A66 $2 "Lord Sidmouth," 1818 2.10 2.10
Nos. 393-396 (4) 4.65 4.25

London 1980 Intl. Stamp Exhib., May 6-14.

Gina Swainson, Miss World, 1979-80, Arms of Bermuda — A67

1980, May 8 *Perf. 14*
397 A67 8c shown .30 .30
398 A67 20c After crowning ceremony .40 .40
399 A67 50c Welcome home party .80 .80
400 A67 $1 In carriage 1.75 1.75
Nos. 397-400 (4) 3.25 3.25

Queen Mother Elizabeth Birthday Issue
Common Design Type

1980, Aug. 4 Wmk. 373 *Perf. 14*
401 CD330 25c multicolored .45 .45

Camden, Prime Minister's House A68

1980, Sept. 24 Litho. *Perf. 14*
402 A68 8c View from satellite .25 .25
403 A68 20c shown .30 .30
404 A68 25c Princess Hotel, Hamilton .30 *.50*
405 A68 50c Government House .60 *1.50*
Nos. 402-405 (4) 1.45 2.55

Commonwealth Finance Ministers Meeting, Bermuda, Sept.

18th Century Kitchen A69

1981, May 21 Wmk. 373 *Perf. 14*
406 A69 8c shown .25 .25
407 A69 25c Gathering Easter lilies .40 .40
408 A69 30c Fisherman .55 .55
409 A69 40c Stone cutting, 19th cent. .75 .75
410 A69 50c Onion shipping, 19th cent. .90 .90
411 A69 $1 Ships, 17th cent. 1.75 1.75
Nos. 406-411 (6) 4.60 4.60

Royal Wedding Issue
Common Design Type

1981, July 22 Wmk. 373 *Perf. 14*
412 CD331 30c Bouquet .30 .30
413 CD331 50c Charles .60 .60
414 CD331 $1 Couple 1.10 1.10
Nos. 412-414 (3) 2.00 2.00

Girl Helping Blind Man Cross Street — A70

1981, Sept. 28 Litho. *Perf. 14*
415 A70 10c shown .25 .25
416 A70 25c Kayaking, Paget Island .30 .30
417 A70 30c Mountain climbing, St. David's Island .35 .35
418 A70 $1 Duke of Edinburgh .75 .75
Nos. 415-418 (4) 1.65 1.65

Duke of Edinburgh's Awards, 25th anniv.

Conus Species A71

1982, May 13 Wmk. 373 *Perf. 14*
419 A71 10c shown .70 .25
420 A71 25c Bursa finlayi 1.40 1.40
421 A71 30c Sconsia striata 1.75 1.75
422 A71 $1 Murex pterynotus lightbourni 4.50 4.50
Nos. 419-422 (4) 8.35 7.90

Bermuda Regiment A72

1982, June 17 Litho. Wmk. 373
423 A72 10c Color guard .80 .25
424 A72 25c Queen's birthday parade 1.25 1.00
425 A72 30c Governor inspecting honor guard 1.60 1.60
426 A72 40c Beating the retreat 1.75 1.75
427 A72 50c Ceremonial gunners 1.75 1.75
428 A72 $1 Royal visit, 1975 3.00 3.00
Nos. 423-428 (6) 10.15 9.35

Southampton Fort — A73

1982, Nov. 18 Litho. Wmk. 373
429 A73 10c Charles Fort, vert. .30 .30
430 A73 25c Pembroks Fort, vert. .80 .80
431 A73 30c shown .90 .90
432 A73 $1 Smiths and Pagets Forts 2.10 2.10
Nos. 429-432 (4) 4.10 4.10

Arms of Sir Edwin Sandys (1561-1629) A74

Coats of Arms: 25c, Bermuda Company. 50c, William Herbert, 3rd Earl of Pembroke (1584-1630). $1, Sir George Somers (1554-1610).

1983, Apr. 14 Litho. *Perf. 13½*
433 A74 10c multicolored .45 .25
434 A74 25c multicolored 1.40 1.25
435 A74 50c multicolored 2.50 2.50
436 A74 $1 multicolored 3.50 3.50
Nos. 433-436 (4) 7.85 7.50

See Nos. 457-460, 474-477.

Fitted Dinghies — A75

Old and modern boats.

1983, July 21 Wmk. 373 *Perf. 14*
437 A75 12c multicolored .55 .25
438 A75 30c multicolored .75 .75
439 A75 40c multicolored .85 .85
440 A75 $1 multicolored 2.00 2.00
Nos. 437-440 (4) 4.15 3.85

Manned Flight Bicentenary — A76

Designs: 12c, Curtiss Jenny, 1919 (first flight over Bermuda). 30c, Stinson Pilot Radio, 1930 (first completed US-Bermuda flight). 40c, Cavalier, 1937 (first scheduled passenger flight). $1, USS Los Angeles airship moored to USS Patoka, 1925.

1983, Oct. 13 Litho. *Perf. 14*
441 A76 12c multicolored .80 .30
442 A76 30c multicolored 1.60 1.60
443 A76 40c multicolored 1.90 1.90
444 A76 $1 multicolored 3.25 3.25
Nos. 441-444 (4) 7.55 7.05

Newspaper and Postal Services, 200th Anniv. — A77

1984, Jan. 26 Litho. *Perf. 14*
445 A77 12c Joseph Stockdale .45 .25
446 A77 30c First Newspaper .75 .75
447 A77 40c Stockdale's Postal Service, horiz. .95 .95
448 A77 $1 "Lady Hammond," horiz. 3.50 3.50
Nos. 445-448 (4) 5.65 5.45

375th Anniv. of Bermuda Settlement — A78

Designs: 12c, Thomas Gates, George Somers. 30c, Jamestown, Virginia, US. 40c, Sea Venture shipwreck. $1, Fleet leaving Plymouth, England.

1984, May 3 Litho. Wmk. 373
449 A78 12c multicolored .25 .25
450 A78 30c multicolored .70 .70
451 A78 40c multicolored 1.25 1.25
452 A78 $1 multicolored 3.00 3.00
a. Souv. sheet of 2, #450, 452 6.00 6.00
Nos. 449-452 (4) 5.20 5.20

1984 Summer Olympics A79

1984, July 19 Litho. *Perf. 14*
453 A79 12c Swimming, vert. .50 .25
454 A79 30c Track & field .95 .95
455 A79 40c Equestrian, vert. 1.60 1.60
456 A79 $1 Sailing 3.50 3.50
Nos. 453-456 (4) 6.55 6.30

Arms Type of 1983

1984, Sept. 27 Litho. *Perf. 13½*
457 A74 12c Southampton .75 .25
458 A74 30c Smith 1.50 1.25
459 A74 40c Devonshire 1.90 1.90
460 A74 $1 St. George 4.25 4.25
Nos. 457-460 (4) 8.40 7.65

Architecture, Buttery — A80

1985, Jan. 24 Litho. *Perf. 13½x13*
461 A80 12c shown .40 .25
462 A80 30c Rooftops 1.10 1.00
463 A80 40c Chimneys 1.25 1.25
464 A80 $1.50 Archway 4.50 4.50
Nos. 461-464 (4) 7.25 7.00

Audubon Birth Bicentenary — A81

1985, Mar. 21 Wmk. 373 *Perf. 14*
465 A81 12c Osprey, vert. 2.75 .85
466 A81 30c Yellow-crowned night heron, vert. 2.75 1.25
467 A81 40c Great egret 3.25 1.60
468 A81 $1.50 Bluebird, vert. 5.25 5.25
Nos. 465-468 (4) 14.00 8.95

Queen Mother 85th Birthday Issue
Common Design Type

Designs: 12c, Queen Consort, 1937. 30c, With grandchildren, 80th birthday. 40c, At Clarence House, 83rd birthday. $1.50, Holding Prince Henry. No. 473, In coach with Prince Charles.

Perf. 14½x14
1985, June 7 Wmk. 384
469 CD336 12c gray, bl & blk .35 .35
470 CD336 30c multicolored .70 .70
471 CD336 40c multicolored 1.10 1.10
472 CD336 $1.50 multicolored 3.50 3.50
Nos. 469-472 (4) 5.65 5.65

Souvenir Sheet
473 CD336 $1 multicolored 4.25 4.25

Arms Type of 1983

Coats of Arms: 12c, James Hamilton, 2nd Marquess of Hamilton (1589-1625). 30c, William Paget, 4th Lord Paget (1572-1629). 40c, Robert Rich, 2nd Earl of Warwick (1587-1658). $1.50, Hamilton, 1957.

1985, Sept. 19 Litho. *Perf. 13½*
474 A74 12c multicolored .90 .25
475 A74 30c multicolored 1.75 1.10
476 A74 40c multicolored 2.10 2.10
477 A74 $1.50 multicolored 5.00 5.00
Nos. 474-477 (4) 9.75 8.45

Halley's Comet A82

1985, Nov. 21 Wmk. 384 *Perf. 14½*
478 A82 15c Bermuda Archipelago 1.10 .35
479 A82 40c Nuremberg Chronicles, 1493 2.10 2.10
480 A82 50c Peter Apian woodcut, 1532 2.50 2.50

481 A82 $1.50 Painting by Samuel Scott (c.1702-72) 4.75 4.75
Nos. 478-481 (4) 10.45 9.70

Shipwrecks — A83

1986 Wmk. 384 *Perf. 14*

Without date imprint

482 A83 3c Constellation, 1943 .80 *1.10*
483 A83 5c Early Riser, 1876 .30 .30
484 A83 7c Madiana, 1903 .65 *2.50*
485 A83 10c Curlew, 1856 .30 .30
486 A83 12c Warwick, 1619 .65 .30
487 A83 15c HMS Vixen, 1890 .45 .45
488 A83 20c San Pedro, 1594 1.10 .55
489 A83 25c Alert, 1877 .75 *3.00*
490 A83 40c North Carolina, 1880 .80 *1.25*
491 A83 50c Mark Antonie, 1777 1.60 *3.25*
492 A83 60c Mary Celestia, 1864 1.75 1.75
493 A83 $1 L'Herminie, 1839 2.50 2.50
494 A83 $1.50 Caesar, 1818 6.00 *7.00*
495 A83 $2 Lord Amherst, 1778 5.75 5.75
496 A83 $3 Minerva, 1849 9.25 9.25
497 A83 $5 Caraquet, 1923 15.00 15.00
498 A83 $8 HMS Pallas, 1783 24.00 24.00
Nos. 482-498 (17) 71.65 78.25

See Nos. 545-546. For surcharges see Nos. 598-600.

Inscribed "1989" or "1990"

1989-90

482a A83 3c 1990 1.75 *3.00*
488a A83 20c 1990 3.00 *4.50*
493a A83 $1 1989 1.50 1.50
495a A83 $2 1989 2.50 *4.50*
496a A83 $3 1989 4.50 *8.25*
Nos. 482a-496a (5) 13.25 *21.75*

Issued: Nos. 493a-496a, 7/89; Nos. 482a, 483a, 1/8/90.

Inscribed "1992"

1992 Litho. Wmk. 373 *Perf. 14*

485a A83 10c 2.40 2.40
487a A83 15c 3.00 3.00
488b A83 20c 3.00 3.00
489a A83 25c 3.00 3.00
492a A83 60c 5.00 5.00
497a A83 $5 20.00 20.00
498a A83 $8 30.00 30.00
Nos. 485a-498a (7) 66.40 66.40

Queen Elizabeth II 60th Birthday

Common Design Type

15c, Age 3. 40c, With the Earl of Rosebury, Oaks May Meeting, Epsom, 1954. 50c, With Prince Philip, state visit,1979. 60c, At the British embassy in Paris, state visit, 1972. $1.50, Visiting Crown Agents' offices, 1983.

1986, Apr. 21 Wmk. 384 *Perf. 14½*

499 CD337 15c scar, blk & sil .25 .25
500 CD337 40c ultra & multi .65 .65
501 CD337 50c green & multi .80 .80
502 CD337 60c violet & multi .95 .95
503 CD337 $1.50 rose vio & multi 2.25 2.25
Nos. 499-503 (5) 4.90 4.90

AMERIPEX '86 — A84

1986, May 22 *Perf. 14*

504 A84 15c No. 452a 1.60 .40
505 A84 40c No. 307 2.50 .85
506 A84 50c No. 441 2.50 1.25
507 A84 $1 No. 339 4.00 3.25
Nos. 504-507 (4) 10.60 5.75

Souvenir Sheet

508 A84 1.50 Statue of Liberty, S.S. Queen of Bermuda 11.50 11.50

Statue of Liberty, cent.

No. 378 Surcharged

Perf. 14x14½

1986, Dec. 4 Photo. Wmk. 373

509 A62 90c on $3 multi 8.75 8.75

Exists with double surcharge. Value $110.

Transport Railway, c. 1931-1947 — A85

Wmk. 373

1987, Jan. 22 Litho. *Perf. 14*

510 A85 15c Front Street, c. 1940 2.25 .40
511 A85 40c Springfield Trestle 2.75 1.40
512 A85 50c No. 101, Bailey's Bay Sta. 2.75 1.90
513 A85 $1.50 No. 31, ship Prince David 4.25 4.25
Nos. 510-513 (4) 12.00 7.95

Paintings by Winslow Homer (1836-1910) A86

1987, Apr. 30 *Perf. 14½*

514 A86 15c Bermuda Settlers, 1901 .90 .40
515 A86 30c Bermuda, 1900 1.25 .65
516 A86 40c Bermuda Landscape, 1901 1.50 .90
517 A86 50c Inland Water, 1901 1.75 1.00
518 A86 $1.50 Salt Kettle, 1899 3.25 3.25
Nos. 514-518 (5) 8.65 6.20

Booklet Stamps

519 A86 40c like 15c 1.90 1.90
520 A86 40c like 30c 1.90 1.90
521 A86 40c like No. 516 1.90 1.90
522 A86 40c like 50c 1.90 1.90
523 A86 40c like $1.50 1.90 1.90
a. Bklt. pane, 2 each #519-523 18.00
Complete booklet, #523a 18.00

Nos. 519-523 printed in strips of 5 within pane. "ER" at lower left.

Intl. Flights Inauguration — A87

1987, June 18 *Perf. 14*

524 A87 15c Sikorsky S-42B, 1937 2.50 .25
525 A87 40c Shorts S-23 Cavalier 3.75 .95
526 A87 50c S-42B Bermuda Clipper 4.00 1.10
527 A87 $1.50 Cavalier, Bermuda Clipper 7.25 7.25
Nos. 524-527 (4) 17.50 9.55

Bermuda Telephone Company, Cent. — A88

1987, Oct. 1 Litho. Wmk. 384

528 A88 15c Telephone poles on wagon 1.10 .25
529 A88 40c Operators 2.25 1.00
530 A88 50c Telephones 2.50 1.10
531 A88 $1.50 Satellite, fiber optics, world 4.25 4.25
Nos. 528-531 (4) 10.10 6.60

Horse-drawn Commercial Vehicles — A89

1988, Mar. 3 Litho. *Perf. 14*

532 A89 15c Mail wagon, c. 1869 .45 .25
533 A89 40c Open cart, c. 1823 1.00 1.00
534 A89 50c Closed cart, c. 1823 1.25 1.25
535 A89 $1.50 Two-wheel wagon, c. 1930 3.75 3.75
Nos. 532-535 (4) 6.45 6.25

Old Garden Roses A90

1988, Apr. 21 Wmk. 373

536 A90 15c Old blush 1.25 .40
537 A90 30c Anna Olivier 1.75 .70
538 A90 40c Rosa chinensis semperflorens, vert. 1.90 1.25
539 A90 50c Archduke Charles 2.00 1.75
540 A90 $1.50 Rosa chinensis viridiflora, vert. 4.00 4.00
Nos. 536-540 (5) 10.90 8.10

See Nos. 561-575.

Lloyds of London, 300th Anniv.

Common Design Type

18c, Loss of the H.M.S. Lutine, 1799. 50c, Cable ship Sentinel. 60c, The Bermuda, Hamilton, 1931. $2, Valerian, lost during a hurricane, 1926.

1988, Oct. 13 Litho. Wmk. 384

541 CD341 18c multi 1.00 .30
542 CD341 50c multi, horiz. 1.75 .80
543 CD341 60c multi, horiz. 2.00 1.00
544 CD341 $2 multi 3.50 3.50
Nos. 541-544 (4) 8.25 5.60

Shipwreck Type of 1986

1988 Litho. Wmk. 384 *Perf. 14*

545 A83 18c like 7c 5.50 3.50
546 A83 70c like $1.50 6.25 5.00

Issue dates: 18c, Sept. 22; 70c, Oct. 27.

Military Uniforms — A91

18c, Devonshire Parish Militia, 1812. 50c, 71st Regiment Highlander, 1831-34. 60c, Cameron Highlander, 1942. $2, Troop of Horse, 1774.

1988, Nov. 10 Wmk. 373 *Perf. 14½*

547 A91 18c multicolored 1.75 .40
548 A91 50c multicolored 2.50 1.50
549 A91 60c multicolored 2.75 1.60
550 A91 $2 multicolored 5.75 5.75
Nos. 547-550 (4) 12.75 9.25

Ferry Service A92

1989 Litho. Wmk. 384 *Perf. 14*

551 A92 18c Corona .60 .40
552 A92 50c Rowboat ferry 1.10 1.10
553 A92 60c St. George's Ferry 1.25 1.25
554 A92 $2 Laconia 4.00 4.00
Nos. 551-554 (4) 6.95 6.75

Photography, Sesquicent. A93

Perf. 14x14½

1989, May 11 Litho. Wmk. 373

555 A93 18c Morgan's Is. 1.20 .40
556 A93 30c Front Street, Hamilton (cannon in square) 1.10 .60
557 A93 50c Front Street (seascape) 1.75 1.60
558 A93 60c Crow Lane, Hamilton Harbor 1.90 1.75
559 A93 70c Hamilton Harbor (shipbuilding) 2.25 2.25
560 A93 $1 Dockyard 2.40 2.40
Nos. 555-560 (6) 10.60 9.00

Old Garden Roses Type of 1988

1989, July 13 *Perf. 14*

561 A90 18c Agrippina 1.40 .40
562 A90 30c Smith's Parish 1.25 .65
563 A90 50c Champney's pink cluster 1.90 1.60
564 A90 60c Rosette delizy 2.10 1.75
565 A90 $1.50 Rosa bracteata 3.50 3.50
Nos. 561-565 (5) 10.15 7.90

Nos. 561-562 vert.

Old Garden Roses Type of 1988 with Royal Cipher Instead of Queen's Silhouette

1989, July 13 Booklet Stamps

566 A90 50c like No. 562 2.75 *3.00*
567 A90 50c like No. 540 2.75 *3.00*
568 A90 50c like No. 561 2.75 *3.00*
569 A90 50c like No. 538 2.75 *3.00*
570 A90 50c like No. 563 2.75 *3.00*
571 A90 50c like No. 536 2.75 *3.00*
572 A90 50c like No. 564 2.75 *3.00*
573 A90 50c like No. 537 2.75 *3.00*
574 A90 50c like No. 565 2.75 *3.00*
575 A90 50c like No. 539 2.75 *3.00*
a. Bklt. pane of 10, #566-575 27.50
Complete booklet, #575a 30.00

Bermuda Library, 150th Anniv. A94

1989, Sept. 14 *Perf. 13½x14*

576 A94 18c Hamilton Main Library .40 .40
577 A94 50c St. George's, The Old Rectory 1.10 1.10
578 A94 60c Springfield, Somerset Library 1.25 1.25
579 A94 $2 Cabinet Building 4.50 4.50
Nos. 576-579 (4) 7.25 7.25

Commonwealth Postal Conference — A95

1989, Nov. 3 Wmk. 384 ***Perf. 14***

580 A95 18c No. 1 1.75 .40
581 A95 50c No. 2 2.50 1.00
582 A95 60c Type A4 2.75 1.60
583 A95 $2 No. 6 4.50 4.50
Nos. 580-583 (4) 11.50 7.50

For overprints see Nos. 594-597.

Fairylands, Bermuda, c. 1890, by Ross Sterling Turner A96

Paintings: 50c, *Shinebone Alley, c. 1953*, by Ogden M. Pleissner. 60c, *Salt Kettle, 1916*, by Prosper Senat. $2, *St. George's, 1934*, by Jack Bush.

1990, Apr. 19

590 A96 18c multicolored .90 .40
591 A96 50c multicolored 1.60 1.60
592 A96 60c multicolored 1.60 1.60
593 A96 $2 multicolored 4.25 4.25
Nos. 590-593 (4) 8.35 7.85

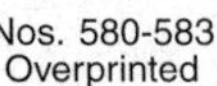
Nos. 580-583 Overprinted

1990, May 3

594 A95 18c multicolored 1.60 .40
595 A95 50c multicolored 2.10 1.75
596 A95 60c multicolored 2.40 2.10
597 A95 $2 multicolored 4.25 4.25
Nos. 594-597 (4) 10.35 8.50

Stamp World London '90.

Nos. 486, 491, 494 Surcharged

1990, Aug. 13

598 A83 30c on 12c No. 486 2.50 2.50
599 A83 55c on 50c No. 491 3.25 3.25
600 A83 80c on $1.50 No. 494 4.00 *5.75*
Nos. 598-600 (3) 9.75 *11.50*

Nova Scotia-Bermuda Cable, Cent. — A97

1990, Oct. 18 Litho. Unwmk.

601 A97 20c Office .85 .40
602 A97 55c Cableship SS Westmeath 2.50 1.60
603 A97 70c Radio station, 1928 2.50 2.50
604 A97 $2 Cableship Sir Eric Sharp 5.75 5.75
Nos. 601-604 (4) 11.60 10.25

Nos. 601-602 with Added Inscription: "BUSH-MAJOR / 16 MARCH 1991"

1991, Mar. Unwmk. ***Perf. 14***

605 A97 20c like #601 2.50 2.00
606 A97 55c like #602 4.50 4.50

Carriages A98

Designs: 20c, Two-seat pony cart, c. 1805. 30c, Varnished rockaway, c. 1830. 55c, Vis-a-Vis Victoria, c. 1895. 70c, Semi-formal phaeton, c. 1900. 80c, Pony runabout, c. 1905. $1, Ladies' phaeton, c. 1910.

Perf. 14x14½

1991, Mar. 21 Litho. Wmk. 373

607 A98 20c green & multi .90 .40
608 A98 30c bl gray & multi 1.00 .85
609 A98 55c dk car & multi 1.90 1.40
610 A98 70c blue & multi 2.75 2.75
611 A98 80c yel org & multi 3.00 3.00
612 A98 $1 dk gray & multi 3.25 3.25
Nos. 607-612 (6) 12.80 11.65

Paintings A99

Designs: 20c, Bermuda by Prosper Senat, vert. 55c, Bermuda Cottage by Frank Allison. 70c, Old Maid's Lane by Jack Bush, vert. $2, St. George's by Ogden M. Pleissner.

Perf. 14x13½

1991, May 16 Litho. Wmk. 373

613 A99 20c multicolored 1.25 .40
614 A99 55c multicolored 2.50 1.90
615 A99 70c multicolored 3.00 3.00
616 A99 $2 multicolored 6.75 6.75
Nos. 613-616 (4) 13.50 12.05

Elizabeth & Philip, Birthdays

Common Design Types

1991, June 20 Wmk. 384 ***Perf. 14½***

617 CD346 55c multicolored 2.00 2.00
618 CD345 70c multicolored 2.00 2.00
a. Pair, #617-618 + label 4.00 4.00

Bermuda in World War II A100

Designs: 20c, Floating drydock. 55c, Kindley Air Field. 70c, Trans-atlantic air route, Boeing 314. $2, Censored trans-atlantic mail.

1991, Sept. 19 Wmk. 373 ***Perf. 14***

619 A100 20c multicolored 2.25 .45
620 A100 55c multicolored 3.50 2.40
621 A100 70c multicolored 4.25 4.25
622 A100 $2 multicolored 7.25 7.25
Nos. 619-622 (4) 17.25 14.35

Queen Elizabeth II's Accession to the Throne, 40th Anniv.

Common Design Type

1992, Feb. 6

623 CD349 20c multicolored .85 .40
624 CD349 30c multicolored 1.00 .75
625 CD349 55c multicolored 1.60 1.40
626 CD349 70c multicolored 2.25 2.25
627 CD349 $1 multicolored 2.50 2.50
Nos. 623-627 (5) 8.20 7.30

Age of Exploration — A101

Artifacts: 25c, Rings, medallion. 35c, Ink wells. 60c, Gold pieces. 75c, Bishop button, crucifix. 85c, Pearl earrings and buttons. $1, 8-real coin, jug and measuring cups.

1992, July 23 ***Perf. 13½***

628 A101 25c multicolored 1.60 .55
629 A101 35c multicolored 1.75 1.00
630 A101 60c multicolored 2.75 2.75
631 A101 75c multicolored 3.25 3.25
632 A101 85c multicolored 3.50 3.50
633 A101 $1 multicolored 3.75 3.75
Nos. 628-633 (6) 16.60 14.80

Stained Glass Windows — A102

Designs: 25c, Ship wreck. 60c, Birds in tree. 75c, St. Francis feeding bird. $2, Seashells.

1992, Sept. 24 ***Perf. 14***

634 A102 25c multicolored 1.90 .55
635 A102 60c multicolored 3.50 2.75
636 A102 75c multicolored 4.25 4.00
637 A102 $2 multicolored 9.00 9.00
Nos. 634-637 (4) 18.65 16.30

7th World Congress of Kennel Clubs A103

Perf. 13½x14, 14x13½

1992, Nov. 12 Litho. Wmk. 373

638 A103 25c German shepherd 1.75 .55
639 A103 35c Irish setter 2.40 1.10
640 A103 60c Whippet, vert. 3.25 3.25
641 A103 75c Border terrier, vert. 3.25 3.25
642 A103 85c Pomeranian, vert. 3.75 3.75
643 A103 $1 Schipperke, vert. 4.00 4.00
Nos. 638-643 (6) 18.40 15.90

A104

Tourist Posters — A105

1993, Feb. 25 Wmk. 373 ***Perf. 14***

644 A104 25c Cyclist, carriage, ship 2.40 1.00
645 A105 60c Golf course 3.25 3.25
646 A105 75c Coastline 3.00 3.00
647 A104 $2 Dancers 5.00 5.00
Nos. 644-647 (4) 13.65 12.25

Royal Air Force, 75th Anniv.

Common Design Type

Designs: 25c, Consolidated Catalina. 60c, Supermarine Spitfire. 75c, Bristol Beaufighter. $2, Handley Page Halifax.

1993, Apr. 1

648 CD350 25c multicolored 1.00 .45
649 CD350 60c multicolored 2.25 2.25
650 CD350 75c multicolored 2.75 2.75
651 CD350 $2 multicolored 4.50 4.50
Nos. 648-651 (4) 10.50 9.95

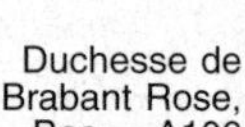
Duchesse de Brabant Rose, Bee — A106

1993, Apr. 1 Wmk. 384

Booklet Stamps

652 A106 10c green & multi .75 *1.60*
653 A106 25c violet & multi .75 .75
a. Booklet pane of 5 3.75
654 A106 50c sepia & multi 2.50 *4.50*
a. Booklet pane, 2 #652, 3 #654 9.00
Complete booklet, #653a, 654a 13.00
655 A106 60c vermilion & multi 1.75 1.90
a. Booklet pane of 5 8.75
Complete booklet, #654a, 655a 18.00
Nos. 652-655 (4) 5.75 *8.75*

Hamilton, Bicent. — A107

Designs: 25c, Modern skyline. 60c, Front Street, ships at left. 75c, Front Street, horse carts. $2, Hamilton Harbor, 1823.

Wmk. 373

1993, Sept. 16 Litho. ***Perf. 14½***

656 A107 25c multicolored 1.75 .55
657 A107 60c multicolored 3.25 3.25
658 A107 75c multicolored 3.25 3.25
659 A107 $2 multicolored 8.25 8.25
Nos. 656-659 (4) 16.50 15.30

Furness Lines — A108

25c, Furness Liv-Aboard Bermuda cruises, vert. 60c, SS Queen of Bermuda entering port. 75c, SS Queen of Bermuda, SS Ocean Monarch. $2, Starlit night aboard ship, vert.

Perf. 15x14, 14x15

1994, Jan. 20 Litho. Wmk. 373

660 A108 25c multicolored .90 .45
661 A108 60c multicolored 2.25 2.25
662 A108 75c multicolored 2.40 2.40
663 A108 $2 multicolored 5.25 5.25
Nos. 660-663 (4) 10.80 10.35

Royal Visit — A109

25c, Queen Elizabeth II. 60c, Queen Elizabeth II, Duke of Edinburgh. 75c, Royal yacht Britannia.

Wmk. 373

1994, Mar. 9 Litho. ***Perf. 13½***

664 A109 25c multicolored 1.50 .60
665 A109 60c multicolored 3.25 3.25
666 A109 75c multicolored 6.50 6.50
Nos. 664-666 (3) 11.25 10.35

Flowering Fruits A110

1994-95 Litho. Wmk. 373 *Perf. 14*

668 A110 5c Peach .45 .45
669 A110 7c Fig .50 .50
670 A110 10c Calabash, vert .50 .50
671 A110 15c Natal plum .80 .40
672 A110 18c Locust & wild honey 3.00 1.50
b. Inscribed "1996" .80 .80
673 A110 20c Pomegranate .80 .45
674 A110 25c Mulberry, vert. 1.10 .60
675 A110 35c Grape, vert. 1.40 .80
676 A110 55c Orange, vert. 1.75 1.10
677 A110 60c Surinam cherry 2.25 1.40
678 A110 75c Loquat 2.50 2.50
679 A110 90c Sugar apple 3.00 3.00
680 A110 $1 Prickly pear, vert. 3.25 3.25
681 A110 $2 Paw paw 5.50 5.50
682 A110 $3 Bay grape 7.75 7.75
683 A110 $5 Banana, vert. 10.50 10.50
684 A110 $8 Lemon 17.00 17.00
Nos. 668-684 (17) 62.05 57.20

Issued: 5c, 7c, 15c, 20c, $8, 7/14/94; 10c, 25c, 35c, 55c, $1, $5, 10/6/94; 18c, 60c, 75c, 90c, $2, $3, 3/23/95. No. 672a, 9/1/96.

1998, Sept. 1 Wmk. 384

668a A110 5c .80 1.25
671a A110 15c 1.40 .50
672a A110 18c 1.40 .50
673a A110 20c 1.40 .60
674a A110 25c 4.00 .60
678a A110 75c 4.00 2.00
679a A110 90c 5.00 2.50
680a A110 $1 6.00 3.75
Nos. 668a-680a (8) 24.00 11.70

No. 672a exists dated "1998."

Issued: Nos. 668a, 671a, 673a-674a, 678a-680a, 9/1/98.

Hospital Care, Cent. — A111

1994, Sept. 15 *Perf. 15x14*

685 A111 25c Child birth 1.25 .45
686 A111 60c Dialysis 2.50 2.50
687 A111 75c Emergency 3.50 3.50
688 A111 $2 Therapy 6.50 6.50
Nos. 685-688 (4) 13.75 12.95

Christmas — A112

1994, Nov. 10 *Perf. 14x15*

689 A112 25c Gombey dancers .90 .45
690 A112 60c Carollers 1.60 1.60
691 A112 75c Marching band 3.25 2.50
692 A112 $2 Natl. dance group 5.75 5.75
Nos. 689-692 (4) 11.50 10.30

Decimalization, 25th Anniv. — A113

Stamps, 1970 coins: 25c, #255, one cent. 60c, #259, five cents. 75c, #262, ten cents. $2, #324, twenty-five cents.

Wmk. 373

1995, Feb. 6 Litho. *Perf. 14*

693 A113 25c multicolored 1.00 .40
694 A113 60c multicolored 1.75 1.75
695 A113 75c multicolored 2.25 2.25
696 A113 $2 multicolored 6.00 6.00
Nos. 693-696 (4) 11.00 10.40

Outdoor Celebrations — A114

Perf. 14x15

1995, May 30 Litho. Wmk. 373

697 A114 25c Kite flying .80 .45
698 A114 60c Majorettes 2.10 2.10
699 A114 75c Portuguese dancers 2.40 2.40
700 A114 $2 Floral float 5.25 5.25
Nos. 697-700 (4) 10.55 10.20

Parliament, 375th Anniv. — A115

Designs: 25c, $1, Bermuda coat of arms.

Perf. 14x13½

1995, Nov. 3 Litho. Wmk. 373

701 A115 25c blue & multi 1.00 .40
702 A115 $1 green & multi 2.25 2.25

See No. 731.

Military Bases A116

Force insignia and: 20c, Ordnance Island Submarine Base. 25c, Royal Naval Dockyard. 60c, Fort Bell and Kindley Field. 75c, Darrell's Island. 90c, US Navy Operating Base. $1, Canadian Forces Station, Daniel's Head.

1995, Dec. 4 *Perf. 14*

703 A116 20c multicolored .75 .75
704 A116 25c multicolored .90 .45
705 A116 60c multicolored 1.90 1.90
706 A116 75c multicolored 2.25 2.25
707 A116 90c multicolored 2.25 2.25
708 A116 $1 multicolored 2.25 2.25
Nos. 703-708 (6) 10.30 9.85

Modern Olympic Games, Cent. — A117

Wmk. 384

1996, May 21 Litho. *Perf. 14*

709 A117 25c Track & field 1.10 .60
710 A117 30c Cycling 4.00 1.60
711 A117 65c Sailing 2.75 2.75
712 A117 80c Equestrian 2.75 2.75
Nos. 709-712 (4) 10.60 7.70

CAPEX '96 A118

Methods of transportation: 25c, Sommerset Express, c. 1900. 60c, Bermuda Railway, 1930's. 75c, First bus, 1946. $2, Early sight-seeing bus, c.1947.

Perf. 13½x14

1996, June 7 Litho. Wmk. 373

713 A118 25c multicolored 1.60 .60
714 A118 60c multicolored 3.25 2.00
715 A118 75c multicolored 3.25 2.40
716 A118 $2 multicolored 6.00 5.75
Nos. 713-716 (4) 14.10 10.75

Panoramas of Hamilton and St. George's, by E. J. Holland, 1933 A119

Hamilton, looking across water from Bostock Hill: No. 717, Palm trees, Furness Line ship coming through Two Rock Passage. No. 718, House, buildings on other side. No. 719, Sailboats on water, Princess Hotel. No. 720, Island, Bermudiana Hotel, Cathedral. No. 721, Coral roads on hillside, city of Hamilton.

St. George's, looking across water from St. David's: No. 722, Island, harbor. No. 723, Sailboat, buildings along shore. No. 724, Sailboat, St. George's Hotel, buildings. No. 725, Hillside, ship. No. 726, Homes on hill top, passage out of harbor.

Perf. 14x14½

1996, May 21 Wmk. 373

Booklet Stamps

717 A119 60c multicolored 2.75 2.75
718 A119 60c multicolored 2.75 2.75
719 A119 60c multicolored 2.75 2.75
720 A119 60c multicolored 2.75 2.75
721 A119 60c multicolored 2.75 2.75
a. Strip of 5, #717-721 14.00 14.00
722 A119 60c multicolored 2.75 2.75
723 A119 60c multicolored 2.75 2.75
724 A119 60c multicolored 2.75 2.75
725 A119 60c multicolored 2.75 2.75
726 A119 60c multicolored 2.75 2.75
a. Strip of 5, #722-726 14.00 14.00
b. Booklet pane, #721a, 726a 28.00
Complete booklet, #726b 30.00

Lighthouses A120

Designs: 30c, Hog Fish Beacon. 65c, Gibbs Hill Lighthouse. 80c, St. David's Lighthouse. $2, North Rock Beacon.

Perf. 14x13½

1996, Aug. 15 Litho. Wmk. 373

727 A120 30c multicolored 2.25 .85
728 A120 65c multicolored 3.00 2.25
729 A120 80c multicolored 3.50 2.75
730 A120 $2 multicolored 5.50 *7.00*
Nos. 727-730 (4) 14.25 *12.85*

See Nos. 737-740.

Bermuda Coat of Arms Type of 1995

Inscribed "Commonwealth Finance Ministers Meeting"

Perf. 14x13½

1996, Sept. 24 Litho. Wmk. 373

731 A115 $1 red & multi 3.50 3.50

Queen Elizabeth II — A121

1996, Nov. 7

732 A121 $22 blue & org brn 50.00 *55.00*

Architectural Heritage — A122

Wmk. 384

1996, Nov. 28 Litho. *Perf. 14*

733 A122 30c Waterville 1.10 .55
734 A122 65c Bridge House 1.60 1.60
735 A122 80c Fannie Fox's Cottage 2.00 2.00
736 A122 $2.50 Palmetto House 5.00 5.00
Nos. 733-736 (4) 9.70 9.15

Lighthouse Type of 1996 Redrawn

Wmk. 373

1997, Feb. 12 Litho. *Perf. 14*

737 A120 30c Like #727 2.75 1.10
738 A120 65c Like #728 4.00 2.75
739 A120 80c Like #729 4.50 3.25
740 A120 $2.50 Like #730 8.50 *11.00*
Nos. 737-740 (4) 19.75 *18.10*

Nos. 737-740 each have Hong Kong '97 emblem. No. 738 inscribed "Gibbs Hill Lighthouse c. 1900." No. 739 inscribed "St. David's Lighthouse c. 1900."

Birds A123

Designs: 30c, White-tailed tropicbird. 60c, White-tailed tropicbird, adult, chick, vert. 80c, Cahow, adult, chick, vert. $2.50, Cahow.

Wmk. 384

1997, Apr. 17 Litho. *Perf. 14*

741 A123 30c multicolored 1.10 .75
742 A123 60c multicolored 2.25 1.90
743 A123 80c multicolored 3.00 2.75
744 A123 $2.50 multicolored 6.75 *7.50*
Nos. 741-744 (4) 13.10 12.90

See Nos. 798-801.

Queen Elizabeth II and Prince Philip, 50th Wedding Anniv. A124

Perf. 14x14½

1997, Oct. 9 Litho. Wmk. 373

745 A124 30c Queen, crowd 1.00 .75
746 A124 $2 Queen, Prince 5.50 5.50
a. Souvenir sheet of 2, #745-746 6.50 6.50

Education in Bermuda A125

Designs: 30c, Man, children using blocks. 40c, Teacher, students with map. 60c, Boys holding sports trophy. 65c, Students in front of Berkeley Institute. 80c, Students working in lab. 90c, Students in graduation gowns.

Wmk. 384

1997, Dec. 18 Litho. *Perf. 14*

747 A125 30c multicolored .80 .60
748 A125 40c multicolored .90 .90
749 A125 60c multicolored 1.25 1.25
750 A125 65c multicolored 1.25 1.25
751 A125 80c multicolored 1.90 1.90
752 A125 90c multicolored 2.10 2.10
Nos. 747-752 (6) 8.20 8.00

Diana, Princess of Wales (1961-97)

Common Design Type

Various portraits: a. 30c. b, 40c. c, 65c. d, 80c.

Perf. 14x14½

1998, Mar. 31 Litho. Wmk. 373

753 CD355 Sheet of 4, #a.-d. 5.50 5.50

No. 753 sold for $2.15 + 25c, with surtax from international sales being donated to the Princess Diana Memorial Fund and surtax from national sales being donated to designated local charity.

Paintings of the Islands A126

Designs: 30c, Fox's Cottage, St. David's. 40c, East Side, Somerset. 65c, Long Bay Road, Somerset. $2, Flatts Village.

1998, June 4 *Perf. 13½x14*

754 A126 30c multicolored 1.50 .70
755 A126 40c multicolored 1.90 1.25
756 A126 65c multicolored 2.75 2.50
757 A126 $2 multicolored 6.50 *8.50*
Nos. 754-757 (4) 12.65 12.95

Hospitality for Tourists in Bermuda — A127

Designs: 25c, Carriage ride. 30c, Golfer at registration desk. 65c, Maid leaving flowers on hotel bed. 75c, Chefs preparing food. 80c, Waiter serving couple. 90c, Singer, bartender, guests.

Wmk. 384

1998, Sept. 24 Litho. *Perf. 14½*

758 A127 25c multicolored 1.40 .60
759 A127 30c multicolored 2.10 1.10
760 A127 65c multicolored 2.10 1.75
761 A127 75c multicolored 2.10 2.10
762 A127 80c multicolored 2.25 2.25
763 A127 90c multicolored 2.50 2.50
Nos. 758-763 (6) 12.45 10.30

Bermuda's Botanical Gardens, Cent. — A128

Wmk. 373

1998, Oct. 15 Litho. *Perf. 14*

764 A128 30c Agave attenuata 1.75 .70
765 A128 65c Bermuda palmetto tree 3.00 1.25
766 A128 $1 Banyan tree 3.75 3.50
767 A128 $2 Cedar tree 6.00 *8.00*
Nos. 764-767 (4) 14.50 *13.45*

Christmas A129

Children's paintings: 25c, Lizard in Santa hat stringing Christmas lights, vert. 40c, Stairway, wreath on door.

Wmk. 373

1998, Nov. 26 Litho. *Perf. 14*

768 A129 25c multicolored 1.75 1.40
769 A129 40c multicolored 2.25 2.25

Beaches — A130

Wmk. 373

1999, Apr. 29 Litho. *Perf. 13½*

770 A130 30c Shelly Bay 1.25 .50
771 A130 60c Catherine's Bay 1.40 1.25
772 A130 65c Jobson's Cove 1.75 1.40
773 A130 $2 Warwick Long Bay 5.25 5.25
Nos. 770-773 (4) 9.65 8.40

Common Design Type and

First Manned Moon Landing, 30th Anniv. A131

Wmk. 373

1999, July 20 Litho. *Perf. 13*

774 A131 30c Ground station 1.25 .50
775 A131 60c Lift-off, vert. 1.90 1.25
776 A131 75c Aerial view of ground station 2.10 1.75
777 A131 $2 Moon walk, vert. 4.75 *6.25*
Nos. 774-777 (4) 10.00 *9.75*

Souvenir Sheet

Wmk. 384

Perf. 14

778 CD357 65c Looking at earth from moon 8.00 8.00

No. 778 contains one 40mm circular stamp.

Mapmaking — A132

Wmk. 373

1999, Aug. 19 Litho. *Perf. 14*

779 A132 30c Somerset Is., theodolite 1.60 .60
780 A132 65c 1901 street map 2.75 2.75
781 A132 80c Aerial photo, modern street map 3.00 3.00
782 A132 $1 Satellite, island 3.50 4.00
Nos. 779-782 (4) 10.85 10.35

Mail Boxes and Stamps — A133

Wmk. 373

1999, Oct. 5 Litho. *Perf. 14¼*

783 A133 30c Victoria era, #6 1.75 .80
784 A133 75c George V era, #49 2.75 2.75
785 A133 95c George VI era, #121 3.00 3.00
786 A133 $1 Elizabeth II era, #142 3.00 3.00
Nos. 783-786 (4) 10.50 9.55

Pioneers of Progress — A134

No. 787: a, Dr. E. F. Gordon, labor leader. b, Sir Henry Tucker, banker. c, Gladys Morrell, suffragist.

Perf. 13½x13¼

2000, May 1 Litho. Wmk. 373

787 A134 30c Horiz. strip of 3, #a-c 4.00 4.00

See Nos. 933-937, 963-964.

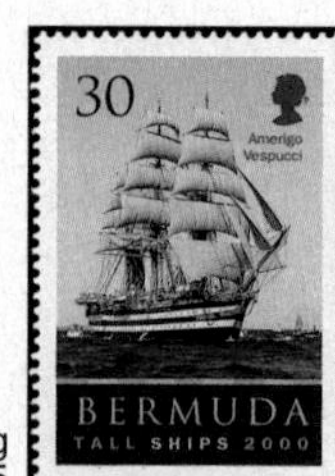

Sailing Ships — A135

Designs: 30c, Amerigo Vespucci. 60c, Europa. 80c Juan Sebastian de Elcano.

2000, May 23 *Perf. 14*

788 A135 30c multi 1.60 .90
789 A135 60c multi 2.25 2.25
790 A135 80c multi 2.75 2.75
Nos. 788-790 (3) 6.60 5.90

Royal Family Birthdays — A136

35c, Prince William, 18th. 40c, Prince Andrew, 40th. 50c, Princess Anne, 50th. 70c, Princess Margaret, 70th. $1, Queen Mother, 100th.

2000, Aug. 7

791 A136 35c multi 1.90 .95
792 A136 40c multi 2.10 1.10
793 A136 50c multi 2.25 1.75
794 A136 70c multi 2.50 2.50
795 A136 $1 multi 3.25 3.25
a. Souvenir sheet, #791-795 13.00 13.00
Nos. 791-795 (5) 12.00 9.55

Christmas A137

Children's art: 30c, Santa Claus and Bermuda onion, by Meghan Jones. 45c, Christmas tree, by Carlita Lodge.

Wmk. 384

2000, Sept. 26 Litho. *Perf. 13¾*

796-797 A137 Set of 2 3.50 3.50

Bird Type of 1997 Redrawn with WWF Emblem

Designs: No. 798, 15c, White-tailed tropic bird. No. 799, 15c, Cahow. No. 800, 20c, Cahow, vert. No. 801, 20c, White-tailed tropic bird, vert.

Wmk. 373

2001, Feb. 1 Litho. *Perf. 14*

798-801 A123 Set of 4 4.50 4.50
801a Miniature sheet, 4 each #798-801 21.00 21.00

Hong Kong 2001 Stamp Exhibition (No. 801a).

Historical Tourist Attractions, St. George's A138

Designs: 35c, King's Castle. 50c, Bridge House. 55c, Whitehall. 70c, Fort Cunningham. 85c, St. Peter's Church. 95c, Water Street.

2001, May 1 *Perf. 13¾*

802-807 A138 Set of 6 16.00 16.00

Boer War, Cent. — A139

Designs: 35c, Crowded boat, plow. 50c, Men, boot last. 70c, Man with children, rings and pin. 95c, Men and women, stamped cover.

2001, June 28 *Perf. 14*

808-811 A139 Set of 4 8.50 8.50

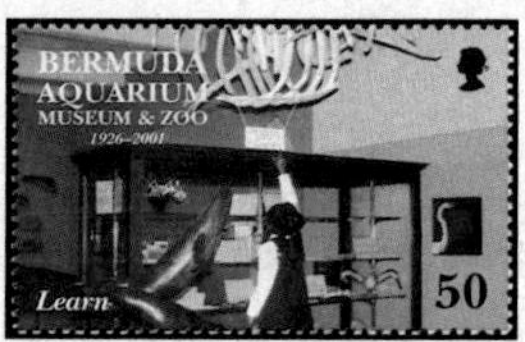

Aquarium, Museum and Zoo, 75th Anniv. — A140

Designs: 35c, Child, sea urchins, starfish, vert. 50c, Child, museum display. 55c, Child, tortoise. 70c, Aquarium. 80c, Diver in aquarium tank, vert. 95c, Turtle, vert.

Perf. 14¾x14¼, 14¼x14¾

2001, Aug. 9 Litho. Wmk. 373

812-817 A140 Set of 6 12.50 12.50

Paintings by Charles Lloyd Tucker — A141

Various paintings: 35c, 70c, 85c, $1.

2001, Oct. 9 *Perf. 14¼x14¾*

818-821 A141 Set of 4 11.50 11.50

Reign Of Queen Elizabeth II, 50th Anniv. Issue

Common Design Type

Designs: Nos. 822, 826a, 10c, Princess Elizabeth with dog, 1952. Nos. 823, 826b, 35c, In 1965. Nos. 824, 826c, 70c, Waving. Nos. 825, 826d, 85c, In 1991. No. 826e, $1, 1955 portrait by Annigoni (38x50mm).

Perf. 14¼x14½, 13¾ (#826e)

2002, Feb. 6 Litho. Wmk. 373

With Gold Frames

822 CD360 10c multicolored .50 .50
823 CD360 35c multicolored 1.25 1.25
824 CD360 70c multicolored 2.75 2.75
825 CD360 85c multicolored 3.50 3.50
Nos. 822-825 (4) 8.00 8.00

Souvenir Sheet

Without Gold Frames

826 CD360 Sheet of 5, #a-e 10.50 10.50

Caves
A142

Designs: 35c, Fantasy Cave. 70c, Crystal Cave. 80c, Prospero's Cave. $1, Cathedral Cave.

Wmk. 373

2002, May 1 Litho. *Perf. 14*
827-830 A142 Set of 4 11.50 11.50

Cricket Cup Match, Cent. — A143

Details from "One Hundred Up," by Robert D. Bassett: No. 831, 35c, Umpire and fielder. No. 832, 35c, Batsman and wicketkeeper. $1, Entire painting, horiz.

Wmk. 373

2002, July 4 Litho. *Perf. 14*
831-832 A143 Set of 2 5.00 5.00

Souvenir Sheet

833 A143 $1 multi 5.25 5.25

See Nos. 869-870.

Queen Mother Elizabeth (1900-2002)
Common Design Type

Designs: Nos. 834, 836a, 30c, Without hat (sepia photograph). Nos. 835, 836b, $1.25, Wearing blue hat.

Perf. 13¾x14¼
2002, Aug. 5 Litho. Wmk. 373
With Purple Frames

834 CD361 30c multicolored 1.25 1.25
835 CD361 $1.25 multicolored 4.00 4.00

Souvenir Sheet
Without Purple Frames
Perf. 14½x14¼

836 CD361 Sheet of 2, #a-b 7.25 7.25

Shells — A144

Designs: 5c, Slit worm-shell. 10c, Netted olive. 20c, Angular triton. 25c, Frog shell. 30c, Colorful Atlantic moon. 35c, Noble wentletrap.40c, Atlantic trumpet triton. 45c, Zigzag scallop. 50c, Bermuda cone. 75c, Very distorted distorsio. 80c, Purple sea snail. 90c, Flame helmet. $1, Scotch bonnet. $2, Gold mouth triton. $3, Bermuda's slit shell. $4, Reticulated cowrie-helmet. $5, Dennison's morum. $8, Sunrise tellin.

2002-03 Litho. Wmk. 373 *Perf. 14*

837	A144	5c multi	.25	.25
838	A144	10c multi	.30	.30
839	A144	20c multi	.55	.55
840	A144	25c multi	.65	.65
841	A144	30c multi	.75	.75
842	A144	35c multi	.90	.90
a.		Inscribed "2008"	.90	.90
843	A144	40c multi	1.10	1.10
844	A144	45c multi	1.25	1.25
845	A144	50c multi	1.50	1.50
846	A144	75c multi	2.00	2.00
847	A144	80c multi	2.25	*2.75*
848	A144	90c multi	2.50	*2.50*
849	A144	$1 multi	2.50	*3.00*
850	A144	$2 multi	5.25	*6.50*
851	A144	$3 multi	8.00	*8.00*
852	A144	$4 multi	9.00	*10.00*
853	A144	$5 multi	10.00	*11.00*
854	A144	$8 multi	17.00	*18.00*
		Nos. 837-854 (18)	65.75	*71.00*

Issued: Nos. 5c, 10c, 35c, 45c, 50c, $8, 9/10/02. 20c, 40c, 80c, 90c, $3, $4, 1/23/03. 25c, 30c, 75c, $1, $2, $5, 3/20/03.

World Peace Day — A145

Dove facing: 35c, Right. 70c, Left.

Wmk. 373

2002, Nov. 7 Litho. *Perf. 14¼*
855-856 A145 Set of 2 5.50 5.50

Bermuda Biological Station for Research, Cent. A146

Designs: 35c, Biological Station and ship, vert. 70c, Fish. 85c, Researcher probing reef. $1, Shrimp, vert.

Wmk. 373

2003, Feb. 4 Litho. *Perf. 14*
857-860 A146 Set of 4 10.00 10.00

Items Made in Bermuda — A147

Designs: 35c, Dolls. 70c, Model of ship. 80c, Wooden sculpture. $1, Silver tankard and goblets.

Perf. 14½x14¼
2003, May 15 Litho. Wmk. 373
861-864 A147 Set of 4 8.00 8.00

See Nos. 880-883, 898-901, 925-928.

Head of Queen Elizabeth II
Common Design Type

Wmk. 373

2003, June 2 Litho. *Perf. 13¾*
865 CD362 $25 multi 55.00 55.00

Coronation of Queen Elizabeth II, 50th Anniv.
Common Design Type

Designs: Nos. 866, 35c, 868a, $1.25, Queen in carriage. Nos. 867, 70c, 868b, $2, Queen with crown at coronation.

Perf. 14¼x14½
2003, June 2 Litho. Wmk. 373
Vignettes Framed, Red Background

866 CD363 35c multicolored .75 .75
867 CD363 $1.25 multicolored 2.50 2.50

Souvenir Sheet
Vignettes Without Frame, Purple Panel

868 CD363 Sheet of 2, #a-b 11.00 11.00

Cricket Cup Type of 2002 with "30th Anniversary CARICOM" Added at Left

Designs: No. 869, 35c, Umpire and fielder. No. 870, 35c, Batsman and wicketkeeper.

Wmk. 373

2003, July 4 Litho. *Perf. 14*
869-870 A143 Set of 2 3.75 3.75

Poinsettias
A148

Bract color: 30c, Red. 45c, White. 80c, Mottled.

Perf. 14½x14¼
2003, Oct. 9 Litho. Wmk. 373
871-873 A148 Set of 3 6.25 6.25

Royal Naval Dockyard — A149

Various views: 25c, 35c, 70c, 85c, 95c, $1.

Wmk. 373

2004, Feb. 19 Litho. *Perf. 13¾*
874-879 A149 Set of 6 14.50 14.50

Items Made in Bermuda Type of 2003

Designs: 35c, Chair. 70c, Pitcher and plate. 80c, Decorative glassware. $1.25, Quilt.

Wmk. 373

2004, May 15 Litho. *Perf. 13¾*
880-883 A147 Set of 4 7.00 7.00

Worldwide Fund for Nature (WWF) — A150

Various depictions of school of bluefin tuna: 10c, 35c, 85c, $1.10.

Wmk. 373

2004, Aug. 19 Litho. *Perf. 14*
884-887 A150 Set of 4 7.25 7.25
887a A150 Sheetlet, 4 each #884-887 30.00

Nos. 884-887 were issued issued both in sheets of 50 (with gutter between panes of 25) and in miniature sheets of 16, with 4 se-tenant strips.

Bermuda Orchid Society, 50th Anniv. — A151

Various orchids: 35c, 45c, 85c, $1.10.

Wmk. 373

2004, Nov. 18 Litho. *Perf. 13¾*
888-891 A151 Set of 4 9.50 9.50

Discovery of Bermuda, 500th Anniv. — A152

Map of Bermuda and: 25c, Compass. 35c, Sextant. 70c, Chronometer. $1.10, Telescope. $1.25, Divider.
$5, Aerial photograph of Bermuda.

Perf. 14x14¾
2005, Jan. 13 Litho. Wmk. 373
892-896 A152 Set of 5 12.50 12.50

Souvenir Sheet

897 A152 $5 multi 14.50 14.50

Items Made in Bermuda Type of 2003

Designs: 35c, Carnival reveler dolls. 70c, Fish and coral sculpture. 85c, Lion and lamb stained glass. $1, Earrings and necklace.

Wmk. 373

2005, May 19 Litho. *Perf. 13¾*
898-901 A147 Set of 4 8.50 8.50

Battle of Trafalgar, Bicent. — A153

Designs: 10c, HMS Victory. 35c, HMS Pickle under construction in Bermuda. 70c, HMS Pickle picking up survivors from the Achille. 85c, HMS Pickle racing back to England.

Wmk. 373, Unwmkd (10c)

2005, June 23 Litho. *Perf. 13¼*
902-905 A153 Set of 4 7.00 7.00

No. 902 has particles of wood from the HMS Victory embedded in the areas covered by a thermographic process that produces a shiny, raised effect.

Birds and Habitats A154

Various birds and: 10c, Sandy beach, 25c, Fresh water pond. 35c, Rocky shore. 70c, Upland forest (blue bird). 85c, Upland forest (owl). $1, Mangroves.

2005, Aug. 18 *Perf. 13¾*
906-911 A154 Set of 6 10.50 10.50

Christmas
A155

Light displays: 30c, Christmas tree. 45c, Dolphin. 80c, Snowman.

Wmk. 373

2005, Oct. 27 Litho. *Perf. 13¾*
912-914 A155 Set of 3 3.75 3.75

Bermuda Electric Light Company, Cent. A156

Designs: 35c, Worker in cherry picker working on overhead electric wires. 70c, Worker in cherry picker. 85c, Worker on elevated walkway near equipment. $1, Building.

2006, Jan. 13 Litho. *Perf. 13¼x13*
915-918 A156 Set of 4 6.00 6.00

Queen Elizabeth II, 80th Birthday A157

Designs: 35c, As child, with dog. 70c, Wearing tiara and small earrings. 85c, Wearing tiara and large earrings. No. 922, $1.25, Wearing blue hat.

No. 923: a, $1.25, Like 70c. b, $2, Like 85c.

Wmk. 373

2006, Apr. 21 Litho. *Perf. 14*

With White Frames

919-922 A157 Set of 4 6.50 6.50

Souvenir Sheet

Without White Frames

923 A157 Sheet of 2, #a-b 6.75 6.75

Map of Bermuda A158

2006, May 27 *Perf. 13¾x13¼*

924 A158 $1.10 multi 2.25 2.25
a. Souvenir sheet of 1 2.75 2.75

Washington 2006 World Philatelic Exhibition.

Items Made in Bermuda Type of 2003

Designs: 35c, Jar of honey. 70c, Stonecutters, by Sharon Wilson. 85c, I've Caught Some Whoppers, sculpture by Desmond Fountain. $1.25, Bottle of perfume.

2006, June 22 *Perf. 13x13¼*

925-928 A147 Set of 4 6.50 6.50

Christmas A159

Various wreaths: 30c, 35c, 45c, 80c.

Wmk. 373

2006, Oct. 12 Litho. *Perf. 13¾*

929-932 A159 Set of 4 4.50 4.50

Pioneers of Progress Type of 2000

Teachers: No. 933, 35c, Millie Neversen (1883-1975). No. 934, 35c, Edith (1880-1978) and Matilda Crawford (1879-1948). No. 935, 35c, May Francis (1899-1985). No. 936, 35c, Francis L. Patton (1843-1932). No. 937, 35c, Adele Tucker (1868-1971).

Perf. 13¾x13½

2007, Feb. 15 Litho. Wmk. 373

933-937 A134 Set of 5 4.00 4.00

Spirit of Bermuda A160

Various views of sloop: 10c, 35c, 70c, 85c, $1.10, $1.25.

Perf. 13¼x13½

2007, May 17 Litho. Wmk. 373

938-943 A160 Set of 6 9.00 9.00

Voyage of Deliverance From Bermuda to Jamestown, Va. — A161

Ship and coastline with panel colors of: 35c, Olive green. $1.10, Blue.

Perf. 12½x12¾

2007, June 21 Litho. Wmk. 373

944-945 A161 Set of 2 3.25 3.25

Jamestown, Va., 400th anniv.

Scouting, Cent. A162

Designs: 35c, 1930 photograph of Bishop's Own Cubs, hand with compass. 70c, 1930 photograph of Lord Robert Baden-Powell inspecting Cubs, hands lashing rope. 85c, 1930 photograph of Scout parade, hands of trumpeter. $1.10, Dance of Kaa, hands tying knot.

No. 950, vert.: a, $1.25, Emblem of Bermuda Scouts. b, $2, Baden-Powell inspecting Cubs.

2007, Aug. 23 *Perf. 13¾*

946-949 A162 Set of 4 6.00 6.00

Souvenir Sheet

950 A162 Sheet of 2, #a-b 7.50 7.50

Poster Art for Troubador Acts A163

Designs: 35c, Celeste & Harris. 70c, Calypsos Hubert Smith, Sydney Bean, Erskine Zuill, Four Deuces. 85c, Calypso Varieties from Bermuda. $1.10, The Talbot Brothers.

Wmk. 373

2008, Mar. 19 Litho. *Perf. 13¾*

951-954 A163 Set of 4 6.75 6.75

Bermuda No. X1, 160th Anniv. — A164

Panel color: 35c, Brown. 70c, Gray blue. 85p, Gold. $1.25, Silver

Wmk. 373

2008, Apr. 23 Litho. *Perf. 13¾*

955-958 A164 Set of 4 6.75 6.75

Local Scenes A165

Designs: (35c), Deep Bay, West Pembroke. (70c), Spanish Point Park. (85c), Flatts Inlet. (95c), Tucker's Town Bay.

Die Cut Perf. 12x12½

2008, May 1 Litho. Unwmk.

Booklet Stamps

Self-Adhesive

959 A165 (35c) multi .70 .70
a. Booklet pane of 10 7.00
960 A165 (70c) multi 1.40 1.40
a. Booklet pane of 10 14.00
961 A165 (85c) multi 1.75 1.75
a. Booklet pane of 10 17.50
962 A165 (95c) multi 1.90 1.90
a. Booklet pane of 10 19.00
Nos. 959-962 (4) 5.75 5.75

No. 959 is inscribed "Postage Paid Local;" No. 960, "Postage Paid Zone 1;" No. 961, "Postage Page Zone 2;" No. 962, "Postage Paid Zone 3."

Pioneers of Progress Type of 2000

Designs: No. 963, 35c, Dr. Pauulu Roosevelt Brown Kamarakafego (1932-2007), political activist. No. 964, 35c, Dame Lois Browne-Evans (1927-2007), attorney general.

Perf. 13¾x13½

2008, June 11 Wmk. 373

963-964 A134 Set of 2 2.00 2.00

2008 Summer Olympics, Beijing A166

Designs: 10c, Running. 35c, Swimming. 70c, Equestrian. 85c, Yachting.

Perf. 12½x13

2008, July 23 Wmk. 373

965-968 A166 Set of 4 4.25 4.25

Lighted Christmas Decorations — A167

Various decorations: 30c, 35c, 45c, 80c.

Wmk. 406

2008, Oct. 1 Litho. *Perf. 13½*

969-972 A167 Set of 4 4.00 4.00

Settlement of Bermuda, 400th Anniv. — A168

Old and modern: 35c, City photographs. 70c, Harbor scenes. 85c, Harbor scenes, diff. $1.25, Maps.

Perf. 12½x12¾

2009, Jan. 22 Litho. Wmk. 406

973-976 A168 Set of 4 8.00 8.00

First Man on the Moon, 40th Anniv. A169

Designs: 35c, Aerial view of tracking station, Cooper's Island. 70c, Antenna at tracking station, Cooper's Island. 85c, Apollo 11 Lunar Module. 95c, Space Shuttle (STS 126). $1.25, International Space Station.

$1.10, Lunar Module on Moon, vert.

Wmk. 406

2009, Apr. 16 Litho. *Perf. 13¼*

977-981 A169 Set of 5 9.00 9.00

Souvenir Sheet

Perf. 13x13¼

982 A169 $1.10 multi 3.00 3.00

No. 982 contains one 40x60mm stamp.

Marathon Derby, Cent. A170

Designs: 35c, Athlete with trophy and cup. 70c, Athlete with trophy, window at left. 85c, Motorcyclist following runner. $1.10, Woman racing with men.

2009, May 21 *Perf. 14*

983-986 A170 Set of 4 7.00 7.00

Atlantic Challenge 2009 Tall Ship Races — A171

Ships: 35c, Concordia. 70c, Picton Castle. 85c, Jolie Brise, horiz. 95c, Tecla. $1.10, Europa. $1.25, Etoile, horiz.

Perf. 13¾x13¼, 13¼x13¾

2009, June 11 Litho. Wmk. 373

987-992 A171 Set of 6 12.00 12.00

Bermuda Theater Boycott, 50th Anniv. A172

Designs: 35c, People. 70c, Stylized people, vert. 85c, Sculpture, vert. $1.25, Photograph of protestors.

2009, July 2 Wmk. 406 *Perf. 12½*

993-996 A172 Set of 4 8.00 8.00

Christmas — A173

Christmas tree ornaments: 30c, Basket. 35c, Angel. 70c, Basket, diff. 85c, Angel, diff.

Perf. 14x13¾

2009, Sept. 24 Litho. Wmk. 406

997-1000 A173 Set of 4 5.25 5.25

Girl Guides, Cent. — A174

Girl Guides: 35c, At ceremony. 70c, Camping. 85c, Marching. $1.10, With parade float.

$1.25, Bermuda's first black Girl Guides unit.

Perf. 14x14¾

2010, Feb. 18 Litho. Wmk. 406

1001-1004 A174 Set of 4 7.00 7.00

Souvenir Sheet

1005 A174 $1.25 multi 3.00 3.00

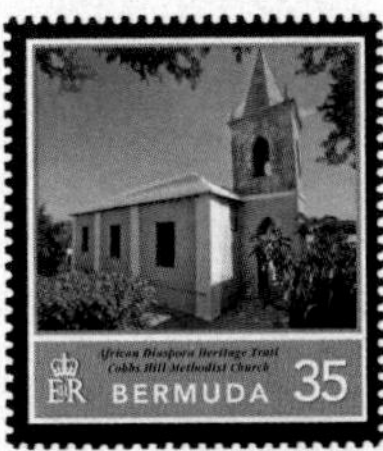

African Diaspora Heritage Trail — A175

Designs: 35c, Cobbs Hill Methodist Church. 70c, Bermudian Heritage Museum. 85c, St. Peter's Church. $1.10, Barr's Bay Park.

Perf. 13x12½

2010, May 20 Litho. Wmk. 406

1006-1009 A175 Set of 4 7.00 7.00

Worldwide Fund for Nature (WWF) — A176

Lined seahorse: 35c, Head. 70c, Pair of seahorses. 85c, Pair of seahorses in seaweed. $1.25, Adults and juveniles.

Wmk. 406

2010, June 17 Litho. *Perf. 14*

1010-1013 A176 Set of 4 8.00 8.00

1013a Sheet of 16, 4 each #1010-1013 32.00 32.00

Dockyard Apprentices A177

Designs: 35c, Hull of boat under construction, plumb bob. 70c, Dockyard gates, gears. 85c, Worker and equipment, wooden rudder pattern. $1.10, Apprentices, tools.

Wmk. 406

2010, Sept. 23 Litho. *Perf. 14*

1014-1017 A177 Set of 4 7.00 7.00

Service of Queen Elizabeth II and Prince Philip — A178

Designs: 10c, Queen Elizabeth II. 35c, Queen and Prince Philip. 70c, Queen and Prince Philip, diff. 85c, Queen and Prince Philip, diff. $1.10, Queen and Prince Philip, diff. $1.25, Prince Philip.

$2.50, Queen and Prince Philip, diff.

Perf. 13¼

2011, Mar. 3 Litho. Unwmk.

1018-1023 A178 Set of 6 8.75 8.75

1023a Sheet of 6, #1018-1023, + 3 labels 8.75 8.75

Souvenir Sheet

1024 A178 $2.50 multi 5.00 5.00

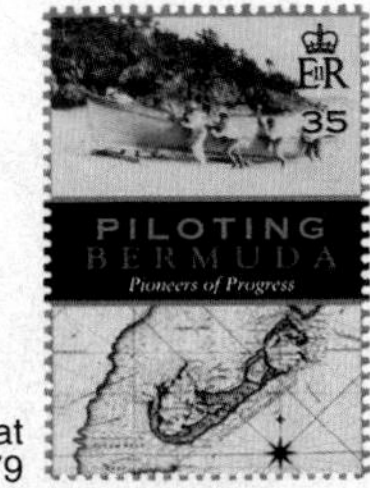

Boat Piloting — A179

Designs: 35c, People dragging boat ashore, nautical chart. 70c, Boats. 85c, Boat, sailor. $1.10, Boat in water, sailors and children on shore.

Perf. 14x14¼

2011, May 19 Wmk. 406

1025-1028 A179 Set of 4 6.00 6.00

Casemate Barracks — A180

Designs: 35c, Casemate Barracks, Great Eastern Storehouse and Commissioner's House, 1857, painting by Gaspard Le Marchant Tupper. 70c, Casemate Barracks and Victualling Yard, 1857, painting by Tupper. 85c, Casemate Barracks and Bermuda Dockyard, 1856, painting by unknown artist. $1.25, 1899 photograph of Casemate Barracks and Lower Ordnance Yard.

Perf. 14¼x14¾

2011, July 21 Wmk. 406

1029-1032 A180 Set of 4 6.50 6.50

Miniature Sheet

Wedding of Prince William and Catherine Middleton — A181

No. 1033 — Couple: a, 35c, Holding hands. b, 70c, Waving in coach, horiz. c, 85c, In automobile, horiz. d, $1.25, Kissing.

2011, Sept. 1 *Perf. 14x14¼*

1033 A181 Sheet of 4, #a-d 6.50 6.50

Reign of Queen Elizabeth II, 60th Anniv. — A182

Various photographs of Queen Elizabeth II: 10c, 35c, 70c, 85c, $1.10, $1.25.

$2.50, Queen Elizabeth II wearing crown.

2012, Feb. 9 Unwmk. *Perf. 13¼*

1034-1039 A182 Set of 6 8.75 8.75

1039a Souvenir sheet of 6, #1034-1039, + 3 labels 8.75 8.75

Souvenir Sheet

1040 A182 $2.50 multi 5.00 5.00

Bermuda Postal Service, 200th Anniv. — A183

Designs: 25c, Postmaster William B. Perot, Bermuda #X1. 35c, Ferry, 1800s, Bermuda #1. 70c, Mail carriage, 1920s, Bermuda #56. 95c, Flying boat, 1930s, Bermuda #109A. $1.10, Mail van, 1960s, Bermuda #225. $1.25, Envelope, binary digits.

2012, Apr. 19 Wmk. 406 *Perf. 13*

1041-1046 A183 Set of 6 9.25 9.25

Paintings — A184

Designs: 35c, South Shore, Bermuda, by Thomas Anschutz. 70c, St. George's, by Ogden Pleissner. 80c, Front Street, 1922, by André Biéler. $1.10, Street Scene, Bermuda (Elliott Street), by Dorothy Austen Stevens. $1.25, La Maison du Gouverneur, by Albert Gleizes, vert. $1.65, The Welcoming Smile, by Frank Small, vert.

Perf. 13¼x13¾, 13¾x13¼

2012, July 12

1047-1052 A184 Set of 6 12.00 12.00

Masterworks Foundation, 25th anniv.

St. Peter's Church, 400th Anniv. — A185

Designs: 35c, Clock tower. 95c, Chandelier and ceiling. $1.10, Bronze plaque for graveyard for blacks and slaves. $1.25, Church exterior.

2012, Oct. 18 *Perf. 13¾x13¼*

1053-1056 A185 Set of 4 7.50 7.50

Items Commemorating British Coronations — A186

Coronation of Queen Elizabeth II, 60th Anniv. — A187

Various items commemorating the coronation of: 10c, Queen Victoria. 35c, King Edward VII. 70c, King George V. 85c, King George VI. $1.10, Queen Elizabeth II.

2013, Feb. 21 *Perf. 14*

1057-1061 A186 Set of 5 6.25 6.25

Souvenir Sheet

Perf. 14¾x14¼

1062 A187 $2.50 multi 5.00 5.00

Beaches — A188

Designs: 35c, Jobson's Cove Beach, Warwick. $1.25, Southlands Beach, Warwick. $1.50, Astwood Park Beach. $1.65, Warwick Long Bay Beach.

2013, May 16 *Perf. 13¾*

1063-1066 A188 Set of 4 9.50 9.50

Gombey Dancers — A189

Various Gombey dancers with frame color of: 35c, Blue. $1.25, Green. $1.50, Red. $1.65, Black.

2013, July 18 *Perf. 14*

1067-1070 A189 Set of 4 9.50 9.50

POSTAL-FISCAL STAMP

"Revenue Revenue" PF1

1936 Typo. Wmk. 4 *Perf. 14*

Chalky Paper

AR1 PF1 12sh6p org & grayish blk 1,250. *1,750.*

Revenue cancel 75.00

#AR1 was authorized for postal use from Feb. 1 through May, 1937 and during Nov. and Dec. 1937. Used values are for examples with dated postal cancels indicating usage during the authorized periods. Beware of bogus and improperly dated favor cancels.

WAR TAX STAMPS

No. 42 Overprinted

1918 **Wmk. 3** ***Perf. 14***
MR1 A11 1p rose red 1.25 *2.00*

No. 42a Overprinted

1920
MR2 A11 1p carmine 2.40 *3.00*

BHUTAN

bü-'tän

LOCATION — Eastern Himalayas
GOVT. — Kingdom
AREA — 18,000 sq. mi.
POP. — 1,951,965(?) (1999 est.)
CAPITAL — Thimphu

100 Chetrum = 1 Ngultrum or Rupee

Watermark

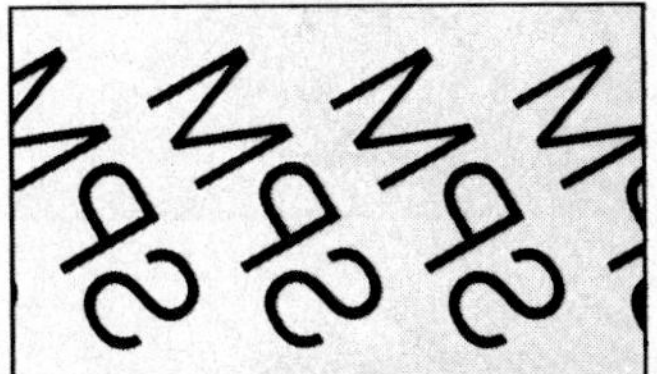

Wmk. 388 — Multiple "SPM"

Catalogue values for all unused stamps in this country are for Never Hinged items.

Postal Runner — A1

Designs: 3ch, 70ch, Archer. 5ch, 1.30nu, Yak. 15ch, Map of Bhutan, portrait of Druk Gyalpo (Dragon King) Ugyen Wangchuk (1867-1902) and Paro Dzong (fortress-monastery). 33ch, Postal runner. All horiz. except 2ch and 33ch.

Perf. 14x14½, 14½x14

1962 Litho. Unwmk.

No.	Type	Value	Color	Unused	Used
1	A1	2ch	red & gray	.30	.30
2	A1	3ch	red & ultra	.35	.35
3	A1	5ch	green & brown	1.90	1.90
4	A1	15ch	red, blk & org yel	.30	.30
5	A1	33ch	blue grn & lil	.35	.35
6	A1	70ch	dp ultra & lt blue	1.00	1.00
7	A1	1.30nu	blue & black	2.40	2.40
			Nos. 1-7 (7)	6.60	6.60

Nos. 1-7 were issued for inland use in April, 1962, and became valid for international mail on Oct. 10, 1962.

For overprint & surcharges see Nos. 42, 72-73.

Refugee Year Emblem and Arms of Bhutan A2

1962, Oct. 10 ***Perf. 14½x14***

No.	Type	Value	Color	Unused	Used
8	A2	1nu	dk blue & dk car rose	1.50	1.50
9	A2	2nu	yel grn & red lilac	5.25	5.25

World Refugee Year. For surcharges see Nos. 68-69.

Equipment of Ancient Warrior — A3

Boy Filling Grain Box and Wheat Emblem — A4

1963 Unwmk. ***Perf. 14x14½***

No.	Type	Value	Color	Unused	Used
10	A3	33ch	multicolored	.45	.45
11	A3	70ch	multicolored	.90	.90
12	A3	1.30nu	multicolored	2.25	2.25
			Nos. 10-12 (3)	3.60	3.60

Bhutan's membership in Colombo Plan.

1963, July 15 ***Perf. 13½x14***

No.	Type	Value	Color	Unused	Used
13	A4	20ch	lt blue, yel & red brn	1.00	1.00
14	A4	1.50nu	rose lil, bl & red brn	2.10	2.10

FAO "Freedom from Hunger" campaign. For surcharge see No. 117M.

Masked Dancer — A5

Various Bhutanese Dancers (Five Designs; 2ch, 5ch, 20ch, 1nu, 1.30nu vert.)

1964, Apr. 16 ***Perf. 14½x14, 14x14½***

No.	Type	Value	Color	Unused	Used
15	A5	2ch	multicolored	.30	.30
16	A5	3ch	multicolored	.30	.30
17	A5	5ch	multicolored	.30	.30
18	A5	20ch	multicolored	.30	.30
19	A5	33ch	multicolored	.30	.30
20	A5	70ch	multicolored	.30	.30
21	A5	1nu	multicolored	1.10	1.10
22	A5	1.30nu	multicolored	1.25	1.25
23	A5	2nu	multicolored	1.90	1.90
			Nos. 15-23 (9)	6.05	6.05

For surcharges & overprints see nos. 70-71, 74-75, 129A, 129G, C1-C3, C11-C13.

Stone Throwing A6

Sport: 5ch, 33ch, Boxing. 1nu, 3nu, Archery. 2nu, Soccer.

1964, Oct. 10 Litho. ***Perf. 14½***

No.	Type	Value	Color	Unused	Used
24	A6	2ch	emerald & multi	.30	.30
25	A6	5ch	orange & multi	.30	.30
26	A6	15ch	brt citron & multi	.30	.30
27	A6	33ch	rose lil & multi	.30	.30
28	A6	1nu	multicolored	1.00	1.00
29	A6	2nu	rose lilac & multi	1.60	1.60
a.			Souv. sheet, #28-29	16.00	16.00
30	A6	3nu	lt blue & multi	2.25	2.25
			Nos. 24-30 (7)	6.05	6.05

18th Olympic Games, Tokyo, Oct. 10-25. See No. B4.

Nos. 24-30 exist imperf. Value $17.50. No. 29a exists imperf. Value, $16.

Flags of the World at Half-mast — A7

1964, Nov. 22 Unwmk. ***Perf. 14½***

Flags in Original Colors

No.	Type	Value	Color	Unused	Used
31	A7	33ch	steel gray	.45	.45
32	A7	1nu	silver	1.10	1.10
33	A7	3nu	gold	3.00	3.00
a.			Souv. sheet, perf. 13½ or imperf.	8.00	8.00
			Nos. 31-33 (3)	4.55	4.55

Issued in memory of those who died in the service of their country. Nos. 31-33 exist imperf. Value $20.

No. 33a contains 2 stamps similar to Nos. 32-33.

For overprints see Nos. 44, 46.

Flowers — A8

1965, Jan. 6 Litho. ***Perf. 13***

No.	Type	Value	Color	Unused	Used
34	A8	2ch	Primrose	.25	.25
35	A8	5ch	Gentian	.25	.25
36	A8	15ch	Primrose	.25	.25
37	A8	33ch	Gentian	.25	.25
38	A8	50ch	Rhododendron	.90	.90
39	A8	75ch	Peony	.90	.90
40	A8	1nu	Rhododendron	.90	.90
41	A8	2nu	Peony	2.25	2.25
			Nos. 34-41 (8)	5.95	5.95

For overprints see No. 43, 45, C4-C5, C14-C15.

Nos. 5, 40, 32, 41 and 33 Overprinted: "WINSTON CHURCHILL 1874-1965"

1965, Feb. 27

No.	Type	Value	Color	Unused	Used
42	A1	33ch	bl grn & lilac	.70	.70
43	A8	1nu	pink, grn & dk gray	1.10	1.10
44	A7	1nu	silver & multi	.95	.95
45	A8	2nu	sepia, yel & grn	1.25	1.25
46	A7	3nu	gold & multi	1.60	1.60
			Nos. 42-46 (5)	5.60	5.60

Issued in memory of Sir Winston Churchill (1874-1965), British statesman. The overprint is in three lines on Nos. 42-43 and 45; in two lines on Nos. 43 and 46.

Nos. 44, 46 exist imperf. Value, both, $4.50.

Skyscraper, Pagoda and World's Fair Emblem — A9

Designs: 10ch, 2nu, Pieta by Michelangelo and statue of Khmer Buddha. 20ch, Skyline of NYC and Bhutanese village. 33ch, George Washington Bridge, NY, and foot bridge, Bhutan.

1965, Apr. 21 Litho. ***Perf. 14½***

No.	Type	Value	Color	Unused	Used
47	A9	1ch	blue & multi	.25	.25
48	A9	10ch	green & multi	.25	.25
49	A9	20ch	rose lilac & multi	.25	.25
50	A9	33ch	bister & multi	.25	.25
51	A9	1.50nu	bister & multi	2.00	2.00
52	A9	2nu	multicolored	3.00	3.00
a.			Souv. sheet, perf. 13½ or imperf.	8.00	8.00
			Nos. 47-52 (6)	6.00	6.00

Nos. 47-52 exist imperf.; value $5.00.

No. 52a contains two stamps similar to Nos. 51-52.

For overprints see Nos. 87-87B.

Telstar, Short-wave Radio and ITU Emblem — A10

Designs (ITU Emblem and): 2nu, Telstar and Morse key. 3nu, Syncom and ear phones.

1966, Mar. 2 Litho. ***Perf. 14½***

No.	Type	Value	Color	Unused	Used
53	A10	35ch	multicolored	.25	.25
54	A10	2nu	multicolored	.80	.80
55	A10	3nu	multicolored	1.40	1.40
			Nos. 53-55 (3)	2.45	2.45

Cent. (in 1965) of the ITU. Souvenir sheets exist containing two stamps similar to Nos. 54-55, perf. 13½ and imperf. Value, 2 sheets, $7.50.

Leopard — A11

Animals: 1ch, 4nu, Asiatic black bear. 2ch, 3nu, Leopard. 4ch, 2nu, Pigmy hog. 8ch, 75ch, Tiger. 10ch, 1.50nu, Dhole (Asiatic hunting dog). 1nu, 5nu, Takin (goat).

1966, Mar. 24 Litho. ***Perf. 13***

No.	Type	Value	Color	Unused	Used
56	A11	1ch	yellow & blk	.25	.25
57	A11	2ch	pale grn & blk	.25	.25
58	A11	4ch	lt citron & blk	.25	.25
59	A11	8ch	lt blue & blk	.25	.25
60	A11	10ch	lt lilac & blk	.35	.35
61	A11	75ch	lt yel grn & blk	.50	.50
62	A11	1nu	lt green & blk	1.25	1.25
63	A11	1.50nu	lt bl grn & blk	.90	.90
64	A11	2nu	dull org & blk	1.25	1.25
65	A11	3nu	bluish lil & blk	1.75	1.75
66	A11	4nu	lt green & blk	2.25	2.25
67	A11	5nu	pink & black	3.25	3.25
			Nos. 56-67 (12)	12.50	12.50

For surcharges see Nos. 115C, 115E, 115I, 117N, 117P, 129B, 129J. For overprints see Nos. C6-C10, C16-C20.

Nos. 6-9, 20-23 Surcharged

1965(?) ***Perf. 14½x14, 14x14½***

No.	Type	Value	Color	Unused	Used
68	A2	5ch	on 1nu	*47.50*	*40.00*
69	A2	5ch	on 2nu	*47.50*	*40.00*
70	A5	10ch	on 70ch	*16.00*	*12.00*
71	A5	10ch	on 2nu	*16.00*	*12.00*
72	A1	15ch	on 70ch	*12.00*	*8.00*
73	A1	15ch	on 1.30nu	*12.00*	*8.00*
74	A5	20ch	on 1nu	*16.00*	*12.00*
75	A5	20ch	on 1.30nu	*16.00*	*12.00*
			Nos. 68-75 (8)	*183.00*	*144.00*

The surcharges on Nos. 68-69 contain two bars at left and right obliterating the denomination on both sides of the design. Four bars on Nos. 72-73.

Simtokha Dzong A12

Tashichho Dzong — A13

Daga Dzong A14

Designs: 5ch, Rinpung Dzong. 50ch, Tongsa Dzong. 1nu, Lhuntsi Dzong.

Perf. 14½x14 (A12), 13½ (A13, A14)

1966-70 Photo.

No.	Type	Value	Color	Unused	Used
76	A12	5ch	orange brn ('67)	*4.00*	*2.40*
77	A13	10ch	dk grn & rose vio ('68)	*4.00*	*2.40*
78	A12	15ch	brown	*4.00*	*3.25*
79	A12	20ch	green	*4.00*	*3.25*
80	A13	50ch	blue grn ('68)	*2.00*	*1.75*
81	A14	75ch	dk bl & ol gray ('70)	*3.25*	*1.25*

82	A14	1nu dk vio & vio bl ('70)	3.25	1.25
		Nos. 76-82 (7)	24.50	15.55

Sizes: 5ch, 15ch, 20ch, 37x20½mm. 10ch, 53½x28½mm. 50ch, 35½x25½mm.

King Jigme Wangchuk — A14a

Coins: 1.30nu, 3nu, 5nu, reverse.

Litho. & Embossed on Gold Foil

1966, July 8 Die Cut *Imperf.*

83	A14a	10ch green	.80	.80
83A	A14a	25ch green	.80	.80
83B	A14a	50ch green	1.25	1.25
83C	A14a	1nu red	2.00	2.00
83D	A14a	1.30nu red	2.75	2.75
83E	A14a	2nu red	3.50	3.50
83F	A14a	3nu red	4.75	4.75
83G	A14a	4nu red	6.50	6.50
83H	A14a	5nu red	8.00	8.00
		Nos. 83-83H (9)	30.35	30.35

See Nos. 98-98B.

Abominable Snowman — A14b

1966 Photo. *Perf. 13½*

84	A14b	1ch multicolored	.35	.35
84A	A14b	2ch multi, diff.	.35	.35
84B	A14b	3ch multi, diff.	.35	.35
84C	A14b	4ch multi, diff.	.35	.35
84D	A14b	5ch multi, diff.	.35	.35
84E	A14b	15ch like #84	.35	.35
84F	A14b	30ch like #84A	.35	.35
84G	A14b	40ch like #84B	.35	.35
84H	A14b	50ch like #84C	.35	.35
84I	A14b	1.25nu like #84D	.50	.50
84J	A14b	2.50nu like #84	1.10	1.10
84K	A14b	3nu like #84A	1.20	1.20
84L	A14b	5nu like #84B	2.00	2.00
84M	A14b	6nu like #84C	2.00	2.00
84N	A14b	7nu like #84D	2.00	2.00
		Nos. 84-84N (15)	11.95	11.95

Issue dates: 1ch, 2ch, 3ch, 4ch, 5ch, 15ch, 30ch, 40ch, 50ch, Oct. 12; others, Nov. 15. Exist imperf.

For overprints see Nos. 93-93G. For surcharges see Nos. 115D, 115K, 115O, 115P, 117I, 117S.

Flowers A14c

Designs: 3ch, 50ch, Lilium sherriffiae. 5ch, 1nu, Meconopsis dhwoju. 7ch, 2.50nu, Rhododendron chaetomallum. 10ch, 4nu, Pleione hookeriana. 5nu, Rhododendron giganteum.

1967, Feb. 9 Litho. *Perf. 13*

85	A14c	3ch multicolored	.35	.35
85A	A14c	5ch multicolored	.35	.35
85B	A14c	7ch multicolored	.35	.35
85C	A14c	10ch multicolored	.35	.35

Gray Background

85D	A14c	50ch multicolored	.35	.35
85E	A14c	1nu multicolored	.60	.60
85F	A14c	2.50nu multicolored	1.40	1.40
85G	A14c	4nu multicolored	2.25	2.25
85H	A14c	5nu multicolored	2.75	2.75
		Nos. 85-85H (9)	8.75	8.75

For surcharges see Nos. 115F, 115L.

Boy Scouts — A14d

1967, Mar. 28 Photo. *Perf. 13½*

86	A14d	5ch Planting tree	.35	.35
86A	A14d	10ch Cooking	.35	.35
86B	A14d	15ch Mountain climbing	.35	.35

Emblem, Border in Gold

86C	A14d	50ch like #86	.55	.55
86D	A14d	1.25nu like #86A	1.15	1.15
86E	A14d	4nu like #86B	3.25	3.25
f.		Souv. sheet of 2, #86D, 86E	8.00	8.00
		Nos. 86-86E (6)	6.00	6.00

Exist imperf. Value: set $6.50; souvenir sheet $8.

See Nos. 89-89E for overprints. For surcharges see Nos. 115G, 117J, 129K.

Nos. 50-52, 52a Ovptd.

Perfs. as Before

1967, May 25 Litho.

87	A9	33ch on #50	1.20	1.20
87A	A9	1.50nu on #51	1.25	1.25
87B	A9	2nu on #52	1.60	1.60
c.		Souv. sheet of 2, on #52a	7.25	7.25
		Nos. 87-87B (3)	4.05	4.05

Nos. 87-87B exist imperf. Value: set $8; souvenir sheet $8.

Airplanes — A14f

1967, June 26 Litho. *Perf. 13½*

88	A14f	45ch Lancaster	1.00	1.00
88A	A14f	2nu Spitfire	2.00	2.00
88B	A14f	4nu Hurricane	7.50	7.50
c.		Souv. sheet of 2, #88A, 88B	6.50	6.50
		Nos. 88-88B (3)	10.50	10.50

Churchill and Battle of Britain. Exist imperf. Value: set $7.50; souvenir sheet $10.

For surcharges see Nos. 117Q, 117T.

Nos. 86-86D, 86e Overprinted "WORLD JAMBOREE / IDAHO, U.S.A. / AUG. 1-9,/67"

1967, Aug. 8 Photo. *Perf. 13½*

89	A14d	5ch Planting tree	.25	.25
89A	A14d	10ch Cookout	.25	.25
89B	A14d	15ch Mountain climbing	.30	.30
89C	A14d	50ch like #89	.35	.35
89D	A14d	1.25nu like #89A	.95	.95
89E	A14d	4nu like #89B	3.25	3.25
f.		Souv. sheet of 2, #89D, 89E	6.50	6.50
		Nos. 89-89E (6)	5.35	5.35

No. 89Ef sold for 6.25nu. Exist imperf. Value: set $16; souvenir sheet $8.

Girl Scouts — A14g

1967, Sept. 28 Photo. *Perf. 13½*

90	A14g	5ch Painting	.25	.25
90A	A14g	10ch Making music	.25	.25
90B	A14g	15ch Picking fruit	.30	.30

Emblem, Border in Gold

90C	A14g	1.50nu like #90	.75	.75
90D	A14g	2.50nu like #90A	1.50	1.50
90E	A14g	5nu like #90B	3.25	3.25
f.		Souv. sheet of 2, #90D, 90E	7.50	7.50
		Nos. 90-90E (6)	6.30	6.30

Exist imperf. Value: set $8.50; souvenir sheet $10.

For surcharge see No. 266.

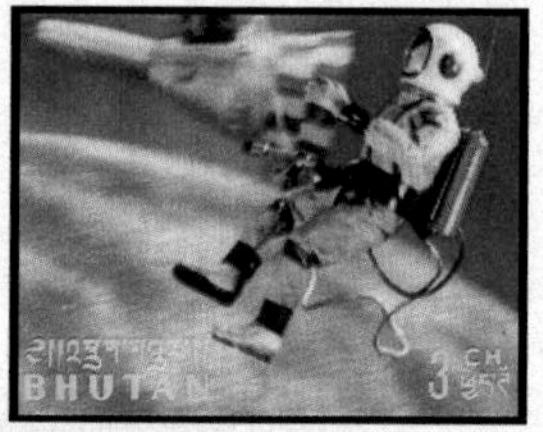

Astronaut, Space Capsule — A14h

Astronaut walking in space and: 5ch, 30ch, 4nu, Orbiter, Lunar modules docked. 7ch, 50ch, 5nu, Lunar module. 10ch, 1.25nu, 9nu, Other astronauts.

1967, Oct. 30 Litho. *Imperf.*

91	A14h	3ch multi	.30	.30
91A	A14h	5ch multi	.30	.30
91B	A14h	7ch multi	.30	.30
91C	A14h	10ch multi	.40	.40
m.		Souv. sheet of 4, #91-91C	8.00	8.00
91D	A14h	15ch multi	.50	.50
91E	A14h	30ch multi	1.10	1.10
91F	A14h	50ch multi	1.90	1.90
91G	A14h	1.25nu multi	4.50	4.50
n.		Souv. sheet of 4, #91D-91G	12.00	12.00
91H	A14h	2.50nu multi	2.75	2.75
91I	A14h	4nu multi	4.50	4.50
91J	A14h	5nu multi	5.50	5.50
91K	A14h	9nu multi	9.75	9.75
o.		Souv. sheet of 4, #91H-91K	20.00	20.00
		Nos. 91-91K (12)	31.80	31.80

Nos. 91H-91K are airmail. Simulated 3-dimensions using a plastic overlay.

For other space issues see designs A15a, A15e.

Pheasants — A14i

Designs: 1ch, 2nu, Tragopan satyra. 2ch, 4nu, Lophophorus sclateri.. 4ch, 5nu, Lophophorus impejanus. 8ch, 7nu, Lophura leucomelanos. 15ch, 9nu, Crossoptilon crossoptilon.

1968 Photo. *Perf. 13½*

92	A14i	1ch multicolored	.25	.25
92A	A14i	2ch multicolored	.25	.25
92B	A14i	4ch multicolored	.25	.25
92C	A14i	8ch multicolored	.25	.25
92D	A14i	15ch multicolored	.25	.25

Border in Gold

92E	A14i	2nu multicolored	.75	.75
92F	A14i	4nu multicolored	1.00	1.00
92G	A14i	5nu multicolored	1.25	1.25
92H	A14i	7nu multicolored	1.75	1.75
92I	A14i	9nu multicolored	2.10	2.10
		Nos. 92-92I (10)	8.10	8.10

Issue dates: 1ch, 2ch, 4ch, 8ch, 15ch, 2nu, 4nu, 7nu, Jan 20; 5nu, 9nu, Apr. 23.

Unauthorized imperfs exist. Value, $13.

For surcharges see Nos. 115H, 117R, 117V, 129D, 129L.

Nos. 84G, 84I, 84K, 84M Ovptd. in Black on Silver

a

b

Perfs. as Before

1968, Feb. 16 Photo.

Overprint Type "a"

93	A14b	40ch on #84G	1.50	1.50
93A	A14b	1.25nu on #84I	1.75	1.75
93B	A14b	3nu on #84K	2.25	2.25
93C	A14b	6nu on #84M	3.00	3.00

Overprint Type "b"

93D	A14b	40ch on #84G	1.50	1.50
93E	A14b	1.25nu on #84I	1.75	1.75
93F	A14b	3nu on #84K	2.25	2.25
93G	A14b	6nu on #84M	3.00	3.00
		Nos. 93-93G (8)	17.00	17.00

Exist imperf. Value, $40.

Snow Lion — A14j

1968, Mar. 14 Photo. *Perf. 12½*

94	A14j	2ch Elephant	.35	.35
94A	A14j	3ch Garuda	.35	.35
94B	A14j	4ch Monastery Tiger	.35	.35
94C	A14j	5ch Wind Horse	.35	.35
94D	A14j	15ch Snow Lion	.35	.35
94E	A14j	20ch like #94	.35	.35
94F	A14j	30ch like #94A	.35	.35
94G	A14j	50ch like #94B	.35	.35
94H	A14j	1.25nu like #94C	.45	.45
94I	A14j	1.50nu like #94	.45	.45
94J	A14j	2nu like #94D	.80	.80
94K	A14j	2.50nu like #94A	.80	.80
94L	A14j	4nu like #94B	1.50	1.50
94M	A14j	5nu like #94C	2.00	2.00
94N	A14j	10nu like #94D	3.75	3.75
		Nos. 94-94N (15)	12.55	12.55

Nos. 94I, 94K-94N are airmail. All exist imperf.

For surcharges see Nos. 115, 115M, 115Q, 117-117E, 129C, C35-C36.

Butterflies A14k

Designs: 15ch, Catagramma sorana. 50ch, Delias hyparete. 1.25nu, Anteos maerula. 2nu, Ornithoptera priamus urvilleanus. 3nu, Euploea mulciber. 4nu, Morpho rhetenor. 5nu, Papilio androgeous. 6nu, Troides magellanus.

1968, May 20 Litho. *Imperf.*

No.	Type	Value	Description	Unused	Used
95	A14k	15ch	multi	.85	.85
95A	A14k	50ch	multi	1.20	1.20
95B	A14k	1.25nu	multi	2.40	2.40
95C	A14k	2nu	multi	3.50	3.50
h.			Souv. sheet of 4, #95-95C	15.00	15.00
95D	A14k	3nu	multi	4.00	4.00
95E	A14k	4nu	multi	4.50	4.50
95F	A14k	5nu	multi	5.50	5.00
95G	A14k	6nu	multi	5.75	5.75
i.			Souv. sheet of 4, #95D-95G	22.50	22.50
			Nos. 95-95G (8)	27.70	27.20

Souv. sheets issued Oct. 23. Nos. 95D-95G, 95Gi are airmail. Simulated 3-dimensions using a plastic overlay.

Paintings — A14m

1968 Litho. & Embossed *Imperf.*

No.	Type	Value	Description	Unused	Used
96	A14m	2ch	Van Gogh	.25	.25
96A	A14m	4ch	Millet	.25	.25
96B	A14m	5ch	Monet	.25	.25
96C	A14m	10ch	Corot	.25	.25
p.			Souv. sheet of 4, #96-96C	1.60	1.60
96D	A14m	45ch	like #96	.25	.25
96E	A14m	80ch	like #96A	.35	.35
96F	A14m	1.05nu	like #96B	.45	.45
96G	A14m	1.40nu	like #96C	.60	.60
q.			Souv. sheet of 4, #96D-96G	2.40	2.40
96H	A14m	1.50nu	like #96	.65	.65
96I	A14m	2nu	like #96	.85	.85
96J	A14m	2.50nu	like #96A	1.10	1.10
96K	A14m	3nu	like #96A	1.25	1.25
96L	A14m	4nu	like #96B	1.50	1.50
96M	A14m	5nu	like #96C	1.60	1.60
r.			Souv. sheet of 4, #96I, 96K-96M	4.00	4.00
96N	A14m	6nu	like #96B	2.25	2.25
96O	A14m	8nu	like #96C	2.75	2.75
s.			Souv. sheet of 4, #96H, 96J, 96N-96O	8.00	8.00
			Nos. 96-96O (16)	14.60	14.60

Issued: nos. 96-96G, 96I, 96K-96M, 7/8; Nos. 96Cp, 96Gq, 96Mr, 8/5; others, 8/28.

Nos. 96H, 96J, 96N-96O are airmail.

See Nos. 114-114O, 144-144G.

Summer Olympics, Mexico, 1968 A14n

1968, Oct. 1 Photo. *Perf. 13½*

No.	Type	Value	Description	Unused	Used
97	A14n	5ch	Discus	.25	.25
97A	A14n	45ch	Basketball	.25	.25
97B	A14n	60ch	Javelin	.25	.25
97C	A14n	80ch	Shooting	.25	.25
97D	A14n	1.05nu	like #97	.25	.25
97E	A14n	2nu	like #97B	.25	.25
97F	A14n	3nu	like #97C	.45	.45
97G	A14n	5nu	Soccer	.75	.75
h.			Souv. sheet of 2, #97D, 97G	2.50	2.50
			Nos. 97-97G (8)	2.70	2.70

Exist imperf. Value: set $4.25; souvenir sheet $2.75.

For surcharges see Nos. 129E, B5-B7.

Coin Type of 1966 Overprinted

Embossed on Gold Foil

1968, Nov. 12 Die Cut *Imperf.*

No.	Type	Value	Description	Unused	Used
98	A14a	15ch	green	.35	.35
98A	A14a	33ch	green	.50	.50
98B	A14a	9nu	green	11.00	11.00
			Nos. 98-98B (3)	11.85	11.85

Human Rights Year.

Birds A14p

2ch, 20ch, 1.50nu, Crimson-winged laughing thrush. 3ch, 30ch, 2.50nu, Ward's trogon. 4ch, 50ch, 4nu, Grey peacock-pheasant. 5ch, 1.25nu, 5nu, Rufous necked hornbill. 15ch, 2nu, 10nu, Myzornis.

1968-69 Photo. *Perf. 12½*

No.	Type	Value	Description	Unused	Used
99	A14p	2ch	multi	.25	.25
99A	A14p	3ch	multi, vert.	.25	.25
99B	A14p	4ch	multi	.25	.25
99C	A14p	5ch	multi, vert.	.25	.25
99D	A14p	15ch	multi	.30	.30
99E	A14p	20ch	multi	.35	.35
99F	A14p	30ch	multi, vert.	.40	.40
99G	A14p	50ch	multi	.40	.40
99H	A14p	1.25nu	multi, vert.	.60	.60
99I	A14p	1.50nu	multi	.75	.75
99J	A14p	2nu	multi	1.00	1.00
99K	A14p	2.50nu	multi, vert.	1.00	1.00
99L	A14p	4nu	multi	1.25	1.25
99M	A14p	5nu	multi, vert.	1.75	1.75
99N	A14p	10nu	multi	3.25	3.25
			Nos. 99-99N (15)	12.05	12.05

Issued: 2c-5ch, 15ch, 30ch, 50ch, 12/7; 20ch, 1.25nu, 2nu, 12/28; others, 1/29/69.

1.50nu, 2.50nu, 4nu, 5nu, 10nu are airmail.

Exist imperf. Value $17.50.

For surcharges see Nos. 115A-115B, 115I, 115M, 115R, 117F-117G, 117K, 117O, 129H.

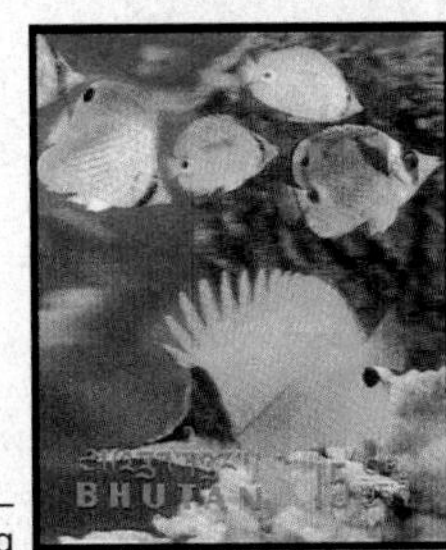

Fish — A14q

1969, Feb. 27 Litho. *Imperf.*

No.	Type	Value	Description	Unused	Used
100	A14q	15ch	multicolored	1.60	1.60
100A	A14q	20ch	multi, diff.	2.10	2.10
100B	A14q	30ch	multi, diff.	3.25	3.25
100C	A14q	5nu	multi, diff.	4.25	4.25
100D	A14q	6nu	multi, diff.	5.25	5.25
100E	A14q	7nu	multi, diff.	6.25	6.25
f.			Souv. sheet, #100B-100E	18.00	18.00
			Nos. 100-100E (6)	22.70	22.70

Nos. 100C-100E are airmail. Simulated 3-dimensions using a plastic overlay.

Insects — A14r

1969, Apr. 10 Litho. *Imperf.*

No.	Type	Value	Description	Unused	Used
101	A14r	10ch	multicolored	.90	.90
101A	A14r	75ch	multi, diff.	1.50	1.50
101B	A14r	1.25nu	multi, diff.	2.00	2.00
101C	A14r	2nu	multi, diff.	3.75	3.75
h.			Souv. sheet, #101-101C	25.00	25.00
101D	A14r	3nu	multi, diff.	5.00	5.00
101E	A14r	4nu	multi, diff.	3.00	3.00
101F	A14r	5nu	multi, diff.	3.75	3.75
101G	A14r	6nu	multi, diff.	5.00	5.00
i.			Souv. sheet, #101D-101G	20.00	20.00
			Nos. 101-101G (8)	24.90	24.90

Nos. 101D-101G, 101i are airmail. Stamps from souvenir sheets have inscription at lower right. Simulated 3-dimensions using a plastic overlay.

Admission to UPU — A14s

1969, May 2 Photo. *Perf. 13*

No.	Type	Value	Description	Unused	Used
102	A14s	5ch	multi	.25	.25
102A	A14s	10ch	multi	.25	.25
102B	A14s	15ch	multi	.25	.25
102C	A14s	45ch	multi	.25	.25
102D	A14s	60ch	multi	.25	.25
102E	A14s	1.05nu	multi	.30	.30
102F	A14s	1.40nu	multi	.40	.40
102G	A14s	4nu	multi	1.10	1.10
			Nos. 102-102G (8)	3.05	3.05

Exist imperf. Value $5.50.

For surcharges see Nos. 117H, 117L, 117U, 129.

History of Steel Making — A14t

Designs: 2ch, Pre-biblical. 5ch, Damascus sword. 15ch, 3nu, Saugus Mill. 45ch, Beehive coke ovens. 75ch, 4nu, Bessemer converter. 1.50nu, 5nu, Rolling mill. 1.75nu, Steel mill. 2nu, 6nu, Future applications.

Litho. on Steel Foil

1969, June 2 *Imperf.*

Without Gum

No.	Type	Value	Description	Unused	Used
103	A14t	2ch	multicolored	.60	.60
103A	A14t	5ch	multicolored	.60	.60
103B	A14t	15ch	multicolored	.60	.60
m.			Souv. sheet, #103A-103B	2.50	2.50
103C	A14t	45ch	multicolored	.60	.60
n.			Souv. sheet, #103, 103C	2.50	2.50
103D	A14t	75ch	multicolored	.60	.60
103E	A14t	1.50nu	multicolored	1.25	1.25
103F	A14t	1.75nu	multicolored	1.75	1.75
o.			Souv. sheet, #103E-103F	3.00	3.00
103G	A14t	2nu	multicolored	2.50	2.50
p.			Souv. sheet, #103D, 103G	3.00	3.00
103H	A14t	3nu	multicolored	3.00	3.00
103I	A14t	4nu	multicolored	3.50	3.50
103J	A14t	5nu	multicolored	4.00	4.00
q.			Souv. sheet, #103I-103J	8.00	8.00
103K	A14t	6nu	multicolored	5.50	5.50
r.			Souv. sheet, #103H,103K	10.00	10.00
			Nos. 103-103K (12)	24.50	24.50

Nos. 103H-103K, 103q, 103r are airmail. Souv. sheets issued June 30.

Birds — A14u

1969, Aug. 5 Litho. *Imperf.*

No.	Type	Value	Description	Unused	Used
104	A14u	15ch	Owl	6.50	6.50
104A	A14u	50ch	Red birds	6.50	6.50
104B	A14u	1.25nu	Hawk	6.50	6.50
104C	A14u	2nu	Penguin	6.50	6.50
h.			Souv. sheet, #104-104C	45.00	45.00
104D	A14u	3nu	Macaws	6.50	6.50
104E	A14u	4nu	Bird of paradise	3.75	3.75
104F	A14u	5nu	Duck	4.25	4.25
104G	A14u	6nu	Pheasant	4.75	4.75
i.			Souv. sheet, #104D-104G	45.00	45.00
			Nos. 104-104G (8)	45.25	45.25

Nos. 104D-104G, 104Gi are airmail. Simulated 3-dimensions using a plastic overlay. Souv. sheets issued Aug. 28.

Buddhist Prayer Banners — A14v

Litho. on Cloth

1969, Sep. 30 *Imperf.*

Self-adhesive

Sizes: 15ch, 75ch, 2nu, 57x57mm, 5nu, 6nu, 70x37mm

No.	Type	Value	Description	Unused	Used
105	A14v	15ch	multicolored	10.00	10.00
105A	A14v	75ch	multi, diff.	13.00	13.00
105B	A14v	2nu	multi, diff.	15.00	15.00
105C	A14v	5nu	multi, diff.	19.00	19.00
105D	A14v	6nu	multi, diff.	22.50	22.50
			Nos. 105-105D (5)	79.50	79.50

Souvenir Sheet

No.	Description	Unused	Used
105E	Sheet of 3	75.00	75.00

No. 105E shows denominations of 75ch, 5nu, 6nu with design elements of Nos. 105A, 105C, 105D with gray frame. Exists perf. 13½.

Mahatma Gandhi — A15

1969, Oct. 2 Litho. *Perf. 13x13½*

No.	Type	Value	Description	Unused	Used
106	A15	20ch	light blue & brn	.85	.85
107	A15	2nu	lemon & brn olive	5.00	5.00

Mohandas K. Gandhi (1869-1948), leader in India's struggle for independence.

Apollo 11 Moon Landing — A15a

Designs: 3ch, Separation from third stage. 5ch, Entering lunar orbit. 15ch, Lunar module separating from orbiter. 20ch, 3nu, Astronaut standing on lunar module's foot pad. 25ch, Astronaut, lunar module on moon. 45ch, Astronaut, flag. 50ch, 4nu, Setting up experiments. 1.75nu, Lunar module docking with orbiter. 5nu, Lift-off from Cape Canaveral. 6nu, Recovery at sea.

1969 Litho. *Imperf.*

No.	Type	Value	Description	Unused	Used
108	A15a	3ch	multi	.30	.30
108A	A15a	5ch	multi	.30	.30
108B	A15a	15ch	multi	.30	.30
108C	A15a	20ch	multi	.55	.55
m.			Souv. sheet, #108-108C	13.50	13.50
108D	A15a	25ch	multi	.70	.70
108E	A15a	45ch	multi	1.10	1.10
108F	A15a	50ch	multi	1.25	1.25
108G	A15a	1.75nu	multi	4.00	4.00
n.			Souv. sheet, #108D-108G	18.00	18.00
108H	A15a	3nu	multi	3.50	3.50
108I	A15a	4nu	multi	4.50	4.50
108J	A15a	5nu	multi	5.75	5.75
108K	A15a	6nu	multi	6.75	6.75
o.			Souv. sheet, #108H-108K	35.00	35.00
			Nos. 108-108K (12)	29.00	29.00

Nos. 108H-108K, 108Ko are airmail. Simulated 3-dimensions using a plastic overlay.

"Aldrin" misspelled on No. 108o.

Issue dates: Nos. 108-108G, Nov. 3; Nos. 108H-108K, Nov. 20; Souv. sheets, Dec. 20.

Paintings
A15b

1970, Jan. 19 Litho. *Imperf.*
109 A15b 5ch Clouet .30 .30
109A A15b 10ch van Eyck .30 .30
109B A15b 15ch David .30 .30
109C A15b 2.75nu Rubens 2.50 2.50
h. Souv. sheet, #109-109C 13.50 13.50
109D A15b 3nu Homer 3.00 3.00
109E A15b 4nu Gentileschi 4.50 4.50
109F A15b 5nu Raphael 6.25 6.25
109G A15b 6nu Ghirlandaio 7.50 7.50
i. Souv. sheet, #109D-109G 13.50 13.50
Nos. 109-109G (8) 24.65 24.65

Nos. 109D-109G, 109Gi are airmail. Simulated 3-dimensions using a plastic overlay. Souv. sheets issued Feb. 25.

Various Forms of Mail Transport, UPU Headquarters, Bern — A15c

1970, Feb. 27 Photo. *Perf. 13½*
110 A15c 3ch ol grn & gold .65 .65
111 A15c 10ch red brn & gold .65 .65
112 A15c 20ch Prus bl & gold .65 .65
113 A15c 2.50nu dp mag & gold 2.25 2.25
Nos. 110-113 (4) 4.20 4.20

New Headquarters of Universal Postal Union, Bern, Switzerland.
Exist imperf. Value $12.
For surcharge see No. 129I.

Painting Type of 1968

Paintings of flowers.

Litho. & Embossed

1970, May 6 *Imperf.*
114 A14m 2ch Van Gogh .35 .35
114A A14m 3ch Redon .35 .35
114B A14m 5ch Kuroda .35 .35
114C A14m 10ch Renoir .40 .40
p. Souv. sheet, #114-114C 2.00 2.00
114D A14m 15ch Renoir, diff. .40 .40
114E A14m 75ch Monet .40 .40
114F A14m 80ch like #114 .80 .80
114G A14m 90ch like #114A .80 .80
114H A14m 1nu La Tour .80 .80
114I A14m 1.10nu like #114B .80 .80
114J A14m 1.40nu Oudot .80 .80
q. Souv. sheet, #114D, 114E, 114H, 114J 3.50 3.50
114K A14m 1.40nu like #114C .80 .80
r. Souv. sheet, #114F, 114G, 114I, 114K 5.75 5.75
114L A14m 1.60nu like #114D 1.20 1.20
114M A14m 1.70nu like #114E 1.50 1.50
114N A14m 3nu like #114H 1.60 1.60
114O A14m 3.50nu like #114J 2.25 2.25
s. Souv. sheet, #114L-114O 8.00 8.00
Nos. 114-114O (16) 13.60 13.60

Nos. 114F-114G, 114I, 114K-114O are airmail.

Stamps of 1966-69 Surcharged

1970, June 19
115 A14j 20ch on 2nu, #94J *4.25 4.25*
115A A14p 20ch on 2nu, #99J *4.25 4.25*
115B A14p 20ch on 2.50nu, #99K *4.25 4.25*
115C A11 20ch on 3nu, #65 *4.25 4.25*
115D A14b 20ch on 3nu, #84K *4.25 4.25*
115E A11 20ch on 4nu, #66 *4.25 4.25*
115F A14c 20ch on 4nu, #85G *4.25 4.25*
115G A14d 20ch on 4nu, #86E *4.25 4.25*
115H A14i 20ch on 4nu, #92F *4.25 4.25*
115I A14p 20ch on 4nu, #99L *4.25 4.25*
115J A11 20ch on 5nu, #67 *4.25 4.25*
115K A14b 20ch on 5nu, #84L *4.25 4.25*
115L A14c 20ch on 5nu, #85H *4.25 4.25*
115M A14j 20ch on 5nu, #94M *4.25 4.25*
115N A14p 20ch on 5nu, #99M *4.25 4.25*
115O A14b 20ch on 6nu, #84M *4.25 4.25*
115P A14b 20ch on 7nu, #84N *4.25 4.25*
115Q A14j 20ch on 10nu, #94N *4.25 4.25*
115R A14p 20ch on 10nu, #99N *4.25 4.25*
Nos. 115-115R (19) *80.75 80.75*

Nos. 115B, 115I, 115M-115N, 115Q-115R are airmail.

Animals — A15d

1970, Oct. 15 Litho. *Imperf.*
116 A15d 5ch African elephant 1.00 1.00
116A A15d 10ch Leopard 1.00 1.00
116B A15d 20ch Ibex 1.40 1.40
116C A15d 25ch Tiger 1.40 1.40
116D A15d 30ch Abominable snowman 1.40 1.40
116E A15d 40ch Water buffalo 1.40 1.40
116F A15d 65ch Rhinoceros 3.50 3.50
116G A15d 75ch Giant pandas 3.50 3.50
116H A15d 85ch Snow leopard 4.25 4.25
116I A15d 2nu Young deer 5.00 5.00
116J A15d 3nu Wild boar, vert. 5.75 5.75
116K A15d 4nu Collared bear, vert. 2.75 2.75
116L A15d 5nu Takin 3.50 3.50
Nos. 116-116L (13) 35.85 35.85

Nos. 116I-116L are airmail. Simulated 3-dimensions using a plastic overlay.

Stamps of 1963-69 Surcharged

1970, Nov. 2
117 A14j 5ch on 30ch, #94F *1.00 1.00*
117A A14j 5ch on 50ch, #94G *1.00 1.00*
117B A14j 5ch on 1.25nu, #94H *1.00 1.00*
117C A14j 5ch on 1.50nu, #94I *1.00 1.00*
117D A14j 5ch on 2nu, #94J *1.00 1.00*
117E A14j 5ch on 2.50nu, #94K *1.00 1.00*
117F A14p 20ch on 30ch, #99F *4.25 4.25*
117G A14p 20ch on 50ch, #99G *4.25 4.25*
117H A14s 20ch on 1.05nu, #102E *4.25 4.25*
117I A14b 20ch on 1.25nu, #84I *4.25 4.25*
117J A14d 20ch on 1.25nu, #86D *4.25 4.25*
117K A14p 20ch on 1.25nu, #99H *4.25 4.25*
117L A14s 20ch on 1.40nu, #102F *4.25 4.25*
117M A4 20ch on 1.50nu, #14 *4.25 4.25*
117N A11 20ch on 1.50nu, #63 *4.25 4.25*
117O A14p 20ch on 1.50nu, #99I *4.25 4.25*
117P A11 20ch on 2nu, #64 *4.25 4.25*
117Q A14f 20ch on 2nu, #88A *4.25 4.25*
117R A14i 20ch on 2nu, #92E *4.25 4.25*
117S A14b 20ch on 2.50nu, #84J *4.25 4.25*
117T A14f 20ch on 4nu, #88B *4.25 4.25*
117U A14s 20ch on 4nu, #102G *4.25 4.25*
117V A14i 20ch on 7nu, #92H *4.25 4.25*
Nos. 117-117V (23) *78.25 78.25*

Nos. 117C, 117E, 117O are airmail.

Conquest of Space — A15e

Designs: 2ch, Jules Verne's "From the Earth to the Moon." 5ch, V-2 rocket. 15ch, Vostok. 25ch, Mariner 2. 30ch, Gemini 7. 50ch, Lift-off. 75ch, Edward White during space walk. 1.50nu, Apollo 13. 2nu, View of Earth from moon. 3nu, Another galaxy. 6nu, Moon, Earth, Sun, Mars, Jupiter. 7nu, Future space station.

1970 Litho. *Imperf.*
118 A15e 2ch multi .75 .75
118A A15e 5ch multi .75 .75
118B A15e 15ch multi .75 .75
118C A15e 25ch multi 1.25 1.25
m. Souv. sheet, #118-118C 10.00 10.00
118D A15e 30ch multi 1.50 1.50
118E A15e 50ch multi 2.00 2.00
118F A15e 75ch multi 2.50 2.50
118G A15e 1.50nu multi 2.75 2.75
n. Souv. sheet, #118D-118G 15.00 15.00
118H A15e 2nu multi 3.25 3.25
118I A15e 3nu multi 4.75 4.75
118J A15e 6nu multi 6.25 6.25
118K A15e 7nu multi 8.00 8.00
o. Souv. sheet, #118H-118K 30.00 30.00
Nos. 118-118K (12) 34.50 34.50

Issued: Nos. 118-118G, 11/9; Nos. 118H-118K, 11/30. Souv. sheets, Dec. 18. Nos. 118H-118K are airmail. Simulated 3-dimensions using a plastic overlay.
See Nos. 127-127C. For surcharge see No. 129F.

Wangdiphodrang Dzong and Bridge
A15f

1971-72 Photo. *Perf. 13½*
119 A15f 2ch gray 1.50 1.50
120 A15f 3ch deep red lilac 1.60 1.60
121 A15f 4ch violet 1.75 1.75
122 A15f 5ch dark green .65 .65
123 A15f 10ch orange brown .90 .90
124 A15f 15ch deep blue 1.25 1.25
125 A15f 20ch deep plum 1.75 1.75
Nos. 119-125 (7) 9.40 9.40

Issued: 5ch-20ch, 2/22; 2ch-4ch, 4/72.

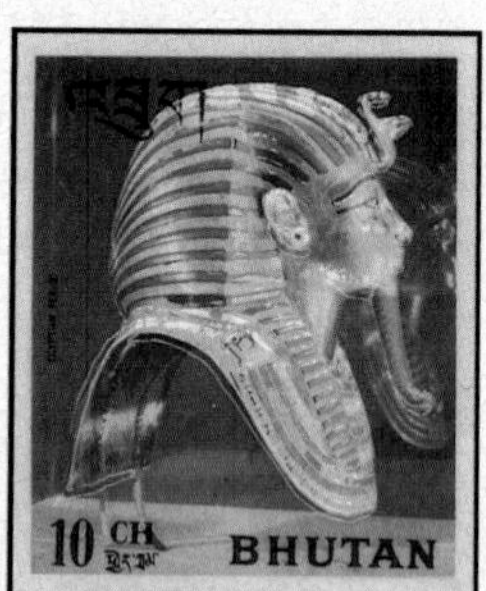

Funeral Mask of King Tutankhamen
A15g

History of Sculpture: 75ch, Winged Bull. 1.25nu, Head of Zeus. 2nu, She-wolf Suckling Romulus and Remus, horiz. 3nu, Head of Cicero. 4nu, Head of David, by Michaelangelo. 5nu, Age of Bronze, by Rodin. 6nu, Head of Woman, by Modigliani.

1971, Feb. 27 Litho. *Imperf.*
Self-adhesive
126 A15g 10ch multi .70 .70
126A A15g 75ch multi .85 .85
126B A15g 1.25nu multi 1.75 1.75
126C A15g 2nu multi 2.75 2.75
h. Souv. sheet, #126-126C 6.50 6.50
126D A15g 3nu multi 4.75 4.75
126E A15g 4nu multi 5.75 5.75
126F A15g 5nu multi 7.75 7.75
126G A15g 6nu multi 5.75 5.75
i. Souv. sheet, #126D-126G 16.00 16.00
Nos. 126-126G (8) 30.05 30.05

Stamps are plastic heat molded into three dimensions. Nos. 126D-126G are airmail.

Conquest of Space Type of 1970

Designs: 10ch, 2.50nu, Lunokhod 1. 1.70nu, 4nu, Apollo 15.

1971, Mar. 20 Litho. *Imperf.*
127 A15e 10ch multi .30 .30
127A A15e 1.70nu multi 2.10 2.10
127B A15e 2.50nu multi 5.25 5.25
127C A15e 4nu multi 5.00 5.00
d. Souv. sheet of 4, #127-127C 27.50 27.50
Nos. 127-127C (4) 12.65 12.65

Nos. 127B-127C are airmail. Simulated 3-dimensions using a plastic overlay.

Antique Automobiles — A15h

2ch, Mercedes Benz, Germany. 5ch, Ford, US. 10ch, Alfa Romeo, Italy. 15ch, Cord, US. 20ch, Hispano Suiza, Spain. 30ch, Invicta, Britain. 60ch, Renault, France. 75ch, Talbot, Britain. 85ch, Mercer, US. 1nu, Sunbeam, Britain. 1.20nu, Austrian Daimler. 1.55nu, Bugatti, Italy. 1.80nu, Simplex, US. 2nu, Amilcar, France. 2.50nu, Bentley, Britain. 4nu, Morris Garage, Britain. 6nu, Duesenberg, US. 7nu, Aston Martin, Britain. 9nu, Packard, US. 10nu, Rolls Royce, Britain.

1971 Litho. *Imperf.*
128-128S A15h Set of 20 37.50 37.50

Issued: Nos. 128-128F, 5/20; Nos. 128G-128N, 6/10; Nos. 128O-128S, 7/5. Nos. 128O-128S are airmail. Simulated 3-dimensions using a plastic overlay.
"Romeo" misspelled.

Stamps of 1964-71 Surcharged

1971, July 1
129 A14s 55ch on 60ch, #102D 2.50 2.50
129A A5 55ch on 1.30nu, #22 2.50 2.50
129B A11 55ch on 3nu, #65 2.50 2.50
129C A14j 55ch on 4nu, #94L 2.50 2.50
129D A14i 55ch on 5nu, #92G 2.50 2.50
129E A14n 90ch on 1.05nu, #97D 3.00 3.00
129F A15e 90ch on 1.70nu, #127A 10.00 10.00
129G A5 90ch on 2nu, #23 2.50 2.50
129H A14p 90ch on 2nu, #99J 4.00 4.00
129I A15c 90ch on 2.50nu, #113 3.00 3.00
129J A11 90ch on 4nu, #66 3.00 3.00
129K A14d 90ch on 4nu, #86E 4.00 4.00
129L A14i 90ch on 9nu, #92I 4.00 4.00
Nos. 129-129L (13) 46.00 46.00

No. 129C is airmail. No. 129F comes with lines 8mm or 18mm long.

UN Emblem and Bhutan Flag — A16

Designs (Bhutan Flag and): 10ch, UN Headquarters, NY. 20ch, Security Council Chamber and mural by Per Krohg. 3nu, General Assembly Hall.

1971, Sept. 21 Photo. *Perf. 13½*

No.	Type	Description	Unused	Used
130	A16	5ch gold, bl & multi	.25	.25
131	A16	10ch gold & multi	.25	.25
132	A16	20ch gold & multi	.25	.25
133	A16	3nu gold & multi	.75	.75
		Nos. 130-133,C21-C23 (7)	3.80	3.80

Bhutan's admission to the UN. Exist imperf. Values, unused or used: set $6.

For overprints see Nos. 140-143. For surcharge see No. 252.

Boy Scout Crossing Stream in Rope Sling — A17

Emblem & Boy Scouts: 20ch, 2nu, mountaineering. 50ch, 6nu, reading map. 75ch, as 10ch.

1971, Nov. 30 Litho. *Perf. 13½*

No.	Type	Description	Unused	Used
134	A17	10ch gold & multi	.25	.25
135	A17	20ch gold & multi	.25	.25
136	A17	50ch gold & multi	.25	.25
137	A17	75ch silver & multi	.50	.50
138	A17	2nu silver & multi	.50	.50
139	A17	6nu silver & multi	2.25	2.25
a.		Souv. sheet of 2, #138-139 + 2 labels	4.50	4.50
		Nos. 134-139 (6)	4.00	4.00

60th anniv. of the Boy Scouts. Exist imperf. Value $7.50.

For overprint and surcharge see Nos. 253, 383.

Nos. 130-133 Overprinted in Gold

1971, Dec. 23

No.	Type	Description	Unused	Used
140	A16	5ch gold & multi	.30	.30
141	A16	10ch gold & multi	.30	.30
142	A16	20ch gold & multi	.30	.30
143	A16	3nu gold & multi	.60	.60
		Nos. 140-143,C24-C26 (7)	4.50	4.50

World Refugee Year. Exist imperf. Values: set unused $10, used $9.

The Bathing Girl by Renoir A17a

Designs: 20ch, A Bar at the Follies, by Manet, horiz. 90ch, Mona Lisa, by da Vinci. 1.70nu, Cart of Father Juniet, by Rousseau, horiz. 2.50nu, The Gleaners, by Millet, horiz. 4.60nu, White Horse, by Gaugin. 5.40nu, The Dancing Lesson, by Degas. 6nu, After the Rain, by Guillaumin, horiz.

1972 Litho. & Embossed *Imperf.*

No.	Type	Description	Unused	Used
144	A17a	15ch multi	.50	.50
144A	A17a	20ch multi	.75	.75
144B	A17a	90ch multi	.85	.85
144C	A17a	1.70nu multi	1.50	1.50
144D	A17a	2.50nu multi	1.50	1.50
h.		Souv. sheet of 4, #144-144B, 144D	7.00	7.00
144E	A17a	4.60nu multi	2.25	2.25
144F	A17a	5.40nu multi	2.75	2.75
144G	A17a	6nu multi	2.75	2.75
i.		Souv. sheet of 4, #144C, 144E-144G	8.00	8.00
		Nos. 144-144G (8)	12.85	12.85

Issued: Nos. 144-144B, 144D, 1/29; others, 2/28.

Nos. 144C, 144E-144G are airmail.

Famous Men A17b

1972, Apr. 17 Litho. *Imperf.*
Self-adhesive

No.	Type	Description	Unused	Used
145	A17b	10ch John F. Kennedy	.60	.60
145A	A17b	15ch Gandhi	.75	.75
145B	A17b	55ch Churchill	1.10	1.10
145C	A17b	2nu De Gaulle	1.25	1.25
145D	A17b	6nu Pope John XVIII	2.00	2.00
145E	A17b	8nu Eisenhower	2.75	2.75
f.		Souv. sheet, #145B-145E	8.00	8.00
		Nos. 145-145E (6)	8.45	8.45

Nos. 145C-145E are airmail. Stamps are plastic heat molded into three dimensions.

Book Year Emblem A17c

1972, May 15 Photo. *Perf. 13½x13*

No.	Type	Description	Unused	Used
146	A17c	2ch multicolored	.25	.25
146A	A17c	3ch multicolored	.25	.25
146B	A17c	5ch multicolored	.25	.25
146C	A17c	20ch multicolored	.25	.25
		Nos. 146-146C (4)	1.00	1.00

International Book Year.

1972 Summer Olympics, Munich — A17d

1972, June 6 Photo. *Perf. 13½*

No.	Type	Description	Unused	Used
147	A17d	10ch Handball	.25	.25
147A	A17d	15ch Archery	.25	.25
147B	A17d	20ch Boxing	.25	.25
147C	A17d	30ch Discus	.25	.25
147D	A17d	35ch Javelin	.25	.25
147E	A17d	45ch Shooting	.25	.25
147F	A17d	1.35nu like #147A	.80	.80
147G	A17d	7nu like #147	1.25	1.25
h.		Souv. sheet of 3, #147D, 147F-147G	3.00	3.00
		Nos. 147-147G (8)	3.55	3.55

Nos. 147D, 147F-147G are airmail and have a gold border.

Exist imperf. Value: set $6; souvenir sheet $5.

For overprint see No. 384.

Apollo 11 Type of 1969

Apollo 16: 15ch, Lift-off, vert. 20ch, Achieving lunar orbit. 90ch, Astronauts Young, Mattingly, Duke, vert. 1.70nu, Lunar module. 2.50nu, Walking on moon. 4.60nu, Gathering rock samples. 5.40nu, Apollo 16 on launch pad, vert. 6nu, Looking at earth, vert.

1972, Sept. 1 Litho. *Imperf.*

No.	Type	Description	Unused	Used
148	A15a	15ch multi	1.25	1.25
148A	A15a	20ch multi	1.25	1.25
148B	A15a	90ch multi	1.25	1.25
148C	A15a	1.70nu multi	1.75	1.75
148D	A15a	2.50nu multi	2.25	2.25
h.		Souv. sheet of 4, #148-148B, 148D	15.00	15.00
148E	A15a	4.60nu multi	3.00	3.00
148F	A15a	5.40nu multi	3.50	3.50
148G	A15a	6nu multi	4.75	4.75
i.		Souv. sheet of 4, #148C, 148E-148G	25.00	25.00
		Nos. 148-148G (8)	19.00	19.00

Nos. 148C, 148E-148G are airmail. Simulated 3-dimensions using a plastic overlay.

Dogs A17f

1972-73 Photo. *Perf. 13½*

No.	Type	Description	Unused	Used
149	A17f	2ch Pointer	.25	.25
149A	A17f	3ch Irish Setter	.25	.25
149B	A17f	5ch Lhasa Apso, vert	.25	.25
149C	A17f	10ch Dochi	.25	.25
149D	A17f	15ch Damci	.25	.25
149E	A17f	15ch Collie	.25	.25
149F	A17f	20ch Basset hound	.25	.25
149G	A17f	25ch Damci, diff	.25	.25
149H	A17f	30ch Fox terrier	.25	.25
149I	A17f	55ch Lhasa Apso, diff.	.25	.25
149J	A17f	99ch Boxer	.25	.25
149K	A17f	2.50nu St. Bernard	.50	.50
149L	A17f	4nu Cocker Spaniel	2.00	2.00
o.		Souv. sheet of 3, #149J-149L, perf. 14	5.50	5.50
149M	A17f	8nu Damci, diff.	2.50	2.50
p.		Souv. sheet of 2, #149I, 149M, perf. 14	5.50	5.50
		Nos. 149-149M (14)	7.75	7.75

Souvenir Sheet
Perf. 14

No.	Type	Description	Unused	Used
149N	A17f	18nu Poodle	12.00	12.00

Issued: Nos. 149B-149D, 149G, 149I, 149M, 149p, 10/5; Nos. 149-149A, 149E-149F, 149H, 149J-149L, 149o, 1/1/73; No. 149N, 1/15/73. No. 149N is airmail. All exist imperf.

For surcharges & overprints see Nos. 268-269, 385.

Roses — A17g

1973, Jan. 30 Photo. *Perf. 13½*
Scented Paper

No.	Type	Description	Unused	Used
150	A17g	15ch Wendy Cussons	.25	.25
150A	A17g	25ch Iceberg	.25	.25
150B	A17g	30ch Marchioness of Urquio	.25	.25
150C	A17g	3nu Pink parfait	.80	.80
150D	A17g	6nu Roslyn	1.50	1.50
150E	A17g	7nu Blue moon	1.75	1.75
f.		Souv. sheet, #150D-150E	3.00	3.00
		Nos. 150-150E (6)	4.80	4.80

Nos. 150D-150E are airmail. Exist imperf. Value: set $10; souvenir sheet $8.

Apollo 11 Type of 1969

Apollo 17: 10ch, Taking photographs on moon. 15ch, Setting up experiments. 55ch, Earth. 2nu, Driving lunar rover. 7nu, Satellite. 9nu, Astronauts Cernan, Evans, Schmitt.

1973, Feb. 28 Litho. *Imperf.*
Size: 50x49mm

No.	Type	Description	Unused	Used
151	A15a	10ch multicolored	1.25	1.25
151A	A15a	15ch multicolored	1.25	1.25
151B	A15a	55ch multicolored	1.50	1.50
151C	A15a	2nu multicolored	2.00	2.00
f.		Souv. sheet of 4, #151-151C	12.00	12.00
151D	A15a	7nu multicolored	6.00	6.00
151E	A15a	9nu multicolored	8.00	8.00
g.		Souv. sheet of 2, #151D-151E	40.00	40.00
		Nos. 151-151E (6)	20.00	20.00

Simulated 3-dimensions using a plastic overlay. Nos. 151D-151E are airmail. No. 151g is circular, 160mm in diameter.

Phonograph Records

A17h

Recordings: 10ch, Bhutanese History. 25ch, Royal Bhutan Anthem. 1.25nu, Bhutanese History (English). 3nu, Bhutanese History (Bhutanese), Folk Song No. 1. 7nu, Folk Song No. 1. 8nu, Folk Song No. 2. 9nu, History in English, Folk Songs Nos. 1 & 2.

Diameter: Nos. 152-152B, 152D-152E, 69mm, Nos. 152C, 152F, 100mm

1973, Apr. 15 Self-adhesive

No.	Type	Description	Unused	Used
152	A17h	10ch yel on red	*15.00*	*15.00*
152A	A17h	25ch gold on grn	*20.00*	*20.00*
152B	A17h	1.25nu sil on bl	*30.00*	*30.00*
152C	A17h	3nu sil on pur	*85.00*	*85.00*
152D	A17h	7nu sil on blk	*50.00*	*50.00*
152E	A17h	8nu red on white	*75.00*	*75.00*
152F	A17h	9nu blk on yel	*125.00*	*125.00*
		Nos. 152-152F (7)	*400.00*	*400.00*

Nos. 152C, 152F are airmail.

A 6nu stamp, silver on green, exists but was not issued. Value, unused $900.

King Jigme Dorji Wangchuk (d. 1972) A17i

Embossed on Gold Foil

1973, May 2 Die Cut *Imperf.*

No.	Type	Description	Unused	Used
153	A17i	10ch orange	.45	.45
153A	A17i	25ch red	.50	.50
153B	A17i	3nu green	1.10	1.10
153C	A17i	6nu blue	2.25	2.25
153D	A17i	8nu purple	3.00	3.00
e.		Souv. sheet of 2, #153C-153D	6.00	6.00
		Nos. 153-153D (5)	7.30	7.30

Nos. 153C-153D are airmail.

Mushrooms — A17j

Different mushrooms.

1973, Sept. 25 Litho. *Imperf.*
154 A17j 15ch multicolored *.50 .50*
154A A17j 25ch multicolored *.50 .50*
154B A17j 30ch multicolored *.50 .50*
154C A17j 3nu multicolored *5.00 5.00*
f. Souv. sheet, #154-154C *20.00 20.00*
154D A17j 6nu multicolored *12.50 12.50*
154E A17j 7nu multicolored *14.00 14.00*
g. Souv. sheet, #154D-154E *80.00 80.00*
Nos. 154-154E (6) 33.00 33.00

Simulated 3-dimensions using a plastic overlay. Nos. 154D-154E are airmail.

Bhutanese Mail Service — A17k

Designs: 5ch, 6nu, Letter carrier at mail box. 10ch, 5nu, Postmaster, letter carrier. 15ch, Sacking mail. 25ch, Mailtruck. 1.25nu, Sorting mail. 3nu, Hand-delivered mail.

1973, Nov. 14 Photo. *Perf. 13½*
155 A17k 5ch multi .25 .25
155A A17k 10ch multi .25 .25
155B A17k 15ch multi .25 .25
155C A17k 25ch multi .25 .25
155D A17k 1.25nu multi .25 .25
155E A17k 3nu multi .75 .75
155F A17k 5nu multi 1.25 1.25
155G A17k 6nu multi 1.50 1.50
h. Souv. sheet, #155F-155G 5.50 5.50
Nos. 155-155G (8) 4.75 4.75

Indipex '73. Nos. 155F-155G are airmail. All exist imperf. Values: set $7; souvenir sheet $6.50.
For surcharges and overprint see Nos. 267, 382, C37-C38.

King Jigme Singye Wangchuk and Royal Crest — A18

Designs (King and): 25ch, 90ch, Flag of Bhutan. 1.25nu, Wheel with 8 good luck signs. 2nu, 4nu, Punakha Dzong, former winter capital. 3nu, 5nu, Crown. 5ch, same as 10ch.

1974, June 2 Litho. *Perf. 13½*
157 A18 10ch maroon & multi .25 .25
158 A18 25ch gold & multi .25 .25
159 A18 1.25nu multi .25 .25
160 A18 2nu gold & multi .40 .40
161 A18 3nu multi .50 .50
Nos. 157-161 (5) 1.65 1.65

Souvenir Sheets

Perf. 13½, Imperf.

162 Sheet of 2 3.00 3.00
a. A18 5ch maroon & multi .50
b. A18 5nu red orange & multi 2.50
163 Sheet of 2 3.00 3.00
a. A18 90ch gold & multi .90
b. A18 4nu gold & multi 2.10

Coronation of King Jigme Singye Wangchuk, June 2, 1974.

Mailman on Horseback A19

Old and New Locomotives A20

Designs (UPU Emblem, Carrier Pigeon and): 3ch, Sailing and steam ships. 4ch, Old biplane and jet. 25ch, Mail runner and jeep.

1974, Oct. 9 Litho. *Perf. 14½*
164 A19 1ch grn & multi .60 .60
165 A20 2ch lilac & multi .60 .60
166 A20 3ch ocher & multi .60 .60
167 A20 4ch yel grn & multi .60 .60
168 A20 25ch salmon & multi .60 .60
Nos. 164-168,C27-C29 (8) 5.50 5.50

Centenary of Universal Postal Union. Issued in sheets of 50 and sheets of 5 plus label with multicolored margin. Exist imperf. Values, unused or used: set $6.

Family and WPY Emblem — A21

1974, Dec. 17 *Perf. 13½*
169 A21 25ch bl & multi .25 .25
170 A21 50ch org & multi .25 .25
171 A21 90ch ver & multi .30 .30
172 A21 2.50nu brn & multi .65 .65
a. Souvenir sheet, 10nu 2.75 2.75
Nos. 169-172 (4) 1.45 1.45

For surcharge see No. 254.

Sephisa Chandra — A22

Indigenous butterflies: 2ch, Lethe kansa. 3ch, Neope bhadra. 4ch, Euthalia duda. 5ch, Vindula erota. 10ch, Bhutanitis Lidderdale. 3nu, Limenitis zayla. 5nu, Delis thysbe. 10nu, Dabasa gyas.

1975, Sept. 15 Litho. *Perf. 14½*
173 A22 1ch multicolored .30 .30
174 A22 2ch multicolored .30 .30
175 A22 3ch multicolored .30 .30
176 A22 4ch multicolored .30 .30
177 A22 5ch multicolored .30 .30
178 A22 10ch multicolored .30 .30
179 A22 3nu multicolored .75 .75
180 A22 5nu multicolored 1.60 1.60
Nos. 173-180 (8) 4.15 4.15

Souvenir Sheet

Perf. 13

181 A22 10nu multicolored 3.00 3.00

For surcharges see Nos. 255-256.

Apollo and Apollo-Soyuz Emblem — A23

Design: No. 183, Soyuz and emblem.

1975, Dec. 1 Litho. *Perf. 14x13½*
182 A23 10nu multicolored 3.00 3.00
183 A23 10nu multicolored 3.00 3.00
a. Souvenir sheet of 2, 15nu 6.00 6.00

Apollo Soyuz link-up in space, July 17. Nos. 182-183 printed se-tenant in sheets of 10. No. 183a contains two 15nu stamps similar to Nos 182-183. Exist imperf.
For surcharges see Nos. 257-258.

Jewelry — A24

Designs: 2ch, Coffee pot, bell and sugar cup. 3ch, Container and drinking horn. 4ch, Pendants and box cover. 5ch, Painter. 15ch, Silversmith. 20ch, Wood carver with tools. 1.50nu, Mat maker. 5nu, 10nu, Printer.

1975, Dec. 17 *Perf. 14½*
184 A24 1ch multicolored .30 .30
185 A24 2ch multicolored .30 .30
186 A24 3ch multicolored .30 .30
187 A24 4ch multicolored .30 .30
188 A24 5ch multicolored .30 .30
189 A24 15ch multicolored .30 .30
190 A24 20ch multicolored .30 .30
191 A24 1.50nu multicolored .35 .35
192 A24 10nu multicolored 2.25 2.25
Nos. 184-192 (9) 4.70 4.70

Souvenir Sheet

Perf. 13

193 A24 5nu multicolored 4.25 4.25

Handicrafts and craftsmen.
For surcharges see No. 259, 381.

King Jigme Singye Wangchuk A25

Designs: 25ch, 90ch, 1nu, 2nu, 4nu, like 15ch. 1.30nu, 3nu, 5nu, Coat of arms. Sizes (Diameter): 15ch, 1nu, 1.30nu, 38mm. 25ch, 2nu, 3nu, 49mm. 90ch, 4nu, 5nu, 63mm.

Lithographed, Embossed on Gold Foil

1975, Nov. 11 *Imperf.*
194 A25 15ch emerald *.65 .65*
195 A25 25ch emerald *.90 .90*
196 A25 90ch emerald *1.40 1.40*
197 A25 1nu bright carmine *1.50 1.50*
198 A25 1.30nu bright carmine *1.90 1.90*
199 A25 2nu bright carmine *2.10 2.10*
200 A25 3nu bright carmine *2.75 2.75*
201 A25 4nu bright carmine *4.75 4.75*
202 A25 5nu bright carmine *6.00 6.00*
Nos. 194-202 (9) 21.95 21.95

King Jigme Singye Wangchuk's 20th birthday.

Rhododendron Cinnabarinum A28

Rhododendron: 2ch, Campanulatum. 3ch, Fortunei. 4ch, Red arboreum. 5ch, Pink arboreum. 1nu, Falconeri. 3nu, Hodgsonii. 5nu, Keysii. 10nu, Cinnabarinum.

1976, Feb. 15 Litho. *Perf. 15*
203 A28 1ch rose & multi .25 .25
204 A28 2ch lt grn & multi .25 .25
205 A28 3ch gray & multi .25 .25
206 A28 4ch lil & multi .25 .25
207 A28 5ch ol gray & multi .25 .25
208 A28 1nu brn org & multi .30 .30
209 A28 3nu ultra & multi .90 .90
210 A28 5nu gray & multi 1.40 1.40
Nos. 203-210 (8) 3.85 3.85

Souvenir Sheet

Perf. 13½

211 A28 10nu multicolored 3.75 3.75

For surcharge see No. 260.

Slalom and Olympic Games Emblem — A29

Olympic Games Emblem and: 2ch, 4-men bobsled. 3ch, Ice hockey. 4ch, Cross-country skiing. 5ch, Figure skating, women's. 2nu, Downhill skiing. 4nu, Speed skating. 6nu, Ski jump. 10nu, Figure skating, pairs.

1976, Mar. 29 Litho. *Perf. 13½*
212 A29 1ch multicolored .25 .25
213 A29 2ch multicolored .25 .25
214 A29 3ch multicolored .25 .25
215 A29 4ch multicolored .25 .25
216 A29 5ch multicolored .25 .25
217 A29 2nu multicolored .40 .40
218 A29 4nu multicolored .90 .90
219 A29 10nu multicolored 2.50 2.50
Nos. 212-219 (8) 5.05 5.05

Souvenir Sheet

220 A29 6nu multicolored 2.75 2.75

12th Winter Olympic Games, Innsbruck, Austria, Feb. 4-15.
For surcharges see Nos. 261-262.
Exist imperf. Values, unused or used: set 7.50; souvenir sheet $7.50.

Ceremonial Masks — A29a

Various masks.

1976, Apr. 23 Litho. *Imperf.*
220A A29a 5ch multi .40 .40
220B A29a 10ch multi .40 .40
220C A29a 15ch multi .40 .40
220D A29a 20ch multi .40 .40
220E A29a 25ch multi, horiz. .40 .40
220F A29a 30ch multi, horiz. .40 .40
220G A29a 35ch multi, horiz. .40 .40
220H A29a 1nu multi, horiz. 2.40 2.40
220I A29a 2nu multi, horiz. 2.75 2.75
220J A29a 2.50nu multi, horiz. 2.75 2.75
220K A29a 3nu multi, horiz. 3.25 3.25
Nos. 220A-220K (11) 13.95 13.95

Souvenir Sheets

220L A29a 5nu like #220C 5.50 5.00
220M A29a 10nu like #220F 12.50 12.50

Simulated 3-dimensions using a plastic overlay. Nos. 220H-220M are airmail.
Sizes of stamps: No. 220L, 59x70mm, No. 220M, 69x57mm.

Orchid A30

Designs: Various flowers.

1976, May 29 Litho. *Perf. 14½*

No.	Type	Description	Unused	Used
221	A30	1ch multicolored	.25	.25
222	A30	2ch multicolored	.25	.25
223	A30	3ch multicolored	.25	.25
224	A30	4ch multicolored	.25	.25
225	A30	5ch multicolored	.25	.25
226	A30	2nu multicolored	.70	.70
227	A30	4nu multicolored	1.25	1.25
228	A30	6nu multicolored	2.00	2.00
		Nos. 221-228 (8)	5.20	5.20

Souvenir Sheet

Perf. 13½

No.	Type	Description	Unused	Used
229	A30	10nu multicolored	4.00	4.00

For surcharges see Nos. 263-264.

Double Carp Design A31

Designs: Various symbolic designs and Colombo Plan emblem.

1976, July 1 Litho. *Perf. 14½*

No.	Type	Description	Unused	Used
230	A31	3ch red & multi	.25	.25
231	A31	4ch ver & multi	.25	.25
232	A31	5ch multicolored	.25	.25
233	A31	25ch bl & multi	.25	.25
234	A31	1.25nu multicolored	.35	.35
235	A31	2nu yel & multi	.60	.60
236	A31	2.50nu vio & multi	.75	.75
237	A31	3nu multicolored	.90	.90
		Nos. 230-237 (8)	3.60	3.60

Colombo Plan, 25th anniversary.
For surcharge see No. 265.

Bandaranaike Conference Hall — A32

1976, Aug. 16 Litho. *Perf. 13½*

No.	Type	Description	Unused	Used
238	A32	1.25nu multicolored	.80	.80
239	A32	2.50nu multicolored	1.90	1.90

5th Summit Conference of Non-aligned Countries, Colombo, Sri Lanka, Aug. 9-19.

Elizabeth II — A33

Liberty Bell — A34

Spirit of St. Louis — A35

Bhutanese Archer, Olympic Rings — A36

Designs: No. 242, Alexander Graham Bell. No. 245, LZ 3 Zeppelin docking, 1907. No. 246, Alfred B. Nobel.

1978, Nov. 15 Litho. *Perf. 14½*

No.	Type	Description	Unused	Used
240	A33	20nu multicolored	4.00	4.00
241	A34	20nu multicolored	5.25	5.25
242	A33	20nu multicolored	5.25	5.25
243	A35	20nu multicolored	5.25	5.25
244	A36	20nu multicolored	5.25	5.25
245	A35	20nu multicolored	6.75	6.75
246	A33	20nu multicolored	5.75	5.75
		Nos. 240-246 (7)	37.50	37.50

25th anniv. of coronation of Elizabeth II; American Bicentennial; cent. of 1st telephone call by Alexander Graham Bell; Charles A. Lindbergh crossing the Atlantic, 50th anniv.; Olympic Games; 75th anniv. of the Zeppelin; 75th anniv. of Nobel Prize. Seven souvenir sheets exist, each 25nu, commemorating same events with different designs. Size: 103x80mm. Value $50.

Issues of 1967-1976 Surcharged with New Value and Bars

Perforations and Printing as Before

1978

No.	Type	Description	Unused	Used
252	A16	25ch on 3nu (#133)		
253	A17	25ch on 6nu (#139)		
254	A21	25ch on 2.50nu (#172)		
255	A22	25ch on 3nu (#179)		
256	A22	25ch on 5nu (#180)		
257	A23	25ch on 10nu (#182)		
258	A23	25ch on 10nu (#183)		
259	A24	25ch on 10nu (#192)		
260	A28	25ch on 5nu (#210)		
261	A29	25ch on 4nu (#218)		
262	A29	25ch on 10nu (#219)		
263	A30	25ch on 4nu (#227)		
264	A30	25ch on 6nu (#228)		
265	A31	25ch on 2.50nu (#236)		
266	A14g	25ch on 5nu (#90E)		
267	A17k	25ch on 3nu (#155E)		
268	A17f	25ch on 4nu (#149L)		
269	A17f	25ch on 8nu (#149M)		
		Nos. 252-269, C31-C38 (26)	120.00	120.00

Mother and Child, IYC Emblem — A37

IYC Emblem and: 5nu, Mother and two children. 10nu, Boys with blackboards and stylus.

1979, June Litho. *Perf. 14x13½*

No.	Type	Description	Unused	Used
289	A37	2nu multicolored	.65	.65
290	A37	5nu multicolored	1.75	1.75
291	A37	10nu multicolored	3.00	3.00
a.		Souv. sheet of 3, #289-291 + label, perf. 15x13½	7.00	7.00
		Nos. 289-291 (3)	5.40	5.40

International Year of the Child.
Exist imperf. Values: set $8; souvenir sheet $11.
For overprints see Nos. 761-763.

Conference Emblem and Dove — A38

10nu, Emblem and Bhutanese symbols.

1979, Sept. 3 Litho. *Perf. 14x13½*

No.	Type	Description	Unused	Used
292	A38	25ch multicolored	.25	.25
293	A38	10nu multicolored	3.25	3.25

6th Non-Aligned Summit Conference, Havana, August 1979.

Silver Rattle, Dorji A39

Antiques: 10ch, Silver handbell, Dilbu, vert. 15ch, Cylindrical jar, Jadum, vert. 25ch, Ornamental teapot, Jamjee. 1nu, Leather container, Kem, vert. 1.25nu, Brass teapot, Jamjee. 1.70nu, Vessel with elephant-head legs, Sangphor, vert. 2nu, Teapot with ornamental spout, Jamjee, vert. 3nu, Metal pot on claw-shaped feet, Yangtho, vert. 4nu, Dish inlaid with precious stones, Battha. 5nu, Metal circular flask, Chhap, vert.

1979, Dec. 17 Photo. *Perf. 14*

No.	Type	Description	Unused	Used
294	A39	5ch multicolored	.25	.25
295	A39	10ch multicolored	.25	.25
296	A39	15ch multicolored	.25	.25
297	A39	25ch multicolored	.25	.25
298	A39	1nu multicolored	.45	.45
299	A39	1.25nu multicolored	.50	.50
300	A39	1.70nu multicolored	.70	.70
301	A39	2nu multicolored	.90	.90
302	A39	3nu multicolored	1.25	1.25
303	A39	4nu multicolored	1.60	1.60
304	A39	5nu multicolored	2.25	2.25
		Nos. 294-304 (11)	8.65	8.65

Hill, Rinpiang Dzong — A40

Hill Statue, Stamps of Bhutan and: 2nu, Dzong. 5nu, Ounsti Dzong. 10nu, Lingzi Dzong, Gt. Britain Type 81. 20nu, Rope bridge, Penny Black.

1980, Mar 15 Litho. *Perf. 14x13½*

No.	Type	Description	Unused	Used
305	A40	1nu multicolored	.40	.40
306	A40	2nu multicolored	.75	.75
307	A40	5nu multicolored	2.00	2.00
308	A40	10nu multicolored	3.75	3.75
		Nos. 305-308 (4)	6.90	6.90

Souvenir Sheet

No.	Type	Description	Unused	Used
309	A40	20nu multicolored	11.00	11.00

Sir Rowland Hill (1795-1879), originator of penny postage.
Exist imperf. Values, unused or used: set $7; souvenir sheet $9.

Kichu Lhakhang Monastery, Phari — A41

Guru Padma Sambhava's Birthday: Monasteries.

1981, July 11 Litho. *Perf. 14*

No.	Type	Description	Unused	Used
310	A41	1nu Dungtse, Phari, vert	.25	.25
311	A41	2nu shown	.40	.40
312	A41	2.25nu Kurjey	.60	.60
313	A41	3nu Tangu, Thimphu	.70	.70
314	A41	4nu Cheri, Thimphu	.95	.95
315	A41	5nu Chorten, Kora	1.40	1.40
316	A41	7nu Tak-Tsang, Phari, vert	1.75	1.75
		Nos. 310-316 (7)	6.05	6.05

Prince Charles and Lady Diana — A42

1981, Sept. 10 Litho. *Perf. 14½*

No.	Type	Description	Unused	Used
317	A42	1nu St. Paul's Cathedral	.80	.80
318	A42	5nu like #317	2.00	2.00
319	A42	20nu shown	3.00	3.00
320	A42	25nu like #319	3.25	3.25
		Nos. 317-320 (4)	9.05	9.05

Souvenir Sheet

No.	Type	Description	Unused	Used
321	A42	20nu Wedding procession	3.00	3.00

Royal wedding. Nos. 318-319 issued in sheets of 5 plus label.
For surcharges see Nos. 471-475.
Exist imperf. Values, unused or used: set $16; souvenir sheet $9.

Orange-bellied Chloropsis — A43

1982, Apr. 19 Litho. *Perf. 14*

No.	Type	Description	Unused	Used
322	A43	2nu shown	.70	.70
323	A43	3nu Monal pheasant	1.75	1.75
324	A43	5nu Ward's trogon	2.50	2.50
325	A43	10nu Mrs. Gould's sunbird	2.75	2.75
		Nos. 322-325 (4)	7.70	7.70

Souvenir Sheet

No.	Type	Description	Unused	Used
326	A43	25nu Maroon oriole	7.50	7.50

1982 World Cup — A44

Designs: Various soccer players.

1982, June 25 Litho. *Perf. 14½x14*

327	A44	1nu multicolored	.25	.25
328	A44	2nu multicolored	.60	.60
329	A44	3nu multicolored	.90	.90
330	A44	20nu multicolored	5.25	5.25
		Nos. 327-330 (4)	7.00	7.00

Souvenir Sheets

331	A44	25nu multicolored	6.00	6.00
331A	A44	25nu multicolored	6.00	6.00

Nos. 331-331A have margins continuing design and listing finalists (No. 331, Algeria-Honduras; No. 331A, Hungary-Yugoslavia).

For surcharges see Nos. 481-485.

21st Birthday of Princess Diana — A45

1982, Aug.

332	A45	1nu St. James' Palace	.50	.50
332A	A45	10nu Diana, Charles	4.50	4.50
332B	A45	15nu Windsor Castle	8.00	8.00
333	A45	25nu Wedding	12.00	12.00
		Nos. 332-333 (4)	25.00	25.00

Souvenir Sheet

334	A45	20nu Diana	16.00	7.50

10nu-15nu issued only in sheets of 5 + label.

For overprints and surcharges see Nos. 361-363, 455-459, 476-480.

Exist imperf. Values unused or used: set $25; souvenir sheet $20.

Scouting Year A46

1982, Aug. 23 Litho. *Perf. 14*

335	A46	3nu Baden-Powell, vert.	.80	.80
336	A46	5nu Eating around fire	1.50	1.50
337	A46	15nu Reading map	4.50	4.50
338	A46	20nu Pitching tents	5.50	5.50
		Nos. 335-338 (4)	12.30	12.30

Souvenir Sheet

339	A46	25nu Mountain climbing	8.00	8.00

For surcharges see Nos. 450-454, 559-563.

Exist imperf. Values unused or used: set $25; souvenir sheet $16.

Rama and Cubs with Mowgli — A47

Scenes from Disney's The Jungle Book.

1982, Sept. 1 *Perf. 11*

340	A47	1ch multicolored	.25	.25
341	A47	2ch multicolored	.25	.25
342	A47	3ch multicolored	.25	.25
343	A47	4ch multicolored	.25	.25
344	A47	5ch multicolored	.25	.25
345	A47	10ch multicolored	.25	.25
346	A47	30ch multicolored	.25	.25
347	A47	2nu multicolored	.40	.40
348	A47	20nu multicolored	6.00	6.00
		Nos. 340-348 (9)	8.15	8.15

Souvenir Sheets

Perf. 13½

349	A47	20nu Baloo and Mowgli in forest	6.50	6.50
350	A47	20nu Baloo and Mowgli floating	6.50	6.50

George Washington Surveying — A48

1982, Nov. 15 Litho. *Perf. 15*

351	A48	50ch shown	.25	.25
352	A48	1nu FDR, Harvard	.30	.30
353	A48	2nu Washington at Valley Forge	.35	.35
354	A48	3nu FDR, family	.50	.50
355	A48	4nu Washington, Battle of Monmouth	.70	.70
356	A48	5nu FDR, White House	1.00	1.00
357	A48	15nu Washington, Mt. Vernon	2.50	2.50
358	A48	20nu FDR, Churchill, Stalin	3.25	3.25
		Nos. 351-358 (8)	8.85	8.85

Souvenir Sheets

359	A48	25nu Washington, vert.	4.50	4.50
360	A48	25nu FDR, vert.	4.50	4.50

Washington and Franklin D. Roosevelt.

Exist imperf. Values unused or used: set $12; souvenir sheet each $6.

Nos. 332-334 Overprinted: "ROYAL BABY / 21.6.82"

1982, Nov. 19 *Perf. 14½x14*

361	A45	1nu multicolored	.25	.25
361A	A45	10nu multicolored	2.50	2.50
361B	A45	15nu multicolored	3.50	3.50
362	A45	25nu multicolored	5.75	5.75
		Nos. 361-362 (4)	12.00	12.00

Souvenir Sheet

363	A45	20nu multicolored	7.50	7.50

Birth of Prince William of Wales, June 21.

Exist imperf. Values unused or used: set $17; souvenir sheet $12.

500th Birth Anniv. of Raphael A51

Portraits.

1983, Mar. 23 *Perf. 13½*

375	A51	1nu Angelo Doni	.30	.30
376	A51	4nu Maddalena Doni	1.10	1.10
377	A51	5nu Baldassare Castiglione	1.50	1.50
378	A51	20nu La Donna Velata	6.00	6.00
		Nos. 375-378 (4)	8.90	8.90

Souvenir Sheets

379	A51	25nu Expulsion of Heliodorus	8.00	8.00
380	A51	25nu Mass of Bolsena	8.00	8.00

Exist imperf. Values unused or used: set $9; souvenir sheets each $6.25.

Nos. 184, 155F, 139, 184, 147G, 149M Surchd. or Ovptd.: "Druk Air"

1983, Feb. 11

381	A24	30ch on 1ch multi	2.00	2.00
382	A17k	5nu multicolored	2.75	2.75
383	A17	6nu multicolored	3.00	3.00
384	A17d	7nu multicolored	4.25	4.25
385	A17f	8nu multicolored	4.50	4.50
		Nos. 381-385 (5)	16.50	16.50

Druk Air Service inauguration. Overprint of 8nu all caps. Nos. 382, 384 air mail.

Manned Flight Bicentenary — A52

1983, Aug. 15 Litho. *Perf. 15*

386	A52	50ch Dornier Wal	.25	.25
387	A52	3nu Savoia-Marchetti S-66	.95	.95
388	A52	10nu Hawker Osprey	2.50	2.50
389	A52	20nu Ville de Paris	5.00	5.00
		Nos. 386-389 (4)	8.70	8.70

Souvenir Sheet

390	A52	25nu Balloon Captif	7.50	7.50

Exist imperf. Values unused or used: set $9; souvenir sheet $7.

Buddhist Symbols — A53

1983, Aug. 11 Litho. *Perf. 13½*

391	A53	25ch Sacred vase	.25	.25
392	A53	50ch Five Sensory Symbols	.25	.25
393	A53	2nu Seven Treasures	.40	.40
394	A53	3nu Five Sensory Organs	.85	.85
395	A53	8nu Five Fleshes	1.90	1.90
396	A53	9nu Sacrificial cake	2.50	2.50
a.		Souv. sheet of 6, #391-396	7.50	7.50
		Nos. 391-396 (6)	6.15	6.15

Size of Nos. 393, 396: 45x40mm.

World Communications Year (1983) — A54

Various Disney characters and history of communications.

1984, Apr. 10 Litho. *Perf. 14½x14*

397	A54	4ch multicolored	.25	.25
398	A54	5ch multicolored	.25	.25
399	A54	10ch multicolored	.25	.25
400	A54	20ch multicolored	.25	.25
401	A54	25ch multicolored	.25	.25
402	A54	50ch multicolored	.25	.25
403	A54	1nu multicolored	.50	.50
404	A54	5nu multicolored	1.50	1.50
405	A54	20nu multicolored	4.25	4.25
		Nos. 397-405 (9)	7.75	7.75

Souvenir Sheets

Perf. 14x14½

406	A54	20nu Donald Duck on phone, horiz.	5.50	5.50
407	A54	20nu Mickey Mouse on TV	5.50	5.50

1984 Winter Olympics — A55

1984, June 16 *Perf. 14*

408	A55	50ch Skiing	.30	.30
409	A55	1nu Cross-country skiing	.40	.40
410	A55	3nu Speed skating	.75	.75
411	A55	20nu Bobsledding	4.00	4.00
		Nos. 408-411 (4)	5.45	5.45

Souvenir Sheet

412	A55	25nu Hockey	6.25	6.25

Exist imperf. Values unused or used: set $7; souvenir sheet $7.

Golden Langur (WWF) A56

Locomotives A57

1984, June 10 Litho. *Perf. 14½*

413	A56	50ch shown	.70	.70
414	A56	1nu Group in tree, horiz.	.70	.70
415	A56	2nu Family, horiz.	1.75	1.75
416	A56	4nu Group walking	3.25	3.25
		Nos. 413-416 (4)	6.40	6.40

Souvenir Sheets

417	A56	20nu Snow leopard	8.00	8.00
418	A56	25nu Yak	8.00	8.00
419	A56	25nu Blue sheep, horiz.	8.00	8.00

1984, July 16

420	A57	50ch Sans Pareil, 1829	.25	.25
421	A57	1nu Planet, 1830	.30	.30
422	A57	3nu Experiment, 1832	.65	.65
423	A57	4nu Black Hawk, 1835	1.00	1.00
424	A57	5.50nu Jenny Lind, 1847	1.25	1.25
425	A57	8nu Semmering-Bavaria, 1851	1.75	1.75
426	A57	10nu Great Northern #1, 1870	2.10	2.10
427	A57	25nu German Natl. Tinder, 1880	5.50	5.50
		Nos. 420-427 (8)	12.80	12.80

Souvenir Sheets

428	A57	20nu Darjeeling Himalayan Railway, 1984	5.00	5.00
429	A57	20nu Sondermann Freight, 1896	5.00	5.00
430	A57	20nu Crampton's locomotive, 1846	5.00	5.00
431	A57	20nu Erzsebet, 1870	5.00	5.00

Nos. 424-427 horiz.

Classic Cars A58

1984, Aug. 29 Litho. *Perf. 14*

432	A58	50ch Riley Sprite, 1936	.25	.25
433	A58	1nu Lanchester, 1919	.30	.30
434	A58	3nu Itala, 1907	.70	.70
435	A58	4nu Morris Oxford Bullnose, 1913	1.00	1.00
436	A58	5.50nu Lagonda LG6, 1939	1.25	1.25
437	A58	6nu Wolseley, 1903	1.40	1.40
438	A58	8nu Buick Super, 1952	1.60	1.60
439	A58	20nu Maybach Zeppelin, 1933	3.75	3.75
		Nos. 432-439 (8)	10.25	10.25

Souvenir Sheets

440	A58	25nu Simplex, 1912	5.00	5.00
441	A58	25nu Renault, 1901	5.00	5.00

Summer Olympic Games — A59

1984, Oct. 27 **Litho.**

442 A59 15ch Women's archery .25 .25
443 A59 25ch Men's archery .25 .25
444 A59 2nu Table tennis .65 .65
445 A59 2.25nu Basketball .95 .95
446 A59 5.50nu Boxing 1.25 1.25
447 A59 6nu Running 1.50 1.50
448 A59 8nu Tennis 2.25 2.25
Nos. 442-448 (7) 7.10 7.10

Souvenir Sheet

449 A59 25nu Archery 6.75 6.75

For overprints see Nos. 537-544.
Exist imperf. Values unused or used: set $8; souvenir sheet $7.

Nos. 335-339 Surcharged with New Values and Bars in Black or Silver

1985 **Litho.** ***Perf. 14***

450 A46 10nu on 3nu multi 2.50 2.25
451 A46 10nu on 5nu multi 2.50 2.25
452 A46 10nu on 15nu multi 2.50 2.25
453 A46 10nu on 20nu multi 2.50 2.25
Nos. 450-453 (4) 10.00 9.00

Souvenir Sheet

454 A46 20nu on 25nu multi 6.00 6.00

Nos. 332, 332A, 332B, 333-334 Surcharged with New Values and Bars

1985, Feb. 28

455 A45 5nu on 1nu multi 1.45 1.30
456 A45 5nu on 10nu multi 1.45 1.30
457 A45 5nu on 15nu multi 1.45 1.30
458 A45 40nu on 25nu multi 11.00 11.00
Nos. 455-458 (4) 15.35 14.90

Souvenir Sheet

459 A45 25nu on 20nu multi 11.00 11.00

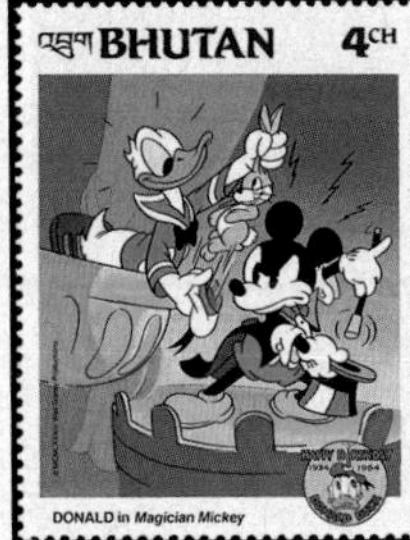

50th Anniv. of Donald Duck — A60

1984, Dec. 10 **Litho.** ***Perf. 13½x14***

460 A60 4ch Magician Mickey .25 .25
461 A60 5ch Slide, Donald, Slide .25 .25
462 A60 10ch Donald's Golf Game .25 .25
463 A60 20ch Mr. Duck Steps Out .25 .25
464 A60 25ch Lion Around .25 .25
465 A60 50ch Alpine Climbers .25 .25
466 A60 1nu Flying Jalopy .25 .25
467 A60 5nu Frank Duck 1.00 1.00
468 A60 20nu Good Scouts 4.50 4.50
Nos. 460-468 (9) 7.25 7.25

Souvenir Sheets

469 A60 20nu Three Caballeros 6.00 6.00
470 A60 20nu Sea Scouts 6.00 6.00

Exist imperf. Values unused or used: set $12; souvenir sheets each $7.

Nos. 317-321 Surcharged with New Values and Bars

1985, Feb. 28 **Litho.** ***Perf. 14½***

471 A42 10nu on 1nu multi 4.50 4.00
472 A42 10nu on 5nu multi 4.50 4.00
473 A42 10nu on 20nu multi 4.50 4.00
474 A42 10nu on 25nu multi 4.50 4.00
Nos. 471-474 (4) 18.00 16.00

Souvenir Sheet

475 A42 30nu on 20nu multi 11.00 11.00

Nos. 361, 361A, 361B, 362-363 Surcharged with New Values and Bars

1985, Feb. 28 ***Perf. 14½x14***

476 A45 5nu on 1nu multi 1.45 1.30
477 A45 5nu on 10nu multi 1.45 1.30
478 A45 5nu on 15nu multi 1.45 1.30
479 A45 40nu on 25nu multi 11.00 11.00
Nos. 476-479 (4) 15.35 14.90

Souvenir Sheet

480 A45 25nu on 20nu multi 11.00 9.00

Nos. 327-331A Surcharged with New Values and Bars in Black or Silver

1985, June

481 A44 5nu on 1nu multi 2.25 2.00
482 A44 5nu on 2nu multi 2.25 2.00
483 A44 5nu on 3nu multi 2.25 2.00
484 A44 5nu on 20nu multi 2.25 2.00
Nos. 481-484 (4) 9.00 8.00

Souvenir Sheets

485 A44 20nu on 25nu multi 4.50 4.25
485A A44 20nu on 25nu multi 4.50 4.25

Mask Dance of the Judgement of Death — A61

1985, Apr. 27 ***Perf. 13½***

486 A61 5ch Shinje Choe-gyel .35 .35
487 A61 35ch Raksh Lango .35 .35
488 A61 50ch Druelgo .35 .35
489 A61 2.50nu Pago .50 .50
490 A61 3nu Telgo .70 .70
491 A61 4nu Due Nakcung .90 .90
492 A61 5nu Lha Karpo 1.00 1.00
a. Souv. sheet, #486-487, 491-492 4.50 4.50
493 A61 5.50nu Nyalbum 1.25 1.25
494 A61 6nu Khimda Pelkyi 1.40 1.40
Nos. 486-494 (9) 6.80 6.80

For overprints see Nos. 764-772.

Monasteries A62

1984, Dec. 1 **Litho.** ***Perf. 12***

495 A62 10ch Domkhar .30 .30
496 A62 25ch Shemgang .30 .30
497 A62 50ch Chapcha .30 .30
498 A62 1nu Tashigang .30 .30
499 A62 2nu Pungthang Chhug .45 .45
500 A62 5nu Dechhenphoda 1.00 1.00
Nos. 495-500 (6) 2.65 2.65

For surcharges, see Nos. 1344-1347B.

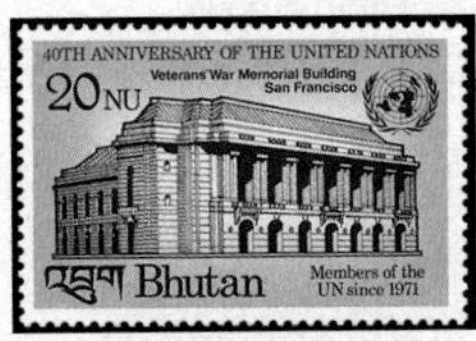

Veteran's War Memorial Building, San Francisco A63

1985, Oct. 24 **Litho.** ***Perf. 14***

502 A63 50ch Flags of Bhutan, UN, vert. .25 .25
503 A63 15nu Headquarters, NY, vert. 2.75 2.75
504 A63 20nu shown 3.75 3.75
Nos. 502-504 (3) 6.75 6.75

Souvenir Sheet

505 A63 25nu UN Human Rights Declaration 6.50 6.50

UN, 40th anniv.

Audubon Birth Bicentenary — A64

Illustrations of North American bird species by Audubon.

1985

506 A64 50ch Anas breweri .25 .25
507 A64 1nu Lagopus lagopus .35 .35
508 A64 2nu Charadrius montanus .55 .55
509 A64 3nu Gavia stellata .60 .60
510 A64 4nu Canachites canadensis .90 .90
511 A64 5nu Mergus cucullatus 1.00 1.00
512 A64 15nu Olor buccinator 2.50 2.50
513 A64 20nu Bucephala clangula 4.00 4.00
Nos. 506-513 (8) 10.15 10.15

Souvenir Sheets

514 A64 25nu Accipiter striatus 5.00 5.00
515 A64 25nu Parus bicolor 5.00 5.00

Issued: Nos. 507, 510-512, 514, 11/15; Nos. 506, 508-509, 513, 515, 12/6.
Exist imperf. Values unused or used: set $20; souvenir sheets, each $7.50.

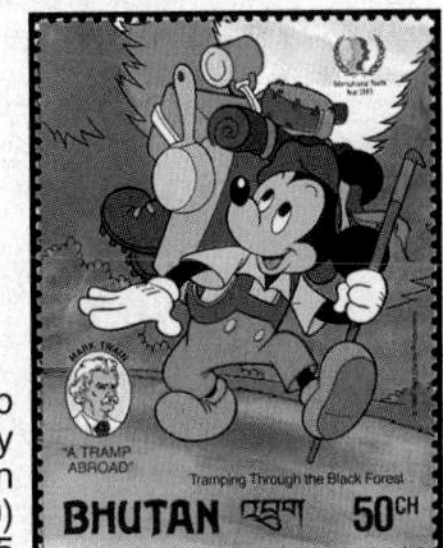

A Tramp Abroad, by Mark Twain (1835-1910) A65

Walt Disney animated characters.

1985, Nov. 15

516 A65 50ch multicolored .30 .25
517 A65 2nu multicolored .50 .50
518 A65 5nu multicolored 1.10 1.10
519 A65 9nu multicolored 2.00 2.00
520 A65 20nu multicolored 4.25 4.25
Nos. 516-520 (5) 8.15 8.10

Souvenir Sheet

521 A65 25nu Goofy, Mickey Mouse 6.50 6.50

Intl. Youth Year.
For overprints see Nos. 554, 556-557.

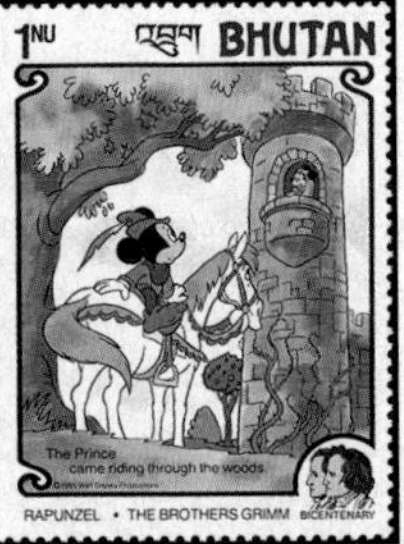

Rapunzel, by Jacob and Wilhelm Grimm A66

Walt Disney animated characters.

1985, Nov. 15

522 A66 1nu multicolored .25 .25
523 A66 4nu multicolored .75 .75
524 A66 7nu multicolored 1.40 1.40
525 A66 8nu multicolored 1.75 1.75
526 A66 15nu multicolored 3.00 3.00
Nos. 522-526 (5) 7.15 7.15

Souvenir Sheet

527 A66 25nu multicolored 6.50 6.50

No. 525 printed in sheets of 8.
For overprints see Nos. 553, 555, 558.

First South Asian Regional Cooperation Summit, Dec. 7-8, Dacca, Bangladesh A67

1985, Dec. 8 ***Perf. 14***

528 A67 50ch multicolored .25 .25
529 A67 5nu multicolored 1.00 1.00

Seven Precious Attributes of the Universal King — A68

1986, Feb. 12 **Litho.** ***Perf. 13x12½***

530 A68 30ch Wheel .25 .25
531 A68 50ch Gem .25 .25
532 A68 1.25nu Queen .25 .25
533 A68 2nu Minister .45 .45
534 A68 4nu Elephant .80 .80
535 A68 6nu Horse 1.25 1.25
536 A68 8nu General 1.60 1.60
Nos. 530-536 (7) 4.85 4.85

Nos. 442-443, 445-449 Ovptd. with Medal, Winners' Names and Countries. No. 449 Ovptd. for Men's and Women's Events

1986, May 5 **Litho.** ***Perf. 14***

537 A59 15ch Hyang Soon Seo, So. Korea .25 .25
538 A59 25ch Darrell Pace, US .25 .25
539 A59 2.25nu US .45 .45
540 A59 5.50nu Mark Breland, US 1.10 1.10
541 A59 6nu Daley Thompson, Britain 1.25 1.25
542 A59 8nu Stefan Edberg, Sweden 1.60 1.60
Nos. 537-542 (6) 4.90 4.90

Souvenir Sheets

543 A59 25nu Hyang Soon Seo 5.00 5.00
544 A59 25nu Darrel Pace 5.00 5.00

Kilkhor Mandalas, Deities — A69

Religious art: 10ch, 1nu, Phurpa, ritual dagger. 25ch, 3nu, Amitayus in wrath. 50ch, 5nu, Overpowering Deities. 75ch, 7nu, Great Wrathful One, Guru Rinpoche.

1986, June 17 ***Perf. 13½***

545 A69 10ch multicolored .50 .50
546 A69 25ch multicolored .50 .50
547 A69 50ch multicolored .50 .50
548 A69 75ch multicolored .50 .50
549 A69 1nu multicolored .50 .50
550 A69 3nu multicolored .65 .65
551 A69 5nu multicolored 1.10 1.10
552 A69 7nu multicolored 1.60 1.60
Nos. 545-552 (8) 5.85 5.85

Nos. 525, 519, 526, 520, 521 and 527 Ovptd. with AMERIPEX '86 Emblem

1986, June 16 **Litho.** ***Perf. 14***

553 A66 8nu multi 1.40 1.40
554 A65 9nu multi 2.25 2.25
555 A66 15nu multi 3.50 3.50
556 A65 20nu multi 4.50 4.50
Nos. 553-556 (4) 11.65 11.65

Souvenir Sheets

557 A65 25nu #521 6.00 6.00
558 A66 25nu #527 6.00 6.00

Nos. 335-339 Overprinted

1986, July 23 Litho. *Perf. 14*

559 A46 3nu multi 1.90 1.90
560 A46 5nu multi 3.75 3.75
561 A46 15nu multi 10.00 10.00
562 A46 20nu multi 14.00 14.00
Nos. 559-562 (4) 29.65 29.65

Souvenir Sheet

563 A46 25nu multi 15.00 15.00

A70

A71

Halley's Comet — A72

Designs: 50ch, Babylonian tablet fragments, 2349 B.C. sighting. 1nu, 17th cent. print, A.D. 66 sighting. 2nu, French silhouette art, 1835 sighting. 3nu, Bayeux Tapestry, 1066 sighting. 4nu, Woodblock, 684 sighting. 5nu, Illustration from Bybel Printen, 1650. 15nu, 1456 Sighting, Cancer constellation. 20nu, Delft plate, 1910 sighting. No. 572, Comet over Himalayas. No. 573, Comet over domed temple Dug-gye Jong.

1986, Nov. 4 Litho. *Perf. 15*

564 A70 50ch multicolored .30 .30
565 A70 1nu multicolored .30 .30
566 A71 2nu multicolored .45 .45
567 A70 3nu multicolored .60 .60
568 A70 4nu multicolored .90 .90
569 A71 5nu multicolored 1.10 1.10
570 A70 15nu multicolored 3.00 3.00
571 A70 20nu multicolored 4.50 4.50
Nos. 564-571 (8) 11.15 11.15

Souvenir Sheets

572 A72 25nu multicolored 5.00 5.00
573 A72 25nu multicolored 5.00 5.00

Exist imperf. Values unused or used: set $20; souvenir sheets, each $11.

A73

Statue of Liberty, Cent. — A74

Statue and ships: 50ch, Mircea, Romania. 1nu, Shalom, Israel. 2nu, Leonardo da Vinci, Italy. 3nu, Libertad, Argentina. 4nu, France, France. 5nu, SS United States, US. 15nu, Queen Elizabeth II, England. 20nu, Europa, West Germany. No. 582, Statue. No. 583, Statue, World Trade Center.

1986, Nov. 4

574 A73 50ch multicolored .25 .25
575 A73 1nu multicolored .25 .25
576 A73 2nu multicolored .45 .45
577 A73 3nu multicolored .65 .65
578 A73 4nu multicolored .80 .80
579 A73 5nu multicolored 1.10 1.10
580 A73 15nu multicolored 3.00 3.00
581 A73 20nu multicolored 4.50 4.50
Nos. 574-581 (8) 11.00 11.00

Souvenir Sheets

582 A74 25nu multicolored 5.00 5.00
583 A74 25nu multi, diff. 5.00 5.00

Exist imperf. Values unused or used: set $11; souvenir sheets each $6.

Discovery of America, 500th Anniv. — A75

1987, May 25 Litho. *Perf. 14*

584 A75 20ch Santa Maria .90 .90
585 A75 25ch Queen Isabella .90 .90
586 A75 50ch Ship, flying fish .90 .90
587 A75 1nu Columbus's coat of arms 1.75 1.75
588 A75 2nu Christopher Columbus 3.00 3.00
589 A75 3nu Landing in the New World 4.50 4.50
a. Miniature sheet of 6, #584-589 16.00 16.00
Nos. 584-589 (6) 11.95 11.95

Souvenir Sheets

590 A75 20ch Pineapple 2.50 2.50
591 A75 25ch Indian hammock 2.50 2.50
592 A75 50ch Tobacco plant 2.50 2.50
593 A75 1nu Flamingo 2.50 2.50
594 A75 2nu Navigator, astrolabe, 15th cent. 2.50 2.50
595 A75 3nu Lizard 2.50 2.50
596 A75 5nu Iguana 2.50 2.50

All stamps are vertical except those contained in Nos. 591, 595 and 596. Stamps from No. 589a have white background.

Exist imperf. Values unused or used: set $18; souvenir sheets each $4.

CAPEX '87 — A76

Locomotives.

1987, June 15

597 A76 50ch Canadian Natl. U1-f .25 .25
598 A76 1nu Via Rail L.R.C. .25 .25
599 A76 2nu Canadian Natl. GM GF-30t .45 .45
600 A76 3nu Canadian Natl. 4-8-4 .75 .75
601 A76 8nu Canadian Pacific 4-6-2 1.75 1.75
602 A76 10nu Via Express passenger train 1.90 1.90
603 A76 15nu Canadian Nat. Turbotrain 2.50 2.50
604 A76 20nu Canadian Pacific Diesel-Electric Express 3.25 3.25
Nos. 597-604 (8) 11.10 11.10

Souvenir Sheet

605 A76 25nu Royal Hudson 4-6-4 5.50 5.50
606 A76 25nu Canadian Natl. 4-8-4, diff. 5.50 5.50

Two Faces, Sculpture by Marc Chagall (1887-1984) A77

Paintings: 1nu, At the Barber's. 2nu, Old Jew with Torah. 3nu, Red Maternity. 4nu, Eve of Yom Kippur. 5nu, The Old Musician. 6nu, The Rabbi of Vitebsk. 7nu, Couple at Dusk. 9nu, The Artistes. 10nu, Moses Breaking the Tablets of the Law. 12nu, Bouquet with Flying Lovers. 20nu, In the Sky of the Opera.

No. 619, Romeo and Juliet. No. 620, Magician of Paris. No. 621, Maternity. No. 622, The Carnival for Aleko: Scene II. No. 623, Visit to the Grandparents. No. 624, The Smolensk Newspaper. No. 625, The Concert. No. 626, Composition with Goat. No. 627, Still Life. No. 628. The Red Gateway. No. 629, Cow with Parasol. No. 630, Russian Village.

1987, Dec. 17 Litho. *Perf. 14*

607-618 A77 Set of 12 20.00 20.00

Size: 110x95mm

Imperf

619-630 A77 25nu Set of 12 65.00 65.00

1988 Winter Olympics, Calgary — A78

Emblem and Disney animated characters as competitors in Olympic events.

1988, Feb. 15 Litho. *Perf. 14*

631 A78 50ch Slalom .30 .30
632 A78 1nu Downhill skiing .30 .30
633 A78 2nu Ice hockey .50 .50
634 A78 4nu Biathlon 1.00 1.00
635 A78 7nu Speed skating 1.75 1.75
636 A78 8nu Figure skating 2.00 2.00
637 A78 9nu Figure skating, diff. 2.40 2.40
638 A78 20nu Bobsled 5.00 5.00
Nos. 631-638 (8) 13.25 13.25

Souvenir Sheets

639 A78 25nu Ski jumping 6.25 6.25
640 A78 25nu Ice dancing 6.25 6.25

Transportation Innovations — A79

1988, Mar. 31

641 A79 50ch Pullman Pioneer, 1865 .25 .25
642 A79 1nu Stephenson's Rocket, 1829 .25 .25
643 A79 2nu Pierre L'Allement's Velocipede, 1866 .35 .35
644 A79 3nu Benz Velocipede, 1886 .50 .50
645 A79 4nu Volkswagen Beetle, c. 1960 .60 .60
646 A79 5nu Natchez Vs. Robert E. Lee, 1870 .70 .70
647 A79 6nu American La France, 1910 .90 .90
648 A79 7nu USS Constitution, 1787, vert. 1.00 1.00
649 A79 9nu Bell Rocket Belt, 1961, vert. 1.45 1.45
650 A79 10nu Trevithick Locomotive, 1804 1.50 1.50
Nos. 641-650 (10) 7.50 7.50

Souvenir Sheets

651 A79 25nu Concorde jet 6.00 6.00
652 A79 25nu Mallard, 1938, vert. 6.00 6.00
653 A79 25nu Shinkansen 6.00 6.00
654 A79 25nu TGV, 1981 6.00 6.00

1988 Summer Olympics, Seoul A80

7nu-20nu vert.

1989, Feb. 15 Litho.

655 A80 50ch Women's gymnastics .25 .25
656 A80 1nu Tae kwon do .25 .25
657 A80 2nu Shot put .35 .35
658 A80 4nu Women's volleyball .75 .75
659 A80 7nu Basketball 1.25 1.25
660 A80 8nu Soccer 1.50 1.50
661 A80 9nu Women's high jump 1.75 1.75
662 A80 20nu Running 3.75 3.75
Nos. 655-662 (8) 9.85 9.85

Souvenir Sheets

663 A80 25nu Archery, vert. 5.00 5.00
664 A80 25nu Fencing 5.00 5.00

Exist imperf. Values unused or used: set $10; souvenir sheets each $5.

Paintings by Titian — A81

Designs: 50ch, *Gentleman with a Book.* 1nu, *Venus and Cupid, with a Lute Player.* 2nu, *Diana and Actaeon.* 3nu, *Cardinal Ippolito dei Medici.* 4nu, *Sleeping Venus.* 5nu, *Venus Risen from the Waves.* 6nu, *Worship of Venus.* 7nu, *Fete Champetre.* 10nu, *Perseus and Andromeda.* 15nu, *Danae.* 20nu, *Venus at the Mirror.* 25nu, *Venus and the Organ Player.* No. 677, *The Pardo Venus,* horiz. No. 678, *Venus and Cupid, with an Organist.* No. 679, *Miracle of the Irascible Son.* No. 680, *Diana and Callisto.* No. 681, *Saint John the Almsgiver.* No. 682, *Danae with the Shower of Gold,* horiz. No. 683, *Bacchus and Ariadne.* No. 684, *Venus Blindfolding Cupid.* No. 685, *Portrait of Laura Dianti.* No. 686, *Venus of Urbino.* No. 687, *Portrait of Johann Friedrich.* No. 688, *Mater Dolorosa with Raised Hands.*

Perf. 13½x14, 14x13½

1989, Feb. 15 Litho.

665 A81 50ch multicolored .25 .25
666 A81 1nu multicolored .30 .30
667 A81 2nu multicolored .50 .50
668 A81 3nu multicolored .70 .70
669 A81 4nu multicolored .85 .85
670 A81 5nu multicolored 1.25 1.25
671 A81 6nu multicolored 1.40 1.40
672 A81 7nu multicolored 1.60 1.60
673 A81 10nu multicolored 2.10 2.10
674 A81 15nu multicolored 3.25 3.25
675 A81 20nu multicolored 4.00 4.00
676 A81 25nu multicolored 5.00 5.00
Nos. 665-676 (12) 21.20 21.20

Souvenir Sheets

677-688 A81 25nu Set of 12 60.00 60.00

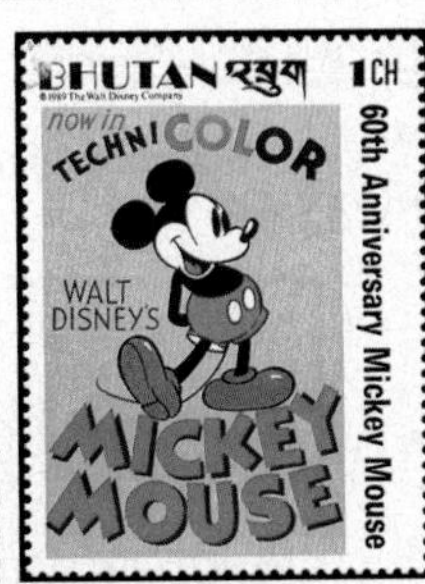

Mickey Mouse, 60th Anniv. (in 1988) — A82

Movie posters: 1ch, Mickey Mouse, 1930s. 2ch, *Barnyard Olympics,* 1932. 3ch, *Society Dog Show,* 1939. 4ch, *Fantasia,* 1980s re-release. 5ch, *The Mad Dog,* 1932. 10ch, *A Gentleman's Gentleman,* 1941. 50ch, *Symphony hour,* 1942. 10nu, *The Moose Hunt,* 1931. 15nu, *Wild Waves,* 1929. 20nu, *Mickey in Arabia,* 1932. 25nu, *Tugboat Mickey,* 1940. 30nu, *Building a Building,* 1933.

No. 701, *The Mad Doctor,* 1933. No. 702, *The Meller Drammer,* 1933. No. 703, *Ye Olden Days,* 1933. No. 704, *Mickey's Good Deed,* 1932. No. 705, *Mickey's Pal Pluto,* 1933. No. 706, *Trader Mickey,* 1932. No. 707, *Touchdown Mickey,* 1932. No. 708, *Steamboat Willie,* 1928. No. 709, *The Whoopee Party,* 1932. No. 710, *Mickey's Nightmare,* 1932. No. 711, *The Klondike Kid,* 1932. No. 712, *The Wayward Canary,* 1932.

1989, June 20 Litho. *Perf. 13½x14*

689-700 A82 Set of 12 22.50 22.50

Souvenir Sheets

701-712 A82 25nu Set of 12 65.00 65.00

Mushrooms — A83

Designs: 50ch, Tricholoma pardalotum. 1nu, Suillus placidus. 2nu, Boletus regius. 3nu, Gomphidius glutinosus. 4nu, Boletus calopus. 5nu, Suillus grevillei. 6nu, Boletus appendiculatus. 7nu, Lactarius torminosus. 10nu, Macrolepiota rhacodes. 15nu, Amanita rubescens. 20nu, Amanita phalloides. No. 724, Amanita citrina.

No. 725, Russula aurata. No. 726, Gyroporus castaneus. No. 727, Cantharellus cibarius. No. 728, Boletus rhodoxanthus. No. 729, Paxillus involutus. No. 730, Gyroporus cyanescens. No. 731, Lepista nuda. No. 732, Dentinum repandum. No. 733, Lepista saeva. No. 734, Hydnum imbricatum. No. 735, Xerocomus subtomentosus. No. 736, Russula olivacea.

1989, Aug. 22 Litho. *Perf. 14*

713	A83	50ch multicolored	.25	.25
714	A83	1nu multicolored	.25	.25
715	A83	2nu multicolored	.40	.40
716	A83	3nu multicolored	.65	.65
717	A83	4nu multicolored	.80	.80
718	A83	5nu multicolored	1.00	1.00
719	A83	6nu multicolored	1.10	1.10
720	A83	7nu multicolored	1.40	1.40
721	A83	10nu multicolored	2.00	2.00
722	A83	15nu multicolored	3.00	3.00
723	A83	20nu multicolored	4.00	4.00
724	A83	25nu multicolored	5.00	5.00
		Nos. 713-724 (12)	19.85	19.85

Souvenir Sheets

725	A83	25nu multicolored	5.50	5.50
726	A83	25nu multicolored	5.50	5.50
727	A83	25nu multicolored	5.50	5.50
728	A83	25nu multicolored	5.50	5.50
729	A83	25nu multicolored	5.50	5.50
730	A83	25nu multicolored	5.50	5.50
731	A83	25nu multicolored	5.50	5.50
732	A83	25nu multicolored	5.50	5.50
733	A83	25nu multicolored	5.50	5.50
734	A83	25nu multicolored	5.50	5.50
735	A83	25nu multicolored	5.50	5.50
736	A83	25nu multicolored	5.50	5.50
		Nos. 725-736 (12)	66.00	66.00

Intl. Maritime Organization, 30th Anniv. — A84

Ships: 50ch, Spanish galleon *La Reale,* 1680. 1 nu, Submersible *Turtle,* 1776. 2nu, *Charlote Dundas,* 1802. 3nu, *Great Eastern,* c. 1858. 4nu, HMS *Warrior,* 1862. 5nu, Mississippi steamer, 1884. 6nu, *Preussen,* 1902. 7nu, USS *Arizona,* 1915. 10nu, *Bluenose,* 1921. 15nu, Steam trawler, 1925. 20nu, American liberty ship, 1943. No. 748, S.S. *United States,* 1952.

Each 25nu: No. 749, Moran tug, c. 1950. No. 750, Sinking of the *Titanic,* 1912. No. 751, U-boat, c. 1942. No. 752, Japanese warship *Yamato,* 1944. No. 753, HMS *Dreadnought.* No. 754, S.S. *Normandie,* c. 1933, and a Chinese junk. No. 755, HMS *Victory,* 1805. No. 756, USS *Monitor,* 1862. No. 757, *Cutty Sark,* 1869. No. 758, USS *Constitution.* No. 759, HMS *Resolution.* No. 760, Chinese junk.

1989, Aug. 24 Litho. *Perf. 14*

737	A84	50ch multicolored	.25	.25
738	A84	1nu multicolored	.40	.40
739	A84	2nu multicolored	.75	.75
740	A84	3nu multicolored	1.00	1.00
741	A84	4nu multicolored	1.25	1.25
742	A84	5nu multicolored	1.40	1.40
743	A84	6nu multicolored	1.90	1.90
744	A84	7nu multicolored	2.00	2.00
745	A84	10nu multicolored	2.50	2.50
746	A84	15nu multicolored	3.50	3.50
747	A84	20nu multicolored	4.25	4.25
748	A84	25nu multicolored	5.75	5.75
		Nos. 737-748 (12)	24.95	24.95

Souvenir Sheets

749-760 A84 Set of 12 66.00 66.00

Nos. 289-291 Overprinted: WORLD / AIDS DAY

1988, Dec. 1 Litho. *Perf. 14x13½*

761	A37	2nu multicolored	.60	.60
762	A37	5nu multicolored	1.40	1.40
763	A37	10nu multicolored	3.50	3.50
		Nos. 761-763 (3)	5.50	5.50

Nos. 486-494 Ovptd. in Silver: AISA-PACIFIC EXPOSITION / FUKUOKA '89

1989, Mar. 17 *Perf. 13½*

764	A61	5ch multicolored	.25	.25
765	A61	35ch multicolored	.25	.25
766	A61	50ch multicolored	.25	.25
767	A61	2.50nu multicolored	.45	.45
768	A61	3nu multicolored	.55	.55
769	A61	4nu multicolored	.70	.70
770	A61	5nu multicolored	.95	.95
771	A61	5.50nu multicolored	1.00	1.00
772	A61	6nu multicolored	1.10	1.10
		Nos. 764-772 (9)	5.50	5.50

This set exists overprinted in Japanese.

Chhukha Hydroelectric Project — A85

1988, Oct. 21 Litho. *Perf. 13½*

773 A85 50ch multicolored .50 .50

Jawaharlal Nehru (1889-1964), Indian Prime Minister A85a

1989, Nov. 14 Photo. *Perf. 14*

773A A85a 100ch olive brown .40 .40

Denomination is shown as 1.00ch in error.

Birds A86

Designs: 50ch, Larger goldenbacked woodpecker. 1nu, Black-naped monarch. 2nu, White-crested laughing thrush. 3nu, Blood-pheasant. 4nu, Blossom-headed parakeet. 5nu, Rosy minivet. 6nu, Chestnut-headed tit babbler. 7nu, Blue pitta. 10nu, Black-naped oriole. 15nu, Green magpie. 20nu, Indian three-toed kingfisher. No. 785, Ibisbill.

Each 25nu:No. 786, Great pied hornbill. No. 787, Himalayan redbreasted falconet. No. 788, Lammergeier. No. 789, Large racket-tailed drongo. No. 790, Fire-tailed sunbird. No. 791, Indian crested swift. No. 792, White-eared pheasant. No. 793, Satyr tragopan. No. 794, Wallcreeper. No. 795, Fairy bluebird. No. 796, Little spiderhunter. No. 797, Spotted forktail. Nos. 774-779 vert.

1989, Nov. 22 Litho. *Perf. 14*

774	A86	50ch multicolored	.25	.25
775	A86	1nu multicolored	.40	.40
776	A86	2nu multicolored	.75	.75
777	A86	3nu multicolored	1.00	1.00
778	A86	4nu multicolored	1.25	1.25
779	A86	5nu multicolored	1.40	1.40
780	A86	6nu multicolored	1.90	1.90
781	A86	7nu multicolored	2.00	2.00
782	A86	10nu multicolored	2.50	2.50
783	A86	15nu multicolored	3.50	3.50
784	A86	20nu multicolored	4.25	4.25
785	A86	25nu multicolored	5.75	5.75
		Nos. 774-785 (12)	24.95	24.95

Souvenir Sheets

786-797 A86 Set of 12 60.00 60.00

Steam Locomotives — A87

Designs: 50ch, *Best Friend of Charleston,* 1830, US 1nu, Class U, 1949, France. 2nu, *Consolidation,* 1866, US. 3nu, *Luggage Engine,* 1843, Great Britain. 4nu, Class 60-3 Shay, 1913, US. 5nu, *John Bull,* 1831, US. 6nu, *Hercules,* 1837, US. 7nu, Eight-wheel tank engine, 1874, Great Britain. 10nu, *The Illinois,* 1852, US. 15nu, German State 4-6-4, 1935. 20nu, American Standard, 1865. No. 809, Class Ps-4, 1926, US.

Each 25nu: No. 810, *Puffing Billy,* 1814, Great Britain. No. 811, Stephenson's *Rocket,* 1829, Great Britain. No. 812, *Cumberland,* 1845, US, vert. No. 813, *John Stevens,* 1849, US, vert. No. 814, No. 22 Baldwin Locomotive Works, 1873, US, No. 815, *Ariel,* 1877, US. No. 816, 1899 *No. 1301* Webb Compound Engine, Great Britain. No. 817, 1893 *No. 999* Empire State Express, US. No. 818, 1923 Class K-36, US. No. 819, 1935 Class A4, Great Britain. No. 820, 1935 Class A, US. No. 821, 1943 Class P-1, US.

1990, Jan. 30

798	A87	50ch multi	.25	.25
799	A87	1nu multi	.25	.25
800	A87	2nu multi	.40	.40
801	A87	3nu multi	.65	.65
802	A87	4nu multi	.80	.80
803	A87	5nu multi	1.00	1.00
804	A87	6nu multi	1.10	1.10
805	A87	7nu multi	1.40	1.40
806	A87	10nu multi	2.00	2.00
807	A87	15nu multi	3.00	3.00
808	A87	20nu multi	4.00	4.00
809	A87	25nu multi	5.00	5.00
		Nos. 798-809 (12)	19.85	19.85

Souvenir Sheets

810-821 A87 Set of 12 60.00 60.00

Butterflies A88

Designs: 50ch, Charaxes harmodius. 1nu, Prioneris thestylis. 2nu, Sephisa chandra. 3nu, Penthema usarda. 4nu, Troides aecus. 5nu, Polyura eudamippus. 6nu, Polyura dolon. 7nu, Neope bhadra. 10nu, Delias descombesis. 15nu, Childreni childrena. 20nu, Kallima inachus. No. 833, Elymnias malelas.

No. 834, Red lacewing. No. 835, Bhutan glory. No. 836, Great eggfly. No. 837, Kaiser-I-Hind. No. 838, Chestnut tiger. No. 839, Common map. No. 840, Swallowtail. No. 841, Jungle glory. No. 842, Checkered swallowtail. No. 843, Common birdwing. No. 844, Blue banded peacock. No. 845, Camberwell beauty.

1990, Jan. 30 Litho. *Perf. 14*

822	A88	50ch multicolored	.25	.25
823	A88	1nu multicolored	.25	.25
824	A88	2nu multicolored	.45	.45
825	A88	3nu multicolored	.75	.75
826	A88	4nu multicolored	.90	.90
827	A88	5nu multicolored	1.10	1.10
828	A88	6nu multicolored	1.25	1.25
829	A88	7nu multicolored	1.50	1.50
830	A88	10nu multicolored	2.25	2.25
831	A88	15nu multicolored	3.50	3.50
832	A88	20nu multicolored	4.75	4.75
833	A88	25nu multicolored	5.75	5.75
		Nos. 822-833 (12)	22.70	22.70

Souvenir Sheets

834	A88	25nu multicolored	5.00	5.00
835	A88	25nu multicolored	5.00	5.00
836	A88	25nu multicolored	5.00	5.00
837	A88	25nu multicolored	5.00	5.00
838	A88	25nu multicolored	5.00	5.00
839	A88	25nu multicolored	5.00	5.00
840	A88	25nu multicolored	5.00	5.00
841	A88	25nu multicolored	5.00	5.00
842	A88	25nu multicolored	5.00	5.00
843	A88	25nu multicolored	5.00	5.00
844	A88	25nu multicolored	5.00	5.00
845	A88	25nu multicolored	5.00	5.00
		Nos. 834-845 (12)	60.00	60.00

Nos. 822-824, 826-827, 830-831, 834-835, 844-845 are vert.

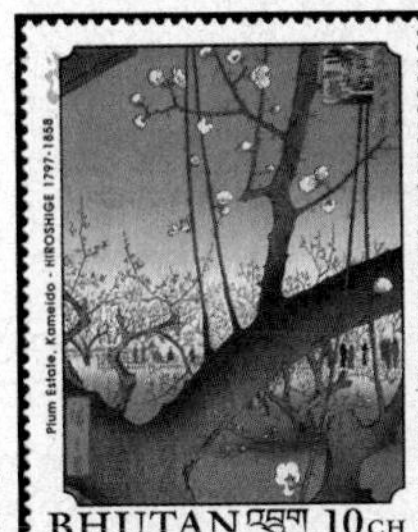

Paintings by Hiroshige A89

10ch, Plum Estate, Kameido. 20ch, Yatsumi Bridge. 50ch, Ayase River and Kanegafuchi. 75ch, View of Shiba Coast. 1nu, Grandpa's Teahouse, Meguro. 2nu, Kameido Tenjin Shrine. 6nu, Yoroi Ferry, Koami-cho. 7nu, Sakasai Ferry. 10nu, Fukagawa Lumberyards. 15nu, Suido Bridge & Surugadai. 20nu, Meguro Drum Bridge, Sunset Hill. #857, Atagoshita & Yabu Lane.

Each 25nu: No. 858, Towboats Along the Yotsugi-dori Canal. No. 859, Minowa, Kanasugi, Mikawashima. No. 860, Horikiri Iris Garden. No. 861, Fukagawa Susaki & Jumantsubo. No. 862, Suijin Shrine & Massaki on the Sumida River. No. 863, New Year's Eve Foxfires at the Changing Tree, Oji. No. 864, Nihonbashi, Clearing After Snow. No. 865, View to the North from Asukayama. No. 866, Komakata Hall & Azuma Bridge. No. 867, The City Flourishing, Tanabata Festival. No. 868, Suruga-cho. No. 869, Sudden Shower over Shin-Ohashi Bridge & Atake.

1990, May 21 Litho. *Perf. 13½*

846	A89	10ch multicolored	.25	.25
847	A89	20ch multicolored	.25	.25
848	A89	50ch multicolored	.25	.25
849	A89	75ch multicolored	.25	.25
850	A89	1nu multicolored	.25	.25
851	A89	2nu multicolored	.40	.40
852	A89	6nu multicolored	1.40	1.40
853	A89	7nu multicolored	1.50	1.50
854	A89	10nu multicolored	2.25	2.25
855	A89	15nu multicolored	3.50	3.50
856	A89	20nu multicolored	4.50	4.50
857	A89	25nu multicolored	5.25	5.25
		Nos. 846-857 (12)	20.05	20.05

Souvenir Sheets

858-869 A89 Set of 12 62.50 62.50

Hirohito (1901-1989) and enthronement of Akihito as emperor of Japan.

Orchids — A90

Designs: 10ch, Renanthera monachica. 50ch, Vanda coerulea. 1nu, Phalaenopsis violacea. 2nu, Dendrobium nobile. 5nu, Vandopsis lissochiloides. 6nu, Paphiopedilum rothschildianum. 7nu, Phalaenopsis schilleriana.

9nu, Paphiopedilum insigne. 10nu, Paphiopedilum bellatulum. 20nu, Doritis pulcherrima. 25nu, Cymbidium giganteum. 35nu, Phalaenopsis mariae.

No. 882, Vanda coerulescens. No. 883, Vandopsis parishi. No. 884, Dendrobium aphyllum. No. 885, Phalaenopsis amabilis. No. 886, Paphiopedilum haynaldianum. No. 887, Dendrobium loddigesii. No. 888, Vanda alpina. No. 889, Phalaenopsis equestris. No. 890, Vanda cristata. No. 891, Phalaenopsis cornu cervi. No. 892, Paphiopedilum niveum. No. 893, Dendrobium margaritaceum.

1990, Apr. 6 Litho. *Perf. 14*

870 A90 10ch multicolored .25 .25
871 A90 50ch multicolored .25 .25
872 A90 1nu multicolored .25 .25
873 A90 2nu multicolored .45 .45
874 A90 5nu multicolored 1.00 1.00
875 A90 6nu multicolored 1.25 1.25
876 A90 7nu multicolored 1.40 1.40
877 A90 9nu multicolored 1.75 1.75
878 A90 10nu multicolored 1.90 1.90
879 A90 20nu multicolored 3.50 3.50
880 A90 25nu multicolored 4.25 4.25
881 A90 35nu multicolored 5.75 5.75
Nos. 870-881 (12) 22.00 22.00

Souvenir Sheets

882 A90 30nu multicolored 6.00 6.00
883 A90 30nu multicolored 6.00 6.00
884 A90 30nu multicolored 6.00 6.00
885 A90 30nu multicolored 6.00 6.00
886 A90 30nu multicolored 6.00 6.00
887 A90 30nu multicolored 6.00 6.00
888 A90 30nu multicolored 6.00 6.00
889 A90 30nu multicolored 6.00 6.00
890 A90 30nu multicolored 6.00 6.00
891 A90 30nu multicolored 6.00 6.00
892 A90 30nu multicolored 6.00 6.00
893 A90 30nu multicolored 6.00 6.00
Nos. 882-893 (12) 72.00 72.00

EXPO '90 Intl. Garden and Greenery Exposition, Osaka, Apr. 1-Dec. 31.

G.P.O., Thimphu — A90a

1990, May 29 Photo. *Perf. 14*

893A A90a 1nu multicolored .75 .75

Penny Black, 150th Anniv. A90b

Penny Black and: 50ch, Bhutan #1. 1nu, Oldenburg #1. 2nu, Bergedorf #3. 4nu, German Democratic Republic #48. 5nu, Brunswick #1. 6nu, Basel #3L1. 8nu, Geneva #2L1. 10nu, Zurich #1L1. No. 902, France #3. 20nu, Vatican City #1. 25nu, Israel #1. No. 905, Japan #1.

Each 15nu: Penny Black and: No. 906a, Mecklenburg-Schwerin #1. b, Mecklenburg-Strelitz #1. No. 907a, Germany #5, #9. b, Prussia #2. No. 908a, Hamburg #1. b, North German Confederation #1, #7. No. 909a, Baden #1. b, Wurttemberg #1. No. 910a, Heligoland #1. b, Hanover #1. No. 911a, Thurn & Taxis #3. b, Thurn & Taxis #42. No. 912a, Schleswig-Holstein #1. b, Lubeck #5.

Each 30nu: No. 913, Saxony #1. No. 914, Berlin #9N1. No. 915, No other stamp. No. 916, US #1. No. 917, Bavaria #1.

1990, Oct. 9 *Perf. 14*

894 A90b 50ch multicolored .25 .25
895 A90b 1nu multicolored .25 .25
896 A90b 2nu multicolored .30 .30
897 A90b 4nu multicolored .65 .65
898 A90b 5nu multicolored .80 .80
899 A90b 6nu multicolored 1.00 1.00
900 A90b 8nu multicolored 1.25 1.25
901 A90b 10nu multicolored 1.50 1.50
902 A90b 15nu multicolored 2.50 2.50
903 A90b 20nu multicolored 3.00 3.00
904 A90b 25nu multicolored 3.75 3.75
905 A90b 30nu multicolored 4.75 4.75
Nos. 894-905 (12) 20.00 20.00

Souvenir Sheets

Sheets of 2 (#906-912) or 1

906-912 A90b Set of 7 40.00 40.00
913-917 A90b Set of 5 25.00 25.00

Stamp World London '90.

Panda Bear A91

Tiger A92

Endangered wildlife of Asia.

1990 *Perf. 14*

918 A91 50ch multi, diff. .30 .25
919 A91 1nu multi, diff. .40 .40
920 A91 2nu multi, diff. .60 .60
921 A91 3nu shown 1.00 1.00
922 A91 4nu multi, diff. 1.25 1.25
923 A92 5nu shown 1.40 1.40
924 A91 6nu multi, diff. 1.60 1.60
925 A91 7nu multi, diff. 1.90 1.90
926 A92 10nu Elephant 2.50 2.50
927 A91 15nu multi, diff. 3.50 3.50
928 A92 20nu Barking deer 4.75 4.75
929 A92 25nu Snow leopard 5.75 5.75
Nos. 918-929 (12) 24.95 24.90

Souvenir Sheets

930 A92 25nu Rhinoceros 5.50 5.50
931 A92 25nu Clouded leopard 5.50 5.50
932 A92 25nu Asiatic wild dog 5.50 5.50
933 A92 25nu Himalayan shou 5.50 5.50
934 A92 25nu Golden cat 5.50 5.50
935 A92 25nu Himalayan musk deer 5.50 5.50
936 A91 25nu multi, diff. 5.50 5.50
937 A92 25nu Asiatic black bear 5.50 5.50
938 A92 25nu Gaur 5.50 5.50
939 A92 25nu Pygmy hog 5.50 5.50
940 A92 25nu Wolf 5.50 5.50
941 A92 25nu Sloth bear 5.50 5.50
Nos. 930-941 (12) 66.00 66.00

Nos. 919-920 and 927 vert.

Buddhist Musical Instruments — A93

1990, Sept. 29 Litho. *Perf. 13½x13*

942 A93 10ch Dungchen .25 .25
943 A93 20ch Dungkar .25 .25
944 A93 30ch Roim .25 .25
945 A93 50ch Tinchag .25 .25
946 A93 1nu Dradu & drilbu .25 .25
947 A93 2nu Gya-ling .40 .40
948 A93 2.50nu Nga .50 .50
a. Souv. sheet, #943, 945, 947-948 3.00 3.00
949 A93 3.50nu Kang-dung .75 .75
a. Souv. sheet, #942, 944, 946, 949 3.00 3.00
Nos. 942-949 (8) 2.90 2.90

Year of the Girl Child — A94

1990, Dec. 8

950 A94 50ch shown .25 .25
951 A94 20nu Young girl 4.00 4.00

Wonders of the World — A95

Walt Disney characters viewing: 1ch, Temple of Artemis, Ephesus. 2ch, Statue of Zeus, Olympia. 3ch, Egyptian pyramids. 4ch, Lighthouse, Alexandria. 5ch, Mausoleum at Halicarnassus. 10ch, Colossus of Rhodes. 50ch, Hanging gardens of Babylon. 5nu, Mauna Loa volcano, Hawaii. 6nu, Carlsbad Caverns, New Mexico. 10nu, Rainbow Bridge, Utah. 15nu, Grand Canyon of the Colorado, Arizona. 20nu, Old Faithful geyser, Wyoming. 25nu, Giant sequoias, California. 30nu, Crater Lake and Wizard Island, Oregon. 5nu, 6nu, 10nu, 15nu, 20nu, 25nu, 30nu are horiz.

Each 25nu, Walt Disney characters viewing: No. 966, Great Wall of China, horiz. No. 967, Mosque of St. Sophia, Istanbul, Turkey. No. 968, The Leaning Tower of Pisa, Italy. No. 969, Colosseum, Rome. No. 970, Stonehenge, England. No. 971, Catacombs of Alexandria, Egypt. No. 972, Porcelain Tower, Nanking, China, horiz. No. 973, The Panama Canal, horiz. No. 974, Golden Gate Bridge, San Francisco, horiz. No. 975, Sears Tower, Chicago, horiz. No. 976, Gateway Arch, St. Louis. No. 977, Alcan Highway, Alaska and Canada, horiz. No. 978, Hoover Dam, Nevada. No. 979, Empire State Building, New York.

1991, Feb. 2 Litho. *Perf. 14*

952 A95 1ch multicolored .25 .25
953 A95 2ch multicolored .25 .25
954 A95 3ch multicolored .25 .25
955 A95 4ch multicolored .25 .25
956 A95 5ch multicolored .25 .25
957 A95 10ch multicolored .25 .25
958 A95 50ch multicolored .25 .25
959 A95 5nu multicolored 1.40 1.40
960 A95 6nu multicolored 1.75 1.75
961 A95 10nu multicolored 2.25 2.25
962 A95 15nu multicolored 3.00 3.00
963 A95 20nu multicolored 4.25 4.25
964 A95 25nu multicolored 4.50 4.50
965 A95 30nu multicolored 6.00 6.00
Nos. 952-965 (14) 24.90 24.90

Souvenir Sheets

Perf. 14x13½, 13½x14

966-979 A95 Set of 14 63.00 63.00

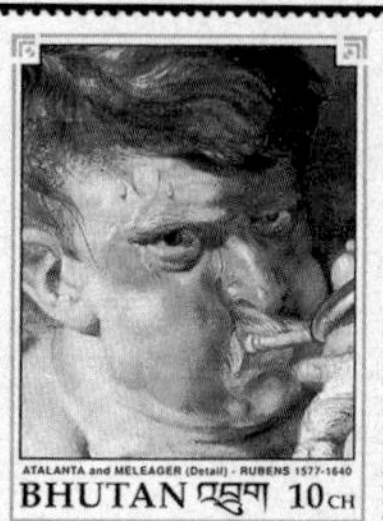

Peter Paul Rubens (1577-1640), Painter A96

Entire paintings or different details from: 10ch, 5nu, 6nu, 10nu, No. 992, Atalanta and Meleager. 50ch, Fall of Phaethon. 1nu, No. 993, Feast of Venus Verticordia. 2nu, Achilles Slaying Hector. 3nu, No. 994, Arachne Punished by Minerva. 4nu, No. 995, Jupiter Receives Psyche on Olympus. 7nu, Venus in Vulcan's Furnace. 20nu, No. 996, Briseis Returned to Achilles. 30nu, No. 997, Mars and Rhea Sylvia. No. 998, Venus Shivering. No. 999, Ganymede and the Eagle. No. 1000, Origin of the Milky Way. No. 1001, Adonis and Venus. No. 1002, Hero and Leander. No. 1003, Fall of the Titans.

Nos. 992-1003, each 25nu.

Nos. 994, 996-997, 1000-1003 are horiz.

1991, Feb. 2

980 A96 10ch multicolored .40 .40
981 A96 50ch multicolored .40 .40
982 A96 1nu multicolored .50 .50
983 A96 2nu multicolored .60 .60
984 A96 3nu multicolored .90 .90
985 A96 4nu multicolored 1.15 1.15
986 A96 5nu multicolored 1.40 1.40
987 A96 6nu multicolored 1.50 1.50
988 A96 7nu multicolored 1.60 1.60
989 A96 10nu multicolored 2.50 2.50
990 A96 20nu multicolored 3.75 3.75
991 A96 30nu multicolored 5.50 5.50
Nos. 980-991 (12) 20.20 20.20

Souvenir Sheets

992-1003 A96 Set of 12 75.00 75.00

Vincent Van Gogh (1853-1890), Painter — A97

Paintings: 10ch, Cottages, Reminiscence of the North. 50ch, Head of a Peasant Woman with Dark Cap. 1nu, Portrait of a Woman in Blue. 2nu, The Midwife. 8nu, Vase with Hollyhocks. 10nu, Portrait of a Man with a Skull Cap. 12nu, Agostina Segatori Sitting in the Cafe du Tambourin. 15nu, Vase with Daisies and Anemones. 18nu, Fritillaries in a Copper Vase. 20nu, Woman Sitting in the Grass. 25nu, On the Outskirts of Paris, horiz. 30nu, Chrysanthemums and Wild Flowers in a Vase.

Each 30nu: No. 1016, Le Moulin de la Galette. No. 1017, Bowl with Sunflowers, Roses and Other Flowers, horiz. No. 1018, Poppies and Butterflies. No. 1019, Trees in the Garden of Saint-Paul Hospital. No. 1020, Le Moulin de Blute Fin. No. 1021, Le Moulin de la Galette, diff. No. 1022, Vase with Peonies. No. 1023, Vase with Zinnias. No. 1024, Fishing in the Spring, Pont de Clichy, horiz. No. 1025, Village Street in Auvers, horiz. No. 1026, Vase with Zinnias and Other Flowers, horiz. No. 1027, Vase with Red Poppies.

1991, July 22 Litho. *Perf. 13½*

1004 A97 10ch multicolored .30 .30
1005 A97 50ch multicolored .30 .30
1006 A97 1nu multicolored .30 .30
1007 A97 2nu multicolored .40 .40
1008 A97 8nu multicolored 1.60 1.60
1009 A97 10nu multicolored 2.00 2.00
1010 A97 12nu multicolored 2.50 2.50
1011 A97 15nu multicolored 3.00 3.00
1012 A97 18nu multicolored 4.00 4.00
1013 A97 20nu multicolored 4.25 4.25
1014 A97 25nu multicolored 5.00 5.00
1015 A97 30nu multicolored 6.25 6.25
Nos. 1004-1015 (12) 29.90 29.90

Size: 76x102mm, 102x76mm

Imperf

1016-1027 A97 Set of 12 84.00 84.00

History of World Cup Soccer — A98

Winning team pictures, plays or possible future site: 50ch, Uruguay, 1930. 1nu, Italy, 1934. 2nu, Italy, 1938. 3nu, Uruguay, 1950. 5nu, West Germany, 1954. 10nu, Brazil, 1958. 20nu, Brazil, 1962. 25nu, England, 1966. 29nu, Brazil, 1970. 30nu, West Germany, 1974. 31nu, Argentina, 1978. 32nu, Italy, 1982. 33nu, Argentina, 1986. 34nu, West Germany, 1990. 35nu, Los Angeles Coliseum, 1994.

Players, each 30nu: No. 1043, Claudio Caniggia, Argentina, vert. No. 1044, Salvatore Schillaci, Italy, vert. No. 1045, Roberto Baggio, Italy, vert. No. 1046, Peter Shilton, England, vert. No. 1047, Lothar Matthaus, West Germany, vert. No. 1048, Paul Gascoigne, England, vert.

1991, Aug. 1 Litho. *Perf. 13½*

1028 A98 50ch multi .25 .25
1029 A98 1nu multi .25 .25
1030 A98 2nu multi .35 .35
1031 A98 3nu multi .60 .60
1032 A98 5nu multi .90 .90
1033 A98 10nu multi 1.90 1.90
1034 A98 20nu multi 3.75 3.75
1035 A98 25nu multi 4.50 4.50
1036 A98 29nu multi 5.50 5.50
1037 A98 30nu multi 5.50 5.50
1038 A98 31nu multi 5.75 5.75

1039 A98 32nu multi 6.00 6.00
1040 A98 33nu multi 6.25 6.25
1041 A98 34nu multi 6.25 6.25
1042 A98 35nu multi 6.50 6.50
Nos. 1028-1042 (15) 54.25 54.25

Souvenir Sheets

1043-1048 A98 Set of 6 40.00 40.00

Phila Nippon '91 — A99

1991, Nov. 16 ***Perf. 13***
1049 A99 15nu multicolored 3.50 3.50

Education in Bhutan A100

1992, Mar. 5 **Photo.** ***Perf. 13½***
1050 A100 1nu multicolored 1.00 1.00

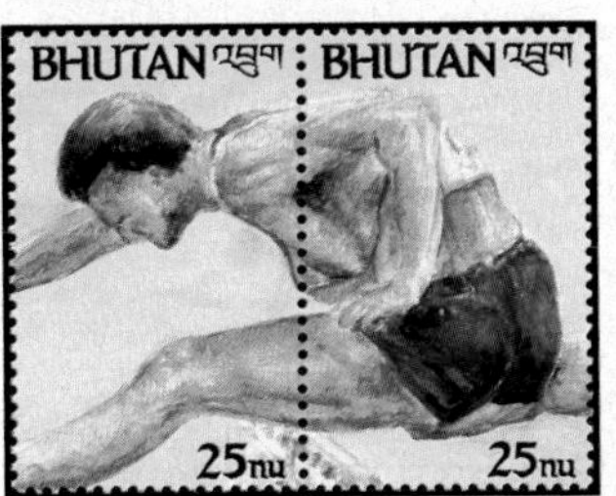

A101

1992 Summer Olympics, Barcelona — A102

1992, July 24 **Litho.** ***Perf. 12***
1051 A101 25nu Pair, #a.-b. 9.75 9.75

Souvenir Sheet

1052 A102 25nu Archer 6.75 6.75

German Reunification — A103

1992, Oct. 3 **Litho.** ***Perf. 12***
1053 A103 25nu multicolored 3.00 3.00

Souvenir Sheet

1054 A103 25nu multicolored 3.00 3.00

Stamp from No. 1054 does not have white inscription or border.

Bhutan Postal Service, 30th Anniv. A104

Designs: 1nu, Mail truck, plane. 3nu, Letter carrier approaching village. 5nu, Letter carrier emptying mail box.

1992, Oct. 9
1055 A104 1nu multicolored .30 .30
1056 A104 3nu multicolored .40 .40
1057 A104 5nu multicolored .75 .75
Nos. 1055-1057 (3) 1.45 1.45

Environmental Protection — A105

Designs: a, 7nu, Red panda. b, 20nu, Takin. c, 15nu, Black-necked crane, blue poppy. d, 10nu, One-horned rhinoceros.

1993, July 1 **Litho.** ***Perf. 14***
1058 A105 Sheet of 4, #b.-e. 9.00 9.00

No. 1058 was delayed from its originally scheduled release in 1992, although some examples were made available to the trade at that time.

A106

A107

1992, Sept. 18 ***Perf. 12***
1059 A106 15nu Ship 2.50 2.50
1060 A106 20nu Portrait 3.25 3.25

Souvenir Sheet

1061 A106 25nu like #1060 5.00 5.00

Discovery of America, 500th anniv.
Stamp from No. 1061 does not have silver inscription or white border.

1992, Nov. 11 **Litho.** ***Perf. 12***

Reign of King Jigme Singye Wangchuk, 20th Anniv.: a, 1nu, Man tilling field, factory. b, 5nu, Airplane. c, 10nu, House, well. d, 15nu, King.
20nu, People, flag, King, horiz.

1062 A107 Block of 4, #a.-d. 6.00 6.00

Souvenir Sheet

1063 A107 20nu multicolored 6.00 6.00

Intl. Volunteer Day — A108

a, 1.50nu, White inscription. b, 9nu, Green inscription. c, 15nu, Red inscription.

1992, Dec. 5 **Litho.** ***Perf. 14***
1067 A108 Block of 4, #a.-c. + label 5.00 5.00

Medicinal Plants — A109

1993, Jan. 1 **Litho.** ***Perf. 12***
1068 A109 1.50nu Meconopsis grandis prain .40 .40
1069 A109 7nu Meconopsis sp. 1.10 1.10
1070 A109 10nu Meconopsis wallichii 1.40 1.40
1071 A109 12nu Meconopsis horridula 1.90 1.90
1072 A109 20nu Meconopsis discigera 3.25 3.25
Nos. 1068-1072 (5) 8.05 8.05

Souvenir Sheet

1073 A109 25nu Meconopsis horridula, diff. 6.00 6.00

Miniature Sheet

Lunar New Year — A110

1993, Feb. 22 **Litho.** ***Perf. 14***
1074 A110 25nu multicolored 7.75 7.75

Exists with overprint "ROCKPEX '93 KAOH-SIUNG" in sheet margin.

No. 1074 Surcharged "TAIPEI '93" in Silver and Black

1993, Aug. 14 **Litho.** ***Perf. 14***
1075 A110 30nu on 25nu 7.75 7.75

Paintings A111

Designs: No. 1076, 1ch, No. 1081, 15ch, No. 1086, 1nu, The Love Letter, by Jean-Honoré Fragonard. No. 1077, 2ch, No. 1082, 25ch, No. 1087, 1.25nu, The Writer, by Vittore Carpaccio. No. 1078, 3ch, No. 1083, 50ch, No. 1088, 2nu, Mademoiselle Lavergne, by Jean-Etienne Liotard. No. 1079, 5ch, No. 1084, 60ch, No. 1089, 3nu, Portrait of Erasmus, by Hans Holbein, the Younger. No. 1080, 10ch, No. 1085, 80ch, No. 1090, 6nu, Woman Writing a Letter, by Gerard Terborch.

Color of frames and text outlines: Nos. 1076-1080, bronze, Nos. 1081-1085, silver, Nos. 1086-1090, gold.

1993, May 2 **Photo.** ***Perf. 13½***
1076-1090 A111 Set of 15 8.00 —
1090a Souvenir sheet, #1088-1089, with bronze frames and text outlines, imperf. 6.50 —

Nos. 1076-1090, 1090a were prepared and distributed in 1974 but were not made valid until 1993. Nos. 1088-1090 are air mail.

Door Gods — A112

1993, Dec. 17 **Litho.** ***Perf. 12***
1091 A112 1.50nu Namtheo-Say .35 .35
1092 A112 5nu Pha-Ke-Po .95 .95
1093 A112 10nu Chen-Mi-Jang 1.90 1.90
1094 A112 15nu Yul-Khor-Sung 2.75 2.75
Nos. 1091-1094 (4) 5.95 5.95

Flowers — A113

Designs: No. 1095a, 1nu, Rhododendron mucronatum. b, 1.5nu. Anemone rupicola. c, 2nu, Polemonium coeruleum. d, 2.5nu, Rosa marophylla. e, 4nu, Paraquilegia microphylla. f, 5nu, Aquilegia nivalis. g, 6nu, Geranium wallichianum. h, 7nu, Rhodendron campanulatum. i, 9nu, Viola suavis. j, 10nu, Cyananthus lobatus.
13nu, Red flower, horiz.

1994, Jan. 1 ***Perf. 13***
1095 A113 Strip of 10, #a.-j. 10.00 10.00

Souvenir Sheet

1096 A113 13nu multicolored 3.50 3.50

New Year 1994 (Year of the Dog) — A114

1994, Feb. 11 **Litho.** ***Perf. 14***
1097 A114 11.50nu multi 1.75 1.75

Souvenir Sheet

1098 A114 20nu like #1097 3.50 3.50

Hong Kong '94.

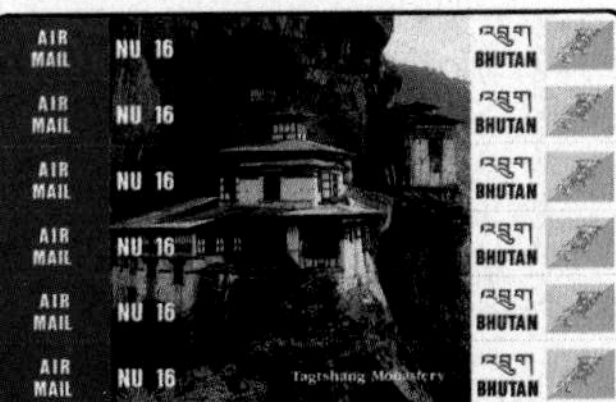

Stamp Cards — A115

Designs: 16nu, Tagtshang Monastery. 20nu, Map of Bhutan.

Rouletted 26 on 2 or 3 Sides

1994, Aug. 15 Litho.

Self-Adhesive

Cards of 6 + 6 labels

1099 A115 16nu #a.-f. 12.00 12.00
1100 A115 20nu #a.-f. 13.00 13.00

Individual stamps measure 70x9mm and have a card backing. Se-tenant labels inscribed "AIR MAIL."

Souvenir Sheet

First Manned Moon Landing, 25th Anniv. — A116

a, 30nu, Astronaut on moon. b, 36nu, Space shuttle, earth, moon.

1994, Nov. 11 Litho. *Perf. 14x14½*
1101 A116 Sheet of 2, #a.-b. 12.00 12.00

Nos. 1101a, 1101b have holographic images. Soaking in water may affect the holograms.

Souvenir Sheet

Victory Over Tibet-Mongol Army, 350th Anniv. — A117

Battle scene: a, Mounted officer. b, Hand to hand combat, soldiers in yellow or blue armor. c, Soldier on gray horse. d, Soldiers in red, drummer, horn player.

1994, Dec. 17 Litho. *Perf. 12½*

Granite Paper

1102 A117 15nu Sheet of 4, #a.-d. 6.00 6.00

Souvenir Sheet

Bridges — A118

a, 15nu, Tower Bridge, London, cent. b, 16nu, Wangdue Bridge, Bhutan, 250th anniv.

1994, Nov. 11 *Perf. 12*
1103 A118 Sheet of 2, #a.-b. 4.50 4.50

1994 World Cup Soccer Championships, US — A119

1994, July 17 Litho. *Perf. 12*
1104 A119 15nu multicolored 2.00 2.00

Souvenir Sheet

World Tourism Year — A120

Scenes of Bhutan: a, 1.50nu, Paro Valley. b, 5nu, Chorten Kora. c, 10nu, Thimphu Tshechu. d, 15nu, Wangdue Tshechu.

1995, Apr. 2 Litho. *Perf. 12*
1105 A120 Sheet of 4, #a.-d. 5.00 5.00

Miniature Sheet

New Year 1995 (Year of the Boar) — A121

Symbols of Chinese Lunar New Year: a, 10ch, Rat. b, 20ch, Ox. c, 30ch, Tiger. d, 40ch, Rabbit. e, 1nu, Dragon. f, 2nu, Snake. g, 3nu, Horse. h, 4nu, Sheep. i, 5nu, Monkey. j, 7nu, Rooster. k, 8nu, Dog. l, 9nu, Boar.

10nu, Wood Hog.

1995, Mar. 2
1106 A121 #a.-l. 6.00 6.00

Souvenir Sheet

1107 A121 10nu multicolored 2.00 2.00

No. 1107 is a continuous design.

A122

Flowers: 9nu, Pleione praecox. 10nu, Primula calderina. 16nu, Primula whitei. 18nu, Notholirion macrophyllum.

1995, May 2 Litho. *Perf. 12*
1108-1111 A122 Set of 4 5.50 5.50

A123

UN, 50th Anniv.: a, 1.5nu, Human resources development. b, 9nu, Health & population. c, 10nu, Water & sanitation. d, 5nu, Transport & communications. e, 16nu, Forestry & environment. f, 18nu, Peace & security. g, 11.5nu, UN in Bhutan.

1995, June 26 *Perf. 14*
1112 A123 Strip of 7 8.00 8.00

Miniature Sheet of 6

Singapore '95 — A124

Birds — No. 1113: a, 1nu, Himalayan pied kingfisher. b, 2nu, Blyth's tragopan. c, 3nu, Long-tailed minivet. d, 10nu, Red junglefowl. e, 15nu, Black-capped sibia. f, 20nu, Red-billed chough.

No. 1114, Black-neck crane.

1995, June 2 Litho. *Perf. 12*
1113 A124 #a.-f. + 3 labels 3.50 3.50

Souvenir Sheet

1114 A124 20nu multicolored 2.50 2.50

Traditional Crafts — A125

1nu, Drying parchment. 2nu, Making tapestry. 3nu, Restoring archaeological finds. 10nu, Weaving textiles. 15nu, Sewing garments. No. 1120, 20nu, Carving wooden vessels.

No. 1121, Mosaic.

1995, Aug. 15 Litho. *Perf. 14*
1115-1120 A125 Set of 6 5.50 5.50

Souvenir Sheet

1121 A125 20nu multicolored 3.25 3.25

New Year 1996 (Year of the Rat) — A126

Designs: a, Monkey. b, Rat, fire. c, Dragon.

1996, Jan. 1 Litho. *Perf. 14*
1122 A126 10nu Sheet of 3, #a.-c. 4.00 4.00

Butterflies A127

a, 2nu, Blue pansy. b, 3nu, Blue peacock. c, 5nu, Great Mormon. d, 10nu, Fritillary. e, 15nu, Blue duke. f, 25nu, Brown Gorgon.

No. 1124, 30nu, Xanthomelas. No. 1124A, 30 nu, Fivebar swordtail.

1996, May 2 Litho. *Perf. 14*
1123 A127 Sheet of 6, #a.-f. 6.00 6.00

Souvenir Sheets

1124-1124A A127 Set of 2 6.50 6.50

1996 Summer Olympic Games, Atlanta A128

5nu, Silver 300n coin, soccer. 7nu, Silver 300n coin, basketball. 10nu, Gold 5s coin, judo. 15nu, Archery.

1996, June 15 Litho. *Perf. 14*
1125-1127 A128 Set of 3 3.00 3.00

Souvenir Sheet

1128 A128 15nu multicolored 3.50 3.50

Olymphilex '96.

Folktales — A129

Designs: a, 1nu, The White Bird. b, 2nu, Sing Sing Lhamo and the Moon. c, 3nu, The Hoopoe. d, 5nu, The Cloud Fairies. e, 10nu, The Three Wishes. f, 20nu, The Abominable Snowman.

1996, Apr. 15 *Perf. 12*
1129 A129 Sheet of 6, #a.-f. 3.00 3.00

Souvenir Sheet

1130 A129 25nu like #1129d 3.00 3.00

Locomotives — A130

No. 1131, each 20nu: a, 0-6-4 Tank engine (Chile). b, First Pacific locomotive in Europe (France). c, 4-6-0 Passenger engine (Norway). d, Atlantic type express (Germany). e, 4-Cylinder 4-6-0 express (Belgium). f, Standard type "4" diesel-electric (England).

No. 1132, each 20nu: a, Standard 0-6-0 Goods engine (India). b, Main-line 1,900 horsepower diesel-electric (Finland). c, 0-8-0 Shunting tank engine (Russia). d, Alco "PA-1" diesel-electric (US). e, "C11" Class 2-6-4 branch passenger tank engine (Japan). f, "Settebello" deluxe high-speed electric train (Italy).

No. 1133, 70nu, Class "KD" 0-6-0 Goods locomotive, 1900 (Sweden). No. 1134, 70nu, Shinkansen "New Railway" series 200 (Japan).

1996, Nov. 25 Litho. *Perf. 14*

Sheets of 6, #a-f

1131-1132 A130 Set of 2 20.00 20.00

Souvenir Sheets

1133-1134 A130 Set of 2 15.00 15.00

Penny Black — A131

Litho. & Embossed

1996, Dec. 17 *Perf. 13½*
1135 A131 140nu black & gold 10.00 10.00

A132

Winter Olympic Medalists: 10nu, Vegard Ulvang, cross-country skiing, 1992. 15nu, Kristi Yamaguchi, figure skating, 1992. 25nu, Markus Wasmeier, giant slalom, 1994. 30nu, Georg Hackl, luge, 1992.

No. 1140: a, Andreas Ostler, 2-man bobsled, 1952. b, Wolfgang Hoppe, 4-man bobsled, 1984. c, Stein Eriksen, giant slalom, 1952. d, Alberto Tomba, giant slalom, 1988.

Each 70nu: No. 1141, Henri Oreiller, downhill, 1948. No. 1142, Eduard Scherrer, 4-man bobsled, 1924.

1997, Jan. 1 ***Perf. 14***

1136-1139 A132 Set of 4 7.50 7.50
1140 A132 15nu Strip of 4, #a.-d. 5.50 5.50

Souvenir Sheets

1141-1142 A132 Set of 2 14.50 14.50

No. 1140 was issued in sheets of 8 stamps.

A133

Insects and Arachnids: a, 1ch, Apis laboriosa smith. b, 2ch, Neptunides polychromus. c, 3ch, Conocephalus maculctus. d, 4ch, Blattidae. e, 5ch, Dytiscus marginalis. f, 10ch, Dynastes hercules. g, 15ch, Hippodamia. h, 20ch, Sarcophaga haemorrhoidalis. i, 25ch, Lucanus cervus. j, 30ch, Caterpillar. k, 35ch, Lycia hirtaria. l, 40ch, Clytarlus pennatus. m, 45ch, Ephemera denica. n, 50ch, Gryllus campestris. o, 60ch, Deilephila elpenor. p, 65ch, Gerris. q, 70ch, Agrion splendens. r, 80ch, Tachyta nana. s, 90ch, Eurydema pulchra. t, 1nu, Hadrurus hirsutus. u, 1.50nu, Vespa germanica. v, 2nu, Pyrops. w, 2.50nu, Mantis religiosa. x, 3nu, Araneus diadematus. y, 3.50nu, Atrophaneura.

15nu, Melolontha.

1997, Jan. 15 ***Perf. 13***

1143 A133 Sheet of 25, #a.-y. 6.50 6.50

Souvenir Sheet

1144 A133 15nu multicolored 4.00 4.00

Hong Kong '97 — A134

Wildlife: a, Thalarctos maritimus. b, Phascolarctos cinereus. c, Selenarctos thibetanus. d, Ailurus fulgens.

20nu, Ailuropoda melanoleuca.

1997, Feb. 1 **Litho.** ***Perf. 14***

1145 A134 10nu Sheet of 4, #a.-d. 5.50 5.50

Souvenir Sheet

1146 A134 20nu multicolored 3.50 3.50

Signs of the Chinese Zodiac — A135

No. 1147: a, 1ch, Mouse. b, 2ch, Ox. c, 3ch, Tiger. d, 4ch, Rabbit. e, 5nu, Dragon. f, 6nu, Snake. g, 7nu, Horse. h, 8nu, Sheep. i, 90ch, Monkey. j, 10nu, Rooster. k, 11nu, Dog. l, 12nu, Pig.

20nu, Ox, diff.

1997, Feb. 8 **Litho.** ***Perf. 14***

1147 A135 Sheet of 12, #a.-l. + label 9.50 9.50

Souvenir Sheet

1148 A135 20nu multicolored 5.50 5.50

Fauna A136

Cuon alpinus: No. 1149: a, Adult, hind legs off ground. b, Adult walking right. c, Mother nursing young. d, Two seated.

Endangered species: No. 1150: a, Lynx. b, Red panda. c, Takin. d, Musk deer. e, Snow leopard. f, Golden langur. g, Tiger. h, Muntjac. i, Marmot.

No. 1151, 70nu, Pseudois nayaur. No. 1152, 70nu, Ursus thibetanus.

1997, Apr. 24

1149 A136 10nu Block or strip of 4, #a.-d. 5.50 5.50
1150 A136 10nu Sheet of 9, #a.-i. 8.00 8.00

Souvenir Sheets

1151-1152 A136 Set of 2 14.50 14.50

World Wildlife Fund (No. 1149).

No. 1149 issued in sheets of 12 stamps.

UNESCO, 50th Anniv. A137

No. 1153: a, Mount Hungshan, China. b, Mausoleum of first Qin Emperor, China. c, Imperial Bronze Dragon, China. d, Tikal Natl. Park, Guatemala. e, Evora, Portugal. f, Shirakami-Sanchi, Japan. g, Paris, France. h, Valley Below the Falls, Plitvice Lakes Natl. Park, Croatia.

Sites in Germany: No. 1154: a, Cathedral, Bamberg. b, Bamberg. c, St. Michael's Church, Hildesheim. d, Potsdam Palace. e, Potsdam Church. f, Lubeck. g, Quedlinberg. h, Benedictine Church, Lorsch.

No. 1155, 60nu, Goslar, Germany, horiz. No. 1156, 60nu, Cathedral, Comenzada, Portugal, horiz.

1997, May 15

Sheets of 8 + Label

1153 A137 10nu #a.-h. 9.00 9.00
1154 A137 15nu #a.-h. 11.00 11.00

Souvenir Sheets

1155-1156 A137 Set of 2 13.50 13.50

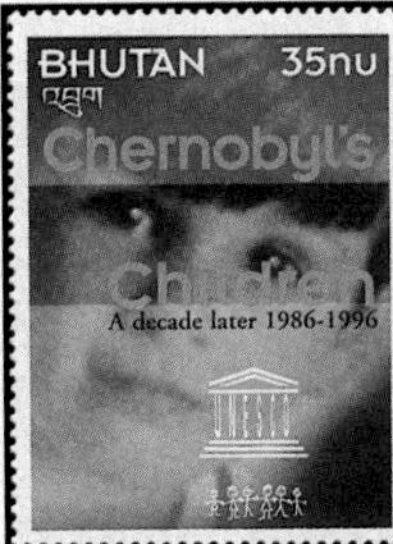

Chernobyl Disaster, 10th Anniv. A138

1997, May 2 **Litho.** ***Perf. 13½x14***

1157 A138 35nu UNESCO 4.75 4.75

Dogs — A139 Cats — A140

Designs: 10nu, Dalmatian. 15nu, Siberian husky. 20nu, Saluki. 25nu, Shar pei.

No. 1162: a, Dandie Dinmont terrier. b, Chinese crested. c, Norwich terrier. d, Basset hound. e, Cardigan welsh corgi. f, French bulldog.

60nu, Hovawart.

1997, July 15 ***Perf. 14***

1158-1161 A139 Set of 4 5.00 5.00
1162 A139 20nu Sheet of 6, #a.-f. 9.00 9.00

Souvenir Sheet

1163 A139 60nu multicolored 4.50 4.50

1997, July 15

Designs: 10nu, Turkish angora. 15nu, Oriental shorthair. 20nu, British shorthair. 25nu, Burmese.

No. 1168: a, Japanese bobtail. b, Ceylon. c, Exotic. d, Rex. e, Ragdoll. f, Russian blue.

60nu, Tonkinese.

1164-1167 A140 Set of 4 5.00 5.00
1168 A140 15nu Sheet of 6, #a.-f. 9.00 9.00

Souvenir Sheet

1169 A140 60nu multicolored 4.50 4.50

1998 World Cup Soccer, France A141

English players: 5nu, Pearce. 10nu, Gascoigne. 15nu, Beckham. 20nu, McManaman. 25nu, Adams. 30nu, Ince.

World Cup captains, horiz.: No. 1176: a, Maradona, Argentina, 1986. b, Alberto, Brazil, 1970. c, Dunga, Brazil, 1994. d, Moore, England, 1966. e, Walter, Germany, 1954. f, Matthaus, Germany, 1990. g, Beckenbauer, Germany, 1974. h, Passarella, Argentina, 1978.

Winning teams, horiz.: No. 1177: a, Italy, 1938. b, W. Germany, 1954. c, Uruguay, 1958. d, England, 1966. e, Argentina, 1978. f, Brazil, 1962. g, Italy, 1934. h, Brazil, 1970. i, Uruguay, 1930.

No. 1178, 35nu, Philippe Albert, Belgium. No. 1179, 35nu, Salvatore (Toto) Schillaci, Italy, horiz.

Perf. 13½x14, 14x13½

1997, Oct. 9 **Litho.**

1170-1175 A141 Set of 6 8.00 8.00

Sheets of 8 or 9

1176 A141 10nu #a.-h. + label 6.25 6.25
1177 A141 10nu #a.-i. 7.00 7.00

Souvenir Sheets

1178-1179 A141 Set of 2 8.75 8.75

Friendship Between India and Bhutan A142

3nu, Jawaharlal Nehru, King Jigme Dorji Wangchuk. 10nu, Rajiv Gandhi, King Jigme Singye Wangchuk.

20nu, Indian Pres. R. V. Venkataraman, King Jigme Singye Wangchuk.

1998 **Litho.** ***Perf. 13x13½***

1180 A142 3nu multicolored .40 .40
1181 A142 10nu multicolored .90 .90

Souvenir Sheet

1182 A142 20nu multicolored 2.00 2.00

No. 1182 contains one 76x35mm stamp.

A143

Indepex '97: No. 1183: a, 3nu, Buddha seated with legs crossed. b, 15nu, Buddha seated with legs down. c, 7nu, Gandhi with hands folded. d, 10nu, Gandhi.

No. 1184, 15nu, Buddha. No. 1185, 15nu, Gandhi holding staff.

1998 ***Perf. 13½x13***

1183 A143 Sheet of 4, #a.-d. 2.50 2.50

Souvenir Sheets

1184-1185 A143 Set of 2 3.50 3.50

India's independence, 50th anniv.

A144

New Year 1998 (Year of the Tiger): 3nu, Stylized tiger walking right.

Tigers: No. 1187: a, 5nu, Lying down. b, 15nu, Adult walking forward. c, 17nu, Cub walking over rocks.

20nu, Adult up close.

1998, Feb. 28 **Litho.** ***Perf. 14***

1186 A144 3nu multicolored .25 .25
1187 A144 Sheet of 4, #a.-c., #1186 3.50 3.50

Souvenir Sheet

1188 A144 20nu multicolored 2.40 2.40

WHO, 50th Anniv. A145

1998, Apr. 7 **Litho.** ***Perf. 13½***

1189 A145 3nu multicolored .25 .25
1190 A145 10nu multicolored .70 .70

Souvenir Sheet

Perf. 14

1191 A145 15nu Mother, child 1.10 1.10

Safe Motherhood. No. 1191 contains one 35x35mm stamp.

Mother Teresa (1910-97) A146

No. 1191A, Mother Teresa, Princess Diana.
No. 1192: a, Portrait (shown). b, Holding child. c, Holding starving infant. d, Seated among nuns. e, Looking down at sick. f, With hands folded in prayer. g, With Pope John Paul II. h, Portrait, diff.
No. 1193: a, like No. 1191A. b, like No. 1192g.

1998, May 25 Litho. *Perf. 13½*

1191A A146 10nu multi 4.50 4.50
1192 A146 10nu Sheet of 9, #a.-h., 1191A 9.00 9.00

Souvenir Sheet of 2

1193 A146 25nu #a.-b. 3.00 3.00

No. 1193 contains two 38x43mm stamps.

Birds — A147

No. 1194: a, 10ch, Red-billed chough. b, 30ch, Great hornbill. c, 50ch, Singing lark. d, 70ch, Chestnut-flanked white-eye. e, 90ch, Magpie-robin. f, 1nu, Mrs. Gould's sunbird. g, 2nu, Tailorbird. h, 3nu, Duck. i, 5nu, Spotted cuckoo. j, 7nu, Gold crest. k, 9nu, Common mynah. l, 10nu, Green cochoa.
15nu, Turtle dove.

1998, July 28 Litho. *Perf. 13*

1194 A147 Sheet of 12, #a.-l. 5.00 5.00

Souvenir Sheet

1195 A147 15nu multicolored 2.00 2.00

No. 1195 contains one 40x30mm stamp.

New Year 1999 (Year of the Rabbit) A148

1999, Jan. 1 Litho. *Perf. 13*

1196 A148 4nu White rabbit .35 .35
1197 A148 15nu Brown rabbit 1.25 1.25

Souvenir Sheet

Perf. 13½

1198 A148 20nu Rabbit facing forward 2.25 2.25

No. 1198 contains one 35x35mm stamp.

King Jigme Singye Wangchuk, 25th Anniv. of Coronation — A149

Various portraits, background color — No. 1199: a, Blue. b, Yellow. c, Orange. d, Green.
No. 1200, Bright pink background.

1999, June 2 Litho. *Perf. 12¼*

1199 A149 25nu Sheet of 4, #a.-d. 7.00 7.00

Souvenir Sheet

1200 A149 25nu multicolored 1.90 1.90

Trains A150

Designs: 5nu, Early German steam. 10nu, EID 711 electric. 20nu, Steam engine. 30nu, Trans Europe Express, Germany.
No. 1205: a, Bullet train, Japan, 1964. b, 2-D-2 Class 26, South Africa, 1953. c, Super Chief, US, 1946. d, Magleus Magnet, Japan, 1991. e, The Flying Scotsman, UK, 1922. f, Kodama Train, Japan, 1958. g, Blue Train, South Africa, 1969. h, Inter-City, Germany, 1960. i, High Speed ET 403, Germany, 1973. j, US Standard 4-4-0, 1855. k, Bayer Garratt, South Africa, 1954. l, Settebello train, Italy, 1953.
No. 1206, each 15nu: a, Diesel-electric, France. b, 6-4-4-6 Pennsylvania RR, US. c, 2-8-2 Steam, Germany. d, Amtrak, US. e, GS&W 2-2-2, Britain. f, Class P steam, Denmark. g, French electric. h, First Japanese locomotive. i, 2-8-2 Germany.
No. 1207, each 15nu: a, Pacific Class 01, Germany. b, Neptune Express, Germany. c, 4-4-0 Steam, Britain. d, Shovelnose streamliner, US. e, German electric. f, Early steam, Germany. g, Union Pacific, US. h, Borsig steam, Germany, 1881. i, Borsig 4-6-4, Germany.
No. 1208, 80nu, Union Pacific electric locomotive E2 streamliner, US. No. 1209, 80nu, Great Northern diesel electric streamliner, US.

1999, July 21 *Perf. 14*

1201-1204 A150 Set of 4 4.50 4.50

Sheet of 12

1205 A150 10nu Sheet of 12, #a.-l. 6.00 6.00

Sheets of 9

1206-1207 A150 Set of 2 13.50 13.50

Souvenir Sheets

1208-1209 A150 Set of 2 8.00 8.00

Paintings by Hokusai (1760-1849) A151

Details or entire paintings — No. 1210, each 15nu: a, Suspension Bridge Between Hida and Etchu. b, Drawings of Women (partially nude). c, Exotic Beauty. d, The Poet Nakamaro in China. e, Drawings of Women (clothed). f, Chinese Poet in Snow.
No. 1211, each 15nu: a, Festive Dancers (with umbrella). b, Drawings of Women (holding book). c, Festive Dancers (man wearing checked pattern). d, Festive Dancers (person wearing black outfit). e, Drawings of Women (holding baby). f, Festive Dancers (woman with scarf tied under chin).
No. 1212, horiz., each 15nu: a, Mount Fuji Seen Above Mist on the Tama River. b, Mount Fuji Seen from Shichirigahama. c, Sea Life (turtle). d, Sea Life (fish). e, Mount Fuji Reflected in a Lake. f, Mount Fuji Seen Through the Piers of Mannenbashi.
Each 80nu: No. 1213, The Lotus Pedestal. No. 1214, Kushunoki Masashige. No. 1215, Peasants Leading Oxen.

1999, July 27 *Perf. 13½x14, 14x13½*

Sheets of 6

1210-1212 A151 Set of 3 18.00 18.00

Souvenir Sheet

1213-1215 A151 Set of 3 18.00 18.00

Souvenir Sheet

IBRA '99, Nuremberg A152

a, 35nu, City view. b, 40nu, Show emblem.

1999, Apr. 27 Litho. *Perf. 13¾*

1216 A152 Sheet of 2, #a.-b. 4.50 4.50

Prehistoric Animals — A153

No. 1217, each 10nu: a, Pterodactylus, Brachiosaurus. b, Pteranodon. c, Anurognathus, Tyrannosaurus. d, Brachiosaurus. e, Corythosaurus. f, Iguanodon. g, Lesothosaurus. h, Allosaurus. i, Velociraptor. j, Triceratops. k, Stegosaurus. l, Compsognatus.
No. 1218, each 10nu: a, Tyrannosaurus, black inscriptions b, Dimorphodon. c, Diplodocus. d, Pterodaustro. e, Tyrannosaurus, white inscriptions. f, Edmontosaurus. g, Apatosaurus. h, Deinonychus. i, Hypsilophodon. j, Oviraptor. k, Stegosaurus, diff. l, Triceratops, diff.
No. 1219: a, Moeritherium. b, Platybelodon. c, Wooly mammoth. d, African elephant. e, Deinonychus, diff. f, Dimorphodon, diff. g, Archaeopteryx. h, Ring-necked pheasant.
Each 80nu: No. 1220, Triceratops, vert. No. 1221, Pteranodon. No. 1222, Hoatzin, vert. No. 1223, Ichthyosaur, vert.

1999, Aug. 10 Litho. *Perf. 14*

Sheets of 12

1217-1218 A153 Set of 2 6.00 6.00

Sheet of 8

1219 A153 20nu a.-h. 9.00 9.00

Souvenir Sheets

1220-1223 A153 Set of 4 22.00 22.00

No. 1221 is incorrectly inscribed "Triceratops" instead of "Pteranodon," and No. 1223 is "Present Day Dolphin" instead of "Ichthysoaur."

Fauna — A154

Designs: a, Musk deer. b, Takin. c, Blue sheep. d, Yak. e, Goral.

1999, Aug. 21 Litho. *Perf. 12¾*

1224 A154 20nu Sheet of 5, #a.-e. + label 8.00 8.00

Birds A155

No. 1225, each 15nu: a, Chestnut-bellied chlorophonia. b, Yellow-faced Amazon parrot. c, White ibis. d, Caique. e, Green jay. f, Tufted coquette. g, Common troupial. h, Purple gallinule. i, Copper-rumped hummingbird.
No. 1226, each 15nu: a, Common egret. b, Rufous-browed peppershrike. c, Glittering-throated emerald. d, Great kiskadee. e, Cuban green woodpecker. f, Scarlet ibis. g, Belted kingfisher. h, Barred antshrike. i, Caribbean parakeet.
No. 1227, vert., each 15nu: a, Rufous-tailed jacamar. b, Scarlet macaw. c, Channel-billed toucan. d, Tricolored heron. e, St. Vincent parrot. f, Blue-crowned motmot. g, Horned screamer. h, Black-billed plover. i, Common meadowlark.
Each 80nu: No. 1228, Toco toucan. No. 1229, Red-billed scythebill, vert. No. 1230, Military macaws, vert.

1999, Oct. 17 Litho. *Perf. 14*

Sheets of 9, #a.-i.

1225-1227 A155 Set of 3 27.00 27.00

Souvenir Sheets

1228-1230 A155 Set of 3 16.00 16.00

Butterflies A156

Designs: 5nu, Sara orange tip. 10nu, Pipe-pine swallowtail. 15nu, Longwings. No. 1234, 20nu, Viceroy. 25nu, Silver-spotted skipper, vert. 30nu, Great spangled fritillary, vert. 35nu, Little copper.
No. 1238, each 20nu: a, Frosted skipper. b, Fiery skipper. c, Banded hairstreak. d, Clouded sulphur. e, Milberts tortoise shell. f, Eastern tailed blue.
No. 1239, each 20nu: a, Zebra swallowtail. b, Colorado hairstreak. c, Pink-edged sulphur. d, Fairy yellow. e, Red-spotted purple. f, Aphrodite.
Each 80nu: No. 1240, Checkered white. No. 1241, Gray hairstreak, vert. No. 1242, Gulf fritillary, vert. No. 1243, Monarch, vert.

1999, Oct. 4 Litho. *Perf. 14*

1231-1237 A156 Set of 7 9.50 9.50

Sheets of 6

1238-1239 A156 Set of 2 16.00 16.00

Souvenir Sheets

1240-1243 A156 Set of 4 22.00 22.00

First Manned Moon Landing, 30th Anniv. — A157

No. 1244, each 20nu: a, Neil A. Armstrong (with name patch). b, Michael Collins. c, Edwin E. Aldrin, Jr. d, Command and service modules. e, Lunar module. f, Aldrin on Moon.
No. 1245, each 20nu: a, X-15 rocket. b, Gemini 8. c, Apollo 11 Saturn V rocket. d, Command and service modules (docked with lunar module). e, Lunar module (docked with command and service modules). f, Aldrin on lunar module ladder.
No. 1246, each 20nu: a, Yuri Gagarin. b, Alan B. Shepard, Jr. c, John H. Glenn, Jr. d, Valentina Tereshkova. e, Edward H. White II. f, Armstrong (no name patch).
Each 80nu: No. 1247, Armstrong, diff. No. 1248, Apollo 11 splashdown. No. 1249, Gemini 8 docked with Agena rocket, horiz.

1999, Nov. 1 Litho. *Perf. 14*

Sheets of 6

1244-1246 A157 Set of 3 25.00 25.00

Souvenir Sheets

1247-1249 A157 Set of 3 16.00 16.00

No. 1249 contains one 57x42mm stamp.

Cats, Horses, Dogs A158

Cats: No. 1250, 5nu, Tortoiseshell. No. 1251, 5nu, Woman and cat. 10nu, Chinchilla Golden Longhair.
No. 1253: a, Russian Blue. b, Birman. c, Devon Rex. d, Pewter Longhair. e, Bombay. f, Sorrel Somali. g, Red Tabby Manx. h, Blue Smoke Longhair. i, Oriental Tabby Shorthair.
70nu, Norwegian Shorthair.

1999, Nov. 15 Litho. *Perf. 14*

1250-1252 A158 Set of 3 3.50 3.50

Sheet of 9

1253 A158 12nu #a.-i. 7.00 7.00

Souvenir Sheet

1254 A158 70nu multicolored 5.00 5.00

1999, Nov. 15

Horses: 15nu, Lipizzaner. 20nu, Andalusian.
No. 1257: a, Przewalski. b, Shetland. c, Dutch Gelderlander. d, Shire. e, Arabian. f, Boulonnais. g, Falabella. h, Orlov Trotter. i, Suffolk Punch.
70nu, Connemara.

1255-1256 A158 Set of 2 3.50 3.50

Sheet of 9

1257 A158 12nu #a.-i. 8.00 8.00

Souvenir Sheet

1258 A158 70nu multicolored 5.00 5.00

1999, Nov. 15

Dogs: 25nu, Weimaraner. 30nu, German Shepherd.
No. 1261: a, Australian Silky Terrier. b, Samoyed. c, Basset Bleu de Gascogne. d, Bernese Mountain Dog. e, Pug. f, Bergamasco. g, Basenji. h, Wetterhoun. i, Drever.
70nu, Labrador Retriever.

1259-1260 A158 Set of 2 6.00 6.00

Sheet of 9

1261 A158 12nu #a.-i. 8.00 8.00

Souvenir Sheet

1262 A158 70nu multicolored 5.00 5.00

Birds, Mushrooms, Anilmals A159

No. 1263, each 20nu: a, Crested lark. b, Ferruginous duck. c, Blood pheasant. d, Laughing thrush. e, Golden eagle. f, Siberian rubythroat.
No. 1264, each 20nu: a, Red-crested pochard. b, Satyr tragopan. c, Lammergeier vulture. d, Kalij pheasant. e, Great Indian hornbill. f, Stork.
No. 1265, each 20nu: a, Rufous-necked hornbill. b, Drongo. c, Himalayan monal pheasant. d, Black-necked crane. e, Little green bee-eater. f, Ibis.
Each 100nu: No. 1266, Siberian rubythroat. No. 1267, Black-naped monarch. No. 1268, Mountain peacock pheasant.

1999, Dec. 17 *Perf. 13¾*

Sheets of 6. #a.-f.

1263-1265 A159 Set of 3 27.00 27.00

Souvenir Sheets

1266-1268 A159 Set of 3 20.00 20.00

1999, Dec. 17

No. 1269, each 20nu: a, Boletus frostii. b, Morchella estculenta. c, Hypomyces lactifuorum. d, Polyporus auricularius. e, Cantahrellus lateritius. f, Volvariella pusilla.
No. 1270, each 20nu: a, Microglossum rufum. b, Lactarius hygrophoroides. c, Lactarius speciousus complex. d, Calostoma cinnabarina. e, Clitocybe clavipes. f, Microstoma floccosa.
No. 1271, each 20nu: a, Mutinus elegans. b, Pholiota squarrosoides. c, Coprinus quadrifudus. d, Clavulinopsis fusiformis. e, Spathularia velutipes. f, Ganoderma lucidum.
Each 100nu: No. 1272, Pholiota aurivella. No. 1273, Ramaria grandis. No. 1274, Oudemansiella lucidum.

Sheets of 6, #a.-f.

1269-1271 A159 Set of 3 27.00 27.00

Souvenir Sheets

1272-1274 A159 Set of 3 20.00 20.00

1999, Nov. 24 Litho. *Perf. 13¾*

No. 1275, each 20nu: a, Otter. b, Tibetan wolf. c, Himalayan black bear. d, Snow leopard. e, Flying s quirrel. f, Red fox.
No. 1276, each 20nu: a, Bharal. b, Lynx. c, Rat snake. d, Elephant. e, Langur. f, Musk deer.
No. 1277, each 20nu: a, Ibex. b, Takin. c, Agama lizard. d, Marmot. e, Red panda. f, Leopard cat.
Each 100nu: No. 1278, Rhinoceros. No. 1279, Cobra. No. 1280, Tiger.

Sheets of 6, #a-f

1275-1277 A159 Set of 3 27.00 27.00

Souvenir Sheets

1278-1280 A159 Set of 3 20.00 20.00

Millennium A160

Frame background color: 10nu, Dark blue green. 20nu, Bright violet.

1999, Dec. 15

1281-1282 A160 Set of 2 2.00 2.00

New Year 2000 (Year of the Dragon) A161

Various dragons. Denominations: 3nu, 5nu, 8nu, 12nu.
15nu, Dragon, vert.

2000

1283-1286 A161 Set of 4 2.50 2.50

Souvenir Sheet

Perf. 12¾

1287 A161 15nu multi 1.50 1.50

No. 1287 contains one 30x40mm stamp.

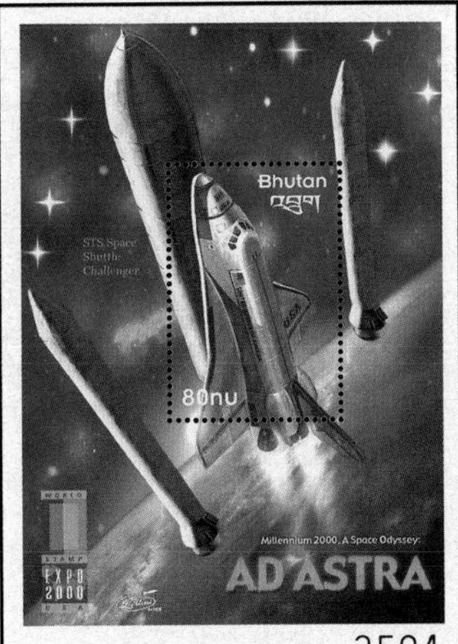

Space — A162

No. 1288, horiz., each 25nu: a, Victor Patsayev. b, Vladislav Volkov. c, Georgi Dobrovolski. d, Virgil Grissom. e, Roger Chaffee. f, Edward White.
No. 1289, horiz., each 25nu: a, NASA shuttle Challenger. b, X-15. c, Buran. d, Hermes. e, X-33 Venturi Star. f, Hope.
No. 1290, horiz., each 25nu: a, Luna 3. b, Ranger 9. c, Lunar Orbiter. d, Lunar Prospector. e, Apollo 11. f, Selene.
Each 80nu: No. 1291, Challenger. No. 1292, Buran. No. 1293, Astronaut on moon.

2000, May 15 Litho. *Perf. 14*

Sheets of 6, #a-f

1288-1290 A162 Set of 3 30.00 30.00

Souvenir Sheets

1291-1293 A162 Set of 3 15.00 15.00

World Stamp Expo 2000, Anaheim.

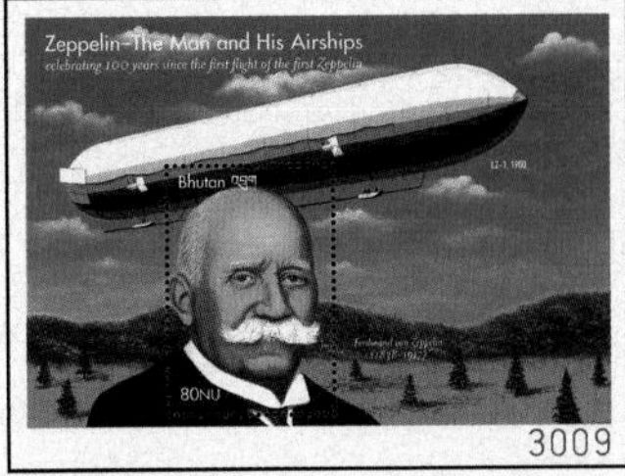

First Zeppelin Flight, Cent. — A163

No. 1294, horiz., each 25nu: a, LZ-1 and hills. b, LZ-9. c, LZ-6 in hangar. d, LZ-10. e, LZ-7. f, LZ-11.
No. 1295, horiz., each 25nu: a, LZ-1 and sky. b, LZ-2 and treetops. c, LZ-3 and ground. d, LZ-127. e, LZ-129. f, LZ-130.
No. 1296, horiz., each 25nu: a, LZ-1 and treetops. b, LZ-2 and mountains. c, LZ-3 and sky. d, LZ-4. e, LZ-5. f, LZ-6.
Each 80nu: No. 1297, Ferdinand von Zeppelin, without hat. No. 1298, Zeppelin with white hat. No. 1299, Zeppelin with black hat.

2000, May 15

Sheets of 6, #a-f

1294-1296 A163 Set of 3 30.00 30.00

Souvenir Sheets

1297-1299 A163 Set of 3 16.00 16.00

Souvenir Sheet

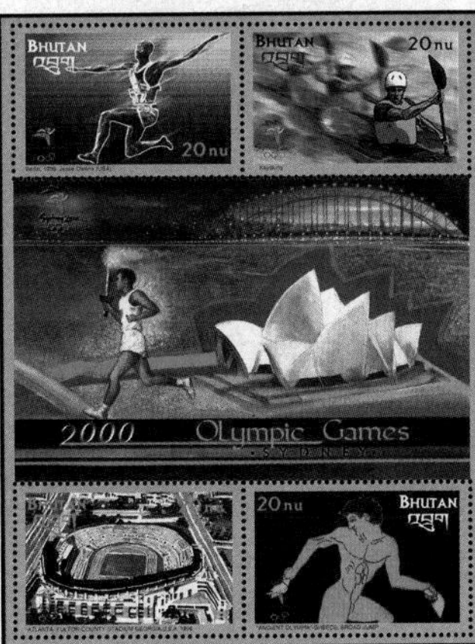

2000 Summer Olympics, Sydney — A164

No. 1300, each 20nu: a, Jesse Owens. b, Kayaking. c, Fulton County Stadium, Atlanta. d, Ancient greek broad jump.

2000, July 24

1300 A164 Sheet of 4, #a-d 5.00 5.00

British Railway System, 175th Anniv. — A165

No. 1301, each 50nu: a, George Stephenson's Rocket. b, London and Birmingham Railway, 1828. c, Northumbrian engine, 1825.
100nu, Stockton and Darlington Railway opening, 1825.

2000, July 31 Litho. *Perf. 14*

1301 A165 Sheet of 3, #a-c 10.00 10.00

Souvenir Sheet

1302 A165 100nu multi 6.50 6.50

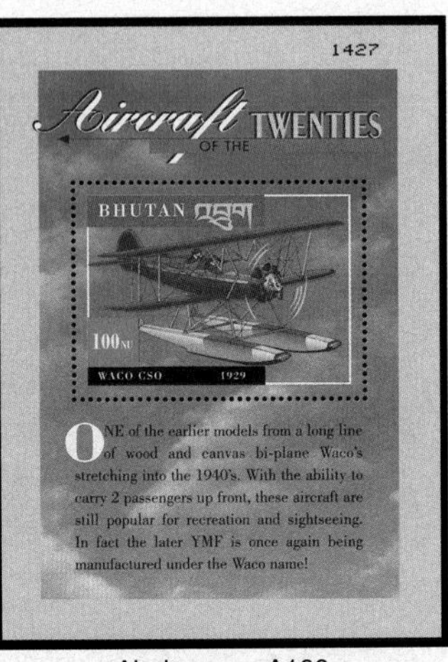

Airplanes — A166

No. 1303, 25nu: a, Laird Commercial. b, Ryan Brougham. c, Cessna AW. d, Travel Air 4000. e, Fairchild F-71. f, Command Aire.
No. 1304, 25nu: a, WACO YMF. b, Piper J4 Cub Coupe. c, Ryan ST-A. d, Spartan Executive. e, Luscombe 8. f, Stinson SR5 Reliant.
No. 1305, 25nu: a, Cessna 195. b, WACO SRE. c, Erco Ercoupe. d, Boeing Stearman. e, Beech Staggerwing. f, Republic Seabee.
No. 1306, 100nu, WACO CSO. No. 1307, 100nu, Curtiss-Wright 19W. No. 1308, 100nu, Grumman G-44 Widgeon.

2000, Aug. 7 *Perf. 13¾*

Sheets of 6, #a-f

1303-1305 A166 Set of 3 26.00 26.00

Souvenir Sheets

1306-1308 A166 Set of 3 18.00 18.00

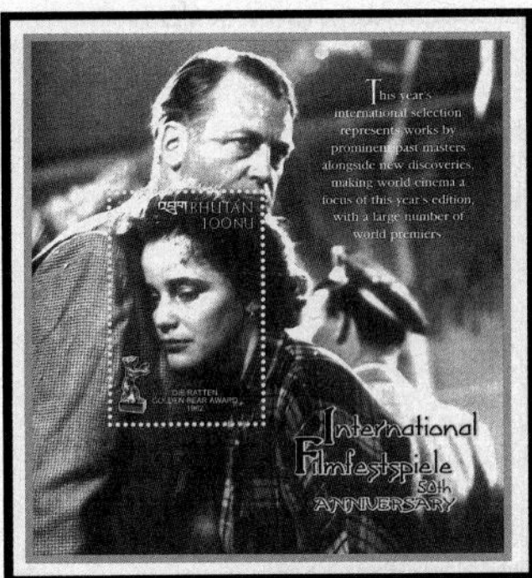

Berlin Film Festival, 50th Anniv. — A167

No. 1309, each 25nu: a, A Kind of Loving. b, Bushido Zankoku Monogatari. c, Hobson's Choice. d, El Lazarillo de Tormes. e, In the Name of the Father. f, Les Cousins.
100nu, Die Ratten.

2000, Aug. 15 *Perf. 14*

1309 A167 Sheet of 6, #a-f 9.00 9.00

Souvenir Sheet

1310 A167 100nu multi 6.50 6.50

Souvenir Sheet

Albert Einstein (1879-1955) — A168

2000, Sept. 1 *Perf. 12x12¼*

1311 A168 100nu multi 7.50 7.50

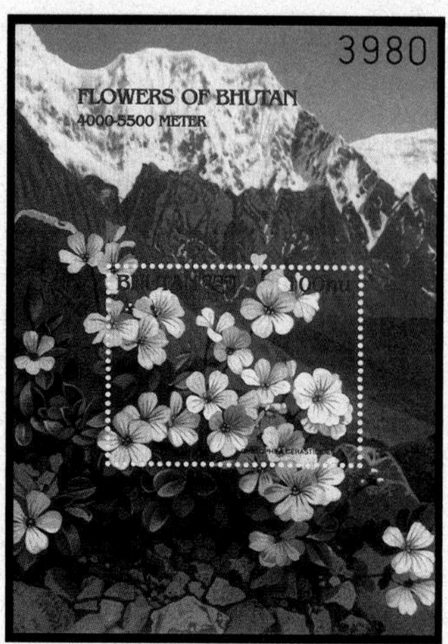

Flowers — A169

No. 1312, 25nu: a, Crinum amoenum. b, Beaumontia grandiflora. c, Trachelospermum lucidum. d, Curcuma aromatica. e, Barleria cristata. f, Holmskioldia sanguinea.

No. 1313, 25nu: a, Meconopsis villosa. b, Salvia hians. c, Caltha palustris. d, Anemone polyanthes. e, Cypripedium cordigerum. f, Cryptochilus luteus.

No. 1314, 25nu: a, Androsace globifera. b, Tanacetum atkinsonii. c, Aster stracheyi. d, Arenaria glanduligera. e, Sibbaldia purpurea. f, Saxifraga parnassifolia.

No. 1315, 100nu, Dendrobium densiflorum, vert. No. 1316, 100nu, Rhododendron arboreum, vert. No. 1317, Gypsophila cerastioides.

Perf. 14¼x14½, 14½x14¼

2000, Sept. 5

Sheets of 6, #a-f

1312-1314 A169 Set of 3 26.00 26.00

Souvenir Sheets

1315-1317 A169 Set of 3 18.00 18.00

St. Thomas Aquinas (1225-1274) A170

2000, Sept. 18 ***Perf. 14x14¾***

1318 A170 25nu multi 1.50 1.50

No. 1318 printed in sheets of 4.

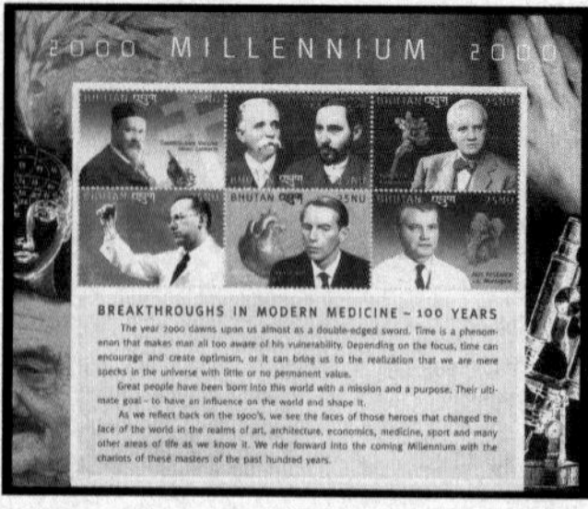

A171

Millennium — A172

Medical pioneers — No. 1319, 25nu: a, Albert Calmette. b, Camillo Golgi and Santiago Ramón y Cajal. c, Alexander Fleming. d, Jonas Salk. e, Christiaan Barnard. f, Luc Montagnier.

Olympic movement — No. 1320, 25nu: a, Baron Pierre de Coubertin. b, 1896 Athens Games. c, Jesse Owens. d, 1972 Munich Games. e, 2000 Sydney Games. f, 2004 Athens Games.

100nu, Paro Taktsang.

2000, Sept. 18 ***Perf. 14***

Sheets of 6, #a-f

1319-1320 A171 Set of 2 18.00 18.00

Souvenir Sheet

1321 A172 100nu multi 6.00 6.00

Souvenir Sheets

Explorers — A173

No. 1322, Christopher Columbus. No. 1323, Capt. James Cook.

2000, Sept. 18

1322-1323 A173 100nu Set of 2 12.00 12.00

Expo 2000, Hanover — A174

No. 1324 — Dzongs: a, 3nu, Trashigang. b, 4nu, Lhuentse. c, 6nu, Gasa. d, 7nu, Punakha. e, 10nu, Trashichhoe. f, 20nu, Paro.

No. 1325 — Flora and Fauna, 10nu: a, Snow leopard, b, Raven. c, Golden langur. d, Rhododendron. e, Black-necked crane. f, Blue poppy.

Perf. 13x13¼ (#1324), 12¾

2000, June 1 **Litho.**

Sheets of 6, #a-f

1324-1325 A174 Set of 2 4.75 4.75

Souvenir Sheet

1326 A174 15nu Temple 1.75 1.75

Size of stamps in Nos. 1325-1326: 40x31mm.

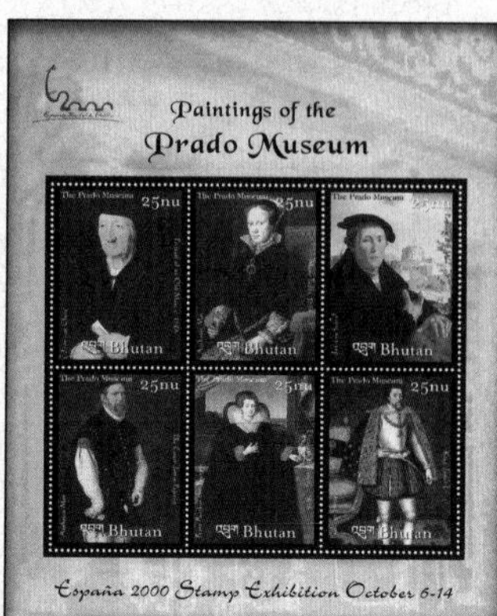

Paintings from the Prado — A175

No. 1327, 25nu: a, Portrait of an Old man, by Joos van Cleve. b, Mary I, by Anthonis Mor. c, Portrait of a Man, by Jan van Scorel. d, The Court Jester Pejerón, by Mor. e, Elizabeth of France, by Frans Pourbus, the Younger. f, King James I, by Paul van Somer.

No. 1328, 25nu: a, Isabella of Portugal, by Titian. b, Lucrecia di Baccia del Fede, the Painter's Wife, by Andrea del Sarto. c, Self-portrait, by Titian. d, Philip II, by Sofonisba Anguisciola. e, Portrait of a Doctor, by Lucia Anguisciola. f, Anna of Austria, by Sofonisba Anguisciola.

No. 1329, 25nu: a, Duchess. b, Child. c, Duke. d, Isidoro Maiquez, by Goya. e, Doña Juana Galarza de Goicoechea, by Goya. f, Ferdinand VII in an Encampment, by Goya. a-c from #1332.

No. 1330, 100nu, Charles V on Horseback at the Battle of Mühlberg. No. 1331, 100nu, The Relief of Genoa, by Antonio de Pereda y Salgado. No. 1332, 100nu, The Duke and Duchess of Osuna With Their Children, by Goya, horiz.

2000, Oct. 6 ***Perf. 12x12¼, 12¼x12***

Sheets of 6, #a-f

1327-1329 A175 Set of 3 32.00 32.00

Souvenir Sheets

1330-1332 A175 Set of 3 21.00 21.00

España 2000 Intl. Philatelic Exhibition.

Indepex 2000 Philatelic Exhibition, India — A176

No. 1333: a, 5nu, Butterfly. b, 8nu, Red jungle fowl. c, 10nu, Zinnia elegans. d, 12nu, Tiger.

15nu, Spotted deer.

2000 **Litho.** ***Perf. 13¾***

1333 A176 Sheet of 4, #a-d 2.00 2.00

Souvenir Sheet

Perf. 13¼x13½

1334 A176 15nu multi 1.90 1.90

New Year 2001 (Year of the Snake) — A177

Various snakes and flowers with panel colors of: 3nu, Light blue. No. 1337a, 10nu, Dark blue. No. 1337b, 15nu, Green. 20nu, Red.

2001 ***Perf. 12¾***

1335-1336 A177 Set of 2 1.50 1.50

Souvenir Sheet

1337 A177 Sheet, #a-b, 1335-1336 3.00 3.00

Souvenir Sheet

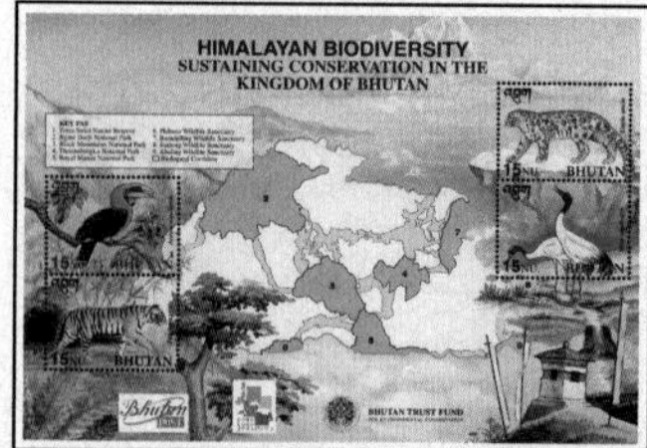

Hong Kong 2001 Stamp Exhibition — A178

No. 1338: a, Uncia uncia. b, Aceros nipalensis. c, Grus nigricollis. d, Panthera tigris.

2001

1338 A178 15nu Sheet of 4, #a-d 4.75 4.75

Intl. Volunteers Year A179

Various children's drawings: 3nu, 4nu, 10nu, 15nu.

2001

1339-1342 A179 Set of 4 2.75 2.75

a. Souvenir sheet, #1339-1342 3.00 3.00

Souvenir Sheet

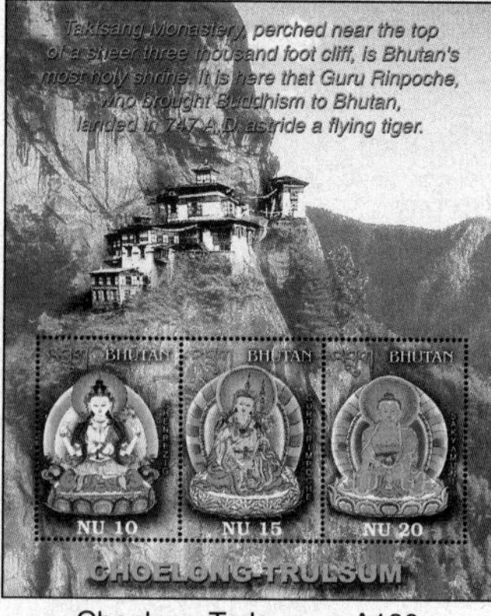

Choelong Trulsum — A180

No. 1343: a, 10nu, Chenrezig. b, 15nu, Guru Rimpoche. c, 20nu, Sakyamuni.

2001, Sept. 23 **Litho.** ***Perf. 13¼***

1343 A180 Sheet of 3, #a-c 3.25 3.25

Nos. 495-498 Surcharged

2001, Oct. 9 **Litho.** ***Perf. 11¾***

1344	A62	4nu on 10ch #495	.50	.50
1345	A62	10nu on 25ch #496	1.00	1.00
1346	A62	15nu on 50ch #497	1.60	1.60
1347	A62	20nu on 1nu #498	2.25	2.25
1347A	A62	4nu on 10ch #495	*3.00*	—
1347B	A62	10nu on 25ch #496	*6.00*	—
		Nos. 1344-1347B (6)	14.35	5.35

Obliterator on Nos. 1347A-1347B has deeper curve than that on Nos. 1344-1345.

Souvenir Sheet

Snow Leopards — A181

No. 1348: a, Face, vert. b, Two leopards. c, Three kittens. d, Leopard walking, vert.

2001, Dec. 17 **Litho.** ***Perf. 13½***

1348 A181 10nu Sheet of 8, 2 each #a-d 3.50 3.50

Souvenir Sheet

Mountains — A182

No. 1349: a, Teri Gang. b, Tsenda Gang. c, Jomolhari. d, Gangheytag. e, Jitchudrake. f, Tse-rim Gang.

2002, Feb. 5 ***Perf. 12¾***
1349 A182 20nu Sheet of 6, #a-f 8.00 8.00

Souvenir Sheet

Orchids — A183

No. 1350: a, Rhomboda lanceolata. b, Odontochilus lanceolatus. c, Zeuxine glandulosa. d, Goodyera schlechtendaliana. e, Anoectochilus lanceolatus. f, Goodyera hipsida.

2002, Apr. 3 ***Perf. 13x13¼***
1350 A183 10nu Sheet of 6 #a-f 4.50 4.50

Souvenir Sheet

Rhododendrons — A184

No. 1351: a, Rhododendron arboreum. b, Rhododendron niveum. c, Rhododendron dalhousiae. d, Rhododendron glaucophyllum. e, Rhododendron barbatum. f, Rhododendron grande.

2002, May 1 ***Perf. 13¾***
1351 A184 15nu Sheet of 6, #a-f, + label 7.50 7.50

New Year 2002 (Year of the Horse) — A185

No. 1352: a, Tan horse. b, White horse.
25nu, Yellow horse, horiz.

2002, Jan. 1 ***Perf. 12¾***
1352 A185 20nu Horiz. pair, #a-b 2.40 2.40

Souvenir Sheet

1353 A185 25nu multi 1.90 1.90

Medicinal Plants — A186

Designs: No. 1354, 10nu, Bombax ceiba. No. 1355, 10nu, Brugmansia suaveolens. No. 1356, 10nu, Podophyllum hexandrum. No. 1357, 10nu, Phytolacca acinosa.

2002, June 2 **Litho.** ***Perf. 12¾***
1354-1357 A186 Set of 4 3.25 3.25
a. Souvenir sheet, #1354-1357 3.50 3.50

United We Stand — A187

2002, Sept. 16 ***Perf. 14***
1358 A187 25nu multi 5.50 5.50

Printed in sheets of 4.

Souvenir Sheet

2002 Winter Olympics, Salt Lake City — A188

No. 1359: a, Ski jumper. b, Cross-country skier.

2002, Sept. 16
1359 A188 50nu Sheet of 2, #a-b 5.50 5.50

Reign of Queen Elizabeth II, 50th Anniv. — A189

No. 1360: a, Wearing blue hat. b, Wearing green and white hat. c, Wearing red violet hat. d, Wearing white hat with blue trim.
90nu, Wearing tiara.

2002, Sept. 16 ***Perf. 14¼***
1360 A189 40nu Sheet of 4, #a-d 7.25 7.25

Souvenir Sheet

1361 A189 90nu multi 6.75 6.75

Intl. Year of Ecotourism — A190

No. 1362: a, Lotus. b, Northern jungle queen butterfly. c, Bengal tiger.
90nu, Peacock.

2002, Oct. 14 ***Perf. 14***
1362 A190 50nu Sheet of 3, #a-c 7.00 7.00

Souvenir Sheet

1363 A190 90nu multi 5.50 5.50

20th World Scout Jamboree, Thailand — A191

No. 1364, horiz.: a, Scout. b, Four scouts. c, Boy saluting, 1908.
90nu, Daniel Beard.

2002, Oct. 14
1364 A191 50nu Sheet of 3, #a-c 7.00 7.00

Souvenir Sheet

1365 A191 90nu multi 5.50 5.50

First Solo Transatlantic Flight, 75th Anniv. — A192

No. 1366: a, Charles Lindbergh and The Spirit of St. Louis. b, Lindbergh.
90nu, Lindbergh, diff.

2002, Oct. 14
1366 A192 75nu Sheet of 2, #a-b 7.00 7.00

Souvenir Sheet

1367 A192 90nu multi 5.00 5.00

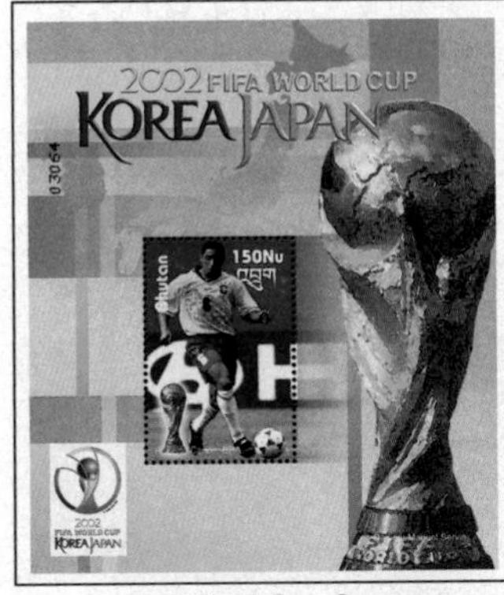

2002 World Cup Soccer Championships, Japan and Korea — A193

No. 1368: a, Zinedine Zidane. b, Michael Owen. c, Miyagi Stadium, Japan. d, Cuauhtemoc Blanco. e, Gabriel Batistuta. f, Incheon Stadium, Korea.
150nu, Roberto Carlos.

2002
1368 A193 25nu Sheet of 6, #a-f 7.00 7.00

Souvenir Sheet

1369 A193 150nu multi 7.00 7.00

A194

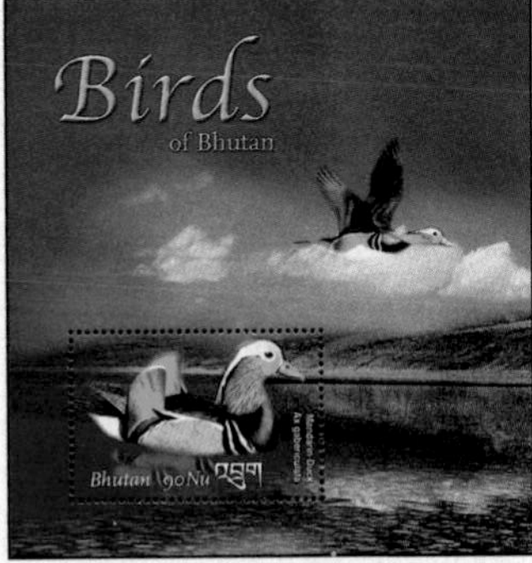

Flora, Fauna and Mushrooms — A195

No. 1370, 25nu — Flowers: a, Primula cawdoriana. b, Meconopsis aculeata. c, Primula wigramiana. d, Primula stuartii. e, Saxifraga andersonii. f, Rheum nobile.

No. 1371, 25nu — Orchids: a, Coelogyne rhodeana. b, Coelogyne virescens. c, Phalaenopsis schilleriana. d, Angraecum eburneum. e, Dendrobium aureum. f, Dendrobium Caesar x Jag.

No. 1372, 25nu — Mushrooms: a, Entire russula. b, March wax cap. c, Fawn tricholoma. d, Sulfur tuft. e, Poplar tricholoma. f, Annatto-colored cortinarius.

No. 1373, 25nu — Butterflies: a, Dead leaf. b, Troides aeacus. c, Atrophaneura latreillei. d, Teinopalpus imperialis. e, Zeuxidia aurelius. f, Euploea dufresne.

No. 1374, 25nu — Birds: a, Yellow-legged gull. b, Sand martin. c, Asian openbill. d, White stork. e, Eurasian oystercatcher. f, Indian pitta.

No. 1375, 25nu — Animals: a, Gaur. b, Hog badger. c, Indian cobra. d, Leopard gecko. e, Gavial. f, Hispid hare.

No. 1376, 90nu, Paris polyphylla. No. 1377, 90nu, Dendrobium chrysotoxum. No. 1378, 90nu, Red tentacle fungus. No. 1379, 90nu, Portia philota. No. 1380, 90nu, Mandarin duck. No. 1381, 90nu, Estuarine crocodile.

2002, Dec. 16 Litho. *Perf. 14*

Sheets of 6, #a-f

1370-1373 A194 Set of 4 25.00 25.00
1374-1375 A195 Set of 2 12.50 12.50

Souvenir Sheets

1376-1379 A194 Set of 4 15.00 15.00
1380-1381 A195 Set of 2 7.50 7.50

Pres. John F. Kennedy (1917-63) — A196

No. 1382: a, As Choate graduate, 1935. b, With John, Jr. c, As congressman, 1946. d, At White House, 1961. e, With wife at tennis court. f, Wife and children at funeral, 1963.
90nu, Portrait.

2003, Feb. 3

1382 A196 25nu Sheet of 6, #a-f 11.00 11.00

Souvenir Sheet

1383 A196 90nu multi 5.00 5.00

Princess Diana (1961-97) — A197

No. 1384: a, Wearing red dress. b, Wearing blue violet dress. c, Wearing black sweater and blue blouse. d, Wearing tiara and yellow gown.
90nu, Wearing red hat.

2003, Feb. 3

1384 A197 40nu Sheet of 4, #a-d 12.00 12.00

Souvenir Sheet

1385 A197 90nu multi 5.00 5.00

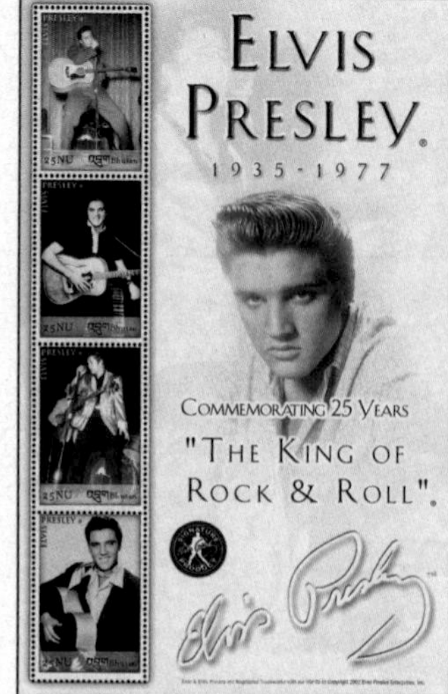

Elvis Presley (1935-77) — A198

No. 1386 — Various photos of Presley with guitar in color of: a, Greenish gray. b, Sepia. c, Bluish gray. d, Lilac.
No. 1387 — Presley without guitar in color of: a, Violet brown. b, Bluish gray. c, Sepia. d, Greenish gray. e, Brown. f, Lilac.

2003, Feb. 3

1386 A198 25nu Sheet of 4, #a-d 6.00 6.00
1387 A198 25nu Sheet of 6, #a-f 9.00 9.00

No. 548 Surcharged

2003, Feb. 25 Litho. *Perf. 13½*

1388 A69 8nu on 75ch multi .60 .60

Souvenir Sheet

New Year 2003 (Year of the Sheep) — A199

No. 1389: a, 15nu, Lambs. b, 20nu, Sheep, vert.

2003, Mar. 3 *Perf. 12½*

1389 A199 Sheet of 2, #a-b 3.00 3.00

Japanese Art — A200

No. 1390, 25nu, vert.: a, Beauty Reading Letter, by Kunisada Utagawa. b, Two Beauties, by Shunsho Katsukawa. c, Beauty Arranging Her Hair, by Doshin Kaigetsudo. d, Dancing, by Kiitsu Suzuki. e, Two Beauties, by Kikumaro Kitagawa. f, Kambun Beauty, by unknown Edo Period artist.

No. 1391, 25nu, vert.: a, Detail of Egret and Willow, by Suzuki. b, Cranes, by Jakuchu Ito. c, Detail of Cranes, by Kiitsu Suzuki. d, Mandarin Ducks Amid Snow-covered Reeds, by Ito. e, Rooster, Hen and Hydrangeas, by Ito. f, Hawk Perched on a Snow-covered Branch, by Zeshin Shibata.

No. 1392, 25nu, vert. — The Thirty-six Poets, by Hoitsu Sakai: a, Poet in black with arms folded. b, Poet in green with object in hand. c, Poet touching head. d, Poets with white, light blue, red and black kimonos. e, Poets with dark blue, black, gray and tan kimonos. f, Poets with white, green, light blue and black kimonos.

No. 1393, 90nu, Detail of Heads of Nine Beauties in a Roundel With Plum Blossom, by Eishi Hosoda. No. 1394, 90nu, Chrysanthemums by a Stream, With Rocks, by Ito. No. 1395, 90nu, Hawk Carrying Off a Monkey, by Shibata.

Perf. 14x14¾, 14¼ (#1392)

2003, Mar. 10

Sheets of 6, #a-f

1390-1392 A200 Set of 3 27.00 27.00

Size: 90x90mm

Imperf

1393-1395 A200 Set of 3 13.50 13.50

Nos. 1390-1391 each contain six 26x77mm stamps; No. 1392 contains six 38x50mm stamps.

Souvenir Sheet

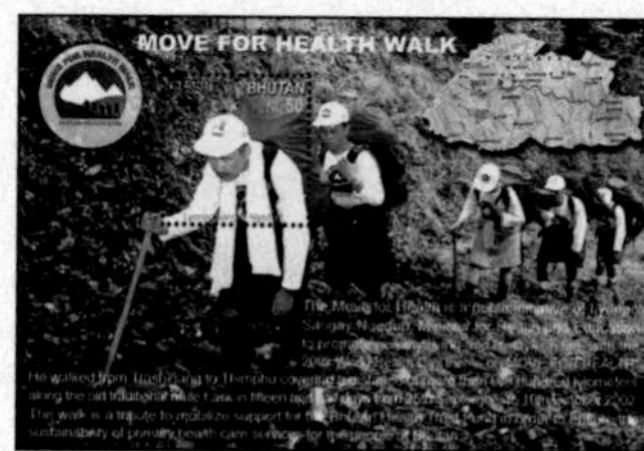

Move for Health Walk — A201

2003, May 19 Litho. *Perf. 13¾*

1396 A201 50nu multi 2.75 2.75

Souvenir Sheet

Education for Every Girl and Boy — A202

No. 1397: a, 5nu, Girl and parrot. b, 5nu, Girl reading book. c, 10nu, Boy and girl. d, 20nu, Girl with soccer ball.

2003, Nov. 11 Litho. *Perf. 12¾*

1397 A202 Sheet of 4, #a-d 2.50 2.50

Souvenir Sheet

Worldwide Fund for Nature (WWF) — A203

No. 1398: a, 2nu, Lophura leucomelanus. b, 5nu, Tragopan blythii. c, 8nu, Tragopan satyra. d, 15nu, Lophophorus impejanus.

2003, Dec. 17

1398 A203 Sheet of 4, #a-d 3.00 3.00

Souvenir Sheet

New Year 2004 (Year of the Monkey) — A204

No. 1399 — Golden langurs: a, Langur with elbow on knee. b, Langur on branch, "Golden Langur" at left. c, Langur with legs spread apart. d, Three langurs.

2004, Jan. 30

1399 A204 10nu Sheet of 4, #a-d 4.00 3.25

2004 Hong Kong Stamp Expo.

FIFA (Fédération Internationale de Football Association), Cent. — A205

No. 1400 — World Cup Champions: a, Brazil, 2002. b, France, 1998.

2004 Litho. *Perf. 11¾x12*

1400 A205 10nu Vert. pair, #a-b 1.50 1.50

Expo 2005, Aichi, Japan — A206

No. 1401 — Masked dancers: a, 10nu, Jugging-cham. b, 10nu, Durdhak-cham. c, 20nu, Nga-cham. d, 20nu, Shazam-cham.
30nu, Buddha.

2005, Mar. 25 Litho. *Perf. 13¼*
1401 A206 Sheet of 4, #a-d 4.00 4.00

Souvenir Sheet
Perf. 12

1402 A206 30nu multi 2.00 2.00

No. 1401 contains four 35x70mm stamps.

Souvenir Sheet

Rotary International, Cent. — A207

2005, Aug. 24 *Perf. 12¾*
1403 A207 85nu multi 7.50 7.50

Miniature Sheet

Pope John Paul II (1920-2005) — A208

No. 1404: a, Pink sky showing below LL corner of vignette, purple mountain sloping upward at right. b, Purple mountain at right slightly above top of Pope's shoulder. c, Purple mountain at right below top of Pope's shoulder. d, Pink frame.

2005, Aug. 24
1404 A208 15nu Sheet of 9, #a-c, 6 #d 13.00 13.00

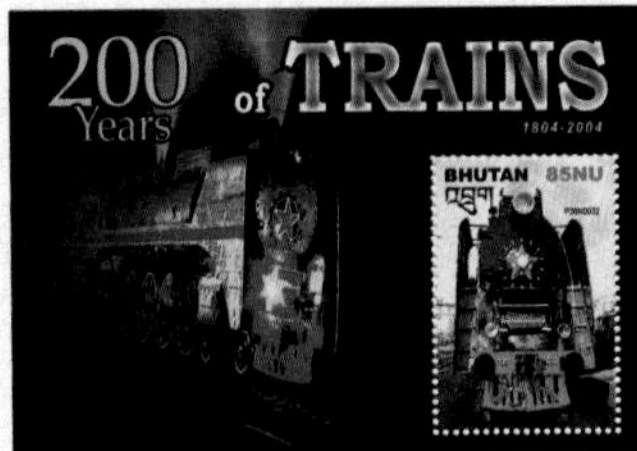

Locomotives — A209

No. 1405, horiz.: a, P36 N0097. b, VIA F 40 6428. c, InterRegio train. d, Amtrak 464.
85nu, P36 N0032.

2005, Aug. 24
1405 A209 30nu Sheet of 4, #a-d 10.00 10.00

Souvenir Sheet

1406 A209 85nu multi 7.50 7.50

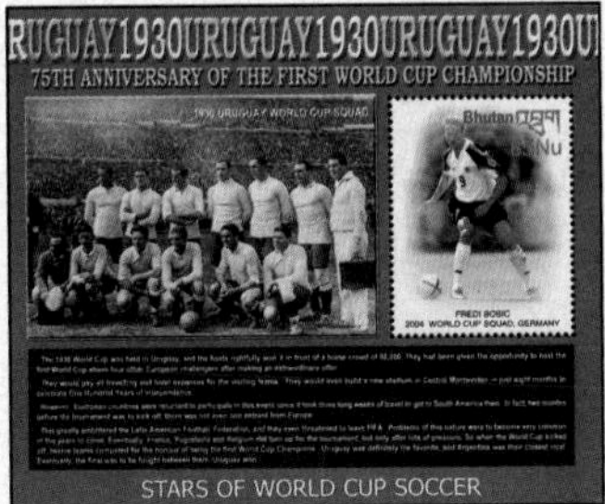

World Cup Soccer Championships, 75th Anniv. — A210

No. 1407: a, Guido Buchwald. b, Mario Basler. c, Torsten Frings.
85nu, Fredi Bobic.

2005, Aug. 24 *Perf. 12¼x12*
1407 A210 40nu Sheet of 3, #a-c 10.00 10.00

Souvenir Sheet

1408 A210 85nu multi 7.50 7.50

No. 298 Surcharged

2005 *Perf. 14*
1409 A39 5nu on 1nu #298 1.00 .40

Souvenir Sheet

New Year 2005 (Year of the Rooster) — A211

No. 1410: a, 15nu, Jungle rooster and hen. b, 20nu, Domestic rooster and hen.

2005 *Perf. 11¾x12*
1410 A211 Sheet of 2, #a-b 2.75 2.75

Japanese Assistance, 20th Anniv. — A212

No. 1411, horiz.: a, Traditional plowing. b, Traditional transplanting. c, Traditional threshing. d, Modern plowing. e, Modern transplanting. f, Modern threshing.
30nu, King Jigme Singye Wangchuk at plow.

2005 *Perf. 11¾x12*
1411 A212 5nu Sheet of 6, #a-f 2.50 2.50

Souvenir Sheet
Perf. 12x11¾

1412 A212 30nu multi 2.50 2.50

Miniature Sheet

My Dream For Peace One Day — A213

No. 1413 — Children's drawings: a, Doves, flags, people, world map. b, Candle, flags. c, Children and jigsaw puzzle. d, Hands, globe, dove. e, Hands, doves, olive branch. f, Globe holding umbrella.

2005, Sept. 21 *Perf. 13¼*
1413 A213 10nu Sheet of 6, #a-f 5.50 5.50

Miniature Sheet

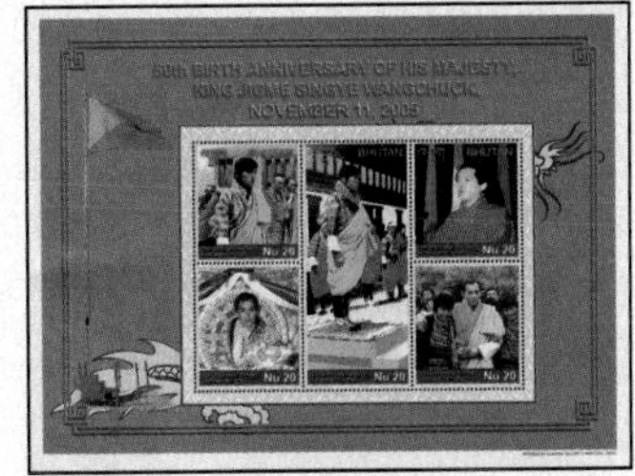

King Jigme Singye Wangchuk, 50th Birthday — A214

No. 1414: a, Standing, with other men. b, At microphone. c, With fruit bowl. d, Shaking hands with man. e, Standing on platform (39x87mm).

2005, Nov. 11 Litho. *Perf. 13¼*
1414 A214 20nu Sheet of 5, #a-e 9.00 9.00

Miniature Sheet

Bridges — A215

No. 1415: a, 10nu, Wachy Bridge. b, 10nu, Chain bridge. c, 10nu, Wooden cantilever bridge. d, 20nu, Mo Chu Bridge. e, 20nu, Langjo Bridge. f, 20nu, Punatshang Chu Bridge.

2005 *Perf. 11¾x12*
1415 A215 Sheet of 6, #a-f 8.00 8.00

New Year 2006 (Year of the Dog) — A216

Designs: Nos. 1416, 1420a, 5nu, St. Bernard. Nos. 1417, 1420b, 10nu, Lhasa Apso. Nos. 1418, 1420c, 15nu, Maltese. Nos. 1419, 1420d, 20nu, Papillon. No. 1420e, 25nu, Husky, vert. (33x68mm).

2006, Feb. 28 Litho. *Perf. 13¼*
Denominations in White or Purple (#1416)

1416-1419 A216 Set of 4 2.50 2.50

Miniature Sheet
Denominations in Yellow

1420 A216 Sheet of 5, #a-e 3.75 3.75

Europa Stamps, 50th Anniv. — A217

Designs: 150nu, Jakar Dzong. 250nu, Archery.

2006 *Perf. 12¾x13½*
1421-1422 A217 Set of 2 20.00 20.00
1422a Souvenir sheet, #1421-1422 20.00 20.00

Nos. 1421-1422, 1422a exist imperf. Values, unused or used: set $25; souvenir sheet $25.

Miniature Sheet

National Symbols — A218

No. 1423: a, 10nu, Raven. b, 10nu, Takins. c, 20nu, Cypress trees. d, 20nu, Blue poppy.

2006 *Perf. 13¼*
1423 A218 Sheet of 4, #a-d 2.75 2.75

A219

New Year 2007 (Year of the Pig) — A220

2007 Litho. *Perf. 12x11¾*

1424 A219 20nu multi 1.00 1.00

Souvenir Sheet

Perf. 13¼

1425 A220 25nu multi 1.25 1.25

Miniature Sheet

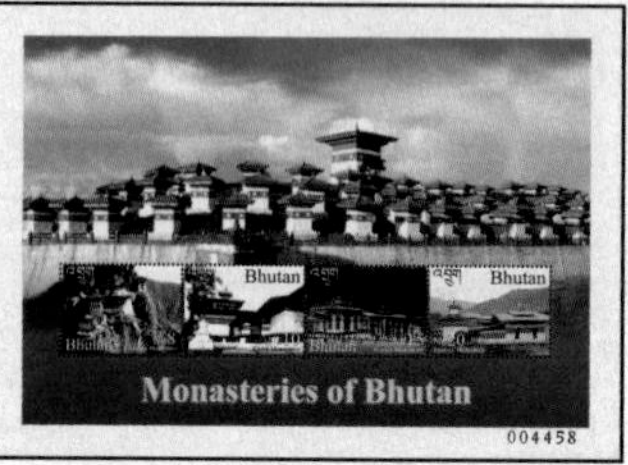

Monasteries — A221

No. 1426: a, 8nu, Taktsang Monastery. b, 10nu, Kichu Monastery. c, 15nu, Kurjey Monastery. d, 20nu, Jambay Monastery.

2007 *Perf. 13¼*

1426 A221 Sheet of 4, #a-d — —

A222

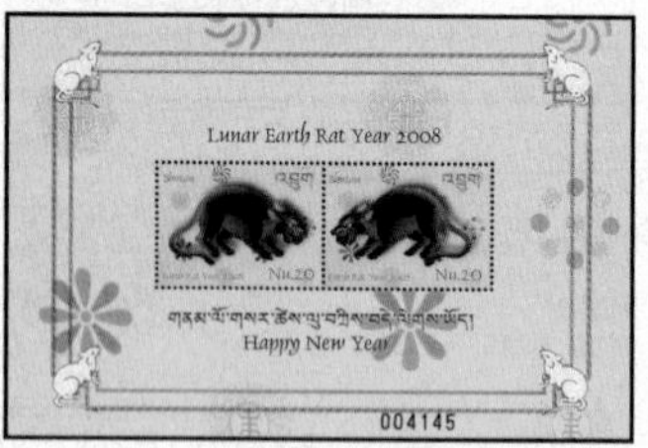

New Year 2008 (Year of the Rat) — A223

No. 1428: a, Rat facing right. b, Rat facing left.

2008

1427 A222 20nu multi 1.00 1.00

Souvenir Sheet

Perf. 13½x13¼

1428 A223 20nu Sheet of 2, #a-b 1.75 1.75

Kings — A224

Kings — A225

In Harmony With Nature — A226

No. 1429 — King: a, 5nu, Ugyen Wangchuck. b, 10nu, Jigme Wangchuck. c, 15nu, Jigme Dorji Wangchuck. d, 20nu, Jigme Singye Wangchuck. e, 25nu, Jigme Khesar Namgyel Wangchuck.

2008 Litho. *Perf. 14¼x14½*

1429 A224 Sheet of 5, #a-e, + label 4.25 4.25

Souvenir Sheets

Imperf

Self-Adhesive

1430 A225 225nu multi 15.00 15.00

1431 A226 225nu multi 15.00 15.00

Nos. 1430-1431 are sealed envelopes containing compact discs. Values are for sealed envelopes containing the discs.

Miniature Sheet

2008 Summer Olympics, Beijing — A227

No. 1432: a, 10nu, Archer aiming arrow. b, 15nu, Archer holding bow. c, 25nu, Dragon, denomination in maroon. d, 25nu, Dragon, denomination in white.

2008 *Perf. 13*

1432 A227 Sheet of 4, #a-d 4.25 4.25

Bhutan at the Smithsonian Folklore Festival — A228

No. 1433: a, Two people wearing Bhutanese masks. b, Archer. c, Farmer plowing. d, Dancers. e, Carver holding knife.

No. 1434, 50nu, Drawing of building. No. 1435, 50nu, Fireworks over building, horiz.

2008 *Perf. 13¼*

1433 A228 20nu Sheet of 5, #a-e 6.00 6.00

Souvenir Sheets

Perf. 14

1434-1435 A228 Set of 2 6.00 6.00

No. 1433 contains five 50x50mm diamond-shaped stamps.

Miniature Sheet

Visit to Bhutan of Indian Prime Minister Manmohan Singh — A229

No. 1436: a, Bhutan Prime Minister Jigme Thinley and Indian Prime Minister Singh shaking hands in front of plaque. b, Thinley and Singh, flags of India and Bhutan. c, Thinley. d, Singh, wearing turban.

2008 Litho. *Perf. 13¼*

1436 A229 25nu Sheet of 4, #a-d 4.75 4.75

Souvenir Sheets

Coronation of King Jigme Khesar Namgyel Wangchuck — A230

Voting for Happiness — A231

2009, Feb. 21 Litho. *Imperf.*

Self-Adhesive

1437 A230 225nu multi 15.00 15.00

1438 A231 225nu multi 15.00 15.00

Nos. 1437-1438 are sealed envelopes containing compact discs. Values are for sealed envelopes containing the discs.

New Year 2009 (Year of the Ox) — A232

Ox with background in: 20nu, Brown. 30nu, Brown black.

2009, Feb. 25 Litho. *Perf. 13*

1439 A232 20nu multi .80 .80

Souvenir Sheet

Perf. 13½

1440 A232 30nu multi 1.25 1.25

No. 1440 contains one 40x30mm stamp.

Punakha Dzong Bridge A233

Designs: 20nu, Entire bridge.

No. 1442: a, Bridge at right. b, Bridge at left.

2009, Mar. 20 *Perf. 12½x12¾*

1441 A233 20nu multi .80 .80

Souvenir Sheet

Perf. 13½x13¼

1442 A233 25nu Sheet of 2, #a-b 2.00 2.00

Souvenir Sheet

July 22, 2009, Total Solar Eclipse — A234

No. 1443 — Solar eclipse, buildings and: a, One man. b, Three men.

2009, June 22 *Perf. 12½*

1443 A234 25nu Sheet of 2, #a-b 2.10 2.10

Miniature Sheet

A235

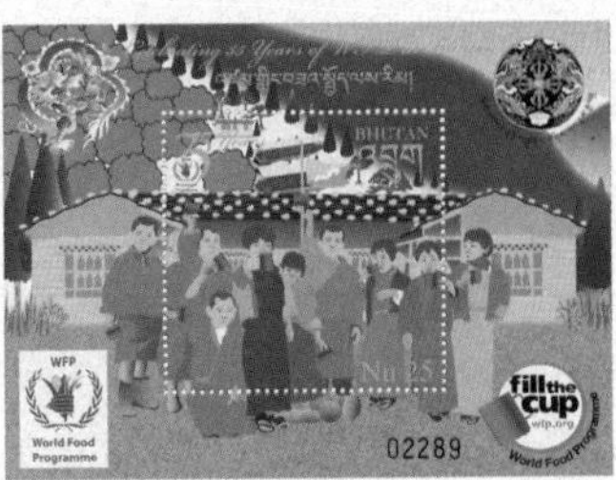

World Food Program in Bhutan, 35th Anniv. — A236

No. 1444: a, 10nu, Child leading oxen carrying rice bags. b, 10nu, Man near oxen carrying ricebags. c, 10nu, Stacked rice bags and vegetable oil boxes. d, 10nu, Farmer with hoe. e, 10nu, Farmers planting crops. f, 10nu, Men removing rocks near house. g, 20nu, Children eating. h, 20nu, Children on food line. i, 20nu, Children studying.
25nu, People holding cups.

2009, June 27 ***Perf. 13¼***
1444 A235 Sheet of 9, #a-i 5.00 5.00

Souvenir Sheet

Perf. 13

1445 A236 25nu multi 1.10 1.10

Miniature Sheet

Textiles — A237

No. 1446: a, Kushuthara. b, Mentse Mathra. c, Lungserma. d, Yathra.

Perf. 12¾x12½

2009, Sept. 28 Litho. Wmk. 388
1446 A237 20nu Sheet of 4, #a-d 3.50 3.50

Worldwide Fund for Nature (WWF) — A238

No. 1447 — Red panda: a, 20nu, Adult and juvenile. b, 20nu, Adult. c, 25nu, Adult and juvenile, diff. d, 25nu, Adult, diff.

2009, Oct. 9 Unwmk. ***Perf. 13½***
1447 A238 Block of 4, #a-d 4.00 4.00

Souvenir Sheets

New Year 2010 (Year of the Tiger) — A239

No. 1448: a, Tiger at night. b, Tiger in daylight.
50nu, Tiger, vert.

Perf. 12½x12¾

2010, Feb. 14 Wmk. 388
1448 A239 30nu Sheet of 2, #a-b 2.60 2.60

Perf. 13¼x13½

1449 A239 50nu multi 2.25 2.25

Worldwide Fund for Nature (WWF).

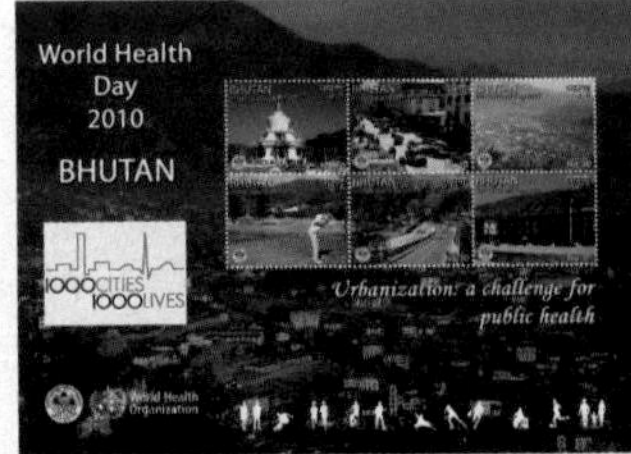

World Health Day — A240

No. 1450: a, Memorial Chorten (temple). b, Thimphu buildings, cars on street. c, Aerial view of Thimphu. d, Golfer. e, Cars on highway. f, Building, clock tower and plaza, Thimphu.
25nu, Jigme Dorji Wangchuk National Referral Hospital, Thimphu.

Perf. 12½x12¾

2010, Apr. 7 Litho. Wmk. 388
1450 A240 10nu Sheet of 6, #a-f 2.75 2.75

Souvenir Sheet

Perf. 14

1451 A240 25nu multi 1.25 1.25

No. 1451 contains one 50x39mm stamp.

16th South Asian Association for Regional Cooperation Summit, Thimphu — A241

No. 1452 — Flag of participating nation: a, Afghanistan. b, Bangladesh. c, Bhutan. d, India. e, Maldive Islands. f, Nepal. g, Pakistan. h, Sri Lanka. 25nu, Leaf, flags of the participating nations.

2010, Apr. 23 Unwmk. ***Perf. 13¼***
1452 A241 10nu Sheet of 8, #a-h 3.75 3.75

Souvenir Sheet

1453 A241 25nu multi 1.25 1.25

No. 1452 contains eight 40x30mm stamps.

A242

A243

A244

A245

King Jigme Khesar Namgyel Wangchuck — A246

No. 1454 — King: a, With bow and arrow. b, Throwing dart. c, Playing soccer with children. d, Playing basketball. e, Holding water polo ball. f, Bicycling.
No. 1455 — King: a, Bending with arms out, in front of children. b, Sitting in doorway with children. c, Standing and waving in middle of group of children. d, Standing in front of children. e, Standing, with hands on wall. f, With girl and baby.
No. 1456 — King: a, with Buddhist monk. b, Writing in book. c, Sitting in doorway with children, diff. d, With hands together touching chin. e, Sitting with children. f, Sitting on wall in front of crowd.
No. 1457 — King with background color of: a, Gold. b, Silver. c, Bronze.

Perf. 13½x13¼

2010, Nov. 1 Unwmk.
1454 A242 10nu Sheet of 6, #a-f 2.75 2.75
1455 A243 10nu Sheet of 6, #a-f 2.75 2.75
1456 A244 20nu Sheet of 6, #a-f 5.50 5.50

Perf.

1457 A245 30nu Sheet of 3, #a-c 4.25 4.25
Nos. 1454-1457 (4) 15.25 15.25

Souvenir Sheet

Perf. 13¼x13½

1458 A246 20nu multi .95 .95

Miniature Sheets

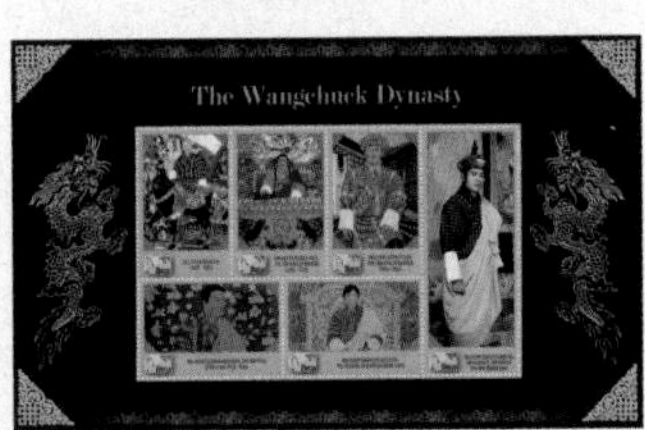

Wangchuck Dynasty Kings — A247

Queens of Bhutan — A248

No. 1459: a, Desi Jigme Namgyel (1825-81) (30x46mm). b, King Ugyen Wangchuck (1826-1926) (30x46mm). c, King Jigme Wangchuck (1905-52) (30x46mm). d, King Jigme Khesar Namgyel Wangchuck (30x76mm). e, King Jigme Dorji Wangchuck (1928-72) (45x30mm). f, King Jigme Singye Wangchuck (45x30mm). No. 1460: a, Queen Ashi Tsendu Lhamo Wangchuck (1886-1922). b, Queen Ashi Phuntsho Choden Wangchuck (1911-2003). c, Queen Ashi Pema Dechen Wangchuck (1918-91). d, Royal Grandmother Ashi Kezang Choeden Wangchuck. e, Queen Mother Ashi Dorji Wangmo Wangchuck. f, Queen Mother Ashi Tshering Pem Wangchuck. g, Queen Mother Ashi Tshering Yangdon Wangchuck. h, Queen Mother Ashi Sangay Choden Wangchuck.

2010, Dec. 17 Unwmk. ***Perf. 14***
1459 A247 15nu Sheet of 6, #a-f 4.00 4.00

Perf. 12¾x12½

Wmk. 388

1460 A248 15nu Sheet of 8, #a-h 5.25 5.25

Souvenir Sheet

New Year 2011 (Year of the Rabbit) — A249

2011, Feb. 3 Wmk. 388 ***Perf. 12¼***
1461 A249 25nu multi 1.10 1.10

Miniature Sheet

Diplomatic Relations Between Bhutan and Japan, 25th Anniv. — A250

No. 1462 — Flags of Bhutan and Japan and: a, Cherry blossoms, Mt. Fuji, flower. b, Bridge in Bhutan. c, Agricultural equipment. d, Farmer inspecting fruit.

Wmk. 388

2011, May 28 Litho. *Perf. 13½*

1462 A250 20nu Sheet of 4, #a-d 3.75 3.75

A251

1958 Visit to Bhutan of Indian Prime Minister Jawaharlal Nehru — A252

No. 1463: a, King Jigme Dorji Wangchuck greeting Nehru. b, Nehru reviewing troops. c, Nehru, King Jigme Dorji Wangchuck and family. d, Meeting.

25nu, Nehru riding ox.

Wmk. 388

2011, Aug. 15 Litho. *Perf. 13½*

1463 A251 10nu Sheet of 4, #a-d 1.75 1.75

Souvenir Sheet

Perf. 13½x14

1464 A252 25nu multi 1.10 1.10

Souvenir Sheet

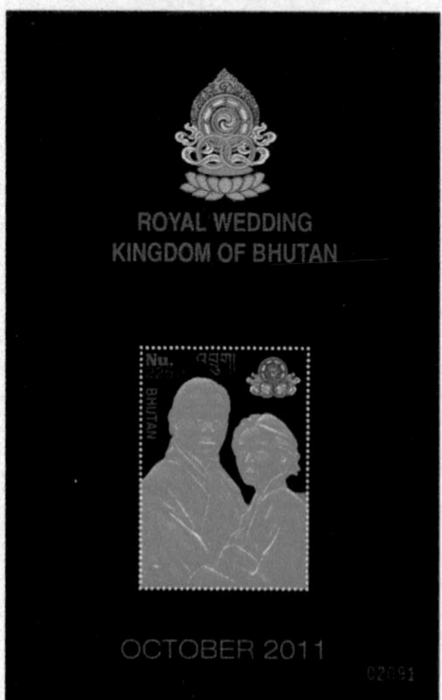

Wedding of King Jigme Khesar Namgyel Wangchuk and Jetsun Pema — A255

Litho. & Embossed With Foil Application

2011, Oct. 9 *Perf. 13¼*

1467 A255 225nu multi 9.25 9.25

Bhutan Post, 50th Anniv. — A256

No. 1468: a, Bhutan #4. b, Bhutan #83H. c, Bhutan #84B. d, Bhutan #105B. e, Bhutan #152B. f, Bhutan #153B.

50nu, Postal messenger running.

2012, Oct. 10 Litho. *Perf. 13¼x13*

1468 A256 20nu Sheet of 6, #a-f 4.50 4.50

Souvenir Sheet

Perf. 13½

1469 A256 50nu multi 1.90 1.90

No. 1469 contains one 40x40mm stamp.

Souvenir Sheets

A257

A258

A259

A260

A261

Wedding of King Jigme Khesar Namgyel Wangchuk and Jetsun Pema, 1st Anniv. — A262

No. 1470 — Royal couple with: a, Trees with green foliage in background. b, Cherry blossoms in background.

2012, Oct. 13 Litho. *Perf. 13*

1470 A257 50nu Sheet of 2, #a-b, + central label 3.75 3.75

Perf.

1471 A258 100nu multi 3.75 3.75

Perf. 13¼

1472 A259 200nu multi 7.50 7.50

1473 A260 200nu multi 7.50 7.50

1474 A261 200nu multi 7.50 7.50

Perf. 14x14½

1475 A262 200nu multi 7.50 7.50

Nos. 1470-1475 (6) 37.50 37.50

New Year 2012 (Year of the Dragon) A263

2013, Jan. 1 Litho. *Perf. 12½x12¾*

1476 A263 20nu shown .75 .75

Souvenir Sheet

Perf. 12

1477 A263 50nu Dragon, diff. 1.90 1.90

No. 1477 contains one 45x35mm stamp.

New Year 2013 (Year of the Snake) A264

2013, Feb. 11 Litho. *Perf. 13x13¼*

1478 A264 20nu shown .75 .75

Souvenir Sheet

1479 A264 50nu Snake, diff. 1.90 1.90

SEMI-POSTAL STAMPS

Nos. 10-12 Surcharged

Perf. 14x14½

1964, Mar. Litho. Unwmk.

B1 A3 33ch + 50ch multi 4.00 4.00

B2 A3 70ch + 50ch multi 4.00 4.00

B3 A3 1.30nu + 50ch multi 4.00 4.00

Nos. B1-B3 (3) 12.00 12.00

9th Winter Olympic Games, Innsbruck, Jan. 29-Feb. 9, 1964.

Olympic Games Type of Regular Issue, 1964

Souvenir Sheet

1964, Oct. 10 *Perf. 13½, Imperf.*

B4 A6 Sheet of 2 20.00 20.00

a. 1nu + 50ch Archery 6.50 6.50

b. 2nu + 50ch Soccer 13.50 13.50

18th Olympic Games, Tokyo, Oct. 10-25.

Nos. 97, 97C, 97E Surcharged

1968, Dec. 7	Photo.	*Perf. 13½*	
B5 A14n	5ch +5ch	.30	.30
B6 A14n	80ch +25ch	.50	.50
B7 A14n	2nu +50ch	1.25	1.25
	Nos. B5-B7 (3)	2.05	2.05

AIR POST STAMPS

Nos. 19-21, 38-39, 63-67 Ovptd.

a

Perfs. as Before

1967, Jan. 10 **Litho.**

Overprint "a"

C1	A5	33ch on #19	.30	.30
C2	A5	70ch on #20	.55	.40
C3	A5	1nu on #21	.65	.55
C4	A8	50ch on #38	.40	.30
C5	A8	75ch on #39	.55	.40
C6	A11	1.50nu on #63	1.00	.90
C7	A11	2nu on #64	1.25	1.25
C8	A11	3nu on #65	1.90	1.75
C9	A11	4nu on #66	2.75	2.50
C10	A11	5nu on #67	3.00	2.75

b

Overprint "b"

C11	A5	33ch on #19	.30	.30
C12	A5	70ch on #20	.50	.40
C13	A5	1nu on #21	.65	.55
C14	A8	50ch on #38	.40	.30
C15	A8	75ch on #39	.50	.40
C16	A11	1.50nu on #63	1.00	.90
C17	A11	2nu on #64	1.50	1.25
C18	A11	3nu on #65	1.90	1.75
C19	A11	4nu on #66	2.75	2.50
C20	A11	5nu on #67	3.50	3.40
		Nos. C1-C20 (20)	25.35	22.85

UN Type of Regular Issue

Bhutan Flag and: 2.50nu, UN Headquarters, NYC. 5nu, Security Council Chamber and mural by Per Krohg. 6nu, General Assembly Hall.

1971, Sept. 21	Photo.	*Perf. 13½*	
C21 A16	2.50nu silver & multi	.45	.45
C22 A16	5nu silver & multi	.85	.85
C23 A16	6nu silver & multi	1.00	1.00
	Nos. C21-C23 (3)	2.30	2.30

Bhutan's admission to the United Nations. Exist imperf.

Nos. C21-C23 Overprinted in Gold: "UNHCR / UNRWA / 1971" like Nos. 145-145C

1971, Dec. 23	Litho.	*Perf. 13½*	
C24 A16	2.50nu silver & multi	.50	.50
C25 A16	5nu silver & multi	1.00	1.00
C26 A16	6nu silver & multi	1.50	1.50
	Nos. C24-C26 (3)	3.00	3.00

World Refugee Year. Exist imperf.

UPU Types of 1974

UPU Emblem, Carrier Pigeon and: 1nu, Mail runner and jeep. 1.40nu, 10nu, Old and new locomotives. 2nu, Old biplane and jet.

1974, Oct. 9	Litho.	*Perf. 14½*	
C27 A19	1nu salmon & multi	.35	.35
C28 A20	1.40nu lilac & multi	.90	.90
C29 A20	2nu multicolored	1.25	1.25
	Nos. C27-C29 (3)	2.50	2.50

Souvenir Sheet

Perf. 13

C30 A20	10nu lilac & multi	5.75	5.75

Cent. of the UPU. Nos. C27-C29 were issued in sheets of 50 and sheets of 5 plus label with multicolored margin. Exist imperf.

Issues of 1968-1974 Surcharged 25ch and Bars

1978 **Perf. & Printing as Before**

C31	A16	25ch on 5nu, #C22	3.00	3.00
C32	A16	25ch on 6nu, #C23	3.00	3.00
C33	A20	25ch on 1.40nu, #C28	4.00	4.00
C34	A20	25ch on 2nu, #C29	4.00	4.00
C35	A14j	25ch on 4nu, #94L	4.00	4.00
C36	A14j	25ch on 10nu, #94N	4.00	4.00
C37	A17k	25ch on 5nu, #155F	4.00	4.00
C38	A17k	25ch on 6nu, #155G	4.00	4.00
		Nos. C31-C38 (8)	30.00	30.00

POSTAL-FISCAL STAMPS

Nos. AR1-AR4 are revenue stamps, authorized for use as postage stamps. After the issue of regular postage stamps in 1962, they served primarily as fiscals, although they appear to have been postally used into 1964.

Dorje (thunderbolt) — PF1

Perf. 12½

1955, Jan. 1	Litho.	Unwmk.	
AR1 PF1	(1ch) blue	1.40	—
AR2 PF1	(2ch) rose red	4.25	—
AR3 PF1	(4ch) green	7.00	—
AR4 PF1	(8ch) orange	19.00	—
	Nos. AR1-AR4 (4)	31.65	

BIAFRA

bē-af-rə

LOCATION — West Africa on the Gulf of Guinea, between Nigeria and Cameroun.
GOVT. — Republic
AREA — 29,848 sq. mi.
POP. — 13,500,000 (1967 est.)
CAPITAL — Enugu

After independence in 1960, Nigeria was torn by ethnic tensions between the Muslim north and the Christian and Animist south. During 1966, two coups, the first staged by Christian Igbo military officers from the oil-rich southeast (Biafra), with a subsequent counter-coup by Muslim officers, resulted in ethnic riots in which more than 30,000 Igbos were killed. Efforts at reconciliation between the regions failed, and on May 30, 1967, Biafra declared its independence. Hostilities between the central government and Biafra began in July, and after a bitter civil war, Biafra surrendered in Jan. 1970, and the region was reunited with Nigeria. Some 1,000,000 Biafrans died during the hostilities, either in battle or from starvation.

12 Pence = 1 Shilling
20 Shillings = 1 Biafran Pound

Catalogue values for all unused stamps in this country are for Never Hinged items.

Values for used stamps are for favor-canceled examples bearing an UMUAHIA postmark with a four-digit year date, rather than the two-digit date used on normal postal cancels. This device is 31mm in diameter, and the city name is 3mm high, both elements larger than postal cancels. Postally used examples sell for much higher prices.

Map of Biafra — A1

Arms, Flag, Date — A2

Mother and Child — A3

Perf. 12½

1968, Feb. 5	Litho.	Unwmk.	
1 A1	2p multi	.25	*.80*
2 A2	4p multi	.25	*.80*
3 A3	1s multi	.25	*2.00*
	Nos. 1-3 (3)	.75	*3.60*

Nigeria Nos. 184-187, 189-197 Overprinted

No. 4

No. 12

Arms in red on Nos. 11-14, 16

1968, Apr. 1

4	A49	½p multi (#184)	1.75	*5.75*
5	A49	1p multi (#185)	2.10	*8.50*
6	A49	1½p multi (#186)	12.00	*17.00*
7	A49	2p multi (#187)	32.50	*62.50*
8	A49	4p multi (#189)	22.50	*62.50*
9	A49	6p multi (#190)	12.00	*16.00*
10	A49	9p multi (#191)	3.75	*4.00*
11	A49	1sh multi (#192)	72.50	*125.00*
12	A49	1sh3p multi (#193)	45.00	*50.00*
13	A49	2sh6p multi (#194)	2.50	*17.00*
14	A49	5sh multi (#195)	2.75	*16.00*
15	A49	10sh multi (#196)	12.00	*50.00*
16	A49	£1 multi (#197)	16.00	*50.00*
		Nos. 4-16 (13)	237.35	*484.25*

Nos. 4-16 were overprinted locally by the Government Printer, Enugu. Overprint errors and varieties exist.

1st Anniv. Indep. — A4

Designs: 4p, Biafran flag, workers, missiles. 1sh, Igbo victim of 1966 Nigerian pogrom. 2sh6p, nurse and refugees. 5sh, Biafran arms, £1 banknote. 10sh, Biafran orphan.

1968, May 30		*Perf. 12½*	
17 A4	4p multi	.25	*.25*
18 A4	1sh multi	.30	*.30*
19 A4	2sh6p multi	.55	*3.00*
20 A4	5sh multi	.75	*3.50*
21 A4	10sh multi	1.25	*4.50*
	Nos. 17-21 (5)	3.10	*11.55*

During 1968 several sets were sold by the Biafran philatelic agents but were not released to post offices within the country and did not perform postal duty: Nigeria Nos. 184 and 185 overprinted "Biafra France Friendship" and surcharged 5sh and £1, respectively. Value, $32.50. Biafra Nos. 17-21 overprinted "Help Biafran Children" and surcharged with additional values. Value, $4. Butterflies and plants, 4 values. Value, $14; later overprinted with Olympic rings and "Mexico Olympics 1968." Value, $14.

2nd Anniv. Indep. — A5

1969, May 30		*Perf. 13¼x13½*	
22 A5	2p multi	2.50	*12.00*
23 A5	4p multi	2.50	*12.00*
24 A5	1sh multi	3.50	*14.00*
25 A5	2sh6p multi	4.00	*27.00*
	Nos. 22-25 (4)	12.50	*65.00*

Souvenir Sheet

26 A5	10sh Biafran children	55.00

No. 26 exists imperf. Value, $65.

No. 26 was numbered on the back. Examples without number are presentation proofs.

Pope Paul VI's Visit to Africa — A6

1969, Aug. 1

27 A6	4p multi, org background	1.00	*4.50*
28 A6	6p multi, blue background	1.00	*11.00*
29 A6	9p multi, green background	1.50	*14.00*

No.	Type	Description	Unused	Used
30	A6	3sh multi, rose car background	5.00	*22.50*
a.		Brown background	75.00	
		Nos. 27-30 (4)	8.50	*52.00*

Souvenir Sheet

No.	Type	Description	Unused	Used
31	A6	10sh multi, mag background	65.00	
a.		Plum background	65.00	

In Dec. 1969 and Jan. 1970, as Biafra was collapsing, three sets were issued by Biafra's philatelic agents but were not available within Biafra: Nos. 27-30 overprinted "Christmas 1969 Peace on Earth and Goodwill to All Men." Value, $9. This overprint also was applied to Nos. 31 and 31a, with denomination surcharged to £1; value, each $40. Nos. 22-26 overprinted "Save Biafra 9th Jan. 1970" with added surtax. Values: set $35, souvenir sheet $45. No. 26 imperf. with this overprint also exists. Nos. 28 and 29 overprinted with UN emblem, "Human Rights" and added surtax. Value, $10.

BOLIVIA

bə-'li-vē-ə

LOCATION — Central South America, separated from the Pacific Ocean by Chile and Peru.
GOVT. — Republic
AREA — 424,165 sq. mi.
POP. — 7,949,933 (1998 est.)
CAPITAL — Sucre (La Paz is the actual seat of government).

100 Centavos = 1 Boliviano
100 Centavos = 1 Peso Boliviano (1963)
100 Centavos = 1 Boliviano (1987)

Catalogue values for unused stamps in this country are for Never Hinged items, beginning with Scott 308 in the regular postage section, Scott C112 in the airpost section, Scott RA5 in the postal tax section, and Scott RAC1 in airpost postal tax section.

On Feb. 21, 1863, the Bolivian Government decreed contracts for carrying the mails should be let to the highest bidder, the service to commence on the day the bid was accepted, and stamps used for the payment of postage. The winner of the contract would be responsible for expenses and would keep the profits. On Mar. 18, the contract was awarded to Sr. Justiniano Garcia and was in effect until Apr. 29, 1863, when it was rescinded. Stamps in the form illustrated above were prepared in denominations of ½, 1, 2 and 4 reales. All values exist in black and in blue. The blue are twice as scarce as the black. Value, black, $75 each.

It is said that used examples exist on covers, but the authenticity of these covers remains to be established.

Condor — A1

A2

A3

72 varieties of each of the 5c, 78 varieties of the 10c, 30 varieties of each of the 50c and 100c.

The plate of the 5c stamps was entirely reengraved 4 times and retouched at least 6 times. Various states of the plate have distinguishing characteristics, each of which is typical of most, though not all the stamps in a sheet. These characteristics (usually termed types) are found in the shading lines at the right side of the globe. a, vertical and diagonal lines. b, diagonal lines only. c, diagonal and horizontal with traces of vertical lines. d, diagonal and horizontal lines. e, horizontal lines only. f, no lines except the curved ones forming the outlines of the globe.

1867-68 Unwmk. Engr. *Imperf.*

No.	Type	Description	Unused	Used
1	A1	5c yel grn, thin paper (a, b)	11.00	*25.00*
a.		5c blue green (a)	11.00	*30.00*
b.		5c deep green (a)	11.00	*30.00*
c.		5c ol grn, thick paper (a)	450.00	450.00
d.		5c yel grn, thick paper (a)	300.00	300.00
e.		5c yel grn, thick paper (b)	300.00	300.00
f.		5c blue green (b)	11.00	*30.00*
2	A1	5c green (d)	10.00	*25.00*
a.		5c green (c)	15.00	*30.00*
b.		5c green (e)	15.00	*30.00*
c.		5c green (f)	15.00	*30.00*
3	A1	5c vio ('68)	375.00	375.00
a.		5c rose lilac ('68)	375.00	375.00
		Revenue cancel		150.00
4	A3	10c brown	400.00	350.00
		Revenue cancel		175.00
5	A2	50c orange	35.00	
		Revenue cancel		15.00
6	A2	50c blue ('68)	*500.00*	
a.		50c dark blue ('68)	*500.00*	
		Revenue cancel		250.00
7	A3	100c blue	80.00	
		Revenue cancel		45.00
8	A3	100c green ('68)	250.00	
a.		100c pale blue grn ('68)	250.00	
		Revenue cancel		175.00

Used values are for postally canceled stamps. Pen cancellations usually indicate that the stamps have been used fiscally and such stamps sell for about one-fifth as much as those with postal cancellations.

The 500c is an essay.

Reprints of Nos. 3,4, 6 and 8 are common. Value, $10 each. Reprints of Nos. 2 and 5 are scarcer. Value, $25 each.

Coat of Arms
A4 A5

1868-69 *Perf. 12*

Nine Stars

No.	Type	Description	Unused	Used
10	A4	5c green	27.50	18.00
11	A4	10c vermilion	45.00	25.00
12	A4	50c blue	70.00	45.00
13	A4	100c orange	80.00	55.00
14	A4	500c black	1,000.	1,000.

Eleven Stars

No.	Type	Description	Unused	Used
15	A5	5c green	18.00	12.00
16	A5	10c vermilion	25.00	20.00
a.		Half used as 5c on cover		600.00
17	A5	50c blue	50.00	40.00
18	A5	100c dp orange	60.00	50.00
19	A5	500c black	*3,500.*	*3,500.*

See Nos. 26-27, 31-34.

Arms and "The Law" — A6

1878 Various Frames *Perf. 12*

No.	Type	Description	Unused	Used
20	A6	5c ultra	15.00	7.00
21	A6	10c orange	12.00	6.00
a.		Half used as 5c on cover		250.00
22	A6	20c green	45.00	10.00
a.		Half used as 10c on cover		200.00
23	A6	50c dull carmine	120.00	30.00
		Nos. 20-23 (4)	192.00	53.00

A7 (11 Stars) A8 (9 Stars)
Numerals Upright

1887 *Rouletted*

No.	Type	Description	Unused	Used
24	A7	1c rose	4.00	3.00
25	A7	2c violet	4.00	3.00
26	A5	5c blue	14.50	8.00
27	A5	10c orange	14.50	8.00
		Nos. 24-27 (4)	37.00	22.00

See No. 37.

1890 *Perf. 12*

No.	Type	Description	Unused	Used
28	A8	1c rose	3.00	2.00
29	A8	2c violet	8.00	4.00
30	A4	5c blue	6.00	2.00
31	A4	10c orange	12.00	3.00
32	A4	20c dk green	25.00	6.00
33	A4	50c red	12.00	8.00
34	A4	100c yellow	25.00	*30.00*
		Nos. 28-34 (7)	91.00	55.00

See Nos. 35-36, 38-39.

1893 Litho. *Perf. 11*

No.	Type	Description	Unused	Used
35	A8	1c rose	6.00	5.00
a.		Imperf. pair	100.00	
b.		Horiz. pair, imperf. vert.	100.00	
c.		Horiz. pair, imperf. btwn.	100.00	
36	A8	2c violet	6.00	5.00
a.		Block of 4 imperf. vert. and horiz. through center	200.00	
b.		Horiz. pair, imperf. btwn.	100.00	
c.		Vert. pair, imperf betwn.	100.00	
37	A7	5c blue	8.00	4.00
a.		Vert. pair, imperf. horiz.	100.00	
b.		Horiz. pair, imperf. btwn.	100.00	
38	A8	10c orange	25.00	8.00
a.		Horiz. pair, imperf. btwn.	100.00	
39	A8	20c dark green	100.00	45.00
a.		Imperf. pair, vert. or horiz.	200.00	
b.		Pair, imperf. btwn., vert. or horiz.	175.00	
		Nos. 35-39 (5)	145.00	67.00

Coat of Arms — A9

1894 Unwmk. Engr. *Perf. 14, 14½*
Thin Paper

No.	Type	Description	Unused	Used
40	A9	1c bister	1.50	1.25
41	A9	2c red orange	3.00	2.25
42	A9	5c green	1.50	1.25
43	A9	10c yellow brn	1.50	1.25
44	A9	20c dark blue	8.00	8.00
45	A9	50c claret	20.00	20.00
46	A9	100c brown rose	40.00	40.00
		Nos. 40-46 (7)	75.50	74.00

Stamps of type A9 on thick paper were surreptitiously printed in Paris on the order of an official and without government authorization. Some of these stamps were substituted for part of a shipment of stamps on thin paper, which had been printed in London on government order.

When the thick paper stamps reached Bolivia they were at first repudiated but afterwards were allowed to do postal duty. A large quantity of the thick paper stamps were fraudulently canceled in Paris with a cancellation of heavy bars forming an oval. Value of unused set: $5.

To be legitimate, stamps of the thick paper stamps must have genuine cancellations of Bolivia. Value, on cover, each $150.

The 10c blue on thick paper is not known to have been issued.

Some examples of Nos. 40-46 show part of a papermakers' watermark "1011."

For overprints see Nos. 55-59.

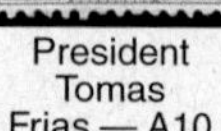

President Tomas Frias — A10

President Jose M. Linares — A11

Pedro Domingo Murillo A12

Bernardo Monteagudo A13

Gen. Jose Ballivian — A14

Gen. Antonio Jose de Sucre — A15

Simon Bolivar — A16

Coat of Arms — A17

1897 Litho. *Perf. 12*

No.	Type	Description	Unused	Used
47	A10	1c pale yellow grn	2.00	2.00
a.		Vert. pair, imperf. horiz.	100.00	
b.		Vert. pair, imperf. btwn.	100.00	
48	A11	2c red	3.00	2.00
49	A12	5c dk green	2.00	2.00
a.		Horiz. pair, imperf. btwn.	100.00	
50	A13	10c brown vio	2.00	2.00
a.		Vert. pair, imperf. btwn.	100.00	
51	A14	20c lake & blk	10.00	5.00
a.		Imperf., pair	100.00	
52	A15	50c orange	10.00	10.00
53	A16	1b Prus blue	20.00	20.00
54	A17	2b red, yel, grn & blk	60.00	*90.00*
		Nos. 47-54 (8)	109.00	*133.00*

Excellent forgeries of No. 54, perf and imperf, exist, some postally used.

Reprint of No. 53 has dot in numeral. Same value.

Nos. 40-44 Handstamped in Violet or Blue

1899 *Perf. 14½*

No.	Type	Description	Unused	Used
55	A9	1c yellow bis	30.00	30.00
56	A9	2c red orange	40.00	*50.00*
57	A9	5c green	17.00	17.00
58	A9	10c yellow brn	30.00	30.00
59	A9	20c dark blue	50.00	*75.00*
		Nos. 55-59 (5)	167.00	202.00

The handstamp is found inverted, double, etc. Values twice the listed amounts. Forgeries of this handstamp are plentiful. "E.F." stands for Estado Federal.

The 50c and 100c (Nos. 45-46) were overprinted at a later date in Brazil. Value, $500.

Antonio José de Sucre — A18

Perf. 11½, 12

1899 Engr. Thin Paper

No.	Type	Description	Unused	Used
62	A18	1c gray blue	5.00	2.00
63	A18	2c brnsh red	5.00	2.00
64	A18	5c dk green	5.00	2.00
65	A18	10c yellow org	4.00	2.00
66	A18	20c rose pink	5.00	2.00

67	A18	50c bister brn	10.00	5.00
68	A18	1b gray violet	8.00	4.00
		Nos. 62-68 (7)	42.00	19.00

1901

69	A18	5c dark red	3.00	2.00

Col. Adolfo Ballivian A19

Eliodoro Camacho A20

President Narciso Campero A21

Jose Ballivian A22

Gen. Andres Santa Cruz — A23

Coat of Arms — A24

1901-02 **Engr.**

70	A19	1c claret	.85	.30
71	A20	2c green	1.00	.50
73	A21	5c scarlet	1.00	.30
74	A22	10c blue	3.00	.50
75	A23	20c violet & blk	2.00	1.00
76	A24	2b brown	7.00	5.00
		Nos. 70-71,73-76 (6)	14.85	7.60

Nos. 73-74 exist imperf. Value, pairs, each $50.

For surcharges see Nos. 95-96, 193.

1904 **Litho.**

77	A19	1c claret	3.00	1.00

In No. 70 the panel above "CENTAVO" is shaded with continuous lines. In No. 77 the shading is of dots.

See Nos. 103-105, 107, 110.

Coat of Arms of Dept. of La Paz — A25

Murillo — A26

Jose Miguel Lanza — A27

Ismael Montes — A28

1909 **Litho.** ***Perf. 11***

78	A25	5c blue & blk	15.00	11.00
79	A26	10c green & blk	15.00	11.00
80	A27	20c orange & blk	15.00	11.00
81	A28	2b red & black	15.00	11.00
		Nos. 78-81 (4)	60.00	44.00

Centenary of Revolution of July, 1809.

Nos. 78-81 exist imperf. and tête bêche. Values: imperf. pairs, each $80; tête bêche pairs, each $95. Nos. 79-81 exist with center inverted. Value, each $95.

Miguel Betanzos A29

Col. Ignacio Warnes A30

Murillo A31

Monteagudo A32

Esteban Arce — A33

Antonio Jose de Sucre — A34

Simon Bolivar — A35

Manuel Belgrano — A36

1909 **Dated 1809-1825** ***Perf. 11½***

82	A29	1c lt brown & blk	1.00	.40
83	A30	2c green & blk	1.50	.60
84	A31	5c red & blk	1.50	.50
85	A32	10c dull bl & blk	2.00	.50
86	A33	20c violet & blk	1.75	.70
87	A34	50c olive bister & blk	2.00	.80
88	A35	1b gray brn & blk	2.50	1.50
89	A36	2b chocolate & blk	2.50	2.00
		Nos. 82-89 (8)	14.75	7.00

War of Independence, 1809-1825.

Nos. 82-89 exist imperf. Value, set of pairs $400.

For surcharge see No. 97.

Warnes A37

Betanzos A38

Arce — A39

Dated 1910-1825

1910 ***Perf. 13x13½***

92	A37	5c green & black	.50	.30
a.		Imperf., pair	15.00	
93	A38	10c claret & indigo	.60	.50
a.		Imperf., pair	50.00	
94	A39	20c dull blue & indigo	1.00	.80
a.		Imperf., pair	20.00	
		Nos. 92-94 (3)	2.10	1.60

War of Independence.

Nos. 92-94 may be found with parts of a papermaker's watermark: "A I & Co/EXTRA STRONG/9303."

Both perf and imperf exist with inverted centers.

Nos. 71 and 75 Surcharged in Black

1911 ***Perf. 11½, 12***

95	A20	5c on 2c green	.75	.30
a.		Inverted surcharge	10.00	10.00
b.		Double surcharge	12.00	10.00
c.		Period after "1911"	4.50	1.50
d.		Blue surcharge	100.00	80.00
e.		Double dsurch., one invtd.	20.00	20.00
96	A23	5c on 20c vio & blk	30.00	30.00
a.		Inverted surcharge	60.00	60.00
b.		Double surch., one invtd.	80.00	
c.		Period after "1911"	40.00	40.00

No. 83 Handstamp Surcharged in Green

97	A30	20c on 2c grn & blk	*2,500.*	

This provisional was issued by local authorities at Villa Bella, a town on the Brazilian border. The 20c surcharge was applied after the stamp had been affixed to the cover. Excellent forgeries of No. 96-97 exist.

"Justice"

A40 A41

1912

Black or Dark Blue Overprint On Revenue Stamps

98	A40	2c green (Bk)	.75	.30
a.		Inverted overprint	15.00	
99	A41	10c ver (Bl)	6.00	1.00
a.		Inverted overprint	20.00	

A42

A43

Red or Black Overprint

Engr.

100	A42	5c orange (R)	.75	.65
a.		Inverted overprint	20.00	
b.		Pair, one without overprint	50.00	
c.		Black overprint	35.00	

Red or Black Surcharge

101	A43	10c on 1c bl (R)	1.00	.60
a.		Inverted surcharge	25.00	
b.		Double surcharge	25.00	
c.		Dbl. surcharge, one invtd.	40.00	
d.		Black surcharge	200.00	150.00
e.		As "d," inverted	250.00	
f.		As "d," double surcharge	225.00	
g.		Pair, one without black surch.	800.00	

Fakes of No. 101d are plentiful.

Revenue Stamp Surcharged

Type 1 —Serifed "1"s in date

Type 2 — Sans-serif "1"s in date

1917 **Litho.**

102		10c on 1c blue, Type 1	*5,000.*	*1,750.*
a.		10c on 1c, Type 2	—	*2,000.*

Design similar to type A43.

1,000 examples of Nos. 102 and 102a were reportedly produced, with 90 percent of the issue being type 1 and the balance type 2. No. 102a also exists with overprint in black. Value, used, $2,500.

Excellent forgeries exist.

Types of 1901 and

Frias — A45

Sucre — A46

Bolivar — A47

1913 **Engr.** ***Perf. 12***

103	A19	1c car rose	.75	.30
104	A20	2c vermilion	.75	.30
105	A21	5c green	1.00	.25
106	A45	8c yellow	1.50	1.00
107	A22	10c gray	1.50	.25
108	A46	50c dull violet	3.00	1.50
109	A47	1b slate blue	6.00	2.00
110	A24	2b black	10.00	5.00
		Nos. 103-110 (8)	24.50	10.60

No. 107, litho., was not regularly issued.

Nine values commemorating the Guaqui-La Paz railroad were printed in 1915 but never issued. Value, set $25.

The original set is engraved. Crude, typographed forgeries exist.

Monolith of Tiahuanacu A48

Mt. Potosí A49

Lake Titicaca — A50

Mt. Illimani — A51

Legislature Building — A53

FIVE CENTAVOS.

Type I — Numerals have background of vertical lines. Clouds formed of dots.

Type II — Numerals on white background. Clouds near the mountain formed of wavy lines.

1916-17 Litho. *Perf. 11½*

No.	Type	Description	Unused	Used
111	A48	½c brown	.40	.30
a.		Horiz. pair, imperf. vert.	50.00	40.00
112	A49	1c gray green	.50	.30
a.		Imperf., pair	40.00	30.00
113	A50	2c car & blk	.50	.30
a.		Imperf., pair	40.00	30.00
b.		Vert. pair, imperf. horiz.	40.00	30.00
c.		Center inverted	*150.00*	*100.00*
d.		Imperf., center inverted	*250.00*	*150.00*
114	A51	5c dk blue (I)	1.25	.30
a.		Imperf., pair	40.00	30.00
b.		Vert. pair, imperf. horiz.	40.00	30.00
c.		Horiz. pair, imperf. vert.	40.00	30.00
115	A51	5c dk blue (II)	1.00	.50
a.		Imperf., pair	40.00	30.00
116	A53	10c org & bl	1.00	.30
a.		Imperf., pair	60.00	40.00
b.		No period after "Legislativo"	1.00	.30
c.		Center inverted	*200.00*	*125.00*
d.		Vertical pair, imperf. between	60.00	50.00
		Nos. 111-116 (6)	4.65	2.00

For surcharges see Nos. 194-196.

Coat of Arms
A54 A55

Printed by the American Bank Note Co.

1919-20 Engr. *Perf. 12*

No.	Type	Description	Unused	Used
118	A54	1c carmine	.40	.30
119	A54	2c dk violet	8.00	4.00
120	A54	5c dk green	.75	.30
121	A54	10c vermilion	.75	.30
122	A54	20c dk blue	2.25	.40
123	A54	22c lt blue	1.40	.90
124	A54	24c purple	.90	.60
125	A54	50c orange	7.00	.70
126	A55	1b red brown	9.00	2.50
127	A55	2b black brn	13.50	6.75
		Nos. 118-127 (10)	43.95	16.75

Printed by Perkins, Bacon & Co., Ltd.

1923-27 Re-engraved *Perf. 13½*

No.	Type	Description	Unused	Used
128	A54	1c carmine ('27)	.40	.30
129	A54	2c dk violet	.40	.30
130	A54	5c dp green	1.00	.30
131	A54	10c vermilion	25.00	18.00
132	A54	20c slate blue	2.50	.50
135	A54	50c orange	5.50	1.50
136	A55	1b red brown	1.50	1.00
137	A55	2b black brown	2.00	.60
		Nos. 128-137 (8)	38.30	22.50

There are many differences in the designs of the two issues but they are too minute to be illustrated or described.

Nos. 128-137 exist imperf. Value, $50 each pair.

See Nos. 144-146, 173-177. For surcharges see Nos. 138-143, 160, 162, 181-186, 236-237.

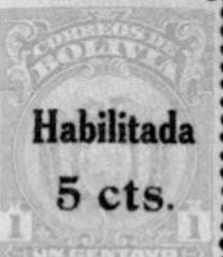

Stamps of 1919-20 Surcharged in Blue, Black or Red

1924 *Perf. 12*

No.	Type	Description	Unused	Used
138	A54	5c on 1c car (Bl)	.40	.30
a.		Inverted surcharge	10.00	6.00
b.		Double surcharge	10.00	6.00
139	A54	15c on 10c ver (Bk)	1.00	.70
a.		Inverted surcharge	12.00	6.00
140	A54	15c on 22c lt bl (Bk)	1.00	.75
a.		Inverted surcharge	12.00	6.00
b.		Double surcharge, one inverted	*16.00*	*6.00*

No. 140 surcharged in red or blue probably are trial impressions. They appear jointly, and with black in blocks.

Same Surcharge on No. 131
Perf. 13½

No.	Type	Description	Unused	Used
142	A54	15c on 10c ver (Bk)	1.00	.30
a.		Inverted surcharge	12.00	6.00

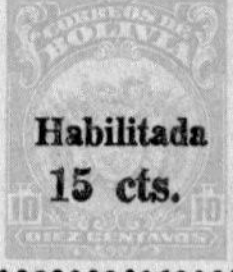

No. 121 Surcharged

Perf. 12

No.	Type	Description	Unused	Used
143	A54	15c on 10c ver (Bk)	1.00	.50
a.		Inverted surcharge	12.00	6.00
b.		Double surcharge	12.00	6.00
		Nos. 138-143 (5)	4.40	2.55

Type of 1919-20 Issue
Printed by Waterlow & Sons
Second Re-engraving

1925 Unwmk. *Perf. 12½*

No.	Type	Description	Unused	Used
144	A54	5c deep green	1.00	.50
145	A54	15c ultra	1.00	.50
146	A54	20c dark blue	1.00	.50
		Nos. 144-146 (3)	3.00	1.50

These stamps may be identified by the perforation.

Miner — A56

Condor Looking Toward the Sea
A57

Designs: 2c, Sower. 5c, Torch of Eternal Freedom. 10c, National flower (kantuta). 15c, Pres. Bautista Saavedra. 50c, Liberty head. 1b, Archer on horse. 2b, Mercury. 5b, Gen. A. J. de Sucre.

1925 Engr. *Perf. 14*

No.	Type	Description	Unused	Used
150	A56	1c dark green	1.50	
151	A56	2c rose	1.50	
152	A56	5c red, *grn*	1.50	.50
153	A56	10c car, *yel*	2.50	1.00
154	A56	15c red brown	.80	.50
155	A57	25c ultra	2.50	1.00
156	A56	50c dp violet	3.00	1.00
157	A56	1b red	5.00	2.50
158	A57	2b orange	6.00	3.00
159	A56	5b black brn	6.00	3.00
		Nos. 150-159 (10)	30.30	

Cent. of the Republic. The 1c and 2c were not released for general use.

Nos. 150-159 exist imperf. Value, $60 each pair.

For surcharges see Nos. C59-C62.

Stamps of 1919-27 Surcharged in Blue, Black or Red

1927

No.	Type	Description	Unused	Used
160	A54	5c on 1c car (Bl)	4.50	3.25
a.		Inverted surcharge	15.00	15.00
b.		Black surcharge	40.00	40.00

Perf. 12

No.	Type	Description	Unused	Used
162	A54	10c on 24c pur (Bk)	4.50	3.25
a.		Inverted surcharge	50.00	50.00
b.		Red surcharge	70.00	70.00

Coat of Arms — A66

Printed by Waterlow & Sons

1927 Litho. *Perf. 13½*

No.	Type	Description	Unused	Used
165	A66	2c yellow	.50	.35
166	A66	3c pink	.90	.90
167	A66	4c red brown	.75	.75
168	A66	20c lt ol grn	1.00	.35
169	A66	25c deep blue	1.00	.50
170	A66	30c violet	1.50	1.50
171	A66	40c orange	2.00	2.00
172	A66	50c dp brown	2.00	1.00
173	A55	1b red	2.50	2.00
174	A55	2b plum	4.00	3.50
175	A55	3b olive grn	4.50	4.50
176	A55	4b claret	7.50	6.00
177	A55	5b bister brn	8.00	6.50
		Nos. 165-177 (13)	36.15	29.85

For overprints and surcharges see Nos. 178-180, 208, 211-212.

Type of 1927 Issue Overprinted

1927

No.	Type	Description	Unused	Used
178	A66	5c dark green	.50	.30
179	A66	10c slate	.75	.30
180	A66	15c carmine	.75	.35
		Nos. 178-180 (3)	2.00	.95

Exist with inverted overprint. Value $30 each.

Stamps of 1919-27 Surcharged

1928 *Perf. 12, 12½, 13½*

Red Surcharge

No.	Type	Description	Unused	Used
181	A54	15c on 20c #122	15.00	15.00
a.		Inverted surcharge	22.50	22.50
182	A54	15c on 20c #132	15.00	15.00
a.		Inverted surcharge	25.00	25.00
b.		Black surcharge	45.00	
183	A54	15c on 20c #146	250.00	160.00

Black Surcharge

No.	Type	Description	Unused	Used
184	A54	15c on 24c #124	2.25	1.25
a.		Inverted surcharge	8.00	8.00
b.		Blue surcharge	75.00	
185	A54	15c on 50c #125	90.00	*400.00*
a.		Inverted surcharge	120.00	
186	A54	15c on 50c #135	1.75	1.25
a.		Inverted surcharge	10.00	10.00
		Nos. 181-186 (6)	374.00	592.50

Condor — A67

Hernando Siles — A68

Map of Bolivia — A69

Printed by Perkins, Bacon & Co., Ltd.

1928 Engr. *Perf. 13½*

No.	Type	Description	Unused	Used
189	A67	5c green	1.50	.25
190	A68	10c slate	.50	.25
191	A69	15c carmine lake	3.00	.25
		Nos. 189-191 (3)	5.00	.75

Nos. 104, 111, 113, Surcharged in Various Colors

1930 *Perf. 12, 11½*

No.	Type	Description	Unused	Used
193	A20	1c on 2c (Bl)	2.00	2.00
a.		"0.10" for "0.01"	35.00	35.00
194	A50	3c on 2c (Br)	2.00	2.00
195	A48	25c on ½c (Bk)	2.00	2.00
196	A50	25c on 2c (V)	2.00	2.00
		Nos. 193-196 (4)	8.00	8.00

The lines of the surcharges were spaced to fit the various shapes of the stamps. The surcharges exist inverted, double, etc.

Trial printings were made of the surcharges on Nos. 193 and 194 in black and on No. 196 in brown.

Mt. Potosi — A70

Mt. Illimani — A71

Eduardo Abaroa — A72

Map of Bolivia — A73

Sucre — A74

Bolivar — A75

1931 Engr. *Perf. 14*

No.	Type	Description	Unused	Used
197	A70	2c green	2.00	1.00
198	A71	5c light blue	2.00	.30
199	A72	10c red orange	2.00	.30
200	A73	15c violet	4.50	.40
201	A73	35c carmine	3.00	1.25
202	A73	45c orange	3.00	1.25
203	A74	50c gray	1.50	1.00
204	A75	1b brown	2.50	1.40
		Nos. 197-204 (8)	20.50	6.90

No. 198 exists imperf.

See Nos. 207, 241. For surcharges see Nos. 209-210.

Symbols of 1930 Revolution — A76

1931 Litho. *Perf. 11*

No.	Type	Description	Unused	Used
205	A76	15c scarlet	6.00	1.00
a.		Pair, imperf. between	25.00	
206	A76	50c brt violet	1.50	1.25
a.		Pair, imperf. between	30.00	

Revolution of June 25, 1930.
For surcharges see Nos. 239-240.

Map Type of 1931
Without Imprint

1932 Litho.

No.	Type	Description	Unused	Used
207	A73	15c violet	4.00	.35

Stamps of 1927-31 Surcharged

1933 *Perf. 13½, 14*

No.	Type	Description	Unused	Used
208	A66	5c on 1b red	1.00	.50
a.		Without period after "Cts"	3.00	3.00
209	A73	15c on 35c car	.50	.50
a.		Inverted surcharge	30.00	20.00
210	A73	15c on 45c orange	.60	.60
a.		Inverted surcharge	30.00	20.00

211 A66 15c on 50c dp brn 2.00 .50
212 A66 25c on 40c orange 1.00 .50
Nos. 208-212 (5) 5.10 2.60

The hyphens in "13-7-33" occur in three positions: type 1, both hypens in middle (shown); type 2, both hypens on base line of numbers; type 3, left hypen in middle, right hyphen on base line. Values are the same for all types.

Coat of Arms — A77

1933 **Engr.** ***Perf. 12***
213 A77 2c blue green .50 .30
214 A77 5c blue .50 .30
215 A77 10c red 1.00 .75
216 A77 15c deep violet .50 .30
217 A77 25c dark blue 1.50 .75
Nos. 213-217 (5) 4.00 2.40

For surcharges see Nos. 233-235, 238.

Mariano Baptista — A78

Map of Bolivia — A79

1935
218 A78 15c dull violet .75 .50

1935
219 A79 2c dark blue .50 .30
220 A79 3c yellow .50 .30
221 A79 5c vermilion .50 .30
222 A79 5c blue grn .50 .30
223 A79 10c black brn .50 .30
224 A79 15c deep rose .50 .30
225 A79 15c ultra .50 .30
226 A79 20c yellow grn 1.00 .60
227 A79 25c lt blue 1.50 .30
228 A79 30c deep rose 1.00 .60
229 A79 40c orange 2.25 1.00
230 A79 50c gray violet 2.25 1.00
231 A79 1b yellow 1.25 .60
232 A79 2b olive brown 3.00 1.50
Nos. 219-232 (14) 15.75 7.70

Regular Stamps of 1925-33 Surcharged in Black

1937 ***Perf. 11, 12, 13½***
233 A77 5c on 2c bl grn .30 .30
234 A77 15c on 25c dk bl .50 .50
235 A77 30c on 25c dk bl .80 .80
236 A55 45c on 1b red brn 1.00 1.00
237 A55 1b on 2b plum 1.00 1.00
a. "1" missing 15.00 15.00
238 A77 2b on 25c dk bl 1.00 1.00

"Comunicaciones" on one line

239 A76 3b on 50c brt vio 2.00 2.00
a. "3" of value missing 20.00 20.00
240 A76 5b on 50c brt vio 3.00 3.00
Nos. 233-240 (8) 9.60 9.60

Exist inverted, double, etc.

President Siles — A80

1937 **Unwmk.** ***Perf. 14***
241 A80 1c yellow brown .50 .50

Native School — A81

Oil Wells — A82

Modern Factories A83

Torch of Knowledge A84

Map of the Sucre-Camiri R. R. — A85

Allegory of Free Education — A86

Allegorical Figure of Learning — A87

Symbols of Industry — A88

Modern Agriculture — A89

1938 **Litho.** ***Perf. 10½, 11***
242 A81 2c dull red .80 .60
243 A82 10c pink .90 .50
244 A83 15c yellow grn 1.40 .40
245 A84 30c yellow 1.75 .60
246 A85 45c rose red 3.00 1.25
247 A86 60c dk violet 2.50 1.25
248 A87 75c dull blue 2.00 1.75
249 A88 1b lt brown 4.50 1.00
250 A89 2b bister 4.00 1.50
Nos. 242-250 (9) 20.85 8.85

For surcharge see No. 314.

Llamas — A90

Vicuna — A91

Coat of Arms — A92

Cocoi Herons — A93

Chinchilla — A94

Toco Toucan — A95

Condor — A96

Jaguar — A97

1939, Jan. 21 ***Perf. 10½, 11½x10½***
251 A90 2c green 1.50 .75
252 A90 4c fawn 1.50 .75
253 A90 5c red violet 1.50 .75
254 A91 10c black 1.50 .75
255 A91 15c emerald 3.00 1.25
256 A91 20c dk slate grn 3.00 1.25
257 A92 25c lemon 1.50 .75
258 A92 30c dark blue 1.50 .75
259 A93 40c vermilion 2.50 1.00
260 A93 45c gray 2.50 1.00
261 A94 60c rose red 2.50 1.00
262 A94 75c slate blue 2.50 1.00
263 A95 90c orange 5.00 1.25
264 A95 1b blue 5.00 1.25
265 A96 2b rose lake 7.00 1.25
266 A96 3b dark violet 10.00 1.75
267 A97 4b brown org 10.00 1.75
268 A97 5b gray brown 11.50 2.00
Nos. 251-268 (18) 73.50 20.25

All but 20c exist imperf. Value, each pair $40.

Imperf. counterfeits with altered designs exist of some values.

For surcharges see Nos. 315-317.

Flags of 21 American Republics — A98

1940, Apr. **Litho.** ***Perf. 10½***
269 A98 9b multicolored 4.50 2.25

Pan American Union, 50th anniversary.

Statue of Murillo — A99

Urns of Murillo and Sagarnaga — A100

Dream of Murillo — A101

Murillo — A102

1941, Apr. 15
270 A99 10c dull vio brn .25 .25
271 A100 15c lt green .50 .30
a. Imperf., pair 25.00
b. Double impression 8.00 8.00
272 A101 45c carmine rose .50 .25
a. Double impression 10.00 10.00
273 A102 1.05b dk ultra .80 .40
Nos. 270-273 (4) 2.05 1.20

130th anniv. of the execution of Pedro Domingo Murillo (1759-1810), patriot.

For surcharge see No. 333.

First Stamp of Bolivia and 1941 Airmail Stamp — A103

1942, Oct. **Litho.** ***Perf. 13½***
274 A103 5c pink 1.00 1.00
275 A103 10c orange 1.00 1.00
276 A103 20c yellow grn 1.50 1.00
277 A103 40c carmine rose 1.50 1.00
278 A103 90c ultra 3.00 2.25
279 A103 1b violet 5.00 3.75
280 A103 10b olive bister 20.00 16.00
Nos. 274-280 (7) 33.00 26.00

1st School Phil. Exposition held in La Paz, Oct., 1941.

Gen. Ballivian Leading Cavalry Charge, Battle of Ingavi — A104

1943 **Photo.** ***Perf. 12½***
281 A104 2c lt blue grn .30 .25
282 A104 3c orange .30 .25
283 A104 25c deep plum .60 .35
284 A104 45c ultra .60 .35
285 A104 3b scarlet 1.40 .70
286 A104 4b brt rose lilac 1.50 .80
287 A104 5b black brown 1.50 .90
Nos. 281-287 (7) 6.20 3.60

Souvenir Sheets

Perf. 13, Imperf.

288 A104 Sheet of 4 6.00 6.00
289 A104 Sheet of 3 15.00 15.00

Centenary of the Battle of Ingavi, 1841. No. 288 contains 4 stamps similar to Nos. 281-284, No. 289 three stamps similar to Nos. 285-287.

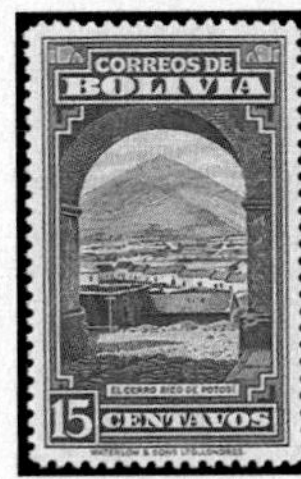

Potosi A107

Quechisla A108

Miner — A109

Dam A110

Mine Interior A111

Chaquiri Dam A112

Entrance to Pulacayo Mine A113

1943 **Engr.** ***Perf. 12½***

290 A107 15c red brown .50 .30
291 A108 45c vio blue .60 .30
292 A109 1.25b brt rose vio 1.00 .50
293 A110 1.50b emerald .80 .50
294 A111 2b brown blk 1.00 .70
295 A112 2.10b lt blue 1.00 .70
296 A113 3b red orange 4.00 1.10
Nos. 290-296 (7) 8.90 4.10

General José Ballivián and Cathedral at Trinidad A114

1943, Nov. 18

297 A114 5c dk green & brn .50 .30
298 A114 10c dull pur & brn .50 .30
299 A114 30c rose red & brn .50 .30
300 A114 45c brt ultra & brn .75 .50
301 A114 2.10b dp org & brn 1.50 1.00
Nos. 297-301,C91-C95 (10) 6.40 4.30

Department of Beni centenary.

"Honor, Work, Law" — A115

"United for the Country" — A116

1944 **Litho.** ***Perf. 13½***

302 A115 20c orange .30 .30
303 A115 90c ultra .30 .30
304 A116 1b brt red vio .30 .30
305 A116 2.40b dull brown .30 .30

1945

306 A115 20c green .30 .30
307 A115 90c dp rose .50 .30
Nos. 302-307,C96-C99 (10) 3.35 2.80

Nos. 302-307 were issued to commemorate the Revolution of Dec. 20, 1943.

Catalogue values for unused stamps in this section, from this point to the end of the section, are for Never Hinged items.

Leopold Benedetto Vincenti, Joseph Ignacio de Sanjines and Bars of Anthem — A117

1946, Aug. 21 **Litho.** ***Perf. 10½***

308 A117 5c rose vio & blk .40 .25
309 A117 10c ultra & blk .40 .25
310 A117 15c blue grn & blk .40 .25
311 A117 30c vermilion & brn .40 .25
a. Souv. sheet of 1, imperf. 3.00 2.50
312 A117 90c dk blue & brn .60 .30
313 A117 2b black & brn 1.00 .50
a. Souv. sheet of 1, imperf. 6.00 5.00
Nos. 308-313 (6) 3.20 1.80

Adoption of Bolivia's natl. anthem, cent. Nos. 311a and 313a sold for 4b over face.

Nos. 248 and 262 Surcharged in Carmine, Black or Orange

1947, Mar. 12 ***Perf. 10½, 11***

314 A87 1.40b on 75c (C) .50 .30
315 A94 1.40b on 75c (Bk) .50 .30
316 A94 1.40b on 75c (C) .50 .30
317 A94 1.40b on 75c (O) .50 .30
Nos. 314-317,C112 (5) 2.50 1.45

People Attacking Presidential Palace — A118

1947, Sept. **Litho.** ***Perf. 13½***

318 A118 20c blue grn .25 .25
319 A118 50c lilac rose .30 .25
320 A118 1.40b grnsh bl .30 .25
321 A118 3.70b dull org 1.00 .30
322 A118 4b violet 1.00 .30
323 A118 10b olive 3.00 1.00
Nos. 318-323,C113-C117 (11) 7.80 4.15

1st anniv. of the Revolution of July 21, 1946. Nos. 318-323 exist imperf. Value, each pair $40.

Arms of Bolivia and Argentina A119

1947, Oct. 23

324 A119 1.40b deep orange .50 .25

Meeting of Presidents Enrique Hertzog of Bolivia and Juan D. Peron of Argentina at Yacuiba on Oct. 23, 1947. Exist imperf.
See No. C118.

Statue of Christ above La Paz — A120

2b, Child kneeling before cross of Golgotha. 3b, St. John Bosco. No. 328, Virgin of Copacabana. No. 329, Pope Pius XII blessing University of La Paz.

1948, Sept. 26 **Unwmk.** ***Perf. 11½***

325 A120 1.40b blue & yel 1.00 .25
326 A120 2b yel grn & sal 1.25 .50
327 A120 3b green & gray 2.50 .50
328 A120 5b violet & sal 2.50 .75
329 A120 5b red brn & lt grn 4.00 1.00
Nos. 325-329,C119-C123 (10) 19.20 6.50

3rd Inter-American Cong. of Catholic Education.

Map and Emblem of Bolivia Auto Club — A125

Pres. Gregorio Pacheco, Map and Post Horn — A126

1948, Oct. 20

330 A125 5b indigo & salmon 3.00 1.00

Intl. Automobile Races of South America, Sept.-Oct. 1948. See No. C124.

1950, Jan. 2 **Litho.** ***Perf. 11½***

331 A126 1.40b violet blue .70 .25
332 A126 4.20b red .80 .25
Nos. 331-332,C125-C127 (5) 4.00 1.25

75th anniv. of the UPU.

No. 273 Surcharged in Black

1950 ***Perf. 10½***

333 A102 2b on 1.05b dk ultra .60 .25

Crucifix and View of Potosi — A127

Symbols of United Nations — A128

Perf. 11½

1950, Sept. 14 **Litho.** **Unwmk.**

334 A127 20c violet .30 .25
335 A127 30c dp orange .30 .25
336 A127 50c lilac rose .30 .25
337 A127 1b carmine .30 .25
338 A127 2b blue .50 .25
339 A127 6b chocolate .60 .30
Nos. 334-339 (6) 2.30 1.55

400th anniv. of the appearance of a crucifix at Potosi. Exist imperf.

1950, Oct. 24

340 A128 60c ultra 2.50 .50
341 A128 2b green 3.75 .50
Nos. 340-341,C138-C139 (4) 10.50 2.00

5th anniv. of the UN, Oct. 24, 1945.

Gate of the Sun and Llama A129

Church of San Francisco — A130

40c, Avenue Camacho. 50c, Consistorial Palace. 1b, Legislative Palace. 1.40b, Communications Bldg. 2b, Arms. 3b, La Gasca ordering Mendoza to found La Paz. 5b, Capt. Alonso de Mendoza founding La Paz. 10b, Arms; portrait of Mendoza.

1951, Mar. **Engr.** ***Perf. 12½***

Center in Black

342 A129 20c green .60 .25
343 A130 30c dp orange .60 .25
344 A129 40c bister brn .60 .25
345 A129 50c dk red .60 .25
346 A129 1b dp purple .60 .25
347 A129 1.40b dk vio blue .60 .25
348 A129 2b dp purple .60 .25
349 A129 3b red lilac .75 .40
a. Sheet, Nos. 345, 346, 348, 349 3.50 3.50
b. As "a," imperf. 3.50 3.50
350 A129 5b dk red 1.00 .50
a. Sheet, Nos. 344, 347, 350 3.50 3.50
b. As "a," imperf. 3.50 3.50
351 A129 10b sepia 1.50 .50
a. Sheet, Nos. 342, 343, 351 3.50 3.50
b. As "a," imperf. 3.50 3.50
Nos. 342-351,C140-C149 (20) 16.95 8.50

400th anniv. of the founding of La Paz.
For surcharges see Nos. 393-402.

Boxing A131

Perf. 12½

1951, July 1 **Unwmk.** **Engr.**

352 A131 20c shown .60 .25
353 A131 50c Tennis .60 .25
354 A131 1b Diving .60 .25
355 A131 1.40b Soccer .60 .25
356 A131 2b Skiing 1.75 .60
357 A131 3b Handball 3.00 1.00
a. Sheet, #352-353, 356-357 7.00 7.00
b. As "a," imperf. 7.00 7.00
358 A131 4b Cycling 4.00 2.00
a. Sheet, #354-355, 358 7.00 7.00
b. As "a," imperf. 7.00 7.00
Nos. 352-358,C150-C156 (14) 32.90 12.20

The stamps were intended to commemorate the 5th athletic championship matches held at La Paz, October 1948.

An imperforate souvenir sheet denominated 54b, depicting Nos. 354, 654 and 659 with simulated perforations, was issued March 24, 1982, to celebrate the España '82 World Cup soccer championship games. Value $50.

A souvenir sheet denominated 2b, containing No. 356 perf 14¼, was issued June 15, 1988, to mark the 1988 Calgary Winter Olympic Games. Value $25.

Eagle and Flag of Bolivia A132

1951, Nov. 5 **Litho.** ***Perf. 11½***

Flag in Red, Yellow and Green.

359 A132 2b aqua .40 .25
360 A132 3.50b ultra .40 .25
361 A132 5b purple .40 .25
362 A132 7.50b gray 1.00 .30
363 A132 15b dp car 1.00 .30
364 A132 30b sepia 2.00 .65
Nos. 359-364 (6) 5.20 2.00

Cent. of the adoption of Bolivia's natl. flag.

Eduardo Abaroa — A133

Queen Isabella I — A134

1952, Mar. ***Perf. 11***

365 A133 80c dk carmine .30 .25
366 A133 1b red orange .30 .25
367 A133 2b emerald .50 .30
368 A133 5b ultra .75 .40
369 A133 10b lilac rose 2.00 .50
370 A133 20b dk brown 2.50 1.00
Nos. 365-370,C157-C162 (12) 21.05 7.45

73rd anniv. of the death of Eduardo Abaroa.

1952, July 16 Unwmk. *Perf. 13½*

371 A134 2b vio bl .55 .25
372 A134 6.30b carmine 1.00 .25
Nos. 371-372,C163-C164 (4) 6.55 1.75

Birth of Isabella I of Spain, 500th anniv.

Columbus Lighthouse — A135

1952, July 16 Litho.

373 A135 2b vio bl, *bl* .50 .25
374 A135 5b car, *sal* 2.00 .50
375 A135 9b emer, *grn* 3.00 1.00
Nos. 373-375,C165-C168 (7) 10.00 2.95

An imperforate souvenir sheet denominated 1,000,000b, depicting No. 374 with simulated perforations, was issued May 12, 1986, to mark the 500th anniversary of the discovery of America. Value $30.

Miner — A136

1953, Apr. 9

376 A136 2.50b vermilion .50 .25
377 A136 8b violet .50 .25

Nationalization of the mines.

Gualberto Villarroel, Victor Paz Estenssoro and Hernan Siles Zuazo A137

1953, Apr. 9 *Perf. 11½*

378 A137 50c rose lil .40 .25
379 A137 1b brt rose .40 .25
380 A137 2b vio bl .50 .25
381 A137 3b lt grn .50 .25
382 A137 4b yel org 1.50 .40
383 A137 5b dl vio .50 .25
Nos. 378-383,C169-C175 (13) 9.60 3.75

Revolution of Apr. 9, 1952, 1st anniv.

Map of Bolivia and Cow's Head — A138

25b, 85b, Map and ear of wheat.

1954, Aug. 2 *Perf. 12x11½*

384 A138 5b car rose .30 .25
385 A138 17b aqua .40 .25
386 A138 25b chalky blue .50 .25
387 A138 85b blk brn 1.50 .40
Nos. 384-387,C176-C181 (10) 9.85 2.90

Nos. 384-385 for the agrarian reform laws of 1953-54. Nos. 386-387 for the 1st National Congress of Agronomy. Exist imperf.

Oil Refinery A139

1955, Oct. 9 Unwmk. *Perf. 12x11½*

388 A139 10b ultra & lt ultra .50 .25
389 A139 35b rose car & rose .50 .25
390 A139 40b dk & lt yel grn .60 .25
391 A139 50b red vio & lil rose .60 .25
392 A139 80b brn & bis brn .80 .25
Nos. 388-392,C182-C186 (10) 14.20 5.70

Nos. 388-392 exist imperf. Value, set of pairs $250.

Nos. 342-351, Surcharged with New Values and Bars in Ultramarine

1957, Feb. 14 Engr. *Perf. 12½*

Center in Black

393 A129 50b on 3b red lilac .30 .25
394 A129 100b on 2b dp pur .30 .25
395 A129 200b on 1b dp pur .30 .25
396 A129 300b on 1.40b dk vio bl .30 .25
397 A129 350b on 20c green .50 .30
398 A129 400b on 40c bis brn .75 .30
399 A130 600b on 30c dp org .80 .40
400 A129 800b on 50c dk red 1.00 .50
401 A129 1000b on 10b sepia 1.50 .60
402 A129 2000b on 5b dk red 2.25 1.00
Nos. 393-402 (10) 8.00 4.10

See Nos. C187-C196.

CEPAL Building, Santiago de Chile, and Meeting Hall in La Paz — A140

1957, May 15 Litho. *Perf. 13*

403 A140 150b gray & ultra .30 .25
404 A140 350b bis brn & gray .60 .25
405 A140 550b chlky bl & brn .90 .25
406 A140 750b dp rose & grn 1.25 .30
407 A140 900b grn & brn blk 2.00 .60
Nos. 403-407,C197-C201 (10) 20.55 6.75

7th session of the C. E. P. A. L. (Comision Economica para la America Latina de las Naciones Unidas), La Paz. Nos. 403-407 exist imperf. Value, set of pairs $250.

For surcharges see Nos. 482-484,

Presidents Siles Zuazo and Aramburu A141

1957, Dec. 15 Unwmk. *Perf. 11½*

408 A141 50b dp red org & org .70 .25
409 A141 350b dp blue & blue 1.00 .25
410 A141 1000b dp brn & brn rose 2.00 .30
Nos. 408-410,C202-C204 (6) 9.20 1.80

Opening of the Santa Cruz-Yacuiba Railroad and the meeting of the Presidents of Bolivia and Argentina. Nos. 408-410, C202-C204 exist imperf. Value, set of pairs $160.

For surcharge see No. 699.

Flags of Bolivia and Mexico and Presidents Hernan Siles Zuazo and Adolfo Lopez Mateos A142

1960, Jan. 30 Litho. *Perf. 11½*

411 A142 350b olive .50 .25
412 A142 600b red brown 1.00 .30
413 A142 1500b black brown 2.50 .60
Nos. 411-413,C205-C207 (6) 10.50 3.65

Issued for an expected visit of Mexico's President Adolfo Lopez Mateos. On sale Jan. 30-Feb. 1, 1960.

Indians and Mt. Illimani A143

1960, Mar. 26 Unwmk.

414 A143 500b olive bister 1.10 .50
415 A143 1000b blue 3.25 .70
416 A143 2000b brown 5.00 1.10
417 A143 4000b green 7.75 5.00
Nos. 414-417,C208-C211 (8) 54.60 25.30

Refugee Children — A144

1960, Apr. 7 *Perf. 11½*

418 A144 50b brown .35 .25
419 A144 350b claret .50 .25
420 A144 400b steel blue .80 .30
421 A144 1000b gray brown 1.75 .75
422 A144 3000b slate green 8.50 1.50
Nos. 418-422,C212-C216 (10) 21.15 7.50

World Refugee Year, 7/1/59-6/30/60.

For surcharges see Nos. 454-458, 529.

Jaime Laredo A145

1960, Aug. 15 Litho. *Perf. 11½*

423 A145 100b olive .70 .25
424 A145 350b deep rose .70 .25
425 A145 500b Prus green 1.50 .30
426 A145 1000b brown 2.50 .70
427 A145 1500b violet blue 3.50 1.00
428 A145 5000b gray 7.50 4.00
Nos. 423-428,C217-C222 (12) 45.65 14.50

Issued to honor violinist Jaime Laredo.

For surcharge see No. 485.

Rotary Emblem and Nurse with Children — A146

1960, Nov. 19 *Perf. 11½*

429 A146 350b multi .45 .25
430 A146 500b multi .65 .40
431 A146 600b multi 1.10 .40
432 A146 1000b multi 1.75 .60
Nos. 429-432,C223-C226 (8) 15.20 6.65

Issued for the Children's Hospital, sponsored by the Rotary Club of La Paz.

For surcharges see Nos. 486-487.

Designs from Gate of the Sun A147 A148

Designs: Various prehistoric gods and ornaments from Tiahuanacu excavations.

Surcharged in Black or Dark Red Gold Background

1960, Dec. 16 *Perf. 13x12, 12x13*

Sizes: 21x23mm, 23x21mm

433 A147 50b on ½c red .90 .45
434 A147 100b on 1c red .45 .25
435 A147 200b on 2c blk 2.00 .40
436 A147 300b on 5c grn (DR) .75 .40
437 A147 350b on 10c grn 1.25 1.10
438 A148 400b on 15c ind 1.25 .40
439 A148 500b on 20c red .75 .40
440 A148 500b on 50c red 1.00 .40
441 A148 600b on 22½c grn 1.00 .60
442 A148 600b on 60c vio 1.50 .60
443 A148 700b on 25c vio 1.50 .60
444 A148 700b on 1b grn 1.75 1.20
445 A148 800b on 30c red 1.50 .50
446 A148 900b on 40c grn 1.50 .50
447 A148 1000b on 2b bl 2.50 1.00
448 A148 1800b on 3b gray 10.00 7.00

Perf. 11

Size: 49½x23mm

449 A148 4000b on 4b gray 95.00 60.00

Perf. 11x13½

Size: 49x53mm

450 A147 5000b on 5b gray 20.00 15.00
Nos. 433-450 (18) 144.60 90.80

Nos. 433-450 were not regularly issued without surcharge. Value, set $60.

The decree for Nos. 433-450 stipulated that 7 were for air mail (500b on 50c, 600b on 60c, 700b on 1b, 1000b, 1800b, 4000b and 5000b), but the overprinting failed to include "Aereo."

The 800b surcharge also exists on the 1c red and gold. This was not listed in the decree. Value $20.

An imperforate 1,000,000b souvenir sheet, depicting the 5c and 3b values of the unissued set was issued May 12, 1986, to commemorate Halley's Comet. Value $75.

For surcharges see Nos. 528, 614.

Miguel de Cervantes A149

Nuflo de Chaves A150

1961, Nov. Photo. *Perf. 13x12½*

451 A149 600b ocher & dl vio 1.00 .40

Cervantes' appointment as Chief Magistrate of La Paz. See No. C230.

1961, Nov. Unwmk.

452 A150 1500b dk bl, *buff* 2.00 .75

Founding of Santa Cruz de la Sierra, 400th anniv. See Nos. 468, C246. For surcharge see No. 533.

People below Eucharist Symbol — A151

1962, Mar. 19 Litho. *Perf. 10½*

453 A151 1000b gray grn, red & yel 2.00 .75

4th Natl. Eucharistic Congress, Santa Cruz, 1961. See No. C231.

Nos. 418-422 Surcharged Horizontally with New Value and Bars or Greek Key Border Segment

No. 454

No. 455

No. 456

Nos. 457-458

1962, June ***Perf. 11½***

454 A144 600b on 50b brown 2.50 .75
455 A144 900b on 350b claret .65 .25
456 A144 1000b on 400b steel blue .80 .50
457 A144 2000b on 1000b gray brn 1.25 .80
458 A144 3500b on 3000b slate grn 2.00 1.40
Nos. 454-458,C232-C236 (10) 16.95 9.70

Old value obliterated with two short bars on No. 454; four short bars on Nos. 455-456 and Greek key border on Nos. 457-458. The Greek key obliteration comes in two positions: two full "keys" on top, and one full and two half keys on top.

Flowers — A152

1962, June 28 **Litho.** ***Perf. 10½***

459 A152 200b Hibiscus 1.10 .30
460 A152 400b Bicolored vanda 1.75 .30
461 A152 600b Lily 2.00 .50
462 A152 1000b Orchid 3.50 .50
Nos. 459-462,C237-C240 (8) 25.35 7.00

Bolivia's Armed Forces — A153

Anti-Malaria Emblem — A154

1962, Sept. 5 ***Perf. 11½***

463 A153 400b Infantry .25 .25
464 A153 500b Cavalry .75 .25
465 A153 600b Artillery .50 .30
466 A153 2000b Engineers 1.50 .40
Nos. 463-466,C241-C244 (8) 9.85 3.95

1962, Oct. 4

467 A154 600b dk & lt vio & yel .90 .30

WHO drive to eradicate malaria. See No. C245.

Portrait Type of 1961

Design: 600b, Alonso de Mendoza.

1962 **Photo.** ***Perf. 13x12½***

468 A150 600b rose vio, *bluish* 1.00 .50

Soccer and Flags A155

Design: 1b, Goalkeeper catching ball, vert.

1963, Mar. 21 **Litho.** ***Perf. 11½***
Flags in National Colors

469 A155 60c gray 1.50 .40
470 A155 1b gray 3.00 .60

21st South American Soccer Championships. See Nos. C247-C248.

An imperforate 20b souvenir sheet, depicting Nos. 469 and C247 with simulated perforations, was issued April 28, 1980, to commemorate the Argentina 1978 and España 1982 World Cup championship soccer games. Value $45.

Two imperforate souvenir sheets commemorating España '82 were issued Aug. 11, 1981. One depicts Nos. 469 and 654 with simulated perforations and is denominated 14.80b (value $75). The other depicts No. 470 with simulated perforations (value$45).

Globe and Wheat Emblem A156

1963, Aug. 1 **Unwmk.** ***Perf. 11½***

471 A156 60c dk bl, bl & yel .75 .30

"Freedom from Hunger" campaign of the FAO. See No. C249.

Oil Derrick and Chart — A157

Designs: 60c, Map of Bolivia. 1b, Students.

1963, Dec. 21 **Litho.** ***Perf. 11½***

472 A157 10c green & dk brn .50 .30
473 A157 60c ocher & dk brn 1.00 .30
474 A157 1b dk blue, grn & yel 1.50 .30
Nos. 472-474,C251-C253 (6) 9.50 2.95

Revolution of Apr. 9, 1952, 10th anniv.

Flags of Bolivia and Peru A158

1966, Aug. 10 **Wmk. 90** ***Perf. 13½***
Flags in National Colors

475 A158 10c black & tan .40 .25
476 A158 60c black & lt grn .60 .30
477 A158 1b black & gray .80 .50
478 A158 2b black & rose 1.10 .75
Nos. 475-478,C254-C257 (8) 7.15 3.95

Marshal Andrés Santa Cruz (1792-1865), president of Bolivia and of Peru-Bolivian Confederation.

Children — A159

Perf. 13½

1966, Dec. 16 **Unwmk.** **Litho.**

479 A159 30c ocher & sepia .75 .25

Issued to help poor children. See No. C258.

Map and Flag of Bolivia and Generals Ovando and Barrientos A160

1966, Dec. 16 **Litho.** ***Perf. 13½***
Flag in Red, Yellow and Green

480 A160 60c violet brn & tan 2.00 .30
481 A160 1b dull grn & tan 1.10 .30

Issued to honor Generals Rene Barrientos Ortuno and Alfredo Ovando C., co-Presidents, 1965-66. See Nos. C259-C260.

Various Issues 1957-60 and Type A161 Surcharged

No. 403 Surcharged

1966, Dec. 21

482 A140 20c on 150b gray & ultra .85 .30

Nos. 405-406 Surcharged

483 A140 30c on 550b chlky bl & brn .85 .25
484 A140 2.80b on 750b dp rose & grn 2.25 .75

No. 424 Surcharged

485 A145 60c on 350b dp rose 1.25 .30

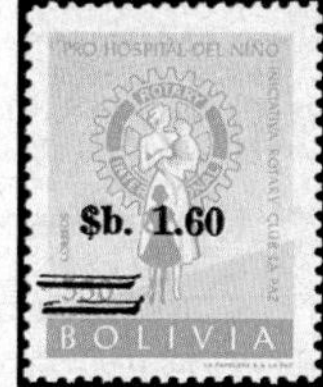

Nos. 429-430 Surcharged

486 A146 1.60b on 350b multi 2.25 .75
487 A146 2.40b on 500b multi 2.25 1.00

Revenue Stamps of 1946 Surcharged

488 A161 20c on 5b red .65 .30

Revenue Stamps of 1946 Surcharged

Revenue Stamps of 1946 Surcharged

489 A161 60c on 2b grn 1.25 .30

490 A161 1b on 10b brn 1.25 .50

491 A161 1.60b on 50c vio 1.25 .50
Nos. 482-491,C261-C272 (22) 36.60 14.25

For surcharge see No. C272.

Sower A162

"Macheteros" A163

1967, Sept. 20 **Litho.** ***Perf. 13½x13***

492 A162 70c multicolored .75 .30

50th anniv. of Lions Intl. See Nos. C273-C273a.

1968, June 24 ***Perf. 13½x13***

Designs (Folklore characters): 60c, Chunchos. 1b, Wiphala. 2b, Diablada.

493 A163 30c gray & multi .50 .25
494 A163 60c sky bl & multi .70 .30
495 A163 1b gray & multi 1.00 .30
496 A163 2b gray ol & multi 2.25 .50
a. Souvenir sheet of 4, #493-496, imperf 27.50 27.50
Nos. 493-496,C274-C277 (8) 14.45 3.70

Issued to publicize the 9th Congress of the Postal Union of the Americas and Spain.

Arms of Tarija — A164

Pres. Gualberto Villaroel — A165

1968, Oct. 29 **Litho.** ***Perf. 13½x13***

497 A164 20c pale sal & multi .55 .25
498 A164 30c gray & multi .55 .25
499 A164 40c dl yel & multi .55 .25
500 A164 60c lt yel grn & multi .55 .25
Nos. 497-500,C278-C281 (8) 9.20 4.05

Battle of Tablada sesquicentennial.

1968, Nov. 6 **Unwmk.**

501 A165 20c sepia & org 1.00 .30
502 A165 30c sepia & dl bl grn 1.00 .30
503 A165 40c sepia & dl rose 1.00 .30
504 A165 50c sepia & yel grn 1.25 .30
505 A165 1b sepia & ol bister 1.50 .30
Nos. 501-505 (5) 5.75 1.50

4th centenary of the founding of Cochabamba. See Nos. C282-C286.

ITU Emblem A166

1968, Dec. 3 Litho. *Perf. 13x13½*
506 A166 10c gray, blk & yel .50 .25
507 A166 60c org, blk & ol 1.10 .55

Cent. (in 1965) of the ITU. See Nos. C287-C288.

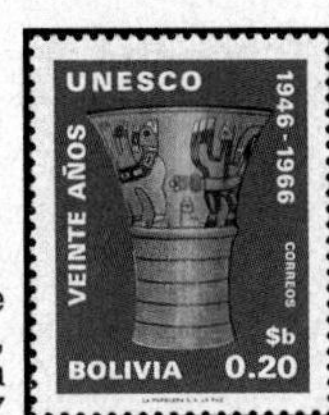

Polychrome Painted Clay Cup, Inca Period — A167

1968, Nov. 14 *Perf. 13½x13*
508 A167 20c dk bl grn & multi .75 .25
509 A167 60c vio bl & multi 1.00 .50

20th anniv. (in 1966) of UNESCO. See Nos. C289-C290.

John F. Kennedy A168

1968, Nov. 22 *Perf. 13x13½*
510 A168 10c yel grn & blk .75 .25
511 A168 4b vio & blk 3.75 1.90
a. Souvenir sheet of 1, type of #511 2.50 2.50

See Nos. C291-C292.

Tennis Player — A169

1968, Dec. 10 *Perf. 13x13½*
512 A169 10c gray, blk & lt brn .75 .35
513 A169 20c yel, blk & lt brn 1.25 .50
514 A169 30c ultra, blk & lt brn 1.25 .50
a. Souvenir sheet #512-514, imperf 2.50 2.50
Nos. 512-514 (3) 3.25 1.35

32nd South American Tennis Championships, La Paz, 1965. See Nos. C293-C294.

Issue of 1863 — A170

1968, Dec. 23 Litho. *Perf. 13x13½*
515 A170 10c yel grn, brn & blk 1.00 .25
516 A170 30c lt bl, brn & blk 1.10 .50
517 A170 2b gray, brn & blk 2.00 .60
a. Souvenir sheet #515-517, imperf 10.00 10.00
Nos. 515-517,C295-C297 (6) 13.10 4.60

Cent. of Bolivian postage stamps. See Nos. C295-C297.

Rifle Shooting A171

Sports: 50c, Equestrian. 60c, Canoeing.

1969, Oct. 29 Litho. *Perf. 13x13½*
518 A171 40c red brn, org & blk .75 .55
519 A171 50c emer, red & blk 1.10 .55
520 A171 60c bl, emer & blk 1.10 .55
a. Souvenir sheet #518-520, imperf 30.00 30.00
Nos. 518-520,C299-C301 (6) 12.45 5.60

19th Olympic Games, Mexico City, 10/12-27/68.

Temenis Laothoe Violetta A172

Butterflies: 10c, Papilio crassus. 20c, Catagramma cynosura. 30c, Eunica eurota flora. 80c, Ituna phenarete.

1970, Apr. 24 Litho. *Perf. 13x13½*
521 A172 5c pale lil & multi 2.50 1.25
522 A172 10c pink & multi 4.50 2.00
523 A172 20c gray & multi 4.50 2.00
524 A172 30c yel & multi 4.50 2.00
525 A172 80c multicolored 4.50 2.00
a. Souvenir sheet #521-523, imperf 45.00 45.00
Nos. 521-525,C302-C306 (10) 60.50 28.75

A souvenir sheet exists containing 3 imperf. stamps similar to Nos. 521-523. Black marginal inscription. Size: 129½x80mm. Value $45.

Boy Scout — A173

Design: 10c, Girl Scout planting rose bush.

1970, June 17 *Perf. 13½x13*
526 A173 5c multicolored .45 .30
527 A173 10c multicolored .60 .30
Nos. 526-527,C307-C308 (4) 2.70 1.40

Honoring the Bolivian Scout movement.

A 1,000,000b imperforate souvenir sheet, depicting No. 526 with simulated perforations, was issued May 12, 1986, to mark the explosion of the U.S. Space Shuttle Challenger. Value $30.

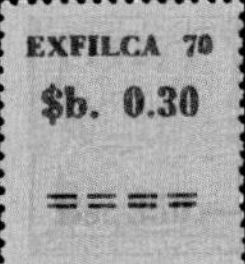

No. 437 Surcharged Red

1970, Dec. 6 Litho. *Perf. 13x12*
528 A147 30c on 350b on 10c .60 .40

EXFILCA 70, 2nd Interamerican Philatelic Exhib., Caracas, Venezuela, Nov. 27-Dec. 6.

Nos. 455 and 452 Surcharged in Black or Red

1970, Dec. Photo. *Perf. 11½*
529 A144 60c on 900b on 350b .60 .40
533 A150 1.20b on 1500b (R) .90 .70

Amaryllis Yungacensis A174

Bolivian Flowers: 30c, Amaryllis escobar uriae, horiz. 40c, Amaryllis evansae, horiz. 2b, Gymnocalycium chiquitanum.

Perf. 13x13½, 13½x13

1971, Aug. 9 Litho. Unwmk.
534 A174 30c gray & multi .60 .25
535 A174 40c multi .60 .30
536 A174 50c multi .90 .50
537 A174 2b multi 2.00 1.00
a. Souvenir sheet of 4, #534, 535, C310, C312, imperf 15.00 15.00
b. Souvenir sheet of 4, #536, 537, C311, C313, imperf 15.00 15.00
Nos. 534-537,C310-C313 (8) 16.10 8.55

Sica Sica Church, EXFILIMA Emblem — A175

1971, Nov. 6 *Perf. 14x13½*
538 A175 20c red & multi .60 .30

EXFILIMA '71, 3rd Inter-American Philatelic Exhibition, Lima, Peru, Nov. 6-14.

A176

Design: Pres. Hugo Banzer Suarez.

1972, Jan. 24 Litho. *Perf. 13½*
539 A176 1.20b blk & multi 2.00 .50

Bolivia's development, 8/19/71-1/24/72.

A177

Folk Dances: 20c, Chiriwano de Achocalla. 40c, Rueda Chapaca. 60c, Kena-kena. 1b, Waca Thokori.

1972, Mar. 23 Litho. *Perf. 13½x13*
540 A177 20c red & multi .40 .25
541 A177 40c rose lil & multi .60 .40
542 A177 60c cream & multi .80 .40
543 A177 1b citron & multi 1.10 .60
a. Souvenir sheet of 4, #540, 541, C315, imperf 35.00 35.00
b. Souvenir sheet of 4, #542, 543, C314 imperf 35.00 35.00
Nos. 540-543,C314-C315 (6) 5.75 2.25

Madonna and Child by B. Bitti — A178

Bolivian paintings: 10c, Nativity, by Melchor Perez de Holguin. 50c, Coronation of the Virgin, by G. M. Berrio. 70c, Harquebusier, anonymous. 80c, St. Peter of Alcantara, by Holguin.

1972 Litho. *Perf. 14x13½*
544 A178 10c gray & multi .40 .25
545 A178 50c sal & multi .60 .30
546 A178 70c lt grn & multi .70 .30
547 A178 80c buff & multi .90 .40
548 A178 1b multi 1.50 .50
a. Souvenir sheet of 2, #548, C318, imperf 45.00 45.00
b. Souvenir sheet of 4, #C317, C318 imperf 45.00 45.00
Nos. 544-548,C316-C319 (9) 10.60 3.15

Issue dates: 1b, Aug. 17; others, Dec. 4.

An imperforate 20b souvenir sheet. depicting No. 548 with simulated perforations, was issued March 16, 1979, to mark the International Year of the Child. Value $45.

An imperf 1b souvenir sheet, depicting No. 548 with simulated perforations, was issued Aug. 1, 1982, to celebrate Christmas. Value $65.

A 2b souvenir sheet containing No. 548, perf 13¼ was issued Dec. 16, 1987, for Christmas. Value $30.

Tarija Cathedral, EXFILBRA Emblem — A179

1972, Aug. 26
549 A179 30c multi .60 .30

4th Inter-American Philatelic Exhibition, EXFILBRA, Rio de Janeiro, Brazil, 8/26-9/2.

Echinocactus Notocactus A180

Designs: Various cacti.

1973, Aug. 6 Litho. *Perf. 13½*
550 A180 20c crim & multi .70 .30
551 A180 40c multi .70 .30
552 A180 50c multi .90 .30
553 A180 70c multi 1.10 .60
a. Souvenir sheet of 2, #553, C321, imperf 40.00 40.00
b. Souvenir sheet of 4, #551, C323 imperf 40.00 40.00
Nos. 550-553,C321-C323 (7) 8.40 3.30

Power Station, Santa Isabel A181

Designs: 20c, Tin industry. 90c, Bismuth industry. 1b, Natural gas plant.

1973, Nov. 26 Litho. *Perf. 13½*

554	A181	10c gray & multi	1.40	.30
555	A181	20c tan & multi	1.40	.30
556	A181	90c lt grn & multi	1.75	.30
557	A181	1b yel & multi	1.75	.30
		Nos. 554-557,C324-C325 (6)	12.55	2.05

Bolivia's development.

Cattleya Nobilior — A182

Orchids: 50c, Zygopetalum bolivianum. 1b, Huntleya melagris.

1974, May 15 *Perf. 13½*

558	A182	20c gray & multi	1.10	.50
559	A182	50c lt bl & multi	1.75	.50
560	A182	1b cit & multi	2.25	.50
a.		Souvenir sheet of 2, #558, C328, imperf	50.00	20.00
b.		Souvenir sheet of 4, #559, 560 imperf	50.00	20.00
		Nos. 558-560,C327-C330 (7)	30.10	6.50

For surcharge see No. 704.

Four imperforate souvenir sheets were issued May 31, 1974, to publicize 1975-77 Bolivian philatelic expositions. They depict: 14.90b, Nos. 18, 544 and C330; 15.50b, Nos. 18, 545 and C329; 16b, Nos. 18 and C320; 16.70b, Nos. 18, 547 and C327. Value, each $5. These sheets were later (Sept. 21) overprinted for various 1974 special events. Vale, set of 4: unused $275; used $150.

UPU and Philatelic Exposition Emblems — A183

1974, Oct. 9

561	A183	3.50b grn, blk & bl	1.90	.75

Centenary of Universal Postal Union: PRENFIL-UPU Philatelic Exhibition, Buenos Aires, Oct. 1-12; EXPO-UPU Philatelic Exhibition, Montevideo, Oct. 20-27.

Gen. Sucre, by I. Wallpher A184

1974, Dec. 9 Litho. *Perf. 13¾*

562	A184	5b multicolored	2.25	1.00

Sesquicentennial of the Battle of Ayacucho.

An imperforate 5b souvenir sheet, depicting No. 562 with simulated perforations, was issued Dec. 31, 1982, to honor Peter Paul Reubens. Value $50.

An imperforate 1,000,000b souvenir sheet, containing No. 562 perf 13¼, was issued Sept. 25, 1986, to mark the Seoul Summer Olympic Games. Value $40.

Lions Emblem and Steles A185

1975, Mar. 17 Litho. *Perf. 13½*

563	A185	30c red & multi	.75	.35

Lions Intl. in Bolivia, 25th anniv.

España 75 Emblem A186

1975, Mar.

564	A186	4.50b yel, red & blk	1.65	.60

Espana 75 International Philatelic Exhibition, Madrid, Apr. 4-13.

Emblem A187

1975 Litho. *Perf. 13½*

565	A187	2.50b lil, blk & sil	1.25	.50

First meeting of Postal Ministers, Quito, Ecuador, March 1974, and for the Cartagena Agreement.

Four 20b imperforate souvenir sheets were issued in March 1975 to publicize 1975-77 Bolivian stamp exhibitions. Each depicts No. 14, with Nos. 562, 563, 564 or 565. Value, each $5. These sheets were also overprint to commemorate special events of 1974. Value, set $175.

Two of the unoverprinted 1974 sheets, those depicting Nos. 563 and 564, were overprinted in April 1981 to commemorate the 150th anniv. of the death of Símon Bolívar. Value, each $5. These sheets were also overprinted to mark the 50th anniv. of the first Bolivia-Brazil flight. Value, each $5.

Pando Coat of Arms — A188

Designs: Departmental coats of arms.

1975, July 16 Litho. *Perf. 13½*

566	A188	20c shown	.65	.30
567	A188	2b Chuquisaca	1.25	.50
568	A188	3b Cochabamba	1.75	.75
		Nos. 566-568,C336-C341 (9)	12.25	6.15

Sesquicentennial of Republic of Bolivia.

Simón Bolívar — A189

Presidents and Statesmen of Bolivia: 30c, Victor Paz Estenssoro. 60c, Tomas Frias. 1b, Ismael Montes. 2.50b, Aniceto Arce. 7b, Bautista Saavedra. 10b, Jose Manuel Pando. 15b, Jose Maria Linares. 50b, Simon Bolivar.

1975 Litho. *Perf. 13½*

Size: 24x32mm

569	A189	30c multi	.30	.25
569A	A189	60c multi	.30	.25
570	A189	1b multi	.40	.25
571	A189	2.50b multi	1.00	.50
572	A189	7b multi	2.50	1.00
573	A189	10b multi	4.00	3.00
574	A189	15b multi	5.00	3.50

Size: 28x39mm

575	A189	50b multi	20.00	12.00
		Nos. 569-575,C346-C353 (16)	69.90	40.30

Sesquicentennial of Republic of Bolivia.

An imperforate 20b souvenir sheet, depicting No. 575 with simulated perforations, was issued Oct. 13, 1980, to celebrate the 1980 Lake Placid Winter Olympic Games. Value $20.

An imperforate 10b souvenir sheet, depicting No. 573 with simulated perforations, was issued March 24, 1982, to commemorate the España '82 World Cup soccer championship games. Value $35.

"EXFIVIA 75" A190

1975, Dec. 1 Litho. *Perf. 13½*

576	A190	3b multicolored	1.50	1.10
a.		Souvenir sheet	4.50	4.50

EXFIVIA 75, 1st Bolivian Philatelic Exposition. No. 576a contains one stamp similar to #576 with simulated perfs. Sold for 5b.

No. 576a was overprinted in 1981 for EXFIVA 77 and EXFILMAR 79. Value $5.

An imperforate 20b souvenir sheet, depicting No. 576 with simulated perforations, was issued June 1, 1978, commemorating the 75th anniv. of the Nobel Prize (in 1976). Value $85.

A191

Chiang Kai-shek, flags of Bolivia and China.

1976, Apr. 4 Litho. *Perf. 13½*

577	A191	2.50b multi, red circle	5.00	1.50
578	A191	2.50b multi, bl circle	5.00	1.50

Pres. Chiang Kai-shek of China (1887-1975).

Erroneous red of sun's circle on Chinese flag of No. 577 was corrected on No. 578 with a dark blue overlay.

A192

1976, Apr. Litho. *Perf. 13½*

579	A192	50c Naval insignia	.75	.50

Navy anniversary.

Geological Map, Pickax and Lamp — A193

1976, May

580	A193	4b multicolored	2.00	1.00

Bolivian Geological Institute.

Lufthansa Jet, Bolivian and German Colors A194

1976, May

581	A194	3b multicolored	2.00	1.00

Lufthansa, 50th anniversary.

An imperforate 20b souvenir sheet, depicting No. 581 with simulated perforations, was issued June 1, 1978, to celebrate the Argentina 78 World Cup. Value $35.

An imperforate 20b souvenir sheet, depicting No. 581 with simulated perforations, was issues Oct. 13, 1980. to Celebrate the 1980 Lake Placid Winter Olympic Games. Value $50.

Boy Scout and Scout Emblem — A195

1976, May Litho. *Perf. 13½*

582	A195	1b multicolored	1.00	.65

Bolivian Boy Scouts, 60th anniversary.

An imperfoate 125,000b souvenir sheet, depicting Nos. 582 and 683 with simulated perforations, was issued June 24, 1985, to mark the 75th anniv. of the Boy Scouts. Value $10. This sheet was overprinted, surcharged 1,500,000b and reissued Apr. 18, 1986, to honor the 1987/88 World Jamboree in Australia. Value $20.

Battle Scene, US Bicentennial Emblem — A196

1976, May 25

583	A196	4.50b bis & multi	3.25	1.10
a.		Souenir sheet of 1	30.00	30.00

American Bicentennial.

No. 583a contains one stamp similar to No. 583 with simulated perforations. Size: 130x80mm.

Three imperforate souvenir sheets, each denominated 20b, depicting No. 583 with simulated perforations and various historic U.S. motifs, were issued Dec. 20, 1976, to commemorate the U.S. Bicentennial. Value, each $6.

Family, Map of Bolivia — A197

Vicente Bernedo — A198

1976 *Perf. 13½*

584	A197	2.50b multicolored	1.00	.50

National Census 1976.

1976, Oct.

585	A198	1.50b multicolored	.60	.40

Brother Vicente Bernedo de Potosi (1544-1619), missionary to the Indians.

Four imperforate souvenir sheets, each denominated 20b, depicting No. 585 with simulated perforations, were issued Dec. 20,

1976, celebrating various themes. These comprise: 75th anniv. Nobel prize, value $50; 1976 Montreal Summer Olympics, value $25; U.S. Bicentennial / Space, value $35; 100th anniv. telephone, 25th anniv. United Nations, 110th anniv. ITU, value $35.

Policeman with Dog, Rainbow over La Paz — A199

1976, Oct.

586 A199 2.50b multicolored 1.10 .80

Bolivian Police, 150 years of service.

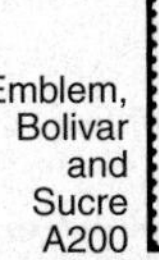

Emblem, Bolivar and Sucre A200

1976, Nov. 18 Litho. *Perf. 13½*

587 A200 1.50b multicolored 1.10 .60

Intl. Congress of Bolivarian Societies.

Pedro Poveda, View of La Paz — A201

1976, Dec.

588 A201 1.50b multicolored .85 .50

Pedro Poveda (1874-1936), educator.

A202

Boy and Girl — A203

1976, Dec. 17 *Perf. 10½*

594	A202	20c brown	.50	.30
595	A202	1b ultra	.80	.30
596	A202	1.50b green	1.25	.60
		Nos. 594-596 (3)	2.55	1.20

1977, Feb. 4 Litho. *Perf. 13½*

599 A203 50c multicolored .60 .30

Christmas 1976, and for 50th anniversary of the Inter-American Children's Institute.

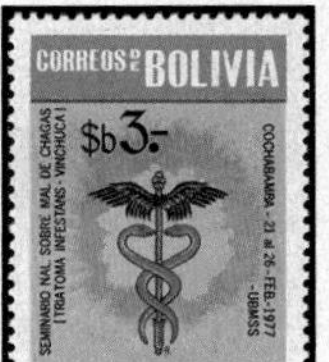

Staff of Aesculapius A204

Supreme Court, Sucre A205

1977, Mar. 18 Litho. *Perf. 13½x13*

600 A204 3b multicolored 1.50 .30

National Seminar on Chagas' disease, Cochabamba, Feb. 21-26.

1977, May 3

Designs: 4b, Manuel Maria Urcullu, first President of Supreme Court. 4.50b, Pantaleon Dalence, President 1883-1889.

601	A205	2.50b multi	.60	.30
602	A205	4b multi	.90	.30
603	A205	4.50b multi	1.25	.30
		Nos. 601-603 (3)	2.75	.90

Sesquicentennial of Bolivian Supreme Court.

Newspaper Mastheads A206

Map of Bolivia, Tower and Flag A207

Designs: 2.50b, Alfredo Alexander and Hoy, horiz. 3b, Jose Carrasco and El Diario, horiz. 4b, Demetrio Canelas and Los Tiempos. 5.50b, Frontpage of Presencia.

1977, June Litho. *Perf. 13½*

604	A206	1.50b multi	.50	.30
605	A206	2.50b multi	.60	.30
606	A206	3b multi	.80	.30
607	A206	4b multi	.90	.40
608	A206	5.50b multi	1.25	.60
		Nos. 604-608 (5)	4.05	1.90

Bolivian newspapers and their founders.

1977, June

609 A207 3b multi .90 .30

90th anniversary of Oruro Club.

Games' Poster — A208

Tin Miner and Emblem — A209

1977, Oct. 20 Litho. *Perf. 13½*

610 A208 5b blue & multi 1.75 .50

8th Bolivian Games, La Paz, Oct. 1977.

Four imperforate souvenir sheets, each denominated 20b, depicting No. 610 with simulated perforations were issued June 1, 1978. Each sheet celebrated an upcoming philatelic exhibition: Honduras '78; Capex '78; Praga '78; and Philaserdica '79. Value, each $15.

1977, Oct. 31 Litho. *Perf. 13*

611 A209 3b multicolored 1.25 .50

Bolivian Mining Corp., 25th anniv.

Miners, Globe, Tin Symbol — A210

Map of Bolivia, Radio Masts — A211

1977, Nov. 3

612 A210 6b silver & multi 2.00 .75

Intl. Tin Symposium, La Paz, Nov. 14-21.

Two souvenir sheets, denominated 1,000,000b, containing No. 612 perf 13¼, were issued Sept. 25, 1986, to commemorate the Uncia-Antofagasto railway. Value, each $30.

1977, Nov. 11

613 A211 2.50b blue & multi 1.00 .50

Radio Bolivia, ASBORA, 50th anniversary.

No. 450 Surcharged in Black

1977, Nov. 25 Litho. *Perf. 11x13½*

614 A147 5b on 5000b on 5b 5.00 2.00

EXFIVIA '77 Philatelic Exhibition, Cochabamba.

Eye, Compass, Book of Law — A212

1978, May 3 Litho. *Perf. 13½x13*

615 A212 5b multi 1.10 .30

Audit Department, 50th anniversary.

Mt. Illimani A213

Pre-Columbian Monolith A214

Design: 1.50b, Mt. Cerro de Potosi.

Perf. 11x10½, 10½x11

1978, June 1 Litho.

616	A213	50c bl & Prus bl	.30	.25
617	A214	1b brn & lemon	.50	.25
618	A213	1.50b red & bl gray	.60	.30
		Nos. 616-618 (3)	1.40	.80

Andean Countries, Staff of Aesculapius — A215

1978, June 1 *Perf. 10½x11*

626 A215 2b org & blk .75 .30

Health Ministers of Andean Countries, 5th meeting.

Map of Americas with Bolivia — A216

1978, June 1

627 A216 2.50b dp ultra & red .80 .30

World Rheumatism Year.

For surcharges see Nos. 697, 972.

Central Bank Building — A217

Jesus and Children — A218

1978, July 26 Litho. *Perf. 13½*

628 A217 7b multi 1.90 .50

50th anniversary of Bank of Bolivia.

1979, Feb. 20 Litho. *Perf. 13½*

629 A218 8b multicolored 1.90 .50

International Year of the Child.

An imperforate 20b souvenir sheet, depicting No. 629 with simulated perforations, was issued March 16, 1979, for the International Year of the Child. Value $50.

An imperforate 20b souvenir sheet, depicting Nos. 599 and 629 with simulated perforations, was issued April 28, 1980, marking the Year of the Child. Value $25.

Antofagasta Cancel — A219

Eduardo Abaroa, Chain — A220

Designs: 1b, La Chimba cancel. 1.50b, Mejillones cancel. 5.50b, View of Antofagasta, horiz. 6.50b, Woman in chains, symbolizing captive province. 8b, Map of Antofagasta Province, 1876. 10b, Arms of province.

1979, Mar. 23 Litho. *Perf. 10½*

630	A219	50e buff & blk	.50	.25
631	A219	1b pink & blk	.60	.40
632	A219	1.50b pale grn & blk	.70	.40

Perf. 13½

633	A220	5.50b multi	1.10	.50
634	A220	6.50b multi	1.60	.50
635	A220	7b multi	1.60	.50
636	A220	8b multi	1.60	.60
637	A220	10b multi	2.10	.90
		Nos. 630-637 (8)	9.80	4.05

Loss of Antofagasta coastal area to Chile, cent.

For surcharge see No. 696.

An imperforate 1000b souvenir sheet, depicting No. 637 with simulated perforations, was issued March 26, 1984, to mark the 1984 World Postal Congress in Hamburg. Value $25.

Emblem and Map of Bolivia — A221

Gymnast — A222

1979, Mar. 26 *Perf. 13½x13*

638 A221 3b multicolored 1.50 .70

Radio Club of Bolivia.

1979, Mar. 27 *Perf. 13x13½, 13½x13*

6.50b, Runner and Games emblem, horiz.

639	A222	6.50b multi	1.90	.80
640	A222	10b multi	2.75	1.00
a.		Souvenir sheet of one	8.25	8.25

Southern Cross Sports Games, Bolivia, Nov. 3-12, 1978.

No. 640a contains No. 640 with simulated perforations. Sold for 20b. Size: 80x130mm.

For surcharge see No. 965.

No. 640a was overprinted in two versions in 1981, the first overprint commemorating the 10th anniv. of the Santa Cruz Philatelic Center, the second celebrating the 10th anniv. of the Bolivian Philatelic Federation. Value, each $5.

Two imperforate 20b souvenir sheets, one depicting No. 639, the other No. 640, both with simulated perforations, were issued March 16, 1979, to mark the 1980 Olympic Games. Values, each $30.

Two imperforate souvenir sheets, each denominated 20b, one depicting No. 639, the other No. 640, both with simulated perforations, were issued Oct. 13, 1980, to commemorate the 1980 Moscow Olympic Games. Values, each $75.

Bulgaria No. 1 — A223

1979, Mar. 30 ***Perf. 10½***
641 A223 2.50b multi 1.40 .50

PHILASERDICA '79 International Philatelic Exhibition, Sofia, Bulgaria, May 18-27.

For surcharge see No. 694.

EXFILMAR Emblem — A224

1979, Apr. 2
642 A224 2b multi 2.25 .50

Bolivian Maritime Philatelic Exhibition, La Paz, Nov. 18-28.

For surcharge see No. 698.

OAS Emblem, Map of Bolivia — A226

1979, Oct. 22 Litho. ***Perf. 14x13½***
644 A226 6b multi 1.75 .50

Organization of American States, 9th Congress, La Paz, Oct.-Nov.

Franz Tamayo — A227

Bolivian and Japanese Flags, Hospital — A228

UN Emblem and Meeting — A229

Radio Tower and Waves — A230

1979, Dec.
645 A227 2.80b blk & gray 1.25 .50
646 A228 5b multi 1.25 .50
648 A229 5b multi 1.00 .50
649 A230 6b multi 1.25 .50
Nos. 645-649 (4) 4.75 2.00

Franz Tamayo, lawyer, birth centenary; Japanese-Bolivian health care cooperation; CEPAL, 18th Congress, La Paz, Sept. 18-26; Bolivian National Radio, 50th anniversary.

For surcharge see No. 695.

An imperforate 500,000b souvenir sheet, depicting No. 645 with simulated perforations, was issued Dec. 1985 to mark the 850th anniv. of Malmonides, Jewish philosopher (1135-1204). Value $10.

Puerto Suarez Iron Ore Deposits A231

1979 Litho. ***Perf. 13½x14***
650 A231 9.50b multi 3.50 .80

Bolivia No. 19, EXFILMAR Emblem, Bolivian Flag — A232

1980 Litho. ***Perf. 13½***
651 A232 4b multi 1.25 .50

EXFILMAR, Bolivian Maritime Philatelic Exhibition, La Paz, Nov. 18-28, 1979.

An imperforate 4b souvenir sheet, depicting No. 651 with simulated perforations, was issued Dec. 31, 1982, to commemorate space exploration. Value $75.

Juana Azurduy on Horseback A233

1980 Litho. ***Perf. 14x13½***
652 A233 4b multi 1.25 .50

Juana Azurduy de Padilla, independence fighter, birth bicentenary.

A souvenir sheet containing No. 652 perforated 13¼ was issued Oct. 19, 1990, to commemorate the 700th anniv. of the Swiss Confederation.

La Salle and World Map A234

1980 ***Perf. 13½x14***
653 A234 9b multi 2.00 .80

St. Jean Baptiste de la Salle (1651-1719), educator.

For surcharge see No. 966.

"Victory" in Chariot, Madrid, Exhibition Emblem, Flags of Bolivia and Spain A235

1980, Oct. Litho. ***Perf. 13½x14***
654 A235 14b multi 3.00 1.50

ESPAMER '80 Stamp Exhibition, Madrid.

Map of South America, Flags of Argentina, Bolivia and Peru — A236

1980, Oct. ***Perf. 14x13½***
655 A236 2b multi 1.10 .40

Ministers of Public Works and Transport of Argentina, Bolivia and Peru meeting.

Santa Cruz-Trinidad Railroad, Inauguration of Third Section — A237

1980, Oct.
656 A237 3b multi 1.75 .70

An imperforate 1500b souvenir sheet, depicting No. 656 and the 50c value of the unissued 1915 set, both with simulated perforations, was issued June 20, 1984, to mark the World Postal Congress in Hamburg. Value $30.

Flag on Provincial Map — A238

Perf. 14x13½, 13½x14
1981, May 11 **Litho.**
657 A238 1b Soldier, flag, map *25.00 30.00*
658 A238 3b Flag, map *25.00 30.00*
659 A238 40b shown 15.00 5.00
660 A238 50b Soldier, civilians, horiz. 15.00 5.00
Nos. 657-660 (4) 80.00 70.00

July 17 Revolution memorial.

An imperforate 40b souvenir sheet, depicting No. 659 with simulated perforations, was issued March 24, 1982, to honor Princess Diana. Value $30.

Parrots — A239

1981, May 11 ***Perf. 14x13½***
661 A239 4b Ara macao 1.00 .50
662 A239 7b Ara chloroptera 1.60 .80
663 A239 8b Ara ararauna 2.00 1.00
664 A239 9b Ara rubrogenys 2.10 1.00
665 A239 10b Ara auricollis 2.10 1.00
666 A239 12b Anodorhynchus hyacinthinus 3.00 1.40
667 A239 15b Ara militaris 3.50 1.75
668 A239 20b Ara severa 4.25 2.10
Nos. 661-668 (8) 19.55 9.55

Christmas 1981 — A240

1981, Dec. 7 Litho. ***Perf. 10½***
669 A240 1b Virgin and Child, vert. .30 .25
670 A240 2b Child, star .60 .25

American Airforces Commanders' 22nd Conference, Buenos Aires — A241

1982, Apr. 12 Litho. ***Perf. 13½***
671 A241 14b multi 3.25 1.25

75th Anniv. of Cobija — A242

1982, July 8 Litho. ***Perf. 13½***
672 A242 28b multi 1.10 .50

Simon Bolivar Birth Bicentenary (1983) A243

1982, July 12
673 A243 18b multi .80 .40

1983 World Telecommunications Year — A244

1982, July 15

674 A244 26b Receiving station 1.00 .50

An imperforate 1b souvenir sheet, depicting No. 674 with simulated perforations, was issued March 20, 1987, to honor Wernher von Braun. Value $60.

1982 World Cup — A245

1982, July 21 ***Perf. 11***

675 A245 4b shown .50 .30
676 A245 100b Final Act, by Picasso 5.00 1.75

For surcharge see No. 701.

Two imperforate souvenir sheets, each denominated 104b, were issued Aug. 1, 1982, to celebrate España '82. The first depicts No. 676 with a stamp similar to No. 675, both with simulated perforations. Value $35. The second depicts No. 677 with simulated perforations. Value $65.

Two imperforate souvenir sheets were issued Dec. 31, 1982, to commemorate the victory of the Italian team in the España '82 World Cup games. One depicts Nos. 675 and 676 with simulated perfs and is denominated 104b. The second depicts Nos. 676 and 677 and is denominated 116b. Values, each $30.

Girl Playing Piano — A246

1982, July 25 ***Perf. 13½***

677 A246 16b Boy playing soccer, vert. 1.50 .75
678 A246 20b shown 2.00 1.00

An imperforate 200b souvenir sheet, depicting Nos. 678 and 629 with simulated perforations, was issued Sept. 16, 1983, for the International Year of the Child. Value $75.

An imperforate 27,500b souvenir sheet, depicting No. 678 with simulated perfs, was issued April 4, 1985, to mark the International Year of the Child. Value $50.

Bolivian-Chinese Agricultural Cooperation, 1972-1982 — A247

1982, Aug. 12

679 A247 30b multi 1.25 .75

First Bolivian-Japanese Gastroenterology Conference, La Paz, Jan. — A248

1982, Aug. 26

680 A248 22b multi 2.00 .80

A249

1982, Aug. 31 Litho. ***Perf. 14x13½***

681 A249 19b Stamps 1.75 .60

10th Anniv. of Bolivian Philatelic Federation.

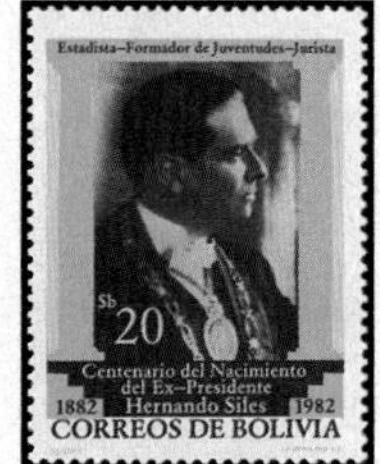

A250

1982, Sept. 1

682 A250 20b tan & dk brown 1.00 .50

Pres. Hernando Siles, birth centenary.

Scouting Year — A251

Cochabamba Philatelic Center, 25th Anniv. — A252

1982, Sept. 3 ***Perf. 11***

683 A251 5b Baden-Powell .50 .30

For surcharge see No. 703.

1982, Sept. 14

684 A252 3b multicolored .50 .30

For surcharge see No. 700.

Cochabamba Superior Court of Justice Sesquicentennial — A253

1982 Litho. ***Perf. 13½***

685 A253 10b multicolored .60 .30

For surcharge see No. 970.

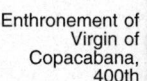

Enthronement of Virgin of Copacabana, 400th Anniv. — A254

1982, Nov. 15 Litho. ***Perf. 13½***

686 A254 13b multicolored .60 .30

For surcharge see No. 971.

Navy Day — A255

1982, Nov. 17

687 A255 14b Port Busch Naval Base .55 .35

An imperforate 1,000,000b souvenir sheet, depicting No. 687 with simulated perforations, was issued Jan. 5, 1987, to mark the 500th anniv. of Columbus' discovery of America. Value $20.

A256

A257

1982, Nov. 19 ***Perf. 11***

688 A256 10b green & gray .90 .30

Christmas. For surcharge see No. 702.

An imperforate 1,000,000b souvenir sheet, depicting No. 688 with simulated perforations, was issued Dec.24, 1986, for Christmas. Value $27.50.

1983, Feb. 13 Litho. ***Perf. 13½***

689 A257 50b multicolored 2.00 1.00

10th Youth Soccer Championship, Jan. 22-Feb. 13.

A 2b souvenir sheet containing Nos. 689 and 726, both perf 13¼, was issued Dec. 15, 1988, to mark the Italia 1990 World Cup. Value $25.

EXFIVIA '83 Philatelic Exhibition A258

1983, Nov. 5 Litho. ***Perf. 13½***

690 A258 150b brown carmine 1.50 .75

An imperforate 1000b souvenir sheet, depicting Nos. 690 and 356 with simulated perforations, was issued March 26, 1984, to mark the 1984 Sarajevo Winter Olympic Games. Value $27.50.

An imperforate 500,000b souvenir sheet, depicting No. 690 with simulated perforartions, was issued Dec. 3, 1985, to celebrate Halley's Comet. Value $30.

Visit of Brazilian Pres. Joao Figueiredo, Feb. — A259

1984, Feb. 7 Litho. ***Perf. 13½x14***

691 A259 150b multicolored .80 .60

Simon Bolivar Entering La Paz, by Carmen Baptista A260

Paintings of Bolivar: 50b, Riding Horse, by Mulato Gil de Quesada, vert.

Perf. 14x13½, 13½x14

1984, Mar. 30

692 A260 50b multi .30 .25
693 A260 200b multi 1.00 .50

An imperforate 1500b souvenir sheet, depicting No. 692 with simulated perforations, was issued June 20, 1984, to mark the 1984 Los Angeles Summer Olympic Games. Value $20.

A 2b souvenir sheet containing No. 692, perf. 13¼, was issued Dec. 16, 1987, to mark the 1988 Seoul Summer Olympc Games. Value $25.

Types of 1957-79 Surcharged

1984, Mar.

694 A223 40b on 2.50b #641 .40 .25
695 A227 40b on 2.80b #645 .40 .25
696 A219 60b on 1.50b #632 .40 .25
697 A216 60b on 2.50b #627 .40 .25
698 A224 100b on 2b #642 .50 .30
699 A141 200b on 350b #409 1.25 .50
Nos. 694-699 (6) 3.35 1.80

See No. 972 for surcharge similar to No. 697.

Nos. 675, 683-684, 688, C328 Surcharged

1984, June 27 Litho. ***Perf. 11***

700 A252 500b on 3b #684 1.25 .60
701 A245 1000b on 4b #675 2.50 1.25
702 A256 2000b on 10b #688 5.00 2.50
703 A251 5000b on 5b #683 13.00 9.00

Perf. 13½

704 A182 10,000b on 3.80b #C328 16.00 10.00
Nos. 700-704 (5) 37.75 23.35

An imperforate 500,000b souvenir sheet, depicting No. 704 with simulated perforations, was issued Dec. 31, 1985, picturing Raphael's *The Three Graces.* Value $20.

Road Safety Education — A261

Cartoons.

1984, Sept. 7 Litho. *Perf. 11*

705 A261 80b Jaywalker .50 .25
706 A261 120b Motorcycle policeman, ambulance .50 .25

Jose Eustaquio Mendez, 200th Birth Anniv. — A262

Paintings: 300b, Birthplace, by Jorge Campos. 500b, Mendez Leading the Battle of La Tablada, by M. Villegas, horiz.

Perf. 14x13½, 13½x14

1984, Sept. 19

707 A262 300b multi .50 .25
708 A262 500b multi .50 .25

1983 World Cup Soccer Championships, Mexico — A263

Chasqui, Postal Runner — A264

Sponsoring shoe-manufacturers' trademarks and: 100b, 200b, Outline map of Bolivia, natl. colors. 600b, World map, soccer ball.

1984, Oct. 26 *Perf. 11*

709 A263 100b multi .70 .25
710 A263 200b multi .70 .25
711 A263 600b multi, horiz. .70 .25
Nos. 709-711 (3) 2.10 .75

An imperforate 125,000b souvenir sheet, depicting No. 711 with simulated perforations, was issued June 24, 1985, to mark the 1984 Los Angeles Summer Olympic Games. Value $20.

1985

712 A264 11000b vio bl 1.00 .40

For surcharge see No. 962.

Intl. Year of Professional Education A265

Intl. Anti-Polio Campaign A266

1985, Apr. 25

713 A265 2000b Natl. Manual Crafts emblem .40 .25

For surcharges see Nos. 721-722, 959.

1985, May 22

714 A266 20000b lt bl & vio .75 .25

Endangered Wildlife — A267

1985, May 22

715 A267 23000b Altiplano boliviano 1.50 .50
716 A267 25000b Sarcorhamphus gryphus 1.00 .50
717 A267 30000b Blastocaros dichotomus 1.25 .50
Nos. 715-717 (3) 3.75 1.50

Nos. 716-717 vert.
For surcharge see No. 963.

Dona Vicenta Juaristi Eguino (b. 1785), Independence Heroine — A268

1985, Oct. Litho. *Perf. 13½*

718 A268 300000b multi 1.40 .60

UN, 40th Anniv. — A269

1985, Oct. 24 *Perf. 11*

719 A269 1000000b bl & gold 4.50 1.00

For surcharge see No. 964.

A 3b souvenir sheet containing No. 719, perforated 12½x11½, was issued Nov. 30, 1991, to promote world peace. Value $10.

A270

1985, Nov.

720 A270 200000b multi 1.25 .60

Soccer Team named "The Strongest," 75th anniv.

No. 713 Surcharged

1986 Litho. *Perf. 11*

721 A265 200000b on 2000b .80 .30
722 A265 5000000b on 2000b 10.00 5.00

A271

1986

723 A271 300000 Emblems, vert. .75 .30
724 A271 550000 Pique trademark, vert. 1.50 .60
725 A271 1000000 Azteca Stadium 2.50 1.50
726 A271 2500000 World cup, vert. 8.00 2.50
Nos. 723-726 (4) 12.75 4.90

1986 World Cup Soccer Championships.
For surcharges see Nos. 961, 1257-1258.

A 1,000,000b souvenir sheet containing No. 723 perforated 13¼ was issued Sept. 25, 1986, to mark the World Cup finals in Mexico City. Value $30.

A 2b souvenir sheet containing Nos. 723 and 739, perf 13¼ was issued Jan. 25, 1989, to mark the Italia 1990 World Cup championships. Value $25.

Intl. Youth Year
A272 A273

1986

727 A272 150000b brt car rose .50 .30
728 A272 500000b bl grn 1.25 .60
729 A273 3000000b multi 7.50 3.00
Nos. 727-729 (3) 9.25 3.90

Inscribed 1985.
For surcharge see No. 958.

Alfonso Sobieta Viaduct, Carretera Quillacollo, Confital A274

1986 *Perf. 13½*

730 A274 400000 int bl & gray 1.25 .50

Inter-American Development Bank, 25th anniv.

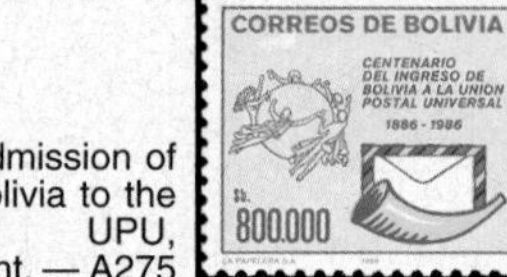

Admission of Bolivia to the UPU, Cent. — A275

1986, Apr. 3 *Perf. 11*

731 A275 800000 multi 1.60 1.00

A 2b souvenir sheet containing No. 731 perforated 13¼ was issued Dec. 7, 1989, to honor the 500th anniv. of the Imperial Reichspost. Value $50.

Postal Workers Soc., 50th Anniv. — A276

1986, Sept. 5

732 A276 2000000 brn & pale brn 5.50 2.00

For surcharge see No. 967.

Founding of Trinidad, 300th Anniv. A277

1986, May 25 *Perf. 13½x14*

733 A277 1400000 Bull and Rider, by Vaca 3.00 1.50

For surcharge see No. 960.

Bolivian Philatelic Federation, 15th Anniv. — A278

1986, Nov. 28

734 A278 600000b No. 19 1.50 .50

Death of a Priest, by Jose Antonio Zampa — A279

Intl. Peace Year — A280

1986, Nov. 21 *Perf. 13¾x13½*

735 A279 400000b multi 1.50 .50

1986, Sept. 16 *Perf. 11*

736 A280 200000 yel grn & pale grn .60 .30

Natl. Oil Corp. (YPBF), 50th Anniv. — A281

1986, Dec. 22 Litho. *Perf. 11*

737 A281 1000000b multi 3.00 1.10

For surcharge see No. 1259.

A282

Photograph of a Devil-mask Dancer, by Jimenez Cordero.

Perf. 13¾x13½

1987, Feb. 13 Litho.

738 A282 20c multi 1.10 .40

February 10th Society, cent. (in 1985).

A283

Perf. 13¾x13½

1987, Mar. 20 Litho.

739 A283 30c Crossed flags 1.10 .50

State Visit of Richard von Weizsacker, Pres. of Germany, Mar. 20.

A 2b souvenir sheet containing No. 739 perforated 13¼ was issued Dec. 16, 1987, to commemorate the 750th anniv. of the founding of Berlin. Value $35.

A 2b souvenir sheet containing No. 739 perforated 13¼ was issued March 18, 1990, to promote world peace. Value $15.

State Visit of King Juan Carlos of Spain, May 20 A284

1987, May 20 *Perf. 13½x13¾*

740 A284 60c Natl. arms 1.75 .80

A 2b souvenir sheet containing No. 740 perforated 13¼ was issued Dec. 15, 1988, to mark the Summer Olympic Games in Seoul (1988) and Barcelona (1992). Value $25.

EXFIVIA '87 — A285

Mount Potosi, 18th cent. engraving.

1987, Oct. Litho. *Perf. 13½*
741 A285 50c multi 2.50 .75

See No. 750.

Wildlife Conservation A286

1987, Oct.

742	A286	20c Condor	.80	.30
743	A286	20c Tapir	.80	.30
744	A286	30c Vicuna	1.50	.50
745	A286	30c Armadillo	1.50	.50
746	A286	40c Spectacled bears	2.00	.70
747	A286	60c Toucans	2.50	.90
		Nos. 742-747 (6)	9.10	3.20

Wildlife in danger of extinction.

A 2b souvenir sheet containing No. 742 perforated 13½ was issued Dec. 7, 1989, to mark the 20th anniv. of the Apollo XI moon landing. Value $20.

A 3b souvenir sheet containing No. 742 perforated 13x13¾ was issued Nov. 30, 1991, to honor Otto Lilienthal and Lilienthal '91. Value $12.

A 3b souvenir sheet containing No. 742 perforated 13½ was issued July 6, 1992, to mark various aviation anninersaries. Value $15.

ESPAMER '87, La Coruna A287

1987, Oct. Litho. *Perf. 14x13½*

748	A287	20c Nina, stern of Santa Maria	.70	.40
749	A287	20c Bow of Santa Maria, Pinta	.70	.40
a.		Pair, #748-749	3.00	3.00

No. 749a has a continuous design.

A 2b souvenir sheet containing No. 749a, perforated 13¼ around and imperforate between, was issued Aug. 15, 1988, to celebrate the 500th anniv. of the discovery of America and the 1992 Barcelona Summer Olympic Games. Value $20.

EXFIVIA Type of 1987

Photograph of Mt. Potosi by Jimenez Cordero.

1987, Aug. 5 Litho. *Perf. 13½*
750 A285 40c multi 1.75 .50

Musical Instruments — A288

1987, Dec. 3 *Perf. 13½x14, 14x13½*

751	A288	50c Zampona and quena (wind instruments)	1.50	.50
752	A288	1b Charango, vert.	3.00	1.40

A289

State Visit of Pope John Paul II A290

Pontiff, religious architecture and art: No. 753, Cathedral of Kings, Beni. No. 754, Carabuco Church. No. 755, Tihuanacu Church. No. 756, St. Francis's Church, Sucre. No. 757, St. Joseph's of Chiquitos Church. 40c, Cobija Chapel, vert. No. 759, Jayu Kcota Church. No. 760, Cochabamba Cathedral, vert. 60c, St. Francis's Basilica, La Paz, vert. No. 762, Christ of Machaca Church. No. 763, St. Lawrence's Church, Potosi, vert. No. 764, *The Holy Family,* by Rubens, vert. No. 765, *The Virgin of Copacabana,* statue, vert. No. 766, Vallegrande Church. No. 767, Tarija Cathedral, vert. No. 768, Concepcion Church.

1988 Litho. *Perf. 13½x14, 14x13½*

753	A289	20c multi	.50	.30
754	A289	20c multi	.50	.30
755	A289	20c multi	.50	.30
756	A289	30c multi	.80	.30
757	A289	30c multi	.80	.30
758	A289	40c multi	1.25	.50
759	A289	50c multi	1.50	.60
760	A289	50c multi	1.50	.60
761	A289	60c multi	1.75	.60
762	A289	70c multi	1.90	.60
763	A289	70c multi	1.90	.60
764	A289	80c multi	2.25	.80
765	A289	80c multi	2.25	.80
766	A289	80c multi	2.25	.80
767	A289	1.30b multi	3.25	1.50
768	A289	1.30b multi	3.25	1.50
769	A290	1.50b shown	4.50	2.00
		Nos. 753-769 (17)	30.65	12.40

Issue dates: 1.50b, May 9; others, Mar. 3.

A 2b souvenir sheet containing No. 764 perforated 13¼ was issued July 16, 1989, to honor Peter Paul Reubens. Value $50.

A 2b souvenir sheet containing No. 764 perforated 13¼ was issued June 2, 1990, to mark the 350th anniv. of the death of artist Peter Paul Reubens (1577-1640). Value $35.

An imperforate souvenir sheet depicting Nos. 769 and 901F with simulated perforations was issued Oct. 20, 1994. Value $5.

An imperforate souvenir sheet depicting Nos. 769 and 934 with simulated perforations was issued Nov. 9, 1994, to celebrate Christmas. Value $25.

Visit of Pres. Jose Sarney of Brazil A291

1988, Aug. 2 Litho. *Perf. 13½x14*
770 A291 50c multi 1.10 .50

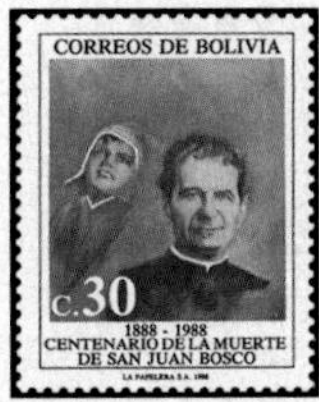

St. John Bosco (1815-1888) A292

1988, Aug. 16 *Perf. 13½*
771 A292 30c multi .80 .30

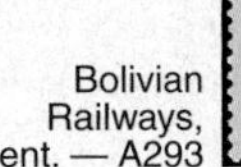

Bolivian Railways, Cent. — A293

Design: 1b, Steam locomotive from the La Paz-Beni line, made by Marca Shy Ohio, Natl. Railway Museum, Sucre.

1988, Aug. 29
772 A293 1b multi 3.00 1.00

Nataniel Aguirre (b. 1888), Author — A294

Department of Pando, 50th Anniv. — A295

1988, Sept. 14 Litho. *Perf. 13½*
773 A294 1b blk & beige 2.00 1.00

1988, Sept. 26 *Perf. 13½*

Designs: 40c, *Columna Porvenir,* memorial to the Battle of Bahio. 60c, Siringuero rubber production (worker sapping latex from *Hevea brasiliensis*).

774	A295	40c multi	.90	.50
775	A295	60c multi	1.50	.70

A296

A297

1988, Sept. 27
776 A296 1.50b multi 4.00 2.00

1988 Summer Olympics, Seoul.

A 2b souvenir sheet containing No. 776 perforated 13¼ was issued Jan. 25, 1989, to honor the German gold medal winners in the equestrian competition at the 1988 Seoul Summer Olympic Games. Value $20.

An imperforate souvenir sheet depicting Nos. 776 and 85, with simulated perforations, was issued July 4, 1995, to mark the 1996 Atlanta Summer Olympic Games. Value $8.

1988

Designs: 70c, Archbishop Bernardino de Cardenas (1579-1668). 80c, Mother Rosa Gattorno (1831-1900), founder of the Sisters of Santa Ana.

777	A297	70c multi	1.75	.90
778	A297	80c multi	2.00	.90

Issue dates: 70c, Oct. 20, 80c, Oct. 14.

Ministry of Transportation & Communications A298

1988, Oct. 24 Litho. *Perf. 14x13½*
779 A298 2b deep car, blk & pale olive grn 4.50 2.00

Army Communications, 50th Anniv. (in 1987) — A299

1988, Nov. 29 Litho. *Perf. 13½*
780 A299 70c multi 2.00 .90

Bolivian Automobile Club, 50th Anniv. A300

1988, Dec. 29 Litho. *Perf. 13½*
781 A300 1.50b multi 3.00 1.50

An imperforate souvenir sheet depicting No. 781 with simulated perforations was issued July 12, 1995, to mark the first anniv. of the death of Ayrton Senna, Brazilian Formula-1 race driver. Value $8.

Flowering Plants and Emblems A301

50c, Orchid, BULGARIA '89 emblem. 60c, Kantuta blossoms, ITALIA '90 emblem. 70c, *Heliconia humilis,* Albertville '86 emblem. 1b, Hoffmanseggia, Barcelona '92 Games emblem. 2b, Puya raymondi, Seoul '88 Games and five-ring emblems.

1989, Feb. 17 Litho. *Perf. 13½*

782	A301	50c multi, vert.	1.60	.50
783	A301	60c multi	2.00	.55
784	A301	70c multi, vert.	3.00	1.25
785	A301	1b multi, vert.	4.00	1.50
786	A301	2b multi, vert.	7.00	3.00
		Nos. 782-786 (5)	17.60	6.80

A 2b souvenir sheet containing No. 783 perforated 13¼ was issued May 18, 1990, to mark the Italia 1990 World Cup games. Value $20.

A 2b souvenir sheet, containing two No. 783, perforated 13¼ aound and imperforate between, was issued Aug. 2, 1990, marking Italia 1990 and picturing the final Germany-Argentina match. Value $20.

Two 2b souvenir sheets, one containing No. 784 perforated 13¼x13½, the other containing two No. 784, perforated 13¼x13½ around and imperforate between, were issued Dec. 27, 1990, to mark the 1992 Albertville Winter Olympic Games. Value, each $10.

A 3b souvenir sheet containing No. 785 perforated 13¾x13, was issued July 6, 1992, to mark Barcelona 1992, Atlanta 1996 and Berlin 2000 Olympic Games. Value $10.

Radio FIDES, 50th Anniv. A302

1989, Feb. 2
787 A302 80c multi 2.00 .80

Gold Quarto of 1852 A303

1989, Feb. 9 *Perf. 13½x14*
788 A303 1b multi 2.25 1.00

A 3b souvenir sheet containing No. 788 perforated 11¾x12½, was issued April 30, 1993, to mark the 40th anniv. of silver coinage in the

German Federal Republic. Value $10. A second sheet, also denominated 3b, depicting No. 788 in tan, rather than blue, and with different marginal design, was issued July 26. Value $12.

French Revolution, Bicent. — A304

1989, June 23 Litho. *Perf. 14x13½*

789 A304 70c red, blk & blue 2.00 .70

Uyuni Township, Cent. — A305

1989, July 9 Litho. *Perf. 14x13½*

790 A305 30c bl, blk & gray 1.25 .40

Noel Kempff Mercado Natl. Park, Santa Cruz — A306

1.50b, Federico Ahlfeld Falls, Pauserna River. 3b, *Ozotoceros bezcarticus* (deer).

1989, Sept. 24 Litho. *Perf. 13½x14*

791 A306 1.50b multicolored 3.50 1.50
792 A306 3b multicolored 7.00 3.00

UPAEP — A306a

1989, Oct. 12 Litho. *Perf. 13½*

792A A306a 50c Metalworking 3.00 .60
792B A306a 1b Temple of Kalasasaya 6.00 1.10

See Nos. 808-809

A 2b souvenir sheet containing Nos. 792A and 792B, perforated 13¼ around and imperforate between, was issued June 2, 1990, to celebrate the 500th anniv. of the discovery of America, UPAE and Expo '92 Sevila. Value $25.

State Visit by Dr. Carlos Andres Perez, Pres. of Venezuela — A306b

1989, Oct. 14

792C A306b 2b multi 3.50 1.50

See Nos. 825-826, 832.

City of Potosi — A306c

1989, Nov. 10 Litho. *Perf. 13½*

792D A306c 60c Cobija Arch 1.50 .60
792E A306c 80c Mint 2.00 1.00
f. Pair, #792D-792E 5.00 2.00

Christmas — A307

Paintings: 40c, *Andean Stillwaters,* by Arturo Borda. 60c, *The Virgin of the Roses,* anonymous. 80c, *The Conquistador,* by Jorge de la Reza. 1b, *Native Harmony,* by Juan Rimsa. 1.50b, *Woman with Jug,* by Cecilio Guzman de Rojas. 2b, *Bloom of Tenderness,* by Gil Imana. Nos. 794-798 vert.

1989, Dec. 18 *Perf. 13½x14, 14x13½*

793 A307 40c multicolored 1.10 .50
794 A307 60c multicolored 1.60 .60
795 A307 80c multicolored 2.25 .80
796 A307 1b multicolored 2.50 1.00
797 A307 1.50b multicolored 3.75 1.50
798 A307 2b multicolored 4.75 2.00
Nos. 793-798 (6) 15.95 6.40

A 3b souvenir sheet containing No. 797, perforated 12½x11¾, was issued Jan. 27, 19930 to commemorate the 200th anniv. of the Louvre. Value $20.

A308

1990, Jan. 23 Litho. *Perf. 13½*

799 A308 80c multicolored 1.75 .70

Fight against drug abuse.

A309

Great Britain #1, Sir Rowland Hill, Bolivia #1

1990, May 13 *Perf. 14x13½*

800 A309 4b multicolored 6.00 3.00

Penny Black, 150th anniv.

World Cup Soccer Championships, Italy — A310

1990, June 16 *Perf. 13½*

801 A310 2b Stadium, Milan 3.25 1.40
802 A310 6b Game 10.00 4.50

A 3b souvenir sheet containing No. 801 perforated 13x13¾ and 817 perforated 11½x12½ was issued July 6, 1992, to honor World Cup soccer. Value $10.

Organization of American States, Cent. — A311

1990, Apr. 14

803 A311 80c dark bl & brt bl 2.25 .70

A312

1990, Apr. 16

804 A312 1.20b multi 3.00 1.25

A313

1990 Litho. *Perf. 14x13½*

805 A313 70c Telecommunications 1.50 .90

A 3b souvenir sheet containing No. 805 perforated 12½x11¾ was issued on April 27, 1992, on the theme of the creation of the Milky Way. Value $15.

A 3b souvenir sheet containing No. 805 perforated 12½x11¾ was issued on Feb. 17, 1993, to mark the 450th anniv. of the death of astronomer Nikolaus Kopernikus (1473-1543). Value $12.

National Chamber of Commerce, Cent. — A314

1990, June

806 A314 50c gold, blk & bl 1.25 .60

Cochabamba Social Club, Cent. — A315

1990, Sept. 14 Litho. *Perf. 13½*

807 A315 40c multicolored .90 .40

UPAEP Type of 1989

Perf. 13½x14, 14x13½

1990, Oct. 12 Litho.

808 A306a 80c Huts 4.50 .80
809 A306a 1b Mountains, lake, vert. 6.00 1.00

A317

1990, Oct. 19 *Perf. 14x13½*

810 A317 1.20b multicolored 2.00 1.00

Magistrate's District of Larecaja, 400th Anniv.

A318

1990, Oct. 12 *Perf. 14x13½*

811 A318 2b multicolored 3.00 1.50

Discovery of America, 500th anniv. (in 1992).

German Reunification A319

1990, Nov. 19 Litho. *Perf. 14x13½*

812 A319 2b multicolored 3.50 1.50

An imperforate 5b souvenir sheet depicting No. 812 with simulated perforations was issued Nov. 20, 1990, to celebrate German reunification and the Philatelia '90 philatelic exhibition in Berlin. Exists with either black or red control number. Value, each $15.

A 3b souvenir sheet containing No. 812, perforated 12½x11½ was issued April 27, 1992, to commemorate the 200th anniv. of the port of Brandenburg. Value $12.

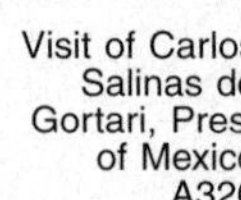

Visit of Carlos Salinas de Gortari, Pres. of Mexico A320

Design: 80c, Visit of Rodrigo Borja Cevallos, Pres. of Ecuador.

1990, Dec. 13 Litho. *Perf. 13½*

813 A320 60c multicolored 2.00 .80
814 A320 80c multicolored 2.25 .80

4th Congress of the Andean Presidents — A321

1990, Nov. 29 *Perf. 13½x14*

815 A321 1.50b multicolored 2.50 1.00

Exfivia '90 — A322

1990, Dec. 9 ***Perf. 13½***
816 A322 40c dk blue .80 .30

Christmas — A323

1990, Nov. 20 ***Perf. 11***
817 A323 50c multicolored .90 .30

Express Mail Service A324

1990, Dec. 14 ***Perf. 13½x14***
818 A324 1b multicolored 1.50 .50

A 3b souvenir sheet containing No. 818, perforated 11¾x12½ was issued Dec. 31, 1993, honoring Dr. Hermann Oberth. Value $15.

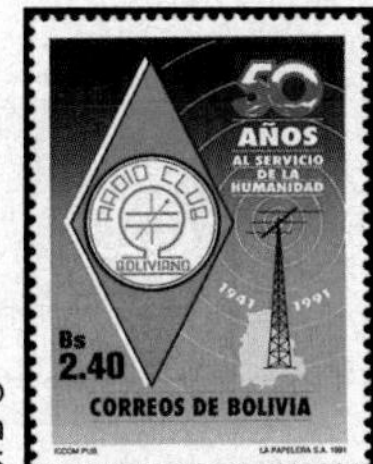

Bolivian Radio Club, 50th Anniv. — A325

1991, Mar. 1 Litho. ***Perf. 14x13½***
819 A325 2.40b multicolored 3.25 1.50

End of Chaco War, 56th Anniv. — A326

Map of Heroes of Chaco Highway.

1991, June 14 Litho. ***Perf. 14x13½***
820 A326 60c multicolored 1.00 .50

National Museums — A327

1991, June 13 ***Perf. 13½***
821 A327 50c Archaeology 1.00 .50
822 A327 50c Art 1.00 .50
823 A327 1b Ethnology, Folklore 1.50 .75
a. Strip of 3, #821-823 2.40 2.40

Espamer '91.

A328

Our Lady of Peace, Metropolitan Cathedral.

1991, July 15 Litho. ***Perf. 14x13½***
824 A328 1.20b multicolored 2.25 .75

Presidential State Visit Type of 1989

Jaime Paz Zamora, Pres. of Bolivia and: No. 825, Dr. Carlos Saul Menem, Pres. of Argentina. No. 826, Dr. Luis Alberto Lacalle, Pres. of Uruguay.

1991 ***Perf. 13½x14***
825 A306b 1b multicolored 1.75 .60
826 A306b 1b multicolored 1.75 .60

Issue dates: No. 825, Aug. 5; No. 826, Aug. 12.

A329

Tremarctos ornatus.

1991, May 31 ***Perf. 13½***
827 A329 30c Adult, 2 cubs 2.75 1.00
828 A329 30c Adult's head 2.75 1.00
829 A329 30c Adult on tree limb 2.75 1.00
830 A329 30c Adult, cubs on tree limb 2.75 1.00
Nos. 827-830 (4) 11.00 4.00

World Wildlife Fund.

A330

1991, Aug. 21 Litho. ***Perf. 14x13½***
831 A330 70c multicolored 1.25 .50

Bolivian Philatelic Federation, 20th anniv.

Presidential State Visit Type of 1989

Design: 50c, Jaime Paz Zamora, Pres. of Bolivia and Alberto Fujimori, Pres. of Peru.

1991, Aug. 29 ***Perf. 13½x14***
832 A306b 50c multicolored .90 .40

A331

1991, Nov. 19 Litho. ***Perf. 14x13½***
833 A331 50c multicolored .80 .40

National census.

America Issue — A332

UPAEP emblem and: 60c, First Discovery of Chuquiago, 1535, by Arturo Reque M. 1.20c, Founding of the City of La Paz, 1548, by J. Rimsa, vert.

1991, Oct. 12 ***Perf. 13½x14, 14x13½***
834 A332 60c multicolored 2.50 .60
835 A332 1.20b multicolored 5.00 1.10

First National Grand Prix Auto and Motorcycle Race — A332a

1991, Sept. 5 Litho. ***Perf. 14x13½***
835A A332a 50c multicolored 1.00 .50

ECOBOL, Postal Security System — A333

1991, Sept. 9 ***Perf. 13½x14***
836 A333 1.40b multicolored 2.00 .75

Simon Bolivar — A334

1992, Feb. 15 Litho. ***Perf. 13½***
837 A334 1.20b buff, brn & org brn 2.00 .75

Exfilbo '92.

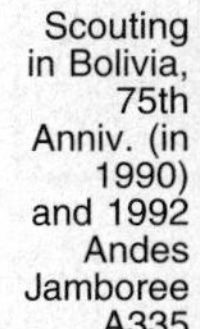
Scouting in Bolivia, 75th Anniv. (in 1990) and 1992 Andes Jamboree A335

1992, Jan. 13 ***Perf. 13½x14***
838 A335 1.20b multicolored 2.25 1.00

Dated 1991.

An imperforate souvenir sheet, depicting Nos. 838, 936 and type of 683 valued 2b, was issued Nov. 7, 1994. Value $5.

Christmas A336

Paintings: 2b, Landscape, by Daniel Pena y Sarmiento. 5b, Woman with Fruit, by Cecilio Guzman de Rojas. 15b, Native Mother, by Crespo Gastelu.

1991, Dec.19 Litho. ***Perf. 13½***
839 A336 2b multicolored 3.25 1.50
840 A336 5b multicolored 7.00 3.00
841 A336 15b multicolored 20.00 9.00
Nos. 839-841 (3) 30.25 13.50

Pacific Ocean Access Pact Between Bolivia and Peru A337

Designs: 1.20b, Pres. Zamora raising flag, vert. 1.50b, Pres. Jaime Paz Zamora of Bolivia and Pres. Alberto Fujimori, Peru. 1.80b, Shoreline of access zone near Ilo, Peru.

1992, Mar. 23 ***Perf. 14x13½, 13½x14***
842 A337 1.20b multicolored *4.50* 1.00
843 A337 1.50b multicolored *5.25* 1.00
844 A337 1.80b multicolored *6.25* 1.25
Nos. 842-844 (3) *16.00* 3.25

Expo '92, Seville A338

1992, Apr. 15 ***Perf. 13½x14***
845 A338 30c multicolored .60 .35
846 A338 50c Columbus' ships 1.00 .50

Miraflores Rotary Club, District 4690, Mt. Illimani A339

1992, Apr. 30 Litho. ***Perf. 13½***
847 A339 90c multicolored 1.40 .70

Prof. Elizardo Perez, Founder of Ayllu of Warisata School, Birth Cent. — A340

1992, June 6 Litho. ***Perf. 13½***
848 A340 60c multicolored .90 .50

Government Palace, Sucre — A341

1992, July 10 Litho. ***Perf. 13½x14***
849 A341 50c multicolored 1.50 .50

A342

1992, Sept. 11 ***Perf. 14x13½***
850 A342 50c multicolored .75 .50

Los Tiempos Newpaper, 25th anniv.

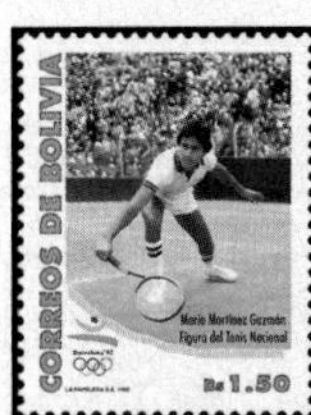

A343

Mario Martinez Guzman, tennis player.

1992, Aug. 9 ***Perf. 13½***

851 A343 1.50b multicolored 2.00 1.00

1992 Summer Olympics, Barcelona.

A 3b souvenir sheet containing No. 851, perforated 14x13, was issued Jan. 27, 1993, to mark the Barcelona 1992 and Atlanta 1996 Olympic Games. Value $30.

First Intl. Whitewater Canoe Regatta, Bermejo River A343a

1992, Sept. 17 **Litho.** ***Perf. 13½***

851A A343a 1.20b multicolored 2.00 1.00

1994 World Cup Soccer Championships, US — A344

1992, Oct. 2 **Litho.** ***Perf. 13½***

852 A344 1.20b multicolored 3.50 1.50

A 3b souvenir sheet containing No. 852, perf 13x13¾, was issued Dec. 31, 1993, to mark the 1994 World Cup. Value $10.

Oruro Technical University, Cent. — A345

1992, Oct. 15 ***Perf. 13½x14***

853 A345 50c multicolored 1.00 .50

Interamerican Institute for Agricultural Cooperation, 50th Anniv. — A346

1992, Oct. 7 ***Perf. 13½***

854 A346 1.20b Chenopodium quinoa 2.00 1.00

Discovery of America, 500th Anniv. A347

Paintings: 60c, Columbus departing from Palos, vert. 2b, Columbus with Caribbean natives.

1992, Oct. 1 ***Perf. 14x13½, 13½x14***

855 A347 60c multicolored 1.00 .50
856 A347 2b multicolored 2.75 1.50

Battle of Ingavi, 150th Anniv. (in 1991) A348

1992, Nov. 18 **Litho.** ***Perf. 13½x14***

857 A348 1.20b sepia & black 2.75 .80

12th Bolivian Games, Cochabamba and Santa Cruz — A349

1992, Nov. 13

858 A349 2b multicolored 3.00 1.25

Fauna, Events A350

Event emblem and fauna: 20c, Beni Dept., sesquicentennial, caiman. 50c, Polska '93, paca. 1b, Bangkok '93, chinchilla. 2b, 1994 Winter Olympics, Lillehammer, Norway, anteater. 3b, Brandenburg Gate, jaguar. 4b, Brasiliana '93, hummingbird, vert. 5b, 1994 World Cup Soccer Championships, US, piranhas.

1992, Nov. 18 **Litho.** ***Perf. 13½***

859 A350 20c multicolored .50 .25
860 A350 50c multicolored 1.00 .40
861 A350 1b multicolored 1.50 .75
862 A350 2b multicolored 3.00 1.25
863 A350 3b multicolored 5.00 2.00
864 A350 4b multicolored 6.00 2.50
865 A350 5b multicolored 8.00 3.50
Nos. 859-865 (7) 25.00 10.65

A 3b souvenir sheet containing No. 862 perforated 13x13¾ was issued Dec. 31, 1993, to mark the 1994 Lillehammer Winter Olympic Games. Value $30.

A 4b souvenir sheet depicting Nos. 864 and C224 with simulated perforations was issued July 3, 1995, to recognize Rotary International and to promote nature conservation. Value $10.

Christmas — A350a

Designs: 1.20b, Man in canoe, star. 2.50b, Star over churches. 6b, Flowers, church, infant on hay.

1992, Dec. 1 **Litho.** ***Perf. 13½***

865A A350a 1.20b multi 1.60 .50
865B A350a 2.50b multi 3.25 1.25
865C A350a 6b multi 8.75 3.25
Nos. 865A-865C (3) 13.60 5.00

A351

A352

Nicolaus Copernicus (1473-1543), Polish Astronomer: 50c, Santa Ana Intl. astrometrical observatory, Tarija, horiz.

Perf. 13x13½, 13½x13

1993, Feb. 18 **Litho.**

866 A351 50c multicolored .70 .30
867 A351 2b black 2.50 .80

An imperforate 3.50b souvenir sheet depicting Nos. 867 and 923 with simulated perforations was issued Oct. 21, 1994. Value $10.

1993, Apr. 14 **Litho.** ***Perf. 13½***

868 A352 60c multicolored 1.10 .40

Beatification of Mother Nazaria.

12th Bolivar Games A353

1993, Apr. 24 ***Perf. 13½x14***

869 A353 2.30b multicolored 2.75 1.10

Bolivia #C240, Brazil #3 A354

1993, May 31

870 A354 2.30b multicolored 3.00 1.10

First Brazilian Stamp, 150th anniv.

A355

Eternal Father, by Gaspar de la Cueva.

1993, June 9 **Litho.** ***Perf. 13½***

871 A355 1.80b multicolored 2.75 1.00

A356

1993, July 31 **Litho.** ***Perf. 14x13½***

872 A356 50c Virgin of Urkupina .80 .35

City of Quillacollo, 400th anniv.

Pedro Domingo Murillo Industrial School A357

1993, Aug. 4 ***Perf. 13½***

873 A357 60c multicolored .85 .35

Butterflies A358

1993, June 4 ***Perf. 13½x14***

874 A358 60c Archaeoprepona demophon 1.25 .40
875 A358 60c Morpho sp. 1.25 .40
876 A358 80c Papilio sp. 1.60 .75
877 A358 80c Historis odius 1.60 .75
878 A358 80c Euptoieta hegesia 1.60 .75
879 A358 1.80b Morpho deidamia 3.50 1.00
880 A358 1.80b Papilio thoas 3.50 1.00
881 A358 1.80b Danaus plexippus 3.50 1.00
882 A358 2.30b Caligo sp. 4.75 1.25
883 A358 2.30b Anaea marthesia 4.75 1.25
884 A358 2.30b Rothschildia sp. 4.75 1.25
885 A358 2.70b Heliconius sp. 7.25 1.50
886 A358 2.70b Marpesia corinna 7.25 1.50
887 A358 2.70b Prepona chromus 7.75 1.50
888 A358 3.50b Heliconius sp., diff. 11.00 2.75
889 A358 3.50b Siproeta epaphus 11.00 2.75
a. Sheet of 16, #874-889 97.50 92.50
Nos. 874-889 (16) 76.30 19.80

Pan-American Health Organization, 90th Anniv. — A359

1993, Oct. 13 **Litho.** ***Perf. 13½***

890 A359 80c multicolored 1.00 .50

An imperforate souvenir sheet depicting Nos. 890 and 789 with simulated perforations was issued July 8, 1995, to honor Louis Pasteur. Value $10.

Archaeological Finds — A360

Location of cave paintings: No. 891, Oruro. No. 892, Santa Cruz, vert. No. 893, Beni, vert. No. 894, Chuquisaca, vert. No. 895, Chuquisaca. No. 896, Potosi. No. 897, La Paz, vert. No. 898, Tarija, vert. No. 899, Cochabamba.

1993, Sept. 28

891 A360 80c multicolored 2.25 .40
892 A360 80c multicolored 2.25 .40
893 A360 80c multicolored 2.25 .40
894 A360 80c multicolored 2.25 .40
895 A360 80c multicolored 2.25 .40
896 A360 80c multicolored 2.25 .40
897 A360 80c multicolored 2.25 .40
898 A360 80c multicolored 2.25 .40
899 A360 80c multicolored 2.25 .40
Nos. 891-899 (9) 20.25 3.60

America Issue — A361

1993, Oct. 9 **Litho.** ***Perf. 13½***

900 A361 80c Saimiri sciureus 1.50 .50
901 A361 2.30b Felis pardalis 4.50 1.50

Famous People — A361a

Designs: 50c, Yolanda Bedregal, poet. 70c, Simon Martinic, President of Cochabamba Philatelic Center. 90c, Eugenio von Boeck, politician, President of Bolivian Philatelic Federation. 1b, Marina Nunez del Prado, sculptor.

1993, Nov. 17 Litho. *Perf. 11*

901A A361a 50c sepia .50 .30
901B A361a 70c sepia .80 .30
901C A361a 90c sepia 1.25 .50
901D A361a 1b sepia 1.25 .50
Nos. 901A-901D (4) 3.80 1.60

Christmas — A361b

Paintings: 2.30b, Adoration of the Shepherds, by Leonardo Flores. 3.50b, Virgin with Child and Saints, by unknown artist. 6b, Virgin of the Milk, by Melchor Perez de Holguin.

1993, Dec. 8 *Perf. 14x13½*

901E A361b 2.30b multicolored 4.00 1.10
901F A361b 3.50b multicolored 6.00 1.50
901G A361b 6b multicolored 10.00 3.00
Nos. 901E-901G (3) 20.00 5.60

Town of Riberalta, Cent. — A362

1994, Feb. 3 Litho. *Perf. 13½*

902 A362 2b multicolored 2.50 .80

World Population Day — A363

1994, Feb. 17 Litho. *Perf. 13½*

903 A363 2.30b multicolored 3.50 1.25

A364

1994, Feb. 21 *Perf. 13½*

904 A364 2b buff & multi 2.25 .80
905 A364 2.30b multi 2.75 1.25

Inauguration of Pres. Gonzalo Sanchez de Lozada.

A365

1994 World Cup Soccer Championships, US: 80c, Mascot. 1.80b, Bolivia, Uruguay. 2.30b, Bolivia, Venezuela. No. 909, Part of Bolivian team, goalies in black. No. 910, Part of Bolivian team, diff. 2.70b, Bolivia, Ecuador. 3.50b, Bolivia, Brazil.

1994, Mar. 22

906 A365 80c multicolored 1.00 .40
907 A365 1.80b multicolored 2.00 1.00
908 A365 2.30b multicolored 3.00 1.25
909 A365 2.50b multicolored 3.00 1.25
910 A365 2.50b multicolored 3.00 1.25
a. Pair, #909-910 8.00 8.00
911 A365 2.70b multicolored 3.25 1.25
912 A365 3.50b multicolored 4.25 1.75
Nos. 906-912 (7) 19.50 8.15

An imperforate souvenir sheet depicting Nos. 907-908 and 911-912 with simulated perforations was issued May 9, 1994. Value $10. On Sept. 18, this sheet was re-released with the overprint "Brasil Campeon." Value $10.

SOS Children's Village, Bolivia — A366

1994, Apr. 12 Litho. *Perf. 13½*

913 A366 2.70b multicolored 3.00 1.25

Catholic Archdiocese La Paz, 50th Anniv. — A367

Churches, priests: 1.80b, Church of San Pedro, Msgr. Jorge Manrique Hurtado. 2b, Archbishop Abel I. Antezana y Rojas, Church of the Sacred Heart of Mary, vert. 3.50b, Msgr. Luis Sainz Hinojosa, Church of Santo Domingo, vert.

1994, July 12 Litho. *Perf. 13½*

914 A367 1.80b multicolored 2.75 .80
915 A367 2b multicolored 3.25 1.00
916 A367 3.50b multicolored 6.00 1.75
Nos. 914-916 (3) 12.00 3.55

A368

Design: 2b, Pres. Victor Paz Estenssoro.

1994, Oct. 2 Litho. *Perf. 13½*

917 A368 2b multicolored 2.25 1.00

A369

1994, Oct. 9

918 A369 1.80b No. 46 1.90 .90

Battle of Ft. Boqueron A370

Col. Manuel Marzana Oroza, battle scene.

1994, Oct. 6

919 A370 80c multicolored 1.25 .40

San Borja, 300th Anniv. A371

1994, Oct. 14

920 A371 1.60b Erythrina fusca 1.75 .60

America Issue — A372

Old, new methods of postal transport: 1b, Streetcar, van. 5b, Airplane, ox cart.

1994, Oct. 12

921 A372 1b multicolored 1.25 .40
922 A372 5b multicolored 5.25 2.25

1994 Solar Eclipse — A373

1994 Oct. 21

923 A373 3.50b multicolored 3.75 1.25

Environmental Protection — A374

Trees: 60c, Buddleja coriacea. 1.80b, Bertholletia exelsa. 2b, Schinus molle, horiz. 2.70b, Polylepis racemosa. 3, Tabebuia chrysantha. 3.50b, Erythrina falcata, horiz.

1994, Sept. 21

924 A374 60c multicolored .75 .25
925 A374 1.80b multicolored 1.60 .75
926 A374 2b multicolored 1.90 .80
927 A374 2.70b multicolored 2.50 1.25
928 A374 3b multicolored 3.25 1.50
929 A374 3.50b multicolored 3.50 1.75
Nos. 924-929 (6) 13.50 6.30

An imperforate souvenir sheet depicting Nos. 925 and 928 with simulated perforations was issued Nov. 3, 1994. Value $12.

Gen. Antonio Jose de Sucre (1795-1830) A375

1995, Jan. 25 Litho. *Perf. 13½*

930 A375 1.80b shown 2.25 .90
931 A375 3.50b diff. background 4.00 1.25

A377

1994, Nov. 25 Litho. *Perf. 13½*

933 A377 2b Tarija girl 2.25 .70
934 A377 5b High plateau child 5.75 1.75
935 A377 20b Eastern girl 22.50 6.75
Nos. 933-935 (3) 30.50 9.20

Christmas.

A378

1994, Nov. 28 Litho. *Perf. 13½*

936 A378 1.80b multicolored 2.00 1.00

Pan-American Scout Jamboree, Cochabamba

Cathedral of St. Anne — A379

1995, Apr. 21 Litho. *Perf. 13½*

937 A379 1.90b black & multi 2.25 1.00
938 A379 2.90b blue & multi 3.00 1.25

Yacuma-Beni Province, cent.

Franciscans at Copacabana Natl. Sanctuary, Cent. — A380

1995, May 2

939 A380 60c gray & multi 1.25 .30
940 A380 80c bister & multi 1.75 .35

A381

1995 Litho. *Perf. 13½*

941 A381 2b multicolored 2.00 1.00

Peace Between Bolivia and Paraguay. Dated 1994.

A382

1995, July 25

942 A382 2.40b multicolored 2.75 1.10

Andes Development Corporation (CAF), 25th anniv.

50th Anniv. of Publication of "Nationalism and the Colonial Age," by Carlos Montenegro (1904-53) A383

1995, Aug. 8

943 A383 1.20b pink & black 2.75 .60

A384

1995, Sept. 26

944 A384 1b multicolored 2.00 .60

FAO, 50th anniv.

A385

1995, Oct. 24 ***Perf. 14½***

945 A385 2.90b multicolored 2.25 1.25

UN, 50th anniv.

America Issue A386

1995, Nov. 21 ***Perf. 14***

946 A386 5b Condor 5.00 2.00
947 A386 5b Llamas 5.00 2.00
a. Pair, #946-947 10.00 10.00

ICAO, 50th Anniv. — A387

1995, Dec. 4 ***Perf. 13½x13***

948 A387 50c multicolored 1.25 .40

Temple of Samaipata — A388

Archaeological finds and: a, 1.90b, Top of ruins. b, 1b, Top of ruins, diff. c, 2.40b, Lower excavation. d, 2b, Floor, tiers.

1995, Dec. 4 ***Perf. 13x13½***

949 A388 Block of 4, #a.-d. 12.00 10.00

No. 949 is a continuous design.

Taquiña Brewery, Cent. — A389

1995, Dec. 8 ***Perf. 14***

950 A389 1b multicolored 2.50 .60

Christmas A390

Paintings: 1.20b, The Annunciation, by Cima da Conegliano. 3b, The Nativity, by Hans Baldung. 3.50b, Adoration of the Magi, by Rogier van der Weyden.

1995, Dec. 15 ***Perf. 14x13½***

951 A390 1.20b multicolored 1.25 .50
952 A390 3b multicolored 3.00 1.10
953 A390 3.50b multicolored 3.75 1.40
Nos. 951-953 (3) 8.00 3.00

Natl. Anthem, 150th Anniv. — A391

Designs: 1b, J.I. de Sanjines, lyricist. 2b, B. Vincenti, composer.

1995, Dec. 18 **Litho.** ***Perf. 13½***

954 A391 1b multicolored 1.40 .70
955 A391 2b multicolored 2.50 1.40
a. Pair, #954-955 5.00 5.00

Decree to Abolish Abuse of Indian Labor, 50th Anniv. — A392

Designs: 1.90b, Modern representations of industry, Gov. Gualberto Villarroel. 2.90, Addressing labor policies, silhouettes of people rejoicing.

1996, Jan. 26 ***Perf. 14***

956 A392 1.90b multicolored 2.00 1.00
957 A392 2.90b multicolored 3.00 1.50
a. Pair, #956-957 6.00 6.00

Nos. 639, 653, 685-686, 712-713, 715, 719, 726, 729, 732-733, C332, C348 Srchd.

Perfs. and Printing Methods as Before

1996

958 A273 50c on 3,000,000b #729 .50 .25
959 A265 60c on 2000b #713 .70 .25
960 A277 60c on 1,400,000b #733 .70 .25
961 A271 1b on 2,500,000b #726 1.00 .50
962 A264 1.50b on 11,000b #712 1.50 .60
963 A267 2.50b on 23,000b #715 2.50 1.00
964 A269 3b on 1,000,000b #719 2.75 1.25
965 A222 3.50b on 6.50b #639 3.25 1.40
966 A234 3.50b on 9b #653 3.25 1.40
967 A276 3.50b on 2,000,000b #732 3.25 1.40
968 AP67 3.80b on 3.80b #C332 3.25 1.40
969 A189 20b on 3.80b #C348 18.00 8.00
970 A253 20b on 10b #685 18.00 8.00
971 A254 20b on 13b #686 18.00 8.00
Nos. 958-971 (14) 76.65 33.70

Size and location of surcharge varies.

No. 627 Surcharged

1996 **Litho.** ***Perf. 10½***

972 A216 60c on 2.50b multi .90 .25

See No. 697 for similar surcharge.

10th Summit of the Chiefs of State and Government (Rio Group), Cochabamba A393

Designs: 2.50b, Stylized person. 3.50b, Stylized globe surrounded by lines.

1996, Sept. 4 ***Perf. 14***

973 A393 2.50b multicolored 2.25 .90
974 A393 3.50b multicolored 3.25 1.25

Anniversaries A394

50c, Natl. Bank of Bolivia, 125th anniv. 1b, Jose Joaquin de Lemoine (1776-1851), first postal administrator, vert.

1996, Dec. 8 **Litho.** ***Perf. 13½***

975 A394 50c multicolored .50 .25
976 A394 1b multicolored 1.00 .40

Summit of the Americas to Sustain Development A395

1996, Dec. 8 ***Perf. 14x13½***

977 A395 2.50b brown & multi 2.25 1.00
978 A395 5b black & multi 4.50 2.00

CARE in Bolivia, 20th Anniv. — A396

1996, Dec. 19 ***Perf. 13½***

979 A396 60c Family, horiz. .50 .25
980 A396 70c shown .60 .30

Natl. Symphony Orchestra, 50th Anniv. — A397

1996, Dec. 24

981 A397 1.50b shown 1.75 .75
982 A397 2b String instruments 2.10 1.10
a. Pair, #981-982 2.50 2.50

No. 982a is a continuous design.

Tourism in Oruro A398

Designs: 50c, Miners' Monument, vert. 60c, Folklore costume, vert. 1b, Virgin of Socavon, vert. 1.50b, Sajama mountains. 2.50b, Chipaya child, building, vert. 3b, Raul Shaw, "Moreno."

1997, Feb. 3 **Litho.** ***Perf. 14½***

983 A398 50c multicolored .50 .50
984 A398 60c multicolored .75 .75
985 A398 1b multicolored 1.25 1.25
986 A398 1.50b multicolored 1.25 1.25
987 A398 2.50b multicolored 2.00 2.00
988 A398 3b multicolored 3.00 3.00
Nos. 983-988 (6) 8.75 8.75

Dated 1996.

Tourism in Chuquisaca — A399

Designs: 60c, La Glorieta. 1b, Governor's Palace, vert. No. 991, Dinosaur tracks. No. 992, House of Liberty. 2b, Tarabaqueno, vert. 3b, Statue of Juana Azurduy of Padilla, vert.

1997, Jan. 30 ***Perf. 13½x14, 14x13½***

989	A399	60c multicolored	.45	.45
990	A399	1b multicolored	.70	.70
991	A399	1.50b multicolored	1.50	1.50
992	A399	1.50b multicolored	1.50	1.50
993	A399	2b multicolored	2.00	2.00
994	A399	3b multicolored	3.00	3.00
		Nos. 989-994 (6)	9.15	9.15

Dated 1996.

Tourism in Tarija A400

Designs: 50c, House of Culture, Dorada, vert. 60c, Church of Entre Rios, vert. 80c, San Luis Falls. 1b, Monument to the Chaco War. 3b, Temple, Statue of the Virgin Mary, Chaguaya. 20b, Eustaquio Mendez house, monument.

1997, Jan. 24 ***Perf. 14x13½, 13½x14***

995	A400	50c multicolored	.50	.30
996	A400	60c multicolored	.65	.35
997	A400	80c multicolored	.85	.55
998	A400	1b multicolored	1.10	.65
999	A400	3b multicolored	3.25	1.90
1000	A400	20b multicolored	20.00	11.00
		Nos. 995-1000 (6)	26.35	14.75

Dated 1996.

Visit of French Pres. Jacques Chirac A401

Design: Bolivian Pres. Gonzalo Sanchez de Lozada, Chirac.

1997, Mar. 15 ***Perf. 14***

1001	A401	4b multicolored	4.00	4.00

Salesian Order in Bolivia, Cent. — A402

Designs: 1.50b, St. John Bosco (1815-88), church. 2b, Statue of St. John Bosco talking with boy, church.

1997, Apr. 29 **Litho.** ***Perf. 13½***

1002	A402	1.50b multicolored	1.50	1.50
1003	A402	2b multicolored	2.00	2.00

UNICEF, 50th Anniv. A403

Children's drawings: 50c, Houses, children on playground. 90c, Child running, cactus, rock, lake. 1b, Boys, girls arm in arm across globe. 2.50b, Girl on swing, others in background.

1997

1004	A403	50c multicolored	.50	.45
1005	A403	90c multicolored	.85	.75
1006	A403	1b multicolored	.85	.75
1007	A403	2.50b multicolored	2.40	2.10
		Nos. 1004-1007 (4)	4.60	4.05

Department of La Paz — A404

Tourism: 50c, Mt. Chulumani, Las Yungas, vert. 80c, Inca monolith, vert. 1.50b, City, Mt. Illimani, vert. 2b, Gate of the Sun, Tiwanacu. 2.50b, Traditional dancers, vert. 10b, Virgin of Copacabana, reed boat.

1997, May 28 **Litho.** ***Perf. 13½***

1008	A404	50c multicolored	.50	.45
1009	A404	80c multicolored	.75	.70
1010	A404	1.50b multicolored	1.40	1.25
1011	A404	2b multicolored	1.75	1.60
1012	A404	2.50b multicolored	2.25	2.00
1013	A404	10b multicolored	9.25	8.50
		Nos. 1008-1013 (6)	15.90	14.50

1997 America Cup Soccer Championships, Bolivia — A405

1998 World Cup Soccer Championships, France — A406

1997, June 13

1014	A405	3b multicolored	3.00	3.00
1015	A406	5b multicolored	5.00	5.00

National Congress A407

1997, July 8 **Litho.** ***Perf. 13½***

1016	A407	1b multicolored	.80	.40

America Issue — A408

Women in traditional costumes: 5b, From valley region. 15b, From eastern Bolivia.

1997, July 14 **Litho.** ***Perf. 13½***

1017	A408	5b multicolored	5.00	5.00
1018	A408	15b multicolored	14.00	14.00

Mercosur (Common Market of Latin America) A409

1997, Sept. 26

1019	A409	3b multicolored	2.75	2.00

See Argentina No. 1975, Brazil No. 2646, Paraguay No. 2565, Uruguay No. 1681.

Christmas A410

Paintings: 2b, Virgen del Cerro, by unknown artist. 5b, Virgen de la Leche, by unknown artist. 10b, The Holy Family, by Melchor Pérez de Holguin.

1997, Dec. 19 **Litho.** ***Perf. 13½***

1020	A410	2b multicolored	2.00	1.00
1021	A410	5b multicolored	5.00	2.50
1022	A410	10b multicolored	10.00	5.00
		Nos. 1020-1022 (3)	17.00	8.50

Diana, Princess of Wales (1961-97) A411

1997, Dec. 29

1023	A411	2b Portrait, vert.	2.00	1.40
1024	A411	3b In mine field	2.75	2.10

Visit of Prime Minister of Spain A412

Hugo Banzer Suarez, Pres. of Bolivia and José Maria Aznar.

1998, Mar. 16

1025	A412	6b multicolored	6.00	3.50

Bolivian Society of Engineers, 75th Anniv. A413

1998, Apr. 28

1026	A413	3.50b multicolored	3.00	1.50

A414 A415

1998, Apr. 30 **Litho.** ***Perf. 13½***

1027	A414	5b multicolored	4.00	2.25

Rotary Intl. in Bolivia, 70th anniv.

1998, July 9

America Issue: 4b, Letter Carriers, 1942, horiz.

1028	A415	3b multicolored	2.50	1.25
1029	A415	4b multicolored	3.50	1.50

Famous Men — A416

1.50b, Werner Guttentag Tichauer, bibliographer. 2b, Dr. Martin Cardenas Hermosa, botanist. 3.50b, Adrian Patiño Carpio, composer.

1998, July 10

1030	A416	1.50b brown	1.00	.50
1031	A416	2b green, vert	1.50	.75
1032	A416	3.50b black, vert	2.40	.90
		Booklet, 4 each #1030-1032	50.00	
		Nos. 1030-1032 (3)	4.90	2.15

Regions in Bolivia A417

Beni: 50c, Victoria regia. 1b, Calliandra. 1.50b, White Tajibo tree, vert. 3.50b, Amazon mask. 5b, Nutria. 7b, King vulture.

1998, Oct. 11 **Litho.** ***Perf. 13½***

1033	A417	50c black & multi	.30	.25
1034	A417	1b black & multi	.75	.40
1035	A417	1.50b black & multi	1.25	.70
1036	A417	3.50b black & multi	3.00	1.50
1037	A417	5b black & multi	4.25	2.00
1038	A417	7b black & multi	5.75	4.00
		Nos. 1033-1038 (6)	15.30	8.85

Pando: 50c, Acre River. 1b, Sloth climbing bamboo tree, vert. 1.50b, Bahia Arroyo, vert. 4b, Boa. 5b, Family of capybaras. 7b, Houses, palm trees, vert.

1039	A417	50c green & multi	.50	.30
1040	A417	1b green & multi	.75	.40
1041	A417	1.50b green & multi	1.25	.70
1042	A417	4b green & multi	3.25	1.75
1043	A417	5b green & multi	4.50	2.00
1044	A417	7b green & multi	6.50	4.00
		Nos. 1039-1044 (6)	16.75	9.15
		Nos. 1033-1044 (12)	32.05	18.00

Women of Bolivia — A418

First Lady Yolanda Prada de Banzer and: 1.50b, Women working in fields, making pottery, weaving. 2b, Women working on computer, standing at blackboard.

1998, Oct. 11

1045	A418	1.50b multicolored	1.10	.60
1046	A418	2b multicolored	1.75	1.00
	a.	Pair, #1045-1046	4.00	4.00

America Issue.

City of La Paz, 450th Anniv. A419

1998, Oct. 14

1047 A419 2b Plaza de Laja Church 2.00 1.00

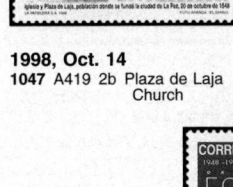

A420

1998, Nov. 6 Litho. ***Perf. 13½x13¾***

1048 A420 3.50b blue & yellow 2.75 .75

Organization of American States, 50th anniv.

A421

1998, Nov. 12 ***Perf. 13¼x13½***

1049 A421 2b multicolored 1.50 .50

Bolivian Philatelic Federation, 25th anniv., Espamer '98, Buenos Aires.

A422

Christmas: 2b, Child's drawing of church. 6b, Pope John Paul II. 7b, John Paul II, Mother Teresa.

Perf. 13¼x13½, 13½x13¼

1998, Nov. 26

1050 A422 2b multi, horiz. 1.60 .50
1051 A422 6b multi 3.75 1.75
1052 A422 7b multi 4.50 2.00
Nos. 1050-1052 (3) 9.85 4.25

UPU, 125th Anniv. A423

1999, Jan. 26 Litho. ***Perf. 13½***

1053 A423 3.50b multicolored 3.00 .70

AFC Soccer Club, 75th Anniv. — A424

1999, Apr. 22 Litho. ***Perf. 13½***

1054 A424 5b multicolored 4.50 2.25

Geneva Convention and Bolivian Red Cross, 50th Anniv. A425

1999, May 18

1055 A425 5b multicolored 4.25 1.25

Bernardo Guarachi, First Bolivian to Reach Summit of Mt. Everest A426

1999, May 25

1056 A426 6b multicolored 6.00 3.00

Special Olympics of Bolivia, 30th Anniv. — A427

Designs: 2b, Medalists on podium. 2.50b, Winners of swimming event, running event.

1999

1057 A427 2b multicolored 1.50 .50
1058 A427 2.50b multicolored 1.75 .60

Japanese Immigration to Bolivia, Cent. — A428

Designs: 3b, Golden Pavilion, Kyoto. 6b, Sun setting across water, vert.

1999, June 3

1059 A428 3b multicolored 2.25 .70
1060 A428 6b multicolored 4.50 1.75

Bolivian Cinema, 100th Anniv. A429

1999 Litho. ***Perf. 13½***

1061 A429 50c Hacia la Gloria, 1932-33 .50 .25
1062 A429 50c Jonas y la Ballena Rosada, 1995 .50 .25
1063 A429 1b Wara Wara, 1929 .80 .45
1064 A429 1b Vuelve Sebastiana, 1953 .80 .45
1065 A429 3b La Campana del Chaco, 1933 2.25 .75
1066 A429 3b La Vertiente, 1958 2.25 .75
1067 A429 6b Yawar Mallku, 1969 5.00 2.00
1068 A429 6b Mi Socio, 1982 5.00 2.00
a. Sheet of 8, #1061-1068 18.00 18.00
Nos. 1061-1068 (8) 17.10 6.90

SOS Children's Village, 50th Anniv. — A430

1999, July 8

1069 A430 3.50b multicolored 2.50 1.40

Intl. Day Against Illegal Drugs A431

Perf. 13¼x13½

1999, June 26 Litho.

1070 A431 3.50b multicolored 2.50 1.40

Completion of Bolivian-Brazilian Gas Pipeline — A432

Designs: 3b, Presidents of Bolivia and Brazil, map of pipeline. 6b, Presidents, gas flame.

1999, July 1 Litho. ***Perf. 13½***

1071 A432 3b multicolored 3.00 1.25
1072 A432 6b multicolored 6.00 2.75

La Paz Lions Club, 50th Anniv. — A433

1999 ***Perf. 13½x13¼***

1073 A433 3.50b multicolored 2.50 1.40

Cochabamba Tourism — A434

50c, Mt. Tunari. 1b, Cochabamba Valley. 2b, Container from Omerque culture, idol from Pachamama culture. 3b, Totora. 5b, Composer Teofilo Vargas Candia. 6b, Statue of Jesus Christ.

1999 ***Perf. 13½x13¾, 13¾x13½***

1074 A434 50c multi .45 .25
1075 A434 1b multi .85 .40
1076 A434 2b multi, vert. 1.40 .60
1077 A434 3b multi 1.90 .85
1078 A434 5b multi, vert. 3.00 1.25
1079 A434 6b multi, vert. 3.50 1.50
Nos. 1074-1079 (6) 11.10 4.85

Potosí Tourism A435

50c, Tarapaya Lake. 1b, Obverse and reverse of 1827 Bolivian coin. 2b, Mt. Chorolque. 3b, Lake, llama, birds. 5b, "Mestizo Woman with a Cigarette Case," by Teofilo Loaiza. 6b, Alfredo Dominguez Romero, musician.

Perf. 13¾x13½, 13½x13¾

1999 Litho.

1080 A435 50c multi, vert. .45 .25
1081 A435 1b multi .85 .40
1082 A435 2b multi 1.40 .60
1083 A435 3b multi 1.90 .85
1084 A435 5b multi, vert. 3.00 1.25
1085 A435 6b multi, vert. 3.50 1.50
Nos. 1080-1085 (6) 11.10 4.85

America Issue, A New Millennium Without Arms — A436

1999 ***Perf. 13½x13¼***

1086 A436 3.50b shown 3.00 1.50
1087 A436 3.50b Globe, flower 3.00 1.50

Christmas A437

2b, Children, Christmas tree. 6b, The Birth of Jesus, by Gaspar Miguel de Berrios. 7b, Our Families of the World, by Omar Medina.

1999 ***Perf. 13¼x13½, 13½x13¼***

1088 A437 2b multi 1.30 .50
1089 A437 6b multi, vert. 3.50 1.40
1090 A437 7b multi, vert. 4.50 1.60
Nos. 1088-1090 (3) 9.30 3.50

Discovery of Brazil, 500th Anniv. A438

2000 Litho. ***Perf. 13½x13¾***

1091 A438 5b multi 4.00 1.50

2000 Doble Copacabana Bicycle Race — A439

Various views of racers.

2000

1092 A439 1b multi .90 .50
1093 A439 3b multi 2.00 1.10
1094 A439 5b multi 4.00 1.60
1095 A439 7b multi 6.00 2.25
Nos. 1092-1095 (4) 12.90 5.45

Sgt. Maximiliano Paredes Military School, Cent. — A440

2000 Litho. ***Perf. 13½x13¾***

1096 A440 2.50b multi 2.00 1.00

Federal Republic of Germany, 50th Anniv. (in 1999) A441

2000

1097 A441 6b multi 4.50 1.25

Paintings of Cecilio Guzmán de Rojas (1900-51) — A442

Designs: 1b, Self-portrait, vert. 2.50b, Triunfo de la Naturaleza. 5b, Andina, vert. 6b, Riña de Estudiantes.

2000 ***Perf. 13¾x13½, 13½x13¾***

1098-1101 A442 Set of 4 10.00 4.00

Artifacts from Natl. Archaeological Museum — A443

Artifacts from: No. 1102, 50c, Pando. No. 1103, 50c, Potosí. 70c, Beni. 90c, Tarija. No. 1106, 1b, Chuquisaca. No. 1107, 1b, Oruro. 3b, Cochabamba. 5b, Santa Cruz. 20b, La Paz.

2000 ***Perf. 11¼x11***

1102-1110 A443 Set of 9 24.00 12.00

America Issue, Fight Against AIDS — A444

Designs: No. 1111, 3.50b, Symbols for male and female in whirlwind. No. 1112, 3.50b, Man, woman, clouds, brick wall.

2000 ***Perf. 13¼x13½***

1111-1112 A444 Set of 2 7.00 2.50

Victor Agustin Ugarte, Soccer Player — A445

2000, Apr. 24 Litho. ***Perf. 13½x13¼***

1113 A445 3b multi 2.50 1.00

Santa Cruz Tourism A446

Designs: 50c, Fountains, Parque el Arenal. 1b, Ox cart. 2b, Writers Raúl Otero Reiche, Gabriel René Moreno, Hernando Sanabria Fernández. 3b, Virgin of Cotoca, vert. 5b, Anthropomorphic vessel, vert. 6b, Speothos venaticus.

Perf. 13½x13¾, 13¾x13½

2000, Apr. 28

1114-1119 A446 Set of 6 14.00 6.25

Javier del Granado (1913-96), Writer — A447

2000, May 26 Litho. ***Perf. 13¼x13½***

1120 A447 3b multi 2.50 .90

Millennium — A448

2000 Litho. ***Perf. 13½x13¼***

1121 A448 5b multi 3.00 1.00

Sovereign Military Order of Malta, 900th Anniv. — A449

2000 ***Perf. 13¾x13½***

1122 A449 6b multi 4.25 1.25

Christmas — A450

Angels from Calamarca Church: 3b, Gabriel. 5b, Angel of Virtue. 10b, Angel with spike of grain.

2000

1123-1125 A450 Set of 3 12.50 4.25

Holy Year 2000 — A451

Holy Year emblem and: 4b, Basilica de San Francisco, La Paz. 6b, Wheat stalks, barbed wire.

2000 Litho. ***Perf. 13½x13¼***

1126-1127 A451 Set of 2 8.00 3.00

Promotion of Philately A452

National Symbols A453

Designs: 50c, Man carying first day covers up stairs. 1b, Child, six stamps. 1.50b, Stamp collector. 2b, Child, three stamps. 2.50b, Envelope in bin. 10b, Patuju bandera, current national flower. 20b, La kantuta, previous national flower. 30b, Coat of arms, 1825. 50b, Coat of arms, 1826. 100b, Coat of arms, 1851.

2001 Litho. ***Perf. 10½***

1128	A452 50c green		.30	.25
1129	A452 1b green		.50	.30
1130	A452 1.50b green		.80	.50
1131	A452 2b green		1.00	.70
1132	A452 2.50b green		1.25	.80
a.	Horiz. strip, #1128-1132, + label		8.00	8.00

Perf. 13¾x13½

1133	A453 10b multi	8.00	4.00
1134	A453 20b multi	17.50	8.00
1135	A453 30b multi	25.00	12.00
1136	A453 50b multi	37.50	25.00
1137	A453 100b multi	75.00	40.00
	Nos. 1128-1137 (10)	166.85	91.55

Issued: 50c, 1b, 1.50b, 2b, 2.50b, 6/12; 10b, 6/29; 20b, 6/8; 30b, 5/16; 50b, 3/16; 100b, 4/16.

Bolivia - European Union Cooperation, 25th Anniv. — A454

2001, May 8 Litho. ***Perf. 13½x13¾***

1138 A454 6b multi 4.25 1.25

Law and Political Science Faculty of San Andres University, 171st Anniv. — A455

2001, May 18 ***Perf. 13¾x13½***

1139 A455 6b multi 4.25 1.25

Muela del Diablo A457

2001, July 6 Litho. ***Perf. 13½x13¾***

1141 A457 1.50b multi 1.25 .40

2001 Census — A458

2001, Aug. 1 ***Perf. 11***

1142	Horiz. strip of 5	8.00	8.00
a.	A458 1b purple & multi	1.00	.30
b.	A458 1.50b red & multi	1.10	.40
c.	A458 1.50b green & multi	1.10	.40
d.	A458 2.50b blue & multi	2.00	.65
e.	A458 3b violet & multi	2.40	.70

Butterflies and Insects A459

Butterflies: No. 1143, 1b, Heliconinae. 1.50b, Philaethria dido. No. 1145, 2.50b, Diathria clymene. No. 1146, 5b, Arctiidae. No. 1147, 6b, Morpho godarti. No. 1148, 6b, Caligo idomineus.

Insects: No. 1149, 1b, Orthopteridae. No. 1150, 2.50b, Mantidae. No. 1151, 3b, Tropidacris latreillei. 4b, Dynastidae. No. 1153, 5b, Acrocinus longimanus. No. 1154, 5b, Lucanidae.

Perf. 13¼x13½

2001, Aug. 30 Litho.

1143-1148 A459 Set of 6 16.50 6.75

1149-1154 A459 Set of 6 16.50 6.75

21st Inter-American Scout Conference A460

2001, Sept. 13 ***Perf. 13¾x13½***

1155 A460 3.50b multi 3.50 2.25

America Issue, UNESCO World Heritage Sites — A461

Designs: 1.50b, Door from Church of St. Francis, Potosi, vert. 5b, Tiwanakwu monoliths.

Perf. 13¾x13½, 13½x13¾

2001, Sept. 26

1156-1157 A461 Set of 2 7.00 4.00

Breast Cancer Prevention A462

2001, Oct. 18 Litho. ***Perf. 13¼x13½***

1158 A462 1.50b multi 1.50 1.00

Christmas — A463

Sculptures by Gaspar de la Cueva: 3b, St. Mary Magdalene. 5b, St. Apolonia. 10b, St. Teresa of Avila.

2001, Nov. 15 ***Perf. 13½x13¼***

1159-1161 A463 Set of 3 16.00 9.25

Joaquin Gantier, Historian, and Casa de la Libertad — A464

2001, Nov. 20

1162 A464 4b multi 3.75 2.00

Bolivian-Belgian Cooperation — A465

2001, Nov. 21 ***Perf. 13¼x13½***
1163 A465 6b multi 6.00 2.50

Meeting of Bolivian and Peruvian Presidents A466

Arms of Bolivia and Peru and: 50c, Dam, aerial view of Lake Titicaca. 3b, Bridge, Route from La Paz, Bolivia to Ilo, Peru.

2002, Jan. 26 ***Perf. 13¾x13½***
1164-1165 A466 Set of 2 3.25 1.75

Mauro Nuñez, Composer, Cent. of Birth — A467

No. 1166: a, 1b, Musical score and stringed instruments. b, 6b, Musical score and Nuñez.

2002, Jan. 29
1166 A467 Horiz. pair, #a-b 6.50 4.50

Naming of Oruro Carnival as UNESCO Masterpiece of Oral and Intangible Heritage of Humanity A468

Dances: 50c, Diablada. 1.50b, Morenada. 2.50b, Caporales. 5b, Tobas. No. 1171, 7b, Suri Sikuri, vert. No. 1172, 7b, Pujllay, vert.

Perf. 13¼x13½, 13½x13¼
2002, Feb. 8
1167-1172 A468 Set of 6 20.00 14.00

Butterfly and insect Type of 2001
Miniature Sheet

No. 1173: a, Urania leilus. b, Tropidacris latreillei. c, Papilio cresphontes. d, Acrocinus longimanus. e, Preponia buckleyana. f, Half of Thysannia agripyna, denomination at left. g, Half of Thysannia agripyna, denomination at right. h, Lucanidae. i, Nymphalidae. j, Dynastidae. k, Nymphalidae-heliconinae. l, Orthopteridae.

2002, Feb. 15 ***Perf. 13¼x13½***
1173 A459 3b Sheet of 12, #a-l 32.50 32.50

3rd Intl. Theater Festival, La Paz — A469

2002, Mar. 21 ***Perf. 13¾x13½***
1174 A469 3b multi 3.00 1.25

Intl. Year of Mountains and Intl. Year of Ecotourism A470

Designs: 80c, Viscachas Mountain, Potosi Department. 1b, Tree, Cochabamba Department, vert. 1.50, Mount Huayna Potosi, La Paz Department. No. 1178, 2.50b, Mt. Sajama, Oruro Department, vert. No. 1179, 2.50b, Mt. Payachatas, Oruro Department.

Perf. 13¼x13½, 13½x13¼
2002, Apr. 2
1175-1179 A470 Set of 5 7.75 3.00

Dr. Gunnar Mendoza, Historian A471

2002, May 25 ***Perf. 13¼x13½***
1180 A471 4b multi 3.25 2.00

Gen. Germán Busch Military Aviation College, 50th Anniv. — A472

Designs: 4b, Airplane over mountains. 5b, Two airplanes, vert. 6b, Three helicopters.

Perf. 13¼x13½, 13½x13¼
2002, June 14
1181-1183 A472 Set of 3 12.00 8.00

Museo de la Recoleta, Sucre, 400th Anniv. — A473

2002, July 12 ***Perf. 13¾x13½***
1184 A473 4b multi 3.25 2.00

Birds — A474

Designs: 50c, Neochen jubata. 4b, Falco deiroleucus. 6b, Dryocopus schulzi.

2002, July 12 ***Perf. 13½x13¼***
1185-1187 A474 Set of 3 9.00 5.50

Cefilco Philatelic Co., Cochabamba (50c), Bolivian Philatelic Federation, 30th anniv. (4b), Phila Korea 2002 World Stamp Exhibition, Seoul (6b).

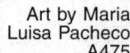

Art by Maria Luisa Pacheco A475

Designs: 70c, Untitled work, vert. 80c, Cordillera, 1967, vert. 5b, Cerros, 1967.

Perf. 13½x13¼, 13¼x13½
2002, July 29
1188-1190 A475 Set of 3 5.25 3.25

Sculptures by Marina Nuñez del Prado — A476

Designs: 70c, Madona India. 80c Madre India. 5b, Venus Negra.

2002, July 29 Litho. ***Perf. 13½x13¼***
1191-1193 A476 Set of 3 5.25 3.25

Armando Alba Zambrana (1901-74), Historian A477

Perf. 13¼x13½
2002, Aug. 30 **Litho.**
1194 A477 3b multi 2.75 1.75

Pan-American Health Organization, Cent. — A478

2002, Apr. 24 ***Perf. 13½x13¾***
1195 A478 3b multi 2.75 1.75

America Issue, Education A479

Students: 1b, In classroom. 2.50b, At computer.

2002, Oct. 11 ***Perf. 13¼x13½***
1196-1197 A479 Set of 2 3.50 2.25

Alcide d'Orbigny (1802-57), Naturalist A480

Designs: 1b, D'orbigny and man and woman in native costumes, vert. 4b, D'Orbigny and boat. 6b, Portrait, vert.

Perf. 13¾x13½, 13½x13¾
2002, Sept. 26
1198-1200 A480 Set of 3 9.00 5.50

Christmas — A481

Designs: 3b, Madonna and Child. 5b, Andean nativity. 6b, Adoration of the Magi.

Perf. 13½x13¼
2002, Nov. 14 **Litho.**
1201-1203 A481 Set of 3 10.00 7.50

Apolinar Camacho (1917-2002), Composer A482

2003, Jan. 10 ***Perf. 13¾x13½***
1204 A482 2.50b multi 1.75 1.25

Battle of Bahia, Cent. (in 2002) — A483

No. 1205: a, 50c, One statue. b, 1b, Three statues.

2003, May 5 Litho. ***Perf. 13½x13¼***
1205 A483 Pair, #a-b 1.50 .80

Permanent Assembly for Human Rights in Bolivia, 25th Anniv. — A484

2003, June 5
1206 A484 6b blue 4.00 1.75

Central Bank of Bolivia, 75th Anniv. — A485

2003, July 18 ***Perf. 13¾x13½***
1207 A485 4b multi 2.50 1.10

Constitutional Tribunal, 5th Anniv. — A486

2003, July 25 ***Perf. 13¼x13½***
1208 A486 1.50b multi 1.10 .50

Indigenous Flora and Fauna — A487

No. 1209: a, 6b, Quinoa. b, 7b, Llamas.

2003, Sept. 23

1209 A487 Pair, #a-b 9.00 7.00

Republic of Panama, Cent. A488

2003, Nov. 3 Litho. ***Perf. 13½x13¾***

1210 A488 7b multi 4.25 2.00

13th Iberoamerican Heads of State Summit, Santa Cruz de la Sierra — A489

No. 1211: a, Flags, Western hemisphere. b, Flags, Eastern hemisphere.

2003, Nov. 7

1211 A489 6b Horiz. pair, #a-b 8.00 2.50

Porfirio Díaz Machicao (1909-81), Rosendo Villalobos (1859-1932), and Msgr. Juan Quiros (1914-92) — A490

Virgin of Guadalupe A491

2003 ***Perf. 13½x13¾, 13¾x13½***

1212 A490 6b multi 4.00 2.00

1213 A491 6b multi 4.00 2.00

a. Pair, #1212-1213 10.00 10.00

Bolivian Language Academy, 75th anniv. (No. 1212), La Plata Archdiocese, 450th anniv. (No. 1213).

Issued: No. 1212, 11/12; No. 1213, 11/25.

Christmas A492

Paintings depicting the Adoration of the Shepherds by: 1.50b, Leonardo Flores, vert. 6b, Bernardo Bitti, vert. 7b, Melchor Pérez de Holguín.

Perf. 13¾x13½, 13½x13¾

2003, Dec. 16

1214-1216 A492 Set of 3 8.50 4.25

Pontificate of Pope John Paul II, 25th Anniv. A493

Designs: 1b, Pope waving, vert. 1.50b, Painting, vert. 5b, Pope blessing Indians. 6b, Pope waving, diff., vert. 7b, Photograph, vert.

20b, Arms of Bolivia and Vatican City, Pope John Paul II, aerial view of Vartican City, #1013, 1161.

2003 ***Perf. 13¾x13½, 13½x13¾***

1217-1221 A493 Set of 5 12.50 11.50

Imperf

Size: 150x110mm

1222 A493 20b multi 12.50 11.50

Arco Iris Foundation, 10th Anniv. — A494

2004, Apr. 4 Litho. ***Perf. 13¾x13½***

1223 A494 1.80b multi 1.25 .50

Academy of Military History, 25th Anniv. — A495

2004, Oct. 19 Litho. ***Perf. 13¾x13½***

1224 A495 1b multi .60 .30

2004 Summer Olympics, Athens — A496

Designs: 1.50b, Shooting, gymnastics, judo. 7b, Track, swimming.

2004, Nov. 8

1225-1226 A496 Set of 2 3.50 1.50

Christmas A497

Designs: 1.50b, Nativity. 3b, Shepherd praying. 6b, Candle.

2004, Dec. 16

1227-1229 A497 Set of 3 4.50 1.75

La Paz Journalist's Association, 75th Anniv. — A498

2004, Dec. 23

1230 A498 1.50b multi .75 .40

America Issue - Environmental Protection A499

Designs: 5b, Palm tree. 6b, Parrots.

2004, Dec. 30

1231-1232 A499 Set of 2 6.00 2.75

Rotary International, Cent. — A500

No. 1233 — Emblem of Rotary International and: a, Emblem of PolioPlus, map of Bolivia. b, Paul Harris, flag of Bolivia.

2005, Mar. 4 Litho. ***Perf. 13¼x13½***

1233 A500 3b Horiz. pair, #a-b 4.50 1.50

Projects of Bolivia and the European Union A501

Designs: 5b, PRAS PANDO, Pando water and drainage project. 6b, PRAEDAC, Chapare alternate development program, vert.

Perf. 13¼x13½, 13½x13¼

2005, Mar. 16

1234-1235 A501 Set of 2 5.50 2.00

Textiles — A502

Designs: 50c, Aguayo Calamarca. 1b, Aqsu Bolivar. 1.50b, Incuña Camacho. No. 1239, 6b, Llixlla Challa. No. 1240, 6b, Unku Santo Lago Titicaca, horiz.

Perf. 13½x13¼, 13¼x13½

2005, Apr. 1

1236-1240 A502 Set of 5 7.75 3.25

Marshal Otto Felipe Braun — A503

2005, May 20 ***Perf. 13¾x13½***

1241 A503 6b multi 3.25 1.25

Birds — A504

Designs: 1b, Harpia harpyja. 1.50b, Penelope dabbenei. 7b, Aulacorhynchus coeruleicinctus.

2005, June 28 ***Perf. 13½x13¼***

1242-1244 A504 Set of 3 5.00 1.50

Interexpo '05, Dominican Republic (1b), Bolivian Philatelic Federation, 35th anniv. (1.50b), Washington 2006 Intl. Philatelic Exhibition (7b).

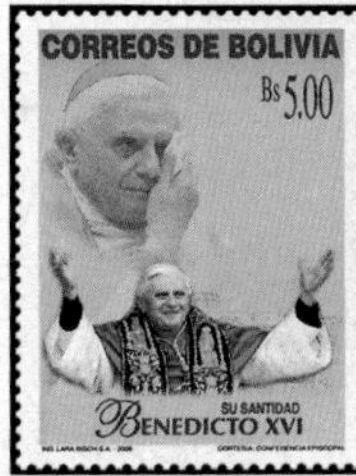

Pope John Paul II (1920-2005) — A505

Pope Benedict XVI — A506

2005, Aug. 1 Litho. ***Perf. 13½x13¾***

1245 A505 5b multi 2.50 1.25

Perf. 13¾x13½

1246 A506 5b multi 2.50 1.25

Pacific War, 125th Anniv. A507

Perf. 13½x13¾

2005, Aug. 17 **Litho.**

1247 A507 5b multi 3.00 1.25

Publication of *Don Quixote,* by Miguel de Cervantes, 400th Anniv. — A508

2005, Aug. 26
1248 A508 4b multi 2.50 1.00

America Issue — Fight Against Poverty A509

Paintings by Gilka Wara Libermann: 6b, Mother and child. 7b, Sailboat and fish skeleton.

2005, Aug. 26
1249-1250 A509 Set of 2 8.50 4.00

Gen. Ildefonso Murguia and Presidential Escort Regiment A510

2005, Sept. 3 Litho. ***Perf. 13¾x13½***
1251 A510 2b multi 1.25 .50

Presidential Escort Regiment, 184th anniv.

Tourism A511

2005, Sept. 27 ***Perf. 13½x13¾***
1252 A511 6b multi 3.25 1.50

Environmental Protection League — A512

2005, Oct. 5
1253 A512 6b multi 3.25 1.50

Miniature Sheet

Stamp Day — A513

No. 1254: a, 2b, Unissued Bolivian stamps of 1863. b, 2b, Imperf. Bolivia #C7. c, 2b, Brazil #1, stamp similar to Great Britain #1. d, 4b, Bolivia #2-3. e, 4b, Bolivia #C25. f, 4b, Bolivia #740.

2005, Oct. 9 ***Perf. 13¼x13½***
1254 A513 Sheet of 6, #a-f 12.50 5.00

Christmas A514

Designs: 1.50b on 60c, Magi on camels, Star of Bethlehem. 3b on 80c, Holy Family.

2005, Oct. 9 Litho. ***Perf. 13¾x13½***
1255-1256 A514 Set of 2 2.50 1.10

Dark gray and dark blue portions of the designs of Nos. 1255-1256 were overprinted on unissued stamps.

Nos. 724, 725, 737 Surcharged

Methods and Perfs As Before

2006, Feb. 12
1257 A271 1b on 1,000,000b #725 .55 .50
1258 A271 2b on 550,000b #724 1.10 1.00
1259 A281 2.50b on 1,000,000b #737 1.40 1.25
Nos. 1257-1259 (3) 3.05 2.75

Size and location of surcharge varies.

National Faculty of Engineering, Cent. — A515

2006, July 4 Litho. ***Perf. 13½x13¾***
1260 A515 6b multi 2.75 1.75

Pres. Evo Morales Ayma — A516

President: 1.50b, Waving. 5b, With flag. 6b, Wearing traditional Indian costume.

2006, Aug. 15 ***Perf. 13¾x13½***
1261-1263 A516 Set of 3 4.50 4.00

Bolivian Red Cross — A517

2006, Aug. 16
1264 A517 5b multi 2.50 1.50

Bolivia Post Corporation, 15th Anniv. — A518

Incan post runner and envelopes in: 1b, Green. 1.50b, Blue.

Perf. 13½x13¼

2006, Aug. 21 Litho.
1265-1266 A518 Set of 2 1.00 .65

Miniature Sheet

Stamp Day — A519

No. 1267: a, 1.50b, Boy Scouts viewing exhibits at Exfivia 75. b, 1.50b, Stamp collector with open album. c, 1.50b, Bolivia #189, Honduras #C1052i. d, 6b, People viewing exhibits at Exfilmar 80. e, 6b, Bolivia #1247, Iceland #990a. f, 6b, Bolivia #C240, Dominican Republic #1308a.

2006, Aug. 24 ***Perf. 13½x13¾***
1267 A519 Sheet of 6, #a-f 9.25 8.00

History of the National Flag — A520

Designs: 1.50b, Legislative Palace and flag of 1851. 5b, Exterior of Casa de la Libertad and flag of 1826. 6b, Interior of Casa de la Libertad, flag of 1825.

2006, Sept. 21 ***Perf. 13¾x13½***
1268-1270 A520 Set of 3 5.25 4.00

Franciscan Order in Tarija, 400th Anniv. — A521

Designs: No. 1271, 2b, Franciscan monk and donkey. No. 1272, 2b, Exterior of San Francisco Church. No. 1273, 6b, Interior of San Francisco Basilica, vert. No. 1274, 6b, Painting of Virgin Mary and angels, vert.

Perf. 13½x13¾, 13¾x13½

2006, Oct. 2
1271-1274 A521 Set of 4 8.50 5.00

Nos. 1271 and 1273 are dated "2005."

First Flight of Alberto Santos-Dumont, Cent. — A522

2006, Oct. 23 ***Perf. 13½x13¾***
1275 A522 1.50b multi .70 .50

Oruro, 400th Anniv. A523

2006, Oct. 23
1276 A523 4b multi 2.00 1.00

Puerto Bahia, Cent. A524

Designs: 1b, Avenida 9 de Febrero. 1.50b, German Busch Plaza. 2.50b, Chestnut tree, vert. 3b, Potosí Plaza. 4b, Bahía Pando River. 6b, Bolivia-Brazil Friendship Bridge. 7b, Avenida del Puerto, vert.

Perf. 13½x13¾, 13¾x13½

2006, Nov. 24 Litho.
1277-1283 A524 Set of 7 8.00 6.25

America Issue, Energy Conservation
A525

Designs: 3b, Fluorescent light bulb on flower stalk, doctor, patient and people. 4b, Light bulb containing money.

2006, Dec. 4 Litho. ***Perf. 13¾x13½***
1284-1285 A525 Set of 2 4.00 2.00

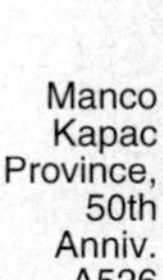
Manco Kapac Province, 50th Anniv.
A526

Designs: 5b, Ruins of astronomical observatory. 6b, Copacabana Church. 7b, Boat on Lake Titicaca.

2006, Dec. 4 ***Perf. 13½x13¾***
1286-1288 A526 Set of 3 9.00 5.00

No. 1288 is dated "2003."

Deserts and Desertification — A527

Designs: 1.50b, Mine degradation in Potosi Department. 2b, Gullies, Tarija Department. 3b, Terraces, La Paz. 4b, Deforested area, Caranavi.

2006, Dec. 4
1289-1292 A527 Set of 4 6.00 3.25

Endangered Animals
A528

Designs: 1b, Vicuna. 1.50b, Caiman, horiz. 5b, Caiman, diff., horiz. 7b, Vicuna, horiz.

Perf. 13¾x13½, 13½x13¾
2006, Dec. 4
1293-1296 A528 Set of 4 6.75 4.25

Christmas
A529

Designs: 4b, Virgin of Rosario. 5b, Adoration of the Magi. 6b, Adoration of the Shepherds.

2006, Dec. 4 ***Perf. 13¾x13½***
1297-1299 A529 Set of 3 6.75 4.25

Birds — A530

Designs: 2.50b, Toucan, Pando Department. 3.50b, Horned curassow, Santa Cruz Department. 6b, Blue bird, Pando Department. 7b, Harpy eagle, Santa Cruz Department.

2006, Dec. 11
1300-1303 A530 Set of 4 9.00 6.00

Dogs — A531

Designs: 1b, Miniature schnauzer. 3b, Husky. 4b, Boxer. 6b, Mixed-breed.

2006, Dec. 21
1304-1307 A531 Set of 4 6.00 3.75

36th Lions International Forum for Latin America and the Caribbean, Cochabamba — A532

2007, Jan. 7 Litho. ***Perf. 13½x13¾***
1308 A532 6b multi 3.00 1.60

Treaty of Rome, 50th Anniv. — A533

No. 1309: a, 3.50b, Map of Europe. b, 7b, European Union flag.

2007, Mar. 27
1309 A533 Horiz. pair, #a-b 5.00 3.00

Cochabamba Philatelic Center (CEFILCO), 50th Anniv — A534

Designs: 50c, Brochures on philately for young people. 1b, Arnold Glaeser, first President of CEFILCO, Bolivia #C270. 2.50b, Bolivia #901B, 1999 CEFILCO stamp catalogue. 3b, Philatelists Franz Steimbach and Oscar Roca.

No. 1314: a, 3.50b, Cochabamba Cathedral and monument. b, 6b, Sculpture of Christ, Cochabamba Cathedral.

2007, Apr. 18
1310-1313 A534 Set of 4 3.00 2.00
1314 A534 Horiz. pair, #a-b 3.75 2.75

Charangos
A535

Designs: 4b, Charangos, Bolivian arms. 6b, Charango, mountain, horiz.

Perf. 13¾x13½, 13½x13¾
2007, Apr. 27
1315-1316 A535 Set of 2 3.25 2.75

Bolivian Red Cross, 90th Anniv.
A536

2007, May 24 ***Perf. 13½x13¾***
1317 A536 2.50b multi 1.40 .70

Francis Harrington, Founder of American Institute, La Paz — A537

2007, May 30 Litho.
1318 A537 7.50b multi 3.50 2.10

American Institute, cent.

Natl. Chamber of Industry, 75th Anniv. — A538

No. 1319: a, 9b, Gears, map of Bolivia. b, 12b, Gears.

2007, June 28
1319 A538 Horiz. pair, #a-b 10.00 6.00

Santa Cruz Zoo — A539

Cats: 6b, Jaguar. 9b, Puma.

2007 ***Perf. 13¾x13½***
1320-1321 A539 Set of 2 7.00 4.50

Scouting, Cent.
A540

Designs: 7.50b, Lord Robert Baden-Powell blowing kudu horn. 8.50b, Scouting emblem, vert.

2007 ***Perf. 13½x13¾, 13¾x13½***
1322-1323 A540 Set of 2 6.75 5.00

57th Conference of the Chiefs of American Air Forces, Santa Cruz de la Sierra — A541

2007 ***Perf. 13½x13¾***
1324 A541 10.50b multi 7.00 5.75

Birds — A542

Designs: 4b, Opisthocomus hoazin, La Paz Department. No. 1326, 5.50b,Tunqui, La Paz Department, horiz. No. 1327, 5.50b, Ara ararauna, Santa Cruz Department, horiz. 7.50b, Porphyrula martinica, Santa Cruz Department, horiz.

2007 ***Perf. 13¾x13½, 13½x13¾***
1325-1328 A542 Set of 4 9.00 6.25

Issued: Nos. 1325-1326, 7/28; Nos. 1327-1328, 7/20.

Birds Type of 2007

Designs: 3.50b, Cyclarhis guyanensis, Tarija Department, horiz. 4b, Egretta alba, Cochabamba Department. 5.50b, Ramphastos toco, Beni Department, horiz. No. 1332, 6.50b, Bubo virginianus, Cochabamba Department. No. 1333, 6.50b, Trogon melanurus, Pando Department. No. 1334, 6.50b, Falco sparverius, Potosí Department, horiz. No. 1335, 6.50b, Hymantopus mexicanus, Oruro Department. No. 1336, 7.50b, Opisthocomus hoazin, Beni Department, horiz. No. 1337, 7.50b, Platalea ajaja, Oruro Department, horiz. No. 1338, 8.50b, Sarcoramphus papa, Tarija Department, horiz. No. 1339, 8.50b, Momotus momota, Chuquisaca Department, horiz. No. 1340, 9b, Tinamotis pentlandii, Potosí Department. No. 1341, 9b, Chlorostilbon aureoventris, Chuquisaca Department. 10.50b, Ardea cocoi, Pando Department.

Perf. 13½x13¾, 13¾x13½
2008 Litho.
1329-1342 A542 Set of 14 35.00 35.00

Issued: Nos. 1329, 1338, 8/20; Nos. 1330, 1332, 8/21; Nos. 1333, 1342, 8/22; Nos. 1331, 1336, 8/23; Nos. 1334, 1340, 8/24; Nos. 1339, 1341, 8/27; Nos. 1335, 1337, 8/28.

Death of Ernesto "Che" Guevara in Bolivia, 40th Anniv.
A543

Designs: 30b, Autograph of Guevara. 50b, Various images of Guevara, vert.

Perf. 13½x13¾, 13¾x13½
2007, Oct. 8
1343-1344 A543 Set of 2 30.00 30.00

Bolivian Air Force, 50th Anniv. A544

Anniversary emblem and: 7.50b, Planes on ground. 9b, Plane in flight.

2007, Oct. 12 *Perf. 13½x13¾*
1345-1346 A544 Set of 2 6.50 6.00

Intl. Civil Aviation Day A545

Airplane and: 6.50b, Globe. 8.50b, World map.

2007, Dec. 10
1347-1348 A545 Set of 2 7.00 6.50

America Issue, Education For All — A546

No. 1349: a, 3b, Three schoolgirls in classroom. b, 5b, Text, map of Bolivia. c, 6b, Teacher and student. d, 9b, School building, girl and flowers.

Perf. 13¼x13½
2007, Dec. 12 **Litho.**
1349 A546 Block of 4, #a-d 8.50 6.00

Tourism A547

Designs: 2b, Maragua Syncline, Chuquisaca Department. 2.50b, Festuca grass pasturelands, Oruro Department. 3.50b, Lagoon, Pando Department. 5b, Lake on Beni River, Beni Department. No. 1354, Manuripi River, Beni Department. No. 1355, Valley, Tarija Department. No. 1356, Zongo Valley, La Paz Department. No. 1357, Trees along Orthon River, Pando Department. No. 1358, Tornado in Sajama Valley, Oruro Department, vert. No. 1359, Sucre Bridge over Pilcomayo River, Chuquisaca Department. No. 1360, Cactus, Isla del Pescador, Potosí Department, vert. 10b, Chapare River, Cochabamba Department. No. 1362, Trichocereus camarguensis, Tarija Department. No. 1363, Uyuni Salt Flats, Potosí Department. 20b, Lake Caimán, Santa Cruz Department. 30b, Zongo, La Paz Department, vert. 50b, Plaza Sucre, Cochabamba Department. 100b, Arcoiris Waterfall, Santa Cruz Department, vert.

Perf. 13½x13¾, 13¾x13½
2007 **Litho.**

1350	A547	2b	multi	.55	.55
1351	A547	2.50b	multi	.65	.65
1352	A547	3.50b	multi	.95	.95
1353	A547	5b	multi	1.40	1.40
1354	A547	5.50b	multi	1.50	1.50
1355	A547	5.50b	multi	1.50	1.50
1356	A547	5.50b	multi	1.50	1.50
1357	A547	7.50b	multi	2.00	2.00
1358	A547	7.50b	multi	2.00	2.00
1359	A547	9b	multi	2.40	2.40
1360	A547	9b	multi	2.40	2.40
1361	A547	10b	multi	2.60	2.60
1362	A547	10.50b	multi	2.75	2.75
1363	A547	10.50b	multi	2.75	2.75
1364	A547	20b	multi	5.25	5.25
1365	A547	30b	multi	8.00	8.00
1366	A547	50b	multi	16.00	16.00
1367	A547	100b	multi	40.00	40.00
		Nos. 1350-1367 (18)		94.20	94.20

Issued: Nos. 1352-1355, 1357, 1362, 12/13; Nos. 1350, 1351, 1356, 1358-1361, 1363-1367, 12/14.

Christmas — A548

No. 1368: a, 3.50b, Holy Family. b, 4b, Adoration of the Shepherds. c, 6.50b, Epiphany.

Perf. 13¾x13½
2007, Dec. 19 **Litho.**
1368 A548 Horiz. strip of 3, #a-c 4.00 4.00

World Post Day — A549

2008, Jan. 15
1369 A549 1b multi .40 .30

Dated 2007.

Bolivian Episcopal Commission of Pastoral Social Charities, 50th Anniv. — A550

Designs: 10b, Jesus, icons, people, map of Bolivia and South America. 15b, Church and indigenous people, vert.

Perf. 13½x13¾, 13¾x13½
2008, Jan. 24
1370-1371 A550 Set of 2 11.00 8.50

Jesuit Church, Santa Cruz A551

Various views of church: 5b, 9b.

2008, Feb. 15 *Perf. 13½x13¾*
1372-1373 A551 Set of 2 4.50 3.75

Dated 2007.

Cochabamba Rotary Club, 80th Anniv. (in 2007) — A552

2008, Mar. 7 *Perf. 13¾x13½*
1374 A552 20b multi 6.25 5.25

Dated 2007.

Superior Court of Oruro, 150th Anniv. (in 2005) — A553

2008, Apr. 5
1375 A553 20b multi 8.50 7.00

Dated 2007.

The Strongest Soccer Team, Cent. — A554

No. 1376: a, 1.50b, Team emblem. b, 2.50b, Team crest. c, 5.50b, Trophy. d, 6.50b, 1908 team.

2008, Apr. 11 *Perf. 13½x13¾*
1376 A554 Block of 4, #a-d 7.00 6.00

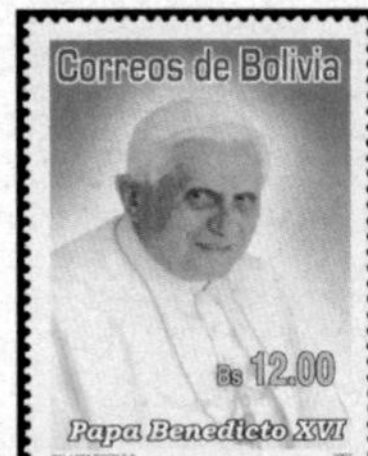

Pope Benedict XVI — A555

Pope Benedict XVI wearing: 12b, White vestments. 15b, Colored vestments.

2008, May 29 **Litho.** *Perf. 13¾x13½*
1377-1378 A555 Set of 2 11.00 9.00

Dated 2007.

Mountain, Soccer Stadium and Ball A556

2008, June 13 *Perf. 13½x13¾*
1379 A556 3b multi 1.25 1.00

Protest against FIFA proposal to ban international soccer matches at altitudes above 2500 meters.

Sucre Rebellion of May 25, 1809 A557

Designs: 1.50b, Clock tower. 5.50b, Liberty Belltower. 7.50b, Clock tower, building with anniversary banner. 9b, San Francisco Xavier University.

2008, June 18
1380-1383 A557 Set of 4 8.00 8.00

Superintendent of Banks and Financial Institutions, 80th Anniv. — A558

Designs: 3b, Emblem. 7b, Building, vert.

Perf. 13½x13¾, 13¾x13½
2008, July 10
1384-1385 A558 Set of 2 4.25 3.50

Acquisition of MA-60 Airplanes by Bolivian Air Force — A559

Airplane: 1.50b, In flight. 9b, On ground.

2008, Aug. 14 *Perf. 13½x13¾*
1386-1387 A559 Set of 2 4.00 4.00

Intl. Year of the Potato A560

Potato varieties and their blossoms: 1.50b, Luk'i Negra. 5.50b, Sani Imilla. 7.50b, Saq'ampaya. 10.50b, Waych'a.

2008, Oct. 10
1388-1391 A560 Set of 4 10.00 10.00

Map of Bolivia and Envelopes — A561

2009, May 1 **Litho.** *Perf. 13½x13¾*
1392 A561 1.50b multi .75 .60

No. 1392 paid an additional postage fee for mail that was to be handled by private postal services in Bolivia.

Nationalization of Entel, 1st Anniv. — A562

Designs: 2b, Emblem. 3b, Emblem and people, horiz.

Perf. 13¾x13½, 13½x13¾

2009, May 5
1393-1394 A562 Set of 2 2.25 2.25

Rainbow Foundation, 15th Anniv. — A563

2009, May 11 ***Perf. 13½x13¾***
1395 A563 5b multi 2.25 2.25

Marshal Sucre National University, Cent. — A564

2009, June 6
1396 A564 3b multi 1.25 1.00

Solidarity With Cuba A565

2009, June 10
1397 A565 7.50b multi 3.25 3.25

Inter-American Development Bank, 50th Anniv. — A566

2009, June 22 ***Perf. 13¾x13½***
1398 A566 5b multi 2.25 2.25

La Paz Revolution, Bicent. — A567

2009, July 14
1399 A567 2b multi .90 .90

Ayllu and Normal School, Warisata, 75th Anniv. A568

2009, Aug. 2 ***Perf. 13½x13¾***
1400 A568 2.50b multi 1.10 1.10

National Institute of Health Laboratories, Cent. — A569

2009, Aug. 4 ***Perf. 13¾x13½***
1401 A569 1.50b multi .70 .70

Venezuela National High School, Cent. — A570

Designs: 1b, Medals. 3b, School building.

2009, Aug. 10 ***Perf. 13½x13¾***
1402-1403 A570 Set of 2 1.75 1.75

Enrique Lindemann B Educational Unit — A571

2009, Aug. 19 **Litho.**
1404 A571 3.50b multi 1.50 1.50

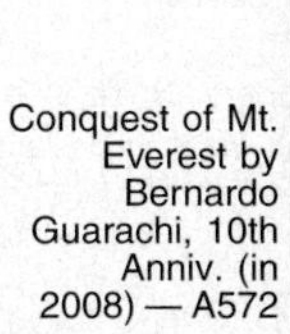

Conquest of Mt. Everest by Bernardo Guarachi, 10th Anniv. (in 2008) — A572

Guarachi, first Bolivian to reach summit of Mt. Everest wearing: 50c, Ski cap. 7b, Red parka, horiz.

Perf. 13¾x13½, 13½x13¾

2009, Aug. 28
1405-1406 A572 Set of 2 3.50 3.50

San Ramon Home for the Elderly, Cent. A573

2009, Oct. 26 ***Perf. 13½x13¾***
1407 A573 2b multi .90 .90

16th Bolivarian Games, Sucre — A574

Designs: 1.50b, Emblem. 9b, Emblem, diff.

2009, Nov. 14 ***Perf. 13¾x13½***
1408-1409 A574 Set of 2 4.00 4.00

America Issue — A575

Children playing with traditional toys: 1b, Top. 7b, Kite.

2009, Nov. 20
1410-1411 A575 Set of 2 3.00 3.00

Japan Intl. Cooperation Agency in Bolivia, 30th Anniv. — A576

Various agency workers with Bolivians: 1b, 1.50b, 3b, 9b.

2009, Dec. 4 ***Perf. 13½x13¾***
1412-1415 A576 Set of 4 5.50 5.50

Dated 2008.

Bolivian Philatelic Federation, 38th Anniv. — A577

2009, Dec. 10
1416 A577 3.50b multi 1.50 1.50

Christmas A578

Designs: 7b, Flight into Egypt. 9b, Jesus in manger.

Perf. 13¾x13½

2009, Dec. 21 **Litho.**

1417-1418 A578 Set of 2 5.75 4.75

Re-election of Pres. Evo Morales Ayma — A579

Pres. Morales: 12.50b, Holding poles. 9b, Waving.

2010, Jan. 20 **Litho.** ***Perf. 13¾x13½***
1419-1420 A579 Set of 2 3.50 3.50

Airplane and Letter to France A580

2010, Mar. 15 ***Perf. 13½x13¾***
1421 A580 9b multi 3.25 3.25

First airmail flight from the Pyrenees to the Andes, 80th anniv.

Global Warming — A581

Mt. Chacaltaya with: 2.50b, Little snow cover. 10b, More snow cover.

2010, Apr. 20
1422-1423 A581 Set of 2 4.50 4.50

Túpac Katari (c. 1750-81), and Wife, Bartolina Sisa (c. 1750-82), Leaders of Rebellion of Indigenous People — A582

2010, Apr. 25 ***Perf. 13¾x13½***
1424 A582 1.50b brown .60 .60

Bolivian Traditions A583

Designs: 1.50b, Items associated with All Saint's Day. 10.50b, Ekeko, god of abundance.

2010, May 10 ***Perf. 13½x13¾***
1425-1426 A583 Set of 2 5.00 5.00

Masks — A584

Designs: 1b, Pepino. 2b, Moreno. 9b, Chuncho. 10b, Kusillo.

2010, May 10 ***Perf. 13¾x13½***
1427-1430 A584 Set of 4 12.50 12.50

Flowers — A585

No. 1431: a, Flowers. b, Flowers and butterfly.

2010, May 27 ***Perf. 13½x13¾***
1431 A585 1.50b Horiz. pair, #a-b 1.00 1.00

Rose, Barbed Wire, Rainer and José Luis Ibsen A586

2010, Aug. 31
1432 A586 3b multi 1.00 1.00

Rainer Ibsen (1949-72), and his father, José Luis (1925-73), were kidnapped and murdered political prisoners of the Banzer regime.

Bolivian Army, 200th Anniv. A587

Flags and: 3.50b, Bulldozer and tank. 9b, Military leaders and battle scene.

2010, Aug. 31
1433-1434 A587 Set of 2 4.25 4.25

2010 Youth Olympics, Singapore — A588

Emblem and: 2b, Soccer player, cyclist. 9b, Swimmer, runner.

2010, Sept. 8 **Litho.** ***Perf. 13½x13¾***
1435-1436 A588 Set of 2 3.75 3.75

Declaration of Independence of Cochabamba, Bicent. — A589

2010, Sept. 10 ***Perf. 13¾x13½***
1437 A589 9b multi 3.00 3.00

Rebellion Against Spanish Rule of Santa Cruz, Bicent. A590

2010, Sept. 20 ***Perf. 13½x13¾***
1438 A590 5b multi 1.75 1.75

America Issue, National Symbols — A591

No. 1439 — Government Palace, La Paz and: a, 2.50b, Andean condor, Bolivian national bird. b, 5b, Patuju, Bolivian national flower.

2010, Oct. 20
1439 A591 Horiz. pair, #a-b 2.50 2.50

Military Engineering School, 60th Anniv. — A592

2010, Oct. 26
1440 A592 7b multi 2.75 2.75

Endangered Species A593

Designs: 1b, Puya raimondii. 2b, Leopardus jacobita, horiz. 2.50b, Atelopus tricolor, horiz. 3.50b, Anairetes alpinus, horiz.

Perf. 13¾x13½, 13½x13¾
2010, Nov. 1
1441-1444 A593 Set of 4 3.75 3.75

Rebellion Against Spanish Rule of Potosí, Bicent. A594

2010, Nov. 10 ***Perf. 13½x13¾***
1445 A594 3.50b multi 1.10 1.10

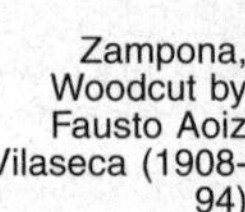
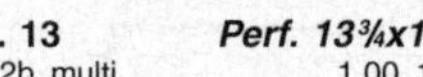

Zampona, Woodcut by Fausto Aoiz Vilaseca (1908-94) A595

2010, Dec. 13 ***Perf. 13¾x13½***
1446 A595 2b multi 1.00 1.00

Christmas A596

Items in Santa Clara Museum of Religious Art, Sucre: 3b, Archangel Michael, wooden sculpture. 9b, Adoration of the Shepherds, painting, horiz.

Perf. 13¾x13½, 13½x13¾
2010, Dec. 17
1447-1448 A596 Set of 2 5.00 5.00

Jaime Escalante (1930-2010), Bolivian-born American High School Mathematics Teacher — A597

2011, Jan. 20 ***Perf. 13½x13¾***
1449 A597 2b multi 1.00 1.00

Fruits A598

Designs: 1.50b, Oranges (naranja). 5.50b, Mangos. 7.50b, Papayas. 9b, Avocados (palta). 10.50b, Bananas (platano).

2011
1450-1454 A598 Set of 5 12.00 12.00

Nos. 1450-1454 paid an additional postage fee for mail that was to be handled by private postal services in Bolivia.

Grains — A599

Designs: 1b, Chenopodium quinoa. 2b, Amaranthus. 2.50b, Chenopodium pallidicaule. 5b, Lupinus mutabilis.

2011, July 5 ***Perf. 13¾x13½***
1455-1458 A599 Set of 4 4.00 4.00

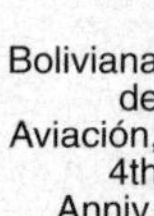

Boliviana de Aviación, 4th Anniv. A600

2011, July 22 ***Perf. 13½x13¾***
1459 A600 3b multi 1.25 1.25

Bolivian Cooperation With Cuba — A601

Designs: 2b, Doctor administering eye examination on patient. 2.50b, People in map of bolivia, dove, vert. 3b, Teacher and adult student.

Perf. 13½x13¾, 13¾x13½
2011, Sept. 2
1460-1462 A601 Set of 3 2.75 2.75

Intl. Registry of Bolivian Ships, 10th Anniv. A602

Designs: 1.50b, Barge. 9b, Bolivian Navy boat.

2011, Sept. 2 ***Perf. 13½x13¾***
1463-1464 A602 Set of 2 4.00 4.00

Blood Donation Campaign — A603

2011, Sept. 15
1465 A603 3b multi 1.25 1.25

Postal Union of the Americas, Spain and Portugal (UPAEP), Cent. — A604

2011, Oct. 6 ***Perf. 13¾x13½***
1466 A604 9b multi 3.25 3.25

Endangered Fish — A605

Designs: 1b, Orestias agassii. 1.50b, Cichla pleiozona. 3b, Colossoma macropomum. 9b, Orestias luteus.

2011, Oct. 21 ***Perf. 13½x13¾***
1467-1470 A605 Set of 4 6.50 6.50

National Institute of Statistics, 75th Anniv. A606

2011, Oct. 25
1471 A606 9b multi 3.25 3.25

Mailboxes — A607

Designs: 1.50b, Rectangular mailbox. 9b, Mailbox with rounded top.

2011, Dec. 6
1472-1473 A607 Set of 2 4.00 4.00

Christmas A608

Children's drawings: 1b, Child, star, Christmas tree, gifts, by Sarah Laura Zailes Azeñas. 9b, Children and Christmas tree, by Adriana Nahir Peñaloza Cusi, horiz.

Perf. 13¾x13½, 13½x13¾

2011, Dec. 7
1474-1475 A608 Set of 2 3.75 3.75

Human Rights A609

2011, Dec. 9 ***Perf. 13½x13¾***
1476 A609 9b multi 3.25 3.25

Intl. Year of Forests — A610

Emblem and: 2.50b, Bertholletia excelsa. 3b, Swietenia macrophylla.

2011, Dec. 11 ***Perf. 13¾x13½***
1477-1478 A610 Set of 2 2.00 2.00

Traditional Cuisine — A611

Designs: 1b, Saice. 1.50b, Majao. 2.50b, Silpancho. 9b, Plato Paceño.

2011, Dec. 16 ***Perf. 13½x13¾***
1479-1482 A611 Set of 4 5.25 5.25

Coca Production — A612

Designs: 50c, Coca plantation and products using coca. 9b, Coca leaves and berries, vert.

Perf. 13½x13¾, 13¾x13½

2011, Dec. 19
1483-1484 A612 Set of 2 3.75 3.75

Yacimentos Petroliferos Fiscales Bolivianos Corporation, 75th Anniv. — A613

Designs: 50c, Line of workers. 9b, Dionisio Foianini, nationalizer of Bolivian oil fields, oil derrick, workers with Bolivian flag, vert.

2011, Dec. 21
1485-1486 A613 Set of 2 3.50 3.50

Coin Commemorating New Bolivian Constitution — A614

2012, Jan. 20 ***Perf. 13¾x13½***
1487 A614 3b multi 1.25 1.25

Bolivia's Seacoast Claim — A615

2012, Mar. 12
1488 A615 5b multi 2.50 2.50

Year Against Violence Towards Children and Adolescents — A616

2012, Apr. 12 ***Perf. 13½x13¾***
1489 A616 3.50b multi 1.50 1.50

Workers A617

Designs: 50c, Sugar cane cutter (zafra). 1b, Seamstresses (fabril). 3b, Miner (minero). 5b, Petroleum worker (petrolero), vert.

Perf. 13½x13¾, 13¾x13½

2012, May 1
1490-1493 A617 Set of 4 4.00 4.00

42nd General Assembly of Organization of American States, Cochabamba A618

2012, May 7 ***Perf. 13¾x13½***
1494 A618 10b multi 3.00 3.00

World Internet Day — A619

Designs: 1b, Map of Western Hemisphere, "@." 1.50b, Stylized globe, pointing finger icon. 3b, "@" and emblems of internet websites.

2012, May 17 **Litho.**
1495-1497 A619 Set of 3 2.50 2.50

Heroic Resistance of Cochabamba Women, Bicent. — A620

2012, May 22 ***Perf. 13¾x13½***
1498 A620 1.50b multi .75 .75

Domesticated Animals — A621

Designs: 50c, Chickens (gallina). 1b, Burro. 3b, Sheep (oveja). 5b, Rabbit (conejo).

2012, May 28 ***Perf. 13½x13¾***
1499-1502 A621 Set of 4 4.00 4.00

Dinosaurs and Their Tracks — A622

Designs: 50c, Theropod. 1.50b, Ankylosaurus. 3b, Sauropod. 5b, Stegosaurus.

2012, June 8 **Litho.**
1503-1506 A622 Set of 4 3.75 3.75

Emblem of the Attorney General A623

2012, June 25
1507 A623 3.50b multi 1.50 1.50

Minerals A624

Designs: 1b, Andorite. 1.50b, Bismuthinite. 2b, Amethyst. 5b, Cassiterite.

2012, July 11
1508-1511 A624 Set of 4 3.75 3.75

Folk Dances — A625

Designs: 50c, Ch'utas. 1b, Llamerada. 1.50b, Kullawada. 2b, Caporales. 10b, Morenada.

2012, July 24 ***Perf. 13¾x13½***
1512-1516 A625 Set of 5 6.00 6.00

Television Show "La Bicicleta de los Huanca," 25th Anniv. A626

2012, Aug. 17 ***Perf. 13½x13¾***
1517 A626 4b multi 1.75 1.75

Bolivian Dishes A627

Designs: 50c, Locro de Gallina. 1b, Mondongo. 1.50b, K'ala Phurka. 5b, Charquekan.

2012, Sept. 18
1518-1521 A627 Set of 4 3.25 3.25

Orchids A628

Designs: 50c, Vasqueziella boliviana. 1.50b, Masdevallia yungasensis. 3b, Cattleya rex. 5b, Restrepia vasquezii.

2012, Sept. 19
1522-1525 A628 Set of 4 4.00 4.00

Congressional Library, Cent. — A629

2012, Sept. 21
1526 A629 3.50b multi 1.50 1.50

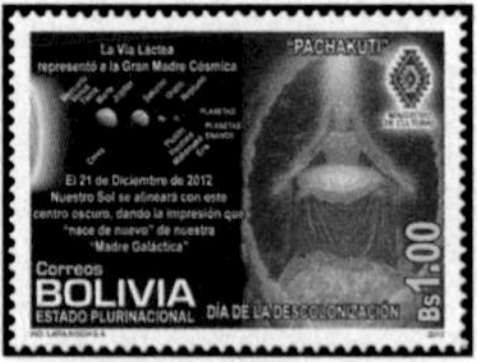

Decolonization Day — A630

Designs: 1b, Mother Earth and alignment of planets (end of Mayan calendar cycle). 1.50b, 1492 discovery of America by Christopher Columbus, vert. 2.50b, Amazonian collective marriage ceremony, vert.

Perf. 13½x13¾, 13¾x13½
2012, Oct. 6
1527-1529 A630 Set of 3 2.00 2.00

America Issue — A631

Myths and legends: 1b, La Palliri. 5b, El amor maldito transformalo en culebra (Cursed love transformed into a snake).

2012, Oct. 12 ***Perf. 13¾x13½***
1530-1531 A631 Set of 2 2.50 2.50

Intl. Year of Sustainable Energy For All — A632

Emblem and: 1b, Christ of Peace statue, Cochabamba, wind generators, power lines. 3.50b, Mountain, solar panels.

2012, Oct. 25 **Litho.**
1532-1533 A632 Set of 2 2.00 2.00

Leaders of 1781 Siege of La Paz A633

Designs: 50c, Tupac Katari (c. 1750-81), and torture of prisoner. 1.50b, Micaela Bastidas (1745-81), Bartolina Sisa (c. 1750-82), wife of Katari, vert. 3b, Katari and Sisa.

Perf. 13½x13¾, 13¾x13½
2012, Oct.
1534-1536 A633 Set of 3 2.00 2.00

Mentisan Ointment, 75th Anniv. A634

2012, Nov. 6 ***Perf. 13½x13¾***
1537 A634 30b multi 12.50 12.50

Christmas A635

Children's art: 1.50b, Bolivians and Holy Family, by Wara Bascopé Céspedes. 2.50b, Christmas tree, by Stefany Gissell Robles.

2012, Nov. 12 ***Perf. 13¾x13½***
1538-1539 A635 Set of 2 1.75 1.75

Avelino Siñani - Elizardo Pérez Education Law, 2nd Anniv. A636

2012, Dec. 14 ***Perf. 11¼x11***
1540 A636 2.50b multi 1.00 1.00

Quinoa Cultivation A637

Quinoa seeds and: 1b, Chenopodium quinoa plants. 3.50b, Quinoa harvesters, horiz. 4b, Quinoa plants in field, horiz.

Perf. 13¾x13½, 13½x13¾
2012, Dec. 18
1541-1543 A637 Set of 3 3.25 3.25

AIR POST STAMPS

Aviation School
AP1 AP2

1924, Dec. **Unwmk.** **Engr.** ***Perf. 14***
C1 AP1 10c ver & blk 1.00 .50
a. Inverted center *2,500.*
C2 AP1 15c carmine & blk 2.00 2.00
C3 AP1 25c dk bl & blk 1.50 1.00
C4 AP1 50c orange & blk 10.00 5.00
C5 AP2 1b red brn & blk 3.00 3.00
C6 AP2 2b blk brn & blk 20.00 10.00
C7 AP2 5b dk vio & blk 25.00 20.00
Nos. C1-C7 (7) 62.50 41.50

Natl. Aviation School establishment.

These stamps were available for ordinary postage. Nos. C1, C3, C5 and C6 exist imperforate. Value, $400. each pair.

Proofs of the 2b with inverted center exist imperforate and privately perforated. Value, *$2,750.*

For overprints and surcharges see Nos. C11-C23, C56-C58.

Emblem of Lloyd Aéreo Boliviano AP3

1928 **Litho.** ***Perf. 11***
C8 AP3 15c green 2.50 1.50
a. Imperf., pair 70.00 60.00
C9 AP3 20c dark blue 4.00 3.25
C10 AP3 35c red brown 3.25 2.50
Nos. C8-C10 (3) 9.75 7.25

No. C8 exists imperf. between. Value, $60 pair.

For surcharges see Nos. C24-C26, C53-C55.

Graf Zeppelin Issues

Nos. C1-C5 Surcharged or Overprinted in Various Colors

Nos. C11, C19

Nos. C12-C18, C20-C23

1930, May 6 ***Perf. 14***
C11 AP1 5c on 10c ver & blk (G) 20.00 20.00
C12 AP1 10c ver & blk (Bl) 20.00 20.00
C13 AP1 10c ver & blk (Br) *2,500.* *2,500.*
C14 AP1 15c car & blk (V) 20.00 20.00
C15 AP1 25c dk bl & blk (R) 20.00 20.00
C16 AP1 50c org & blk (Br) 20.00 20.00
C17 AP1 50c org & blk (R) *1,000.* *1,000.*
C18 AP2 1b red brn & blk (gold) 350.00 350.00

Experts consider the 50c with gold or silver overprint and 5c with black to be trial color proofs.

Nos. C11-C18 exist with the surcharges inverted, double, or double with one inverted, but the regularity of these varieties is questioned.

See notes following No. C23.

Surcharged or Overprinted in Bronze Inks of Various Colors

C19 AP1 5c on 10c ver & blk (G) 120.00 *150.00*
a. Inverted surcharge 200.00 —
C20 AP1 10c ver & blk (Bl) 100.00 *150.00*
a. Inverted surcharge — —
C21 AP1 15c car & blk (V) 100.00 *150.00*
a. Inverted surcharge 150.00 —
C22 AP1 25c dk bl & blk (cop) 100.00 *150.00*
a. Inverted surcharge 150.00 —
C23 AP2 1b red brn & blk (gold) *700.00* *900.00*
a. Inverted surcharge — —
Nos. C19-C23 (5) 1,120. *1,500.*

Flight of the airship Graf Zeppelin from Europe to Brazil and return via Lakehurst, NJ.

Nos. C19 to C23 were intended for use on postal matter forwarded by the Graf Zeppelin.

No. C18 was overprinted with light gold or gilt bronze ink. No. C23 was overprinted with deep gold bronze ink. Nos. C13 and C17 were overprinted with trial colors but were sold with the regular printings. The 5c on 10c is known surcharged in black and in blue.

No. C8-C10 Surcharged

1930, May 6 ***Perf. 11***
C24 AP3 1.50b on 15c 80.00 80.00
a. Inverted surcharge 300.00 300.00
b. Comma instead of period after "1" 100.00 100.00
C25 AP3 3b on 20c 80.00 80.00
a. Inverted surcharge 350.00 350.00
b. Comma instead of period after "3" 125.00 125.00
C26 AP3 6b on 35c *80.00* *80.00*
a. Inverted surcharge 375.00 375.00
b. Comma instead of period after "6" 125.00 125.00
Nos. C24-C26 (3) 240.00 240.00

Airplane and Bullock Cart — AP6

Airplane and River Boat — AP7

1930, July 24 **Litho.** ***Perf. 14***
C27 AP6 5c dp violet 1.50 1.10
C28 AP7 15c red 1.50 1.10
C29 AP7 20c yellow 1.10 .90
C30 AP6 35c yellow grn 1.00 .75
C31 AP7 50c deep blue 2.50 1.50
C32 AP6 1b lt brown 3.50 1.75
C33 AP7 2b deep rose 4.50 2.50
C34 AP6 3b slate 8.00 6.00
Nos. C27-C34 (8) 23.60 15.60

Nos. C27 to C34 exist imperforate. Value, $60 each pair.

For surcharge see No. C52.

Air Service Emblem AP8

1932, Sept. 16 ***Perf. 11***
C35 AP8 5c ultra 3.25 2.40
C36 AP8 10c gray 2.00 1.50
C37 AP8 15c dark rose 2.00 1.50
C38 AP8 25c orange 2.00 1.50
C39 AP8 30c green 1.25 .80
C40 AP8 50c violet 3.25 2.50
C41 AP8 1b dk brown 3.25 2.50
Nos. C35-C41 (7) 17.00 12.70

Map of Bolivia — AP9

1935, Feb. 1 **Engr.** ***Perf. 12***
C42 AP9 5c brown red .30 .30
C43 AP9 10c dk green .30 .30
C44 AP9 20c dk violet .30 .30

C45 AP9 30c ultra .30 .30
C46 AP9 50c orange .50 .50
C47 AP9 1b bister brn .50 .50
C48 AP9 1½b yellow 1.25 .75
C49 AP9 2b carmine 1.25 1.00
C50 AP9 5b green 1.50 1.25
C51 AP9 10b dk brown 5.00 1.75
Nos. C42-C51 (10) 11.20 6.95

Nos. C1, C4, C10, C30 Srchd. in Red (#C52-C56) or Green (#C57-C58) — c

1937, Oct. 6 ***Perf. 11, 14***
C52 AP6 5c on 35c yel grn .50 .40
a. "Carreo" 30.00 30.00
b. Inverted surcharge 20.00
C53 AP3 20c on 35c red brn .75 .60
a. Inverted surcharge 20.00 20.00
C54 AP3 50c on 35c red brn 1.50 1.00
a. Inverted surcharge 50.00 50.00
C55 AP3 1b on 35c red brn 2.00 1.50
a. Inverted surcharge 25.00 20.00
C56 AP1 2b on 50c org & blk 2.50 2.00
a. Inverted surcharge 20.00 15.00
C57 AP1 12b on 10c ver & blk 15.00 10.00
a. Inverted surcharge 75.00 50.00
C58 AP1 15b on 10c ver & blk 15.00 10.00
a. Inverted surcharge 75.00 30.00

Regular Postage Stamps of 1925 Surcharged in Green or Red — d

Perf. 14
C59 A56 (d) 3b on 50c dp vio (G) 5.00 5.00
C60 A56 (d) 4b on 1b red (G) 5.00 5.00
C61 A57 (c) 5b on 2b org (G) 6.00 6.00
a. Double surcharge 175.00
C62 A56 (d) 10b on 5b blk brn 8.50 7.00
a. Double surcharge 50.00
Nos. C52-C62 (11) 61.75 48.50

No. C59-C62 exist with inverted surcharge, No. C62a with black and black and red surcharges.

Courtyard of Potosi Mint — AP10

Emancipated Woman AP12

Pincers, Torch and Good Will Principles AP15

Airplane over Field AP13

Airplanes and Liberty Monument AP14

Airplane over River AP16

Emblem of New Government AP17

Transport Planes over Map of Bolivia AP18

1938, May **Litho.** ***Perf. 10½***
C63 AP10 20c deep rose .60 .30
C64 AP11 30c gray .60 .30
C65 AP12 40c yellow .70 .40
C66 AP13 50c yellow grn .60 .30
C67 AP14 60c dull blue .75 .40
C68 AP15 1b dull red .75 .40
C69 AP16 2b bister 1.50 .50
C70 AP17 3b lt brown 2.25 1.00
C71 AP18 5b dk violet 3.00 1.00
Nos. C63-C71 (9) 10.75 4.60

40c, 1b, 2b exist imperf.

Chalice — AP19

Virgin of Copacabana AP20

Jesus Christ — AP21

Church of San Francisco, La Paz AP22

St. Anthony of Padua — AP23

1939, July 19 **Litho.** ***Perf. 13½, 10½***
C72 AP19 5c dull violet .75 .50
a. Pair, imperf. between 80.00
C73 AP20 30c lt bl grn 1.00 .50
C74 AP21 45c violet bl 1.00 .50
a. Vertical pair, imperf. between 90.00
C75 AP22 60c carmine 1.50 .75
C76 AP23 75c vermilion 1.50 1.25
C77 AP23 90c deep blue 1.50 .60
C78 AP22 2b dull brown 2.50 .50
C79 AP21 4b deep plum 3.00 1.00
C80 AP20 5b lt blue 7.00 .80
C81 AP19 10b yellow 12.00 1.25
Nos. C72-C81 (10) 31.75 7.65

2nd National Eucharistic Congress.
For surcharge see No. C112.

Plane over Lake Titicaca — AP24

Mt. Illimani and Condor — AP25

1941, Aug. 21 ***Perf. 13½***
C82 AP24 10b dull green 15.00 2.00
C83 AP24 20b light ultra 7.00 2.50
C84 AP25 50b rose lilac 15.00 5.00
C85 AP25 100b olive bister 25.00 8.00
Nos. C82-C85 (4) 62.00 17.50

Counterfeits exist.
A souvenir sheet containing Nos. C84 and 356, perforated 13¼ and 14¼ respectively, was issued Dec. 16, 1987, to mark the 1988 Calgary Winter Olympic Games. Value $20.

Liberty and Clasped Hands — AP26

1942, Nov. 12
C86 AP26 40c rose lake .50 .50
C87 AP26 50c ultra .50 .50
C88 AP26 1b orange brn 1.50 .75
C89 AP26 5b magenta 2.00 .60
a. Double impression 90.00
C90 AP26 10b dull brn vio 6.50 3.50
Nos. C86-C90 (5) 11.00 5.85

Conference of Chancellors, Jan. 15, 1942.

Ballivián Type of Regular Issue

General José Ballivián; old and modern transportation.

1943, Nov. 18 **Engr.** ***Perf. 12½***
C91 A114 10c rose vio & brn .30 .25
C92 A114 20c emerald & brn .30 .25
C93 A114 30c rose car & brn .30 .25
C94 A114 3b blue & brn .75 .40
C95 A114 5b black & brn 1.00 .75
Nos. C91-C95 (5) 2.65 1.75

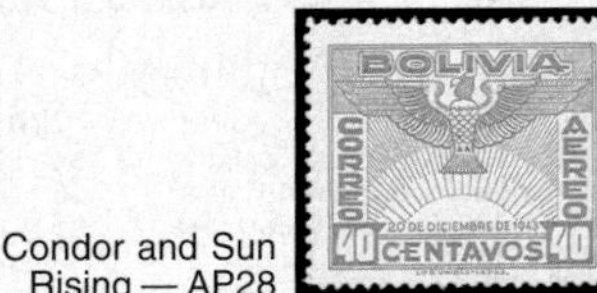
Condor and Sun Rising — AP28

Plane — AP29

1944, Sept. 19 **Litho.** ***Perf. 13½***
C96 AP28 40c red violet .25 .25
C97 AP28 1b blue violet .30 .25
C98 AP29 1.50b yellow green .30 .25
C99 AP29 2.50b dk gray blue .50 .25
Nos. C96-C99 (4) 1.30 .95

Revolution of Dec. 20, 1943.

Map of Natl. Airways — AP30

Map of Bolivian Air Lines — AP31

1945, May 31 ***Perf. 11***
C100 AP30 10c red .30 .25
a. Imperf., pair 25.00
C101 AP30 50c yellow .30 .25
a. Imperf., pair 30.00
C102 AP30 90c lt green .40 .30
a. Imperf., pair 30.00
C103 AP30 5b lt ultra 1.00 .50
C104 AP30 20b deep brown 2.00 1.00
Nos. C100-C104 (5) 4.00 2.30

10th anniversary of first flight, La Paz to Tacna, Peru, by Panagra Airways.
For surcharges see Nos. C128-C129.

1945, Sept. 15 ***Perf. 13½***
Centers in Red and Blue
C105 AP31 20c violet .25 .25
C106 AP31 30c orange brn .25 .25
C107 AP31 50c brt blue grn .25 .25
C108 AP31 90c brt violet .25 .25
C109 AP31 2b blue .40 .25
C110 AP31 3b magenta .50 .25
C111 AP31 4b olive bister .90 .50
Nos. C105-C111 (7) 2.80 2.00

Founding of Lloyd Aéreo Boliviano, 20th anniv.

Catalogue values for unused stamps in this section, from this point to the end of the section, are for Never Hinged items.

No. C76 Surcharged in Blue

1947, Mar. 23
C112 AP23 1.40b on 75c ver .50 .25

Mt. Illimani — AP32

1947, Sept. 15 **Litho.** ***Perf. 11½***
C113 AP32 1b rose car .25 .25
C114 AP32 1.40b emerald .30 .25
a. Imperf, pair 20.00
C115 AP32 2.50b blue .40 .30
a. Imperf, pair 20.00
C116 AP32 3b dp orange .50 .50
C117 AP32 4b rose lilac .50 .50
Nos. C113-C117 (5) 1.90 1.70

1st anniv. of the Revolution of July 21, 1946.
For surcharge see No. C137.

Bolivia/Argentina Arms Type

1947, Oct. 23 ***Perf. 13½***
C118 A119 2.90b ultra .60 .45
a. Imperf., pair 30.00
b. Perf. 10½ 7.50 6.00

Statue of Christ Type

Designs: 2.50b, Statue of Christ above La Paz. 3.70b, Child kneeling before cross. No. C121, St. John Bosco. No. C122, Virgin of Copacabana. 13.60b, Pope Plus XII blessing University of La Paz.

1948, Sept. 26 ***Perf. 11½***
C119 A120 2.50b ver & yellow 1.10 .75
C120 A120 3.70b rose & cream 1.40 .75
C121 A120 4b rose lil & gray 1.60 .50
C122 A120 4b lt ultra & sal 1.60 .50
C123 A120 13.60b ultra & lt grn 2.25 1.00
Nos. C119-C123 (5) 7.25 3.50

Bolivia Auto Club Type

1948, Oct.
C124 A125 10b emerald & salmon 8.00 1.25

Pacheco Type of Regular Issue

1950, Jan. 2 **Unwmk.**
C125 A126 1.40b orange brown .75 .25
C126 A126 2.50b orange 1.00 .25
C127 A126 3.30b rose violet .75 .25
Nos. C125-C127 (3) 2.50 .60

75th anniv. of the UPU.
No. C126 exists imperf. Value, pair $25.

Nos. C100 and C104 Surcharged in Black

1950, May 31 ***Perf. 11***
C128 AP30 4b on 10c red .50 .30
a. Inverted surcharge 35.00 35.00
C129 AP30 10b on 20b dp brn 1.00 .50
a. Inverted surcharge 35.00 35.00

Panagra air services in Bolivia, 15th anniv.

L. A. B. Plane — AP35

1950, Sept. 15 **Litho.** ***Perf. 13½***
C130 AP35 20c red orange .30 .25
C131 AP35 30c purple .50 .25
C132 AP35 50c green .50 .25
C133 AP35 1b orange .50 .25
C134 AP35 3b ultra .50 .25
C135 AP35 15b carmine 2.00 .50
C136 AP35 50b chocolate 3.75 1.00
Nos. C130-C136 (7) 8.05 2.75

25th anniv. of the founding of Lloyd Aero Boliviano. 30c, 50c, 15b exist imperforate.
No. C132 exists without imprint at bottom of stamp.

No. C116 Surcharged in Black

1950, Sept. 24 ***Perf. 11½***
C137 AP32 1.40b on 3b dp org 1.00 .50

1st anniv. of the ending of the Civil War of Aug. 24-Sept. 24, 1949.
Exists with inverted and double surcharge.

UN Type of Regular Issue

1950, Oct. 24 **Unwmk.**
C138 A128 3.60b crimson rose 1.50 .50
C139 A128 4.70b black brown 2.75 .50

La Paz Type of Regular Issue

20c, Gate of the Sun and llama. 30c, Church of Old San Francisco. 40c, Avenue Camacho. 50c, Consistorial Palace. 1b, Legislative Palace. 2b, Communications Bldg. 3b, Arms. 4b, La Gasca ordering Mendoza to found La Paz. 5b, Capt. Alonso de Mendoza founding La Paz. 10b, Arms; portrait of Mendoza.

1951, Mar. 1 **Engr.** ***Perf. 12½***
Center in Black
C140 A129 20c carmine .60 .25
C141 A130 30c dk vio bl .60 .25
C142 A129 40c dark blue .60 .25
C143 A129 50c blue green .60 .25
C144 A129 1b red .60 .30
C145 A129 2b red orange 1.00 .60
C146 A129 3b deep blue 1.00 .60
C147 A129 4b vermilion 1.00 .60
a. Souvenir sheet of 4 3.50 3.50
b. As "a," imperf. 3.50 3.50
C148 A129 5b dark green 1.50 .75
a. Souvenir sheet of 3 3.50 3.50
b. As "a," imperf. 3.50 3.50
C149 A129 10b red brown 2.00 1.50
a. Souvenir sheet of 3 3.50 3.50
b. As "a," imperf. 3.50 3.50
Nos. C140-C149 (10) 9.50 5.15

Nos. C147a-C147b contain #C143-C145, C147; Nos. C148a-C148b contain #C142, C146, C148; Nos. C149a-C149b contain #C140, C141, C149.
For surcharges see Nos. C187-C196.

Athletic Type of Regular Issue

20c, Horsemanship. 30c, Basketball. 50c, Fencing. 1b, Hurdling. 2.50b, Javelin throwing. 3b, Relay race. 5b, La Paz stadium.

1951, Aug. 23 **Unwmk.**
Center in Black
C150 A131 20c purple 1.00 .25
C151 A131 30c rose vio 1.50 .30
C152 A131 50c dp red org 2.00 .50
C153 A131 1b chocolate 2.00 .30
C154 A131 2.50b orange 3.25 1.25
C155 A131 3b black brn 5.00 2.00
a. Souv. sheet, #C153-C155 10.00 10.00
b. As "a," imperf. 10.00 10.00
C156 A131 5b red 7.00 3.00
a. Souv. sheet of 4, #C150-C152, C156 10.00 10.00
b. As "a," imperf. 10.00 10.00
Nos. C150-C156 (7) 21.75 7.55

Eduardo Abaroa Type

1952, Mar. 24 **Litho.** ***Perf. 11***
C157 A133 70c rose red .50 .25
C158 A133 2b orange yel .60 .25
C159 A133 3b yellow green .60 .25
C160 A133 5b blue 2.00 .50
C161 A133 50b rose lilac 4.00 1.50
C162 A133 100b gray black 7.00 2.00
a. Perf. 14 60.00 30.00
Nos. C157-C162 (6) 14.70 4.60

Queen Isabella I Type

1952, July 16 ***Perf. 13½***
C163 A134 50b emerald 1.50 .50
C164 A134 100b brown 3.50 .75

Nos. C163-C164 exist imperforate. Value, $40 each pair.
An imperforate 500,000b souvenir sheet depicting No. C164 with simulated perforations was issued Dec. 31, 1985, to mark the 500th anniv. of the discovery of America. Value $20.

Columbus Lighthouse Type

1952, July 16
C165 A135 2b rose lilac, *salmon* 1.00 .30
C166 A135 3.70b blue grn, *bl* 1.00 .30
C167 A135 4.40b orange, *salmon* 1.00 .30
C168 A135 20b dk brn, *cream* 1.50 .30
Nos. C165-C168 (4) 4.50 1.20

No. C168 exists imperforate. Value, $60 pair.

Revolution Type and

Soldiers — AP43

Perf. 13½ (AP43), 11½ (A137)
1953, Apr. 9 **Litho.**
C169 A137 3.70b chocolate .55 .25
C170 AP43 6b red violet .55 .25
C171 A137 9b brown rose .55 .25
C172 A137 10b aqua .55 .25
C173 A137 16b vermilion 1.10 .30
C174 AP43 22.50b dk brown 1.40 .50
C175 A137 40b gray 1.10 .30
Nos. C169-C175 (7) 5.25 1.90

Nos. C169-C170 and C174 exist imperf. Value, $40 each pair.

Map and Peasant Type and

Pres. Victor Paz Estenssoro Embracing Indian — AP45

1954, Aug. 2 ***Perf. 12x11½***
C176 AP45 20b orange brn .30 .25
C177 A138 27b brt pink .50 .25
C178 A138 30b red org .60 .25
C179 A138 45b violet brn 1.00 .25
C180 AP45 100b blue grn 1.25 .25
C181 A138 300b yellow grn 3.50 .50
Nos. C176-C181 (6) 7.15 1.60

AP45 for 3rd Inter-American Indian Cong. A138 agrarian reform laws of 1953-54.
Nos. C176-C180 exist imperf. Value, $25 each pair.
For surcharge see No. C261.

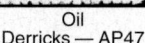

Oil Derricks — AP47

Map of South America and Bolivian National Arms — AP48

1955, Oct. 9 ***Perf. 10½***
C182 AP47 55b dk & lt grnsh bl .50 .25
C183 AP47 70b dk gray & gray .60 .30
C184 AP47 90b dk & lt grn 1.10 .40
Perf. 13
C185 AP47 500b red lilac 4.00 1.25
C186 AP47 1000b blk brn & fawn 5.00 2.25
Nos. C182-C186 (5) 11.20 4.40

For surcharge see No. C262.

Nos. C140-C149 Surcharged in Black or Carmine

1957 **Engr.** ***Perf. 12½***
Center in Black
C187 A129 100b on 3b (C) .50 .25
C188 A129 200b on 2b .50 .25
C189 A129 500b on 4b .50 .25
C190 A129 600b on 1b .50 .25
C191 A129 700b on 20c .75 .30
C192 A129 800b on 40c (C) .90 .30
C193 A130 900b on 30c (C) 1.25 .25
C194 A129 1800b on 50c (C) 1.25 .75
C195 A129 3000b on 5b (C) 3.00 1.50
C196 A129 5000b on 10b (C) 5.00 2.25
Nos. C187-C196 (10) 14.15 6.35

See Nos. 393-402.

Unwmk.
1957, May 25 **Litho.** ***Perf. 12***
C197 AP48 700b lilac & vio 1.50 .35
C198 AP48 1200b pale brn 2.50 .75
C199 AP48 1350b rose car 3.00 1.00
C200 AP48 2700b blue grn 3.50 1.25
C201 AP48 4000b violet bl 5.00 1.75
Nos. C197-C201 (5) 15.50 5.10

Nos. C197-C201 exist imperf. Value, $50 each pair.
For surcharges see Nos. C263-C265.

Type of Regular Issue, 1957

1957, Dec. 19 ***Perf. 11½***
C202 A141 600b dp magenta & pink 1.00 .30
C203 A141 700b violet blue & blue 1.50 .30
C204 A141 900b dk green & pale green 3.00 .40
Nos. C202-C204 (3) 5.50 1.00

Type of Regular Issue, 1960

1960, Jan. 30
C205 A142 400b rose claret 1.50 .75
C206 A142 800b slate blue 2.00 .75
C207 A142 2000b slate 3.00 1.00
Nos. C205-C207 (3) 6.50 2.50

Gate of the Sun, Tiahuanacu AP49

Uprooted Oak Emblem AP50

1960, Mar. 26 **Litho.** ***Perf. 11½***
C208 AP49 3000b gray 4.50 2.50
C209 AP49 5000b orange 6.50 2.50
C210 AP49 10,000b rose cl 8.50 6.00
C211 AP49 15,000b blue violet 18.00 7.00
Nos. C208-C211 (4) 37.50 18.00

1960, Apr. 7 ***Perf. 11½***
C212 AP50 600b ultra .75 .60
C213 AP50 700b lt red brn .90 .60
C214 AP50 900b dk bl grn 1.10 .75
C215 AP50 1800b violet 2.50 1.00
C216 AP50 2000b gray 4.00 1.50
Nos. C212-C216 (5) 9.25 4.45

WRY, July 1, 1959-June 30, 1960.
No. C215 exists with "1961" overprint in dark carmine, but was not regularly issued in this form.

Jaime Laredo Type

Laredo facing left, Bolivia in color.

Perf. 11½
1960, Aug. 15 **Unwmk.** **Litho.**
C217 A145 600b rose vio 2.50 .50
C218 A145 700b ol gray 2.50 .50
C219 A145 800b vio brn 3.25 .75
C220 A145 900b dk bl 5.00 1.25
C221 A145 1800b green 6.00 2.00
C222 A145 4000b dk gray 10.00 3.00
Nos. C217-C222 (6) 29.25 8.00

Issued to honor the violinist Jaime Laredo.
For surcharges see Nos. C266-C267.

Children's Hospital Type of 1960

1960, Nov. 21 ***Perf. 11½***
C223 A146 600b multi 1.00 .50
C224 A146 1000b multi 1.75 .50
C225 A146 1800b multi 2.50 1.00
C226 A146 5000b multi 6.00 3.00
Nos. C223-C226 (4) 11.25 5.00

For surcharges see No. C268-C269.

Pres. Paz Estenssoro and Pres. Getulio Vargas of Brazil AP52

1960, Dec. 14 **Litho.** ***Perf. 11½***
C227 AP52 1200b on 10b org & blk 2.00 .75

Exists with surcharge inverted. Value, $75.
No. C227 without surcharge was not regularly issued, although a decree authorizing its circulation was published. Value, $2.
Postally used counterfeits of surcharge exist.

Pres. Paz Estenssoro and Pres. Frondizi of Argentina AP53

4000b, Flags of Bolivia and Argentina.

1961, May 23 ***Perf. 10½***

C228	AP53	4000b brn, red, yel, grn & bl	3.00	1.50
C229	AP53	6000b dk grn & blk	3.00	1.50

Visit of the President of Argentina, Dr. Arturo Frondizi, to Bolivia.

For surcharge see No. C309.

Miguel de Cervantes — AP54

1961, Oct. **Photo.** ***Perf. 13***

C230	AP54	1400b pale grn & dk ol grn	1.50	.60

Cervantes' appointment as Chief Magistrate of La Paz. See No. 451.

Virgin of Cotoca and Symbol of Eucharist — AP55

1962, Mar. 19 **Litho.** ***Perf. 10½***

C231	AP55	1400b brn, pink & yel	1.75	.75

4th Natl. Eucharistic Cong., Santa Cruz, 1961.

Nos. C212-C216 Surcharged

1962, June **Unwmk.** ***Perf. 11½***

C232	AP50	1200b on 600b	2.25	1.00
C233	AP50	1300b on 700b	1.50	1.00
C234	AP50	1400b on 900b	2.00	1.00
C235	AP50	2800b on 1,800b	2.00	1.50
C236	AP50	3000b on 2,000b	2.00	1.50
		Nos. C232-C236 (5)	9.75	6.00

The overprinted segment of Greek key border on Nos. C232-C236 comes in two positions: two full "keys" on top, and one full and two half keys on top.

Flower Type of 1962

Flowers: 100b, 1800b, Cantua buxifolia. 800b, 10,000b, Cantua bicolor.

1962, June 28 **Litho.** ***Perf. 10½***

Flowers in Natural Colors

C237	A152	100b dk bl	1.00	.25
C238	A152	800b green	2.00	.40
C239	A152	1800b violet	4.00	.75
a.		Souvenir sheet of 3	14.00	14.00
C240	A152	10,000b dk bl	10.00	4.00
		Nos. C237-C240 (4)	17.00	5.35

No. C239a contains 3 imperf. stamps similar to Nos. C237-C239, but with the 1,800b background color changed to dark violet blue.

For surcharges see Nos. C270-C271.

Planes and Parachutes AP56

1200b, 5000b, Plane and oxcart. 2000b, Aerial photography (plane over South America).

1962, Sept. 5 **Litho.** ***Perf. 11½***

Emblem in Red, Yellow & Green

C241	AP56	600b blk & bl	.60	.25
C242	AP56	1200b multi	1.50	.50
C243	AP56	2000b multi	1.75	.75
C244	AP56	5000b multi	3.00	1.25
		Nos. C241-C244 (4)	6.85	2.70

Armed Forces of Bolivia.

An imperforate 200b souvenir sheet depicting No. C241 with simulated perforations was issued Sept. 16, 1983, to clebrate 200 years of manned flight. Value $50.

Malaria Type of 1962

Design: Inscription around mosquito, laurel around globe.

1962, Oct. 4

C245	A154	2000b ind, grn & yel	3.50	1.00

Type of Regular Issue, 1961

Design: Pedro de la Gasca (1485-1567).

1962 **Unwmk.** **Photo.** ***Perf. 13x12½***

C246	A150	1200b brn, *yel*	1.00	.50

Condor, Soccer Ball and Flags — AP57

1.80b, Map of Bolivia, soccer ball, goal and flags.

1963, Mar. 21 **Litho.** ***Perf. 11½***

C247	AP57	1.40b multi	3.00	1.25
C248	AP57	1.80b multi	3.00	1.25

21st South American Soccer Championships.

An imperforate 20b souvenir sheet depicting No. C248 with simulated perforations was issued March 16, 1979 to celebrate the 1979 World Cup soccer championship games. Value $40.

Two imperforate 20b souvenir sheets, one containing No. C247 and the other containing No. C248, both with simulated perforations, were issued Oct. 13, 1980, to mark various World Cup competitions. Value, each $45.

Freedom from Hunger Type

Design: Wheat, globe and wheat emblem.

1963, Aug. 1 **Unwmk.** ***Perf. 11½***

C249	A156	1.20b dk grn, bl & yel	1.75	1.00

Alliance for Progress Emblem — AP58

1963, Nov. 15 ***Perf. 11½***

C250	AP58	1.20b dl yel, ultra & grn	2.50	1.00

2nd anniv. of the Alliance for Progress, which aims to stimulate economic growth and raise living standards in Latin America.

Type of Regular Issue, 1963

1.20b, Ballot box and voters. 1.40b, Map and farmer breaking chain. 2.80b, Miners.

1963, Dec. 21 ***Perf. 11½***

C251	A157	1.20b gray, dk brn & rose	1.50	.30
C252	A157	1.40b bister & grn	2.00	.50
C253	A157	2.80b slate & buff	3.00	1.25
		Nos. C251-C253 (3)	6.50	2.05

Andrés Santa Cruz — AP59

Perf. 13½

1966, Aug. 10 **Wmk. 90** **Litho.**

C254	AP59	20c dp bl	.40	.25
C255	AP59	60c dp grn	.60	.30
C256	AP59	1.20b red brn	1.25	.60
C257	AP59	2.80b black	2.00	1.00
		Nos. C254-C257 (4)	4.25	2.15

Cent. (in 1965) of the death of Marshal Andrés Santa Cruz (1792-1865), pres. of Bolivia and of Peru-Bolivia Confederation.

Children Type of 1966

Design: 1.40b, Mother and children.

1966, Dec. 16 **Unwmk.** ***Perf. 13½***

C258	A159	1.40b gray bl & blk	3.00	1.00

Co-Presidents Type of Regular Issue

1966, Dec. 16 **Litho.** ***Perf. 12½***

Flag in Red, Yellow and Green

C259	A160	2.80b gray & tan	3.00	1.25
C260	A160	10b sep & tan	4.00	2.00
a.		Souvenir sheet of 4	14.00	14.00

No. C260a contains 4 imperf. stamps similar to Nos. 480-481 and C259-C260. Dark green marginal inscription. Size: 135x82mm.

Various Issues 1954-62 Surcharged with New Values and Bars

On No. C177

1966, Dec. 21

C261	A138	10c on 27b	.75	.30
a.		Agraria/Agraria	20.00	10.00

On No. C182

C262	AP47	10c on 55b	.75	.30

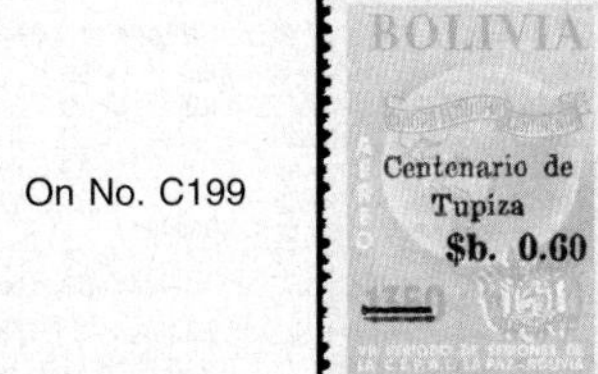

On No. C199

C263	AP48	60c on 1350b	1.00	.50

On No. C200

C264	AP48	2.80b on 2700b	5.00	3.00

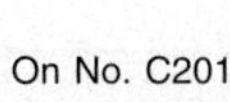

On No. C201

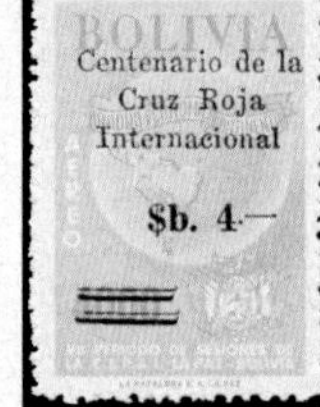

C265	AP48	4b on 4000b	2.50	.70

On No. C219

C266	A145	1.20b on 800b	1.50	.75

On No. C222

C267	A145	1.40b on 4,000b	1.50	.75

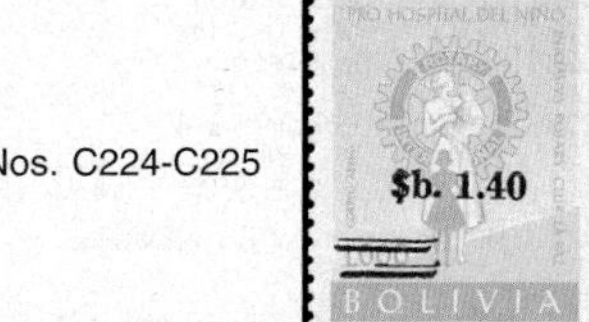

Nos. C224-C225

C268	A146	1.40b on 1,000b	1.75	.75
C269	A146	1.40b on 1,800b	1.75	.75

Nos. C238-C239

C270	A152	1.20b on 800b	2.25	.50
C271	A152	1.20b on 1,800b	2.25	.50

Revenue Stamp of 1946 Surcharged

C272	A161	1.20b on 1b dk bl	1.50	.50
		Nos. C261-C272 (12)	22.50	9.30

Lions Emblem and Pre-historic Sculptures AP60

1967, Sept. 20 **Litho.** ***Perf. 13x13½***

C273	AP60	2b red & multi	1.50	.75
a.		Souvenir sheet of 2	8.00	8.00

50th anniv. of Lions Intl. No. C273a contains 2 imperf. stamps similar to Nos. 492 and C273.

Folklore Type of Regular Issue

Folklore characters: 1.20p, Pujllay. 1.40p, Ujusiris. 2p, Morenada. 3p, Auki-aukis.

1968, June 24 ***Perf. 13½x13***

C274	A163	1.20b lt yel grn & multi	1.00	.45
C275	A163	1.40b gray & multi	1.50	.45
C276	A163	2b dk ol bis & multi	3.00	.45

C277 A163 3b sky bl & multi 4.50 1.00
a. Souvenir sheet of 4, #C274-C277 imperf 25.00 25.00
Nos. C274-C277 (4) 10.00 2.35

Moto Mendez — AP61

1968, Oct. 29 Litho. *Perf. 13½x13*
C278 AP61 1b multi .90 .30
C279 AP61 1.20b multi 1.10 .50
C280 AP61 2b multi 2.00 .75
C281 AP61 4b multi 3.00 1.50
Nos. C278-C281 (4) 7.00 3.05

Battle of Tablada sesquicentennial.

Pres. Gualberto Villarroel AP62

1968, Nov. 6 *Perf. 13x13½*
C282 AP62 1.40b org & blk 1.10 .30
C283 AP62 3b lt bl & blk 2.00 .75
C284 AP62 4b rose & blk 2.50 1.00
C285 AP62 5b gray grn & blk 3.00 1.10
C286 AP62 10b pale pur & blk 6.00 2.50
Nos. C282-C286 (5) 14.60 5.65

4th centenary of Cochabamba.

ITU Type of Regular Issue

1968, Dec. 3 Litho. *Perf. 13x13½*
C287 A166 1.20b gray, blk & yel 1.50 .50
C288 A166 1.40b bl, blk & gray ol 1.50 .50

UNESCO Emblem — AP63

1968, Nov. 14 *Perf. 13½x13*
C289 AP63 1.20b pale vio & blk 1.50 .35
C290 AP63 2.80b yel grn & blk 2.50 .75

20th anniv. (in 1966) of UNESCO.

Kennedy Type of Regular Issue

1968, Nov. 22 Unwmk.
C291 A168 1b grn & blk .75 .30
C292 A168 10b scar & blk 6.00 3.75
a. 7.50 7.50 7.50

No. C292a contains one imperf. stamp similar to No. C291. Dark violet marginal inscription. Size: 131x81½mm.

Tennis Type of Regular Issue

1968, Dec. 10 *Perf. 13x13½*
C293 A169 1.40b org, blk & lt brn 1.50 .60
C294 A169 2.80b sky bl, blk & lt brn 2.50 1.00
a. Souvenir sheet of 1 #C293, imperf 15.00 15.00

A 1,000,000b souvenir sheet containing Nos. C294 and 353, perforated 13¼ and 14¼ respectively, was issued Sept. 25, 1986, with a tennis theme. Value $30.

Stamp Centenary Type

Design: 1.40b, 2.80b, 3b, Bolivia No. 1.

1968, Dec. 23 Litho. *Perf. 13x13½*
C295 A170 1.40b org, grn & blk 2.00 .75
C296 A170 2.80b pale rose, grn & blk 3.50 1.25
C297 A170 3b lt vio, grn & blk 3.50 1.25
a. Souvenir sheet of 3, #C295-C297, imperf 10.00 10.00
Nos. C295-C297 (3) 9.00 3.25

An imperforate 20b souvenir sheet depicting No. C297 with simulated perforations was issued March 16, 1979, to mark the 100th anniv. of the death of Sir Rowland Hill (1795-1879), inventor of the postage stamp. Value $50.

Two additional imperforate 20b souvenir sheets, one depicting Nos. C297 and C358, with Bolivia Nos. 14 and 19 and Great Britain No. 1, the other depicting Nos. C297, C11, C12, C17, a trial color surcharge on No. C4, and Great Britain No. 1, were issued April 28, 1980, to mark the 100th anniv. of the death of Sir Rowland Hill. Value, both sheets $60.

Franklin D. Roosevelt — AP64

1969, Oct. 29 Litho. *Perf. 13½x13*
C298 AP64 5b brn, blk & buff 3.50 2.00

Olympic Type of Regular Issue

Sports: 1.20b, Woman runner, vert. 2.80b, Discus thrower, vert. 5b, Hurdler.

Perf. 13½x13, 13x13½
1969, Oct. 29 Litho.
C299 A171 1.20b yel grn, bis & blk 1.50 .60
C300 A171 2.80b red, org & blk 3.50 1.10
C301 A171 5b bl, lt bl, red & blk 4.50 2.25
a. Souvenir sheet of 3, #C299-C301 imperf 30.00 30.00
Nos. C299-C301 (3) 9.50 3.95

Two imperforate 20b souvenir sheets depicting Nos. C300 and C301 with simulated perforations were issued April 28, 1980, to commemorate the 1980 Moscow Olympics. Value, both sheets $75.

An imperforate 200b souvenir sheet depicting Nos. C300 and 639 with simulated perforations was issued Sept. 16, 1983, to mark the 1983 Los Angeles Summer Olympic Games. Value $25.

An imperforate 27,500b souvenir sheet depicting No. C299 with simulated perforations was issued April 4, 1985, to mark the 1984 Los Angeles Summer Olympic Games. Value $25.

A 2b souvenir sheet containing Nos. C299 and 712, perforated 13¼, was issued April 13, 1987, to mark the 1988 Seoul Summer Olympic Games. Value $20.

An additional 2b souvenir sheet containing No. C300, perforated 13¼, was issued Aug. 15, 1988, to mark the Seoul Olympics. Value $30.

Butterfly Type of Regular Issue

1b, Metamorpha dido wernichei. 1.80b, Heliconius felix. 2.80b, Morpho casica. 3b, Papilio yuracares. 4b, Heliconius melitus.

1970, Apr. 24 Litho. *Perf. 13x13½*
C302 A172 1b sal & multi 4.00 2.00
C303 A172 1.80b lt bl & multi 6.00 3.00
C304 A172 2.80b multi 9.00 4.50
C305 A172 3b multi 9.00 4.50
C306 A172 4b multi 12.00 5.50
a. Souvenir sheet of 3, #C302-C304 25.00 25.00
Nos. C302-C306 (5) 40.00 19.50

A souvenir sheet exists containing 3 imperf. stamps similar to Nos. C302-C304. Black marginal inscription. Size: 129½x80mm.

Scout Type of Regular Issue

Designs: 50c, Boy Scout building brick wall. 1.20b, Bolivian Boy Scout emblem.

1970, June 17 Litho. *Perf. 13½x13*
C307 A173 50c yel & multi .75 .30
C308 A173 1.20b multi .90 .50

No. C228 Surcharged

1970, Dec. Litho. *Perf. 10½*
C309 AP53 1.20b on 4000b multi .90 .30

Flower Type of Regular Issue

Bolivian Flowers: 1.20b, Amaryllis pseudopardina, horiz. 1.40b, Rebutia kruegeri. 2.80b, Lobivia pentlandii, horiz. 4b, Rebutia tunariensis.

Perf. 13x13½, 13½x13
1971, Aug. 9 Litho. Unwmk.
C310 A174 1.20b multi 1.50 .75
C311 A174 1.40b multi 2.50 1.25
C312 A174 2.80b multi 3.50 1.50
C313 A174 4b multi 4.50 3.00
Nos. C310-C313 (4) 12.00 6.50

Folk Dance Type of Regular Issue

1972, Mar. 23 Litho. *Perf. 13½x13*
C314 A177 1.20b Kusillo 1.10 .30
a. Souvenir sheet of 3, #542-543, C314 imperf 50.00 50.00
C315 A177 1.40b Taquirari 1.75 .30
a. Souvenir sheet of 3, #540-541, C315 imperf 50.00 50.00

Painting Type of Regular Issue

Bolivian Paintings: 1.40b, Portrait of Chola Paceña, by Cecilio Guzman de Rojas. 1.50b, Adoration of the Kings, by G. Gamarra. 1.60b, Adoration of Pachamama (mountain), by A. Borda. 2b, The Kiss of the Idol, by Guzman de Rojas.

1972 Litho. *Perf. 13½*
C316 A178 1.40b multi 1.50 .30
C317 A178 1.50b multi 1.50 .30
C318 A178 1.60b multi 1.50 .30
a. Souvenir sheet of 2, #548, C318 imperf 60.00 60.00
C319 A178 2b multi 2.00 .50
a. Souvenir sheet of 2, #C317, C319, imperf 60.00 60.00
Nos. C316-C319 (4) 6.50 1.40

Issued: 1.40b, Dec. 4; others Aug. 17.

An imperforate 20b souvenir sheet depicting No. C318 with simulated perforations was issued March 16, 1979, to mark the 1980 Olympic Games. Value $25.

An imperforate 1.50b souvenir sheet depicting No. C317 with simulated perforations was issued Aug. 1, 1982, for Christmas 1982. Value $60.

An imperforate 200b souvenir sheet depicting Nos. C318 and 616 with simulated perforations was issued Sept. 16, 1983, to celebrate the 1984 Sarajevo Winter Olympic Games. Value $30.

An imperforate 7500b souvenir sheet depicting No. C319 with simulated perforations was issued Nov. 12, 1984, to honor Peter Paul Reubens (pictures *Diana and Calisto*). Value $50.

An imperforate 1b souvenir sheet depicting No. C319 with simulated perforations was issued March 20, 1987, to honor Peter Paul Reubens (pictures *Juno and Argus*). Value $25.

Bolivian Coat of Arms AP65

1972, Dec. 4 *Perf. 13½x13¾*
C320 AP65 4b lt bl & multi 3.50 1.50

An imperforate 20b souvenir sheet depicting Nos. C320 and 651 with simulated perforations was issued Oct. 13, 1980, to celebrate the 1980 Lake Placid Winter Olympic Games. Value $75.

An imperforate 4b souvenir sheet depicting No. C320 with simulated perforations was issued Aug. 11, 1981, to celebrate the wedding of Prince Charles and Lady Diana. Value $25.

An imperforate 4b souvenir sheet depicting No. C320 with simulated perforations was issued March 24, 1982, to honor Princess Diana. Value $25.

An imperforate 7500b souvenir sheet depicting Nos. C320 and 703 with simulated perforations was issued Nov. 12, 1984, to mark the 1984 Sarajevo Winter Olympic Games. Value $50.

An imperforate 500,000b souvenir sheet depicting No. C320 with simulated perforations was issued Dec. 3, 1985, to mark the World Chess Congress. Value $65.

A 1,000,000b souvenir sheet containing Nos. C320 and 616 perforated 13¼ was issued Sept. 25, 1986, to mark the 1988 Calgary Winter Olympic Games. Value $30.

A 2b souvenir sheet containing No. C320 perforated 13¼ was issued April 13, 1987, to mark the 1988 Calgary Winter Olympic Games. Value $27.50.

A 2b souvenir sheet containing No. C320 perforated 13¼ was issued Dec. 16, 1987, to honor U.S. and Soviet space flights. Value $25.

A 2b souvenir sheet containing No. C320 perforated 13¼ was issued July 16, 1989, to commemorate the 200th anniv. of the French Revolution. Value $20.

A 2b souvenir sheet containing No. C320 perforated 13¼ was issued May 18, 1990, to mark the 700th anniv. of the Swiss Confederation. Value $40.

Cactus Type of Regular Issue

Designs: Various cacti.

1973, Aug. 6 Litho. *Perf. 13½*
C321 A180 1.20b tan & multi 1.00 .30
C322 A180 1.90b org & multi 1.50 .50
C323 A180 2b multi 2.50 1.00
Nos. C321-C323 (3) 5.00 1.80

Development Type of Regular Issue

1.40b, Highway 1Y4. 2b, Rail car on bridge.

1973, Nov. 26 Litho. *Perf. 13½*
C324 A181 1.40b salmon & multi 2.50 .35
C325 A181 2b multi 3.75 .50

A 2b souvenir sheet containing No. C325 perforated 13¼ was issued June 15, 1988, to mark the 1931 Bentley/Zug auto/train race in England. Value $35.

Santos-Dumont and 14-Bis Plane — AP66

1973, July 20
C326 AP66 1.40b yel & blk 1.50 .60

Alberto Santos-Dumont (1873-1932), Brazilian aviation pioneer.

Orchid Type of 1974

Orchids: 2.50b, Cattleya luteola, horiz. 3.80b, Stanhopaea. 4b, Catasetum, horiz. 5b, Maxillaria.

1974 Litho. *Perf. 13½*
C327 A182 2.50b multi 3.00 .50
C328 A182 3.80b rose & multi 5.00 1.00
C329 A182 4b multi 8.00 1.50
C330 A182 5b sal & multi 9.00 2.00
Nos. C327-C330 (4) 25.00 5.00

Air Force Emblem, Plane over Map of Bolivia AP67

Designs: 3.80b, Plane over Andes. 4.50b, Triple decker and jet. 8b, Rafael Pabon and double decker. 15b, Jet and "50."

1974 Litho. *Perf. 13x13½*
C331 AP67 3b multi 1.50 .60
C332 AP67 3.80b multi 2.25 1.00
C333 AP67 4.50b multi 2.25 1.00
C334 AP67 8b multi 3.50 2.00
C335 AP67 15b multi 6.25 2.75
Nos. C331-C335 (5) 15.75 7.35

Bolivian Air Force, 50th anniv. Nos. C331-C335 exist imperf. Value, $40 each pair.

For surcharge see No. 968.

Coat of Arms Type of 1975

Designs: Departmental coats of arms.

1975, July 16 Litho. *Perf. 13½*

C336 A188	20c	Beni	.50	.25
C337 A188	30c	Tarija	.50	.25
C338 A188	50c	Potosi	.70	.30
C339 A188	1b	Oruro	1.40	.80
C340 A188	2.50b	Santa Cruz	2.75	1.25
C341 A188	3b	La Paz	2.75	1.75
		Nos. C336-C341 (6)	8.60	4.60

LAB Emblem — AP68

Bolivia on Map of Americas AP69

Map of Bolivia, Plane and Kyllmann AP70

1975 Litho. *Perf. 13½*

C342 AP68	1b	gold, bl & blk	.75	.50
C343 AP69	1.50b	multi	.90	.50
C344 AP70	2b	multi	1.25	.60
		Nos. C342-C344 (3)	2.90	1.60

Lloyd Aereo Boliviano, 50th anniversary, founded by Guillermo Kyllmann.

Bolivar, Presidents Perez and Banzer, and Flags — AP71

1975, Aug. 4 Litho. *Perf. 13½*

C345 AP71 3b gold & multi 2.50 1.00

Visit of Pres. Carlos A. Perez of Venezuela.

Eight imperforate souvenir sheets, each denominated 5.50b, depicting No. 19 with various contemporaneous Bolivian stamps with simulated perforations were issued on Nov. 7, 1975, celebrating various anniversaries and philatelic events. These comprise: No. 345, Innsbruck 1976, value $25; No. C345, Interphil '76, value $6; No. C350, Concorde/Zeppelin, value $50; No. C350, Wien '75, value $6; No. C3251, U.S. Bicentennial, value $30; No. C351, Hafnia '76, value $6; No C352, Montreal Olympics/Argentina '78, value $35; No. C352, Exfilmo '75, value $6. Four of these sheets were overprinted in April 1981 for WIPA 81 (value $5), Espamer 81 (value $5), Philatokyo 81 (value $5) and Philexfrance 1982 (value $12.50).

An imperforate 25b souvenir sheet depicting No. C345 with simulated perforations was issued June 1, 1978, to commemorate the 25th anniv. of the coronation of Queen Elizabeth II. Value $25.

Bolivar Type of 1975

Presidents and Statesmen of Bolivia: 50c, Rene Barrientos O. 2b, Francisco B. O'Connor. 3.80b, Gualberto Villarroel. 4.20b, German Busch. 4.50b, Hugo Banzer Suarez. 20b, José Ballivian. 30b, Andres de Santa Cruz. 40b, Antonio Jose de Sucre.

1975 Litho. *Perf. 13½*

Size: 24x33mm

C346 A189	50c	multi	.50	.25
C347 A189	2b	multi	1.40	.50
C348 A189	3.80b	multi	1.50	.80
C349 A189	4.20b	multi	2.00	1.00

Size: 28x39mm

C350 A189 4.50b multi 2.50 1.00

Size: 24x33mm

C351 A189	20b	multi	6.50	4.00
C352 A189	30b	multi	10.00	5.00
C353 A189	40b	multi	12.00	7.00
		Nos. C346-C353 (8)	36.40	19.50

For surcharge see No. 969.

An imperforate 20b souvenir sheet depicting No. C353 with simulated perforations was issued March 16, 1979, to commemorate the 75th anniv. of powered flight. Value $40.

An imperforate 54b souvenir sheet depicting Nos. C346 and C358 with simulated perforations was issued April 28, 1980, to celebrate the 1980 Lake Placid Winter Olympics. Value $25.

UPU Emblem AP72

1975, Dec. 7 Litho. *Perf. 13½*

C358 AP72 25b blue & multi		6.00	4.00
a.	Souvenir sheet of 1, imperf	20.00	20.00

Cent. of UPU (in 1974).

No. C358a contains a single No. C358, imperforate with simulated perforations. Size: 130x80mm.

An imperforate 25b souvenir sheet depicting No. C358 with simulated perforations was issued Jan. 1, 1978, to recognize Charles Lindbergh and Zeppelin flights. Value $100.

POSTAGE DUE STAMPS

D1

1931 Unwmk. Engr. *Perf. 14, 14½*

J1	D1	5c	ultra	1.75	*3.50*
J2	D1	10c	red	2.50	*3.50*
J3	D1	15c	yellow	2.50	*5.00*
J4	D1	30c	deep green	2.50	*6.00*
J5	D1	40c	deep violet	6.00	*8.00*
J6	D1	50c	black brown	12.00	*15.00*
			Nos. J1-J6 (6)	27.25	*41.00*

Symbol of Youth D2

Torch of Knowledge D3

Symbol of the Revolution of May 17, 1936 — D4

1938 Litho. *Perf. 11*

J7	D2	5c	deep rose	1.75	1.50
a.			Pair, imperf. between	10.00	
J8	D3	10c	green	2.00	1.50
J9	D4	30c	gray blue	2.00	1.60
			Nos. J7-J9 (3)	5.75	4.60

POSTAL TAX STAMPS

Worker — PT1

Imprint: "LITO. UNIDAS LA PAZ."

Perf. 13½x10½, 10½, 13½

1939 Litho. Unwmk.

RA1 PT1 5c dull violet		1.00	.50
a.	Double impression	15.00	15.00

Redrawn

Imprint: "TALL. OFFSET LA PAZ."

1940 *Perf. 12x11, 11*

RA2 PT1 5c violet		.75	.30
a.	Horizontal pair, imperf. between	3.00	2.00
b.	Imperf. horiz., pair	10.00	
c.	Double impression	15.00	10.00

Tax of Nos. RA1-RA2 was for the Workers' Home Building Fund.

Communications Symbols — PT2

1944-45 Litho. *Perf. 10½*

RA3 PT2	10c	salmon	.75	.30
RA4 PT2	10c	blue ('45)	.75	.30

A 30c orange inscribed "Centenario de la Creacion del Departmento del Beni" was issued in 1946 and required to be affixed to all air and surface mail to and from the Department of Beni in addition to regular postage. Values: unused $1; used 50¢.Five higher denominations in the same scenic design were used for local revenue purposes.

Catalogue values for unused stamps in this section, from this point to the end of the section, are for Never Hinged items.

Type of 1944 Redrawn

1947-48 Unwmk. *Perf. 10½*

RA5 PT2	10c	carmine	2.50	.25
RA6 PT2	10c	org yel ('48)	2.50	.25
RA7 PT2	10c	yel brn ('48)	2.50	.25
RA8 PT2	10c	emerald ('48)	2.50	.25
		Nos. RA5-RA8 (4)	10.00	1.00

Post horn and envelope reduced in size.

Condor, Envelope and Post Horn — PT3

1951-52

RA9 PT3 20c deep orange		.70	.30
a.	Imperf., pair	25.00	
RA10 PT3 20c green ('52)		.70	.30
a.	Imperf., pair	25.00	
RA11 PT3 20c blue ('52)		.70	.30
a.	Imperf., pair	25.00	
	Nos. RA9-RA11 (3)	2.10	.90

For surcharges see Nos. RA17-RA18.

Communication Symbols — PT4

1952-54 *Perf. 13½, 10½, 10½x12*

RA12 PT4	50c	green	.70	.25
RA13 PT4	50c	carmine	1.00	.25
RA14 PT4	3b	green	.70	.30
RA15 PT4	3b	olive bister	.85	.30
RA16 PT4	5b	violet ('54)	2.50	1.00
		Nos. RA12-RA16 (5)	5.75	2.10

For surcharges see Nos. RA21-RA22.

No. RA10 and Type of 1951-52 Surcharged with New Value in Black

1953 *Perf. 10½*

RA17 PT3	50c on 20c green	.60	.25
RA18 PT3	50c on 20c red vio	.60	.25

Postman Blowing Horn — PT5

1954-55 Unwmk. *Perf. 10½*

RA19 PT5	1b	brown	1.25	.25
RA20 PT5	1b	car rose ('55)	1.25	.25

Nos. RA19-RA20 exist imperf. Value, $25 each pair.

Nos. RA15 and RA14 Surcharged in Black

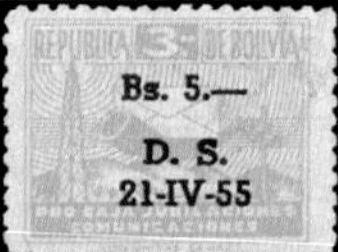

1955 *Perf. 10½, 10½x12*

RA21 PT4	5b on 3b olive bister	1.00	.25
RA22 PT4	5b on 3b green	2.00	.30

Tax of Nos. RA3-RA22 was for the Communications Employees Fund.

No. RA21 is known with surcharge in thin type of different font and with comma added after "55." Value, $10.

Plane over Airport — PT6

Planes — PT7

Perf. 10½, 12, 13½

1955 Unwmk. Litho.

RA23 PT6 5b dp ultra		1.00	.30
a.	Vertical pair imperf. between	30.00	

Perf. 11½

RA24 PT7 10b light green 1.00 .30

PT8

PT9

1955 Litho. *Perf. 10½*

RA25 PT8 5b red		15.00	10.00
a.	Imperf., pair	40.00	

Perf. 12

RA26 PT9 20b dark brown 1.10 .30

Tax of Nos. RA23-RA26 was for the building of new airports.

General Alfredo Ovando and Three Men — PT10

1970, Sept. 26 Litho. *Perf. 13x13½*

RA27	PT10	20c black & red	.70	.30

See No. RAC1.

Pres. German Busch PT11

1971, May 13 Litho. *Perf. 13x13½*

RA28	PT11	20c lilac & black	.70	.30

AIR POST POSTAL TAX STAMPS

Catalogue values for unused stamps in this section are for Never Hinged items.

Type of Postal Tax Issue

Design: 30c, General Ovando and oil well.

1970, Sept. 26 Litho. *Perf. 13x13½*

RAC1	PT10	30c blk & grn	.80	.30

Pres. Gualberto Villarroel, Refinery PTAP1

1971, May 25 Litho. *Perf. 13x13½*

RAC2	PTAP1	30c lt bl & blk	1.00	.30

Type of 1971 Inscribed: "XXV ANIVERSARIO DE SU GOBIERNO"

1975 Litho. *Perf. 13x13½*

RAC3	PTAP1	30c lt bl & blk	10.00	2.75

BOSNIA & HERZEGOVINA

'bäz-nē-ə and ˌhert-sə-gō-'vē-nə

LOCATION — Between Dalmatia and Serbia

GOVT. — Provinces of Turkey under Austro-Hungarian occupation, 1879-1908; provinces of Austria-Hungary 1908-1918

AREA — 19,768 sq. mi.

POP. — 2,000,000 (approx. 1918)

CAPITAL — Sarajevo

Following World War I Bosnia and Herzegovina united with the kingdoms of Montenegro and Serbia, and Croatia, Dalmatia and Slovenia, to form the Kingdom of Yugoslavia (See Yugoslavia.)

100 Novcica (Neukreuzer) = 1 Florin (Gulden)

100 Heller = 1 Krone (1900)

Watermark

Wmk. 91 — BRIEF-MARKEN or (from 1890) ZEITUNGS-MARKEN in Double-lined Capitals, Across the Sheet

Coat of Arms — A1

Type I — The heraldic eaglets on the right side of the escutcheon are entirely blank. The eye of the lion is indicated by a very small dot, which sometimes fails to print.

Type II — There is a colored line across the lowest eaglet. A similar line sometimes appears on the middle eaglet. The eye of the lion is formed by a large dot which touches the outline of the head above it.

Type III — The eaglets and eye of the lion are similar to type I. Each tail feather of the large eagle has two lines of shading and the lowest feather does not touch the curved line below it. In types I and II there are several shading lines in these feathers, and the lowest feather touches the curved line.

Varieties of the Numerals

2 NOVCICA:
A — The "2" has curved tail. All are type I.
B — The "2" has straight tail. All are type II.

15 NOVCICA:
C — The serif of the "1" is short and forms a wide angle with the vertical stroke.
D — The serif of the "1" forms an acute angle with the vertical stroke.

The numerals of the 5n were retouched several times and show minor differences, especially in the flag.

Other Varieties

½ NOVCICA:
There is a black dot between the curved ends of the ornaments near the lower spandrels.
G — This dot touches the curve at its right. Stamps of this (1st) printing are litho.
H — This dot stands clear of the curved lines. Stamps of this (2nd) printing are typo.

10 NOVCICA:
Ten stamps in each sheet of type II show a small cross in the upper section of the right side of the escutcheon.

Perf. 9 to 13½ and Compound

1879-94 Litho. Wmk. 91

Type I

1	A1	½n blk (type II) ('94)	26.00	*50.00*
2	A1	1n gray	16.00	2.50
c.		1n gray lilac		3.00
4	A1	2n yellow	24.00	1.60
5	A1	3n green	27.50	3.25
6	A1	5n rose red	47.50	.55
7	A1	10n blue	160.00	1.60
8	A1	15n brown (D)	160.00	10.25
a.		15n brown (C)	360.00	50.00
9	A1	20n gray green ('93)	625.00	14.00
10	A1	25n violet	140.00	12.00
		Nos. 1-10 (9)	1,226.	95.75

No. 2c was never issued. It is usually canceled by blue pencil marks and "mint" examples generally have been cleaned.

Perf. 10½ to 13 and Compound

1894-98 Typo.

Type II

1a	A1	½n black	17.50	*25.00*
2a	A1	1n gray	5.75	1.60
4a	A1	2n yellow	3.25	.80
5a	A1	3n green	5.75	1.75
6a	A1	5n rose red	140.00	.90
7a	A1	10n blue	8.00	1.25
b.		Pair, imperf btw, perf 10½ all around		*12,500.*
8b	A1	15n brown	7.25	4.75
9a	A1	20n gray green	8.00	6.00
10a	A1	25n violet	9.50	15.00
		Nos. 1a-10a (9)	205.00	57.05

Type III

6b	A1	5n rose red ('98)	8.00	.85

All the preceding stamps exist in various shades.

Nos. 1a to 10a were reprinted in 1911 in lighter colors, on very white paper and perf. 12½. Value, set $32.50.

A2

A3

Perf. 10½, 12½ and Compound

1900 Typo.

11	A2	1h gray black	.25	.25
12	A2	2h gray	.25	.25
13	A2	3h yellow	.25	.25
14	A2	5h green	.25	.25
15	A2	6h brown	.40	.25
16	A2	10h red	.25	.25
17	A2	20h rose	150.00	12.50
18	A2	25h blue	1.20	1.20
19	A2	30h bister brown	150.00	14.50
20	A2	40h orange	200.00	17.00
21	A2	50h red lilac	.80	.80
22	A3	1k dark rose	1.10	.65
23	A3	2k ultra	1.60	*2.00*
24	A3	5k dull blue grn	3.75	*6.75*
		Nos. 11-24 (14)	510.10	56.90

All values of this issue except the 3h exist on ribbed paper.

Nos. 17, 19 and 20 were reprinted in 1911. The reprints are in lighter colors and on whiter paper than the originals. Reprints of Nos. 17 and 19 are perf. 10½ and those of No. 20 are perf. 12½. Value each $5. Reprints also exist imperf.

Numerals in Black

1901-04 *Perf. 12½*

25	A2	20h pink ('02)	1.00	.60
26	A2	30h bister brn ('03)	1.00	.60
27	A2	35h blue	1.50	.95
a.		35h ultramarine	*175.00*	9.50
28	A2	40h orange ('03)	1.25	1.00
29	A2	45h grnsh blue ('04)	1.25	1.00
		Nos. 25-29 (5)	6.00	4.15

Nos. 11-16, 18, 21-29 exist imperf. Most of Nos. 11-29 exist perf. 6½; compound with 12½; part perf.; in pairs imperf. between. These were supplied only to some high-ranking officials and never sold at any P.O.

View of Deboj A4

The Carsija at Sarajevo — A5

Designs: 2h, View of Mostar. 3h, Pliva Gate, Jajce. 5h, Narenta Pass and Prenj River. 6h, Rama Valley. 10h, Vrbas Valley. 20h, Old Bridge, Mostar. 25h, Bey's Mosque, Sarajevo. 30h, Donkey post. 35h, Jezero and tourists' pavilion. 40h, Mail wagon. 45h, Bazaar at Sarajevo. 50h, Postal car. 2k, St. Luke's Campanile, Jajce. 5k, Emperor Franz Josef.

Perf. 6½, 9½, 10½ and 12½, also Compounds

1906 Engr. Unwmk.

30	A4	1h black	.25	.25
31	A4	2h violet	.25	.25
32	A4	3h olive	.25	.25
33	A4	5h dark green	.35	.25
34	A4	6h brown	.25	*.30*
a.		Perf. 13½	.85	1.25
35	A4	10h carmine	.45	.25
36	A4	20h dark brown	.90	.45
a.		Perf. 13½	2.50	3.50
37	A4	25h deep blue	1.75	1.60
38	A4	30h green	1.75	.80
39	A4	35h myrtle green	1.75	.80
40	A4	40h orange red	1.75	.80
41	A4	45h brown red	1.75	2.00
42	A4	50h dull violet	2.50	2.00
43	A5	1k maroon	6.50	3.50
44	A5	2k gray green	8.00	*12.00*
45	A5	5k dull blue	5.00	*8.00*
		Nos. 30-45 (16)	33.45	*33.50*

Nos. 30-45 exist imperf. Value, set $91.35 unused, $107 canceled. Many perforation varieties exist. See the *Scott Classic Specialized Catalogue of Stamps and Covers 1840-1940* for detailed listings.

For overprints and surcharges see Nos. 126, B1-B4.

Birthday Jubilee Issue

Designs of 1906 Issue, with "1830-1910" in Label at Bottom

1910 *Perf. 12½*

46	A4	1h black	.40	.40
47	A4	2h violet	.40	.40
48	A4	3h olive	.40	.40
49	A4	5h dark green	.40	.40
50	A4	6h orange brn	.40	.40
51	A4	10h carmine	.85	.25
52	A4	20h dark brown	1.60	*2.50*
53	A4	25h deep blue	2.50	*4.25*
54	A4	30h green	2.50	*4.25*
55	A4	35h myrtle grn	2.50	*4.25*
56	A4	40h orange red	2.50	*5.00*
57	A4	45h brown red	3.50	*8.50*
58	A4	50h dull violet	4.25	*8.50*
59	A5	1k maroon	5.00	*8.50*
60	A5	2k gray green	16.00	*34.00*
61	A5	5k dull blue	1.60	*10.00*
		Nos. 46-61 (16)	44.80	*92.00*

80th birthday of Emperor Franz Josef.

Scenic Type of 1906

Views: 12h, Jaice. 60h, Konjica. 72h, Vishegrad.

1912

62	A4	12h ultra	6.00	*7.25*
63	A4	60h dull blue	3.50	*5.00*
64	A4	72h carmine	12.00	*24.00*
		Nos. 62-64 (3)	21.50	*36.25*

Value, imperf set, $120.

See Austria for similar designs inscribed "FELDPOST" instead of "MILITARPOST."

Emperor Franz Josef
A23 A24

A25

A26

1912-14 Various Frames

65	A23	1h olive green	.40	.25
66	A23	2h brt blue	.40	.25
67	A23	3h claret	.40	.25
68	A23	5h green	.40	.25
69	A23	6h dark gray	.40	.25
70	A23	10h rose car	.40	.25
71	A23	12h dp olive grn	.55	.40
72	A23	20h orange brn	3.00	.25
73	A23	25h ultra	1.60	.25
74	A23	30h orange red	1.60	.25
75	A24	35h myrtle grn	1.90	.25
76	A24	40h dk violet	5.25	.25
77	A24	45h olive brn	2.40	.40
78	A24	50h slate blue	2.75	.25
79	A24	60h brown vio	1.60	.25
80	A24	72h dark blue	4.00	*6.00*
81	A25	1k brn vio, *straw*	9.75	.85
82	A25	2k dk gray, *bl*	8.50	.85
83	A26	3k carmine, *grn*	10.00	*12.00*
84	A26	5k dk vio, *gray*	20.00	*32.50*
85	A25	10k dk ultra, *gray* ('14)	100.00	*140.00*
		Nos. 65-85 (21)	175.30	196.25

Value, imperf set, $375.

For overprints and surcharges see Nos. 127, B5-B8, Austria M1-M21.

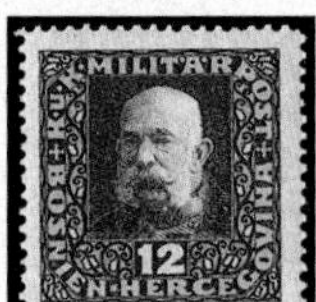

A27

A28

1916-17 ***Perf. 12½***

No.	Type	Description	Unused	Used
86	A27	3h dark gray	.25	*.40*
87	A27	5h olive green	.25	*.60*
88	A27	6h violet	.25	*.75*
89	A27	10h olive brown	1.60	*3.25*
a.		10h bister	2.40	3.75
90	A27	12h blue gray	.30	*.95*
91	A27	15h car rose	.25	.25
92	A27	20h brown	.40	*.95*
93	A27	25h blue	.25	*.95*
94	A27	30h dark green	.25	*.95*
95	A27	40h vermilion	.25	*.95*
96	A27	50h green	.25	*.95*
97	A27	60h lake	.25	*.95*
98	A27	80h orange brn	1.50	.80
a.		Perf. 11½	3.50	*8.00*
99	A27	90h dark violet	1.10	*1.60*
a.		Perf. 11½	1,050.	—
101	A28	2k claret, *straw*	.75	*3.25*
102	A28	3k green, *bl*	1.50	*4.00*
103	A28	4k carmine, *grn*	6.50	*13.50*
104	A28	10k dp vio, *gray*	21.00	*40.00*
		Nos. 86-104 (18)	36.90	*75.05*

Value, imperf set: hinged $275; never hinged $500.

For overprints see Nos. B11-B12.

Emperor Karl I

A29 A30

1917 ***Perf. 12½***

No.	Type	Description	Unused	Used
105	A29	3h olive gray	.25	*.30*
a.		Perf. 11½	125.00	*250.00*
b.		Perf. 12½x11½	24.00	*55.00*
106	A29	5h olive green	.25	*.30*
107	A29	6h violet	.40	*.95*
108	A29	10h orange brn	.25	.25
a.		Perf. 11½x12½	160.00	*350.00*
b.		Perf. 11½	160.00	*425.00*
109	A29	12h blue	.35	*.95*
110	A29	15h brt rose	.25	.25
111	A29	20h red brown	.25	.25
112	A29	25h ultra	.65	*.80*
113	A29	30h gray green	.25	*.40*
114	A29	40h olive bis	.25	*.40*
115	A29	50h dp green	.65	*.80*
116	A29	60h car rose	.55	*.80*
a.		Perf. 11½	30.00	*67.50*
117	A29	80h steel blue	.30	*.75*
118	A29	90h dull violet	1.25	*2.10*
119	A30	2k carmine, *straw*	1.00	.85
120	A30	3k green, *bl*	21.00	*27.50*
121	A30	4k carmine, *grn*	7.50	*16.00*
122	A30	10k dp violet, *gray*	4.00	*14.50*
		Nos. 105-122 (18)	39.40	*68.15*

Value, imperf set, $140.

Nos. 47 and 66 Overprinted in Red

1918

No.	Type	Description	Unused	Used
126	A4	2h violet	.60	*1.75*
b.		Inverted overprint	60.00	
d.		Double overprint	35.00	
f.		Double overprint, one inverted	30.00	
127	A23	2h bright blue	.60	*1.75*
a.		Pair, one without overprint		—
b.		Inverted overprint	60.00	
c.		Double overprint	35.00	
d.		Double overprint, one inverted	30.00	

Emperor Karl I — A31

1918 **Typo.** ***Perf. 12½, Imperf.***

No.	Type	Description	Unused	Used
128	A31	2h orange	12.00	
129	A31	3h dark green	12.00	
130	A31	5h lt green	12.00	
131	A31	6h blue green	12.00	
132	A31	10h brown	12.00	
133	A31	20h brick red	12.00	
134	A31	25h ultra	12.00	
135	A31	45h dk slate	12.00	
136	A31	50h lt bluish grn	12.00	
137	A31	60h blue violet	12.00	
138	A31	70h ocher	12.00	
139	A31	80h rose	12.00	
140	A31	90h violet brn	12.00	

Engr.

No.	Type	Description	Unused	Used
141	A30	1k ol grn, *grnsh*	*2,100.*	
		Nos. 128-140 (13)	156.00	

Nos. 128-141 were prepared for use in Bosnia and Herzegovina, but were not issued there. They were sold after the Armistice at the Vienna post office for a few days.

SEMI-POSTAL STAMPS

Nos. 33 and 35 Surcharged in Red

1914, Nov. 1 **Unwmk.** ***Perf. 12½***

No.	Type	Description	Unused	Used
B1	A4	7h on 5h dk grn	.45	*.85*
B2	A4	12h on 10h car	.45	*.85*

Three varieties of the surcharge include "4" with open top, narrow "4" and wide "4." See the *Scott Classic Specialized Catalogue of Stamps and Covers* for detailed listings.

Nos. B1-B2 exist with double and inverted surcharges. Values, double surcharge, each: unused $25, never hinged $40. Values, inverted surcharge, each: unused $30, never hinged $50.

Nos. 33, 35 Surcharged in Red or Blue

1915, July 10 ***Perf. 12½***

No.	Type	Description	Unused	Used
B3	A4	7h on 5h (R)	12.00	*17.00*
a.		Perf. 9¼	200.00	*250.00*
B4	A4	12h on 10h (Bl)	.40	*.60*

Nos. B3-B4 exist with double and inverted surcharges. Value about $30 each.

Nos. 68, 70 Surcharged in Red or Blue

1915, Dec. 1

No.	Type	Description	Unused	Used
B5	A23	7h on 5h (R)	.85	*2.40*
a.		"1915" at top and bottom	42.50	*77.50*
B6	A23	12h on 10h (Bl)	1.75	*4.75*
a.		Surcharged "7 Heller."	47.50	*100.00*

Nos. B5-B6 are found in four types differing in length of surcharge lines. See the *Scott Classic Specialized Catalogue of Stamps and Covers* for detailed listings.

Nos. B5-B6 exist with double and inverted surcharges. Values, each: unused $25, never hinged $42.50.

Nos. B5a and B6a exist double and inverted.

Nos. 68, 70 Surcharged in Red or Blue

1916. Feb. 1

No.	Type	Description	Unused	Used
B7	A23	7h on 5h (R)	.85	*.85*
B8	A23	12h on 10h (Bl)	.85	*.90*

The oerprint on Nos. B7-B8 is found in two types, differing in length of surcharge lines. See the *Scott Classic Specialized Catalogue of Stamps and Covers* for detailed listings.

Nos. B7-B8 exist with double and inverted surcharges. Value $20 each.

Wounded Soldier — SP1 Blind Soldier — SP2

1916, July 10 **Engr.**

No.	Type	Description	Unused	Used
B9	SP1	5h (+ 2h) green	1.10	*2.10*
B10	SP2	10h (+ 2h) magenta	1.75	*3.00*

Nos. B9-B10 exist imperf. Value, set $200.

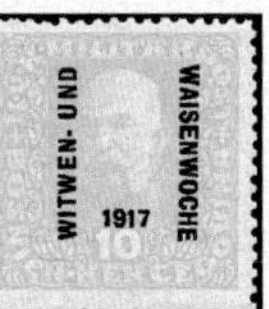

Nos. 89, 89a, 91 Overprinted

1917, May 9

No.	Type	Description	Unused	Used
B11	A27	10h bister (#89a)	.30	*.30*
B12	A27	15h carmine rose	.30	*.60*

Nos. B11-B12 exist imperf. Value set $190.

Nos. B11-B12 exist with double and inverted overprint. Value $15-20 each.

Design for Memorial Church at Sarajevo SP3

Archduke Francis Ferdinand — SP4

Duchess Sophia and Archduke Francis Ferdinand SP5

1917, June 20 **Typo.** ***Perf. 12½***

No.	Type	Description	Unused	Used
B13	SP3	10h violet black	.40	*.40*
B14	SP4	15h claret	.40	*.40*
B15	SP5	40h deep blue	.40	*.40*
		Nos. B13-B15 (3)	1.20	1.20

Assassination of Archduke Ferdinand and Archduchess Sophia. Sold at a premium of 2h each, which helped build a memorial church at Sarajevo.

Exist perf 11½. See Scott Classic Specialized catalogue for detailed listings.

Exist imperf. Value set, $37.50.

Blind Soldier — SP6

Emperor Karl I — SP8

Design: 15h, Wounded soldier.

1918, Mar. 1 **Engr.** ***Perf. 12½***

No.	Type	Description	Unused	Used
B16	SP6	10h (+ 10h) grnsh bl	.60	*1.60*
B17	SP6	15h (+ 10h) red brn	.60	*1.60*

#B16-B17 exist imperf. Value, set $80.

1918, July 20 **Typo.** ***Perf. 12½x13***

Design: 15h, Empress Zita.

No.	Type	Description	Unused	Used
B18	SP8	10h gray green	.50	*1.25*
B19	SP8	15h brown red	.50	*1.25*
B20	SP8	40h violet	.50	*1.25*
		Nos. B18-B20 (3)	1.50	*3.75*

Sold at a premium of 10h each which went to the "Karl's Fund."

Nos. B18-B20 exist imperf. Value, set: $140.

POSTAGE DUE STAMPS

D1

D2

1904 **Unwmk.** ***Perf. 12½***

No.	Type	Description	Unused	Used
J1	D1	1h black, red & yel	.85	.35
J2	D1	2h black, red & yel	.85	.35
J3	D1	3h black, red & yel	.85	.35
J4	D1	4h black, red & yel	.85	.35
J5	D1	5h black, red & yel	4.25	.35
J6	D1	6h black, red & yel	.85	.35
J7	D1	7h black, red & yel	6.00	*4.25*
J8	D1	8h black, red & yel	6.00	2.60
J9	D1	10h black, red & yel	.85	.35
J10	D1	15h black, red & yel	.85	.35
J11	D1	20h black, red & yel	6.75	.35
J12	D1	50h black, red & yel	3.50	.45
J13	D1	200h black, red & grn	30.00	3.50
		Nos. J1-J13 (13)	62.45	13.95
		Set, never hinged	140.00	

Nos. J1-J13 exists with a wide variety of perforations. See the *Scott Classic Specialized Catalogue of Stamps and Covers* for detailed listings.

Nos. J1-J13 also exist perf. 10½, 9¼, 6¼, and in various compound combinations.

Value, imperf set: hinged $125; never hinged $300.

For overprints and surcharges see Western Ukraine Nos. 61-72, Yugoslavia Nos. 1LJ23-1LJ26.

1916-18 ***Perf. 12½***

No.	Type	Description	Unused	Used
J14	D2	2h red ('18)	.40	*1.60*
J15	D2	4h red ('18)	.25	*1.60*
J16	D2	5h red	.40	*1.60*
J17	D2	6h red ('18)	.25	*1.60*
J18	D2	10h red	.40	*1.60*
J19	D2	15h red	3.50	*10.00*
J20	D2	20h red	.45	*1.60*
J21	D2	25h red	1.25	*4.25*
J22	D2	30h red	1.00	*4.25*
J23	D2	40h red	9.50	*24.00*
J24	D2	50h red	30.00	*72.50*

J25	D2	1k dark blue	6.25	*13.00*
J26	D2	3k dark blue	22.50	*45.00*
		Nos. J14-J26 (13)	76.15	*182.60*
		Set, never hinged	200.00	

Nos. J25-J26 have colored numerals on a white tablet.

Value, imperf. set, $240.

For surcharges see Italy Nos. NJ1-NJ7, Yugoslavia 1LJ1-1LJ13.

NEWSPAPER STAMPS

Bosnian Girl — N1

1913 Unwmk. *Imperf.*

P1	N1	2h ultra	.85	*1.25*
P2	N1	6h violet	2.50	*3.75*
P3	N1	10h rose	3.00	*3.75*
P4	N1	20h green	3.50	*4.25*
		Nos. P1-P4 (4)	9.85	13.00

After Bosnia and Herzegovina became part of Yugoslavia, stamps of type N1 perf., and imperf. copies surcharged with new values, were used as regular postage stamps. See Yugoslavia Nos. 1L21-1L22, 1L43-1L45.

SPECIAL HANDLING STAMPS

"Lightning" — SH1

1916 Unwmk. Engr. *Perf. 12½*

QE1	SH1	2h vermilion	.30	.85
a.		Perf. 11½x12½	425.00	250.00
QE2	SH1	5h deep green	.45	1.25
a.		Perf. 11½	17.50	42.50

For surcharges see Italy Nos. NE1-NE2.

BOSNIA & HERZEGOVINA (MUSLIM GOVT)

ˈbäz-nē-ə and ˌhert-sə-gō-ˈvē-nə

LOCATION — Bordering on Croatia, Seribia & Montenegro.
GOVT. — Republic
CAPITAL — Sarajevo

Formerly part of Yugoslavia. Proclamation of independence in 1992 was followed by protracted civil war that was ended by the Dayton Peace Agreement of Nov. 21, 1995.

While Dinars were the official currency until 6/22/98, a currency pegged to the German mark was in use for some time prior to that. Stamps are denominated in pfennigs and marks in 11/97.

100 Paras = 1 Dinar
100 Pfennig = 1 Mark (6/22/98)

Catalogue values for all unused stamps in this country are for Never Hinged items.

Muslim Government in Sarajevo

Natl. Arms — A50

Denominations: 100d, 500d, 1000d, 5000d, 10,000d, 20,000d, 50,000d.

1993, Oct. 27 Litho. *Imperf.*
Booklet Stamps

200-206	A50	Set of 7	19.00	19.00

Nos. 200-206 each were available in bklts. of 50 (10 strips of 5).

1984 Winter Olympic Games, Sarajevo, 10th Anniv. — A51

No. 207, Games emblem. No. 208a, 100,000d, Four man bobsled. No. 208b, 200,000d, Hockey.

1994, Feb. 8

207	A51	50,000d org & blk	2.50	2.50

Souvenir Sheet

208	A51	Sheet of 2, #a.-b.	11.50	11.50

No. 208 contains 45x27mm stamps.

Souvenir Sheet

Bairam Festival A52

Various illustrations from Koran: a, 400d. b, 600d.

1995, May 12 *Perf. 14*

209	A52	Sheet of 2, #a.-b.	18.50	18.50

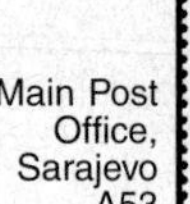

Main Post Office, Sarajevo A53

Designs: 10d, Facade. 20d, 30d, Demolished interior. 35d, 50d, Pre-civil war exterior. 100d, 200d, Post-war exterior.

1995, June 12

210-216	A53	Set of 7	9.50	9.50
216a		Pane of 7	14.00	14.00

No. 216a sold unattached in booklet covers.

Bosnian History A54

Designs: 35d, Historical map, 10th-15th cent. 100d, Tomb, vert. 200d, Arms, Kotromanic Dynasty, vert. 300d, Charter by Ban Kulin, 1189.

1995, Aug. 12 *Perf. 11½*

217-220	A54	Set of 4	11.00	11.00

Peace & Freedom, Europa A55

1995, Sept. 25

221	A55	200d multicolored	*4.25*	*4.25*

A56 A57

1995, Sept. 25

222	A56	100d multicolored	2.00	2.00

World Post Day.

1995, Oct. 12

Flowers: No. 223: a, 100d, Simphyandra hofmannii. b, 200d, Lilium bosniacum.

223	A57	Pair, #a.-b.	5.50	5.50

Fish A58

No. 224: a, 100d, Aulopyge hugeli. b, 200d, Paraphoxinus alepidotus.

1995, Oct. 12

224	A58	Pair, #a.-b.	5.50	5.50

Children's Week A59

1995, Oct. 12

225	A59	100d multicolored	2.00	2.00

Electric Tram System, Sarajevo, Cent. A60

1995, Oct. 12

226	A60	200d multicolored	3.75	3.75

Bridges A61

Designs: 20d, Kozija, Sarajevo. 30d, Arslanagica, Trebinje. 35d, Latinska, Sarajevo. 50d, Old Bridge, Mostar. 100d, Visegrad.

1995, Dec. 12

227-231	A61	Set of 5	4.25	4.25

Christmas A62

Designs: 100d, Visiting friends. 200d, Madonna and Child, vert.

1995, Dec. 24

232-233	A62	Set of 2	5.25	5.25

A63 A64

Designs: 30d, Queen Jelena's tomb.

1995, Dec. 31

234	A63	30d multicolored	.70	.70

1995, Dec. 31

Design: Husein Gradascevic (1802-33).

235	A64	35d multicolored	.70	.70

Mirza Safvet Basagic (1870-1934) — A65

1995, Dec. 31

236	A65	100d multicolored	1.75	1.75

Religious Diversity A66

1995, Dec. 31

237	A66	35d multicolored	.70	.70

Destruction of Olympic Stadium, Sarajevo — A67

35d, Stadium, various skaters. 100d, Stadium ablaze, vert.

1995, Dec. 31

238-239	A67	Set of 2	3.00	3.00

Famous Women — A68

Europa: 80d, Bahrija Hadzic (1904-93), opera singer. 120d, Nasiha Hadzic (1932-95), writer.

1996, Apr. 15 ***Perf. 15***
240-241 A68 Set of 2 *4.50 4.50*

UNICEF, 50th Anniv. — A69

Designs: a, 50d, Child stepping on land mine. b, 150d, Child's handprint.

1996, Apr. 15 ***Perf. 11½***
242 A69 Pair, #a.-b. 4.00 4.00

Bobovac Castle — A70 Bairam Festival — A71

1996, May 5 ***Perf. 11½***
243 A70 35d multicolored .70 .70

1996, May 5 ***Perf. 14***
244 A71 80d multicolored 1.50 1.50

No. 244 was issued in sheets of 2. Value $3.50.

Sarajevo Town Hall, Cent. A72

1996, May 5 ***Perf. 11½***
245 A72 80d multicolored 1.40 1.40

Bosnian Journalists Assoc., Cent. A73

1996, May 5
246 A73 100d multicolored 2.10 2.10

Essen '96, Intl. Philatelic Expo A74

1996, May 25 ***Perf. 11½***
247 A74 200d multicolored 3.75 3.75

1996 Summer Olympic Games, Atlanta — A75

No. 248: a, 120d, Baron de Coubertin. b, 80d, Olympic Torch. c, 30d, Runners. d, 35d, Atlanta Games emblem.

1996, May 25
248 A75 Block of 4, #a.-d. 5.00 5.00

Background of No. 248 differs with location on sheet.

Alexander Graham Bell's Telephone, 120th Anniv. A76

1996, July 10 ***Perf. 11½***
249 A76 80d multicolored 1.50 1.50

Extension of Privleges to Dubrovnik by Ban Stepan II, 1333 A77

1996, July 10
250 A77 100d multicolored 1.90 1.90

Use of Mail Vans in Bosnia, Cent. A78

1996, July 10
251 A78 120d multicolored 2.00 2.00

Flowers — A79

No. 252: a, 30d, Campanula hercegovina. b, 35d, Iris bosniaca.

1996, July 10
252 A79 Pair, #a.-b. 1.40 1.40

Printed checkerwise on the sheet.

Dogs A80

No. 253: a, 35d, Barak. b, 80d, Tornjak.

1996, July 10
253 A80 Pair, #a.-b. 2.50 2.50

Printed checkerwise on the sheet.

SOS Children's Village, Sarajevo — A81

1996, Sept. 1
254 A81 100d multicolored 1.75 1.75

A83

A84

Traditional costumes — No. 255: a, 50d, Moslem, Bjelasnice. b, 80d, Croatian. c, 100d, Moslem, Sarajevo.

Uniforms — No. 256: a, 35d, Bogomil soldier. b, 80d, Austro-Hungarian rifleman. c, 100d, Turkish light cavalry. d, 120d, Medieval Bosnian king.

1996, Sept. 20
255 A83 Strip of 3, #a.-c. + label 3.75 3.75
256 A84 Strip of 4, #a.-d. 6.00 6.00

Winter Festival, Sarajevo A85

1996, Nov. 25
257 A85 100d multicolored 1.75 1.75

Bosnia Day — A86

1996, Nov. 25
258 A86 120d Map, natl. arms 2.25 2.25

Christmas A87

1996, Dec. 21
259 A87 100d multicolored 2.00 2.00

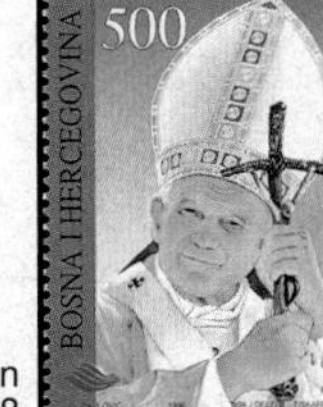

Visit by Pope John Paul II — A88

1996, Dec. 21 ***Perf. 14***
260 A88 500d multicolored 10.00 10.00

Archaeological Finds — A89

Designs: 35d, Paleolithic rock carving, Badanj. 50d, Neolithic ceramic head, Butmir. 80d, Bronze age bird wagon, Glasinac.

Walls of Daorson, Illyria — No. 264: a, 100d, Walls, rock face at L. b, 120d, Low wall outside city wall.

1997, Mar. 31 ***Perf. 15***
261-263 A89 Set of 3 3.00 3.00

Souvenir Sheet

264 A89 Sheet of 2, #a.-b. 4.25 4.25

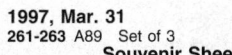

Children's Week — A90

Bairam Festival — A91

1997, Apr. 15 ***Perf. 11½***
265 A90 100d multicolored 1.75 1.75

1997, Apr. 15 ***Perf. 11½***
266 A91 200d Ferhad Pasha Mosque 3.75 3.75

A92

1997, Apr. 25 ***Perf. 14***
267 A92 100d multicolored 1.75 1.75

Mujaga Komadina (1839-1925), mayor of Mostar.

A93

Europa (Myths & Legends): 100d, Trojan warriors, map. 120d, Man on prayer mat, castle from The Miraculous Spring of Ajvatovica.

1997, May 3 ***Perf. 11½***
268-269 A93 Set of 2 *4.25 4.25*

Greenpeace, 25th Anniv. — A94

Rainbow Warrior, inscribed: a, 35d, Grace. b, 80d, Dorreboom. c, 100d, Beltra. d, 120d, Morgan.

1997, May 25
270 A94 Block or strip of 4, #a.-d. 8.00 8.00

Third Intl. Film Festival, Sarajevo A95

1997, June 15
271 A95 110d multicolored 2.25 2.25

Mediterranean Games, Bari — A96

Designs: 40d, Games emblem. 130d, Boxing, basketball, kick boxing.

1997, June 15
272-273 A96 Set of 2 3.25 3.25

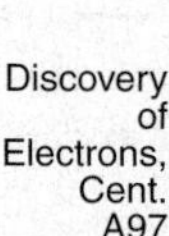

Discovery of Electrons, Cent. A97

1997, June 25
274 A97 40d multicolored 1.00 1.00

Vasco da Gama's Voyage Around Africa, 500th Anniv. — A98

1997, June 25
275 A98 110d multicolored 2.00 2.00

Stamp Day — A99

1997, June 25
276 A99 130d multicolored 2.40 2.40

Railroads in Bosnia & Herzegovina, 125th Anniv. — A100

1997, June 25
277 A100 150d multicolored 3.00 3.00

Fauna — A101 A102

No. 278: a, 40d, Dinaromys bogdanovi. b, 80d, Triturus alpestris.
No. 279: a, 40d, Oxytropis prenja. b, 110d, Dianthus freynii.

1997, Aug. 25
278 A101 Pair, #a.-b. 2.50 2.50
279 A101 Pair, #a.-b. 3.25 3.25

1997, Aug. 25

World Peace Day: a, 50d, Sweden, Switzerland, Australia & other flags. b, 60d, Flags, globe showing Europe, Africa. c, 70d, Flags, globe showing North & South America. d, 110d, US, UK, Canadian & other flags.

280 A102 Strip of 4, #a.-d. 5.50 5.50

Great Sarajevo Fire, 300th Anniv. — A103

1997, Sept. 15
281 A103 110d multicolored 2.25 2.25

Architecture — A104

Designs: 40d, House with attic. 50d, Tiled stove, door. 130d, Three-storied house.

1997, Sept. 15
282-284 A104 Set of 3 4.00 4.00

Italian Pioneer Corps Aid in Reconstruction of Sarajevo — A105

1997, Nov. 1 ***Perf. 14***
285 A105 1.40m multicolored 2.50 2.50

Famous Men A106

1.30m, Augustin Tin Ujevic (1891-1955), writer. 2m, Zaim Imamovic (1920-94), singer, vert.

1997, Nov. 1 ***Perf. 11½***
286-287 A106 Set of 2 6.25 6.25

Diana, Princess of Wales (1961-97) — A107

1997, Nov. 3 ***Perf. 14***
288 A107 2.50m multicolored 4.25 4.25

Gnijezdo, by Fikret Libovac A108

Sarajevo Library, by Nusret Pasic A109

1997, Nov. 6 ***Perf. 11½***
289-290 A108-A109 Set of 2 2.25 2.25

Samac-Sarajevo Railway, 50th Anniv. — A110

1997, Nov. 17 ***Perf. 14***
291 A110 35pf multicolored .70 .70

A111 A112

Religious Holidays: 50pf, Nativity Scene, Orthodox Christmas. No. 293, 1.10m, Wreath on door, Christmas. No. 294, 1.10m, Pupils before teacher, Hagada.

1997, Dec. 22 ***Perf. 11½***
292-294 A111 Set of 3 5.00 5.00

1998, Jan. 15 ***Perf. 14***

Designs: a, 35pf, Sports. b, 1m, Games emblem.

295 A112 Sheet of 2, #a.-b. 2.50 2.50

1998 Winter Olympic Games, Nagano.

Bairam Festival — A113

1998, Jan. 28
296 A113 1m Mosque fountain 1.90 1.90

Ahmed Muradbegovic (1898-1972), Writer — A114

1998, Mar. 20
297 A114 1.50m multicolored 3.00 3.00

Fortified Towns — A115

No. 298: a, 35pf, Zvornik. b, 70pf, Bihac. c, 1m, Pocitelj. d, 1.20m, Gradacac.

1998, Mar. 20
298 A115 Booklet pane of 4, #a.-d. 6.50 6.50
Complete booklet, #298 6.50

A116 A117

1998, May 5 ***Perf. 11½***
299 A116 1.10m multicolored *3.50 3.50*

Intl. Theater Festival, Sarajevo, Europa.

1998, May 5

Former Presidents of Univ. of Arts and Science: 40pf, Branislav Durdev (1908-93). 70pf, Alojz Benac (1914-92). 1.30m, Edhem Camo (1909-96).

300-302 A117 Set of 3 4.50 4.50

A118 A119

Ciconia Ciconia — No. 303: a, 70pf, Three in water. b, 90pf, Two in flight. c, 1.10m, Two in nest. d, 1.30m, Adult, chicks.

1998, May 5
303 A118 Strip of 4, #a.-d. 7.50 7.50

1998, May 22
304 A119 2m Sheet with 2 labels 3.75 3.75

World Congress of Intl. League of Humanists, Sarajevo.

1998 World Cup Soccer Championships, France — A120

50pf, Soccer balls. 1m, Map, soccer ball. 1.50m, Asim Ferhatovic Hase (1934-87), soccer player.

1998, May 22 ***Perf. 14½***
305-307 A120 Set of 3 5.50 5.50

A121

A122

1998, July 20 ***Perf. 11½***
308 A121 1.10m multicolored 2.25 2.25

Sarajevo Tunnel, 5th anniv.

1998, July 30

Mushrooms: 50pf, Morchella esculenta. 80pf, Cantharellus cibarius. 1.10m, Boletus edulis. 1.35m, Amanita caesarea.

309-312 A122 Set of 4 7.00 7.00

Paris Subway A123

1998, Aug. 30
313 A123 2m violet blue & green 3.50 3.50

Henri Dunant — A124

1998, Sept. 14 ***Perf. 14***
314 A124 50pf multicolored 1.00 1.00

Intl. Red Cross fight against tuberculosis.

Cities — A125

1998, Sept. 24
315 A125 5pf Travnik .30 .30
316 A125 38pf Sarajevo .65 .65

Chess — A126

Bosnian players — No. 317: a, 20pf, Woman at chess board. b, 40pf, Silver medal team, 31st Chess Olympiad. c, 60pf, Women's team, 32nd Chess Olympiad. d, 80pf, Men, Women's teams, 11th European Chess Championships.

1998, Sept. 24
317 A126 Sheet of 4, #a.-d. 3.75 3.75

A127

A128

1998, Oct. 9 ***Perf. 11½***
318 A127 1m multicolored 1.75 1.75

World Post Day.

1998, Oct. 23
319 A128 80pf Musical instruments 1.50 1.50

Intl. Day of Disabled Persons A129

1998, Dec. 3
320 A129 1m multicolored 1.75 1.75

Mt. Bjelasnica A130

1998, Dec. 3
321 A130 1m multicolored 1.75 1.75

Universal Declaration of Human Rights, 50th Anniv. — A131

1998, Dec. 10 ***Perf. 14½***
322 A131 1.35m multicolored 2.50 2.50

New Year A132

Christmas — A133

Designs: 1m, Child's drawing. 1.50m, Fr. Andeo Zvizdovic (1420?-98).

1998, Dec. 18 ***Perf. 11½***
323 A132 1m multicolored 2.25 2.25
324 A133 1.50m multicolored 2.25 2.25

School Anniversaries — A134

Designs: No. 325, 40pf, First Sarajevo High School, 120th anniv. No. 326, 40pf, Sarajevo University, 50th anniv., vert.

1999, Apr. 22 **Litho.** ***Perf. 11¾***
325-326 A134 Set of 2 1.40 1.40

Flora and Fauna A135

80pf, Pigeons. 1.10m, Knautia sarajevensis.

1999, Apr. 22 **Litho.** ***Perf. 11¾***
327-328 A135 Set of 2 4.25 4.25

First Manned Moon Landing, 30th Anniv. — A136

1999, May 20 **Litho.** ***Perf. 11¾***
329 A136 2m multicolored 3.50 3.50

Una River — A137

1999, May 20
330 A137 2m multicolored *4.25 4.25*

Europa

Gorazde A137a

1999, June 9 **Litho.** ***Perf. 14x14¼***
330A A137a 40pf multi .70 .70

World Environmental Protection Day — A138

1999, June 15 **Litho.** ***Perf. 11¾***
331 A138 80pf Buna River Well-spring 1.50 1.50

Philex France 99 — A139

1999, June 15
332 A139 2m multicolored 3.50 3.50

Special Olympics A140

1999, June 15
333 A140 50pf multicolored .90 .90

Bosnia & Herzegovina Postage Stamps, 120th Anniv. — A141

1999, July 1
334 A141 1m multicolored 2.00 2.00

UPU, 125th Anniv. — A142

1999, July 1 **Litho.** ***Perf. 11¾***
335 A142 1.50m multi 3.00 3.00

Minerals A143

Designs: 40pf, Tuzlite. 60pf, Siderite. 1.20m, Hijelofan. 1.80m, Quartz, vert.

1999, July 27 **Litho.** ***Perf. 11¾***
336-339 A143 Set of 4 7.75 7.75

Dzuzovi Mehmed Pasha Sokolovic Koran Manuscript A144

1999, Sept. 23
340 A144 1.50m multicolored 2.50 2.50

Kursumli Medresa Library, Founded 1537 — A145

1999, Sept. 23
341 A145 1m multicolored 1.75 1.75

Radiology in Bosnia & Herzegovina, Cent. — A146

1999, Oct. 5
342 A146 90pf multicolored 1.75 1.75

Handija Kasevljakovic (1888-1959), Historian — A147

1999, Oct. 5
343 A147 1.30m multicolored 2.25 2.25

25th European Chess Club Cup Finals — A148

1999, Oct. 29 Litho. *Perf. 14*
344 A148 1.10m multicolored 2.25 2.25

Hvalov Zbornik, Book in Glagolitic Text — A149

1999, Sept. 23 Litho. *Perf. 11¾*
345 A149 1.10m multicolored 2.00 2.00

Sarajevo Summit A150

1999, July 29 Litho. *Perf. 14*
346 A150 2m multi 3.75 3.75

Expo 2000, Hanover A151

1999, Nov. 9 Litho. *Perf. 11¾*
347 A151 1m multi 1.75 1.75

Painting by Afan Ramic A152

1999, Nov. 25
348 A152 1.20m multi 2.00 2.00

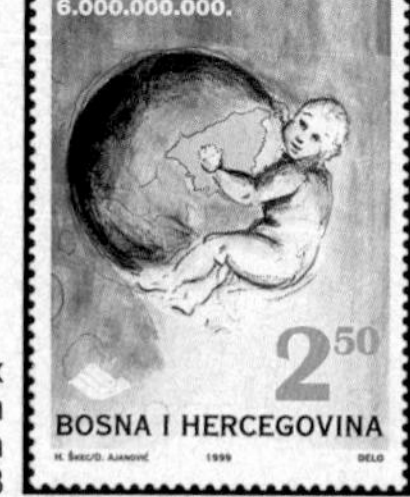

Birth of Six Billionth Person A153

1999, Nov. 25 *Perf. 14*
349 A153 2.50m multi 4.75 4.75

Souvenir Sheet

Bjelasnica Weather Observatory, 105th Anniv. — A154

1999, Dec. 15
350 A154 1.10m multi 2.00 2.00

Sarajevo Philharmonic A155

Sarajevo Intl. Music Festival A156

1999, Dec. 20
351 A155 40pf multi .75 .75
352 A156 1.10m multi 1.75 1.75

Mehmed Spaho (1883-1939), Politician — A157

2000, Mar. 15 *Perf. 11¾*
353 A157 1m multi 1.90 1.90

Bairam Festival — A158

2000, Mar. 15
354 A158 1.10m multi 2.25 2.25

Amateur Radio in Bosnia and Herzegovina, 50th Anniv. — A159

2000, Mar. 15
355 A159 1.50m multi 3.00 3.00

Oriental Institute, Sarajevo, 50th Anniv. — A160

2000, Mar. 15
356 A160 2m multi 4.00 4.00

Souvenir Sheet

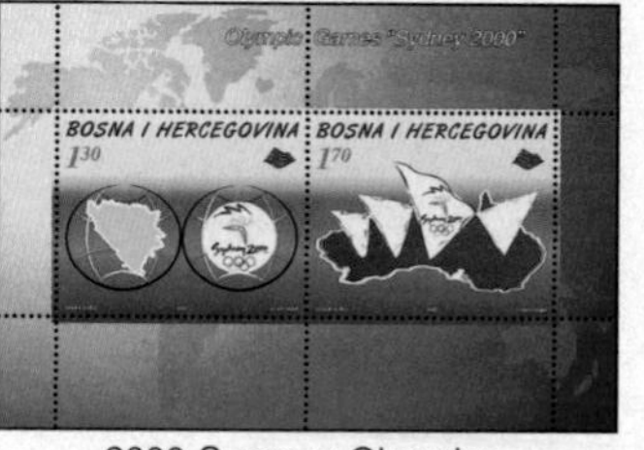

2000 Summer Olympics, Sydney — A161

Emblem of Sydney Olympics and map of: a, 1.30m, Bosnia & Herzegovina. b, 1.70m, Australia.

2000, Apr. 10 Litho. *Perf. 14¾*
357 A161 Sheet of 2, #a-b 6.25 6.25

Europa, 2000
Common Design Type

2000, May 9 *Perf. 11¾*
358 CD17 2m multi *4.75 4.75*

Birds A162

1m, Gyps fulvus. 1.50m, Platalea leucorodia.

2000, May 9 Litho. *Perf. 11¾*
359-360 A162 Set of 2 5.00 5.00

Lake Boracko A163

River Una Emeralds — A164

2000, May 9
361 A163 40pf multi .85 .85
362 A164 1m multi 1.90 1.90

World Environmental Protection Day.

Souvenir Sheet

Greenpeace — A165

a, 50pf, Fish. b, 60pf, Lobster. c, 90pf, Anemones. d, 1.50m, Diver on shipwreck.

2000, May 9 *Perf. 11¾x11½*
363 A165 Sheet of 4, #a-d 7.00 7.00

First Zeppelin Flight, Cent. A166

2000, June 10 *Perf. 11¾*
364 A166 1.50m multi 3.00 3.00

Cities — A167

2000, June 9 Litho. *Perf. 14*
365 A167 50pf Zenica 1.15 1.15
366 A167 1m Mostar 1.50 1.50
367 A167 1.10m Bihac 1.75 1.75
368 A167 1.50m Tuzla, vert. 2.50 2.50
Nos. 365-368 (4) 6.90 6.90

Vranduk A168

Kraljeva Sutjeska A169

2000, Sept. 20 *Perf. 11¾x11½*
369 A168 1.30m multi 2.00 2.00
370 A169 1.50m multi 3.00 3.00

The Adventures of Tom Sawyer, by Mark Twain A170

2000, Sept. 20
371 A170 1.50m multi 3.00 3.00

Souvenir Sheet

Millennium — A171

2000, Sept. 20 ***Perf. 11¾***

372 A171 2m multi 4.00 4.00

No. 372 contains one 29x57mm 80pf "stamp," and one 57x57mm 1.20m "stamp," but both lack the country name, which appears only in the sheet margin.

Intl. Children's Week — A172

2000, Oct. 5 ***Perf. 11½x11¾***

373 A172 1.60m multi 3.25 3.25

Paintings A173

Paintings by: 60pf, J. Mujezinovic. 80pf, I. Seremet.

2000, Oct. 5 ***Perf. 11¾x11½***

374-375 A173 Set of 2 2.75 2.75

UN High Commissioner for Refugees, 50th Anniv. — A174

2000, Dec. 14 ***Perf. 11¾x11½***

376 A174 1m multi 2.00 2.00

Cities — A175

2001, Mar. 22 ***Perf. 14***

377	A175	10pf Tesanj, vert.	.25	.25
378	A175	20pf Bugojno	.40	.40
379	A175	30pf Konjic	.50	.50
380	A175	35pf Zivinice	1.00	1.00
381	A175	2m Cazin	3.75	3.75
		Nos. 377-381 (5)	5.90	5.90

Animals — A176

No. 382, vert.: a, 90pf, Alcedo atthis. b, 1.10m, Bombycilla garrulus. No. 383: a, 1.10m, Equus caballus facing right. b, 1.90m, Equus caballus facing left.

2001, Mar. 22 **Litho.** ***Perf. 11¾***

382 A176 Horiz. pair, #a-b 4.50 4.50

Perf. 11¾x11½

383 A176 Horiz. pair, #a-b 5.00 5.00

Walt Disney (1901-66) — A177

Perf. 11½x11¾

2001, Mar. 22 **Litho.**

384 A177 1.10m multi 2.00 2.00

Shell Fossils — A178

Denominations in: a, 1.30m, Blue. b, 1.80m, Black.

2001, Mar. 22 ***Perf. 11¾x11½***

385 A178 Horiz. pair, #a-b 6.25 6.25

Souvenir Sheet

Comic Strips — A179

Inscriptions: a, Ti si moje janje. b, Ti si moj medo. c, Ti si moja maca. d, Ti si moj cvijet. e, Ti si moje pile.

2001, Mar. 22 **Litho.** ***Perf. 11¾***

Granite Paper

386 A179 30pf Sheet of 5, #a-e 3.00 3.00

See No. 419.

Souvenir Sheet

Europa — A180

2001, Apr. 10 ***Perf. 11½x11¾***

387 A180 2m multi 4.00 4.00

Souvenir Sheet

Bosnia Institute, Sarajevo — A181

2001, May 25 **Litho.** ***Perf. 14***

388 A181 1.10m multi 2.25 2.25

Souvenir Sheet

Emir Balic, Mostar Bridge Diver — A182

2001, May 30 ***Perf. 11½x11¾***

389 A182 2m multi 4.00 4.00

14th Mediterranean Games, Tunis — A183

2001, May 30 **Litho.** ***Perf. 14x14¼***

390 A183 1.30m multi 2.50 2.50

Ferrari Race Cars — A184

No. 391: a, 40pf, 15954 625 F1. b, 60pf, 1970 312 B. c, 1.30m, 1978 312 T3. d, 1.70m, 1983 126 C3.

2001, June 20 **Litho.** ***Perf. 14x14¼***

391 A184 Block of 4, #a-d 7.25 7.25

Zeljeznic, Soccer Champions — A185

2001, July 18

392 A185 1m multi 1.75 1.75

Nobel Prizes, Cent. A186

2001, July 18

393 A186 1.50m multi 3.00 3.00

Charlie Chaplin (1889-1977) A187

2001, July 18 ***Perf. 14x13¾***

394 A187 1.60m multi 3.25 3.25

Art by Edin Numankadic — A188

Perf. 12½x12¾

2001, Sept. 10 **Litho.**

395 A188 80pf multi 1.50 1.50

Portions of the design were applied by a thermographic process producing a shiny, raised effect.

David, by Michelangelo, 500th Anniv. — A189

2001, Sept. 10

396 A189 2m multi 3.75 3.75

Portions of the design were applied by a thermographic process producing a shiny, raised effect.

Breastfeeding Week — A190

2001, Oct. 1 **Litho.** ***Perf. 14***

397 A190 1.10m multi 2.25 2.25

World Post Day — A191

2001, Oct. 9
398 A191 1.30m multi 3.50 3.50

Horse-drawn Mail Delivery Railcar — A192

2001, Oct. 30 Litho. *Perf. 14¼x14*
399 A192 1.10m multi 2.25 2.25

Alija Bejtic (1920-81), Historian — A193

2001, Nov. 10 Litho. *Perf. 14*
400 A193 80pf multi 1.50 1.50

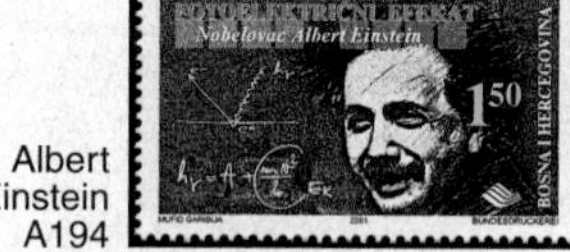

Albert Einstein A194

2001, Dec. 14
401 A194 1.50m multi 3.00 3.00

Musical Group "Indexi" A195

2002, Apr. 5 Litho. *Perf. 14*
402 A195 38pf multi .75 .75

Mustafa Ejubovic (Sejh Jujo, 1651-1707), Writer — A196

2002, Apr. 15 Litho. *Perf. 13¾x14*
403 A196 1m multi 1.75 1.75

Juraj Neidhardt (1901-79), Architect A197

2002, Apr. 15 *Perf. 14x13¾*
404 A197 1m multi 1.75 1.75

Dr. Sevala Zildzic-Iblizovic (1903-78) — A198

2002, Apr. 15 *Perf. 13¾x14*
405 A198 1.30m multi 2.75 2.75

Sarajevo's Candidacy to Host 2010 Winter Olympics — A199

2002, Apr. 15 Litho. *Perf. 13¾x14*
406 A199 1.50m multi 3.00 3.00

Intl. Earth Day — A200

2002, Apr. 15 Litho. *Perf. 13¾*
407 A200 2m multi 3.50 3.50

Bosnia & Herzegovina Scouting Organization, 80th Anniv. — A201

2002, Apr. 20 Litho. *Perf. 14x13¾*
408 A201 1m multi 2.00 2.00

Europa — A202

2002, Apr. 20 *Perf. 13¾x14*
409 A202 2.50m multi *5.00 5.00*

Independence, 10th Anniv. — A203

2002, Apr. 20 *Perf. 14x13¾*
410 A203 2.50m multi 4.75 4.75

Souvenir Sheet

Sarajevo Fire Fighters — A204

2002, Apr. 20 *Perf. 13¾x14*
411 A204 2.20m multi 4.25 4.25

Flowers — A205

Designs: 1m, Gentiana dinarica. 1.50m, Aquilegia dinarica.

2002, Apr. 20 Litho. *Perf. 13¾x14*
412-413 A205 Set of 2 5.00 5.00

Butterflies — A206

Designs: 1.50m, Parnassus apollo. 2.50m, Iphiclides podalirius.

2002, Apr. 20 Litho. *Perf. 13¾x14*
414-415 A206 Set of 2 7.50 7.50

Traditional Food A207

2002, June 28 Litho. *Perf. 14*
416 A207 1.10m multi 2.25 2.25

30th Una River Regatta A208

2002, June 28
417 A208 1.30m multi 2.75 2.75

Souvenir Sheet

Ships — A209

No. 418: a, 1.20m, Galley. b, 1.80m, Galleon.

2002, June 28
418 A209 Sheet of 2, #a-b 6.00 6.00

Comic Strips Type of 2001

Inscriptions: a, Ako mi se ne javis! b, Ako me ne volis! c, Ako ti dosadujem! d, Ako me ne odgovoris! e, Ako me foliras.

2002, June 28
419 A179 40pf Sheet of 5, #a-e 4.00 4.00

Napredak, Croatian Cultural Organization, Cent. — A210

Perf. 13¾x13½
2002, Sept. 14 Litho.
420 A210 1m multi 2.00 2.00

Mountaineering, Cent. — A211

2002, Sept. 14 *Perf. 13½x13¾*
421 A211 1m multi 1.75 1.75

Sarajevo Synagogue, Cent. A212

2002, Sept. 14
422 A212 2m multi 4.00 4.00

Miniature Sheet

Handicrafts — A213

No. 423: a, 80pf, Ironsmithing. b, 1.10m, Basketry. c, 1.20m, Filigree. d, 1.30m, Embroidery.

2002, Oct. 10
423 A213 Sheet of 4, #a-d 8.50 8.50

Bosnia & Herzegovina Flag — A214

2002, Nov. 20
424 A214 1m multi 2.00 2.00

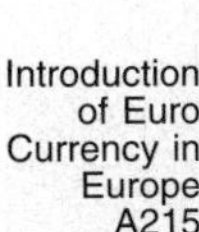

Introduction of Euro Currency in Europe A215

2002, Nov. 20
425 A215 2m multi 3.75 3.75

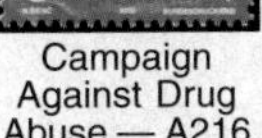

Campaign Against Drug Abuse — A216

Mak Dizdar (1917-71), Writer — A218

Mother and Child Institute — A217

2002, Dec. 10 ***Perf. 14***
426 A216 10pf multi .60 .60

2002, Dec. 10
427 A217 38pf multi 1.10 1.10

2002, Dec. 10
428 A218 1m multi 2.00 2.00

Coins — A219

Paintings by Mersad Berber (b. 1940) — A220

Coins from reign of: 20pf, King Tvrtko (1376-91). 30pf, King Stjepan Tomas (1443-61). 50pf, King Stjepan Tomasevic (1461-63).

2002, Dec. 10
429-431 A219 Set of 3 1.75 1.75

2002, Dec. 10 ***Perf. 13¾ (40pf), 14***

Designs: 40pf, Horse's head (34x34mm). 1.10m, Portrait of a woman. 1.50m, Angel statue, two women, horiz.

432-434 A220 Set of 3 6.25 6.25

Archbishop Josip Stadler (1843-1918) — A221

2003, Jan. 24 **Litho.** ***Perf. 14***
435 A221 50pf multi 2.00 2.00

No. 435 was sold by the post offices of the Moslem Administration as well as the Croat Administration.

Preporod, Bosnian Cultural Association, Cent. — A222

2003, Feb. 20 **Litho.** ***Perf. 13x13¼***
436 A222 1m multi 2.00 2.00

Portions of the design were applied by a thermographic process producing a shiny, raised effect.

2006 European Foresters' Competition in Nordic Skiing, Sarajevo — A223

2003, Feb. 20 ***Perf. 13¼x13½***
437 A223 1m multi 1.75 1.75

Mother and Child, by Omer Mujadzic (1903-91) A224

2003, Mar. 31 ***Perf. 13¼***
438 A224 70pf multi 1.50 1.50

Svetozar Zimonjic (1928-99), Electrical Engineer — A225

2003, Mar. 31 ***Perf. 13½x13¼***
439 A225 90pf multi 1.75 1.75

Bosnian Sitting Volleyball Team, 2002 World Champions — A226

2003, Mar. 31 ***Perf. 13½x13***
440 A226 1m multi 2.00 2.00

Flowers — A227

No. 441: a, Leontopodium alpinum (38mm diameter). b, Gentiana symphyandra.

2003, Mar. 31 ***Perf. 12¾***
441 A227 90pf Pair, #a-b 3.75 3.75

Europa — A228

2003, May 9 ***Perf. 13½x13¼***
442 A228 2.50m multi 4.75 4.75
a. Booklet pane of 4 19.00 —
Complete booklet, #442a 25.00

Visit of Pope John Paul II — A229

Perf. 13¼x13½
2003, June 22 **Litho.**
443 A229 1.50m multi 3.00 3.00

Discovery of Structure of DNA, 50th Anniv. — A230

2003, June 30 ***Perf. 13***
444 A230 50pf multi 1.00 1.00

Souvenir Sheet

San Monstruma, Comic Strip by Enki Bilal — A231

Designs: a, Man on roof of building (30x24mm). b, Hotel and street (30x24mm). c, Man and woman (40x26mm). d, Woman and two men (40x26mm).

Perf. 13¼ (#a, b), 13 (#c, d)
2003, June 30
445 A231 50pf Sheet of 4, #a-d 4.00 4.00

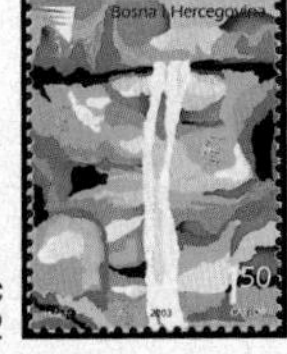

Skakavac Waterfall — A232

2003, Sept. 30 **Litho.** ***Perf. 13½***
446 A232 1.50m multi 3.00 3.00

Printed in sheets of 8 + 2 labels.

Decorations in Cekrekci Musilhudin Mosque — A233

Decorations in Hajji Sinan Dervish Convent — A234

2003, Sept. 30 ***Perf. 13¼***
447 A233 1m multi 2.00 2.00
Perf. 13¼
448 A234 2m multi 4.00 4.00

Children's Week A235

2003, Oct. 3 ***Perf. 13¼x13½***
449 A235 50pf multi 1.00 1.00

Self-Adhesive
Serpentine Die Cut 12½
450 A235 50pf multi *24.00 24.00*

Souvenir Sheet

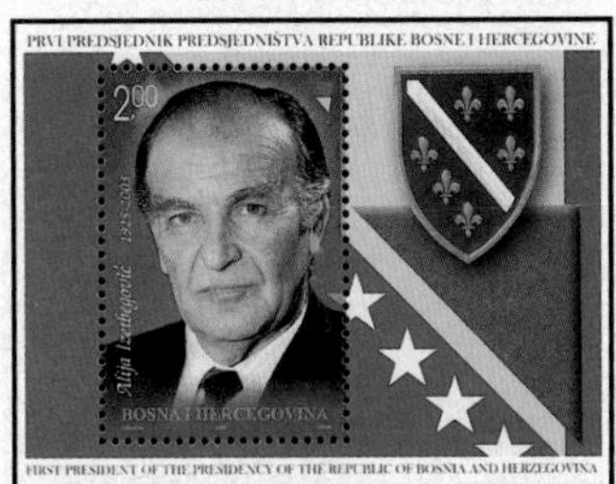

Pres. Alija Izetbegovic (1925-2003) — A236

2003, Nov. 27 ***Perf. 13½x13¼***
451 A236 2m multi 4.00 4.00

Souvenir Sheet

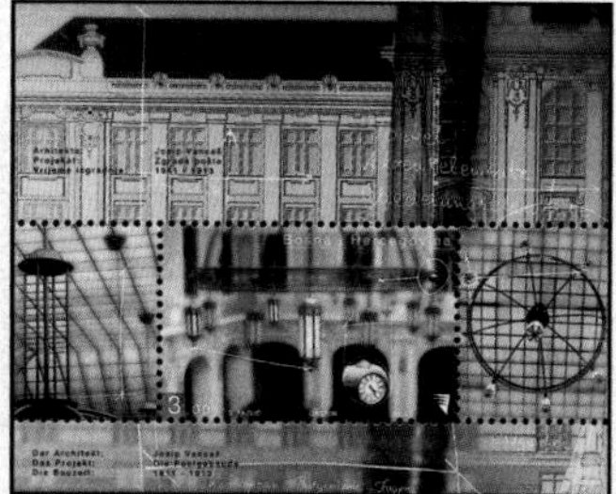

Sarajevo Post Office, by Josip Vancas, 90th Anniv. — A237

2003, Nov. 27 ***Perf. 13***
452 A237 3m multi 6.00 6.00

Animals — A238

Designs: 30pf, Rupicapra rupicapra balcanica. 50pf, Ursus arctos bosniensis.

2003, Dec. 9 ***Perf. 13¼***
453-454 A238 Set of 2 2.75 2.75

Christmas A239

2003, Dec. 18 **Litho.** ***Perf. 13¼***
455 A239 20pf multi .45 .45

Pleminitas II, by Dzevad Hozo — A240

2003, Dec. 18 ***Perf. 13½x13¼***
456 A240 10pf multi .35 .35

Painting by Ibrahim Ljubovic — A241

2003, Dec. 20 ***Perf. 12½***
457 A241 1.50m multi 3.00 3.00

Powered Flight, Cent. A242

Perf. 13¼x13½
2003, Dec. 20 **Litho.**
458 A242 1m multi 2.00 2.00

Bayram Festival — A243

2004, Jan. 19 **Litho.** ***Perf. 13¼***
459 A243 50pf multi 1.00 1.00

Ban Kulin, 800th Anniv. of Death — A244

2004, Jan. 26 ***Perf. 12½***
460 A244 50pf multi 1.00 1.00

Love A245

2004, Feb. 2 ***Perf. 13***
461 A245 2m multi 4.00 4.00

Values are for stamps with surrounding selvage.

Sarajevo Winter Olympics, 20th Anniv. — A246

2004, Feb. 7 ***Perf. 13¼***
462 A241 1.50m multi + 2 flanking labels 2.50 2.50

Cities A247

Designs: 20pf, Jajce, vert. 50pf, Jablanica. 2m, Stolac. 4m, Gradacac, vert. 5m, Fojnica.

2004 ***Perf. 13½x13¼, 13¼x13½***

463	A247	20pf multi	.40	.40
464	A247	50pf multi	1.00	1.00
465	A247	2m multi	3.75	3.75
466	A247	4m multi	7.75	7.75
467	A247	5m multi	10.00	10.00
		Nos. 463-467 (5)	22.90	22.90

Issued: 20pf, 50pf, 4/5; 2m, 3/15; 4m, 5m, 2/23.

FIFA (Fédération Internationale de Football Association), Cent. — A248

2004, Mar. 31 ***Perf. 13***
468 A248 2m multi 4.00 4.00

Flora — A249

No. 469 — Orchids: a, 1.50m, Cattleya intermedia. b, 2m, Brassavola David Sander.
No. 470 — Succulents: a, 1.50m, Aloe barbadensis. b, 2.50, Carnegiea gigantea.

2004, Mar. 31 ***Perf. 13½x13¼***
Vert. Pairs, #a-b
469-470 A249 Set of 2 13.00 13.00

Zodiac Signs — A250

Nos. 471 and 472: a, Aries. b, Taurus. c, Gemini. d, Cancer. e, Leo. f, Virgo. g, Libra. h, Scorpio. i, Sagittarius. j, Capricorn. k, Aquarius. l, Pisces.

2004, Apr. 15 ***Perf. 13¼***
471 A250 50pf Sheet of 12, #a-l 11.50 11.50

Booklet Stamps
Self-Adhesive
Serpentine Die Cut 12½

472 Booklet of 12 12.50 12.50
a.-l. A250 50pf Any single .90 .90

Europa — A251

No. 473: a, 1m, Clock on skis. b, 1.50m, Clocks at beach.

2004, Apr. 26 ***Perf. 13½x13¼***
473 A251 Pair, #a-b 5.00 5.00
c. Booklet pane, 3 each #473a-473b *14.50* 14.50
Complete booklet, #473c *16.00* 16.00

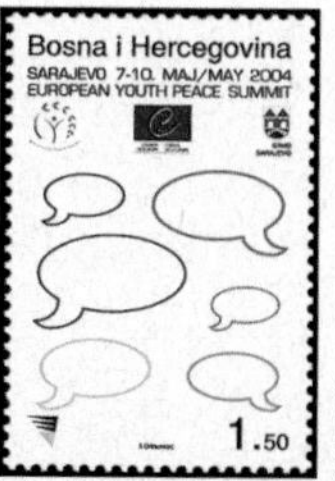

European Youth Peace Summit — A252

2004, Apr. 26 **Litho.**
474 A252 1.50m multi 3.25 3.25

Greetings — A253

2004, May 15 ***Perf. 13***
475 Horiz. pair, #a-b, with alternating labels 4.00 4.00
a. A253 50pf Clown and balloons 1.00 1.00
b. A253 1.50m Bride and groom 3.00 3.00

Souvenir Sheet

Bees — A254

No. 476: a, On flower. b, In flight.

2004, May 15 ***Perf. 13x13¼***
476 A254 2m Sheet of 2, #a-b 7.50 7.50

Reconstruction of Old Bridge, Mostar — A255

Old Bridge: 50pf, Close-up. 1m, From distance, horiz.

Perf. 13½x13¼, 13¼x13½
2004, June 23
477-478 A255 Set of 2 3.25 3.25
478a Souvenir sheet, #477-478, perf. 13 3.25 3.25

No. 478a is rouletted in five sections with stamps which have printer's inscription at bottom, in the central section.

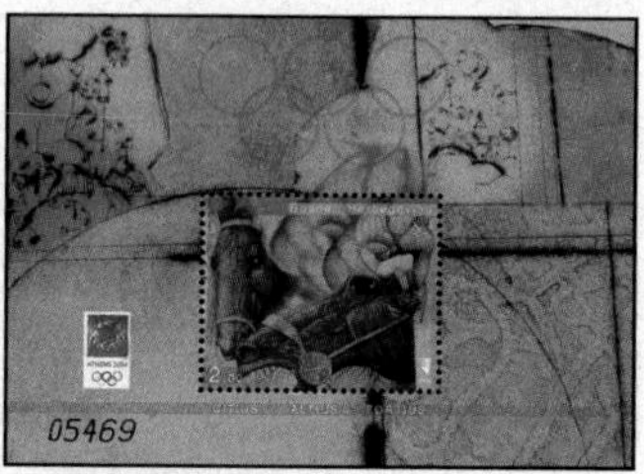

2004 Summer Olympics, Athens — A256

2004, July 5 ***Perf. 13***
479 A256 2m multi 4.00 4.00

10th Sarajevo Film Festival — A257

2004, July 26 ***Perf. 13½x13¼***
480 A257 1.50m multi 2.50 2.50

Cities Type of 2004 and

A258

Designs: 10pf, Brcko. 20pf, Livno, vert. 30pf, Visoko. 1m, Sanski Most, vert.

2004, Dec. 31 **Litho.** ***Perf. 13***

481	A258 10pf multi	.25	.25
482	A247 20pf multi	.45	.45
483	A258 30pf multi	.55	.55
484	A258 1m multi	1.75	1.75
	Nos. 481-484 (4)	3.00	3.00

The New Year, by Adin Hebib — A259

2004, Dec. 31
485 A259 1m multi 1.50 1.50

European Cultural Convention, 50th Anniv. — A260

2004, Dec. 31
486 A260 1.50m multi 3.00 3.00

Windows, by Safet Zec A261

2004, Dec. 31
487 A261 2m multi 3.25 3.25

Nikola Sop (1904-82), Poet — A262

2004, Dec. 31
488 A262 3m multi 4.75 4.75

Family Houses A263

House of: No. 489, 1m, Svrzo family (blue denomination). No. 490, 1m, Despic family (red denomination).

2004, Dec. 31
489-490 A263 Set of 2 3.25 3.25

Chamber Theater 55, Sarajevo, 50th Anniv. A264

2005, Mar. 7 **Litho.** ***Perf. 13***
491 A264 40pf multi .75 .75

Jablanica Hydroelectric Plant, 50th Anniv. — A265

2005, Mar. 7
492 A265 60pf multi 1.25 1.25

Electric Lighting and Trams in Sarajevo, 110th Anniv. — A266

2005, Mar. 7
493 A266 2m multi 4.00 4.00

Izet Kiko Sarajlic (1930-2002), Poet — A267

2005, Mar. 10
494 A267 1m multi 2.00 2.00

Hasan Kikic (1905-42), Writer — A268

2005, Mar. 10
495 A268 1.50m multi 3.00 3.00

Europa A269

Designs: No. 496, 2m, Baklava (denomination in black). No. 497, 2m, Stuffed onions (denomination in white).

2005, Apr. 20
496-497 A269 Set of 2 7.00 7.00
a. Souvenir sheet, #496-497 7.00 7.00

Roses — A270

Designs: 80pf, Rosa damascena. 1.20m, Rosa alba.

2005, Apr. 20 **Litho.** ***Perf. 13***
498-499 A270 Set of 2 4.00 4.00

Fauna A271

Designs: 2m, Tetrao urogalius. 3m, Castor fiber.

2005, Apr. 20 **Litho.** ***Perf. 13***
500-501 A271 Set of 2 10.00 10.00

Nos. 500-501 each printed in sheets of 8 + 2 labels.

Mediterranean Games, Almería, Spain — A272

2005, May 20 **Litho.** ***Perf. 13***
502 A272 1m multi 2.00 2.00

Sarajevo Music Academy, 50th Anniv. A273

2005, May 31
503 A273 1m multi 2.00 2.00

Friendship Between Sarajevo and Doha, Qatar A274

2005, June 30
504 A274 2m multi 3.75 3.75

See Qatar No. 1000.

Srebrenica Massacre, 10th Anniv. — A275

2005, July 1 **Litho.** ***Perf. 13***
505 A275 1m multi 2.00 2.00

Mail Services A276

Running mailman with letter and: 10pf, Mail van, EMS emblem. 20pf, Printing press. 30pf, Text. 50pf, Bosnia & Herzegovina #327.

2005, Sept. 1

506	A276 10pf multi	.25	.25
507	A276 20pf multi	.45	.45
508	A276 30pf multi	.60	.60
509	A276 50pf multi	.95	.95
	Nos. 506-509 (4)	2.25	2.25

Fruit — A277

Designs: 1m, Pyrus communis. 1.50m, Orange carica. 2m, Ficus carica. 2.50m, Prunus domestica. 5m, Prunus avium.

2005, Sept. 1

510	A277 1m multi	2.00	2.00
511	A277 1.50m multi	3.00	3.00
512	A277 2m multi	4.00	4.00
513	A277 2.50m multi	5.25	5.25
514	A277 5m multi	9.75	9.75
	Nos. 510-514 (5)	24.00	24.00

Aladza Mosque, Foca — A278

2005, Sept. 15 **Litho.** ***Perf. 13***
515 A278 1m multi 2.00 2.00

Zitomislici Moanastery, Mostar — A279

2005, Sept. 15
516 A279 1m multi 2.00 2.00

St. Mark the Evangelist Monastery, Plehan — A280

2005, Sept. 15
517 A280 1m multi 2.00 2.00

The Bay, by Hakija Kulenovic (1905-87) — A281

2005, Sept. 15
518 A281 2m multi 4.00 4.00

Souvenir Sheet

Cartoon Characters — A282

No. 502: a, Girl and dogs. b, Windsurfing hedgehog.

2005, Sept. 15
519 A282 50pf Sheet of 2, #a-b 2.00 2.00

Trade Unions in Bosnia & Herzegovina, Cent. — A283

2005, Sept. 15 Litho. *Perf. 13*
520 A283 1m multi 2.00 2.00

Bogomil Culture A284

Designs: No. 521, 50pf, Ban Kulin (1180-1203). No. 522, 50pf, King Tvrtko I Kotromanic (1353-91). 1m, Stone carving of Bogomil burning at stake. 2m, Bull of Pope Eugene IV.

2005, Oct. 10 *Perf. 13¾x13¼*
521-524 A284 Set of 4 8.00 8.00

2004 Exhibition at Bosniac Institute, Istanbul — A285

Designs: 70pf, Exhibit hall. 4m, Entryway and exhibits.

2005, Nov. 15 *Perf. 13*
525-526 A285 Set of 2 9.50 9.50

Nos. 525-526 each printed in sheets of 8 + 2 labels.

Dayton Peace Accords, 10th Anniv. — A286

2005, Nov. 21 *Perf. 13¾x13¼*
527 A286 1.50m multi 3.00 3.00

Printed in sheets of 8 + label.

End of World War II, 60th Anniv. — A287

2005, Nov. 25
528 A287 1m multi 2.00 2.00

Europa Stamps, 50th Anniv. (in 2006) A288

No. 529: a, Flags and Western Hemisphere. b, Flags and Eastern Hemisphere. c, Map of Europe and 1-euro coin. d, Stars and chess organization emblems.

2005, Nov. 30 *Perf. 13*
529 Horiz. strip of 4 22.00 22.00
a.-d. A288 3m Any single 5.00 5.00
e. Souvenir sheet, #529a-529d 22.00 22.00

No. 529e exists imperf. Value $30.

World Vision — A289

2005, Dec. 3 *Perf. 13¾x13¼*
530 A289 50pf multi 1.75 1.75

Souvenir Sheet

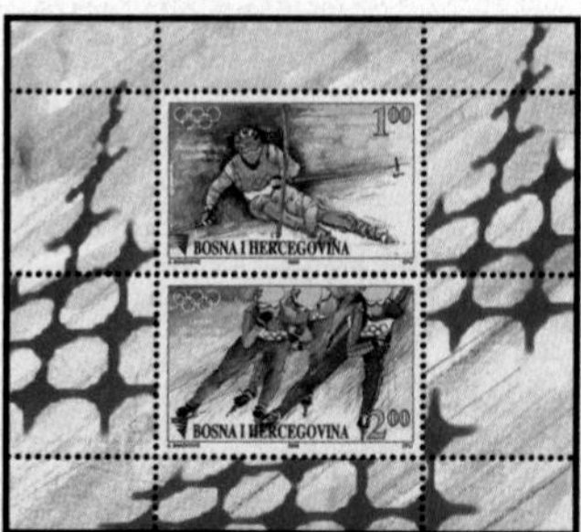

2006 Winter Olympics, Turin — A290

No. 531: a, 1m, Skiing. b, 2m, Speed skating.

2006, Feb. 1 Litho. *Perf. 13*
531 A290 Sheet of 2, #a-b 6.00 6.00

Tourism A291

Designs: No. 532, 1m, Treskavica, Trnovo. No. 533, 1m, Raft in water, Gorazde, vert.

Perf. 13¼x13¾, 13¾x13¼
2006, Mar. 10
532-533 A291 Set of 2 4.00 4.00

Souvenir Sheet

Automobiles — A292

No. 534: a, 50pf, 1935 Mercedes-Benz 500k Cabriolet B. b, 50pf, 1939 Dodge D11 Graber Cabriolet. c, 1m, 1929, Mercedes-Benz SS Schwarzer. d, 2m, 1939 Bugatti T57 Ventoux.

2006, Apr. 5 *Perf. 13*
534 A292 Sheet of 4, #a-d 8.25 8.25

Europa A293

Designs: No. 535, 2m, Upper arc of circle, denomination at left. No. 536, 2m, Lower arc of circle, denomination at right.

2006, Apr. 5 *Perf. 13*
535-536 A293 Set of 2 8.00 8.00
536a Souvenir sheet, #535-536 8.00 8.00

Fauna and Fungi — A294

Designs: 1.50m, Formica rufa. 3m, Sarcosphaera crassa.

2006, Apr. 20 *Perf. 13¾x13¼*
537-538 A294 Set of 2 9.00 9.00

Prisoners of War Association, 10th Anniv. — A295

2006, May 9 *Perf. 13¼x13¾*
539 A295 1m multi 2.00 2.00

Bosnia & Herzegovina Art Gallery, 60th Anniv. — A296

2006, May 20 *Perf. 13*
540 A296 1m multi 2.00 2.00

Isak Samokovlija (1889-1955), Writer, and Samuel, the Porter — A297

2006, May 20
541 A297 1m multi 2.00 2.00

Academicians — A298

Designs: No. 542, 1m, Muhamed Kadic (1906-83). No. 543, 1m, Mustafa Kamaric (1906-73).

2006, May 20 Litho. *Perf. 13*
542-543 A298 Set of 2 4.25 4.25

Sarajevo Soccer Team, 60th Anniv. A299

2006, June 10 Litho. *Perf. 13½*
544 A299 1m multi 2.00 2.00
a. Booklet pane of 2 5.00 5.00

A circle of perforations is in the middle of the stamp.

2006 World Cup Soccer Championships, Germany — A300

2006, June 10
545 A300 3m multi 6.00 6.00
a. Booklet pane of 2 12.00 12.00
Complete booklet, #544a, 545a 18.00

A circle of perforations is in the middle of the stamp.

49th European Junior Table Tennis Championships A301

2006, July 5 *Perf. 13*

546 A301 1m multi 2.00 2.00

Breza Basilica Archaelogical Site — A302

2006, Sept. 10 *Perf. 13¼x13¾*

547 A302 1m multi 2.00 2.00

Semiz Ali Pasha's Mosque, Praca — A303

2006, Sept. 10 *Perf. 13¾x13¼*

548 A303 1m multi 2.00 2.00

Souvenir Sheet

Cartoon Characters From "Ptice Kao Mi" — A304

No. 549: a, Red bird. b, Yellow bird.

2006, Sept. 10 **Litho.**

549 A304 50pf Sheet of 2, #a-b 2.00 2.00

Vegetables — A305

Designs: 10pf, Potatoes (Solanum tuberosum). 20pf, Cauliflower (Brassica oleracea var. botrytis). 30pf, Savoy cabbage (Brassica oleracea var. sabauda). 40pf, Cabbage (Brassica oleracea var. capitata). 50pf, Garlic (Allium sativum). 1m, Carrots (Dauctus carota).

2006, Mar. **Litho.** *Perf. 13½x13¾*

550 A305 10pf multi .25 .25
551 A305 20pf multi .40 .40
552 A305 30pf multi .60 .60
553 A305 40pf multi .95 .95
554 A305 50pf multi 1.10 1.10
555 A305 1m multi 2.10 2.10
Nos. 550-555 (6) 5.40 5.40

Wild Animals A306

Designs: 1.50m, Lepus europaeus. 2m, Capreolus capreolus. 2.50m, Anas sp., horiz. 4m, Vulpes vulpes. 5m, Canis lupus, horiz.

Perf. 13¾x13¼, 13¼x13¾

2006, June 30

556 A306 1.50m multi 3.00 3.00
557 A306 2m multi 3.75 3.75
558 A306 2.50m multi 5.00 5.00
559 A306 4m multi 7.75 7.75
560 A306 5m multi 9.50 9.50
Nos. 556-560 (5) 29.00 29.00

Each stamp printed in sheets of 8 + label.

Children's Week — A307

2006, Oct. 6 *Die Cut*

Self-Adhesive

561 A307 50pf multi 1.00 1.00

Elci Ibrahim-Pasha Madrassa, Travnik, 300th Anniv. — A308

2006, Oct. 25 *Perf. 13¼x13¾*

562 A308 1m multi 2.00 2.00

Tuzla University, 30th Anniv. — A309

2006, Oct. 25 *Perf. 13¾x13¼*

563 A309 1m multi 2.00 2.00

Nobel Laureates A310

Designs: 1m, Vladimir Prelog (1906-98), 1975 Chemistry laureate. 2.50m, Ivo Andric (1892-1975), 1961 Literature laureate.

2006, Oct. 25

564-565 A310 Set of 2 7.00 7.00

Museum Exhibits — A311

2006, Nov. 24 *Perf. 13*

566 A311 1m multi 2.00 2.00

Trains A312

Designs: 50pf, Steam locomotive. 1m, Electric train.

2006, Nov. 24 **Litho.**

567-568 A312 Set of 2 3.00 3.00

Sarajevo National Opera, 60th Anniv. — A313

2007, Feb. 15 *Perf. 13¾x13¼*

569 A313 50pf multi 1.00 1.00

Prokos Lake A314

2007, Feb. 15 *Perf. 13¼x13¾*

570 A314 2.50m multi 5.00 5.00

Europa A315

Scouts and: No. 571, 2m, Backpacks. No. 572, 2m. Tent and campfire.

2007, Feb. 15 *Perf. 13*

571-572 A315 Set of 2 8.00 8.00
572a Souvenir sheet, #571-572 + 2 labels 8.00 8.00
572b Booklet pane, 2 each #571-572 + label 15.00 —
Complete booklet, #572b 15.00

Scouting, cent. Nos. 571-572 each were printed in sheets of 8 + label.

Domesticated Animals — A316

Designs: 10pf, Ovis aries. 20pf, Capra hircus. 30pf, Bos taurus. 40pf, Equus asinus. 70pf, Equus caballus. 1m, Felis silvestris.

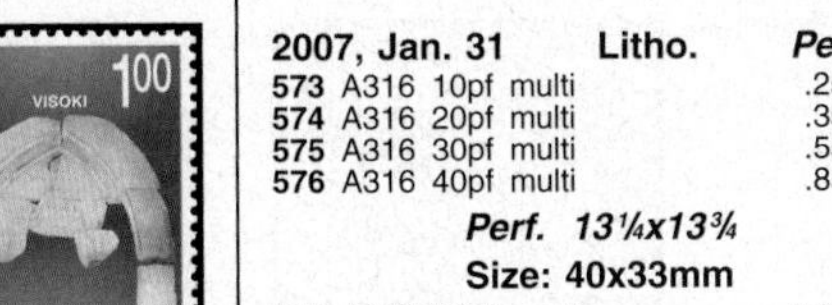

2007, Jan. 31 **Litho.** *Perf. 13*

573 A316 10pf multi .25 .25
574 A316 20pf multi .35 .35
575 A316 30pf multi .55 .55
576 A316 40pf multi .85 .85

Perf. 13¼x13¾

Size: 40x33mm

577 A316 70pf multi 1.40 1.40
578 A316 1m multi 1.90 1.90
Nos. 573-578 (6) 5.30 5.30

Nos. 573-578 each printed in sheets of 8 + label.

Knautia Travnicensis A317

Sciurus Vulgaris A318

2007, Mar. 15 *Perf. 13*

579 A317 80pf multi 1.60 1.60
580 A318 1.20m multi 2.40 2.40

Nos. 579-580 each printed in sheets of 8 + label.

Kozarac A319

2007, Mar. 15 *Perf. 13¾x13¼*

581 A319 1m multi 2.00 2.00

Dr. Abdulah Nakas Hospital, 140th Anniv. A320

2007, Apr. 10 *Perf. 13¼x13¾*

582 A320 1.50m sil & maroon 2.75 2.75

Madrassa, Cazin, 140th Anniv. — A321

2007, Apr. 10 *Perf. 13*

583 A321 2m multi 4.00 4.00

Fountain, Tuzla — A322

Fountain, Mostar A323

Fountain, Sanski Most — A324

Fountain, Sarajevo A325

Fountain Near Bey's Mosque A326

Perf. 13¾x13¼, 13¼x13¾

2007, Apr. 10

584	A322	1.50m multi	2.75	2.75
585	A323	2m multi	3.75	3.75
586	A324	2.50m multi	4.75	4.75
587	A325	4m multi	7.50	7.50
588	A326	5m multi	9.25	9.25
	Nos. 584-588 (5)		28.00	28.00

Nos. 584-588 each printed in sheets of 8 + label.

Gajret Newspaper, Cent. — A327

2007, Apr. 16 ***Perf. 13***

589 A327 1m multi 2.00 2.00

Gazi Husrev-Begova Library — A328

2007, Apr. 16

590 A328 1.50m multi 3.00 3.00

Islamic Sciences Faculty, Sarajevo, 30th Anniv. A329

2007, Apr. 16

591 A329 2m multi 4.00 4.00

Pocitelj Art Colony A330

2007, May 4 Litho. *Perf. 13¼x13¾*

592 A330 1m multi 2.00 2.00

Painting by Ismet Rizvic A331

2007, May 4 Litho. *Perf. 13*

593 A331 1.50m multi 3.00 3.00

Bear Figurine, 3500 B.C. A332

2007, June 1 *Perf. 13¼x13¾*

594 A332 1m multi 2.00 2.00

Karel Parik (1857-1942), Architect — A333

2007, June 6 *Perf. 13*

595 A333 2.50m multi 5.00 5.00

Karate — A334

2007, July 2 Litho. *Perf. 13*

596 A334 1m multi 2.00 2.00

Zulfikar Zuko Dzumhur (1920-89), Cartoonist A335

2007, July 2

597 A335 1m multi 2.00 2.00

Sarajevo University Medical Faculty, 61st Anniv. A336

2007, July 2

598 A336 1m multi 2.00 2.00

Sepp Blatter, Fédération Internationale de Football Association (FIFA) President — A337

Juan Antonio Samaranch, Former Pres. of Intl. Olympic Committee — A338

Perf. 13¼x13¾

2007, Sept. 20 Litho.

599 A337 2m multi 4.00 4.00

600 A338 2m multi 4.00 4.00

Honorary Ambassadors of Sport and Culture of Peace.

Fortress, Samobor A339

Perf. 13¾x13¼

2007, Sept. 28 Litho.

601 A339 1m multi 2.00 2.00

Ecology A340

Children's art by: No. 602, 50pf, Amira Halilovic. No. 603, 50pf, Maida Hasanic.

2007, Sept. 28 *Perf. 13*

602-603 A340 Set of 2 2.00 2.00

603a Souvenir sheet, #602-603 2.00 2.00

Meat Pie A341

2007, Oct. 1 *Perf. 13½*

604 A341 2m multi 4.00 4.00

Values are for stamps with surrounding selvage.

Stegosaurus — A342

2007, Nov. 15 *Perf. 13¼x13¾*

605 A342 2m multi 4.00 4.00

Space Flight of Dog, Laika, on Sputnik 2, 50th Anniv. — A343

2007, Nov. 15 *Perf. 13¾x13¼*

606 A343 3m multi 6.25 6.25

Bosnian University Sports Association, 60th Anniv. — A344

2007, Dec. 3 *Perf. 13*

607 A344 50pf multi 1.00 1.00

Printed in sheets of 4.

Bosnian Handball Team, 60th Anniv. — A345

2007, Dec. 31

608 A345 50pf multi 1.00 1.00

Merhamet Charitable Organization, 95th Anniv. — A346

2008, Feb. 15

609 A346 70pf multi 1.40 1.40

Europa
A347

Designs: 2m, Letter, candle, quill pen. 3m, Person writing on postcard.

2008, Mar. 8 Litho. *Perf. 13½x13¾*

610-611	A347	Set of 2	10.00	10.00
611a		Souvenir sheet, #610-611	10.00	10.00

University of Sarajevo College of Pharmacy — A348

2008, Feb. 15 Litho. *Perf. 13*

612 A348 2m multi 4.00 4.00

Local Cuisine
A349

Designs: 1m, Shishkebabs. 2m, Apple stuffed with whipped cream.

2008, Feb. 15 *Perf. 13¼x13¾*

613-614 A349 Set of 2 6.25 6.25

Nos. 613-614 each were printed in sheets of 8 + label.

Blood Transfusion Institute, Sarajevo, 50th Anniv.
A350

2008, Mar. 8 *Perf. 13*

615 A350 1.50m multi 3.00 3.00

Intl. Women's Day — A351

2008, Mar. 8

616 A351 2m multi 4.00 4.00

Printed in sheets of 8 + label.

Bosanska Krupa — A352

Velika Kladusa
A353

2008, Mar. 8

617	A352	70pf multi	1.50	1.50
618	A353	1m multi	2.00	2.00

Nos. 617-618 each were printed in sheets of 8 + label.

Sarajevo Shooting Club, 60th Anniv.
A354

2008, Apr. 10

619 A354 1.50m multi 3.00 3.00

Universal Esperanto Association, Cent. — A355

2008, Apr. 10

620 A355 1.50m multi 3.00 3.00

2008 Summer Olympics, Beijing
A356

Designs: 1m, Judo. 1.50m, Track and field.

2008, May 5 *Perf. 13¾x13¼*

621-622 A356 Set of 2 4.25 4.25

Nos. 621-622 each were printed in sheets of 8 + label.

Motorcycles
A357

Designs: No. 623, 1.50m, Jawa Trail 90. No. 624, 1.50m, Ural-3.

2008, May 5 *Perf. 13*

623-624 A357 Set of 2 5.50 5.50

Vjetrenica Cave
A358

2008, June 10 Litho.

625 A358 1m multi 2.00 2.00

Stabilization and Association Agreement with European Union — A359

2008, June 16

626 A359 70pf multi 1.40 1.40

Krivaja House, Zavidovici
A360

2008, July 1 *Perf. 13¾x13¼*

627 A360 2.50m multi 5.00 5.00

Pond Flora and Fauna
A361

Designs: 1.50m, Nymphaea alba. 2m, Rana esculenta.

2008, July 1 *Perf. 13*

628-629 A361 Set of 2 7.00 7.00

Nos. 628-629 each were printed in sheets of 9 + label.

Musalla, Kamengrad
A362

Ostrovica
A363

2008, July 11

630	A362	1m multi	2.00	2.00
631	A363	1.50m multi	3.00	3.00

Turritella Turris Fossil Shell
A364

2008, Sept. 1 *Perf. 13¼x13¾*

632 A364 1.50m multi 3.00 3.00

Printed in sheets of 8 + label.

Friendship Between Bosnia and Herzegovina and Kuwait — A365

2008, Sept. 9 *Perf. 13*

633 A365 3m multi 6.25 6.25

Sarajevo Ski Club, 80th Anniv.
A366

2008, Nov. 1 *Perf. 13¼x13¾*

634 A366 2m multi 4.00 4.00

Printed in sheets of 8 + label.

Fauna — A367

Designs: 5pf, Lynx lynx. 70pf, Accipiter gentilis. 5m, Strigiformes.

2008, Dec. 15 *Perf. 13¾x13¼*

635-637 A367 Set of 3 8.75 8.75

Douglas Fir
A368

Birch
A369

Cypress
A370

2008, Dec. 15 *Perf. 13¼x13¾*

638	A368	70c multi	1.25	1.25
639	A369	70c multi	1.25	1.25
640	A370	70c multi	1.25	1.25
		Nos. 638-640 (3)	3.75	3.75

Europa
A371

Designs: 2m, Planets. 3m, Space telescope.

2009, Sept. 10 **Litho.** ***Perf. 13***
641-642 A371 Set of 2 10.00 10.00
642a Souvenir sheet of 2, #641-642, + 2 labels 10.00 10.00

Intl. Year of Astronomy.

Intl. Day of Missing Persons A372

2009, Aug. 30 **Litho.** ***Perf. 13***
643 A372 20pf multi .50 .50

Hirundo Rustica A373

2009, Sept. 10 ***Perf. 13¼x13***
644 A373 70pf multi 1.40 1.40

Printed in sheets of 8 + label.

Historical Archives of Sarajevo Museum — A374

2009, Sept. 10 ***Perf. 13***
645 A374 70pf multi 1.25 1.25

Academic Culture Center of Sarajevo University, 60th Anniv. — A375

2009, Sept. 10 ***Perf. 13¼x13***
646 A375 1m multi 1.75 1.75

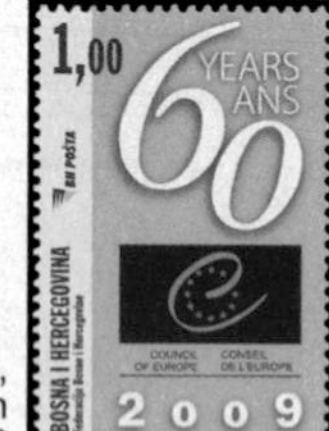

Council of Europe, 60th Anniv. — A376

2009, Sept. 10 ***Perf. 13x13¼***
647 A376 1m multi 1.75 1.75

Sarajevo Museum, 60th Anniv. A377

2009, Sept. 10 ***Perf. 13***
648 A377 1m multi 1.75 1.75

Bosnian Coffee — A378

2009, Sept. 10 **Litho.**
649 A378 1m multi 1.75 1.75

Printed in sheets of 8 + label.

Charles Darwin (1809-82), Naturalist — A379

2009, Sept. 10 ***Perf. 13¼x13***
650 A379 2m multi 4.00 4.00

World Track and Field Championships, Berlin — A380

Designs: 1.50m, Runners. 2m, Stylized runners.

2009, Sept. 10
651-652 A380 Set of 2 6.75 6.75
652a Souvenir sheet, #651-652 6.75 6.75

Children's Week A381

2009, Oct. 1 ***Perf. 13***
653 A381 70pf multi 1.40 1.40

Pansies A382

2009, Oct. 9 ***Perf. 13¼x13***
654 A382 1m multi 1.75 1.75

Printed in sheets of 8 + label.

Sarajevo Canton Tribunal, 130th Anniv. A383

2009, Oct. 9 ***Perf. 13***
655 A383 1m multi 2.00 2.00

Postal Cooperation Between Bosnia & Herzegovina and Turkey — A384

2009, Oct. 9
656 A384 2m multi 3.50 3.50

See Turkey No. 3191.

Strawberries — A385

2009, Oct. 9
657 A385 5m multi 10.00 10.00

Franciscan Theological College, Sarajevo, Cent. — A386

2009, Dec. 7 **Litho.**
658 A386 1m multi 1.75 1.75

Printed in sheets of 8 + label.

Franciscan Order, 800th Anniv. A387

2009, Dec. 7
659 A387 1.50m multi 2.75 2.75

Printed in sheets of 8 + label.

Sign Language A388

2009, Dec. 7 ***Perf. 13¼x13***
660 A388 1.50m multi 3.00 3.00

Souvenir Sheet

2010 Winter Olympics, Vancouver — A389

No. 661: a, 1.50m, Skier, ski jumper, speed skater, ice hockey players, biathlete. b, 2m, Figure skater, snowboarder, ice hockey player, bobsledders.

2010, Feb. 12 ***Perf. 13x13¼***
661 A389 Sheet of 2, #a-b 7.00 7.00

Old City, Srebrenik A390

Ostrozac Castle A391

2010, Mar. 22 ***Perf. 13***
662 A390 70pf multi 1.50 1.50
663 A391 1m multi 2.00 2.00

Nos. 662-663 each were printed in sheets of 8 + label.

Taxus Baccata A392

Aesculus Hippocastanum — A393

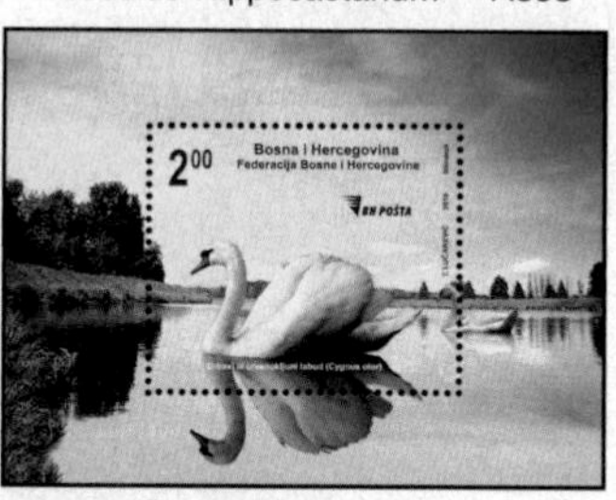

Cygnus Olor — A394

2010, Apr. 12 **Litho.** ***Perf. 13***
664 A392 1m multi 2.00 2.00
665 A393 1m multi 2.00 2.00

Souvenir Sheet

666 A394 2m multi 4.00 4.00

Nos. 664-665 each were printed in sheets of 8 + label.

Folk Ballad "Hasanaganica" — A395

2010, Apr. 26 ***Perf. 13¼x13***
667 A395 1m multi 1.75 1.75

Printed in sheets of 8 + label.

Europa — A396

No. 668: a, 1m, Dragon. b, 1.50m, Little Blu (knight).

2010, Apr. 26 *Perf. 13x13¼*

668 A396 Horiz. pair, #a-b 5.00 5.00
c. Souvenir sheet, #668a-668b 5.00 5.00
d. Booklet pane, 3 each #668a-668b, perf. 13x13¼ on 2 or 3 sides 15.00 —
Complete booklet, #668d 15.00

Ajvatovica, 500th Anniv. — A397

2010, June 15 *Perf. 13*

669 A397 1.50m multi 3.00 3.00

Robert Schumann (1810-56), Composer — A398

Frédéric Chopin (1810-49), Composer — A399

2010, Oct. 18 Litho. *Perf. 13¼x13*

670 A398 1m multi 1.75 1.75
671 A399 1.50m multi 2.50 2.50

Nos. 670-671 each were printed in sheets of 8 + label.

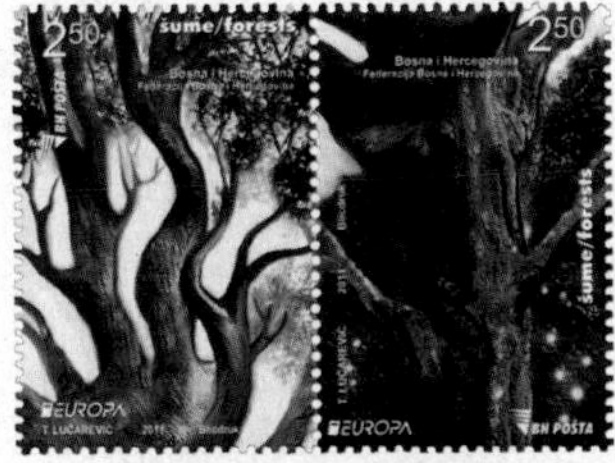

Europa — A400

No. 672 — Tree with denomination at: a, Upper left. b, Upper right.

2011, May 9 *Perf. 13x13¼*

672 A400 2.50m Horiz. pair, #a-b 8.50 8.50
c. Souvenir sheet, #672a-672b 8.50 8.50
d. Booklet pane of 6, 3 each #672a-672b, perf. 13x13¼ on 2 or 3 sides 25.00 —

Intl. Year of Forests. No. 672d was sold with, but not attached to, a booklet cover.

Gentiana Jasnae A401

Passer Domesticus — A402

2011, May 26 *Perf. 13*

673 A401 2m multi 3.75 3.75

Souvenir Sheet

674 A402 2.50m multi 4.75 4.75

No. 673 was printed in sheets of 8 + label.

Apparition of the Virgin Mary at Medjugorje, 30th Anniv. — A403

Litho. With Foil Application

2011, May 26

675 A403 2.50m multi 4.25 4.25

Printed in sheets of 8 + label.

Souvenir Sheet

First Man in Space, 50th Anniv. — A404

2011, May 26 **Litho.**

676 A404 2m multi 3.50 3.50

Arms of Duke Stjepan Vukcic Kosaca (1404-66) A405

2011, June 6 Litho. *Perf. 13¼x13*

677 A405 1m multi 1.60 1.60

Printed in sheets of 8 + label.

Campaign Against AIDS, 30th Anniv. — A406

2011, June 6 Litho. *Perf. 13*

678 A406 70pf multi 1.25 1.25

Hutovo Blato Nature Park — A407

2011, Sept. 20

679 A407 70pf multi 1.10 1.10

No. 679 was printed in sheets of 8 + label.

Astacus Astacus A408

2011, Sept. 20

680 A408 1.50m multi 2.50 2.50

No. 680 was printed in sheets of 8 + label.

Writers A409

Designs: 1m, Skender Kulenovic (1910-78). 1.50m, Mesa Selimovic (1910-82).

2011, Oct. 7 *Perf. 13¼x13*

681-682 A409 Set of 2 4.25 4.25

Nos. 681-682 each were printed in sheets of 8 + label.

Fridtjof Nansen (1861-1930), Polar Explorer and Diplomat — A410

2011, Oct. 25 *Perf. 13x13¼*

683 A410 1.50m multi 2.50 2.50

Souvenir Sheet

Sinking of the Titanic, Cent. — A411

2012, May 29 Litho. *Perf. 13*

684 A411 2.50m multi 4.25 4.25

Souvenir Sheet

Locomotives — A412

No. 685: a, 1m, Locomotive 55-99. b, 1.50m, Locomotive 83-180.

2012, May 29 *Perf. 13¼x13*

685 A412 Sheet of 2, #a-b 4.25 4.25

Europa — A413

No. 686: a, Sarajevo. b, Mountains, waterfalls, rowboat, monument.

2012, May 29 *Perf. 13x13¼*

686 A413 2.50m Horiz. pair, #a-b 8.50 8.50
c. Souvenir sheet of 2, #686a-686b 8.50 8.50
d. Booklet pane of 6, 3 each #686a-686b, perf. 13x13¼ on 2 or 3 sides 25.00 —
Complete booklet, #686d 25.00

Miniature Sheet

Flowers — A414

No. 687: a, Three Viola odorata. b, Two Primula veris. c, Two Helleborus. d, Two Galanthus. e, Two Crocus sativa. f, Viola odorata and bubbles. g, Cluster of Primula veris and leaves. h, Two Helleborus and leaves. i, Two Galanthus and rock crystal. j, Crocus sativa and rock crystal.

2012, June 7 *Perf. 13*

687 A414 70pf Sheet of 10, #a-j 12.00 12.00

Rustempasic Castle, Bugojno — A415

2012, June 22

688 A415 2m multi 3.50 3.50

Printed in sheets of 8 + label.

Old Sections of Cities A416

No. 689: a, Tesanj. b, Buzim.

2012, June 25 *Perf. 13¼x13*

689 A416 20pf Vert. pair, #a-b .80 .80

Sports A417

2012, July 10 ***Perf. 13x13¼***
690 A417 2.50m multi 4.00 4.00

Printed in sheets of 8 + label.

La Benevolencia Jewish Organization, 120th Anniv. — A418

2012, Sept. 10 ***Perf. 13***
691 A418 70pf multi 1.25 1.25

No. 691 was printed in sheets of 8 + label.

Snakes — A419

Designs: 1m, Vipera ammodytes. 1.50m, Vipera berus bosniensis.

2012, Sept. 10
692-693 A419 Set of 2 4.50 4.50

Nos. 692-693 each were printed in sheets of 8 + label.

Children's Week A420

2012, Oct. 1
694 A420 70pf multi 1.25 1.25

Printed in sheets of 8 + label.

Intorduction of Euro Currency in Europe, 10th Anniv. — A421

2012, Oct. 1
695 A421 2m multi 3.50 3.50

Marine Life A422

No. 696: a, Various fish. b, Seahorse and fish. c, Sstarfish. d, Crab and fish. e, Jellyfish and fish.

2012, Nov. 27
696 Horiz. strip of 5 4.75 4.75
a.-e. A422 70pf Any single .95 .95

Souvenir Sheet

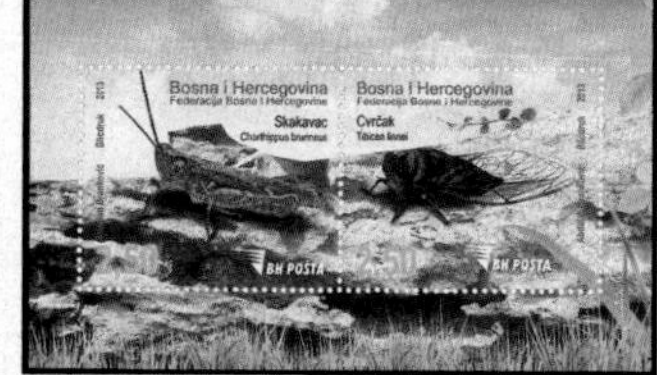
Insects — A423

No. 697: a, Chorthippus brunneus. b, Tibicen linnei.

2013, Mar. 15
697 A423 2.50m Sheet of 2, #a-b 6.75 6.75

Old City, Kljuc — A424

2013, Mar. 20
698 A424 70pf multi .95 .95

Europa — A425

No. 699 — Postal van: a, Facing left. b, Facing right.

2013, May 9 ***Perf. 13¼x13***
699 A425 2.50m Horiz. pair, #a-b 7.00 7.00
c. Souvenir sheet of 2, #699a-699b 7.00 7.00
d. Booklet pane of 6, 3 each #699a-699b, perf. 13¼x13 on 2 or 3 sides 21.00 —

No. 699d was sold with, but unattached to, a booklet cover.

Composers A426

Designs: No. 700, 2m, Giuseppe Verdi (1813-1901). No. 701, 2m, Richard Wagner (1813-83).

2013, May 22 ***Serpentine Die Cut 11***
Self-Adhesive
700-701 A426 Set of 2 5.50 5.50

Nos. 700-701 were printed in sheets of 8 + central label.

17th Mediterranean Games, Mersin, Turkey — A427

2013, June 20 ***Perf. 13***
702 A427 1m multi 1.40 1.40

Friends of Nature Postal Workers Lodge, 60th Anniv. A428

2013, July 29 **Litho.** ***Perf. 13***
703 A428 70pf multi .95 .95

Architecture — A429

No. 704: a, Velagicevina guest house, Blagaj. b, Guest house, Fojnica.

2013, July 29 **Litho.** ***Perf. 13***
704 A429 90pf Horiz. pair, #a-b 2.50 2.50

Souvenir Sheet

Seventh World Paragliding Accuracy Championships, Bjelasnica — A430

2013, July 29 **Litho.** ***Perf. 13***
705 A430 1.50m multi 2.10 2.10

BOSNIA & HERZEGOVINA (CROAT ADMIN)

Bosnian Croat Administration Located In Mostar

(Herceg Bosna)

100 Paras = 1 Dinar (1993)
100 Lipa = 1 Kuna (1994)
100 pfennig = 1 Mark (6/22/98)

Catalogue values for all unused stamps in this country are for Never Hinged items.

A1

1993, May 12 **Litho.** ***Perf. 14***
1 A1 2000d multicolored 2.00 2.00

Our Lady of Peace Shrine, Medjugorje.

A2

Silvije Kranjcevic (1865-1908), poet: 500d, Waterfall, gate at Jajce. 1000d, Old bridge, Mostar, horiz.

1993
2-4 A2 Set of 3 2.00 2.00

Issued: 200d, 5/20; 500d, 5/18; 1000d, 5/15.

Census in Bosnia & Herzegovina, 250th Anniv. — A3

1993, May 24
5 A3 100d Medieval gravestone .50 .50

Madonna of the Grand Duke, by Raphael — A4

1993, Dec. 3
6 A4 6000d multicolored 3.50 3.50

Christmas.

Paintings, by Gabrijel Jurkic (1886-1974) — A5

Europa: a, 3500d, Uplands in Bloom. b, 5000d, Wild Poppy.

1993, Dec. 6
7 A5 Pair, #a.-b. *11.00 11.00*

Kravica Waterfalls A6

1993, Dec. 7
8 A6 3000d multicolored 1.90 1.90

Grand Duke Hrvoje Vukcic-Hrvatinic (1350-1416) — A7

1993, Dec. 8
9 A7 1500d multicolored 1.50 1.50

Pleham Monastery A8

1993, Dec. 15
10 A8 2200d multicolored 1.50 1.50

Formation of Bosnian Croat Administration A9

1994, Feb. 10
11 A9 10,000d multicolored 6.00 6.00

Bronze Cross, Rama A10

1994, Nov. 28
12 A10 2.80k multicolored 2.00 2.00

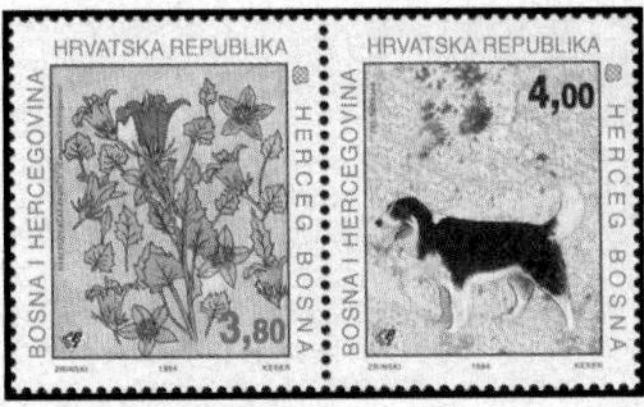
Flora & Fauna — A11

a, 3.80k, Campanula hercegovina. b, 4k, Dog.

1994, Nov. 30
13 A11 Pair, #a.-b. 5.00 5.00

Hutovo Wetlands A12

1994, Dec. 2
14 A12 80 l multicolored 1.00 1.00

Europa — A13

Transportation: a, 8k, Bicycles, 1885. b, 10k, 1901 Mercedes.

1994, Dec. 5
15 A13 Pair, #a.-b. *12.50 12.50*

City of Ljubuski, 550th Anniv. — A14

1994, Dec. 8
16 A14 1k multicolored .65 .65

Dr. Nikolic Franciscan Hospital, Nova Bila, 2nd Anniv. — A15

1994, Dec. 12
17 A15 5k multicolored 3.00 3.00

UN, 50th Anniv. — A16

1995, Oct. 24 ***Rouletted***
Self-Adhesive
18 A16 1.50k Card of 10 55.00 55.00

Color ranges from pale pink at UL of card to dark rose at LR of card. Each stamp is numbered at LR.

Christmas — A17

1995, Dec. 4 ***Perf. 14***
19 A17 5.40k multicolored 3.00 3.00

Kraljeva Sutjeska Monastery A18

1995, Dec. 7
20 A18 3k multicolored 1.50 1.50

Cities — A19

Europa — A20

Monasteries: 2k, Srebrenica. 4k, Mostar.

1995
21-22 A19 Set of 2 4.00 4.00
Issued: 2k, 12/20; 4k, 12/12.

1995, Dec. 28
23 A20 6.50k multicolored *25.00 25.00*

A21

Europa — A22

1996, June 24
24 A21 10k multicolored 6.00 6.00
a. Booklet pane of 4 24.00
Complete booklet, #24a 24.00

Apparitions at Medugorje, 15th anniv.

1996, July 20
25 A22 2.40k multicolored *2.50 2.50*

Queen Katarina Kosaca Kotromanic.

A23

1996, July 23
26 A23 1.40k multicolored 1.25 1.25

Franciscan Monastery, Siroki Brijeg, 150th anniv.

A24

Virgin Mary.

1996, Aug. 14 ***Rouletted***
Self-Adhesive
27 A24 2k multicolored 3.50 3.50
a. Card of 10 37.50 37.50
28 A24 9k multicolored 11.50 11.50
a. Card of 5 + 5 labels 60.00 60.00

Nos. 27-28 Surcharged

1996, Oct. 21 ***Rouletted***
Self-Adhesive
29 A24 1.10k on 2k multi *20.00* —
a. Card of 10 *165.00*
30 A24 1.10k on 9k multi *45.00* —
a. Card of 5 + 5 labels *165.00*

Taipei '96 Philatelic Exhibition.

Christmas — A25

Europa — A26

1996, Dec. 8 **Litho.** ***Perf. 14***
31 A25 2.20k multicolored 1.25 1.25

1997, Apr. 4

Myths & legends: a, 2k, St. George slaying the dragon. b, 5k, Zeus coming to Europa disguised as a bull.

32 A26 Pair, #a.-b. *5.50 5.50*
No. 32b is 39x34mm.

A27

A28

1997, Apr. 12
33 A27 3.60k multicolored 2.00 2.00
a. Pane of 4 8.75

Visit of Pope John Paul II.

1997, Apr. 20
34 A28 1.40k Samatorje Church .80 .80

Flora & Fauna — A29

Designs: 1k, Ardea purpurea. 2.40k, Symphyandra hofmannii.

1997
35-36 A29 Set of 2 2.00 2.00
Issued: 1k, 11/19. 2.40k, 11/17.

Christmas A30

1997, Dec. 1
37 A30 1.40k multicolored .80 .80

World Animated Film Festival A31

1998, Apr. 1
38 A31 6.50k multicolored *4.75 4.75*

Europa.

Hercegovina, 550th Anniv. — A32

1998, Apr. 8
39 A32 2.30k multicolored 1.25 1.25

City of Livno, 1100th Anniv. — A33

1998, Apr. 9
40 A33 1.20k multicolored .70 .70

Sibiraea Croatica — A34

Gyps Fulvus — A35

1998, Nov. 9
41 A34 1.40k multicolored 1.00 1.00

1998, Nov. 16
42 A35 2.40m multicolored 1.40 1.40

A36

A37

1998, Dec. 2
43 A36 5.40k Christmas 2.75 2.75

1999, Mar. 26 **Litho.** ***Perf. 14***
44 A37 40pf Native attire .75 .75

A. B. Simic (1898-1925) — A38

1999, Mar. 29
45 A38 30pf multi .65 .65

Bobovac Castle — A39

1999, Mar. 30
46 A39 10pf multi .30 .30

Europa — A40

1999, Mar. 31
47 A40 1.50m Blidinje Park *4.00 4.00*

Dianthus Freynii — A41

1999, Oct. 11 **Litho.** ***Perf. 14***
48 A41 80pf multi 1.75 1.75

Martes Martes — A42

1999, Oct. 15
49 A42 40pf multi .80 .80

Stolac Castle — A43

1999, Nov. 3
50 A43 10pf multi .30 .30

Christmas — A44

1999, Nov. 22
51 A44 30pf multi .75 .75

Nikola Sop (1904-82), Writer — A45

World Health Day — A46

2000, Apr. 5 **Litho.** ***Perf. 14***
52 A45 40pf multi .75 .75

2000, Apr. 7
53 A46 40pf multi .75 .75

Europa — A47

2000, May 9
54 A47 1.80m multi *5.25 5.25*

Brother Lovro Karaula (1800-75) A48

Quercus Sessilis A49

2000, May 19
55 A48 80pf multi 1.50 1.50

2000, Aug. 16
56 A49 1.50m multi 3.00 3.00

Anguilla Anguilla — A50

2000, Aug. 18
57 A50 80pf multi 1.50 1.50

16th European Chess Club Cup — A51

30th Intl. Chess Tournament A52

2000, Sept. 23
58 A51 80pf multi 1.50 1.50
59 A52 80pf multi 1.50 1.50

Tomislavgrad Monastery A53

2000, Sept. 26
60 A53 1.50m multi 3.00 3.00

Woman From Kraljeva Sutjeska — A54

2000, Sept. 27
61 A54 40pf multi .90 .90

Fight Against AIDS A55

Christmas A56

2000, Dec. 1
62 A55 80pf multi 1.75 1.75

2000, Dec. 4
63 A56 40pf multi .90 .90

Fish — A57

Designs: 30pf, Chondrostoma phoxinus. 1.50m, Salmo marmoratus.

2001
64-65 A57 Set of 2 3.50 3.50

Europa — A58

Designs: 1.10m, Tihaljina spring. 1.80m, Pliva waterfall.

2001, Mar. 31
66-67 A58 Set of 2 *6.00 6.00*

Execution of Zrinski and Frankopan, 330th Anniv. — A59

No. 68: a, Petar Zrinski (1621-71). b, Fran Krsto Frankopan (1643-71).

2001, Apr. 30 **Litho.** ***Perf. 14***
68 A59 40pf Vert. pair, #a-b 1.50 1.50

16th Century Galley — A60

2001, June 15
69 A60 1.80m multi 3.00 3.00

Boat From Neretva River Valley — A61

2001, June 20 ***Perf. 14x14¼***
70 A61 80pf multi 1.75 1.75

Souvenir Sheet

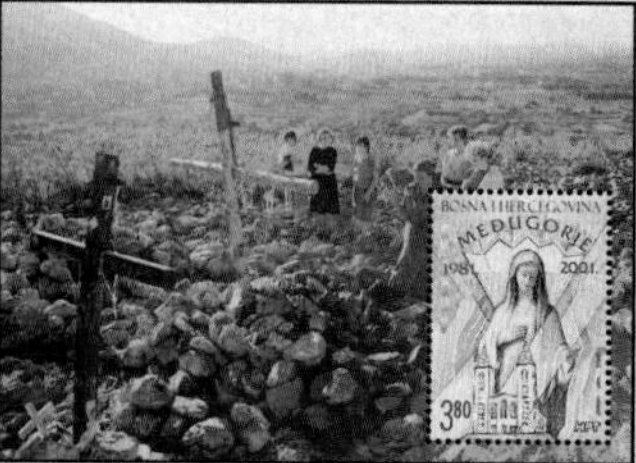

Apparition of the Virgin Mary at Medjugorje, 20th Anniv. — A62

2001, June 24
71 A62 3.80m multi 6.50 6.50

Our Lady of Kondzilo — A63

2001, Aug. 15 ***Perf. 14***
72 A63 80pf multi 1.50 1.50

Computers, 50th Anniv. — A64

No. 73: a, Denomination in red. b, Denomination in black and white.

2001, Sept. 9
73 A64 40pf Horiz. pair, #a-b 1.60 1.60

Mars Odyssey Mission — A65

2001, Sept. 9
74 A65 1.50m multi + label 3.00 3.00

Father Slavko Barbaric (1946-2000), Priest at Medjugorje — A66

2001, Nov. 24
75 A66 80pf multi 1.60 1.60

Walt Disney (1901-66), Animated Film Producer A67

2001, Dec. 5
76 A67 1.50m multi 3.00 3.00

Christmas A68

2001, Dec. 8
77 A68 40pf multi .75 .75

Nobel Prizes, Cent. — A69

2001, Dec. 10 **Litho.** ***Perf. 14***
78 A69 1.80m multi 3.50 3.50

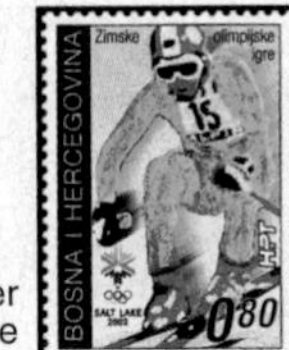
2002 Winter Olympics, Salt Lake City — A70

2002, Feb. 4 **Litho.** ***Perf. 14***
79 A70 80pf multi 1.50 1.50

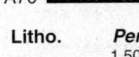

Intl. Year of Mountains — A71

2002, Mar. 11 **Litho.** ***Perf. 14***
80 A71 40pf multi + label .75 .75

First Written Record of Mostar, 550th Anniv. — A72

2002, Apr. 3
81 A72 30pf multi .65 .65

Europa — A73

Designs: 80pf, Clown, lion and mouse. 1.50m, Clowns, juggler, circus tent.

2002, Apr. 5
82-83 A73 Set of 2 *6.50 6.50*

Leonardo da Vinci (1452-1519) — A74

2002, Apr. 15
84 A74 40pf multi 1.25 1.25

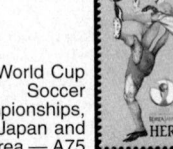

2002 World Cup Soccer Championships, Japan and Korea — A75

2002, May 22
85 A75 1.50m multi 3.00 3.00

Father Didak Buntic (1871-1922) — A76

2002, June 5
86 A76 80pf multi 1.60 1.60

Humac Tablet — A77

2002, June 13
87 A77 40pf multi *.80 .80*

Marilyn Monroe (1926-62), Actress — A78

2002, Aug. 5
88 A78 40pf multi *.80 .80*

Elvis Presley (1935-77) — A79

Television, 75th Anniv. — A80

2002, Aug. 16
89 A79 1.50m multi 3.25 3.25

2002, Sept. 7
90 A80 1.50m multi 2.75 2.75

Stamp Day — A81

2002, Sept. 9
91 A81 80pf multi 1.60 1.60

Croatian Cultural Association Napredak, Cent. — A82

2002, Sept. 14
92 A82 40pf multi .75 .75

European Bocce Championships, Grude — A83

2002, Oct. 8
93 A83 1.50m multi 2.75 2.75

Viola Beckiana — A84

2002, Oct. 21
94 A84 30pf multi .80 .80

Vanessa Atalanta — A85

2002, Oct. 25
95 A85 80pf multi 1.50 1.50

Christmas — A86

2002, Dec. 4
96 A86 40pf multi .85 .85

Archdiocesan Gymnasium, Travnik, 120th Anniv. — A87

2002, Dec. 14
97 A87 80pf multi 1.50 1.50

A 50pf stamp commemorating Archbishop Josip Stadler was jointly issued by the post offices of the Croat Administration and the Muslim Government. It is listed as No. 435 in the listings of the Muslim Government issues.

Franciscan Secondary School, Siroki Brijeg — A88

2003, Feb. 26 **Litho.** ***Perf. 14***
98 A88 40pf multi .80 .80

Europa — A89

2003, Apr. 5
99 A89 1.80m multi 4.50 4.50

Printed in sheets of 8 stamps + label.

Abjuration of the Bogomil Heresy at Bilino Polje, 800th Anniv. — A90

2003, Apr. 8
100 A90 50pf multi .90 .90

Post Office of the Croat Administration, 10th Anniv. — A91

2003, May 12
101 A91 80pf multi 1.60 1.60

World Wine Day A92

2003, May 25
102 A92 1.50m multi 2.75 2.75

Flora & Fauna — A93

Designs: 50pf, Oxytropis prenja. 2m, Alectoris graeca.

2003 Litho. *Perf. 14*
103 A93 50pf multi 1.25 1.25
104 A93 2m multi 3.50 3.50

Issued: 50pf, 6/10; 2m, 6/16.

Visit of Pope John Paul II — A94

2003, June 22 *Perf. 13¼x13½*
105 A94 1.50m multi 3.00 3.00

Father Matija Divkovic (1563-1631), First Bosnian Writer — A95

2003, June 24 *Perf. 14*
106 A95 3.80m multi 7.00 7.00

Woman From Rama — A96

Jewelry From Neum — A97

2003, Aug. 20 Litho. *Perf. 14*
107 A96 50pf multi 1.00 1.00
108 A97 70pf multi 1.25 1.25

Cross on Mt. Krizevac, 70th Anniv. — A98

2003, Sept. 14
109 A98 80pf multi 1.75 1.75

Ban Stjepan II Kotromanic, 650th Anniv. of Death — A99

2003, Sept. 28
110 A99 20pf multi .45 .45

Teleprinter, 75th Anniv. A100

2003, Oct. 9 Litho. *Perf. 14*
111 A100 1.50m blk & red brn 3.00 3.00

World Post Day.

Alberto Fortis, Writer of Dalmatian Travelogue, 200th Anniv. of Death — A101

2003, Oct. 21
112 A101 50pf multi 1.00 1.00

Intl. Children's Day — A102

2003, Nov. 20
113 A102 1m multi 2.00 2.00

Christmas A103

2003, Dec. 4
114 A103 50pf multi 1.25 1.25

Powered Flight A104

2003, Dec. 17
115 A104 2m multi 4.00 4.00

Intl. Investment Conference A105

2004, Jan. 23
116 A105 5m silver 9.00 9.00

St. Valentine's Day — A106

2004, Feb. 14
117 A106 10pf multi .75 .75

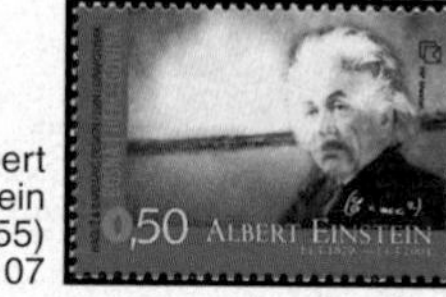

Albert Einstein (1879-1955) A107

2004, Mar. 14
118 A107 50pf multi 1.25 1.25

Hand Tattoos A108

2004, Mar. 20
119 A108 50pf multi 1.10 1.10

Flora & Fauna Type of 2003

Designs: 1m, Aquilegia dinarica. 1.50m, Salamandra atra prenjensis.

2004, Mar. 30
120 A93 1m multi 2.00 2.00
121 A93 1.50m multi 3.25 3.25

Europa — A109

No. 122: a, 1.50m, Skis of skier at hill, 2m, Fins of swimmer at beach.

2004, Apr. 5 Litho. *Perf. 14*
122 A109 Horiz. pair, #a-b *8.00 8.00*

Printed in sheets of 4 pairs + 2 labels.

Father Andrija Kacic Miosic (1704-60), Poet — A110

2004, Apr. 17
123 A110 70pf dk ol bis & brn 1.40 1.40

A111

A112

2004, June 12
124 A111 2m multi 3.75 3.75
a. Miniature sheet of 4 16.00 16.00

European Soccer Championships, Portugal.

2004, June 27
125 A112 70pf multi 1.40 1.40

Kocerin Tablet, 600th anniv.

Moon Landing, 35th Anniv. — A113

2004, July 20
126 A113 1m multi 2.10 2.10

Reconstruction of Old Bridge, Mostar — A114

2004, July 23
127 A114 50pf multi 1.25 1.25

Buna River Water Wheel A115

2004, Sept. 9 Litho. *Perf. 14*
128 A115 1m multi 2.10 2.10

World Post Day — A116

2004, Oct. 9
129 A116 1.50m multi 3.00 3.00

Printed in sheets of 8 + label.

Savings Day — A117

2004, Oct. 31
130 A117 50pf multi 1.00 1.00

Printed in sheets of 8 + label.

Karl Benz (1844-1929), Automobile Manufacturer — A118

2004, Nov. 25
131 A118 1.50m multi 3.00 3.00

Printed in sheets of 8 + label.

Christmas — A119

No. 132: a, 50pf, Journey to Bethlehem. b, 1m, Christmas trees, man with gift.

2004, Dec. 4
132 A119 Horiz. pair, #a-b 3.00 3.00

Woman From Kupres — A120

2005, Feb. 20
133 A120 1.50m multi 3.00 3.00

Birds — A121

No. 134: a, Egretta garzetta. b, Himantopus himantopus. c, Merops apiaster. d, Alcedo atthis.

2005, Mar. 2
134 A121 1m Block of 4, #a-d 8.25 8.25

Flowers — A122

Designs: No. 135, 50pf, Gentiana dinarica. No. 136, 50pf, Petteria ramentacea.

2005, Mar. 2
135-136 A122 Set of 2 2.00 2.00

Zrinjski Soccer Team, Cent. — A123

No. 137: a, Three players, denomination at right. b, Two players, denomination at left.

2005, Mar. 15 Litho. *Perf. 14*
137 A123 3m Pair, #a-b 12.00 12.00

Easter — A124

2005, Mar. 27
138 A124 50pf multi 1.00 1.00

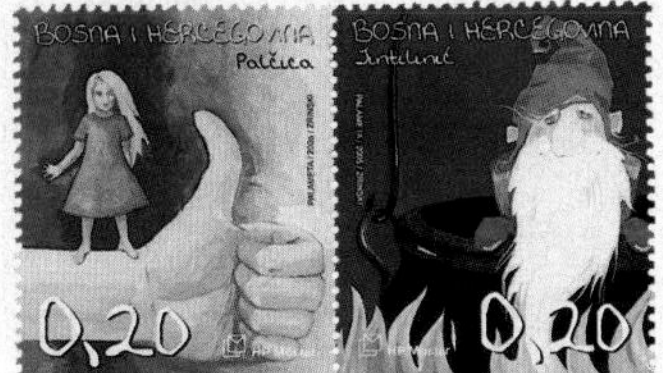

Fairy Tales — A125

No. 139: a, Palcica (Thumbelina, by Hans Christian Andersen). b, Tintilinic, by Ivana Brlic Mazuranic.

2005, Apr. 2
139 A125 20pf Pair, #a-b .90 .90

Europa — A126

No. 140: a, Wine bottle, knife, cutting board, garlic, ham, cheese, and bread. b, Cruet, grapes, bread, nuts and cheese.

2005, Apr. 5
140 Pair 7.50 7.50
a.-b. A126 2m Either single 2.50 2.50
c. Souvenir sheet, 2 each #140a-140b 16.00 16.00

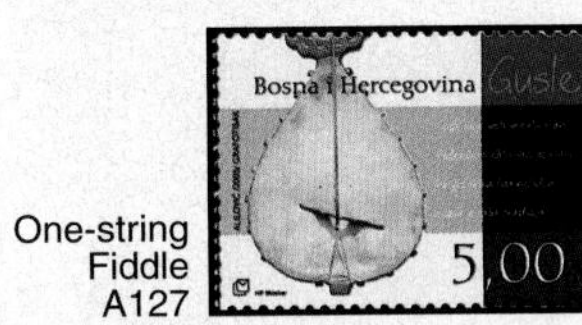

One-string Fiddle A127

2005, May 10 Litho. *Perf. 14*
141 A127 5m multi 9.25 9.25

Vjetrenica Cave — A128

2005, June 5 Litho. *Perf. 14*
142 A128 1m multi 2.00 2.00

World Environment Day.

Metkovic — Mostar Rail Line — A129

2005, June 14
143 A129 50pf multi 1.00 1.00

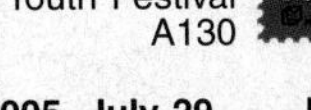

Medjugorje Youth Festival A130

2005, July 29 Litho. *Perf. 14*
144 A130 1m multi 2.00 2.00

Father Grgo Martic (1822-1905), Writer — A131

2005, Aug. 30
145 A131 1m multi 2.00 2.00

Trumpet A132

2005, Oct. 1 Litho. *Perf. 14*
146 A132 50pf multi 1.00 1.00

Printed in sheets of 8 + label.

Dayton Peace Accords, 10th Anniv. — A133

2005, Nov. 21
147 A133 1.50m multi 3.00 3.00

Printed in sheets of 8 + label.

Brother Slavko Barbaric (1946-2000) A134

2005, Nov. 24
148 A134 1m multi 2.00 2.00

Printed in sheets of 8 + label.

Christmas — A135

Designs: No. 149, 50pf, Madonna and Child. No. 150, 50pf, Christmas tree.

2005, Dec. 4
149-150 A135 Set of 2 2.00 2.00

Nos. 149-150 each printed in sheets of 8 + label.

Europa Stamps, 50th Anniv. — A136

No. 151: a, Map of Europe, "50." b, Map of Europe in flowers, envelope. c, Map of Europe in examples of #99. d, Flags, flower, "50."

2006, Jan. 15
151 Horiz. strip of 4 15.00 15.00
a.-d. A136 2m Any single 3.25 3.25
e. Souvenir sheet, #151a-151d 15.00 15.00

World Wetlands Day — A137

2006, Feb. 2
152 A137 1m multi 2.00 2.00

Printed in sheets of 8 + label.

Europa — A138

No. 153: a, Footprints and "integration." b, Faces.

2006, Apr. 5
153 A138 2m Pair, #a-b 7.50 7.50
c. Souvenir sheet, 2 each #153a-153b 15.00 15.00

No. 153 printed in sheets containing 4 pairs and 2 labels.

Earth Day — A139

2006, Apr. 22
154 A139 1m multi 2.00 2.00

World Press Freedom Day — A140

2006, May 3
155 A140 50pf multi 1.00 1.00

World Telecommunications Day — A141

2006, May 17
156 A141 1m multi 2.00 2.00

Apparition of the Virgin Mary at Medjugorje, 25th Anniv. — A142

Designs: No. 157, Statue of Virgin Mary, church at night. No. 158, Statue with halo. No. 159, Statue and cross. No. 160, Statue, church and tent. No. 161, People and church.

2006, June 18 Litho. *Perf. 14*
Booklet Stamps

157 A142 1m multi 1.90 1.90
158 A142 1m multi 1.90 1.90
159 A142 1m multi 1.90 1.90
160 A142 1m multi 1.90 1.90
161 A142 1m multi 1.90 1.90
a. Booklet pane, 2 each #157-161 19.00 —
Complete booklet, #161a 19.00

Parish of Uzdol, 150th Anniv. — A143

2006, June 24
162 A143 50pf multi 1.00 1.00

Printed in sheets of 8 + label.

Nikola Tesla (1856-1943), Electrical Engineer — A144

2006, July 9
163 A144 2m multi 4.00 4.00

Medieval Tombstones A145

2006, Sept. 9
164 A145 20pf multi .45 .45

European Car-Free Day — A146

2006, Sept. 22
165 A146 1m multi 2.00 2.00

Printed in sheets of 8 + label.

Women's Jewelry in Franciscan Monastery Museum, Humac — A147

2006, Oct. 9
166 A147 5m multi 10.00 10.00

Flowers — A148

No. 167: a, Cerastium dinaricum. b, Papaver kerneri.

2006, Nov. 1
167 A148 20pf Horiz. pair, #a-b .75 .75

Birds —A148a

Designs: No. 167C, 70pf, Podiceps cristatus. No. 167D, 70pf, Acrocephalus scirpaceus. No. 167E, 70pf, Upupa epops. No. 167F, 70pf, Alauda arvensis.

2006, Nov. 1 Litho. *Perf. 14*
167C-167F A148a Set of 4 5.50 5.50

A148b

Christmas — A148c

2006, Dec. 1 Litho. *Perf. 14*
167G A148b 50pf multi 1.00 1.00
167H A148c 1m multi 1.75 1.75

Nos. 167G-167H each were printed in sheets of 8 + label.

Valentine's Day — A149

2007, Feb. 14 Litho. *Perf. 14*
168 A149 10pf multi .45 .45

Miniature Sheet

Tornjak Dog — A150

No. 169: a, Head of dog facing right. b, Head of dog facing left. c, Entire dog facing right. d, Entire dog facing left.

2007, Feb. 22
169 A150 70pf Sheet of 4, #a-d 5.25 5.25

Mak Dizdar (1917-71), Poet — A151

2007, Mar. 21
170 A151 1m multi 2.00 2.00

Europa — A152

No. 171: a, Clasped hands. b, Knot.

2007, Apr. 5
171 A152 3m Pair, #a-b 11.00 11.00
c. Miniature sheet, 2 each #171a-171b 22.00 22.00

Scouting, cent.

Souvenir Sheet

Arbor Day — A153

2007, Apr. 25
172 A153 2.10m multi 4.50 4.50

Gabela Archaeological Site — A154

2007, May 12
173 A154 1.50m multi 3.00 3.00

Iris — A155

Irises and Ship — A156

2007, May 22
174 A155 2m multi 4.25 4.25

Souvenir Sheet

175 A156 3m multi 6.25 6.25

Apparition of the Virgin Mary at Medjugorje, 26th Anniv. — A157

No. 176: a, Statue of Virgin Mary. b, Hands holding rosary. c, People near statue of Virgin Mary. d, Steeple and statue of Virgin Mary. e, Statue of priest holding crucifix.

2007, June 1 Booklet Stamps
176 Horiz. strip of 5 10.00 10.00
a.-e. A157 1m Any single 1.00 1.00
f. Booket pane of 10, 2 each #176a-176e 20.00 —
Complete booklet, #176f 20.00

Bishop Marko Dobretic (c. 1707-84) — A158

2007, June 13
177 A158 60pf multi 1.25 1.25

Boljuni Cemetery — A159

2007, Sept. 23 Litho. *Perf. 14*
178 A159 20pf multi .45 .45

Printed in sheets of 8 + label.

World Bowling Championships, Grude — A160

2007, Sept. 24
179 A160 5m black & red 10.00 10.00

Printed in sheets of 8 + label.

Distaff and Spindle — A161

2007, Oct. 9
180 A161 70pf multi 1.40 1.40

Printed in sheets of 8 + label.

Birds of Hutovo Blato — A162

No. 181: a, Streptopelia turtur. b, Anas crecca. c, Anas platyrhynchos. d, Fulica atra.

2007, Nov. 1
181 A162 2m Block of 4, #a-d 17.00 17.00

Flora of Blidinje Nature Park — A163

Designs: No. 182, Gentiana lutea. No. 183, Vaccinium vitis-idaea.

2007, Nov. 1
182 A163 3m multi 6.25 6.25

Souvenir Sheet

183 A163 3m multi 6.25 6.25

Christmas and New Year's Day — A164

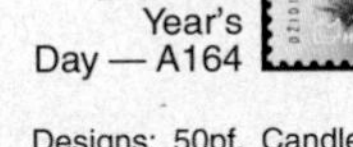

Designs: 50pf, Candles and wreath. 70pf, Christmas tree near steps.

2007, Dec. 1
184-185 A164 Set of 2 2.40 2.40

Nos. 184-185 each printed in sheets of 8 + label.

Bishop Andjeo Kraljevic (1807-79) A165

2007, Dec. 28
186 A165 1m multi 2.00 2.00

Easter — A166

2008, Mar. 23 **Litho.** ***Perf. 14***
187 A166 70pf multi 1.50 1.50

Croatian Cultural Days — A167

2008, Mar. 25
188 A167 10pf multi .45 .45

Europa — A168

Designs: No. 189, 3m, Airmail envelope folded into paper airplane. No. 190, 3m, Letter and fountain pen.

2008, Apr. 5
189-190 A168 Set of 2 12.00 12.00
190a Miniature sheet, 2 each #189-190 24.00 24.00

Helmet of Illyrian Warrior — A169

Litho. & Embossed

2008, May 12 ***Perf. 14***
191 A169 2.10m multi 3.50 3.50

Printed in sheets of 8 + 2 labels.

Grave of Rabbi Moshe Danon — A170

2008, May 21
192 A170 1.50m multi 2.50 2.50

Souvenir Sheet

Achillea Millefolium and Andrija Simic (1833-1905), Outlaw — A171

2008, May 22
193 A171 2.90m multi 5.00 5.00

Apparition of the Virgin Mary at Medjugorje, 27th Anniv. — A172

No. 194: a, Dove, cross, cloud. b, Dove, Virgin Mary. c, Bible, crucified Jesus, praying hands. d, Hands, church. e, Virgin Mary, child, dove.

2008, June 1
194 Horiz. strip of 5 10.00 10.00
a.-e. A172 1m Any single 2.00 2.00

Brotnjo Vintage Days — A173

Color of grapes: 50pf, Purple. 70pf, Red.

2008, Sept. 9 **Litho.** ***Perf. 14***
195-196 A173 Set of 2 2.25 2.25

Zaostrog Monastery — A174

2008, Oct. 4
197 A174 1m multi 1.90 1.90

Tobacco Cutter — A175

2008, Oct. 9
198 A175 2m multi 3.75 3.75

Printed in sheets of 8 + label.

Zepce, 550th Anniv. — A176

2008, Oct. 14
199 A176 1.50m multi 3.00 3.00

Intl. Year of the Potato — A177

Solanum tuberosum: 60pf, Plant and tubers. 5m, Flower.

2008, Nov. 1
200 A177 60pf multi 1.10 1.10

Souvenir Sheet

201 A177 5m multi 9.25 9.25

Birds — A178

No. 202: a, Accipiter gentilis. b, Bubo bubo. c, Circaetus gallicus. d, Falco tinnunculus.

2008, Nov. 1
202 A178 1.50m Block of 4, #a-d 11.50 11.50

Father Leo Petrovic (1883-1945), Professor — A179

2008, Nov. 15
203 A179 1m multi 2.50 2.50

Christmas A180

New Year's Day — A181

2008, Dec. 1

204 A180 70pf multi 1.40 1.40
205 A181 70pf multi 1.40 1.40

Siroki Brijeg Soccer Team, 60th Anniv. — A182

Players and team emblem: 70pf, Sepia photograph. 2.10m, Full color and black-and-white photographs.

2008, Dec. 12

206 A182 70pf multi 1.40 1.40

Souvenir Sheet

207 A182 2.10m multi 4.00 4.00

No. 207 contains one 35x30mm stamp.

Daffodil Day — A183

2009, Mar. 21 Litho. *Perf. 14*

208 A183 20pf brt pink & yel .45 .45

Campaign against breast cancer.

Intl. Water Day — A184

No. 209: a, Waterfall on Pliva River. b, Mills along river.

2009, Mar. 22

209 A184 70pf Horiz. pair, #a-b 2.50 2.50

Council of Europe, 60th Anniv. — A185

European Court of Human Rights, 50th Anniv. A186

2009, Apr. 1

210 A185 1.50m multi 2.75 2.75
211 A186 1.50m multi 2.75 2.75

Europa A187

No. 212 — Planets and: a, Galileo Galilei (1564-1642), astronomer. b, Telescope.

2009, Apr. 5 Litho. & Embossed

212 A187 3m Vert. pair, #a-b 10.00 10.00

Intl. Year of Astronomy. Printed in sheets containing two pairs.

Seal of Duke Stipan Vukcic Kosaca — A188

2009, May 12 Litho. *Perf. 14*

213 A188 1.50m multi 2.50 2.50

Printed in sheets of 8 + label.

Field of Tanacetum Balsamita — A189

2009, May 22

214 A189 2.10m shown 3.25 3.25

Souvenir Sheet

215 A189 2.10m Flowers, woman's head 3.25 3.25

Guca Gora Franciscan Monastery, 150th Anniv. A190

2009, May 30

216 A190 70pf multi 1.25 1.25

Printed in sheets of 8 + central label.

Apparition of the Virgin Mary at Medjugorje, 28th Anniv. — A191

No. 217: a, Virgin Mary. b, Virgin Mary and church. c, Steeples and hand raising crucifix. d, Cross and path. e, Church.

2009, June 1 *Perf. 14*

Booklet Stamps

217 Horiz. strip of 5 7.50 7.50
a.-e. A191 1m Any single 1.50 1.50
f. Booklet pane of 10, 2 each #217a-217e 15.00 —
Complete booklet, #217f 15.00

10th Mediterranean Film Festival A192

2009, Sept. 1

218 A192 70pf multi 1.25 1.25

Franciscan Order, 800th Anniv. — A193

No. 219: a, Monk's rope cincture. b, Shrine.

2009, Oct. 4 Litho. *Perf. 14*

219 A193 1m Horiz. pair, #a-b 3.50 3.50

Wooden Hope Chest — A194

2009, Oct. 9

220 A194 70pf multi 1.25 1.25

Gorica Livno Franciscan Monastery, 150th Anniv. — A195

2009, Nov. 1

221 A195 60pf multi 1.10 1.10

Prunus Domestica A196

Prunus domestica: No. 222, Fruit on branch. No. 223, Blossoms and fruit.

2009, Nov. 1

222 A196 5m multi 7.50 7.50

Souvenir Sheet

223 A196 5m multi 7.50 7.50

Birds of Hutovo Blato — A197

No. 224: a, Coturnix coturnix. b, Cucuclus canorus. c, Rallus aquaticus. d, Nycticorax nycticorax.

2009, Nov. 1

224 A197 1.50m Block or strip of 4, #a-d 9.25 9.25

Christmas A198

New Year's Day — A199

2009, Dec. 1

225 A198 70pf multi 1.25 1.25
226 A199 70pf multi 1.25 1.25

2010 Winter Olympics, Vancouver A200

Designs: 70pf, Shown. 1.50m, Maple leaf on skis.

2010, Feb. 1

227-228 A200 Set of 2 3.50 3.50

Nos. 227-228 each were printed in sheets of 8 + 2 labels.

Intl. Women's Day — A201

2010, Mar. 8

229 A201 20pf multi .45 .45

Friar Martin Nedic (1810-95), Poet — A202

2010, Apr. 1

230 A202 2.10m multi 3.25 3.25

Europa — A203

Stylized child with: No. 231, 3m, Kite. No. 232, 3m, Pinwheel.

2010, Apr. 5

231-232 A203 Set of 2 10.00 10.00
232a Sheet of 4, 2 each #231-232 20.00 20.00

Ravlica Cave Archaeological Site — A204

2010, May 12 Litho. *Perf. 14*
233 A204 1.50m multi 2.75 2.75

Souvenir Sheet

Linden Tree in Slavic Mythology — A205

2010, May 22
234 A205 5m multi 7.50 7.50

Apparition of the Virgin Mary at Medjugorje, 29th Anniv. A206

No. 235: a, Flags, church and crowd. b, Statue and crowd. c, Hand holding rosary. d, Cross and crowd. e, Statue and crosses on hillside.

2010, June 1 Booklet Stamps
235 Vert. strip of 5 9.50 9.50
a.-e. A206 1m Any single 1.90 1.90
f. Booklet pane of 10, 2 each #235a-235e 19.00 19.00
Complete booklet, #235f 19.00 19.00

Matrix Croatica General Assembly, Citluk — A207

2010, June 19
236 A207 1m red & black 1.50 1.50

Printed in sheets of 8 + 2 labels.

Mother Teresa (1910-97), Humanitarian A208

2010, Aug. 27 Litho. *Perf. 14*
237 A208 2.10m blue 4.00 4.00

Intl. Day for Habitat Protection — A209

No. 238: a, Lake Prokosko. b, Lake Prokosko and Triturus alpestris reiseri.

2010, Oct. 6
238 A209 1m Horiz. pair, #a-b 3.75 3.75

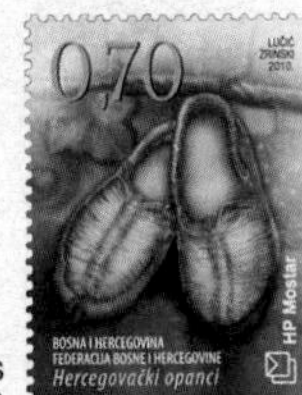

Peasant's Shoes — A210

2010, Oct. 9
239 A210 70pf multi 1.40 1.40

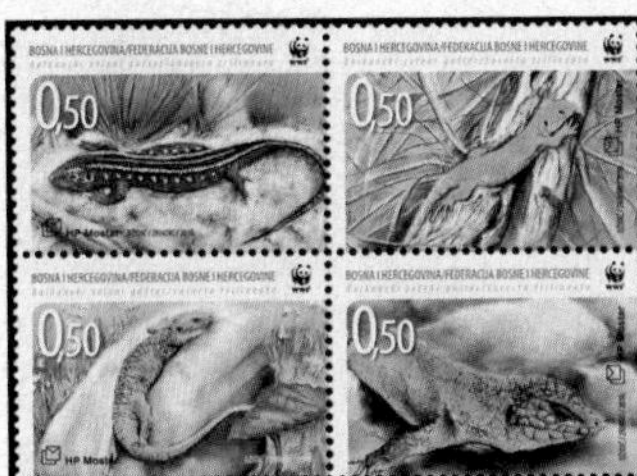

Worldwide Fund for Nature — A211

No. 240 — Lacerta trilineata: a, With black coloring, on rock. b, Climbing tree. c, With green coloring, on rock. d, Head.

2010, Nov. 1
240 A211 50pf Block of 4, #a-d 3.50 3.50

Mushrooms — A212

No. 241: a, Lycoperdon perlatum. b, Amanita muscaria.

2010, Nov. 1
241 A212 2.10m Horiz. pair, #a-b 8.25 8.25

Father Slavko Barbaric (1946-2000), Investigator of Medjugorje Apparitions — A213

2010, Nov. 24
242 A213 1m multi 1.90 1.90

Christmas A214

New Year 2011 — A215

2010, Dec. 1
243 A214 70pf multi 1.25 1.25
244 A215 70pf multi 1.25 1.25

Printing of First Croatian Book in Bosnia & Herzegovina, 400th Anniv. A216

2011, Feb. 21
245 A216 70pf multi 1.10 1.10

World Meteorological Day — A217

2011, Mar. 23
246 A217 20pf multi .40 .40

Easter A218

2011, Apr. 1
247 A218 70pf multi 1.10 1.10

Europa — A219

No. 248 — Forest with: a, Green panels. b, Red panels.

2011, Apr. 5
248 A219 3m Pair, #a-b 10.00 10.00
c. Souvenir sheet of 4, 2 each #248a-248b 20.00 20.00

Intl. Year of Forests. No. 248 was printed in sheets containing four pairs and two central labels.

First Man in Space, 50th Anniv. — A220

2011, Apr. 12
249 A220 10pf multi .40 .40

Diagram of Early Christian Basilica, Cim — A221

2011, May 12
250 A221 1.50m multi 3.00 3.00

Rudjer Boskovic (1711-87), Astronomer A222

2011, May 18
251 A222 2.10m multi 4.00 4.00

Souvenir Sheet

Hawthorn Branch — A223

2011, May 22
252 A223 5m multi 7.25 7.25

Apparition of the Virgin Mary at Medjugorje, 30th Anniv. — A224

No. 253: a, Wooden cross and rosary beads. b, Church. c, Sculpture of crucified Jesus. d, Statue of Virgin Mary.

Litho. & Embossed

2011, June 1 *Perf. 14x13¾*
253 A224 1m Block of 4, #a-d 7.50 7.50
e. Souvenir sheet of 4, #253a-253d 7.50 7.50
f. Booklet pane, 2 #253 + 2 labels 15.00 —
Complete booklet, #253f 15.00

St. Anthony of Padua (1195-1231) A225

2011, June 13 Litho. *Perf. 14*
254 A225 1m multi 2.00 2.00

World Bicycle Day — A226

2011, July 16 Litho. *Perf. 14*
255 A226 70pf green 1.15 1.15

Skopaljska Gracanica Parish, Cent. — A227

2011, Aug. 13
256 A227 50pf multi .75 .75

Beatification of the Blessed Martyrs of Drina — A228

2011, Sept. 24
257 A228 70pf multi 1.00 1.00

Fibulae A229

2011, Oct. 9
258 A229 1m multi 1.60 1.60

World Post Day. No. 258 was printed in sheets of 8 + label.

Fridtjof Nansen (1861-1930), Polar Explorer and Diplomat — A230

2011, Oct. 10
259 A230 1.50m multi 2.25 2.25

Fruit — A231

No. 260: a, Punica granatum. b, Ficus carica.

2011, Nov. 1
260 A231 2m Horiz. pair, #a-b 6.00 6.00

Lynx Lynx — A232

No. 261 — Panel color: a, Green. b, Red. c, Orange. d, Blue violet.

2011, Nov. 1
261 A232 3m Block of 4, #a-d 18.00 18.00

Christmas A233

New Year 2012 A234

2011, Dec. 1
262 A233 70pf multi 1.00 1.00
263 A234 70pf multi 1.00 1.00

Latin Grammar Book, by Toma Babic, 300th Anniv. of Publication A235

2012, Feb. 21
264 A235 70pf multi 1.00 1.00

Cheese Produced at Trappist Monasteries A236

2012, Mar. 21
265 A236 2.10m multi 3.00 3.00

Europa — A237

No. 266 — Sites in Mostar: a, Duke Stjepan Kosaca Lodge. b, Old Bridge.

2012, Apr. 5
266 A237 3m Pair, #a-b 9.50 9.50
c. Souvenir sheet of 4, 2 each #266a-266b 19.00 19.00

No. 266 was printed in sheets of 4 pairs + 2 labels.

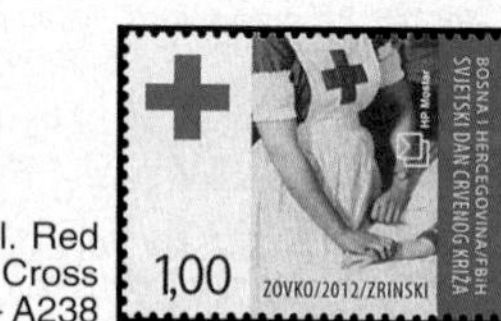

Intl. Red Cross Day — A238

2012, May 8
267 A238 1m red & black 1.75 1.75

Monument to God Mithra, Konjic A239

2012, May 12
268 A239 70pf multi 1.25 1.25

Souvenir Sheet

Carpinus Betulus — A240

2012, May 22
269 A240 3m multi 4.50 4.50

Nobel Laureates Ivo Andric (1892-1975) and Vladimir Prelog (1906-98) — A241

2012, May 23
270 A241 1.50m multi 2.25 2.25

Apparition of the Virgin Mary at Medjugorje, 31st Anniv. — A242

2012, June 1
271 A242 1m multi 1.75 1.75

Walled Towns — A243

No. 272: a, Visoko. b, Blagaj.

2012, June 22
272 A243 60pf Pair, #a-b 1.75 1.75

Father Nikola Simovic (1839-1912), Vicar General — A244

2012, Sept. 10
273 A244 1m multi 1.60 1.60

Printed in sheets of 8 + central label.

Sargija — A245

2012, Oct. 9
274 A245 20pf multi .40 .40

3rd Cent. B.C. Coins From Daorson — A246

No. 275 — Obverse and reverse of coin: a, With verdigris (green oxidation). b, Without verdigris.

2012, Oct. 31 **Litho. & Embossed**
275 A246 5m Pair, #a-b 15.00 15.00

Savings Day. No. 275 was printed in sheets containing two pairs.

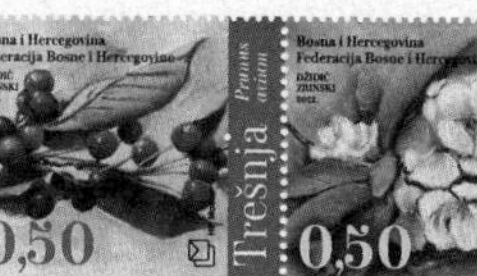

Prunus Avium — A247

Prunus avium: a, Fruit. b, Blossoms.

2012, Nov. 1 **Litho.**
276 A247 50pf Pair, #a-b 1.60 1.60

Printed in sheets containing 4 pairs + 2 labels

Snakes — A248

No. 277: a, Natrix natrix. b, Zamenis longissimus. c, Vipera ammodytes. d, Vipera berus.

2012, Nov. 1 ***Perf. 14***
277 A248 2m Block of 4, #a-d 12.00 12.00

Christmas A249

New Year's Day — A250

2012, Dec. 1
278 A249 70pf multi 1.10 1.10
279 A250 70pf multi 1.10 1.10

Edict of Milan, 1700th Anniv. — A251

2013, Jan. 26
280 A251 90pf multi 1.25 1.25

Printed in sheets of 8 + central label.

New Year 2013 (Year of the Snake) A252

2013, Feb. 10 ***Perf. 14***
281 A252 20pf multi .30 .30

Kulin (1163-1204), Ban of Bosnia — A253

2013, Mar. 1
282 A253 1.50m multi 2.00 2.00

Printed in sheets of 8 + 2 labels.

Europa — A254

No. 283: a, Postal van. b, Postal moped.

2013, Apr. 5 ***Perf. 14¼x14***
283 A254 3m Horiz. pair, #a-b 8.00 8.00
c. Souvenir sheet of 4, 2 each #283a-283b 16.00 16.00

No. 283 was printed in sheets containing 4 pairs + 2 labels.

Intl. Firefighter's Day — A255

2013, May 4 ***Perf. 14***
284 A255 70pf multi .95 .95

Cemetery Stone, Monastery of St. John, Livno — A256

2013, May 12
285 A256 10pf multi .25 .25

Postage Stamps of Croat Administration, 20th Anniv. — A257

Litho. With Foil Application
Perf. 13¾x14 Syncopated

2013, May 12
286 A257 2.10m multi 3.00 3.00

Printed in sheets of 9 + label.

Souvenir Sheet

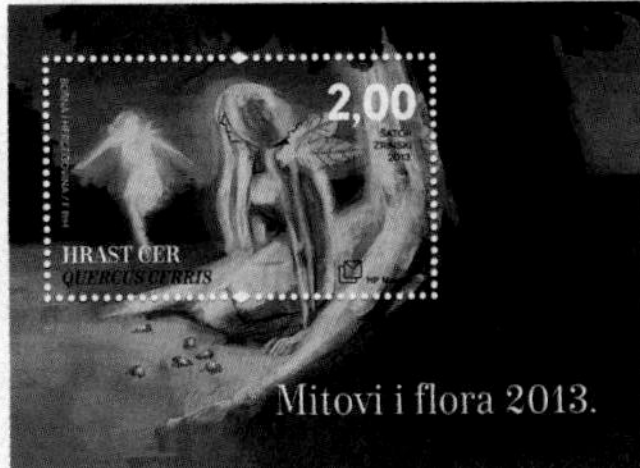

Quercus Cerris — A258

Perf. 13¾x14 Syncopated

2013, May 22 **Litho.**
287 A258 2m multi 2.75 2.75

Apparition of the Virgin Mary at Medjugorje, 32nd Anniv. A259

2013, June 1 **Litho.** ***Perf. 14***
288 A259 1m multi 1.40 1.40

Friar Radoslav Glavas (1867-1913), Writer — A260

2013, July 20 **Litho.** ***Perf. 14x14¼***
289 A260 1m multi 1.40 1.40

BOSNIA & HERZEGOVINA (SERB ADMIN)

Bosnian Serb Administration Located In Banja Luka

(Republika Srpska)

100 Paras = 1 Dinar

100pfennig = 1 mark (6/22/98)

Catalogue values for all unused stamps in this country are for Never Hinged items.

Stamps of Yugoslavia Surcharged

No. 3

No. 3a

No. 4

No. 9

No. 11

1992, Oct. 26 **Litho.** ***Perf. 12½***
1 A559 5d on 10p #2004 2.10 2.10
2 A559 30d on 3d #2015 *225.00 225.00*
3 A559 50d on 40p #2007a, perf. 13½ 2.10 2.10
a. Thick bars in obliterator 9.00 9.00
b. On #2007, perf 12½ — —
4 A559 60d on 20p #2005 2.40 2.40
5 A559 60d on 30p #2006 2.40 2.40
6 A559 100d on 1d #2013 2.40 2.40
7 A559 100d on 2d #2014a, perf. 13½ 2.40 2.40
a. On #2014, perf 12½ — —
8 A559 100d on 3d #2015 2.40 2.40
9 A621 300d on 5d #2017a, perf. 13½ 2.40 2.40
a. On #2017, perf 12½ — —
10 A620 500d on 50p #2008 2.40 2.40
11 A619 500d on 60p #2009 2.40 2.40
a. On #2009 perf. 13½ *110.00 110.00*
Nos. 1-11 (11) *248.40 248.40*

Obliterator on Nos. 1, 3 and 9 has thin bars.

Musical Instrument — A1

Designs: 10d, 20d, 30d, 5000d, 6000d, 10,000d, Stringed instrument. 50d, 100d, 20,000d, 30,000d, Coat of arms, vert. 500d, 50,000d, Monastery.

1993 ***Perf. 13¼, 12½ (#19)***
12 A1 10d blk & org yel 6.50 6.50
13 A1 20d blk & blue .30 .30
14 A1 30d blk & salmon .75 .75
15 A1 50d blk & ver .75 .75
16 A1 100d blk & ver 2.00 2.00
17 A1 500d blk & blue 4.25 4.25
18 A1 5000d blk & lilac .35 .35
19 A1 6000d blk & yel .35 .35
20 A1 10,000d blk & vio bl 4.50 4.50
a. Perf. 12½ 3.50 3.50
21 A1 20,000d blk & ver 1.25 1.25
22 A1 30,000d blk & ver 2.00 2.00
23 A1 50,000d blk & lilac 2.00 2.00
Nos. 12-23 (12) 25.00 25.00

Nos. 12-17 dated 1992, others dated 1993. Issued: Nos. 12-17, 1/11; others 6/8.

For surcharges see Nos. 24-26, 34-36, 41-45, F9

Nos. 15-16 Surcharged

1993, June 15
24 A1 7500d on 50d #15 2.75 2.75
25 A1 7500d on 100d #16 2.75 2.75
26 A1 9000d on 50d #15 3.75 3.75
Nos. 24-26 (3) 9.25 9.25

Referendum, May 15-16, 1993.

A2

Symbol of St. John, the Evangelist.

1993, Aug. 16 ***Perf. 13¼***
27 A2 (A) vermilion .90 .90

A3

1994, Jan. 9 ***Perf. 14***
28 A3 1d Icon of St. Stefan 9.00 9.00

King Peter I Karageorge A4

1994, May 28
29 A4 80p sepia 4.25 4.25

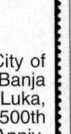

City of Banja Luka, 500th Anniv. A5

1994, July 18
30 A5 1.20d multicolored 5.50 5.50

Nos. 31-32 have been reserved for surcharges on Nos. 13, 21. The editors would like to examine these stamps.

Madonna & Child, Cajnica Church — A6

1994, Sept. 1
33 A6 1d multicolored 4.50 4.50

Nos. 18, 20, 23 Surcharged

1994, Nov. 1 ***Perf. 13¼***
34 A1 (A) on 5000d #18 1.60 1.60
35 A1 40p on 10,000d #20 1.60 1.60
a. On #20a 3.50 3.50
36 A1 2d on 50,000d #23 1.60 1.60
a. Perf 12½ 22.50 22.50
Nos. 34-36,F9 (4) 6.40 6.40

No. 34 sold for 20p on day of issue.

Mostanica Monastery A7

Designs: 60p, Tavna Monastery, vert. 1.20d, Zitomislic Monastery, vert.

1994 ***Perf. 14***
37-39 A7 Set of 3 12.00 12.00

Issued: 60p, 11/11; 1d, 12/31; 1.20d, 12/28.

Flora & Fauna A8

No. 40: a, Shore lark. b, Dinaromys bogdanovi. c, Edraianthus niveus. d, Aquilegia dinarica.

1996, Mar. 1 ***Perf. 13¾***
40 A8 1.20d Block of 4, #a.-d. 7.00 7.00

Nos. 14-16, 19, 22 Surcharged

1996, July 1 *Perf. 13¼*

41 A1 70p on 30d #14 .65 .65
42 A1 1d on 100d #16 .85 .85
43 A1 2d on 30,000d #22 1.75 1.75
44 A1 3d on 50d #15 2.75 2.75

Perf. 12½

45 A1 5d on 6000d #19 4.75 4.75
Nos. 41-45 (5) 10.75 10.75

Relay Station, Mt. Kozara — A9

1.20d, Drina River Bridge, Srbinje, horiz. 2d, Mt. Romanija relay station. 5d, Stolice relay station, Mt. Maljevica. 10d, Visegrad Bridge, horiz.

1996, Sept. 20 *Perf. 14*

46 A9 (A) multicolored .30 .30
47 A9 1.20d multicolored .75 .75
48 A9 2d multicolored 1.50 1.50
49 A9 5d multicolored 3.50 3.50
50 A9 10d multicolored 7.00 7.00
Nos. 46-50,F10 (6) 13.80 13.80

No. 46 sold for 30p on day of issue.

Church, Bashcharsi A10

1997, July 7 *Perf. 13¾*

51 A10 2.50d multicolored 2.25 2.25

Mihailo Pupin (1848-1935), Electrical Engineer A11

1997, July 14

52 A11 2.50d multicolored 2.25 2.25

A12

A13

Flowers: No. 53, Oxytropis compestris. No. 54, Primula kitaibeliana. No. 55, Pedicularis hoermanniana. No. 56, Knautia sarajevensis.

1997, Sept. 12

53-56 A12 3.20d Set of 4 9.00 9.00

1997, Nov. 1 *Perf. 13¾*

Famous Men: A, Branko Copic (1915-85). 1.50d, Mesa Selimovic (1910-82). 3d, Aleksa Santic (1868-1924). 5d, Peter Kocic (1873-1916). 10d, Ivo Andric (1892-1975).

57 A13 A multicolored .45 .45
58 A13 1.50d multicolored .75 .75
59 A13 3d multicolored 1.90 1.90
60 A13 5d multicolored 3.25 3.25
61 A13 10d multicolored 6.00 6.00
Nos. 57-61,F11 (6) 13.10 13.10

No. 57 sold for 60p on day of issue.

A14

Europa — A15

2.50d, Lutra lutra. 4.50d, Capreolus capreolus. 6.50d, Ursus arctos.

1997, Nov. 12

62-64 A14 Set of 3 7.50 7.50

1997, Nov. 12

Stories & legends: 2.50d, Two queens. 6.50d, Prince on horseback.

65-66 A15 Set of 2 *30.00 30.00*

Diana, Princess of Wales (1961-97) — A16

"Diana" in: a, Roman letters. b, Cyrillic letters.

1997, Dec. 22

67 A16 3.50d Pair, #a.-b. 20.00 20.00

1998 World Cup Soccer Championships, France — A17

Players, country flags (each 90p) — No. 68: a, Brazil. b, Morocco. c, Norway. d, Scotland. e, Italy. f, Chile. g, Austria. h, Cameroun.

No. 69: a, France. b, Saudi Arabia. c, Denmark. d, South Africa. e, Spain. f, Nigeria. g, Paraguay. h, Bulgaria.

No. 70: a, Netherlands. b, Belgium. c, Mexico. d, South Korea. e, Germany. f, US. g, Yugoslavia. h, Iran.

No. 71: a, Romania. b, England. c, Tunisia. d, Colombia. e, Argentina. f, Jamaica. g, Croatia. h, Japan.

1998, May 5 **Sheets of 8 + label**

68-71 A17 Set of 4 75.00 75.00

Europa — A18

Natl. festivals, each 7.50d: No. 72, Instrument at R. No. 73, Instrument at L.

1998, June 9

72-73 A18 Set of 2 *27.00 27.00*

Icons, Chelandari Monastery A19

Various icons: 50p, 70p, 1.70d, 2d.

1998

74-77 A19 Set of 4 11.50 11.50

Buildings — A20

Designs: 15pf, Bijeljina. 20pf, Sokolac. A, Banja Luka. 75pf, Prijedor. 2m, Brcko, vert. 4.50m, Zvornik, vert. 10m, Doboj.

1999, Mar. 15 **Litho.** *Perf. 13¾*

78-84 A20 Set of 7 36.00 36.00

No. 80 has black "A." It sold for 50pf on day of issue. See No. F12.

Air Srpska Airplanes A21

Airplane: No. 85, 50pf, In clouds. No. 86, 50pf, Over lake. 75pf, Over rocks. 1.50m, Over lake, diff.

1999, Mar. 26 **Litho.** *Perf. 13¾*

85-88 A21 Set of 4 7.50 7.50

World Table Tennis Championships, Belgrade — A22

Designs: 1m, Cracked globe as ball. 2m, Table, paddle, ball.

1999, Apr. 19

89-90 A22 Set of 2 9.25 9.25

Issued in sheets of 8 + label.

Europa — A23

Natl. Parks: 1.50m, Kozara. 2m, Peruchitsa.

1999, May 4

91-92 A23 Set of 2 *175.00 175.00*

Anniversaries — A24

No. 93, each 50pf: a, Gorazde incorporation document. b, Dobrin Monastery (denomination at UL). c, Illuminated letter. d, Zitomislic Monastery. e, Gomionica Monastery (2 steeples). f, Madonna and Child icon. g, St. Nicholas icon. h, Holy trinity icon.

1999, May 26 **Litho.** *Perf. 13¾*

93 A24 Sheet of 8, #a-h, + label 8.50 8.50

Dabrobosanska and Zahumskohercegovacka Archbishopric, 780th anniv., Gorazde Printing Press, 480th anniv.

Fish — A25

No. 94: a, 50pf, Salmo trutta m. fario. b, 50pf, Salmo trutta m. lacustris. c, 75pf, Hucho hucho. d, 1m, Thymallus thymallus.

1999, June 17

94 A25 Horiz. strip of 4, #a-d, + central label 6.75 6.75

Issued in sheets of 5 strips with different labels.

Man on the Moon, 30th Anniv. — A26

Designs: 1m, Equipment on moon. 2m, Astronaut, lunar module.

1999, July 21

95-96 A26 Set of 2 6.75 6.75

Issued in sheets of 8 + 1 label.

UPU, 125th Anniv. — A27

Designs: 75pf, Pencil. 1.25m, Arc and map.

1999, Sept. 9

97-98 A27 Set of 2 4.75 4.75

Issued in sheets of 8 + 1 label.

Icons — A28

No. 99, each 50pf: a, Madonna and Child (black denomination at UL). b, Madonna and Child (white denomination at UL). c, Madonna and Child (white denomination at LR). d, Saint with cross. e, Pieta. f, Christ enters Jerusalem (on donkey). g, St. Jovan (with scroll). h, Sts. Sava and Simeon.

1999, Oct. 29

99 A28 Sheet of 8, #a-h, + label 7.75 7.75

Millennium A29

a, Egyptians, obelisk. b, Hourglass. c, Iron bell. d, Locomotive, steamship. e, Balloon, airplanes, automobiles. f, Man on the moon.

1999, Nov. 22

100 Booklet pane of 6 17.00 17.00
a.-e. A29 50pf Any single 2.75 2.75
f. A29 1m multi 4.50 4.50
Booklet, #100 17.50 17.50

See No. 126.

Postal Services in Serbian Territory, 135th Anniv. — A30

1999, Dec. 23

101 A30 50pf shown 1.10 1.10

Souvenir Sheet

102 A30 3m Postriders on bridge 90.00 90.00

Prince Stephen Nemanja — A31

2000, Feb. 29

103 A31 1.50m multi 3.50 3.50

Issued in sheets of 8 + 1 label.

Flora — A32

1m, Prunus domestica. 2m, Corylus avellana.

2000, Mar. 22

104-105 A32 Set of 2 6.25 6.25

Issued in sheets of 8 + 1 label.

Bridges — A33

No. 106, Brod (deer at left). No. 107, Pavlovica (horses and birds). No. 108, Zepce (bird at right). No. 109, Zvornik (bird at left).

2000, Apr. 12

106-109 A33 1m Set of 4 8.75 8.75

Issued in sheets of 8 + 1 label.

Jovan Ducic (1871-1943), Writer — A34

2000, Apr. 26 **Litho.** ***Perf. 13¾***

110 A34 20pf multi .60 .60

Common Design Type and

Europa — A35

2000, May 5 **Litho.** ***Perf. 13¾***

111 CD17 1.50m multi *60.00 60.00*
112 A35 2.50m multi *75.00 75.00*

Banja Luka Province, Cent. — A36

2000, May 26 **Litho.** ***Perf. 13¾***

113 A36 1.50m multi 3.50 3.50

European Soccer Championships A37

Various players. Denominations: 1m, 2m.

2000, June 14

114-115 A37 Set of 2 7.00 7.00

Souvenir Sheet

116 A37 6m Players, map 21.00 21.00

No. 116 contains one 35x42mm stamp.

Nevesinje Rebellion, 125th Anniv. — A38

2000, July 12

117 A38 1.50m multi 3.50 3.50

2000 Summer Olympics, Sydney A39

Map of Australia and: No. 118, 50pf, Handball. No. 119, 50pf, Basketball. No. 120, 50pf, Hurdles. No. 121, 50pf, Volleyball.
2m, Emu, kangaroo, Australian arms.

2000, Sept. 6

118-121 A39 Set of 4 4.50 4.50

Souvenir Sheet

122 A39 2m multi + label 4.50 4.50

No. 122 contains one 42x35mm stamp.

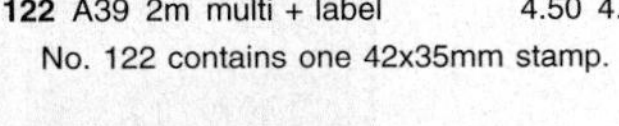

Locomotives A40

No. 123 — Locomotive from: a, 1848. b, 1865. c, 1930. d, 1990.

2000, Oct. 4 **Litho.** ***Perf. 13¾***

123 Horiz. strip of 4 + central label 10.50 10.50
a.-c. A40 50pf Any single 2.00 2.00
d. A40 1m multi 4.00 4.00

Protected Species — A41

Designs: 1m, Leontopodium alpinum. 2m, Proteus anguinus, horiz.

2000, Oct. 31

124-125 A41 Set of 2 6.75 6.75

Millennium Type of 1999

No. 126: a, Ship. b, Glassblowers. c, Blacksmith. d, Printers. e, James Watt, steam engine, steam-powered vehicle. f, Satellites. g, People on shore, ships (105x55mm).

2000, Nov. 22

126 Booklet pane of 7 + label 12.00 12.00
a.-f. A29 50pf Any single 1.25 1.25
g. A29 3m multi 5.25 5.25
Booklet, #126 13.50 13.50

Icons — A42

Icons from: No. 127, 50pf, 1577-78. No. 128, 50pf, 1607-08. No. 129, 1m, 1577-78. No. 130, 1m, Unknown year.

2000, Dec. 20

127-130 A42 Set of 4 6.25 6.25

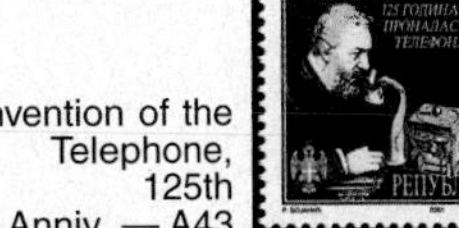

Invention of the Telephone, 125th Anniv. — A43

2001, Feb. 27

131 A43 1m multi 2.10 2.10

Manned Space Flight, 40th Anniv. — A44

Designs: 1m, Yuri Gagarin, Vostok 1. 3m, Gagarin, Earth, rocket lift-off.

2001, Mar. 29

132 A44 1m multi 2.10 2.10

Souvenir Sheet

133 A44 3m multi 9.00 9.00

No. 133 contains one 53x35mm stamp.

Vlado Milosevic, Composer A45

Europa A46

2001, Apr. 11

134 A45 50pf multi 1.25 1.25

2001, May 4 ***Perf. 13¾***

Designs: Nos. 135, 137a, 1m, Skakavac Waterfall. No. 136, 137b, 2m, Turjanica River.

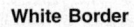

White Border

135-136 A46 Set of 2 *8.25 8.25*

Light Blue Border

Perf. 13¾ Vert.

137 A46 Vert. pair, #a-b *17.00 17.00*

No. 137 printed in panes of 3 pairs which were sold with a booklet cover, but unattached to it.

Butterflies — A47

Designs: No. 138, 50pf, Maniola jurtina. No. 139, 50pf, Pyrgus malvae. No. 140, 1m, Papilio machaon. No. 141, 1m, Lycaena pylaeas.

2001, June 19 ***Perf. 13¾***

138-141 A47 Set of 4 7.00 7.00

Kostajnica A48

Srbinje — A49

2001, Sept. 5 **Litho.** ***Perf. 13¾***

142 A48 25pf multi .65 .65
143 A49 1m multi 2.00 2.00

Issued: 25pf, 9/5. 1m, 9/20.

Karate Championships A50

2001, Sept. 5

144 A50 1.50m multi 3.00 3.00

A51

A51a

A51b

A51c

Costumes

2001, July 17 **Litho.** ***Perf. 13¾***

145 A51 50pf multi 1.00 1.00
146 A51a 50pf multi 1.00 1.00
147 A51b 1m multi 2.25 2.25
148 A51c 1m multi 2.25 2.25
Nos. 145-148 (4) 6.50 6.50

A52 A53

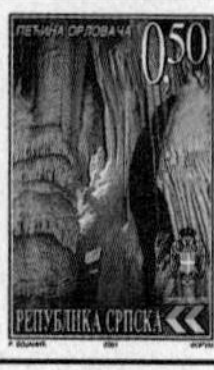

A54 A55

Caves

A56 A57

2001, Sept. 20 ***Perf. 13¾ Vert.***

149	Booklet pane of 6	6.50	
a.	A52 50pf Rastusha Cave	1.00	1.00
b.	A53 50pf Vaganska Cave	1.00	1.00
c.	A54 50pf Pavlova Cave	1.00	1.00
d.	A55 50pf Orlovacha Cave	1.00	1.00
e.	A56 50pf Ledana Cave	1.00	1.00
f.	A57 50pf Pod Jelikom Cave	1.00	1.00

Building Type of 1999 with Red "A"

2001, Oct. 23 **Litho.** ***Perf. 13¾***

150 A20 A Banja Luka 1.00 1.00

No. 150 sold for 50pf on day of issue. "A" on No. 80 is in black.

Nobel Prizes, Cent. — A58

Designs: 1m, Alfred Nobel (1833-96). 2m, Ivo Andric (1892-1975), 1961 Literature laureate.

2001, Oct. 23

151-152 A58 Set of 2 6.25 6.25

Each stamp printed in sheets of 8 + central label.

Bardacha-Srbac — A59

Lake Klinje — A60

2001, Nov. 15

153 A59 1m multi 2.10 2.10
154 A60 1m multi 2.10 2.10

Each stamp printed in sheets of 8 + central label.

Art A61

Designs: No. 155, 50pf, Belgrade Suburb, by Kosta Hakman (1899-1961). No. 156, 50pf, Djerdap, by Todor Shvrakic (1882-1931). No. 157, 50pf, Still Life With Parrot, by Jovan Bijelic (1884-1964), vert. No. 158, 50pf, Adela, by Miodrag Vujacic Mirski (1932-97), vert.

2001, Dec. 5

155-158 A61 Set of 4 4.25 4.25

Each stamp printed in sheets of 8 + central label.

Christmas A62

2001, Dec. 5

159 A62 1m multi 2.10 2.10

Printed in sheets of 8 + central label.

Borac Soccer Team, 75th Anniv. — A63

2001, Dec. 24

160 A63 1.50m multi 3.00 3.00

Printed in sheets of 8 + central label.

Serb Administration, 10th Anniv. — A64

Designs: 50pf, Arms, vert. 1m, Flag.

2002, Jan. 10

161-162 A64 Set of 2 3.00 3.00

Nos. 161-162 were each printed in sheets of 8 + central label. A number has been reserved for an additional item in this set.

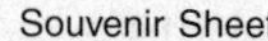

Souvenir Sheet

Serb Administration, 10th Anniv. — A65

2002, Jan. 10 **Litho.** ***Perf. 13¾***

163 A65 2m multi 4.25 4.25

War on Terrorism — A66

Designs: 1m, Hand holding snake. 2m, Globe, eyes, guns.

2002, Jan. 29 **Litho.** ***Perf. 13¾***

164 A66 1m multi 2.00 2.00

Souvenir Sheet

165 A66 2m multi 4.00 4.00

No. 164 printed in sheets of 8 + central label. No. 165 contains one 35x46mm stamp.

2002 Winter Olympics, Salt Lake City — A67

Designs: 50pf, Ski jumper. 1m, Bobsled.

2002, Feb. 13

166-167 A67 Set of 2 3.00 3.00

Each stamp printed in sheets of 8 + label.

Serbian Sarajevo — A68

Serbian Brod — A69

2002

168 A68 50pf multi 1.00 1.00
169 A69 2m multi 4.00 4.00

Issued: 50pf, 3/5. 2m, 4/18.

Education, Cent. — A70

2002, Mar. 5

170 A70 1m multi 2.00 2.00

Printed in sheets of 8 + central label.

Charles Lindbergh's Non-stop Solo Trans-Atlantic Flight, 75th Anniv. — A71

2002, Apr. 11

171 A71 1m multi 2.00 2.00

Printed in sheets of 8 + central label.

Europa — A72

Designs: 1m, Horses and clown. 1.50m, Elephants and clowns.

2002, Apr. 30 **Litho.** ***Perf. 13¾***

172-173 A72 Set of 2 *5.50 5.50*

Pink Border

173A	Vert. pair	*9.00*	*9.00*
b.	A72 1m Like #172, imperf. at top	*2.50*	*2.50*
c.	A72 1.50m Like #173, imperf. at bottom	*5.00*	*5.00*

No. 173A printed in sheets of 3 pairs which were sold in a booklet cover, but unattached to it.

2002 World Cup Soccer Championships, Japan and Korea — A73

Designs: 50pf, Two players. 1m, Two players, diff.

2002, May 31

174-175 A73 Set of 2 3.00 3.00

Resorts — A74

Designs: 25pf, Banja Slatina. 50pf, Banja Mljechanica. 75pf, Banja Vilina Vlas. 1m, Banja Laktashi. 1.50m, Banja Vruchica. 5m, Banja Dvorovi.

2002, July 5

176-181 A74 Set of 6 17.00 17.00

See No. 225. Compare with Nos. 241-242.

Artifacts — A75

Designs: No. 182, 50pf, Greco-Illyrian helmet, 4th-5th cent. No. 183, 50pf, Glassware, 14th cent. No. 184, 1m, Silver snake heads, 4th-5th cent. No. 185, 1m, Inscriptions on stone, 12th cent.

2002, Sept. 5
182-185 A75 Set of 4 6.00 6.00

Mushrooms A76

No. 186: a, Boletus regius. b, Macrolepiota procera. c, Amanita caesarea. d, Craterellus cornucopioides.

2002, Oct. 17 Litho. ***Perf. 13¾***
186 Horiz. strip of 4, #a-d, + central label 6.00 6.00
a.-b. A76 50pf Any single 1.15 1.15
c.-d. A76 1m Any single 1.60 1.60

Nature Protection — A77

Designs: 50pf, Maglic. 1m, Klekovacha.

2002, Nov. 26 Litho. ***Perf. 13¾***
187-188 A77 Set of 2 3.00 3.00

Art — A78

Designs: No. 189, 50pf, Crno Jezero pod Durmitorom, by Lazar Drijaca, 1935. No. 190, 50pf, Petar Popovic Pecija, by Spiro Bocaric, 1933, vert. No. 191, 1m, Zembiljeva Ulica, by Branko Sotra, 1937. No. 192, 1m, Ptice u Pejzazu, by Milan Sovilj, 2000.

2002, Dec. 18
189-192 A78 Set of 4 6.00 6.00

Souvenir Sheet

Showing of First Film in Bosnia, Cent. — A79

2003, Feb. 13 Litho. ***Perf. 13¾***
193 A79 3m multi 6.00 6.00

Alekse Santic (1868-1924), Writer — A80

2003, Mar. 5
194 A80 1m multi 2.10 2.10

Easter — A80a

Designs: 50pf, Crucifixion. 1m, Resurrection of Christ, by Matthias Grünewald.

2003, Mar. 28
195-196 A80a Set of 2 3.00 3.00

Souvenir Sheet

First Ascent of Mt. Everest, 50th Anniv. — A81

No. 197: a, Mt. Everest. b, Mt. Everest and mountain climber.

2003, Apr. 16 Litho. ***Perf. 13¾***
197 A81 1.50m Sheet of 2, #a-b 6.00 6.00

Europa — A82

Designs: 1m, Man affixing poster to wall. 1.50m, Hand and poster.

2003, May 5 ***Perf. 13¾***
198 A82 1m multi 2.50 2.50
a. Perf. 13¾, imperf. at top 5.50 5.50
b. Perf. 13¾, imperf. at bottom 6.00 6.00
199 A82 1.50m multi 3.50 3.50
a. Perf. 13¾, imperf. at bottom 7.00 7.00
b. Perf. 13¾, imperf. at top 8.00 8.00

A sheet of six containing one each of Nos. 198b and 199b and two each of Nos. 198a and 199a was sold in, but unattached to, a booklet cover.

Horses — A83

Designs: No. 200, 50pf, Arabian. No. 201, 50pf, Two Lippizaners. No. 202, 1m, Bosansko-brdski. No. 203, 1m, Two Posavacs.

2003, June 9 ***Perf. 13¾***
200-203 A83 Set of 4 6.00 6.00

A84

Visit of Pope John Paul II — A85

2003, June 22 ***Perf. 13¾***
204 A84 1.50m multi 5.50 5.50
Perf. 13½x13¾
205 A85 1.50m multi 3.00 3.00

No. 204 was printed in sheets of 8 stamps + central label.

Orders — A86

Different orders with background colors of: 50pf, Brown. 1m, Blue.

2003, July 11 ***Perf. 13¾x13***
206-207 A86 Set of 2 3.00 3.00

Fight Against Terrorism — A87

2003, Aug. 14 Litho. ***Perf. 13¾x13***
208 A87 1m multi 2.00 2.00

Leo Tolstoy (1828-1910), Writer — A88

2003, Sept. 25 Litho. ***Perf. 13¾x13***
209 A88 1m multi 2.00 2.00

Printed in sheets of 8 + label.

Nature Protection — A89

Designs: 50pf, Bear eating fish, Ugar River. 1m, Drina River.

2003, Oct. 21
210-211 A89 Set of 2 3.00 3.00

Each stamp printed in sheet of 8 + label.

Icons — A90

No. 212: a, St. Sava and Martyr Barbara (shown). b, St. Lazarus, 1658. c, Crowning of Mary in Heaven, by Dimitrije Bacevic. d, Holy Family.

2003, Nov. 19 ***Perf. 13x13¾***
212 Horiz. strip of 4 + central label 6.00 6.00
a.-b. A90 50pf Either single 1.15 1.15
c.-d. A90 1m Either single 1.90 1.90

New Year's Day — A91

Designs: 50pf, Child and snowman. 1m, Santa Claus and reindeer.

2003, Dec. 5 ***Perf. 13¾x13***
213-214 A91 Set of 2 3.00 3.00

Each stamp printed in sheet of 8 + label.

Powered Flight, Cent. — A92

Designs: 50pf, Wright Brothers, Wright Flyer. 1m, Count Ferdinand von Zeppelin, Graf Zeppelin.

2003, Dec. 17 ***Perf. 13x13¾***
215-216 A92 Set of 2 3.00 3.00

Souvenir Sheet

First Serbian Rebellion, Bicent. — A93

No. 217 — Rebels: a, Denomination at UL. b, Denomination at LR.

2004, Feb. 5 ***Perf. 13¾x13***
217 A93 1.50m Sheet of 2, #a-b 6.00 6.00

Souvenir Sheet

2004 Summer Olympics, Athens — A94

No. 218 — Chariot race: a, Denomination at UL. b, Denomination at UR.

2004, Mar. 2 ***Perf. 13x13¾***
218 A94 1.50m Sheet of 2, #a-b 6.00 6.00

Albert Einstein (1879-1955) A95

2004, Mar. 12

219 A95 1.50m multi 3.00 3.00

Printed in sheets of 8 + label.

Easter — A96

Paintings by: 50pf, Konstantinos Xenopoulos, 1961. 1m, Eremija Profeta.

2004, Apr. 2

220-221 A96 Set of 2 3.00 3.00

Europa — A97

Designs: Nos. 222, 224a, 224b, 1m, White water rafting. Nos. 223, 224c, 224d, 1.50m, Paragliding.

2004, May 5 Litho. ***Perf. 13¾x13***

White Border

222-223 A97 Set of 2 5.25 5.25

Light Blue Border

Perf. 13¾x13 on 3 Sides

224 Sheet of 6, #224b, 224d, 2 each #224a, 224c 21.00 21.00

a. A97 1m Imperf. at top 3.00 3.00
b. A97 1m Imperf. at bottom 3.00 3.00
c. A97 1.50m Imperf. at bottom 4.00 4.00
d. A97 1.50m Imperf. at top 4.00 4.00

Nos. 222-223 each were printed in sheets of 8 + label. No. 224 was sold in booket cover but was not attached to it.

Resorts Type of 2002

2004, May 10 ***Perf. 13¾***

225 A74 20pf Kulasi 1.00 1.00
a. Dated "2006" 1.00 1.00

Milutin Milankovic (1879-1958), Astronomer — A98

2004, May 28 ***Perf. 13¾x13***

226 A98 1m multi 2.00 2.00

Printed in sheets of 8 + label.

European Soccer Championships, Portugal — A99

2004, June 8 ***Perf. 13x13¾***

227 A99 1.50m multi 3.00 3.00

Printed in sheets of 8 + label.

2004 Summer Olympics, Athens A100

Athens Olympics emblem and: No. 228, 50pf, Shot put, Greek ruins. No. 229, 50pf, Hurdle, Greek ruins. No. 230, 1m, Runners, Greek ruins. No. 231, 1m, Runners, horses.

2004, July 12

228-231 A100 Set of 4 4.00 4.00

Nos. 228-230 each were printed in sheets of 8 + label. No. 231 was printed in sheet of 3 + 3 labels.

Nature Protection A101

Designs: 50pf, Arctostaphylos uva-ursi. 1m, Monticola saxatilis.

2004, Aug. 27 Litho. ***Perf. 13¾x13***

232-233 A101 Set of 2 3.25 3.25

Each stamp printed in sheets of 8 + label.

Minerals A102

Designs: No. 234, 50pf, Antimonite (shown). No. 235, 50pf, Pyrite (Prussian blue background). No. 236, 1m, Sphalerite. No. 237, 1m, Quartz, vert.

2004, Sept. 14 ***Perf. 13¾***

234-237 A102 Set of 4 6.00 6.00

Each stamp printed in sheets of 8 + label.

Michael Pupin (1858-1935), Physicist — A103

2004, Oct. 9 Litho. ***Perf. 13¾x13½***

238 A103 1m multi 2.00 2.00

Printed in sheets of 8 + label.

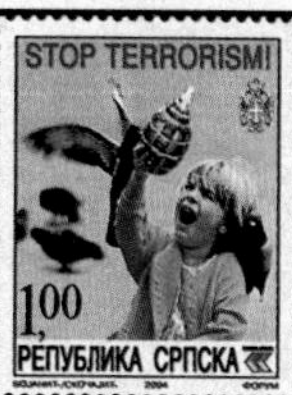

Fight Against Terrorism — A104

2004, Oct. 21

239 A104 1m multi 2.00 2.00

Printed in sheets of 8 + label.

Flowers — A105

No. 240: a, Digitalis grandiflora. b, Arnica montana. c, Rosa pendulina. d, Gentiana lutea.

2004, Nov. 18 Litho. ***Perf. 13¾x13***

240 Horiz. strip of 4 + central label 6.00 6.00

a.-b. A105 50pf Either single 1.10 1.10
c.-d. A105 1m Either single 1.60 1.60

Banja Mljechanica Resort — A106

Banja Laktashi Resort — A107

2004, Dec. 6 ***Perf. 13¾***

241 A106 50pf multi 1.00 1.00
242 A107 1m multi 2.00 2.00

Compare No. 241 with No. 177, which has red in sky and a black roof. Compare No. 242 with No. 179, which has a blue sky.

Christmas A108

2004, Dec. 7 ***Perf. 13x13¾***

243 A108 1m multi 2.00 2.00

Printed in sheets of 8 + label.

Paintings by Milenko Atanatskovic A109

Designs: 50c, Serbian Farmer, Semberije. 1m, Beledija, Stara Opstina, (house) horiz.

2005, Feb. 7 ***Perf. 13¾x13, 13x13¾***

244-245 A109 Set of 2 3.00 3.00

Each stamp printed in sheets of 8 + label.

Janj River Waterfall A110

Perf. 13¼x13¾

2005, Mar. 22 **Litho.**

246 A110 1m multi 2.00 2.00

Printed in sheets of 8 + label.

Europa A111

Designs: Nos. 247, 249a, 249b, 1m, Cooking pots near fire. Nos. 248. 249c, 249d, 1.50m, Food on table.

2005, Apr. 4 ***Perf. 13¼x13¾***

Tan Bottom Panel

247-248 A111 Set of 2 5.75 5.75

Green Bottom Panel

Perf. 13¼x13¾ on 3 Sides

249 Sheet of 6, #249b, 249d, 2 each #249a, 249c 13.50 13.50

a. A111 1m Imperf. at top 2.00 2.00
b. A111 1m Imperf. at bottom 2.00 2.00
c. A111 1.50m Imperf. at top 2.75 2.75
d. A111 1.50m Imperf. at bottom 2.75 2.75

Nos. 247-248 each were printed in sheets of 8 + label. No. 249 was issued with, but not attached to, a booklet cover.

Easter — A112

2005, Apr. 18 ***Perf. 13¾x13¼***

250 A112 50pf multi 1.10 1.10

Printed in sheets of 8 + label.

Pope John Paul II (1920-2005) A113

Pope John Paul II: 1.50m, Praying. 5m, With arms open.

2005, Apr. 21 Litho. ***Perf. 13x13¾***

251 A113 1.50m multi 3.00 3.00

Souvenir Sheet

252 A113 5m multi 10.00 10.00

No. 251 printed in sheets of 8 + label.

Vipers A114

No. 253: a, Vipera berus berus. b, Vipera ursinii. c, Vipera berus bosniensis. d, Vipera ammodytes.

Perf. 13¼x13¾

2005, June 23 **Litho.**

253 Horiz. strip of 4 + central label 6.00 6.00
a.-b. A114 50pf Either single .90 .90
c.-d. A114 1m Either single 1.75 1.75

Disneyland, 50th Anniv. — A115

Designs: 50pf, Sleeping Beauty Castle. 1m, Buildings.

2005, July 15 ***Perf. 13¾x13¼***

254-255 A115 Set of 2 3.00 3.00

Nos. 254-255 each printed in sheets of 8 + label.

Bulls — A116

2005, Aug. 5 **Litho.** ***Perf. 13¼x13¾***

256 A116 1.50m multi 3.00 3.00

Printed in sheets of 8 + label.

European Philatelic Cooperation, 50th Anniv. (in 2006) — A117

Designs: No. 257, 1.95m, Perucica (stream). No. 258, 1.95m, Rafters. No. 259, 1.95m, Old Bridge, Mostar. No. 260, 1.95m, Drina River multi-arch stone bridge.

2005, Aug. 30 ***Perf. 13¾x13¼***

257-260 A117 Set of 4 15.00 15.00
260a Sheet of 4, #257-260 15.00 15.00

Europa stamps, 50th anniv. (in 2006).

Nos. 257-260 each printed in sheets of 8 + label.

2005 European Basketball Championships — A118

No. 261 — Background colors: a, Green. b, Indigo. c, Blue. d, Red. e, Yellow brown.

Perf. 13¼x13¾

2005, Sept. 16 **Litho.**

261 Strip of 5 5.00 5.00
a.-e. A118 50pf Any single .85 .85

Museum of the Serb Republic, 75th Anniv. — A119

National Theater, 75th Anniv. A120

2005, Sept. 26 ***Perf. 13¾x13¼***

262 A119 1m multi 2.00 2.00

Perf. 13¼x13¾

263 A120 1m multi 2.00 2.00

Nos. 262-263 each printed in sheets of 8 + label.

Souvenir Sheet

Visegrad-Mokra Gora Railroad — A121

No. 264: a, 50pf, Train and tunnel. b, 1m, Train and station.

2005, Oct. 3 ***Perf. 13¼x13¾***

264 A121 Sheet of 2, #a-b 3.00 3.00

Intl. Aeronautics Federation, Cent. — A122

2005, Oct. 14

265 A122 1.50m multi 3.00 3.00

Printed in sheets of 8 + label.

Dayton Peace Accords, 10th Anniv. — A123

2005, Nov. 21 ***Perf. 13¾x13¼***

266 A123 1.50m multi 3.00 3.00

Printed in sheets of 8 + label.

Banja Guber Resort — A124

2005, Nov. 23 ***Perf. 13¾***

267 A124 50pf multi 1.10 1.10

Nature Protection — A125

Birds: 50pf, Crex crex. 1m, Platalea leucorodia.

2005, Nov. 25 ***Perf. 13¾x13¼***

268-269 A125 Set of 2 3.25 3.25

Nos. 268-269 each printed in sheets of 8 + label.

Liberation of Jasenovac Concentration Camp, 60th Anniv. A126

2005, Dec. 15 ***Perf. 13¼x13¾***

270 A126 50pf multi 1.00 1.00

Printed in sheets of 8 + label.

Wolfgang Amadeus Mozart (1756-91), Composer — A127

2006, Jan. 27 ***Perf. 13¾x13¼***

271 A127 1.50m multi 3.00 3.00

Printed in sheets of 8 + label.

Branka Sotre (1906-60), Painter — A128

2006, Jan. 31

272 A128 1m multi 2.00 2.00

Printed in sheets of 8 + label.

2006 Winter Olympics, Turin — A129

Designs: 50pf, Biathlon. 1m, Alpine skier.

2006, Feb. 10 ***Perf. 13¼x13¾***

273-274 A129 Set of 2 3.00 3.00

Nos. 273-274 each printed in sheets of 8 + label.

Flowers A130

No. 275: a, Saxifraga prenja. b, Asperula hercegovina. c, Oxytropis prenja. d, Campanula hercegovina.

Perf. 13¼x13¾

2006, Mar. 14 **Litho.**

275 Strip of 4 + central label 6.00 6.00
a.-b. A130 50pf Either single .85 .85
c.-d. A130 1m Either single 1.60 1.60

Printed in sheets of 24 containing six of each stamp + a central label.

Europa A131

Designs: Nos. 276, 278a, 278b, 1m, Person crying. Nos. 277, 2778c, 278d, 1.50m, People holding hands.

2006, Apr. 5 ***Perf. 13¼x13¾***

White Backgrounds

276-277 A131 Set of 2 5.50 5.50

Yellow Backgrounds

Perf. 13¼x13¾ on 3 Sides

278 Sheet of 6, #278a, 278d, 2 each #278b, 278c 18.00 18.00
a. A131 1m Imperf. at top 2.00 2.00
b. A131 1m Imperf. at bottom 2.00 2.00
c. A131 1.50m Imperf. at top 3.50 3.50
d. A131 1.50m Imperf. at bottom 3.50 3.50

Nos. 276-277 each printed in sheets of 8 + label. No. 278 was issued with, but not attached to, a booklet cover.

Easter A132

2006, Apr. 14 ***Perf. 13¼x13¾***

279 A132 70pf multi 1.50 1.50

Printed in sheets of 8 + label.

2006 World Cup Soccer Championships, Germany — A133

No. 280: a, 50pf, Players and soccer ball. b, 1m, Soccer ball, German flag, stadium. 3m, Player and soccer ball.

2006, June 9

280 A133 Pair, #a-b 3.00 3.00

Souvenir Sheet

281 A133 3m multi 6.00 6.00

No. 280 printed in sheets containing 4 of each stamp + label. No. 281 contains one 35x27mm stamp.

Vidovdan Race, Brcko — A134

2006, June 28

282 A134 1m multi 2.00 2.00

Printed in sheets of 8 + label.

Souvenir Sheet

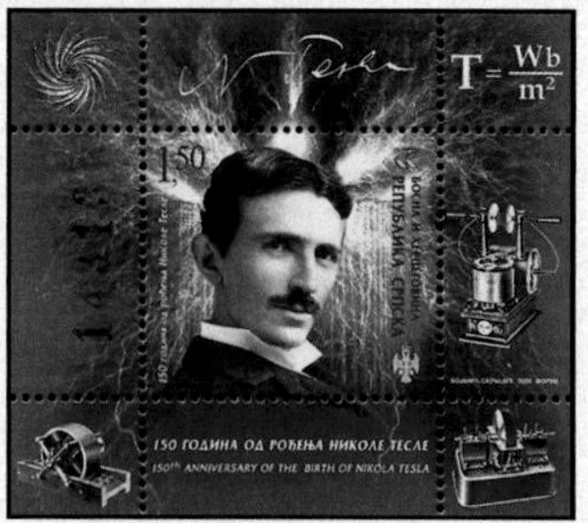

Nikola Tesla (1856-1943), Inventor — A135

2006, July 10
283 A135 1.50m multi 3.00 3.00

See No. 288A.

Nature Protection A136

Designs: 50pf, Tetrao urogallus. 1m, Rupicapra rupicapra.

2006, Sept. 19
284-285 A136 Set of 2 3.25 3.25

Children's Theater, 50th Anniv. A137

2006, Oct. 14 Litho. ***Perf. 13¼x13¾***
286 A137 1m multi 2.00 2.00

Printed in sheets of 8 + label.

A138

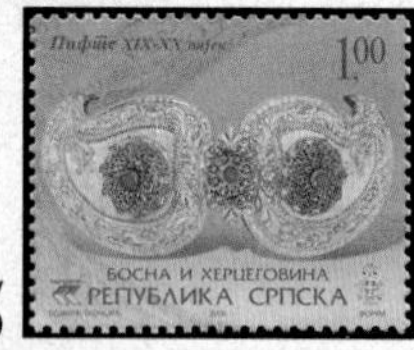

Jewelry A139

2006, Nov. 28
287 A138 1m multi 2.00 2.00
288 A139 1m multi 2.00 2.00

Each stamp printed in sheets of 8 + label.

Tesla Type of 2006

2006, Dec. 29 Litho. ***Perf. 13¾***
Size: 25x23mm
288A A135 70pf multi 1.50 1.50

Johann Wolfgang von Goethe (1749-1832), Poet — A140

Perf. 13¼x13¾
2007, Mar. 22 Litho.
289 A140 1.50m multi 3.00 3.00

Printed in sheets of 8 + label.

Easter — A141

2007, Apr. 10 ***Perf. 13¾x13¼***
290 A141 70pf multi 1.50 1.50

Printed in sheets of 8 + label.

Leonardo da Vinci (1452-1519), Painter — A142

No. 291, 70pf — Head of Isabella d'Este with text in: a, Cyrillic letters. b, Latin letters.

No. 292, 1m — Sketch of St. Peter with text in: a, Cyrillic letters. b, Latin letters.

2007, Apr. 16 ***Perf. 13¾x13¼***
Pairs, #a-b
291-292 A142 Set of 2 6.75 6.75

Nos. 291-292 each printed in sheets of 4 pairs + label.

Europa A143

Designs: Nos. 293, 295a, 295b, 1m, Scouts and tents. Nos. 294, 295c, 295d, 1.50m, Scouts on expedition.

2007, May 3 ***Perf. 13¼x13¾***
Green Background
293-294 A143 Set of 2 5.50 5.50

Rose Violet Background
Perf. 13¼x13¾ on 3 Sides

295 Sheet of 6, #295a, 295d, 2 each #295b, 295c 17.50 17.50
a. A143 1m Imperf. at top 2.25 2.25
b. A143 1m Imperf. at bottom 2.25 2.25
c. A143 1.50m Imperf. at top 3.50 3.50
d. A143 1.50m Imperf. at bottom 3.50 3.50

Scouting, cent. Nos. 293-294 were each printed in sheets of 8 + label. No. 295 was issued with, but not attached to, a booklet cover.

Monasteries A144

Designs: 70pf, Liplje Monastery. 1m, Dobricevo Monastery.

2007, June 5 ***Perf. 13¼x13¾***
296-297 A144 Set of 2 3.25 3.25

Nos. 296-297 were each printed in sheets of 8 + label.

Post Office and Church, Obudovac A145

Municipal Building, Prijedor A146

Fire House, Kozarac A147

Town Square, Bijeljina A148

Deventa A149

Foca A150

Cultural Club, Laktasi A151

Building, Srebrenica A152

Cultural Club, Sipovo — A153

Municipal Building, Mrkonjic Grad — A154

Old City, Trebinje A155

Zvornik A156

2007 Litho. ***Perf. 13¾***

298	A145	10pf multi	.25	.25
299	A146	20pf multi	.45	.45
300	A147	20pf multi	.45	.45
301	A148	20pf multi	.45	.45
302	A149	20pf multi	.45	.45
303	A150	20pf multi	.45	.45
304	A151	20pf multi	.45	.45
305	A152	70pf multi	1.50	1.50
306	A153	1.50m multi	3.00	3.00
307	A154	1.50m multi	3.00	3.00
308	A155	2m multi	4.00	4.00
309	A156	5m multi	10.00	10.00
		Nos. 298-309 (12)	24.45	24.45

Issued: 10pf, 7/7; 70pf, 6/20; others, 6/9.

A157

A158

A159

Dogs — A160

2007, July 5 ***Perf. 13¼x13¾***

310 Horiz. strip of 4 + central label 6.00 6.00
a. A157 70pf multi 1.50 1.50
b. A158 70pf multi 1.50 1.50
c. A159 70pf multi 1.50 1.50
d. A160 70pf multi 1.50 1.50

Ban Svetislav Milosavljevic (1882-1960) A161

2007, Sept. 7 ***Perf. 13¾x13¼***
311 A161 1.50m multi 3.00 3.00

Souvenir Sheet

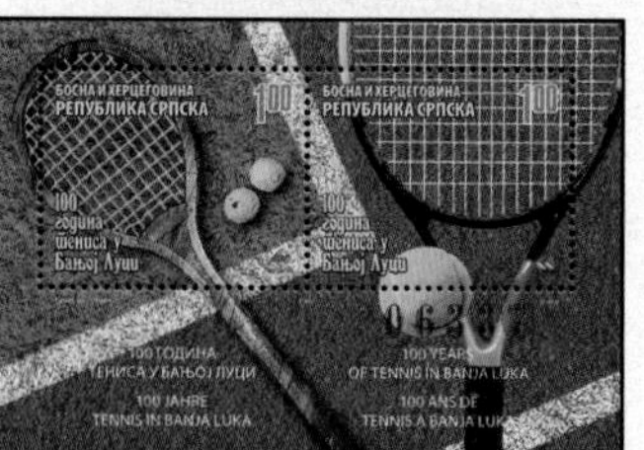

Tennis in Banja Luka, Cent. — A162

No. 312: a, Wooden racquet, old balls. b, Modern racquet and ball.

2007, Sept. 14 ***Perf. 13¾***
312 A162 1m Sheet of 2, #a-b 3.75 3.75

Launch of Sputnik 1, 50th Anniv. — A163

2007, Oct. 4 Litho. ***Perf. 13¾x13¼***
313 A163 1.50m multi 3.00 3.00

Printed in sheets of 8 + label.

Pine Cones — A164

Designs: 70pf, Picea abies. 1m, Picea omorica.

2007, Nov. 9
314-315 A164 Set of 2 3.50 3.50

Nos. 314-315 each printed in sheets of 8 + label.

Filip Visnjic Library, 75th Anniv. — A165

2007, Nov. 26 ***Perf. 13¼x13¾***
316 A165 70pf multi 1.50 1.50

Printed in sheets of 8 + label.

New Year 2008 — A166

Designs: No. 317, 70pf, Snowman. No. 318, 70pf, Christmas tree.

Perf. 13¾x13¼
2007, Dec. 10 **Litho.**
317-318 A166 Set of 2 2.75 2.75

Nos. 317-318 were each printed in sheets of 8 + label.

Serb Republic Adminstrative Center — A167

2007, Dec. 20
319 A167 70pf multi 1.50 1.50

Samac Post Office, 125th Anniv. A168

2008, Feb. 28 **Litho.** ***Perf. 14***
320 A168 1.40m multi 2.75 2.75

Printed in sheets of 8 + label.

Self-Portrait of Vincent Van Gogh (1853-90), Painter — A169

2008, Mar. 28 **Litho.** ***Perf. 14x14¼***
321 A169 1.50m multi 3.00 3.00

Printed in sheets of 8 + label.

Souvenir Sheet

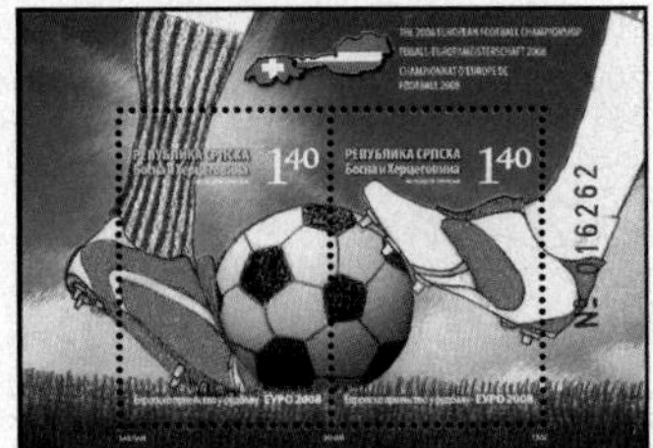

UEFA Euro 2008 Soccer Championships, Austria and Switzerland — A170

No. 322: a, Foot to left of soccer ball. b, Foot to right of soccer ball.

2008, Apr. 18 ***Perf. 13x13½***
322 A170 1.40m Sheet of 2, #a-b 5.50 5.50

Europa — A171

Letter and: Nos. 323, 325a, 325b, 1m, Quill pen and inkwell. Nos. 324, 325c, 325d, 2m, Hand with pencil.

2008, Apr. 24 ***Perf. 14***
Stamps With White Frames
323-324 A171 Set of 2 6.00 6.00

Stamps With Tan Frames
Perf. 13x13½ on 3 Sides
325 Sheet, #325a, 325d, 2 each #325b-325c 18.50 18.50
a. A171 1m Imperf. at top 2.00 2.00
b. A171 1m Imperf. at bottom 2.00 2.00
c. A171 2m Imperf. at top 4.00 4.00
d. A171 2m Imperf. at bottom 4.00 4.00

Nos. 323-324 each were printed in sheets of 8 + label.

Djurdjevdan Festival A172

2008, May 8 **Litho.** ***Perf. 13***
326 A172 1.50m multi 3.00 3.00

Printed in sheets of 8 + label.

A173

A174

A175

Personalized Stamps A176

2008, May 13 ***Serpentine Die Cut 10***
Self-Adhesive
327 A173 70pf multi 1.40 1.40
328 A174 70pf multi 1.40 1.40
329 A175 70pf multi 1.40 1.40
330 A176 70pf multi 1.40 1.40
Nos. 327-330 (4) 5.60 5.60

Images shown in frames of Nos. 327-330 are generic and could be personalized.

Banja Luka Carnival — A177

2008, May 15 ***Perf. 13***
331 A177 1.50m multi 3.00 3.00

Mushrooms — A178

No. 332: a, Gyromitra esculenta. b, Amanita muscaria. c, Amanita pantherina. d, Amanita phalloides.

2008, May 26 ***Perf. 13x13¼***
332 Horiz. strip of 4 + central label 5.50 5.50
a.-d. A178 70pf Any single 1.40 1.40

Charles Darwin (1809-82), Naturalist, and Birds — A179

2008, July 1 ***Perf. 13***
333 A179 1.50m multi 3.00 3.00

Development by Darwin of theory of evolution, 150th anniv.

Flowers
A180 A181

Designs: 50pf, Gentiana verna. 1.50m, Galanthus nivalis. 2m, Viola odorata. 5m, Centaurea cyanus.

2008, July 7 **Litho.** ***Perf. 13***
334 A180 50pf multi .95 .95
335 A181 1.50m multi 2.75 2.75
336 A180 2m multi 4.00 4.00
337 A180 5m multi 9.50 9.50
Nos. 334-337 (4) 17.20 17.20

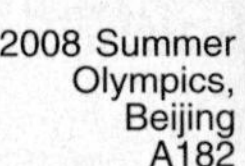

2008 Summer Olympics, Beijing A182

Map of China and: 70pf, High jump, National Stadium. 2.10m, Swimmer on starting platform, Aquatics Center.
3.10m, Gymnast.

2008, July 16
338-339 A182 Set of 2 5.50 5.50

Souvenir Sheet
340 A182 3.10m multi 6.00 6.00

Nos. 338 and 339 each were printed in sheets of 8 + label.

Birds — A183

Designs: No. 341, 1m, Strix aluco. No. 342, 1m, Ciconia ciconia.

2008, Aug. 12
341-342 A183 Set of 2 4.00 4.00

Nos. 341 and 342 each were printed in sheets of 8 + label.

Monasteries A184

Monastery at: No. 343, 1m, Gracanica (shown). No. 344, 1m, Tvrdos.

2008, Sept. 10
343-344 A184 Set of 2 4.00 4.00

Nos. 343 and 344 each were printed in sheets of 8 + label.

Souvenir Sheet

Bosnian Serb Pres. Milan Jelic (1956-2007) — A185

2008, Sept. 20
345 A185 2.10m multi 4.00 4.00

Orient Express, 125th Anniv. A186

2008, Oct. 3 Litho. *Perf. 13*

346 A186 1.40m multi	2.75	2.75

Printed in sheets of 8 + label.

Alfred Nobel (1833-96), Inventor and Philanthropist A187

2008, Oct. 21

347 A187 1.50m multi	3.00	3.00

Printed in sheets of 8 + label.

Jovan Jovanovich Zmaj (1833-1904), Poet — A188

2008, Nov. 24

348 A188 1.50m multi	3.00	3.00

Printed in sheets of 8 + label.

Christmas A189

2008, Dec. 26

349 A189 1m multi	2.00	2.00

Printed in sheets of 8 + label.

1984 Sarajevo Winter Olympics, 25th Anniv. — A190

2009, Feb. 13

350 A190 1.50m multi	3.00	3.00

Printed in sheets of 8 + label.

Explorers and Ships — A191

Designs: 70pf, Amerigo Vespucci (1454-1512). 1.50m, Marco Polo (1254-1324).

2009, Mar. 7

351-352 A191 Set of 2	4.50	4.50

Nos. 351-352 each were printed in sheets of 8 + label.

Buildings A192

Designs; 1m, European Court of Human Rights. 1.50m, Council of Europe Building.

2009, Mar. 25

353-354 A192 Set of 2	5.00	5.00

European Court of Human Rights, 50th anniv., Council of Europe, 60th anniv. Nos. 353-354 each were printed in sheets of 8 + label.

Animals — A193

Designs: 20pf, Meles meles. 70pf, Sciurus vulgaris. 1m, Vulpes vulpes.

2009, Apr. 15

355 A193 20pf multi	.50	.50
a. Perf. 13¾	1.75	1.75
356 A193 70pf multi	2.25	2.25
357 A193 1m multi	1.40	1.40
Nos. 355-357 (3)	4.15	4.15

Issued: No. 355a, 12/10.

Dinosaurs A194

Designs: 70pf, Triceratops. 1.50m, Diplodocus.

2009, Mar. 13 Litho. *Perf. 13*

358-359 A194 Set of 2	4.50	4.50

Nos. 358-359 each were printed in sheets of 8 + label.

Europa A195

Designs: Nos. 360, 362a, 362b, 362c, 1m, Observatory. Nos. 361, 362d, 362e, 362f, 2m, Telescope and star chart.

2009, Apr. 23 *Perf. 13*

Stamp Size: 35x26mm

360-361 A195 Set of 2	6.50	6.50

Souvenir Sheet

Stamp Size: 38x27mm

Perf. 13¼x13 on 2 or 3 Sides

362 Sheet of 6	21.00	21.00
a. A195 1m Imperf. at right	2.50	2.50
b A195 1m Imperf. at left	2.50	2.50
c. A195 1m Imperf. at right and bottom	2.50	2.50
d. A195 2m Imperf. at left	4.50	4.50
e. A195 2m Imperf. at right	4.50	4.50
f. A195 2m Imperf. at left and bottom	4.50	4.50

Intl. Year of Astronomy. Nos. 360-361 each were printed in sheets of 8 + label.

Souvenir Sheet

World Rafting Championships, Banja Luka — A196

No. 363 — Rafters with: a, All paddles in water. b, Two paddles out of water.

2009, May 15 *Perf. 13¾*

363 A196 1.50m Sheet of 2, #a-b	6.00	6.00

Paja Jovanovic (1859-1957), Painter — A197

2009, June 16 *Perf. 13¾x13¼*

364 A197 1.40m multi	3.00	3.00

Printed in sheets of 8 + label.

Portraits of Amedeo Modigliani (1884-1920) A198

2009, July 11 *Perf. 13¼x13¾*

365 A198 1.50m multi	3.00	3.00

Printed in sheets of 8 + label.

Cats — A199

No. 366: a, Siamese (shown). b, Tabby (broom in background). c, Russian blue (flower pot with flowers in background). d, Persian (large pot in background).

2009, Aug. 19

366 Horiz. strip of 4 + central label	6.00	6.00
a.-d. A199 70pf Any single	1.45	1.45

Forts — A200

Fort at: 20pf, Doboj. 70pf, Zvornik. 1m, Kastel.

2009 Litho. *Perf. 13¾*

367 A200 20pf multi	.45	.45
368 A200 70pf multi	1.60	1.60
369 A200 1m multi	2.25	2.25
Nos. 367-369 (3)	4.30	4.30

Issued: 20pf, 7/23; 70pf, 1m, 9/25.

Insects A201

Designs: No. 370, 1m, Coccinellidae. No. 371, 1m, Odonata. No. 372, 1m, Lucanus cervus.

2009, Sept. 9 Litho. *Perf. 13¼x13¾*

370-372 A201 Set of 3	6.00	6.00

Nos. 370-372 each were printed in sheets of 8 + label.

Skoda 1937 Locomotive A202

Rama Locomotive A203

UNRRA 22 Locomotive A204

JZ 83-056 Locomotive A205

2009, Nov. 10

373 A202 70pf multi	1.40	1.40
374 A203 70pf multi	1.40	1.40
375 A204 80pf multi	1.60	1.60
376 A205 80pf multi	1.60	1.60
Nos. 373-376 (4)	6.00	6.00

Nos. 373-376 each were printed in sheets of 8 + label.

Automobiles A206

Designs: No. 377, 70pf, Red Citroen 2CV. No. 378, 70pf, Yellow Fiat 500. 80pf, Volkswagen Beetle.

2009, Nov. 17

377-379 A206 Set of 3	4.50	4.50

Nos. 377-379 each were printed in sheets of 8 + label.

Christmas and New Year's Day — A207

Designs: No. 380, 60pf, Santa Claus. No. 381, 60pf, Snowman.

2009, Dec. 4 *Perf. 13¾x13¼*

380-381 A207 Set of 2	2.75	2.75

Nos. 380-381 each were printed in sheets of 8 + label.

Zvornik, 600th Anniv. — A208

2010, Jan. 26 ***Perf. 13¼x13¾***

382 A208 70pf multi 1.50 1.50

Printed in sheets of 8 + label.

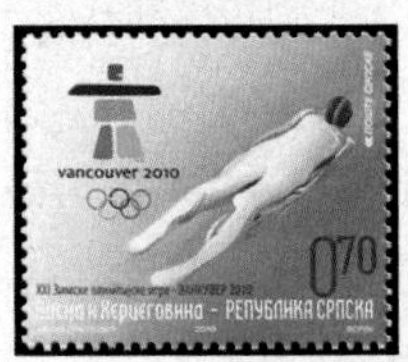

2010 Winter Olympics, Vancouver A209

Designs: 70pf, Luge. 1.50m, Figure skating.

2010, Feb. 5

383-384 A209 Set of 2 4.50 4.50

Nos. 383-384 each were printed in sheets of 8 + label.

Frédéric Chopin (1810-49), Composer A210

2010, Mar. 1 ***Perf. 13¾x13¼***

385 A210 1.50m multi 3.25 3.25

Printed in sheets of 8 + label.

Mesa Selimovic (1910-82), Writer — A211

2010, Apr. 20

386 A211 1m multi 2.00 2.00

Printed in sheets of 8 + label.

Europa A212

Children's books: Nos. 387, 389a, 389b, 389c, 1m, Flying. Nos. 388, 389d, 389e, 389f, 2m, On tree.

2010, May 7 Litho. ***Perf. 13x13¾***

387-388 A212 Set of 2 4.00 4.00

Perf. 13x13¾ on 2 or 3 Sides

389 Sheet of 6 12.00 12.00
- ***a.*** A212 1m Imperf. at top 1.40 1.40
- ***b.*** A212 1m Imperf. at bottom 1.40 1.40
- ***c.*** A212 1m Imperf. at bottom and right 1.40 1.40
- ***d.*** A212 2m Imperf. at top 2.60 2.60
- ***e.*** A212 2m Imperf. at top and right 2.60 2.60
- ***f.*** A212 2m Imperf. at bottom 2.60 2.60

Nos. 387-388 each were printed in sheets of 8 + label. No. 389 was sold with, but unattached to, a booklet cover.

2010 World Cup Soccer Championships, South Africa — A213

Designs: No. 390, 1.50m, Player with arms raised. No. 391, 1.50m, Player dribbling ball.

2010, May 25 ***Perf. 13x13¾***

390-391 A213 Set of 2 6.00 6.00

Nos. 390-391 each were printed in sheets of 8 + label.

Animals A214

Old Weapons A215

2010, May 28 ***Perf. 13¾***

392 A214 10pf Hedgehog .40 .40
393 A214 50pf Boar 1.00 1.00
394 A214 90pf Wolf 1.75 1.75
395 A214 1m Bear 2.00 2.00
Nos. 392-395 (4) 5.15 5.15

2010, June 15

396 A215 1.80m Knives 3.50 3.50
397 A215 2m Guns 4.00 4.00
398 A215 5m Iron mace 9.50 9.50
Nos. 396-398 (3) 17.00 17.00

Nos. 396-398 each were printed in sheets of 8 + label.

Endangered Flora — A216

No. 399: a, Rhododendron hirsutum. b, Edrainthus sutjeske. c, Trollius europaeus. d, Pancicia serbica.

2010, June 17 ***Perf. 13x13¾***

399 Horiz. strip of 4 + central label .50 5.50
- ***a.-d.*** A216 70pf Any single 1.40 1.40

Fragments of Roman Monuments A217

Monument fragment showing: 70pf, People. 1.50m, Text.

2010, June 30

400-401 A217 Set of 2 4.50 4.50

Nos. 400-401 each were printed in sheets of 8 + label.

50th Trumpet Festival, Guca, Serbia A218

2010, Aug. 13 Litho. ***Perf. 13x13¾***

402 A218 1.50m multi 3.00 3.00

Printed in sheets of 8 + label. See Serbia No. 516.

Day of Fallen and Missing Persons — A219

2010, Sept. 15 ***Perf. 13¾x13***

403 A219 90pf multi 2.00 2.00

Printed in sheets of 8 + label.

A220

Fish — A221

2010, Sept. 23 ***Perf. 13¼x13¾***

404 A220 1m multi 2.00 2.00
405 A221 1m multi 2.00 2.00

Nos. 404-405 each were printed in sheets of 8 + label.

Serb Republic Museum, Banja Luka, 80th Anniv. — A222

2010, Sept. 24 ***Perf. 13¾x13***

406 A222 90pf multi 1.75 1.75

Printed in sheets of 8 + label.

Banja Luka Gymnasium, 115th Anniv. A223

2010, Oct. 4 ***Perf. 13x13¾***

407 A223 90pf multi 1.75 1.75

Printed in sheets of 8 + label.

Souvenir Sheet

World Post Day — A224

No. 408: a, 70pf, Detail from Bosnia & Herzegovina #41. b, 1.40m, Marija Zvijezda Trappist Monastery, Banja Luka, detail from Bosnia & Herzegovina #41.

2010, Oct. 9 **Litho.**

408 A224 Sheet of 2, #a-b 4.00 4.00

St. Nicholas and Christmas Stocking A225

2010, Nov. 24

409 A225 1m multi 2.00 2.00

Printed in sheets of 8 + label.

Souvenir Sheet

St. Basil of Ostrog (1610-71) — A226

No. 410: a, 70pf, Ostrog Monastery. b, 1.40m, St. Basil of Ostrog.

2010, Dec. 28 ***Perf. 13¾***

410 A226 Sheet of 2, #a-b 4.00 4.00

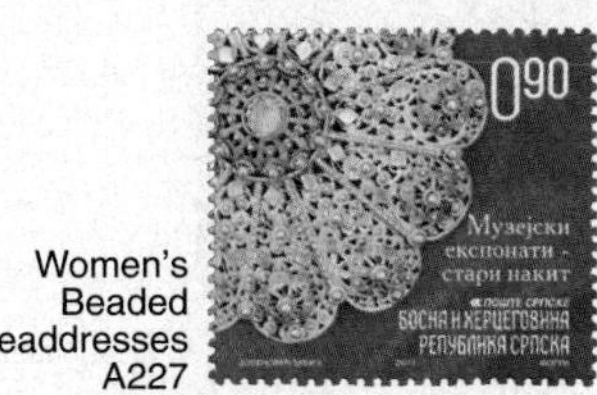

Women's Beaded Headdresses A227

Various headdresses with denomination at: No. 411, 90pf, UR. No. 412, 90pf, UL.

2011, Jan. 24 ***Perf. 13x13¾***

411-412 A227 Set of 2 3.50 3.50

Nos. 411-412 each were printed in sheets of 8 + label.

Milan Budimir (1891-1975), Philosopher A228

2011, Feb. 11 ***Perf. 13¾x13***

413 A228 90pf multi 1.75 1.75

Printed in sheets of 8 + label.

Awarding of Nobel Prize in Chemistry to Marie Curie, Cent. — A229

2011, Mar. 8 Litho. ***Perf. 13¾x13¼***

414 A229 1.50m multi 3.00 3.00

Printed in sheets of 8 + central label.

Europa A230

Forest scene with: Nos. 415, 417a, 417b, 417c, 1m, Deer and rabbit. Nos. 416, 417d, 417e, 417f, 2m, Fox and bear.

2011, Apr. 6 ***Perf. 13x13¾***

415-416 A230 Set of 2 6.00 6.00

Perf. 13x13¾ on 2 or 3 Sides

417 Sheet of 6 18.00 18.00
- *a.* A230 1m Imperf. at top 2.00 2.00
- *b.* A230 1m Imperf. at bottom 2.00 2.00
- *c.* A230 1m Imperf. at bottom and right 2.00 2.00
- *d.* A230 2m Imperf. at top 4.00 4.00
- *e.* A230 2m Imperf. at top and right 4.00 4.00
- *f.* A230 2m Imperf. at bottom 4.00 4.00

Intl. Year of Forests. Nos. 415-416 each were printed in sheets of 8 + label. No. 417 was sold with, but unattached to, a booklet cover.

Animals — A231

2011, Apr. 20 **Litho.** ***Perf. 13¾***

418 A231 10pf Rabbit .25 .25
419 A231 20pf Weasel .40 .40
420 A231 50pf Otter .90 .90
421 A231 90pf Lynx 1.75 1.75
Nos. 418-421 (4) 3.30 3.30

Birds — A232

No. 422: a, Aythya ferina. b, Alcedo atthis. c, Cygnus olor. d, Podiceps nigricollis

2011, May 10 ***Perf. 13¼x13¾***

422 Horiz. strip of 4 + central label 7.00 7.00
- *a.-d.* A232 90pf Any single 1.75 1.75

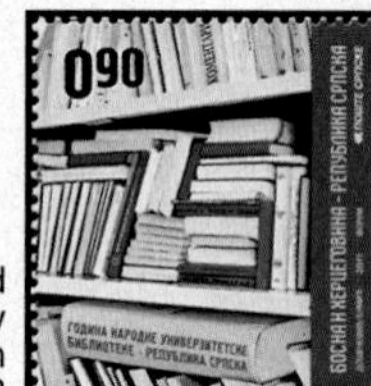

National and University Library, 75th Anniv. — A233

2011, May 17 ***Perf. 13¾x13¼***

423 A233 90pf multi 1.75 1.75

Printed in sheets of 8 + label.

Souvenir Sheet

European Kayak and Canoe Championships, Banja Luka. — A234

No. 424: a, 1.50m, Canoeist. b, 2.30m, Kayaker.

2011, June 7 ***Perf. 13¾***

424 A234 Sheet of 2, #a-b 7.25 7.25

Book Illuminations A235

Various book illuminations.

2011, June 15 ***Perf. 13¾***

Denomination Color

425 A235 1.50m brown 3.00 3.00
426 A235 2.30m blue green 4.50 4.50
427 A235 5m buff 9.50 9.50
Nos. 425-427 (3) 17.00 17.00

Intl. Youth Year — A236

2011, June 30 ***Perf. 13¾x13¼***

428 A236 90pf multi 1.75 1.75

Printed in sheets of 8 + label.

Locomotives A237

Designs: No. 429, 90pf, DMV 801. No. 430, 90pf, DMV 802. No. 431, 90pf, DHL 720-001. No. 432, 90pf, DHL 740-108.
3m, DHL L458-096.

2011, July 1 ***Perf. 13¼x13¾***

429-432 A237 Set of 4 7.00 7.00

Souvenir Sheet

Perf. 13¾

433 A237 3m multi 6.00 6.00

Nos. 429-432 each were printed in sheets of 8 + label. No. 433 contains one 35x29mm stamp.

Birds — A238

Designs: 90pf, Buteo buteo. 1.50m, Accipiter gentilis.

2011, Sept. 15 ***Perf. 13¼x13¾***

434-435 A238 Set of 2 4.75 4.75

Fridtjof Nansen (1861-1930), Polar Explorer and Diplomat — A239

2011, Oct. 10 ***Perf. 13¾x13¼***

436 A239 1.50m multi 3.00 3.00

No. 436 was printed in sheets of 8 + central label.

Franz Liszt (1811-86), Composer A240

2011, Oct. 22

437 A240 1.50m multi 3.00 3.00

No. 437 was printed in sheets of 8 + central label.

Novak Djokovic, Tennis Player, and Wimbledon Singles Trophy — A241

2011, Nov. 30

438 A241 90pf multi *4.00 4.00*

No. 438 was printed in sheets of 8 + central label.

Ivo Andric (1892-1975), 1961 Nobel Literature Laureate A242

2011, Dec. 10 ***Perf. 13¼x13¾***

439 A242 90pf multi 1.75 1.75

No. 439 was printed in sheets of 8 + central label.

Roald Amundsen's Expedition to South Pole, Cent. — A243

Amundsen and: 1.50m, Expedition member Helmer Hanssen near Norwegian flag at South Pole. 2m, Dog sled, Norwegian flag and map of expedition's route.

2011, Dec. 14 ***Perf. 13¼x13¾***

440 A243 1.50m multi 3.00 3.00

Souvenir Sheet

Perf. 13¾

441 A243 2m multi 4.00 4.00

No. 440 was printed in sheets of 8 + central label. No. 441 contains one 35x29mm stamp.

New Year 2012 (Year of the Dragon) A244

2012, Feb. 14 ***Perf. 13¼x13¾***

442 A244 90pf multi 3.25 3.25

No. 442 was printed in sheets of 8 + central label.

Postal Service of the Serbian Administration of Bosnia & Herzegovina, 15th Anniv. A245

2012, Feb. 23

443 A245 90pf multi 1.75 1.75

No. 443 was printed in sheets of 8 + central label.

A246

A247

A248

Architecture A249

2012, Mar. 9 ***Perf. 13x13¼***

444 Horiz. strip of 4 + central label 7.00 7.00
- *a.* A246 90pf multi 1.75 1.75
- *b.* A247 90pf multi 1.75 1.75
- *c.* A248 90pf multi 1.75 1.75
- *d.* A249 90pf multi 1.75 1.75

Transportation Disasters A250

Designs: No. 445, 1.50m, Titanic. No. 446, 1.50m, Hindenburg.

2012, Apr. 23 ***Perf. 13¼x13¾***

445-446 A250 Set of 2 6.00 6.00

Sinking of the Titanic, cent.; Burning of the Hindenburg, 75th anniv. Nos. 445-446 each were printed in sheets of 8 + central label.

Europa A251

Forest scene with: Nos. 447, 449a, 449b, 449c, 1m, River rafters. Nos. 448, 449d, 449e, 449f, 2m, Hikers.

2012, Apr. 26 ***Perf. 13x13¾***

447-448 A251 Set of 2 4.00 4.00

Perf. 13x13¾ on 2 or 3 Sides

449 Sheet of 6 12.00 12.00
- *a.* A251 1m Imperf. at top 1.40 1.40
- *b.* A251 1m Imperf. at bottom 1.40 1.40
- *c.* A251 1m Imperf. at top and right 1.40 1.40
- *d.* A251 2m Imperf. at top 2.60 2.60
- *e.* A251 2m Imperf. at bottom 2.60 2.60
- *f.* A251 2m Imperf. at bottom and right 2.60 2.60

Nos. 447-448 each were printed in sheets of 8 + label. No. 449 was sold with, but unattached to, a booklet cover.

Musical Instruments — A252

2012, May 17 ***Perf. 13¾***

450 A252 10pf Dvojnice .35 .35
451 A252 20pf Rognjaca .35 .35
452 A252 35pf Gusle .65 .65
Nos. 450-452 (3) 1.35 1.35

European Nature Protection A253

No. 453: a, 90pf, Stone pinnacles. b, 1.50m, Janja River waterfalls.

2012, May 29 ***Perf. 13x13¾***
453 A253 Vert. pair, #a-b 5.00 5.00

Printed in sheets containing 4 pairs + 2 labels

Animals — A254

2012, June 12 ***Perf. 13¾***
454 A254 50pf Otter .95 .95
455 A254 90pf Lynx 1.75 1.75

Trees — A255

No. 456: a, Quercus (oak). b, Fraxinus (ash). c, Tilia (linden). d, Betula (birch).

2012, June 13 ***Perf. 13x13¼***
456 Horiz. strip of 4 + flanking label 7.00 7.00
a.-d. A255 90pf Any single 1.75 1.75

Slavija Boxing Club, 50th Anniv. — A256

2012, Sept. 15 **Litho.**
457 A256 90pf multi 1.75 1.75

Printed in sheets of 8 + central label.

Airplanes A257

Designs: 90pf, Fizir FN biplane. 1.50m, Ikarus IK-2.

2012, Sept. 19 ***Perf. 13x13¾***
458-459 A257 Set of 2 4.50 4.50

Nos. 458-459 each were printed in sheets of 8 + central label.

Souvenir Sheet

Amateur Film Making in Banja Luka, 75th Anniv. — A258

2012, Oct. 26 ***Perf. 13¾***
460 A258 2.30m multi 4.25 4.25

Vuk Karadzic (1787-1864), Linguist A259

2012, Nov. 7 ***Perf. 13x13¼***
461 A259 1.50m multi 2.75 2.75

Printed in sheets of 8 + central label.

Sub-machine Guns — A260

Designs: 10pf, MP 40. 20pf, PPSh-41. 35pf, Sten Mk II.

2013, Jan. 10 ***Perf. 13¾***
462 A260 10pf multi .25 .25
463 A260 20pf multi .30 .30
464 A260 35pf multi .50 .50
Nos. 462-464 (3) 1.05 1.05

Chess Pieces — A261

Designs: 50pf, Black rook, White bishop. 90pf, Black knight, White pawn. 2.30m, Black queen, White king.

2013, Jan. 10
465 A261 50pf multi .70 .70
466 A261 90pf multi 1.25 1.25
467 A261 2.30m multi 3.25 3.25
Nos. 465-467 (3) 5.20 5.20

JZ 73 Steam Locomotive A262

JZ 85 Steam Locomotive A263

JZ 92 Steam Locomotive A264

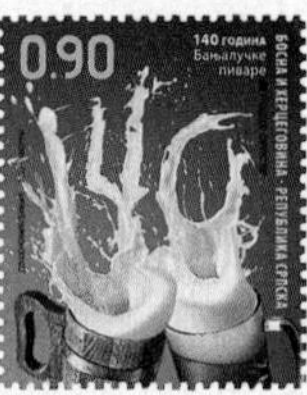

Kloze Steam Locomotive A265

2013, Feb. 7 ***Perf. 13¼x13¾***
468 A262 90pf multi 1.25 1.25
469 A263 90pf multi 1.25 1.25
470 A264 90pf multi 1.25 1.25
471 A265 90pf multi 1.25 1.25
Nos. 468-471 (4) 5.00 5.00

Nos. 468-471 each were printed in sheets of 8 + central label.

Banja Luka Brewery, 140th Anniv. — A266

2013, Mar. 6 ***Perf. 13¾x13¼***
472 A266 90pf multi 1.25 1.25

No. 472 was printed in sheets of 8 + central label.

Europa A267

Old postal truck: Nos. 473, 475a, 475b, 475c, 1m, Facing right. Nos. 474, 475d, 475e, 475f, 2m, Facing left.

2013, July 12 ***Perf. 13x13¾***
473-474 A267 Set of 2 4.00 4.00

Perf. 13x13¾ on 2 or 3 Sides

475 Sheet of 6 12.00 12.00
a. A267 1m Imperf. at top 1.40 1.40
b. A267 1m Imperf. at bottom 1.40 1.40
c. A267 1m Imperf. at top and right 1.40 1.40
d. A267 2m Imperf. at top 2.60 2.60
e. A267 2m Imperf. at bottom 2.60 2.60
f. A267 2m Imperf. at bottom and right 2.60 2.60

Nos. 473-474 each were printed in sheets of 8 + central label.

Giuseppe Verdi (1813-1901), Composer A268

Richard Wagner (1813-83), Composer A269

2013, July 17 ***Perf. 13x13¾***
476 A268 1.50m multi 2.10 2.10
477 A269 1.50m multi 2.10 2.10

Nos. 476-477 each were printed in sheets of 8 + central label.

Souvenir Sheet

Edict of Milan, 1700th Anniv. — A270

No. 478: a, Bust of Emperor Constantine. b, Chrismon and wreath.

2013, July 19 ***Perf. 13¾***
478 A270 1.50m Sheet of 2, #a-b 4.25 4.25

Glas Newspaper, 70th Anniv. — A271

2013, July 30 ***Perf. 13¾x13***
479 A271 90pf multi 1.25 1.25

No. 479 was printed in sheets of 8 + central label.

Souvenir Sheet

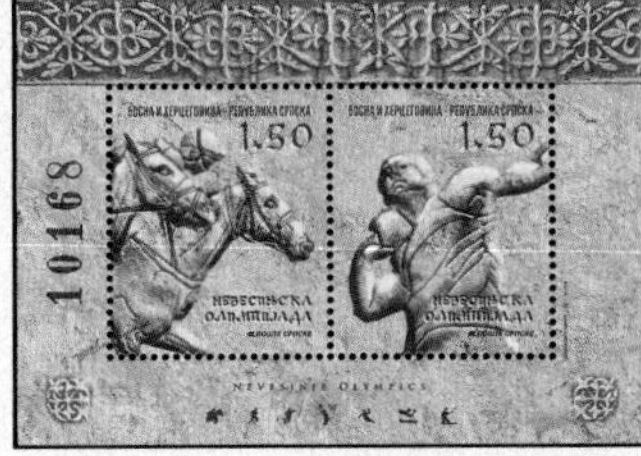

Nevesinje Olympics — A272

No. 480: a, Horse racing. b, Shot put.

2013, Aug. 29 **Litho.** ***Perf. 13¾***
480 A272 1.50m Sheet of 2, #a-b 4.25 4.25

REGISTRATION STAMPS

No. 19 Surcharged

1994, Nov. 1 **Litho.** ***Perf. 13¼***
F9 A1 (P) on 6,000d #19 1.60 1.60

No. F9 sold for 40p on day of issue.

Relay Station Type of 1996

Kraljica relay station, Mt. Ozren.

1996, Sept. 20 ***Perf. 14***
F10 A9 (R) multicolored .75 .75

No. F10 sold for 90p on day of issue.

Famous Men Type of 1997

1997, Nov. 1 ***Perf. 13¾***
F11 A13 (R) Jovan Ducic (1871-1943) .75 .75

No. F11 sold for 90p on day of issue.

Building Type of 1999

1999, Mar. 15 **Litho.** ***Perf. 13¾***
F12 A20 (R) Trebinje 2.00 2.00

No. F12 sold for 1m on day of issue.

POSTAL TAX STAMPS

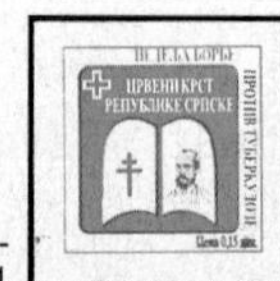

Robert Koch (1843-1910) — PT1

1997, Sept. 14 Litho. ***Imperf.***
Self-Adhesive

RA1 PT1 15p red & blue 1.25 1.25

Obligatory on mail 9/14-21.

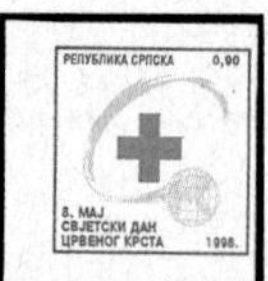

Red Cross — PT2

1998, May 5 Self-Adhesive

RA2 PT2 90p multicolored 1.25 1.25

Obligatory on mail 5/5-15.

Fight Against Tuberculosis PT3

1998, Sept. 14 ***Perf. 10¾***

RA3 PT3 75pf multicolored 1.25 1.25

Obligatory on mail 9/14-21.

Red Cross — PT4

1999, May 8 Litho. ***Perf. 10¾***

RA4 PT4 10pf multi 1.25 1.25

Obligatory on mail 5/8-5/15.

Red Cross — PT5

1999, Sept. 14 Litho. ***Perf. 10¾***

RA5 PT5 10pf multi .60 .60

Obligatory on mail 9/14-21.

Red Cross — PT6

2000, May 8 Litho. ***Perf. 10¾***

RA6 PT6 10pf multi 1.25 1.25

Obligatory on mail 5/8-5/15.

Red Cross — PT7

2000, Sept. 14 Litho. ***Perf. 10¾***

RA7 PT7 10pf multi 1.25 1.25

Obligatory on mail 9/14-21.

Red Cross — PT8

2001, May 8 Litho. ***Perf. 10¾***

RA8 PT8 10pf multi 1.25 1.25

Obligatory on mail 5/8-5/15.

Anti-Tuberculosis Week — PT9

2001, Sept. 14 Litho. ***Perf. 10½***

RA9 PT9 10pf multi 1.25 1.25

Obligatory on mail 9/14-9/21.

Red Cross — PT10

2002, May 8 Litho. ***Perf. 10¾***

RA10 PT10 10pf multi 1.20 1.20

Obligatory on mail 5/8-5/15.

Fight Against Tuberculosis — PT11

2002, Sept. 14 Litho. ***Perf. 10¾***

RA11 PT11 10pf multi 1.20 1.20

Obligatory on mail 9/14-9/21.

Red Cross — PT12

2003, May 8 Litho. ***Perf. 10¾***

RA12 PT12 10pf multi 1.20 1.20

Obligatory on mail 5/8-5/15.

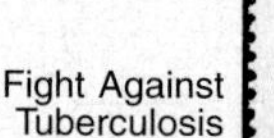

Fight Against Tuberculosis PT13

2003, Sept. 14 Litho. ***Perf. 10¾***

RA13 PT13 10pf multi 1.20 1.20
a. Imperf. 2.40 2.40

Obligatory on mail 9/14-9/21.

Red Cross — PT14

2004, May 8 Litho. ***Perf. 10¾***

RA14 PT14 10pf multi .85 .85
a. Imperf. 2.00 2.00

Obligatory on mail 5/8-5/15.

Fight Against Tuberculosis PT15

2004, Sept. 14 Litho. ***Perf. 10¾***

RA15 PT15 10pf multi .85 .85
a. Imperf. 2.00 2.00

Obligatory on mail 9/14-9/21.

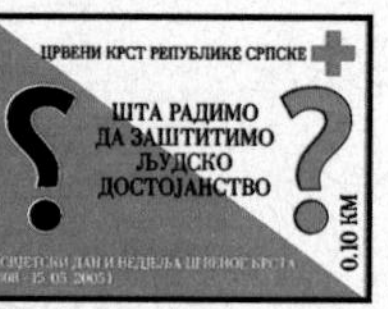

Red Cross — PT16

2005, May 8 Litho. ***Imperf.***
Self-Adhesive

RA16 PT16 10pf red & black .80 .80

Obligatory on mail 5/8-5/15.

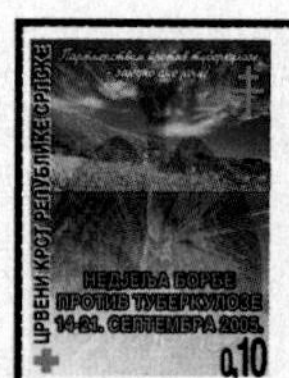

Fight Against Tuberculosis PT17

Rouletted 16½

2005, Sept. 14 Litho.

RA17 PT17 10pf multi .75 .75
a. Imperf. 1.00 1.00

Obligatory on mail 9/14-9/21.

PT18

PT19

2006, May 8 Litho. ***Perf. 10***

RA18 PT18 20pf multi .70 .70
a. Imperf. 1.40 1.40

Red Cross. Obligatory on mail 5/8-5/15.

2006, Sept. 14 ***Perf. 10¾***

RA19 PT19 20pf multi .70 .70
a. Imperf. 1.40 1.40

Fight against tuberculosis. Obligatory on mail 9/14-9/21.

PT20

PT21

2007, May 8 Litho. ***Perf. 10***

RA20 PT20 20pf multi .60 .60
a. Imperf. 1.40 1.40

Red Cross. Obligatory on mail May 8-15.

2007, Sept. 14 ***Perf. 10***

RA21 PT21 20pf multi .60 .60
a. Imperf. 1.40 1.40

Fight against tuberculosis. Obligatory on mail Sept. 14-21.

Hands — PT22

2008, May 8 Litho. ***Perf. 10***

RA22 PT22 20pf multi .90 .90
a. Imperf. .90 .90

Red Cross. Obligatory on mail May 8-15.

PT23

PT24

2008, Sept. 14 Litho. ***Perf. 10***

RA23 PT23 20pf multi .90 .90
a. Imperf. .90 .90

Fight against tuberculosis. Obligatory on mail Sept. 14-21.

2009, May 8 ***Perf. 10¾***

RA24 PT24 20pf multi .90 .90
a. Imperf. .90 .90

Red Cross. Obligatory on mail May 8-15.

Fight Against Tuberculosis PT25

2009, Sept. 14 Litho. ***Perf. 10¾x11***

RA25 PT25 20pf multi .90 .90
a. Imperf. .90 .90

Obligatory on mail Sept. 14-21.

Red Cross — PT26

2010, May 8 Litho. *Perf. 10¾*

RA26 PT26 20pf multi .90 .90
a. Imperf. .90 .90

Obligatory on mail May 8-15.

Fight Against Tuberculosis PT27

2010, Sept. 14 Litho. *Perf. 10¾*

RA27 PT27 20pf multi .90 .90
a. Imperf. .90 .90

Obligatory on mail Sept. 14-21.

Red Cross — PT28

2011, May 8 *Perf. 10*

RA28 PT28 20pf multi .80 .80
a. Perf. 10 horiz. .80 .80

Obligatory on mail May 8-15.

Fight Against Tuberculosis — PT29

2011, Sept. 14

RA29 PT29 20pf multi .80 .80
a. Imperf. .80 .80

Obligatory on mail Sept. 14-21.

Red Cross — PT30

2012, May 8 *Perf. 9*

RA30 PT30 20pf multi .80 .80
a. Imperf. .80 .80

Obligatory on mail May 8-15.

Fight Against Tuberculosis PT31

2012, Sept. 14 Litho. *Perf. 9*

RA31 PT31 20pf multi .30 .30
a. Imperf. .30 .30

Obligatory on mail Sept. 14-21.

Red Cross, 150th Anniv. — PT32

2013, May 8 Litho. *Perf. 9*

RA32 PT32 20pf multi .30 .30
a. Imperf. .30 .30

Obligatory on mail May 8-15.

BOTSWANA

bä-ˈswä-nə

LOCATION — In central South Africa, north of the Republic of South Africa, east of Namibia and bounded on the north by the Caprivi Strip of Namibia and on the east by Zimbabwe.
GOVT. — Independent republic
AREA — 222,000 sq. mi.
POP. — 1,561,973 (July 2004 est.)
CAPITAL — Gaborone

The former Bechuanaland Protectorate became an independent republic, September 30, 1966, taking the name Botswana.

100 Cents = 1 Rand
100 Thebe = 1 Pula (1976)

Catalogue values for all unused stamps in this country are for Never Hinged items.

National Assembly Building — A1

Designs: 5c, Abattoir, Lobatsi. 15c, Dakota plane. 35c, State House, Gaborone.

Unwmk.

1966, Sept. 30 Photo. *Perf. 14*

1 A1 2½c multicolored .30 .25
a. Imperf., pair *425.00*
2 A1 5c multicolored .40 .25
3 A1 15c multicolored 1.10 .30
4 A1 35c multicolored .75 .60
Nos. 1-4 (4) 2.55 1.40

Establishment of Republic of Botswana.

Bechuanaland Protectorate Nos. 180-193 Overprinted

Perf. 14x14½, 14½x14

1966, Sept. 30 Wmk. 314

5 A15 1c multicolored .55 .25
6 A15 2c multicolored .65 .90
7 A15 2½c multicolored .65 .25
8 A15 3½c yel, blk, sep & pink .90 .35
9 A15 5c multicolored .90 *1.75*
10 A15 7½c multicolored .90 *2.40*
11 A15 10c multicolored 1.25 .35
12 A15 12½c multicolored 4.00 *4.50*
13 A15 20c gray & brown 1.00 1.50
14 A15 25c yel & dk brn 1.00 *2.75*
15 A15 35c dp org & ultra 1.25 *3.00*
16 A15 50c lt ol grn & sep 1.00 .95
17 A15 1r ocher & black 1.25 *1.90*
18 A15 2r blue & brown 2.25 *3.75*
Nos. 5-18 (14) 17.55 24.60

European Golden Oriole — A2

Birds: 2c, African hoopoe. 3c, Ground-scraper thrush. 4c, Blue waxbill. 5c, Secretary bird. 7c, Yellow-billed hornbill. 10c, Crimson-breasted shrike. 15c, Malachite kingfisher. 20c, Fish eagle. 25c, Gray lourie. 35c, Scimitar bill. 50c, Knob-billed duck. 1r, Crested barbet. 2r, Didrio cuckoo.

Perf. 14x14½

1967, Jan. 3 Photo. Unwmk.

19 A2 1c gray & multi .40 .25
20 A2 2c lt blue & multi .60 .25
21 A2 3c yel green & multi .75 .25
22 A2 4c salmon & multi .75 .35
23 A2 5c pink & multi .75 .40
24 A2 7c slate & multi .80 .70
25 A2 10c emerald & multi .80 .80
26 A2 15c lt green & multi 12.00 1.50
27 A2 20c ultra & multi 12.00 1.90
28 A2 25c green & multi 7.50 2.40
29 A2 35c multicolored 10.00 3.00
30 A2 50c dl yel & multi 4.50 4.50
31 A2 1r dl grn & multi 11.00 6.00
32 A2 2r org brn & multi 12.50 *17.50*
Nos. 19-32 (14) 74.35 39.80

University Buildings and Graduates — A3

1967, Apr. 7 *Perf. 14x14½*

33 A3 3c yel, sepia & dp blue .25 .25
34 A3 7c blue, sepia & dp bl .25 .25
35 A3 15c dull rose, sepia & dp bl .25 .25
36 A3 35c lt vio, sepia & dp bl .25 .25
Nos. 33-36 (4) 1.00 1.00

1st conferment of degrees by the University of Botswana, Lesotho and Swaziland at Roma, Lesotho.

Chobe Bush Bucks A4

Designs: 7c, Sable antelopes. 35c, Fishing on the Chobe River.

1967, Oct. 2 Photo. *Perf. 14*

37 A4 3c multicolored .60 .25
38 A4 7c multicolored .60 .25
39 A4 35c multicolored 1.50 *1.75*
Nos. 37-39 (3) 2.70 2.25

Publicity for Chobe Game Reserve.

Human Rights Flame and Arms of Botswana — A5

Design elements rearranged on 15c, 25c.

1968, Apr. 8 Litho. *Perf. 13½x13*

40 A5 3c brown red & multi .25 .25
41 A5 15c emerald & multi .25 *.45*
42 A5 25c yellow & multi .40 *.55*
Nos. 40-42 (3) .90 1.25

International Human Rights Year.

Rock Painting A6

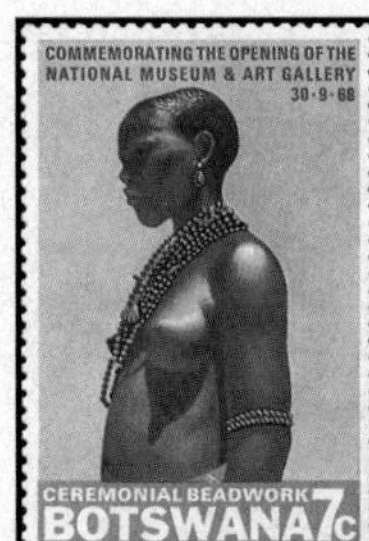

Girl Wearing Ceremonial Beads — A7

Designs: 10c, Baobab Trees, by Thomas Baines (34x25mm). 15c, National Museum and Art Gallery (71½x19mm).

Perf. 13x13½ (3c, 10c); Perf. 12½ (7c); Perf. 12½x13 (15c)

1968, Sept. 30 Litho.

43 A6 3c multicolored .35 .25
44 A7 7c multicolored .40 .40
45 A6 10c multicolored .40 .35
46 A6 15c multicolored .75 *1.60*
a. Souv. sheet of 4, #43-46, perf. 13½ 2.25 *3.00*
Nos. 43-46 (4) 1.90 2.60

Opening of the National Museum and Art Gallery, Gaborone, Sept. 30, 1968.

African Nativity Scene A8

1968, Nov. 11 Unwmk. *Perf. 13x14*

47 A8 1c car & multi .25 .25
48 A8 2c brown & multi .25 .25
49 A8 5c green & multi .25 .25
50 A8 25c dp violet & multi .25 *.50*
Nos. 47-50 (4) 1.00 1.25

Christmas.

Boy Scout, Botswana Scout Emblem and Lion — A9

Botswana Boy Scout emblem, lion and: 15c, Boy Scouts cooking, vert. 25c, Boy Scouts around campfire.

1969, Aug. 21 Litho. *Perf. 13½*

51 A9 3c emerald & multi .30 .25
52 A9 15c lt brown & multi .90 *1.10*
53 A9 25c dk brown & multi 1.25 *1.40*
Nos. 51-53 (3) 2.45 2.75

22nd World Scouting Conf., Helsinki, Finland, Aug. 21-27.

Mother, Child and Star of Bethlehem — A10

Diamond Treatment Plant, Orapa — A11

1969, Nov. 6 *Perf. 14½x14*

54 A10 1c dk brn & lt blue .25 .25
55 A10 2c dk brn & apple grn .25 .25
56 A10 4c dk brn & dull yel .25 .25
57 A10 35c dk brn & vio blue .25 .25
a. Souv. sheet, #54-57, perf 14½ 1.10 1.10
Nos. 54-57 (4) 1.00 1.00

Christmas.

1970, Mar. 23 ***Perf. 14½x14, 14x14½***

Designs: 7c, Copper and nickel mining, Selebi-Pikwe. 10c, Copper and nickel mining and metal bars, Selebi-Pikwe, horiz. 35c, Orapa diamond mine and diamonds, horiz.

No.	Type	Description	Unused	Used
58	A11	3c multicolored	.80	.35
59	A11	7c multicolored	1.50	.35
60	A11	10c multicolored	3.00	.25
61	A11	35c multicolored	4.25	2.00
		Nos. 58-61 (4)	9.55	2.95

Botswana development program.

Mr. Micawber and Charles Dickens A12

Charles Dickens (1812-70), English novelist and: 7c, Scrooge. 15c, Fagin. 25c, Bill Sykes.

1970, July 7 **Litho.** ***Perf. 11***

No.	Type	Description	Unused	Used
62	A12	3c gray green & multi	.25	.25
63	A12	7c multicolored	.30	.25
64	A12	15c brown & multi	.65	.55
65	A12	25c dp violet & multi	1.00	.85
a.		Souvenir sheet of 4, #62-65	5.00	5.00
		Nos. 62-65 (4)	2.20	1.90

UN Headquarters, Emblem — A13

1970, Oct. 24 **Litho.** ***Perf. 11***

No.	Type	Description	Unused	Used
66	A13	15c ultra, red & silver	1.00	.50

United Nations' 25th anniversary.

Toys A14

1970, Nov. 3 **Litho.** ***Perf. 14***

No.	Type	Description	Unused	Used
67	A14	1c Crocodile	.25	.25
68	A14	2c Giraffe	.25	.25
69	A14	7c Elephant	.25	.25
70	A14	25c Rhinoceros	.90	.90
a.		Souvenir sheet of 4, #67-70	2.10	2.10
		Nos. 67-70 (4)	1.65	1.65

Christmas.

Sorghum A15

1971, Apr. 6 **Litho.** ***Perf. 14***

No.	Type	Description	Unused	Used
71	A15	3c shown	.25	.25
72	A15	7c Millet	.25	.25
73	A15	10c Corn	.25	.25
74	A15	35c Peanuts	1.10	1.10
		Nos. 71-74 (4)	1.85	1.85

Ox Head and Botswana Map — A16

Map of Botswana and: 4c, Cogwheels and waves. 7c, Zebra rampant. 10c, Tusk and corn. 20c, Coat of arms of Botswana.

1971, Sept. 30 ***Perf. 14½x14***

No.	Type	Description	Unused	Used
75	A16	3c yel grn, blk & brn	.25	.25
76	A16	4c lt blue, blk & bl	.25	.25
77	A16	7c orange & blk	.25	.25
78	A16	10c yellow & multi	.35	.25
79	A16	20c blue & multi	.90	*2.40*
		Nos. 75-79 (5)	2.00	3.40

5th anniversary of independence.

King Bringing Gift — A17

Christmas: 2c, King bringing gift. 7c, Kneeling King with gift. 20c, Three Kings and star.

1971, Nov. 11 ***Perf. 14***

No.	Type	Description	Unused	Used
80	A17	2c brt rose & multi	.25	.25
81	A17	3c lt blue & multi	.25	.25
82	A17	7c brt pink & multi	.25	.25
83	A17	20c vio blue & multi	.25	.60
a.		Souvenir sheet of 4, #80-83	1.50	1.50
		Nos. 80-83 (4)	1.00	1.35

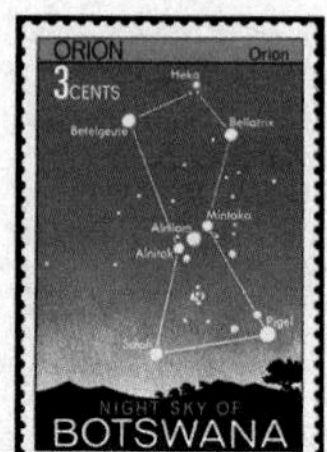

Constellation Orion — A18

Night sky over Botswana: 7c, Scorpio. 10c, Centaur. 20c, Southern Cross.

1972, Apr. 24 **Litho.** ***Perf. 14***

No.	Type	Description	Unused	Used
84	A18	3c dp org, bl grn & blk	.75	.75
85	A18	7c org, blue & blk	1.25	1.25
86	A18	10c org, green & blk	2.00	2.00
87	A18	20c emer, vio bl & blk	4.25	4.25
		Nos. 84-87 (4)	8.25	8.25

Gubulawayo Cancel and Map of Trail — A19

Cross, Map of Botswana, Bells — A20

Sections of Mafeking-Gubulawayo Trail and: 4c, Bechuanaland Protectorate No. 65. 7c, Mail runners. 20c, Mafeking 638 killer cancellation.

1972, Aug. 21 ***Perf. 13½x13***

No.	Type	Description	Unused	Used
88	A19	3c cream & multi	.25	.25
89	A19	4c cream & multi	.25	.25
90	A19	7c cream & multi	.55	.55
91	A19	20c cream & multi	1.40	1.40
a.		Souvenir sheet of 4	20.00	20.00
		Nos. 88-91 (4)	2.45	2.45

84th anniv. of Mafeking to Gubulawayo runner post. No. 91a contains one each of Nos. 88-91, arranged vertically to show map of trail. No. 91a exists with pale buff background omitted. Value, $700.

Compare with design A89.

1972, Nov. 6 **Litho.** ***Perf. 14***

Cross, map of Botswana and: 3c, Candle. 7c, Christmas tree. 20c, Star and holly.

No.	Type	Description	Unused	Used
92	A20	2c yellow & multi	.25	.25
93	A20	3c pale lilac & multi	.25	.25
94	A20	7c yel green & multi	.25	.25
95	A20	20c pink & multi	.25	.25
a.		Souvenir sheet of 4, #92-95	2.00	2.00
		Nos. 92-95 (4)	1.00	1.00

Christmas.

Chariot of the Sun, Trundholm, Denmark — A21

WMO Emblem and: 3c, Thor, Norse thunder god, vert. 7c, Ymir, Icelandic frost giant, vert. 20c, Odin on 8-legged horse Sleipnir.

1973, Mar. 23 **Litho.** ***Perf. 14***

No.	Type	Description	Unused	Used
96	A21	3c orange & multi	.25	.25
97	A21	4c yellow & multi	.30	.25
98	A21	7c ultra & multi	.55	.25
99	A21	20c gold & multi	1.50	1.10
		Nos. 96-99 (4)	2.60	1.85

Intl. meteorological cooperation, cent.

Livingstone and Boat on Lake Ngwami — A22

Design: 20c, Livingstone and his meeting with Henry Stanley.

1973, Sept. 10 **Litho.** ***Perf. 13½x14***

No.	Type	Description	Unused	Used
100	A22	3c gray & multi	.35	.30
101	A22	20c yel green & multi	1.25	1.25

Dr. David Livingstone (1813-1873), medical missionary and explorer.

Shepherd and Flock — A23

Christmas: 3c, Ass and foal, African huts, vert. 7c, African mother, child and star, vert. 20c, Tribal meeting (kgotla), symbolic of Wise Men.

1973, Nov. 12 **Litho.** ***Perf. 14½***

No.	Type	Description	Unused	Used
102	A23	3c multicolored	.25	.25
103	A23	4c multicolored	.25	.25
104	A23	7c multicolored	.25	.25
105	A23	20c multicolored	.25	*.75*
		Nos. 102-105 (4)	1.00	1.50

Gaborone Campus, Botswana A24

Designs: 7c, Kwaluseni Campus, Swaziland. 20c, Roma Campus, Lesotho. 35c, Map and flags of Botswana, Swaziland & Lesotho.

1974, May 8 **Litho.** ***Perf. 14***

No.	Type	Description	Unused	Used
106	A24	3c lt blue & multi	.25	.25
107	A24	7c yel green & multi	.25	.25
108	A24	20c yel green & multi	.25	.25
109	A24	35c brt blue & multi	.25	.25
		Nos. 106-109 (4)	1.00	1.00

10th anniversary of the University of Botswana, Lesotho and Swaziland.

UPU Emblem, Mail Vehicles — A25

UPU, cent.: 3c, Post Office, Palapye, c. 1889. 7c, Bechuanaland police camel post, 1900. 20c, 1920 and 1974 planes.

1974, May 22 **Litho.** ***Perf. 13½x14***

No.	Type	Description	Unused	Used
110	A25	2c car & multi	.80	.55
111	A25	3c green & multi	.80	.55
112	A25	7c brown & multi	1.25	.90
113	A25	20c blue & multi	3.50	3.25
		Nos. 110-113 (4)	6.35	5.25

Gems and Minerals A26

1974, July 1 **Photo.** ***Perf. 14x13***

No.	Type	Description	Unused	Used
114	A26	1c Amethyst	.65	*2.00*
115	A26	2c Agate	.65	*2.00*
116	A26	3c Quartz	.70	*.75*
117	A26	4c Niccolite	.80	.55
118	A26	5c Moss agate	.80	*1.10*
119	A26	7c Agate	1.25	.60
120	A26	10c Stilbite	2.50	.60
121	A26	15c Moshaneng banded marble	3.00	*3.25*
122	A26	20c Gem diamonds	5.50	4.00
123	A26	25c Chrysotile	6.75	2.75
124	A26	35c Jasper	7.00	4.75
125	A26	50c Moss quartz	6.50	*7.00*
126	A26	1r Citrine	11.00	*10.00*
127	A26	2r Chalcopyrite	27.50	20.00
		Nos. 114-127 (14)	74.60	59.35

For surcharges see Nos. 155-168.

Stapelia Variegata — A27

Pres. Sir Seretse Khama — A28

Flowers of Botswana: 7c, Hibiscus lunarifolius. 15c, Ceratotheca triloba. 20c, Nerine laticoma.

1974, Nov. 4 **Litho.** ***Perf. 14***

No.	Type	Description	Unused	Used
128	A27	2c multicolored	.30	*.45*
129	A27	7c multicolored	.65	.25
130	A27	15c multicolored	1.25	*1.75*
131	A27	20c multicolored	1.75	*2.25*
a.		Souvenir sheet of 4, #128-131	4.50	4.50
		Nos. 128-131 (4)	3.95	4.70

1975, Mar. 24 **Photo.** ***Perf. 13½x13***

No.	Type	Description	Unused	Used
132	A28	4c olive & multi	.25	.25
133	A28	10c yellow & multi	.25	.25
134	A28	20c ultra & multi	.30	.30
135	A28	35c brown & multi	.50	.50
a.		Souvenir sheet of 4, #132-135	1.50	*1.75*
		Nos. 132-135 (4)	1.30	1.30

10th anniv. of self-government.

Ostrich and Rock Painting A29

Paintings and animals: 10c, Rhinoceros. 25c, Hyena. 35c, Scorpion.

1975, June 23 **Litho.** ***Perf. 14x14½***

No.	Type	Description	Unused	Used
136	A29	4c yel green & multi	1.60	.25
137	A29	10c buff & multi	2.10	.25
138	A29	25c blue & multi	3.25	1.00
139	A29	35c lilac & multi	5.25	1.75
a.		Souvenir sheet of 4, #136-139	20.00	20.00
		Nos. 136-139 (4)	12.20	3.25

Rock paintings from Tsodilo Hills.

Map of British Bechuanaland A30

Chiefs Sebele, Bathoen and Khama A31

Design: 10c, Khama the Great, antelope.

Perf. 14½x14, 14x14½

1975, Oct. 31			**Litho.**	
140	A30	6c buff & multi	.50	.25
141	A30	10c rose & multi	.55	.25
142	A31	25c lt green & multi	1.25	1.00
		Nos. 140-142 (3)	2.30	1.50

Establishment of Protectorate, 90th anniv. (6c); Khama the Great (1828-1923), centenary of his accession as chief (10c); visit of the chiefs of the Bakwena, Bangwaketse and Bamangwato tribes to London, 80th anniv. (25c).

Aloe Marlothii — A32

Christmas: 10c, Aloe lutescens. 15c, Aloe zebrina. 25c, Aloe littoralis.

1975, Nov. 3		**Litho.**	***Perf. 14½x14***	
143	A32	3c multicolored	.30	.25
144	A32	10c multicolored	.90	.25
145	A32	15c multicolored	1.25	*1.75*
146	A32	25c multicolored	2.40	*2.75*
		Nos. 143-146 (4)	4.85	5.00

Traditional Musical Instruments — A33

Designs: 4c, Drum. 10c, Hand piano. 15c, Segankuru (violin). 25c, Kudu signal horn.

1976, Mar. 1		**Litho.**	***Perf. 14***	
147	A33	4c yellow & multi	.25	.25
148	A33	10c lilac & multi	.35	.25
149	A33	15c dull yel & multi	.45	*.65*
150	A33	25c lt blue & multi	.55	*1.40*
		Nos. 147-150 (4)	1.60	2.55

1-pula Bank Note with Seretse Khama A34

Reverse of Bank Notes: 10c, Basket weaver, hut builder. 15c, Antelopes. 25c, National Assembly building.

1976, June 28		**Litho.**	***Perf. 14***	
151	A34	4c rose & multi	.25	.25
152	A34	10c brt green & multi	.25	.25
153	A34	15c yel green & multi	.30	.30
154	A34	25c blue & multi	.45	.45
a.		Souvenir sheet of 4, #151-154	2.75	*4.00*
		Nos. 151-154 (4)	1.25	1.25

First national currency.

Nos. 114-127 Surcharged in Black or Gold

Type I

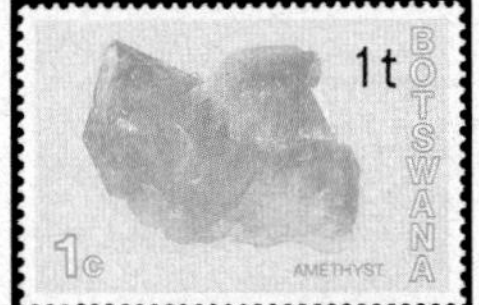

Type II

Type I surcharge: Thick numerals and "t."
Type II surcharge: Thin numerals and "t."

Type I

1976, Aug. 23		**Photo.**	***Perf. 14x13***	
155	A26	1t on 1c multi	2.40	.70
156	A26	2t on 2c multi	2.40	.70
157	A26	3t on 3c multi (G)	1.80	.60
158	A26	4t on 4c multi	2.75	.45
159	A26	5t on 5c multi	2.75	.45
160	A26	7t on 7c multi	1.40	*2.50*
161	A26	10t on 10c multi	1.75	.80
162	A26	15t on 15c multi (G)	5.50	2.40
163	A26	20t on 20c multi	7.50	.80
164	A26	25t on 25c multi	6.00	1.25
165	A26	35t on 35c multi	5.50	4.50
166	A26	50t on 50c multi	8.75	*9.00*
167	A26	1p on 1r multi	9.50	*9.75*
168	A26	2p on 2r multi (G)	13.50	11.50
		Nos. 155-168 (14)	71.50	45.40

1977, July 15			**Type II**	
155a	A26	1t on 1c multi	2.60	.80
156a	A26	2t on 2c multi	2.60	.80
158a	A26	4t on 4c multi	3.00	.80
159a	A26	5t on 5c multi	3.00	.80
162a	A26	15t on 15c multi (G)	7.00	1.50
163a	A26	20t on 20c multi (G)	9.00	1.50
		Nos. 155a-163a (6)	27.20	6.20

The government printer in Pretoria applied the typographed type I surcharge. Enschede applied the lithographed type II surcharge.

Cattle Industry A35

Designs: 10t, Antelope, tourism, vert. 15t, Schoolhouse and children, education. 25t, Rural weaving, vert. 35t, Mining industry, vert.

1976, Sept. 30		**Litho.**	***Perf. 14x14½***	
		Textured Paper		
169	A35	4t multicolored	.25	.25
170	A35	10t multicolored	.35	.35
171	A35	15t multicolored	.55	.55
172	A35	25t multicolored	.75	.75
173	A35	35t multicolored	1.00	1.00
		Nos. 169-173 (5)	2.90	2.90

10th anniversary of independence.

Colophospermum Mopane — A36

Trees: 4t, Baikiaea plurijuga. 10t, Sterculia rogersii. 25t, Acacia nilotica. 40t, Kigelia africana.

1976, Nov. 1		**Litho.**	***Perf. 13***	
174	A36	3t multicolored	.40	.30
175	A36	4t multicolored	.40	.30
176	A36	10t multicolored	.55	.45
177	A36	25t multicolored	1.10	.95
178	A36	40t multicolored	1.90	1.50
		Nos. 174-178 (5)	4.35	3.50

Christmas.

Pres. Seretse Khama and Elizabeth II — A37

Designs: 25t, Coronation coach in procession. 40t, Recognition scene.

1977, Feb. 7		**Litho.**	***Perf. 12***	
179	A37	4t multicolored	.25	.25
180	A37	25t multicolored	.25	.30
181	A37	40t multicolored	.40	.50
		Nos. 179-181 (3)	.90	1.05

Reign of Queen Elizabeth II, 25th anniv.

Clawless Otter — A38

World Wildlife Fund Emblem and: 4t, Serval. 10t, Bat-eared foxes. 25t, Pangolins. 40t, Brown hyena.

1977, June 6		**Litho.**	***Perf. 14***	
182	A38	3t multicolored	*8.50*	*1.00*
183	A38	4t multicolored	*8.50*	*1.00*
184	A38	10t multicolored	*10.50*	*1.00*
185	A38	25t multicolored	*22.50*	*4.25*
186	A38	40t multicolored	*30.00*	*14.00*
		Nos. 182-186 (5)	*80.00*	*21.25*

Endangered wildlife.

Khama Memorial A39

Designs: 4t, Gcwihaba Caverns. 15t, Green's (expedition) tree. 20t, Mmajojo ruins. 25t, Ancient morabaraba board. 35t, Matsieng's footprints.

1977, Aug. 22		**Litho.**	***Perf. 14***	
187	A39	4t multicolored	.25	.25
188	A39	5t multicolored	.25	.25
189	A39	15t multicolored	.40	.40
190	A39	20t multicolored	.50	.50
191	A39	25t multicolored	.80	.80
192	A39	35t multicolored	1.10	1.10
a.		Souvenir sheet of 6, #187-192	4.75	4.75
		Nos. 187-192 (6)	3.30	3.30

Historical sites and national monuments.

Lilies — A40

Birds — A41

Designs: 3t, Hypoxis Itida. 5t, Haemanthus magnificus. 10t, Boophane disticha. 25t, Vellozia retinervis. 40t, Ammocharis coranica.

1977, Nov. 7		**Litho.**	***Perf. 14***	
193	A40	3t sepia & multi	.25	.25
194	A40	5t gray & multi	.25	.25
195	A40	10t multicolored	.30	.30
196	A40	25t multicolored	.50	*.65*
197	A40	40t multicolored	1.00	*1.25*
		Nos. 193-197 (5)	2.30	2.70

Christmas.

1978, July 3		**Photo.**	***Perf. 14***	
198	A41	1t Black korhaan	.80	*1.10*
199	A41	2t Marabou storks	1.00	*1.10*
200	A41	3t Red-billed hoopoe	.80	*.80*
201	A41	4t Carmine bee-eaters	1.00	*1.00*
202	A41	5t African jacana	.80	.35
203	A41	7t Paradise flycatcher	1.40	*2.75*
204	A41	10t Bennett's woodpecker	2.25	.50
205	A41	15t Red bishop	1.75	*2.75*
206	A41	20t Crowned plovers	2.00	*1.90*
207	A41	25t Giant kingfishers	.80	*2.75*
208	A41	30t White-faced ducks	.80	.60
209	A41	35t Green-backed heron	.80	*3.00*
210	A41	45t Black-headed herons	1.75	*2.75*
211	A41	50t Spotted eagle owl	9.00	4.25
212	A41	1p Gabar goshawk	4.25	4.25
213	A41	2p Martial eagle	5.25	7.50
214	A41	5p Saddlebill storks	14.50	*16.00*
		Nos. 198-214 (17)	48.95	53.35

For surcharges see Nos. 289-290.

Tawana Making Kaross (Garment) A42

Designs: 5t, Map of Okavango Delta. 15t, Bushman collecting roots. 20t, Herero woman milking cow. 25t, Yei pulling mokoro (boat). 35t, Mbukushu fishing.

1978, Sept. 11		**Litho.**	***Perf. 14***	
		Textured Paper		
215	A42	4t multicolored	.25	*.30*
216	A42	5t multicolored	.25	.25
217	A42	15t multicolored	.25	*.40*
218	A42	20t multicolored	.45	*.65*
219	A42	25t multicolored	.55	*.60*
220	A42	35t multicolored	.65	*1.60*
a.		Souvenir sheet of 6, #215-220	3.00	*3.50*
		Nos. 215-220 (6)	2.40	*3.80*

People of the Okavango Delta.

Caralluma Lutea — A43

Boy at Sip Well — A44

Flowers: 10t, Hoodia lugardii. 15t, Ipomoea transvaalensis. 25t, Ansellia gigantea.

1978, Nov. 6				
221	A43	5t multicolored	.40	.25
222	A43	10t multicolored	.65	.35
223	A43	15t multicolored	1.10	.60
224	A43	25t multicolored	1.25	.90
		Nos. 221-224 (4)	3.40	2.10

Christmas.

1979, Mar. 30 **Litho.** ***Perf. 14***

Water Development: 5t, Watering pit. 10t, Hand-dug well and goats. 25t, Windmill, well and cattle. 40t, Modern drilling rig.

225	A44	3t multicolored	.25	.25
226	A44	5t multicolored	.25	.25
227	A44	10t multicolored	.25	.25
228	A44	25t multicolored	.25	.25
229	A44	40t multicolored	.30	.30
		Nos. 225-229 (5)	1.30	1.30

Botswana Pot — A45

Handicrafts: 10t, Clay buffalo. 25t, Woven covered basket. 40t, Beaded bag.

1979, June 11		**Litho.**	***Perf. 14***	
230	A45	5t multicolored	.25	.25
231	A45	10t multicolored	.25	.25
232	A45	25t multicolored	.25	.25
233	A45	40t multicolored	.60	.60
a.		Souvenir sheet of 4, #230-233	1.75	1.75
		Nos. 230-233 (4)	1.35	1.35

Bechuanaland No. 6, Rowland Hill — A46

Sir Rowland Hill (1795-1879), originator of penny postage, and: 25t, Bechuanaland Protectorate No. 107. 45t, Botswana No. 20.

1979, Aug. 27 Litho. ***Perf. 13½***

234 A46 5t rose & black .25 .25
235 A46 25t multicolored .35 .35
236 A46 45t multicolored .50 .50
Nos. 234-236 (3) 1.10 1.10

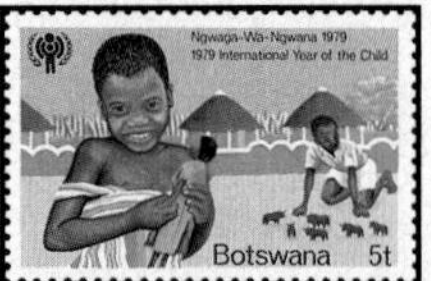

Children Playing A47

Design: 10t, Child playing with rag doll, and IYC emblem, vert.

1979, Sept. 24 ***Perf. 14***

237 A47 5t multicolored .25 .25
238 A47 10t multicolored .25 .25

International Year of the Child.

Ximenia Caffra — A48

Christmas: 10t, Sclerocarya caffra. 15t, Hexalobus monopetalus. 25t, Ficus soldanella.

1979, Nov. 12 Litho. ***Perf. 14***

239 A48 5t multicolored .25 .25
240 A48 10t multicolored .25 .25
241 A48 15t multicolored .30 .30
242 A48 25t multicolored .55 .55
Nos. 239-242 (4) 1.35 1.35

Flap-Necked Chameleon A49

1980, Mar. 3 Litho. ***Perf. 14***

243 A49 5t shown .95 .85
244 A49 10t Leopard tortoise .95 .85
245 A49 25t Puff adder 1.60 1.60
246 A49 40t White-throated monitor 2.25 *3.00*
Nos. 243-246 (4) 5.75 6.30

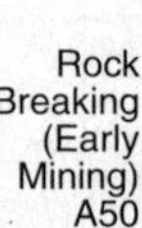

Rock Breaking (Early Mining) A50

1980, July 7 Litho. ***Perf. 13½x14***

247 A50 5t shown .45 .35
248 A50 10t Ore hoisting .55 .40
249 A50 15t Ore transport 1.10 1.00
250 A50 20t Ore crushing 1.40 1.10
251 A50 25t Smelting 1.50 1.10
252 A50 35t Tools, products 2.00 1.50
Nos. 247-252 (6) 7.00 5.45

Chiwele and the Giant — A51

Folktales: 10t, Kgori Is Not Deceived. 30t, Nyambi's Wife and Crocodile. 45t, Clever Hare, horiz.

Perf. 14, 14½ (10t, 30t)

1980, Sept. 8

253 A51 5t multicolored .25 .25

Size: 28x36mm

254 A51 10t multicolored .25 .25
255 A51 30t multicolored .50 .50

Size: 44x26mm

256 A51 45t multicolored .80 .80
Nos. 253-256 (4) 1.80 1.80

Game Watching — A52

1980, Oct. 6 Litho. ***Perf. 14***

257 A52 5t multicolored .70 .40

World Tourism Conf., Manila, Sept. 27.

Christmas — A53

1980, Nov. 3 Litho. ***Perf. 14***

258 A53 5t shown .25 .25
259 A53 10t Acacia nilotica .30 .25
260 A53 25t Acacia erubescens .60 .35
261 A53 40t Dichrostachys cinerea 1.10 .55
Nos. 258-261 (4) 2.25 1.40

Heinrich von Stephan, Bechuanaland Protectorate No. 150, Botswana No. 111 — A55

Design: 20t, Von Stephan, Bechuanaland Protectorate No. 151, Botswana No. 112.

1981, Jan. 7 ***Perf. 14***

266 A55 6t multicolored .85 .50
267 A55 20t multicolored 1.90 *2.25*

Von Stephan (1831-1897), founder of UPU.

Emperor Dragonfly — A56

1981, Feb. 23 Litho. ***Perf. 14***

268 A56 6t shown .30 .25
269 A56 7t Praying mantis .30 .25
270 A56 10t Elegant grasshopper .35 .25
271 A56 20t Dung beetle .90 .65
272 A56 30t Citrus swallowtail butterfly 1.50 1.10
273 A56 45t Mopane worm 2.25 1.75
a. Souv. sheet of 6, #268-273 9.00 9.00
Nos. 268-273 (6) 5.60 4.25

Blind Basket Weaver A57

1981, Apr. 6 Litho. ***Perf. 14***

274 A57 6t Seamstress .25 .25
275 A57 20t shown .75 .35
276 A57 30t Carpenter 1.00 .45
Nos. 274-276 (3) 2.00 1.05

International Year of the Disabled.

Woman Reading Letter (Literacy Campaign) — A58

1981, June 8

277 A58 6t shown .25 .25
278 A58 7t Man sending telegram .25 .25
279 A58 20t Boy, newspaper .60 .25
280 A58 30t Father and daughter reading .80 .35
Nos. 277-280 (4) 1.90 1.10

Pres. Seretse Khama (1921-80) and Flag A59

Portrait and various local buildings: 6t, 10t, 45t..

1981, July 13

281 A59 6t multicolored .25 .25
282 A59 10t multicolored .25 .25
283 A59 30t multicolored .50 .50
284 A59 45t multicolored .75 .75
Nos. 281-284 (4) 1.75 1.75

Cattle in Agricultural Show — A60

1981, Sept. 21 Litho. ***Perf. 14½***

285 A60 6t Plowing .30 .25
286 A60 20t shown .40 .25
287 A60 30t Meat Commission .55 .40
288 A60 45t Vaccine Institute .75 .60
Nos. 285-288 (4) 2.00 1.50

Nos. 204, 209 Surcharged

1981, Sept. 1 Photo. ***Perf. 14***

289 A41 25t on 35t multicolored 5.50 4.00
290 A41 30t on 10t multicolored 5.50 4.00

Christmas — A61

Designs: Water lilies.

1981, Nov. 11 Litho.

291 A61 6t Nymphaea caerulea .30 .25
292 A61 10t Nymphoides indica .40 .25
293 A61 25t Nymphaea lotus 1.10 .95
294 A61 40t Ottelia kunenensis 1.25 2.50
Nos. 291-294 (4) 3.05 3.95

Children's Drawings — A62

1982, Feb. 15 Litho. ***Perf. 14½x14***

295 A62 6t Cattle .70 .45
296 A62 10t Kgotla meeting .90 .55
297 A62 30t Village 2.25 2.00
298 A62 45t Huts 2.25 2.25
Nos. 295-298 (4) 6.10 5.25

Traditional Houses — A63

1982, May 3 Litho. ***Perf. 14***

299 A63 6t Common type .50 .25
300 A63 10t Kgatleng .60 .25
301 A63 30t Northeastern 2.75 1.25
302 A63 45t Sarwa 2.75 3.25
Nos. 299-302 (4) 6.60 5.00

Red-billed Teals — A64

Perf. 14x14½, 14½x14

1982, Aug. 2 Photo.

303 A64 1t Masked weaver 1.25 *1.75*
304 A64 2t Lesser double-collared sunbirds 1.40 *1.75*
305 A64 3t White-fronted bee-eaters 1.40 *1.75*
306 A64 4t Ostriches 1.40 *1.75*
307 A64 5t Grey-headed gulls 1.40 *1.75*
308 A64 6t Pygmy geese 1.40 .45
309 A64 7t Cattle egrets 1.40 .25
310 A64 8t Lanner falcon 3.00 1.60
311 A64 10t Yellow-billed storks 1.40 .25
312 A64 15t shown 3.75 .30
313 A64 20t Barn owls 8.25 4.00
314 A64 25t Hamerkops 4.50 .85
315 A64 30t Stilts 5.25 1.00
316 A64 35t Blacksmith plovers 5.25 .90
317 A64 45t Wattled plover 5.25 2.00
318 A64 50t Crowned guinea-fowl 7.25 2.75
319 A64 1p Cape vultures 13.00 *14.00*
320 A64 2p Augur bustards 14.50 *19.00*
Nos. 303-320 (18) 81.05 56.10

Nos. 303-311 vert.

For surcharges see Nos. 401-403.

Christmas — A65

Designs: Mushrooms.

1982, Nov. 2 Litho. *Perf. 14½*
321 A65 7t Shaggy mane 3.50 .90
322 A65 15t Orange milk 5.50 1.75
323 A65 35t Panther 8.75 4.25
324 A65 50t King boletus 11.00 12.50
Nos. 321-324 (4) 28.75 19.40

A66

1983, Mar. 14 Litho. *Perf. 14*
325 A66 7t Pres. Quett Masire .25 .25
326 A66 15t Dancers .25 .25
327 A66 35t Melbourne Conference Center .70 *.75*
328 A66 45t Heads of State meeting .80 *1.10*
Nos. 325-328 (4) 2.00 2.35

Commonwealth Day.

Endangered Species — A67

1983, Apr. 19 Litho. *Perf. 14x14½*
329 A67 7t Wattle crane 5.00 .50
330 A67 15t Aloe lutescens 4.25 .90
331 A67 35t Roan antelope 5.00 3.00
332 A67 50t Hyphaene ventricosa 6.00 5.75
Nos. 329-332 (4) 20.25 10.15

Wooden Spoons — A68

1983, June 18 Litho. *Perf. 14*
333 A68 7t shown .45 .25
334 A68 15t Jewelry .75 .40
335 A68 35t Ox-hide milk bag 1.90 .95
336 A68 50t Decorated knives 2.25 1.10
a. Souvenir sheet of 4, #333-336 10.00 10.00
Nos. 333-336 (4) 5.35 2.70

Christmas A69

Designs: Dragonflies.

1983, Nov. 7 Litho. *Perf. 14½x14*
337 A69 6t Pantala flavescens 1.50 .25
338 A69 15t Anax imperator 3.00 .40
339 A69 25t Trithemis arteriosa 3.50 .80
340 A69 45t Chlorolestes elegans 4.50 *5.25*
Nos. 337-340 (4) 12.50 6.70

Mining Industry — A70

1984, Mar. 19 Litho. *Perf. 14½*
341 A70 7t Diamonds 3.75 .85
342 A70 15t Lime 3.75 1.25
343 A70 35t Copper, nickel, vert. 6.00 4.25
344 A70 50t Coal, vert. 7.00 *11.00*
Nos. 341-344 (4) 20.50 17.35

Traditional Transport A71

1984, June 16 Litho. *Perf. 14½x14*
345 A71 7t Man riding ox .30 .30
346 A71 25t Sled 1.25 1.10
347 A71 35t Wagon 1.40 1.40
348 A71 50t Cart 2.50 2.25
Nos. 345-348 (4) 5.45 5.05

Intl. Civil Aviation Org., 40th Anniv. — A72

1984, Oct. 8 Litho. *Perf. 14x13½*
349 A72 7t Avro 504 1.25 .25
350 A72 10t Westland Wessex 1.75 .40
351 A72 15t Junkers 52-3M 2.75 1.10
352 A72 25t Dragon Rapide 3.50 2.00
353 A72 35t DC-3 4.00 4.00
354 A72 50t F27 Fokker Friendship 4.25 *7.00*
Nos. 349-354 (6) 17.50 14.75

Christmas A73

Butterflies.

1984, Nov. 5 Litho. *Perf. 14½x14*
355 A73 7t Papilio demodocus 4.00 .30
356 A73 25t Byblia acheloia 6.50 2.00
357 A73 35t Hypolimnas missipus 6.75 4.00
358 A73 50t Graphium taboranus 9.00 *12.00*
Nos. 355-358 (4) 26.25 18.30

Traditional & Exotic Foods — A74

Bechuanaland No. 4 — A75

1985, Mar. 18 Litho. *Perf. 14½*
359 A74 7t Man preparing seswaa .65 .30
360 A74 15t Woman preparing bogobe .90 .55
361 A74 25t Girl eating madilla 1.25 1.00
362 A74 50t Woman collecting caterpillars 2.10 2.10
a. Souvenir sheet of 4, #359-362 11.50 11.50
Nos. 359-362 (4) 4.90 3.95

Southern African Development Coordination Conference, 5th anniv.

1985, June 24

Postage stamp cent.: 15t, Bechuanaland Protectorate No. 72. 25t, Bechuanaland Protectorate No. 106. 35t, Bechuanaland No. 199, 50t, Botswana No. 1, horiz.

363 A75 7t multicolored 1.60 .30
364 A75 15t multicolored 1.60 .60
365 A75 25t multicolored 2.40 1.25
366 A75 35t multicolored 3.25 2.25
367 A75 50t multicolored 5.00 5.00
Nos. 363-367 (5) 13.85 9.40

Police Centenary A76

Designs: 7t, Bechuanaland Border Police, 1885-95. 10t, Bechuanaland Mounted Police, 1894-1902. 25t, Bechuanaland Protectorate Police, 1903-66. 50t, Botswana Motorcycle Police, 1966-85.

1985, Aug. 5 *Perf. 14½x14*
368 A76 7t multicolored 3.25 .60
369 A76 10t multicolored 3.25 .70
370 A76 25t multicolored 5.00 1.25
371 A76 50t multicolored 10.00 5.75
Nos. 368-371 (4) 21.50 8.30

Edible Wild Cucumbers A77

1985, Nov. 4
372 A77 7t Cucumis metuliferus 2.00 .65
373 A77 15t Acanthosicyos naudinianus 2.00 1.00
374 A77 25t Coccinia sessifolia 3.25 1.90
375 A77 50t Momordica balsamina 6.00 6.00
Nos. 372-375 (4) 13.25 9.55

Christmas.

Declaration of Protectorate, Cent. — A78

1985, Dec. 30 Litho. *Perf. 14x14½*
376 A78 7t Heads of state meet 1.40 .25
377 A78 15t Declaration reading, 1885 1.40 .60
378 A78 25t Mackenzie and Khama 1.75 1.25
379 A78 50t Map 3.75 3.75
a. Souvenir sheet of 4, #376-379 18.00 18.00
Nos. 376-379 (4) 8.30 5.85

Halley's Comet — A79

1986, Mar. 24 *Perf. 14½x14*
380 A79 7t Comet over Serowe 1.50 .25
381 A79 15t Over Bobonong 1.50 .90
382 A79 35t Over Gomare swamps 3.00 2.25
383 A79 50t Over Thamaga, Letlhakeng 4.50 4.50
Nos. 380-383 (4) 10.50 7.90

Milk Containers — A80

1986, June 23 *Perf. 14½*
384 A80 8t Leather bag .40 .25
385 A80 15t Ceramic pots .50 .40
386 A80 35t Wood pot 1.00 1.00
387 A80 50t Woman, pots 1.40 1.40
Nos. 384-387 (4) 3.30 3.05

Souvenir Sheet

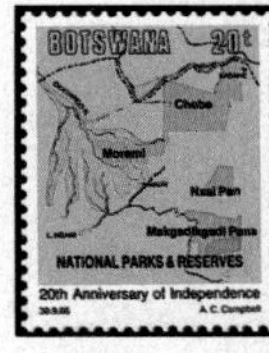

Natl. Independence, 20th Anniv. — A81

No. 388: a, Map of natl. parks and reserves. b, Morupule Power Station. c, Cattle, Kgalagadi. d, Natl. Assembly.

1986, Sept. 30 Litho. *Perf. 14½x14*
388 Sheet of 4 7.00 7.00
a.-d. A81 20t any single 1.75 1.75

Flowers of the Okavango Swamps — A82

1986, Nov. 3 Litho. *Perf. 14x14½*
389 A82 8t Ludwigia stogonifera 3.00 .25
390 A82 15t Sopubia mannii 3.00 1.60
391 A82 35t Commelina diffusa 5.75 4.00
392 A82 50t Hibiscus diversifolius 7.50 7.50
Nos. 389-392 (4) 19.25 13.35

Christmas.

Traditional Medicine A83

1987, Mar. 2 Litho. *Perf. 14½x14*
393 A83 8t Professional diviners 1.60 .25
394 A83 15t Lightning prevention 1.60 1.25
395 A83 35t Rainmaker 4.00 3.50
396 A83 50t Bloodletting 5.75 5.75
Nos. 393-396 (4) 12.95 10.75

UN Child Survival Campaign — A84

1987, June 1
397 A84 8t Oral rehydration therapy .85 .25
398 A84 15t Growth monitoring .85 .75
399 A84 35t Immunization 2.10 2.10
400 A84 50t Breast-feeding 2.75 2.75
Nos. 397-400 (4) 6.55 5.85

Nos. 308, 311 and 318 Surcharged

Perf. 14x14½, 14½x14
1987, Apr. 1 Photo.
401 A64 3t on 6t No. 308 4.00 1.25
402 A64 5t on 10t No. 311 4.00 1.25
403 A64 20t on 50t No. 318 5.50 2.75
Nos. 401-403 (3) 13.50 5.25

Wildlife Conservation — A85

1987, Aug. 3 ***Perf. 14***

404	A85	1t Cape fox	.40	*1.00*
405	A85	2t Lechwe	.75	*1.75*
406	A85	3t Zebra	.40	1.00
407	A85	4t Duiker	.40	*1.10*
408	A85	5t Banded mon-goose	.40	*1.10*
409	A85	6t Rusty-spotted ge-net	.40	*1.10*
410	A85	8t Hedgehog	.50	.25
411	A85	10t Scrub hare	.50	.25
412	A85	12t Hippopotamus	4.25	4.00
413	A85	15t Suricate	3.00	2.50
414	A85	20t Caracal	1.00	.55
415	A85	25t Steenbok	1.10	1.10
416	A85	30t Gemsbok	2.00	1.25
417	A85	35t Square-lipped rhi-no	2.75	2.50
418	A85	40t Mountain reed-buck	2.25	1.75
419	A85	50t Rock dassie	1.40	*1.75*
420	A85	1p Giraffe	2.75	*3.25*
421	A85	2p Tsessebe	5.50	*6.00*
422	A85	3p Side-striped jackal	9.00	*10.00*
423	A85	5p Hartebeest	14.50	*17.00*
		Nos. 404-423 (20)	53.25	59.20

For surcharges see Nos. 480-482, 506-509.

Wetland Grasses — A86

1987, Oct. 26 ***Perf. 14x14½***

424	A86	8t Cyperus articu-latus	.85	.25
425	A86	15t Miscanthus junceus	.85	.60
426	A86	30t Cyperus alopecuroides	1.60	1.10
427	A86	1p Typha latifolia	5.75	5.75
a.		Souvenir sheet of 4, #424-427	9.75	9.75
		Nos. 424-427 (4)	9.05	7.70

Christmas, preservation of the Okavango and Kuando-Chobe River wetlands.

Early Cultivation Techniques A87

1988, Mar. 14 Litho. ***Perf. 14½x14***

428	A87	8t Digging stick	1.00	.25
429	A87	15t Iron hoe	1.00	.55
430	A87	35t Wooden plow	1.75	1.40
431	A87	50t Communal plant-ing, Lesotla	2.50	2.25
		Nos. 428-431 (4)	6.25	4.45

World Wildlife Fund — A88

Designs: WWF emblem and various red lechwe, Kobus leche.

1988, June 6 Litho. ***Perf. 14½x14***

432	A88	10t Adult wading	1.75	.25
433	A88	15t Adult, sun	2.40	.90
434	A88	35t Cow, calf	5.25	2.40
435	A88	75t Herd	10.00	12.50
		Nos. 432-435 (4)	19.40	16.05

Runner Post, Cent. — A89

Routes and: 10t, Gubulawayo, Bechuanaland, cancellation dated Aug. 21 '88. 15t, Bechuanaland Protectorate No. 65. 30t, Pack traders. 60t, Mafeking killer cancel No. 638.

1988, Aug. 22 Litho. ***Perf. 14½***

436	A89	10t multicolored	.90	.25
437	A89	15t multicolored	.90	.50
438	A89	30t multicolored	1.75	1.25
439	A89	60t multicolored	3.00	3.00
a.		Souvenir sheet of 4, #436-439	15.00	15.00
		Nos. 436-439 (4)	6.55	5.00

Printed in a continuous design picturing the Mafeking-Gubulawayo route and part of the Shoshong runner post route.

State Visit of Pope John Paul II, Sept. 13 — A90

Natl. Museum and Art Gallery, Gaborone, 20th Anniv. — A91

1988, Sept. 13 Litho. ***Perf. 14x14½***

440	A90	10t Map, portrait	1.75	.25
441	A90	15t Portrait	1.75	.50
442	A90	30t Map, portrait, diff.	3.50	1.10
443	A90	80t Portrait, diff.	7.25	6.50
		Nos. 440-443 (4)	14.25	8.35

1988, Sept. 30 ***Perf. 14½***

444	A91	8t Museum	.45	.35
445	A91	15t Pottery, c. 400-1300	.55	.50
446	A91	30t Buffalo bellows	1.10	.90
447	A91	60t Children, mobile mu-seum	2.00	2.00
		Nos. 444-447 (4)	4.10	3.75

Flowering Plants of Southeastern Botswana — A92

1988, Oct. 31 Litho. ***Perf. 14x14½***

448	A92	8t Grewia flava	.45	.30
449	A92	15t Cienfuegosia digitata	.45	.40
450	A92	40t Solanum seaforthi-anum	1.25	1.00
451	A92	75t Carissa bispinosa	2.10	2.10
		Nos. 448-451 (4)	4.25	3.80

Christmas.

Traditional Grain Storage — A93

1989, Mar. 13 Litho. ***Perf. 14x14½***

452	A93	8t Sesigo basket granary	.95	.30
453	A93	15t Letlole daga grana-ry	1.50	.70
454	A93	30t Sefalana bisque granary	2.10	1.00
455	A93	60t Serala granaries	3.25	3.25
		Nos. 452-455 (4)	7.80	5.25

Slaty Egrets A94

1989, July 5 ***Perf. 15x14***

456	A94	8t Nesting	.60	.25
457	A94	15t Young	1.25	.35
458	A94	30t Adult in flight	1.75	1.10
459	A94	60t Two adults	3.50	3.25
a.		Souvenir sheet of 4, #456-459	8.25	8.25
		Nos. 456-459 (4)	7.10	4.95

Children's Drawings A95

1989, Sept. 4 ***Perf. 14½x14, 14x14½***

460	A95	10t Ephraim Seeletso	.85	.30
461	A95	15t Neelma Bhatia, vert.	.85	.65
462	A95	30t Thabo Habana	1.25	1.25
463	A95	1p Thabo Olesitse	4.00	4.00
		Nos. 460-463 (4)	6.95	6.20

Star and Orchids — A96

1989, Oct. 30 Litho. ***Perf. 14x14½***

464	A96	8t Eulophia angolen-sis	1.10	.25
465	A96	15t Eulophia herer-oensis	1.40	1.00
466	A96	30t Eulophia speciosa	2.75	2.00
467	A96	60t Eulophia petersii	6.25	*8.50*
		Nos. 464-467 (4)	11.50	11.75

Christmas.

Anniversaries — A97

Designs: 8t, Bechuanaland Protectorate #201. 15t, Voter at ballot box. 30t, Map & flags of nations at SADCC conference. 60t, Great Britain #1.

1990, Mar. 5 Litho. ***Perf. 14½***

468	A97	8t multicolored	1.75	.25
469	A97	15t multicolored	1.75	.85
470	A97	30t multicolored	3.50	2.40
471	A97	60t multicolored	4.50	*8.00*
		Nos. 468-471 (4)	11.50	11.50

25th anniv. of self government (8t); 1st elections, 25th anniv. (15t); Southern African Development Coordination Conference (SADCC), 10th anniv. (30t); and Penny Black, 150th anniv. (60t).

Stamp World London '90 — A98

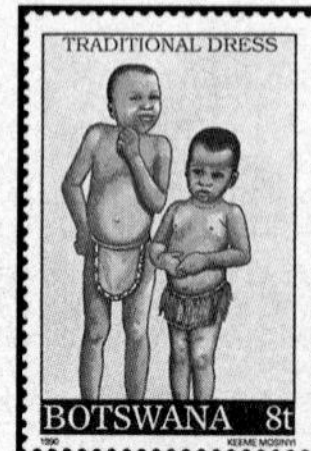

Traditional Dress — A99

Aspects of the telecommunications industry.

1990, May 3

472	A98	8t Training	.75	.30
473	A98	15t Transmission	.75	.70
474	A98	30t Public telephone	1.25	1.25
475	A98	2p Testing circuitry	6.50	6.50
		Nos. 472-475 (4)	9.25	8.75

1990, Aug. 1 Litho. ***Perf. 14***

476	A99	8t Children	.55	.25
477	A99	15t Young woman	.85	.50
478	A99	30t Man	1.50	.75
479	A99	2p Adult woman	5.75	*7.25*
a.		Souvenir sheet of 4, #476-479	11.50	11.50
		Nos. 476-479 (4)	8.65	8.75

Nos. 404 & 412 Surcharged

No. 409 Surcharged

1990, Apr. 27

480	A85	10t on 1t No. 404	1.50	.40
481	A85	20t on 6t No. 409	2.25	1.40
482	A85	50t on 12t No. 412	5.25	*6.75*
		Nos. 480-482 (3)	9.00	8.55

Flowering Trees — A100

1990, Oct. 30 Litho. ***Perf. 14***

483	A100	8t Acacia nigrescens	1.20	.30
484	A100	15t Peltophorum afri-canum	1.20	.60
485	A100	30t Burkea africana	1.50	1.25
486	A100	2p Pterocarpus angolensis	7.75	*9.00*
		Nos. 483-486 (4)	11.65	11.15

Christmas.

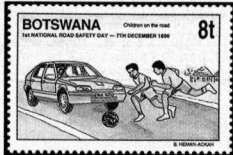

Natl. Road Safety Day A101

1990, Dec. 7 Litho. ***Perf. 14½***

487	A101	8t Children playing on road	3.25	.60
488	A101	15t Accident	3.25	1.90
489	A101	30t Livestock on road	5.25	5.25
		Nos. 487-489 (3)	11.75	7.75

Petroglyphs A102

Various petroglyphs.

1991, Mar. 4 Litho. ***Perf. 14x14½***

Textured Paper

490	A102	8t multicolored	2.50	.60
491	A102	15t multicolored	3.00	1.25
492	A102	30t multicolored	3.75	2.40
493	A102	2p multicolored	9.00	9.00
		Nos. 490-493 (4)	18.25	13.25

Natl. Census — A103

1991, June 3 Litho. *Perf. 14*

494 A103 8t Children playing 1.40 .25

Perf. 14½

495 A103 15t Houses 1.60 .80

Perf. 14x14½

496 A103 30t Children in schoolyard 2.00 1.40
497 A103 2p Children, hospital 9.00 *11.00*
Nos. 494-497 (4) 14.00 13.45

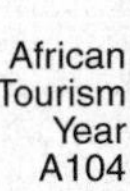

African Tourism Year A104

1991, Sept. 30 Litho. *Perf. 14*

498 A104 8t Tourists, elephants 4.00 1.40
499 A104 15t Birds, crocodiles 4.75 1.25
500 A104 35t Airplane, fish eagles 8.00 5.25

Size 26x43mm

501 A104 2p Okavango Delta 10.00 *11.00*
Nos. 498-501 (4) 26.75 18.90

No. 501 incorporates designs of Nos. 498-500.

Christmas — A105

Seed pods: 8t, Harpagophytum procumbens. 15t, Tylosema esculentum. 30t, Abrus precatorius. 2p, Kigelia africana.

1991, Nov. 4 Litho. *Perf. 14*

502 A105 8t multicolored 1.25 .25
503 A105 15t multicolored 1.75 .70
504 A105 30t multicolored 2.75 1.25
505 A105 2p multicolored 5.25 *8.50*
Nos. 502-505 (4) 11.00 10.70

Nos. 406, 409 & 412 Surcharged

1992, Mar. 9 Litho. *Perf. 14*

506 A85 8t on 12t No. 412 3.00 1.40
507 A85 10t on 12t No. 412 3.00 1.40
508 A85 25t on 6t No. 409 3.50 2.75
509 A85 40t on 3t No. 406 4.00 *5.50*
Nos. 506-509 (4) 13.50 11.05

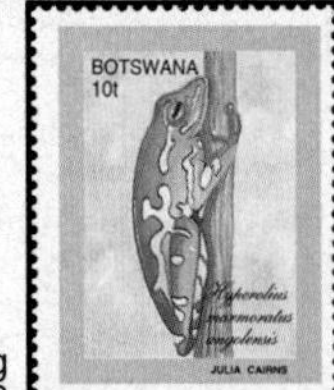

Climbing Frogs — A106

Designs: 8t, Cacosternum boettgeri, horiz. 10t, Hyperolius marmoratus angolensis. 40t, Bufo fenoulheti, horiz. 1p, Hyperolius.

1992, Mar. 23 *Perf. 14½x14, 14x14½*

510 A106 8t multicolored 1.20 .60
511 A106 10t multicolored 1.20 .60
512 A106 40t multicolored 2.25 2.75
513 A106 1p multicolored 5.00 *8.00*
Nos. 510-513 (4) 9.65 11.95

Botswana Railways A107

Designs: 10t, Deluxe air-conditioned coaches. 25t, BD1 locomotive. 40t, Deluxe coach interio. 2p, Locomotive pulling air-conditioned coaches.

1992, June 29 Litho. *Perf. 14*

514 A107 10t multi 1.75 .70
515 A107 25t multi, vert. 2.75 1.40
516 A107 40t multi, vert. 3.25 1.90
517 A107 2p multi 4.25 *8.50*
a. Souv. sheet of 4, #514-517 + label 15.00 15.00
Nos. 514-517 (4) 12.00 12.50

Wild Animals A108

1992, Aug. 3 Litho. *Perf. 14½*

518 A108 1t Cheetah .45 *2.00*
519 A108 2t Spring hares .45 *2.00*
520 A108 4t Blackfooted cat .80 *2.00*
521 A108 5t Striped mouse .80 *1.75*
522 A108 10t Oribi 1.10 .30
523 A108 12t Pangolin 1.75 *3.00*
524 A108 15t Aardwolf 1.75 .60
525 A108 20t Warthog 1.75 .50
526 A108 25t Ground squirrels 1.75 .30
527 A108 35t Honey badger 2.00 .45
528 A108 40t Common mole rat 2.00 .45
529 A108 45t Wild dogs 2.00 .45
530 A108 50t Water mongoose 2.00 .55
531 A108 80t Klipspringer 3.00 2.75
532 A108 1p Lesser bushbaby 3.00 2.75
533 A108 2p Bushveld elephant shrew 4.50 4.00
534 A108 5p Zorilla 6.50 *7.50*
535 A108 10p Vervet monkey 9.50 *12.00*
Nos. 518-535 (18) 45.10 43.35

For surcharges see Nos. 594A-597.

A109

Ferns — A110

1992, Aug. 7 *Perf. 14x15*

536 A109 10t Boxer .65 .25
537 A109 50t Four sprinters 1.30 .85
538 A109 1p Two boxers 3.00 *3.50*
539 A109 2p Three runners 5.00 *6.50*
a. Souvenir sheet of 4, #536-539 11.00 11.00
Nos. 536-539 (4) 9.95 11.10

1992 Summer Olympics, Barcelona.

1992, Nov. 23 Litho. *Perf. 14½*

540 A110 10t Adiantum incisum .80 .25
541 A110 25t Actiniopteris radiata 1.00 .60
542 A110 40t Ceratopteris cornuta 1.40 1.50
543 A110 1.50p Pellaea calomelanos 5.25 *7.50*
Nos. 540-543 (4) 8.45 9.85

Christmas.

Organizations A111

10t, Lions Intl., conquering blindness. 15t, Red Cross Society. 25t, Ecumenical Decade, churches in solidarity with women. 35t, Round Table supporting the deaf. 40t, Rotary Intl. 50t, Botswana Christian Council.

1993, Mar. 29 Litho. *Perf. 14*

544 A111 10t multi, vert. 1.10 .25
545 A111 15t multi 1.10 .70
546 A111 25t multi, vert. 1.25 .80
547 A111 35t multi 1.75 1.60
548 A111 40t multi, vert. 1.75 1.90
549 A111 50t multi 2.00 *3.00*
Nos. 544-549 (6) 8.95 8.25

Botswana Railway, Cent. A112

Designs: 10t, Engine No. 1, 6th class 4-6-0, Bechuanaland Railways. 40t, Engine No. 317, 19th class 4-8-2. 50t, Engine No. 256, 12th class 4-8-2. 1.50p, Engine No. 71, 7th class 4-8-0, Rhodesia Railways.

1993, May 24 Litho. *Perf. 15x14*

550 A112 10t multicolored .85 .50
551 A112 40t multicolored 2.10 .85
552 A112 50t multicolored 2.10 1.10
553 A112 1.50p multicolored 4.00 *5.00*
a. Souvenir sheet of 4, #550-553 9.25 9.25
Nos. 550-553 (4) 9.05 7.45

Eagles — A113

1993, Aug. 30 Litho. *Perf. 14½*

554 A113 10t Long crested eagle 1.50 .45
555 A113 25t Snake eagle 2.75 .80
556 A113 50t Bateleur eagle 3.25 2.25
557 A113 1.50p Secretary bird 5.00 *6.50*
Nos. 554-557 (4) 12.50 10.00

Christmas A114

1993, Oct. 25 Litho. *Perf. 14x14½*

558 A114 12t Aloe zebrina .55 .25
559 A114 25t Croton megalobotrys .80 .40
560 A114 50t Boophane disticha 1.25 1.00
561 A114 1p Euphorbia davyi 3.00 *3.75*
Nos. 558-561 (4) 5.60 5.40

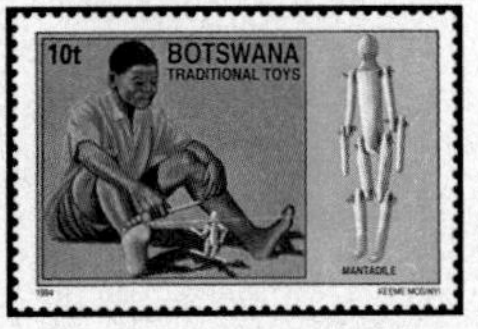

Traditional Children's Toys A115

1994, Mar. 28 Litho. *Perf. 14½*

562 A115 10t Mantadile .65 .25
563 A115 40t Dikgomo tsa mimopa 1.00 .50
564 A115 50t Sefuu-fuu 1.35 .75
565 A115 1p Mantlwane 1.90 *3.25*
Nos. 562-565 (4) 4.90 4.75

ICAO, 50th Anniv. A116

Perf. 14½x14, 14x14½

1994, June 30 Litho.

566 A116 10t Inside control tower .65 .25
567 A116 25t Fire engine 1.00 .50
568 A116 40t Baggage carts, vert. 1.35 .75
569 A116 50t Control tower, vert. 1.90 *3.25*
Nos. 566-569 (4) 4.90 4.75

A117

Environmental Protection: 10t, Flamingos, Sua Pan, vert. 35t, Makgadikgadi Pan trees. 50t, Zebra, Makgadikgadi Palm trees, vert. 2p, Map of Makgadikgadi Pans.

1994, Sept. 26 Litho. *Perf. 14*

570 A117 10t multicolored 1.40 .50
571 A117 35t multicolored 1.40 .50
572 A117 50t multicolored 1.75 1.10
573 A117 2p multicolored 6.00 *6.75*
Nos. 570-573 (4) 10.55 8.85

Christmas A118

Edible fruits: 10t, Ziziphus mucronata. 25t, Strychnos cocculoides. 40t, Bauhinia petersiana. 50t, Schinziphyton rautaneii.

1994, Oct. 24

574 A118 10t multicolored .85 .25
575 A118 25t multicolored .85 .50
576 A118 40t multicolored 1.00 1.10
577 A118 50t multicolored 1.25 1.40
Nos. 574-577 (4) 3.95 3.25

See Nos. 587-590.

Traditional Fishing A119

1995, Apr. 3 Litho. *Perf. 14*

578 A119 15t Spear .90 .30
579 A119 40t Hook 1.25 .75
580 A119 65t Net 2.00 1.60
581 A119 80t Basket 2.25 *2.50*
Nos. 578-581 (4) 6.40 5.15

UN, 50th Anniv. — A120

1995, Oct. 16 Litho. *Perf. 14*

582 A120 20t FAO .65 .25
583 A120 50t World Food Program .90 .45
584 A120 80t Development Plan 1.25 1.00
585 A120 1p UNICEF 1.50 *2.00*
Nos. 582-585 (4) 4.30 3.70

World Wildlife Fund A121

No. 586 — Hyaena brunnea: a, 20t, Adult walking right. b, 50t, Two young. c, 80t, Adult finding eggs. d, 1p, Two young, adult resting.

1995, Nov. 6

586 A121 Strip of 4, #a.-d. 6.75 6.75

No. 586 was issued in miniature sheets of 4 each.

Christmas Type of 1994

1995, Nov. 27 Litho. *Perf. 14*

587 A118 20t Adenia glauca .65 .30
588 A118 50t Pterodiscus ngamicus .95 .60
589 A118 80t Sesamothamnus lugardii 1.60 1.75
590 A118 1p Fockea multiflora 1.75 *2.50*
Nos. 587-590 (4) 4.95 5.15

Traditional Weapons A122

1996, Mar. 25 Litho. *Perf. 14*

591 A122 20t Spears .50 .25
592 A122 50t Axes .70 .50
593 A122 80t Shield, knob-kerries 1.10 1.10
594 A122 1p Knives, cases 1.40 *2.00*
Nos. 591-594 (4) 3.70 3.85

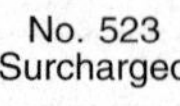

No. 523 Surcharged

Nos. 518-520 Surcharged

1994-96 Litho. *Perf. 14½*

594A A108 10t on 12t No. 523 18.00 3.00
595 A108 20t on 2t No. 519 1.90 .80
596 A108 30t on 1t No. 518 2.10 1.40
597 A108 70t on 4t No. 520 3.25 *7.00*
Nos. 594A-597 (4) 25.25 12.20

Issued: No. 594A, 8/1/94; others, 2/12/96.

Radio, Cent. — A123

Designs: 20t, Child listening to early radio. 50t, Mobile unit, transmitter. 80t, Local police. 1p, Radio Botswana at the Kgotila.

1996, June 3 Litho. *Perf. 14*

598 A123 20t multicolored .50 .25
599 A123 50t multicolored .75 .45
600 A123 80t multicolored 1.40 1.10
601 A123 1p multicolored 1.00 *1.75*
Nos. 598-601 (4) 3.65 3.55

Modern Olympic Games, Cent. — A124

Designs: 20t, Hand holding torch, laurel wreath, Olympic rings. 50t, Pierre de Coubertin. 80t, Map, flag of Botswana, athletes. 1p, Ruins of original Olympic Stadium, Olympia.

1996, July 19 Litho. *Perf. 14*

602 A124 20t multicolored .70 .40
603 A124 50t multicolored .95 .60
604 A124 80t multicolored 1.40 1.40
605 A124 1p multicolored 1.60 *2.10*
Nos. 602-605 (4) 4.65 4.50

Worthy Causes — A125

Adansonia Digitata — A126

Designs: 20t, Family planning education, Welfare Association. 30t, Skills for the blind, Pudulogong Rehabilitation Center. 50t, Collection of seeds, Forestry Association. 70t, Secretarial class, YWCA. 80t, Day care center, Council of Women. 1p, SOS Children's Village, Tlokweng.

1996, Sept. 23 Litho. *Perf. 14*

606 A125 20t multicolored .30 .25
607 A125 30t multicolored .40 .25
608 A125 50t multicolored .70 .70
609 A125 70t multicolored .90 .90
610 A125 80t multicolored 1.00 1.10
611 A125 1p multicolored 1.10 *1.90*
Nos. 606-611 (6) 4.40 5.10

1996, Nov. 4 Litho. *Perf. 14*

612 A126 20t Leaf, flower .45 .25
613 A126 50t Fruit .70 .40
614 A126 80t Tree in leaf 1.10 1.10
615 A126 1p Tree without leaves 1.25 *1.75*
Nos. 612-615 (4) 3.50 3.50

Christmas.

Francistown, Cent. — A127

Designs: 20t, Tati Hotel. 50t, Railway station. 80t, Company manager's house. 1p, Monarch Mine.

1997, Apr. 21 Litho. *Perf. 14*

616 A127 20t multicolored .70 .30
617 A127 50t multicolored .75 .65
618 A127 80t multicolored 1.25 1.25
619 A127 1p multicolored 1.40 *2.00*
Nos. 616-619 (4) 4.10 4.20

Birds — A128

Designs: 5t, Pel's fishing owl. 10t, Gymnogene. 15t, Meyers parrot. 20t, Harlequin quail. 25t, Marico sunbird. 30t, Kurrichane thrush. 40t, Redheaded finch. 50t, Buffalo weaver. 60t, Sacred ibis. 70t, Cape shoveller. 80t, Greater honeyguide. 1p, Woodland kingfisher. 1.25p, Purple heron. 1.50p, Yellowbilled oxpecker. 2p, Shafttailed whydah. 2.50p, White stork. 5p, Ovambo sparrowhawk. 10p, Spotted crake.

1997, Aug. 4 Litho. *Perf. 13½*

620 A128 5t multi, vert. .25 *1.00*
621 A128 10t multi .25 *1.00*
622 A128 15t multi, vert. .25 *1.00*
623 A128 20t multi .25 *1.00*
624 A128 25t multi .25 1.00
625 A128 30t multi .25 *1.00*
626 A128 40t multi, vert. .30 *.70*
627 A128 50t multi, vert. .35 *.45*
628 A128 60t multi .40 *.90*
629 A128 70t multi .60 *.90*
630 A128 80t multi .90 *.90*
631 A128 1p multi 1.25 *.90*
632 A128 1.25p multi, vert. 1.50 1.50
633 A128 1.50p multi 1.75 *2.00*
634 A128 2p multi, vert. 2.75 2.25
635 A128 2.50p multi, vert. 3.25 2.75
636 A128 5p multi, vert. 5.50 4.00
637 A128 10p multi, vert. 10.00 7.50
Nos. 620-637 (18) 30.05 30.75

Botswana Railway, Cent. — A129

Designs: 35t, Bechuanaland Rail, 1897. 50t, Elephants on the tracks. 80t, First locomotives in Bechuanaland, Cape of Good Hope 4-6-0. 1p, 4-6-4+4-6-4 Beyer Garratt. 2p, New BD3 locomotive. 2.50p, Fantuzzi Container Stacker.

1997, July 12 Litho. *Perf. 14x14½*

638 A129 35t multicolored .60 .35
639 A129 50t multicolored .70 .50
640 A129 80t multicolored 1.00 .70
641 A129 1p multicolored 1.10 1.10
642 A129 2p multicolored 1.40 *1.60*
643 A129 2.50p multicolored 1.90 *2.10*
Nos. 638-643 (6) 6.70 6.35

A130

Queen Elizabeth II and Prince Philip, 50th wedding anniv.: No. 644, Prince in casual attire. No. 645, Queen wearing white & blue hat. No. 646, Queen with horse. No. 647, Prince with horse. No. 648, Prince, Queen. No. 649, Princess Ann in riding attire.

10p, Queen, Prince riding in open carriage.

Wmk. 373

1997, Sept. 22 Litho. *Perf. 13*

644 A130 35t multicolored .30 .30
645 A130 35t multicolored .30 .30
a. Pair, #644-645 .60 .60
646 A130 2p multicolored 1.75 1.75
647 A130 2p multicolored 1.75 1.75
a. Pair, #646-647 3.50 3.50
648 A130 2.50p multicolored 2.10 2.10
649 A130 2.50p multicolored 2.10 2.10
a. Pair, #648-649 4.25 4.25
Nos. 644-649 (6) 8.30 8.30

Souvenir Sheet

650 A130 10p multicolored 7.50 7.50

A131

Christmas (Combretum):, 35t, Zeyheri. 1p, Apiculatum. 2p, Molle. 2.50p, Imberbe.

1997, Nov. 10 Unwmk. *Perf. 14*

651 A131 35t multicolored .40 .25
652 A131 1p multicolored 1.10 .50
653 A131 2p multicolored 2.25 2.25
654 A131 2.50p multicolored 2.75 2.75
Nos. 651-654 (4) 6.50 5.75

Tourism A132

1998, Mar. 23

655 A132 35t Baobab trees .30 .30
656 A132 1p Crocodile .85 .65
657 A132 2p Stalactites, vert. 1.75 1.75
658 A132 2.50p Tourists, vert. 2.10 2.10
Nos. 655-658 (4) 5.00 4.80

Diana, Princess of Wales (1961-97)
Common Design Type

Portraits: 35t, No. 663a, Wearing red (without hat). 1p, No. 663b, Wearing red with hat. 2p, No. 663c, Wearing white (hand on face). No. 662, Greeting people.

1998, June 1 Wmk. 373 *Perf. 13*

659 CD355 35t multicolored .25 .25
660 CD355 1p multicolored .65 .50
661 CD355 2p multicolored 1.25 1.25
662 CD355 2.50p multicolored 1.60 1.60
Nos. 659-662 (4) 3.75 3.60

Souvenir Sheet

663 CD355 2.50p Sheet of 4, #662, 663a-663c 6.50 6.50

Textiles A133

Christmas A134

Designs: 35t, Tapestry of a village. 55t, Woman arranging materials on ground. 1p, Tapestry of African map, animals, huts, people. 2p, Woman seated at loom.

2.50p, Tapestry of elephants and trees, horiz.

Perf. 14x13½

1998, Sept. 28 Litho. Unwmk.

664 A133 35t multicolored .55 .30
665 A133 55t multicolored .75 .40
666 A133 1p multicolored 1.40 1.40
667 A133 2p multicolored 1.75 *2.50*
Nos. 664-667 (4) 4.45 4.60

Souvenir Sheet

Perf. 13½

668 A133 2.50p multicolored 4.00 4.00

1998, Nov. 30 Litho. *Perf. 13x13½*

Berries: 35t, Ficus ingens. 55t, Ficus pygmaea. 1p, Ficus abutilifolia. 2.50p, Ficus sycomorus.

669 A134 35t multicolored .65 .30
670 A134 55t multicolored .90 .45
671 A134 1p multicolored 1.30 .50
672 A134 2.50p multicolored 1.90 *3.50*
Nos. 669-672 (4) 4.75 4.75

Tourism A135

Designs: 35t, Rock paintings. 55t, Salt pan. 1p, Rock paintings, diff. 2p, Baobab tree.

1999, May 24 Litho. *Perf. 13½x14*

673 A135 35t multi .60 .40
674 A135 55t multi .90 .45

Perf. 14x13½

675 A135 1p multi, vert. 1.15 1.40
676 A135 2p multi, vert. 1.30 *2.50*
Nos. 673-676 (4) 3.95 4.75

Souvenir Sheet

Southern African Development Community Day — A136

1999, Aug. 17 **Litho.** ***Perf. 14¼***
677 A136 5p multi 5.75 5.75

UPU, 125th Anniv. A137

1999, Oct. 9 **Litho.** ***Perf. 14¼***
678 A137 2p multicolored 2.50 2.50

Mpule Kwelagobe, Miss Universe 1999 — A138

1999, Dec. 1 ***Perf. 14½***

679	A138	35t	With crown, vert.	.50	.25
680	A138	1p	With head-dress	.80	.50
681	A138	2p	In swimsuit, vert.	1.75	1.00
682	A138	2.50p	With Botswana sash	2.10	1.25
683	A138	15p	With leopard	9.00	*13.00*
a.			Souvenir sheet of 5, #679-683	15.00	15.00
			Nos. 679-683 (5)	14.15	16.00

River Scenes A139

Designs: 35t, Bird over river. 1p, Hippopotami in river, vert. 2p, Bird, man in canoe. 2.50p, Elephant on shore, vert.

2000, Apr. 5 **Litho.** ***Perf. 14***

684	A139	35t	multi	.50	.25
685	A139	1p	multi	.75	.75
686	A139	2p	multi	1.25	1.25
687	A139	2.50p	multi	1.60	*2.25*
			Nos. 684-687 (4)	4.10	4.50

Moths A140

Designs: 35t, Mopane. 70t, Wild silk. 1p, Crimson-speckled footman. 2p, African lunar. 15p, Speckled emperor.

2000, July 19 **Litho.** ***Perf. 12½***
688-692 A140 Set of 5 11.00 *13.00*
692a Souvenir sheet, #688-692 17.00 *19.00*

Literacy Decade A141

Designs: 35t, Mother and child. 70t, Old men learning to read. 2p, Man unaware of fire danger. 2.50p, Man at ATM machine.

2000, Aug. 23 ***Perf. 12***
693-696 A141 Set of 4 + labels 4.00 4.00

Kings and Presidents A142

Designs: 35t, Sebele I of Bakwena, Bathoen I of Bangwaketse, Khama III of Bangwato (60x40mm). 1p, Sir Seretse Khama. 2p, Sir Ketumile J. Masire. 2.50p, Festus G. Mogae.

Litho. & Embossed

2000, Sept. 29 ***Perf. 14***
697-700 A142 Set of 4 4.00 4.00

Botswana Flying Mission — A143

Designs: 35t, Two men, plane with yellow stripes. 1.75p, Plane, nurses, people. 2p, Plane in air, natives in boats. 2.50p, Plane, donkey cart.

2000, Nov. 3 **Litho.** ***Perf. 13½***
701-704 A143 Set of 4 5.00 5.00
704a Horiz. strip of 4, #701-704, + central label 5.75 5.75

Wetlands Fauna A144

Designs: 35t, Hippopotamus. 1p, Tiger fish, tilapia. 1.75p, Wattled crane, painted reed frog, vert. 2p, Vervet monkey, Pels fishing owl, vert. 2.50p, Sitatunga, Nile crocodile, red lechwe.

2000, Dec. 6 **Litho.** ***Perf. 13¾***
705-709 A144 Set of 5 6.00 *6.50*
709a Souvenir sheet, #705-709, perf. 13½ 6.25 *6.75*
709b As "a," with emblem of Hong Kong 2001 Stamp Exhibition in margin 6.75 *7.25*

Issued: No. 709b, 1/2/01.

See Nos. 726-730, 761-765, 775-779.

Diamonds — A145

Cut diamond and: 35t, Uncut diamonds. 1.75p, Mine. 2p, Diamond grader. 2.50p, Pendant and ring.

Serpentine Die Cut 10

2001, Feb. 1 **Litho.**

Self-Adhesive

710-713 A145 Set of 4 7.00 *8.00*

Unused value is for stamps with surrounding selvage.

Kgalagadi Transfrontier Park A146

Designs: 35t, Pygmy falcons. 1p, Leopard. 2p, Gemsboks, flags of Botswana and South Africa. 2.50p, Bat-eared fox.

2001, May 12 **Litho.** ***Perf. 13x13¼***
714-717 A146 Set of 4 5.50 5.50
717a Souvenir sheet #715, 717 4.00 4.00

See South Africa Nos. 1252-1255.

Basketry A147

Designs: 35t, Shown. 1p, Tall basket with triangles and chevrons. 2p, Basket weaver. 2.50p, Spherical basket.

2001, July 30 ***Perf. 13¼***
718-721 A147 Set of 4 4.00 4.00
721a Souvenir sheet, #718-721 4.00 4.00

Sky Views A148

Natives and pictures of sun on horizon: 50t, 1p, 2p, 10p.

2001, Sept. 28 ***Perf. 13½***
722-725 A148 Set of 4 6.75 6.75

Wetlands Fauna Type of 2000

Designs: 50t, Water monitor, carmine bee-eaters. 1.75p, Buffalos. 2p, Savanna baboons, vert. 2.50p, Lion, vert. 3p, African elephants.

2001, Dec. 12 **Litho.** ***Perf. 13¾***
726-730 A144 Set of 5 6.50 6.50
730a Souvenir sheet, #726-730, perf. 13½ 6.50 6.50

Snakes A149

Designs: 50t, Black mamba. 1.75p, Spitting cobra, vert. 2.50p, Puff adder. 3p, Boomslang, vert.

2002, Mar. 22 ***Perf. 14x13¼, 13¼x14***
731-734 A149 Set of 4 5.25 *5.50*

Pottery A150

Pots: 50t, Mbukushu. 2p, Sekgatla. 2.50p, Setswana. 3p, Kalanga.

2002, May 31 **Litho.** ***Perf. 13¾***
735-738 A150 Set of 4 4.75 4.75

Reign of Queen Elizabeth II, 50th Anniv. A151

Mammals A152

Queen Elizabeth II: 55t, Wearing crown, horiz. 2.75p, Holding flowers.

2002, July 25 ***Perf. 13x13¼, 13¼x13***
739-740 A151 Set of 2 3.75 *4.00*

Perf. 13½x13¼, 13¼x13½

2002, Aug. 5 **Photo.**

Designs: 5t, Tree squirrel. 10t, Black-backed jackal. 20t, African wild cat. 30t, Slender mongoose, horiz. 40t, African civet, horiz. 55t, Elephant. 90t, Reedbuck. 1p, Kudu. 1.45p, Waterbuck. 1.95p, Sable, horiz. 2.20p, Sitatunga, horiz. 2.75p, Porcupine, horiz. 3.30p, Serval, horiz. 4p, Antbear, horiz. 5p, Bush pig, horiz. 15p, Chakma baboon.

741	A152	5t	multi	.25	.25
742	A152	10t	multi	.25	.25
743	A152	20t	multi	.25	.25
744	A152	30t	multi	.25	.30
745	A152	40t	multi	.25	.30
746	A152	55t	multi	.25	.30
747	A152	90t	multi	.40	.40
748	A152	1p	multi	.45	.40
749	A152	1.45p	multi	.65	.75
750	A152	1.95p	multi	.90	1.00
751	A152	2.20p	multi	1.00	1.00
752	A152	2.75p	multi	1.25	1.00
753	A152	3.30p	multi	1.50	1.25
754	A152	4p	multi	1.90	2.25
755	A152	5p	multi	2.75	2.50
756	A152	15p	multi	8.00	6.00
			Nos. 741-756 (16)	20.30	18.20

For surcharges see Nos. 813A-813B.

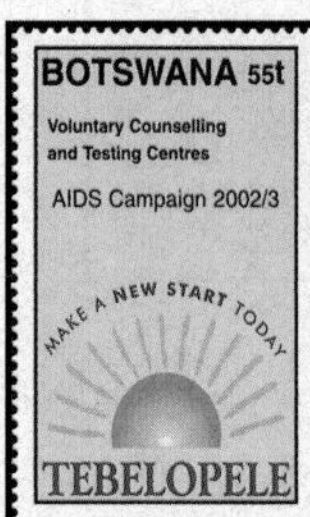

2002-03 AIDS Campaign — A153

Designs: 55t, Voluntary counseling and testing centers. 1.10p, Prevention of mother to child transmission. 2.75p, Stigma and discrimination. 3.30p, Orphan care.

2002, Dec. 1 **Litho.** ***Perf. 14x14¼***
757-760 A153 Set of 4 6.25 6.25

Wetlands Fauna Type of 2000

Wildlife in the Makgadikgadi Pans: 55t, Aardwolf. 1.10p, Blue wildebeest. 2.50p, Zebras, vert. 2.75p, Flamingos, vert. 3.30p, Pelican.

2002, Dec. 18 ***Perf. 13¾***
761-765 A144 Set of 5 8.00 8.00
765a Souvenir sheet, #761-765, perf. 13½ 8.50 *8.75*

Tourist Attractions A154

Designs: 55t, Hill of Lovers. 2.20p, Sand dunes, Bokspits. 2.75p, Moremi Waterfalls, vert. 3.30p, Entrance of Gcwihaba Cave.

2003, Mar. 27 Litho. *Perf. 13¾*
766-769 A154 Set of 4 5.00 5.00

Beetles — A155

Designs: 55t, Ngwale. 2.20p, Kgomo-ya-buru. 2.75p, Kgomo-ya-pula. 3.30p, Lebitse. 5.50p, Kgaladuwa.

2003, Nov. 12 Litho. *Perf. 13*
770-773 A155 Set of 4 6.00 6.00

Souvenir Sheet

774 A155 5.50p multi 6.00 *6.25*

Wetlands Fauna Type of 2000

Fauna of the Limpopo River Valley: 55t, Giraffe. 1.45p, Black eagle, Nile crocodile, vert. 2.50p, Ostrich, vert. 2.75p, Klipspringer. 3.30p, Serval cat.

2003, Dec. 23 Litho. *Perf. 13¾*
775-779 A144 Set of 5 8.50 8.50
779a Souvenir sheet, #775-779, perf. 13½ 8.50 8.50

Contemporary Art — A156

Designs: 55t, People and Birds. 1.45p, Stylized trees. 2.75p, Stylized tree. 3.30p, Snake.

2004, Apr. 29 *Perf. 13¾*
780-783 A156 Set of 4 6.00 6.00

Traditional Lifestyles — A157

Designs: 80t, Masimo. 2.10p, Kgotla. 3.90p, Moraka. 4.70p, Legae.

2004, June 30 Litho. *Perf. 14*
784-787 A157 Set of 4 7.75 7.75

World Post Day — A158

Designs: 80t, Child placing letter in mail box. 2.10p, Children reading letter. 3.90p, Mailman and car. 4.70p, Woman reading letter.

2004, Oct. 9 Litho. *Perf. 14x14¾*
788-791 A158 Set of 4 7.75 7.75

Birds A159

Designs: 5p, Cattle egrets, national bird of Botswana.

No. 793: a, 40t, Peregrine falcons, national bird of Angola. b, 50t, African fish eagles, national bird of Zambia. c, 60t, African fish eagles, national bird of Zimbabwe. d, 70t, Bar-tailed trogons. e, 80t, Purple-crested louries, national bird of Swaziland. f, 1p, African fish eagles, national bird of Namibia. g, 2p, Blue cranes, national bird of South Africa.

2004, Oct. 9 Litho. *Perf. 14*
792 A159 5p multi 2.75 2.75

Miniature Sheet

793 A159 Sheet of 8, #a-g, #792 7.00 7.00

See Namibia No. 1052, South Africa No. 1342, Swaziland Nos. 727-735, Zambia No. 1033, and Zimbabwe No. 975.

Christmas A160

Flowers: 80t, Pterodiscus speciosus. 2.10p, Bulbine narcissifolia. 3.90p, Babiana hypogea. 4.70p, Hibiscus micranthus.

2004, Dec. 8 *Perf. 13*
794-797 A160 Set of 4 7.00 7.00

Historic Buildings A161

Designs: 80t, Blackbeard's Store, Phalatswe, 1899. 2.10p, Primary School, 1899. 3.90p, Telegraph Office, Phalatswe, 1899. 4.70p, Magistrate's Court, Phalatswe, 1899.

2005, Mar. 21 Litho. *Perf. 14¾x14*
798-801 A161 Set of 4 6.75 6.75

Food Crops — A162

Designs: 80t, Beans. 2.10p, Millet. 3.90p, Sorghum. 4.70p, Watermelon.

2005, June 15 Litho. *Perf. 13¾*
802-805 A162 Set of 4 5.00 5.00

Worldwide Fund for Nature (WWF) — A163

Black-footed cat: 80t, With dead bird. 2.10p, Looking left. 3.90p, Adult and kitten. 4.70p, Close-up of head.

2005, Oct. 25 Litho. *Perf. 13¼x13½*
806-809 A163 Set of 4 5.00 5.00
809a Sheet, 2 each #806-809 10.00 10.00

Christmas A164

Doves and pigeons: 80t, Namaqua dove. 2.10p, Red-eyed dove. 3.90p, Laughing doves. 4.70p, Green pigeons

2005, Dec. 20 *Perf. 14x14¾*
810-813 A164 Set of 4 5.00 5.00

No. 747 Surcharged

No. 750 Surcharged

Methods and Perfs As Before

2006, Apr. 26
813A A152 80t on 90t #747 — —
813B A152 2.10p on 1.95p #750 —

Fish A165

Designs: 80t, Nembwe. 2.10p, Tiger fish. 3.90p, Pike. 4.70p, Spotted squeaker.

2006, May 30 Litho. *Perf. 13¼x13¾*
814-817 A165 Set of 4 5.00 5.00

Tswana Cattle — A166

Designs: 1.10p, Oxen. 2.60p, Cows and calves. 4.10p, Bulls. 4.90p, Horn shapes.

2006, Sept. 4 Litho. *Perf. 13¾x13¼*
818-821 A166 Set of 4 5.00 5.00

Independence, 40th Anniv. — A167

Maps of Botswana showing: 1.10p, Primary and secondary roads. 2.60p, Population distribution. 4.10p, Mines and coal resources. 4.90p, National parks and reserves.

Perf. 13¼x13¾

2006, Sept. 29 Litho.
822-825 A167 Set of 4 4.00 4.00
825a Souvenir sheet, #822-825 4.00 4.00

Christmas A168

Flora: 1.10p, Hyphaene petersiana tree. 2.60p, Phoenix reclinata tree. 4.10p, Hyphaene petersiana fruit. 4.90p, Phoenix reclinata fruit.

2006, Dec. 1 *Perf. 13¾x13¼*
826-829 A168 Set of 4 4.25 4.25

Kingfishers A169

Designs: 1.10p, Pied kingfisher. 2.60p, Malachite kingfisher. 4.10p, Woodland kingfisher. 4.90p, Brown-hooded kingfisher.

Perf. 13¾x13¼

2007, Mar. 31 Litho.
830-833 A169 Set of 4 4.25 4.25

Mushrooms — A170

Designs: 1.10p, False parasols. 2.60p, Bushveld bolete. 4.10p, Lacquered bracket fungus. 4.90p, Collared earthstars.

2007, July 30 Litho. *Perf. 13½x13¾*
834-837 A170 Set of 4 4.25 4.25

Miniature Sheet

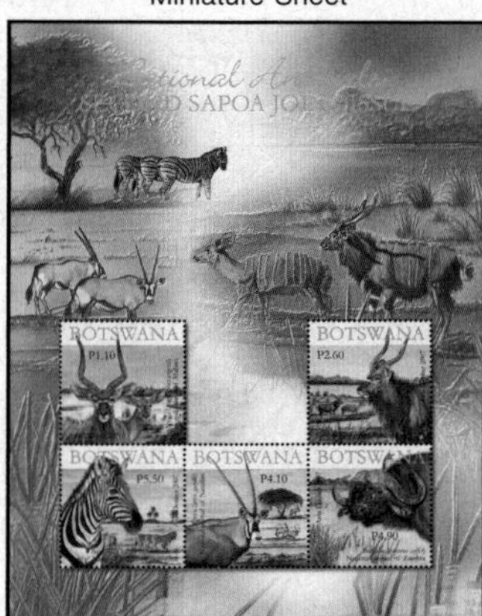

National Animals — A171

No. 838: a, 1.10p, Nyala (Malawi). b, 2.60p, Nyala (Zimbabwe). c, 4.10p, Oryx (Namibia). d, 4.90p, Buffalo (Zambia). e, 5.50p, Bruschell's zebra (Botswana).

Litho. With Foil Application

2007, Oct. 9 *Perf. 13¾*
838 A171 Sheet of 5, #a-e 6.00 6.00

See Malawi No. 752, Namibia Nos. 1141-1142, Zambia Nos. 1097-1101, Zimbabwe Nos. 1064-1068.

University of Botswana, 25th Anniv. A172

Anniversary emblem and: 1.10p, Library. 2.60p, Campus appeal. 4.10p, Okavango research. 4.90p, Old and new infrastructure.

2007, Oct. 13 Litho. *Perf. 14*
839-842 A172 Set of 4 4.50 4.50

Butterflies A173

Designs: 10t, Mimosa sapphire. 20t, Bushveld orange-tip. 30t, African monarch. 40t, Common black-eye. 50t, Brown playboy. 1p, Sapphire. B, Dwarf blue. 2p, Large blue emperor. A, Scarlet tip. 3p, Apricot playboy. 4p, Blue pansy. 5p, Black-striped hairtail. 10p, Natal barred blue. 20p, Foxy charaxes.

2007, Nov. 1 Litho. *Perf. 13½x13¾*

843	A173	10t multi	.30	.30
844	A173	20t multi	.30	.30
845	A173	30t multi	.30	.30
846	A173	40t multi	.30	.30
847	A173	50t multi	.30	.30
848	A173	1p multi	.45	.45
849	A173	B multi	.55	.55
850	A173	2p multi	.90	.90
851	A173	A multi	1.20	1.20
852	A173	3p multi	1.30	1.30
853	A173	4p multi	1.90	1.90
854	A173	5p multi	2.25	2.25
855	A173	10p multi	4.50	4.50
856	A173	20p multi	9.00	9.00
	Nos. 843-856 (14)		23.55	23.55

On day of issue, No. 849 sold for 1.10p; No. 851 for 2.60p.

Art — A174

Designs: 1.10p, Dancer, by Boitshepo Lesego. 2.60p, Baobab Tree, by Philip Huebsch. 4.10p, Child Playing with Dolls, by Giel Kgamane. 4.90p, Donkeys Tired After Hard Work, by Tineni Kepaletswe, horiz. 5.50p, Donkeys in the City, by Andrew Jones, horiz.

2008, Mar. 28 *Perf. 14*
857-861 A174 Set of 5 5.75 5.75

Elephants A175

Elephants and: 1.10p, Hunters. 2.60p, Tourists in boat. 4.10p, Botswana villagers. 4.90p, Riders.

2008, June 20 Litho. *Perf. 14*
862-865 A175 Set of 4 4.00 4.00

2008 Summer Olympics, Beijing — A176

Designs: 1.10p, Runners. 2.60p, Boxing.

2008, Aug. 8 *Perf. 14¼*
866-867 A176 Set of 2 1.25 1.25

National Museum, 40th Anniv. A177

Designs: 1.10p, Launch of Pitse Ya Naga (mobile museum), 1978. 2.60p, Opening of Botanical Garden, 1988, vert. 4.10p, Opening of new museum galleries, 2008. 4.90p, Tsodilo Hills rock drawings, 1998. 5.50p, Official opening, 1968, vert.

2008, Sept. 29
868-872 A177 Set of 5 5.25 5.25

Events of 2008 — A178

Designs: 4.10p, Premiere of movie filmed in Botswana, *The No. 1 Ladies Detective Agency*. 4.90p, Launch of Heart Foundation of Botswana, vert. 5.50p, Launch of Diamond Trading Company.

2008, Oct. 30
873-875 A178 Set of 3 3.75 3.75

Beetles A179

Designs: 1.10p, Small green dung beetle. 2.60p, Lunate ladybird. 4.10p, Garden fruit chafer. 4.90p, Darkling beetle.

2008, Dec. 1 *Perf. 14x13¼*
876-879 A179 Set of 4 3.25 3.25

Endangered Birds — A180

Designs: 1.10p, Lesser flamingos. 2.60p, Gray crowned cranes, horiz. 4.10p, Wattled cranes, horiz. 4.90p, Blue cranes, horiz.

2009, June 5 Litho. *Perf. 14*
880-883 A180 Set of 4 3.75 3.75

Children A181

Inscriptions: 1.10p, Education. 2.60p, Sanitation, vert. 4.10p, Inoculation, vert. 4.90p, Orphan care.

2009, Sept. 11 Litho. *Perf. 14*
884-887 A181 Set of 4 4.00 4.00

Night Sky Over Botswana — A182

Botswana landscapes and: 1.10p, Southern Cross constellation, giraffes. 2.60p, Meteorite, native hunters. 4.10p, Moon, native dancers. 4.90p, Solar eclipse, lions.

2009, Nov. 18 *Perf. 13½x13¾*
888-891 A182 Set of 4 4.00 4.00

Honey Bees A183

Apis mellifera: 1.10p, Bee at flower. 2.60p, Bees on honeycomb. 4.10p, Beehive. 4.90p, Bees at flower.

2010, Mar. 25 Litho. *Perf. 14x13¼*
892-895 A183 Set of 4 3.75 3.75

2010 World Cup Soccer Championships, South Africa — A184

Soccer players, ball, 2010 World Cup mascot and flag of: Nos. 896, 905a, 1.10p, Botswana. Nos. 897, 905b, 2.60p, Namibia. Nos. 898, 905c, 3p, South Africa. Nos. 899, 905d, 4p, Zimbabwe. Nos. 900, 905e, 4.10p, Malawi. Nos. 901, 905f, 4.90p, Swaziland. Nos. 902, 905g, 5.50p, Mauritius. Nos. 903, 905h, 6.60p, Lesotho. Nos. 904, 905i, 8.20p, Zambia.

2010, Apr. 9 *Perf. 13¾*
On Plain Paper With Olive Brown Background
896-904 A184 Set of 9 12.00 12.00
On Gold-faced Paper
905 A184 Sheet of 9, #a-i 12.00 12.00

See Lesotho No. , Malawi No. 753, Mauritius No. , Namibia No. 1188, South Africa No. 1403, Swaziland Nos. 794-803, Zambia Nos. 1115-1118, and Zimbabwe Nos. 1112-1121.

Energy — A185

Designs: 2.60p, Family watching television. 4.10p, Botswanan with cell phone, solar panel outside of house. 5.50p, Man on locomotive. 6.10p, People and compact fluorescent lightbulb, horiz.

2010, Oct. 8 *Perf. 14*
906-909 A185 Set of 4 5.75 5.75

Nocturnal Animals — A185a

Designs: 2.60p, Spring hare. 3p, Fruit bat. 4.10p, Pearl spotted owl. 5.50p, Aardwolf, horiz. 5.60p, Porcupine. 6.10p, Civet, horiz.

Perf. 13¼x13, 13x13¼
2010, Dec. 1 Litho.
Granite Paper
909A-909F A185a Set of 6 8.25 8.25

An additional souvenir sheet exists with this set. The editors would like to examine any example of it.

Flowers — A186

Designs: 2.60p, Ipomoea obscura. 4.10p, Xenostegia tridentata. 5.50p, Ipomoea magnusiana. 6.10p, Ipomoea bolusiana.

2011, Mar. 11 *Perf. 13¼x13¾*
910-913 A186 Set of 4 5.50 5.50

Worldwide Fund for Nature (WWF) A187

Southern white rhinoceros: 2.60p, One rhinoceros facing left. 4.10p, Two rhinoceroses facing forward. 5.50p, Two rhinoceroses facing left. 6.10p, One rhinoceros facing forward, another facing right.

2011, Nov. 21 *Perf. 14x13¼*
914-917 A187 Set of 4 5.00 5.00
917a Souvenir sheet of 4, #914-917 5.00 5.00

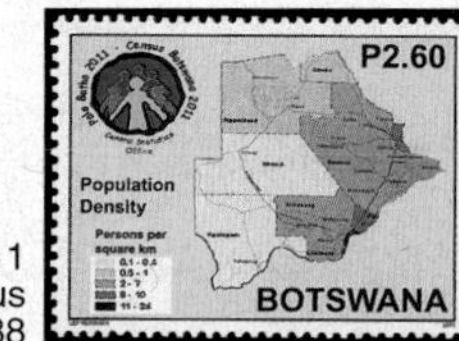
2011 Census A188

Emblem of 2011 Census and: 2.60p, Map of Botswana showing population density. 4.10p, Graduates, road, communications tower. 5.50p, Bar graph showing males and females in age groupings, vert. 6.20p, Population growth graph, vert.

2011, Sept. 9 *Perf. 14x13¼, 13¼x14*
918-921 A188 Set of 4 5.25 5.25

Malaria Prevention A189

Inscriptions: 2.60p, Spraying of houses. 4.10p, Using anti-malaria medicines. 5.50p,

Keeping surroundings clean. 6.10p, Sleeping under treated mosquito nets.

2011, Oct. 25 *Perf. 13¼x14*

922-925	A189	Set of 4	5.00	5.00

Myths and Legends A191

Designs: 3.20p, Matsieng. 4p, All the Stars in Heaven. 4.10p, Tumtumbolosa, horiz. 4.90p, Kgwanyape, horiz. 5.50p, Nonyane, horiz. 6.60p, How Death Came to the World.

Perf. 13¾x13¼, 13¼x13¾

2012 **Litho.**

930-935	A191	Set of 6	7.25	7.25

POSTAGE DUE STAMPS

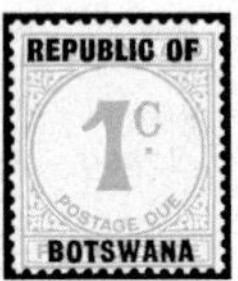

Bechuanaland Protectorate Nos. J10-J12 Overprinted

Perf. 14

1967, Mar. 1 **Wmk. 4** **Typo.**

J1	D2	1c carmine rose	.35	*3.00*
J2	D2	2c dull violet	.35	*3.00*
J3	D2	5c olive green	.45	*3.00*
		Nos. J1-J3 (3)	1.15	*9.00*

Elephant — D1

Perf. 13½

1971, June 9 **Litho.** **Unwmk.**

J4	D1	1c carmine rose	1.75	*4.50*
J5	D1	2c violet blue	2.10	*5.00*
J6	D1	6c sepia	3.25	*7.50*
J7	D1	14c green	6.25	*11.00*
		Nos. J4-J7 (4)	13.35	*28.00*

Zebra — D2

1978 *Perf. 12½*

J8	D2	1t red orange & black	1.25	*1.75*
J9	D2	2t emerald & black	1.25	*1.75*
J10	D2	4t red & black	1.25	*1.75*
J11	D2	10t dark blue & black	1.25	*1.75*
J12	D2	16t brown & black	1.25	*1.75*
		Nos. J8-J12 (5)	6.25	*8.75*

1984 *Perf. 14½x14*

J8a	D2	1t	1.50	*2.00*
J9a	D2	2t	1.50	*2.00*
J10a	D2	4t	1.50	*2.00*
J11a	D2	10t	1.50	*2.00*
J12a	D2	16t	1.50	*2.00*
		Nos. J8a-J12a (5)	7.50	*10.00*

1989, Apr. 1 *Perf. 14½*

J8b	D2	1t	.50	*.65*
J9b	D2	2t	.50	*.65*
J10b	D2	4t	.50	*.65*
J11b	D2	10t	.50	*.65*
J12b	D2	16t	.75	*1.00*
		Nos. J8b-J12b (5)	2.75	*3.60*

The design is the same size on the 1984 and 1989 issues, but the grass of Nos. J8b-J12b is lower and less defined than on previous issues. The paper is wider on the 1989 issue.

1994, Dec. 1 *Perf. 14*

J8c	D2	1t	1.00	1.00
J9c	D2	2t	1.00	1.00
J10c	D2	4t	1.00	1.00
J11c	D2	10t	1.00	1.00
J12c	D2	16t	1.00	1.00
		Nos. J8c-J12c (5)	5.00	5.00

See note after No. J12b.

BRAZIL

brə-'zil

Brasil (after 1918)

LOCATION — On the north and east coasts of South America, bordering on the Atlantic Ocean.
GOVT. — Republic
AREA — 3,286,000 sq. mi.
POP. — 157,070,163 (1996)
CAPITAL — Brasilia

Brazil was an independent empire from 1822 to 1889, when a constitution was adopted and the country became officially known as The United States of Brazil.

1000 Reis = 1 Milreis
100 Centavos = 1 Cruzeiro (1942)
100 Centavos = 1 Cruzado (1986)
100 Centavos = 1 Cruzeiro (1990)
(Cruzeiro Real 8/2/93-7/1/94)
100 Centavos = 1 Real (7/1/94)

Catalogue values for unused stamps in this country are for Never Hinged items, beginning with Scott 680 in the regular postage section, Scott B12 in the semi-postal section, Scott C66 in the airpost section, Scott RA2 in the postal tax section, and Scott RAB1 in the postal tax semi-postal section.

Values for unused stamps are for examples with original gum as defined in the catalogue introduction except for Nos. 1-38 and 42-52 which are valued without gum.

Watermarks

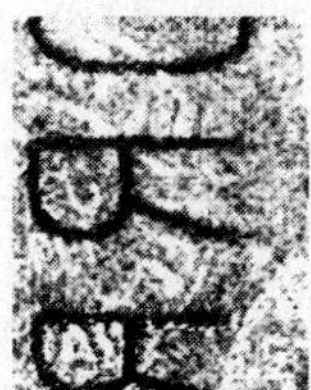
Wmk. 97 — "CORREIO FEDERAL REPUBLICA DOS ESTADOS UNIDOS DO BRAZIL" in Sheet

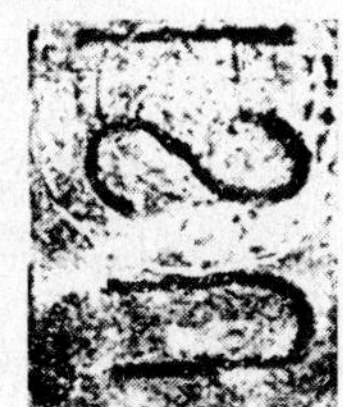
Wmk. 98 — "IMPOSTO DE CONSUMO REPUBLICA DOS ESTADOS UNIDOS DO BRAZIL" in Sheet

Wmk. 99 — "CORREIO"

Wmk. 100 — "CASA DA MOEDA" in Sheet

Because of the spacing of this watermark, a few stamps in each sheet may show no watermark.

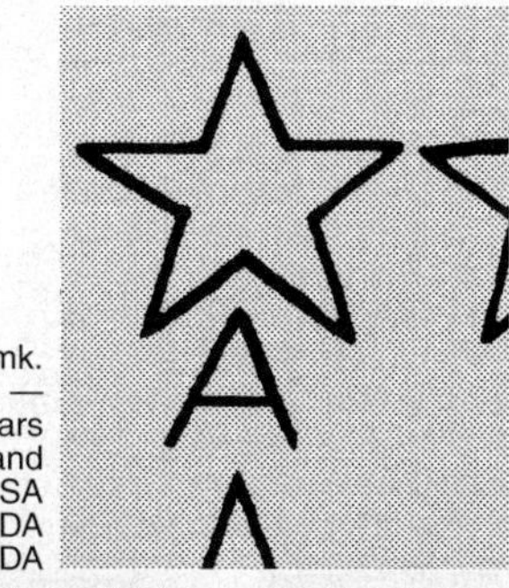
Wmk. 101 — Stars and CASA DA MOEDA

Wmk. 116 — Crosses and Circles

Wmk. 127 — Quatrefoils

Wmk. 193 — ESTADOS UNIDOS DO BRASIL

Wmk. 206 — Star-framed CM, Multiple

Wmk. 218 — E U BRASIL Multiple, Letters 8mm High

Wmk. 221 — ESTADOS UNIDOS DO BRASIL, Multiple, Letters 6mm High

Wmk. 222 — CORREIO BRASIL and 5 Stars in Squared Circle

Wmk. 236 — Coat of Arms in Sheet

Watermark (reduced illustration) covers 22 stamps in sheet.

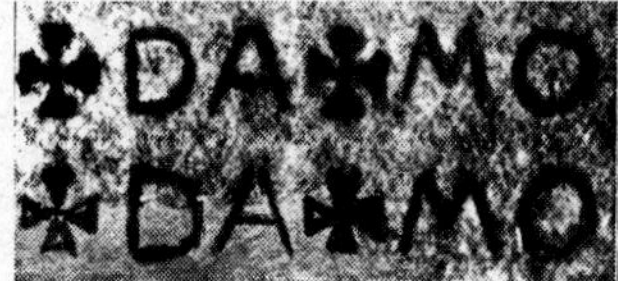
Wmk. 245 — Multiple "CASA DA MOEDA DO BRASIL" and Small Formee Cross

Wmk. 249 — "CORREIO BRASIL" multiple

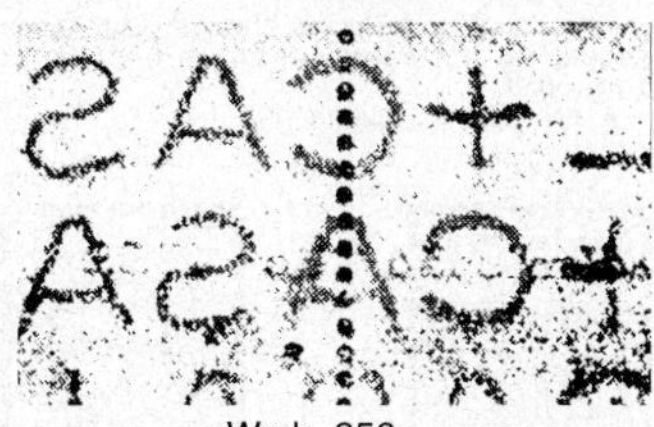
Wmk. 256 — "CASA+DA+MOEDA+DO+BRAZIL" in 8mm Letters

Wmk. 264 — "*CORREIO*BRASIL*" Multiple, Letters 7mm High

Wmk. 267 — "*CORREIO*BRASIL*" Multiple in Small Letters 5mm High

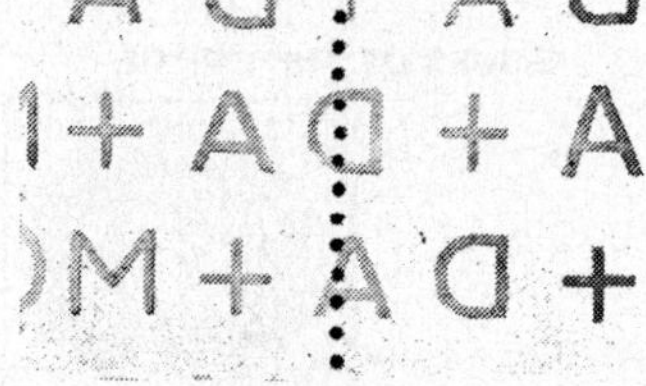
Wmk. 268 — "CASA+DA+MOEDA+DO+BRASIL" in 6mm Letters

Wmk. 270 — Wavy Lines and Seal

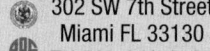

Wmk. 271 — Wavy Lines

Wmk. 281 — Wavy Lines

ISSUES OF THE EMPIRE

A1

Fine Impressions
Grayish or Yellowish Paper
Unwmk.

1843, Aug. 1 **Engr.** ***Imperf.***

1	A1	30r black	4,500.	550.
c.		Pair, #1-2		*950,000.*
2	A1	60r black	600.	300.
3	A1	90r black	4,000.	1,400.

Nos. 1-3 were issued with gum, but very few unused examples retain even a trace of their original gum. Stamps with original gum command substantial premiums.

Fine impressions are true black and have background lathework complete. Intermediate impressions are grayish black and have weaker lathework in the background. These sell for somewhat less than fine impressions. Worn impressions have white areas in the background surrounding the numerals due to plate wear affecting especially the lathework. These examples sell for somewhat less than intermediate impressions.

Most examples of Nos. 1-3 also exist on white paper, usually thin and somewhat translucent. Such examples are scarce and command premiums. For detailed listings, see the Scott Classic Specialized catalogue

A2

A3

Grayish or Yellowish Paper

1844-46

7	A2	10r black	125.00	25.00
8	A2	30r black	160.00	35.00
9	A2	60r black	125.00	25.00
10	A2	90r black	1,000.	120.00
11	A2	180r black	4,500.	1,800.
12	A2	300r black	6,500.	2,000.
13	A2	600r black	6,000.	2,200.

Nos. 8, 9 and 10 exist on thick paper and are considerably scarcer.

Grayish or Yellowish Paper

1850, Jan. 1

21	A3	10r black	30.00	*42.50*
22	A3	20r black	92.50	*120.00*
23	A3	30r black	12.00	3.50
24	A3	60r black	12.00	3.00
25	A3	90r black	100.00	14.50
26	A3	180r black	100.00	65.00
27	A3	300r black	400.00	72.50
28	A3	600r black	500.00	110.00

No. 22 used is generally found precanceled with a single horizontal line in pen or blue crayon or with two diagonal pen lines. Value precanceled without gum, $75.

All values except the 90r were reprinted in 1910 on very thick paper.

1854

37	A3	10r blue	14.50	14.50
38	A3	30r blue	40.00	*60.00*

A4

1861

39	A4	280r red	175.00	120.00
40	A4	430r yellow	250.00	175.00

Nos. 39-40 have been reprinted on thick white paper with white gum. They are printed in aniline inks and the colors are brighter than those of the originals.

1866 ***Perf. 13½***

42	A3	10r blue	125.00	*150.00*
43	A3	20r black	1,100.	500.00
44	A3	30r black	350.00	190.00
45	A3	30r blue	*800.00*	*925.00*
46	A3	60r black	140.00	30.00
47	A3	90r black	725.00	350.00
48	A3	180r black	925.00	350.00
49	A4	280r red	800.00	800.00
50	A3	300r black	750.00	400.00
51	A4	430r yellow	725.00	425.00
52	A3	600r black	725.00	300.00

Fraudulent perforations abound. Purchases should be accompanied by certificates of authenticity.

A 10r black is questioned.

A5

A6

A7

A8

A8a

A9

Emperor Dom Pedro — A9a

Thick or Thin White Wove Paper

1866, July 1 ***Perf. 12***

53	A5	10r vermilion	14.50	6.00
54	A6	20r red lilac	25.00	3.50
a.		20r dull violet	80.00	30.00
56	A7	50r blue	35.00	3.00
57	A8	80r slate violet	92.50	6.00
58	A8a	100r blue green	35.00	1.90
a.		100r yellow green	35.00	1.90
59	A9	200r black	120.00	10.00
a.		Half used as 100r on cover		*1,750.*
60	A9a	500r orange	250.00	42.50
		Nos. 53-60 (7)	572.00	72.90

The 10r and 20r exist imperf. on both white and bluish paper. Some authorities consider them proofs.

Nos. 58 and 65 are found in three types.

Bluish Paper

53a	A5	10r	600.00	500.00
54b	A6	20r	190.00	30.00
56a	A7	50r	250.00	30.00
57a	A8	80r	300.00	35.00
58b	A8a	100r Type II	1,000.	140.00
d.		A8a 100r Type I	*9,000.*	—

1876-77 ***Rouletted***

61	A5	10r vermilion ('77)	72.50	42.50
62	A6	20r red lilac ('77)	85.00	35.00
63	A7	50r blue ('77)	85.00	12.00
64	A8	80r violet ('77)	210.00	25.00
65	A8a	100r green	50.00	1.50
66	A9	200r black ('77)	100.00	9.25
a.		Half used as 100r on cover		*1,000.*
67	A9a	500r orange	225.00	50.00
		Nos. 61-67 (7)	827.50	175.25

A10

A11

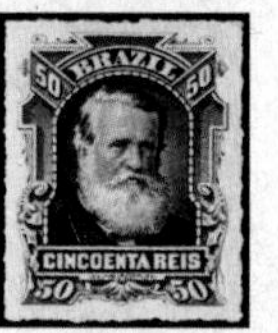

A12

A13

A14

A15

A16

A17

A18

A19

A20

1878-79 ***Rouletted***

68	A10	10r vermilion	14.50	3.50
69	A11	20r violet	19.00	3.00
70	A12	50r blue	30.00	2.50
71	A13	80r lake	35.00	12.00
72	A14	100r green	35.00	1.50
73	A15	200r black	175.00	21.00
a.		Half used as 100r on cover		*1,000.*
74	A16	260r dk brown	100.00	27.50
75	A18	300r bister	100.00	7.25
a.		One-third used as 100r on cover		*10,000.*
76	A19	700r red brown	190.00	100.00
77	A20	1000r gray lilac	225.00	47.50
		Nos. 68-77 (10)	923.50	225.75

1878, Aug. 21 ***Perf. 12***

78	A17	300r orange & grn	100.00	25.00

Nos. 68-78 exist imperforate.

A21

A22

A23

Small Heads
Laid Paper
Perf. 13, 13½ and Compound

1881, July 15

79	A21	50r blue	140.00	21.00
80	A22	100r olive green	600.00	35.00
81	A23	200r pale red brn	600.00	140.00
a.		Half used as 100r on cover		*2,100.*

On Nos. 79 and 80 the hair above the ear curves forward. On Nos. 83 and 88 it is drawn backward. On the stamps of the 1881 issue the beard is smaller than in the 1882-85 issues and fills less of the space between the neck and the frame at the left.

See No. 88.

A24 A25

A26

A27

Two types each of the 100 and 200 reis.

100 REIS:

Type I — Groundwork formed of diagonal crossed lines and horizontal lines.

Type II — Groundwork formed of diagonal crossed lines and vertical lines.

200 REIS:

Type I — Groundwork formed of diagonal and horizontal lines.

Type II — Groundwork formed of diagonal crossed lines.

Larger Heads
Laid Paper
Perf. 12½ to 14 and Compound

1882-84

82	A24	10r black	12.00	*25.00*
83	A25	100r ol grn, type I	42.50	3.50
b.		100r dark green, type II	250.00	14.50
84	A26	200r pale red brn, type I	100.00	27.50
a.		Half used as 100r on cover		*1,300.*
85	A27	200r pale rose, type II	55.00	5.50
a.		Diag. half used as 100r on cover		950.00
		Nos. 82-85 (4)	209.50	61.50

See No. 86.

A28

A29

A30

Three types of A29

Type I — Groundwork of horizontal lines.

Type II — Groundwork of diagonal crossed lines.

Type III — Groundwork solid.

Perf. 13, 13½, 14 and Compound

1884-85

86 A24 10r orange 3.00 2.50
87 A28 20r slate green 35.00 3.50
a. 20r olive green 35.00 3.50
b. Half used as 10r on newspaper *3,500.*
88 A21 50r bl, head larger 35.00 3.50
90 A29 100r lilac, type I 150.00 3.00
a. 100r lilac, type II 450.00 75.00
b. 100r lilac, type III 325.00 55.00
91 A30 100r lilac 200.00 5.00
Nos. 86-91 (5) 423.00 17.50

A31

A32

Southern Cross A33

Crown A34

Perf. 13, 13½, 14 and Compound

1885

92 A31 100r lilac 125.00 3.00

Compare design A31 with A35.

1887

93 A32 50r chalky blue 35.00 5.00
94 A33 300r gray blue 250.00 30.00
95 A34 500r olive 140.00 14.00
Nos. 93-95 (3) 425.00 49.00

A35

A36

Entrance to Bay of Rio de Janeiro — A37

1888

96 A35 100r lilac 72.50 1.90
a. Imperf., pair 150.00 *175.00*
97 A36 700r violet 80.00 *110.00*
98 A37 1000r dull blue 300.00 110.00
Nos. 96-98 (3) 452.50 221.90

Issues of the Republic

Southern Cross — A38

Wove Paper, Thin to Thick

Perf. 12½ to 14, 11 to 11½, and 12½ to 14x11 to 11½, Rough or Clean-Cut

Engraved; Typographed (#102)

1890-91

99 A38 20r gray green 2.50 1.90
a. 20r blue green 2.50 1.90
b. 20r emerald 19.00 7.00
100 A38 50r gray green 6.25 1.90
a. 50r olive green 14.00 7.00
b. 50r yellow green 14.00 7.00
c. 50r dark slate green 8.25 4.00
d. Horiz. pair, imperf. btwn. —
101 A38 100r lilac rose 450.00 6.00
102 A38 100r red lil, redrawn 30.00 1.90
a. Tete beche pair *25,000.* *19,000.*
103 A38 200r purple 10.00 1.90
a. 200r violet 12.00 2.50
b. 200r violet blue 27.50 3.50
c. Half used as 100r on cover 875.00
104 A38 300r dark violet 90.00 6.00
a. 300r gray 90.00 10.00
b. 300r gray blue 100.00 10.00
c. 300r slate violet 175.00 30.00
105 A38 500r olive bister 21.00 9.50
a. 500r olive gray 21.00 11.50
106 A38 500r slate 21.00 13.50
107 A38 700r fawn 19.00 *19.00*
a. 700r chocolate 24.00 26.00
108 A38 1000r bister 17.50 3.50
a. 1000r yellow buff 35.00 8.50
Nos. 99-108 (10) 667.25 65.10

The redrawn 100r may be distinguished by the absence of the curved lines of shading in the left side of the central oval. The pearls in the oval are not well aligned and there is less shading at right and left of "CORREIO" and "100 REIS."

A 100 reis stamp of type A38 but inscribed "BRAZIL" instead of "E. U. DO BRAZIL" was not placed in issue but postmarked copies are known. A reprint on thick paper was made in 1910.

No. 101 exists imperf., not regularly issued.

For surcharges see Nos. 151-158.

Liberty Head
A39 A40

Perf. 12½ to 14, 11 to 11½ and 12½ to 14x11 to 11½

1891, May 1 **Typo.**

109 A39 100r blue & red 42.50 1.90
a. Frame inverted 125.00 110.00
b. Tete beche pair 850.00 *925.00*
c. 100r ultra & red 42.50 1.90

Perf. 11, 11½, 13, 13½, 14 and Compound

1893, Jan. 18 **Litho.**

111 A40 100r rose 75.00 1.75

A41

A41a

Sugarloaf Mountain

A42

A42a

Liberty Head

Hermes — A43

Perf. 11 to 11½, 12½ to 14 and 12½ to 14x11 to 11½

1894-97 **Unwmk.**

112 A41 10r rose & blue 2.50 .90
113 A41a 10r rose & blue 2.50 .90
114 A41a 20r orange & bl ('97) 1.40 .40
115 A41a 50r dk blue & blue 13.00 1.60
116 A42 100r carmine & blk 5.00 .50
118 A42a 200r orange & blk 1.25 .50
d. Half used as 100r on cover 850.00
119 A42a 300r green & blk 19.00 .70
120 A42a 500r blue & blk 30.00 2.00
121 A42a 700r light lilac & blk 20.00 2.00
122 A43 1000r green & vio 72.50 2.00
124 A43 2000r blk & gray lil 85.00 20.00
Nos. 112-124 (11) 252.15 31.50

The head of No. 116 exists in five types. See Nos. 140-150A, 159-161, 166-171d.

1889 Issue of Newspaper Stamps Surcharged (Type N1)

a

b

c

1898 **Green Surcharge** ***Rouletted***

125 (b) 700r on 500r yel 8.50 *12.00*
126 (c) 1000r on 700r yel 42.50 35.00
a. Surcharged "700r" 850.00 1,000.
127 (c) 2000r on 1000r yel 35.00 18.00
128 (c) 2000r on 1000r brn 25.00 7.25

Violet Surcharge

129 (a) 100r on 50r brn yel 2.50 *55.00*
130 (c) 100r on 50r brn yel 77.50 57.50
131 (c) 300r on 200r blk 4.00 1.40
a. Double surcharge 190.00 325.00

The surcharge on No. 130 is handstamped. The impression is blurred and lighter in color than on No. 129. The two surcharges differ most in the shapes and serifs of the figures "1."

Counterfeits exist of No. 126a.

Black Surcharge

132 (b) 200r on 100r violet 4.00 1.40
a. Double surcharge 95.00 *200.00*
b. Inverted surcharge 95.00 *200.00*
132C (b) 500r on 300r car 6.50 3.50
133 (b) 700r on 500r green 9.50 2.40

Blue Surcharge

134 (b) 500r on 300r car 7.50 6.25

Red Surcharge

135 (c) 1000r on 700r ultra 27.50 17.00
a. Inverted surcharge 240.00 —

Surcharged on 1890-94 Issues

d

e

Perf. 11 to 14 and Compound

Black Surcharge

136 N3(e) 20r on 10r blue 3.75 7.00
137 N2(d) 200r on 100r red lilac 25.00 17.00
a. Double surcharge 275.00 300.00

Surcharge on No. 137 comes blue to deep black.

Blue Surcharge

138 N3(e) 50r on 20r green 9.50 11.50

Red Surcharge

139 N3(e) 100r on 50r green 21.00 24.00
a. Blue surcharge 15.00

The surcharge on 139a exists inverted, and in pair, one without surcharge.

Types of 1894-97

1899 ***Perf. 5½-7 and 11-11½x5½-7***

140 A41a 10r rose & bl 6.00 *14.00*
141 A41a 20r orange & bl 9.25 9.25
142 A41a 50r dk bl & lt bl 12.00 *37.50*
143 A42 100r carmine & blk 20.00 5.50
144 A42a 200r orange & blk 12.00 3.50
145 A42a 300r green & blk 75.00 8.75
Nos. 140-145 (6) 134.25 78.50

Perf. 8½-9½, 8½-9½x11-11½

146 A41a 10r rose & bl 6.00 3.50
147 A41a 20r orange & bl 19.00 3.50
147A A41a 50r dk bl & bl 160.00 35.00
148 A42 100r carmine & blk 37.50 1.75
149 A42a 200r orange & blk 19.00 1.25
150 A42a 300r green & blk 75.00 6.00
150A A43 1000r green & vio 160.00 15.00
Nos. 146-150A (7) 476.50 66.00

Nos. 140-150A are valued with perfs just cut into the design on one or two sides. Expect some irregularity of the perforations.

Issue of 1890-93 Surcharged in Violet or Magenta

Perf. 11 to 11½, 12½ to 14 and Compound

1899, June 25

151 A38 50r on 20r gray grn 2.50 *3.50*
a. Double surcharge 150.00 150.00
152 A38 100r on 50r gray grn 2.50 *3.50*
b. Double surcharge 125.00 125.00
153 A38 300r on 200r pur 9.25 *14.50*
a. Double surcharge 300.00 —
b. Pair, one without surcharge 500.00 —
154 A38 500r on 300r ultra, perf. 13 22.50 8.75
a. 500r on 300r gray lilac 35.00 10.00
b. Pair, one without surcharge 500.00 *575.00*
c. 500r on 300r slate violet 45.00 17.00
155 A38 700r on 500r ol bis 30.00 7.00
a. Pair, one without surcharge 500.00 —
156 A38 1000r on 700r choc 22.50 7.00
157 A38 1000r on 700r fawn 22.50 7.00
a. Pair, one without surcharge 500.00 *575.00*
158 A38 2000r on 1000r bister (perf 11-11½) 37.50 5.25
a. 2000r on 1000r yel buff (perf 13) 60.00 5.25
b. Pair, one without surcharge 500.00 *575.00*
Nos. 151-158 (8) 149.25 56.50

Types of 1894-97

Perf. 11, 11½, 13 and Compound

1900

159 A41a 50r green 13.00 .70
160 A42 100r rose 25.00 .35
a. Frame around inner oval 125.00 4.75
161 A42a 200r blue 14.50 .40
Nos. 159-161 (3) 52.50 1.45

Three types exist of No. 161, all of which have the frame around inner oval.

Cabral Arrives at Brazil — A44

Independence Proclaimed — A45

"Emancipation of Slaves" — A46

Allegory, Republic of Brazil — A47

1900, Jan. 1 Litho. *Perf. 12½*
162 A44 100r red 7.25 5.75
a. Imperf., pair 400.00 500.00
163 A45 200r green & yel 7.25 5.75
164 A46 500r blue 7.25 5.75
165 A47 700r emerald 7.25 5.75
Nos. 162-165 (4) 29.00 23.00

Discovery of Brazil, 400th anniversary.

Types of 1894-97
Wmk. (97? or 98?)

1905 *Perf. 11, 11½*
166 A41a 10r rose & bl 7.00 4.75
167 A41a 20r orange & bl 12.50 2.40
168 A41a 50r green 25.00 3.50
169 A42 100r rose 32.50 1.25
170 A42a 200r dark blue 19.00 1.25
171 A42a 300r green & blk 65.00 2.40
Nos. 166-171 (6) 161.00 15.55

Positive identification of Wmk. 97 or 98 places stamp in specific watermark groups below.

Wmk. 97
166b A41a 10r rose & blue 37.50 19.00
167b A41a 20r orange & blue 37.50 9.50
168b A41a 50r green 72.50 9.50
169b A42 100r rose 250.00 35.00
170b A42a 200r dark blue 150.00 4.75
171b A42a 300r green & blk 450.00 35.00
171A A43 1000r green & vio 350.00 35.00
Nos. 166b-171A (7) 1,347. 147.75

Wmk. 98
166c A41a 10r rose & blue 50.00 50.00
167c A41a 20r orange & blue 100.00 24.00
168c A41a 50r green 200.00 35.00
169c A42 100r rose 100.00 4.75
170c A42a 200r dark blue 150.00 4.75
171d A42a 300r green & blk 350.00 35.00
Nos. 166c-171d (6) 950.00 153.50

Allegory, Pan-American Congress A48

1906, July 23 Litho. Unwmk.
172 A48 100r carmine rose 30.00 30.00
173 A48 200r blue 75.00 10.00

Third Pan-American Congress.

Aristides Lobo A48a

Benjamin Constant A49

Pedro Alvares Cabral A50

Eduardo Wandenkolk A51

Manuel Deodoro da Fonseca A52

Floriano Peixoto A53

Prudente de Moraes A54

Manuel Ferraz de Campos Salles A55

Francisco de Paula Rodrigues Alves — A56

Liberty Head — A57

A58

A59

1906-16 Engr. *Perf. 12*
174 A48a 10r bluish slate 1.10 .25
175 A49 20r aniline vio 1.10 .25
176 A50 50r green 1.10 .25
a. Booklet pane of 6 ('08) 47.50 *150.00*
177 A51 100r anil rose 2.50 .25
a. Imperf. vert., coil ('16) 4.75 .40
b. Booklet pane of 6 ('08) 95.00 *150.00*
178 A52 200r blue 2.50 .25
a. Booklet pane of 6 ('08) 72.50 *150.00*
179 A52 200r ultra ('15) 2.50 .40
a. Imperf. vert., coil ('16) 2.50 .40
180 A53 300r gray blk 3.75 .80
181 A54 400r olive grn 37.50 2.40
182 A55 500r dk violet 7.50 .80
183 A54 600r olive grn ('10) 4.25 1.60
184 A56 700r red brown 7.50 3.50
185 A57 1000r vermilion 42.50 1.25
186 A58 2000r yellow grn 25.00 .80
187 A58 2000r Prus blue ('15) 13.00 1.25
188 A59 5000r carmine rose 10.00 2.40
Nos. 174-188 (15) 161.80 16.45

Allegorical Emblems: Liberty, Peace, Industry, etc. — A60

1908, July 14
189 A60 100r carmine 24.00 1.75

National Exhibition, Rio de Janeiro.

Emblems of Peace Between Brazil and Portugal A61

1908, July 14
190 A61 100r red 11.00 1.25

Opening of Brazilian ports to foreign commerce, cent. Medallions picture King Carlos I of Portugal and Pres. Affonso Penna of Brazil.

Bonifacio, Bolivar, Hidalgo, O'Higgins, San Martin, Washington — A62

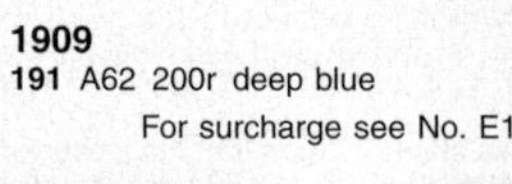

1909
191 A62 200r deep blue 13.50 1.50

For surcharge see No. E1.

Nilo Peçanha A63

Baron of Rio Branco A64

1910, Nov. 15
192 A63 10,000r brown 11.00 3.00

1913-16
193 A64 1000r deep green 5.00 .50
194 A64 1000r slate ('16) 29.00 .80

Cabo Frio — A65

Perf. 11½
1915, Nov. 13 Litho. Wmk. 99
195 A65 100r dk grn, *yelsh* 5.00 4.00

Founding of the town of Cabo Frio, 300th anniversary.

Bay of Guajara A66

1916, Jan. 5
196 A66 100r carmine 11.00 6.00

City of Belem, 300th anniversary.

Revolutionary Flag — A67

1917, Mar. 6
197 A67 100r deep blue 18.00 8.50

Revolution of Pernambuco, Mar. 6, 1817.

Rodrigues Alves — A68

Unwmk.
1917, Aug. 31 Engr. *Perf. 12*
198 A68 5000r red brown 80.00 12.50

Liberty Head
A69 A70

Perf. 12½, 13, 13x13½.
1918-20 Typo. Unwmk.
200 A69 10r orange brn .70 .30
201 A69 20r slate .70 .30
202 A69 25r ol gray ('20) .70 .30
203 A69 50r green 40.00 4.00
204 A70 100r rose 2.25 .30
a. Imperf., pair —
205 A70 300r red orange 25.00 4.00
206 A70 500r dull violet 25.00 4.00
Nos. 200-206 (7) 94.35 13.20

1918-20 Wmk. 100
207 A69 10r red brown 8.00 2.00
a. Imperf., pair —
207B A69 20r slate 1.90 1.90
c. Imperf., pair —
208 A69 25r ol gray ('20) 1.00 .65
209 A69 50r green 1.90 .65
210 A70 100r rose 62.50 .65
a. Imperf., pair —
211 A70 200r dull blue 8.00 .65
212 A70 300r orange 62.50 5.00
213 A70 500r dull violet 62.50 9.50
214 A70 600r orange 3.50 *9.50*
Nos. 207-214 (9) 211.80 30.50

Because of the spacing of this watermark, a few stamps in each sheet may show no watermark.

"Education" — A72

1918 Engr. *Perf. 11½*
215 A72 1000r blue 8.00 .30
216 A72 2000r red brown 35.00 10.00
217 A72 5000r dark violet 10.00 10.00
Nos. 215-217 (3) 53.00 20.30

Watermark note below No. 257 also applies to Nos. 215-217.

See Nos. 233-234, 283-285, 404, 406, 458, 460. For surcharge see No. C30.

Railroad A73

"Industry" A74

"Aviation" A75

Mercury A76

"Navigation" — A77

Perf. 13½x13, 13x13½
1920-22 Typo. Unwmk.
218 A73 10r red violet 1.00 .50
219 A73 20r olive green 1.00 .50
220 A74 25r brown violet .90 .50
221 A74 50r blue green 1.10 .50
222 A74 50r orange brn ('22) 1.90 .50
223 A75 100r rose red 3.75 .50
224 A75 100r orange ('22) 10.00 .50
225 A75 150r violet ('21) 1.90 .50
226 A75 200r blue 6.00 .50
227 A75 200r rose red ('22) 10.50 .50
228 A76 300r olive gray 17.00 .65

229 A76 400r dull blue ('22) 30.00 4.25
230 A76 500r red brown 24.00 .65
Nos. 218-230 (13) 109.05 10.55

See Nos. 236-257, 265-266, 268-271, 273-274, 276-281, 302-311, 316-322, 326-340, 357-358, 431-434, 436-441, 461-463B, 467-470, 472-474, 488-490, 492-494. For surcharges see Nos. 356-358, 376-377.

Perf. 11, 11½

Engr. Wmk. 100

231 A77 600r red orange 2.75 .50
232 A77 1000r claret 7.00 .30
a. Perf. 8½ 50.00 9.50
233 A72 2000r dull violet 27.50 .95
234 A72 5000r brown 21.00 11.00
Nos. 231-234 (4) 58.25 12.75

Nos. 233 and 234 are inscribed "BRASIL CORREIO." Watermark note below No. 257 also applies to Nos. 231-234.

See No. 282.

King Albert of Belgium and President Epitacio Pessoa A78

1920, Sept. 19 Engr. *Perf. 11½x11*

235 A78 100r dull red 1.00 1.00

Visit of the King and Queen of Belgium.

Types of 1920-22 Issue

Perf. 13x13½, 13x12½

1922-29 Typo. Wmk. 100

236 A73 10r red violet .30 .25
237 A73 20r olive green .30 .25
238 A75 20r gray violet ('29) .30 .25
239 A74 25r brown violet .35 .25
240 A74 50r blue grn 4.25 *45.00*
241 A74 50r org brn ('23) .50 .40
242 A75 100r rose red 30.00 .50
243 A75 100r orange ('26) .65 .25
244 A75 100r turq grn ('28) .65 .25
245 A75 150r violet 2.50 .50
246 A75 200r blue 400.00 15.00
247 A75 200r rose red .50 .25
248 A75 200r ol grn ('28) 3.50 3.75
249 A76 300r olive gray 2.50 .30
250 A76 300r rose red ('29) .40 .30
251 A76 400r blue 2.50 .25
252 A76 400r orange ('29) 1.00 3.25
253 A76 500r red brown 10.00 .65
254 A76 500r ultra ('29) 14.50 .25
255 A76 600r brn org ('29) 12.00 4.50
256 A76 700r dull vio ('29) 12.00 2.50
257 A76 1000r turq bl ('29) 14.50 1.00
Nos. 236-257 (22) 513.20 *79.90*

Because of the spacing of the watermark, a few stamps in each sheet show no watermark.

A booklet exists with panes of 6 (2x3), created from the left margin blocks of sheet stamps of Nos. 241, 243, 247, 249 and 253. Once removed from the booklet, they cannot be separately identified.

"Agriculture" — A79

1922 Unwmk. *Perf. 13x13½*

258 A79 40r orange brown .70 .50
259 A79 80r grnsh blue .50 *3.25*

See Nos. 263, 267, 275.

Declaration of Ypiranga — A80

Dom Pedro I and Jose Bonifacio — A81

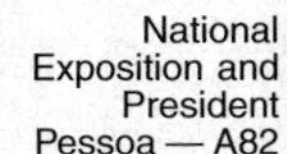

National Exposition and President Pessoa — A82

Unwmk.

1922, Sept. 7 Engr. *Perf. 14*

260 A80 100r ultra 5.00 .75
261 A81 200r red 7.00 .50
262 A82 300r green 7.00 .50
Nos. 260-262 (3) 19.00 1.75

Cent. of independence and Natl. Exposition of 1922.

Agriculture Type of 1922

Perf. 13½x12

1923 Wmk. 100 Typo.

263 A79 40r orange brown .75 *7.50*

Brazilian Army Entering Bahia — A83

Unwmk.

1923, July 12 Litho. *Perf. 13*

264 A83 200r rose 11.00 6.50

Centenary of the taking of Bahia from the Portuguese.

Types of 1920-22 Issue

Perf. 13x13½

1924 Typo. Wmk. 193

265 A73 10r red violet 9.00 7.50
266 A73 20r olive green 10.50 7.50
267 A79 40r orange brown 7.50 2.75
268 A74 50r orange brown 10.00 *30.00*
269 A75 100r orange 7.50 .75
270 A75 200r rose 10.50 .75
271 A76 400r blue 8.00 4.75
Nos. 265-271 (7) 63.00 *54.00*

Arms of Equatorial Confederation, 1824 — A84

Unwmk.

1924, July 2 Litho. *Perf. 11*

272 A84 200r bl, blk, yel, & red 4.00 2.75
a. Red omitted 350.00 350.00

Centenary of the Equatorial Confederation.

Chemically bleached fakes of No. 272a are more common than the genuine error. Expertization is advised.

Types of 1920-22 Issue

Perf. 9½ to 13½ and Compound

1924-28 Typo. Wmk. 101

273 A73 10r red violet .75 .35
274 A73 20r olive gray .75 .35
275 A79 40r orange brn .75 .35
276 A74 50r orange brn .75 .35
277 A75 100r red orange 2.25 .35
278 A75 200r rose 1.00 .35
279 A76 300r ol gray ('25) 10.00 1.25
280 A76 400r blue 6.00 .50
281 A76 500r red brown 15.00 .50

Engr.

282 A77 600r red orange ('26) 2.50 .35
283 A72 2000r dull vio ('26) 7.50 .75
284 A72 5000r brown ('26) 22.50 .85
285 A72 10,000r rose ('28) 30.00 2.00
Nos. 273-285 (13) 99.75 8.30

Nos. 283-285 are inscribed "BRASIL CORREIO."

Ruy Barbosa — A85

1925 Wmk. 100 *Perf. 11½*

286 A85 1000r claret 6.25 1.75

1926 Wmk. 101

287 A85 1000r claret 2.10 .40

"Justice" — A86

Scales of Justice and Map of Brazil — A87

Perf. 13½x13

1927, Aug. 11 Typo. Wmk. 206

288 A86 100r deep blue 1.10 .65
289 A87 200r rose .95 .40

Founding of the law courses, cent.

Liberty Holding Coffee Leaves — A88

1928, Feb. 5

290 A88 100r blue green 1.75 .80
291 A88 200r carmine 1.10 .50
292 A88 300r olive black 9.00 .40
Nos. 290-292 (3) 11.85 1.70

Introduction of the coffee tree in Brazil, bicent.

Official Stamps of 1919 Surcharged in Red or Black

Perf. 11, 11½

1928 Wmk. 100 Engr.

293 O3 700r on 500r org 8.00 8.00
a. Inverted surcharge 210.00 210.00
294 O3 1000r on 100r rose red (Bk) 4.75 .60
295 O3 2000r on 200r dull bl 6.50 1.00
296 O3 5000r on 50r grn 6.50 1.60
297 O3 10,000r on 10r ol grn 30.00 2.50
Nos. 293-297 (5) 55.75 13.70

Nos. 293-297 were used for ordinary postage.

Stamps in the outer rows of the sheets are often without watermark.

Ruy Barbosa — A89

Perf. 9, 9½x11, 11, and Compound

1929 Wmk. 101

300 A89 5000r blue violet 20.00 .95

See Nos. 405, 459. For surcharge see No. C29.

Types of 1920-22 Issue

Perf. 13½x12½

1929 Typo. Wmk. 218

302 A75 20r gray violet .40 .25
303 A75 50r red brown .40 .25
304 A75 100r turq green .55 .25
305 A75 200r olive green 22.50 5.00
306 A76 300r rose red 1.10 .25
307 A76 400r orange 1.25 *2.00*
308 A76 500r ultra 14.00 .65
309 A76 600r brown org 16.00 1.25
310 A76 700r dp violet 4.25 .25
311 A76 1000r turq blue 7.50 .25
Nos. 302-311 (10) 67.95 10.40

Wmk. 218 exists both in vertical alignment and in echelon.

Wmk. in echelon

302a A75 20r .50 .40
303a A75 50r 140.00 75.00
306a A76 300r 1.25 1.25
308a A76 500r 200.00 47.50
311a A76 1000r 10.00 11.00

Architectural Fantasies
A90 A91

Architectural Fantasy — A92

Perf. 13x13½

1930, June 20 Wmk. 206

312 A90 100r turq blue 2.00 1.25
313 A91 200r olive gray 3.25 .80
314 A92 300r rose red 5.50 1.25
Nos. 312-314 (3) 10.75 3.30

Fourth Pan-American Congress of Architects and Exposition of Architecture.

Types of 1920-22 Issue

1930 Wmk. 221 *Perf. 13x12½*

316 A75 20r gray violet .40 .35
317 A75 50r red brown .40 .35
318 A75 100r turq blue .80 .35
319 A75 200r olive green 4.75 1.25
320 A76 300r rose red .95 .35
321 A76 500r ultra 2.40 .35
322 A76 1000r turq blue 40.00 1.50
Nos. 316-322 (7) 49.70 4.50

Imperforates

From 1930 to 1947, imperforate or partly perforated sheets of nearly all commemorative and some definitive issues were obtainable.

Types of 1920-22 Issue

Perf. 11, 13½x13, 13x12½

1931-34 Typo. Wmk. 222

326 A75 10r deep brown .25 .25
327 A75 20r gray violet .25 .25
328 A74 25r brn vio ('34) .25 1.25
330 A75 50r blue green .25 .25
331 A75 50r red brown .25 .25
332 A75 100r orange .50 .25
334 A75 200r dp carmine 1.00 .40
335 A76 300r olive green 1.40 .25
336 A76 400r ultra 3.00 .25
337 A76 500r red brown 6.00 .25
338 A76 600r brown org 6.50 .25
339 A76 700r deep violet 6.50 .25
340 A76 1000r turq blue 21.00 .25
Nos. 326-340 (13) 47.15 4.40

Getulio Vargas and Joao Pessoa A93

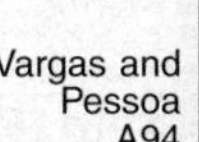

Vargas and Pessoa A94

Oswaldo Aranha
A95 A96

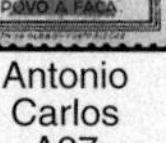

Antonio Carlos A97
Pessoa A98

Vargas — A99

Unwmk.

1931, Apr. 29 Litho. *Perf. 14*

No.	Type	Description	Unused	Used
342	A93	10r + 10r lt bl	.25	*13.00*
343	A93	20r + 20r yel brn	.25	*9.50*
344	A95	50r + 50r bl grn, red & yel	.25	*.40*
a.		Red missing at left	.90	*1.60*
345	A93	100r + 50r orange	.55	.45
346	A93	200r + 100r green	.55	.45
347	A94	300r + 150r multi	.55	.45
348	A93	400r + 200r dp rose	1.90	1.00
349	A93	500r + 250r dk bl	1.40	1.10
350	A93	600r + 300r brn vio	.95	*13.00*
351	A94	700r + 350r multi	1.75	.90
352	A96	1000r + 500r brt grn, red & yel	3.75	.55
353	A97	2000r + 1000r gray blk & red	15.00	.80
354	A98	5000r + 2500r blk & red	32.50	13.50
355	A99	10000r + 5000r brt grn & yel	80.00	24.00
		Nos. 342-355 (14)	139.65	79.10

Revolution of Oct. 3, 1930. Prepared as semi-postal stamps, Nos. 342-355 were sold as ordinary postage stamps with stated surtax ignored.

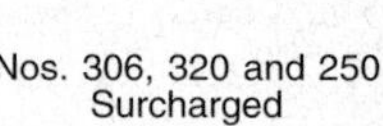

Nos. 306, 320 and 250 Surcharged

Perf. 13½x12½

1931, July 20 Wmk. 218

No.	Type	Description	Unused	Used
356	A76	200r on 300r rose red	1.75	1.25
a.		Wmk. in echelon	30.00	30.00
b.		Inverted surcharge	47.50	

Perf. 13x12½

Wmk. 221

No.	Type	Description	Unused	Used
357	A76	200r on 300r rose red	.50	.25
a.		Inverted surcharge	55.00	55.00

Perf. 13½x12½

Wmk. 100

No.	Type	Description	Unused	Used
358	A76	200r on 300r rose red	92.50	92.50

Map of South America Showing Meridian of Tordesillas — A100

Joao Ramalho and Tibiriça A101

Martim Affonso de Souza A102

King John III of Portugal A103

Disembarkation of M. A. de Souza at Sao Vicente — A104

Wmk. 222

1932, June 3 Typo. *Perf. 13*

No.	Type	Description	Unused	Used
359	A100	20r dk violet	.40	.50
360	A101	100r black	.60	.50
361	A102	200r purple	1.25	.40
362	A103	600r red brown	2.10	2.25

Engr.

Wmk. 101

Perf. 9½, 11, 9½x11

No.	Type	Description	Unused	Used
363	A104	700r ultra	3.50	2.75
		Nos. 359-363 (5)	7.85	6.40

1st colonization of Brazil at Sao Vicente, in 1532, under the hereditary captaincy of Martim Affonso de Souza.

Revolutionary Issue

Map of Brazil — A105

Soldier and Flag — A106

Allegory: Freedom, Justice, Equality A107

Soldier's Head A108

"LEX" and Sword A109

Symbolical of Law and Order — A110

Symbolical of Justice — A111

Perf. 11½

1932, Sept. Litho. Unwmk.

No.	Type	Description	Unused	Used
364	A105	100r brown org	.55	2.40
365	A106	200r dk car	.45	.85
366	A107	300r gray green	2.40	4.25
367	A108	400r dark blue	8.75	8.75
368	A105	500r blk brn	8.75	8.75
369	A107	600r red	8.75	8.75
370	A106	700r violet	4.25	*8.75*
371	A108	1000r orange	2.10	*8.75*
372	A109	2000r dark brn	17.00	*24.00*
373	A110	5000r yellow grn	21.00	*40.00*
374	A111	10000r plum	24.00	*45.00*
		Nos. 364-374 (11)	98.00	160.25

Issued by the revolutionary forces in the state of Sao Paulo during the revolt of September, 1932. Subsequently the stamps were recognized by the Federal Government and placed in general use.

Excellent counterfeits of Nos. 373 and 374 exist. Favor cancels, applied at a later date, abound.

City of Vassouras and Illuminated Memorial — A112

Wmk. 222

1933, Jan. 15 Typo. *Perf. 12*

No.	Type	Description	Unused	Used
375	A112	200r rose red	1.40	1.10

City of Vassouras founding, cent.

Nos. 306, 320 Surcharged

Perf. 13½x12½

1933, July 28 Wmk. 218

No.	Type	Description	Unused	Used
376	A76	200r on 300r rose red	1.00	1.00
a.		Wmk. 218 in echelon (No. 306a)	19.00	19.00
b.		Wmk. 100 (No. 250)	140.00	140.00

Perf. 13x12½

Wmk. 221

No.	Type	Description	Unused	Used
377	A76	200r on 300r rose red	.65	.65
a.		Inverted surcharge	42.50	
b.		Double surcharge	42.50	

Religious Symbols and Inscriptions — A113

Wmk. 222

1933, Sept. 3 Typo. *Perf. 13*

No.	Type	Description	Unused	Used
378	A113	200r dark red	1.00	.85

1st Natl. Eucharistic Congress in Brazil.

"Flag of the Race" A114

1933, Aug. 18

No.	Type	Description	Unused	Used
379	A114	200r deep red	2.00	.85

The raising of the "Flag of the Race" and the 441st anniv. of the sailing of Columbus from Palos, Spain, Aug. 3, 1492.

Republic Figure, Flags of Brazil and Argentina — A115

Wmk. 101

1933, Oct. 7 Engr. *Perf. 11½*

No.	Type	Description	Unused	Used
380	A115	200r blue	.45	.35

Thick Laid Paper

1933, Dec. Wmk. 236 *Perf. 11, 11½*

No.	Type	Description	Unused	Used
381	A115	400r green	1.50	1.25
382	A115	600r brt rose	5.00	6.75
383	A115	1000r lt violet	7.25	4.75
		Nos. 380-383 (4)	14.20	13.10

Visit of President Justo of the Argentina to Brazil, Oct. 2-7, 1933.

Allegory: "Faith and Energy" — A116

Allegory of Flight — A117

1933 Typo. Wmk. 222

No.	Type	Description	Unused	Used
384	A116	200r dark red	.30	.25
385	A116	200r dark violet	.85	.25

See Nos. 435, 471, 491.

Wmk. 236

1934, Apr. 15 Engr. *Perf. 12*

No.	Type	Description	Unused	Used
386	A117	200r blue	.80	.65

1st Natl. Aviation Congress at Sao Paulo.

A118

Wmk. 222

1934, May 12 Typo. *Perf. 11*

No.	Type	Description	Unused	Used
387	A118	200r dark olive	.40	.40
388	A118	400r carmine	2.25	2.25
389	A118	700r ultra	2.40	2.25
390	A118	1000r orange	6.00	1.00
		Nos. 387-390 (4)	11.05	5.90

7th Intl. Fair at Rio de Janeiro.

Christ of Corcovado A119

1934, Oct. 20

No.	Type	Description	Unused	Used
392	A119	300r dark red	4.25	4.25
a.		Tete beche pair	17.00	17.00
393	A119	700r ultra	17.00	17.00
a.		Tete beche pair	72.50	72.50

Visit of Eugenio Cardinal Pacelli, later Pope Pius XII, to Brazil.

The three printings of Nos. 392-393, distinguishable by shades, sell for different prices.

José de Anchieta A120

Thick Laid Paper

1934, Nov. 8 Wmk. 236 *Perf. 11, 12*

394 A120 200r yellow brown .90 .60
395 A120 300r violet .75 .40
396 A120 700r blue 3.00 3.00
397 A120 1000r lt green 6.00 1.75
Nos. 394-397 (4) 10.65 5.75

Jose de Anchieta, S.J. (1534-1597), Portuguese missionary and "father of Brazilian literature."

A121

"Brazil" and "Uruguay" — A122

Wmk. 222

1935, Jan. 8 Typo. *Perf. 11*

398 A121 200r orange 1.10 .55
399 A122 300r yellow 1.40 1.25
400 A122 700r ultra 5.00 5.00
401 A121 1000r dk violet 13.00 8.00
Nos. 398-401 (4) 20.50 14.80

Visit of President Terra of Uruguay.

View of Town of Igarassu A123

1935, July 1

402 A123 200r maroon & brn 1.60 .55
403 A123 300r vio & olive brn 1.60 .45

Captaincy of Pernambuco founding, 400th anniv.

Types of 1918-29
Thick Laid Paper
Perf. 9½, 11, 12, 12x11

1934-36 Engr. Wmk. 236

404 A72 2000r violet 12.50 .60
405 A89 5000r blue vio ('36) 17.00 1.25
406 A72 10000r claret ('36) 15.00 1.75
Nos. 404-406 (3) 44.50 3.60

No. 404 is inscribed "BRASIL CORREIO."

Revolutionist A124

Bento Gonçalves da Silva — A125

Duke of Caxias A126

Perf. 11, 12

1935, Sept. 20-1936, Jan.

407 A124 200r black 1.40 1.40
408 A124 300r rose lake 1.40 .80
409 A125 700r dull blue 4.50 6.50
410 A126 1000r light violet 5.00 4.00
Nos. 407-410 (4) 12.30 12.70

Centenary of the "Ragged" Revolution.

Federal District Coat of Arms A127

Wmk. 222

1935, Oct. 19 Typo. *Perf. 11*

411 A127 200r blue 4.00 4.00

8th Intl. Sample Fair held at Rio de Janeiro.

Coutinho's Ship — A128

Arms of Fernandes Coutinho — A129

1935, Oct. 25

412 A128 300r maroon 3.00 1.25
413 A129 700r turq blue 5.50 3.75

400th anniversary of the establishment of the first Portuguese colony at Espirito Santo by Vasco Fernandes Coutinho.

Gavea, Rock near Rio de Janeiro A130

1935, Oct. 12 Wmk. 245 *Perf. 11*

414 A130 300r brown & vio 2.75 2.00
415 A130 300r blk & turq bl 2.75 2.00
416 A130 300r Prus bl & ultra 2.75 2.00
417 A130 300r crimson & blk 2.75 2.00
Nos. 414-417 (4) 11.00 8.00

"Child's Day," Oct. 12.

Viscount of Cairu — A131

Perf. 11, 12x11

1936, Jan. 20 Engr. Wmk. 236

418 A131 1200r violet 10.00 6.00

Jose da Silva Lisboa, Viscount of Cairu (1756-1835).

View of Cametá A132

1936, Feb. 26 *Perf. 11, 12*

419 A132 200r brown orange 1.75 1.40
420 A132 300r green 1.75 1.00

300th anniversary of the founding of the city of Cameta, Dec. 24, 1635.

Coining Press A133

Thick Laid Paper

1936, Mar. 24 *Perf. 11*

421 A133 300r pur brn, *cr* 1.25 1.25

1st Numismatic Cong. at Sao Paulo, Mar., 1936.

Carlos Gomes — A134

"Il Guarany" — A135

Thick Laid Paper

1936, July 11 *Perf. 11, 11x12*

422 A134 300r dull rose 1.00 .70
423 A134 300r black brown 1.00 .70
424 A135 700r ocher 3.25 2.00
425 A135 700r blue 3.75 2.75
Nos. 422-425 (4) 9.00 6.15

Birth cent. of Antonio Carlos Gomes, who composed the opera "Il Guarany."

Scales of Justice — A136

Wmk. 222

1936, July 4 Typo. *Perf. 11*

426 A136 300r rose 2.00 .65

First National Judicial Congress.

Federal District Coat of Arms A137

1936, Nov. 13 Typo. Wmk. 249

427 A137 200r rose red 1.25 .65

Ninth International Sample Fair held at Rio de Janeiro.

Eucharistic Congress Seal — A138

1936, Dec. 17 Wmk. 245 *Perf. 11½*

428 A138 300r grn, yel, bl & blk 1.25 .60

2nd Natl. Eucharistic Congress in Brazil.

Botafogo Bay A139

Thick Laid Paper
Wmk. 236

1937, Jan. 2 Engr. *Perf. 11*

429 A139 700r blue 1.60 .80
430 A139 700r black 1.60 .80

Birth cent. of Francisco Pereira Passos, engineer who planned the modern city of Rio de Janeiro.

Types of 1920-22, 1933
Perf. 11, 11½ and Compound

1936-37 Typo. Wmk. 249

431 A75 10r deep brown .25 .25
432 A75 20r dull violet .25 .25
433 A75 50r blue green .25 .25
434 A75 100r orange .50 .25
435 A116 200r dk violet 1.50 .25
436 A76 300r olive green .50 .25
437 A76 400r ultra 1.25 .25
438 A76 500r lt brown 1.75 .25
439 A76 600r brn org ('37) 9.00 .25
440 A76 700r deep violet 7.00 .25
441 A76 1000r turq blue 7.75 .25
Nos. 431-441 (11) 30.00 2.75

Massed Flags and Star of Esperanto A140

1937, Jan. 19

442 A140 300r green 1.75 .90

Ninth Brazilian Esperanto Congress.

Bay of Rio de Janeiro A141

1937, June 9 Unwmk. *Perf. 12½*

443 A141 300r orange red & blk 1.00 .75
444 A141 700r blue & dk brn 2.50 .75

2nd South American Radio Communication Conf. held in Rio, June 7-19.

Globe — A142

Perf. 11, 12

1937, Sept. 4 Wmk. 249

445 A142 300r green 1.50 .65

50th anniversary of Esperanto.

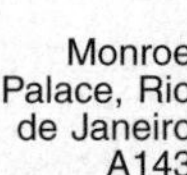

Monroe Palace, Rio de Janeiro A143

Botanical Garden, Rio de Janeiro — A144

1937, Sept. 30 Unwmk. *Perf. 12½*

446 A143 200r lt brn & bl 1.00 .50
447 A144 300r org & ol grn 1.00 .50
448 A143 2000r grn & cerise 13.00 13.00
449 A144 10000r lake & indigo 70.00 60.00
Nos. 446-449 (4) 85.00 74.00

Brig. Gen. Jose da Silva Paes — A145

1937, Oct. 11 Wmk. 249 *Perf. 11½*

450 A145 300r blue 1.00 .50

Bicentenary of Rio Grande do Sul.

Eagle and Shield — A146

1937, Dec. 2 Typo. *Perf. 11*

451 A146 400r dark blue 2.75 .60

150th anniversary of the US Constitution.

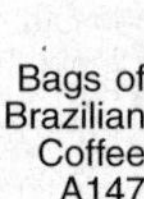

Bags of Brazilian Coffee A147

Frame Engraved, Center Typographed

1938, Jan. 17 Unwmk. *Perf. 12½*

452 A147 1200r multicolored 6.25 .50

Arms of Olinda A148

Perf. 11, 11x11½

1938, Jan. 24 Engr. Wmk. 249

453 A148 400r violet .80 .35

4th cent. of the founding of the city of Olinda.

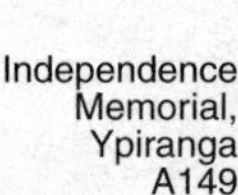

Independence Memorial, Ypiranga A149

1938, Jan. 24 Typo. *Perf. 11*

454 A149 400r brown olive 1.00 .50

Proclamation of Brazil's independence by Dom Pedro, Sept. 7, 1822.

Iguaçu Falls — A150

Perf. 12½

1938, Jan. 10 Unwmk. Engr.

455 A150 1000r sepia & yel brn 3.00 1.75
456 A150 5000r ol blk & grn 27.50 22.50

Couto de Magalhaes A151

Perf. 11, 11x11½

1938, Mar. 17 Wmk. 249

457 A151 400r dull green .80 .40

General Couto de Magalhaes (1837-1898), statesman, soldier, explorer, writer, developer.

Types of 1918-38

Perf. 11, 12x11, 12x11½, 12

1938 Engr. Wmk. 249

458 A72 2000r blue violet 12.00 .30
459 A89 5000r violet blue 45.00 .50
a. 5000r deep blue 37.50 .50
460 A72 10000r rose lake 55.00 1.50
Nos. 458-460 (3) 112.00 2.30

No. 458 is inscribed "BRASIL CORREIO."

Types of 1920-22

1938 Wmk. 245 Typo. *Perf. 11*

461 A75 50r blue green 1.40 1.10
462 A75 100r orange 3.25 1.10
463 A76 300r olive green 1.40 3.00
463A A76 400r ultra 225.00 150.00
463B A76 500r red brown 1.40 *60.00*
Nos. 461-463B (5) 232.45 215.20

National Archives Building A152

1938, May 20 Wmk. 249

464 A152 400r brown .75 .40

Centenary of National Archives.

Souvenir Sheets

Sir Rowland Hill — A153

1938, Oct. 22 *Imperf.*

465 A153 Sheet of 10 20.00 20.00
a. 400r dull green, single stamp 1.25 1.25

Brazilian Intl. Philatelic Exposition (Brapex).

Issued in sheets measuring 106x118mm. A few perforated sheets exist.

President Vargas — A154

1938, Nov. 10 *Perf. 11*

Without Gum

466 A154 Sheet of 10 27.50 27.50
a. 400r slate blue, single stamp 1.75 1.75

Constitution of Brazil, set up by President Vargas, Nov. 10, 1937. Size: 113x135½mm.

Types of 1920-33

1939 Typo. Wmk. 256 *Perf. 11*

467 A75 10r red brown 1.00 1.00
468 A75 20r dull violet 2.00 .30
469 A75 50r blue green 1.50 .30
470 A75 100r yellow org 1.50 .30
471 A116 200r dk violet 3.00 .30
472 A76 400r ultra 3.00 .30
473 A76 600r dull orange 4.50 .30
474 A76 1000r turq blue 20.00 .30
Nos. 467-474 (8) 36.50 3.10

View of Rio de Janeiro — A155

1939, June 14 Engr. Wmk. 249

475 A155 1200r dull violet 2.25 .25

View of Santos — A156

1939, Aug. 23

476 A156 400r dull blue .50 .40

Centenary of founding of Santos.

Chalice Vine and Blossoms — A157

1939, Aug. 23

477 A157 400r green 1.60 .35

1st South American Botanical Congress held in January, 1938.

Eucharistic Congress Seal — A158

1939, Sept. 3

478 A158 400r rose red .60 .45

Third National Eucharistic Congress.

Duke of Caxias, Army Patron — A159

1939, Sept. 12 Photo. *Rouletted*

479 A159 400r deep ultra .60 .45

Issued for Soldiers' Day.

A159a

A159b

A159c

A159d

Designs: 400r, George Washington. 800r, Emperor Pedro II. 1200r, Grover Cleveland. 1600r, Statue of Friendship, given by US.

Unwmk.

1939, Oct. 7 Engr. *Perf. 12*

480 A159a 400r yellow orange .70 .30
481 A159b 800r dark green .35 .25
482 A159c 1200r rose car .70 .25
483 A159d 1600r dark blue .70 .30
Nos. 480-483 (4) 2.45 1.10

New York World's Fair.

Benjamin Constant
A160

Fonseca on Horseback
A162

Manuel Deodoro da Fonseca and President Vargas
A161

Wmk. 249

1939, Nov. 15 Photo. *Rouletted*

484	A160	400r deep green	.85	.50
485	A161	1200r chocolate	1.10	.50

Engr. *Perf. 11*

486	A162	800r gray black	.65	.50
		Nos. 484-486 (3)	2.60	1.50

Proclamation of the Republic, 50th anniv.

President Roosevelt, President Vargas and Map of the Americas
A163

1940, Apr. 14

487	A163	400r slate blue	1.00	.55

Pan American Union, 50th anniversary.

Types of 1920-33

1940-41 Typo. Wmk. 264 *Perf. 11*

488	A75	10r red brown	.80	.80
489	A75	20r dull violet	.80	.80
489A	A75	50r blue grn ('41)	1.50	*1.75*
490	A75	100r yellow org	2.50	.50
491	A116	200r violet	7.50	.50
492	A76	400r ultra	7.50	.25
493	A76	600r dull orange	10.00	.50
494	A76	1000r turq blue	22.50	.50
		Nos. 488-494 (8)	53.10	*5.60*

Map of Brazil — A164

1940, Sept. 7 Engr.

495	A164	400r carmine	.50	.50
a.		Unwmkd.	50.00	30.00

9th Brazilian Congress of Geography held at Florianopolis.

Victoria Regia Water Lily — A165

President Vargas — A166

Relief Map of Brazil — A167

1940, Oct. 30 Wmk. 249 *Perf. 11*
Without Gum

496	A165	1000r dull violet	1.40	1.75
a.		Sheet of 10	14.50	*35.00*
497	A166	5000r red	10.00	10.00
a.		Sheet of 10	125.00	*175.00*
498	A167	10,000r slate blue	15.00	7.50
a.		Sheet of 10	160.00	*175.00*
		Nos. 496-498 (3)	26.40	19.25

New York World's Fair.

All three sheets exist unwatermarked and also with papermaker's watermark of large globe and "AMERICA BANK" in sheet. A few imperforate sheets also exist.

Joaquim Machado de Assis — A168

Pioneers and Buildings of Porto Alegre — A169

1940, Nov. 1

499	A168	400r black	.65	.25

Birth centenary of Joaquim Maria Machado de Assis, poet and novelist.

1940, Nov. 2 Wmk. 264

500	A169	400r green	.60	.30

Colonization of Porto Alegre, bicent.

Proclamation of King John IV of Portugal — A173

1940, Dec. 1 Wmk. 249

501	A173	1200r blue black	2.50	.50

800th anniv. of Portuguese independence and 300th anniv. of the restoration of the monarchy.

No. 501 was also printed on paper with papermaker's watermark of large globe and "AMERICA BANK." Unwatermarked copies are from these sheets. Value of unwatermarked stamps, $150.

Brazilian Flags and Head of Liberty — A175

Wmk. 256

1940, Dec. 18 Engr. *Perf. 11*

502	A175	400r dull violet	.70	.25
b.		Unwmkd.	22.50	22.50

Wmk. 245

502A	A175	400r dull violet	75.00	50.00

10th anniv. of the inauguration of President Vargas.

Calendar Sheet and Inscription "Day of the Fifth General Census of Brazil" — A176

Wmk. 256

1941, Jan. 14 Typo. *Perf. 11*

503	A176	400r blue & red	.40	.25

Wmk. 245

504	A176	400r blue & red	3.00	1.00

Fifth general census of Brazil.

King Alfonso Henriques
A177

Father Antonio Vieira
A178

Salvador Corrêia de Sa e Benevides — A179

President Carmona of Portugal and President Vargas
A180

Wmk. 264

1940-41 Photo. *Rouletted*

504A	A177	200r pink	.25	.25
505	A178	400r ultra	.25	.25
506	A179	800r brt violet	.40	.25
506A	A180	5400r slate grn	2.75	.70

Wmk. 249

507	A177	200r pink	8.50	3.25
507A	A178	400r ultra	40.00	25.00
508	A180	5400r slate grn	8.50	4.25
		Nos. 504A-508 (7)	60.65	33.95

Portuguese Independence, 800th anniv.

For surcharge & overprint see nos. C45, C47.

Jose de Anchieta
A181

Amador Bueno
A182

Wmk. 264

1941, Aug. 1 Engr. *Perf. 11*

509	A181	1000r gray violet	4.00	.80

Society of Jesus, 400th anniversary.

1941, Oct. 20 *Perf. 11½*

510	A182	400r black	1.00	.40

300th anniv. of the acclamation of Amador Bueno (1572-1648) as king of Sao Paulo.

Air Force Emblem
A183

1941, Oct. 20 *Perf. 11*

511	A183	5400r slate green	5.00	2.50

Issued in connection with Aviation Week, as propaganda for the Brazilian Air Force.

Petroleum
A184

Agriculture
A185

Steel Industry
A186

Commerce
A187

Marshal Peixoto
A188

Count of Porto Alegre
A189

Admiral J. A. C. Maurity
A190

"Armed Forces"
A191

Vargas — A192

1941-42 Wmk. 264 Typo. *Perf. 11*

512	A184	10r yellow brn	.50	.40
513	A184	20r olive grn	.50	.40
514	A184	50r olive bis	.50	.40
515	A184	100r blue grn	.90	.40
516	A185	200r brown org	1.60	.40
517	A185	300r lilac rose	.50	.40
518	A185	400r grnsh blue	3.00	.40
519	A185	500r salmon	.50	.40
520	A186	600r violet	1.50	.40
521	A186	700r brt rose	.50	.40
522	A186	1000r gray	3.00	.40
523	A186	1200r dl blue	5.50	.40
524	A187	2000r gray vio	4.50	.40

Engr.

525	A188	5000r blue	9.25	1.75
526	A189	10,000r rose red	16.00	.50
527	A190	20,000r dp brown	15.00	1.25
528	A191	50,000r red ('42)	47.50	11.00
529	A192	100,000r blue ('42)	1.00	*12.00*
		Nos. 512-529 (18)	111.75	31.70

Nos. 512 to 527 and later issues come on thick or thin paper. The stamps on both papers also exist with three vertical green lines printed on the back, a control mark.

See Nos. 541-587, 592-593, 656-670.

Bernardino de Campos
A193

Prudente de Morais
A194

1942, May 25

533 A193 1000r red 2.00 .80
534 A194 1200r blue 6.00 .60

100th anniversary of the birth of Bernardino de Campos and Prudente de Morais, lawyers and statesmen of Brazil.

Head of Indo-Brazilian Bull — A195

1942, May 1 Wmk. 264 ***Perf. 11½***

535 A195 200r blue .75 .40
536 A195 400r orange brn .75 .40
a. Wmk. 267 75.00 75.00

2nd Agriculture and Livestock Show of Central Brazil held at Uberaba.

Outline of Brazil and Torch of Knowledge
A196

Map of Brazil Showing Goiania
A197

Wmk. 264

1942, July 5 Typo. ***Perf. 11***

537 A196 400r orange brn .65 .40

8th Brazilian Congress of Education.

1942, July 5

538 A197 400r lt violet .65 .45

Founding of Goiania city.

Seal of Congress
A198

1942, Sept. 20 Wmk. 264

539 A198 400r olive bister 1.00 .30
a. Wmk. 267 45.00 45.00

4th Natl. Eucharistic Cong. at Sao Paulo.

Types of 1941-42

1942-47 Wmk. 245 ***Perf. 11***

541 A184 20r olive green .50 *1.40*
542 A184 50r olive bister .50 .40
543 A184 100r blue grn 3.00 2.50
544 A185 200r brown org 1.50 .50
545 A185 400r grnsh blue 1.50 .40
546 A186 600r lt violet 4.50 .40
547 A186 700r brt rose .60 *1.25*
548 A186 1200r dl blue 5.00 .40
549 A187 2000r gray vio ('47) 15.00 .40

Engr.

550 A188 5000r blue 25.00 .40
551 A189 10,000r rose red 15.00 .50
552 A190 20,000r dp brn ('47) 12.50 1.40
553 A192 100,000r blue 15.00 15.00
Nos. 541-553 (13) 99.60 24.95

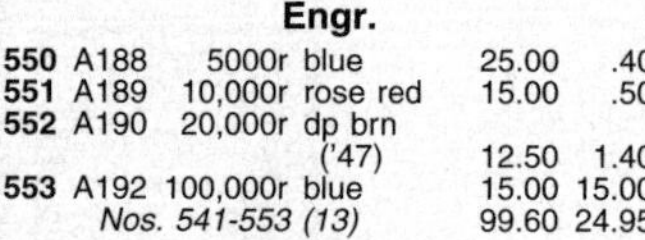

Types of 1941-42

1941-47 Typo. Wmk. 268 ***Perf. 11***

554 A184 20r olive grn 1.00 .45
555 A184 50r ol bis ('47) 1.00 .45
556 A184 100r bl grn ('43) 1.00 .45
557 A185 200r brn org ('43) 1.00 .45
558 A185 300r lilac rose ('43) 1.00 .45
559 A185 400r grnsh bl ('42) 1.00 .45
560 A185 500r sal ('43) 1.00 .45
561 A186 600r violet 1.00 .45
562 A186 700r brt rose ('45) 1.00 *5.50*
563 A186 1000r gray 3.75 .45
564 A186 1200r dp bl ('44) 4.00 .45
565 A187 2000r gray vio ('43) 10.00 .45

Engr.

566 A188 5000r blue ('43) 12.50 .45
567 A189 10,000r rose red ('43) 15.00 .45
568 A190 20,000r dp brn ('42) 27.50 .90
569 A191 50,000r red ('42) 30.00 4.00
a. 50,000r dark brown red ('47) 22.50 15.00
570 A192 100,000r blue 1.40 *5.50*
Nos. 554-570 (17) 113.15 21.75

Types of 1941-42

1942-47 Typo. Wmk. 267

573 A184 20r ol grn ('43) .60 .45
574 A184 50r ol bis ('43) .60 .45
575 A184 100r bl grn ('43) .60 .45
576 A185 200r brn org ('43) 1.50 .45
577 A185 400r grnsh blue .60 .45
578 A185 500r sal ('43) 125.00 45.00
579 A186 600r violet ('43) 45.00 4.50
580 A186 700r brt rose ('47) .90 *45.00*
581 A186 1000r gray ('44) 4.00 .40
582 A186 1200r dl bl 4.00 .40
583 A187 2000r gray vio 7.50 .40

Engr.

584 A188 5000r blue 7.50 .40
585 A189 10,000r rose red ('44) 15.00 2.00
586 A190 20,000r dp brn ('45) 16.00 .90
587 A191 50,000r red ('43) 60.00 10.00
Nos. 573-587 (15) 288.80 111.25

1942 Typo. Wmk. 249

592 A184 100r bl grn 10.00 *20.00*
593 A186 600r violet 4.00 4.50

Map Showing Amazon River — A199

1943, Mar. 19 Wmk. 267 ***Perf. 11***

607 A199 40c orange brown .60 .50

Discovery of the Amazon River, 400th anniv.

Reproduction of Brazil Stamp of 1866 — A200

1943, Mar. 28 Wmk. 267

608 A200 40c violet .85 .45
a. Wmk. 268 *1,200.*

Centenary of city of Petropolis.

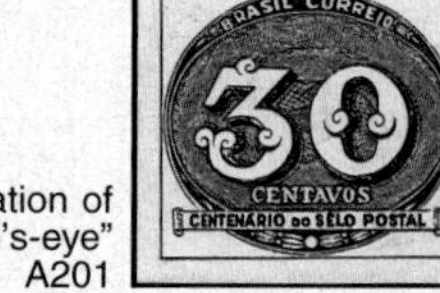

Adaptation of 1843 "Bull's-eye"
A201

1943, Aug. 1 Engr. ***Imperf.***

609 A201 30c black .70 .40
610 A201 60c black .85 .40
611 A201 90c black .70 .40
Nos. 609-611 (3) 2.25 1.20

Cent. of the 1st postage stamp of Brazil. The 30c and 90c exist unwatermarked; values $25 and $65.

Souvenir Sheet

A202

Wmk. 281 Horizontally or Vertically

1943 Engr. ***Imperf.***

Without Gum

612 A202 Sheet of 3 26.00 26.00
a. 30c black 6.75 6.75
b. 60c black 6.75 6.75
c. 90c black 6.75 6.75

Ubaldino do Amaral — A203

"Justice" — A204

Perf. 11, 12

1943, Aug. 27 Typo. Wmk. 264

613 A203 40c dull slate green .75 .30
a. Wmk. 267 50.00 20.00

Birth centenary of Ubaldino do Amaral, banker and statesman.

1943, Aug. 30 Wmk. 267

614 A204 2cr bright rose 1.75 1.75

Centenary of Institute of Brazilian Lawyers.

Indo-Brazilian Bull — A205

1943, Aug. 30 Engr.

615 A205 40c dk red brn 1.00 .55

9th Livestock Show at Bahia.

José Barbosa Rodrigues — A206

1943, Nov. 13 Typo.

616 A206 40c bluish grn 1.25 .30

Birth cent. of Jose Barbosa Rodrigues, botanist.

Charity Hospital, Santos
A207

1943, Nov. 7 Engr.

617 A207 1cr blue .80 .45

400th anniv. of Charity Hospital, Santos.

Pedro Americo de Figueiredo e Melo (1843-1905), Artist-hero and Statesman — A208

Wmk. 267

1943, Dec. 16 Typo. ***Perf. 11***

618 A208 40c brown orange .75 .30

Gen. A. E. Gomes Carneiro
A209

1944, Feb. 9 Engr.

619 A209 1.20cr rose 1.25 .45

50th anniversary of the Lapa siege.

Statue of Baron of Rio Branco — A210

1944, May 13 Typo.

620 A210 1cr blue .75 .30

Statue of the Baron of Rio Branco unveiling.

Duke of Caxias
A211

1944, May 13 Unwmk. ***Perf. 12***

Granite Paper

621 A211 1.20cr bl grn & pale org 3.00 .40

Centenary of pacification of Sao Paulo and Minas Gerais in an independence movement in 1842.

YMCA Seal — A212

1944, June 7 Litho. *Perf. 11*
Granite Paper

622 A212 40c dp bl, car & yel .50 .25

Centenary of Young Men's Christian Assn.

Chamber of Commerce Rio Grande — A213

Wmk. 268

1944, Sept. 25 Engr. *Perf. 12*

623 A213 40c lt yellow brn 1.10 .25

Centenary of the Chamber of Commerce of Rio Grande.

Martim F. R. de Andrada A214

1945, Jan. 30 *Perf. 11*

624 A214 40c blue .50 .25

Centenary of the death of Martim F. R. de Andrada, statesman.

Meeting of Duke of Caxias and David Canabarro A215

1945, Mar. 19 Photo.

625 A215 40c ultra .50 .25

Pacification of Rio Grande do Sul, cent.

Globe and "Esperanto" — A216

1945, Apr. 16

626 A216 40c lt blue grn .65 .40

10th Esperanto Congress, Rio, Apr. 14-22.

Baron of Rio Branco's Bookplate A217

1945, Apr. 20 Wmk. 268 *Perf. 11*

627 A217 40c violet 1.00 .30

Cent. of the birth of Jose Maria da Silva Paranhos, Baron of Rio Branco.

Tranquility A218

Glory — A219

Victory A220

Peace A221

Cooperation — A222

Rouletted 7

1945, May 8 Engr. Wmk. 268

628	A218	20c dk rose vio	.25	.25
629	A219	40c dk carmine	.25	.25
630	A220	1cr dull orange	.80	.45
631	A221	2cr steel blue	.95	.65
632	A222	5cr green	3.50	.60
		Nos. 628-632 (5)	5.75	2.20

Victory of the Allied Nations in Europe.

Nos. 628-632 exist on thin card, imperf. and unwatermarked.

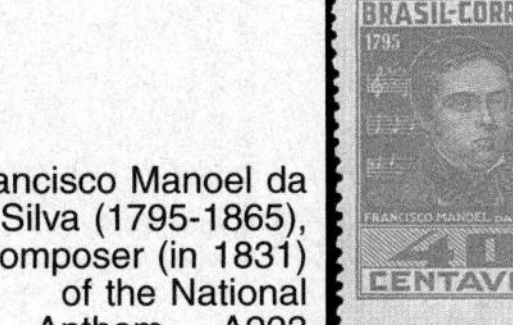

Francisco Manoel da Silva (1795-1865), Composer (in 1831) of the National Anthem — A223

Wmk. 245

1945, May 30 Typo. *Perf. 12*

633 A223 40c brt rose .65 .35
a. Wmk. 268 15.00 15.00

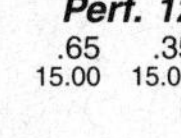

Bahia Institute of Geography and History A224

1945, May 30 Wmk. 268 *Perf. 11*

634 A224 40c lt ultra .75 .25

50th anniv. of the founding of the Institute of Geography and History at Bahia.

Emblems of 5th Army and B.E.F.
A225 A226

U.S. Flag and Shoulder Patches A227

Brazilian Flag and Shoulder Patches A228

Victory Symbol and Shoulder Patches — A229

1945, July 18 Litho.

635	A225	20c multicolored	.35	.30
636	A226	40c multicolored	.35	.30
637	A227	1cr multicolored	1.50	.50
638	A228	2cr multicolored	2.25	.70
639	A229	5cr multicolored	3.75	.80
		Nos. 635-639 (5)	8.20	2.60

Honoring the Brazilian Expeditionary Force and the US 5th Army Battle against the Axis in Italy.

Radio Tower and Map — A230

1945, Sept. 3 Engr.

640 A230 1.20cr gray .60 .25

Third Inter-American Conference on Radio Communications.

No. 640 was reproduced on a souvenir card with blue background and inscriptions. Size: 145x161mm.

A 40c lilac stamp, picturing the International Bridge between Argentina and Brazil and portraits of Presidents Justo and Vargas, was prepared late in 1945. It was not issued, but later was sold, without postal value, to collectors. Value, 60 cents.

Admiral Luiz Felipe Saldanha da Gama (1846-1895) — A231

1946, Apr. 7

641 A231 40c gray black .50 .50

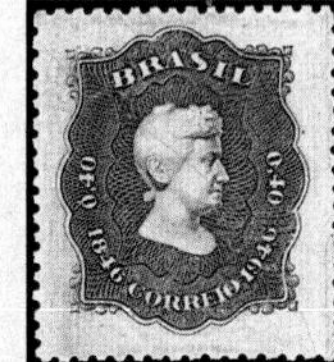

Princess Isabel d'Orleans-Braganca Birth Cent. — A232

1946, July 29 Unwmk.

642 A232 40c black .50 .50

Post Horn, V and Envelope — A233

Post Office, Rio de Janeiro A234

Bay of Rio de Janeiro and Plane A235

Wmk. 268

1946, Sept. 2 Litho. *Perf. 11*

643 A233 40c blk & pale org .25 .25

Perf. 12½

Engr. Unwmk.

Center in Ultramarine

644	A234	2cr slate	.65	.25
645	A234	5cr orange brn	3.25	1.25
646	A234	10cr dk violet	3.75	.60

Center in Brown Orange

647	A235	1.30cr dk green	.40	.40
648	A235	1.70cr car rose	.40	.40
649	A235	2.20cr dp ultra	.65	.50
		Nos. 643-649 (7)	9.35	3.65

5th Postal Union Congress of the Americas and Spain.

No. 643 was reproduced on a souvenir card. Size: 188x239mm. Sold for 10cr.

Liberty — A236

Perf. 11x11½

1946, Sept. 18 Wmk. 268

650 A236 40c blk & gray .35 .25
a. Unwmkd. 150.00

Adoption of the Constitution of 1946.

Columbus Lighthouse, Dominican Republic — A237

1946, Sept. 14 Litho. *Perf. 11*

651 A237 5cr Prus grn 12.00 2.75

Orchid — A238

1946, Nov. 8 Wmk. 268

652 A238 40c ultra, red & yel .60 .30
a. Unwmkd. 55.00

4th National Exhibition of Orchids, Rio de Janeiro, November, 1946.

Gen. A. E. Gomes Carneiro — A239

Perf. 10½x12

1946, Dec. 6 Engr. Unwmk.

653 A239 40c deep green .30 .25

Centenary of the birth of Gen. Antonio Ernesto Gomes Carneiro.

Brazilian Academy of Letters A240

1946, Dec. 14 *Perf. 11*

654 A240 40c blue .40 .25

50th anniv. of the foundation of the Brazilian Academy of Letters, Rio de Janeiro.

Antonio de Castro Alves (1847-1871), Poet — A241

1947, Mar. 14 Litho. Wmk. 267

655 A241 40c bluish green .25 .25

Types of 1941-42, Values in Centavos or Cruzeiros

1947-54 Wmk. 267 Typo. *Perf. 11*

656	A184	2c olive	.25	.25
657	A184	5c yellow brn	.25	.25
658	A184	10c green	.25	.25
659	A185	20c brown org	.25	.25
660	A185	30c dk lil rose	.60	.25
661	A185	40c blue	.30	.25
b.		Wmk. 268	1,250.	150.00
661A	A185	50c salmon	.60	.25
662	A186	60c lt violet	1.00	.25
663	A186	70c brt rose ('54)	.40	.25
664	A186	1cr gray	1.00	.25
665	A186	1.20cr dull blue	2.50	.25
a.		Wmk. 268	11.00	9.00
666	A187	2cr gray violet	5.00	.25
		Engr.		
667	A188	5cr blue	12.00	.25
668	A189	10cr rose red	10.00	.25
		Perf. 11, 13		
669	A190	20cr deep brn	25.00	.75
670	A191	50cr red	50.00	.50
		Nos. 656-670 (16)	109.40	4.75

The 5, 20, 50cr also exist with perf. 12-13.

Pres. Gonzalez Videla of Chile A242

1947, June 26 Unwmk. *Perf. 12x11*

671 A242 40c dk brown orange .30 .25

Visit of President Gabriel Gonzalez Videla of Chile, June 1947.

A souvenir folder contains four impressions of No. 671, and measures 6½x8¼ inches.

"Peace" and Western Hemisphere A243

1947, Aug. 15 *Perf. 11x12*

672 A243 1.20cr blue .35 .25

Inter-American Defense Conference at Rio de Janeiro, August-September, 1947.

Pres. Harry S. Truman, Map and Statue of Liberty A244

1947, Sept. 1 Typo. *Perf. 12x11*

673 A244 40c ultra .35 .25

Visit of US President Harry S Truman to Brazil, Sept. 1947.

Pres. Eurico Gaspar Dutra — A245

Wmk. 268

1947, Sept. 7 Engr. *Perf. 11*

674	A245	20c green	.30	.25
675	A245	40c rose carmine	.30	.25
676	A245	1.20cr deep blue	.35	.25
		Nos. 674-676 (3)	.95	.75

The souvenir sheet containing Nos. 674-676 is listed as No. C73A. See No. 679.

Mother and Child — A246

1947, Oct. 10 Typo. Unwmk.

677 A246 40c brt ultra .35 .25

Issued to mark Child Care Week, 1947.

Arms of Belo Horizonte — A247

1947, Dec. 12 Engr. Wmk. 267

678 A247 1.20cr rose carmine .35 .25

50th anniversary of the founding of the city of Belo Horizonte.

Dutra Type of 1947

1948 Engr. Wmk. 267

679 A245 20c green 3.75 3.75

Catalogue values for unused stamps in this section, from this point to the end of the section, are for Never Hinged items.

Globe — A248

1948, July 10 Litho.

680 A248 40c dl grn & pale lil .65 .30

International Exposition of Industry and Commerce, Petropolis, 1948.

Arms of Paranagua A249

1948, July 29

681 A249 5cr bister brown 5.00 .80

300th anniversary of the founding of the city of Paranagua, July 29, 1648.

Child Reading Book — A250

1948, Aug. 1

682 A250 40c green .45 .25

National Education Campaign.

No. 682 was reproduced on a souvenir card. Size: 124x157mm.

Tiradentes A251

Symbolical of Cancer Eradication A252

1948, Nov. 12

683 A251 40c brown orange .45 .25

200th anniversary of the birth of Joaquim José da Silva Xavier (Tiradentes).

1948, Dec. 14

684 A252 40c claret .50 .25

Anti-cancer publicity.

Adult Student A253

1949, Jan. 3 Wmk. 267 *Perf. 12x11*

685 A253 60c red vio & pink .60 .25

Campaign for adult education.

"Battle of Guararapes," by Vitor Meireles — A254

1949, Feb. 15 *Perf. 11½x12*

686 A254 60c lt blue 1.75 .70

2nd Battle of Guararapes, 300th anniv.

Church of Sao Francisco de Paula — A255

Manuel de Nobrega — A256

Perf. 11x12

1949, Mar. 8 Unwmk. Engr.

687 A255 60c dark brown .60 .25
a. Souvenir sheet 62.50 30.00

Bicentenary of city of Ouro Fino, state of Minas Gerais.

No. 687a contains one imperf. stamp similar to No. 687, with dates in lower margin. Size: 70x89mm.

1949, Mar. 29 *Imperf.*

688 A256 60c violet .60 .30

Founding of the City of Salvador, 400th anniv.

Emblem of Brazilian Air Force and Plane A257

1949, June 18
689 A257 60c blue violet .60 .25

Issued to honor the Brazilian Air Force.

Star and Angel — A258

1949 Wmk. 267 Litho. *Perf. 11x12*
690 A258 60c pink .55 .25

1st Ecclesiastical Cong., Salvador, Bahia.

Globe A259

1949, Oct. 31 Typo. *Perf. 12x11*
691 A259 1.50cr blue .75 .25

75th anniv. of the UPU.

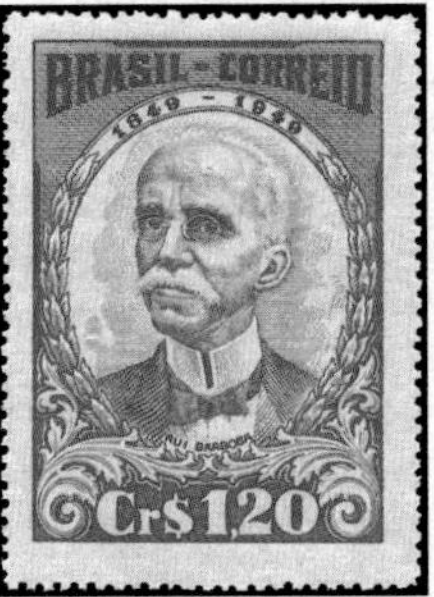
Ruy Barbosa A260

Unwmk.
1949, Dec. 14 Engr. *Perf. 12*
692 A260 1.20cr rose carmine 1.00 .30

Centenary of birth of Ruy Barbosa.

Joaquim Cardinal Arcoverde A. Cavalcanti, Birth Centenary — A261

Perf. 11x12
1950, Feb. 27 Litho. Wmk. 267
693 A261 60c rose .65 .25

Grapes and Factory A262

1950, Mar. 15 *Perf. 12x11*
694 A262 60c rose lake .55 .25

75th anniversary of Italian immigration to the state of Rio Grande do Sul.

Virgin of the Globe — A263

1950, May 31 *Perf. 11x12*
695 A263 60c blk & lt bl .50 .25

Establishment in Brazil of the Daughters of Charity of St. Vincent de Paul, cent.

Globe and Soccer Players — A264

1950, June 24
696 A264 60c ultra, bl & gray 1.50 .60

4th World Soccer Championship.

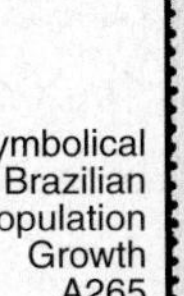
Symbolical of Brazilian Population Growth A265

1950, July 10 Typo. *Perf. 12x11*
697 A265 60c rose lake .55 .25

Issued to publicize the 6th Brazilian census.

Dr. Oswaldo Cruz — A266

1950, Aug. 23 Litho. *Perf. 11x12*
698 A266 60c orange brown .65 .25

5th International Congress of Microbiology.

View of Blumenau and Itajai River A267

Perf. 12x11
1950, Sept. 9 Wmk. 267
699 A267 60c bright pink .65 .25

Centenary of the founding of Blumenau.

Amazonas Theater, Manaus A268

1950, Sept. 27
700 A268 60c light brn red .45 .25

Centenary of Amazonas Province.

Arms of Juiz de Fora — A269

1950, Oct. 24 *Perf. 11x12*
701 A269 60c carmine .60 .30

Centenary of the founding of Juiz de Fora.

Post Office at Recife A270

1951, Jan. 10 Typo. *Perf. 12x11*
702 A270 60c carmine .35 .25
703 A270 1.20cr carmine .55 .25

Opening of the new building of the Pernambuco Post Office.

Arms of Joinville — A271

1951, Mar. 9 *Perf. 11x12*
704 A271 60c orange brown 1.10 .25

Centenary of the founding of Joinville.

Jean-Baptiste de La Salle — A272

1951, Apr. 30 Litho.
705 A272 60c blue .60 .25

Birth of Jean-Baptiste de La Salle, 300th anniv.

Heart and Flowers — A273

1951, May 13 Engr.
706 A273 60c deep plum .70 .25

Mother's Day, May 14, 1951.

Sylvio Romero — A274

1951, Apr. 21 Litho.
707 A274 60c dl vio brn .45 .25

Romero (1851-1914), poet and author.

Joao Caetano, Stage and Masks A275

1951, July 9 *Perf. 12x11*
708 A275 60c lt gray bl .45 .25

1st Brazilian Theater Cong., Rio, July 9-13, 1951.

Orville A. Derby — A276

1951, July 23 *Perf. 11x12*
709 A276 2cr slate .70 .35

Centenary of the birth (in New York State) of Orville A. Derby, geologist.

First Mass Celebrated in Brazil — A277

1951, July 25
710 A277 60c dl brn & buff .45 .25

4th Inter-American Congress on Catholic Education, Rio de Janeiro, 1951.

Euclides Pinto Martins A278

1951, Aug. 16 ***Perf. 12x11***

711 A278 3.80cr brn & citron 3.50 .55

1st flight from NYC to Rio, 29th anniv.

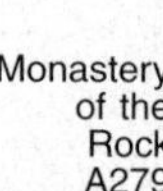

Monastery of the Rock A279

1951, Sept. 8

712 A279 60c dl brn & cream .50 .25

Founding of Vitoria, 4th centenary.

Santos-Dumont and Model Plane Contest — A280

Dirigible and Eiffel Tower — A281

Perf. 11x12

1951, Oct. 19 **Wmk. 267** **Litho.**

713 A280 60c salmon & dk brn .85 .35

Unwmk. **Engr.**

714 A281 3.80cr dark purple 2.75 .40

Week of the Wing and 50th anniv. of Santos-Dumont's flight around the Eiffel Tower.

In December 1951, Nos. 713 and 714 were privately overprinted: "Exposicao Filatelica Regional Distrito Federal 15-XII-1951 23-XII-1951." These were attached to souvenir sheets bearing engraved facsimiles of Nos. 38, 49 and 51, which were sold by Clube Filatelico do Brasil to mark its 20th anniversary. The overprinted stamps on the sheets were canceled, but 530 "unused" sets were sold by the club.

Farmers and Ear of Wheat — A282

1951, Nov. 10 **Litho.** **Wmk. 267**

715 A282 60c dp grn & gray .60 .30

Festival of Grain at Bage, 1951.

Map and Open Bible A283

1951, Dec. 9 ***Perf. 12x11***

716 A283 1.20cr brn org .90 .40

Issued to publicize the Day of the Bible.

Queen Isabella — A284

Henrique Oswald — A285

1952, Mar. 10 ***Perf. 11x12***

717 A284 3.80cr lt bl 1.10 .35

500th anniversary of the birth of Queen Isabella I of Spain.

1952, Apr. 22

718 A285 60c brown .45 .25

Oswald (1852-1931), composer.

Vicente Licinio Cardoso — A286

1952, May 2

719 A286 60c gray blue .55 .25

4th Brazilian Homeopathic Congress.

Map and Symbol of Labor — A287

1952, Apr. 30

720 A287 1.50cr brnsh pink .45 .25

5th International Labor Organization Conference for American Countries.

Gen. Polidoro da Fonseca — A288

Portraits: 5cr, Baron de Capanema. 10cr, Minister Eusebio de Queiros.

Unwmk.

1952, May 11 **Engr.** ***Perf. 11***

721	A288 2.40cr lt car		.60	.25
722	A288 5cr blue		4.00	.30
723	A288 10cr dk bl grn		4.00	.30
	Nos. 721-723 (3)		8.60	.85

Centenary of telegraph in Brazil.

Luiz de Albuquerque M. P. Caceres — A289

Perf. 11x12

1952, June 8 **Litho.** **Wmk. 267**

724 A289 1.20cr vio bl .45 .25

200th anniversary of the founding of the city of Mato Grosso.

Symbolizing the Glory of Sports — A290

1952, July 21 ***Perf. 12x11***

725 A290 1.20cr dp bl & bl 1.10 .45

Fluminense Soccer Club, 50th anniversary.

José Antonio Saraiva — A291

1952, Aug. 16 ***Perf. 11x12***

726 A291 60c lil rose .50 .25

Centenary of the founding of Terezina, capital of Piaui State.

Emperor Dom Pedro — A292

1952, Sept. 3 **Wmk. 267**

727 A292 60c lt bl & blk .50 .25

Issued for Stamp Day and the 2nd Philatelic Exhibition of Sao Paulo.

Flag-encircled Globe — A293

1952, Oct. 24 ***Perf. 13½***

728 A293 3.80cr blue 1.75 .60

Issued to publicize United Nations Day.

View of Sao Paulo, Sun and Compasses — A294

1952, Nov. 8 **Litho.** ***Perf. 12x11***

729 A294 60c dl bl, yel & gray grn .50 .25

City Planning Day.

Father Diogo Antonio Feijo — A295

1952, Nov. 9 ***Perf. 11x12***

730 A295 60c Fawn .55 .25

Rodolpho Bernardelli and His "Christ and the Adultress" A297

1952, Dec. 18 ***Perf. 12x11***

732 A297 60c gray blue .50 .25

Bernardelli, sculptor and painter, birth cent.

Map of Western Hemisphere and View of Rio de Janeiro — A298

1952, Sept. 20

733 A298 3.80cr vio brn & lt grn 1.50 .35

2nd Congress of American Industrial Medicine, Rio de Janeiro, 1952.

Arms and Head of Pioneer A299

Coffee, Cotton and Sugar Cane — A300

Designs: 2.80cr, Jesuit monk planting tree. 3.80cr, 5.80cr, Spiral, symbolizing progress.

1953, Jan. 25 **Litho.** ***Perf. 11***

734	A299	1.20cr ol brn & blk brn	2.00	.35
735	A300	2cr olive grn & yel	3.25	.35
736	A300	2.80cr red brn & dp org	2.25	.35
737	A300	3.80cr dk brn & yel grn	1.90	.25
738	A300	5.80cr int bl & yel grn	1.40	.25
		Nos. 734-738 (5)	10.80	1.55

400th anniversary of Sao Paulo.

Used copies of No. 734 exist with design inverted.

Ledger and Winged Cap A301

1953, Feb. 22 ***Perf. 12x11***

739 A301 1.20cr dl brn & fawn .45 .25

6th Brazilian Accounting Congress.

Joao Ramalho — A302

Wmk. 264

1953, Apr. 8 **Engr.** ***Perf. 11½***

740 A302 60c blue .40 .25

Founding of the city of Santo Andre, 4th cent.

Aarao Reis and Plan of Belo Horizonte A303

1953, May 6 **Photo.**

741 A303 1.20cr red brn .40 .25

Aarao Leal de Carvalho Reis (1853-1936), civil engineer.

A304

1953, May 16

742 A304 1.50cr Almirante Saldanha .60 .30

4th globe-circling voyage of the training ship Almirante Saldanha.

A305

Joaquim Jose Rodrigues Torres, Viscount of Itaborai.

1953, July 5 **Photo.**

743 A305 1.20cr violet .40 .25

Centenary of the Bank of Brazil.

Lamp and Rio-Petropolis Highway — A306

1953, July 14

744 A306 1.20cr gray .45 .25

10th Intl. Congress of Nursing, Petropolis, 1953.

Bay of Rio de Janeiro A307

1953, July 15

745 A307 3.80cr dk bl grn .65 .25

Issued to publicize the fourth World Congress of Baptist Youth, July 1953.

Arms of Jau and Map A308

1953, Aug. 15 **Engr.**

746 A308 1.20cr purple .45 .25

Centenary of the city of Jau.

Ministry of Health and Education Building, Rio — A309

1953, Aug. 1

747 A309 1.20cr dp grn .45 .25

Day of the Stamp and the first Philatelic Exhibition of National Education.

Maria Quiteria de Jesus Medeiros — A310

1953, Aug. 21 **Photo.**

748 A310 60c vio bl .30 .25

Centenary of the death of Maria Quiteria de Jesus Medeiros (1792-1848), independence heroine.

Pres. Odria of Peru — A311

1953, Aug. 25

749 A311 1.40cr rose brn .40 .25

Issued to publicize the visit of Gen. Manuel A. Odria, President of Peru, Aug. 25, 1953.

Duke of Caxias Leading his Troops — A312

Designs: 1.20cr, Caxias' tomb. 1.70cr, 5.80cr, Portrait of Caxias. 3.80cr, Arms of Caxias.

Engr. (60c, 5.80cr); Photo.

1953, Aug. 25

750 A312	60c dp grn	.40	.25
751 A312	1.20cr dp claret	.50	.25
752 A312	1.70cr slate grn	.50	.25
753 A312	3.80cr rose brn	1.40	.25
754 A312	5.80cr gray vio	.90	.25
	Nos. 750-754 (5)	3.70	1.25

150th anniversary of the birth of Luis Alves de Lima e Silva, Duke of Caxias.

Quill Pen, Map and Tree — A313

1953, Sept. 12 **Photo.**

755 A313 60c ultra .45 .25

5th National Congress of Journalism.

Horacio Hora — A314

1953, Sept. 17 **Litho.** **Wmk. 267**

756 A314 60c org & dp plum .40 .25

Horacio Pinto de Hora (1853-1890), painter.

Pres. Somoza of Nicaragua — A315

1953, Sept. 24 **Photo.** **Wmk. 264**

757 A315 1.40cr dk vio brn .40 .25

Issued to publicize the visit of Gen. Anastasio Somoza, president of Nicaragua.

Auguste de Saint-Hilaire A316

1953, Sept. 30

758 A316 1.20cr dk brn car .60 .30

Centenary of the death of Auguste de Saint-Hilaire, explorer and botanist.

Jose Carlos do Patrocinio — A317

1953, Oct. 9 **Photo.**

759 A317 60c dk slate gray .40 .25

Jose Carlos do Patrocinio, (1853-1905), journalist and abolitionist.

Clock Tower, Crato — A318

1953, Oct. 17

760 A318 60c blue green .40 .25

Centenary of the city of Crato.

Joao Capistrano de Abreu — A319

1953, Oct. 23

761 A319	60c dull blue	.25	.25
762 A319	5cr purple	2.10	.30

Joao Capistrano de Abreu (1853-1927), historian.

Allegory: "Justice" — A320

1953, Nov. 17

763 A320	60c indigo	.45	.25
764 A320	1.20cr dp magenta	.45	.25

50th anniv. of the Treaty of Petropolis.

Farm Worker in Wheat Field — A321

1953, Nov. 29 **Photo.** ***Perf. 11½***

766 A321 60c dk green .45 .25

3rd Natl. Wheat Festival, Erechim, 1953.

Teacher and Pupils — A322

1953, Dec. 14
767 A322 60c red .45 .25

First National Conference of Primary School Teachers, Salvador, 1953.

Zacarias de Gois e Vasconsellos A323

Design: 5cr, Porters with trays of coffee beans.

1953-54 **Photo.**
768 A323 2cr org brn & blk, *buff* ('54) 1.75 .40
a. White paper 3.00 .40
769 A323 5cr dp org & blk 1.75 .40

Centenary of the state of Parana.

Alexandre de Gusmao — A324

1954, Jan. 13
770 A324 1.20cr brn vio .45 .25

Gusmao (1695-1753), statesman, diplomat and writer.

Symbolical of Sao Paulo's Growth — A325

Arms and View of Sao Paulo A326

Designs: 2cr, Priest, settler and Indian. 2.80cr, José de Anchieta.

1954, Jan. 25 ***Perf. 11½x11***
771 A325 1.20cr dk vio brn 1.00 .50
a. Buff paper 4.00 1.00

Engr.

772 A325 2cr lilac rose 1.50 .60
773 A325 2.80cr pur gray 1.75 1.00

Perf. 11x11½

774 A326 3.80cr dl grn 2.00 .50
a. Buff paper 4.00 2.00
775 A326 5.80cr dl red 2.25 .60
a. Buff paper 10.00 .75
Nos. 771-775 (5) 8.50 3.20

400th anniversary of Sao Paulo.

J. Fernandes Vieira, A. Vidal de Negreiros, A. F. Camarao and H. Dias — A327

Perf. 11x11½

1954, Feb. 18 **Photo.** **Unwmk.**
776 A327 1.20cr ultra .50 .25

300th anniversary of the recovery of Pernambuco from the Dutch.

Sao Paulo and Minerva A328

1954, Feb. 24
777 A328 1.50cr dp plum .55 .30

10th International Congress of Scientific Organizations, Sao Paulo, 1954.

Stylized Grapes, Jug and Map A329

Monument of the Immigrants A330

1954, Feb. 27 **Photo.** ***Perf. 11½x11***
778 A329 40c dp claret .50 .25

Grape Festival, Rio Grande do Sul.

1954, Feb. 28
779 A330 60c dp vio bl .45 .25

Unveiling of the Monument to the Immigrants of Caxias do Sul.

First Brazilian Locomotive — A331

Perf. 11x11½

1954, Apr. 30 **Unwmk.**
781 A331 40c carmine .80 .25

Centenary of the first railroad engine built in Brazil.

Pres. Chamoun of Lebanon — A332

1954, May 12 **Photo.** ***Perf. 11½x11***
782 A332 1.50cr maroon .50 .30

Visit of Pres. Camille Chamoun of Lebanon.

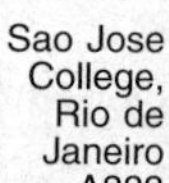

Sao Jose College, Rio de Janeiro A333

J. B. Champagnat Marcelin — A334

Apolonia Pinto — A335

1954, June 6 ***Perf. 11x11½, 11½x11***
783 A333 60c purple .30 .25
784 A334 120cr vio blue .30 .25

50th anniversary of the founding of the Marist Brothers in Brazil.

1954, June 21 **Photo.**
785 A335 1.20cr bright green .40 .25

Apolonia Pinto (1854-1937), actress.

Adm. Margues Tamandare — A336

Portraits: 2c, 5c, 10c, Admiral Margues Tamandare. 20c, 30c, 40c, Oswaldo Cruz. 50c, 60c, 90c, Joaquim Murtinho. 1cr, 1.50cr, 2cr, Duke of Caxias. 5cr, 10cr, Ruy Barbosa. 20cr, 50cr, Jose Bonifacio.

1954-60 **Wmk. 267** ***Perf. 11x11½***
786 A336 2c vio blue .30 .25
787 A336 5c org red .30 .25
788 A336 10c brt green .30 .25
789 A336 20c magenta .30 .25
790 A336 30c dk gray grn .50 .25
791 A336 40c rose red 1.00 .25
792 A336 50c violet 1.00 .25
793 A336 60c gray grn .35 .25
794 A336 90c orange ('55) .70 .25
795 A336 1cr brown .60 .25
796 A336 1.50cr blue .30 .25
a. Wmk. 264 75.00 30.00
797 A336 2cr dk bl grn ('56) 2.75 .25
798 A336 5cr rose lil ('56) 7.50 .25
799 A336 10cr lt grn ('60) 3.75 .25
800 A336 20cr crim rose ('59) 2.50 .25
801 A336 50cr ultra ('59) 9.50 .25
Nos. 786-801 (16) 31.65 4.00

See Nos. 890, 930-933.

Boy Scout Waving Flag (Statue) — A337

Baltasar Fernandes, Explorer — A338

1954, Aug. 2 **Unwmk.** ***Perf. 11½x11***
802 A337 1.20cr vio bl .80 .25

Intl. Boy Scout Encampment, Sao Paulo.

1954, Aug. 15
803 A338 60c dk red .45 .30

300th anniversary of city of Sorocaba.

Adeodato Giovanni Cardinal Piazza — A339

Our Lady of Aparecida, Map of Brazil — A340

1954, Sept. 2
804 A339 4.20cr red org 1.00 .35

Visit of Adeodato Cardinal Piazza, papal legate to Brazil.

1954

Design: 1.20cr, Virgin standing on globe.

805 A340 60c claret .55 .35
806 A340 1.20cr vio bl .40 .35

No. 805 was issued for the 1st Cong. of Brazil's Patron Saint (Our Lady of Aparecida); No. 806, the cent. of the proclamation of the dogma of the Immaculate Conception. Both stamps also for the Marian Year.

Issue dates: 60c, Sept. 6; 1.20cr, Sept. 8.

Benjamin Constant and Hand Reading Braille A341

1954, Sept. 27 **Photo.** **Unwmk.**
807 A341 60c dk grn .45 .25

Centenary of the founding of the Benjamin Constant Institute.

River Battle of Riachuelo — A342

Admiral F. M. Barroso A343

Dr. Christian F. S. Hahnemann A344

1954, Oct. 6 ***Perf. 11x11½, 11½x11***
808 A342 40c redsh brown .40 .25
809 A343 60c purple .30 .25

Admiral Francisco Manoel Barroso da Silva (1804-82).

1954, Oct. 8 ***Perf. 11½x11***
810 A344 2.70cr dk green .75 .35

1st World Cong. of Homeopathic Medicine.

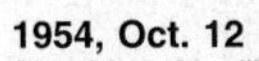

Nizia Floresta — A345

Ears of Wheat — A346

1954, Oct. 12

811 A345 60c lilac rose .45 .25

Reburial of the remains of Nizia Floresta (Dio Nizia Pinto Lisboa), writer and educator.

1954, Oct. 22

812 A346 60c olive green .50 .30

4th National Wheat Festival, Carazinho.

Basketball Player and Ball-Globe A347

Allegory of the Spring Games A348

1954, Oct. 23 **Photo.**

813 A347 1.40cr orange red .85 .35

Issued to publicize the second World Basketball Championship Matches, 1954.

Perf. 11½x11

1954, Nov. 6 **Wmk. 267**

814 A348 60c red brown .55 .25

Issued to publicize the 6th Spring Games.

San Francisco Hydroelectric Plant — A349

1955, Jan. 15 ***Perf. 11x11½***

815 A349 60c brown org .40 .25

Issued to publicize the inauguration of the San Francisco Hydroelectric Plant.

Itutinga Hydroelectric Plant — A350

1955, Feb. 3

816 A350 40c blue .40 .25

Issued to publicize the inauguration of the Itutinga Hydroelectric Plant at Lavras.

Rotary Emblem and Bay of Rio de Janeiro — A351

1955, Feb. 23 ***Perf. 12x11½***

817 A351 2.70cr slate gray & blk 1.60 .35

Rotary International, 50th anniversary.

Fausto Cardoso Palace A352

1955, Mar. 17 ***Perf. 11x11½***

818 A352 40c henna brown .40 .40

Centenary of Aracaju.

Aviation Symbols A353

1955, Mar. 13 **Photo.** ***Perf. 11½***

819 A353 60c dark gray green .45 .25

Issued to publicize the third National Aviation Congress at Sao Paulo, Mar. 6-13.

Arms of Botucatu A354

1955, Apr. 14

820 A354 60c orange brn .30 .25

821 A354 1.20cr brt green .40 .25

Centenary of Botucatu.

Young Racers at Starting Line A355

Perf. 11½

1955, Apr. 30 **Photo.** **Unwmk.**

823 A355 60c orange brn .50 .25

5th Children's Games.

Marshal Hermes da Fonseca — A356

Congress Altar, Sail and Sugarloaf Mountain — A357

1955, May 12 **Wmk. 267**

824 A356 60c purple .40 .25

Marshal Hermes da Fonseca, birth cent.

Engraved; Photogravure (2.70cr)

1955, July 17 **Unwmk.** ***Perf. 11½***

Designs: 2.70cr, St. Pascoal. 4.20cr, Aloisi Benedetto Cardinal Masella.

Granite Paper

825 A357 1.40cr green .35 .25

826 A357 2.70cr deep claret .40 .25

827 A357 4.20cr blue .90 .30

Nos. 825-827 (3) 1.65 .80

36th World Eucharistic Cong. in Rio de Janeiro.

Girl Gymnasts A358

1955, Nov. 12 **Engr.**

Granite Paper

828 A358 60c rose lilac .40 .25

Issued to publicize the 7th Spring Games.

José B. Monteiro Lobato, Author A359

1955, Dec. 8 **Granite Paper**

829 A359 40c dark green .40 .25

Adolfo Lutz — A360

Lt. Col. Vilagran Cabrita — A361

1955, Dec. 18 **Granite Paper**

830 A360 60c dk green .40 .25

Centenary of the birth of Adolfo Lutz, public health pioneer.

1955, Dec. 22 **Photo.** **Wmk. 267**

831 A361 60c violet blue .40 .25

First Battalion of Engineers, cent.

Salto Grande Hydroelectric Dam A362

1956, Jan. 15 **Unwmk.** ***Perf. 11½***

Granite Paper

832 A362 60c brick red .40 .25

Arms of Mococa — A363

Wmk. 256

1956, Apr. 17 **Photo.** ***Perf. 11½***

833 A363 60c brick red .40 .25

Centenary of Mococa, Sao Paulo.

"G" and Globe — A364

1956, Apr. 14 **Unwmk.**

Granite Paper

834 A364 1.20cr violet blue .75 .25

18th Intl. Geographic Cong., Rio, Aug. 1956.

Girls' Foot Race A365

1956, Apr. 28 **Photo.**

Granite Paper

835 A365 2.50cr brt blue .55 .25

6th Children's Games.

Plane over Map of Brazil — A366

1956, June 12 **Wmk. 267** ***Perf. 11½***

836 A366 3.30cr brt vio bl .70 .25

National Airmail Service, 25th anniv.

Fireman Rescuing Child A367

1956, July 2 **Wmk. 264**

837 A367 2.50cr crimson 1.00 .35

a. Buff paper 3.25 3.00

Centenary of the Fire Brigade.

Map of Brazil and Open Book A368

1956, Sept. 8 **Wmk. 267**

838 A368 2.50cr brt vio bl .45 .25

50th anniversary of the arrival of the Marist Brothers in Northern Brazil.

Church and Monument, Franca — A369

1956, Sept. 7 **Engr.**

839 A369 2.50cr dk blue .45 .25

Centenary of city of Franca, Sao Paulo.

Woman Hurdler A370

1956, Sept. 22 Photo. Unwmk.

Granite Paper

840 A370 2.50cr dk car .80 .30

Issued to publicize the 8th Spring Games.

Forest and Map of Brazil — A371

1956, Sept. 30 Wmk. 267 *Perf. 11½*

841 A371 2.50cr dk green .50 .25

Issued to publicize education in forestry.

Baron da Bocaina A372

1956, Oct. 8 Engr. Wmk. 268

842 A372 2.50cr reddish brown .45 .30

Centenary of the birth of Baron da Bocaina, who introduced the special delivery mail system to Brazil.

Marbleized Paper

Paper with a distinct wavy-line or marbleized watermark (which Brazilians call *marmorizado* paper) has been found on many stamps of Brazil, 1956-68, including Nos. 843-845, 847, 851-854, 858-858A, 864, 878, 880, 882, 884, 886-887, 896, 909, 918, 920-921, 925-928, 936-939, 949, 955-958, 960, 962-964, 978-979, 983, 985-987, 997-998, 1002-1003, 1005, 1009-1012, 1017, 1024, 1026, 1055, 1075, 1078, 1082, C82, C82a, C83-C87, C96, C99, C109.

Quantities are much less than those of stamps on regular paper.

Panama Stamp Showing Pres. Juscelino Kubitschek A373

1956, Oct. 12 Photo. Wmk. 267

843 A373 3.30cr green & blk .80 .30

Issued on America Day, Oct. 12, to commemorate the meeting of the Presidents and the Pan-American Conference at Panama City, July 21-22.

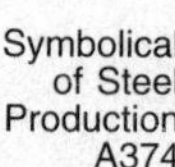

Symbolical of Steel Production A374

Wmk. 267

1957, Jan. 31 Photo. *Perf. 11½*

844 A374 2.50cr chocolate .60 .25

2nd expansion of the National Steel Company at Volta Redonda.

Joaquim E. Gomes da Silva — A375

1957, Mar. 1 Photo. Unwmk.

Granite Paper

845 A375 2.50cr dk bl grn .50 .25

Centenary of the birth (in 1856) of Joaquim E. Gomes da Silva.

Allan Kardec A376

Wmk. 268

1957, Apr. 18 Engr. *Perf. 11½*

846 A376 2.50cr dk brown .50 .25

Issued in honor of Allan Kardec, pen name of Leon Hippolyto Denizard Rivail, and for the centenary of the publication of his "Codification of Spiritism."

Boy Gymnast A377

1957, Apr. 27 Photo. Unwmk.

Granite Paper

847 A377 2.50cr lake .70 .25

7th Children's Games.

Pres. Craveiro Lopes — A378

1957, June 7 Engr. Wmk. 267

848 A378 6.50cr blue .80 .25

Visit of Gen. Francisco Higino Craveiro Lopes, President of Portugal.

Stamp of 1932 — A379

1957, July 9 Photo.

849 A379 2.50cr rose .50 .25

25th anniv. of the movement for a constitution.

St. Antonio Monastery, Pernambuco — A380

1957, Aug. 24 Engr. Wmk. 267

850 A380 2.50cr deep magenta .40 .25

300th anniv. of the emancipation of the Franciscan province of St. Antonio in Pernambuco State.

Volleyball — A381

1957, Sept. 28 Photo. *Perf. 11½*

851 A381 2.50cr dull org red .95 .30

Issued for the 9th Spring Games.

Basketball — A382

1957, Oct. 12

852 A382 3.30cr org & brt grn 1.10 .30

2nd Women's International Basketball Championship, Rio de Janeiro.

Count of Pinhal and Sao Carlos A383

1957, Nov. 4 Wmk. 267 *Perf. 11½*

853 A383 2.50cr rose .60 .30

Centenary of the city of Sao Carlos and honoring the Count of Pinhal, its founder.

Auguste Comte — A384

1957, Nov. 15

854 A384 2.50cr dk red brn .50 .25

Centenary of the death of Auguste Comte, French mathematician and philosopher.

Radio Station A385

1957, Dec. 10 Wmk. 268

855 A385 2.50cr dk green .50 .25

Opening of Sarapui Central Radio Station.

Admiral Tamandare and Warship A386

Design: 3.30cr, Aircraft carrier.

1957-58 Photo.

856 A386 2.50cr light blue .55 .25

Engr.

857 A386 3.30cr green ('58) .75 .25

150th anniversary of the birth of Admiral Joaquin Marques de Tamandare, founder of the Brazilian navy.

Coffee Plant and Symbolic "R" — A387

Wmk. 267

1957-58 Photo. *Perf. 11½*

858 A387 2.50cr magenta .60 .40

Unwmk.

Granite Paper

858A A387 2.50cr magenta ('58) .55 .40

Centenary (in 1956) of the city of Ribeirao Preto in Sao Paulo state.

Dom John VI — A388

1958, Jan. 28 Engr. Wmk. 268

859 A388 2.50cr magenta .55 .25

150th anniversary of the opening of the ports of Brazil to foreign trade.

Bugler A389

1958, Mar. 18 Wmk. 267

860 A389 2.50cr red .65 .40

Brazilian Marine Corps, 150th anniv.

Station at Rio and Locomotive of 1858 — A390

Wmk. 267

1958, Mar. 29 Photo. *Perf. 11½*
861 A390 2.50cr red brn .80 .35

Central Railroad of Brazil, cent.

Court House — A391

1958, Apr. 1 Engr. Wmk. 256
862 A391 2.50cr green .45 .25

150th anniv. of the Military Superior Court.

Emblem and Brazilian Pavilion A392

1958, Apr. 17 Wmk. 267
863 A392 2.50cr dk blue .55 .35

World's Fair, Brussels, Apr. 17-Oct. 19.

High Jump — A393

1958, Apr. 20 Photo. Unwmk.
Granite Paper
864 A393 2.50cr crimson rose .55 .30

8th Children's Games.

Marshal Mariano da Silva Rondon A394

1958, Apr. 19 Engr. Wmk. 267
865 A394 2.50cr magenta .50 .25

Issued to honor Marshal Mariano da Silva Rondon and the "Day of the Indian."

Hydroelectric Station — A395

1958, Apr. 28 Wmk. 267 *Perf. 11½*
866 A395 2.50cr magenta .50 .25

Opening of Sao Paulo State power plant.

National Printing Plant A396

1958, May 22 Photo.
867 A396 2.50cr redsh brn .50 .25

150th anniversary of the founding of the National Printing Plant.

Marshal Osorio — A397

1958, May 24
868 A397 2.50cr brt violet .50 .25

150th anniversary of the birth of Marshal Manoel Luiz Osorio.

Pres. Ramon Villeda Morales — A398

1958, June 7 Engr. *Perf. 11½*
869 A398 6.50cr dk green 3.25 1.00
a. Wmk. 268 15.00 3.00

Visit of Pres. Ramon Villeda Morales of Honduras.

Fountain — A399

1958, June 13
870 A399 2.50cr dk green .50 .25

Botanical Garden, Rio de Janeiro, 150th anniv.

Symbols of Agriculture A400

1958, June 18 Photo.
871 A400 2.50cr rose carmine .50 .25

50th anniv. of Japanese immigration to Brazil.

Prophet Joel — A401

1958, June 21 Engr.
872 A401 2.50cr dk blue .50 .25

Bicentenary of the Cathedral of Bom Jesus at Matosinhos.

Stylized Globe A402

1958, July 10 Photo.
873 A402 2.50cr dk brown .50 .25

Intl. Investment Conference, Belo Horizonte.

Julio Bueno Brandao — A403

1958, Aug. 1 Wmk. 268 *Perf. 11½*
874 A403 2.50cr red brown .50 .25

Centenary of the birth of Julio Bueno Brandao, President of Minas Gerais.

Palacio Tiradentes (House of Congress) A404

1958, July 24 Engr.
875 A404 2.50cr sepia .50 .25

47th Interparliamentary Conference, Rio de Janeiro, July 24-Aug. 1.

Presidential Palace, Brasilia — A405

1958, Aug. 8 Photo. Wmk. 267
876 A405 2.50cr ultra .45 .25

Issued to publicize the construction of Brazil's new capital, Brasilia.

Freighters A406

1958, Aug. 22
877 A406 2.50cr blue .60 .25

Brazilian merchant marine.

Joaquim Caetano da Silva A407

1958, Sept. 2 Unwmk.
Granite Paper
878 A407 2.50cr redsh brn .50 .25

Joaquim Caetano da Silva, scientist & historian.

Giovanni Gronchi — A408

1958, Sept. 4 Engr. Wmk. 268
879 A408 7cr dk blue .80 .25

Visit of Italy's President Giovanni Gronchi to Brazil.

Archers — A409

Perf. 11½
1958, Sept. 21 Photo. Unwmk.
Granite Paper
880 A409 2.50cr red org .55 .25

Issued to publicize the 10th Spring Games.

Elderly Couple — A410

1958, Sept. 27 Wmk. 267
881 A410 2.50cr magenta .50 .25

Day of the Old People, Sept. 27.

Machado de Assis — A411

1958, Sept. 28 Unwmk.
882 A411 2.50cr red brn .45 .25

50th anniversary of the death of Joaquim Maria Machado de Assis, writer.

Pres. Vargas and Oil Derrick
A412

1958, Oct. 6 **Wmk. 268**
883 A412 2.50cr blue .75 .25

5th anniv. of Pres. Getulio D. Vargas' oil law.

Globe — A413

Wmk. 267
1958, Nov. 14 **Photo.** ***Perf. 11½***
884 A413 2.50cr blue .50 .25

7th Inter-American Congress of Municipalities.

Gen. Lauro Sodré — A414

1958, Nov. 15 **Engr.**
885 A414 3.30cr green .50 .25

Cent. of the birth of Gen. Lauro Sodré.

UN Emblem — A415

1958, Dec. 26 **Photo.** ***Perf. 11½***
886 A415 2.50cr brt blue .50 .25

10th anniv. of the signing of the Universal Declaration of Human Rights.

Soccer Player — A416

1959, Jan. 20
887 A416 3.30cr emer & red brn .75 .30

World Soccer Championships of 1958.

Railroad Track and Map — A417

1959, Apr. **Wmk. 267** ***Perf. 11½***
888 A417 2.50cr dp orange .80 .25

Centenary of the linking of Patos and Campina Grande by railroad.

Pres. Sukarno of Indonesia — A418

1959, May 20
889 A418 2.50cr blue .50 .25

Visit of President Sukarno of Indonesia.

Dom John VI — A419

Boy Polo Players — A420

Perf. 10½x11½
1959, June 12 **Wmk. 267**
890 A419 2.50cr crimson .60 .25

1959, June 13 ***Perf. 11½***
891 A420 2.50cr orange brn .55 .25

9th Children's Games.

Loading Freighter — A421

1959, July 10
892 A421 2.50cr dk green .50 .25

Honoring the merchant marine.

Organ and Emblem — A422

1959, July 16 **Photo.**
893 A422 3.30cr magenta .50 .25

Bicentenary of the Carmelite Order in Brazil.

Joachim Silverio de Souza — A423

1959, July 20 ***Perf. 11½***
894 A423 2.50cr red brown .50 .25

Birth centenary of Joachim Silverio de Souza, first bishop of Diamantina, Minas Gerais.

Symbolic Road — A424

1959, Sept. 27 **Wmk. 267**
895 A424 3.30cr bl grn & ultra .50 .25

11th International Roadbuilding Congress.

Woman Athlete — A425

1959, Oct. 4
896 A425 2.50cr lilac rose .50 .25

11th Spring Games.

Map of Parana A426

1959, Sept. 27
897 A426 2.50cr dk green .50 .25

Founding of Londrina, Parana, 25th anniv.

Globe and Snipes — A427

1959, Oct. 22 ***Perf. 11½***
898 A427 6.50cr dull grn .50 .25

World Championship of Snipe Class Sailboats, Porto Alegre, won by Brazilian yachtsmen.

Cross of Lusitania — A428

1959, Oct. 24 **Engr.**
899 A428 6.50cr dull blue .50 .25

4th Intl. Conf. on Brazilian-Portuguese Studies, University of Bahia, Aug. 10-20.

Factory Entrance and Order of Southern Cross — A429

1959, Nov. 19 **Photo.**
900 A429 3.30cr orange red .50 .25

Pres. Vargas Gunpowder Factory, 50th anniv.

Corcovado Christ, Globe and Southern Cross — A430

1959, Nov. 26 ***Perf. 11½***
901 A430 2.50cr blue .50 .25

Universal Thanksgiving Day.

Burning Bush A431

1959, Dec. 24 **Wmk. 267**
902 A431 3.30cr lt grn .50 .25

Centenary of Presbyterian work in Brazil.

Piraja da Silva and Schistosoma Mansoni — A432

1959, Dec. 28
903 A432 2.50cr rose violet .80 .25

25th anniv. of the discovery and identification of schistosoma mansoni, a parasite of the fluke family, by Dr. Piraja da Silva.

Luiz de Matos A433

1960, Jan. 3 **Photo.**
904 A433 3.30cr red brown .50 .25

Birth centenary of Luiz de Matos.

Zamenhof — A434

1960, Mar. 10 **Wmk. 267** ***Perf. 11½***
905 A434 6.50cr emerald .75 .25

Lazarus Ludwig Zamenhof (1859-1917), Polish oculist who invented Esperanto in 1887.

Adél Pinto — A435

1960, Mar. 19 **Engr.** **Wmk. 268**
906 A435 11.50cr rose red .50 .25

Centenary of the birth of Adél Pinto, civil engineer and railroad expert.

Presidential Palace, Colonnade — A436

Design: 27cr, Plan of Brasilia (like No. C98).

Perf. 11x11½

1960 **Photo.** **Wmk. 267**
907 A436 2.50cr brt green .45 .25

Size: 105x46½mm

908 A436 27cr salmon 1.75 1.00
Nos. 907-908,C95-C98 (6) 3.70 2.25

No. 907 for the inauguration of Brazil's new capital, Brasilia, Apr. 21, 1960.
No. 908 for the birthday of Pres. Juscelino Kubitschek and has a 27cr in design of No. C98, flanked by the chief design features of Nos. 907, C95-C97, with Kubitschek signature below. Issued in sheets of 4 with wide horizontal gutter.
Issued: 2.50cr, 4/21; 27cr, 9/12.

Grain, Coffee, Cotton and Cacao — A437

Paulo de Frontin — A438

Perf. 11½x11

1960, July 28 **Wmk. 267**
909 A437 2.50cr brown .50 .25

Centenary of Ministry of Agriculture.

1960, Oct. 12 **Wmk. 268**
910 A438 2.50cr orange red .50 .25

Cent. of the birth of Paulo de Frontin, engineer.

Woman Athlete Holding Torch — A439

1960, Oct. 18 ***Perf. 11½x11***
911 A439 2.50cr blue grn .50 .25

12th Spring Games.

Volleyball and Net — A440

Locomotive Wheels — A441

Perf. 11½x11

1960, Nov. 12 **Wmk. 268**
912 A440 11cr blue .50 .25

International Volleyball Championships.

1960, Oct. 15 ***Perf. 11½x11***
913 A441 2.50cr ultra 1.00 .35

10th Pan-American Railroad Congress.

Symbols of Flight A442

1960, Dec. 16 **Photo.** ***Perf. 11½***
914 A442 2.50cr brn & yel .50 .25

Intl. Fair of Industry and Commerce, Rio.

Emperor Haile Selassie — A443

1961, Jan. 31 ***Perf. 11½x11***
915 A443 2.50cr dk brown .50 .25

Visit of Emperor Haile Selassie of Ethiopia to Brazil, Dec. 1960.

Map of Brazil, Open Book and Sacred Heart Emblem A444

Perf. 11x11½

1961, Mar. 13 **Wmk. 268**
916 A444 2.50cr blue .50 .25

50th anniv. of the operation in Brazil of the Order of the Blessed Heart of Mary.

Map of Guanabara — A445

1961, Mar. 27 **Wmk. 267**
917 A445 7.50cr org brn .50 .25

Promulgation of the constitution of the state of Guanabara.

Arms of Agulhas Negras — A446

Brazil and Senegal Linked on Map — A447

Design: 3.30cr, Dress helmet and sword.

Perf. 11½x11

1961, Apr. 23 **Wmk. 267**
918 A446 2.50cr green .35 .25
919 A446 3.30cr rose car .35 .25

Sesquicentennial of the Agulhas Negras Military Academy.

1961, Apr. 28 **Photo.**
920 A447 27cr ultra .55 .25

Visit of Afonso Arinos, Brazilian foreign minister, to Senegal to attend its independence ceremonies.

View of Ouro Preto, 1711 A448

1961, June 6 ***Perf. 11x11½***
921 A448 1cr orange .50 .25

250th anniversary of Ouro Preto.

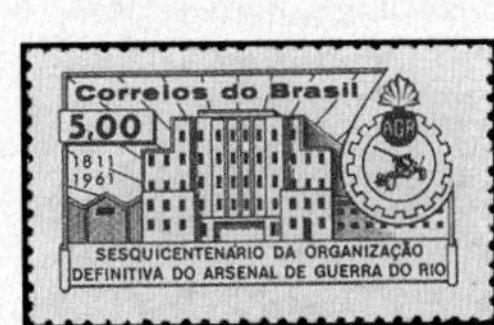

War Arsenal A449

1961, June 20 **Wmk. 256**
924 A449 5cr dk red brn .50 .25

War Arsenal, Rio de Janeiro, 150th anniv.

Coffee Bean and Branch — A450

Rabindranath Tagore — A451

Perf. 11½x11

1961, June 26 **Wmk. 267**
925 A450 20cr redsh brn 1.60 .25

8th Directorial Committee meeting of the Intl. Coffee Convention, Rio, June 26.

1961, July 28 **Photo.** **Wmk. 267**
926 A451 10cr rose car .50 .25

Rabindranath Tagore, Indian poet, birth cent.

Stamp of 1861 and Map of English Channel A452

Design: 20cr, 430r stamp of 1861 and map of Netherlands.

1961, Aug. 1 ***Perf. 11x11½***
927 A452 10cr rose 1.10 .25
928 A452 20cr salmon pink 3.75 .25

Centenary of 1861 stamp issue.

Portrait Type of 1954-60
Designs as Before

1961 **Wmk. 268** ***Perf. 11x11½***
930 A336 1cr brown 1.60 .40
931 A336 2cr dk bl grn 2.40 .40
932 A336 5cr red lilac 7.25 .25
933 A336 10cr emerald 14.50 .25
Nos. 930-933 (4) 25.75 1.30

1cr, 5cr, 10cr have patterned background.

Sun, Clouds, Rain and Weather Symbols — A453

Dedo de Deus Peak — A454

1962, Mar. 23 ***Perf. 11½x11***
936 A453 10cr red brown 1.50 .50

World Meteorological Day, Mar. 23.

1962, Apr. 14 **Photo.** **Wmk. 267**
937 A454 8cr emerald .55 .35

50th anniversary of the climbing of Dedo de Deus (Finger of God) peak.

Dr. Gaspar Vianna and Leishmania Protozoa — A455

1962, Apr. 24 ***Perf. 11x11½***
938 A455 8cr blue .50 .25

Discovery by Gaspar Oliveiro Vianna (1885-1914) of a cure for leishmaniasis, 50th anniv.

Henrique Dias A456

1962, June 18 **Wmk. 267**
939 A456 10cr dk vio brn .55 .35

300th anniversary of the death of Henrique Dias, Negro military leader who fought against the Dutch and Spaniards.

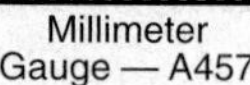

Millimeter Gauge — A457 Sailboats, Snipe Class — A458

1962, June 26 ***Perf. 11½x11***
940 A457 100cr car rose .80 .25

Centenary of the introduction of the metric system in Brazil.

1962, July 21 **Photo.** **Wmk. 267**
941 A458 8cr Prus green .50 .25

Commemorating the 13th Brazilian championships for Snipe Class sailing.

Julio Mesquita A459

1962, Aug. 18 ***Perf. 11x11½***
942 A459 8cr dull brown 1.25 .25

Julio Mesquita, journalist and founder of a Sao Paulo newspaper, birth cent.

Empress Leopoldina — A460

1962, Sept. 7 ***Perf. 11½x11***
943 A460 8cr rose claret .50 .25

140th anniversary of independence.

Buildings, Brasilia — A461

Perf. 11x11½
1962, Oct. 24 **Wmk. 267**
944 A461 10cr orange .55 .35

51st Interparliamentary Conf., Brasilia.

Pouring Ladle — A462

1962, Oct. 26 ***Perf. 11½x11***
945 A462 8cr orange .50 .25

Inauguration of the Usiminas State Iron and Steel Foundry at Belo Horizonte, Minas Gerais.

UPAE Emblem A463

1962, Nov. 19 ***Perf. 11x11½***
946 A463 8cr bright magenta .75 .25

Founding of the Postal Union of the Americas and Spain, UPAE, 50th anniv.

Chimney and Cogwheel Forming "10" — A464

1962, Nov. 26 ***Perf. 11½x11***
947 A464 10cr lt blue grn .50 .25

Natl. Economic and Development Bank, 10th anniv.

Quintino Bocaiuva A465 Soccer Player and Globe A466

Perf. 11½x11
1962, Dec. 27 **Photo.** **Wmk. 267**
948 A465 8cr brown org .55 .35

Bocaiuva, journalist, 50th death anniv.

1963, Jan. 14
949 A466 10cr blue grn .80 .25

World Soccer Championship of 1962.

Carrier Pigeon — A467

1963, Jan. **Unwmk.** **Litho.** ***Perf. 14***
950 A467 8cr yel, dk bl, red & grn .60 .25

Souvenir Sheet

Imperf

951 A467 100cr yel, dk bl, red & grn 4.25 4.25

300 years of Brazilian postal service.
Issue dates: 8cr, Jan. 25; 100cr, Jan. 31.

Severino Neiva — A468

Perf. 10½x11½
1963, Jan. 31 **Photo.** **Wmk. 267**
952 A468 8cr brt vio .50 .25

Radar Tracking Station and Rockets — A469 "Cross of Unity" — A470

Perf. 11½x11
1963, Mar. 15 **Wmk. 268**
953 A469 21cr lt ultra .50 .25

International Aeronautics and Space Exhibition, Sao Paulo.

1963 **Wmk. 267** ***Perf. 11½x11***
954 A470 8cr red lilac .50 .25

Vatican II, the 21st Ecumenical Council of the Roman Catholic Church.

"ABC" in Geometric Form — A471

1963, Apr. 22 **Photo.** **Wmk. 267**
955 A471 8cr brt bl & lt bl .50 .25

Education Week, Apr. 22-27, 3-year alphabetization program.

Basketball Player — A472

1963, May 15
956 A472 8cr dp lilac rose .75 .25

4th International Basketball Championships, Rio de Janeiro, May 10-25, 1963.

Games Emblem A473 "OEA" and Map of the Americas A474

1963, May 22 ***Perf. 11½x11***
957 A473 10cr car rose .65 .25

4th Pan American Games, Sao Paulo.

1963, June 6
958 A474 10cr org & dp org .65 .35

15th anniversary of the charter of the Organization of American States.

José Bonifacio de Andrada — A475

1963, June 13
959 A475 8cr dk brown .50 .25

Bicentenary of the birth of José Bonifacio de Andrada e Silva, statesman.

Wheat A476

Perf. 11x11½
1963, June 18 **Photo.** **Wmk. 267**
960 A476 10cr blue .65 .30

FAO "Freedom from Hunger" campaign.

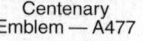

Centenary Emblem — A477 Joao Caetano — A478

1963, Aug. 19 ***Perf. 11½x11***
961 A477 8cr yel org & red .60 .25

Centenary of International Red Cross.

1963, Aug. 24 ***Perf. 11½x11***
962 A478 8cr slate .50 .25

Death centenary of Joao Caetano, actor.

Symbols of Agriculture, Industry and Atomic Energy — A479

Hammer Thrower — A480

1963, Aug. 28
963 A479 10cr car rose .50 .25

Atomic Development Law, 1st anniv.

1963, Sept. 13
964 A480 10cr gray .85 .35

Intl. College Students' Games, Porto Alegre.

Marshal Tito — A481

Compass Rose, Map of Brazil and View of Rio — A482

1963, Sept. 19
965 A481 80cr sepia 1.10 .50

Visit of Marshal Tito of Yugoslavia.

1963, Sept. 20
966 A482 8cr lt blue grn .50 .25

8th International Leprology Congress.

Oil Derrick and Storage Tank A483

1963, Oct. 3 *Perf. 11x11½*
967 A483 8cr dk slate grn .50 .25

Petrobras, the natl. oil company, 10th anniv.

"Spring Games" A484

1963, Nov. 5 **Photo.** **Wmk. 267**
968 A484 8cr yel & org .50 .25

1963 Spring Games.

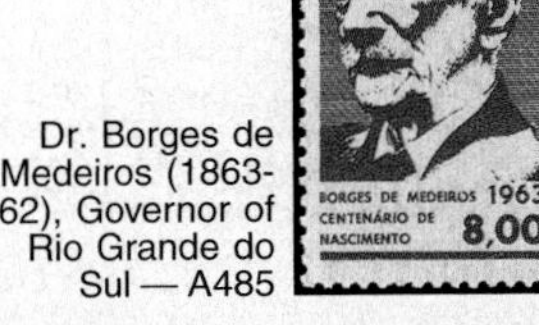

Dr. Borges de Medeiros (1863-1962), Governor of Rio Grande do Sul — A485

1963, Nov. 29 *Perf. 11½x11*
969 A485 8cr red brown .50 .25

Sao Joao del Rei A486

1963, Dec. 8 *Perf. 11x11½*
970 A486 8cr violet blue .50 .25

250th anniversary of Sao Joao del Rei.

Dr. Alvaro Alvim A487

1963, Dec. 19
971 A487 8cr dk gray .60 .25

Alvaro Alvim (1863-1928), X-ray specialist and martyr of science.

Viscount de Mauá — A488

Mandacaru Cactus and Emblem — A489

1963, Dec. 28 *Perf. 11½x11*
972 A488 8cr rose car .50 .25

Sesquicentennial of the birth of Viscount de Mauá, founder of first Brazilian railroad.

1964, Jan. 23 **Photo.** **Wmk. 267**
973 A489 8cr dull green .50 .25

Bank of Northeast Brazil, 10th anniv.

Coelho Netto — A490

Lauro Müller — A491

1964, Feb. 21 *Perf. 11½x11*
974 A490 8cr brt violet .50 .25

Birth centenary of Coelho Netto, writer.

1964, Mar. 8 **Wmk. 267**
975 A491 8cr dp orange .45 .25

Lauro Siverino Müller, politician and member of the Brazilian Academy of Letters, birth cent.

Child Holding Spoon A492

1964, Mar. 25 *Perf. 11x11½*
976 A492 8cr yel brn & yel .50 .25

Issued for "School Meals Week."

Chalice Rock — A493

Allan Kardec — A494

1964, Apr. 9 **Engr.** *Perf. 11½x11*
977 A493 80cr red orange .60 .25

Issued for tourist publicity.

1964, Apr. 18 **Photo.**
978 A494 30cr slate green 1.00 .85

Cent. of "O Evangelho" (Gospel) of the codification of Spiritism.

Heinrich Lübke — A495

Pope John XXIII — A496

Perf. 11½x11

1964, May 8 **Photo.** **Wmk. 267**
979 A495 100cr red brown 1.10 .35

Visit of President Heinrich Lübke of Germany.

1964, June 29 **Wmk. 267**
980 A496 20cr dk car rose .50 .25
a. Unwmkd. 2.00 .25

Issued in memory of Pope John XXIII.

Pres. Senghor of Senegal — A497

1964, Sept. 19 **Wmk. 267**
981 A497 20cr dk brown .50 .25

Visit of Leopold Sedar Senghor, President of Senegal.

Botafogo Bay and Sugarloaf Mountain — A498

Designs: 100cr, Our Lady of Penha Church, vert. 200cr, Copacabana beach.

Perf. 11x11½, 11½x11

1964-65 **Photo.**
983 A498 15cr org & bl .50 .40
984 A498 100cr brt grn & red brn, *yel* .60 .40
985 A498 200cr black & red 2.25 .50
a. Souvenir sheet of 3 ('65) 15.00 *17.50*
Nos. 983-985 (3) 3.35 1.30

4th cent. of Rio de Janeiro.

No. 985a contains three imperf. stamps similar to Nos. 983-985, but printed in brown. Sold for 320cr. Issued Dec. 30, 1965.

A souvenir card containing one lithographed facsimile of No. 984, imperf., exists, but has no franking value. Size: 100x125mm. Sold by P.O. for 250cr.

Pres. Charles de Gaulle A499

Pres. John F. Kennedy A500

1964, Oct. 13 *Perf. 11½x11*
986 A499 100cr orange brn .70 .25

Visit of Charles de Gaulle, President of France, Oct. 13-15.

1964, Oct. 24 **Photo.** **Wmk. 267**
987 A500 100cr slate .60 .30

"Prophet" by Lisboa — A501

1964, Nov. 18 *Perf. 11½x11*
988 A501 10cr slate .50 .25

150th death anniv. of the sculptor Antonio Francisco Lisboa, "O Aleijadinho" (The Cripple).

Antonio Goncalves Dias — A502

Designs: 30cr, Euclides da Cunha. 50cr, Prof. Angelo Moreira da Costa Lima. 200cr, Tiradentes. 500cr, Dom Pedro I. 1000cr, Dom Pedro II.

1965-66 **Wmk. 267** *Perf. 11x11½*

989	A502	30cr brt bluish grn ('66)	4.00	.25
989A	A502	50cr dull brn ('66)	3.50	.25
990	A502	100cr blue	1.50	.25
991	A502	200cr brown org	7.00	.25
992	A502	500cr red brown	42.50	.45
992A	A502	1000cr sl bl ('66)	110.00	1.60
		Nos. 989-992A (6)	168.50	3.05

Statue of St. Sebastian, Guanataro Bay — A503

The Arches A504

Design: 35cr, Estacio de Sa (1520-67), founder of Rio de Janeiro.

1965 **Photo.** *Perf. 11½*
Size: 24x37mm
993 A503 30cr bl & rose red .55 .25

Lithographed and Engraved
Perf. 11x11½

994 A504 30cr lt bl & blk .55 .35

Photo. *Perf. 11½*
Size: 21x39mm

995 A503 35cr blk & org .25 .25
a. Souvenir sheet of 3 12.00 12.00
Nos. 993-995 (3) 1.35 .85

4th cent. of Rio de Janeiro.
No. 995a contains three imperf. stamps similar to Nos. 993-995, but printed in deep orange. Size: 130x79mm. Sold for 100cr.
Issued: No. 993, 3/5; No. 994, 11/30; No. 995, 7/28; No. 995a, 12/30.

Sword and Cross — A505

1965, Apr. 15 Wmk. 267 *Perf. 11½*
996 A505 120cr gray .55 .35

1st anniv, of the democratic revolution.

Vital Brazil — A506

1965, Apr. 28 Wmk. 267 *Perf. 11½*
997 A506 120cr deep orange .55 .35

Centenary of birth of Vital Brazil, M.D.
A souvenir card containing one impression similar to No. 997, imperf., exists, printed in dull plum. Sold by P.O. for 250cr. Size: 114x180mm.

Shah of Iran — A507

1965, May 5 **Photo.**
998 A507 120cr rose claret .50 .25

Commemorating the visit of Shah Mohammed Riza Pahlavi of Iran.

Marshal Mariano da Silva Rondon — A508

1965, May 7 **Engr.**
999 A508 30cr claret .50 .25

Marshal Mariano da Silva Rondon (1865-1958), explorer and expert on Indians.

Lions' Emblem — A509

1965, May 14 **Photo.**
1000 A509 35cr pale vio & blk .50 .25

12th convention of the Lions Clubs of Brazil, Rio de Janeiro, May 11-16.

ITU Emblem, Old and New Communication Equipment — A510

1965, May 21 *Perf. 11½*
1001 A510 120cr yellow & grn .60 .25

Centenary of the ITU.

Epitácio Pessoa — A511

1965, May 23 **Photo.**
1002 A511 35cr blue gray .50 .25

Epitácio da Silva Pessoa (1865-1942), jurist, president of Brazil, 1919-22.

Statue of Admiral Barroso — A512

1965, June 11
1003 A512 30cr blue .50 .25

Cent. of the naval battle of Riachuelo.
A souvenir card containing one lithographed facsimile of No. 1003, imperf., exists. Size: 100x139½mm.

José de Alencar and Indian Princess — A513

1965, June 24 *Perf. 11½x11*
1004 A513 30cr deep plum .50 .25

Centenary of the publication of "Iracema" by Joséde Alencar.
A souvenir card containing one lithographed facsimile of No. 1004, printed in rose red and imperf., exists. Size: 100x141½mm.

Winston Churchill A514

1965, June 25 *Perf. 11x11½*
1005 A514 200cr slate 1.25 .25

Scout Jamboree Emblem — A515

1965, July 17 Photo. *Perf. 11¾*
1006 A515 30cr dull bl grn .60 .35

1st Pan-American Boy Scout Jamboree, Fundao Island, Rio de Janeiro, July 15-25.

ICY Emblem A516

1965, Aug. 25 Wmk. 267 *Perf. 11½*
1007 A516 120cr dl bl & blk .60 .25

International Cooperation Year, 1965.

Leoncio Correias — A517

Emblem — A518

1965, Sept. 1 *Perf. 11½x11*
1008 A517 35cr slate grn .50 .25

Leoncio Correias, poet, birth cent.

1965, Sept. 4
1009 A518 30cr brt rose .50 .25

Eighth Biennial Fine Arts Exhibition, Sao Paulo, Nov.-Dec., 1965.

Pres. Saragat of Italy — A519

1965, Sept. 11 Photo. Wmk. 267
1010 A519 100cr slate grn, *pink* .50 .25

Visit of Pres. Giuseppe Saragat of Italy.

Grand Duke and Duchess of Luxembourg — A520

1965, Sept. 17 *Perf. 11x11½*
1011 A520 100cr brn olive .50 .25

Visit of Grand Duke Jean and Grand Duchess Josephine Charlotte of Luxembourg.

Biplane — A521

1965, Oct. 8 Photo. *Perf. 11½x11*
1012 A521 35cr ultra .50 .25

3rd Aviation Week Philatelic Exhibition, Rio.
A souvenir card carries one impression of this 35cr, imperf. Size: 102x140mm. Sold for 100cr.

Flags of OAS Members A522

1965, Nov. 17 *Perf. 11x11½*
1013 A522 100cr brt bl & blk .50 .25

2nd meeting of OAS Foreign Ministers, Rio.

"Coffee Beans" — A524

King Baudouin and Queen Fabiola of Belgium — A523

1965, Nov. 18
1014 A523 100cr gray .50 .25

Visit of King and Queen of Belgium.

Perf. 11½x11
1965, Dec. 21 Photo. Wmk. 267
1015 A524 30cr brown .60 .25

Brazilian coffee publicity.

Conveyor and Loading Crane A525

1966, Apr. 1 *Perf. 11x11½*
1016 A525 110cr tan & dk sl grn .60 .35

Opening of the new terminal of the Rio Doce Iron Ore Company at Tubarao.

Pouring Ladle and Steel Beam — A526

Prof. de Rocha Dissecting Cadaver — A527

Perf. 11½x11

1966, Apr. 16 Photo. Wmk. 267

1017 A526 30cr blk, *dp org* .50 .25

25th anniv. of the National Steel Company (nationalization of the steel industry).

1966, Apr. 26

1018 A527 30cr brt bluish grn .80 .35

50th anniv. of the discovery and description of Rickettsia Prowazeki, the cause of typhus fever, by Prof. Henrique de Rocha Lima.

Battle of Tuiuti A528

Perf. 11x11½

1966, May 24 Photo. Wmk. 267

1019 A528 30cr gray grn .65 .25

Centenary of the Battle of Tuiuti.

Symbolic Water Cycle — A529

Pres. Shazar of Israel — A530

1966, July 1 ***Perf. 11½x11***

1020 A529 100cr lt brn & bl .65 .25

Hydrological Decade (UNESCO), 1965-74.

1966, July 18 Photo. Wmk. 267

1021 A530 100cr ultra .55 .35

Visit of Pres. Zalman Shazar of Israel.

Imperial Academy of Fine Arts — A531

Perf. 11x11½

1966, Aug. 12 Engr. Wmk. 267

1022 A531 100cr red brown 1.50 .35

150th anniversary of French art mission.

Military Service Emblem A532

1966, Sept. 6 Photo. ***Perf. 11x11½***

1023 A532 30cr yel, ultra & grn .50 .25

a. With commemorative border 6.25 6.25

New Military Service Law.

No. 1023a issued in sheets of 4. It carries at left a 30cr, design A532, in deeper tones of yellow and ultramarine, Wmk. 264. Without gum. Sold for 100cr.

Ruben Dario — A533

Perf. 11½x11

1966, Sept. 20 Photo. Wmk. 267

1024 A533 100cr brt rose lilac .50 .25

Ruben Dario (pen name of Felix Ruben Garcia Sarmiento (1867-1916), Nicaraguan poet, newspaper correspondent and diplomat.

Ceramic Candlestick from Santarém — A534

1966, Oct. 6 ***Perf. 11x11½***

1025 A534 30cr dk brn, *salmon* .50 .25

Centenary of Goeldi Museum at Belem.

Arms of Santa Cruz — A535

Perf. 11½x11

1966, Oct. 15 Photo. Wmk. 267

1026 A535 30cr slate grn .50 .25

1st Natl. Tobacco Exposition, Santa Cruz.

UNESCO Emblem A536

1966, Oct. 24 Engr. ***Perf. 11½***

1027 A536 120cr black 1.50 .40

a. With commemorative border 15.00 15.00

20th anniv. of UNESCO. No. 1027a issued in sheets of 4. It carries at right a design similar to No. 1027. Unwatermarked granite paper, without gum. Sold for 150cr.

Captain Antonio Correia Pinto and Map of Lages — A537

Cross of Lusitania and Southern Cross — A538

Perf. 11½x11

1966, Nov. 22 Photo. Wmk. 267

1028 A537 30cr salmon pink .50 .25

Arrival of Capt. Antonio Correia Pinto, bicent.

1966, Dec. 4 ***Perf. 11½***

1029 A538 100cr blue green .60 .35

LUBRAPEX 1966 philatelic exhibition at the National Museum of Fine Arts, Rio.

Madonna and Child — A539

A540

Perf. 11½x11

1966, Dec. Photo. Wmk. 267

1030 A539 30cr blue green .50 .25

Perf. 11½

1031 A540 35cr salmon & ultra .40 .25

a. 150cr salmon & ultra 5.50 *6.50*

Christmas 1966.

No. 1031a measures 46x103mm and is printed in sheets of 4. It is inscribed "Pax Hominibus" (but not "Brasil Correio") and carries the Madonna shown on No. 1031. Issued without gum.

Issued: 30cr, 12/8; 35cr, 12/22; 150cr, 12/28.

Arms of Laguna A541

1967, Jan. 4 Engr. ***Perf. 11x11½***

1032 A541 60cr sepia .50 .25

Centenary of the Post and Telegraph Agency of Laguna, Santa Catarina.

Railroad Bridge A542

1967, Feb. 16 Photo. Wmk. 267

1033 A542 50cr deep orange 1.00 .30

Centenary of the Santos-Jundiai railroad.

Black Madonna of Czestochowa, Polish Eagle and Cross — A543

1967, Mar. 12 ***Perf. 11x11½***

1034 A543 50cr yel, bl & rose red .80 .35

Adoption of Christianity in Poland, 1,000th anniv.

Research Rocket A544

Anita Garibaldi A545

1967, Mar. 23 ***Perf. 11½x11***

1035 A544 50cr blk & brt bl 1.10 .25

World Meteorological Day, March 23.

Perf. 11x11½

1967-69 Photo. Wmk. 267

Portraits: 1c, Mother Joana Angelica. 2c, Marilia de Dirceu. 3c, Dr. Rita Lobato. 6c, Ana Neri. 10c, Darcy Vargas.

1036 A545 1c dp ultra .40 .25

1037 A545 2c red brn .40 .25

1038 A545 3c brt grn .40 .25

1039 A545 5c black .70 .25

1040 A545 6c brown .70 .25

1041 A545 10c dk slate grn 2.00 .25

Nos. 1036-1041 (6) 4.60 1.50

Issued: 1c, 5/3; 2c, 8/14; 3c, 6/7; 5c, 4/14; 6c, 5/14/67; 10c, 6/18/69.

VARIG Airlines — A546

1967, May 8 ***Perf. 11½x11***

1046 A546 6c brt bl & blk .55 .35

40th anniversary of VARIG Airlines.

Lions Emblem and Globes A547

1967, May 9 Engr. ***Perf. 11x11½***

1047 A547 6c green .55 .35

a. Souvenir sheet 10.00 *7.50*

50th anniv. of Lions Intl. No. 1047a contains one imperf. stamp similar to No. 1047. Sold for 15c.

Madonna and Child, by Robert Feruzzi — A548

1967, May 14 Photo. *Perf. 11½x11*

1048 A548 5c violet .55 .35
a. 15c Souvenir sheet 11.00 *7.00*

Mother's Day. No. 1048a contains one 15c imperf. stamp in design of No. 1048.

Prince Akihito and Princess Michiko A549

1967, May 25 *Perf. 11x11½*

1049 A549 10c black & pink .55 .35

Visit to Brazil of Crown Prince Akihito and Princess Michiko of Japan.

Carrier Pigeon and Radar Screen A550

Brother Vicente do Salvador A551

Perf. 11½x11

1967, June 20 Photo. Wmk. 267

1050 A550 10c sl & brt pink .50 .25

Commemorating the opening of the Communications Ministry in Brasilia.

1967, June 28 Engr.

1051 A551 5c brown .50 .25

400th birth anniv. of Brother Vicente do Salvador (1564-1636), founder of Franciscan convent in Rio de Janeiro, and historian.

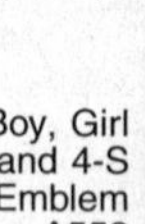

Boy, Girl and 4-S Emblem A552

1967, July 12 Photo. *Perf. 11½*

1052 A552 5c green & blk .50 .25

National 4-S (4-H) Day.

Möbius Strip A553

1967, July 21 *Perf. 11x11½*

1053 A553 5c brt bl & blk .50 .25

6th Brazilian Mathematical Congress.

Fish A554

1967, Aug. 1 *Perf. 11½*

1054 A554 5c slate .55 .35

Bicentenary of city of Piracicaba.

Golden Rose and Papal Arms — A555

1967, Aug. 15

1055 A555 20c mag & yel 2.00 .70

Offering of a golden rose by Pope Paul VI to the Virgin Mary of Fatima (Our Lady of Peace), Patroness of Brazil.

General Sampaio A556

King Olaf of Norway A557

1967, Aug. 25 Engr. *Perf. 11½x11*

1056 A556 5c blue .50 .25

Honoring General Antonio de Sampaio, hero of the Battle of Tutui.

1967, Sept. 8 Photo.

1057 A557 10c brown org .50 .25

Visit of King Olaf of Norway.

Sun over Sugar Loaf, Botafogo Bay A558

Nilo Peçanha A559

Photogravure and Embossed

1967, Sept. 25 Wmk. 267 *Perf. 11½*

1058 A558 10c blk & dp org .50 .25

22nd meeting of the Intl. Monetary Fund, Intl. Bank for Reconstruction and Development, Intl. Financial Corporation and Intl. Development Assoc.

Perf. 11½x11

1967, Oct. 1 Photo. Wmk. 267

1059 A559 5c brown violet .50 .25

Peçanha (1867-1924), Pres. of Brazil 1909-10.

Virgin of the Apparition and Basilica of Aparecida — A560

Cockerel, Festival Emblem — A561

1967, Oct. 11 *Perf. 11½*

1060 A560 5c ultra & dl yel .55 .35
a. Souvenir sheet of 2 25.00 *15.00*

250th anniv. of the discovery of the statue of Our Lady of the Apparition, now in the National Basilica of the Apparition at Aparecida do Norte.

No. 1060a contains imperf. 5c and 10c stamps similar to No. 1060. Issued Dec. 27, 1967, for Christmas.

Engraved and Photogravure

1967, Oct. 16 *Perf. 11½x11*

1061 A561 20c black & multi .90 .70

Second International Folksong Festival.

Balloon, Plane and Rocket A562

Perf. 11x11½

1967, Oct. 18 Photo. Unwmk.

1062 A562 10c blue .90 .50
a. 15c souvenir sheet 45.00 *29.00*

Week of the Wing, Oct. 18-23. No. 1062a contains one imperf. 15c stamp similar to No. 1062 and was issued Oct. 23.

Pres. Arthur Bernardes — A563

Portraits of Brazilian Presidents: 20c, Campos Salles. 50c, Wenceslau Pereira Gomes Braz. 1cr, Washington Pereira de Souza Luiz. 2cr, Castello Branco.

Perf. 11x11½

1967-68 Photo. Wmk. 267

1063 A563 10c blue .50 .25
1064 A563 20c dk red brn 1.50 .25

Engr.

1065 A563 50c black ('68) 13.50 .25
1066 A563 1cr lil rose ('68) 20.00 .35
1067 A563 2cr emerald ('68) 4.00 .30
Nos. 1063-1067 (5) 39.50 1.40

Carnival of Rio — A564

Ships, Anchor and Sailor — A565

1967, Nov. 22 *Perf. 11½x11*

1070 A564 10c lem, ultra & pink .55 .35
a. 15c souvenir sheet 20.00 12.50

Issued for International Tourist Year, 1967. No. 1070a contains a 15c imperf. stamp in design of No. 1070. Issued Nov. 24.

1967, Dec. 6

1071 A565 10c ultra .55 .35

Issued for Navy Week.

Christmas Decorations A566

1967, Dec. 8 *Perf. 11½*

1072 A566 5c car, yel & bl .50 .25

Christmas 1967.

Olavo Bilac, Planes, Tank and Aircraft Carrier A567

Perf. 11x11½

1967, Dec. 16 Photo. Wmk. 267

1073 A567 5c brt blue & yel .55 .35

Issued for Reservists' Day and to honor Olavo Bilac, sponsor of compulsory military service.

Rodrigues de Carvalho — A568

1967, Dec. 18 Engr. *Perf. 11½x11*

1074 A568 10c green .50 .25

Cent. of the birth of Rodrigues de Carvalho, poet and lawyer.

Orlando Rangel A569

1968, Feb. 29 Photo. *Perf. 11x11½*

1075 A569 5c lt grnsh bl & blk .70 .40

Orlando de Fonseca Rangel, pioneer of pharmaceutical industry in Brazil, birth cent.

Virgin of Paranagua and Diver — A570

Map of Brazil Showing Manaus — A571

1968, Mar. 9 ***Perf. 11½x11***
1076 A570 10c dk sl grn & brt yel grn .70 .40

250th anniversary of the first underwater explorations at Paranagua.

1968, Mar. 13 Photo. Wmk. 267
1077 A571 10c yel, grn & red .70 .40

Free port of Manaus on the Amazon River.

Human Rights Flame — A572

Paul Harris and Rotary Emblem — A573

1968, Mar. 21 ***Perf. 11½x11***
1078 A572 10c blue & salmon .70 .40

International Human Rights Year.

1968, Apr. 19 Litho. Unwmk.
Without Gum
1079 A573 20c grn & org brn 2.00 1.25

Paul Percy Harris (1868-1947), founder of Rotary International.

Pedro Alvares Cabral and his Fleet — A574

Design: 20c, First Mass celebrated in Brazil.

1968 Without Gum ***Perf. 11½***
1080 A574 10c multicolored 1.40 .75
1081 A574 20c multicolored 1.50 .90

500th anniversary of the birth of Pedro Alvares Cabral, navigator, who took possession of Brazil for Portugal.
Issue dates: 10c, Apr. 22; 20c, July 11.

College Arms — A575

1968, Apr. 22 Photo. Wmk. 267
1082 A575 10c vio bl, red & gold 1.00 .60

Centenary of St. Luiz College, Sao Paulo.

Motherhood, by Henrique Bernardeli A576

1968, May 12 Litho. Unwmk.
Without Gum
1083 A576 5c multicolored .70 .40

Issued for Mother's Day.

Harpy Eagle A577

Photogravure and Engraved
1968, May 28 Wmk. 267
1084 A577 20c brt bl & blk 5.00 .75

Sesquicentennial of National Museum.

Brazilian and Japanese Women — A578

1968, June 28 Litho. Unwmk.
Without Gum
1085 A578 10c yellow & multi 1.00 .60

Commemorating the inauguration of Varig's direct Brazil-Japan airline.

Horse Race A579

Perf. 11x11½
1968, July 16 Litho. Unwmk.
Without Gum
1086 A579 10c multicolored .80 .35

Centenary of the Jockey Club of Brazil.

Musician Wren A580

Designs: 10c, Red-crested cardinal, vert. 50c, Royal flycatcher, vert.

Perf. 11½x11, 11x11½
1968-69 Engr. Wmk. in Sheet
Without Gum
1087 A580 10c multi ('69) 1.60 .45
1088 A580 20c multicolored 1.75 .45
1089 A580 50c multicolored 3.50 .80
Nos. 1087-1089 (3) 6.85 1.70

Some stamps in each sheet of Nos. 1087-1089 show parts of a two-line papermaker's watermark: "WESTERPOST / INDUSTRIA BRASILEIRA" with diamond-shaped emblem between last two words. Entire watermark appears in one sheet margin. Value, set $45.
Issued: 10c, 8/20/69; 20c, 7/9/68; 50c, 8/2/68.

Mailbox and Envelope A581

Photogravure and Engraved
1968, Aug. 1 Wmk. 267 ***Perf. 11***
1091 A581 5c citron, blk & grn .50 .25

Stamp Day, 1968 and for 125th anniv. of the 1st Brazilian postage stamps.

Emilio Luiz Mallet — A582

Seal of Portuguese Literary School — A584

1968, Aug. 25 Engr. Wmk. 267
1092 A582 10c pale purple .50 .25

Honoring Marshal Emilio Luiz Mallet, Baron of Itapevi, patron of the marines.

Map of South America — A583

1968, Sept. 5 Photo.
1093 A583 10c deep orange .50 .25

Visit of President Eduardo Frei of Chile.

Perf. 11½x11

Photogravure and Engraved
1968, Sept. 10 ***Perf. 11½***
1094 A584 5c pink & grn .50 .25

Centenary of Portuguese Literary School.

Map of Brazil and Telex Tape A585

1968, Sept. Photo. ***Perf. 11x11½***
1095 A585 20c citron & brt grn .90 .40

Linking of 25 Brazilian cities by teletype.

Soldiers' Heads on Medal — A586

Perf. 11½x11
1968, Sept. 24 Litho. Unwmk.
Without Gum
1096 A586 5c blue & gray .55 .35

8th American Armed Forces Conference.

Clef, Notes and Sugarloaf Mountain A587

1968, Sept. 30 ***Perf. 11½***
Without Gum
1097 A587 6c blk, yel & red .90 .45

Third International Folksong Festival.

Catalytic Cracking Plant A588

1968, Oct. 4 Without Gum
1098 A588 6c blue & multi .85 .60

Petrobras, the natl. oil company, 15th anniv.

Child Protection — A589

Whimsical Girl — A590

5c, School boy walking toward the sun.

Perf. 11½x11, 11x11½
1968, Oct. 16 Litho. Unwmk.
Without Gum
1099 A590 5c gray & lt bl .75 .45
1100 A589 10c brt bl, dk red & blk .90 .40
1101 A590 20c multicolored 1.10 .40
Nos. 1099-1101 (3) 2.75 1.25

22nd anniv. of UNICEF.

Children with Books
A591

1968, Oct. 23 ***Perf. 11x11½***
Without Gum

1102 A591 5c multicolored .55 .35

Book Week.

UN Emblem and Flags — A592

1968, Oct. 24 ***Perf. 11½x11***
Without Gum

1103 A592 20c black & multi 1.10 .60

20th anniv. of WHO.

Jean Baptiste Debret, Self-portrait — A593

Perf. 11x11½
1968, Oct. 30 **Litho.** **Unwmk.**
Without Gum

1104 A593 10c dk gray & pale yel .70 .40

Jean Baptiste Debret, (1768-1848), French painter who worked in Brazil (1816-31). Design includes his "Burden Bearer."

Queen Elizabeth II
A594

1968, Nov. 4 ***Perf. 11½***
Without Gum

1105 A594 70c lt bl & multi 3.00 1.60

Visit of Queen Elizabeth II of Great Britain.

Francisco Braga — A595

Perf. 11½x11
1968, Nov. 19 **Wmk. 267**

1106 A595 5c dull red brn .80 .40

Cent. of the birth of Antonio Francisco Braga, composer of the Hymn of the Flag.

Brazilian Flag — A596

1968, Nov. 19 **Unwmk.** ***Perf. 11½***
Without Gum

1107 A596 10c multicolored .80 .45

Issued for Flag Day.

Clasped Hands and Globe
A597

Perf. 11x11½
1968, Nov. 25 **Typo.** **Unwmk.**
Without Gum

1108 A597 5c multicolored .50 .50

Issued for Voluntary Blood Donor's Day.

Old Locomotive — A598

1968, Nov. 28 **Litho.** ***Perf. 11½***
Without Gum

1109 A598 5c multicolored 2.00 .80

Centenary of the Sao Paulo Railroad.

Bell — A599

Francisco Caldas, Jr. — A600

Design: 6c, Santa Claus and boy.

1968 **Without Gum** ***Perf. 11½x11***

1110 A599 5c multicolored .55 .40
1111 A599 6c multicolored .55 .40

Christmas 1968.
Issue dates: 5c, Dec. 12; 6c, Dec. 20.

1968, Dec. 13 **Without Gum**

1112 A600 10c crimson & blk .50 .25

Cent. of the birth of Francisco Caldas, Jr., journalist and founder of Correio de Povo, newspaper.

Map of Brazil, War Memorial and Reservists' Emblem — A601

Perf. 11x11½
1968, Dec. 16 **Photo.** **Wmk. 267**

1113 A601 5c bl grn & org brn .70 .35

Issued for Reservists' Day.

Radar Antenna — A602

Viscount of Rio Branco — A603

Perf. 11½x11
1969, Feb. 28 **Litho.** **Unwmk.**
Without Gum

1114 A602 30c ultra, lt bl & blk 1.40 .90

Inauguration of EMBRATEL, satellite communications ground station bringing US television to Brazil via Telstar.

1969, Mar. 16 **Without Gum**

1115 A603 5c black & buff .55 .40

José Maria da Silva Paranhos, Viscount of Rio Branco (1819-1880), statesman.

St. Gabriel — A604

1969, Mar. 24 **Without Gum**

1116 A604 5c multicolored .75 .40

Honoring St. Gabriel as patron saint of telecommunications.

Shoemaker's Last and Globe — A605

Perf. 11x11½
1969, Mar. 29 **Litho.** **Unwmk.**
Without Gum

1117 A605 5c multicolored .50 .50

4th Intl. Shoe Fair, Novo Hamburgo.

Allan Kardec
A606

1969, Mar. 31 **Photo.** **Wmk. 267**

1118 A606 5c brt grn & org brn .55 .35

Allan Kardec (pen name of Leon Hippolyto Denizard Rivail, 1803-1869), French physician and spiritist.

Men of 3 Races and Arms of Cuiabá
A607

1969, Apr. 8 **Litho.** **Unwmk.**
Without Gum

1119 A607 5c black & multi .55 .35

250th anniversary of the founding of Cuiabá, capital of Matto Grosso.

State Mint — A608

1969, Apr. 11 ***Perf. 11½***
Without Gum

1120 A608 5c olive bister & org .85 .50

Opening of the state money printing plant.

Brazilian Stamps and Emblem
A609

Perf. 11x11½
1969, Apr. 30 **Litho.** **Unwmk.**
Without Gum

1121 A609 5c multicolored .55 .35

Sao Paulo Philatelic Society, 50th anniv.

St. Anne, Baroque Statue
A610

1969, May 8 ***Perf. 11½***
Without Gum

1122 A610 5c lemon & multi .90 .60

Issued for Mother's Day.

ILO Emblem
A611

Perf. 11x11½
1969, May 13 **Photo.** **Wmk. 267**

1123 A611 5c dp rose red & gold .50 .25

50th anniv. of the ILO.

Diving Platform and Swimming Pool — A612

Mother and Child at Window — A613

Lithographed and Photogravure
Perf. 11½x11

1969, June 13 **Unwmk.**
Without Gum

1124 A612 20c bis brn, blk & bl grn 1.10 .70

40th anniversary of the Cearense Water Sports Club, Fortaleza.

1969 **Litho.** ***Perf. 11½***

Designs: 20c, Modern sculpture by Felicia Leirner. 50c, "The Sun Sets in Brasilia," by Danilo di Prete. 1cr, Angelfish, painting by Aldemir Martins.

Size: 24x36mm

1125 A613 10c orange & multi 1.25 .40

Size: 33x34mm

1126 A613 20c red & multi 1.25 .80

Size: 33x53mm

1127 A613 50c yellow & multi 4.00 2.25

Without Gum

1128 A613 1cr gray & multi 3.00 1.75
Nos. 1125-1128 (4) 9.50 5.20

10th Biennial Art Exhibition, Sao Paulo, Sept.-Dec. 1969.

Angelfish
A614

No. 1130: 10c, Tetra. 15c, Piranha. 20c, Megalamphodus megalopterus. 30c, Black tetra.

Wmk. 267

1969, July 21 **Litho.** ***Perf. 11½***

1129 A614 20c multicolored 1.25 .60

Souvenir Sheet

Fish — A615

1969, July 24 **Unwmk.** ***Imperf.***

1130 A615 Sheet of 4 10.00 10.00
a. 10c yellow & multi 2.00 2.00
b. 15c bright blue & multi 2.00 2.00
c. 20c green & multi 2.00 2.00
d. 30c orange & multi 2.00 2.00

Issued to publicize the work of ACAPI, an organization devoted to the preservation and development of fish in Brazil.
No. 1130 contains four 38½x21mm stamps.

L. O. Teles de Menezes
A616

Mailman
A617

Perf. 11½x11

1969, July 26 **Photo.** **Wmk. 267**

1131 A616 50c dp org & bl grn 2.00 1.25

Centenary of Spiritism press in Brazil.

1969, Aug. 1

1132 A617 30c blue 1.75 1.00

Issued for Stamp Day.

Map of Brazil
A618

Railroad Bridge
A619

Gen. Tasso Fragoso — A620

Without Gum

Perf. 11½

1969, Aug. 25 **Unwmk.** **Litho.**

1133 A618 10c lt ultra, grn & yel .50 .25

Perf. 11x11½

1134 A619 20c multicolored 1.60 .60

With Gum

Perf. 11½x11

Engr. **Wmk. 267**

1135 A620 20c green 1.60 .70
Nos. 1133-1135 (3) 3.70 1.55

No. 1133 honors the Army as guardian of security; No. 1134, as promoter of development. No. 1135 the birth centenary of Gen. Tasso Fragoso.

Jupia Dam, Parana River
A621

Perf. 11½

1969, Sept. 10 **Litho.** **Unwmk.**
Without Gum

1136 A621 20c lt blue & multi 1.10 .80

Inauguration of the Jupia Dam, part of the Urubupunga hydroelectric system serving Sao Paulo.

Gandhi and Spinning Wheel
A622

1969, Oct. 2 ***Perf. 11x11½***

1137 A622 20c yellow & blk .90 .45

Mohandas K. Gandhi (1869-1948), leader in India's fight for independence.

Santos Dumont, Eiffel Tower and Module Landing on Moon — A623

1969, Oct. 17 ***Perf. 11½***
Without Gum

1138 A623 50c dk bl & multi 2.40 1.50

Man's first landing on the moon, July 20, 1969. See note after US No. C76.

Smelting Plant
A624

1969, Oct. 26 **Unwmk.** ***Perf. 11½***
Without Gum

1139 A624 20c multicolored .85 .60

Expansion of Brazil's steel industry.

Steel Furnace
A625

1969, Oct. 31 **Litho.**
Without Gum

1140 A625 10c yellow & multi .85 .60

25th anniversary of Acesita Steel Works.

Water Vendor, by J. B. Debret — A626

Design: 30c, Street Scene, by Debret.

1969-70 **Without Gum**

1141 A626 20c multicolored 2.25 .75
1141A A626 30c multicolored 2.25 1.25

Jean Baptiste Debret (1768-1848), painter.
Issued: 20c, 11/5/69; 30c, 5/19/70.

Exhibition Emblem — A627

1969, Nov. 15 ***Perf. 11½x11***
Without Gum

1142 A627 10c multicolored .70 .25

ABUEXPO 69 Philatelic Exposition, Sao Paulo, Nov. 15-23.

Plane — A628

1969, Nov. 23 **Without Gum**

1143 A628 50c multicolored 4.50 2.00

Publicizing the year of the expansion of the national aviation industry.

Pelé Scoring
A629

1969-70 **Without Gum**

1144 A629 10c multicolored .85 .85

Souvenir Sheet
Imperf

1145 A629 75c multi ('70) 15.00 4.50

Commemorating the 1,000th goal scored by Pele, Brazilian soccer player.
No. 1145 contains one imperf. stamp with simulated perforations.
Issued: 10c, 11/28/69; 75c, 1/23/70.

Madonna and Child from Villa Velha Monastery
A630

Perf. 11½

1969, Dec. **Unwmk.** **Litho.**

1146 A630 10c gold & multi .80 .25

Souvenir Sheet
Imperf

1147 A630 75c gold & multi *40.00 40.00*

Christmas 1969.
No. 1147 has simulated perforations.
Issue dates: 10c, Dec. 8; 75c, Dec. 18.

Destroyer and Submarine — A631

Perf. 11x11½

1969, Dec. 9 Engr. Wmk. 267

1148 A631 5c bluish gray .70 .35

Issued for Navy Day.

Dr. Herman Blumenau A632

1969, Dec. 26 ***Perf. 11½***

1149 A632 20c gray grn 1.50 .60

Dr. Herman Blumenau (1819-1899), founder of Blumenau, Santa Catarina State.

Carnival Scene — A633

Sugarloaf Mountain, Mask, Confetti and Streamers A634

Designs: 5c, Jumping boy and 2 women, vert. 20c, Clowns. 50c, Drummer.

1969-70 Litho. Unwmk.

Without Gum

1150	A633	5c multicolored	.70	.45
1151	A633	10c multicolored	.70	.45
1152	A633	20c multicolored	.85	.55
1153	A634	30c multicolored	5.00	2.50
1154	A634	50c multicolored	4.75	1.60
		Nos. 1150-1154 (5)	12.00	5.55

Carioca Carnival, Rio de Janeiro.

Issued: nos. 1150-1152, 12/29; others, 2/5/70.

Opening Bars of "Il Guarani" with Antonio Carlos Gomes Conducting A635

1970, Mar. 19 Litho. ***Perf. 11½***

Without Gum

1155 A635 20c blk, yel, gray & brn .75 .40

Centenary of the opera Il Guarani, by Antonio Carlos Gomes.

Church of Penha A636

1970, Apr. 6 Unwmk. ***Perf. 11½***

Without Gum

1156 A636 20c black & multi .50 .25

400th anniversary of the Church of Penha, State of Espirito Santo.

Assembly Building A637

10th anniv. of Brasilia: 50c, Reflecting Pool. 1cr, Presidential Palace.

1970, Apr. 21 Without Gum

1157	A637	20c multicolored	1.00	.50
1158	A637	50c multicolored	2.50	1.75
1159	A637	1cr multicolored	2.50	1.75
		Nos. 1157-1159 (3)	6.00	4.00

Symbolic Water Design A638

1970, May 5 Unwmk. ***Perf. 11½***

Without Gum

1161 A638 50c multicolored 2.50 3.00

Publicizing the Rondon Project for the development of the Amazon River basin.

Marshal Manoel Luiz Osorio and Osorio Arms — A639

1970, May 8 Without Gum

1162 A639 20c multicolored 1.50 1.00

Commemorating the inauguration of the Marshal Osorio Historical Park.

Madonna, from San Antonio Monastery, Rio de Janeiro A640

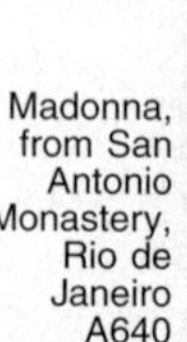

1970, May 10 Without Gum

1163 A640 20c multicolored .65 .50

Issued for Mother's Day.

Detail from Brasilia Cathedral — A641

1970, May 27 Engr. Wmk. 267

1164 A641 20c lt yellow grn .50 .30

8th National Eucharistic Congress, Brasilia.

Census Symbol — A642

Perf. 11½

1970, June 22 Unwmk. Litho.

Without Gum

1165 A642 20c green & yel .85 .85

Publicizing the 8th general census.

Soccer Cup, Maps of Brazil and Mexico A643

Swedish Flag and Player Holding Rimet Cup — A644

Designs: 2cr, Chilean flag and soccer. 3cr, Mexican flag and soccer.

1970 Without Gum

1166	A643	50c blk, lt bl & gold	1.10	1.10
1167	A644	1cr pink & multi	3.50	1.60
1168	A644	2cr gray & multi	6.00	1.60
1169	A644	3cr multicolored	5.25	1.25
		Nos. 1166-1169 (4)	15.85	5.55

9th World Soccer Championships for the Jules Rimet Cup, Mexico City, May 30-June 21. No. 1166 honors Brazil's victory.

Issued: No. 1166, 6/24; Nos. 1167-1169, 8/4.

Corcovado Christ and Map of South America A645

1970, July 18 Without Gum

1170 A645 50c brn, dk red & bl 4.00 3.50

6th World Cong. of Marist Brothers' Alumni.

Pandia Calogeras, Minister of War — A646

Perf. 11½x11

1970, Aug. 25 Photo. Unwmk.

1171 A646 20c blue green 1.00 .60

Brazilian Military Emblems and Map A647

Perf. 11x11½

1970, Sept. 8 Litho. Unwmk.

Without Gum

1172 A647 20c gray & multi .70 .70

25th anniv. of victory in World War II.

Annunciation (Brazilian Primitive Painting) A648

1970, Sept. 29 ***Perf. 11½***

Without Gum

1173 A648 20c multicolored 1.25 1.00

Issued for St. Gabriel's (patron saint of communications) Day.

Boy in Library — A649

1970, Oct. 23 Without Gum

1174 A649 20c multicolored 1.25 1.00

Issued to publicize Book Week.

UN Emblem — A650

1970, Oct. 24 Without Gum

1175 A650 50c dk bl, lt bl & sil 1.25 1.25

25th anniversary of the United Nations.

Rio de Janeiro, 1820 — A651

Designs: 50c, LUBRAPEX 70 emblem. 1cr, Rio de Janeiro with Sugar Loaf Mountain, 1970. No. 1179, like 20c.

1970, Oct. Without Gum

1176 A651 20c multicolored 2.25 1.00
1177 A651 50c yel brn & blk 5.00 2.25
1178 A651 1cr multicolored 6.00 2.75
Nos. 1176-1178 (3) 13.25 6.00

Souvenir Sheet

Imperf

1179 A651 1cr multicolored 30.00 25.00

LUBRAPEX 70, 3rd Portuguese-Brazilian Phil. Exhib., Rio de Janeiro, Oct. 24-31.
Issued: Nos. 1176-1178, 10/27; No. 1179, 10/31.

Holy Family by Candido Portinari A652

1970, Dec. Litho. *Perf. 11½*
Without Gum

1180 A652 50c multicolored 1.50 1.50

Souvenir Sheet

Imperf

1181 A652 1cr multicolored 60.00 60.00

Christmas 1970. No. 1181 contains one stamp with simulated perforations.
Issue dates: 50c, Dec. 1; 1cr, Dec. 8.

Battleship — A653

1970, Dec. 11 Litho. *Perf. 11½*
Without Gum

1182 A653 20c multicolored 1.50 .85

Navy Day.

CIH Emblem — A654

1971, Mar. 28 Litho. *Perf. 11½*
Without Gum

1183 A654 50c black & red 2.00 2.25

3rd Inter-American Housing Cong., 3/27-4/3.

Links Around Globe — A655

1971, Mar. 31 Litho. *Perf. 12½x11*
Without Gum

1184 A655 20c grn, yel, blk & red 1.00 .60

Intl. year against racial discrimination.

Morpho Melacheilus — A656

Design: 1cr, Papilio thoas brasiliensis.

Perf. 11x11½

1971, Apr. 28 Litho. Unwmk.
Without Gum

1185 A656 20c multicolored 1.60 .75
1186 A656 1cr multicolored 7.50 4.50

Madonna and Child — A657

1971, May 9 Litho. *Perf. 11½*
Without Gum

1187 A657 20c multicolored 1.00 .50

Mother's Day, 1971.

Basketball A658

1971, May 19 Without Gum

1188 A658 70c multicolored 2.50 1.40

6th World Women's Basketball Championship.

Map of Trans-Amazon Highway — A659

Perf. 11½

1971, July 1 Unwmk. Litho.
Without Gum

1189 40c multicolored 9.50 4.00
1190 1cr multicolored 9.50 8.00
a. A659 Pair, #1189-1190 20.00 20.00

Trans-Amazon Highway. No. 1190a printed in sheets of 28 (4x7). Horizontal rows contain 2 No. 1190a with a label between. Each label carries different inscription.

Man's Head, by Victor Mairelles de Lima A661

Stamp Day: 1cr, Arab Violinist, by Pedro Américo.

1971, Aug. 1

1191 A661 40c pink & multi 2.00 .90
1192 A661 1cr gray & multi 4.75 1.75

Duke of Caxias and Map of Brazil A662

1971, Aug. 23 Photo.

1193 A662 20c yel grn & red brn .80 .95

Army Week.

Anita Garibaldi — A663

1971, Aug. 30 Litho.
Without Gum

1194 A663 20c multicolored .60 .50

Anita Garibaldi (1821-1849), heroine in liberation of Brazil.

Xavante Jet and Santos Dumont's Plane, 1910 — A664

1971, Sept. 6 Without Gum

1195 A664 40c yellow & multi 2.25 1.00

First flight of Xavante jet plane.

Flags and Map of Central American Nations — A665

"71" in French Flag Colors — A666

1971, Sept. 15 Without Gum

1196 A665 40c ocher & multi 1.50 .70

Sesquicentennial of the independence of Central American nations.

1971, Sept. 16 Without Gum

1197 A666 1.30cr ultra & multi 2.00 1.25

French Exhibition.

Black Mother, by Lucilio de Albuquerque A667

Archangel Gabriel A668

1971, Sept. 28 Without Gum

1198 A667 40c multicolored 1.00 .60

Centenary of law guaranteeing personal freedom starting at birth.

1971, Sept. 29 *Perf. 11½x11*
Without Gum

1199 A668 40c multicolored 1.00 .75

St. Gabriel's Day.

Bridge over River A669

Children's Drawings: 35c, People crossing bridge. 60c, Woman with hat.

1971, Oct. 25 *Perf. 11½*
Without Gum

1200 A669 35c pink, bl & blk 1.40 .50
1201 A669 45c black & multi 1.40 .50
1202 A669 60c olive & multi 1.40 .50
Nos. 1200-1202 (3) 4.20 1.50

Children's Day.

Werkhäuserii Superba — A670

1971, Nov. 16 Without Gum

1203 A670 40c blue & multi 3.25 1.40

In memory of Carlos Werkhauser, botanist.

Greek Key Pattern "25" — A671

1971, Dec. 3 **Without Gum**

1204 A671 20c black & blue 1.50 1.25
1205 A671 40c black & org 1.50 1.25
a. Pair, #1204-1205 3.50 3.50

25th anniversary of SENAC (national apprenticeship system) and SESC (commercial social service).

Gunboat A672

1971, Dec. 8 *Perf. 11*
Without Gum

1206 A672 20c blue & multi 1.10 .60

Navy Day.

Cross and Circles — A673

1971, Dec. 11

1207 A673 20c car & blue .60 .60
1208 A673 75c silver & gray .75 *4.00*
1209 A673 1.30cr blk, yel, grn & bl 6.00 3.00
Nos. 1207-1209 (3) 7.35 *7.60*

Christmas 1971.

Washing of Bonfim Church, Salvador, Bahia — A674

Designs: 40c, Grape Festival, Rio Grande do Sul. 75c, Festival of the Virgin of Nazareth, Belém. 1.30cr, Winter Arts Festival, Ouro Preto.

1972, Feb. 18 **Litho.** *Perf. 11½x11*
Without Gum

1210 A674 20c silver & multi 3.25 1.00
1211 A674 40c silver & multi 3.25 1.00
1212 A674 75c silver & multi 4.00 2.75
1213 A674 1.30cr silver & multi 8.50 4.00
Nos. 1210-1213 (4) 19.00 8.75

Pres. Lanusse and Flag of Argentina A675

1972, Mar. 13 *Perf. 11x11½*
Without Gum

1214 A675 40c blue & multi 3.25 3.75

Visit of Lt. Gen. Alejandro Agustin Lanusse, president of Argentina.

Presidents Castello Branco, Costa e Silva and Garrastazu Medici — A676

1972, Mar. 29 **Without Gum**

1215 A676 20c emerald & multi 1.75 .80

Anniversary of 1964 revolution.

Post Office Emblem — A677

Perf. 11½x11

1972, Apr. 10 **Photo.** **Unwmk.**

1216 A677 20c red brown 3.50 .25

No. 1216 is luminescent.

Pres. Thomaz and Portuguese Flag — A678

1972, Apr. 22 **Litho.** *Perf. 11*
Without Gum

1217 A678 75c ol brn & multi 3.00 2.25

Visit of Pres. Americo Thomaz of Portugal to Brazil, Apr. 22-27.

Soil Research (CPRM) A679

1972, May 3 *Perf. 11½*
Without Gum

1218 A679 20c shown 1.75 .60
1219 A679 40c Offshore oil rig 2.75 1.00
1220 A679 75c Hydroelectric dam 2.75 1.60
1221 A679 1.30cr Iron ore production 4.25 2.00
Nos. 1218-1221 (4) 11.50 5.20

Industrial development. Stamps are inscribed with names of industrial firms.
See Nos. 1228-1229.

Souvenir Sheet

Poster for Modern Art Week 1922 — A680

1972, May 5

1222 A680 1cr black & car 75.00 75.00

50th anniversary of Modern Art Week.

Mailman, Map of Brazil and Letters A681

Designs: 45c, "Telecommunications", vert. 60c, Tropospheric scatter system. 70c, Road map of Brazil and worker.

1972, May 26 **Without Gum**

1223 A681 35c blue & multi 2.00 .50
1224 A681 45c silver & multi 2.00 1.75
1225 A681 60c black & multi 2.00 1.50
1226 A681 70c multicolored 3.00 1.50
Nos. 1223-1226 (4) 9.00 5.25

Unification of communications in Brazil.

Development Type of 1972 and

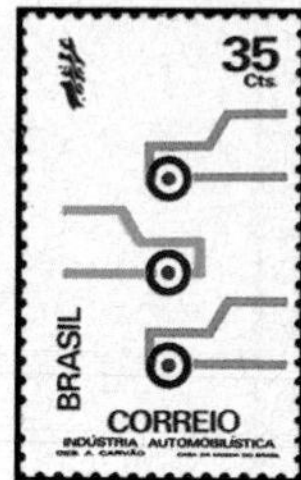

Automobiles — A682

Perf. 11x11½, 11½x11

1972, June 21 **Photo.**

1227 A682 35c shown 1.25 .60

Litho.

1228 A679 45c Ships 1.25 .70
1229 A679 70c Ingots 1.25 .70
Nos. 1227-1229 (3) 3.75 2.00

Industrial development. The 35c is luminescent.

Soccer — A683

75c, Folk music. 1.30cr, Plastic arts.

Perf. 11½x11

1972, July 7 **Photo.** **Unwmk.**

1230 A683 20c black & yel 1.50 .75
1231 A683 75c black & ver 3.00 5.25
1232 A683 1.30cr black & ultra 6.25 4.50
Nos. 1230-1232 (3) 10.75 10.50

150th anniv. of independence. No. 1230 publicizes the 1972 sports tournament, a part of independence celebrations. Luminescent.

Souvenir Sheet

Shout of Independence, by Pedro Americo de Figueiredo e Melo — A684

1972, July 19 **Litho.** *Perf. 11½*
Without Gum

1233 A684 1cr multicolored 9.50 *12.00*

4th Interamerican Philatelic Exhibition, EXFILBRA, Rio de Janeiro, Aug 26-Sept. 2.

Figurehead A685

Brazilian folklore: 60c, Gauchos dancing fandango. 75c, Acrobats (capoeira). 1.15cr, Karajá (ceramic) doll. 1.30cr, Mock bullfight (bumba meu boi).

1972, Aug. 6 **Without Gum**

1234 A685 45c multicolored .70 .40
1235 A685 60c org & multi 2.10 1.90
1236 A685 75c gray & multi .70 .40
1237 A685 1.15cr multicolored .70 .70
1238 A685 1.30cr yellow & multi 6.50 2.50
Nos. 1234-1238 (5) 10.70 5.90

Map of Brazil, by Diego Homem, 1568 A686

Designs: 1cr, Map of Americas, by Nicholas Visscher, 1652. 2cr, Map of Americas, by Lopo Homem, 1519.

1972, Aug. 26 **Litho.** *Perf. 11½*
Without Gum

1239 A686 70c multicolored .80 .65
1240 A686 1cr multicolored 13.00 1.25
1241 A686 2cr multicolored 5.25 1.90
Nos. 1239-1241 (3) 19.05 3.80

4th Inter-American Philatelic Exhibition, EXFILBRA, Rio de Janeiro, Aug. 26-Sept. 2.

Dom Pedro Proclaimed Emperor, by Jean Baptiste Debret — A687

Designs: 30c, Founding of Brazil (people with imperial flag), vert. 1cr, Coronation of Emperor Dom Pedro, vert. 2cr, Dom Pedro commemorative medal. 3.50cr, Independence Monument, Ipiranga.

1972, Sept. 4 Litho. *Perf. 11½x11*

1242 A687 30c yellow & grn 1.60 1.25
1243 A687 70c pink & rose lil 1.25 1.25
1244 A687 1cr buff & red brn 10.00 1.25
1245 A687 2cr pale yel & blk 6.75 1.25
1246 A687 3.50cr gray & blk 9.50 4.00
Nos. 1242-1246 (5) 29.10 9.00

Sesquicentennial of independence.

Souvenir Sheet

"Automobile Race" — A688

1972, Nov. 14 *Perf. 11½*

1247 A688 2cr multicolored 17.50 17.50

Emerson Fittipaldi, Brazilian world racing champion.

Numeral and Post Office Emblem — A689

Möbius Strip A689a

Perf. 11½x11

1972-75 Unwmk. Photo.

1248 A689 5c orange .55 .25
a. Wmk. 267 .30 .25
1249 A689 10c brown ('73) 1.75 .25
a. Wmk. 267 6.00 .25
1250 A689 15c brt blue ('75) .30 .25
1251 A689 20c ultra 2.75 .25
1252 A689 25c sepia ('75) .40 .25
1253 A689 30c dp carmine 1.75 .25
1254 A689 40c dk grn ('73) .30 .25
1255 A689 50c olive 2.25 .25
1256 A689 70c red lilac ('75) .60 .25

Engr. *Perf. 11½*

1257 A689a 1cr lilac ('74) 2.25 .25
1258 A689a 2cr grnsh bl ('74) 3.00 .25
1259 A689a 4cr org & vio ('75) 7.50 .25
1260 A689a 5cr brn, car & buff ('74) 6.50 .25
1261 A689a 10cr grn, blk & buff ('74) 13.00 .40
Nos. 1248-1261 (14) 42.90 3.65

The 5cr and 10cr have beige lithographed multiple Post Office emblem underprint.

Nos. 1248-1261 are luminescent. Nos. 1248a and 1249a are not.

Hand Writing "Mobral" A690

Designs: 20c, Multiracial group and population growth curve. 1cr, People and hands holding house. 2cr, People, industrial scene and upward arrow.

1972, Nov. 28 Litho. *Perf. 11½*
Without Gum

1262 A690 10c black & multi .60 .60
1263 A690 20c black & multi 1.25 .70
1264 A690 1cr black & multi 12.00 .60
1265 A690 2cr black & multi 2.75 .70
Nos. 1262-1265 (4) 16.60 2.60

Publicity for: "Mobral" literacy campaign (10c); Centenary of census (20c); Housing and retirement fund (1cr); Growth of gross national product (2cr).

Congress Building, Brasilia, by Oscar Niemeyer, and "Os Guerreiros," by Bruno Giorgi — A691

1972, Dec. 4 Without Gum

1266 A691 1cr blue, blk & org 15.00 9.00

Meeting of Natl. Cong., Brasilia, Dec. 4-8.

Holy Family (Clay Figurines) — A692

1972, Dec. 13 Photo. *Perf. 11½x11*

1267 A692 20c ocher & blk 1.00 .60

Christmas 1972. Luminescent.

Retirement Plan — A693

Designs: No.1269, School children and traffic lights, horiz. 70c, Dr. Oswaldo Cruz with Red Cross, caricature. 2cr, Produce, fish and cattle, horiz.

Perf. 11½x11, 11x11½

1972, Dec. 20 Litho.
Without Gum

1268 A693 10c blk, bl & dl org .60 .60
1269 A693 10c orange & multi 1.25 1.25
1270 A693 70c blk, red & brn 11.00 4.75
1271 A693 2cr green & multi 19.00 8.00
Nos. 1268-1271 (4) 31.85 14.60

Publicity for: Agricultural workers' assistance program (No. 1268); highway and transportation development (No. 1269); centenary of the birth of Dr. Oswaldo Cruz (1872-1917), Director of Public Health Institute (70c); agricultural and cattle export (2cr). Nos. 1268-1271 are luminescent.

Sailing Ship, Navy A694

Designs: 10c, Monument, Brazilian Expeditionary Force. No. 1274, Plumed helmet, Army. No. 1275, Rocket, Air Force.

Lithographed and Engraved

1972, Dec. 28 *Perf. 11x11½*
Without Gum

1272 A694 10c brn, dk brn & blk 2.00 2.00
1273 A694 30c lt ultra, grn & blk 2.00 2.00
1274 A694 30c yel grn, bl grn & blk 2.00 2.00
1275 A694 30c lilac, mar & blk 2.00 2.00
a. Block of 4, #1272-1275 8.50 8.50

Armed Forces Day.

Rotary Emblem and Cogwheels A695

Perf. 11½

1973, Mar. 21 Litho. Unwmk.

1276 A695 1cr ultra, grnsh bl & yel 2.50 2.25

Rotary International serving Brazil 50 years.

Swimming — A696

Designs: No. 1278, Gymnastics. No. 1279, Volleyball, vert.

1973 Photo. *Perf. 11x11½, 11½x11*

1277 A696 40c brt bl & red brn .55 .55
1278 A696 40c green & org brn 3.00 .50
1279 A696 40c violet & org brn 1.00 .50
Nos. 1277-1279 (3) 4.55 1.55

Issued: No. 1277, 4/19; No. 1278, 5/22; No.1279, 10/15.

Flag of Paraguay A697

Perf. 11½

1973, Apr. 27 Litho. Unwmk.

1280 A697 70c multicolored 2.25 1.75

Visit of Pres. Alfredo Stroessner of Paraguay, Apr. 25-27.

"Communications" — A698

Designs: 1cr, Neptune, map of South America and Africa.

1973, May 5 *Perf. 11x11½*

1281 A698 70c multicolored 1.00 .80
1282 A698 1cr multicolored 5.00 3.00

Inauguration of the Ministry of Communications Building, Brasilia (70c); and of the first underwater telephone cable between South America and Europe, Bracan 1 (1cr).

Congress Emblem — A699

1973, May 19 *Perf. 11½x11*

1283 A699 1cr orange & pur 5.00 3.75

24th Congress of the International Chamber of Commerce, Rio de Janeiro, May 19-26.

Swallowtailed Manakin — A700

Birds: No. 1285, Orange-backed oriole. No. 1286, Brazilian ruby (hummingbird).

1973 Litho. *Perf. 11x11½*

1284 A700 20c multicolored 1.40 .50
1285 A700 20c multicolored 1.40 .50
1286 A700 20c multicolored 1.40 .50
Nos. 1284-1286 (3) 4.20 1.50

Issued: No. 1284, 5/26; No. 1285, 6/6; No. 1286, 6/19.

Tourists A701

1973, June 28 Litho. *Perf. 11x11½*

1287 A701 70c multicolored 1.50 1.00

National Tourism Year.

Conference at Itu — A702

1973 *Perf. 11½x11*

1288 A702 20c shown 1.00 .45
1289 A702 20c Decorated wagon 1.00 .45
1290 A702 20c Indian 1.00 .45
1291 A702 20c Graciosa Road 1.00 .45
Nos. 1288-1291 (4) 4.00 1.80

Centenary of the Itu Convention (No. 1288); sesquicentennial of the July 2 episode (No. 1289); 400th anniversary of the founding of Niteroi (No. 1290); centenary of Graciosa Road (No. 1291).

Issue dates: No. 1291, July 29; others July 2.

Satellite and Multi-spectral Image A703

Designs: 70c, Official opening of Engineering School, 1913. 1cr, Möbius strips and "IMPA."

1973, July 11 ***Perf. 11½***

1292 A703 20c black & multi .55 .50
1293 A703 70c dk blue & multi 3.00 .90
1294 A703 1cr lilac & multi 4.25 .90
Nos. 1292-1294 (3) 7.80 2.30

Institute for Space Research (20c); School of Engineering, Itajubá, 60th anniversary (70c); Institute for Pure and Applied Mathematics (1cr).

Santos-Dumont and 14-Bis Plane — A704

Santos-Dumont and: 70c, No. 6 Balloon and Eiffel Tower. 2cr Demoiselle plane.

Lithographed and Engraved

1973, July 20 ***Perf. 11x11½***

1295 A704 20c lt grn, brt grn & brn .85 .30
1296 A704 70c yel, rose red & brn 2.00 1.50
1297 A704 2cr bl, vio bl & brn 3.50 1.50
Nos. 1295-1297 (3) 6.35 3.30

Centenary of the birth of Alberto Santos-Dumont (1873-1932), aviation pioneer.

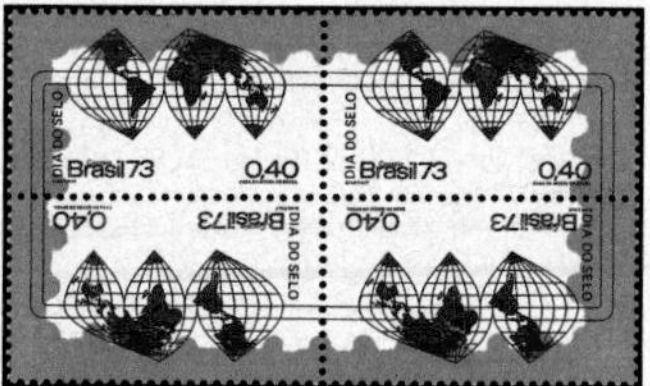

Mercator Map — A705

Designs: No. 1298, "BRASIL" within white background. No. 1299, Right half of "0" in "40" overlays red border. No. 1299A, "B" in "BRASIL" touches red. No. 1299B, Top edge of "0" in "40" overlays red border.

Photogravure and Engraved

1973, Aug. 1 **Wmk. 267**

1298 40c red & black 5.00 5.00
1299 40c red & black 3.00 3.00
1299A 40c red & black 9.00 5.00
1299B 40c red & black 6.00 6.00
c. A705 Block of 4, #1298-1299B 45.00 30.00

Stamp Day. Nos. 1298-1299B are printed se-tenant horizontally and tête bêche vertically in sheets of 55.

Gonçalves Dias (1823-1864), Poet — A706

Perf. 11½x11

1973, Aug. 10 **Wmk. 267**

1300 A706 40c violet & blk 1.00 .70

Souvenir Sheet

Copernicus and Sun — A707

Perf. 11x11½

1973, Aug. 15 **Litho.** **Unwmk.**

1301 A707 1cr multicolored 22.50 22.50

500th anniversary of the birth of Nicolaus Copernicus (1473-1543), Polish astronomer.

Folklore Festival Banner — A708

1973, Aug. 22 ***Perf. 11½***

1302 A708 40c ultra & multi 1.00 .60

Folklore Day, Aug. 22.

Masonic Emblem A709

1973, Aug. 24 **Photo.** ***Perf. 11x11½***

1303 A709 1cr Prus blue 4.00 2.50

Free Masons of Brazil, 1822-1973.

Nature Protection — A710

Designs: No. 1305, Fire protection. No. 1306, Aviation safety. No. 1307, Safeguarding cultural heritage.

1973, Sept. 20 **Litho.** ***Perf. 11x11½***

1304 A710 40c brt grn & multi 1.00 .65
1305 A710 40c dk blue & multi 1.00 .65
1306 A710 40c lt blue & multi 1.00 .65
1307 A710 40c pink & multi 1.00 .65
Nos. 1304-1307 (4) 4.00 2.60

Souvenir Sheet

St. Gabriel and Proclamation of Pope Paul VI — A711

Lithographed and Engraved

1973, Sept. 29 **Unwmk.** ***Perf. 11½***

1308 A711 1cr bister & blk 24.00 11.00

1st National Exhibition of Religious Philately, Rio de Janeiro, Sept. 29-Oct. 6.

St. Teresa — A712

Photogravure and Engraved

Perf. 11½x11

1973, Sept. 30 **Wmk. 267**

1309 A712 2cr dk org & brn 4.50 3.00

St. Teresa of Lisieux, the Little Flower (1873-1897), Carmelite nun.

Monteiro Lobato and Emily A713

Perf. 11½

1973, Oct. 12 **Litho.** **Unwmk.**

1310 A713 40c shown 1.25 .60
1311 A713 40c Aunt Nastacia 1.25 .60
1312 A713 40c Snubnose, Peter and Rhino 1.25 .60
1313 A713 40c Viscount de Sabugosa 1.25 .60
1314 A713 40c Dona Benta 1.25 .60
a. Block of 5 + label 6.00 6.00

Monteiro Lobato, author of children's books.

Soapstone Sculpture of Isaiah (detail) A714

Baroque Art in Brazil: No. 1316, Arabesque, gilded wood carving, horiz. 70c, Father José Mauricio Nuñes Garcia and music score. 1cr, Church door, Salvador, Bahia. 2cr, Angels, church ceiling painting by Manoel da Costa Athayde, horiz.

1973, Nov. 5

1315 A714 40c multicolored 1.90 .45
1316 A714 40c multicolored 1.90 .45
1317 A714 70c multicolored 3.50 2.10
1318 A714 1cr multicolored 7.75 2.50
1319 A714 2cr multicolored 7.75 3.00
Nos. 1315-1319 (5) 22.80 8.50

Old and New Telephones — A715

1973, Nov. 28 ***Perf. 11x11½***

1320 A715 40c multicolored .50 .35

50th anniv. of Brazilian Telephone Co.

Symbolic Angel A716

1973, Nov. 30 ***Perf. 11½***

1321 A716 40c ver & multi .65 .35

Christmas 1973.

River Boats A717

1973, Nov. 30 **Litho.** ***Perf. 11x11½***

1322 A717 40c "Gaiola" .50 .35
1323 A717 70c "Regatao" 2.00 1.05
1324 A717 1cr "Jangada" 7.50 3.00
1325 A717 2cr "Saveiro" 7.50 2.50
Nos. 1322-1325 (4) 17.50 6.90

Nos. 1322-1325 are luminescent.

Scales of Justice A718

1973, Dec. 5 ***Perf. 11½***

1326 A718 40c magenta & vio .80 .40

To honor the High Federal Court, created in 1891. Luminescent.

José Placido de Castro — A719

Scarlet Ibis and Victoria Regia — A720

Lithographed and Engraved

Perf. 11½x11

1973, Dec. 12 **Wmk. 267**

1327 A719 40c lilac rose & blk .75 .40

Centenary of the birth of Jose Placido de Castro, liberator of the State of Acre.

Perf. 11½x11

1973, Dec. 28 **Litho.** **Unwmk.**

Designs: 70c, Jaguar and spathodea campanulata. 1cr, Scarlet macaw and carnauba palm. 2cr, Rhea and coral tree.

1328 A720 40c brown & multi 1.25 .50
1329 A720 70c brown & multi 3.00 1.75
1330 A720 1cr bister & multi 3.00 .40
1331 A720 2cr bister & multi 12.00 4.00
Nos. 1328-1331 (4) 19.25 6.65

Nos. 1328-1331 are luminescent.

Saci Perere, Mocking Goblin — A721

Characters from Brazilian Legends: 80c, Zumbi, last chief of rebellious slaves. 1cr, Chico Rei, African king. 1.30cr, Little Black Boy of the Pasture. 2.50cr, Iara, Queen of the Waters.

Perf. 11½x11

1974, Feb. 28 **Litho.** **Unwmk.**

Size: 21x39mm

1332 A721 40c multicolored .60 .40
1333 A721 80c multicolored .80 .50
1334 A721 1cr multicolored 1.75 .50

Perf. 11½

Size: 32½x33mm

1335 A721 1.30cr multicolored 4.50 1.00
1336 A721 2.50cr multicolored 13.00 3.00
Nos. 1332-1336 (5) 20.65 5.40

Nos. 1332-1336 are luminescent.

Pres. Costa e Silva Bridge A722

1974, Mar. 11
1337 A722 40c multicolored .80 .35

Inauguration of the Pres. Costa e Silva Bridge, Rio Niteroi, connecting Rio de Janeiro and Guanabara State.

"The Press" A723

1974, Mar. 25 ***Perf. 11½***
1338 A723 40c shown .60 .35
1339 A723 40c "Radio" .60 .35
1340 A723 40c "Television" .60 .35
Nos. 1338-1340 (3) 1.80 1.05

Communications Commemorations: No. 1338, bicentenary of first Brazilian newspaper, published in London by Hipolito da Costa; No. 1339, founding of the Radio Sociedade do Rio de Janeiro by Roquette Pinto; No. 1340, installation of first Brazilian television station by Assis Chateaubriand. Luminescent.

"Reconstruction" — A724

1974, Mar. 31
1341 A724 40c multicolored .90 .55

10 years of progress. Luminescent.

Corcovado Christ, Marconi, Colors of Brazil and Italy — A725

1974, Apr. 25 Litho. ***Perf. 11½***
1342 A725 2.50cr multi 7.50 4.25

Guglielmo Marconi (1874-1937), Italian physicist and inventor. Luminescent.

Stamp Printing Press, Stamp Designing A726

1974, May 6
1343 A726 80c multicolored 1.40 .50

Brazilian mint.

World Map, Indian, Caucasian and Black Men — A727

World Map and: No. 1345, Brazilians. No. 1346, Cabin & German horseback rider. No. 1347, Italian farm wagon. No. 1348, Japanese woman & torii.

1974, May 3 **Unwmk.**
1344 A727 40c multicolored .45 .35
1345 A727 40c multicolored .45 .35
1346 A727 2.50cr multicolored 4.00 1.00
1347 A727 2.50cr multicolored 8.50 1.00
1348 A727 2.50cr multicolored 4.00 1.00
Nos. 1344-1348 (5) 17.40 3.70

Ethnic and migration influences in Brazil.

Sandstone Cliffs, Sete Cidades National Park — A728

Tourist publicity: 80c, Ruins of Cathedral of Sao Miguel das Missões.

Lithographed and Engraved
1974, June 8 ***Perf. 11x11½***
1349 A728 40c multicolored 1.00 .60
1350 A728 80c multicolored 1.00 .60

Souvenir Sheet

Soccer — A729

1974, June 20 Litho. ***Perf. 11½***
1351 A729 2.50cr multi 17.00 17.00

World Cup Soccer Championship, Munich, June 13-July 7.

Church and College, Caraça A730

1974, July 6 Litho. ***Perf. 11x11½***
1352 A730 40c multicolored .80 .50

College (Seminary) of Caraça, bicent.

Wave on Television Screen A731

1974, July 15 ***Perf. 11½***
1353 A731 40c black & blue .50 .50

TELEBRAS, Third Brazilian Congress of Telecommunications, Brasilia, July 15-20.

Fernao Dias Paes A732

1974, July 21 ***Perf. 11½***
1354 A732 20c green & multi .45 .45

3rd centenary of the expedition led by Fernao Dias Paes exploring Minas Gerais and the passage from South to North in Brazil.

Mexican Flag — A733

1974, July 24 Litho. ***Perf. 11½***
1355 A733 80c multicolored 3.50 1.40

Visit of Pres. Luis Echeverria Alvares of Mexico, July 24-29.

Flags of Brazil and Germany A734

1974, Aug. 5 ***Perf. 11x11½***
1356 A734 40c multicolored .90 .90

World Cup Soccer Championship, 1974, victory of German Federal Republic.

Souvenir Sheet

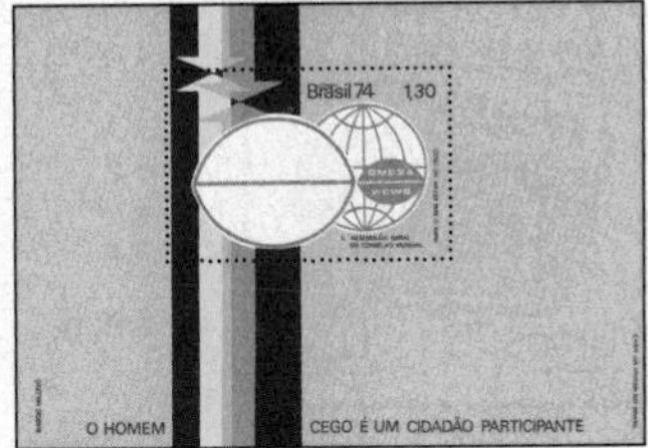

Congress Emblem — A735

1974, Aug. 7 ***Perf. 11½***
1357 A735 1.30cr multi 1.75 *2.50*

5th World Assembly of the World Council for the Welfare of the Blind, Sao Paulo, Aug. 7-16. Stamp and margin inscribed in Braille with name of Assembly.

Raul Pederneiras (1874-1953, Journalist, Professor of Law and Fine Arts), Caricature by J. Carlos — A736

Lithographed and Engraved
1974, Aug. 15 ***Perf. 11½x11***
1358 A736 40c buff, blk & ocher .45 .45

Society Emblem and Landscape — A737

1974, Aug. 19 Litho. ***Perf. 11x11½***
1359 A737 1.30cr multi 1.90 1.10

13th Congress of the International Union of Building and Savings Societies.

Souvenir Sheet

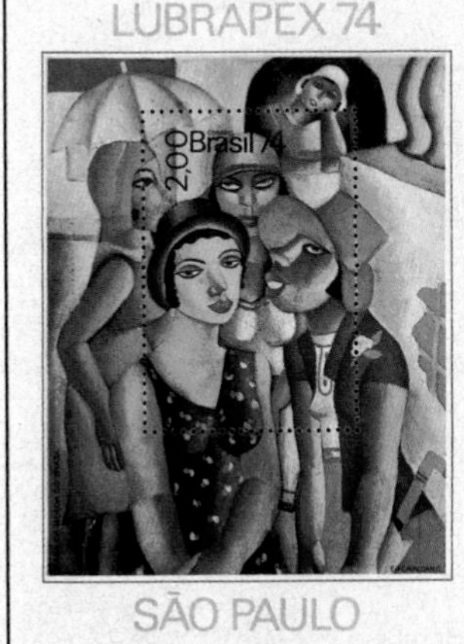

Five Women, by Di Cavalcanti — A738

1974, Aug. 26 Litho. ***Perf. 11½***
1360 A738 2cr multicolored 6.00 *7.50*

LUBRAPEX 74, 5th Portuguese-Brazilian Phil. Exhib., Sao Paulo, Nov. 26-Dec. 4.

"UPU" and World Map A739

1974, Oct. 9 Litho. ***Perf. 11½***
1361 A739 2.50cr blk & brt bl 7.00 3.00

Centenary of Universal Postal Union.

Hammock (Antillean Arawak Culture) A740

Bilro Lace — A741

Singer of "Cord" Verses — A742

Ceramic Figure by Master Vitalino — A743

1974, Oct. 16 Litho. *Perf. 11½*

1362 A740 50c deep rose lilac 2.25 .50
1363 A741 50c lt & dk blue 2.75 .50
1364 A742 50c yel & red brn .70 .50
1365 A743 50c brt yel & dk brn .90 .50
Nos. 1362-1365 (4) 6.60 2.00

Popular Brazilian crafts.

Branch of Coffee A744

1974, Oct. 27 Unwmk. *Perf. 11*

1366 A744 50c multicolored 1.25 .70

Centenary of city of Campinas.

Hornless Tabapua A745

Animals of Brazil: 1.30cr, Creole horse. 2.50cr, Brazilian mastiff.

1974, Nov. 10 *Perf. 11½*

1367 A745 80c multi 1.50 1.00
1368 A745 1.30cr multi 1.50 1.00
1369 A745 2.50cr multi 11.00 3.50
Nos. 1367-1369 (3) 14.00 5.50

Christmas — A746

1974, Nov. 18 *Perf. 11½x11*

1370 A746 50c Angel 1.00 .40

Solteira Island Hydroelectric Dam — A747

1974, Nov. 11 *Perf. 11½*

1371 A747 50c black & yellow 2.00 .60

Inauguration of the Solteira Island Hydroelectric Dam over Parana River.

The Girls, by Carlos Reis — A748

1974, Nov. 26

1372 A748 1.30cr multi .90 .60

LUBRAPEX 74, 5th Portuguese-Brazilian Phil. Exhib., Sao Paulo, Nov. 26-Dec. 4.

Youths, Judge, Scales A749

1974, Dec. 20 Litho. *Perf. 11½*

1373 A749 90c yel, red & bl .50 .50

Juvenile Court of Brazil, 50th anniversary.

Long Distance Runner — A750

1974, Dec. 23

1374 A750 3.30cr multi .90 .90

Sao Silvestre long distance running, 50th anniversary.

News Vendor, 1875, Masthead, 1975 A751

1975, Jan. 4

1375 A751 50c multicolored 1.75 .90

Newspaper "O Estado de S. Paulo," cent.

Sao Paulo Industrial Park A752

Designs: 1.40cr, Natural rubber industry, Acre. 4.50cr, Manganese mining, Amapá.

1975, Jan. 24 Litho. *Perf. 11x11½*

1376 A752 50c vio bl & yel 1.50 .50
1377 A752 1.40cr yellow & brn .75 .50
1378 A752 4.50cr yellow & blk 7.00 .50
Nos. 1376-1378 (3) 9.25 1.50

Economic development.

Fort of the Holy Cross A753

Colonial forts: No. 1380, Fort of the Three Kings. No. 1381, Fort of Monteserrat. 90c, Fort of Our Lady of Help.

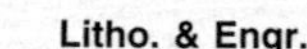

Litho. & Engr.

1975, Mar. 14 *Perf. 11½*

1379 A753 50c yel & red brn .60 .25
1380 A753 50c yel & red brn .60 .25
1381 A753 50c yel & red brn .60 .25
1382 A753 90c yel & red brn .70 .25
Nos. 1379-1382 (4) 2.50 1.00

House on Stilts, Amazon Region A754

Designs: 50c, Modern houses and plan of Brasilia. 1.40cr, Indian hut, Rondonia. 3.30cr, German-style cottage (Enxaimel), Santa Catarina.

1975, Apr. 18 Litho. *Perf. 11½*

1383 A754 50c yel & multi 2.50 2.50
1384 A754 50c yel & multi 16.00 10.00
a. Pair, #1383-1384 18.50 12.50
1385 A754 1cr yel & multi 1.60 .35
1386 A754 1.40cr yel & multi 6.00 2.50
1387 A754 1.40cr yel & multi .95 .95
a. Pair, #1386-1387 7.00 3.75
1388 A754 3.30cr yel & multi 1.50 1.25
1389 A754 3.30cr yel & multi 6.75 4.50
a. Pair, #1388-1389 8.25 5.75
Nos. 1383-1389 (7) 35.30 22.05

Brazilian architecture. Nos. 1383, 1386, 1388 have yellow strip at right side, others at left.

Fish — A755

1975, May 2 Litho. *Perf. 11½*

1390 A755 50c Astronotus ocellatus .85 .40
1391 A755 50c Colomesus psitacus .85 .25
1392 A755 50c Phallocerus caudimaculatus .85 .40
1393 A755 50c Symphysodon discus .85 .50
Nos. 1390-1393 (4) 3.40 1.55

Soldier's Head in Brazil's Colors, Plane, Rifle and Ship — A756

1975, May 8 *Perf. 11½x11*

1394 A756 50c vio bl & multi .60 .40

In honor of the veterans of World War II, on the 30th anniversary of victory.

Brazilian Otter — A757

Nature protection: 70c, Brazilian pines, horiz. 3.30cr, Marsh cayman, horiz.

1975, June 17 Litho. *Perf. 11½*

1395 A757 70c bl, grn & blk 1.75 .60
1396 A757 1cr multi .90 .60
1397 A757 3.30cr multi .90 .60
Nos. 1395-1397 (3) 3.55 1.80

Petroglyphs, Stone of Ingá — A758

Marjoara Vase, Pará — A759

Vinctifer Comptoni, Petrified Fish A760

1975, July 8 Litho. *Perf. 11½*

1398 A758 70c multicolored 1.00 .40
1399 A759 1cr multicolored .45 .40
1400 A760 1cr multicolored .45 .40
Nos. 1398-1400 (3) 1.90 1.20

Archaeological discoveries.

Immaculate Conception, Franciscan Monastery, Vitoria — A761

1975, July 15

1401 A761 3.30cr blue & multi 1.25 .95

Holy Year 1975 and 300th anniv. of establishment of the Franciscan Province in Southern Brazil.

Post and Telegraph Ministry — A762

1975, Aug. 8 Engr. *Perf. 11½*

1402 A762 70c dk carmine .90 .40

Stamp Day 1975.

Dances A763

Designs: No. 1403, Sword Dance, Minas Gerais. No. 1404, Umbrella Dance, Pernambuco. No. 1405, Warrior's Dance, Alagoas.

1975, Aug. 22 Litho. *Perf. 11½*

1403 A763 70c gray & multi .55 .40
1404 A763 70c pink & multi .55 .40
1405 A763 70c yellow & multi .55 .40
Nos. 1403-1405 (3) 1.65 1.20

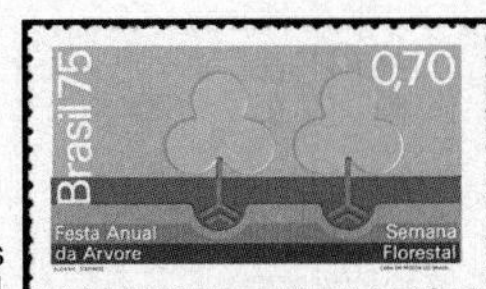

Trees A764

1975, Sept. 15 ***Perf. 11x11½***
1406 A764 70c multicolored .45 .30

Annual Tree Festival.

Globe, Radar and Satellite — A765

1975, Sept. 16 ***Perf. 11½***
1407 A765 3.30cr multi .90 .90

Inauguration of 2nd antenna of Tangua Earth Station, Rio de Janeiro State.

Woman Holding Flowers and Globe A766

1975, Sept. 23
1408 A766 3.30cr multi 1.25 1.25

International Women's Year 1975.

Tile, Railing and Column, Alcantara A767

Cross and Monastery, Sao Cristovao — A768

Historic cities: No. 1411, Jug and Clock Tower, Goiás, vert.

1975, Sept. 27 **Litho.** ***Perf. 11½***
1409 A767 70c multicolored .70 .50
1410 A768 70c multicolored .70 .50
1411 A768 70c multicolored .70 .50
Nos. 1409-1411 (3) 2.10 1.50

"Books teach how to live" A769

1975, Oct. 23 **Litho.** ***Perf. 11½***
1412 A769 70c multicolored .40 .40

Day of the Book.

ASTA Congress Emblem A770

1975, Oct. 27 ***Perf. 11x11½***
1413 A770 70c multicolored .40 .35

American Society of Travel Agents, 45th World Congress, Rio, Oct. 27-Nov. 1.

Angels A771

1975, Nov. 11
1414 A771 70c red & brown .40 .35

Christmas 1975.

Map of Americas, Waves — A772

1975, Nov. 19 ***Perf. 11½x12***
1415 A772 5.20cr gray & multi 4.00 2.50

2nd Interamerican Conference of Telecommunications (CITEL), Rio, Nov. 19-27.

Dom Pedro II — A773

1975, Dec. 2 **Engr.** ***Perf. 12***
1416 A773 70c violet brown 1.00 .55

Dom Pedro II (1825-1891), emperor of Brazil, birth sesquicentennial.

People and Cross A774

1975, Nov. 27 **Litho.** ***Perf. 11x11½***
1417 A774 70c lt bl & dp bl .65 .65

National Day of Thanksgiving.

Tourism A775

Designs: No. 1418, Guarapari Beach, Espirito Santo. No. 1419, Salt Stone beach, Piaui. No. 1420, Cliffs, Rio Grande Do Sul.

1975, Dec. 19 **Litho.** ***Perf. 11½***
1418 A775 70c multicolored .40 .40
1419 A775 70c multicolored .40 .40
1420 A775 70c multicolored .40 .40
Nos. 1418-1420 (3) 1.20 1.20

Triple Jump, Games Emblem A776

1975, Dec. 22 ***Perf. 11x11½***
1421 A776 1.60cr bl grn & blk .50 .50

Triple jump world record by Joao Carlos de Oliveira in 7th Pan-American Games, Mexico City, Oct. 12-26.

UN Emblem and Headquarters — A777

1975, Dec. 29 ***Perf. 11½***
1422 A777 1.30cr dp bl & vio bl .35 .35

United Nations, 30th anniversary.

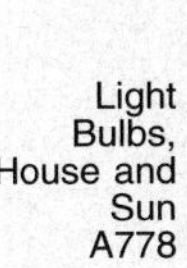

Light Bulbs, House and Sun A778

Energy conservation: No. 1424, Gasoline drops, car and sun.

1976, Jan. 16
1423 A778 70c multicolored .70 .30
1424 A778 70c multicolored .70 .30

Concorde A779

1976, Jan. 21 **Litho.** ***Perf. 11x11½***
1425 A779 5.20cr bluish black .70 .40

First commercial flight of supersonic jet Concorde from Paris to Rio, Jan. 21.

Souvenir Sheet

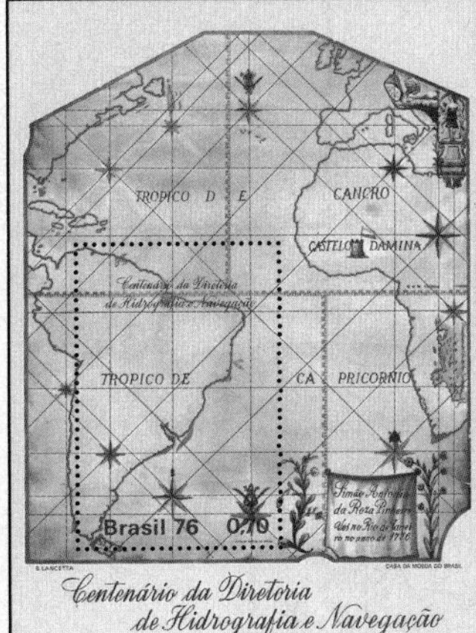

Nautical Map of South Atlantic, 1776 — A780

1976, Feb. 2 ***Perf. 11½***
1426 A780 70c salmon & multi 2.50 2.50

Centenary of the Naval Hydrographic and Navigation Institute.

Telephone Lines, 1876 Telephone — A781

1976, Mar. 10 **Litho.** ***Perf. 11x11½***
1427 A781 5.20cr orange & blue 1.00 .60

Centenary of first telephone call by Alexander Graham Bell, March 10, 1876.

Eye and Exclamation Point — A782

Kaiapo Body Painting — A783

1976, Apr. 7 **Litho.** ***Perf. 11½x11***
1428 A782 1cr vio red brn & brn .75 .75

World Health Day: "Foresight prevents blindness."

1976, Apr. 19 **Litho.** ***Perf. 11½***

Designs: No. 1430, Bakairi ceremonial mask. No. 1431, Karajá feather headdress.

1429 A783 1cr light violet & multi .30 .25
1430 A783 1cr light violet & multi .30 .25
1431 A783 1cr light violet & multi .30 .25
Nos. 1429-1431 (3) .90 .75

Preservation of indigenous culture.

Itamaraty Palace, Brasilia A784

1976, Apr. 20
1432 A784 1cr multicolored 1.00 .70

Diplomats' Day. Itamaraty Palace, designed by Oscar Niemeyer, houses the Ministry of Foreign Affairs.

Watering Can over Stones, by José Tarcisio A785

Fingers and Ribbons, by Pietrina Checcacci A786

1976, May 14 **Litho.** ***Perf. 11½***
1433 A785 1cr multi .30 .25
1434 A786 1.60cr multi .30 .25

Modern Brazilian art.

Basketball — A787

Olympic Rings and: 1.40cr, Yachting. 5.20cr, Judo.

1976, May 21 Litho. *Perf. 11½*

1435 A787 1cr emerald & blk .35 .25
1436 A787 1.40cr dk blue & blk .35 .25
1437 A787 5.20cr orange & blk .60 .30
Nos. 1435-1437 (3) 1.30 .80

21st Olympic Games, Montreal, Canada, July 17-Aug. 1.

Orchid — A788

Nature protection: No. 1439, Golden-faced lion monkey.

1976, June 4 *Perf. 11½x11*

1438 A788 1cr multicolored .75 .25
1439 A788 1cr multicolored .75 .25

Film Camera, Brazilian Colors — A789

1976, June 19

1440 A789 1cr vio bl, brt grn & yel .40 .40

Brazilian film industry.

Bahia Woman — A790

Designs: 10c, Oxcart driver, horiz. 20c, Raft fishermen, horiz. 30c, Rubber plantation worker. 40c, Cowboy, horiz. 50c, Gaucho. 80c, Gold panner. 1cr, Banana plantation worker. 1.10cr, Grape harvester. 1.30cr, Coffee picker. 1.80cr, Farmer gathering wax palms. 2cr, Potter. 5cr, Sugar cane cutter. 7cr, Salt mine worker. 10cr, Fisherman. 15cr, Coconut seller. 20cr, Lacemaker.

Perf. 11½x11, 11x11½

1976-78 Photo.

1441 A790 10c red brown ('77) .30 .25
1442 A790 15c brown .50 .50
1443 A790 20c violet blue .30 .25
1444 A790 30c lilac rose .30 .25
1445 A790 40c orange ('77) .40 .25
1446 A790 50c citron .75 .25
1447 A790 80c slate green .50 .25
1448 A790 1cr black .30 .25
1449 A790 1.10cr magenta ('77) .30 .25
1450 A790 1.30cr red ('77) .30 .25
1451 A790 1.80cr dk vio bl ('78) .30 .25

Engr.

1452 A790 2cr brown ('77) 3.00 .25
1453 A790 5cr dk pur ('77) 5.50 .25
1454 A790 7cr violet 11.00 .25
1455 A790 10cr yel grn ('77) 7.00 .25
1456 A790 15cr gray grn ('78) 2.75 .25
1457 A790 20cr blue 7.00 .25
Nos. 1441-1457 (17) 40.50 4.50

See Nos. 1653-1657.

Fish A791

Designs: No. 1460, Hyphessobrycon innesi. No. 1461, Copeina arnoldi. No. 1462, Prochilodus insignis. No. 1463, Crenicichla lepidota. No. 1464, Ageneiosus. No. 1465, Corydoras reticulatus.

1976, July 12 Litho. *Perf. 11x11½*

1460 A791 1cr multi .80 .55
1461 A791 1cr multi .80 .55
1462 A791 1cr multi .80 .55
1463 A791 1cr multi .80 .55
1464 A791 1cr multi .80 .55
1465 A791 1cr multi .80 .55
a. Block of 6, #1460-1465 5.00 5.00

Santa Marta Lighthouse A792

1976, July 29 Engr. *Perf. 12x11½*

1466 A792 1cr blue .60 .30

300th anniversary of the city of Laguna.

Children on Magic Carpet A793

1976, Aug. 1 Litho. *Perf. 11½x12*

1467 A793 1cr multicolored .40 .30

Stamp Day.

Nurse's Lamp and Head A794

1976, Aug. 12 Litho. *Perf. 11½*

1468 A794 1cr multicolored .40 .30

Brazilian Nurses' Assoc., 50th anniv.

Puppet, Soldier — A795

Designs: 1.30cr, Girl's head. 1.60cr, Hand with puppet head on each finger, horiz.

1976, Aug. 20

1469 A795 1cr multi .30 .30
1470 A795 1.30cr multi .30 .30
1471 A795 1.60cr multi .30 .30
Nos. 1469-1471 (3) .90 .90

Mamulengo puppet show.

Winner's Medal — A796

1976, Aug. 21

1472 A796 5.20cr multi .90 .60

27th International Military Athletic Championships, Rio de Janeiro, Aug. 21-28.

Family Protection — A797

1976, Sept. 12

1473 A797 1cr lt & dk blue .40 .30

National organizations SENAC and SESC helping commercial employees to improve their living standard, both commercially and socially.

Dying Tree — A798

1976, Sept. 20 Litho. *Perf. 11½*

1474 A798 1cr gray & multi .35 .25

Protection of the environment.

Atom Symbol, Electron Orbits A799

1976, Sept. 21

1475 A799 5.20cr multi .90 .60

20th General Conference of the International Atomic Energy Agency, Rio de Janeiro, Sept. 21-29.

Train in Tunnel A800

1976, Sept. 26

1476 A800 1.60cr multi .55 .25

Sao Paulo subway, 1st in Brazil.

St. Francis and Birds A801

1976, Oct. 4

1477 A801 5.20cr multi .90 .50

St. Francis of Assisi, 750th death anniv.

Ouro Preto School of Mining — A802

1976, Oct. 12 Engr. *Perf. 12x11½*

1478 A802 1cr dk vio 1.00 .60

Ouro Preto School of Mining, centenary.

Three Kings A803

Designs: Children's drawings.

1976, Nov. 4 Litho. *Perf. 11½*

1479 A803 80c shown .40 .30
1480 A803 80c Santa Claus on donkey .40 .30
1481 A803 80c Virgin and Child and Angels .40 .30
1482 A803 80c Angels with candle .40 .30
1483 A803 80c Nativity .40 .30
a. Strip of 5, #1479-1483 2.00 2.00

Christmas 1976.

Souvenir Sheet

30,000 Reis Banknote — A804

1976, Nov. 5 Litho. *Perf. 11½*

1484 A804 80c multicolored 1.50 *2.50*

Opening of 1000th branch of Bank of Brazil, Barra do Bugres, Mato Grosso.

Virgin of Monte Serrat, by Friar Agostinho A805

St. Joseph, 18th Century Wood Sculpture — A806

5.60cr, The Dance, by Rodolfo Bernadelli, 19th cent. 6.50cr, The Caravel, by Bruno Giorgi, 20th cent. abstract sculpture.

1976, Nov. 5

1485 A805 80c multi .30 .25
1486 A806 5cr multi .80 .50
1487 A805 5.60cr multi .80 .50
1488 A806 6.50cr multi .80 .50
Nos. 1485-1488 (4) 2.70 1.75

Development of Brazilian sculpture.

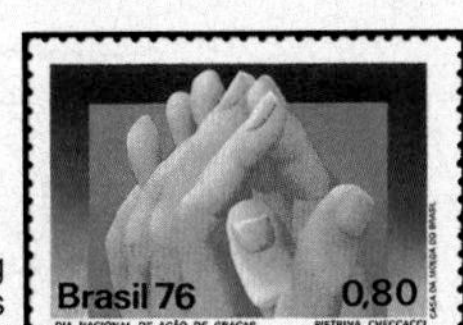

Praying Hands A807

1976, Nov. 25

1489 A807 80c multicolored .40 .30

National Day of Thanksgiving.

Sailor, 1840 — A808

Design: 2cr, Marine's uniform, 1808.

1976, Dec. 13 Litho. ***Perf. 11½x11***

1490 A808 80c multicolored .40 .30
1491 A808 2cr multicolored .40 .30

Brazilian Navy.

"Natural Resources and Development" — A809

1976, Dec. 17 ***Perf. 11½***

1492 A809 80c multicolored .35 .25

Brazilian Bureau of Standards, founded 1940.

Wheel of Life — A810

Designs: 5.60cr, Beggar, sculpture by Agnaldo dos Santos. 6.50cr, Benin mask.

1977, Jan. 14

1493 A810 5cr multi .95 .50
1494 A810 5.60cr multi .95 .50
1495 A810 6.50cr multi 2.00 .50
Nos. 1493-1495 (3) 3.90 1.50

FESTAC '77, 2nd World Black and African Festival, Lagos, Nigeria, Jan. 15-Feb. 12.

A811

1977, Jan. 20 Litho. ***Perf. 11½***

1496 A811 6.50cr bl & yel grn 1.00 .80

Rio de Janeiro International Airport.

Seminar Emblem with Map of Americas — A812

1977, Feb. 6

1497 A812 1.10cr gray, vio bl & bl 1.00 .25

6th Inter-American Budget Seminar.

Salicylate, Microphoto A813

1977, Apr. 10 Litho. ***Perf. 11½***

1498 A813 1.10cr multi .40 .25

International Rheumatism Year.

Lions International Emblem A814

1977, Apr. 16

1499 A814 1.10cr multi .40 .25

25th anniv. of Brazilian Lions Intl.

Heitor Villa Lobos A815

1977, Apr. 26 ***Perf. 11x11½***

1500 A815 1.10cr shown .35 .25
1501 A815 1.10cr Chiquinha Gonzaga .35 .25
1502 A815 1.10cr Noel Rosa .35 .25
Nos. 1500-1502 (3) 1.05 .75

Brazilian composers.

Farmer and Worker — A816

Medicine Bottles and Flask — A817

1977, May 8 Litho. ***Perf. 11½***

1503 A816 1.10cr grn & multi .45 .25
1504 A817 1.10cr lt & dk grn .45 .25

Support and security for rural and urban workers (No. 1503) and establishment in 1971 of Medicine Distribution Center (CEME) for low-cost medicines (No. 1504).

Churchyard Cross, Porto Seguro — A818

Views, Porto Seguro: 5cr, Beach and boats. 5.60cr, Our Lady of Pena Chapel. 6.50cr, Town Hall.

1977, May 25 Litho. ***Perf. 11½***

1505 A818 1.10cr multi .25 .25
1506 A818 5cr multi 1.75 .40
1507 A818 5.60cr multi .75 .40
1508 A818 6.50cr multi 1.00 .40
Nos. 1505-1508 (4) 3.75 1.45

Cent. of Brazil's membership in UPU.

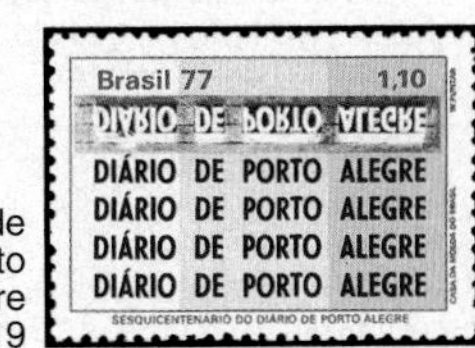

Diario de Porto Alegre A819

1977, June 1

1509 A819 1.10cr multi .40 .25

Diario de Porto Alegre, newspaper, 150th anniv.

Blue Whale A820

1977, June 3

1510 A820 1.30cr multi 2.00 .30

Protection of marine life.

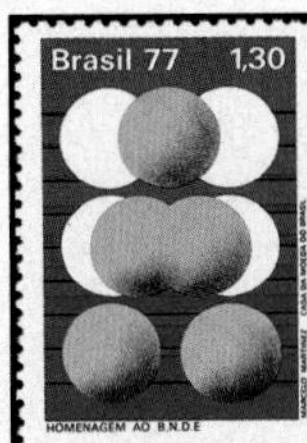

"Life and Development" A821

1977, June 20

1511 A821 1.30cr multi .35 .25

National Development Bank, 25th anniv.

Train Leaving Tunnel A822

1977, July 8 Engr. ***Perf. 11½***

1512 A822 1.30cr black .80 .25

Centenary of Sao Paulo-Rio de Janeiro railroad.

Shells — A823

Caduceus, Formulas for Water and Fluoride — A824

Designs: No. 1513, Vasum cassiforme. No. 1514, Strombus goliath. No. 1515, Murex tenuivaricosus.

1977, July 14 **Litho.**

1513 A823 1.30cr blue & multi .75 .25
1514 A823 1.30cr brown & multi .75 .25
1515 A823 1.30cr green & multi .75 .25
Nos. 1513-1515 (3) 2.25 .75

1977, July 15 ***Perf. 11½x11***

1516 A824 1.30cr multi .35 .25

3rd Intl. Odontology Congress, Rio, 7/15-21.

Masonic Emblem, Map of Brazil — A825

1977, July 18 ***Perf. 11½***

1517 A825 1.30cr bl, lt bl & blk .40 .25

50th anniversary of the founding of the Brazilian Grand Masonic Lodge.

"Stamps Don't Sink or Lose their Way" — A826

1977, Aug. 1

1518 A826 1.30cr multi .40 .25

Stamp Day 1977.

Dom Pedro's Proclamation
A827

1977, Aug. 11 Litho. *Perf. 11½*

1519 A827 1.30cr multi .40 .25

150th anniversary of Brazilian Law School.

Horses and Bulls — A828

Brazilian folklore: No. 1521, King on horseback. No. 1522, Joust, horiz.

Perf. 11½x11, 11x11½

1977, Aug. 20 Litho.

1520 A828 1.30cr ocher & multi .30 .25
1521 A828 1.30cr blue & multi .30 .25
1522 A828 1.30cr yel & multi .30 .25
Nos. 1520-1522 (3) .90 .75

Brazilian Colonial Coins
A829

Designs: No. 1523, 2000-reis doubloon. No. 1524, 640r pataca. No. 1525, 20r copper "vintem."

1977, Aug. 31 *Perf. 11½*

1523 A829 1.30cr vio bl & multi .35 .25
1524 A829 1.30cr dk red & multi .35 .25
1525 A829 1.30cr yel & multi .35 .25
Nos. 1523-1525 (3) 1.05 .75

Pinwheel
A830

Neoregelia Carolinae
A831

1977, Sept. 1

1526 A830 1.30cr multi .40 .25

National Week.

1977, Sept. 21 Litho. *Perf. 11½*

1527 A831 1.30cr multi .75 .30

Nature preservation.

Pen, Pencil, Letters — A832

1977, Oct. 15 Litho. *Perf. 11½*

1528 A832 1.30cr multi .40 .25

Primary education, sesquicentennial.

Dome and Telescope
A833

1977, Oct. 15

1529 A833 1.30cr multi .45 .25

National Astrophysics Observatory, Brasópolis, sesquicentennial.

"Jahu" Hydroplane (Savoia Marchetti S-55) — A834

Design: No. 1531, PAX, dirigible.

1977, Oct. 17

1530 A834 1.30cr multi .40 .30
1531 A834 1.30cr multi .40 .30

50th anniv. of crossing of South Atlantic by Joao Ribeiro de Barros, Genoa-Sao Paulo (No. 1530) and 75th anniv. of the PAX airship (No. 1531).

A835

1977, Oct. 24

1532 A835 1.30cr Il'Guarani .40 .25

Book Day and to honor Jose Martiniano de Alencar, writer, jurist.

A836

1977, Nov. 5 Litho. *Perf. 11½*

1533 A836 1.30cr Waves .50 .25

Amateur Radio Operators' Day.

Christmas
A837

Folk art: 1.30cr, Nativity. 2cr, Annunciation. 5cr, Nativity.

1977, Nov. 10

1534 A837 1.30cr bister & multi .25 .25
1535 A837 2cr bister & multi .30 .25
1536 A837 5cr bister & multi .65 .25
Nos. 1534-1536 (3) 1.20 .75

A838

1977, Nov. 19

1537 A838 1.30cr Emerald .60 .25
1538 A838 1.30cr Topaz .60 .25
1539 A838 1.30cr Aquamarine .60 .25
Nos. 1537-1539 (3) 1.80 .75

PORTUCALE 77, 2nd International Topical Exhibition, Porto, Nov. 19-20.

A839

1977, Nov. 24 Litho. *Perf. 11½*

1540 A839 1.30cr Angel, cornucopia .40 .25

National Thanksgiving Day.

Army's Railroad Construction Battalion — A840

Civilian services of armed forces: No. 1542, Navy's Amazon flotilla. No. 1543, Air Force's postal service (plane).

1977, Dec. 5

1541 A840 1.30cr multi .50 .25
1542 A840 1.30cr multi .50 .25
1543 A840 1.30cr multi .50 .25
Nos. 1541-1543 (3) 1.50 .75

Varig Emblem, Jet
A841

1977, Dec. *Perf. 11x11½*

1544 A841 1.30cr bl & blk .35 .25

50th anniversary of Varig Airline.

Brazilian Architecture
A842

Designs: 2.70cr, Sts. Cosme and Damiao Church, Igaracu. 7.50cr, St. Bento Monastery Church, Rio de Janeiro. 8.50cr, Church of St. Francis of Assisi, Ouro Preto. 9.50cr, St. Anthony Convent Church, Joao Pessoa.

1977, Dec. 8

1545 A842 2.70cr multi .25 .40
1546 A842 7.50cr multi 1.25 .40
1547 A842 8.50cr multi 1.25 .40
1548 A842 9.50cr multi 1.25 .50
Nos. 1545-1548 (4) 4.00 1.70

Woman Holding Sheaf — A843

1977, Dec. 19 *Perf. 11½*

1549 A843 1.30cr multi .35 .25

Brazilian diplomacy.

Soccer Ball and Foot — A844

Designs: No. 1551, Soccer ball in net. No. 1552, Symbolic soccer player.

1978, Mar. 1 Litho. *Perf. 11½*

1550 A844 1.80cr multi .50 .25
1551 A844 1.80cr multi .50 .25
1552 A844 1.80cr multi .50 .25
Nos. 1550-1552 (3) 1.50 .75

11th World Cup Soccer Championship, Argentina, June 1-25.

"La Fosca" on La Scala Stage and Carlos Gomes
A845

1978, Feb. 9

1553 A845 1.80cr multi .40 .25

Bicentenary of La Scala in Milan, and to honor Carlos Gomes (1836-1893), Brazilian composer.

Symbols of Postal Mechanization — A846

1978, Mar. 15 Litho. *Perf. 11½*

1554 A846 1.80cr multi .40 .25

Opening of Postal Staff College.

Hypertension Chart — A847

1978, Apr. 4
1555 A847 1.80cr multi .40 .25

World Health Day, fight against hypertension.

Waves from Antenna Uniting World — A848

1978, May 17 Litho. ***Perf. 12x11½***
1556 A848 1.80cr multi .40 .25

10th World Telecommunications Day.

Brazilian Canary A849

Birds: 8.50cr, Cotinga. 9.50cr, Tanager fastuosa.

1978, June 5 ***Perf. 11½x12***
1557 A849 7.50cr multi 1.50 .75
1558 A849 8.50cr multi 1.50 .75
1559 A849 9.50cr multi 1.50 .75
Nos. 1557-1559 (3) 4.50 2.25

Inocencio Serzedelo Correa and Manuel Francisco Correa, 1893 — A850

1978, June 20 Litho. ***Perf. 11x11½***
1560 A850 1.80cr multi .40 .25

85th anniversary of Union Court of Audit.

Post and Telegraph Building A851

1978, June 22 ***Perf. 11½***
1561 A851 1.80cr multi .40 .40

Souvenir Sheet

Imperf

1562 A851 7.50cr multi 1.00 2.00

Inauguration of Post and Telegraph Building (ECT), Brasilia, and for BRAPEX, 3rd Brazilian Philatelic Exhibition, Brasilia, June 23-28 (No. 1562).

Ernesto Geisel, President of Brazil — A852

1978, June 22 Engr. ***Perf. 11½***
1563 A852 1.80cr dull green .40 .25

Savoia-Marchetti S-64, Map of South Atlantic — A853

1978, July 3 Litho.
1564 A853 1.80cr multi .45 .25

50th anniv. of 1st crossing of South Atlantic by Carlos del Prete and Arturo Ferrarin.

Symbolic of Smallpox Eradication A854

1978, July 25
1565 A854 1.80cr multi .40 .25

Eradication of smallpox.

Brazil No. 68 — A855

1978, Aug. 1
1566 A855 1.80cr multi .40 .25

Stamp Day, centenary of the "Barba Branca" (white beard) issue.

Stormy Sea, by Seelinger A856

1978, Aug. 4
1567 A856 1.80cr multi .40 .25

Helios Seelinger, painter, birth centenary.

Musicians and Instruments A857

Designs: No. 1568, Guitar players. No. 1569, Flutes. No. 1570, Percussion instruments.

1978, Aug. 22 Litho. ***Perf. 11½***
1568 A857 1.80cr multi .30 .25
1569 A857 1.80cr multi .30 .25
1570 A857 1.80cr multi .30 .25
Nos. 1568-1570 (3) .90 .75

Children at Play A858

1978, Sept. 1 Litho. ***Perf. 11½***
1571 A858 1.80cr multi .40 .25

National Week.

Collegiate Church A859

1978, Sept. 6 Engr.
1572 A859 1.80cr red brn .45 .25

Restoration of patio of Collegiate Church, Sao Paulo.

Justice by A. Geschiatti A860

1978, Sept. 18 Litho.
1573 A860 1.80cr blk & olive .40 .25

Federal Supreme Court, sesquicentennial.

Iguacu National Park — A861

Design: No. 1574, Iguacu Falls. No. 1575, Yellow ipe.

1978, Sept. 21
1574 A861 1.80cr multi .35 .25
1575 A861 1.80cr multi .35 .25

Stages of Intelsat Satellite A862

1978, Oct. 9 Litho. ***Perf. 11½***
1576 A862 1.80cr multi .40 .25

Brazilian Flags A863

Designs: No. 1577, Flag of the Order of Christ. No. 1578, Principality of Brazil. No. 1579, United Kingdom. No. 1580, Imperial Brazil. No. 1581, National flag (current).

1978, Oct. 13
1577 A863 1.80cr multi .95 .70
1578 A863 1.80cr multi .95 .70
1579 A863 1.80cr multi .95 .70
1580 A863 8.50cr multi .95 .70
1581 A863 8.50cr multi .95 .70
a. Block of 5, #1577-1581 + label 7.50 6.50
Nos. 1577-1581 (5) 4.75 3.50

7th LUBRAPEX Philatelic Exhibition, Porto Alegre.

Mail Transportation — A864

Designs: No. 1582, Mail street car. No. 1583, Overland mail truck. No. 1584, Mail delivery truck. 7.50cr. Railroad mail car. 8.50cr, Mail coach. 9.50cr, Post riders.

1978, Oct. 21 ***Perf. 11x11½***
1582 A864 1.80cr multi .70 .70
1583 A864 1.80cr multi .70 .70
1584 A864 1.80cr multi .70 .70
1585 A864 7.50cr multi .70 .70
1586 A864 8.50cr multi .70 .70
1587 A864 9.50cr multi .70 .70
a. Block of 6, #1582-1587 6.75 6.75

18th UPU Congress, Rio de Janeiro, 1979.

Gaucho Herding Cattle, and Cactus — A865

1978, Oct. 23 ***Perf. 11½x11***
1588 A865 1.80cr multi .30 .25

Joao Guimaraes Rosa, poet and diplomat, 70th birthday.

Landscape Paintings A866

Designs: No. 1589, St. Anthony's Hill, by Nicholas A. Taunay. No. 1590, Castle Hill, by Victor Meirelles. No. 1591, View of Sabara, by Alberto da Veiga Guignard. No. 1592, View of Pernambuco, by Frans Post.

1978, Nov. 6 Litho. ***Perf. 11½***
1589 A866 1.80cr multi .30 .25
1590 A866 1.80cr multi .30 .25
1591 A866 1.80cr multi .30 .25
1592 A866 1.80cr multi .30 .25
Nos. 1589-1592 (4) 1.20 1.00

Christmas A867

Angel with: No. 1593, Harp. No. 1594, Lute. No. 1595, Oboe.

1978, Nov. 10
1593 A867 1.80cr multi .40 .25
1594 A867 1.80cr multi .40 .25
1595 A867 1.80cr multi .40 .25
Nos. 1593-1595 (3) 1.20 .75

Symbolic Candles — A868

1978, Nov. 23

1596 A868 1.80cr blk, gold & car .35 .25

National Thanksgiving Day.

Red Crosses and Activities A869

1978, Dec. 5 Litho. *Perf. 11x11½*

1597 A869 1.80cr blk & red .35 .25

70th anniversary of Brazilian Red Cross.

Paz Theater, Belem A870

Designs: 12cr, José de Alencar Theater, Fortaleza. 12.50cr, Municipal Theater, Rio de Janeiro.

1978, Dec. 6 *Perf. 11½*

1598 A870 10.50cr multi .90 .30
1599 A870 12cr multi .90 .30
1600 A870 12.50cr multi .90 .30
Nos. 1598-1600 (3) 2.70 .90

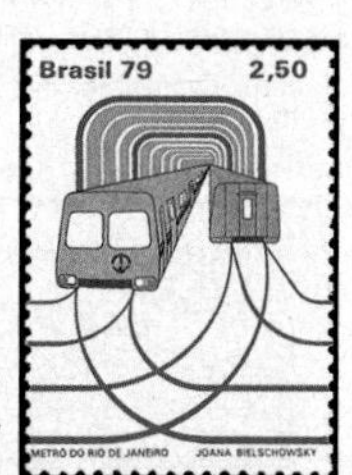

Subway Trains — A871

1979, Mar. 5 Litho. *Perf. 11½*

1601 A871 2.50cr multi .60 .25

Inauguration of Rio subway system.

Old and New Post Offices A872

Designs: No. 1603, Old and new mail boxes. No. 1604, Manual and automatic mail sorting. No. 1605, Old and new planes. No. 1606, Telegraph and telex machine. No. 1607, Mailmen's uniforms.

1979, Mar. 20 Litho. *Perf. 11x11½*

1602 A872 2.50cr multi .35 .25
1603 A872 2.50cr multi .35 .25
1604 A872 2.50cr multi .35 .25
1605 A872 2.50cr multi .35 .25
1606 A872 2.50cr multi .35 .25
1607 A872 2.50cr multi .35 .25
a. Block of 6, #1602-1607 2.10 2.10

10th anniv. of the new Post and Telegraph Dept., and 18th Universal Postal Union Cong., Rio de Janeiro, Sept.-Oct., 1979.

O'Day 23 Class Yacht A873

Yachts and Stamp Outlines: 10.50cr, Penguin Class. 12cr, Hobie Cat Class. 12.50cr, Snipe Class.

1979, Apr. 18 Litho. *Perf. 11x11½*

1608 A873 2.50cr multi .40 .40
1609 A873 10.50cr multi .75 .40
1610 A873 12cr multi .75 .40
1611 A873 12.50cr multi .90 .40
Nos. 1608-1611 (4) 2.80 1.60

Brasiliana '79, 3rd World Thematic Stamp Exhibition, Sao Conrado, Sept. 15-23.

Children, IYC Emblem — A874

1979, May 23 Litho. *Perf. 11½*

1612 A874 2.50cr multi .35 .25

Intl. Year of the Child & Children's Book Day.

Giant Water Lily — A875

Designs: 12cr, Amazon manatee. 12.50cr, Arrau (turtle).

1979, June 5 Litho. *Perf. 11½*

1613 A875 10.50cr multi 1.60 .60
1614 A875 12cr multi 1.60 .60
1615 A875 12.50cr multi 1.60 .60
Nos. 1613-1615 (3) 4.80 1.80

Amazon National Park, nature conservation.

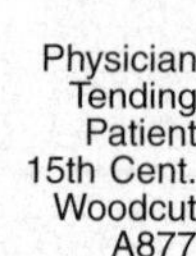

Bank Emblem A876

1979, June 7

1616 A876 2.50cr multi .35 .25

Northwest Bank of Brazil, 25th anniversary.

Physician Tending Patient 15th Cent. Woodcut A877

1979, June 30

1617 A877 2.50cr multi .35 .25

Natl. Academy of Medicine, 150th anniv.

Flower made of Hearts — A878

1979, July 8 Litho. *Perf. 11½*

1618 A878 2.50cr multi .45 .25

35th Brazilian Cardiology Congress.

Souvenir Sheet

Hotel Nacional, Rio de Janeiro — A879

1979, July 16

1619 A879 12.50cr multi 1.50 1.50

Brasiliana '79 comprising 1st Inter-American Exhibition of Classical Philately and 3rd World Topical Exhibition, Rio de Janeiro, Sept. 15-23.

Cithaerias Aurora A880

Moths: 10.50cr, Evenus regalis. 12cr, Caligo eurilochus. 12.50cr, Diaethria clymena janeira.

1979, Aug. 1

1620 A880 2.50cr multi .50 .25
1621 A880 10.50cr multi .90 .50
1622 A880 12cr multi 1.25 .50
1623 A880 12.50cr multi 2.25 .60
Nos. 1620-1623 (4) 4.90 1.85

Stamp Day 1979.

EMB-121 Xingo A881

1979, Aug. 19 Litho. *Perf. 11½*

1624 A881 2.50cr vio blue .35 .25

Embraer, Brazilian aircraft comp., 10th anniv.

A882

Natl. emblem over landscape.

1979, Sept. 12

1625 A882 3.20cr multi .45 .25

National Week.

A883

1979, Sept. 8 Litho. *Perf. 11½*

1626 A883 2.50cr multi .35 .25

Statue of Our Lady of the Apparition, 75th anniversary of coronation.

"UPU," Envelope and Mail Transport A884

"UPU" and: No. 1628, Post Office emblems. 10.50cr, Globe. 12cr, Flags of Brazil and UN. 12.50cr, UPU emblem.

1979, Sept. 12 *Perf. 11x11½*

1627 A884 2.50cr multi .30 .30
1628 A884 2.50cr multi .30 .30
1629 A884 10.50cr multi .60 .60
1630 A884 12cr multi .80 .80
1631 A884 12.50cr multi .80 .80
Nos. 1627-1631 (5) 2.80 2.80

18th UPU Cong., Rio, Sept.-Oct. 1979.

Pyramid Fountain, Rio de Janeiro — A885

Fountains: 10.50cr, Facade, Marilia, Ouro Preto, horiz. 12cr, Boa Vista, Recife.

Perf. 12x11½, 11½x12

1979, Sept. 15

1632 A885 2.50cr multi .30 .25
1633 A885 10.50cr multi .65 .50
1634 A885 12cr multi .75 .60
Nos. 1632-1634 (3) 1.70 1.35

Brasiliana '79, 1st Interamerican Exhibition of Classical Philately.

Church of the Glory A886

Landscapes by Leandro Joaquim: 12cr, Whale hunting on Guanabara Bay. 12.50cr, Boqueirao Lagoon and Carioca Aqueduct.

1979, Sept. 15 *Perf. 11½*

1635	A886	2.50cr multi	.40	.30
1636	A886	12cr multi	.70	.60
1637	A886	12.50cr multi	.70	.60
		Nos. 1635-1637 (3)	1.80	1.50

Brasiliana '79, 3rd World Topical Exhibition, Sao Conrado, Sept. 15-23.

World Map A887

1979, Sept. 20

1638	A887	2.50cr multi	.35	.25

3rd World Telecommunications Exhibition, Geneva, Sept. 20-26.

"UPU" and UPU Emblem — A888

1979, Oct. 9 **Litho.** *Perf. 11½x11*

1639	A888	2.50cr multi	.30	.30
1640	A888	10.50cr multi	.65	.65
1641	A888	12cr multi	.70	.70
1642	A888	12.50cr multi	.70	.70
		Nos. 1639-1642 (4)	2.35	2.35

Universal Postal Union Day.

IYC Emblem, Feather Toy A889

IYC Emblem and Toys: No. 1644, Bumble bee, ragdoll. No. 1645, Flower, top. No. 1646, Wooden acrobat.

1979, Oct. 12 *Perf. 11½*

1643	A889	2.50cr multi	.30	.25
1644	A889	3.20cr multi	.30	.30
1645	A889	3.20cr multi	.30	.30
1646	A889	3.20cr multi	.30	.30
		Nos. 1643-1646 (4)	1.20	1.15

International Year of the Child.

Christmas A890

Designs: No. 1647, Adoration of the Magi. No. 1648, Nativity. No. 1649 Jesus and the Elders in the Temple.

1979, Nov. 12 **Litho.** *Perf. 11½*

1647	A890	3.20cr multi	.40	.25
1648	A890	3.20cr multi	.40	.25
1649	A890	3.20cr multi	.40	.25
		Nos. 1647-1649 (3)	1.20	.75

Souvenir Sheet

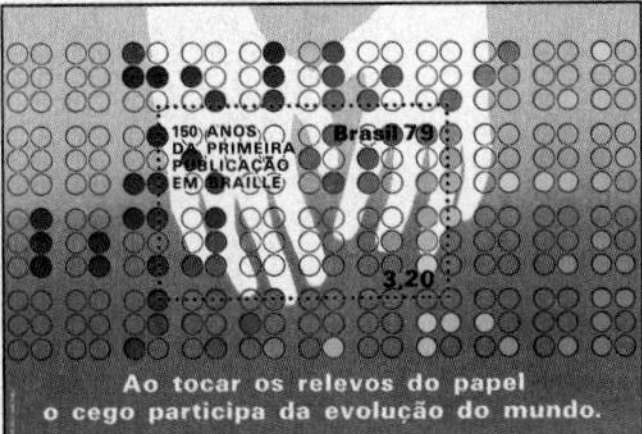

Hands Reading Braille — A891

Lithographed and Embossed

1979, Nov. 20. *Perf. 11½*

1650	A891	3.20cr multi	1.00	1.50

Publication of Braille script, 150th anniversary. Margin shows extension of stamp design with Braille printed and embossed.

Thanksgiving A892

1979, Nov. 22

1651	A892	3.20cr Wheat harvester	.35	.25

Steel Mill — A893

1979, Nov. 23

1652	A893	3.20cr multi	.40	.25

COSIPA Steelworks, Sao Paulo, 25th anniversary.

Type of 1976

Designs: 70c, Women grinding coconuts. 2.50cr, Basket weaver. 3.20cr, River boatman. 21cr, Harvesting ramie (China grass). 27cr, Man leading pack mule. 3.20cr, 27cr, horiz.

Photogravure, Engraved (21cr)

1979 *Perf. 11x11½, 11½x11*

1653	A790	70c gray green	.40	.25
1654	A790	2.50cr sepia	.40	.25
1655	A790	3.20cr blue	.40	.25
1656	A790	21cr purple	1.75	.25
1657	A790	27cr sepia	2.75	.25
		Nos. 1653-1657 (5)	5.70	1.25

A894

Designs: 2cr, Coconuts. 3cr, Mangoes. 4cr, Corn. 5cr, Onions. 7cr, Oranges. 10cr, Maracuja. 12cr, Pineapple. 15cr, Bananas. 17cr, Guarana. 20cr, Sugar cane. 24cr, Beekeeping. 30cr, Silkworm. 34cr, Cacao. 38cr, Coffee. 42cr, Soybeans. 45cr, Mandioca. 50cr, Wheat. 57cr, Peanuts. 66cr, Grapes. 100cr, Cashews. 140cr, Tomatoes. 200cr, Mamona. 500cr, Cotton.

1980-83 **Photo.** *Perf. 11½x11*

1658	A894	2cr yel brn ('82)	.30	.25
1659	A894	3cr red ('82)	.30	.25
1660	A894	4cr orange	.30	.25
1661	A894	5cr dk pur ('82)	.30	.25
1662	A894	7cr org ('81)	.30	.25
1663	A894	10cr bl grn ('82)	.30	.25
1664	A894	12cr dk grn ('81)	.30	.25
1665	A894	15cr gldn brn ('83)	.30	.25
1666	A894	17cr brn org ('82)	.40	.25
1667	A894	20cr olive ('82)	.40	.25
1668	A894	24cr bis ('82)	2.25	.25
1669	A894	30cr blk ('82)	3.50	.25
1670	A894	34cr brown	8.00	.25
1671	A894	38cr red ('83)	7.00	.25
1672	A894	42cr green	15.00	.75
1673	A894	45cr sepia ('83)	.75	.25
1674	A894	50cr yel org ('82)	.40	.25
1675	A894	57cr brn ('83)	6.00	.25
1676	A894	66cr pur ('81)	9.50	.25
1677	A894	100cr dk red brn ('81)	4.00	.25
1678	A894	140cr red ('82)	6.00	.25

Engr.

1678A	A894	200cr grn ('82)	5.00	.25
1679	A894	500cr brn ('82)	5.50	.25
		Nos. 1658-1679 (23)	76.10	6.25

See Nos. 1934-1941.

Plant Inside Raindrop — A896

Light bulb containing: 17cr+7cr, Sun. 20cr+8cr, Windmill. 21cr+9cr, Dam.

1980, Jan. 2 **Litho.** *Perf. 12*

1680	A896	3.20cr multi	.30	.30
1681	A896	24cr (17 + 7)	.40	.35
1682	A896	28cr (20 + 8)	2.50	.90
1683	A896	30cr (21 + 9)	3.50	1.00
		Nos. 1680-1683 (4)	6.70	2.55

Nos. 1681-1683 were originally intended to be sold as semi-postal stamps but were actually issued as regular postage stamps, sold and valid for the combined denominations appearing on each stamp.

Anthracite Industry A897

1980, Mar. 19 **Litho.** *Perf. 11½*

1684	A897	4cr multi	.40	.25

Map of Americas, Symbols of Development — A898

1980, Apr. 14 **Litho.** *Perf. 11x11½*

1685	A898	4cr multi	.35	.25

21st Assembly of Inter-American Development Bank Governors, Rio, Apr. 14-16.

Tapirape Mask, Mato Grosso A899

1980, Apr. 18 *Perf. 11½*

1686	A899	4cr shown	.30	.25
1687	A899	4cr Tukuna mask, Amazonas, vert.	.30	.25
1688	A899	4cr Kanela mask, Maranhao, vert.	.30	.25
		Nos. 1686-1688 (3)	.90	.75

Brazilian Television, 30th Anniversary A900

1980, May 5 **Litho.** *Perf. 11½*

1689	A900	4cr multicolored	.35	.25

Duke of Caxias, by Miranda — A901

1980, May 7

1690	A901	4cr multicolored	.45	.25

Duke of Caxias, death centenary.

The Worker, by Candido Portinari — A902

Paintings: 28cr, Mademoiselle Pogany, by Constantin Brancusi. 30cr, The Glass of Water, by Francisco Aurelio de Figueiredo.

1980, May 18

1691	A902	24cr multi	1.25	.60
1692	A902	28cr multi	1.50	.60
1693	A902	30cr multi	2.25	.65
		Nos. 1691-1693 (3)	5.00	1.85

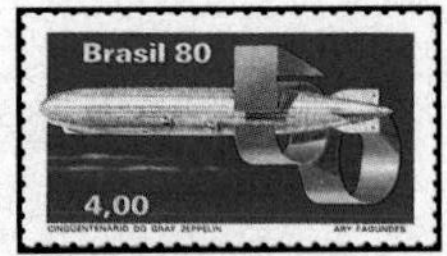

Graf Zeppelin, 50th Anniversary of Atlantic Crossing A903

1980, June **Litho.** *Perf. 11x11½*

1694	A903	4cr multicolored	.50	.25

Pope John Paul II, St. Peter's, Rome, Congress Emblem A904

Pope, Emblem and Brazilian Churches: No. 1696, Fortaleza, vert. 24cr, Apericida 28cr, Rio de Janeiro. 30cr, Brasilia.

1980, June 24 *Perf. 12*

1695	A904	4cr multi	.40	.25
1696	A904	4cr multi	.40	.25
1697	A904	24cr multi	1.50	.50
1698	A904	28cr multi	1.50	.50
1699	A904	30cr multi	3.00	.50
		Nos. 1695-1699 (5)	6.80	2.00

Visit of Pope John Paul II to Brazil, June 30-July 12; 10th National Eucharistic Congress, Fortaleza, July 9-16.

1st Airmail Flight across the South Atlantic, 50th Anniv. A905

1980, June Litho. *Perf. 11x11½*
1700 A905 4cr multicolored .50 .25

Souvenir Sheet

Yacht Sail, Exhibition Emblem — A906

1980, June *Perf. 11½*
1701 A906 30cr multi 1.60 1.60

Brapex IV Stamp Exhib., Fortaleza, June 13-21.

Rowing, Moscow '80 Emblem A907

1980, June 30

1702	A907 4cr shown	.40	.25
1703	A907 4cr Target shooting	.40	.25
1704	A907 4cr Bicycling	.40	.25
	Nos. 1702-1704 (3)	1.20	.75

22nd Summer Olympic Games, Moscow, July 19-Aug. 3.

Rondon Community Works Project A908

1980, July 11
1705 A908 4cr multicolored .35 .25

Helen Keller and Anne Sullivan A909

1980, July 28
1706 A909 4cr multicolored .45 .25

Helen Keller (1880-1968), blind deaf writer and lecturer taught by Anne Sullivan (1867-1936).

Souvenir Sheet

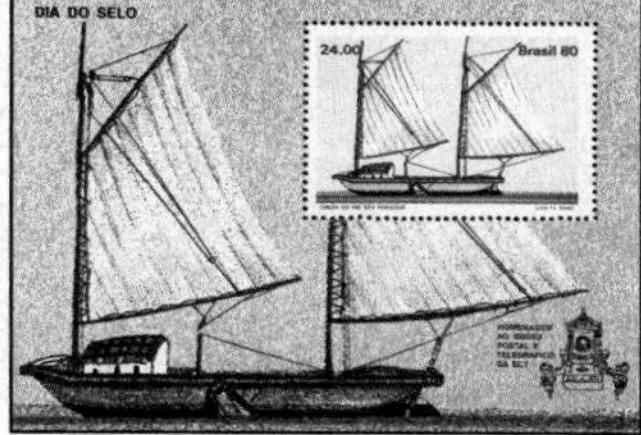

Sáo Francisco River Canoe — A910

1980, Aug. 1 Litho. *Perf. 11½*
1707 A910 24cr multi 2.00 2.25

Stamp Day.

Microscope, Red Cross, Insects, Brick and Tile Houses — A911

1980, Aug. 5 *Perf. 11½x11*
1708 A911 4cr multi .40 .25

National Health Day.

EMBRATEL, 15th Anniversary — A912

1980, Sept. 16 Litho. *Perf. 12*
1709 A912 5cr multi .40 .25

Souvenir Sheet

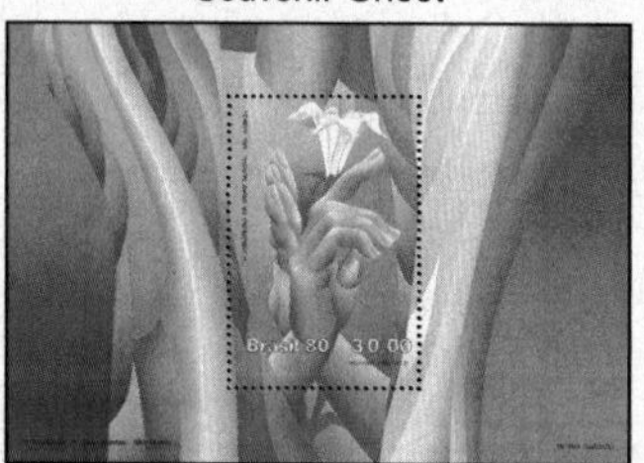

A913

1980, Sept. 29 *Perf. 11½x12*
1710 A913 30cr multi 2.00 1.50

St. Gabriel World Union, 6th congress.

Orchids A914

Designs: No. 1711, Cattleya amethystoglossa. No. 1712, Laelia cinnabarina. 24cr, Zygopetalu, crinitum. 28cr, Laelia tenebrosa.

1980, Oct. 3 *Perf. 11½*

1711	A914 5cr multi	.40	.25
1712	A914 5cr multi	.40	.25
1713	A914 24cr multi	2.00	.70
1714	A914 28cr multi	2.00	.70
	Nos. 1711-1714 (4)	4.80	1.90

Espamer 80, American-European Philatelic Exhibition, Madrid, Oct. 3-12.

Parrots — A915

Designs: No. 1715, Amazona brazilensis. No. 1716, Amazona Vinacea. No. 1717, Touit melanonota. No. 1718, Amazona pretrei.

1980, Oct. 18 Litho. *Perf. 12*

1715	A915 5cr multi	.40	.25
1716	A915 5cr multi	.40	.25
1717	A915 28cr multi	2.00	.70
1718	A915 28cr multi	2.00	.70
	Nos. 1715-1718 (4)	4.80	1.90

Lubrapex '80 Stamp Exhib., Lisbon, Oct. 18-26.

Captain Rodrigo, Hero of Erico Verissimo's "O Continento" A916

1980, Oct. 23
1719 A916 5cr multi .35 .25

Book Day.

Christmas A917

1980, Nov. 5
1720 A917 5cr Flight into Egypt .45 .25

Sound Waves and Oscillator Screen A918

1980, Nov. 7
1721 A918 5cr multi .40 .25

Telebras Research Center inauguration.

Carvalho Viaduct, Paranagua-Curitiba Railroad — A919

1980, Nov. 10
1722 A919 5cr multi .50 .25

Engineering Club centenary.

A920

1980, Nov. 18 Litho. *Perf. 11½*
1723 A920 5cr Portable chess board .45 .35

Postal chess contest.

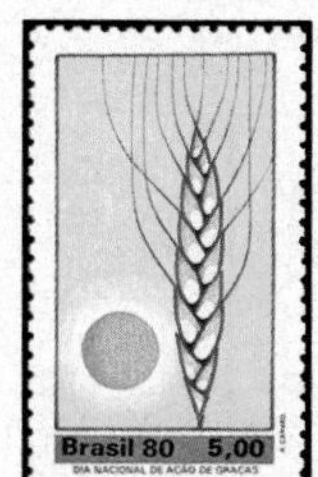

A921

1980, Nov. 27 *Perf. 11½x11*
1724 A921 5cr Sun, wheat .35 .25

Thanksgiving 1980

Father Anchieta Writing "Virgin Mary, Mother of God" on Sand of Iperoig Beach — A922

1980, Dec. 8 *Perf. 12*
1725 A922 5cr multi .45 .25

Antonio Francisco Lisboa (O Aleijadinho), 250th Birth Anniv. — A923

No. 1726 — Paintings of the life of Christ: a, Mount of Olives. b, Arrest in the Garden. c, Flagellation. d, Crown of Thorns. e, Christ Carrying the Cross (shown). f, Crucifixion.

1980, Dec. 29

1726	Block of 6	3.00	3.00
a.-f.	A923 5cr any single	.45	.25

Agricultural Productivity — A924

1981, Jan. 2 Litho. *Perf. 11x11½*

1727	A924 30cr shown	1.40	.35
1728	A924 35cr Domestic markets	1.25	.30
1729	A924 40cr Exports	1.25	.35
	Nos. 1727-1729 (3)	3.90	1.00

Boy Scout and Campfire A925

1981, Jan. 22 Litho. *Perf. 11x11½*

1730	A925 5cr shown	.35	.25
1731	A925 5cr Scouts cooking	.35	.25
1732	A925 5cr Scout, tents	.35	.25
	Nos. 1730-1732 (3)	1.05	.75

4th Pan-American Scout Jamboree.

Souvenir Sheet

Dept. of Posts & Telegraphs, 50th anniv. — A926

1981, Mar. 11 Litho. *Perf. 11*

1733	Sheet of 3	5.50	5.50
a.	A926 30cr Mailman, 1930	1.25	1.25
b.	A926 35cr Mailman, 1981	1.25	1.25
c.	A926 40cr Telegram messenger, 1930	1.25	1.25

Souvenir Sheet

The Hunter and the Jaguar, by Felix Taunay (1795-1881) — A927

1981, Apr. 10 Litho. *Perf. 11*

1734	A927 30cr multi	1.40	*2.00*

Lima Barreto and Rio de Janeiro, 1900 A928

1981, May 13 Litho. *Perf. 11½*

1735	A928 7cr multi	.40	.25

Lima Barreto, writer, birth centenary.

Maraca Indian Funerary Urn — A929

1981, May 18

1736	A929 7cr shown	.50	.25
1737	A929 7cr Marajoara triangular jug	.50	.25
1738	A929 7cr Tupi-Guarani bowl	.50	.25
	Nos. 1736-1738 (3)	1.50	.75

Hummingbirds — A930

Designs: No. 1739, Lophornis magnifica. No. 1740, Phaethornis pretrei. No. 1741, Chrysolampis mosquitus. No. 1742, Heliactin cornuta.

1981, May 22 *Perf. 11½*

1739	A930 7cr multi	.75	.30
1740	A930 7cr multi	.75	.30
1741	A930 7cr multi	.75	.30
1742	A930 7cr multi	.75	.30
	Nos. 1739-1742 (4)	3.00	1.20

Rotary Emblem and Faces A931

1981, May 31

1743	A931 7cr Emblem, hands	.25	.25
1744	A931 35cr shown	1.10	.90

72nd Convention of Rotary Intl., Sao Paulo.

Environmental Protection — A932

1981, June 5 *Perf. 12*

1745	A932 7cr Fish	.65	.25
1746	A932 7cr Forest	.65	.25
1747	A932 7cr Clouds (air)	.65	.25
1748	A932 7cr Village (soil)	.65	.25
a.	Block of 4, #1745-1748	4.00	4.00

Biplane, 1931 (Airmail Service, 50th Anniv.) A933

1981, June 10 *Perf. 11½*

1749	A933 7cr multi	.60	.25

Madeira-Mamore Railroad, 50th Anniv. of Nationalization — A934

1981, July 10 Litho. *Perf. 11x11½*

1750	A934 7cr multi	.50	.25

66th Intl. Esperanto Congress, Brasilia A935

1981, July 26 *Perf. 12*

1751	A935 7cr green & blk	.35	.25

No. 79 A936

1981, Aug. 1

1752	A936 50cr shown	1.60	.35
1753	A936 55cr No. 80	1.60	.35
1754	A936 60cr No. 81	1.60	.35
	Nos. 1752-1754 (3)	4.80	1.05

Stamp Day; cent. of "small head" stamps.

Institute of Military Engineering, 50th Anniv. — A937

1981, Aug. 11 Litho. *Perf. 11½*

1755	A937 12cr multi	.35	.25

Reisado Dancers A938

1981, Aug. 22

1756	A938 50cr Dancers, diff.	1.25	.30
1757	A938 55cr Sailors	1.25	.30
1758	A938 60cr shown	1.25	.30
	Nos. 1756-1758 (3)	3.75	.90

Intl. Year of the Disabled A939

1981, Sept. 17 Litho. *Perf. 11½*

1759	A939 12cr multi	.40	.25

Flowers of the Central Plateau A940

1981, Sept. 21 Litho. *Perf. 12*

1760	A940 12cr Palicourea rigida	.50	.25
1761	A940 12cr Dalechampia caperonioides	.50	.25
1762	A940 12cr Cassia clausseni, vert.	.50	.25
1763	A940 12cr Eremanthus sphaerocephalus, vert.	.50	.25
	Nos. 1760-1763 (4)	2.00	1.00

Virgin of Nazareth Statue — A941

1981, Oct. 10 Litho. *Perf. 12*

1764	A941 12cr multi	.35	.25

Candle Festival of Nazareth, Belem.

Christ the Redeemer Statue, Rio de Janeiro, 50th Anniv. — A942

1981, Oct. 12

1765	A942 12cr multi	.30	.25

World Food Day A943

1981, Oct. 16

1766	A943 12c multi	.30	.25

75th Anniv. of Santos-Dumont's First Flight — A944

1981, Oct. 23 Litho. *Perf. 12*

1767	A944 60cr multi	1.25	.40

Father José de Santa Rita Durao, Titlepage of his Epic Poem Caramuru, Diego Alvares Correia (Character) — A945

1981, Oct. 29

1768	A945 12cr multi	.35	.25

Caramuru publication 200th anniv.; World Book Day.

Christmas A946

Designs: Creches and figurines.

1981, Nov. 10 Litho. *Perf. 12*

1769	A946 12cr multi	.30	.25
1770	A946 50cr multi	1.40	.25
1771	A946 55cr multi, vert.	1.40	.25
1772	A946 60cr multi, vert.	1.40	.35
	Nos. 1769-1772 (4)	4.50	1.10

State Flags A947

No. 1773: a, Alagoas. b, Bahia. c, Federal District. d, Pernambuco. e, Sergipe.

1981, Nov. 19

1773	Block of 5 + label	2.25	2.25
a.-e.	A947 12cr, any single	.35	.25

Label shows arms of Brazil.

See Nos. 1830, 1892, 1962, 2037, 2249, 2726-2727.

Thanksgiving A948

1981, Nov. 26 Litho. *Perf. 11½*
1776 A948 12cr multi .30 .25

Ministry of Labor, 50th Anniv. A949

1981, Nov. 26
1777 A949 12cr multi .35 .25

School of Engineering, Itajuba — A950

1981, Nov. 30 *Perf. 11x11½*
1778 A950 15cr lt grn & pur .50 .25

Theodomiro C. Santiago, founder, birth centenary.

Sao Paulo State Police Sesquicentennial A951

1981, Dec. 15 Litho. *Perf. 12*
1779 A951 12cr Policeman with saxophone .35 .25
1780 A951 12cr Mounted policemen .35 .25

Army Library Centenary A952

1981, Dec. 17
1781 A952 12cr multi .30 .25

Souvenir Sheet

A953

1981, Dec. 18 *Perf. 11*
1782 A953 180cr multi 6.25 6.25

Philatelic Club of Brazil, 50th anniv.

Brigadier Eduardo Gomes A954

1982, Jan. 20 Litho. *Perf. 11x11½*
1783 A954 12cr blue & blk .40 .25

Birth Centenary of Henrique Lage, Industrialist — A956

1982, Mar. 14 Litho. *Perf. 11½*
1785 A956 17cr multi .70 .25

1982 World Cup Soccer A957

Designs: Various soccer players.

1982, Mar. 19
1786 A957 75cr multi 1.50 .60
1787 A957 80cr multi 1.50 .60
1788 A957 85cr multi 1.50 .60
Nos. 1786-1788 (3) 4.50 1.80

Souvenir Sheet
Imperf

1789 Sheet of 3 7.50 7.50
a. A957 100cr like #1786 2.00 1.50
b. A957 100cr like #1787 2.00 1.50
c. A957 100cr like #1788 2.00 1.50

TB Bacillus Cent. — A958

1982, Mar. 24 *Perf. 12*
1790 A958 90cr Microscope, lung 3.50 1.00
1791 A958 100cr Lung, pills 3.50 1.00
a. Pair, #1790-1791 7.00 2.25

Souvenir Sheet

A959

1982, Apr. 17 Litho. *Perf. 11*
1792 A959 Sheet of 3 12.00 12.00
a. 75cr Laelia Purpurata 2.75 2.25
b. 80cr Oncidium flexuosum 2.75 2.25
c. 85cr Cleistes revoluta 2.75 2.25

BRAPEX V Stamp Exhibition, Blumenau.

Oil Drilling Centenary A960

1982, Apr. 18 *Perf. 11½*
1793 A960 17cr multi .40 .25

400th Birth Anniv. of St. Vincent de Paul A961

1982, Apr. 24 Litho. *Perf. 11½*
1794 A961 17cr multi .40 .25

Seven Steps of Guaira (Waterfalls) A962

1982, Apr. 29
1795 A962 17cr Fifth Fall .30 .25
1796 A962 21cr Seventh Fall .50 .25

Ministry of Communications, 15th Anniv. — A963

1982, May 15
1797 A963 21cr multi .35 .25

Museology Course, Natl. Historical Museum, 50th Anniv. A964

1982, May 18
1798 A964 17cr blk & sal pink .45 .25

Vale de Rio Doce Mining Co. — A965

1982, June 1
1799 A965 17cr Gears .45 .25

Martin Afonso de Souza Reading Charter to Settlers A966

1982, June 3 Litho. *Perf. 11½*
1800 A966 17cr multi .50 .25

Town of Sao Vincente, 450th anniv.

Armadillo A967

1982, June 4
1801 A967 17cr shown .65 .25
1802 A967 21cr Wolves .75 .25
1803 A967 30cr Deer 2.25 .30
Nos. 1801-1803 (3) 3.65 .80

Film Strip and Award A968

1982, June 19
1804 A968 17cr multi .45 .25

20th anniv. of Golden Palm award for The Promise Keeper, Cannes Film Festival.

Souvenir Sheet

50th Anniv. of Constitutionalist Revolution — A969

1982, July 9 Litho. *Perf. 11*
1805 A969 140cr multi 4.50 4.50

Church of Our Lady of O'Sabara — A970

Baroque Architecture, Minas Gerais State: No. 1807, Church of Our Lady of the Rosary, Diamantina. No. 1808, Town Square, Mariana.

1982, July 16 *Perf. 11½*
1806 A970 17cr multi .50 .25
1807 A970 17cr multi, horiz. .50 .25
1808 A970 17cr multi, horiz. .50 .25
Nos. 1806-1808 (3) 1.50 .75

St. Francis of Assisi, 800th Birth Anniv. — A971

1982, July 24
1809 A971 21cr multi .45 .25

Stamp Day and Centenary of Pedro II "Large Head" Stamps A972

1982, Aug. 1

1810 A972 21cr No. 82 .45 .25

Port of Manaus Free Trade Zone A973

1982, Aug. 15 ***Perf. 11x11½***

1811 A973 75cr multi 1.10 .45

Scouting Year — A974

1982, Aug. 21 Litho. ***Perf. 11***

1812 A974 Sheet of 2 9.00 9.00
a. 185cr Scout 4.50 4.50
b. 85cr Baden-Powell 4.50 4.50

Orixas Folk Costumes of African Origin A975

1982, Aug. 21 ***Perf. 11½***

1813 A975 20cr Iemanja .45 .25
1814 A975 20cr Xango .45 .25
1815 A975 20cr Oxumare .45 .25
Nos. 1813-1815 (3) 1.35 .75

10th Anniv. of Central Bank of Brazil Currency Museum A976

Designs: No. 1816, 1645 12-florin coin, obverse and reverse. No. 1817, 1822 Emperor Pedro 6.40-reis coronation coin.

1982, Aug. 31

1816 A976 25cr multi .35 .25
1817 A976 25cr multi .35 .25

Dom Pedro Proclaiming Independence — A977

1982, Sept. 1

1818 A977 25cr multi .50 .30

National Week.

A978

A979

1982, Oct. 4

1819 A978 85cr Portrait 1.25 .60

St. Theresa of Avila (1515-1582).

1982, Oct. 15 Litho. ***Perf. 11½x11***

1820 A979 75cr Instruments 2.00 1.75
1821 A979 80cr Dancers 2.00 1.75
1822 A979 85cr Musicians 2.00 1.75
a. Souv. sheet, #1820-1822, perf 11 7.50 7.50
Nos. 1820-1822 (3) 6.00 5.25

Lubrapex '82, 4th Portuguese-Brazilian Stamp Exhibition. Stamps in No. 1822a are without "LUBRAPEX 82."

Aviation Industry Day A980

1982, Oct. 17 ***Perf. 12***

1823 A980 24cr Embraer EMB-312 trainer plane .45 .25

Bastos Tigre, Poet, Birth Centenary, and "Saudade" Text A981

1982, Oct. 29

1824 A981 24cr multi .35 .25

Book Day.

10th Anniv. of Brazilian Telecommunications Co. — A982

1982, Nov. 9 Litho. ***Perf. 11½***

1825 A982 24cr multi .40 .25

Christmas A983

Children's Drawings.

1982, Nov. 10

1826 A983 24cr Nativity 1.10 .30
1827 A983 24cr Angels 1.10 .30
1828 A983 30cr Nativity, diff. 1.10 .30
1829 A983 30cr Flight into Egypt 1.10 .30
Nos. 1826-1829 (4) 4.40 1.20

State Flags Type of 1981

No. 1830: a, Ceara. b, Espirito Santo. c, Paraiba. d, Grande de Norte. e, Rondonia.

1982, Nov. 19

1830 Block of 5 + label 8.00 8.00
a.-e. A947 24cr any single 1.60 .40

Thanksgiving — A985

1982, Nov. 25

1835 A985 24cr multi .50 .25

Homage to the Deaf — A986

1982, Dec. 1

1836 A986 24cr multi .40 .25

Naval Academy Bicentenary A987

Training Ships: No. 1837, Brazil. No. 1838, Benjamin Constant. No. 1839, Almirante Saldanha.

1982, Dec. 14

1837 A987 24cr multi .80 .25
1838 A987 24cr multi .80 .25
1839 A987 24cr multi .80 .25
Nos. 1837-1839 (3) 2.40 .75

Souvenir Sheet

No. 12 — A988

1982, Dec. 18 Litho. ***Perf. 11***

1840 A988 200cr multi 6.00 6.00

BRASILIANA '83 Intl. Stamp Exhibition, Rio de Janeiro, July 29-Aug. 7.

Brasiliana '83 Carnival A989

1983, Feb. 9 Litho. ***Perf. 11½***

1841 A989 24cr Samba drummers .40 .25
1842 A989 130cr Street parade 2.25 1.00
1843 A989 140cr Dancer 2.25 1.00
1844 A989 150cr Male dancer 2.25 1.00
Nos. 1841-1844 (4) 7.15 3.25

Antarctic Expedition A990

1983, Feb. 20 Litho. ***Perf. 11½***

1845 A990 150cr Support ship Barano de Teffe 4.00 .75

50th Anniv. of Women's Rights — A991

1983, Mar. 8

1846 A991 130cr multi 1.50 .60

Itaipu Hydroelectric Power Station Opening — A992

1983, Mar. Litho. ***Perf. 12***

1847 A992 140cr multi 2.50 .50

Cancer Prevention A993

Designs: 30cr, Microscope. 38cr, Antonio Prudente, Paulista Cancer Assoc. founder, Camargo Hospital.

1983, Apr. 18

1848 A993 30cr multi .50 .35
1849 A993 38cr multi .50 .35
a. Pair, #1848-1849 1.25 1.25

Martin Luther (1483-1546) A994

1983, Apr. 18

1850 A994 150cr pale grn & blk 1.75 .50

Agricultural Research A995

1983, Apr. 26 Litho. ***Perf. 11½***

1851 A995 30cr Chestnut tree .50 .25
1852 A995 30cr Genetic research .50 .25
1853 A995 38cr Tropical soy beans .60 .25
Nos. 1851-1853 (3) 1.60 .75

Father Rogerio Neuhaus (1863-1934), Centenary of Ordination — A996

1983, May 3 *Perf. 11½x11*
1854 A996 30cr multi .35 .25

30th Anniv. of Customs Cooperation Council — A997

1983, May 5 *Perf. 11x11½*
1855 A997 30cr multi .35 .25

World Communications Year — A998

1983, May 17 Litho. *Perf. 11½*
1856 A998 250cr multi 4.25 .55

Toucans A999

1983, May 21

1857	A999	30cr Tucanucu	1.25	.35
1858	A999	185cr White-breasted	3.75	1.00
1859	A999	205cr Green-beaked	4.00	1.00
1860	A999	215cr Black-beaked	4.50	1.00
		Nos. 1857-1860 (4)	13.50	3.35

Souvenir Sheet

Resurrection, by Raphael (1483-1517) — A1000

1983, May 25 *Perf. 11*
1861 A1000 250cr multi 6.00 6.00

Hohenzollern 980 Locomotive, 1875 — A1001

Various locomotives.

1983, June 12 Litho. *Perf. 11½*

1862	A1001	30cr shown	1.10	.50
1863	A1001	30cr Baldwin #1, 1881	1.10	.50
1864	A1001	38cr Fowler #1, 1872	1.10	.60
		Nos. 1862-1864 (3)	3.30	1.60

9th Women's Basketball World Championship A1002

1983, July 24 Litho. *Perf. 11½x11*
1865 A1002 30cr Players, front view .40 .25
1866 A1002 30cr Players, rear view .40 .25

Simon Bolivar (1783-1830) — A1003

1983, July 24 *Perf. 12*
1867 A1003 30cr multi .50 .25

Children's Polio and Measles Vaccination Campaign — A1004

1983, July 25
1868 A1004 30cr Girl, measles .40 .25
1869 A1004 30cr Boy, polio .40 .25

A1005

1983, July 28 *Perf. 11½x11*
1870 A1005 30cr Goddess Minerva, computer tape .45 .25

20th Anniv. of Master's program in engineering.

A1006

Guanabara Bay.

1983, July 29 **Engr.**

1871	A1006	185cr No. 1	1.90	.75
1872	A1006	205cr No. 2	1.90	.75
1873	A1006	215cr No. 3	1.90	.75
		Nos. 1871-1873 (3)	5.70	2.25

Souvenir Sheet

Perf. 11

1874		Sheet of 3	12.00	13.50
a.	A1006	185cr No. 1	3.00	3.75
b.	A1006	205cr No. 2	3.00	3.75
c.	A1006	215cr No. 3	3.00	3.75

BRASILIANA '83 Intl. Stamp Show, Rio de Janeiro, July 29-Aug. 7.

Stamps in No. 1874 have unframed denomination at bottom of the stamps. The background scene is enlarged to cover all 3 stamps in a continuous design.

Souvenir Sheets

A set of five 2000cr souvenir sheets also exist for BRASILIANA '83. These picture early flying attempts, Ademar Ferreira da Silva, Olympic gold medal winner, Soccer, Formula 1 auto racing, and Gold medal winners in Olympic sailing. Value $35 each.

Souvenir Sheet

The First Mass in Brazil, by Vitor Meireles (1833-1903) — A1007

1983, Aug. 18 *Perf. 11*
1875 A1007 250cr multi 5.50 4.00

EMB-120 Brasilia Passenger Plane A1008

1983, Aug. 19 *Perf. 12*
1876 A1008 30cr multi .50 .30

Vision of Don Bosco Centenary A1009

1983, Aug. 30
1877 A1009 130cr multi 1.00 .35

Independence Week — A1010

1983, Sept. 1 Litho. *Perf. 11½*
1878 A1010 50cr multi .50 .25

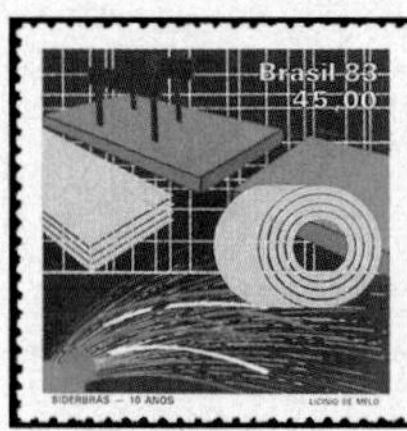

National Steel Corp., 10th Anniv. A1011

1983, Sept. 17 Litho. *Perf. 11½*
1879 A1011 45cr multi .60 .25

Cactus A1012

1983, Sept. 12 Litho. *Perf. 11½*

1880	A1012	45cr Pilosocereus gounellei	1.10	.25
1881	A1012	45cr Melocactus bahiensis	1.10	.25
1882	A1012	57cr Cereus jamacaru	1.40	.25
		Nos. 1880-1882 (3)	3.60	.75

50th Anniv. of the 1st National Eucharistic Congress A1013

1983, Oct. 12 Litho. *Perf. 11½*
1883 A1013 45cr multi .50 .25

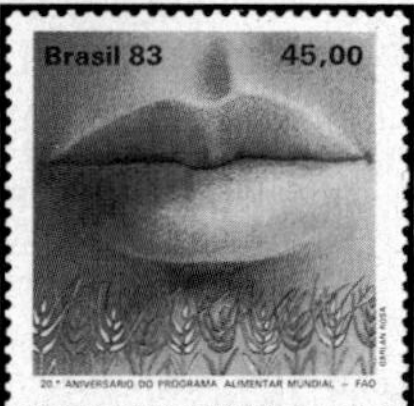

World Food Program A1014

1983, Oct. 14 Litho. *Perf. 11½*
1884 A1014 45cr Mouth, grain .50 .25
1885 A1014 57cr Fish, sailboat .60 .25

Souvenir Sheet

Louis Breguet, Death Centenary — A1015

1983, Oct. 27 Litho. *Perf. 11*

1886 A1015 376cr Telegraph transmitter 10.00 10.00

Christmas 1983 A1016

17th-18th Cent. Statues: 45cr, Our Lady of the Angels. 315cr, Our Lady of the Parturition. 335cr, Our Lady of Joy. 345cr, Our Lady of the Presentation.

1983, Nov. 10 Litho. *Perf. 11½*

1887 A1016 45cr multi .50 .30
1888 A1016 315cr multi 2.00 1.00
1889 A1016 335cr multi 2.00 1.00
1890 A1016 345cr multi 2.00 1.00
Nos. 1887-1890 (4) 6.50 3.30

Marshal Mascarenhas Birth Centenary — A1017

1983, Nov. 13 Litho. *Perf. 11½*

1891 A1017 45cr Battle sites .35 .25

Commander of Brazilian Expeditionary Force in Italy.

State Flags Type of 1981

No. 1892: a, Amazonas. b, Goias. c, Rio. d, Mato Grosso Do Sol. e, Parana.

1983, Nov. 17 Litho. *Perf. 11½*

1892 Block of 5 + label 3.75 3.75
a.-e. A947 45cr any single .60 .40

Thanksgiving — A1018

1983, Nov. 24 Litho. *Perf. 12*

1896 A1018 45cr Madonna, wheat .40 .25

Manned Flight Bicentenary A1019

1983, Dec. 15 Litho. *Perf. 12*

1897 A1019 345cr Montgolfiere balloon, 1783 6.00 2.00

Ethnic Groups A1020

1984, Jan. 20 Litho. *Perf. 12*

1898 A1020 45cr multi .35 .25

50th anniv. of publication of Masters and Slaves, sociological study by Gilberto Freyre.

Centenary of Crystal Palace, Petropolis A1021

1984, Feb. 2

1899 A1021 45cr multi .35 .25

Souvenir Sheet

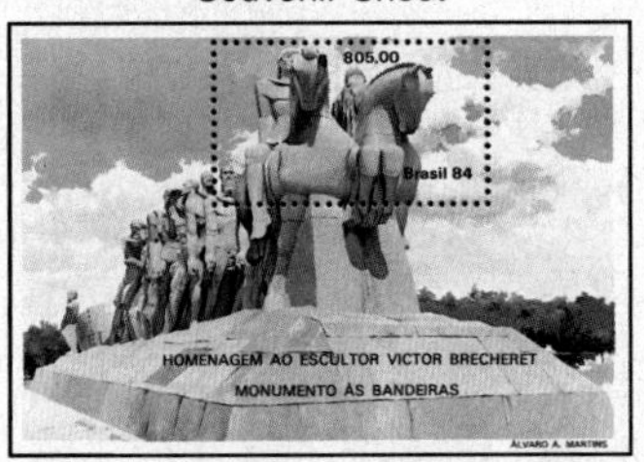

Flags (Sculpture with 40 Figures), by Victor Brecheret (b. 1894) — A1022

1984, Feb. 22 Litho. *Perf. 11*

1900 A1022 805cr multi 3.25 3.25

Naval Museum Centenary A1023

1984, Mar. 23 Litho. *Perf. 11½*

1901 A1023 620cr Figurehead, frigate, 1847 1.50 .70

Slavery Abolition Centenary A1024

1984, Mar. 25

1902 A1024 585cr Broken chain, raft 1.10 .55
1903 A1024 610cr Freed slave 1.25 .60

Souvenir Sheet

Visit of King Carl XVI Gustaf of Sweden — A1025

1984, Apr. 2 *Perf. 11*

1904 A1025 2105cr multi 6.00 6.00

1984 Summer Olympics A1026

1984, Apr. 13 *Perf. 11½*

1905 A1026 65cr Long jump .40 .30
1906 A1026 65cr 100-meter race .40 .30
1907 A1026 65cr Relay race .40 .30
1908 A1026 585cr Pole vault 1.00 .40
1909 A1026 610cr High jump 1.10 .40
1910 A1026 620cr Hurdles 1.10 .40
a. Block of 6, #1905-1910 4.50 4.50

Voters Casting Ballots, Symbols of Labor A1027

Pres. Getulio Vargas Birth Centenary: Symbols of Development.

1984, Apr. 19 Litho. *Perf. 11½*

1911 A1027 65cr shown .30 .25
1912 A1027 65cr Oil rig, blast furnace .30 .25
1913 A1027 65cr High-tension towers .30 .25
Nos. 1911-1913 (3) .90 .75

Columbus, Espana '84 Emblem — A1028

1984, Apr. 27

1914 A1028 65cr Pedro Cabral .50 .25
1915 A1028 610cr shown 2.00 .70

Map of Americas, Heads — A1029

1984, May 7 Litho. *Perf. 11½*

1916 A1029 65cr multi .30 .25

Pan-American Association of Finance and Guarantees, 8th Assembly.

Lubrapex '84 — A1030

18th Century Paintings, Mariana Cathedral.

1984, May 8 *Perf. 11½x11*

1917 A1030 65cr Hunting scene .35 .30
1918 A1030 585cr Pastoral scene .90 .50
1919 A1030 610cr People under umbrellas 1.00 .50
1920 A1030 620cr Elephants 1.25 .50
Nos. 1917-1920 (4) 3.50 1.80

Souvenir Sheet

Intl. Fedn. of Soccer Associations, 80th Anniv. — A1031

1984, May 21 *Perf. 11*

1921 A1031 2115cr Globe 6.00 6.00

Matto Grosso Lowland Fauna A1032

1984, June 5 Litho. *Perf. 11½*

1922 Strip of 3 2.10 2.10
a. A1032 65cr Deer .70 .30
b. A1032 65cr Jaguar .70 .30
c. A1032 80cr Alligator .70 .30

First Letter Mailed in Brazil, by Guido Mondin — A1033

1984, June 8 *Perf. 12x11½*

1923 A1033 65cr multi .40 .25

Postal Union of Americas and Spain, first anniv. of new headquarters.

Brazil-Germany Air Service, 50th Anniv. — A1034

1984, June 19

1924 610cr Dornier-Wal seaplane 1.50 .70
1925 620cr Steamer Westfalen 1.50 .70
a. A1034 Pair, #1924-1925 3.00 3.00

Woolly Spider Monkey, World Wildlife Fund Emblem — A1036

1984, July 6 *Perf. 11½*

1926 A1036 65cr Mother, baby 2.25 .90
1927 A1036 80cr Monkey 2.25 .90

Agriculture Type of 1980

Designs: 65cr, Rubber tree. 80cr, Brazil nuts. 120cr, Rice. 150cr, Eucalyptus. 300cr, Pinha da Parana. 800cr, Carnauba. 1000cr, Babacu. 2000cr, Sunflower.

Photogravure (65, 80, 120, 150cr), Engraved

1984-85 *Perf. 11x11½*

1934 A894 65cr lilac .30 .25
1935 A894 80cr brn red .80 .50
1936 A894 120cr dk sl bl .75 .25
1937 A894 150cr green .50 .25
1938 A894 300cr rose mag 2.00 .30
1939 A894 800cr grnsh bl 2.00 .30
1940 A894 1000cr lemon 2.00 .25
1941 A894 2000cr yel org ('85) 2.50 .40
Nos. 1934-1941 (8) 10.85 2.50

Marajo Isld. Buffalo A1037

1984, July 9 **Litho.** *Perf. 12*

1942 Strip of 3 1.60 1.60
a. A1037 65cr Approaching stream .50 .30
b. A1037 65cr Standing on bank .50 .30
c. A1037 80cr Drinking .50 .30

Continuous design.

Banco Economico Sesquicentenary — A1038

1984, July 13 *Perf. 11½*

1943 A1038 65cr Bank, coins .30 .25

Historic Railway Stations A1039

1984, July 23 **Litho.** *Perf. 11½*

1944 A1039 65cr Japeri .70 .30
1945 A1039 65cr Luz, vert. .70 .30
1946 A1039 80cr Sao Joao del Rei .70 .30
Nos. 1944-1946 (3) 2.10 .90

Souvenir Sheet

A1040

1984, Aug. 13 *Perf. 11*

1947 A1040 585cr Girl scout 4.00 4.00

Girl Scouts in Brazil, 65th anniv.

A1041

1984, Aug. 21 **Litho.** *Perf. 11½*

1948 A1041 65cr Couple sheltered from rain .30 .25

Housing project bank, 20th anniv.

Independence Week — A1042

Children's Drawings.

1984, Sept. 3

1949 A1042 100cr Explorer & ship .30 .25
1950 A1042 100cr Sailing ships .30 .25
1951 A1042 100cr "BRASIL" mural .30 .25
1952 A1042 100cr Children under rainbow .30 .25
Nos. 1949-1952 (4) 1.20 1.00

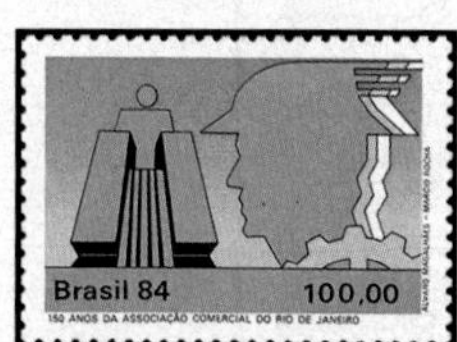

Rio de Janeiro Chamber of Commerce Sesquicentenary — A1043

1984, Sept. 10

1953 A1043 100cr Monument, worker silhouette .30 .25

Death Sesquicentenary of Don Pedro I (IV of Portugal) — A1044

1984, Sept. 23 *Perf. 12x11½*

1954 A1044 1000cr Portrait 3.50 1.50

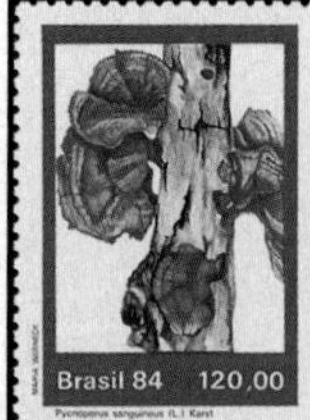

Local Mushrooms A1045

1984, Oct. 22 *Perf. 11½*

1955 A1045 120cr Pycnoporus sanguineus .60 .25
1956 A1045 1050cr Calvatia sp 2.25 1.25
1957 A1045 1080cr Pleurotus sp, horiz. 2.25 1.25
Nos. 1955-1957 (3) 5.10 2.75

Book Day — A1046

1984, Oct. 23 *Perf. 11½*

1958 A1046 120cr Girl in open book .30 .25

New State Mint Opening — A1047

1984, Nov. 1

1959 A1047 120cr multi .35 .25

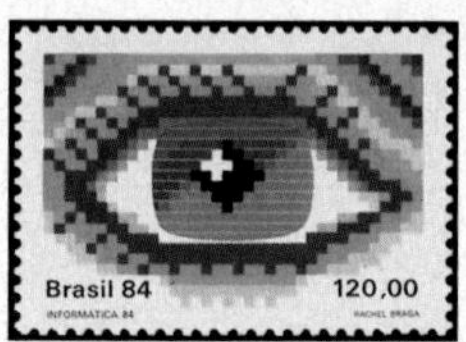

Informatics Fair & Congress A1048

1984, Nov. 5 **Litho.** *Perf. 12*

1960 A1048 120cr Eye, computer terminal .60 .25

Org. of American States, 14th Assembly A1049

1984, Nov. 14

1961 A1049 120cr Emblem, flags .35 .25

State Flags Type of 1981

No. 1962: a, Maranhaio. b, Mato Grosso. c, Minas Gerais. d, Piaui. e, Santa Catarina.

1984, Nov. 19 *Perf. 11½*

1962 Block of 5 + label 3.25 3.25
a.-e. A947 120cr, any single .65 .40

Thanksgiving 1984 — A1051

1984, Nov. 22

1963 A1051 120cr Bell tower, Brasilia .35 .25

Christmas 1984 A1052

Paintings: No. 1964, Nativity, by Djanira. No. 1965, Virgin and Child, by Glauco Rodrigues. No. 1966, Flight into Egypt, by Paul Garfunkel. No. 1967, Nativity, by Di Cavalcanti.

1984, Dec. 3 **Litho.** *Perf. 12*

1964 A1052 120cr multi .40 .30
1965 A1052 120cr multi .40 .30
1966 A1052 1050cr multi 2.25 .60
1967 A1052 1080cr multi 2.25 .60
Nos. 1964-1967 (4) 5.30 1.80

40th Anniv., International Civil Aviation Organization — A1053

1984, Dec. 7 **Litho.** *Perf. 12*

1968 A1053 120cr Aircraft, Earth globe .50 .25

25th Anniv., North-Eastern Development — A1054

1984, Dec. 14 **Litho.** *Perf. 12*

1969 A1054 120cr Farmer, field .30 .25

Emilio Rouede A1055

Painting: Church of the Virgin of Safe Travels, by Rouede.

1985, Jan. 22 **Litho.** *Perf. 12*

1970 A1055 120cr multi .40 .25

BRASILSAT — A1056

1985, Feb. 8 **Litho.** *Perf. 11½x12*

1971 A1056 150cr Satellite, Brazil .45 .25

Metropolitan Railways — A1057

1985, Mar. 2 Litho. *Perf. 11x11½*
1972 A1057 200cr Passenger trains .60 .25

Brasilia Botanical Gardens A1058

1985, Mar. 8 Litho. *Perf. 11½x12*
1973 A1058 200cr Caryocar brasiliense .45 .25

40th Anniv., Brazilian Paratroops A1059

1985, Mar. 8 Litho. *Perf. 11½x12*
1974 A1059 200cr Parachute drop .50 .25

Natl. Climate Awareness Program — A1060

1985, Mar. 18 Litho. *Perf. 11½x12*
1975 A1060 500cr multi .50 .25

Pure Bred Horses A1061

1985, Mar. 19 Litho. *Perf. 12*
1976 A1061 1000cr Campolina 2.00 .75
1977 A1061 1500cr Marajoara 2.00 .75
1978 A1061 1500cr Mangalarga marchador 2.00 .75
Nos. 1976-1978 (3) 6.00 2.25

Ouro Preto — A1062

1985, Apr. 18 Litho. *Perf. 11½x12*
1979 A1062 220cr shown .40 .25
1980 A1062 220cr St. Miguel des Missoes .40 .25
1981 A1062 220cr Olinda .40 .25
Nos. 1979-1981 (3) 1.20 .75

Polivolume, by Mary Vieira — A1063

1985, Apr. 20 Litho.
1982 A1063 220cr multi .40 .25

Rio Branco Inst., 40th anniv.

Natl. Capital, Brasilia, 25th Anniv. — A1064

1985, Apr. 22 Litho.
1983 A1064 220cr Natl. Theater, acoustic shell .30 .25
1984 A1064 220cr Catetinho Palace, JK Memorial .30 .25

A1065

A1065a

1985-86 Photo. *Perf. 11½*
1985 A1065 50cr lake .25 .25
1986 A1065 100cr dp vio .25 .25
1987 A1065 150cr violet .25 .25
1988 A1065 200cr ultra .25 .25
1989 A1065 220cr green .45 *.95*
1990 A1065 300cr royal bl .25 .25
1991 A1065 500cr olive blk .40 .30
1992 A1065a 1000cr brn ol ('86) .25 .25
1993 A1065a 2000cr brt grn ('86) .40 .25
1994 A1065a 3000cr dl vio .50 .25
1995 A1065a 5000cr brown 1.75 .25
Nos. 1985-1995 (11) 5.00 3.50

Marshal Rondon, 120th Birth Anniv. A1066

1985, May 5 *Perf. 11x11½*
1996 A1066 220cr multi .40 .25

Educator, protector of the Indians, building superintendent of telegraph lines.

Candido Fontoura (1885-1974) A1067

1985, May 14 *Perf. 12x11½*
1997 A1067 220cr multi .35 .25

Pioneer of the Brazilian pharmaceutical industry.

Brapex VI — A1068

Cave paintings: No. 1998, Deer, Cerca Grande. No. 1999, Lizards, Lapa do Caboclo. No. 2000, Running deer, Grande Abrigo de Santana do Riacho.

1985, May 18 *Perf. 11½x11*
1998 A1068 300cr multi .25 .25
1999 A1068 300cr multi .25 .25
2000 A1068 2000cr multi 1.10 .50
a. Souvenir sheet of 3, #1998-2000, perf. 10½x11 3.50 3.50
Nos. 1998-2000 (3) 1.60 1.00

Wildlife Conservation — A1069

Birds in Marinho dos Abrolhos National Park: No. 2001, Fregata magnificens. No. 2002, Sula dactylatra. No. 2003, Anous stolidus. No. 2004, Pluvialis squatarola.

1985, June 5 *Perf. 11½x12*
2001 A1069 220cr multi .80 .25
2002 A1069 220cr multi .80 .25
2003 A1069 220cr multi .80 .25
2004 A1069 2000cr multi 2.40 .30
Nos. 2001-2004 (4) 4.80 1.05

A1070

UN infant survival campaign: No. 2005, Mother breastfeeding infant. No. 2006, Hand, eyedropper, children.

1985, June 11 *Perf. 12x11½*
2005 A1070 220cr multi .50 .25
2006 A1070 220cr multi .50 .25
a. Pair, #2005-2006 1.25 1.25

A1071

1985, June 22 Litho. *Perf. 11½x11*
2007 A1071 220cr multi .35 .25

Sea Search & Rescue.

Souvenir Sheet

World Cup Soccer, Mexico, 1986 — A1072

1985, June 23 *Perf. 11*
2008 A1072 2000cr multi 7.00 7.00

Intl. Youth Year — A1073

1985, June 28 *Perf. 12*
2009 A1073 220cr Circle of children .40 .25

11th Natl. Eucharistic Congress A1074

1985, July 16 *Perf. 12x11½*
2010 A1074 2000cr Mosaic, Priest raising host .90 .50

Director Humberto Mauro, Scene from Sangue Mineiro, 1929 — A1075

1985, July 27
2011 A1075 300cr multi .60 .25

Cataguases Studios, 60th anniv.

Escola e Sacro Museum, Convent St. Anthony, Joao Pessoa, Paraiba A1076

1985, Aug. 5 *Perf. 11½x12*
2012 A1076 330cr multi .40 .25

Paraiba State 400th anniv.

Inconfidencia Museum
A1077

1985, Aug. 11 ***Perf. 12x11½***
2013 A1077 300cr shown .25 .25
2014 A1077 300cr Museum of History & Diplomacy .25 .25

Revolutionary, by Guido Mondin — A1078

1985, Aug. 14
2015 A1078 330cr multi .30 .25

Cabanagem Insurrection, 150th anniv.

AMX Subsonic Air Force Fighter Plane
A1079

1985, Aug. 19 ***Perf. 11½x12***
2016 A1079 330cr multi .30 .25

AMX Project, joint program with Italy.

16th-17th Century Military Uniforms
A1080

1985, Aug. 26 ***Perf. 12x11½***
2017 A1080 300cr Captain, crossbowman .30 .25
2018 A1080 300cr Harquebusier, sergeant .30 .25
2019 A1080 300cr Musketeer, pikeman .30 .25
2020 A1080 300cr Fusilier, pikeman .30 .25
Nos. 2017-2020 (4) 1.20 1.00

Bento Goncalves and Insurrectionist Cavalry on Southern Battlefields, by Guido Mondin — A1081

1985, Sept. 20 ***Perf. 11½x12***
2021 A1081 330cr multi .40 .25

Farrouphilha Insurrection, 150th anniv.

Aparados da Serra National Park
A1082

1985, Sept. 23
2022 A1082 3100cr Ravine 1.10 .50
2023 A1082 3320cr Mountains 1.10 .55
2024 A1082 3480cr Forest, waterfall 1.10 .55
Nos. 2022-2024 (3) 3.30 1.60

President-elect Tancredo Neves, Natl. Congress, Alvorada Palace, Supreme Court — A1083

1985, Oct. 10 Litho. ***Perf. 11x11½***
2025 A1083 330cr multi .30 .25

FEB, Postmark
A1084

1985, Oct. 10 ***Perf. 11½x12***
2026 A1084 500cr multi .30 .25

Brazilian Expeditionary Force Postal Service, 41st anniv.

Rio de Janeiro-Niteroi Ferry Service, 150th Anniv. — A1085

1985, Oct. 14 ***Perf. 11½x12***
2027 A1085 500cr Segunda .40 .25
2028 A1085 500cr Terceira .40 .25
2029 A1085 500cr Especuladora .40 .25
2030 A1085 500cr Urca .40 .25
Nos. 2027-2030 (4) 1.60 1.00

Muniz M-7 Inaugural Flight, 50th Anniv. — A1086

1985, Oct. 22
2031 A1086 500cr multi .50 .25

UN 40th Anniv.
A1087

Natl. Press System
A1088

1985, Oct. 24 ***Perf. 11½x11***
2032 A1087 500cr multi .30 .25

1985, Nov. 7
2033 A1088 500cr multi .30 .25

Diario de Pernambuco, newspaper, 160th anniv.

Christmas 1985
A1089

1985, Nov. 11 ***Perf. 11½x12***
2034 A1089 500cr Christ in Manger .30 .25
2035 A1089 500cr Adoration of the Magi .30 .25
2036 A1089 500cr Flight to Egypt .30 .25
Nos. 2034-2036 (3) .90 .75

State Flags Type of 1981

No. 2037: a, Para. b, Rio Grande do Sul. c, Acre. d, Sao Paulo.

1985, Nov. 19 ***Perf. 12***
2037 Block of 4 1.60 .60
a.-d. A947 500cr, any single .40 .25

Thanksgiving Day — A1091

1985, Nov. 28 ***Perf. 12x11½***
2038 A1091 500cr Child gathering wheat .30 .25

Economic Development of Serra dos Carajas Region — A1092

1985, Dec. 11 Litho. ***Perf. 11½x12***
2039 A1092 500cr multi .35 .25

Fr. Bartholomeu Lourenco de Gusmao (1685-1724), Inventor, the Aerostat — A1093

1985, Dec. 19 Litho. ***Perf. 11x11½***
2040 A1093 500cr multi .40 .25

A1094

The Trees, by Da Costa E Silva (b. 1885), poet.

1985, Dec. 20 Litho. ***Perf. 12x11½***
2041 A1094 500cr multi .30 .25

Values for used commemoratives issued after 1985 and for used souvenir sheets are for favor-canceled examples. Postally used examples are worth more.

Souvenir Sheet

A1095

1986, Mar. 3 Litho. ***Perf. 11***
2042 A1095 10000cr multi 6.00 6.00

1986 World Cup Soccer Championships, Mexico. LUBRAPEX '86, philatelic exhibition.

Halley's Comet — A1096

1986, Apr. 11 Litho. ***Perf. 11½x12***
2043 A1096 50c multi .40 .25

Commander Ferraz Antarctic Station, 2nd Anniv. — A1097

1986, Apr. 25
2044 A1097 50c multi .40 .25

Labor Day — A1098

1986, May 1 Litho. *Perf. 12x11½*
2045 A1098 50c multi .30 .25

Maternity, by Henrique Bernardelli (1858-1936) A1099

1986, May 8
2046 A1099 50c multi .30 .25

Amnesty Intl., 25th Anniv. A1100

1986, May 28 Litho. *Perf. 11½x12*
2047 A1100 50c multi .40 .25

Butterflies A1101

1986, June 5 *Perf. 12x11½*

2048	A1101	50c Pyrrhopyge rufi-cauda	.50	.25
2049	A1101	50c Prepona eugenes diluta	.50	.25
2050	A1101	50c Pierriballia mandel mo-lione	.50	.25
		Nos. 2048-2050 (3)	1.50	.75

Score from Opera "Il Guarani" and Antonio Carlos Gomes (1836-1896), Composer — A1102

1986, July 11 *Perf. 11½x12*
2051 A1102 50c multi .40 .25

Natl. Accident Prevention Campaign — A1103

1986, July 30 Litho. *Perf. 11½x11*
2052 A1103 50c Lineman .35 .25

Souvenir Sheet

Stamp Day — A1104

1986, Aug. 1 *Perf. 11*
2053 A1104 5cz No. 53 2.50 2.50

Brazilian Phil. Soc., 75th anniv., and Dom Pedro II issue, Nos. 53-60, 120th anniv.

Architecture A1105

Designs: 10c, House of Garcia D'Avila, Nazare de Mata, Bahia. 20c, Church of Our Lady of the Assumption, Anchieta Village. 50c, Fort Reis Magos, Natal. 1cz, Pilgrim's Column, Alcantara Village, 1648. 2cz, Cloisters, St. Francis Convent, Olinda. 5cz, St. Anthony's Chapel, Sao Roque. 10cz, St. Lawrence of the Indians Church, Niteroi. 20cz, Principe da Beiro Fort, Mato Dentro. 50cz, Jesus of Matozinhos Church, vert. 100cz, Church of our Lady of Sorrow, Campanha. 200cz, Casa dos Contos, Ouro Preto. 500cz, Antiga Alfandega, Belem, Para.

Perf. 11½x11, 11x11½

1986-88 Photo.

2055	A1105	10c sage grn	.30	.25
2057	A1105	20c brt blue	.30	.25
2059	A1105	50c orange	.70	.25
a.		Litho., perf. 13 ('88)	6.50	.70
2064	A1105	1cz golden brn	.40	.25
2065	A1105	2cz dull rose	.60	.25
a.		Litho., perf. 13 ('88)	2.00	.25
2067	A1105	5cz lt olive grn	1.50	.60
a.		Litho., perf. 13 ('88)	2.25	.25
2068	A1105	10cz slate blue	1.25	.50
a.		Litho., perf. 13 ('88)	4.75	.50
2069	A1105	20cz lt red brn	1.75	1.00
2070	A1105	50cz brn org	3.50	2.50
2071	A1105	100cz dull grn	3.75	3.00
2072	A1105	200cz deep blue	3.75	2.75
2073	A1105	500cz dull red brn	3.50	1.75
		Nos. 2055-2073 (12)	21.30	13.35

Issued: 10c, 8/11; 20c, 12/8; 50c, 8/19; 1cz, 11/19; 2cz, 11/9; 5cz, 12/30; 10cz, 6/2/87; 20cz, 50cz, 9/18/87; 100cz, 12/21/87; 200cz, 5/9/88; 500cz, 11/22/88.

Famous Men — A1106

Designs: No. 2074, Juscelino Kubitschek de Oliveira, president 1956-61, and Alvorado Palace, Brasilia. No. 2075, Octavio Mangabeira, statesman, and Itamaraty Palace, Rio de Janeiro, horiz.

1986 *Perf. 12x11½, 11½x12*
2074 A1106 50c multi .30 .25
2075 A1106 50c multi .30 .25

Issued: No. 2074, Aug. 21; No. 2075, Aug. 27.

World Gastroenterology Congress, Sao Paulo — A1107

1986, Sept. 7 *Perf. 11½x12*
2076 A1107 50c multi .30 .25

Federal Broadcasting System, 50th Anniv. — A1108

1986, Sept. 15 *Perf. 12x11½*
2077 A1108 50c multi .40 .25

Intl. Peace Year — A1109

Painting (detail): War and Peace, by Candido Portinari.

1986, Sept. 16
2078 A1109 50c multi .30 .25

Famous Men — A1111

Federal Savings Bank, 125th Anniv. — A1112

Ernesto Simoes Filho (b. 1886), Publisher of A Tarde A1110

1986, Oct. 4 Litho. *Perf. 11½x12*
2079 A1110 50c multi .30 .25

Designs: No. 2080, Title page from manuscript, c. 1683-94, by Gregorio Mattos e Guerra (b. 1636), author. No. 2081, Manuel Bandeira (1886-1968), poet, text from I'll Go Back to Pasargada.

1986, Oct. 29 *Perf. 11½x11*
2080 A1111 50c lake & beige .25 .25
2081 A1111 50c lake & dl grn .25 .25

1986, Nov. 4 *Perf. 12x11½*
2082 A1112 50c multi .30 .25

Flowering Plants A1113

Glauber Rocha, Film Industry Pioneer A1114

Perf. 12x11½, 11½x12

1986, Sept. 23

2083	A1113	50c Urera mitis	.25	.25
2084	A1113	6.50cz Couroupita guyanensis	.70	.40
2085	A1113	6.90cz Bauhinia variegata, horiz.	.90	.40
		Nos. 2083-2085 (3)	1.85	1.05

1986, Nov. 20 *Perf. 12x11½*
2086 A1114 50c multi .45 .25

LUBRAPEX '86 — A1115

Cordel Folk Tales: No. 2087, Romance of the Mysterious Peacock. No. 2088, History of the Empress Porcina.

1986, Nov. 21 *Perf. 11x12*

2087	A1115	6.90cz multi	.80	.40
2088	A1115	6.90cz multi	.80	.40
a.		Souvenir sheet of 2, #2087-2088, perf. 11	2.75	2.75

Christmas A1116

Birds: 50c, And Christ child. 6.50cz, And tree. 7.30cz, Eating fruit.

1986, Nov. 10 *Perf. 11½x12*

2089	A1116	50c multi	.40	.25
2090	A1116	6.50cz multi	1.10	.50
2091	A1116	7.30cz multi	1.40	.60
		Nos. 2089-2091 (3)	2.90	1.35

Military Uniforms, c. 1930 — A1117

Designs: No. 2092, Navy lieutenant commander, dreadnought Minas Gerais. No. 2093, Army flight lieutenant, WACO S.C.O. biplane, Fortaleza Airport.

1986, Dec. 15 *Perf. 12x11½*
2092 A1117 50c multi .30 .25
2093 A1117 50c multi .30 .25

Fortaleza Air Base, 50th anniv. (No. 2093).

Bartolomeu de Gusmao Airport, 50th Anniv. — A1118

1986, Dec. 26
2094 A1118 1cz multi .45 .25

Heitor Villa Lobos (1887-1959), Conductor A1119

1987, Mar. 5 Litho. *Perf. 12x11½*
2095 A1119 1.50cz multi .45 .25

Natl. Air Force C-130 Transport Plane, Flag, the Antarctic A1120

1987, Mar. 9 *Perf. 11x11½*
2096 A1120 1cz multi .60 .25

Antarctic Project.

Special Mail Services A1121

1987, Mar. 20 *Perf. 12x11½*
2097 A1121 1cz Rural delivery .30 .25
2098 A1121 1cz Intl. express .30 .25

TELECOM '87, Geneva A1122

1987, May 5 *Perf. 11½x12*
2099 A1122 2cz Brasilsat, wave, globe .35 .25

10th Pan American Games, Indianapolis, Aug. 7-25—A1123

1987, May 20 *Perf. 12x11½*
2100 A1123 18cz multi 1.75 1.00

Natl. Fine Arts Museum, 150th Anniv A1124

1987, Jan. 13 *Perf. 11½x12*
2101 A1124 1cz multi .45 .25

Marine Conservation — A1125

1987, June 5
2102 A1125 2cz Eubalaena australis .65 .30
2103 A1125 2cz Eretmochelys imbricata .65 .30

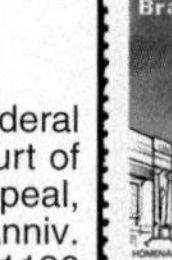

Federal Court of Appeal, 40th Anniv. A1126

1987, June 15
2104 A1126 2cz multi .30 .25

Military Club, Cent. — A1127

1987, June 26 *Perf. 12x11½*
2105 A1127 3cz multi .35 .25

Agriculture Institute of Campinas, Cent. A1128

1987, June 27 *Perf. 11½x12*
2106 A1128 2cz multi .35 .25

Entomological Society, 50th Anniv. — A1129

1987, July 17
2107 A1129 3cz Zoolea lopiceps .55 .25
2108 A1129 3cz Fulgora servillei .55 .25

Natl. Tourism Year A1130

Designs: No. 2109, Monuments and Sugarloaf Mountain, Rio de Janeiro. No. 2110, Colonial church, sailboats, parrot, cashews.

1987, Aug. 4
2109 A1130 3cz multi .30 .25
2110 A1130 3cz multi .30 .25

Royal Portuguese Cabinet of Literature, 150th Anniv. — A1131

1987, Aug. 27 *Perf. 12x11½*
2111 A1131 30cz ver & brt grn 1.25 .95

Sport Club Intl. A1132

Championship soccer clubs, Brazil's Gold Cup: b, Sao Paulo. c, Guarani. d, Regatas do Flamengo.

1987, Aug. 29 *Perf. 11½x12*
2112 Block of 4 1.40 .70
a.-d. A1132 3cz any single .25 .25

St. Francis Convent, 400th Anniv. A1133

1987, Oct. 4
2113 A1133 4cz multi .35 .25

Jose Americo de Almeida, Author A1134

Design: Characters from romance novel, "A Bagaceira," 1928, and portrait of author.

1987, Oct. 23 Litho. *Perf. 11x11½*
2114 A1134 4cz multi .30 .25

Spanish Galleons Anchored in Recife Port, 1537 A1135

1987, Nov. 12 Litho. *Perf. 11½x12*
2115 A1135 5cz Harbor entrance .35 .25

Recife City, 450th anniv.

Thanksgiving A1136

1987, Nov. 26 *Perf. 12x11½*
2116 A1136 5cz multi .35 .25

Christmas 1987 A1137

1987, Nov. 30 *Perf. 11½x12*
2117 A1137 6cz Shepherd and flock .30 .25
2118 A1137 6cz Christmas pageant .30 .25
2119 A1137 6cz Six angels .30 .25
Nos. 2117-2119 (3) .90 .75

Pedro II College, 150th Anniv. — A1138

Gold pen Emperor Pedro II used to sign edict establishing the school, and Senator Bernardo Pereira de Vasconcellos, founder.

1987, Dec. 2
2120 A1138 6cz multi .35 .25

Natl. Orchid Growers' Soc., 50th Anniv. A1139

1987, Dec. 3
2121 A1139 6cz Laelia lobata veitch .60 .25
2122 A1139 6cz Cattleya guttata lindley .60 .25

Marian Year — A1140

Statue of Our Lady and Basilica at Fatima, Portugal.

1987, Dec. 20 *Perf. 12x11½*
2123 A1140 50cz multi 1.75 1.00

Exhibit of the Statue of Our Lady of Fatima in Brazil.

Descriptive Treatise of Brazil, by Gabriel S. de Sousa, 400th Anniv. — A1141

1987, Dec. 21 Litho. *Perf. 11x11½*
2124 A1141 7cz multi .40 .25

Natl. Archives, 150th Anniv. A1142

Design: Text from illuminated Gregorian canticle and computer terminal.

1988, Jan. 5 ***Perf. 11½x12***
2125 A1142 7cz multi .35 .25

Opening of Brazilian Ports to Ships of Friendly Nations, 180th Anniv. A1143

1988, Jan. 28 ***Perf. 11x11½***
2126 A1143 7cz multi .30 .25

Souvenir Sheet

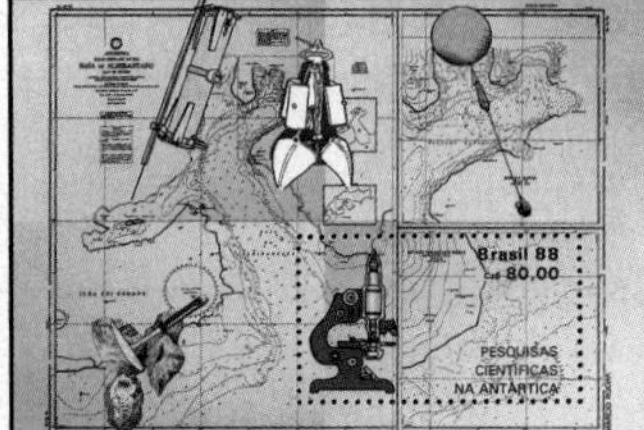

Antarctic Research — A1144

1988, Feb. 9 **Litho.** ***Perf. 11***
2127 A1144 80cz multi 2.75 2.75

Energy Resources A1145

1988, Mar. 15 **Litho.** ***Perf. 12x11½***
2128 A1145 14cz Electricity .30 .25
2129 A1145 14cz Fossil fuels .30 .25

Souvenir Sheet

Brazilians as Formula 1 World Champions in 1981, 1983, 1987 — A1146

1988, Mar. 30 ***Perf. 11***
2130 A1146 300cz multi 7.50 5.50

Jose Bonifacio, Armorial and Masonic Emblems A1147

1988, Apr. 6 ***Perf. 12x11½***
2131 A1147 20cz multi .50 .30

Jose Bonifacio de Andrada e Silva (c. 1763-1838), geologist and prime minister under Pedro I who supported the movement for independence from Portugal and was exiled for opposing the emperor's advisors.

Abolition of Slavery, Cent. — A1148

Telecom '88 — A1149

Designs: 20cz, Declaration and quill pen. 50cz, Slave ship and maps of African coastline and slave trade route between Africa and South America.

1988, May 12 **Litho.** ***Perf. 12x11½***
2132 A1148 20cz multi .45 .25
2133 A1148 50cz multi .45 .50

1988, May 16 ***Perf. 11½x11***
2134 A1149 50cz multi 1.00 .50

Jesus of Matosinhos Sanctuary A1150

1988, May 16 ***Perf. 11½x12***
2135 A1150 20cz shown .45 .25
2136 A1150 50cz Pilot plan of Brazilia .90 .45
2137 A1150 100cz Salvador historic district 1.10 .90
Nos. 2135-2137 (3) 2.45 1.60

LUBRAPEX '88. World heritage list.

Japanese Immigrants in Brazil, 80th Anniv. — A1151

1988, June 18 **Litho.** ***Perf. 11½x11***
2138 A1151 100cz multi 1.00 .60

A1152

A1153

1988, July 1 **Photo.** ***Perf. 13***
2139 A1152 (A) brt blue 3.00 .25
a. Perf 11x11½ 3.00 .25

No. 2139 met the first class domestic letter postage rate (28cz).
See Nos. 2201, 2218.

1988, July 14 **Litho.** ***Perf. 12x11½***
2140 A1153 20cz Judo .70 .25

1988 Summer Olympics, Seoul.

Wildlife Conservation — A1154

1988, July 24 ***Perf. 11½x12***
2141 A1154 20cz Myrmecophaga tridactyla .40 .25
2142 A1154 50cz Chaetomys subspinosus .65 .25
2143 A1154 100cz Speothos venaticus 1.10 .35
Nos. 2141-2143 (3) 2.15 .85

Souvenir Sheet

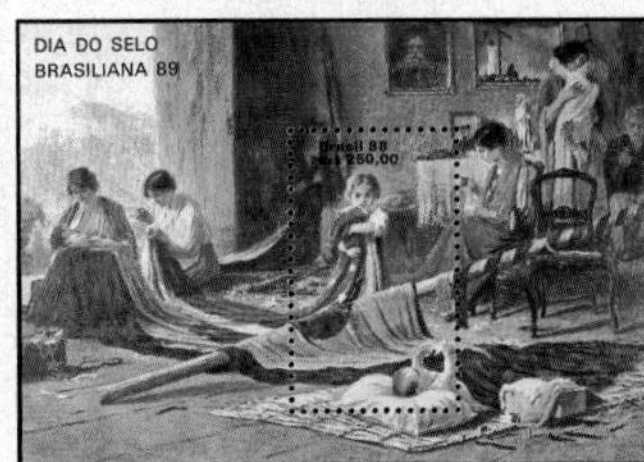

The Motherland, 1919 by Pedro Bruno — A1155

1988, Aug. 1 **Litho.** ***Perf. 11***
2144 A1155 250cz multi 5.00 5.00

Stamp Day, BRASILIANA '89.

Natl. Confederation of Industries, 50th Anniv. — A1156

1988, Aug. 12 ***Perf. 11½x12***
2145 A1156 50cz multi .40 .25

Soccer Clubs A1157

No. 2146, Recife, Pernambuco. No. 2147, Coritiba, Parana. 100cz, Gremio, Porto Alegre, Rio Grando do Sul. 200cz, Fluminense, Rio de Janeiro.

1988, Sept. 29 ***Perf. 11½x12***
2146 A1157 50cz multi .75 .35
2147 A1157 50cz multi .40 .35
2148 A1157 100cz multi .40 .35
2149 A1157 200cz multi .40 .35
a. Block of 4, #2146-2149 3.00 3.00

Poems, 1888 A1158

Portraits and text: 50cz, *O Ateneu,* by Raul Pompeia. 100cz, *Poesias,* by Olavo Bilac.

1988, Oct. 28 ***Perf. 11x11½***
2150 A1158 50cz multi .35 .25
2151 A1158 100cz multi .45 .25

Souvenir Sheet

1988 Democratic Constitution for the Union of the People and the State — A1159

1988, Oct. 5 **Litho.** ***Perf. 11***
2152 A1159 550cz Government building 3.75 3.75

Origami Art A1160

1988, Nov. 11 **Litho.** ***Perf. 11½x12***
2153 A1160 50cz Abbey, nuns .45 .25
2154 A1160 100cz Nativity .45 .25
2155 A1160 200cz Santa Claus, presents .70 .40
Nos. 2153-2155 (3) 1.60 .90

Christmas.

ARBRAFEX Philatelic Exhibition of Argentina and Brazil — A1161

1988, Nov. 26
2156 A1161 400cz multi 3.00 1.00

Fresh-water Fish — A1162

Designs: a, Gasteropelecus. b, Osteoglossum ferreirai. c, Moenkhausia. d, Xavantei. e, Ancistrus hoplogenys. f, Brochis splendens. Se-tenant in a continuous design.

1988, Nov. 29 **Litho.** ***Perf. 11½x12***
2157 Block of 6 2.50 2.50
a.-f. A1162 55cz any single .25 .30

Souvenir Sheet

BRAPEX '88, Ecological Preservation — A1163

1988, Dec. 10 ***Perf. 11***
2158 Sheet of 3 11.00 11.00
a. A1163 100cz Parrot 1.00 .50
b. A1163 250cz Plant 2.50 1.25
c. A1163 400cz Egret 4.00 2.00

Satellite Dishes — A1164

Performing Arts — A1165

1988, Dec. 20 ***Perf. 12x11½***
2159 A1164 70cz multi .35 .25

Ansat 10-Earth satellite station communication.

1988, Dec. 21
2160 A1165 70cz multi .50 .25

Court of Justice, Bahia, 380th Anniv. A1166

1989, Mar. 10 Litho. ***Perf. 11½x12***
2161 A1166 25c multi .50 .30

Public Library Year A1167

1989, Mar. 13 ***Perf. 11½***
2162 A1167 25c Library, Bahia, 1811 .50 .30

Brazilian Post & Telegraph Enterprise, 20th Anniv. A1168

No. 2163 — Intl. and domestic postal services: a, Facsimile transmission (Post-Grama). b, Express mail (EMS). c, Parcel post (Sedex). d, Postal savings (CEFPostal).

1989, Mar. 20 ***Perf. 11½x12***
2163 Block of 4 2.50 1.50
a.-d. A1168 25c any single .55 .35

Souvenir Sheet

Ayrton Senna, 1988 Formula 1 World Champion — A1169

1989, Mar. 23
2164 A1169 2cz multi 16.00 16.00

Environmental Conservation A1170

1989, Apr. 6 Litho. ***Perf. 12x11½***
2165 A1170 25c multi .40 .25

Mineira Inconfidencia Independence Movement, Bicent. — A1171

Designs: a, Pyramid, hand. b, Figure of a man, houses. c, Destruction of houses.

1989, Apr. 21 ***Perf. 11½x12***
2166 Strip of 3 1.50 1.00
a.-b. A1171 30c any single .40 .30
c. A1171 40c multi .60 .40

First rebellion against Portuguese dominion.

Military School, Rio de Janeiro, Cent. A1172

1989, May 6 Litho. ***Perf. 11½x12***
2167 A1172 50c multi .55 .40

Flowering Plants A1173

Designs: 50c, Pavonia alnifolia. 1cz, Worsleya rayneri. 1.50cz, Heliconia farinosa.

1989, June 5 ***Perf. 11½x12, 12x11½***
2168 A1173 50c multi .90 .60
2169 A1173 1cz multi 1.75 1.25
2170 A1173 1.50cz multi 2.25 1.75
Nos. 2168-2170 (3) 4.90 3.60

Nos. 2169-2170 vert.

Barreto and Recife Law School, Pedro II Square A1174

1989, June 7 ***Perf. 11x11½***
2171 A1174 50c multi .85 .50

Tobias Barreto (b. 1839), advocate of Germanization of Brazil.

Cultura Broadcasting System, 20th Anniv. — A1175

1989, June 27 Litho. ***Perf. 11½x12***
2172 A1175 50c multi .80 .45

Aviation A1176

1989, July 7
2173 A1176 50c Ultra-light aircraft .50 .40
2174 A1176 1.50cz Eiffel Tower, *Demoiselle* 1.75 1.10

Flight of Santos-Dumont's *Demoiselle,* 80th anniv (1.50cz).

Indigenous Flora — A1177

Designs: 10c, Dichorisandra, vert. 20c, Quiabentia zehnteri. 50c, Bougainvillea glabra. 1cz, Impatiens specie. 2cz, Chorisia crispiflora. 5cz, Hibiscus trilineatus.

1989 Photo. ***Perf. 11x11½, 11½x11***
2176 A1177 10c multi .25 .25
2177 A1177 20c multi .25 .25
2178 A1177 50c multi .60 .45
2179 A1177 1cz multi 1.10 .85
2180 A1177 2cz multi .25 .25
2181 A1177 5cz multi .70 .50
Nos. 2176-2181 (6) 3.15 2.55

Issued: 10c, July 4; 20c, June 21; 50c, June 26; 1cz, June 19; 2cz, 5cz, Dec. 4.
No. 2181 vert.
See Nos. 2259-2273.

Souvenir Sheet

Largo da Carioca, by Nicolas Antoine Taunay — A1179

1989, July 7 Litho. ***Perf. 11***
2197 A1179 3cz multi 5.00 5.00

PHILEXFRANCE '89, French revolution bicent.

Cut and Uncut Gemstones A1180

1989, July 12 Litho. ***Perf. 12x11½***
2198 A1180 50c Tourmaline .60 .30
2199 A1180 1.50cz Amethyst 1.25 .90

Souvenir Sheet

Paco Imperial, Rio de Janeiro, and Map — A1181

1989, July 28 ***Perf. 11***
2200 A1181 5cz multi 6.50 6.50

BRASILANA '89.

Type of 1988 Redrawn

1989, July 26 Photo. ***Perf. 13***
Size: 17x21mm
2201 A1152 (A) org & brt blue 4.50 .50
Complete booklet, strip of 10 #2201 45.00

Size of type and postal emblem are smaller on No. 2201; "1e PORTE" is at lower left.
No. 2201 met the first class domestic letter postage rate (cz).

Pernambuco Commercial Assoc., 150th Anniv. — A1182

1989, Aug. 1 Litho. ***Perf. 11½x12***
2202 A1182 50c multi .50 .30

Photography, 150th Anniv. — A1183

1989, Aug. 14
2203 A1183 1.50cz multi 1.50 1.10

1st Hydroelecric Power Station in South America, Marmelos-o, Cent. — A1184

1989, Sept. 5 Litho. ***Perf. 11½x12***
2204 A1184 50c multi .45 .25

Conchs Endemic to the Brazilian Coast A1185

Designs: 50c,Voluta ebraea. 1cz, Morum matthewsi. 1.50cz, Agaronia travassosi.

1989, Sept. 8
2205 A1185 50c multi .30 .25
2206 A1185 1cz multi .60 .45
2207 A1185 1.50cz multi 1.10 .65
Nos. 2205-2207 (3) 2.00 1.35

Wildlife conservation.

America Issue A1186

UPAE emblem and pre-Columbian stone carvings: 1cz, Muiraquita ritual statue, vert. 4cz, Ceramic brazier under three-footed votive urn.

Perf. 12x11½, 11½x12
1989, Oct. 12 Litho.
2208 A1186 1cz multicolored .55 .35
2209 A1186 4cz multicolored 2.10 1.40

Discovery of America 500th anniv. (in 1992).

A1187

Hologram and: a. *Lemons,* by Danilo di Prete. b. *O Indio E A Suacuapara,* by sculptor Victor Brecheret. c. Francisco Matarazzo.

1989, Oct. 14 ***Perf. 11***
Souvenir Sheet
2210 A1187 Sheet of 3 5.50 5.50
a. 2cz multicolored 1.10 .80
b. 3cz multicolored 1.75 1.25
c. 5cz multicolored 2.50 2.00

Sao Paulo 20th intl. art biennial.

A1188

Writers, residences and quotes: No. 2211, Casimiro de Abreu (b. 1839). No. 2212, Cora Coralina (b. 1889). No. 2213, Joaquim Machado de Assis (b. 1839).

1989, Oct. 26 ***Perf. 11½x11***

2211 A1188 1cz multicolored .65 .40
2212 A1188 1cz multicolored .65 .40
2213 A1188 1cz multicolored .65 .40
Nos. 2211-2213 (3) 1.95 1.20

Federal Police Department, 25th Anniv. — A1189

1989, Nov. 9 ***Perf. 11½x12***

2214 A1189 1cz multicolored .45 .25

Christmas A1190

1989, Nov. 10 ***Perf. 12x11½***

2215 A1190 70c Heralding angel .30 .25
2216 A1190 1cz Holy family .35 .25

Thanksgiving Day — A1191

1989, Nov. 23

2217 A1191 1cz multicolored .40 .25

Type of 1988 Redrawn
Size: 22x26mm

1989, Nov. 6 Photo. ***Perf. 13x13½***

2218 A1152 (B) org & dark red 7.25 4.50

Size of type and postal emblem are smaller on No. 2218; "1e PORTE" is at lower left.

No. 2218 met the first class intl. letter postage rate, initially at 9cz.

Souvenir Sheet

Proclamation of the Republic, Cent. — A1192

1989, Nov. 19 Litho. ***Perf. 11***

2225 A1192 15cz multicolored 6.00 6.00

Bahia Sports Club, 58th Anniv. A1193

1989, Nov. 30 ***Perf. 11½x12***

2226 A1193 50c Soccer .45 .25

Yellow Man, by Anita Malfatti (b. 1889) A1194

1989, Dec. 2 ***Perf. 12x11½***

2227 A1194 1cz multicolored .45 .25

Bahia State Public Archives, Cent. — A1195

1990, Jan. 16 Litho. ***Perf. 11½x12***

2228 A1195 2cz multicolored .35 .25

Brazilian Botanical Soc., 40th Anniv. A1196

1990, Jan. 21

2229 A1196 2cz Sabia, Caatinga .25 .25
2230 A1196 13cz Pau, Brazil 1.60 1.10

Churches A1197

Designs: 2cz, St. John the Baptist Cathedral, Santa Cruz do Sul, vert. 3cz, Our Lady of Victory Church, Oeiras. 5cz, Our Lady of the Rosary Church, Ouro Preto, vert.

1990, Feb. 5 ***Perf. 12x11½, 11½x12***

2231 A1197 2cz multicolored .25 .25
2232 A1197 3cz multicolored .35 .25
2233 A1197 5cz multicolored .50 .30
Nos. 2231-2233 (3) 1.10 .80

Lloyd's of London in Brazil, Cent. A1198

1990, Feb. 19 Litho. ***Perf. 11½x12***

2234 A1198 3cz multicolored .35 .25

Souvenir Sheet

Antarctic Research Program — A1199

1990, Feb. 22 Litho. ***Perf. 11***

2235 A1199 20cz Fauna, map 3.50 3.50

Vasco da Gama Soccer Club A1200

1990, Mar. 5

2236 A1200 10cz multicolored .60 .40

Lindolfo Collor (b. 1890), Syndicated Columnist, and Labor Monument A1201

1990, Mar. 7

2237 A1201 20cz multicolored 1.10 .70

Pres. Jose Sarney — A1202

1990, Mar. 8 ***Perf. 12x11½***

2238 A1202 20cz chalky blue 1.25 .70

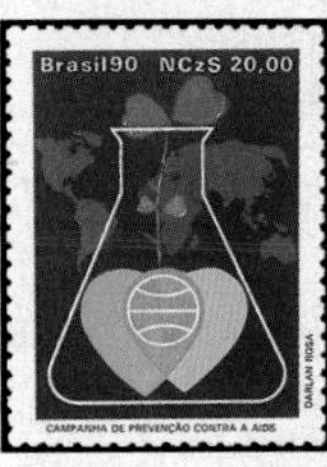
AIDS Prevention A1203

1990, Apr. 6 ***Perf. 12x11½***

2239 A1203 20cz multicolored 1.40 .50

Souvenir Sheet

Penny Black, 150th Anniv. — A1204

No. 2240: 20cr, Dom Pedro, Brazil No. 1. 100cr, Queen Victoria, Great Britain No. 1.

1990, May 3 Litho. ***Perf. 11***

2240 A1204 Sheet of 2 4.25 4.25
a. 20cr multicolored 1.25 1.00
b. 100cr multicolored 3.00 2.50

Central Bank, 25th Anniv. A1205

1990, Mar. 30 Litho. ***Perf. 11½x12***

2241 A1205 20cr multicolored 1.00 .50

Amazon River Postal Network, 21st Anniv. A1207

1990, Apr. 20 ***Perf. 11x11½***

2243 A1207 20cr multicolored 1.10 .50

Souvenir Sheet

World Cup Soccer Championships, Italy — A1208

1990, May 12 Litho. ***Perf. 12x11½***

2244 A1208 120cr multicolored 5.00 5.00

22nd Congress of the Intl. Union of Highway Transportation — A1209

1990. May 14 ***Perf. 11½x12***

2245 A1209 20cr multicolored 1.20 .75
2246 A1209 80cr multicolored 2.50 1.50
a. Pair, #2245-2246 3.75 2.75

No. 2246a has a continuous design.

Imperial Crown, 18th Cent. — A1210

Designs: No. 2248, Our Lady of Immaculate Conception, 18th cent.

1990, May 18 ***Perf. 12x11½***

2247 A1210 20cr shown .80 .50
2248 A1210 20cr multicolored .80 .50

Imperial Museum, 50th anniv.(No. 2247). Mission Museum, 50th anniv. (No. 2248).

State Flags Type of 1981

1990, May 20 *Perf. 11½x12*

2249 A947 20cr Tocantins .75 .55

Army Geographical Service, Cent. — A1212

1990, May 30 *Perf. 11x11½*

2250 A1212 20cr multicolored 1.00 .50

Film Personalities — A1213

1990, June 19 *Perf. 11½x12*

2251 A1213 25cr Adhemar Gonzaga .80 .60
2252 A1213 25cr Carmen Miranda .80 .60
2253 A1213 25cr Carmen Santos .80 .60
2254 A1213 25cr Oscarito .80 .60
a. Block of 4, #2251-2254 3.20 2.40

France-Brazil House, Rio de Janeiro — A1214

1990, July 14 Litho. *Perf. 11½x11*

2255 A1214 50cr multicolored 2.00 1.10

See France No. 2226.

World Men's Volleyball Chmpships. A1215

Intl. Literacy Year A1217

CBA 123 A1216

1990, July 28 Litho. *Perf. 12x11½*

2256 A1215 10cr multicolored .70 .25

1990, July 30 *Perf. 11½x12*

2257 A1216 10cr multicolored .50 .25

1990, Aug. 22 *Perf. 12x11½*

2258 A1217 10cr multicolored .50 .25

Flora Type of 1989

Designs: 1cr, Like #2179. 2cr, Like #2180. 5cr, Like #2181. 10cr, Tibouchina granulosa. 20cr, Cassia macranthera. No. 2264, Clitoria fairchildiana. No. 2265, Tibouchina mutabilis. 100cr, Erythrina crista-galli. 200cr, Jacaranda mimosifolia. 500cr, Caesalpinia peltophoroides. 1000, Pachira aquatica. 2000, Hibiscus pernambucensis. 5000, Triplaris surinamensis. 10,000, Tabebuia heptaphylla. 20,000, Erythrina speciosa.

Perf. 11x11½, 11½x11

1989-93 **Photo.**

2259 A1177 1cr multi .50 .25
2260 A1177 2cr multi .50 .25
2261 A1177 5cr multi .50 .25
2262 A1177 10cr multi .50 .25
2263 A1177 20cr multi .50 .25
2264 A1177 50cr multi .50 .25
2265 A1177 50cr multi 1.00 .40
2266 A1177 100cr multi, perf. 13 .50 .35
2267 A1177 200cr multi .50 .60
2268 A1177 500cr multi .50 1.50
2269 A1177 1000cr multi .50 .25
2270 A1177 2000cr multi .50 .25
2271 A1177 5000cr multi 1.00 1.00
2272 A1177 10,000cr multi .90 1.75
2273 A1177 20,000cr multi .90 2.50
Nos. 2259-2273 (15) 9.30 10.10

Issued: 1cr, 11/8/90; 2cr, 11/12/90; 5cr, 11/16/90; No. 2264, 6/1/89; 10cr, 4/18/90; 20cr, 5/4/90; 100cr, 8/24/90; 200cr, 6/16/91; 500cr, 5/14/91; 1000cr, 9/2/92; 2000cr, 9/8/92; 5000cr, 10/16/92; 10,000cr, 11/16/92; 20,000cr, 4/25/93; No. 2265, 10/20/93.

Granbery Institute, Cent. A1218

1990, Sept. 8 Litho. *Perf. 11½x12*

2279 A1218 13cr multicolored .70 .30

18th Panamerican Railroad Congress — A1219

1990, Sept. 9

2280 A1219 95cr multicolored 3.50 2.00

Embratel, 25th Anniv. — A1220

1990, Sept. 21

2281 A1220 13cr multicolored .70 .30

LUBRAPEX '90 A1221

Statues by Ceschiatti and Giorgi (No. 2283).

1990, Sept. 22

2282 A1221 25cr As Banhistas .80 .55
2283 A1221 25cr Os Candangos .80 .55
2284 A1221 100cr Evangelista Sao Joao 1.75 1.10
2285 A1221 100cr A Justica 1.75 1.10
a. Block of 4, #2282-2285 6.00 6.00
b. Souv. sheet of 4, #2282-2285 9.00 9.00

Praia Do Sul Wildlife Reserve A1222

1990, Oct. 12

2286 A1222 15cr Flowers .60 .35
2287 A1222 105cr Shoreline 3.00 2.00
a. Pair, #2286-2287 4.50 3.00

Discovery of America, 500th anniv. (in 1992).

Natl. Library, 180th Anniv. A1223

Writers: No. 2289, Guilherme de Almeida (1890-1969). No. 2290, Oswald de Andrade (1890-1954).

1990, Oct. 29 Litho. *Perf. 11x11½*

2288 A1223 15cr multicolored .60 .30
2289 A1223 15cr multicolored .60 .30
2290 A1223 15cr multicolored .60 .30
Nos. 2288-2290 (3) 1.80 .90

Natl. Tax Court, Cent. A1224

1990, Nov. 7 Litho. *Perf. 11½x12*

2291 A1224 15cr multicolored .70 .35

Christmas A1225

Architecture of Brasilia: No. 2292, National Congress. No. 2293, Television tower.

1990, Nov. 20

2292 A1225 15cr multicolored .70 .35
2293 A1225 15cr multicolored .70 .35

A1226 A1227

1990, Dec. 13 Litho. *Perf. 12x11½*

2294 A1226 15cr multicolored .40 .25

Organization of American States, cent.

1990, Dec. 14

2295 A1227 15cr multicolored .45 .25

First Flight of Nike Apache Missile, 25th anniv.

Colonization of Sergipe, Founding of Sao Cristovao, 400th Anniv. — A1228

1990, Dec. 18 Litho. *Perf. 11½x12*

2296 A1228 15cr multicolored .45 .25

World Congress of Physical Education A1229

1991, Jan. 7 *Perf. 11½x12*

2297 A1229 17cr multicolored .50 .25

Rock in Rio II — A1230

1991, Jan. 9 *Perf. 12x11½*

2298 A1230 25cr Cazuza .75 .50
2299 A1230 185cr Raul Seixas 2.25 .60
a. Pair, #2298-2299 3.50 1.40
Complete booklet, pane of 12 21.00

Printed in panes of 12.

Ministry of Aviation, 50th Anniv. A1231

1991, Jan. 20 *Perf. 11x11½*

2300 A1231 17cr multicolored .45 .25

Carnivals A1232

1991, Feb. 8 Litho. *Perf. 12x11½*

2301 A1232 25cr Olinda .30 .25
2302 A1232 30cr Salvador .30 .25
2303 A1232 280cr Rio de Janeiro 4.00 2.25
Nos. 2301-2303 (3) 4.60 2.75

Visit to Antarctica by Pres. Collor — A1233

1991, Feb. 20

2304 A1233 300cr multicolored 4.50 2.25

Hang Gliding World Championships — A1234

1991, Feb. 24 *Perf. 11½x12*

2305 A1234 36cr multicolored .70 .35

11th Pan American Games, 25th Summer Olympics A1235

1991, Mar. 30 Litho. *Perf. 11½x12*
2306 A1235 36cr Sailing .45 .30
2307 A1235 36cr Rowing .45 .30
2308 A1235 300cr Swimming 3.00 2.00
a. Block of 3, #2306-2308 + label 4.50 4.50

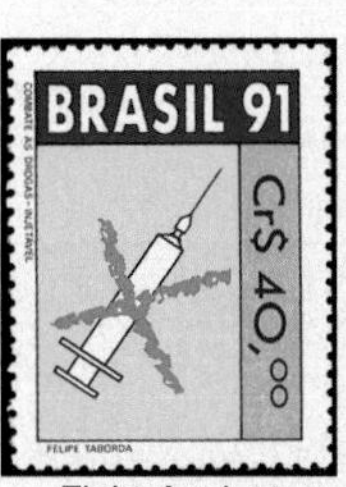

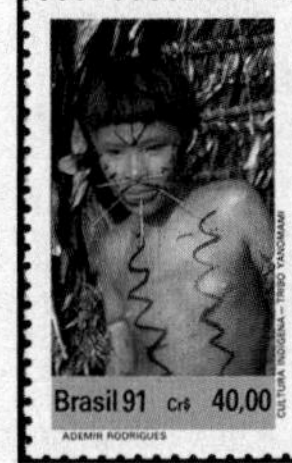

Fight Against Drugs — A1236
Yanomami Indian Culture — A1237

1991, Apr. 7 Litho. *Perf. 12x11½*
2309 A1236 40cr Drugs .60 .35
2310 A1236 40cr Alcohol .60 .35
2311 A1236 40cr Smoking .60 .35
Nos. 2309-2311 (3) 1.80 1.05

1991, Apr. 19 *Perf. 11½x11, 11x11½*
2312 A1237 40cr shown .50 .30
2313 A1237 400cr Indian, horiz. 5.00 3.25

Journal of Brazil, Cent. A1238

1991, Apr. 8 Litho. *Perf. 11x11½*
2314 A1238 40cr multicolored .60 .35

Neochen Jubata (Orinoco Goose) — A1239

1991, June 5 Litho. *Perf. 12x11½*
2315 A1239 45cr multi .70 .25

UN Conference on Development.

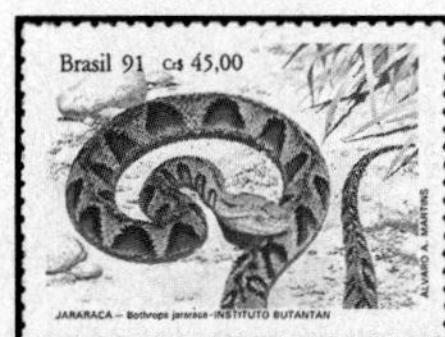

Snakes & Dinosaurs A1240

1991, June 6 *Perf. 11½x12*
2316 A1240 45cr Bothrops jararaca .40 .25
2317 A1240 45cr Corallus caninus .40 .25
a. Pair, #2316-2317 1.00 .80
2318 A1240 45cr Teropods .40 .25
2319 A1240 350cr Sauropods 2.75 1.75
a. Pair, #2318-2319 4.00 3.00
Nos. 2316-2319 (4) 3.95 2.50

Flag of Brazil — A1241

1991, June 10 Photo. *Perf. 13x13½*
2320 A1241 A multicolored 4.00 .25

Valued at domestic letter rate on day of issue.
Exists with inscription at lower right. Same value.

Fire Pumper A1242

1991, July 2 Litho. *Perf. 11½x12*
2321 A1242 45cr multicolored .60 .25

Tourism A1243

Map location and: 45cr, Painted stones, Roraima. 350cr, Dedo de Deus Mountain, Rio De Janeiro.

1991, July 6 *Perf. 11x11½*
2322 A1243 45cr multicolored .30 .25
2323 A1243 350cr multicolored 2.50 1.50

Labor Laws, 50th Anniv. A1244

1991, Aug. 11 *Perf. 11½x12*
2324 A1244 45cr multicolored .45 .25

Leonardo Mota, Birth Cent. A1245

1991, Aug. 22
2325 A1245 45cr buff, blk & red .45 .25

Folklore Festival.

Jose Basilio da Gama (1741-1795), Poet — A1246

Designs: No. 2327, Fagundes Varela (b. 1841), poet. No. 2328, Jackson de Figueiredo (b. 1891), writer.

1991, Aug. 29
2326 A1246 45cr multicolored .40 .25
2327 A1246 50cr multicolored .50 .25
2328 A1246 50cr multicolored .50 .25
Nos. 2326-2328 (3) 1.40 .75

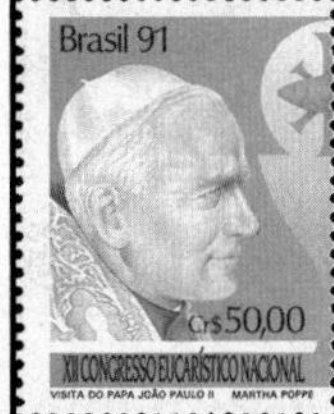

12th Natl. Eucharistic Congress A1247

1991, Oct. 6 Litho. *Perf. 12x11½*
2329 A1247 50cr Pope John Paul II .45 .25
2330 A1247 400cr Map, crosses 1.40 .90
a. Pair, #2329-2330 3.00 2.50

Visit by Pope John Paul II.

First Brazilian Constitution, Cent. — A1248

1991, Oct. 7 *Perf. 11½x12*
2331 A1248 50cr multicolored .60 .25

Telecom '91 — A1249

1991, Oct. 8 *Perf. 12x11½*
2332 A1249 50cr multicolored .60 .25

Sixth World Forum and Exposition on Telecommunications, Geneva, Switzerland.

America Issue A1250

UPAEP emblem and explorers: 50cr, Ferdinand Magellan (c. 1480-1521). 400cr, Francisco de Orellana (c. 1490-c. 1546).

1991, Oct. 12 *Perf. 11½x12*
2333 A1250 50cr multicolored .30 .25
2334 A1250 400cr multicolored 2.50 1.25

Discovery of America, 500th anniv. (in 1992).

A1251 A1252

BRAPEX VIII (Orchids and Hummingbirds): 50cr, Colibri serrirostris, Cattleya warneri. No. 2336, Chlorostilbon aureoventris, Rodriguezia venusta. No. 2337, Clytolaema rubricauda, Zygopetalum intermedium. No. 2338a, 50cr, Colibri serrirostris. b, 50cr, Chlorostilbon aureoventris. c, 500cr, Clytolaema rubricauda.

1991, Oct. 29 Litho. *Perf. 12x11½*
2335 A1251 50cr multicolored .80 .25
2336 A1251 65cr multicolored .80 .25
2337 A1251 65cr multicolored .80 .25
Nos. 2335-2337 (3) 2.40 .75

Souvenir Sheet

2338 A1251 Sheet of 3, #a.-c. 10.00 10.00

1991, Oct. 29 Litho. *Perf. 11½x11*
2339 A1252 400cr multicolored 1.25 .65

Lasar Segall, artist, birth cent.

Bureau of Agriculture and Provision of Sao Paulo, Cent. — A1253

1991, Nov. 11 *Perf. 12x11½*
2340 A1253 70cr multicolored 1.25 .25

First Civilian Presidents, Birth Sesquicentennials — A1254

Designs: 70cr, Manuel de Campos Salles. 90cr, Prudente de Moraes Barros.

1991, Nov. 14 *Perf. 11½x12*
2341 A1254 70cr multi .50 .25
2342 A1254 90cr multi .50 .25
a. Pair, #2341-2342 1.00 1.00

Christmas A1255

1991, Nov. 20 *Perf. 12x11½*
2343 A1255 70cr multicolored 1.00 .25

Thanksgiving A1256

1991, Nov. 28
2344 A1256 70cr multicolored .35 .25

Military Police A1257

1991, Dec. 1 *Perf. 11½x12*
2345 A1257 80cr multicolored .35 .25

Souvenir Sheet

Emperor Dom Pedro (1825-1891) — A1258

No. 2346: a, 80cr, Older age. b, 800cr, Wearing crown.

Litho. & Engr.

1991, Nov. 29 *Perf. 11*

2346 A1258 Sheet of 2, #a.-b. 4.00 4.00

BRASILIANA 93.

Churches A1259

Designs: No. 2347, Presbyterian Church, Rio de Janeiro. No. 2348, First Baptist Church, Niteroi.

1992, Jan. 12 Litho. *Perf. 12x11½*

2347 A1259 250cr multicolored 1.00 .25
2348 A1259 250cr multicolored 1.00 .25

1992 Summer Olympics, Barcelona A1260

Medalists in shooting, Antwerp, 1920: 300cr, Afranio Costa, silver. 2500cr, Guihlherme Paraense, gold.

1992, Jan. 28 *Perf. 11½x12*

2349 A1260 300cr multicolored 2.00 .75
2350 A1260 2500cr multicolored 8.50 3.00

Port of Santos, Cent. A1261

1992, Feb. 3 Litho. *Perf. 11½*

2351 A1261 300cr multicolored .80 .35

Fauna of Fernando de Noronha Island A1262

1992, Feb. 25 Litho. *Perf. 11½x12*

2352 A1262 400cr White-tailed tropicbirds .75 .35
2353 A1262 2500cr Dolphins 3.50 1.75

Earth Summit, Rio de Janeiro.

Yellow Amaryllis — A1263

1992, Feb. 27 Photo. *Perf. 13½*

2354 A1263 (A) multicolored 3.00 .25

No. 2354 met the second class domestic letter postage rate of 265cr on date of issue.

ARBRAFEX '92, Argentina-Brazil Philatelic Exhibition — A1264

Designs: No. 2355, Gaucho throwing bola at rhea. No. 2356, Man playing accordion, couple dancing. No. 2357, Couple in horse-drawn cart, woman. 1000cr, Gaucho throwing lasso at steer.

No. 2358c, 250cr, like No. 2356. d, 500cr, like No. 2355. e, 1500cr, like No. 2358.

1992, Mar. 20 Litho. *Perf. 11½x12*

2355 A1264 250cr multi .40 .30
2356 A1264 250cr multi .40 .30
2357 A1264 250cr multi .40 .30
2358 A1264 1000cr multi 1.25 .80
a. Block of 4, Nos. 2355-2358 3.25 3.25

Souvenir Sheet

2358B A1264 Sheet of 4, #2357, 2358c-2358e 17.50 17.50

1992 Summer Olympics, Barcelona A1265

1992, Apr. 3 *Perf. 12x11½*

2359 A1265 300cr multicolored 1.00 .30

Discovery of America, 500th Anniv. A1266

1992, Apr. 24 *Perf. 11½x12*

2360 A1266 500cr Columbus' fleet 1.00 .40
2361 A1266 3500cr Columbus, map 4.00 1.50
a. Pair, #2360-2361 5.00 3.00

Telebras Telecommunications System — A1267

1992, May 5 *Perf. 11x11½*

2362 A1267 350cr multicolored .50 .25

Installation of 10 million telephones.

Langsdorff Expedition to Brazil, 170th Anniv. A1268

Designs: No. 2363, Aime-Adrien Taunay, natives. No. 2364, Johann Moritz Rugendas, monkey. No. 2365, Hercule Florence, flowering plant. 3000cr, Gregory Ivanovitch Langsdorff, map.

1992, June 2 *Perf. 11½x12*

2363 A1268 500cr multicolored .45 .25
2364 A1268 500cr multicolored .45 .25
2365 A1268 500cr multicolored .45 .25
2366 A1268 3000cr multicolored 3.00 1.50
Nos. 2363-2366 (4) 4.35 2.25

UN Conf. on Environmental Development, Rio.

UN Conference on Environmental Development, Rio de Janeiro — A1269

Globe and: No. 2367, Flags of Sweden and Brazil. No. 2368, City, grain, mountain and tree. 3000cr, Map of Brazil, parrot, orchid.

1992, June 3 Litho. *Perf. 11x11½*

2367 A1269 450cr multicolored .35 .25
2368 A1269 450cr multicolored .35 .25
2369 A1269 3000cr multicolored 3.00 1.50
Nos. 2367-2369 (3) 3.70 2.00

Ecology A1270

Designs: No. 2370, Flowers, waterfall, and butterflies. No. 2371, Butterflies, canoe, and hummingbirds. No. 2372, Boy taking pictures of tropical birds. No. 2373, Armadillo, girl picking fruit.

1992, June 4 *Perf. 11½x12*

2370 A1270 500cr multicolored .60 .25
2371 A1270 500cr multicolored .60 .25
2372 A1270 500cr multicolored .60 .25
2373 A1270 500cr multicolored .60 .25
a. Strip of 4, #2370-2373 3.75 3.75
Complete booklet, #2373a 3.75

UN Conf. on Environmental Development, Rio.

Floral Paintings by Margaret Mee — A1271

1992, June 5 *Perf. 12x11½*

2374 A1271 600cr Nidularium innocentii .80 .40
2375 A1271 600cr Canistrum exiguum .80 .40
2376 A1271 700cr Canistrum cyathiforme .80 .40
2377 A1271 700cr Nidularium rubens .80 .40
Nos. 2374-2377 (4) 3.20 1.60

UN Conf. on Environmental Development, Rio.

Souvenir Sheet

Joaquim Jose da Silva Xavier (1748-1792), Patriot — A1272

Litho. & Engr.

1992, Apr. 21 *Perf. 11*

2378 A1272 3500cr multicolored 5.00 5.00

Souvenir Sheet

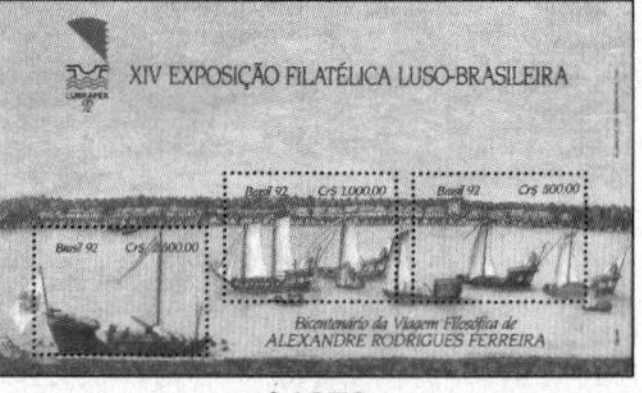

A1273

Expedition of Alexandre Rodrigues Ferreira, Bicent.: a, 500cr, Sailing ships, gray and green hulls. b, 1000cr, Sailing ships, red hulls. c, 2500cr, Sailing ship at shore.

1992, May 9 Litho. *Perf. 11½x12*

2379 A1273 Sheet of 3, #a.-c. 5.75 5.75

Lubrapex '92.

A1274 A1275

1992, June 5 Litho. *Perf. 12x11½*

2380 A1274 600cr Hummingbird .65 .25

Diabetes Day.

1992, July 13 Litho. *Perf. 11½x11*

2381 A1275 550cr multicolored 1.00 .25

Volunteer firemen of Joinville.

A1276

Serra da Capivara National Park: No. 2382, Leopard, animals, map of park. No. 2383, Canyon, map of Brazil.

1992, July 17 *Perf. 12x11½*

2382 A1276 550cr multicolored .80 .25
2383 A1276 550cr multicolored .80 .25
a. Pair, #2382-2383 1.75 1.25

A1277

1992, July 24
2384 A1277 550cr multicolored .75 .25

Financing for studies and projects.

Natl. Service for Industrial Training, 50th Anniv. — A1278

1992, Aug. 5 ***Perf. 11½x12***
2385 A1278 650cr multicolored .75 .35

Fortresses A1279

1992, Aug. 19 Litho. ***Perf. 11½x12***
2386 A1279 650cr Santa Cruz .50 .30
2387 A1279 3000cr Santo Antonio 1.75 1.25

Masonic Square, Compass and Lodge A1280

1992, Aug. 20
2388 A1280 650cr multicolored .60 .30

Brazilian Assistance Legion, 50th Anniv. — A1281

1992, Aug. 28 ***Perf. 12x11½***
2389 A1281 650cr multicolored .50 .30

Hospital of Medicine and Orthopedics A1282

1992, Sept. 11
2390 A1282 800cr multicolored .50 .30

Merry Christmas A1283

1992, Nov. 20 ***Perf. 11½***
2391 A1283 (1) multicolored 1.25 .50

No. 2391 met the first class domestic letter postage rate of 1090cr on day of issue.

Writers A1284

Designs: No. 2392, Graciliano Ramos (1892-1953). No. 2393, Menotti del Picchia (1892-1988). 1000cr, Assis Chateaubriand (1892-1968).

Perf. 12x11½, 11½x12
1992, Oct. 29 **Litho.**
2392 A1284 900cr multi, vert. .40 .25
2393 A1284 900cr multi, vert. .40 .25
2394 A1284 1000cr multi .50 .30
Nos. 2392-2394 (3) 1.30 .80

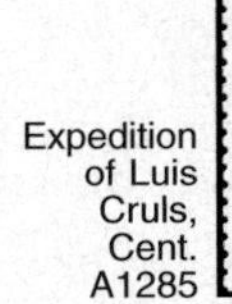

Expedition of Luis Cruls, Cent. A1285

1992, Nov. 11 ***Perf. 11½x12***
2395 A1285 900cr multicolored .60 .25

Brazillian Program for Quality and Productivity A1286

1992, Nov. 12
2396 A1286 1200cr multicolored .60 .30

Souvenir Sheet

Tourism Year in the Americas — A1287

a, 1200cr, Mountains, coastline. b, 9000cr, Sugarloaf Mt., aerial tram, Rio de Janeiro.

1992, Nov. 18 Litho. ***Perf. 11½x12***
2397 A1287 Sheet of 2, #a.-b. 3.00 3.00

Brasiliana '93.

Sister Irma Dulce A1288

1993, Mar. 13 Litho. ***Perf. 11½x12***
2398 A1288 3500cr multicolored .50 .35

Souvenir Sheet

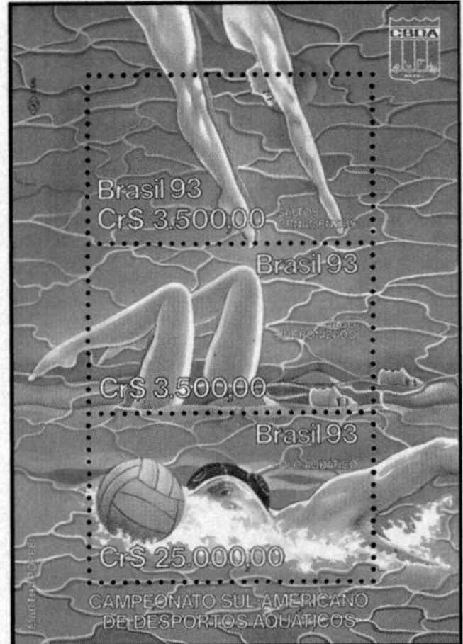

Water Sports Championships of South America — A1289

Designs: a, 3500cr, Diver. b, 3500cr, Synchronized swimmers. c, 25,000cr, Water polo.

1993, Mar. 21 Litho. ***Perf. 11***
2399 A1289 Sheet of 3, #a.-c. 4.00 4.00

Curitiba, 300th Anniv. A1290

1993, Mar. 29
2400 A1290 4500cr multicolored .60 .60

Health and Preservation of Life — A1291

Red Cross emblem and: No. 2401, Bleeding heart, flowers. No. 2402, Cancer symbol, breast. No. 2403, Brain waves, rainbow emerging from head.

1993, Apr. 7 Litho. ***Perf. 12x11½***
2401 A1291 4500cr multicolored .40 .30
2402 A1291 4500cr multicolored .40 .30
2403 A1291 4500cr multicolored .40 .30
a. Strip of 3, #2401-2403 1.25 1.25

Pedro Americo, 150th Birth Anniv. — A1292

Paintings: 5500cr, A Study of Love, 1883. No. 2405, David and Abizag, 1879, horiz. No. 2406, Seated Nude, 1882.

1993, Apr. 29 ***Perf. 12x11½, 11½x12***
2404 A1292 5500cr multi .60 .30
2405 A1292 36,000cr multi 3.00 1.75
2406 A1292 36,000cr multi 3.00 1.75
Nos. 2404-2406 (3) 6.60 3.80

Natl. Flag — A1292a

1993, May 26 Litho. ***Die Cut***
Self-adhesive
2407 A1292a A multicolored 2.00 .35

No. 2407 valued at first class domestic letter rate of 9570cr on day of issue.

Beetles A1293

1993, June 5 Litho. ***Perf. 11½x12***
2408 A1293 8000cr Dynastes hercules .35 .35
2409 A1293 55,000cr Batus barbicornis 2.50 1.75

3rd Iberian-American Conference of Chiefs of State and Heads of Government, Salvador — A1294

1993, July 15 Litho. ***Perf. 11x11½***
2410 A1294 12,000cr multi .50 .25

1st Brazilian Postage Stamps, 150th Anniv. — A1295

Litho. & Engr.
1993, July 30 ***Perf. 12x11½***
2411 A1295 30,000cr No. 1 .70 .40
2412 A1295 60,000cr No. 2 1.50 .60
2413 A1295 90,000cr No. 3 2.25 1.00
a. Souvenir sheet of 3, #2411-2413, wmk. 268 22.50 22.50
Nos. 2411-2413 (3) 4.45 2.00

No. 2413a sold for 200,000cr and was issued without gum. Stamps in No. 2413a do not have imprint at bottom.

Union of Portuguese Speaking Capitals A1296

No. 2414: a, 15,000cr, Brasilia. b, 71,000cr, Rio de Janiero.

1993, July 30 Litho. ***Perf. 11½x12***
2414 A1296 Pair, #a.-b. 3.25 2.00

No. 2414 printed in continuous design.

Monica & Friends, by Mauricio de Sousa A1297

Monica, Cebolinha, Cascao, Magali, and Bidu: a, Engraving die. b, Reading proclamation, king, No. 1. c, Writing and sending letter, No. 2. d, Receiving letter, No. 3.

1993, Aug. 1

2415 A1297 (1) Strip of 4, #a.-d. 9.00 9.00
Complete booklet, #2415 9.00

First Brazilian postage stamps, 150th anniv. Nos. 2415a-2415d paid the first class rate (9600cr)on day of issue.

Brazilian Post, 330th Anniv. A1298

No. 2416 — Postal buildings: a, Imperial Post Office, Rio de Janeiro. b, Petropolis. c, Central office, Rio de Janeiro. d, Niteroi.

1993, Aug. 3 Litho. ***Perf. 11½x12***

2416 A1298 20,000cr Block of 4, #a.-d. 3.00 3.00

Brazilian Engineering Schools — A1299

Designs: No. 2417, School of Engineering, Federal University, Rio de Janeiro. No. 2418, Polytechnical School, University of Sao Paulo.

1993, Aug. 24 Litho. ***Perf. 11x11½***

2417 A1299 17cr multicolored .65 .35
2418 A1299 17cr multicolored .65 .35

Preservation of Sambaquis Archaelogical Sites — A1300

1993, Sept. 19 ***Perf. 12x11½***

2419 A1300 17cr Two artifacts .45 .25
2420 A1300 17cr Six artifacts .45 .25

Ulysses Guimaraes, Natl. Congress — A1301

1993, Oct. 6 Litho. ***Perf. 11x11½***

2421 A1301 22cr multicolored .45 .45

A1302 A1303

1993, Oct. 8 Litho. ***Perf. 12x11½***

2422 A1302 22cr multicolored .45 .45

Virgin of Nazare Religious Festival, bicent.

1993, Oct. 13 Litho. ***Perf. 11½x11***

Endangered birds (America Issue): 22cr, Anodorhynchus hyacinthinus, anodorhynchus glaucus, anodorhynchus leari. 130cr, Cyanopsitta spixii.

2423 A1303 22cr multicolored .80 .35
2424 A1303 130cr multicolored 2.50 1.00

A1304

Composers.

1993, Oct. 19 Litho. ***Perf. 12x11½***

2425 A1304 22cr Vinicius de Moraes .35 .25
2426 A1304 22cr Pixinguinha .35 .25

A1307

Poets: No. 2427, Mario de Andrade (1893-1945). No. 2428, Alceu Amoroso Lima (Tristao de Athayde) (1893-1983). No. 2429, Gilka Machado (1893-1980).

1993, Oct. 29 Litho. ***Perf. 12x11½***

2427 A1307 30cr multicolored .30 .30
2428 A1307 30cr multicolored .30 .30
2429 A1307 30cr multicolored .30 .30
Nos. 2427-2429 (3) .90 .90

Natl. Book Day.

Brazil-Portugal Treaty of Consultation and Friendship, 40th Anniv. — A1308

1993, Nov. 3 Litho. ***Perf. 11½x12***

2430 A1308 30cr multicolored .35 .30

See Portugal No. 1980.

Image of the Republic — A1309

Photo. & Engr.

1993, Nov. 3 ***Perf. 13***

2431 A1309 (B) multicolored 4.25 1.75

Valued at first class international letter rate (178.70 cr) on day of issue.

2nd Intl. Biennial of Comic Strips A1310

Cartoon drawings: No. 2432, Nho-Quim. No. 2433, Benjamin. No. 2434, Lamparina. No. 2435, Reco-Reco, Bolao, Azeitona.

1993, Nov. 11 Litho. ***Perf. 11½x12***

2432 A1310 (1) multicolored 1.60 .50
2433 A1310 (1) multicolored 1.60 .50
2434 A1310 (1) multicolored 1.60 .50
2435 A1310 (1) multicolored 1.60 .50
a. Block of 4, #2432-2435 6.50 6.50

Valued at first class domestic letter rate (30.20 cr) on day of issue.

Launching of First Brazilian-Built Submarine — A1311

1993, Nov. 18 ***Perf. 11½***

2436 A1311 240cr multicolored 2.50 2.50

Christmas A1312

1993, Nov. 20

2437 A1312 (1) multicolored 1.25 .80

Valued at first class domestic letter rate (30.20 cr) on day of issue.

First Fighter Group, 50th Anniv. A1313

1993, Dec. 18 Litho. ***Perf. 11½***

2438 A1313 42cr multicolored .70 .35

Convent of Merces, 340th Anniv. A1314

1994, Jan. 31 Litho. ***Perf. 11½x12***

2439 A1314 58cr multicolored .45 .30

Mae Menininha of Gantois, Birth Cent. — A1315

1994, Feb. 10 Litho. ***Perf. 11x11½***

2440 A1315 80cr multicolored .50 .50

Intl. Olympic Committee, Cent. A1316

1994, Feb. 17 ***Perf. 11½x12***

2441 A1316 (1) multicolored 3.00 2.00

No. 2441 valued at first class international letter rate (446.30 cr) on day of issue.

Natl. Flag — A1317

1994, Jan. 31 Litho. ***Die Cut***

Self-Adhesive

2442 A1317 (1) multicolored 1.75 .40

No. 2442 valued at first class domestic letter rate (55.90 cr) on day of issue.

Birds — A1318

Designs: 10cr, Notiochelidon cyanoleuca. 20cr, Buteo magnirostris. 50cr, Turdus rufiventris. 100cr, Columbina talpacoti. 200cr, Vanellus chilensis. 500cr, Zonotrichia capensis.

1994 Photo. ***Perf. 11x11½***

2443 A1318 10cr multi .45 .25
2444 A1318 20cr multi .45 .25
2445 A1318 50cr multi .45 .25
2446 A1318 100cr multi .45 .25
2447 A1318 200cr multi .45 .25
2448 A1318 500cr multi 1.25 .30
Nos. 2443-2448 (6) 3.50 1.55

Issued: 10cr, 3/17; 20cr, 3/9; 50cr, 3/1; 100cr, 200cr, 4/4; 500cr, 4/13.

See Nos. 2484-2494.

Image of the Republic — A1318a

Self-Adhesive

Die Cut

1994, May 10 Litho.

2449 A1318a (1) blue .75 .25
2450 A1318a (3) claret 1.50 .65

Size: 25x35mm

Perf. 12x11½

2451 A1318a (4) green 3.00 1.00
2452 A1318a (5) henna brown 6.00 1.25
Nos. 2449-2452 (4) 11.25 3.15

Nos. 2449, 2450, 2451, 2452 valued 131.37cr, 321.14cr, 452.52cr, 905.05cr on day of issue.

Prince Henry the Navigator (1394-1460) — A1319

1994, Mar. 4 Litho. ***Perf. 11½x12***
2463 A1319 635cr multicolored 4.00 2.25

See Macao No. 719, Portugal No. 1987.

America Issue A1320

Postal vehicles: 110cr, Bicycle, country scene. 635cr, Motorcycle, city scene.

1994, Mar. 18
2464 A1320 110cr multicolored .40 .25
2465 A1320 635cr multicolored 4.00 1.50

Father Cicero Romao Batista, 150th Birth Anniv. A1321

1994, Mar. 24 ***Perf. 11x11½***
2466 A1321 (1) multicolored 1.50 .75

No. 2466 valued at first class domestic letter rate (98.80 cr) on day of issue.

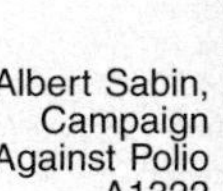

Albert Sabin, Campaign Against Polio A1322

1994, Apr. 7 ***Perf. 11½x12***
2467 A1322 160cr multicolored 1.00 .35

Carlos Castello Branco, Journalist A1323

1994, Apr. 14
2468 A1323 160cr multicolored .45 .30

Karl Friedrich Phillip von Martius, Naturalist A1324

Flowers: No. 2469, Euterpe oleracea. No. 2470, Jacaranda paucifoliolata. No. 2471, Barbacernia tomentosa.

1994, Apr. 24 ***Perf. 12x11½***
2469 A1324 (1) multicolored .90 .45
2470 A1324 (1) multicolored .90 .45
2471 A1324 (1) multicolored 3.00 1.50
Nos. 2469-2471 (3) 4.80 2.40

Nos. 2469-2470 were valued at first class domestic letter rate (144 cr) on day of issue. No. 2471 valued at first class intl. letter rate (860 cr) on day of issue.

Monkeys — A1326

No. 2474, Leontopithecus rosalia. No. 2475, Saguinus imperator. No. 2476, Saguinus bicolor.

1994, May 24
2474 A1326 (1) multicolored 3.75 1.75
2475 A1326 (1) multicolored 1.25 .60
2476 A1326 (1) multicolored 1.25 .60
Nos. 2474-2476 (3) 6.25 2.95

Nos. 2474-2476 were valued at first class domestic letter rate (207.03 cr) on day of issue.

1994 World Cup Soccer Championships, US — A1327

1994, May 19 ***Perf. 11½x12***
2477 A1327 (1) multicolored 4.00 4.00

No. 2477 was valued at first class intl. rate (1378.32 cr) on day of issue.
Soccer in Brazil, cent.

Souvenir Sheet

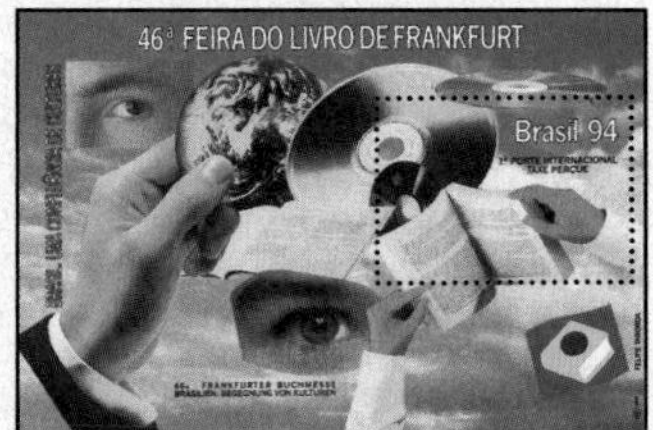

46th Frankfurt Intl. Book Fair — A1328

1994, May 27
2478 A1328 (1) multicolored 5.00 5.00

No. 2478 was valued at first class intl. rate (1523.83 cr) on day of issue.

Natl. Literacy Program — A1329

Designs: No. 2479, Pencil, buildings. No. 2480, Pencil, people on television, people watching. No. 2481, Classroom, pencil. No. 2482, Pencils crossed over fingerprint, map of Brazil.

1994, June 3 Litho. ***Perf. 12x11½***
2479 A1329 (1) multicolored 1.10 .55
2480 A1329 (1) multicolored 1.10 .55
2481 A1329 (1) multicolored 1.10 .55
2482 A1329 (1) multicolored 1.10 .55
Nos. 2479-2482 (4) 4.40 2.20

Nos. 2479-2482 were valued at first class domestic letter rate (233.05 cr) on day of issue.

Souvenir Sheet

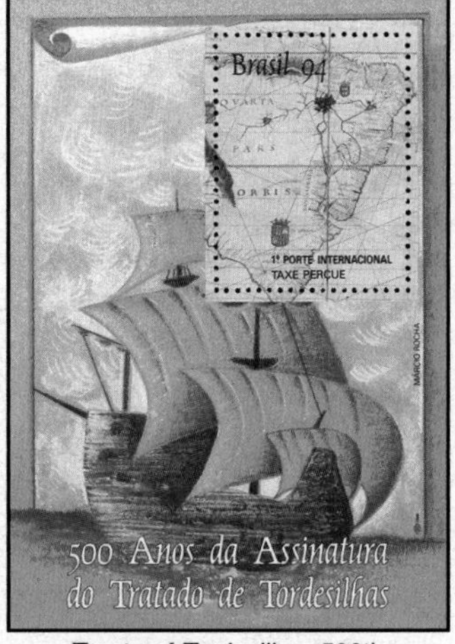

Treaty of Tordesillas, 500th Anniv. — A1330

1994, June 7
2483 A1330 (1) multicolored 3.50 3.50

No. 2483 was valued at first class intl. letter rate (1689.02 cr) on day of issue.

Bird Type of 1994 and

A1330a

Designs: 1c, Like No. 2443. 2c, Like No. 2444. 5c, Like No. 2445. 10c, Like No. 2446. 15c, Sicalis flaveola. 20c, Like No. 2447. No. 2490, Tyrannus savana. 50c, Like No. 2448. 1r, Fumarius rufus.
No. 2498, Myiozetestes similis. No. 2499, Volantia jacarina.

Perf. 11x11½, 13 (15c), 12½13 (22c)
1994-2001 Photo.
2484 A1318 1c multi .40 .25
2485 A1318 2c multi .40 .25
2486 A1318 5c multi .40 .25
2487 A1318 10c multi .40 .25
2488 A1330a 15c multi .90 .35
2489 A1318 20c multi .90 .40
2490 A1318 22c multi .65 .50
a. Inscribed "1999" 1.90 .80
2491 A1318 50c multi 2.75 1.00
2494 A1318 1r multi 5.25 2.25
Nos. 2484-2494 (9) 12.05 5.50

Size: 21x27mm
Self-Adhesive
Serpentine Die Cut 5¾

2498 A1318 22c multi .85 .50
2499 A1318 (22c) multi 1.25 .50
a. Inscribed "2000" 10.00 —

No. 2499 is inscribed "1o PORTE NATIONAL" and was valued at 22c on day of issue.
No. 2490 has 1998 year date; No. 2499 has 1997 year date.
Issued: 1c, 2c, 5c, 20c, 20c, 50c, 1r, 7/1/94; 11/16/95; No. 2490, 10/13/97; No. 2498, 2/16/98; No. 2499, 7/22/97; No. 2490a, 11/99; No. 2499a, 1/01.

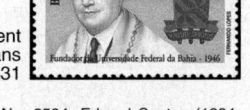

Prominent Brazilians A1331

Designs: No. 2504, Edgard Santos (1894-1962), surgeon, educator. No. 2505, Oswaldo Aranha (1894-1960), politician. No. 2507, Otto Lara Resende (1922-92), writer, educator.

1994, July 5 Litho. ***Perf. 11½x12***
2504 A1331 (1) multicolored 1.50 .60
2505 A1331 (1) multicolored 1.50 .60
2506 A1331 (1) multicolored 1.50 .60
Nos. 2504-2506 (3) 4.50 1.80

Nos. 2504-2506 were valued at first class domestic letter rate (12c) on day of issue.

A1332 A1333

1994, July 15 ***Perf. 12x11½***
2507 A1332 12c multicolored 1.10 .30

Petrobras, 40th anniv.

Litho. & Engr.
1994, July 26 ***Perf. 11½***
2508 A1333 12c multicolored .80 .30

Brazilian State Mint, 300th anniv.

Campaign Against Famine & Misery A1334

1994, July 27 Litho. ***Perf. 11½x12***
2509 A1334 (1) Fish .90 .35
2510 A1334 (1) Bread .90 .35

Nos. 2509-2510 were valued at first class domestic letter rate (12c) on day of issue.

Institute of Brazilian Lawyers, 150th Anniv. A1335

1994, Aug. 11
2511 A1335 12c multicolored .70 .35

Intl. Year of the Family A1336

1994, Aug. 16 ***Perf. 11½***
2512 A1336 84c multicolored 3.50 2.00

Maternity Hospital of Sao Paulo, Cent. A1337

1994, Aug. 26 ***Perf. 11½x12***
2513 A1337 12c multicolored 1.50 .35

Vincente Celestino (1894-1968), Singer — A1338

1994, Sept. 12

2514 A1338 12c multicolored 1.40 .35

"Contos da Carochinha," First Brazilian Children's Book, Cent. — A1339

No. 2515: Fairy tales: a, Joao e Maria (Hansel & Gretel). b, Dona Baratinha. c, Puss 'n Boots. d, Tom Thumb.

1994, Oct. 5 Litho. ***Perf. 11½x12***

2515 Block of 4 9.00 9.00
a.-b. A1339 12c any single 1.40 .70
c.-d. A1339 84c any single 3.00 2.00

Brazilian Literature A1340

Portraits: No. 2516, Tomas Antonio Gonzaga (1744-1809?), poet. No. 2517, Fernando de Azevedo (1894-1974), author.

1994, Oct. 5 ***Perf. 11½***

2516 A1340 12c multicolored .75 .30
2517 A1340 12c multicolored .75 .30

St. Clare of Assisi (1194-1253) A1341

1994, Oct. 19 ***Perf. 12x11½***

2518 A1341 12c multicolored .70 .30

Ayrton Senna (1960-1994), Race Car Driver — A1342

No. 2519: a, McClaren Formula 1 race car, Brazilian flag. b, Fans, Senna. c, Flags, race cars, Senna.

1994, Oct. 24 ***Perf. 11½x12***

2519 Triptych 9.50 9.50
a.-b. A1342 12c any single 2.25 1.10
c. A1342 84c multicolored 4.75 2.75

Institute of History & Geography of Sao Paulo, Cent. A1343

1994, Nov. 1

2520 A1343 12c multicolored .70 .30

Popular Music A1344

Designs: No. 2521, Music from "The Sea," by Dorival Caymmi. No. 2522, Adoniran Barbosa (1910-82), samba composer.

1994, Nov. 5 ***Perf. 11½***

2521 A1344 12c multicolored .75 .30
2522 A1344 12c multicolored .75 .30

Christmas A1345

No. 2523 — Folk characters: a, Boy wearing Santa coat, pot on head. b, Worm in apple. c, Man, animals singing. d, Shoe on tree stump, man with pipe holding pen.

1994, Dec. 1 Litho. ***Perf. 11½***

2523 Block of 4 4.00 4.00
a. A1345 84c multicolored 2.40 1.10
b.-d. A1345 12c any single .35 .35
e. Booklet pane, #2523 + 4 labels *17.50*
Complete booklet, #2523e *20.00*

Souvenir Sheet

Brazil, 1994 World Cup Soccer Champions — A1346

1994, Dec. 5 ***Perf. 12x11½***

2524 A1346 2.14r multicolored 8.00 8.00

Louis Pasteur (1822-95) A1347

1995, Feb. 19 Litho. ***Perf. 11½x12***

2525 A1347 84c multicolored 2.75 2.75

Historical Events A1348

Designs: No. 2526, Capture of Monte Castello, 50th anniv. No. 2527, End of the Farroupilha Revolution, 150th anniv.

1995, Feb. 21

2526 A1348 12c multicolored .70 .30
2527 A1348 12c multicolored .70 .30

Pres. Itamar Franco — A1349

FAO, 50th Anniv. — A1350

1995, Mar. 22 Litho. ***Perf. 12x11½***

2528 A1349 12c multicolored .75 .30

1995, Apr. 3 ***Perf. 11½x11***

2529 A1350 84c multicolored 2.50 2.50

Famous Men A1351

Designs: No. 2530, Alexandre de Gusmao (1695-1753), diplomat. No. 2531, Francisco Brandao, Viscount of Jequitinhonha (1794-1870), lawyer, abolitionist. 15c, Jose da Silva Paranhos, Jr., Baron of Rio Branco (1845-1912), politician, diplomat.

1995, Apr. 28 ***Perf. 11½x12***

2530 A1351 12c multicolored .75 .30
2531 A1351 12c multicolored .75 .30
2532 A1351 15c multicolored .75 .35
Nos. 2530-2532 (3) 2.25 .95

Guglielmo Marconi (1874-1937), Radio Transmitting Equipment — A1352

1995, May 5 Litho. ***Perf. 11½x12***

2533 A1352 84c multicolored 2.75 2.10

Radio, cent.

Friendship Between Brazil & Japan A1353

1995, May 29

2534 A1353 84c multicolored 2.75 1.75

Endangered Birds — A1354

1995, June 5 ***Perf. 12x11½***

2535 A1354 12c Tinamus solitarius .85 .30
2536 A1354 12c Mitu mitu .85 .30

June Festivals — A1355

Designs: No. 2537, Couples dancing at Campina Grande, "Greatest St. John's Party of the World." No. 2538, Bride, bridegroom, festivities, Caruaru.

1995, June 11 ***Perf. 11½x12***

2537 A1355 12c multicolored .75 .30
2538 A1355 12c multicolored .75 .30

St. Anthony of Padua (1195-1231) — A1356

1995, June 13

2539 A1356 84c multicolored 3.00 1.90

See Portugal No. 2054.

Souvenir Sheet

Louis and Auguste Lumiere, Camera — A1357

1995, June 21

2540 A1357 2.14r multicolored 8.50 8.50

Motion pictures, cent.

New Currency, The Real, 1st Anniv. — A1358

1995, July 1 Litho. ***Perf. 12x11½***

2541 A1358 12c multicolored .80 .30

Volleyball, Cent. — A1359

1995, July 8

2542 A1359 15c multicolored 1.60 .50

Dinosaurs A1360

1995, July 23 ***Perf. 11½x12***

2543 A1360 15c Angaturama limai 1.10 .35
2544 A1360 1.50r Titanosaurus 4.25 1.50

Traffic Safety Program A1361

Designs: 12c, Test dummy without seat belt hitting windshield. 71c, Auto hitting alcoholic beverage glass.

1995, July 25

2545 A1361 12c multicolored .50 .30
2546 A1361 71c multicolored 2.50 1.65

Souvenir Sheet

Roberto Burle Marx, Botanist — A1362

No. 2547: a, 15c, Calathea burle-marxii. b, 15c, Vellozia burle-marxii. c, 1.50r, Heliconia aemygdiana.

1995, Aug. 4 **Litho.** ***Perf. 12x11½***

2547 A1362 Sheet of 3, #a.-c. 8.50 8.50

Singapore '95.

Parachute Infantry Brigade, 50th Anniv. — A1363

1995, Aug. 23

2548 A1363 15c multicolored 1.25 .35

Paulista Museum, Cent. A1364

1995, Sept. 5 ***Perf. 11½***

2549 A1364 15c multicolored .75 .35

Lighthouses A1365

1995, Sept. 28

2550 A1365 15c Olinda 1.60 .35
2551 A1365 15c Sao Joao 1.60 .35
2552 A1365 15c Santo Antonio da Barra 1.60 .35
Nos. 2550-2552 (3) 4.80 1.05

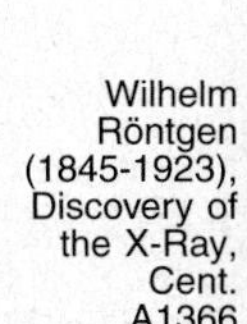

Wilhelm Röntgen (1845-1923), Discovery of the X-Ray, Cent. A1366

1995, Sept. 30

2553 A1366 84c multicolored 3.00 2.00

Lubrapex '95, 15th Brazilian-Portuguese Philatelic Exhibition — A1367

Wildlife scene along Tiete River: 15c, No. 2556a, Bird, otter with fish. 84c, No. 2556b, Birds, river boat.

1995, Sept. 30 ***Perf. 12x11½***

2554 A1367 15c multicolored .50 .35
2555 A1367 84c multicolored 3.00 2.00

Souvenir Sheet

2556 A1367 1.50r Sheet of 2, #a.-b. 12.00 12.00

No. 2556 is a continuous design.

Flamengo Regatta Soccer Club — A1368

1995, Oct. 6 ***Perf. 11x11½***

2557 A1368 15c multicolored 1.00 .35

America Issue A1369

Outdoor scenes: 15c, Trees, mushrooms, alligator, lake. 84c, Black-neck swans on lake, false swans in air.

1995, Oct. 12 **Litho.** ***Perf. 11½x12***

2558 A1369 15c multicolored 1.00 .40
2559 A1369 84c multicolored 3.00 1.40
a. Pair, #2558-2559 4.00 4.00

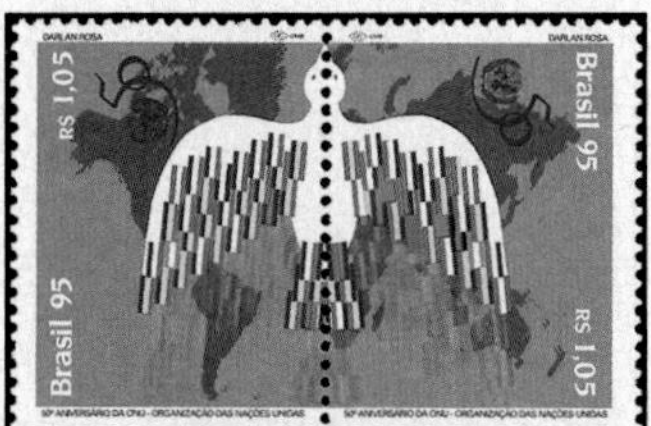

UN, 50th Anniv. — A1370

1995, Oct. 24 ***Perf. 12x11½***

2560 1.05r multicolored 3.25 2.25
2561 1.05r multicolored 3.25 2.25
a. A1370 Pair, No. 2560-2561 6.75 6.75

Writers — A1372

Designs: No. 2562, Eca de Queiroz (1845-1900), village. No. 2563, Rubem Braga (1913-90), beach, Rio de Janeiro. 23c, Carlos Drummond de Andrade (1902-87), letters.

1995, Oct. 27 ***Perf. 12x11***

2562 A1372 15c multicolored 1.00 .60
2563 A1372 15c multicolored 1.00 .60
2564 A1372 23c multicolored 1.25 .85
Nos. 2562-2564 (3) 3.25 2.05

Souvenir Sheet

Death of Zumbi Dos Palmares, Slave Resistance Leader, 300th Anniv. — A1373

1995, Nov. 20 ***Perf. 12x11½***

2565 A1373 1.05r multicolored 6.00 6.00

2nd World Short Course Swimming Championships — A1374

No. 2566: a, Freestyle. b, Backstroke. c, Butterfly. d, Breaststroke.

1995, Nov. 30 ***Perf. 11½x12***

2566 A1374 23c Block of 4, #a.-d. 3.25 3.25

Christmas A1375

No. 2567: a, 23c, Cherub looking right, stars. b, 15c, Cherub looking left, stars.

1995, Dec. 1 ***Perf. 11½***

2567 A1375 Pair, #a.-b.+2 labels 2.50 2.50

Botafogo Soccer and Regatta Club A1376

1995, Dec. 8 ***Perf. 11x11½***

2568 A1376 15c multicolored 1.10 .35

Diário de Pernambuco Newspaper, 170th Anniv. — A1377

1995, Dec. 14 **Litho.** ***Perf. 12x11½***

2569 A1377 23c multicolored 1.60 .75

Souvenir Sheet

Amazon Theatre, Cent. — A1378

1996, Feb. 27

2570 A1378 1.23r multicolored 7.00 7.00

Francisco Prestes Maia, Politician, Birth Cent. A1379

1996, Mar. 19 ***Perf. 11½x12***

2571 A1379 18c multicolored 1.25 .40

Irineu Bornhausen, Governor of Santa Catarina, Birth Cent. — A1380

1996, Mar. 25 ***Perf. 11x11½***

2572 A1380 27c multicolored 1.50 .55

Paintings A1381

Designs: No. 2573, Boat with Little Flags and Birds, by Alfredo Volpi. No. 2574, Ouro Preto Landscape, by Alberto da Veiga Guignard.

1996, Apr. 15 ***Perf. 12x11½***

2573 A1381 15c multicolored 1.10 .30
2574 A1381 15c multicolored 1.10 .30

UNICEF, 50th Anniv. A1382

1996, Apr. 16 ***Perf. 11½***

2575 A1382 23c multicolored 1.50 .50

Portuguese Discovery of Brazil, 500th Anniv. (in 2000) — A1383

1996, Apr. 22 *Perf. 12x11½*

2576 A1383 1.05r multicolored 4.50 2.25

See No. 2626.

Israel Pinheiro da Silva, Politician, Business Entrepeneur, Birth Cent. — A1384

1996, Apr. 23 *Perf. 11½x12*

2577 A1384 18c multicolored 1.10 .40

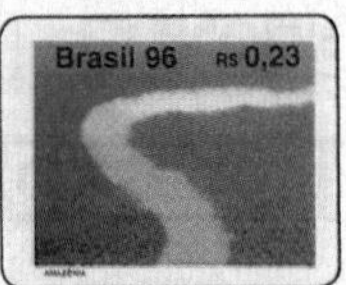

Tourism A1385

Designs: No. 2578, Amazon River. No. 2579, Swampland area. No. 2580, Sail boat, northeastern states. No. 2581, Sugarloaf, Guanabara Bay. No.2582, Iguacu Falls.

1996, Apr. 24 *Die Cut*

Self-Adhesive

2578	A1385	23c multicolored	1.25	.50
2579	A1385	23c multicolored	1.25	.50
2580	A1385	23c multicolored	1.25	.50
2581	A1385	23c multicolored	1.25	.50
2582	A1385	23c multicolored	1.25	.50
a.		Strip of 5, #2578-2582	6.25	

Hummingbirds — A1386

Espamer '96: 15c, Topaza pella. 1.05r, Stephanoxis lalandi. 1.15r, Eupetomena macroura.

1996, May 4 **Litho.** *Perf. 11½*

2583	A1386	15c multicolored	1.75	.50
2584	A1386	1.05r multicolored	7.50	3.00
2585	A1386	1.15r multicolored	7.50	3.00
		Nos. 2583-2585 (3)	16.75	6.50

1996 Summer Olympic Games, Atlanta A1387

1996, May 21

2586	A1387	18c Marathon	.90	.40
2587	A1387	23c Gymnastics	1.00	.50
2588	A1387	1.05r Swimming	3.75	2.00
2589	A1387	1.05r Beach volley-ball	3.75	2.00
		Nos. 2586-2589 (4)	9.40	4.90

Souvenir Sheet

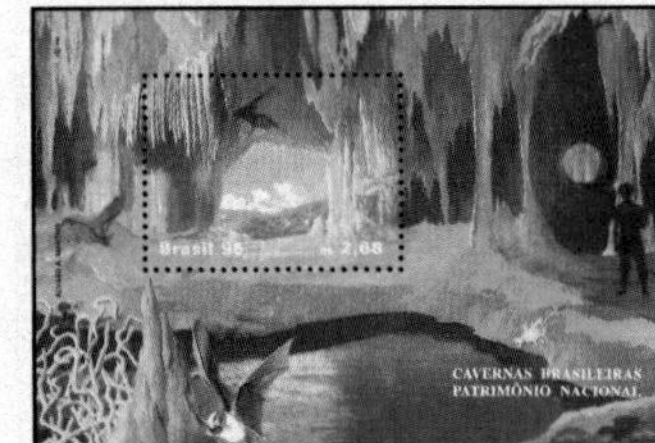

Brazilian Caverns — A1388

1996, June 5 *Perf. 11½x12*

2590 A1388 2.68r multicolored 12.00 12.00

Americas Telecom '96 — A1389

1996, June 10 *Perf. 11½*

2591 A1389 1.05r multicolored 5.50 2.75

Souvenir Sheet

World Day to Fight Desertification — A1390

1996, June 17 *Perf. 12x11½*

2592 A1390 1.23r multicolored 8.00 8.00

Fight Against Drug Abuse A1391

1996, June 26 *Perf. 11½x12*

2593 A1391 27c multicolored 3.00 .65

Year of Education A1392

1996, July 10 *Perf. 12x11½*

2594 A1392 23c multicolored 1.25 .55

Princess Isabel, 150th Birth Anniv. A1393

1996, July 29 *Perf. 11½x12*

2595 A1393 18c multicolored 1.25 .40

Carlos Gomes (1836-96), Composer A1394

1996, Sept. 16 *Perf. 11½*

2596 A1394 50c multicolored 2.00 1.25

15th World Orchid Conference A1395

Designs: No. 2597, Promenaea stapelioides. No. 2598, Cattleya eldorado. No. 2599, Cattleya loddigesii.

1996, Sept. 17

2597	A1395	15c multicolored	3.00	.60
2598	A1395	15c multicolored	3.00	.60
2599	A1395	15c multicolored	3.00	.60
		Nos. 2597-2599 (3)	9.00	1.80

Apparition of Virgin Mary at La Salette, 150th Anniv. A1396

1996, Sept. 19

2600 A1396 1r multicolored 3.00 2.25

Souvenir Sheet

Popular Legends — A1397

No. 2601: a, 23c, "Cuca" walking from house. b, 1.05r, "Boitatá," snake of life. c, 1.15r, "Caipora," defender of ecology.

1996, Sept. 28 *Perf. 11x10½*

2601 A1397 Sheet of 3, #a.-c. 8.00 8.00

BRAPEX '96.

23rd Sao Paulo Intl. Biennial Exhibition A1398

No. 2602: a, Marilyn Monroe by Andy Warhol, vert. b, The Scream, by Edvard Munch, vert. c, Abstract, by Louise Bourgeois, vert. d, Woman Drawing, by Pablo Picasso.

1996, Oct. 5 *Perf. 12x11½*

2602 A1398 55c Block of 4, #a.-d. 27.50 27.50

Traditional Costumes A1400

America issue: 50c, Man dressed as cowboy. 1r, Woman dressed in baiana clothes.

1996, Oct. 12 **Litho.** *Perf. 11½*

2604	A1400	50c multicolored	2.50	1.00
2605	A1400	1r multicolored	4.75	2.25

Christmas A1401

1996, Nov. 4 **Litho.** *Perf. 12x11½*

2606 A1401 1st multicolored 2.40 .60

No. 2606 was valued at 23c on day of issue.

José Carlos (1884-1950), Caricaturist A1402

1996, Nov. 22

2607 A1402 1st multicolored 2.40 .60

No. 2607 was valued at 23c on day of issue.

Tourism A1403

Designs: No. 2608, Ipiranga Monument, Sao Paulo. No. 2609, Hercílio Luz Bridge, Florianópolis. No. 2610, Natl. Congress Building, Brasília. No. 2611, Pelourinho, Salvador. No. 2612, Ver-o-Peso Market, Belém.

Serpentine Die Cut

1996, Dec. 9 **Photo.**

Self-Adhesive

2608	A1403	1st multicolored	1.20	.75
2609	A1403	1st multicolored	1.20	.75
2610	A1403	1st multicolored	1.20	.75
2611	A1403	1st multicolored	1.20	.75
2612	A1403	1st multicolored	1.20	.75
a.		Strip of 5, #2608-2612	6.00	

Nos. 2608-2612 are inscribed "1o PORTE NACIONAL," and were valued 23c on day of issue. Selvage surrounding each stamp in No. 2612a is rouletted.

Rio de Janeiro, Candidate for 2004 Summer Olympic Games A1404

1997, Jan. 17 Litho. *Perf. 11½*
2613 A1404 1st multicolored 3.50 2.25

No. 2613 is inscribed "1o PORTE INTERNACIONAL" and was valued at 1.05r on day of issue.

The Postman A1405

1997, Jan. 25
2614 A1405 1st multicolored 1.50 .75

America issue. No. 2614 is inscribed "1o PORTE NACIONAL" and was valued at 23c on day of issue.

Antonio de Castro Alves (1847-71), Poet A1406

1997, Mar. 14
2615 A1406 15c multicolored 1.10 .50

Marquis of Tamandaré, Naval Officer, Death Cent. — A1407

1997, Mar. 19 *Perf. 11x11½*
2616 A1407 23c multicolored 1.00 .50

Stamp Design Contest Winner A1408

1997, Mar. 20 *Perf. 11½x12*
2617 A1408 15c "Joy Joy" 3.00 .35

World Day of Water — A1409

1997, Mar. 22 *Perf. 12x11½*
2618 A1409 1.05r multicolored 3.00 2.10

Brazilian Airplanes A1410

Designs: No. 2619, EMB-145. No. 2620, AMX. No. 2621, EMB-312 H Super Tucano. No. 2622, EMB-120 Brasilia. No. 2623, EMB-312 Tucano.

1997, Mar. 27 Litho. *Die Cut*
Self-Adhesive

2619 A1410 15c multicolored .60 .25
2620 A1410 15c multicolored .60 .25
2621 A1410 15c multicolored .60 .25
2622 A1410 15c multicolored .60 .25
2623 A1410 15c multicolored .60 .25
a. Strip of 5, #2619-2623 3.00

Campaign Against AIDS — A1411

1997, Apr. 7 Litho. *Perf. 12x11½*
2624 A1411 23c multicolored 1.25 .50

Souvenir Sheet

Indian Culture — A1412

Weapons of the Xingu Indians.

1997, Apr. 16 *Perf. 11x11½*
2625 A1412 1.15r multicolored 3.00 3.00

Portuguese Discovery of Brazil, 500th Anniv. Type

1997, Apr. 22 *Perf. 12x11½*
2626 A1383 1.05r like #2576 2.75 2.25

No. 2576 has green background and blue in lower right corner. No. 2626 has those colors reversed and is inscribed "BRASIL 97" at top.

Pixinguinha (1897-1973), Composer, Musician — A1413

1997, Apr. 23
2627 A1413 15c multicolored .80 .35

Souvenir Sheet

Brazilian Claim to Trindade Island, Cent. — A1414

1997, May 7 *Perf. 11½x11*
2628 A1414 1.23r multicolored 3.50 3.50

Human Rights — A1415

1997, May 13 *Perf. 12x11½*
2629 A1415 18c multicolored .80 .35

Souvenir Sheet

Brazilian Antarctic Program — A1416

1997, May 13
2630 A1416 2.68r multicolored 8.00 8.00

Fruits and Nuts — A1417

Designs: 1c, Oranges. 2c, Bananas. 5c, Papayas. 10c, Pineapple. Nos. 2635, 2636L, Cashews. Nos. 2636, 2636Q, Sugar apple. No. 2636A, Grapes. Nos. 2636B, 2636M, 2636R, Watermelon. 50c, Surinam cherry (pitanga), 51c, Coconuts. 80c, Apples. 82c, Lemons. 1r, Strawberries.

1997-99 Litho. *Serpentine Die Cut*
Self-Adhesive

2631 A1417 1c multi .45 .45
2632 A1417 2c multi .45 .45
2633 A1417 5c multi .45 .45
2634 A1417 10c multi, vert. 1.50 .45
2635 A1417 20c multi, vert. 3.00 1.50
2636 A1417 20c multi, vert. 1.50 .45
2636A A1417 22c multi .60 .45
2636B A1417 (22c) multi 1.25 .45
2636C A1417 50c multi .90 .45
2636D A1417 51c multi, vert. 2.50 1.75
2636E A1417 80c multi, vert. 5.50 1.50
2636F A1417 82c multi, vert. 9.50 6.00
2636G A1417 1r multi, vert. 2.50 .90
Nos. 2631-2636G (13) 30.10 15.25

Issued: (22c), 5/28; 1c, 6/97; 2c, 10c, No. 2635, 7/97; 5c, 8/97; 1r, 8/3; 22c, 10/3; No. 2636, 51c, 80c, 82c, 1/15/98; 50c, 11/26/99.

No. 2636B is inscribed "1o PORTE NATIONAL" and was valued at 22c on day of issue.

Fruits and Nuts Type of 1997-99

1998-99 Litho. *Die Cut*
Self-Adhesive

2636H A1417 1c multi .75 .75
2636I A1417 2c multi 1.50 1.25
2636J A1417 5c multi 2.75 1.50
2636K A1417 10c multi, vert. 6.00 2.50
2636L A1417 20c multi, vert. 13.00 3.00
2636M A1417 (22c) multi 16.00 2.00
Nos. 2636H-2636M (6) 40.00 11.00

Microperfed
Without Gum

2636N A1417 1c multi *.50 .50*
2636O A1417 5c multi *4.50 4.50*
2636P A1417 10c multi, vert. *6.00 6.00*
2636Q A1417 20c multi, vert. *8.00 8.00*
2636R A1417 (31c) multi *11.00 11.00*
2636S A1417 51c multi, vert. *16.00 16.00*
2636T A1417 80c multi, vert. *24.00 24.00*
2636U A1417 1r multi, vert. *30.00 30.00*
Nos. 2636N-2636U (8) 100.00 100.00

Issued: 2636H-2636L, 1998. No. 2636M, 1999.

Issued: Nos. 2636N-2636Q, 9/28/99; No. 2636R, 9/12/99; No. 2636S, 9/22/99; Nos. 2636T, 2636U, 9/15/99.

A1418

Amazon Flora and Fauna — A1419

Designs: No. 2637, Swietenia macropylla. No. 2638, Arapaima gigas.

1997, June 5 Litho. *Perf. 11½x12*
2637 A1418 27c multicolored 1.10 .40
2638 A1419 27c multicolored 1.10 .40

Fr. José de Anchieta (1534-97), Missionary in Brazil — A1420

Design: No. 2640, Fr. António Vieira (1608-97), missionary in Brazil, diplomat.

1997, June 9 *Perf. 12*
2639 A1420 1.05r multicolored 3.50 2.00
2640 A1420 1.05r multicolored 3.50 2.00

See Portugal Nos. 2168-2169.

Tourism A1421

Designs: No. 2641, Parnaíba River Delta. No. 2642, Lencóis Maranhenses Park.

1997, June 20 *Perf. 11½x12*

2641 A1421 1st multicolored 3.25 2.00
2642 A1421 1st multicolored 3.25 2.00

Nos. 2641-2642 are inscribed "1o PORTE INTERNACIONAL TAXE PERCUE" and were each valued at on day of issue.

Brazilian Academy of Literature, Cent. A1422

1997, July 20

2643 A1422 22c multicolored 1.25 .50

Emiliano de Cavalcanti (1897-1976), Painter A1423

1997, Sept. 16 **Litho.** *Perf. 11½*

2644 A1423 31c multicolored 1.10 .65

2nd World Meeting of the Pope with Families, Rio de Janeiro A1424

1997, Sept. 22 *Perf. 11½x12*

2645 A1424 1.20r multicolored 6.00 2.50

A1425

1997, Sept. 26 *Perf. 12x11½*

2646 A1425 80c multicolored 3.00 1.60

MERCOSUR (Common Market of Latin America). See Argentina #1975, Bolivia #1019, Paraguay #2565, Uruguay #1681.

A1426

1997, Sept. 27

2647 A1426 22c multicolored .80 .45

End of Canudos War, cent.

Integration of MERCOSUR Communications by Telebras, 25th Anniv. — A1427

1997, Oct. 6 *Perf. 11½*

2648 A1427 80c multicolored 4.00 2.25

Composers — A1428

Designs: No. 2649, Oscar Lorenzo Fernandez (1897-1948). No. 2650, Francisco Mignone (1897-1986).

1997, Oct. 7 *Perf. 11x11½*

2649 A1428 22c multicolored .80 .45
2650 A1428 22c multicolored .80 .45

Marist Brothers Presence in Brazil, Cent. A1429

1997, Oct. 22

2651 A1429 22c multicolored 1.00 .45

Christmas A1430

1997, Nov. 5 *Perf. 12x11½*

2652 A1430 22c multicolored 1.00 .45

Education and Citizenship — A1431

1997, Dec. 10 *Perf. 11x11½*

2653 A1431 31c blue & yellow 1.10 .65

City of Belo Horizonte, Cent. A1432

1997, Dec. 12 *Perf. 11½x12*

2654 A1432 31c multicolored 1.10 .65

Citzenship A1433

Map of Brazil and: No. 2655, Education, stack of books. No. 2656, Employment, worker's papers. No. 2657, Agriculture, oranges. No. 2658, Health, stethoscope, vert. No. 2659, Culture, clapboard with musical notes, artist's paint brush, vert.

1997, Dec. 20 *Die Cut*

Self-Adhesive

Booklet Stamps

2655 A1433 22c multicolored .90 .45
2656 A1433 22c multicolored .90 .45
2657 A1433 22c multicolored .90 .45
2658 A1433 22c multicolored .90 .45
2659 A1433 22c multicolored .90 .45
a. Bklt. pane, 2 ea #2655-2659 10.00

The peelable paper backing of No. 2659a serves as a booklet cover.

Gems — A1434

1998, Jan. 22 *Perf. 12x11½*

2660 A1434 22c Alexandrite 1.50 .60
2661 A1434 22c Cat's eye chrysoberyl 1.50 .60
2662 A1434 22c Indicolite 1.50 .60
a. Strip of 3, #2660-2662 4.50 2.75

Famous Brazilian Women A1435

America Issue: No. 2663, Elis Regina, singer. No. 2664, Clementina de Jesus, singer. No. 2665, Dulcina de Moraes, actress. No. 2666, Clarice Lispector, writer.

1998, Mar. 11 *Perf. 11½*

2663 A1435 22c multicolored .80 .45
2664 A1435 22c multicolored .80 .45
2665 A1435 22c multicolored .80 .45
2666 A1435 22c multicolored .80 .45
a. Block of 4, #2663-2666 3.25 3.25

Education — A1436

1998, Mar. 19 *Perf. 12x11½*

2667 31c Children at desks .70 .70
2668 31c Teacher at blackboard .70 .70
a. A1436 Pair, #2667-2668 1.40 1.40

Cruz e Sousa (1861-98), Poet A1437

1998, Mar. 19 **Litho.** *Perf. 11½x12*

2669 A1437 36c multicolored 1.00 .65

Discovery of Brazil, 500th Anniv. — A1438

Designs: No. 2670, 1519 map showing natives, vegetation, fauna. No. 2671, Caravel from Cabral's fleet.

1998, Apr. 22 *Perf. 12x11½*

2670 1.05r multicolored 3.00 1.40
2671 1.05r multicolored 3.00 1.40
a. A1438 Pair, #2670-2671 6.00 6.00

Volunteer Work A1439

Designs: a, Caring for sick man. b, Caring for sick child. c, Fighting forest fire. c, Child's hand holding adult's finger.

1998, May 5 *Perf. 11½x12*

2672 A1439 31c Block of 4, #a.-d. 4.00 4.00

Brazilian Circus — A1440

No. 2673 — Piolin the clown: a, Looking through circle. b, Standing in ring. c, With outside of tent to the left. d, With inside of tent to the right.

1998, May 18 *Perf. 12x11½*

2673 A1440 31c Block of 4, #a.-d. 4.00 4.00

Intl. Year of the Ocean A1441

No. 2674 — Pictures, drawings of marine life: a, Turtle. b, Tail fin of whale. c, Barracuda. d, Jellyfish, school of fish. e, School of fish, diver. f, Dolphins. g, Yellow round fish. h, Two whales. i, Two black-striped butterfly fish. j, Orange & yellow fish. k, Manatee. l, Yellow-striped fish. m, Blue & yellow fish. n, Several striped fish. o, Fish with wing-like fins. p, Manta ray. q, Two fish swimming in opposite directions. r, Long, thin fish, coral. s, Moray eel. t, Yellow & black butterfly fish, coral. u, Starfish, fish. v, Crab, coral. w, Black & orange fish, coral. x, Sea horse, coral.

1998, May 22 *Perf. 11½x12*

Sheet of 24

2674 A1441 31c #a.-x. 25.00 25.00

Expo '98.

1998 World Cup Soccer Championships, France — A1442

No. 2675 — Paintings by: a, Gregorio Gruber. b, Mario Gruber. c, Maciej Babinski. d, Cildo Meireles, vert. e, Claudio Tozzi, vert. f, Antonio Henrique Amaral, vert. g, Jose Roberto Aguilar. h, Nelson Leirner. i, Wesley Duke Lee. j, Mauricio Nogueira Lima, vert. k, Zelio Alves Pinto, vert. l, Aldemir Martins, vert. m, Ivald Granato. n, Carlos Vergara. o, Joao Camara, vert. p, Roberto Magalhaes, vert. q, Guto Lacaz, vert. r, Glauco Rodrigues, vert. s, Leda Catunda. t, Tomoshige Kusuno. u, Jose Zaragoza. v, Luiz Zerbine, vert. w, Antonio Peticov, vert. x, Marcia Grostein, vert.

1998, May 28 ***Perf. 11½x12, 12x11½***
2675 A1442 22c Sheet of 24, #a.-x. 22.50 22.50

Feijoada, Traditional Cuisine A1443

1998, June 1 ***Perf. 11½***
2676 A1443 31c multicolored 1.10 .50

Preservation of Flora and Fauna — A1444

Designs: No. 2677, Araucaria angustifolia. No. 2678, Cyanocorax caeruleus.

1998, June 5 ***Perf. 11½x12***
2677 A1444 22c multicolored 1.50 .60
2678 A1444 22c multicolored 1.50 .60
a. Pair, #2677-2678 3.00 1.40

Launching of Submarine Tapajó A1445

1998, June 5
2679 A1445 51c multicolored 2.00 .75

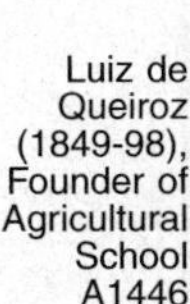

Luiz de Queiroz (1849-98), Founder of Agricultural School A1446

1998, June 6 ***Perf. 11½***
2680 A1446 36c multicolored 1.40 .75

Benedictine Monastery, Sao Paulo, 400th Anniv. A1447

1998, July 10 **Litho.** ***Perf. 11½x12***
2681 A1447 22c multicolored 1.25 .65

Alberto Santos-Dumont (1873-1932), Aviation Pioneer — A1448

Designs: No. 2682, Balloon "Brazil." No. 2683, Dirigible Nr. 1, Santos-Dumont at controls.

1998, July 18
2682 A1448 31c multicolored .80 .40
2683 A1448 31c multicolored .80 .40
a. Pair, #2682-2683 1.75 1.10

Brazilian Cinema, Cent. (in 1997) A1449

No. 2684: a, Guanabara Bay, by Lumière, 1897. b, Taciana Reiss in "Limite," by Mário Peixoto, 1931. c, Actors in (Chanchada), from "A Dupla do Barulho," by Carlos Manga, 1953. d, Films produced by Vera Cruz pictures, caricature of Mazzaropi from "The Dream Factory." e, Glauber Rocha's "New Cinema". f, International film festival awards won by Brazilian films.

1998, July 24 ***Perf. 11½***
2684 A1449 31c Block of 6, #a.-f. 10.00 10.00

Rodrigo Melo Franco de Andrade (1898-1969), and Church of Our Lady of the Rosary, Ouro Preto — A1450

1998, Aug. 17 ***Perf. 11x11½***
2685 A1450 51c multicolored 1.60 .65

Luís da Camara Cascudo (1898-1986), Writer — A1451

1998, Aug. 22
2686 A1451 22c multicolored 1.40 .40

42nd Aeronautical Pentathlon World Championship A1452

No. 2687: a, Fencing. b, Running. c, Swimming. d, Shooting. e, Basketball.

1998, Aug. 22 ***Perf. 12x11½***
2687 A1452 22c Strip of 5, #a.-e. 4.00 4.00

Missionary Cross, Ruins of the Church of Sao Miguel das Missoes — A1453

1998, Sept. 17 ***Perf. 11½x12***
2688 A1453 80c multicolored 2.50 1.00

24th Sao Paulo Art Biennial — A1454

No. 2689: a, Biennial emblem, by José Leonilson. b, Tapuia Dance, by Albert von Eckhout. c, The Schoolboy, by Vincent van Gogh. d, Portrait of Michel Leiris, by Francis Bacon. e, The King's Museum, by René Magritte. f, Urutu, by Tarsila do Amaral. g, Facade with Arcs, Circle and Fascia, by Alfredo Volpi. h, The Raft of the Medusa, by Asger Jorn.

1998, Sept. 22
2689 A1454 31c Block of 8, #a.-h. 10.00 10.00

Nos. 2689b, 2689h have horiz. designs placed vert. on stamps.

Child and Citizenship Stamp Design Contest Winner A1455

1998, Oct. 9
2690 A1455 22c multicolored 1.10 .30

Reorganization of Maritime Mail from Portugal to Brazil, Bicent. — A1456

1998, Oct. 9
2691 A1456 1.20r multicolored 3.00 1.50

See Portugal Nos. 2271-2272.

Dom Pedro I (1798-1834) A1457

1998, Oct. 13 ***Perf. 11½***
2692 A1457 22c multicolored .75 .25

Frisco's Mango Refreshment Promotional Stamp — A1458

Serpentine Die Cut

1998, Oct. 15 **Photo.**

Self-Adhesive

2693 A1458 36c multicolored 5.00 4.00

No. 2693 is valid on all mail, but must be used on mail entries to Frisco on Faustao's Truck raffle.

Flowers A1459

No. 2694: a, Solanum lycocarpum. b, Cattleya walkeriana. c, Kielmeyera coriacea.

1998, Oct. 23 **Litho.** ***Perf. 11½***
2694 A1459 31c Strip of 3, #a.-c. 3.00 3.00

Humanitarians — A1460

No. 2695: a, Mother Teresa (1910-97). b, Friar Galvao (1739-1822). c, Herbert José de Souza "Betinho" (b. 1935). d, Friar Damiao (1898-1997).

1998, Oct. 25
2695 A1460 31c Block of 4, #a.-d. 4.00 4.00

Sergio Motta, Former Minister of Communications, Natl. Telecommunications Agency Headquarters, Brasilia — A1461

1998, Nov. 5 ***Perf. 12x11½***
2696 A1461 31c multicolored 1.40 .35

Christmas — A1462

1998, Nov. 19 ***Perf. 11½x12***
2697 A1462 22c multicolored 1.00 .30

Domestic Animals A1463

Designs: No. 2698, Moxotó goat. No. 2699, Brazilian donkey. No. 2700, Junqueira ox. No. 2701, Brazilian terrier. No. 2702, Brazilian shorthair cat.

1998, Nov. 20 ***Die Cut***

Booklet Stamps

Self-Adhesive

2698	A1463 22c multi		1.10	.60
2699	A1463 22c multi		1.10	.60
2700	A1463 22c multi		1.10	.60
2701	A1463 22c multi, vert.		1.10	.60
2702	A1463 22c multi, vert.		1.10	.60
a.	Bklt. pane, 2 ea #2698-2702		11.00	

No. 2702a is a complete booklet.

Universal Declaration of Human Rights, 50th Anniv. — A1464

1998, Dec. 9 ***Perf. 12x11½***

2703 A1464 1.20r multicolored 3.25 1.25

Natal, 400th Anniv. A1465

Perf. 11x11½, 11½x11

1999, Jan. 6 **Litho.**

2704	A1465 31c Wise Men's Fortress	1.25	.40
2705	A1465 31c Mother Luiza Lighthouse, vert.	1.25	.40

Program for Evaluating Resources in Brazil's Exclusive Economic Zone A1466

No. 2706: a, Satellite, St. Peter and St. Paul Archipelago. b, Bird on buoy. c, Fishing boat. d, Sea turtle. e, Dolphin. f, Diver.

1999, Mar. 5 ***Perf. 11½x12***

2706 A1466 31c Block of 6, #a.-f. 10.00 10.00

Australia '99 World Stamp Expo.

UPU, 125th Anniv. A1467

No. 2707: a, Stamp vending machines from 1940s and 1998. b, Vending machines, 1906, 1998. c, Collection boxes, 1870, 1973. d, Federal Government's 1998 Quality Award.

1999, Mar. 19 ***Perf. 11½***

2707 A1467 31c Block of 4, #a.-d. 3.50 3.50

Reorganization of Brazilian Posts and Telegraphs, 30th anniv.

City of Salvador, 450th Anniv. — A1468

1999, Mar. 29 Litho. ***Perf. 11½x12***

2708 A1468 1.05r multi 5.50 2.00

Dinosaurs' Valley A1469

1999, Apr. 17 Litho. ***Perf. 11½x12***

2709 A1469 1.05r multicolored 3.00 1.25

Fort of Santo Amaro da Barra Grande — A1470

1999, Apr. 21 Litho. ***Perf. 11½x12***

2710 A1470 22c multicolored 1.00 .25

Souvenir Sheet

Discovery of Brazil, 500th Anniv. (in 2000) — A1471

1999, Apr. 22 Litho. ***Perf. 11½x11***

2711 A1471 2.68r multi 7.00 7.00

Lubrapex 2000.

6th Air Transportation Squadron, 30th Anniv. — A1472

1999, May 12 Litho. ***Perf. 11x11½***

2712 A1472 51c multicolored 2.00 .50

Holy Spirit Feast, Planaltina — A1473

1999, May 21 ***Perf. 12x11½***

2713 A1473 22c multicolored .90 .25

Historical and Cultural Heritage A1474

No. 2714 — Views of cities: a, Ouro Preto. b, Olinda. c, Sao Luís.

1999, June 2 ***Perf. 11½x11***

2714 A1474 1.05r Sheet of 3, #a.-c. 7.50 7.50

PhilexFrance '99, World Philatelic Exhibition.

Sao Paolo State Institute for Technological Research, Cent. — A1475

1999, June 24 Litho. ***Perf. 11½x12***

2715 A1475 36c multicolored 1.10 .40

Flight of Alberto Santos-Dumont's Dirigible No. 3, Cent. — A1476

1999, July 20

2716 A1476 1.20r multicolored 4.00 1.75

Forest Fire Prevention A1477

No. 2717: a, Anteater. b, Flower. c, Leaf. d, Burnt trunk.

Serpentine Die Cut 6

1999, Aug. 1 **Litho.**

Self-Adhesive

2717	Block of 4	7.00	
a.-d.	A1477 51c Any single	1.75	.75

No. 2717 is printed on recycled paper impregnated with burnt wood odor.

Souvenir Sheet

America Issue, A New Millennium Without Arms — A1478

No. 2718: a, Hands of adult and child drawing dove. b, Overturned tank.

1999, Aug. 6 Litho. ***Perf. 12x11½***

2718 A1478 90c Sheet of 2, #a.-b. 4.75 4.75

Issued with rouletted tab at right showing Universal Product Code.

Political Amnesty, 20th Anniv. — A1479

1999, Aug. 18

2719 A1479 22c multicolored .75 .25

Famous Brazilians — A1480

Designs: 22c, Joaquim Nabuco (1849-1910), politician and diplomat. 31c, Ruy Barbosa (1849-1923), politician and justice for International Court.

1999, Aug. 19 Litho. ***Perf. 11½x12***

2720	A1480 22c multicolored	.80	.25
2721	A1480 31c multicolored	.80	.35

Fish — A1481

No. 2722: a, 22c, Salminus maxillosus. b, 31c, Brycon microlepsus. c, 36c, Acestrorhynchus pantaneiro. d, 51c, Hyphessobrycon eques. e, 80c, Rineloricaria. f, 90c, Leporinus macrocephalus. g, 1.05r, Abramites. h, 1.20r, Ancistrus.

1999, Aug. 20 Litho. ***Perf. 11½x12***

2722 A1481 Sheet of 8, #a.-h. 10.00 10.00

China 1999 World Philatelic Exhibition. No. 2722h has a holographic image. Soaking in water may affect hologram.

Mercosur Cultural Heritage Day A1482

1999, Sept. 17 Litho. ***Perf. 11½x12***

2723 A1482 80c multi 3.50 1.75

Water Resources — A1483

No. 2724: a, Ecological station, Aguas Emendadas. b, House on water's edge, boat. c, Cedro Dam. d, Orós Dam.

1999, Oct. 21
2724 A1483 31c Block of 4, #a.-d. 3.50 3.50

National Library of Rio de Janeiro Bookplate A1484

1999, Oct. 29 Litho. *Perf. 12x11½*
2725 A1484 22c multi .80 .25

State Flag Type of 1981

1999, Nov. 19 Litho. *Perf. 11½x12*
2726 A947 31c Amapá .70 .35
2727 A947 36c Roraima .70 .35

Antonio Carlos Jobim (1927-94), Composer A1485

1999, Nov. 22
2728 A1485 31c multi .85 .35

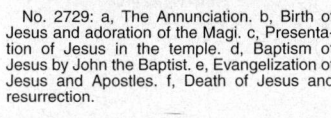

Christianity, 2000th Anniv. — A1486

No. 2729: a, The Annunciation. b, Birth of Jesus and adoration of the Magi. c, Presentation of Jesus in the temple. d, Baptism of Jesus by John the Baptist. e, Evangelization of Jesus and Apostles. f, Death of Jesus and resurrection.

1999, Nov. 26 Litho. *Perf. 11½*
2729 A1486 22c Block of 6, #a-f 7.50 7.50

New Middle School Education System — A1487

1999, Dec. 2 *Perf. 11x11½*
2730 A1487 31c multi .85 .35

Itamaraty Palace, Rio A1488

Litho. & Engr.

1999, Dec. 6 *Perf. 11½x12*
2731 A1488 1.05r pale yel & brn 3.00 1.25

New Year 2000 — A1489

2000, Jan. 1 Litho.
2732 A1489 90c multi 2.00 1.25

National School Book Program A1490

2000, Feb. 7 *Perf. 11x11½*
2733 A1490 31c multi .60 .35

Aviatrixes — A1491

No. 2734: a, Ada Rogato (1920-86). b, Thereza de Marzo (1903-86). c, Anésia Pinheiro (1904-99).

2000, Mar. 8 *Perf. 11½x12*
2734 A1491 22c Horiz. strip of 3, #a-c 1.40 1.40

Regional Cuisine — A1492

a, Moqueca Capixaba. b, Moqueca Baiana.

2000, Mar. 24
2735 A1492 1.05r Pair, #a-b 3.25 3.25

Gilberto Freyre (1900-87), Sociologist — A1493

2000, Mar. 24
2736 A1493 36c multi .55 .40

UIT Telecom A1494

2000, Apr. 9 Litho. *Perf. 11½*
2737 A1494 51c multi .85 .55

Discovery of Brazil, 500th anniv.

Discovery of Brazil, 500th Anniv. — A1495

No. 2738: a, Two sailors, three natives, parrot. b, Sailor, ships, four natives. c, Sailors, natives, sails. d, Sailor and natives inspecting tree.

2000, Apr. 11 Litho. *Perf. 11½x12*
2738 A1495 31c Block of 4, #a-d 2.75 2.75

See Portugal Nos. 2354-2357.

Discovery of Brazil, 500th Anniv. — A1496

2000, Apr. 11 Litho. *Perf. 11½*
2739 A1496 31c multi + label *17.00 17.00*

Printed in sheets of 9 stamps + 9 labels that could be personalized. Sheets sold for 5r.

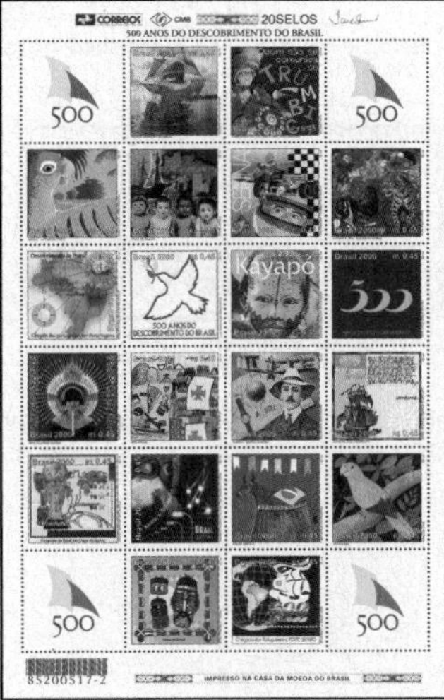

Discovery of Brazil, 500th Anniv. — A1497

No. 2740: a, Brazilian flag as sails of ship. b, Man with pineapple, telephone dial, horn. c, Parrot and ships. d, Ship, map of Brazil, children. e, Race car driver Ayrton Senna. f, Flora and fauna. g, Map of Brazil, compass roses. h, Dove. i, Native with decorated face. j, Stylized "500." k, Native with feathered headdress. l, Children's drawing. m, Aviator Alberto Santos Dumont. n, Ship, manuscript. o, World Cup trophies, soccer player and ball, map. p, Fiber optic cables, street lights. q, Bull with Brazilian flag. r, Parrot. s, Native masks. t, Ship, Brazil highlighted on globe.

2000, Apr. 22 Litho. *Perf. 11½*
2740 A1497 45c Sheet of 20, #a-t, + 4 labels 18.00 18.00

Brazil Trade Net Website, 2nd Anniv. A1498

2000, May 11 Litho. *Perf. 11½*
2741 A1498 27c multi .60 .30

National Coastal Management Program — A1499

2000, May 16 Litho. *Perf. 11½*
2742 A1499 40c multi .85 .40

Souvenir Sheet

Expo 2000, Hanover — A1500

No. 2743: a, Map of Western Brazil. b, Map of Eastern Brazil. c, Gold and gemstones.

2000, May 19 Litho. *Perf. 10¾x11*
2743 A1500 1.30r #a-c 6.75 6.75

Oswaldo Cruz Foundation, Cent. — A1501

2000, May 25 *Perf. 11½x12*
2744 A1501 40c multicolored .70 .40

Africa Day A1502

2000, May 25 *Perf. 11½*
2745 A1502 1.10r multi 2.50 1.50

Sailing Feats of Amyr Klink A1503

No. 2746: a, First crossing of South Atlantic by rowboat, 1984. b, Solo circumnavigation of Antarctica, 1999.

2000, May 27
2746 A1503 1r Vert. pair, #a-b 4.50 4.50

Juiz de Fora, 150th Anniv. — A1504

2000, May 31 ***Perf. 11½x12***
2747 A1504 60c multi .90 .60

Sports — A1505

Serpentine Die Cut 5¾
2000 **Photo.**
Self-Adhesive
2748 A1505 27c Hanggliding .90 .35
2749 A1505 27c Surfing .90 .35
2750 A1505 40c Mountain climbing .90 .50
2751 A1505 40c Skateboarding .90 .50
Nos. 2748-2751 (4) 3.60 1.70

Issued: Nos. 2748, 2750, 6/1; No. 2749, 8/1; No. 2751, 7/1.

Environmental Protection — A1506

No. 2752: a, Trees. b, Trees, Felis tigrina in background. c, Heads of two Felis tigrina, two white flowers. d, Felis tigrina, one white flower.

2000, June 5 ***Perf. 11½***
2752 A1506 40c Block of 4, #a-d 4.25 4.25

Ships — A1507

No. 2753: a, Cisne Branco. b, Brasil.

2000, June 11 Litho. ***Perf. 11x11½***
2753 A1507 27c Pair, #a-b 1.00 .60

Souvenir Sheets

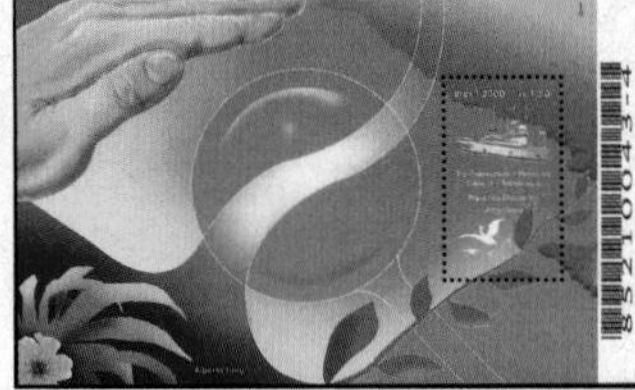
Military Presence in Amazonia — A1508

2000, June 11 Litho. ***Perf. 11½x11***
2754 A1508 1.50r multi 2.25 2.25

Barcode is separated from the sheet margin by a row of microperfs.

America Issue — A1509

No. 2755: a, Campaign against AIDS. b, Natl. anti-drug week.

2000, June 19 ***Perf. 12x11½***
2755 A1509 1.10r Sheet of 2, #a-b 3.25 3.25

Barcode is separated from the sheet margin by a row of microperfs.

Anísio Teixeira (1900-71), Educator — A1510

2000, July 12 Litho. ***Perf. 11½x12***
2756 A1510 45c multi .80 .55

Children's and Teenagers Statute, 10th Anniv. — A1511

2000, July 13 ***Perf. 12x11½***
2757 A1511 27c multi .60 .35

Natl. Movement of Street Boys and Girls, 15th Anniv. — A1512

2000, July 13
2758 A1512 40c multi .90 .50

Gustavo Capanema (1900-54), Politician — A1513

2000, Aug. 10 Litho. ***Perf. 11½x12***
2759 A1513 60c multi 1.25 .75

Milton Campos, Politician — A1514

2000, Aug. 16
2760 A1514 1r multi 2.50 1.10

World Ozone Layer Protection Day — A1515

2000, Sept. 16 ***Perf. 12x11½***
2761 A1515 1.45r multi 3.50 2.00

Fruit — A1516

Serpentine Die Cut 5¾
2000, Sept. 21 **Litho.**
Self-Adhesive
2762 A1516 27c Cupuacu .50 .30
2763 A1516 40c Soursop .75 .45

2000 Summer Olympics, Sydney — A1517

No. 2764: a, Pommel horse. b, Weight lifting. c, Discus. d, Men's rings. e, Sprinting. f, Javelin. g, Rhythmic gymnastics. h, Field hockey. i, Volleyball. j, Synchronized swimming. k, Judo. l, Wrestling. m, Cycling. n, Rowing. o, Parallel bars. p, Equestrian. q, Pole vault. r, Fencing. s, Shooting. t, Taekwondo.

No. 2765: a, Archery. b, Beach volleyball. c, Boxing. d, Soccer. e, Canoeing. f, Handball. g, Diving. h, Rhythmic gymnastics. i, Badminton. j, Swimming. k, Hurdles. l, Pentathlon. m, Basketball. n, Tennis. o, Marathon. p, High jump. q, Long jump. r, Triple jump. s, Triathlon. t, Yachting.

2000, Sept. 23 Litho. ***Perf. 11½x12***
2764 Sheet of 20 + 4 labels 15.00 15.00
a.-t. A1517 40c Any single .70 .70
2765 Sheet of 20 + 4 labels 15.00 15.00
a.-t. A1517 40c Any single .70 .70

Organ Donation and Transplantation — A1519

No. 2766: a, Doctor holding heart. b, Heart, hands, body with organs outlined.

2000, Sept. 27
2766 A1519 1.50r Horiz. pair, #a-b 4.00 4.00

Masks and Puppets A1520

Designs: No. 2767, 27c, Chinese puppet. No. 2768, 27c, Brazilian mask.

2000, Oct. 9
2767-2768 A1520 Set of 2 .90 .60

Brazil-People's Republic of China diplomatic relations, 25th anniv. See People's Republic of China Nos. 3053-3054.

Race Car Drivers A1521

Designs: 1.30r, Francisco "Chico" Landi (1907-89). 1.45r, Ayrton Senna (1960-94).

2000, Oct. 12 ***Perf. 11x11½***
2769-2770 A1521 Set of 2 4.00 4.00

Telecourse 2000 Project A1522

2000, Oct. 13 Litho. ***Perf. 11½x12***
2771 A1522 27c multi .60 .30

Airplanes A1523

No. 2772: a, EMB 145 AEW. b, Super Tucano. c, AMX-T. d, ERJ 135. e, ERJ 170. f, ERJ 145. g, ERJ 190. h, EMB 145 RS/MP. i, ERJ 140. j, EMB 120.

2000, Oct. 23 Litho. ***Die Cut***
Self-Adhesive
2772 Pane of 10 7.50
a.-j. A1523 27c Any single .75 .30

Christmas — A1524

No. 2773: a, Hand of Jesus, star of Bethlehem. b, Mary, baby Jesus. c, Hand of Jesus, fish, boats on Sea of Galilee. d, Jesus, Sea of Galilee. e, Hand of Jesus, mountain, trees, Earth. f, Jesus, Earth.

2000, Nov. 23 ***Perf. 11½***

2773 Block of 6 4.00 4.00
a.-f. A1524 27c Any single .65 .40

Light and Sound Project — A1525

2000, Dec. 2 ***Perf. 12x11½***

2774 A1525 1.30r multi 2.25 1.50

Settlement of Brazil-French Guiana Border Dispute, Cent. — A1526

2000, Dec. 12 ***Perf. 11½x12***

2775 A1526 40c multi .65 .45

Advent of New Millennium — A1527

Designs: Nos. 2776, 2779a, 40c, Chalice and eucharist. Nos. 2777, 2779b, 1.30r, Star of David, menorah, Torah, tablets. Nos. 2778, 2779c, 1.30r, Minaret, dome of mosque, Holy Ka'aba.

2001, Jan. 1 ***Perf. 11x11½***

2776-2778 A1527 Set of 3 7.00 7.00

Souvenir Sheet

2779 A1527 Sheet of 3, #a-c 5.00 5.00

Nos. 2779a-2779c lack white border. On No. 2779, barcode is separated from sheet margin by a row of rouletting.

Pan-American Scout Jamboree, Foz do Iguaçu — A1528

No. 2780: a, Flags, map, emblems. b, Scouts in canoe, waterfall.

2001, Jan. 7 ***Perf. 12x11½***

2780 A1528 1.10r Horiz. pair, #a-b 2.75 2.75

New Year 2001 (Year of the Snake) — A1529

Litho. & Embossed

2001, Jan. 24 ***Perf. 11½***

2781 A1529 1.45r multi 2.00 2.00

Hong Kong 2001 Stamp Exhibition.

Venomous Animals A1530

No. 2782: a, Dirphya sp. b, Megalopyge sp. c, Phoneutria sp. d, Tityus bahiensis. e, Crotalus durissus. f, Micrurus corallinus. g, Lachesis muta. h, Bothrops jararaca.

2001, Feb. 23 Litho. ***Perf. 11½x12***

2782 Sheet of 8 4.50 4.50
a.-h A1530 40c Any single .55 .40

Butantan Institute, cent.

Brazilian Publishing Industry — A1531

2001, Mar. 5 ***Perf. 11x11½***

2783 A1531 27c multi .45 .30

Special Exports Program — A1532

2001, Mar. 5 ***Perf. 11½x12***

2784 A1532 1.30r multi 1.50 1.50

National Library, 190th Anniv. — A1533

Litho. & Engr.

2001, Mar. 26 ***Perf. 11½x12***

2785 A1533 27c multi .40 .25

Council for Scientific and Technical Development — A1534

2001, Apr. 17

2786 A1534 40c blue .50 .50

Soccer Teams — A1535

Designs: No. 2787, Regatas Vasco da Gama. No. 2788, Palmeiras. No. 2789, Gremio. No. 2790, Sao Paolo. No. 2791, Santos. No. 2792, Regatas do Flamengo.

2001 Litho. ***Perf. 12x11½***

2787	A1535	70c multi	.90	.90
2788	A1535	70c multi	.90	.90
2789	A1535	70c multi	.90	.90
2790	A1535	70c multi	.90	.90
2791	A1535	1r multi	1.10	1.10
2792	A1535	1r multi	1.10	1.10
	Nos. 2787-2792 (6)		5.80	5.80

Numbers have been reserved for additional stamps in this set. Numbers may change.

Issued: No. 2787, 8/21; No. 2788, 8/26; No. 2789, 9/10; No. 2790, 12/16; No. 2791, 4/20. No. 2792, 11/28.

Intl. Culture of Peace Year — A1536

2001, May 3 Litho. ***Perf. 12x11½***

2794 A1536 1.10r multi 1.40 .95

Murilo Mendes (1901-75), Poet — A1537

2001, May 13 ***Perf. 11x11½***

2795 A1537 40c multi .60 .35

Minas Commercial Association, Cent. A1538

2001, May 16 ***Perf. 11½***

2796 A1538 40c multi .60 .35

World Tobacco-free Day — A1539

2001, May 31 ***Perf. 12x11½***

2797 A1539 40c multi .60 .35

José Lins do Rego (1901-87), Writer — A1540

2001, May 31 ***Perf. 11x11½***

2798 A1540 60c multi .70 .50

Souvenir Sheet

Worldwide Fund for Nature (WWF) — A1541

Parrots: a, Anodorhynchus hyacinthinus. b, Aratinga solstitialis auricapilla. c, Pyrrhura cruentata. d, Amazona xanthops.

2001, June 3 ***Perf. 11½***

2799 A1541 1.30r Sheet of 4, #a-d 6.50 6.50

Barbosa Lima Sobrinho (1897-2000), Journalist A1542

2001, June 6

2800 A1542 40c multi .60 .35

Beaches A1543

No. 2801: a, Jericoacoara. b, Ponta Negra. c, Rosa.

2001, June 13 ***Perf. 11x11½***

2801 Horiz. strip of 3 2.40 2.40
a.-c. A1543 40c Any single .70 .50

Issued in sheets of 25 stamps containing 10 each of Nos. 2801a-2801b and 5 of No. 2801c.

Souvenir Sheet

Automobiles — A1544

No. 2802: a, 1959 Romi Isetta. b, 1965 DKW Vemag. c, 1962 Renault Gordini. d, 1959 Volkswagen 1200. e, 1964 Simca Chambord. f, 1961 Aero-Willys.

2001, June 16 ***Perf. 11½x12***

2802 A1544 1.10r Sheet of 6, #a-f 7.25 7.25

Bernardo Sayao (1901-59), Politician A1545

2001, June 18 ***Perf. 11½***

2803 A1545 60c multi 1.10 .50

Eleazar de Carvalho (1912-96), Composer A1546

2001, July 1

2804 A1546 45c multi .75 .35

Souvenir Sheet

Third French Tennis Open Victory of Gustavo Kuerten — A1547

2001, July 10

2805 A1547 1.30r multi 2.25 2.25

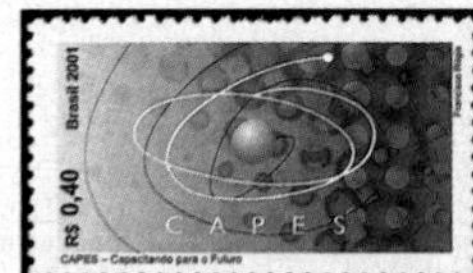

Academic Qualifications Coordinating Institution, 50th Anniv. — A1548

2001, July 11 ***Perf. 11x11½***

2806 A1548 40c multi .70 .35

Pedro Aleixo, Politician, Cent. of Birth A1549

2001, Aug. 1 ***Perf. 11½***

2807 A1549 55c multi 1.00 .50

Solidarity Community Programs — A1550

No. 2808: a, Map on man. b, Man on map.

2001, Aug. 25

2808 A1550 55c Horiz. pair, #a-b 1.60 1.60

World Conference Against Racism, Durban, South Africa — A1551

2001, Aug. 30 ***Perf. 12x11½***

2809 A1551 1.30r multi 1.60 1.10

See South Africa Nos. 1261-1262.

Musical Instruments A1552

Designs: 1c, Drum (Tambourin). 5c, Saxophone. 10c, Ukulele. 40c, Flute. 50c, Rebec. 55c, Guitar. 60c, Drum. 70c, Guitar (viola caipira). 1r, Trombone.

2001 **Litho.** ***Serpentine Die Cut 5¾***

Self-Adhesive

2810	A1552	1c multi	.40	.25
2811	A1552	5c multi	.40	.25
2812	A1552	10c multi	.40	.25
2813	A1552	40c multi	.50	.30
2814	A1552	50c multi	.60	.35
2815	A1552	55c multi	.80	.45
2816	A1552	60c multi	.80	.45
2817	A1552	70c multi	1.25	.60
2818	A1552	1r multi	1.90	.75
	Nos. 2810-2818 (9)		7.05	3.65

Booklet Stamp

Self-Adhesive

Die Cut

2818A A1552 40c multi — —

b. Booklet pane of 5 —

Issued: Nos. 2810-2818, 9/20. No. 2818A, 10/15.

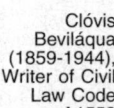

Clóvis Beviláqua (1859-1944), Writer of Civil Law Code A1553

2001, Oct. 4 **Litho.** ***Perf. 11½***

2819 A1553 55c multi .90 .50

Year of Dialogue Among Civilizations A1554

2001, Oct. 9 ***Perf. 12x11½***

2820 A1554 1.30r multi 1.75 1.10

Souvenir Sheet

Commercial Aircraft — A1555

No. 2821: a, Junkers F-13. b, Douglas C-47. c, Dornier Wal. d, Lockheed Constellation. e, Convair 340. f, Caravelle.

2001, Oct. 23 **Litho.** ***Perf. 11½x12***

2821 A1555 55c Sheet of 6, #a-f 4.75 4.75

Barcode is separated from sheet margin by a row of rouletting.

Cecília Meireles (1901-64), Poet — A1556

2001, Nov. 7 **Litho.** ***Perf. 11x11½***

2822 A1556 55c multi .90 .50

America Issue - Bom Jesus de Matosinhos Sanctuary, UNESCO World Heritage Site — A1557

2001, Nov. 9 ***Perf. 11½x12***

2823 A1557 1.30r multi 1.40 1.00

Madalena Caramuru, First Literate Woman in Brazil A1558

2001, Nov. 14

2824 A1558 55c multi .90 .50

National Day of Black Consciousness — A1559

2001, Nov. 20

2825 A1559 40c multi .70 .35

Pantanal Flora A1560

No. 2826: a, Caiman crocodilus yacare, Plataleia ajaja. b, Anhinga anhinga. c, Ardea cocoi. d, Jabiru mycteria. e, Pseudoplatystoma fasciatum. f, Leporinus macrocephalus. g, Hydrochoerus hydrochoeris. h, Nasua nasua, Casmerodius albus. i, Eichornia crassipes. j, Porphyrula martinica.

2001, Nov. 20 ***Die Cut Perf. 6¼***

Self-Adhesive

2826 Booklet of 10 7.50

a.-j. A1560 55c Any single .70 .50

See No. 2832.

Christmas A1561

2001, Nov. 23 ***Perf. 11½x12***

2827 A1561 40c multi .70 .35

Souvenir Sheet

Minerals — A1562

No. 2828: a, Topaz jewelry. b, Garnet ring.

2001, Nov. 30 ***Perf. 12x11½***

2828 A1562 1.30r Sheet of 2, #a-b 3.50 3.50

Intl. Day of Disabled Persons — A1563

2001, Dec. 3 ***Perf. 11½***

2829 A1563 1.45r multi 1.75 1.75

Coffee A1564

2001, Dec. 7 ***Perf. 11½x12***
2830 A1564 1.30r multi 1.75 1.25

No. 2830 is impregnated with a coffee scent.

Merchant Ships — A1565

No. 2831: a, Copacabana. b, Flamengo.

2001, Dec. 13 ***Perf. 11x11½***
2831 A1565 55c Horiz. pair, #a-b 1.75 1.75

Pantanal Flora Type of 2001 With "MERCOSUR" Inscription Added

2001, Dec. 21 ***Perf. 11½x12***
2832 A1560 1r Eichornia crassipes 1.00 .85

Kahal Zur Israel, First Synagogue in the Americas A1566

2001, Oct. 21 **Litho.** ***Perf. 11½x12***
2833 A1566 1.30r multi 1.75 1.10

New Year 2002 (Year of the Horse) — A1567

Litho. With Foil Application

2002, Jan. 25 ***Perf. 11½***
2834 A1567 1.45r multi 1.75 1.25

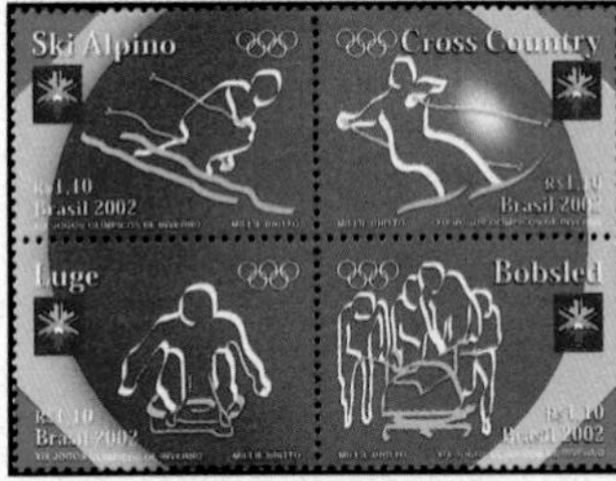

2002 Winter Olympics, Salt Lake City — A1568

No. 2835: a, Alpine skiing. b, Cross-country skiing. c, Luge. d, Bobsled.

2002, Feb. 4 **Litho.** ***Perf. 11½x12***
2835 A1568 1.10r Block of 4, #a-d 5.25 5.25

Lucio Costa (1902-98), Architect A1569

2002, Feb. 27
2836 A1569 55c multi .70 .50

Intl. Women's Day — A1570

2002, Mar. 8 ***Perf. 11½***
2837 A1570 40c multi .70 .35

Sao José do Rio Preto, 150th Anniv. A1571

2002, Mar. 19 ***Perf. 11½x12***
2838 A1571 40c multi .70 .35

Pres. Juscelino Kubitschek (1902-76) — A1572

2002, Apr. 21 **Litho.**
2839 A1572 55c multi .60 .45

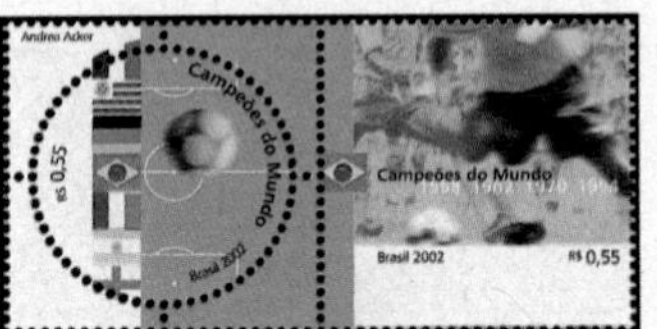

2002 World Cup Soccer Championships, Japan and Korea — A1573

No. 2840: a, Flags, soccer ball, and field (28mm diameter). b, Soccer players, years of Brazilian championships.

2002, Apr. 22 **Photo.** ***Perf. 13¾***
2840 A1573 55c Horiz. pair, #a-b 1.50 1.50

See Argentina No. 2184, France No. 2891, Germany No. 2163, Italy No. 2526, and Uruguay No. 1946.

Progress in Brazilian Education — A1574

No. 2841: a, Children in classroom, globe, letters "a-d." b, Computer, globe, letters "e-h."

2002, Apr. 28 **Litho.** ***Perf. 11½x12***
2841 A1574 40c Horiz. pair, #a-b 1.50 .70

St. Josemaría Escrivá de Balaguer (1902-75) — A1575

2002, May 1
2842 A1575 55c multi .60 .45

Souvenir Sheet

Brazilian Air Force's Esquadrilha da Fumaça Aerobatics Team — A1576

No. 2843: a, T-6 North American. b, T-24 Super Fouga Magister. c, T-25 Universal. d, Two T-27 Tucanos, one flying upside-down. e, T-27 Tucanos, heart-shaped smoke design. f, Blue, green and yellow T-27 Tucano.

2002, May 17
2843 A1576 55c Sheet of 6, #a-f 4.25 4.25

Barcode is separated from sheet margin by a row of rouletting.

Children's Cavalhadinha of Pirenópolis — A1577

No. 2844: a, Procession of virgins and stick-pony riders. b, Stick-pony combat. c, Children wearing masks. d, Musicians and vendor.

2002, May 19 ***Perf. 11x11½***
2844 A1577 40c Block of 4, #a-d 3.00 3.00

Couroupita Guianensis — A1578

Serpentine Die Cut 12¾x13

2002, May 20 **Photo.**

Coil Stamp

Self-Adhesive

2845 A1578 55c multi .70 .45

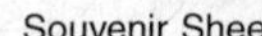
Souvenir Sheet

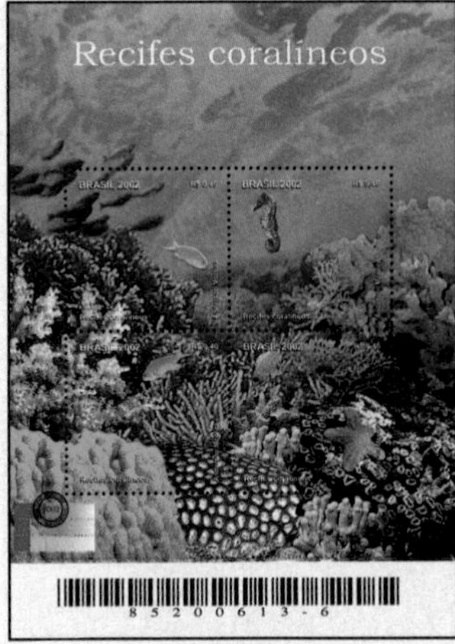

Coral Reefs — A1579

No. 2846 — Coral and: a, Orange fish, school of fish. b, Seahorse. c, Orange fish. d, Orange fish, starfish.

2002, June 5 ***Perf. 11½***
2846 A1579 40c Sheet of 4, #a-d 2.75 2.75

Philakorea 2002 World Stamp Exhibition, Seoul. Barcode is separated from sheet margin by a row of rouletting.

Charity Hospital of Curitiba, 150th Anniv. A1580

2002, June 9 **Litho.** ***Perf. 11x11½***
2847 A1580 70c multi .90 .50

Brazil's Fifth World Cup Soccer Championship A1581

2002, July 2 **Litho.** ***Perf. 12x11½***
2848 A1581 55c multi 1.00 .50

Souvenir Sheet

Preservation of Caatinga Nordestina — A1582

2002, July 14 **Litho.** ***Perf. 10¾x11***
2849 A1582 1.10r multi 2.40 2.40

Fluminense Soccer Team, Cent. — A1583

2002, July 17 Litho. *Perf. 12x11½*
2850 A1583 55c multi .75 .40

Souvenir Sheet

Alberto Santos-Dumont's House, Encantada — A1584

No. 2851: a, House. b, Santos-Dumont and stairway.

2002, July 19 Litho. *Perf. 11¾*
2851 A1584 1r Sheet of 2, #a-b 2.50 2.50

System for the Vigilance of the Amazon Project — A1585

2002, July 27 *Perf. 11½x12*
2852 A1585 1.10r multi 1.40 .75

Jorge Amado (1912-2001), Writer — A1586

2002, Aug. 5 *Perf. 11x11½*
2853 A1586 40c multi .50 .30

Plácido de Castro and Rio Branco Palace A1587

2002, Aug. 6 Litho. *Perf. 11½x12*
2854 A1587 50c multi .50 .35

Acre Revolution, cent.

Souvenir Sheet

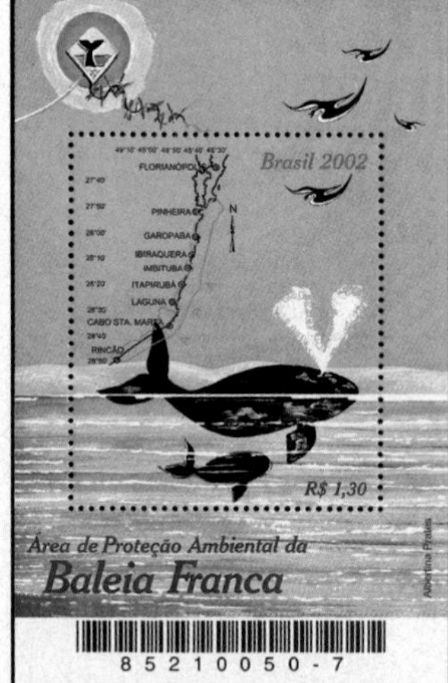

Protected Area for Whales — A1588

2002, Sept. 14 Litho. *Perf. 12x11½*
2855 A1588 1.30r multi 2.75 2.75

Confluence of Rio Solimoes and Rio Negro A1589

2002, Sept. 27 *Perf. 11½*
2856 A1589 45c multi .60 .25

Adhemar Ferreira da Silva (1927-2001), 1952 and 1956 Olympic Triple Jump Gold Medalist — A1590

2002, Sept. 28 *Perf. 11x11½*
2857 A1590 40c multi .60 .25

Motorcycles — A1591

No. 2858: a, YZF-R1. b, CG125 Titan. c, GSX-R1000. d, Daytona 955i Centennial Edition. e, BMW R32 and BMW R 1200 C. f, V-ROD.

2002, Sept. 29 Litho. *Perf. 11½x12*
2858 A1591 60c Sheet of 6, #a-f 4.50 4.50

Locomotives — A1592

No. 2859, Zezé Leoni. 2860, Baroneza.

2002, Sept. 30
2859 55c multicolored .80 .80
2859A 55c multicolored .80 .80
a. Pair, #2859-2859A 2.50 2.50

Tourism in Bonito A1593

2002, Oct. 2 Litho. *Perf. 11½x12*
2860 A1593 1r multi 1.40 .55

Carlos Drummond de Andrade (1902-87), Writer — A1594

2002, Oct. 25 *Perf. 11x11½*
2861 A1594 55c multi .70 .30

America Issue - Youth, Education and Literacy — A1595

2002, Nov. 14 Litho. *Perf. 11½x12*
2862 A1595 1.30r multi 1.60 .95

National Archives — A1596

2002, Nov. 20
2863 A1596 40c multi .70 .30

Sergio Motta Cultural Center A1597

2002, Nov. 24
2864 A1597 45c multi .65 .30

Christmas A1598

2002, Nov. 29
2865 A1598 45c multi .65 .30

Social Security in Brazil, 80th Anniv. A1599

2002, Dec. 3
2866 A1599 45c multi .65 .30

Ethnographic Paintings of Albert Eckhout — A1600

No. 2867: a, Group of natives. b, Woman with basket of flowers. c, Native man with headdress and spears. d, Man with bow and arrows. e, Man with spears. f, Woman with child and basket. g, Woman with headdress and child. h, Man with gun.

2002, Dec. 3 *Perf. 11½*
2867 A1600 45c Block of 8, #a-h 4.75 4.75

Brazil — Iran Diplomatic Relations, Cent. A1601

Flags of Brazil and Iran, and pottery and rug from: No. 2868, 60c, Brazil. No. 2869, 60c, Iran.

2002, Dec. 15 *Perf. 11½x12*
2868-2869 A1601 Set of 2 1.25 .80

See Iran No. 2844.

Musical Instruments — A1602

Designs: 1c, Drum (Atabaque). 5c, Snare drum (Caixa clara). 10c, Trumpet. 20c, Clarinet. 45c, Mandolin (Bandolim). 50c, Tambourine (Pandeiro). 60c, Accordion. 70c, Maraca (Cholcalho). 80c, Xylophone. 1r, Berimbau.

Serpentine Die Cut 5¾

2002-05 Photo.

Self-Adhesive

2869A A1602 1c multi .25 .25
2870 A1602 5c multi .25 .25
2871 A1602 10c multi .25 .25
2872 A1602 20c multi .25 .25
2873 A1602 45c multi .35 .25

2874	A1602	50c multi	.50	.30
2875	A1602	60c multi	.55	.35
2876	A1602	70c multi	.60	.40
2877	A1602	80c multi	.80	.45
2877A	A1602	1r multi	1.10	.55

Die Cut Perf. 12x12¼

2877B	A1602	1c Like #2869A	—	
2877C	A1602	5c like #2870	—	—
2877D	A1602	10c like #2871	.35	.35
2877K	A1602	1r like #2877A	—	—
		Nos. 2869A-2877K (14)	5.25	3.65

Issued: Nos. 2869A-2877A, 2002; Nos. 2877B-2877D, 2877K, 5/2005.

One additional value exists in this set. The editors would like to examine any examples.

Rotary Intl. in Brazil, 80th Anniv. — A1603

2003, Feb. 26 Litho. ***Perf. 12x11½***
2878 A1603 60c multi .70 .35

Waterfalls A1604

Waterfalls: No. 2879, 45c, Itiquira. No. 2880, 45c, Rio Preto.

2003, Mar. 22
2879-2880 A1604 Set of 2 1.00 .60

Souvenir Sheet

Coffee Plantations — A1605

No. 2881: a, Pau d'Alho. b, Ponte Alta.

2003, Apr. 15 ***Perf. 11½***
2881 A1605 1r Sheet of 2, #a-b 2.10 2.10

Independence of East Timor — A1606

2003, May 20 ***Perf. 11½x12***
2882 A1606 1.45r multi 1.40 1.10

America Issue — Medicinal Plants — A1607

No. 2883: a, Macrosiphonia velame. b, Lychnophora ericoides. c, Lafoensia pacari. d, Tabebuia impetiginosa. e, Xylopia aromatica. f, Himatanthus obovatus.

2003, June 2 ***Perf. 11½***
2883 A1607 60c Sheet of 6, #a-f 3.50 3.50

Art Made From Recycled Material — A1608

No. 2884: a, Glass bottles. b, Paper. c, Plastic. d, Metal.

2003, June 5
2884 A1608 60c Block of 4, #a-d 2.50 2.50

Santo Inácio College, Cent. A1609

2003, July 1 ***Perf. 11½x12***
2885 A1609 60c multi .75 .45

Pluft, the Ghost, and Maribel A1610

2003, July 12
2886 A1610 80c multi .90 .55

Ceará State, 400th Anniv. A1611

2003, July 15
2887 A1611 70c multi .85 .50

Souvenir Sheet

Stamp Collecting — A1612

No. 2888: a, Collector's album, Brazil #2 in tongs. b, Portugal #2 in tongs.

2003, Aug. 1 ***Perf. 11½***
2888 A1612 1.30r Sheet of 2, #a-b 2.75 2.75

First Portuguese stamp, 150th anniv., Lubrapex 2003 Philatelic Exhibition.

Souvenir Sheet

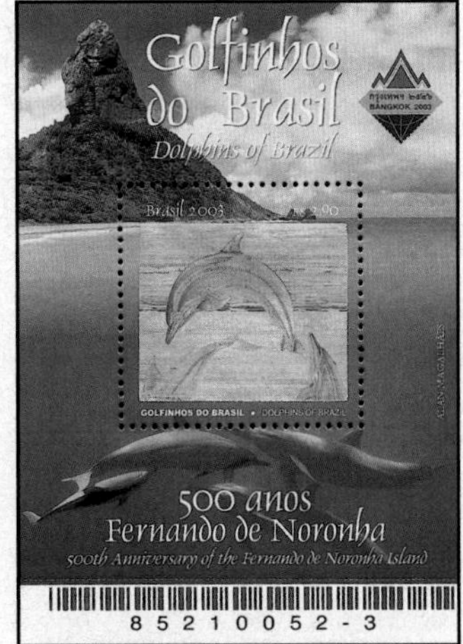

Dolphins — A1613

Litho. with Hologram Applied

2003, Aug. 10 ***Perf. 11½***
2889 A1613 2.90r multi 3.00 3.00

Bangkok 2003 Intl. Philatelic Exhibition.

Barnabite Order in Brazil, Cent. A1614

2003, Aug. 22 Litho. ***Perf. 11½x12***
2890 A1614 45c multi .45 .35

Luis Alves de Lima y Silva, Duque de Caxias (1803-80), Soldier and Politician A1615

2003, Aug. 25
2891 A1615 60c multi .75 .45

Self-Portrait, by Candido Portinari (1903-62) A1616

2003, Sept. 4 Litho. ***Perf. 12x11½***
2892 A1616 80c multi .90 .55

Courtesy on Mass Transit — A1617

Designs: No. 2893, "No Drinking." No. 2894, "Be Peaceful" (dove in triangle).

Serpentine Die Cut 5¾

2003, Sept. 5 Photo.

Self-Adhesive

2893 A1617 (50c) multi .50 .50
2894 A1617 (74c) multi .70 .70

Grémio Soccer Team, Cent. — A1618

2003, Sept. 18 Litho. ***Perf. 12x11½***
2895 A1618 60c multi .55 .45
a. Sheet of 12 + 12 labels 15.00 15.00

No. 2895a sold for 21r. Labels could be personalized.

Antonina - Morretes Railway A1619

2003, Sept. 30 Litho. ***Perf. 11½***
2896 A1619 74c multi .90 .90

Children's Games — A1620

No. 2897: a, Kite flying (Pipa). b, Cricket (Bete). c, Rope jumping (Pula corda). d, Hula hoop (Bambolê).

2003, Oct. 4
2897 A1620 50c Block of 4, #a-d 2.25 2.25

Program Against Hunger A1621

2003, Oct. 9 *Perf. 11½x12*

2898 A1621 50c multi .70 .70

Souvenir Sheet

Export Products — A1622

2003, Oct. 29 *Perf. 11½*

2899 A1622 1.30r multi 1.25 1.25

Christmas — A1623

Frame color: No. 2900, 50c, Green. No. 2901, 50c, Gold.

2003, Oct. 31 *Die Cut Perf. 12*

Self-Adhesive

2900-2901 A1623 Set of 2 1.00 1.00

Marcantonio Vilaça Cultural Space — A1624

2003, Nov. 5 Litho. *Perf. 11½x12*

2902 A1624 74c multi .75 .75

Ary Barroso (1903-64), Songwriter, Television Personality — A1625

2003, Nov. 7

2903 A1625 1.50r multi 1.25 1.25

Congress, 180th Anniv. A1626

2003, Nov. 13

2904 A1626 74c multi .75 .75

Brazil — Lebanon Diplomatic and Cultural Relations A1627

2003, Nov. 21 Litho. *Perf. 12x11½*

2905 A1627 1.75r multi 1.40 1.40

Fight Against AIDS A1628

2003, Dec. 1 Litho. *Perf. 11*

2906 A1628 74c multi 1.00 1.00

Values are for stamps with surrounding selvage.

Paragliding A1629

2003, Dec. 6 *Perf. 11½x12*

2907 A1629 75c multi .75 .75

Capistrano de Abreu (1853-1927), Ethnographer — A1630

2003, Dec. 9

2908 A1630 50c multi .50 .50

Fernando Henrique Cardoso, President from 1995-2002 A1631

2003, Dec. 20 *Perf. 11½*

2909 A1631 74c multi .65 .65

Paintings by Candido Portinari — A1632

Designs: 74c, Boy from Brodowski. 75c, Cowboy.

2003 Litho. *Die Cut Perf. 12x12¼*

Self-Adhesive

2910 A1632 74c black .60 .60
2911 A1632 75c black .65 .65

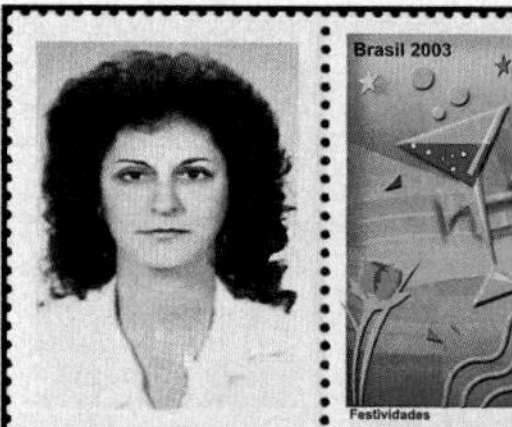

Festivals — A1633

Cats — A1634

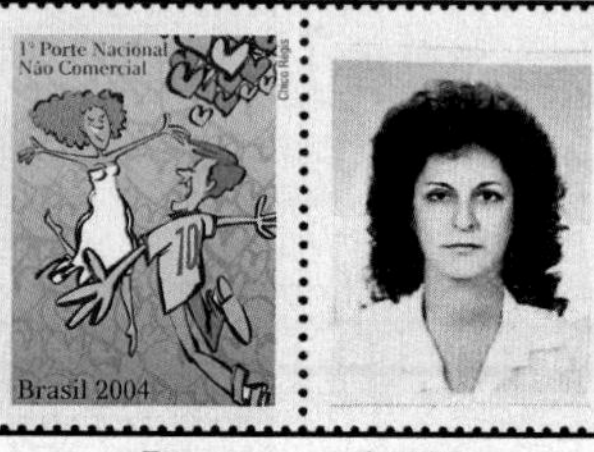

Romance — A1635

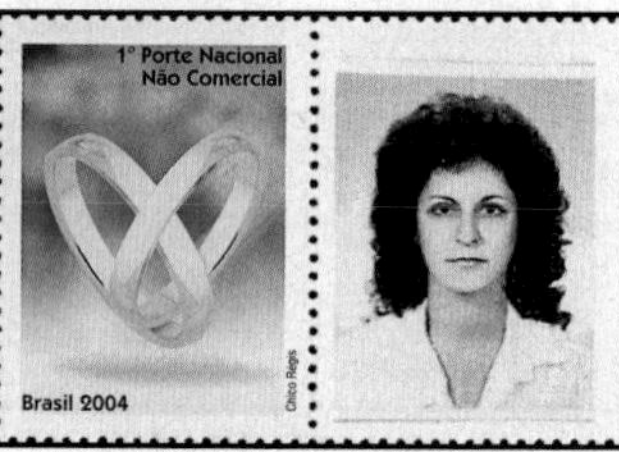

Wedding Rings — A1636

Mata Atlantica — A1637

2003-04 Litho. *Perf. 12x11½*

2912 A1633 45c multi + label 2.00 2.00
2913 A1634 (50c) multi + label 2.00 2.00
2914 A1635 (50c) multi + label 2.00 2.00
2915 A1636 (50c) multi + label 2.00 2.00
2916 A1637 60c multi + label 2.00 2.00
Nos. 2912-2916 (5) 10.00 10.00

Issued: Nos. 2912, 2916, 2003; Nos. 2913-2915, 2004. Nos. 2912-2916 each were printed in sheets of 12 stamps + 12 labels that could be personalized. Each sheet sold for 21r.

Souvenir Sheet

Sao Miguel Arcanjo Chapel, Sao Paolo — A1638

2004, Jan. 17 Litho. *Perf. 12x11½*

2917 A1638 1.50r multi 1.50 1.50

Sao Paolo, 450th Anniv. — A1639

No. 2918: a, Faces. b, Buildings, road. c, Buildings, trees. d, "450."

2004, Jan. 23 *Perf. 11½x12*

2918 Block of 4 3.00 3.00
a.-d. A1639 74c Any single .75 .50

Vicente Scherer (1903-96), Monk, Educator A1640

2004, Feb. 5

2919 A1640 50c multi .65 .65

Bairro da Lapa — A1641

2004, Feb. 19 *Perf. 12x11½*

2920 A1641 75c multi .75 .75

Eudocimus Ruber A1642

2004, Feb. 20 *Perf. 11½x12*

2921 A1642 74c multi 3.50 *3.50*
2921a Sheet of 12 + 12 labels 100.00 *100.00*

No. 2921a sold for 21r. Labels could be personalized.

Potable Water — A1643

2004, Mar. 22 *Perf. 12x11½*

2922 A1643 1.20r multi 1.10 1.10

Orlando Villas Bôas (1914-2002), Advocate of Indian Rights — A1644

2004, Apr. 19

2923 A1644 74c multi .90 .90

FIFA (Fédération Internationale de Football Association), Cent. A1645

2004, May 21 *Perf. 11½*
2924 A1645 1.60r multi 1.60 1.40

92nd Intl. Labor Organization Conference — A1646

2004, June 1 *Perf. 11½x12*
2925 A1646 50c multi .50 .50

Preservation of Mangrove Swamps and Tidal Zones — A1647

No. 2926: a, Ajaja ajaja. b, Pitangus sulphuratus. c, Chasmagnathus granulata. d, Aramides mangle. e, Goniopsis cruentata.

2004, June 5
2926 A1647 1.60r Sheet of 5, #a-e 7.50 7.50

2004 Summer Olympics, Athens — A1648

No. 2927: a, Torch bearer, Rio de Janeiro. b, 2004 Athens Olympics emblem. c, Sailing. d, Track and field.

2004, June 12 *Perf. 11½*
2927 A1648 1.60r Block of 4, #a-d 6.00 6.00

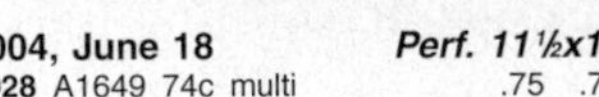

Bonfim Basilica, 250th Anniv. A1649

2004, June 18 *Perf. 11½x12*
2928 A1649 74c multi .75 .75

Folk Festivals — A1650

No. 2929: a, Caprichoso. b, Garantido.

2004, June 28
2929 A1650 74c Horiz. pair, #a-b 1.50 1.50

Brazilian Inventions A1651

Designs: No. 2930, 50c, Telephone card. No. 2931, 50c, Artificial heart valve. No. 2932, 50c, Caller identification system for telephones.

2004, July 15 *Perf. 11½*
2930-2932 A1651 Set of 3 1.25 1.25

Nos. 2930-2932 were printed in sheets containing eight of each stamp.

CBERS-2 Satellite A1652

2004, Aug. 9 **Litho.** *Perf. 11½x12*
2933 A1652 1.75r multi 1.40 1.40

Masonic Traditions — A1653

No. 2934 — Masonic emblem and: a, Pillars. b, Mason with hammer and chisel. c, Book, ladder and symbols. d, Tools.

2004, Aug. 20 **Litho.** *Perf. 11½*
2934 A1653 50c Block of 4, #a-d 1.90 1.90

Paintings by Candido Portinari — A1654

Designs: 55c, Negrinha. 80c, Duas Crianças. 95c, Seated Child with Sheep. 1.15r, Group of Women and Child. 1.50r, Marcel Gontrau.

2004, May 26 *Die Cut Perf. 12x12¼*
Self-Adhesive

2935 A1654 55c multi .40 .40
2936 A1654 80c multi .55 .55
2937 A1654 95c multi .70 .70
2938 A1654 1.15r black .85 .85
2939 A1654 1.50r multi 1.10 1.10
a. Die cut perf. 12x12¼ syncopated ('11) 1.75 1.75
Nos. 2935-2939 (5) 3.60 3.60

Flag and Sculptures — A1655

Chiroxiphia Caudata — A1656

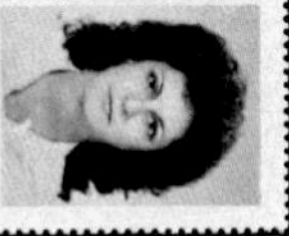

Tourism — A1657

2004 **Litho.** *Perf. 11½x12*
2940 A1655 (80c) multi + label 1.75 1.75
2941 A1656 (80c) multi + label 1.75 1.75
2942 A1657 (80c) multi + label 1.75 1.75
Nos. 2940-2942 (3) 5.25 5.25

Issued: No. 2940, 8/3; No. 2941, 9/22; No. 2942, 10/15. Labels could be personalized.

Nelson Rodrigues (1912-80), Playwright — A1658

2004, Aug. 23 **Litho.** *Perf. 11½x12*
2943 A1658 50c multi .40 .40

Brazil in World War II — A1659

No. 2944: a, Airplane. b, Ship. c, Troops in action. d, Soldier reading letter.

2004, Aug. 25 *Perf. 11½*
2944 A1659 50c Block of 4, #a-d 1.75 1.75

Coronation of Our Lady of Aparecida, Cent. — A1660

2004, Sept. 8 *Perf. 12x11½*
2945 A1660 74c multi .50 .50

Allan Kardec (1804-69), Writer A1661

2004, Oct. 3 *Perf. 11½x12*
2946 A1661 1.60r multi 1.25 1.25

Christmas A1662

2004, Oct. 28 *Die Cut*
Self-Adhesive

2947 A1662 (55c) multi .50 .50
a. Booklet pane of 10 5.00

Porto Alegre Post Office A1663

2004, Oct. 29 *Perf. 11½x12*
2948 A1663 50c multi .40 .40

Cyperus Articulatus A1664

2004, Nov. 23 *Perf. 12x11½*
2949 A1664 1.60r multi 1.40 1.40

Pampulha Architectural Complex — A1665

2004, Dec. 12 *Perf. 11½x12*
2950 A1665 80c multi .65 .65

Nise da Silveira (1905-99), Psychiatrist — A1666

2005, Feb. 15 **Litho.**
2951 A1666 55c multi .45 .45

Rotary International, Cent. — A1667

2005, Mar. 23 ***Perf. 11½***
2952 A1667 1.45r multi 1.10 1.10

Souvenir Sheet

Theobroma Grandiflorum — A1668

No. 2953: a, Fruit on tree. b, Fruit cut open.

2005, Mar. 15
2953 A1668 1.90r Sheet of 2, #a-b 3.25 3.25

Pacific Explorer 2005 World Stamp Expo, Sydney.

Lebanese Immigration to Brazil — A1669

2005, Mar. 31 ***Perf. 11½x12***
2954 A1669 1.75r multi 1.50 1.50

Oscar Niemeyer Museum A1670

2005, Apr. 25
2955 A1670 80c multi .65 .65

Pope John Paul II (1920-2005) A1671

2005, May 18 ***Perf. 11½x11***
2956 A1671 80c multi .70 .70

Souvenir Sheet

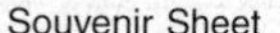
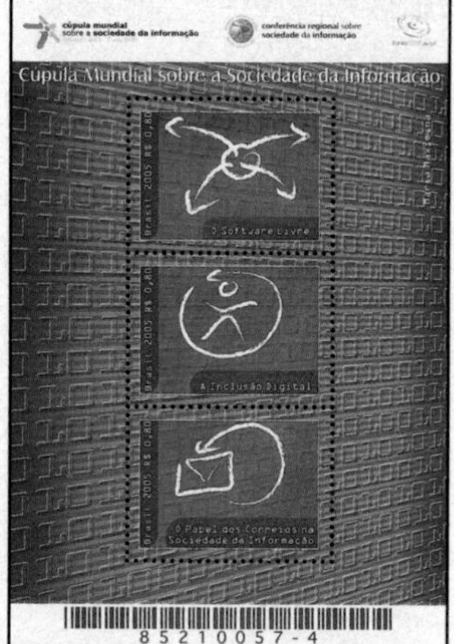
World Summit on the Information Society, Tunis — A1672

No. 2957: a, Circle and arrows. b, Stick figure of person in circle. c, Envelope and arrow.

2005, June 8 **Litho.**
2957 A1672 80c Sheet of 3, #a-c 2.50 2.50

Brazil Year in France A1673

No. 2958, 80c: a, Pankararu Indians. b, Musicians.
No. 2959, 80c: a, Contemporary Dance. b, Vivaldo Lima Stadium
No. 2960, 80c: a, "String" literature. b, Pato na Tucupi and Açai.

2005, June 15 ***Perf. 11½x12***
Pairs, #a-b
2958-2960 A1673 Set of 3 4.25 4.25

Erico Veríssimo (1905-75), Writer — A1674

2005, July 9 ***Perf. 11½x11***
2961 A1674 1.25r multi 1.25 1.25

Mario Quintana (1906-94), Poet A1675

2005, July 30 **Engr.** ***Perf. 11½***
2962 A1675 80c green .80 .80

America Issue — Fight Against Poverty — A1676

2005, Aug. 10 **Litho.** ***Perf. 12x11½***
2963 A1676 80c multi .80 .80

19th Congress of the Postal Union of the Americas, Spain and Portugal — A1677

2005, Aug. 10 ***Die Cut Perf. 12x12¼***
Self-Adhesive
2964 A1677 (85c) multi .75 .75

Royal Road — A1678

No. 2965: a, Map, miner. b, Hikers and cyclist. c, People on horseback, hills and food.

Litho., Litho. & Embossed (#2965a)
2005, Aug. 13 ***Perf. 11½***
2965 A1678 80c Horiz. strip of 3, #a-c 2.25 2.25

Samba Dancer A1679

2005, Aug. 15 **Litho.** ***Perf. 11½x12***
2966 A1679 55c multi .60 .60

Dances — A1680

Parrot and: No. 2967, 80c, Son dancers and Cuban flag. No. 2968, 80c, Samba dancers and Brazilian flag.

2005, Aug. 16 **Litho.** ***Perf. 12x11½***
2967-2968 A1680 Set of 2 1.40 1.40

See Cuba No. 4497-4498.

Sao Francisco River Basin A1681

2005, Sept. 2 ***Perf. 11½x12***
2969 A1681 80c multi .70 .70

Army Staff and Command School, Cent. A1682

2005, Sept. 22
2970 A1682 80c multi .70 .70

Teacher's Day — A1683

Die Cut Perf. 12x12¼
2005, Oct. 15 **Litho.**
Self-Adhesive
2971 A1683 (55c) multi .50 .50

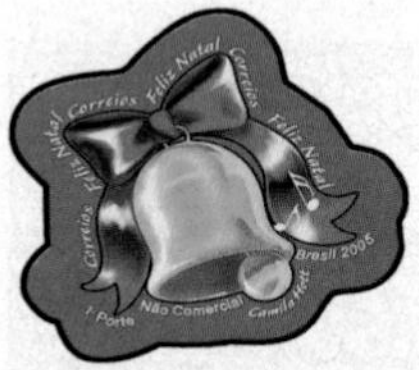
Christmas A1684

2005, Oct. 25 **Litho.** ***Die Cut***
2972 A1684 (55c) multi .50 .50

Souvenir Sheet

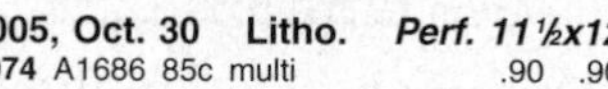
Adoration of the Shepherds, by Oscar Pereira da Silva — A1685

2005, Nov. 24 **Litho.** ***Perf. 12x11½***
2973 A1685 2.90r multi 2.75 2.75

Christmas.

Women's Soccer A1686

2005, Oct. 30 **Litho.** ***Perf. 11½x12***
2974 A1686 85c multi .90 .90

Souvenir Sheet

Salminus Maxillosus — A1687

Litho. & Embossed

2005, Nov. 3 *Perf. 11¾*
2975 A1687 3.10r multi 3.25 3.25

Brazilian Furniture and Furnishings Design — A1688

No. 2976: a, Ceiling light fixtures, by Fernando Prado. b, Ceiling fan, by Indio da Costa Design. c, Chair, by Humberto and Fernando Campana. d, Desk, by Ivan Rezende.

2005, Dec. 12 Litho. *Perf. 11¾*
2976 A1688 85c Block of 4, #a-d 3.25 3.25

Hans Christian Andersen (1805-75), Author A1689

2005, Dec. 14 *Perf. 11½x12*
2977 A1689 55c multi .70 .70

Occupations A1690

Die Cut Perf. 12x12¼

2005, Dec. 19 Photo.

Self-Adhesive

2978 A1690 5c Seamstress .25 .25
a. Die cut perf. 12x12¼ syncopated ('11) .25 .25
2979 A1690 20c Shoemaker .25 .25
a. Die cut perf. 12x12¼ syncopated ('11) .25 .25
2980 A1690 85c Shoe polisher .70 .70
Nos. 2978-2980 (3) 1.20 1.20

See Nos. 2997-2998, 3020A-3020B.

Graffiti Artists — A1691

Designs: No. 2981, 55c, Man with paint sprayer. No. 2982, 55c, Man wearing hat, wavy lines. No. 2983, 55c, Man with cap and spray paint can, horiz.

Perf. 12x11½, 11½x12

2006, Mar. 27 Litho.
2981-2983 A1691 Set of 3 1.75 1.75

Lubrapex 2006, Rio. See No. 2993.

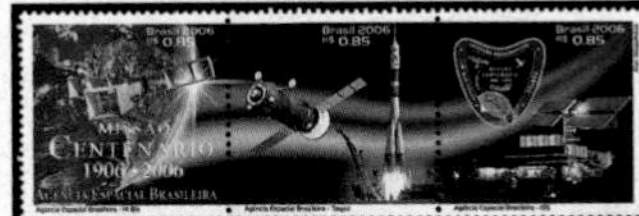

Brazilian Space Agency — A1692

No. 2984: a, Alberto Santos-Dumont's 14bis airplane. b, Soyuz spacecraft. c, Intl. Space Station.

2006, Apr. 3 *Perf. 11½*
2984 A1692 85c Horiz. strip of 3, #a-c 2.50 2.50

Brazilians in flight, cent.

2006 World Cup Soccer Championships, Germany — A1693

2006, Apr. 19
2985 A1693 85c multi .90 .90

Bidu Sayao (1902-99), Opera Singer A1694

2006, May 11
2986 A1694 55c multi .60 .60

World Day of Cultural Diversity for Dialogue and Development A1695

2006, May 21 *Perf. 11½x11*
2987 A1695 1.90r multi 2.00 2.00

2007 Pan American Games, Rio — A1696

2006-07 *Serpentine Die Cut 10¾*

Self-Adhesive

2988 A1696 (85c) multi .90 .90

Perf. 12x11½

2988A A1696 60c multi + label 2.75 2.75

Issued: No. 2988, 8/8/06, No. 2988A, 2007.
No. 2988A was issued in sheets of 12 + 12 labels that could be personalized. Sheets sold for 25r.

Brazilian Paralympic Committee, 11th Anniv. — A1697

2006, Aug. 16 *Perf. 11½x12*
2989 A1697 55c multi .80 .80

Viola de Cocho A1698

2006, Aug. 22
2990 A1698 1.35r multi 1.50 1.50

National Parks and Reserves — A1699

No. 2991: a, Emas National Park. b, Mamirauá Reserve. c, Chapada dos Veadeiros National Park. d, Itatiaia National Park.

Litho. & Embossed

2006, Sept. 4 *Perf. 11½*
2991 A1699 85c Block of 4, #a-d 3.50 3.50

Souvenir Sheet

Cashews — A1700

2006, Sept. 11 Litho. *Die Cut*
2992 A1700 2.90r multi 3.25 3.25

Graffiti Type of 2006

Souvenir Sheet

No. 2993: a, Like #2981. b, Like #2982.

2006, Sept. 11 *Perf. 12x11½*
2993 A1691 1.60r Sheet of 2, #a-b 3.50 3.50

Lubrapex 2006, Rio.

Fernando de Noronha Archipelago A1701

2006, Sept. 27 *Perf. 11½*
2994 A1701 2.50r multi 3.25 3.25

First Flight of Alberto Santos-Dumont's 14bis Airplane, Cent. — A1702

2006, Oct. 23 Litho. *Perf. 11½x12*
2995 A1702 (90c) multi .90 .90

Christmas A1703

2006, Oct. 27 Litho. *Die Cut*

Self-Adhesive

2996 A1703 (60c) multi .65 .65

Glitter was applied to portions of the stamp.

Occupation Type of 2005

Die Cut Perf. 12x12¼

2006, Nov. 6 Photo.

Self-Adhesive

2997 A1690 1c Popcorn vendor .30 .30
a. Die cut perf. 12x12¼ syncopated ('11) .25 .25
2998 A1690 1r Manicurist 1.10 1.10
a. Die cut perf. 12x12¼ syncopated ('11) 1.10 1.10

Souvenir Sheet

Christmas — A1704

No. 2999: a, Shepherds and sheep (25x35mm). b, Angel with horn (36x41mm). c, Holy Family (25x35mm).

Serpentine Die Cut 11½x11

2006, Nov. 9 Litho.
2999 A1704 1.60r Sheet of 3, #a-c 5.00 5.00

A shiny varnish was applied to portions of the design.

America Issue, Energy Conservation — A1705

2006, Nov. 22 *Perf. 11½x12*
3000 A1705 1.75r multi 1.90 1.90

Souvenir Sheet

Sharks — A1706

No. 3001: a, Isurus oxyrinchus and Sphyrna lewini. b, Mustelus schmitti.

Litho., Litho. & Embossed (#3001b)

2006, Nov. 26 ***Perf. 11½***

3001 A1706 1.90r Sheet of 2, #a-b 3.75 3.75

Christmas — A1707

2006, Oct. 30 Litho. ***Perf. 12x11½***

3002 A1707 (55c) multi + label *6.50 6.50*

No. 3002 was printed in sheets of 12 stamps + 12 labels that could be personalized. Sheets sold for 21r.

A1708

Flag and Map of Brazil — A1708a

2007 Litho. ***Perf. 11½x12***

3003 A1708 (90c) multi + label *6.50 6.50*

Perf. 12x11½

3003A A1708a (90c) multi + label *6.50 6.50*

Issued: No. 3003, 2/14; No. 3003A, 10/30. Nos. 3003 and 30003A each were printed in sheets of 12 stamps + 12 labels that could be personalized. Each sheet sold for 25r. See Nos. 3080M-3080N for similar stamps without year date.

Praia Vermelha (Red Beach) — A1708b

Cable Car, Sugarloaf Mountain — A1708c

Guanabara Bay, Sugarloaf Mountain — A1708d

Candelária Church — A1708e

Christ the Redeemer Statue — A1708f

Arcos da Lapa (Carioca Aqueduct) — A1708g

2007, Sept. 24 Litho. ***Perf. 12x12¾***

3003B Block of 6 + 6 labels *13.00 13.00*

c. A1708b (90c) multi + label *2.10 2.10*
d. A1708c (90c) multi + label *2.10 2.10*
e. A1708d (90c) multi + label *2.10 2.10*
f. A1708e (90c) multi + label *2.10 2.10*
g. A1708f (90c) multi + label *2.10 2.10*
h. A1708g (90c) multi + label *2.10 2.10*

Rio de Janeiro tourist attractions. No. 3003B was printed in sheets containing 12 stamps +12 labels, two of each stamp, that could be personalized. Sheets sold for 25r.

2007 Pan American Games, Rio A1709

Designs: No. 3004, (85c), Indoor soccer, bright blue background. No. 3005, (85c), Diving, orange background. No. 3006, (85c), Water polo, blue violet background. No. 3007, (85c), Swimming, yellow orange background. No. 3008, (85c), Synchronized swimming, green background.

Serpentine Die Cut 11

2007, Jan. 19 **Litho.**

Self-Adhesive

3004-3008 A1709 Set of 5 4.50 4.50

Dances A1710

No. 3009: a, Carimbo. b, Frevo.

2007, Feb. 8 ***Perf. 11½***

3009 A1710 (55c) Vert. pair, #a-b 1.90 1.90

Intl. Polar Year — A1711

No. 3010: a, Ship Ary Rongel. b, Commander Ferraz Antarctic Station. c, Emperor penguin, map of Antarctica.

2007, Mar. 13 ***Perf. 11½x12***

3010 A1711 (90c) Horiz. strip of 3, #a-c 3.00 3.00

Path of Father José de Anchieta — A1712

No. 3011: a, Our Lady of the Assumption Church. b, Father José de Anchieta. c, Metropolitan Cathedral, Vitória.

2007, Mar. 19 ***Perf. 12x11½***

3011 A1712 90c Horiz. strip of 3, #a-c 3.00 3.00

Soccer Stadiums — A1713

Designs: 60c, Mangueirao Stadium, Belem. 90c, Serra Dourada Stadium, Goiania. No. 3014, 2.60r, Maracana Stadium, Rio. No. 3015, 2.60r, Pacaembu Stadium, Sao Paulo.

2007, Mar. 25 ***Perf. 11x11½***

3012-3015 A1713 Set of 4 7.00 7.00

Juscelino Kubitschek Bridge, Brasilia A1714

2007, Apr. 21 ***Perf. 11½x12***

3016 A1714 (90c) multi 1.10 1.10

Scouting, Cent. — A1715

2007, Apr. 23 ***Perf. 12x11½***

3017 A1715 2r multi 2.25 2.25

Pope Benedict XVI A1716

2007, May 9 ***Perf. 11½x12***

3018 A1716 90c multi 1.25 1.25

Souvenir Sheet

Shells — A1717

No. 3019: a, Cochlespira elongata. b, Charonia variegata. c, Chicoreus beauii.

Litho. & Embossed

2007, June 5 ***Perf. 12x11½***

3019 A1717 2r Sheet of 3, #a-c 6.75 6.75

Portions of the design were applied by a thermographic process producing a shiny, raised effect.

Diplomatic Relations Between Brazil and Canada, 140th Anniv. — A1718

2007, June 27 Litho. ***Perf. 12¾x12***

3020 A1718 90c multi .95 .95

Occupations Type of 2005

Die Cut Perf. 12x12¼

2007, July 4 **Photo.**

Self-Adhesive

3020A A1690 60c Barber .65 .65
3020B A1690 90c Carpenter .95 .95

Giuseppe Garibaldi (1807-82), Italian Leader A1719

Designs: No. 3021, 1.40r, Ship, Garibaldi on horseback. No. 3022, 1.40r, Garibaldi, ship.

2007, July 4 ***Perf. 12x12¾***

3021-3022 A1719 Set of 2 3.25 3.25
3022a Horiz. pair, #3021-3022 3.25 3.25

See Uruguay Nos. 2196-2197.

Rail Transport A1720

Designs: 1.40r, Rio de Janeiro Metro car. 1.45r, Baroneza steam locomotive. 1.60r, Tram, Santa Teresa.

2007, July 6

3023-3025 A1720 Set of 3 4.75 4.75

Teófilo Ottoni (1807-69), Leader of 1842 Uprising A1721

2007, Aug. 23 Litho. ***Perf. 12x12¾***

3026 A1721 60c multi .75 .75

America Issue, Education for All A1722

2007, Sept. 8

3027 A1722 60c multi .75 .75

Souvenir Sheet

Rose Varieties — A1723

No. 3028: a, High & Magic. b, Caballero. c, Avalanche.

2007, Sept. 29 ***Perf. 12¾x12***

3028 A1723 2.60r Sheet of 3, #a-c 8.75 8.75

Zoo Animals A1724

No. 3029: a, African elephant. b, Tiger. c, Giraffes. d, Parrot. e, African lion. f, Chimpanzee.

2007, Oct. 5 Litho. ***Perf. 12x12¾***

3029 Block or horiz. strip of 6 4.25 4.25

a.-f. A1724 60c Any single .65 .65

Christmas

A1725 A1726

Die Cut Perf. 12x12¼

2007, Oct. 11 Photo.

Self-Adhesive

3030 A1725 (60c) multi .70 .70

3031 A1726 (90c) multi 1.00 1.00

Arrival of Portuguese Royal Family in Brazil, 200th Anniv. — A1727

No. 3032: a, King John VI and ships. b, Royal family and ship.

2008, Jan. 22 Litho. ***Perf. 12x12¾***

3032 A1727 2r Horiz. pair, #a-b 4.50 4.50

See Portugal No. 2973.

Bank of Brazil, 200th Anniv. A1728

2008, Jan. 28

3033 A1728 (90c) multi 1.10 1.10

Opening of Brazilian Ports to Friendly Nations, 200th Anniv. A1729

2008, Jan. 28

3034 A1729 (90c) multi 1.10 1.10

Foreign Trade, 200th Anniv. A1730

2008, Jan. 28

3035 A1730 (90c) multi 1.10 1.10

America Issue - Dancer and Musicians A1731

Die Cut Perf. 12¼x12

2008, Feb. 1 Photo.

Self-Adhesive

3036 A1731 (60c) multi .75 .75

Medical Faculty Bicentenaries — A1732

Buildings at: No. 3037, (90c), Federal University of Bahia. No. 3038, (90c), Federal University of Rio de Janeiro.

2008, Feb. 18 Litho. ***Perf. 12x12¾***

3037-3038 A1732 Set of 2 2.25 2.25

First National Youth Conference, Brasilia — A1733

Die Cut Perf. 12x12¼

2008, Feb. 27 Photo.

Self-Adhesive

3039 A1733 (90c) multi 1.10 1.10

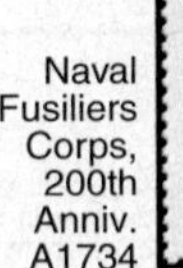

Naval Fusiliers Corps, 200th Anniv. A1734

2008, Mar. 7 Litho. ***Perf. 12x12¾***

3040 A1734 (90c) multi 1.10 1.10

Souvenir Sheet

Architecture of Oscar Niemeyer — A1735

No. 3041: a, Museum of Contemporary Art, Niterói. b, Latin America Memorial, Sao Paolo.

Litho. & Embossed

2008, Mar. 18 ***Perf. 12x11½***

3041 A1735 2.60r Sheet of 2, #a-b 6.25 6.25

Independent Judiciary, 200th Anniv. — A1736

2008, Mar. 27 Litho. ***Perf. 12¾x12***

3042 A1736 (90c) multi 1.10 1.10

Military Justice in Brazil, 200th Anniv. A1737

2008, Apr. 1 ***Perf. 12x12¾***

3043 A1737 (90c) multi 1.10 1.10

Brazilian Press Association, Cent. — A1738

2008, Apr. 7

3044 A1738 (90c) multi 1.10 1.10

Brazilian Heroes — A1739

No. 1739: a, Dom Pedro I (1798-1834). b, Marshal Manuel Deodoro da Fonseca (1827-92). c, Duque de Caxias (1803-80), soldier and politician. d, Admiral Francisco Manuel Barroso (1804-82). e, Admiral Joaquim Marques de Tamandaré (1807-97). f, José Bonifácio (1763-1838), statesman. g, Alberto Santos-Dumont (1873-1932), aviation pioneer. h, Zumbi dos Palmares (1655-95), fugitive slave leader. i, Tiradentes (1746-92), Brazilian independence leader. j, José Plácido de Castro (1873-1908), Acrean Army leader.

2008, Apr. 21 ***Perf. 12x11½***

3045 A1739 (90c) Block of 10, #a-j 11.00 11.00

Police, 200th Anniv. A1740

2008, May 10 ***Perf. 12x12¾***

3046 A1740 (90c) multi 1.10 1.10

Independence Dragoons, 200th Anniv. — A1741

2008, May 10 ***Perf. 12¾x12***

3047 A1741 (90c) multi 1.10 1.10

National Printing Office, 200th Anniv. — A1742

2008, May 10

3048 A1742 (90c) multi 1.10 1.10

Souvenir Sheet

Fauna of Serra do Japi Region — A1743

No. 3049: a, Tangara cayana cayana. b, Consul fabius drurii.

2008, May 16 ***Perf. 11½x12***
3049 A1743 2r Sheet of 2, #a-b 5.00 5.00

Rio de Janeiro Botanical Gardens, 200th Anniv. — A1744

2008, June 13 ***Perf. 12¾x12***
3050 A1744 (60c) multi .75 .75

Souvenir Sheet

Japanese Immigration to Brazil, Cent. — A1745

No. 3051: a, Map of Brazil, ship Kasato-Maru. b, Flags of Brazil and Japan, origami crane.

Litho. With Foil Application
2008, June 18 ***Perf. 12x11½***
3051 A1745 3.50r multi 8.75 8.75

See Japan No. 3028.

French and Brazilian Landscapes — A1746

No. 3052: a, Glacier, France. b, Amazonian forest, Brazil.

2008, June 21 Litho. ***Perf. 11½x12***
3052 Horiz. pair 5.00 5.00
a.-b. A1746 2r Either single 2.50 2.50

Joao Guimaraes Rosa (1908-67), Novelist — A1747

Litho. & Embossed
2008, June 27 ***Perf. 12x11½***
3053 A1747 60c multi .75 .75

Agriculture Ministry, 200th Anniv. — A1748

2008, June 30 Litho. ***Perf. 12¾x12***
3054 A1748 (90c) multi 1.10 1.10

2008 Summer Olympics, Beijing — A1749

No. 3055: a, Mascot Beibei, rhythmic gymnastics. b, Mascot Jingjing, equestrian. c, Mascot Huanhuan, swimming. d, Mascots Nini and Yingying, emblem of 2008 Summer Olympics.

Litho. & Embossed
2008, July 4 ***Perf. 11½***
3055 A1749 65c Block of 4, #a-d 3.25 3.25

Brazilian Cuisine A1750

2008, Aug. 8 Litho. ***Perf. 11½x12***
3056 A1750 90c multi 1.10 1.10

Endangered Animals of the Amazon Region — A1751

Designs: No. 3057, 1r, Pteronura brasiliensis. No. 3058, 1r, Lontra longicaudis. No. 3059, 1r, Trichechus inunguis.

2008, Sept. 5 ***Perf. 11½x12***
3057-3059 A1751 Set of 3 3.50 3.50

Birds — A1752

Designs: No. 3060, Strix virgata. No. 3060A, Celeus obrieni.

2008, Oct. 10 ***Perf. 12x11½***
3060 A1752 1.40r multi 1.25 1.25
3060A A1752 1.40r multi 1.25 1.25

Christmas
A1753 A1754

Die Cut Perf. 12x12¼
2008, Oct. 17 **Photo.**
Self-Adhesive
3061 A1753 (65c) multi .60 .60
3062 A1754 (1r) multi .95 .95

Convent of St. Anthony, 400th anniv. (No. 3061), Franciscan Movement, 800th anniv. (in 2009) (No. 3062).

Provisional Regulations of General Administration of the Posts, 200th Anniv. — A1755

2008, Nov. 22 Litho. ***Perf. 11½x12***
3063 A1755 1r multi .85 .85

Louis Braille (1809-52), Educator of the Blind — A1756

2009, Jan. 4 **Litho. & Embossed**
3064 A1756 2.20r multi 2.00 2.00

Brazilian Leadership in Production of Fuels From Renewable Resources A1757

Serpentine Die Cut 4¾x5
2009, Jan. 13 **Litho.**
Self-Adhesive
3065 A1757 1r multi .85 .85

New Year 2009 (Year of the Ox) — A1758

Litho. & Embossed With Foil Application
2009, Jan. 15 ***Perf. 11½x12***
3066 A1758 2.35r multi 2.00 2.00

Souvenir Sheets

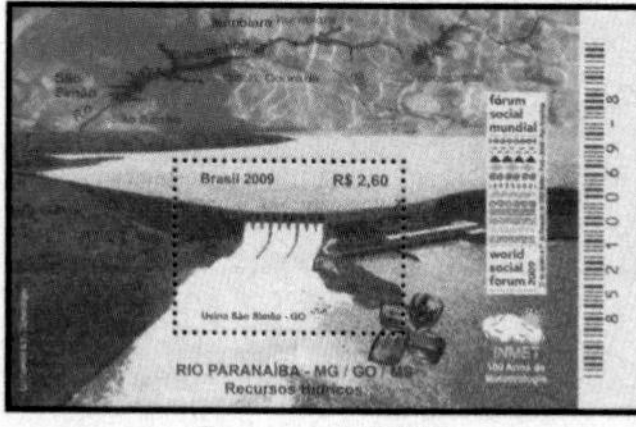

Rivers — A1759

Designs: No. 3067, 2.60r, Sao Simao Hydroelectric Plant, Paranaíba River. No. 3068, 3.85r, Cichla mirianae, Sao Benedito River.

2009, Jan. 27 **Litho.**
3067-3068 A1759 Set of 2 5.75 5.75

Archbishop Helder Camara (1909-99) A1760

2009, Feb. 7 Litho. ***Perf. 11½x12***
3069 A1760 1r multi .85 .85

Map, Flag and Scenes of Pernambuco — A1761

2009, Feb. 21
3070 A1761 (1r) multi + label *2.60 2.60*

No. 3070 was printed in sheets of 12 stamps + 12 labels that could be personalized. Sheets sold for 26r.

Intl. Polar Year — A1762

No. 3071: a, Hydrurga leptonyx. b, Ursus maritimus.

Perf. 11½x11¾
2009, Mar. 18 **Litho.**
3071 A1762 1r Horiz. pair, #a-b 1.90 1.90

Postman A1763

Die Cut Perf. 12¼x12
2009, Mar. 20 **Photo.**
Self-Adhesive
3072 A1763 65c multi .60 .60

Sport Club Internacional Soccer Team, Cent. — A1764

2009, Apr. 4 Litho. ***Perf. 12x11½***
3073 A1764 1r multi .95 .95

Diplomatic Relations Between Brazil and Thailand
A1765

Flowers and buildings: No. 3074, 2.35r, Rhynchostylis gigantea, Grand Palace, Bangkok. No. 3075, 2.35r, Aechmea disticantha, Sao Pedro de Alcântara Cathedral, Petrópolis, Brazil.

2009, Apr. 17
3074-3075 A1765 Set of 2 4.50 4.50

Hercílio Luz Bridge, Florianópolis — A1766

Serra do Rio do Rastro — A1766a

Blumenau — A1766b

Balneário Camboriú — A1766c

Santa Marta Lighthouse, Laguna — A1766d

Windmill, Joinville — A1766e

2009, Apr. 17 Litho. ***Perf. 11½x12***
3076 Block of 6 + 6 labels 32.50 32.50
a. A1766 (1r) multi + label 5.25 5.25
b. A1766a (1r) multi + label 5.25 5.25
c. A1766b (1r) multi + label 5.25 5.25
d. A1766c (1r) multi + label 5.25 5.25
e. A1766d (1r) multi + label 5.25 5.25
f. A1766e (1r) multi + label 5.25 5.25

Santa Catarina tourist attractions. No. 3076 was printed in sheets containing 12 stamps +12 labels, two of each stamp, that could be personalized. Sheets sold for 26r.

Miniature Sheet

Zebu Expo — A1767

No. 3077: a, Bos taurus indicus Indubrasil. b, Bos taurus indicus Nelore Mocho. c, Bos taurus indicus Sindi. d, Bos taurus indicus Tabapua. e, Bos taurus indicus Brahman. f, Bos taurus indicus Nelore. g, Bos taurus indicus Guzerá. h, Bos taurus indicus Gir Leiteiro. i, Zebu Breeders Association of Brazil Headquarters (Sede ABCZ). j, Bos taurus indicus Gir Mocho. k, Bos taurus indicus Gir Dupla Aptidao. l, Zebu Breeders Association of Brazil Exposition Park.

2009, May 3
3077 A1767 Sheet of 12 + 12 labels 65.00 65.00
a.-l. (1r) Any single + label 5.25 5.25

No. 3077 sold for 26r. Labels could be personalized.

Miniature Sheet

Tocantins Tourist Attractions — A1768

No. 3078: a, Morro da Catedral, Jalapao. b, Our Lady of Mercy Cathedral, Porto Nacional. c, Registro Waterfall, Natividade. d, Matriz Church, Natividade. e, Owl, Palmas. f, Araguatins Quay, Araguatins. g, Flower, Palmas. h, Tartaruga Beach, Peixe. i, Velha Waterfall, Jalapao. j, Rafting on Rio Novo, Jalapao. k, Jalapao. l, Graciosa Beach, Palmas.

2009, May 14
3078 A1768 Sheet of 12 + 12 labels 26.00 26.00
a.-l. (1r) Any single + label 2.10 2.10

No. 3078 sold for 26r. Labels could be personalized.

Planes and Coastline — A1769

Two Planes — A1769a

Plane and Smoke — A1769b

Plane and Sun — A1769c

Plane Over Water — A1769d

Planes Over Forest — A1769e

2009, May 15 Litho. ***Perf. 11½x12***
3079 Block of 6 + 6 labels 13.00 13.00
a. A1769 (1r) multi + label 2.10 2.10
b. A1769a (1r) multi + label 2.10 2.10
c. A1769b (1r) multi + label 2.10 2.10
d. A1769c (1r) multi + label 2.10 2.10
e. A1769d (1r) multi + label 2.10 2.10
f. A1769e (1r) multi + label 2.10 2.10

Aerobatics Squadron. No. 3079 was printed in sheets containing 12 stamps +12 labels, two of each stamp, that could be personalized. Sheets sold for 26r.

Miniature Sheet

Rio Grande do Norte Tourist Attractions — A1770

No. 3080: a, Genipabu Beach, Natal. b, Castelo Zé dos Montes, Sítio Novo. c, Pipa Beach, Tibau do Sul. d, Fortalez dos Reis Magos, Natal. e, Rodolfo Fernandes Square, Mossoró. f, Alberto Maranhao Theater, Natal. g, Mae Luiza Lighthouse, Natal. h, Newton Navarro Bridge, Natal. i, Three Wise Men Statue, Natal. j, Ponta Negra Beach, Natal. k, Barra de Cunhaú Beach, Canguaretama. l, Matriz Church, Martins.

2009, July 27
3080 A1770 Sheet of 12 + 12 labels 26.00 26.00
a.-l. (1r) Any single + label 2.10 2.10

No. 3080 sold for 26r. Labels could be personalized.

A1770a

Flag and Map of Brazil — A1770b

2009, Aug. 6 ***Perf. 11½x12***
3080M A1770a (1r) multi + label 2.60 2.60
Perf. 12x11½
3080N A1770b (1r) multi + label 2.60 2.60

Nos. 3080M and 3080N each were printed in sheets of 12 stamps + 12 labels that could be personalized. Each sheet sold for 26r.

Miniature Sheet

Ceará Tourist Attractions — A1771

No. 3081: a, West Coast, Lagoinha. b, Ipú Waterfall. c, Dragao do Mar Arts and Culture Center, Fortaleza. d, José de Alencar Theater, Fortaleza. e, Iracema Statue, Fortaleza. f, Ubajara National Park. g, Statue of Padre Cícero, Juazerio do Norte. h, West Coast, Jericoacara. i, Beira Mar Avenue, Fortaleza. j, Fortim. k, Cedro Dam and Galinha Choco rock, Quixadá. l, Canoa Quebrada.

2009, Aug. 18 ***Perf. 11½x12***
3081 A1771 Sheet of 12 + 12 labels 26.00 26.00
a.-l. (1r) Any single + label 2.10 2.10

No. 3081 sold for 26r. Labels could be personalized.

Books, Khalil Gibran (1883-1931), Poet, and His House in Beirut, Lebanon — A1772

2009, May 5 Litho. ***Perf. 11½x12***
3082 A1772 2.35r multi 2.40 2.40

Telegram
A1773

Die Cut Perf. 12¼x12
2009, Mar. 20 Photo.
3083 A1773 1r multi .90 .90

Brazilian Kickboxing
A1774

Die Cut Perf. 12
2009, May 25 Litho.
Self-Adhesive
3084 A1774 65c multi .70 .70

Edésio Fernandes School of Justice — A1775

2009, May 29 ***Perf. 12x11½***
3085 A1775 1r multi 1.10 1.10

Cooperation in Space Projects With Russia — A1776

2009, June 12 ***Perf. 11½x12***
3086 A1776 2.35r multi 2.50 2.50

Municipal Theater, Rio de Janeiro, Cent. A1777

Litho. With Foil Application

2009, July 14 ***Perf. 11½x11¾***
3087 A1777 (1r) multi 1.10 1.10

Commercial Association of Rio de Janeiro, Bicent. A1778

2009, July 15 Litho. ***Perf. 11½x12***
3088 A1778 1r multi 1.10 1.10

Fruit — A1779

No. 3092: a, Vitis labrusca (purple). b, Prunus persica. c, Prunus salicina. d, Malpighia glabra. e, Vitis labrusca (green). f, Fragaria x ananassa. g, Passiflora edulis. h, Vitis spp. i, Ficus carica. j, Diospyros kaki.

2009, July 23 Litho. ***Perf. 12x11½***
3089 Block of 10 11.00 11.00
a.-j. A1779 (1r) Any single 1.10 1.10

Miniature Sheet

Dutch Presence in Brazil — A1780

No. 3090: a, Prince John Maurice of Nassau-Siegen ("The Brazilian") (1604-79), governor general of Dutch possessions in Brazil. b, Dutch ship Zutphen. c, Dutch pipes. d, Palácio de Friburgo, Recife. e, Palácio do Campo das Princesas, Recife. f, Dutch houses on Rua Aurora, Recife.

2009, Aug. 4 Litho. ***Perf. 12x11½***
3090 A1780 2.20r Sheet of 6, #a-f 14.50 14.50

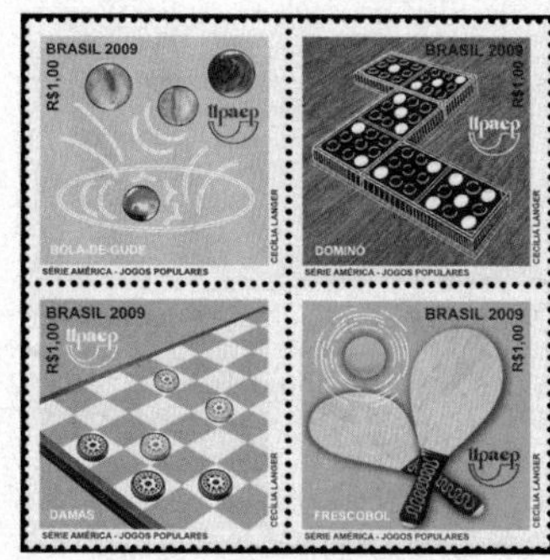

America Issue, Traditional Games — A1781

No. 3091: a, Marbles (bola-de-gude). b, Dominoes. c, Checkers. d, Paddleball.

Litho. & Embossed

2009, Aug. 18 ***Perf. 11½***
3091 A1781 1r Block of 4, #a-d 4.25 4.25

A1782

Minas Gerais Flag and Map, Church in Serro — A1783

2009, Aug. 21 ***Perf. 11½x12***
3092 A1782 (1r) multi + label *2.60 2.60*

Perf. 12x11½
3093 A1783 (1r) multi + label *2.60 2.60*

Nos. 3092 and 3093 each were printed in sheets of 12 samps + 12 labels that could be personalized. Each sheet sold for 26r.

Miniature Sheet

A1784

Sao Paulo Tourist Attractions — A1785

Nos. 3094 and 3095: a, Pateo do Collegio. b, Paulista Avenue. c, Ipiranga Museum. d, Luz Station. e, Santa Ifigênia Viaduct. f, Post Office (Palácio dos Correios). g, Mercado Municipal Paulistano. h, Altino Arantes Building. i, Sao Paulo Cathedral (Catedral da Sé). j, Sao Paulo Museum of Art (MASP). k, Latin America Memorial. l, Octávio Frias de Oliveira Bridge. Stamps from No. 3094 are vertical and from No. 3095, horizontal.

2009, Aug. 29 ***Perf. 12x11½***
3094 A1784 Sheet of 12 + 12 labels *26.00 26.00*
a.-l. (1r) Any single + label *2.10 2.10*

Perf. 11½x12
3095 A1785 Sheet of 12 + 12 labels *26.00 26.00*
a.-l. (1r) Any single + label *2.10 2.10*

Nos. 3094 and 3095 each sold for 26r. Labels could be personalized.

Federal Educational, Professional and Technological Network, Cent. — A1786

Litho. & Embossed

2009, Sept. 23 ***Perf. 11½x12***
3096 A1786 (1r) multi 1.10 1.10

Redrawn With White Border
3096A A1786 (1r) multi + label *6.50 6.50*

No. 3096A was printed in sheets of 12 stamps + 12 labels that could be personalized. Sheets sold for 26r.

Buildings, Historic Center of Sao Luís UNESCO World Heritage Site A1787

2009, Sept. 25 **Litho.**
3097 A1787 (1r) multi 1.10 1.10

Miniature Sheet

Birds — A1788

No. 3098: a, Paroaria coronata. b, Rupicola rupicola. c, Chlorophonia cyanea. d, Porphyrospiza caerulescens. e, Tangara cyanocephala. f, Amblyramphus holosericeus.

2009, Oct. 2
3098 A1788 1r Sheet of 6, #a-f 6.75 6.75

Lubrapex 2009, Evora, Portugal; Birdpex 2010, Antwerp, Belgium.

Carmen Miranda (1909-55), Actress — A1789

2009, Oct. 6 ***Perf. 12x11½***
3099 A1789 2.20r multi 2.60 2.60

Souvenir Sheet

France Year in Brazil — A1790

No. 3100: a, Le Corbusier (1887-1965), architect. b, Brazilian Indian.

Litho. & Engr. (#3100a), Litho. & Embossed (#3100b)

2009, Oct. 7 ***Perf. 11½***
3100 A1790 2.20r Sheet of 2, #a-b 5.25 5.25

Postman on Motorcycle A1791

Mail Bag — A1792

Die Cut Perf. 12¼x12

2009, Oct. 9 **Photo.**

Self-Adhesive

3101 A1791 (65c) multi .75 .75
a. Die cut perf. 12¼x12 syncopated ('11) .70 .70

Die Cut Perf. 12x12¼
3102 A1792 (1r) multi 1.25 1.25
a. Die cut perf. 12x12¼ syncopated ('11) 1.10 1.10

Coritiba Soccer Club, Cent. — A1793

2009, Oct. 12 Litho. ***Perf. 12x11½***
3103 A1793 1.05r multi 1.25 1.25

Sport Club International Soccer Team, Cent. — A1794

2009, Oct. 13
3104 A1794 (1r) multi + label *2.60 2.60*

No. 3104 was printed in sheets of 12 stamps + 12 labels that could be personalized. Sheets sold for 26r.

Souvenir Sheet

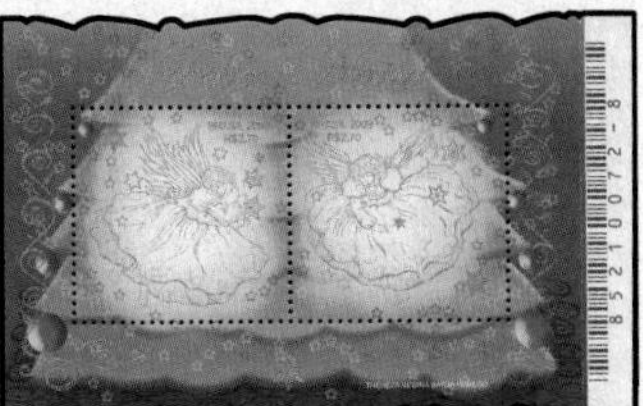

Christmas — A1795

No. 3105 — Angel with denomination at: a, UR. b, UL.

Litho. & Engr.

2009, Oct. 16 ***Perf. 11½***

3105 A1795 2.70r Sheet of 2, #a-b 6.50 6.50

A1796

A1797

A1798

A1799

A1800

A1801

Christmas A1802

Die Cut Perf. 12

2009, Oct. 16 **Litho.**

Self-Adhesive

3106 A1796 (65c) multi .75 .75
3107 A1797 (65c) multi .75 .75
3108 A1798 (65c) multi .75 .75
3109 A1799 (65c) multi .75 .75
3110 A1800 (65c) multi .75 .75
3111 A1801 (65c) multi .75 .75
a. Horiz. strip of 6, #3106-3111 4.50

Die Cut

3112 A1802 (1r) multi 1.25 1.25
Nos. 3106-3112 (7) 5.75 5.75

Bridges — A1803

No. 3113: a, Incheon Bridge, South Korea (denomination at UR). b, Octavio Frias de Oliveira Bridge, Brazil (denomination at UL).

2009, Oct. 30 ***Perf. 11½x11***

3113 A1803 1.05r Horiz. pair, #a-b 2.50 2.50

See South Korea No. 2324.

Soccer — A1804

No. 3114 — Soccer player from: a, Brazil, denomination at UR. b, Brazil, denomination at UL. c, Hong Kong, denomination at LR. d, Hong Kong, denomination at LL.

2009, Nov. 5

3114 A1804 1.05r Block of 4, #a-d 5.00 5.00

See Hong Kong Nos. 1372-1375.

Flag, Map and Scenes of Rondônia — A1805

2009, Dec. 29 **Litho.** ***Perf. 11½x12***

3115 A1805 (1.05r) multi + label *2.60 2.60*

No. 3115 was printed in sheets of 12 stamps + 12 labels that could be personalized. Sheets sold for 26r.

Miniature Sheet

Rio de Janeiro Beach Scenes — A1806

No. 3116 — Flag of Brazil and: a, Praia Vermelha (Red Beach). b, Barra da Tijuca. c, Copacabana. d, Leblon. e, Botafogo. f, Flamengo. g, Ipanema. h, Arpoador. i, Recreio dos Bandeirantes. j, Praia da Reserva. k, Leme. l, Sao Conrado.

2009, Dec. 29

3116 A1806 Sheet of 12 + 12 labels *26.00 26.00*
a.-l. (1.05r) Any single + label *2.10 2.10*

No. 3116 sold for 26r. Labels could be personalized.

Corrida de Reis Race, Cuiabá — A1807

2010, Jan. 10 **Litho.** ***Perf. 11½x12***

3117 A1807 70c multi .75 .75

Miniature Sheet

Brasília Tourist Attractions — A1808

No. 3118: a, Cathedral. b, Palácio da Justiça (Palace of Justice. c, Palácio do Planalto (Palace of the Highlands). d, National Congress. e, Our Lady of Fátima Church. f, Federal Supreme Tribunal Building. g, Museum of the Republic. h, Dois Candangos sculpture. i, Juscelino Kubitschek Bridge. j, Ipé tree on the Esplenade. k, Juscelino Kubitschek Memorial. l, Interior of Cathedral.

2010, Feb. 5

3118 A1808 Sheet of 12 + 12 labels *26.00 26.00*
a.-l. (1.05r) Any single + label *2.10 2.10*

No. 3118 sold for 26r. Labels could be personalized.

Pres. Tancredo de Almeida Neves (1910-85) — A1809

2010, Mar. 10 **Litho.** ***Perf. 11x11½***

3119 A1809 1.05r multi 1.25 1.25

Zilda Arns (1934-2010), Pediatrician and Aid Worker — A1810

2010, Mar. 25 ***Perf. 11½x12***

3120 A1810 1.45r multi 1.75 1.75

Francisco Cândido Xavier (1910-2002), Medium and Writer — A1811

2010, Apr. 2 ***Perf. 12x11½***

3121 A1811 (1.05r) multi 1.25 1.25

Architecture and Monuments of Brasília — A1812

No. 3122: a, Juscelino Kubitschek Memorial. b, Dois Candangos Monument. c, Cathedral of Brasília, horiz. d, Our Lady of Fatima Chapel (Igrejinha), horiz. e, Sculpture at Alvorada Palace. f, National Congress Buildings and ipê tree blossoms.

Perf. 12x11½, 11½x12 (#3122c, 3122d)

2010, Apr. 21

3122 Strip of 6 7.50 7.50
a.-f. A1812 (1.05r) Any single 1.25 1.25

St. Benedict's Monastery, Sorocaba, Paintign by Sonia Vrubleski A1813

2010, Apr. 23 ***Perf. 12x11½***

3123 A1813 (1.05r) multi 1.25 1.25

St. Benedict's Monastery, 350th Anniv.

Souvenir Sheet

Amerigo Vespucci (1454-1512), Navigator — A1814

No. 3124 — Map and ship with: a, Vespucci. b, Vespucci and silhouette of building.

2010, May 10 ***Perf. 11½x12***

3124 A1814 2.40r Sheet of 2, #a-b 5.25 5.25

Fifth World Military Games, Rio A1815

2010, May 12

3125 A1815 2r multi 2.25 2.25

Souvenir Sheet

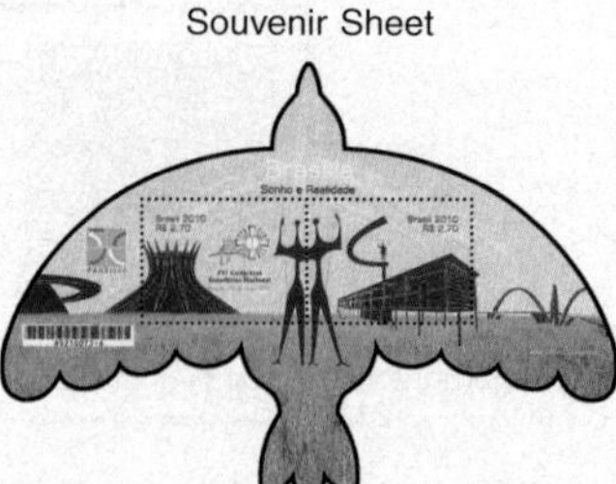

16th National Eucharistic Congress, Brasília — A1816

No. 3126: a, Congress emblem, Cathedral of Brasília, half of Dois Candangos Monument. b, Half of Dois Candangos Monument, Juscelino Kubitschek Moument, Catetinho (first home of Pres. Kubitschek and first building in Brasília).

2010, May 13
3126 A1816 2.70r Sheet of 2, #a-b 6.00 6.00

Church of Our Lady of the Rosary and St. Benedict's Chapel, Cuiabá — A1817

2010, June 4 **Litho.**
3127 A1817 1.10r multi 1.25 1.25

Feast of the Divine Eternal Father, Trinidade A1818

2010, June 6 ***Perf. 12x11½***
3128 A1818 70c multi .80 .80

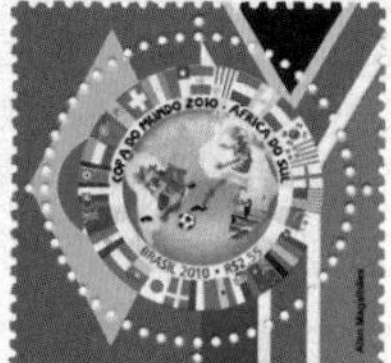

2010 World Cup Soccer Championships, South Africa — A1819

2010, June 11 ***Perf. 11½***
3129 A1819 2.55r multi 3.00 3.00

Values are for stamps with surrounding selvage.

Miniature Sheet

Brasília Tourist Attractions — A1820

No. 3130: a, Juscelino Kubitschek Memorial. b, Brazilian flag on flagpole. c, Catetinho Building. d, Dois Candangos sculpture. e, National Museum. f, Wall of tiles of Athos Bulcao. g, National Congress. h, Television tower. i, Juscelino Kubitschek Bridge. j, Palácio de Alvorada (President's residence). k, Panteao da Pátria (Pantheon of the Fatherland). l, Cathedral.

2010, June 11
3130 A1820 Sheet of 12 + 12 labels 26.00 26.00
a.-l. (1.10r) Any single + label *2.10 2.10*

No. 3130 sold for 26r. Labels could be personalized.

Peter Lund (1801-80), Paleontologist — A1821

2010, June 14 **Litho.** ***Perf. 11½x12***
3131 A1821 1.05r multi 1.25 1.25

Historical and Tourism Sites of Brazil and Syria — A1822

2010, June 28 ***Perf. 11½x12***
3132 A1822 2r multi 2.25 2.25

See Syria No. 1677.

Iguaçu Falls and Flags of Brazil and State of Paraná — A1823

2010, June 29
3133 A1823 (1.10r) multi + label *2.60 2.60*

No. 3133 was printed in sheets of 12 stamps + 12 labels that could be personalized. Sheets sold for 26r.

Miniature Sheet

Pará Tourist Attractions — A1824

No. 3134: a, Atalaia Dunes, Salinópolis. b, Buildings, Belém. c, Mosqueiro Beach Entranceway, Belém. d, Ver-o-Peso Market Complex, Belém. e, Mangal das Garças Park, Belém. f, Docks Station (Estaçao das Docas), Belém. g, Antônio Lemos Palace, Belém. h, Paz Theater, Belém. i, Açai berries and paste. j, House of Eleven Windows (Casa das Onze Janelas), Belém. k, Hangar, Convention Center and Amazon Fair, Belém. l, Our Lady of Nazareth Basilica, Belém.

2010, June 29 **Litho.** ***Perf. 11½x12***
3134 A1824 Sheet of 12 + 12 labels 26.00 26.00
a.-l. (1.10r) Any single + label *2.10 2.10*

No. 3134 sold for 26r. Labels could be personalized.

Souvenir Sheet

Fish of Lake Malawi, Africa — A1825

No. 3135: a, Nimbochromis venustus. b, Ajacobfreibergi eureka. c, Cynotilapia sp.

2010, July 6
3135 A1825 2r Sheet of 3, #a-c 7.00 7.00

English Village in Paranapiacaba — A1826

2010, July 17
3136 A1826 1.05r multi 1.25 1.25

Temple of Abu Simbel, Egypt A1827

2010, July 22
3137 A1827 1.05r multi 1.25 1.25

Ministry of Agriculture, Livestock and Food Supply, 150th Anniv. — A1828

2010, July 28 ***Perf. 12x11½***
3138 A1828 1.05r multi 1.25 1.25

Irineu Evangelista de Sousa, Viscount of Mauá (1813-89), Railroad Entrepreneur — A1829

2010, July 28 ***Perf. 11½x12***
3139 A1829 1.05r multi 1.25 1.25

Ministry of Transportation, 150th anniv.

Victoria Regia — A1830

Victoria Regia Flower — A1831

Parrots — A1832

Jaguar — A1833

Ipé Tree — A1834

Caiman — A1835

Jabiru — A1836

2010, June 26 **Litho.** ***Perf. 11½x12***
3140 Sheet of 12, #a-b, 2 each #c-g, + 12 labels 26.00 26.00

a.	A1830 (1.05r) multi	*2.10*	*2.10*
b.	A1831 (1.05r) multi	*2.10*	*2.10*
c.	A1832 (1.05r) multi	*2.10*	*2.10*
d.	A1833 (1.05r) multi	*2.10*	*2.10*
e.	A1834 (1.05r) multi	*2.10*	*2.10*
f.	A1835 (1.05r) multi	*2.10*	*2.10*
g.	A1836 (1.05r) multi	*2.10*	*2.10*

Pantanal flora and fauna. No. 3140 sold for 30r. Labels could be personalized.

Textile Crops — A1837

No. 3141: a, Gossypium hirsutum (cotton). b, Cocos nucifera (coir). c, Corchorus capsularis (jute).d, Agave sisalana (sisal).

2010, Aug. 12 **Litho. & Engr.**
3141 A1837 2r Block of 4, #a-d 9.25 9.25

Miniature Sheet

Espírito Santo Tourist Attractions — A1838

No. 3142: a, O Frade e a Freira rock formations. b, Moqueca Capixaba (seafood stew). c, Itaúnas Dunes. d, Ponte da Passagem, Vitória. e, Palácio Anchuieta. f, Penha Convent, Vila Velha. g, Caparaó National Park. h, Pedra Azul. i, Pedra da Cebola. j, Guarapari Beach. k, Port of Vitória. l, Curva da Jurema Beach.

2010, Aug. 16 Litho. *Perf. 11½x12*

3142 A1838 Sheet of 12 + 12 labels 26.00 26.00
a.-l. (1.05r) Any single + label *2.10 2.10*

No. 3142 sold for 30r. Labels could be personalized.

A1839

A1840

A1841

Corinthians Paulista Sport Club, Cent. A1842

2010, Sept. 1 Litho. *Perf. 11½x12*

3143 A1839 1.05r multi 1.25 1.25
3144 A1840 (1.05r) multi + label *2.10 2.10*

Perf. 12x11½

3145 A1841 (1.05r) multi + label *2.10 2.10*

Embroidered
Self-Adhesive
Die Cut Perf. 11¾x11½

3146 A1842 8.30r multi 9.75 9.75

Nos. 3144-3145 each were printed in sheets of 12 stamps + 12 labels that sold for 30r. Labels could be personalized.

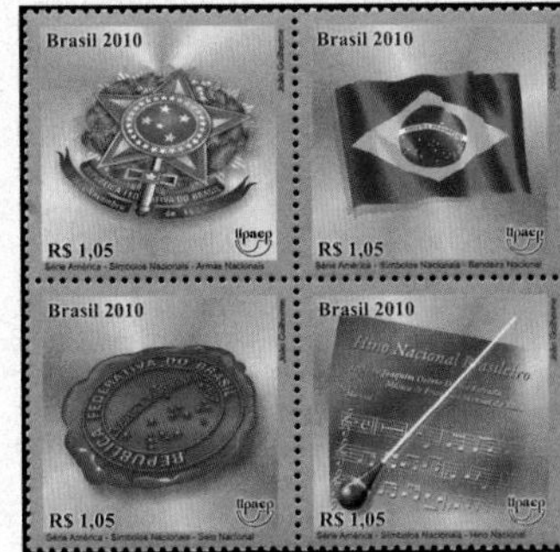

America Issue, National Symbols — A1843

No. 3147: a, National coat of arms. b, National flag. c, National seal. d, National anthem.

2010, Sept. 7 Litho. *Perf. 11½*

3147 A1843 1.05r Block of 4, #a-d 5.00 5.00

13th Conference of Government Postage Stamp Printers' Association, Rio de Janeiro A1844

Litho. & Embossed

2010, Sept. 20 *Perf. 11½*

3148 A1844 2r multi 2.40 2.40

Souvenir Sheet

Intl. Year of Biodiversity — A1845

No. 3149: a, Tomatoes on vine. b, Organic green vegetables.

2010, Sept. 21 Litho. *Perf. 11½x12*

3149 A1845 2.40r Sheet of 2, #a-b 5.75 5.75

Portugal 2010 World Philatelic Exhibition, Lisbon.

Miniature Sheet

Rio de Janeiro Tourist Attractions — A1846

No. 3150: a, Arcos de Lapa (Lapa Arches), Rio de Janeiro. b, Ponte Estalada (Estalada Bridge), Rio des Ostras. c, Imperial Museum, Petrópolis. d, Monumento dos Pracinhas (World War II Soldier's Monument), Rio de Janeiro. e, Santa Rita Church, Paraty. f, Christ the Redeemer Statue, Rio de Janeiro. g, Serra dos Oragaos, Teresópolis. h, Ponte Rio Niterói (Niterói River Bridge), Rio de Janeiro. i, Crystal Palace, Petrópolis. j, Museum of Contemporary Art, Niterói. k, Sao Tomé Lighthouse, Campos dos Goytacazes. l, Metropolitan Cathedral, Rio de Janeiro.

2010, Sept. 27 *Perf. 12x11½*

3150 A1846 Sheet of 12 + 12 labels *26.00 26.00*
a.-l. (1.05r) Any single + label *2.10 2.10*

No. 3150 sold for 30r. Labels could be personalized.

A1847

A1848

Christmas A1849

2010, Oct. 22 *Perf. 11½*

Souvenir Sheet

3151 A1847 2.70r multi 3.25 3.25

Self-Adhesive
Die Cut Perf. 12

3152 A1848 (75c) multi .90 .90
3153 A1849 (1.05r) multi 1.25 1.25

Diplomatic Relations Between Brazil and Zambia — A1850

No. 3154 — Animals and sites in Zambia: a, Leopard. b, Victoria Falls. c, Lion. d, Buffalo. e, Black rhinoceros. f, African elephant.

2010, Oct. 24 *Perf. 11½*

3154 A1850 1.05r Block of 6, #a-f 7.50 7.50

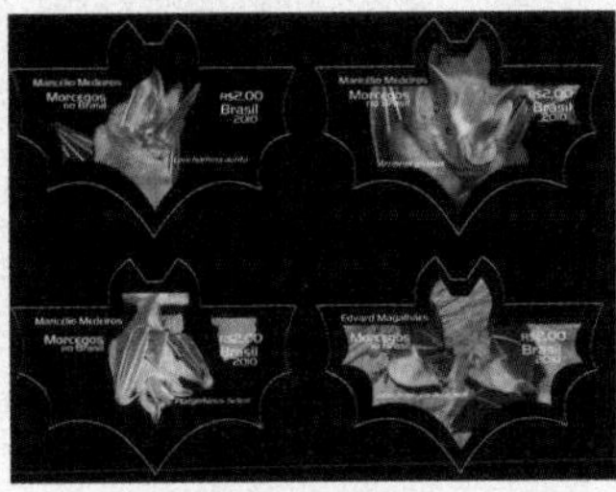

Bats — A1851

No. 3155: a, Lonchorhina aurita. b, Artibeus gnomus. c, Platyrrhinus helleri. d, Lonchophylla dekeyseri.

2010, Oct. 30 *Die Cut*

Self-Adhesive

3155 A1851 Block of 4 9.75
a.-d. 2r Any single 2.40 2.40

A1852

Christmas — A1853

2010, Nov. 30 Litho. *Perf. 11½x12*

3156 A1852 (1.05r) multi + label *2.40 2.40*

Perf. 12x11½

3157 A1853 (1.05r) multi + label *2.40 2.40*

Nos. 3156-3157 each were printed in sheets of 12stamps + 12 labels that sold for 30r. Labels could be personalized.

Miniature Sheet

Goias Tourist Attractions — A1854

No. 3158: a, Vaca Brava Park, Goiânia. b, Waterfalls near Cavalcante. c, Pools, Caldas Novas. d, Rio Quente. e, Praça do Trabalhador (Worker's Square), Goiânia. f, Rio Araguala. g, Mask from Pirenópolis. h, Bosque dos Buritis, Goiânia. i, Waterfalls, Chapada dos Veadeiros National Park. j, Waterfalls, Pirenópolis. k, Basilica, Trinidade. l, Casa de Cora (House of Cora Coralina), Cidade de Goiás.

2010, Dec. 23 *Perf. 11½x12*

3158 A1854 Sheet of 12 + 12 labels *24.00 24.00*
a.-l. (1.05r) Any single + label *2.00 2.00*

No. 3158 sold for 30r. Labels could be personalized.

End of Term of Pres. Luiz Inácio Lula da Silva — A1855

2011, Jan. 1 *Perf. 12x11½*

3159 A1855 2r mulyi 2.40 2.40

Federal Savings Bank, 150th Anniv. A1856

2011, Jan. 12 Litho. *Perf. 11½x12*

3160 A1856 (1.05r) multi 1.25 1.25

Federal Savings Bank, 150th Anniv. — A1857

2011, Jan. 12 ***Perf. 12x11½***
3161 A1857 (1.05r) multi + label 3.00 3.00

No. 3161 was printed in sheets of 12 stamps + 12 labels that sold for 30r. Labels could be personalized.

Father Roberto Landell de Moura (1861-1928), Radio Pioneer — A1858

2011, Jan. 21 ***Perf. 11½x12***
3162 A1858 (1.05r) multi 1.25 1.25

Postal Union of the Americas, Spain and Portugal (UPAEP), Cent. A1859

2011, Mar. 23 ***Perf. 11½***
3163 A1859 1.25r multi 1.60 1.60

Guarani Soccer Team, Cent. — A1860

2011, Apr. 2 ***Perf. 12x11½***
3164 A1860 (1.10r) multi 1.40 1.40

Mariana, 300th Anniv. — A1861

2011, Apr. 8 ***Perf. 11½x12***
3165 A1861 1.10r multi 1.40 1.40

Military Academy of Agulhas Negras, 200th Anniv. A1862

2011, Apr. 15
3166 A1862 1.10r multi 1.40 1.40

Railway Stations A1863

Designs: No. 3167, Luz Station, Sao Paolo. No. 3168, Júlio Prestes Station, Sao Paolo. No. 3169, Central do Brasil Station, Rio de Janeiro, vert.

2011, Apr. 30 ***Perf. 11½x12***
3167 A1863 1.10r multi 1.40 1.40
3168 A1863 1.10r multi 1.40 1.40

Self-Adhesive

Die Cut Perf. 12

3169 A1863 1.10r multi 1.40 1.40

Itaipu Dam A1864

2011, May 6 ***Perf. 11½x12***
3170 A1864 1.10r multi 1.40 1.40

Paraguayan independence, bicent.

Miniature Sheet

Marine Life — A1865

No. 3171: a, Pelagia sp., Phyllorhiza punctata. b, Sepioteuthis sepioidea. c, Octopus insularis. d, Oreaster reticulatus.

2011, June 5
3171 A1865 2.70r Sheet of 4, #a-d 13.50 13.50

PhilaNippon 2011 Intl. Philatelic Exhibition, Yokohama, Japan.

Intl. Elder Abuse Awareness Day — A1866

2011, June 15 ***Perf. 12x11½***
3172 A1866 1.10r multi 1.40 1.40

Assembly of God Churches in Brazil, Cent. — A1867

2011, June 18 ***Perf. 11½x12***
3173 A1867 (1.10r) multi + label *3.25 3.25*

No. 3173 was printed in sheets of 12 stamps + 12 labels that sold for 30r. Labels could be personalized.

Souvenir Sheet

Flora and Fauna of Tijuca National Park — A1868

No. 3174: a, Tangara seledon, Hadrolaelia lobata. b, Thalurania glaucopis, Coendou insidiosus.

2011, July 6 **Litho.**
3174 A1868 5r Sheet of 2, #a-b 13.00 13.00

Intl. Year of Forests, Brasiliana 2013 Intl. Philatelic Exhibition, Rio de Janeiro.

Ouro Preto, 300th Anniv. — A1869

2011, July 8
3175 A1869 1.10r multi 1.40 1.40

Regional Labor Court, Fortaleza — A1870

2011, July 11 ***Perf. 11½x12***
3176 A1870 (1.10r) multi + label *3.25 3.25*

No. 3176 was printed in sheets of 12 stamps + 12 labels that sold for 30r. Labels could be personalized.

Bahia Commercial Association, 200th Anniv. — A1871

2011, July 15 ***Perf. 12x11½***
3177 A1871 1.10r multi 1.40 1.40

Paulo Gracindo (1911-95), Actor — A1872

2011, July 16 ***Perf. 11½x12***
3178 A1872 1.85r multi 2.40 2.40

Sabará, 300th Anniv. — A1873

2011, July 17
3179 A1873 1.10r multi 1.40 1.40

Brazilian Folklore — A1874

Nos. 3180 and 3181: a, Curupira on boar, logger with chainsaw. b, Mother-of-gold (mae-do-ouro), gold panner. c, Dolphin (boto), pregnant woman. d. Headless mule (mula-sem-cabeça), church.

2011, July 23 ***Perf. 11½***
3180 A1874 (1.10r) Block of 4, #a-d 5.50 5.50

Souvenir Sheet

3181 A1874 1.10r Sheet of 4, #a-d 5.50 5.50

Nos. 3180a-3180d are each inscribed "1 Porte Carta Nao Comercial." Brapex 2011, Recife (No. 3181).

Stylized People and Envelope — A1875

Die Cut Perf. 12¼x12 Syncopated

2011, Aug. 5 **Self-Adhesive**
3182 A1875 (1c) dk blue & org brn .25 .25

No. 3182 was for use by impoverished people in the Bolsa Família program on a maximum of five hand-addressed domestic letters weighing no more than 10 grams. Stamps were applied to letters by postal clerks upon verification of the sender's involvement in the program and were not intended for direct sale to customers. The stamp was valid until Sept. 30, 2011.

Diplomatic Relations Between Brazil and Ukraine — A1876

2011, Aug. 24 ***Perf. 11x11½***
3183 A1876 2.55r multi 3.00 3.00

Mogi das Cruzes, 400th Anniv. — A1877

2011, Sept. 1 ***Perf. 11½x12***
3184 A1877 1.10r multi 1.25 1.25

Delivery of Registered Letter — A1878

Die Cut Perf. 12 Syncopated

2011, Sept. 2 **Self-Adhesive**

3185 A1878 (2.80r) multi 3.25 3.25

Sao Paolo Municipal Theater, Cent. — A1879

2011, Sept. 12 ***Perf. 11½x12***

3186 A1879 2r multi 2.40 2.40

Miniature Sheet

Piauí Tourist Attractions — A1880

No. 3187: a, Parnaíba River Delta. b, Rock arch, Serra da Capivara National Park, Sao Raimundo Nonato. c, Metálica Bridge, Teresina. d, Our Lady of Victory Church, Oeiras. e, Carved wooden statues, Teresina. f, Ferry approaching dock, Parnaiba. g, Master Isidoro França Bridge, Teresina. h, Opal jewelry, Pedro II. i, Rio Poty Canyon, Buriti dos Montes. j, Sete Cidades National Park, Piracuruca. k, Barra Grande Beach, Cajueiro da Praia. l, Monument to the Battle of Jenipapo, Campos Maior.

2011, Sept. 12

3187 A1880 Sheet of 12 + 12 labels *35.00 35.00*

a.-l. (1.10r) Any single + label *2.75 2.75*

No. 3187 sold for 30r. Labels could be personalized.

Coelho Rodrigues Court House, Teresina — A1881

2011, Oct. 1 ***Perf. 11½x12***

3188 A1881 (1.10r) multi + label *2.75 2.75*

No. 3188 was printed in sheets of 12 stamps + 12 labels that sold for 30r. Labels could be personalized.

Trees of Brazil — A1882

Nos. 3189 and 3190: a, Tree with small branches and few leaves, text above tree starting with "As árvores nascem." b, Larger tree, text above tree starting with "copas abertas." c, Larger tree, text above tree starting with "devolvendo." d, No text above large tree.

2011, Oct. 3 ***Perf. 11½***

Stamps With White Frames

3189 A1882 (1.10r) Block of 4, #a-d 5.00 5.00

Miniature Sheet

Stamps Without White Frames

3190 A1882 2.70r Sheet of 4, #a-d, + 5 labels 12.50 12.50

On No. 3190, a square of cedar wood is affixed to the back of the central label. The four numbered corner labels illustrate how the stamps can be folded to show the square of cedar wood through the die cut openings replacing the tree trunks that were made in Nos. 3190a-3190c. Two of the corner labels depict stamps from No. 3190, but these labels are not valid for postage.

Mail Recipient Signing for Registered Letter — A1883

Die Cut Perf. 12 Syncopated

2011, Oct. 7 **Self-Adhesive**

3191 A1883 (5.60r) multi 6.50 6.50

America Issue — A1884

No. 3192: a, Imperial era mailbox. b, Republic era mailbox. c, Department of Mail and Telegraphs (DCT) mailbox. d, Mailbox in current use.

Litho. & Engr., Litho. & Embossed (#3192d)

2011, Oct. 9 ***Perf. 11½***

3192 A1884 2r Block of 4, #a-d 9.25 9.25

Diplomatic Relations Between Brazil and Italy — A1885

2011, Oct. 12 Litho. ***Perf. 12x11½***

3193 A1885 2.10r multi 2.40 2.40

A1886

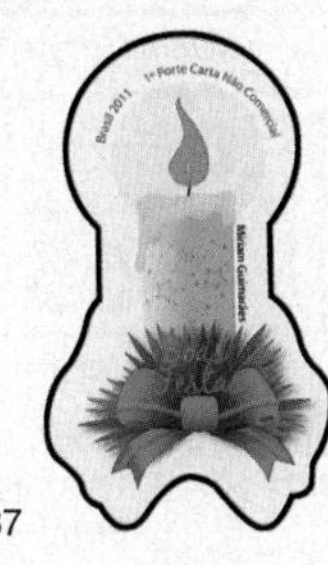

A1887

Christmas A1888

No. 3194: a, Open Bible. b, Closed Bible.

No. 3196 — Ornament color: a, Dark red. b, Purple. c, Green. d, Yellow. e, Blue. f, Red violet.

2011, Oct. 21 ***Perf. 11½***

3194 A1886 2.70r Souvenir sheet of 2, #a-b 6.25 6.25

Self-Adhesive

Die Cut

3195 A1887 (75c) multi .85 .85

3196 Block of 6 7.50

a.-f. A1888 (1.10r) Any single 1.25 1.25

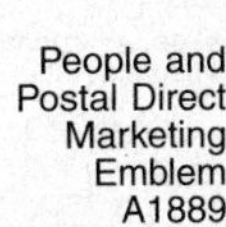

People and Postal Direct Marketing Emblem A1889

Die Cut Perf. 12 Syncopated

2011, Oct. 24 **Self-Adhesive**

3197 A1889 2r multi 2.25 2.25

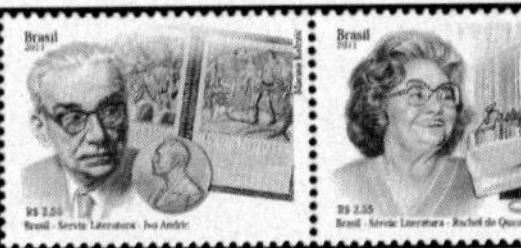

Writers — A1890

No. 3198: a, Ivo Andric (1892-1975), Yugoslavian writer, and Nobel medal. b, Rachel de Queiroz (1910-2003), Brazilian writer.

2011, Oct. 26 ***Perf. 11½x12***

3198 A1890 2.55r Horiz. pair, #a-b 6.00 6.00

See Serbia Nos. 570-571.

Diplomatic Relations Between Belgium and Brazil — A1891

Designs: Nos, 3199, 3201a, 2.55r, Flag bearer and master of ceremonies at Carnaval. Nos. 3200, 3201b, 2.55r, Acarajé de Lansan, No Ilê Oxumarê, painting by Carybé.

2011, Oct. 29 ***Perf. 11x11½***

Stamps With White Frames

3199-3200 A1891 Set of 2 5.75 5.75

Souvenir Sheet

Stamps With Gray Frames

3201 A1891 2.55r Sheet of 2, #a-b 5.75 5.75

Brazilian Philatelic Society, Cent. — A1893

Litho. & Engr.

2011, Nov. 18 ***Perf. 12x11½***

3202 A1893 2.55r copper & black 3.00 3.00

No. 3202 was printed in sheets of 28 stamps + 2 labels.

Dawn in Parana Area, Cyanocorax Caeruleus — A1894

Tree and Cyanocorax Caeruleus — A1895

2011, Nov. 25 Litho. ***Perf. 11½x12***

3203 A1894 (1.10r) multi + label *2.75 2.75*

Perf. 12x11½

3204 A1895 (1.10r) multi + label *2.75 2.75*

Nos. 3203-3204 each were printed in sheets of 12 stamps + 12 labels that sold for 30r. Labels could be personalized.

Mário Lago (1911-2002), Actor — A1896

Litho. & Engr.

2011, Nov. 26 ***Perf. 11½x12***

3205 A1896 1.85r black & bronze 2.10 2.10

Campaign for Prevention of AIDS — A1897

No. 3206: a, Heart, condom, man and woman. b, Condom. c, Hypodermic needle. d, Man and woman looking up. e, Condom, man and woman embracing. f, Heart in hourglass frame. g, AIDS ribbons. h, Condoms and hearts.

2011, Dec. 1 Litho. *Perf. 11½*
3206 A1897 (1.10r) Block of 8, #a-h 10.00 10.00

Diplomatic Relations Between Brazil and Qatar — A1898

Litho. & Embossed
2011, Dec. 19 *Perf. 12x11½*
3207 A1898 2.70r multi 3.00 3.00

Rio de Janeiro Presbyterian Church, 150th Anniv. — A1899

2012, Jan. 12
3208 A1899 1.60r multi 1.90 1.90

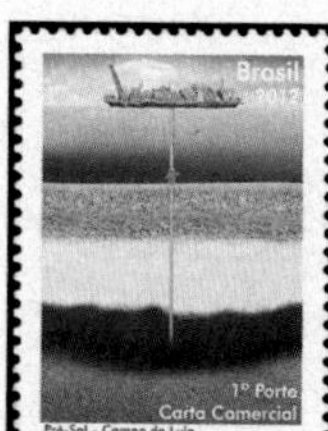

Lula Oil Field — A1900

2012, Jan. 17 Litho.
3209 A1900 (1.10r) multi 1.25 1.25

Bahia Medical Faculty, 200th Anniv. — A1901

2012, Jan. 19 *Perf. 11½x12*
3210 A1901 (1.10r) multi + label *2.75 2.75*

No. 3210 was printed in sheets of 12 stamps + 12 labels that sold for 30r. Labels could be personalized.

Minas Gerais Flag — A1902

Minas Gerais Flag — A1903

2012, Jan. 19 *Perf. 12x11½*
3211 A1902 (1.10r) multi + label *2.75 2.75*
Perf. 11½x12
3212 A1903 (1.10r) multi + label *2.75 2.75*

Nos. 3211-3212 each were printed in sheets of 12 stamps + 12 labels that sold for 30r. Labels could be personalized.

Miniature Sheet

Santa Catarina Tourist Attractions — A1904

No. 3213: a, Hercílio Luz Bridge, Florianópolis. b, Rock arch, Pedra Furada, Urubici. c, Rua des Palmeiras, Joinville. d, Morro dos Conventos, Araranguá. e, Sao Francisco do Sul. f, Monument to Explorers, Chapecó. g, Whale near Siriú Beach, Garopaba. h, Santa Paulina Sanctuary, Nova Trento. i, Balneário Camboriú. j, German Village, Blumenau. k, Port of Itajaí. l, Railroad Museum, Tubarao.

2012, Jan. 19 *Perf. 11½x12*
3213 A1904 Sheet of 12 + 12 labels *35.00 35.00*
a.-l. (1.10r) Any single + label *2.75 2.75*

No. 3213 sold for 30r. Labels could be personalized.

Souvenir Sheet

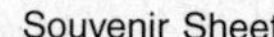

Dorina Nowill Foundation for the Blind — A1905

No. 3214: a, Blind boy. b, Nowill (1919-2010), philantropist.

Litho., Litho. & Embossed (#3214b)
2012, Mar. 11 *Perf. 12x11½*
Without Gum
3214 A1905 2.80r Sheet of 2, #a-b 6.25 6.25

Santos Soccer Team, Cent. — A1906

2012, Apr. 14 Litho. *Perf. 12x11½*
3215 A1906 (1.10r) black & gold 1.25 1.25

América Soccer Team, Cent. — A1907

2012, Apr. 30
3216 A1907 (1.10r) multi 1.25 1.25

Traditional Foods of Brazil and Mexico — A1908

No. 3217: a, Milho e mandioca. b, Pozole.

2012, June 1 *Perf. 11½*
3217 A1908 2.30r Horiz. pair, #a-b 4.75 4.75

See Mexico Nos. 2784-2785.

A1909

Rio + 20 United Nations Conference on Sustainable Development, Rio de Janeiro — A1910

No. 3218: a, Monkey, crocodile, birds, butterflies and armadillo in forest. b, Irrigation of fields near house and water tanks. c, People and dog approaching school building. d, Rio + 20 conference emblem. e, Bird, ecotourists, guide, kayaker. f, Farmers harvesting crops from irrigated field, house, water tank, truck. g, Truck at produce market. h, Garbage truck near apartment buildings and park. i, Bulldozer, logs, man planting saplings. j, Dam, dyanmo, electric power lines and towers. k, Cars at gas station and electric recharging station. l, Train, cable cars, bicycles. m, Green factory, electric train, forklift and crates. n, Swimmer in river, scientists testing water. o, Bus on road, electric train on bridge. p, Handicapped people at telephone, bus stop and crosswalk. q, Indigenous people, boar, fish. r, Garbage trucks at recycling center. s, Birds and crabs in mangrove swamp. t, People on beach, solar panels. u, Wind generators. v, Electric train, ship and shipping containers at port. w, Wildlife warden and fishermen in boats. x, Scuba diver, whale, turtle, jellyfish and marine life.

No. 3219: a, City in droplet, sun, birds, tree, ship, whale, shark and dolphins. b, Bird, fish, bicycle, windmill and hand. c, Earth and city in flower.

2012, June 1 *Perf. 11½x12*
3218 Sheet of 24 26.50 26.50
a.-x. A1909 (1.10r) Any single 1.10 1.10

Souvenir Sheet
Self-Adhesive
Die Cut Perf. 12
3219 A1910 2r Sheet of 3, #a-c 6.00 6.00

Wild Cats A1911

No. 3220: a, Puma yagouaroundi. b, Leopardus pardalis.

2012, June 5 *Perf. 11½*
3220 A1911 (1.10r) Vert. pair, #a-b 2.25 2.25

Wind Turbines A1912

2012, June 15 ***Perf. 11x11½***
3221 A1912 1.85r multi 1.90 1.90

21st LUBRAPEX Philatelic Exhibition, Sao Paolo — A1913

Litho. & Engr.
2012, Aug. 1 ***Perf. 12x11½***
3222 A1913 2.75r silver & blk 2.75 2.75

Medicinal Plants — A1914

No. 3223: a, Carapa guianensis. b, Copaifera martii. c, Ptychopetalum olacoides. d, Uncaria guianensis.

2012, Aug. 5 **Litho.** ***Perf. 11½***
3223 A1914 (1.20r) Block of 4, #a-d 4.75 4.75

America Issue A1915

No. 3224 — Legend of origin of: a, Guaraná. b, Cassava.

2012, Aug. 22
3224 A1915 1.85r Vert. pair, #a-b 3.75 3.75

A1916

Poets — A1917

No. 3225: a, Fernando Pessoa (1888-1935). b, Poetry by Pessoa, ship.
No. 3226: a, Joao da Cruz e Sousa (1861-98). b, Poetry by Cruz e Sousa, bird in flight.

2012, Sept. 7 ***Perf. 12x11½***
3225 A1916 2r Horiz. pair, #a-b 4.00 4.00
3226 A1917 2r Horiz. pair, #a-b 4.00 4.00

LUBRAPEX 2012, Sao Paolo. See Portugal Nos. 3437-3438.

Sao Luís Cathedral, Palace of the Lions, Sao Luís — A1918

2012, Sept. 8 ***Perf. 11½x12***
3227 A1918 1.20r multi 1.25 1.25

Sao Luís, 400th anniv.

Holy Family — A1919

Choir — A1920

Gifts in Post Office Box — A1921

No. 3228: a, Jesus and Virgin Mary. b, St. Joseph.

Litho. With Foil Application
2012, Oct. 17 ***Perf. 12x11½***
Souvenir Sheet
3228 A1919 3.85r Sheet of 2, #a-b 7.75 7.75

Litho.
Die Cut
Self-Adhesive
3229 A1920 (80c) multi .80 .80
3230 A1921 (1.20r) multi 1.25 1.25

Christmas.

Emblems of Postal Bank, Bank of Brazil and Brazilian Postal Service — A1922

Die Cut Perf. 12 Syncopated
2012, Oct. 22 **Litho.**
Self-Adhesive
3231 A1922 (1.20r) multi 1.25 1.25

Souvenir Sheet

Sugarloaf Mountain Aerial Cable Car, Cent. — A1923

No. 3232: a, Sugarloaf Mountain. b, Cable car.

2012, Oct. 27 ***Perf. 11½***
3232 A1923 2.40r Sheet of 2, #a-b 4.75 4.75

Brasiliana 2013 Intl. Philatelic Exhibition, Rio de Janeiro.

Jorge Amado (1912-2001), Writer A1924

2012, Nov. 10
3233 A1924 1.20r multi 1.25 1.25

LUBRAPEX 2012, Sao Paolo.

Quilombo dos Palmares Memorial Park, Uniao dos Palmares — A1925

2012, Nov. 19 ***Perf. 11x11½***
3234 A1925 (1.20r) multi 1.25 1.25

Chinese Immigration to Brazil, 200th Anniv. — A1926

No. 3235: a, Dragon and ship. b, Dragon dancers.

2012, Dec. 10 ***Perf. 11½x12***
3235 A1926 2.90r Horiz. pair, #a-b 5.75 5.75

Luiz Gonzaga (1912-89), Musician A1927

Litho. & Embossed
2012, Dec. 13 ***Perf. 11½***
3236 A1927 (1.20r) multi 1.25 1.25

Sports and Their Venues A1928

No. 3237: a, Horse racing, Gávea Horse Racing Track, Rio de Janeiro. b, Go-karting, Ayrton Senna Kart Track, Interlagos. c, Volleyball, Journalist Felipe Drummond Stadium, Belo Horizonte. d, Auto racing, Nelson Piquet International Racetrack, Brasilia. e, Cycling, Velodrome, Maringá.

2012, Dec. 14 **Litho. & Engr.**
3237 Horiz. strip of 5 10.00 10.00
a.-e. A1928 2r Any single 2.00 2.00

Federal University of Paraná, Cent. — A1929

2012, Dec. 19 **Litho.** ***Perf. 11x11½***
3238 A1929 1.20r multi 1.25 1.25

Miniature Sheet

Brazilian Postal Services, 350th Anniv. — A1930

No. 3239: a, Ship (first postal activities in Brazil, 1663). b, Mail delivery by horseback. c, Building (first postal administration in Brazil, 1798). d, Court postman making delivery, 1835. e, Issuance of Brazil #1, 2 and 3, 1843. f, Issuance of Brazil #7, 8, 9, 10 and 13, 1844. g, Mail collection box, 1845, Brazil #3192a and 3192b. h, Baron Capanema (1824-1908), installer of first electric telegraph system in Brazil, 1852. i, Dial of Bréguet telegraph. j, Workers constructing telegraph line. k, Equipment in telegraph office. l, Issuance of Brazil #59, 1866. m, Construction of first post office in Rio de Janeiro, 1878. n, Pneumatic post mail, 1910. o, Sao Paolo Post Office, 1922. p, Badges (creation of Department of Posts and Telegraphs,1931). q, Mechanical sorting of mail, 1940. r, Postman with bicycle, emblem of Brazil Posts and Telegraphs Company (creation of Brazilian Posts and Telegraphs Company, 1969). s, Postal workers at electronic sorting equipment, 1972. t, Brazil Postal Headquarters, 1978. u, Participation of postal workers in social and environmental projects. v, Mail sorters, postmen, motorcycle, ship. w, Mail deliverers, postal truck (presence of postal service in all towns, 2001). x, 350th anniv. emblem, Brazil Post emblem (2013).

2013, Jan. 25 **Litho.** ***Perf. 11½x12***
3239 A1930 Sheet of 24 30.00 30.00
a.-x. (1.20r) Any single 1.25 1.25

Campaign Against Racial Discrimination — A1931

2013, Mar. 21 **Litho.** ***Perf. 11½x12***
3240 A1931 2r multi 2.00 2.00

America issue.

Souvenir Sheet

Intl. Year of Water Cooperation — A1932

No. 3241 — Half of stylized globe, water stream and: a, Hand. b, Open mouth.

Litho. & Embossed

2013, Mar. 22 ***Perf. 12x11½***

3241 A1932 2.75r Sheet of 2, #a-b 5.50 5.50

World Youth Day, Rio de Janeiro — A1933

2013, Mar. 23 Litho. ***Perf. 12x11½***

3242 A1933 1.20r multi 1.25 1.25

SEMI-POSTAL STAMPS

National Philatelic Exhibition Issue

SP1

Thick Paper

Wmk. Coat of Arms in Sheet (236)

1934, Sept. 16 Engr. ***Imperf.***

B1	SP1	200r + 100r dp claret	1.25	*3.00*
B2	SP1	300r + 100r ver	1.25	*3.00*
B3	SP1	700r + 100r brt bl	8.00	*27.50*
B4	SP1	1000r + 100r blk	8.00	*27.50*
		Nos. B1-B4 (4)	18.50	*61.00*

The surtax was to help defray the expenses of the exhibition. Issued in sheets of 60, inscribed "EXPOSICAO FILATELICA NACIONAL."

Red Cross Nurse and Soldier SP2

Wmk. 222

1935, Sept. 19 Typo. ***Perf. 11***

B5	SP2	200r + 100r pur & red	1.75	1.25
B6	SP2	300r + 100r ol brn & red	2.00	.90
B7	SP2	700r + 100r turq bl & red	12.50	7.00
		Nos. B5-B7 (3)	16.25	9.15

3rd Pan-American Red Cross Conf. Exist imperf.

Three Wise Men and Star of Bethlehem — SP3

Angel and Child — SP4

Southern Cross and Child — SP5

Mother and Child — SP6

Wmk. 249

1939-40 Litho. ***Perf. 10½***

B8	SP3	100r + 100r chlky bl & bl blk	1.60	1.60
a.		Horiz. or vert. pair, imperf. between	40.00	
B9	SP4	200r + 100r brt grnsh bl	2.25	2.10
a.		Horizontal pair, imperf. between	40.00	
B10	SP5	400r + 200r ol grn & ol	1.75	1.10
B11	SP6	1200r + 400r crim & brn red	7.00	3.25
a.		Vertical pair, imperf. between	40.00	
		Nos. B8-B11 (4)	12.60	8.05

Dates of issue: #B8, 12/20/39; #B9-B11, 2/26/40.

Surtax for charitable institutions.

For surcharges see Nos. C55-C59.

Catalogue values for unused stamps in this section, from this point to the end of the section, are for Never Hinged items.

In 1980 three stamps that were intended to be semi-postals were issued as postage stamps at the total combined face value. See Nos. 1681-1683.

Children and Citizenship — SP7

Designs: a, Cutouts of children forming pyramid. b, Man and woman's hands holding onto girl. c, Children going into school. d, Pregnant woman in front of house. e, Children flying paper doves. f, Parent working in garden, child writing letters, doves. g, Breastfeeding. h, Father holding birth certificate, mother holding infant. i, Disabled child on wheelchair ramp. j, Mother, father with sick child. k, Stylized child, pencil, letters. l, Hands above and below pregnant woman. m, Two families of different races. n, Small child playing large guitar. o, People looking to baby on pedestal. p, Children, book, "Statute of Children and Adolescent."

1997, Nov. 20 Litho. ***Perf. 12x11½***

B12	Sheet of 16	15.00	15.00
a.-p.	SP7 22c +8c any single	.80	.70

Surcharge for Natl. Fund for Children and Adolescents.

Stampin' the Future Children's Stamp Design Contest Winners — SP8

Art by: a, Jonas Sampaio de Freitas. b, Clarissa Cazane. c, Caio Ferreira Guimaraes de Oliveira. d, Milena Karoline Ribeiro Reis.

2000, Jan. 1 Litho. ***Perf. 11½x12***

B13 SP8 22c + 8c Block of 4, #a-d 3.00 3.00

Children's Hope SP9

Designs: No. B14, Child and family activities. No. B15, Children reading, painting, dancing.

2002, July 26 Litho. ***Perf. 11½x12***

B14	SP9	(80c) +10c multi	.85	.85
B15	SP9	(80c) +10c multi	.85	.85
a.		Pair, #B14-B15	1.90	1.90

AIR POST STAMPS

Nos. O14-O29 Surcharged

SERVICO AEREO 200 Rs.

1927, Dec. 28 Unwmk. ***Perf. 12***

C1	O2	50r on 10r	.45	.35
a.		Inverted surcharge	325.00	
b.		Top ornaments missing	75.00	
C2	O2	200r on 1000r	2.25	*4.50*
a.		Double surcharge	325.00	
C3	O2	200r on 2000r	1.40	*10.00*
a.		Double surcharge	750.00	
b.		Double surcharge, one inverted	750.00	
C4	O2	200r on 5000r	1.75	1.40
a.		Double surcharge	325.00	—
b.		Double surcharge, one inverted	350.00	
c.		Triple surcharge	450.00	
C5	O2	300r on 500r	1.75	2.25
C6	O2	300r on 600r	.85	.90
b.		Pair, one without surch.	—	
C6A	O2	500r on 10r	400.00	425.00
C7	O2	500r on 50r	1.75	.70
a.		Double surcharge	300.00	—
C8	O2	1000r on 20r	1.40	.45
a.		Double surcharge	300.00	—
C9	O2	2000r on 100r	3.00	1.75
a.		Pair, one without surcharge	—	
b.		Double surcharge	300.00	
C10	O2	2000r on 200r	4.00	1.75
C11	O2	2000r on 10,000r	3.50	.70
C12	O2	5000r on 20,000r	10.00	4.00
C13	O2	5000r on 50,000r	10.00	4.00
C14	O2	5000r on 100,000r	32.50	30.00
C15	O2	10,000r on 500,000r	35.00	20.00
C16	O2	10,000r on 1,000,000r	45.00	37.50
		Nos. C1-C6,C7-C16 (16)	154.60	120.25

Nos. C1, C1b, C7, C8 and C9 have small diamonds printed over the numerals in the upper corners.

Monument to de Gusmao — AP1

Santos-Dumont's Airship — AP2

Augusto Severo's Airship "Pax" — AP3

Santos-Dumont's Biplane "14 Bis" — AP4

Ribeiro de Barros's Seaplane "Jahu" — AP5

Perf. 11, 12½x13, 13x13½

1929 Typo. Wmk. 206

C17	AP1	50r blue grn	.35	.25
C18	AP2	200r red	1.40	.25
C19	AP3	300r brt blue	2.25	.25
C20	AP4	500r red violet	2.50	.25
C21	AP5	1000r orange brn	9.00	.40
		Nos. C17-C21 (5)	15.50	1.40

See Nos. C32-C36. For surcharges see Nos. C26-C27.

Bartholomeu de Gusmao — AP6

Augusto Severo — AP7

Alberto Santos-Dumont AP8

Perf. 9, 11 and Compound

1929-30 Engr. Wmk. 101

C22	AP6	2000r lt green ('30)	14.00	.50
C23	AP7	5000r carmine	16.00	1.25
C24	AP8	10,000r olive grn	16.00	1.75
		Nos. C22-C24 (3)	46.00	3.50

Nos. C23-C24 exist imperf.

See Nos. C37, C40.

Allegory: Airmail Service between Brazil and the US — AP9

1929 Typo. Wmk. 206

C25 AP9 3000r violet 14.00 1.75

Exists imperf. See Nos. C38, C41. For surcharge see No. C28.

Nos. C18-C19 Surcharged in Blue or Red

1931, Aug. 16 ***Perf. 12½x13½***

C26 AP2 2500r on 200r (Bl) 30.00 25.00
C27 AP3 5000r on 300r (R) 35.00 30.00

No. C25 Surcharged

1931, Sept. 2 ***Perf. 11***

C28 AP9 2500r on 3000r vio 27.50 *27.50*
a. Inverted surcharge 160.00 —
b. Surch. on front and back 160.00

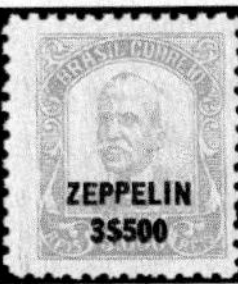

Regular Issues of 1928-29 Surcharged

1932, May Wmk. 101 ***Perf. 11, 11½***

C29 A89 3500r on 5000r gray lil 27.50 27.50
C30 A72 7000r on 10,000r rose 27.50 27.50
b. Horiz. pair, imperf. between *750.00*

Imperforates

Since 1933, imperforate or partly perforated sheets of nearly all of the airmail issues have become available.

Flag and Airplane AP10

Wmk. 222

1933, June 7 Typo. ***Perf. 11***

C31 AP10 3500r grn, yel & dk bl 6.50 2.00

See Nos. C39, C42.

1934 Wmk. 222

C32 AP1 50r blue grn 2.75 2.75
C33 AP2 200r red 3.25 .85
C34 AP3 300r brt blue 8.00 2.40
C35 AP4 500r red violet 3.25 .85
C36 AP5 1000r orange brn 11.00 .85
Nos. C32-C36 (5) 28.25 7.70

1934 Wmk. 236 Engr. ***Perf. 12x11***

Thick Laid Paper

C37 AP6 2000r lt green 6.75 1.75

Types of 1929, 1933

Perf. 11, 11½, 12

1937-40 Typo. Wmk. 249

C38 AP9 3000r violet 25.00 2.25
C39 AP10 3500r grn, yel & dk bl 4.50 2.00

Engr.

C40 AP7 5000r ver ('40) 9.00 2.00
Nos. C38-C40 (3) 38.50 6.25

Watermark note after No. 501 also applies to No. C40.

Types of 1929-33

Perf. 11, 11½x12

1939-40 Typo. Wmk. 256

C41 AP9 3000r violet 2.40 .90
C42 AP10 3500r bl, dl grn & yel ('40) 2.40 .80

Map of the Western Hemisphere Showing Brazil — AP11

1941, Jan. 14 Engr. ***Perf. 11***

C43 AP11 1200r dark brown 3.25 .65

5th general census of Brazil.

No. 506A Overprinted in Carmine

1941, Nov. 10 Wmk. 264 ***Rouletted***

C45 A180 5400r slate grn 3.25 1.25
a. Overprint inverted 140.00

President Varges' new constitution, 4th anniv.

Nos. 506A and 508 Surcharged in Black

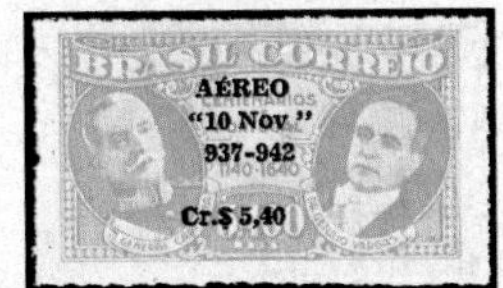

1942, Nov. 10 Wmk. 264

C47 A180 5.40cr on 5400r sl grn 2.75 1.90
a. Wmk. 249 225.00 140.00
b. Surcharge inverted 60.00 75.00

President Vargas' new constitution, 5th anniv. The status of No. C47a is questioned.

Southern Cross and Arms of Paraguay AP12

Wmk. 270

1943, May 11 Engr. ***Perf. 12½***

C48 AP12 1.20cr lt gray blue 2.00 1.40

Issued in commemoration of the visit of President Higinio Morinigo of Paraguay.

Map of South America — AP13

1943, June 30 Wmk. 271 ***Perf. 12½***

C49 AP13 1.20cr multi 2.00 1.00

Visit of President Penaranda of Bolivia.

Numeral of Value AP14

1943, Aug. 7

C50 AP14 1cr blk & dull yel 3.00 2.00
a. Double impression 30.00
C51 AP14 2cr blk & pale grn 4.25 2.00
a. Double impression 40.00
C52 AP14 5cr blk & pink 5.00 2.50
Nos. C50-C52 (3) 12.25 6.50

Centenary of Brazil's first postage stamps.

Souvenir Sheet

AP15

Without Gum ***Imperf.***

C53 AP15 Sheet of 3 50.00 50.00
a. 1cr black & dull yellow 15.00 15.00
b. 2cr black & pale green 15.00 15.00
c. 5cr black & pink 15.00 15.00

100th anniv. of the 1st postage stamps of Brazil and the 2nd Phil. Exposition (Brapex). Printed in panes of 6 sheets, perforated 12½ between. Each sheet is perforated on two or three sides. Size approximately 155x155mm.

Law Book — AP16

1943, Aug. 13 ***Perf. 12½***

C54 AP16 1.20cr rose & lil rose .80 .40

2nd Inter-American Conf. of Lawyers.

No. B10 Surcharged in Red, Carmine or Black

1944, Jan. 3 Wmk. 249 ***Perf. 10½***

C55 SP5 20c on 400r+200r (R) 1.75 .75
C56 SP5 40c on 400r+200r (Bk) 3.75 .85
C57 SP5 60c on 400r+200r (C) 4.00 .85
C58 SP5 1cr on 400r+200r (Bk) 5.75 1.00
C59 SP5 1.20cr on 400r+200r (C) 8.75 .85
Nos. C55-C59 (5) 24.00 4.30

No. C59 is known with surcharge in black but its status is questioned.

Bartholomeu de Gusmao and the "Aerostat" — AP17

Wmk. 268

1944, Oct. 23 Engr. ***Perf. 12***

C60 AP17 1.20cr rose carmine .55 .25

Week of the Wing.

L. L. Zamenhof AP18

1945, Apr. 16 Litho. ***Perf. 11***

C61 AP18 1.20cr dull brown .45 .30

Esperanto Congress held in Rio, Apr. 14-22.

Map of South America — AP19

Baron of Rio Branco — AP20

1945, Apr. 20

C62 AP19 1.20cr gray brown .35 .25
C63 AP20 5cr rose lilac .95 .40

Centenary of the birth of José Maria de Silva Paranhos, Baron of Rio Branco.

Dove and Flags of American Republics AP21

Perf. 12x11

1947, Aug. 15 Engr. Unwmk.

C64 AP21 2.20cr dk blue green .35 .25

Inter-American Defense Conference at Rio de Janeiro August-September, 1947.

Santos-Dumont Monument, St. Cloud, France — AP22

1947, Nov. 15 Typo. ***Perf. 11x12***

C65 AP22 1.20cr org brn & ol 1.00 .50

Issued to commemorate the Week of the Wing and to honor the Santos-Dumont monument which was destroyed in World War II.

Catalogue values for unused stamps in this section, from this point to the end of the section, are for Never Hinged items.

Bay of Rio de Janeiro and Rotary Emblem — AP23

1948, May 16 Engr. *Perf. 11*

C66 AP23 1.20cr deep claret .80 .55
C67 AP23 3.80cr dull violet 1.60 .55

39th convention of Rotary Intl., Rio.

Hotel Quitandinha, Petropolis — AP24

1948, July 10 Litho. Wmk. 267

C68 AP24 1.20cr org brn .45 .45
C69 AP24 3.80cr violet 1.25 .45

International Exposition of Industry and Commerce, Petropolis, 1948.

Musician and Singers AP25

1948, Aug. 13 Engr. Unwmk.

C70 AP25 1.20cr blue 1.25 .45

National School of Music, cent.

Luis Batlle Berres AP26

1948, Sept. 2 Typo.

C71 AP26 1.70cr blue .55 .30

Visit of President Luis Batlle Berres of Uruguay, September, 1948.

Merino Ram AP27

Perf. 12x11

1948, Oct. 10 Wmk. 267

C72 AP27 1.20cr dp orange .85 .50

Intl. Livestock Exposition at Bagé.

Eucharistic Congress Seal — AP28

Unwmk.

1948, Oct. 23 Engr. *Perf. 11*

C73 AP28 1.20cr dk car rose .55 .30

5th Natl. Eucharistic Cong., Porto Alegre, Oct. 24-31.

Souvenir Sheet

AP28a

1948, Dec. 14 Engr. *Imperf.*
Without Gum

C73A AP28a Sheet of 3 80.00 90.00

No. C73A contains one each of Nos. 674-676. Issued in honor of President Eurico Gasper Dutra and the armed forces. Exists both with and without number on back. Measures 130x75mm.

Church of Prazeres, Guararapes — AP29

Perf. 11½x12

1949, Feb. 15 Litho. Wmk. 267

C74 AP29 1.20cr pink 2.40 1.00

Second Battle of Guararapes, 300th anniv.

Thomé de Souza Meeting Indians — AP30

Perf. 11x12

1949, Mar. 29 Engr. Unwmk.

C75 AP30 1.20cr blue 1.25 .35

Founding of the City of Salvador, 400th anniv.

A souvenir folder, issued with No. C75, has an engraved 20cr red brown postage stamp portraying John III printed on it, and a copy of No. C75 affixed to it and postmarked. Paper is laid, and size of folder front is 100x150mm. Value, $5.

Franklin D. Roosevelt AP31

1949, May 20 Unwmk. *Imperf.*

C76 AP31 3.80cr deep blue 1.10 1.10
a. Souvenir sheet 29.00 29.00

No. C76a measures 85x110mm, with deep blue inscriptions in upper and lower margins. It also exists with papermaker's watermark. Value, $25.

Joaquim Nabuco (1849-1910), Lawyer and Writer — AP32

1949, Aug. 30 *Perf. 12*

C77 AP32 3.80cr rose lilac .80 .50
a. Wmk. 256, imperf. 25.00

Maracanã Stadium AP33

Soccer Player and Flag — AP34

Perf. 11x12, 12x11

1950, June 24 Litho. Wmk. 267

C78 AP33 1.20cr ultra & salmon 1.10 .60
C79 AP34 5.80cr bl, yel grn & yel 3.75 1.00

4th World Soccer Championship, Rio.

AP35

Symbolical of Brazilian population growth.

1950, July 10 *Perf. 12x11*

C80 AP35 1.20cr red brown .50 .25

Issued to publicize the 6th Brazilian census.

AP36

Design: J. B. Marcelino Champagnat.

1956, Sept. 8 Engr. *Perf. 11½*

C81 AP36 3.30cr rose lilac .50 .25

50th anniversary of the arrival of the Marist Brothers in Northern Brazil.

Santos-Dumont's 1906 Plane — AP37

1956 Photo.

C82 AP37 3cr dk blue grn 1.50 .30
C83 AP37 3.30cr brt ultra .30 .25
C84 AP37 4cr dp claret .80 .25
C85 AP37 6.50cr red brown .30 .25
C86 AP37 11.50cr orange red 2.50 .35
Nos. C82-C86 (5) 5.40 1.40

Souvenir Sheet

C86A AP37 Sheet of 4 17.00 9.00
b. 3cr dark carmine 2.00 .90

1st flight by Santos-Dumont, 50th anniv. Issued: No. C86A, 10/14; others 10/16.

Lord Baden-Powell AP38

1957, Aug. 1 Unwmk.
Granite Paper

C87 AP38 3.30cr deep red lilac .85 .25

Centenary of the birth of Lord Baden-Powell, founder of the Boy Scouts.

UN Emblem, Soldier and Map of Suez Canal Area AP39

Wmk. 267

1957, Oct. 24 Engr. *Perf. 11½*

C88 AP39 3.30cr dark blue .50 .25

Brazilian contingent of the UN Emergency Force.

Basketball Player — AP40

1959, May 30 Photo. *Perf. 11½*

C89 AP40 3.30cr brt red brn & bl .60 .30

Brazil's victory in the World Basketball Championships of 1959.

Symbol of Flight AP41

1959, Oct. 21 Wmk. 267

C90 AP41 3.30cr deep ultra .60 .25

Issued to publicize Week of the Wing.

Caravelle AP42

1959, Dec. 18 *Perf. 11½*

C91 AP42 6.50cr ultra .50 .25

Inauguration of Brazilian jet flights.

Pres. Adolfo Lopez Mateos — AP43

1960, Jan. 19 Photo. Wmk. 267

C92	AP43 6.50cr brown	.50	.25

Issued to commemorate the visit of President Adolfo Lopez Mateos of Mexico.

Pres. Dwight D. Eisenhower AP44

1960, Feb. 23 ***Perf. 11½***

C93	AP44 6.50cr deep orange	.60	.25

Visit of Pres. Dwight D. Eisenhower.

World Refugee Year Emblem — AP45

1960, Apr. 7 Wmk. 268

C94	AP45 6.50cr blue	.50	.25

WRY, July 1, 1959-June 30, 1960.

Type of Regular Issue and

Tower at Brasilia — AP46

Designs: 3.30cr, Square of the Three Entities. 4cr, Cathedral. 11.50cr, Plan of Brasilia.

Perf. 11x11½, 11½x11

1960, Apr. 21 Photo. Wmk. 267

C95	A436 3.30cr violet	.30	.25
C96	A436 4cr blue	.40	.25
C97	AP46 6.50cr rose carmine	.40	.25
C98	A436 11.50cr brown	.40	.25
	Nos. C95-C98 (4)	1.50	1.00

Inauguration of Brazil's new capital, Brasilia, Apr. 21, 1960.

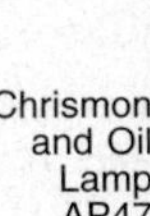

Chrismon and Oil Lamp AP47

1960, May 16 ***Perf. 11x11½***

C99	AP47 3.30cr lilac rose	.50	.25

7th Natl. Eucharistic Congress at Curitiba.

Cross, Sugarloaf Mountain and Emblem — AP48

1960, July 1 Wmk. 267

C100	AP48 6.50cr brt blue	.50	.25

10th Cong. of the World Baptist Alliance, Rio.

Boy Scout — AP49 Caravel — AP50

1960, July 23 ***Perf. 11½x11***

C101	AP49 3.30cr orange ver	.60	.25

Boy Scouts of Brazil, 50th anniversary.

1960, Aug. 5 Engr. Wmk. 268

C102	AP50 6.50cr black	.50	.25

Prince Henry the Navigator, 500th death anniv.

Maria E. Bueno AP51

1960, Dec. 15 Photo. ***Perf. 11x11½***

C103	AP51 60cr pale brown	.75	.25

Victory at Wimbledon of Maria E. Bueno, women's singles tennis champion.

War Memorial, Sugarloaf Mountain and Allied Flags — AP52

1960, Dec. 22 Wmk. 268

C104	AP52 3.30cr lilac rose	.60	.25

Reburial of Brazilian servicemen of WW II.

Power Line and Map — AP53 Malaria Eradication Emblem — AP54

1961, Jan. 20 ***Perf. 11½x11***

C105	AP53 3.30cr lilac rose	.60	.25

Inauguration of Three Marias Dam and hydroelectric station in Minas Gerais.

1962, May 24 Wmk. 267 Engr.

C106	AP54 21cr blue	.50	.25

WHO drive to eradicate malaria.

F. A. de Varnhagen — AP55

1966, Feb. 17 Photo. Wmk. 267

C107	AP55 45cr red brown	.50	.25

Francisco Adolfo de Varnhagen, Viscount of Porto Seguro (1816-1878), historian and diplomat.

Map of the Americas and Alliance for Progress Emblem AP56

1966, Mar. 14 ***Perf. 11x11½***

C108	AP56 120cr grnsh bl & vio bl	.75	.25

5th anniv. of the Alliance for Progress.

A souvenir card contains one impression of No. C108, imperf. Size: 113x160mm.

Nun and Globe — AP57 Face of Jesus from Shroud of Turin — AP58

1966, Mar. 25 Photo. ***Perf. 11½x11***

C109	AP57 35cr violet	.50	.25

Centenary of the arrival of the teaching Sisters of St. Dorothea.

1966, June 3 Photo. Wmk. 267

C110	AP58 45cr brown org	.50	.25

Issued to commemorate Vatican II, the 21st Ecumenical Council of the Roman Catholic Church, Oct. 11, 1962-Dec. 8, 1965.

A souvenir card contains one impression of No. C110, imperf. Size: 100x39mm.

Admiral Mariz e Barros — AP59 "Youth" by Eliseu Visconti — AP60

1966, June 13 Photo. Wmk. 267

C111	AP59 35cr red brown	.50	.25

Death centenary of Admiral Antonio Carlos Mariz e Barros, who died in the Battle of Itaperu.

1966, July 31 ***Perf. 11½x11***

C112	AP60 120cr red brown	.75	.30

Birth centenary of Eliseu Visconti, painter.

SPECIAL DELIVERY STAMPS

No. 191 Surcharged

1930 Unwmk. ***Perf. 12***

E1	A62 1000r on 200r dp blue	6.50	2.00
a.	Inverted surcharge	500.00	

POSTAGE DUE STAMPS

D1

D2

1889 Unwmk. Typo. ***Rouletted***

J1	D1 10r carmine	2.10	1.40
J2	D1 20r carmine	3.25	2.00
J3	D1 50r carmine	5.50	4.00
J4	D1 100r carmine	2.10	1.40
J5	D1 200r carmine	65.00	15.00
J6	D1 300r carmine	6.75	*8.00*
J7	D1 500r carmine	6.75	*8.00*
J8	D1 700r carmine	11.00	*14.00*
J9	D1 1000r carmine	11.00	10.00
	Nos. J1-J9 (9)	113.45	63.80

Counterfeits are common.

1890

J10	D1 10r orange	.65	.30
J11	D1 20r ultra	.65	.30
J12	D1 50r olive	1.40	.30
J13	D1 200r magenta	6.75	.60
J14	D1 300r blue green	3.25	1.50
J15	D1 500r slate	4.50	3.00
J16	D1 700r purple	5.25	*7.75*
J17	D1 1000r dk violet	6.50	5.00
	Nos. J10-J17 (8)	28.95	18.75

Counterfeits are common.

Perf. 11 to 11½, 12½ to 14 and Compound

1895-1901

J18	D2 10r dk blue ('01)	2.10	1.25
J19	D2 20r yellow grn	8.75	3.00
J20	D2 50r yellow grn ('01)	11.00	5.50
J21	D2 100r brick red	7.25	1.25
J22	D2 200r violet	6.75	.60
a.	200r gray lilac ('98)	13.00	2.00
J23	D2 300r dull blue	4.00	2.25
J24	D2 2000r brown	13.00	13.00
	Nos. J18-J24 (7)	52.85	26.85

1906 Wmk. 97

J25	D2 100r brick red	8.75	3.00

Wmk. (97? or 98?)

J26	D2 200r violet	8.75	1.25
a.	Wmk. 97	350.00	85.00
b.	Wmk. 98	14.50	50.00

D3

D4

1906-10 Unwmk. Engr. ***Perf. 12***

J28	D3 10r slate	.25	.25
J29	D3 20r brt violet	.25	.25
J30	D3 50r dk green	.30	.25
J31	D3 100r carmine	2.00	.60
J32	D3 200r dp blue	1.10	.30
J33	D3 300r gray blk	.40	.60
J34	D3 400r olive grn	1.40	.90
J35	D3 500r dk violet	40.00	40.00
J36	D3 600r violet ('10)	1.40	*3.00*
J37	D3 700r red brown	35.00	30.00
J38	D3 1000r red	1.60	*3.25*
J39	D3 2000r green	5.25	5.50
J40	D3 5000r choc ('10)	1.60	*24.00*
	Nos. J28-J40 (13)	90.55	108.90

Perf. 12½, 11, 11x10½

1919-23 **Typo.**

J41 D4 5r red brown .30 .25
J42 D4 10r violet .60 .25
J43 D4 20r olive gray .30 .25
J44 D4 50r green ('23) .30 .25
J45 D4 100r red 1.75 1.10
J46 D4 200r blue 8.75 2.10
J47 D4 400r brown ('23) 1.75 1.60
Nos. J41-J47 (7) 13.75 5.80

Perf. 12½, 12½x13½

1924-35 **Wmk. 100**

J48 D4 5r red brown .25 .25
J49 D4 100r red .85 .70
J50 D4 200r slate bl ('29) 1.25 .50
J51 D4 400r dp brn ('29) 1.50 1.00
J52 D4 600r dk vio ('29) 1.75 1.10
J53 D4 600r orange ('35) .75 .50
Nos. J48-J53 (6) 6.35 4.05

1924 **Wmk. 193** ***Perf. 11x10½***

J54 D4 100r red 55.00 55.00
J55 D4 200r slate blue 6.00 6.00

Perf. 11x10½, 13x13½

1925-27 **Wmk. 101**

J56 D4 20r olive gray .25 .25
J57 D4 100r red 1.25 .35
J58 D4 200r slate blue 4.50 .50
J59 D4 400r brown 3.25 2.00
J60 D4 600r dk violet 5.50 3.25
Nos. J56-J60 (5) 14.75 6.35

Wmk. E U BRASIL Multiple (218)

1929-30 ***Perf. 12½x13½***

J61 D4 100r light red .50 .25
J62 D4 200r blue black 1.75 .50
J63 D4 400r brown 1.75 .50
J64 D4 1000r myrtle green 1.75 .75
Nos. J61-J64 (4) 5.75 2.00

Perf. 11, 12½x13, 13

1931-36 **Wmk. 222**

J65 D4 10r lt violet ('35) .25 .25
J66 D4 20r black ('33) .25 .25
J67 D4 50r blue grn ('35) .50 .25
J68 D4 100r rose red ('35) .50 .25
J69 D4 200r sl blue ('35) 2.00 .50
J70 D4 400r blk brn ('35) 3.25 2.00
J71 D4 600r dk violet .50 .25
J72 D4 1000r myrtle grn .65 .50
J73 D4 2000r brown ('36) 1.10 1.10
J74 D4 5000r indigo ('36) 1.25 1.00
Nos. J65-J74 (10) 10.25 6.35

1938 **Wmk. 249** ***Perf. 11***

J75 D4 200r slate blue 2.75 1.00

1940 **Typo.** **Wmk. 256**

J76 D4 10r light violet 1.10 1.10
J77 D4 20r black 1.10 1.10
J79 D4 100r rose red 1.10 1.10
J80 D4 200r myrtle green 2.40 1.10
Nos. J76-J80 (4) 5.70 4.40

1942 **Wmk. 264**

J81 D4 10r lt violet .25 .25
J82 D4 20r olive blk .25 .25
J83 D4 50r lt blue grn .25 .25
J84 D4 100r vermilion 1.10 1.10
J85 D4 200r gray blue 1.75 1.75
J86 D4 400r claret 1.10 1.10
J87 D4 600r rose vio .50 .25
J88 D4 1000r dk bl grn .50 .25
J89 D4 2000r dp yel brn 1.75 1.75
J90 D4 5000r indigo .90 .90
Nos. J81-J90 (10) 8.35 7.85

1949 **Wmk. 268**

J91 D4 10c pale rose lilac 2.00 3.25
J92 D4 20r black 27.50 25.00

No. J92 exists in shades of gray ranging to gray olive.

OFFICIAL STAMPS

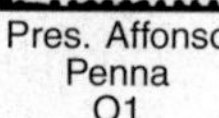

Pres. Affonso Penna
O1

Pres. Hermes da Fonseca
O2

Unwmk.

1906, Nov. 15 **Engr.** ***Perf. 12***

O1 O1 10r org & grn 1.00 .30
O2 O1 20r org & grn 1.25 .30
O3 O1 50r org & grn 1.90 .30
O4 O1 100r org & grn 1.00 .30
O5 O1 200r org & grn 1.25 .30
O6 O1 300r org & grn 4.00 .60
O7 O1 400r org & grn 8.25 2.75
O8 O1 500r org & grn 4.00 1.60
O9 O1 700r org & grn 5.25 3.75
O10 O1 1000r org & grn 5.25 1.25
O11 O1 2000r org & grn 7.50 2.25
O12 O1 5000r org & grn 13.50 1.60
O13 O1 10,000r org & grn 13.50 1.40
Nos. O1-O13 (13) 67.65 16.70

The portrait is the same but the frame differs for each denomination of this issue.

1913, Nov. 15 **Center in Black**

O14 O2 10r gray .40 .55
O15 O2 20r ol grn .40 .55
O16 O2 50r gray .40 .55
O17 O2 100r ver 1.10 .40
O18 O2 200r blue 2.00 .40
O19 O2 500r orange 3.50 .65
O20 O2 600r violet 4.00 2.50
O21 O2 1000r blk brn 5.00 1.75
O22 O2 2000r red brn 7.50 1.75
O23 O2 5000r brown 8.75 3.50
O24 O2 10,000r black 16.00 7.75
O25 O2 20,000r blue 30.00 30.00
O26 O2 50,000r green 55.00 55.00
O27 O2 100,000r org red 200.00 200.00
O28 O2 500,000r brown 325.00 325.00
O29 O2 1,000,000r dk brn 350.00 350.00
Nos. O14-O29 (16) 1,009. 980.35

The portrait is the same on all denominations of this series but there are eight types of the frame.

Pres. Wenceslau Braz — O3

Perf. 11, 11½

1919, Apr. 11 **Wmk. 100**

O30 O3 10r olive green .50 *9.00*
O31 O3 50r green 1.25 1.25
O32 O3 100r rose red 2.00 .85
O33 O3 200r dull blue 3.50 .85
O34 O3 500r orange 9.25 *40.00*
Nos. O30-O34 (5) 16.50 51.95

The official decree called for eleven stamps in this series but only five were issued.
For surcharges see Nos. 293-297.

NEWSPAPER STAMPS

N1

Rouletted

1889, Feb. 1 **Unwmk.** **Litho.**

P1 N1 10r yellow 3.25 7.25
a. Pair, imperf. between 125.00 140.00
P2 N1 20r yellow 9.00 9.00
P3 N1 50r yellow 15.00 12.50
P4 N1 100r yellow 7.50 3.00
P5 N1 200r yellow 3.00 2.50
P6 N1 300r yellow 3.00 2.50
P7 N1 500r yellow 30.00 15.00
P8 N1 700r yellow 3.00 *20.00*
P9 N1 1000r yellow 3.00 *20.00*
Nos. P1-P9 (9) 76.75 91.75

For surcharges see Nos. 125-127.

1889, May 1

P10 N1 10r olive 3.00 1.25
P11 N1 20r green 3.00 1.25
P12 N1 50r brn yel 3.00 1.25
P13 N1 100r violet 4.50 3.00
a. 100r deep violet 7.50 *20.00*
b. 100r lilac 14.00 3.00
P14 N1 200r black 4.50 3.00
P15 N1 300r carmine 17.50 17.50
P16 N1 500r green 75.00 *90.00*
P17 N1 700r pale blue 50.00 *55.00*
a. 700r ultramarine 90.00 *100.00*
b. 700r cobalt 425.00 *450.00*
P18 N1 1000r brown 17.50 *75.00*
Nos. P10-P18 (9) 178.00 247.25

For surcharges see Nos. 128-135.

N2

N3

White Wove Paper Thin to Thick

Perf. 11 to 11½, 12½ to 14 and 12½ to 14x11 to 11½

1890 **Typo.**

P19 N2 10r blue 22.50 10.00
a. 10r ultramarine 22.50 10.00
P20 N2 20r emerald 70.00 20.00
P21 N2 100r violet 22.50 14.00
Nos. P19-P21 (3) 115.00 44.00

For surcharge see No. 137.

1890-93

P22 N3 10r ultramarine 5.00 3.00
a. 10r blue 9.00 4.00
P23 N3 10r ultra, *buff* 3.00 3.00
P24 N3 20r green 10.00 3.00
a. 20r emerald 10.00 3.00
P25 N3 50r yel grn ('93) 25.00 15.00
Nos. P22-P25 (4) 43.00 24.00

For surcharges see Nos. 136, 138-139.

POSTAL TAX STAMPS

Icarus from the Santos-Dumont Monument at St. Cloud, France — PT1

Perf. 13½x12½, 11

1933, Oct. 1 **Typo.** **Wmk. 222**

RA1 PT1 100r deep brown .75 .25

Honoring the Brazilian aviator, Santos-Dumont. Its use was obligatory as a tax on all correspondence sent to countries in South America, the US and Spain. Its use on correspondence to other countries was optional. The funds obtained were used for the construction of airports throughout Brazil.

Catalogue values for unused stamps in this section, from this point to the end of the section, are for Never Hinged items.

Father Joseph Damien and Children
PT2

Perf. 12x11

1952, Nov. 24 **Litho.** **Wmk. 267**

RA2 PT2 10c yellow brown 1.50 .25

1953, Nov. 30

RA3 PT2 10c yellow green 1.50 .25

Father Bento Dias Pacheco — PT3

1954, Nov. 22 **Photo.** ***Perf. 11½***

RA4 PT3 10c violet blue .40 .25

1955-69, Nov. 24

RA5 PT3 10c dk car rose .40 .25
RA6 PT3 10c org red ('57) .40 .25
RA7 PT3 10c dp emer ('58) .40 .25
RA8 PT3 10c red lilac ('61) .40 .25
RA9 PT3 10c choc ('62) .40 .25
RA10 PT3 10c slate ('63) .40 .25
RA11 PT3 2cr dp mag ('64) .40 .25
RA12 PT3 2cr violet ('65) .40 .25
RA13 PT3 2cr orange ('66) .40 .25
RA14 PT3 5c brt yel grn ('68) 2.00 .75
RA15 PT3 5c deep plum ('69) .90 .30

Issued: 11/25, No. RA14; 11/28, No. RA15; others, 11/24.

Eunice Weaver — PT4

1971-73, Nov. 24

RA16 PT4 10c slate green 1.50 .40
RA17 PT4 10c brt rose lil ('73) .50 .25

Father Nicodemos — PT5

1975, Nov. 24 **Litho.** **Unwmk.**

RA18 PT5 10c sepia .50 .25

Father Vicente Borgard (1888-1977) — PT6

1983, Nov. 24 **Photo.** ***Perf. 11½***

RA19 PT6 10cr brown 4.00 3.00

Father Bento Dias Pacheco — PT7

1984, Nov. 24 **Photo.** ***Perf. 11½***

RA20 PT7 30cr deep blue 1.60 .65

1985, Nov. 24 **Litho.**

RA21 PT7 100cr lake 1.25 .35

1986, Nov. 24 **Litho.**

RA22 PT7 10c gray brown .50 .35

1987, Nov. 24 **Photo.**

RA23 PT7 30c sage green .50 .30

Father Santiago Uchoa — PT8

1988, Nov. 24 **Litho.**

RA24 PT8 1.30cz dull red brn .90 .30

See Nos. RA29-RA30.

Fr. Joseph Damien — PT9

1989-92 **Photo.** ***Perf. 11½***

RA25 PT9 2c deep lilac rose .40 .25
RA26 PT9 50c blue .40 .25

Perf. 12½

RA27 PT9 3cr green .40 .25
RA28 PT9 30cr brown .40 .25
Nos. RA25-RA28 (4) 1.60 1.00

Issued: 2c, Nov. 24; 50c, Nov. 24, 1990; 3cr, Nov. 24, 1991; 30cr, Nov. 24, 1992.

Father Santiago Uchoa Type of 1988

1993, Nov. 24 **Photo.** ***Perf. 12½***

RA29 PT8 50c blue .40 .25

1994, Nov. 24

RA30 PT8 1c dull lake .40 .30

The tax was for the care and treatment of lepers.
Use of Nos. RA2-RA30 was required for one week.

POSTAL TAX SEMI-POSTAL STAMP

Catalogue values for unused stamps in this section are for Never Hinged items.

Icarus — PTSP1

Wmk. 267

1947, Nov. 15 Typo. *Perf. 11*

RAB1	PTSP1 40c + 10c brt red	1.50	.35
a.	Pair, imperf. between	*350.00*	

Aviation Week, November 15-22, 1947, and compulsory on all domestic correspondence during that week.

BRITISH ANTARCTIC TERRITORY

'bri-tish ˌant-'ärk-tik 'ter-ə-ˌtōr-ē

LOCATION — South Atlantic Ocean between 20-80 degrees longitude and south of 60 degrees latitude
GOVT. — British territory
POP. — About 300 scientific staff at research stations.

This territory includes Graham Land (Palmer Peninsula), South Shetland Islands and South Orkney Islands. Formerly part of Falkland Islands Dependency.

12 Pence = 1 Shilling
20 Shillings = 1 Pound
100 Pence = 1 Pound (1971)

Catalogue values for all unused stamps in this country are for Never Hinged items.

M. V. Kista Dan — A1

1p, Skiers hauling load. 1½p, Muskeg (tractor). 2p, Skiers. 2½p, Beaver seaplane. 3p, R.R.S. John Biscoe. 4p, Camp scene. 6p, H.M.S. Protector. 9p, Dog sled. 1sh, Otter skiplane. 2sh, Huskies & aurora australis. 2sh6p, Helicopter. 5sh, Snocat (truck). 10sh, R.R.S. Shackleton. £1, Map of Antarctica.

Perf. 11x11½

1963, Feb. 1 Engr. Wmk. 314

1	A1	½p dark blue	1.00	*2.00*
2	A1	1p brown	1.40	.95
3	A1	1½p plum & red	1.40	1.60
4	A1	2p rose violet	2.00	.95
5	A1	2½p dull green	3.25	1.50
6	A1	3p Prus blue	3.75	1.60
7	A1	4p sepia	2.75	1.75
8	A1	6p dk blue & olive	4.75	2.50
9	A1	9p olive	3.75	2.25
10	A1	1sh steel blue	4.25	1.00
11	A1	2sh dl vio & bis	20.00	10.00
12	A1	2sh6p blue	22.50	15.00
13	A1	5sh rose red & org	27.50	20.00
14	A1	10sh grn & vio bl	50.00	27.50
15	A1	£1 black & blue	52.50	52.50
		Nos. 1-15 (15)	200.80	141.10

See No. 24. For surcharges see Nos. 25-38.

Common Design Types pictured following the introduction.

Churchill Memorial Issue
Common Design Type

1966, Jan. 24 Photo. *Perf. 14*

16	CD319	½p bright blue	.85	3.25
17	CD319	1p green	3.00	3.25
18	CD319	1sh brown	20.00	6.50
19	CD319	2sh violet	22.50	7.00
		Nos. 16-19 (4)	46.35	20.00

Lemaire Channel, Iceberg and Adelie Penguins A2

Designs: 6p, Weather sonde and operator. 1sh, Muskeg (tractor) pulling tent equipment. 2sh, Surveyors with theodolite.

1969, Feb. 6 Litho.

20	A2	3½p blue, vio bl & blk	3.50	3.00
21	A2	6p emer, blk & dp org	1.75	*2.50*
22	A2	1sh ultra, blk & ver	1.75	*2.00*
23	A2	2sh grnsh bl, blk & och	1.75	*3.00*
		Nos. 20-23 (4)	8.75	*10.50*

25 years of continuous scientific work in the Antarctic.

Type of 1963

£1, H.M.S. Endurance and helicopter.

1969, Dec. 1 Engr. *Perf. 11x11½*

24	A1	£1 black & rose red	190.00	160.00

Nos. 1-14 Surcharged in Decimal Currency; Three Bars Overprinted

1971, Feb. 15 Wmk. 314

25	A1	½p on ½p	.65	*3.50*
26	A1	1p on 1p	1.00	1.00
27	A1	1½p on 1½p	1.25	.80
28	A1	2p on 2p	1.25	.50
29	A1	2½p on 2½p	3.25	2.50
30	A1	3p on 3p	2.25	.80
31	A1	4p on 4p	2.50	.80
32	A1	5p on 6p	4.50	3.50
33	A1	6p on 9p	16.00	8.00
34	A1	7½p on 1sh	17.00	9.25
35	A1	10p on 2sh	17.00	12.00
36	A1	15p on 2sh6p	17.00	12.00
37	A1	25p on 5sh	20.00	15.00
38	A1	50p on 10sh	30.00	30.00
		Nos. 25-38 (14)	133.65	99.65

Map of Antarctica, Aurora Australis, Explorers — A3

Map of Antarctica, Aurora Australis and: 4p, Sea gulls. 5p, Seals. 10p, Penguins.

Litho. & Engr.

1971, June 23 *Perf. 14x13*

39	A3	1½p multicolored	6.00	2.00
40	A3	4p multicolored	15.00	5.00
41	A3	5p multicolored	10.00	8.50
42	A3	10p multicolored	22.50	10.00
		Nos. 39-42 (4)	53.50	25.50

10th anniv. of the Antarctic Treaty pledging peaceful uses of and scientific cooperation in Antarctica.

Silver Wedding Issue, 1972
Common Design Type

Design: Queen Elizabeth II, Prince Philip, seals and emperor penguins.

1972, Dec. 13 Photo. *Perf. 14x14½*

43	CD324	5p rose brn & multi	3.25	2.60
44	CD324	10p olive & multi	4.50	3.50

Capt. Cook and "Resolution" — A4

Polar Explorers and their Crafts: 1p, Thaddeus von Bellingshausen and "Vostok." 1½p, James Weddell and "Jane." 2p, John Biscoe and "Tula." 2½p, J. S. C. Dumont d'Urville and "Astrolabe." 3p, James Clark Ross and "Erebus." 4p, C. A. Larsen and "Jason." 5p, Adrien de Gerlache and "Belgica." 6p, Otto Nordenskjöld and "Antarctic." 7½p, W. S. Bruce and "Scotia." 10p, Jean-Baptiste Charcot and "Pourquoi Pas?" 15p, Ernest Shackleton and "Endurance." 25p, Hubert Wilkins and airplane "San Francisco." 50p, Lincoln Ellsworth and airplane "Polar Star." £1, John Rymill and "Penola."

Wmk. 373

1975-80 Litho. *Perf. 14½*

45	A4	½p multi	.90	*2.90*
46	A4	1p multi ('78)	.75	*2.50*
47	A4	1½p multi ('78)	.75	*2.50*
48	A4	2p multi ('79)	2.50	*3.50*
49	A4	2½p multi ('79)	2.50	*3.50*
50	A4	3p multi ('79)	3.00	*3.75*
52	A4	5p multi ('79)	3.00	*4.00*
55	A4	10p multi ('79)	2.25	*3.75*
56	A4	15p multi ('79)	1.50	*2.50*
57	A4	25p multi ('79)	1.50	1.60
58	A4	50p multi ('79)	2.40	3.25
59	A4	£1 multi ('78)	5.00	2.50
		Nos. 45-59 (12)	26.05	36.25

1973, Feb. 14 Wmk. 314

45a	A4	½p multi	*1.50*	*2.75*
46a	A4	1p multi	*2.75*	*4.25*
47a	A4	1½p multi	*11.50*	*5.50*
48a	A4	2p multi	2.50	2.25
49a	A4	2½p multi	2.00	*2.25*
50a	A4	3p multi	1.10	*2.25*
51a	A4	4p multi	1.10	*2.25*
52a	A4	5p multi	1.25	*2.25*
53a	A4	6p multi	1.50	*2.25*
54a	A4	7½p multi	1.75	*3.00*
55a	A4	10p multi	3.00	*3.50*
56a	A4	15p multi	6.00	5.00
57a	A4	25p multi	3.75	*5.00*
58a	A4	50p multi	3.00	*5.50*
59a	A4	£1 multi	5.25	*9.50*
		Nos. 45a-59a (15)	47.95	57.50

1980 Wmk. 373 *Perf. 12*

51	A4	4p multi	.65	*2.00*
53	A4	6p multi	1.00	*3.50*
54	A4	7½p multi	1.50	*4.00*
55b	A4	10p multi	.75	*3.50*
56b	A4	15p multi	.75	*3.50*
57b	A4	25p multi	1.25	*3.00*
58b	A4	50p multi	2.40	*2.90*
59b	A4	£1 multi	4.75	*4.50*
		Nos. 51-59b (8)	13.05	26.90

Princess Anne's Wedding Issue
Common Design Type

1973, Nov. 14 Wmk. 314 *Perf. 14*

60	CD325	5p ocher & multi	.40	.30
61	CD325	15p blue grn & multi	.85	.80

Wedding of Princess Anne and Capt. Mark Phillips, Nov. 14, 1973. Nos. 60-61 were not available locally until Dec. 23, 1973, and first-day covers bear that date.

Churchill and Map of Churchill Peninsula A5

Design: 15p, Churchill and "Trepassey" of Operation Tabarin, 1943.

1974, Nov. 30 Litho. *Perf. 14*

62	A5	5p multicolored	1.75	1.75
63	A5	15p multicolored	3.00	3.00
a.		Souvenir sheet of 2, #62-63	15.00	15.00

Sir Winston Churchill (1874-1965).

Humpback Whale — A6

Wmk. 373

1977, Jan. 4 Litho. *Perf. 14*

64	A6	2p Sperm whale	6.50	4.50
65	A6	8p Fin whale	7.50	5.00
66	A6	11p shown	7.75	5.00
67	A6	25p Blue whale	8.50	6.75
		Nos. 64-67 (4)	30.25	21.25

Conservation of whales.

Prince Philip in Antarctica, 1956-57 — A7

Designs: 11p, Coronation oath. 33p, Queen before taking oath.

1977, Feb. 7 *Perf. 13½x14*

68	A7	6p multicolored	.70	.50
69	A7	11p multicolored	.80	.60
70	A7	33p multicolored	2.10	.80
		Nos. 68-70 (3)	3.60	1.90

25th anniv. of the reign of Elizabeth II.

Elizabeth II Coronation Anniversary Issue
Common Design Types
Souvenir Sheet

Unwmk.

1978, June 2 Litho. *Perf. 15*

71	Sheet of 6	6.00	6.00
a.	CD326 25p Black bull of Clarence	1.00	1.00
b.	CD327 25p Elizabeth II	1.00	1.00
c.	CD328 25p Emperor penguin	1.00	1.00

No. 71 contains 2 se-tenant strips of Nos. 71a-71c, separated by horizontal gutter with commemorative and descriptive inscriptions and showing central part of coronation procession with coach.

Macaroni Penguins — A8

Perf. 13½x14

1979, Jan. 14 Litho. Wmk. 373

72	A8	3p shown	11.00	11.00
73	A8	8p Gentoo	3.25	3.25
74	A8	11p Adelie	3.50	3.50
75	A8	25p Emperor	4.75	4.75
		Nos. 72-75 (4)	22.50	22.50

John Barrow, Tula, Society Emblem A9

Royal Geographical Society Sesquicentennial (Past Presidents and Expedition Scenes): 7p, Clement Markham 11p, Lord Curzon. 15p, William Goodenough. 22p, James Wordie. 30p, Raymond Priestley.

Wmk. 373

1980, Dec. 1 Litho. *Perf. 13½*

76	A9	3p multicolored	.25	.25
77	A9	7p multicolored	.25	.25
78	A9	11p multicolored	.35	.35
79	A9	15p multicolored	.45	.45
80	A9	22p multicolored	.65	.65
81	A9	30p multicolored	.85	.85
		Nos. 76-81 (6)	2.80	2.80

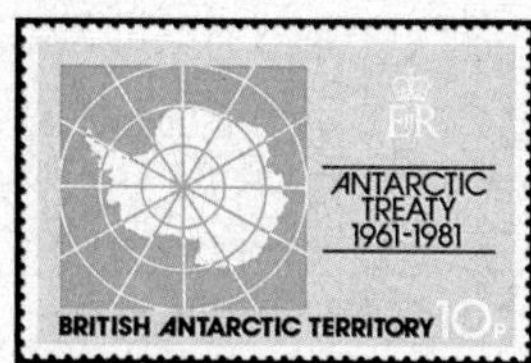

20th Anniv. of Antarctic Treaty — A10

1981, Dec. 1 ***Perf. 13½x14***
82 A10 10p Map .25 *.65*
83 A10 13p Conservation research .40 *.75*
84 A10 25p Satellite image mapping .70 *.80*
85 A10 26p Global geophysics .75 *.80*
Nos. 82-85 (4) 2.10 3.00

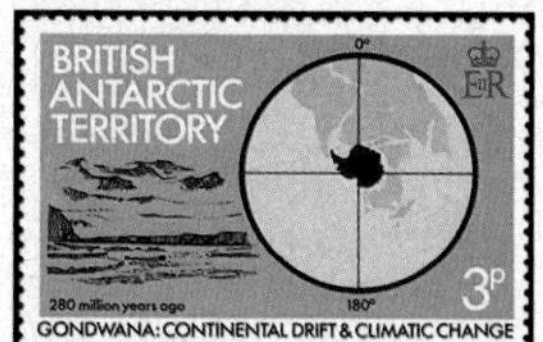

Continental Drift and Climatic Change — A11

1982, Mar. 8 **Litho.** ***Perf. 13½x14***
86 A11 3p Land, water .30 *.35*
87 A11 6p Shrubs .35 *.45*
88 A11 10p Dinosaur .35 *.55*
89 A11 13p Volcano .50 *.65*
90 A11 25p Trees .65 *.75*
91 A11 26p Penguins .65 *.75*
Nos. 86-91 (6) 2.80 3.50

Princess Diana Issue
Common Design Type

1982, July 1 **Litho.** ***Perf. 14½x14***
92 CD333 5p Arms .40 .25
93 CD333 17p Diana, by Bryan Organ .90 .70
94 CD333 37p Wedding 1.50 1.00
95 CD333 50p Portrait 2.50 1.50
Nos. 92-95 (4) 5.30 3.45

10th Anniv. of Convention for Conservation of Antarctic Seals — A12

1983, Jan. 3 **Litho.**
96 A12 5p shown .35 .35
97 A12 10p Weddell seals .50 .50
98 A12 13p Elephant seals .60 .60
99 A12 17p Fur seals .75 .75
100 A12 25p Ross seal .80 .80
101 A12 34p Crabeater seals 1.40 1.40
Nos. 96-101 (6) 4.40 4.40

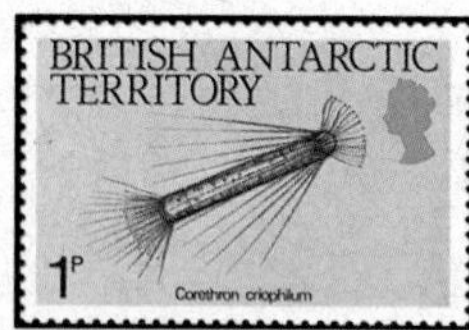

Corethron Criophilum — A13

1p, shown. 2p, Desmonema gaudichaudi. 3p, Tomopteris carpenteri. 4p, Pareuchaeta antarctica. 5p, Antarctomysis maxima. 6p, Antarcturus signiensis. 7p, Serolis comuta. 8p, Parathemisto gaudichaudii. 9p, Bovallia gigantea. 10p, Euphausia superba. 15p, Colossendeis australis. 20p, Todarodes sagittatus. 25p, Notothenia neglecta. 50p, Chaenocephalus aceratus. £1, Lobodon carcinophagus. £3, Antarctic marine food chain.

1984, Mar. 15 **Litho.** ***Perf. 14***
102 A13 1p multicolored .85 *1.60*
103 A13 2p multicolored .90 *1.60*
104 A13 3p multicolored .90 *1.60*
105 A13 4p multicolored 1.00 *1.60*
106 A13 5p multicolored 1.00 *1.60*
107 A13 6p multicolored 1.00 *1.60*
108 A13 7p multicolored 1.00 *1.60*
109 A13 8p multicolored 1.00 *1.60*
110 A13 9p multicolored 1.00 *1.60*
110A A13 10p multicolored 1.00 *1.60*
111 A13 15p multicolored 1.00 *1.60*
112 A13 20p multicolored 1.10 *1.60*
113 A13 25p multicolored 1.10 *1.60*
114 A13 50p multicolored 1.75 *2.00*
115 A13 £1 multicolored 2.25 *2.50*
116 A13 £3 multicolored 6.50 *6.50*
Nos. 102-116 (16) 23.35 *31.80*

Manned Flight Bicentenary — A14

1983, Dec. 17 **Wmk. 373**
117 A14 5p De Havilland Twin Otter .30 .30
118 A14 13p De Havilland Single Otter .55 .55
119 A14 17p Consolidated Canso .70 .70
120 A14 50p Lockheed Vega 2.10 2.10
Nos. 117-120 (4) 3.65 3.65

British-Graham Land Expedition, 1934-1937 — A15

Designs: 7p, M. Y. Penola in Stella Creek. 22p, Northern base, Winter Island. 27p, D. H. Fox Moth at southern base, Barry Island. 54p, Dog team near Ablation Point, George VI Sound.

1985, Mar. 23 **Litho.** ***Perf. 14½***
121 A15 7p multicolored .55 .55
122 A15 22p multicolored .90 .90
123 A15 27p multicolored 1.10 1.10
124 A15 54p multicolored 2.10 2.10
Nos. 121-124 (4) 4.65 4.65

A16

Naturalists, fauna and flora: 7p, Robert McCormick (1800-1890), Catharacta Skua Maccormicki. 22p, Sir Joseph Dalton Hooker (1817-1911), Deschampsea antarctica. 27p, Jean Rene C. Quoy (1790-1869), Lagenorhynchus cruciger. 54p, James Weddell (1787-1834), Leptonychotes weddelli.

1985, Nov. 4 **Litho.** ***Perf. 14½***
125 A16 7p multicolored 1.75 1.75
126 A16 22p multicolored 2.25 *3.25*
127 A16 27p multicolored 2.50 *3.25*
128 A16 54p multicolored 3.25 *4.50*
Nos. 125-128 (4) 9.75 12.75

A17

Halley's comet.

1986, Jan. 6 **Wmk. 373** ***Perf. 14***
129 A17 7p Edmond Halley 1.75 *1.50*
130 A17 22p Halley Station 2.25 *2.75*
131 A17 27p Trajectory, 1531 2.50 *3.25*
132 A17 54p Giotto space probe 3.25 *5.25*
Nos. 129-132 (4) 9.75 12.75

Intl. Glaciological Society, 50th Anniv. — A18

Different snowflakes.

1986, Dec. 6 **Wmk. 384** ***Perf. 14½***
133 A18 10p dp blue & lt bl .65 *1.00*
134 A18 24p blue grn & lt bl grn .85 *1.50*
135 A18 29p dp rose lil & lt lil .95 *1.75*
136 A18 58p dp vio & pale vio blue 2.10 *2.75*
Nos. 133-136 (4) 4.55 7.00

Capt. Robert Falcon Scott, CVO RN (1868-1912) A19

Designs: 24p, The Discovery at Hut Point, 1902-1904. 29p, Cape Evans Hut, 1911-1913. 58p, South Pole, 1912.

1987, Mar. 19 **Litho.** **Wmk. 373**
137 A19 10p multicolored .80 *.95*
138 A19 24p multicolored 1.40 *2.00*
139 A19 29p multicolored 1.60 *2.40*
140 A19 58p multicolored 2.25 *3.25*
Nos. 137-140 (4) 6.05 8.60

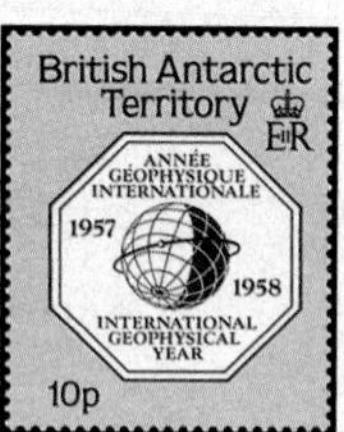

Intl. Geophysical Year, 30th Anniv. — A20

1987, Dec. 25 **Wmk. 384**
141 A20 10p Emblem .55 *.70*
142 A20 24p Port Lockroy .85 *1.40*
143 A20 29p Argentine Islands 1.10 *1.60*
144 A20 58p Halley Bay 2.00 *2.60*
Nos. 141-144 (4) 4.50 6.30

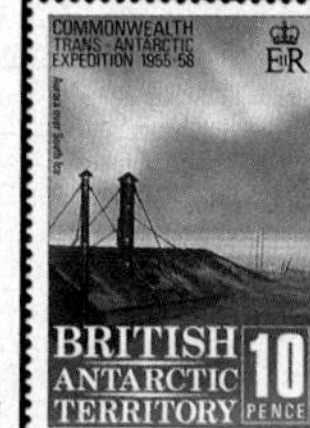

Commonwealth Trans-Antarctic Expedition — A21

1988, Mar. 19 ***Perf. 14***
145 A21 10p Aurora over South Ice .35 .35
146 A21 24p Otter aircraft .80 .80
147 A21 29p Seismic ice-depth sounding .95 .95
148 A21 58p Sno-cat over crevasse 1.90 1.90
Nos. 145-148 (4) 4.00 4.00

Lichens A22

1989, Mar. 25 **Wmk. 373**
149 A22 10p Xanthoria elegans 1.00 1.00
150 A22 24p Usnea aurantiaco-atra 2.00 2.00
151 A22 29p Cladonia chlorophaea 2.25 *2.50*
152 A22 58p Umbilicaria antarctica 3.50 *4.00*
Nos. 149-152 (4) 8.75 *9.50*

Fossils A23

1990, Apr. 2 **Litho.** **Wmk. 384**
153 A23 1p Archaeocyath 1.50 1.50
154 A23 2p Brachiopod 1.50 1.50
155 A23 3p Trilobite *(Triplagnostus)* 1.60 1.60
156 A23 4p Trilobite *(Lyriaspis)* 1.75 1.75
157 A23 5p Gymnosperm 1.75 1.75
158 A23 6p Fern 1.75 1.75
159 A23 7p Belemnite 1.75 1.90
160 A23 8p Ammonite *(Sanmartinoceras)* 1.75 1.90
161 A23 9p Bivalve *(Pinna)* 1.75 1.90
162 A23 10p Bivalve *(Aucellina)* 1.75 1.90
163 A23 20p Bivalve *(Trigonia)* 3.00 *3.50*
164 A23 25p Gastropod 3.00 *3.50*
165 A23 50p Ammonite *(Ainoceras)* 4.00 *5.00*
166 A23 £1 Ammonite *(Gunnarites)* 7.00 *9.00*
167 A23 £3 Crayfish 10.00 *12.00*
Nos. 153-167 (15) 43.85 *50.45*

Queen Mother, 90th Birthday
Common Design Types

1990, Aug. 4 **Wmk. 384** ***Perf. 14x15***
170 CD343 26p Wedding portrait, 1923 1.50 1.50

Perf. 14½
171 CD344 £1 Family portrait, 1940 5.25 5.25

Age of Dinosaurs A24

1991, Mar. 27 **Wmk. 373** ***Perf. 14***
172 A24 12p Late Cretaceous forest 1.50 1.50
173 A24 26p Hypsilophodont dinosaur 2.50 2.50
174 A24 31p Frilled shark 2.75 2.75
175 A24 62p Mosasaur, plesiosaur 4.75 4.75
Nos. 172-175 (4) 11.50 11.50

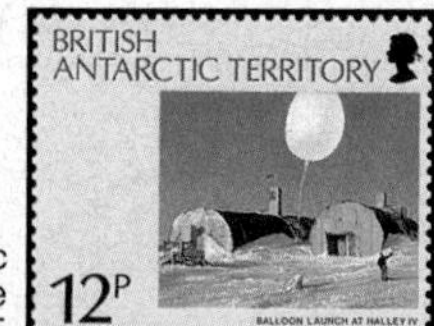

Antarctic Ozone Hole — A25

1991, Mar. 30 ***Perf. 14½x14***
176 A25 12p Launching weather balloon 1.25 *1.90*
177 A25 26p Measuring ozone 2.00 *3.00*
178 A25 31p Ozone hole over Antarctica 2.50 *3.25*
179 A25 62p Airplane, chemical studies 4.50 *5.00*
Nos. 176-179 (4) 10.25 *13.15*

Antarctic Treaty, 30th Anniv. — A26

1991, June 24 ***Perf. 14½***
180 A26 12p Dry valley 1.50 1.50
181 A26 26p Mapping ice sheet 2.25 2.25

182 A26 31p BIOMASS emblem 2.75 2.75
183 A26 62p Ross seal 4.50 4.50
Nos. 180-183 (4) 11.00 11.00

Royal Research Ship James Clark Ross — A27

Designs: 12p, HMS Erebus and Terror in Antarctic by John W. Carmichael. 26p, Launch of RRS James Clark Ross. 62p, Scientific research.

1991, Dec. 10 ***Perf. 14x14½***

184 A27 12p multicolored 1.25 *1.75*
185 A27 26p multicolored 2.25 *3.00*
186 A27 31p shown 2.75 *3.50*
187 A27 62p multicolored 4.50 *5.25*
Nos. 184-187 (4) 10.75 *13.50*

Inscribed in Blue

1991, Dec. 24

188 A27 12p like #184 1.75 *2.25*
189 A27 26p like #185 2.25 *3.25*
190 A27 31p like #186 2.75 *4.25*
191 A27 62p like #187 4.75 *5.25*
Nos. 188-191 (4) 11.50 *15.00*

Seals and Penguins A28

1992, Oct. 20 ***Perf. 13½***

192 A28 4p Ross seal 1.50 *1.75*
193 A28 5p Adelie penguin 1.50 *1.75*
194 A28 7p Weddell seal 1.50 *1.75*
195 A28 29p Emperor penguin 3.00 *3.75*
196 A28 34p Crabeater seal 2.75 *3.75*
197 A28 68p Chinstrap penguin 3.50 *4.25*
Nos. 192-197 (6) 13.75 *17.00*

World Wildlife Fund.

Lower Atmospheric Phenomena A29

Perf. 14x14½

1992, Dec. 22 Litho. Wmk. 373

198 A29 14p Sun pillar at Faraday 1.25 *1.75*
199 A29 29p Halo with iceberg 2.25 *2.25*
200 A29 34p Lee wave cloud 2.75 *3.00*
201 A29 68p Nacreous clouds 4.50 *5.00*
Nos. 198-201 (4) 10.75 *12.00*

Research Ships A30

Wmk. 373

1993, Dec. 13 Litho. ***Perf. 14***

202 A30 1p SS Fitzroy 1.75 *2.50*
203 A30 2p HMS William Scoresby 2.50 2.50
204 A30 3p SS Eagle 2.50 2.50
205 A30 4p MV Trepassey 2.50 2.50
206 A30 5p RRS John Biscoe (I) 2.50 2.50
207 A30 10p MV Norsel 3.00 *3.25*
208 A30 20p HMS Protector 3.75 *4.00*
209 A30 30p MV Oluf Sven 4.25 *4.75*
210 A30 50p RRS John Biscoe (II), RRS Shackleton 5.25 *6.00*
a. Souvenir sheet of 1 5.00 *5.25*
211 A30 £1 MV Tottan 7.00 *7.25*
a. Souvenir sheet of 1 8.00 *8.00*
212 A30 £3 MV Perla Dan 15.00 *17.00*
213 A30 £5 HMS Endurance (I) 27.50 *29.00*
Nos. 202-213 (12) 77.50 *88.75*

No. 210a for Hong Kong '97. Issued 2/3/97.
No. 211a for return of Hong Kong to China. Issued 7/1/97.

Operation Taberin, 50th Anniv. — A31

Designs: 15p, Bransfield House and Post Office, Port Lockroy. 31p, Survey team, Hope Bay. 36p, Dog team, Hope Bay. 72p, SS Fitzroy, HMS William Scoresby at sea.

Wmk. 373

1994, Mar. 19 Litho. ***Perf. 14***

214 A31 15p multicolored 1.75 *2.25*
215 A31 31p multicolored 3.00 *3.25*
216 A31 36p multicolored 3.50 *3.75*
217 A31 72p multicolored 4.75 *5.00*
Nos. 214-217 (4) 13.00 *14.25*

Old and New Transportation — A32

Designs: 15p, Huskies. 24p, DeHavilland DHC-2 Turbo Beaver, British Antarctic Survey. 31p, Dogs, cargo being taken from aircraft. 36p, DHC-6 Twin Otter, sled team. 62p, DHC-6 in flight. 72p, DHC-6 taxiing down runway.

1994, Mar. 21

218 A32 15p multicolored 1.25 1.25
219 A32 24p multicolored 1.75 1.75
220 A32 31p multicolored 2.00 *2.25*
221 A32 36p multicolored 2.25 *2.50*
222 A32 62p multicolored 3.00 *3.50*
223 A32 72p multicolored 3.75 *4.00*
Nos. 218-223 (6) 14.00 15.25

Ovptd. with Hong Kong '94 Emblem

1994, Feb. 18

224 A32 15p on #218 1.50 1.50
225 A32 24p on #219 2.00 2.00
226 A32 31p on #220 2.25 2.50
227 A32 36p on #221 2.50 2.75
228 A32 62p on #222 3.50 3.75
229 A32 72p on #223 4.25 4.50
Nos. 224-229 (6) 16.00 17.00

Antarctic Food Chain — A33

a, Crabeater seals. b, Blue whale. c, Wandering albatross. d, Mackeral icefish. e, Krill. f, Squid.

1994, Nov. 29

230 A33 35p Sheet of 6, #a-f 15.00 15.00

Geological Structures A34

Designs: 17p, Hauberg Mountains, folded sedimentary rocks. 35p, Arrowsmith Peninsula, dikes cross-cutting granite. 40p, Colbert Mountains, columnar jointing in volcanic rocks. 76p, Succession Cliffs, flat-lying sedimentary rocks.

Perf. 14x14½

1995, Nov. 28 Litho. Wmk. 373

231 A34 17p multicolored 2.00 2.00
232 A34 35p multicolored 3.25 3.25
233 A34 40p multicolored 3.50 *4.00*
234 A34 76p multicolored 5.25 *6.00*
Nos. 231-234 (4) 14.00 *15.25*

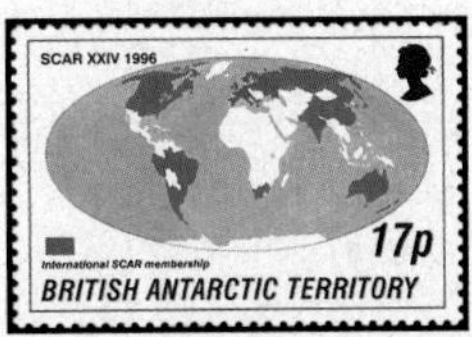

Scientific Committee on Antarctic Research (SCAR) — A35

Designs: 17p, World map showing SCAR member countries. 35p, Earth sciences. 40p, Atmospheric sciences. 76p, Life sciences. £1, Cambridge, August 1996.

Wmk. 384

1996, Mar. 23 Litho. ***Perf. 14***

235 A35 17p multicolored 1.75 1.75
236 A35 35p multicolored 2.75 2.75
237 A35 40p multicolored 3.00 3.00
238 A35 76p multicolored 4.50 4.50
Nos. 235-238 (4) 12.00 12.00

Souvenir Sheet

239 A35 £1 multicolored 9.00 9.00

Queen Elizabeth II, 70th Birthday

Common Design Type

Various portraits of Queen: 17p, Pink outfit. 35p, In formal dress, tiara. 40p, Blue outfit. 76p, Red coat.

Wmk. 384

1996, Nov. 25 Litho. ***Perf. 14½***

240 CD354 17p multicolored 1.75 .90
241 CD354 35p multicolored 2.25 1.50
242 CD354 40p multicolored 2.50 2.50
243 CD354 76p multicolored 4.00 4.00
Nos. 240-243 (4) 10.50 8.90

Whales A36

Wmk. 373

1996, Nov. 25 Litho. ***Perf. 14***

244 A36 17p Killer whale 1.50 1.00
245 A36 35p Sperm whale 2.25 1.50
246 A36 40p Minke whale 3.75 2.50
247 A36 76p Blue whale 4.75 4.00
Nos. 244-247 (4) 12.25 9.00

Souvenir Sheet

248 A36 £1 Humpback whale 11.00 11.00

Christmas — A37

Penguins in snow: 17p, Sledding. 35p, Caroling. 40p, Throwing snowballs. 76p, Ice skating.

Wmk. 384

1997, Dec. 22 Litho. ***Perf. 14½***

249 A37 17p multicolored 3.25 2.00
250 A37 35p multicolored 5.00 3.50
251 A37 40p multicolored 5.75 5.00
252 A37 76p multicolored 7.00 *7.50*
Nos. 249-252 (4) 21.00 18.00

History of Mapping — A38

Maps of Antarctic and: 16p, Surveyor looking through theodolite, 1902-03. 30p, Cartographer, 1949. 35p, Man using radar rangefinder, 1964. 40p, Satellite, 1981. 65p, Tripod, hand held remote control device, 1993.

Wmk. 373

1998, Mar. 19 Litho. ***Perf. 14***

253 A38 16p multicolored 2.25 2.00
254 A38 30p multicolored 2.75 2.25
255 A38 35p multicolored 3.25 2.75
256 A38 40p multicolored 3.50 *3.75*
257 A38 65p multicolored 4.50 *5.00*
Nos. 253-257 (5) 16.25 15.75

Diana, Princess of Wales (1961-97)

Common Design Type

a, Wearing sun glasses. b, In white top. c, Up close. d, Wearing blue-green blazer.

1998, Mar. 31 ***Perf. 14½x14***

258 CD355 35p Sheet of 4, #a-d 6.25 6.25

No. 258 sold for £1.40 + 20p, with surtax and 50% of profit from total sales being donated to the Princess Diana Memorial Fund.

Antarctic Clothing Through the Ages — A39

Man outfitted for cold weather: 30p, Holding shovel, sailing ship, 1843. 35p, With dog, sailing ship, 1900. 40p, With sketch pad, tripod, dog, steamer ship, 1943. 65p, Wearing red suit, penguins, ship, 1998.

Perf. 14½x14

1998, Nov. 30 Litho. Wmk. 373

259 A39 30p multicolored 4.25 3.25
260 A39 35p multicolored 4.50 3.50
261 A39 40p multicolored 4.75 4.50
262 A39 65p multicolored 7.00 6.75
Nos. 259-262 (4) 20.50 18.00

Birds A40

Designs: 1p, Sheathbill. 2p, Antarctic prion. 5p, Adelie penguin. 10p, Emperor penguin. 20p, Antarctic tern. 30p, Black bellied storm petrel. 35p, Antarctic fulmar. 40p, Blue eyed shag. 50p, McCormick's skua. £1, Kelp gull. £3, Wilson's storm petrel. £5, Brown skua.

1998 ***Perf. 14***

263 A40 1p multicolored 1.25 1.25
264 A40 2p multicolored 1.25 1.25
265 A40 5p multicolored 1.40 1.40
266 A40 10p multicolored 1.50 1.50
267 A40 20p multicolored 1.75 1.75
268 A40 30p multicolored 2.25 2.25
269 A40 35p multicolored 2.50 2.50
270 A40 40p multicolored 3.00 3.00
271 A40 50p multicolored 4.00 4.00
272 A40 £1 multicolored 5.00 5.00
273 A40 £3 multicolored 10.00 10.00
274 A40 £5 multicolored 16.00 16.00
Nos. 263-274 (12) 49.90 49.90

Fish — A41

Wmk. 373

1999, Nov. 14 Litho. *Perf. 13½*

275 A41	10p Mackerel icefish		2.00	1.50
276 A41	20p Toothfish		3.00	2.00
277 A41	25p Borch		3.50	2.50
278 A41	50p Marbled notothen		5.00	3.50
279 A41	80p Bernach		6.00	6.00
	Nos. 275-279 (5)		19.50	15.50

Survey Discoveries — A42

15p, Map of crustal microplates of West Antarctica. 30p, Lead levels in ice. 35p, Gigantism in marine invertebrates. 40p, Ozone hole. 70p, Electric field associated with aurora.

Wmk. 373

1999, Dec. 18 Litho. *Perf. 14*

280 A42	15p multi, vert.	4.25	2.00
281 A42	30p multi, vert.	4.75	2.75
282 A42	35p multi	5.00	3.00
283 A42	40p multi	5.25	3.25
284 A42	70p multi	6.75	6.00
	Nos. 280-284 (5)	26.00	17.00

Sir Ernest Shackleton (1874-1922), Polar Explorer — A43

Designs: 35p, Wreck of the Endurance. 40p, Ocean Camp on ice floe. 65p, Launching the James Caird from Elephant Island.

2000, Feb. 10 Wmk. 373

285 A43	35p multi	7.00	3.50
286 A43	40p multi	7.50	3.50
287 A43	65p multi	8.50	5.50
	Nos. 285-287 (3)	23.00	12.50

See Falkland Islands Nos. 758-760, South Georgia and South Sandwich Islands Nos. 254-256.

The Stamp Show 2000, London — A44

Commonwealth Trans-Antarctic Exhibition of 1955-58: a, Map of route. b, Expedition at South Pole, 1958. c, MV Magga Dan. d, Sno-cat repair camp. e, Sno-cat over crevasse. f, Seismic explosion.

Perf. 13¼x13¾

2000, May 22 Litho. Wmk. 373

288 A44	37p Sheet of 6, #a-f	70.00	70.00

Survey Ships A45

Designs: 20p, RRS Bransfield unloading near Halley, vert. 33p, Supply boat Tula and RRS Ernest Shackleton, vert. 37p, RRS Bransfield. 43p, RRS Ernest Shackleton.

Wmk. 373

2000, Nov. 30 Litho. *Perf. 14*

289-292 A45	Set of 4	22.50	22.50

Composing of Antarctic Symphony, by Sir Peter Maxwell Davies — A46

Designs: No. 293, 37p, RRS James Clark Ross and track cut through ice. No. 294, 37p, Iceberg. No. 295, 43p, Camp on Jones Ice Shelf. No. 296, 43p, Iceberg, diff.

2000, Dec. 4

293-296 A46	Set of 4	20.00	20.00

Port Lockroy — A47

Designs: 33p, Visitors near building, penguins, flagpole, 2001. 37p, Visitors on rocks below building, ship in water, 2001. 43p, Port Lockroy building, 1945. 65p, Laboratory interior, 1945.

Perf. 13¾x14

2001, Nov. 29 Litho. Wmk. 373

297-300 A47	Set of 4	22.50	22.50

British National Antarctic Expedition of 1901-04, Cent. A48

Designs: 33p, Map of expedition's route, vert. 37p, Capt. Robert Falcon Scott (1868-1912), vert. 43p, First Antarctic balloon ascent, 1902. 65p, Emperor penguin chick, vert. 70p, Ernest Shackleton, Scott, Edward Adrian Wilson, sleds at southernmost point of expedition. 80p, Discovery trapped in ice.

2001, Dec. 5 Wmk. 384 *Perf. 14*

301-306 A48	Set of 6	24.00	24.00

Reign Of Queen Elizabeth II, 50th Anniv. Issue

Common Design Type

Designs: Nos. 307, 311a, 20p, Princess Elizabeth making first broadcast. Nos. 308, 311b, 37p, At Garter ceremony, 1998. Nos. 309, 311c, 43p, In 1952. Nos. 310, 311d, 50p, In 1996. No. 311e, 50p, 1955 portrait by Annigoni (38x50mm).

Perf. 14¼x14½, 13¾ (#311e)

2002, Feb. 6 Litho. Wmk. 373

With Gold Frames

307 CD360	20p multicolored	1.50	1.50
308 CD360	37p multicolored	2.75	2.75
309 CD360	43p multicolored	3.00	3.00
310 CD360	50p multicolored	3.75	3.75
	Nos. 307-310 (4)	11.00	11.00

Souvenir Sheet

Without Gold Frames

311 CD360	Sheet of 5, #a-e	14.00	14.00

Queen Mother Elizabeth (1900-2002)

Common Design Type

Designs: 40p, Without hat (sepia photograph). 45p, Wearing blue green hat.

No. 314: a, 70p, Wearing feathered hat (black and white photograph). b, 95p, Wearing dark blue hat.

Wmk. 373

2002, Aug. 5 Litho. *Perf. 14¼*

With Purple Frames

312 CD361	40p multicolored	3.00	3.00
313 CD361	45p multicolored	3.25	3.25

Souvenir Sheet

Without Purple Frames

Perf. 14½x14¼

314 CD361	Sheet of 2, #a-b	13.00	13.00

Commission for the Conservation of Antarctic Marine Living Resources, 20th Anniv. — A49

No. 315: a, Map of Antarctica, vessel monitoring satellite. b, Wandering albatross, fishing boat. c, Icefish, toothfish and crabeater seal. d, Krill and phytoplankton.

Perf. 13½x13¾

2002, Oct. 22 Litho. Wmk. 373

315	Vert. strip of 4	13.00	13.00
a.-d.	A49 37p Any single	3.00	3.00

Scottish National Antarctic Expedition, 1902-04 — A50

Designs: 30p, Map of oceanographic cruises of the Scotia, vert. 40p, Bagpiper Gilbert Kerr and Emperor penguin. 45p, SY Scotia, vert. 70p, Meteorological observations, cent. 95p, William Speirs Bruce, vert. £1, Omond House, Laurie Island.

Wmk. 373

2002, Dec. 5 Litho. *Perf. 14*

316-321 A50	Set of 6	27.50	27.50

Head of Queen Elizabeth II

Common Design Type

Wmk. 373

2003, June 2 Litho. *Perf. 13¾*

322 CD362	£2 multi	10.00	10.00

Coronation of Queen Elizabeth II, 50th Anniv.

Common Design Type

Designs: Nos. 323, 40p, 325a, Queen in carriage. Nos. 324, 45p, 325b, 95p, Queen and family on Buckingham Palace balcony.

Perf. 14¼x14½

2003, June 2 Litho. Wmk. 373

Vignettes Framed, Red Background

323 CD363	40p multicolored	3.25	3.25
324 CD363	45p multicolored	3.75	3.75

Souvenir Sheet

Vignettes Without Frame, Purple Panel

325 CD363	95p Sheet of 2, #a-b	15.00	15.00

Worldwide Fund for Nature (WWF) A51

Blue whale: 40p, Underwater. No. 327, 45p, Tail above water. No. 328, 45p, Two whales underwater. 70p, Two whales at surface.

Wmk. 373

2003, Dec. 5 Litho. *Perf. 14*

326-329 A51	Set of 4	10.00	10.00
329a	Sheet, 4 each #326-329	42.50	42.50

Bases and Postmarks A52

Bases: 1p, G, Admiralty Bay. 2p, B, Deception Island. 5p, D, Hope Bay. 22p, F, Argentine Islands. 25p, E, Stonington Island. 40p, A, Port Lockroy. 45p, H, Signy. 50p, N, Anvers Island. 95p, R, Rothera. £1, T, Adelaide Island. £3, Y, Horseshoe Island. £5, Z, Hailey Bay.

2003, Dec. 8 Wmk. 373 *Perf. 14*

330 A52	1p multi	.40	.40
331 A52	2p multi	.50	.50
332 A52	5p multi	.60	.60
333 A52	22p multi	1.00	1.00
334 A52	25p multi	1.10	1.10
335 A52	40p multi	1.75	1.75
336 A52	45p multi	2.00	2.00
337 A52	50p multi	2.10	2.10
338 A52	95p multi	4.00	4.00
339 A52	£1 multi	4.25	4.25
340 A52	£3 multi	12.50	12.50
341 A52	£5 multi	20.00	20.00
	Nos. 330-341 (12)	50.20	50.20

Climate Change A53

No. 342, 24p: a, Map of Antarctica showing annual temperature trends since 1950. b, Larsen Ice Shelf.

No. 343, 42p: a, Graph of ice core age and warmth. b, Ice core drilling.

No. 344, 50p: a, Graph of rise of mean summer air temperatures at Faraday Station. b, Pearlwort.

Wmk. 373

2004, Dec. 9 Litho. *Perf. 14*

Vert. Pairs, #a-b

342-344 A53	Set of 3	17.00	17.00

Petrels A54

Designs: 25p, Cape petrel. 42p, Snow petrel. 75p, Wilson's storm petrel. £1, Antarctic petrel.

No. 349 — Southern giant petrel: a, In flight, name at right. b, In flight, name at left. c, Close-up of head, bird in flight. d, With wings extended above nest. e, Adult and chick. f, Chick.

2005, Jan. 23 *Perf. 13¾*

345-348 A54	Set of 4	17.00	17.00

Souvenir Sheet

349 A54	50p Sheet of 6, #a-f	18.00	18.00

Ships Named Endurance A55

Designs: 42p, Endurance, 1914-15. 50p, HMS Endurance, 1968-90. £1, HMS Endurance, 1991-present.

2005, Jan. 24 *Perf. 14¾x14*

350-352 A55	Set of 3	15.00	15.00

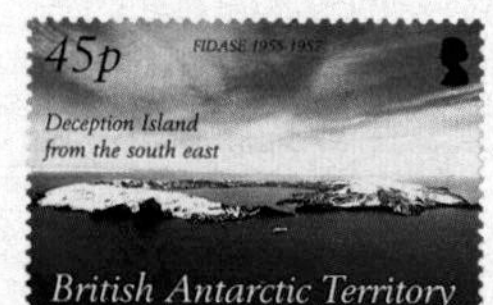

Falkland Islands and Dependencies Aerial Survey Expedition, 50th Anniv. — A56

Designs: 45p, Deception Island. 55p, Hunting Lodge. 80p, Bell 47 helicopter. £1, Canso Flying Boat.

Wmk. 373

2005, Dec. 19 Litho. *Perf. 14*

353-356 A56 Set of 4 17.50 17.50

Halley VI Research Station Design Competition — A57

Designs: No. 357, 45p, Concept of Faber Maunsell. No. 358, 45p, Concept of Buro Hoppold. 55p, Concept by Hopkins. 80p, Laws Building of Halley V Research Station.

Wmk. 373

2005, Dec. 22 Litho. *Perf. 14*

357-360 A57 Set of 4 14.00 14.00

Dogs of Sir Ernest Shackleton — A58

Designs: No. 361, 45p, Shackleton and puppies. No. 362, 45p, Samson, Shakespeare and Surley, horiz. 55p, Ice kennels around ship, Endurance, horiz. £1, Training on sea ice.

2005, Dec. 22

361-364 A58 Set of 4 13.00 13.00

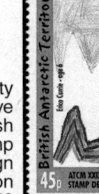

Antarctic Treaty Consultative Meeting Scottish Children's Stamp Design Competition A59

Winning designs by: No. 365, 45p, Erica Currie. No. 366, 45p, Meghan Joyce. 55p, Lorna MacDonald. £1, Danielle Dalgleish.

2006, Feb. 26

365-368 A59 Set of 4 14.00 14.00

Queen Elizabeth II, 80th Birthday A60

Queen: 45p, As child. Nos. 370, 373a, 55p, Wearing crown. Nos. 371, 373b, 80p, Wearing red hat. £1, Without head covering.

Wmk. 373

2006, Apr. 21 Litho. *Perf. 14*

With White Frames

369-372 A60 Set of 4 17.50 17.50

Souvenir Sheet

Without White Frames

373 A60 Sheet of 2, #a-b 10.00 10.00

Seals A61

Designs: 25p, Elephant seals. 50p, Crabeater seals. 60p, Weddell seals. £1.05, Leopard seal.

Perf. 14¼x14¾

2006, Dec. 16 Litho. Wmk. 373

374-377 A61 Set of 4 20.00 20.00

Icebergs A62

Various icebergs: 25p, 50p, 60p, £1.05.

Wmk. 373

2007, Nov. 14 Litho. *Perf. 13¾*

378-381 A62 Set of 4 11.00 11.00

Marine Invertebrates — A63

Designs: 25p, Sea lemon. 50p, Antarctic sea anemone. 60p, Sea spider. £1.05, Sea star.

2007, Nov. 14 *Perf. 14*

382-385 A63 Set of 4 12.00 12.00

Souvenir Sheet

Intl. Polar Year — A64

2007, Nov. 14 *Perf.*

386 A64 £2 multi 10.00 10.00

Explorers and Ships A65

Designs: 1p, James Weddell (1787-1834), Jane and Beaufoy. 2p, Sir James Clark Ross (1800-62), Erebus and Terror. 5p, Neil Alison Mackintosh (1900-74), Discovery II. 27p, Sir Douglas Mawson (1882-1958), Discovery. 55p, Captain James Cook (1728-79), Resolution. Nos. 392, 399a, Captain Egeberg Borchgrevink (1864-1934), Southern Cross. Nos. 393, 399b, Dr. William Speirs Bruce (1867-1921), Scotia. Nos. 394, 399c, Captain Robert Falcon Scott (1868-1912), Discovery. Nos. 395, 399d, Sir Ernest Shackleton (1874-1922), Endurance. £1.10, John Riddoch Rymill (1905-68), Penola. £2.50, Captain Victor Marchesi (1914-2006), William Scoresby. £5, Sir Vivian Fuchs (1908-99), Magga Dan.

Wmk. 406

2008, Nov. 17 Litho. *Perf. 14*

387	A65	1p multi	.25	.25
388	A65	2p multi	.25	.25
389	A65	5p multi	.25	.25
390	A65	27p multi	.80	.80
391	A65	55p multi	1.60	1.60
392	A65	65p multi	1.90	1.90
393	A65	65p multi	1.90	1.90
394	A65	65p multi	1.90	1.90
395	A65	65p multi	1.90	1.90
396	A65	£1.10 multi	3.25	3.25
397	A65	£2.50 multi	7.50	7.50
398	A65	£5 multi	15.00	15.00
		Nos. 387-398 (12)	36.50	36.50

Souvenir Sheet

399 Sheet of 4 7.75 7.75
a.-d. A65 (65p) Any single 1.90 1.90

Nos. 399a-399d are inscribed "Airmail Letter."

A66

A67

A68

A69

Aurora Australis A70

2008, Nov. 17 Wmk. 373

400 Horiz. strip of 5 9.50 9.50

a.	A66 65p multi	1.90	1.90
b.	A67 65p multi	1.90	1.90
c.	A68 65p multi	1.90	1.90
d.	A69 65p multi	1.90	1.90
e.	A70 65p multi	1.90	1.90

Fossil Ferns A71

Map of Antarctica and: 55p, Lophosoria cupulatus. 65p, Cladophlebis oblonga. No. 403, £1.10, Pachypteris indica. No. 404, £1.10, Aculea acicularis.

2008, Nov. 17 *Perf. 14*

401-404 A71 Set of 4 10.00 10.00

Naval Aviation, Cent. A72

Designs: No. 405, 10p, Fairey Seafox. No. 406, 10p, Westland Lynx helicopter. No. 407, 90p, Supermarine Walrus. No. 408, 90p, Westland Wasp helicopter.
£2, HMA No. 1 Mayfly airship.

Wmk. 406

2009, Jan. 1 Litho. *Perf. 14*

405-408 A72 Set of 4 6.00 6.00

Souvenir Sheet

409 A72 £2 multi 6.00 6.00

Worldwide Fund for Nature (WWF) — A73

Crabeater seal: 27p, On ice. 65p, Head poking through hole in ice. £1.10, Two seals on ice. £1.50, Underwater.

Wmk. 406

2009, Nov. 6 Litho. *Perf. 14*

410-413 A73 Set of 4 12.00 12.00
413a Sheet of 16, 4 each #410-413 48.00 48.00

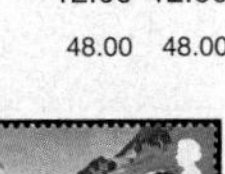

Antarctic Treaty, 50th Anniv. — A74

No. 414, 27p: a, Antarctic fur seal. b, Humpback whale.
No. 415, 55p: a, Southern giant petrel. b, Gentoo penguins.
No. 416, 65p: a, Giant squid. b, Jellyfish.

2009, Nov. 6 *Perf. 14*

Horiz. Pairs, #a-b

414-416 A74 Set of 3 10.00 10.00

Miniature Sheet

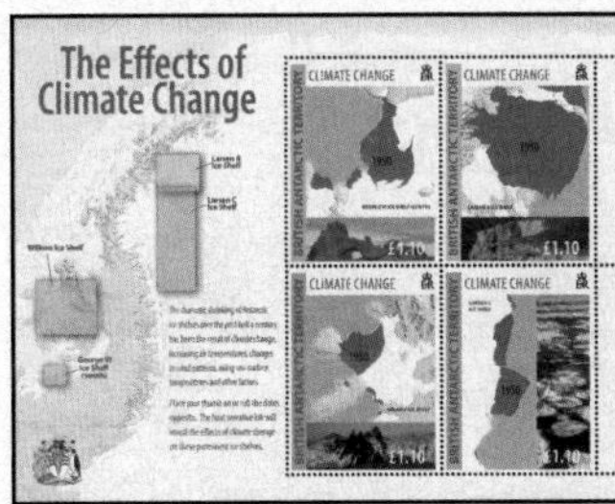

Effects of Climate Change — A75

No. 417 — Maps showing present day and 1950 extents of: a, George VI Ice Shelf (South). b, Larsen B Ice Shelf. c, Wilkins Ice Shelf. d, Larsen C Ice Shelf.

2009, Nov. 26 *Perf. 13¼x13½*

417 A75 £1.10 Sheet of 4, #a-d 14.50 14.50

Marine Life A76

Designs: No. 418, 27p, Polychaete worm. No. 419, 27p, Button worm. No. 420, 27p, Sponge. No. 421, 27p, Amphipod.
No. 422: a, Solitary coral. b, Amphipod, diff. c, Comb jellyfish. d, Basket star.

Wmk. 406

2010, Dec. 3 Litho. *Perf. 14*

418-421 A76 Set of 4 3.50 3.50

Souvenir Sheet

Perf. 13¼

422 A76 £1.15 Sheet of 4, #a-d 14.50 14.50

No. 422 contains four 36x36mm stamps.

Birds — A77

No. 423, 27p: a, South polar skua. b, Adélie penguin.

No. 424, 70p: a, Gray-headed albatross. b, Emperor penguin.

No. 425, £1.15: a, Kelp gull. b, Antarctic petrel.

2010, Dec. 3 ***Perf. 14***

Horiz. Pairs, #a-b

423-425 A77 Set of 3 13.50 13.50

Miniature Sheets

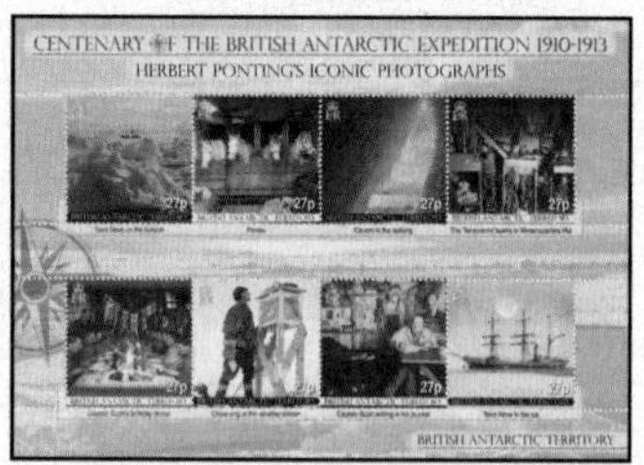

Photographs of 1910-13 British Antarctic Expedition — A78

No. 426, 27p: a, Ship, Terra Nova, on horizon. b, Ponies. c, Cavern in iceberg. d, "Tenements" bunks in Winterquarters hut. e, Capt. Robert Falcon Scott's birthday dinner. f, Observing at the weather station. g, Capt. Scott writing in his journal. h, Terra Nova in the ice.

No. 427, 60p: a, Terra Nova in harbor. b, Lieutenant Rennick leading pony. c, Matterhorn Berg. d, Nelson at work in the lab. e, Capt. Scott on skis. f, Chris (dog) and gramophone. g, Motorized tractor and load passing Inaccessible Island. h, Polar party at the South Pole.

2010, Dec. 3 ***Perf. 13¼***

Sheets of 8, #a-h

426-427 A78 Set of 2 22.00 22.00

Miniature Sheets

A79

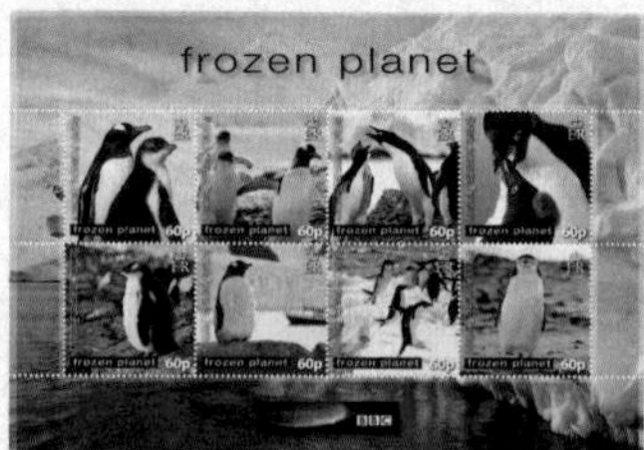

Filming in British Antarctic Territory of *Frozen Planet* Television Series — A80

No. 428: a, Close-up of head of seal. b, Seal with head on rock. c, Head of seal on back in snow. d, Seal in water. e, Dorsal fin of killer whales. f, Head of killer whale and four other killer whales with heads below water. g, Two killer whales with heads abovve water. h, Dorsal fins of two killer whales.

No. 429: a, Adult and juvenile penguin. b, Three penguins walking. c, Four penguins, one with beak open. d, Adult penguin feeding juvenile. e, Juvenile penguin on rock facing left. f, Penguin and ship. g, Group of penguins jumping from water to ice. h, Chinstrap penguin facing forward.

2011, Nov. 17

428 A79 27p Sheet of 8, #a-h 6.75 6.75
429 A80 60p Sheet of 8, #a-h 15.00 15.00

Miniature Sheets

A81

A82

Science in the Antarctic — A83

No. 430: a, Building (sepia-toned). b, Building (color). c, Scientists preparing weather balloon for flight (sepia-toned), vert. d, Scientist preparing weather ballon for flight (color), vert. e, Two scientists on boat preparing equipment (sepia-toned), vert. f, Scientific equipment on cable (color), vert. g, Two skiers, iceberg (sepia-toned). h, Scientists in small boat (color).

No. 431 (color images): a, Airplane. b, Scientist spraying water into air. c, Scientist opening weather station. d, British Antarctic Survey Advanced Ionospheric Sounder.

No. 432 (sepia-toned images): a, Scientist, microscope and bottles. b, Scientist at weather station. c, Equipment in storage. d, Scientist looking through telescope.

2011, Nov. 17 ***Perf. 14***

430	A81	27p Sheet of 8, #a-h	6.75	6.75
431	A82	70p Sheet of 4, #a-d	8.75	8.75
432	A83	£1.15 Sheet of 4, #a-d	14.50	14.50
		Nos. 430-432 (3)	30.00	30.00

A84

A85

A86

A87

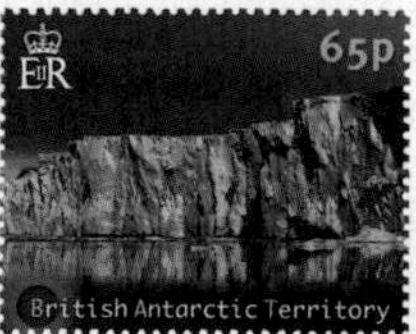

A88

A89

A90

A91

A92

Glaciers and Icesheets A93

2012, Dec. 21 ***Perf. 13¾***

433		Horiz. strip of 5	10.50	10.50
a.	A84	65p multi	2.10	2.10
b.	A85	65p multi	2.10	2.10
c.	A86	65p multi	2.10	2.10
d.	A87	65p multi	2.10	2.10
e.	A88	65p multi	2.10	2.10
434		Horiz. strip of 5	12.50	12.50
a.	A89	75p multi	2.50	2.50
b.	A90	75p multi	2.50	2.50
c.	A91	75p multi	2.50	2.50
d.	A92	75p multi	2.50	2.50
e.	A93	75p multi	2.50	2.50

British Graham Land Expedition, 75th Anniv. — A94

No. 435, 40p: a, Boat on shore with three crew members. b, Two boats on dock.

No. 436, 40p: a, Dog. b, Dog and expedition member.

No. 437, 50p: a, Airplane, dog, expedition members. b, Airplane on water.

No. 438, 50p: a, Ship, denomination in white at LR. b, Ship, denomination in black at UR.

£1.20, Ship "Penola."

2012, Dec. 21 ***Perf. 13¾***

Horiz. Pairs, #a-b

435-438 A94 Set of 4 12.00 12.00

Souvenir Sheet

Perf. 14x14¾

439 A94 £1.20 multi 4.00 4.00

No. 439 contains one 49x33mm stamp.

Souvenir Sheet

HMS Protector — A95

2012, Dec. 21 ***Perf. 14¼x15***

440 A95 £3.50 multi 11.50 11.50

Souvenir Sheet

Naming of Queen Elizabeth Land — A96

2013, Mar. 18 ***Perf. 14¾x14***

441 A96 £3 multi 9.25 9.25

SEMI-POSTAL STAMPS

Antarctic Heritage SP1

Designs: 17p+3p, Capt. James Cook, HMS Resolution. 35p+15p, Sir James Clark Ross, HMS Erebus, HMS Terror. 40p+10p, Capt. Robert Falcon Scott. 76p+4p, Sir Ernest Shackleton, HMS Endurance trapped in ice.

Wmk. 384

1994, Nov. 23 **Litho.** ***Perf. 14½***

B1	SP1	17p + 3p multi	2.50	2.50
B2	SP1	35p + 15p multi	3.50	3.50
B3	SP1	40p + 10p multi	3.50	3.50
B4	SP1	76p + 4p multi	6.50	6.50
		Nos. B1-B4 (4)	16.00	16.00

Surtax for United Kingdom Antarctic Heritage Trust.

AIR POST STAMPS

Penguins — AP1

No. C1: a, Two Emperors. b, Macaroni. c, Adult Gentoo. d, Two Adelies. e, Adult Chinstrap. f, Juvenile Gentoo. g, Two emperors, horizon. h, Juvenile Chinstrap. i, Seven Adelies. j, Adult and juvenile Gentoos. k, Two Macaronis. l, Emperor.

Wmk. 373

2003, Dec. 8 Litho. ***Perf. 13¼***

C1 AP1 (40p) Sheet of 12, #a-l 29.00 29.00

Penguins — AP2

Nos. C2 and C3: a, Chinstrap chick. b, Head of Emperor. c, Adelie with wings extended. d, Head of Chinstrap. e, Head of Macaroni, red country name. f, Gentoo adult feeding juvenile. g, Emperor chick. h, Adelie on nest. i, Two Emperors and mountain. j, Gentoo. k, Two Adelies. l, Two Emperor juveniles.

Wmk. 373

2006, Nov. 8 Litho. ***Perf. 13¼***

C2 AP2 (50p) Sheet of 12, #a-l 26.00 26.00

Self-Adhesive

Unwmk.

Die Cut Perf. 9x9½

C3 AP2 (50p) Booklet pane of 12, #a-l 26.00 26.00

Miniature Sheet

Penguins — AP3

No. C4: a, Head of Chinstrap. b, Adult Gentoo and two chicks. c, Macaroni with open beak. d, Chinstrap with open beak and wings extended. e, Two Emperors. f, Adelie chicks. g, Chinstrap with wings extended. h, Gentoo with open beak. i, Macaroni. j, Adult Emperor and chick. k, Two Adelies. l, Emperor chick.

Wmk. 373

2008, Nov. 17 Litho. ***Perf. 13¼***

C4 AP3 (55p) Sheet of 12, #a-l 19.50 19.50

RRS James Clark Ross — AP4

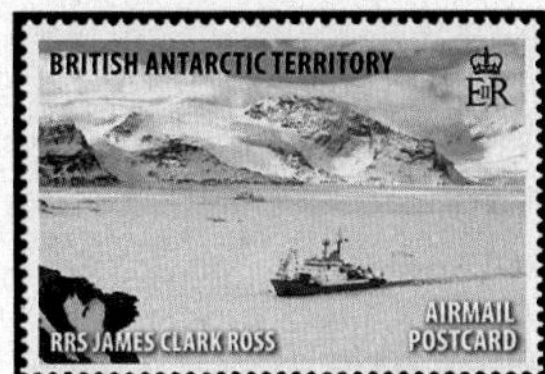

RRS James Clark Ross — AP5

RRS Bransfield — AP6

RRS Bransfield — AP7

RRS Ernest Shackleton — AP8

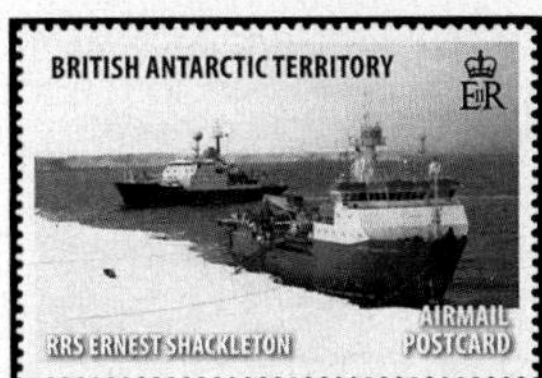

RRS Ernest Shackleton — AP9

Design: £1.15, RRS James Clark Ross and penguin.

Perf. 14¼x14¾

2011, Nov. 17 Wmk. 406

C5	AP4	(60p)	multi	1.90	1.90
C6	AP5	(60p)	multi	1.90	1.90
C7	AP6	(60p)	multi	1.90	1.90
C8	AP7	(60p)	multi	1.90	1.90
C9	AP8	(60p)	multi	1.90	1.90
C10	AP9	(60p)	multi	1.90	1.90
		Nos. C5-C10 (6)		11.40	11.40

Souvenir Sheet

Perf. 13¼

C11 AP4 £1.15 multi 3.75 3.75

Coil Stamps

Self-Adhesive

Size: 33x22mm

Unwmk.

Die Cut Perf. 13¼x12¾

C12	AP4	(60p)	multi	1.90	1.90
C13	AP5	(60p)	multi	1.90	1.90
C14	AP6	(60p)	multi	1.90	1.90
C15	AP7	(60p)	multi	1.90	1.90
C16	AP8	(60p)	multi	1.90	1.90
C17	AP9	(60p)	multi	1.90	1.90
a.		Horiz. coil strip of 6, #C12-C17		11.50	
		Nos. C12-C17 (6)		11.40	11.40

Gentoo Penguins AP10

Adelie Penguin AP11

Chinstrap Penguin AP12

Adelie Penguin AP13

Gentoo Penguin — AP14

Die Cut Perf. 13¼x13½

2012, Nov. 16

Coil Stamps

Self-Adhesive

C18	AP10	(65p)	multi	2.10	2.10
C19	AP11	(65p)	multi	2.10	2.10
C20	AP12	(65p)	multi	2.10	2.10
C21	AP13	(65p)	multi	2.10	2.10
C22	AP14	(65p)	multi	2.10	2.10
a.		Vert. strip of 5, #C18-C22		10.50	
		Nos. C18-C22 (5)		10.50	10.50

BRITISH CENTRAL AFRICA

'bri-tish 'sen-trəl 'a-fri-kə

LOCATION — Central Africa, on the west shore of Lake Nyassa

GOVT. — British territory, under charter to the British South Africa Company

AREA — 37,800 sq. mi.

POP. — 1,639,329

CAPITAL — Zomba

In 1907 the name was changed to Nyasaland Protectorate, and stamps so inscribed replaced those of British Central Africa.

12 Pence = 1 Shilling

20 Shillings = 1 Pound

Rhodesia Nos. 2, 4-19 Overprinted in Black

1891-95 Unwmk. ***Perf. 14***

1	A1	1p	black	12.00	*9.00*
2	A2	2p	gray green & ver	13.00	*5.00*
a.			Half used as 1p on cover ('95)		*7,000.*
3	A2	4p	red brn & blk	13.00	*6.25*
4	A1	6p	ultramarine	60.00	24.00
5	A1	6p	dark blue	16.00	*10.00*
6	A2	8p	rose & blue	20.00	*35.00*
7	A1	1sh	bis brown	27.50	18.00
8	A1	2sh	vermilion	42.50	*60.00*
9	A1	2sh6p	gray lilac	80.00	*105.00*
10	A2	3sh	brn & grn ('95)	85.00	*85.00*
11	A2	4sh	gray & ver ('93)	85.00	*105.00*
12	A1	5sh	yellow	100.00	*100.00*
13	A1	10sh	green	190.00	*230.00*
14	A3	£1	blue	1,000.	*800.00*
15	A3	£2	rose red	1,200.	*1,500.*
16	A3	£5	yel green	2,250.	—
17	A3	£10	red brown	*4,500.*	*5,500.*
		Nos. 1-13 (13)		744.00	*792.25*

High values with fiscal cancellation are fairly common and can be purchased at a small fraction of the above values. This applies to subsequent issues also. The most common fiscal marking consists of an undated double-circle cancel with the words "BRITISH CENTRAL AFRICA" between the circles, and a town name in the center. This cancel exists in various sizes and is usually applied in black.

For surcharge see No. 20.

Rhodesia Nos. 13-14 Surcharged in Black

1892-93

18	A2	3sh on 4sh gray & ver ('93)	400.00	400.00
19	A1	4sh on 5sh yellow	100.00	*110.00*

No. 2 Surcharged in Black, with Bar

1895

20	A2	1p on 2p	27.50	*55.00*
a.		Double surcharge	*9,500.*	*7,000.*

A double surcharge, without period after "Penny," and measuring 16mm instead of 18mm, is from a trial printing made at Blantyre. Value, $650.

A4

Coat of Arms of the Protectorate — A5

1895 Unwmk. Typo. ***Perf. 14***

21	A4	1p	black	19.00	16.00
22	A4	2p	green & black	45.00	14.50
23	A4	4p	org & black	80.00	52.50
24	A4	6p	ultra & black	85.00	10.00
25	A4	1sh	rose & black	100.00	42.50
26	A5	2sh6p	vio & black	325.00	375.00
27	A5	3sh	yel & black	190.00	60.00
28	A5	5sh	olive & blk	250.00	250.00
29	A5	£1	org & black	1,150.	800.00
30	A5	£10	ver & black	*6,750.*	*4,800.*
31	A5	£25	bl grn & blk	*14,500.*	—
		Nos. 21-28 (8)		1,094.	820.50

1896 Wmk. 2

32	A4	1p	black	4.25	*8.00*
33	A4	2p	green & black	18.00	6.00
34	A4	4p	org brown & blk	30.00	*21.00*
35	A4	6p	ultra & black	45.00	16.00
36	A4	1sh	rose & black	45.00	22.00

Wmk. 1 Sideways

37	A5	2sh6p	vio rose & blk	180.00	*160.00*
38	A5	3sh	yel & black	160.00	67.50
39	A5	5sh	olive & blk	225.00	*240.00*
40	A5	£1	blue & blk	1,100.	600.00
41	A5	£10	ver & blk	*10,000.*	*4,800.*
42	A5	£25	bl grn & blk	*19,000.*	—
		Nos. 32-39 (8)		707.25	*540.50*

A6

A7

1897-1901 Wmk. 2

43	A6	1p	ultra & black	4.00	1.50
44	A6	1p	rose & violet ('01)	3.50	.80
45	A6	2p	yel & black	2.50	2.50
46	A6	4p	car rose & blk	8.00	2.25
47	A6	4p	ol green & violet ('01)	11.00	*13.50*
48	A6	6p	green & black	60.00	5.25
49	A6	6p	red brown & violet ('01)	7.00	3.75
50	A6	1sh	gray lilac & blk	13.50	8.50

Wmk. 1

51	A7	2sh6p	ultra & blk	85.00	*50.00*
52	A7	3sh	gray grn & blk	300.00	*325.00*
53	A7	4sh	car rose & blk	100.00	*100.00*

54 A7 10sh ol & black 250.00 *275.00*
55 A7 £1 dp vio & blk 425.00 200.00
56 A7 £10 org & black *7,000.* *2,500.*
Nos. 43-54 (12) 844.50 *788.05*

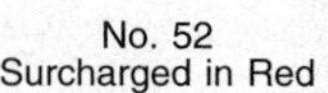

No. 52 Surcharged in Red

1897

57 A7 1p on 3sh 9.50 *15.00*
a. "PNNEY" 7,500. 5,500.
b. "PENN" 3,750. 2,750.
c. Double surcharge 650.00 1,100.

A8

Type I — The vertical framelines are not continuous between stamps.

Type II — The vertical framelines are continuous between stamps.

1898, Mar. 11 Unwmk. *Imperf.*

Type I

Control on Reverse

58 A8 1p ver & ultra — 145.00
a. 1p ver & deep ultra 5,500. 150.00
b. No control on reverse 4,750. 220.00
c. Control double 525.00
d. Control on front *3,900.*
e. Pair, one without oval *30,000.*

Type II

Control on Reverse

f. 1p ver & ultra — 800.00

No Control on Reverse

g. 1p grayish blue & ver, initials on back 12,000. 1,100.
h. No initials 6,000.
i. Oval inverted 30,000.
j. Oval double —
k. Pair, with 3 ovals —

Perf. 12

Type I

Control on Reverse

59 A8 1p ver & ultra 5,000. 30.00
a. 1p ver & deep ultra — 47.50
b. Two diff. controls on reverse — 800.00

No Control on Reverse

d. 1p ver & ultra 4,750. 115.00

There are 30 types of each setting of Nos. 58-59.

No. 58 issued without gum.

Control consists of figures or letters.

Initials are of Postmaster General (J.G. or J.T.G.).

A9

King Edward VII — A10

1903-04 Wmk. 2

60 A9 1p car & black 9.50 2.25
61 A9 2p vio & dull vio 4.50 2.25
62 A9 4p blk & gray green 3.25 *11.00*
63 A9 6p org brn & blk 4.00 *4.00*
64 A9 1sh pale blue & blk ('04) 5.00 *15.00*

Wmk. 1

65 A10 2sh6p gray green 65.00 *100.00*
66 A10 4sh vio & dl vio 90.00 *105.00*
67 A10 10sh blk & gray green 190.00 *300.00*
68 A10 £1 scar & blk 360.00 250.00
69 A10 £10 ultra & blk *7,750.* *4,500.*
Nos. 60-68 (9) 731.25 *789.50*

1907 Wmk. 3

70 A9 1p car & black 8.50 3.50
71 A9 2p vio & dull vio *16,000.*
72 A9 4p blk & gray grn *16,000.*
73 A9 6p org brn & blk 40.00 *60.00*

Nos. 71-72 were not issued.

British Central Africa stamps were replaced by those of Nyasaland Protectorate in 1908.

BRITISH EAST AFRICA

'bri-tish 'ēst 'a-fri-kə

LOCATION — East coast of Africa; modern Kenya. Included all of the territory in East Africa under British control.

Postage stamps were issued by the Imperial British East Africa Company (IBEAC) in May 1900. Transferred to the Crown as a Protectorate July 1, 1895. Postal administration amalgamated with Uganda in 1901 with new stamps issued in July 1903 inscribed 'East Africa and Uganda Protectorates.'

16 Annas = 1 Rupee

A1

A2

Queen Victoria — A3

1890 Wmk. 30 *Perf. 14*

1 A1 ½a on 1p lilac 350.00 240.00
2 A2 1a on 2p grn & car rose 575.00 350.00
3 A3 4a on 5p lilac & bl 600.00 375.00

Sun and Crown Symbolical of "Light and Liberty"

A4 A5

1890-94 Unwmk. Litho. *Perf. 14*

14 A4 ½a bister brown 1.25 *15.00*
b. ½a deep brown 1.00 *8.50*
c. As "b," horiz. pair, imperf. btwn. *1,925.* 775.00
d. As "b," vert. pair, imperf. btwn. 1,200. 600.00
15 A4 1a blue green 8.00 *12.00*
16 A4 2a vermilion 4.50 *5.25*
17 A4 2½a black, *yel* ('91) 5.50 *6.00*
a. Horiz. pair, imperf. btwn. 6,000.
18 A4 3a black, *red* ('91) 5.50 *12.00*
b. Horiz. pair, imperf. btwn. 1,100 525.00
c. Vert. pair, imperf. btwn. 850.00 450.00
19 A4 4a yellow brown 3.00 *11.00*
20 A4 4½a brown vio ('91) 3.00 *21.00*
b. 4½a gray violet ('91) 42.50 18.00
c. Horiz. pair, imperf. btwn. 2,100. 1,200.
d. Vert. pair, imperf. btwn. 1,200. 600.00
21 A4 5a black, *blue* ('94) 1.50 *13.00*
22 A4 7½a black ('94) 1.50 *19.00*
23 A4 8a blue 6.75 *11.50*
24 A4 8a gray 350.00 *350.00*
25 A4 1r rose 7.50 *11.00*
26 A4 1r gray 275.00 *275.00*
27 A5 2r brick red 17.00 *42.50*
28 A5 3r gray violet 12.00 *60.00*
29 A5 4r ultra 15.00 *60.00*
30 A5 5r gray green 37.50 *85.00*
Nos. 14-30 (17) 754.50 *1,009.*

Some of the paper used for this issue had a papermaker's watermark and parts of it often can be seen on the stamps.

Values for Nos. 14c, 14d, 18b, 18c, 20c, 20d, unused, are for examples with little or no original gum. Stamps with natural straight edges are almost as common as fully perforated stamps from the early printings of Nos. 14-30, and for all printings of the rupee values. Values about the same.

For surcharges and overprints see Nos. 31-53.

1890-93 *Imperf.*

Values for Pairs except No. 19b.

14a A4 ½a bister brown 1,200. 450.
14e A4 ½a deep brown 1,700. 725.
15a A4 1a blue green 3,300. 850.
16a A4 2a vermilion 2,750. 975.
17d A4 2½a black, *bright yellow* 1,200. 550.
18a A4 3a black, *red* 1,150. 500.
19a A4 4a yel brown 3,000. 1,350.
19b A4 4a gray 1,500. 1,700.
20a A4 4½a dull violet 1,950. 550.
23a A4 8a blue 5,700. 1,150.
25a A4 1r rose 14,500. 1,300.

A6

Handstamped Surcharges

1891 *Perf. 14*

31 A6 ½a on 2a ver ("A.D.") 14,000. 1,000.
a. Double surcharge *10,000.*
32 A6 1a on 4a yel brn ("A.B.") 21,000. 2,300.

Validation initials are shown in parentheses. See note below No. 35.

Manuscript Surcharges

1891-95

33 A6 ½a on 2a ver ("A.B.") 17,000. 1,050.
a. "½ Annas" ("A.B.") 1,200.
b. Initialed "A.D." 6,500.
34 A6 ½a on 3a blk, *red* ("T.E.C.R.") 700. 60.
b. Initialed "A.B." 14,000. 2,750.
34A A6 1a on 3a blk, *red* ("V.H.M.") 13,000. 2,250.
c. Initialed "T.E.C.R." 23,000. 3,250.
35 A6 1a on 4a yel brn ("A.B.") 12,000. 2,200.

The manuscript initials on Nos. 31-35, given in parentheses, stand for Andrew Dick, Archibald Brown, Victor H. Mackenzie (1891) and T.E.C. Remington (1895).

Three persons applied the surcharge to No. 33, and two persons applied the surcharge to No. 35, resulting in different types.

A7

1894 Printed Surcharges

36 A7 5a on 8a blue 85.00 *110.00*
37 A7 7½a on 1r rose 85.00 *110.00*

Stamps of 1890-94 Handstamped in Black

1895

38 A4 ½a deep brown 90.00 30.00
b. Inverted overprint *6,000.*
39 A4 1a blue green 200.00 135.00
40 A4 2a vermilion 220.00 115.00
41 A4 2½a black, *yel* 220.00 67.50
42 A4 3a black, *dull red* 105.00 60.00
43 A4 4a yel brown 62.50 42.50
44 A4 4½a gray violet 250.00 120.00
a. 4½a brown violet 1,450. 1,150.
45 A4 5a black, *blue* 300.00 170.00
b. Inverted overprint *4,500.*
46 A4 7½a black 150.00 100.00
47 A4 8a blue 115.00 90.00
b. Inverted overprint *7,200.*
48 A4 1r rose 67.50 60.00
49 A5 2r brick red 550.00 300.00
50 A5 3r gray violet 275.00 160.00
b. Inverted overprint
51 A5 4r ultra 250.00 200.00
52 A5 5r gray green 525.00 *325.00*
Nos. 38-52 (15) 3,380. 1,975.

Forgeries exist.

Double Overprints

38a A4 ½a 550. 525.
39a A4 1a 600. 550.
40a A4 2a 800. 575.
41a A4 2½a 800. 525.
43a A4 4a 575. 550.
44b A4 4½a gray violet 850. 675.
44c A4 4½a brown violet 3,300. 2,400.
45a A4 5a 1,100. 1,000.
46a A4 7½a 800. 675.
47a A4 8a 725. 725.
48a A4 1r 675. 675.
50a A5 3r 1,100. 1,100.
51a A5 4r 1,000. 1,000.
52a A5 5r 1,600. 1,600.

Surcharged in Red

1895

53 A4 2½a on 4½a gray vio 225.00 90.00
a. Double overprint (#44b) 1,200. 1,050.

Stamps of India 1874-95 Overprinted or Surcharged

a

b

c

1895 Wmk. Star (39)

54 A17 ½a green 8.50 *6.75*
55 A19 1a maroon 8.00 *7.25*
56 A20 1a6p bister brn 5.25 *5.00*
57 A21 2a ultra 8.50 3.75
58 A28 2a6p green 12.00 3.25
59 A20(a) 2½a on 1a6p bis brn 115.00 57.50
a. "½" without fraction line 135.00
d. As "a," "1" of "½" invtd. 1,100. 725.00
62 A22 3a orange 20.00 *13.50*
63 A23 4a olive green 50.00 37.50
a. 4a slate green 32.00 26.00
64 A25 8a red violet 35.00 *60.00*
a. 8a red lilac 110.00 85.00
65 A26 12a vio, *red* 27.50 *40.00*
66 A27 1r gray 115.00 80.00
67 A29 1r car & grn 55.00 *160.00*
a. Dbl. ovpt., one sideways 525.00 1,100.
68 A30 2r bis & rose 110.00 *180.00*
69 A30 3r grn & brn 135.00 *200.00*
70 A30 5r vio & ultra 160.00 *200.00*
a. Double overprint 2,750.

Wmk. Elephant's Head (38)

71 A14 6a bister 50.00 *60.00*
Nos. 54-59,62-71 (16) 914.75 *1,114.*

Varieties of the overprint include "Brit1sh," "Br1tish," "Afr1ca," "Biitish," "Bpitish," inverted "a" for "t," "Eas" for "East," and letter "B" handstamped. See the *Scott Specialized Catalogue of Stamps and Covers* for detailed listings.

No. 59 is surcharged in bright red; surcharges in brown red were prepared for the UPU, but not regularly issued as stamps. See note following No. 93.

Queen Victoria and British Lions — A8

1896-1903 Engr. Wmk. 2 *Perf. 14*

72	A8	½a yel green	5.00	1.00
73	A8	1a carmine	13.00	.50
a.		1a red	11.00	.50
74	A8	1a dp rose ('03)	27.50	5.00
75	A8	2a chocolate	10.00	7.00
76	A8	2½a dark blue	16.00	2.25
77	A8	3a gray	8.50	*12.00*
78	A8	4a deep green	8.00	4.25
79	A8	4½a orange	15.00	*20.00*
80	A8	5a dk ocher	9.25	7.00
81	A8	7½a lilac	9.00	*27.00*
82	A8	8a olive gray	9.50	7.00
83	A8	1r ultra	130.00	80.00
a.		1r pale blue	75.00	30.00
84	A8	2r red orange	80.00	35.00
85	A8	3r deep violet	80.00	40.00
86	A8	4r lake	72.50	85.00
87	A8	5r dark brown	70.00	50.00
		Nos. 72-87 (16)	563.25	383.00

Zanzibar Nos. 38-40, 44-46 Overprinted in Black

1897 Wmk. Rosette (71)

88	A2	½a yel grn & red	67.50	55.00
89	A2	1a indigo & red	115.00	110.00
90	A2	2a red brn & red	47.50	26.00
91	A2	4½a org & red	60.00	37.50
92	A2	5a bister & red	67.50	42.50
93	A2	7½a lilac & red	60.00	42.50
a.		Ovptd. on front and back		—
		Nos. 88-93 (6)	417.50	313.50

The 1a with red overprint, which includes a period after "Africa", was sent to the UPU, but never placed in use. Nos. 88, 90-93 and 95-100 also exist with period (in black) in sets sent to the UPU. Some experts consider these essays.

Black Ovpt. on Zanzibar #39, 42
New Value Surcharged in Red

1897

95	A2(a)	2½a on 1a	135.00	80.00
a.		Black overprint double	7,800.	
96	A2(b)	2½a on 1a	300.00	130.00
97	A2(c)	2½a on 1a	160.00	90.00
a.		Black overprint double	7,800.	
98	A2(a)	2½a on 3a	135.00	67.50
99	A2(b)	2½a on 3a	300.00	120.00
100	A2(c)	2½a on 3a	160.00	75.00
		Nos. 95-100 (6)	1,190.	562.50

A special printing of the 2½a surcharge on the 1a and 3a stamps was made for submission to the U.P.U. Stamps have a period after "Africa" in the overprint, and the surcharges included a "2" over "1" error in the fraction of the surcharge. These stamps were never placed in use. The fraction error appears on both the 1a and 3a stamps. Value, each, $1,500.

A10

1898 Wmk. 1 Engr.

102a	A10	1r 1r dull blue ('01)	95.00	47.50
103	A10	2r orange	130.00	130.00
104	A10	3r dk violet	170.00	*180.00*
105	A10	4r carmine	475.00	*550.00*
106	A10	5r black brown	425.00	*500.00*
107	A10	10r bister	425.00	*550.00*
108	A10	20r yel green	1,000.	*2,000.*
109	A10	50r lilac	2,000.	*7,500.*
		Nos. 102a-107 (6)	1,720.	*1,957.*

Nos. 102-109 are often found with fiscal or Court Fee cancels. Stamps with these cancels can be purchased at a fraction of these values.

The stamps of this country were superseded by the stamps of East Africa and Uganda Protectorate.

BRITISH GUIANA

'bri-tish gē-'a-nə, -'ä-nə

LOCATION — On the northeast coast of South America
GOVT. — British Crown Colony
AREA — 83,000 sq. mi.
POP. — 628,000 (estimated 1964)
CAPITAL — Georgetown

British Guiana became the independent state of Guyana May 26, 1966.

100 Cents = 1 Dollar

Catalogue values for unused stamps in this country are for Never Hinged items, beginning with Scott 242 in the regular postage section and Scott J1 in the postage due section.

Values for unused stamps are for examples with original gum except for Nos. 6-12 and 35-53, which are valued without gum. Very fine examples of all stamps from No. 6 on will have four clear margins. Inferior examples sell at much reduced prices, depending on the condition of the individual stamp.

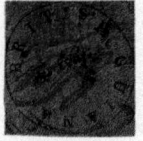

A1

1850-51 Typeset Unwmk. *Imperf.*

1	A1	2c blk, *pale rose,* cut to shape ('51)		*275,000.*
2	A1	4c black, *orange*		*75,000.*
		Cut to shape		*12,000.*
a.		4c black, *yellow*		*100,000.*
		Cut to shape		*17,500.*
3	A1	4c blk, *yellow* (pelure)		*110,000.*
		Cut to shape		*18,500.*
4	A1	8c black, *green*		*50,000.*
		Cut to shape		*12,000.*
5	A1	12c black, *blue*		*21,500.*
		Cut to shape		*8,000.*
a.		12c black, *pale blue*		*27,500.*
		Cut to shape		*9,750.*
b.		12c black, *indigo*		*27,500.*
		Cut to shape		*9,250.*
c.		"1" of "12" omitted, cut to shape		*200,000.*

These stamps were initialed before use by the Deputy Postmaster General or by one of the clerks of the Colonial Postoffice at Georgetown. The following initials are found: — E. T. E. D(alton); E. D. W(ight); G. B. S(mith); H. A. K(illikelley); W. H. L(ortimer). As these stamps are type-set there are several types of each value.

Ship and Motto of Colony — A2

1852 Litho.

6	A2	1c black, *magenta*	*10,000.*	*6,750.*
7	A2	4c black, *blue*	*18,500.*	*10,500.*

Both 1c and 4c are found in two types. Examples with paper cracked or rubbed sell for much less.

Some examples are initialed E. D. W(ight).

The reprints are on thicker paper and the colors are brighter. They are perforated 12½ and imperforate. Value $20 each.

Seal of the Colony — A3

Without Line above Value

1853-59 *Imperf.*

8	A3	1c vermilion	6,000.	1,750.

A proof of No. 8 exists in reddish brown, value about $850.

Full or Partial White Line Above Value

9	A3	1c red (I)	4,800.	1,750.
10	A3	4c blue	2,400.	750.00
a.		4c dark blue	4,250.	975.00
b.		4c pale blue	1,750.	650.00

On No. 9, "ONE CENT" varies from 11 to 13mm in width.

No. 10 Retouched; White Line above Value Removed

11	A3	4c blue	3,250.	925.00
a.		4c dark blue	6,000.	1,400.
b.		4c pale blue	2,150.	850.00

Reprints of Nos. 8 and 10 are on thin paper, perf. 12½ or imperf. The 1c is orange red, the 4c sky blue.

1860

Numerals in Corners Framed

12	A3	4c blue	5,500.	750.00

A4

1856 Typeset *Imperf.*

13	A4	1c black, *magenta*		—
14	A4	4c black, *magenta*		*15,000.*
a.		4c black, *rose carmine*	*45,000.*	*18,500.*
15	A4	4c black, *blue*		*100,000.*
16	A4	4c black, *blue, paper colored through*		*140,000.*

These stamps were initialed before being issued and the following initials are found: — E. T. E. D.; E. D. W.; W. H. L.; C. A. W. No. 13 is unique.

A5

Wide space between value and "Cents"

1860-61 Litho. *Perf. 12*

Thick Paper

17	A5	1c brown red ('61)	500.00	115.00
18	A5	1c pink	3,500.	300.00
19	A5	2c orange	350.00	65.00
20	A5	8c rose	825.00	130.00
21	A5	12c gray	750.00	55.00
a.		12c lilac	850.00	55.00
22	A5	24c green	1,600.	85.00

All denominations of type A5 above four cents are expressed in Roman numerals.

Bisects and trisects are found on covers. These were not officially authorized.

The reprints of the 1c pink are perforated 12½; the other values have not been reprinted.

1862-65 Thin Paper

23	A5	1c brown	925.00	275.00
24	A5	1c black ('63)	160.00	65.00
25	A5	2c orange	150.00	65.00
26	A5	8c rose ('63)	300.00	85.00
27	A5	12c lilac	400.00	55.00
28	A5	24c green	1,600.	110.00

Perf. 12½ and 13

29	A5	1c black	80.00	25.00
30	A5	2c orange	95.00	27.50
31	A5	8c rose	350.00	97.50
32	A5	12c lilac	1,075.	140.00
33	A5	24c green	875.00	80.00

Medium Paper

33A	A5	1c black ('64)	70.00	55.00
33B	A5	2c deep orange ('64)	90.00	32.50
33C	A5	8c pink ('64)	300.00	80.00
33D	A5	12c lilac ('65)	1,250.	130.00
33E	A5	24c green ('64)	375.00	65.00
f.		24c deep green	450.00	90.00

Perf. 10

34	A5	12c gray lilac	800.00	97.50

Imperfs. are proofs. See Nos. 44-62.

A6

A7

A8

A9

A10

A11

1862 Typeset *Rouletted*

35 A6 1c black, *rose* *5,400.* *850.*
Unsigned 650.
36 A7 1c black, *rose* *7,000.* *1,400.*
Unsigned 750.
37 A8 1c black, *rose* *9,750.* *1,400.*
Unsigned 1,200.
38 A6 2c black, *yellow* *5,500.* *450.*
Unsigned 2,400.
39 A7 2c black, *yellow* *7,000.* *550.*
Unsigned 2,750.
40 A8 2c black, *yellow* *9,750.* *925.*
Unsigned 3,500.
41 A9 4c black, *blue* *8,000.* *1,400.*
Unsigned 1,400.
42 A10 4c black, *blue* *10,750.* *2,000.*
Unsigned —
a. Without inner lines *8,000.* *1,400.*
As "a," unsigned 1,300.
43 A11 4c black, *blue* *6,000.* *1,100.*
Unsigned 1,175.

Nos. 35-43 were typeset, in sheets of 24 each. They were initialed before use "R. M. Ac. R. G.," being the initials of Robert Mather, Acting Receiver General.

The initials are in black on the 1c and in red on the 2c. An alkali was used on the 4c stamps, which, destroying the color of the paper, caused the initials to appear to be written in white.

Uninitialed stamps are remainders, few sheets having been found.

Stamps with roulette on all sides are valued higher.

Narrow space between value and "Cents"

1860 Thick Paper Litho. *Perf. 12*

44 A5 4c blue 450.00 80.00
c. 4c deep blue 800.00 120.00

Thin Paper

44A A5 4c pale blue 150.00 42.50
d. 4c blue 170.00 55.00

Perf. 12½ and 13

44B A5 4c blue 115.00 32.50

Medium Paper

1863-68 *Perf. 12½ and 13*

45 A5 1c black ('66) 80.00 40.00
46 A5 2c orange 85.00 10.00
47 A5 4c gray blue ('64) 100.00 25.00
48 A5 8c rose ('68) 400.00 27.50
49 A5 12c lilac ('67) 650.00 50.00
Nos. 45-49 (5) 1,315. 152.50

1866-71 *Perf. 10*

50 A5 1c black 24.00 8.50
51 A5 2c orange 60.00 5.00
52 A5 4c blue 130.00 11.00
a. Half used as 2c on cover *7,500.*
53 A5 8c rose 300.00 37.50
a. Diagonal half used as 4c on cover —
54 A5 12c lilac 300.00 27.50
a. Third used as 4c on cover —
Nos. 50-54 (5) 814.00 89.50

1875-76 *Perf. 15*

58 A5 1c black 65.00 9.00
59 A5 2c orange 185.00 17.00
60 A5 4c blue 300.00 120.00
61 A5 8c rose 325.00 110.00
62 A5 12c lilac 925.00 100.00
Nos. 58-62 (5) 1,800. 356.00

Seal of Colony
A12 A13

1863 *Perf. 12*

63 A12 24c yellow green 275.00 15.50
a. 24c green 350.00 25.00

Perf. 12½ to 13

64 A12 6c blue 200.00 72.50
65 A12 24c green 275.00 16.00
66 A12 48c deep red 425.00 80.00
a. 48c rose 450.00 80.00
Nos. 63-66 (4) 1,175. 184.00

1866 *Perf. 10*

67 A12 6c blue 200.00 40.00
a. 6c ultramarine 215.00 67.50
68 A12 24c yellow green 275.00 9.00
a. 24c green 375.00 11.00
69 A12 48c rose red 400.00 37.50
Nos. 67-69 (3) 875.00 86.50

For surcharges see Nos. 83-92.

1875 *Perf. 15*

70 A12 6c ultra 1,075. 150.00
71 A12 24c yellow green 800.00 42.50
a. 24c deep green 1,600. 120.00

1876 Typo. Wmk. 1 *Perf. 14*

72 A13 1c slate 3.25 1.75
a. Perf. 14x12½ 225.00
73 A13 2c orange 92.50 4.00
74 A13 4c ultra 150.00 15.00
a. Perf. 12½ 1,450. 250.00
75 A13 6c chocolate 100.00 12.75
76 A13 8c rose 160.00 1.00
77 A13 12c lilac 75.00 2.50
78 A13 24c green 80.00 4.00
79 A13 48c red brown 160.00 50.00
80 A13 96c bister 575.00 325.00
Nos. 72-80 (9) 1,395. 416.00

See Nos. 107-111. For surcharges see Nos. 93-95, 98-101.

Stamps Surcharged by Brush-like Pen Lines

Type a

Type b

Type c

Type d

Surcharge Types:
Type a — Two horiz. lines.
Type b — Two lines, one horiz., one vert.
Type c — Three lines, two horiz., one vert.
Type d — One horiz. line.

On Nos. 75 and 67

1878 *Perf. 10, 14*

82 A13(a) (1c) on 6c choc 52.50 *140.00*
83 A12(b) (1c) on 6c blue 250.00 90.00
84 A13(b) (1c) on 6c choc 425.00 135.00

On Nos. O3, O8-O10

85 A13(c) (1c) on 4c ultra 425.00 120.00
a. Type b *50,000.* *6,000.*
86 A13(c) (1c) on 6c choc 650.00 135.00
87 A5(c) (2c) on 8c rose *4,800.* 400.00
88A A13(b) (2c) on 8c rose 600.00 240.00

On Nos. O1, O3, O6-O7

89 A5(d) (1c) on 1c blk 300.00 90.00
89A A5(d) (2c) on 8c rose
90 A13(d) (1c) on 1c sl 220.00 80.00
91 A13(d) (2c) on 2c org 450.00 80.00

The provisional values of Nos. 82 to 91 were established by various official decrees. The horizontal lines crossed out the old value, "OFFICIAL," or both.

The existence of No. 89A has been questioned by specialists. The editors would like to see authenticated evidence of its existence.

Nos. 69 and 80 Surcharged with New Values in Black

No. 92

No. 93

No. 94

No. 95

1881

92 A12 1c on 48c red 55.00 6.00
93 A13 1c on 96c bister 6.00 *10.00*
94 A13 2c on 96c bister 18.50 *22.00*
95 A13 2c on 96c bister 80.00 *150.00*
Nos. 92-95 (4) 159.50 *188.00*

Nos. O4, O5 and Unissued Official Stamps Surcharged with New Values

No. 96

No. 97

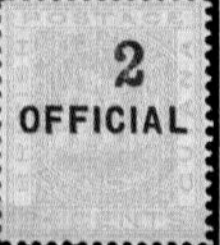

Nos. 98, 100

Nos. 99, 101

No. 102

1881

96 A5 1c on 12c lilac (#O4) 155.00 85.00
97 A13 1c on 48c red brn 215.00 140.00
98 A13 2c on 12c lilac 700.00 500.00
99 A13 2c on 12c lilac 100.00 55.00
a. "2" inverted
b. "2" double *950.00* 550.00
100 A13 2c on 24c green 925.00 *925.00*
101 A13 2c on 24c green 110.00 65.00
a. "2" inverted
d. Double surcharge 1,325.
102 A12 2c on 24c green (#O5) 375.00 185.00

A27

Typeset

ONE AND TWO CENTS.
Type I — Ship with three masts.
Type II — Brig with two masts.

"SPECIMEN"

Perforated Diagonally across Stamp

1882 Unwmk. *Perf. 12*

103 A27 1c black, *lil rose,* I 75.00 35.00
a. Horiz. pair, imperf between *10,000.*
104 A27 1c black, *lil rose,* II 75.00 35.00
a. Without "Specimen" 1,200. 525.00
105 A27 2c black, *yel,* I 95.00 60.00
a. Without "Specimen" 975.00 650.00
b. Diagonal half used as 1c on cover —
106 A27 2c black, *yel,* II 110.00 65.00
a. Without "Specimen" 975.00 650.00
Nos. 103-106 (4) 355.00 195.00

Nos. 103-106 were typeset, 12 to a sheet, and, to prevent fraud on the government, the word *"Specimen"* was perforated across them before they were issued. There were 2 settings of the 1c and 3 settings of the 2c, thus there are 24 types of the former and 36 of the latter.

Type of 1876

1882 Typo. Wmk. 2 *Perf. 14*

107 A13 1c slate 16.00 .40
108 A13 2c orange 52.50 .35
a. "2 CENTS" double *11,500.*
109 A13 4c ultra 110.00 6.50
110 A13 6c brown 6.00 8.00
111 A13 8c rose 130.00 1.00
Nos. 107-111 (5) 314.50 16.25

"INLAND REVENUE" Overprint and Surcharged in Black

A28

A29

4 CENTS and $4
Type I — Figure "4" is 3mm high.
Type II — Figure "4" is 3½mm high.

Type I

Type II

6 CENTS
Type I — Top of "6" is flat.
Type II — Top of "6" turns downward.

1889

112 A28 1c lilac 3.00 .55
113 A28 2c lilac 2.75 2.75
114 A28 3c lilac 1.60 .40
115 A28 4c lilac, I 13.00 .45
116 A28 4c lilac, II 24.00 7.50
117 A28 6c lilac, I 23.00 8.50
118 A28 6c lilac, II 15.00 6.50
119 A28 8c lilac 1.90 .65
120 A28 10c lilac 7.25 3.25
121 A28 20c lilac 26.00 22.50
122 A28 40c lilac 42.50 32.50
123 A28 72c lilac 80.00 *72.50*
124 A28 $1 green 575.00 *650.00*
125 A28 $2 green 275.00 *300.00*
126 A28 $3 green 275.00 *300.00*
127 A28 $4 green, I 650.00 *775.00*
127A A28 $4 green, II 2,200. *2,750.*
128 A28 $5 green 400.00 *425.00*
Nos. 112-128 (18) 4,615. 5,358.

For surcharges see Nos.129, 148-151B.

No. 113 Surcharged "2" in Red

1889

129 A29 2c on 2c lilac 5.50 .55

Inverted and double surcharges of "2" were privately made.

A30

A31

1889-1903 Typo.

130 A30 1c lilac & gray 8.00 3.50
131 A30 1c green ('90) 1.10 .25
131A A30 1c gray grn ('00) 2.10 *6.00*
132 A30 2c lilac & org 5.50 .25
133 A30 2c lil & rose ('00) 4.00 .40
134 A30 2c vio & blk, *red* ('01) 2.00 .25
135 A30 4c lilac & ultra 5.50 4.00
a. 4c lilac & blue 25.00 4.00
136 A30 5c ultra ('91) 3.75 .25
137 A30 6c lilac & mar 8.50 *25.00*
a. 6c lilac & brown 42.50 27.50
138 A30 6c gray blk & ultra ('02) 8.00 *13.50*
139 A30 8c lilac & rose 18.50 4.00
140 A30 8c lil & blk ('90) 7.50 2.25
141 A30 12c lilac & vio 10.00 4.00
142 A30 24c lilac & grn 7.50 4.00
143 A30 48c lilac & ver 30.00 13.00
144 A30 48c dk gray & lil brn ('01) 35.00 35.00
a. 48c gray & purple brown 60.00 50.00
145 A30 60c gray grn & car ('03) 75.00 *250.00*
146 A30 72c lil & org brn 34.00 *55.00*
a. 72c lilac & yellow brown 77.50 *90.00*
147 A30 96c lilac & carmine 80.00 *85.00*
a. 96c lilac & rose 90.00 *100.00*
Nos. 130-147 (19) 345.95 *505.65*

Stamps of the 1889-1903 issue with pen or revenue cancellation sell for a small fraction of the above quotations.

See Nos. 160-177.

1890 Red Surcharge

148 A31 1c on $1 grn & blk 3.00 .50
a. Double surcharge *300.00* *170.00*
149 A31 1c on $2 grn & blk 2.50 1.10
a. Double surcharge *120.00* —
150 A31 1c on $3 grn & blk 3.25 1.50
a. Double surcharge *160.00* —
151 A31 1c on $4 grn & blk, type I 5.50 *12.00*
a. Double surcharge *150.00*
151B A31 1c on $4 grn & blk, type II 15.00 *40.00*
c. Double surcharge
Nos. 148-151B (5) 29.25 *55.10*

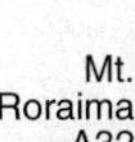

Mt. Roraima A32

Kaieteur (Old Man's) Falls — A33

1898 **Wmk. 1** **Engr.**

152 A32 1c car & gray blk 9.25 2.50
153 A33 2c indigo & brn 35.00 4.50
a. Horiz. pair, imperf. between *16,500.*
b. 2c blue & brown 40.00 4.50
154 A32 5c brown & grn 57.50 6.50
155 A33 10c red & blue blk 30.00 32.50
156 A32 15c blue & red brn 37.50 26.00
Nos. 152-156 (5) 169.25 72.00

60th anniv. of Queen Victoria's accession to the throne.

Nos. 154-156 Surcharged in Black

1899

157 A32 2c on 5c brn & grn 4.00 3.25
a. Without period 185.00 140.00
158 A33 2c on 10c red & bl black 4.00 2.75
a. "GENTS" 70.00 *92.50*
b. Inverted surcharge *750.00* *875.00*
c. Without period 25.00 *65.00*
159 A32 2c on 15c bl & red brown 4.00 1.50
a. Without period 80.00 *80.00*
b. Double surcharge *1,100.* *1,500.*
c. Inverted surcharge 875.00 *1,100.*
Nos. 157-159 (3) 12.00 7.50

There are many slight errors in the setting of this surcharge, such as: small "E" in "CENTS"; no period and narrow "C"; comma between "T" and "S"; dash between "TWO" and "CENTS"; comma between "N" and "T."

Ship Type of 1889-1903

1905-10 **Wmk. 3**

Chalky Paper

160 A30 1c gray green 12.00 1.35
a. Booklet pane of 6
161 A30 2c vio & blk, *red* 5.50 .25
162 A30 4c lilac & ultra 8.50 *15.00*
163 A30 5c lil & blue, *bl* 4.25 *8.00*
164 A30 6c gray black & ultra 18.00 *50.00*
165 A30 12c lilac & vio 27.50 *55.00*
166 A30 24c lil & grn ('06) 4.50 *5.50*
167 A30 48c gray & vio brn 17.00 *27.50*
168 A30 60c gray grn & car rose 17.00 *110.00*
169 A30 72c lil & org brn ('07) 40.00 *85.00*
170 A30 96c blk & red, *yel*('06) 42.50 *55.00*
Nos. 160-170 (11) 196.75 *412.60*

The 2c-60c exist on ordinary paper. See *Scott Classic Specialized Catalogue of Stamps and Covers.*

Ordinary Paper

A34

Black Overprint

171 A34 $2.40 grn & vio *210.00* *500.00*

Ship Type of 1889-1903
Ordinary Paper

Type I

Type II

TWO CENTS
Type I — Only the upper right corner of the flag touches the mast.
Type II — The entire right side of the flag touches the mast.

1907-10

171A A30 1c blue green ('10) 16.00 3.00
172 A30 2c red, type I 21.00 1.10
b. 2c red, type II 10.50 .25
174 A30 4c brown & vio 3.50 1.35
175 A30 5c blue 18.50 6.00
176 A30 6c gray & black 16.00 8.50
177 A30 12c orange & vio 5.00 6.50
Nos. 171A-177 (6) 80.00 26.45

George V — A35

1913-17 ***Perf. 14***

178 A35 1c green 4.50 .90
a. bl grn ('17) 1.90 .30
179 A35 2c scarlet 3.75 .25
a. 2c carmine 1.60 .25
180 A35 4c brn & red vio 7.50 .40
181 A35 5c ultra 2.25 1.25
182 A35 6c gray & black 3.75 2.75
183 A35 12c org & vio 1.75 1.25

Chalky Paper

184 A35 24c dl vio & grn 4.25 *5.00*
185 A35 48c blk & vio brn 30.00 21.00
186 A35 60c grn & car 20.00 *60.00*
187 A35 72c dl vio & org brn 60.00 *100.00*

Surface Colored Paper

188 A35 96c blk & red, *yel* 32.50 *65.00*

Paper Colored Through

189 A35 96c blk & red, *yel* ('16) 22.50 *65.00*
Nos. 178-189 (12) 192.75 *322.80*

The 72c and late printings of the 2c and 5c are from redrawn dies. The ruled lines behind the value are thin and faint, making the tablet appear lighter than before. The shading lines in other parts of the stamps are also lighter. Several paper shades of No. 189 exist.

1921-27 **Wmk. 4**

191 A35 1c green 5.75 .40
192 A35 2c rose red 6.50 .30
193 A35 2c dp vio ('23) 3.00 .25
194 A35 4c brn & vio 5.75 .25
195 A35 6c ultra 3.75 .40
196 A35 12c org & vio 3.50 2.00

Chalky Paper

197 A35 24c dl vio & grn 2.75 *5.50*
198 A35 48c blk & vio brn ('26) 12.00 4.50
199 A35 60c grn & car ('26) 12.50 *57.50*
200 A35 72c dl vio & brn org 37.50 *80.00*
201 A35 96c blk & red, *yel* ('27) 27.50 *55.00*
Nos. 191-201 (11) 120.50 *206.10*

Plowing a Rice Field — A36

Indian Shooting Fish — A37

Kaieteur Falls — A38

Georgetown, Public Buildings A39

1931, July 21 **Engr.** ***Perf. 12½***

205 A36 1c blue green 3.00 1.75
206 A37 2c dk brown 2.75 .25
207 A38 4c car rose 2.50 .60
208 A39 6c ultra 3.00 *3.50*
209 A38 $1 violet 55.00 *65.00*
Nos. 205-209 (5) 66.25 *71.10*
Set, never hinged 100.00

Cent. of the union of Berbice, Demerara and Essequibo to form the Colony of British Guiana.

A40

A41

Gold Mining — A42

Kaieteur Falls — A43

Shooting Logs over Falls — A44

Stabroek Market — A45

Sugar Cane in Punts — A46

Forest Road — A47

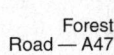

Victoria Regia Lilies — A48

Mt. Roraima — A49

Sir Walter Raleigh and Son — A50

Botanical Gardens A51

1934, Oct. 1 ***Perf. 12½***

210 A40 1c green .75 *2.25*
211 A41 2c brown 1.75 1.90
212 A42 3c carmine .50 .25
b. Perf. 12½x13½ ('43) 1.10 *1.10*
c. Perf. 13x13½ ('49) .75 .25
213 A43 4c vio black 2.50 3.75
a. Vert. pair, imperf. horiz. *20,000.* *20,000.*
214 A44 6c dp ultra 5.50 *7.50*
215 A45 12c orange .25 .25
a. Perf. 13½x13 ('51) .70 *1.25*
216 A46 24c rose violet 4.50 *12.00*
217 A47 48c black 10.00 *10.00*
218 A43 50c green 15.00 *22.50*
219 A48 60c brown 32.50 *32.00*
220 A49 72c rose violet 1.60 *2.75*
221 A50 96c black 37.50 *37.50*
222 A51 $1 violet 52.50 50.00
Nos. 210-222 (13) 164.85 *182.65*
Set, never hinged 290.00

See Nos. 236, 238, 240.

Common Design Types pictured following the introduction.

Silver Jubilee Issue
Common Design Type

1935, May 6 ***Perf. 13½x14***

223 CD301 2c gray blk & ultra .35 .25
224 CD301 6c blue & brown 1.50 *5.50*
225 CD301 12c indigo & grn 6.50 *9.75*
226 CD301 24c brt vio & ind 10.00 *20.00*
Nos. 223-226 (4) 18.35 35.50
Set, never hinged 27.50

Coronation Issue
Common Design Type

1937, May 12 ***Perf. 13½x14***

227 CD302 2c brown .25 .25
228 CD302 4c gray black .65
229 CD302 6c bright ultra .55 *2.15*
Nos. 227-229 (3) .80 3.05
Set, never hinged 1.60

A52

A53

A54

A55

A56

A57

A58

Victoria Regia Lilies and Jacanas — A59

1938-52 Engr. Wmk. 4 *Perf. 12½*

230 A52 1c green .25 .25
b. Perf. 14x13 ('49) .65 *1.00*
231 A53 2c violet blk, perf. 13x14 ('49) .40 .25
b. Perf. 12½ .50 .25
232 A54 4c black & rose, perf. 13x14 ('52) .65 .25
a. Perf. 12½ .90 .40
c. Vert. pair, imperf. between *30,000. 30,000.*
233 A55 6c deep ultra, perf. 13x14 ('49) 1.50 .40
a. Perf. 12½ 1.00 .25
234 A56 24c deep green 2.75 .25
a. Wmk. upright 20.00 12.50
235 A53 36c purple 3.50 .25
a. Perf. 13x14 ('51) 3.00 .40
236 A47 48c orange yel .90 .60
a. Perf. 14x13 ('51) 1.25 2.25
237 A57 60c brown 13.50 10.00
238 A50 96c brown vio 8.00 *3.25*
a. Perf. 12½x13½ ('44) 8.75 *13.00*
239 A58 $1 deep violet 17.50 .55
a. Perf. 14x13 ('51) 300.00 *700.00*
240 A49 $2 rose vio ('45) 12.50 *27.50*
a. Perf. 14x13 ('50) 16.00 *37.50*
241 A59 $3 orange brn ('45) 27.50 *40.00*
a. Perf. 14x13 ('52) 29.50 *55.00*
Nos. 230-241 (12) 88.95 *83.55*
Set, never hinged 90.00

The watermark on No. 234 is sideways.

Catalogue values for unused stamps in this section, from this point to the end of the section, are for Never Hinged items.

Peace Issue
Common Design Type

1946, Oct. 21 *Perf. 13½x14*

242 CD303 3c carmine .25 *.45*
243 CD303 6c deep blue .80 *.95*

Silver Wedding Issue
Common Design Types

1948, Dec. 20 Photo. *Perf. 14x14½*

244 CD304 3c scarlet .25 *.45*

Engr.
Perf. 11½x11

245 CD305 $3 orange brown 24.00 *28.00*

UPU Issue
Common Design Types

Engr.; Name Typo. on 6c and 12c
Perf. 13½, 11x11½

1949, Oct. 10 Wmk. 4

246 CD306 4c rose carmine .25 *.55*
247 CD307 6c indigo 1.90 2.00
248 CD308 12c orange .25 *.75*
249 CD309 24c blue green .25 *.90*
Nos. 246-249 (4) 2.65 4.20

University Issue
Common Design Types

1951, Feb. 16 Engr. *Perf. 14x14½*

250 CD310 3c carmine & black .55 *.55*
251 CD311 6c dp ultra & black .55 *.70*

Coronation Issue
Common Design Type

1953, June 2 *Perf. 13½x13*

252 CD312 4c carmine & black .45 .25

G. P. O., Georgetown A60

Indian Shooting Fish — A61

Designs: 2c, Botanical gardens. 3c, Victoria regia lilies and jacanas. 5c, Map. 6c, Rice combine. 8c, Sugar cane entering factory. 12c, Felling greenheart tree. 24c, Bauxite mining. 36c, Mt. Roraima. 48c, Kaieteur Falls. 72c, Arapaima (fish). $1, Toucan. $2, Dredging gold. $5, Coat of Arms.

Engr., Center Litho. on $1
Perf. 12½x13, 13

1954, Dec. 1 Wmk. 4

253 A60 1c black .25 .25
254 A60 2c dark green .25 .25
255 A60 3c red brn & ol 3.75 .25
256 A61 4c violet 1.50 .25
257 A60 5c black & red 1.75 .25
258 A60 6c yellow green 1.00 .25
259 A60 8c ultramarine .40 .25
260 A61 12c brown & black 1.25 .30
261 A60 24c orange & black 4.50 .25
262 A60 36c black & rose 6.00 1.00
263 A61 48c red brn & ultra 1.00 *1.25*
264 A61 72c emerald & rose 14.00 3.00
265 A60 $1 blk, yel, grn & sal 17.00 2.50
266 A60 $2 magenta 22.50 7.00
267 A61 $5 black & ultra 21.00 *30.00*
Nos. 253-267 (15) 96.15 *47.05*

See Nos. 279-287.

Clasped Hands — A62

Perf. 14½x14

1961, Oct. 23 Photo. Wmk. 314

268 A62 5c sal pink & brown .25 .25
269 A62 6c lt blue grn & brown .25 .25
270 A62 30c lt orange & brown .45 .40
Nos. 268-270 (3) .95 .90

Fourth annual History and Culture Week.

Freedom from Hunger Issue
Common Design Type

1963, July 22 *Perf. 14x14½*

271 CD314 20c lilac .45 .25

Red Cross Centenary Issue
Common Design Type

Wmk. 314

1963, Sept. 2 Litho. *Perf. 13*

272 CD315 5c black & red .25 .25
273 CD315 20c ultra & red .80 .55

Queen Types of 1954

Engr.; Center Litho. on $1
Perf. 12½x13, 13

1963-65 Wmk. 314

279 A60 3c red brn & ol ('65) 4.00 2.50
280 A60 5c black & red ('64) .40 .25
281 A61 12c brown & blk ('64) .50 .25
282 A60 24c orange & black 4.50 .25
283 A60 36c black & rose .80 .25
284 A61 48c red brn & ultra 1.75 *3.00*
285 A61 72c emerald & rose 5.00 *22.50*
286 A60 $1 blk, yel, grn & sal 8.25 1.50
287 A60 $2 magenta 13.50 *15.00*
Nos. 279-287 (9) 38.70 *45.50*

Weight Lifter A63

1964, Oct. 1 Photo. *Perf. 13x13½*

290 A63 5c orange .25 .25
291 A63 8c blue .25 .25
292 A63 25c carmine rose .45 .45
Nos. 290-292 (3) .95 .95

18th Olympic Games, Tokyo, Oct. 10-25.

ITU Issue
Common Design Type
Perf. 11x11½

1965, May 17 Litho. Wmk. 314

293 CD317 5c emerald & olive .25 .25
294 CD317 25c lt blue & brt pink .35 .30

Intl. Cooperation Year Issue
Common Design Type

1965, Oct. 25 Wmk. 314 *Perf. 14½*

295 CD318 5c blue grn & claret .25 .25
296 CD318 25c lt vio & green .40 .35

Winston Churchill and St. George's Cathedral, Georgetown — A64

1966, Jan. 24 Photo. *Perf. 14x14½*

297 A64 5c multicolored .75 .25
298 A64 25c dp blue, blk & gold 2.40 .70

Sir Winston Leonard Spencer Churchill (1874-1965), statesman and WWII leader.

Royal Visit Issue
Common Design Type

1966, Feb. 4 Litho. *Perf. 11x12*

299 CD320 3c violet blue .95 .80
300 CD320 25c dark car rose 2.40 .80

POSTAGE DUE STAMPS

Catalogue values for unused stamps in this section are for Never Hinged items.

D1

Perf. 13½x14

1940-55 Typo. Wmk. 4

J1 D1 1c green, *chalky paper* ('52) 1.50 *22.50*
a. Wmk. 4a (error) 140.00
J2 D1 2c black, *chalky paper* ('52) 4.00 *10.00*
a. Wmk. 4a (error) 145.00
J3 D1 4c ultra ('52) .35 *14.00*
a. Wmk. 4a (error) 145.00
J4 D1 12c carmine, *chalky paper* ('55) 17.50 *45.00*
Nos. J1-J4 (4) 23.35 *91.50*

The 1940 printings of Nos. J1-J2 and J4 are on ordinary paper. For detailed listings, see the Scott Classic Specialized catalogue.

WAR TAX STAMP

Regular Issue No. 179 Overprinted

1918, Jan. 4 Wmk. 3 *Perf. 14*

MR1 A35 2c scarlet 1.90 .25

The relative positions of "War" and "Tax" vary throughout the sheet.

OFFICIAL STAMPS

Counterfeit overprints exist.

No. 50 Overprinted in Red

1875 Unwmk. *Perf. 10*

O1 A5 1c black 75.00 26.00
a. Horiz. pair, imperf btwn. 22,500.

Nos. 51, 53-54, 68 Overprinted in Black

O2 A5 2c orange 300.00 17.50
O3 A5 8c rose 375.00 150.00
O4 A5 12c lilac 3,500. 600.00
O5 A12 24c green 2,750. 325.00

For surcharges see Nos. 87, 89, 89A, 96, 102.

Nos. 72-76 Overprinted "OFFICIAL" Similar to #O2-O5

1877 Wmk. 1 *Perf. 14*

O6 A13 1c slate 350.00 70.00
a. Vert. pair, imperf btwn. *27,500.*
O7 A13 2c orange 160.00 18.00
O8 A13 4c ultramarine 140.00 35.00
O9 A13 6c chocolate 6,600. 725.00
O10 A13 8c rose 2,400. 550.00

The type A13 12c lilac, 24c green and 48c red brown overprinted "OFFICIAL" were never placed in use. A few examples of the 12c and 24c have been seen but the 48c is only known surcharged with new value for provisional use in 1881. See Nos. 97-101.

For surcharges see #85-86, 88A, 90-91.

BRITISH HONDURAS

'bri-tish hän-'dur-əs

LOCATION — Central America bordering on Caribbean on east, Mexico on north and Guatemala on west.
GOVT. — British Crown Colony
AREA — 8,867 sq. mi.
POP. — 130,000 (est. 1972)
CAPITAL — Belmopan

Before British Honduras became a colony (subordinate to Jamaica) in 1862, it was a settlement under British influence. In 1884 it became an independent colony. In 1973 the colony changed its name to Belize.

12 Pence = 1 Shilling
100 Cents = 1 Dollar (1888)

Catalogue values for unused stamps in this country are for Never Hinged items, beginning with Scott 127 in the regular postage section, Scott J1 in the postage due section.

Values for unused stamps are for examples with original gum as defined in the catalogue introduction. Very fine examples of Nos. 1-37 will have perforations touching the design on at least one side due to the narrow spacing of the stamps on the plates. Stamps with perfs clear of the design on all four sides are extremely scarce and will command higher prices.

Queen Victoria — A1

1866 Unwmk. Typo. *Perf. 14*
1 A1 1p pale blue 72.50 72.50
a. Horiz. pair, imperf. btwn.
2 A1 6p rose 425.00 195.00
3 A1 1sh green 400.00 145.00

The 6p and 1sh were printed only in a sheet with the 1p. The 1p was later printed in sheets without the 6p and 1sh. The 1sh is known in se-tenant gutter pairs with the 1p and the 6p.

1872 Wmk. 1 *Perf. 12½*
4 A1 1p pale blue 100.00 24.00
5 A1 3p reddish brn 180.00 90.00
6 A1 6p rose 400.00 55.00
7 A1 1sh green 500.00 32.50
a. Horiz. pair, imperf. btwn. *27,500.*

For surcharges see Nos. 18-19.
No. 7a is unique and has faults.

1877-79 *Perf. 14*
8 A1 1p blue 87.50 22.50
a. Horiz. strip of 3, imperf. btwn. *27,500.*
9 A1 3p brown 170.00 24.00
10 A1 4p violet ('79) 300.00 10.00
11 A1 6p rose ('78) 500.00 225.00
12 A1 1sh green 325.00 13.50

For surcharges see Nos. 20-21, 29.

1882-87 Wmk. 2
13 A1 1p blue ('84) 67.50 18.00
14 A1 1p rose ('84) 27.50 16.00
a. Diagonal half used as ½p on cover —
b. 1p carmine 60.00 22.50
15 A1 4p violet 100.00 5.75
16 A1 6p yellow ('85) 325.00 240.00
17 A1 1sh gray ('87) 300.00 200.00

For surcharges see Nos. 22-26, 28-35.

Stamps of 1872-87 Surcharged in Black

1888 Wmk. 1 *Perf. 12½*
18 A1 2c on 6p rose 350.00 275.00
19 A1 3c on 3p brown *20,000.* *6,500.*

Perf. 14
20 A1 2c on 6p rose 190.00 180.00
a. Diagonal half used as 1c on cover *300.00*
b. Double surcharge 2,700. —
c. "2" with curved tail 3,500. —
21 A1 3c on 3p brown 110.00 *120.00*

Wmk. 2
22 A1 2c on 1p rose 11.00 *35.00*
a. Diagonal half used as 1c on cover 220.00
b. Double surcharge 1,100. 1,100.
c. Inverted surcharge 4,500. 4,000.
23 A1 10c on 4p violet 70.00 20.00
a. Inverted surcharge
24 A1 20c on 6p yellow 35.00 *42.50*
25 A1 50c on 1sh gray 475.00 *725.00*

No. 25 with Additional Surcharge in Red or Black

26 A1 2c (R) on 50c on 1sh gray 60.00 *115.00*
a. "TWO" in black *18,750.* *15,000.*
b. "TWO" double (Blk + R) *18,750.* *16,000.*
c. Diagonal half used as 1c on cover 350.00

Stamps of 1872-87 Srchd. in Black — c

1888-89
28 A1 2c on 1p rose .80 *2.75*
a. Diagonal half used as 1c on cover 110.00
29 A1 3c on 3p brown 4.00 1.75
30 A1 10c on 4p violet 22.50 1.00
a. Double surcharge *3,500.*
31 A1 20c on 6p yel ('89) 18.00 15.00
32 A1 50c on 1sh gray 35.00 *105.00*
Nos. 28-32 (5) 80.30 *125.50*

For other examples of this surcharge see Nos. 36, 47. For overprint see No. 51.

No. 30 with Additional Surcharge in Black or Red

1891
33 A1 6c (Blk) on 10c on 4p 1.75 *2.25*
a. "6" and bar inverted *4,500.* *1,200.*
b. "6" only inverted *6,500.*
34 A1 6c (R) on 10c on 4p 1.90 *2.50*
a. "6" and bar inverted *725.00* *725.00*
b. "6" only inverted *6,500.*

Stamps similar to No. 33 but with "SIX" instead of "6," both with and without bar, were prepared but not regularly issued.
See No. 37.

No. 29 with Additional Surcharge in Black

35 A1 5c on 3c on 3p brown 1.60 *2.00*
a. Double surcharge of "Five" and bar 450.00 *850.00*

Black Surcharge, Type "c"
36 A1 6c on 3p blue 4.25 *22.00*

No. 36 with Additional Surcharge like Nos. 33-34 in Red

1891
37 A1 15c (R) on 6c on 3p blue 16.00 *35.00*
a. Double surcharge —

A8

1891-98 Wmk. 2 *Perf. 14*
38 A8 1c green 3.00 1.50
39 A8 2c carmine rose 4.00 .30
40 A8 3c brown 9.50 5.00
41 A8 5c ultra ('95) 14.50 .90
42 A8 6c ultramarine 13.00 2.50
43 A8 10c vio & grn ('95) 14.00 *15.00*
44 A8 12c vio & green 3.25 3.00
45 A8 24c yellow & blue 6.75 *21.00*
46 A8 25c red brn & grn ('98) 95.00 *160.00*
Nos. 38-46 (9) 163.00 *209.20*

Numeral tablet on Nos. 43-46 has lined background with colorless value and "c."
For overprints see Nos. 48-50.

Type of 1866 Surcharged Type "c"

1892
47 A1 1c on 1p green 1.00 *1.90*

Regular Issue Overprinted in Black

1899 Overprint 12mm Long
48 A8 5c ultramarine 25.00 3.00
a. "BEVENUE" 150.00 *175.00*
49 A8 10c lilac & green 15.00 *20.00*
a. "BEVENUE" 300.00 *425.00*
c. "REVENU" 725.00
50 A8 25c red brn & grn 3.75 *42.50*
a. "BEVENUE" 175.00 *425.00*
c. "REVE UE" 2,700.
51 A1 50c on 1sh gray (No. 32) 235.00 450.00
a. "BEVENUE" 5,500. 6,000.
Nos. 48-51 (4) 278.75 *515.50*

Two lengths of the overprint are found on the same pane: 12mm (43 to the pane) and 11mm (17 to the pane). The "U" is found in both a tall, narrow type and the more common small type.

A9

1899-1901
52 A9 5c gray blk & ultra, *bl* ('00) 19.50 3.00
53 A9 10c vio & grn ('01) 13.50 *9.00*
54 A9 50c grn & car rose 30.00 *72.50*
55 A9 $1 grn & car rose 100.00 *155.00*
56 A9 $2 green & ultra 150.00 *200.00*
57 A9 $5 green & black 400.00 *500.00*
Nos. 52-57 (6) 713.00 *939.50*

Numeral tablet on Nos. 53-54 has lined background with colorless value and "c."

King Edward VII — A10

1902-04 Typo. Wmk. 2
58 A10 1c gray grn & grn ('04) 2.25 *27.50*
59 A10 2c vio & blk, *red* 1.25 .40
60 A10 5c gray blk & ultra, *blue* 14.00 .70
61 A10 20c dl vio & vio ('04) 12.00 *20.00*
Nos. 58-61 (4) 29.50 *48.60*

1904-06 Chalky Paper Wmk. 3
62 A10 1c green 2.25 *2.75*
63 A10 2c vio & blk, *red* 1.75 .40
64 A10 5c blk & ultra, *bl* ('05) 2.10 .25
65 A10 10c vio & grn ('06) 5.25 *16.00*
67 A10 25c vio & org ('06) 9.50 *55.00*
68 A10 50c grn & car rose ('06) 24.00 *90.00*
69 A10 $1 grn & car rose ('06) 70.00 *100.00*
70 A10 $2 grn & ultra ('06) 150.00 *200.00*
71 A10 $5 grn & blk ('06) 375.00 *425.00*
Nos. 62-71 (9) 639.85 *889.40*

The 1c and 2c exist also on ordinary paper.

1909 Ordinary Paper
72 A10 2c carmine 14.00 .25
73 A10 5c ultramarine 2.50 .25

1911
74 A10 25c black, *green* 6.50 *55.00*

Numeral tablet on Nos. 61, 65-68, 74 has lined background with colorless value and "c."

King George V
A11 A12

1913-17 Wmk. 3 *Perf. 14*
75 A11 1c green 4.50 1.75
76 A11 2c scarlet 5.00 1.75
Complete booklet of 100 #76, in blocks of 10 (5x2) 4,500.
a. 2c carmine 5.00 1.25
77 A11 3c orange ('17) 1.25 .25
Complete booklet of 100 #77, in blocks of 10 (5x2) —
78 A11 5c ultra 2.50 1.10

Chalky Paper
79 A12 10c dl vio & ol grn 4.50 *8.00*
80 A12 25c blk, *gray grn* 1.50 *14.50*
a. 25c black, *emerald* 2.10 *34.00*
b. 25c blk, *bl grn*, olive back 6.00 *13.50*
81 A12 50c vio & ultra, *bl* 26.00 *17.50*
82 A11 $1 black & scar 27.50 *65.00*
83 A11 $2 grn & dull vio 85.00 *100.00*
84 A11 $5 vio & blk, *red* 290.00 *325.00*
Nos. 75-84 (10) 447.75 *534.85*

See No. 91. For overprints see Nos. MR2-MR5.

With Moire Overprint in Violet

1915
85 A11 1c green 4.50 *22.00*
a. 1c yellow green .65 *19.00*
86 A11 2c carmine 4.25 .60
87 A11 5c ultramarine .40 *7.25*
Nos. 85-87 (3) 9.15 *29.85*

For 'War' overprint see No. MR1.

Peace Commemorative Issue

Seal of Colony and George V
A13

1921, Apr. 28 Engr.
89 A13 2c carmine 5.50 1.00
Never hinged 10.00

Similar to A13 but without "Peace Peace"

1922 Wmk. 4
90 A13 4c dark gray 11.00 1.25
Never hinged 18.50

Type of 1913-17

1921 Typo. Wmk. 4
91 A11 1c green 7.00 *14.00*

A14

1922-33 Typo. Wmk. 4
92 A14 1c green ('29) 14.00 6.50
93 A14 2c dark brown 2.00 2.00
Complete booklet of 100 #93, in blocks of 10 (5x2) —

94 A14 2c rose red ('27) 7.50 2.00
Complete booklet of 100 #94, in blocks of 10 (5x2) —
95 A14 3c orange ('33) 32.50 5.00
96 A14 4c gray ('29) 19.00 1.00
97 A14 5c ultramarine 2.00 .70

Chalky Paper

98 A14 10c olive grn & lil 3.50 .40
99 A14 25c black, *emerald* 2.00 *9.00*
100 A14 50c ultra & vio, *bl* 5.75 *16.00*
101 A14 $1 scarlet & blk 15.00 *27.50*
102 A14 $2 red vio & grn 45.00 *120.00*

Wmk. 3

103 A14 25c black, *emerald* 8.00 *55.00*
104 A14 $5 blk & vio, *red* 275.00 *300.00*
Nos. 92-104 (13) 431.25 *545.10*

For surcharges see Nos. B1-B5.

Common Design Types pictured following the introduction.

Silver Jubilee Issue
Common Design Type
Perf. 11x12

1935, May 6 Engr. Wmk. 4
108 CD301 3c black & ultra 2.00 .60
109 CD301 4c indigo & grn 4.50 *4.25*
110 CD301 5c ultra & brn 2.25 *2.50*
111 CD301 25c brn vio & ind 6.50 *8.00*
Nos. 108-111 (4) 15.25 *15.35*
Set, never hinged 24.00

Coronation Issue
Common Design Type

1937, May 12 *Perf. 13½x14*
112 CD302 3c deep orange .25 .25
113 CD302 4c gray black .35 .35
114 CD302 5c bright ultra .60 *1.75*
Nos. 112-114 (3) 1.20 2.35
Set, never hinged 2.00

Mayan Figures A15

Chicle Tapping — A16

Cohune Palm — A17

Local Products A18

Grapefruit Industry A19

Mahogany Logs in River — A20

Sergeant's Cay — A21

Dory — A22

Chicle Industry A23

Court House, Belize — A24

Mahogany Cutting — A25

Seal of Colony — A26

1938 *Perf. 11x11½, 11½x11*
115 A15 1c green & violet .25 *1.75*
116 A16 2c car & black .25 *1.25*
a. Perf. 12 ('47) 2.75 1.25
117 A17 3c brown & dk vio .50 *1.00*
118 A18 4c green & black .50 *.90*
119 A19 5c slate bl & red vio 1.10 1.00
120 A20 10c brown & yel grn 1.25 .80
121 A21 15c blue & brown 2.25 .90
122 A22 25c green & ultra 1.75 1.50
123 A23 50c dk vio & blk 9.00 4.25
124 A24 $1 ol green & car 17.50 10.00
125 A25 $2 rose lake & ind 21.00 *25.00*
126 A26 $5 brn & carmine 22.50 *37.50*
Nos. 115-126 (12) 77.85 *85.85*
Set, never hinged 175.00

Issued: 3c-5c, 1/10; 1c, 2c, 10c-50c, 2/14; $1-$5, 2/28.

Catalogue values for unused stamps in this section, from this point to the end of the section, are for Never Hinged items.

Peace Issue
Common Design Type
Perf. 13½x14

1946, Sept. 9 Engr. Wmk. 4
127 CD303 3c brown .25 .25
128 CD303 5c deep blue .25 .25

Silver Wedding Issue
Common Design Types

1948, Oct. 1 Photo. *Perf. 14x14½*
129 CD304 4c dark green .25 *.70*

Engraved; Name Typographed
Perf. 11½x11
130 CD305 $5 light brown 22.50 52.50

St. George's Cay — A27

H.M.S. Merlin — A28

1949, Jan. 10 Engr. *Perf. 12½*
131 A27 1c green & ultra .25 1.25
132 A27 3c yel brn & dp blue .25 1.50
133 A27 4c purple & brn ol .25 1.75
134 A28 5c dk blue & brown 1.75 .75
135 A28 10c vio brn & blue grn 1.75 .45
136 A28 15c ultra & emerald 1.75 .45
Nos. 131-136 (6) 6.00 6.15

Battle of St. George's Cay, 150th anniv.

UPU Issue
Common Design Types
Perf. 13½, 11x11½

1949, Oct. 10 Engr. Wmk. 4
137 CD306 4c blue green .40 .40
138 CD307 5c indigo 1.50 .60
139 CD308 10c chocolate .55 3.00
140 CD309 25c blue .90 .75
Nos. 137-140 (4) 3.35 4.75

University Issue
Common Design Types

1951, Feb. 16 Engr. *Perf. 14x14½*
141 CD310 3c choc & purple .55 1.50
142 CD311 10c choc & green .85 .65

Coronation Issue
Common Design Type

1953, June 2 *Perf. 13½x13*
143 CD312 4c dk green & black .55 .40

Arms — A29

Maya — A30

Designs: 2c, Tapir. 3c, Legislative Council Chamber and mace. 4c, Pine industry. 5c, Spiny lobster. 10c, Stanley Field Airport. 15c, Mayan frieze. 25c, Blue butterfly. $1, Armadillo. $2, Hawkesworth Bridge. $5, Pine Ridge orchid.

1953-57 Engr. *Perf. 13½*
144 A29 1c gray blk & green .25 .50
a. Perf. 13½x13 .60 .25
145 A29 2c gray blk & brn, perf. 14 ('57) .75 .25
a. Perf. 13½ .40 2.25
b. Perf. 13½x13 .25 .60
146 A29 3c mag & rose lil, perf. 14 ('57) .25 .25
a. Perf. 13½ .40 .25
b. Perf. 13½x13 5.75 13.50
147 A29 4c grn & dk brn .60 .40
148 A29 5c car & ol brn, perf. 14 ('57) .40 .25
a. Perf. 13½ .25 .25
149 A29 10c ultra & bl gray .25 .25
a. Perf. 13½x13 .25 .25
150 A29 15c vio & yel grn .25 *.25*
151 A29 25c brown & ultra 7.00 3.50
152 A30 50c purple & brown 12.00 3.00
153 A29 $1 red brn & sl bl 6.00 6.00
154 A29 $2 gray & car 7.25 5.00
155 A30 $5 blue gray & pur 50.00 17.50
Nos. 144-155 (12) 85.00 37.15

Issued: 5c, 5/15; 2c, 3c, 9/18, perf. 13½, 9/2.
For overprints see Nos. 159-166.

View of Belize, 1842 — A31

Designs: 10c, Public seals, 1860 and 1960. 15c, Tamarind Tree, Newtown Barracks.

Perf. 11½x11

1960, July 1 Wmk. 314
156 A31 2c green .40 .70
157 A31 10c carmine .55 .25
158 A31 15c blue .70 .70
Nos. 156-158 (3) 1.65 1.65

Cent. of the establishment of a local PO.

Nos. 145-146 and 149-150 Overprinted: "NEW CONSTITUTION/1960"

1961, Mar. 1 Wmk. 4 *Perf. 14, 13*
159 A29 2c gray black & brn .30 .25
160 A29 3c mag & rose lilac .40 .25
161 A29 10c ultra & blue gray .40 .25
162 A29 15c violet & yel green .55 .35
Nos. 159-162 (4) 1.65 1.10

Nos. 144, 149, 151 and 152 Overprinted: "HURRICANE/HATTIE"

1962, Jan. 15 *Perf. 13*
163 A29 1c gray black & green .25 *.65*
164 A29 10c ultra & blue gray .45 .25
165 A29 25c brown & ultra 2.00 1.00
166 A30 50c purple & brown .75 1.25
Nos. 163-166 (4) 3.45 3.15

Hurricane Hattie struck Belize, Oct. 31, 1961.

Great Curassow A32

Birds: 2c, Red-legged honeycreeper. 3c, American jacana. 4c, Great kiskadee. 5c, Scarlet-rumped tanager. 10c, Scarlet macaw. 15c, Massena trogon. 25c, Redfooted booby. 50c, Keel-billed toucan. $1, Magnificent frigate bird. $2, Rufoustailed jacamar. $5, Montezuma oropendola.

Perf. 14x14½

1962, Apr. 2 Photo. Wmk. 314
Birds in Natural Colors; Black Inscriptions
167 A32 1c yellow 1.25 1.00
168 A32 2c gray 2.00 .30
a. Green omitted *450.00*
169 A32 3c lt yel green 3.25 3.00
a. Dark grn (legs) omitted *475.00*
170 A32 4c lt gray 3.25 3.25
171 A32 5c buff 3.00 .30
172 A32 10c beige 4.25 .30
a. Blue omitted *575.00*
173 A32 15c pale lemon 1.50 .45
174 A32 25c bluish gray & pink 5.00 .50
175 A32 50c pale blue 6.50 *.65*
b. Blue (beak & claw) omitted —
176 A32 $1 blue 10.00 1.50
177 A32 $2 pale gray 18.00 5.25
178 A32 $5 light blue 27.50 17.50
Nos. 167-178 (12) 85.50 34.00

For overprints see Nos. 182-186, 195-199.

1967 Wmk. 314 Sideways
Colors as 1962 Issue
167a A32 1c .25 .60
168b A32 2c .40 1.10
170a A32 4c 1.75 *2.00*
171a A32 5c .50 .25
172b A32 10c .50 .25
173a A32 15c .50 .25
175a A32 50c 2.25 *3.50*
Nos. 167a-175a (7) 6.15 7.95

Issued: 1, 4, 5, 50c, 2/16; 2, 10, 15c, 11/28.

Freedom from Hunger Issue
Common Design Type

1963, June 4 *Perf. 14x14½*
179 CD314 22c green .65 .25

Red Cross Centenary Issue
Common Design Type
Wmk. 314

1963, Sept. 2 Litho. *Perf. 13*
180 CD315 4c black & red .25 1.00
181 CD315 22c ultra & red .75 1.25

Nos. 167, 169, 170, 172 and 174 Overprinted

1964 Photo. *Perf. 14x14½*
182 A32 1c multicolored .25 .40
a. Yellow omitted *200.00*
183 A32 3c multicolored .75 .40
184 A32 4c multicolored .75 .40
185 A32 10c multicolored .75 .25
186 A32 25c multicolored 1.00 .75
Nos. 182-186 (5) 3.50 2.20

Attainment of self-government.

ITU Issue
Common Design Type
Perf. 11x11½

1965, May 17 Litho. Wmk. 314

187	CD317	2c ver & green	.25	.25
188	CD317	50c yel & red lilac	.60	.60

Intl. Cooperation Year Issue
Common Design Type

1965, Oct. 25 ***Perf. 14½***

189	CD318	1c bl grn & claret	.25	.25
190	CD318	22c lt violet & green	.35	.30

Churchill Memorial Issue
Common Design Type

1966, Jan. 24 Photo. ***Perf. 14***

Design in Black, Gold and Carmine Rose

191	CD319	1c bright blue	.25	.50
192	CD319	4c green	.50	.30
193	CD319	22c brown	.80	.30
194	CD319	25c violet	1.00	.70
		Nos. 191-194 (4)	2.55	1.80

Bird Type of 1962 Overprinted: "DEDICATION OF SITE / NEW CAPITAL / 9th OCTOBER 1965"
Wmk. 314 Sideways

1966, July 1 ***Perf. 14x14½***

195	A32	1c multicolored	.30	.30
196	A32	3c multicolored	.60	.65
197	A32	4c multicolored	.60	.65
198	A32	10c multicolored	.60	.30
199	A32	25c multicolored	.75	.50
		Nos. 195-199 (5)	2.85	2.40

Citrus Grove — A33

10c, Half Moon Cay & Lighthouse Reef. 22c, Hidden Valley Falls & Mountain Pine Ridge. 25c, Xunantunich Mayan ruins in Cayo district.

Perf. 14x14½

1966, Oct. 1 Photo. Wmk. 314

200	A33	5c multicolored	.25	.25
201	A33	10c multicolored	.25	.25
202	A33	22c multicolored	.25	.25
203	A33	25c multicolored	.25	.50
		Nos. 200-203 (4)	1.00	1.25

1st British Honduras stamp issue, cent.

International Tourist Year — A34

1967, Dec. 4 ***Perf. 12½***

204	A34	5c Sailfish	.25	.40
205	A34	10c Deer	.25	.25
206	A34	22c Jaguar	.40	.25
207	A34	25c Tarpon	.40	.50
		Nos. 204-207 (4)	1.30	1.40

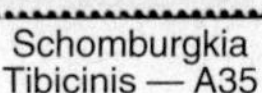

Schomburgkia Tibicinis — A35

Belizean Patriots' Memorial, Belize City, and Human Rights Flame — A36

Orchids: 10c, Maxillaria tenuifolia. 22c, Bletia purpurea. 25c, Sobralia macrantha.

Inscribed: "20th Anniversary of E.C.L.A."

Perf. 14½x14

1968, Apr. 16 Photo. Wmk. 314

208	A35	5c violet & multi	.60	.60
209	A35	10c green & multi	.85	.85
210	A35	22c multicolored	1.00	1.00
211	A35	25c olive & multi	1.50	1.50
		Nos. 208-211 (4)	3.95	3.95

20th anniv. of the Economic Commission for Latin America. See Nos. 226-229, 255-258.

Perf. 13x13½

1968, July 15 Litho. Wmk. 314

Design: 50c, Mayan motif stele, monument at new capital site and Human Rights flame.

212	A36	22c multicolored	.25	.25
213	A36	50c multicolored	.25	.25

International Human Rights Year.

Jewfish A37

Designs: 2c, White-lipped peccary. 3c, Grouper (sea bass). 4c, Collared anteater. 5c, Bonefish. 10c, Paca. 15c, Dolphinfish. 25c, Kinkajou. 50c, Yellow-and-green-banded muttonfish. $1, Tayra. $2, Great barracudas. $5, Mountain lion.

Perf. 13x12½

1968, Oct. 15 Litho. Unwmk.

214	A37	1c yellow & multi	.40	.25
215	A37	2c brt yel & multi	.25	.25
216	A37	3c pink & multi	.25	.25
217	A37	4c brt grn & multi	.25	1.25
218	A37	5c brick red & multi	.25	1.25
219	A37	10c lilac & multi	.25	.25
220	A37	15c org yel & multi	2.00	.25
221	A37	25c multicolored	.40	.50
222	A37	50c bl grn & multi	.85	1.25
223	A37	$1 ocher & multi	2.75	1.50
224	A37	$2 violet & multi	2.75	2.50
225	A37	$5 ultra & multi	14.00	7.00
		Nos. 214-225 (12)	24.40	16.50

See Nos. 234-240, Belize 327-339.
For overprints see Nos. 251-254, 281-282.

Orchid Type of 1968
Inscribed "Orchids of Belize"

Designs: 5c, Rhyncholaetia digbyana. 10c, Cattleya bowringiana. 22c, Lycaste cochleatum. 25c, Coryanthes speciosum.

Perf. 14½x14

1969, Apr. 9 Photo. Wmk. 314

226	A35	5c Prus blue & multi	1.00	.50
227	A35	10c olive bis & multi	1.25	.30
228	A35	22c yellow grn & multi	1.50	.30
229	A35	25c violet blue & multi	1.75	1.75
		Nos. 226-229 (4)	5.50	2.85

Hardwood Trees — A38

1969, Sept. 1 Litho. ***Perf. 14***

230	A38	5c Ziricote	.25	.25
231	A38	10c Rosewood	.25	.25
232	A38	22c Mayflower	.25	.25
233	A38	25c Mahogany	.35	.35
		Nos. 230-233 (4)	1.10	1.10

Timber industry of British Honduras. Issued in sheets of 9 (3x3) on simulated wood background.

Fish-Animal Type of 1968
Designs: ½c, Crana (fish). Others as before.

Wmk. 314 Sideways (½c, 2c, $5), Upright (3c, 5c, 10c)

1969-72 Litho. ***Perf. 13x12½***

234	A37	½c vio bl, yel & blk	.25	.25
235	A37	½c citron, blk & bl ('71)	2.50	1.50
236	A37	2c brt yel, blk & grn ('72)	3.75	3.75
237	A37	3c pink & multi ('72)	2.00	3.25
a.		Wmk. sideways ('72)	4.00	6.00
238	A37	5c brick red & multi ('72)	2.00	3.25
239	A37	10c lilac & multi ('72)	2.00	3.25
a.		Wmk. sideways ('72)	4.00	7.00
240	A37	$5 ultra & multi ('70)	9.00	9.00
		Nos. 234-240 (7)	21.50	24.25

For overprints see Nos. 251-252.

Virgin and Child, by Giovanni Bellini — A39

Christmas: 22c, 25c, Adoration of the Kings, by Veronese.

1969, Nov. 1 Litho. ***Perf. 14***

247	A39	5c multicolored	.25	.25
248	A39	15c dp orange & multi	.25	.25
249	A39	22c lilac rose & multi	.25	.25
250	A39	25c emerald & multi	.25	.25
		Nos. 247-250 (4)	1.00	1.00

Nos. 238-239 and Type of 1968 Overprinted "POPULATION/ CENSUS 1970"
Wmk. 314 Sideways

1970, Feb. 2 Photo. ***Perf. 13x12½***

251	A37	5c brick red & multi	.25	.25
252	A37	10c lilac & multi	.25	.25
253	A37	15c org yel & multi	.35	.25
254	A37	25c multicolored	.35	.25
		Nos. 251-254 (4)	1.20	1.00

Orchid Type of 1968 Inscribed: "Orchids of Belize"
Wmk. 314

1970, Apr. 2 Litho. ***Perf. 14***

255	A35	5c Black	.75	.25
256	A35	15c White butterfly	1.00	.25
257	A35	22c Swan	1.40	.25
258	A35	25c Butterfly	1.50	.75
		Nos. 255-258 (4)	4.65	1.50

Santa Maria Tree and Wood (Calophyllum Brasiliense) A40

Nativity, by Arthur Hughes A41

Hardwood Trees and Woods: 15c, Nargusta (terminalia amazonia). 22c, Cedar (cedrela mexicana). 25c, Sapodilla (achras sapota).

1970, Sept. 7 ***Perf. 14***

259	A40	5c multicolored	.40	.25
260	A40	15c multicolored	.65	.25
261	A40	22c multicolored	.80	.25
262	A40	25c multicolored	.80	.65
		Nos. 259-262 (4)	2.65	1.40

1970, Nov. 2 ***Perf. 14***

Christmas: 5c, 15c, 50c, Mystic Nativity, by Botticelli.

263	A41	½c black & multi	.25	.25
264	A41	5c brown & multi	.25	.25
265	A41	10c multicolored	.25	.25
266	A41	15c slate bl & multi	.25	.25
267	A41	22c dk green & multi	.30	.25
268	A41	50c black & multi	.50	.50
		Nos. 263-268 (6)	1.80	1.75

Legislative Assembly House A42

Designs: 5c, View of South Side of Belize. 10c, Government Plaza, Belmopan. 22c, Magistrates' Court. 25c, Police Headquarters. 50c, New General Post Office.

1971, Jan. 30 Litho. ***Perf. 13½x14***

Size: 59x22mm

269	A42	5c multicolored	.25	.25
270	A42	10c multicolored	.25	.25

Size: 37x21½mm

271	A42	15c multicolored	.25	.25
272	A42	22c multicolored	.30	.25
273	A42	25c multicolored	.35	.25
274	A42	50c multicolored	.55	.65
		Nos. 269-274 (6)	1.95	1.90

New capital at Belmopan.

Tabebuia Chrysantha — A43

Flowers: 5c, 22c, Hymenocallis littoralis. 10c, 25c, Hippeastrum equestre. 15c, like ½c.

1971, Mar. 27 Litho. ***Perf. 14***

275	A43	½c vio blue & multi	.25	.25
276	A43	5c olive & multi	.25	.25
277	A43	10c violet & multi	.25	.25
278	A43	15c multicolored	.35	.30
279	A43	22c multicolored	.35	.30
280	A43	25c lt brown & multi	.35	.40
		Nos. 275-280 (6)	1.80	1.75

Easter.

Type of 1968 Overprinted: "RACIAL EQUALITY / YEAR — 1971"
Perf. 13x12½

1971, June 14 Litho. Wmk. 314

281	A37	10c lilac & multi	.45	.25
282	A37	50c blue green & multi	1.40	.30

Intl. year against racial discrimination.

Tubroos (Enterolobium Cyclocarpum) A44

Hardwood Trees of Belize: 15c, Yemeri (Vochysia hondurensis). 26c, Billyweb (Sweetia panamensis). 50c, Logwood (Haematoxylum campechiaum).

Queen's Head in Silver

1971, Aug. 16 ***Perf. 14***

283	A44	5c green, brn & blk	.90	.25
284	A44	15c multicolored	1.25	.40
285	A44	26c multicolored	1.75	.45
286	A44	50c multicolored	2.50	2.50
a.		Souvenir sheet of 4, #283-286	8.00	8.00
		Nos. 283-286 (4)	6.40	3.60

Verrazano-Narrows Bridge, New York, and Quebec Bridge, Canada — A45

Bridges of the World: ½c, Hawksworth Bridge connecting San Ignacio and Santa Helena and Belcan Bridge, Belize, Br. Honduras. 26c, London Bridge in 1871, and at Lake Havasu City, Ariz., in 1971. 50c, Belize-Mexico Bridge and Belize Swing Bridge.

1971, Sept. 23 **Litho.**

287 A45 ½c multicolored .25 .25
288 A45 5c multicolored .45 .25
289 A45 26c multicolored 1.10 .25
290 A45 50c multicolored 1.40 1.40
Nos. 287-290 (4) 3.20 2.15

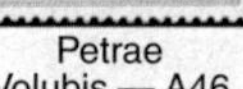

Petrae Volubis — A46

Seated Jade Figure — A47

Wild Flowers: 15c, Vochysia hondurensis. 26c, Tabebuia pentaphylla. 50c, Erythrina americana.

1972, Feb. 28

Flowers in Natural Colors; Black Inscriptions

292 A46 6c lilac & yellow .25 .25
293 A46 15c lt blue & pale grn .45 .40
294 A46 26c pink & lt blue .75 .50
295 A46 50c orange & lt grn 1.25 1.25
Nos. 292-295 (4) 2.70 2.40

Easter.

Perf. 14x13½, 13½x14

1972, May 22 **Unwmk.**

Mayan Carved Jade, 4th-8th centuries: 6c, Dancing priest. 16c, Sun god's head, horiz. 26c, Priest on throne and sun god's head. 50c, Figure and mask.

296 A47 3c rose red & multi .35 .25
297 A47 6c vio bl & multi .40 .30
298 A47 16c brown & multi .60 .50
299 A47 26c ol grn & multi .85 .80
300 A47 50c purple & multi 1.75 1.75
Nos. 296-300 (5) 3.95 3.60

Black inscription with details of designs on back of stamps.

Banak (Virola Koschnyi) — A48

Hardwood Trees of Belize: 5c, Quamwood (Schizolobium parahybum). 16c, Waika chewstick (Symphonia globulifera). 26c, Mammee-apple (Mammea americana). 50c, My lady (Aspidosperma megalocarpon).

1972, Aug. 21 **Wmk. 314** ***Perf. 14***

Queen's Head in Gold

301 A48 3c brt pink & multi .35 .25
302 A48 5c gray & multi .35 .25
303 A48 16c green & multi .65 .25
304 A48 26c lemon & multi .85 .35
305 A48 50c lt violet & multi 1.75 1.75
Nos. 301-305 (5) 3.95 2.85

Silver Wedding Issue, 1972

Common Design Type

Design: Queen Elizabeth II, Prince Philip and Belize orchids.

1972, Nov. 20 **Photo.** ***Perf. 14x14½***

306 CD324 26c slate grn & multi .35 .35
307 CD324 50c violet & multi .55 .55

Baron Bliss Day A49

Festivals of Belize: 10c, Labor Day boat race. 26c, Carib Settlement Day dance. 50c, Pan American Day parade.

1973, Mar. 9 **Litho.** ***Perf. 14½***

308 A49 3c dull blue & black .25 .25
309 A49 10c red & multi .25 .25
310 A49 26c ver & multi .50 .40
311 A49 50c black & multi 1.00 1.00
Nos. 308-311 (4) 2.00 1.90

SEMI-POSTAL STAMPS

Regular Issue of 1921-29 Surcharged in Black or Red

1932 **Wmk. 4** ***Perf. 14***

B1 A14 1c + 1c green 2.00 *12.00*
B2 A14 2c + 2c rose red 2.00 *12.00*
B3 A14 3c + 3c orange 2.50 *25.00*
B4 A14 4c + 4c gray (R) 13.00 *27.50*
B5 A14 5c + 5c ultra 7.50 *15.00*
Nos. B1-B5 (5) 27.00 *91.50*

The surtax was for a fund to aid sufferers from the destruction of the city of Belize by a hurricane in Sept. 1931.

POSTAGE DUE STAMPS

Catalogue values for unused stamps in this section are for Never Hinged items.

D1

1923-64 **Typo.** **Wmk. 4** ***Perf. 14***

J1 D1 1c black 1.25 *26.00*
J2 D1 2c black 1.25 *22.50*
J3 D1 4c black 2.50 *19.00*
Nos. J1-J3 (3) 5.00 *67.50*

Nos. J1-J3 were re-issued on chalky paper in 1956. Values shown are for the 1956 issue. The 1923 issue, on yellowish thin ordinary paper, sells for $7.25 unused, $42.50 used. The 1c was reprinted in 1964 on white, ordinary paper. Value, $37.50 unused, $45 used.

Perf. 13½x13, 13½x14

1965-72 **Wmk. 314**

J4 D1 2c black ('72) 4.00 *6.50*
J5 D1 4c black 2.00 *8.00*

WAR TAX STAMPS

Nos. 85, 75 and 77 Overprinted

1916-17 **Wmk. 3** ***Perf. 14***

With Moire Overprint

MR1 A11 1c green .80 2.50
a. "WAR" inverted 300.00 *350.00*

Without Moire Overprint

MR2 A11 1c green ('17) 1.75 *5.50*
MR3 A11 3c orange ('17) 5.50 9.50
a. Double overprint 425.00 425.00
Nos. MR1-MR3 (3) 8.05 17.50

Nos. 75 and 77 Overprinted

1918

MR4 A11 1c green .25 *.40*
MR5 A11 3c orange 1.00 *3.00*

BRITISH INDIAN OCEAN TERRITORY

ˈbri-tish ˈin-dē-ən ˈō-chən ˈter-ə-ˌtōr-ē

LOCATION — Indian Ocean
GOVT. — British Dependency
POP. — 0

B.I.O.T. was established Nov. 8, 1965. This island group lies 1,180 miles north of Mauritius. It consisted of Chagos Archipelago (chief island: Diego Garcia), Aldabra, Farquhar and Des Roches Islands until June 23, 1976, when the last three named islands were returned to Seychelles.

There is no permanent population on the islands. There are military personnel located there.

100 Cents = 1 Rupee
100 Pence = 1 Pound (1990)

Catalogue values for all unused stamps in this country are for Never Hinged items.

Seychelles Nos. 198-202, 204-212 Overprinted

Perf. 14½x14, 14x14½

1968, Jan. 17 Photo. Wmk. 314
Size: 24x31, 31x24mm

1 A17 5c multicolored 1.25 *1.90*
2 A17 10c multicolored .25 .25
3 A17 15c multicolored .25 .25
4 A17 20c multicolored .25 .25
5 A17 25c multicolored .25 .25
6 A18 40c multicolored .30 .25
7 A18 45c multicolored .30 .40
8 A17 50c multicolored .30 .40
9 A17 75c multicolored .75 .50
10 A18 1r multicolored .90 .50
11 A18 1.50r multicolored 2.25 2.00
12 A18 2.25r multicolored 3.50 *5.00*
13 A18 3.50r multicolored 3.50 *6.00*
14 A18 5r multicolored 12.50 10.00

Perf. 13x14
Size: 22½x39mm

15 A17 10r multicolored 24.00 24.00
Nos. 1-15 (15) 50.55 51.95

Lascar A1

Marine Fauna: 10c, Hammerhead shark, vert. 15c, Tiger shark. 20c, Sooty eagle ray. 25c, Butterflyfish, vert. 30c, Robber crab. 40c, Green carangue. 45c, Needlefish, vert. 50c, Barracuda. 60c, Spotted pebble crab. 75c, Parrotfish. 85c, Rainbow runner (fish). 1r, Giant hermit crab. 1.50r, Humphead. 2.25r, Rock cod. 3.50r, Black marlin. 5r, Whale shark, vert. 10r, Lionfish.

Perf. 14x13½, 13½x14; 14 (30c, 60c, 85c)

1968-73 Litho. Wmk. 314

16 A1 5c multicolored .90 1.75
a. Wmk. upright ('73) 1.25 5.50
17 A1 10c multicolored .35 *1.10*
18 A1 15c multicolored .35 *1.40*
19 A1 20c multicolored .35 *.90*
20 A1 25c multicolored .90 .90
21 A1 30c multi ('70) 4.25 4.25
22 A1 40c multicolored 1.10 .35
23 A1 45c multicolored 2.50 2.50
24 A1 50c multicolored 1.10 .65
25 A1 60c multi ('70) 4.25 4.25
26 A1 75c multicolored 2.75 2.75
27 A1 85c multi ('70) 5.25 5.25
28 A1 1r multicolored 1.75 1.10
29 A1 1.50r multicolored 2.75 2.75
30 A1 2.25r multicolored 13.50 12.50
31 A1 3.50r multicolored 4.25 4.25
32 A1 5r multicolored 13.50 12.00
33 A1 10r multicolored 10.00 9.50
Nos. 16-33 (18) 69.80 68.15

No. 16 has watermark sideways.

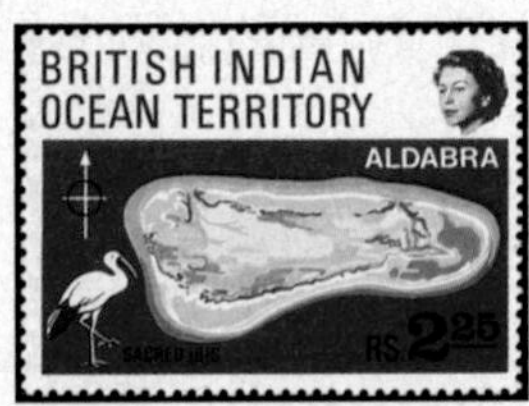

Aldabra Atoll and Sacred Ibis — A2

1969, July 10 Litho. *Perf. 13½x13*

34 A2 2.25r vio blue & multi 2.50 2.00

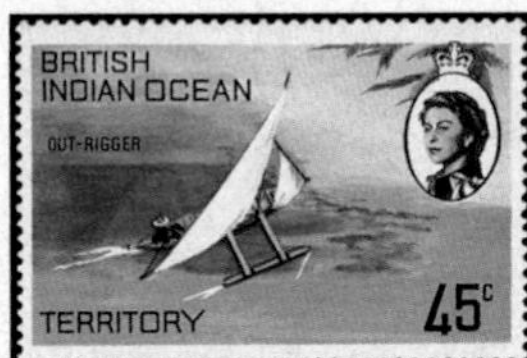

Outrigger Canoe — A3

75c, Beaching canoe. 1r, Merchant ship Nordvaer. 1.50r, Yacht, Isle of Farquhar.

Perf. 13½x14

1969, Dec. 15 Litho. Wmk. 314

35 A3 45c multicolored .40 .40
36 A3 75c multicolored .75 .75
37 A3 1r multicolored 1.10 1.10
38 A3 1.50r multicolored 1.75 1.75
Nos. 35-38 (4) 4.00 4.00

Giant Land Tortoise — A4

Designs: 75c, Aldabra lily. 1r, Aldabra tree snail. 1.50r, Dimorphic egrets.

1971, Feb. 1 Litho. Wmk. 314

39 A4 45c multicolored 3.00 2.50
40 A4 75c multicolored 3.50 2.50
41 A4 1r multicolored 4.00 2.50
42 A4 1.50r multicolored 14.00 11.00
Nos. 39-42 (4) 24.50 18.50

Aldabra Nature Reserve.

Society Coat of Arms and Flightless Rail — A5

1971, June 30 Litho. *Perf. 13½*

43 A5 3.50r multicolored 16.50 11.00

Opening of Royal Society Research Station at Aldabra.

Acropora Formosa A6

Corals: 60c, Goniastrea pectinata. 1r, Fungia fungites. 1.75r, Tubipora musica.

1972, Mar. 1

44 A6 40c blue & multi 3.75 3.75
45 A6 60c brt pink & multi 4.25 4.25
46 A6 1r blue & multi 4.25 4.25
47 A6 1.75r brt pink & multi 5.75 5.75
Nos. 44-47 (4) 18.00 18.00

Common Design Types pictured following the introduction.

Silver Wedding Issue, 1972
Common Design Type

Design: Queen Elizabeth II, Prince Philip, flightless rail and sacred ibis.

1972, Nov. 20 Photo. *Perf. 14x14½*

48 CD324 95c multicolored 1.25 .50
49 CD324 1.50r violet & multi 1.25 .50

Crucifixion, 17th Century — A7 Upsidedown Jellyfish — A8

Paintings, Ethiopian Manuscripts, 17th Century: 75c, 1.50r, Joseph and Nicodemus burying Jesus. 1r, Like 45c.

1973, Apr. 9 Litho. *Perf. 14*

50 A7 45c buff & multi .30 *.40*
51 A7 75c buff & multi .35 *.55*
52 A7 1r buff & multi .50 .40
53 A7 1.50r buff & multi .90 .70
a. Souvenir sheet of 4, #50-53 2.40 *2.40*
Nos. 50-53 (4) 2.05 2.05

Easter.

1973, Nov. 12 Litho. Wmk. 314

54 A8 50c shown 4.75 4.00
55 A8 1r Butterflies 5.25 4.00
56 A8 1.50r Spider 5.50 4.00
Nos. 54-56 (3) 15.50 12.00

Nordvaer and July 14, 1969 Cancel — A9

2.50r, Nordvaer offshore and cancel.

1974, July 14

57 A9 85c multicolored 1.00 .95
58 A9 2.50r multicolored 2.00 1.75

Nordvaer traveling post office, 5th anniv.

Terebra Maculata and Terebra Subulata — A10

Sea Shells: 75c, Turbo marmoratus. 1r, Drupa rubusidaeus. 1.50r, Cassis rufa.

1974, Nov. 12 Litho. *Perf. 13½x14*

59 A10 45c multicolored 2.75 1.40
60 A10 75c multicolored 3.00 1.60
61 A10 1r multicolored 3.25 1.90
62 A10 1.50r multicolored 3.50 2.10
Nos. 59-62 (4) 12.50 7.00

Aldabra Drongo — A11 Grewia Salicifolia — A12

Birds: 10c, Malagasy coucal. 20c, Red-headed forest fody. 25c, Fairy tern. 30c, Crested tern. 40c, Brown booby. 50c, Noddy tern. 60c, Gray heron. 65c, Blue-faced booby. 95c, Malagasy white-eye. 1r, Green-backed heron. 1.75r, Lesser frigate bird. 3.50r, White-tailed tropic bird. 5r, Souimanga sunbird. 10r, Malagasy turtledove. Nos. 69, 71-77 horiz.

1975, Feb. 28 Wmk. 314 *Perf. 14*

63 A11 5c buff & multi 1.50 *3.50*
64 A11 10c lt ultra & multi 1.50 *3.50*
65 A11 20c dp yel & multi 1.50 *3.50*
66 A11 25c ultra & multi 1.50 *3.50*
67 A11 30c dl yel & multi 1.50 *3.50*
68 A11 40c bis & multi 1.50 *3.50*
69 A11 50c lt blue & multi 1.50 *3.75*
70 A11 60c yel & multi 1.50 *3.75*
71 A11 65c yel grn & multi 1.50 *3.75*
72 A11 95c citron & multi 1.50 *3.75*
73 A11 1r bister & multi 1.50 *3.75*
74 A11 1.75r yel & multi 2.50 *9.00*
75 A11 3.50r blue & multi 3.25 *9.00*
76 A11 5r pale sal & multi 4.50 *8.00*
77 A11 10r brt yel & multi 8.50 *14.00*
Nos. 63-77 (15) 35.25 *79.75*

1975, July 10 Litho. Wmk. 314

Native Plants: 65c, Cassia aldabrensis. 1r, Hypoestes aldabrensis. 1.60r, Euphorbia pyrifolia.

78 A12 50c multicolored .65 *1.10*
79 A12 65c multicolored .70 *1.25*
80 A12 1r multicolored .85 *1.25*
81 A12 1.60r multicolored 1.25 *1.75*
Nos. 78-81 (4) 3.45 *5.35*

Nature protection.

Aldabra and Compass Rose — A13

Maps of Islands: 1r, Desroches. 1.50r, Farquhar. 2r, Diego Garcia.

1975, Nov. 8 Litho. *Perf. 13½x14*

82 A13 50c blk, blue & grn 1.00 1.00
83 A13 1r green & multi 1.10 1.10
84 A13 1.50r blk, ultra & grn 1.40 1.40
85 A13 2r blk, lilac & grn 1.50 1.50
a. Souvenir sheet of 4, #82-85 10.00 *13.00*
Nos. 82-85 (4) 5.00 5.00

British Indian Ocean Territory, 10th anniv.

Crimson Speckled Moth — A14

Insects: 1.20r, Dysdercus fasciatus. 1.50r, Sphex torridus. 2r, Oryctes rhinoceros.

1976, Mar. 22 Litho. Wmk. 373

86 A14 65c multicolored 1.25 1.25
87 A14 1.20r multicolored 1.75 1.50
88 A14 1.50r multicolored 2.10 1.75
89 A14 2r multicolored 3.25 1.75
Nos. 86-89 (4) 8.35 6.25

Exhibition Emblem and No. 37 — A15

1990, May 3 Wmk. 373 *Perf. 14*

90 A15 15p No. 62	7.00	6.25
91 A15 20p No. 89	7.50	6.50
92 A15 34p No. 85	11.00	9.25
93 A15 54p shown	13.50	11.50
Nos. 90-93 (4)	39.00	33.50

Stamp World London '90.

Birds — A16

1990, May 3 Wmk. 384 *Perf. 14*

94 A16 15p White-tailed tropic birds	1.40	*2.25*
95 A16 20p Turtle doves	1.50	*2.25*
96 A16 24p Greater frigate birds	2.75	*2.25*
97 A16 30p Little green herons	2.00	*2.50*
98 A16 34p Greater sand plovers	2.25	*2.50*
99 A16 41p Crab plovers	2.25	*2.50*
100 A16 45p Crested terns	4.25	*3.00*
101 A16 54p Lesser crested terns	3.25	*3.75*
102 A16 62p Fairy terns	3.25	*3.75*
103 A16 71p Red-footed boobies	3.50	*5.75*
104 A16 80p Indian mynahs	3.50	*4.50*
105 A16 £1 Madagascar fodies	4.75	*5.25*
Nos. 94-105 (12)	34.65	*40.25*

For overprints see Nos. 145-146.

Queen Mother, 90th Birthday
Common Design Types

Designs: 24p, Lady Elizabeth Bowes-Lyon, 1923. £1, Queen, Princesses Elizabeth & Margaret, 1940.

1990, Aug. 4 Wmk. 384 *Perf. 14x15*

106 CD343 24p multicolored	7.75	7.25

Perf. 14½

107 CD344 £1 brown & black	13.00	14.00

British Indian Ocean Territory, 25th Anniv. — A17

1990, Nov. 8 Litho. *Perf. 14*

108 A17 20p Flag	6.50	6.50
109 A17 24p Coat of arms	6.50	6.50

Souvenir Sheet

110 A17 £1 Map	13.00	13.00

Govt. Services A18

Wmk. 373

1991, June 3 Litho. *Perf. 14*

111 A18 20p Postal service	2.50	2.50
112 A18 24p Royal Marines	2.75	2.75
113 A18 34p Police station, officers	4.75	4.50
114 A18 54p Customs service	6.25	6.00
Nos. 111-114 (4)	16.25	15.75

Visiting Ships A19

1991, Nov. 8

115 A19 20p Survey ship Experiment, 1786	3.25	3.25
116 A19 24p US Brig Pickering, 1819	3.50	3.50
117 A19 34p SMS Emden, 1914	4.75	4.75
118 A19 54p HMS Edinburgh, 1988	5.75	5.75
Nos. 115-118 (4)	17.25	17.25

Queen Elizabeth II's Accession to the Throne, 40th Anniv.
Common Design Type

Wmk. 373

1992, Feb. 6 Litho. *Perf. 14*

119 CD349 15p multicolored	3.50	*3.00*
120 CD349 20p multicolored	4.25	*3.25*
121 CD349 24p multicolored	6.00	*4.25*
122 CD349 34p multicolored	5.50	*5.25*
123 CD349 54p multicolored	5.50	*5.25*
Nos. 119-123 (5)	24.75	*21.00*

Aircraft A20

Wmk. 384

1992, Oct. 23 Litho. *Perf. 14*

124 A20 20p Catalina	2.25	2.00
125 A20 24p Nimrod	2.75	2.75
126 A20 34p P-3 Orion	3.25	3.25
127 A20 54p B-52	4.25	4.25
Nos. 124-127 (4)	12.50	12.25

Christmas — A21

Paintings: 5p, The Mystical Marriage of St. Cathrin, by Correggio. 24p, Madonna and Child by unknown artist. 34p, Madonna and Child by unknown artist, diff. 54p, The Birth of Jesus, by Kaspar Jele.

1992, Nov. 27 *Perf. 14½*

128 A21 5p multicolored	.75	.75
129 A21 24p multicolored	1.50	1.50
130 A21 34p multicolored	2.00	2.00
131 A21 54p multicolored	2.50	2.50
Nos. 128-131 (4)	6.75	6.75

Coconut Crab A22

Wmk. 384

1993, Mar. 3 Litho. *Perf. 14*

132 A22 10p Crab, coconut	2.50	2.50
133 A22 10p Large crab	2.50	2.50
134 A22 10p Two crabs	2.50	2.50
135 A22 15p Crab on tree trunk	3.00	3.00
Nos. 132-135 (4)	10.50	10.50

World Wildlife Fund.

Royal Air Force, 75th Anniv.
Common Design Type

Airplanes: No. 136, Vickers Virginia. 24p, Bristol Bulldog. 34p, Short Sunderland. 54p, Bristol Blenheim IV.

No. 140: a, Douglas Dakota. b, Gloster Javelin. c, Blackburn Beverley. d, Vickers VC10.

1993, Apr. 1 Wmk. 373

136 CD350 20p multicolored	1.25	1.25
137 CD350 24p multicolored	1.60	1.60
138 CD350 34p multicolored	1.90	1.90
139 CD350 54p multicolored	3.25	3.25
Nos. 136-139 (4)	8.00	8.00

Souvenir Sheet of 4

140 CD350 20p #a.-d.	9.50	9.50

Flowers — A23

Christmas: 20p, Stachytarpheta urticifolia. 24p, Ipomea pes-caprae. 34p, Sida pusilla. 54p, Catharanthus roseus.

Wmk. 373

1993, Nov. 22 Litho. *Perf. 14½*

141-144 A23 Set of 4	7.50	7.50

Nos. 96, 105 Ovptd. with Hong Kong '94 Emblem

Wmk. 384

1994, Feb. 18 Litho. *Perf. 14*

145 A16 24p multicolored	5.50	3.00
146 A16 £1 multicolored	8.00	*8.50*

A24

18th Cent. Maps and Charts: a, 20p, Sketch of Diego Garcia. b, 24p, Plan of harbor, Chagos Island or Diego Garcia, by Lt. Archibald Blair. c, 34p, Chart of Chagos Archipelago, by Lt. Blair. d, 44p, Plan of part of Chagos Island or Diego Garcia, from survey made by the Drake. e, 54p, Plan of Chagos Island or Diego Garcia, by M. Aa Fontaine.

1994, June 1 Wmk. 373

147 A24 Strip of 5, #a.-e.	11.00	11.00

Butterflies — A25

1994, Aug. 16 Wmk. 384

148 A25 24p Junonia villida	3.00	3.00
149 A25 30p Petrelaea dana	3.50	3.50
150 A25 56p Hypolimnas misippus	4.50	4.50
Nos. 148-150 (3)	11.00	11.00

Sharks A26

1994, Nov. 1 Wmk. 373

151 A26 15p Nurse	4.25	3.50
152 A26 20p Silver tip	4.25	3.50
153 A26 24p Black tip reef	4.75	3.75
154 A26 30p Oceanic white tip	5.50	4.75
155 A26 35p Black tip	6.50	6.00
156 A26 41p Smooth hammerhead	6.50	6.00
157 A26 46p Lemon	6.50	6.00
158 A26 55p White tip reef	7.75	6.25
159 A26 65p Tiger	7.75	6.25
a. Souvenir sheet of 1	5.00	5.00
160 A26 74p Indian sand tiger	8.00	7.25
a. Souvenir sheet of 1	7.00	7.00
161 A26 80p Great hammerhead	9.00	8.00
162 A26 £1 Great white	10.00	9.00
Nos. 151-162 (12)	80.75	70.25

No. 159a for Hong Kong '97. Issued 2/3/97.

No. 160a for return of Hong Kong to China. Issued 7/1/97.

End of World War II, 50th Anniv.
Common Design Types

20p, War graves, memorial cross, Diego Garcia. 24p, 6-inch naval gun, Cannon Point. 30p, Sunderland flying boat, 230 Squadron. 56p, HMIS Clive.

£1, Reverse of War Medal 1939-45.

Wmk. 373

1995, May 8 Litho. *Perf. 14*

163 CD351 20p multicolored	2.00	2.00
164 CD351 24p multicolored	2.25	2.25
165 CD351 30p multicolored	2.75	2.75
166 CD351 56p multicolored	3.75	3.75
Nos. 163-166 (4)	10.75	10.75

Souvenir Sheet

167 CD352 £1 multicolored	5.50	5.50

Game Fish A27

1995, Oct. 6 Wmk. 384

168 A27 20p Dolphinfish	2.00	2.00
169 A27 24p Sailfish	2.10	2.10
170 A27 30p Wahoo	3.00	3.00
171 A27 56p Striped marlin	4.25	4.25
Nos. 168-171 (4)	11.35	11.35

Sea Shells A28

20p, Terebra crenulata. 24p, Bursa bufonia. 30p, Nassarius papillosus. 56p, Lopha cristagalli.

1996, Jan. 8 Wmk. 373 *Perf. 14*

172 A28 20p multicolored	2.10	2.10
173 A28 24p multicolored	2.25	2.25
174 A28 30p multicolored	2.75	2.75
175 A28 56p multicolored	5.00	5.00
Nos. 172-175 (4)	12.10	12.10

Queen Elizabeth II, 70th Birthday
Common Design Type

Various portraits of Queen, scenes of British Indian Ocean Territory: 20p, View to north from south end of lagoon. 24p, Manager's House, Peros Banhos. 30p, Wireless station, Peros Banhos. 56p, Sunset scene.

£1, Wearing crown, formal dress.

Perf. 14x14½

1996, Apr. 22 Wmk. 384

176 CD354 20p multicolored	.95	.95
177 CD354 24p multicolored	1.10	1.10
178 CD354 30p multicolored	1.20	1.20
179 CD354 56p multicolored	2.00	2.00
Nos. 176-179 (4)	5.25	5.25

Souvenir Sheet

180 CD354 £1 multicolored	6.00	6.00

Turtles
A29

1996, Sept. 2 **Wmk. 373**

181	A29 20p Loggerhead	1.90	1.90
182	A29 24p Leatherback	2.00	2.00
183	A29 30p Hawksbill	2.75	2.75
184	A29 56p Green	3.50	3.50
	Nos. 181-184 (4)	10.15	10.15

Uniforms — A30

Designs: 20p, British representative. 24p, Royal Marine officer. 30p, Royal Marine in camouflage. 56p, Police dog handler, female police officer.

1996, Dec. ***Perf. 14***

185	A30 20p multicolored	1.50	1.50
186	A30 24p multicolored	2.00	2.00
187	A30 30p multicolored	2.50	2.50
188	A30 56p multicolored	3.25	3.25
	Nos. 185-188 (4)	9.25	9.25

Queen Elizabeth II and Prince Philip, 50th Wedding Anniv. — A31

No. 189, Queen up close. No. 190, 4-horse team fording river. No. 191, Queen riding in open carriage. No. 192, Prince Philip up close. No. 193, Prince driving 4-horse team, Prince, Queen near jeep. No. 194, Queen on horseback, castle in distance.

£1.50, Queen, Prince riding in open carriage.

1997, July 10 ***Perf. 14½x14***

189	A31 20p multicolored	2.00	2.00
190	A31 20p multicolored	2.00	2.00
a.	Pair, #189-190	4.00	4.00
191	A31 24p multicolored	2.00	2.00
192	A31 24p multicolored	2.00	2.00
a.	Pair, #191-192	4.00	4.00
193	A31 30p multicolored	2.00	2.00
194	A31 30p multicolored	2.00	2.00
a.	Pair, #193-194	4.00	4.00
	Nos. 189-194 (6)	12.00	12.00

Souvenir Sheet

195	A31 £1.50 multicolored	11.50	11.50

Ocean Wave '97, Naval Exercise — A32

Designs: a, HMS Richmond, HMS Beaver. b, HMS Illustrious. c, HMS Beaver. d, RFA Sir Percivale, HMY Britannia, HMS Beaver. e, HMY Britannia. f, HMS Richmond, HMS Beaver, HMS Gloucester. g, HMS Richmond. h, HMS Illustrious (aerial view). i, HMS Sheffield. j, RFA Diligence, HMS Trenchant. k, HMS Illustrious, RFA Fort George, HMS Gloucester. l, HMS Richmond, HMS Beaver, HMS Gloucester.

1997, Dec. 1 **Litho.** ***Perf. 14x14½***

196	A32 24p Sheet of 12, #a.-l.	22.50	22.50

Diana, Princess of Wales (1961-97)
Common Design Type

Various portraits: a, 26p, shown. b, 26p, Close-up. c, 34p. d, 60p.

1998, Mar. 31 ***Perf. 14½x14***

197	CD355 Sheet of 4, #a.-d.	6.50	6.50

No. 197 sold for £1.46 + 20p, with surtax and 50% of profits from total sale being donated to the Princess Diana Memorial Fund.

Royal Air Force, 80th Anniv.
Common Design Type of 1993
Re-inscribed

Designs: 26p, Blackburn Iris, 1930-34. 34p, Gloster Gamecock, 1926-33. 60p, North American Sabre F86, 1953-56. 80p, Avro Lincoln, 1945-55.

No. 202: a, Sopwith Baby, 1915-19. b, Martinsyde Elephant, 1916-19. c, De Havilland Tiger Moth, 1932-55. d, North American Mustang III, 1943-47.

1998, Apr. 1 **Wmk. 384** ***Perf. 14***

198	CD350 26p multicolored	1.60	1.60
199	CD350 34p multicolored	1.90	1.90
200	CD350 60p multicolored	3.25	3.25
201	CD350 80p multicolored	4.25	4.25
	Nos. 198-201 (4)	11.00	11.00

Souvenir Sheet

202	CD350 34p Sheet of 4, #a.-d.	10.00	10.00

Intl. Year of the Ocean
A33

Dolphins and whales: No. 203, Striped dolphin. No. 204, Bryde's whale. No. 205, Pilot whale. No. 206, Spinner dolphin.

Wmk. 373

1998, Dec. 7 **Litho.** ***Perf. 14***

203	A33 26p multicolored	4.00	4.00
204	A33 26p multicolored	4.00	4.00
205	A33 34p multicolored	4.00	4.00
206	A33 34p multicolored	4.00	4.00
	Nos. 203-206 (4)	16.00	16.00

Sailing Ships — A34

2p, Bark "Westminster," 1837. 15p, "Sao Cristovao," Spain, 1589. 20p, Clipper ship "Sea Witch," US, 1849. 26p, HMS "Royal George," 1778. 34p, Clipper ship "Cutty Sark," 1883. 60p, British East India Co. ship "Mentor," 1789. 80p, HM brig "Trinculo," 1809. £1, Paddle steamer "Enterprise," 1825. £1.15, Privateer "Confiance," France, 1800. £2, British East India Co. ship "Kent," 1820.

Wmk. 373

1999, Feb. 1 **Litho.** ***Perf. 14***

207	A34 2p multicolored	.65	.65
208	A34 15p multicolored	1.25	1.25
209	A34 20p multicolored	1.50	1.50
210	A34 26p multicolored	1.75	1.75
211	A34 34p multicolored	2.25	2.25
212	A34 60p multicolored	3.50	3.50
213	A34 80p multicolored	4.25	4.25
214	A34 £1 multicolored	5.25	5.25
215	A34 £1.15 multicolored	5.75	5.75
216	A34 £2 multicolored	9.00	9.00
	Nos. 207-216 (10)	35.15	35.15

Tea Race, 1872
A35

a, Cutty Sark (up close). b, Thermopylae (in distance).

Wmk. 384

1999, Mar. 19 **Litho.** ***Perf. 14***

217	A35 60p Sheet of 2, #a.-b.	12.50	12.50

Australia '99 World Stamp Expo.

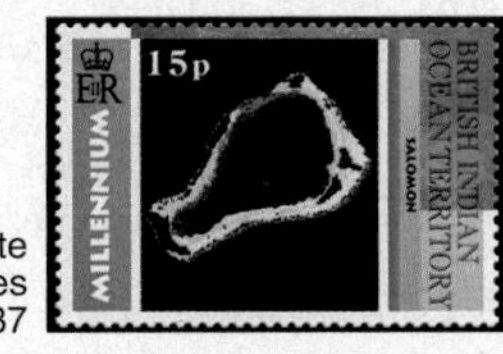
The Stamp Show 2000, London — A36

Winning photos in photography contest: a, 26p, Field vole by Colin Sargent. b, 34p, Puffin, by P. J. Royal. c, 55p, Red fox, by Jim Wilson. d, £1, Robin, by Harry Smith.

Perf. 14½x14¼

2000, May 22 **Litho.** **Wmk. 373**

218	A36 Sheet of 4, #a-d	12.00	12.00

Satellite Images
A37

Designs: 15p, Salomon Atoll. 20p, Egmont Atoll. 60p, Blenheim Reef. 80p, Diego Garcia.

Wmk. 373

2000, July 3 **Litho.** ***Perf. 14***

219-222	A37 Set of 4	11.00	11.00

Queen Mother, 100th Birthday — A38

Designs: 26p, Blue hat. 34p, Blue green hat. No. 225: a, 55p, Blue hat. £1, Yellow hat.

2000, Aug. 4 **Wmk. 373** ***Perf. 13¾***

223-224	A38 Set of 2	4.75	4.75

Souvenir Sheet

225	A38 Sheet of 2, #a-b	9.50	9.50

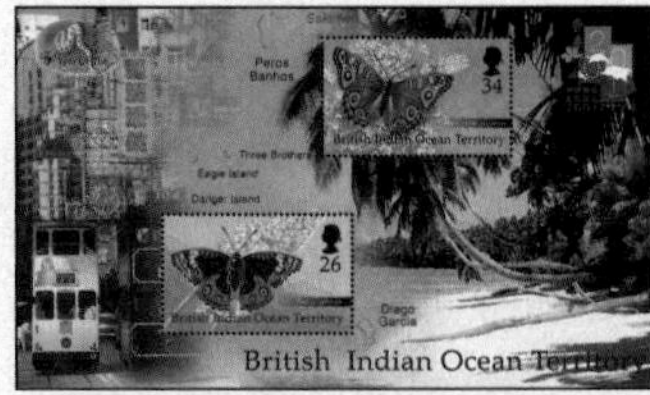
Flowers — A39

Designs: 26p, Delonix regia. 34p, Barringtonia asiatica. 60p, Zephyranthes rosea.

2000, Dec. 4 ***Perf. 14½x14¼***

226-228	A39 Set of 3	8.50	8.50

Souvenir Sheet

New Year 2001 (Year of the Snake) — A40

Butterflies: a, 26p, Precis orithya. b, 34p, Junonia villida chagoensis.

Perf. 14 ¼

2001, Feb. 1 **Litho.** **Wmk. 373**

229	A40 Sheet of 2, #a-b	7.50	7.50

Hong Kong 2001 Stamp Exhibition.

Souvenir Sheet

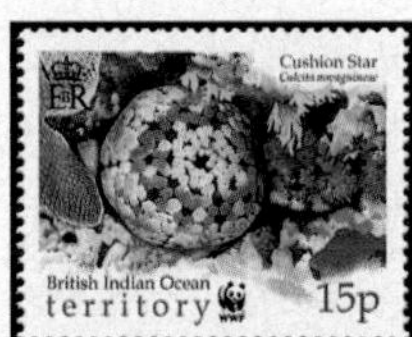
Royal Navy Submarines, Cent. — A41

No. 230: a, 26p, HMS Turbulent. b, 26p, HMS Churchill. c, 34p, HMS Resolution. d, 34p, HMS Vanguard. e, 60p, HMS Otter. f, 60p, HMS Oberon. Size of Nos. 230e-230f: 75x30mm.

Perf. 14¼x14½

2001, May 28 **Litho.** **Wmk. 373**

230	A41 Sheet of 6, #a-f	17.50	17.50

Worldwide Fund for Nature (WWF)
A42

Starfish: 15p, Cushion star. 26p, Azure sea star. 34p, Crown-of-thorns. 56p, Banded bubble star.

Wmk. 373

2001, Aug. 1 **Litho.** ***Perf. 13¾***

231-234	A42 Set of 4	9.00	9.00
234a	Strip, #231-234	10.00	10.00

Plants — A43

Designs: 10p, Catharanthus roseus, horiz. 26p, Scadoxus mutiflora. 34p, Striga asiatica. 60p, Argusia argentia, horiz. 70p, Euphorbia cyathophora, horiz.

2001, Sept. 24 ***Perf. 13¾x14¼***

235	A43 26p multi	2.25	2.25
a.	Perf. 14½	2.25	2.25

236 A43 34p multi 2.50 2.50
a. Perf. 14½ 2.50 2.50

Souvenir Sheet

Perf. 14½

237 Sheet, #a-c, 235a, 236a 10.00 10.00
a. A43 10p multi .60 .60
b. A43 60p multi 2.50 2.50
c. A43 70p multi 3.00 3.00

Souvenir Sheet

Birdlife International World Bird Festival — A44

Crab plover: a, Resting. b, Eating crab, vert. c, Close-up of head, vert. d, In flight. e, Standing on one leg.

2001, Oct. 1 ***Perf. 14½***
238 A44 50p Sheet of 5, #a-e 13.00 13.00

Reign Of Queen Elizabeth II, 50th Anniv. Issue

Common Design Type

Designs: Nos. 239, 243a, 10p, Princess Elizabeth, 1943. Nos. 240, 243b, 25p, In 1967. Nos. 241, 243c, 35p, With Prince Philip, 1947. Nos. 242, 243d, 55p, Wearing tiara. No. 243e, 75p, 1955 portrait by Annigoni (38x50mm).

Perf. 14¼x14½, 13¾ (#243e)

2002, Feb. 6 Litho. Wmk. 373

With Gold Frames

239 CD360 10p multicolored .75 .75
240 CD360 25p multicolored 2.00 2.00
241 CD360 35p multicolored 2.75 2.75
242 CD360 55p multicolored 4.50 4.50
Nos. 239-242 (4) 10.00 10.00

Souvenir Sheet

Without Gold Frames

243 CD360 Sheet of 5, #a-e 12.00 12.00

Souvenir Sheet

Red-footed Booby — A45

No. 244: a, Head of bird with brown feathers. b, Bird in flight, vert. c, Bird on nest, vert. d, Close-up of bird with white and black feathers. e, Chick.

Wmk. 373

2002, June 17 Litho. *Perf. 14½*
244 A45 50p Sheet of 5, #a-e 16.00 16.00

Queen Mother Elizabeth (1900-2002)

Common Design Type

Designs: 26p, Wearing hat (sepia photograph). No. 246, £1, Wearing blue green hat.
No. 247: a, £1, Wearing feathered hat (black and white photograph). b, £1, Wearing dark blue hat.

Wmk. 373

2002, Aug. 5 Litho. *Perf. 14¼*

With Purple Frames

245 CD361 26p multicolored 1.25 1.25
246 CD361 £1 multicolored 5.25 5.25

Souvenir Sheet

Without Purple Frames

Perf. 14½x14¼

247 CD361 Sheet of 2, #a-b 13.00 13.00

Friends of the Chagos, 10th Anniv. — A46

Various reef fish: 2p, 15p, 26p, 34p, 58p, £1. £1.90, Fish.

Perf. 14¼x14½

2002, Oct. 3 Litho. Wmk. 373
248-253 A46 Set of 6 14.00 14.00

Souvenir Sheet

254 A46 £1.90 multi 11.50 11.50

No. 254 is a parcel post stamp.

Sea Slugs — A47

Designs: 2p, Halgerda tesselata. 15p, Notodoris minor. 26p, Nembrotha lineolata. 50p, Chromodoris quadricolor. 76p, Glossodoris cincta. £1.10, Chromodoris cf. leopardus.

Wmk. 373

2003, Mar. 17 Litho. *Perf. 13¼*
255-260 A47 Set of 6 16.00 16.00

Head of Queen Elizabeth II

Common Design Type

Wmk. 373

2003, June 2 Litho. *Perf. 13¾*
261 CD362 £2.50 multi 12.50 12.50

Coronation of Queen Elizabeth II, 50th Anniv.

Common Design Type

Designs: Nos. 262, 264a, £1, Queen wearing crown. Nos. 263, 264b, £2, Queen with family.

Perf. 14¼x14½

2003, June 2 Litho. Wmk. 373

Vignettes Framed, Red Background

262 CD363 £1 multicolored 5.50 5.50
263 CD363 £2 multicolored 10.50 10.50

Souvenir Sheet

Vignettes Without Frame, Purple Panel

264 CD363 Sheet of 2, #a-b 15.00 15.00

Prince William, 21st Birthday

Common Design Type

No. 265: a, William on polo pony at right. b, William with Prince Charles at left.

Wmk. 373

2003, June 21 Litho. *Perf. 14¼*
265 Horiz. pair 9.00 9.00
a. CD364 50p multi 3.25 3.25
b. CD364 £1 multi 5.00 5.00

Powered Flight, Cent. — A48

Designs: No. 266, 34p, De Havilland Mosquito. No. 267, 34p, Avro Lancaster Dambuster. No. 268, 58p, Supermarine Spitfire. No. 269, 58p, Hawker Hurricane. No. 270, 76p, Lockheed C-130 Hercules. No. 271, 76p, Vickers Armstrong Wellington.
No. 272: a, Boeing E-3A Sentry AWACS. b, Boeing B-17 Flying Fortress. c, Lockheed P3 Orion. d, Consolidated B-24 Liberator. e, Lockheed C-141 Starlifter. f, Supermarine Walrus. g, Short Sunderland. h, Supermarine Stranraer. i, PBY Catalina. j, Supermarine Sea Otter.
Illustration reduced.

Wmk. 373

2003, July 18 Litho. *Perf. 14*

Stamp + Label

266-271 A48 Set of 6 16.00 16.00

Miniature Sheet

272 A48 26p Sheet of 10, #a-j 16.00 16.00

Fisheries Patrol — A49

No. 273: a, 34p, M. V. Pacific Marlin. b, 34p, Marlin. c, 58p, Skipjack tuna. d, 58p, Yellowfin tuna. e, 76p, Swordfish. f, 76p, Bigeye tuna.

Wmk. 373

2004, Feb. 16 Litho. *Perf. 14¼*
273 A49 Sheet of 6, #a-f 18.00 18.00

Birds A50

Designs: 2p, Madagascar fody. 14p, Barred ground dove. 20p, Indian mynah. 26p, Cattle egret. 34p, Fairy tern. 58p, Masked booby. 76p, Greater frigatebird. 80p, White-tailed tropicbird. £1.10, Little green heron. £1.34, Pacific golden plover. £1.48, Garganey teal. £2.50, Bar-tailed godwit.

Wmk. 373

2004, June 21 Litho. *Perf. 14*
274 A50 2p multi .30 .30
275 A50 14p multi .65 .65
276 A50 20p multi .95 .95
277 A50 26p multi 1.10 1.10
278 A50 34p multi 1.50 1.50
279 A50 58p multi 2.50 2.50
280 A50 76p multi 3.25 3.25
281 A50 80p multi 3.50 3.50
282 A50 £1.10 multi 5.00 5.00
283 A50 £1.34 multi 6.00 6.00
284 A50 £1.48 multi 7.25 7.25
285 A50 £2.50 multi 11.00 11.00
Nos. 274-285 (12) 43.00 43.00

Crabs A51

Designs: 26p, Coconut crab. 34p, Land crab. 76p, Rock crab. £1.10, Ghost crab.

Wmk. 373

2004, Dec. 20 Litho. *Perf. 14*
286-289 A51 Set of 4 14.50 14.50

Turtles A52

Designs: No. 290, 26p, Green turtle hatchling. No. 291, 26p, Hawksbill turtle hatchlings. No. 292, 34p, Hawksbill turtle's head. No. 293, 34p, Green turtle's head. 76p, Hawksbill turtle swimming. £1.10, Green turtle swimming.
£1.70, Like £1.10.

2005, Feb. 14
290-295 A52 Set of 6 15.00 15.00

Souvenir Sheet

296 A52 £1.70 multi 10.00 10.00

Battle of Trafalgar, Bicent. — A53

Designs: No. 297, 26p, HMS Phoebe. No. 298, 26p, Tower Sea Service pistol, 1796. No. 299, 34p, HMS Harrier. No. 300, 34p, Royal Navy Boatswain, 1805. No. 301, 76p, Portrait of Adm. Horatio Nelson. No. 302, 76p, HMS Victory, horiz.
No. 303: a, HMS Minotaur, ship in distance. b, HMS Spartiate.

Wmk. 373, Unwmkd. (#302)

2005, May 6 *Perf. 13¼*
297-302 A53 Set of 6 16.00 16.00

Souvenir Sheet

303 A53 £1.10 Sheet of 2, #a-b 10.00 10.00

No. 302 has particles of wood from the HMS Victory embedded in the areas covered by a thermographic process that produces a raised, shiny effect.

Miniature Sheet

End of World War II, 60th Anniv. — A54

No. 304: a, 26p, HMAS Wollongong. b, 26p, Dutch tanker Ordina, HMIS Bengal attacked by Japanese surface raiders. c, 26p, HMS Pathfinder arrives at Diego Garcia. d, 26p, HMS Lossie rescues 112 survivors from Australian freighter Nellore. e, 26p, US Liberty Ship Jean Nicolet sunk by HIJMS I-8. f, 34p, Gen. Douglas MacArthur. g, 34p, Gen. Bernard L. Montgomery. h, 34p, Gen. George S. Patton. i, 34p, British Prime Minister Winston Churchill. j, 34p, Pres. Franklin D. Roosevelt.

Wmk. 373

2005, June 26 Litho. *Perf. 13¾*
304 A54 Sheet of 10, #a-j 16.00 16.00

Sharks and Rays A55

Designs: No. 305, 26p, Blacktip reef shark. No. 306, 26p, Gray reef shark. No. 307, 34p, Silvertip shark. No. 308, 34p, Spotted eagle ray. No. 309, 34p, Tawny nurse shark. No. 310, 34p, Manta ray. 76p, Porcupine ray. £2, Feathertail stingray.

2005, Aug. 15 ***Perf. 13½x13¾***
305-312 A55 Set of 8 26.00 26.00

Battle of Trafalgar, Bicent. — A56

Designs: 26p, HMS Victory. 34p, Ships in battle, horiz. £2, Admiral Horatio Nelson.

Perf. 13¼

2005, Oct. 18 Litho. Unwmk.
313-315 A56 Set of 3 14.00 14.00

Miniature Sheet

British Indian Ocean Territory, 40th Anniv. — A57

No. 316: a, Crab, palm fronds. b, Two crabs. c, White birds. d, Black bird, map of Indian Ocean area. e, Fish, blue starfish. f, Two triggerfish, corals. g, Angelfish, corals. h, Turtle, map of British Indian Ocean Territory.

Perf. 14¾x14¼

2005, Nov. 8 Wmk. 373

316 A57 34p Sheet of 8, #a-h 17.00 17.00

Queen Elizabeth II, 80th Birthday A58

Queen: 26p, As young woman, wearing military cap. 34p, As young woman, diff. 76p, Wearing tiara. £1.10, Wearing kerchief.

No. 321: a, Like 34p. b, Like 76p.

Wmk. 373

2006, Apr. 21 Litho. *Perf. 14*

317-320 A58 Set of 4 13.00 13.00

Souvenir Sheet

321 A58 £1 Sheet of 2, #a-b 10.50 10.50

Miniature Sheet

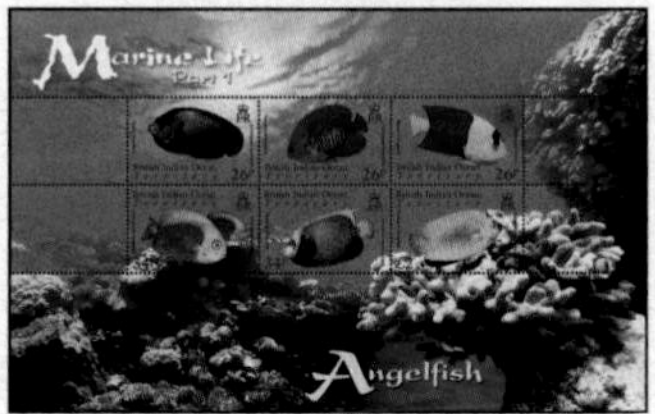

Angelfish — A59

No. 322: a, 26p, Dusky angelfish. b, 26p, Twospined angelfish. c, 26p, Bicolor angelfish. d, 34p, Orangeback angelfish. e, 34p, Emperor angelfish. f, £2, Threespot angelfish.

No. 323: a, 26p, Melon butterflyfish. b, 26p, Raccoon butterflyfish. c, 26p, Scrawled butterflyfish. d, 34p, Longnose butterflyfish. e, 34p, Threadfin butterflyfish. f, £2, Masked bannerfish.

No. 324: a, 54p, Common parrotfish. b, 54p, Daisy parrotfish. c, 54p, Bicolor parrotfish. d, 54p, Bridled parrotfish. e, 90p, Indian Ocean steephead parrotfish. f, 90p, Male and female ember parrotfish.

2006-07

322 A59 Sheet of 6, #a-f 19.00 19.00
323 A59 Sheet of 6, #a-f 15.00 15.00
324 A59 Sheet of 6, #a-f 18.00 18.00

Issued: No. 322, 5/29; No. 323, 7/31; No. 324, 3/29/07.

Miniature Sheet

BirdLife International — A60

No. 325: a, 26p, Great frigatebird. b, 26p, Black-naped terns. c, 26p, Yellow-billed tropicbirds. d, 26p, White terns. e, 26p, Brown noddies. f, £2, Red-footed boobies.

2006, Oct. 6 *Perf. 13¾*

325 A60 Sheet of 6, #a-f 13.50 13.50

Wedding of Queen Elizabeth II and Prince Philip, 60th Anniv. — A61

Designs: No. 326, 54p, Couple. No. 327, 54p, Coach in procession. No. 328, 90p, Couple, diff. No. 329, 90p, Wedding ceremony.

£2.14, Couple, diff.

Wmk. 373

2007, June 1 Litho. *Perf. 13¾*

326-329 A61 Set of 4 11.50 11.50

Souvenir Sheet

Perf. 14

330 A61 £2.14 multi 8.50 8.50

No. 330 contains one 43x58mm stamp.

Charles Darwin (1809-82), Naturalist A62

Designs: No. 331, 54p, Darwin and wildlife. No. 332, 54p, HMS Beagle. No. 333, 90p, Coral reef. No. 334, 90p, Turtles.

Wmk. 373

2007, July 23 Litho. *Perf. 13¼*

331-334 A62 Set of 4 12.00 12.00

BirdLife International — A63

Designs: No. 335, 54p, Pomarine skua chasing white-tailed tropic bird. No. 336, 54p, Two Pomarine skuas in flight. No. 337, 54p, Two Pomarine skuas on beach. No. 338, 54p, Pomarine skua attacking red-footed booby in flight, boobies on land. No. 339, 90p, Pomarine skua attacking black-necked terns in flight. No. 340, Pomarine skua on water.

2007, Oct. 1 *Perf. 12½x13*

335-340 A63 Set of 6 16.50 16.50

Miniature Sheet

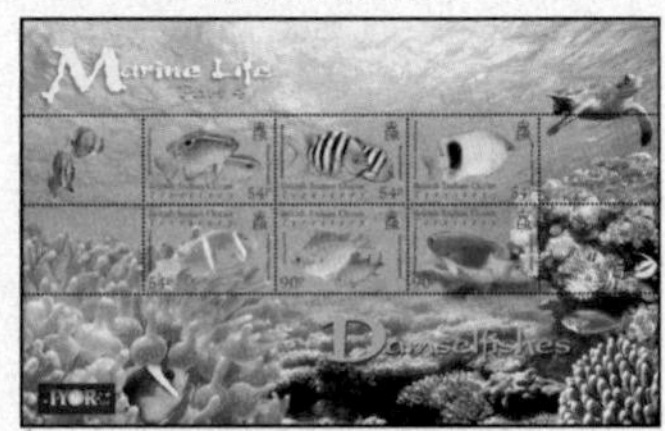

Damselfish — A64

No. 341: a, 54p, One-spot demoiselle. b, 54p, Banded sergeant. c, 54p, Johnston Island damsel. d, 54p, Chagos anemonefish. e, 90p, Black-axil chromis. f, 90p, Caerulean damsel.

Wmk. 373

2008, Jan. 30 Litho. *Perf. 14*

341 A64 Sheet of 6, #a-f 16.00 16.00

Military Uniforms — A65

Designs: No. 342, 27p, Royal Marines. No. 343, 27p, Royal Engineers. No. 344, 54p, Officer, East India Company Army. No. 345, 54p, Sepoys, East India Company Army. No. 346, 54p, Sergeant, Royal Military Police. No. 347, 54p, Artillery Corps.

2008, Mar. 3

342-347 A65 Set of 6 11.00 11.00

A66

Royal Air Force, 90th Anniv. — A67

Designs: No. 348, 27p, Avro 504. No. 349, 27p, Short Sunderland. No. 350, 27p, Vickers VC10. No. 351, 27p, De Havilland Mosquito. 54p, English Electric Canberra.

£1.72, King George V, Marshal of the Royal Air Force.

Wmk. 373

2008, Apr. 1 Litho. *Perf. 14*

348-352 A66 Set of 5 6.50 6.50

Souvenir Sheet

353 A67 £1.72 black 7.00 7.00

Nos. 348-352 each were printed in sheets of 8 + central label.

End of World War I, 90th Anniv. — A68

Soldiers and their letters home: No. 354, 50p, Sergeant Major Francis Proud. No. 355, 50p, Second Lieutenant Eric Heaton. No. 356, 50p, Private Dennis Harry Wilson. No. 357, 50p, Second Lieutenant Eric Rose. No. 358, 50p, Second Lieutenant Charles Roberts. No. 359, 50p, Private Harry Lamin.

£1, Wreath of Remembrance.

Wmk. 406

2008, Sept. 16 Litho. *Perf. 14*

354-359 A68 Set of 6 11.00 11.00

Souvenir Sheet

360 A68 £1 multi 3.75 3.75

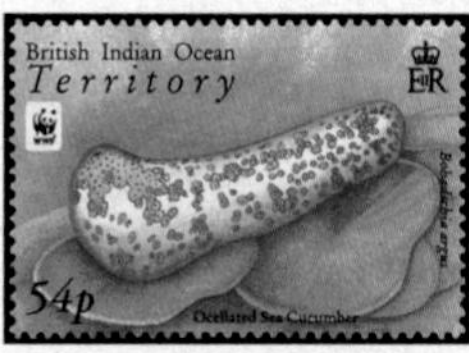

Worldwide Fund For Nature (WWF) — A69

Designs: No. 361, 54p, Ocellated sea cucumber. No. 362, 54p, Pineapple sea cucumber. No. 363, 90p, Graeffe's sea cucumber. No. 364, 90p, Dark green sea cucumber.

Wmk. 373

2008, Dec. 1 Litho. *Perf. 14*

361-364 A69 Set of 4 10.00 10.00
a. Sheet of 16, 4 each #361-364 40.00 40.00

Ships A70

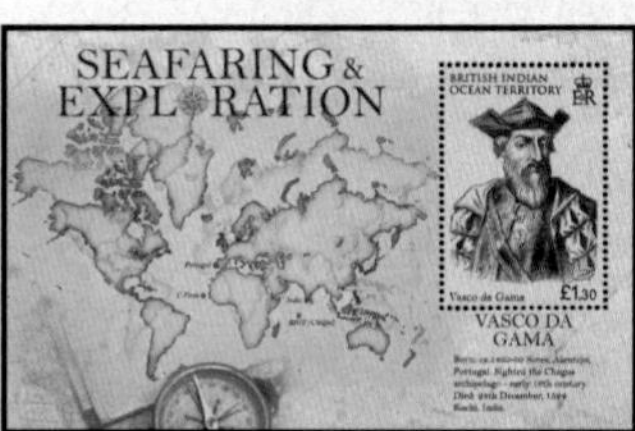

Vasco da Gama (c. 1460-1524), Explorer — A71

Designs: No. 365, 54p, HMS Victory. No. 366, 54p, HMS Endeavour. No. 367, 54p, HMS Beagle. No. 368, 54p, SS Windsor Castle. No. 369, 54p, HMS Edinburgh. No. 370, 54p, SMS Fürst Bismarck.

Wmk. 406

2009, Mar. 9 Litho. *Perf. 14*

365-370 A70 Set of 6 9.75 9.75

Souvenir Sheet

371 A71 £1.30 multi 4.00 4.00

Naval Aviation, Cent. A72

Royal Navy aircraft: No. 372, 27p, Short S.38 and ship. No. 373, 27p, Sopwith Pup. No. 374, 54p, Supermarine Scimitar and ship. No. 375, 54p, Westland Wessex helicopter and ship.

£1.72, Squadron Commander E. H. Dunning landing airplane on HMS Furious, 1917.

2009, Apr. 17

372-375 A72 Set of 4 4.75 4.75

Souvenir Sheet

376 A72 £1.72 multi 5.00 5.00

Nos. 372-375 each were printed in sheets of 8 + central label.

Space Exploration A73

Designs: No. 377, 54p, Early rockets Corporal and Private. No. 378, 54p, Flying Bedstead, 1964. No. 379, 54p, Apollo launch site, 1969. No. 380, 54p, Space Shuttle STS-71 launch, 1995. 90p, ESA Columbus laboratory, STS-122, 2008.

£1.50, Astronaut on Moon, painting by Capt. Alan Bean, vert.

2009, July 20 *Perf. 13¼*

377-381 A73 Set of 5 13.50 13.50

Souvenir Sheet

Perf. 13x13¼

382 A73 £1.50 multi 7.25 7.25

No. 382 contains one 40x60mm stamp. Nos. 377-381 each were printed in sheets of 6.

Flora, Fauna and Sites — A74

Designs: 1p, Two-band anemonefish. 2p, Angelfish. 5p, Royal poinciana flowers. 12p, Beach morning glories. 27p, Bay cedar flowers. 45p, Scaevola bush flowers. 54p, Madagascan red fodies. 90p, Greater frigatebirds. £1.30, Sharks Cove. £1.72, Turtle Cove. £2.64, Hawksbill turtles. £3.02 Sticklefin lemon sharks.

Wmk. 406

2009, Oct. 5 Litho. *Perf. 13¾*

383 A74 1p multi .25 .25
384 A74 2p multi .25 .25
385 A74 5p multi .25 .25
386 A74 12p multi .40 .40
387 A74 27p multi .90 .90
388 A74 45p multi 1.50 1.50
389 A74 54p multi 1.75 1.75
390 A74 90p multi 3.00 3.00
391 A74 £1.30 multi 4.25 4.25
392 A74 £1.72 multi 5.75 5.75
393 A74 £2.64 multi 8.75 8.75
394 A74 £3.02 multi 10.00 10.00
a. Sheet of 12, #383-394 37.00 37.00
Nos. 383-394 (12) 37.05 37.05

Fungi — A75

Designs: No. 395, 54p, Entoloma sp. No. 396, 54p, Lentinus sp. No. 397, 90p, Leucocoprinus sp. No. 398, 90p, Pycnoporus sp.

2009, Dec. 7 *Perf. 13¼*

395-398 A75 Set of 4 14.50 14.50

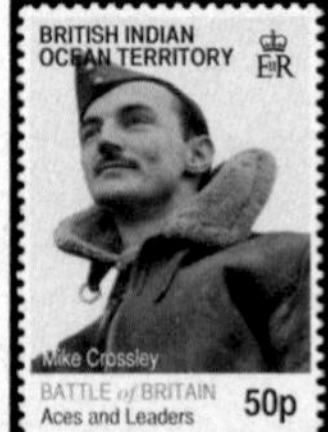

Battle of Britain, 70th Anniv. — A76

British leaders and aces: No. 399, 50p, Mike Crossley. No. 400, 50p, Bob Doe. No. 401, 50p, Sir Hugh Dowding. No. 402, 50p, Ginger Lacey. No. 403, 50p, Eric Lock. No. 404, 50p, Bob Stanford Tuck.

£1.50, Sir Douglas Bader.

Perf. 12¾x13

2010, Mar. 18 Litho. Wmk. 406

399-404 A76 Set of 6 9.50 9.50

Souvenir Sheet

405 A76 £1.50 black & gray 5.25 5.25

Nos. 399-405 each were printed in sheets of 6.

Souvenir Sheet

Great Britain No. 161 — A77

2010, May 8 *Perf. 14*

406 A77 £1.50 multi 5.25 5.25

Accession to throne of King George V, cent.; London 2010 Intl. Stamp Exhibition.

Battles and Sieges A78

Designs: No. 407, 50p, Battle of Hastings, 1066. No. 408, 50p, Battle of Agincourt, 1415. No. 409, 50p, Battle of Bosworth, 1485. No. 410, 50p, Battle of Naseby, 1645. No. 411, 50p, Battle of Culloden, 1746. No. 412, 50p, Battle of Waterloo, 1815. No. 413, 50p, Battle of the Alma, 1854. No. 414, 50p, Battle of Rorke's Drift, 1879. No. 415, 50p, Siege of Mafeking, 1899. No. 416, 50p, Battle of the Somme, 1916. No. 417, 50p, Battle of El Alamein, 1942. No. 418, 50p, Normandy Landings, 1944.

Wmk. 406

2010, Sept. 30 Litho. *Perf. 13¼*

407-418 A78 Set of 12 21.00 21.00

Service of Queen Elizabeth II and Prince Philip — A79

Designs: No. 419, 54p, Queen Elizabeth II. No. 420, 54p, Queen and Prince Philip, black-and-white photograph, Queen at left. No. 421, 54p, Queen and Prince Philip, black-and-white photograph, Queen at right. No. 422, 54p, Queen and Prince Philip, color photograph, Queen at left. No. 423, 54p, Queen and Prince Philip, color photograph, Queen at right. No. 424, 54p, Prince Philip.

£3.02, Queen and Prince Philip, diff.

Perf. 13¼

2011, Mar. 1 Litho. Unwmk.

419-424 A79 Set of 6 12.00 12.00
424a Sheet of 6, #419-424, + 3 labels 12.00 12.00

Souvenir Sheet

425 A79 £3.02 multi 11.00 11.00

Souvenir Sheet

Wedding of Prince William and Catherine Middleton — A80

Perf. 14¾x14

2011, Apr. 29 Wmk. 406

426 A80 £3 multi 11.00 11.00

Wedding of Prince William and Catherine Middleton — A81

Designs: No. 427, 54p, Couple in carriage waving. No. 428, 54p, Couple kissing, vert. No. 429, 90p, Couple in car after wedding. No. 430, 90p, Couple holding hands, vert.

Wmk. 406

2011, Aug. 1 Litho. *Perf. 12½*

427-430 A81 Set of 4 9.50 9.50

Royal British Legion, 90th Anniv. A82

Poppy at left and: No. 431, 50p, Poppies on crosses. No. 432, 50p, Lines from poem "In Flanders Fields," poppy field. No. 433, 50p, Shadow of soldier, Glorious Dead Cenotaph, London. No. 434, 50p, War graves. No. 435, 50p, Poppy drop. No. 436, 50p, Poppy appeal. No. 437, 50p, Ex-servicemen. No. 438, 50p, Festival of Remembrance. £1.50, Soldiers and sailors at attention.

Perf. 13¼x13½

2011, Nov. 11 Wmk. 406

431-438 A82 Set of 8 12.50 12.50

Souvenir Sheet

439 A82 £1.50 multi 4.75 4.75

Reign of Queen Elizabeth II, 60th Anniv. — A83

Queen Elizabeth II wearing: No. 440, 54p, Pearl necklace, no tiara (black-and-white photograph). No. 441, 54p, Blue hat (color photograph). No. 442, 54p, Red dress (color photograph). No. 443, 54p, Tiara and necklace (color photograph). No. 444, 54p, Tiara (black-and-white photograph). No. 445, 54p, Eyeglasses (color photograph).

£3.02, Queen Elizabeth II wearing red dress, diff.

2012, Feb. 6 *Perf. 13¼*

440-445 A83 Set of 6 10.50 10.50
445a Souvenir sheet of 6, #440-445 10.50 10.50

Souvenir Sheet

446 A83 £3.02 multi 9.75 9.75

BRUNEI

'brü-ˌnī

LOCATION — On the northwest coast of Borneo
GOVT. — Independent state
AREA — 2,226 sq. mi.
POP. — 322,982 (1999 est.)
CAPITAL — Bandar Seri Begawan

Brunei became a British protectorate in 1888. A treaty between the sultan and the British Government in 1979 provided for independence in 1983.

100 Cents (Sen) = 1 Dollar

Catalogue values for unused stamps in this country are for Never Hinged items, beginning with Scott 62.

Watermarks

Wmk. 385 — CARTOR

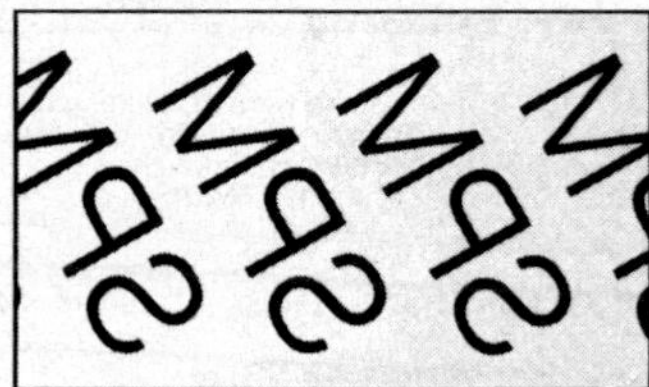

Wmk. 388 — Multiple "SPM"

Syncopated Perforation

Type A (first stamp #555): On 2 longer sides, oval holes equal in width to 3 holes which are the 11th hole from the top and 10th hole from the bottom.

Labuan Stamps of 1902-03 Overprinted or Surcharged in Red

1906 Unwmk. *Perf. 12 to 16*

1 A38 1c violet & blk 47.50 *65.00*
a. Black overprint *2,500. 3,000.*
2 A38 2c on 3c brn & blk 6.50 *19.00*
a. "BRUNEI." double *4,500. 3,000.*
b. "TWO CENTS." double *6,500.*
3 A38 2c on 8c org & blk 32.50 *80.00*
a. "TWO CENTS." double *13,000.*
b. "TWO CENTS." omitted, in pair with normal *14,500.*
4 A38 3c brown & blk 38.50 *100.00*
5 A38 4c on 12c yel & black 7.00 *6.00*
6 A38 5c on 16c org brn & green 55.00 *90.00*
7 A38 8c orange & blk 14.00 *37.50*
8 A38 10c on 16c org brn & green 7.75 *26.00*
9 A38 25c on 16c org brn & green 125.00 *150.00*
10 A38 30c on 16c org brn & green 125.00 *150.00*
11 A38 50c on 16c org brn & green 125.00 *150.00*
12 A38 $1 on 8c org & blk 125.00 *150.00*
Nos. 1-12 (12) 708.75 *1,023.*

The 25c surcharge reads: "25 CENTS."

Scene on Brunei River — A1

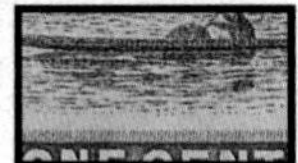
Type I

Type II

Two Types of 1908 1c, 3c:
Type I — Dots form bottom line of water shading. (Double plate.)
Type II — Dots removed. (Single plate.)

1907-21 Engr. Wmk. 3 *Perf. 14*

No.	Type	Description	Unused	Used
13	A1	1c yel green & blk	2.75	*13.00*
14	A1	1c green (II) ('08)	.70	*2.50*
a.		Type I ('19)	1.00	*2.75*
15	A1	2c red & black	3.75	*5.25*
16	A1	2c brn & blk ('11)	4.75	*1.50*
17	A1	3c red brn & blk	12.50	*26.00*
18	A1	3c car (I) ('08)	7.25	1.75
a.		Type II ('17)	120.00	*45.00*
19	A1	4c lilac & blk	9.00	*12.00*
20	A1	4c claret ('12)	5.75	.90
21	A1	5c ultra & blk	60.00	*110.00*
22	A1	5c org & blk ('08)	8.50	8.50
23	A1	5c orange ('16)	19.00	25.00
24	A1	8c orange & blk	9.00	*27.50*
25	A1	8c blue ('08)	8.50	*13.00*
26	A1	8c ultra ('16)	7.25	*32.50*
27	A1	10c dk green & blk	5.25	*9.00*
28	A1	10c violet, *yel* ('12)	4.50	2.10
29	A1	25c yel brn & blue	37.50	*57.50*
30	A1	25c violet ('12)	6.75	*22.50*
31	A1	30c black & pur	30.00	26.00
32	A1	30c org & red vio ('12)	11.00	*14.50*
33	A1	50c brown & grn	18.00	*27.50*
34	A1	50c blk, *grn* ('12)	32.50	*77.50*
35	A1	50c blk, *grnsh bl* ('21)	10.00	*42.50*
36	A1	$1 slate & red	72.50	*110.00*
37	A1	$1 red & blk, *bl* ('12)	25.00	*57.50*
38	A1	$5 lake, *grn* ('08)	200.00	*300.00*
39	A1	$25 blk, *red* ('08)	650.00	*1,200.*
		Nos. 13-38 (26)	611.70	*1,026.*

Used value for No. 39 is for a canceled-to-order example dated before December 1941. CTOs dated later are worth about half the value given.

Stamps of 1908-21 Overprinted in Four Lines in Black

1922

No.	Type	Description	Unused	Used
14b	A1	1c green	7.75	*42.50*
16a	A1	2c brown & black	7.75	*50.00*
18b	A1	3c carmine	8.75	*55.00*
20a	A1	4c claret	15.50	*60.00*
23a	A1	5c orange	21.00	*65.00*
28a	A1	10c violet, *yellow*	8.00	*65.00*
30a	A1	25c violet	17.00	*100.00*
35a	A1	50c greenish blue	60.00	*175.00*
37a	A1	$1 red & black, *blue*	90.00	*225.00*
		Nos. 14b-37a (9)	235.75	*837.50*

Industrial fair, Singapore, Mar. 31-Apr. 15

Type of 1907 Issue

1924-37 Wmk. 4

No.	Type	Description	Unused	Used
43	A1	1c black ('26)	1.25	.90
44	A1	2c deep brown	1.25	*9.00*
45	A1	2c green ('33)	2.40	1.25
46	A1	3c green	1.25	*7.75*
47	A1	4c claret brown	1.75	1.50
48	A1	4c orange ('29)	2.40	1.25
49	A1	5c orange	8.25	2.00
50	A1	5c lt gray ('31)	21.00	14.00
51	A1	5c brown ('33)	21.00	1.20
52	A1	8c ultra ('27)	7.25	6.00
53	A1	8c gray ('33)	19.00	.90
54	A1	10c violet, *yel* ('37)	21.00	*32.50*
55	A1	25c dk violet ('31)	14.00	*15.00*
56	A1	30c org & red vio ('31)	25.00	*19.00*
57	A1	50c black, *grn* ('31)	13.00	*17.50*
58	A1	$1 red & blk, *bl* ('31)	29.00	*90.00*
		Nos. 43-58 (16)	188.80	*219.75*

For overprints see Nos. N1-N20.

Dwellings in Town of Brunei
A2

1924-31

No.	Type	Description	Unused	Used
59	A2	6c black	17.00	12.00
60	A2	6c red ('31)	8.00	*13.00*
61	A2	12c blue	5.50	*11.00*
		Nos. 59-61 (3)	30.50	*36.00*

See note after Nos. N1-N19.

Catalogue values for unused stamps in this section, from this point to the end of the section, are for Never Hinged items.

Types of 1907-24

1947-51 Engr. *Perf. 14*

No.	Type	Description	Unused	Used
62	A1	1c brown	.65	*2.50*
63	A1	2c gray	.75	*6.00*
a.		Perf. 14½x13½ ('50)	2.40	*5.25*
64	A2	3c dark green	1.20	*6.50*
65	A1	5c deep orange	1.00	*1.75*
a.		Perf. 14½x13½ ('50)	4.75	*17.00*
66	A2	6c gray black	1.25	*6.00*
67	A1	8c scarlet	.60	*1.50*
a.		Perf. 13 ('51)	.65	*10.00*
68	A1	10c violet	2.25	.40
a.		Perf. 14½x13½ ('50)	2.40	6.50
69	A1	15c brt ultra	2.10	*.90*
70	A1	25c red violet	3.25	1.25
a.		Perf. 14½x13½ ('51)	3.50	*11.00*
71	A1	30c dp org & gray blk	3.00	1.25
a.		Perf. 14½x13½ ('51)	2.40	*16.00*
72	A1	50c black	4.75	1.00
a.		Perf. 13 ('50)	2.10	*19.00*
73	A1	$1 scar & gray blk	12.00	.90
74	A1	$5 red org & grn ('48)	20.00	*22.50*
75	A1	$10 dp claret & gray blk ('48)	85.00	35.00
		Nos. 62-75 (14)	137.80	*87.45*

Sultan Ahmed and Pile Dwellings
A3

1949, Sept. 22 Wmk. 4 *Perf. 13*

No.	Type	Description	Unused	Used
76	A3	8c car & black	1.50	1.50
77	A3	25c red orange & pur	1.50	*1.90*
78	A3	50c blue & black	1.50	*1.90*
		Nos. 76-78 (3)	4.50	5.30

25th anniv. of the reign of Sultan Ahmed Tajudin Akhazul Khair Wad-din.

Common Design Types pictured following the introduction.

UPU Issue

Common Design Types

Engr.; Name Typo. on 15c and 25c

1949, Oct. 10 *Perf. 13½, 11x11½*

No.	Type	Description	Unused	Used
79	CD306	8c rose car	1.25	*1.75*
80	CD307	15c indigo	4.00	2.00
81	CD308	25c red lilac	1.25	*1.50*
82	CD309	50c slate	1.25	*1.50*
		Nos. 79-82 (4)	7.75	6.75

Sultan Omar Ali Saifuddin — A4

River Kampong
A5

Perf. 13½x13

1952, Mar. 1 Engr. Wmk. 4

Center in Black

No.	Type	Description	Unused	Used
83	A4	1c black	.25	.60
84	A4	2c red orange	.25	.60
85	A4	3c red brown	.25	.35
86	A4	4c green	.25	.25
87	A4	6c gray	.60	.25
88	A4	8c carmine	.60	.60
89	A4	10c olive brown	.25	.25
90	A4	12c violet	6.00	.25
91	A4	15c blue	4.00	.25
92	A4	25c purple	3.00	.25
93	A4	50c ultramarine	3.00	.35

Perf. 13

No.	Type	Description	Unused	Used
94	A5	$1 dull green	1.75	1.75
95	A5	$2 red	5.50	3.00
96	A5	$5 deep plum	22.50	8.50
		Nos. 83-96 (14)	48.20	17.25

See Nos. 101-114.

Mosque and Sultan Omar
A6

1958, Sept. 24 Wmk. 314 *Perf. 13*

Center in Black

No.	Type	Description	Unused	Used
97	A6	8c dull green	.25	*.70*
98	A6	15c carmine rose	.40	.25
99	A6	35c rose violet	.50	*1.10*
		Nos. 97-99 (3)	1.15	*2.05*

Opening of the Brunei Mosque.

Freedom from Hunger Issue

Common Design Type with Portrait of Sultan Omar

1963, June 4 Photo. *Perf. 14x14½*

No.	Type	Description	Unused	Used
100	CD314	12c sepia	3.25	2.25

Types of 1952 On Ordinary Paper

Wmk. 314 Upright

1964-70 Engr. *Perf. 13½x13*

Center in Black

No.	Type	Description	Unused	Used
101	A4	1c black	.60	*.90*
102	A4	2c red orange	1.75	.25
103	A4	3c red brown	1.75	.75
104	A4	4c green	.35	.25
105	A4	6c gray	3.50	.25
c.		6c black ('69)	9.00	*9.50*
106	A4	8c dk carmine	1.20	.25
107	A4	10c olive brown	.80	.25
108	A4	12c violet	1.75	.25
109	A4	15c blue	.65	.25
110	A4	25c purple	9.00	.25
111	A4	50c ultramarine	3.00	.25
b.		50c bright ultra ('69)	7.25	1.50

Perf. 13

No.	Type	Description	Unused	Used
112	A5	$1 dull green ('68)	3.50	*7.50*
		Nos. 101-112 (12)	27.85	11.40

On Whiter, Glazed Paper

Wmk. 314 Upright

1969-72 *Perf. 13½x13*

Center in Black

No.	Type	Description	Unused	Used
101a	A4	1c black ('69)	2.10	3.25
c.		1c slate gray ('72)	.25	*2.75*
102a	A4	2c red org ('70)	3.00	.25
103a	A4	3c red brn ('70)	3.00	.25
104a	A4	4c green ('70)	.60	.25
c.		4c emerald & black ('71)	1.75	*4.75*
105a	A4	6c gray ('69)	.40	.35
106a	A4	8c dk carmine ('70)	1.20	.25
c.		8c brownish red & black ('71)	4.00	*5.50*
107a	A4	10c olive brn ('70)	3.25	.25
c.		10c pale brn & gray ('71)	4.25	*5.00*
108a	A4	12c violet ('70)	15.00	1.20
109a	A4	15c blue ('69)	.75	.25
110a	A4	25c purple ('70)	17.00	7.75
c.		Reddish violet & black ('71)	18.00	1.50
111a	A4	50c br ultra ('70)	17.00	4.75
c.		50c indigo & gray ('71)	14.00	4.75

Perf. 13

No.	Type	Description	Unused	Used
112a	A5	$1 dull green ('70)	10.00	8.50
113	A5	$2 red ('70)	45.00	25.00
114	A5	$5 deep plum ('70)	55.00	42.50
		Nos. 101a-114 (14)	173.30	94.80

Wmk. 314 Sideways

1972-73 *Perf. 13½x13*

Center in Black

No.	Type	Description	Unused	Used
102b	A4	2c red orange	4.00	*12.50*
103b	A4	3c red brown	2.75	.65
104b	A4	4c green	.80	*1.50*
105b	A4	6c black	3.50	.55
106b	A4	8c dark carmine	5.25	*11.00*
107b	A4	10c olive brown	1.40	.75
108b	A4	12c violet	2.50	*3.75*
109b	A4	15c blue	2.75	*3.50*
		Nos. 102b-109b (8)	22.95	*34.20*

Issue dates: 2c, 8c, May 9, 1973, others, Nov. 17, 1972.

The following six sets are Common Design Types but with the portrait of Sultan Omar.

ITU Issue

Perf. 11x11½

1965, May 17 Litho. Wmk. 314

No.	Type	Description	Unused	Used
116	CD317	4c red lil & org brn	.25	.25
117	CD317	75c orange & emer	1.50	1.50

Intl. Cooperation Year Issue

1965, Oct. 25 *Perf. 14½*

No.	Type	Description	Unused	Used
118	CD318	4c blue grn & claret	.25	.25
119	CD318	15c lt violet & grn	.60	.60

Churchill Memorial Issue

1966, Jan. 24 Photo. *Perf. 14*

No.	Type	Description	Unused	Used
120	CD319	3c multicolored	.30	.25
121	CD319	10c multicolored	.85	.75
122	CD319	15c multicolored	1.60	1.50
123	CD319	75c multicolored	5.25	4.75
		Nos. 120-123 (4)	8.00	7.25

World Cup Soccer Issue

1966, July 4 Litho. *Perf. 14*

No.	Type	Description	Unused	Used
124	CD321	4c multicolored	.30	.25
125	CD321	75c multicolored	1.10	.75

WHO Headquarters Issue

1966, Sept. 20 Litho. *Perf. 14*

No.	Type	Description	Unused	Used
126	CD322	12c multicolored	.35	.25
127	CD322	25c multicolored	1.00	.75

UNESCO Anniversary Issue

1966, Dec. 1 Litho. Wmk. 314

No.	Type	Description	Unused	Used
128	CD323	4c "Education"	.50	.40
129	CD323	15c "Science"	1.25	1.00
130	CD323	75c "Culture"	3.25	*6.00*
		Nos. 128-130 (3)	5.00	*7.40*

State Religious Building and Sultan Hassanal Bolkiah
A7

1967, Dec. 19 Photo. *Perf. 12½*

No.	Type	Description	Unused	Used
131	A7	4c violet & multi	.25	.25
132	A7	10c red & multi	.25	.25
133	A7	25c orange & multi	.30	.30
134	A7	50c lt violet & multi	.45	.45
		Nos. 131-134 (4)	1.25	1.25

A three-stamp set (12c, 25c, 50c) showing views of the new Language and Communications Headquarters was prepared and announced for release in April, 1968. The Crown Agents distributed sample sets, but the stamps were not issued. Later, Nos. 144-146 were issued instead.

Sultan Hassanal Bolkiah, Brunei Mosque and Flags
A8

Sultan Hassanal Bolkiah Installation: 12c, Sultan, Mosque and flags, horiz.

Perf. 13x14, 14x13

1968, July 9 Photo. Unwmk.

No.	Type	Description	Unused	Used
135	A8	4c green & multi	.25	*.50*
136	A8	12c dp bister & multi	.35	*1.50*
137	A8	25c violet & multi	.85	*2.00*
		Nos. 135-137 (3)	1.45	*4.00*

Sultan Hassanal Bolkiah A9

Wmk. 314

1968, July 15 Litho. *Perf. 12*

138 A9 4c multicolored .25 *.35*
139 A9 12c multicolored .25 *.75*
140 A9 25c multicolored .50 *1.25*
Nos. 138-140 (3) 1.00 *2.35*

Sultan Hassanal Bolkiah's birthday.

Coronation of Sultan Hassanal Bolkiah, Aug. 1, 1968 — A10

1968, Aug. 1 Photo. *Perf. 14½x14*

141 A10 4c Prus blue & multi .25 .25
142 A10 12c rose lilac & multi .25 *.50*
143 A10 25c multicolored .55 *.90*
Nos. 141-143 (3) 1.05 *1.65*

A11

Hall of Language and Culture — A12

Perf. 13½, 12½x13½ (A12)

1968, Sept. 29 Photo. Wmk. 314

144 A11 10c blue grn & multi .30 *1.90*
145 A12 15c ocher & multi .30 *.40*
146 A12 30c ultra & multi .60 *1.00*
Nos. 144-146 (3) 1.20 *3.30*

Opening of the Hall of Language and Culture and of the Broadcasting and Information Department Building. Nos. 144-146 are overprinted "1968" and 4 bars over the 1967 date. They were not issued without this overprint.

Human Rights Flame and Struggling Man — A13

Unwmk.

1968, Dec. 16 Litho. *Perf. 14*

147 A13 12c green, yel & blk .25 .25
148 A13 25c ultra, yel & blk .25 .25
149 A13 75c dk plum, yel & blk .55 *2.00*
Nos. 147-149 (3) 1.05 *2.50*

International Human Rights Year.

Sultan and WHO Emblem A14

1968, Dec. 19 Litho. *Perf. 14*

150 A14 4c lt blue, org & blk .30 .30
151 A14 15c brt purple, org & blk .45 *.65*
152 A14 25c olive, org & blk .90 *1.25*
Nos. 150-152 (3) 1.65 *2.20*

20th anniv. of the WHO.

Sultan Hassanal Bolkiah, Pengiran Shahbandar and Oil Rig — A15

Perf. 14x13

1969, July 10 Photo. Wmk. 314

153 A15 12c green & multi .85 .50
154 A15 40c dk rose brn & multi 1.25 *2.00*
155 A15 50c violet & multi 1.75 *2.00*
Nos. 153-155 (3) 3.85 *4.50*

Installation of Pengiran Shahbandar as Second Minister (Di-Galong Sahibol Mal).

Royal Assembly Hall and Council Chamber — A16

Design: 50c, Front view of buildings.

Unwmk.

1969, Sept. 23 Litho. *Perf. 15*

156 A16 12c multicolored .25 .25
157 A16 25c multicolored .30 *.50*
158 A16 50c violet & pink .75 *2.75*
Nos. 156-158 (3) 1.30 *3.50*

Opening of the Royal Assembly Hall and Council Chamber.

Youth Center — A17

1969, Dec. 20 Litho. Wmk. 314

159 A17 6c lt org, blk & dull vio .25 *1.00*
160 A17 10c cit, blk & dl Prus grn .30 .25
161 A17 30c yel green, blk & brn .75 *1.00*
Nos. 159-161 (3) 1.30 *2.25*

Opening of Youth Center, Mar. 15, 1969.

Helicopter and Emblem — A18

Designs: 10c, Soldier and emblem, vert. 75c, Patrol boat and emblem.

1971, May 31 Litho. *Perf. 14*

162 A18 10c green & multi .90 .35
163 A18 15c Prus blue & multi 2.10 .80
164 A18 75c lt ultra & multi 4.50 *7.50*
Nos. 162-164 (3) 7.50 *8.65*

10th anniv. of Royal Brunei Malay Reg.

50th Anniv. of the Royal Brunei Police Force — A19

1971, Aug. 14 *Perf. 14½*

165 A19 10c Superintendent .55 .50
166 A19 15c Constable .90 .75
167 A19 50c Traffic policeman 2.75 *6.25*
Nos. 165-167 (3) 4.20 *7.50*

Sultan, Heir Apparent and View of Brunei — A20

Portraits and: 25c, View of Brunei with Mosque. 50c, Mosque and banner.

1971, Aug. 27 Litho. Wmk. 314

168 A20 15c multicolored .45 .25
169 A20 25c multicolored .80 *1.00*
170 A20 50c multicolored 1.50 *5.25*
Nos. 168-170 (3) 2.75 *6.50*

Installation of Sultan Hassanal Bolkiah's brother Muda Omar Ali Saifuddin as heir apparent (Perdana Wazir).

Brass and Copper Goods A21

Designs: 12c, Basketware. 15c, Leather goods. 25c, Silverware. 50c, Brunei Museum.

1972, Feb. 29 *Perf. 13½x14*

Size: 37x21mm

Portrait in Black

171 A21 10c brn, sal & yel grn .40 .40
172 A21 12c org, yel & green .50 .50
173 A21 15c dk grn, emer & org .55 .55
174 A21 25c brown, org & slate 1.60 1.60

Size: 58x21mm

175 A21 50c dull blue & multi 3.25 *6.00*
Nos. 171-175 (5) 6.30 *9.05*

Opening of Brunei Museum.

Queen Elizabeth II, Sultan and View — A22

Queen Elizabeth II, Sultan Hassanal Bolkiah and: 15c, View of Brunei. 25c, Mosque and barge. 50c, Royal Assembly Hall.

1972, Feb. 29 Photo. *Perf. 13x13½*

176 A22 10c lt brown & multi .85 .45
177 A22 15c lt blue & multi .90 .90
178 A22 25c lt green & multi 2.40 2.25
179 A22 50c dull purple & multi 4.50 *7.75*
Nos. 176-179 (4) 8.65 *11.35*

Visit of Queen Elizabeth II, Feb. 29.

Bangunan Secretariat (Government Buildings) — A23

Sultans Omar Ali Saifuddin and Hassanal Bolkiah: 15c, Istana Darul Hana (Sultan's residence). 25c, View of capital. 50c, View of new Mosque.

1972, Oct. 4 Litho. *Perf. 13½*

180 A23 10c org, blk & green .40 .40
181 A23 15c green & multi .55 .55
182 A23 25c ultra & multi .90 .90
183 A23 50c rose red & multi 2.00 *2.50*
Nos. 180-183 (4) 3.85 *4.35*

Change of capital's name from Brunei to Bandar Seri Begawan, Oct. 4, 1970.

Beverley Plane Landing — A24

Design: 25c, Blackburn Beverley plane dropping supplies by parachute, vert.

Perf. 14x13½, 13½x14

1972, Nov. 15 Litho.

184 A24 25c blue & multi 2.50 2.00
185 A24 75c ultra & multi 5.50 5.25

Opening of Royal Air Force Museum, Hendon, London.

Silver Wedding Issue, 1972

Common Design Type

Design: Queen Elizabeth II, Prince Philip; girl and boy with traditional gifts.

1972, Nov. 20 Photo. *Perf. 14x14½*

186 CD324 12c multi .25 .25
187 CD324 75c multi .40 *.60*

INTERPOL Emblem and Headquarters, Paris — A25

Design: 50c, similar to 25c.

1973, Sept. 7 Litho. *Perf. 14x14½*

188 A25 25c emerald & multi 1.90 1.25
189 A25 50c multicolored 2.10 1.50

50th anniv. of Intl. Criminal Police Org. (INTERPOL).

Princess Anne and Mark Phillips — A26

1973, Nov. 14 Litho. *Perf. 13½*

190 A26 25c vio blue & multi .25 .25
191 A26 50c red lilac & multi .35 .35

Wedding of Princess Anne and Capt. Mark Phillips, Nov. 14, 1973.

Churchill Painting Outdoors A27

Sultan Hassanal Bolkiah A28

Design: 50c, Churchill making "V" sign.

Perf. 14x13½

1973, Dec. 31 Litho. Wmk. 314

192 A27 12c car rose & multi .25 .25
193 A27 50c dk green & multi .55 1.50

Winston Churchill Memorial Exhibition.

Wmk. 314 Sideways

1974, July 15 Photo. *Perf. 13x15*

194 A28 4c blue grn & multi .25 *.25*
195 A28 5c dull blue & multi .25 *.35*
196 A28 6c olive grn & multi 4.00 *7.50*
197 A28 10c lt violet & multi .35 *.25*
b. Watermark upright ('76) 4.25 1.75
198 A28 15c brown & multi 3.00 *.50*
199 A28 20c buff & multi .35 *.25*
b. Watermark upright ('76) 4.25 4.25
200 A28 25c olive & multi .45 *.25*
b. Watermark upright ('76) 4.25 *4.25*
201 A28 30c multicolored .45 *.25*
202 A28 35c gray & multi .45 *.25*
203 A28 40c multicolored .45 *.25*
204 A28 50c yel brn & multi .45 *.25*
205 A28 75c multicolored .70 *4.25*
206 A28 $1 dull org & multi 1.75 *4.25*
207 A28 $2 multicolored 2.75 *13.00*
208 A28 $5 silver & multi 3.50 *21.00*
209 A28 $10 gold & multi 6.00 *37.50*
Nos. 194-209 (16) 25.15 *90.35*

Issue date: Nos. 197b-200b, Apr. 12.

1975, Aug. 13 Wmk. 373

194a A28 4c .35 *2.75*
195a A28 5c .35 *2.75*
196a A28 6c 6.00 *7.50*
197a A28 10c .35 *.25*
Complete booklet, 4 x #195a, 8 x #197a 6.00
198a A28 15c .65 *2.00*
199a A28 20c .65 *1.75*
200a A28 25c .75 *1.75*
201a A28 30c .65 *2.25*
202a A28 35c .45 *2.25*
203a A28 40c .60 *2.50*
204a A28 50c 1.00 *.75*
205a A28 75c .90 *3.75*
206a A28 $1 1.75 *3.75*
207a A28 $2 4.75 *10.00*
208a A28 $5 6.00 *20.00*
209a A28 $10 30.00 *37.50*
Nos. 194a-209a (16) 55.20 *101.50*

For surcharge see No. 225.

Brunei Airport A29

Design: 75c, Sultan Hassanal Bolkiah in uniform and jet over airport.

Perf. 14x14½, 12½x13 (75c)

1974, July 18 Litho. Wmk. 314

Size: 44x28mm

215 A29 50c multicolored 1.40 1.00

Size: 47x36mm

216 A29 75c multicolored 1.60 1.40

Opening of Brunei Airport.

UPU Emblem A30

1974, Oct. 28 *Perf. 14½*

217 A30 12c orange & multi .25 .25
218 A30 50c blue & multi .50 *1.50*
219 A30 75c emerald & multi .75 *1.75*
Nos. 217-219 (3) 1.50 *3.50*

Centenary of Universal Postal Union.

Winston Churchill A31

Design: 75c, Churchill smoking cigar.

1974, Nov. 30 Wmk. 373 *Perf. 14*

220 A31 12c vio blue, blue & gold .25 .25
221 A31 75c dk green, black & gold 1.00 1.50

Sir Winston Churchill (1874-1965).

Boeing 737 Planes at Airport A32

Designs: 35c, Boeing 737 over Bandar Seri Begawan Mosque. 75c, Boeing 737 in flight. All planes with crest of Royal Brunei Airlines.

Perf. 12½x12

1975, May 14 Unwmk.

222 A32 12c multicolored .85 .30
223 A32 35c multicolored 2.25 *3.50*
224 A32 75c multicolored 4.00 *4.75*
Nos. 222-224 (3) 7.10 *8.55*

Inauguration of Royal Brunei Airlines.

No. 196a Surcharged in Silver

Perf. 13x15

1976, Aug. 16 Photo. Wmk. 373

225 A28 10c on 6c multicolored 3.50 3.50
a. 10c on 6c, wmk 314 sideways (#196) 5.00 3.50

British Royal Coat of Arms — A33

20c, Imperial State Crown. 75c, Elizabeth II.

Wmk. 373

1977, June 7 Litho. *Perf. 14*

226 A33 10c dk blue & multi .25 .25
227 A33 20c purple & multi .25 .25
228 A33 75c yellow & multi .65 .65
Nos. 226-228 (3) 1.15 1.15

25th anniv. of the reign of Elizabeth II.

Coronation of Elizabeth II A34

20c, Elizabeth II with coronation regalia. 75c, Departure from Westminster Abbey (coach).

1978, June 2 Litho. *Perf. 13½x13*

229 A34 10c multicolored .25 .25
230 A34 20c multicolored .25 .25
231 A34 75c multicolored .60 *.90*
Nos. 229-231 (3) 1.10 *1.40*

25th anniv. of coronation of Elizabeth II.

Sultan's Coat of Arms — A35

Coronation of Sultan Hassanal Bolkiah, 10th Anniv.: 20c, Ceremony. 75c, Royal crown.

1978, Aug. 1 Wmk. 373 *Perf. 12*

232 A35 10c multicolored .25 .25
233 A35 20c multicolored .45 .25
234 A35 75c multicolored 1.25 *3.50*
a. Souvenir sheet of 3, #232-234 19.00 *22.50*
Nos. 232-234 (3) 1.95 *4.00*

Struggling Man, Human Rights Flame — A36

1978, Dec. 10 Litho. *Perf. 14*

235 A36 10c red, black & yel .25 .25
236 A36 20c violet, black & yel .25 .25
237 A36 75c olive, black & yel .70 *3.00*
Nos. 235-237 (3) 1.20 *3.50*

Universal Declaration of Human Rights, 30th anniversary.

Children and IYC Emblem A37

1979, June 30 Wmk. 373 *Perf. 14*

238 A37 10c shown .25 .25
239 A37 $1 IYC emblem 1.40 *2.75*

Telisai Earth Satellite Station A38

Designs: 20c, Radar screen and satellite. 75c, Cameraman, telex operator, telephone.

1979, Sept. 23 Litho. *Perf. 14½x14*

240 A38 10c multicolored .25 .25
241 A38 20c multicolored .45 *.55*
242 A38 75c multicolored .90 *3.25*
Nos. 240-242 (3) 1.60 *4.05*

Hajeer Emblem — A39

1979, Nov. 21

243 A39 10c multicolored .25 .25
244 A39 20c multicolored .35 .35
245 A39 75c multicolored .85 *2.25*
a. Souvenir sheet of 3, #243-245 6.50 *8.00*
Nos. 243-245 (3) 1.45 *2.85*

Hegira, 1400th anniversary.

A40

A41

1980 Litho. *Perf. 14*

246 A40 10c Installation ceremony .25 .25
247 A40 10c Ceremony, diff. .25 .25
248 A40 75c Jefri Bolkiah 1.00 *2.50*
249 A40 75c Sufri Bolkiah 1.00 *2.25*
Nos. 246-249 (4) 2.50 *5.25*

Installation of Jefri Bolkiah and Sufri Bolkiah as Wizars (Ministers of State for Royalty) 1st anniv. Issued: Nos. 246, 248, 11/8; others, 12/6.

1981, Jan. 19 Litho. *Perf. 12x11½*

255 A41 10c Umbrella .45 .45
256 A41 15c Dagger, shield .45 .45
257 A41 20c Spears .50 .50
258 A41 30c Gold pouch .75 .75

Size: 22½x40mm

Perf. 14x13½

259 A41 50c Headdress 1.40 *5.00*
a. Souvenir sheet of 5, #255-259 6.75 *8.00*
Nos. 255-259 (5) 3.55 *7.15*

A42

A43

1981, May 17 Litho. *Perf. 13x13½*

260 A42 10c car rose & black .70 .30
261 A42 75c dp violet & black 2.75 5.00

13th World Telecommunications Day.

Perf. 12½x12, 12 (75c)

1981, July 15 Litho.

Deep Rose Lilac Background

262 A43 10c Dagger, case .35 .30
263 A43 15c Rifle, powder pouch .35 .30
264 A43 20c Spears .35 .30
265 A43 30c Sword, tunic, shield .50 .45
266 A43 50c Horns .85 *2.50*

Size: 28½x45mm

267 A43 75c Gold bowl, table 1.50 *4.75*
Nos. 262-267 (6) 3.90 *8.60*

See Nos. 278-289.

Royal Wedding Issue
Common Design Type

1981, July 29 ***Perf. 14***

268 CD331 10c Bouquet .25 .25
269 CD331 $1 Charles .65 *1.50*
270 CD331 $2 Couple 1.25 *2.75*
Nos. 268-270 (3) 2.15 *4.50*

World Food Day — A44

Intl. Year of the Disabled — A45

1981, Oct. 16 **Litho.** ***Perf. 12***

271 A44 10c Fishermen 1.25 .25
272 A44 $1 Produce 6.00 *8.00*

1981, Dec. 16 **Wmk. 373** ***Perf. 12***

273 A45 10c Blind man .90 .30
274 A45 20c Sign language 1.75 1.00
275 A45 75c Man in wheelchair 3.50 *7.00*
Nos. 273-275 (3) 6.15 *8.30*

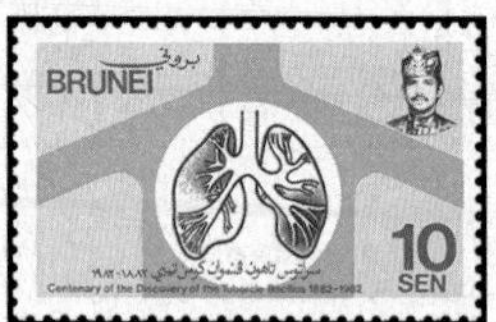

TB Bacillus Centenary — A46

1982, Mar. 24 ***Perf. 12, 13½ (75c)***

276 A46 10c Lungs .75 .35
277 A46 75c Bacillus, microscope 3.75 *5.75*

Type of 1981

1982, May 31 **Litho.** ***Perf. 12½x12***

Deep Magenta Background

278 A43 10c shown .35 .30
279 A43 15c Pedestal urn .35 .30
280 A43 20c Silver bowl .35 .30
281 A43 30c Candle .75 *.90*
282 A43 50c Gold pipe 1.10 *2.75*

Size: 28x44mm

Perf. 13½

283 A43 75c Silver pointer 1.50 *4.25*
Nos. 278-283 (6) 4.40 *8.80*

1982, July 15 **Litho.** ***Perf. 12½x12***

Violet Background

284 A43 10c Urn .35 .30
285 A43 15c Crossed banners .70 .60
286 A43 20c Golden fan .80 .60
287 A43 30c Lid .90 *1.75*
288 A43 50c Sword, sheath 2.00 *3.75*

Size: 28x44mm

Perf. 12

289 A43 75c Golden chalice pole 2.50 *4.75*
Nos. 284-289 (6) 7.25 *11.75*

A47

1983, Mar. 14 **Litho.** ***Perf. 13½***

290 A47 10c Flag .25 *.75*
291 A47 20c Omar Ali Saifuddin Mosque .35 *.85*
292 A47 75c Oil well 1.50 *1.25*
293 A47 $2 Sultan Bolkiah 4.25 4.25
a. Block of 4, #290-293 6.00 *7.00*

Commonwealth Day.

World Communications Year — A48

1983, July 15 **Litho.** ***Perf. 13½***

294 A48 10c Mail delivery .25 .25
295 A48 75c Teletype, phone 1.25 *1.40*
296 A48 $2 Dish antenna, satellite, TV 3.25 *3.50*
Nos. 294-296 (3) 4.75 5.15

Opening of Hassanal Bolkiah National Stadium — A49

1983, Sept. 23 **Litho.** ***Perf. 12***

297 A49 10c Soccer, vert. .75 .25
298 A49 75c Runners, vert. 2.75 2.75
299 A49 $1 shown 3.50 4.50
Nos. 297-299 (3) 7.00 7.50

Size, Nos. 297-298: 26x33mm.

Fishing Industry — A50

1983, Sept. 23 **Litho.** ***Perf. 13½***

300 A50 10c Shrimp, lobster 1.60 .25
301 A50 50c Pacific jacks 4.50 2.10
302 A50 75c Parrotfish, flatfish 4.50 *4.75*
303 A50 $1 Tuna 5.00 *6.00*
Nos. 300-303 (4) 15.60 *13.10*

State Assembly Building — A51

Map of Southeast Asia, Flag — A52

Sultan Hassanal Bolkiah — A53

1984, Jan. 1 **Litho.** ***Perf. 13***

304 A51 10c shown .25 .25
305 A51 20c State Secretariat building .50 .25
306 A51 35c New Law Court .90 .75
307 A51 50c Liquid natural gas well 2.00 1.50
308 A51 75c Omar Ali Saifuddin Mosque 2.25 2.00
309 A51 $1 Sultan's Palace 2.50 2.50
310 A52 $3 shown 7.75 7.50
a. Souvenir sheet of 7, #304-310 17.50 17.50
Nos. 304-310 (7) 16.15 14.75

Souvenir Sheets

311 Sheet of 4, Constitution signing, 1959 3.25 *4.75*
a.-d. A53 25c any single .60 *.75*
312 Sheet of 4, Brunei U.K. Friendship Agreement, 1979 3.25 *4.75*
a.-d. A53 25c any single .60 *.75*

Forestry Resources — A54

1984, Apr. 21 **Litho.** ***Perf. 13½***

313 A54 10c Forests, enrichment planting 1.50 .35
314 A54 50c Water resources 3.50 2.75
315 A54 75c Recreation forest 4.75 4.75
316 A54 $1 Wildlife 7.25 8.00
Nos. 313-316 (4) 17.00 *15.85*

Philakorea 1984 — A55

Litho. & Engr.

1984, Oct. 22 ***Perf. 13***

317 A55 10c No. 93 .75 .25
a. Souvenir sheet of 1 .90 .90
318 A55 75c No. 27 2.00 2.75
a. Souvenir sheet of 1 2.25 2.00
319 A55 $2 1895 local stamp 5.00 *8.00*
a. Souvenir sheet of 1 5.00 4.75
Nos. 317-319 (3) 7.75 *11.00*

Brunei Admission to Intl. Organizations A56

1985, Sept. 23 **Litho.** ***Perf. 13***

320 A56 50c UN 1.00 1.00
321 A56 50c Commonwealth 1.00 1.00
322 A56 50c ASEAN 1.00 1.00
323 A56 50c OIC 1.00 1.00
a. Souv. sheet, #320-323 + label 7.50 *8.00*
Nos. 320-323 (4) 4.00 4.00

Intl. Youth Year A57

1985, Oct. 17 ***Perf. 12***

324 A57 10c shown 1.75 1.50
325 A57 75c Industry, education 6.50 6.50
326 A57 $1 Public Service 7.50 7.50
Nos. 324-326 (3) 15.75 15.50

Intl. Day of Solidarity with the Palestinian People A58

1985, Nov. 29 ***Perf. 12x12½***

327 A58 10c lt blue & multi 2.75 .25
328 A58 50c pink & multi 4.50 2.00
329 A58 $1 lt green & multi 7.25 7.25
Nos. 327-329 (3) 14.50 9.50

Natl. Scout Jamboree, Dec. 14-20 — A59

Sultan Hassanal Bolkiah — A60

1985, Dec. 14 ***Perf. 13½***

330 A59 10c Scout handshake .75 .25
331 A59 20c Semaphore 1.25 .50
332 A59 $2 Jamboree emblem 4.75 4.50
Nos. 330-332 (3) 6.75 5.25

1985-86 **Wmk. 233** ***Perf. 13½x14½***

333 A60 10c multi .25 .25
334 A60 15c multi .25 .25
Complete booklet, 4 ea. #333, 334 3.00
335 A60 20c multi .25 .25
336 A60 25c multi .30 .30
337 A60 35c multi ('86) .40 .40
338 A60 40c multi ('86) .45 .45
339 A60 50c multi ('86) .55 .55
340 A60 75c multi ('86) .85 .85

Size: 35x42mm

Perf. 14

341 A60 $1 multi ('86) 1.25 1.25
342 A60 $2 multi ('86) 3.00 *3.00*
343 A60 $5 multi ('86) 5.75 *7.00*
344 A60 $10 multi ('86) 11.50 *15.00*
Nos. 333-344 (12) 24.80 *29.55*

Issued: Nos. 333-336, Dec. 23; Nos. 337-340, Jan. 15; Nos. 341-343, Feb. 23; No. 344, Mar. 29.

Admission to Intl. Organizations A61

Wmk. Carter (385)

1986, Apr. 30 **Litho.** ***Perf. 13***

345 A61 50c WMO .75 .75
346 A61 50c ITU .75 .75
347 A61 50c UPU .75 .75
348 A61 50c ICAO .75 .75
a. Souv. sheet, #345-348 + label 7.00 7.00
Nos. 345-348 (4) 3.00 *3.00*

Royal Brunei Armed Forces, 25th Anniv. A62

1986, May 31 Unwmk. *Perf. 13½*

349 Strip of 4 25.00 25.00
a. A62 10c In combat 4.75 4.75
b. A62 20c Communications 5.25 5.25
c. A62 50c Air and sea defense 6.75 6.75
d. A62 75c On parade, Royal Palace 8.25 8.25

Royal Ensigns — A63

No. 350, Tunggul charok buritan, Pisang-pisang, Alam bernaga, Sandaran. No. 351, Dadap, Tunggul kawan, Ambal, Payong ubor-ubor, Sapu-sapu ayeng and Rawai lidah. No. 352, Ula-ula besar, Payong haram, Sumbu layang. No. 353, Payong ubor-ubor tiga ringkat and Payong tinggi. No. 354, Panji-panji, Chogan istiadat, Chogan ugama. No. 355, Lambang duli yang maha mulia and Mahligai.

1986 Litho. *Perf. 12½*

350 A63 10c multicolored .50 .25
351 A63 10c multicolored .50 .25
352 A63 75c multicolored 1.75 1.40
353 A63 75c multicolored 1.75 1.40
354 A63 $2 multicolored 3.75 *4.00*
355 A63 $2 multicolored 3.75 *4.00*
Nos. 350-355 (6) 12.00 *11.30*

Intl. Peace Year — A64

1986, Oct. 24 Litho. *Perf. 12*

356 A64 50c Peace doves 1.00 1.00
357 A64 75c Hands 1.50 1.50
358 A64 $1 Peace symbols 2.00 2.00
Nos. 356-358 (3) 4.50 4.50

Natl. Anti-Drug Campaign Posters — A65

Brass Artifacts — A66

1987, Mar. 15 Litho. *Perf. 12*

359 A65 10c Jail 2.75 1.00
360 A65 75c Noose 6.00 *7.00*
361 A65 $1 Execution 8.00 *9.00*
Nos. 359-361 (3) 16.75 *17.00*

1987, July 15

362 A66 50c Kiri (kettle) 1.00 1.00
363 A66 50c Langguai (bowl) 1.00 1.00
364 A66 50c Badil (cannon) 1.00 1.00
365 A66 50c Pelita (lamp) 1.00 1.00
Nos. 362-365 (4) 4.00 4.00

See Nos. 388-391.

Dewan Bahasa Dan Pustaka, 25th Anniv. — A67

1987, Sept. 29 *Perf. 13½x13*

366 A67 Strip of 3 4.25 4.25
a. 10c multicolored .75 .75
b. 50c multicolored .90 .90
c. $2 multicolored 2.75 2.75

Language and Literature Bureau.

ASEAN, 20th Anniv. — A68

1987, Aug. 8 Litho. *Perf. 14x13½*

367 A68 20c Map .50 .40
368 A68 50c Year dates .90 .85
369 A68 $1 Flags, emblem 2.00 1.75
Nos. 367-369 (3) 3.40 3.00

World Food Day A70

Fruit: a, Artocarpus odoratissima. b, Canarium odontophyllum mig. c, Litsea garciae. d, Mangifera foetida lour.

1987, Oct. 31 *Perf. 12½*

370 Strip of 4 4.25 4.25
a.-d. A70 50c any single 1.00 1.00

See Nos. 374, 405, 423, 457-460.

Intl. Year of Shelter for the Homeless A71

Various houses.

1987, Nov. 28 Litho. *Perf. 13*

371 A71 50c multi .85 *1.00*
372 A71 75c multi, diff. 1.40 *1.50*
373 A71 $1 multi, diff. 2.00 *2.25*
Nos. 371-373 (3) 4.25 *4.75*

Fruit Type of 1987
Without FAO Emblem, Dated 1988

Fruit: a, Durio. b, Durio oxleyanus. c, Durio graveolens (cross section at L). d, Durio graveolens (cross section at R).

1988, Jan. 30 Litho. *Perf. 12*

374 Strip of 4 4.25 *4.75*
a.-d. A70 50c, any single 1.00 *1.10*

Opening of Malay Technology Museum — A72

1988, Feb. 29 *Perf. 12½x12*

375 A72 10c Wooden lathe .40 *.50*
376 A72 75c Water wheel, buffalo 1.00 *1.10*
377 A72 $1 Bird caller in blind 2.10 *2.25*
Nos. 375-377 (3) 3.50 *3.85*

Handwoven Cloth — A73

Designs: 10c, Kain Beragi Bunga Sakah-Sakah Dan Bunga Cengkih. 20c, Kain Jong Sarat. 25c, Kain Si Pugut. 40c, Kain Si Pugut Bunga Berlapis. 75c, Kain Si Lobang Bangsi Bunga Belitang Kipas.

1988, Apr. 30 Litho. *Perf. 12*

378 A73 10c multicolored .25 .25
379 A73 20c org brown & blk .25 .25
380 A73 25c multicolored .35 .35
381 A73 40c multicolored .70 .70
382 A73 75c multicolored 1.50 1.50
a. Souvenir sheet of 5, #378-382 + label 5.00 5.00
Nos. 378-382 (5) 3.05 3.05

1988, Sept. 29 Litho. *Perf. 12*

Designs: 10c, Kain Beragi. 20c, Kain Bertabur. 25c, Kain Sukma Indra. 40c, Kain Si Pugut Bunga Bersusup. 75c, Kain Beragi Si Lobang Bangsi Bunga Cendera Kesuma.

383 A73 10c multicolored .25 .25
384 A73 20c multicolored .25 .25
385 A73 25c multicolored .30 .30
386 A73 40c multicolored .50 .50
387 A73 75c multicolored .90 *1.25*
a. Souvenir sheet of 5, #383-387 5.50 *6.00*
Nos. 383-387 (5) 2.20 *2.55*

Brass Artifacts Type of 1987

1988, June 30 Litho. *Perf. 12*

388 A66 50c Celapa (repousse box) .80 .80
389 A66 50c Gangsa (footed plate) .80 .80
390 A66 50c Periok (lidded pot) .80 .80
391 A66 50c Lampong (candle-stick) .80 .80
Nos. 388-391 (4) 3.20 3.20

Coronation of Sultan Hassanal Bolkiah, 20th Anniv. — A74

1988, Aug. 1 Litho. *Perf. 14*

392 A74 20c shown .30 .25
393 A74 75c Reading from the Koran 1.10 1.10

Size: 26x62mm

Perf. 12½x13

394 A74 $2 In full regalia 2.50 2.50
a. Souvenir sheet of 3, #392-394 5.25 5.25
Nos. 392-394 (3) 3.90 3.85

Eradicate Malaria, WHO 40th Anniv. — A75

1988, Dec. 17 Litho. *Perf. 14x13½*

395 A75 25c Mosquito 1.40 .40
396 A75 35c Extermination 1.75 .70
397 A75 $2 Microscope, infected blood cells 4.00 4.00
Nos. 395-397 (3) 7.15 5.10

Natl. Day A76

1989, Feb. 23 Litho. *Perf. 12*

Size of 60c: 22x54½mm

398 A76 20c Sultan Bolkiah, officials .25 .25
399 A76 30c Honor guard .40 .25
400 A76 60c Fireworks, palace, vert. .85 .50
401 A76 $2 Religious ceremony 3.60 3.00
a. Souvenir sheet of 4, #398-401 6.75 6.75
Nos. 398-401 (4) 5.10 4.00

Independence from Britain, 5th anniv.

Solidarity with the Palestinians — A77

1989, Apr. 1 Litho. *Perf. 13½*

402 A77 20c shown .90 .25
403 A77 75c Map, flag 2.25 1.40
404 A77 $1 Dome of the Rock 4.00 2.50
Nos. 402-404 (3) 7.15 4.15

Fruit Type of 1987
Without FAO Emblem, Dated 1989

Designs: a, Daemonorops fissa. b, Eleiodoxa conferia. c, Salacca zalacca. d, Calamus ornatus.

1989, Oct. 31 Litho. *Perf. 12*

405 Strip of 4 10.00 10.00
a.-d. A70 60c any single 2.25 2.25

Oil and Gas Industry, 60th Anniv. A79

1989, Dec. 28 *Perf. 13½*

406 A79 20c Oil well pump 3.25 .60
407 A79 60c Tanker 5.50 3.00
408 A79 90c Offshore rig 5.75 4.00
409 A79 $1 Rail transport 5.75 4.00
410 A79 $2 Offshore platform 11.00 9.50
Nos. 406-410 (5) 31.25 21.10

Brunei Museum, 25th Anniv. A80

1990, Jan. 1 Litho. *Perf. 12x12½*

411 A80 30c Exhibits 2.75 1.00
412 A80 60c Official opening, 1965 4.00 3.00
413 A80 $1 Museum exterior 4.75 4.25
Nos. 411-413 (3) 11.50 8.25

Intl. Literacy Year A81

1990, July 15 Litho. *Perf. 12x12½*

414 A81 15c multicolored 1.00 .50
415 A81 90c multicolored 4.50 4.50
416 A81 $1 multicolored 4.50 4.50
Nos. 414-416 (3) 10.00 9.50

Tarsier — A82

1990, Sept. 29 Litho. *Perf. 12*

417 A82 20c shown 2.00 .75
418 A82 60c Eating leaves 3.75 3.75
419 A82 90c Climbing tree 5.25 5.25
Nos. 417-419 (3) 11.00 9.75

Fight Against AIDS — A83

1990, Dec. 1 Litho. *Perf. 13*

420 A83 20c shown 3.50 .90
421 A83 30c AIDS transmission 4.50 2.75
422 A83 90c Tombstone, skulls 11.50 *12.50*
Nos. 420-422 (3) 19.50 *16.15*

Fruit Type of 1987
Without FAO Emblem, Dated 1990

Fruit: a, Willoughbea (uncut core). b, Willoughbea (core cut in half). c, Willoughbea angustifolia.

1990, Dec. 31 *Perf. 12½*

423 Strip of 3 12.00 12.00
a.-c. A70 60c any single 3.50 3.50

Proboscis Monkey, World Wildlife Fund — A84

1991, Mar. 30 Litho. *Perf. 13½x14*

424 A84 15c shown 2.75 1.10
425 A84 20c Head, facing 3.00 1.40
426 A84 50c Sitting on branch 5.50 4.75
427 A84 60c Adult with young 5.75 5.75
Nos. 424-427 (4) 17.00 13.00

Teacher's Day A85

Design: 90c, Teacher at blackboard.

1991, Sept. 23 Litho. *Perf. 13½x14*

428 A85 60c multicolored 3.50 3.50
429 A85 90c multicolored 5.00 *5.50*

Brunei Beauty A86

1991, Oct. 1 Litho. *Perf. 13*

430 A86 30c Three immature 2.50 1.40
431 A86 60c Female 4.00 3.75
432 A86 $1 Adult male 5.25 4.75
Nos. 430-432 (3) 11.75 9.90

Happy Family Campaign — A87

1991, Nov. 30 Litho. *Perf. 13*

433 A87 20c Family, graduating son 1.25 .75
434 A87 60c Mothers, children 2.75 2.50
435 A87 90c Adults, children, heart 3.75 *4.25*
Nos. 433-435 (3) 7.75 *7.50*

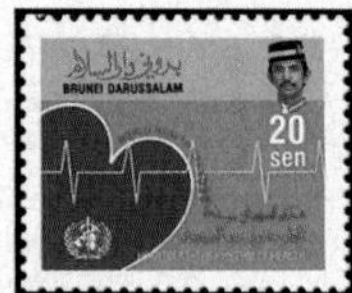

World Health Day — A88

1992, Apr. 7 Litho. *Perf. 13*

436 A88 20c multicolored 2.00 .65
437 A88 50c multi, diff. 3.50 3.50

Size: 48x28mm

438 A88 75c multi, diff. 5.00 *6.50*
Nos. 436-438 (3) 10.50 *10.65*

Brunei-Singapore and Brunei-Malaysia-Philippines Fiber Optic Submarine Cables — A89

1992, Apr. 28 Litho. *Perf. 12*

439 A89 20c Map 2.75 .60
440 A89 30c Diagram 3.00 1.60
441 A89 90c Submarine cable 5.50 *6.75*
Nos. 439-441 (3) 11.25 *8.95*

Visit ASEAN Year — A90

Designs: a, 20c, Sculptures. b, 60c, Judo exhibition. c, $1, Sculptures, diff.

1992, June 30 Litho. *Perf. 13½x14*

442 A90 Strip of 3, #a.-c. 9.00 9.00

ASEAN, 25th Anniv. — A91

A92

1992, Aug. 8 Litho. *Perf. 14*

443 A91 20c shown 1.75 .75
444 A91 60c Building 3.75 3.00
445 A91 90c Views of member states 4.50 4.25
Nos. 443-445 (3) 10.00 8.00

1992, Oct. 5 *Perf. 14x13½*

Sultan in various forms of dress and: No. 446a, Coronation procession. b, Airport. c, New Law Court, Sultan's Palace. d, Ship and Brunei University. e, Mosque, buildings.

446 A92 25c Strip of 5, #a.-e. 11.00 11.00

Sultan Hassanal Bolkiah's Accession to the Throne, 25th Anniv.

Birds A93

Designs: No. 447, Crested wood partridge, vert. No. 448, Long-tailed parakeet, vert. No. 449, Chestnut-breasted malkoha. No. 450, Asian paradise flycatcher, vert. No. 451, Magpie robin, vert. No. 452, White-rumped shama. No. 453, Great argus pheasant, vert. No. 454, Malay lorikeet, vert. No. 455, Black and red broadbill, vert.

Perf. 14x13½, 13½x14

1992-93 Litho.

447 A93 30c multicolored 1.25 .75
448 A93 30c multicolored 1.25 .75
449 A93 30c multicolored 1.40 .75
450 A93 60c multicolored 2.10 2.10
451 A93 60c multicolored 2.75 2.75
452 A93 60c multicolored 2.75 2.75
453 A93 $1 multicolored 3.50 3.50
454 A93 $1 multicolored 4.50 4.50
455 A93 $1 multicolored 4.50 4.50
Nos. 447-455 (9) 24.00 22.35

Issued: Nos. 447, 450, 453, 12/30/92; Nos. 448, 451, 454, 1/27/93; others, 5/3/93.

Natl. Day, 10th Anniv. — A94

10th anniv. emblem and: a, 10c, Natl. flag. b, 20c, Hands supporting inscription. c, 30c, Natl. day emblems, 1985-93. d, 60c, Emblem with star, crossed swords.

1994, June 16 Litho. *Perf. 13*

456 A94 Strip of 4, #a.-d. 5.50 5.50

Fruit Type of 1987
Without FAO Emblem, Dated 1994

No. 457, Nephelium mutabile. No. 458, Nephelium xerospermoides. No. 459, Nephelium spp. No. 460, Nephelium macrophyllum.

1994, Aug. 8 Litho. *Perf. 13½x13*

457 A70 60c multicolored 2.00 2.00
458 A70 60c multicolored 2.00 2.00
459 A70 60c multicolored 2.00 2.00
460 A70 60c multicolored 2.00 2.00
Nos. 457-460 (4) 8.00 8.00

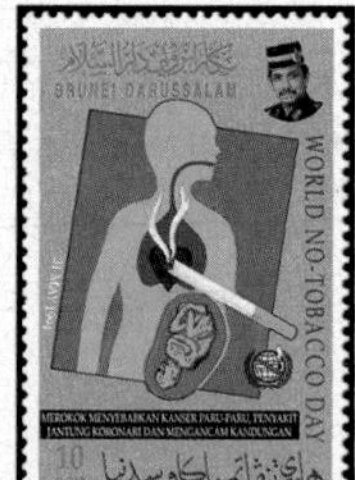

A95

World Stop Smoking Day: 10c, Cigarette, lung, fetus over human figure. 15c, People throwing away tobacco, cigarettes, pipe. $2, Arms around world crushing out cigarettes.

1994, Sept. 1 Litho. *Perf. 13½x13*

461 A95 10c multicolored .50 .25
462 A95 15c multicolored .50 .25
463 A95 $2 multicolored 7.00 *7.25*
Nos. 461-463 (3) 8.00 *7.75*

A96

Girl Guides in Brunei, 40th anniv.: a, Leader. b, Girl receiving award. c, Girl reading. d, Girls in various costumes. e, Girls camping out.

1994, Oct. 7 *Perf. 13½*

464 A96 40c Strip of 5, #a.-e. 11.00 11.00

Royal Brunei Airlines, 20th Anniv. A97

Airplanes: 10c, Twin-engine propeller. 20c, Passenger jet attached to tow bar. $1, Passenger jet in air.

1994, Nov. 18 Litho. *Perf. 13½*

465 A97 10c multicolored .80 .45
466 A97 20c multicolored 1.40 .60
467 A97 $1 multicolored 4.50 4.25
Nos. 465-467 (3) 6.70 5.30

Intl. Day Against Drug Abuse — A98

Healthy people wearing traditional costumes: 20c, 60c, $1.

1994, Dec. 30 Litho. *Perf. 13½*

468 A98 Strip of 3, #a.-c. 8.50 8.50

No. 468 is a continuous design.

City of Bandar Seri Begawan, 25th Anniv. A100

Aerial view of city: 30c, In 1970. 50c, In 1980, with details of significant buildings. $1, In 1990.

1995, Oct. 4 Litho. *Perf. 13½*

481 A100 30c multicolored 1.50 .55
482 A100 50c multicolored 2.00 1.75
483 A100 $1 multicolored 3.00 *3.25*
Nos. 481-483 (3) 6.50 *5.55*

A101

UN headquarters: 20c, Delegates in General Assembly. 60c, Security Council. 90c, Exterior.

1995, Oct. 24 *Perf. 14½x14*

484 A101 20c multicolored .60 .30
485 A101 60c multicolored 1.40 1.40

Size: 27x44mm

486 A101 90c multicolored 2.50 2.50
Nos. 484-486 (3) 4.50 4.20

UN, 50th anniv.

A102

University of Brunei, 10th Anniv.: 30c, Students in classroom. 50c, Campus buildings. 90c, Sultan in procession.

1995, Oct. 28 *Perf. 13x13½*
487 A102 30c multicolored .75 .40
488 A102 50c multicolored 1.20 .95
489 A102 90c multicolored 2.25 *2.50*
Nos. 487-489 (3) 4.20 *3.85*

A103

Royal Brunei Police, 75th Anniv.: 25c, Policemen in various uniforms. 50c, Various tasks performed by police. 75c, Sultan reviewing police.

1996, Feb. 10 Litho. *Perf. 13½x13*
490 A103 25c multicolored 1.50 .50
491 A103 50c multicolored 2.00 1.60
492 A103 75c multicolored 3.50 *4.25*
Nos. 490-492 (3) 7.00 *6.35*

A104

World Telecommunications Day: 20c, Cartoon telephone, cordless telephone. 35c, Globe, telephone dial surrounded by communication devices. $1, Signals transmitting from earth, people communicating.

1996, May 17 Litho. *Perf. 13½*
493 A104 20c multicolored .90 .35
494 A104 35c multicolored 1.60 .65
495 A104 $1 multicolored 3.50 *4.00*
Nos. 493-495 (3) 6.00 *5.00*

A105

Sultan: No. 496, Among people, in black attire. No. 497, Waving, in yellow attire. No. 498, In blue shirt. No. 499, Among people, wearing cream-colored robe.
$1, Hand raised in yellow attire.

1996, July 15 Litho. *Perf. 13*
496 A105 50c multicolored 1.50 *1.90*
497 A105 50c multicolored 1.50 *1.90*
498 A105 50c multicolored 1.50 *1.90*
499 A105 50c multicolored 1.50 *1.90*
Nos. 496-499 (4) 6.00 *7.60*

Souvenir Sheet

500 A105 $1 multicolored 5.00 5.00

Sultan Paduka Seri Baginda, 50th birthday.
A souvenir sheet of five $50 stamps exists. Value $650.

A106

Terns.

1996, Nov. 11 Litho. *Perf. 13½*
501 A106 20c Black-naped tern 1.00 .70
502 A106 30c Roseate tern 1.00 .70
503 A106 $1 Bridle tern 3.00 3.00
Nos. 501-503 (3) 5.00 *4.40*

No. 502 is spelled "Roslate" on stamp.

Sultan Hassanal Bolkiah
A107 A108

Perf. 14x13½

1996, Oct. 9 Litho. Wmk. 387

Background Color

504 A107 10c yellow green .25 .25
505 A107 15c pale pink .30 .25
506 A107 20c lilac pink .45 .40
507 A107 30c salmon .65 .60
508 A107 50c yellow .95 .85
509 A107 60c pale green 1.10 1.00
510 A107 75c blue 1.25 1.10
511 A107 90c lilac 1.50 1.40
512 A108 $1 pink 2.00 1.75
513 A108 $2 orange yellow 4.00 3.50
514 A108 $5 light blue 8.25 8.00
515 A108 $10 bright yellow 17.00 16.00
Nos. 504-515 (12) 37.70 35.10

Flowers
A109

1997, May 29 Litho. *Perf. 12*
516 A109 20c Acanthus ebracteatus .70 .30
517 A109 30c Lumnitzera littorea .90 .45
518 A109 $1 Nypa fruticans 2.40 *3.00*
Nos. 516-518 (3) 4.00 *3.75*

Marine Life
A110

Designs: No. 519, Bohadschia argus. No. 520, Oxycomanthus bennetti. No. 521, Heterocentrotus mammillatus. No. 522, Linckia laevigata.

1997, Dec. 15 Litho. *Perf. 12*
519 A110 60c multicolored 1.25 1.25
520 A110 60c multicolored 1.25 1.25
521 A110 60c multicolored 1.25 1.25
522 A110 60c multicolored 1.25 1.25
Nos. 519-522 (4) 5.00 5.00

Asian and Pacific Decade of Disabled Persons (1993-2002) — A111

Designs: 20c, Silhouettes of people, hands finger spelling "Brunei," children. 50c, Fireworks over city, blind people participating in arts, crafts, music. $1, Handicapped people playing sports.

1998, Mar. 31 Litho. *Perf. 13x13½*
523 A111 20c multicolored .65 .30
524 A111 50c multicolored 1.10 1.10
525 A111 $1 multicolored 1.75 *2.00*
Nos. 523-525 (3) 3.50 *3.40*

ASEAN, 30th Anniv. — A112

Designs: No. 526, Night scene of Sultan's Palace, buildings, map of Brunei. No. 527, Flags of ASEAN nations. No. 528, Daytime scenes of Sultan's Palace, transportation methods, buildings in Brunei.

1998, Aug. 8 Litho. *Perf. 13½*
526 A112 30c multicolored 1.25 1.25
527 A112 30c multicolored 1.25 1.25
528 A112 30c multicolored 1.25 1.25
Nos. 526-528 (3) 3.75 3.75

Sultan Hassanal Bolkiah, 30th Anniv. of Coronation — A113

Designs: 60c, In procession, saluting, on throne. 90c, Sultan Omar Ali Saifuddin standing, Sultan Hassanal Bolkiah on throne. $1, Procession.

1998, Aug. 1 Litho. *Perf. 12*
529 A113 60c multicolored 1.10 .70
530 A113 90c multicolored 1.60 1.60
531 A113 $1 multicolored 1.90 1.90
a. Souvenir sheet, #529-531 5.75 5.75
Nos. 529-531 (3) 4.60 4.20

A114 A115

Investiture of Crown Prince Al-Muhtadee Billah: $1, Signing document. $2, Formal portrait. $3, Arms of the Crown Prince.

1998, Aug. 10
532 A114 $1 multicolored 1.60 1.60
533 A114 $2 multicolored 3.00 3.00
534 A114 $3 multicolored 4.00 4.00
a. Souvenir sheet, #532-534 10.00 10.00
Nos. 532-534 (3) 8.60 8.60

1998, Sept. 29 *Perf. 13x13½*

30c, Hands clasped, woman, man. 60c, Dollar sign over book, arrows, "7.45AM." 90c, Silhouettes of people seated at table, standing, scales.

535 A115 30c multicolored .85 .55
536 A115 60c multicolored 1.25 1.25
537 A115 90c multicolored 1.90 *2.00*
Nos. 535-537 (3) 4.00 *3.80*

Civil Sevice Day, 5th anniv.

A116

Kingfishers.

1998, Nov. 11 Litho. *Perf. 13½x13*
538 A116 20c Blue-eared 1.00 .65
539 A116 30c Common 1.25 .65
540 A116 60c White-collared 1.75 1.50
541 A116 $1 Stork-billed 2.50 *2.75*
Nos. 538-541 (4) 6.50 *5.55*

A117

National Day, 15th Anniv.: 20c, Boat docks, residential area. 60c, Methods of communications. 90c, Buildings, roadways, tower, oil rig.

1999, Feb. 23 Litho. *Perf. 13*
542 A117 20c multicolored .60 .40
543 A117 60c multicolored 1.25 1.10
544 A117 90c multicolored 2.50 *2.75*
a. Souvenir sheet, #542-544 5.00 *5.50*
Nos. 542-544 (3) 4.35 *4.25*

20th Sea Games, 1999 — A119

No. 549: a, Field hockey, cycling. b, Basketball, soccer. c, Tennis, track and field. d, Billiards. e, Bowling.
No. 550: a, Shooting. b, Golf, squash. c, Boxing. d, Kick fighting, badminton, ping pong. e, Swimming, rowing.
$1, Shooting, tennis, running, soccer, cycling, basketball.

1999, Aug. 7 Litho. *Perf. 14¼*

Strips of 5, #a.-e.

549-550 A119 20c each 6.00 6.00

Souvenir Sheet

551 A119 $1 multicolored 4.25 4.25

No. 551 contains one 35x35mm stamp.

UPU, 125th Anniv. — A120

20c, Handshake, globe, letters. 30c, Emblems of UPU, Brunei Post. 75c, Postal workers & services.

1999, Oct. 9 Litho. *Perf. 14*
552 A120 20c multicolored .60 .25
553 A120 30c multicolored .90 .70
554 A120 75c multicolored 1.75 *1.90*
Nos. 552-554 (3) 3.25 *2.85*

Millennium
A121

No. 555: a, Building with clock, children at computer. b, Building with red roof, man and woman at computer. c, Building with gray roof, mosque. d, Map of park. e, Airplane and ships. f, Satellite dishes.

Perf. 13¾x13½ Syncopated Type A

2000, Feb. 1 **Litho.**

555 A121 20c Strip of 6, #a-f 4.00 4.00
g. Souvenir sheet, #555 5.00 5.00

Flowers A122

Designs: 30c, Rafflesia pricei. 50c, Rhizanthes lowi. 60c, Nepenthes rafflesiana.

2000, Oct. 2 **Litho.** ***Perf. 14¼x14***

556-558 A122 Set of 3 4.00 4.00

Asia-Pacific Economic Cooperation A123

Designs: 20c, Satellite dish, people at computers. 30c, Food processing enterprises. 60c, Eco-tourism (flower and bridge).

2000, Nov. 15 ***Perf. 13½x13***

559 A123 20c multi .75 .40
a. Booklet pane of 1 .75
560 A123 30c multi .90 .50
a. Booklet pane of 1 .90
561 A123 60c multi 1.75 *1.90*
a. Booklet pane of 1 1.75
Booklet, #559a-561a 3.50
b. Souvenir sheet, #559-561 4.25 *5.00*

The 20th Century — A124

No. 562 — Scenes from: a, 1901-20. b, 1921-40. c, 1941-60. d, 1961-80. e, 1981-99.

Perf. 13¾x13½ Syncopated Type A

2000, Feb. 23 **Litho.**

562 Strip of 5 5.00 5.00
a.-e. A124 30c Any single .90 .90

Turtles A125

No. 563: a, Green turtle. b, Hawksbill turtle. c, Olive Ridley turtle.

2000, Nov. 16 ***Perf. 13¼x13***

563 Strip of 3 5.00 5.00
a.-c. A125 30c Any single .90 .90

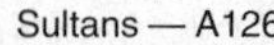
Sultans — A126

No. 564: a, Hashim Jalilul Alam. b, Muhammad Jamalul Alam II. c, Ahmed Tajudin. d, Haji Omar Ali Saifuddin. e, Haji Hassanal Bolkiah.

2000, July 15 **Litho.** ***Perf. 13¾***

564 Horiz. strip of 5 10.00 10.00
a.-e. A126 60c Any single 1.75 1.75
f. Souvenir sheet, #564, perf. 14¼x14 12.00 12.00
g. Booklet pane of 1, #564a 3.50
h. Booklet pane of 1, #564b 3.50
i. Booklet pane of 1, #564c 3.50
j. Booklet pane of 1, #564d 3.50
k. Booklet pane of 1, #564e 3.50
Booklet, #564g-564k 30.00

Visit Brunei Year — A127

Designs: 20c, People in boat. 30c, Houses on pilings. 60c, Shown.

2001, Mar. 14 ***Perf. 14¼x13¾***

565-567 A127 Set of 3 5.00 5.00

Sultan Hassanal Bolkiah, 55th Birthday — A128

No. 568: a, Navy blue uniform. b, Light blue uniform. c, Robes. d, Camouflage uniform. e, White uniform.

No. 569, Casual shirt.

Perf. 12¼

2001, July 15 **Litho.** **Unwmk.**

568 Horiz. strip of 5 4.00 4.00
a.-e. A128 55c Any single .75 .75

Souvenir Sheet

Perf. 12

569 A128 55c multi 4.25 4.25

No. 569 contains one 40x70mm stamp.

International Youth Camp 2001 — A129

No. 570: a, Scout, administering first aid. b, Girls, tents. c, Scouts and leader.

2001, Aug. 5 **Wmk. 388** ***Perf. 12¼***

570 Horiz. strip of 3 3.50 3.50
a.-c. A129 30c Any single .85 .85
d. Souvenir sheet, #570 6.00 6.00

First Intl. Islamic Expo A130

No. 571: a, Jewelry, cane. b, Mosque exterior. c, Computer, satellite dishes. d, Mosque interior.

2001, Aug. 18 **Wmk. 388** ***Perf. 12***

571 Horiz. strip of 4 2.40 2.40
a.-d. A130 20c Any single .60 .60

Visit Brunei Year A131

No. 572: a, Bridge. b, Waterfall. c, Aerial view of city. d, Dock.

Perf. 13¼x13½

2001, Sept. 1 **Unwmk.**

572 Horiz. strip of 4 3.50 3.50
a.-d. A131 20c Any single .80 .80

Year of Dialogue Among Civilizations A132

No. 573: a, Emblem. b, Two abstract heads. c, Cubist-style head, native. d, Multicolored leaves.

2001, Oct. 9 **Unwmk.** ***Perf. 12***

573 Horiz. strip of 4 3.50 3.50
a.-d. A132 30c Any single .80 .80

Worldwide Fund for Nature (WWF) — A133

No. 574 — Bulwer's pheasant: a, Male and female. b, Male. c, Female and chicks. d, Female.

2001, Nov. 1 **Wmk. 388** ***Perf. 12***

574 Horiz. strip of 4 3.50 3.50
a.-d. A133 30c Any single .80 .70

Jabatan Telekom Brunei, 50th Anniv. — A134

No. 575: a, People, old telecommunications equipment. b, Anniversary emblem. c, Women, computer, new services.

2002 **Litho.** ***Perf. 12¼***

575 A134 50c Horiz. strip of 3, #a-c 3.00 3.00
a.-c. A134 50c Any single .90 *1.00*

Survey Department, 50th Anniv. — A135

No. 576: a, "50." b, Headquarters. c, Surveyor.

2002, July **Litho.** ***Perf. 12¼***

576 Horiz. strip of 3 3.00 3.00
a.-c. A135 50c Any single .90 *1.00*

Yayasan Sultan Haji Hassanal Bolkiah, 10th Anniv. — A136

No. 577: a, Stilt house community. b, Mosque. c, School and children. d, Buildings.

2002, Oct. 5 ***Perf. 12¾x12½***

577 Horiz. strip of 4 2.50 2.50
a.-d. A136 10c Any single .55 .55

Anti-Corruption Bureau, 20th Anniv. — A137

No. 578: a, Anti-Corruption Bureau buildings. b, City skyline. c, Posters.

2002, Nov. 19 **Litho.** ***Perf. 13***

578 Horiz. strip of 3 2.25 2.25
a.-c. A137 20c Any single .65 .65

Medicinal Plants — A138

No. 579: a, Melastoma malabathricum. b, Etlingera solaris. c, Dillenia suffruticosa. d, Costus speciosus.

2003 ***Perf. 12¾x12½***

579 Horiz. strip of 4 3.25 3.25
a.-d. A138 20c Any single .75 .75

ASEAN - Japan Exchange Year — A139

No. 580: a, Drums. b, Tops. c, Kites.

2003, Dec. 13 **Litho.** ***Perf. 13***

580 Horiz. strip of 3 2.25 2.25
a.-c. A139 20c Any single .65 .65

National Day, 20th Anniv. — A140

No. 581: a, Sultan Hassanal Bolkiah at UN. b, Military officer. c, Man reading from scroll. d, Emblem.

2004, Feb. 23 ***Perf. 12¼***

581 Horiz. strip of 4 2.25 2.25
a.-d. A140 20c Any single .65 .65
e. Souvenir sheet, #581 5.00 5.00

Brunei National Philatelic Society — A141

No. 582: a, Magnifying glass, #A1. b, Magnifying glass, tongs, perforation gauge, stamps. c, Brunei stamps and cancels

2004, Mar. 27 ***Perf. 12¾x12½***
582 Horiz. strip of 3 2.25 2.25
a.-c. A141 25c Any single .65 .65

Wedding of Crown Prince Haji al-Muhtadee Billah and Sarah Salleh — A142

No. 583: a, Dark shadows on background below and to right of Sultan Bolkiah's picture and between picture frames. b, Dark shadows on background below "Darussalam" and to left of Crown Prince's picture frame.

2004, Sept. 9 **Litho.** ***Perf. 12***
583 A142 99c Horiz. pair, #a-b, + central label 3.00 3.00

Sultan Hassanal Bolkiah, 60th Birthday — A143

No. 584 — Photographs of Sultan at various activities with panel color of: a, Red violet. b, Rose (women at LL). c, Orange. d, Red (men at LL). e, Green. b, Prussian blue.
$60, Sultan at activities.

2006, July 15 **Litho.** ***Perf. 12½***
584 Horiz. strip of 6 5.25 5.25
a.-f. A143 60c Any single .85 .85
g. Souvenir sheet, #584 5.25 5.25

Souvenir Sheet

Perf. 13¾x13½

585 A143 $60 black 150.00 150.00

No. 585 contains one 100x91mm stamp.

A144

Brunei Postal Service, Cent. — A145

No. 586: a, General Post Office, Bandar Seri Begawan. b, Kuala Belait Post Office. c, Tutong Post Office. d, Bangar Post Office, Temburong.
No. 587 — Children's drawings: a, Airplane, mailbox, letters, packages, globe. b, Postal worker, Postal Service, emblem, post office scenes. c, Cycle of mail delivery. d, Postal worker, letters, buildings, mailbox. e, Globe, letter with wings, children. f, Globe, flags, airplane.

2006, Oct. 11 **Litho.** ***Perf. 13¾x13¼***
586 Horiz. strip of 4 5.75 5.75
a.-d. A144 100c Any single 1.40 1.40
e. Souvenir sheet, #586a-586d 6.00 6.00
587 A145 100c Sheet of 6, #a-f 12.00 12.00

Marine Life — A146

Designs: No. 588, 60c, Orange-striped triggerfish. No. 589, 60c, Leaf scorpionfish.
No. 590: a, Chambered nautilus. b, Spotted boxfish.

Perf. 13½x12x13½x13½

2007, Feb. 6
588-589 A146 Set of 2 2.50 2.50

Souvenir Sheet

Perf. 13½x13¼

590 A146 $1 Sheet of 2, #a-b 3.25 3.25

Dated 2006. See Malaysia Nos. 1139-1141.

Sultan Hassanal Bolkiah
A147 A148

2007, Feb. 23 ***Perf. 13¼***

Background Color

591 A147 10c light blue .25 .25
592 A147 15c bright green .35 .25
593 A147 20c lilac .35 .30
594 A147 30c blue .45 .45
595 A147 50c orange .90 .75
596 A147 60c red 1.00 .90
597 A147 75c green 1.10 1.10
598 A147 90c brt yel grn 1.40 1.40

Perf. 13¼x13¾

599 A148 $1 blue 1.50 1.50
600 A148 $2 purple 3.00 3.00
601 A148 $5 green 7.75 7.75
602 A148 $10 yellow 16.00 16.00
Nos. 591-602 (12) 34.05 33.65

Bubungan Dua Belas (House of 12 Roofs), Bukit Subok, Cent. — A149

Designs: 30c, House from foot of hill. 60c, Aerial view of house. $1, Early black-and-white picture of house.

2007, July 23 **Litho.** ***Perf. 13½x13¼***
603-605 A149 Set of 3 2.75 2.75
605a Souvenir sheet of 3, #603-605 3.00 3.00

Bubungan Dua Belas was the residence of the British High Commissioner.

Public Works Department, Cent. — A150

No. 606: a, Modern building. b, Riverfront building. c, Centenary emblem.

2007, Aug. 30 ***Perf. 13¼***
606 A150 75c Horiz. strip of 3, #a-c 3.50 3.50

Miniature Sheet

Association of South East Asian Nations (ASEAN), 40th Anniv. — A151

No. 607: a, Secretariat Building, Bandar Seri Begawan, Brunei. b, Yangon Post Office, Myanmar. c, National Museum of Cambodia. d, Malacañang Palace, Philippines. e, Fatahillah Museum, Jakarta, Indonesia. f, National Museum of Singapore. g, Typical house, Laos. h, Vimanmek Mansion, Bangkok, Thailand. i, Malayan Railway Headquarters Building, Kuala Lumpur, Malaysia. j, Presidential Palace, Hanoi, Viet Nam.

2007, Nov. 21
607 A151 20c Sheet of 10, #a-j 3.25 3.25

See Burma No. 370, Cambodia No. 2339, Indonesia Nos. 2120-2121, Laos Nos. 1717-1718, Malaysia No. 1170, Philippines Nos. 3103-3105, Singapore No. 1265, Thailand No. 2315, and Viet Nam Nos. 3302-3311.

Movement of Capital From Kampong Air to Bandar Seri Begawan, Cent. — A152

Designs: 20c, Istana Majlis. 30c, Istana Kota. 60c, Bandar Brunei. 100c, Bandar Seri Begawan.

2008, Apr. 24 **Litho.** ***Perf. 13¼***
608-611 A152 Set of 4 3.25 3.25

Coronation of Sultan Hassanal Bolkiah, 40th Anniv. — A153

No. 612 — Coronation ceremony: a, Sultan with hand raised. b, Parade. c, Crowning of Sultan. d, Sultan wearing crown.
$40, Parade, diff.

2008, Aug. 1 ***Perf. 12¾x12½***
612 Horiz. strip of 4 2.40 2.40
a.-d. A153 40c Any single .60 .60

Souvenir Sheet

Perf. 12

613 A153 $40 multi 60.00 60.00

No. 613 contains one 45x70mm stamp.

Omar Ali Saifuddien Mosque, 50th Anniv. — A154

No. 614: a, Opening ceremony (green panels). b, Sultan Hassanal Bolkiah (blue panels). c, Worshipers (orange panels). d, Aerial view of mosque (red violet panels).
$50, Mosque, diff.

2008, Sept. 26 ***Perf. 14½x14***
614 Horiz. strip of 4 2.75 2.75
a.-d. A154 50c Any single .65 .65
e. Souvenir sheet of 4, #614a-614d 2.75 2.75

Souvenir Sheet

Litho. With Foil Application

Perf. 13¾x13½

615 A154 $50 multi 70.00 70.00

No. 615 contains one 44x72mm stamp.

Health Services, Cent. — A155

Designs: No. 616, 10c, Pediatric examination. No. 617, 10c, Magnetic resonance imaging machine, operating room. $1, First government hospital in Brunei town.

2008, Oct. 9 **Litho.** ***Perf. 13¼***
616-618 A155 Set of 3 1.75 1.75

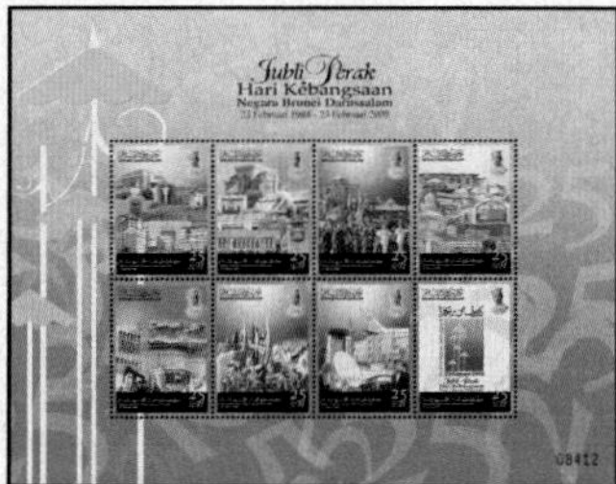

25th National Day — A156

Nos. 619 and 620: a, Buildings, blue sky. b, Buildings, green sky. c, Buildings, military parade, red sky. d, Buildings, buff sky. e, Oil facilities, blue violet sky. f, People with flags, red violet sky. g, Buildings, airplane, satellite dish, brown orange sky. h, Emblem.

$25, Sultans Hassanal Bolkiah and Omar Ali Saifuddin, horiz.

2009, Feb. 23 ***Perf. 13¼***

Stamps With Blue Frames

619 A156 25c Sheet of 8, #a-h 2.60 2.60

Stamps With White Frames

620 A156 25c Sheet of 8, #a-h 2.60 2.60

Souvenir Sheet

621 A156 $25 multi 32.50 32.50

No. 621 contains one 102x72mm stamp.

Orchids — A157

No. 622: a, Dendrobium secundum. b, Bulbophyllum sp. c, Phalaenopsis cornucervi.
No. 623: a, Bulbophyllum beccarii. b, Vanda hastifera. c, Corybas pictus.

Litho. & Embossed

2009, Dec. 9 ***Perf. 14***

622 Horiz. strip of 3 1.90 1.90
a. A157 10c multi .25 .25
b. A157 20c multi .30 .30
c. A157 $1 multi 1.40 1.40
623 Horiz. strip of 3 1.90 1.90
a. A157 10c multi .25 .25
b. A157 20c multi .30 .30
c. A157 $1 multi 1.40 1.40

Modern Land Administration, Cent. — A158

No. 624: a, People at Land Administration office. b, Surveyors at construction site. c, Two men, house.

2010, June 23 **Litho.** ***Perf. 13½***

624 Horiz. strip of 3 1.90 1.90
a. A158 10c multi .25 .25
b. A158 20c multi .30 .30
c. A158 $1 multi 1.40 1.40

Liquid Natural Gas, 40th Anniv. of Production (in 2009) — A159

No. 625: a, Tanker in harbor. b, Control rooms. c, Workers and pipelines.

2010, July 7 ***Perf. 13½x14***

625 Horiz. strip of 3 1.75 1.75
a.-c. A159 40c Any single .55 .55

Miniature Sheet

Sultan Hassanal Bolkiah, 65th Birthday — A160

No. 626 — Sultan and other people with panel color of: a, Dull violet. b, Golden brown. c, Green. d, Blue green. e, Dark brown. f, Rose.

2011, July 15 ***Perf. 14x14¼***

626 A160 65c Sheet of 6, #a-f 6.50 6.50

A $65 souvenir sheet was sold only with special packaging for more than face value.

Dewan Bahasa Dan Pustaka Library, 50th Anniv. A161

2011, Sept. 17 ***Perf. 12¾***

627 Horiz. strip of 3 2.75 2.75
a. A161 20c Books .35 .35
b. A161 50c Libraries .80 .80
c. A161 $1 Men 1.60 1.60

Farmers and Fishermen Day — A162

No. 628: a, Fishermen at work. b, Farm products.

2011, Nov. 1

628 A162 20c Horiz. pair, #a-b .65 .65

A163

Rice Production A164

No. 629 — Inscription "Towards Self-Sufficiency In Rice Production 20%" and: a, Rice plants, arrow with "20%." b, Sultan Hassanal Bolkiah. c, Sultan in rice field.
No. 630 — Inscription "To Commemorate Large Scale Rice Planting" and: a, Sultan driving motorized farm equipment. b, Rice field. c, Sultan planting rice.

2011, Nov. 1 ***Perf. 12¾***

629 Horiz. strip of 3 1.10 1.10
a.-c. A163 20c Any single .35 .35
630 Horiz. strip of 3 1.10 1.10
a.-c. A164 20c Any single .35 .35

Royal Brunei Armed Forces, 50th Anniv. (in 2011) — A165

No. 631 — Sultan Hassanal Bolkiah in various uniforms with frame color of: a, Golden brown. b, Dark gray. c, Red. d, Light gray. e, Blue.

2012, May 31 ***Perf. 13¼***

631 Horiz. strip of 5 4.00 4.00
a.-e. A165 50c Any single .80 .80

OCCUPATION STAMPS

Issued under Japanese Occupation

Stamps and Types of 1908-37 Hstmpd. in Violet, Red Violet, Blue or Red

Perf. 14, 14x11½ (#N7)

1942-44 **Wmk. 4**

N1 A1 1c black 11.00 *28.00*
N2 A1 2c green 75.00 *140.00*
N3 A1 2c dull orange 7.50 *11.00*
N4 A1 3c green 45.00 *92.50*
N5 A1 4c orange 6.00 *16.00*
N6 A1 5c brown 7.00 *16.00*
N7 A2 6c slate gray 85.00 *275.00*
N8 A2 6c red 900.00 775.00
N9 A1 8c gray (RV) 1,200. *1,050.*
N10 A2 8c carmine 11.00 *15.00*
N11 A1 10c violet, *yel* 14.00 *32.50*
N12 A2 12c blue 42.50 *32.50*
N13 A2 15c ultra 32.50 *32.50*
N14 A1 25c dk violet 40.00 *70.00*
N15 A1 30c org & red vio 150.00 *290.00*
N16 A1 50c blk, *green* 60.00 *85.00*
N17 A1 $1 red & blk, *bl* 85.00 *110.00*

Wmk. 3

N18 A1 $5 lake, *green* 1,400. *2,750.*
N19 A1 $25 black, *red* 1,500. *2,750.*

Overprints vary in shade. Nos. N3, N7, N10 and N13 without overprint are not believed to have been regularly issued.

No. N1 Surcharged in Red

1944 **Wmk. 4** ***Perf. 14***

N20 A1 $3 on 1c black *15,000.* 7,500.
a. On No. 43 10,000. —

BULGARIA

ˌbəl-ˈgar-ē-ə

LOCATION — Southeastern Europe bordering on the Black Sea on the east and the Danube River on the north
GOVT. — Republic
AREA — 42,855 sq. mi.
POP. — 8,194,772 (1999 est.)
CAPITAL — Sofia

In 1885 Bulgaria, then a principality under the suzerainty of the Sultan of Turkey, was joined by Eastern Rumelia. Independence from Turkey was obtained in 1908.

100 Centimes = 1 Franc
100 Stotinki = 1 Lev (1881)

Catalogue values for unused stamps in this country are for Never Hinged items, beginning with Scott 293 in the regular postage section, Scott B1 in the semi-postal section, Scott C15 in the airpost section, Scott CB1 in the airpost semi-postal section, Scott E1 in the special delivery section, Scott J47 in the postage due section, Scott O1 in the officials section, and Scott Q1 in the parcel post section.

Watermarks

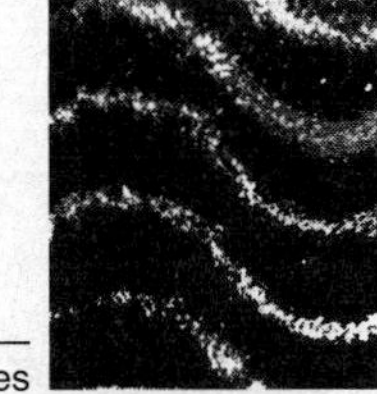

Wmk. 145 — Wavy Lines

Wmk. 168 — Wavy Lines and EZGV in Cyrillic

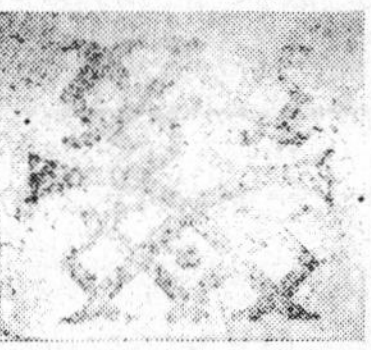

Wmk. 275 — Entwined Curved Lines

Lion of Bulgaria
A1 A2 A3

Perf. 14½x15

1879, May 1 **Wmk. 168** **Typo.**

Laid Paper

1 A1 5c black & orange 160.00 57.50
2 A1 10c black & green 900.00 200.00
3 A1 25c black & violet 440.00 40.00
a. Imperf.
4 A1 50c black & blue 800.00 160.00
5 A2 1fr black & red 95.00 40.00

1881, Apr. 10

6 A3 3s red & silver 32.50 6.50
7 A3 5s black & orange 32.50 6.50
a. Background inverted *2,400.*
8 A3 10s black & green 175.00 20.00
9 A3 15s dp car red & green 175.00 20.00
10 A3 25s black & violet 900.00 100.00
11 A3 30s blue & fawn 32.50 16.00

1882, Dec. 4

12 A3 3s orange & yel 1.60 .80
a. Background inverted *4,000.* *4,000.*
13 A3 5s green & pale green 12.50 1.20
a. 5s rose & pale rose (error) *3,000.* *3,000.*
14 A3 10s rose & pale rose 16.00 1.20
15 A3 15s red vio & pale lil 16.00 1.20
16 A3 25s blue & pale blue 14.50 1.60
17 A3 30s violet & grn 14.50 1.20
18 A3 50s blue & pink 14.50 1.20
Nos. 12-18 (7) 89.60 8.40

See Nos. 207-210, 286.

Surcharged in Black, Carmine or Vermilion

A4

A5

1884, May 1 Typo. Surcharge

19 A4 3s on 10s rose (Bk) 240.00 80.00
20 A4 5s on 30s blue & fawn (C) 160.00 100.00
20A A4 5s on 30s bl & fawn (Bk) *2,800.* *2,250.*
21 A5 15s on 25s blue (C) 175.00 100.00

On some values the surcharge may be found inverted or double.

1885, Apr. 5 Litho. Surcharge

21B A4 3s on 10s rose (Bk) 80.00 80.00
21C A4 5s on 30s bl & fawn (V) 80.00 80.00
21D A5 15s on 25s blue (V) 145.00 100.00
22 A5 50s on 1fr blk & red (Bk) 550.00 360.00

Forgeries of Nos. 19-22 are plentiful.

Word below left star in oval has 5 letters
A6

Third letter below left star is "A"
A7

1885, May 25

23 A6 1s gray vio & pale gray 28.00 9.50
24 A7 2s sl grn & pale gray 28.00 6.75

Word below left star has 4 letters
A8

Third letter below left star is "b" with cross-bar in upper half
A9

A10

1886-87

25 A8 1s gray vio & pale gray 2.00 .40
26 A9 2s sl grn & pale gray 2.00 .40
27 A10 1 l black & red ('87) 57.50 7.25
Nos. 25-27 (3) 61.50 8.05

For surcharge see No. 40.

A11

Perf. 10½, 11, 11½, 13, 13½

1889 Wove Paper Unwmk.

28 A11 1s lilac 1.60 .40
29 A11 2s gray 2.40 1.20
30 A11 3s bister brown 1.60 .40
31 A11 5s yellow green 12.00 .30
a. Vert. pair, imperf. btwn.
32 A11 10s rose 12.00 .80
33 A11 15s orange 80.00 .80
34 A11 25s blue 12.00 .80
35 A11 30s dk brown 13.50 .80
36 A11 50s green .80 .40
37 A11 1 l orange red .80 .80
Nos. 28-37 (10) 136.70 6.70

The 10s orange is a proof.

Nos. 28-34 exist imperforate. Value, set $225.

See Nos. 39, 41-42. For overprints and surcharges see Nos. 38, 55-56, 77-81, 113.

No. 35 Surcharged in Black

1892, Jan. 26

38 A11 15s on 30s brn 40.00 1.60
a. Inverted surcharge *70.00* *52.50*

1894 *Perf. 10½, 11, 11½*

Pelure Paper

39 A11 10s red 7.00 2.00
a. Imperf. *57.50*

No. 26 Surcharged in Red

Wmk. Wavy Lines (168)

1895, Oct. 25 *Perf. 14½x15*

Laid Paper

40 A9 1s on 2s 1.20 .40
a. Inverted surcharge 8.00 6.50
b. Double surcharge *62.50* *62.50*
c. Pair, one without surcharge *125.00* *125.00*

This surcharge on No. 24 is a proof.

Wmk. Coat of Arms in the Sheet

1896, Apr. 30 *Perf. 11½, 13*

Wove Paper

41 A11 2 l rose & pale rose 3.25 2.40
42 A11 3 l black & buff 4.75 5.50

Coat of Arms
A14

Cherry Wood Cannon
A15

1896, Feb. 2 *Perf. 13*

43 A14 1s blue green .35 .25
44 A14 5s dark blue .35 .25
45 A14 15s purple .60 .30
46 A14 25s red 5.75 1.00
Nos. 43-46 (4) 7.05 1.80

Baptism of Prince Boris.

Examples of Nos. 41-46 from sheet edges show no watermark.

Nos. 43, 45-46 were also printed on rough unwatermarked paper.

1901, Apr. 20 Litho. Unwmk.

53 A15 5s carmine 1.50 1.10
54 A15 15s yellow green 1.50 1.10

Insurrection of Independence in April, 1876, 25th anniversary.

Exist imperf. Forgeries exist.

Nos. 30 and 36 Surcharged in Black

1901, Mar. 24 Typo.

55 A11 5s on 3s bister brn 2.50 1.60
a. Inverted surcharge 45.00 45.00
b. Pair, one without surcharge *70.00* *70.00*
56 A11 10s on 50s green 2.50 1.60
a. Inverted surcharge 50.00 50.00
b. Pair, one without surcharge *72.50* *72.50*

Tsar Ferdinand — A17

Type I

Type II

ONE LEV:

Type I — The numerals in the upper corners have, at the top, a sloping serif on the left side and a short straight serif on the right.

Type II — The numerals in the upper corners are of ordinary shape without the serif at the right.

1901, Oct. 1-1905 Typo. *Perf. 12½*

57 A17 1s vio & gray blk .25 .25
58 A17 2s brnz grn & ind .25 .25
a. Imperf.
59 A17 3s orange & ind .25 .25
60 A17 5s emerald & brn 2.25 .25
61 A17 10s rose & blk 1.50 .25
62 A17 15s claret & gray blk .80 .25
63 A17 25s blue & blk .80 .25
64 A17 30s bis & gray blk 18.00 .30
65 A17 50s dk blue & brn 1.00 .25
66 A17 1 l red org & brnz grn, type I 2.50 1.25
67 A17 1 l brn red & brnz grn, II ('05) 55.00 4.00
68 A17 2 l carmine & blk 5.00 .85
69 A17 3 l slate & red brn 6.00 2.25
Nos. 57-69 (13) 93.60 10.65

For surcharges see Nos. 73, 83-85, 87-88.

Fighting at Shipka Pass — A18

1902, Aug. 29 Litho. *Perf. 11½*

70 A18 5s lake 3.00 1.00
71 A18 10s blue green 3.00 1.00
72 A18 15s blue 12.00 5.00
Nos. 70-72 (3) 18.00 7.00

Battle of Shipka Pass, 1877.

Imperf. copies are proofs.

Excellent forgeries of Nos. 70 to 72 exist.

No. 62 Surcharged in Black

1903, Oct. 1 *Perf. 12½*

73 A17 10s on 15s 6.00 .40
a. Inverted surcharge *57.50* *50.00*
b. Double surcharge *57.50* *50.00*
c. Pair, one without surcharge *100.00* *100.00*
d. 10s on 10s rose & black *325.00* *325.00*

Ferdinand in 1887 and 1907 — A19

1907, Aug. 12 Litho. *Perf. 11½*

74 A19 5s deep green 17.50 1.75
75 A19 10s red brown 25.00 1.75
76 A19 25s deep blue 60.00 3.50
Nos. 74-76 (3) 102.50 7.00

Accession to the throne of Ferdinand I, 20th anniversary.

Nos. 74-76 imperf. are proofs. Nos. 74-76 exist in pairs imperforate between.

Stamps of 1889 Overprinted

1909

77 A11 1s lilac 1.60 .70
a. Inverted overprint 21.00 17.50
b. Double overprint, one inverted 24.00 24.00
78 A11 5s yellow green 1.60 .70
a. Inverted overprint 25.00 25.00
b. Double overprint 25.00 25.00

With Additional Surcharge

79 A11 5s on 30s brown (Bk) 2.75 .70
a. "5" double
b. "1990" for "1909" *700.00* *550.00*
80 A11 10s on 15s org (Bk) 2.75 .95
a. Inverted surcharge 17.50 17.50
b. "1909" omitted *27.50* *27.50*
81 A11 10s on 50s dk grn (R) 2.75 .95
a. "1990" for "1909" 100.00 100.00
b. Black surcharge 52.50 52.50

Nos. 62 & 64 Surcharged with Value Only

83 A17 5s on 15s (Bl) 2.40 .80
a. Inverted surcharge 21.00 21.00
84 A17 10s on 15s (Bl) 6.25 .55
a. Inverted surcharge 21.00 21.00
85 A17 25s on 30s (R) 8.00 1.25
a. Double surcharge 75.00 75.00
b. "2" of "25" omitted 87.50 87.50
c. Blue surcharge *300.00* *175.00*

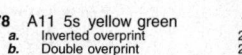

Nos. 59 and 62 Surcharged in Blue

1910, Oct.

87 A17 1s on 3s 4.25 1.60
a. "1910" omitted 21.00
88 A17 5s on 15s 4.25 1.60

Tsar Assen's Tower (Crown over lion)
A20

Tsar Ferdinand
A21

City of Trnovo
A22

Tsar Ferdinand
A23

Ferdinand
A24

Isker River
A25

Ferdinand
A26

Rila Monastery (Crown at UR)
A27

Tsar and Princes — A28

Ferdinand in Robes of Ancient Tsars — A29

Monastery of Holy Trinity — A30

View of Varna — A31

1911, Feb. 14 Engr. *Perf. 12*

No.	Type	Value	Description	Unused	Used
89	A20	1s	myrtle green	.25	.25
90	A21	2s	car & blk	.25	.25
91	A22	3s	lake & blk	.45	.25
92	A23	5s	green & blk	1.60	.25
93	A24	10s	dp red & blk	2.50	.25
94	A25	15s	brown bister	5.75	.25
95	A26	25s	ultra & blk	.55	.25
96	A27	30s	blue & blk	5.75	.25
97	A28	50s	ocher & blk	30.00	.25
a.			Center inverted		*2,700.*
98	A29	1 l	chocolate	13.50	.25
99	A30	2 l	dull pur & blk	3.25	.50
100	A31	3 l	blue vio & blk	15.00	3.75
			Nos. 89-100 (12)	78.85	6.75

See Nos. 114-120, 161-162. For overprints and surcharges see Nos. 104-112, 188, B8, Greece N167-N178, N182-N187, Thrace 16-21, Romania 2N1-2N4.

Tsar Ferdinand — A32

1912, Aug. 2 Typo. *Perf. 12½*

No.	Type	Value	Description	Unused	Used
101	A32	5s	olive green	15.00	2.00
a.		5s	pale green	*325.00*	*150.00*
102	A32	10s	claret	7.00	3.50
103	A32	25s	slate	10.00	5.50
			Nos. 101-103 (3)	32.00	11.00

25th year of reign of Tsar Ferdinand.

Nos. 89-95 Overprinted in Various Colors

1913, Aug. 6 Engr.

No.	Type	Value	Description	Unused	Used
104	A20	1s	myrtle grn (C)	.50	.25
105	A21	2s	car & blk (Bl)	2.00	.25
107	A22	3s	lake & blk (Bl Bk)	2.00	.25
108	A23	5s	grn & blk (R)	.50	.25
109	A24	10s	dp red & blk (Bk)	.50	.25
110	A25	15s	brown bis (G)	2.50	1.50
111	A26	25s	ultra & blk (R)	8.00	2.50
			Nos. 104-111 (7)	16.00	5.25

Victory over the Turks in Balkan War of 1912-1913.

No. 95 Surcharged in Red

1915, July 6

No.	Type	Description	Unused	Used
112	A26	10s on 25s	.95	.25

No. 28 Surcharged in Green

No.	Type	Description	Unused	Used
113	A11	3s on 1s lilac	9.50	4.50

Types of 1911 Re-engraved

1915, Nov. 7 *Perf. 11½, 14*

No.	Type	Value	Description	Unused	Used
114	A20	1s	dk bl grn	.25	.25
115	A23	5s	grn & brn vio	3.25	.25
116	A24	10s	red brn & brnsh blk	.25	.25
117	A25	15s	olive green	.25	.25
118	A26	25s	indigo & blk	.25	.25
119	A27	30s	ol grn & red brn	.25	.25
120	A29	1 l	dark brown	.40	.30
			Nos. 114-120 (7)	4.90	1.80

Widths: No. 114 is 19½mm; No. 89, 18½mm. No. 118 is 19¼mm; No. 95, 18¼mm. No. 120 is 20mm; No. 98, 19mm. The re-engraved stamps also differ from the 1911 issue in many details of design. Nos. 114-120 exist imperforate.

The 5s exists in two types: I, 20x29.3mm, green and brown violet; II, 19.5x29mm, dark green and brown. There are a number of minor design differences between the two types. The editors would welcome any information that Bulgarian specialists can provide on this and similar varieties on stamps of this period.

The 5s and 10s exist perf. 14x11½.

For Nos. 114-116 and 118 overprinted with Cyrillic characters and "1916-1917," see Romania Nos. 2N1-2N4.

Coat of Arms — A33

Peasant and Bullock — A34

Soldier and Mt. Sonichka — A35

View of Nish — A36

Town and Lake Okhrida — A37

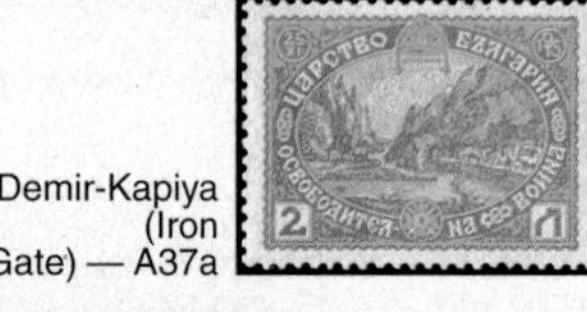

Demir-Kapiya (Iron Gate) — A37a

View of Gevgeli — A38

Perf. 11½, 12½x13, 13x12½

1917-19 Typo.

No.	Type	Value	Description	Unused	Used
122	A33	5s	green	.30	.25
123	A34	15s	slate	.25	.25
124	A35	25s	blue	.25	.25
125	A36	30s	orange	.25	.25
126	A37	50s	violet	.50	.30
126A	A37a	2 l	brn org ('19)	.50	.35
127	A38	3 l	claret	1.75	1.75
			Nos. 122-127 (7)	3.80	3.40

Liberation of Macedonia. A 1 l dark green was prepared but not issued. Value $1.65.

For surcharges see Nos. B9-B10, B12.

View of Veles — A39

Monastery of St. Clement at Okhrida — A40

1918 *Perf. 13x14*

No.	Type	Value	Description	Unused	Used
128	A39	1s	gray	.25	.25
129	A40	5s	green	.25	.25

Tsar Ferdinand A41

Plowing with Oxen A42

1918, July 1 *Perf. 12½x13*

No.	Type	Value	Description	Unused	Used
130	A41	1s	dark green	.80	.25
131	A41	2s	dark brown	.80	.25
132	A41	3s	indigo	1.60	.25
133	A41	10s	brown red	1.60	.25
			Nos. 130-133 (4)	4.80	1.00

Ferdinand's accession to the throne, 30th anniv.

1919 *Perf. 13½x13*

No.	Type	Value	Description	Unused	Used
134	A42	1s	gray	.25	.25

Sobranye Palace — A43

Tsar Boris III — A44

1919 *Perf. 11½x12, 12x11½*

No.	Type	Value	Description	Unused	Used
135	A43	1s	black	.25	.25
137	A43	2s	olive green	.25	.25

For surcharges see Nos. 186, B1.

1919, Oct. 3

No.	Type	Value	Description	Unused	Used
138	A44	3s	orange brn	.25	.25
139	A44	5s	green	.25	.25
140	A44	10s	rose red	.25	.25
141	A44	15s	violet	.25	.25
142	A44	25s	deep blue	.25	.25
143	A44	30s	chocolate	.25	.25
144	A44	50s	yellow brn	.25	.25
			Nos. 138-144 (7)	1.75	1.75

1st anniv. of enthronement of Tsar Boris III. Nos. 135-144 exist imperforate.

For surcharges see Nos. 187, B2-B7.

Birthplace of Vazov at Sopot and Cherrywood Cannon — A47

"The Bear Fighter"-a Character from "Under the Yoke" — A48

Ivan Vazov in 1870 and 1920 A49

Vazov — A50

Homes of Vazov at Plovdiv and Sofia A51

The Monk Paisii — A52

1920, Oct. 20 Photo. *Perf. 11½*

No.	Type	Value	Description	Unused	Used
147	A47	30s	brown red	.25	.25
148	A48	50s	dark green	.25	.25
149	A49	1 l	drab	.25	.30
150	A50	2 l	light brown	1.20	.65
151	A51	3 l	black violet	1.90	.75
152	A52	5 l	deep blue	2.40	1.50
			Nos. 147-152 (6)	6.25	3.70

70th birthday of Ivan Vazov (1850-1921), Bulgarian poet and novelist.

Several values of this series exist imperforate and in pairs imperforate between.

Tsar Ferdinand

A53 A54

Mt. Shar — A55

Bridge over Vardar River — A56

View of Ohrid — A57

Perf. 13x14, 14x13

1921, June 11 **Typo.**

153	A53	10s claret	.25	.25
154	A54	10s claret	.25	.25
155	A55	10s claret	.25	.25
156	A56	10s rose lilac	.25	.25
157	A57	20s blue	.70	.25
		Nos. 153-157 (5)	1.70	1.25

Nos. 153-157 were intended to be issued in 1915 to commemorate the liberation of Macedonia. They were not put in use until 1921. A 50s violet was prepared but never placed in use. Value $1.75.

View of Sofia — A58

"The Liberator," Monument to Alexander II A59

Monastery at Shipka Pass — A62

Tsar Boris III — A63

Harvesting Grain — A64

Tsar Assen's Tower (No crown over lion) — A65

Rila Monastery (Rosette at upper right) — A66

1921-23 **Engr.** ***Perf. 12***

158	A58	10s blue gray	.25	.25
159	A59	20s deep green	.25	.25
160	A63	25s blue grn ('22)	.25	.25
161	A22	50s orange	.25	.25
162	A22	50s dk blue ('23)	4.00	2.50
163	A62	75s dull vio	.25	.25
164	A62	75s dp blue ('23)	.30	.25
165	A63	1 l carmine	.30	.25
166	A63	1 l dp blue ('22)	.30	.25
167	A64	2 l brown	.30	1.00
168	A65	3 l brown vio	1.40	1.10
169	A66	5 l lt blue	3.75	1.25
170	A63	10 l violet brn	9.50	2.10
		Nos. 158-170 (13)	21.10	9.95

For surcharge see No. 189.

Bourchier in Bulgarian Costume A67

James David Bourchier A68

View of Rila Monastery A69

1921, Dec. 31

171	A67	10s red orange	.25	.25
172	A67	20s orange	.25	.25
173	A68	30s dp gray	.25	.25
174	A68	50s bluish gray	.25	.25
175	A68	1 l dull vio	.25	.25
176	A69	1½ l olive grn	.25	.25
177	A69	2 l deep green	.25	.25
178	A69	3 l Prus blue	.60	.25
179	A69	5 l red brown	1.00	.50
		Nos. 171-179 (9)	3.35	2.50

Death of James D. Bourchier, Balkan correspondent of the London Times.

For surcharges see Nos. B13-B16.

Postage Due Stamps of 1919-22 Surcharged — a

1924

182	D6	10s on 20s yellow	.25	.25
183	D6	20s on 5s gray grn	.25	.25
a.		20s on 5s emerald	*30.00*	*30.00*
184	D6	20s on 10s violet	.25	.25
185	D6	20s on 30s orange	.25	.25
		Nos. 182-185 (4)	1.00	1.00

Nos. 182 to 185 were used for ordinary postage.

Regular Issues of 1919-23 Surcharged in Blue or Red

b

c

186	A43 (a)	10s on 1s black (R)	.25	.25
187	A44 (b)	1 l on 5s emer (Bl)	.25	.25
188	A22 (c)	3 l on 50s dk bl (R)	.25	.25
189	A63 (b)	6 l on 1 l car (Bl)	.60	.25
		Nos. 186-189 (4)	1.35	1.00

The surcharge of No. 188 comes in three types: normal, thick and thin.

Nos. 182, 184-189 exist with inverted surcharge.

Lion of Bulgaria A70 A71

Tsar Boris III — A72

New Sofia Cathedral — A73

Harvesting A74

1925 **Typo.** ***Perf. 13, 11½***

191	A70	10s red & bl, *pink*	.40	.25
192	A70	15s car & org, *blue*	.40	.25
193	A70	30s blk & buff	.40	.25
a.		Cliche of 15s in plate of 30s		
194	A71	50s choc, *green*	.40	.25
195	A72	1 l dull green	.95	.25
196	A73	2 l dk grn & buff	1.90	.25
197	A74	4 l lake & yellow	1.90	.25
		Nos. 191-197 (7)	6.35	1.75

Several values of this series exist imperforate and in pairs imperforate between.

See Nos. 199, 201. For overprint see No. C2.

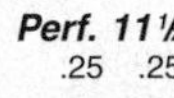

Cathedral of Sveta Nedelya, Sofia, Ruined by Bomb — A75

1926 ***Perf. 11½***

198	A75	50s gray black	.25	.25

A76

A77

Type A72 Re-engraved. (Shoulder at left does not touch frame)

1926

199	A76	1 l gray	.45	.25
a.		1 l green	.45	.25
201	A76	2 l olive brown	.70	.25

Center Embossed

202	A77	6 l dp bl & pale lemon	1.90	.25
203	A77	10 l brn blk & brn org	4.75	1.75
		Nos. 199-203 (4)	7.80	2.50

For overprints see Nos. C1, C3-C4.

Christo Botev — A78

1926, June 2

204	A78	1 l olive green	.55	.25
205	A78	2 l slate violet	1.20	.25
206	A78	4 l red brown	1.20	.35
		Nos. 204-206 (3)	2.95	.85

Botev (1847-76), Bulgarian revolutionary, poet.

Lion Type of 1881 Redrawn

1927-29 ***Perf. 13***

207	A3	10s dk red & drab	.25	.25
208	A3	15s blk & org ('29)	.25	.25
209	A3	30s dk bl & bis brn ('28)	.25	.25
a.		30s indigo & buff	.25	.25
210	A3	50s blk & rose red ('28)	.25	.25
		Nos. 207-210 (4)	1.00	1.00

Scott 207-210 have less detailed scrollwork surrounding the central lion, which is also less detailed than Scott 1-18.

Tsar Boris III — A79

1928, Oct. 3 ***Perf. 11½***

211	A79	1 l olive green	.90	.25
212	A79	2 l deep brown	1.00	.25

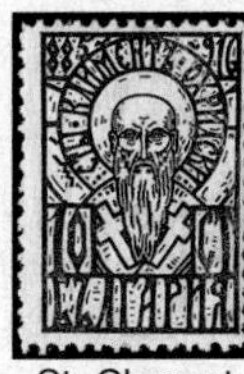

St. Clement A80

Konstantin Miladinov A81

George S. Rakovski A82

Drenovo Monastery A83

Paisii — A84

Tsar Simeon — A85

Lyuben Karavelov A86

Vassil Levski A87

Georgi Benkovski A88

Tsar Alexander II A89

1929, May 12

213	A80	10s dk violet	.25	.25
214	A81	15s violet brn	.40	.40
215	A82	30s red	.25	.25
216	A83	50s olive grn	.25	.25
217	A84	1 l orange brn	1.00	.25
218	A85	2 l dk blue	1.15	.25
219	A86	3 l dull green	2.50	.45
220	A87	4 l olive brown	4.00	.25
221	A88	5 l brown	2.50	.35
222	A89	6 l Prus green	3.75	.90
		Nos. 213-222 (10)	16.05	3.60

Millenary of Tsar Simeon and 50th anniv. of the liberation of Bulgaria from the Turks.

Royal Wedding Issue

Tsar Boris and Fiancee, Princess Giovanna A90

Queen Ioanna and Tsar Boris — A91

1930, Nov. 12 ***Perf. 11½***

223	A90	1 l green	.35	.25
224	A91	2 l dull violet	.35	.30
225	A90	4 l rose red	.35	.30
226	A91	6 l dark blue	.35	.40
		Nos. 223-226 (4)	1.40	1.25

Fifty-five copies of a miniature sheet incorporating one each of Nos. 223-226 were printed and given to royal, governmental and diplomatic personages.

Tsar Boris III
A92 A93

Perf. 11½, 12x11½, 13

1931-37 **Unwmk.**

No.	Type	Denomination	Unused	Used
227	A92	1 l blue green	.25	.25
228	A92	2 l carmine	.40	.25
229	A92	4 l red org ('34)	.75	.25
230	A92	4 l yel org ('37)	.25	.25
231	A92	6 l deep blue	.70	.25
232	A92	7 l dp bl ('37)	.25	.25
233	A92	10 l slate blk	8.75	.70
234	A92	12 l lt brown	.40	.25
235	A92	14 l lt brn ('37)	.30	.25
236	A93	20 l claret & org brn	1.00	.45
		Nos. 227-236 (10)	13.05	3.15

Nos. 230-233 and 235 have outer bars at top and bottom as shown on cut A92; Nos. 227-229 and 234 are without outer bars.

See Nos. 251, 279-280, 287. For surcharge see No. 252.

Balkan Games Issues

Gymnast A95

Soccer — A96

Riding — A97

Swimmer A100

"Victory" A101

Designs: 6 l, Fencing. 10 l, Bicycle race.

1931, Sept. 18 *Perf. 11½*

No.	Type	Denomination	Unused	Used
237	A95	1 l lt green	1.25	.50
238	A96	2 l garnet	1.75	.50
239	A97	4 l carmine	3.25	.75
240	A95	6 l Prus blue	7.50	1.25
241	A95	10 l red org	20.00	3.75
242	A100	12 l dk blue	70.00	16.00
243	A101	50 l olive brn	65.00	36.00
		Nos. 237-243 (7)	168.75	58.75

1933, Jan. 5

No.	Type	Denomination	Unused	Used
244	A95	1 l blue grn	2.50	.95
245	A96	2 l blue	4.00	1.10
246	A97	4 l brn vio	6.00	1.10
247	A95	6 l brt rose	12.50	1.50
248	A95	10 l olive brn	90.00	20.00
249	A100	12 l orange	150.00	37.50
250	A101	50 l red brown	400.00	160.00
		Nos. 244-250 (7)	665.00	222.15

Nos. 244-250 were sold only at the philatelic agency.

Boris Type of 1931 Outer Bars at Top and Bottom Removed

1933 *Perf. 13*

No.	Type	Denomination	Unused	Used
251	A92	6 l deep blue	.80	.25

Type of 1931 Surcharged in Blue

1934

No.	Type	Denomination	Unused	Used
252	A92	2 (l) on 3 l ol brn	7.25	.25

Soldier Defending Shipka Pass A102

Shipka Battle Memorial A103

Color-Bearer A104

Veteran of the War of Liberation, 1878 — A105

Widow and Orphans — A106

Perf. 10½, 11½

1934, Aug. 26 **Wmk. 145**

No.	Type	Denomination	Unused	Used
253	A102	1 l green	.70	.40
254	A103	2 l pale red	.70	.25
255	A104	3 l bister brn	2.40	1.25
256	A105	4 l dk carmine	2.00	.60
257	A104	7 l dk blue	2.75	2.25
258	A106	14 l plum	17.00	8.00
		Nos. 253-258 (6)	25.55	12.75

Shipka Pass Battle memorial unveiling.

An unwatermarked miniature sheet incorporating one each of Nos. 253-258 was put on sale in 1938 in five cities at a price of 8,000 leva. Printing: 100 sheets. Value: $1,500.

1934, Sept. 21

No.	Type	Denomination	Unused	Used
259	A102	1 l bright green	.70	.40
260	A103	2 l dull orange	.70	.25
261	A104	3 l yellow	2.40	1.25
262	A105	4 l rose	2.00	.60
263	A104	7 l blue	2.75	2.25
264	A106	14 l olive bister	17.00	8.00
		Nos. 259-264 (6)	25.55	12.75

An unwatermarked miniature sheet incorporating one each of Nos. 259-263 was issued. Value: $1,500.

Velcho A. Djamjiyata A108

Capt. G. S. Mamarchev A109

1935, May 5 *Perf. 11½*

No.	Type	Denomination	Unused	Used
265	A108	1 l deep blue	2.00	.40
266	A109	2 l maroon	2.00	.60

Bulgarian uprising against the Turks, cent.

Soccer Game — A110

Cathedral of Alexander Nevski — A111

Soccer Team — A112

Symbolical of Victory — A113

Player and Trophy — A114

The Trophy — A115

1935, June 14

No.	Type	Denomination	Unused	Used
267	A110	1 l green	12.00	.90
268	A111	2 l blue gray	12.00	1.40
269	A112	4 l crimson	12.00	2.25
270	A113	7 l brt blue	20.00	7.00
271	A114	14 l orange	20.00	9.00
272	A115	50 l lilac brn	300.00	125.00
		Nos. 267-272 (6)	376.00	145.55

5th Balkan Soccer Tournament.

Gymnast on Parallel Bars A116

Youth in "Yunak" Costume A117

Girl in "Yunak" Costume A118

Pole Vaulting A119

Stadium, Sofia — A120

Yunak Emblem — A121

1935, July 10

No.	Type	Denomination	Unused	Used
273	A116	1 l green	6.00	1.10
274	A117	2 l lt blue	6.00	1.10
275	A118	4 l carmine	8.00	2.25
276	A119	7 l dk blue	8.00	3.50
277	A120	14 l dk brown	10.00	4.00
278	A121	50 l red	170.00	80.00
		Nos. 273-278 (6)	208.00	91.95

8th tournament of the Yunak Gymnastic Organization at Sofia, July 12-14.

Boris Type of 1931

1935 **Wmk. 145** *Perf. 12½, 13*

No.	Type	Denomination	Unused	Used
279	A92	1 l green	.55	.25
280	A92	2 l carmine	35.00	.25

Janos Hunyadi A122

King Ladislas Varnenchik A123

Varna Memorial A124

King Ladislas III — A125

Battle of Varna, 1444 — A126

1935, Aug. 4 *Perf. 10½, 11½*

No.	Type	Denomination	Unused	Used
281	A122	1 l brown org	3.75	1.50
282	A123	2 l maroon	3.75	1.75
283	A124	4 l vermilion	22.50	6.75
284	A125	7 l dull blue	3.75	2.25
285	A126	14 l green	4.00	2.00
		Nos. 281-285 (5)	37.75	14.25

Battle of Varna, and the death of the Polish King, Ladislas Varnenchik (1424-44). Nos. 281-285 exist imperf. Value, set $50.

Lion Type of 1881

1935 **Wmk. 145** *Perf. 13*

No.	Type	Denomination	Unused	Used
286	A3	10s dk red & drab	.70	.25

Boris Type of 1933 Outer Bars at Top and Bottom Removed

1935

No.	Type	Denomination	Unused	Used
287	A92	6 l gray blue	1.25	.25

Dimitr Monument
A127

Haji
Dimitr — A128

Haji Dimitr
and Stefan
Karaja
A129

Taking the
Oath — A130

Birthplace of
Dimitr
A131

1935, Oct. 1 Unwmk. *Perf. 11½*

288	A127	1 l	green	2.50	.45
289	A128	2 l	brown	3.50	.90
290	A129	4 l	car rose	10.00	2.75
291	A130	7 l	blue	12.00	6.00
292	A131	14 l	orange	15.00	4.50
			Nos. 288-292 (5)	43.00	14.60

67th anniv. of the death of the Bulgarian patriots, Haji Dimitr and Stefan Karaja. Nos. 288-292 exist imperf.

Catalogue values for unused stamps in this section, from this point to the end of the section, are for Never Hinged items.

A132

A133

1936-39 *Perf. 13x12½, 13*

293	A132	10s	red org ('37)	.30	.25
294	A132	15s	emerald	.30	.25
295	A133	30s	maroon	.30	.25
296	A133	30s	yel brn ('37)	.30	.25
297	A133	30s	Prus bl ('37)	.30	.25
298	A133	50s	ultra	.30	.25
299	A133	50s	dk car ('37)	.30	.25
300	A133	50s	slate grn ('39)	.30	.25
			Nos. 293-300 (8)	2.40	2.00

Meteorological
Station, Mt.
Moussalla
A134

Peasant Girl
A135

Town of
Nessebr
A136

1936, Aug. 16 Photo. *Perf. 11½*

301	A134	1 l	purple	4.00	1.90
302	A135	2 l	ultra	4.00	2.25
303	A136	7 l	dark blue	8.00	3.75
			Nos. 301-303 (3)	16.00	7.90

4th Geographical & Ethnographical Cong., Sofia, Aug. 1936.

Sts. Cyril and
Methodius
A137

Displaying the
Bible to the
People
A138

1937, June 2

304	A137	1 l	dk green	.60	.30
305	A137	2 l	dk plum	.65	.30
306	A138	4 l	vermilion	.80	.30
307	A137	7 l	dk blue	4.25	1.60
308	A138	14 l	rose red	4.75	1.90
			Nos. 304-308 (5)	11.05	4.40

Millennium of Cyrillic alphabet.

Princess
Marie Louise
A139

Tsar Boris III
A140

1937, Oct. 3

310	A139	1 l	yellow green	.70	.25
311	A139	2 l	brown red	.70	.25
312	A139	4 l	scarlet	.70	.40
			Nos. 310-312 (3)	2.10	.90

Issued in honor of Princess Marie Louise.

1937, Oct. 3

313	A140	2 l	brown red	1.00	.45

19th anniv. of the accession of Tsar Boris III to the throne. See No. B11.

National Products Issue

Peasants
Bundling Wheat
A141

Sunflower
A142

Wheat — A143

Chickens and
Eggs — A144

Cluster of
Grapes — A145

Rose and
Perfume
Flask — A146

Strawberries
A147

Girl Carrying
Grape Clusters
A148

Rose — A149

Tobacco
Leaves — A150

1938 *Perf. 13*

316	A141	10s	orange	.25	.25
317	A141	10s	red org	.25	.25
318	A142	15s	brt rose	.50	.25
319	A142	15s	deep plum	.50	.25
320	A143	30s	golden brn	.40	.25
321	A143	30s	copper brn	.40	.25
322	A144	50s	black	1.00	.25
323	A144	50s	indigo	1.00	.25
324	A145	1 l	yel grn	1.00	.25
325	A145	1 l	green	1.00	.25
326	A146	2 l	rose pink	1.00	.25
327	A146	2 l	rose brn	1.00	.25
328	A147	3 l	dp red lil	2.00	.25
329	A147	3 l	brn lake	2.00	.25
330	A148	4 l	plum	1.50	.25
331	A148	4 l	golden brn	1.50	.25
332	A149	7 l	vio blue	3.00	1.50
333	A149	7 l	dp blue	3.00	1.50
334	A150	14 l	dk brown	5.00	1.90
335	A150	14 l	red brn	5.00	1.90
			Nos. 316-335 (20)	31.30	10.80

Several values of this series exist imperforate.

Crown Prince Simeon
A151 A153

Designs: 2 l, Same portrait as 1 l, value at lower left. 14 l, similar to 4 l, but no wreath.

1938, June 16

336	A151	1 l	brt green	.30	.25
337	A151	2 l	rose pink	.30	.25
338	A153	4 l	dp orange	.40	.25
339	A151	7 l	ultra	1.25	.40
340	A153	14 l	dp brown	1.50	.50
			Nos. 336-340 (5)	3.75	1.65

First birthday of Prince Simeon.
Nos. 336-340 exist imperf. Value, set $15.

Tsar Boris III
A155 A156

Various Portraits of Tsar.

1938, Oct. 3

341	A155	1 l	lt green	.25	.25
342	A156	2 l	rose brown	.95	.25
343	A156	4 l	golden brn	.30	.25
344	A156	7 l	brt ultra	.50	.50
345	A156	14 l	deep red lilac	.55	.50
			Nos. 341-345 (5)	2.55	1.75

Reign of Tsar Boris III, 20th anniv.
Nos. 341-345 exist imperf. Value, set $40.

Early
Locomotive
A160

Designs: 2 l, Modern locomotive. 4 l, Train crossing bridge. 7 l, Tsar Boris in cab.

1939, Apr. 26

346	A160	1 l	yel green	.50	.30
347	A160	2 l	copper brn	.50	.30
348	A160	4 l	red orange	3.00	1.50
349	A160	7 l	dark blue	9.00	4.00
			Nos. 346-349 (4)	13.00	6.10

50th anniv. of Bulgarian State Railways.

Post Horns and
Arrows — A164

Central Post
Office,
Sofia — A165

1939, May 14 Typo.

350	A164	1 l	yellow grn	.30	.25
351	A165	2 l	brt carmine	.40	.25

Establishment of the postal system, 60th anniv.

Gymnast on
Bar — A166

Yunak
Emblem — A167

Discus Thrower — A168

Athletic Dancer — A169

Weight Lifter — A170

1939, July 7 **Photo.**

352	A166	1 l yel grn & pale grn	.45	.35
353	A167	2 l brt rose	.50	.35
354	A168	4 l brn & gldn brn	.90	.45
355	A169	7 l dk bl & bl	3.00	1.50
356	A170	14 l plum & rose vio	14.00	10.00
		Nos. 352-356 (5)	18.85	12.65

9th tournament of the Yunak Gymnastic Organization at Sofia, July 4-8.

Tsar Boris III — A171

Bulgaria's First Stamp — A172

1940-41 **Typo.**

356A	A171	1 l dl grn ('41)	.80	.25
357	A171	2 l brt crimson	.80	.25

1940, May 19 **Photo.** ***Perf. 13***

20 l, Similar design, scroll dated "1840-1940."

358	A172	10 l olive black	2.50	2.00
359	A172	20 l indigo	2.50	2.00

Cent. of 1st postage stamp.
Nos. 358-359 exist imperf. Value, set $100.

Peasant Couple and Tsar Boris — A174

Flags over Wheat Field and Tsar Boris — A175

Tsar Boris and Map of Dobrudja A176

1940, Sept. 20

360	A174	1 l slate green	.25	.25
361	A175	2 l rose red	.25	.25
362	A176	4 l dark brown	.40	.25
363	A176	7 l dark blue	1.00	.65
		Nos. 360-363 (4)	1.90	1.40

Return of Dobrudja from Romania.

Fruit A177

Bees and Flowers A178

Plowing A179

Shepherd and Sheep A180

Tsar Boris III — A181

Perf. 10, 10½x11½, 11½, 13

1940-44 **Typo.** **Unwmk.**

364	A177	10s red orange	.25	.25
365	A178	15s blue	.25	.25
366	A179	30s olive brn ('41)	.25	.25
367	A180	50s violet	.25	.25
368	A181	1 l brt green	.25	.25
369	A181	2 l rose car	.25	.25
370	A181	4 l red orange	.25	.25
371	A181	6 l red vio ('44)	.30	.25
372	A181	7 l blue	.30	.25
373	A181	10 l blue grn ('41)	.30	.25
		Nos. 364-373 (10)	2.65	2.50

See Nos. 373A-377, 440. For overprints see Nos. 455-463, C31-C32.

1940-41 **Wmk. 145** ***Perf. 13***

373A	A180	50s violet ('41)	.25	.25
374	A181	1 l brt grn	.25	.25
375	A181	2 l rose car	.25	.25
376	A181	7 l dull blue	.45	.25
377	A181	10 l blue green	.65	.25
		Nos. 373A-377 (5)	1.85	1.25

Watermarked vertically or horizontally.

P. R. Slaveikov A182

Sofronii, Bishop of Vratza A183

Saint Ivan Rilski — A184

Martin S. Drinov — A185

Monk Khrabr — A186

Kolio Ficheto — A187

1940, Sept. 23 **Photo.** **Unwmk.**

378	A182	1 l brt bl grn	.25	.25
379	A183	2 l brt carmine	.25	.25
380	A184	3 l dp red brn	.25	.25
381	A185	4 l red orange	.25	.25
382	A186	7 l deep blue	1.60	.60
383	A187	10 l dp red brn	2.40	.85
		Nos. 378-383 (6)	5.00	2.45

Liberation of Bulgaria from the Turks in 1878.

Johannes Gutenberg A188

N. Karastoyanov, 1st Bulgarian Printer A189

1940, Dec. 16

384	A188	1 l slate green	.35	.35
385	A189	2 l orange brown	.35	.35

500th anniv. of the invention of the printing press and 100th anniv. of the 1st Bulgarian printing press.

Christo Botev — A190

Monument to Botev — A192

Botev with his Insurgent Band — A191

1941, May 3

386	A190	1 l dark blue green	.25	.25
387	A191	2 l crimson rose	.30	.25
388	A192	3 l dark brown	1.00	.45
		Nos. 386-388 (3)	1.55	.95

Christo Botev, patriot and poet.

Palace of Justice, Sofia — A193

20 l, Workers' hospital. 50 l, National Bank.

1941-43 **Engr.** ***Perf. 11½***

389	A193	14 l lt gray brn ('43)	.25	.25
390	A193	20 l gray grn ('43)	.70	.25
391	A193	50 l lt bl gray	3.25	2.10
		Nos. 389-391 (3)	4.20	2.60

Macedonian Woman — A196

City of Okhrida — A200

Outline of Macedonia and Tsar Boris III A197

View of Aegean Sea — A198

Poganovski Monastery A199

1941, Oct. 3 **Photo.** ***Perf. 13***

392	A196	1 l slate grn	.25	.25
393	A197	2 l crimson	.25	.25
394	A198	2 l red org	.25	.25
395	A199	4 l org brn	.25	.25
396	A200	7 l dp gray bl	1.40	1.25
		Nos. 392-396 (5)	2.40	2.25

Issued to commemorate the acquisition of Macedonian territory from neighboring countries.

Peasant Working in a Field — A201

Designs: 15s, Plowing. 30s, Apiary. 50s, Women harvesting fruit. 3 l, Shepherd and sheep. 5 l, Inspecting cattle.

1941-44

397	A201	10s dk violet	.25	.25
398	A201	10s dk blue	.25	.25
399	A201	15s Prus blue	.25	.25
400	A201	15s dk ol brn	.25	.25
401	A201	30s red orange	.25	.25
402	A201	30s dk slate grn	.25	.25
403	A201	50s blue vio	.25	.25
404	A201	50s red lilac	.25	.25
405	A201	3 l henna brn	.40	.25
406	A201	3 l dk brn ('44)	1.40	1.10
407	A201	5 l sepia	.50	.50
408	A201	5 l vio bl ('44)	1.40	1.10
		Nos. 397-408 (12)	5.70	4.95

Girls Singing — A207

Boys in Camp — A208

Raising Flag — A209

Folk Dancers — A211

Camp Scene A210

1942, June 1 **Photo.**

409	A207	1 l dk bl grn	.25	.25
410	A208	2 l scarlet	.25	.25
411	A209	4 l olive gray	.25	.25
412	A210	7 l deep blue	.25	.25
413	A211	14 l fawn	.90	.75
		Nos. 409-413 (5)	1.90	1.75

National "Work and Joy" movement.

Wounded Soldier — A212

Soldier's Farewell A213

4 l, Aiding wounded soldier. 7 l, Widow & orphans at grave. 14 l, Tomb of Unknown Soldier. 20 l, Queen Ioanna visiting wounded.

1942, Sept. 7

414 A212 1 l slate grn .25 .25
415 A213 2 l brt rose .25 .25
416 A213 4 l yel org .25 .25
417 A213 7 l dark blue .25 .25
418 A213 14 l brown .25 .25
419 A213 20 l olive blk .25 .25
Nos. 414-419 (6) 1.50 1.50

Issued to aid war victims. No. 419 was printed in sheets of 50, alternating with 50 labels.

Legend of Kubrat — A218

Cavalry Charge — A219

Designs: 30s, Rider of Madara. 50s, Christening of Boris I. 1 l, School, St. Naum. 2 l, Crowning of Tsar Simeon by Boris I. 3 l, Golden era of Bulgarian literature. 4 l, Sentencing of the Bogomil Basil. 5 l, Proclamation of 2nd Bulgarian Empire. 7 l, Ivan Assen II at Trebizond. 10 l, Deporting the Patriarch Jeftimi. 14 l, Wandering minstrel. 20 l, Monk Paisii. 30 l, Monument, Shipka Pass.

1942, Oct. 12

420 A218 10s bluish blk .25 .25
421 A219 15s Prus grn .25 .25
422 A219 30s dk rose vio .25 .25
423 A219 50s indigo .25 .25
424 A219 1 l slate grn .25 .25
425 A219 2 l crimson .25 .25
426 A219 3 l brown .25 .25
427 A219 4 l orange .25 .25
428 A219 5 l grnsh blk .25 .25
429 A219 7 l dk blue .25 .25
430 A219 10 l brown blk .25 .25
431 A219 14 l olive blk .25 .25
432 A219 20 l henna brn .40 .30
433 A219 30 l black .70 .40
Nos. 420-433 (14) 4.10 3.70

Tsar Boris III A234

Designs: Various portraits of Tsar.

Perf. 13, Imperf.

1944, Feb. 28 Photo. Wmk. 275

Frames in Black

434 A234 1 l olive grn .25 *.40*
435 A234 2 l red brown .25 *.40*
436 A234 4 l brown .25 *.40*
437 A234 5 l gray vio .80 *1.20*
438 A234 7 l slate blue .85 *1.60*
Nos. 434-438 (5) 2.40 *4.00*

Tsar Boris III (1894-1943).

Tsar Simeon II — A239

Perf. 11½, 13

1944, June 12 Typo. Unwmk.

439 A239 3 l red orange .30 .25

Shepherd Type of 1940

1944

440 A180 50s yellow green .25 .25

Parcel Post Stamps of 1944 Overprinted in Black or Orange

1945, Jan. 25 ***Perf. 11½***

448 PP5 1 l dk carmine .25 .25
449 PP5 7 l rose lilac .25 .25
450 PP5 20 l org brn .25 .25
451 PP5 30 l dk brn car .25 .25
452 PP5 50 l red orange .25 .25
453 PP5 100 l blue (O) .60 .25

Overprint reads: "Everything for the Front."

No. 448 with Additional Surcharge of New Value in Black

454 PP5 4 l on 1 l dk car .25 .25
Nos. 448-454 (7) 2.10 1.75

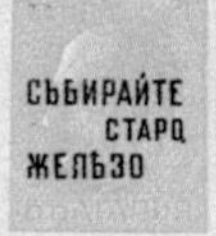

Nos. 368 to 370 Overprinted in Black

1945, Mar. 15 ***Perf. 11½, 13***

455 A181 1 l brt green .40 .25
456 A181 2 l rose carmine .95 .25
457 A181 4 l red orange 1.40 .25

Overprint reads: "Collect old iron."

Overprinted in Black

458 A181 1 l brt green .40 .25
459 A181 2 l rose carmine .65 .25
460 A181 4 l red orange .95 .25

Overprint reads: "Collect discarded paper."

Overprinted in Black

461 A181 1 l brt green .40 .25
462 A181 2 l rose carmine .65 .25
463 A181 4 l red orange .95 .25
Nos. 455-463 (9) 6.75 2.25

Overprint reads: "Collect all kinds of rags."

Oak Tree — A245

Imperf., Perf. 11½.

1945 Litho. Unwmk.

464 A245 4 l vermilion .25 .25
465 A245 10 l blue .25 .25

Imperf

466 A245 50 l brown lake .25 .25
Nos. 464-466 (3) .75 .75

Slav Congress, Sofia, March, 1945.

A246

A247

A248

A249

A251

A252

A253

A254

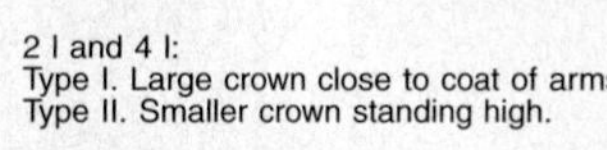

2 l and 4 l:
Type I. Large crown close to coat of arms.
Type II. Smaller crown standing high.

1945-46 Photo. ***Perf. 13***

469 A246 30s yellow grn .25 .25
470 A247 50s peacock grn .25 .25
471 A248 1 l dk green .25 .25
472 A249 2 l choc (I) .25 .25
a. Type II .25 .25
473 A249 4 l dk blue (I) .25 .25
a. Type II .25 .25
475 A251 5 l red violet .25 .25
476 A251 9 l slate gray .25 .25
477 A252 10 l Prus blue .25 .25
478 A253 15 l brown .25 .25
479 A254 20 l carmine .25 .25
480 A254 20 l gray blk .25 .25
Nos. 469-480 (11) 2.75 2.75

Breaking Chain — A255

1 Lev Coin — A256

Water Wheel — A257

Coin and Symbols of Agriculture and Industry — A258

Unwmk.

1945, June 4 Litho. ***Imperf.***

Laid Paper

481 A255 50 l brn red, *pink* .25 .25
482 A255 50 l org, *pink* .25 .25
483 A256 100 l gray bl, *pink* .25 .25
484 A256 100 l brn, *pink* .25 .25
485 A257 150 l dk ol gray, *pink* .85 .25
486 A257 150 l dl car, *pink* .85 .25
487 A258 200 l dp bl, *pink* 1.25 .70
488 A258 200 l ol grn, *pink* 1.25 .70
Nos. 481-488 (8) 5.20 2.90

Souvenir Sheets

489 Sheet of 4 6.00 3.50
a. A255 50 l violet blue .60 .25
b. A256 100 l violet blue .60 .25
c. A257 150 l violet blue .60 .25
d. A258 200 l violet blue .60 .25
490 Sheet of 4 6.00 3.50
a. A255 50 l brown orange .60 .25
b. A256 100 l brown orange .60 .25
c. A257 150 l brown orange .60 .25
d. A258 200 l brown orange .60 .25

Publicizing Bulgaria's Liberty Loan.

Olive Branch — A260

1945, Sept. 1 Typo. ***Perf. 13***

491 A260 10 l org brn & yel grn .25 .25
492 A260 50 l dull red & dp grn .40 .25

Victory of Allied Nations, World War II.

September 9, 1944 — A261

Numeral, Broken Chain — A262

1945, Sept. 7

493 A261 1 l gray green .25 .25
494 A261 4 l deep blue .25 .25
495 A261 5 l rose lilac .25 .25
496 A262 10 l lt blue .25 .25
497 A262 20 l brt car .25 .25
498 A261 50 l brt bl grn .70 .25
499 A261 100 l orange brn .80 .50
Nos. 493-499 (7) 2.75 2.00

1st anniv. of Bulgaria's liberation.

Old Postal Savings Emblem — A263

Child Putting Coin in Bank — A265

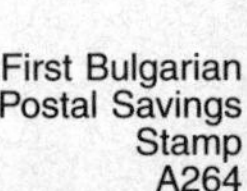

First Bulgarian Postal Savings Stamp A264

Postal Savings Building, Sofia — A266

1946, Apr. 12

500	A263	4 l brown org	.25	.25
501	A264	10 l dk olive	.25	.25
502	A265	20 l ultra	.45	.25
503	A266	50 l slate gray	.90	.90
		Nos. 500-503 (4)	1.85	1.65

50th anniv. of Bulgarian Postal Savings.

Refugee Children A267

Nurse Assisting Wounded Soldier A269

Wounded Soldier A268

35 l, 100 l, Red Cross hospital train.

1946, Apr. 4 **Cross in Carmine**

504	A267	2 l dk olive	.25	.25
505	A268	4 l violet	.25	.25
506	A267	10 l plum	.25	.25
507	A268	20 l ultra	.25	.25
508	A269	30 l brown org	.25	.25
509	A268	35 l gray blk	.25	.25
510	A269	50 l violet brn	.50	.25
511	A268	100 l gray brn	1.25	1.10
		Nos. 504-511 (8)	3.25	2.85

See Nos. 553-560.

Advancing Troops A271

Grenade Thrower — A272

Attacking Planes — A274

Designs: 5 l, Horse-drawn cannon. 9 l, Engineers building pontoon bridge. 10 l, 30 l, Cavalry charge. 40 l, Horse-drawn supply column. 50 l, Motor transport column. 60 l, Infantry, tanks and planes.

1946, Aug. 9 **Typo.** **Unwmk.**

512	A271	2 l dk red vio	.25	.25
513	A272	4 l dk gray	.25	.25
514	A271	5 l dk org red	.25	.25
515	A274	6 l black brn	.25	.25
516	A271	9 l rose lilac	.25	.25
517	A271	10 l dp violet	.25	.25
518	A271	20 l dp blue	.40	.25
519	A271	30 l red org	.40	.25
520	A271	40 l dk ol bis	.50	.25
521	A271	50 l dk green	.50	.25
522	A271	60 l red brown	.65	.50
		Nos. 512-522 (11)	3.95	3.00

Bulgaria's participation in World War II.

Arms of Russia and Bulgaria A279

Lion Rampant A280

1946, May 23

523	A279	4 l red orange	.25	.25
525	A279	20 l turq green	.25	.25

Congress of the Bulgarian-Soviet Association, May 1946. The 4 l exists in dk car rose and 20 l in blue, value, set $17.

1946, May 25 ***Imperf.***

526	A280	20 l blue	.70	.55

Day of the Postage Stamp, May 26, 1946.

Alekandr Stamboliski A281

Flags of Albania, Romania, Bulgaria and Yugoslavia A282

1946, June 13 ***Perf. 12***

527	A281	100 l red orange	8.75	8.75

23rd anniversary of the death of Alekandr Stamboliski, agrarian leader.

1946, July 6 ***Perf. 11½***

528	A282	100 l black brown	1.50	1.00

1946 Balkan Games.

Sheet of 100 arranged so that all stamps are tete beche vert. and horiz., except 2 center rows in left pane which provide 10 vert. pairs that are not tete beche vert.

St. Ivan Rilski — A283

A286

A284

A285

Views of Rila Monastery A287

1946, Aug. 26

529	A283	1 l red brown	.25	.25
530	A284	4 l black brn	.25	.25
531	A285	10 l dk green	.25	.25
532	A286	20 l dp blue	.40	.25
533	A287	50 l dk red	1.50	1.00
		Nos. 529-533 (5)	2.65	2.00

Millenary of Rila Monastery.

People's Republic

A288

1946, Sept. 15 **Typo.**

534	A288	4 l brown lake	.25	.25
535	A288	20 l dull blue	.25	.25
536	A288	50 l olive bister	.25	.25
		Nos. 534-536 (3)	.75	.75

No. 535 is inscribed "BULGARIA" in Latin characters.

Referendum of Sept. 8, 1946, resulting in the establishment of the Bulgarian People's Republic.

Partisan Army — A289

Snipers — A290

Soldiers: Past and Present — A291

Design: 30 l, Partisans advancing.

1946, Dec. 2

537	A289	1 l violet brn	.25	.25
538	A290	4 l dull grn	.25	.25
539	A291	5 l chocolate	.25	.25
540	A290	10 l crimson	.25	.25
541	A289	20 l ultra	.35	.25
542	A290	30 l olive bister	.35	.25
543	A291	50 l black	.50	.35
		Nos. 537-543 (7)	2.20	1.85

Relief Worker and Children — A294

Child with Gift Parcels — A295

Waiting for Food Distribution A296

Mother and Child A297

1946, Dec. 30

545	A294	1 l dk vio brn	.25	.25
546	A295	4 l brt red	.25	.25
547	A295	9 l olive bis	.25	.25
548	A294	10 l slate gray	.25	.25
549	A296	20 l ultra	.25	.25
550	A297	30 l dp brn org	.25	.25
551	A296	40 l maroon	.25	.25
552	A294	50 l peacock grn	.65	.65
		Nos. 545-552 (8)	2.40	2.40

"Bulgaria" is in Latin characters on No. 548.

Red Cross Types of 1946

1947, Jan. 31 **Cross in Carmine**

553	A267	2 l olive bister	.25	.25
554	A268	4 l olive black	.25	.25
555	A267	10 l blue grn	.25	.25
556	A268	20 l brt blue	.25	.25
557	A269	30 l yellow grn	.50	.50
558	A268	35 l grnsh gray	.50	.50
559	A269	50 l henna brn	.85	.85
560	A268	100 l dark blue	1.25	1.25
		Nos. 553-560 (8)	4.10	4.10

Laurel Branch, Allied and Bulgarian Emblems A298

Dove of Peace A299

1947, Feb. 28

561	A298	4 l olive	.25	.25
562	A299	10 l brown red	.25	.25
563	A299	20 l deep blue	.25	.25
		Nos. 561-563 (3)	.75	.75

Return to peace at the close of World War II. "Bulgaria" in Latin characters on No. 563.

A302

Guerrilla Fighters A303 A304

1947, Jan. 21 ***Perf. 11½***

567	A302	10 l choc & brn org	.55	.40
568	A303	20 l dk bl & bl	.55	.40
569	A304	70 l dp claret & rose	40.00	37.50
		Nos. 567-569 (3)	41.10	38.30

Issued to honor the anti-fascists.

Hydroelectric Station A305

Miner — A306

Symbols of Industry — A307

Tractor A308

1947, Aug. 6

570	A305	4 l olive green	.25	.25
571	A306	9 l red brown	.25	.25
572	A307	20 l deep blue	.45	.25
573	A308	40 l olive brown	.85	.55
		Nos. 570-573 (4)	1.80	1.30

Exhibition Building A309

Former Home of Alphonse de Lamartine A310

Symbols of Agriculture and Horticulture A311

Perf. 11x11½, 11½x11

1947, Aug. 31 Litho. Unwmk.

574	A309	4 l scarlet	.25	.25
575	A310	9 l brown lake	.25	.25
576	A311	20 l brt ultra	.25	.25
		Nos. 574-576 (3)	.75	.75

Plovdiv Intl. Fair, 1947. See No. C54.

Basil Evstatiev Aprilov — A312

1947, Oct. 19 Photo. *Perf. 11*

577	A312	40 l brt ultra	.70	.25

Cent. of the death of Basil Evstatiev Aprilov, educator and historian. See No. 603.

Bicycle Race — A313

Basketball A314

Chess A315

Balkan Games: 20 l, Soccer players. 60 l, Four flags of participating nations.

1947, Sept. 29 Typo. *Perf. 11½*

578	A313	2 l plum	.25	.25
579	A314	4 l dk olive grn	.25	.25
580	A315	9 l orange brn	3.50	3.50
581	A315	20 l brt ultra	1.40	.25
582	A315	60 l violet brn	2.75	1.25
		Nos. 578-582 (5)	8.15	5.50

People's Theater, Sofia A316

National Assembly A317

Central Post Office, Sofia A318

Presidential Mansion A319

1947-48 Typo. *Perf. 12½*

583	A316	50s yellow grn	.25	.25
584	A317	50s yellow grn	.25	.25
585	A318	1 l green	.25	.25
586	A319	1 l green	.25	.25
587	A316	2 l brown lake	.25	.25
588	A317	2 l lt brown	.25	.25
589	A316	4 l deep blue	.25	.25
590	A317	4 l deep blue	.25	.25
591	A316	9 l carmine	.35	.25
592	A317	20 l deep blue	.75	.30
		Nos. 583-592 (10)	3.10	2.55

On Nos. 583-592 inscription reads "Bulgarian Republic." No. 592 is inscribed in Latin characters.

Redrawn

Added to inscription

593	A318	1 l green	.25	.25
594	A318	2 l brown lake	.25	.25
595	A318	4 l deep blue	.25	.25
		Nos. 593-595 (3)	.75	.75

Cyrillic inscription beneath design on Nos. 593-595 reads "Bulgarian People's Republic."

Geno Kirov — A320

Actors' Portraits: 1 l, Zlatina Nedeva. 2 l, Ivan Popov. 3 l, Athanas Kirchev. 4 l, Elena Snejina. 5 l, Stoyan Bachvarov.

Perf. 10½

1947, Dec. 8 Unwmk. Litho.

596	A320	50s bister brn	.25	.25
597	A320	1 l lt blue grn	.25	.25
598	A320	2 l slate green	.25	.25
599	A320	3 l dp blue	.25	.25
600	A320	4 l scarlet	.25	.25
601	A320	5 l red brown	.25	.25
		Nos. 596-601,B22-B26 (11)	4.60	3.65

National Theater, 50th anniversary.

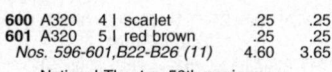

Merchant Ship "Fatherland" — A321

1947, Dec. 19

602	A321	50 l Prus bl, *cream*	1.00	.75

B. E. Aprilov — A322

Worker — A323

1948, Feb. 19 *Perf. 11*

603	A322	4 l brn car, *cream*	.25	.25

Centenary of the death of Basil Evstatiev Aprilov, educator and historian.

1948, Feb. 29 Photo. *Perf. 11½x12*

604	A323	4 l dp blue, *cream*	.25	.25

2nd Bulgarian Workers' Congress.

Self-education A324

Accordion Player — A325

Factory Recess — A326

Girl Throwing Basketball — A327

1948, Mar. 31 Photo.

605	A324	4 l red	.25	.25
606	A325	20 l deep blue	.25	.25
607	A326	40 l dull green	.50	.25
608	A327	60 l brown	1.25	.75
		Nos. 605-608 (4)	2.25	1.50

Nicholas Vaptzarov — A328

Portraits: 9 l, P. K. Iavorov. 15 l, Christo Smirnenski. 20 l, Ivan Vazov. 45 l, P. R. Slaveikov.

1948, May 18 Litho. *Perf. 11*

Cream Paper

611	A328	4 l brt ver	.25	.25
612	A328	9 l lt brown	.25	.25
613	A328	15 l claret	.25	.25
614	A328	20 l deep blue	.35	.35
615	A328	45 l green	.45	.45
		Nos. 611-615 (5)	1.55	1.55

Soviet Soldier — A329

Civilians Offering Gifts to Soldiers A330

Designs: 20 l, Soldiers, 1878 and 1944. 60 l, Stalin and Spasski Tower.

1948, July 5 Photo. Cream Paper

616	A329	4 l brown org	.25	.25
617	A330	10 l olive grn	.25	.25
618	A330	20 l dp blue	.30	.25
619	A329	60 l olive brn	1.00	1.00
		Nos. 616-619 (4)	1.80	1.75

The Soviet Army.

Demeter Blagoev — A331

Monument to Bishop Andrey A332

9 l, Gabriel Genov. 60 l, Marching youths.

1948, Sept. 6 Litho. Cream Paper

620	A331	4 l dk brown	.25	.25
621	A331	9 l brown org	.25	.25
622	A332	20 l dp blue	.40	.25
623	A332	60 l brown	.90	.70
		Nos. 620-623 (4)	1.80	1.45

No. 623 is inscribed in Cyrillic characters. Natl. Insurrection of 1923, 25th anniv.

Christo Smirnenski A333

Battle of Grivitza, 1877 A334

1948, Oct. 2 Photo. *Perf. 11½*

Cream Paper

624	A333	4 l blue	.25	.25
625	A333	16 l red brown	.25	.25

Christo Smirnenski, poet, 1898-1923.

1948, Nov. 1

626	A334	20 l blue	.25	.25
		Nos. 626,C56-C57 (3)	1.85	1.50

Romanian-Bulgarian friendship.

Bath, Gorna Banya — A335

Bath, Bankya — A336

Mineral Bath, Sofia
A337

Maliovitza
A338

1948-49 Typo. *Perf. 12½*

No.	Type	Value	Color	Unused	Used
627	A335	2 l	red brown	.25	.25
628	A336	3 l	red orange	.25	.25
629	A337	4 l	deep blue	.25	.25
630	A338	5 l	violet brown	.25	.25
631	A336	10 l	red violet	.40	.25
632	A338	15 l	olive grn ('49)	1.20	.25
633	A335	20 l	deep blue	1.75	.25
			Nos. 627-633 (7)	4.35	1.75

Latin characters on No. 633. See No. 653.

Emblem of the Republic — A339

1948-50

No.	Type	Value	Color	Unused	Used
634	A339	50s	red orange	.25	.25
634A	A339	50s	org brn ('50)	.25	.25
635	A339	1 l	green	.25	.25
636	A339	9 l	black	.40	.25
			Nos. 634-636 (4)	1.15	1.00

Botev's Birthplace, Kalofer
A340

Christo Botev — A341

Designs: 9 l, Steamer "Radetzky." 15 l, Kalofer village. 20 l, Botev in uniform. 40 l, Botev's mother. 50 l, Pen, pistol and wreath.

Cream Paper

Perf. 11x11½, 11½

1948, Dec. 21 Photo.

No.	Type	Value	Color	Unused	Used
638	A340	1 l	dk green	.25	.25
639	A341	4 l	violet brn	.25	.25
640	A340	9 l	violet	.25	.25
641	A340	15 l	brown	.25	.25
642	A341	20 l	blue	.25	.25
643	A340	40 l	red brown	.50	.25
644	A341	50 l	olive blk	.65	.50
			Nos. 638-644 (7)	2.40	2.00

Botev, Bulgarian natl. poet, birth cent.

Lenin — A342

Lenin Speaking — A343

1949, Jan. 24 Unwmk. *Perf. 11½*

Cream Paper

No.	Type	Value	Color	Unused	Used
645	A342	4 l	brown	.35	.25
646	A343	20 l	brown red	.50	.25

25th anniversary of the death of Lenin.

Road Construction
A344

Designs: 5 l, Tunnel construction. 9 l, Locomotive. 10 l, Textile worker. 20 l, Female tractor driver. 40 l, Workers in truck.

1949, Apr. 6 *Perf. 10½*

Inscribed: "CHM"

Cream Paper

No.	Type	Value	Color	Unused	Used
647	A344	4 l	dark red	.25	.25
648	A344	5 l	dark brown	.25	.25
649	A344	9 l	dk slate grn	.55	.25
650	A344	10 l	violet	.55	.25
651	A344	20 l	dull blue	1.25	.80
652	A344	40 l	brown	2.00	1.10
			Nos. 647-652 (6)	4.85	2.90

Honoring the Workers' Cultural Brigade.

Type of 1948 Redrawn
Country Name and "POSTA" in Latin Characters

1949 Typo. *Perf. 12½*

No.	Type	Value	Color	Unused	Used
653	A337	20 l	deep blue	1.90	.25

Miner — A345

1949 *Perf. 11x11½*

No.	Type	Value	Color	Unused	Used
654	A345	4 l	dark blue	.25	.25

A347

Prime Minister George Dimitrov, 1882-1949
A348

1949, July 10 Photo.

No.	Type	Value	Color	Unused	Used
656	A347	4 l	red brown	.50	.25
657	A348	20 l	dark blue	1.00	.25

Power Station — A349

Grain Towers — A350

Farm Machinery — A351

Tractor Parade
A352

Agriculture and Industry
A353

1949, Aug. 5 *Perf. 11½x11, 11x11½*

No.	Type	Value	Color	Unused	Used
658	A349	4 l	olive green	.25	.25
659	A350	9 l	dark red	.25	.25
660	A351	15 l	purple	.50	.50
661	A352	20 l	blue	1.10	.75
662	A353	50 l	orange brn	3.75	1.60
			Nos. 658-662 (5)	5.85	3.35

Bulgaria's Five Year Plan.

Grenade and Javelin Throwers — A354

Hurdlers
A355

Motorcycle and Tractor
A356

Boy and Girl Athletes — A357

1949, Sept. 5

No.	Type	Value	Color	Unused	Used
663	A354	4 l	brown orange	.60	.25
664	A355	9 l	olive green	1.40	.55
665	A356	20 l	violet blue	2.75	1.50
666	A357	50 l	red brown	6.25	2.75
			Nos. 663-666 (4)	11.00	5.05

A358

Frontier Guards — A359

1949, Oct. 31

No.	Type	Value	Color	Unused	Used
667	A358	4 l	chestnut brn	.45	.45
668	A359	20 l	gray blue	1.25	.55

See No. C60.

George Dimitrov — A360

Allegory of Labor — A361

Laborers of Both Sexes — A362

Workers and Flags of Bulgaria and Russia — A363

Perf. 11½

1949, Dec. 13 Photo. Unwmk.

No.	Type	Value	Color	Unused	Used
669	A360	4 l	orange brn	.25	.25
670	A361	9 l	purple	.25	.25
671	A362	20 l	dull blue	.70	.60
672	A363	50 l	red	1.40	1.10
			Nos. 669-672 (4)	2.60	2.20

Joseph V. Stalin — A364

Stalin and Dove — A365

1949, Dec. 21

No.	Type	Value	Color	Unused	Used
673	A364	4 l	deep orange	.50	.25
674	A365	40 l	rose brown	1.25	.55

70th anniv. of the birth of Joseph V. Stalin.

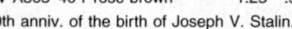

Kharalamby Stoyanov — A366

Railway Strikers
A367

Communications Strikers — A368

1950, Feb. 15

No.	Type	Value	Color	Unused	Used
675	A366	4 l	yellow brown	.25	.25
676	A367	20 l	violet blue	.45	.25
677	A368	60 l	brown olive	1.10	.70
			Nos. 675-677 (3)	1.80	1.20

30th anniv. (in 1949) of the General Railway and Postal Employees' Strike of 1919.

Miner — A369

Locomotive A370

Shipbuilding — A371

Tractor A372

Stalin Central Heating Plant — A374

Textile Worker — A375

Farm Machinery A373

1950-51 ***Perf. 11½, 13***

No.	Type	Value	Color	Unused	Used
678	A369	1 l	olive	.25	.25
679	A370	2 l	gray blk	.25	.25
680	A371	3 l	gray blue	.25	.25
681	A372	4 l	dk blue grn	2.50	.60
682	A373	5 l	henna brn	.50	.25
682A	A373	9 l	gray blk ('51)	.25	.25
683	A374	10 l	dp plum ('51)	.35	.25
684	A375	15 l	dk car ('51)	.50	.25
685	A375	20 l	dk blue ('51)	.85	.50
			Nos. 678-685 (9)	5.70	2.85

No. 685 is inscribed in Latin characters. See Nos. 750-751A.

Vassil Kolarov (1877-1950) — A377

1950, Mar. 6 ***Perf. 11½***

Size: 21½x31½mm

No.	Type	Value	Color	Unused	Used
686	A377	4 l	red brown	.25	.25

Size: 27x39½mm

No.	Type	Value	Color	Unused	Used
687	A377	20 l	violet blue	.70	.70

No. 687 has altered frame and is inscribed in Latin characters.

Stanislav Dospevski, Self-portrait A378

King Kaloyan and Desislava A379

Plowman Resting, by Christo Stanchev A380

Statue of Dimtcho Debelianov, by Ivan Lazarov — A381

"Harvest," by V. Dimitrov — A382

Design: 9 l, Nikolai Pavlovich, self-portrait.

1950, Apr. 15 ***Perf. 11½***

No.	Type	Value	Color	Unused	Used
688	A378	1 l	dk olive grn	.50	.25
689	A379	4 l	dk red	2.00	.55
690	A378	9 l	chocolate	2.00	.55
691	A380	15 l	brown	3.25	1.00
692	A380	20 l	deep blue	5.00	2.50
693	A381	40 l	red brown	6.25	3.50
694	A382	60 l	deep orange	8.75	5.00
			Nos. 688-694 (7)	27.75	13.35

Latin characters on No. 692.

Ivan Vazov (1850-1921), Poet and Birthplace A383

1950, June 26

No.	Type	Value	Color	Unused	Used
695	A383	4 l	olive green	.25	.25

Road Building A384

Men of Three Races and "Stalin" Flag — A385

Perf. 11½x11, 11x11½

1950, Sept. 19

No.	Type	Value	Color	Unused	Used
696	A384	4 l	brown red	.25	.25
697	A385	20 l	violet blue	.75	.25

2nd National Peace Conference.

Molotov, Kolarov, Stalin and Dimitrov A386

Spasski Tower and Flags — A387

Russian and Bulgarian Women — A388

Loading Russian Ship — A389

Perf. 11½

1950, Oct. 10 Unwmk. Photo.

No.	Type	Value	Color	Unused	Used
698	A386	4 l	brown	.25	.25
699	A387	9 l	rose carmine	.25	.25
700	A388	20 l	gray blue	.60	.25
701	A389	50 l	dk grnsh blue	2.50	.95
			Nos. 698-701 (4)	3.60	1.70

2nd anniversary of the Soviet-Bulgarian treaty of mutual assistance.

St. Constantine Sanatorium — A390

2 l, 10 l, Children at seashore. 5 l, Rest home.

1950 **Typo.**

No.	Type	Value	Color	Unused	Used
702	A390	1 l	dark green	.25	.25
703	A390	2 l	carmine	.25	.25
704	A390	5 l	deep orange	.25	.25
705	A390	10 l	deep blue	.40	.25
			Nos. 702-705 (4)	1.15	1.00

Originally prepared in 1945 as "Sunday Delivery Stamps," this issue was released for ordinary postage in 1950. Compare with Nos. RA16-RA18.

Runners — A393

1950, Aug. 21 Photo. ***Perf. 11***

No.	Type	Value	Design	Unused	Used
706	A393	4 l	shown	.80	.40
707	A393	9 l	Cycling	.80	.80
708	A393	20 l	Shot put	1.20	1.20
709	A393	40 l	Volleyball	2.40	2.40
			Nos. 706-709 (4)	5.20	4.80

Marshal Fedor I. Tolbukhin — A394

Natives Greeting Tolbukhin A395

Perf. 11½x11, 11x11½

1950, Dec. 10 Photo. Unwmk.

No.	Type	Value	Color	Unused	Used
710	A394	4 l	claret	.25	.25
711	A395	20 l	dk blue	1.50	.25

The return of Dobrich and part of the province of Dobruja from Romania to Bulgaria.

Dimitrov's Birthplace A396

George Dimitrov A397 A398

Various Portraits, Inscribed

Design: 2 l, Dimitrov Museum, Sofia.

1950, July 2 ***Perf. 10½***

No.	Type	Value	Color	Unused	Used
712	A396	50s	olive grn	.25	.25
713	A397	50s	brown	.25	.25
714	A397	1 l	redsh brn	.50	.25
715	A396	2 l	gray	.50	.25
716	A397	4 l	claret	1.00	.25
717	A397	9 l	red brown	1.40	.50
718	A398	10 l	brown red	1.50	.70
719	A396	15 l	olive gray	1.50	.70
720	A396	20 l	dark blue	4.00	1.25
			Nos. 712-720,C61 (10)	17.90	7.90

1st anniversary of the death of George Dimitrov, statesman. No. 720 is inscribed in Latin characters.

A. S. Popov — A400

1951, Feb. 10

No.	Type	Value	Color	Unused	Used
722	A400	4 l	red brown	.25	.25
723	A400	20 l	dark blue	1.50	.25

No. 723 is inscribed in Latin characters.

Arms of Bulgaria
A401 A402

1950 Unwmk. Typo. *Perf. 13*

724 A401 2 l dk brown .25 .25
725 A401 3 l rose .25 .25
726 A402 5 l carmine .25 .25
727 A402 9 l aqua .25 .25
Nos. 724-727 (4) 1.00 1.00

Nos. 724-727 were prepared in 1947 for official use but were issued as regular postage stamps Oct. 1, 1950.

Heroes Chankova, Antonov-Malchik, Dimitrov and Dimitrova — A403

Stanke Dimitrov-Marek A404

George Kirkov A405

George Dimitrov at Leipzig A406

Natcho Ivanov and Avr. Stoyanov A407

9 l, Anton Ivanov. 15 l, Christo Michailov.

1951, Mar. 25 Photo. *Perf. 11½*

728 A403 1 l red violet .25 .25
729 A404 2 l dk red brn .25 .25
730 A405 4 l car rose .25 .25
731 A405 9 l orange brn 1.00 .25
732 A405 15 l olive brn 1.75 .55
733 A406 20 l dark blue 2.40 1.10
734 A407 50 l olive gray 5.25 1.90
Nos. 728-734 (7) 11.15 4.55

First Bulgarian Tractor A408

First Steam Roller — A409

First Truck — A410

Bulgarian Embroidery — A411

15 l, Carpet. 20 l, Tobacco & roses. 40 l, Fruits.

Perf. 11x10½

1951, Mar. 30 Photo. Unwmk.

735 A408 1 l olive brn .25 .25
736 A409 2 l violet .55 .25
737 A410 4 l red brown 1.00 .25
738 A411 9 l purple 1.50 .25
739 A409 15 l deep plum 2.00 .55
740 A411 20 l violet blue 3.00 .55
741 A410 40 l deep green 5.00 1.25

Perf. 13

Size: 23x18½mm

742 A408 1 l purple .25 .25
743 A409 2 l Prus green .55 .25
744 A410 4 l red brown .55 .25
Nos. 735-744 (10) 14.65 4.10

For surcharges, see Nos. 894, 973.

Turkish Attack on Mt. Zlee Dol A412

Designs: 4 l, Georgi Benkovski speaking to rebels. 9 l, Cherrywood cannon of 1876 and Russian cavalry, 1945. 20 l, Rebel, 1876 and partisan, 1944. 40 l, Benkovski and Dimitrov.

1951, May 3 *Perf. 10½*

Cream Paper

745 A412 1 l redsh brown .25 .25
746 A412 4 l dark green .25 .25
747 A412 9 l violet brown 1.25 .75
748 A412 20 l deep blue 1.75 1.25
749 A412 40 l dark red 2.50 1.75
Nos. 745-749 (5) 6.00 4.25

75th anniv. of the "April" revolution.

Industrial Types of 1950

1951 *Perf. 13*

750 A369 1 l violet .25 .25
751 A370 2 l dk brown .25 .25
751A A372 4 l dk yel grn .75 .25
Nos. 750-751A (3) 1.25 .75

Demeter Blagoev Addressing 1891 Congress at Busludja — A413

1951 Photo. *Perf. 11*

752 A413 1 l purple .40 .25
753 A413 4 l dark green .70 .25
754 A413 9 l deep claret 1.40 .60
Nos. 752-754 (3) 2.50 1.10

60th anniversary of the first Congress of the Bulgarian Social-Democratic Party.

See Nos. 1174-1176.

Day Nursery A414

Designs: 4 l, Model building construction. 9 l, Playground. 20 l, Children's town.

1951, Oct. 10 Unwmk.

755 A414 1 l brown .25 .25
756 A414 4 l deep plum .50 .25
757 A414 9 l blue green 1.50 .60
758 A414 20 l deep blue 2.50 1.40
Nos. 755-758 (4) 4.75 2.50

Children's Day, Sept. 25, 1951.

Order of Labor
A415 A416

1952, Feb. 1 *Perf. 13*

Reverse of Medal

759 A415 1 l red brown .25 .25
760 A415 4 l blue green .25 .25
761 A415 9 l dark blue .45 .25

Obverse of Medal

762 A416 1 l carmine .25 .25
763 A416 4 l green .25 .25
764 A416 9 l purple .45 .25
Nos. 759-764 (6) 1.90 1.50

No. 764 has numeral at lower left and different background.

Workers and Symbols of Industry — A417

Design: 4 l, Flags, Dimitrov, Chervenkov.

1951, Dec. 29 *Perf. 11*

Inscribed: "16 XII 1951"

765 A417 1 l olive black .25 .25
766 A417 4 l chocolate .25 .25

Third Congress of Bulgarian General Workers' Professional Union.

Dimitrov and Chemical Works — A418

George Dimitrov and V. Chervenkov — A419

Portrait: 80s, Dimitrov.

Unwmk.

1952, June 18 Photo. *Perf. 11*

767 A418 16s brown .75 .55
768 A419 44s brown carmine 1.10 .55
769 A418 80s brt blue 2.40 1.10
Nos. 767-769 (3) 4.25 2.20

70th anniv. of the birth of George Dimitrov.

Vassil Kolarov Dam — A420

1952, May 16 *Perf. 13*

770 A420 4s dark green .25 .25
771 A420 12s purple .25 .25
772 A420 16s red brown .25 .25
773 A420 44s rose brown 1.10 .25
774 A420 80s brt blue 3.25 .25
Nos. 770-774 (5) 5.10 1.25

No. 774 is inscribed in Latin characters.

Republika Power Station — A421

1952, June 30 *Perf. 13, Pin Perf.*

775 A421 16s dark brown .25 .25
776 A421 44s magenta 2.00 .25

Nikolai I. Vapzarov A422

Designs: Various portraits.

1952, July 23 *Perf. 10½*

777 A422 16s rose brown .25 .25
778 A422 44s dk red brn 1.75 .25
779 A422 80s dk olive brn 3.75 1.25
Nos. 777-779 (3) 5.75 1.75

10th anniversary of the death of Nikolai I. Vapzarov, poet and revolutionary.

Dimitrov and Youth Conference — A423

16s, Resistance movement incident. 44s, Frontier guards & industrial scene. 80s, George Dimitrov & young workers.

1952, Sept. 1 *Perf. 11x11½*

780 A423 2s brown carmine .25 .25
781 A423 16s purple .55 .25
782 A423 44s dark green 1.00 .55
783 A423 80s dark brown 2.10 1.10
Nos. 780-783 (4) 3.90 2.15

40th anniv. of the founding conference of the Union of Social Democratic Youth.

Assault on the Winter Palace — A424

Designs: 8s, Volga-Don Canal. 16s, Symbols of world peace. 44s, Lenin and Stalin. 80s, Himlay hydroelectric station.

Perf. 11½

1952, Nov. 6 Unwmk. Photo.

Dated: "1917-1952"

784 A424 4s red brown .35 .25
785 A424 8s dark green .35 .25
786 A424 16s dark blue 1.10 .35
787 A424 44s brown 1.40 .35
788 A424 80s olive brown 2.75 1.90
Nos. 784-788 (5) 5.95 3.10

35th anniv. of the Russian revolution.

Vassil Levski — A425

Design: 44s, Levski and comrades.

1953, Feb. 19 ***Perf. 11***
Cream Paper

789	A425	16s brown	.25	.25
790	A425	44s brown blk	.50	.25

80th anniv. of the death of Levski, patriot.

Ferrying Artillery and Troops into Battle A426

Soldier A427

Mother and Children A428

Designs: 44s, Victorious soldiers. 80s, Soldier welcomed. 1 l, Monuments.

1953, Mar. 3 ***Perf. 10½***

791	A426	8s Prus green	.25	.25
792	A427	16s dp brown	.45	.25
793	A426	44s dk slate grn	.80	.25
794	A426	80s dull red brn	3.25	2.50
795	A426	1 l black	3.25	2.25
		Nos. 791-795 (5)	8.00	5.50

Bulgaria's independence from Turkey, 75th anniv.

1953, Mar. 9

796	A428	16s slate green	.25	.25
797	A428	16s bright blue	.25	.25

Women's Day.

Woodcarvings at Rila Monastery
A429 A430

Designs: 12s, 16s, 28s, Woodcarvings, Rila Monastery. 44s, Carved Ceilings, Trnovo. 80s, 1 l, 4 l, Carvings, Pasardjik.

1953 Unwmk. Photo. ***Perf. 13***

798	A429	2s gray brown	.25	.25
799	A430	8s dk slate grn	.25	.25
800	A430	12s brown	.25	.25
801	A430	16s rose lake	.40	.25
802	A429	28s dk olive grn	.50	.25
803	A430	44s dk brown	.80	.25
804	A430	80s ultra	1.40	.25
805	A430	1 l violet blue	2.75	.40
806	A430	4 l rose lake	6.00	1.50
		Nos. 798-806 (9)	12.60	3.65

For surcharge see No. 1204.

Karl Marx — A431

"Das Kapital" — A432

1953, Apr. 30 ***Perf. 10½***

807	A431	16s bright blue	.25	.25
808	A432	44s deep brown	.65	.25

70th anniversary of the death of Karl Marx.

Labor Day Parade — A433

Joseph V. Stalin — A434

1953, Apr. 30 ***Perf. 13***

809	A433	16s brown red	.35	.35

Labor Day, May 1, 1953.

1953, May 23 ***Perf. 13x13½***

810	A434	16s dark gray	.65	.25
811	A434	16s dark brown	.65	.25

Death of Joseph V. Stalin, Mar. 5, 1953.

Georgi Delchev — A435

Battle Scene — A436

Peasants Attacking Turkish Troops A437

1953, Aug. 8 ***Perf. 13***

812	A435	16s dark brown	.25	.25
813	A436	44s purple	.65	.25
814	A437	1 l deep claret	.95	.25
		Nos. 812-814 (3)	1.85	.75

50th anniv. of the Ilinden Revolt (Nos. 812, 814) and the Preobrazhene Revolt (No. 813).

Soldier and Rebels A438

44s, Soldier guarding industrial construction.

1953, Sept. 18

815	A438	16s deep claret	.25	.25
816	A438	44s greenish blue	1.00	.25

Army Day.

George Dimitrov and Vassil Kolarov A439

Designs: 16s, Citizens in revolt. 44s, Attack.

1953, Sept. 22

817	A439	8s olive gray	.25	.25
818	A439	16s dk red brn	.50	.25
819	A439	44s cerise	1.00	.25
		Nos. 817-819 (3)	1.75	.75

September Revolution, 30th anniversary.

Demeter Blagoev — A440

Portraits: 44s, G. Dimitrov and D. Blagoev.

1953, Sept. 21

820	A440	16s brown	.70	.25
821	A440	44s red brown	1.00	.25

50th anniversary of the formation of the Social Democratic Party.

Railway Viaduct A441

Pouring Molten Metal — A442

Designs: 16s, Welder and storage tanks. 80s, Harvesting machine.

1953, Oct. 17

826	A441	8s brt blue	.25	.25
827	A441	16s grnsh blk	.25	.25
828	A442	44s brown red	.75	.25
829	A441	80s orange	1.00	.75
		Nos. 826-829 (4)	2.25	1.50

Month of Bulgarian-Russian friendship.

Belladonna A443

Kolarov Library, Sofia A444

Medicinal Flowers: 4s, Jimson weed. 8s, Sage. 12s, Dog rose. 16s, Gentian. 20s, Poppy. 28s, Peppermint. 40s, Bear grass. 44s, Coltsfoot. 80s, Cowslip. 1 l, Dandelion. 2 l, Foxglove.

1953 Unwmk. Photo. ***Perf. 13***
White or Cream Paper

830	A443	2s dull blue	.25	.25
831	A443	4s brown org	.25	.25
832	A443	8s blue grn	.25	.25
833	A443	12s brown org	.25	.25
834	A443	12s blue grn	.25	.25
835	A443	16s violet blue	.25	.25
836	A443	16s dp red brn	.65	.65
837	A443	20s car rose	.25	.25
838	A443	28s dk gray grn	.90	.90
839	A443	40s dark blue	1.00	1.00
840	A443	44s brown	1.00	1.00
841	A443	80s yellow brn	2.00	2.00
842	A443	1 l henna brn	4.75	1.10
843	A443	2 l purple	8.50	3.00
a.		Souvenir sheet	57.50	50.00
		Nos. 830-843 (14)	20.55	11.40

No. 843a contains 12 stamps, one of each denomination above, printed in dark green. Size: 161x172mm. Sold for 6 leva.

1953, Dec. 16

854	A444	44s brown	.50	.25

75th anniversary of the founding of the Kolarov Library, Sofia.

Singer and Accordionist A445

Lenin and Stalin A446

1953, Dec. 26

855	A445	16s shown	.85	.85
856	A445	44s Dancers	.85	.85

1954, Mar. 13 **Cream Paper**

Designs: 44s, Lenin statue. 80s, Lenin mausoleum, Moscow. 1 l, Lenin.

857	A446	16s brown	.25	.25
858	A446	44s rose brown	.70	.25
859	A446	80s blue	1.00	.25
860	A446	1 l dp olive grn	1.50	1.00
		Nos. 857-860 (4)	3.45	1.75

30th anniversary of the death of Lenin.

Demeter Blagoev and Followers A447

Design: 44s, Blagoev at desk.

1954, Apr. 28 **Cream Paper**

861	A447	16s dp red brn	.25	.25
862	A447	44s black brn	.65	.25

30th anniv. of the death of Demeter Blagoev.

George Dimitrov — A448

Dimitrov and Refinery A449

1954, June 11

863	A448	44s lake, *cream*	.40	.25
864	A449	80s brown, *cream*	1.20	.55

5th anniv. of the death of George Dimitrov.

Train Leaving Tunnel — A450

1954, July 30

865	A450	44s dk grn, *cream*	1.50	.65
866	A450	44s blk brn, *cream*	1.50	.65

Day of the Railroads, Aug. 1, 1954.

Miner at Work — A451

1954, Aug. 19

867	A451	44s grnsh blk, *cream*	.40	.40

Miners' Day.

Academy of Science A452

1954, Oct. 27

868 A452 80s black, *cream* 1.25 .65

85th anniversary of the foundation of the Bulgarian Academy of Science.

Horsemanship — A454

16s, 44s, 2 l, vert.

1954, Dec. 21

869 A454	16s Gymnastics	1.10	.30
870 A454	44s Wrestling	1.40	.65
871 A454	80s shown	3.00	1.25
872 A454	2 l Skiing	4.75	3.75
	Nos. 869-872 (4)	10.25	5.95

Welcoming Liberators A455

Soldier's Return — A456

28s, Refinery. 44s, Dimitrov & Workers. 80s, Girl & boy. 1 l, George Dimitrov.

1954, Oct. 4 **Cream Paper**

873 A455	12s brown car	.25	.25
874 A455	16s dp carmine	.25	.25
875 A455	28s indigo	.25	.25
876 A455	44s redsh brn	.25	.25
877 A456	80s deep blue	1.10	.50
878 A456	1 l dark green	1.10	.50
	Nos. 873-878 (6)	3.20	2.00

10th anniversary of Bulgaria's liberation.

Recreation at Workers' Rest Home — A457

Metal Worker and Furnace — A458

80s, Dimitrov, Blagoev, Kirkov.

Unwmk.

1954, Dec. 28 **Photo.** ***Perf. 13***

Cream Paper

879 A457	16s dark green	.25	.25
880 A458	44s brown orange	.55	.25
881 A457	80s dp violet blue	.95	.25
	Nos. 879-881 (3)	1.75	.75

50th anniversary of Bulgaria's trade union movement.

Geese — A459

Designs: 4s, Chickens. 12s, Hogs. 16s, Sheep. 28s, Telephone building. 44s, Communist party headquarters. 80s, Apartment buildings. 1 l, St. Kiradgieff Mills.

1955-56

882 A459	2s dk blue grn	.25	.25
883 A459	4s olive green	.95	.25
884 A459	12s dk red brn	1.25	.25
885 A459	16s brown orange	2.10	.25
886 A459	28s violet blue	.95	.25
887 A459	44s lil red, *cream*	2.00	.25
a.	44s brown red	4.50	1.00
888 A459	80s dk red brown	2.50	.25
889 A459	1 l dk blue green	5.00	.25
	Nos. 882-889 (8)	15.00	2.00

Issued: No. 887, 4/20/56; others, 2/19/55.

Textile Worker A460

Mother and Child — A461

Design: 16s, Woman feeding calf.

1955, Mar. 5

890 A460	12s dark brown	.25	.25
891 A460	16s dark green	.25	.25
892 A461	44s dk car rose	.85	.25
893 A461	44s blue	.85	.25
	Nos. 890-893 (4)	2.20	1.00

Women's Day, Mar. 8, 1955.

No. 744 Surcharged in Blue

Type I

Type II

Two overprint types: I, overprint in blue-black, "16" 4mm high, thin font; II, overprint in blue, "16" 5mm high, thick font.

1955, Mar. 8 ***Perf. 13***

894 A410	16s on 4 l red brown, Type I	1.75	.40
a.	Type II	1.75	.40

May Day Demonstration of Workers — A462

Design: 44s, Three workers and globe.

1955, Apr. 23 **Photo.**

895 A462	16s car rose	.25	.25
896 A462	44s blue	.65	.25

Labor Day, May 1, 1955.

Sts. Cyril and Methodius A463

Designs: 8s, Paisii Hilendarski. 16s, Nicolas Karastoyanov's printing press. 28s, Christo Botev. 44s, Ivan Vazov. 80s, Demeter Blagoev and socialist papers. 2 l, Blagoev printing plant, Sofia.

1955, May 21 **Cream Paper**

897 A463	4s deep blue	.25	.25
898 A463	8s olive	.25	.25
899 A463	16s black	.25	.25
900 A463	28s henna brn	.25	.25
901 A463	44s brown	.60	.25
902 A463	80s rose red	1.10	.25
903 A463	2 l black	3.00	.95
	Nos. 897-903 (7)	5.70	2.45

Creation of the Cyrillic alphabet, 1100th anniv. Latin lettering at bottom on Nos. 901-903.

Sergei Rumyantzev A464

Mother and Children A465

16s, Christo Jassenov. 44s, Geo Milev.

1955, June 30 **Unwmk.** ***Perf. 13***

Cream Paper

904 A464	12s orange brn	.25	.25
905 A464	16s lt brown	.25	.25
906 A464	44s grnsh blk	1.75	.70
	Nos. 904-906 (3)	2.25	1.20

30th anniv. of the deaths of Sergei Rumyanchev, Christo Jassenov and Geo Milev. Latin lettering at bottom of No. 906.

1955, July 30

907 A465 44s brn car, *cream* .85 .25

World Congress of Mothers in Lausanne, 1955.

Young People of Three Races — A466

1955, July 30

908 A466 44s blue, *cream* .85 .25

5th World Festival of Youth in Warsaw, July 31-Aug. 14.

Friedrich Engels and Book — A467

1955, July 30

909 A467 44s brown .85 .25

60th anniv. of the death of Friedrich Engels.

Entrance to Fair, 1892 — A468

Statuary Group at Fair, 1955 — A469

Designs: 44s, "Fruit of our Land." 80s, Woman holding Fair emblem.

1955, Aug. 31 **Cream Paper**

910 A468	4s deep brown	.25	.25
911 A469	16s dk car rose	.25	.25
912 A468	44s olive blk	.25	.25
913 A469	80s deep blue	1.10	.25
	Nos. 910-913 (4)	1.85	1.00

16th International Plovdiv Fair. Latin lettering on Nos. 912-913.

Friedrich von Schiller — A470

44s, Adam Mickiewicz. 60s, Hans Christian Andersen. 80s, Baron de Montesquieu. 1 l, Miguel de Cervantes. 2 l, Walt Whitman.

1955, Oct. 31 **Cream Paper**

914 A470	16s brown	.45	.25
915 A470	44s brown red	.90	.25
916 A470	60s Prus blue	1.25	.25
917 A470	80s black	1.50	.55
918 A470	1 l rose violet	3.00	1.25
919 A470	2 l olive green	3.75	3.00
	Nos. 914-919 (6)	10.85	5.55

Various anniversaries of famous writers. Nos. 918 and 919 are issued in sheets alternating with labels without franking value. The labels show title pages for Leaves of Grass and Don Quixote in English and Spanish, respectively. Latin lettering on Nos. 915-919.

A471

A472

A473

2s, Karl Marx Industrial Plant. 4s, Alekandr Stamboliski Dam. 16s, Bridge over Danube. 44s, Friendship Monument. 80s, I. V. Michurin. 1 l, Vladimir V. Mayakovsky.

1955, Dec. 1 **Unwmk.**

920 A471	2s slate blk	.25	.25
921 A471	4s deep blue	.25	.25
922 A471	16s dk blue grn	.25	.25
923 A472	44s red brown	.25	.25
924 A473	80s dark green	.85	.25
925 A473	1 l gray blk	1.10	.25
	Nos. 920-925 (6)	2.95	1.50

Russian-Bulgarian friendship.

Library Seal — A474

Krusto Pishurka A475

Portrait: 44s, Bacho Kiro.

1956, Feb. 10 *Perf. 11x10½*
926 A474 12s car lake, *cream* .25 .25
927 A475 16s dp brn, *cream* .25 .25
928 A475 44s slate blk, *cream* .85 .25
Nos. 926-928 (3) 1.35 .75

100th anniversary of the National Library. Latin lettering at bottom of No. 928.

Canceled to Order

Beginning about 1956, some issues were sold in sheets canceled to order. Values in second column when much less than unused are for "CTO" examples. Postally used stamps are valued at slightly less than, or the same as, unused.

Quinces — A476

8s, Pears. 16s, Apples. 44s, Grapes.

1956 **Photo.** *Perf. 13*
929 A476 4s carmine 1.60 .25
930 A476 8s blue green .60 .25
931 A476 16s lilac rose 1.90 .25
932 A476 44s deep violet 1.90 .25
Nos. 929-932 (4) 6.00 1.00

Latin lettering on No. 932. See Nos. 964-967. For surcharge see No. 1364.

Cherrywood Cannon A477

1956, Apr. 28 *Perf. 11x10½*
933 A477 16s shown .25 .25
934 A477 44s Cavalry attack .65 .25

April Uprising against Turkish rule, 80th anniv.

Demeter Blagoev (1856-1924), Writer, Birthplace A478

1956, May 30 *Perf. 11*
935 A478 44s Prus blue 1.25 .25

Cherries — A479

1956 **Unwmk.** *Perf. 13*
936 A479 2s shown .25 .25
937 A479 12s Plums .25 .25
938 A479 28s Peaches .25 .25
939 A479 80s Strawberries 1.10 .25
Nos. 936-939 (4) 1.85 1.00

Latin lettering on No. 939.

Gymnastics A480

Pole Vaulting A481

Designs: 12s, Discus throw. 44s, Soccer, 80s, Basketball. 1 l, Boxing.

Perf. 11x10½, 10½x11

1956, Aug. 29
940 A480 4s brt ultra .40 .25
941 A480 12s brick red .50 .25
942 A481 16s yellow brn .60 .25
943 A481 44s dark green 1.40 .65
944 A480 80s dark red brn 2.10 1.40
945 A481 1 l deep magenta 3.00 1.75
Nos. 940-945 (6) 8.00 4.55

Latin lettering on Nos. 943-945.
16th Olympic Games at Melbourne, Nov. 22-Dec. 8, 1956.

Tobacco, Rose and Distillery — A482

1956, Sept. 1 *Perf. 13*
946 A482 44s deep carmine 1.25 1.25
947 A482 44s olive green 1.25 1.25

17th International Plovdiv Fair.

People's Theater A483

Design: 44s, Dobri Woinikoff and Sawa Dobroplodni, dramatists.

1956, Nov. 16 **Unwmk.**
948 A483 16s dull red brown .25 .25
949 A483 44s dark blue green .65 .25

Bulgarian Theater centenary.

Benjamin Franklin — A484

Cyclists, Palms and Pyramids — A485

Portraits: 20s, Rembrandt. 40s, Mozart. 44s, Heinrich Heine. 60s, Shaw. 80s, Dostoevski. 1 l, Ibsen. 2 l, Pierre Curie.

1956, Dec. 29
950 A484 16s dark olive grn .25 .25
951 A484 20s brown .25 .25
952 A484 40s dark car rose .25 .25
953 A484 44s dark violet brn .60 .25
954 A484 60s dark slate .75 .25
955 A484 80s dark brown 1.10 .25
956 A484 1 l bluish grn 2.00 .75
957 A484 2 l Prus green 4.50 1.25
Nos. 950-957 (8) 9.70 3.50

Great personalities of the world.

1957, Mar. 6 **Photo.** *Perf. 10½*
958 A485 80s henna brown 1.25 .60
959 A485 80s Prus green 1.25 .60

Fourth Egyptian bicycle race.

Woman Technician A486

Designs: 16s, Woman and children. 44s, Woman feeding chickens.

1957, Mar. 8
960 A486 12s deep blue .25 .25
961 A486 16s henna brown .25 .25
962 A486 44s slate green .45 .25
Nos. 960-962 (3) .95 .75

Women's Day. Latin lettering on 44s.

"New Times" Review — A487

1957, Mar. 8 **Unwmk.**
963 A487 16s deep carmine .35 .35

60th anniversary of the founding of the "New Times" review.

Fruit Type of 1956

4s, Quinces. 8s, Pears. 16s, Apples. 44s, Grapes.

1957 **Photo.** *Perf. 13*
964 A476 4s yellow green .25 .25
965 A476 8s brown orange .25 .25
966 A476 16s rose red .25 .25
967 A476 44s orange yellow 1.10 .25
Nos. 964-967 (4) 1.85 1.00

Latin lettering on No. 967. For surcharge see No. 1364.

Sts. Cyril and Methodius — A488

1957, May 22 *Perf. 11*
968 A488 44s olive grn & buff 1.25 .25

Centenary of the first public veneration of Sts. Cyril and Methodius, inventors of the Cyrillic alphabet.

Basketball A489

1957, June 20 **Photo.** *Perf. 10½x11*
969 A489 44s dark green 2.10 .55

10th European Basketball Championship at Sofia.

Dancer and Spasski Tower, Moscow — A490

1957, July 18 *Perf. 13*
970 A490 44s blue .70 .25

Sixth World Youth Festival in Moscow.

George Dimitrov (1882-1949) — A491

1957, July 18
971 A491 44s deep carmine 1.25 .25

Vassil Levski — A492

1957, July 18 *Perf. 11*
972 A492 44s grnsh black .85 .25

120th anniversary of the birth of Vassil Levski, patriot and national hero.

No. 742 Surcharged in Carmine

1957 **Unwmk.** *Perf. 13*
973 A408 16s on 1 l purple .25 .25

Trnovo and Lazarus L. Zamenhof A493

1957, July 27
974 A493 44s slate green 1.25 .25

50th anniv. of the Bulgarian Esperanto Society and the 70th anniv. of Esperanto.
For surcharge see No. 1235.

Bulgarian Veteran of 1877 War and Russian Soldier — A494

Design: 44s, Battle of Shipka Pass.

1957, Aug. 13
975 A494 16s dk blue grn .25 .25
976 A494 44s brown .65 .25

80th anniversary of Bulgaria's liberation from the Turks. Latin lettering on No. 976.

Woman Planting Tree — A495

Red Deer in Forest — A496

16s, Dam, lake and forest. 44s, Plane over forest. 80s, Fields on edge of forest.

1957, Sept. 16 **Photo.** ***Perf. 13***

977 A495 2s deep green .25 .25
978 A496 12s dark brown .25 .25
979 A496 16s Prus blue .25 .25
980 A496 44s Prus green .60 .25
981 A496 80s yellow green .95 .25
Nos. 977-981 (5) 2.30 1.25

Latin lettering on Nos. 980 and 981.

Lenin — A497

Designs: 16s, Cruiser "Aurora." 44s, Dove over map of communist area. 60s, Revolutionaries and banners. 80s, Chemical plant.

1957, Oct. 29 ***Perf. 11***

982 A497 12s chocolate .85 .25
983 A497 16s Prus green 1.75 .55
984 A497 44s deep blue 2.40 1.10
985 A497 60s dk car rose 4.00 1.50
986 A497 80s dark green 6.25 2.00
Nos. 982-986 (5) 15.25 5.40

40th anniv. of the Communist Revolution. Latin lettering on Nos. 984-985.

Globes A498

1957, Oct. 4 ***Perf. 13***

987 A498 44s Prus blue .70 .25

4th Intl. Trade Union Cong., Leipzig, 10/4-15.

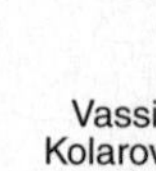

Vassil Kolarov Hotel A499

Bulgarian Health Resorts: 4s, Skis and Pirin Mountains. 8s, Old house at Koprivspitsa. 12s, Rest home at Velingrad. 44s, Momin-Prochod Hotel. 60s, Nesebr Hotel, shoreline and peninsula. 80s, Varna beach scene. 1 l, Hotel at Varna.

1958 **Photo.** ***Perf. 13***

988 A499 4s blue .25 .25
989 A499 8s orange brn .25 .25
990 A499 12s dk green .25 .25
991 A499 16s green .25 .25
992 A499 44s dk blue grn .25 .25
993 A499 60s deep blue .25 .25
994 A499 80s fawn .40 .25
995 A499 1 l dk red brn .55 .25
Nos. 988-995 (8) 2.45 2.00

Latin lettering on 44s, 60s, 80s, and 1 l.
Issue dates: Nos. 991-994, 1/20; others, 7/5.
For surcharges see Nos. 1200, 1436.

Mikhail I. Glinka — A500

Portraits: 16s, Jan A. Komensky (Comenius). 40s, Carl von Linné. 44s, William Blake. 60s, Carlo Goldoni. 80s, Auguste Comte.

1957, Dec. 30

996 A500 12s dark brown .50 .25
997 A500 16s dark green .50 .25
998 A500 40s Prus blue 1.25 .30
999 A500 44s maroon 1.25 .35
1000 A500 60s orange brown 2.00 .65
1001 A500 80s deep plum 4.75 3.00
Nos. 996-1001 (6) 10.25 4.80

Famous men of other countries. Latin lettering on Nos. 999-1001.

Young Couple, Flag, Dimitrov — A501

People's Front Salute — A502

1957, Dec. 28 ***Perf. 11***

1002 A501 16s carmine rose .25 .25

10th anniversary of Dimitrov's Union of the People's Youth.

1957, Dec. 28

1003 A502 16s dk violet brn .25 .25

15th anniversary of the People's Front.

Hare A503

12s, Red deer (doe), vert. 16s, Red deer (stag). 44s, Chamois. 80s, Brown bear. 1 l, Wild boar.

Perf. 10½

1958, Apr. 5 **Unwmk.** **Photo.**

1004 A503 2s lt & dk ol grn .55 .25
1005 A503 12s sl grn & red brn .95 .30
1006 A503 16s bluish grn & dk red brn 1.50 .40
1007 A503 44s blue & brown 1.75 .65
1008 A503 80s bis & dk brn 2.10 .90
1009 A503 1 l stl bl & dk brn 2.50 1.50
Nos. 1004-1009 (6) 9.35 4.00

Value, imperf. set $10.

Marx and Lenin A504

Designs: 16s, Marchers and flags. 44s, Lenin blast furnaces.

1958, July 2 ***Perf. 11***

1010 A504 12s dark brown .25 .25
1011 A504 16s dark carmine .25 .25
1012 A504 44s dark blue 2.10 .80
Nos. 1010-1012 (3) 2.60 1.30

Bulgarian Communist Party, 7th Congress.

Wrestlers — A505

1958, June 20 ***Perf. 10½***

1013 A505 60s dk carmine rose 1.75 1.40
1014 A505 80s deep brown 2.10 1.60

World Wrestling Championship, Sofia.

Chessmen and Globe A506

Perf. 10½

1958, July 18 **Unwmk.** **Photo.**

1015 A506 80s grn & yel grn 12.00 10.00

5th World Students' Chess Games, Varna.

Conference Emblem A507

1958, Sept. 24

1016 A507 44s blue .85 .25

World Trade Union Conference of Working Youth, Prague, July 14-20.

Swimmer A508

1958 Students' Games: 28s, Dancer, vert. 44s, Volleyball, vert.

1958, Sept. 19 ***Perf. 11x10½***

1017 A508 16s bright blue .25 .25
1018 A508 28s brown orange .55 .25
1019 A508 44s bright green .75 .25
Nos. 1017-1019 (3) 1.55 .75

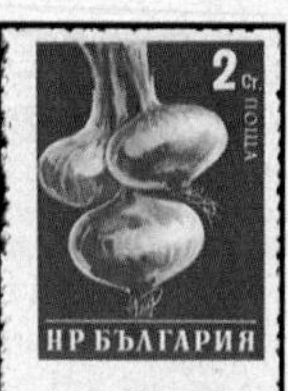

Onions — A509

Vegetables: 12s, Garlic. 16s, Peppers. 44s, Tomatoes. 80s, Cucumbers. 1 l, Eggplant.

1958, Sept. 20 ***Perf. 13***

1020 A509 2s orange brown .25 .25
1021 A509 12s Prus blue .25 .25
1022 A509 16s dark green .25 .25
1023 A509 44s deep carmine .25 .25
1024 A509 80s deep green 1.25 .25
1025 A509 1 l brt purple 1.40 .25
Nos. 1020-1025 (6) 3.65 1.50

Value, imperf. set $8.50.
See No. 1072. For surcharge see No. 1201.

Plovdiv Fair Building A510

1958, Sept. 14 **Unwmk.** ***Perf. 11***

1026 A510 44s deep carmine .85 .25

18th International Plovdiv Fair.

Attack — A511

44s, Fighter dragging wounded man.

1958, Sept. 23 **Photo.** ***Perf. 11***

1027 A511 16s orange ver .25 .25
1028 A511 44s lake 1.00 .25

35th anniv. of the September Revolution.

Emblem, Brussels Fair — A512

1958, Oct. 13 ***Perf. 11***

1029 A512 1 l blk & brt blue 8.75 8.75

Brussels World's Fair, Apr. 17-Oct. 19.
Exists imperf. Value, $85.

Runner at Finish Line — A513

Woman Throwing Javelin A514

60s, High jumper. 80s, Hurdler. 4 l, Shot putter.

1958, Nov. 30

1030 A513 16s red brn, *pnksh* .75 .35
1031 A514 44s olive, *yelsh* .85 .55
1032 A514 60s dk bl, *bluish* 1.50 .65
1033 A514 80s dp grn, *grnsh* 1.90 1.00
1034 A513 4 l dp rose cl, *pnksh* 11.50 6.50
Nos. 1030-1034 (5) 16.50 9.05

1958 Balkan Games.
Latin lettering on Nos. 1032-1033.

Christo Smirnenski A515

1958, Dec. 22

1035 A515 16s dark carmine .35 .35

Christo Smirnenski (1898-1923), poet.

Girls Harvesting — A516

Girl Tending Calves A517

16s, Boy & girl laborers. 40s, Boy pushing wheelbarrow. 44s, Headquarters building.

1959, Nov. 29 **Photo.**

1036 A516 8s dk olive green .25 .25
1037 A517 12s redsh brown .25 .25
1038 A516 16s violet brown .25 .25
1039 A517 40s Prus blue .25 .25
1040 A516 44s deep carmine 1.25 .25
Nos. 1036-1040 (5) 2.25 1.25

4th Congress of Dimitrov's Union of People's Youth.

UNESCO Building, Paris A518

1959, Mar. 28 **Unwmk.** ***Perf. 11***

1041 A518 2 l dp red lilac, *cream* 3.25 1.50

Opening of UNESCO Headquarters, Paris, Nov. 3, 1958. Value imperf. $6.50.

Skier — A519

1959, Mar. 28 ***Perf. 11***

1042 A519 1 l blue, *cream* 2.10 1.10

Forty years of skiing in Bulgaria.

Soccer Players — A520

1959, Mar. 25

1043 A520 2 l chestnut, *cream* 3.00 1.50

1959 European Youth Soccer Championship.

Russian Soldiers Installing Telegraph Wires — A521

First Bulgarian Postal Coach A522

Designs: 60s, Stamp of 1879. 80s, First Bulgarian automobile. 1 l, Television tower. 2 l, Strike of railroad and postal workers, 1919.

1959, May 4

1044 A521 12s dk grn & cit .45 .25
1045 A522 16s deep plum .55 .25
1046 A521 60s dk brn & yel 1.00 .55
1047 A522 80s hn brn & sal 1.10 .55
1048 A521 1 l blue 2.25 .65
1049 A522 2 l dk red brown 4.00 2.50
Nos. 1044-1049 (6) 9.35 4.75

80th anniv. of the Bulgarian post. Latin lettering on Nos. 1046-1049.

Two imperf. souvenir sheets exist with olive borders and inscriptions. One contains one copy of No. 1046 in black & ocher, and measures 92x121mm. The other sheet contains one copy each of Nos. 1044-1045 and 1047-1048 in changed colors: 12s, olive green & ocher; 16s, deep claret & ocher; 80s, dark red & ocher; 1 l, olive & ocher. Each sheet sold for 5 leva. Value, each $65.

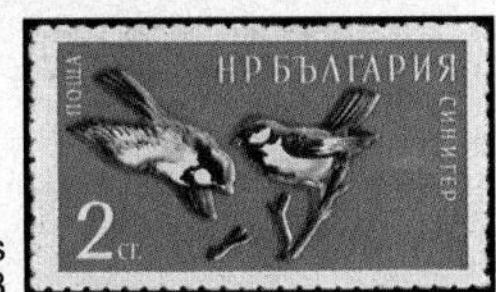

Great Tits A523

Birds: 8s, Hoopoe. 16s, Great spotted woodpecker, vert. 45s, Gray partridge, vert. 60s, Rock partridge. 80s, European cuckoo.

1959, June 30 **Photo.**

1050 A523 2s olive & sl grn .25 .25
1051 A523 8s dp orange & blk .70 .25
1052 A523 16s chestnut & dk brn .70 .25
1053 A523 45s brown & blk 1.50 .60
1054 A523 60s dp blue & gray 3.00 .85
1055 A523 80s dp bl grn & gray 4.25 1.50
Nos. 1050-1055 (6) 10.40 3.70

Bagpiper — A524

12s, Acrobats. 16s, Girls exercising with hoops. 20s, Male dancers. 80s, Ballet dancers. 1 l, Ceramic pitcher. 16s, 20s, 80s are horiz.

1959, Aug. 29 **Unwmk.** ***Perf. 11***

Surface-colored Paper

1056 A524 4s dk olive .25 .25
1057 A524 12s scarlet .25 .25
1058 A524 16s maroon .25 .25
1059 A524 20s dk blue .45 .25
1060 A524 80s brt green .90 .45
1061 A524 1 l brown org 1.90 .70
Nos. 1056-1061 (6) 4.00 2.15

7th International Youth Festival, Vienna. Latin inscriptions on Nos. 1060-1061.

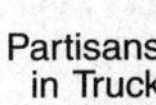

Partisans in Truck A525

Designs: 16s, Partisans and soldiers shaking hands. 45s, Steel mill. 60s, Tanks. 80s, Harvester. 1.25 l, Children with flag, vert.

1959, Sept. 8

1062 A525 12s red & Prus grn .25 .25
1063 A525 16s red & dk pur .25 .25
1064 A525 45s red & int bl .25 .25
1065 A525 60s red & ol grn .25 .25
1066 A525 80s red & brn .80 .25
1067 A525 1.25 l red & dp brn 1.40 1.10
Nos. 1062-1067 (6) 3.20 2.35

15th anniversary of Bulgarian liberation.

Soccer A526

1959, Oct. 10 **Unwmk.** ***Perf. 11***

1068 A526 1.25 l dp green, *yel* 6.75 4.50

50 years of Bulgarian soccer.

Stamp exists imperf in changed colors. Value $19 unused, $7.50 canceled.

Batak Defenders A527

1959, Aug. 8

1069 A527 16s deep claret .40 .40

300th anniv. of the settlement of Batak.

Post Horn and Letter — A528

Design: 1.25 l, Dove and letter.

1959, Nov. 23

1070 A528 45s emerald & blk .65 .25
1071 A528 1.25 l lt blue, red & blk 1.10 .25

Intl. Letter Writing Week Oct. 5-11.

Type of 1958 Surcharged in Dark Blue

Design: Tomatoes.

1959 **Photo.** ***Perf. 13***

1072 A509 45s on 44s scarlet 1.25 .25

Bird-shaped Lyre — A529

1960, Feb. 23 **Unwmk.** ***Perf. 10½***

1073 A529 80s shown .75 .25
1074 A529 1.25 l Lyre 1.40 .25

50th anniv. of Bulgaria's State Opera.

N. I. Vapzarov — A530

Parachute and Radio Tower — A531

1959, Dec. 14 ***Perf. 11***

1075 A530 80s yel grn & red brn .85 .25

Vapzarov, poet and patriot, 50th birth anniv.

1959, Dec. 3 **Photo.**

1076 A531 1.25 l dp grnsh bl & yel 3.00 1.10

3rd Cong. of Voluntary Participants in Defense.

Cotton Picker — A532

Harvester Combine A533

Designs: 2s, Kindergarten. 4s, Woman doctor and child. 10s, Woman milking cow. 12s, Woman holding tobacco leaves. 15s, Woman working loom. 16s, Industrial plants, Dimitrovgrad. 25s, Rural electrification. 28s, Woman picking sunflowers. 40s, "Cold-well" hydroelectric dam. 45s, Miner. 60s, Foundry worker. 80s. Woman harvesting grapes. 1 l, Worker and peasant with cogwheel. 1.25 l, Industrial worker. 2 l, Party leader.

1959-61 **Photo.** ***Perf. 13***

1077 A533 2s brn org ('60) .25 .25
1077A A532 4s gldn brn ('61) .25 .25
1078 A532 5s dk green .25 .25
1079 A533 10s red brn ('61) .25 .25
1080 A532 12s red brown .25 .25
1081 A532 15s red lil ('60) .25 .25
1082 A533 16s dp vio ('60) .25 .25
1083 A533 20s orange .25 .25
1084 A532 25s brt blue ('60) .25 .25
1085 A532 28s brt green .25 .25
1086 A533 40s brt grnsh bl .50 .25
1087 A532 45s choc ('60) .25 .25
1088 A533 60s scarlet .70 .25
1089 A532 80s olive ('60) .90 .25
1090 A532 1 l maroon .90 .25
1090A A533 1.25 l dull bl ('61) 3.00 .50
1091 A532 2 l dp car ('60) 2.00 .40
Nos. 1077-1091 (17) 10.75 4.65

Early completion of the 5-year plan (in 1959).

For surcharges see Nos. 1192-1199, 1202-1203.

L. L. Zamenhof
A534

1959, Dec. 5 Unwmk. *Perf. 11*

1092	A534	1.25 l	dk grn & yel grn	1.25	.80

Lazarus Ludwig Zamenhof (1859-1917), inventor of Esperanto.

Path of Lunik 3 — A535

1960, Mar. 28 *Perf. 11*

1093	A535	1.25 l	Prus bl & brt yel	6.50	4.75

Flight of Lunik 3 around moon. Value, imperf. $9

Skier
A536

1960, Apr. 15 Litho.

1094	A536	2 l	ultra, blk & brn	1.25	.45

8th Winter Olympics, Squaw Valley, CA, Feb. 18-29. Value, imperf. $3.50 unused, $1 canceled.

Vela Blagoeva
A537

Portraits: 28s, Anna Maimunkova. 45s, Vela Piskova. 60s, Rosa Luxemburg. 80s, Klara Zetkin. 1.25 l, N. K. Krupskaya.

1960, Apr. 27 Photo. *Perf. 11*

1095	A537	16s	rose & red brn	.25	.25
1096	A537	28s	citron & olive	.25	.25
1097	A537	45s	ol grn & sl grn	.25	.25
1098	A537	60s	lt bl & Prus bl	.25	.25
1099	A537	80s	red org & dp brn	.70	.25
1100	A537	1.25 l	dull yel & olive	1.00	.25
			Nos. 1095-1100 (6)	2.70	1.50

International Women's Day, Mar. 8, 1960.

Lenin — A538

1960, May 12

1101	A538	16s	shown	1.60	.25
1102	A538	45s	Lenin sitting	3.00	.25

90th anniversary of the birth of Lenin.

A539

1960, June 3 *Perf. 11*

1103	A539	1.25 l	yel & slate grn	1.75	.70

Seventh European Women's Basketball championships.

A541

1960, June 29 Litho.

1105	A541	16s	Parachutist	.75	.45
1106	A541	1.25 l	Parachutes	2.25	.65

5th International Parachute Championships.

Yellow Gentian — A542

5s, Tulips. 25s, Turk's-cap lily. 45s, Rhododendron. 60s, Lady's-slipper. 80s, Violets.

1960, July 27 Photo. *Perf. 11*

1107	A542	2s	beige, grn & yel	.25	.25
1108	A542	5s	yel grn, grn & car rose	.45	.25
1109	A542	25s	pink, grn & org	.60	.25
1110	A542	45s	pale lil, grn & rose lil	.75	.25
1111	A542	60s	yel, grn & org	1.90	.75
1112	A542	80s	gray, grn & vio bl	2.10	1.10
			Nos. 1107-1112 (6)	6.05	2.85

Soccer
A543

12s, Wrestling. 16s, Weight lifting. 45s, Woman gymnast. 80s, Canoeing. 2 l, Runner.

1960, Aug. 29 Unwmk. *Perf. 11*

Athletes' Figures in Pink

1113	A543	8s	brown	.25	.25
1114	A543	12s	violet	.25	.25
1115	A543	16s	Prus blue	.25	.25
1116	A543	45s	deep plum	.25	.25
1117	A543	80s	blue	.50	.25
1118	A543	2 l	deep green	1.75	.80
			Nos. 1113-1118 (6)	3.25	2.05

17th Olympic Games, Rome, 8/25-9/11. Value, set imperf. in changed colors, $9.50.

Globes — A544

Unwmk.

1960, Oct. 12 Photo. *Perf. 11*

1125	A544	1.25 l	blue & ultra	.85	.25

15th anniversary of the World Federation of Trade Unions.

Alexander Popov
A545

1960, Oct. 12

1126	A545	90s	blue & blk	1.25	.25

Centenary of the birth of Alexander Popov, radio pioneer.

Bicyclists
A546

1960, Sept. 22

1127	A546	1 l	yel, red org & blk	1.75	.85

The 10th Tour of Bulgaria Bicycle Race.

Jaroslav Vésin
A547

1960, Nov. 22 Unwmk. *Perf. 11*

1128	A547	1 l	brt citron & ol grn	5.00	1.10

Birth centenary of Jaroslav Vesin, painter.

UN Headquarters A548 — Costume of Kyustendil A549

1961, Jan. 14 Photo. *Perf. 11*

1129	A548	1 l	brown & yel	2.25	1.00
a.			Souvenir sheet	12.00	12.00

15th anniv. of the UN. No. 1129 sold for 2 l. Value, imperf. $7.50.

No. 1129a sold for 2.50 l and contains one copy of No. 1129, imperf, in dark olive and pink.

1961, Jan. 28

Regional Costumes: 16s, Pleven. 28s, Sliven. 45s, Sofia. 60s, Rhodope. 80s, Karnobat.

1130	A549	12s	sal, sl grn & yel	.25	.25
1131	A549	16s	pale lil, brn vio & buff	.25	.25
1132	A549	28s	pale grn, sl grn & rose	.25	.25
1133	A549	45s	blue & red	.65	.25
1134	A549	60s	grnsh bl, Prus bl & yel	1.00	.25
1135	A549	80s	yel, sl grn & pink	1.25	.45
			Nos. 1130-1135 (6)	3.65	1.70

Theodor Tiro (Fresco)
A550

Designs: 60s, Boyana Church. 1.25 l, Duchess of Dessislava (fresco).

1961, Jan. 28 Photo.

1136	A550	60s	yel grn, blk & grn	1.10	.50
1137	A550	80s	yel, sl grn & org	1.40	.65
1138	A550	1.25 l	yel grn, hn brn & buff	2.00	1.10
			Nos. 1136-1138 (3)	4.50	2.25

700th anniv. of murals in Boyana Church.

Clock Tower, Vratsa — A551

Wooden Jug — A552

Designs: 12s, Clock tower, Bansko. 20s, Anguchev House, Mogilitsa. 28s, Oslekov House, Koprivspitsa, horiz. 40s, Pasha's house. Melnik, horiz. 45s, Lion sculpture. 60s, Man on horseback, Madara. 80s, Fresco, Bratchkovo monastery. 1 l, Tsar Assen coin.

1961, Feb. 25 Unwmk. *Perf. 11*

Denomination and Stars in Vermilion

1139	A551	8s	olive grn	.25	.25
1140	A551	12s	lt violet	.25	.25
1141	A552	16s	dk red brn	.25	.25
1142	A551	20s	brt blue	.25	.25
1143	A551	28s	grnsh blue	.25	.25
1144	A551	40s	red brown	.25	.25
1145	A552	45s	olive gray	.25	.25
1146	A552	60s	slate	.60	.25
1147	A552	80s	dk olive gray	1.25	.25
1148	A552	1 l	green	1.50	.25
			Nos. 1139-1148 (10)	5.10	2.50

Capercaillie
A553

Birds: 4s, Dalmatian pelican. 16s, Ring-necked pheasant. 80s, Great bustard. 1 l, Lammergeier. 2 l, Hazel hen.

1961, Mar. 31

1149	A553	2s	blk, sal & Prus grn	.30	.25
1150	A553	4s	blk, yel grn & org	.30	.25
1151	A553	16s	brn, lt grn & org	.40	.30
1152	A553	80s	brn, bluish grn & yel	2.25	1.25
1153	A553	1 l	blk, lt bl & yel	3.00	1.60
1154	A553	2 l	brn, bl & yel	4.00	1.90
			Nos. 1149-1154 (6)	10.25	5.55

Radio Tower and Winged Anchor A554

1961, Apr. 1 Unwmk. *Perf. 11*
1155 A554 80s brt green & blk .85 .25

50th anniv. of the Transport Workers' Union.

T. G. Shevchenko A555

1961, Apr. 27
1156 A555 1 l olive & blk 5.50 3.75

Centenary of the death of Taras G. Shevchenko, Ukrainian poet.

Water Polo — A556

Designs: 5s, Tennis. 16s, Fencing. 45s, Throwing the discus. 1.25 l, Sports Palace. 2 l, Basketball. 5 l, Sports Palace, different view. 5s, 16s, 45s and 1.25 l, are horizontal.

1961, May 15 Black Inscriptions
1157 A556 4s lt ultra .40 .25
1158 A556 5s orange ver .40 .25
1159 A556 16s olive grn .40 .25
1160 A556 45s dull blue .40 .25
1161 A556 1.25 l yellow brn 3.00 .25
1162 A556 2 l lilac 3.75 1.25
Nos. 1157-1162 (6) 8.35 2.50

Souvenir Sheet

Imperf

1163 A556 5 l yel grn, dl bl & yel 17.00 14.50

1961 World University Games, Sofia, Aug. 26-Sept. 3.
Value, Nos. 1157-1162 in changed colors, imperf. $9.

Monk Seal A557

Black Sea Fauna: 12s, Jellyfish. 16s, Dolphin. 45s, Black Sea sea horse, vert. 1 l, Starred sturgeon. 1.25 l, Thornback ray.

1961, June 19 *Perf. 11*
1164 A557 2s green & blk .25 .25
1165 A557 12s Prus grn & pink .25 .25
1166 A557 16s ultra & vio bl .25 .25
1167 A557 45s lt blue & brn 1.40 .90
1168 A557 1 l yel grn & Prus grn 3.00 1.90
1169 A557 1.25 l lt vio bl & red brn 3.75 3.25
Nos. 1164-1169 (6) 8.90 6.80

Hikers — A558

Designs: 4s, "Sredetz" hostel, horiz. 16s, Tents. 1.25 l, Mountain climber.

1961, Aug. 25 Litho. *Perf. 11*
1170 A558 4s yel grn, yel & blk .25 .25
1171 A558 12s lt bl, cr & blk .25 .25
1172 A558 16s green, cr & blk .25 .25
1173 A558 1.25 l bister, cr & blk .65 .25
Nos. 1170-1173 (4) 1.40 1.00

"Know Your Country" campaign.

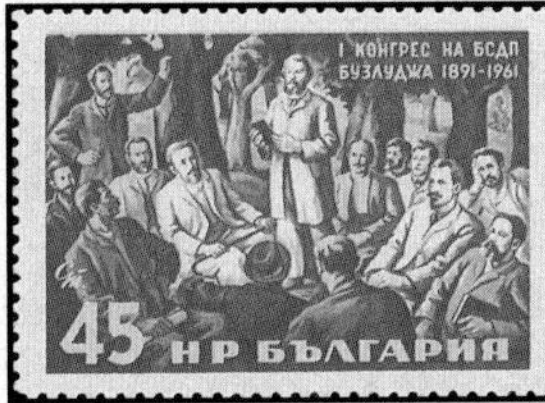

Demeter Blagoev Addressing 1891 Congress at Busludja — A559

1961, Aug. 5 Photo.
1174 A559 45s dk red & buff .25 .25
1175 A559 80s blue & pink .55 .25
1176 A559 2 l dk brn & pale cit 1.40 .50
Nos. 1174-1176 (3) 2.20 1.00

70th anniversary of the first Congress of the Bulgarian Social-Democratic Party.

The Golden Girl A560

Fairy Tales: 8s, The Living Water. 12s, The Golden Apple. 16s, Krali-Marko, hero. 45s, Samovila-Vila, Witch. 80s, Tom Thumb.

1961, Oct. 10 Unwmk. *Perf. 11*
1177 A560 2s blue, blk & org .25 .25
1178 A560 8s rose lil, blk & gray .50 .25
1179 A560 12s bl grn, blk & pink .50 .25
1180 A560 16s red, blk, bl & gray .75 .25
1181 A560 45s ol grn, blk & pink 1.40 .50
1182 A560 80s ocher, blk & dk car 2.10 .60
Nos. 1177-1182 (6) 5.50 2.10

Caesar's Mushroom A561

Designs: Various mushrooms.

1961, Dec. 20 Photo. *Perf. 11*
Denominations in Black
1183 A561 2s lemon & red .25 .25
1184 A561 4s ol grn & red brn .25 .25
1185 A561 12s bister & red brn .25 .25
1186 A561 16s lilac & red brn .25 .25
1187 A561 45s car rose & yel .45 .25
1188 A561 80s brn org & sepia .75 .45
1189 A561 1.25 l vio & dk brn 1.25 .40
1190 A561 2 l org brn & brn 1.75 .90
Nos. 1183-1190 (8) 5.20 3.00

Value, denomination in dark grn, imperf set $13 unused or canceled.

Miladinov Brothers and Title Page — A562

1961, Dec. 21 Unwmk. *Perf. 10½*
1191 A562 1.25 l olive & blk 1.25 .50

Publication of "Collected Folksongs" by the Brothers Miladinov, Dimitri and Konstantin, cent.

Nos. 1079-1085, 1087, 992, 1023, 1090-1091 and 806 Surcharged

In Black — No. 1192

In Black — No. 1193

In Red — No. 1195

In Red — No. 1197

In Violet — No. 1204

1962, Jan. 1
1192 A533 1s on 10s red brown .25 .25
1193 A532 1s on 12s red brown .25 .25
1194 A532 2s on 15s red lilac .25 .25
1195 A533 2s on 16s dp vio (R) .25 .25
1196 A533 2s on 20s orange .25 .25
a. "2 CT." on 2 lines .25 .25
1197 A532 3s on 25s brt bl (R) .25 .25
a. Black surcharge 10.00 10.00
1198 A532 3s on 28s brt grn (R) .25 .25
1199 A532 5s on 45s chocolate .35 .25
1200 A499 5s on 44s dk bl grn (R) .25 .25
1201 A509 5s on 44s dp car (V) .25 .25
1202 A532 10s on 1 l maroon .50 .25
1203 A532 20s on 2 l dp car 1.00 .55
1204 A430 40s on 4 l rose lake (V) 2.50 1.10
Nos. 1192-1204 (13) 6.60 4.40

Freighter "Varna" A563

Designs: 5s, Tanker "Komsomoletz." 20s, Liner "G. Dimitrov."

1962, Mar. 1 Photo. *Perf. 10½*
1205 A563 1s lt grn & brt bl .25 .25
1206 A563 5s lt blue & grn .25 .25
1207 A563 20s gray bl & grnsh bl 1.25 .25
Nos. 1205-1207 (3) 1.75 .75

Dimitrov Working as Printer — A564

Roses — A565

13s, Griffin, emblem of state printing works.

1962, Mar. 19 Unwmk.
1208 A564 2s ver, blk & yel .25 .25
1209 A564 13s red org, blk & yel .65 .25

80th anniversary (in 1961) of the George Dimitrov state printing works.

1962, Mar. 28
Various Roses in Natural Colors
1210 A565 1s deep violet .25 .25
1211 A565 2s salmon & dk car .25 .25
1212 A565 3s gray & car .25 .25
1213 A565 4s dark green .45 .25
1214 A565 5s ultra .85 .25
1215 A565 6s bluish grn & dk car 1.10 .60
1216 A565 8s citron & car 2.75 1.25
1217 A565 13s blue 4.50 3.00
Nos. 1210-1217 (8) 10.40 6.10

For overprint and surcharges see Nos. 1281-1283.

Malaria Eradication Emblem and Mosquito A566

Design: 20s, Malaria eradication emblem.

1962, Apr. 19
1218 A566 5s org brn, yel & blk .65 .25
1219 A566 20s emerald, yel & blk 1.50 .60

WHO drive to eradicate malaria.
Value, imperf. $5 unused, $1.50 canceled.

Lenin and First Issue of Pravda A567

1962, May 4 Unwmk. *Perf. 10*
1220 A567 5s deep rose & slate 1.60 .95

50th anniversary of Pravda, Russian newspaper founded by Lenin.

Blackboard and Book — A568

1962, May 21 Photo.
1221 A568 5s Prus bl, blk & yel .40 .25

The 1962 Teachers' Congress.

Soccer Player and Globe
A569

1962, May 26 ***Perf. 10½***

1222 A569 13s brt grn, blk & lt brn 1.75 .65

World Soccer Championship, Chile, May 30-June 17. Value, imperf. in changed colors, $3.25 unused or canceled.

George Dimitrov
A570

1962, June 18 **Photo.**

1223 A570 2s dark green .40 .25
1224 A570 5s turq blue 1.00 .25

80th anniv. of the birth of George Dimitrov (1882-1949), communist leader and premier of the Bulgarian Peoples' Republic.

Bishop — A571

1962, July 7 **Unwmk.** ***Perf. 10½***

1225 A571 1s shown .25 .25
1226 A571 2s Rook .25 .25
1227 A571 3s Queen .25 .25
1228 A571 13s Knight 1.50 .55
1229 A571 20s Pawn 2.50 .85
Nos. 1225-1229 (5) 4.75 2.15

15th Chess Olympics, Varna. Nos. 1225-1229 were also issued imperf in changed colors. Value, $7.50 unused.

An imperf. souvenir sheet contains one 20s horizontal stamp showing five chessmen. Size: 75x66mm. Value, $13 unused.

Rila Mountain
A572

Designs: 2s, Pirin mountain. 6s, Nesebr, Black Sea. 8s, Danube. 13s, Vidin Castle. 1 l, Rhodope mountain.

1962-63 ***Perf. 13***

1230 A572 1s dk blue grn .25 .25
1231 A572 2s blue .25 .25
1232 A572 6s grnsh blue .25 .25
1233 A572 8s lilac .25 .25
1234 A572 13s yellow grn 1.25 .25
1234A A572 1 l dp green ('63) 6.00 1.40
Nos. 1230-1234A (6) 8.25 2.65

No. 974 Surcharged in Red

1962, July 14 ***Perf. 13***

1235 A493 13s on 44s slate grn 4.50 3.00

25th Bulgarian Esperanto Congress, Burgas, July 14-16.

Girl and Festival Emblem
A573

Design: 5s, Festival emblem.

1962, Aug. 18 **Photo.** ***Perf. 10½***

1236 A573 5s green, lt bl & pink .25 .25
1237 A573 13s lilac, lt bl & gray 1.00 .25

8th Youth Festival for Peace and Friendship, Helsinki, July 28-Aug. 6, 1962.

Parnassius Apollo — A574

1962, Sept. 13
Various Butterflies in Natural Colors

1238 A574 1s pale cit & dk grn .25 .25
1239 A574 2s rose & brown .25 .25
1240 A574 3s buff & red brn .25 .25
1241 A574 4s gray & brown .25 .25
1242 A574 5s lt gray & brn .40 .25
1243 A574 6s gray & black .90 .25
1244 A574 10s pale grn & blk 3.00 .95
1245 A574 13s buff & red brn 4.00 2.40
Nos. 1238-1245 (8) 9.30 4.85

Planting Machine — A575

2s, Electric locomotive. 3s, Blast furnace. 13s, Blagoev, Dimitrov & Communist flag.

1962, Nov. 1 ***Perf. 11½***

1246 A575 1s bl grn & dk ol grn .25 .25
1247 A575 2s bl & Prus bl .25 .25
1248 A575 3s carmine & brn .25 .25
1249 A575 13s plum, red & blk 1.10 .25
Nos. 1246-1249 (4) 1.85 1.00

Bulgarian Communist Party, 8th Congress.

Title Page of "Slav-Bulgarian History" — A576

Paisii Hilendarski Writing History
A577

1962, Dec. 8 **Unwmk.** ***Perf. 10½***

1250 A576 2s olive grn & blk .25 .25
1251 A577 5s brown org & blk .25 .25

200th anniv. of "Slav-Bulgarian History."

Aleco Konstantinov (1863-1897), Writer
A578

1963, Mar. 5 **Photo.** ***Perf. 11½***

1252 A578 5s red, grn & blk .40 .25

Printed with alternating red brown and black label showing Bai Ganu, hero from Konstantinov's books.

A579

Sofia University — A580

No. 1255, Levski Stadium, Sofia. No. 1256, Arch, Nissaria. No. 1257, Parachutist.

1963, Feb. 20 **Unwmk.** ***Perf. 10***

1253 A579 1s brown red .25 .25
1254 A580 1s red brown .25 .25
1255 A580 1s blue green .25 .25
1256 A580 1s dark green .25 .25
1257 A580 1s brt blue .25 .25
Nos. 1253-1257 (5) 1.25 1.25

Vassil Levski
A581

1963, Apr. 11 **Photo.**

1258 A581 13s grnsh blue & buff 1.75 .55

90th anniversary of the death of Vassil Levski, revolutionary leader in the fight for liberation from the Turks.

Boy, Girl and Dimitrov — A582

13s, Girl with book & boy with hammer.

1963, Apr. 25 **Unwmk.** ***Perf. 11½***

1259 A582 2s org, ver, red brn & blk .25 .25
1260 A582 13s bluish grn, brn & blk .65 .25

10th Congress of Dimitrov's Union of the People's Youth.

Red Squirrel — A583

2s, Hedgehog. 3s, European polecat. 5s, Pine marten. 13s, Badger. 20s, Otter. 2s, 3s, 5s, 13s, horiz.

1963, Apr. 30 **Red Numerals**

1261 A583 1s grn & brn, *grnsh* .25 .25
1262 A583 2s grn & blk, *yel* .25 .25
1263 A583 3s grn & brn, *bis* .25 .25
1264 A583 5s vio & red brn, *lil* .90 .25
1265 A583 13s red brn & blk, *pink* 2.75 1.10
1266 A583 20s blk & brn, *blue* 4.25 1.60
Nos. 1261-1266 (6) 8.65 3.70

Sun Coast Promenade
A584

Black Sea Resorts: 2s, 3s, 13s, Views of Gold Sand. 5s, 20s, Sun Coast.

1963, Mar. 12 **Unwmk.** ***Perf. 13***

1267 A584 1s blue .25 .25
1268 A584 2s vermilion .25 .25
1269 A584 2s car rose 2.50 1.25
1270 A584 3s ocher .25 .25
1271 A584 5s lilac .25 .25
1272 A584 13s blue green .55 .25
1273 A584 20s green 1.10 .25
Nos. 1267-1273 (7) 5.15 2.75

Freestyle Wrestling
A585

Design: 20s, Freestyle wrestling, horiz.

1963, May 31 ***Perf. 11½***

1274 A585 5s yel bister & blk .40 .25
1275 A585 20s org brn & blk 1.25 .25

15th International Freestyle Wrestling Competitions, Sofia.

"Women for Peace"
A586

1963, June 24 **Unwmk.** ***Perf. 11½***

1276 A586 20s blue & blk 1.25 .25

World Congress of Women, Moscow, June 24-29.

Esperanto Emblem and Arms of Sofia — A587

1963, June 29 **Photo.**

1277 A587 13s multicolored 1.25 .25

48th World Esperanto Congress, Sofia, Aug. 3-10.

Moon, Earth and Lunik 4 — A588

2s, Radar equipment. 3s, Satellites and moon.

1963, July 22

1278 A588 1s ultra .25 .25
1279 A588 2s red lilac .25 .25
1280 A588 3s greenish blue .25 .25
Nos. 1278-1280 (3) .75 .75

Russia's rocket to the moon, Apr. 2, 1963.

Nos. 1211-1212 and 1215 Ovptd. or Srchd. in Green, Ultra or Black

1963, Aug. 31 ***Perf. 10½***

1281 A565 2s (G) .35 .25
1282 A565 5s on 3s (U) .75 .25
1283 A565 13s on 6s 1.40 .35
Nos. 1281-1283 (3) 2.50 .85

Intl. Stamp Fair, Riccione, Aug. 31.

Women's Relay Race — A589

2s, Hammer thrower. 3s, Women's long jump. 5s, Men's high jump. 13s, Discus thrower.

Perf. 11½

1963, Sept. 13 Photo. Unwmk.

Flags in National Colors

1284 A589 1s slate green .25 .25
1285 A589 2s purple .25 .25
1286 A589 3s Prus blue .25 .25
1287 A589 5s maroon .85 .55
1288 A589 13s chestnut brn 3.00 2.25
Nos. 1284-1288 (5) 4.60 3.55

Balkan Games. A multicolored, 50s, imperf. souvenir sheet shows design of women's relay race. Size: 74x70mm. Value, $5 unused.

"Slav-Bulgarian History" — A590

1963, Sept. 19 ***Perf. 10½***

1289 A590 5s sal pink, slate & yel .40 .40

5th International Slavic Congress.

Revolutionists A591

1963, Sept. 22 ***Perf. 11½***

1290 A591 2s brt red & blk .25 .25

40th anniv. of the September Revolution.

Christo Smirnenski A592

1963, Oct. 28 ***Perf. 10½***

1291 A592 13s pale lilac & indigo .85 .25

Christo Smirnenski, poet, 65th birth anniv.

Columbine A593

1963, Oct. 9 Photo. ***Perf. 11½***

1292 A593 1s shown .25 .25
1293 A593 2s Edelweiss .25 .25
1294 A593 3s Primrose .25 .25
1295 A593 5s Water lily .25 .25
1296 A593 6s Tulips .25 .25
1297 A593 8s Larkspur .80 .25
1298 A593 10s Alpine clematis 1.60 .25
1299 A593 13s Anemone 3.00 .60
Nos. 1292-1299 (8) 6.65 2.35

Horses — A594

Designs: 2s, Charioteer and chariot. 3s, Trumpeters. 5s, Woman carrying tray with food. 13s, Man holding bowl. 20s, Woman in armchair. Designs are from a Thracian tomb at Kazanlik.

1963, Dec. 28 Unwmk. ***Perf. 10½***

1300 A594 1s gray, org & dk red .30 .25
1301 A594 2s gray, ocher & pur .30 .25
1302 A594 3s gray, dl yel & sl grn .30 .25
1303 A594 5s pale grn, ocher & brn .30 .25
1304 A594 13s pale grn, bis & blk .75 .35
1305 A594 20s pale grn, org & dk car 1.50 .55
Nos. 1300-1305 (6) 3.45 1.90

World Map and Emblem A595

Designs: 2s, Blood transfusion. 3s, Nurse bandaging injured wrist. 5s, Red Cross nurse. 13s, Henri Dunant.

1964, Jan. 27 ***Perf. 10½***

1306 A595 1s lem, blk & red .25 .25
1307 A595 2s ultra, blk & red .25 .25
1308 A595 3s gray, sl, blk & red .25 .25
1309 A595 5s brt bl, blk & red .25 .25
1310 A595 13s org yel, blk & red .90 .25
Nos. 1306-1310 (5) 1.90 1.25

Centenary of International Red Cross.

Speed Skating A596

Sports: 2s, 50s, Women's figure skating. 3s, Cross-country skiing. 5s, Ski jump. 10s, Ice hockey goalkeeper. 13s, Ice hockey players.

1964, Feb. 21 Unwmk. ***Perf. 10½***

1311 A596 1s grnsh bl, ind & ocher .25 .25
1312 A596 2s brt pink, ol grn & dk sl grn .25 .25
1313 A596 3s dl grn, dk grn & brn .25 .25
1314 A596 5s bl, blk & yel brn .25 .25
1315 A596 10s gray, org & blk .70 .25
1316 A596 13s lil, blk & lil rose 1.00 .45
Nos. 1311-1316 (6) 2.70 1.70

Miniature Sheet

Imperf

1317 A596 50s gray, Prus grn & pink 5.00 5.00

9th Winter Olympic Games, Innsbruck, Jan. 29-Feb. 9, 1964.

Mask of Nobleman, 2nd Century A597

2s, Thracian horseman. 3s, Ceramic jug. 5s, Clasp & belt. 6s, Copper kettle. 8s, Angel. 10s, Lioness. 13s, Scrub woman, contemporary sculpture.

1964, Mar. 14 Photo. ***Perf. 10½***

Gray Frame

1318 A597 1s dp green & red .25 .25
1319 A597 2s ol gray & red .25 .25
1320 A597 3s bister & red .25 .25
1321 A597 5s indigo & red .25 .25
1322 A597 6s org brn & red .45 .25
1323 A597 8s brn red & red .75 .25
1324 A597 10s olive & red .75 .25
1325 A597 13s gray ol & red 1.10 .45
Nos. 1318-1325 (8) 4.05 2.20

2,500 years of Bulgarian art.

"The Unborn Maid" A598

Fairy Tales: 2s, Grandfather's Glove. 3s, The Big Turnip. 5s, The Wolf and the Seven Kids. 8s, Cunning Peter. 13s, The Wheat Cake.

1964, Apr. 17 Unwmk. ***Perf. 10½***

1326 A598 1s bl grn, red & org brn .25 .25
1327 A598 2s ultra, ocher & blk .25 .25
1328 A598 3s cit, red & blk .25 .25
1329 A598 5s dp rose, brn & blk .25 .25
1330 A598 8s yel grn, red & blk .25 .25
1331 A598 13s lt vio bl, grn & blk 1.50 .25
Nos. 1326-1331 (6) 2.75 1.50

Ascalaphus Otomanus A599

Insects: 2s, Nemoptera coa., vert. 3s, Saga natalia (grasshopper). 5s, Rosalia alpina, vert. 13s, Anisoplia austriaca, vert. 20s, Scolia flavitrons.

1964, May 16 Photo. ***Perf. 11½***

1332 A599 1s brn org, yel & blk .25 .25
1333 A599 2s dl bl grn, bis & blk .25 .25
1334 A599 3s gray, grn & blk .25 .25
1335 A599 5s lt ol grn, blk & vio .25 .25
1336 A599 13s vio, bis & blk 1.75 .25
1337 A599 20s gray bl, yel & blk 2.50 .85
Nos. 1332-1337 (6) 5.25 2.10

Soccer — A600

Designs: 13s, Women's volleyball. 60s, Map of Europe and European Women's Volleyball Championship Cup (rectangular, size: 60x69mm).

1964, June 8 Unwmk. ***Perf. 11½***

1338 A600 2s bl, dk bl, ocher & red .25 .25
1339 A600 13s bl, dk bl, ocher & red 1.00 .40

Miniature Sheet

Imperf

1340 A600 60s ultra, ocher, red & gray 4.25 3.00

Levski Physical Culture Assoc., 50th anniv.

Peter Beron and Title Page of Primer — A601

1964, June 22 ***Perf. 11½***

1341 A601 20s red brn & dk brn, *grysh* 2.75 2.75

140th anniversary of the publication of the first Bulgarian primer.

Robert Stephenson's "Rocket" Locomotive, 1825 — A602

Designs: 2s, Modern steam locomotive. 3s, Diesel locomotive. 5s, Electric locomotive. 8s, Freight train on bridge. 13s, Diesel locomotive and tunnel.

1964, July 1 Photo. ***Perf. 11½***

1342 A602 1s multicolored .25 .25
1343 A602 2s multicolored .25 .25
1344 A602 3s multicolored .25 .25
1345 A602 5s multicolored .25 .25
1346 A602 8s multicolored .60 .25
1347 A602 13s multicolored 1.50 .25
Nos. 1342-1347 (6) 3.10 1.50

German Shepherd — A603

1964, Aug. 22 **Photo.**

1348 A603 1s shown .25 .25
1349 A603 2s Setter .25 .25
1350 A603 3s Poodle .35 .25
1351 A603 4s Pomeranian .45 .25
1352 A603 5s St. Bernard .60 .25
1353 A603 6s Terrier .85 .55
1354 A603 10s Pointer 3.50 1.75
1355 A603 13s Dachshund 5.75 3.00
Nos. 1348-1355 (8) 12.00 6.55

Partisans — A604

Designs: 2s, People welcoming Soviet army. 3s, Russian aid to Bulgaria. 4s, Blast furnace, Kremikovski. 5s, Combine. 6s, Peace demonstration. 8s, Sentry. 13s, Demeter Blagoev and George Dimitrov.

1964, Sept. 9 **Unwmk.** ***Perf. 11½***
Flag in Red

1356 A604 1s lt & dp ultra .25 .25
1357 A604 2s ol bis & dp ol .25 .25
1358 A604 3s rose lil & mar .25 .25
1359 A604 4s lt vio & vio .25 .25
1360 A604 5s org & red brn .25 .25
1361 A604 6s bl & dp bl .25 .25
1362 A604 8s lt grn & grn .25 .25
1363 A604 13s fawn & red brn .80 .25
Nos. 1356-1363 (8) 2.55 2.00

20th anniv. of People's Government of Bulgaria.

No. 967 Surcharged

1964, Sept. 13 ***Perf. 13***

1364 A476 20s on 44s org yel 1.75 .65

International Plovdiv Fair.

Gymnast on Parallel Bars — A606

Sports: 2s, Long jump. 3s, Woman diver. 5s, Soccer. 13s, Women's volleyball. 20s, Wrestling.

1964, Oct. 10 ***Perf. 11½***

1366 A606 1s pale grn, grn & red .25 .25
1367 A606 2s pale vio, vio bl & red .25 .25
1368 A606 3s bl grn, brn & red .25 .25
1369 A606 5s pink, pur & red .25 .25
1370 A606 13s bl, Prus grn & red .85 .25
1371 A606 20s yel, grn & red 1.60 .45
Nos. 1366-1371 (6) 3.45 1.70

18th Olympic Games, Tokyo. Oct. 10-25. See No. B27.

Vratcata Mountain Road — A607

Bulgarian Views: 2s, Ritlite mountain road. 3s, Pines, Maliovica peak. 4s, Pobitite rocks. 5s, Erkupria. 6s, Rhodope mountain road.

1964, Oct. 26 **Photo.** ***Perf. 12½x13***

1372 A607 1s dk slate grn .25 .25
1373 A607 2s brown .25 .25
1374 A607 3s grnsh blue .25 .25
1375 A607 4s dk red brn .25 .25
1376 A607 5s deep green .25 .25
1377 A607 6s blue violet .75 .25
Nos. 1372-1377 (6) 2.00 1.50

Mail Coach, Plane and Rocket A608

1964, Oct. 3 **Unwmk.** ***Perf. 11½***

1378 A608 20s greenish blue 1.25 .50

First national stamp exhibition, Sofia, Oct. 3-18. Issued in sheets of 12 stamps and 12 labels (woman's head and inscription, 5x5) arranged around one central label showing stylized bird design. No. 1378 with label, value $2.50.

Exists imperf.

Students Holding Book — A609

1964, Dec. 30 **Photo.**

1379 A609 13s lt blue & blk .85 .45

8th Intl. Students' Congress, Sofia.

500-Year-Old Walnut Tree at Golemo Drenovo — A610

Designs: Various old trees.

1964, Dec. 28

1380 A610 1s blk, buff & cl brn .25 .25
1381 A610 2s blk, pink & dp cl .25 .25
1382 A610 3s blk, yel & dk brn .25 .25
1383 A610 4s blk, lt bl & Prus bl .25 .25
1384 A610 10s blk, pale grn & grn .70 .25
1385 A610 13s blk, pale bis & dk ol grn 1.00 .25
Nos. 1380-1385 (6) 2.70 1.50

Soldiers' Monument A611

1965, Jan. 1 **Unwmk.**

1386 A611 2s red & black .40 .40

Bulgarian-Soviet friendship.

Olympic Medal Inscribed "Olympic Glory" A612

1965, Jan. 27 **Photo.** ***Perf. 11½***

1387 A612 20s org brn, gold & blk 1.25 .65

Bulgarian victories in the 1964 Olympic Games.

"Victory Over Fascism" A613

13s, "Fight for Peace" (dove and globe).

1965, Apr. 16 ***Perf. 11½***

1388 A613 5s gray, blk & ol bis .25 .25
1389 A613 13s gray, blk & blue .60 .25

Victory over Fascism, 5/9/45, 20th anniv.

Vladimir M. Komarov and Section of Globe — A614

Designs: 2s, Konstantin Feoktistov. 5s, Boris B. Yegorov. 13s, Komarov, Feoktistov and Yegorov. 20s, Spaceship Voskhod.

1965, Feb. 15 **Photo.**

1390 A614 1s pale lil & dk bl .25 .25
1391 A614 2s lt bl, ind & dl vio .25 .25
1392 A614 5s pale grn, grn & ol grn .25 .25
1393 A614 13s pale pink, dp rose & mar .65 .25
1394 A614 20s lt bl, vio bl, grnsh bl & yel 1.25 .25
Nos. 1390-1394 (5) 2.65 1.25

Russian 3-man space flight, Oct. 12-13, 1964.

Imperfs in changed colors. Four low values se-tenant. Value, set $4 unused, $1 canceled.

Bullfinch — A615

Birds: 2s, European golden oriole. 3s, Common rock thrush. 5s, Barn swallow. 8s, European roller. 10s, European goldfinch. 13s, Rosy pastor starling. 20s, Nightingale.

1965, Apr. 20 **Unwmk.** ***Perf. 11½***
Birds in Natural Colors

1395 A615 1s blue green .25 .25
1396 A615 2s rose lilac .25 .25
1397 A615 3s rose .25 .25
1398 A615 5s brt blue .25 .25
1399 A615 8s citron .55 .45
1400 A615 10s gray 2.25 .65
1401 A615 13s lt vio blue 2.25 1.25
1402 A615 20s emerald 4.50 2.75
Nos. 1395-1402 (8) 10.55 6.10

Black Sea Fish A616

1965, June 10 **Photo.** ***Perf. 11½***
Gray Frames

1403 A616 1s Sting ray .25 .25
1404 A616 2s Belted bonito .25 .25
1405 A616 3s Hogfish .25 .25
1406 A616 5s Gurnard .25 .25
1407 A616 10s Scad 1.50 .25
1408 A616 13s Turbot 2.25 .50
Nos. 1403-1408 (6) 4.75 1.75

Plane, Bus, Train, Ship and Whale A617

1965, Apr. 30

1409 A617 13s multicolored 1.25 .75

4th Intl. Conf. of Transport, Dock and Fishery Workers, Sofia, May 10-14.

ITU Emblem and Communications Symbols — A618

1965, May 17

1410 A618 20s multicolored 1.25 .60

Centenary of the ITU.

Col. Pavel Belyayev and Lt. Col. Alexei Leonov — A619

Design: 20s, Leonov floating in space.

1965, May 20 **Unwmk.**

1411 A619 2s gray, dull bl & dk brn .40 .25
1412 A619 20s multicolored 3.25 1.40

Space flight of Voskhod 2 and the first man floating in space, Lt. Col. Alexei Leonov.

ICY Emblem A620

1965, May 15 **Photo.**

1413 A620 20s orange, olive & blk 1.25 .70

International Cooperation Year, 1965.

Corn — A621

Marx and Lenin — A622

1965, Apr. 1 ***Perf. 12½x13***

1414 A621 1s shown .25 .25
1415 A621 2s Wheat .25 .25
1416 A621 3s Sunflowers .25 .25
1417 A621 4s Sugar beet .25 .25
1418 A621 5s Clover .25 .25
1419 A621 10s Cotton .80 .25
1420 A621 13s Tobacco 1.25 .25
Nos. 1414-1420 (7) 3.30 1.75

1965, June ***Perf. 10½***

1421 A622 13s red & dk brn 1.75 .25

6th Conference of Postal Ministers of Communist Countries, Peking, June 21-July 15.

Film and UNESCO Emblem A623

1965, June 30

1422 A623 13s dp bl, blk & lt gray .85 .25

Balkan Film Festival, Varna.

Ballerina — A624

1965, July 10 **Photo.**

1423 A624 5s dp lil rose & blk 1.75 1.75

2nd Intl. Ballet Competition, Varna.

Map of Balkan Peninsula and Dove with Letter A625

Col. Pavel Belyayev and Lt. Col. Alexei Leonov — A626

2s, Sailboat and modern buildings. 3s, Fish and plants. 13s, Symbolic sun and rocket. 40s, Map of Balkan Peninsula and dove with letter (like 1s).

1965 ***Perf. 10½***

1424 A625 1s sil, dp ultra & yel .25 .25
1425 A625 2s sil, pur & yel .25 .25
1426 A625 3s gold, grn & yel .25 .25
1427 A625 13s gold, hn brn & yel .90 .90
1428 A626 20s sil, bl & brn 1.50 1.50
Nos. 1424-1428 (5) 3.15 3.15

Miniature Sheet

Imperf

1429 A625 40s gold & brt bl 3.75 2.10

Balkanphila 1965 Philatelic Exhibition, Varna, Aug. 7-15, and visit of Russian astronauts Belyayev and Leonov.

Value, No. 1428 imperf. in changed colors, $1.75.

Issued: 20s, 40s, 8/7; others, 7/23.

Woman Gymnast — A627

Designs: 2s, Woman gymnast on parallel bars. 3s, Weight lifter. 5s, Automobile and chart. 10s, Women basketball players. 13s, Automobile and map of rally.

1965, Aug. 14 ***Perf. 10½***

1430 A627 1s crim, brn & blk .25 .25
1431 A627 2s rose vio, dp cl & blk .25 .25
1432 A627 3s dp car, brn & blk .25 .25
1433 A627 5s fawn, red brn & blk .35 .25
1434 A627 10s dp lil rose, dp cl & blk .65 .25
1435 A627 13s lilac, claret & blk .90 .25
Nos. 1430-1435 (6) 2.65 1.50

Sports events in Bulgaria during May-June, 1965.

No. 989 Surcharged

1965, Aug. 12 ***Perf. 13***

1436 A499 2s on 8s orange brn, surcharge 36mm wide 2.25 2.00
a. Surcharge 32mm wide 7.50 7.50

1st Natl. Folklore Competition, Aug. 12-15.

Escaping Prisoners — A628

Fruit — A629

1965, July 23 ***Perf. 10½***

1437 A628 2s slate .40 .40

40th anniversary of the escape of political prisoners from Bolshevik Island.

1965, July 1 ***Perf. 13***

1438 A629 1s Apples .25 .25
1439 A629 2s Grapes .25 .25
1440 A629 3s Pears .25 .25
1441 A629 4s Peaches .25 .25
1442 A629 5s Strawberries .25 .25
1443 A629 6s Walnuts .30 .25
Nos. 1438-1443 (6) 1.55 1.50

Horsemanship — A630

1965, Sept. 30 **Unwmk.** ***Perf. 10½***

1444 A630 1s Dressage .25 .25
1445 A630 2s Three-day test .25 .25
1446 A630 3s Jumping .25 .25
1447 A630 5s Race .55 .25
1448 A630 10s Steeplechase 2.50 1.10
1449 A630 13s Hurdle race 2.75 1.60
Nos. 1444-1449 (6) 6.55 3.70

See No. B28.

Smiling Children — A631

Designs: 2s, Two girl Pioneers. 3s, Bugler. 5s, Pioneer with model plane. 8s, Two singing girls in national costume. 13s, Running boy.

1965, Oct. 24 **Photo.**

1450 A631 1s dk bl grn & yel grn .25 .25
1451 A631 2s vio & deep rose .25 .25
1452 A631 3s olive & lemon .25 .25
1453 A631 5s dp blue & bister .25 .25
1454 A631 8s olive bister & org .45 .25
1455 A631 13s rose car & vio 1.10 .35
Nos. 1450-1455 (6) 2.55 1.60

Dimitrov Pioneer Organization.

U-52 Plane over Trnovo A632

2s, 1L-14 over Plovdiv. 3s, Mi-4 Helicopter over Dimitrovgrad. 5s, Tu-104 over Ruse. 13s, IL-18 over Varna. 20s, Tu-114 over Sofia.

1965, Nov. 25 ***Perf. 10½***

1456 A632 1s gray, blue & red .25 .25
1457 A632 2s gray, lilac & red .25 .25
1458 A632 3s gray, grnsh bl & red .25 .25
1459 A632 5s gray, orange & red .25 .25
1460 A632 13s gray, bister & red 1.10 .25
1461 A632 20s gray, lt grn & red 1.60 .45
Nos. 1456-1461 (6) 3.70 1.70

Development of Bulgarian Civil Air Transport.

IQSY Emblem, and Earth Radiation Zones A633

Designs (IQSY Emblem and): 2s, Sun with corona. 13s, Solar eclipse.

1965, Dec. 15 **Photo.** ***Perf. 10½***

1462 A633 1s grn, yel & ultra .25 .25
1463 A633 2s yel, red lil & red .25 .25
1464 A633 13s bl, yel & blk .85 .25
Nos. 1462-1464 (3) 1.35 .75

International Quiet Sun Year, 1964-65.

"North and South Bulgaria" A634

1965, Dec. 6

1465 A634 13s brt yel grn & blk .85 .55

Union of North and South Bulgaria, cent.

"Martenitsa" Emblem — A635

"Spring" in Folklore: 2s, Drummer. 3s, Bird ornaments. 5s, Dancer "Lazarka." 8s, Vase with flowers. 13s, Bagpiper.

1966, Jan. 10 **Photo.** ***Perf. 10½***

1466 A635 1s rose lil, vio bl & gray .25 .25
1467 A635 2s gray, blk & crim .25 .25
1468 A635 3s red, vio & gray .25 .25
1469 A635 5s lil, blk & crimson .25 .25
1470 A635 8s rose lil, brn & pur .50 .25
1471 A635 13s bl, blk & rose lilac .85 .25
Nos. 1466-1471 (6) 2.35 1.50

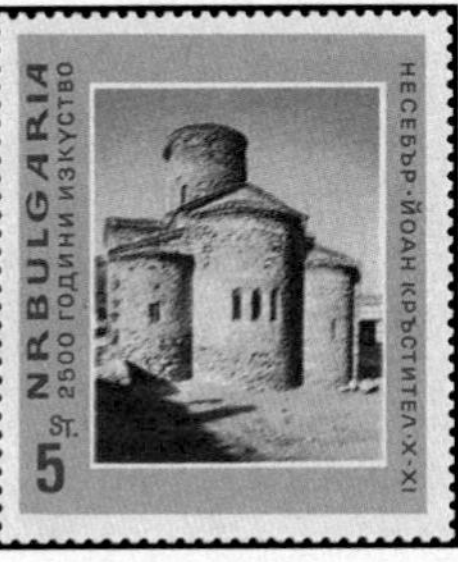

Church of St. John the Baptist, Nessebr A636

Designs: 1s, Christ, fresco from Bojana Church. 2s, Ikon "Destruction of Idols," horiz. 3s, Bratchkovo Monastery. 4s, Zemen Monastery, horiz. 13s, Nativity, ikon from Arbanassi. 20s, Ikon "Virgin and Child," 1342.

1966, Feb. 25 **Litho.** ***Perf. 11½***

1472 A636 1s gray & multi *5.00* *1.75*
1473 A636 2s gray & multi .35 .25
1474 A636 3s multicolored .35 .25
1475 A636 4s multicolored .35 .25
1476 A636 5s multicolored .35 .25
1477 A636 13s gray & multi .70 .25
1478 A636 20s multicolored 1.40 .50
Nos. 1472-1478 (7) *8.50* *3.50*

2,500 years of art in Bulgaria.

Georgi Benkovski and T. Kableshkov — A637

1s, Proclamation of April Uprising, Koprivstitsa. 3s, Dedication of flag, Panaguriste. 5s, V. Petleshkov, Z. Dyustabanov. 10s, Botev landing at Kozlodui. 13s, P. Volov, Ilarion Dragostinov.

1966, Mar. 3 **Photo.** ***Perf. 10½***

Center in Black

1479 A637 1s red brn & gold .25 .25
1480 A637 2s brt red & gold .25 .25
1481 A637 3s ol grn & gold .25 .25
1482 A637 5s steel bl & gold .25 .25
1483 A637 10s brt rose lil & gold .25 .25
1484 A637 13s lt vio & gold .75 .25
Nos. 1479-1484 (6) 2.00 1.50

April Uprising against the Turks, 90th anniv.

Sofia Zoo Animals A638

1966, May 23 **Litho.**

1485 A638 1s Elephant .25 .25
1486 A638 2s Tiger .25 .25
1487 A638 3s Chimpanzee .25 .25

1488 A638 4s Siberian ibex .25 .25
1489 A638 5s Polar bear .75 .25
1490 A638 8s Lion 1.10 .50
1491 A638 13s Bison 2.75 1.25
1492 A638 20s Kangaroo 3.75 1.90
Nos. 1485-1492 (8) 9.35 4.90

WHO Headquarters, Geneva — A639

1966, May 3 Photo.
1493 A639 13s deep blue & silver 1.00 .40

Inauguration of the WHO Headquarters, Geneva.

Worker A640

1966, May 9 Photo. *Perf. 10½*
1494 A640 20s gray & rose 1.25 .70

Sixth Trade Union Congress.

Yantra River Bridge, Biela — A641

No. 1496, Maritsa River Bridge, Svilengrad. No. 1497, Fountain, Samokov. No. 1498, Ruins of Fort, Kaskovo. 8s, Old Fort, Ruse. 13s, House, Gabrovo.

1966, Feb. 10 Photo. *Perf. 13*
1495 A641 1s Prus blue .25 .25
1496 A641 1s brt green .25 .25
1497 A641 2s olive green .25 .25
1498 A641 2s dk red brown .25 .25
1499 A641 8s red brown .35 .25
1500 A641 13s dark blue .60 .25
Nos. 1495-1500 (6) 1.95 1.50

Souvenir Sheet

Moon Allegory — A642

1966, Apr. 29 *Imperf.*
1501 A642 60s blk, plum & sil 4.25 3.50

1st Russian soft landing on the moon by Luna 9, Feb. 3, 1966.

Steamer Radetzky and Bugler — A643

1966, May 28 *Perf. 10½*
1502 A643 2s multicolored .25 .25

90th anniv. of the participation of the Danube steamer Radetzky in the uprising against the Turks.

Standard Bearer Nicola Simov-Kuruto A644

1966, May 30
1503 A644 5s bister, green & olive .40 .25

Hero of the Turkish War.

UNESCO Emblem A645

1966, June 8
1504 A645 20s gold, blk & ver 1.00 .50

20th anniv. of UNESCO.

Youth Federation Badge — A646

1966, June 6 Photo. *Perf. 10½*
1505 A646 13s silver, bl & blk .85 .25

7th Assembly of the Intl. Youth Federation.

Soccer — A647

Various soccer scenes. 50s, Jules Rimet Cup.

1966, June 27
1506 A647 1s gray, yel brn & blk .25 .25
1507 A647 2s gray, crim & blk .25 .25
1508 A647 5s gray, ol bis & blk .25 .25
1509 A647 13s gray, ultra & blk .55 .25
1510 A647 20s gray, Prus bl & blk 1.00 .25
Nos. 1506-1510 (5) 2.30 1.25

Miniature Sheet
Imperf

1511 A647 50s gray, dp lil rose & gold 3.75 2.50

World Soccer Cup Championship, Wembley, England, July 11-30. Size of No. 1511: 60x64mm.

Woman Javelin Thrower — A648

No. 1513, Runner. No. 1514, Young man and woman carrying banners, vert.

1966 Photo. *Perf. 10½*
1512 A648 2s grn, yel & ver .25 .25
1513 A648 13s dp grn, yel & sal pink .75 .25
1514 A648 13s bl, lt bl & salmon .75 .25
Nos. 1512-1514 (3) 1.75 .75

Nos. 1512-1513: 3rd Spartacist Games; issued Aug. 10. No. 1514: 3rd congress of the Bulgarian Youth Federation; issued May 25.

Wrestlers Nicolas Petrov and Dan Kolov — A649

1966, July 29
1515 A649 13s bis brn, dk brn & lt ol grn .85 .50

3rd International Wrestling Championships.

Map of Balkan Countries, Globe and UNESCO Emblem — A650

1966, Aug. 26 *Perf. 10½x11½*
1516 A650 13s ultra, lt grn & pink .85 .25

First Congress of Balkanologists.

Children with Building Blocks A651

2s, Bunny & teddy bear with book. 3s, Children as astronauts. 13s, Children with pails & shovel.

1966, Sept. 1 *Perf. 10½*
1517 A651 1s dk car, org & blk .25 .25
1518 A651 2s emerald, blk & red brn .25 .25
1519 A651 3s ultra, org & blk .25 .25
1520 A651 13s blue, rose & blk 1.10 .25
Nos. 1517-1520 (4) 1.85 1.00

Children's Day.

Yuri A. Gagarin and Vostok 1 — A652

Designs: 2s, Gherman S. Titov, Vostok 2. 3s, Andrian G. Nikolayev, Pavel R. Popovich, Vostoks 3 & 4. 5s, Valentina Tereshkova, Valeri Bykovski, Vostoks 5 & 6. 8s, Vladimir M. Komarov, Boris B. Yegorov, Konstantin Feoktistov, Voskhod 1. 13s, Pavel Belyayev, Alexei Leonov, Voskhod 2.

1966, Sept. 29 Photo. *Perf. 11½x11*
1521 A652 1s slate & gray .25 .25
1522 A652 2s plum & gray .25 .25
1523 A652 3s yel brn & gray .25 .25
1524 A652 5s brn red & gray .25 .25
1525 A652 8s ultra & gray .25 .25
1526 A652 13s Prus bl & gray .80 .25
Nos. 1521-1526,B29 (7) 3.65 2.05

Russian space explorations.

St. Clement, 14th Century Wood Sculpture A653

1966, Oct. 27 Photo. *Perf. 11½x11*
1527 A653 5s red, buff & brown .85 .85

1050th anniversary of the birth of St. Clement of Ochrida.

Metodi Shatorov A654

Portraits: 3s, Vladimir Trichkov. 5s, Valcho Ivanov. 10s, Raiko Daskalov. 13s, General Vladimir Zaimov.

1966, Nov. 8 *Perf. 11x11½*
Gold Frame, Black Denomination
1528 A654 2s crimson & bl vio .25 .25
1529 A654 3s magenta & blk .25 .25
1530 A654 5s car rose & dk bl .25 .25
1531 A654 10s orange & olive .50 .25
1532 A654 13s red & brown .65 .25
Nos. 1528-1532 (5) 1.90 1.25

Fighters against fascism.

George Dimitrov — A655

Steel Worker — A656

1966, Nov. 14 Photo. *Perf. 11½x11*
1533 A655 2s magenta & blk .25 .25
1534 A656 20s fawn, gray & blk .90 .25

Bulgarian Communist Party, 9th Congress.

Deer's Head Drinking Cup A667

Gold Treasure: 2s, 6s, 10s, Various Amazon's head jugs. 3s, Ram's head cup. 5s, Circular plate. 8s, Deer's head cup. 13s, Amphora. 20s, Ram drinking horn.

1966, Nov. 28 *Perf. 12x11½*
Vessels in Gold and Brown; Black Inscriptions
1535 A667 1s gray & violet .25 .25
1536 A667 2s gray & green .25 .25
1537 A667 3s gray & dk bl .25 .25
1538 A667 5s gray & red brn .25 .25
1539 A667 6s gray & Prus bl .25 .25
1540 A667 8s gray & brn ol 1.40 .25
1541 A667 10s gray & sepia 1.40 .25

1542 A667 13s gray & dk vio bl 1.40 .45
1543 A667 20s gray & vio brn 1.60 .45
Nos. 1535-1543 (9) 7.05 2.65

The gold treasure from the 4th century B.C. was found near Panagyurishte in 1949.

Tourist House, Bansko — A668

Tourist Houses: No. 1545, Belogradchik. No. 1546, Triavna. 20s, Rila.

1966, Nov. 29 Photo. *Perf. 11x11½*

1544 A668 1s dark blue .25 .25
1545 A668 2s dark green .25 .25
1546 A668 2s brown red .25 .25
1547 A668 20s lilac .65 .25
Nos. 1544-1547 (4) 1.40 1.00

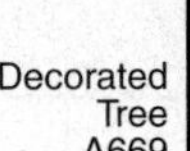

Decorated Tree A669

Design: 13s, Jug with bird design.

1966, Dec. 12 *Perf. 11*

1548 A669 2s grn, pink & gold .25 .25
1549 A669 13s brn lake, rose, emer & gold .65 .25

New Year, 1967.

Pencho Slaveikov, Author — A670

Portraits: 2s, Dimcho Debeljanov, author. 3s, P. H. Todorov, author. 5s, Dimitri Dobrovich, painter. 8s, Ivan Markvichka, painter. 13s, Ilya Bezhkov, painter.

1966, Dec. 15 *Perf. 10½x11*

1550 A670 1s blue, olive & org .25 .25
1551 A670 2s org, brn & gray .25 .25
1552 A670 3s olive, bl & org .25 .25
1553 A670 5s gray, red brn & org .25 .25
1554 A670 8s lilac, dk gray & bl .40 .25
1555 A670 13s blue, vio & lil .55 .25
Nos. 1550-1555 (6) 1.95 1.50

Dahlia — A671

Flowers: No. 1557, Clematis. No. 1558, Foxglove. No. 1559, Narcissus. 3s, Snowdrop. 5s, Petunia. 13s, Tiger lily. 20s, Bellflower.

Flowers in Natural Colors

1966, Dec. 29

1556 A671 1s gray & lt brn .25 .25
1557 A671 1s gray & dull bl .25 .25
1558 A671 2s gray & dull lil .25 .25
1559 A671 2s gray & brown .25 .25
1560 A671 3s gray & dk grn .35 .25
1561 A671 5s gray & dp ultra .50 .25
1562 A671 13s gray & brown 1.25 .30
1563 A671 20s gray & ultra 1.50 .35
Nos. 1556-1563 (8) 4.60 2.15

Ringnecked Pheasant — A672

Game: 2s, Rock partridge. 3s, Gray partridge. 5s, Hare. 8s, Roe deer. 13s, Red deer.

1967, Jan. 28 *Perf. 11x10½*

1564 A672 1s lt ultra, dk brn & ocher .25 .25
1565 A672 2s pale yel grn & dk grn .25 .25
1566 A672 3s lt bl, blk & cr .25 .25
1567 A672 5s lt grn & blk .95 .45
1568 A672 8s pale bl, dk brn & ocher 2.50 .95
1569 A672 13s bl & dk brn 2.75 1.60
Nos. 1564-1569 (6) 6.95 3.75

Bulgaria No. 1, 1879 — A673

1967, Feb. 4 Photo. *Perf. 10½*

1570 A673 10s emerald, blk & yel 2.25 1.60

Bulgarian Philatelic Union, 10th Congress.

Thracian Coin, 6th Century, B.C. — A674

Coins: 2s, Macedonian tetradrachma, 2nd cent. B.C. 3s, Tetradrachma of Odessus, 2nd cent. B.C. 5s, Philip II of Macedonia, 4th cent., B.C. 13s, Thracian King Seuthus VII, 4th cent., B.C., obverse and reverse. 20s, Apollonian coin, 5th cent., B.C., obverse and reverse.

1967, Mar. 30 *Perf. 11½x11*

Size: 25x25mm

1571 A674 1s brn, blk & sil .25 .25
1572 A674 2s red lil, blk & sil .25 .25
1573 A674 3s grn, blk & sil .25 .25
1574 A674 5s brn org, blk & sil .40 .30

Size: 37½x25mm

1575 A674 13s brt bl, blk & brnz 1.40 .60
1576 A674 20s vio, blk & sil 2.25 1.00
Nos. 1571-1576 (6) 4.80 2.65

Partisans Listening to Radio — A675

Design: 20s, George Dimitrov addressing crowd and Bulgarian flag.

1967, Apr. 20 *Perf. 11x11½*

1577 A675 1s red, gold, buff & sl grn .25 .25
1578 A675 20s red, gold, dl red, grn & blk 1.10 .25

25th anniversary of the Union of Patriotic Front Organizations.

Nikolas Kofardjiev A676

2s, Petko Napetov. 5s, Petko D. Petkov. 10s, Emil Markov. 13s, Traitcho Kostov.

1967, Apr. 24 *Perf. 11½x11*

1579 A676 1s brn red, gray & blk .25 .25
1580 A676 2s ol grn, gray & blk .25 .25
1581 A676 5s brn, gray & blk .25 .25
1582 A676 10s dp bl, gray & blk .25 .25
1583 A676 13s mag, gray & blk .95 .25
Nos. 1579-1583 (5) 1.95 1.25

Fighters against fascism.

Symbolic Flower and Flame — A677

1967, May 18 Photo. *Perf. 11x11½*

1584 A677 13s gold, yel & lt grn .85 .25

First Cultural Congress, May 18-19.

Gold Sand Beach and ITY Emblem A678

20s, Hotel, Pamporovo. 40s, Nessebr Church.

1967, June 12 Photo. *Perf. 11x11½*

1585 A678 13s ultra, yel & blk .55 .25
1586 A678 20s Prus bl, blk & buff .85 .25
1587 A678 40s brt grn, blk & ocher 2.10 .55
Nos. 1585-1587 (3) 3.50 1.05

International Tourist Year, 1967.

Angora Cat — A679

Cats: 2s, Siamese, horiz. 3s, Abyssinian. 5s, Black European. 13s, Persian, horiz. 20s, Striped domestic.

Perf. 11½x11, 11x11½

1967, June 19

1588 A679 1s dl vio, dk brn & buff .25 .25
1589 A679 2s ol, sl & brt bl .25 .25
1590 A679 3s dull blue & brn .45 .25
1591 A679 5s grn, blk & yel 1.25 .25
1592 A679 13s dl red brn, sl & org 1.50 .25
1593 A679 20s gray grn, brn & buff 2.40 .45
Nos. 1588-1593 (6) 6.10 1.70

Scene from Opera "The Master of Boyana" by K. Iliev A680

Songbird on Keyboard — A681

1967, June 19

1594 A680 5s gray, vio bl & dp car .45 .25
1595 A681 13s gray, dp car & dk bl 1.40 .25

3rd Intl. Competition for Young Opera Singers.

George Kirkov (1867-1919), Revolutionist — A682

1967, June 24 *Perf. 11x11½*

1596 A682 2s rose red & dk brn .25 .25

Symbolic Tree and Stars — A683

1967, July 28 Photo. *Perf. 11½x11*

1597 A683 13s dp bl, car & blk .85 .25

11th Congress of Dimitrov's Union of the People's Youth.

Roses and Distillery A684

Designs: No. 1599, Chick and incubator. No. 1600, Cucumbers and hothouse. No. 1601, Lamb and sheep farm. 3s, Sunflower and oil mill. 4s, Pigs and pig farm. 5s, Hops and hop farm. 6s, Corn and irrigation system. 8s, Grapes and Bolgar tractor. 10s, Apples and cultivated tree. 13s, Bees and honey. 20s, Bee, blossoms and beehives.

1967 *Perf. 11x11½*

1598 A684 1s multicolored .25 .25
1599 A684 1s dk car, yel & blk .25 .25
1600 A684 2s vio, lt grn & blk .25 .25
1601 A684 2s brt grn, gray & blk .25 .25
1602 A684 3s yel grn, yel & blk .25 .25
1603 A684 4s brt pur, yel & blk .25 .25
1604 A684 5s ol bis, yel grn & blk .25 .25
1605 A684 6s ol, brt grn & blk .25 .25
1606 A684 8s grn, bis & blk .25 .25
1607 A684 10s multicolored .45 .25
1608 A684 13s grn, bis brn & blk .70 .25
1609 A684 20s grnsh bl, brt pink & blk .90 .25
Nos. 1598-1609 (12) 4.30 3.00

Issue dates: Nos. 1598-1601, 1607, 1609, July 15; Nos. 1602-1606, 1608, July 24.

Map of Communist Countries, Spasski Tower A685

2s, Lenin speaking to soldiers. 3s, Fighting at Wlodaja, 1918. 5s, Marx, Engels & Lenin. 13s, Oil refinery. 20s, Vostok communication satellite.

1967, Aug. 25 *Perf. 11*

1610 A685 1s multicolored .25 .25
1611 A685 2s magenta & olive .25 .25
1612 A685 3s mag & dull vio .25 .25
1613 A685 5s magenta & red .25 .25
1614 A685 13s magenta & ultra .55 .25
1615 A685 20s magenta & blue .80 .25
Nos. 1610-1615 (6) 2.35 1.50

Russian October Revolution, 50th anniv.

Rod, "Fish" and Varna A686

1967, Aug. 29 **Photo.** *Perf. 11*

1616 A686 10s multicolored .70 .25

7th World Angling Championships, Varna.

Skiers and Winter Olympics' Emblem — A687

Sports and Emblem: 2s, Ski jump. 3s, Biathlon. 5s, Ice hockey. 13s, Figure skating couple.

1967, Sept. 20 **Photo.** *Perf. 11*

1617 A687 1s dk bl grn, red & blk .25 .25
1618 A687 2s ultra, blk & ol .25 .25
1619 A687 3s vio brn, bl & blk .25 .25
1620 A687 5s green, yel & blk .25 .25
1621 A687 13s vio bl, blk & buff .75 .25
Nos. 1617-1621,B31 (6) 5.00 1.85

10th Winter Olympic Games, Grenoble, France, Feb. 6-18, 1968.

Mountain Peaks — A688

1967, Sept. 25 **Engr.** *Perf. 11½*

1622 A688 1s Bogdan .25 .25
1623 A688 2s Czerny .25 .25
1624 A688 3s Ruen, vert. .25 .25
1625 A688 5s Persenk .25 .25
1626 A688 10s Botev .25 .25
1627 A688 13s Rila, vert. .40 .25
1628 A688 20s Vihren .75 .25
Nos. 1622-1628 (7) 2.40 1.75

George Rakovski A689

1967, Oct. 20 **Photo.** *Perf. 11*

1629 A689 13s yellow grn & blk .85 .40

Centenary of the death of George Rakovski, revolutionary against Turkish rule.

Yuri A. Gagarin, Valentina Tereshkova and Alexei Leonov — A690

Designs: 2s, Lt. Col. John H. Glenn, Jr., and Maj. Edward H. White. 5s, Earth and Molniya 1. 10s, Gemini 6 and 7. 13s, Luna 13 moon probe. 20s, Gemini 10 and Agena rocket.

1967, Nov. 25

1630 A690 1s Prus bl, blk & yel .25 .25
1631 A690 2s dl bl, blk & dl yel .25 .25
1632 A690 5s vio bl, grnsh bl & blk .25 .25
1633 A690 10s dk bl, blk & red .60 .25
1634 A690 13s grnsh bl, brt yel & blk .95 .25
1635 A690 20s dl bl, blk & red 1.25 .25
Nos. 1630-1635 (6) 3.55 1.50

Achievements in space exploration.

Various Views of Trnovo A691

1967, Dec. 5 **Photo.** *Perf. 11*

1636 A691 1s multicolored .25 .25
1637 A691 2s multicolored .25 .25
1638 A691 3s multicolored .25 .25
1639 A691 5s multicolored .25 .25
1640 A691 13s multicolored .50 .25
1641 A691 20s multicolored .85 .25
Nos. 1636-1641 (6) 2.35 1.50

Restoration of the ancient capital Veliko Trnovo.

Ratchenitza Folk Dance, by Ivan Markvichka — A692

1967, Dec. 9

1642 A692 20s gold & gray grn 1.75 1.40

Belgo-Bulgarian Philatelic Exposition, Brussels, Dec. 9-10. Printed in sheets of 8 stamps and 8 labels. No. 1642 with label, value $2.25.

Cosmos 186 and 188 Docking — A693

40s, Venera 4 and orbits around Venus.

1968, Jan.

1643 A693 20s multi 1.00 .25
1644 A693 40s multi, horiz. 2.00 .50

Docking maneuvers of the Russian spaceships Cosmos 186 and Cosmos 188, Nov. 1, 1967, and the flight to Venus of Venera 4, June 12-Nov. 18, 1967.

Crossing the Danube, by Orenburgski — A694

Paintings: 2s, Flag of Samara, by J. Veschin, vert. 3s, Battle of Pleven by Orenburgski. 13s, Battle of Orlovo Gnezdo, by N. Popov, vert. 20s, Welcome for Russian Soldiers, by D. Gudienov.

1968, Jan. 25 **Photo.** *Perf. 11*

1645 A694 1s gold & dk green .25 .25
1646 A694 2s gold & dk blue .25 .25
1647 A694 3s gold & chocolate .25 .25
1648 A694 13s gold & dk vio .80 .25
1649 A694 20s gold & Prus grn 1.10 .25
Nos. 1645-1649 (5) 2.65 1.25

90th anniv. of the liberation from Turkey.

Shepherds, by Zlatyn Boyadjiev — A695

Paintings: 2s, Wedding dance, by V. Dimitrov, vert. 3s, Partisans' Song, by Ilya Petrov. 5s, Portrait of Anna Penchovich, by Nikolai Pavlovich, vert. 13s, Self-portrait, by Zachary Zograf, vert. 20s, View of Old Plovdiv, by T. Lavrenov. 60s, St. Clement of Ochrida, by A. Mitov.

1967, Dec. **Litho.** *Perf. 11½*

Size: 45x38mm, 38x45mm

1650 A695 1s gray & multi .25 .25
1651 A695 2s gray & multi .25 .25

Size: 55x35mm

1652 A695 3s gray & multi .30 .25

Size: 38x45mm, 45x38mm

1653 A695 5s gray & multi .70 .25
1654 A695 13s gray & multi 1.50 .30
1655 A695 20s gray & multi 2.10 .70
Nos. 1650-1655 (6) 5.10 2.00

Miniature Sheet

Size: 65x84mm

Imperf

1656 A695 60s multicolored 5.00 3.00

Marx Statue, Sofia — A696

1968, Feb. 20 **Photo.** *Perf. 11*

1657 A696 13s black & red .85 .25

150th anniversary of birth of Karl Marx.

Maxim Gorky — A697

1968, Feb. 20

1658 A697 13s ver & grnsh blk .85 .25

Maxim Gorky (1868-1936), Russian writer.

Folk Dancers — A698

5s, Runners. 13s, Doves. 20s, Festival poster, (head, flowers, birds). 40s, Globe & Bulgaria No. 1 under magnifying glass.

1968, Mar. 20

1659 A698 2s multicolored .25 .25
1660 A698 5s multicolored .25 .25
1661 A698 13s multicolored .45 .25
1662 A698 20s multicolored .80 .25
1663 A698 40s multicolored 1.75 .65
Nos. 1659-1663 (5) 3.50 1.65

9th Youth Festival for Peace and Friendship, Sofia, July 28-Aug. 6.

Bellflower — A699

1968, Apr. 25 *Perf. 11*

1664 A699 1s shown .25 .25
1665 A699 2s Gentian .25 .25
1666 A699 3s Crocus .25 .25
1667 A699 5s Iris .25 .25
1668 A699 10s Dog-tooth violet .25 .25
1669 A699 13s Sempervivum 1.25 .25
1670 A699 20s Dictamnus 1.60 .40
Nos. 1664-1670 (7) 4.10 1.90

"The Unknown Hero," Tale by Ran Bosilek A700

Design: 20s, The Witch and the Young Man (Hans Christian Andersen fairy tale.)

1968, Apr. 25 **Photo.** *Perf. 10½*

1671 A700 13s black & multi .45 .25
1672 A700 20s black & multi .80 .45

Bulgarian-Danish Philatelic Exhibition.

Memorial Church, Shipka — A701

1968, May 3
1673 A701 13s multi + label .85 .25

Bulgarian Stamp Exhibition in Berlin. No. 1673 with label, value $1.25.

Show Jumping A702

Olympic Rings and: 1s, Gymnast on bar. 3s, Fencer. 10s, Boxer. 13s, Woman discus thrower.

1968, June 24 Photo. *Perf. 10½*
1674 A702 1s red & black .25 .25
1675 A702 2s gray, blk & rose brn .25 .25
1676 A702 3s mag, gray & blk .25 .25
1677 A702 10s grnsh bl, blk & lem .55 .25
1678 A702 13s vio bl, gray & pink 1.25 .45
Nos. 1674-1678,B33 (6) 4.45 2.00

19th Olympic Games, Mexico City, 10/12-27.

Battle of Buzluja A703

Design: 13s, Haji Dimitr and Stefan Karaja.

1968, July 1
1679 A703 2s silver & red brn .25 .25
1680 A703 13s gold & sl grn .65 .25

Centenary of the death of the patriots Haji Dimitr and Stefan Karaja.

Lakes of Smolian — A704

Sofia Zoo, 80th Anniv. — A705

Bulgarian Scenes: 2s, Ropotamo Lake. 3s, Erma-Idreloto mountain pass. 8s, Isker River dam. 10s, Slanchev Breg (sailing ship). 13s, Cape Caliacra. 40s, Old houses, Sozopol. 2 l, Chudnite Skali ("Strange Mountains").

1968 Photo. *Perf. 13*
1681 A704 1s Prus green .25 .25
1682 A704 2s dark green .25 .25
1683 A704 3s dark brown .25 .25
1684 A704 8s olive green .25 .25
1685 A704 10s redsh brown .25 .25
1686 A704 13s dk olive grn .40 .25
1687 A704 40s Prus blue 1.10 .40
1688 A704 2 l sepia 6.00 1.25
Nos. 1681-1688 (8) 8.75 3.15

1968, July 29 *Perf. 10½*
1689 A705 1s Cinereous vulture .25 .25
1690 A705 2s Crowned crane .25 .25
1691 A705 3s Zebra .25 .25
1692 A705 5s Cheetah .55 .25
1693 A705 13s Indian python 2.40 .90
1694 A705 20s African crocodile 3.25 1.50
Nos. 1689-1694 (6) 6.95 3.40

Human Rights Flame — A706

1968, July 8
1695 A706 20s dp blue & gold 1.00 .50

International Human Rights Year, 1968.

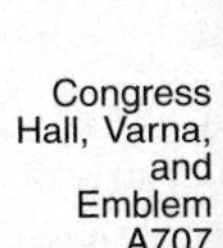

Congress Hall, Varna, and Emblem A707

1968, Sept. 17 Photo. *Perf. 10½*
1696 A707 20s bister, grn & red .85 .25

56th International Dental Congress, Varna.

Flying Swans A708

Rose A709

Designs: 2s, Jug. 20s, Five Viking ships.

1968 Photo. *Perf. 10½*
1697 A709 2s green & ocher 1.40 1.00
1698 A708 5s dp blue & gray 1.40 1.00
1699 A709 13s dp plum & lil rose 1.40 1.00
a. Pair, #1698, 1699 + label 3.00 3.00
1700 A708 20s dp vio & gray 1.40 1.00
a. Pair, #1697, 1700 + label 3.00 3.00
Nos. 1697-1700 (4) 5.60 4.00

Cooperation with the Scandinavian countries. Issued: 5s, 13s, Sept. 12; 2s, 20s, Nov. 22.

Stag Beetle — A710

No. 1702, Ground beetle (Procerus scabrosus). No. 1703, Ground beetle (Calosoma sycophania). No. 1704, Scarab beetle, horiz. No. 1705, Saturnid moth, horiz.

Perf. 12½x13, 13x12½
1968, Aug. 26
1701 A710 1s brown olive .25 .25
1702 A710 1s dark blue .25 .25
1703 A710 1s dark green .25 .25
1704 A710 1s orange brown .25 .25
1705 A710 1s magenta .25 .25
Nos. 1701-1705 (5) 1.25 1.25

Turks Fighting Insurgents, 1688 — A711

1968, Aug. 22 *Perf. 10½*
1706 A711 13s multicolored .85 .25

280th anniversary of the Tchiprovtzi insurrection.

Christo Smirnenski (1898-1923), Poet — A712

1968, Sept. 28 Litho. *Perf. 10½*
1707 A712 13s gold, red org & blk .85 .25

Dalmatian Pelican — A713

Birds: 2s, Little egret. 3s, Crested grebe. 5s, Common tern. 13s, European spoonbill. 20s, Glossy ibis.

1968, Oct. 28 Photo.
1708 A713 1s silver & multi .25 .25
1709 A713 2s silver & multi .40 .25
1710 A713 3s silver & multi .50 .25
1711 A713 5s silver & multi .80 .25
1712 A713 13s silver & multi 2.00 1.60
1713 A713 20s silver & multi 4.00 2.00
Nos. 1708-1713 (6) 7.95 4.60

Srebirna wild life reservation.

Carrier Pigeon A714

1968, Oct. 19
1714 A714 20s emerald 1.00 .65
a. Sheet of 4 + labels 8.50 2.75

2nd Natl. Stamp Exhib. in Sofia, Oct. 25-Nov. 15. No. 1714a contains 4 No. 1714 and 5 labels. No. 1714 with label, value $1.25.

Man and Woman from Silistra A715

Regional Costumes: 2s, Lovech. 3s, Yambol. 13s, Chirpan. 20s, Razgrad. 40s, Ihtiman.

1968, Nov. 20 Litho. *Perf. 13½*
1715 A715 1s dp org & multi .25 .25
1716 A715 2s Prus bl & multi .25 .25
1717 A715 3s multicolored .25 .25
1718 A715 13s multicolored .50 .25
1719 A715 20s multicolored .90 .40
1720 A715 40s green & multi 2.25 .70
Nos. 1715-1720 (6) 4.40 2.10

St. Arsenius A716

10th cent. Murals & Icons: 2s, Procession with relics of St. Ivan Rilsky, horiz. 3s, St. Michael Torturing the Soul of the Rich Man. 13s, St. Ivan Rilski. 20s, St. John. 40s, St. George. 1 l, Procession meeting relics of St. Ivan Rilsky, horiz.

Perf. 11½x12½, 12½x11½
1968, Nov. 25 Photo.
1721 A716 1s gold & multi .25 .25
1722 A716 2s gold & multi .25 .25
1723 A716 3s gold & multi .25 .25
1724 A716 13s gold & multi .65 .25
1725 A716 20s gold & multi 1.95 .55
1726 A716 40s gold & multi 2.50 1.00
Nos. 1721-1726 (6) 5.85 2.55

Souvenir Sheet
Imperf
1727 A716 1 l gold & multi 5.50 4.00

Millenium of Rila Monastery. No. 1727 also: Sofia 1969 Intl. Phil. Exhib., May 31-June 8, 1969. No. 1727 contains one stamp, size: 57x51mm.

Medlar A717

Herbs: No. 1729, Camomile. 2s, Lily-of-the-valley. 3s, Belladonna. 5s, Mallow. 10s, Buttercup. 13s, Poppies. 20s, Thyme.

1969, Jan. 2 Litho. *Perf. 10½*
1728 A717 1s blk, grn & org red .25 .25
1729 A717 1s black, grn & yel .25 .25
1730 A717 2s blk, emer & grn .25 .25
1731 A717 3s black & multi .25 .25
1732 A717 5s black & multi .25 .25
1733 A717 10s black, grn & yel .25 .25
1734 A717 13s black & multi .55 .25
1735 A717 20s black, lil & grn 1.25 .25
Nos. 1728-1735 (8) 3.30 2.00

Silkworms and Spindles A718

Designs: 2s, Silkworm, cocoons and pattern. 3s, Cocoons and spinning wheel. 5s, Cocoons, woof-and-warp diagram. 13s, Silk moth, Cocoon and spinning frame. 20s, Silk moth, eggs and shuttle.

1969, Jan. 30 Photo. *Perf. 10½*
1736 A718 1s bl, grn, sl & blk .25 .25
1737 A718 2s dp car, sil & blk .25 .25
1738 A718 3s Prus bl, sil & blk .25 .25
1739 A718 5s pur, ver, sil & blk .25 .25
1740 A718 13s red lil, ocher, sil & blk .50 .25
1741 A718 20s grn, org, sil & blk .85 .25
Nos. 1736-1741 (6) 2.35 1.50

Bulgarian silk industry.

Attack and Capture of Emperor Nicephorus A719

Designs (Manasses Chronicle): No. 1742, 1s, Death of Ivan Asen. No. 1746, 3s, Khan Kroum feasting after victory. No. 1748, 13s, Invasion of Bulgaria by Prince Sviatoslav of Kiev. No. 1750, 20s, Russian invasion and campaigns of Emperor John I Zimisces, c. 972 A.D. No. 1752, 40s, Tsar Ivan Alexander, Jesus and Constantine Manasses.

Horizontal designs: No. 1743, 1s, Kings Nebuchadnezzar, Balthazar, Darius and Cyrus. No. 1745, 2s, Kings Cambyses, Gyges and Darius. No. 1747, 5s, King David and Tsar Ivan Alexander. No. 1749, 13s, Persecution of Byzantine army after battle of July 26, 811. No. 1751, 20s, Christening of Bulgarian Tsar Boris, 865. No. 1753, 60s, Arrival of Tsar Simeon in Constantinople and his succeeding surprise attack on that city.

1969 Photo. ***Perf. 14x13½, 13½x14***

1742 A719 1s multicolored .25 .25
1743 A719 1s multicolored .25 .25
1744 A719 2s multicolored .25 .25
1745 A719 2s multicolored .25 .25
1746 A719 3s multicolored .25 .25
1747 A719 5s multicolored .25 .25
1748 A719 13s multicolored .55 .25
1749 A719 13s multicolored .55 .25
1750 A719 20s multicolored 1.10 .25
1751 A719 20s multicolored 1.10 .25
1752 A719 40s multicolored 2.00 .55
1753 A719 60s multicolored 3.75 .55
Nos. 1742-1753 (12) 10.55 3.60

Sts. Cyril and Methodius, Mural, Troian Monastery A720

1969, Mar. 23

1754 A720 28s gold & multi 1.75 1.00

Post Horn — A721

Designs: 13s, Bulgaria Nos. 1 and 534. 20s, Street fighting at Stackata, 1919.

1969, Apr. 15 Photo. ***Perf. 10½***

1755 A721 2s green & yel .25 .25
1756 A721 13s multicolored .70 .25
1757 A721 20s dk bl & lt bl .85 .25
Nos. 1755-1757 (3) 1.80 .75

Bulgarian postal administration, 90th anniv.

The Fox and the Rabbit A722

Puppet theater characters and illustrations from children's books: 2s, Boy reading to hedgehog and squirrel. 13s, Two birds and frog singing together.

1969, Apr. 21

1758 A722 1s emer, org & blk .25 .25
1759 A722 2s org, lt bl & blk .25 .25
1760 A722 13s lt bl, ol & blk .40 .25
Nos. 1758-1760 (3) .90 .75

Issued for Week of Children's Books and Arts.

ILO Emblem — A723

1969, Apr. 28

1761 A723 13s dull grn & blk .60 .25

50th anniv. of the ILO.

St. George and SOFIA 69 Emblem A724

Designs: 2s, Virgin Mary and St. John Bogoslov. 3s, Archangel Michael. 5s, Three Saints. 8s, Jesus Christ. 13s, Sts. George and Dimitrie. 20s, Christ, the Almighty. 40s, St. Dimitrie. 60s, The 40 Martyrs. 80s, The Transfiguration.

1969, Apr. 30 ***Perf. 11x12***

1762 A724 1s gold & multi .25 .25
1763 A724 2s gold & multi .25 .25
1764 A724 3s gold & multi .25 .25
1765 A724 5s gold & multi .30 .25
1766 A724 8s gold & multi .30 .25
1767 A724 13s gold & multi .50 .25
1768 A724 20s gold & multi .75 .30
1769 A724 40s gold & multi 2.10 1.20
a. Sheet of 4 9.00 7.75
1770 A724 60s gold & multi 2.75 1.60
1771 A724 80s gold & multi 3.75 2.00
Nos. 1762-1771 (10) 11.20 6.60

Old Bulgarian art from the National Art Gallery. No. 1769a contains 4 of No. 1769 with center gutter showing Alexander Nevski Shrine. See note on SOFIA 69 after Nos. C112-C120.

St. Cyril Preaching A725

Design: 28s, St. Cyril and followers.

1969, June 20 Litho. ***Perf. 10½***

1772 A725 2s sil, grn & red .25 .25
1773 A725 28s sil, dk bl & red 1.75 .85

St. Cyril (827-869), apostle to the Slavs, inventor of Cyrillic alphabet. Issued in sheets of 25 with se-tenant labels; Cyrillic inscription on label of 2s, Glagolitic inscription on label of 28s.

St. Sophia Church — A726

Sofia Through the Ages: 1s, Roman coin with inscription "Ulpia Serdica." 2s, Roman coin with Aesculapius Temple. 4s, Bojana Church. 5s, Sobranie Parliament. 13s, Vasov National Theater. 20s, Alexander Nevski Shrine. 40s, Clement Ochrida University. 1 l, Coat of arms.

1969, May 25 ***Perf. 13x12½***

1774 A726 1s gold & blue .25 .25
1775 A726 2s gold & ol grn .25 .25
1776 A726 3s gold & red brn .25 .25
1777 A726 4s gold & purple .25 .25
1778 A726 5s gold & plum .25 .25
1779 A726 13s gold & brt grn .30 .25
1780 A726 20s gold & vio bl .45 .25
1781 A726 40s gold & dp car 1.25 .30
Nos. 1774-1781 (8) 3.25 2.05

Souvenir Sheet

Imperf

1782 A726 1 l grn, gold & red 3.75 3.25

Historic Sofia in connection with the International Philatelic Exhibition, Sofia, 5/31-6/8.

No. 1782 contains one 43½x43½mm stamp. Emblems of 8 preceding philatelic exhibitions in metallic ink in margin; gold inscription.

No. 1782 was overprinted in green "IBRA 73" and various symbols, and released May 4, 1973, for the Munich Philatelic Exhibition. Value $150. The overprint also exists in gray. Value $50.

St. George A727

1969, June 9 Litho. ***Perf. 11½***

1783 A727 40s sil, blk & pale rose 2.10 1.00

38th FIP Congress, June 9-11.

Hand Planting Sapling A728

1969, Apr. 28 Photo. ***Perf. 11***

1784 A728 2s ol grn, blk & lilac .25 .25

25 years of the reforestation campaign.

Partisans — A729

Designs: 2s, Combine harvester. 3s, Dam. 5s, Flutist and singers. 13s, Factory. 20s, Lenin, Dimitrov, Russian and Bulgarian flags.

1969, Sept. 9

1785 A729 1s blk, pur & org .25 .25
1786 A729 2s blk, ol bis & org .25 .25
1787 A729 3s blk, bl grn & org .25 .25
1788 A729 5s blk, brn red & org .25 .25
1789 A729 13s blk, bl & org .50 .25
1790 A729 20s blk, brn & org .85 .25
Nos. 1785-1790 (6) 2.35 1.50

25th anniversary of People's Republic.

Women Gymnasts — A730

1969, Sept. Photo. ***Perf. 11***

1791 A730 2s shown .25 .25
1792 A730 20s Wrestlers .80 .30

Third National Spartakiad.

Tchanko Bakalov Tcherkovski, Poet. Birth Cent. — A731

1969, Sept. 6

1793 A731 13s multicolored .70 .25

Woman Gymnast A732

2s, Two women with hoops. 3s, Woman with hoop. 5s, Two women with spheres.

1969, Oct.

Gymnasts in Light Gray

1794 A732 1s green & dk blue .25 .25
1795 A732 2s blue & dk blue .25 .25
1796 A732 3s emer & sl grn .25 .25
1797 A732 5s orange & pur .25 .25
Nos. 1794-1797,B35-B36 (6) 3.20 1.75

World Championships for Artistic Gymnastics, Varna.

The Priest Rilski, by Zachary Zograf A733

Paintings from the National Art Gallery. 2s, Woman at Window, by Vasil Stoilov. 3s, Workers at Rest, by Nenko Balkanski, horiz. 4s, Woman Dressing (Nude), by Ivan Nenov. 5s, Portrait of a Woman, by N. Pavlovich. 13s, Falstaff, by Duzunov Kr. Sarafov. No. 1804, Portrait of a Woman, by N. Mihajlov, horiz. No. 1805, Workers at Mealtime, by Stojan Sotirov, horiz. 40s, Self-portrait, by Tcheno Togorov.

Perf. 11½x12, 12x11½

1969, Nov. 10

1798 A733 1s gold & multi .25 .25
1799 A733 2s gold & multi .25 .25
1800 A733 3s gold & multi .25 .25
1801 A733 4s gold & multi .25 .25
1802 A733 5s gold & multi .25 .25
1803 A733 13s gold & multi .50 .25
1804 A733 20s gold & multi 1.25 .40
1805 A733 20s gold & multi 1.25 .40
1806 A733 40s gold & multi 2.50 1.00
Nos. 1798-1806 (9) 6.75 3.30

Roman Bronze Wolf — A734

Design: 2s, Roman statue of woman, found at Silistra, vert.

1969, Oct. Photo. *Perf. 11*

1807 A734 2s sil, ultra & gray .25 .25
1808 A734 13s sil, dk grn & gray .90 .40

City of Silistra's 1,800th anniversary.

Worker and Factory A735

1969 *Perf. 13*

1809 A735 6s ultra & blk .25 .25

25th anniversary of the Engineering Corps.

European Hake — A736

Designs: No. 1811, Deep-sea fishing trawler. Fish: 2s, Atlantic horse mackerel. 3s, Pilchard. 5s, Dentex macrophthalmus. 10s, Chub mackerel. 13s, Otolithes macrognathus. 20s, Lichia vadigo.

1969 *Perf. 11*

1810 A736 1s ol grn & blk .25 .25
1811 A736 1s ultra, ind & gray .25 .25
1812 A736 2s lilac & blk .25 .25
1813 A736 3s vio bl & blk .25 .25
1814 A736 5s rose cl, pink & blk .50 .25
1815 A736 10s gray & blk 1.10 .25
1816 A736 13s ver, sal & blk 1.60 .25
1817 A736 20s ocher & black 2.75 .25
Nos. 1810-1817 (8) 6.95 2.00

Marin Drinov A737

1969, Nov. 10 Litho. *Perf. 11*

1818 A737 20s black & red org .85 .25

Centenary of the Bulgarian Academy of Science, founded by Marin Drinov.

Trapeze Artists — A738

Circus Performers: 2s, Jugglers. 3s, Jugglers with loops. 5s, Juggler and bear on bicycle. 13s, Woman and performing horse. 20s, Musical clowns.

1969 Photo. *Perf. 11*

1819 A738 1s dk blue & multi .25 .25
1820 A738 2s dk green & multi .25 .25
1821 A738 3s dk violet & multi .25 .25
1822 A738 5s multicolored .25 .25
1823 A738 13s multicolored .60 .25
1824 A738 20s multicolored 1.10 .25
Nos. 1819-1824 (6) 2.70 1.50

Pavel Bania Sanatorium A739

Health Resorts: 5s, Chisar Sanatorium. 6s, Kotel Children's Sanatorium. 20s, Narechen Polyclinic.

1969, Dec. Photo. *Perf. 10½-14*

1825 A739 2s blue .25 .25
1826 A739 5s ultra .25 .25
1827 A739 6s green .25 .25
1828 A739 20s emerald .65 .25
Nos. 1825-1828 (4) 1.40 1.00

G. S. Shonin, V. N. Kubasov and Spacecraft A740

Designs: 2s, A. V. Filipchenko, V. N. Volkov, V. V. Gorbatko and spacecraft. 3s, Vladimir A. Shatalov, Alexei S. Yeliseyev and spacecraft. 28s, Three spacecraft in orbit.

1970, Jan. Photo. *Perf. 11*

1829 A740 1s rose car, ol grn & blk .25 .25
1830 A740 2s bl, dl cl & blk .25 .25
1831 A740 3s grnsh bl, vio & blk .25 .25
1832 A740 28s vio bl, lil rose & lt bl 1.10 .25
Nos. 1829-1832 (4) 1.85 1.00

Russian space flights of Soyuz 6, 7 and 8, Oct. 11-13, 1969.

Khan Krum and Defeat of Emperor Nicephorus, 811 — A741

Bulgarian History: 1s, Khan Asparuch and Bulgars crossing the Danube (679). 3s, Conversion of Prince Boris to Christianity, 865. 5s, Tsar Simeon and battle of Akhelo, 917. 8s, Tsar Samuel defeating the Byzantines, 976. 10s, Tsar Kaloyan defeating Emperor Baldwin, 1205. 13s, Tsar Ivan Assen II defeating Greek King Theodore Komnine, 1230. 20s, Coronation of Tsar Ivailo, 1277.

1970, Feb. *Perf. 10½*

1833 A741 1s gold & multi .25 .25
1834 A741 2s gold & multi .25 .25
1835 A741 3s gold & multi .25 .25
1836 A741 5s gold & multi .25 .25
1837 A741 8s gold & multi .25 .25
1838 A741 10s gold & multi .50 .25
1839 A741 13s gold & multi .65 .25
1840 A741 20s gold & multi 1.25 .25
Nos. 1833-1840 (8) 3.65 2.00

See Nos. 2126-2133.

Bulgarian Pavilion, EXPO '70 — A742

1970 *Perf. 12½*

1841 A742 20s brown, sil & org 1.75 1.10

EXPO '70 International Exposition, Osaka, Japan, Mar. 15-Sept. 13, 1970.

Soccer — A743

Designs: Various views of soccer game.

1970, Mar. 4 Photo. *Perf. 12½*

1842 A743 1s blue & multi .25 .25
1843 A743 2s rose car & multi .25 .25
1844 A743 3s ultra & multi .25 .25
1845 A743 5s green & multi .25 .25
1846 A743 20s emerald & multi .90 .25
1847 A743 40s red & multi 2.10 .45
Nos. 1842-1847 (6) 4.00 1.70

9th World Soccer Championships for the Jules Rimet Cup, Mexico City, May 30-June 21, 1970. See No. B37.

Lenin (1870-1924) — A744

1970, Apr. 22

1848 A744 2s shown .25 .25
1849 A744 13s Portrait .55 .25
1850 A744 20s Writing 1.40 .25
Nos. 1848-1850 (3) 2.20 .75

Tephrocactus Alexanderi V. Bruchii — A745

Cacti: 2s, Opuntia drummondii. 3s, Hatiora cilindrica. 5s, Gymnocalycium vatteri. 8s, Heliantho cereus grandiflorus. 10s, Neochilenia andreaeana. 13s, Peireskia vargasii v. longispina. 20s, Neobesseya rosiflora.

1970 Photo. *Perf. 12½*

1851 A745 1s multicolored .25 .25
1852 A745 2s dk green & multi .25 .25
1853 A745 3s multicolored .25 .25
1854 A745 5s blue & multi .25 .25
1855 A745 8s brown & multi .45 .30
1856 A745 10s vio bl & multi 1.75 .40
1857 A745 13s brn red & multi 2.25 .75
1858 A745 20s purple & multi 2.50 .95
Nos. 1851-1858 (8) 7.95 3.40

Rose — A746

Designs: Various Roses.

1970, June 5 Litho. *Perf. 13½*

1859 A746 1s gray & multi .25 .25
1860 A746 2s gray & multi .25 .25
1861 A746 3s gray & multi .25 .25
1862 A746 4s gray & multi .25 .25
1863 A746 5s gray & multi .40 .25
1864 A746 13s gray & multi .65 .40
1865 A746 20s gray & multi 2.00 .65
1866 A746 28s gray & multi 3.50 .95
Nos. 1859-1866 (8) 7.55 3.25

Gold Bowl A747

Designs: Various bowls and art objects from Gold Treasure of Thrace.

1970, June 15 Photo. *Perf. 12½*

1867 A747 1s blk, bl & gold .25 .25
1868 A747 2s blk, lt vio & gold .25 .25
1869 A747 3s blk, ver & gold .25 .25
1870 A747 5s blk, yel grn & gold .25 .25
1871 A747 13s blk, org & gold 1.25 .25
1872 A747 20s blk, lil & gold 1.40 .25
Nos. 1867-1872 (6) 3.65 1.50

EXPO Emblem, Rose and Bulgarian Woman — A748

Designs (EXPO Emblem and): 2s, Three women. 3s, Woman and fruit. 28s, Dancers. 40s, Mt. Fuji and pavilions.

1970, June 20

1873 A748 1s gold & multi .25 .25
1874 A748 2s gold & multi .25 .25
1875 A748 3s gold & multi .25 .25
1876 A748 28s gold & multi 1.10 .30
Nos. 1873-1876 (4) 1.85 1.05

Miniature Sheet

Imperf

1877 A748 40s gold & multi 1.75 .85

EXPO '70 International Exposition, Osaka, Japan, Mar. 15-Sept. 13. No. 1877 contains one stamp with simulated perforations.

Ivan Vasov A749

1970, Aug. 1 Photo. *Perf. 12½*

1878 A749 13s violet blue .85 .25

Ivan Vasov, author, 120th birth anniv.

UN Emblem — A750

1970, Aug. 1

1879 A750 20s Prus bl & gold .85 .25

25th anniversary of the United Nations.

George Dimitrov — A751

1970, June 8

1880 A751 20s blk, gold & org 1.25 .25

BZNC (Bulgarian Communist Party), 70th anniv.

Retriever A752

Dogs: 1s, Golden retriever, horiz. 3s, Great Dane. 4s, Boxer. 5s, Cocker spaniel. 13s, Doberman pinscher. 20s, Scottish terrier. 28s, Russian greyhound, horiz.

1970	**Photo.**	***Perf. 12½***		
1881	A752	1s multicolored	.25	.25
1882	A752	2s multicolored	.25	.25
1883	A752	3s multicolored	.25	.25
1884	A752	4s multicolored	.40	.25
1885	A752	5s multicolored	.40	.25
1886	A752	13s multicolored	1.10	.40
1887	A752	20s multicolored	2.75	.95
1888	A752	28s multicolored	3.25	1.10
		Nos. 1881-1888 (8)	8.65	3.70

Volleyball A753

No. 1890, Two women players. No. 1891, Woman player. No. 1892, Man player.

1970, Sept.	**Photo.**	***Perf. 12½***		
1889	A753	2s dk red brn, bl & blk	.25	.25
1890	A753	2s ultra, org & blk	.25	.25
1891	A753	20s Prus bl, yel & blk	1.00	.25
1892	A753	20s grn, yel & blk	1.00	.25
		Nos. 1889-1892 (4)	2.50	1.00

World Volleyball Championships.

Enrico Caruso and "I Pagliacci" by Ruggiero Leoncavallo — A754

Opera Singers and Operas: 2s, Christina Morfova and "The Bartered Bride" by Bedrich Smetana. 3s, Peter Reitchev and "Tosca" by Giacomo Puccini. 10s, Svetana Tabakova and "The Flying Dutchman" by Richard Wagner. 13s, Katia Popova and "The Masters" by Paroshkev Hadjev. 20s, Feodor Chaliapin and "Boris Godunov" by Modest Musorgski.

1970, Oct. 15	**Photo.**	***Perf. 14***		
1893	A754	1s black & multi	.25	.25
1894	A754	2s black & multi	.25	.25
1895	A754	3s black & multi	.25	.25
1896	A754	10s black & multi	.25	.25
1897	A754	13s black & multi	.60	.25
1898	A754	20s black & multi	1.60	.25
		Nos. 1893-1898 (6)	3.20	1.50

Honoring opera singers in their best roles.

Ivan Assen II Coin — A755

Coins from 14th Century with Ruler's Portrait: 2s, Theodor Svetoslav. 3s, Mikhail Chichman. 13s, Ivan Alexander and Mikhail Assen. 20s, Ivan Sratsimir. 28s, Ivan Chichman (initials).

1970, Nov.		***Perf. 12½***		
1899	A755	1s buff & multi	.25	.25
1900	A755	2s gray & multi	.25	.25
1901	A755	3s multicolored	.25	.25
1902	A755	13s multicolored	.40	.25
1903	A755	20s lt blue & multi	1.00	.25
1904	A755	28s multicolored	1.40	.40
		Nos. 1899-1904 (6)	3.55	1.65

Fire Protection A756

1970	**Litho.**	***Perf. 12½***		
1905	A756	1s Fireman	.25	.25
1906	A756	3s Fire engine	.25	.25

Bicyclists A757

1970		**Photo.**		
1907	A757	20s grn, yel & pink	.85	.25

20th Bulgarian bicycle race.

Congress Emblem — A758

1970				
1908	A758	13s gold & multi	.70	.25

7th World Congress of Sociology, Varna, Sept. 14-19.

Ludwig van Beethoven A759

1970				
1909	A759	28s lil rose & dk bl	2.50	1.10

Beethoven (1770-1827), composer.

Friedrich Engels — A760

1970	**Photo.**	***Perf. 12½***		
1910	A760	13s ver, tan & brn	.85	.25

Friedrich Engels (1820-1895), German socialist, collaborator of Karl Marx.

Miniature Sheets

Luna 16 A761

Russian moon mission: 80s, Lunokhod 1, unmanned vehicle on moon, horiz.

1970	**Photo.**	***Imperf.***		
1911	A761	80s plum, sil, blk & bl	5.00	5.00
1912	A761	1 l vio bl, sil & red	7.00	4.75

No. 1911 , Lunokhod 1, Nov. 10-17. No. 1912, Luna 16 mission, Sept. 12-24.

Issue dates: 80s, Dec. 18; 1 l, Nov. 10.

Snowflake — A762

1970, Dec. 15	**Photo.**	***Perf. 12½x13***		
1913	A762	2s ultra & multi	.25	.25

New Year 1971.

Birds and Flowers A763

Folk Art: 2s, Bird and flowers. 3s, Flying birds. 5s, Birds and flowers. 13s, Sun. 20s, Tulips and pansies.

1971, Jan. 25		***Perf. 12½x13½***		
1914	A763	1s multicolored	.25	.25
1915	A763	2s multicolored	.25	.25
1916	A763	3s multicolored	.25	.25
1917	A763	5s multicolored	.25	.25
1918	A763	13s multicolored	.25	.25
1919	A763	20s multicolored	.75	.25
		Nos. 1914-1919 (6)	2.00	1.50

Spring 1971.

Girl, by Zeko Spiridonov A764

Modern Bulgarian Sculpture: 2s, Third Class (people looking through train window), by Ivan Funev. 3s, Bust of Elin Pelin, by Marko Markov. 13s, Bust of Nina, by Andrej Nikolov. 20s, Monument to P. K. Yavorov (kneeling woman), by Ivan Lazarov. 28s, Engineer, by Ivan Funev. 1 l, Refugees, by Sekul Krimov, horiz.

1970, Dec. 28		***Perf. 12½***		
1920	A764	1s gold & vio	.25	.25
1921	A764	2s gold & dk ol grn	.25	.25
1922	A764	3s gold & rose brn	.25	.25
1923	A764	13s gold & dk grn	.50	.25
1924	A764	20s gold & red brn	.90	.25
1925	A764	28s gold & dk brn	1.40	.25
		Nos. 1920-1925 (6)	3.55	1.50

Souvenir Sheet

Imperf

1926	A764	1 l gold, dk brn & buff	3.50	3.00

Runner A765

Design: 20s, Woman putting the shot.

1971, Mar. 13	**Photo.**	***Perf. 12½x13***		
1927	A765	2s brown & multi	.25	.25
1928	A765	20s dp grn, org & blk	1.50	.40

2nd European Indoor Track and Field Championships.

Bulgarian Secondary School, Bolgrad — A766

Educators: 20s, Dimiter Mitev, Prince Bogoridi and Sava Radoulov.

1971, Mar. 16		***Perf. 12½***		
1929	A766	2s silver, brn & grn	.25	.25
1930	A766	20s silver, brn & vio	1.10	.25

First Bulgarian secondary school, 1858, in Bolgrad, USSR.

Communards — A767

1971, Mar. 18	**Photo.**	***Perf. 12½x13***		
1931	A767	20s rose magenta & blk	.85	.25

Centenary of the Paris Commune.

Dimitrov Facing Goering, Quotation, FIR Emblem — A768

1971, Apr. 11 *Perf. 12½*

1932 A768 2s grn, gold, blk & red .25 .25
1933 A768 13s plum, gold, blk & red 1.10 .25

Intl. Fed. of Resistance Fighters (FIR), 20th anniv.

George S. Rakovski (1821-1867), Revolutionary Against Turkish Rule — A769

1971, Apr. 14

1934 A769 13s olive & blk brn .70 .25

Edelweiss Hotel, Borovets A770

2s, Panorama Hotel, Pamporovo. 4s, Boats at Albena, Black Sea. 8s, Boats at Rousalka. 10s, Shtastlivetsa Hotel, Mt. Vitosha.

1971 *Perf. 13*

1935 A770 1s brt green .25 .25
1936 A770 2s olive gray .25 .25
1937 A770 4s brt blue .25 .25
1938 A770 8s blue .25 .25
1939 A770 10s bluish green .45 .25
Nos. 1935-1939 (5) 1.45 1.25

Technological Progress — A771

Designs: 1s, Mason with banner, vert. 13s, Two men and doves, vert.

1971, Apr. 20 Photo. *Perf. 12½*

1940 A771 1s gold & multi .25 .25
1941 A771 2s gray blue & multi .25 .25
1942 A771 13s lt green & multi .85 .25
Nos. 1940-1942 (3) 1.35 .75

10th Cong. of Bulgarian Communist Party.

Panayot Pipkov and Anthem A772

1971, May 20

1943 A772 13s sil, blk & brt grn .85 .25

Panayot Pipkov, composer, birth cent.

Mammoth A773

Prehistoric Animals: 2s, Bear, vert. 3s, Hipparion (horse). 13s, Platybelodon. 20s, Dinotherium, vert. 28s, Saber-tooth tiger.

1971, May 29 *Perf. 12½*

1944 A773 1s dull bl & multi .25 .25
1945 A773 2s lilac & multi .25 .25
1946 A773 3s multicolored .25 .25
1947 A773 13s multicolored 1.10 .40
1948 A773 20s dp grn & multi 2.50 1.00
1949 A773 28s multicolored 3.50 1.25
Nos. 1944-1949 (6) 7.85 3.40

Khan Asparuch Crossing Danube, 679 A.D., by Boris Angelushev — A774

Historical Paintings: 3s, Reception at Trnovo, by Ilya Petrov. 5s, Chevartov's Troops at Benkovsky, by P. Morozov. 8s, Russian Gen. Gurko and People in Sofia, 1878, by D. Gudjenko. 28s, People Greeting Red Army, by S. Venov.

1971, Mar. 6 *Perf. 13½x14*

1950 A774 2s gold & multi .25 .25
1951 A774 3s gold & multi .25 .25
1952 A774 5s gold & multi .25 .25
1953 A774 8s gold & multi .40 .25
a. Souv. sheet of 4, #1950-1953 1.75 .85
1954 A774 28s gold & multi 3.75 1.10
Nos. 1950-1954 (5) 4.90 2.10

In 1973, No. 1953a was surcharged 1 lev and overprinted "Visitez la Bulgarie," airline initials and emblems, and, on the 5s stamp, "Par Avion."

Freed Black, White and Yellow Men — A775

1971, May 20 Photo. *Perf. 12½*

1955 A775 13s blue, blk & yel .85 .25

Intl. Year against Racial Discrimination.

Map of Europe, Championship Emblem — A776

"XXX" Supporting Barbell — A777

1971, June 19

1956 A776 2s lt blue & multi .25 .25
1957 A777 13s yellow & multi 1.10 .25

30th European Weight Lifting Championships, Sofia, June 19-27.

Facade, Old House, Koprivnica — A778

Designs: Decorated facades of various old houses in Koprivnica.

1971, July 10 Photo. *Perf. 12½*

1958 A778 1s green & multi .25 .25
1959 A778 2s brown & multi .25 .25
1960 A778 6s violet & multi .25 .25
1961 A778 13s dk red & multi .65 .25
Nos. 1958-1961 (4) 1.40 1.00

Frontier Guard and German Shepherd A779

1971, July 31 *Perf. 13*

1962 A779 2s green & ol grn .25 .25

25th anniversary of the Frontier Guards.

Congress of Busludja, Bas-relief — A780

1971, July 31 *Perf. 12½*

1963 A780 2s dk red & ol grn .25 .25

80th anniversary of the first Congress of the Bulgarian Social Democratic party.

Young Woman, by Ivan Nenov — A781

Paintings: 2s, Lazarova in Evening Gown, by Stefan Ivanov. 3s, Performer in Dress Suit, by Kyril Zonev. 13s, Portrait of a Woman, by Detchko Uzunov. 20s, Woman from Kalotina, by Vladimir Dimitrov. 40s, Gorjanin (Mountain Man), by Stoyan Venev.

1971, Aug. 2 *Perf. 14x13½*

1964 A781 1s green & multi .25 .25
1965 A781 2s green & multi .25 .25
1966 A781 3s green & multi .25 .25
1967 A781 13s green & multi .75 .25
1968 A781 20s green & multi 1.25 .50
1969 A781 40s green & multi 2.10 .90
Nos. 1964-1969 (6) 4.85 2.40

National Art Gallery.

Wrestlers A782

Designs: 13s, Wrestlers.

1971, Aug. 27 *Perf. 12½*

1970 A782 2s green, blk & bl .25 .25
1971 A782 13s red org, blk & bl .65 .25

European Wrestling Championships.

Young Workers — A783

1971 Photo. *Perf. 13*

1972 A783 2s dark blue .25 .25

25th anniv. of the Young People's Brigade.

Post Horn Emblem A784

1971, Sept. 15 *Perf. 12½*

1973 A784 20s dp green & gold .85 .40

8th meeting of postal administrations of socialist countries, Varna.

FEBS Waves Emblem — A785

1971, Sept. 20

1974 A785 13s black, red & mar .85 .40

7th Congress of European Biochemical Association (FEBS), Varna.

Statue of Republic A786

Design: 13s, Bulgarian flag.

1971, Sept. 20 *Perf. 13x12½*

1975 A786 2s gold, yel & dk red .25 .25
1976 A786 13s gold, grn & red .65 .25

Bulgarian People's Republic, 25th anniv.

Cross Country Skiing and Winter Olympics Emblem A787

Sport and Winter Olympics Emblem: 2s, Downhill skiing. 3s, Ski jump and skiing. 4s, Women's figure skating. 13s, Ice hockey. 28s, Slalom skiing. 1 l, Torch and stadium.

1971, Sept. 25 ***Perf. 12½***

1977	A787	1s dk green & multi	.25	.25
1978	A787	2s vio blue & multi	.25	.25
1979	A787	3s ultra & multi	.25	.25
1980	A787	4s dp plum & multi	.25	.25
1981	A787	13s dk blue & multi	.60	.25
1982	A787	28s multicolored	1.60	.55
		Nos. 1977-1982 (6)	3.20	1.80

Miniature Sheet

Imperf

1983	A787	1 l multicolored	3.50	1.60

11th Winter Olympic Games, Sapporo, Japan, Feb. 3-13, 1972.

Factory, Botevgrad A788

Industrial Buildings: 2s, Petro-chemical works, Pleven, vert. 10s, Chemical works, Vratsa. 13s, Maritsa-Istok Power Station, Dimitrovgrad. 40s, Electronics works, Sofia.

1971 **Photo.** ***Perf. 13***

1984	A788	1s violet	.25	.25
1985	A788	2s orange	.25	.25
1986	A788	10s deep purple	.25	.25
1987	A788	13s lilac rose	.50	.25
1988	A788	40s deep brown	1.40	.25
		Nos. 1984-1988 (5)	2.65	1.25

UNESCO Emblem A789

1971, Nov. 4 ***Perf. 12½***

1989	A789	20s lt bl, blk, gold & red	.85	.25

25th anniv. of UNESCO.

Soccer Player, by Kyril Zonev (1896-1971) A790

Paintings by Kyril Zonev: 2s, Landscape, horiz. 3s, Self-portrait. 13s, Lilies. 20s, Landscape, horiz. 40s, Portrait of a Young Woman.

1971, Nov. 10 ***Perf. 11x12***

1990	A790	1s gold & multi	.25	.25
1991	A790	2s gold & multi	.25	.25
1992	A790	3s gold & multi	.25	.25
1993	A790	13s gold & multi	.40	.25
1994	A790	20s gold & multi	1.25	.40
1995	A790	40s gold & multi	2.00	.50
		Nos. 1990-1995 (6)	4.40	1.90

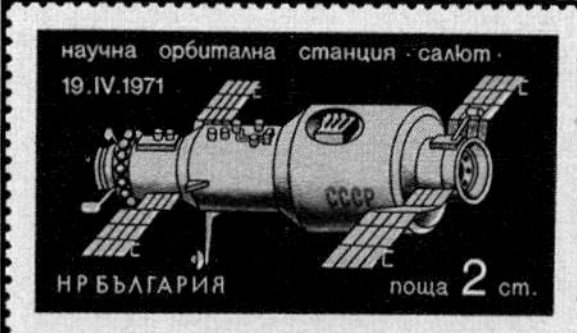

Salyut Space Station — A791

Astronauts Dobrovolsky, Volkov and Patsayev — A792

Designs: 13s, Soyuz 11 space transport. 40s, Salyut and Soyuz 11 joined.

1971, Dec. 20 ***Perf. 12½***

1996	A791	2s dk grn, yel & red	.25	.25
1997	A791	13s multicolored	.40	.25
1998	A791	40s dk blue & multi	1.90	.60
		Nos. 1996-1998 (3)	2.55	1.10

Souvenir Sheet

Imperf

1999	A792	80s multicolored	2.50	1.90

Salyut-Soyuz 11 space mission, and in memory of the Russian astronauts Lt. Col. Georgi T. Dobrovolsky, Vladislav N. Volkov and Victor I. Patsayev, who died during the Soyuz 11 space mission, June 6-30, 1971.

Oil Tanker Vihren — A793

1972, Jan. 8 **Photo.** ***Perf. 12½***

2000	A793	18s lil rose, vio & blk	1.25	.40

Bulgarian shipbuilding industry.

Goce Delchev A794

5s, Jan Sandanski. 13s, Damjan Gruev.

1972, Jan. 21 **Photo.** ***Perf. 12½***

2001	A794	2s brick red & blk	.25	.25
2002	A794	5s green & blk	.25	.25
2003	A794	13s lemon & blk	.35	.25
		Nos. 2001-2003 (3)	.85	.75

Centenary of the births of Bulgarian patriots Delchev (1872-1903) and Sandanski, and of Macedonian Gruev (1871-1906).

Gymnast with Hoop, Medals — A795

13s, Gymnast with ball, medals. 70s, Gymnasts with hoops, medals.

1972, Feb. 10

2004	A795	13s multicolored	.90	.25
2005	A795	18s multicolored	1.25	.25

Miniature Sheet

Imperf

2006	A795	70s multicolored	3.75	3.00

5th World Women's Gymnastic Championships, Havana, Cuba.

View of Melnik, by Petar Mladenov — A796

Paintings from National Art Gallery: 2s, Plower, by Pencho Georgiev. 3s, Funeral, by Alexander Djendov. 13s, Husband and Wife, by Vladimir Dimitrov. 20s, Nursing Mother, by Nenko Balkanski. 40s, Paisii Hilendarski Writing History, by Koio Denchev.

1972, Feb. 20 ***Perf. 13½x14***

2007	A796	1s green & multi	.25	.25
2008	A796	2s green & multi	.25	.25
2009	A796	3s green & multi	.25	.25
2010	A796	13s green & multi	.40	.25
2011	A796	20s green & multi	1.50	.25
2012	A796	40s green & multi	2.50	.55
		Nos. 2007-2012 (6)	5.15	1.80

Paintings from National Art Gallery.

Worker — A797

1972, Mar. 7 ***Perf. 12½***

2013	A797	13s silver & multi	.70	.30

7th Bulgarian Trade Union Congress.

Singing Harvesters A798

Designs: Paintings by Vladimir Dimitrov.

1972, Mar. 31 ***Perf. 11½x12, 12x11½***

2014	A798	1s shown	.25	.25
2015	A798	2s Harvester	.25	.25
2016	A798	3s Women Diggers	.25	.25
2017	A798	13s Fabric Dyers	.55	.25
2018	A798	20s "My Mother"	1.00	.25
2019	A798	40s Self-portrait	2.10	.45
		Nos. 2014-2019 (6)	4.40	1.70

Vladimir Dimitrov, painter, 90th birth anniv.

"Your Heart is your Health" — A799

1972, Apr. 30 ***Perf. 12½***

2020	A799	13s red, blk & grn	1.25	.55

World Health Day.

St. Mark's Basilica and Wave — A800

Design: 13s, Ca' D'Oro and wave.

1972, May 6 ***Perf. 13x12½***

2021	A800	2s ol grn, bl grn & lt bl	.25	.25
2022	A800	13s red brn, vio & lt grn	1.10	.25

UNESCO campaign to save Venice.

Dimitrov in Print Shop, 1901 — A801

Designs: Life of George Dimitrov.

1972, May 8 **Photo.** ***Perf. 12½***

2023	A801	1s shown	.25	.25
2024	A801	2s Dimitrov as leader of 1923 uprising	.25	.25
2025	A801	3s Leipzig trial, 1933	.25	.25
2026	A801	5s As Communist functionary, 1935	.25	.25
2027	A801	13s As leader and teacher, 1948	.25	.25
2028	A801	18s Addressing youth rally, 1948	.65	.25
2029	A801	28s With Pioneers, 1948	1.00	.25
2030	A801	40s Mausoleum	1.60	.45
2031	A801	80s Portrait	4.25	.70
	a.	Souvenir sheet	6.00	3.50
		Nos. 2023-2031 (9)	8.75	2.90

90th anniversary of the birth of George Dimitrov (1882-1949), communist leader.

No. 2031a contains one imperf. stamp similar to No. 2031, but in different colors.

Value, No. 2031 imperf. in slightly changed colors, $8.50.

Paisii Hilendarski A802

Design: 2s, Flame and quotation.

1972, May 12

2032	A802	2s gold, grn & brn	.25	.25
2033	A802	13s gold, grn & brn	1.10	.25

Paisii Hilendarski (1722-1798), monk, writer of Bulgarian-Slavic history.

Canoeing, Motion and Olympic Emblems — A803

Designs (Motion and Olympic emblems and): 2s, Gymnastics. 3s, Swimming, women's. 13s, Volleyball. 18s, Jumping. 40s, Wrestling. 80s, Stadium and sports.

1972, June 25

Figures of Athletes in Silver & Black

2034 A803 1s lt blue & multi .25 .25
2035 A803 2s orange & multi .25 .25
2036 A803 3s multicolored .25 .25
2037 A803 13s yellow & multi .25 .25
2038 A803 18s multicolored .60 .25
2039 A803 40s pink & multi 1.60 .40
Nos. 2034-2039 (6) 3.20 1.65

Miniature Sheet

Imperf

Size: 62x60mm

2040 A803 80s gold, ver & yel 3.50 2.00

20th Olympic Games, Munich, 8/26-9/11.

Angel Kunchev A804

1972, June 30 Photo. ***Perf. 12½***
2041 A804 2s mag, dk pur & gold .30 .30

Centenary of the death of Angel Kunchev, patriot and revolutionist.

Zlatni Pyassatsi A805

1972, Sept. 16
2042 A805 1s shown .25 .25
2043 A805 2s Drouzhba .25 .25
2044 A805 3s Slunchev Bryag .25 .25
2045 A805 13s Primorsko .25 .25
2046 A805 28s Roussalka 1.10 .35
2047 A805 40s Albena 1.50 .45
Nos. 2042-2047 (6) 3.60 1.80

Bulgarian Black Sea resorts.

Bronze Medal, Olympic Emblems, Canoeing — A806

Olympic Emblems and: 2s, Silver medal, broad jump. 3s, Gold medal, boxing. 18s, Gold medal, wrestling. 40s, Gold medal, weight lifting.

1972, Sept. 29
2048 A806 1s Prus bl & multi .25 .25
2049 A806 2s dk green & multi .25 .25
2050 A806 3s orange brn & multi .25 .25
2051 A806 18s olive & multi .90 .25
2052 A806 40s multicolored 1.90 .75
Nos. 2048-2052 (5) 3.55 1.75

Bulgarian victories in 20th Olympic Games. For overprint see No. 2066.

Stoj Dimitrov — A807

Resistance Fighters: 2s, Cvetko Radoinov. 3s, Bogdan Stivrodski. 5s, Mirko Aliev. 13s, Nedelyo Nikolov.

1972, Oct. 30 Photo. ***Perf. 12½x13***
2053 A807 1s olive & multi .25 .25
2054 A807 2s multicolored .25 .25
2055 A807 3s multicolored .25 .25
2056 A807 5s multicolored .25 .25
2057 A807 13s multicolored .45 .25
Nos. 2053-2057 (5) 1.45 1.25

"50 Years USSR" A808

1972, Nov. 3 Photo. ***Perf. 12½x13***
2058 A808 13s gold, red & yel .70 .25

50th anniversary of Soviet Union.

Turk's-cap Lily — A809

Protected Plants: 2s, Gentian. 3s, Sea daffodil. 4s, Globe flower. 18s, Primrose. 23s, Pulsatilla vernalis. 40s, Snake's-head.

1972, Nov. 25 ***Perf. 12½***

Flowers in Natural Colors

2059 A809 1s olive bister .25 .25
2060 A809 2s olive bister .25 .25
2061 A809 3s olive bister .25 .25
2062 A809 4s olive bister .25 .25
2063 A809 18s olive bister .45 .25
2064 A809 23s olive bister 1.00 .30
2065 A809 40s olive bister 2.00 .50
Nos. 2059-2065 (7) 4.45 2.05

No. 2052 Overprinted in Red

1972, Nov. 27
2066 A806 40s multicolored 2.10 .55

Bulgarian weight lifting Olympic gold medalists.

Dobri Chintulov A810

1972, Nov. 28 Photo. ***Perf. 12½***
2067 A810 2s gray, dk & lt grn .35 .35

Chintulov, writer, 150th birth anniv.

Forehead Band — A811

Designs (14th-19th Century Jewelry): 2s, Belt buckles. 3s, Amulet. 8s, Pendant. 23s, Earrings. 40s, Necklace.

1972, Dec. 27 Engr. ***Perf. 14x13½***
2068 A811 1s red brn & blk .25 .25
2069 A811 2s emerald & blk .25 .25
2070 A811 3s Prus bl & blk .25 .25
2071 A811 8s dk red & blk .45 .25
2072 A811 23s red org & multi 1.25 .45
2073 A811 40s violet & blk 2.00 1.00
Nos. 2068-2073 (6) 4.45 2.45

Skin Divers A812

Designs: 2s, Shelf-1 underwater house and divers. 18s, Diving bell and diver, vert. 40s, Elevation balloon and divers, vert.

1973, Jan. 24 Photo. ***Perf. 12½***
2074 A812 1s lt bl, blk & yel .25 .25
2075 A812 2s blk, bl & org yel .25 .25
2076 A812 18s blk, Prus bl & dl org .60 .25
2077 A812 40s blk, ultra & bister 1.50 .45
Nos. 2074-2077 (4) 2.60 1.20

Bulgarian deep-sea research in the Black Sea.

A souvenir sheet of four contains imperf. 20s stamps in designs of Nos. 2074-2077 with colors changed. Sold for 1 l. Value $6.50 unused, $3 canceled.

Execution of Levski, by Boris Angelushev A813

20s, Vassil Levski, by Georgi Danchev.

1973, Feb. 19 ***Perf. 13x12½***
2078 A813 2s dull rose & Prus grn .25 .25
2079 A813 20s dull grn & brn 1.50 .25

Centenary of the death of Vassil Levski (1837-1873), patriot, executed by the Turks.

Kukersky Mask, Elhovo Region — A814

Kukersky Masks at pre-Spring Festival: 2s, Breznik. 3s, Hissar. 13s, Radomir. 20s, Karnobat. 40s, Pernik.

1973, Feb. 26 ***Perf. 12½***
2080 A814 1s dp rose & multi .25 .25
2081 A814 2s emerald & multi .25 .25
2082 A814 3s violet & multi .25 .25
2083 A814 13s multicolored .60 .25
2084 A814 20s multicolored .70 .25
2085 A814 40s multicolored 3.75 1.75
Nos. 2080-2085 (6) 5.80 3.00

Nicolaus Copernicus — A815

1973, Mar. 21 Photo. ***Perf. 12½***
2086 A815 28s ocher, blk & claret 2.10 1.00

500th anniversary of the birth of Nicolaus Copernicus (1473-1543), Polish astronomer.

Vietnamese Worker and Rainbow A816

1973, Apr. 16
2087 A816 18s lt blue & multi .70 .25

Peace in Viet Nam.

A817

Wild flowers.

1973, May Photo. ***Perf. 13***
2088 A817 1s Poppy .25 .25
2089 A817 2s Daisy .25 .25
2090 A817 3s Peony .25 .25
2091 A817 13s Centaury .55 .25
2092 A817 18s Corn cockle 5.25 2.50
2093 A817 28s Ranunculus 2.10 .80
Nos. 2088-2093 (6) 8.65 4.30

A818

1973, June 2
2094 A818 2s pale grn, buff & brn .25 .25
2095 A818 18s pale brn, gray & grn 1.10 .55

Christo Botev (1848-1876), poet.

Asen Halachev and Revolutionists — A819

2s, "Suffering Worker."

1973, June 6 Photo. ***Perf. 13***
2096 A819 1s gold, red & blk .25 .25
2097 A819 2s gold, org & dk brn .25 .25

50th anniversary of Pleven uprising.

Muskrat A820

Perf. 12½x13, 13x12½

1973, June 29 **Litho.**

2098 A820 1s shown .25 .25
2099 A820 2s Racoon .25 .25
2100 A820 3s Mouflon, vert. .25 .25
2101 A820 12s Fallow deer, vert. .50 .25
2102 A820 18s European bison 1.60 .70
2103 A820 40s Elk 5.50 2.40
Nos. 2098-2103 (6) 8.35 4.10

Aleksandr Stamboliski — A821

1973, June 14 **Photo.** ***Perf. 12½***

2104 A821 18s dp brown & org .35 .25
a. 18s orange 4.75 1.40

Aleksandr Stamboliski (1879-1923), leader of Peasants' Party and premier.

Trade Union Emblem — A822

Stylized Sun, Olympic Rings — A823

1973, Aug. 27 **Photo.** ***Perf. 12½***

2105 A822 2s yellow & multi .25 .25

8th Congress of World Federation of Trade Unions, Varna, Oct. 15-22.

1973, Aug. 29 ***Perf. 13***

28s, Emblem of Bulgarian Olympic Committee & Olympic rings. 80s, Soccer, emblems of Innsbruck & Montreal 1976 Games, horiz.

2106 A823 13s multicolored 1.25 .60
2107 A823 28s multicolored 2.50 .80

Souvenir Sheet

2108 A823 80s multicolored 5.50 3.25

Olympic Congress, Varna. No. 2108 contains one stamp. It also exists imperf, Value $21; also with violet margin, imperf, Value $120.

Revolutionists with Communist Flag — A824

Designs: 5s, Revolutionists on flatcar blocking train. 13s, Raising Communist flag, vert. 18s, George Dimitrov and Vassil Kolarov.

1973, Sept. 22 **Photo.** ***Perf. 12½***

2109 A824 2s magenta & multi .25 .25
2110 A824 5s magenta & multi .25 .25
2111 A824 13s magenta & multi .40 .25
2112 A824 18s magenta & multi 1.25 .40
Nos. 2109-2112 (4) 2.15 1.15

50th anniv. of the September Revolution.

Warrior Saint A825

Murals from Boyana Church: 1s, Tsar Kaloyan and 2s, his wife Dessislava. 5s, "St. Wystratti." 10s, Tsar Constantine Assen. 13s, Deacon Laurentius. 18s, Virgin Mary. 20s, St. Ephraim. 28s, Jesus. 80s, Jesus in the Temple, horiz.

1973, Sept. 24

2113 A825 1s gold & multi .25 .25
2114 A825 2s gold & multi .25 .25
2115 A825 3s gold & multi .25 .25
2116 A825 5s gold & multi .45 .25
2117 A825 10s gold & multi .75 .30
2118 A825 13s gold & multi .85 .45
2119 A825 18s gold & multi 1.40 .70
2120 A825 20s gold & multi 1.60 .85
2121 A825 28s gold & multi 5.25 1.40
Nos. 2113-2121 (9) 11.05 4.70

Miniature Sheet

Imperf

2122 A825 80s gold & multi 6.75 6.75

No. 2122 contains one stamp with simulated perforations.

Christo Smirnenski — A826

1973, Sept. 29 **Photo.** ***Perf. 12½***

2123 A826 1s multicolored .25 .25
2124 A826 2s vio blue & multi .25 .25

Christo Smirnenski (1898-1923), poet.

Human Rights Flame — A827

1973, Oct. 10

2125 A827 13s dk bl, red & gold .60 .25

Universal Declaration of Human Rights, 25th anniv.

Bulgarian History Type

1s, Tsar Theodor Svetoslav receiving Byzantine envoys. 2s, Tsar Mihail Shishman's army in battle with Byzantines. 3s, Tsar Ivan Alexander's victory at Russocastro. 4s, Patriarch Euthimius at the defense of Turnovo. 5s, Tsar Ivan Shishman leading horsemen against the Turks. 13s, Momchil attacking Turks at Umour. 18s, Tsar Ivan Stratsimir meeting King Sigismund's crusaders. 28s, The Boyars Balik, Theodor & Dobrotitsa, meeting ship bringing envoys from Anne of Savoy.

1973, Oct. 23 ***Perf. 13***

Silver and Black Vignettes

2126 A741 1s olive bister .25 .25
2127 A741 2s Prus blue .25 .25
2128 A741 3s lilac .25 .25
2129 A741 4s green .25 .25
2130 A741 5s violet .25 .25
2131 A741 13s orange & brn .50 .25
2132 A741 18s olive green .75 .25
2133 A741 28s yel brn & brn 2.00 .85
Nos. 2126-2133 (8) 4.50 2.60

Finn Class — A828

Sailboats: 2s, Flying Dutchman. 3s, Soling class. 13s, Tempest class. 20s, Class 470. 40s, Tornado class.

1973, Oct. 29 **Litho.** ***Perf. 13***

2134 A828 1s ultra & multi .25 .25
2135 A828 2s green & multi .25 .25
2136 A828 3s dk blue & multi .25 .25
2137 A828 13s dull vio & multi .50 .25
2138 A828 20s gray bl & multi .90 .50
2139 A828 40s dk blue & multi 3.50 2.75
Nos. 2134-2139 (6) 5.65 4.25

Value, set imperf. in changed colors, $17.

Village, by Bencho Obreshkov — A829

Paintings: 2s, Mother and Child, by Stoyan Venev. 3s, Rest (woman), by Tsenko Boyadjiev. 13s, Flowers in Vase, by Sirak Skitnik. 18s, Meri Kuneva (portrait), by Ilya Petrov. 40s, Winter in Plovdiv, by Zlatyu Boyadjiev. 13s, 18s, 40s, vert.

Perf. 12½x12, 12x12½

1973, Nov. 10

2140 A829 1s gold & multi .25 .25
2141 A829 2s gold & multi .25 .25
2142 A829 3s gold & multi .25 .25
2143 A829 13s gold & multi .45 .25
2144 A829 18s gold & multi .70 .25
2145 A829 40s gold & multi 3.75 1.25
Nos. 2140-2145 (6) 5.65 2.50

Souvenir Sheet

Paintings by Stanislav Dospevski: a, Domnica Lambreva. b, Self-portrait. Both vert.

2146 Sheet of 2 5.50 3.50
a. A829 50s gold & multi 1.40 1.00
b. A829 50s gold & multi 1.40 1.00

Bulgarian paintings. No. 2146 commemorates the 150th birth anniv. of Stanislav Dospevski.

Souvenir Sheet

Soccer — A830

1973, Dec. 10 **Photo.** ***Perf. 13***

2147 A830 28s multicolored 5.50 4.75

No. 2147 sold for 1 l. Exists overprinted for Argentina 78. Value $9.50.

Angel and Ornaments A831

1s, Attendant facing right. 2s, Passover table and lamb. 3s, Attendant facing left. 8s, Abraham and ornaments. 13s, Adam and Eve. 28s, Expulsion from Garden of Eden.

1974, Jan. 21 **Photo.** ***Perf. 13***

2148 A831 1s fawn, yel & brn .25 .25
2149 A831 2s fawn, yel & brn .25 .25
2150 A831 3s fawn, yel & brn .25 .25
a. Strip of 3, #2148-2150 .50 .25
2151 A831 5s slate grn & yel .25 .25
2152 A831 8s slate grn & yel .25 .25
a. Pair, #2151-2152 .65 .50
2153 A831 13s lt brown, yel & ol .30 .25
2154 A831 28s lt brown, yel & ol .50 .30
a. Pair, #2153-2154 1.60 .70
Nos. 2148-2154 (7) 2.05 1.80

Woodcarvings from Rozhen Monastery, 19th century.

Lenin, by N. Mirtchev — A832

18s, Lenin visiting Workers, by W. A. Serov.

1974, Jan. 28 **Litho.** ***Perf. 12½x12***

2155 A832 2s ocher & multi .25 .25
2156 A832 18s ocher & multi .80 .30

50th anniversary of the death of Lenin.

1974, Jan. 28

Demeter Blagoev at Rally, by G. Kowachev.

2157 A832 2s multicolored .25 .25

50th anniversary of the death of Demeter Blagoev, founder of Bulgarian Communist Party.

Domestic Animals A833

1974, Feb. 1 Photo. *Perf. 13*

2158 A833 1s Sheep .25 .25
2159 A833 2s Goat .25 .25
2160 A833 3s Pig .25 .25
2161 A833 5s Cow .25 .25
2162 A833 13s Buffalo cow .80 .25
2163 A833 20s Horse 2.25 .75
Nos. 2158-2163 (6) 4.05 2.00

Comecon Emblem A834

1974, Feb. 11 Photo. *Perf. 13*

2164 A834 13s silver & multi .70 .25

25th anniversary of the Council of Mutual Economic Assistance.

Soccer — A835

Designs: Various soccer action scenes.

1974, Mar. Photo. *Perf. 13*

2165 A835 1s dull green & multi .25 .25
2166 A835 2s brt green & multi .25 .25
2167 A835 3s slate grn & multi .25 .25
2168 A835 13s olive & multi .25 .25
2169 A835 28s blue grn & multi .80 .55
2170 A835 40s emerald & multi 2.25 .90
Nos. 2165-2170 (6) 4.05 2.45

Souvenir Sheet

2171 A835 1 l green & multi 4.25 2.25

World Soccer Championship, Munich, June 13-July 7. No. 2171 exists imperf. Value $100.

Salt Production A836

Children's Paintings: 1s, Cosmic Research for Peaceful Purposes. 3s, Fire Dancers. 28s, Russian-Bulgarian Friendship (train and children). 60s, Spring (birds).

1974, Apr. 15 Photo. *Perf. 13*

2172 A836 1s lilac & multi .25 .25
2173 A836 2s lt green & multi .25 .25
2174 A836 3s blue & multi .25 .25
2175 A836 28s slate & multi 2.40 1.25
Nos. 2172-2175 (4) 3.15 2.00

Souvenir Sheet

Imperf

2176 A836 60s blue & multi 3.50 2.75

Third World Youth Philatelic Exhibition, Sofia, May 23-30. No. 2176 contains one stamp with simulated perforations.

Folk Singers — A837

Designs: 2s, Folk dancers (men). 3s, Bagpiper and drummer. 5s, Wrestlers. 13s, Runners (women). 18s, Gymnast.

1974, Apr. 25 *Perf. 13*

2178 A837 1s vermilion & multi .25 .25
2179 A837 2s org brn & multi .25 .25
2180 A837 3s brn red & multi .25 .25
2181 A837 5s blue & multi .25 .25
2182 A837 13s ultra & multi .90 .30
2183 A837 18s violet bl & multi .45 .25
Nos. 2178-2183 (6) 2.35 1.55

4th Amateur Arts and Sports Festival

Flowers A838

1974, May Photo. *Perf. 13*

2184 A838 1s Aster .25 .25
2185 A838 2s Petunia .25 .25
2186 A838 3s Fuchsia .25 .25
2187 A838 18s Tulip .50 .25
2188 A838 20s Carnation 1.00 .40
2189 A838 28s Pansy 2.50 .85
Nos. 2184-2189 (6) 4.75 2.25

Souvenir Sheet

2190 A838 80s Sunflower 3.00 2.00

Automobiles and Emblems — A839

1974, May 15 Photo. *Perf. 13*

2191 A839 13s multicolored .60 .25

International Automobile Federation (FIA) Spring Congress, Sofia, May 20-24.

Old and New Buildings, UNESCO Emblem A840

1974, June 15

2192 A840 18s multicolored .60 .25

UNESCO Executive Council, 94th Session, Varna.

Postrider A841

Designs: 18s, First Bulgarian mail coach. 28s, UPU Monument, Bern.

1974, Aug. 5

2193 A841 2s ocher, blk & vio .25 .25
2194 A841 18s ocher, blk & grn .65 .25

Souvenir Sheet

2195 A841 28s ocher, blk & bl 2.50 1.90

UPU cent. No. 2195 exists imperf. Value $75.

Pioneer and Komsomol Girl — A842

Designs: 2s, Pioneer and birds. 60s, Emblem with portrait of George Dimitrov.

1974, Aug. 12

2196 A842 1s green & multi .25 .25
2197 A842 2s blue & multi .25 .25

Souvenir Sheet

2198 A842 60s red & multi 2.10 2.10

30th anniversary of Dimitrov Pioneer Organization, Septemvrilche.

"Bulgarian Communist Party" — A843

Symbolic Designs: 2s, Russian liberators. 5s, Industrialization. 13s, Advanced agriculture and husbandry. 18s, Scientific and technical progress.

1974, Aug. 20

2199 A843 1s blue gray & multi .25 .25
2200 A843 2s blue gray & multi .25 .25
2201 A843 5s gray & multi .25 .25
2202 A843 13s gray & multi .50 .25
2203 A843 18s gray & multi .65 .25
Nos. 2199-2203 (5) 1.90 1.25

30th anniversary of the People's Republic.

Gymnast on Parallel Bars — A844

Design: 13s, Gymnast on vaulting horse.

1974, Oct. 18 Photo. *Perf. 13*

2204 A844 2s multicolored .25 .25
2205 A844 13s multicolored .50 .25

18th Gymnastic Championships, Varna.

Souvenir Sheet

Symbols of Peace — A845

1974, Oct. 29 Photo. *Perf. 13*

2206 A845 Sheet of 4 2.50 1.10
a. 13s Doves .25 .25
b. 13s Map of Europe .25 .25
c. 13s Olive Branch .25 .25
d. 13s Inscription .25 .25

1974 European Peace Conference. "Peace" in various languages written on Nos. 2206a-2206c. Sold for 60s. Exists imperf. Value $95.

No. 2206 was overprinted "Europa" and various cities and dates in 1979. Value $60.

Nib and Envelope — A846

1974, Nov. 20

2207 A846 2s yellow, blk & grn .25 .25

Introduction of postal zone numbers.

Flowers A847

1974, Dec. 5

2208 A847 2s emerald & multi .25 .25

St. Todor, Ceramic Icon — A848

Designs: 2s, Medallion, Veliko Turnovo. 3s, Carved capital. 5s, Silver bowl. 8s, Goblet. 13s, Lion's head finial. 18s, Gold plate with Cross. 28s, Breastplate with eagle.

1974, Dec. 18 Photo. *Perf. 13*

2209 A848 1s orange & multi .25 .25
2210 A848 2s pink & multi .25 .25
2211 A848 3s blue & multi .25 .25
2212 A848 5s lt vio & multi .25 .25
2213 A848 8s brown & multi .25 .25
2214 A848 13s multicolored .50 .25
2215 A848 18s red & multi .60 .25
2216 A848 28s ultra & multi 1.75 .95
Nos. 2209-2216 (8) 4.10 2.70

Art works from 9th-12th centuries.

Fruit Tree Blossoms — A849

1975, Jan. Photo. *Perf. 13*

2217 A849 1s Apricot .25 .25
2218 A849 2s Apple .25 .25
2219 A849 3s Cherry .25 .25
2220 A849 19s Pear .45 .25
2221 A849 28s Peach 1.10 .25
Nos. 2217-2221 (5) 2.30 1.25

Tree and Book A850

1975, Mar. 25 Photo. *Perf. 13*

2222 A850 2s gold & multi .25 .25

Forestry High School, 50th anniversary.

Souvenir Sheet

Farmers' Activities (Woodcuts) — A851

1975, Mar. 25

2223 A851 Sheet of 4 1.25 .75
a. 2s Farmer with ax and flag
b. 5s Farmers on guard
c. 13s Dancing couple
d. 18s Woman picking fruit

Bulgarian Agrarian Peoples Union, 75th anniv.

Michelangelo, Self-portrait A852

13s, Night, horiz. 18s, Day, horiz. Both designs after sculptures from Medici Tomb, Florence.

1975

2224 A852 2s plum & dk blue .25 .25
2225 A852 13s vio bl & plum .45 .25
2226 A852 18s brown & green 1.10 .25
Nos. 2224-2226 (3) 1.80 .75

Souvenir Sheet

2227 A852 2s olive & red 1.75 1.75

Michelangelo Buonarotti (1475-1564), Italian sculptor, painter and architect. No. 2227 issued to publicize ARPHILA 75 Intl. Phil. Exhib., Paris, June 6-16. Sheet sold for 60s.

Issued: Nos. 2224-2226, 3/28; No. 2227, 3/31.

Souvenir Sheet

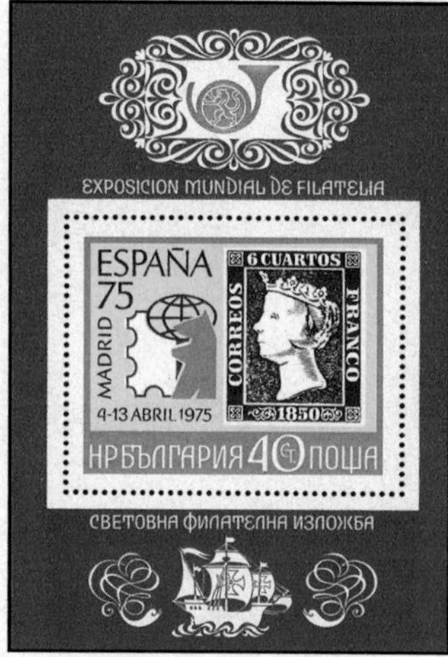

Spain No. 1 and España 75 Emblem — A853

1975, Apr. 4

2228 A853 40s multicolored 6.00 4.75

Espana 75 International Philatelic Exhibition, Madrid, Apr. 4-13.

Gabrov Costume A854

Regional Costumes: 3s, Trnsk. 5s, Vidin. 13s, Gocedelchev. 18s, Risen.

1975, Apr. Photo. *Perf. 13*

2229 A854 2s blue & multi .25 .25
2230 A854 3s emerald & multi .25 .25
2231 A854 5s orange & multi .25 .25
2232 A854 13s olive & multi .65 .25
2233 A854 18s multicolored 1.25 .40
Nos. 2229-2233 (5) 2.65 1.40

Red Star and Arrow — A855

Design: 13s, Dove and broken sword.

1975, May 9

2234 A855 2s red, blk & gold .25 .25
2235 A855 13s blue, blk & gold .50 .25

Victory over Fascism, 30th anniversary.

Standard Kilogram and Meter — A856

1975, May 9 *Perf. 13x13½*

2236 A856 13s silver, lil & blk .35 .25

Cent. of Intl, Meter Convention, Paris, 1875.

IWY Emblem, Woman's Head — A857

1975, May 20 Photo. *Perf. 13*

2237 A857 13s multicolored .35 .25

International Women's Year 1975.

Ivan Vasov — A858

Design: 13s, Ivan Vasov, seated.

1975, May

2238 A858 2s buff & multi .25 .25
2239 A858 13s gray & multi .40 .25

125th birth anniversary of Ivan Vasov.

Nikolov and Sava Kokarechkov — A859

2s, Mitko Palaouzov, Ivan Vassilev. 5s, Nicolas Nakev, Stevtcho Kraychev. 13s, Ivanka Pachkoulova, Detelina Mintcheva.

1975, May 30

2240 A859 1s multicolored .25 .25
2241 A859 2s multicolored .25 .25
2242 A859 5s multicolored .25 .25
2243 A859 13s multicolored .30 .25
Nos. 2240-2243 (4) 1.05 1.00

Teen-age resistance fighters, killed during World War II.

Mother Feeding Child, by John E. Millais A861

Etchings: 2s, The Dead Daughter, by Goya. 3s, Reunion, by Beshkov. 13s, Seated Nude, by Renoir. 20s, Man in a Fur Hat, by Rembrandt. 40s, The Dream, by Daumier, horiz. 1 l, Temptation, by Dürer.

Photogravure and Engraved

1975, Aug. *Perf. 12x11½, 11½x12*

2248 A861 1s yel grn & multi .25 .25
2249 A861 2s orange & multi .25 .25
2250 A861 3s lilac & multi .25 .25
2251 A861 13s lt blue & multi .40 .25
2252 A861 20s ocher & multi .65 .25
2253 A861 40s rose & multi 1.75 .45
Nos. 2248-2253 (6) 3.55 1.70

Souvenir Sheet

2254 A861 1 l emerald & multi 3.50 2.10

World Graphics Exhibition.

Letter "Z" from 12th Century Manuscript A862

Initials from Illuminated Manuscripts: 2s, "B" from 17th cent. prayerbook. 3s, "V" from 16th cent. Bouhovo Gospel. 8s, "B" from 14th cent. Turnovo collection. 13s, "V" from Dobreisho's Gospel, 13th cent. 18s, "E" from 11th cent. Enina book of the Apostles.

1975, Aug. Litho. *Perf. 11½*

2255 A862 1s multicolored .25 .25
2256 A862 2s multicolored .25 .25
2257 A862 3s multicolored .25 .25
2258 A862 8s multicolored .25 .25
2259 A862 13s multicolored .45 .25
2260 A862 18s multicolored 1.25 .25
Nos. 2255-2260 (6) 2.70 1.50

Bulgarian art.

Whimsical Globe — A863

1975, Aug. Photo. *Perf. 13*

2261 A863 2s multicolored .25 .25

Festival of Humor and Satire.

Lifeboat Dju IV and Gibraltar-Cuba Route — A864

1975, Aug. 5 Photo. *Perf. 13*

2262 A864 13s multicolored .40 .25

Oceanexpo 75, 1st Intl. Ocean Exhib., Okinawa, July 20, 1975-Jan. 18, 1976.

Sts. Cyril and Methodius — A865

Sts. Constantine and Helena — A866

St. Sophia Church, Sofia, Woodcut by V. Zahriev — A867

1975, Aug. 21

2263 A865 2s ver, yel & brn .25 .25
2264 A866 13s green, yel & brn .40 .25

Souvenir Sheet

2265 A867 50s orange & multi 1.75 1.10

Balkanphila V, philatelic exhibition, Sofia, Sept. 27-Oct. 5.

Peace Dove and Map of Europe — A868

1975, Nov. **Photo.** ***Perf. 13***

2266 A868 18s ultra, rose & yel .70 .35

European Security and Cooperation Conference, Helsinki, Finland, July 30-Aug. 1. No. 2266 printed in sheets of 5 stamps and 4 labels, arranged checkerwise.

Acherontia Atropos — A869

Designs: Moths.

1975 **Photo.** ***Perf. 13***

2267 A869 1s Acherontia atropos .25 .25
2268 A869 2s Daphnis nerii .25 .25
2269 A869 3s Smerinthus ocellata .25 .25
2270 A869 10s Deilephila nicea .40 .25
2271 A869 13s Choerocampa elpenor .75 .40
2272 A869 18s Macroglossum fuciformis 1.75 .65
Nos. 2267-2272 (6) 3.65 2.05

Soccer Player — A870

1975, Sept. 21

2273 A870 2s multicolored .25 .25

8th Inter-Toto (soccer pool) Soccer Championships, Varna.

Constantine's Rebellion Against the Turks, 1403 — A871

Designs (Woodcuts): 2s, Campaign of Vladislav III, 1443-1444. 3s, Battles of Turnovo, 1598 and 1686. 10s, Battle of Liprovsko, 1688. 13s, Guerrillas, 17th century. 18s, Return of exiled peasants.

1975, Nov. 27 **Photo.** ***Perf. 13***

2274 A871 1s bister, grn & blk .25 .25
2275 A871 2s blue, car & blk .25 .25
2276 A871 3s yellow, lil & blk .25 .25
2277 A871 10s orange, grn & blk .25 .25
2278 A871 13s green, lil & blk .50 .25
2279 A871 18s pink, grn & blk .85 .25
Nos. 2274-2279 (6) 2.35 1.50

Bulgarian history.

Red Cross and First Aid — A872

Design: 13s, Red Cross and dove.

1975, Dec. 1

2280 A872 2s red brn, red & blk .25 .25
2281 A872 13s bl grn, red & blk .40 .25

90th anniversary of Bulgarian Red Cross.

Egyptian Galley A873

Historic Ships: 2s, Phoenician galley. 3s, Greek trireme. 5s, Roman galley. 13s, Viking longship. 18s, Venetian galley.

1975, Dec. 15 **Photo.** ***Perf. 13***

2282 A873 1s multicolored .25 .25
2283 A873 2s multicolored .25 .25
2284 A873 3s multicolored .25 .25
2285 A873 5s multicolored .25 .25
2286 A873 13s multicolored .45 .25
2287 A873 18s multicolored .90 .25
Nos. 2282-2287 (6) 2.35 1.50

See Nos. 2431-2436, 2700-2705.

Souvenir Sheet

Ethnographical Museum, Plovdiv — A874

1975, Dec. 17

2288 Sheet of 3 7.50 4.00
a. A874 80s grn, yel & dark brn 2.25 1.10

European Architectural Heritage Year. No. 2288 contains 3 stamps and 3 labels showing stylized bird.

Dobri Hristov — A875

1975, Dec. ***Perf. 13***

2289 A875 5s brt green, yel & brn .25 .25

Dobri Hristov, musician, birth centenary.

United Nations Emblem — A876

1975, Dec.

2290 A876 13s gold, blk & mag .40 .40

United Nations, 30th anniversary.

Glass Ornaments — A877

13s, Peace dove, decorated ornament.

1975, Dec. 22 **Photo.** ***Perf. 13***

2291 A877 2s brt violet & multi .25 .25
2292 A877 13s gray & multi .25 .25

New Year 1976.

Downhill Skiing — A878

Designs (Winter Olympic Games Emblem and): 2s, Cross country skier, vert. 3s, Ski jump. 13s, Biathlon, vert. 18s, Ice hockey, vert. 23s, Speed skating, vert. 80s, Figure skating, pair, vert.

1976, Jan. 30 ***Perf. 13½***

2293 A878 1s silver & multi .25 .25
2294 A878 2s silver & multi .25 .25
2295 A878 3s silver & multi .25 .25
2296 A878 13s silver & multi .45 .25
2297 A878 18s silver & multi .55 .25
2298 A878 23s silver & multi 1.40 .50
Nos. 2293-2298 (6) 3.15 1.75

Souvenir Sheet

2299 A878 80s silver & multi 3.00 1.90

12th Winter Olympic Games, Innsbruck, Austria, Feb. 4-15.

Electric Streetcar, Sofia, 1976 — A879

Design: 13s, Streetcar and trailer, 1901.

1976, Jan. 12 **Photo.** ***Perf. 13½x13***

2300 A879 2s gray & multi .25 .25
2301 A879 13s gray & multi .55 .25

75th anniversary of Sofia streetcars.

Stylized Bird — A880

5s, Dates "1976," "1956" & star. 13s, Hammer & sickle. 50s, George Dimitrov.

1976, Mar. 1 ***Perf. 13***

2302 A880 2s gold & multi .25 .25
2303 A880 5s gold & multi .25 .25
2304 A880 13s gold & multi .25 .25
Nos. 2302-2304 (3) .75 .75

Souvenir Sheet

2305 A880 50s gold & multi 1.75 3.00

11th Bulgarian Communist Party Congress.

A. G. Bell and Telephone, 1876 — A881

1976, Mar. 10

2306 A881 18s dk brn, yel & ocher .60 .25

Centenary of first telephone call by Alexander Graham Bell, Mar. 10, 1876.

Mute Swan — A882

Waterfowl: 2s, Ruddy shelduck. 3s, Common shelduck. 5s, Garganey teal. 13s, Mallard. 18s, Red-crested pochard.

1976, Mar. 27 **Litho.** ***Perf. 11½***

2307 A882 1s vio bl & multi .25 .25
2308 A882 2s yel grn & multi .25 .25
2309 A882 3s blue & multi .25 .25
2310 A882 5s multicolored 1.40 .25
2311 A882 13s purple & multi 1.50 .70
2312 A882 18s green & multi 4.00 2.10
Nos. 2307-2312 (6) 7.65 3.80

Guerrillas — A883

Designs (Woodcuts by Stoev): 2s, Peasants with rifle and proclamation. 5s, Raina Knaginia with horse and guerrilla. 13s, Insurgents with cherrywood cannon.

1976, Apr. 5 **Photo.** ***Perf. 13***

2313 A883 1s multicolored .25 .25
2314 A883 2s multicolored .25 .25
2315 A883 5s multicolored .25 .25
2316 A883 13s multicolored .25 .25
Nos. 2313-2316 (4) 1.00 1.00

Centenary of uprising against Turkey.

Guard and Dog A884

13s, Men on horseback, observation tower.

1976, May 15

2317 A884 2s multicolored .25 .25
2318 A884 13s multicolored .25 .25

30th anniversary of Border Guards.

Construction Worker — A885

1976, May 20

2319 A885 2s multicolored .25 .25

Young Workers Brigade, 30th anniversary.

Busludja, Bas-relief A886

Design: 5s, Memorial building.

1976, May 28 Photo. *Perf. 13*

2320 A886 2s green & multi .25 .25
2321 A886 5s violet bl & multi .25 .25

First Congress of Bulgarian Social Democratic Party, 85th anniversary.

Memorial Building — A887

2s, AES Complex. 8s, Thermal power plant. 10s, Chemical plant. 13s, Chemical plant (diff.). 20s, Hydroelectric station.

1976, Apr. 7

2322 A887 5s green .25 .25
2323 A887 8s maroon .25 .25
2324 A887 10s green .25 .25
2325 A887 13s violet .65 .25
2326 A887 20s brt green .90 .25
Nos. 2322-2326 (5) 2.30 1.25

Five-year plan accomplishments.

Children Playing Around Table — A888

Kindergarten Children: 2s, with doll carriage & hobby horse. 5s, playing ball. 23s, in costume.

1976, June 15

2327 A888 1s green & multi .25 .25
2328 A888 2s yellow & multi .25 .25
2329 A888 5s lilac & multi .25 .25
2330 A888 23s rose & multi .40 .25
Nos. 2327-2330 (4) 1.15 1.00

Demeter Blagoev — A889

1976, May 28

2331 A889 13s bluish blk, red & gold .60 .25

Demeter Blagoev (1856-1924), writer, political leader, 120th birth anniversary.

Christo Botev — A890

1976, May 25

2332 A890 13s ocher & slate grn .60 .25

Christo Botev (1848-1876), poet, death centenary. Printed se-tenant with yellow green and ocher label, inscribed with poem.

Boxing, Montreal Olympic Emblem — A891

Designs (Montreal Olympic Emblem): 1s, Wrestling, horiz. 3s, 1 l, Weight lifting. 13s, One-man kayak. 18s, Woman gymnast. 28s, Woman diver. 40s, Woman runner.

1976, June 25

2333 A891 1s orange & multi .25 .25
2334 A891 2s multicolored .25 .25
2335 A891 3s lilac & multi .25 .25
2336 A891 13s multicolored .25 .25
2337 A891 18s multicolored .50 .25
2338 A891 28s blue & multi .70 .25
2339 A891 40s lemon & multi 1.40 .50
Nos. 2333-2339 (7) 3.60 2.00

Souvenir Sheet

2340 A891 1 l orange & multi 2.50 1.75

21st Olympic Games, Montreal, Canada, July 17-Aug. 1.

Belt Buckle — A892

Thracian Art (8th-4th Centuries): 2s, Brooch. 3s, Mirror handle. 5s, Helmet cheek cover. 13s, Gold ornament. 18s, Lion's head (harness decoration). 20s, Knee guard. 28s, Jeweled pendant.

1976, July 30 Photo. *Perf. 13*

2341 A892 1s brown & multi .25 .25
2342 A892 2s blue & multi .25 .25
2343 A892 3s multicolored .25 .25
2344 A892 5s claret & multi .25 .25
2345 A892 13s purple & multi .35 .25
2346 A892 18s multicolored .40 .25
2347 A892 20s multicolored .55 .25
2348 A892 28s multicolored .90 .25
Nos. 2341-2348 (8) 3.20 2.00

Souvenir Sheet

Composite of Bulgarian Stamp Designs — A893

1976, June 5

2349 A893 50s red & multi 3.00 1.25

International Federation of Philately (F.I.P.), 50th anniversary and 12th Congress.

Partisans at Night, by Ilya Petrov — A894

Paintings: 5s, Old Town, by Tsanko Lavenov. 13s, Seated Woman, by Petrov, vert. 18s, Seated Boy, by Petrov, vert. 28s, Old Plovdiv, by Lavrenov, vert. 80s, Ilya Petrov, self-portrait, vert.

1976, Aug. 11 Photo. *Perf. 14*

2350 A894 2s multicolored .25 .25
2351 A894 5s multicolored .25 .25
2352 A894 13s ultra & multi .45 .25
2353 A894 18s multicolored .65 .25
2354 A894 28s multicolored 1.00 .25
Nos. 2350-2354 (5) 2.60 1.25

Souvenir Sheet

2354A A894 80s multicolored 2.25 1.75

Souvenir Sheet

Olympic Sports and Emblems — A895

1976, Sept. 6 Photo. *Perf. 13*

2355 A895 Sheet of 4 2.50 1.50
a. 25s Weight Lifting .50 .25
b. 25s Rowing .50 .25
c. 25s Running .50 .25
d. 25s Wrestling .50 .25

Medalists, 21st Olympic Games, Montreal.

Souvenir Sheet

Fresco and UNESCO Emblem — A896

1976, Dec. 3

2356 A896 50s red & multi 2.25 1.00

UNESCO, 30th anniv.

"The Pianist" by Jendov — A897

Designs (Caricatures by Jendov): 5s, Imperialist "Trick or Treat." 13s, The Leader, 1931.

1976, Sept. 30 Photo. *Perf. 13*

2357 A897 2s green & multi .25 .25
2358 A897 5s purple & multi .25 .25
2359 A897 13s magenta & multi .30 .25
Nos. 2357-2359 (3) .80 .75

Alex Jendov (1901-1953), caricaturist.

Fish and Hook — A898

1976, Sept. 21 Photo. *Perf. 13*

2360 A898 5s multicolored .25 .25

World Sport Fishing Congress, Varna.

St. Theodore A899

Frescoes: 3s, St. Paul. 5s, St. Joachim. 13s, Melchizedek. 19s, St. Porphyrius. 28s, Queen. 1 l, The Last Supper.

1976, Oct. 4 Litho. *Perf. 12x12½*

2361 A899 2s gold & multi .25 .25
2362 A899 3s gold & multi .25 .25
2363 A899 5s gold & multi .25 .25
2364 A899 13s gold & multi .45 .25

2365 A899 19s gold & multi .50 .25
2366 A899 28s gold & multi .95 .25
Nos. 2361-2366 (6) 2.65 1.50

Miniature Sheet

Perf. 12

2367 A899 1 l gold & multi 2.50 1.50

Zemen Monastery frescoes, 14th cent.

Document A900

1976, Oct. 5

2368 A900 5s multicolored .25 .25

State Archives, 25th anniversary.

Cinquefoil A901

1976, Oct. 14 Photo. *Perf. 13*

2369 A901 1s Chestnut .25 .25
2370 A901 2s Cinquefoil .25 .25
2371 A901 5s Holly .25 .25
2372 A901 8s Yew .25 .25
2373 A901 13s Daphne .50 .25
2374 A901 23s Judas tree .85 .25
Nos. 2369-2374 (6) 2.35 1.50

Dimitri Polianov — A902

1976, Nov. 19

2375 A902 2s dk purple & ocher .25 .25

Dimitri Polianov (1876-1953), poet.

Christo Botev, by Zlatyu Boyadjiev A903

Paintings: 2s, Partisan Carrying Cherrywood Cannon, by Ilya Petrov. 3s, "Necklace of Immortality" (man's portrait), by Detchko Uzunov. 13s, "April 1876," by Georgi Popoff. 18s, Partisans, by Stoyan Venev. 60s, The Oath, by Svetlin Ruseff.

1976, Dec. 8

2376 A903 1s bister & multi .25 .25
2377 A903 2s bister & multi .25 .25
2378 A903 3s bister & multi .25 .25
2379 A903 13s bister & multi .25 .25
2380 A903 18s bister & multi .35 .25
Nos. 2376-2380 (5) 1.35 1.25

Souvenir Sheet

Imperf

2381 A903 60s gold & multi 1.75 1.00

Uprising against Turkish rule, centenary.

"Pollution" and Tree A904

Design: 18s, "Pollution" obscuring sun.

1976, Nov. 10 *Perf. 13*

2382 A904 2s ultra & multi .25 .25
2383 A904 18s blue & multi .50 .25

Protection of the environment.

Congress Emblem — A904a

Flags — A904b

1976, Nov. 28 Photo. *Perf. 13*

2384 A904a 2s multicolored .25 .25
2384A A904b 13s multicolored .40 .25

33rd BSIS Cong. (Bulgarian Socialist Party).

Tobacco Workers, by Stajkov A905

Paintings by Stajkov: 2s, View of Melnik. 13s, Shipbuilder.

1976, Dec. 16 Photo. *Perf. 13*

2385 A905 1s multicolored .25 .25
2386 A905 2s multicolored .25 .25
2387 A905 13s multicolored .30 .25
Nos. 2385-2387 (3) .80 .75

Veselin Stajkov (1906-1970), painter.

Snowflake — A906

1976, Dec. 20

2388 A906 2s silver & multi .25 .25

New Year 1977.

Zachary Stoyanov (1851-1889), Historian — A907

1976, Dec. 30

2389 A907 2s multicolored .25 .25

Bronze Coin of Septimus Severus — A908

Roman Coins: 2s, 13s, 18s, Bronze coins of Caracalla, diff. 23s, Copper coin of Diocletian.

1977, Jan. 28 Photo. *Perf. 13½x13*

2390 A908 1s gold & multi .25 .25
2391 A908 2s gold & multi .25 .25
2392 A908 13s gold & multi .25 .25
2393 A908 18s gold & multi .45 .25
2394 A908 23s gold & multi .70 .25
Nos. 2390-2394 (5) 1.90 1.25

Coins struck in Serdica (modern Sofia).

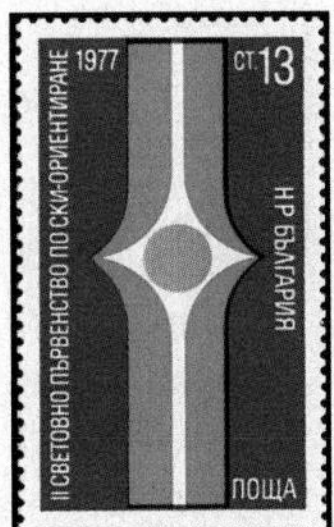

Skis and Compass — A909

1977, Feb. 14 *Perf. 13*

2395 A909 13s ultra, red & lt bl .50 .25

2nd World Ski Orienteering Championships.

Tourist Congress Emblem — A910

1977, Feb. 24 Photo. *Perf. 13*

2396 A910 2s multicolored .25 .25

5th Congress of Bulgarian Tourist Organization.

Bellflower A911

Designs: Various bellflowers.

1977, Mar. 2

2397 A911 1s yellow & multi .25 .25
2398 A911 2s rose & multi .25 .25
2399 A911 3s lt blue & multi .25 .25
2400 A911 13s multicolored .40 .25
2401 A911 43s yellow & multi 1.50 .30
Nos. 2397-2401 (5) 2.65 1.30

Vasil Kolarov — A912

1977, Mar. 21 Photo. *Perf. 13*

2402 A912 2s blue & black .25 .25

Vasil Kolarov (1877-1950), politician.

Union Congress Emblem — A913

1977, Mar. 25

2403 A913 2s multicolored .25 .25

8th Bulgarian Trade Union Cong., Apr. 4-7.

Wolf — A914

Wild Animals: 2s, Red fox. 10s, Weasel. 13s, European wildcat. 23s, Jackal.

1977, May 16 Litho. *Perf. 12½x12*

2404 A914 1s multicolored .25 .25
2405 A914 2s multicolored .25 .25
2406 A914 10s multicolored .40 .25
2407 A914 13s multicolored .70 .40
2408 A914 23s multicolored 1.50 .75
Nos. 2404-2408 (5) 3.10 1.90

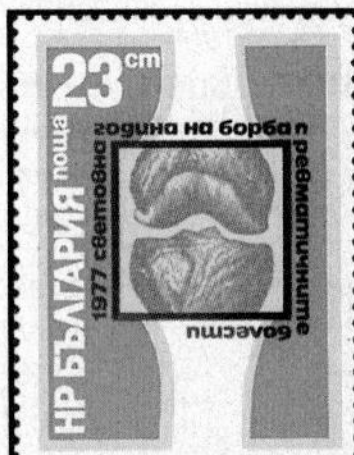

Diseased Knee — A915

1977, Mar. 31 Photo. *Perf. 13*

2409 A915 23s multicolored .85 .25

World Rheumatism Year.

Writers' Congress Emblem A916

1977, June 7

2410 A916 23s lt bl & yel grn 1.25 .25

International Writers Congress: "Peace, the Hope of the Planet." No. 2410 printed in sheets of 8 stamps and 4 labels with signatures of participating writers.

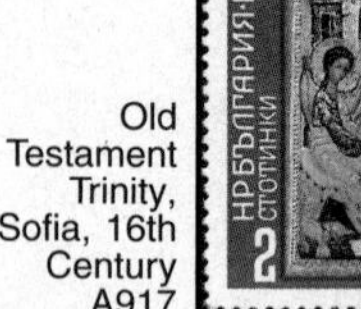
Old Testament Trinity, Sofia, 16th Century A917

Icons: 1s, St. Nicholas, Nessebur, 13th cent. 3s, Annunciation, Royal Gates, Veliko Turnovo, 16th cent. 5s, Christ Enthroned, Nessebur, 17th cent. 13s, St. Nicholas, Elena, 18th cent. 23s, Presentation of the Virgin, Rila Monastery, 18th cent. 35s, Virgin and Child, Tryavna, 19th cent. 40s, St. Demetrius on Horseback, Provadia, 19th cent. 1 l, The 12 Holidays, Rila Monastery, 18th cent.

1977, May 10 Photo. *Perf. 13*

2411	A917	1s black & multi	.25	.25
2412	A917	2s green & multi	.25	.25
2413	A917	3s brown & multi	.25	.25
2414	A917	5s blue & multi	.25	.25
2415	A917	13s olive & multi	.45	.25
2416	A917	23s maroon & multi	.70	.25
2417	A917	35s green & multi	1.10	.35
2418	A917	40s dp ultra & multi	1.60	.55
		Nos. 2411-2418 (8)	4.85	2.40

Miniature Sheet

Imperf

2419 A917 1 l gold & multi 3.75 3.25

Bulgarian icons. See Nos. 2615-2619.

Souvenir Sheet

St. Cyril — A918

1977, June 7 Photo. *Perf. 13*

2420 A918 1 l gold & multi 3.00 3.00

St. Cyril (827-869), reputed inventor of Cyrillic alphabet.

Congress Emblem — A919

1977, May 9

2421 A919 2s red, gold & grn .25 .25

13th Komsomol Congress.

Newspaper Masthead — A920

1977, June 3 Photo. *Perf. 13*

2422 A920 2s multicolored .25 .25

Cent. of Bulgarian daily press and 50th anniv. of Rabotnichesko Delo newspaper.

Patriotic Front Emblem — A921

1977, May 26

2423 A921 2s gold & multi .25 .25

8th Congress of Patriotic Front.

Weight Lifting — A922

1977, June 15

2424 A922 13s dp brown & multi .40 .25

European Youth Weight Lifting Championships, Sofia, June.

Women Basketball Players — A923

1977, June 15 *Perf. 13*

2425 A923 23s multicolored .85 .25

7th European Women's Basketball Championships.

Wrestling — A924

Games Emblem and: 13s, Running. 23s, Basketball. 43s, Women's gymnastics.

1977, Apr. 15

2426	A924	2s multicolored	.25	.25
2427	A924	13s multicolored	.25	.25
2428	A924	23s multicolored	.85	.25
2429	A924	43s multicolored	1.25	.40
		Nos. 2426-2429 (4)	2.60	1.15

UNIVERSIADE '77, University Games, Sofia, Aug. 18-27.

TV Tower, Berlin — A925

1977, Aug. 12 Litho. *Perf. 13*

2430 A925 25s blue & dk blue .85 .25

SOZPHILEX 77 Philatelic Exhibition, Berlin, Aug. 19-28.

Ship Type of 1975

Historic Ships: 1s, Hansa cog. 2s, Santa Maria, caravelle. 3s, Golden Hind, frigate. 12s, Santa Catherina, carrack. 13s, La Corone, galleon. 43s, Mediterranean galleass.

1977, Aug. 29 Photo. *Perf. 13*

2431	A873	1s multicolored	.25	.25
2432	A873	2s multicolored	.25	.25
2433	A873	3s multicolored	.25	.25
2434	A873	12s multicolored	.30	.25
2435	A873	13s multicolored	.30	.25
2436	A873	43s multicolored	1.25	.30
		Nos. 2431-2436 (6)	2.60	1.55

Ivan Vasov National Theater A926

Buildings, Sofia: 13s, Party Headquarters. 23s, House of the People's Army. 30s, Clement Ochrida University. 80s, National Gallery. 1 l, National Assembly.

1977, Aug. 30 Photo. *Perf. 13*

2437	A926	12s red, *gray*	.25	.25
2438	A926	13s red brn, *gray*	.40	.25
2439	A926	23s blue, *gray*	.65	.25
2440	A926	30s olive, *gray*	.95	.30
2441	A926	80s violet, *gray*	2.00	.90
2442	A926	1 l claret, *gray*	2.50	1.10
		Nos. 2437-2442 (6)	6.75	3.05

Map of Europe A927

1977, June 10

2443 A927 23s brown, bl & grn .85 .25

21st Congress of the European Organization for Quality Control, Varna.

Union of Earth and Water, by Rubens A928

Rubens Paintings: 23s, Venus and Adonis. 40s, Pastoral Scene (man and woman). 1 l, Portrait of a Lady in Waiting.

1977, Sept. 23 Litho. *Perf. 12*

2444	A928	13s gold & multi	.70	.25
2445	A928	23s gold & multi	1.25	.25
2446	A928	40s gold & multi	1.25	.35
		Nos. 2444-2446 (3)	3.20	.85

Souvenir Sheet

2447 A928 1 l gold & multi 4.25 2.40

Peter Paul Rubens (1577-1640).

George Dimitrov A929

1977, June 17 Photo. *Perf. 13*

2448 A929 13s red & deep claret .60 .25

George Dimitrov (1882-1947).

Flame with Star — A930

1977, May 17

2449 A930 13s gold & multi .40 .25

3rd Bulgarian Culture Congress.

Smart Pete on Donkey, by Ilya Beshkov — A931

1977, May 19

2450 A931 2s multicolored .25 .25

11th National Festival of Humor and Satire Gabrovo.

Elin Pelin — A932

Writers: 2s, Pelin (Dimitur Ivanov Stojanov, (1877-1949). 5s, Peju K. Jaworov (1878-1914).

Artists: 13s, Boris Angelushev (1902-1966), 23s, Ceno Todorov (Ceno Todorov Dikov, 1877-1953). Each printed with label showing scenes from authors' works or illustrations by the artists.

1977, Aug. 26 Photo. *Perf. 13*

2451	A932	2s gold & brown	.25	.25
2452	A932	5s gold & gray grn	.25	.25
2453	A932	13s gold & claret	.50	.25
2454	A932	23s gold & blue	.85	.25
		Nos. 2451-2454 (4)	1.85	1.00

13th Canoe World Championships — A933

1977, Sept. 1 Photo. *Perf. 13*
2455 A933 2s shown .25 .25
2456 A933 23s 2-man canoe .85 .25

Albena, Black Sea — A933a

1977, Oct. 5 Photo. *Perf. 13*
2456A A933a 35s shown 1.25 .50
2456B A933a 43s Rila Monastery 1.50 .55

Sheet contains 4 each plus label.

Dr. Pirogov — A934

1977, Oct. 14 Photo. *Perf. 13*
2457 A934 13s olive, ocher & brn .40 .25

Centenary of visit by Russian physician N. J. Pirogov during war of liberation from Turkey.

Peace Decree, 1917 — A935

13s, Lenin, 1917. 23s, "1917" as a flame.

1977, Oct. 21
2458 A935 2s black, buff & red .25 .25
2459 A935 13s multicolored .55 .25
2460 A935 23s multicolored .75 .25
Nos. 2458-2460 (3) 1.55 .75

60th anniv. of Russian October Revolution.

Old Soldier with Grandchild A936

Designs (Festival Posters): 13s, "The Bugler." 23s, Liberation Monument, Sofia (detail). 25s, Samara flag.

1977, Sept. 30
2461 A936 2s multicolored .25 .25
2462 A936 13s multicolored .40 .25
2463 A936 23s multicolored .70 .25
2464 A936 25s multicolored .85 .40
Nos. 2461-2464 (4) 2.20 1.15

Liberation from Turkish rule, centenary.

Souvenir Sheet

Games' and Sports Emblems — A937

1977, Aug. 10 Photo. *Perf. 13½x13*
2465 A937 1 l multicolored 2.50 2.00

University Games '77, Sofia.

Conference Building — A938

1977, Sept. 12 *Perf. 13½*
2466 A938 23s multicolored .85 .25

64th Interparliamentary Union Conf., Sofia.

Bulgarian Worker's Newspaper, Anniversaries A939

1977, Sept. 12 Photo. *Perf. 13*
2467 A939 2s yel grn, blk & red .25 .25

Ornament A940

New Year 1978: 13s, Different ornament.

1977, Dec. 1
2468 A940 2s gold & multi .25 .25
2469 A940 13s silver & multi .40 .25

Railroad Bridge — A941

1977, Nov. 9
2470 A941 13s green, yel & gray .70 .25

Transport Organization, 50th anniversary.

A942

1977, Nov. 15
2471 A942 8s gold & vio brn .25 .25

Petko Ratchev Slaveikov (1827-95), poet, birth sesquicentennial. No. 2471 printed in sheets of 8 stamps and 8 labels in 4 alternating vertical rows.

A943

Designs: 23s, Soccer player and Games' emblem. 50s, Soccer players.

1978, Jan. 30 Photo. *Perf. 13*
2472 A943 13s multicolored .65 .25
2473 A943 23s multicolored 1.10 .25

Souvenir Sheet

2474 A943 50s ultra & multi 2.25 1.90

11th World Cup Soccer Championship, Argentina, June 1-25.

Todor Zhivkov and Leonid I. Brezhnev A944

1977, Sept. 7 Photo. *Perf. 13*
2475 A944 18s gold, car & brn .50 .25

Bulgarian-Soviet Friendship. No. 2475 issued in sheets of 3 stamps and 3 labels.

Ostankino Tower, Moscow, Bulgarian Post Emblem — A945

1978, Mar. 1
2476 A945 13s multicolored .40 .25

Comecon Postal Organization (Council of Mutual Economic Assistance), 20th anniv.

Leo Tolstoy — A946

Shipka Pass Monument — A947

5s, Fedor Dostoevski. 13s, Ivan Sergeevich Turgenev. 23s, Vasili Vasilievich Vereshchagin. 25s, Giuseppe Garibaldi. 35s, Victor Hugo.

1978, Mar. 28 Photo. *Perf. 13*
2477 A946 2s yellow & dk grn .25 .25
2478 A946 5s lemon & brown .25 .25
2479 A946 13s tan & sl grn .25 .25
2480 A946 23s gray & vio brn .40 .25
2481 A946 25s yel grn & blk .50 .25
2482 A946 35s lt bl & vio bl .95 .50
Nos. 2477-2482 (6) 2.60 1.75

Souvenir Sheet

2483 A947 50s multicolored 1.25 .90

Bulgaria's liberation from Ottoman rule, cent.

Bulgarian and Russian Colors A948

1978, Mar. 18
2484 A948 2s multicolored .25 .25

30th anniv. of Russo-Bulgarian co-operation.

Heart and WHO Emblem A949

1978, May 12
2485 A949 23s gray, red & org .85 .25

World Health Day, fight against hypertension.

Goddess A950

Ceramics (2nd-4th Cent.) & Exhibition Emblem: 5s, Mask of bearded man. 13s, Vase. 23s, Vase. 35s, Head of Silenus. 53s, Cock.

1978, Apr. 26
2486 A950 2s green & multi .25 .25
2487 A950 5s multicolored .25 .25
2488 A950 13s multicolored .45 .25
2489 A950 23s multicolored 1.10 .25
2490 A950 35s multicolored 1.50 .45
2491 A950 53s carmine & multi 2.50 .55
Nos. 2486-2491 (6) 6.05 2.00

Philaserdica Philatelic Exhibition.

Nikolai Roerich, by Svyatoslav Roerich — A951

"Mind and Matter," by Andrei Nikolov — A952

1978, Apr. 5

2492 A951 8s multicolored .25 .25
2493 A952 13s multicolored .50 .25

Nikolai K. Roerich (1874-1947) and Andrei Nikolov (1878-1959), artists.

Bulgarian Flag and Red Star — A953

1978, Apr. 18

2494 A953 2s vio blue & multi .25 .25

Bulgarian Communist Party Congress.

Young Man, by Albrecht Dürer A954

Paintings: 23s, Bathsheba at Fountain, by Rubens. 25s, Portrait of a Man, by Hans Holbein the Younger. 35s, Rembrandt and Saskia, by Rembrandt. 43s, Lady in Mourning, by Tintoretto. 60s, Old Man with Beard, by Rembrandt. 80s, Knight in Armor, by Van Dyck.

1978, June 19 Photo. *Perf. 13*

2495 A954 13s multicolored .25 .25
2496 A954 23s multicolored .50 .25
2497 A954 25s multicolored .50 .25
2498 A954 35s multicolored .75 .25
2499 A954 43s multicolored .95 .25
2500 A954 60s multicolored 1.60 .40
2501 A954 80s multicolored 2.00 .65
Nos. 2495-2501 (7) 6.55 2.30

Dresden Art Gallery paintings.

Doves and Festival Emblem — A955

1978, May 31

2502 A955 13s multicolored .40 .25

11th World Youth Festival, Havana, 7/28-8/5.

Fritillaria Stribrnyi — A956

Rare Flowers: 2s, Fritillaria drenovskyi. 3s, Lilium rhodopaeum. 13s, Tulipa urumoffii. 23s, Lilium jankae. 43s, Tulipa rhodopaea.

1978, June 27

2503 A956 1s multicolored .25 .25
2504 A956 2s multicolored .25 .25
2505 A956 3s multicolored .25 .25
2506 A956 13s multicolored .35 .25
2507 A956 23s multicolored .65 .25
2508 A956 43s multicolored 1.40 .50
Nos. 2503-2508 (6) 3.15 1.75

Yacht Cor Caroli and Map of Voyage A957

1978, May 19 Photo. *Perf. 13*

2509 A957 23s multicolored 1.75 .25

First Bulgarian around-the-world voyage, Capt. Georgi Georgiev, 12/20/76-12/20/77.

Market, by Naiden Petkov — A958

Views of Sofia: 5s, Street, by Emil Stoichev. 13s, Street, by Boris Ivanov. 23s, Tolbukhin Boulevard, by Nikola Tanev. 35s, National Theater, by Nikola Petrov. 53s, Market, by Anton Mitov.

1978, Aug. 28 Litho. *Perf. 12½x12*

2510 A958 2s multicolored .25 .25
2511 A958 5s multicolored .25 .25
2512 A958 13s multicolored .25 .25
2513 A958 23s multicolored .40 .25
2514 A958 35s multicolored .75 .25
2515 A958 53s multicolored 1.25 .40
Nos. 2510-2515 (6) 3.15 1.65

Miniature Sheet

Sleeping Venus, by Giorgione — A959

1978, Aug. 7 Photo. *Imperf.*

2516 A959 1 l multicolored 2.25 .85

View of Varna — A960

1978, July 13 Photo. *Perf. 13*

2517 A960 13s multicolored .70 .55

63rd Esperanto Cong., Varna, 7/29-8/5.

Black Woodpecker A961

Woodpeckers: 2s, Syrian. 3s, Three-toed. 13s, Middle spotted. 23s, Lesser spotted. 43s, Green.

1978, Sept. 1

2518 A961 1s multicolored .40 .25
2519 A961 2s multicolored .40 .25
2520 A961 3s multicolored .40 .25
2521 A961 13s multicolored .75 .40
2522 A961 23s multicolored 1.25 .55
2523 A961 43s multicolored 2.75 1.25
Nos. 2518-2523 (6) 5.95 2.95

"September 1923" — A962

1978, Sept. 5

2524 A962 2s red & brn .25 .25

55th anniversary of September uprising.

Souvenir Sheet

A963

a, National Theater, Sofia. b, Festival Hall, Sofia. c, Charles Bridge, Prague. d, Belvedere Palace, Prague.

Photogravure and Engraved

1978, Sept. 1 *Perf. 12x11½*

2525 Sheet of 4 2.50 1.00
a. A963 40s multi .60 .25
b. A963 40s multi .60 .25
c. A963 40s multi .60 .25
d. A963 40s multi .60 .25

PRAGA '78 and PHILASERDICA '79 Philatelic Exhibitions.

Black and White Hands, Human Rights Emblem — A964

1978, Oct. 3 Photo. *Perf. 13x13½*

2526 A964 13s multicolored .40 .25

Anti-Apartheid Year.

Gotse Deltchev — A965

1978, Aug. 1 Photo. *Perf. 13*

2527 A965 13s multicolored .50 .25

Gotse Deltchev (1872-1903), patriot.

Bulgarian Calculator — A966

1978, Sept. 3

2528 A966 2s multicolored .25 .25

International Sample Fair, Plovdiv.

Guerrillas — A967

1978, Aug. 1

2529 A967 5s blk & rose red .25 .25

Ilinden and Preobrazhene revolts, 75th anniv.

"Pipe Line" and Flags A968

1978, Oct. 3

2530 A968 13s multicolored .40 .25

Construction of gas pipe line from Orenburg to Russian border.

A969

1978, Oct. 4 *Perf. 13x13½*
2531 A969 13s Three acrobats .40 .25

3rd World Acrobatic Championships, Sofia, Oct. 6-8.

A970

1978, Sept. 18 Photo. *Perf. 13*
2532 A970 2s dp claret & ocher .25 .25

Christo G. Danov (1828-1911), 1st Bulgarian publisher. No. 2532 printed with se-tenant label showing early printing press.

Insurgents, by Todor Panajotov — A971

1978, Sept. 20
2533 A971 2s multicolored .25 .25

Vladaja mutiny, 60th anniversary.

A972

1978, Oct. 11 Photo. *Perf. 13*
2534 A972 13s dk brn & org red .40 .25

Salvador Allende (1908-1973), president of Chile.

A973

1978, Oct. 18
2535 A973 23s Human Rights flame .85 .25

Universal Declaration of Human Rights, 30th anniversary.

A974

Burgarian Paintings: 1s, Levski and Matei Mitkaloto, by Kalina Tasseva. 2s, "Strength for my Arm" by Zlatyu Boyadjiev. 3s, Rumena, woman military leader, by Nikola Mirchev, horiz. 13s, Kolju Ficeto, by Elza Goeva. 23s, Family, National Revival Period, by Naiden Petkov.

Perf. 12x12½, 12½x12

1978, Oct. 25 **Litho.**

2536	A974	1s multicolored	.25	.25
2537	A974	2s multicolored	.25	.25
2538	A974	3s multicolored	.25	.25
2539	A974	13s multicolored	.50	.25
2540	A974	23s multicolored	.65	.25
		Nos. 2536-2540 (5)	1.90	1.25

1300th anniversary of Bulgaria (in 1981).

From late 1978 to 1991, imperf varieties, some overprinted, exist for many sets and souvenir sheets. These were distributed in limited numbers and are described in footnotes following the listed issues.

Souvenir Sheet

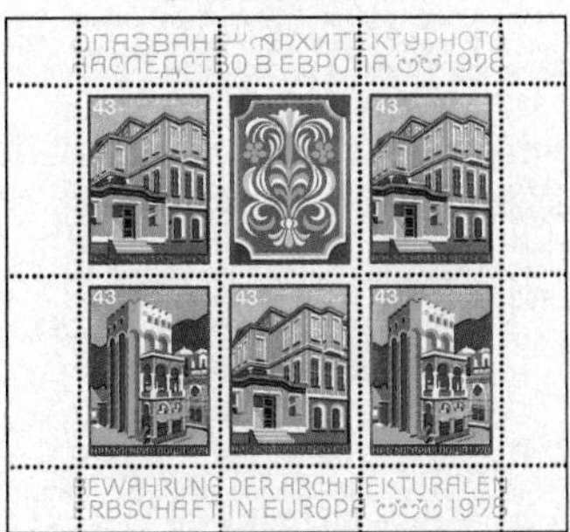

A975

Designs: a, Tourism building, Plovdiv. b, Chrelo Tower, Rila Cloister.

1978, Nov. 1 Photo. *Perf. 13*

2541	Sheet of 5 + label	4.75	2.40
a.	A975 43s multicolored	.85	.35
b.	A975 43s multicolored	.85	.35

Conservation of European architectural heritage. No. 2541 contains 3 No. 2541a & 2 No. 2541b.

Exists overprinted "Essen 1978." Value $37.50.

Ferry, Map of Black Sea with Route A976

1978, Nov. 1 Photo. *Perf. 13*
2542 A976 13s multicolored .40 .25

Opening of Ilychovsk-Varna Ferry.

Bird, from Marble Floor, St. Sofia Church — A977

1978, Nov. 20
2543 A977 5s multicolored .25 .25

3rd Bulgaria '78, National Philatelic Exhibition, Sofia. Printed se-tenant with label showing emblems of Bulgaria '78 and Philaserdica '79.

Initial, 13th Century Gospel — A978

Designs: 13s, St. Cyril, miniature, 1567. 23s, Book cover, 16th century. 80s, St. Methodius, miniature, 13th century.

1978, Dec. 15 Photo. *Perf. 13*

2544	A978	2s multicolored	.25	.25
2545	A978	13s multicolored	.25	.25
2546	A978	23s multicolored	.75	.25
		Nos. 2544-2546 (3)	1.25	.75

Souvenir Sheet

2547 A978 80s multicolored 2.00 1.25

Cent. of the Cyril and Methodius Natl. Library.

Bulgaria No. 53 A979

Bulgarian Stamps: 13s, #534. 23s, #968. 35s, #1176, vert. 53s, #1223, vert. 1 l, #1.

1978, Dec. 30

2548	A979	2s ol grn & red	.25	.25
2549	A979	13s ultra & rose car	.25	.25
2550	A979	23s rose lil & ol grn	.35	.25
2551	A979	35s brt bl & blk	.65	.25
2552	A979	53s ver & sl grn	1.10	.35
		Nos. 2548-2552 (5)	2.60	1.35

Souvenir Sheet

2553 A979 1 l multicolored 1.75 1.25

Philaserdica '79, International Philatelic Exhibition, Sofia, May 18-27, 1979, and centenary of Bulgarian stamps. No. 2553 exists imperf. Value $17.50.

A larger (63mmx61mm) souvenir sheet was issued in 1979, containing one 1 l stamp, perf 13. Value $4.50. A second souvenir sheet (92mmx125mm), containing one 5 l stamp, perf 13, with reproductions of many stamps of the first Bulgarian issue, was also issued in 1979. Value $35.

See Nos. 2560-2564.

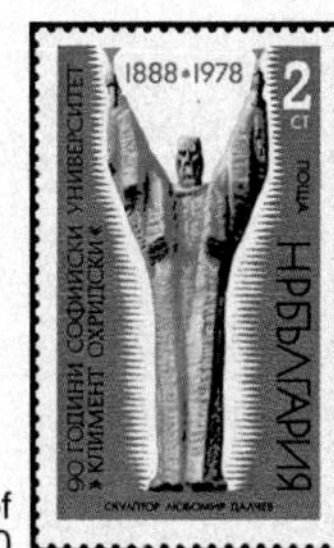

St. Clement of Ochrida — A980

1978, Dec. 8
2554 A980 2s multicolored .25 .25

Clement of Ochrida University, 90th anniv.

Ballet Dancers A981

1978, Dec. 22
2555 A981 13s multicolored .40 .25

Bulgarian ballet, 50th anniversary.

Nikola Karastojanov — A982

1978, Dec. 12
2556 A982 2s multicolored .35 .35

Nikola Karastojanov (1778-1874), printer. No. 2556 printed se-tenant with label showing printing press.

Christmas Tree Made of Birds — A983

1978, Dec. 22

2557	A983	2s shown	.25	.25
2558	A983	13s Post horn	.25	.25

New Year 1979.

COMECON Building, Moscow, Members' Flags — A984

1979, Jan. 25 Photo. *Perf. 13*
2559 A984 13s multicolored .40 .25

Council for Mutual Economic Aid (COMECON), 30th anniversary.

Philaserdica Type of 1978

Designs as Before

1979, Jan. 30

2560	A979	2s brt bl & red	.25	.25
2561	A979	13s grn & dk car	.25	.25
2562	A979	23s org brn & multi	.45	.25
2563	A979	35s dl red & blk	.75	.35
2564	A979	53s vio & dk ol	1.40	.55
		Nos. 2560-2564 (5)	3.10	1.65

Philaserdica '79.

Bank Building, Commemorative Coin — A985

1979, Feb. 13

2565 A985 2s yel, gray & silver .25 .25

Centenary of Bulgarian People's Bank.

Aleksandr Stamboliski A986

1979, Feb. 28

2566 A986 2s orange & dk brn .25 .25

Aleksandr Stamboliski (1879-1923), leader of peasant's party and premier.

Flower with Child's Face, IYC Emblem — A987

1979, Mar. 8

2568 A987 23s multicolored .85 .25

International Year of the Child.

Stylized Heads, World Association Emblem — A988

1979, Mar. 20

2569 A988 13s multicolored .40 .25

8th World Cong. for the Deaf, Varna, June 20-27.

"75" and Trade Union Emblem — A989

1979, Mar. 20

2570 A989 2s slate grn & org .25 .25

75th anniversary of Bulgarian Trade Unions.

Souvenir Sheet

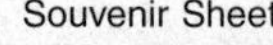

Sculptures in Sofia — A990

Designs: 2s, Soviet Army Monument (detail). 5s, Mother and Child, Central Railroad Station. 13s, 23s, 25s, Bas-relief from Monument of the Liberators.

1979, Apr. 2 Photo. *Perf. 13*

2571 A990 Sheet of 5 + label 2.00 1.25
- *a.* 2s multicolored .25 .25
- *b.* 5s multicolored .25 .25
- *c.* 13s multicolored .35 .25
- *d.* 23s multicolored .50 .25
- *e.* 25s multicolored .65 .25

Centenary of Sofia as capital.

Rocket Launch, Space Flight Emblems A991

Intercosmos & Bulgarian-USSR Flight Emblems and: 25s, Link-up, horiz. 35s, Parachute descent. 1 l, Globe, emblems & orbit, horiz.

1979, Apr. 11

2572 A991 12s multicolored .25 .25
2573 A991 25s multicolored .85 .25
2574 A991 35s multicolored 1.10 .40
Nos. 2572-2574 (3) 2.20 .90

Souvenir Sheet

2575 A991 1 l multicolored 1.75 1.00

1st Bulgarian cosmonaut on Russian space flight.

A slightly larger imperf. sheet similar to No. 2575 with control numbers at bottom and rockets at sides exists. $125.

Georgi Ivanov A992

Design: 13s, Rukavishnikov and Soviet cosmonaut Georgi Ivanov.

1979, May 14 Photo. *Perf. 13*

2576 A992 2s multicolored .25 .25
2577 A992 13s multicolored .65 .25

Col. Rukavishnikov, 1st Bulgarian astronaut.

Souvenir Sheet

Thracian Gold-leaf Collar — A993

1979, May 16

2578 A993 1 l multicolored 3.50 2.25

48th International Philatelic Federation Congress, Sofia, May 16-17.

Post Horn, Carrier Pigeon, Jet, Globes and UPU Emblem — A994

Designs (Post Horn, Globes and ITU Emblem): 5s, 1st Bulgarian and modern telephones. 13s, Morse key and teleprinter. 23s, Old radio transmitter and radio towers. 35s, Bulgarian TV tower and satellite. 50s, Ground receiving station

1979, May 8 *Perf. 13½x13*

2579 A994 2s multicolored .25 .25
2580 A994 5s multicolored .25 .25
2581 A994 13s multicolored .25 .25
2582 A994 23s multicolored .65 .25
2583 A994 35s multicolored .90 .35
Nos. 2579-2583 (5) 2.30 1.35

Souvenir Sheet

Perf. 13

2584 A994 50s vio, blk & gray 2.25 1.40

Intl. Telecommunications Day and cent. of Bulgarian Postal & Telegraph Services. Size of stamp in No. 2584: 39x28mm. No. 2584 exists imperf. Value $17.

Hotel Vitosha-New Otani — A996

1979, May 20

2586 A996 2s ultra & pink .25 .25

Philaserdica '79 Day.

Horseman Receiving Gifts, by Karellia and Boris Kuklievi — A997

1979, May 23

2587 A997 2s multicolored .25 .25

Bulgarian-Russian Friendship Day.

A998

Man on Donkey, by Boris Angeloushev.

1979, May 23 Photo. *Perf. 13½*

2588 A998 2s multicolored .25 .25

12th National Festival of Humor and Satire, Gabrovo.

A999

Durer Engravings: 13s, Four Women. 23s, Three Peasants. 25s, The Cook and his Wife. 35s, Portrait of Helius Eobanus Hessus. 80s, Rhinoceros, horiz.

Lithographed and Engraved

1979, May 31 *Perf. 14x13½*

2589 A999 13s multicolored .35 .25
2590 A999 23s multicolored .55 .25
2591 A999 25s multicolored .65 .25
2592 A999 35s multicolored .95 .25
Nos. 2589-2592 (4) 2.50 1.00

Souvenir Sheet

Imperf

2593 A999 80s multicolored 2.00 1.25

Albrecht Durer (1471-1528), German engraver and painter.

R. Todorov (1879-1916) — A1000

Bulgarian Writers: No. 2595, Dimitri Dymov (1909-66). No. 2596, S. A. Kostov (1879-1939).

1979, June 26 Photo. *Perf. 13*

2594 A1000 2s multicolored .25 .25
2595 A1000 2s slate grn & yel grn .25 .25
2596 A1000 2s dp claret & yel .25 .25
Nos. 2594-2596 (3) .75 .75

Nos. 2594-2596 each printed se-tenant with label showing title page or character from writer's work.

Moscow '80 Emblem, Runners A1001

Moscow '80 Emblem and: 13s, Pole vault, horiz. 25s, Discus. 35s, Hurdles, horiz. 43s, High jump, horiz. 1 l, Long jump.

1979, May 15 ***Perf. 13***

No.	Type	Value	Color	Unused	Used
2597	A1001	2s	multicolored	.25	.25
2598	A1001	13s	multicolored	.25	.25
2599	A1001	25s	multicolored	.60	.25
2600	A1001	35s	multicolored	1.25	.35
2601	A1001	43s	multicolored	1.75	.45
2602	A1001	1 l	multicolored	3.25	.95
			Nos. 2597-2602 (6)	7.35	2.50

Souvenir Sheet

No.	Type	Value	Color	Unused	Used
2602A	A1001	2 l	multicolored	7.50	4.00

22nd Summer Olympic Games, Moscow, July 19-Aug. 3, 1980.

Rocket — A1002

5s, Flags of USSR and Bulgaria. 13s, "35."

1979, Sept. 4 **Photo.**

No.	Type	Value	Color	Unused	Used
2603	A1002	2s	multicolored	.25	.25
2604	A1002	5s	multicolored	.25	.25
2605	A1002	13s	multicolored	.25	.25
			Nos. 2603-2605 (3)	.75	.75

35th anniversary of liberation.

Moscow '80 Emblem, Gymnast A1003

Moscow '80 Emblem & gymnasts.

1979, July 31 **Photo.** ***Perf. 13***

No.	Type	Value	Color	Unused	Used
2606	A1003	2s	multi	.25	.25
2607	A1003	13s	multi, horiz.	.25	.25
2608	A1003	25s	multi	.65	.25
2609	A1003	35s	multi	.95	.35
2610	A1003	43s	multi	1.25	.35
2611	A1003	1 l	multi	2.75	1.00
			Nos. 2606-2611 (6)	6.10	2.45

Souvenir Sheet

No.	Type	Value	Color	Unused	Used
2612	A1003	2 l	multicolored	7.75	4.00

22nd Summer Olympic Games, Moscow, July 19-Aug. 3, 1980.

A1004

1979, July 8 **Photo.** ***Perf. 13***

No.	Type	Value	Color	Unused	Used
2613	A1004	13s	ultra & blk	.35	.35

Theater Institute, 18th Congress.

A1005

1979, July 17

No.	Type	Value	Color	Unused	Used
2614	A1005	8s	multicolored	.25	.25

Journalists' Vacation House, Varna, 20th Anniv.

Icon Type of 1977

Virgin and Child from: 13s, 23s, Nesebar, 16th cent., diff. 35s, 43s, Sozopol, 16th cent., diff. 53s, Samokov, 19th cent. Inscribed 1979.

1979, Aug. 7 **Litho.** ***Perf. 12½***

No.	Type	Value	Color	Unused	Used
2615	A917	13s	multicolored	.25	.25
2616	A917	23s	multicolored	.50	.25
2617	A917	35s	multicolored	.75	.25
2618	A917	43s	multicolored	1.00	.25
2619	A917	53s	multicolored	1.40	.45
			Nos. 2615-2619 (5)	3.90	1.45

A1006

1979, Aug. 9 **Photo.** ***Perf. 13x13½***

No.	Type	Value	Color	Unused	Used
2620	A1006	2s	Anton Besenschek	.25	.25

Bulgarian stenography centenary.

A1007

1979, Aug. 28 ***Perf. 13***

No.	Type	Value	Color	Unused	Used
2621	A1007	2s	multicolored	.25	.25

Bulgarian Alpine Club, 50th anniv.

Public Health Ordinance — A1008

1979, Aug. 31 ***Perf. 13½***

No.	Type	Value	Color	Unused	Used
2622	A1008	2s	multicolored	.25	.25

Public Health Service centenary. No. 2622 printed with label showing Dimitar Mollov, founder.

Isotope Measuring Device — A1009

1979, Sept. 8 ***Perf. 13½x13***

No.	Type	Value	Color	Unused	Used
2623	A1009	2s	multicolored	.25	.25

International Sample Fair, Plovdiv.

Games' Emblem A1010

1979, Sept. 20 ***Perf. 13***

No.	Type	Value	Color	Unused	Used
2624	A1010	5s	multicolored	.25	.25

Universiada '79, World University Games, Mexico City, Sept.

Sofia Locomotive Sports Club, 50th Anniversary — A1011

1979, Oct. 2

No.	Type	Value	Color	Unused	Used
2625	A1011	2s	blue & org red	.25	.25

Ljuben Karavelov (1837-1879), Poet and Freedom Fighter — A1012

1979, Oct. 4 **Photo.** ***Perf. 13***

No.	Type	Value	Color	Unused	Used
2626	A1012	2s	blue & slate grn	.25	.25

A1013

1979, Oct. 20

No.	Type	Value	Color	Unused	Used
2627	A1013	2s	Biathlon	.25	.25
2628	A1013	13s	Speed skating	.40	.25
2629	A1013	23s	Downhill skiing	.65	.25
2630	A1013	43s	Luge	1.25	.40
			Nos. 2627-2630 (4)	2.55	1.15

Souvenir Sheet

Imperf

No.	Type	Value	Color	Unused	Used
2631	A1013	1 l	Slalom	2.50	1.50

13th Winter Olympic Games, Lake Placid, NY, Feb. 12-24.

No. 2631 exists overprinted "Lake Placid 1980," with serial number. Value $125.

A1014

Decko Uzunov, 80th Birthday: 12s, Apparition in Red. 13s, Woman from Thrace. 23s, Composition.

1979, Oct. 31 ***Perf. 14***

No.	Type	Value	Color	Unused	Used
2632	A1014	12s	multicolored	.50	.25
2633	A1014	13s	multicolored	.50	.25
2634	A1014	23s	multicolored	.75	.25
			Nos. 2632-2634 (3)	1.75	.75

Swimming, Moscow '80 Emblem — A1016

1979, Nov. 30 **Photo.** ***Perf. 13***

No.	Type	Value	Color	Unused	Used
2636	A1016	2s	Two-man kayak, vert.	.25	.25
2637	A1016	13s	Swimming, vert.	.25	.25
2638	A1016	25s	shown	.60	.25
2639	A1016	35s	One-man kayak	1.25	.25
2640	A1016	43s	Diving, vert	1.50	.60
2641	A1016	1 l	Diving, vert., diff.	3.50	1.00
			Nos. 2636-2641 (6)	7.35	2.60

Souvenir Sheet

No.	Type	Value	Color	Unused	Used
2642	A1016	2 l	Water polo, vert.	7.75	4.00

22nd Summer Olympic Games, Moscow, July 19-Aug. 3, 1980.

Nikola Vapzarov — A1017

1979, Dec. 7 **Photo.** ***Perf. 13***

No.	Type	Value	Color	Unused	Used
2643	A1017	2s	claret & rose	.25	.25

Vapzarov (1909-1942), poet and freedom fighter. No. 2643 printed with label showing smokestacks.

The First Socialists, by Bojan Petrov — A1018

Paintings: 13s, Demeter Blagoev Reading Newspaper, by Demeter Gjudshenov, 1892. 25s, Workers' Party March, by Sotir Sotirov, 1917. 35s, Dawn in Plovdiv, by Johann Leviev, vert.

Perf. 12½x12, 12x12½

1979, Dec. 10 **Litho.**

No.	Type	Value	Color	Unused	Used
2644	A1018	2s	multicolored	.25	.25
2645	A1018	13s	multicolored	.40	.25
2646	A1018	25s	multicolored	.65	.25
2647	A1018	35s	multicolored	.90	.25
			Nos. 2644-2647 (4)	2.20	1.00

Sharpshooting, Moscow '80 Emblem
A1019

1979, Dec. 22 Photo. *Perf. 13*

2648 A1019 2s shown .25 .25
2649 A1019 13s Judo, horiz. .25 .25
2650 A1019 25s Wrestling, horiz. .60 .25
2651 A1019 35s Archery 1.25 .35
2652 A1019 43s Fencing, horiz. 1.50 .75
2653 A1019 1 l Fencing 3.50 1.40
Nos. 2648-2653 (6) 7.35 3.25

Souvenir Sheet

2654 A1019 2 l Boxing 7.75 5.00

Procession with Relics, 11th Century Fresco
A1020

Frescoes of Sts. Cyril and Methodius, St. Clement's Basilica, Rome: 13s, Reception by Pope Hadrian II. 23s, Burial of Cyril the Philosopher, 18th century. 25s, St. Cyril. 35s, St. Methodius.

1979, Dec. 25

2655 A1020 2s multicolored .25 .25
2656 A1020 13s multicolored .35 .25
2657 A1020 23s multicolored .50 .25
2658 A1020 25s multicolored .65 .25
2659 A1020 35s multicolored .90 .25
Nos. 2655-2659 (5) 2.65 1.25

Bulgarian Television Emblem — A1021

1979, Dec. 29 *Perf. 13½*

2660 A1021 5s violet bl & lt bl .25 .25

Bulgarian television, 25th anniversary. No. 2660 printed with label showing Sofia television tower.

Doves in Girl's Hair
A1022

Design: 2s, Children's heads, mosaic, vert.

1979 *Perf. 13*

2661 A1022 2s multicolored .25 .25
2662 A1022 13s multicolored .35 .35

International Year of the Child. Issue dates: 2s, July 17; 13s, Dec. 14.

Puppet on Horseback, IYC Emblem — A1023

1980, Jan. 22 Photo. *Perf. 13*

2663 A1023 2s multicolored .25 .25

UNIMA, Intl. Puppet Theater Organization, 50th anniv. (1979); Intl. Year of the Child (1979).

Thracian Rider, Votive Tablet, 3rd Century — A1024

National Archaeological Museum Centenary; 13s, Deines stele, 5th century B.C.

1980, Jan. 29 Photo. *Perf. 13x13½*

2664 A1024 2s brown & gold .25 .25
2665 A1024 13s multicolored .25 .25

A miniature sheet was issued March 27, 1980, containing six 13s stamps, perf 13, which spelled out "EUROPA." Size 130mmx118mm. Value $35.

Dimitrov Meeting Lenin in Moscow, by Alexander Poplilov
A1026

1980, Mar. 28 *Perf. 12x12½*

2667 A1026 13s multicolored .35 .35

Lenin, 110th birth anniversary.

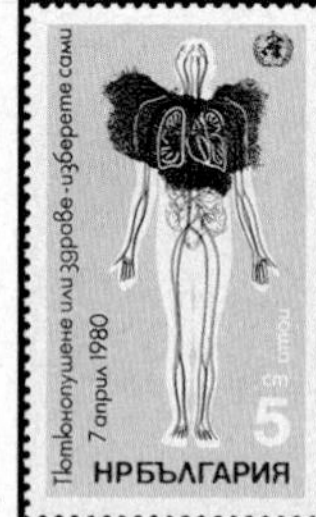

A1027

Circulatory system, lungs enveloped in smoke.

1980, Apr. 7 *Perf. 13*

2668 A1027 5s multicolored .25 .25

World Health Day fight against cigarette smoking.

A1027a

1980, Apr. 10 Photo. *Perf. 13*

2669 A1027a 2s Basketball .25 .25
2670 A1027a 13s Soccer .25 .25
2671 A1027a 25s Hockey .75 .35
2672 A1027a 35s Cycling 1.10 .55
2673 A1027a 43s Handball 1.75 .75
2674 A1027a 1 l Volleyball 3.25 1.10
Nos. 2669-2674 (6) 7.35 3.25

Souvenir Sheet

2675 A1027a 2 l Weightlifting 8.50 5.50

22nd Summer Olympic Games, Moscow, July 19-Aug. 3, 1980.

Souvenir Sheet

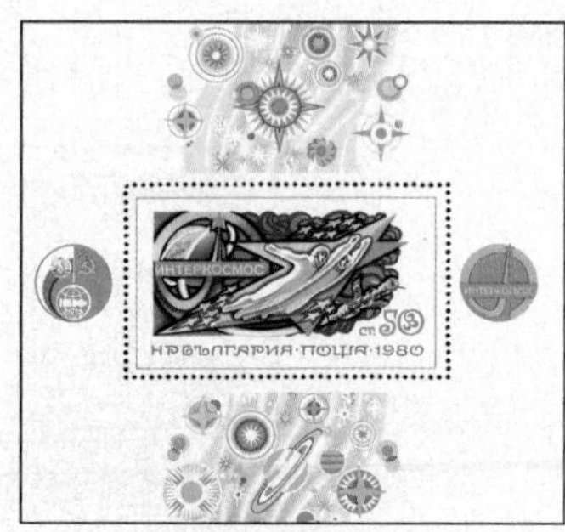

Intercosmos Emblem, Cosmonauts — A1028

1980, Apr. 22 *Perf. 12*

2676 A1028 50s multicolored 1.75 .80

Intercosmos cooperative space program.

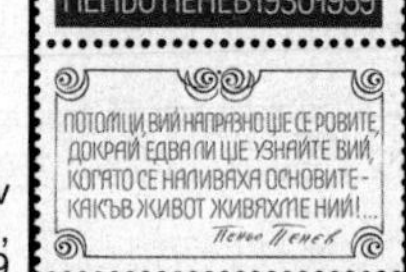

Penio Penev (1930-1959), Poet — A1029

1980, Apr. 22 Photo. *Perf. 13*

2677 A1029 5s multicolored .25 .25

Se-tenant with label showing quote from author's work.

Penny Black — A1030

1980, Apr. 24 *Perf. 13*

2678 A1030 25s dark red & sepia .85 .60

London 1980 International Stamp Exhibition, May 6-14; printed se-tenant with label showing Rowland Hill between every two stamps.

No. 2678 was overprinted "UPU 1984" in 1982. Value $3.

Demeter H. Tchorbadjiiski, Self-portrait — A1031

1980, Apr. 29

2679 A1031 5s shown .25 .25
2680 A1031 13s "Our People" .25 .25

Nikolai Giaurov — A1032

1980, Apr. 30

2681 A1032 5s multicolored .25 .25

Nikolai Giaurov (b. 1930), opera singer; printed se-tenant with label showing Boris Godunov.

Raising Red Flag Reichstag Building, Berlin — A1033

Armistice, 35th Anniversary: 13s, Soviet Army memorial, Berlin-Treptow.

1980, May 6 *Perf. 13x13½*

2682 A1033 5s multicolored .25 .25
2683 A1033 13s multicolored .25 .25

Numeral — A1034

1979 *Perf. 14*

2684 A1034 2s ultra .25 .25
2685 A1034 5s rose car .25 .25

A1034a

1980, May 12 Photo. *Perf. 13*

2685A A1034a 5s multicolored .25 .25

75th Anniv. of Teachers' Union.

A1035

1980, May 14 Photo. *Perf. 13*

2686	A1035	13s multicolored	.40	.40

Warsaw Pact, 25th anniv.

A1036

Statues.

1980, June 10

2687	A1036	2s multicolored	.25	.25
2688	A1036	13s multicolored	.40	.35
2689	A1036	25s multicolored	.80	.60
2690	A1036	35s multicolored	1.40	.80
2691	A1036	43s multicolored	1.75	1.10
2692	A1036	1 l multicolored	3.00	1.50
		Nos. 2687-2692 (6)	7.60	4.60

Souvenir Sheet

2693	A1036	2 l multicolored	7.75	4.00

22nd Summer Olympic Games, Moscow, July 19-Aug. 3.

In 1981 a souvenir sheet was issued, containing one 50s stamp, perf 13, depicting Olympic medal and lion. Size 100mmx105mm. Value $18.50.

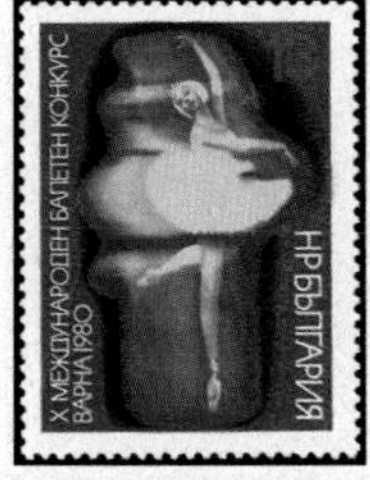

A1037

1980, Sept. Photo. *Perf. 13*

2694	A1037	13s multicolored	.40	.25

10th Intl. Ballet Competition, Varna.

Hotel Europa, Sofia A1038

Hotels: No. 2696, Bulgaria, Burgas, vert. No. 2697, Plovdiv, Plovdiv. No. 2698, Riga, Russe, vert. No. 2699, Varna, Djuba.

1980, July 11

2695	A1038	23s lt ultra & multi	.50	.25
2696	A1038	23s orange & multi	.50	.25
2697	A1038	23s gray & multi	.50	.25
2698	A1038	23s blue & multi	.50	.25
2699	A1038	23s yellow & multi	.50	.25
		Nos. 2695-2699 (5)	2.50	1.25

See No. 2766.

Ship Type of 1975

Ships of 16th, 17th Centuries: 5s, Christ of Lubeck, galleon. 8s, Roman galley. 13s, Eagle, Russian galleon. 23s, Mayflower. 35s, Maltese galley. 53s, Royal Louis, galleon.

1980, July 14

2700	A873	5s multicolored	.25	.25
2701	A873	8s multicolored	.25	.25
2702	A873	13s multicolored	.25	.25
2703	A873	23s multicolored	.50	.25
2704	A873	35s multicolored	.85	.25
2705	A873	53s multicolored	1.40	.40
		Nos. 2700-2705 (6)	3.50	1.65

On Aug. 28, 1980, a miniature sheet of six stamps, denominated 5s to 45s, perf 13, was issued. Size: 115mmx135mm. Inscribed "ESSEN 1980" in selvage and serially numbered. Value $55.

Int'l Year of the Child, 1979 — A1040

Designs: Children's drawings and IYC emblem. 43s, Tower. 5s, 25s, 43s, vert.

Perf. 12½x12, 12x12½

1980, Sep. 1 Litho.

2708	A1040	3s multicolored	.25	.25
2709	A1040	5s multicolored	.25	.25
2710	A1040	8s multicolored	.25	.25
2711	A1040	13s multicolored	.25	.25
2712	A1040	25s multicolored	.55	.25
2713	A1040	35s multicolored	.70	.25
2714	A1040	43s multicolored	.95	.25
		Nos. 2708-2714 (7)	3.20	1.75

Helicopter, Missile Transport, Tank — A1041

1980, Sept. 23 Photo. *Perf. 13*

2715	A1041	3s shown	.25	.25
2716	A1041	5s Jet, radar, rocket	.25	.25
2717	A1041	8s Helicopter, ships	.25	.25
		Nos. 2715-2717 (3)	.75	.75

Bulgarian People's Army, 35th anniversary.

St. Anne, by Leonardo da Vinci A1042

Da Vinci Paintings: 8s, 13s, Annunciation (diff.). 25s, Adoration of the Kings. 35s, Lady with the Ermine. 50s, Mona Lisa.

1980, Oct. 10

2718	A1042	5s multicolored	.25	.25
2719	A1042	8s multicolored	.25	.25
2720	A1042	13s multicolored	.25	.25
2721	A1042	25s multicolored	.65	.25
2722	A1042	35s multicolored	.90	.25
		Nos. 2718-2722 (5)	2.30	1.25

Souvenir Sheet

Imperf

2723	A1042	50s multicolored	1.25	.40

International Peace Conference, Sofia — A1043

1980, Sept. 4 Photo. *Perf. 13*

2724	A1043	25s multicolored	.50	.25

Yordan Yovkov (1880-1937), Writer — A1044

1980, Sept. 19

2725	A1044	5s multicolored	.25	.25

Se-tenant with label showing scene from Yovkov's work.

International Samples Fair, Plovdiv — A1045

1980, Sept. 24 *Perf. 13½x13*

2726	A1045	5s multicolored	.25	.25

On Oct. 1, 1980, a souvenir sheet containing one perf 13 50s stamp depicting a map of Europe and dove, was issued. Size: 80mmx80mm). Serially numbered. Value $30.

Blooming Cacti — A1045a

1980, Nov. 4 Photo. *Perf. 13*

2726A	A1045a	5s multicolored	.25	.25
2726B	A1045a	13s multicolored	.25	.25
2726C	A1045a	25s multicolored	.75	.25
2726D	A1045a	35s multicolored	1.10	.45
2726E	A1045a	53s multicolored	2.00	.55
		Nos. 2726A-2726E (5)	4.35	1.75

Souvenir Sheet

25th Anniv. of Bulgarian UN Membership — A1045b

1980, Nov. 25

2726F	A1045b	60s multicolored	3.50	3.00

World Ski Racing Championship, Velingrad — A1046

1981, Jan. 17 Photo. *Perf. 13*

2727	A1046	43s multicolored	1.00	.40

Hawthorn A1047

Designs: Medicinal herbs.

1981, Jan.

2728	A1047	3s shown	.25	.25
2729	A1047	5s St. John's wort	.25	.25
2730	A1047	13s Common elder	.25	.25
2731	A1047	25s Blackberries	.75	.25
2732	A1047	35s Lime	1.10	.25
2733	A1047	43s Wild briar	1.50	.45
		Nos. 2728-2733 (6)	4.10	1.70

Slalom — A1048

1981, Feb. 27 Photo. *Perf. 13*

2734	A1048	43s multicolored	1.00	.40

Evian Alpine World Ski Cup Championship, Borovets.

Nuclear Traces, Research Institute — A1049

1981, Mar. 10 *Perf. 13½x13*

2735 A1049 13s gray & blk .35 .35

Nuclear Research Institute, Dubna, USSR, 25th anniversary.

Congress Emblem — A1050

1981, Mar. 12 *Perf. 13½*

2736 A1050 5s shown .25 .25
2737 A1050 13s Stars .25 .25
2738 A1050 23s Teletape .60 .25
Nos. 2736-2738 (3) 1.10 .75

Souvenir Sheet

2739 A1050 50s Demeter Blagoev, George Dimitrov 1.25 .75

12th Bulgarian Communist Party Congress. Nos. 2736-2738 each printed se-tenant with label.

Paintings by Zachary Zograf — A1050a

1981, Mar. 23 Photo. *Perf. 12x12½*

2739A A1050a 5s multicolored .25 .25
2739B A1050a 13s multicolored .40 .25
2739C A1050a 23s multicolored .75 .25
2739D A1050a 25s multicolored .90 .25
2739E A1050a 35s multicolored 1.25 .25
Nos. 2739A-2739E (5) 3.55 1.25

Nos. 2739A-2739C are vert.

EXPO '81, Plovdiv — A1050b

1981, Apr. 7

2739F A1050b 5s multicolored .25 .25
2739G A1050b 8s multicolored .25 .25
2739H A1050b 13s multicolored .70 .25
2739J A1050b 25s multicolored 1.40 .25
2739K A1050b 53s multicolored 2.50 .70
Nos. 2739F-2739K (5) 5.10 1.70

Centenary of Bulgarian Shipbuilding — A1050c

1981, Apr. 15 Photo. *Perf. 13*

2739L A1050c 35s Georgi Dimitrov, liner 1.00 .25
2739M A1050c 43s 5th from RMS, freighter 1.25 .45
2739N A1050c 53s Khan Asparuch, tanker 1.60 .55
Nos. 2739L-2739N (3) 3.85 1.25

On May 15, 1980, a souvenir sheet commemorating the 125th anniv. of the European Danube Commission was issued. It contains two 25s stamps depicting ships, perf 13, was issued. Size: 90mmx124mm. Serially numbered. Value $22.50.

A miniature sheet containing eight perf 13 35s stamps depicting ships, was issued Sept. 25, 1981. Size: 109mmx176mm. Value $20.

Arabian Horse A1051

Various breeds.

1980, Nov. 27 Litho. *Perf. 12½x12*

2740 A1051 3s multicolored .25 .25
2741 A1051 5s multicolored .25 .25
2742 A1051 13s multicolored .80 .25
2743 A1051 23s multicolored 1.40 .25
2744 A1051 35s multicolored 2.40 .25
Nos. 2740-2744 (5) 5.10 1.25

Vassil Stoin, Ethnologist, Birth Centenary — A1052

1980, Dec. 5 Photo. *Perf. 13½x13*

2745 A1052 5s multicolored .25 .25

12th Bulgarian Communist Party Congress — A1052a

1980, Dec. 26 Photo. *Perf. 13x13½*

2745A A1052a 5s Party symbols .25 .25

New Year A1053

1980, Dec. 8 *Perf. 13*

2746 A1053 5s shown .25 .25
2747 A1053 13s Cup, date .25 .25

Culture Palace, Sofia A1053a

1981, Mar. 13 Photo. *Perf. 13*

2747A A1053a 5s multicolored .25 .25

Vienna Hofburg Palace A1054

1981, May 15 Photo. *Perf. 13*

2748 A1054 35s multicolored .85 .25

WIPA 1981 Intl. Philatelic Exhibition, Vienna, May 22-31.

34th Farmers' Union Congress — A1055

1981, May 18 *Perf. 13½*

2749 A1055 5s shown .25 .25
2750 A1055 8s Flags .25 .25
2751 A1055 13s Flags, diff. .25 .25
Nos. 2749-2751 (3) .75 .75

Wild Cat — A1056

1981, May 27

2752 A1056 5s shown .25 .25
2753 A1056 13s Boar .50 .25
2754 A1056 23s Mouflon .85 .25
2755 A1056 25s Mountain goat .95 .25
2756 A1056 35s Stag 1.25 .25
2757 A1056 53s Roe deer 2.25 .50
Nos. 2752-2757 (6) 6.05 1.75

Souvenir Sheet

Perf. 13½x13

2758 A1056 1 l Stag, diff. 2.50 1.25

EXPO '81 Intl. Hunting Exhibition, Plovdiv. Nos. 2752-2757 each se-tenant with labels showing various hunting rifles. No. 2758 contains one stamp, size: 48½x39mm.

25th Anniv. of UNESCO Membership A1057

1981, June 11 *Perf. 13*

2759 A1057 13s multicolored .35 .35

Hotel Type of 1980

1981, July 13 Photo. *Perf. 13*

2766 A1038 23s Veliko Tirnovo Hotel .50 .25

Flying Figure, Sculpture by Velichko Minekov — A1059

Bulgarian Social Democratic Party Buzludja Congress, 90th Anniv. (Minkov Sculpture): 13s, Advancing Female Figure.

1981, July 16 *Perf. 13½*

2767 A1059 5s multicolored .25 .25
2768 A1059 13s multicolored .25 .25

Kukeri, by Georg Tschapkanov A1060

1981, May 28 Photo. *Perf. 13*

2769 A1060 5s multicolored .25 .25

13th Natl. Festival of Humor and Satire.

Statistics Office Centenary A1061

1981, June 9

2770 A1061 5s multicolored .25 .25

Gold Dish A1063

Designs: Goldsmiths' works, 7th-9th cent.

1981, July 21

2772 A1063 5s multicolored .25 .25
2773 A1063 13s multicolored .25 .25
2774 A1063 23s multicolored .50 .25
2775 A1063 25s multicolored .60 .35
2776 A1063 35s multicolored .85 .50
2777 A1063 53s multicolored 1.40 .60
Nos. 2772-2777 (6) 3.85 2.20

35th Anniv. of Frontier Force — A1064

1981, July 28 *Perf. 13½x13*

2778 A1064 5s multicolored .25 .25

1300th Anniv. of First Bulgarian State — A1065

Designs: No. 2779, Sts. Cyril and Methodius. No. 2780, 9th cent. bas-relief. 8s, Floor plan, Round Church, Preslav, 10th cent. 12s, Four Evangelists of King Ivan Alexander, miniature, 1356. No. 2783, King Ivan Asen II memorial column. No. 2784, Warriors on horseback. 16s, April uprising, 1876. 23s, Russian liberators, Tirnovo. 25s, Social Democratic Party founding, 1891. 35s, September uprising, 1923. 41s, Fatherland Front. 43s, Prime Minister George Dimitrov, 5th Communist Party Congress, 1948. 50s, Lion, 10th cent. bas-relief. 53s, 10th Communist Party Congress. 55s, Kremikovski Metalurgical Plant. 1 l, Brezhnev, Gen. Todor Zhivkov.

1981, Aug. 10

2779 A1065 5s multicolored .25 .25
2780 A1065 5s multicolored .25 .25
2781 A1065 8s multicolored .25 .25
2782 A1065 12s multicolored .25 .25
2783 A1065 13s multicolored .25 .25
2784 A1065 13s multicolored .25 .25
2785 A1065 16s multicolored .45 .25
2786 A1065 23s multicolored .50 .25
2787 A1065 25s multicolored .60 .25
2788 A1065 35s multicolored .85 .25
2789 A1065 41s multicolored 1.00 .45
2790 A1065 43s multicolored 1.10 .45
2791 A1065 53s multicolored 1.40 .50
2792 A1065 55s multicolored 1.40 .50
Nos. 2779-2792 (14) 8.80 4.40

Souvenir Sheets

2793 A1065 50s multicolored 1.00 .75
2794 A1065 1 l multicolored 2.75 1.90

European Volleyball Championship A1066

1981, Sept. 16 *Perf. 13*

2795 A1066 13s multicolored .35 .35

Pegasus, Bronze Sculpture (Word Day) — A1067

1981, Oct. 2

2796 A1067 5s olive & cream .25 .25

World Food Day — A1068

1981, Oct. 16

2797 A1068 13s multicolored .35 .35

Professional Theater Centenary A1069

1981, Oct. 30

2798 A1069 5s multicolored .25 .25

Anti-Apartheid Year — A1070

1981, Dec. 2

2799 A1070 5s multicolored .25 .25

Espana '82 World Cup Soccer — A1071

Designs: Various soccer players.

1981, Dec.

2800 A1071 5s multicolored .25 .25
2801 A1071 13s multicolored .25 .25
2802 A1071 43s multicolored .70 .25
2803 A1071 53s multicolored .95 .35
Nos. 2800-2803 (4) 2.15 1.10

Heritage Day A1072

1981, Nov. 21 **Photo.** *Perf. 13*

2804 A1072 13s multicolored .25 .25

Souvenir Sheet

2804A A1072 60s multicolored 8.50 1.90

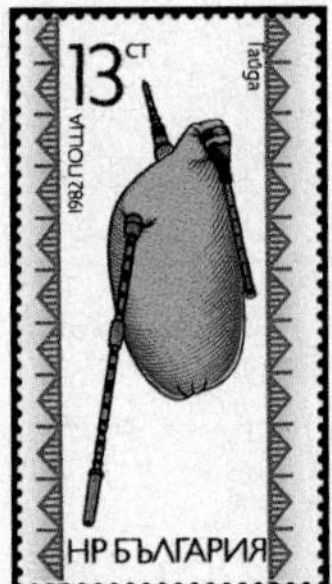

Bagpipe — A1073

1982, Jan. 14

2805 A1073 13s shown .25 .25
2806 A1073 25s Flutes .40 .25
2807 A1073 30s Rebec .50 .25
2808 A1073 35s Flute, recorder .55 .25
2809 A1073 44s Mandolin .75 .30
Nos. 2805-2809 (5) 2.45 1.30

Public Libraries and Reading Rooms, 125th Anniv — A1074

1982, Jan. 20

2810 A1074 5s dk grn .25 .25

Souvenir Sheet

Intl. Decade for Women (1975-1985) — A1075

1982, Mar. 8

2811 A1075 1 l multicolored 1.75 1.00

New Year 1982 A1076

1981, Dec. 22 **Photo.** *Perf. 13*

2812 A1076 5s Ornament .25 .25
2813 A1076 13s Ornament, diff. .25 .25

The Sofia Plains, by Nicolas Petrov (1881-1916) — A1077

1982, Feb. 10 *Perf. 12½*

2814 A1077 5s shown .25 .25
2815 A1077 13s Girl Embroidering .25 .25
2816 A1077 30s Fields of Peshtera .50 .25
Nos. 2814-2816 (3) 1.00 .75

35th Anniv. of UNICEF (1981) — A1078

Mother and Child Paintings.

1982, Feb. 25 *Perf. 14*

2817 A1078 53s Vladimir Dimitrov 1.50 .55
2818 A1078 53s Basil Stoilov 1.50 .55
2819 A1078 53s Ivan Milev 1.50 .55
2820 A1078 53s Liliana Russeva 1.50 .55
Nos. 2817-2820 (4) 6.00 2.20

Figures, by Vladamir Dimitrov (1882-1961) — A1079

1982, Mar. 8 **Litho.**

2821 A1079 5s shown .25 .25
2822 A1079 8s Landscape .25 .25
2823 A1079 13s View of Istanbul .25 .25
2824 A1079 25s Harvesters, vert. .50 .25
2825 A1079 30s Woman in a Landscape, vert. .60 .25
2826 A1079 35s Peasant Woman, vert. .75 .30
Nos. 2821-2826 (6) 2.60 1.55

Souvenir Sheet

2827 A1079 50s Self-portrait 1.25 .95

No. 2827 contains one stamp, size: 54x32mm.

Trade Union Congress — A1080

1982, Apr. 8 **Photo.** *Perf. 13½*

2828 A1080 5s Dimitrov reading union paper .25 .25
2829 A1080 5s Culture Palace .25 .25

Nos. 2828-2829 se-tenant with label showing text.

Marsh Snowdrop A1081

Designs: Medicinal plants.

1982, Apr. 10 **Photo.** *Perf. 13*

2830 A1081 3s shown .25 .25
2831 A1081 5s Chicory .25 .25
2832 A1081 8s Chamaenerium angustifolium .25 .25
2833 A1081 13s Solomon's seal .35 .25
2834 A1081 25s Violets .80 .25
2835 A1081 35s Centaury 1.25 .35
Nos. 2830-2835 (6) 3.15 1.60

Cosmonauts' Day — A1082

1982, Apr. 12 *Perf. 13½*

2836 A1082 13s Salyut-Soyuz link-up .35 .35

Se-tenant with label showing K.E. Tsiolkovsky (space pioneer).

Souvenir Sheet

SOZFILEX Stamp Exhibition — A1083

1982, May 7 *Perf. 13*

2837 A1083 50s Dimitrov, emblems 3.00 1.25

14th Komsomol Congress (Youth Communists) — A1084

1982, May 25

2838 A1084 5s multicolored .25 .25

PHILEXFRANCE '82 Intl. Stamp Exhibition, Paris, June 11-21 — A1085

1982, May 28

2839 A1085 42s France #1, Bulgaria #1 .85 .30

19th Cent. Fresco A1086

Designs: Various floral pattern frescoes.

1982, June 8 *Perf. 11½*

2840	A1086	5s red & multi	.25	.25
2841	A1086	13s green & multi	.25	.25
2842	A1086	25s violet & multi	.50	.25
2843	A1086	30s ol grn & multi	.65	.25
2844	A1086	42s blue & multi	1.00	.30
2845	A1086	60s brown & multi	1.25	.50
		Nos. 2840-2845 (6)	3.90	1.80

Souvenir Sheet

George Dimitrov (1882-1949), First Prime Minister — A1087

1982, June 15 *Perf. 13*

2846 A1087 50s multicolored 1.25 .50

9th Congress of the National Front — A1088

1982, June 21 **Photo.** *Perf. 13*

2847 A1088 5s Dimitrov .25 .25

35th Anniv. of Balkan Bulgarian Airline — A1089

1982, June 28 *Perf. 13½x13*

2848 A1089 42s multicolored .85 .30

A1090

1982, July 15 *Perf. 13*

2849 A1090 13s multicolored .40 .25

Nuclear disarmament.

A1091

1982, July **Photo.** *Perf. 13*

2850 A1091 5s multicolored .25 .25
2851 A1091 13s multicolored .25 .25

Souvenir Sheet

2852 A1091 1 l multicolored 1.75 1.00

Ludmila Zhivkova (b. 1942), artist.

5th Congress of Bulgarian Painters — A1092

1982, July 27 *Perf. 13½*

2853 A1092 5s multicolored .25 .25

Se-tenant with label showing text.

Flag of Peace Youth Assembly — A1093

Various children's drawings. Frame & inscriptions: 3s, red, 5s, blue, 8s, pale green, 13s, gold.

1982, Aug. 10 *Perf. 14*

2853A	A1093	3s multicolored	.25	.25
2853B	A1093	5s multicolored	.25	.25
2853C	A1093	8s multicolored	.25	.25
2853D	A1093	13s multicolored	.25	.25
		Nos. 2853A-2853D (4)	1.00	1.00

Souvenir Sheet

Perf. 14, Imperf.

2853E A1093 50s In balloon 3.25 .35

See Nos. 2864-2870, 3052-3058, 3321-3327.

10th Anniv. of UN Conference on Human Environment, Stockholm — A1093a

1982, Nov. 10 *Perf. 13*

2854 A1093a 13s dk blue & grn .35 .35

A1094

Designs: No. 2855, Park Hotel Moskva, Sofia. No. 2856, Tchernomore, Varna.

1982, Oct. 20 **Photo.** *Perf. 13*

2855 A1094 32s lt blue & multi .75 .25
2856 A1094 32s pink & multi .75 .25

A1095

1982, Nov. 4

2857 A1095 13s Cruiser Aurora, Vostok I .35 .35

October Revolution, 65th anniv.

60th Anniv. of Institute of Communications A1096

1982, Dec. 9

2858 A1096 5s ultra .25 .25

60th Anniv. of USSR A1097

1982, Dec. 9

2859 A1097 13s multicolored .35 .35

The Piano, by Pablo Picasso (1881-1973) A1098

Perf. 11½x12½

1982, Dec. 24 **Litho.**

2860	A1098	13s shown	.25	.25
2861	A1098	30s Portrait of Jacqueline	.70	.25
2862	A1098	42s Maternity	1.25	.45
		Nos. 2860-2862 (3)	2.20	.95

Souvenir Sheet

2863 A1098 1 l Self-portrait 2.75 .75

Children's Drawings Type of 1982

Various children's drawings. 8s, 13s, 50s vert. 3s has pale violet frame & inscriptions, 5s orange frame & inscriptions.

1982, Dec. 28 *Perf. 14*

2864	A1093	3s multicolored	.25	.25
2865	A1093	5s multicolored	.25	.25
2866	A1093	8s multicolored	.25	.25
2867	A1093	13s multicolored	.25	.25
2868	A1093	25s multicolored	.65	.25
2869	A1093	30s multicolored	.70	.25
		Nos. 2864-2869 (6)	2.35	1.50

Souvenir Sheet

Perf. 14, Imperf.

2870 A1093 50s Shaking hands 2.75 .35

New Year A1100

1982, Dec. 28 **Photo.** *Perf. 13*

2872 A1100 5s multicolored .25 .25
2873 A1100 13s multicolored .25 .25

A1101

1982, Dec. 28

2874 A1101 25s Robert Koch .65 .25
2875 A1101 30s Simon Bolivar .65 .25
2876 A1101 30s Rabindranath Tagore (1861-1941) .65 .25
Nos. 2874-2876 (3) 1.95 .75

No. 2874 also for TB bacillus cent.

A1102

1983, Jan. 10 Photo. ***Perf. 13x13½***

2877 A1102 5s olive & brown .25 .25

Vassil Levski (1837-73), revolutionary.

Universiade Games — A1103

1983, Feb. 15 ***Perf. 13***

2878 A1103 30s Downhill skiing .70 .25

Fresh-water Fish — A1104

1983, Mar. 24 Photo. ***Perf. 13½x13***

2879 A1104 3s Pike .25 .25
2880 A1104 5s Sturgeon .25 .25
2881 A1104 13s Chub .25 .25
2882 A1104 25s Perch 1.00 .25
2883 A1104 30s Catfish 1.00 .25
2884 A1104 42s Trout 1.25 .55
Nos. 2879-2884 (6) 4.00 1.80

Karl Marx (1818-1883) A1105

1983, Apr. 5 ***Perf. 13x13½***

2885 A1105 13s multicolored .35 .35

Jaroslav Hasek (1883-1923) — A1106

1983, Apr. 20 Photo. ***Perf. 13***

2886 A1106 13s multicolored .35 .35

Martin Luther (1483-1546) A1107

1983, May 10

2887 A1107 13s multicolored .50 .50

55th Anniv. of Komsomol Youth Movement — A1108

1983, May 13

2888 A1108 5s "PMC" .25 .25

A1109

National costumes.

1983, May 17 Litho. ***Perf. 14***

2889 A1109 5s Khaskovo .25 .25
2890 A1109 8s Pernik .25 .25
2891 A1109 13s Burgas .25 .25
2892 A1109 25s Tolbukhin .95 .25
2893 A1109 30s Blagoevgrad 1.10 .25
2894 A1109 42s Topolovgrad 1.40 .25
Nos. 2889-2894 (6) 4.20 1.50

A1111

6th Intl. Satire and Humor Biennial, Gabrovo: Old Man Feeding Chickens.

1983, May 20

2900 A1111 5s multicolored .25 .25

Christo Smirnensky (1898-1983), Poet — A1112

1983, May 25

2901 A1112 5s multicolored .25 .25

17th Intl. Geodesists' Congress A1113

1983, May 27

2902 A1113 30s Emblem .60 .25

Interarch '83 Architecture Exhibition, Sofia — A1114

1983, June 6

2903 A1114 30s multicolored .70 .25

8th European Chess Championships, Plovdiv A1115

1983, June 20 Photo. ***Perf. 13***

2904 A1115 13s Chess pieces, map of Europe .40 .40

Souvenir Sheet

BRASILIANA '83 Philatelic Exhibition — A1116

Brazilian and Bulgarian stamps

1983, June 24

2905 A1116 1 l multicolored 2.25 1.40

Social Democratic Party Congress of Russia, 80th Anniv. — A1118

Design: Lenin addressing congress.

1983, July 29 Photo. ***Perf. 13***

2907 A1118 5s multicolored .25 .25

Ilinden-Preobrazhensky Insurrection, 80th Anniv. — A1119

1983, July 29

2908 A1119 5s Gun, dagger, book .25 .25

Institute of Mining and Geology, Sofia, 30th Anniv. — A1120

1983, Aug. 10

2909 A1120 5s multicolored .25 .25

60th Anniv. of September 1923 Uprising — A1121

1983, Aug. 19

2910 A1121 5s multicolored .25 .25
2911 A1121 13s multicolored .25 .25

Angora Cat A1123

1983, Sept. 26 ***Perf. 13***

2917 A1123 5s shown .25 .25
2918 A1123 13s Siamese .50 .25
2919 A1123 20s Abyssinian, vert. .80 .25
2920 A1123 25s Persian .80 .25
2921 A1123 30s European, vert. 1.10 .50
2922 A1123 42s Indochinese 1.50 .55
Nos. 2917-2922 (6) 4.95 2.05

Animated Film Festival — A1124

1983, Sept. 15 Photo. ***Perf. 14x13½***

2923 A1124 5s Articulation layout .25 .25

Trevethick's Engine, 1804 — A1125

Locomotives: 13s, Blenkinsop's Prince Royal, 1810. 42s, Hedley's Puffing Billy, 1812. 60s, Adler (first German locomotive), 1835.

1983, Oct. 20 ***Perf. 13***

2924	A1125	5s multicolored	.25	.25
2925	A1125	13s multicolored	.70	.25
2926	A1125	42s multicolored	2.00	.70
2927	A1125	60s multicolored	2.75	.80
		Nos. 2924-2927 (4)	5.70	2.00

See Nos. 2983-2987.

Souvenir Sheet

Liberation Monument, Plovdiv — A1126

1983, Nov. 4

2928 A1126 50s multicolored 1.25 .75

Philatelic Federation, 90th anniv.

Sofia Opera, 75th Anniv. — A1127

1983, Dec. 2 ***Perf. 13x13½***

2929 A1127 5s Mask, lyre, laurel .25 .25

Composers' Assoc., 50th Anniv. — A1128

Composers: 5s, Ioan Kukuzel (14th cent.) 8s, Atanasov. 13s, Petko Stainov. 20s, Veselin Stodiov. 25s, Liubomir Pipkov. 30s, Pancho Vladigerov. Se-tenant with labels showing compositions.

1983, Dec. 5

2930	A1128	5s multicolored	.25	.25
2931	A1128	8s multicolored	.25	.25
2932	A1128	13s multicolored	.25	.25
2933	A1128	20s multicolored	.30	.25
2934	A1128	25s multicolored	.40	.25
2935	A1128	30s multicolored	.50	.25
		Nos. 2930-2935 (6)	1.95	1.50

New Year 1984 A1129

1983, Dec. 10 ***Perf. 13***

2936 A1129 5s multicolored .25 .25

Angelo Donni, by Raphael A1130

1983, Dec. 22 ***Perf. 14***

2937	A1130	5s shown	.25	.25
2938	A1130	13s Cardinal	.25	.25
2939	A1130	30s Baldassare Castiglioni	.45	.25
2940	A1130	42s Donna Belata	.70	.30
		Nos. 2937-2940 (4)	1.65	1.05

Souvenir Sheet

2941 A1130 1 l Sistine Madonna 1.75 1.25

Bat, World Wildlife Emblem — A1131

Various bats and rodents.

1983, Dec. 30 ***Perf. 13***

2942	A1131	12s multicolored	.75	.35
2943	A1131	13s multicolored	.95	.55
2944	A1131	20s multicolored	1.25	.75
2945	A1131	30s multicolored	1.75	1.00
2946	A1131	42s multicolored	2.75	1.25
		Nos. 2942-2946 (5)	7.45	3.90

Dmitri Mendeleev (1834-1907), Russian Chemist — A1132

1984, Mar. 14

2947 A1132 13s multicolored .35 .25

Ljuben Karavelov, Poet and Freedom Fighter, Birth Sesquicentenary A1133

1984, Jan. 31 ***Perf. 13x13½***

2948 A1133 5s multicolored .25 .25

Tanker Gen. V.I. Zaimov A1137

1984, Mar. 22 ***Perf. 13½***

2959	A1137	5s shown	.25	.25
2960	A1137	13s Mesta	.25	.25
2961	A1137	25s Veleka	.55	.25
2962	A1137	32s Ferry	.80	.25
2963	A1137	42s Cargo ship Rossen	1.25	.45
		Nos. 2959-2963 (5)	3.10	1.45

Souvenir Sheet

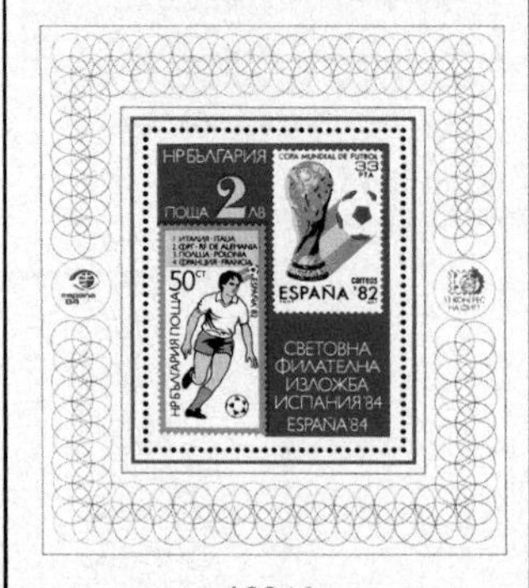

World Cup Soccer Commemorative of 1982, Spain No. 2281 — A1137a

1984, Apr. 18 Photo. ***Perf. 13x13½***

2963A A1137a 2 l multicolored 6.50 5.00

ESPANA '84.

Dove with Letter over Globe — A1138

1984, Apr. 24 ***Perf. 13***

2964 A1138 5s multicolored .25 .25

World Youth Stamp Exhibition, Pleven, Oct. 5-11.

Berries — A1139

1984, May 5

2965	A1139	5s Cherries	.25	.25
2966	A1139	8s Strawberries	.25	.25
2967	A1139	13s Blackberries	.25	.25
2968	A1139	20s Raspberries	.50	.25
2969	A1139	42s Currants	1.40	.40
		Nos. 2965-2969 (5)	2.65	1.40

A1140

1984, May 23

2970 A1140 13s Athlete, doves .35 .35

6th Republican Spartikiade games,

A1142

1984, June 12

2972 A1142 5s Folk singer, drum .25 .25

6th amateur art festival.

Bulgarian-Soviet Relations, 50th Anniv. — A1143

1984, June 27

2973 A1143 13s Initialed seal .35 .35

Doves and Pigeons A1144

1984, July 6 Litho. ***Perf. 14***

2974	A1144	5s Rock dove	.25	.25
2975	A1144	13s Stock dove	.25	.25
2976	A1144	20s Wood pigeon	.55	.25
2977	A1144	30s Turtle dove	.80	.25
2978	A1144	42s Domestic pigeon	1.25	.45
		Nos. 2974-2978 (5)	3.10	1.45

1st Natl. Communist Party Congress, 60th Anniv. — A1145

1984, May 18 Photo. ***Perf. 13½x13***

2979 A1145 5s multicolored .25 .25

Souvenir Sheet

Intl. Stamp Exhibition, Essen, May 26-31 — A1146

Europa Conf. stamps: a, 1980. b, 1981.

1984, May 22 *Perf. 13x13½*
2980 A1146 Sheet of 2 *7.50 5.00*
a.-b. 1.50 l multi *3.50 2.50*

Mount Everest A1147

1984, May 31 *Perf. 13*
2981 A1147 5s multicolored .25 .25

1st Bulgarian Everest climbing expedition, Apr. 20-May 9.

Souvenir Sheet

UPU Congress, Hamburg — A1148

1984, June 11 *Perf. 13½x13*
2982 A1148 3 l Sailing ship *7.50 5.00*

Locomotives Type of 1983

1984, July 31 *Perf. 13*
2983 A1125 13s Best Friend of Charleston, 1830, US .40 .25
2984 A1125 25s Saxonia, 1836, Dresden .65 .40
2985 A1125 30s Lafayette, 1837, US .80 .45
2986 A1125 42s Borsig, 1841, Germany 1.25 .65
2987 A1125 60s Philadelphia, 1843, Austria 1.90 .95
Nos. 2983-2987 (5) 5.00 2.70

September 9 Revolution, 40th Anniv. — A1149

1984, Aug. 4
2988 A1149 5s K, production quality emblem .25 .25
2989 A1149 20s Victory Monument, Sofia .45 .25
2990 A1149 30s Star, "9" .60 .45
Nos. 2988-2990 (3) 1.30 .95

Paintings by Nenko Balkanski (1907-1977) — A1150

1984, Sept. 17 *Perf. 14*
2991 A1150 5s Boy Playing Harmonica, vert. .25 .25
2992 A1150 30s A Paris Window, vert. .85 .40
2993 A1150 42s Double Portrait 1.10 .55
Nos. 2991-2993 (3) 2.20 1.20

Souvenir Sheet

2994 A1150 1 l Self-portrait, vert. 2.25 1.50

MLADPOST '84 International Youth Stamp Exhibition, Pleven — A1151

Buildings in Pleven: 5s, Mausoleum to Russian soldiers, 1877-78 Russo-Turkish War. 13s, Panorama Building.

1984, Sept. 20 *Perf. 13*
2995 A1151 5s multicolored .25 .25
2996 A1151 13s multicolored .30 .25

Septembrist Young Pioneers Org., 40th Anniv. — A1152

1984, Sept. 21 **Photo.** *Perf. 13*
2997 A1152 5s multicolored .25 .25

Nikola Vapzarov A1153

1984, Oct. 2
2998 A1153 5s maroon & pale yel .25 .25

Natl. Soccer, 75th Anniv. A1154

1984, Oct. 3
2999 A1154 42s multicolored .85 .40

Souvenir Sheet

MLADPOST '84 — A1155

1984, Oct. 5 **Photo.** *Perf. 13*
3000 A1155 50s multicolored 1.10 .50

Bridges and Maps — A1156

1984, Oct. 5 **Photo.** *Perf. 13½x13*
3001 A1156 5s Devil's Bridge, Arda River .25 .25
3002 A1156 13s Koljo-Fitscheto, Bjala .55 .25
3003 A1156 30s Asparuchow, Warna 1.00 .55
3004 A1156 42s Bebresch Highway Bridge, Botevgrad 1.75 .75
Nos. 3001-3004 (4) 3.55 1.80

Souvenir Sheet

3005 A1156 1 l Bridge of Friendship, Russia 5.50 2.75

Intl. Olympic Committee, 90th Anniv. — A1158

1984, Oct. 24 **Photo.** *Perf. 13*
3007 A1158 13s multicolored .35 .25

A1159

Pelecanus crispus.

1984, Nov. 2
3008 A1159 5s Adult, young .50 .30
3009 A1159 13s Two adults .95 .45
3010 A1159 20s Adult in water 1.50 .75
3011 A1159 32s In flight 3.25 1.25
Nos. 3008-3011 (4) 6.20 2.75

World Wildlife Fund.

A1160

1984, Nov. 2
3012 A1160 5s multicolored .25 .25

Anton Ivanov (1884-1942), labor leader.

Women's Socialist Movement, 70th Anniv. — A1161

1984, Nov. 9
3013 A1161 5s multicolored .25 .25

Telecommunication Towers — A1162

1984, Nov. 23
3014 A1162 5s Snezhanka .25 .25
3015 A1162 1 l Orelek 1.90 1.00

Snowflakes, New Year 1985 — A1163

1984, Dec. 5
3016 A1163 5s Doves, posthorns .25 .25
3017 A1163 13s Doves, blossom .25 .25

Paintings by Stoyan Venev (b. 1904) — A1164

1984, Dec. 10 **Litho.**
3018 A1164 5s September Nights .25 .25
3019 A1164 30s Man with Three Medals .70 .45
3020 A1164 42s The Best 1.25 .60
Nos. 3018-3020 (3) 2.20 1.30

Butterflies A1165

1984, Dec. 14 *Perf. 11½*

3021 A1165 13s Inachis io .25 .25
3022 A1165 25s Papilio machaon .65 .35
3023 A1165 30s Brintesia circe .85 .45
3024 A1165 42s Anthocaris cardamines 1.25 .60
3025 A1165 60s Vanessa atalanta 1.75 .90
Nos. 3021-3025 (5) 4.75 2.55

Souvenir Sheet

3026 A1165 1 l Limenitis populi 2.25 1.00

A1166

1984, Dec. 18 Photo. *Perf. 13x13½*

3027 A1166 13s multicolored .35 .25

Cesar Augusto Sandino (1895-1934), Nicaraguan freedom fighter.

A1167

1984, Dec. 28 Litho. *Perf. 14*

3028 A1167 5s The Three Graces .25 .25
3029 A1167 13s Cupid and the Graces .35 .25
3030 A1167 30s Original Sin .70 .35
3031 A1167 42s La Fornarina 1.00 .50
Nos. 3028-3031 (4) 2.30 1.35

Souvenir Sheet

3032 A1167 1 l Galatea 2.25 1.00

Raphael, 500th birth anniv. (1983).

Cruise Ship Sofia, Maiden Voyage — A1168

1984, Dec. 29 Photo. *Perf. 13*

3033 A1168 13s blue, dk bl & yel .35 .25

Predators A1170

1985, Jan. 17

3035 A1170 13s Conepatus leuconotus .30 .25
3036 A1170 25s Prionodon linsang .60 .30
3037 A1170 30s Ictonix striatus .75 .45
3038 A1170 42s Hemigalus derbyanus 1.10 .60
3039 A1170 60s Galidictis fasciata 1.50 .90
Nos. 3035-3039 (5) 4.25 2.50

Nikolai Liliev (1885-1960), Poet, UNESCO Emblem — A1171

1985, Jan. 25

3040 A1171 30s multicolored .60 .35

Zviatko Radojnov (1895-1942), Labor Leader — A1172

1985, Jan. 29

3041 A1172 5s dk red & dk brn .25 .25

Dr. Assen Zlatarov (1885-1936), Chemist A1173

1985, Feb. 14

3042 A1173 5s multicolored .25 .25

Souvenir Sheet

Akademik, Research Vessel — A1174

1985, Mar. 1

3043 A1174 80s multicolored 1.75 1.00

UNESCO Intl. Oceanographic Commission, 25th anniv.

Souvenir Sheet

Lenin — A1175

1985, Mar. 12

3044 A1175 50s multicolored 1.00 .65

A1176

1985, Mar. 19

3045 A1176 13s multicolored .25 .25

Warsaw Treaty Org., 30th anniv.

A1177

Composers.

1985, Mar. 25

3046 A1177 42s Bach 1.50 .55
3047 A1177 42s Mozart 1.50 .55
3048 A1177 42s Tchaikovsky 1.50 .55
3049 A1177 42s Mussorgsky 1.50 .55
3050 A1177 42s Verdi 1.50 .55
3051 A1177 42s Kutev 1.50 .55
Nos. 3046-3051 (6) 9.00 3.30

Children's Drawings Type of 1982

Inscribed 1985. Various children's drawings.

1985, Mar. 26 Litho. *Perf. 14*

3052 A1093 5s multicolored .25 .25
3053 A1093 8s multicolored .25 .25
3054 A1093 13s multicolored .30 .25
3055 A1093 20s multicolored .45 .25
3056 A1093 25s multicolored .50 .30
3057 A1093 30s multicolored .60 .40
Nos. 3052-3057 (6) 2.35 1.70

Souvenir Sheet

3058 A1093 50s Children dancing, vert. 2.00 .80

3rd Flag of Peace Intl. Assembly, Sofia. No. 3058 exists imperf. with blue control number, same value.

St. Methodius, 1100th Death Anniv. — A1179

1985, Apr. 6 Photo. *Perf. 13*

3059 A1179 13s multicolored .60 .25

Victory Parade, Moscow, 1945 — A1180

13s, 11th Infantry on parade, Sofia. 30s, Soviet soldier, orphan. 50s, Soviet flag-raising, Berlin.

1985, Apr. 30 *Perf. 13½*

3060 A1180 5s multicolored .25 .25
3061 A1180 13s multicolored .35 .25
3062 A1180 30s multicolored .70 .40
Nos. 3060-3062 (3) 1.30 .90

Souvenir Sheet

Perf. 13

3063 A1180 50s multicolored 1.10 .50

Defeat of Nazi Germany, end of World War II, 40th anniv. Nos. 3060-3062 printed se-tenant with labels picturing Soviet (5s, 30s) and Bulgarian medals of honor.

7th Intl. Humor and Satire Biennial — A1181

1985, Apr. 30 *Perf. 13½*

3064 A1181 13s yel, sage grn & red .25 .25

No. 3064 printed se-tenant with label picturing Gabrovo Cat emblem.

Intl. Youth Year — A1182

1985, May 21 *Perf. 13*

3065 A1182 13s multicolored .25 .25

Ivan Vazov (1850-1921), Poet — A1183

1985, May 30 *Perf. 13½*

3066 A1183 5s tan & sepia .25 .25

No. 3066 printed se-tenant with label picturing Vasov's birthplace in Sopot.

Soviet War Memorial, Haskovo City Arms A1184

1985, June 1 *Perf. 13*

3067 A1184 5s multicolored .25 .25

Haskovo millennium.

12th World Youth Festival, Moscow — A1185

1985, June 25

3068 A1185 13s multicolored .25 .25

Indira Gandhi (1917-1984), Prime Minister of India — A1186

1985, June 26

3069 A1186 30s org yel, sep & ver .60 .30

Vasil Aprilov, Founder — A1187

1985, June 30

3070 A1187 5s multicolored .25 .25

1st secular school, Gabrovo, 150th anniv.

INTERSTENO '85 — A1188

1985, June 30

3071 A1188 13s multicolored .25 .25

Congress for the Intl. Union of Stenographers and Typists, Sofia.

Alexander Nevski Cathedral A1189

1985, July 9

3072 A1189 42s multicolored .80 .40

World Tourism Org., general assembly, Sofia.

UN, 40th Anniv. A1190

1985, July 16

3073 A1190 13s multicolored .25 .25

A1191

1985, July 16

3074 A1191 13s multicolored .25 .25

Admission of Bulgaria to UN, 30th anniv.

Roses — A1192

1985, July 20 **Litho.**

3075	A1192	5s	Rosa damascena	.25	.25
3076	A1192	13s	Rosa trakijka	.25	.25
3077	A1192	20s	Rosa radiman	.35	.25
3078	A1192	30s	Rosa marista	.55	.35
3079	A1192	42s	Rosa valentina	.90	.45
3080	A1192	60s	Rosa maria	1.25	.70
a.			Min. sheet of 6, #3075-3080	4.00	2.25
			Nos. 3075-3080 (6)	3.55	2.25

Helsinki Conference, 10th Anniv. — A1193

1985, Aug. 1 **Photo.**

3081 A1193 13s multicolored .40 .25

European Swimming Championships, Sofia — A1194

1985, Aug. 2 **Litho.** *Perf. 12½*

3082	A1194	5s	Butterfly stroke	.25	.25
3083	A1194	13s	Water polo, vert.	.25	.25
3084	A1194	42s	Diving, vert.	1.10	.60
3085	A1194	60s	Synchronized swimming	1.50	.70
			Nos. 3082-3085 (4)	3.10	1.80

The 60s exists with central design inverted.

Natl. Tourism Assoc., 90th Anniv. A1195

1985, Aug. 15 **Photo.** *Perf. 13*

3086 A1195 5s multicolored .25 .25

1986 World Cup Soccer Championships, Mexico A1196

Various soccer plays.

1985, Aug. 29 *Perf. 13*

3087	A1196	5s	multicolored	.25	.25
3088	A1196	13s	multicolored	.25	.25
3089	A1196	30s	multicolored	.85	.25
3090	A1196	42s	multicolored	1.00	.45
			Nos. 3087-3090 (4)	2.35	1.20

Souvenir Sheet

3091 A1196 1 l multi, horiz. 2.25 1.25

Union of Eastern Rumelia and Bulgaria, 1885 — A1197

1985, Aug. 29 *Perf. 14x13½*

3092 A1197 5s multicolored .25 .25

Computer Design Portraits — A1198

1985, Sept. 23 *Perf. 13*

3093	A1198	5s	Boy	.25	.25
3094	A1198	13s	Youth	.25	.25
3095	A1198	30s	Cosmonaut	.50	.30
			Nos. 3093-3095 (3)	1.00	.80

Intl. Exhibition of the Works of Youth Inventors, Plovdiv.

St. John the Baptist Church, Nessebar A1199

Natl. restoration projects: 13s, Tyrant Hreljo Tower, Rila Monastery. 35s, Soldier, fresco, Ivanovo Rock Church. 42s, Archangel Gabriel, fresco, Bojana Church. 60s, Thracian Woman, fresco, Tomb of Kasanlak, 3rd century B.C. 1 l, The Horseman of Madara, bas-relief.

1985, Sept. 25 **Litho.** *Perf. 12½*

3096	A1199	5s	multicolored	.25	.25
3097	A1199	13s	multicolored	.25	.25
3098	A1199	35s	multicolored	.80	.40
3099	A1199	42s	multicolored	1.00	.50
3100	A1199	60s	multicolored	1.50	.75
			Nos. 3096-3100 (5)	3.80	2.15

Souvenir Sheet

Imperf

3101 A1199 1 l multicolored 1.90 1.00

UNESCO, 40th anniv.

Souvenir Sheet

Ludmila Zhishkova Cultural Palace, Sofia — A1200

1985, Oct. 8 *Perf. 13*

3102 A1200 1 l multicolored 1.60 1.00

UNESCO 23rd General Assembly, Sofia.

Colosseum, Rome — A1201

1985, Oct. 15 Photo. *Perf. 13½*

3103 A1201 42s multicolored .75 .40

ITALIA '85. No. 3103 printed se-tenant with label picturing the exhibition emblem.

Souvenir Sheet

Cultural Congress, Budapest — A1202

Designs: No. 3104a, St. Cyril, patron saint of Europe. No. 3104b, Map of Europe. No. 3104c, St. Methodius, patron saint of Europe.

Perf. 13, 13 Vert. (#3104b)

1985, Oct. 22 Photo.

3104 A1202 Sheet of 3 3.50 1.75

a.-c. 50s, any single 1.00 .60

Helsinki Congress, 10th anniv.

Exists imperf with serial number. Value $42.50.

Flowers — A1203

1985, Oct. 22 Photo. *Perf. 13x13½*

3105 A1203 5s Gladiolus hybridy .25 .25

3106 A1203 5s Iris germanica .25 .25

3107 A1203 5s Convolvulus tricolor .25 .25

Nos. 3105-3107 (3) .75 .75

See Nos. 3184-3186.

Historic Sailing Ships A1204

1985, Oct. 28 Photo. *Perf. 13*

3108 A1204 5s Dutch .25 .25

3109 A1204 12s Sea Sovereign, Britain .25 .25

3110 A1204 20s Mediterranean .25 .25

3111 A1204 25s Royal Prince, Britain .55 .25

3112 A1204 42s Mediterranean 1.00 .60

3113 A1204 60s British battleship 1.60 .65

Nos. 3108-3113 (6) 3.90 2.25

Souvenir Sheet

PHILATELIA '85, Cologne — A1205

Designs: a, Cologne Cathedral. b, Alexander Nevski Cathedral, Sofia.

1985, Nov. 4 *Imperf.*

3114 A1205 Sheet of 2 1.40 .65

a.-b. 30s, any single .60 .30

Conspiracy to Liberate Bulgaria from Turkish Rule, 150th Anniv. — A1206

Freedom fighters and symbols: No. 3115, Georgi Stojkov Rakowski (1820-76). No. 3116, Batscho Kiro (1835-76). No. 3117, Sword, Bible & hands.

1985, Nov. 6 *Perf. 13*

3115 A1206 5s multicolored .25 .25

3116 A1206 5s multicolored .25 .25

3117 A1206 13s multicolored .25 .25

Nos. 3115-3117 (3) .75 .75

Liberation from Byzantine Rule, 800th Anniv. — A1207

Paintings: 5s, The Revolt 1185, by G. Bogdanov. 13s, The Revolt 1185, by Alexander Tersiev. 30s, Battle Near Klokotnitza, by B. Grigorov and M. Ganowski. 42s, Velika Tarnovo Town Wall, by Zanko Lawrenov. 1 l, St. Dimitriev Church, 12th cent.

1985, Nov. 15 Litho.

3118 A1207 5s multicolored .25 .25

3119 A1207 13s multicolored .35 .25

3120 A1207 30s multicolored .70 .40

3121 A1207 42s multicolored 1.00 .55

Nos. 3118-3121 (4) 2.30 1.45

Souvenir Sheet

Imperf

3122 A1207 1 l multicolored 2.00 1.00

Souvenir Sheet

BALKANPHILA '85 — A1208

1985, Nov. 29 Photo. *Perf. 13*

3123 A1208 40s Dove, posthorn .85 .65

Intl. Post and Telecommunications Development Program — A1209

1985, Dec. 2

3124 A1209 13s multicolored .25 .25

Anton Popov (1915-1942), Freedom Fighter — A1210

1985, Dec. 11 Photo. *Perf. 13*

3125 A1210 5s lake .25 .25

New Year 1986 A1211

1985, Dec. 11 Photo. *Perf. 13*

3126 A1211 5s Doves, snowflake .25 .25

3127 A1211 13s Doves .25 .25

Hunting Dogs and Prey — A1212

5s, Pointer, partridge. 8s, Irish setter, pochard. 13s, English setter, mallard. 20s, Cocker spaniel, woodcock. 25s, German pointer, rabbit. 30s, Balkan hound, boar. 42s, Shorthaired dachshund, fox.

1985, Dec. 27 Litho. *Perf. 13x12½*

3128 A1212 5s multicolored .25 .25

3129 A1212 8s multicolored .25 .25

3130 A1212 13s multicolored .25 .25

3131 A1212 20s multicolored .25 .25

3132 A1212 25s multicolored .50 .25

3133 A1212 30s multicolored .70 .25

3134 A1212 42s multicolored 1.50 .50

Nos. 3128-3134 (7) 3.70 2.00

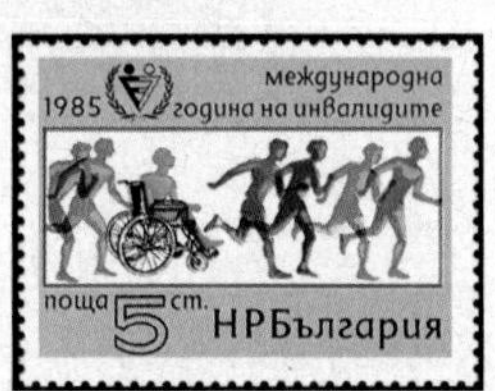

Intl. Year of the Handicapped — A1213

1985, Dec. 30 Photo. *Perf. 13*

3135 A1213 5s multicolored .25 .25

George Dimitrov (1882-1949) — A1214

1985, Dec. 30 Photo. *Perf. 13*

3136 A1214 13s brn lake .35 .25

7th Intl. Communist Congress, Moscow.

UN Child Survival Campaign — A1215

1986, Jan. 21 Photo. *Perf. 13*

3137 A1215 13s multicolored .35 .25

UNICEF, 40th anniv.

Demeter Blagoev (1856-1924) A1216

1986, Jan. 28 Photo. *Perf. 13*

3138 A1216 5s dk lake, car & dk red .25 .25

Intl. Peace Year A1217

1986, Jan. 31 *Perf. 13½*

3139 A1217 5s multicolored .25 .25

Orchids — A1218

1986, Feb. 12 Litho. *Perf. 13x12½*

3140 A1218 5s Dactylorhiza romana .25 .25

3141 A1218 13s Epipactis palustris .25 .25

3142 A1218 30s Ophrys cornuta .50 .40

3143 A1218 32s Limodorum abortivum .50 .40

3144 A1218 42s Cypripedium calceolus .60 .50

3145 A1218 60s Orchis papilionacea 1.25 .60

a. Min. sheet of 6, #3140-3145 3.50 1.60

Nos. 3140-3145 (6) 3.35 2.40

Hares and Rabbits
A1219

1986, Feb. 24 *Perf. 12½x12*

3146 A1219 5s multicolored .25 .25
3147 A1219 25s multicolored .45 .25
3148 A1219 30s multicolored .65 .40
3149 A1219 32s multicolored .80 .40
3150 A1219 42s multicolored 1.00 .50
3151 A1219 60s multicolored 1.40 .80
Nos. 3146-3151 (6) 4.55 2.60

Exist imperf. Value, set $10.

Bulgarian Eagle, Newspaper, 140th Anniv. — A1220

Front page of 1st issue & Ivan Bogorov, journalist.

1986, Feb. 2 **Photo.** *Perf. 13*

3152 A1220 5s multicolored .25 .25

Souvenir Sheet

Halley's Comet — A1221

Comet's orbit in the Solar System: a, 1980. b, 1910-86. c, 1916-70. d, 1911.

1986, Mar. 7 *Perf. 13½x13*

3153 Sheet of 4 1.90 1.25
a.-d. A1221 25s, any single .40 .30

Exists imperf. Value $15.

A1222

1986, Mar. 12 *Perf. 13x13½*

3154 A1222 5s dp bl & bl .25 .25

Vladimir Bachev (1935-1967), poet.

A1223

1986, Mar. 17 *Perf. 13*

3155 A1223 5s Wavy lines .25 .25
3156 A1223 8s Star .25 .25
3157 A1223 13s Worker .25 .25
Nos. 3155-3157 (3) .75 .75

Souvenir Sheet

Imperf

3158 A1223 50s Scaffold, flags .70 .50

13th Natl. Communist Party Congress.

Souvenir Sheet

1st Manned Space Flight, 25th Anniv. — A1224

Designs: a, Vostok I, 1961. b, Yuri Gagarin (1934-68), Russian cosmonaut.

1986, Mar. 28 *Perf. 13½x13*

3159 Sheet of 2 1.90 1.00
a.-b. A1224 50s, any single 1.00 .50

Exists imperf. Value $20.

April Uprising against the Turks, 110th Anniv. — A1225

Monuments: 5s, 1876 Uprising monument, Panagjuriste. 13s, Christo Botev, Vraca.

1986, Mar. 30 *Perf. 13*

3160 A1225 5s multicolored .25 .25
3161 A1225 13s multicolored .25 .25

A1225a

Levsky-Spartak Sports Club, 75th Anniv. — A1226

1986 *Perf. 13*

3161A A1225a 5s multicolored .25 .25

Souvenir Sheet

Imperf

3162 A1226 50s Rhythmic gymnastics .90 .50

Issue dates: 5s, Dec. 50s, May 12.

A1227

1986, May 19 *Perf. 13*

3163 A1227 5s Congress emblem .25 .25
3164 A1227 8s Emblem on globe .25 .25
3165 A1227 13s Flags .25 .25
Nos. 3163-3165 (3) .75 .75

35th Congress of Bulgarian farmers, Sofia.

A1228

1986, May 27 *Perf. 13x13½*

3166 A1228 13s multicolored .25 .25

Conference of Transport Ministers from Socialist Countries.

17th Intl. Book Fair, Sofia — A1229

1986, May 28

3167 A1229 13s blk, brt red & grysh blk .25 .25

1986 World Cup Soccer Championships, Mexico — A1230

Various soccer plays; attached labels picture Mexican landmarks.

1986, May 30 *Perf. 13½*

3168 A1230 5s multi, vert. .25 .25
3169 A1230 13s multicolored .30 .25
3170 A1230 20s multicolored .40 .25
3171 A1230 30s multicolored .60 .35
3172 A1230 42s multicolored .85 .45
3173 A1230 60s multi, vert. 1.40 .65
Nos. 3168-3173 (6) 3.80 2.20

Souvenir Sheet

Perf. 13

3174 A1230 1 l Azteca Stadium 2.00 1.00

Exist imperf. Value: set $7; souvenir sheet $15.

Treasures of Preslav — A1231

Gold artifacts: 5s, Embossed brooch. 13s, Pendant with pearl cross, vert. 20s, Crystal and pearl pendant. 30s, Embossed shield. 42s, Pearl and enamel pendant, vert. 60s, Enamel shield.

1986, June 7 *Perf. 13½x13, 13x13½*

3175 A1231 5s multicolored .25 .25
3176 A1231 13s multicolored .25 .25
3177 A1231 20s multicolored .35 .25
3178 A1231 30s multicolored .55 .30
3179 A1231 42s multicolored .75 .40
3180 A1231 60s multicolored 1.00 .60
Nos. 3175-3180 (6) 3.15 2.05

World Fencing Championships, Sofia, July 25-Aug. 3 — A1232

1986, July 25 **Photo.** *Perf. 13*

3181 A1232 5s Head cut, lunge .25 .25
3182 A1232 13s Touche .25 .25
3183 A1232 25s Lunge, parry .45 .25
Nos. 3181-3183 (3) .95 .75

Flower Type of 1985

1986, July 29 *Perf. 13x13½*

3184 A1203 8s Ipomoea tricolor .25 .25
3185 A1203 8s Anemone coronaria .25 .25
3186 A1203 32s Lilium auratum .55 .30
Nos. 3184-3186 (3) 1.05 .80

A1233

1986, Aug. 25

3187 A1233 42s sepia, sal brn & lake .80 .45

STOCKHOLMIA '86. No. 3187 printed in sheets of 3 + 3 labels picturing folk art.

Miniature Sheet

A1234

Environmental Conservation: a, Ciconia ciconia. b, Nuphar lutea. c, Salamandra salamandra. d, Nymphaea alba.

1986, Aug. 25 **Litho.** *Perf. 14*

3188 Sheet of 4 + label 3.75 3.50
a.-d. A1234 30s any single .60 .35

No. 3188 is a miniature sheet containing a center label picturing the oldest oak tree in Bulgaria, Granit Village.

Exists imperf. Value $17.50.

Natl. Arms, Building of the Sobranie — A1235

1986, Sept. 13 Photo. *Perf. 13*
3189 A1235 5s Prus grn, yel grn & red .25 .25

People's Republic of Bulgaria, 40th anniv.

15th Postal Union Congress — A1236

1986, Sept. 24
3190 A1236 13s multicolored .25 .25

Natl. Youth Brigade Movement, 40th Anniv. — A1237

1986, Oct. 4
3191 A1237 5s multicolored .25 .25

Intl. Organization of Journalists, 10th Congress A1238

1986, Oct. 13
3192 A1238 13s blue & dark blue .25 .25

Sts. Cyril and Methodius, Disciples — A1239

1986, Oct. 23 *Perf. 13½*
3193 A1239 13s dark brown & buff .25 .25

Sts. Cyril and Methodius in Bulgaria, 1100th anniv. No. 3193 se-tenant with inscribed label.

Telephones in Bulgaria, Cent. — A1240

1986, Nov. 5 *Perf. 13*
3194 A1240 5s multicolored .25 .25

World Weight Lifting Championships — A1241

1986, Nov. 6
3195 A1241 13s multicolored .25 .25

Ships A1242

1986, Nov. 20
3196 A1242 5s King of Prussia .25 .25
3197 A1242 13s East Indiaman, 18th cent. .25 .25
3198 A1242 25s Shebek, 18th cent. .45 .25
3199 A1242 30s St Paul .55 .30
3200 A1242 32s Topsail schooner, 18th cent. .60 .30
3201 A1242 42s Victory .80 .40
Nos. 3196-3201 (6) 2.90 1.75

European Security and Cooperation Congress, Vienna — A1243

Various buildings and emblems: a, Bulgaria. b, Austria. c, Donau Park, UN.

Perf. 13, Imperf. x13 (#3202b)
1986, Nov. 27
3202 Souvenir sheet of 3 3.25 1.50
a.-c. A1243 50s any single 1.00 .50

Exists imperf. bearing control number. Value $27.50.

Rogozen Thracian Pitchers A1244

1986, Dec. 5 *Perf. 13*
3203 A1244 10s Facing left .25 .25
3204 A1244 10s Facing right .25 .25
a. Block, #3203-3204 + 2 labels .65 .65

Union of Bulgarian Philatelists, 14th Congress.

Exist imperf. Value, block $1.

New Year 1987 A1245

1986, Dec. 9
3205 A1245 5s shown .25 .25
3206 A1245 13s Snow flakes .25 .25

Home Amateur Radio Operators in Bulgaria, 60th Anniv. — A1246

1986, Dec. 10
3207 A1246 13s multicolored .25 .25

Miniature Sheet

Paintings by Bulgarian Artists — A1247

a, Red Tree, by Danail Dechev (1891-1962). b, Troopers Confront Two Men, by Ilya Beshkov (1901-58). c, View of Melnik, by Veselin Stajkov (1906-70). d, View of Houses through Trees, by Kyril Zonev (1896-1961).

1986, Dec. 10 Litho. *Perf. 14*
3208 A1247 Sheet of 4 2.50 1.25
a.-b. 25s any single .55 .30
c.-d. 30s any single .65 .35

Sofia Academy of Art, 90th anniv.

Augusto Cesar Sandino (1893-1934), Nicaraguan Revolutionary, and Flag — A1248

1986, Dec. 16 Photo. *Perf. 13*
3209 A1248 13s multicolored .25 .25

Sandinista movement in Nicaragua, 25th anniv.

Smoyan Mihylovsky (b. 1856), Writer — A1249

Ran Bossilek (b. 1886) A1250

Title Page from Bulgarian Folk Songs of the Miladinov Brothers — A1251

Annivs. and events: No. 3211, Pentcho Slaveyckov (b. 1861), writer. No. 3212, Nickola Atanassov (b. 1886), musician.

1986, Dec. 17
3210 A1249 5s multicolored .25 .25
3211 A1249 5s multicolored .25 .25
3212 A1249 8s multicolored .25 .25
3213 A1250 8s multicolored .25 .25
3214 A1251 10s multicolored .25 .25
Nos. 3210-3214 (5) 1.25 1.25

Paintings by Titian — A1252

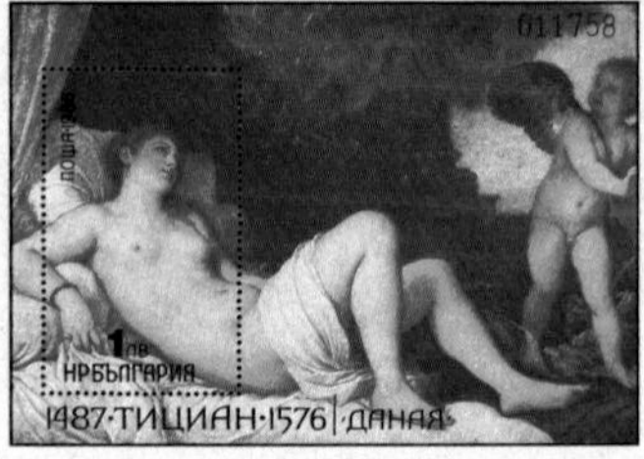

A1253

Various portraits.

1986, Dec. 23 Litho. *Perf. 14*
3215 A1252 5s multicolored .25 .25
3216 A1252 13s multicolored .35 .25
3217 A1252 20s multicolored .45 .25
3218 A1252 30s multicolored .65 .30
3219 A1252 32s multicolored .75 .30
3220 A1252 42s multicolored .90 .40
a. Min. sheet of 6, #3215-3220 3.00 1.50
Nos. 3215-3220 (6) 3.35 1.75

Souvenir Sheet
3221 A1253 1 l multicolored 2.75 1.00

Rayko Daskalov (b. 1886), Politician A1254

1986, Dec. 23 Photo. *Perf. 13*
3222 A1254 5s deep claret .25 .25

Sports Cars — A1255

1986, Dec. 30 Litho. *Perf. 13½*

3223	A1255	5s	1905 Fiat	.25	.25
3224	A1255	10s	1928 Bugatti	.25	.25
3225	A1255	25s	1936 Mercedes	.45	.30
3226	A1255	32s	1952 Ferrari	.60	.35
3227	A1255	40s	1985 Lotus	.75	.45
3228	A1255	42s	1986 McLaren	.80	.45
			Nos. 3223-3228 (6)	3.10	2.05

Varna Railway Inauguration, 120th Anniv. — A1257

1987, Jan. 19 Photo. *Perf. 13½*

3229	A1257	5s	multicolored	.25	.25
a.			Perf. 11	.40	.40

Dimcho Debelianov (1887-1916), Poet — A1258

1987, Jan. 20 Photo. *Perf. 13*

3230	A1258	5s	blue, dull yel & dp blue	.25	.25

L.L. Zamenhof, Creator of Esperanto — A1259

1987, Feb. 12

3231	A1259	13s	multicolored	.25	.25

Mushrooms A1260

1987, Feb. 6 Litho. *Perf. 11½*

3232	A1260	5s	Amanita rubescens	.25	.25
3233	A1260	20s	Boletus regius	.35	.25
3234	A1260	30s	Leccinum aurantiacum	.50	.35
3235	A1260	32s	Coprinus comatus	.55	.40
3236	A1260	40s	Russula vesca	.75	.50
3237	A1260	60s	Cantharellus cibarius	1.00	.60
a.			Min. sheet of 6, #3232-3237	5.25	
			Nos. 3232-3237 (6)	3.40	2.35

10th Natl. Trade Unions Congress A1261

1987, Mar. 20 Photo. *Perf. 13*

3238	A1261	5s	dark red & violet	.25	.25

Rogozen Thracian Treasure A1262

Embossed and gilded silver artifacts: 5s, Plate, Priestess Auge approaching Heracles. 8s, Pitcher, lioness attacking stag. 20s, Plate, floral pattern. 30s, Pitcher, warriors on horseback dueling. 32s, Urn, decorative pattern. 42s, Pitcher (not gilded), winged horses.

1987, Mar. 31

3239	A1262	5s	multicolored	.25	.25
3240	A1262	8s	multicolored	.25	.25
3241	A1262	20s	multicolored	.25	.25
3242	A1262	30s	multicolored	.25	.25
3243	A1262	32s	multicolored	.40	.25
3244	A1262	42s	multicolored	.60	.25
			Nos. 3239-3244 (6)	2.00	1.50

Miniature Sheet

Modern Architecture — A1263

Designs: a, Ludmila Zhivkova conf. center, Varna. b, Ministry of Foreign Affairs, Sofia. c, Interpred Building, Sofia. d, Hotel, Sandanski.

1987, Apr. 7 *Perf. 13½x13*

3245		Sheet of 4	2.50	1.50
a.-d.	A1263	30s any single	.60	.35

Exists imperf. with black control number. Value $15.

European Freestyle Wrestling Championships A1264

1987, Apr. 22 *Perf. 13*

3246	A1264	5s	multicolored	.25	.25
3247	A1264	13s	multi, diff.	.40	.25

CAPEX '87, Toronto A1265

1987, Apr. 24

3248	A1265	42s	multicolored	1.00	.40

10th Congress of the Natl. Front — A1266

1987, May 11

3249	A1266	5s	multicolored	.25	.25

15th Communist Youth Congress — A1267

1987, May 13

3250	A1267	5s	George Dimitrov	.25	.25

8th Intl. Humor and Satire Biennial, Gabrovo — A1268

1987, May 15 *Perf. 13x13½*

3251	A1268	13s	multicolored	.35	.25

13th World Rhythmic Gymnastics Championships, Varna — A1269

Gymnasts.

1987, Aug. 5 Photo. *Perf. 13*

3252	A1269	5s	Maria Gigova	.25	.25
3252A	A1269	8s	Iliana Raeva	.25	.25
3252B	A1269	13s	Anelia Ralenkova	.30	.25
3252C	A1269	25s	Pilyana Georgieva	.55	.30
3252D	A1269	30s	Lilia Ignatova	.65	.40
3252E	A1269	42s	Bianca Panova	.90	.50
			Nos. 3252-3252E (6)	2.90	1.95

Souvenir Sheet

Perf. 13x13½

3252F	A1269	1 l	Neshka Robeva, coach	2.50	1.50

Exists imperf. with black control number. Value $8.50.

Vassil Kolarov — A1270

1987, June 3 *Perf. 13*

3253	A1270	5s	dk red, yel & dk bl	.25	.25

Stela Blagoeva (b. 1887) — A1271

1987, June 4

3254	A1271	5s	pink & sepia	.25	.25

Rabotnichesko Delo Newspaper, 60th Anniv. — A1272

1987, May 28

3255	A1272	5s	black & lake	.25	.25

Deer A1273

1987, June 23 Litho.

3256	A1273	5s	Capreolus capreolus, vert.	.25	.25
3257	A1273	10s	Alces alces	.25	.25
3258	A1273	32s	Dama dama, vert.	.65	.25
3259	A1273	40s	Cervus nippon, vert.	.95	.30
3260	A1273	42s	Cervus elaphus	.95	.30
3261	A1273	60s	Rangifer tarandus, vert.	1.20	.45
a.			Min. sheet, #3256-3261, imperf	5.50	3.00
			Nos. 3256-3261 (6)	4.25	1.80

Vassil Levski (1837-73) A1274

Various portraits.

1987, June 19 Photo.

3262	A1274	5s	red brn & dark grn	.25	.25
3263	A1274	13s	dark grn & red brn	.25	.25

Namibia Day A1275

1987, July 8

3264	A1275	13s	org, blk & dark red	.30	.25

Georgi Kirkov (1867-1919), Revolutionary A1276

1987, July 17 ***Perf. 13x13½***
3265 A1276 5s claret & dp claret .25 .25

Bees and Plants — A1277

1987, July 29 **Litho.** ***Perf. 13***
3266 A1277 5s Phacelia tanacetifolia .25 .25
3267 A1277 10s Helianthus annuus .25 .25
3268 A1277 30s Robinia pseudoacacia .60 .35
3269 A1277 32s Lavandula vera .65 .40
3270 A1277 42s Tilia parvifolia .90 .50
3271 A1277 60s Onobrychis sativa 1.10 .70
a. Min. sheet of 6, #3266-3271 4.75 2.75
Nos. 3266-3271 (6) 3.75 2.45

BULGARIA '89 — A1278

1987, Sept. 3 ***Perf. 13½x13***
3272 A1278 13s No. 1 .45 .25

HAFNIA '87 — A1279

1987, Sept. 8 ***Perf. 13***
3273 A1279 42s multicolored .75 .45

No. 3273 issued in sheets of 3 plus 2 labels picturing emblems of the HAFNIA '87 and BULGARIA '89 exhibitions, and 1 label with background similar to Denmark Type A32 with castle instead of denomination.

Portrait of a Girl, by Stefan Ivanov — A1280

Paintings in the Sofia City Art Galler: 8s, Grape-gatherer, by Bencho Obreshkov. 20s, Portrait of a Lady with a Hat, by David Perets. 25s, Listeners of Marimba, by Kiril Tsonev. 32s, Boy with an Harmonica, by Nenko Balkanski. 60s, Rumyana, by Vasil Stoilov.

1987, Sept. 15 **Litho.** ***Perf. 14***
3274 A1280 5s shown .25 .25
3275 A1280 8s multicolored .25 .25
3276 A1280 20s multicolored .40 .25
3277 A1280 25s multicolored .50 .25
3278 A1280 32s multicolored .60 .25
3279 A1280 60s multicolored 1.00 .25
Nos. 3274-3279 (6) 3.00 1.50

Intl. Atomic Energy Agency, 30th Anniv. A1281

1987, Sept. 15 **Photo.** ***Perf. 13½x13***
3280 A1281 13s red, lt blue & emer .35 .25

Songbirds A1282

1987, Oct. 12 **Litho.** ***Perf. 12½x12***
3281 A1282 5s Troglodytes troglodytes .25 .25
3282 A1282 13s Emberiza citrinella .25 .25
3283 A1282 20s Sitta europaea .35 .25
3284 A1282 30s Turdus merula .55 .30
3285 A1282 42s Coccothraustes coccothraustes .85 .35
3286 A1282 60s Cinclus cinclus 1.20 .45
a. Min. sheet of 6, #3281-3286 3.25 2.25
Nos. 3281-3286 (6) 3.45 1.85

Balkan War, 75th Anniv. A1283

1987, Sept. 15 **Photo.** ***Perf. 13½***
3287 A1283 5s buff, blk & brt org .25 .25

Newspaper Anniversaries — A1283a

1987, Sept. 24 **Photo.** ***Perf. 13***
3287A A1283a 5s multicolored .25 .25

Rabotnik, 95th anniv., *Rabotnicheski Vstnik,* 90th anniv. and *Rabotnichesko Delo,* 60th anniv.

October Revolution, Russia, 70th Anniv. — A1284

Lenin and: 5s, Revolutionary. 13s, Cosmonaut.

1987, Oct. 27 **Photo.** ***Perf. 13***
3288 A1284 5s rose brn & red org .25 .25
3289 A1284 13s brt ultra & red org .25 .25

1988 Winter Olympics, Calgary A1285

1987, Oct. 27 **Litho.** ***Perf. 13x13½***
3290 A1285 5s Biathlon .25 .25
3291 A1285 13s Slalom .25 .25
3292 A1285 30s Women's figure skating .60 .30
3293 A1285 42s 4-Man bobsled .80 .50
Nos. 3290-3293 (4) 1.90 1.30

Souvenir Sheet

3294 A1285 1 l Ice hockey 2.00 1.50

No. 3294 exists imperf. Value $8.50.

Souvenir Sheet

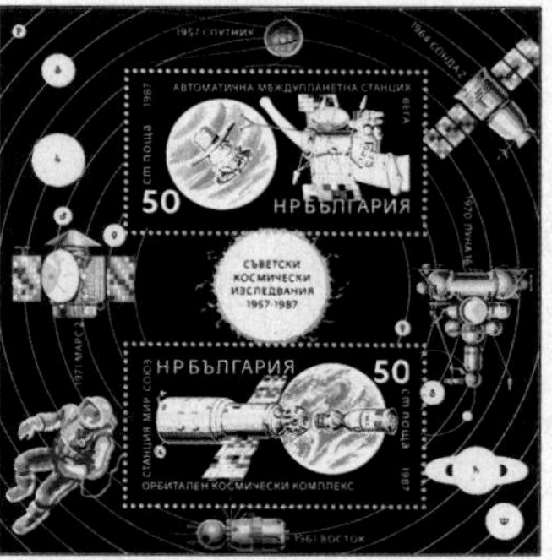

Soviet Space Achievements, 1957-87 — A1286

Designs: No. 3295a, Vega probe. No. 3295b, Mir-Soyuz Space Station.

1987, Dec. 24 **Photo.** ***Perf. 13½x13***
3295 A1286 Sheet of 2 3.00 1.50
a.-b. 50s any single 1.25 .75

Exists imperf. Value $15.

New Year 1988 A1287

Sofia stamp exhibition emblem within folklore patterns.

1987, Dec. 25 ***Perf. 13***
3296 A1287 5s multicolored .25 .25
3297 A1287 13s multi, diff. .35 .25

Souvenir Sheet

European Security Conferences — A1288

Conferences held in Helsinki, 1973, and Vienna, 1987: a, Helsinki Conf. Center. b, Map of Europe. c, Vienna Conf. Center.

Perf. 13x13½ on 2 or 4 Sides

1987, Dec. 30
3298 Sheet of 3 4.25 3.00
a.-c. A1288 50s any single 1.50 .75

Exists imperf. Value $17.

A1289

1988, Jan. 20
3299 A1289 5s multicolored .25 .25

Christo Kabaktchiev (b. 1878), party leader.

A1290

Marine flowers.

1988, Jan. 25 **Litho.** ***Perf. 12***
3300 A1290 5s Scilla bythynica .25 .25
3301 A1290 10s Geum rhodopaeum .25 .25
3302 A1290 13s Caltha polypetala .25 .25
3303 A1290 25s Nymphoides peltata .25 .25
3304 A1290 30s Cortusa matthioli .40 .25
3305 A1290 42s Stratiotes aloides .60 .45
a. Min. sheet of 6, #3300-3305 1.75 1.50
Nos. 3300-3305 (6) 2.00 1.70

Liberation of Bulgaria, 110th Anniv. A1291

1988, Feb. 15 **Photo.** ***Perf. 13***
3306 A1291 5s Officer, horse .25 .25
3307 A1291 13s Soldiers .35 .25

8th Intl. Civil Servants Congress, Sofia — A1292

1988, Mar. 22 **Photo.** ***Perf. 13***
3308 A1292 13s multicolored .30 .25

State Railways, Cent. — A1293

Locomotives: 5s, Jantra, 1888. 13s, Christo Botev, 1905. 25s, 0-10-1, 1918. 32s, 4-12-1 heavy duty, 1943. 42s, Diesel, 1964. 60s, Electric, 1979.

1988, Mar. 25 **Litho.** ***Perf. 11***
3309 A1293 5s multicolored .25 .25
3310 A1293 13s multicolored .25 .25
3311 A1293 25s multicolored .50 .30
3312 A1293 32s multicolored .65 .35
3313 A1293 42s multicolored .80 .45
3314 A1293 60s multicolored 1.00 .60
a. Min. sheet of 6, #3309-3314 3.50 2.00
Nos. 3309-3314 (6) 3.45 2.20

Ivan Nedyalkov (1880-1925)
A1294

Postal workers, heroes of socialism: 8s, Delcho Spasov (1918-43). 10s, Nikola Ganchev (1915-43). 13s, Ganka Stoyanova Rasheva (1921-44).

1988, Mar. 31 Photo. *Perf. 13½x13*

3315 A1294 5s buff & dark rose brn .25 .25
3316 A1294 8s pale ultra & violet blue .25 .25
3317 A1294 10s pale olive grn & olive grn .25 .25
3318 A1294 13s pale pink & lake .25 .25
Nos. 3315-3318 (4) 1.00 1.00

Georgi Traikov (b. 1898), Statesman
A1295

1988, Apr. 8 Litho. *Perf. 13x13½*

3319 A1295 5s orange & brn .25 .25

Intl. Red Cross and Red Crescent Organizations, 125th Annivs. — A1296

1988, Apr. 26 Photo. *Perf. 13*

3320 A1296 13s multicolored .25 .25

Children's Drawings Type of 1982

Designs: 5s, Girl wearing a folk costume, vert. 8s, Painter at easel, vert. 13s, Children playing. 20s, Ringing bells for peace. 32s, Accordion player, vert. 42s, Cosmonaut, vert. 50s, Assembly emblem.

1988, Apr. 28 Litho. *Perf. 14*

3321 A1093 5s multicolored .25 .25
3322 A1093 8s multicolored .25 .25
3323 A1093 13s multicolored .25 .25
3324 A1093 20s multicolored .30 .25
3325 A1093 32s multicolored .65 .25
3326 A1093 42s multicolored .80 .25
Nos. 3321-3326 (6) 2.50 1.50

Souvenir Sheet

3327 A1093 50s multicolored 1.10 .60

4th Intl. Children's Assembly, Sofia.
No. 3327 exists imperf. Value $2.50.

Karl Marx
A1297

1988, May 5 *Perf. 13*

3328 A1297 13s multicolored .30 .25

Birds — A1297a

Designs: No. 3328A, Ciconia ciconia. No. 3328B, Larus argentatus. No. 3328C, Ardea cinerea. No. 3328D, Corvus corone cornix. 10s, Accipiter gentillis. 42s, Bubo bubo.

1988, May 6 Litho. *Perf. 13x13½*

3328A A1297a 5s multicolored .25 .25
3328B A1297a 5s multicolored .25 .25
3328C A1297a 8s multicolored .30 .25
3328D A1297a 8s multicolored .30 .25
3328E A1297a 10s multicolored .50 .25
3328F A1297a 42s multicolored 1.50 .50
Nos. 3328A-3328F (6) 3.10 1.75

Dated 1987.

Sofia Zoo
A1298

1988, May 20

3329 A1298 5s Loxodonta africana .25 .25
3330 A1298 13s Ceratotherium simum .25 .25
3331 A1298 25s Lycaon pictus .50 .30
3332 A1298 30s Pelecanus onocrotalus .65 .35
3333 A1298 32s Bucorvus abissinicus .70 .40
3334 A1298 42s Nyctea scandiaca .90 .55
a. Min. sheet of 6, #3329-3334 3.75 1.75
Nos. 3329-3334 (6) 3.25 2.10

FINLANDIA '88 — A1299

1988, June 7

3335 A1299 30s Finland No. 1 .70 .35

No. 3335 printed in miniature sheets of 3 plus 3 labels picturing skyline, SOFIA '89 and FINLANDIA '88 exhibition emblems.
Exists imperf. Value $.90

2nd Joint USSR-Bulgaria Space Flight — A1300

1988, June 7

3336 A1300 5s shown .25 .25
3337 A1300 13s Rocket, globe .30 .25

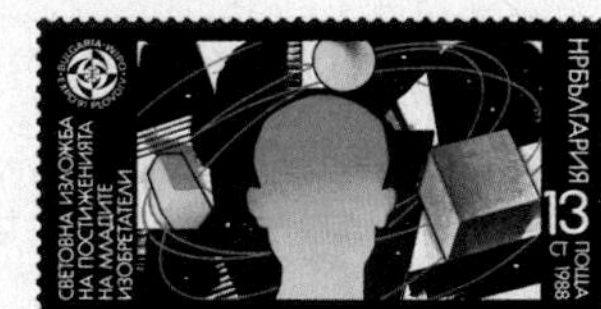

EXPO '91, Plovdiv — A1301

1988, June 7 *Perf. 13½x13*

3338 A1301 13s multicolored .30 .25

1988 European Soccer Championships — A1302

1988, June 10 *Perf. 13*

3339 A1302 5s Corner kick .25 .25
3340 A1302 13s Heading the ball .25 .25
3341 A1302 30s Referee, player .55 .35
3342 A1302 42s Player holding trophy .85 .55
Nos. 3339-3342 (4) 1.90 1.40

Souvenir Sheet

3343 A1302 1 l Stadium 2.25 1.25

No. 3343 exists imperf. Value $16.50

Paintings by Dechko Usunov (1899-1986)
A1303

Designs: 5s, Portrait of a Young Girl. 13s, Portrait of Maria Wassilewa. 30s, Self-portrait.

1988, June 14 *Perf. 13x13½*

3344 A1303 5s multicolored .25 .25
3345 A1303 13s multicolored .30 .25
3346 A1303 30s multicolored .70 .35
Nos. 3344-3346 (3) 1.25 .85

Souvenir Sheet

1st Woman in Space, 25th Anniv. — A1304

1988, June 16 *Perf. 13½x13*

3347 A1304 1 l multicolored 2.40 1.50

Valentina Tereshkova's flight, June 16-19, 1963.
Exists imperf. Value $15.

Kurdzhali Region Religious Art — A1305

Designs: 5s, St. John the Baptist, 1592. 8s, St. George Slaying the Dragon, 1841.

1988, June 27 *Perf. 13x13½*

3348 A1305 5s multicolored .25 .25
3349 A1305 8s multicolored .25 .25

1988 Summer Olympics, Seoul — A1306

1988, July 25 Litho. *Perf. 13*

3350 A1306 5s High jump .25 .25
3351 A1306 13s Weight lifting .25 .25
3352 A1306 30s Greco-Roman wrestling .50 .30
3353 A1306 42s Rhythmic gymnastics .75 .30
Nos. 3350-3353 (4) 1.75 1.10

Souvenir Sheet

3354 A1306 1 l Volleyball 2.40 1.25

No. 3354 exists imperf. Value $15.

Dimitr and Karaja
A1307

1988, July 25 Litho. *Perf. 13*

3355 A1307 5s blk, dark olive bister & grn .25 .25

120th anniv. of the deaths of Haji Dimitr and Stefan Karaja, patriots killed during the Balkan Wars.

Problems of Peace and Socialism, 30th Anniv. — A1308

1988, July 26 Photo.

3356 A1308 13s multicolored .25 .25

Paintings in the Ludmila Zhivkova Art Gallery
A1309

Paintings: No. 3357, Harbor, Algiers, by Albert Marquet (1875-1947). No. 3358, Portrait of Hermine David in the Studio, by Jules Pascin (1885-1930). No. 3359, Madonna with Child and Sts. Sebastian and Rocco, by Giovanni Rosso (1494-1540). No. 3360, The Barren Tree, by Roland Oudot (1879-1982).

1988, July 27 Litho. *Perf. 14*

3357 A1309 30s multicolored .60 .40
3358 A1309 30s multicolored .60 .40
3359 A1309 30s multicolored .60 .40
3360 A1309 30s multicolored .60 .40
Nos. 3357-3360 (4) 2.40 1.60

St. Clement of Ohrid University, Sofia, 100th Anniv. — A1310

1988, Aug. 22 ***Perf. 13***

3361 A1310 5s blk & pale yel .25 .25

PRAGA '88 A1311

1988, Aug. 22

3362 A1311 25s Czechoslovakia #2 in vermilion .60 .30

Printed in miniature sheets of 3 plus 3 labels picturing skyline, PRAGA '88 and SOFIA '89 exhibition emblems.

Exists imperf.

OLYMPHILEX '88 — A1312

1988, Sept. 1

3363 A1312 62s Korea No. 1 1.25 .75

Printed in miniature sheets of 3 plus 3 labels picturing skyline, OLYMPHILEX '88 and SOFIA '89 exhibition emblems.

Exists imperf.

A1313

1988, Sept. 15

3364 A1313 5s dp bl, lt bl & red .25 .25

Kremikovtsi steel mill, 25th anniv.

A1314

1988, Sept. 16 ***Perf. 13½x13***

3365 A1314 13s dark red & ultra .25 .25

80th Interparliamentary Conference.

Transportation Commission 80th Congress — A1315

1988, Oct. 17

3366 A1315 13s deep lil rose & blk .25 .25

Kurdzhali Region Artifacts A1316

5s, Earthenware bowl, 13th-14th cent. 8s, Medieval fortification, Gorna Krepost Village, vert.

1988, Sept. 20 ***Perf. 13***

3367 A1316 5s multicolored .25 .25
3368 A1316 8s multicolored .25 .25

Chiprovo Uprising, 300th Anniv. — A1317

1988, Sept. 23

3369 A1317 5s multicolored .25 .25

Bears A1318

Designs: 5s, Ursus arctos. 8s, Thalassarctos maritimus. 13s, Melursus ursinus. 20s, Helarctos malayanus. 32s, Selenarctos thibetanus. 42s, Tremarctos ornatus.

1988, Sept. 26 ***Perf. 12½***

3370 A1318 5s multicolored .25 .25
3371 A1318 8s multicolored .25 .25
3372 A1318 13s multicolored .30 .25
3373 A1318 20s multicolored .45 .25
3374 A1318 32s multicolored .70 .40
3375 A1318 42s multicolored .95 .50
a. Min. sheet of 6, #3370-3375 3.25 1.50
Nos. 3370-3375 (6) 2.90 1.90

ECOFORUM for Peace — A1319

1988, Oct. 29 ***Perf. 13***

3376 A1319 20s multicolored .40 .25

PLOVDIV '88 — A1320

Design: Amphitheater ruins, PRAGA '88 and PLOVDIV '88 emblems.

1988, Nov. 2

3377 A1320 5s multicolored .25 .25

Exists in imperf. sheet of six.

Radio & Television Authority, 25th Anniv. — A1321

1988, Nov. 17 **Litho.** ***Perf. 13***

3378 A1321 5s multicolored .25 .25

BULGARIA '89 — A1321a

1988, Nov. 22 **Litho.** ***Perf. 13***

3379 A1321a 42s No. 1 .75 .60

Printed in miniature sheets of 3+3 labels picturing exhib. emblem and conf. center.

Exists imperf.

Danube Cruise Excursion Industry, 40th Anniv. — A1321b

1988, Nov. 25 ***Perf. 13½x13***

3380 Sheet of 2 5.00 2.75
a. A1321b 1 l *Russia* 2.50 1.40
b. A1321b 1 l *Aleksandr Stamboliski* 2.50 1.40

Exists imperf. Value $21.

Traffic Safety — A1321c

1988, Nov. 28

3381 A1321c 5s multicolored .25 .25

New Year 1989 — A1321d

1988, Dec. 20 ***Perf. 13***

3382 A1321d 5s shown .25 .25
3383 A1321d 13s multi, diff. .35 .25

Hotels in Winter A1322

1988, Dec. 19 **Litho.** ***Perf. 13½x13***

3384 A1322 5s shown .25 .25
3385 A1322 8s multi, diff. .25 .25
3386 A1322 13s multi, diff. .30 .25
3387 A1322 30s multi, diff. .50 .25
Nos. 3384-3387 (4) 1.30 1.00

Souvenir Sheet

Soviet Space Shuttle Energija-Buran A1322a

1988, Dec. 28 ***Perf. 13½x13***

3387A A1322a 1 l dark blue 2.50 1.50

Exists imperf. Value $15.

BULGARIA '89 — A1322b

Traditional modes of postal conveyance.

1988, Dec. 29 ***Perf. 13½x13***

3387B A1322b 25s Mail coach .50 .30
3387C A1322b 25s Biplane .50 .30
3387D A1322b 25s Truck .50 .30
3387E A1322b 25s Steam packet .50 .30
Nos. 3387B-3387E (4) 2.00 1.20

Philatelic Exhibitions — A1323

1989 **Litho.** ***Perf. 13***

3388 A1323 42s France No. 1 1.00 .50
3389 A1323 62s India No. 200 1.50 .80

BULGARIA '89 and PHILEXFRANCE '89 (42s) or INDIA '89 (62s).

Nos. 3388-3389 each printed in sheets of 3 + 3 labels picturing skylines, BULGARIA '89 and PHILEXFRANCE or INDIA exhibition labels. Exist in sheets of 4 also. Exist imperf.

Issue dates: 42s, Feb. 23; 62s, Jan. 14.

Souvenir Sheet

Universiade Winter Games, Sofia — A1324

Designs: a, Downhill skiing. b, Ice hockey. c, Cross-country skiing. d, Speed skating.

1989, Jan. 30 **Litho.** ***Imperf.***
Simulated Perforations

3390 Sheet of 4 2.25 1.00
a.-d. A1324 25s multicolored .50 .25

No. 3390 exists imperf. without simulated perforations and containing black control number. Value $15.

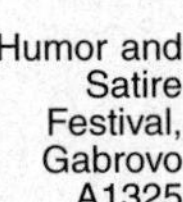

Humor and Satire Festival, Gabrovo A1325

1989, Feb. 7 ***Perf. 13½x13***

3391 A1325 13s Don Quixote .30 .25

Endangered Plant Species — A1326

Designs: 5s, Ramonda serbica. 10s, Paeonia maskula. 25s, Viola perinensis. 30s, Dracunculus vulgaris. 42s, Tulipa splendens. 60s, Rindera umbellata.

1989, Feb. 22 ***Perf. 13x13½***

3392 A1326 5s multicolored .25 .25
3393 A1326 10s multicolored .25 .25
3394 A1326 25s multicolored .50 .30
3395 A1326 30s multicolored .60 .35
3396 A1326 42s multicolored .85 .50
3397 A1326 60s multicolored 1.25 .70
a. Min. sheet of 6, #3392-3397 4.25 2.50
Nos. 3392-3397 (6) 3.70 2.35

World Wildlife Fund A1327

Bats.

1989, Feb. 27 ***Perf. 13***

3398 A1327 5s Nyctalus noctula .30 .35
3399 A1327 13s Rhinolophus ferrumequinum .60 .45
3400 A1327 30s Myotis myotis 1.60 .55
3401 A1327 42s Vespertilio murinus 3.25 .95
a. Min. sheet of 4, #3398-3401 6.75 6.75
Nos. 3398-3401 (4) 5.75 2.30

Aleksandr Stamboliski (1879-1923), Premier — A1328

1989, Mar. 1 ***Perf. 13½x13***

3402 A1328 5s brt org & blk .25 .25

Souvenir Sheet

Soviet-Bulgarian Joint Space Flight, 10th Anniv. — A1329

Designs: a, Liftoff. b, Crew.

1989, Apr. 10 ***Perf. 13***

3403 A1329 Sheet of 2 2.40 1.25
a.-b. 50s any single 1.10 .60

Exists imperf. Value $15.

EXPO '91 Young Inventors Exhibition, Plovdiv — A1330

1989, Apr. 20 ***Perf. 13½x13***

3404 A1330 5s multicolored .25 .25

Petko Enev (b. 1889) A1331

Stanke Dimitrov Marek (b. 1889) — A1332

1989, Apr. 28 ***Perf. 13½x13, 13x13½***

3405 A1331 5s scarlet & black .25 .25
3406 A1332 5s scarlet & black .25 .25

Icons — A1333

Paintings by Bulgarian artists: No. 3407, Archangel Michael, by Dimiter Molerov. No. 3408, Mother and Child, by Toma Vishanov. No. 3409, St. John, by Vishanov. No. 3410, St. Dimitri, by Ivan Terziev.

1989, Apr. 28 ***Perf. 13x13½***

3407 A1333 30s multicolored .60 .35
3408 A1333 30s multicolored .60 .35
3409 A1333 30s multicolored .60 .35
3410 A1333 30s multicolored .60 .35
Nos. 3407-3410 (4) 2.40 1.40

Nos. 3408, 3410 exist in sheets of four. Nos. 3407-3410 exist in souvenir sheets of four and together in one sheet of four, imperf.

Photocopier A1334

1989, May 5

3411 A1334 5s shown .25 .25
3412 A1334 8s Computer .50 .25
3413 A1334 35s Telephone .80 .45
3414 A1334 42s Dish receiver .90 .50
Nos. 3411-3414 (4) 2.45 1.45

Bulgarian Communications, 110th anniv. Nos. 3411-3413 exist in imperf. sheets of six.

Souvenir Sheet

58th FIP Congress — A1335

1989, May 22

3415 A1335 1 l Charioteer 2.25 1.00

Exists imperf. Value $15.

1st Communist Party Congress in Bulgaria, 70th Anniv. — A1336

1989, June 15

3416 A1336 5s mar, blk & dk red .25 .25

Famous Men — A1337

No. 3417, Ilya Blaskov. No. 3418, Sofronii, Bishop of Vratza. No. 3419, Vassil Aprilov (b. 1789), educator, historian. No. 3420, Christo Jassenov (1889-1925). No. 3421, 10s, Stoyan Zagorchinov (1889-1969).

1989

3417 A1337 5s black & gray ol .25 .25
3418 A1337 5s blk, brn blk & pale green .25 .25
3419 A1337 8s lt blue, blk & vio blk .30 .25
3420 A1337 8s tan, blk & dark red brown .25 .25
3421 A1337 10s blk, pale pink & gray blue .30 .25
Nos. 3417-3421 (5) 1.35 1.25

Issued: Nos. 3417-3418, June 15; No. 3419, Aug. 1; No. 3420, Sept. 25; 10s, Aug. 5.

French Revolution, Bicent. — A1338

1989, June 26 ***Perf. 13½x13***

3422 A1338 13s Anniv. emblem .25 .25
3423 A1338 30s Jean-Paul Marat .60 .35
3424 A1338 42s Robespierre .85 .50
Nos. 3422-3424 (3) 1.70 1.10

7th Army Games — A1339

1989, June 30 *Perf. 13*

3425 A1339 5s Gymnast .25 .25
3426 A1339 13s Equestrian .30 .25
3427 A1339 30s Running .50 .40
3428 A1339 42s Shooting .70 .50
Nos. 3425-3428 (4) 1.75 1.40

22nd World Canoe and Kayak Championships, Plovdiv — A1340

1989, Aug. 11 **Litho.** *Perf. 13*

3429 A1340 13s Woman paddling .30 .25
3430 A1340 30s Man rowing .60 .25

Photography, 150th Anniv. — A1341

1989, Aug. 29 *Perf. 13½x13*

3431 A1341 42s blk, buff & yel .95 .45

September 9 Revolution, 45th Anniv. — A1342

1989, Aug. 30 *Perf. 13*

3432 A1342 5s Revolutionaries .25 .25
3433 A1342 8s Couple embracing .25 .25
3434 A1342 13s Faces in a crowd .25 .25
Nos. 3432-3434 (3) .75 .75

Natural History Museum, Cent. A1343

1989, Aug. 31

3435 A1343 13s multicolored .30 .25

Postal Workers Killed in World War II — A1343a

Designs: 5s, L.D. Dardjikov. 8s, I.B. Dobrev. 10s, N.P. Antonov.

1989, Sept. 22 **Litho.** *Perf. 13*

3436 A1343a 5s multicolored .25 .25
3437 A1343a 8s multicolored .25 .25
3438 A1343a 13s multicolored .30 .25
Nos. 3436-3438 (3) .80 .75

12th Shipping Unions Congress (FIATA) — A1344

1989, Sept. 25 **Litho.** *Perf. 13½x13*

3439 A1344 42s light bl & dark bl 1.00 .45

Jawaharlal Nehru, 1st Prime Minister of Independent India — A1346

1989, Oct. 10

3440 A1346 13s blk, pale yel & brn .30 .25

Souvenir Sheet

European Ecology Congress — A1347

1989, Oct. 12 *Perf. 13*

3441 A1347 Sheet of 2 4.75 4.75
a. 50s multicolored 1.50 .85
b. 1 l multicolored 2.50 1.40

Souvenir sheet exists imperf. Value $18.50.

Snakes A1368

Designs: 5s, Eryx jaculus turcicus. 10s, Elaphe longissima. 25s, Elaphe situla. 30s, Elaphe quatuorlineata. 42s, Telescopus fallax. 60s, Coluber rubriceps.

1989, Oct. 20 **Litho.** *Perf. 13*

3491 A1368 5s multicolored .25 .25
3492 A1368 10s multicolored .25 .25
3493 A1368 25s multicolored .55 .30
3494 A1368 30s multicolored .65 .35
3495 A1368 42s multicolored .90 .50
3496 A1368 60s multicolored 1.25 .70
a. Min. sheet of 6, #3491-3496 4.25 2.00
Nos. 3491-3496 (6) 3.85 2.35

Intl. Youth Science Fair, Plovdiv, 1989 — A1369

1989, Nov. 4

3497 A1369 13s multicolored .25 .25

1990 World Soccer Championships, Italy — A1370

Various athletes: No. 3502a, Athletes facing right. No. 3502b, Athletes facing left.

1989, Dec. 1

3498 A1370 5s shown .25 .25
3499 A1370 13s multi, diff. .30 .25
3500 A1370 30s multi, diff. .70 .35
3501 A1370 42s multi, diff. 1.00 .50
Nos. 3498-3501 (4) 2.25 1.35

Souvenir Sheet

3502 Sheet of 2 2.40 1.10
a.-b. A1370 50s any single 1.10 .55

No. 3502 exists imperf. Value $15.

Air Sports A1371

1989, Dec. 8

3503 A1371 5s Glider planes .25 .25
3504 A1371 13s Hang glider .30 .25
3505 A1371 30s Sky diving .70 .35
3506 A1371 42s Three sky divers 1.00 .50
Nos. 3503-3506 (4) 2.25 1.35

82nd General conference of the FAI, Varna.

Traffic Safety A1372

1989, Dec. 12

3507 A1372 5s multicolored .25 .25

New Year 1990 — A1373

1989, Dec. 25 **Litho.** *Perf. 13*

3508 A1373 5s Santa's sleigh .25 .25
3509 A1373 13s Snowman .30 .25

Cats A1374

No. 3510, Persian. No. 3511, Tiger. 8s, Tabby. No. 3513, Himalayan. No. 3514, Persian, diff. 13s, Siamese. Nos. 3511, 3514-3515 vert.

Perf. 13½x13, 13x13½

1989, Dec. 26 **Background Color**

3510 A1374 5s gray .25 .25
3511 A1374 5s yellow .25 .25
3512 A1374 8s orange .25 .25
3513 A1374 10s blue .25 .25
3514 A1374 10s brown orange .25 .25
3515 A1374 13s red .30 .25
Nos. 3510-3515 (6) 1.55 1.50

Explorers and Their Ships — A1375

1990, Jan. 17 *Perf. 13*

3516 A1375 5s Columbus .25 .25
3517 A1375 8s da Gama .25 .25
3518 A1375 13s Magellan .25 .25
3519 A1375 32s Drake .60 .35
3520 A1375 42s Hudson .75 .50
3521 A1375 60s Cook 1.00 .70
a. Min. sheet of 6, #3516-3521 3.75 1.75
Nos. 3516-3521 (6) 3.10 2.30

Natl. Esperanto Movement, Cent. — A1376

1990, Feb. 23 **Litho.** *Perf. 13*

3522 A1376 10s multicolored .35 .25

Paintings by Foreign Artists in the Natl. Museum A1377

Artists: No. 3523, Suzanna Valadon (1867-1938). No. 3524, Maurice Brianchon (1899-1978). No. 3525, Moise Kisling (1891-1953). No. 3526, Giovanni Beltraffio (1467-1516).

1990, Mar. 23 *Perf. 14*

3523 A1377 30s multicolored .65 .40
3524 A1377 30s multicolored .65 .40
3525 A1377 30s multicolored .65 .40
3526 A1377 30s multicolored .65 .40
Nos. 3523-3526 (4) 2.60 1.60

1990 World Soccer Championships, Italy — A1378

Various athletes.

1990, Mar. 26 *Perf. 13*

3527 A1378 5s multicolored .25 .25
3528 A1378 13s multi, diff. .30 .25
3529 A1378 30s multi, diff. .70 .40
3530 A1378 42s multi, diff. .95 .50
Nos. 3527-3530 (4) 2.20 1.40

Souvenir Sheet

3531 Sheet of 2 2.40 1.25
a. A1378 50s Three players 1.10 .60
b. A1378 50s Two players 1.10 .60

No. 3531 exists imperf. Value $12.50.

Bavaria No. 1 A1379

1990, Apr. 6 Litho. *Perf. 13*
3532 A1379 42s vermilion & blk 1.00 .50

ESSEN '90, Germany, Apr. 12-22. No. 3532 printed in sheets of 3 + 3 labels.

Souvenir Sheet

Penny Black, 150th Anniv. — A1380

1990, Apr. 10
3533 Sheet of 2 2.50 1.25
a. A1380 50s Great Britain #1 1.20 .60
b. A1380 50s Sir Rowland Hill 1.20 .60

Cooperative Farming in Bulgaria, Cent. — A1381

1990, Apr. 17
3534 A1381 5s multicolored .25 .25

Dimitar Chorbadjiski-Chudomir (1890-1967) — A1382

1990, Apr. 24
3535 A1382 5s multicolored .25 .25

Labor Day, Cent. — A1383

1990, May 1 *Perf. 13x13½*
3536 A1383 10s multicolored .25 .25

ITU, 125th Anniv. — A1384

1990, May 13 Litho. *Perf. 13½x13*
3537 A1384 20s bl, red & blk .50 .25

Belgium No. 1 A1385

1990, May 23 *Perf. 13*
3538 A1385 30s multicolored .75 .40

Belgica '90. No. 3538 printed in sheets of 3 + 3 labels.

Lamartine (1790-1869), French Poet — A1386

1990, June 15 *Perf. 13½x13*
3539 A1386 20s multicolored .45 .25

Dinosaurs — A1387

1990, June 19 *Perf. 12½*
3540 A1387 5s Brontosaurus .25 .25
3541 A1387 8s Stegosaurus .25 .25
3542 A1387 13s Edaphosaurus .30 .25
3543 A1387 25s Rhamphorhynchus .60 .30
3544 A1387 32s Protoceratops .80 .40
3545 A1387 42s Triceratops 1.10 .55
a. Min. sheet of 6, #3540-3545 3.50 1.60
Nos. 3540-3545 (6) 3.30 2.00

1992 Summer Olympic Games, Barcelona — A1388

1990, July 13 *Perf. 13½x13*
3546 A1388 5s Swimming .25 .25
3547 A1388 13s Handball .30 .25
3548 A1388 30s Hurdling .75 .40
3549 A1388 42s Cycling 1.10 .55
Nos. 3546-3549 (4) 2.40 1.45

Souvenir Sheet

3550 Sheet of 2 3.50 1.25
a. A1388 50s Tennis, forehand 1.50 .60
b. A1388 50s Tennis, backhand 1.50 .60

No. 3550 exists imperf. Value $10.

Butterflies A1389

1990, Aug. 8 Litho. *Perf. 13*
3551 A1389 5s Zerynthia Polyxena .25 .25
3552 A1389 10s Panaxia quadripunctaria .25 .25
3553 A1389 20s Proserpinus proserpina .25 .25
3554 A1389 30s Hyles lineata .25 .25
3555 A1389 42s Thecla betulae .50 .25
3556 A1389 60s Euphydryas cynthia 1.75 .60
a. Min. sheet of 6, #3551-3556 3.50 1.75
Nos. 3551-3556 (6) 3.25 1.85

Airplanes — A1390

1990, Aug. 30 Litho. *Perf. 13½x13*
3557 A1390 5s Airbus A-300 .25 .25
3558 A1390 10s Tu-204 .25 .25
3559 A1390 25s Concorde .30 .25
3560 A1390 30s DC-9 .40 .30
3561 A1390 42s Il-86 .70 .40
3562 A1390 60s Boeing 747 1.20 .55
a. Min. sheet of 6, #3557-3562 3.50 2.00
Nos. 3557-3562 (6) 3.10 2.00

Exarch Joseph I (1840-1915), Religious Leader — A1391

1990, Sept. 27 *Perf. 13*
3563 A1391 5s blk, pur & grn .25 .25

Intl. Traffic Safety Year A1392

1990, Oct. 9 Litho. *Perf. 13*
3564 A1392 5s multicolored .25 .25

Olymphilex '90, Varna — A1393

1990, Oct. 16 *Perf. 13x13½*
3565 A1393 5s Shot put .25 .25
3566 A1393 13s Discus .25 .25
3567 A1393 42s Hammer throw .90 .55
3568 A1393 60s Javelin 1.25 .70
a. Souv. sheet of 4, #3565-3568, imperf. 13.00 7.50
Nos. 3565-3568 (4) 2.65 1.75

Space Exploration — A1394

Designs: 5s, Sputnik, 1957, USSR. 8s, Vostok, 1961, USSR. 10s, Voshkod 2, 1965, USSR. 20s, Apollo-Soyuz, 1975, US-USSR. 42s, Space Shuttle Columbia, 1981, US. 60s, Galileo, 1989-1996, US. 1 l, Apollo 11 Moon landing, 1969, US.

1990, Oct. 22 *Perf. 13½x13*
3569 A1394 5s multicolored .25 .25
3570 A1394 8s multicolored .25 .25
3571 A1394 10s multicolored .25 .25
3572 A1394 20s multicolored .40 .25
3573 A1394 42s multicolored .90 .55
3574 A1394 60s multicolored 1.25 .70
Nos. 3569-3574 (6) 3.30 2.25

Souvenir Sheet

3575 A1394 1 l multicolored 2.50 1.50

No. 3575 exists imperf. Value $8.50.

St. Clement of Ohrid — A1395

1990, Nov. 29 Litho. *Perf. 13*
3576 A1395 5s multicolored .25 .25

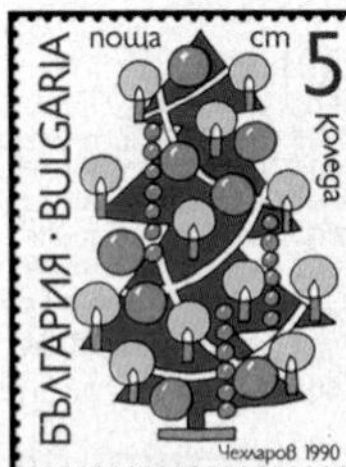

Christmas A1396

1990, Dec. 25 Litho. *Perf. 13*
3577 A1396 5s Christmas tree .25 .25
3578 A1396 20s Santa Claus .40 .25

European Figure Skating Championships, Sofia — A1397

1991, Jan. 18 *Perf. 13½x13*
3579 A1397 15s multicolored .35 .25

Farm Animals A1398

1991-92 *Perf. 14x13½*

3581 A1398 20s Sheep .25 .25
3582 A1398 25s Goose .25 .25
3583 A1398 30s Hen, chicks .35 .25
3584 A1398 40s Horse .35 .25
3585 A1398 62s Goat .55 .30
3586 A1398 86s Sow .80 .50
3587 A1398 95s Goat .55 .30
3588 A1398 1 l Donkey .75 .40
3589 A1398 2 l Bull 1.50 .50
3590 A1398 5 l Turkey 3.00 1.25
3591 A1398 10 l Cow 5.00 1.75
Nos. 3581-3591 (11) 13.35 6.00

Issued: 20s, 25s, 40s, 86s, 1 l, 8/21; 10 l, 2/22; 95s, 5/5/92; others, 2/11/91.

Mushrooms A1399

1991, Mar. 19 *Perf. 12½x13*

3597 A1399 5s Amanita phalloides .25 .25
3598 A1399 10s Amanita verna .25 .25
3599 A1399 20s Amanita pantherina .25 .25
3600 A1399 32s Amanita muscaria .40 .30
3601 A1399 42s Gyromitra esculenta .45 .35
3602 A1399 60s Boletus satanas .70 .50
a. Min. sheet of 6, #3597-3602 3.25 1.50
Nos. 3597-3602 (6) 2.30 1.90

French Impressionists A1400

Designs: 20s, Good Morning, by Gauguin. 43s, Madame Dobini, by Degas. 62s, Peasant Woman, by Pissarro. 67s, Woman with Black Hair, by Manet. 80s, Blue Vase, by Cezanne. 2 l, Jeanny Samari, by Renoir. 3 l, Self portrait, by Van Gogh.

1991, Apr. 1 *Perf. 13*

3603 A1400 20s multicolored .25 .25
3604 A1400 43s multicolored .50 .40
3605 A1400 62s multicolored .70 .55
3606 A1400 67s multicolored .80 .60
3607 A1400 80s multicolored .90 .75
3608 A1400 2 l multicolored 2.00 1.75
Nos. 3603-3608 (6) 5.15 4.30

Miniature Sheet

3609 A1400 3 l multicolored 4.00 2.75

Swiss Confederation, 700th Anniv. — A1401

1991, Apr. 11

3610 A1401 62s multicolored .75 .55

Philatelic Review, Cent. — A1402

1991, May 7 **Litho.** *Perf. 13*

3611 A1402 30s multicolored .45 .25

Europa — A1403

1991, May 10 *Perf. 13x13½*

3612 A1403 43s Meteosat *.70 .40*
3613 A1403 62s Ariane rocket *1.00 .55*

Horses — A1404

1991, May 21 *Perf. 13x12½*

3614 A1404 5s Przewalski's horse .25 .25
3615 A1404 10s Tarpan .25 .25
3616 A1404 25s Arabian .25 .25
3617 A1404 35s Arabian .45 .30
3618 A1404 42s Shetland pony .55 .35
3619 A1404 60s Draft horse .70 .50
a. Min. sheet of 6, #3614-3619 3.25 1.50
Nos. 3614-3619 (6) 2.45 1.90

EXPO 91, Plovdiv — A1405

1991, June 6 **Litho.** *Perf. 13½x13*

3620 A1405 30s multicolored .45 .30

Wolfgang Amadeus Mozart A1406

1991, July 2 *Perf. 13*

3621 A1406 62s multicolored 1.00 .55

Space Shuttle Missions, 10th Anniv. A1407

1991, July 23 **Litho.** *Perf. 13*

3622 A1407 12s Columbia .25 .25
3623 A1407 32s Challenger .30 .25
3624 A1407 50s Discovery .40 .25
3625 A1407 86s Atlantis, vert. .75 .40
3626 A1407 1.50 l Buran, vert. 1.25 .60
3627 A1407 2 l Atlantis, diff., vert. 1.50 .75
Nos. 3622-3627 (6) 4.45 2.50

Souvenir Sheet

3628 A1407 3 l US shuttle, earth 3.00 2.00

No. 3628 exists imperf. Value $6.25.

1992 Winter Olympics, Albertville A1408

1991, Aug. 7 **Litho.** *Perf. 13x13½*

3629 A1408 30s Luge .40 .30
3630 A1408 43s Slalom skiing .50 .40
3631 A1408 67s Ski jumping .85 .60
3632 A1408 2 l Biathlon 2.50 1.75
Nos. 3629-3632 (4) 4.25 3.05

Souvenir Sheet

3633 A1408 3 l Two-man bobsled 3.00 2.00

No. 3633 exists imperf. Value $7.

Sheraton Sofia Hotel Balkan A1409

1991, Sept. 6 **Litho.** *Perf. 13*

3634 A1409 62s multicolored 1.25 .55

Printed in sheets of 3 + 3 labels.

Dogs — A1410

1991, Oct. 11 *Perf. 13x13½*

3635 A1410 30s Japanese .25 .25
3636 A1410 43s Chihuahua .25 .25
3637 A1410 62s Pinscher .55 .30
3638 A1410 80s Yorkshire terrier .70 .35
3639 A1410 1 l Chinese .90 .45
3640 A1410 3 l Pug 2.00 1.25
a. Min. sheet of 6, #3635-3640 5.75 2.75
Nos. 3635-3640 (6) 4.65 2.85

Cologne '91, Intl. Philatelic Exhibition A1411

1991, Oct. 21 *Perf. 13*

3641 A1411 86s multicolored 1.20 .75

Printed in sheets of 3 + 3 labels.

Souvenir Sheet

Brandenburg Gate, Bicent. — A1412

1991, Oct. 23

3642 A1412 4 l multicolored 2.00 2.00

Exists imperf. Value $6.75.

Phila Nippon '91 A1413

1991, Nov. 11

3643 A1413 62s Japan #1 .75 .55

Printed in sheets of 3 + 3 labels.

Bulgarian Railroad, 125th Anniv. — A1414

1991, Nov. 30

3644 A1414 30s Locomotive .45 .30
3645 A1414 30s Passenger car .45 .30

Medicinal Plants — A1415

Designs: 30s, Pulsatilla vernalis. 40s, Pulsatilla pratensis. 55s, Pulsatilla halleri. 60s, Aquilegia nigricans. 1 l, Hippophae rhamnoides. 2 l, Ribes nigrum.

1991, Nov. 20 **Litho.** *Perf. 13*

3646 A1415 30s +15s label .40 .25
3647 A1415 40s multicolored .35 .25
3648 A1415 55s multicolored .50 .25
3649 A1415 60s multicolored .55 .30
3650 A1415 1 l multicolored .90 .45
3651 A1415 2 l multicolored 1.75 .90
a. Min. sheet of 6, #3646-3651 4.75 2.50
Nos. 3646-3651 (6) 4.45 2.40

No. 3646 printed se-tenant with label. No. 3651a sold for 5 l, but does not contain the 15s label printed with No. 3646.

Basketball, Cent. A1416

1991, Dec. 6 *Perf. 13½x13*

3652 A1416 43s Ball below rim .40 .25
3653 A1416 62s Ball at rim .60 .40
3654 A1416 90s Ball in cylinder .90 .55
3655 A1416 1 l Ball in basket 1.00 .65
Nos. 3652-3655 (4) 2.90 1.85

El Greco, 450th Birth Anniv. — A1417

Paintings: 43s, Christ Carrying the Cross. 50s, Holy Family with St. Anne. 60s, St. John the Evangelist and St. John the Baptist. 62s, St. Andrew and St. Francis. 1 l, Holy Family with St. Mary Magdalene. 2 l, Cardinal Nino de Guevara. 3 l, Holy Family with St. Anne (detail).

1991, Dec. 13 *Perf. 13*

3656 A1417 43s multicolored .45 .25
3657 A1417 50s multicolored .55 .30
3658 A1417 60s multicolored .65 .35
3659 A1417 62s multicolored .70 .40
3660 A1417 1 l multicolored 1.10 .55
3661 A1417 2 l multicolored 2.00 1.00
Nos. 3656-3661 (6) 5.45 2.85

Souvenir Sheet

3662 A1417 3 l multicolored 3.00 2.00

No. 3662 contains one 43x53mm stamp.

Christmas — A1418

1991, Dec. 18

3663 A1418 30s Snowman, candle, bell, heart .25 .25
3664 A1418 62s Star, angel, flower, house, tree 1.00 .25

Marine Mammals — A1419

Designs: 30s, Phogophoca graenlandica. 43s, Orcinus orca. 62s, Odobenus rosmarus. 68s, Tursiops truncatus. 1 l, Monachus monachus. 2 l, Phocaena phocaena.

1991, Dec. 24

3665 A1419 30s multicolored .25 .25
3666 A1419 43s multicolored .40 .25
3667 A1419 62s multicolored .60 .40
3668 A1419 68s multicolored .65 .40
3669 A1419 1 l multicolored 1.00 .65
3670 A1419 2 l multicolored 2.00 1.25
a. Min. sheet of #3665-3670 5.00 3.00
Nos. 3665-3670 (6) 4.90 3.20

Settlement of Jews in Bulgaria, 500th Anniv. — A1420

1992, Mar. 5 **Litho.** *Perf. 13*

3671 A1420 1 l multicolored 1.75 .90

Gioacchino Rossini (1792-1868), Composer — A1421

1992, Mar. 11

3672 A1421 50s multicolored .65 .35

Plovdiv Fair, Cent. — A1422

1992, Mar. 25

3673 A1422 1 l buff & black 1.00 .75

Fiat Croma — A1423

Automobiles.

1992, Mar. 26 *Perf. 13½x13*

3674 A1423 30s Volvo 740 .25 .25
3675 A1423 45s Ford Escort .45 .30
3676 A1423 50s shown .50 .30
3677 A1423 50s Mercedes 600 .50 .30
3678 A1423 1 l Peugeot 605 1.00 .55
3679 A1423 2 l BMW 316 1.50 .90
Nos. 3674-3679 (6) 4.20 2.60

Francisco de Orellana A1424

Explorers: No. 3681, Vespucci. No. 3682, Magellan. No. 3683, Gonzalo Jimenez de Quesada (1500-1579). 2 l, Drake. 3 l, Pedro de Valdivia (1500-1553). 4 l, Columbus.

1992, Apr. 22 **Litho.** *Perf. 13*

3680 A1424 50s multicolored .25 .25
3681 A1424 50s multicolored .25 .25
3682 A1424 1 l multicolored .60 .35
3683 A1424 1 l multicolored .60 .35
3684 A1424 2 l multicolored 1.25 .90
3685 A1424 3 l multicolored 1.90 1.40
Nos. 3680-3685 (6) 4.85 3.50

Souvenir Sheet

3686 A1424 4 l multicolored 3.25 1.50

Granada '92 A1425

1992, Apr. 23

3687 A1425 62s multicolored .55 .30

No. 3687 printed in sheets of 3 + 3 labels.

Discovery of America, 500th Anniv. — A1426

1992, Apr. 24

3688 1 l Ships, map .90 .45
3689 2 l Columbus, ship 2.40 .90
a. A1426 Pair, #3688-3689 4.00 2.10

Europa.

SOS Children's Village A1427

1992, June 15 **Litho.** *Perf. 13*

3690 A1427 1 l multicolored .80 .50

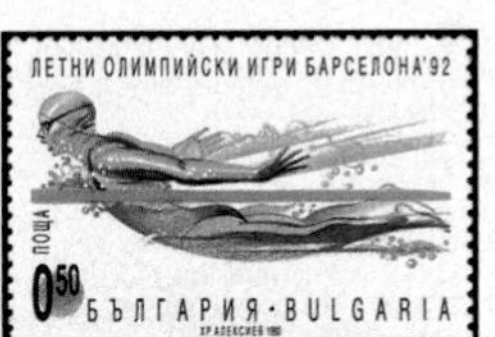

1992 Summer Olympics, Barcelona — A1428

1992, July 15 *Perf. 13½x13*

3691 A1428 50s Swimming .35 .25
3692 A1428 50s Long jump .35 .25
3693 A1428 1 l High jump .70 .45
3694 A1428 3 l Gymnastics 2.00 1.40
Nos. 3691-3694 (4) 3.40 2.35

Souvenir Sheet

Perf. 13x13½

3695 A1428 4 l Torch, vert. 3.00 1.75

Motorcycles — A1429

Designs: 30s, 1902 Laurin & Klement. No. 3697, 1928 Puch 200 Luxus. No. 3698, 1931 Norton CS1. 70s, 1950 Harley Davidson. 1 l, 1986 Gilera SP 01. 2 l, 1990 BMW K1.

1992, July 30 *Perf. 13*

3696 A1429 30s multicolored .25 .25
3697 A1429 50s multicolored .30 .25
3698 A1429 50s multicolored .30 .25
3699 A1429 70s multicolored .40 .25
3700 A1429 1 l multicolored .60 .30
3701 A1429 2 l multicolored 1.25 .65
Nos. 3696-3701 (6) 3.10 1.95

Genoa '92 Intl. Philatelic Exhibition A1430

1992, Sept. 18 *Perf. 13*

3702 A1430 1 l multicolored .70 .35

This is a developing set. Numbers may change.

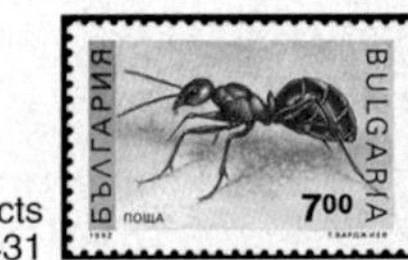

Insects A1431

1992 **Litho.** *Perf. 14x13½*

3710 A1431 1 l Dragonfly *.25*
3711 A1431 2 l Mayfly *.45*
3712 A1431 3 l Locust *.55*
3713 A1431 4 l Stag beetle *.80*
3714 A1431 5 l Carrion beetle *1.00*
3715 A1431 7 l Ant *1.50*
3716 A1431 20 l Bee *4.00*
3717 A1431 50 l Praying mantis *10.50*
Nos. 3710-3717 (8) *19.05*

Issued: 7, 20 l, 9/25; 3, 50 l, 11/30; 1, 2, 4, 5 l, 12/15/93.

A1432

1992, Sept. 30 *Perf. 13*

3719 A1432 1 l blk, pink & rose .90 .45

Higher Institute of Architecture and Building, 50th anniv.

A1433

Trees: No. 3720, Quercus mestensis. No. 3721, Aesculus hippocastanum. No. 3722, Quercus thracica. No. 3723, Pinus peuce. 2 l, Acer heldreichii. 3 l, Pyrus bulgarica.

1992, Oct. 16 **Litho.** *Perf. 13*

3720 A1433 50s multicolored .30 .25
3721 A1433 50s multicolored .30 .25
3722 A1433 1 l multicolored .60 .30
3723 A1433 1 l multicolored .60 .30
3724 A1433 2 l multicolored 1.25 .65
3725 A1433 3 l multicolored 2.00 1.00
Nos. 3720-3725 (6) 5.05 2.75

Ethnographical Museum, Cent. — A1434

1992, Oct. 23

3726 A1434 1 l multicolored .90 .45

Tanker Bulgaria — A1435

1992, Oct. 30 Litho. *Perf. 13*

3727 A1435 30s Freighter Bulgaria .25 .25
3728 A1435 50s Castor .30 .25
3729 A1435 1 l Hero of Sevastopol .60 .30
3730 A1435 2 l shown 1.00 .65
3731 A1435 2 l Aleko Constantinov 1.25 .65
3732 A1435 3 l Varna 2.00 1.00
Nos. 3727-3732 (6) 5.40 3.10

Bulgarian Merchant Fleet, Cent.

Bulgaria, Member of the Council of Europe — A1436

1992, Nov. 6 Litho. *Perf. 13*

3733 A1436 7 l multicolored 4.00 2.00

Souvenir Sheet

4th World Congress of Popular Sports, Varna — A1437

1992, Nov. 17 Litho. *Perf. 13*

3734 A1437 4 l multicolored 2.75 2.75

Christmas A1438

1992, Dec. 1 *Perf. 13½x13*

3735 A1438 1 l Santa Claus .50
3736 A1438 7 l Madonna & Child 4.00

Wild Cats — A1439

1992, Dec. 18 Litho. *Perf. 13*

3737 A1439 50s Panthera pardus .25 .25
3738 A1439 50s Acinonyx jubatus .25 .25
3739 A1439 1 l Panthera onca .50 .25
3740 A1439 2 l Panthera tigris 1.25 .50
3741 A1439 2 l Felis concolor 1.25 .50
3742 A1439 3 l Panthera leo 1.50 .60
Nos. 3737-3742 (6) 5.00 2.35

Sports A1440

1992, Dec. 18

3743 A1440 50s Baseball .35 .25
3744 A1440 50s Cricket .35 .25
3745 A1440 1 l Polo .75 .25
3746 A1440 1 l Harness racing .75 .25
3747 A1440 2 l Field hockey 1.00 .70
3748 A1440 3 l Football 2.00 .90
Nos. 3743-3748 (6) 5.20 2.60

Owls A1441

1992, Dec. 23

3749 A1441 30s Aegolius funereus .25 .25
3750 A1441 50s Strix aluco .25 .25
3751 A1441 1 l Asio otus .50 .25
3752 A1441 2 l Otus scops 1.25 .50
3753 A1441 2 l Asio flammeus 1.25 .50
3754 A1441 3 l Tyto alba 1.50 .65
Nos. 3749-3754 (6) 5.00 2.40

Nos. 3749, 3751, 3753-3754 are vert.

Paintings Depicting History of Bulgaria A1442

Artists: 50s, Dimiter Gyudzhenov. 1 l, 3 l, Nikolai Pavlovich. 2 l, Dimiter Panchev. 4 l, Mito Ganovski.

1992, Dec. 28

3755 A1442 50s multicolored .35 .25
3756 A1442 1 l multicolored .65 .25
3757 A1442 2 l multicolored 1.40 .60
3758 A1442 3 l multicolored 2.00 .90
Nos. 3755-3758 (4) 4.40 2.00

Souvenir Sheet

3759 A1442 4 l multicolored, vert. 2.50

Archeological Museum, Cent. — A1443

1993, Jan. 1 Litho. *Perf. 13x13½*

3760 A1443 1 l multicolored .75 .25

1993 World Biathlon Championships, Borovetz — A1444

1993, Feb. 5

3761 A1444 1 l Woman aiming rifle .50 .30
3762 A1444 7 l Skiing 5.00 1.75

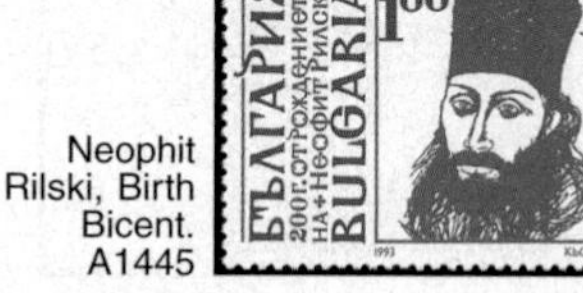

Neophit Rilski, Birth Bicent. A1445

1993, Apr. 22 Litho. *Perf. 13½x13*

3763 A1445 1 l henna brn & ol bis .75 .25

Contemporary Art — A1446

Europa: 3 l, Sculpture of centaur, by Georgi Chapkinov. 8 l, Painting of geometric forms, by D. Bujukliski.

1993, Apr. 29 *Perf. 13x13½*

3764 A1446 3 l multicolored 1.50 .55
3765 A1446 8 l multicolored 2.50 1.10

Fish A1447

1993, June 29 Litho. *Perf. 13*

3766 A1447 1 l C.a.j. bicaudatus .25 .25
3767 A1447 2 l Mollienesia velifera .40 .25
3768 A1447 3 l Aphyosemion bivittatum .60 .25
3769 A1447 3 l Pterophyllum eimekei .80 .25
3770 A1447 4 l Symphysodon discus 1.00 .30
3771 A1447 8 l Trichogaster leeri 2.00 .50
Nos. 3766-3771 (6) 5.05 1.80

Fruit — A1448

1993, July 8 *Perf. 13x13½*

3772 A1448 1 l Malus domestica .25 .25
3773 A1448 2 l Pyrus sativa .45 .25
3774 A1448 2 l Persica vulgaris .45 .25
3775 A1448 3 l Cydonia oblonga .60 .25
3776 A1448 5 l Punica granatum 1.25 .30
3777 A1448 7 l Ficus carica 1.75 .50
Nos. 3772-3777 (6) 4.75 1.80

Claudio Monteverdi (1567-1643), Composer — A1449

1993, July 20 Litho. *Perf. 13½x13*

3778 A1449 1 l multicolored .50

17th World Summer Games for the Deaf A1450

1993, July 20 *Perf. 13*

3779 A1450 1 l shown .25 .25
3780 A1450 2 l Swimming .50 .25
3781 A1450 3 l Cycling .75 .25
3782 A1450 4 l Tennis 1.00 .30
Nos. 3779-3782 (4) 2.50 1.05

Souvenir Sheet

3783 A1450 5 l Soccer 1.00 1.00

Miniature Sheet

A1451

Council of Preslav, Cyrillic Alphabet in Bulgaria, 1100th Anniv.: a, Baptism of Christian convert. b, Tsar Boris I (852-889). c, Tsar Simeon (893-927). d, Battle between Bulgarians and Byzantines.

1993, Sept. 16 Litho. *Perf. 13½x13*

3784 A1451 5 l Sheet of 4, #a.-d. 4.00 4.00

Alexander of Battenberg (1857-93), Prince of Bulgaria — A1452

1993, Sept. 23 *Perf. 13x13½*

3785 A1452 3 l multicolored .65 .25

Peter I. Tchaikovsky (1840-93) A1453

1993, Sept. 30 *Perf. 13½x13*

3786 A1453 3 l multicolored .65 .25

Small Arms — A1454

1993, Oct. 22 Litho. *Perf. 13½x14*

3787 A1454 1 l Crossbow, 16th cent. .25 .25
3788 A1454 2 l Pistol, 18th cent. .40 .25
3789 A1454 3 l Luger, 1908 .60 .25
3790 A1454 3 l Pistol, 1873 .60 .25
3791 A1454 5 l Rifle, 1938 1.10 .30
3792 A1454 7 l Kalashnikov, 1947 1.60 .60
Nos. 3787-3792 (6) 4.55 1.90

Isaac Newton (1643-1727) A1455

1993, Oct. 29 *Perf. 13½x13*
3793 A1455 1 l multicolored *.25* .25

Organized Philately in Bulgaria, Cent. A1456

1993, Nov. 16
3794 A1456 1 l multicolored *.25* .25

Ecology A1457

1993, Nov. 17
3795 A1457 1 l shown *.25* .25
3796 A1457 7 l Ecology *1.60* .50

Game Animals A1458

1993, Nov. 25
3797 A1458 1 l Anas platrhynchos *.25* .25
3798 A1458 1 l Phasianus colchicus *.25* .25
3799 A1458 2 l Vulpes vulpes *.35* .25
3800 A1458 3 l Capreolus capreolus *.50* .40
3801 A1458 6 l Lepus europaeus *1.00* .50
3802 A1458 8 l Sus scrofa *1.40* .60
Nos. 3797-3802 (6) *3.75* 2.25

Christmas A1459

Signs of Zodiac on sundial: No. 3803a, Taurus, Gemini, Cancer. b, Libra, Virgo, Leo.
No. 3804a, Aquarius, Pisces, Aries. b, Capricorn, Sagittarius, Scorpio.

1993, Dec. 1
3803 A1459 1 l Pair, #a.-b. *.35* .25
3804 A1459 7 l Pair, #a.-b. *2.50* .70

When placed together, Nos. 3803-3804 form a complete sundial.

Regional Folk Costumes for Men
A1460 A1461

1993, Dec. 16 **Litho.** *Perf. 13½x14*
3805 A1460 1 l Sofia *.25* .25
3806 A1461 1 l Plovdiv *.25* .25
3807 A1460 2 l Belogradchik *.25* .25
3808 A1460 3 l Shumen *.30* .25
3809 A1461 3 l Oryakhovitsa *.40* .25
3810 A1461 8 l Kurdzhali *1.25* .40
Nos. 3805-3810 (6) *2.70* 1.65

1994 Winter Olympics, Lillehammer A1462

1994, Feb. 8 *Perf. 13*
3811 A1462 1 l Freestlye skiing *.25* .25
3812 A1462 2 l Speed skating *.30* .25
3813 A1462 3 l 2-Man luge *.40* .25
3814 A1462 4 l Hockey *.80* .25
Nos. 3811-3814 (4) *1.75* 1.00

Souvenir Sheet

3815 A1462 5 l Downhill skiing *.75* .75

Nikolai Pavlovich (1835-94) A1463

1994, Feb. 16 *Perf. 13½x13*
3816 A1463 3 l multicolored *.50* .25

Dinosaurs — A1464

1994, Apr. 27 **Litho.** *Perf. 13*
3817 A1464 2 l Plesiosaurus *.60* .55
3818 A1464 3 l Iguanodon *.60* .55
3819 A1464 3 l Archaeopteryx *.60* .55
3820 A1464 4 l Edmontonia *.60* .55
3821 A1464 5 l Styracosaurus *.60* .55
3822 A1464 7 l Tyrannosaurus Rex *1.00* .55
Nos. 3817-3822 (6) *4.00*

1994 World Cup Soccer Championships, US — A1465

Players in championships of : 3 l, Chile, 1962. 6 l, England, 1966. 7 l, Mexico, 1970. 9 l, West Germany, 1974. No. 3827a, Mexico, 1986, vert. b, US, 1994.

1994, Apr. 28
3823 A1465 3 l multicolored *.25* .25
3824 A1465 6 l multicolored *1.00* .25
3825 A1465 7 l multicolored *1.10* .25
3826 A1465 9 l multicolored *1.50* 1.25
Nos. 3823-3826 (4) *3.85* 2.00

Souvenir Sheet

3827 A1465 5 l Sheet of 2, #a.-b. *1.75* 1.75

For No. 3827 with inscription reading up along the left margin, see No. 3851.

Europa A1466

European Discoveries: 3 l, Axis of symmetry. 15 l, Electrocardiogram.

1994, Apr. 29 **Litho.** *Perf. 13½*
3828 A1466 3 l multicolored *1.00* .25
3829 A1466 15 l multicolored *3.50* 1.25

Boris Hristov (1914-93) — A1467

1994, May 18 **Litho.** *Perf. 13*
3830 A1467 3 l brown & bister *.50* .45

Cricetus Cricetus A1468

Designs: 3 l, In nest. 7 l, Emerging from burrow. 10 l, Standing on hind legs. 15 l, Finding berry.

1994, Sept. 23 **Litho.** *Perf. 13*
3831 A1468 3 l multicolored *.60* .40
3832 A1468 7 l multicolored *1.00* .50
3833 A1468 10 l multicolored *1.50* .65
3834 A1468 15 l multicolored *2.25* 1.00
Nos. 3831-3834 (4) *5.35* 2.55

World Wildlife Fund.

Space Program — A1469

1994, Nov. 4 **Litho.** *Perf. 13*
3835 A1469 3 l multicolored *.45* .45

Intl. Olympic Committee, Cent. — A1470

1994, Nov. 7
3836 A1470 3 l multicolored *.45* .45

Icons — A1471

1994, Nov. 24 **Litho.** *Perf. 13x13½*
3837 A1471 2 l Christ *.25* .25
3838 A1471 3 l Christ, the healer *.45* .25
3839 A1471 5 l Crucifixion *.45* .25
3840 A1471 7 l Archangel Michael *1.00* .35
3841 A1471 8 l Sts. Cyril, Methodius *1.25* .45
3842 A1471 15 l Madonna & Child *2.50* .45
Nos. 3837-3842 (6) *5.90* 2.00

Christmas A1472

1994, Dec. 1
3843 A1472 3 l Ancient coin *.50* .25
3844 A1472 15 l Coin, diff. *2.50* 1.40

Roses A1473

1994, Dec. 12 *Perf. 13*

Color of Rose

3845 A1473 2 l yellow *.30* .25
3846 A1473 3 l rose red *.50* .25
3847 A1473 5 l white *.80* .25
3848 A1473 7 l salmon *1.10* .45
3849 A1473 10 l carmine *1.75* .45
3850 A1473 15 l orange & yellow *2.50* .45
Nos. 3845-3850 (6) *6.95* 2.10

No. 3827 with Addtl. Inscription in Left Sheet Margin

1994, Dec. 15 **Litho.** *Perf. 13*

Souvenir Sheet

3851 A1465 5 l Sheet of 2, #a.-b. *18.00* *18.00*

Trams — A1474

1994, Dec. 29
3852 A1474 1 l Model 1912 *.25* .25
3853 A1474 2 l Model 1928 *.25* .25
3854 A1474 3 l Model 1931 *.45* .25
3855 A1474 5 l Model 1942 *.70* .25
3856 A1474 8 l Model 1951 *1.50* .50
3857 A1474 10 l Model 1961 *1.75* .60
Nos. 3852-3857 (6) *4.90* 2.10

Vassil Petleshkov (1845-76), Revolutionary — A1475

1995, Feb. 27 Litho. *Perf. 13½x13*

3858	A1475	3 l multicolored	*.50*	.25

End of World War II, 50th Anniv. — A1476

Europa: 15 l, Dove holding olive branch standing on gun barrel.

1995, May 3 Litho. *Perf. 13*

3859	A1476	3 l multicolored	*1.25*	.50
3860	A1476	15 l multicolored	*2.75*	1.25

Men's World Volleyball League, Cent. — A1477

Designs: a, 10 l, Player digging ball. b, 15 l, Player spiking ball, vert.

1995, May 25 Litho. *Perf. 13*

3861	A1477	Sheet of 2, #a.-b.	*3.25*	1.60

Souvenir Sheet

European Nature Conservation Year — A1478

Designs: a, 10 l, Pancratium maritimum. b, 15 l, Aquila heliaca.

1995, June 23 Litho. *Perf. 13*

3862	A1478	Sheet of 2, #a.-b.	4.50	4.50

Antarctic Wildlife — A1479

1 l, Euphausia superba. 2 l, Chaenocephalus. 3 l, Physeter catodon. 5 l, Leptonychotes weddelli. 8 l, Stercorarius skua. 10 l, Aptenodytes forsteri, vert.

1995, June 29

3863	A1479	1 l multicolored	*.25*	.25
3864	A1479	2 l multicolored	*.25*	.25
3865	A1479	3 l multicolored	*.35*	.25
3866	A1479	5 l multicolored	*.60*	.25
3867	A1479	8 l multicolored	*1.00*	.50
3868	A1479	10 l multicolored	*1.50*	.60
		Nos. 3863-3868 (6)	*3.95*	2.10

Stephan Stambolov (1854-95), Revolutionary Leader, Politician — A1480

1995, July 6 Litho. *Perf. 13*

3869	A1480	3 l multicolored	*.50*	.45

1996 Summer Olympics, Atlanta A1481

Designs: 3 l, Pole vault. 7 l, High jump. 10 l, Women's long jump. 15 l, Track.

1995, July 17

3870	A1481	3 l multicolored	*.35*	.25
3871	A1481	7 l multicolored	*.90*	.45
3872	A1481	10 l multicolored	*1.25*	.45
3873	A1481	15 l multicolored	*2.50*	.45
		Nos. 3870-3873 (4)	*5.00*	1.60

Legumes — A1482

1995, July 31

3874	A1482	2 l Pisum sativum	*.60*	.45
3875	A1482	3 l Glicine	*.60*	.45
3876	A1482	3 l Cicer arietinum	*.60*	.45
3877	A1482	4 l Spinacia oleracea	*.60*	.35
3878	A1482	5 l Arachis hypogaea	*.60*	.35
3879	A1482	15 l Lens esculenta	*2.00*	.45
		Nos. 3874-3879 (6)	*5.00*	2.50

Organized Tourism in Bulgaria, Cent. — A1483

1995, Aug. 21 Litho. *Perf. 13*

3880	A1483	3 l multicolored	*.45*	.45

Vassil Zahariev (1895-1971), Graphic Artist — A1484

Designs: 2 l, Woodcut of a man. 3 l, Woodcut of building in valley. 5 l, Self-portrait. 10 l, Carving of two women.

1995, Sept. 4 Litho. *Perf. 13*

3881	A1484	2 l multicolored	*.25*	.25
3882	A1484	3 l multicolored	*.50*	.25
3883	A1484	5 l multicolored	*.75*	.35
3884	A1484	10 l multicolored	*1.50*	.75
		Nos. 3881-3884 (4)	*3.00*	1.60

UN, 50th Anniv. A1485

1995, Sept. 12

3885	A1485	3 l multicolored	*.45*	.45

Airplanes — A1486

1995, Sept. 26 Litho. *Perf. 13*

3886	A1486	3 l PO-2	*.35*	.25
3887	A1486	5 l Li-2	*.60*	.25
3888	A1486	7 l JU52-3M	*.85*	.45
3889	A1486	10 l FV-58	*1.25*	.45
		Nos. 3886-3889 (4)	*3.05*	1.40

Motion Pictures, Cent. — A1487

Designs: 2 l, Charlie Chaplin, Mickey Mouse. 3 l, Marilyn Monroe, Marlene Dietrich. 5 l, Humphrey Bogart. 8 l, Sophia Loren, Liza Minnelli. 10 l, Toshiro Mifune. 15 l, Katya Paskaleva.

1995, Oct. 16

3890	A1487	2 l multicolored	*.25*	.25
3891	A1487	3 l multicolored	*.35*	.25
3892	A1487	5 l multicolored	*.45*	.25
3893	A1487	8 l multicolored	*1.20*	.25
3894	A1487	10 l multicolored	*1.50*	.25
3895	A1487	15 l multicolored	*2.00*	.60
		Nos. 3890-3895 (6)	*5.75*	1.85

Minerals A1488

1995, Nov. 20 Litho. *Perf. 13*

3896	A1488	1 l Agate	*.25*	.25
3897	A1488	2 l Sphalerite	*.25*	.25
3898	A1488	5 l Calcite	*.70*	.25
3899	A1488	7 l Quartz	*1.00*	.25
3900	A1488	8 l Pyromorphite	*1.20*	.45
3901	A1488	10 l Almandine	*1.50*	.45
		Nos. 3896-3901 (6)	*4.90*	1.90

Christmas A1489

1995, Dec. 8 Litho. *Perf. 13*

3902	A1489	3 l shown	*.50*	.25
3903	A1489	15 l Magi	*2.00*	.25

Southern Fruit, by Cyril Tsonev (1896-1961) — A1490

1996, Jan. 25 Litho. *Perf. 13*

3904	A1490	3 l multicolored	*.45*	.45

Martin Luther (1483-1546) — A1491

1996, Feb. 5

3905	A1491	3 l multicolored	*.45*	.45

Historic Buildings A1492

Monasteries: 3 l, Preobragenie. 5 l, Arapovsky. 10 1, Drianovo. 20 l, Bachkovo. 25 l, Troyan. 40 l, Zografski.

1996, Feb. 28 *Perf. 14x13½*

3906	A1492	3 l green	*.25*	.25
3907	A1492	5 l red	*.25*	.25
3908	A1492	10 l blue	*.40*	.25
3909	A1492	20 l yellow orange	*1.00*	.35
3910	A1492	25 l brown	*1.20*	.55
3911	A1492	40 l purple	*2.00*	.70
		Nos. 3906-3911 (6)	*5.10*	2.35

5th Meeting of European Bank for Reconstruction and Development A1493

1996, Apr. 15 Litho. *Perf. 13*

3912	A1493	7 l shown	*.50*	.25
3913	A1493	30 l Building, diff.	*2.00*	.95

Conifers A1494

Designs: 5 l, Taxus baccata. 8 l, Abies alba. 10 l, Picea abies. 20 l, Pinus silvestris. 25 l, Pinus heldreichii. 40 l, Juniperus excelsa.

1996, Apr. 23 *Perf. 13½x13*

3914 A1494 5 l multicolored *.25* .25
3915 A1494 8 l multicolored *.25* .25
3916 A1494 10 l multicolored *.50* .25
3917 A1494 20 l multicolored *1.00* .25
3918 A1494 25 l multicolored *1.20* .25
3919 A1494 40 l multicolored *2.00* .25
Nos. 3914-3919 (6) *5.20* 1.50

A1495

10 l, People in distress. 40 l, Khristo Botev (1848-1876), poet, patriot, horiz.

1996, May 1 *Perf. 13*

3920 A1495 10 l multicolored *.50* .25
3921 A1495 40 l multicolored *2.00* 1.10

April Uprising, death of Khristo Botev, 120th anniv.

A1496

Uniforms: 5 l, Light brown dress uniform. 8 l, Brown combat, helmet. 10 l, Brown uniform, holding gun with fixed bayonet. 20 l, Early red, blue dress uniform. 25 l, Officer's early green dress uniform. 40 l, Soldier's green uniform.

1996, May 6

3922 A1496 5 l multicolored *.25* .25
3923 A1496 8 l multicolored *.25* .25
3924 A1496 10 l multicolored *.25* .25
3925 A1496 20 l multicolored *.85* .25
3926 A1496 25 l multicolored *1.50* .80
3927 A1496 40 l multicolored *1.90* .95
Nos. 3922-3927 (6) *5.00* 2.75

Republic of Bulgaria, 50th Anniv. — A1497

1996, May 13 **Litho.** *Perf. 13½*

3928 A1497 10 l multicolored *.45* .45

Famous Women A1498

Europa: 10 l, Elisaveta Bagriana (1893-1990), poet. 40 l, Katia Popova (1924-66), opera singer.

1996, May 29 **Litho.** *Perf. 13*

3929 A1498 10 l multicolored *1.25* 1.25
Complete booklet, 5 #3929 *8.25*
3930 A1498 40 l multicolored *2.75* 2.75
Complete booklet, 5 #3930 *15.00*

A1499

10 l, Soccer player. 15 l, Soccer player, diff.

1996, June 4 **Souvenir Sheet**

3931 A1499 Sheet of 2, #a.-b. *2.00* .85

Euro '96, European Soccer Championships, Great Britain.

A1500

1996, July 4

3932 A1500 5 l Wrestling *.25* .25
3933 A1500 8 l Boxing *.25* .25
3934 A1500 10 l Women's shot put *.75* .25
3935 A1500 25 l Women sculling *1.40* .60
Nos. 3932-3935 (4) *2.65* 1.35

Souvenir Sheet

3936 A1500 15 l Pierre de Coubertin *1.25* 1.25

1996 Summer Olympic Games, Atlanta. Olymphilex '96 (No. 3936).

Crabs A1501

Designs: 5 l, Gammarus arduus. 10 l, Asellus aquaticus. 12 l, Astacus astacus. 25 l, Palaemon serratus. 30 l, Cumella limicola. 40 l, Carcinus mediterraneus.

1996, July 30

3937 A1501 5 l multicolored *2.00* .75
3938 A1501 10 l multicolored *.35* .25
3939 A1501 12 l multicolored *.50* .25
3940 A1501 25 l multicolored *.85* .25
3941 A1501 30 l multicolored *.85* .25
3942 A1501 40 l multicolored *.85* .25
Nos. 3937-3942 (6) *5.40* 2.00

Francisco Goya (1746-1828) A1502

Entire paintings or details: 8 l, Young Woman with a Letter. 26 l, The Third of May, 1808. 40 l, Neighboring Women on a Balcony.

No. 3947: a, 10 l, The Clothed Maja. b, 15 l, The Naked Maja.

1996, July 9 **Litho.** *Perf. 13*

3943 A1502 5 l multicolored *.25* .25
3944 A1502 8 l multicolored *.25* .25
3945 A1502 26 l multicolored *1.25* .70
3946 A1502 40 l multicolored *2.10* 1.10
Nos. 3943-3946 (4) *3.85* 2.30

Souvenir Sheet

Perf. 13½x13

3947 A1502 Sheet of 2, #a.-b. *1.50* 1.50

No. 3947 contains two 54x29mm stamps.

Souvenir Sheet

St. John of Rila (876-946), Founder of Rila Monastery — A1503

1996, Sept. 3

3948 A1503 10 l multicolored *.75* .75

Bulgarian Renaissance Houses A1504

Various multi-level houses.

1996, Sept. 12 **Litho.** *Perf. 14x13½*

Background Color

3949 A1504 10 l buff *.25* .25
3950 A1504 15 l orange yellow *.25* .25
3951 A1504 30 l yellow green *.75* .25
3952 A1504 50 l red lilac *1.25* .25
3953 A1504 60 l apple green *2.00* .75
3954 A1504 100 l green blue *3.00* 1.10
Nos. 3949-3954 (6) *7.50* 2.85

Steam Locomotives — A1505

1996, Sept. 24 *Perf. 13*

3955 A1505 5 l 1836 *.25* .25
3956 A1505 10 l 1847 *.50* .25
3957 A1505 12 l 1848 *.60* .25
3958 A1505 26 l 1876 *1.40* .25
Nos. 3955-3958 (4) *2.75* 1.00

Natl. Gallery of Art, Cent. A1506

1996, Oct. 14 **Litho.** *Perf. 13*

3959 A1506 15 l multicolored *.75* .75

Defeat of Byzantine Army by Tsar Simeon, 1100th Anniv. — A1507

10 l, Sword hilt, soldiers on horseback. 40 l, Sword blade, dagger, fallen soldiers.

1996, Oct. 21

3960 A1507 10 l multicolored *.50* .25
3961 A1507 40 l multicolored *2.00* .25
a. Pair, #3960-3961 *2.25* 2.25

No. 3961 is a continuous design.

UNICEF, 50th Anniv. — A1508

Children's drawings: 7 l, Diver, fish. 15 l, Circus performers. 20 l, Boy, artist's pallete. 60 l, Women seated at table.

1996, Nov. 18 **Litho.** *Perf. 13*

3962 A1508 7 l multicolored *.25* .25
3963 A1508 15 l multicolored *.80* .25
3964 A1508 20 l multicolored *1.10* .55
3965 A1508 60 l multicolored *3.25* 1.40
Nos. 3962-3965 (4) *5.40* 2.45

A1509

1996, Nov. 26

3966 A1509 15 l Candles on tree *.75* .25
3967 A1509 60 l Church *3.50* 1.50

Christmas.

A1510

Painting of Old Bulgarian Town, by Tsanko Lavrenov (1896-1978).

1996, Dec. 11 **Litho.** *Perf. 13*

3968 A1510 15 l multicolored *.75* .25

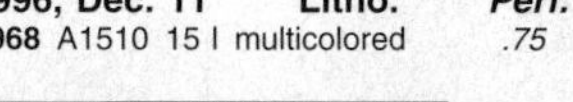

Puppies A1511

1997, Feb. 25 **Litho.** *Perf. 13*

3969 A1511 5 l Pointer *.25* .25
3970 A1511 7 l Chow chow *.30* .25
3971 A1511 25 l Carakachan dog *1.00* .25
3972 A1511 50 l Basset hound *2.00* 1.00
Nos. 3969-3972 (4) *3.55* 1.75

Alexander Graham Bell (1847-1922) — A1512

1997, Mar. 10

3973 A1512 30 l multicolored *.75* .45

Ivan Milev (1897-1927), Painter — A1513

Paintings: 5 l, Boy drinking from jar. 15 l, Person with head bowed holding up hand. 30 l, Woman. 60 l, Woman carrying child.

1997, Mar. 20

3974	A1513	5 l	multicolored	*.25*	.25
3975	A1513	15 l	multicolored	*.25*	.25
3976	A1513	30 l	multicolored	*.60*	.25
3977	A1513	60 l	multicolored	*1.50*	.45
			Nos. 3974-3977 (4)	*2.60*	1.20

Stories and Legends — A1514

Europa: 120 l, "March" lady in folk costume, symbol of spring. 600 l, St. George.

1997, Apr. 14

3978	A1514	120 l	multicolored	*2.00*	*.90*
3979	A1514	600 l	multicolored	*2.50*	*1.10*

Konstantin Kissimov (1897-1965), Actor — A1515

1997, Apr. 16

3980	A1515	120 l	multicolored	*.25*	.25

A1516

A1517

1997, Apr. 21

3981	A1516	60 l	multicolored	*.25*	.25

Heinrich von Stephan (1831-97).

1997, May 2 ***Perf. 13½***

Historical Landmarks: 80 l, Nessebar. 200 l, Ivanovo Rock Churches. 300 l, Boyana Church. 500 l, Madara horseman. 600 l, Tomb of Sveshtari. 1000 l, Tomb of Kazanlak.

3982	A1517	80 l	brn & multi	*.25*	.25
3983	A1517	200 l	pur & multi	*.25*	.25
3984	A1517	300 l	bis & multi	*.30*	.25
3985	A1517	500 l	grn & multi	*.45*	.25
3986	A1517	600 l	yel & multi	*.75*	.30
3987	A1517	1000 l	org & multi	*1.00*	.40
			Nos. 3982-3987 (6)	*3.00*	1.70

Composers A1518

Designs: a, Gaetano Donizetti (1797-1848). b, Franz Schubert (1797-1828). c, Felix Mendelssohn (1809-1847). d, Johannes Brahms (1833-1897).

1997, May 29 Litho. ***Perf. 13½x13***

3988	A1518	120 l	Sheet of 4, #a.-d.	*1.50*	1.10

Plants in Bulgaria's Red Book — A1519

Designs: 80 l, Trifolium rubens. 100 l, Tulipa hageri. 120 l, Inula spiraeifolia. 200 l, Paeonia tenuifolia.

1997, June 24 ***Perf. 13***

3989	A1519	80 l	multicolored	*.25*	.25
3990	A1519	100 l	multicolored	*.25*	.25
3991	A1519	120 l	multicolored	*.25*	.25
3992	A1519	200 l	multicolored	*.75*	.25
			Nos. 3989-3992 (4)	*1.50*	1.00

A1520

1997, June 29 Litho. ***Perf. 13***

3993	A1520	120 l	multicolored	*.25*	.25

Civil aviation in Bulgaria, 50th anniv.

A1521

1997, July 3

3994	A1521	120 l	multicolored	*.25*	.25

Evlogy Georgiev (1819-97), banker, philanthropist.

Sofia '97, Modern Pentathlon World Championship — A1522

60 l, Equestrian cross-country, running. 80 l, Fencing, swimming. 100 l, Running, women's fencing. 120 l, Men's shooting, diving. 200 l, Equestrian jumping, women's shooting.

1997, July 25

3995	A1522	60 l	multicolored	*.40*	.35
3996	A1522	80 l	multicolored	*.40*	.35
3997	A1522	100 l	multicolored	*.40*	.35
3998	A1522	120 l	multicolored	*.40*	.35
3999	A1522	200 l	multicolored	*.40*	.35
			Nos. 3995-3999 (5)	*2.00*	1.75

City of Moscow, 850th Anniv. — A1523

1997, July 30

4000	A1523	120 l	multicolored	*.60*	.60

No. 4000 is printed se-tenant with label for Moscow '97 Intl. Philatelic Exhibition.

Diesel Engine, Cent. A1524

1997, Sept. 8 Litho. ***Perf. 13½x13***

4001	A1524	80 l	Boat	*.25*	.25
4002	A1524	100 l	Tractor	*.25*	.25
4003	A1524	120 l	Truck	*.50*	.25
4004	A1524	200 l	Forklift	*1.20*	.25
			Nos. 4001-4004 (4)	*2.20*	1.00

43rd General Assembly of Atlantic Club of Bulgaria — A1525

Designs: a, Goddess Tyche. b, Eagle on sphere. c, Building, lion statue, denomination UL. d, Building, denomination UR.

1997, Oct. 2 ***Perf. 13***

4005	A1525	120 l	Sheet of 4, #a.-d.	*1.75*	1.50

Miguel de Cervantes (1547-1616) — A1526

1997, Oct. 15

4006	A1526	120 l	multicolored	*.45*	.45

Asen Raztsvetnikov (1897-1951), Poet, Writer — A1527

1997, Nov. 5

4007	A1527	120 l	multicolored	*.25*	.25

Tsar Samuel (d. 1014), Ascension to Throne, 1000th Anniv. A1528

1997, Nov. 18 ***Perf. 13½x13***

4008	A1528	120 l	Inscription	*.25*	.25
4009	A1528	600 l	Tsar, soldiers	*1.75*	.70
a.			Pair, #4008-4009	*2.25*	2.25

Christmas A1529

Designs: 120 l, Snow-covered houses, stars inside shape of Christmas tree, animals. 600 l, Nativity scene.

1997, Dec. 8 ***Perf. 13x13½***

4010	A1529	120 l	multicolored	*.40*	.25
4011	A1529	600 l	multicolored	*1.75*	.75

1998 Winter Olympic Games, Nagano A1530

Designs: 60 l, Speed skating. 80 l, Skiing. 120 l, Biathlon. 600 l, Pairs figure skating.

1997, Dec. 17 ***Perf. 13½x13***

4012	A1530	60 l	multicolored	*.25*	.25
4013	A1530	80 l	multicolored	*.25*	.25
4014	A1530	120 l	multicolored	*.25*	.25
4015	A1530	600 l	multicolored	*2.25*	1.10
			Nos. 4012-4015 (4)	*3.00*	1.85

For overprint see No. 4029.

Coat of Arms of Bulgaria A1531

1997, Dec. 22 Litho. ***Perf. 13½x13***

4016	A1531	120 l	multicolored	*.35*	.25

Souvenir Sheet

Bulgarian Space Program, 25th Anniv. — A1532

1997, Dec. 22 ***Perf. 13***

4017	A1532	120 l	multicolored	*.85*	.85

Christo Botev (1848-76), Revolutionary, Poet — A1533

1998, Jan. 6 Litho. ***Perf. 13***

4018	A1533	120 l	multicolored	*.25*	.25

Bertolt Brecht (1898-1956), Playwright
A1534

1998, Feb. 10
4019 A1534 120 l multicolored .25 .25

Bulgarian Telegraph Agency, Cent.
A1535

1998, Feb. 13
4020 A1535 120 l multicolored .25 .25

Illustrations by Alexander Bozhinov (1878-1968)
A1536

Designs: a, Bird wearing bonnet. b, Black bird wearing hat. c, Grandfather Frost, children. d, Girl among flowers looking upward at rain.

1998, Feb. 24 ***Perf. 13½x13***
4021 A1536 120 l Sheet of 4, #a.-d. 1.25 .50

A1537

1998, Feb. 27 ***Perf. 13***
4022 A1537 120 l Prince Alexander .25 .25
4023 A1537 600 l Monument 1.50 .50
a. Pair, #4022-4023 2.00 2.00

Bulgarian independence from Turkey, 120th anniv.

Easter — A1538

1998, Mar. 27 **Litho.** ***Perf. 13***
4024 A1538 120 l multicolored .25 .25

Bulgarian Olympic Committee, 75th Anniv. — A1539

1998, Mar. 30
4025 A1539 120 l multicolored .25 .25

PHARE (Intl. Post and Telecommunications Program) — A1540

1998, Apr. 24 **Litho.** ***Perf. 13***
4026 A1540 120 l multicolored .35 .25

National Days and Festivals — A1541

Europa: 120 l, Girls with flowers, "Enyovden." 600 l, Masked men with bells, "Kukery."

1998, Apr. 27
4027 A1541 120 l multicolored .50 .25
4028 A1541 600 l multicolored 3.00 2.25

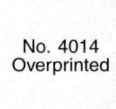

No. 4014 Overprinted

1998, Apr. 29 ***Perf. 13½x13***
4029 A1530 120 l multicolored 3.25 3.25

Dante and Virgil in Hell, by Eugene Delacroix (1798-1863)
A1542

1998, Apr. 30
4030 A1542 120 l multicolored .35 .25

A1543

1998, May 15 ***Perf. 13***
4031 A1543 120 l multicolored .25 .25

Soccer Team of Central Sports Club of the Army, 50th anniv.

A1544

Cats: 60 l, European tabby. 80 l, Siamese. 120 l, Exotic shorthair. 600 l, Birman.

1998, May 25
4032 A1544 60 l multicolored .25 .25
4033 A1544 80 l multicolored .25 .25
4034 A1544 120 l multicolored .25 .25
4035 A1544 600 l multicolored 1.40 1.25
Nos. 4032-4035 (4) 2.15 2.00

Are You Jealous?, by Paul Gauguin (1848-1903) — A1545

1998, June 4
4036 A1545 120 l multicolored .30 .25

Neophit Hylendarsky-Bozvely (1745-1848), Priest, Author — A1546

1998, June 4
4037 A1546 120 l multicolored .35 .25

1998 World Cup Soccer Championships, France — A1547

Lion mascot with soccer ball, various stylized soccer plays.

1998, June 10
4038 A1547 60 l multicolored .25 .25
4039 A1547 80 l multicolored .25 .25
4040 A1547 120 l multicolored .35 .25
4041 A1547 600 l multicolored 1.60 .60
Nos. 4038-4041 (4) 2.45 1.35

Souvenir Sheet

4042 A1547 120 l Mascot, Eiffel Tower .75 .75

A. Aleksandrov's Flight on Mir, 10th Anniv. — A1548

1998, June 17 **Litho.** ***Perf. 13***
4043 A1548 120 l multicolored .35 .35

Lisbon '98 — A1549

Designs: a, Map showing route around Cape of Good Hope, Vasco da Gama (1460-1524). b, Sailing ship, map of Africa.

1998, June 23
4044 A1549 600 l Sheet of 2, #a.-b. + 2 labels 3.50 2.25

Helicopters — A1550

80 l, Focke Wulf FW61, 1937. 100 l, Sikorsky R-4, 1943. 120 l, Mil Mi-12 (V-12), 1970. 200 l, McDonnell-Douglas MD-900, 1995.

1998, July 7 **Litho.** ***Perf. 13***
4045 A1550 80 l multicolored .25 .25
4046 A1550 100 l multicolored .30 .30
4047 A1550 120 l multicolored .40 .40
4048 A1550 200 l multicolored .55 .55
Nos. 4045-4048 (4) 1.50 1.50

Souvenir Sheet

Intl. Year of the Ocean — A1551

Monachus monachus.

1998, July 14 **Litho.** ***Perf. 13***
4049 A1551 120 l multicolored 3.25 1.60

Dimitr Talev (1898-1966), Writer — A1552

1998, Sept. 14
4050 A1552 180 l multicolored .45 .45

A1553

1998, Sept. 22
4051 A1553 180 l multicolored .45 .45

Declaration of Bulgarian Independence, 90th anniv.

A1554

Butterflies, flowers: 60 l, Limenitis redukta, ligularia sibirica. 180 l, Vanessa cardui, anthemis macrantha. 200 l, Vanessa atalanta, trachelium jacquinii. 600 l, Anthocharis gruneri, geranium tuberosum.

1998, Sept. 24

4052	A1554	60 l	multicolored	.25	.25
4053	A1554	180 l	multicolored	.40	.25
4054	A1554	200 l	multicolored	.50	.50
4055	A1554	600 l	multicolored	1.60	1.60
	Nos. 4052-4055 (4)			2.75	2.60

Christo Smirnenski (1898-1923), Poet — A1555

1998, Sept. 29

4056 A1555 180 l multicolored .45 .45

Universal Declaration of Human Rights, 50th Anniv. — A1556

1998, Oct. 26 Litho. *Perf. 13*

4057 A1556 180 l multicolored .45 .45

Giordano Bruno (1548-1600), Philosopher — A1557

1998, Oct. 26

4058 A1557 180 l multicolored .45 .45

Greetings Stamps A1558

No. 4059, Man diving through flaming heart, "I Love You." No. 4060, Baby emerging from chalice, "Happy Birthday." No. 4061, Grape vine, bird, wine coming from vat, "Happy Holiday." No. 4062, Waiter carrying tray with glass & ttle of wine, "Happy Name Day."

1998, Nov. 11

4059	A1558	180 l	multi	.50	.50
4060	A1558	180 l	multi, vert.	.50	.50
4061	A1558	180 l	multi, vert.	.50	.50
4062	A1558	180 l	multi, vert.	.50	.50
	Nos. 4059-4062 (4)			2.00	2.00

See No. 4628.

Christmas A1559

1998, Dec. 2 Litho. *Perf. 13½x13*

4063 A1559 180 l multicolored .45 .45

Ivan Geshov (1849-1924), Finance Minister — A1560

1999, Feb. 8 Litho. *Perf. 13*

4064 A1560 180 l multicolored .35 .35

Third Bulgarian State, 120th Anniv. — A1561

Designs: a, Reflection of National Assembly. b, Men, paper, Council of Ministers. c, Scales of Justice, Supreme Court of Appeal. d, Coins, Bulgarian Natl. Bank. e, Soldiers, Bulgarian Army. f, Lion, lightpost, Sofia, capital of Bulgaria.

1999, Feb. 10

4065 A1561 180 l Sheet of 6, #a.-f. 2.50 2.50

Bulgarian Culture and Art — A1562

180 l, Georgy Karakashev (1899-1970), set designer. 200 l, Bencho Obreshkov (1899-1970), artist. 300 l, Assen Naydenov (1899-1995), conductor. 600 l, Pancho Vladiguerov (1899-1978), composer.

1999, Mar. 12 Litho. *Perf. 13*

4066	A1562	180 l	multicolored	.25	.25
4067	A1562	200 l	multicolored	.25	.25
4068	A1562	300 l	multicolored	.75	.75
4069	A1562	600 l	multicolored	1.50	.85
	Nos. 4066-4069 (4)			2.75	2.10

Bulgaria '99 — A1562a

Parrots: a, Trichoglossus haematodus. b, Platycercus eximius. c, Melopsittacus undulatus. d, Ara chloroptera.

1999, Mar. 15 Litho. *Perf. 13x13¼*
Sheet of 4

4069A A1562a 600 l #a.-d. 17.00 17.00

NATO, 50th Anniv. — A1563

1999, Mar. 29 Litho. *Perf. 13*

4070 A1563 180 l multicolored .35 .35

Easter A1564

1999, Apr. 1

4071 A1564 180 l multicolored .35 .35

National Parks and Nature Preserves — A1565

Europa: 180 l, Duck, pond, Ropotamo Preserve. 600 l, Ibex, waterfall, Central Balkan Natl. Park.

1999, Apr. 13 Litho. *Perf. 13*

4072	A1565	180 l	multicolored	.75	.25
4073	A1565	600 l	multicolored	1.75	.95

IBRA '99, Intl. Philatelic Exhibition, Nuremberg — A1566

1999, Apr. 15

4074 A1566 600 l multicolored 1.50 .75

No. 4074 is divided in half by vert. simulated perfs. and was issued in sheets of 3 + 3 labels.

Council of Europe, 50th Anniv. — A1567

1999, May 5 Litho. *Perf. 13*

4075 A1567 180 l multicolored 1.00 1.00

Foreign Culture and Art — A1567a

Designs: 180 l, Honoré de Balzac (1799-1850), novelist. 200 l, Johann Wolfgang von Goethe (1749-1832), poet. 250 l, Aleksandr Pushkin (1799-1837), poet. 600 l, Diego Velázquez (1599-1660), painter.

1999, May 18

4076	A1567a	180 l	multi	.25	.25
4077	A1567a	200 l	multi	.80	.80
4078	A1567a	300 l	multi	.80	.80
4078A	A1567a	600 l	multi	1.75	1.75
	Nos. 4076-4078A (4)			3.60	3.60

Bicycles — A1568

Designs: 180 l, Large front-wheeled bicycle, 1867. 200 l, Multi-gear bicycle. 300 l, BMX racing bike. 600 l, Mountain racing bike.

1999, June 1 Litho. *Perf. 13¼*

4079	A1568	180 l	multicolored	.25	.25
4080	A1568	200 l	multicolored	.25	.25
4081	A1568	300 l	multicolored	.85	.85
4082	A1568	600 l	multicolored	1.75	1.75
	Nos. 4079-4082 (4)			3.10	3.10

Sts. Cyril and Methodius — A1569

Various paintings of Sts. Cyril and Methodius standing side by side with denomination at: a, UL. b, UR. c, LL. d, LR.

1999, June 15 Litho. *Perf. 13¼*

4083 A1569 600 l Sheet of 4, #a.-d. 13.00 11.00

Bulgaria '99, European Philatelic Exhibition.

Flowers A1570

a, Oxytropis urumovii. b, Campanula transsilvanica. c, Iris reichenbachii. d, Gentiana punctata.

1999, July 20

4084 A1570 60s Sheet of 4, #a.-d. 13.00 13.00

Bulgaria '99, European Philatelic Exhibition.

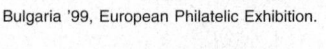

Mushrooms — A1571

Designs: a, 10s, Russula virescens. b, 18s, Agaricus campestris. c, 20s, Hygrophorus russula. d, 60s, Lepista nuda.

1999, July 27

4085 A1571 Sheet of 4, #a.-d. 2.75 2.75

Souvenir Sheet

Total Solar Eclipse, Aug. 11, 1999 — A1572

1999, Aug. 10 *Perf. 13*

4086 A1572 20s multicolored 1.50 1.50

A1573

1999, Sept. 23 **Litho.** *Perf. 13*

4087 A1573 18s multicolored .25 .25

Organized agrarian movement in Bulgaria, 100th anniv.

Souvenir Sheet of 4

A1574

Lion (portion) and: a, No. J2. b, Dove and letter. c, Eastern hemisphere. d, Western hemisphere.

1999, Oct. 5 *Perf. 13x13½*

4088 A1574 60s #a.-d. 10.00 10.00

Bulgaria '99, UPU 125th anniv.

Birds, Eggs and Nests — A1575

8s, Lanius minor. 18s, Turdus viscivorus. 20s, Prunella modularis. 60s, Emberiza hortulana.

1999, Oct. 6 *Perf. 13*

4089 A1575 8s multicolored .25 .25
4090 A1575 18s multicolored .25 .25
4091 A1575 20s multicolored .25 .25
4092 A1575 60s multicolored 1.90 1.90
Nos. 4089-4092 (4) 2.65 2.65

Endangered Turtles — A1576

10s, Testudo graeca. 18s, Emys orbicularis. 30s, Testudo hermanni. 60s, Mauremys caspica.

1999, Oct. 8 *Perf. 13*

4093 A1576 10s multicolored .25 .25
4094 A1576 18s multicolored .25 .25
4095 A1576 30s multicolored .85 .85
4096 A1576 60s multicolored 1.50 1.50
Nos. 4093-4096 (4) 2.85 2.85

Olympic Sports A1577

1999, Oct. 10

4097 A1577 10s Boxing .25 .25
4098 A1577 20s High jump .25 .25
4099 A1577 30s Weight lifting .85 .85
4100 A1577 60s Wrestling 1.50 1.50
Nos. 4097-4100 (4) 2.85 2.85

Fountains — A1578

Fountains from: 1s, Sopotski Monastery. 8s, Karlovo. 10s, Koprivshchitsa. 18s, Sandanski. 20s, Karlovo. 60s, Sokolski Monastery.

1999 **Litho.** *Perf. 13½x14*

Fountain Color

4101 A1578 1s bister .25 .25
4102 A1578 8s green .25 .25
4103 A1578 10s brown .25 .25
4104 A1578 18s light blue .30 .30
4105 A1578 20s dark blue .35 .35
4109 A1578 60s brown 1.00 1.00
Nos. 4101-4109 (6) 2.40 2.40

Issued: 8s, 60s, 11/22/99; others, 1999.

2003, Mar. *Perf. 12¾ Syncopated*

4101a A1578 1s .25 .25
4102a A1578 8s .25 .25
4103a A1578 10s .25 .25
4104a A1578 18s .25 .25
4105a A1578 20s .25 .25
4109a A1578 60s .65 .65
Nos. 4101a-4109a (6) 1.90 1.90

Police Trade Unions' European Council, 10th Anniv. — A1579

1999, Nov. 8 **Litho.** *Perf. 13*

4113 A1579 18s multi .35 .35

A1580 A1581

Various gold artifacts from Panagyurishte.

1999, Nov. 15 *Perf. 13½x14*

4114 A1580 2s multi .25 .25
4115 A1580 3s multi .25 .25
4116 A1580 5s multi .25 .25
4117 A1580 30s multi .50 .50
4118 A1580 1 l multi 1.60 1.60
Nos. 4114-4118 (5) 2.85 2.85

Perf. Perf. 12¾ Syncopated

2003, Mar.

4114a A1580 2s .25 .25
4115a A1580 3s .25 .25
4116a A1580 5s .25 .25
4117a A1580 30s .30 .30
4118a A1580 1 l 1.10 1.10
Nos. 4114a-4118a (5) 2.15 2.15

1999, Nov. 22 *Perf. 13*

4119 A1581 18s Icon, 1600 .35 .35
4120 A1581 60s Icon, 1607 1.25 1.25

Scouting A1582

10s, Scout, campfire. 18s, Scout assisting another. 30s, Salute. 60s, Scouts, cross.

1999, Dec. 6

4121 A1582 10s multi .25 .25
4122 A1582 18s multi .40 .40
4123 A1582 30s multi .65 .65
4124 A1582 60s multi 1.25 1.25
Nos. 4121-4124 (4) 2.55 2.55

Expo 2005, Japan — A1583

1999, Dec. 21 *Perf. 13*

4125 A1583 18s multi .30 .30

Start of Negotiations for Bulgaria's Entry into European Community — A1584

2000, Feb. 15 **Litho.** *Perf. 13*

4126 A1584 18s multi 1.00 1.00

Souvenir Sheet

Ciconia Ciconia — A1585

2000, Mar. 22

4127 A1585 60s multi 2.40 1.40

Petar Beron (1800-71), Scientist — A1586

Zakhari Stoyanov (1850-89), Writer — A1586a

Kolyo Ficheto (1800-81), Architect — A1586b

2000, Mar. 30 **Litho.** *Perf. 13¼*

4128 A1586 10s multi .25 .25
4129 A1586a 20s multi .45 .45
4130 A1586b 50s multi 1.10 1.10
Nos. 4128-4130 (3) 1.80 1.80

Europa A1587

2000, Apr. 26 **Litho.** *Perf. 13*

4131 A1587 18s shown *.60 .60*
4132 A1587 60s Madonna and child at R *2.40 2.40*

2000 Summer Olympics, Sydney — A1588

2000, Apr. 28 *Perf. 13¼x13*

4133 A1588 10s Judo .25 .25
4134 A1588 18s Tennis .30 .30
4135 A1588 20s Shooting .35 .35
4136 A1588 60s Long jump 1.00 1.00
Nos. 4133-4136 (4) 1.90 1.90

Bulgarian Art A1589

Designs: No. 4137, Friends, by Assen Vassilev (1900-81). No. 4138, Landscape from Veliko Turnovo, by Ivan Hristov (1900-87). No. 4139, At the Fountain, sculpture by Ivan Funev (1900-83). No. 4140, All Souls' Day, by Pencho Georgiev (1900-40).

2000, May 23 *Perf. 13*

4137 A1589 18s multi .40 .40
4138 A1589 18s multi .40 .40
4139 A1589 18s multi .40 .40
4140 A1589 18s multi .40 .40
Nos. 4137-4140 (4) 1.60 1.60

Souvenir Sheet

Fairy Tales — A1590

Designs: a, Puss in Boots, by Charles Perrault. b, Little Red Riding Hood, by the Brothers Grimm. c, Thumbelina, by Hans Christian Andersen.

2000, May 23 *Perf. 13¼x13*
4141 A1590 18s Sheet of 3, #a-c + 3 labels 1.50 1.50

Expo 2000, Hanover — A1591

2000, May 31 *Perf. 13*
4142 A1591 60s multi + label 1.40 1.40

Birth and Death Anniversaries — A1592

Designs: 10s, Johann Gutenberg, inventor of movable type (c. 1400-68). 18s, Johann Sebastian Bach, composer (1685-1750). 20s, Guy de Maupassant, writer (1850-93). 60s, Antoine de Saint-Exupéry, writer (1900-44).

2000, June 20

4143	A1592	10s multi	.25	.25
4144	A1592	18s multi	.40	.40
4145	A1592	20s multi	.50	.50
4146	A1592	60s multi	1.40	1.40
	Nos. 4143-4146 (4)		2.55	2.55

Airships — A1593

Designs: 10s, Le Jaune over Paris. 18s, LZ-13 Hansa over Cologne. 20s, N-1 Norge over Rome. 60s, Graf Zeppelin over Sofia.

2000, July 3 **Litho.** *Perf. 13¼*

4147	A1593	10s multi	.25	.25
4148	A1593	18s multi	.40	.40
4149	A1593	20s multi	.50	.50
4150	A1593	60s multi	1.40	1.40
	Nos. 4147-4150 (4)		2.55	2.55

Ivan Vazov (1850-1921), Writer — A1594

2000, July 9
4151 A1594 18s multi .40 .40

Souvenir Sheet

European Security and Cooperation Conference, Helsinki, 25th Anniv. — A1595

No. 4152: a, Hands. b, Three "e's."

2000, July 19 **Litho.** *Perf. 13*
4152 A1595 20s Sheet of 2, #a-b 2.50 2.50

Churches A1596

Panel colors: 22s, Blue. 24s, Red violet. 50s, Bister. 65s, Bright green. 3 l, Brown. 5 l, Red.

2000, Sept. 1 *Perf. 14x13¾*
4153-4158 A1596 Set of 6 16.00 16.00

Perf. Perf. 12¾ Syncopated

2003, Mar.

4153a	A1596	22s	.25	.25
4154a	A1596	24s	.55	.55
4155a	A1596	50s	.55	.55
4156a	A1596	65s	.75	.75
	Nos. 4153a-4156a (4)		2.10	2.10

Animals A1597

Designs: 10s, Capra ibex. 22s, Ovis ammon. 30s, Bison bonasus. 65s, Bos grunniens.

2000, Sept. 25 *Perf. 13*
4159-4162 A1597 Set of 4 2.50 1.60

Flowers — A1598

Designs: 10s, Gladiolus segetum. 22s, Hepatica nobilis. 30s, Adonis vernalis. 65s, Anemone pavonina.

2000, Oct. 17 *Perf. 13x13¼*
4163-4166 A1598 Set of 4 2.50 1.60

European Convention on Human Rights, 50th Anniv. A1599

2000, Nov. 3 **Litho.** *Perf. 13¼x13*
4167 A1599 65s multi 2.00 2.00

Bulgarian Orders — A1600

Designs: 12s, Bravery. 22s, St. Alexander. 30s, Citizen's merit. 65s, Sts. Cyril and Methodius.

2000, Nov. 28 *Perf. 13*
4168-4171 A1600 Set of 4 2.75 2.75

Souvenir Sheet

Christianity, 2000th Anniv. — A1601

No. 4172: a, 22s, St. Boris Michael (2000 at UL). b, 22s, St. Sofroni Vrachanski (2000 at LL). c, 65s, Madonna and Child (2000 at UL). d, 65s, Exarch Antim I (2000 at LL).

2000, Nov. 28 *Perf. 13¼x13*
4172 A1601 Sheet of 4, #a-d 4.00 4.00

First Bulgarian Law, 120th Anniv. — A1602

2000, Dec. 8 *Perf. 13x13¼*
4173 A1602 22s multi .50 .50

Advent of New Millennium — A1603

2001, Jan. 8 *Perf. 13x12¾*
4174 A1603 22s multi .50 .50

Souvenir Sheet

Electrified City Transport in Bulgaria, Cent. — A1604

No. 4175: a, 22s, Streetcar. b, 65s, Two streetcars.

2001, Jan. 12 *Perf. 13*
4175 A1604 Sheet, 2 each #4175a-4175b 4.00 4.00

Viticulture A1605

Wine glass, wine grapes and buildings: 12s, Muscat, Evxinograd Palace. 22s, Gumza, Baba Vida Fortress. 30s, Wide Melnik, houses in Melnik. 65s, Mavroud, Assenova Fortress.

2001, Feb. 7
4176-4179 A1605 Set of 4 2.75 2.75

Souvenir Sheet

Bulgaria and the Information Society — A1606

No. 4180: a, 22s, Circuits, "@" character. b, 65s, Letters, Dr. John Atanasov (1903-95), computer pioneer.

2001, Mar. 1 *Perf. 13¼x13*
4180 A1606 Sheet, #a-b 27.50 20.00

Souvenir Sheet

"Atlantic" Values, 10th Anniv. — A1607

2001, Apr. 4 *Perf. 13x12¾*
4181 A1607 65s multi 4.00 4.00

Europa
A1608

Designs: 22s, Aerial view of Rila Lakes. 65s, Rock bridges, Rhodope Mountains.

2001, Apr. 18 *Perf. 12¾x13*
4182-4183 A1608 Set of 2 *20.00 15.00*

Todor Kableshkov (1851-1876), Organizer of 1876 April Uprising — A1609

2001, May 1 *Perf. 13*
4184 A1609 22s multi .50 .50

Protected Species Neophron Percnopterus — A1610

Designs: 12s, Juvenile in flight. 22s, Juvenile with mouth open. 30s, Adult and chick. 65s, Adult and eggs.

2001, May 21 **Litho.** *Perf. 13*
4185-4188 A1610 Set of 4 2.75 2.75

Souvenir Sheet

Athletes — A1611

No. 4189: a, 22s, Georgi Asparuchov (1943-71), soccer player. b, 30s, Dan Kolov (1892-1940), wrestler. c, 65s, Krum Lekarski (1898-1981), equestrian.

2001, June 29
4189 A1611 Sheet of 3, #a-c, + 3 labels 2.50 2.50

UN High Commissioner for Refugees, 50th Anniv. — A1612

2001, July 11
4190 A1612 65s multi 1.40 1.40

Writers
A1613

Designs: 22s, Aleksandr Zhendov (1901-53). 65s, Ilya Beshkov (1901-58).

2001, July 24
4191-4192 A1613 Set of 2 2.00 2.00

Constitutional Court, 10th Anniv. — A1614

2001, Oct. 3
4193 A1614 25s multi .50 .50

Souvenir Sheet

Sofia Summit 2001 — A1615

Flags of various countries: a, 12s. b, 24s. c, 25s. d, 65s.

2001, Oct. 5 *Perf. 13¼x13*
4194 A1615 Sheet of 4, #a-d 5.00 5.00

Year of Dialogue Among Civilizations
A1616

2001, Oct. 9 *Perf. 13*
4195 A1616 65s multi 1.25 1.25

Souvenir Sheet

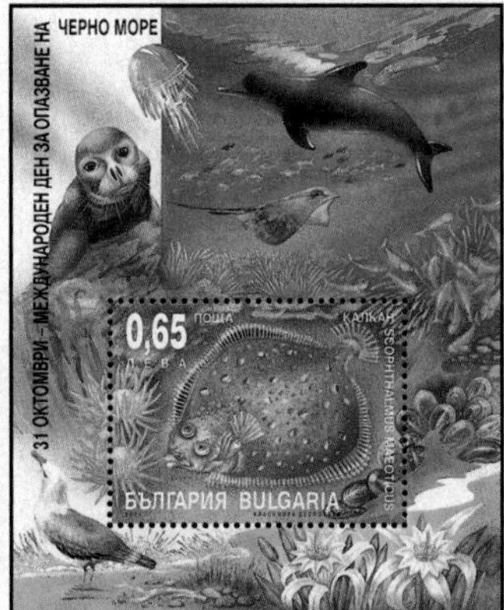

Intl. Black Sea Preservation Day — A1617

2001, Oct. 31
4196 A1617 65s multi 2.00 2.00

Christmas
A1618

2001, Nov. 19
4197 A1618 25s multi .50 .50

Lighthouses
A1619

Designs: 25s, Shabla. 32s, Kaliakra.

2001, Nov. 19 *Perf. 14x13½*
4198-4199 A1619 Set of 2 1.00 1.00

2003, Mar. *Perf. 12¾ Syncopated*
4198a-4199a A1619 Set of 2 1.00 1.00

A souvenir sheet containing Nos. 4198a and 4199a dated "2013" and 2 labels was produced in limited quantities and released 8/15/13.

Souvenir Sheet

Zograf Monastery, Mount Athos, Greece — A1620

No. 4200: a, 25s, Monastery. b, 65s, Icon of St, George.

2001, Nov. 27
4200 A1620 Sheet of 2, #a-b 2.50 2.50

Cartoons — A1621

2001, Dec. 12 **Litho.** *Perf. 13¼x13*
4201 A1621 25s multi + label .60 .60

Printed in sheets of 3 stamps and labels.

Vincenzo Bellini (1801-35), Italian Composer — A1622

2001, Dec. 17 *Perf. 13*
4202 A1622 25s multi .60 .60

Builders of the Bulgarian State
A1623

Designs: 10s, Ancient Bulgarian calendar. 25s, Khans Kubrat (632-51) and Asparukh (681-700). 30s, Khans Krum (803-14) and Omurtag (814-31). 65s, King Boris I (852-89) and Tsar Simeon I (893-927).

2001, Dec. 21
4203-4206 A1623 Set of 4 3.00 3.00

Introduction of Euro Currency in 12 European Nations — A1624

2002, Jan. 3
4207 A1624 65s multi 1.50 1.50

UN Disarmament Committee, 50th Anniv. — A1625

2002, Jan. 23
4208 A1625 25s multi .60 .60

Souvenir Sheet

Balkanmax 2002 — A1626

No. 4209: a, 25s, Natural bridge. b, 65s, Buteo rufinus.

2002, Jan. 29
4209 A1626 Sheet of 2, #a-b 25.00 25.00

2002 Winter Olympics, Salt Lake City
A1627

Designs: 25s, Figure skater. 65s, Speed skater.

2002, Feb. 5 *Perf. 13¼x13*
4210-4211 A1627 Set of 2 2.00 2.00

10th Natl. Antarctic Expedition — A1628

2002, Mar. 20
4212 A1628 25s multi + label .60 .60

Issued in sheets of 3 stamps and 3 different labels.

Europa A1629

Circus performers: 25s, Elephant trainer. 65s, Clown.

2002, Mar. 22 ***Perf. 13***
4213-4214 A1629 Set of 2 *2.50 2.50*

See No. 4629 for clown stamp without "Europa" inscription..

Famous Bulgarians — A1630

Designs: 25s, Veselin Stoyanov (1902-69), composer. 34s, Angel Karaliichev (1902-72), writer.

2002, Mar. 27 ***Perf. 13¼x13***
4215-4216 A1630 Set of 2 1.25 1.25

Paintings — A1631

Designs: 10s, Industrial Landscape, by Vasil Barakov, vert. 25s, Illustration for book *Under the Yoke*, by Boris Angelushev. 65s, The Balcony and the Canary, by Ivan Nenov, vert.

2002, Apr. 17 ***Perf. 13***
4217-4219 A1631 Set of 3 2.25 2.25

Stamp Designers A1632

Designs: 25s, Stefan Kanchev (1915-2001). 65s, Alexander Popilov (1916-2001).

2002, Apr. 26 ***Perf. 13¼x13***
4220-4221 A1632 Set of 2 2.00 2.00

Fruits and Vegetables A1633

Designs: 10s, Cucumis melo. 25s, Citrullus lanatus. 27s, Cucurbita pepo. 65s, Lagenaria siceraria.

2002, May 8 Litho. ***Perf. 13¼x13***
4222-4225 A1633 Set of 4 3.00 3.00

Roosters A1634

Designs: 10s, Bankivski, vert. 20s, Leghorn. 25s, Bergich Crower. 65s, Plymouth Rock, vert.

2002, May 10 ***Perf. 13x13¼, 13¼x13***
4226-4229 A1634 Set of 4 2.75 2.75

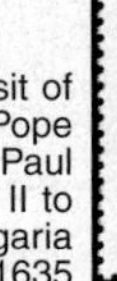

Visit of Pope John Paul II to Bulgaria A1635

2002, May 24 Litho. ***Perf. 13***
4230 A1635 65s multi 2.00 2.00

Souvenir Sheet

Chess — A1636

No. 4231: a, 25s, Chess pieces. b, 65s, Hand moving piece.

2002, May 27
4231 A1636 Sheet of 2, #a-b 2.00 2.00

Admission to Council of Europe, 10th Anniv. A1637

2002, May 29
4232 A1637 25s multi .60 .60

Carvings by Peter Kushlev A1638

Designs: 6s, Rabbit and fawn. 12s, Deer. 36s, Bird. 44s, Boar.

Perf. 13¾x13½
2002, Aug. 12 Litho.
4233-4236 A1638 Set of 4 2.25 2.25

Perf. Perf. 12¾ Syncopated
2003, Mar.
4233a-4236a A1638 Set of 4 2.25 2.25

Ships A1639

Designs: 12s, Maria Luisa. 36c, Percenk. 49c, Kaliakra. 65c, Sofia.

2002, Oct. 18 ***Perf. 13¼x13***
4237-4240 A1639 Set of 4 3.00 3.00

Christmas A1640

2002, Nov. 20
4241 A1640 36s multi .80 .80

Souvenir Sheet

Invitation to Join NATO — A1641

2002, Nov. 21 ***Perf. 13***
4242 A1641 65s multi 3.00 3.00

Souvenir Sheet

Start of European Security and Cooperation Negotiations, 30th Anniv. — A1642

2002, Nov. 22 ***Perf. 13¼x13***
4243 A1642 65s multi 2.50 2.50

Tsars A1643

Designs: 18s, Samuel (d. 1014). 36s, Peter II (d. 1197), Assen (d. 1196). 49s, Kaloyan (d. 1207). 65s, Ivan Assen II (d. 1241).

2002, Dec. 6 Litho. ***Perf. 13¼x13***
4244-4247 A1643 Set of 4 3.50 3.50

See Nos. 4272, 4288-4290.

Europalia, European Culture Festival — A1644

2003, Jan. 10 Litho. ***Perf. 13***
4248 A1644 65s multi 1.50 1.50

Paintings A1645

Designs: 18s, Rose Pickers, by Stoyan Sotirov (1903-84). 36s, The Blind Rebec Player, by Ilya Petrov (1903-75). 65s, Pig Tender, by Zlatyo Boyadjiev (1903-76).

2003, Jan. 28
4249-4251 A1645 Set of 3 2.50 2.50

Souvenir Sheet

Science Fiction — A1646

2003, Feb. 7
4252 A1646 65s multi 2.00 2.00

Re-establishment of the Bulgarian State, 125th Anniv. — A1647

2003, Feb. 28 Litho. ***Perf. 13***
4253 A1647 36s multi .80 .80

Rescue of Bulgarian Jews, 60th Anniv. — A1648

2003, Mar. 10
4254 A1648 36s multi .80 .80

Europa — A1649

No. 4255: a, 36s, Woman and birds. b, 65s, Legs, chicken, pig and dog.

2003, Mar. 17
4255 A1649 Vert. pair, #a-b *2.50 2.50*

Souvenir Sheet

Vincent van Gogh (1853-90), Painter — A1650

2003, Mar. 19 *Perf. 13x13¼*
4256 A1650 65s multi 1.40 1.40

Prehistoric Animals A1651

2003, Apr. 24 *Perf. 13*
4257 Horiz. strip of 4 4.00 4.00
a. A1651 30s Pterodactylus .60 .60
b. A1651 36s Gorgosaurus .75 .75
c. A1651 49s Mesosaurus 1.00 1.00
d. A1651 65s Monoclonius 1.40 1.40
Booklet, #4257 5.00

Bulgaria 2003 Philatelic Exhibition — A1652

2003, May 15
4258 A1652 36s multi .80 .80

Bees A1653

Designs: 20s: Apis mellifera. 30s, Anthidium manicatum. 36s, Bombus subterraneus. 65s, Xylocopa violacea.

2003, June 17 **Litho.** *Perf. 13¼x13*
4259-4262 A1653 Set of 4 3.00 3.00

Water Plants — A1654

Designs: 20s, Butomus umbellatus. 36s, Sagittaria sagittifolia. 50s, Menyanthes trifoliata. 65s, Iris pseudacorus.

2003, July 25 **Litho.** *Perf. 13*
4263-4266 A1654 Set of 4 3.50 3.50

Goce Delchev (1872-1903), Patriot — A1655

2003, Aug. 1
4267 A1655 36s multi .80 .80

Ilinden and Preobrazhene Revolts, cent.

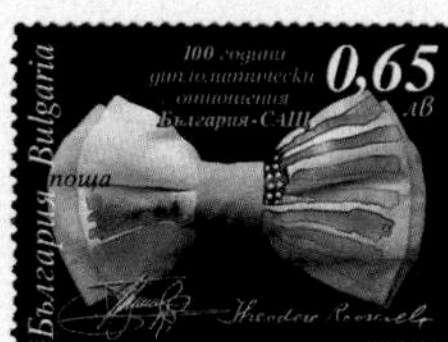

Bulgaria — United States Diplomatic Relations, Cent. A1656

2003, Sept. 19 **Litho.** *Perf. 13*
4268 A1656 65s multi 1.40 1.40

Intl Years of Fresh Water, Mountains and Ecotourism — A1657

2003, Sept. 19
4269 A1657 65s multi + label 1.50 1.50

Printed in sheets of 3 + 3 different labels.

John Atanassov (1903-95), Computer Pioneer — A1658

2003, Oct. 3 **Litho.** *Perf. 13*
4270 A1658 65s multi + label 2.00 2.00

2003 European Team Chess Championships, Plovdiv — A1659

2003, Oct. 10
4271 A1659 65s multi 1.40 1.40

Tsar Type of 2002

Design: Tsar Ivan Shishman (d. 1396).

2003, Oct. 18
4272 A1643 65s multi 1.40 1.40

Bulgarian Olympic Committee, 80th Anniv. — A1660

New Olympic sports: 20s, Taekwondo. 36s, Mountain biking. 50s, Softball. 65s, Canoe slalom.

2003, Oct. 18
4273-4276 A1660 Set of 4 3.50 3.50

Christmas A1661

2003, Nov. 24 *Perf. 13x13¼*
4277 A1661 65s multi 1.40 1.40

Coaches — A1662

Designs: 30s, Man and coach. 36s, Man and woman in coach. 50s, Woman, dog and coach. 65s, Man, woman and coach.

2003, Nov. 28 *Perf. 13*
4278-4281 A1662 Set of 4 3.75 3.75

FIFA (Fédération Internationale de Football Association), Cent. (in 2004) — A1663

Designs: 20s, FIFA emblem. 25s, Soccer match. 36s, Soccer match, rules. 50s, FIFA Fair Play Trophy, vert. 65s, FIFA World Player Trophy, vert.

2003, Dec. 12
4282-4286 A1663 Set of 5 4.00 4.00

Re-establisment of Masons in Bulgaria, 10th Anniv. — A1664

2003, Dec. 22 **Litho.** *Perf. 13*
4287 A1664 80s multi 1.60 1.60

Tsar Type of 2002

Designs: 30s, Tsar Ivan Alexander (r. 1331-71). 45s, Despot Dosrotitsa (r. 1360-85). 80s, Tsar Ivan Strazhimir (r. 1371-96).

2003, Dec. 23
4288-4290 A1643 Set of 3 3.00 3.00

Butterflies A1665

Designs: 40s, Noctua tertia. 45s, Rethera komarovi. 55s, Symtomis marjana. 80s, Arctia caja.

2004, Jan. 15 *Perf. 12¾ Syncopated*
4291-4294 A1665 Set of 4 4.25 4.25

Perf. 14x13½

4291a-4294a A1655 Set of 4 28.00 28.00

Issued: Nos 4291a-4294a, Oct.

A souvenir sheet containing Nos. 4291-4294 with inscriptions commemorating the Australia 2013 and Thailand 2013 World Stamp Exhibitions was produced in limited quantities.

Intl. Masquerade Festival, Pernik — A1666

2004, Jan. 23 *Perf. 13*
4295 A1666 80s multi + label 1.60 1.60

Printed in sheets of 3 +3 labels.

Bulgarian Chairmanship of Organization for Security and Cooperation in Europe — A1667

2004, Jan. 30
4296 A1667 80s multi 1.50 1.50

Ivan Vazov National Theater, Cent. — A1668

2004, Feb. 19
4297 A1668 45s multi + label 1.00 1.00

Famous Men A1669

Designs: 45s, Atanas Dalchev (1904-78), poet. 80s, Lubomir Pipkov (1904-74), composer.

2004, Mar. 25
4298-4299 A1669 Set of 2 2.50 2.50

Admission to NATO — A1670

2004, Apr. 2
4300 A1670 80s multi 2.00 2.00

Souvenir Sheet

Flight of Georgi Ivanov, First Bulgarian in Space, 25th Anniv. — A1671

2004, Apr. 15
4301 A1671 80s multi 1.50 1.50

Souvenir Sheet

Turnovo Constitution and Restoration of Bulgarian State, 125th Anniv. — A1672

2004, Apr. 16
4302 A1672 45s multi 5.00 5.00

"Bulgarian Dream" Program A1673

2004, May 3
4303 A1673 45s multi .90 .90

Souvenir Sheet

Salvador Dali (1904-89), Artist — A1674

2004, May 12 **Litho.** ***Perf. 13***
4304 A1674 80s multi 3.00 3.00

Artists — A1675

Designs: 45s, Boris Ivanov (1904-93) and Lyuben Dimitrov (1904-2000). 80s, Vassil Stylov (1904-90) and Stoyan Venev (1904-89).

2004, May 21
4305-4306 A1675 Set of 2 2.50 2.50

Europa — A1676

Designs: 45s, Skiers on mountain. 80s, Parachutist near seaside resort.

2004, May 27
4307-4308 A1676 Set of 2 *2.50 2.50*
4308a Booklet pane, 2 each #4307-4308 *5.00* —
Complete booklet, 2 #4308a *10.00*

Complete booklet contains one pane with illustrated margins at right and one pane with illustrated margins at left.

Soccer Players — A1677

No. 4309: a, Christo Stoychkov wearing collared shirt, player holding trophy. b, Georgi Asparuchov wearing uncollared shirt, players wearing green and black shorts. c, Krassimir Balakov wearing collared shirt, players wearing white and yellow shirts. d, Nilola Kotkov wearing uncollared shirt, players wearing white shorts.

2004, June 2
4309 A1677 45s Block of 4, #a-d 4.00 4.00

Souvenir Sheet

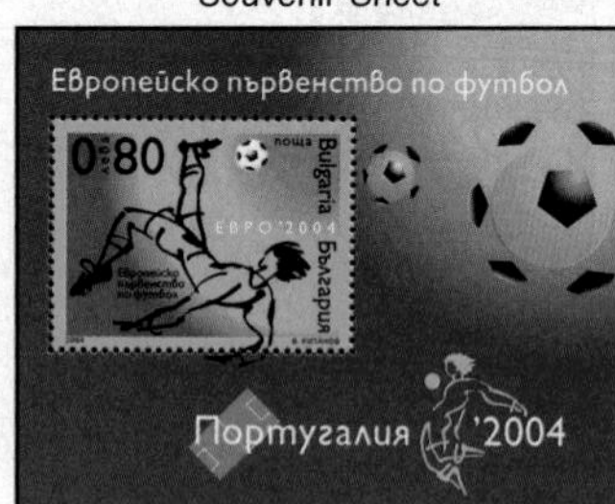

European Soccer Championships, Portugal — A1678

2004, June 11
4310 A1678 80s multi 1.50 1.50

Bulgaria — Austria Diplomatic Relations, 125th Anniv. — A1679

2004, June 23 **Litho.** ***Perf. 13***
4311 A1679 80s multi 1.50 1.50

Interior Ministry, 125th Anniv. — A1680

2004, June 26
4312 A1680 45s multi 1.00 1.00

Souvenir Sheet

Bulgarian Postal Service, 125th Anniv. — A1681

2004, July 16
4313 A1681 45s multi + label 5.00 5.00

Souvenir Sheet

Ecology — A1682

No. 4314: a, 45s, Milvus milvus. b, 80s, Blennius ocellaris.

2004, July 28
4314 A1682 Sheet of 2, #a-b 4.25 4.25

2004 Summer Olympics, Athens — A1683

Olympic rings, torch bearer, torch, map of Bulgaria showing route of torch bearers going to Olympics in: 10s, Berlin, 1936. 20s, Munich, 1972. 45s, Moscow, 1980. 80s, Athens, 2004.

2004, Aug. 5
4315-4318 A1683 Set of 4 3.25 3.25

Bulgarian Navy, 125th Anniv. — A1684

Designs: 10s, Steamer "Krum." 25s, Torpedo boat "Druski." 45s, Mine sweeper "Christo Botev." 80s, Frigate "Smeli."

2004, Aug. 6
4319-4322 A1684 Set of 4 3.25 3.25

Masons in Bulgaria, 125th Anniv. A1685

2004, Sept. 20 **Litho.** ***Perf. 13***
4323 A1685 45s multi 5.00 5.00

Famous Bulgarians — A1686

Designs: 10s, Patriarch Ephtimius Turnovski (1327-1402). 20s, Princes Fruzhin (1393-1460) and Constantine (1396-1422). 45s, Georgi Peyachevich (1655-1725) and Peter Partchevich (1612-74), uprising leaders. 80s, Paisii Hilendarski (1722-73), historian.

2004, Nov. 15
4324-4327 A1686 Set of 4 3.50 3.50

Miniature Sheet

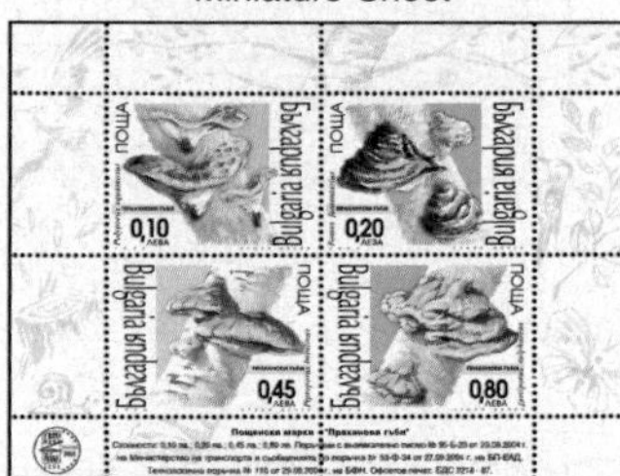

Mushrooms — A1687

No. 4328: a, 10s, Polyporus squamosus. b, 20s, Fomes fomentarius. 45s, Piptoporus betulinus. 80s, Laetiporus sulphureus.

2004, Nov. 17
4328 A1687 Sheet of 4, #a-d 3.50 3.50

Worldwide Fund for Nature (WWF) — A1688

No. 4329: a, Two fish, blue background. b, One fish, yellow green background. c, One fish, light blue background. d, Large fish eating small fish, green background.

2004, Nov. 18
4329 Horiz. strip of 4 7.50 7.50
a.-d. A1688 80s Any single 1.60 1.60
Complete booklet, 2 #4329 16.00

Christmas — A1689

2004, Nov. 24
4330 A1689 45s multi 1.00 1.00

Souvenir Sheet

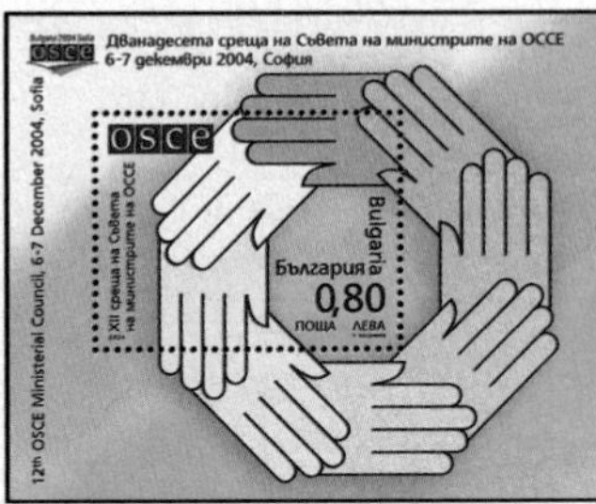

Organization for Security and Cooperation in Europe Ministerial Council Meeting, Sofia — A1690

2004, Dec. 6 **Litho.** ***Perf. 13***
4331 A1690 80s multi 1.50 1.50

Self-Portrait of Geo Milev (1895-1925), Artist, Writer — A1691

2005, Jan. 17
4332 A1691 45s multi 1.00 1.00

Rotary International, Cent. — A1692

2005, Feb. 23
4333 A1692 80s multi 1.60 1.60

Souvenir Sheet

Cinema History — A1693

No. 4334: a, 10s, Charlie Chaplin in "The Gold Rush." b, 20s, "The Battleship Potemkin." c, 45s, Marlene Dietrich in "The Blue Angel." d, 80s, Vassil Ghendov in "Bulgaran is a Gallant Man."

2005, Feb. 25 ***Perf. 13x13¼***
4334 A1693 Sheet of 4, #a-d 3.25 3.25

Souvenir Sheet

Bulgarian Exarchate, 135th Anniv. — A1694

2005, Mar. 11 ***Perf. 13***
4335 A1694 45s multi 3.00 3.00

Volunteers for Europe A1695

2005, Mar. 16
4336 A1695 80s multi 1.60 1.60

Panayot Hitov (1830-1912) and Philip Totyo (1830-1907), Revolutionaries A1696

2005, Mar. 21
4337 A1696 45s multi 1.00 1.00

Souvenir Sheet

Polar Explorers — A1697

No. 4338: a, 45s, Admiral Robert Peary (1856-1920). b, 80s, Roald Amundsen (1872-1928).

2005, Mar. 23
4338 A1697 Sheet of 2, #a-b 2.50 2.50

Souvenir Sheet

Fire Trucks — A1698

No. 4339: a, 10s, 1936 Peugeot. b, 20s, 1935 Mercedes. 45s, 1934 Magirus. 80s, 1925 Renault.

2005, Apr. 2 **Litho.** ***Perf. 13***
4339 A1698 Sheet of 4, #a-d 3.25 3.25

Souvenir Sheet

Hans Christian Andersen (1805-75), Author — A1699

2005, May 20
4340 A1699 80s multi 1.60 1.60

Souvenir Sheet

Introduction of Cyrillic Alphabet to European Union — A1700

2005, May 24
4341 A1700 80s multi 1.60 1.60

Souvenir Sheet

Trains — A1701

No. 4342: a, 45s, Series 46 locomotive. b, 80s, DMV Series 10.

2005, May 26
4342 A1701 Sheet, 2 each #4342a-4342b 5.00 5.00

Child's Drawing of the Radetski A1702

2005, May 27 **Litho.** ***Perf. 13***
4343 A1702 45s multi 1.00 1.00

Europa A1703

No. 4344: a, Plates of food, apple, gourd. b, Plates of food, wine glass, tomato, scallions.

2005, May 28

4344	Pair	*2.50*	*2.50*
a.	A1703 45s green & multi	*.90*	*.90*
b.	A1703 80s red & multi	*1.50*	*1.50*
c.	Booklet pane, 2 each #4344a-4344b	*5.00*	—
	Complete booklet, 2 #4344c	*10.00*	

European Philatelic Cooperation, 50th Anniv. (in 2006) — A1704

Designs: 45s, Two stylized people. 80s, Rectangle of stylized people.

2005, May 28
4345-4346 A1704 Set of 2 2.50 2.50

Europa stamps, 50th anniv. (in 2006).

Dragonflies A1705

Designs: 10s, Cordulegaster bidentata. 20s, Erythromma najas, horiz. 45s, Sympetrum pedemontanum, horiz. 80s, Brachytron pratense.

2005, June 29
4347-4350 A1705 Set of 4 3.25 3.25

Elias Canetti (1905-94), 1981 Nobel Laureate in Literature — A1706

2005, July 25
4351 A1706 80s multi 1.75 1.75

Spiders A1707

Designs: 10s, Synema globosum. 20s, Argiope bruennichi. 45s, Eresus cinnaberinus. 80s, Araneus diadematus.

2005, July 29
4352-4355 A1707 Set of 4 3.25 3.25

Organized Tourism in Bulgaria, 110th Anniv. — A1708

2005, Aug. 26 **Litho.** ***Perf. 13***
4356 A1708 45s multi .70 .70

Union of Bulgaria and Eastern Rumelia, 120th Anniv. — A1709

2005, Sept. 6
4357 A1709 45s multi .70 .70

Women's Folk Costumes A1710

Clothing from region of: 20s, Sofia. 25s, Pleven. 45s, Sliven. 80s, Stara Zagora.

2005, Oct. 15 **Litho.** ***Perf. 13***
4358-4361 A1710 Set of 4 2.50 2.50

Souvenir Sheet

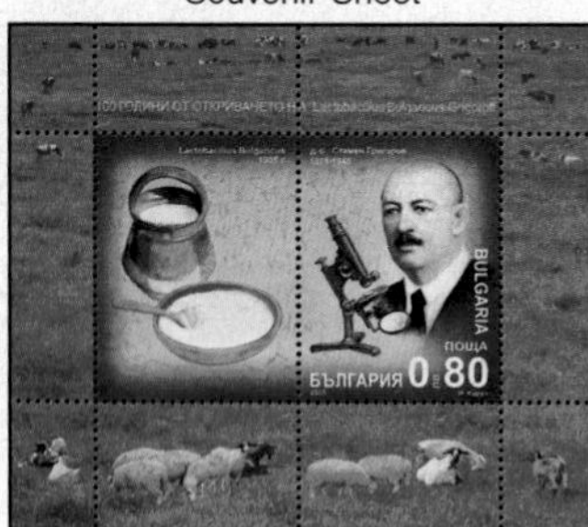

Stamen Grigoroff (1878-1945) and Microscope — A1711

2005
4362 A1711 80s multi + label 1.25 1.25
a. As #4362, with owl added in UR of stamp, imperf. 12.00 12.00

Grigoroff's discovery of Lactobacillus bulgaricus grigoroff, cent.

Issued: No. 4362, 10/21; No. 4362a, 12/2.

No. 4362a has simulated perforations and a perforated serial number.

Antoaneta Stefanova, Female World Chess Champion — A1712

2005, Nov. 10
4363 A1712 80s multi 1.10 1.10

Christmas — A1713

2005, Nov. 30
4364 A1713 45s multi .70 .70

Souvenir Sheet

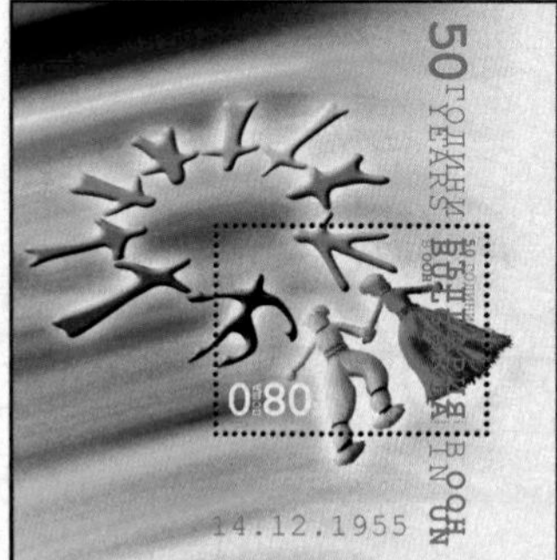

Admission to the United Nations, 50th Anniv. — A1714

2005, Dec. 14 **Litho.** ***Perf. 13***
4365 A1714 80s multi 1.10 1.10

Builders of the Bulgarian State — A1715

Designs: 10s, Illarion Makariopolski (1812-75) and Antim I (1816-88), religious leaders. 20s, Georgi Rakovski (1821-67) and Vassil Levski (1837-73), revolutionaries. 45s, Ljuben Karavelov (1834-79) and Christo Botev (1848-76), poets. 80s, Panayot Volov (1850-76) and Pavel Bobekov (1852-77), revolutionaries.

2005, Dec. 20
4366-4369 A1715 Set of 4 2.40 2.40

Roses — A1716

Designs: 54s, Rosa pendulina. 1.50 l, Rosa gallica. 2 l, Rosa spinosissima. 10 l, Rosa arvenis.

Perf. 13x12¾ Syncopated

2006, Jan. 23 **Litho.**
4370 A1716 54s multi .75 .75
4371 A1716 1.50 l multi 2.25 2.25
4372 A1716 2 l multi 3.00 3.00
4373 A1716 10 l multi 14.00 14.00
Nos. 4370-4373 (4) 20.00 20.00

Wolfgang Amadeus Mozart (1756-91), Composer — A1717

2006, Jan. 27 ***Perf. 13***
4374 A1717 1 l multi + label 7.00 7.00

Famous Bulgarian Philatelists — A1718

Designs: 35s, Ellin Pellin (1877-1949), novelist. 55s, Lazar Dobrich (1881-1970), circus performer. 60s, Boris Christov (1914-93), opera singer. 1 l, Bogomil Nonev (1920-2002), writer.

2006, Jan. 31 **Litho.**
Stamp + Label
4375-4378 A1718 Set of 4 3.75 3.75

Souvenir Sheet

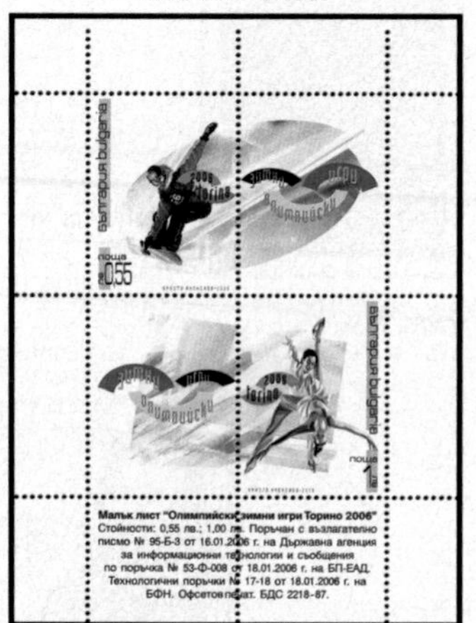

2006 Winter Olympics, Turin — A1719

No. 4379: a, 55s, Snowboarding. b, 1 l, Figure skating.

2006, Feb. 10 ***Perf. 13x13¼***
4379 A1719 Sheet of 2, #a-b 2.25 2.25

Souvenir Sheet

Bulgarian Antarctic Cartography, 10th Anniv. — A1720

2006, Feb. 28 ***Perf. 13***
4380 A1720 1 l multi 1.50 1.50

Battle of Nicopolis, 610th Anniv. — A1721

2006, Mar. 14
4381 A1721 1.50 l multi 2.25 2.25

Souvenir Sheet

Ecology — A1722

No. 4382: a, 55s, Martes martes. b, 1.50 l, Ursus arctos.

2006, Mar. 28 ***Perf. 13½x13¼***
4382 A1722 Sheet of 2, #a-b + label 2.60 2.60

Europa A1723

Designs: 55c, Person holding star. 1 l, Flower.

Perf. 12¾x13 Syncopated

2006, Apr. 25
4383 A1723 55c multi 1.00 1.00
4384 A1723 1 l multi 2.00 2.00

Booklet Stamps

Perf. 13

4385 A1723 55c multi 4.50 4.50
4386 A1723 1 l multi 9.25 9.25
a. Booklet pane, 4 each #4385-4386 55.00 —
Complete booklet, #4386a 57.50
Nos. 4383-4386 (4) 16.75 16.75

Souvenir Sheet

Meeting of NATO Foreign Ministers, Sofia — A1724

2006, Apr. 27 ***Perf. 13***
4387 A1724 1.50 l multi 2.00 2.00

Trud Newspaper, 70th Anniv. — A1725

2006, Apr. 28

4388 A1725 55s multi 1.50 1.50

Souvenir Sheet

Vesselin Topalov, World Chess Champion — A1726

2006, May 4 ***Perf. 13***

4389 A1726 1.50 l multi 2.00 2.00

Exists imperf. with perforated serial number. Value $12.

Palace of Culture, Sofia, 25th Anniv. — A1727

2006, May 5 ***Perf. 13¼x13***

4390 A1727 55s multi + label 1.50 1.50

Birds A1728

Designs: 10s, Circus aeruginosus. 35s, Circus cyaneus. 55s, Circus macrourus. 1 l, Circus pygargus.

2006, May 9 ***Perf. 13***

4391-4394 A1728 Set of 4 3.00 3.00

Nikola Vaptsarov Naval Academy, 125th Anniv. — A1729

2006, May 20 ***Perf. 13¼x13***

4395 A1729 55s multi .75 .75

Souvenir Sheet

2006 World Cup Soccer Championships, Germany — A1730

2006, June 9

4396 A1730 1 l multi 1.40 1.40

Bulgarian Membership in UNESCO, 50th Anniv. — A1731

2006, June 29 ***Perf. 13***

4397 A1731 1 l multi 1.40 1.40

Gena Dimitrova (1941-2005), Opera Singer — A1732

2006, July 18 **Litho.** ***Perf. 13¼***

4398 A1732 1 l multi 1.40 1.40

Flowers A1733

No. 4399: a, Saponaria stranjensis. b, Trachystemon orientalis. c, Hypericum calycinum. d, Rhododendron ponticum.

2006, July 28 ***Perf. 13***

4399 Horiz. strip of 4 3.00 3.00

a. A1733 10s multi .25 .25

b. A1733 35s multi .45 .45

c. A1733 55s multi .70 .70

d. A1733 1 l multi 1.40 1.40

No. 4399 printed in sheets of 2 strips which are tete-beche.

Bulgarian Automobiles — A1734

Designs: 10s, 1995 Rover Maestro. 35s, 1967 Moskvich. 55s, 1967 Bulgaralpine. 1 l, 1967 Bulgarrenault.

2006, Sept. 29 **Litho.** ***Perf. 13***

4400-4403 A1734 Set of 4 3.00 3.00

Souvenir Sheet

Return of the Prodigal Son, by Rembrandt (1606-69) — A1735

2006, Oct. 25

4404 A1735 1 l multi 1.40 1.40

Paintings by Bulgarian Artists — A1736

Designs: 10s, All Souls Day, by Ivan Murkvitchka. 35s, Sozopol - Houses, by Veselin Staykov. 55s, Sofia in Winter, by Nikola Petrov. 1 l, Portrait of T. Popova, by Georgi Popov.

2006, Oct. 27 ***Perf. 13x13¼***

4405-4408 A1736 Set of 4 3.25 3.25

World Sambo Championships, Sofia — A1737

2006, Nov. 3 ***Perf. 13***

4409 A1737 55s multi .90 .90

Souvenir Sheet

Postal Vans — A1738

2006, Nov. 17 ***Perf. 13¼***

4410 A1738 1 l multi + label 9.00 9.00

Christmas — A1739

2006, Nov. 24 ***Perf. 13¼x13***

4411 A1739 55s multi .90 .90

2007 Admission of Bulgaria and Romania into European Union — A1740

Designs: 55s, Flags of Bulgaria and Romania, map of Europe, European Union ballot box. 1.50 l, "EU" in colors of Bulgarian and Romanian flags.

2006, Nov. 29 ***Perf. 13***

4412-4413 A1740 Set of 2 3.25 3.25

4413a Souvenir sheet, #4412-4413 3.25 3.25

See Bulgaria Nos.

Peter Dimkov (1886-1981), Naturopath — A1741

2006, Dec. 20

4414 A1741 55s multi .90 .90

Builders of the Bulgarian State — A1742

Designs: 10s, Gen. Danail Nikolaev (1852-1942), Gen. Racho Petrov (1861-1942). 35s, Petko Karavelov (1843-1903), Marin Drinov (1838-1906). 55s, Dr. Konstantin Stoylov (1853-1901), Stefan Stambolov (1854-95). 1 l, Prince Alexander I (1857-93).

2006, Dec. 21

4415-4418 A1742 Set of 4 3.25 3.25

Souvenir Sheet

Opening of New Terminal at Sofia Airport — A1743

2006, Dec. 27 **Litho.**

4419 A1743 55s multi 2.00 2.00

Exists imperf. with perforated serial number. Value, $17.50.

Souvenir Sheet

Admission to European Union — A1744

2007, Jan. 31 ***Perf. 13¼***

4420 A1744 1.50 l multi 2.00 2.00

Emilian Stanev (1907-79), Novelist — A1745

2007, Feb. 28 ***Perf. 13***

4421 A1745 55s multi + label .75 .75

Treaty of Rome, 50th Anniv. A1746

2007, Mar. 23 ***Perf. 13¼x13***

4422 A1746 1 l multi 1.40 1.40

Stage Actors — A1747

Designs: 10s, Ivan Dimov (1897-1965). 55s, Sava Ognyanov (1876-1933). 1 l, Krustyo Sarafov (1876-1952).

2007, Mar. 27 ***Perf. 13***

4423-4425 A1747 Set of 3 2.50 2.50

Souvenir Sheet

Launch of Sputnik 1, 50th Anniv. — A1748

2007, Apr. 25 Litho. ***Perf. 13¼x13***

4426 A1748 1 l multi 1.40 1.40

Europa — A1749

Nos. 4427 and 4428: a, 55s, Scouts around campfire. b, 1.50 l, Scouts reading map.

2007, Apr. 26 ***Perf. 13 Syncopated***

Size: 39x28mm

4427 A1749 Pair, #a-b 3.00 3.00

Booklet Stamps

Size: 31x23mm

Perf. 13

4428 A1749 Pair, #a-b 3.00 3.00

c. Booklet pane, 4 each #4428a-4428b 12.00 —

Complete booklet, #4428c 12.00

Scouting, cent.

Military Aircraft A1750

Designs: 10s, DAR 3, 1937. 35s, DAR 9, 1939. 55s, KB 309, 1939. 1 l, KB 11A, 1940

2007, Apr. 27 ***Perf. 13¼x13***

4429-4432 A1750 Set of 4 3.00 3.00

Death of King Boris I, 1100th Anniv. A1751

2007, May 2

4433 A1751 55s multi .80 .80

Poets and Painters A1752

Designs: 10s, Dimcho Debelyanov (1887-1916), poet. 35s, Nenko Balkanski (1907-77), painter. 55s, Vera Lukova (1907-74), painter. 1 l, Theodor Trayanov (1882-1945), poet.

2007, May 23 ***Perf. 13***

4434-4437 A1752 Set of 4 3.00 3.00

European Conference of Transportation Ministers, Sofia — A1753

2007, May 30 ***Perf. 13x13¼***

4438 A1753 1 l multi 1.60 1.60

Monasteries — A1754

Designs: 63s, Lozenski Monastery. 75s, Obradovski Monastery. 1.20 l, Kremikovski Monastery. 2.20 l, Chepinski Monastery.

Perf. 12½x12¾ Syncopated

2007, May 30

Color Behind Denomination

4439 A1754 63s yel orange .90 .90

4440 A1754 75s green 1.25 1.25

4441 A1754 1.20 l red 1.90 1.90

4442 A1754 2.20 l blue 3.50 3.50

Nos. 4439-4442 (4) 7.55 7.55

Souvenir Sheet

Diplomatic Relations Between Bulgaria and Azerbaijan, 15th Anniv. — A1755

2007, June 1 ***Perf. 13***

4443 A1755 1 l multi 1.60 1.60

Excavations of San Clemente Basilica, Rome, 150th Anniv. — A1756

2007, May 21 Litho. ***Perf. 13***

4444 A1756 1 l multi 1.60 1.60

Flowers — A1757

Designs: 10s, Onosma thracica. 45s, Astracantha aitosensis. 55s, Veronica krumovii. 1 l, Verbascum adrianopolitanum.

Perf. 13x12½ Syncopated

2007, July 6

4445-4448 A1757 Set of 4 3.50 3.50

Vassil Levski (1837-73), Patriot — A1758

2007, July 18 ***Perf. 13***

4449 A1758 55s multi .80 .80

World Youth 470 Class Yachting Championships, Bourgas A1759

2007, July 21

4450 A1759 1 l multi 2.00 2.00

Battle of Stara Zagora, 130th Anniv. — A1760

2007, July 31

4451 A1760 55s multi .80 .80

2007 Rugby World Cup, France A1761

2007, Sept. 5 ***Perf. 13¼***

4452 A1761 55s multi .80 .80

Souvenir Sheet

Ropotamo Reserve, 15th Anniv. — A1762

No. 4453: a, 55s, Lutra lutra. b, 1 l, Haliaeetus albicilla.

2007, Sept. 10

4453 A1762 Sheet of 2, #a-b 2.50 2.50

Miniature Sheet

Endangered Birds — A1763

No. 4454: a, 10s, Alcedo atthis. b, 35s, Tichodroma muraria. c, 55s, Bombycilla garrulus. d, 1 l, Phoenicopterus ruber.

2007, Sept. 11 ***Perf. 13***
4454 A1763 Sheet of 4, #a-d 3.25 3.25

Great Lodge of the Old Freemasons of Bulgaria, 10th Anniv. — A1764

2007, Sept. 21
4455 A1764 55s multi .90 .90

Souvenir Sheet

Bulgaria Post Exchange and Sorting Center, Sofia — A1765

2007, Oct. 9 Litho. ***Perf. 13¼***
4456 A1765 55s multi .80 .80

World Post Day.

Ivan Hadjiiski (1907-44), Psychologist A1766

2007, Oct. 12 ***Perf. 13***
4457 A1766 55s multi .80 .80

Christmas A1767

2007, Nov. 27 Litho. ***Perf. 13***
4458 A1767 55s multi .85 .85

Sports Champions A1768

Designs: 10s, Rumyana Neykova, European 2000-meter skiff rowing champion. 35s, Stanka Zlateva, world freestyle wrestling champion. 1 l, Stefka Kostadinova, women's world record-holder in high jump.

2007, Dec. 19 ***Perf. 13½x13***
4459-4461 A1768 Set of 3 2.25 2.25

Military Reconnaisance in Bulgaria, Cent. — A1769

2007, Dec. 20 ***Perf. 13x13¼***
4462 A1769 55s multi .85 .85

Christo Botev (1848-76), Poet — A1770

2008, Jan. 6 Litho. ***Perf. 13***
4463 A1770 55s multi .85 .85

Souvenir Sheet

Intl. Polar Year — A1771

No. 4464: a, 55s, Polar bear. b, 1 l, Penguins.

2008, Jan. 30 ***Perf. 13¼***
4464 A1771 Sheet of 2, #a-b, + 2 labels 2.40 2.40

Bulgarian Antarctic expeditions, 20th anniv.

Souvenir Sheet

2008 Summer Olympics, Beijing — A1772

No. 4465: a, 55s, One volleyball player. b, 1 l, Two volleyball players.

2008, Feb. 25 Litho. ***Perf. 13***
4465 A1772 Sheet of 2, #a-b 2.40 2.40

Independence, 130th Anniv. — A1773

2008, Feb. 29
4466 A1773 55s multi 1.10 1.10

Europa — A1774

Cover with stamp and: Nos. 4467, 4468, Postman. Nos. 4469, 4470, Bird.

2008, Apr. 22

4467	A1774 55s grn & multi	.90	.90
4468	A1774 55s lilac & multi	.90	.90
a.	Booklet pane of 4	3.60	—
4469	A1774 1 l blue & multi	1.60	1.60
4470	A1774 1 l org yel & multi	1.60	1.60
a.	Booklet pane of 4	6.40	—
	Complete booklet, #4468a, 4470a	10.00	
	Nos. 4467-4470 (4)	5.00	5.00

Stamps in booket panes are tete-beche.

Military Aviators — A1775

No. 4471 — Airplane and: a, 55s, Capt. Dimitri Spisarevski (1918-43). b, 1 l, Gen. Stoyan Stoyanov (1913-97).

2008, Apr. 25
4471 A1775 Horiz. pair, #a-b 2.75 2.75

Art — A1776

Designs: 10s, Painting by Boris Kotsev (1908-59). 35s, Nude, by Eliezer Alsheh (1908-78). 55s, Nude, by Vera Nedkova (1908-96). 1 l, Sculpture by Asen Peikov (1908-73).

2008, May 7
4472-4475 A1776 Set of 4 3.75 3.75

Sofia Zoo, 120th Anniv. — A1777

No. 4476: a, 10s, Csalithrix geoffroyi. b, 20s, Hippopotamus amphibius. c, 35s, Camelus bactrianus. d, 55s, Suricata suricata. e, 60s, Ara ararauna. f, 1 l, Lynx lynx.
No. 4477, Like No. 4476d.

2008, May 14 ***Perf. 13***
4476 A1777 Sheet of 6, #a-f 5.00 5.00

Souvenir Sheet

Imperf

4477 A1777 55s multi *27.50 27.50*

No. 4477 has simulated perforations. Bulgaria 2009 European Philatelic Exhibition.

Souvenir Sheet

Central Sports Club of the Army (CSKA) Soccer Team, 60th Anniv. — A1778

2008, May 7 Litho. ***Perf. 13½x13¼***
4478 A1778 55s multi .90 .90

Souvenir Sheet

Space Flight of Alexander Alexandrov, 20th Anniv. — A1779

2008, June 9 Litho. ***Perf. 13***
4479 A1779 1 l multi 1.75 1.75

Union of Bulgarian Philatelists, 70th Anniv. — A1780

2008, June 16 Litho. ***Perf. 13***

Stamp With White Border

4480 A1780 60s multi 1.00 1.00

An imperforate souvenir sheet containing No. 4480 with a colored background sold for well above face value.

Souvenir Sheet

Wildlife of Strandzha Nature Park — A1781

No. 4481: a, 60s, Canis aureus. b, 1.50 l, Aquila pomarina, vert.

2008, July 21 Litho. ***Perf. 13¼***
4481 A1781 Sheet of 2, #a-b 3.50 3.50

Relations Between Bulgaria and European Economic Community, 20th Anniv. — A1782

2008, July 30 ***Perf. 13***
4482 A1782 1 l multi 1.75 1.75

Railroad Anniversaries — A1783

No. 4483: a, Orient Express passenger car, coat of arms of Paris, Munich and Vienna. b, Locomotive of Bulgarian State Railways, coat of arms of Belgrade, Sofia and Istanbul.

2008, Sept. 11
4483 Pair 3.50 3.50
a. A1783 60s multi 1.00 1.00
b. A1783 1.50 l multi 2.40 2.40

Orient Express and Bulgarian State Railways, 130th anniv. No. 4483 printed in sheets containing four of each stamp + one label.

Nikola (1893-1947) and Dimitar Petkov (1858-1907), Politicians — A1784

2008, Sept. 18 **Litho.** ***Perf. 13***
4484 A1784 60s multi 1.00 1.00

Souvenir Sheet

Tsar Ferdinand (1861-1948) — A1785

2008, Sept. 22 ***Perf. 13x13¼***
4485 A1785 60s multi 1.00 1.00

Proclamation of Bulgarian independence, cent.

Destruction of the Knights Templar, 700th Anniv. — A1786

2008, Sept. 30 ***Perf. 13***
4486 A1786 1 l multi 1.75 1.75

Ferrari Race Cars — A1787

2008, Oct. 16
4487 Pair 2.75 2.75
a. A1787 60s 2008 Ferrari 1.00 1.00
b. A1787 1 l 1952 Ferrari 1.60 1.60

An imperforate souvenir sheet of the 60s stamp with simulated perforations exists.

Red Cross in Bulgaria, 130th Anniv. — A1788

2008, Oct. 24
4488 A1788 60s multi 1.00 1.00

Christmas A1789

2008, Nov. 21
4489 A1789 60s multi 1.00 1.00

Monastery Icons — A1790

No. 4490 — Madonna and Child icons from: a, Rila Monastery, 12th cent. b, Troyan Monastery, 18th cent. c, Bachkovo Monastery, 14th cent.

2008, Nov. 21
4490 Horiz. strip of 3 3.50 3.50
a. A1790 50s multi .75 .75
b. A1790 60s multi 1.20 1.20
c. A1790 1 l multi 1.50 1.50

An imperf. souvenir sheet of the 60s stamp with simulated perforations exists.

Sofia St. Clement of Ohrid University, 120th Anniv. — A1791

2008, Nov. 25
4491 A1791 60s multi 1.00 1.00

Famous Men — A1792

No. 4492: a, Andranik Ozanian (1865-1927), Armenian general who particpated in Balkan Wars. b, Peyo Yavorov (1878-1914), Bulgarian poet.

2008, Dec. 10
4492 Horiz. pair 3.50 3.50
a. A1792 60s multi 1.00 1.00
b. A1792 1.50 l multi 2.40 2.40

See Armenia No. 789.

Bulgaria 2009 European Stamp Exhibition A1793

2009, Jan. 23
4493 A1793 60s multi 1.00 1.00

Famous Men Born in 1809 — A1794

Designs: 10s, Abraham Lincoln (1809-65), US President. 50s, Nikolai Gogol (1809-52), writer. 60s, Charles Darwin (1809-82), naturalist. 1 l, Edgar Allan Poe (1809-49), writer.

2009, Feb. 6
4494-4497 A1794 Set of 4 3.50 3.50

An imperf. souvenir sheet of No. 4496 with simulated perforations exists.

Birds — A1795

Designs: Nos. 4498a, 4499a, 60s, Scolopax rusticola. Nos. 4498b, 4499b, 1 l, Monticola saxatilis.

2009, Mar. 2 ***Perf. 13***
4498 A1795 Horiz. pair, #a-b 2.50 2.50

Souvenir Sheet

Imperf

4499 A1795 Sheet of 2, #a-b 3.00 3.00

No. 4499 has simulated perforations. See Serbia Nos. 457-458.

Amethyst A1796

2009, Mar. 24 **Litho.** ***Perf. 13x13¼***
4500 A1796 60s multi .85 .85

Natl. Museum of Natural History, 120th anniv. An imperf. souvenir sheet with simulated perforations exists.

Hagia Sofia Church and St. Alexander Nevsky Cathedral, Sofia — A1797

2009, Mar. 25 ***Perf. 13***
4501 A1797 60s multi .85 .85

Sofia as Bulgarian capital, 130th anniv.

Souvenir Sheet

Preservation of Polar Regions and Glaciers — A1798

No. 4502: a, 60s, Penguins, head of narwhal. b, 1.50 l, Body of narwhal, polar bear, seal, white-tailed eagle, icebreaker.

2009, Mar. 27
4502 A1798 Sheet of 2, #a-b 3.25 3.25

NATO Anniversaries — A1799

No. 4503 — NATO emblem and flags making up number: a, 60s, "60" (60th anniv. of NATO). b, 1.50s, "5" (5th anniv. of Bulgarian membership in NATO).

2009, Mar. 30
4503 A1799 Horiz. pair, #a-b 3.00 3.00

Bicycles A1800

Various bicycles.

2009, Mar. 31
4504 Horiz. strip of 4 3.00 3.00
a. A1800 10s multi .25 .25
b. A1800 50s multi .65 .65
c. A1800 60s multi .85 .85
d. A1800 1 l multi 1.25 1.25

An imperf. souvenir sheet of the 60s with simulated perforations exists.

Souvenir Sheet

Space Flight of First Bulgarian Cosmonaut Georgi Ivanov, 30th Anniv. — A1801

2009, Apr. 9 ***Perf. 13¼x13***

4505 A1801 60s multi 1.00 1.00

Souvenir Sheet

Restoration of the Bulgarian State, 130th Anniv. — A1802

No. 4506 — Arms of: a, 60s, 1879. b, 1 l, 1997.

2009, Apr. 15

4506 A1802 Sheet of 2, #a-b 2.50 2.50

Cacti — A1803

No. 4507: a, 10s, Rathbunia alamosensis. b, 50s, Mammilaria pseudoperbella. c, 60s, Obregonia degenerii. d, 1.50 l, Astrophitum mayas.

2009, Apr. 24 ***Perf. 13***

4507 A1803 Horiz. strip of 4, #a-d 4.00 4.00

An imperf souvenir sheet of the 60s with simulated perforations exists.

Europa A1804

Designs: Nos. 4508, 4510, 60s, IC342 galaxy. Nos. 4509, 4511, 1.50 l, M31 (Andromeda galaxy).

2009, Apr. 28 ***Perf. 13 Syncopated***

Size: 28x40mm

4508-4509 A1804 Set of 2 3.00 3.00

Size: 25x36mm

Perf. 13x13¼

4510-4511 A1804 Set of 2 3.00 3.00

4511a Souvenir sheet, 2 each #4510-4511 6.00 6.00

4511b Booklet pane of 4, #4510, 3 #4511 7.25 —

4511c Booklet pane of 4, #4511, 3 #4510 4.75 —

Complete booklet, #4511b, 4511c 12.00

Intl. Year of Astronomy. Nos. 4508-4509 were printed in sheets of 5 + label.

Introduction of the Euro, 10th Anniv. — A1805

2009, May 20 ***Perf. 13***

4512 A1805 1 l multi 1.50 1.50

Art — A1806

Designs: 10s, Landscape, by Vassil Ivanov (1909-75). 50s, Three Vases, by Georgi Kolarov (1909-96). 60s, The Black Sea, by Alexander Mutaffov (1879-1957). 1 l, Cast Shadows, by Konstantin Sturkelov (1889-1961).

2009, May 27 **Litho.**

4513-4516 A1806 Set of 4 3.25 3.25

Lokomotiv Sofia Soccer Team, 80th Anniv. — A1807

2009, May 28 ***Perf. 13¼x13***

4517 A1807 60s multi .85 .85

Owls — A1808

No. 4518: a, 10s, Bubo bubo. b, 50s, Athene noctua. c, 60s, Strix uralensis. d, 1.50 l, Glaucidium passerinum.

2009, May 30 ***Perf. 13x13¼***

4518 A1808 Horiz. strip or block of 4, #a-d 4.00 4.00

Souvenir Sheet

Supermoto European Cup, Pleven — A1809

2009, June 16

4519 A1809 60s multi .85 .85

Captain Petko Voivoda (1844-1900), Hajduk Leader — A1810

2009, June 17 ***Perf. 13***

4520 A1810 60s multi .85 .85

Todor Burmov (1834-1906), First Bulgarian Prime Minister — A1811

2009, June 26

4521 A1811 60s multi .85 .85

Ministry of Internal Affairs, 130th anniv.

Souvenir Sheet

Bulgarian Post and Communications Department, 130th Anniv. — A1812

No. 4522 — Hands: a, 60s, Opening air mail letter. b, 1 l, Holding telephone.

2009, June 29 ***Perf. 13¼x13***

4522 A1812 Sheet of 2, #a-b 2.40 2.40

Souvenir Sheet

First Man on the Moon, 40th Anniv. — A1813

2009, July 20

4523 A1813 60s multi .90 .90

Bulgarian Academy of Science, 140th Anniv. — A1814

2009, Oct. 9 **Litho.** ***Perf. 13***

4524 A1814 60s multi .95 .95

Souvenir Sheet

Diplomatic Relations Between Bulgaria and Italy, 130th Anniv. — A1815

2009, Oct. 15 ***Perf. 13¼x13***

4525 A1815 1 l multi 1.60 1.60

See Italy No. 2970.

Souvenir Sheet

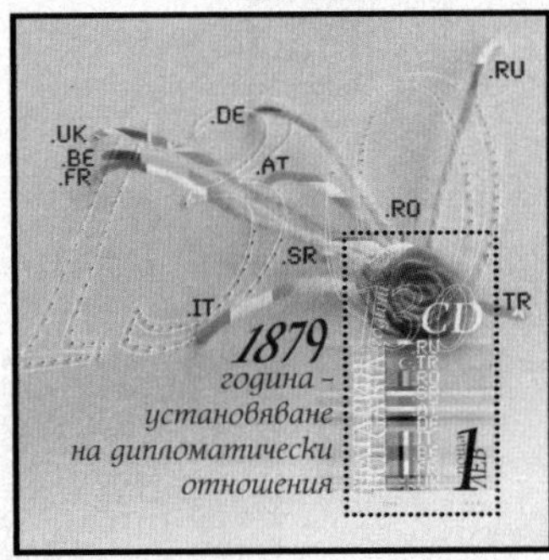

First Establishment of Diplomatic Relations With Foreign Countries, 130th Anniv. — A1816

2009, Nov. 1 ***Perf. 13x13¼***

4526 A1816 1 l multi 1.75 1.75

Bulgarian National Television, 50th Anniv. — A1817

2009, Nov. 14 ***Perf. 13¼x13***

4527 A1817 60s multi .95 .95

Military Aviation — A1818

No. 4528: a, Fokker E. III and Capt. Marko Parvanov (1892-1962). b, Assen Jordanoff (1896-1967), aeronautical engineer, and Jordanoff 1.

2009, Nov. 18 ***Perf. 13***

4528 Horiz. pair 2.50 2.50

a. A1818 60s multi .95 .95

b. A1818 1 l multi 1.50 1.50

Nikola Vapzarov (1909-42), Poet — A1819

2009, Nov. 20
4529 A1819 60s multi .95 .95

Christmas A1820

2009, Nov. 20
4530 A1820 60s multi .95 .95

Dimitar Miladinov (1810-62), Poet — A1821

2010, Jan. 7 **Litho.** ***Perf. 13***
4531 A1821 60s multi .85 .85

Bulgarian National Radio, 75th Anniv. — A1822

2010, Jan. 25 ***Perf. 13x13¼***
4532 A1822 60s multi .85 .85

Souvenir Sheet

2010 Winter Olympics, Vancouver — A1823

No. 4533: a, 60s, Luge. b, 1 l, Snowboarding.

2010, Feb. 5 ***Perf. 13½x13***
4533 A1823 Sheet of 2, #a-b 2.25 2.25

Souvenir Sheet

Frédéric Chopin (1810-49), Composer — A1824

No. 4534 — Chopin with: a, G line of musical staff below blue frame line at bottom. b, Beam connecting four notes below blue frame line below Chopin's tie and lapel.

2010, Mar. 1 ***Perf. 13***
4534 A1824 1 l Sheet of 2, #a-b, + 4 labels 3.00 3.00

Souvenir Sheet

Peonies — A1825

No. 4535: a, Paeonia suffruticosa subsp. rockii. b, Paeonia officinalis "Rubra Plena."

2010, Mar. 23
4535 A1825 60s Sheet of 2, #a-b 1.75 1.75

Miniature Sheet

Military Commanders — A1826

No. 4536: a, General Georgi Vazov (1860-1934), denomination at left. b, General Ivan Fichev (1860-1931). c, General Stilyan Kovachev (1860-1939). d, Colonel Vladimir Serafimov (1860-1934), denomination at right. e, General Dimitar Geshev (1860-1922).

2010, Mar. 26
4536 A1826 60s Sheet of 5, #a-e, + label 4.25 4.25

Souvenir Sheet

FIDE World Chess Championship Match, Sofia — A1827

2010, Apr. 22
4537 A1827 1 l multi 1.40 1.40

Europa A1828

Children's book, tree and: 60s, House, flowers, bird. 1.50s, Rabbit, insect, owl.

2010, Apr. 23 **Litho.** ***Perf. 13***
4538 Horiz. pair 3.00 3.00
a. A1828 60s multi, 29x40mm, with white frame .85 .85
b. A1828 1.50 l multi, 29x40mm, with white frame 2.10 2.10

Perf. 13x13¼

4539 Booklet pane of 2 + central label *3.00 3.00*
a. A1828 60s multi, 25x36mm, with white frame *.85 .85*
b. A1828 1.50 l multi, 25x36mm, with white frame *2.10 2.10*
Complete booklet, 4 #4539 *12.00*

Souvenir Sheet

Perf. 13

4540 Sheet of 2 3.00 3.00
a. A1828 60s multi, 32x43mm, without white frame .85 .85
b. A1828 1.50 l multi, 32x43mm, without white frame 2.10 2.10

Expo 2010, Shanghai — A1829

2010, Apr. 30 **Litho.** ***Perf. 13***
4541 A1829 1.40 l multi 1.90 1.90

Diplomatic Relations Between Bulgaria and Spain, Cent. A1830

2010, May 4 ***Perf. 13½x13***
4542 A1830 1 l multi 1.40 1.40

Souvenir Sheet

Intl. Day of Biological Diversity — A1831

2010, May 21 ***Perf. 13¼x13***
4543 A1831 1.50 l multi 1.90 1.90

Souvenir Sheets

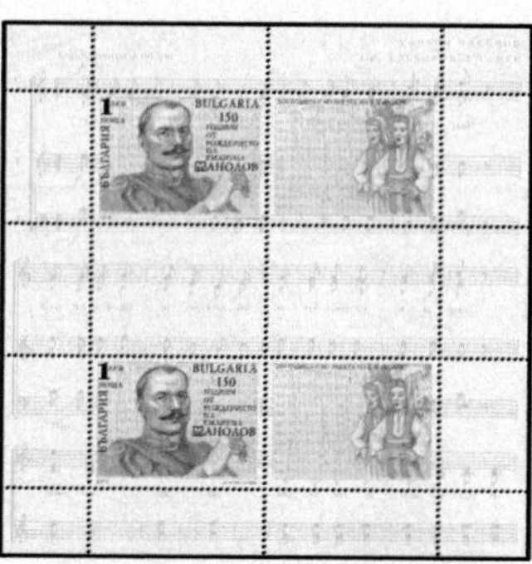

Emanuil Manolov (1860-1902), Composer — A1832

Robert Schumann (1810-56), Composer — A1833

No. 4544 — Manolov with: a, Notes above blue frame line at top and below blue frame line at bottom. b, No notes above blue frame line at top, tails of quarter notes below blue frame at bottom.

No. 4545 — Schumann with: a, F line of musical staff below blue frame line at bottom. b, Lines of musical staff and notes below blue frame line at bottom.

2010, June 8 **Litho.** ***Perf. 13***
4544 A1832 1 l Sheet of 2, #a-b, + 4 labels 2.50 2.50
4545 A1833 1 l Sheet of 2, #a-b, + 4 labels 2.50 2.50

Souvenir Sheet

Bulgarian Shepherd — A1834

2010, June 9 ***Imperf.***
4546 A1834 60s multi *.75 .75*

Balkanfila Philatelic Exhibition, Plovdiv.

Souvenir Sheet

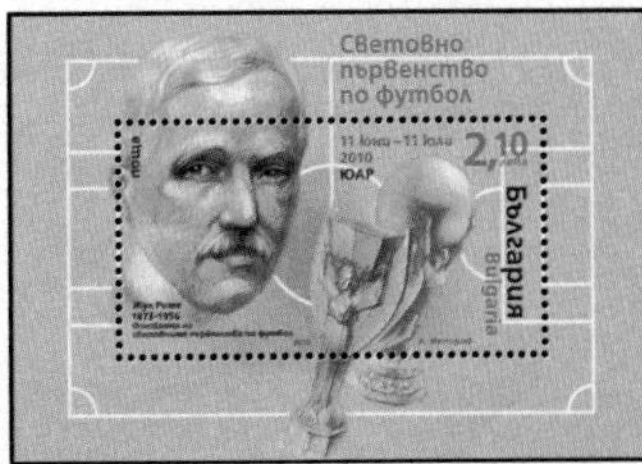

2010 World Cup Soccer Championships, South Africa — A1835

2010, June 10 *Perf. 13¼x13*
4547 A1835 2.10 l multi 2.60 2.60

St. Prokopi Varnenski, 200th Anniv. of Death — A1836

2010, June 16 *Perf. 13*
4548 A1836 60s multi .80 .80

Paintings by Jaroslav Veshin (1860-1915) — A1837

No. 4549: a, Maneuvers, 1899. b, Returning from the Market, 1898.

2010, July 23 *Perf. 13¼x13*
4549 A1837 1 l Vert. pair, #a-b, + central label 2.75 2.75

Souvenir Sheet

Alphonse Mucha (1860-1939), Illustrator — A1838

No. 4550: a, Summer, Autumn (denomination at left). b, Winter, Spring (denomination at right).

2010, July 23 *Perf. 13¼*
4550 A1838 1 l Sheet of 2, #a-b, + central label 2.75 2.75

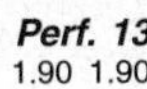

Youth Olympics, Singapore A1839

2010, July 30 *Perf. 13*
4551 A1839 1.40 l multi 1.90 1.90

Unification of Bulgaria, 125th Anniv. — A1840

2010, Sept. 3 **Litho.** *Perf. 13*
4552 A1840 60s multi .80 .80

These imperforate souvenir sheets with simulated perforations, released in late 2010, were produced in limited quantities.

Miniature Sheet

Pandas — A1841

No. 4553: a, 10s, Head of Ailuropoda melanoleuca. b, 60s, Ailuropoda melanoleuca. c, 1 l, Ailurus fulgens. d, 1.50 l, Head of Ailurus fulgens.

2010, Oct. 28 **Litho.** *Perf. 13*
4553 A1841 Sheet of 4, #a-d 5.00 5.00

Military Aircraft — A1842

Designs: 50s, Jak-23. 65s, MiG-15. 1 l, MiG-29.

2010, Nov. 12
4554-4556 A1842 Set of 3 3.00 3.00

Christmas — A1843

2010, Nov. 19
4557 A1843 65s multi .90 .90

Miniature Sheet

Tourist Attractions of Northeastern Bulgaria — A1844

No. 4558: a, 10s, Carvings from Thracian Tomb of Sveshtari. b, 50s, Balchik Palace. c, 65s, Srebarna Nature Reserve. d, 1 l, Pobiti Kamani Geological Formation.

2010, Nov. 24 *Perf. 13x13¼*
4558 A1844 Sheet of 4, #a-d 3.25 3.25

Zachary Zograf (1810-53), Painter — A1845

2010, Nov. 26 *Perf. 13*
4559 A1845 1.50 l multi 2.10 2.10

Diplomatic Relations Between Bulgaria and Cuba, 50th Anniv. — A1846

No. 4560: a, 65s, Cuban flag, San Cristobal Church, Havana. b, 1.40 l, Bulgarian flag, St. Alexander Nevsky Cathedral, Sofia.

2010, Dec. 10
4560 A1846 Horiz. pair, #a-b 2.75 2.75

Hydrurga Leptonyx and Map of Antarctica A1847

2011, Jan. 7 *Perf. 12¾ Syncopated*
4561 A1847 58s multi .80 .80

A souvenir sheet containing 2 stamps + 2 labels was printed in 2013 in limited quantities.

Princess Clementine and 9th Plovdiv Infantry Regiment — A1848

2011, Jan. 24 *Perf. 13*
4562 A1848 65s multi + label .90 .90

9th Plovdiv Infantry Regiment, 125th anniv. Printed in sheets of 4 + 4 labels.

Vanga (Vangelia Pandeva Dimitrova) (1911-96), Mystic A1849

2011, Jan. 31 **Litho.**
4563 A1849 65s multi .90 .90

April Fools' Day — A1850

2011, Apr. 1
4564 A1850 65s multi + label 1.00 1.00

Fictional discovery of the Planet of Gabrovo, 35th anniv. Gabrovo is Bulgarian town hosting a humor festival. Printed in sheets of 4 stamps + 4 labels. Horizontal stamp + label strips are tete-beche within the sheet.

Souvenir Sheet

Atlantic Club of Bulgaria, 20th Anniv. — A1851

2011, Apr. 11
4565 A1851 1 l multi 1.50 1.50

Souvenir Sheet

Space Achievements of the Soviet Union, 50th Anniv. — A1852

No. 4566: a, 65s, First manned space flight by Yuri Gagarin. b, 1.50 l, First probe to Venus, Venera 1.

2011, Apr. 12 ***Perf. 13x13¼***
4566 A1852 Sheet of 2, #a-b 3.25 3.25

Europa — A1853

Forest and: 65s, Capreolus capreolus in winter. 1.50 l, Scolopax rusticola.

2011, Apr. 28 Litho. ***Perf. 13***
Size: 29x54mm

4567 A1853 65s multi .95 .95
4568 A1853 1.50 l multi 2.25 2.25
a. Souvenir sheet, #4567-4568, perf. 13x13¼ 3.25 3.25

Booklet Stamps
Size: 24x44mm
Perf. 13

4569 A1853 65s multi .95 .95
4570 A1853 1.50 l multi 2.25 2.25
a. Booklet pane of 4, 2 each #4569-4570 6.50 —
Complete booklet, 2 #4570a 13.00

Intl. Year of Forests

Souvenir Sheet

Serdica Edict of Religious Toleration, 1700th Anniv. — A1854

2011, Apr. 30 ***Perf. 13¼x13***
4571 A1854 65s multi .95 .95

Competition Protection Commission, 20th Anniv. — A1855

2011, May 2 ***Perf. 13x12¾***
4572 A1855 65s multi .95 .95

This imperforate souvenir sheet with simulated perforations, released in May 2011, was produced in limited quantities. Compare with Type A1905.

Miniature Sheet

Tourist Attractions of North Central Bulgaria — A1856

No. 4573: a, 65s, Bear and Woodpecker, Boatin Reserve. b, 65s, Gold ring of Tsar Kaloyan, Church of the Forty Holy Martyrs, Veliko Turnovo. c, 1 l, Glozhene Monastery. d, 1 l, Woman at Etar Architectural and Ethnographic Complex, Gabrovo.

2011, June 10 ***Perf. 13x13¼***
4573 A1856 Sheet of 4, #a-d 5.00 5.00

Miniature Sheet

Fish of the Danube River — A1857

No. 4574: a, 65s, Stizostedion lucioperca, Esox lucius, Aspius aspius, Hucho hucho. b, 65s, Abramis brama, Barbus barbus, Ctenopharyngodon idella, Cyprinus carpio, Carassius carassius. c, 1 l, Acipenser ruthenus, Huso huso. d, 1 l, Silurus glanis, Lota lota.

2011, June 29 ***Perf. 13¼x13***
4574 A1857 Sheet of 4, #a-d 5.00 5.00

Victory of Khan Krum at Battle of Pliska, 1200th Anniv. A1858

2011, July 26
4575 A1858 65s multi .95 .95

Miniature Sheet

Poisonous Mushrooms — A1859

No. 4576: a, 65s, Rhodophyllus sinuatus. b, 65s, Inocybe patouillardii. c, 1 l, Russula emetica. d, 1 l, Omphalotus olearius.

2011, July 29 ***Perf. 13***
4576 A1859 Sheet of 4, #a-d 5.00 5.00

Souvenir Sheet

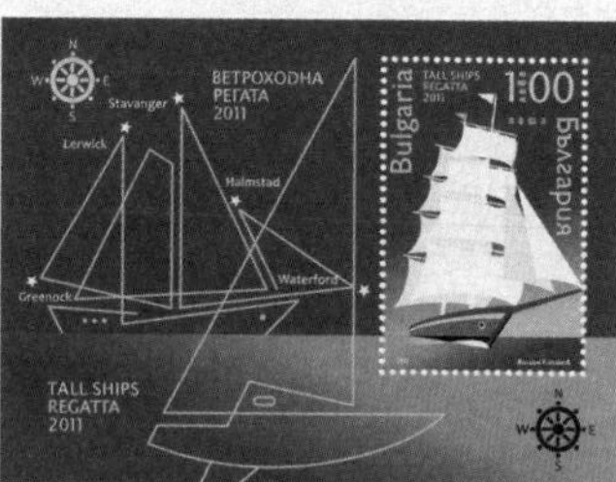

Waterford, Ireland to Halmstad, Sweden Tall Ships Regatta — A1860

2011, Aug. 25 ***Perf. 13¼***
4577 A1860 1 l multi 1.40 1.40

Souvenir Sheet

Fridtjof Nansen (1861-1930), Arctic Explorer — A1861

2011, Oct. 10 Litho. ***Perf. 13x13¼***
4578 A1861 1 l multi 1.40 1.40

Franz Liszt (1811-86), Composer — A1862

2011, Oct. 21 ***Perf. 13***
4579 A1862 1 l multi + label 1.40 1.40

Printed in sheets of 2 + 2 labels.

Souvenir Sheet

First Bulgarian Railway Line, 145th Anniv. — A1863

No. 4580: a, 65s, William Gladstone (1809-98), British prime minister. b, 1 l, Rail carriage. c, 1.50 l. Locomotive.

2011, Oct. 27 ***Perf. 13¼x13***
4580 A1863 Sheet of 3, #a-c, + label 4.50 4.50

Miniature Sheet

Dogs Launched Into Space — A1864

No. 4581: a, 65s, Laika (Nov. 3, 1957). b, 65s, Belka and Strelka (Aug. 19, 1960). c, 1 l, Chernushka (Mar. 9, 1961). d, 1 l, Zvezdochka (Mar. 25, 1961).

2011, Oct. 28 ***Perf. 13¼x13***
4581 A1864 Sheet of 4, #a-d 4.75 4.75

A souvenir sheet containing an imperforate example of No. 4581a exists from a limited printing.

First Bulgarians in Dakar Rally, South America — A1865

2011, Oct. 29 ***Perf. 13***
4582 A1865 1.50 l multi + label 2.10 2.10

Printed in sheets of 2 + 2 labels.

Souvenir Sheet

Intl. Black Sea Action Day — A1866

No. 4583: a, Scomber scombrus. b, Mytilus galloprovincialis.

2011, Oct. 31 ***Perf. 13x13¼***
4583 A1866 1 l Sheet of 2, #a-b 3.00 3.00

Yosif Tsankov (1911-71), Composer — A1867

2011, Nov. 7 **Litho.** ***Perf. 13¼x13***
4584 A1867 65s multi + label .95 .95

Christmas A1868

2011, Nov. 17 ***Perf. 13x13¼***
4585 A1868 65s multi .90 .90

Military Medical Academy, 120th Anniv. — A1869

2011, Dec. 1 ***Perf. 13¼x13***
4586 A1869 65s multi .90 .90

Flowers A1870

Designs: 65s, Shown. 1 l, Flowers, diff., vert.

2012, Mar. 16 ***Perf. 13 Syncopated***
4587-4588 A1870 Set of 2 2.25 2.25

Disbanding of the Knights Templar, 700th Anniv. — A1871

2012, Mar. 22 ***Perf. 13¼x13***
4589 A1871 65s multi .90 .90

No. 4589 was printed in sheets of 5 + label.

Famous People — A1872

Designs: No. 4590, 65s, Dimcho Debelyanov (1887-1916), poet. No. 4591, 65s, Anton Mitov (1862-1930), painter. No. 4592, 1 l, Yana Yazova (1912-74), writer. No. 4593, 1 l, Petya Dubarova (1962-79), poet.

2012, Mar. 28 ***Perf. 13x13¼***
4590-4593 A1872 Set of 4 4.50 4.50

Europa A1873

Landmarks in Veliko Turnovo: Nos. 4594, 4596a, 65s, Baldwin Tower. Nos. 4595, 4596b, 1.50 l, Patriarchal Cathedral of Tsaravets.

Perf. 13 Syncopated

2012, Apr. 4 **Litho.**
4594-4595 A1873 Set of 2 3.00 3.00

Souvenir Sheet

Perf. 13

4596 A1873 Sheet of 2, #a-b 3.00 3.00
c. Booklet pane of 4, #4596a, perf. 13 on 3 sides *4.50* —
d. Booklet pane of 4, #4596b, perf. 13 on 3 sides *10.50* —
Complete booklet, #4596c-4596d *17.50* —

20th National Antarctic Expedition — A1874

2012, Apr. 7 ***Perf. 13¼x13***
4597 A1874 1.40 l multi + label 1.90 1.90

No. 4597 was printed in sheets of 2 + 2 labels. A 65s imperf. souvenir sheet with simulated perfoations was produced in limited quantities.

Souvenir Sheet

Sinking of the Titanic, Cent. — A1875

2012, Apr. 10
4598 A1875 1.40 l multi 1.90 1.90

Airplane Bombardment of Edirne Railway Station, Cent. — A1876

2012, Apr. 12 ***Perf. 13x13¼***
4599 A1876 65s multi .90 .90

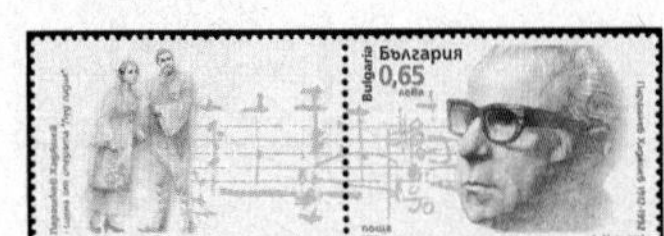

Parashkev Hadjiev (1912-92), Composer — A1877

2012, Apr. 27 ***Perf. 13¼x13***
4600 A1877 65s multi + label .90 .90

Bulgarian Admission to Council of Europe, 20th Anniv. — A1878

2012, May 7 ***Perf. 13x13¼***
4601 A1878 1 l multi 1.25 1.25

Stara Zagora Stone Relief Lion, 9th-11th Cent. A1879

2012, May 16 ***Perf. 13***
4602 A1879 65s multi .85 .85

Souvenir Sheet

Association of Bulgarian Enterprises for Intl. road Transport and Roads, 50th Anniv. — A1880

2012, May 30 ***Perf. 13¼x13***
4603 A1880 2.10 l multi 2.75 2.75

Souvenir Sheet

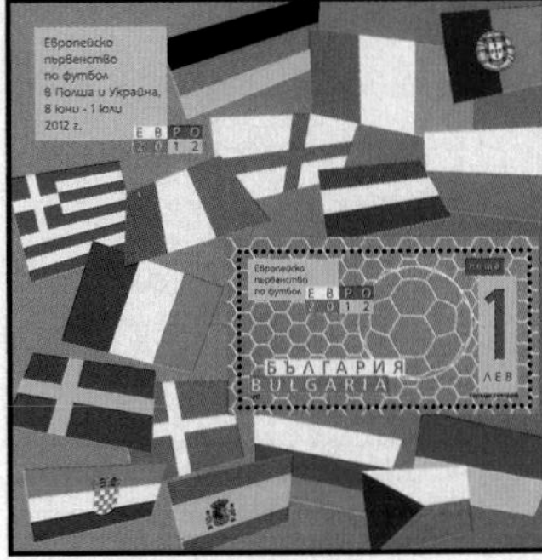

2012 European Soccer Championships, Poland and Ukraine — A1881

2012, June 8 **Litho.** ***Perf. 13¼***
4604 A1881 1 l multi 1.25 1.25

Miniature Sheet

Thorny Plants — A1882

No. 4605: a, 65s, Silybum marianum and butterfly. b, 65s, Carduus acanthoides and bee. c, 1 l, Centaurea solstitialis and ladybug. d, 1 l, Dipsacus laciniatus and beetle.

2012, June 14 ***Perf. 13***
4605 A1882 Sheet of 4, #a-d 4.25 4.25

Slavonic-Bulgarian History, by St. Paisios of Hilandar, 250th Anniv. of Publication — A1883

2012, June 22
4606 A1883 65s multi .85 .85

Miniature Sheet

Tourist Attractions of Northwestern Bulgaria — A1884

No. 4607: a, 65s, Plate and goblet from Rogozen Treasure archaeological find. b, 65s, Drawings from Magura Cave. c, 1 l, Meshchiite Tower, Vratsa. d, 1 l, Baba Vida Fortress, Vidin.

2012, July 12 ***Perf. 13x13¼***
4607 A1884 Sheet of 4, #a-d 4.25 4.25

Souvenir Sheet

2012 Summer Olympics, London — A1885

2012, July 16 ***Perf. 13¼x13***
4608 A1885 1.50 l multi 1.90 1.90

Vassil Levski (1837-73), National Hero — A1886

2012, July 18
4609 A1886 65s multi .85 .85

Claude Debussy (1862-1918), Composer — A1887

2012, Aug. 22 ***Perf. 13***
4610 A1887 1 l multi + label 1.60 1.60

Plovdiv Fair, 120th Anniv. — A1888

2012, Sept. 24
4611 A1888 65s multi .85 .85

Ivan Stoyanovich (1862-1947), Revolutionary Leader A1889

2012, Sept. 25
4612 A1889 65s multi .85 .85

Monument of Liberty, Ruse, by Arnoldo Zocchi (1862-1940) A1890

2012, Oct. 10 ***Perf. 13x13¼***
4613 A1890 1 l blue 1.40 1.40

Souvenir Sheet

Flora and Fauna of Parangalitsa Preserve — A1891

No. 4614: a, 65s, Primula deorum. b, 1.50 l, Felis silvestris silvestris.

2012, Oct. 18 ***Perf. 13***
4614 A1891 Sheet of 2, #a-b 3.00 3.00

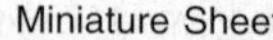

Miniature Sheet

Railroad Mail Cars — A1892

No. 4615: a, 65s, First mail car (blue and red), ships on river. b, 65s, Green and red mail car used from 1888-1904, post offices. c, 1 l, Brown mail car used from 1895-1930, picture postcard depicting Plovdiv area costumes. d, 1 l, Green mail car used from 1909-35, railway map.

2012, Oct. 22
4615 A1892 Sheet of 4, #a-d, + 2 labels 4.50 4.50

This imperforate souvenir sheet with simulated perforations, released in October 2012, was produced in limited quantities.

A1893

Horses — A1894

No. 4616: a, 65s, Andalusian horse. b, 1 l, Arabian horse.

No. 4617: a, 65s, Irish tinker horse. b, 1 l, Haflinger pony.

2012, Oct. 28
4616 A1893 Pair, #a-b 2.25 2.25
4617 A1894 Pair, #a-b 2.25 2.25

Nos. 4616-4617 each were printed in sheets containing two horizontal pairs and 2 labels.

Ministry of Railways, Posts and Telegraph, Cent. — A1895

2012, Oct. 30
4618 A1895 65s multi .85 .85

Discovery of Artifacts From Grave of Khan Kubrat, Cent. — A1896

2012, Nov. 7
4619 A1896 1 l multi 1.40 1.40

Christmas A1897

2012, Nov. 20
4620 A1897 65s multi .85 .85

Intl. Year of Chemistry — A1898

2012, Nov. 28 **Litho.**
4621 A1898 65s multi .85 .85

Diplomatic Relations Between Bulgaria and Kazakhstan, 20th Anniv. — A1899

No. 4622: a, 65s, Gold rhyton with design of deer's head, 4th cent. B.C. b, 1.40 l, Gold buckle depicting bird and deer, 8th-7th cent. B.C.

2012, Dec. 12
4622 A1899 Pair, #a-b 2.75 2.75

Printed in sheets containing 3 pairs. See Kazakhstan No. 689.

Souvenir Sheet

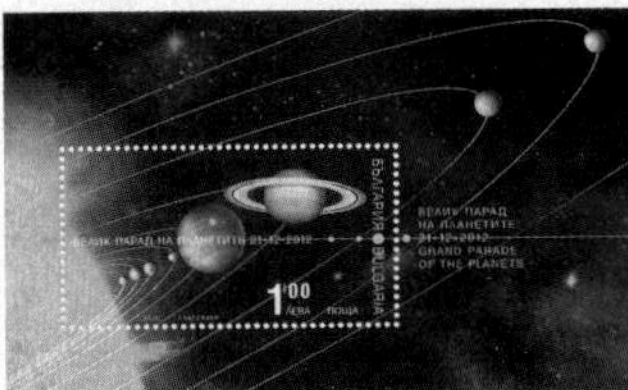

Planetary Alignment of Dec. 21, 2012 — A1900

2012, Dec. 21 *Perf. 13¼x13*
4623 A1900 1 l multi 1.40 1.40

Tourism A1901

2013, Jan. 4 *Perf. 13*
4624 A1901 1 l multi 1.40 1.40

Maritime Administration, 130th Anniv. — A1902

2013, Feb. 28 *Perf. 13¼x13*
4625 A1902 65s multi + label .90 .90

Souvenir Sheet

General M. D. Skobelev on Horse, by N. D. Dimitriev-Orenburgsky — A1903

2013, Mar. 5 *Perf. 13x13¼*
4626 A1903 1.40 l multi 1.90 1.90

End of Russo-Turkish War, 135th anniv. See Russia No. 7436.

An 65s imperforate sheet of type A1903 was printed in limited quantities and issued on Oct. 25.

Salvation of Bulgarian Jews, 70th Anniv. — A1904

2013, Mar. 10
4627 A1904 1.40 l multi + label 1.90 1.90

Printed in sheets containing 2 stamps + 2 labels.

Bird, Grapes and Wine Vat Greetings Type of 1998

Perf. 13 Syncopated

2013, Mar. 29 **Litho.**
4628 A1558 65s multi .85 .85

No. 4214 Redrawn With Bulgarian Inscription at Lower Left Instead of "Europa"

2013, Mar. 29 *Perf. 13 Syncopated*
4629 A1629 65s multi .85 .85

Rabbit Mail Carrier A1905

2013, Mar. 29 *Perf. 13 Syncopated*
4630 A1905 65s multi .85 .85

See footnote after No. 4572.

Bells — A1906

2013, Mar. 29
4631 A1906 1 l multi 1.40 1.40

Cherno More Soccer Team, Cent. — A1907

2013, Mar. 29 *Perf. 13¼x13*
4632 A1907 65s multi .85 .85

No. 4632 was printed in sheets of 3 + label.

Slavia Soccer Team, Cent. — A1908

2013, Apr. 5 *Perf. 13¼x13*
4633 A1908 65s multi .90 .90

No. 4633 was printed in sheets of 3 + label.

This imperforate souvenir sheet with simulated perforations, released in Apr. 2013, was produced in limited quantities.

Miniature Sheet

Balkan Wars, Cent. — A1909

Designs: a, 65s, Bulgairan Army in battle. b, 65s, Victory Arch. c, 1 l, Surrender of Adrianople, Mar. 13, 1913. d, 1 l, Tsar Ferdinand on horse.

2013, Apr. 16 **Litho.** *Perf. 13¼x13*
4634 A1909 Sheet of 4, #a-d 4.50 4.50

CSKA Soccer Team, 65th Anniv. — A1910

2013, Apr. 23
4635 A1910 65s multi .90 .90

No. 4635 was printed in sheets of 3 + label.

Europa — A1911

Bulgarian postal van: Nos. 4636, 4640a, 65s, Facing lower left corner, area in red behind denomination. Nos. 4637, 4640b, 1.50 l, Facing lower right corner, with red triangle at lower left. No. 4638, Like No. 4636, with olive green area behind denomination. No. 4639, Like No. 4637, with blue triangle at lower left.

2013, Apr. 24 *Perf. 13x13¼*

Stamps With White Frames

4636 A1911 65s multi .90 .90
4637 A1911 1.50 l multi 2.00 2.00

Booklet Stamps

Perf. 13 on 3 Sides

4638 A1911 65s multi .90 .90
a. Booklet pane of 4 3.60 —
4639 A1911 1.50 l multi 2.00 2.00
a. Booklet pane of 4 8.00 —
Complete booklet, #4638a, 4639a 12.00

Souvenir Sheet

Stamps Without White Frame

Perf. 13x13¼

4640 A1911 Sheet of 2, #a-b 3.00 3.00

Souvenir Sheet

Bulgarian State Railways, 125th Anniv. — A1912

2013, May 14 *Perf. 13*
4641 A1912 1.40 l multi + label 1.90 1.90

Richard Wagner (1813-83), Composer — A1913

2013, May 22 *Perf. 13¼x13*
4642 A1913 1 l multi + label 1.40 1.40

Souvenir Sheet

Birds in Mantaritsa Nature Reserve — A1914

2013, May 22 **Litho.**
4643 A1914 1.50 l multi 2.10 2.10

St. Ivan Rilski University of Mining and Geology, 60th Anniv. — A1915

2013, May 28 *Perf. 13x13¼*
4644 A1915 65s multi .90 .90

SOS Children's Villages — A1916

2013, May 30 ***Perf. 13***
4645 A1916 65s multi .90 .90

Souvenir Sheet

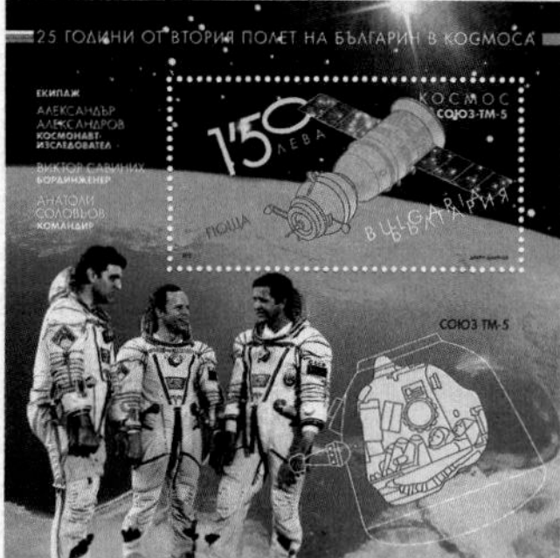

Soyuz TM-5 Space Flight of Alexander Alexandrov, 25th Anniv. — A1917

2013, May 30 ***Perf. 13¼x13***
4646 A1917 1.50 l multi 2.10 2.10

Souvenir Sheet

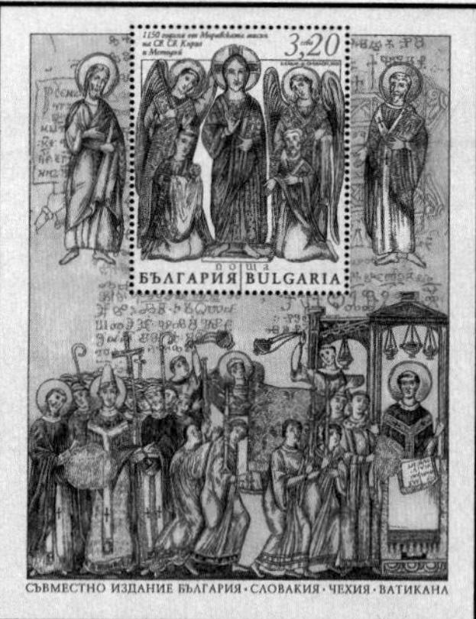

Mission of Sts. Cyril and Methodius to Slavic Lands, 1150th Anniv. — A1918

2013, June 12 ***Perf. 13x13¼***
4647 A1918 3.20 l multi 4.50 4.50

See Czech Republic No. 3573, Slovakia No. 666 and Vatican City No. 1536.

Miniature Sheet

Tourist Attractions in Southwestern Bulgaria — A1919

No. 4648: a, 65s, Building in Kovachevitsa. b, 65s, Wildlife in Skakavitsa Reserve. c, 1 l, Fresco, Zemen Monastery. d, 1 l, Church of St. Petka of the Saddlers, Vassil Levski (1837-73), national hero.

2013, June 17
4648 A1919 Sheet of 4, #a-d 4.50 4.50

Souvenir Sheet

Tsar Boris III (1894-1943) — A1920

2013, Aug. 30 **Litho.** ***Perf. 13¼***
4649 A1920 1.50 l multi 2.10 2.10

Diplomatic Relations Between Bulgaria and the United States, 110th Anniv. — A1921

2013, Sept. 12 **Litho.** ***Perf. 13¼x13***
4650 A1921 1.40 l multi 1.90 1.90

Botev-Plovdiv Soccer Team, Cent — A1922

2013, Oct. 25 **Litho.** ***Perf. 13***
4651 A1922 65s multi .90 .90

Cat Breeds — A1923

No. 4652: a, 65s, Siamese. b, 1 l, Birman.
No. 4653, horiz.: a, 65s, Scottish Fold. b, 1 l, Somali.

Perf. 13¼x13, 13x13¼
2013, Oct. 26 **Litho.**
Pairs, #a-b
4652-4653 A1923 Set of 2 4.50 4.50

Miniature Sheet

Orchids — A1924

No. 4654: a, 65s, Cymbidium tridioides. b, 65s, Dendrobium fimbriatum var. occulatum. c, 1 l, Epidendrum radicans. d, 1 l, Dendrobium nobile.

2013, Oct. 26 **Litho.** ***Perf. 13***
4654 A1924 Sheet of 4, #a-d 4.50 4.50

Souvenir Sheet

Green Balkans Association, 25th Anniv. — A1925

2013, Oct. 27 **Litho.** ***Perf. 13½x13¼***
4655 A1925 1 l multi 1.40 1.40

Sofia Metro, 15th Anniv. A1926

No. 4656 — Metro cars and: a, Serdika Fortress, Sofia coat of arms. b, Lion's Bridge Station. c, Station, Sofia coat of arms.

2013, Nov. 22 **Litho.** ***Perf. 13x13¼***

4656	Booklet pane of 3 + label	4.50	—
a.	A1926 65s multi	.95	.95
b.	A1926 1 l multi	1.40	1.40
c.	A1926 1.50 l multi	2.10	2.10
	Complete booklet, #4656	4.50	

Christmas — A1927

2013, Nov. 22 **Litho.** ***Perf. 13x13¼***
4657 A1927 65s multi .95 .95

SEMI-POSTAL STAMPS

Catalogue values for unused stamps in this section are for Never Hinged items.

Regular Issues of 1911-20 Surcharged

a

b

c

Perf. 11½x12, 12x11½
1920, June 20 **Unwmk.**

B1	A43 (a)	2s + 1s ol grn	.25	.25
B2	A44 (b)	5s + 2½s grn	.25	.25
B3	A44 (b)	10s + 5s rose	.25	.25
B4	A44 (b)	15s + 7½s vio	.25	.25
B5	A44 (b)	25s + 12½s dp bl	.25	.25
B6	A44 (b)	30s + 15s choc	.25	.25
B7	A44 (b)	50s + 25s yel brn	.25	.25
B8	A29 (c)	1 l + 50s dk brn	.45	.25
B9	A37a (a)	2 l + 1 l brn org	.45	.40
B10	A38 (a)	3 l + 1½ l claret	1.20	.80
		Nos. B1-B10 (10)	3.85	3.20

Surtax aided ex-prisoners of war. Value, Nos. B1-B7 imperf., $7.75.

Tsar Boris Type of 1937
Souvenir Sheet

1937, Nov. 22 **Photo.** ***Imperf.***
B11 A140 2 l + 18 l ultra 10.00 *20.00*

19th anniv. of the accession of Tsar Boris III to the throne.

Stamps of 1917-21 Surcharged in Black

1939, Oct. 22 ***Perf. 12½, 12***

B12	A34	1 l + 1 l on 15s slate	.25	.25
B13	A69	2 l + 1 l on 1½ l ol grn	.35	.35
B14	A69	4 l + 2 l on 2 l dp grn	.40	.40
B15	A69	7 l + 4 l on 3 l Prus bl	1.25	*1.50*
B16	A69	14 l + 7 l on 5 l red brn	1.75	*2.00*
		Nos. B12-B16 (5)	4.00	*4.50*

Surtax aided victims of the Sevlievo flood. The surcharge on #B13-B16 omits "leva."

Map of Bulgaria SP2

1947, June 6 **Typo.** ***Perf. 11½***
B17 SP2 20 l + 10 l dk brn red & grn .85 .85

30th Jubilee Esperanto Cong., Sofia, 1947.

Postman — SP3

Radio Towers — SP6

#B19, Lineman. #B20, Telephone operators.

1947, Nov. 5

B18	SP3	4 l + 2 l ol brn	.25	.25
B19	SP3	10 l + 5 l brt red	.25	.25
B20	SP3	20 l + 10 l dp ultra	.25	.25
B21	SP6	40 l + 20 l choc	1.20	1.20
		Nos. B18-B21 (4)	1.95	1.95

Christo Ganchev — SP7

Actors' Portraits: 10 l+6 l, Adriana Budevska. 15 l+7 l, Vasil Kirkov. 20 l+15 l, Sava Ognianov. 30 l+20 l, Krostyu Sarafov.

1947, Dec. 8 **Litho.** ***Perf. 10½***

B22	SP7	9 l + 5 l Prus grn	.35	.25
B23	SP7	10 l + 6 l car lake	.35	.25
B24	SP7	15 l + 7 l rose vio	.35	.25

B25 SP7 20 l + 15 l ultra .55 .40

B26 SP7 30 l + 20 l vio brn 1.50 1.00

Nos. B22-B26 (5) 3.10 2.15

National Theater, 50th anniversary.

Souvenir Sheet

Olympic Emblem — SP8

1964, Oct. 10 Litho. *Imperf.*

B27 SP8 40s + 20s bis, red & bl 5.25 1.75

18th Olympic Games, Tokyo, Oct. 10-25.

Horsemanship Type of 1965

Miniature Sheet

1965, Sept. 30 Photo. *Imperf.*

B28 A630 40s + 20s Hurdle race 5.25 1.75

Space Exploration Type of 1966

Designs: 20s+10s, Yuri A. Gagarin, Alexei Leonov and Valentina Tereshkova. 30s+10s, Rocket and globe.

1966, Sept. 29 Photo. *Perf. 11½x11*

B29 A652 20s + 10s pur & gray 1.60 .55

Miniature Sheet

B30 A652 30s + 10s gray, fawn & blk 3.50 1.10

Winter Olympic Games Type of 1967

Sports and Emblem: 20s+10s, Slalom. 40s+10s, Figure skating couple.

1967, Sept. Photo. *Perf. 11*

B31 A687 20s + 10s multi 3.25 .60

Souvenir Sheet

Imperf

B32 A687 40s + 10s multi 3.25 .85

Type of Olympic Games Issue, 1968

Designs: 20s+10s, Rowing. 50s+10s, Stadium, Mexico City, and communications satellite.

1968, June 24 Photo. *Perf. 10½*

B33 A702 20s + 10s vio bl, gray & pink 1.90 .55

Miniature Sheet

Imperf

B34 A702 50s + 10s gray, blk & Prus bl 3.50 1.50

Sports Type of Regular Issue, 1969

Designs: 13s+5s, Woman with ball. 20s+10s, Acrobatic jump.

Gymnasts in Light Gray

1969, Oct. Photo. *Perf. 11*

B35 A732 13s + 5s brt rose & vio .95 .25

B36 A732 20s + 10s citron & bl grn 1.25 .50

Miniature Sheet

Soccer Ball — SP9

1970, Mar. 4 Photo. *Imperf.*

B37 SP9 80s + 20s multi 3.50 1.75

9th World Soccer Championships for the Jules Rimet Cup, Mexico City, May 30-June 21, 1970.

Souvenir Sheet

Yuri A. Gagarin — SP10

1971, Apr. 12 Photo. *Imperf.*

B38 SP10 40s + 20s multi 3.25 1.10

10th anniversary of the first man in space.

SP11

Bulgarian lion, magnifying glass, stamp tongs

1971, July 10 Photo. *Perf. 12½*

B39 SP11 20s + 10s brn org, blk & gold 1.60 .40

11th Congress of Bulgarian Philatelists, Sofia, July, 1971.

SP12

Toys: a, Skateboarding. b, Doll, ball. c, Rope. d, Train set.

Souvenir Sheet

1989, Nov. 10 Litho. *Perf. 13x13½*

B40 Sheet of 4 3.00 1.40

a.-d. SP12 30s +15s any single .65 .35

For the benefit of the Children's Foundation. Exists imperf. Value $8.75.

AIR POST STAMPS

Regular Issues of 1925-26 Overprinted in Various Colors

1927-28 Unwmk. *Perf. 11½*

C1 A76 2 l ol (R) ('28) 1.60 1.60

C2 A74 4 l lake & yel (Bl) 3.00 1.60

C3 A77 10 l brn blk & brn org (G) ('28) 47.50 10.00

Overprinted Vertically and Surcharged with New Value

C4 A77 1 l on 6 l dp bl & pale lem (C) 1.60 1.60

a. Inverted surcharge *340.00 275.00*

b. Pair, one without surcharge *440.00*

Nos. C1-C4 (4) 53.70 14.80

Nos. C2-C4 overprinted in changed colors were not issued, value set $14.

Dove Delivering Message AP1

Junkers Plane, Rila Monastery AP2

1931, Oct. 28 Typo.

C5 AP1 1 l dk green .45 .25

C6 AP1 2 l maroon .45 .25

C7 AP1 6 l dp blue .60 .40

C8 AP1 12 l carmine 1.25 .40

C9 AP1 20 l dk violet 1.25 .80

C10 AP1 30 l dp orange 2.40 1.60

C11 AP1 50 l orange brn 3.50 2.75

Nos. C5-C11 (7) 9.90 6.45

Counterfeits exist. See Nos. C15-C18.

1932, May 9

C12 AP2 18 l blue grn 72.50 40.00

C13 AP2 24 l dp red 50.00 30.00

C14 AP2 28 l ultra 30.00 25.00

Nos. C12-C14 (3) 152.50 95.00

Catalogue values for unused stamps in this section, from this point to the end of the section, are for Never Hinged items.

1938, Dec. 27

C15 AP1 1 l violet brown .35 .25

C16 AP1 2 l green .40 .25

C17 AP1 6 l deep rose 1.25 .50

C18 AP1 12 l peacock blue 1.40 .55

Nos. C15-C18 (4) 3.40 1.55

Counterfeits exist.

Mail Plane — AP3

Plane over Tsar Assen's Tower — AP4

Designs: 4 l, Plane over Bachkovski Monastery. 6 l, Bojurishte Airport, Sofia. 10 l, Plane, train and motorcycle. 12 l, Planes over Sofia Palace. 16 l, Plane over Pirin Valley. 19 l, Plane over Rila Monastery. 30 l, Plane and Swallow. 45 l, Plane over Sofia Cathedral. 70 l, Plane over Shipka Monument. 100 l, Plane and Royal Cipher.

1940, Jan. 15 Photo. *Perf. 13*

C19 AP3 1 l dk green .25 .25

C20 AP4 2 l crimson 2.25 .25

C21 AP4 4 l red orange .25 .25

C22 AP3 6 l dp blue .50 .25

C23 AP4 10 l dk brown .50 .25

C24 AP3 12 l dull brown 1.00 .25

C25 AP3 16 l brt bl vio 1.10 .50

C26 AP3 19 l sapphire 1.50 .75

C27 AP4 30 l rose lake 2.25 1.00

C28 AP4 45 l gray violet 5.50 1.25

C29 AP4 70 l rose pink 5.50 1.75

C30 AP4 100 l dp slate bl 18.50 5.00

Nos. C19-C30 (12) 39.10 11.75

Nos. 368 and 370 Overprinted in Black

1945, Jan. 26

C31 A181 1 l bright green .25 .25

C32 A181 4 l red orange .25 .25

A similar overprint on Nos. O4, O5, O7 and O8 was privately applied.

Type of Parcel Post Stamps of 1944 Surcharged or Overprinted in Various Colors

Imperf

C37 PP5 10 l on 100 l dl yel (Bl) .25 .25

C38 PP5 45 l on 100 l dl yel (C) .30 .25

C39 PP5 75 l on 100 l dl yel (G) 1.00 .25

C40 PP5 100 l dl yel (V) 1.00 .35

Nos. C37-C40 (4) 2.55 1.10

Plane and Sun — AP16

Pigeon with Letter — AP17

Plane, Letter AP18

Wings, Posthorn AP19

Winged Letter — AP20

Plane, Sun — AP21

Pigeon, Posthorn AP22

Mail Plane AP23

Conventionalized Figure Holding Pigeon — AP24

1946, July 15 Litho. *Perf. 13*

C41 AP16	1 l dull lilac	.25	.25
C42 AP16	2 l slate gray	.25	.25
C43 AP17	4 l violet blk	.25	.25
C44 AP18	6 l blue	.25	.25
C45 AP19	10 l turq green	.25	.25
C46 AP19	12 l yellow brn	.25	.25
C47 AP20	16 l rose violet	.25	.25
C48 AP19	19 l carmine	.25	.25
C49 AP21	30 l orange	.25	.25
C50 AP22	45 l lt ol grn	.25	.25
C51 AP22	75 l red brown	.60	.25
C52 AP23	100 l slate blk	1.60	.60
C53 AP24	100 l red	1.60	.60
	Nos. C41-C53 (13)	6.30	3.95

No. C47 exists imperf. Value $90.

People's Republic

Plane over Plovdiv AP25

1947, Aug. 31 Photo. *Imperf.*

C54 AP25 40 l dull olive grn 1.60 1.60

Plovdiv International Fair, 1947.

Baldwin's Tower — AP26

1948, May 23 Litho. *Perf. 11½*

C55 AP26 50 l ol brn, *cr* 1.75 1.75

Stamp Day and the 10th Congress of Bulgarian Philatelic Societies, June 1948.

Romanian and Bulgarian Parliament Buildings AP27

Romanian and Bulgarian Flags, Bridge over Danube AP28

1948, Nov. 3 Photo.

C56 AP27 40 l ol gray, *cr* .50 .35
C57 AP28 100 l red vio, *cr* 1.10 .90

Romanian-Bulgarian friendship.

Mausoleum of Pleven — AP29

1949, June 26

C58 AP29 50 l brown 5.00 5.00

7th Congress of Bulgarian Philatelic Associations, June 26-27, 1949.

Symbols of the UPU — AP30

Frontier Guard and Dog — AP31

1949, Oct. 10 *Perf. 11½*

C59 AP30 50 l violet blue 2.50 1.40

75th anniv. of the UPU.

1949, Oct. 31

C60 AP31 60 l olive black 3.75 3.75

Dimitrov Mausoleum AP32

1950, July 3 *Perf. 10½*

C61 AP32 40 l olive brown 7.00 3.50

1st anniv. of the death of George Dimitrov.

Belogradchic Rocks — AP33

Air View of Plovdiv Fair — AP34

Designs: 16s, Beach, Varna. 20s, Harvesting grain. 28s, Rila monastery. 44s, Studena dam. 60s, View of Dimitrovgrad. 80s, View of Trnovo. 1 l, University building, Sofia. 4 l, Partisans' Monument.

1954, Apr. 1 Unwmk. *Perf. 13*

C62 AP33	8s olive black	.25	.25
C63 AP34	12s rose brown	.25	.25
C64 AP33	16s brown	.25	.25
C65 AP33	20s brn red, *cream*	.25	.25
C66 AP33	28s dp bl, *cream*	.30	.25
C67 AP33	44s vio brn, *cream*	.40	.25
C68 AP33	60s red brn, *cream*	.70	.30
C69 AP34	80s dk grn, *cream*	.80	.35
C70 AP33	1 l dk bl grn, *cream*	2.50	.70
C71 AP34	4 l deep blue	5.50	2.00
	Nos. C62-C71 (10)	11.20	4.85

Glider on Mountainside AP35

60s, Glider over airport. 80s, Three gliders.

1956, Oct. 15 Photo.

C72 AP35	44s brt blue	.40	.25
C73 AP35	60s purple	.75	.25
C74 AP35	80s dk blue grn	1.25	.80
	Nos. C72-C74 (3)	2.40	1.30

30th anniv. of glider flights in Bulgaria.

Passenger Plane — AP36

1957, May 21 Unwmk. *Perf. 13*

C75 AP36 80s deep blue 1.50 .55

10th anniv. of civil aviation in Bulgaria.

Sputnik 3 over Earth AP37

1958, Nov. 28 *Perf. 11*

C76 AP37 80s brt grnsh blue 6.00 4.50

International Geophysical Year, 1957-58. Value, imperf. $17.50.

Lunik 1 Leaving Earth for Moon — AP38

1959, Mar. *Perf. 10½*

C77 AP38 2 l brt blue & ocher 8.50 7.75

Launching of 1st man-made satellite to orbit moon. Value, imperf. in slightly different colors, $15.00 unused, $5.25 canceled.

Statue of Liberty and Tu-110 Airliner AP39

Perf. 10½

1959, Nov. 11 Photo. Unwmk.

C78 AP39 1 l violet bl & pink 3.50 2.75

Visit of Khrushchev to US. Value, imperf. $10.

Lunik 2 and Moon — AP40

1960, June 23 Litho. *Perf. 11*

C79 AP40 1.25 l blue, blk & yel 6.50 3.00

Russian rocket to the Moon, Sept. 12, 1959.

Sputnik 5 and Dogs Belka and Strelka — AP41

1961, Jan. 14 Photo. *Perf. 11*

C80 AP41 1.25 l brt grnsh bl & org 6.00 3.75

Russian rocket flight of Aug. 19, 1960.

Maj. Yuri A. Gagarin and Vostok 1 AP42

1961, Apr. 26 Unwmk.

C81 AP42 4 l grnsh bl, blk & red 6.00 3.50

First manned space flight, Apr. 12, 1961.

Soviet Space Dogs AP43

1961, June 28 *Perf. 11*

C82 AP43 2 l slate & dk car 5.00 2.75

Venus-bound Rocket — AP44

1961, June 28

C83 AP44 2 l brt bl, yel & org 9.50 6.00

Soviet launching of the Venus space probe, 2/12/61.

Maj. Gherman Titov AP45

Design: 1.25 l, Spaceship Vostok 2.

1961, Nov. 20 Photo. *Perf. 11x10½*

C84 AP45 75s dk ol grn & gray grn 3.50 1.90
C85 AP45 1.25 l vio bl, lt bl & pink 4.25 1.90

1st manned space flight around the world, Maj. Gherman Titov of Russia, 8/6-7/61.

Iskar River Narrows AP46

Designs: 2s, Varna and sailboat. 3s, Melnik. 10s, Trnovo. 40s, Pirin mountains.

1962, Feb. 3 Unwmk. *Perf. 13*

C86 AP46	1s bl grn & gray bl	.25	.25
C87 AP46	2s blue & pink	.25	.25
C88 AP46	3s brown & ocher	.35	.25
C89 AP46	10s black & lemon	.65	.25
C90 AP46	40s dk green & green	1.90	.40
	Nos. C86-C90 (5)	3.40	1.40

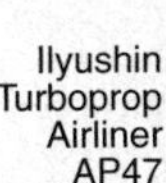

Ilyushin Turboprop Airliner AP47

1962, Aug. 18 *Perf. 11*

C91 AP47 13s blue & black 1.25 .50

15th anniversary of TABSO airline.

Konstantin E. Tsiolkovsky and Rocket Launching — AP48

Design: 13s, Earth, moon and rocket on future flight to the moon.

1962, Sept. 24 *Perf. 11*

C92 AP48 5s dp green & gray 2.50 1.25
C93 AP48 13s ultra & yellow 3.50 2.25

13th meeting of the International Astronautical Federation.

Maj. Andrian G. Nikolayev — AP49

Designs: 2s, Lt. Col. Pavel R. Popovich. 40s, Vostoks 3 and 4 in orbit.

1962, Dec. 9 **Photo.** **Unwmk.**

C94 AP49 1s bl, sl grn & blk .25 .25
C95 AP49 2s bl grn, grn & blk .55 .25
C96 AP49 40s dk bl grn, pink & blk 3.50 1.75
Nos. C94-C96 (3) 4.30 2.25

First Russian group space flight of Vostoks 3 and 4, Aug. 12-15, 1962.

Spacecraft "Mars 1" Approaching Mars — AP50

Design: 13s, Rocket launching spacecraft, Earth, Moon and Mars.

1963, Mar. 5 **Unwmk.** *Perf. 11*

C97 AP50 5s multicolored .75 .50
C98 AP50 13s multicolored 1.75 .75

Launching of the Russian spacecraft "Mars 1," Nov. 1, 1962.

Lt. Col. Valeri F. Bykovski AP51

Designs: 2s, Lt. Valentina Tereshkova. 5s, Globe and trajectories.

1963, Aug. 26 **Unwmk.** *Perf. 11½*

C99 AP51 1s pale vio & Prus bl .30 .30
C100 AP51 2s citron & red brn .30 .30
C101 AP51 5s rose & dk red .30 .30
Nos. C99-C101 (3) .90 .90

The space flights of Valeri Bykovski, June 14-19, and Valentina Tereshkova, first woman cosmonaut, June 16-19, 1963. An imperf. souvenir sheet contains one 50s stamp showing Spasski tower and globe in lilac and red brown. Light blue border with red brown inscription. Size: 77x67mm. Value $4. See No. CB3.

Nos. C99-C100 Surcharged in Magenta or Green

1964, Aug. 22

C102 AP51 10s on 1s (M) .50 .25
C103 AP51 20s on 2s 1.25 .40

International Space Exhibition in Riccione, Italy. Overprint in Italian on No. C103.

St. John's Monastery, Rila — AP52

13s, Notre Dame, Paris; French inscription.

1964, Dec. 22 **Photo.** *Perf. 11½*

C104 AP52 5s pale brn & blk .25 .25
C105 AP52 13s lt ultra & sl bl 1.25 .25

The philatelic exhibition at St. Ouen (Seine) organized by the Franco-Russian Philatelic Circle and philatelic organizations in various People's Democracies.

Paper Mill, Bukijovtz AP53

10s, Metal works, Plovdiv. 13s, Metal works, Kremikovtsi. 20s, Oil refinery, Stara-Zagora. 40s, Fertilizer plant, Stara-Zagora. 1 l, Rest home, Meded.

1964-68 **Unwmk.** *Perf. 13*

C106 AP53 8s grnsh blue .25 .25
C107 AP53 10s red lilac .25 .25
C108 AP53 13s brt violet .45 .25
C109 AP53 20s slate blue 1.00 .25
C110 AP53 40s dk olive grn 1.50 .25
C111 AP53 1 l red ('68) 2.75 .55
Nos. C106-C111 (6) 6.20 1.80

Issue dates: 1 l, May 6. Others, Dec. 7.

Three-master AP54

Means of Communication: 2s, Postal coach. 3s, Old steam locomotive. 5s, Early cars. 10s, Montgolfier balloon. 13s, Early plane. 20s, Jet planes. 40s, Rocket and satellites. 1 l, Postrider.

1969, Mar. 31 **Photo.** *Perf. 13x12½*

C112 AP54 1s gray & multi .25 .25
C113 AP54 2s gray & multi .25 .25
C114 AP54 3s gray & multi .25 .25
C115 AP54 5s gray & multi .25 .25
C116 AP54 10s gray & multi .25 .25
C117 AP54 13s gray & multi .50 .25
C118 AP54 20s gray & multi 1.00 .50
C119 AP54 40s gray & multi 1.75 .75
Nos. C112-C119 (8) 4.50 2.75

Miniature Sheet
Imperf

C120 AP54 1 l gold & org 3.50 2.25

SOFIA 1969 Philatelic Exhibition, Sofia, May 31-June 8.

Veliko Turnovo — AP55

Designs: Historic buildings in various cities.

1973, July 30 **Photo.** *Perf. 13*

C121 AP55 2s shown .25 .25
C122 AP55 13s Roussalka .30 .25
C123 AP55 20s Plovdiv 3.00 1.50
C124 AP55 28s Sofia 1.25 .25
Nos. C121-C124 (4) 4.80 2.25

Aleksei A. Leonov and Soyuz AP56

Designs: 18s, Thomas P. Stafford and Apollo. 28s, Apollo and Soyuz over earth. 1 l, Apollo Soyuz link-up.

1975, July 15

C125 AP56 13s blue & multi .50 .25
C126 AP56 18s purple & multi .75 .25
C127 AP56 28s multicolored 1.75 .50
Nos. C125-C127 (3) 3.00 1.00

Souvenir Sheet

C128 AP56 1 l violet & multi 3.75 2.25

Apollo Soyuz space test project (Russo-American cooperation), launching July 15; link-up July 17.

Balloon Over Plovdiv — AP57

1977, Sept. 3

C129 AP57 25s yellow, brn & red .85 .25

Alexei Leonov Floating in Space — AP58

Designs: 25s, Mariner 6, US spacecraft. 35s, Venera 4, USSR Venus probe.

1977, Oct. 14 **Photo.** *Perf. 13½*

C130 AP58 12s multicolored .25 .25
C131 AP58 25s multicolored .90 .25
C132 AP58 35s multicolored 1.40 .55
Nos. C130-C132 (3) 2.55 1.05

Space era, 20 years.

TU-154, Balkanair Emblem AP59

1977 *Perf. 13*

C133 AP59 35s ultra & multi 1.50 .65

30th anniv. of Bulgarian airline, Balkanair. Issued in sheets of 6 stamps + 3 labels (in lilac) with inscription and Balkanair emblem.

Baba Vida Fortress AP60

Design: 35s, Peace Bridge, connecting Rousse, Bulgaria, with Giurgiu, Romania.

1978 **Photo.** *Perf. 13*

C134 AP60 25s multicolored .80 .80
C135 AP60 35s multicolored 1.20 1.20

The Danube, European Intercontinental Waterway. Issued in sheets containing 5 each of Nos. C134-C135 and 2 labels, one showing course of Danube, the other hydrofoil and fish.

Red Cross AP61

1978, Mar. **Photo.** *Perf. 13*

C136 AP61 25s multicolored .85 .25

Centenary of Bulgarian Red Cross.

AP62

Clock towers.

1979, June 5 **Litho.** *Perf. 12x12½*

C137 AP62 13s Byalla Cherkva .25 .25
C138 AP62 23s Botevgrad .50 .25
C139 AP62 25s Pazardgick .50 .25
C140 AP62 35s Grabovo .75 .25
C141 AP62 53s Tryavna 1.40 .50
Nos. C137-C141 (5) 3.40 1.50

1980, Oct. 22 **Photo.** *Perf. 12x12½*

C142 AP62 13s Bjala .25 .25
C143 AP62 23s Rasgrad .60 .45
C144 AP62 25s Karnabat .70 .25
C145 AP62 35s Serlievo .85 .45
C146 AP62 53s Berkovitza 1.40 .60
Nos. C142-C146 (5) 3.80 2.00

AP63

1980
C147 AP63 13s shown .25 .25
C148 AP63 25s Parachutist .80 .25

15th World Parachute Championships, Kazanluk.

DWVY-1 Aircraft — AP64

1981, June 27 Litho. *Perf. 12½*
C149 AP64 5s shown .25 .25
C150 AP64 12s LAS-7 .25 .25
C151 AP64 25s LAS-8 .60 .25
C152 AP64 35s DAR-1 .75 .25
C153 AP64 45s DAR-3 1.10 .35
C154 AP64 55s DAR-9 1.40 .45
Nos. C149-C154 (6) 4.35 1.80

AP65

1983, June 28
C155 Sheet of 2 2.50 1.60
a. AP65 50s Valentina Tereshkova 1.25 .80
b. AP65 50s Svetlana Savitskaya 1.25 .80

Women in space, 20th anniv.

AP66

1983, July 20 Photo. *Perf. 13*
C156 AP66 5s TV tower, Tolbukhin .25 .25
C157 AP66 13s Postwoman .25 .25
C158 AP66 30s TV tower, Mt. Botev .60 .30
a. Strip of 3, #C156-C158 1.25 .65

World Communications Year. Emblems of World Communications Year, Bulgarian Post, UPU and ITU on attached margins.

Souvenir Sheet

Geophysical Map of the Moon, Russia's Luna I, II and III Satellites — AP67

1984, Oct. 24 Photo. *Perf. 13*
C159 AP67 1 l multicolored 2.50 1.25

Conquest of Space.

Intl. Civil Aviation Org., 40th Anniv. — AP68

1984, Dec. 21 Photo. *Perf. 13*
C160 AP68 42s Balkan Airlines jet 1.00 .50

Balkan Airlines — AP69

Design: Helicopter MU-8, passenger jet TU-154 and AN-21 transport plane.

1987, Aug. 25 Photo.
C161 AP69 25s multicolored .50 .30

2nd Joint Soviet-Bulgarian Space Flight — AP70

Cosmonauts: A. Aleksandrov, A. Solovov and V. Savinich.

1989, June 7 Litho. *Perf. 13½x13*
C162 AP70 13s multicolored .35 .25

AIR POST SEMI-POSTAL STAMPS

Catalogue values for unused stamps in this section are for Never Hinged items.

Statue of Liberty, Plane and Bridge SPAP1

Perf. 11½.
1947, May 24 Unwmk. Litho.
CB1 SPAP1 70 l + 30 l red brn 1.60 1.60

5th Philatelic Congress, Trnovo, and CIPEX, NYC, May, 1947.

Bulgarian Worker SPAP2

1948, Feb. 28 Photo. *Perf. 12x11½.*
CB2 SPAP2 60 l henna brn, *cream* .45 .35

2nd Bulgarian Workers' Congress, and sold by subscription only, at a premium of 16 l over face value.

Type of Air Post Stamps, 1963

Valeri Bykovski & Valentina Tereshkova.

1963, Aug. 26 Unwmk. *Perf. 11½*
CB3 AP51 20s + 10s pale bluish grn & dk grn 2.00 .45

See note after No. C101.

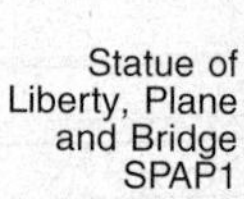

SPECIAL DELIVERY STAMPS

Catalogue values for unused stamps in this section are for Never Hinged items.

Postman on Bicycle SD1

Postman on Motorcycle SD3

Mail Car — SD2

1939 Unwmk. Photo. *Perf. 13*
E1 SD1 5 l deep blue 1.20 .25
E2 SD2 6 l copper brn .25 .25
E3 SD3 7 l golden brn .35 .25
E4 SD2 8 l red orange 1.20 .25
E5 SD1 20 l bright rose 2.50 .40
Nos. E1-E5 (5) 5.50 1.40

POSTAGE DUE STAMPS

D1

Large Lozenge Perf. 5½ to 6½
1884 Typo. Unwmk.
J1 D1 5s orange 875.00 110.00
J2 D1 25s lake 340.00 52.50
J3 D1 50s blue 47.50 32.50
Nos. J1-J3 (3) 1,262. 195.00

1886 *Imperf.*
J4 D1 5s orange 440.00 20.00
J5 D1 25s lake 640.00 20.00
J6 D1 50s blue 20.00 17.50
Nos. J4-J6 (3) 1,100. 57.50

1887 *Perf. 11½*
J7 D1 5s orange 60.00 9.50
J8 D1 25s lake 20.00 6.00
J9 D1 50s blue 24.00 16.00
Nos. J7-J9 (3) 104.00 31.50

Same, Redrawn
24 horizontal lines of shading in upper part instead of 30 lines

1892 *Perf. 10½, 11½*
J10 D1 5s orange 40.00 6.00
J11 D1 25s lake 20.00 6.00

D2

1893 Pelure Paper
J12 D2 5s orange 47.50 20.00

D3

D4

1895 *Imperf.*
J13 D3 30s on 50s blue 35.00 9.50
Perf. 10½, 11½
J14 D3 30s on 50s blue 40.00 9.50

Wmk. Coat of Arms in the Sheet
1896 *Perf. 13*
J15 D4 5s orange 20.00 3.25
J16 D4 10s purple 12.00 2.75
J17 D4 30s green 9.50 2.40
Nos. J15-J17 (3) 41.50 8.40

Nos. J15-J17 are also known on unwatermarked paper from the edges of sheets.

In 1901 a cancellation, "T" in circle, was applied to Nos. 60-65 and used provisionally as postage dues.

D5

D6

1901-04 Unwmk. *Perf. 11½*
J19 D5 5s dl rose .80 .50
J20 D5 10s yel grn 1.60 .50
J21 D5 20s dl bl ('04) 12.00 .50
J22 D5 30s vio brn 4.00 .50
J23 D5 50s org ('02) 9.50 9.50
Nos. J19-J23 (5) 27.90 11.50

Nos. J19-J23 exist imperf. and in pairs imperf. between. Value, imperf., $250.

1915 Unwmk. *Perf. 11½*
Thin Semi-Transparent Paper
J24 D6 5s green .50 .25
J25 D6 10s purple .50 .25
J26 D6 20s dl rose .50 .25
J27 D6 30s dp org 2.75 .25
J28 D6 50s dp bl .95 .25
Nos. J24-J28 (5) 5.20 1.25

1919-21 *Perf. 11½, 12x11½*
J29 D6 5s emerald .25 .25
a. 5s gray green ('21) .30 .25
J30 D6 10s violet .25 .25
a. 10s light violet ('21) .25 .25
J31 D6 20s salmon .25 .25
a. 20s yellow .25 .25
J32 D6 30s orange .25 .25
a. 30s red orange ('21) .65 .65
J33 D6 50s blue .25 .25
J34 D6 1 l emerald ('21) .25 .25
J35 D6 2 l rose ('21) .25 .25
J36 D6 3 l brown org ('21) .35 .25
Nos. J29-J36 (8) 2.10 2.00

Stotinki values of the above series surcharged 10s or 20s were used as ordinary postage stamps. See Nos. 182-185.

The 1919 printings are on thicker white paper with clean-cut perforations, the 1921 printings on thicker grayish paper with rough perforations.

Most of this series exist imperforate and in pairs imperforate between.

Heraldic Lion — D7

1932, Aug. 15 Thin Paper
J37 D7 1 l olive bister 1.60 1.00
J38 D7 2 l rose brown 1.60 1.00
J39 D7 6 l brown violet 3.50 1.20
Nos. J37-J39 (3) 6.70 3.20

Lion of Trnovo — D8

National Arms — D9

1933, Apr. 10
J40 D8 20s dk brn .25 .25
J41 D8 40s dp bl .25 .25
J42 D8 80s car rose .25 .25
J43 D9 1 l org brn 1.60 .50
J44 D9 2 l olive 1.60 .75

J45 D9 6 l dl vio .80 .30
J46 D9 14 l ultra 1.20 .50
Nos. J40-J46 (7) 5.95 2.80

Catalogue values for unused stamps in this section, from this point to the end of the section, are for Never Hinged items.

National Arms — D10

1947, June	**Typo.**	***Perf. 10½***	
J47 D10	1 l chocolate	.25	.25
J48 D10	2 l deep claret	.25	.25
J49 D10	8 l deep orange	.30	.25
J50 D10	20 l blue	.95	.25
	Nos. J47-J50 (4)	1.75	1.00

Arms of the People's Republic — D11

1951		***Perf. 11½x10½***	
J51 D11	1 l chocolate	.25	.25
J52 D11	2 l claret	.25	.25
J53 D11	8 l red orange	.50	.40
J54 D11	20 l deep blue	1.25	1.00
	Nos. J51-J54 (4)	2.25	1.90

OFFICIAL STAMPS

Catalogue values for unused stamps in this section are for Never Hinged items.

Bulgarian Coat of Arms
O1 O2

1942	**Unwmk.**	**Typo.**	***Perf. 13***	
O1	O1	10s yel grn	.25	.25
O2	O1	30s red	.25	.25
O3	O1	50s bister	.25	.25
O4	O2	1 l vio bl	.25	.25
O5	O2	2 l dk grn	.25	.25
O6	O2	3 l lilac	.25	.25
O7	O2	4 l rose	.25	.25
O8	O2	5 l carmine	.25	.25
		Nos. O1-O8 (8)	2.00	2.00

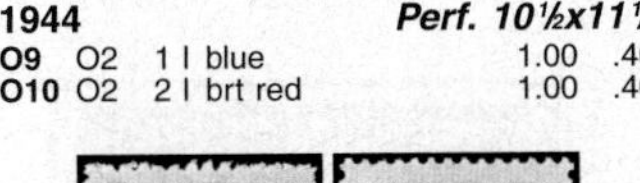

1944		***Perf. 10½x11½***	
O9 O2	1 l blue	1.00	.40
O10 O2	2 l brt red	1.00	.40

Lion Rampant
O3 O4

O5

1945		***Imperf.***	
O11 O5	1 l pink	.25	.25

Perf. 10½x11½, Imperf.			
O12 O3	2 l blue green	.25	.25
O13 O4	3 l bister brown	.25	.25
O14 O4	4 l light ultra	.25	.25
O15 O5	5 l brown lake	.25	.25
	Nos. O11-O15 (5)	1.25	1.25

In 1950, four stamps prepared for official use were issued as regular postage stamps. See Nos. 724-727.

PARCEL POST STAMPS

Catalogue values for unused stamps in this section are for Never Hinged items.

Weighing Packages — PP1

Parcel Post — PP2

Designs: 3 l, 8 l, 20 l, Parcel post truck. 4 l, 6 l, 10 l, Motorcycle.

Perf. 12½x13½, 13½x12½

1941-42	**Photo.**	**Unwmk.**	
Q1 PP1	1 l slate grn	.25	.25
Q2 PP2	2 l crimson	.25	.25
Q3 PP2	3 l dull brn	.25	.25
Q4 PP2	4 l red org	.25	.25
Q5 PP1	5 l deep blue	.25	.25
Q6 PP1	5 l slate grn ('42)	.25	.25
Q7 PP2	6 l red vio	.25	.25
Q8 PP2	6 l henna brn ('42)	.25	.25
Q9 PP1	7 l dark blue	.25	.25
Q10 PP1	7 l dk brn ('42)	.25	.25
Q11 PP2	8 l brt bl grn	.25	.25
Q12 PP2	8 l green ('42)	.25	.25
Q13 PP2	9 l olive gray	.25	.25
Q14 PP2	9 l dp olive ('42)	.25	.25
Q15 PP2	10 l orange	.25	.25
Q16 PP2	20 l gray vio	.40	.25
Q17 PP2	30 l dull blk	.55	.25
Q18 PP2	30 l sepia ('42)	.50	.25
	Nos. Q1-Q18 (18)	5.20	4.50

Arms of Bulgaria — PP5

1944	**Litho.**	***Imperf.***	
Q21 PP5	1 l dk carmine	.25	.25
Q22 PP5	3 l blue grn	.25	.25
Q23 PP5	5 l dull bl grn	.25	.25
Q24 PP5	7 l rose lilac	.25	.25
Q25 PP5	10 l deep blue	.25	.25
Q26 PP5	20 l orange brn	.25	.25
Q27 PP5	30 l dk brn car	.25	.25
Q28 PP5	50 l red orange	.30	.25
Q29 PP5	100 l blue	.50	.25
	Nos. Q21-Q29 (9)	2.55	2.25

For overprints and surcharges see Nos. 448-454, C37-C40.

POSTAL TAX STAMPS

The use of stamps Nos. RA1 to RA18 was compulsory on letters, etc., to be delivered on Sundays and holidays. The money received from their sale was used toward maintaining a sanatorium for employees of the post, telegraph and telephone services.

View of Sanatorium PT1

Sanatorium, Peshtera PT2

1925-29	**Unwmk.**	**Typo.**	***Perf. 11½***	
RA1	PT1	1 l blk, *grnsh bl*	2.75	.25
RA2	PT1	1 l chocolate ('26)	2.75	.25
RA3	PT1	1 l orange ('27)	3.00	.30
RA4	PT1	1 l pink ('28)	4.50	.30
RA5	PT1	1 l vio, *pnksh* ('29)	4.75	.30
RA6	PT2	2 l blue green	.35	.25
RA7	PT2	2 l violet ('27)	.35	.25
RA8	PT2	5 l deep blue	3.00	.80
RA9	PT2	5 l rose ('27)	3.75	.40
		Nos. RA1-RA9 (9)	25.20	3.10

St. Constantine Sanatorium PT3

1930-33			
RA10 PT3	1 l red brn & ol grn	4.00	.25
RA11 PT3	1 l ol grn & yel ('31)	.50	.25
RA12 PT3	1 l red vio & ol brn ('33)	.50	.25
	Nos. RA10-RA12 (3)	5.00	.75

Trojan Rest Home PT4

Sanatorium PT5

1935	**Wmk. 145**	***Perf. 11, 11½***	
RA13 PT4	1 l choc & red org	.30	.25
RA14 PT4	1 l emer & indigo	.30	.25
RA15 PT5	5 l red brn & indigo	1.40	.35
	Nos. RA13-RA15 (3)	2.00	.85

St. Constantine Sanatorium PT6

2 l, Children at seashore. 5 l, Rest home.

1941	**Unwmk.**	**Photo.**	***Perf. 13***	
RA16	PT6	1 l dark olive green	.25	.25
RA17	PT6	2 l red orange	.25	.25
RA18	PT6	5 l deep blue	.30	.25
		Nos. RA16-RA18 (3)	.80	.75

See Nos. 702-705 for same designs in smaller size issued as regular postage.

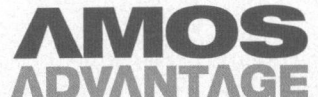

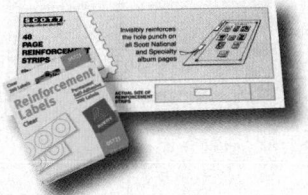

BURKINA FASO

bur-ˈkē-nə-ˈfä-sō

Upper Volta

LOCATION — Northwestern Africa, north of Ghana
GOVT. — Republic
AREA — 105,869 sq. mi.
POP. — 11,575,898 (1999 est.)
CAPITAL — Ouagadougou

In 1919 the French territory of Upper Volta was detached from the southern section of Upper Senegal and Niger and made a separate colony. In 1933 the colony was divided among its neighbors: French Sudan, Ivory Coast, and Niger Territory. The Republic of Upper Volta was proclaimed December 11, 1958; the name was changed to Burkina Faso on August 4, 1984.

100 Centimes = 1 Franc

Catalogue values for unused stamps in this country are for Never Hinged items, beginning with Scott 70 in the regular postage section, Scott B1 in the semi-postal section, Scott C1 in the airpost section, Scott J21 in the postage due section, and Scott O1 in the official section.

See French West Africa Nos. 67, 84 for additional stamps inscribed "Haute Volta" and "Afrique Occidentale Francaise."

Stamps and Types of Upper Senegal and Niger, 1914-17, Overprinted in Black or Red

1920-28 Unwmk. *Perf. 13½x14*

1 A4 1c brn vio & vio .25 .40
2 A4 2c gray & brn vio (R) .25 .40
3 A4 4c blk & bl .30 .50
4 A4 5c yel grn & bl grn .90 .80
5 A4 5c ol brn & dk brn ('22) .25 .40
6 A4 10c red org & rose 1.40 1.60
7 A4 10c yel grn & bl grn ('22) .30 .50
Complete booklet, 20 #7 9,250.
8 A4 10c claret & bl ('25) .80 .80
a. Overprint omitted 240.00
9 A4 15c choc & org .75 .80
Complete booklet, 20 #9 3,250.
10 A4 20c brn vio & blk (R) 1.10 1.20
11 A4 25c ultra & bl 1.40 1.10
12 A4 25c blk & bl grn ('22) .75 .75
a. Overprint omitted 200.00
13 A4 30c ol brn & brn (R) 2.90 3.50
14 A4 30c red org & rose ('22) 1.50 2.25
15 A4 30c vio & brn red ('25) 1.25 1.60
16 A4 30c dl grn & bl grn ('27) 1.25 1.60
17 A4 35c car rose & vio 1.00 1.60
18 A4 40c gray & car rose 1.00 1.60
19 A4 45c bl & brn (R) 1.00 1.60
20 A4 50c blk & grn 3.00 3.50
21 A4 50c ultra & bl ('22) 1.20 1.75
22 A4 50c red org & bl ('25) 1.25 1.60
a. Double surcharge, one inverted 1,275. 1,250.
23 A4 60c org red ('26) .80 1.25
24 A4 65c bis & pale bl ('28) 1.60 2.50
25 A4 75c org & brn 1.40 .90
26 A4 1fr brn & brn vio 1.40 2.00
27 A4 2fr grn & bl 1.90 2.40
28 A4 5fr vio & blk (R) 4.00 5.50
Nos. 1-28 (28) 34.90 44.40

No. 9 Surcharged in Various Colors

1922

29 A4 0,01c on 15c (Bk) 1.00 1.60
a. Double surcharge 175.00 250.00
30 A4 0,02c on 15c (Bl) 1.00 1.60
31 A4 0,05c on 15c (R) 1.00 1.60
Nos. 29-31 (3) 3.00 4.80

Type of 1920 Surcharged

1922

32 A4 60c on 75c vio, *pnksh* .90 1.25

Stamps and Types of 1920 Surcharged with New Value and Bars

1924-27

33 A4 25c on 2fr grn & bl .80 1.00
34 A4 25c on 5fr vio & blk .80 1.00
35 A4 65c on 45c bl & brn ('25) 1.20 1.60
36 A4 85c on 75c org & brn ('25) 1.60 2.40
37 A4 90c on 75c brn red & sal pink ('27) 1.60 2.40
38 A4 1.25fr on 1fr dp bl & lt bl (R) ('26) 1.25 2.00
39 A4 1.50fr on 1fr dp bl & ultra ('27) 2.75 3.50
40 A4 3fr on 5fr dl red & brn org ('27) 4.50 5.50
41 A4 10fr on 5fr ol grn & lil rose ('27) 14.50 18.50
42 A4 20fr on 5fr org brn & vio ('27) 21.00 28.00
Nos. 33-42 (10) 50.00 65.90

Hausa Chief — A5

Hausa Woman — A6

Hausa Warrior A7

1928 Typo. *Perf. 13½x14*

43 A5 1c indigo & grn .25 .40
44 A5 2c brn & lil .25 .40
45 A5 4c blk & yel .30 .50
46 A5 5c indigo & gray bl .30 .50
47 A5 10c indigo & pink .90 1.25
48 A5 15c brn & bl 1.40 1.90
49 A5 20c brn & grn 1.40 1.60
50 A6 25c brn & yel 1.90 2.40
51 A6 30c dp grn & grn 1.90 2.40
52 A6 40c blk & pink 1.90 2.00
53 A6 45c brn & blue 2.50 3.25
54 A6 50c blk & grn 2.25 2.40
55 A6 65c indigo & bl 2.75 3.25
56 A6 75c blk & lil 2.40 2.75
57 A6 90c brn red & lil 2.75 3.25

Perf. 14x13½

58 A7 1fr brn & grn 2.40 2.75
59 A7 1.10fr indigo & lil 2.75 4.00
60 A7 1.50fr ultra & grysh 3.50 4.50
61 A7 2fr blk & bl 4.00 4.75
62 A7 3fr brn & yel 4.00 4.75
63 A7 5fr brn & lil 4.00 4.75
64 A7 10fr blk & grn 20.00 26.00
65 A7 20fr blk & pink 30.00 32.50
Nos. 43-65 (23) 93.80 112.25

Common Design Types pictured following the introduction.

Colonial Exposition Issue
Common Design Types

1931 Engr. *Perf. 12½*
Country Name Typo. in Black

66 CD70 40c dp grn 4.00 4.00
67 CD71 50c violet 4.75 4.75
68 CD72 90c red org 4.75 4.75
69 CD73 1.50fr dull blue 5.50 5.50
Nos. 66-69 (4) 19.00 19.00

Catalogue values for unused stamps in this section, from this point to the end of the section, are for Never Hinged items.

Republic

President Ouezzin Coulibaly — A8

1959 Unwmk. Engr. *Perf. 13*

70 A8 25fr black & magenta .50 .40

1st anniv. of the proclamation of the Republic; Ouezzin Coulibaly, Council President, who died in December, 1958.

Imperforates
Most Upper Volta stamps from 1959 onward exist imperforate in issued and trial colors, and also in small presentation sheets in issued colors.

Deer Mask and Deer — A9

Animal Masks: 1fr, 2fr, 4fr, Wart hog. 5fr, 6fr, 8fr, Monkey. 10fr, 15fr, 20fr, Buffalo. 25fr, Coba (antelope). 30fr, 40fr, 50fr, Elephant. 60fr, 85fr, Secretary bird.

1960

71 A9 30c rose & violet .25 .25
72 A9 40c buff & dp claret .25 .25
73 A9 50c bl grn & gray ol .25 .25
74 A9 1fr red, blk & red brn .25 .25
75 A9 2fr emer, yel grn & dk grn .25 .25
76 A9 4fr bl, vio & ind .25 .25
77 A9 5fr ol bis, red & brn .25 .25
78 A9 6fr grnsh bl & vio brn .25 .25
79 A9 8fr org & red brn .25 .25
80 A9 10fr lt yel grn & plum .25 .25
81 A9 15fr org, ultra & brn .55 .25
82 A9 20fr green & ultra .55 .35
83 A9 25fr bl, emer & dp claret .70 .35
84 A9 30fr dk bl grn, blk & brn .90 .35
85 A9 40fr ultra, ind & dk car 1.10 .50
86 A9 50fr brt pink, brn & grn 1.50 .50
87 A9 60fr org brn & bl 1.75 .65
88 A9 85fr gray ol & dk bl 2.75 1.00
Nos. 71-88 (18) 12.30 6.45

C.C.T.A. Issue
Common Design Type

1960 Engr. *Perf. 13*

89 CD106 25fr vio bl & slate .45 .40

Emblem of the Entente — A9a

Pres. Maurice Yameogo — A10

1960 Photo. *Perf. 13x13½*

90 A9a 25fr multicolored .60 .40

Council of the Entente.

1960, May 1 Engr. *Perf. 13*

91 A10 25fr dk vio brn & slate .25 .25

Flag, Village and Couple — A11

1960, Aug. 5 Unwmk. *Perf. 13*

92 A11 25fr red brn, blk & red .45 .40

Proclamation of independence, Aug. 5, 1960.

World Meteorological Organization Emblem — A12

1961, May 4

93 A12 25fr blk, bl & red 1.00 .45

First World Meteorological Day.

Arms of Republic — A13

1961, Dec. 8 Photo. *Perf. 12x12½*

94 A13 25fr multicolored .45 .40

The 1961 independence celebrations.

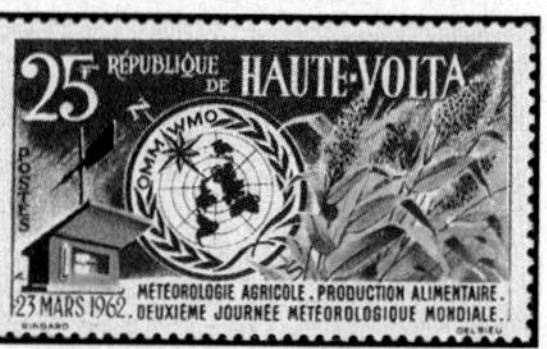

WMO Emblem, Weather Station and Sorghum Grain — A14

1962, Mar. 23 Unwmk. *Perf. 13*

95 A14 25fr dk bl, emer & brn 1.10 .55

UN 2nd World Meteorological Day, Mar. 23.

Hospital and Nurse — A15

1962, June 23 *Perf. 13x12*
96 A15 25fr multicolored .90 .55

Founding of Upper Volta Red Cross.

Buffalos at Water Hole — A16

Designs: 10fr, Lions, horiz. 15fr, Defassa waterbuck. 25fr, Arly reservation, horiz. 50fr, Diapaga reservation, horiz. 85fr, Buffon's kob.

Perf. 12½x12, 12x12½

1962, June 30 **Engr.**
97 A16 5fr sepia, bl & grn .45 .25
98 A16 10fr red brn, grn & yel .50 .40
99 A16 15fr sepia, grn & yel 1.50 .65
100 A16 25fr vio brn, bl & grn 1.50 .65
101 A16 50fr vio brn, bl & grn 2.25 1.50
102 A16 85fr red brn, bl & grn 5.50 2.90
Nos. 97-102 (6) 11.70 6.35

Abidjan Games Issue
Common Design Type

Designs: 20fr, Soccer. 25fr, Bicycling. 85fr, Boxing. All horiz.

1962, July 21 **Photo.** *Perf. 12½x12*
103 CD109 20fr multicolored .55 .35
104 CD109 25fr multicolored .85 .55
105 CD109 85fr multicolored 1.75 .90
Nos. 103-105 (3) 3.15 1.80

African-Malgache Union Issue
Common Design Type

1962, Sept. 8 **Unwmk.**
106 CD110 30fr red, bluish grn & gold 1.50 .90

Weather Map and UN Emblem A17

1963, Mar. 23 *Perf. 12x12½*
107 A17 70fr multicolored 1.60 .70

3rd World Meteorological Day, Mar. 23.

Friendship Games, Dakar, Apr. 11-21 — A18

1963, Apr. 11 **Engr.** *Perf. 13*
108 A18 20fr Basketball .45 .30
109 A18 25fr Discus .65 .30
110 A18 50fr Judo 1.40 .55
Nos. 108-110 (3) 2.50 1.15

Amaryllis A19

Flowers: 50c, Hibiscus. 1fr, Oldenlandia grandiflora. 1.50fr, Rose moss (portulaca). 2fr, Tobacco. 4fr, Morning glory. 5fr, Striga senegalensis. 6fr, Cowpea. 8fr, Lepidagathis heudelotiana. 10fr, Spurge. 25fr, Argyreia nervosa. 30fr, Rangoon creeper. 40fr, Water lily. 50fr, White plumeria. 60fr, Crotalaria retusa. 85fr, Hibiscus.

1963 **Photo.**
111 A19 50c multi, vert. .25 .25
112 A19 1fr multi, vert. .25 .25
113 A19 1.50fr multi, vert. .25 .25
114 A19 2fr multi, vert. .25 .25
115 A19 4fr multi, vert. .25 .25
116 A19 5fr multi, vert. .30 .30
117 A19 6fr multi, vert. .45 .30
118 A19 8fr multi, vert. .45 .30
119 A19 10fr multi, vert. .45 .30
120 A19 15fr multi .50 .45
121 A19 25fr multi .75 .45
122 A19 30fr multi 1.00 .45
123 A19 40fr multi 1.60 .75
124 A19 50fr multi 1.75 .75
125 A19 60fr multi 2.50 1.25
126 A19 85fr multi 3.50 1.50
Nos. 111-126 (16) 14.50 8.05

Centenary Emblem and Globe — A20

Scroll — A21

1963, Oct. 21 **Unwmk.** *Perf. 12*
127 A20 25fr multicolored 1.00 .75

Centenary of International Red Cross.

1963, Dec. 10 **Photo.** *Perf. 13x12½*
128 A21 25fr dp claret, gold & bl .80 .50

15th anniv. of the Universal Declaration of Human Rights.

Sound Wave Patterns A22

1964, Jan. 16 *Perf. 12½x13*
129 A22 25fr multicolored .60 .35

Upper Volta's admission to the ITU.

Recording Rain Gauge and WMO Emblem A23

1964, Mar. 23 **Engr.** *Perf. 13*
130 A23 50fr dk car rose, grn & bl 1.20 .80

4th World Meteorological Day, Mar. 23.

World Connected by Letters and Carrier Pigeon — A24

60fr, World connected by letters and jet plane.

1964, Mar. 29 **Photo.** *Perf. 13x12*
131 A24 25fr gray brn & ultra .65 .35
132 A24 60fr gray brn & org 1.10 .90

Upper Volta's admission to the UPU.

IQSY Emblem and Seasonal Allegories — A25

1964, Aug. 17 **Engr.** *Perf. 13*
133 A25 30fr grn, ocher & car .90 .65

International Quiet Sun Year.

Cooperation Issue
Common Design Type

1964, Nov. 7 **Unwmk.** *Perf. 13*
134 CD119 70fr dl bl grn, dk brn & car 1.25 .75

Hotel Independance, Ouagadougou — A26

1964, Dec. 11 **Litho.** *Perf. 12½x13*
135 A26 25fr multicolored 2.25 .90

Pigmy Long-tailed Sunbird — A27

Comoe Waterfall — A28

1965, Mar. 1 **Photo.** *Perf. 13x12½*
Size: 22x36mm
136 A27 10fr shown 1.25 .45
137 A27 15fr Olive-bellied Sunbird 1.60 .60
138 A27 20fr Splendid Sunbird 3.00 .90
Nos. 136-138,C20 (4) 28.35 10.95

1965 **Engr.** *Perf. 13*

25fr, Great Waterfall of Banfora, horiz.

139 A28 5fr yel grn, bl & red brn .30 .25
140 A28 25fr dk red, brt bl & grn .90 .30
Nos. 139-140 (2) 1.20 .55

Soccer — A29

Abraham Lincoln — A30

Designs: 25fr, Boxing gloves and ring. 70fr, Tennis rackets, ball and net.

1965, July 15 **Unwmk.** *Perf. 13*
141 A29 15fr brn, red & dk grn .40 .25
142 A29 25fr pale org, bl & brn .60 .35
143 A29 70fr dk car & brt grn 1.50 .80
Nos. 141-143 (3) 2.50 1.40

1st African Games, Brazzaville, July 18-25.

1965, Nov. 3 **Photo.** *Perf. 13x12½*
144 A30 50fr green & multi 1.00 .50

Centenary of death of Abraham Lincoln.

Pres. Maurice Yameogo — A31

1965, Dec. 11 **Photo.** *Perf. 13x12½*
145 A31 25fr multicolored .60 .30

Mantis A32

Wart Hog — A33

1966 *Perf. 13x12½, 12½x13*
146 A33 1fr Nemopistha imperatrix .35 .25
147 A33 2fr Ball python .25 .25
148 A32 3fr shown .35 .25
149 A32 4fr Grasshopper .60 .25
150 A33 5fr shown .25 .25
151 A32 6fr Scorpion .90 .25
152 A33 8fr Green monkey .55 .25
153 A32 10fr Dromedary .45 .25
154 A33 15fr Leopard 1.00 .35
155 A32 20fr Cape buffalo 1.25 .35
156 A33 25fr Hippopotamus 1.40 .45
157 A32 30fr Agama lizard 1.10 .50
158 A33 45fr Common puff adder 2.50 .60
159 A33 50fr Chameleon 2.75 .80
160 A33 60fr Ugada limbata 2.75 .90
161 A33 85fr Elephant 3.50 1.25
Nos. 146-161 (16) 19.95 7.20

Headdress — A34

25fr, Plumed headdress. 60fr, Male dancer.

1966, Apr. 9 **Photo.** *Perf. 13x12½*
162 A34 20fr yel grn, choc & red .60 .25
163 A34 25fr multicolored .70 .35
164 A34 60fr org, dk brn & red 1.60 .60
Nos. 162-164 (3) 2.90 1.20

Intl. Negro Arts Festival, Dakar, Senegal, 4/1-24.

Pô Church A35

Design: No. 166, Bobo-Dioulasso Mosque.

1966, Apr. 15 *Perf. 12½x13*
165 A35 25fr multicolored .60 .35
166 A35 25fr bl, cream & red brn .60 .35

The Red Cross Helping the World — A36

1966, June Photo. *Perf. 13x12½*

167 A36 25fr lemon, blk & car .80 .40

Issued to honor the Red Cross.

Boy Scouts in Camp A37

15fr, Two Scouts on a cliff exploring the country.

1966, June 15 *Perf. 12½x13*

168 A37 10fr multicolored .50 .25
169 A37 15fr blk, bis brn, & dl yel .50 .25

Issued to honor the Boy Scouts.

Cow Receiving Injection A38

1966, Aug. 16 Photo. *Perf. 12½x13*

170 A38 25fr yel, blk & blue 1.40 .60

Campaign against cattle plague.

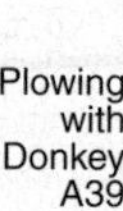

Plowing with Donkey A39

Design: 30fr, Crop rotation, Kamboince Experimental Station.

1966, Sept. 15 Photo. *Perf. 12½x13*

171 A39 25fr multicolored .65 .35
172 A39 30fr multicolored .65 .35

Natl. and rural education; 3rd anniv. of the Kamboince Experimental Station (No. 172).

UNESCO Emblem and Map of Africa A40

UNICEF Emblem and Children A41

1966, Dec. 10 Engr. *Perf. 13*

173 A40 50fr brt bl, blk & red .95 .60
174 A41 50fr dk vio, dp lil & dk red .95 .60

20th anniv. of UNESCO and of UNICEF.

Arms of Upper Volta — A42

Symbols of Agriculture, Industry, Men and Women — A43

1967, Jan. 2 Photo. *Perf. 12½x13*

175 A42 30fr multicolored .75 .25

Europafrica Issue

1967, Feb. 4 Photo. *Perf. 12½*

176 A43 60fr multicolored 1.50 .65

Scout Handclasp and Jamboree Emblem A44

5fr, Jamboree emblem, Scout holding hat.

1967, June 8 Photo. *Perf. 12½x13*

177 A44 5fr multicolored .50 .25
178 A44 20fr multicolored .95 .50

12th Boy Scout World Jamboree, Farragut State Park, Idaho, Aug. 1-9. See No. C41.

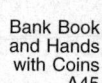

Bank Book and Hands with Coins A45

1967, Aug. 22 Engr. *Perf. 13*

179 A45 30fr slate grn, ocher & olive .65 .35

National Savings Bank.

Mailman on Bicycle — A46

1967, Oct. 15 Engr. *Perf. 13*

180 A46 30fr dk bl, emer & brn 1.00 .45

Stamp Day.

Monetary Union Issue

Common Design Type

1967, Nov. 4 Engr. *Perf. 13*

181 CD125 30fr dk vio & dl bl .70 .35

View of Nizier A47

Olympic Emblem and: 50fr, Les Deux-Alps, vert. 100fr, Ski lift and view of Villard-de-Lans.

1967, Nov. 28

182 A47 15fr brt bl, grn & brn .50 .30
183 A47 50fr brt bl & slate grn .90 .45
184 A47 100fr brt bl, grn & red 2.10 1.25
Nos. 182-184 (3) 3.50 2.00

10th Winter Olympic Games, Grenoble, France, Feb. 6-18, 1968.

White and Black Men Holding Human Rights Emblem A48

1968, Jan. 2 Photo. *Perf. 12½x13*

185 A48 20fr brt bl, gold & dp car .70 .25
186 A48 30fr grn, gold & dp car .80 .35

International Human Rights Year.

Administration School and Student — A49

1968, Feb. 2 Engr. *Perf. 13*

187 A49 30fr ol bis, Prus bl & brt grn .70 .35

National School of Administration.

WHO Emblem and Sick People A50

1968, Apr. 8 Engr. *Perf. 13*

188 A50 30fr ind, brt bl & car rose .70 .35
189 A50 50fr brt bl, sl grn & lt brn .95 .50

WHO, 20th anniversary.

Telephone Office, Bobo-Dioulasso — A51

1968, Sept. 30 Photo. *Perf. 12½x12*

190 A51 30fr multicolored .95 .45

Opening of the automatic telephone office in Bobo-Dioulasso.

Weaver A52

1968, Oct. 30 Engr. *Perf. 13*

Size: 36x22mm

191 A52 30fr magenta, brn & ocher .70 .30

See No. C58.

Grain Pouring over World, Plower and FAO Emblem — A53

1969, Jan. 7 Engr. *Perf. 13*

192 A53 30fr slate, vio bl & maroon .70 .35

UNFAO world food program.

Automatic Looms and ILO Emblem A54

1969, Mar. 15 Engr. *Perf. 13*

193 A54 30fr brt grn, mar & indigo .75 .45

ILO, 50th anniversary.

Smith A55

1969, Apr. 3 Engr. *Perf. 13*

Size: 36x22mm

194 A55 5fr magenta & blk .35 .25

See No. C64.

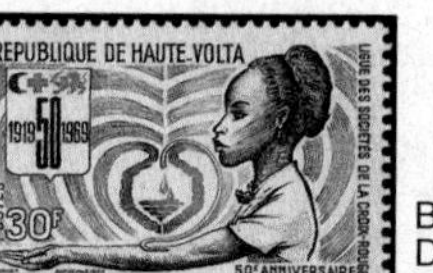

Blood Donor A56

1969, May 15 Engr. *Perf. 13*

195 A56 30fr blk, bl & car 1.00 .60

League of Red Cross Societies, 50th anniv.

Nile Pike — A57

Fish: 20fr, Nannocharax gobioides. 25fr, Hemigrammocharax polli. 55fr, Alestes luteus. 85fr, Micralestes voltae.

1969 Engr. *Perf. 13*

Size: 36x22mm

196 A57 20fr brt bl, brn & yel 1.50 .70
197 A57 25fr slate, brn & dk brn 1.60 .70
198 A57 30fr dk olive & blk 1.70 .60
199 A57 55fr dk grn, yel & ol 2.00 .90
200 A57 85fr slate brn & pink 4.00 1.90
Nos. 196-200,C66-C67 (7) 18.05 8.20

Development Bank Issue

Common Design Type

1969, Sept. 10 Engr. *Perf. 13*

201 CD130 30fr sl grn, grn & ocher .70 .30

Millet A58

Design: 30fr, Cotton.

1969, Oct. 30 Photo. *Perf. 12½x13*

202 A58 15fr dk brn, grn & yel .50 .25
203 A58 30fr dp claret & brt bl .60 .35
Nos. 202-203,C73-C74 (4) 6.10 2.10

ASECNA Issue

Common Design Type

1969, Dec. 12 Engr. *Perf. 13*

204 CD132 100fr brown 1.75 1.00

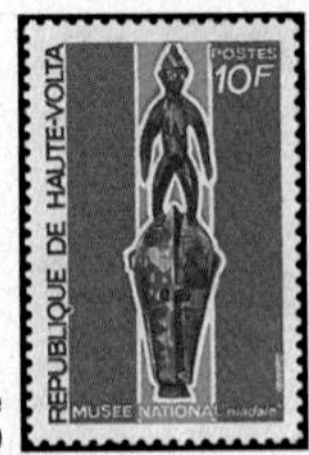

Niadale Mask — A59

Carvings from National Museum: 30fr, Niaga. 45fr, Man and woman, Iliu Bara. 80fr, Karan Weeba figurine.

1970, Mar. 5 Engr. *Perf. 13*

207 A59 10fr dk car rose, org & dk brn .30 .25
209 A59 30fr dk brn, brt vio & grnsh bl .50 .25
211 A59 45fr yel grn, brn & bl 1.00 .45
212 A59 80fr pur, rose lil & brn 1.75 .70
Nos. 207-212 (4) 3.55 1.65

African Huts and European City — A60

1970, Apr. 25 Engr. *Perf. 13*

213 A60 30fr dk brn, red & bl .75 .45

Issued for Linked Cities' Day.

Mask for Nebwa Gnomo Dance A61

Designs: 8fr, Cauris dancers, vert. 20fr, Gourmantchés dancers, vert. 30fr, Larllé dancers.

1970, May 7 Photo. *Perf. 13*

214 A61 5fr lt brn, vio bl & blk .45 .25
215 A61 8fr org brn, car & blk .70 .25
216 A61 20fr dk brn, sl grn & ocher .90 .25
217 A61 30fr dp car, dk gray & brn 1.10 .35
Nos. 214-217 (4) 3.15 1.10

Education Year Emblem, Open Book and Pupils A62

Design: 90fr, Education Year emblem, telecommunication and education symbols.

1970, May 14 *Perf. 12½x12*

218 A62 40fr black & multi .60 .25
219 A62 90fr olive & multi 1.40 .60

International Education Year.

UPU Headquarters Issue

Abraham Lincoln, UPU Headquarters and Emblem — A63

1970, May 20 Engr. *Perf. 13*

220 A63 30fr dk car rose, ind & red brn .70 .25
221 A63 60fr dk bl grn, vio & red brn 1.25 .50

See note after CD133, Common Design section.

Ship-building Industry — A64

45fr, Chemical industry. 80fr, Electrical industry.

1970, June 15

222 A64 15fr brt pink, red brn & blk .90 .40
223 A64 45fr emerald, dp bl & blk 1.00 .40
224 A64 80fr red brn, claret & blk 2.00 .70
Nos. 222-224 (3) 3.90 1.50

Hanover Fair.

Cattle Vaccination A65

1970, June 30 Photo. *Perf. 13*

225 A65 30fr Prus bl, yel & sepia 1.00 .50

National Veterinary College.

Vaccination and Red Cross — A66

1970, Aug. 28 Engr. *Perf. 12½x13*

226 A66 30fr chocolate & car 1.00 .50

Issued for the Upper Volta Red Cross.
For surcharge see No. 252.

Europafrica Issue

Nurse with Child, by Frans Hals — A67

Paintings: 30fr, Courtyard of a House in Delft, by Pieter de Hooch. 150fr, Christina of Denmark, by Hans Holbein. 250fr, Courtyard of the Royal Palace at Innsbruck, Austria, by Albrecht Dürer.

1970, Sept. 25 Litho. *Perf. 13x14*

227 A67 25fr multicolored .80 .25
228 A67 30fr multicolored .95 .45
229 A67 150fr multicolored 3.50 1.25
230 A67 250fr multicolored 6.00 1.75
Nos. 227-230 (4) 11.25 3.70

Citroen A68

Design: 40fr, Old and new Citroen cars.

1970, Oct. 16 Engr. *Perf. 13*

231 A68 25fr ol brn, mar & sl grn 1.40 .50
232 A68 40fr brt grn, plum & sl 1.75 .85

57th Paris Automobile Salon.

Professional Training Center A69

1970, Dec. 10 Engr. *Perf. 13*

233 A69 50fr grn, bis & brn .80 .40

Opening of Professional Training Center under joint sponsorship of Austria and Upper Volta.

Upper Volta Arms and Soaring Bird — A70

1970, Dec. 10 Photo.

234 A70 30fr lt blue & multi .45 .25

Tenth anniversary of independence, Dec. 11.

Political Maps of Africa — A71

1970, Dec. 14 Litho. *Perf. 13½*

235 A71 50fr multicolored .80 .45

10th anniv. of the declaration granting independence to colonial territories and countries.

Beingolo Hunting Horn — A72

Musical Instruments: 15fr, Mossi guitar, vert. 20fr, Gourounsi flutes, vert. 25fr, Lunga drums.

1971, Mar. 1 Engr. *Perf. 13*

236 A72 5fr blue, brn & car .50 .25
237 A72 15fr grn, crim rose & brn 1.00 .25
238 A72 20fr car rose, bl & gray 1.75 .25
239 A72 25fr brt grn, red brn & ol gray 2.00 .50
Nos. 236-239 (4) 5.25 1.25

Voltaphilex I, National Phil. Exhibition.

Four Races — A73

1971, Mar. 21 Engr. *Perf. 13*

240 A73 50fr rose cl, lt grn & dk brn 1.60 .50

Intl. year against racial discrimination.

Telephone and Globes A74

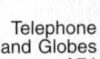

1971, May 17 Engr. *Perf. 13*

241 A74 50fr brn, gray & dk pur 1.00 .40

3rd World Telecommunications Day.

Cane Field Worker, Banfora Sugar Mill — A75

Cotton and Voltex Mill Emblem — A76

1971, June 24 Photo. *Perf. 13*

242 A75 10fr multicolored .25 .25
243 A76 35fr multicolored .50 .25

Industrial development.

Gonimbrasia Hecate — A77

Butterflies and Moths: 2fr, Hamanumida daedalus. 3fr, Ophideres materna. 5fr, Danaus chyrsippus. 40fr, Hypolimnas misippus. 45fr, Danaus petiverana.

1971, June 30

244 A77 1fr blue & multi .35 .25
245 A77 2fr lt lilac & multi .60 .25
246 A77 3fr multicolored .80 .25
247 A77 5fr gray & multi 1.75 .35
248 A77 40fr ocher & multi 10.00 2.00
249 A77 45fr multicolored 14.00 2.50
Nos. 244-249 (6) 27.50 5.60

Kabuki Actor — A78

40fr, African mask and Kabuki actor.

1971, Aug. 12 Photo. *Perf. 13*

250 A78 25fr multicolored .50 .25
251 A78 40fr multicolored .70 .35

Philatokyo 71, Philatelic Exposition, Tokyo, Apr. 19-29.

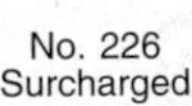

No. 226 Surcharged

1971 Engr. *Perf. 12½x13*

252 A66 100fr on 30fr choc & car 1.60 .85

10th anniversary of Upper Volta Red Cross.

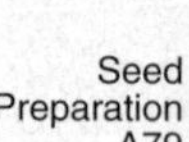

Seed Preparation A79

Designs: 75fr, Old farmer with seed packet, vert. 100fr, Farmer in rice field.

1971, Sept. 30 Photo. *Perf. 13*

253 A79 35fr ocher & multi .50 .25
254 A79 75fr lt blue & multi .90 .30
255 A79 100fr brown & multi 1.10 .60
Nos. 253-255 (3) 2.50 1.15

National campaign for seed protection.

Outdoor Classroom A80

Design: 50fr, Mother learning to read.

1971, Oct. 14

256 A80 35fr multicolored .65 .25
257 A80 50fr multicolored .80 .50

Women's education.

Joseph Dakiri, Soldiers Driving Tractors — A81

40fr, Dakiri & soldiers gathering harvest.

1971, Oct. 13 *Perf. 12x12½*

258 A81 15fr blk, yel & red brn .70 .25
259 A81 40fr blue & multi 1.00 .50

Joseph Dakiri (1938-1971), inaugurator of the Army-Aid-to-Agriculture Program.

Spraying Lake, Fly, Man Leading Blind Women A82

1971, Nov. 26 Photo. *Perf. 13*

260 A82 40fr dk brn, yel & bl .90 .50

Drive against onchocerciasis, roundworm infestation.
For surcharge see No. 295.

Children and UNICEF Emblem — A84

1971, Dec. 11 *Perf. 13*

262 A84 45fr red, bister & blk .75 .50

UNICEF, 25th anniv.

Peulh House A85

Upper Volta Houses: 20fr, Gourounsi house. 35fr, Mossi houses. 45fr, Bobo house, vert. 50fr, Dagari house, vert. 90fr, Bango house, interior.

Perf. 13x13½, 13½x13

1971-72 Photo.

263 A85 10fr ver & multi .25 .25
264 A85 20fr multicolored .45 .25
265 A85 35fr brt grn & multi .70 .45
266 A85 45fr multi ('72) .70 .35
267 A85 50fr multi ('72) .85 .45
268 A85 90fr multi ('72) 1.40 .60
Nos. 263-268 (6) 4.35 2.35

Town Halls of Bobo-Dioulasso and Chalons-sur-Marne — A86

1971, Dec. 23 *Perf. 13x12½*

269 A86 40fr yellow & multi .95 .60

Kinship between the cities of Bobo-Dioulasso, Upper Volta, and Chalons-sur-Marne, France.

Louis Armstrong — A87

1972, May 17 *Perf. 14x13*

270 A87 45fr multicolored 6.00 1.00

Black musician. See No. C104.

Red Crescent, Cross and Lion Emblems A88

1972, June 23 *Perf. 13x14*

271 A88 40fr yellow & multi .75 .50

World Red Cross Day. See No. C105.

Coiffure of Peulh Woman — A89

Designs: Various hair styles.

1972, July 23 Litho. *Perf. 13*

272 A89 25fr blue & multi .40 .25
273 A89 35fr emerald & multi .70 .25
274 A89 75fr yellow & multi 1.60 .65
Nos. 272-274 (3) 2.70 1.15

Classroom A90

15fr, Clinic. 20fr, Factory. 35fr, Cattle. 40fr, Plowers.

1972, Oct. 30 Engr. *Perf. 13*

275 A90 10fr sl grn, lt grn & choc .25 .25
276 A90 15fr brt grn, brn org & brn .25 .25
277 A90 20fr bl, lt brn & grn .45 .25
278 A90 35fr grn, brn & brt bl .80 .25
279 A90 40fr choc, pink & sl grn .80 .25
Nos. 275-279,C106 (6) 3.55 2.05

2nd Five-Year Plan.

West African Monetary Union Issue
Common Design Type

1972, Nov. 2

280 CD136 40fr brn, bl & gray .60 .25

Lottery Office and Emblem A91

1972, Nov. 6 Litho.

281 A91 35fr multicolored .75 .35

5th anniversary of National Lottery.

Domestic Animals — A92

1972, Dec. 4 Litho. *Perf. 13½x12½*

282 A92 5fr Donkeys .25 .25
283 A92 10fr Geese 1.00 .25
284 A92 30fr Goats 1.50 .35
285 A92 50fr Cow 1.90 .50
286 A92 65fr Dromedaries 2.75 .70
Nos. 282-286 (5) 7.40 2.05

Mossi Woman's Hair Style, and Village — A93

1973, Jan. 24 Engr. *Perf. 13*

287 A93 5fr slate grn, org & choc .25 .25
288 A93 40fr bl, org & chocolate .70 .25

Eugene A. Cernan and Lunar Module A94

65fr, Ronald E. Evans & splashdown. 100fr, Capsule, in orbit & interior, horiz. 150fr, Harrison H. Schmitt & lift-off. 200fr, Conference & moon-buggy. 500fr, Moon-buggy & capsule, horiz.

Perf. 12½x13½, 13½x12½

1973, Mar. 29 Litho.

289 A94 50fr multi .50 .25
290 A94 65fr multi .70 .35
291 A94 100fr multi 1.00 .45
292 A94 150fr multi 1.25 .50
293 A94 200fr multi 2.00 .70
Nos. 289-293 (5) 5.45 2.25

Souvenir Sheet

294 A94 500fr multi 5.00 3.75

Apollo 17 moon mission.

No. 260 Srchd. in Red

1973, Apr. 7 Photo. *Perf. 13*

295 A82 45fr on 40fr multi .75 .45

WHO, 25th anniversary.

Scout Bugler A95

1973, July 18 Litho. *Perf. 12½x13*

296 A95 20fr multicolored .40 .25
Nos. 296,C160-C163 (5) 4.30 2.25

African Postal Union Issue
Common Design Type

1973, Sept. 12 Engr. *Perf. 13*

297 CD137 100fr brt red, mag & dl yel 1.25 .70

Pres. Kennedy, Saturn 5 on Assembly Trailer A96

Pres. John F. Kennedy (1917-1963) and: 10fr, Atlas rocket carrying John H. Glenn. 30fr, Titan 2 rocket and Gemini 3 capsule.

1973, Sept. 12 Litho. *Perf. 12½x13*

298 A96 5fr multicolored .25 .25
299 A96 10fr multicolored .25 .25
300 A96 30fr multicolored .45 .25
Nos. 298-300,C167-C168 (5) 4.85 2.85

Cross-examination — A97

Designs: 65fr, "Diamond Ede." 70fr, Forensic Institute. 150fr, Robbery scene.

1973, Sept. 15 *Perf. 13x12½*

301 A97 50fr multicolored .70 .25
302 A97 65fr multicolored .70 .25
303 A97 70fr multicolored .85 .35
304 A97 150fr multicolored 1.40 .60
Nos. 301-304 (4) 3.65 1.45

Interpol, 50th anniversary. See No. C170.

Market Place, Ouagadougou — A98

40fr, Swimming pool, Hotel Independence.

1973, Sept. 30

305 A98 35fr multicolored .45 .25
306 A98 40fr multicolored .60 .35
Nos. 305-306,C171 (3) 2.45 1.40

Tourism. See No. C172.

Protestant Church — A99

Design: 40fr, Ouahigouya Mosque.

1973, Sept. 28 ***Perf. 13x12½***

307 A99 35fr multicolored .45 .25
308 A99 40fr multicolored .45 .25
Nos. 307-308,C173 (3) 3.40 1.75

Houses of worship.

Kiembara Dancers A100

Folklore: 40fr, Dancers.

1973, Nov. 30 Litho. ***Perf. 12½x13***

309 A100 35fr multicolored .45 .25
310 A100 40fr multicolored .50 .25
Nos. 309-310,C174-C175 (4) 4.60 1.95

Yuri Gagarin and Aries — A101

Famous Men and their Zodiac Signs: 10fr, Lenin and Taurus. 20fr, John F. Kennedy, rocket and Gemini. 25fr, John H. Glenn, orbiting capsule and Cancer. 30fr, Napoleon and Leo. 50fr, Goethe and Virgo. 60fr, Pelé and Libra. 75fr, Charles de Gaulle and Scorpio. 100fr, Beethoven and Sagittarius. 175fr, Conrad Adenauer and Capricorn. 200fr, Edwin E. Aldrin, Jr. (Apollo XI) and Aquarius. 250fr, Lord Baden-Powell and Pisces.

1973, Dec. 15 Litho. ***Perf. 13x14***

311 A101 5fr multicolored .25 .25
312 A101 10fr multicolored .25 .25
313 A101 20fr multicolored .25 .25
314 A101 25fr multicolored .25 .25
315 A101 30fr multicolored .35 .25
316 A101 50fr multicolored .35 .25
317 A101 60fr multicolored .55 .25
318 A101 75fr multicolored .85 .35
319 A101 100fr multicolored .85 .35
320 A101 175fr multicolored 1.40 .55
321 A101 200fr multicolored 1.75 .55
322 A101 250fr multicolored 2.25 .70
Nos. 311-322 (12) 9.35 4.25

See Nos. C176-C178.

Rivera with Italian Flag and Championship '74 Emblem — A102

40fr, World Cup, soccer ball, World Championship '74 emblem & Pelé with Brazilian flag.

1974, Jan. 15 ***Perf. 13x12½***

323 A102 5fr multicolored .25 .25
324 A102 40fr multicolored .45 .25
Nos. 323-324,C179-C181 (5) 4.10 1.80

10th World Cup Soccer Championship, Munich, June 13-July 7.

Charles de Gaulle A103

40fr, De Gaulle memorial. 60fr, Pres. de Gaulle.

1974, Feb. 4 Litho. ***Perf. 12½x13***

325 A103 35fr multicolored .50 .25
326 A103 40fr multicolored .70 .25
327 A103 60fr multicolored .90 .35
a. Strip of 3, Nos. 325-327 2.25 .75
Nos. 325-327,C183 (4) 6.35 2.60

Gen. Charles de Gaulle (1890-1970), president of France. See No. C184.

N'Dongo and Cameroun Flag A104

World Cup, Emblems and: 20fr, Kolev and Bulgarian flag. 50fr, Keita and Mali flag.

1974, Mar. 19

328 A104 10fr multicolored .25 .25
329 A104 20fr multicolored .25 .25
330 A104 50fr multicolored .45 .25
Nos. 328-330,C185-C186 (5) 4.30 2.10

10th World Cup Soccer Championship, Munich, June 13-July 7.

Map and Flags of Members A105

1974, May 29 Photo. ***Perf. 13x12½***

331 A105 40fr blue & multi .75 .50

15th anniversary of the Council of Accord.

UPU Emblem and Mail Coach — A106

1974, July 23 Litho. ***Perf. 13½***

332 A106 35fr Mail coach .45 .25
333 A106 40fr Steamship .45 .25
334 A106 85fr Mailman .90 .45
Nos. 332-334,C189-C191 (6) 6.95 3.80

Universal Postal Union centenary.
For overprints see Nos. 339-341, C197-C200.

Soccer Game, Winner Italy, in France, 1938 — A107

World Cup, Game and Flags: 25fr, Uruguay, in Brazil, 1950. 50fr, East Germany, in Switzerland, 1954.

1974, Sept. 2 Litho. ***Perf. 13½***

335 A107 10fr multicolored .25 .25
336 A107 25fr multicolored .25 .25
337 A107 50fr multicolored .45 .25
Nos. 335-337,C193-C195 (6) 6.20 3.50

World Cup Soccer winners.

Map and Farm Woman — A108

1974, Oct. 2 Litho. ***Perf. 13x12½***

338 A108 35fr yellow & multi .75 .50

Kou Valley Development.

Nos. 332-334 Overprinted in Red

1974, Oct. 9

339 A106 35fr multicolored .55 .25
340 A106 40fr multicolored .80 .35
341 A106 85fr multicolored .90 .50
Nos. 339-341,C197-C199 (6) 9.75 4.50

Universal Postal Union centenary.

Flowers, by Pierre Bonnard A109

Flower Paintings by: 10fr, Jan Brueghel. 30fr, Jean van Os. 50fr, Van Brussel.

1974, Oct. 31 Litho. ***Perf. 12½x13***

342 A109 5fr multicolored .25 .25
343 A109 10fr multicolored .25 .25
344 A109 30fr multicolored .25 .25
345 A109 50fr multicolored .45 .25
Nos. 342-345,C201 (5) 4.70 2.10

Churchill as Officer of India Hussars — A110

Churchill: 75fr, As Secretary of State for Interior. 100fr, As pilot. 125fr, meeting with Roosevelt, 1941. 300fr, As painter. 450fr, and "HMS Resolution."

1975, Jan. 11 ***Perf. 13½***

346 A110 50fr multicolored .50 .25
347 A110 75fr multicolored .60 .25
348 A110 100fr multicolored .90 .35
349 A110 125fr multicolored 1.00 .45
350 A110 300fr multicolored 2.75 1.25
Nos. 346-350 (5) 5.75 2.55

Souvenir Sheet

351 A110 450fr multicolored 4.75 1.75

Sir Winston Churchill, birth centenary.

US No. 619 and Minutemen — A111

US Stamps: 40fr, #118 and Proclamation of Independence. 75fr, #798 and Signing the Constitution. 100fr, #703 and Surrender at Yorktown. 200fr, #1003 and George Washington. 300fr, #644 and Surrender of Burgoyne at Saratoga. 500fr, #63, 68, 73, 157, 179, 228 and 1483a.

1975, Feb. 17 Litho. ***Perf. 11***

352 A111 35fr multicolored .45 .25
353 A111 40fr multicolored .45 .25
354 A111 75fr multicolored .80 .25
355 A111 100fr multicolored 1.00 .35
356 A111 200fr multicolored 2.00 .60
357 A111 300fr multicolored 3.00 .95
Nos. 352-357 (6) 7.70 2.65

Souvenir Sheet

Imperf

358 A111 500fr multicolored 7.50 2.25

American Bicentennial.

"Atlantic" No. 2670, 1904-12 — A112

Locomotives from Mulhouse, France, Railroad Museum: 25fr, No. 2029, 1882. 50fr, No. 2129, 1882.

1975, Feb. 28 Litho. *Perf. 13x12½*

359 A112 15fr multicolored .50 .25
360 A112 25fr multicolored .80 .25
361 A112 50fr multicolored 1.40 .25
Nos. 359-361,C203-C204 (5) 6.95 1.75

French Flag and Renault Petit Duc, 1910 — A113

Flags and Old Cars: 30fr, US and Ford Model T, 1909. 35fr, Italy and Alfa Romeo "Le Mans," 1931.

1975, Apr. 6 *Perf. 14x13½*

362 A113 10fr multicolored .25 .25
363 A113 30fr multicolored .45 .25
364 A113 35fr multicolored .50 .25
Nos. 362-364,C206-C207 (5) 5.20 1.95

Washington and Lafayette — A114

American Bicentennial: 40fr, Washington reviewing troops at Valley Forge. 50fr, Washington taking oath of office.

1975, May 6 Litho. *Perf. 14*

365 A114 30fr multicolored .25 .25
366 A114 40fr multicolored .45 .25
367 A114 50fr multicolored .70 .25
Nos. 365-367,C209-C210 (5) 7.15 4.15

Souvenir Sheet

367A A114 500fr multicolored 5.25 2.25

Schweitzer and Pelicans — A115

15fr, Albert Schweitzer and bateleur eagle.

1975, May 25 Litho. *Perf. 13½*

368 A115 5fr multicolored .30 .25
369 A115 15fr multicolored .90 .25
Nos. 368-369,C212-C214 (5) 7.45 2.85

Albert Schweitzer, birth centenary.

Apollo and Soyuz Orbiting Earth — A116

Design: 50fr, Apollo and Soyuz near link-up.

1975, July 18

370 A116 40fr multicolored .45 .25
371 A116 50fr multicolored .60 .25
Nos. 370-371,C216-C218 (5) 6.70 2.65

Apollo-Soyuz space test project, Russo-American cooperation, launched July 15, link-up July 17.

Maria Picasso Lopez, Artist's Mother A117

Paintings by Pablo Picasso (1881-1973): 60fr, Self-portrait. 90fr, First Communion.

1975, Aug. 7

372 A117 50fr multicolored .45 .25
373 A117 60fr multicolored .60 .25
374 A117 90fr multicolored 1.10 .25
Nos. 372-374,C220-C221 (5) 8.90 2.60

Expo '75 Emblem and Tanker, Idemitsu Maru — A118

Oceanographic Exposition, Okinawa: 25fr, Training ship, Kaio Maru. 45fr, Firefighting ship, Hiryu. 50fr, Battleship, Yamato. 60fr, Container ship, Kamakura Maru.

1975, Sept. 26 Litho. *Perf. 11*

375 A118 15fr multicolored .25 .25
376 A118 25fr multicolored .45 .25
377 A118 45fr multicolored .60 .25
377A A118 50fr multicolored .90 .45
378 A118 60fr multicolored 1.00 .45
Nos. 375-378,C223 (6) 5.70 2.55

Woman, Globe and IWY Emblem — A119

1975, Nov. 20 Photo. *Perf. 13*

379 A119 65fr multicolored .90 .60

International Women's Year.

Msgr. Joanny Thevenoud and Cathedral — A120

65fr, Father Guillaume Templier & Cathedral.

1975, Nov. 20 Engr. *Perf. 13x12½*

380 A120 55fr grn, blk & dl red .90 .45
381 A120 65fr blk, org & dl red 1.00 .60

75th anniv. of the Evangelization of Upper Volta.

Farmer's Hat, Hoe and Emblem A121

1975, Dec. 10 Photo. *Perf. 13x13½*

382 A121 15fr buff & multi .25 .25
383 A121 50fr lt green & multi .80 .45

Development of the Volta valleys.

Sledding and Olympic Emblem — A122

Innsbruck Background, Olympic Emblem and: 45fr, Figure skating. 85fr, Skiing.

1975, Dec. 16 Litho. *Perf. 13½*

384 A122 35fr multicolored .45 .25
385 A122 45fr multicolored .60 .25
386 A122 85fr multicolored .90 .45
Nos. 384-386,C225-C226 (5) 4.80 2.10

12th Winter Olympic Games, Innsbruck, Austria, Feb. 4-15, 1976.

Gymnast and Olympic Emblem — A123

1976, Mar. 17

387 A123 40fr Gymnastics .45 .25
388 A123 50fr Sailing .60 .25
389 A123 100fr Soccer 1.10 .45
Nos. 387-389,C228-C229 (5) 4.85 1.85

21st Olympic Games, Montreal, Canada, July 17-Aug. 1.

Olympic Emblem and Sprinters A124

Olympic Emblem and: 55fr, Equestrian. 75fr, Hurdles.

1976, Mar. 25 Litho. *Perf. 11*

390 A124 30fr multicolored .35 .25
391 A124 55fr multicolored .60 .25
392 A124 75fr multicolored .80 .25
Nos. 390-392,C231-C232 (5) 4.90 1.80

21st Olympic Games, Montreal.

For overprints see nos. 420-422, C245-C247.

Blind Woman and Man — A125

1976, Apr. 7 Engr. *Perf. 13*

393 A125 75fr dk brn, grn & org 1.00 .45
394 A125 250fr dk brn, ocher & org 2.75 1.50

Drive against onchocerciasis, roundworm infestation.

"Deutschland" over Friedrichshafen — A126

Airships: 40fr, "Victoria Louise" over sailing ships. 50fr, "Sachsen" over German countryside.

1976, May 11 Litho. *Perf. 11*

395 A126 10fr multicolored .25 .25
396 A126 40fr multicolored .45 .25
397 A126 50fr multicolored .80 .35
Nos. 395-397,C234-C236 (6) 8.00 3.05

75th anniversary of the Zeppelin.

Viking Lander and Probe on Mars — A127

Viking Mars project: 55fr, Viking orbiter in flight. 75fr, Titan rocket start for Mars, vert.

1976, June 24 *Perf. 13½*

398 A127 30fr multicolored .25 .25
399 A127 55fr multicolored .55 .25
400 A127 75fr multicolored .90 .25
Nos. 398-400,C238-C239 (5) 6.85 2.15

World Map, Arms of Upper Volta A128

Design: 100fr, World map, arms and dove.

1976, Aug. 19 Litho. *Perf. 12½*

401 A128 55fr brown & multi .55 .25
402 A128 100fr blue & multi 1.25 .60

5th Summit Conference of Non-aligned Countries, Colombo, Sri Lanka, Aug. 9-19.

Bicentennial, Interphil 76 Emblems and Washington at Battle of Trenton — A129

90fr, Bicentennial, Interphil 76 emblems, Seat of Government, Pennsylvania.

1976, Sept. 30 *Perf. 13½*

403 A129 60fr multicolored	.70	.25
404 A129 90fr multicolored	1.10	.25
Nos. 403-404,C241-C243 (5)	7.55	2.50

American Bicentennial, Interphil 76, Philadelphia, Pa., May 29-June 6.

UPU and UN Emblems — A130

1976, Dec. 8 **Engr.** *Perf. 13*

405 A130 200fr red, olive & blue 2.25 1.25

UN Postal Administration, 25th anniv.

Arms of Tenkodogo A131

Coats of Arms: 20fr, 100fr, Ouagadougou.

1977, May 2 **Litho.** *Perf. 13*

406 A131 10fr multicolored	.25	.25
407 A131 20fr multicolored	.25	.25
408 A131 65fr multicolored	.70	.25
409 A131 100fr multicolored	.90	.45
Nos. 406-409 (4)	2.10	1.20

Bronze Statuette — A132

Design: 65fr, Woman with bowl, bronze.

1977, June 13 **Photo.** *Perf. 13*

410 A132 55fr multicolored	.60	.25
411 A132 65fr multicolored	1.00	.35

Nos. 410-411 issued in sheets and coils with black control number on every 5th stamp.

Granaries A133

1977, June 20 **Photo.** *Perf. 13½x13*

412 A133 5fr Samo	.25	.25
413 A133 35fr Boromo	.35	.25
414 A133 45fr Banfora	.55	.25
415 A133 55fr Mossi	.75	.25
Nos. 412-415 (4)	1.90	1.00

Handbags A134

1977, June 20

416 A134 30fr Gouin	.35	.25
417 A134 40fr Bissa	.35	.25
418 A134 60fr Lobi	.60	.25
419 A134 70fr Mossi	.60	.35
Nos. 416-419 (4)	1.90	1.10

Nos. 390-392 Overprinted in Gold

(a)

(b)

(c)

1977, July 4 **Litho.** *Perf. 11*

420 A124 (a) 30fr multicolored	.45	.25
421 A124 (b) 55fr multicolored	.55	.45
422 A124 (c) 75fr multicolored	.70	.60
Nos. 420-422,C245-C246 (5)	4.70	3.00

Winners, 21st Olympic Games.

Crinum Ornatum — A135

Haemanthus Multiflorus A136

Hannoa Undulata A137

Designs: Flowers, flowering branches and wild fruits. 175fr, 300fr, horiz.

1977 **Litho.** *Perf. 12½*

423 A137 2fr Cordia myxa	.25	.25
424 A137 3fr Opilia celtidifolia	.35	.25
425 A135 15fr Crinum ornatum	.55	.25
426 A136 25fr Haemanthus multiflorus	.60	.25
427 A137 50fr Hannoa undulata	.90	.45
428 A135 90fr Cochlospermum planchonii	1.40	.55
429 A135 125fr Clitoria ternatea	2.25	.60
430 A136 150fr Cassia alata	2.00	1.25
431 A136 175fr Nauclea latifolia	2.25	1.40
432 A136 300fr Bombax costatum	3.50	1.75
433 A135 400fr Eulophia cucullata	5.25	2.00
Nos. 423-433 (11)	19.30	9.00

Issued: 25fr, 150fr, 175fr, 300fr, 8/1; 2fr, 3fr, 50fr, 8/8; 15fr, 90fr, 125fr, 400fr, 8/23.

De Gaulle and Cross of Lorraine A138

Designs: 200fr, King Baudouin of Belgium.

1977, Aug. 16 *Perf. 13½x14*

434 A138 100fr multicolored	3.00	.65
435 A138 200fr multicolored	2.25	.65

Elizabeth II A139

Designs: 300fr, Elizabeth II taking salute. 500fr, Elizabeth II after Coronation.

1977, Aug. 16

436 A139 200fr multicolored	2.25	.65
437 A139 300fr multicolored	3.00	.90

Souvenir Sheet

438 A139 500fr multicolored 5.00 2.00

25th anniv. of reign of Queen Elizabeth II. For overprints see Nos. 478-480.

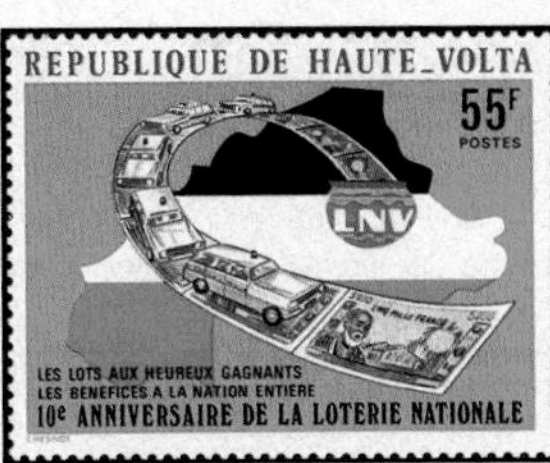

Lottery Tickets, Cars and Map of Upper Volta in Flag Colors — A140

1977, Sept. 16 **Photo.** *Perf. 13*

439 A140 55fr multicolored .70 .50

10th anniversary of National Lottery.

Selma Lagerlof, Literature — A141

Nobel Prize Winners: 65fr, Guglielmo Marconi, physics. 125fr, Bertrand Russell, literature. 200fr, Linus C. Pauling, chemistry. 300fr, Robert Koch, medicine. 500fr, Albert Schweitzer, peace.

1977, Sept. 22 **Litho.** *Perf. 13½*

440 A141 55fr multicolored	.90	.25
441 A141 65fr multicolored	.55	.25
442 A141 125fr multicolored	1.10	.35
443 A141 200fr multicolored	2.00	.65
444 A141 300fr multicolored	3.50	.95
Nos. 440-444 (5)	8.05	2.45

Souvenir Sheet

445 A141 500fr multicolored 6.00 1.90

The Three Graces, by Rubens A142

Paintings by Peter Paul Rubens (1577-1640): 55fr, Heads of Black Men, horiz. 85fr, Bathsheba at the Fountain. 150fr, The Drunken Silenus. 200fr, 300fr, Life of Maria de Medicis, diff.

1977, Oct. 19 **Litho.** *Perf. 14*

446 A142 55fr multicolored	.55	.25
447 A142 65fr multicolored	.65	.25
448 A142 85fr multicolored	.80	.25
449 A142 150fr multicolored	1.40	.55
450 A142 200fr multicolored	2.25	.70
451 A142 300fr multicolored	3.25	1.00
Nos. 446-451 (6)	8.90	3.00

Lenin in His Office A143

85fr, Lenin Monument, Kremlin. 200fr, Lenin with youth. 500fr, Lenin & Leonid Brezhnev.

1977, Oct. 28 Litho. *Perf. 12*

452 A143 10fr multicolored .45 .25
453 A143 85fr multicolored 1.40 .45
454 A143 200fr multicolored 2.75 1.10
455 A143 500fr multicolored 6.25 2.90
Nos. 452-455 (4) 10.85 4.70

Russian October Revolution, 60th anniv.

Stadium and Brazil No. C79 — A144

Stadium and: 65fr, Brazil #1144. 125fr, Gt. Britain #458. 200fr, Chile #340. 300fr, Switzerland #350. 500fr, Germany #1147.

1977, Dec. 30 Litho. *Perf. 13½*

456 A144 55fr multicolored .40 .25
457 A144 65fr multicolored .50 .25
458 A144 125fr multicolored 1.00 .35
459 A144 200fr multicolored 1.75 .50
460 A144 300fr multicolored 2.60 .85
Nos. 456-460 (5) 6.25 2.20

Souvenir Sheet

461 A144 500fr multicolored 5.00 1.90

11th World Cup Soccer Championship, Argentina.
For overprints see Nos. 486-491.

Jean Mermoz and Seaplane — A145

History of Aviation: 75fr, Anthony H. G. Fokker. 85fr, Wiley Post. 90fr, Otto Lilienthal, vert. 100fr, Concorde. 500fr, Charles Lindbergh and "Spirit of St. Louis."

1978, Jan. 2 Litho. *Perf. 13½*

462 A145 65fr multicolored .65 .25
463 A145 75fr multicolored .70 .25
464 A145 85fr multicolored .90 .25
465 A145 90fr multicolored 1.10 .25
466 A145 100fr multicolored 1.25 .50
Nos. 462-466 (5) 4.60 1.50

Souvenir Sheet

467 A145 500fr multicolored 5.25 1.90

Crataeva Religiosa — A146

1978, Feb. 28 Litho. *Perf. 12½*

468 A146 55fr Spider tree .70 .40
469 A146 75fr Fig tree .90 .60

Souvenir Sheet

Virgin and Child, by Rubens — A147

1978, May 24 Litho. *Perf. 13½x14*

470 A147 500fr multicolored 5.25 1.90

Peter Paul Rubens (1577-1640).

Antenna and ITU Emblem A148

1978, May 30 *Perf. 13*

471 A148 65fr silver & multi .70 .50

10th World Telecommunications Day.

Fetish Gate of Bobo — A149

1978, July 10 Litho. *Perf. 13½*

472 A149 55fr Bobo fetish .70 .35
473 A149 65fr Mossi fetish .90 .50

Capt. Cook and "Endeavour" — A150

Capt. James Cook (1728-1779) and: 85fr, Death on Hawaiian beach. 250fr, Navigational instruments. 350fr, "Resolution."

1978, Sept. 1 Litho. *Perf. 14½*

474 A150 65fr multicolored .70 .25
475 A150 85fr multicolored .90 .25
476 A150 250fr multicolored 2.40 .70
477 A150 350fr multicolored 3.25 1.00
Nos. 474-477 (4) 7.25 2.20

Nos. 436-438 Overprinted in Silver

1978, Oct. 24 Litho. *Perf. 13½x14*

478 A139 200fr multicolored 1.75 1.10
479 A139 300fr multicolored 2.50 1.75

Souvenir Sheet

480 A139 500fr multicolored 4.75 4.25

25th anniversary of Coronation of Queen Elizabeth II. Overprint in 3 lines on 200fr, in 2 lines on 300fr and 500fr.
Nos. 478-480 exist with overprint in metallic red.

Trent Castle, by Dürer — A151

Paintings by Albrecht Durer (1471-1528): 150fr, Virgin and Child with St. Anne, vert. 250fr, Sts. George and Eustachius, vert. 350fr, Hans Holzschuher, vert.

Perf. 14x13½, 13½x14

1978, Nov. 20 Litho.

481 A151 65fr multicolored .70 .25
482 A151 150fr multicolored 1.40 .45
483 A151 250fr multicolored 2.50 .90
484 A151 350fr multicolored 3.50 1.25
Nos. 481-484 (4) 8.10 2.85

Human Rights Emblem A152

1978, Dec. 10 Litho. *Perf. 12½*

485 A152 55fr multicolored 1.00 .60

Universal Declaration of Human Rights, 30th anniv.

Nos. 456-461 Overprinted in Silver

(a)

(b)

(c)

(d)

(e)

(f)

1979, Jan. 4 Litho. *Perf. 13½*

486 A144(a) 55fr multicolored .50 .35
487 A144(b) 65fr multicolored .60 .45
488 A144(c) 125fr multicolored 1.25 .70
489 A144(d) 200fr multicolored 1.75 .95
490 A144(e) 300fr multicolored 2.50 1.50
Nos. 486-490 (5) 6.60 3.95

Souvenir Sheet

491 A144(f) 500fr multicolored 4.75 4.25

Winners, World Soccer Cup Championships 1950-1978.

Radio Station A153

Design: 65fr, Mail plane at airport.

1979, Mar. 30 Litho. *Perf. 12½*

492 A153 55fr multicolored .50 .25
493 A153 65fr multicolored .70 .45

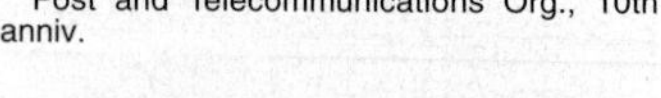

Post and Telecommunications Org., 10th anniv.

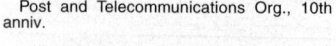

Teacher and Pupils, IYC Emblem — A154

1979, Apr. 9 *Perf. 13½*

494 A154 75fr multicolored 1.00 .60

International Year of the Child.

Telecommunications — A155

1979, May 17 Litho. *Perf. 13*
495 A155 70fr multicolored .70 .45

11th Telecommunications Day.

Basketmaker and Upper Volta No. 111 — A156

Design: No. 497, Map of Upper Volta, Concorde, truck and UPU emblem.

1979, June 8 Photo.
496 A156 100fr multicolored 3.50 2.40
497 A156 100fr multicolored 3.50 2.40

Philexafrique II, Libreville, Gabon, June 8-17. Nos. 496, 497 each printed in sheets of 10 and 5 labels showing exhibition emblem.

Synodontis Voltae A157

Fresh-water Fish: 50fr, Micralestes comoensis. 85fr, Silurus.

1979, June 10 Litho. *Perf. 12½*
498 A157 20fr multicolored .75 .25
499 A157 50fr multicolored 1.50 .25
500 A157 85fr multicolored 2.00 .60
Nos. 498-500 (3) 4.25 1.10

Rowland Hill, Train and Upper Volta No. 60 — A158

Sir Rowland Hill (1795-1879), originator of penny postage, Trains and Upper Volta Stamps: 165fr, #59. 200fr, #57. 300fr, #56. 500fr, #55.

1979, June Litho. *Perf. 13½*
501 A158 65fr multicolored .70 .25
502 A158 165fr multicolored 1.75 .55
503 A158 200fr multicolored 2.00 .65
504 A158 300fr multicolored 3.50 1.00
Nos. 501-504 (4) 7.95 2.45

Souvenir Sheet

505 A158 500fr multicolored 5.25 1.90

Wildlife Fund Emblem and Protected Animals — A159

1979, Aug. 30 Litho. *Perf. 14½*
506 A159 30fr Waterbuck 1.40 .25
507 A159 40fr Roan antelope 2.00 .25
508 A159 60fr Caracal 2.75 .30
509 A159 100fr African bush elephant 3.75 .80
510 A159 175fr Hartebeest 6.00 1.00
511 A159 250fr Leopard 14.00 1.25
Nos. 506-511 (6) 29.90 3.85

Adult Students and Teacher — A160

Design: 55fr, Man reading book, vert.

1979, Sept. 8 *Perf. 12½x13, 13x12½*
512 A160 55fr multicolored .50 .45
513 A160 250fr multicolored 2.50 1.50

World Literacy Day.

Map of Upper Volta, Telephone Receiver and Lines, Telecom Emblem — A161

1979, Sept. 20 *Perf. 13x12½*
514 A161 200fr multicolored 1.90 .95

3rd World Telecommunications Exhibition, Geneva, Sept. 20-26.

King Vulture — A162

1979, Oct. 26 Litho. *Perf. 13*
515 A162 5fr King vulture 1.00 .25
516 A162 10fr Hoopoe 1.00 .25
517 A162 15fr Bald vulture 1.10 .25
518 A162 25fr Egrets 1.75 .35
519 A162 35fr Ostrich 2.60 .45
520 A162 45fr Crowned crane 3.25 .55
521 A162 125fr Eagle 7.25 1.90
Nos. 515-521 (7) 17.95 4.00

Control Tower, Emblem, Jet — A163

1979, Dec. 12 Photo. *Perf. 13x12½*
522 A163 65fr multicolored .90 .60

ASECNA (Air Safety Board), 20th anniv.

Central Bank of West African States — A164

1979, Dec. 28 Litho. *Perf. 12½*
523 A164 55fr multicolored .70 .45

Eugene Jamot, Map of Upper Volta, Tsetse Fly — A165

1979, Dec. 28 *Perf. 13x13½*
524 A165 55fr multicolored 2.25 .80

Eugene Jamot (1879-1937), discoverer of sleeping sickness cure.

UPU Emblem, Upper Volta Type D4 under Magnifier A166

1980, Feb. 26 Litho. *Perf. 12½x13*
525 A166 55fr multicolored .80 .35

Stamp Day.

World Locomotive Speed Record, 25th Anniversary A167

1980, Mar. 30 Litho. *Perf. 12½*
526 A167 75fr multicolored 2.00 .60
527 A167 100fr multicolored 2.75 1.25

Pres. Sangoule Lamizana, Pope John Paul II, Cardinal Pau Zoungrana, Map of Upper Volta — A168

1980, May 10 Litho. *Perf. 12½*
528 A168 65fr multicolored 2.50 .60

Size: 21x36mm

529 A168 100fr Pope John Paul II 3.25 1.50

Visit of Pope John Paul II to Upper Volta.

A169

A170

1980, May 17 *Perf. 13x12½*
530 A169 50fr multicolored .60 .35

12th World Telecommunications Day.

1980, June 12 Litho. *Perf. 13*
531 A170 65fr Sun and earth .60 .35
532 A170 100fr Solar energy 1.00 .45

Downhill Skiing, Lake Placid '80 Emblem — A171

1980, June 26 *Perf. 14½*
533 A171 65fr Downhill skiing .50 .25
534 A171 100fr Women's downhill 1.00 .30
535 A171 200fr Figure skating 2.00 .50
536 A171 350fr Slalom, vert. 3.25 1.00
Nos. 533-536 (4) 6.75 2.05

Souvenir Sheet

537 A171 500fr Speed skating 5.25 1.90

12th Winter Olympic Game Winners, Lake Placid, NY, Feb. 12-24.

Europafrica Issue

Map of Europe and Africa, Jet — A172

1980, July 14 Litho. *Perf. 13*
538 A172 100fr multicolored 1.20 .60

Hand Holding Back Sand Dune — A173

Operation Green Sahel: 55fr, Hands holding seedlings.

1980, July 18
539 A173 50fr multicolored .60 .25
540 A173 55fr multicolored .80 .45

Gourmantche Chief Initiation — A174

1980, Sept. 12 **Litho.** ***Perf. 14***

541 A174 30fr Gourmantche chief initiation .50 .25
542 A174 55fr Moro Naba, Mossi Emperor .70 .30
543 A174 65fr Princess Guimbe Quattara, vert. 1.00 .30
Nos. 541-543 (3) 2.20 .85

A175

Gourounsi mask, conference emblem.

1980, Oct. 6 ***Perf. 13½x13***

544 A175 65fr multicolored .80 .45

World Tourism Conf., Manila, Sept. 27.

A176

1980, Nov. 5 **Litho.** ***Perf. 12½***

545 A176 55fr Agriculture .40 .25
546 A176 65fr Transportation .50 .35
547 A176 75fr Dam, highway .60 .35
548 A176 100fr Industry 1.00 .50
Nos. 545-548 (4) 2.50 1.45

West African Economic Council, 5th anniv.

20th Anniv. of Independence — A177

1980, Dec. 11 ***Perf. 13***

549 A177 500fr multicolored 5.25 3.00

Madonna and Child, by Raphael — A178

Christmas: Paintings of Madonna and Child, by Raphael.

1980, Dec. 22 ***Perf. 12½***

550 A178 60fr multicolored .50 .25
551 A178 150fr multicolored 1.40 .50
552 A178 250fr multicolored 2.25 .80
Nos. 550-552 (3) 4.15 1.55

West African Postal Union, 5th Anniv. — A179

1980, Dec. 24 **Photo.** ***Perf. 13½***

553 A179 55fr multicolored .75 .45

Dung Beetle A180

Perf. 13x13½, 13½x13

1981, Mar. 10 **Litho.**

554 A180 5fr Dung beetle .60 .25
555 A180 10fr Crickets .60 .25
556 A180 15fr Termites 1.25 .25
557 A180 20fr Praying mantis, vert. 2.25 .25
558 A180 55fr Emperor moth 4.00 .45
559 A180 65fr Locust, vert. 4.50 .60
Nos. 554-559 (6) 13.20 2.05

Antelope Mask, Kouroumba A181

Designs: Various ceremonial masks.

1981, Mar. 20 **Litho.** ***Perf. 13***

560 A181 45fr multicolored .60 .25
561 A181 55fr multicolored .70 .35
562 A181 85fr multicolored 1.00 .50
563 A181 105fr multicolored 1.25 .60
Nos. 560-563 (4) 3.55 1.70

Notre Dame of Kologh' Naba College, 25th Anniv. A182

1981, Mar. 30

564 A182 55fr multicolored .60 .25

Heinrich von Stephan, UPU Founder, Birth Sesquicentennial — A183

1981, May 4 **Litho.** ***Perf. 13***

565 A183 65fr multicolored .75 .45

13th World Telecommunications Day — A184

1981, May 17 ***Perf. 13½x13***

566 A184 90fr multicolored .80 .50

Diesel Train, Abidjan-Niger Railroad — A185

Designs: Trains.

1981, July 6 **Litho.** ***Perf. 13***

567 A185 25fr Diesel train .40 .25
568 A185 30fr Gazelle .70 .25
569 A185 40fr Belier .80 .35
Nos. 567-569 (3) 1.90 .85

Tree Planting Month A186

1981, July 15

570 A186 70fr multicolored 1.10 .50

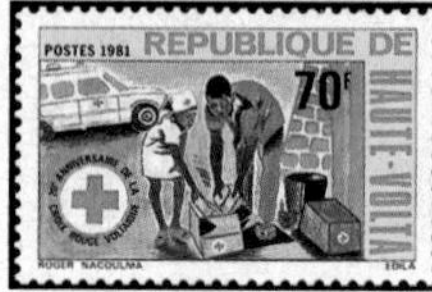

Natl. Red Cross, 20th Anniv. A187

1981, July 31 ***Perf. 12½x13***

571 A187 70fr multicolored 1.00 .50

Intl. Year of the Disabled — A188

1981, Aug. 20 **Litho.** ***Perf. 13x12½***

572 A188 70fr multicolored 1.00 .45

View of Koudougou A189

1981, Sept. 3 **Litho.** ***Perf. 12½***

573 A189 35fr Koudougou .40 .25
574 A189 45fr Toma .50 .25
575 A189 85fr Volta Noire 1.00 .30
Nos. 573-575 (3) 1.90 .80

World Food Day — A190

1981, Oct. 16 ***Perf. 13***

576 A190 90fr multicolored 1.10 .70

Elephant A191

Designs: Various protected species.

1981, Oct. 21 **Photo.** ***Perf. 14***

577 A191 5fr multicolored .60 .25
578 A191 15fr multicolored .90 .25
579 A191 40fr multicolored 1.50 .35
580 A191 60fr multicolored 3.00 .60
581 A191 70fr multicolored 3.25 .95
Nos. 577-581 (5) 9.25 2.40

Fight Against Apartheid — A192

1981, Dec. 9 **Litho.** ***Perf. 12½***

582 A192 90fr red orange 1.00 .50

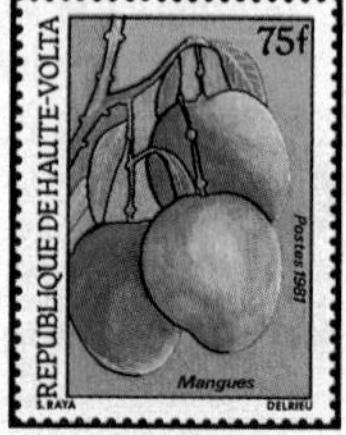

Mangoes — A193

1981, Dec. 15 ***Perf. 13x13½, 13½x13***

583 A193 20fr Papayas, horiz. .60 .25
584 A193 35fr Fruits, vegetables, horiz. .55 .25
585 A193 75fr Mangoes, vert. .90 .50
586 A193 90fr Melons, horiz. 1.00 .70
Nos. 583-586 (4) 3.05 1.70

Guinea Hen — A194

West African Rice Development Assoc., 10th Anniv. — A195

Designs: Breeding animals. 10fr, 25fr, 70fr, 250fr, 300fr horiz.

1981, Dec. 22 ***Perf. 13***

587 A194 10fr Donkey .35 .25
588 A194 25fr Pig .55 .25
589 A194 70fr Cow 1.00 .25
590 A194 90fr Guinea hen 1.10 .45
591 A194 250fr Rabbit 3.00 1.10
Nos. 587-591 (5) 6.00 2.30

Souvenir Sheet

592 A194 300fr Sheep 5.25 4.75

1981, Dec. 29

593 A195 90fr multicolored 1.10 .50

20th Anniv. of World Food Program — A196

1982, Jan. 18

594 A196 50fr multicolored .60 .25

Traditional Houses — A197

1982, Apr. 23 Litho. *Perf. 12½*

595 A197 30fr Morhonaba Palace, vert. .25 .25
596 A197 70fr Bobo .70 .25
597 A197 100fr Gourounsi 1.10 .35
598 A197 200fr Peulh 2.00 .80
599 A197 250fr Dagari 2.50 .90
Nos. 595-599 (5) 6.55 2.55

14th World Telecommunications Day — A198

1982, May 17

600 A198 125fr multicolored 1.20 .60

Water Lily — A199

1982, Sept. 22 *Perf. 13x12½*

601 A199 25fr Water lily .35 .25
602 A199 40fr Kapoks .60 .25
603 A199 70fr Frangipani .90 .25
604 A199 90fr Cochlospermum planchonii 1.25 .45
605 A199 100fr Cotton 1.25 .45
Nos. 601-605 (5) 4.35 1.65

African Postal Union A200

1982, Oct. 7

606 A200 70fr multicolored .60 .25
607 A200 90fr multicolored 1.00 .50

25th Anniv. of Cultural Aid Fund — A201

1982, Nov. 10 *Perf. 12½x13*

608 A201 70fr multicolored .80 .45

Map, Hand Holding Grain, Steer Head A202

1982 *Perf. 12½*

609 A202 90fr multicolored .95 .45

Traditional Hairstyle A203

1983, Jan. Litho. *Perf. 12½*

610 A203 90fr lt green & multi .90 .35
611 A203 120fr lt blue & multi 1.25 .45
612 A203 170fr pink & multi 1.90 .70
Nos. 610-612 (3) 4.05 1.50

For overprints see Nos. 884-886.

8th Film Festival, Ouagadougou — A204

1983, Feb. 10 Litho. *Perf. 13x12½*

613 A204 90fr Scene 1.40 .80
614 A204 500fr Filmmaker Dumarou Ganda 7.00 3.50

UN Intl. Drinking Water and Sanitation Decade, 1981-90 — A205

1983, Apr. 21 Litho. *Perf. 13½x13*

615 A205 60fr Water drops .50 .25
616 A205 70fr Carrying water 1.00 .50

Manned Flight Bicentenary A206

Portraits and Balloons: 15fr, J.M. Montgolfier, 1783. 25fr, Etienne Montgolfier's balloon, 1783, Pilatre de Rozier. 70fr, Charles & Roberts flight, 1783, Jacques Charles. 90fr, Flight over English Channel, John Jeffries. 100fr, Testu-Brissy's horseback flight, Wilhemine Reichardt. 250fr, Andree's Spitzbergen flight, 1897, S.A. Andree. 300fr, Piccard's stratosphere flight, 1931, August Piccard.

No. 623A, J. M. and J. E. Montgolfier, balloon, horiz. No. 623B, John Wise, balloon.

1983, Apr. 15 Litho. *Perf. 13½*

617 A206 15fr multicolored .25 .25
618 A206 25fr multicolored .25 .25
619 A206 70fr multicolored .70 .25
620 A206 90fr multicolored .90 .30
621 A206 100fr multicolored 1.10 .35
622 A206 250fr multicolored 2.50 .80
Nos. 617-622 (6) 5.70 2.20

Souvenir Sheet

623 A206 300fr multicolored 3.50 1.25

Size: 57x39mm

623A A206 1500fr gold & multi — —

Souvenir Sheet

623B A206 1500fr gold & multi — —

No. 623 contains one stamp 38x47mm. Nos. 621-623 airmail.

No. 623B contains one 39x57mm stamp. Nos. 623A-623B are airmail.

World Communications Year — A207

1983, May 26 Litho. *Perf. 12½*

624 A207 30fr Man reading letter .25 .25
625 A207 35fr Like No. 624 .50 .25
626 A207 45fr Aircraft over stream .70 .25
627 A207 90fr Girl on telephone .90 .40
Nos. 624-627 (4) 2.35 1.15

Fishing Resources A208

1983, July 28 Litho. *Perf. 13*

628 A208 20fr Synadontis gambiensis .60 .25
629 A208 30fr Palmotochromis .80 .25
630 A208 40fr Boy fishing, vert. 1.00 .35
631 A208 50fr Fishing with net 1.10 .35
632 A208 75fr Fishing with basket 1.75 .45
Nos. 628-632 (5) 5.25 1.65

Anti-deforestation — A209

1983, Sept. 13 Litho. *Perf. 13*

633 A209 10fr Planting saplings .25 .25
634 A209 50fr Tree nursery .50 .25
635 A209 100fr Prevent forest fires 1.10 .25
636 A209 150fr Woman cooking 2.00 .60
637 A209 200fr Prevent felling, vert. 2.25 .90
Nos. 633-637 (5) 6.10 2.25

Fresco Detail, by Raphael — A210

Paintings: 120fr, Self-portrait, by Pablo Picasso, 1901, vert. 185fr, Self-portrait at the palette, by Manet, 1878, vert. 350fr, Fresco Detail, diff., by Raphael. 500fr, Goethe, by George Oswald May, 1779, vert.

1983, Nov. Litho. *Perf. 13*

638 A210 120fr multicolored 1.75 .45
639 A210 185fr multicolored 1.75 .60
640 A210 300fr multicolored 3.00 .80
641 A210 350fr multicolored 3.50 1.00
642 A210 500fr multicolored 4.50 1.50
Nos. 638-642 (5) 14.50 4.35

25th Anniv. of the Republic A211

1983, Dec. 9 Litho. *Perf. 14*

643 A211 90fr Arms .70 .25
644 A211 500fr Family, flag 4.50 1.75

A212

1984, May 29 Litho. *Perf. 12½*

645 A212 90fr multicolored .80 .30
646 A212 100fr multicolored .90 .40

Council of Unity, 25th anniv.

Scouting — A213

1984, June 15 Litho. *Perf. 13½*

647 A213 25fr Polystictus leoninus 3.00 .30
648 A213 185fr Pterocarpus Lucens 4.00 .60
649 A213 200fr Phlebopus colossus sudanicus 5.00 .70
650 A213 250fr Cosmos sulphureus 6.00 .75
651 A213 300fr Trametes versicolor 6.50 1.00
652 A213 400fr Ganoderma lucidum 7.50 1.50
Nos. 647-652 (6) 32.00 4.85

Souvenir Sheet

653 A213 600fr Leucocoprinus cepaestipes 6.25 2.25

Nos. 651-653 are airmail. For overprints see Nos. 669-674.

Wildlife A214

Wildlife — A215

1984, July 19

654 A214 15fr Cheetah, four cubs 1.50 .50
655 A214 35fr Two adults 2.50 .75

656 A214 90fr One adult 2.75 1.00
657 A214 120fr Cheetah, two cubs 3.00 1.25
658 A214 300fr Baboons 3.50 1.10
659 A214 400fr Vultures 3.50 1.25
Nos. 654-659 (6) 16.75 5.85

Souvenir Sheet

660 A215 1000fr Antelopes 10.00 2.00

World Wildlife Fund (Nos. 654-657); Rotary Intl. (Nos. 658, 660); Natl. Boy Scouts (No. 659). Nos. 658-660 are airmail.

Sailing Ships and Locomotives — A216

1984, Aug. 14 *Perf. 12½*

661 A216 20fr Maiden Queen .25 .25
662 A216 40fr CC 2400 ch .45 .25
663 A216 60fr Scawfell .70 .25
664 A216 100fr PO 1806 1.00 .25
665 A216 120fr Harbinger 1.25 .45
666 A216 145fr Livingstone 1.40 .60
667 A216 400fr True Briton 4.25 1.50
668 A216 450fr Pacific C51 4.50 1.10
Nos. 661-668 (8) 13.80 4.65

Burkina Faso

Natl. Defense — A216a

Design: 120fr, Capt. Sankara, crowd, horiz.

1984, Nov. 21 **Litho.** *Perf. 13½*

668A A216a 90fr multicolored 50.00 —
668B A216a 120fr multicolored 72.50 —

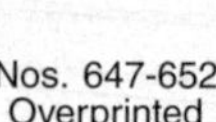

Nos. 647-652 Overprinted

1985, Mar. 5 **Litho.** *Perf. 13½*

669 A213 25fr multicolored .50 .25
670 A213 185fr multicolored 3.25 1.10
671 A213 200fr multicolored 5.00 1.50
672 A213 250fr multicolored 4.50 1.60
673 A213 300fr multicolored 6.00 2.25
674 A213 400fr multicolored 7.50 3.00
Nos. 669-674 (6) 26.75 9.70

A217

Designs: 5fr, 120fr, Flag. 15fr, 150fr, Natl. Arms, vert. 90fr, 185fr, Map.

1985, Mar. 8 **Litho.** *Perf. 12½*

675 A217 5fr multicolored .50 .25
676 A217 15fr multicolored .50 .25
677 A217 90fr multicolored 2.40 1.10
678 A217 120fr multicolored 2.40 1.10
679 A217 150fr multicolored 3.25 1.40
680 A217 185fr multicolored 3.75 1.60
Nos. 675-680 (6) 12.80 5.70

Nos. 678-680 are airmail.

1986 World Cup Soccer Championships, Mexico — A218

Various soccer plays and Aztec artifacts.

1985, Apr. 20 **Litho.** *Perf. 13*

681 A218 25fr multicolored .40 .25
682 A218 45fr multicolored .50 .25
683 A218 90fr multicolored 1.00 .45
684 A218 100fr multicolored 1.10 .55
685 A218 150fr multicolored 1.60 .90
686 A218 200fr multicolored 2.25 1.25
687 A218 250fr multicolored 3.00 1.60
Nos. 681-687 (7) 9.85 5.25

Souvenir Sheet

688 A218 500fr multicolored 7.75 1.25

Nos. 681-685 vert. No. 684-688 are airmail. No. 688 contains one 40x32mm stamp.

Motorcycle, Cent. — A220

1985, May 26

689 A220 50fr Steam tricycle, G.A. Long .65 .25
690 A220 75fr Pope .95 .35
691 A220 80fr Manet-90 1.10 .45
692 A220 100fr Ducati 1.50 .55
693 A220 150fr Jawa 2.10 .90
694 A220 200fr Honda 3.00 1.25
695 A220 250fr B.M.W. 3.50 1.60
Nos. 689-695 (7) 12.80 5.35

Nos. 692-695 are airmail.

Reptiles A221

1985, June 20

696 A221 5fr Chamaeleon dilepis .25 .25
697 A221 15fr Agama stellio .25 .25
698 A221 35fr Lacerta Lepida .70 .25
699 A221 85fr Hiperolius marmoratus 1.90 .35
700 A221 100fr Echis leucogaster 1.90 .35
701 A221 150fr Kinixys erosa 2.50 .55
702 A221 250fr Python regius 4.00 .90
Nos. 696-702 (7) 11.50 2.90

Nos. 696-697 vert. Nos. 700-702 are airmail.

A222

Queen Mother, 85th Birthday A222a

75fr, On pony bobs. 85fr, Wedding, 1923. 500fr, Holding infant Elizabeth, 1926. 600fr, Coronation of King George VI, 1937. 1000fr, Christening of Prince William, 1982. No. 707A, Christening of Prince Harry, 1985.

1985, June 21 *Perf. 13½*

703 A222 75fr multicolored .90 .45
704 A222 85fr multicolored 1.00 .45
705 A222 500fr multicolored 5.00 2.50
706 A222 600fr multicolored 6.50 3.00
Nos. 703-706 (4) 13.40 6.40

Litho. & Embossed

Perf. 13¼

706A A222a 1500fr gold & multi 16.00 —

Souvenir Sheets

Litho.

707 A222 1000fr multi 10.00 10.00

Litho. & Embossed

707A A222a 1500fr gold & multi 16.00 —

Nos. 705-707A are airmail.

Vintage Autos and Aircraft — A223

1985, June 21

708 A223 5fr Benz Victoria, 1893 .25 .25
709 A223 25fr Peugeot 174, 1927 .45 .25
710 A223 45fr Louis Bleriot .60 .25
711 A223 50fr Breguet 14 .70 .25
712 A223 500fr Bugatti Coupe Napoleon T41 Royale 5.50 2.50
713 A223 500fr Airbus A300-P4 4.75 2.50
714 A223 600fr Mercedes-Benz 540K, 1938 6.00 3.00
715 A223 600fr Airbus A300B 6.00 3.00
Nos. 708-715 (8) 24.25 12.00

Souvenir Sheet

716 A223 1000fr Louis Bleriot, Karl Benz 10.00 10.00

Automobile, cent. Nos. 712-716 are airmail.

Audubon Birth Bicent. A224

Illustrations of No. American bird species by Audubon and scouting trefoil.

1985, June 21

717 A224 60fr Aix sponsa .70 .25
718 A224 100fr Mimus polyglotos 1.00 .50
719 A224 300fr Icterus galbula 3.00 1.40
720 A224 400fr Sitta carolinensis 4.00 1.90
721 A224 500fr Asyndesmus lewis 5.50 2.40
722 A224 600fr Buteo cagopus 6.50 2.75
Nos. 717-722 (6) 20.70 9.20

Souvenir Sheet

723 A224 1000fr Columba leucocephala 11.00 8.50

Nos. 721-723 are airmail.

ARGENTINA '85, Buenos Aires — A225

Various equestrians.

1985, July 5 *Perf. 13*

724 A225 25fr Gaucho, piebald .40 .25
725 A225 45fr Horse and rider, Andes Mountains .65 .25
726 A225 90fr Rodeo 1.25 .55
727 A225 100fr Hunting gazelle 1.25 .55
728 A225 150fr Gauchos, 3 horses 1.90 .90
729 A225 200fr Rider beside mount 2.50 1.40
730 A225 250fr Contest 3.25 1.60
Nos. 724-730 (7) 11.20 5.50

Souvenir Sheet

731 A225 500fr Foal 6.50 1.40

Nos. 727-731 are airmail.

Locomotives — A226

1985, July 23

732 A226 50fr 105-30 electric, tank wagon .80 .25
733 A226 75fr Diesel shunting locomotive 1.00 .25
734 A226 80fr Diesel locomotive 1.10 .25
735 A226 100fr Diesel railcar 1.50 .25
736 A226 150fr No. 6093 1.90 .35
737 A226 200fr No. 105 diesel railcar 2.50 .45
738 A226 250fr Diesel, passenger car 3.75 .60
Nos. 732-738 (7) 12.55 2.40

Nos. 735-738 are airmail.

Artifacts — A227

Designs: 10fr, 4-legged jar, Tikare. 40fr, Lidded pot with bird handles, P. Bazega. 90fr, Mother and child, bronze statue, Ouagadougou. 120fr, Drummer, bronze statue, Ouagadougou.

1985, July 27 *Perf. 13x12½*

739-742 A227 Set of 4 5.25 1.50

No. 742 is airmail.

Fungi — A228

1985, Aug. 8 *Perf. 13*

743	A228	15fr Philiota mutabilis	.30	.25
744	A228	20fr Hypholoma (nematoloma) fasciculare	.45	.25
745	A228	30fr Ixocomus granulatus	.55	.25
746	A228	60fr Agaricus campestris	1.10	.35
747	A228	80fr Trachypus scaber	1.60	.70
748	A228	150fr Armillaria mellea	2.50	1.00
749	A228	250fr Marasmius scorodonius	5.50	2.50
		Nos. 743-749 (7)	12.00	5.30

Nos. 748 is airmail.

ITALIA '85 A228a

Paintings by Botticelli: 25fr, Virgin and Child. 45fr, Portrait of a Man. 90fr, Mars and Venus. 100fr, Birth of Venus. 150fr, Allegory of the Calumny. 200fr, Pallas and the Centaur. 250fr, Allegory of Spring. 500fr, The Virgin of Melagrana.

1985, Oct. 25 Litho. *Perf. 12½x13*

749A	A228a	25fr multicolored	.50	.25
749B	A228a	45fr multicolored	.80	.25
749C	A228a	90fr multicolored	1.90	.50
749D	A228a	100fr multicolored	2.10	.65
749E	A228a	150fr multicolored	2.75	1.00
749F	A228a	200fr multicolored	3.25	1.25
749G	A228a	250fr multicolored	3.75	1.50
		Nos. 749A-749G (7)	15.05	5.40

Souvenir Sheet

749H	A228a	500fr multicolored	6.00	4.00

No. 749D-749H are airmail.

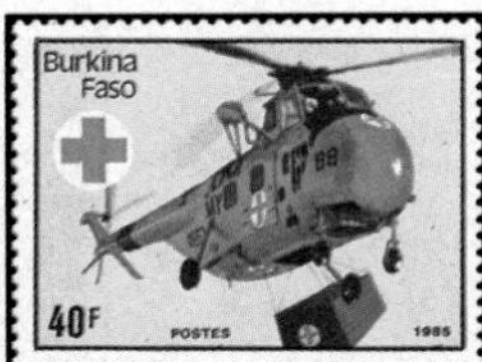

Intl. Red Cross in Burkina Faso, 75th Anniv. A229

1985, Nov. 10

750	A229	40f Helicopter	1.60	.25
751	A229	85fr Ambulance	1.90	.45
752	A229	150fr Henri Dunant	3.50	.90
753	A229	250fr Physician, patient	6.50	1.50
		Nos. 750-753 (4)	13.50	3.10

Nos. 752-753 are vert. and airmail.

Child Survival A230

1986, Jan. 6

754	A230	90fr Breast-feeding	1.25	.50

Dated 1985.

Dodo Carnival — A231

1986, Jan. 6 *Perf. 12½*

755	A231	20fr Three children, drummer	.25	.25
756	A231	25fr Lion, 4 dancers	.30	.25
757	A231	40fr Two dancers, two drummers	.55	.25
758	A231	45fr Three dancers	.65	.25
759	A231	90fr Zebra, ostrich, dancers	1.25	.50
760	A231	90fr Elephant, dancer	1.25	.50
		Nos. 755-760 (6)	4.25	2.00

Dated 1985.

Christopher Columbus (1451-1506) — A232

Columbus: 250fr, At Court of King of Portugal, the Nina. 300fr, Using astrolable, the Santa Maria. 400fr, Imprisonment at Hispanola, 1500, the Santa Maria. 450fr, At San Salvador, 1492, the Pinta. 1000fr, Fleet departing Palos harbor, 1492.

1986, Feb. 10 *Perf. 13½*

761	A232	250fr multicolored	2.75	1.25
762	A232	300fr multicolored	3.50	1.40
763	A232	400fr multicolored	4.50	1.75
764	A232	450fr multicolored	4.75	2.10
		Nos. 761-764 (4)	15.50	6.50

Souvenir Sheet

765	A232	1000fr multicolored	10.50	7.50

Nos. 764-765 are airmail. Dated 1985.

Railroad Construction — A233

1986, Feb. 10

766	A233	90fr Man, woman carrying rail	1.00	.45
767	A233	120fr Laying rails	1.10	.60
768	A233	185fr Diesel train on new tracks	1.90	.95
769	A233	500fr Adler locomotive, 1835	4.75	2.50
		Nos. 766-769 (4)	8.75	4.50

Souvenir Sheet

770	A233	1000fr Electric train, Series 290 diesel	10.50	7.50

German Railways, sesquicentennial. Nos. 769-770 are airmail. Dated 1985.

Intl. Peace Year — A234

1986, Oct. 10 Photo. *Perf. 12½x13*

771	A234	90fr blue	1.75	.55

World Health by the Year 2000 — A235

Designs: 100fr, Primary care medicine. 150fr, Mass inoculations.

1986, Aug. 8 Litho. *Perf. 13*

772	A235	90fr multicolored	1.10	.40

Size: 26x38mm

Perf. 12½x13

773	A235	100fr multicolored	1.10	.50
774	A235	120fr multicolored	1.60	.55
		Nos. 772-774 (3)	3.80	1.45

Insects — A236

1986, Sept. 10 Litho. *Perf. 12½x13*

775	A236	15fr Phryneta aurocinta	.35	.25
776	A236	20fr Sternocera interrupta	.35	.25
777	A236	40fr Prosoprocera lactator	.90	.35
778	A236	45fr Gonimbrasia hecate	.95	.35
778A	A236	85fr Charaxes epijasius	1.90	.70
		Nos. 775-778A (5)	4.45	1.90

World Post Day — A237

1986, Oct. 9 *Perf. 13*

779	A237	120fr multicolored	1.75	.70

UN Child Survival Campaign — A238

Designs: 30fr, Mother feeding child. 60fr, Adding medicines to food. 90fr, Nurse vaccinating child. 120fr, Nurse weighing child.

1986, Oct. 8 Litho. *Perf. 11½x12*

780	A238	30fr multicolored	.50	.25
781	A238	60fr multicolored	.80	.35
782	A238	90fr multicolored	1.10	.50
783	A238	120fr multicolored	1.60	.60
		Nos. 780-783 (4)	4.00	1.70

Mammals A239

Designs: 50fr, Warthog. 65fr, Hyena. 90fr, Antelope. 100fr, Gazelle. 120fr, Bushbuck. 145fr, Kudu. 500fr, Gazelle, diff.

1986, Nov. 3 Litho. *Perf. 13x12½*

784	A239	50fr multicolored	.75	.25
784A	A239	65fr multicolored	1.00	.30
784B	A239	90fr multicolored	1.40	.40
784C	A239	100fr multicolored	1.60	.50
784D	A239	120fr multicolored	1.90	.55
784E	A239	145fr multicolored	2.25	.65
784F	A239	500fr multicolored	7.50	2.40
		Nos. 784-784F (7)	16.40	5.05

Traditional Dances — A240

Designs: 10fr, Namende. 25fr, Mouhoun. 90fr, Houet. 105fr, Seno. 120fr, Ganzourgou.

1986, Nov. 3 Litho. *Perf. 12½x13*

785	A240	10fr multicolored	.50	.25
785A	A240	25fr multicolored	.50	.25
785B	A240	90fr multicolored	2.25	.55
785C	A240	105fr multicolored	2.25	.65
785D	A240	120fr multicolored	2.50	.70
		Nos. 785-785D (5)	8.00	2.40

Hairstyles A241

1986, Nov. 4 Litho. *Perf. 12½x13*

788	A241	35fr Peul	.50	.25
789	A241	75fr Dafing	1.00	.40
790	A241	90fr Peul, diff.	1.60	.50
791	A241	120fr Mossi	1.75	.65
792	A241	185fr Peul, diff.	2.50	.90
		Nos. 788-792 (5)	7.35	2.70

10th African Film Festival — A242

1987, Feb. 21 Litho. *Perf. 12x12½*

793	A242	90fr Maps, cameras	1.25	.70
794	A242	120fr Jolson, cameramen	2.25	.90
795	A242	185fr Charlie Chaplin	3.75	1.40
		Nos. 793-795 (3)	7.25	3.00

60th Anniv. of the film *The Jazz Singer* (120fr); 10th anniv. of the death of Charlie Chaplin (185fr).

Intl Women's Day — A243

1987, Mar. 8 *Perf. 13½*

796 A243 90fr multicolored 1.40 .50

Flora — A244

1987, June 6 Litho. *Perf. 12½x13*

797 A244 70fr Calotropis procera 1.00 .35
798 A244 75fr Acacia seyal 1.00 .35
799 A244 85fr Parkia biglobosa 1.25 .55
800 A244 90fr Sterospernum kunthianum 1.25 .55
801 A244 100fr Dichrostachys cinerea 1.60 .55
802 A244 300fr Combretum paniculatum 4.00 1.75
Nos. 797-802 (6) 10.10 4.10

Fight Against Leprosy — A245

Raoul Follereau (1903-1977) and: 90fr, Doctors examining African youth. 100fr, Laboratory research. 120fr, Gerhard Hansen (1841-1912), microscope, bacillus under magnification. 300fr, Follereau embracing cured leper.

1987, Aug. 6 *Perf. 13*

803 A245 90fr multicolored 1.40 .50
804 A245 100fr multicolored 1.50 .50
805 A245 120fr multicolored 1.75 .60
806 A245 300fr multicolored 4.00 1.50
Nos. 803-806 (4) 8.65 3.10

World Environment Day — A246

1987, Aug. 18 Litho. *Perf. 13x12½*

807 A246 90fr shown 1.25 .50
808 A246 145fr Emblem, huts 2.00 .90

Pre-Olympic Year — A247

1987, Aug. 31 *Perf. 12½*

809 A247 75fr High jump .95 .45
810 A247 85fr Tennis, vert. 1.00 .45
811 A247 90fr Ski jumping 1.10 .60
812 A247 100fr Soccer 1.25 .60
813 A247 145fr Running 1.60 .80
814 A247 350fr Pierre de Coubertin, tennis, vert. 4.50 2.00
Nos. 809-814 (6) 10.40 4.90

Pierre de Coubertin (1863-1937).

World Post Day — A248

1987, Oct. 5 Litho. *Perf. 12½x13*

815 A248 90fr multicolored 1.25 .70

Fight Against Apartheid — A249

1987, Nov. 11 Litho. *Perf. 13*

816 A249 90fr shown 1.25 .50
817 A249 100fr Luthuli, book, 1962 1.40 .55

Albert John Luthuli (1898-1967), South African reformer, author and 1960 Nobel Peace Prize winner. No. 817 incorrectly inscribed "1899-1967."

Traditional Costumes — A250

1987, Dec. 4 Litho. *Perf. 11½x12*

818 A250 10fr Dagari .25 .25
819 A250 30fr Peul .40 .25
820 A250 90fr Mossi 1.25 .25
821 A250 200fr Senoufo 2.25 1.10
822 A250 500fr Mossi 6.25 2.75
Nos. 818-822 (5) 10.40 4.60

Traditional Musical Instruments A251

Perf. 12x11½, 11½x12

1987, Dec. 4 **Litho.**

823 A251 20fr Xylophone .30 .25
824 A251 25fr 3-Stringed lute, vert. .30 .25
825 A251 35fr Zither .40 .25
826 A251 90fr Conical drum 1.00 .45
827 A251 1000fr Calabash drum, vert. 12.00 6.50
Nos. 823-827 (5) 14.00 7.70

Intl. Year of Shelter for the Homeless — A252

1987, Dec. 4 Litho. *Perf. 13*

828 A252 90fr multicolored 1.25 .55

Five-year Natl. Development Plan — A253

1987, Dec. 15 *Perf. 13½*

829 A253 40fr Small businesses .50 .25
830 A253 55fr Agriculture .70 .25
831 A253 60fr Constructing schools .70 .25
832 A253 90fr Transportation and communications 1.10 .45
833 A253 100fr Literacy 1.25 .55
834 A253 120fr Animal husbandry 1.60 .60
Nos. 829-834 (6) 5.85 2.35

World Health Organization, 40th Anniv. — A254

1988, Mar. 31 Litho. *Perf. 12½x13*

835 A254 120fr multicolored 1.60 .55

1988 Summer Olympics, Seoul A255

1988, May 5 *Perf. 13x12½*

836 A255 30fr shown .40 .25
837 A255 160fr Torch, vert. 1.90 .70
838 A255 175fr Soccer 2.10 .80
839 A255 235fr Volleyball, vert. 3.00 1.10
840 A255 450fr Basketball, vert. 5.25 2.25
Nos. 836-840 (5) 12.65 5.10

Souvenir Sheet

Perf. 12½x13

841 A255 500fr Runners 6.50 5.25

No. 841 contains one stamp, size: 40x52mm plus two labels.

Ritual Masks A256

1988, May 30 Litho. *Perf. 13*

842 A256 10fr Epervier, Houet .25 .25
843 A256 20fr Jeunes Filles, Oullo .30 .25
844 A256 30fr Bubale, Houet .50 .25
845 A256 40fr Forgeron, Mouhoun .50 .25
846 A256 120fr Nounouma, Ouri 1.60 .55
847 A256 175fr Chauve-souris, Ouri 2.10 .90
Nos. 842-847 (6) 5.25 2.45

Nos. 842-846 vert.

Handicrafts A257

1988, Aug. 22 Litho. *Perf. 13½*

848 A257 5fr Kieriebe ceramic pitcher, vert. .25 .25
849 A257 15fr Mossi basket .25 .25
850 A257 25fr Gurunsi chair .25 .25
851 A257 30fr Bissa basket .30 .25
852 A257 45fr Ougadougou leather box .65 .25
853 A257 85fr Ougadougou bronze statue, vert. .80 .35
854 A257 120fr Ougadougou leather valise 1.25 .55
Nos. 848-854 (7) 3.75 2.15

World Post Day — A258

1988, Oct. 9 Litho. *Perf. 13*

855 A258 120fr multicolored 1.40 .55

Aquatic Fauna A259

1988, Oct. 31 *Perf. 12*

856 A259 70fr Angler martin .80 .25
857 A259 100fr Mormyrus rume 1.10 .45
858 A259 120fr Frog 1.50 .55
859 A259 160fr Duck 2.10 .70
Nos. 856-859 (4) 5.50 1.95

Civil Rights and Political Activists A260

Designs: 80fr, Mohammed Ali Jinnah (1876-1948), 1st Governor General of Pakistan. 120fr, Mahatma Gandhi (1869-1948), India. 160fr, John F. Kennedy. 235fr, Martin Luther King, Jr.

1988, Nov. 22 Litho. *Perf. 14*

860 A260 80fr multicolored .90 .35
861 A260 120fr multicolored 1.40 .55
862 A260 160fr multicolored 1.75 .70
863 A260 235fr multicolored 2.25 1.10
Nos. 860-863 (4) 6.30 2.70

No. 863 is airmail.

A261

Christmas — Stained-glass windows: 120fr, Adoration of the shepherds. 160fr, Adoration of the Magi. 450fr, Madonna and child. 1000fr, Flight into Egypt.

1988, Dec. 2 *Perf. 12*

864 A261 120fr multicolored 1.25 .50
865 A261 160fr multicolored 1.90 .65
866 A261 450fr multicolored 4.75 1.90
867 A261 1000fr multicolored 9.50 4.75
Nos. 864-867 (4) 17.40 7.80

A262

No. 869, Ababacar Makharam. No. 870, Jean Tchissoukou. No. 871, Paulin Vieyra.

1989, Feb. 25 Litho. *Perf. 14*

868 A262 75fr shown 1.10 .35
869 A262 500fr multicolored 7.50 2.25
870 A262 500fr multicolored 7.50 2.25
871 A262 500fr multicolored 7.50 2.25
Nos. 868-871 (4) 23.60 7.10

Souvenir Sheet

872 Sheet of 3 26.50 16.00
a.-c. A262 500fr like #869-871, inscribed in gold 4.75 2.25

Panafrican Film Festival (FESPACO), 20th anniv. Nos. 869-872 are airmail.

World Fight Against AIDS A263

1989, Apr. 7 Litho. *Perf. 13*

873 A263 120fr multicolored 1.25 .50

Council for Rural Development, 30th Anniv. — A264

1989, May 3 Litho. *Perf. 15x14*

874 A264 75fr multicolored .90 .45

Parasitic Plants — A265

Legumes and cereals: 20fr, Striga generiodes. 50fr, Striga hermonthica. 235fr, Striga aspera. 450fr, Alectra vogelii.

1989, Oct. 9 Litho. *Perf. 11½*

Granite Paper

875 A265 20fr multicolored .25 .25
876 A265 50fr multicolored .50 .40
877 A265 235fr multicolored 2.40 1.10
878 A265 450fr multicolored 4.75 2.00
Nos. 875-878 (4) 7.90 3.75

Dogs A266

1989, Oct. 9 *Perf. 15x14½*

879 A266 35fr Sahel .35 .25
880 A266 50fr Puppy .65 .25
881 A266 60fr Hunting dog .80 .25
882 A266 350fr Guard dog 4.00 1.75
Nos. 879-882 (4) 5.80 2.50

Solidarity with the Palestinian People — A267

1989, Nov. 15 *Perf. 13*

883 A267 120fr Monument, Place de la Palestine 1.50 .55

Nos. 610-612 Overprinted

1988, Dec. 21 Litho. *Perf. 12½*

884 A203 90fr multicolored .90 .35
885 A203 120fr multicolored 1.10 .55
886 A203 170fr multicolored 1.75 .80
Nos. 884-886 (3) 3.75 1.70

Visit of Pope John Paul II A268

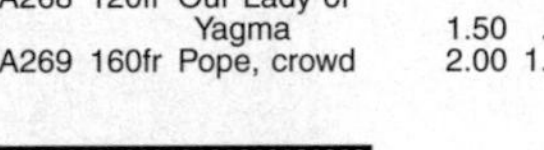

1990, Jan. 1 Litho. *Perf. 15x14*

887 A268 120fr Our Lady of Yagma 1.50 .55
888 A269 160fr Pope, crowd 2.00 1.00

150th Anniv. of the Postage Stamp A269

1990, Mar. 20 Litho. *Perf. 15x14*

889 A269 120fr multicolored 1.40 .60

Souvenir Sheet

Perf. 14x15

890 A269 500fr Penny Black, ship 4.75 4.50

Stamp World London '90.

World Cup Soccer Championships, Italy — A270

1990, Apr. 26 Litho. *Perf. 11½*

891 A270 30fr multicolored .30 .25
892 A270 150fr multi, diff. 2.10 .70

Souvenir Sheet

893 A270 1000fr multi, horiz. 10.00 8.50

Intl. Literacy Year A271

1990, July 10 Litho. *Perf. 13*

894 A271 40fr multicolored .50 .25
895 A271 130fr multicolored 1.60 .60

Mushrooms — A272

1990, May 17 Litho. *Perf. 11½*

896 A272 10fr Cantharellus cibarius .30 .25
897 A272 15fr Psalliota bispora .50 .25
898 A272 60fr Amanita caesarea 1.10 .80
899 A272 190fr Boletus badius 3.50 1.75
a. Souv. sheet of 4, #896-899 21.00 6.25
Nos. 896-899 (4) 5.40 3.05

Intl. Exposition of Handicrafts — A273

1990, Sept. 25 Litho. *Perf. 13*

900 A273 35fr Masks, fans, vert. .30 .25
901 A273 45fr shown .40 .25
902 A273 270fr Rattan chair, vert. 2.50 1.25
Nos. 900-902 (3) 3.20 1.75

Gen. Charles de Gaulle (1890-1970) A274

1990, Nov. 22 Litho. *Perf. 13*

903 A274 200fr multicolored 2.40 .90

Minerals A275

1991, Feb. 4 Litho. *Perf. 15x14*

904 A275 20fr Quartz .35 .25
905 A275 50fr Granite .60 .25
906 A275 280fr Amphibolite 3.50 1.40
Nos. 904-906 (3) 4.45 1.90

African Film Festival — A276

1991, Feb. 20 *Perf. 11½*

907 A276 150fr multicolored 2.10 .90

Souvenir Sheet

908 A276 1000fr Award 16.00 10.00

Fight Against Drugs — A277

1991, Feb. 20

909 A277 130fr multicolored 1.40 .60

Samuel F.B. Morse (1791-1872), Inventor — A278

1991, May 17 Litho. *Perf. 13*

910 A278 200fr multicolored 2.10 .90

Native Girl — A279

1991-93 Litho. *Perf. 14½x15*

911 A279 5fr gray & multi .25 .25
912 A279 10fr yellow & multi .25 .25
913 A279 25fr lilac rose & multi .25 .25
914 A279 50fr red lilac & multi .25 .25
915 A279 130fr blue & multi 1.25 .55
916 A279 150fr multicolored 1.50 .60
920 A279 200fr multicolored 1.90 .80
922 A279 330fr orange & multi 3.25 1.40
Nos. 911-922 (8) 8.90 4.35

Issued: 150fr, 200fr, 6/20/91; 130fr, 330fr, 1/15/93; 5-50fr, 5/3/94.

Flowers A280

1991, July 31 Litho. *Perf. 11½*

926 A280 5fr Grewia tenax .25 .25
927 A280 15fr Hymenocardia acide .25 .25
928 A280 60fr Cassia sieberiana, vert. .65 .25
929 A280 100fr Adenium obesum 1.00 .40
930 A280 300fr Mitragyna inermis 3.00 1.25
Nos. 926-930 (5) 5.15 2.40

Traditional Dance Costumes A281

1991, Aug. 20 *Perf. 12½*

931 A281 75fr Warba 1.10 .40
932 A281 130fr Wiskamba 1.90 .70
933 A281 280fr Pa-zenin 3.50 1.50
Nos. 931-933 (3) 6.50 2.60

World Post Day — A282

1991, Oct. 9 *Perf. 13½*

934 A282 130fr multicolored 1.40 .50

Cooking Utensils A283

1992, Jan. 8 Litho. *Perf. 11½*

935 A283 45fr Pancake fryer .50 .25
936 A283 130fr Cooking pot, vert. 1.50 .55
937 A283 310fr Mortar & pestle, vert. 3.50 1.25
938 A283 500fr Ladle, calabash 6.00 2.00
Nos. 935-938 (4) 11.50 4.05

1992 African Soccer Championships, Senegal — A284

1992, Jan. 17 *Perf. 13½*

939 A284 50fr Yousouf Fofana .65 .25
940 A284 100fr Francois-Jules Bocande 1.25 .40

Souvenir Sheet

Perf. 13x12½

941 A284 500fr Trophy 5.50 2.00

UN Decade For the Handicapped — A285

1992, Mar. 31 Litho. *Perf. 12½*

942 A285 100fr multicolored 1.10 .40

World Health Day — A286

1992, Apr. 7 *Perf. 13*

943 A286 330fr multicolored 4.25 1.40

Discovery of America, 500th Anniv. A287

1992, Aug. 12 Litho. *Perf. 12½*

944 A287 50fr Columbus, Santa Maria 1.00 .25
945 A287 150fr Ships, natives 2.50 .65

Souvenir Sheet

946 A287 350fr Map 6.50 1.50

Genoa '92. No. 946 contains one 52x31mm stamp.

A288

Insects.

1992, Aug. 17 *Perf. 15x14*

947 A288 20fr Dysdercus voelkeri .25 .25
948 A288 40fr Rhizopertha dominica .55 .25
949 A288 85fr Orthetrum microstigma 1.10 .35
950 A288 500fr Apis mellifera 6.50 2.25
Nos. 947-950 (4) 8.40 3.10

A289

Christmas: 10fr, Boy, creche. 130fr, Children decorating creche. 1000fr, Boy holding painting of Madonna and Child.

1992, Dec. 21 Litho. *Perf. 11½*

951 A289 10fr multicolored .25 .25
952 A289 130fr multicolored 1.40 .50
953 A289 1000fr multicolored 11.00 4.00
Nos. 951-953 (3) 12.65 4.75

Invention of the Diesel Engine, Cent. A290

1993, Jan. 25 Litho. *Perf. 11½*

954 A290 1000fr multicolored 12.00 4.00

The date of issue is in question.

Paris '94, Philatelic Exhibition A291

1993, July 15

955 A291 400fr multicolored 5.00 1.75
956 A291 650fr multi, diff. 7.00 2.75

African Film Festival — A292

Designs: 250fr, Monument to the cinema. 750fr, M. Douta (1919-1991), comedian, horiz.

Perf. 11½x12, 12x11½

1993, Feb. 16 Litho.

957 A292 250fr multicolored 3.00 1.00
958 A292 750fr multicolored 9.00 3.00

Birds — A293

100fr, Mycteria ibis. 200fr, Leptoptilos crumeniferus. 500fr, Ephippiorhynchus senegalensis.

1993, Mar. 31 *Perf. 11½x12*

959 A293 100fr multicolored 1.10 .40
960 A293 200fr multicolored 2.10 .80
961 A293 500fr multicolored 5.50 2.00
a. Souvenir sheet of 3, #959-961 15.00 4.75
Nos. 959-961 (3) 8.70 3.20

No. 961a sold for 1200fr.

1994 World Cup Soccer Championships, U.S. — A294

1993, Apr. 8 *Perf. 15*

962 A294 500fr shown 6.50 2.00
963 A294 1000fr Players, US flag 13.50 4.00

Fruit Trees — A295

150fr, Saba senegalensis, vert. 300fr, Butyrospermum parkii. 600fr, Adansonia digitata, vert.

1993, June 2 Litho. *Perf. 11½*

964 A295 150fr multicolored 1.75 .95
965 A295 300fr multicolored 3.50 1.90
966 A295 600fr multicolored 7.50 4.00
Nos. 964-966 (3) 12.75 6.85

Traditional Jewelry A296

1993, Sept. 25 Litho. *Perf. 11½*

967 A296 200fr Ring for hair 2.00 .85
968 A296 250fr Agate necklace, vert. 2.50 1.00
969 A296 500fr Bracelet 5.00 2.00
Nos. 967-969 (3) 9.50 3.85

Gazella Rufifrons A297

1993, Dec. 10 Litho. *Perf. 14½*

970 A297 30fr shown 1.75 .50
971 A297 40fr Two facing left 2.00 .50
972 A297 60fr Two standing 3.00 1.50
973 A297 100fr Young gazelle 7.50 2.75
a. Souvenir sheet, #970-973 8.50 6.50
Nos. 970-973 (4) 14.25 5.25

World Wildlife Fund (Nos. 970-973). No. 973a sold for 400fr.

Kingfishers — A298

1994, Mar. 8 Litho. *Perf. 11½*

974 A298 600fr Halcyon senegalensis 5.25 1.75
975 A298 1200fr Halcyon chelicuti 12.00 3.75

Souvenir Sheet

976 A298 2000fr Ceyx picta 19.00 9.75

1994 World Cup Soccer Championships, U.S. — A299

1994, Mar. 28

977 A299 1000fr Players, US map 6.25 3.00
978 A299 1800fr Soccer ball, players 10.50 5.25
a. Souvenir sheet of 1 12.00 8.50

No. 978a sold for 2000fr.

First Manned Moon Landing, 25th Anniv. — A300

1994, July 15 Litho. *Perf. 11½*

979 A300 750fr Astronaut, flag 4.50 1.90
980 A300 750fr Lunar module, earth 4.50 1.90
a. Pair, #979-980 9.25 3.75

No. 980a is a continuous design.

First Stamp Exhibition, Paris, 1994 A301

1994, Apr. 28

981 A301 1500fr Dogs 8.25 4.75
a. Souvenir sheet of 1 12.00 8.25

Legumes — A302

40fr, Hibiscus sabdariffa. 45fr, Solanum aethiopicum. 75fr, Solanum melongena. 100fr, Hibiscus esculentus.

1994 Litho. *Perf. 11½*

982 A302 40fr multicolored .25 .25
983 A302 45fr multicolored .35 .25
984 A302 75fr multicolored .60 .25
985 A302 100fr multicolored .75 .25
Nos. 982-985 (4) 1.95 1.00

Intl. Olympic Committee, Cent. — A303

Domestic Animals — A304

1994, Oct. 10 *Perf. 15*

986 A303 320fr multicolored 2.00 .80

1994, Oct. 10 *Perf. 11½*

987 A304 150fr Pig, horiz. .90 .35
988 A304 1000fr Capra hircus 5.50 2.50
989 A304 1500fr Ovis aries, horiz. 8.50 3.75
Nos. 987-989 (3) 14.90 6.60

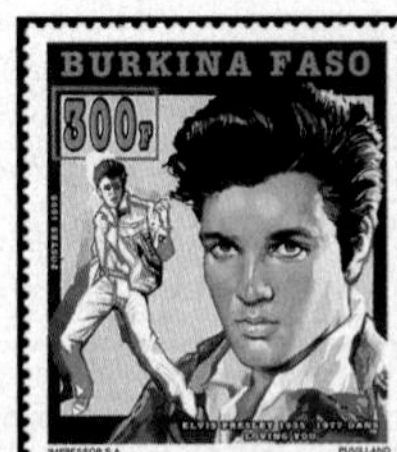

Elvis Presley (1935-77) A305

A305a

Portraits in feature films: 300fr, Loving You. 500fr, Jailhouse Rock. 1000fr, Blue Hawaii. 1500fr, Marilyn Monroe, Presley.

1995 Litho. *Perf. 13½*

990-992	A305	Set of 3	10.00	6.50

Souvenir Sheets

993	A305	1500fr multicolored	8.25	6.50

Litho. & Embossed

993A	A305a	3000fr gold & multi	17.50	11.00

Nos. 990-992 exist in souvenir sheets of one. No. 993 contains one 51x42mm stamp with continuous design. No. 993A, exists in souvenir sheets of silver & multi with different designs in sheet margin.

Issued: No. 993A, 2/24/95.

See Nos. 1012-1015A.

Crocodile — A306

1995, Feb. 6 Litho. *Perf. 15x14½*

994	A306	10fr brown & multi	.25	.25
995	A306	20fr lilac & multi	.25	.25
996	A306	25fr olive brn & multi	.25	.25
997	A306	30fr green & multi	.25	.25
998	A306	40fr red brn & multi	.25	.25
999	A306	50fr gray & multi	.25	.25
1000	A306	75fr gray vio & multi	.35	.25
1001	A306	100fr gray brn & multi	.50	.25
1002	A306	150fr olive & multi	.75	.40
1003	A306	175fr gray bl & multi	.90	.45
1004	A306	250fr brn lake & multi	1.25	.65
1005	A306	400fr bl grn & multi	1.50	1.00
		Nos. 994-1005 (12)	6.75	4.50

World Tourism Organization, 20th Anniv. A307

Designs: 150fr, Man riding donkey, vert. 350fr, Bobo-Dioulasso railroad station. 450fr, Grand Mosque, Bani. 650fr, Gazelle, map.

1995, Jan. 26 Litho. *Perf. 11½*

1006	A307	150fr multicolored	.75	.40
1007	A307	350fr multicolored	1.75	.90
1008	A307	450fr multicolored	2.25	1.10
1009	A307	650fr multicolored	3.25	1.60
		Nos. 1006-1009 (4)	8.00	4.00

FESPACO '95 — A308

Motion pictures: 150fr, "Rabi," Gaston Kabore. 250fr, "Tilai," Idrissa Ouedraogo.

1995 *Perf. 13½*

1010	A308	150fr multicolored	.80	.40
1011	A308	250fr multicolored	1.40	.70

Nos. 1010-1011 exist in souvenir sheets of one. Motion pictures, cent.

Traditional Houses A308a

1995 Litho. *Perf. 13½*

1011A	A308a	70fr Mossi	*1.00*	*.25*
1011B	A308a	100fr Kassena	*1.75*	*.25*
1011C	A308a	200fr Bobo	*3.75*	*.35*
1011D	A308a	250fr Peulh	*4.00*	*.55*
		Nos. 1011A-1011D (4)	*10.50*	*1.40*

Stars of Motion Pictures Type of 1995

Marilyn Monroe in feature films: 400fr, The Joyful Parade. 650fr, The Village Tramp. 750fr, Niagara.

1500fr, The Seven Year Itch. 3000fr, Marilyn Monroe (1926-62).

1995 Litho. *Perf. 13½*

1012-1014	A305	Set of 3	9.00	4.00

Souvenir Sheets

1015	A305	1500fr multicolored	8.25	4.00

Litho. & Embossed

1015A	A305a	3000fr gold & multi	17.50	11.00

Nos. 1012-1014 exist in souvenir sheets of 1. No. 1015 contains one 42x51mm stamp with continuous design. No. 1015A exists in souvenir sheets of silver & multi with different designs in sheet margin.

Birds — A309

Designs: 450fr, Laniarius barbarus. 600fr, Estrilda bengala. 750fr, Euplectes afer.

1995, Apr. 5 Litho. *Perf. 11½*

1016	A309	450fr multicolored	2.50	1.00
1017	A309	600fr multicolored	3.50	1.40
1018	A309	750fr multicolored	4.50	1.75
a.		Souv. sheet, #1016-1018	11.00	4.50
		Nos. 1016-1018 (3)	10.50	4.15

No. 1018a sold for 2000fr.

Reptiles A310

Designs: 450fr, Psammophis sibilans. 500fr, Eryx muelleri. 1500fr, Turtle.

1995, Dec. 31

1019	A310	450fr multicolored	2.75	1.00
1020	A310	500fr multicolored	3.00	1.10
1021	A310	1500fr multicolored	9.25	3.50
		Nos. 1019-1021 (3)	15.00	5.60

1996 Summer Olympics, Atlanta A311

Design: 3000fr, Tennis, diff.

1995, Sept. 20 Litho. *Perf. 13½*

1022	A311	150fr Basketball	.70	.35
1023	A311	250fr Baseball	1.25	.60
1024	A311	650fr Tennis	3.00	1.50
1025	A311	750fr Table tennis	3.50	1.75
a.		Souv. sheet, #1022-1025	50.00	—
		Nos. 1022-1025 (4)	8.45	4.20

Souvenir Sheets

1026	A311	1500fr Equestrian event	7.75	7.00

Litho. & Embossed

1026A	A311	3000fr gold & multi	16.00	10.00

No. 1026A also exists as a silver & multi souvenir sheet with different design in sheet margin. Both the gold & silver stamps also exist together in a souvenir sheet of 2.

Sports Figures A312

Ayrton Senna (1960-94), World Driving Champion — A313

Designs: 300fr, Juan Manuel Fangio, race car driver, 1955 Mercedes W 196. 400fr, Andre Agassi, US tennis player. 500fr, Ayrton Senna (1960-94), race car driver, McLaren MP 4/6 Honda. 1000fr, Michael Schumacher, race car driver, 1995 Benetton B 195.

1500fr, Enzo Ferrari, 412 TR, F40.

1995, Sept. 20

1027	A312	300fr multi	4.50	1.10
1028	A312	400fr multi	1.75	1.60
1029	A312	500fr multi	2.40	2.00
1030	A312	1000fr multi	4.60	4.00
a.		Souvenir sheet of 3, #1027, 1029-1030	14.50	7.25
		Nos. 1027-1030 (4)	13.25	8.70

Souvenir Sheets

1031	A312	1500fr multicolored	*7.75*	*3.50*

Litho. & Embossed

1032	A313	3000fr gold & multi	15.00	10.00

Nos. 1027-1030 exist in souvenir sheets of 1. No. 1031 contains one 55x48mm stamp.

No. 1032 also exists as a silver & multi souvenir sheet with different design in sheet margin. Both the gold and silver stamps also exist together in a souvenir sheet of 2.

For surcharge see No. 1078.

Souvenir Sheets

John Lennon (1940-1980) — A314

Designs: No. 1033, With guitar, circular pattern with name "LENNON," portrait. No. 1034, With guitar, emblem, portrait.

1995 Litho. & Embossed *Perf. 13½*

1033	A314	3000fr gold & multi	16.00	10.00
1034	A314	3000fr gold & multi	16.00	10.00

Nos. 1033-1034 each exist in souvenir sheets of silver & multi. Souvenir sheets of one gold and one silver exist in same designs and one of each design.

1995 Boy Scout Jamboree, Holland A315

Mushrooms: 150fr, Russula nigricans. 250fr, Lepiota rhacodes. 300fr, Xerocomus subtomentos. 400fr, Boletus erythropus. 500fr, Russula sanguinea. 650fr, Amanita rubescens. 750fr, Amanita vaginata. 1000fr, Geastrum sessil.

No. 1043, 1500fr, Amanita muscaria. No. 1044, 1500fr, Morchella esculenta.

1996, Feb. 20 Litho. *Perf. 13½*

1035-1042	A315	Set of 8	17.50	8.00
1041a		Sheet of 4, #1035, 1037, 1040-1041	15.00	12.50
1042a		Sheet of 4, #1036, 1038-1039, 1042	15.00	12.50

Souvenir Sheets

1043-1044	A315	Set of 2	15.00	6.00

Mushrooms — A316

Designs: 175fr, Hygrophore perroquet. 250fr, Pleurote en huitre. 300fr, Pezize (oreille d'ane). 450fr, Clavaire jolie.

1996, Jan. 24

1045-1048	A316	Set of 4	6.50	2.25
1048a		Souv. sheet, #1045-1048	16.00	2.25

Nos. 1045-1048 each exist in souv. sheets of 1.

UN, 50th Anniv. A317

Designs: 500fr, UN headquarters, New York. 1000fr, UN emblem, people, vert.

1995, Dec. 20 *Perf. 11½*

1049	A317	500fr multicolored	2.75	1.25
1050	A317	1000fr multicolored	4.50	2.75

Christmas A318

Designs: 150fr, Christmas tree, children pointing to picture of nativity scene. 450fr, Yagma Grotto. 500fr, Flight into Egypt. 1000fr, Adoration of the Magi.

1995, Dec. 18

1051	A318	150fr multicolored	.80	.40
1052	A318	450fr multicolored	2.40	1.25
1053	A318	500fr multicolored	2.75	1.40
1054	A318	1000fr multicolored	5.25	2.75
		Nos. 1051-1054 (4)	11.20	5.80

Entertainers — A319

Portraits: 150fr, Michael Jackson. 250fr, Prince. 300fr, Madonna. 400fr, Mick Jagger. 500fr, Bob Marley. 650fr, The Beatles. 750fr, Marilyn Monroe. 1000fr, Elvis Presley wearing black jacket. No. 1062, Elvis Presley, smiling. No. 1063, 1500fr, Presley, hand under chin. No. 1064, 1500fr, Stevie Wonder.

1996, May 14 Litho. *Perf. 13½*

1055	A319	150fr multi	*.60*	*.25*
1056	A319	250fr multi	*1.25*	*.25*
1057	A319	300fr multi	*1.75*	*.35*
1058	A319	400fr multi	*2.40*	*.35*
1059	A319	500fr multi	*2.75*	*.50*
1060	A319	650fr multi	*2.75*	*.50*
1061	A319	750fr multi	—	—
1061A	A319	1000fr multi	*6.00*	*.60*

Souvenir Sheets

1062-1064 A319 Set of 3 *18.00 7.50*

Dated 1995.

Butterflies and Insects A320

100fr, Epiphora bauhiniae. 150fr, Kraussella amabile. 175fr, Charaxes epijasius. 250fr, Locusta migratoria.

1996 Litho. *Perf. 13½*

1065	A320	100fr multi, vert.	.70	.25
1066	A320	150fr multi, vert.	1.25	.35
1067	A320	175fr multi, vert.	1.40	.40
1068	A320	250fr multi	1.90	.60
		Nos. 1065-1068 (4)	5.25	1.60

Two souvenir sheets containing Nos. 1065, 1067 and Nos. 1066, 1068, respectively, exist.

Butterflies A321

Designs: 150fr, Morpho rega. 250fr, Hypolymnas misippus. 450fr, Pseudacraea boisduvali. 600fr, Charaxes castor.
1500fr, Antanartia delius.

1996, June 28 Litho. *Perf. 13½*

1069	A321	150fr multicolored	.80	.35
1070	A321	250fr multicolored	1.25	.55
1071	A321	450fr multicolored	2.25	1.00
1072	A321	600fr multicolored	3.25	2.75
		Nos. 1069-1072 (4)	7.55	4.65

Souvenir Sheet

1073	A321	1500fr multicolored	9.25	6.75
a.		Ovptd. in sheet margin	9.25	6.25

Overprint in silver in sheet margin of No. 1073a contains Hong Kong '97 Exhibition emblem and two line inscription in Chinese. Issued in 1997.

Insects — A321a

c, 25fr, Sauterelle. d, 75fr, Schistocerca gregaria. e, 300fr, Pardolata haasi. f, 400fr, Psammomys obesus.

1996, June 28 Litho. *Perf. 13½*

1073B A321a Strip of 4, #c.-f. 5.50 1.40

1998 World Cup Soccer Championships, France — A322

Various soccer plays.

1996 Litho. *Perf. 13*

1074	A322	50fr multi	.25	.25
1075	A322	150fr multi, vert.	.90	.25
1076	A322	250fr multi, vert.	1.50	.55
1077	A322	450fr multi, vert.	2.50	1.00
		Nos. 1074-1077 (4)	5.15	2.05

No. 1028 Ovptd. in Metallic Red

1996 Litho. *Perf. 13½*

1078 A312 400fr multicolored 8.25 .80

No. 1078 exists in souvenir sheet of 1.

Wild Cats — A323

Designs: 100fr, Panthera leo. 150fr, Acinonyx jubatus. 175fr, Lynx caracal. 250fr, Panthera pardus.

1996 *Perf. 12½x12*

1079	A323	100fr multicolored	.75	.25
1080	A323	150fr multicolored	1.10	.30
1081	A323	175fr multicolored	1.25	.35
1082	A323	250fr multicolored	1.90	.45
		Nos. 1079-1082 (4)	5.00	1.35

Summit of France and African Nations, Ouagadougou A323a

1996 Litho. *Perf. 11¾*

1082A	A323a	150fr pink & multi	—	—
1082B	A323a	250fr yel & multi	—	—

Orchids — A324

Various orchids.

1996, Aug. 30 Litho. *Perf. 12½x13*

1083	A324	100fr blue & multi	1.10	.55
1084	A324	175fr lilac & multi	1.50	.95
1085	A324	250fr orange & multi	2.50	1.25
1086	A324	300fr olive & multi	3.00	1.60
		Nos. 1083-1086 (4)	8.10	4.35

UNICEF, 50th Anniv. — A324a

Design: 70fr, Child drinking near water pump, horiz. 75fr, Child reading book. 150fr, Mother nursing child. 250fr, Vaccination of child.

1996 Litho. *Perf. 11¾*

1086A	A324a	70fr multi		—
1086B	A324a	75fr multi	—	—
1086C	A324a	150fr multi	—	—
1086D	A324a	250fr multi	*1.10*	*.50*

Birds — A325

Designs: 500fr, Falco peregrinus. 750fr, Crossoptilon mantchuricum. 1000fr, Branta canadensis. 1500fr, Pelecanus crispus.

1996, June 25 *Perf. 12½x12*

1087	A325	500fr multicolored	*3.00*	*1.00*
1088	A325	750fr multicolored	*3.75*	*1.25*
1089	A325	1000fr multicolored	*5.50*	*1.90*
1090	A325	1500fr multicolored	*8.50*	*2.75*
		Nos. 1087-1090 (4)	*20.75*	*6.90*

Nos. 1087-1090 each printed se-tenant with labels.

Diana, Princess of Wales (1961-97) — A325a

Various portraits, color of sheet margin: No. 1090A, blue. No. 1090K, deep pink.
No. 1090U, 2000fr, In yellow. No. 1090V, 2000fr, Wearing tiara.

1997 Litho. *Perf. 13½*

Sheets of 9

1090A	A325a	150fr #Ab-Aj	9.00	2.40
1090K	A325a	180fr #Kl-Kti	10.00	3.00

Souvenir Sheets

1090U-1090V A325a Set of 2 27.50 7.00

Nos. 1090U-1090V each contain one 41x46mm stamp.

See Nos. 1125U-1128.

Flowers — A325b

Design: 150fr, Cienfuegosia digitata, vert. 175fr, Costus pectabilis. 250fr, Cerathoteca sesamoides, vert. 400fr, Crotalaria retusa, vert.

Perf. 13¼x13, 13x13¼

1997, Dec. 22 Litho.

1090W	A325b	150fr multi	—	—
1090X	A325b	175fr multi	*.80*	*.45*
1090Y	A325b	250fr multi	—	—
1090Z	A325b	400fr multi	*1.90*	*.90*

A326

Various portraits, color of sheet margin: No. 1091, Pale pink. No. 1092, Pale blue. No. 1093, Pale yellow.
No. 1094, 1500fr, In white dress, serving food to child (in sheet margin). No. 1095, 1500fr, Wearing wide-brimmed hat.

1998 Litho. *Perf. 14*

Sheets of 6

1091	A326	425fr #a.-f.	11.00	4.50
1092	A326	530fr #a.-f.	13.00	5.50
1093	A326	590fr #a.-f.	15.00	6.00

Souvenir Sheets

1094-1095 A326 Set of 2 18.00 5.00

Diana, Princess of Wales (1961-97).

A327

1998 Litho. *Perf. 14*

1096 A327 260fr shown 2.00 .30

Souvenir Sheet

1097 A327 1500fr Portrait, diff. 11.00 2.50

Mother Teresa (1910-97). No. 1096 was issued in sheets of 6. Nos. 1096-1097 have birth date inscribed "1907."

Birds — A328

5fr, White-winged triller. 10fr, Golden sparrow. 100fr, American goldfinch. 170fr, Red-legged thrush. 260fr, Willow warbler. 425fr, Blue grosbeak.
No. 1104: a, Bank swallow. b, Kirtland's warbler. c, Long-tailed minivet. d, Blue-gray gnatcatcher. e, Reed-bunting. f, Black-collared apalis. g, American robin. h, Cape long-claw. i, Wood thrush.
No. 1105: a, Song sparrow. b, Dartford warbler. c, Eastern bluebird. d, Rock thrush. e, Northern mockingbird. f, Northern cardinal. g, Eurasian goldfinch. h, Varied thrush. i, Northern oriole.
No. 1106, 1500fr, Golden whistler. No. 1107, 1500fr, Barn swallow, horiz.

1998, Oct. 1 Litho. *Perf. 13½*
1098-1103 A328 Set of 6 7.25 2.00

Sheets of 9

1104 A328 260fr #a.-i. 17.00 4.50
1105 A328 425fr #a.-i. 26.00 8.00

Souvenir Sheets

1106-1107 A328 Set of 2 21.00 6.00

Butterflies and Moths A329

No. 1108: a, Arctia caja. b, Nymphalis antiopa. c, Brahmaea wallichii. d, Issoria lathonia. e, Speyeria cybele. f, Vanessa virginiensis. g, Rothchildia orizaba. h, Cethosia hypsea. i, Marpesia petreus.

No. 1109: a, Agraulis vanillae. b, Junonia coenia. c, Danaus gilippus. d, Polygonia comma. e, Anthocharis cardamines. f, Heliconius aoede. g, Atlides halesus. h, Mesosemia croseus. i, Automeris io.

No. 1110, 1500fr, Papilio xuthus. No. 1111, 1500fr, Pterourus multicaudatus. No. 1112, 1500fr, Pterourus troilus. No. 1113, 1500fr, Papilio machaon.

1998, Oct. 25 Sheets of 9
1108 A329 170fr #a.-i. 11.00 4.00
1109 A329 530fr #a.-i. 30.00 9.00

Souvenir Sheets

1110-1113 A329 Set of 4 42.50 12.00

Nos. 1110-1113 each contain one 56x42mm stamp.

Christmas — A330

Fauna, flora with Christmas items: 100fr, Tersina viridis, holly, vert. 170fr, Citherias menander, present, vert. 260fr, Chrysanthemum, reindeer, sleigh, vert. 425fr, Swallowtail butterfly, greeting card. 530fr, European bee eater, Santa Claus, snowman.

No. 1119, 1500fr, Anthemis tinctoria, sleigh. No. 1120, 1500fr, Papilio ulysses, greeting card.

1998, Dec. 1 Litho. *Perf. 14*
1114-1118 A330 Set of 5 10.00 2.75

Souvenir Sheets

1119-1120 A330 Set of 2 22.00 5.50

Handicrafts A330a

Design: No. 1120A, Wooden carved stool, vert. No. 1120B, Stool with carved heads. 50fr, Peul hat. 70fr, Basket with handle, vert. 75fr, Bronze figurine of woman milk seller and child, vert. No. 1120F, Bronze figurine of Mossi chief on horseback. No. 1120G, Dagari stool. 150fr, Basket, vert. 170fr, Wooden statue, Pasoré region, vert. 260fr, Wooden statue, Kaya region, vert.

1996-98 Litho. *Perf. 11¾*
1120A A330a 25fr multi — —
1120B A330a 25fr multi — —
1120C A330a 50fr multi — —
1120D A330a 70fr multi — —
1120E A330a 75fr multi — —
1120F A330a 100fr multi — —
1120G A330a 100fr multi — —
1120H A330a 150fr multi — —
1120I A330a 170fr multi — —
1120J A330a 260fr multi — —

Issued: No. 1120A, 50fr, 70fr, 75fr, No. 1120F, 150fr, 11/13/96. No. 1120B, 1120G, 170fr, 260f, 6/20/98.

34th Organization for African Unity Summit, Ouagadougou — A330b

1998, May 20 Litho. *Perf. 13x13¼*
1120K A330b 170fr red & multi *.80 .40*
1120L A330b 425fr blue & multi *2.00 .90*

Protected Wildlife — A330c

Designs: 170fr, Leptoptilos crumeniferus. 200fr, Acionyx jubatus. 260fr, Orycteropus afer. 530fr, Struthio camulus. 590fr, Hippopotamus amphibus, horiz.

Perf. 13¼x13, 13x13¼
1998, May 20 Litho.
1120M A330c 170fr multi *.80 .30*
1120N A330c 200fr multi *.90 .35*
1120O A330c 260fr multi *1.10 .50*
1120P A330c 530fr multi *2.50 1.00*
1120Q A330c 590fr multi *2.75 1.25*

15th FESPACO Film Festival — A330d

Film: 150fr, Enfance et Jeunesse. 250fr, Etalon de Yennega.

1997, Feb. 5 Litho. *Perf. 11½x11¾*
1120R A330d 150fr multi *.75 .30*
1120S A330d 250fr multi *1.25 .45*

Wild Animals — A330e

Design: 25fr, Redunca. 50fr, Cob Defassa (Defassa waterbuck). 150fr, Bubale. 250fr, Buffle (buffalo).

Perf. 11½x11¾
1997, Mar. 20 Litho.
1120T A330e 25fr multi *.25 .25*
1120U A330e 50fr multi — —
1120V A330e 150fr multi *.70 .30*
1120W A330e 250fr multi — —
x. Souvenir sheet, #1120T-1120W — —

No. 1120Wx sold for 500fr.

Heinrich Von Stephan (1831-97), Founder of UPU — A320f

1997, Apr. 8 Litho. *Perf. 11¾*
1120Y A320f 250fr multi — —

Trains — A331

No. 1121: a, CDR No. 19, Ireland. b, EMD "F" Series Bo-Bo, US. c, Class 72000, France. d, Class AE 4/4 Bo-Bo, Switzerland. e, Class 277, Spain. f, ET 403 four car train, West Germany. g, Class EM2 Co-Co, UK. h, Europe Dutch Swiss Tee.

No. 1122: a, DF 4 East Wind IV Co-Co, China. b, Union Pacific Railroad, US. c, No. 3.641, Norway. d, Class GE 4/4 Bo-bo, Switzerland. e, Class GE Bo-Bo, South Africa. f, WDM-2 Co-Co, India. g, Kraus Mafeei Co-Co, US. h, RTG Four-car transit, France.

No. 1123, 1500fr, ETR 401 Pendolino, Italy. No. 1124, 1500fr, No. 12 Sarah Siddons, UK.

1998, Nov. 10

Sheets of 8

1121 A331 170fr #a.-h. 11.00 3.00
1122 A331 425fr #a.-h. 27.50 8.00

Souvenir Sheets

1123-1124 A331 Set of 2 22.00 7.50

Intl. Fund for Agricultural Development, 20th Anniv. — A331a

Design: 150fr, Restoration of degraded soils. 400fr, "20," wheat stalk.

Perf. 13½x13¼
1998, Mar. 20 Litho.
1124A A331a 150fr multi *.70 .30*
1125 A331a 400fr multi *1.75 .80*

Masks — A331b

Design: 75fr, Buffalo mask, vert. 150fr, Duck mask. 200fr, Kob mask. 250fr, Mask with panels, vert.

1997, May 20 Litho. *Perf. 13¼*
1125A A331b 75fr multi — —
1125B A331b 150fr multi — —
1125C A331b 200fr multi — —
1125D A331b 250fr multi — —

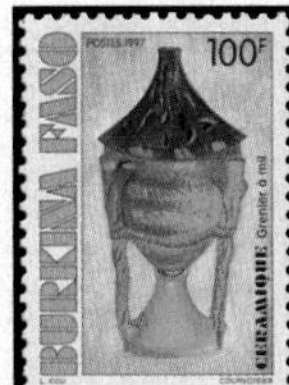

Ceramics — A331c

Design: 100fr, Millet container. 150fr, Decorated covered baking pot. 250fr, Beer mug. 450fr, Vase.

Perf. 11½x11¾
1997, Sept. 11 Litho.
1125E A331c 100fr multi —
1125F A331c 150fr multi — —
1125G A331c 250fr multi —
1125H A331c 450fr multi *2.00 .75*

Fish — A331d

Design: 100fr, Aplocheiolichthys pfaffi. 150fr, Fundulosoma thierryi. 175fr, Sarotherodon galilaeus. 250fr, Epiplatys spilargyreius.

1997, Nov. 20 Litho. *Perf. 13¼*
1125I A331d 100fr multi *.45 .25*
1125J A331d 150fr multi — —
1125K A331d 175fr multi —
1125L A331d 250fr multi —

African Soccer Championships — A331e

Design: 175fr, Goalie making save. 150fr, Four players. 250fr, Soccer player, stylized person holding food bowl, vert. 500fr, Soccer ball, trophy, map of Africa, vert.

Perf. 13x13¼, 13¼x13
1998, Jan. 20 Litho.
1125M A331e 150fr multi *.70 .30*
1125N A331e 175fr multi *.85 .30*
1125O A331e 250fr multi —
1125P A331e 500fr multi —

No. 1125P is dated 1997.

Traditional Costumes — A331f

Design: 150fr, Peulh (Togore). 175fr, Mossi (Banague). 250fr, Peulh (Boodi). 450fr, Bissa (Gangadruku).

1998, Feb. 20 Litho. *Perf. 13½x13*
1125Q A331f 150fr multi *.70 .25*
1125R A331f 175fr multi —
1125S A331f 250fr multi *1.10 .50*
1125T A331f 450fr multi *2.00 .75*

An additional stamps were released in this set. The editors would like to examine them.

Diana, Princess of Wales Type

Designs: 260fr, Diana wearing tiara. 425fr, Diana in white blouse. 590fr, Diana with Pope John Paul II. No. 1127A: various portraits, color of sheet margin is violet.

1500fr, Diana speaking, American Red Cross emblem in sheet margin. 2000fr, Diana wearing Japanese kimono.

1997 Litho. *Perf. 13½*
1125U A325a 260fr multi —
1126 A325a 425fr multi 1.60 1.60
1127 A325a 590fr multi 2.25 1.10

Sheet of 9

1127A A325a 180fr #b-j 6.00 3.00

Souvenir Sheets

1127K A325a 1500fr multi 5.50 2.75
1128 A325a 2000fr multi 7.50 3.75

No. 1127 was issued in sheets of 9. No. 1127K contains one 41x46mm stamp.

Airplanes A332

No. 1129: a, Sukhoi Su-24. b, Yakovlev Yak-38. c, Tupolev Blackjack. d, Antonov An-26. e, Antonov An-22 Anteus. f, Antonov An-124. 1000fr, Ilyushin Il-76T.

1999, Sept. 8 Litho. *Perf. 14*

1129 A332 425fr Sheet of 6, #a.-f. 15.00 9.00

Souvenir Sheet

1130 A332 1000fr multicolored 6.00 4.00

No. 1130 contains one 57x43mm stamp.

Ships A333

No. 1131: a, Portland. b, Goethe. c, Fulton.

No. 1132: a, CSS Nashville. b, Cutty Sark. c, Brilliant. d, Eagle. e, Red Jacket. f, USS Columbia. g, HMS Rose. h, Resolution. i, 1000-ton paquebot. j, Mayflower.

No. 1133: a, USS Tennessee. b, HMS Alacrity. c, Bismarck. d, Yamoto. e, Aurora. f, Iowa class battleship. g, Liberty Ship. h, F209. i, Star. j, Big Eagle.

Each 1000fr: No. 1134, Batavia. No. 1135, Grand Voilier.

1999, Sept. 8 Sheets of 3 and 10

1131 A333 170fr #a.-c. 2.75 1.75
1132 A333 100fr #a.-j. 5.75 3.25
1133 A333 200fr #a.-j. 12.50 6.50

Souvenir Sheets

1134-1135 A333 Set of 2 12.00 6.50

Domesticated Animals — A334

5fr, Tabby cat, vert. 10fr, Chinchilla. 20fr, Yorkshire terriers. 25fr, Cocker spaniels.

No. 1140, vert.: a, Afghan hound. b, Fox terrier. c, Pug. d, Dalmatian. e, Boston terrier. f, Cocker spaniel.

No. 1141: a, American wirehaired. b, Tabby. c, Blue Burmese. d, Abyssinian. e, Lilac Burmese. f, Siamese.

No. 1142, 1000fr, Persian. No. 1143, 1000fr, Japanese bobtail, vert. No. 1144, 1000fr, Labrador retriever, vert. No. 1145, 1000fr, Labrador retrievers, vert.

1999, Oct. 4

1136-1139 A334 Set of 4 1.10 .80

Sheets of 6

1140 A334 260fr #a.-f. 8.50 5.50
1141 A334 530fr #a.-f. 20.00 12.00

Souvenir Sheets

1142-1145 A334 Set of 4 24.00 14.50

Domesticated Animals — A335

No. 1146 — Horses: a, Gelderlander. b, Trait lourd. c, Vladimir. d, Percheron. e, Sumba. f, Dartmoor.

No. 1147 — Dogs: a, French bulldog. b, Bernese. c, Griffon. d, King Charles spaniel. e, Spitz. f, Yorkshire terrier.

No. 1148 — Cats: a, American wirehaired. b, Japanese bobtail. c, Himalayan. d, LaPerm. e, Lilac Siamese colorpoint. f, Norwegian forest cat.

No. 1149, 1000fr, Shetland pony, vert. No. 1150, 1000fr, Basset hound, vert. No. 1151, 1000fr, Japanese bobtail, diff., vert.

1999, Oct. 4 Sheets of 6

1146 A335 170fr #a.-f. 5.25 3.50
1147 A335 425fr #a.-f. 15.00 9.00
1148 A335 590fr #a.-f. 20.00 13.00

Souvenir Sheets

1149-1151 A335 Set of 3 18.00 11.00

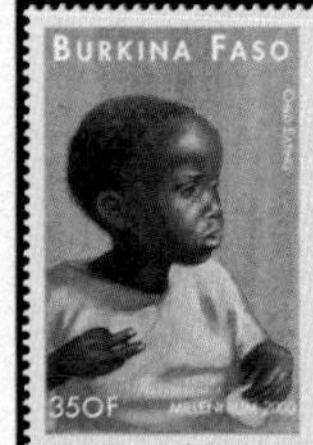

Fight Against Hunger — A337

1999, Dec. Litho. *Perf. 14*

1157 A337 350fr multi 1.75 1.00

Issued in sheets of 5.

FESPACO '99 Film Festival A338

Award winning film: 170fr, Tilai, by Idrissa Ouédraogo. 260fr, Map of Africa, camera, clapper board, vert. 425fr, Buud Yam, by Gaston Kaboré.

1999 Litho. *Perf. 13x13¼, 13¼x13*

1158 A338 170fr multi *.70 .30*
1159 A338 260fr multi *1.25 .45*
1159A A338 425fr multi *2.00 .75*

Issued: 1159A, 2/22/99.

Council of the Entente, 40th Anniv. A338a

Denomination color: 170fr, Black. 260fr, Green.

1999, May 5 Litho. *Perf. 13x13¼*

1160-1161 A338a Set of 2 *1.90 .75*

Lions A338b

Panel colors: 170fr, blue; 260fr, red; 425fr, green; 530fr, orange; 590fr, purple.

1999, May 26 Litho. *Perf. 13x13¼*

1161A-1161E A338b Set of 5 *32.50 3.50*

Philex France 99.

Orchids — A339

No. 1162, each 260fr: a, Angraecum orchid cape. b, Disa kirstenbosck pride. c, Disa blackii. d, Angraecum long icalear. e, Bulbophyllum falcatum. f, Phragmipedium schlimii (two flowers). g, Polystachya affinis. h, Jumellea sagittata (with leaves).

No. 1163, each 260fr: a, Angraecum sesquipedale. b, Oeceoclades maculata. c, Ancistrochilus childianus. d, Polystachyabella. e, Bulbophyllum lepidum. f, Vanilla imperialis. g, Tridactyle tridactylites. h, Eulophia guineensis.

No. 1164, each 260fr: a, Ansellia africana. b, Aerangis luteo-alba. c, Disa uniflora. d, Angraecum distichum. e, Bulbophyllum falcatum. f, Phragmepedium schlimii (pink flower). g, Polystachya affinis. h, Jumellea sagittata (without leaves).

No. 1165, 1500fr, Disa tripetaloides, horiz. No. 1166, 1500fr, Liparis guineensis, horiz. No. 1167, 1500fr, Bolusiella talbotii, horiz.

2000, Jan. 10 Litho. *Perf. 14*

Sheets of 8, #a.-h.

1162-1164 A339 Set of 3 37.50 22.00

Souvenir Sheets

1165-1167 A339 Set of 3 27.50 16.00

Space Exploration A340

No. 1168: a, Robert H. Goddard and 1926 rocket. b, Sputnik 1. c, X-15. d, Chinese, inventors of rockets. e, V-2. f, Explorer 1.

No. 1169: a, Vostok 1. b, Friendship 7. c, Soyuz 1. d, Freedom 7. e, Gemini 4. f, Apollo 7.

No. 1170, horiz.: a, Gemini 8. b, Agena target vehicle. c, Soyuz 11. d, Salyut 1. e, Apollo 18. f, Soyuz 19.

No. 1171, 1500fr, Tacsat satellite. No. 1172, 1500fr, Hubble Space Telescope. No. 1173, 1500fr, Viking Lander, horiz.

2000, Jan. 10 Sheets of 6

1168 A340 350fr #a.-f. 12.50 7.50
1169 A340 425fr #a.-f. 14.50 9.00
1170 A340 530fr #a.-f. 18.00 11.00

Souvenir Sheets

1171-1173 A340 Set of 3 17.00 17.00

No. 1173 contains one 57x42mm stamp.

Peter Pan — A341

Designs: a, 75fr, Fairy, red flowers. b, 75fr, Parrot. c, 75fr, Moon, Wendy, Michael, John. d, 75fr, White flower. e, 80fr, Fairy, pink flower. f, 80fr, Butterflies. g, 80fr, Peter Pan. h, 80fr, Fairy. i, 90fr, Red flower. j, 90fr, Butterflies. k, 90fr, Egret. l, 90fr, White flower. m, 100fr, Mermaid. n, 100fr, Pirate ship, crocodile's tail. o, 100fr, Crocodile's head. p, 100fr, Captain Hook.

2000, Jan. 10 *Perf. 12¼*

1174 A341 Sheet of 16, #a.-p. 8.25 4.25

2000 Summer Olympics, Sydney — A343

No. 1191: a, Hannes Kohlemainen. b, Runner. c, US flag, Fulton County Stadium, Atlanta. d, Discus thrower.

2000, Nov. 12 Litho. *Perf. 14*

1191 A343 350fr Sheet of 4, #a-d 7.75 3.75

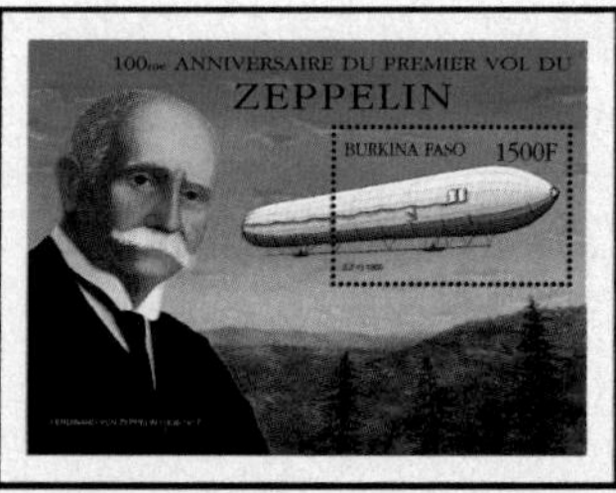

First Zeppelin Flight, Cent. — A344

No. 1192, 350fr: a, LZ-1, b, LZ-2 (dark gray at left). c, LZ-2 (white at left) d, LZ-5. e, LZ-8. f, LZ-7.

No. 1193, 350fr: a, LZ-9. b, LZ-10. c, LZ-11. d, LZ-127. e, LZ-129. f, LZ-130.

No. 1194, 1500fr, LZ-1. No. 1195, 1500fr, LZ-4.

2000, Nov. 12 Sheets of 6, #a-f

1192-1193 A344 Set of 2 26.50 11.00

Souvenir Sheets

1194-1195 A344 Set of 2 18.00 8.00

Berlin Film Festival, 50th Anniv. — A345

No. 1196: a, Le Grand Blond Avec Une Chaussure Noire. b Ruy Guerra. c, Mario Monicelli. d, Mudhur Jaffrey. e, Orökbefogadás. f, Palermo Oder Wolfsburg.

2000, Nov. 12 Litho. *Perf. 14*

Sheet of 6

1196 A345 420fr #a-f 15.00 7.25

Souvenir Sheet

1197 A345 1500fr Platoon 9.25 4.50

Souvenir Sheets

Public Railways, 175th Anniv. — A346

No. 1198: a, George Stephenson, Locomotion No. 1. b, Stourbridge Lion.

No. 1199: a, George Stephenson, Brusselton inclined plane. b, Robert Stephenson, turnpike crossing near Darlington. c, Locomotive built by George Stephenson. d, Experiment passenger coach built by Robert Stephenson.

2000, Nov. 12 Sheets of 2 and 4

1198 A346 550fr #a-b 7.00 3.25
1199 A346 800fr #a-d 17.00 9.25

Fruits — A347

2000	Litho.	Perf. 14¾		
1200	A347	95fr Parkia biglobosa	2.25	.25
1201	A347	100fr Baobab	2.25	.25
1202	A347	170fr Tamarind, horiz.	4.25	.30
1203	A347	425fr Vitellaria paradoxa	9.75	.60
		Nos. 1200-1203 (4)	*18.50*	*1.40*

Issued: 170fr, 2/23.

The editors suspect that other stamps of this type were issued and would like to examine any examples.

Elephants A348

2000, Mar. 22	Litho.	Perf. 14¾		
1204	A348	200fr Facing left	6.50	.35
1205	A348	425fr multi, vert.	13.50	.65
1206	A348	500fr Facing right	19.00	.85
		Nos. 1204-1206 (3)	*39.00*	*1.85*

National Culture Week — A349

Designs: 120fr, Sidari Troupe, Sidéradougou, vert. 130fr, Dancer and drummer, vert. 260fr, Dancer and xylophone player, vert. 425fr, Dancers and drummer. 530fr, Musicians. 590fr, Dancers.

2000	Litho.	Perf. 13½x13, 13x13½		
1207	A349	120fr multi	4.00	.25
1208	A349	130fr multi	4.00	.25
1209	A349	260fr multi	6.25	.45
1210	A349	425fr multi	10.00	.60
1211	A349	530fr multi	12.50	.75
1212	A349	590fr multi	14.50	1.10
		Nos. 1207-1212 (6)	*51.25*	*3.40*

Molluscs and Crustaceans A350

Designs: 30fr, Limnaea natalensis. 170fr, Caelastura teretiscula. 250fr, Achatina achatina. 260fr, Biomphalaria pfeifferi. 425fr, Potamonautes macleay.

2000, Apr. 28	Litho.	Perf. 13x13¼		
1213	A350	30fr multi	.25	.25
1214	A350	170fr multi	6.00	.25
1215	A350	250fr multi	8.75	.35
1216	A350	260fr multi	9.25	.35
1217	A350	425fr multi	15.00	.65
		Nos. 1213-1217 (5)	*39.25*	*1.85*

Belem-Yegre Museum — A351

Designs: 170fr, Dougui mask, vert. 260fr, Main entrance. 425fr, Monuments. 530fr, Tombstone, vert.

2000	Litho.	Perf. 15x14¾, 14¾x15		
1218	A351	170fr multi	3.75	.25
1219	A351	260fr multi	5.75	.35
1220	A351	425fr multi	9.75	.65
1221	A351	530fr multi	11.50	.90
		Nos. 1218-1221 (4)	*30.75*	*2.15*

Items in National Museum — A352

Designs: 170fr, Kurumba statuettes. 260fr, Mossi statuette. 425fr, Loulouka pot. 530fr, Mossi du Kourwéogo statuette. 590fr, San statuette.

2001	Litho.	Perf. 13¼x13		
1222	A352	170fr multi	5.00	.25
1223	A352	260fr multi	7.00	.35
1224	A352	425fr multi	10.00	.65
1224A	A352	530fr multi	14.00	.90
1225	A352	590fr multi	15.00	1.10
		Nos. 1222-1225 (5)	*51.00*	*3.25*

Birds A353

Designs: 25fr, Anaplectes rubriceps. 50fr, Dendrocygna viduata. 95fr, Ploceus cucullatus, vert. 170fr, Bubulcus ibis, vert. 425fr, Campethera masculosa, vert. 590fr, Francolinus bicalcaratus, vert.

2001	Litho.	Perf. 13x13¼, 13¼x13		
1226	A353	25fr multi	1.00	.25
1227	A353	50fr multi	1.60	.25
1227A	A353	95fr multi	3.25	.25
1228	A353	170fr multi	6.00	.25
1228A	A353	425fr multi	16.00	.65
1229	A353	590fr multi	21.00	1.10
		Nos. 1226-1229 (6)	*48.85*	*2.75*

Tourism A354

Designs: 170fr, Karfiguéla Waterfall, vert. 260fr, Sand dune, Oursi. 425fr, Laongo granite sculptures, vert. 530fr, Decorated homes, Tiébélé. 590fr, Sindou Peaks.

2001	Litho.	Perf. 13¼x13, 13x13¼		
1230	A354	170fr multi	3.75	.25
1231	A354	260fr multi	7.50	.35
1232	A354	425fr multi	12.00	.65
1233	A354	530fr multi	13.50	.90
1234	A354	590fr multi	14.00	1.10
		Nos. 1230-1234 (5)	*50.75*	*3.25*

Fish A355

Designs: 25fr, Gymnarchus niloticus. 40fr, Bagrus docmak. 50fr, Hemisynedontis membranenceus. 170fr, Oreochromis niloticus niloticus. 425fr, Lates niloticus. 530fr, Heterotis niloticus.

2001	Litho.	Perf. 13x13½		
1235	A355	25fr multi	1.40	.25
1236	A355	40fr multi	1.75	.25
1237	A355	50fr multi	1.90	.25
1238	A355	170fr multi	6.50	.25
1239	A355	425fr multi	17.00	.65
1240	A355	530fr multi	21.00	.90
		Nos. 1235-1240 (6)	*49.55*	*2.55*

Insects A356

Designs: 5fr, Helicoverpa armigera. 10fr, Poekilocerus bufonius hieroglyphicus. 20fr, Diopsis thoracica. 100fr, Psalydolitta sp. 170fr, Ptinus fur, vert. 200fr, Bruchidius atralineatus, vert. 260fr, Dysdercus sp., vert. 500fr, Lygus lineolaris. 1000fr, Doryphora. 1500fr, Acantboscelides obtectus say, vert.

2002, Apr. 4	Perf. 13x13½, 13½x13	Litho.		
1241	A356	5fr multi	1.00	.25
1242	A356	10fr multi	1.00	.25
1243	A356	20fr multi	1.00	.25
1244	A356	100fr multi	3.00	.75
1245	A356	170fr multi	—	—
1246	A356	200fr multi	4.00	1.00
1247	A356	260fr multi	5.00	1.25
1248	A356	500fr multi	10.00	2.50
1249	A356	1000fr multi	20.00	5.00
1250	A356	1500fr multi	24.00	2.25
		Nos. 1241-1250 (10)	*69.00*	*13.50*

Crafts — A357

Design: 100fr, Long-headed Pouni mask. 170fr, Figurine of Mossi tom-tom player. 425fr, Calao Pouni mask, horiz.

2003, June 30	Litho.	Perf. 13½x13		
1251	A357	100fr multi	2.50	.75
1252	A357	170fr multi	4.00	1.00
		Perf. 13x13½		
1253	A357	425fr multi	14.00	3.50

Intl. Fund for Agricultural Development, 25th Anniv. — A358

2003, Sept. 20	Litho.	Perf. 13x13¼		
1254	A358	170fr multi	5.00	1.25

Burkina Faso - Taiwan Cooperation — A359

Designs: 5fr, 10fr, 20fr, 100fr, 170fr, Kou Valley rice farm. 200fr, 260fr, 425fr, 530fr, 590fr, Bagré Aqueduct.

2003, Oct. 10	Litho.	Perf. 13x13½		
		Frame Color		
1255	A359	5fr red	.50	.25
1256	A359	10fr blue	.50	.25
1257	A359	20fr brown	.50	.25
1258	A359	100fr blue	1.60	.25
1259	A359	170fr black	2.50	.25
1260	A359	200fr dark red	3.25	.55
1261	A359	260fr blue	4.50	.55
1262	A359	425fr brown	8.00	.65
1263	A359	530fr blue	9.00	.90
1264	A359	590fr black	10.00	1.10
		Nos. 1255-1264 (10)	*40.35*	*5.00*

Musical Instruments A360

Design: 30fr, Bwaba balaphone, horiz. 40fr, Nouni flute. 150fr, Mossi funerary drum, horiz.

2004, Mar. 27	Litho.	Perf. 13½x13		
1265	A360	30fr multi		—
1266	A360	40fr multi	1.50	1.50
1268	A360	150fr multi		—

One additional stamp was issued in this set. The editors would like to examine any examples.

National Pardon Day — A361

2004, Mar. 30	Litho.	Perf. 13¼x13		
1269	A361	170fr tan & multi	2.00	2.00
1270	A361	530fr red & multi	4.00	4.00

An additional stamp was issued in this set. The editors would like to examine it.

Tenth Francophone Summit, Ouagadougou A362

2004, Nov. 1	Litho.	Perf. 13½x13		
1271	A362	425fr lil, brn & multi	2.75	2.75
1272	A362	530fr red, grn & multi	3.50	3.50
1273	A362	590fr blue & multi	4.50	4.50
		Nos. 1271-1273 (3)	*10.75*	*10.75*

Mediator of Faso, 10th Anniv. — A363

Design: 100fr, Mediator grasping two men. 330fr, Mediator grasping two men.

2005, Jan. 20	Litho.	Perf. 13½x13		
1274	A363	100fr grn & multi	1.00	1.00
1276	A363	330fr blue & multi	3.00	3.00

Two additional stamps were issued in this set. The editors would like to examine any examples.

Hoes — A363a

Designs: 5p, Peulh hoe, Dou, vert. 10fr, Dagari hoe, eastern region. 30fr, Dagari hoe. 70fr, Mossi plateau hoe. 100fr, Mossi hoe, Zitenga, horiz.

Perf. 13½x13, 13x13½

2005, Nov. 16 **Litho.**

1276B A363a 5fr multi *1.00 1.00*
1276C A363 10fr multi *1.00 1.00*
1276D A363a 30fr multi *1.00 1.00*
1276E A363a 70fr multi *1.00 1.00*
1276F A363a 100fr multi *1.00 1.00*
Nos. 1276B-1276F (5) *5.00 5.00*

Hats — A363b

Designs: 265fr, Peulh du Seno hat, horiz. 300fr, Mossi chief's hat. 500fr, Yatenga banded hat. 690fr, Crooked Yatenga hat.

2005, Nov. 16 **Litho.** ***Perf. 13½x13***

1276G A363b 265fr multi *1.00 1.00*
1276H A363b 300fr multi *1.00 1.00*
1276I A363b 500fr multi *1.00 1.00*
1276J A363b 690fr multi *1.00 1.00*
Nos. 1276G-1276J (4) *4.00 4.00*

See Nos. 1285-1291.

Léopold Sédar Senghor (1906-2001), First President of Senegal — A364

2006, Mar. 2 **Litho.** ***Perf. 13x13½***

1277 A364 100fr red & multi — —
1278 A364 200fr bl grn & multi *1.50 1.50*
1279 A364 1000fr pur & multi — —

Cooperation Between Burkina Faso and Germany — A365

2006 **Litho.** ***Perf. 13x13¼***

1280 A365 200fr multi *2.50 2.50*

Burkina EMS Chronopost, 5th Anniv. — A366

2006, June 9 **Litho.** ***Perf. 13½x13***

1281 A366 200fr org & multi *2.00 2.00*
1282 A366 330fr red brn & multi *3.00 3.00*
1283 A366 690fr red vio & multi *5.00 5.00*

Hats Type of 2005

Design: 5fr, 10fr, 20fr, 40fr, 50fr, 75fr, 1500fr, Peulh du Seno hat, horiz.

2006, Nov. 6 **Litho.** ***Perf. 13x13¼***

1284 A363b 5fr rose & multi —
1285 A363b 10fr lt blue & multi *1.00 1.00*
1286 A363b 20fr org & multi *1.00 1.00*
1287 A363b 40fr blue & multi *1.00 1.00*
1288 A363b 50fr green & multi *1.00 1.00*
1289 A363b 75fr lt blue & multi —
1291 A363b 1500fr yel brn & multi *15.00 15.00*

Dated 2006. One additional stamp was issued in this set. The editors would like to examine any examples.

Lions International, 90th Anniv. — A367

Denomination color: 330fr, Blue; 690fr, Pink.

2007 **Litho.** ***Perf. 13¼***

1292 A367 330fr multi *3.00 3.00*
1293 A367 690fr multi *7.00 7.00*

Wrestling A368

Designs: 5fr, Parade of wrestlers. 30fr, Wrestlers in attack position. 200fr, Wrestlers grabbing each other's thighs, vert. 690fr, Wrestler grabbing opponent's leg.

2008, Mar. 17 **Litho.** ***Perf. 13x13¼***

1294 A368 5fr multi — —
1295 A368 30fr multi — —
1296 A368 200fr multi — —
1297 A368 690fr multi — —

Safari Animals and Shelters A369

Designs: 10fr, Nerwaya Safari hut, lion. 25fr, Express Safari hut, duck. 75fr, Sahel shelter, bird, vert. 100fr, Safari Chasse hut, leopard.

Perf. 13x13¼, 13¼x13

2008, June 6 **Litho.**

1298 A369 10fr multi — —
1299 A369 25fr multi — —
1300 A369 75fr multi — —
1301 A369 100fr multi — —
1302 A369 200fr multi — —

Dances — A370

Designs: 50fr, Bissa dance. 200fr, Gourmatché dance. 500fr, Mossi Kiegba dance. 690fr, Kassena dance.

2008, July 1 **Litho.** ***Perf. 13¼x13***

1303 A370 50fr multi — —
1304 A370 200fr multi — —
1305 A370 500fr multi — —
1306 A370 690fr multi — —

Burkina Faso Federation of Associations for Promotion of the Handicapped — A371

2008, Oct. 31 **Litho.** ***Perf. 13x13¼***

1307 A371 200fr blue & multi — —
1308 A371 690fr green & multi — —

Independence, 48th Anniv. — A372

2008, Dec. 5 **Litho.** ***Perf. 13¼x13***

1309 A372 200fr green & multi — —
1310 A372 690fr blue & multi — —

FESPACO 2009 Film Festival A373

Designs: 690fr, Sembene Ousmane (1923-2007), writer and film director. 1000fr, 40th anniversary emblem.

2009, Feb. 20 ***Perf. 13x13¼***
Granite Paper

1311-1312 A373 Set of 2 *13.00 13.00*

Traditional Foods A374

Designs: 20fr, Millet fritters. 300fr, Tô de mais. 1500fr, Bean fritters.

2009 **Litho.** **Granite Paper**

1313-1315 A374 Set of 3 *14.00 14.00*

Agricultural Work A375

Designs: 200fr, Planting. 690fr, Hoeing. 1000fr, Millet harvesting.

2009 **Litho.** ***Perf. 13x13¼***

1316-1318 A375 Set of 3 10.50 10.50

Traditional Occupations — A376

Designs: 40fr, Blacksmith. 200fr, Weaver. 1500fr, Cotton spinner.

2009 **Litho.** ***Perf. 13x13¼***
Granite Paper

1319-1321 A376 Set of 3 *16.50 16.50*

Transportation — A378

Designs: 30fr, Woman on bicycle. 70fr, Man on donkey cart.

2010, Aug. 16 **Litho.** ***Perf. 13x13¼***

1325-1326 A378 Set of 2 1.10 1.10

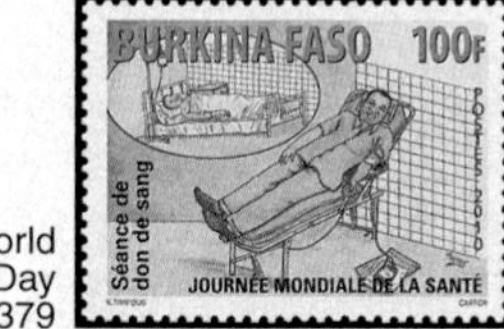

World Health Day A379

Designs: 100fr, Blood donation. 160fr, Campaign against malaria.

2010, Oct. 15 **Granite Paper**

1327-1328 A379 Set of 2 2.00 2.00

Domesticated Animals — A381

Designs: 100fr, Donkey. 265fr, Horse. 300fr, Dromedary.

2011, Feb. 1 **Litho.** ***Perf. 13x13¼***

1331-1333 A381 Set of 3 2.75 2.75

Dated 2010.

Campaign Against AIDS, 30th Anniv. A382

Designs: 200fr, Man, woman, letter carrier with Post Office AIDS campaign poster. 690fr, People in post office, Post Office AIDS campaign poster.

2011, Aug. 8

1334-1335 A382 Set of 2 4.00 4.00

Poultry A383

Designs: 100fr, Ducks (canard). 160fr, Turkeys (dindon). 265fr, Rooster and hen (coq).

2011, Oct. 12

1336-1338 A383 Set of 3 2.25 2.25

Vegetable Cultivation A384

Designs: 30fr, Onions. 70fr, Cabbages. 100fr, Carrots.

2011, Nov. 7
1339-1341 A384 Set of 3 .85 .85

Cooperation Between Burkina Faso and Germany, 50th Anniv. — A385

Background color: 200fr, Blue. 690fr, Yellow orange.

2011, Dec. 23 ***Perf. 14½x14¼***
1342-1343 A385 Set of 2 4.00 4.00

SEMI-POSTAL STAMPS

Catalogue values for unused stamps in this section are for Never Hinged items.

Anti-Malaria Issue
Common Design Type
Perf. 12½x12

1962, Apr. 7 **Engr.** **Unwmk.**
B1 CD108 25fr + 5fr red org .95 .95

Freedom from Hunger Issue
Common Design Type

1963, Mar. 21 ***Perf. 13***
B2 CD112 25fr + 5fr dk grn, bl & brn .95 .95

CAN '96 (African Nations) Soccer Championships — SP1

Designs: 150fr+25fr, Stallions, soccer ball. 250fr+25fr, Map of Africa, soccer player.

1996, Jan. 2 **Litho.** ***Perf. 11½***
B3 SP1 150fr +25fr multi .95 .45
a. Souvenir sheet of 1 2.75 1.40
B4 SP1 250fr +25fr multi 1.50 .75

No. B3a sold for 500fr.

AIR POST STAMPS

Catalogue values for unused stamps in this section are for Never Hinged items.

Plane over Map Showing Air Routes — AP1

200fr, Plane at airport, Ouagadougou. 500fr, Champs Elysees, Ouagadougou.

Unwmk.

1961, Mar. 4 **Engr.** ***Perf. 13***
C1 AP1 100fr multicolored 2.25 1.00
C2 AP1 200fr multicolored 5.75 1.75
C3 AP1 500fr multicolored 14.50 6.25
Nos. C1-C3 (3) 22.50 9.00

Air Afrique Issue
Common Design Type

1962, Feb. 17
C4 CD107 25fr brt pink, dk pur & lt grn .65 .45

UN Emblem and Upper Volta Flag — AP2

Perf. 13½x12½

1962, Sept. 22 **Photo.**
C5 AP2 50fr multicolored .75 .40
C6 AP2 100fr multicolored 1.75 .80

Admission to UN, second anniversary.

Post Office, Ouagadougou — AP3

1962, Dec. 11 ***Perf. 13x12***
C7 AP3 100fr multicolored 1.75 .80

Jet Over Map AP4

1963, June 24
C8 AP4 200fr multicolored 5.00 1.50

First jet flight, Ouagadougou to Paris.
For surcharge see No. C10.

African Postal Union Issue
Common Design Type

1963, Sept. 8 **Unwmk.** ***Perf. 12½***
C9 CD114 85fr dp vio, ocher & red 1.50 .75

No. C8 Surcharged in Red

1963, Nov. 19 ***Perf. 13x12***
C10 AP4 50fr on 200fr multi 1.40 .80

See note after Mauritania No. C26.

Europafrica Issue
Common Design Type

50fr, Sunburst & Europe linked with Africa.

1964, Jan. 6 ***Perf. 12x13***
C11 CD116 50fr multicolored 1.50 .80

Ramses II, Abu Simbel — AP5

1964, Mar. 8 **Engr.** ***Perf. 13***
C12 AP5 25fr dp green & choc .75 .50
C13 AP5 100fr brt bl & brn 2.75 2.00

UNESCO world campaign to save historic monuments of Nubia.

Greek Sculptures AP6

1964, July 1 **Unwmk.** ***Perf. 13***
C14 AP6 15fr Greek Portrait Head .45 .25
C15 AP6 25fr Seated boxer .60 .25
C16 AP6 85fr Victorious athlete 1.40 1.00
C17 AP6 100fr Venus of Milo 2.00 1.10
a. Min. sheet of 4, #C14-C17 10.00 10.00
Nos. C14-C17 (4) 4.45 2.60

18th Olympic Games, Tokyo, Oct. 10-25.

West African Gray Woodpecker AP7

1964, Oct. 1 **Engr.** ***Perf. 13***
C18 AP7 250fr multicolored 10.50 5.50

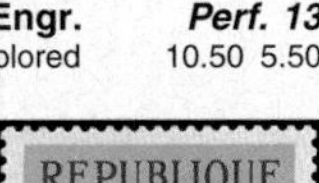

President John F. Kennedy (1917-1963) AP8

1964, Nov. 25 **Photo.** ***Perf. 12½***
C19 AP8 100fr orange, brn & lil 2.25 1.50
a. Souvenir sheet of 4 10.00 8.00

Bird Type of Regular Issue, 1965

1965, Mar. 1 **Photo.** ***Perf. 13***
Size: 27x48mm
C20 A27 500fr Abyssinian roller 22.50 9.00

Earth and Sun — AP9

1965, Mar. 23 **Engr.**
C21 AP9 50fr multicolored 1.25 .50

5th World Meteorological Day.

Hughes Telegraph, ITU Emblem and Dial Telephone — AP10

1965, May 17 **Unwmk.** ***Perf. 13***
C22 AP10 100fr red, sl grn & bl grn 2.50 1.10

ITU, centenary.

Intl. Cooperation Year — AP10a

1965, June 21 **Photo.** ***Perf. 13***
C23 AP10a 25fr multicolored .60 .25
C24 AP10a 100fr multicolored 1.75 .50
a. Min. sheet, 2 each #C23-C24 4.50 3.00

Sacred Sabou Crocodile — AP11

1965, Aug. 9 **Engr.** ***Perf. 13***
C25 AP11 60fr shown 3.25 1.00
C26 AP11 85fr Lion, vert. 3.75 1.10

Early Bird Satellite over Globe — AP12

1965, Sept. 15 **Unwmk.** ***Perf. 13***
C27 AP12 30fr brt bl, brn & brn red .75 .45

Space communications.

Tiros Satellite and Weather Map — AP13

1966, Mar. 23 Engr. *Perf. 13*
C28 AP13 50fr dk car, brt bl & blk 1.25 .65

6th World Meteorological Day.

FR-1 Satellite over Ouagadougou Space Tracking Station — AP14

1966, Apr. 28 *Perf. 13*
C29 AP14 250fr mag, ind & org brn 4.75 2.50

Inauguration of WHO Headquarters, Geneva — AP15

1966, May 3 Photo.
C30 AP15 100fr yel, blk & bl 2.25 .95

Air Afrique Issue

Common Design Type

1966, Aug. 31 Photo. *Perf. 13*
C31 CD123 25fr tan, blk & yel grn .75 .50

Sir Winston Churchill, British Lion and "V" Sign — AP16

1966, Nov. 5 Engr. *Perf. 13*
C32 AP16 100fr slate grn & car rose 2.25 .85

Sir Winston Spencer Churchill (1874-1965), statesman and WWII leader.

Pope Paul VI, Peace Dove, UN General Assembly and Emblem — AP17

1966, Nov. 5
C33 AP17 100fr dk blue & pur 2.25 .85

Pope Paul's appeal for peace before the UN General Assembly, Oct. 4, 1965.

Blind Man and Lions Emblem — AP18

1967, Feb. 28 Engr. *Perf. 13*
C34 AP18 100fr dk vio bl, brt bl & dk brn 2.25 .85

50th anniversary of Lions Intl.

UN Emblem and Rain over Landscape AP19

1967, Mar. 23 Engr. *Perf. 13*
C35 AP19 50fr ultra, dk grn & bl grn 1.25 .60

7th World Meteorological Day.

Diamant Rocket — AP20

French Spacecraft: 20fr, FR-1 satellite, horiz. 30fr, D1-C satellite. 100fr, D1-D satellite, horiz.

1967, Apr. 18 Engr. *Perf. 13*
C36 AP20 5fr brt bl, sl grn & org .25 .25
C37 AP20 20fr lilac & slate blue .55 .25
C38 AP20 30fr red brn, brt bl & emer .75 .25
C39 AP20 100fr emer & dp claret 2.00 .85
Nos. C36-C39 (4) 3.55 1.60

For overprint see No. C69.

Albert Schweitzer (1875-1965), Medical Missionary and Organ Pipes — AP21

1967, May 12 Engr. *Perf. 13*
C40 AP21 250fr claret & blk 4.75 2.50

World Map and 1967 Jamboree Emblem — AP22

1967, June 8 Photo.
C41 AP22 100fr multicolored 1.75 .85

12th Boy Scout World Jamboree, Farragut State Park, Idaho, Aug. 1-9.

Madonna and Child, 15th Century AP23

Paintings: 20fr, Still life by Paul Gauguin. 50fr, Pietà, by Dick Bouts. 60fr, Anne of Cleves, by Hans Holbein the Younger. 90fr, The Money Lender and his Wife, by Quentin Massys (38x40mm). 100fr, Blessing of the Risen Christ, by Giovanni Bellini. 200fr, The Handcart, by Louis Le Nain, horiz. 250fr, The Four Evangelists, by Jacob Jordaens.

Perf. 12½x12, 12x12½, 13½ (90fr)

1967-68 Photo.
C42 AP23 20fr multi ('68) .45 .35
C43 AP23 30fr multi .70 .35
C44 AP23 50fr multi 1.00 .50
C45 AP23 60fr multi ('68) .85 .60
C46 AP23 90fr multi ('68) 1.25 .95
C47 AP23 100fr multi 1.75 1.00
C48 AP23 200fr multi ('68) 3.00 2.10
C49 AP23 250fr multi 4.75 2.50
Nos. C42-C49 (8) 13.75 8.35

See Nos. C70-C72.

African Postal Union Issue, 1967

Common Design Type

1967, Sept. 9 Engr. *Perf. 13*
C50 CD124 100fr multicolored 1.80 .70

Caravelle "Ouagadougou" — AP24

1968, Feb. 29 Engr. *Perf. 13*
C51 AP24 500fr bl, dp cl & blk 11.50 5.50

WMO Emblem, Sun, Rain, Wheat — AP25

1968, Mar. 23 Engr. *Perf. 13*
C52 AP25 50fr dk red, ultra & gray grn 1.25 .50

8th World Meteorological Day.

Europafrica Issue

Clove Hitch — AP25a

1968, July 20 Photo. *Perf. 13*
C53 AP25a 50fr yel bis, blk & dk red 1.00 .55

See note after Niger No. C89.

Vessel in Form of Acrobat with Bells, Colima Culture — AP26

Mexican Sculptures: 30fr, Ballplayer, Veracruz, vert. 60fr, Javelin thrower, Colima, vert. 100fr, Seated athlete with cape, Jalisco.

1968, Oct. 14 Engr. *Perf. 13*
C54 AP26 10fr dk red, ocher & choc .55 .25
C55 AP26 30fr bl grn, brt grn & dk brn .70 .25
C56 AP26 60fr ultra, ol & mar 1.40 .55
C57 AP26 100fr brt grn, bl & mar 1.90 .90
Nos. C54-C57 (4) 4.55 1.95

19th Olympic Games, Mexico City, 10/12-27.

Artisan Type of Regular Issue

1968, Oct. 30 Engr. *Perf. 13*

Size: 48x27mm

C58 A52 100fr Potter 1.60 .75

PHILEXAFRIQUE Issue

Too Late or The Letter, by Armand Cambon AP27

1968, Nov. 22 Photo. *Perf. 12½*
C59 AP27 100fr multicolored 3.50 3.25

PHILEXAFRIQUE, Phil. Exhib., Abidjan, Feb. 14-23, 1969. Printed with alternating rose claret label.

Albert John Luthuli — AP28

Design: No. C61, Mahatma Gandhi.

1968, Dec. 16 Photo. *Perf. 12½*

C60 AP28 100fr dk grn, yel grn & blk 2.00 2.00
C61 AP28 100fr dk grn, yel & blk 2.00 2.00
a. Min. sheet, 2 each #C60-C61 9.00 9.00

Exponents of non-violence.

2nd PHILEXAFRIQUE Issue
Common Design Type

50fr, Upper Volta #59, dancers & musicians.

1969, Feb. 14 Engr. *Perf. 13*

C62 CD128 50fr pur, bl car & brn 4.00 3.75

Weather Sonde, WMO Emblem, Mule and Cattle in Irrigated Field — AP29

1969, Mar. 24 Engr. *Perf. 13*

C63 AP29 100fr dk brn, brt bl & grn 4.25 2.25

9th World Meteorological Day.

Artisan Type of Regular Issue

Design: 150fr, Basket weaver.

1969, Apr. 3 Engr. *Perf. 13*
Size: 48x27mm

C64 A55 150fr brn, bl & blk 2.75 1.25

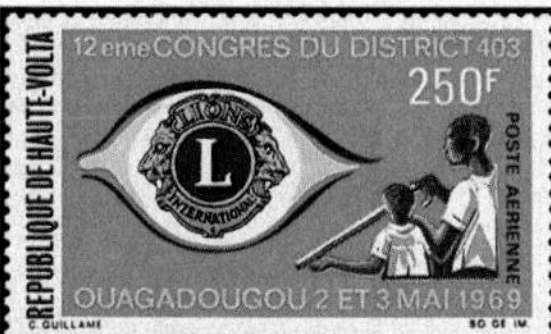

Lions Emblem, Eye and Blind Man — AP30

1969, Apr. 30 Photo.

C65 AP30 250fr red & multi 3.50 1.75

12th Congress of District 403 of Lions Intl., Ouagadougou, May 2-3.

Fish Type of Regular Issue

Designs: 100fr, Phenacogrammus pabrensis. 150fr, Upside-down catfish.

1969 Engr. *Perf. 13*
Size: 48x27mm

C66 A57 100fr slate, pur & yel 2.50 1.00
C67 A57 150fr org brn, gray & slate 4.75 2.40

Earth and Astronaut — AP31

Embossed on Gold Foil

1969 *Die-cut Perf. 10½x10*

C68 AP31 1000fr gold 25.00 25.00

Apollo 8 mission, which put the first man into orbit around the moon, Dec. 21-27, 1968.

No. C39 Overprinted in red with Lunar Landing Module and

1969, July 25 Engr. *Perf. 13*

C69 AP20 100fr emer & dp claret 4.50 4.50

See note after Mali No. C80.

Painting Type of 1967-68

Paintings: 50fr, Napoleon Crossing Great St. Bernard Pass, by Jacques Louis David. 150fr, Napoleon Awarding the First Cross of the Legion of Honor, by Jean-Baptiste Debret. 250fr, Napoleon Before Madrid, by Carle Vernet.

1969, Aug. 18 Photo. *Perf. 12½x12*

C70 AP23 50fr carmine & multi 2.25 1.00
C71 AP23 150fr violet & multi 5.75 2.50
C72 AP23 250fr green & multi 8.00 4.50
Nos. C70-C72 (3) 16.00 8.00

Napoleon Bonaparte (1769-1821).

Agriculture Type of Regular Issue

1969, Oct. 30 Photo. *Perf. 12½x13*
Size: 47½x27mm

C73 A58 100fr Peanuts 1.75 .50
C74 A58 200fr Rice 3.25 1.00

AP32

Tree of Life, symbols of science, agriculture and industry.

1969, Nov. 21 Photo. *Perf. 12x13*

C75 AP32 100fr multicolored 1.25 .80

See note after Mauritania No. C28.

AP33

Designs: 20fr, Lenin. 100fr, Lenin Addressing Revolutionaries in Petrograd, by V. A. Serov, horiz.

1970, Apr. 22 Photo. *Perf. 12½*

C76 AP33 20fr ocher & brn .60 .35
C77 AP33 100fr blk, lt grn & red 1.90 1.25

Lenin (1870-1924), Russian communist leader.

Pres. Roosevelt with Stamp Collection — AP34

10fr, Franklin Delano Roosevelt, vert.

1970, June 4 Photo. *Perf. 12½*

C78 AP34 10fr dk brn, emer & red brn .25 .25
C79 AP34 200fr vio bl, gray & dk car 2.25 1.10

Soccer Game and Jules Rimet Cup — AP35

100fr, Goalkeeper catching ball, globe.

1970, June 4 Engr. *Perf. 13*

C80 AP35 40fr olive, brt grn & brn .60 .45
C81 AP35 100fr blk, lil, brn & grn 1.60 .80

9th World Soccer Championships for the Jules Rimet Cup, Mexico City, 5/30-6/21/70.

EXPO Emblem, Monorail and "Cranes at the Seashore" AP36

Design: 150fr, EXPO emblem, rocket, satellites and "Geisha."

1970, Aug. 7 Photo. *Perf. 12½*

C82 AP36 50fr multicolored 2.25 .80
C83 AP36 150fr green & multi 1.60 1.00

Issued to publicize EXPO '70 International Exhibition, Osaka, Japan, Mar. 15-Sept. 13.

UN Emblem, Dove and Star — AP37

250fr, UN emblem and doves, horiz.

1970, Oct. 2 Engr. *Perf. 13*

C84 AP37 60fr dk bl, bl & grn .50 .35
C85 AP37 250fr dk red brn, vio bl & ol 3.25 1.25

25th anniversary of the United Nations.

Holy Family — AP38

Silver Embossed

1970, Nov. 27 *Die-Cut Perf. 10*

C86 AP38 300fr silver 9.00 9.00

Gold Embossed

C87 AP38 1000fr gold 22.50 22.50

Christmas.

Family and Upper Volta Flag — AP39

Litho.; Gold Embossed

1970, Dec. 10 *Perf. 12½*

C88 AP39 500fr gold, blk & red 7.00 3.75

10th anniversary of independence, Dec. 11.

UN "Key to a Free World" — AP40

1970, Dec. 14 Engr. *Perf. 13*

C89 AP40 40fr red, bister & blue .90 .50

UN Declaration of Independence for Colonial Peoples, 10th anniv.

Gamal Abdel Nasser — AP41

1971, Jan. 30 Photo. *Perf. 12½*

C90 AP41 100fr green & multi 1.20 .50

Nasser (1918-1970), president of Egypt.

Herons, Egyptian Art, 1354 — AP42

250fr, Page from Koran, Egypt, 1368-1388.

1971, May 13 Photo. *Perf. 13*

C91 AP42 100fr multi 1.25 .80
C92 AP42 250fr multi, vert. 4.00 2.00

Olympic Rings and Various Sports — AP43

1971, June 10 Engr. *Perf. 13*
C93 AP43 150fr vio bl & red 3.25 1.60

Pre-Olympic Year.

Boy Scout and Buildings — AP44

1971, Aug. 12 Photo. *Perf. 12½*
C94 AP44 45fr multicolored 1.00 .60

13th Boy Scout World Jamboree, Asagiri Plain, Japan, Aug. 2-10.

De Gaulle, Map of Upper Volta, Cross of Lorraine — AP45

Charles de Gaulle — AP46

1971, Nov. 9 Photo. *Perf. 13x12*
C95 AP45 40fr lt brn, grn & blk .80 .80

Lithographed; Gold Embossed

Perf. 12½

C96 AP46 500fr gold & grn 12.00 11.00

Gen. Charles de Gaulle (1890-1970), president of France.

African Postal Union Issue, 1971

Common Design Type

Design: 100fr, Mossi dancer and UAMPT building, Brazzaville, Congo.

1971, Nov. 13 Photo. *Perf. 13x13½*
C97 CD135 100fr bl & multi 1.50 .70

Gen. Sangoule Lamizana AP47

1971, Dec. 11 *Perf. 12½*
C98 AP47 35fr sep, blk, gold & ultra .90 .60

Inauguration of 2nd Republic of Upper Volta.

Kabuki Actor and Ice Hockey — AP48

1972, Feb. 15 Engr. *Perf. 13*
C99 AP48 150fr red, bl & pur 2.75 1.50

11th Winter Olympic Games, Sapporo, Japan, Feb. 3-13.

Music, by Pietro Longhi AP49

Design: 150fr, Gondolas and general view, by Ippolito Caffi, horiz.

1972, Feb. 28 Photo. *Perf. 13*
C100 AP49 100fr gold & multi 2.25 1.00
C101 AP49 150fr gold & multi 3.25 1.50

UNESCO campaign to save Venice.

Running and Olympic Rings — AP50

Design: 200fr, Discus and Olympic rings.

1972, May 5 Engr. *Perf. 13*
C102 AP50 65fr dp bl, brn & grn .70 .60
C103 AP50 200fr dp bl & brn 2.25 1.50
a. Min. sheet of 2, #C102-C103 3.00 3.00

20th Olympic Games, Munich, 8/26-9/10.

Musician Type of Regular Issue

Design: 500fr, Jimmy Smith and keyboard.

1972, May 17 Photo. *Perf. 14x13*
C104 A87 500fr green & multi 9.00 4.75

Red Crescent Type of Regular Issue

1972, June 23 *Perf. 13x14*
C105 A88 100fr yellow & multi 1.40 .60

2nd Plan Type of Regular Issue

Design: 85fr, Road building machinery.

1972, Oct. 30 Engr. *Perf. 13*
C106 A90 85fr brick red, bl & blk 1.00 .80

Presidents Pompidou and Lamizana — AP51

Design: 250fr, Presidents Pompidou and Lamizana, different design.

1972, Nov. 20 Photo. *Perf. 13*

Size: 48x37mm

C107 AP51 40fr gold & multi 2.25 2.25

Photogravure; Gold Embossed

Size: 56x36mm

C108 AP51 250fr yel grn, dk grn & gold 7.50 7.50

Visit of Pres. Georges Pompidou of France, Nov. 1972.

Skeet-shooting, Scalzone, Italy — AP52

Gold-medal Winners: 40fr, Pentathlon, Peters, Great Britain. 45fr, Dressage, Meade, Great Britain. 50fr, Weight lifting, Talts, USSR. 60fr, Boxing, light-weight, Seales, US. 65fr, Fencing, Ragno-Lonzi, Italy. 75fr, Gymnastics, rings, Nakayama, Japan. 85fr, Gymnastics, Touritcheva, USSR. 90fr, 110m high hurdles, Milburn, US. 150fr, Judo, Kawaguchi, Japan. 200fr, Sailing, Finn class, Maury, France. 250fr, Swimming, Spitz, US (7 gold). 300fr, Women's high jump, Meyfarth, West Germany. 350fr, Field Hockey, West Germany. 400fr, Javelin, Wolfermann, West Germany. No. C124, Women's diving, King, US. No. C125, Cycling, Morelon, France. No. C126, Individual dressage, Linsenhoff, West Germany.

1972-73 Litho. *Perf. 12½*
C109 AP52 35fr multi ('73) .45 .25
C110 AP52 40fr multi .45 .25
C111 AP52 45fr multi ('73) .55 .45
C112 AP52 50fr multi ('73) .55 .45
C113 AP52 60fr multi ('73) .70 .45
C114 AP52 65fr multi .70 .45
C115 AP52 75fr multi ('73) .70 .55
C116 AP52 85fr multi 1.00 .55
C117 AP52 90fr multi ('73) 1.00 .55
C118 AP52 150fr multi ('73) 1.40 .70
C119 AP52 200fr multi 2.10 .80
C120 AP52 250fr multi ('73) 2.25 1.10
C121 AP52 300fr multi 3.50 1.50
C122 AP52 350fr multi ('73) 3.50 1.50
C123 AP52 400fr multi ('73) 3.50 2.00
Nos. C109-C123 (15) 22.35 11.55

Souvenir Sheets

C124 AP52 500fr multi 9.00 5.00
C125 AP52 500fr multi ('73) 9.00 5.00
C126 AP52 500fr multi ('73) 9.00 5.00

20th Olympic Games, Munich.

Nativity, by Della Notte — AP53

Christmas: 200fr, Adoration of the Kings, by Albrecht Dürer.

1972, Dec. 23 Photo. *Perf. 13*
C127 AP53 100fr gold & multi 1.25 .90
C128 AP53 200fr gold & multi 2.75 2.00

Madonna and Child, by Albrecht Dürer AP54

Christmas: 75fr, Virgin Mary, Child and St. John, by Joseph von Führich. 100fr, The Virgin of Grand Duc, by Raphael. 125fr, Holy Family, by David. 150fr, Madonna and Child, artist unknown. 400fr, Flight into Egypt, by Gentile da Fabriano, horiz.

1973, Mar. 22 Litho. *Perf. 12½x13*
C129 AP54 50fr multi .45 .25
C130 AP54 75fr multi .60 .35
C131 AP54 100fr multi .90 .45
C132 AP54 125fr multi 1.10 .55
C133 AP54 150fr multi 1.40 .55
Nos. C129-C133 (5) 4.45 2.15

Souvenir Sheet

C134 AP54 400fr multi 5.25 4.00

Manned Lunar Buggy on Moon — AP55

Moon Exploration: 65fr, Lunakhod, Russian unmanned vehicle on moon. 100fr, Lunar module returning to orbiting Apollo capsule. 150fr, Apollo capsule in moon orbit. 200fr, Space walk. 250fr, Walk in Sea of Tranquillity.

1973, Apr. 30 Litho. *Perf. 13x12½*
C135 AP55 50fr multi .45 .25
C136 AP55 65fr multi .70 .25
C137 AP55 100fr multi 1.00 .45
C138 AP55 150fr multi 1.25 .60
C139 AP55 200fr multi 2.00 .80
Nos. C135-C139 (5) 5.40 2.35

Souvenir Sheet

C140 AP55 250fr multi 3.50 2.50

Giraffes AP56

African Wild Animals: 150fr, Elephants. 200fr, Leopard, horiz. 250fr, Lion, horiz. 300fr, Rhinoceros, horiz. 500fr, Crocodile, horiz.

Perf. 12½x13, 13x12½

1973, May 3 Litho.
C141 AP56 100fr multi 1.10 .35
C142 AP56 150fr multi 1.50 .60
C143 AP56 200fr multi 2.00 1.10
C144 AP56 250fr multi 2.25 1.10
C145 AP56 500fr multi 5.00 2.75
Nos. C141-C145 (5) 11.85 5.90

Souvenir Sheet

C146 AP56 300fr multi 4.00 4.00

Europafrica Issue

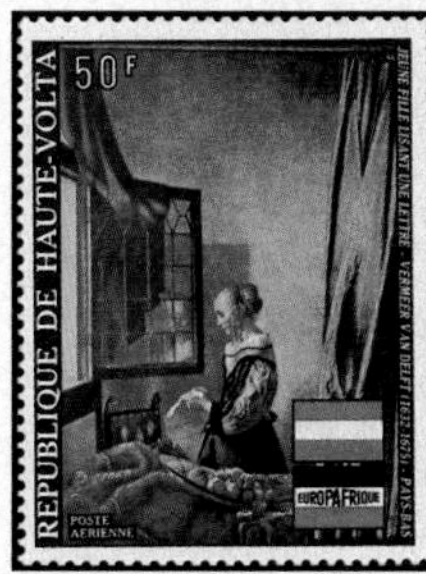

Girl Reading Letter, by Jan Vermeer AP57

Paintings: 65fr, Portrait of a Lady, by Roger van der Weyden. 100fr, Young Lady at her Toilette, by Titian. 150fr, Jane Seymour, by Hans Holbein. 200fr, Mrs. Williams, by John Hoppner. 250fr, Milkmaid, by Jean-Baptiste Greuze.

1973, June 7 Litho. ***Perf. 12½x13***

C147 AP57 50fr multi .45 .25
C148 AP57 65fr multi .70 .25
C149 AP57 100fr multi 1.00 .45
C150 AP57 150fr multi 1.25 .60
C151 AP57 200fr multi 2.00 .80
Nos. C147-C151 (5) 5.40 2.35

Souvenir Sheet

C152 AP57 250fr multi 3.75 1.50

For overprint see No. C165-C166.

Africa Encircled by OAU Flags AP58

1973, June 7

C153 AP58 45fr multi .75 .40

10th anniv. of Org. for African Unity.

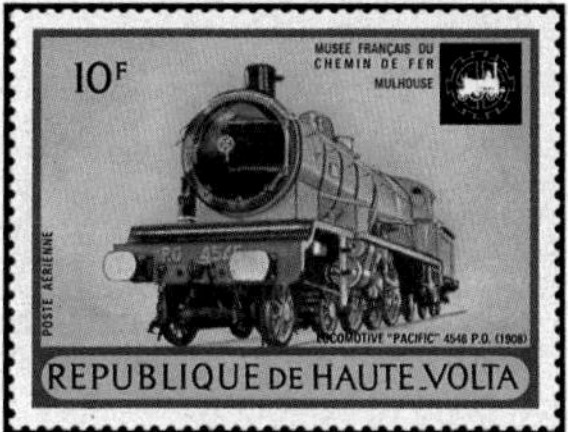

Locomotive "Pacific" 4546, 1908 — AP59

Locomotives from Railroad Museum, Mulhouse, France: 40fr, No. 242, 1927. 50fr, No. 2029, 1882. 150fr, No. 701, 1885-92. 250fr, "Coupe-Vent" No. C145, 1900. 350fr, Buddicomb No. 33, Paris to Rouen, 1884.

1973, June 30 ***Perf. 13x12½***

C154 AP59 10fr multi .25 .25
C155 AP59 40fr multi .55 .25
C156 AP59 50fr multi .60 .25
C157 AP59 150fr multi 2.00 .60
C158 AP59 250fr multi 3.25 1.10
Nos. C154-C158 (5) 6.65 2.45

Souvenir Sheet

C159 AP59 350fr multi 4.00 2.75

Boy Scout Type of 1973

40fr, Flag signaling. 75fr, Skiing. 150fr, Cooking. 200fr, Hiking. 250fr, Studying stars.

1973, July 18 Litho. ***Perf. 12½x13***

C160 A95 40fr multi .45 .25
C161 A95 75fr multi .70 .45
C162 A95 150fr multi 1.25 .60
C163 A95 200fr multi 1.50 .70
Nos. C160-C163 (4) 3.90 1.95

Souvenir Sheet

C164 A95 250fr multi 4.00 1.25

Nos. C148 and C150 Surcharged in Silver

1973, Aug. 16

C165 AP57 100fr on 65fr multi 1.75 1.50
C166 AP57 200fr on 150fr multi 3.50 2.25

Drought relief.

Kennedy Type, 1973

John F. Kennedy and: 200fr, Firing Saturn 1 rocket, Apollo program. 300fr, First NASA manned space capsule. 400fr, Saturn 5 countdown.

1973, Sept. 12 Litho. ***Perf. 12½x13***

C167 A96 200fr multi 1.50 .85
C168 A96 300fr multi 2.40 1.25

Souvenir Sheet

C169 A96 400fr multi 4.25 2.50

10th death anniv. of Pres John F. Kennedy.

Interpol Type of 1973

Souvenir Sheet

Design: Victim in city street.

1973, Sept. 15 ***Perf. 13x12½***

C170 A97 300fr multi 3.25 1.10

Tourism Type of 1973

1973, Sept. 30

C171 A98 100fr Waterfalls 1.40 .80

Souvenir Sheet

C172 A98 275fr Elephant 4.25 1.25

House of Worship Type of 1973

Cathedral of the Immaculate Conception.

1973, Sept. 28

C173 A99 200fr multi 2.50 1.25

Folklore Type of 1973

100fr, 225fr, Bobo masked dancers, diff.

1973, Nov. 30 Litho. ***Perf. 12½x13***

C174 A100 100fr multi 1.40 .50
C175 A100 225fr multi 2.25 .95

Zodiac Type of 1973

Souvenir Sheets

Zodiacal Light and: No. C176, 1st 4 signs of Zodiac. No. C177, 2nd 4 signs. No. C178, Last 4 signs.

1973, Dec. 15 ***Perf. 13x14***

C176 A101 250fr multi 3.00 1.10
C177 A101 250fr multi 3.00 1.10
C178 A101 250fr multi 3.00 1.10

Nos. C176-C178 have multicolored margin showing night sky and portraits: No. C176, Louis Armstrong; No. C177, Mahatma Gandhi; No. C178, Martin Luther King.

Soccer Championship Type, 1974

Championship '74 emblem and: 75fr, Gento, Spanish flag. 100fr, Bereta, French flag. 250fr, Best, British flag. 400fr, Beckenbauer, West German flag.

1974, Jan. 15 Litho. ***Perf. 13x12½***

C179 A102 75fr multi .60 .25
C180 A102 100fr multi .90 .25
C181 A102 250fr multi 1.90 .80
Nos. C179-C181 (3) 3.40 1.25

Souvenir Sheet

C182 A102 400fr multi 8.00 3.25

De Gaulle Type, 1974

300fr, De Gaulle, Concorde, horiz. 400fr, De Gaulle, French space shot.

Perf. 13x12½, 12½x13

1974, Feb. 4 Litho.

C183 A103 300fr multi 4.25 1.75

Souvenir Sheet

C184 A103 400fr multi 7.00 1.90

Soccer Cup Championship Type, 1974

World Cup, Emblems and: 150fr, Brindisis, Argentinian flag. No. C186, Kenko, Zaire flag. No. C187, Streich, East German flag. 400fr, Cruyff, Netherlands flag.

1974, Mar. 19 ***Perf. 12½x13***

C185 A104 150fr multi 1.10 .45
C186 A104 300fr multi 2.25 .90

Souvenir Sheets

C187 A104 300fr multi 4.00 1.50
C188 A104 400fr multi 4.00 1.50

UPU Type, 1974

UPU Emblem and: 100fr, Dove carrying mail. 200fr, Air Afrique 707. 300fr, Dish antenna. 500fr, Telstar satellite.

1974, July 23 ***Perf. 13½***

C189 A106 100fr multi .90 .45
C190 A106 200fr multi 1.75 .90
C191 A106 300fr multi 2.50 1.50
Nos. C189-C191 (3) 5.15 2.85

Souvenir Sheet

C192 A106 500fr multi 4.75 1.90

For overprint see No. C197-C200.

Soccer Cup Winners Type, 1974

World Cup, Game and Flags: 150fr, Brazil, in Sweden, 1958. 200fr, Brazil, in Chile, 1962. 250fr, Brazil, in Mexico, 1970. 450fr, England, in England, 1966.

1974, Sept. 2

C193 A107 150fr multi 1.25 .60
C194 A107 200fr multi 1.75 .90
C195 A107 250fr multi 2.25 1.25
Nos. C193-C195 (3) 5.25 2.75

Souvenir Sheet

C196 A107 450fr multi 4.00 1.90

Nos. C189-C192 Overprinted in Red

1974, Oct. 9

C197 A106 100fr multi 1.50 .80
C198 A106 200fr multi 2.25 1.10
C199 A106 300fr multi 3.75 1.50
Nos. C197-C199 (3) 7.50 3.40

Souvenir Sheet

C200 A106 500fr multi 4.00 1.90

Universal Postal Union, centenary.

Flower Type of 1974

Flower Paintings by: 300fr, Auguste Renoir. 400fr, Carl Brendt.

1974, Oct. 31 Litho. ***Perf. 12½x13***

C201 A109 300fr multi 3.50 1.10

Souvenir Sheet

C202 A109 400fr multi 5.25 1.60

Locomotive Type of 1975

Locomotives from Railroad Museum. Mulhouse, France: 100fr, Crampton No. 80, 1852. 200fr, No. 701, 1885-92. 300fr, "Forquenot," 1882.

1975, Feb. 28 Litho. ***Perf. 13x12½***

C203 A112 100fr multi 1.50 .35
C204 A112 200fr multi 2.75 .65

Souvenir Sheet

C205 A112 300fr multi 5.25 2.25

Old Cars Type, 1975

Flags and Old Cars: 150fr, Germany and Mercedes-Benz, 1929. 200fr, Germany and Maybach, 1936. 400fr, Great Britain and Rolls Royce Silver Ghost, 1910.

1975, Apr. 6 ***Perf. 14x13½***

C206 A113 150fr multi 1.75 .50
C207 A113 200fr multi 2.25 .70

Souvenir Sheet

C208 A113 400fr multi 3.75 1.75

American Bicentennial Type

200fr, Washington crossing Delaware. 300fr, Hessians Captured at Trenton.

1975, May 6 Litho. ***Perf. 14***

C209 A114 200fr multi 2.75 .90
C210 A114 300fr multi 3.00 2.50

Schweitzer Type of 1975

Albert Schweitzer and: 150fr, Toucan. 175fr, Vulturine guinea fowl. 200fr, King vulture. 450fr, Crested corythornis.

1975, May 25 Litho. ***Perf. 13½***

C212 A115 150fr multi 1.75 .70
C213 A115 175fr multi 1.75 .70
C214 A115 200fr multi 2.75 .95
Nos. C212-C214 (3) 6.00 2.35

Souvenir Sheet

C215 A115 450fr multi 6.50 2.25

Apollo Soyuz Type of 1975

100fr, Apollo, Soyuz near link-up. 200fr, Cosmonauts Alexei Leonov, Valeri Kubasov. 300fr, Astronauts Donald K. Slayton, Vance Brand, Thomas P. Stafford. 500fr, Apollo Soyuz emblem, U.S., USSR flags.

1975, July 18 Litho. ***Perf. 13½***

C216 A116 100fr multi 1.00 .25
C217 A116 200fr multi 1.90 .65
C218 A116 300fr multi 2.75 1.25
Nos. C216-C218 (3) 5.65 2.10

Souvenir Sheet

C219 A116 500fr multi 5.25 2.25

Picasso Type of 1975

Picasso Paintings: 150fr, El Prado, horiz. 350fr, Couple in Patio. 400fr, Science and Charity.

1975, Aug. 7

C220 A117 150fr multi 2.25 .60
C221 A117 350fr multi 4.50 1.25

Souvenir Sheet

C222 A117 400fr multi 5.50 1.60

EXPO '75 Type of 1975

Expo '75 emblem and: 150fr, Passenger liner Asama Maru. 300fr, Future floating city Aquapolis.

1975, Sept. 26 Litho. ***Perf. 11***

C223 A118 150fr multi 2.50 .90

Souvenir Sheet

Perf. 13½

C224 A118 300fr multi 3.75 1.25

Winter Olympic Games Type of 1975

Innsbruck Background, Olympic Emblem and: 100fr, Ice hockey. 200fr, Ski jump. 300fr, Speed skating.

1975, Dec. 15 ***Perf. 13½***

C225 A122 100fr multi .95 .45
C226 A122 200fr multi 1.90 .70

Souvenir Sheet

C227 A122 300fr multi 4.50 1.50

Olympic Games Type of 1976

Olympic Emblem and: 125fr, Heavyweight judo. 150fr, Weight lifting. 500fr, Sprint.

1976, Mar. 17 Litho. ***Perf. 13½***

C228 A123 125fr multi 1.10 .35
C229 A123 150fr multi 1.60 .55

Souvenir Sheet

C230 A123 500fr multi 6.00 2.25

Summer Olympic Games Type of 1976

Olympic emblem and: 150fr, Pole vault. 200fr, Gymnast on balance beam. 500fr, Two-man sculls.

1976, Mar. 25 ***Perf. 11***

C231 A124 150fr multi 1.25 .45
C232 A124 200fr multi 1.90 .60

Souvenir Sheet

C233 A124 500fr multi 5.25 2.25

For overprint see No. C245-C247.

Zeppelin Type of 1976

Airships: 100fr, Graf Zeppelin over Swiss Alps. 200fr, LZ-129 over city. 300fr, Graf Zeppelin. 500fr, Zeppelin over Bodensee.

1976, May 11

C234 A126 100fr multi 1.25 .35
C235 A126 200fr multi 2.25 .75
C236 A126 300fr multi 3.00 1.10
Nos. C234-C236 (3) 6.50 2.20

Souvenir Sheet

C237 A126 500fr multi 5.50 2.25

Viking Mars Type of 1976

Designs: 200fr, Viking lander assembly. 300fr, Viking orbiter in descent on Mars. 450fr, Viking in Mars orbit.

1976, June 24 Litho. *Perf. 13½*

C238 A127 200fr multi 1.90 .45
C239 A127 300fr multi 3.25 .95

Souvenir Sheet

C240 A127 450fr multi 5.25 2.25

American Bicentennial Type

Bicentennial and Interphil '76 Emblems and: 100fr, Siege of Yorktown. 200fr, Battle of Cape St. Vincent. 300fr, Peter Francisco's bravery. 500fr, Surrender of the Hessians.

1976, Sept. 30 Litho. *Perf. 13½*

C241 A129 100fr multi 1.00 .35
C242 A129 200fr multi 1.75 .65
C243 A129 300fr multi 3.00 1.00
Nos. C241-C243 (3) 5.75 2.00

Souvenir Sheet

C244 A129 500fr multi 7.25 2.25

Nos. C231-C233 Overprinted in Gold

a. VAINQUEUR 1976 / TADEUSZ SLUSARSKI / POLOGNE
b. VAINQUEUR 1976 / NADIA COMANECI / ROUMANIE

(c)

1976, July 4 Litho. *Perf. 11*

C245 A124(a) 150fr multi 1.25 .70
C246 A124(b) 200fr multi 1.75 1.00

Souvenir Sheet

C247 A124(c) 500fr multi 4.50 2.25

Winners, 21st Olympic Games.

UPU Emblem over Globe — AP60

1978, Aug. 8 Litho. *Perf. 13*

C248 AP60 350fr multi 3.50 2.00

Congress of Paris, establishing UPU, cent.

Jules Verne, Apollo 11 Emblem, Footprint on Moon, Neil Armstrong — AP61

Space Conquest: 50fr, Yuri Gagarin and moon landing. 100fr, Montgolfier hot air balloon and memorial medal, 1783; Bleriot's monoplane, 1909.

1978, Sept. 27 Litho. *Perf. 13x12½*

C249 AP61 50fr multi .55 .25
C250 AP61 60fr multi .60 .25
C251 AP61 100fr multi 1.10 .55
Nos. C249-C251 (3) 2.25 1.05

Anti-Apartheid Year — AP62

1978, Oct. 12 Litho. *Perf. 13*

C252 AP62 100fr blue & multi 1.10 .60

Philexafrique II-Essen Issue

Common Design Types

No. C253, Hippopotamus, Upper Volta #C18. No. C254, Kingfisher, Hanover #1.

1978, Nov. 1 Litho. *Perf. 12½*

C253 CD138 100fr multi 2.40 1.40
C254 CD139 100fr multi 2.40 1.40

Nos. C253-C254 printed se-tenant.

Sun God Horus with Sun — AP63

300fr, Falcon with cartouches, UNESCO emblem.

1978, Dec. 4

C255 AP63 200fr multi 1.75 .80
C256 AP63 300fr multi 2.50 1.25

UNESCO Campaign to safeguard monuments at Philae.

Jules Verne and Balloon — AP64

1978, Dec. 10 Engr. *Perf. 13*

C257 AP64 200fr multi 2.50 1.40

Verne (1828-1905), science fiction writer.

Bicycling, Olympic Rings — AP65

Designs: Bicycling scenes.

1980 *Perf. 14½*

C258 AP65 65fr multi .70 .25
C259 AP65 150fr multi, vert. 1.25 .50
C260 AP65 250fr multi 2.50 .80
C261 AP65 350fr multi 3.50 1.25
Nos. C258-C261 (4) 7.95 2.80

Souvenir Sheet

C262 AP65 500fr multi 6.00 1.90

22nd Summer Olympic Games, Moscow, July 19-Aug. 3.

Nos. C258-C262 Overprinted with Name of Winner and Country

1980, Nov. 22 Litho. *Perf. 14½*

C263 AP65 65fr multi .70 .40
C264 AP65 150fr multi, vert. 1.60 .85
C265 AP65 250fr multi 2.75 1.50
C266 AP65 350fr multi 3.50 1.75
Nos. C263-C266 (4) 8.55 4.50

Souvenir Sheet

C267 AP65 500fr multi 6.00 3.50

1982 World Cup — AP66

Designs: Various soccer players.

1982, June 22 Litho. *Perf. 13½*

C268 AP66 70fr multi .60 .25
C269 AP66 90fr multi .80 .35
C270 AP66 150fr multi 1.40 .50
C271 AP66 300fr multi 2.50 1.00
Nos. C268-C271 (4) 5.30 2.10

Souvenir Sheet

C272 AP66 500fr multi 4.75 1.60

Anniversaries and Events — AP67

1983, June Litho. *Perf. 13½*

C273 AP67 90fr Space Shuttle .80 .25
C274 AP67 120fr World Soccer Cup 1.10 .45
C275 AP67 300fr Cup, diff. 2.50 .80
C276 AP67 450fr Royal Wedding 3.50 1.10
Nos. C273-C276 (4) 7.90 2.60

Souvenir Sheet

C277 AP67 500fr Prince Charles, Lady Diana 4.75 1.75

Pre-Olympics, 1984 Los Angeles — AP68

1983, Aug. 1 Litho. *Perf. 13*

C278 AP68 90fr Sailing .90 .25
C279 AP68 120fr Type 470 1.40 .35
C280 AP68 300fr Wind surfing 2.90 .80
C281 AP68 400fr Wind surfing, diff. 3.75 1.00
Nos. C278-C281 (4) 8.95 2.40

Souvenir Sheet

C282 AP68 500fr Soling Class, Wind surfing 6.00 1.75

Christmas AP69

Rubens Paintings.

1983 Litho. *Perf. 13*

C283 AP69 120fr Adoration of the Shepherds 1.00 .45
C284 AP69 350fr Virgin of the Garland 3.00 .90
C285 AP69 500fr Adoration of the Kings 4.00 1.40
Nos. C283-C285 (3) 8.00 2.75

1984 Summer Olympics — AP70

1984, Mar. 26 Litho. *Perf. 12½*

C286 AP70 90fr Handball, vert. .70 .25
C287 AP70 120fr Volleyball, vert. 1.00 .35
C288 AP70 150fr Handball, diff. 1.40 .45
C289 AP70 250fr Basketball 2.25 .60
C290 AP70 300fr Soccer 2.75 1.00
Nos. C286-C290 (5) 8.10 2.65

Souvenir Sheet

C291 AP70 500fr Volleyball, diff. 4.75 1.75

Local Birds — AP71

1984, May 14 Litho. *Perf. 12½*

C292 AP71 90fr Phoenicopterus roseus 1.40 .55
C293 AP71 185fr Choriotis kori, vert. 2.50 1.25
C294 AP71 200fr Buphagus erythrorhynchus, vert. 2.50 1.40
C295 AP71 300fr Bucorvus leadbeateri 3.50 2.25
Nos. C292-C295 (4) 9.90 5.45

AP72

Famous Men — AP73

Designs: 5fr, Houari Boumediene (1927-1978), president of Algeria 1965-78. 125fr, Gottlieb Daimler (1834-1900), German automotive pioneer, and 1886 Daimler. 250fr, Louis Bleriot (1872-1936), French aviator, first to fly the English Channel in a heavier-than-air craft. 300fr, Abraham Lincoln. 400fr, Henri Dunant (1828-1910), founder of the Red Cross. 450fr, Auguste Piccard (1884-1962), Swiss physicist, inventor of the bathyscaphe Trieste, 1948. 500fr, Robert Baden-Powell (1856-1941), founder of Boy Scouts. 600fr, Anatoli Karpov, Russian chess champion. 1000fr, Paul Harris (1868-1947), founder of Rotary Intl.

1984, May 21 Litho. *Perf. 13½*

C296	AP72	5fr multi	.25	.25
C297	AP72	125fr multi	1.10	.35
C298	AP72	250fr multi	2.25	.60
C299	AP72	300fr multi	2.75	.80
C300	AP72	400fr multi	3.50	1.00
C301	AP72	450fr multi	4.00	1.00
C302	AP72	500fr multi	4.50	1.25
C303	AP72	600fr multi	4.75	1.50
		Nos. C296-C303 (8)	23.10	6.75

Souvenir Sheet

C304	AP73	1000fr multi	9.00	2.00

No. C304 contains one 51x30mm stamp.

Burkina Faso

Butterflies — AP73a

1984, May 23 *Perf. 13½*

C305	AP73a	10fr Graphium pylades	.25	.25
C306	AP73a	120fr Hypolimnas misippus	1.75	.60
C307	AP73a	400fr Danaus chrysippus	5.50	2.25
C308	AP73a	450fr Papilio demodocus	5.75	2.50
		Nos. C305-C308 (4)	13.25	5.60

Philexafrica '85, Lome — AP74

1985, May 20 Litho. *Perf. 13*

C309	AP74	200fr Solar & wind energy	2.40	1.25
C310	AP74	200fr Children	2.40	1.25
a.		Pair, #C309-C310 + label	5.00	2.50

PHILEXAFRICA '85, Lome — AP75

National development: No. C311, Youth. No. C312, Communications and transportation.

1985, Nov. 16 Litho. *Perf. 13*

C311	AP75	250fr multi	4.25	1.50
C312	AP75	250fr multi	4.25	1.50
a.		Pair, #C311-C312 + label	10.50	4.00

Intl. Youth Year (No. C311).

French Revolution, Bicent. — AP76

Designs: 150fr, *Oath of the Tennis Court,* by David. 200fr, *Storming of the Bastille,* by Thevenin. 600fr, *Rouget de Lisle Singing La Marseillaise,* by Pils.

1989, May 3 Litho. *Perf. 13*

C313	AP76	150fr multi	1.75	.70
C314	AP76	200fr multi	2.10	1.00
C315	AP76	600fr multi	7.00	2.75
		Nos. C313-C315 (3)	10.85	4.45

PHILEXFRANCE '89.

POSTAGE DUE STAMPS

Postage Due Stamps of Upper Senegal and Niger, 1914, Overprinted in Black or Red

1920 Unwmk. *Perf. 14x13½*

J1	D2	5c green	.50	.80
J2	D2	10c rose	.50	.80
J3	D2	15c gray	.65	.80
J4	D2	20c brown (R)	.75	.80
J5	D2	30c blue	.75	.80
J6	D2	50c black (R)	1.25	1.60
J7	D2	60c orange	1.25	1.60
J8	D2	1fr violet	1.75	2.50
		Nos. J1-J8 (8)	7.40	9.70

Type of 1914 Issue Surcharged

1927

J9	D2	2fr on 1fr lilac rose	3.25	4.00
J10	D2	3fr on 1fr orange brn	4.00	4.75

D3

1928 Typo.

J11	D3	5c green	.65	.80
J12	D3	10c rose	.80	.80
J13	D3	15c dark gray	1.25	1.60
J14	D3	20c dark brown	1.25	1.60
J15	D3	30c dark blue	1.75	2.50
J16	D3	50c black	3.50	4.00
J17	D3	60c orange	4.50	4.75
J18	D3	1fr dull violet	6.50	7.25
J19	D3	2fr lilac rose	10.50	12.75
J20	D3	3fr orange brn	14.50	18.50
		Nos. J11-J20 (10)	45.20	54.55

Catalogue values for unused stamps in this section, from this point to the end of the section, are for Never Hinged items.

Republic

D4

1962, Jan. 31 *Perf. 14x13½*

Denomination in Black

J21	D4	1fr bright blue	.25	.25
J22	D4	2fr orange	.25	.25
J23	D4	5fr brt vio blue	.25	.25
J24	D4	10fr red lilac	.35	.35
J25	D4	20fr emerald	.80	.80
J26	D4	50fr rose red	1.75	1.75
		Nos. J21-J26 (6)	3.65	3.65

OFFICIAL STAMPS

Catalogue values for unused stamps in this section are for Never Hinged items.

Elephant — O1

Perf. 12½

1963, Feb. 1 Unwmk. Photo.

Center in Sepia

O1	O1	1fr red brown	.25	.25
O2	O1	5fr yel green	.25	.25
O3	O1	10fr deep vio	.25	.25
O4	O1	15fr red org	.35	.35
O5	O1	25fr brt rose lilac	.80	.80
O6	O1	50fr brt green	1.25	1.25
O7	O1	60fr brt red	1.40	1.40
O8	O1	85fr dk slate grn	2.25	2.25
O9	O1	100fr brt blue	3.50	3.50
O10	O1	200fr bright rose	5.25	5.25
		Nos. O1-O10 (10)	15.55	15.55

BURMA

ˈbər-mə

Myanmar

LOCATION — Bounded on the north by China; east by China, Laos and Thailand; south and west by the Bay of Bengal, Bangladesh and India.
GOVT. — Republic
AREA — 261,228 sq. mi.
POP. — 48,081,302 (1999 est.)
CAPITAL — Naypyidaw (Pyinmana)

Burma was part of India from 1826 until April 1, 1937, when it became a self-governing unit of the British Commonwealth and received a constitution. On January 4, 1948, Burma became an independent nation. In 1990 it became the Union of Myanmar.

12 Pies = 1 Anna
16 Annas = 1 Rupee
100 Pyas = 1 Kyat (1953)

Catalogue values for unused stamps in this country are for Never Hinged items, beginning with Scott 35 in the regular postage section and Scott O28 in the official section.

Watermarks

Wmk. 254 — Elephant Heads

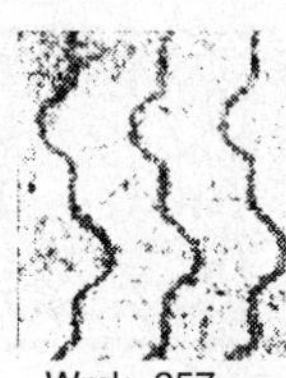
Wmk. 257 — Curved Wavy Lines

Stamps of India 1926-36 Overprinted

1937, Apr. 1 Wmk. 196 *Perf. 14*

1	A46	3p slate	1.25	.25
2	A71	½a green	.65	.25
3	A68	9p dark green	.65	.25
4	A72	1a dark brown	2.75	.25
5	A49	2a ver (small die)	.65	.25
6	A57	2a6p buff	.55	.25
7	A51	3a carmine rose	2.75	.50
8	A70	3a6p deep blue	4.25	.25
9	A52	4a olive green	.75	.25
10	A53	6a bister	.75	.60
11	A54	8a red violet	2.25	.25
12	A55	12a claret	8.50	3.25

Overprinted

13	A56	1r green & brown	35.00	5.00
14	A56	2r brn org & car rose	29.00	*40.00*
15	A56	5r dk violet & ultra	32.50	*45.00*
16	A56	10r car & green	135.00	*125.00*
17	A56	15r ol green & ultra	450.00	225.00
18	A56	25r blue & ocher	750.00	500.00
		Nos. 1-18 (18)	1,457.	946.60
		Set, never hinged	2,475.	

For overprints see Nos. 1N1-1N3, 1N25-1N26, 1N47.

King George VI
A1 A2

Royal Barge — A3

Elephant Moving Teak Log — A4

Farmer Plowing Rice Field — A5

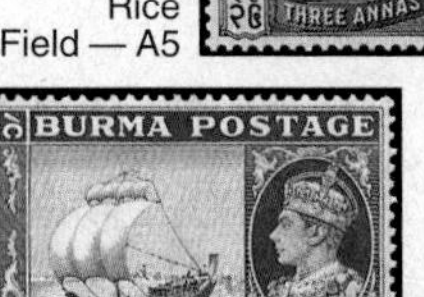

Sailboat on Irrawaddy River — A6

Peacock — A7

George VI — A8

Perf. 13½x14

1938-40 Litho. Wmk. 254

No.	Type	Denom.	Color	Unused	Used
18A	A1	1p	red org ('40)	2.25	1.10
19	A1	3p	violet	.25	*2.60*
20	A1	6p	ultramarine	.25	.25
21	A1	9p	yel green	.90	*1.60*
22	A2	1a	brown violet	.25	.25
23	A2	1½a	turquoise green	.25	*3.25*
24	A2	2a	carmine	1.60	.55
			Perf. 13		
25	A3	2a6p	rose lake	10.00	3.25
26	A4	3a	dk violet	10.00	3.25
27	A5	3a6p	dp bl & brt bl	2.50	*7.75*
28	A2	4a	slate blue, perf. 13½x14	2.00	.25
29	A6	8a	slate green	2.75	.60
			Perf. 13½		
30	A7	1r	brt ultra & dk violet	3.00	1.00
31	A7	2r	dk vio & red brown	16.00	4.75
32	A8	5r	car & dull vio	45.00	*47.50*
33	A8	10r	gray grn & brn	50.00	*80.00*
			Nos. 18A-33 (16)	147.00	157.95
			Set, never hinged	220.00	

See Nos. 51-65. For overprints and surcharges see Nos. 34-50, O15-O27, 1N4-1N11, 1N28-1N30, 1N37-1N46, 1N48-1N49.

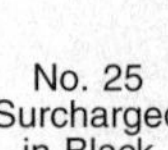

No. 25 Surcharged in Black

1940, May 6 ***Perf. 13***

No.	Type	Description	Unused	Used
34	A3	1a on 2a6p rose lake	3.00	2.75
		Never hinged	4.50	

Centenary of first postage stamp.

Catalogue values for unused stamps in this section, from this point to the end of the section, are for Never Hinged items.

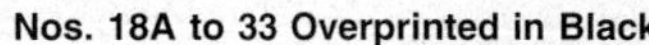

Nos. 18A to 33 Overprinted in Black

a

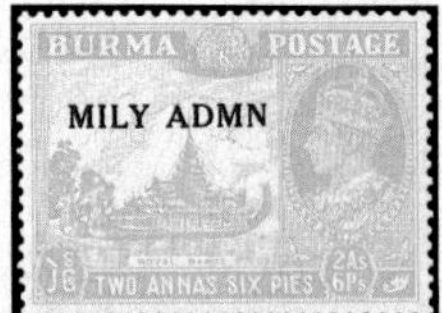

b

1945

No.	Type	Denom.	Color	Unused	Used
35	A1(a)	1p	red orange	.25	.25
a.			Pair, one without overprint	1,850.	
36	A1(a)	3p	violet	.25	*1.60*
37	A1(a)	6p	ultramarine	.25	*.35*
38	A1(a)	9p	yel green	.35	*1.40*
39	A2(a)	1a	brown violet	.25	.25
40	A2(a)	1½a	turq green	.25	.25
41	A2(a)	2a	carmine	.25	.25
42	A3(b)	2a6p	rose lake	2.25	2.50
43	A4(b)	3a	dk violet	1.75	.25
44	A5(b)	3a6p	dp bl & brt bl	.25	*.85*
45	A2(a)	4a	slate blue	.25	*.85*
46	A6(b)	8a	slate green	.25	*1.60*
47	A7(b)	1r	brt ultra & dk vio	.50	*.60*
48	A7(b)	2r	dk vio & red brown	.50	*1.50*
49	A8(b)	5r	car & dull vio	.60	*1.50*
50	A8(b)	10r	gray grn & brn	.60	*1.50*
			Nos. 35-50 (16)	8.80	*15.50*

Types of 1938

Perf. 13½x14

1946, Jan. 1 Litho. Wmk. 254

No.	Type	Denom.	Color	Unused	Used
51	A1	3p	brown	.25	*3.75*
52	A1	6p	violet	.25	*.40*
53	A1	9p	dull green	.25	*5.75*
54	A2	1a	deep blue	.25	.25
55	A2	1½a	salmon	.25	.25
56	A2	2a	rose lake	.25	*.60*
			Perf. 13		
57	A3	2a6p	greenish blue	3.25	*6.75*
58	A4	3a	blue violet	7.00	*9.50*
59	A5	3a6p	ultra & gray blk	2.25	*4.50*
60	A2	4a	rose lil, perf. 13½x14	.60	*1.00*
61	A6	8a	deep magenta	2.00	*6.25*
			Perf. 13½		
62	A7	1r	dp mag & dk vio	2.10	*3.25*
63	A7	2r	salmon & red brn	7.50	6.25
64	A8	5r	red brn & dk grn	8.50	*25.00*
65	A8	10r	dk vio & car	21.00	*37.50*
			Nos. 51-65 (15)	55.70	*111.00*

For overprints see Nos. 70-84, O28-O42.

Burmese Man — A9

Burmese Woman — A10

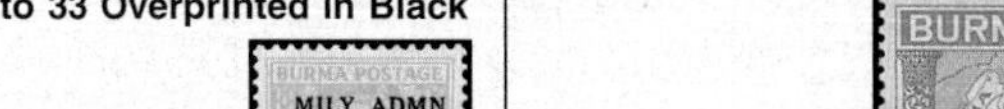

Mythological Chinze — A11

Elephant Hauling Teak — A12

1946, May 2 ***Perf. 13***

No.	Type	Denom.	Color	Unused	Used
66	A9	9p	peacock green	.30	.25
67	A10	1½a	brt violet	.30	.25
68	A11	2a	carmine	.30	.25
69	A12	3a6p	ultramarine	.70	.55
			Nos. 66-69 (4)	1.60	1.30

Victory of the Allied Nations in WWII.

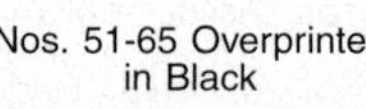

Nos. 51-65 Overprinted in Black

1947, Oct. 1 ***Perf. 13½x14, 13, 13½***

No.	Type	Denom.	Color	Unused	Used
70	A1	3p	brown	1.50	.85
71	A1	6p	violet	.25	*.40*
72	A1	9p	dull green	.25	*.40*
a.			Inverted overprint	26.00	*32.50*
73	A2	1a	deep blue	.25	*.40*
74	A2	1½a	salmon	2.10	.25
75	A2	2a	rose lake	.40	.30
76	A3	2a6p	greenish bl	2.25	1.75
77	A4	3a	blue violet	4.00	2.00
78	A5	3a6p	ultra & gray blk	1.60	*2.75*
79	A2	4a	rose lilac	2.25	.50
80	A6	8a	dp magenta	2.25	3.00
81	A7	1r	dp mag & dk vio	7.50	3.00
82	A7	2r	sal & red brn	7.50	*7.75*
83	A8	5r	red brn & dk grn	7.50	*6.00*
84	A8	10r	dk vio & car	5.00	*6.00*
			Nos. 70-84 (15)	44.60	*35.35*

The overprint is slightly larger on Nos. 76 to 78 and 80 to 84. The Burmese characters read "Interim Government."

Other denominations are known with the overprint inverted or double.

Issues of the Republic

U Aung San Map and Chinze — A13

Perf. 12½x12

1948, Jan. 6 Litho. Unwmk.

No.	Type	Denom.	Color	Unused	Used
85	A13	½a	emerald	.25	.25
86	A13	1a	deep rose	.30	.25
87	A13	2a	carmine	.40	.25
88	A13	3½a	blue	.60	.25
89	A13	8a	lt chocolate	.90	.25
			Nos. 85-89 (5)	2.45	1.25

Attainment of independence, Jan. 4, 1948.

Martyrs' Memorial — A14

1948, July 19 Engr. ***Perf. 14x13½***

No.	Type	Denom.	Color	Unused	Used
90	A14	3p	ultramarine	.25	.25
91	A14	6p	green	.25	.25
92	A14	9p	dp carmine	.25	.25
93	A14	1a	purple	.25	.25
94	A14	2a	lilac rose	.25	.25
95	A14	3½a	dk slate green	.35	.25
96	A14	4a	yel brown	.50	.25
97	A14	8a	orange red	.60	.25
98	A14	12a	claret	.80	.25
99	A14	1r	blue green	1.25	.25
100	A14	2r	deep blue	2.00	.35
101	A14	5r	chocolate	6.00	.80
			Nos. 90-101 (12)	12.75	3.65

1st anniv. of the assassination of Burma's leaders in the fight for independence.

Ball Game (Chinlon) A15

Bell A16

Mythical Bird — A17

Rice Planting A18

Throne — A19

Designs: 6p, Dancer. 9p, Musician. 3a, Spinning. 3a6p, Royal Palace. 4a, Cutting teak. 8a, Plowing rice field.

Perf. 12½ (A15-A17), 12x12½ (A18), 13 (A19)

1949, Jan. 4

No.	Type	Denom.	Color	Unused	Used
102	A15	3p	ultramarine	1.90	.45
103	A15	6p	green	.25	.25
104	A15	9p	carmine	.25	.25
105	A16	1a	red orange	.40	.25
106	A17	2a	orange	1.00	.25
107	A18	2a6p	lilac rose	.40	.25
108	A18	3a	purple	.40	.25
109	A18	3a6p	dk slate grn	.65	.25
110	A16	4a	chocolate	.65	.25
111	A18	8a	carmine	.85	.25
112	A19	1r	blue green	1.60	.25
a.			Perf. 14		2.50
113	A19	2r	deep blue	2.90	.60
114	A19	5r	chocolate	6.50	1.00
115	A19	10r	orange red	14.00	2.00
			Nos. 102-115 (14)	31.75	6.55

See Nos. 122-135, 139-152, O56-O67.

UPU Monument, Bern — A20

1949, Oct. 9 Unwmk. ***Perf. 13***

No.	Type	Denom.	Color	Unused	Used
116	A20	2a	orange	.40	.40
117	A20	3½a	olive grn	.50	.25
118	A20	6a	lilac	.75	.40
119	A20	8a	crimson	1.10	1.10
120	A20	12½a	ultra	2.00	1.25
121	A20	1r	blue green	2.40	1.90
			Nos. 116-121 (6)	7.15	5.30

75th anniv. of the UPU.

Types of 1949

Designs as before.

Perf. 13½x14, 14x13½, 13

1952-53 Litho. Wmk. 254

No.	Type	Denomination / Color	Unused	Used
122	A15	3p brown orange	1.00	.40
123	A15	6p deep plum	.25	.25
124	A15	9p blue	.25	.25
125	A16	1a violet bl	.25	.25
126	A17	2a green ('52)	.90	.25
127	A18	2a6p green	.35	.25
128	A18	3a sal pink ('52)	.35	.25
129	A18	3a6p brown orange	.65	.25
130	A16	4a vermilion	.65	.25
131	A18	8a lt blue ('52)	.80	.50
132	A19	1r rose violet	1.10	.75
133	A19	2r yel green	2.25	1.00
134	A19	5r ultramarine	6.00	2.00
135	A19	10r aquamarine	13.00	4.00
		Nos. 122-135 (14)	27.80	10.65

Map of Burma and Monument — A21

1953, Jan. 4 ***Perf. 14***

No.	Type	Denomination / Color	Unused	Used
136	A21	14p green	.85	.25

Perf. 13

Size: 36½x26mm

No.	Type	Denomination / Color	Unused	Used
137	A21	20p salmon pink	1.10	.30
138	A21	25p ultramarine	1.25	.40

Fifth anniversary of independence.
For surcharge see No. 166.

Types of 1949

Designs: 2p, Dancer. 3p, Musician. 20p, Spinning. 25p, Royal Palace. 30p, Cutting teak. 50p, Plowing rice field.

1954, Jan. 4 ***Perf. 14x13½, 13, 14***

No.	Type	Denomination / Color	Unused	Used
139	A15	1p brown orange	1.40	.25
140	A15	2p plum	.25	.25
141	A15	3p blue	.25	.25
142	A16	5p ultramarine	.25	.25
143	A18	10p yel green	.25	.25
144	A17	15p green	.65	.25
145	A18	20p vermilion	.45	.25
146	A18	25p lt red org	.45	.25
147	A16	30p vermilion	.65	.25
148	A18	50p blue	.75	.25
149	A19	1k rose violet	1.60	.50
150	A19	2k green	2.75	.75
151	A19	5k ultramarine	7.00	1.00
152	A19	10k light blue	17.50	1.50
		Nos. 139-152 (14)	34.20	6.25

For overprints and surcharges see Nos. 163-165, 173-175, O68-O79, O80-O81, O83, O85, O87.

Peace Pagoda, Monks' Hostels and Meeting-cave — A22

Designs: 10p, Sangha (community) of Cambodia. 15p, Council meeting. 50p, Sangha of Thailand. 1k, Sangha of Ceylon. 2k, Sangha of Laos.

1954 Typo. ***Perf. 13***

No.	Type	Denomination / Color	Unused	Used
153	A22	10p deep blue	.25	.25
154	A22	15p deep claret	.35	.25
155	A22	35p dark brown	.70	.30
156	A22	50p green	.90	.40
157	A22	1k carmine	2.00	.50
158	A22	2k violet	3.25	1.00
		Nos. 153-158 (6)	7.45	2.70

6th Buddhist Council, Rangoon, 1954-56.

Marble Markers of 5th Buddhist Council A23

Designs: 40p, Thatbyinnyu Pagoda. 60p, Shwedagon Pagoda, Rangoon. 1.25k, Aerial View of 6th Buddhist Council, Yegu.

Perf. 11x11½

1956, May 24 Litho. Unwmk.

No.	Type	Denomination / Color	Unused	Used
159	A23	20p blue & gray olive	.45	.25
160	A23	40p blue & brt yel grn	.75	.30
161	A23	60p green & lemon	1.10	.50
162	A23	1.25k gray blue & yel	2.25	.90
		Nos. 159-162 (4)	4.55	1.95

2500th anniv. of the Buddhist Era.

Nos. 146, 149-150 Srchd. or Ovptd.

1959, Nov. 9 Wmk. 254 ***Perf. 13, 14***

No.	Type	Denomination / Color	Unused	Used
163	A18	15p on 25p lt red org	.50	.25
164	A19	1k rose violet	1.90	.60
165	A19	2k green	4.00	1.25
		Nos. 163-165 (3)	6.40	2.10

Centenary of Mandalay, former capital.
The two lines of overprint are 4mm apart on No. 163; 7mm on Nos. 164-165.

No. 136 Surcharged

1961, June ***Perf. 14***

No.	Type	Denomination / Color	Unused	Used
166	A21	15p on 14p green	2.50	.40

Children A24

Unwmk.

1961, Dec. 11 Litho. ***Perf. 13***

No.	Type	Denomination / Color	Unused	Used
167	A24	15p claret & rose claret	1.60	.25

15th anniversary of UNICEF.

Runner with Torch — A25

Soccer, Pole Vault and Shot Put — A26

Designs: 50p, Women runners. 1k, Hurdling, weight lifting, boxing, bicycling and swimming.

1961, Dec. 11 Photo. ***Perf. 14x13***

No.	Type	Denomination / Color	Unused	Used
168	A25	15p red & ultra	.35	.25
169	A26	25p dk green & ocher	.60	.25
170	A26	50p vio blue & pink	1.10	.35
171	A25	1k brt green & yel	1.75	.75
		Nos. 168-171 (4)	3.80	1.60

2nd South East Asia Peninsular Games, Rangoon.

Map and Flag of Burma — A27

Wmk. 254

1963, Mar. 2 Engr. ***Perf. 13***

No.	Type	Denomination / Color	Unused	Used
172	A27	15p red	2.50	.25

First anniversary of new government.

Nos. 143 and 148 Overprinted in Violet or Red: "FREEDOM FROM HUNGER"

1963, Mar. 21 Litho.

No.	Type	Denomination / Color	Unused	Used
173	A18	10p yel green (V)	2.75	.45
174	A18	50p blue (R)	2.75	.75

FAO "Freedom from Hunger" campaign.

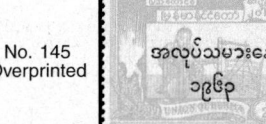

No. 145 Overprinted

1963, May 1

No.	Type	Denomination / Color	Unused	Used
175	A18	20p vermilion	2.40	.50

Issued for May Day.

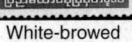

White-browed Fantail — A28

Indian Roller — A29

Birds: 20p, Red-whiskered bulbul. 25p, Crested serpent eagle. 50p, Sarus crane. 1k, Malabar pied hornbill. 2k, Lineated kalij pheasant. 5k, Green peafowl.

Perf. 13½

1964, Apr. 16 Unwmk. Photo.

Size: 25x21mm

No.	Type	Denomination / Color	Unused	Used
176	A28	1p gray	.30	.25
177	A28	2p carmine rose	.45	.25
178	A28	3p blue green	.45	.25

Size: 22x26½mm

No.	Type	Denomination / Color	Unused	Used
179	A29	5p violet blue	.65	.25
180	A29	10p orange brn	.65	.25
181	A29	15p olive	.65	.25

Size: 35x25mm

No.	Type	Denomination / Color	Unused	Used
182	A28	20p rose & brn	1.25	.25

Size: 27x36½mm, 36½x27mm

No.	Type	Denomination / Color	Unused	Used
183	A29	25p yel & brown	1.25	.40
184	A29	50p red, blk & gray	2.25	.50
185	A29	1k gray, ind & yel	5.25	1.00
186	A28	2k pale ol, ind & red	11.50	1.75
187	A29	5k citron, dk bl & red	25.00	4.50
		Nos. 176-187 (12)	49.65	9.90

See Nos. 197-208. For overprints see Nos. O82, O84, O86, O88-O93, O94-O115.

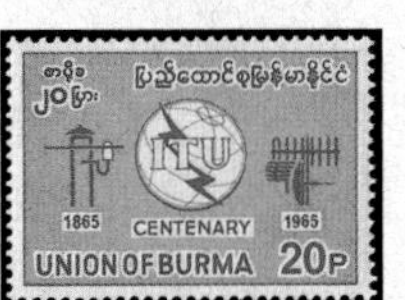

ITU Emblem, Old and New Communication Equipment — A30

1965, May 17 Litho. ***Perf. 15***

Size: 32x22mm

No.	Type	Denomination / Color	Unused	Used
188	A30	20p bright pink	2.00	.25

Perf. 13

Size: 34x24½mm

No.	Type	Denomination / Color	Unused	Used
189	A30	50p dull green	2.75	.50

Centenary of the ITU.

ICY Emblem A31

1965, July 1 Unwmk. ***Perf. 13***

No.	Type	Denomination / Color	Unused	Used
190	A31	5p violet blue	.50	.25
191	A31	10p brown orange	1.25	.25
192	A31	15p olive	3.00	.50
		Nos. 190-192 (3)	4.75	1.00

International Cooperation Year.

Rice Farmer — A32

Cogwheel and Hammer — A33

1966, Mar. 2

No.	Type	Denomination / Color	Unused	Used
193	A32	15p multicolored	2.40	.40

Issued for Farmers' Day.

1967, May 1 Litho. Unwmk.

No.	Type	Denomination / Color	Unused	Used
194	A33	15p lt blue, yel & black	2.40	.50

Issued for Labor Day, May 1.

Aung San, Tractor and Farmers A34

1968, Jan. 4 Unwmk. ***Perf. 13***

No.	Type	Denomination / Color	Unused	Used
195	A34	15p sky bl, blk & ocher	1.90	.40

20th anniversary of independence.

Largest Burmese Pearl — A35

1968, Mar. 4 Litho. ***Perf. 13½x13***

No.	Type	Denomination / Color	Unused	Used
196	A35	15p blue, ultra, gray & yel	3.50	.40

Burmese pearl industry.

Bird Types of 1964 in Changed Sizes

Designs as before.

Unwmk.

1968, July 1 Photo. ***Perf. 14***

Size: 21x17mm

No.	Type	Denomination / Color	Unused	Used
197	A28	1p gray	.45	.30
198	A28	2p carmine rose	.45	.30
199	A28	3p blue green	.65	.40

Size: 23½x28mm

No.	Type	Denomination / Color	Unused	Used
200	A29	5p violet blue	.65	.40
201	A29	10p orange brown	.80	.55
202	A29	15p olive	.90	.60

Size: 38½x21, 21x38½mm

No.	Type	Denomination / Color	Unused	Used
203	A28	20p rose & brown	1.05	.60
204	A29	25p yel & brown	1.50	1.25
205	A29	50p ver, blk, & gray	2.25	1.25
206	A29	1k gray, ind & yel	10.00	1.25
207	A28	2k dull cit, ind & red	13.25	3.00
208	A29	5k yel, dk blue & red	35.00	6.00
		Nos. 197-208 (12)	66.95	15.90

For overprints see Nos. O92-O102.

Wheat — A36

1969, Mar. 2 Litho. ***Perf. 13***

No.	Type	Denomination / Color	Unused	Used
209	A36	15p blue, emerald & yel	2.40	.30

Issued for Peasant's Day.

ILO Emblem A37

1969, Oct. 29 Photo. Wmk. 254

210 A37 15p dk blue grn & gold .70 .25
211 A37 50p dp carmine & gold 1.75 .55

50th anniv. of the ILO.

Soccer — A38

Designs: 25p, Runner, horiz. 50p, Weight lifter. 1k, Women's volleyball.

Perf. 12½x13, 13x12½

1969, Dec. 1 Litho. Wmk. 254

212 A38 15p brt olive & multi .45 .25
213 A38 25p brown & multi .65 .25
214 A38 50p brt green & multi 1.50 .30
215 A38 1k blue, yel grn & blk 2.75 .50
Nos. 212-215 (4) 5.35 1.30

5th South East Asia Peninsular Games, Rangoon.

Burmese Flags and Marching Soldiers — A39

1970, Mar. 27 ***Perf. 13***

216 A39 15p multicolored 2.10 .30

Issued for Armed Forces Day.

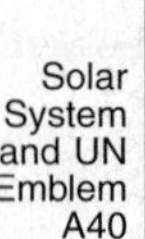

Solar System and UN Emblem A40

1970, June 26 Photo. Unwmk.

217 A40 15p lt ultra & multi 2.10 .40

25th anniversary of the United Nations.

Scroll, Marchers, Peacock Emblem — A41

Designs: 25p, Students' boycott demonstration. 50p, Banner and marchers at Shwedagon Camp.

1970, Nov. 23 Litho. ***Perf. 13x13½***

218 A41 15p ultra & multi .60 .25
219 A41 25p multicolored 1.25 .25
220 A41 50p lt blue & multi 2.10 .45
Nos. 218-220 (3) 3.95 .95

50th National Day (Students' 1920 uprising).

Workers, Farmers, Technicians — A42

15p, Burmese of various races, & flags. 25p, Hands holding document. 50p, Red party flag.

1971, June 28 Litho. ***Perf. 13½***

221 A42 5p blue & multi .45 .25
222 A42 15p blue & multi .80 .25
223 A42 25p blue & multi 1.10 .30
224 A42 50p blue & multi 1.60 .45
a. Souvenir sheet of 4, #221-224 19.00 19.00
Nos. 221-224 (4) 3.95 1.25

1st Congress of Burmese Socialist Program Party.

Child Drinking Milk — A43

UNICEF, 25th Anniv.: 50p, Marionettes.

1971, Dec. 11 ***Perf. 14½***

225 A43 15p lt ultra & multi 1.10 .30
226 A43 50p emerald & multi 2.50 .60

Aung San, Independence Monument, Pinlon — A44

Union Day, 25th Anniv.: 50p, Bogyoke Aung San and people in front of Independence Monument. 1k, Map of Burma with flag pointing to Pinlon, vert.

1972, Feb. 12 ***Perf. 14***

227 A44 15p ocher & multi .45 .25
228 A44 50p blue & multi 1.25 .35
229 A44 1k green, ultra & red 3.00 .55
Nos. 227-229 (3) 4.70 1.15

Burmese and Double Star A45

1972 Litho. ***Perf. 14***

230 A45 15p bister & multi 2.40 .25

Revolutionary Council, 10th anniversary.

"Your Heart is your Health" — A46

1972, Apr. 7 ***Perf. 14x14½***

231 A46 15p yellow, red & black 2.40 .30

World Health Day.

Burmese of Various Ethnic Groups A47

1973, Feb. 12 Litho. ***Perf. 14***

232 A47 15p multicolored 2.40 .25

1973 census.

Casting Vote — A48

Natl. Referendum: 10p, Voters holding map of Burma. 15p, Farmer & soldier holding ballots.

Perf. 14x14½, 14½x14

1973, Dec. 15 Litho.

233 A48 5p deep org & black .80 .25
234 A48 10p blue & multi .80 .25
235 A48 15p blue & multi, vert. .80 .25
Nos. 233-235 (3) 2.40 .75

Open-air Meeting A49

Designs: 15p, Regional flags. 1k, Scales of justice and Burmese emblem.

1974, Mar. 2 Photo. ***Perf. 13***

Size: 80x26mm

236 A49 15p blue & multi .65 .30

Size: 37x25mm

237 A49 50p blue & multi 1.60 .45
238 A49 1k lt blue, bis & blk 2.50 .65
Nos. 236-238 (3) 4.75 1.40

First meeting of People's Parliament.

Messenger Bird and UPU Emblem — A50

UPU Cent.: 20p, Mother reading letter to child, vert. 50p, Simulated block of stamps, vert. 1k, Burmese doll, vert. 2k, Mailman delivering letter to family.

1974, May 22

239 A50 15p grn, lt grn & org .45 .25
240 A50 20p multicolored .70 .25
241 A50 50p green & multi 1.40 .25
242 A50 1k ultra & multi 2.50 .30
243 A50 2k blue & multi 4.50 .85
Nos. 239-243 (5) 9.55 1.90

Children A51

Man and Woman A52

Designs: 3p, Tribal woman. 5p, 15p, Man and woman. 10p, Tribal man and woman (like 1p). 50p, Woman with fan. 1k, Seated woman. 5k, Tribal man with drum.

Perf. 13, 13x13½ (#248-251)

1974-78 Photo.

244 A51 1p rose & lilac rose .30 .25
245 A51 3p dk brown & pink .30 .25
246 A51 5p pink & violet .30 .25
246A A51 10p Prus blue ('76) .30 .25
247 A51 15p lt grn & ol ('75) .35 .25
248 A52 20p lt blue & multi .50 .25
249 A52 50p ocher & multi 2.10 .50
250 A52 1k brt rose & multi 3.25 .80
251 A52 5k ol green & multi 13.25 2.25
Nos. 244-251 (9) 20.65 5.05

For different country names see Nos. 298-303.

IWY Emblem, Woman and Globe A53

IWY: 2k, Symbolic flower, globe and IWY emblem, vert.

1975, Dec. 15 Photo. ***Perf. 13½***

252 A53 50p green & black 1.10 .30
253 A53 2k black & blue 4.00 1.10

Burmese with Raised Fists A54

Constitution Day: 50p, Demonstrators with banners and emblem. 1k, People and map of Burma, emblem.

1976, Jan. 3 ***Perf. 14***

254 A54 20p blue & black .45 .25
255 A54 50p blue, blk & brn 1.10 .45

Size: 56x20mm

256 A54 1k blue & multi 3.00 .70
Nos. 254-256 (3) 4.55 1.40

Students, Campaign Emblem — A55

Abacus A56

Intl. Literacy Year: 50p, Campaign emblem. 1k, Emblem, book and globe.

1976, Sept. 8 Photo. ***Perf. 14***

257 A55 10p salmon & black .55 .25
258 A56 15p blue grn & multi .85 .25
259 A56 50p ultra, org & blk 1.60 .40
260 A55 1k multicolored 3.00 .60
Nos. 257-260 (4) 6.00 1.50

Steam Locomotive A57

Diesel Train Emerging from Tunnel — A58

Cent. of Burma's Railroad: 20p, Early train and oxcart. 25p, Old and new trains approaching station. 50p, Railroad bridge.

1977, May 1 *Perf. 13½*
261 A57 15p multicolored 9.00 1.50

Size: 38x26, 26x38mm

262 A57 20p multicolored 2.75 .50
263 A57 25p multicolored 4.25 .75
264 A57 50p multicolored 5.25 1.50
265 A58 1k multicolored 12.00 2.25
Nos. 261-265 (5) 33.25 6.50

Karaweik Pagoda A59

Design: 1k, Karaweik Pagoda, front view.

1977
266 A59 50p light brown 1.00 .45

Size: 78x25mm

267 A59 1k multicolored 3.75 .75

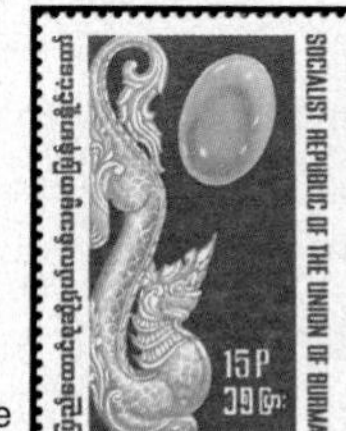

Jade Dragon — A60

Precious Jewelry: 20p, Gold bird with large pearl. 50p, Hand holding pearl necklace with pendant. 1k, Gold dragon, horiz.

1978 **Photo.** *Perf. 13*
268 A60 15p green & yel grn .70 .25
269 A60 20p multicolored 1.40 .25
270 A60 50p multicolored 3.50 .45

Size: 55x20mm
Perf. 14

271 A60 1k multicolored 9.00 .80
Nos. 268-271 (4) 14.60 1.75

Satellite over Map of Asia A61

1979, Feb., 12 **Photo.** *Perf. 13*
272 A61 25p multicolored 2.10 .60

IYC Emblem in Map of Burma — A62

1979, Dec. **Photo.** *Perf. 13½*
273 A62 25p multicolored 1.25 .30
274 A62 50p multicolored 3.75 .60

International Year of the Child.

Weather Balloon, WMO Emblem — A63

1980, Mar. 23 **Photo.** *Perf. 13½*
275 A63 25p shown 1.10 .25
276 A63 50p Weather satellite, cloud 2.40 .45

World Meteorological Day.

Weight Lifting, Olympic Rings A64

1980, Dec. **Litho.** *Perf. 14*
277 A64 20p Weight lifting .85 .25
278 A64 50p Boxing 1.50 .40
279 A64 1k Soccer 2.40 .65
Nos. 277-279 (3) 4.75 1.30

22nd Summer Olympic Games, Moscow, July 19-Aug. 3.

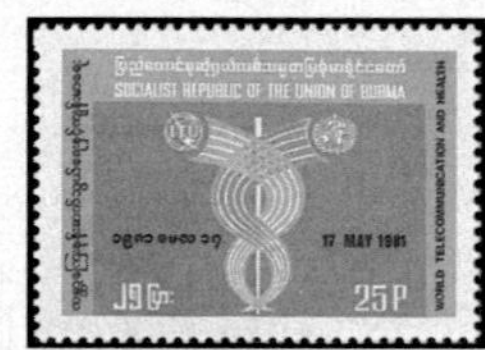

13th World Telecommunications Day — A65

1981, May 17 **Photo.** *Perf. 13½*
280 A65 25p orange & black 3.25 .30

World Food Day A66

1981, Oct. 16 **Photo.** *Perf. 13½*
281 A66 25p Livestock, produce 1.00 .25
282 A66 50p Farmer, rice, produce 1.50 .30
283 A66 1k Emblems 2.50 .50
Nos. 281-283 (3) 5.00 1.05

Intl. Year of the Disabled A67

1981, Dec. 12
284 A67 25p multicolored 3.25 .35

World Communications Year — A68

1983, Sept. 15 **Litho.** *Perf. 14½x14*
285 A68 15p pale blue & black .60 .25
286 A68 25p dull lake & black 1.10 .30
287 A68 50p grn, pale grn, blk & lake 2.75 .65
288 A68 1k buff, blk, beige & yel grn 4.50 .95
Nos. 285-288 (4) 8.95 2.15

Fish, Ship, Globe, FAO Emblem — A69

1983, Oct. 16 **Photo.** *Perf. 14x14½*
289 A69 15p brt blue, bister & blk .50 .25
290 A69 25p yel grn, pale org & blk .90 .25
291 A69 50p org, pale grn & blk 2.50 .80
292 A69 1k yel, ultra & black 4.00 1.60
Nos. 289-292 (4) 7.90 2.90

World Food Day.

Stylized Trees, Hemispheres and Log — A70

1984, Oct. 16 *Perf. 14½x14*
293 A70 15p org, black & blue .55 .25
294 A70 25p pale yel, blk & lt vio .70 .25
295 A70 50p pale pink, blk & lt grn 1.75 .55
296 A70 1k yel, blk & lt rose vio 5.00 1.40
Nos. 293-296 (4) 8.00 2.45

World Food Day.

Intl. Youth Year — A71

1985, Oct. 15 *Perf. 14x14½*
297 A71 15p multicolored 2.40 .30

Types of 1974
Inscribed: Union of Burma

1989 **Photo.** *Perf. 13½*
298 A51 15p olive & lt green .55 .25
298A A52 20p lt blue & multi *125.00* —
299 A52 50p violet & brown 1.10 .40
300 A52 1k multicolored 2.50 .75
Nos. 298,299-300 (3) 4.15 1.40

Issued: 15p, 6/26; 50p, 6/12; 1k, 9/6.

No. 298A was prepared but not issued. A quantity was accidentally supplied to the Shan State post office in July 1995, and these stamps were sold to the public. A limited quantity was subsequently made available to collectors in Yangon.

UNION OF MYANMAR
Inscribed: Union of Myanmar

1990-91 **Photo.** *Perf. 13½*
301 A51 15p olive & lt green .60 .25
301A A52 20p brown, greenish blue & black ('91) *45.00* —
302 A52 50p violet & brown 1.10 .55
303 A52 1k multicolored 1.75 .90

Issued: 15p, May 26; 50p, May 12.

Fountain, Natl. Assembly Park — A74

1990, May 27 **Litho.** *Perf. 14½x14*
304 A74 1k multicolored 7.50 1.00

State Law and Order Restoration Council.

A75

1990, Dec. 20 **Litho.** *Perf. 14x14½*
305 A75 2k multicolored 7.00 1.75

UN Development Program, 40th anniv.

A76

1991, Jan. 26
306 A76 50p Nawata ruby 7.00 .95

Painting of Freedom Fighters — A77

Bronze Statue — A78

1992, Jan. 4 **Litho.** *Perf. 14x14½*
307 A77 50p multicolored 2.50 .60
308 A78 2k multicolored 7.00 2.00

A79

1992, Apr. 10 **Litho.** *Perf. 14x14½*
309 A79 50p multicolored 2.25 .60

National Sports Festival.

A80

1992, Dec. 1 **Litho.** *Perf. 14x14½*
310 A80 50p red 3.00 .50

World Campaign Against AIDS.

A81

1992, Dec. 5 Litho. *Perf. 14x14½*
Background Color

311 A81 50p pink .75 .30
312 A81 1k yellow 1.25 .65
313 A81 3k orange 3.50 1.50
314 A81 5k green 6.50 2.50
Nos. 311-314 (4) 12.00 4.95

Intl. Conference on Nutrition, Rome.

Artifacts — A82

1993, Sept. 1 Litho. *Perf. 14x14½*
315 A82 5k Bird 6.50 2.50
316 A82 10k Statue 13.00 5.00

Natl. Assembly — A83

1993, Jan. 1 Litho. *Perf. 14x14½*
317 A83 50p multicolored .75 .30
318 A83 3k multicolored 3.75 1.50

Equestrian Festival — A84

1993, Oct. 23 Litho. *Perf. 14½x14*
319 A84 3k multicolored 5.50 1.50

A85

1994, June 5 Litho. *Perf. 14*
320 A85 4k multicolored 6.50 2.00

Environment day.

A86

1994, Sept. 15 Litho. *Perf. 14*
321 A86 3k multicolored 5.50 2.00

Union of Solidarity & Development, 1st anniv.

Armed Forces, 50th Anniv. A87

1995, Mar. 27 Litho. *Perf. 14½x14*
322 A87 50p multicolored 1.50 .50

A88

1995, June 26 Litho. *Perf. 14*
323 A88 2k multicolored 3.50 1.50

Prevent drug abuse.

A89

1995, Oct. 17 Litho. *Perf. 14x14½*
324 A89 50p multicolored 2.00 .50

Myanmar motion pictures, 60th anniv.

A90

1995, Oct. 24
325 A90 4k UN, 50th Anniv. 6.50 3.25

A91

1995, Nov. 1
326 A91 50p pink & multi .80 .50
327 A91 2k green & multi 3.25 1.75

University of Yangon (Rangoon), 75th anniv.

Visit Myanmar Year A92

Designs: 50p, Couple in boat on Inlay Lake with food bowl for Buddha, Buddhist monks. 4k, Decorated royal barge on Kandawgyi (Royal Lake), Yangoon. 5k, Royal moat, entrance of Yadanabon (Mandalay), vert.

Perf. 14½x14, 14x14½
1996, Mar. 1 Litho.
328 A92 50p multicolored .85 .50
329 A92 4k multicolored 5.50 3.00
330 A92 5k multicolored 7.00 4.00
Nos. 328-330 (3) 13.35 7.50

UNICEF, 50th Anniv. — A93

Stylized designs: 1k, Mother breastfeeding. 2k, Vaccinating child. 4k, Girls going to school.

1996, Dec. 11 Litho. *Perf. 14x14½*
331 A93 1k multicolored 1.40 1.00
332 A93 2k multicolored 2.75 2.00
333 A93 4k multicolored 5.50 3.00
Nos. 331-333 (3) 9.65 6.00

Intl. Letter Writing Week A94

Designs: 2k, Men in canoe. 5k, Stylized figures forming pyramid, flag, map, vert.

1996, Oct. 7 *Perf. 14½x14, 14x14½*
334 A94 2k multicolored 2.50 2.00
335 A94 5k multicolored 5.50 4.00

A95

1997, July 24 Litho. *Perf. 14x14½*
336 A95 1k blue & multi 1.75 1.50
337 A95 2k yellow & multi 3.50 3.00

Assoc. of Southeast Asian Nations (ASEAN), 30th anniv.

A96

1998, Jan. 4 Litho. *Perf. 14x14½*
338 A96 2k multicolored 3.50 3.50

Independence, 50th anniv.

Musical Instruments A97

1998-2000 Photo. *Perf. 13¼*
339 A97 5k Xylophone 4.75 4.75
340 A97 10k Mon brass gongs 8.75 8.75
341 A97 20k Rakhine (drum) 15.00 15.00
342 A97 30k Harp 22.50 22.50
343 A97 50k Shan pot drum 35.00 35.00
344 A97 100k Kachin brass gong ('00) 50.00 50.00
Nos. 339-344 (6) 136.00 136.00

Issued: 5k, 8/28/98; 100k, 2/12/00.

Decade of Disabled Persons (1993-2002) A98

1998 Litho. *Perf. 14*
345 A98 2k yellow & multi 3.00 3.00
346 A98 5k apple green & multi 6.00 6.00

UPU, 125th Anniv. — A99

1999 Litho. *Perf. 14x14¼*
347 A99 2k blue & multi 3.00 3.00
348 A99 5k purple & multi 6.00 6.00

Independence, 52nd Anniv. — A100

2000
349 A100 2k multi 3.50 3.50

World Meteorological Day — A101

2000 Photo. ***Perf. 14x14¼, 14¼x14***

350 A101 2k Anemometer, vert. 2.75 2.75
351 A101 5k shown 7.00 7.00
352 A101 10k Cloud, sun 12.50 12.50
Nos. 350-352 (3) 22.25 22.25

Diplomatic Relations with People's Republic of China, 50th Anniv. — A102

2000 Litho. ***Perf. 14¼x14***

353 A102 5k multi 9.00 9.00

Myanmar postal officials have declared as "illegal" the following items inscribed "Union of Myanmar."

Sheets of nine stamps of various denominations depicting:

Personalities of the 20th Century, Musical stars, Orchids with Rotary emblems, Mushrooms with Rotary emblems, Cats and dogs with Scout emblems, Chess, Fish, Owls, and Trains (two different).

Sheets of six stamps of various denominations depicting:

Bruce Lee, Horror movie scenes, and Marilyn Monroe (two different).

Souvenir sheets of two stamps of various denominations depicting:

Formula 1 race cars (two different), Golfers (six different), and Classic cars (eight different).

Souvenir sheets of one depicting:

Dutch royal wedding, Bruce Lee (three different), Tiger Woods (three different), Impressionist paintings (six different), Elvis Presley (six different), and Chess (twelve different).

Campaign Against Drugs — A103

2000, June 26 Litho. ***Perf. 14x14¼***

354 A103 2k multi 3.25 3.25

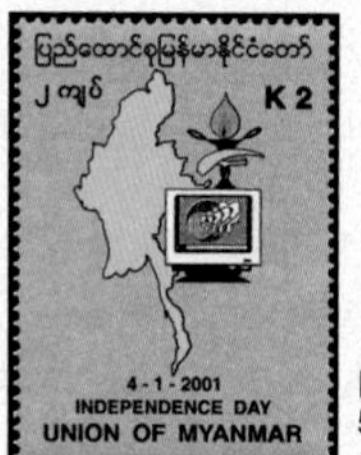

Independence, 53rd Anniv. — A104

2001, Jan. 4

355 A104 2k multi 4.00 4.00

Independence, 54th Anniv. — A105

Inscriptions in: (2k), Burmese. 30k, English.

2002, Jan. 4

356-357 A105 Set of 2 16.00 16.00

Independence, 55th Anniv. — A106

Inscriptions in: (2k), Burmese. 30k, English.

2003, Jan. 4

358-359 A106 Set of 2 *12.00 12.00*

Flora — A107

Designs: No. 360, 30k, Black orchide. No. 361, 30k, Mango.

2004, Feb. 11

360-361 A107 Set of 2 *10.50 10.50*

FIFA (Fédération Internationale de Football Association), Cent. — A108

2004, May 5 ***Perf. 14¼x14***

362 A108 2k multi 4.50 4.50

World Buddhist Summit — A109

Designs: 5k, Emblem, temples. 30k, Emblem, temples, diff.

2004, Dec. 9 Litho. ***Perf. 14¼x14***

363-364 A109 Set of 2 6.25 6.25

Myanmar postal authorities have declared overprints of No. 362 with Burmese inscriptions for the 2006 World Cup to be illegal.

Independence, 59th Anniv. — A110

Statues, star and: (2k), Flag, Burmese inscriptions. 5k, Map, English inscriptions.

2007, Jan. 4 Litho. ***Perf. 14x14¼***

365-366 A110 Set of 2 2.25 2.25

A111

A112

National Convention — A113

2007, Aug. 13 Litho. ***Perf. 14¼x14***

367 A111 20k multi *1.25 1.25*
368 A112 30k multi *2.50 2.50*
369 A113 50k multi *3.00 3.00*
Nos. 367-369 (3) *6.75 6.75*

Miniature Sheet

Association of South East Asian Nations (ASEAN), 40th Anniv. — A114

No. 370: a, Secretariat Building, Bandar Seri Begawan, Brunei. b, National Museum of Cambodia. c, Fatahillah Museum, Jakarta, Indonesia. d, Typical house, Laos. e, Malayan Railway Headquarters Building, Kuala Lumpur, Malaysia. f, Yangon Post Office, Myanmar. g, Malacañang Palace, Philippines. h, National Museum of Singapore. i, Vimanmek Mansion, Bangkok, Thailand. j, Presidential Palace, Hanoi, Viet Nam.

2007, Oct. 19

370 A114 50k Sheet of 10, #a-j *25.00 25.00*

See Brunei No. 607, Cambodia No. 2339, Indonesia Nos. 2120-2121, Laos Nos. 1717-1718, Malaysia No. 1170, Philippines Nos. 3103-3105, Singapore No. 1265, Thailand No. 2315, and Viet Nam Nos. 3302-3311.

A115

Independence, 60th Anniv. — A116

2008, Jan. 4 Litho. ***Perf. 14¼x14***

371 A115 50k multi *1.80 1.80*
372 A116 100k multi *3.00 3.00*

Constitutional Referendum — A117

Designs: No. 373, 100k, Map of Burma, people, statues, ballot box. No. 374, 100k, Line of people casting ballots, statues. 200k, Map of Burma, hand depositing ballot, vert.

Perf. 14¼x14, 14x14¼

2008, May 9 Litho.

373-375 A117 Set of 3 *10.00 10.00*

A118

Independence, 61st Anniv. — A119

2009, Jan. 4 Litho. ***Perf. 14¼x14***

376 A118 200k multi *4.00 4.00*
377 A119 300k multi *6.00 6.00*

The values for the stamps are based on official exchange rates set by the Myanmar government. Actual exchange rates appear to differ significantly.

A120

Independence, 62nd Anniv. — A121

2010, Jan. 4 Litho. *Perf. 14¼x14*

378	A120	100k multi	*10.00*	*10.00*
379	A121	200k multi	*10.00*	*10.00*

Diplomatic Relations Between Myanmar and People's Republic of China, 60th Anniv. — A122

2010, June 8 Litho. *Perf. 14¼x14*

380	A122	100k multi	*7.50*	*7.50*

General Elections — A123

2010, Nov. 7

381	A123	500k multi	*5.00*	*5.00*

Souvenir Sheet

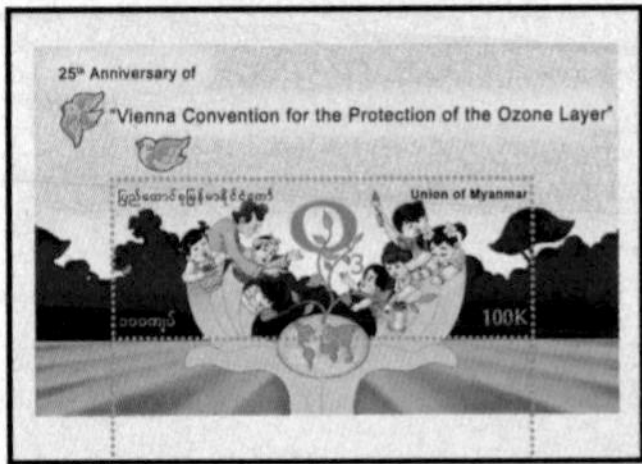

Vienna Convention for the Protection of the Ozone Layer, 25th Anniv. — A124

2010, Nov. 18

382	A124	100k multi	*16.00*	*16.00*

A125

A126

Government Buildings — A127

2011, June 16 Litho. *Perf. 14¼x14*

383	A125	100k multi	*5.00*	*5.00*
384	A126	500k multi	*10.00*	*10.00*
385	A127	500k multi	*10.00*	*10.00*
		Nos. 383-385 (3)	*25.00*	*25.00*

A128

Independence, 64th Anniv. — A129

2012, Jan. 4

386	A128	500k multi	3.00	3.00
387	A129	1200k multi	7.00	7.00

Miniature Sheet

11th ASEAN Telecommunications and Information Technology Ministers Meeting, Nay Pyi Taw — A130

No. 388: a, 100k, Line of flags, emblem, building. b, 100k, Circle of flags around emblem, building. c, 100k, Emblem, buildings in circle. d, 200k, Like #388a. e, 200k, Like #388b. f, 200k, Like #388c.

2012, Mar. 19

388	A130	Sheet of 6, #a-f	8.00	8.00

A131

Second Leaders Retreat of Asian Telecommunications Senior Officials and Asian Telecommunications Regulators Council, Bangkok, Thailand — A132

2012, Oct. 1

389	A131	500k multi	*5.00*	*5.00*
390	A132	500k multi	*5.00*	*5.00*

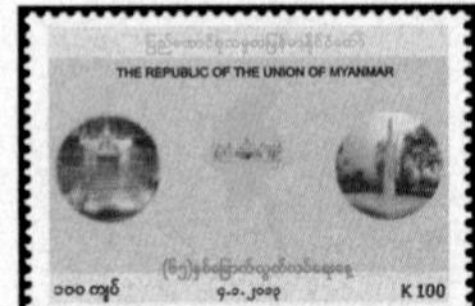

A133

Independence, 65th Anniv. — A134

2013, Jan. 4

391	A133	100k multi	*2.25*	*2.25*
392	A134	100k multi	*2.25*	*2.25*

Diplomatic Relations Between Myanmar and Russia, 65th Anniv. — A135

2013, Apr. 10

393	A135	500k multi	*4.75*	*4.75*

Miniature Sheet

27th South East Asia Games, Naypyidaw — A136

No. 394: a, 100k, Emblem of 2013 Games. b, 100k, Owl holding torch. c, 100k, Two owls. d, 100k, Six owls. e, 500k, Like #394a. f, 500k, Like #394b. g, 500k, Like #394c. h, 500k, Like #394d.

2013, Sept. 2 Litho. *Perf. 14¼x14*

394	A136	Sheet of 8, #a-h	*12.50*	*12.50*

OFFICIAL STAMPS

Stamps of India, 1926-34, Overprinted in Black

1937 Wmk. 196 *Perf. 14*

O1	A46	3p gray	4.25	.25
O2	A71	½a green	15.00	.25
O3	A68	9p dark green	5.25	1.60
O4	A72	1a dark brown	8.50	.30
O5	A49	2a vermilion	18.00	.75
O6	A57	2a6p buff	8.50	3.25
O7	A52	4a olive grn	8.50	.30
O8	A53	6a bister	8.50	*15.00*
O9	A54	8a red violet	8.50	3.25
O10	A55	12a claret	8.50	*12.00*

Overprinted

O11	A56	1r green & brown	24.00	9.50
O12	A56	2r buff & car rose	47.50	*67.50*
O13	A56	5r dk vio & ultra	160.00	70.00
O14	A56	10r car & green	450.00	*250.00*
		Nos. O1-O14 (14)	775.00	*433.95*
		Set, never hinged	825.00	

For overprint see No. 1N27.

Regular Issue of 1938 Overprinted in Black

Perf. 13½x14, 13, 13½

1939 Wmk. 254

O15	A1	3p violet	.35	*.45*
O16	A1	6p ultramarine	.35	*.45*
O17	A1	9p yel green	5.00	*6.25*
O18	A2	1a brown violet	.40	*.50*
O19	A2	1½a turquoise green	4.50	2.75
O20	A2	2a carmine	1.50	.50
O21	A2	4a slate blue	5.50	4.75

Overprinted

O22	A3	2a6p rose lake	24.00	20.00
O23	A6	8a slate green	19.00	5.00
O24	A7	1r brt ultra & dk vio	20.00	7.00
O25	A7	2r dk vio & red brn	37.50	18.00
O26	A8	5r car & dull vio	31.00	*40.00*
O27	A8	10r gray grn & brn	160.00	50.00
		Nos. O15-O27 (13)	309.10	155.65
		Set, never hinged	420.00	

For overprints see Nos. 1N12-1N16, 1N31-1N36, 1NO1.

Catalogue values for unused stamps in this section, from this point to the end of the section, are for Never Hinged items.

Nos. 51-56, 60 Overprinted Like Nos. O15-O21

1946 *Perf. 13½x14*

O28	A1	3p brown	3.75	*5.50*
O29	A1	6p violet	2.75	2.75
O30	A1	9p dull green	.70	*5.75*
O31	A2	1a deep blue	.30	*2.50*
O32	A2	1½a salmon	.30	.40
O33	A2	2a rose lake	.35	*2.25*
O34	A2	4a rose lilac	.35	.90

Nos. 57, 61-65 Ovptd. Like Nos. O22-O27

Perf. 13, 13½

O35	A3	2a6p greenish blue	2.50	*10.50*
O38	A6	8a deep magenta	4.50	*6.25*
O39	A7	1r dp mag & dk vio	1.90	*9.50*
O40	A7	2r salmon & red brn	10.00	*55.00*
O41	A8	5r red brn & dk grn	19.00	*67.50*
O42	A8	10r dk violet & car	20.00	*75.00*
		Nos. O28-O42 (13)	66.40	*243.80*

Nos. O28 to O42 Overprinted in Black

1947

O43	A1	3p brown	2.40	.50
O44	A1	6p violet	4.75	.25
O45	A1	9p dull green	6.25	1.25

O46 A2 1a deep blue 6.25 1.10
O47 A2 1½a salmon 10.50 .60
O48 A2 2a rose lake 6.25 .30
O49 A3 2a6p greenish bl 35.00 18.00
O50 A2 4a rose lilac 24.00 .80
O51 A6 8a dp magenta 24.00 5.00
O52 A7 1r dp mag & dk vio 17.50 3.00
O53 A7 2r sal & red brn 17.50 *25.00*
O54 A8 5r red brn & dk grn 18.00 *25.00*
O55 A8 10r dk vio & car 18.00 *37.50*
Nos. O43-O55 (13) 190.40 118.30

The overprint is slightly larger on Nos. O49 and O51 to O55. The Burmese characters read "Interim Government."

Issues of the Republic

Nos. 102-106, 109-115 Overprinted in Carmine or Black

a. Overprint 13mm long.
b. Overprint 15mm long.

1949 Unwmk. *Perf. 12½, 13*
O56 A15(a) 3p ultra (C) .80 .25
O57 A15(a) 6p green (C) .25 .25
O58 A15(a) 9p carmine .25 .25
O59 A16(a) 1a red orange .25 .25
O60 A17(a) 2a orange .45 .25
O61 A18(b) 3a6p dk sl grn (C) .45 .25
O62 A16(a) 4a chocolate .45 .25
O63 A18(b) 8a carmine .45 .25
O64 A19(b) 1r blue green (C) .80 .25
O65 A19(b) 2r dp blue (C) 1.60 .90
O66 A19(b) 5r chocolate 5.25 1.75
O67 A19(b) 10r orange red 15.00 4.50
Nos. O56-O67 (12) 26.00 9.40

Same Overprint in Black on Nos. 139-142, 144-152
Perf. 14x13½, 13, 14

1954-57 Wmk. 254
O68 A15(a) 1p brown org .25 .25
O69 A15(a) 2p plum .25 .25
O70 A15(a) 3p blue .25 .25
O71 A16(a) 5p ultra .25 .25
O72 A17(a) 15p green .25 .25
O72A A18(b) 20p ver ('57) .40 .25
O73 A18(b) 25p lt red org .40 .25
O74 A16(a) 30p vermilion .40 .25
O75 A18(b) 50p blue 1.00 .30
O76 A19(b) 1k rose violet 1.40 .40
O77 A19(b) 2k green 3.50 .70
O78 A19(b) 5k ultra 5.75 1.10
O79 A19(b) 10k light blue 17.50 3.00
Nos. O68-O79 (13) 31.60 7.50

No. 141 Ovptd. Service

1964 Litho. *Perf. 14*
O80 A15 3p blue *17.50 11.50*

Nos. 139, 141-142, 144, 177-179, 181, 183 Ovptd.

1964-65
Overprint: 11½mm
O81 A15 1p brown orange *8.00 1.00*
O82 A28 2p carmine rose ('65) *7.00 1.00*
O83 A15 3p blue *8.00 1.00*
O84 A28 3p blue green ('65) *7.00 1.00*
O85 A16 5p ultramarine *8.00 1.00*
O86 A28 5p violet blue ('65) *7.00 1.00*
O87 A17 15p green *8.00 1.00*
O88 A28 15p olive ('65) *7.00 1.00*
O89 A29 25p yel & brn ('65) *8.00 1.00*
Nos. O81-O89 (9) *68.00 9.00*

အစိုးရကိစ္စ
#176-178 Ovptd.

အစိုးရကိစ္စ
#181 Ovptd.

1966
Overprint: 15mm
O90 A28 1p black 9.50 3.00
O91 A28 2p carmine rose 9.50 3.00
O92 A28 3p blue green 9.50 3.00
Overprint: 12mm
O93 A29 15p olive 9.50 3.00

Nos. 176-179, 181-187 Overprinted in Black or Red

1967 Unwmk. Photo. *Perf. 13½*
Overprint: 15mm
Size: 25x21mm
O94 A28 1p gray .45 .40
O95 A28 2p carmine rose .80 .50
O96 A28 3p blue green .80 .65
Size: 22x26½mm
O97 A29 5p violet blue 1.00 .70
O98 A29 15p olive 1.00 .80
Size: 35x25mm
O99 A28 20p rose & brown 1.75 .90
Size: 27x36½mm, 36½x27mm
O100 A29 25p yel & brown (R) 2.25 1.00
O101 A29 50p red, blk & gray 3.50 1.25
O102 A29 1k gray, ind & yel (R) 8.50 1.90
O103 A28 2k pale ol, ind & red (R) 14.00 3.00
O104 A29 5k cit, dk bl & red (R) 35.00 15.00
Nos. O94-O104 (11) 69.05 26.10

Similar Overprint on Nos. 197-200, 202-208 in Black or Red

1968 Unwmk. *Perf. 14*
Size: 21x17mm
Overprint: 13mm
O105 A28 1p gray .40 .25
O106 A28 2p carmine rose .80 .25
O107 A28 3p blue green .90 .40
Size: 23½x28mm
Overprint: 15mm
O108 A29 5p violet blue 1.00 .40
O109 A29 15p olive 1.00 .40
Size: 38½x21mm, 21x38½mm
Overprint: 14mm
O110 A28 20p rose & brn 1.60 .50
O111 A29 25p yel & brown (R) 3.25 .50
O112 A29 50p ver, blk & gray 4.00 .75
O113 A29 1k gray, ind & yel (R) 6.25 1.00
O114 A28 2k dl cit, ind & red (R) 10.00 2.00
O115 A29 5k yel, dk bl & red (R) 15.00 5.75
Nos. O105-O115 (11) 44.20 12.20

OCCUPATION STAMPS

Issued by Burma Independence Army (in conjunction with Japanese occupation officials)

Henzada Issue

Stamps of Burma, 1937-40, Overprinted in Black Blue, or Red; Nos. 1, 3, 5 Overprinted in Blue or Black

Henzada Type I

1942, May Wmk. 196 *Perf. 14*
1N1 A46 3p slate 5.00 *25.00*
1N2 A68 9p dark green 30.00 *80.00*
1N3 A49 2a vermilion 130.00 *220.00*

On 1938-40 George VI Issue
Perf. 13½x14
Wmk. 254
1N4 A1 1p red orange 275.00 *400.00*
1N5 A1 3p violet 45.00 *95.00*
1N6 A1 6p ultra 30.00 *65.00*
1N7 A1 9p yel green 1,100.
1N8 A2 1a brown violet 11.00 *50.00*
1N9 A2 1½a turq green 25.00 *85.00*
1N10 A2 2a carmine 25.00 *85.00*
1N11 A2 4a slate blue 50.00 *120.00*

On Official Stamps of 1939
1N12 A1 3p violet 150.00 *300.00*
1N13 A1 6p ultra 175.00 *300.00*
1N14 A2 1½a turq green 200.00 *350.00*
1N15 A2 2a carmine 425.00 550.00
1N16 A2 4a slate blue 1,350.

Authorities believe this overprint was officially applied only to postal stationery and that the adhesive stamps existing with it were not regularly issued. It has been called "Henzada Type II."

Myaungmya Issue

1937 George V Issue Overprinted in Black

Myaungmya Type I

1942, May Wmk. 196 *Perf. 14*
1N25 A68 9p dk green 130.00
1N26 A70 3a6p deep blue 85.00

On Official Stamp of 1937, No. O8
1N27 A53 6a bister 95.00

On 1938-40 George VI Issue
Perf. 13½x14
Wmk. 254
1N28 A1 9p yel green 175.00
1N29 A2 1a brown vio 650.00
1N30 A2 4a sl blue (blk ovpt. over red) 190.00

On Official Stamps of 1939
1N31 A1 3p violet 35.00 *110.00*
1N32 A1 6p ultra 25.00 *80.00*
1N33 A2 1a brown vio 25.00 *65.00*
1N34 A2 1½a turq green 850.00 *1,350.*
1N35 A2 2a carmine 32.50 *120.00*
1N36 A2 4a slate blue 32.50 *95.00*

1938-40 George VI Issue Overprinted

Myaungmya Type II

1942, May
1N37 A1 3p violet 21.00 *90.00*
1N38 A1 6p ultra 60.00 *130.00*
1N39 A1 9p yel green 25.00 *85.00*
1N40 A2 1a brown vio 17.50 *80.00*
1N41 A2 2a carmine 32.50 *100.00*
1N42 A2 4a slate blue 57.50 *130.00*

Nos. 30-31 Overprinted

Myaungmya Type III

1N43 A7 1r brt ultra & dk vio 400.00 *650.00*
1N44 A7 2r dk vio & red brn 210.00 *475.00*

Pyapon Issue

No. 5 and 1938-40 George VI Issue Overprinted

1942, May
1N45 A1 6p ultra 100.00
1N46 A2 1a brown vio 120.00 *300.00*
1N47 A49 2a vermilion 100.00
1N48 A2 2a carmine 160.00 *350.00*
1N49 A2 4a slate blue 850.00 850.00
Nos. 1N45-1N49 (5) 1,330.

Nos. 1N47-1N49 are valued in faulty condition.

Counterfeits of the peacock overprints exist.

OCCUPATION OFFICIAL STAMP

Myaungmya Issue

Burma No. O23 Overprinted in Black

1942, May Wmk. 254 *Perf. 13*
1NO1 A6 8a slate green 110.00

Overprint characters translate: "Office use." Two types of overprint differ mainly in base of peacock which is either 5mm or 8mm.

ISSUED UNDER JAPANESE OCCUPATION

Yano Seal — OS1

Wmk. ABSORBO DUPLICATOR and Outline of Elephant in Center of Sheet

Handstamped

1942, June 1 *Perf. 12x11*
Without Gum
2N1 OS1 1(a) vermilion 50.00 *85.00*

This stamp is the handstamped impression of the personal chop or seal of Shizuo Yano, chairman of the committee appointed to re-establish the Burmese postal system. It was prepared in Rangoon on paper captured from the Burma Government Offices. Not every stamp shows a portion of the watermark.

Farmer Plowing — OS2

Vertically Laid Paper
Without Gum

Wmk. ELEPHANT BRAND and Outline of Trumpeting Elephant Covering Several Stamps

1942, June 15 Litho. *Perf. 11x12*
2N2 OS2 1a scarlet 22.50 *25.00*

See illustration OS4.

Same, Surcharged with New Value

1942, Oct. 15
2N3 OS2 5c on 1a scarlet 22.50 *27.50*

Stamps of Japan, 1937-42, as shown, Handstamp Surcharged with New Value in Black

Rice Harvest A83

General Nogi A84

Power Plant A85

Admiral Togo A86

Diamond Mountains, Korea — A89

Meiji Shrine, Tokyo — A90

Yomei Gate, Nikko — A91

Mount Fuji and Cherry Blossoms A94

Torii of Miyajima Shrine — A96

1942, Sept. Wmk. 257 *Perf. 13*

2N4	A83	¼a on 1s fawn	45.00	*52.50*
2N5	A84	½a on 2s crim	52.50	*55.00*
2N6	A85	¾a on 3s green	85.00	*90.00*
2N7	A86	1a on 5s brn lake	82.50	72.50
2N8	A89	3a on 7s dp green	130.00	*150.00*
2N9	A86	4a on 4s dk green	65.00	72.50
a.		4a on 4s + 2s dk green (#B5)	190.00	*200.00*
2N10	A90	8a on 8s dk pur & pale vio	180.00	180.00
a.		Red surcharge	300.00	*325.00*
2N11	A91	1r on 10s lake	26.00	*30.00*
2N12	A94	2r on 20s ultra	60.00	60.00
a.		Red surcharge	60.00	60.00
2N13	A96	5r on 30s pck bl	17.50	*32.50*
a.		Red surcharge	30.00	*37.50*
		Nos. 2N4-2N13 (10)	743.50	*795.00*

Numerous double, inverted, etc., surcharges exist.

Re-surcharged in Black

1942, Oct. 15

2N14	A83	1c on ¼a on 1s	65.00	65.00
2N15	A84	2c on ½a on 2s	65.00	65.00
2N16	A85	3c on ¾a on 3s	65.00	65.00
a.		"3C." in blue	225.00	
2N17	A86	5c on 1a on 5s	90.00	77.50
2N18	A89	10c on 3a on 7s	160.00	150.00
2N19	A86	15c on 4a on 4s	55.00	*60.00*
2N20	A90	20c on 8a on 8s (#2N10)	825.00	750.00
a.		On #2N10a	400.00	200.00
		Nos. 2N14-2N20 (7)	1,325.	1,232.

No. 2N16a was issued in the Shan States.

Done locally, numerous different handstamps of each denomination can exist.

Stamps of Japan, 1937-42, Handstamp Surcharged with New Value in Black

1942, Oct. 15

2N21	A83	1c on 1s fawn	32.50	24.00
2N22	A84	2c on 2s crim	65.00	42.50
2N23	A85	3c on 3s green	92.50	65.00
a.		"3C." in blue	110.00	*120.00*
2N24	A86	5c on 5s brn lake	100.00	60.00
a.		"5C." in violet	180.00	*200.00*
2N25	A89	10c on 7s dp grn	120.00	82.50
2N26	A86	15c on 4s dk grn	30.00	*30.00*
2N27	A90	20c on 8s dk pur & pale vio	210.00	110.00
		Nos. 2N21-2N27 (7)	650.00	*414.00*

Nos. 2N23a and 2N24a were issued in the Shan States.

Burma State Government Crest — OS3

Unwmk.

1943, Feb. 15 Litho. *Perf. 12*

Without Gum

2N29	OS3	5c carmine	27.50	*32.50*
a.		Imperf.	27.50	*32.50*

This stamp was intended to be used to cover the embossed George VI envelope stamp and generally was sold affixed to such envelopes. It is also known used on private envelopes.

Farmer Plowing — OS4

1943, Mar. Typo. Without Gum

2N30	OS4	1c deep orange	5.00	10.00
2N31	OS4	2c yel green	1.00	*1.20*
2N32	OS4	3c blue	4.00	1.20
a.		Laid paper	24.00	35.00
2N33	OS4	5c carmine	4.00	*7.50*
a.		Small "5c"	27.50	*20.00*
b.		Imperf.	130.00	
2N34	OS4	10c violet brown	7.75	*8.00*
2N35	OS4	15c red violet	1.00	*4.00*
a.		Laid paper	7.25	*25.00*
2N36	OS4	20c dull purple	1.00	*1.20*
2N37	OS4	30c blue green	1.00	*2.50*
		Nos. 2N30-2N37 (8)	24.75	*35.60*

Small "c" in Nos. 2N34 to 2N37.

Burmese Soldier Carving "Independence" OS5

Farmer Rejoicing OS6

Boy with Burmese Flag — OS7

Hyphen-hole Perf., Pin-Perf. x Hyphen-hole Perf.

1943, Aug. 1 Typo.

2N38	OS5	1c orange	1.50	*2.10*
a.		Perf. 11	11.50	*19.50*
2N39	OS6	3c blue	3.00	*3.25*
a.		Perf. 11	12.00	*20.00*
2N40	OS7	5c rose	3.00	*3.50*
a.		Perf. 11	22.50	10.00
		Nos. 2N38-2N40 (3)	7.50	*8.85*

Declaration of the independence of Burma by the Ba Maw government, Aug. 1, 1943.

Burmese Girl Carrying Water Jar — OS8

Elephant Carrying Teak Log — OS9

Watch Tower of Mandalay Palace — OS10

1943, Oct. 1 Litho. *Perf. 12½*

2N41	OS8	1c dp salmon	24.00	18.00
2N42	OS8	2c yel green	1.00	*2.40*
2N43	OS8	3c violet	1.00	*2.75*
2N44	OS9	5c rose	1.00	*1.00*
2N45	OS9	10c blue	2.00	1.25
2N46	OS9	15c vermilion	1.20	*3.50*
2N47	OS9	20c yel green	1.20	*2.10*
2N48	OS9	30c brown	1.20	*2.40*
2N49	OS10	1r vermilion	1.00	*2.40*
2N50	OS10	2r violet	1.00	*2.75*
		Nos. 2N41-2N50 (10)	34.60	*38.55*

No. 2N49 exists imperforate. Canceled to order examples of Nos. 2N42-2N50 same values as unused.

Bullock Cart OS11

Shan Woman OS12

1943, Oct. 1 *Perf. 12½*

2N51	OS11	1c brown	40.00	*47.50*
2N52	OS11	2c yel green	45.00	*47.50*
2N53	OS11	3c violet	7.00	*14.00*
2N54	OS11	5c ultra	2.75	*8.50*
2N55	OS12	10c blue	18.00	*22.50*
2N56	OS12	20c rose	42.50	22.50
2N57	OS12	30c brown	27.50	*75.00*
		Nos. 2N51-2N57 (7)	182.75	*237.50*

For use only in the Shan States. Perak No. N34 also used in Shan States. Canceled-to-order stamps are valued at ½ used value.

Surcharged in Black

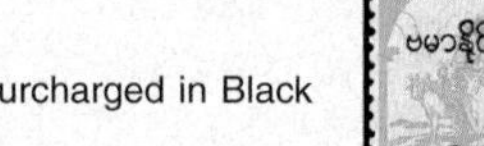

1944, Nov. 1

2N58	OS11	1c brown	4.25	*8.00*
2N59	OS11	2c yel green	1.00	*5.00*
a.		Inverted surcharge	500.00	*850.00*
2N60	OS11	3c violet	2.75	*8.50*
2N61	OS11	5c ultra	2.50	*3.00*
2N62	OS12	10c blue	4.00	3.00
2N63	OS12	20c rose	1.00	*2.00*
2N64	OS12	30c brown	1.00	*2.25*
		Nos. 2N58-2N64 (7)	16.50	*31.75*

Top line of surcharge reads: "Bama naing ngan daw" (Burma State). Bottom line repeats denomination in Burmese. Surcharge applied when the Shan States came under Burmese government administration, Dec. 24, 1943. Canceled-to-order stamps same value as unused.

BURUNDI

bu-'rün-dē

LOCATION — Central Africa, adjoining the ex-Belgian Congo Republic, Rwanda and Tanzania

GOVT. — Republic

AREA — 10,759 sq. mi.

POP. — 5,735,937 (1999 est.)

CAPITAL — Bujumbura

Burundi was established as an independent country on July 1, 1962. With Rwanda, it had been a UN trusteeship territory (Ruanda-Urundi) administered by Belgium. A military coup overthrew the monarchy November 28, 1966.

100 Centimes = 1 Franc

Catalogue values for all unused stamps in this country are for Never Hinged items.

Flower Issue of Ruanda-Urundi, 1953 Overprinted

Perf. 11½

1962, July 1 Unwmk. Photo.

Flowers in Natural Colors

1	A27	25c dk grn & dull org	.25	.25
2	A27	40c grn & salmon	.25	.25
3	A27	60c blue grn & pink	.40	.40
4	A27	1.25fr dk grn & blue	19.00	19.00
5	A27	1.50fr vio & apple grn	.65	.55
6	A27	5fr dp plum & lt bl grn	1.60	1.10
7	A27	7fr dk grn & fawn	2.50	1.90
8	A27	10fr dp plum & pale ol	3.50	3.25
		Nos. 1-8 (8)	28.15	26.70

Animal Issue of Ruanda-Urundi, 1959-61 with Similar Overprint or Surcharge in Black or Violet Blue

Size: 23x33mm, 33x23mm

9	A29	10c multicolored	.25	.25
10	A30	20c multicolored	.25	.25
11	A29	40c multicolored	.25	.25
12	A30	50c multicolored	.25	.25
a.		Larger overprint and bar	1.50	.25
b.		As "a," ovpt. "Royume du Royaume"	12.50	
13	A29	1fr multicolored	.25	.25
14	A30	1.50fr multi (VB)	.25	.25
15	A29	2fr multicolored	.25	.25
16	A30	3fr multicolored	.25	.25
17	A30	3.50fr on 3fr multi	.25	.25
18	A30	4fr on 10fr multi ("XX" 6mm wide)	.30	.25
a.		"XX" 4mm wide	1.40	.60
19	A30	5fr multicolored	.35	.25
20	A30	6.50fr multicolored	.35	.25
a.		Ovpt. "Royume du Royaume"	12.50	
21	A30	8fr multicolored	1.25	.55
a.		Violet blue overprint	2.25	1.25
22	A30	10fr multicolored	1.00	.55

Size: 45x26½mm

23	A30	20fr multicolored	2.50	1.10
24	A30	50fr multi (ovpt. bars 2mm wide)	4.00	1.90
a.		Overprint bars 4mm wide	4.50	2.75
		Nos. 9-24 (16)	12.00	7.10

On No. 12a, "Burundi" is 13mm long; bar is continuous line across sheet. On No. 12, "Burundi" is 10mm; bar is 29mm. No. 12a was issued in 1963.

Two types of overprint exist on 10c, 40c, 1fr and 2fr: I, "du" is below "me"; bar 22½mm. II, "du" below "oy"; bar 20mm.

The 50c and 3fr exist in two types, besides the larger 50c overprint listed as No. 12: I, "du" is closer to "Royaume" than to "Burundi"; bar is less than 29mm; wording is centered above bar. II, "du" is closer to "Burundi"; bar is more than 30mm; wording is off-center leftward.

King Mwami Mwambutsa IV and Royal Drummers — A1

Flag and Arms of Burundi — A2

2fr, 8fr, 50fr, Map of Burundi and King.

Unwmk.

1962, Sept. 27 Photo. *Perf. 14*

No.	Type	Description	Unused	Used
25	A1	50c dull rose car & dk brn	.25	.25
26	A2	1fr dk grn, red & emer	.25	.25
27	A1	2fr brown ol & dk brn	.25	.25
28	A1	3fr vermilion & dk brn	.25	.25
29	A2	4fr Prus bl, red & emer	.25	.25
30	A1	8fr violet & dk brn	.25	.25
31	A1	10fr brt green & dk brn	.25	.25
32	A2	20fr brown, red & emer	.60	.25
33	A1	50fr brt pink & dk brn	1.75	.25
		Nos. 25-33 (9)	4.10	2.25

Burundi's independence, July 1, 1962.
Exist imperf. Value set, $20.
See Nos. 47-50. For overprints see Nos. 45-46, 51-52.

Ruanda-Urundi Nos. 151-152 Srchd.

Photogravure, Surcharge Engraved

1962, Oct. 31 *Perf. 11½*

Inscription in French

No.	Type	Description	Unused	Used
34	A31	3.50fr on 3fr ultra & red	.25	.25
35	A31	6.50fr on 3fr ultra & red	.30	.25
36	A31	10fr on 3fr ultra & red	.65	.35

Inscription in Flemish

No.	Type	Description	Unused	Used
37	A31	3.50fr on 3fr ultra & red	.30	.25
38	A31	6.50fr on 3fr ultra & red	.50	.30
39	A31	10fr on 3fr ultra & red	.65	.35
		Nos. 34-39 (6)	2.65	1.75

Dag Hammarskjold, Secretary General of the United Nations, 1953-61.

King Mwami Mwambutsa IV, Map of Burundi and Emblem — A3

1962, Dec. 10 Photo. *Perf. 14*

No.	Type	Description	Unused	Used
40	A3	8fr yel, bl grn & blk brn	.50	.25
41	A3	50fr gray grn, bl grn & blk brn	2.00	1.00

WHO drive to eradicate malaria.
Exist imperf. Value set, $24.
Stamps of type A3 without anti-malaria emblem are listed as Nos. 27, 30 and 33.

Sowing Seed over Africa — A4

1963, Mar. 21 *Perf. 14x13*

No.	Type	Description	Unused	Used
42	A4	4fr olive & dull pur	.25	.25
43	A4	8fr dp org & dull pur	.25	.25
44	A4	15fr emerald & dull pur	.30	.25
		Nos. 42-44 (3)	.80	.75

FAO "Freedom from Hunger" campaign.

Exist imperf. Value set, $25.

Nos. 27 and 33 Overprinted in Dark Green

1963, June 19 Unwmk. *Perf. 14*

No.	Type	Description	Unused	Used
45	A1	2fr brn olive & dk brn	2.25	2.25
46	A1	50fr brt pink & dk brn	3.50	3.50

Conquest and peaceful use of outer space.

Types of 1962 Inscribed: "Premier Anniversaire" in Red or Magenta

1963, July 1 Photo.

No.	Type	Description	Unused	Used
47	A2	4fr olive, red & emer (R)	.25	.25
48	A1	8fr orange & dk brn (M)	.25	.25
49	A1	10fr lilac & dk brn (M)	.30	.25
50	A2	20fr gray, red & emer (R)	1.00	.25
		Nos. 47-50 (4)	1.80	1.00

First anniversary of independence.
Exist imperf. Value set, $15.

Nos. 26 and 32 Surcharged in Brown

1963, Sept. 24 Unwmk. *Perf. 14*

No.	Type	Description	Unused	Used
51	A2	6.50fr on 1fr multi	.55	.25
52	A2	15fr on 20fr multi	.90	.25

Red Cross Flag over Globe with Map of Africa — A5

1963, Sept. 26 *Perf. 14x13*

No.	Type	Description	Unused	Used
53	A5	4fr emer, car & gray	.25	.25
54	A5	8fr brn ol, car & gray	.40	.25
55	A5	10fr blue, car & gray	.70	.25
56	A5	20fr lilac, car & gray	1.60	.50
		Nos. 53-56 (4)	2.95	1.25

Centenary of International Red Cross.
Exist imperf. Value set, $20.
See No. B7.

"1962", Arms of Burundi, UN and UNESCO Emblems — A6

UN Agency Emblems: 8fr, ITU. 10fr, World Meteorological Organization. 20fr, UPU. 50fr, FAO.

1963, Nov. 4 Unwmk. *Perf. 14*

No.	Type	Description	Unused	Used
57	A6	4fr yel, ol grn & blk	.25	.25
58	A6	8fr pale lil, Prus bl & blk	.35	.25
59	A6	10fr blue, lil & blk	.45	.25
60	A6	20fr yel grn, grn & blk	.90	.25
61	A6	50fr yel, red brn & blk	1.50	.35
a.		Souvenir sheet of 2	5.75	5.75
		Nos. 57-61 (5)	3.45	1.35

1st anniv. of Burundi's admission to the UN. Exist imperf. Value set, $20. No. 61a contains two imperf. stamps with simulated perforations similar to Nos. 60-61. The 20fr stamp shows the FAO and the 50fr the WMO emblems.

UNESCO Emblem, Scales and Map — A7

Designs: 3.50fr, 6.50fr, Scroll, scales and "UNESCO." 10fr, 20fr, Abraham Lincoln, broken chain and scales.

1963, Dec. 10 Litho. *Perf. 14x13½*

No.	Type	Description	Unused	Used
62	A7	50c pink, lt bl & blk	.25	.25
63	A7	1.50fr org, lt bl & blk	.25	.25
64	A7	3.50fr fawn, lt grn & blk	.25	.25
65	A7	6.50fr lt vio, lt grn & blk	.25	.25
66	A7	10fr blue, bis & blk	.30	.25
67	A7	20fr pale brn, ocher, bl & blk	.55	.25
		Nos. 62-67 (6)	1.85	1.50

15th anniv. of the Universal Declaration of Human Rights and the cent. of the American Emancipation Proclamation (Nos. 66-67). Exist imperf. Value set, $6.

Ice Hockey — A8

3.50fr, Women's figure skating. 6.50fr, Torch. 10fr, Men's speed skating. 20fr, Slalom.

Unwmk.

1964, Jan. 25 Photo. *Perf. 14*

No.	Type	Description	Unused	Used
68	A8	50c olive, blk & gold	.25	.25
69	A8	3.50fr lt brown, blk & gold	.25	.25
70	A8	6.50fr pale gray, blk & gold	.60	.25
71	A8	10fr gray, blk & gold	1.50	.30
72	A8	20fr tan, blk & gold	2.00	.50
		Nos. 68-72 (5)	4.60	1.55

Issued to publicize the 9th Winter Olympic Games, Innsbruck, Jan. 29-Feb. 9, 1964. Exist imperf. Value set, $80.

A souvenir sheet contains two stamps (10fr+5fr and 20fr+5fr) in tan, black and gold. Value: perf, $12, unused or used; imperf $13, unused or used.

Canceled to Order

Starting about 1964, values in the used column are for "canceled to order" stamps. Postally used stamps sell for much more.

Impala — A9

Animals: 1fr, 5fr, Hippopotamus, horiz. 1.50fr, 10fr, Giraffe. 2fr, 8fr, Cape buffalo, horiz. 3fr, 6.50fr, Zebra, horiz. 3.50fr, 15fr, Defassa waterbuck. 20fr, Cheetah. 50fr, Elephant. 100fr, Lion.

Perf. 14x13, 13x14

1964, Feb. 10 Litho.

Size: 21½x35mm, 35x21½mm

No.	Type	Description	Unused	Used
73	A9	50c multi	.25	.25
74	A9	1fr multi	.25	.25
75	A9	1.50fr multi	.25	.25
76	A9	2fr multi	.35	.25
77	A9	3fr multi	.50	.25
78	A9	3.50fr multi	.60	.25

Size: 26x42mm, 42x26mm

No.	Type	Description	Unused	Used
79	A9	4fr multi	.25	.25
80	A9	5fr multi	.35	.25
81	A9	6.50fr multi	.40	.35
82	A9	8fr multi	.50	.35
83	A9	10fr multi	.80	.40
84	A9	15fr multi	1.00	.50

Perf. 14

Size: 53x33mm

No.	Type	Description	Unused	Used
85	A9	20fr multi	1.75	.50
86	A9	50fr multi	3.50	.80
87	A9	100fr multi	7.00	1.10
		Nos. 73-87,C1-C7 (22)	30.25	8.70

Exist imperf. Value set (22), $48.

Burundi Dancer — A10

Designs: Various Dancers and Drummers.

Unwmk.

1964, Aug. 21 Litho. *Perf. 14*

Dancers Multicolored

No.	Type	Description	Unused	Used
88	A10	50c gold & emerald	.25	.25
89	A10	1fr gold & vio blue	.25	.25
90	A10	4fr gold & brt blue	.25	.25
91	A10	6.50fr gold & red	.30	.25
92	A10	10fr gold & brt blue	.50	.25
93	A10	15fr gold & emerald	.70	.25
94	A10	20fr gold & red	.95	.50
a.		Souvenir sheet of 3, #92-94	4.25	4.25
		Nos. 88-94 (7)	3.20	2.00

Exist imperf. Value set, $9; souvenir sheet, $5.50.

1965, Sept. 10

Dancers Multicolored

No.	Type	Description	Unused	Used
88a	A10	50c silver & emerald	.25	.25
89a	A10	1fr silver & violet blue	.25	.25
90a	A10	4fr silver & bright blue	.25	.25
91a	A10	6.50fr silver & red	.30	.25
92a	A10	10fr silver & bright blue	.50	.25
93a	A10	15fr silver & emerald	.65	.30
94b	A10	20fr silver & red	.95	.50
c.		Souvenir sheet of 3, #92a-94b	3.50	3.50
		Nos. 88a-94b (7)	3.15	2.05

New York World's Fair, 1964-65.
Exist imperf. Value set, $9; souvenir sheet, $4.

Pope Paul VI and King Mwami Mwambutsa IV — A11

22 Sainted Martyrs — A12

4fr, 14fr, Pope John XXIII and King Mwami.

1964, Nov. 12 Photo. *Perf. 12*

95	A11	50c brt bl, gold & red brn	.25	.25
96	A12	1fr mag, gold & slate	.25	.25
97	A11	4fr pale rose lil, gold & brn	.25	.25
98	A12	8fr red, gold & brn	.30	.25
99	A11	14fr lt grn, gold & brn	.60	.25
100	A11	20fr red brn, gold & grn	.90	.35
		Nos. 95-100 (6)	2.55	1.60

Canonization of 22 African martyrs, 10/18/64. Exist imperf. Value set, $15.

Shot Put — A13

Sports: 1fr, Discus. 3fr, Swimming. 4fr, Running. 6.50fr, Javelin, woman. 8fr, Hurdling. 10fr, Broad jump. 14fr, Diving, woman. 18fr, High jump. 20fr, Vaulting.
3fr, 8fr, 10fr, 18fr, 20fr are horiz.

1964, Nov. 18 Litho. *Perf. 14*

101	A13	50c olive & multi	.25	.25
102	A13	1fr brt pink & multi	.25	.25
103	A13	3fr multi	.25	.25
104	A13	4fr multi	.25	.25
105	A13	6.50fr multi	.25	.25
106	A13	8fr lt bl & multi	.40	.25
107	A13	10fr multi	.45	.25
108	A13	14fr multi	.60	.25
109	A13	18fr bister & multi	.85	.35
110	A13	20fr gray & multi	.90	.60
		Nos. 101-110 (10)	4.45	2.95

18th Olympic Games, Tokyo, Oct. 10-25, 1964. Exist imperf. Value set, $15. See No. B8.

African Purple Gallinule — A14

Birds: 1fr, 5fr, Little bee eater. 1.50fr, 6.50fr, Secretary bird. 2fr, 8fr, Yellow-billed stork. 3fr, 10fr, Congo peacock. 3.50fr, 15fr, African anhinga. 20fr, Saddle-billed stork. 50fr, Abyssinian ground hornbill. 100fr, Crowned crane.

Birds in Natural Colors

1965 Unwmk. *Perf. 14*

Size: 21x35mm

111	A14	50c tan, grn & blk	.25	.25
112	A14	1fr pink, mag & blk	.25	.25
113	A14	1.50fr blue & blk	.25	.25
114	A14	2fr yel grn, dk grn & blk	.25	.25
115	A14	3fr yellow, brn & blk	.25	.25
116	A14	3.50fr yel grn, dk grn & blk	.35	.25

Size: 26x43mm

117	A14	4fr tan, grn & blk	.45	.25
118	A14	5fr pink, mag & blk	.55	.25
119	A14	6.50fr blue & blk	.70	.25
120	A14	8fr yel grn, dk grn & blk	.90	.25
121	A14	10fr yel, brn & blk	1.10	.35
122	A14	15fr yel grn, dk grn & blk	1.75	.35

Size: 33x53mm

123	A14	20fr rose lilac & blk	2.25	.45
124	A14	50fr yellow, brn & blk	4.50	.90
125	A14	100fr green, yel & blk	9.00	1.75
		Nos. 111-125 (15)	22.80	6.30

Issue dates: Nos. 111-116, Mar. 31. Nos. 117-122, Apr. 16. Nos. 123-125, Apr. 30.
For overprints see Nos. 174-184, C35A-C35I.

Relay Satellite and Morse Key — A15

3fr, Telstar & old telephone handpiece. 4fr, Luna satellite & old wall telephone. 6.50fr, Orbiting Geophysical Observatory & radar screen. 8fr, Telstar II & headphones. 10fr, Sputnik II & radar aerial. 14fr, Syncom & transmission aerial. 20fr, Interplanetary Explorer & tracking aerial.

1965, July 3 Litho. *Perf. 13*

126	A15	1fr multi	.25	.25
127	A15	3fr multi	.25	.25
128	A15	4fr multi	.25	.25
129	A15	6.50fr multi	.25	.25
130	A15	8fr multi	.25	.25
131	A15	10fr multi	.25	.25
132	A15	14fr multi	.25	.25
133	A15	20fr multi	.30	.25
		Nos. 126-133 (8)	2.05	2.00

Cent. of the ITU. Exist imperf, Value, set $7.50.
Perf. and imperf. souv. sheets of 2 contain Nos. 131, 133. Size: 120x86mm. Value, both sheets, $7.50.

Globe and ICY Emblem — A16

Designs: 4fr, Map of Africa and UN development emblem. 8fr, Map of Asia and Colombo Plan emblem. 10fr, Globe and UN emblem. 18fr, Map of the Americas and Alliance for Progress emblem. 25fr, Map of Europe and EUROPA emblems. 40fr, Map of Outer Space and satellite with UN wreath.

1965, Oct. 1 Litho. *Perf. 13*

134	A16	1fr ol green & multi	.25	.25
135	A16	4fr dull blue & multi	.25	.25
136	A16	8fr pale yellow & multi	.25	.25
137	A16	10fr lilac & multi	.25	.25
138	A16	18fr salmon & multi	.45	.25
139	A16	25fr gray & multi	.75	.25
140	A16	40fr blue & multi	1.25	.25
a.		Souvenir sheet of 3, #138-140	4.50	4.50
		Nos. 134-140 (7)	3.45	1.75

International Cooperation Year.
Exist imperf. Values: set $7.50; souvenir sheet $5.50.

Protea A17

Flowers: 1fr, 5fr, Crossandra. 1.50fr, 6.50fr, Ansellia. 2fr, 8fr, Thunbergia. 3fr, 10fr, Schizoglossum. 3.50fr, 15fr, Dissotis. 4fr, 20fr, Protea. 50fr, Gazania. 100fr, Hibiscus. 150fr, Markhamia.

1966 Unwmk. *Perf. 13½*

Size: 26x26mm

141	A17	50c multi	.25	.25
142	A17	1fr multi	.25	.25
143	A17	1.50fr multi	.25	.25
144	A17	2fr multi	.25	.25
145	A17	3fr multi	.25	.25
146	A17	3.50fr multi	.25	.25

Size: 31x31mm

147	A17	4fr multi	.25	.25
148	A17	5fr multi	.35	.25
149	A17	6.50fr multi	.45	.25
150	A17	8fr multi	.90	.25
151	A17	10fr multi	1.00	.25
152	A17	15fr multi	1.10	.25

Size: 39x39mm

153	A17	20fr multi	1.60	.25
154	A17	50fr multi	3.50	.30
155	A17	100fr multi	5.25	.50
156	A17	150fr multi	7.50	.70
		Nos. 141-156,C17-C25 (25)	39.60	8.10

Issue dates: Nos. 141-147, Feb. 28; Nos. 148-153, May 18; Nos. 154-156, June 15.
Exist imperf. Value set (25), $55.
For overprints see Nos. 159-173, C27-C35.

Souvenir Sheets

Allegory of Prosperity and Equality Tapestry by Peter Colfs — A18

1966, Nov. 4 Litho. *Perf. 13½*

157	A18	Sheet of 7 (1.50fr)	2.75	.95
a.-g.		Any single	.25	.25
158	A18	Sheet of 7 (4fr)	4.50	1.50
a.-g.		Any single	.25	.25

20th anniv. of UNESCO. Each sheet contains 6 stamps showing a reproduction of the Colfs tapestry from the lobby of the General Assembly Building, NYC, and one stamp with the UNESCO emblem plus a label. The labels on Nos. 157-158 and C26 are inscribed in French or English. The 3 sheets with French inscription have light blue marginal border. The 3 sheets with English inscription have pink border. See No. C26.
Exist imperf. Value each sheet, $15.

Republic

Nos. 141-152, 154-156 Overprinted

1967 Litho. *Perf. 13½*

Size: 26x26mm

159	A17	50c multi	.25	.25
160	A17	1fr multi	.25	.25
161	A17	1.50fr multi	.25	.25
162	A17	2fr multi	.25	.25
163	A17	3fr multi	.25	.25
164	A17	3.50fr multi	.25	.25

Size: 31x31mm

165	A17	4fr multi	1.60	.30
166	A17	5fr multi	.25	.25
167	A17	6.50fr multi	.35	.25
168	A17	8fr multi	.35	.25
169	A17	10fr multi	.60	.25
170	A17	15fr multi	.80	.25

Size: 39x39mm

171	A17	50fr multi	3.50	.90
172	A17	100fr multi	11.00	2.75
173	A17	150fr multi	11.00	2.75
		Nos. 159-173,C27-C35 (24)	57.30	14.95

Nos. 111, 113, 116, 118-125 Overprinted "REPUBLIQUE DU BURUNDI" and Horizontal Bar

1967 Litho. *Perf. 14*

Birds in Natural Colors

Size: 21x35mm

174	A14	50c multi	2.75	2.75
175	A14	1.50fr blue & black	.60	.60
176	A14	3.50fr multi	.75	.75

Size: 26x43mm

177	A14	5fr multi	.90	.90
178	A14	6.50fr blue & black	1.00	1.00
179	A14	8fr multi	1.25	1.25
180	A14	10fr yel, brn & blk	1.75	1.75
181	A14	15fr multi	2.25	2.25

Size: 33x53mm

182	A14	20fr multi	4.00	4.00
183	A14	50fr multi	7.00	7.00
184	A14	100fr multi	12.00	12.00
		Nos. 174-184 (11)	34.25	34.25

Haplochromis Multicolor — A19

Various Tropical Fish.

1967 Photo. *Perf. 13½*

Size: 42x19mm

186	A19	50c multi	.25	.25
187	A19	1fr multi	.25	.25
188	A19	1.50fr multi	.25	.25
189	A19	2fr multi	.30	.25
190	A19	3fr multi	.30	.25
191	A19	3.50fr multi	.40	.25

Size: 50x25mm

192	A19	4fr multi	.60	.25
193	A19	5fr multi	.75	.25
194	A19	6.50fr multi	.85	.25
195	A19	8fr multi	1.40	.25
196	A19	10fr multi	2.25	.25
197	A19	15fr multi	2.75	.25

Size: 59x30mm

198	A19	20fr multi	4.00	.35
199	A19	50fr multi	6.75	.45
200	A19	100fr multi	11.00	.65
201	A19	150fr multi	15.00	1.00
		Nos. 186-201,C46-C54 (25)	96.60	8.25

Issue Dates: Nos. 186-191, Apr. 4; Nos. 192-197, Apr. 28; Nos. 198-201, May 18.

Ancestor Figures, Ivory Coast — A20

African Art: 1fr, Seat of Honor, Southeast Congo. 1.50fr, Antelope head, Aribinda Region. 2fr, Buffalo mask, Upper Volta. 4fr, Funeral figures, Southwest Ethiopia.

1967, June 5 Photo. *Perf. 13½*

202	A20	50c silver & multi	.25	.25
203	A20	1fr silver & multi	.25	.25
204	A20	1.50fr silver & multi	.25	.25
205	A20	2fr silver & multi	.25	.25
206	A20	4fr silver & multi	.25	.25
		Nos. 202-206,C36-C40 (10)	3.70	2.80

Exists imperf. Value set, $9.

Scouts on Hiking Trip — A21

Designs: 1fr, Cooking at campfire. 1.50fr, Lord Baden-Powell. 2fr, Boy Scout and Cub Scout giving Scout sign. 4fr, First aid.

1967, Aug. 9 **Photo.** ***Perf. 13½***

No.	Type	Description	Unused	Used
207	A21	50c silver & multi	.25	.25
208	A21	1fr silver & multi	.35	.25
209	A21	1.50fr silver & multi	.50	.25
210	A21	2fr silver & multi	.65	.25
211	A21	4fr silver & multi	.80	.25
		Nos. 207-211,C41-C45 (10)	12.80	2.65

60th anniv. of the Boy Scouts and the 12th Boy Scout World Jamboree, Farragut State Park, Idaho, Aug. 1-9.
Exists imperf. Value set, $20.

The Gleaners, by Francois Millet A22

Paintings Exhibited at EXPO '67: 8fr, The Water Carrier of Seville, by Velazquez. 14fr, The Triumph of Neptune and Amphitrite, by Nicolas Poussin. 18fr, Acrobat Standing on a Ball, by Picasso. 25fr, Marguerite van Eyck, by Jan van Eyck. 40fr, St. Peter Denying Christ, by Rembrandt.

1967, Oct. 12 **Photo.** ***Perf. 13½***

No.	Type	Description	Unused	Used
212	A22	4fr multi	.25	.25
213	A22	8fr multi	.25	.25
214	A22	14fr multi	.45	.25
215	A22	18fr multi	.50	.25
216	A22	25fr multi	.80	.25
217	A22	40fr multi	1.00	.25
a.		Souvenir sheet of 2, #216-217	2.25	2.25
		Nos. 212-217 (6)	3.25	1.50

EXPO '67 International Exhibition, Montreal, Apr. 28-Oct. 27. Printed in sheets of 10 stamps and 2 labels inscribed in French or English.
Exists imperf. Value: set $5.50; souvenir sheet $2.25.

Place de la Revolution and Pres. Michel Micombero — A23

Designs: 5fr, President Michel Micombero and flag. 14fr, Formal garden and coat of arms. 20fr, Modern building and coat of arms.

1967, Nov. 23 ***Perf. 13½***

No.	Type	Description	Unused	Used
218	A23	5fr multi	.25	.25
219	A23	14fr multi	.40	.25
220	A23	20fr multi	.70	.25
221	A23	30fr multi	.90	.25
		Nos. 218-221 (4)	2.25	1.00

First anniversary of the Republic.
Exists imperf. Value set, $5.

Madonna by Carlo Crivelli — A24

Designs: 1fr, Adoration of the Shepherds by Juan Bautista Mayno. 4fr, Holy Family by Anthony Van Dyck. 14fr, Nativity by Maitre de Moulins.

1967, Dec. 7 **Photo.** ***Perf. 13½***

No.	Type	Description	Unused	Used
222	A24	1fr multi	.25	.25
223	A24	4fr multi	.25	.25
224	A24	14fr multi	.60	.25
225	A24	26fr multi	1.00	.30
a.		Sheetlet of 4, #222-225	3.00	3.00
		Nos. 222-225 (4)	2.10	1.05

Christmas 1967. Exists imperf. Value: set $4; souvenir sheet, $3.50.
Printed in sheets of 25 and one corner label inscribed "Noel 1967" and giving name of painting and painter.

Slalom — A25

10fr, Ice hockey. 14fr, Women's skating. 17fr, Bobsled. 26fr, Ski jump. 40fr, Speed skating. 60fr, Hand holding torch, and Winter Olympics emblem.

1968, Feb. 16 **Photo.** ***Perf. 13½***

No.	Type	Description	Unused	Used
226	A25	5fr silver & multi	.25	.25
227	A25	10fr silver & multi	.30	.25
228	A25	14fr silver & multi	.55	.25
229	A25	17fr silver & multi	.65	.25
230	A25	26fr silver & multi	.95	.25
231	A25	40fr silver & multi	1.20	.25
232	A25	60fr silver & multi	1.65	.25
a.		Souvenir sheet of 2, types of #231-232 inscribed "Poste Aerienne"	3.00	2.25
		Nos. 226-232 (7)	5.55	1.75

Issued to publicize the 10th Winter Olympic Games, Grenoble, France, Feb. 6-18. Issued in sheets of 10 stamps and label.
Exists imperf. Values: set, $10; souvenir sheet, $3.

The Lacemaker, by Vermeer A26

Paintings: 1.50fr, Portrait of a Young Man, by Botticelli. 2fr, Maja Vestida, by Goya, horiz.

1968, Mar. 29 **Photo.** ***Perf. 13½***

No.	Type	Description	Unused	Used
233	A26	1.50fr gold & multi	.25	.25
234	A26	2fr gold & multi	.25	.25
235	A26	4fr gold & multi	.30	.25
		Nos. 233-235,C59-C61 (6)	3.70	2.35

Issued in sheets of 6.
Exists imperf. Value set, $6.50.

Moon Probe A27

Designs: 6fr, Russian astronaut walking in space. 8fr, Mariner satellite, Mars. 10fr, American astronaut walking in space.

1968, May 15 **Photo.** ***Perf. 13½***

Size: 35x35mm

No.	Type	Description	Unused	Used
236	A27	4fr silver & multi	.25	.25
237	A27	6fr silver & multi	.30	.25
238	A27	8fr silver & multi	.40	.25
239	A27	10fr silver & multi	.50	.25
		Nos. 236-239,C62-C65 (8)	5.50	2.35

Issued to publicize peaceful space explorations. Exist imperf. Value, set $7.
A souvenir sheet contains one 25fr stamp in Moon Probe design and one 40fr in Mariner satellite design. Stamp size: 41x41mm. Value: perf $3.50; imperf $4.

Salamis Aethiops A28

Butterflies: 1fr, 5fr, Graphium ridleyanus. 1.50fr, 6.50fr, Cymothoe. 2fr, 8fr, Charaxes eupale. 3fr, 10fr, Papilio bromius. 3.50fr, 15fr, Teracolus annae. 20fr, Salamis aethiops. 50fr, Papilio zonobia. 100fr, Danais chrysippus. 150fr, Salamis temora.

1968 **Size: 30x33½mm**

No.	Type	Description	Unused	Used
240	A28	50c gold & multi	.25	.25
241	A28	1fr gold & multi	.25	.25
242	A28	1.50fr gold & multi	.35	.25
243	A28	2fr gold & multi	.45	.25
244	A28	3fr gold & multi	.60	.25
245	A28	3.50fr gold & multi	.75	.25

Size: 33½x37½mm

No.	Type	Description	Unused	Used
246	A28	4fr gold & multi	.90	.25
247	A28	5fr gold & multi	1.10	.25
248	A28	6.50fr gold & multi	1.60	.25
249	A28	8fr gold & multi	2.00	.25
250	A28	10fr gold & multi	2.75	.30
251	A28	15fr gold & multi	3.50	.35

Size: 41x46mm

No.	Type	Description	Unused	Used
252	A28	20fr gold & multi	4.50	.40
253	A28	50fr gold & multi	7.75	.60
254	A28	100fr gold & multi	15.00	1.00
255	A28	150fr gold & multi	20.00	1.50
		Nos. 240-255,C66-C74 (25)	117.10	12.85

Issue dates: Nos. 240-245, June 7; Nos. 246-251, June 28; Nos. 252-255, July 19.

Women, Along the Manzanares, by Goya — A29

Paintings: 7fr, The Letter, by Pieter de Hooch. 11fr, Woman Reading a Letter, by Gerard Terborch. 14fr, Man Writing a Letter, by Gabriel Metsu.

1968, Sept. 30 **Photo.** ***Perf. 13½***

No.	Type	Description	Unused	Used
256	A29	4fr multi	.25	.25
257	A29	7fr multi	.25	.25
258	A29	11fr multi	.40	.25
259	A29	14fr multi	.50	.25
		Nos. 256-259,C84-C87 (8)	8.05	2.40

International Letter Writing Week.

Exists imperf. Value set, $9.

Soccer — A30

1968, Oct. 24

No.	Type	Description	Unused	Used
260	A30	4fr shown	.25	.25
261	A30	7fr Basketball	.25	.25
262	A30	13fr High jump	.25	.25
263	A30	24fr Relay race	.35	.25
264	A30	40fr Javelin	.75	.30
		Nos. 260-264,C88-C92 (10)	8.45	3.00

19th Olympic Games, Mexico City, Oct. 12-27. Printed in sheets of 8.
Exists imperf. Value set, $15.

Virgin and Child, by Fra Filippo Lippi — A31

Paintings: 5fr, The Magnificat, by Sandro Botticelli. 6fr, Virgin and Child, by Albrecht Durer. 11fr, Madonna del Gran Duca, by Raphael.

1968, Nov. 26 **Photo.** ***Perf. 13½***

No.	Type	Description	Unused	Used
265	A31	3fr multi	.25	.25
266	A31	5fr multi	.25	.25
267	A31	6fr multi	.25	.25
268	A31	11fr multi	.35	.25
a.		Souvenir sheet of 4, #265-268	1.60	1.25
		Nos. 265-268,C93-C96 (8)	3.75	2.25

Christmas 1968. Exist imperf. Value: set (8) $5; souvenir sheets $5.
For overprints see Nos. 272-275, C100-C103.

WHO Emblem and Map of Africa — A32

1969, Jan. 22

No.	Type	Description	Unused	Used
269	A32	5fr gold, dk grn & yel	.25	.25
270	A32	6fr gold, vio & ver	.35	.25
271	A32	11fr gold, pur & red lil	.50	.25
		Nos. 269-271 (3)	1.10	.75

20th anniv. of WHO in Africa.
Exist imperf. Value set, $2.50.

Nos. 265-268 Overprinted in Silver

1969, Feb. 17 Photo. *Perf. 13½*

272 A31 3fr multi .25 .25
273 A31 5fr multi .25 .25
274 A31 6fr multi .35 .25
275 A31 11fr multi .55 .25
Nos. 272-275,C100-C103 (8) 4.15 2.30

Man's 1st flight around the moon by the US spacecraft Apollo 8, Dec. 21-27, 1968. Exist imperf. Value set (8), $6.50.

Map of Africa, and CEPT Emblem A33

Designs: 14fr, Plowing with tractor. 17fr, Teacher and pupil. 26fr, Maps of Europe and Africa and CEPT (Conference of European Postal and Telecommunications Administrations) emblem, horiz.

1969, Mar. 12 Photo. *Perf. 13*

276 A33 5fr multi .25 .25
277 A33 14fr multi .45 .25
278 A33 17fr multi .55 .25
279 A33 26fr multi .90 .25
Nos. 276-279 (4) 2.15 1.00

5th anniv. of the Yaounde (Cameroun) Agreement, creating the European and African-Malgache Economic Community. Exist imperf. Value set, $4.

Resurrection, by Gaspard Isenmann — A34

Paintings: 14fr, Resurrection by Antoine Caron. 17fr, Noli me Tangere, by Martin Schongauer. 26fr, Resurrection, by El Greco.

1969, Mar. 24

280 A34 11fr gold & multi .35 .25
281 A34 14fr gold & multi .45 .25
282 A34 17fr gold & multi .60 .25
283 A34 26fr gold & multi .75 .25
a. Souvenir sheet of 4, #280-283 2.25 2.25
Nos. 280-283 (4) 2.15 1.00

Easter 1969. Exist imperf. Values: set $3; souvenir sheet $2.

Potter — A35

ITU Emblem and: 5fr, Farm workers. 7fr, Foundry worker. 10fr, Woman testing corn crop.

1969, May 17 Photo. *Perf. 13½*

284 A35 3fr multicolored .25 .25
285 A35 5fr multicolored .25 .25
286 A35 7fr multicolored .25 .25
287 A35 10fr multicolored .35 .25
Nos. 284-287 (4) 1.10 1.00

50th anniv. of the ILO. Exist imperf. Value set, $2.50

Industry and Bank's Emblem A36

African Development Bank Emblem and: 17fr, Communications. 30fr, Education. 50fr, Agriculture.

1969, July 29 Photo. *Perf. 13½*

288 A36 10fr gold & multi .30 .25
289 A36 17fr gold & multi .50 .25
290 A36 30fr gold & multi .80 .40
291 A36 50fr gold & multi 1.40 .75
a. Souvenir sheet of 4, #288-291 4.00 4.00
Nos. 288-291 (4) 3.00 1.65

African Development Bank, 5th anniv. Exist imperf. Values: set $7; souvenir sheet $4.50.

Girl Reading Letter, by Vermeer A37

Paintings: 7fr, Graziella (young woman), by Auguste Renoir. 14fr, Woman writing a letter, by Gerard Terborch. 26fr, Galileo Galilei, painter unknown. 40fr, Ludwig van Beethoven, painter unknown.

1969, Oct. 24 Photo. *Perf. 13½*

292 A37 4fr multicolored .25 .25
293 A37 7fr multicolored .25 .25
294 A37 14fr multicolored .45 .25
295 A37 26fr multicolored .75 .25
296 A37 40fr multicolored 1.10 .25
a. Souvenir sheet of 2, #295-296 3.00 3.00
Nos. 292-296 (5) 2.80 1.25

Intl. Letter Writing Week, Oct. 7-13. Exist imperf. Values: set $6; souvenir sheet $3.

Rocket Launching A38

Moon Landing: 6.50fr, Rocket in space. 7fr, Separation of landing module from capsule. 14fr, 26fr, Landing module landing on moon. 17fr, Capsule in space. 40fr, Neil A. Armstrong leaving landing module. 50fr, Astronaut on moon.

1969, Nov. 6 Photo. *Perf. 13½*

297 A38 4fr blue & multi .25 .25
298 A38 6.50fr vio blue & multi .25 .25
299 A38 7fr vio blue & multi .50 .25
300 A38 14fr black & multi 1.00 .25
301 A38 17fr vio blue & multi 1.75 .30
Nos. 297-301,C104-C106 (8) 12.00 2.55

Souvenir Sheet

302 Sheet of 3 13.50 13.50
a. A38 26fr multicolored 1.75 1.75
b. A38 40fr multicolored 2.50 2.50
c. A38 50fr multicolored 3.50 3.50

Exist imperf. Values: set $14; souvenir sheet $15.

See note after Algeria No. 427.

Madonna and Child, by Rubens — A39

Paintings: 6fr, Madonna and Child with St. John, by Giulio Romano. 10fr, Magnificat Madonna, by Botticelli.

1969, Dec. 2 Photo.

303 A39 5fr gold & multi .25 .25
304 A39 6fr gold & multi .25 .25
305 A39 10fr gold & multi .40 .25
a. Souvenir sheet of 3, #303-305 1.25 1.25
Nos. 303-305,C107-C109 (6) 5.60 1.60

Christmas 1969. Exist imperf. Values: set (6) $7; souvenir sheets (2) $6.

Sternotomis Bohemani — A40

Designs: Various Beetles and Weevils.

1970 Size: 39x28mm *Perf. 13½*

306 A40 50c multicolored .25 .25
307 A40 1fr multicolored .25 .25
308 A40 1.50fr multicolored .25 .25
309 A40 2fr multicolored .25 .25
310 A40 3fr multicolored .30 .25
311 A40 3.50fr multicolored .40 .25

Size: 46x32mm

312 A40 4fr multicolored .50 .25
313 A40 5fr multicolored .65 .25
314 A40 6.50fr multicolored .75 .25
315 A40 8fr multicolored .90 .25
316 A40 10fr multicolored 1.50 .25
317 A40 15fr multicolored 2.00 .30

Size: 52x36mm

318 A40 20fr multicolored 3.25 .40
319 A40 50fr multicolored 6.00 .50
320 A40 100fr multicolored 10.50 .75
321 A40 150fr multicolored 15.00 1.00
Nos. 306-321,C110-C118 (25) 78.70 9.90

Issue dates: Nos. 306-313, Jan. 20; Nos. 314-318, Feb. 17; Nos. 319-321, Apr. 3.

Jesus Condemned to Death — A41

Stations of the Cross, by Juan de Aranoa y Carredano: 1.50fr, Jesus carries His Cross. 2fr, Jesus falls the first time. 3fr, Jesus meets His mother. 3.50fr, Simon of Cyrene helps carry the cross. 4fr, Veronica wipes the face of Jesus. 5fr, Jesus falls the second time.

1970, Mar. 16 Photo. *Perf. 13½*

322 A41 1fr gold & multi .25 .25
323 A41 1.50fr gold & multi .25 .25
324 A41 2fr gold & multi .25 .25
325 A41 3fr gold & multi .25 .25
326 A41 3.50fr gold & multi .25 .25
327 A41 4fr gold & multi .25 .25
328 A41 5fr gold & multi .25 .25
a. Souv. sheet, #322-328 + label 1.60 1.60
Nos. 322-328,C119-C125 (14) 7.65 4.15

Easter 1970. Exists imperf. Values: set (14) $10; souvenir sheets (2) $10.

Parade and EXPO '70 Emblem — A42

Designs (EXPO '70 Emblem and): 6.50fr, Aerial view. 7fr, African pavilions. 14fr, Pagoda, vert. 26fr, Recording pavilion and pool. 40fr, Tower of the Sun, vert. 50fr, Flags of participating nations.

1970, May 5 Photo. *Perf. 13½*

329 A42 4fr gold & multi .25 .25
330 A42 6.50fr gold & multi .25 .25
331 A42 7fr gold & multi .25 .25
332 A42 14fr gold & multi .45 .25
333 A42 26fr gold & multi .90 .25
334 A42 40fr gold & multi 1.25 .25
335 A42 50fr gold & multi 1.40 .30
Nos. 329-335 (7) 4.75 1.80

EXPO '70 Intl. Exhibition, Osaka, Japan, Mar. 15-Sept. 13, 1970. Exists imperf. Value $6.

See No. C126.

White Rhinoceros — A43

Fauna: a, i, Camel. c, d, Dromedary. g, r, Okapi. f, m, Addax. j, o, Rhinoceros. l, p, Burundi cow (each animal in 2 different poses).

Map of the Nile: b, Delta and pyramids. e, dhow. h, Falls. k, Blue Nile and crowned crane. n, Victoria Nile and secretary bird. q, Lake Victoria and source of Nile on Mt. Gikizi. Continuous design.

1970, July 8 Photo. *Perf. 13½*

336 Sheet of 18 45.00 24.50
a.-r. A43 7fr any single 2.50 .35

Publicizing the southernmost source of the Nile on Mt. Gikizi in Burundi. Exists imperf. Value $55.

See No. C127.

Winter Wren, Firecrest, Skylark and Crested Lark — A44

Birds: 2fr, 3.50fr, 5fr, vert.; others horiz.

1970, Sept. 30 Photo. *Perf. 13½*

Stamp Size: 44x33mm

337 A44 Block of 4 2.50 .60
a. 2fr Northern shrike .60 .25
b. 2fr European starling .60 .25
c. 2fr Yellow wagtail .60 .25
d. 2fr Bank swallow .60 .25
338 A44 Block of 4 3.00 .70
a. 3fr Winter wren .65 .25
b. 3fr Firecrest .65 .25
c. 3fr Skylark .65 .25
d. 3fr Crested lark .65 .25
339 A44 Block of 4 4.00 .80
a. 3.50fr Woodchat shrike .75 .25
b. 3.50fr Common rock thrush .75 .25
c. 3.50fr Black redstart .75 .25
d. 3.50fr Ring ouzel .75 .25
340 A44 Block of 4 5.50 1.00
a. 4fr European Redstart 1.00 .25
b. 4fr Hedge sparrow 1.00 .25
c. 4fr Gray wagtail 1.00 .25
d. 4fr Meadow pipit 1.00 .25
341 A44 Block of 4 6.50 1.10
a. 5fr Eurasian hoopoe 1.15 .25
b. 5fr Pied flycatcher 1.15 .25
c. 5fr Great reed warbler 1.15 .25
d. 5fr Eurasian kingfisher 1.15 .25
342 A44 Block of 4 7.75 1.25
a. 6.50fr House martin 1.50 .30
b. 6.50fr Sedge warbler 1.50 .30
c. 6.50fr Fieldfare 1.50 .30

d. 6.50fr European Golden oriole 1.50 .30
Nos. 337-342,C132-C137 (12) 152.25 19.20

Nos. 337-342 are printed in sheets of 16.

Library, UN Emblem — A45

Designs: 5fr, Students taking test, and emblem of University of Bujumbura. 7fr, Students in laboratory and emblem of Ecole Normale Superieure of Burundi. 10fr, Students with electron-microscope and Education Year emblem.

1970, Oct. 23

343 A45 3fr gold & multi .25 .25
344 A45 5fr gold & multi .25 .25
345 A45 7fr gold & multi .30 .25
346 A45 10fr gold & multi .40 .25
Nos. 343-346 (4) 1.20 1.00

Issued for International Education Year. Exists imperf. Value set, $1.50.

Pres. and Mrs. Michel Micombero — A46

Designs: 7fr, Pres. Michel Micombero and Burundi flag. 11fr, Pres. Micombero and Revolution Memorial.

1970, Nov. 28 Photo. *Perf. 13½*

347 A46 4fr gold & multi .25 .25
348 A46 7fr gold & multi .35 .25
349 A46 11fr gold & multi .45 .25
a. Souvenir sheet of 3 1.25 1.25
Nos. 347-349 (3) 1.05 .75

4th anniv. of independence. No. 349a contains 3 stamps similar to Nos. 347-349, but inscribed "Poste Aerienne."

Exist imperf. Value: set $1.25; souvenir sheet, $1.25.

See Nos. C140-C142.

Lenin with Delegates A47

Designs (Lenin, Paintings): 5fr, addressing crowd. 6.50fr, with soldier and sailor. 15fr, speaking from balcony. 50fr, Portrait.

1970, Dec. 31 Photo. *Perf. 13½*

Gold Frame

350 A47 3.50fr dk red brown .55 .25
351 A47 5fr dk red brown .70 .25
352 A47 6.50fr dk red brown .85 .25
353 A47 15fr dk red brown 1.40 .40
354 A47 50fr dk red brown 3.50 .50
Nos. 350-354 (5) 7.00 1.65

Lenin's birth centenary (1870-1924). Exist imperf. Value set, $8.

Lion — A48

1971, Mar. 19 Photo. *Perf. 13½*

Size: 38x38mm

355 Strip of 4 2.00 .80
a. A48 1fr Lion .35 .25
b. A48 1fr Cape buffalo .35 .25
c. A48 1fr Hippopotamus .35 .25
d. A48 1fr Giraffe .35 .25
356 Strip of 4 2.75 .90
a. A48 2fr Hartebeest .45 .25
b. A48 2fr Black rhinoceros .45 .25
c. A48 2fr Zebra .45 .25
d. A48 2fr Leopard .45 .25
357 Strip of 4 3.25 1.00
a. A48 3fr Grant's gazelles .55 .25
b. A48 3fr Cheetah .55 .25
c. A48 3fr African white-backed vultures .55 .25
d. A48 3fr Johnston's okapi .55 .25
358 Strip of 4 3.75 1.10
a. A48 5fr Chimpanzee .60 .25
b. A48 5fr Elephant .60 .25
c. A48 5fr Spotted hyenas .60 .25
d. A48 5fr Beisa .60 .25
359 Strip of 4 4.75 1.50
a. A48 6fr Gorilla .95 .30
b. A48 6fr Gnu .95 .30
c. A48 6fr Wart hog .95 .30
d. A48 6fr Cape hunting dog .95 .30
360 Strip of 4 5.75 1.75
a. A48 11fr Sable antelope 1.10 .35
b. A48 11fr Caracal lynx 1.10 .35
c. A48 11fr Ostriches 1.10 .35
d. A48 11fr Bongo 1.10 .35
Nos. 355-360,C146-C151 (12) 90.75 15.70

Nos. 355a-355d, 356a-356d, 357a-357d, 358a-358d and 359a-359d exist with gold line under country name.

For overprints and surcharges see Nos. C152, CB15-CB18.

The Resurrection, by Il Sodoma — A49

Paintings: 6fr, Resurrection, by Andrea del Castagno. 11fr, Noli me Tangere, by Correggio.

1971, Apr. 2

361 A49 3fr gold & multi .25 .25
362 A49 6fr gold & multi .25 .25
363 A49 11fr gold & multi .50 .25
a. Souvenir sheet of 3, #361-363 1.75 1.75
Nos. 361-363,C143-C145 (6) 5.60 1.60

Easter 1971. Exist imperf. Value: set (6) $4.75; souvenir sheets, $5.75.

Young Venetian Woman, by Dürer — A50

Dürer Paintings: 11fr, Hieronymus Holzschuher. 14fr, Emperor Maximilian I. 17fr, Holy Family, from Paumgartner Altar. 26fr, Haller Madonna. 31fr, Self-portrait, 1498.

1971, Sept. 20

364 A50 6fr multicolored .30 .25
365 A50 11fr multicolored .40 .25
366 A50 14fr multicolored .55 .25
367 A50 17fr multicolored 1.00 .40
368 A50 26fr multicolored 1.25 .50
369 A50 31fr multicolored 1.50 .60
a. Souvenir sheet of 2, #368-369 3.50 3.50
Nos. 364-369 (6) 5.00 2.25

International Letter Writing Week. Albrecht Dürer (1471-1528), German painter and engraver.

Exist imperf. Values: set $9; souvenir sheet $4.

Nos. 364-369, 369a Overprinted in Black and Gold: "VIème CONGRES / DE L'INSTITUT INTERNATIONAL / DE DROIT D'EXPRESSION FRANCAISE"

1971, Oct. 8

370 A50 6fr multicolored .25 .25
371 A50 11fr multicolored .35 .25
372 A50 14fr multicolored .50 .25
373 A50 17fr multicolored .75 .25
374 A50 26fr multicolored 1.10 .25
375 A50 31fr multicolored 1.40 .25
a. Souvenir sheet of 2 3.00 3.00
Nos. 370-375 (6) 4.35 1.50

6th Cong. of the Intl. Legal Institute of the French-speaking Area, Bujumbura, 8/10-19. Exists imperf. Values: set $9; souvenir sheet $3.50.

Madonna and Child, by Il Perugino — A51

Paintings of the Madonna and Child by: 5fr, Andrea del Sarto. 6fr, Luis de Morales.

1971, Nov. 2 Photo. *Perf. 13½*

376 A51 3fr dk green & multi .30 .25
377 A51 5fr dk green & multi .30 .25
378 A51 6fr dk green & multi .35 .25
a. Souvenir sheet of 3, #376-378 4.50 4.50
Nos. 376-378,C153-C155 (6) 3.85 1.60

Christmas 1971.

Exist imperf. Value: set (6) $4.50; souvenir sheets, $9.

For surcharges see Nos. B49-B51, CB19-CB21.

Lunar Orbiter A52

Designs: 11fr, Vostok. 14fr, Luna 1. 17fr, Apollo 11 astronaut on moon. 26fr, Soyuz 11. 40fr, Lunar Rover (Apollo 15).

1972, Jan. 15

379 A52 6fr gold & multi .25 .25
380 A52 11fr gold & multi .40 .25
381 A52 14fr gold & multi .60 .25
382 A52 17fr gold & multi .70 .25
383 A52 26fr gold & multi 1.25 .30
384 A52 40fr gold & multi 2.00 .50
a. Souvenir sheet of 6 5.50 5.50
Nos. 379-384 (6) 5.20 1.80

Conquest of space.

No. 384a contains one each of Nos. 379-384 inscribed "APOLLO 16."

Exist imperf. Value: set $11; souvenir sheet, $11.

See No. C156.

Slalom and Sapporo '72 Emblem — A53

Sapporo '72 Emblem and: 6fr, Figure skating, pairs. 11fr, Figure skating, women's. 14fr, Ski jump. 17fr, Ice hockey. 24fr, Speed skating, men's. 26fr, Snow scooter. 31fr, Downhill skiing. 50fr, Bobsledding.

1972, Feb. 3

385 A53 5fr silver & multi .25 .25
386 A53 6fr silver & multi .25 .25
387 A53 11fr silver & multi .35 .25
388 A53 14fr silver & multi .45 .25
389 A53 17fr silver & multi .60 .25
390 A53 24fr silver & multi .75 .25
391 A53 26fr silver & multi .90 .25
392 A53 31fr silver & multi 1.00 .25
393 A53 50fr silver & multi 1.75 .30
Nos. 385-393 (9) 6.30 2.30

11th Winter Olympic Games, Sapporo, Japan, Feb. 3-13. Printed in sheets of 12. See No. C157.

Exists imperf. Value: set $37.50.

Issued: Nos. 385-390, 2/1; Nos. 391-393, 2/21.

Ecce Homo, by Quentin Massys — A54

Paintings: 6.50fr, Crucifixion, by Rubens. 10fr, Descent from the Cross, by Jacopo da Pontormo. 18fr, Pieta, by Ferdinand Gallegos. 27fr, Trinity, by El Greco.

1972, Mar. 20 Photo. *Perf. 13½*

394 A54 3.50fr gold & multi .25 .25
395 A54 6.50fr gold & multi .45 .25
396 A54 10fr gold & multi .70 .25
397 A54 18fr gold & multi 1.50 .25
398 A54 27fr gold & multi 1.75 .25
a. Souv. sheet, #394-398 + label 7.00 7.00
Nos. 394-398 (5) 4.65 1.25

Easter 1972. Printed in sheets of 8 with label.

Exist imperf. Value: set $6; souvenir sheet $7.

Gymnastics, Olympic Rings and "Motion" A55

1972, May 19

399 A55 5fr shown .25 .25
400 A55 6fr Javelin .35 .25
401 A55 11fr Fencing .70 .25
402 A55 14fr Bicycling .90 .25
403 A55 17fr Pole vault 1.10 .25
Nos. 399-403,C158-C161 (9) 11.50 2.60

Souvenir Sheet

404 Sheet of 2 4.00 3.75
a. A55 31fr Discus 1.50 1.50
b. A55 40fr Soccer 1.50 1.50

20th Olympic Games, Munich, 8/26-9/11.

Exist imperf. Values: set (9) $9; souvenir sheet $5.

Prince Rwagasore, Pres. Micombero, Burundi Flag, Drummers A56

7fr, Rwagasore, Micombero, flag, map of Africa, globe. 13fr, Micombero, flag, globe.

1972, Aug. 24 Photo. *Perf. 13½*

405 A56 5fr silver & multi .25 .25
406 A56 7fr silver & multi .25 .25
407 A56 13fr silver & multi .45 .25
a. Souvenir sheet of 3, #405-407 .90 .90
Nos. 405-407,C162-C164 (6) 2.65 1.70

10th anniversary of independence.
Exist imperf. Values: set $3.50; souvenir sheets $2.

Madonna and Child, by Andrea Solario — A57

Paintings of the Madonna and Child by: 10fr, Raphael. 15fr, Botticelli.

1972, Nov. 2

408 A57 5fr lt blue & multi .30 .25
409 A57 10fr lt blue & multi .60 .25
410 A57 15fr lt blue & multi 1.10 .25
a. Souvenir sheet of 3, #408-410 2.75 2.75
Nos. 408-410,C165-C167 (6) 8.00 1.65

Christmas 1972. Sheets of 20 stamps + label.
Exist imperf. Values: set (6) $7; souvenir sheets $8.50.
For surcharges see Nos. B56-B58, CB26-CB28.

Platycoryne Crocea — A58

1972 Size: 33x33mm

411 A58 50c shown .40 .25
412 A58 1fr Cattleya trianaei .50 .25
413 A58 2fr Eulophia cucullata .60 .25
414 A58 3fr Cymbidium hamsey .75 .25
415 A58 4fr Thelymitra pauciflora .90 .25
416 A58 5fr Miltassia 1.25 .25
417 A58 6fr Miltonia 1.50 .25

Size: 38x38mm

418 A58 7fr Like 50c 1.75 .25
419 A58 8fr Like 1fr 2.00 .25
420 A58 9fr Like 2fr 2.50 .25
421 A58 10fr Like 3fr 3.00 .25
Nos. 411-421,C168-C174 (18) 41.90 5.35

Orchids. Issued: Nos. 411-417, 11/6; Nos. 418-421, 11/29.

Henry Morton Stanley — A59

Designs: 7fr, Porters, Stanley's expedition. 13fr, Stanley entering Ujiji.

1973, Mar. 19 Photo. *Perf. 13½*

422 A59 5fr gold & multi .35 .25
423 A59 7fr gold & multi .50 .25
424 A59 13fr gold & multi .85 .25
Nos. 422-424,C175-C177 (6) 5.05 1.60

Exploration of Africa by David Livingstone (1813-1873) and Henry Morton Stanley (John Rowlands; 1841-1904).
Exist imperf. Values: set (6) $4.50; souvenir sheets $3.50.

Crucifixion, by Roger van der Weyden — A60

Easter (Paintings): 5fr, Flagellation of Christ, by Caravaggio. 13fr, The Burial of Christ, by Raphael.

1973, Apr. 10

425 A60 5fr gold & multi .25 .25
426 A60 7fr gold & multi .35 .25
427 A60 13fr gold & multi .65 .25
a. Souvenir sheet of 3, #425-427 3.75 3.00
Nos. 425-427,C178-C180 (6) 5.80 1.65

Exist imperf. Values: set (6) $6; souvenir sheets $7.

INTERPOL Emblem, Flag — A61

Design: 10fr, INTERPOL flag and emblem. 18fr, INTERPOL Headquarters and emblem.

1973, May 19 Photo. *Perf. 13½*

428 A61 5fr silver & multi .25 .25
429 A61 10fr silver & multi .35 .25
430 A61 18fr silver & multi .60 .25
Nos. 428-430,C181-C182 (5) 4.05 1.55

Intl. Criminal Police Organization, 50th anniv.
Exist imperf. Value set, $5.50.

Signs of the Zodiac, Babylon — A62

Designs: 5fr, Greek and Roman gods representing planets. 7fr, Ptolemy (No. 433a) and Ptolemaic solar system. 13fr, Copernicus (No. 434a) and heliocentric system.
a, UL. b, UR. c, LL. d, LR.

1973, July 27 Photo. *Perf. 13½*

431 A62 3fr Block of 4, #a.-d. 1.10 .40
432 A62 5fr Block of 4, #a.-d. 1.75 .60
433 A62 7fr Block of 4, #a.-d. 2.50 .60
434 A62 13fr Block of 4, #a.-d. 3.50 1.00
e. Souvenir sheet of 4, #431-434 25.00 25.00
Nos. 431-434,C183-C186 (8) 31.60 7.60

500th anniversary of the birth of Nicolaus Copernicus (1473-1543), Polish astronomer.
Exist imperf. Values: set (8) $60; souvenir sheets $95.

Flowers and Butterflies — A63

Block of 4 containing 2 flower & 2 butterfly designs. The 1fr, 2fr, 5fr and 11fr have flower designs listed as "a" and "d" numbers, butterflies as "b" and "c" numbers; the arrangement is reversed for the 3fr and 6fr.

1973, Sept. 3 Photo. *Perf. 13*
Stamp Size: 34x41½mm

435 A63 Block of 4 1.75 .40
a. 1fr Protea cynaroides .30 .25
b. 1fr Precis octavia .30 .25
c. 1fr Epiphora bauhiniae .30 .25
d. 1fr Gazania longiscapa .30 .25
436 A63 Block of 4 3.50 .40
a. 2fr Kniphofia .60 .25
b. 2fr Cymothoe coccinata .60 .25
c. 2fr Nudaurelia zambesina .60 .25
d. 2fr Freesia refracta .60 .25
437 A63 Block of 4 5.50 .40
a. 3fr Calotis eupompe .90 .25
b. 3fr Narcissus .90 .25
c. 3fr Cineraria hybrida .90 .25
d. 3fr Cyrestis camillus .90 .25
438 A63 Block of 4 9.00 .40
a. 5fr Iris tingitana 1.50 .25
b. 5fr Pappilio demodocus 1.50 .25
c. 5fr Catopsilia avelaneda 1.50 .25
d. 5fr Nerine sarniensis 1.50 .25
439 A63 Block of 4 10.00 .45
a. 6fr Hypolimnas dexithea 1.75 .25
b. 6fr Zantedeschia tropicalis 1.75 .25
c. 6fr Sandersonia aurantiaca 1.75 .25
d. 6fr Drurya antimachus 1.75 .25
440 A63 Block of 4 12.50 .50
a. 11fr Nymphaea capensis 2.00 .25
b. 11fr Pandoriana pandora 2.00 .25
c. 11fr Precis orythia 2.00 .25
d. 11fr Pelargonium domestica 2.00 .25
Nos. 435-440,C187-C192 (12) 141.25 7.10

Virgin and Child, by Giovanni Bellini — A64

Virgin and Child by: 10fr, Jan van Eyck. 15fr, Giovanni Boltraffio.

1973, Nov. 13 Photo. *Perf. 13*

441 A64 5fr gold & multi .50 .25
442 A64 10fr gold & multi 1.00 .25
443 A64 15fr gold & multi 1.25 .25
a. Souvenir sheet of 3, #441-443 2.50 2.00
Nos. 441-443,C193-C195 (6) 7.50 1.55

Christmas 1973.
Exist imperf. Values: set $8; souvenir sheets $8.
For surcharges see Nos. B59-B61, CB29-CB31.

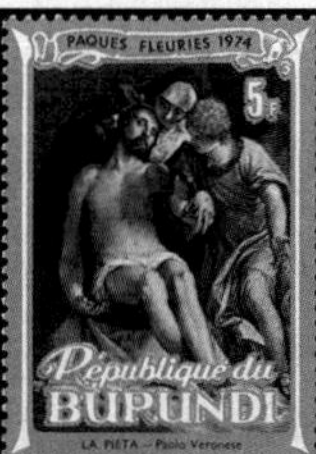

Pietá, by Paolo Veronese — A65

Paintings: 10fr, Virgin and St. John, by van der Weyden. 18fr, Crucifixion, by van der Weyden. 27fr, Burial of Christ, by Titian. 40fr, Pietá, by El Greco.

1974, Apr. 19 Photo. *Perf. 14x13½*

444 A65 5fr gold & multi .25 .25
445 A65 10fr gold & multi .40 .25
446 A65 18fr gold & multi 1.10 .25
447 A65 27fr gold & multi 1.60 .25
448 A65 40fr gold & multi 2.50 .35
a. Souvenir sheet of 5, #444-448 5.75 5.00
Nos. 444-448 (5) 5.85 1.35

Easter 1974.
Exist imperf. Values: set $6.50; souvenir sheet $8.

Fish — A66

1974, May 30 Photo. *Perf. 13*
Stamp Size: 35x35mm

449 A66 Block of 4 4.50 .55
a. 1fr Haplochromis multicolor .80 .25
b. 1fr Pantodon buchholzi .80 .25
c. 1fr Tropheus duboisi .80 .25
d. 1fr Distichodus sexfasciatus .80 .25
450 A66 Block of 4 6.00 .40
a. 2fr Pelmatochromis kribensis .90 .25
b. 2fr Nannaethiops tritaeniatus .90 .25
c. 2fr Polycentropsis abbreviata .90 .25
d. 2fr Hemichromis bimaculatus .90 .25
451 A66 Block of 4 6.50 .65
a. 3fr Ctenopoma acutirostre 1.00 .25
b. 3fr Synodontis angelicus 1.00 .25
c. 3fr Tilapia melanopleura 1.00 .25
d. 3fr Aphyosemion bivittatum 1.00 .25
452 A66 Block of 4 10.00 .70
a. 5fr Monodactylus argenteus 1.60 .25
b. 5fr Zanclus canescens 1.60 .25
c. 5fr Pygoplites diacanthus 1.60 .25
d. 5fr Cephalopholis argus 1.60 .25
453 A66 Block of 4 12.50 .75
a. 6fr Priacanthus arenatus 2.25 .25
b. 6fr Pomacanthus arcuatus 2.25 .25
c. 6fr Scarus guacamaia 2.25 .25
d. 6fr Zeus faber 2.25 .25
454 A66 Block of 4 25.00 1.90
a. 11fr Lactophrys quadricornis 4.50 .45
b. 11fr Balistes vetula 4.50 .45
c. 11fr Acanthurus bahianus 4.50 .45
d. 11fr Holocanthus ciliaris 4.50 .45
Nos. 449-454,C207-C212 (12) 144.00 13.15

Soccer and Cup A67

Designs: Various soccer scenes and cup.

1974, July 4 Photo. *Perf. 13*

455 A67 5fr gold & multi .30 .25
456 A67 6fr gold & multi .40 .25
457 A67 11fr gold & multi .75 .25
458 A67 14fr gold & multi 1.10 .30
459 A67 17fr gold & multi 1.50 .30
a. Souvenir sheet of 3 7.25 6.00
Nos. 455-459,C196-C198 (8) 10.05 2.65

World Soccer Championship, Munich, June 13-July 7. No. 459a contains 3 stamps similar to Nos. C196-C198 without "Poste Aerienne."
Exist imperf. Values: set (8) $8; souvenir sheet $10.

Flags over UPU Headquarters, Bern — A68

No. 460b, G.P.O., Bujumbura. No. 461a, Mailmen ("11F" in UR). No. 461b, Mailmen ("11F" in UL). No. 462a, UPU emblem. No. 462b, Means of transportation. No. 463a, Pigeon over globe showing Burundi. No. 463b, Swiss flag, pigeon over map showing Bern. Pairs are continuous designs.

1974, July 23

460 A68 6fr Pair, #a.-b. .85 .25
461 A68 11fr Pair, #a.-b. 1.25 .25
462 A68 14fr Pair, #a.-b. 1.75 .25
463 A68 17fr Pair, #a.-b. 2.10 .25
c. Souvenir sheet of 8, #460-463 20.00 20.00
Nos. 460-463,C199-C202 (8) 19.95 3.35

Cent. of UPU.
Exist imperf. Value set, $30.

St. Ildefonso Writing Letter, by El Greco A69

Paintings: 11fr, Lady Sealing Letter, by Chardin. 14fr, Titus at Desk, by Rembrandt. 17fr, The Love Letter, by Vermeer. 26fr, The Merchant G. Gisze, by Holbein. 31fr, Portrait of Alexandre Lenoir, by David.

1974, Oct. 1 **Photo.** ***Perf. 13***

468 A69 6fr gold & multi .35 .25
469 A69 11fr gold & multi .60 .30
470 A69 14fr gold & multi .70 .35
471 A69 17fr gold & multi 1.00 .35
472 A69 26fr gold & multi 1.10 .45
473 A69 31fr gold & multi 1.50 .60
a. Souvenir sheet of 2, #472-473 4.00 4.00
Nos. 468-473 (6) 5.25 2.30

International Letter Writing Week, Oct. 6-12.
Exist imperf. Values: set $7; souvenir sheet $4.

Virgin and Child, by Bernaert van Orley — A70

Paintings of the Virgin and Child: 10fr, by Hans Memling. 15fr, by Botticelli.

1974, Nov. 7 **Photo.** ***Perf. 13***

474 A70 5fr gold & multi .65 .25
475 A70 10fr gold & multi 1.20 .25
476 A70 15fr gold & multi 1.50 .25
a. Souvenir sheet of 3, #474-476 4.00 4.00
Nos. 474-476,C213-C215 (6) 8.75 1.75

Christmas 1974. Sheets of 20 stamps and one label.
Exist imperf. Values: set (6) $7.50; souvenir sheets $9.

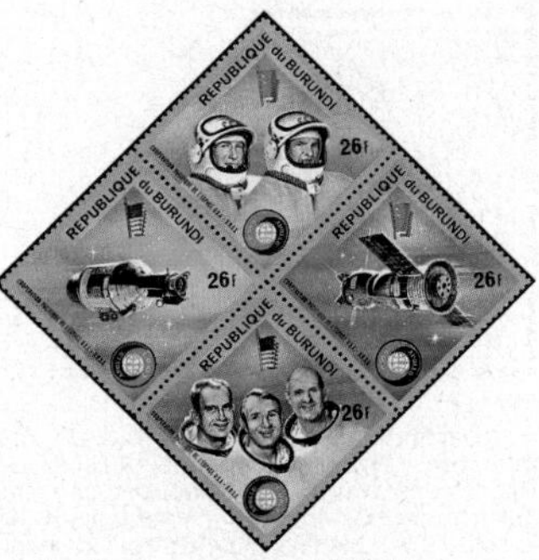

Apollo-Soyuz Space Mission and Emblem — A71

1975, July 10 **Photo.** ***Perf. 13***

477 A71 Block of 4 4.00 2.75
a. 26fr A.A. Leonov, V.N. Kubasov, Soviet flag .65
b. 26fr Soyuz and Soviet flag .65
c. 26fr Apollo and American flag .65
d. 26fr D.K. Slayton, V.D. Brand, T.P. Stafford, American flag .65
478 A71 Block of 4 5.00 3.25
a. 31fr Apollo-Soyuz link-up .95
b. 31fr Apollo, blast-off .95
c. 31fr Soyuz, blast-off .95
d. 31fr Kubasov, Leonov, Slayton, Brand, Stafford .95
Nos. 477-478,C216-C217 (4) 18.00 12.00

Apollo Soyuz space test project (Russo-American cooperation), launching July 15; link-up, July 17.
Exist imperf. Value set, $16.

Addax — A72

1975, July 31 **Photo.** ***Perf. 13½***

479 Strip of 4 1.50 .65
a. A72 1fr shown .30 .25
b. A72 1fr Roan antelope .30 .25
c. A72 1fr Nyala .30 .25
d. A72 1fr White rhinoceros .30 .25
480 Strip of 4 2.40 .65
a. A72 2fr Mandrill .45 .25
b. A72 2fr Eland .45 .25
c. A72 2fr Salt's dik-dik .45 .25
d. A72 2fr Thomson's gazelles .45 .25
481 Strip of 4 4.00 .65
a. A72 3fr African small-clawed otter .65 .25
b. A72 3fr Reed buck .65 .25
c. A72 3fr Indian civet .65 .25
d. A72 3fr Cape buffalo .65 .25
482 Strip of 4 6.00 1.10
a. A72 5fr White-tailed gnu 1.10 .25
b. A72 5fr African wild asses 1.10 .25
c. A72 5fr Black-and-white colobus monkey 1.10 .25
d. A72 5fr Gerenuk 1.10 .25
483 Strip of 4 8.75 1.10
a. A72 6fr Dama gazelle 1.60 .25
b. A72 6fr Black-backed jackal 1.60 .25
c. A72 6fr Sitatungas 1.60 .25
d. A72 6fr Zebra antelope 1.60 .25
484 Strip of 4 12.00 1.10
a. A72 11fr Fennec 2.25 .25
b. A72 11fr Lesser kudus 2.25 .25
c. A72 11fr Blesbok 2.25 .25
d. A72 11fr Serval 2.25 .25
Nos. 479-484,C218-C223 (12) 94.90 11.30

For overprints see Nos. C224-C227.

Jonah, by Michelangelo — A73

Paintings from Sistine Chapel: No. 485b, Libyan Sybil. No. 486a, Prophet Isaiah. No. 486b, Delphic Sybil. No. 487a, Daniel. No. 487b, Cumaean Sybil.

1975, Dec. 3 **Photo.** ***Perf. 13***

485 A73 5fr Pair, #a.-b. 1.50 .50
486 A73 13fr Pair, #a.-b. 3.50 .60
487 A73 27fr Pair, #a.-b. 6.00 .70
c. Souvenir sheet of 6, #485-487 12.00 9.00
Nos. 485-487,C228-C230 (6) 30.50 4.30

Michelangelo Buonarotti (1475-1564), Italian sculptor, painter and architect. Printed in sheets of 18 stamps + 2 labels.

Exist imperf. Values: set (6) $30; souvenir sheets $28.
For surcharges see Nos. B65-B67, CB35-CB37.

Speed Skating — A74

Basketball — A75

Designs (Innsbruck Games Emblem and): 24fr, Figure skating, women's. 26fr, Two-man bobsled. 31fr, Cross-country skiing.

1976, Jan. 23 **Photo.** ***Perf. 14x13½***

491 A74 17fr dp bl & multi .70 .25
492 A74 24fr multi 1.00 .25
493 A74 26fr multi 1.25 .25
494 A74 31fr plum & multi 1.50 .35
a. Souvenir sheet of 3, perf. 13½ 5.50 3.50
Nos. 491-494,C234-C236 (7) 9.35 2.50

12th Winter Olympic Games, Innsbruck, Austria, Feb. 4-15.
No. 494a contains stamps similar to Nos. C234-C236, without "POSTE AERIENNE."
Exist imperf. Values: set (7) $10; souvenir sheets $10.

1976, May 3 **Litho.** ***Perf. 13½***

Montreal Games Emblem and: Nos. 495a, 498b, 499c, Basketball. Nos. 495b, 497a, 499b, Pole vault. Nos. 496a, 497b, 499d, Running. Nos. 496b, 498a, 499a, Soccer.

495 A75 14fr Pair, #a.-b. 1.50 1.00
496 A75 17fr Pair, #a.-b. 2.25 1.50
497 A75 28fr Pair, #a.-b. 3.50 2.25
498 A75 40fr Pair, #a.-b. 9.00 4.00
Nos. 495-498,C237-C239 (7) 34.25 20.90

Souvenir Sheet

499 Sheet of 4 13.50 13.50
a. A75 14fr red & multi 3.00 3.00
b. A75 17fr olive & multi 3.00 3.00
c. A75 28fr blue & multi 3.00 3.00
d. A75 40fr magenta & multi 3.00 3.00

21st Olympic Games, Montreal, Canada, July 17-Aug. 1.
Exist imperf. Values: set (7) $30; souvenir sheets $50.

Virgin and Child, by Dirk Bouts — A76

Virgin and Child by: 13fr, Giovanni Bellini. 27fr, Carlo Crivelli.

1976, Oct. 18 **Photo.** ***Perf. 13½***

504 A76 5fr gold & multi .85 .25
505 A76 13fr gold & multi 1.10 .25
506 A76 27fr gold & multi 2.00 .25
a. Souvenir sheet of 3, #504-506 4.00 3.50
Nos. 504-506,C250-C252 (6) 11.20 1.75

Christmas 1976. Sheets of 20 stamps and descriptive label.
Exist imperf. Values: set (6) $10; souvenir sheets $11.
For surcharges see Nos. B71-B73, CB41-CB43.

St. Veronica, by Rubens A77

Paintings by Rubens: 21fr, Christ on the Cross. 27fr, Descent from the Cross. 35fr, The Deposition.

1977, Apr. 5 **Photo.** ***Perf. 13***

507 A77 10fr gold & multi 1.50 1.50
508 A77 21fr gold & multi 3.00 3.00
509 A77 27fr gold & multi 3.25 3.25
510 A77 35fr gold & multi 4.00 4.00
a. Souvenir sheet of 4 10.00 10.00
Nos. 507-510 (4) 11.75 11.75

Easter 1977. Sheets of 30 stamps and descriptive label. No. 510a contains 4 stamps similar to Nos. 507-510 inscribed "POSTE AERIENNE."
Exist imperf. Values: set $14; souvenir sheet $12.

A78

No. 511a, Alexander Graham Bell. Nos. 511b, Intelsat Satellite, Modern & Old Telephones. No. 512a, Switchboard operator, c. 1910, wall telephone. No. 512b, Intelsat, radar. No. 513a, A.G. Bell, 1st telephone. No. 513b, Satellites around globe, videophone.

1977, May 17 **Photo.** ***Perf. 13***

511 A78 10fr Pair, #a.-b. 1.25 1.25
512 A78 17fr Pair, #a.-b. 2.50 2.50
513 A78 26fr Pair, #a.-b. 4.50 4.50
Nos. 511-513,C253-C254 (5) 13.90 13.90

Centenary of first telephone call by Alexander Graham Bell, Mar. 10, 1876.
Exist imperf. Value set (5), $9.

Buffon's Kob — A80

1977, Aug. 22 **Photo.** ***Perf. 14x14½***

517 Strip of 4 2.25 .25
a. A80 2fr shown .50 .25
b. A80 2fr Marabous .50 .25
c. A80 2fr Brindled gnu .50 .25
d. A80 2fr River hog .50 .25
518 Strip of 4 3.75 .50
a. A80 5fr Zebras .75 .25
b. A80 5fr Shoebill .75 .25
c. A80 5fr Striped hyenas .75 .25
d. A80 5fr Chimpanzee .75 .25
519 Strip of 4 6.00 .60
a. A80 8fr Flamingos 1.25 .25
b. A80 8fr Nile crocodiles 1.25 .25
c. A80 8fr Green mamba 1.25 .25
d. A80 8fr Greater kudus 1.25 .25
520 Strip of 4 12.00 .70
a. A80 11fr Hyrax 2.25 .25
b. A80 11fr Cobra 2.25 .25
c. A80 11fr Jackals 2.25 .25
d. A80 11fr Verreaux's eagles 2.25 .25
521 Strip of 4 17.50 1.00
a. A80 21fr Honey badger 3.25 .25
b. A80 21fr Harnessed antelopes 3.25 .25
c. A80 21fr Secretary bird 3.25 .25
d. A80 21fr Klipspringer 3.25 .25
522 Strip of 4 22.50 1.50
a. A80 27fr African big-eared fox 4.75 .30
b. A80 27fr Elephants 4.75 .30
c. A80 27fr Vulturine guineafowl 4.75 .30
d. A80 27fr Impalas 4.75 .30
Nos. 517-522,C258-C263 (12) 184.50 13.45

Exist imperf.

The Goose Girl, by Grimm — A81

Fairy Tales: 5fr, by Grimm Brothers. 11fr, by Aesop. 14fr, by Hans Christian Andersen. 17fr, by Jean de La Fontaine. 26fr, English fairy tales.

1977, Sept. 14 *Perf. 14*

523 Block of 4 5.50 .65
- *a.* A81 5fr shown 1.00 .25
- *b.* A81 5fr The Two Wanderers 1.00 .25
- *c.* A81 5fr The Man of Iron 1.00 .25
- *d.* A81 5fr Snow White and Rose Red 1.00 .25

524 Block of 4 11.50 .65
- *a.* A81 11fr The Quarreling Cats 2.00 .25
- *b.* A81 11fr The Blind and the Lame 2.00 .25
- *c.* A81 11fr The Hermit and the Bear 2.00 .25
- *d.* A81 11fr The Fox and the Stork 2.00 .25

525 Block of 4 14.50 .65
- *a.* A81 14fr The Princess and the Pea 2.50 .25
- *b.* A81 14fr The Old Tree Mother 2.50 .25
- *c.* A81 14fr The Ice Maiden 2.50 .25
- *d.* A81 14fr The Old House 2.50 .25

526 Block of 4 18.00 1.00
- *a.* A81 17fr The Oyster and the Suitors 3.50 .25
- *b.* A81 17fr The Wolf and the Lamb 3.50 .25
- *c.* A81 17fr Hen with the Golden Egg 3.50 .25
- *d.* A81 17fr The Wolf as Shepherd 3.50 .25

527 Block of 4 24.00 1.25
- *a.* A81 26fr Three Heads in the Well 4.00 .25
- *b.* A81 26fr Mother Goose 4.00 .25
- *c.* A81 26fr Jack and the Beanstalk 4.00 .25
- *d.* A81 26fr Alice in Wonderland 4.00 .25

Nos. 523-527 (5) 73.50 4.20

Exist imperf. Value (set), $80.

Security Council Chamber, UN Nos. 28, 46, 37, C7 — A82

UN Stamps and: 8fr, UN General Assembly, interior. 21fr, UN Meeting Hall.

1977, Oct. 10 **Photo.** *Perf. 13½*

528 A82 Block of 4 3.50 2.50
- *a.* 8fr No. 25 .90 .50
- *b.* 8fr No. C5 .90 .50
- *c.* 8fr No. 23 .90 .50
- *d.* 8fr No. 2 .90 .50

529 A82 Block of 4 5.25 3.50
- *a.* 10fr No. 28 1.00 .75
- *b.* 10fr No. 46 1.00 .75
- *c.* 10fr No. 37 1.00 .75
- *d.* 10fr No. C7 1.00 .75

530 A82 Block of 4 8.75 6.00
- *a.* 21fr No. 45 1.60 1.25
- *b.* 21fr No. 42 1.60 1.25
- *c.* 21fr No. 17 1.60 1.25
- *d.* 21fr No. 13 1.60 1.25
- *e.* Souvenir sheet of 3 4.00 4.00

Nos. 528-530,C264-C266 (6) 41.00 35.50

25th anniv. (in 1976) of the UN Postal Administration. No. 530e contains 8fr in design of No. 529d, 10fr in design of No. 530b, 21fr in design of No. 528c.

Exist imperf. Value (set), $55.

Virgin and Child — A83

Designs: Paintings of the Virgin and Child.

1977, Oct. 31 **Photo.** *Perf. 14x13*

531 A83 5fr By Meliore Toscano 1.10 .30
532 A83 13fr By J. Lombardos 2.25 .60
533 A83 27fr By Emmanuel Tzanes, 1610-1680 3.25 .75
- *a.* Souvenir sheet of 3, #531-533 6.00 6.00

Nos. 531-533,C267-C269 (6) 14.60 6.65

Christmas 1977. Sheets of 24 stamps with descriptive label.

Exist imperf. Values: set (6) $15; souvenir sheets $9.

For surcharges see Nos. B74-B76, CB44-CB46.

Cruiser Aurora, Russia Nos. 211, 303, 1252, 187 — A84

Russian Stamps and: 8fr, Kremlin, Moscow. 11fr, Pokrovski Cathedral, Moscow. 13fr, Labor Day parade, 1977 and 1980 Olympic Games emblem.

1977, Nov. 14 **Photo.** *Perf. 13*

534 A84 Block of 4 4.00 .60
- *a.* 5fr No. 211 .85 .25
- *b.* 5fr No. 303 .85 .25
- *c.* 5fr No. 1252 .85 .25
- *d.* 5fr No. 187 .85 .25

535 A84 Block of 4 7.75 .60
- *a.* 8fr No. 856 1.25 .25
- *b.* 8fr No. 1986 1.25 .25
- *c.* 8fr No. 908 1.25 .25
- *d.* 8fr No. 2551 1.25 .25

536 A84 Block of 4 10.50 .60
- *a.* 11fr No. 3844b 1.75 .25
- *b.* 11fr No. 3452 1.75 .25
- *c.* 11fr No. 3382 1.75 .25
- *d.* 11fr No. 3837 1.75 .25

537 A84 Block of 4 13.00 .90
- *a.* 13fr No. 4446 2.10 .25
- *b.* 13fr No. 3497 2.10 .25
- *c.* 13fr No. 2926 2.10 .25
- *d.* 13fr No. 2365 2.10 .25

Nos. 534-537 (4) 35.25 2.70

60th anniv. of Russian October Revolution.

Exist imperf. Value (set), $30.00.

Ship at Dock, Arms and Flag — A85

Burundi Arms and Flag and: 5fr, Men at lathes. 11fr, Male leopard dance. 14fr, Coffee harvest. 17fr, Government Palace.

1977, Nov. 25 **Photo.** *Perf. 13½*

538 A85 1fr sil & multi .25 .25
539 A85 5fr sil & multi .25 .25
540 A85 11fr sil & multi .70 .25
541 A85 14fr sil & multi 1.10 .25
542 A85 17fr sil & multi 1.40 .30

Nos. 538-542 (5) 3.70 1.30

15th anniversary of independence.

Exist imperf. Value (set), $4.

A86

Paintings of the Virgin and Child by: 13fr, Rubens. 17fr, Solario. 27fr, Tiepolo. 31fr, Gerard David. 40fr, Bellini.

1979, Feb. **Photo.** *Perf. 14x13*

543 A86 13fr multi 1.75 1.10
544 A86 17fr multi 2.10 1.25
545 A86 27fr multi 3.50 2.10
546 A86 31fr multi 4.50 2.75
547 A86 40fr multi 6.00 3.75

Nos. 543-547 (5) 17.85 10.95

Christmas 1978. See Nos. B77-B81, C270, CB47.

Exist imperf. Value (set), $19.

Birds — A87

Designs: 1fr, Buceros abyssinicus. 2fr, Anhinga rufa. 3fr, Melittophagus pusillus. 5fr, Phoeniconais minor. 8fr, Afropavo congenis. 10fr, Porphyrio alba. 20fr, Polemaethus bellicosus. 27fr, Ibis ibis. 50fr, Ephippiorhynchus senegalensis.

1979 **Photo.** *Perf. 13½x13*

548 A87 1fr multicolored .60 .60
549 A87 2fr multicolored .65 .65
550 A87 3fr multicolored .75 .75
551 A87 5fr multicolored 1.10 1.00
552 A87 8fr multicolored 1.90 1.75
553 A87 10fr multicolored 2.25 2.00
554 A87 20fr multicolored 4.75 4.50
555 A87 27fr multicolored 5.25 5.00
556 A87 50fr multicolored 10.50 10.00

Nos. 548-556,C273-C281 (18) 91.50 65.90

See No. 585F.

Mother and Infant, IYC Emblem A88

IYC Emblem and: 20fr, Infant. 27fr, Girl with doll. 50fr, Children in Children's Village.

1979, July 19 **Photo.** *Perf. 14*

557 A88 10fr multi .90 .90
558 A88 20fr multi 2.10 1.75
559 A88 27fr multi 2.75 2.75
560 A88 50fr multi 4.25 4.25

Nos. 557-560 (4) 10.00 9.65

Exist imperf. Value set, $10.

See No. B82.

A89

Virgin and Child by: 20fr, del Garbo. 27fr, Giovanni Penni. 31fr, G. Romano. 50fr, Jacopo Bassano.

1979, Oct. 12

561 A89 20fr multi 2.00 1.00
562 A89 27fr multi 3.75 2.00
563 A89 31fr multi 5.25 2.50
564 A89 50fr multi 6.50 2.75

Nos. 561-564,B83-B86 (8) 39.50 16.50

Christmas 1979. See Nos. C271, CB48.

Exist imperf. Value set (8), $35.

A90

Designs: 20fr, Rowland Hill, Penny Black.

Stamps of Burundi: 27fr, German East Africa Nos. 17, N17. 31fr, Nos. 4, 24. 40fr, Nos. 29, 294. 60fr, Heinrich von Stephan, No. 462.

1979, Nov. 6

565 A90 20fr multi 1.35 .75
566 A90 27fr multi 1.90 1.00
567 A90 31fr multi 2.10 1.10
568 A90 40fr multi 3.50 1.90
569 A90 60fr multi 5.00 2.75

Nos. 565-569 (5) 13.85 7.50

Sir Rowland Hill (1795-1879), originator of penny postage.

Exist imperf. Vale, set $14.

See No. C272.

A91

No. 570: a, 110-meter hurdles. b, Hurdles, Thomas Munkelt. c, Hurdles, R.D.A.

No. 571: a, Discus. b, Discus, V. Rasshchupkin. c, Discus, U.R.S.S.

No. 572: a, Soccer (player preparing to kick ball) b, Soccer (ball in air) c, Soccer, (ball being blocked by hands).

1980, Oct. 24 **Photo.** *Perf. 13x13½*

570 A91 20fr Strip of 3, #a.-c. 10.00 4.00
571 A91 30fr Strip of 3, #a.-c. 16.00 6.00
572 A91 40fr Strip of 3, #a.-c. 23.00 9.50

Nos. 570-572 (3) 49.00 19.50

22nd Summer Olympic Games, Moscow, July 19-Aug. 3.

Exist imperf. Value set, $49.

See No. C282.

Virgin and Child, by Mainardi A92

Christmas 1980 (Paintings): 30fr, Holy Family, by Michelangelo. 40fr, Virgin and Child, by di Cosimo. 45fr, Holy Family, by Fra Bartolomeo.

1980, Dec. 12 **Photo.** *Perf. 13½x13*

579 A92 10fr multi 1.50 .65
580 A92 30fr multi 3.00 1.25
581 A92 40fr multi 6.50 3.00
582 A92 45fr multi 9.00 4.00

Nos. 579-582,B87-B90 (8) 42.10 17.80

Exist imperf. Value set, $45.

See No. CB49.

UPRONA Party National Congress, 1979 — A93

1980, Dec. 29 *Perf. 14x13½*

583 A93 10fr multi .90 .65
584 A93 40fr multi 2.75 2.10
585 A93 45fr multi 3.00 2.40

Nos. 583-585 (3) 6.65 5.15

Exist imperf. Value set, $6.

Birds Type of 1979

Designs: 5fr, Buceros abyssinicus. 30fr, Melittophagus pusillus. 40fr, Phoeniconaias minor. 50fr, Porphyrio alba.

1980 **Photo.** *Perf. 13½x13*

Brown Frame

585A A87 5fr multi —
585C A87 30fr multi —
585D A87 40fr multi —
585F A87 50fr multi — —

Metallic Blue Frame

585L A87 50fr Like #585F — —

Seven additional stamps were issued in this set. The editors would like to examine any examples.

Johannes Kepler, Dish Antenna A94

1981, Feb. 12 *Perf. 14*

586 A94 10fr shown 2.75 1.00
587 A94 40fr Satellite 6.00 1.90
588 A94 45fr Satellite, diff. 8.25 2.50
a. Souvenir sheet of 3, #586-588 17.50 13.00
Nos. 586-588 (3) 17.00 5.40

350th death anniv. of Johannes Kepler and 1st earth satellite station in Burundi.

Exist imperf. Values: set $16; souvenir sheet $19.

Lion A95

1983, Apr. 22 **Photo.** *Perf. 13*

589 A95 2fr shown *4.50 11.00*
590 A95 3fr Giraffes *4.50 11.00*
591 A95 5fr Rhinoceros *6.00 11.00*
592 A95 10fr Cape buffalo *7.50 15.00*
593 A95 20fr Elephant *11.00 15.00*
594 A95 25fr Hippopotamus *15.00 30.00*
595 A95 30fr Zebra *22.50 30.00*
596 A95 50fr Warthog *30.00 55.00*
597 A95 60fr Oryx *15.00 67.50*
598 A95 65fr Wild dog *19.00 75.00*
599 A95 70fr Cheetah *22.50 90.00*
600 A95 75fr Wildebeest *30.00 110.00*
601 A95 85fr Hyena *1,100. 525.00*
Nos. 589-601 (13) 1,287. 1,045.

Nos. 589-601 Overprinted in Silver with World Wildlife Fund Emblem

1983 **Photo.** *Perf. 13*

589a A95 2fr multi *10.00 5.00*
590a A95 3fr multi *10.00 6.00*
591a A95 5fr multi *10.00 6.50*
592a A95 10fr multi *10.00 15.00*
593a A95 20fr multi *25.00 22.50*
594a A95 25fr multi *40.00 27.50*
595a A95 30fr multi *50.00 40.00*
596a A95 50fr multi *75.00 60.00*
597a A95 60fr multi *90.00 67.50*
598a A95 65fr multi *110.00 75.00*
599a A95 70fr multi *130.00 80.00*
600a A95 75fr multi *180.00 90.00*
601a A95 85fr multi *260.00 100.00*
Nos. 589a-601a (13) 1,000. 595.00

Apparently there is speculation in these two sets. Both sets exist imperf, offered at prices 5-7 times the values shown above.

20th Anniv. of Independence, July 1, 1982 — A96

Flags, various arms, map or portrait.

1983 *Perf. 14*

602 A96 10fr multi 1.00 .65
603 A96 25fr multi 3.25 2.25
604 A96 30fr multi 3.75 2.50
605 A96 50fr multi 5.25 3.25
606 A96 65fr multi 6.75 4.50
Nos. 602-606 (5) 20.00 13.15

Exist imperf. Value set, $22.50.

Christmas 1983 — A97

Virgin and Child paintings: 10fr, by Luca Signorelli (1450-1523). 25fr, by Esteban Murillo (1617-1682). 30fr, by Carlo Crivelli (1430-1495). 50fr, by Nicolas Poussin (1594-1665).

1983, Oct. 3 **Litho.** *Perf. 14½x13½*

607 A97 10fr multi 4.50 1.25
608 A97 25fr multi 6.50 1.75
609 A97 30fr multi 12.00 3.50
610 A97 50fr multi 17.00 9.00
Nos. 607-610,B91-B94 (8) 89.50 31.00

Exist imperf. Value set, $110.

See Nos. C285, CB50.

Butterflies — A98

No. 611a, Cymothoe coccinata. No. 611b, Papilio zalmoxis. No. 612a, Asterope pechueli. No. 612b, Papilio antimachus. No. 613a, Papilio hesperus. No. 613b, Bebearia mardania. No. 614a, Euphaedra neophron. No. 614b, Euphaedra perseis. No. 615a, Euphaedra imperialis. No. 615b, Pseudocraea striata.

1984, June 29 **Photo.** *Perf. 13*

611 A98 5fr Pair, #a.-b. 13.00 3.75
612 A98 10fr Pair, #a.-b. 22.00 4.50
613 A98 30fr Pair, #a.-b. 62.50 18.00
614 A98 35fr Pair, #a.-b. 67.50 29.00
615 A98 65fr Pair, #a.-b. 150.00 50.00
Nos. 611-615 (5) 315.00 105.25

Exist imperf. Value set, $1,600.

For surcharges see No. 654D.

19th UPU Congress, Hamburg A99

UPU emblem and: 10fr, German East Africa, #17, N17. 30fr, #4, 24. 35fr, #294, 595. 65fr, Dr. Heinrich von Stephan, #464-465.

1984, July 14 **Litho.** *Perf. 13x13½*

621 A99 10fr multi 2.75 .60
622 A99 30fr multi 6.00 2.75
623 A99 35fr multi 7.25 3.75
624 A99 65fr multi 8.75 4.50
Nos. 621-624 (4) 24.75 11.60

Exist imperf. Value set, $27.50.

See No. C286.

1984 Summer Olympics — A100

Gold medalists: 10fr, Jesse Owens, US, track and field, Berlin, 1936. 30fr, Rafer Johnson, US, decathlon, 1960. 35fr, Bob Beamon, US, long jump, 1968. 65fr, Kipchoge Keino, Kenya, 3000-meter steeplechase, 1972.

1984, Aug. 6 *Perf. 13½x13*

625 A100 10fr multi 2.75 .90
626 A100 30fr multi 7.25 2.75
627 A100 35fr multi 8.75 3.00
628 A100 65fr multi 14.50 6.00
Nos. 625-628 (4) 33.25 12.65

Exist imperf. Value set, $32.50.

See No. C287.

Christmas 1984 — A101

Paintings: 10fr, Rest During the Flight into Egypt, by Murillo (1617-1682). 25fr, Virgin and Child, by R. del Garbo. 30fr, Virgin and Child, by Botticelli (1445-1510). 50fr, The Adoration of the Shepherds, by Giacomo da Bassano (1517-1592).

1984, Dec. 15 *Perf. 13½*

629 A101 10fr multi 3.25 1.00
630 A101 25fr multi 7.50 2.50
631 A101 30fr multi 9.00 3.00
632 A101 50fr multi 13.00 4.75
Nos. 629-632,B95-B98 (8) 60.75 22.50

Exist imperf. Value set (8), $65.

See Nos. C288, CB51.

Flowers — A102

1986, July 31 **Photo.** *Perf. 13x13½*

633 A102 2fr Thunbergia .50 .40
634 A102 3fr Saintpaulia .75 .50
635 A102 5fr Clivia 1.25 .75
636 A102 10fr Cassia 3.25 1.60
637 A102 20fr Strelitzia 6.50 4.00
638 A102 35fr Gloriosa 9.75 5.75
Nos. 633-638,C289-C294 (12) 120.00 77.50

For surcharges see Nos. 654A-654B.

Intl. Peace Year — A103

1986, May 1 **Litho.** *Perf. 14*

639 A103 10fr Rockets as housing 1.00 .55
640 A103 20fr Atom as flower 2.00 1.10
641 A103 30fr Handshake 3.25 2.00
642 A103 40fr Globe, chicks 4.75 2.75
a. Souvenir sheet of 4, #639-642 11.50 6.25
Nos. 639-642 (4) 11.00 6.40

No. 642a exists imperf. Value $11.

Great Lake Nations Economic Community (CEPGI), 10th Anniv. — A104

Outline maps of Lake Tanganyika, CEPGI emblem and: 5fr, Aviation. 10fr, Agriculture. 15fr, Industry. 25fr, Electrification. 35fr, Flags of Burundi, Rwanda and Zaire.

1986, May 1 **Photo.** *Perf. 13½x14½*

643 A104 5fr multi 2.75 .50
644 A104 10fr multi 6.50 1.90
645 A104 15fr multi 10.50 2.50
646 A104 25fr multi 14.50 3.75
647 A104 35fr multi 21.00 60.00
a. Souv. sheet, #643-647 + label 70.00 27.50
Nos. 643-647 (5) 55.25 68.65

No. 647a exists imperf. Value $70.

Intl. Year of Shelter for the Homeless A105

1987, June **Litho.** *Perf. 14*

648 A105 10fr Hovel 2.50 .55
649 A105 20fr Drain pipe shelter 4.50 1.25
650 A105 80fr Shoveling sand 10.00 4.50
651 A105 150fr Children, house model 18.00 7.75
a. Souvenir sheet of 4, #648-651 35.00 17.50
Nos. 648-651 (4) 35.00 14.05

Exist imperf. Values: set $35; souvenir sheet $35.

A106

1987(?) **Litho.** *Perf. 14*

652 A106 5fr shown 1.45 .50
653 A106 20fr Skull, lungs 9.00 2.40
654 A106 80fr Cigarette, face 24.00 7.50
Nos. 652-654 (3) 34.45 10.40

WHO Anti-smoking campaign.

Exist imperf. Value set, $35.

Nos. 633-634 Srchd. in Silver and Black

Methods and Perfs As Before

1989

654A A102 20fr on 2fr #633 —
654B A102 20fr on 3fr #634 —

An additional stamp was issued in this set. The editors would like to examine any example.

No. 613 Surcharged

1989 **Photo.** *Perf. 13*

654D A98 80fr on 30fr, pair #e.-f. —

Numbers have been reserved for additional values in this set.

A107

1990 Litho. *Perf. 14*

No.	Type	Description	Unused	Used
655	A107	5fr red lil & multi	1.15	.30
656	A107	10fr blue & multi	1.75	.50
657	A107	20fr gray & multi	3.25	1.25
658	A107	30fr ol grn & multi	5.25	2.25
659	A107	50fr brt blue & multi	7.25	3.25
660	A107	80fr grn bl & multi	11.50	5.50
a.		Souv. sheet of 6, #655-660, perf. 13½	30.00	15.00
		Nos. 655-660 (6)	30.15	13.05

Visit of Pope John Paul II.
No. 660a exists imperf. Value $37.50.

Animals A108

1991, Oct. 4 Litho. *Perf. 14*

No.	Type	Description	Unused	Used
661	A108	5fr Hippopotamus	1.10	.45
662	A108	10fr Chickens	1.40	.75
663	A108	20fr Lion	3.00	2.10
664	A108	30fr Elephant	4.25	2.25
665	A108	50fr Guinea fowl	6.00	3.75
666	A108	80fr Crocodile	12.00	5.25
a.		Souv. sheet of 6, #661-666, perf. 13½	27.50	17.50
		Nos. 661-666 (6)	27.75	14.55

No. 666a exists imperf. Value $30.

Flowers — A108a

1992, June 2 Litho. *Perf. 14*

No.	Type	Description	Unused	Used
666B	A108a	15fr Impatiens petersiana	3.00	.70
666C	A108a	20fr Lachenalia aloides	4.25	1.40
666D	A108a	30fr Nymphaea lotus	6.75	1.75
666E	A108a	50fr Clivia miniata	8.50	3.00
f.		Souvenir sheet of 4, #666B-666E, perf. 13½	22.50	6.50
		Nos. 666B-666E (4)	22.50	6.85

No. 666Ef exists imperf. Value $22.50.

A109

Native Music and Dancing A110

15fr, Native drummer. 30fr, Two dancers. 115fr, Drummers. 200fr, Five dancers.

1992, Apr. 2 Litho. *Perf. 14*

No.	Type	Description	Unused	Used
667	A109	15fr multicolored	1.25	.40
668	A109	30fr multicolored	2.00	.85
669	A110	115fr multicolored	7.75	2.50
670	A110	200fr multicolored	11.50	4.50
a.		Souvenir sheet	22.50	13.50
		Nos. 667-670 (4)	22.50	8.25

No. 670a contains one each of Nos. 667-668, perf. 13x13½, and Nos. 669-670, perf. 13½x13.
No. 670a exists imperf. Value $22.50.

Independence, 30th Anniv. — A111

30fr, 140fr, People with flag. 85fr, 115fr, Natl. flag. 110fr, 200fr, Monument. 120fr, 250fr, Map.

1992, June 30 Litho. *Perf. 15*

No.	Type	Description	Unused	Used
671	A111	30fr multi	.50	.30
672	A111	85fr multi	1.75	1.10
673	A111	110fr multi, vert.	2.00	1.50
674	A111	115fr multi	2.50	1.90
675	A111	120fr multi, vert.	2.75	2.00
676	A111	140fr multi	3.00	2.25
677	A111	200fr multi, vert.	4.25	3.00
678	A111	250fr multi, vert.	5.25	4.25
		Nos. 671-678 (8)	22.00	16.30

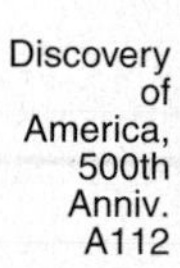

Discovery of America, 500th Anniv. A112

Columbus' fleet, globe and: 200fr, Pre-Columbian artifacts. 400fr, Fruits and vegetables.

1992, Oct. 12 Litho. *Perf. 15*

No.	Type	Description	Unused	Used
679	A112	200fr multicolored	6.50	3.25
680	A112	400fr multicolored	11.00	7.00

Felis Serval A113

1992, Oct. 16

No.	Type	Description	Unused	Used
681	A113	30fr shown	1.10	.50
682	A113	130fr Two seated	5.75	3.25
683	A113	200fr One standing, one lying	8.00	4.25
684	A113	220fr Two faces	10.00	5.50
		Nos. 681-684 (4)	24.85	13.50

World Wildlife Fund.
Each stamp in this set was issued in 1997 with a 50fr surcharge and overprinted 'CAROLOPHILEX 97.' Value, set $120.

Mushrooms A114

Designs: 10fr, Russula ingens. 15fr, Russula brunneorigida. 20fr, Amanita zambiana. 30fr, Russula subfistulosa. 75fr, 85fr, Russula meleagris. 100fr, Russula immaculata. 110fr, like No. 685. 115fr, like No. 686. 120fr, 130fr, Russula sejuncta. 250fr, Afroboletus luteolus.

1992-93 *Perf. 11½x12*

Granite Paper

No.	Type	Description	Unused	Used
685	A114	10fr multicolored	.25	.25
686	A114	15fr multicolored	.40	.25
687	A114	20fr multicolored	.45	.30
688	A114	30fr multicolored	1.00	.90
689	A114	75fr multicolored	2.50	1.90
690	A114	85fr multicolored	3.00	2.50
691	A114	100fr multicolored	4.00	2.75
691A	A114	110fr multicolored	3.50	2.50
691B	A114	115fr multicolored	4.50	3.25
692	A114	120fr multicolored	5.25	3.25
693	A114	130fr multicolored	6.50	3.75
694	A114	250fr multicolored	12.50	7.75
		Nos. 685-694 (12)	43.85	29.35

Issued: 110fr, 115fr, 1993; others, 9/30/92.
For surcharges see Nos. 781-783.

1992 Summer Olympics, Barcelona A115

1992, Nov. 6 *Perf. 15*

No.	Type	Description	Unused	Used
695	A115	130fr Runners	4.00	2.00
696	A115	500fr Hurdler	13.50	8.50

A116

A116a

Christmas (Details of Adoration of the Kings, by Gentile da Fabriano): a, 100fr, Crowd, horses. b, 130fr, Kings. c, 250fr, Nativity scene.

1992, Dec. 7 Litho. *Perf. 11½*

No.	Type	Description	Unused	Used
697	A116	Strip of 3, #a.-c.	11.50	5.00
d.		Souvenir sheet of 3, #697a-697c	11.50	5.50

Nos. 697a-697c have white border. No. 697d has continuous design and sold for 580fr.

1992, Dec. 5 Litho. *Perf. 15*

Designs: 200fr, Emblems. 220fr, Profile of person made from fruits and vegetables.

No.	Type	Description	Unused	Used
697E	A116a	200fr multicolored	8.50	4.00
697F	A116a	220fr multicolored	10.00	5.25

Intl. Conference on Nutrition, Rome.

European Common Market A117

Designs: 130fr, Flags, stars. 500fr, Europe, Africa, clasped hands, stars.

1993, Mar. 29 Litho. *Perf. 15*

No.	Type	Description	Unused	Used
698	A117	130fr multicolored	3.00	1.50
699	A117	500fr multicolored	11.50	7.50

1994 World Cup Soccer Championships, US — A118

Players, stadium, US flag and: 130fr, Statue of Liberty. 200fr, Golden Gate Bridge.

1993, July 5 Litho. *Perf. 15*

No.	Type	Description	Unused	Used
700	A118	130fr multicolored	5.50	2.50
701	A118	200fr multicolored	7.00	3.50

Traditional Musical Instruments — A119

1993, Apr. 30 Litho. *Perf. 15*

No.	Type	Description	Unused	Used
702	A119	200fr Indonongo	3.50	3.25
703	A119	220fr Ingoma	4.00	3.50
704	A119	250fr Ikembe	4.50	3.75
705	A119	300fr Umuduri	5.25	4.50
		Nos. 702-705 (4)	17.25	15.00

A120

A121

1993, June 4 Litho. *Perf. 11½*

No.	Type	Description	Unused	Used
706	A120	130fr Papilio bromius	3.50	3.00
707	A120	200fr Charaxes eupale	5.25	4.50
708	A120	250fr Cymothoe caenis	6.75	6.25
709	A120	300fr Graphium ridleyanus	7.50	6.25
a.		Souvenir sheet of 4, #706-709	25.00	25.00
		Nos. 706-709 (4)	23.00	20.00

No. 709a sold for 980fr.

1993, Dec. 9 *Perf. 14*

No.	Type	Description	Unused	Used
710	A121	100fr Cattle	2.10	1.75
711	A121	120fr Sheep	2.50	2.40
712	A121	130fr Pigs	3.00	2.50
713	A121	250fr Goats	5.00	4.25
		Nos. 710-713 (4)	12.60	10.90

Christmas — A122

Natives adoring Christ Child: a, 100fr, Woman carrying baby, two people kneeling. b, 130fr, With Christ Child. 250fr, c, Woman carrying baby, three other people.

1993, Dec. 10 *Perf. 11½*

No.	Type	Description	Unused	Used
714	A122	Strip of 3, #a.-c.	12.00	12.00
d.		Souvenir sheet of 3, #714a-714c	12.00	12.00

Nos. 714a-714c have white border. No. 714d has continuous design and sold for 580fr.

Rock Stars — A123

1994 Litho. *Perf. 15*

No.	Type	Description	Unused	Used
715	A123	60fr Elvis Presley	2.00	1.75
716	A123	115fr Mick Jagger	4.00	3.50
717	A123	120fr John Lennon	4.00	3.50
718	A123	200fr Michael Jackson	7.25	6.50
a.		Souvenir sheet, #715-718	17.50	16.00
		Nos. 715-718 (4)	17.25	15.25

No. 718a sold for 600fr.

A124

1994, Oct. 10 Litho. *Perf. 15*
719 A124 150fr multicolored 9.00 6.00

Intl. Olympic Committee, cent.

A125

Christmas (Madonna and Child): a, 115fr, Chinese. b, 120fr, Japanese. c, 250fr, Polish.

1994, Dec. 14 Photo. *Perf. 15*
720 A125 Strip of 3, #a.-c. 12.50 12.50
d. Souvenir sheet of 1, #720c 9.00 9.00

A126 A127

115fr, FAO, 50th anniv. 120fr, UN, 50th anniv.

1995, Feb. 21 Litho. *Perf. 11½*
721 A126 115fr multicolored 3.00 3.00
722 A126 120fr multicolored 3.00 3.00

1995 Litho. *Perf. 11½*

Flowers: 15fr, Cassia didymobotrya. 20fr, Mitragyna rubrostipulosa. 30fr, Phytolacca dodecandra. 85fr, Acanthus pubescens. 100fr, Bulbophyllum comatum. 110fr, Angraecum evradianum. 115fr, Eulophia burundiensis. 120fr, Habenaria adolphii.

Granite Paper

723 A127 15fr multicolored .25 .25
724 A127 20fr multicolored .45 .25
725 A127 30fr multicolored .85 .45
726 A127 85fr multicolored 2.00 1.40
727 A127 100fr multicolored 2.50 1.60
728 A127 110fr multicolored 2.75 2.10
729 A127 115fr multicolored 3.50 2.75
730 A127 120fr multicolored 4.25 3.25
Nos. 723-730 (8) 16.55 12.05

Transportation Methods — A128

30fr, Otraco bus. 115fr, Transintra semi truck. 120fr, Arnolac tugboat. 250fr, Air Burundi airplane.

1995, Nov. 16 Litho. *Perf. 11½*
731 A128 30fr multicolored .50 .35
732 A128 115fr multicolored 2.10 1.60
733 A128 120fr multicolored 2.40 1.90
734 A128 250fr multicolored 5.00 4.25
Nos. 731-734 (4) 10.00 8.10

A129

Christmas (African sculpture): a, 100fr, Boy with panga, basket on head. b, 130fr, Boy carrying sheaf of wheat. c, 250fr, Mother, children.

1995, Dec. 26 Litho. *Perf. 11½x12*
735 A129 Strip of 3, #a.-c. 10.00 10.00
d. Souvenir sheet of 3, #735a-735c 11.00 11.00

A130

Athlete, national flag: 130fr, Venuste Niyongabo. 500fr, Arthemon Hatungimana.

1996, June 28 Litho. *Perf. 14*
736 A130 130fr multicolored 3.00 2.75
737 A130 500fr multicolored 9.50 8.50

1996 Summer Olympic Games, Atlanta.

Birds A131

Designs: 15fr, Hagedashia hagedash. 20fr, Alopochen aegyptiacus. 30fr, Haliaeetus vocifer. 120fr, Ardea goliath. 165fr, Balearica regulorum. 220fr, Actophilornis africana.

1996 Litho. *Perf. 14*
740 A131 15fr multicolored .40 .40
741 A131 20fr multicolored .55 .55
742 A131 30fr multicolored .65 .65
743 A131 120fr multicolored 2.00 2.00
744 A131 165fr multicolored 4.00 4.00
745 A131 220fr multicolored 5.50 5.50
Nos. 740-745 (6) 13.10 13.10

Fish of Lake Tanganyika A132

Designs: 30fr, Julidochromis malieri. 115fr, Cyphotilapia frontosa. 120fr, Lamprologus brichardi. 250fr, Synodonis petricola.

1996, June 4 Litho. *Perf. 11¾x11½*
746 A132 30fr multicolored .65 .55
747 A132 115fr multicolored 2.10 2.00
748 A132 120fr multicolored 2.50 2.10
749 A132 250fr multicolored 4.50 4.50
a. Souv. sheet, #746-749, perf 11¾ 11.00 11.00
Nos. 746-749 (4) 9.75 9.15

No. 749a sold for 615fr.

Although ostensibly issued in 1996, this set was not available in the philatelic marketplace until 1999.

SOS Children's Village, 50th Anniv. A133

100fr, Children in Village. 250fr, Children, flags. 270fr, Children around flagpole.

1998, Dec. 26 Litho. *Perf. 14*
750 A133 100fr multicolored 1.00 1.00
751 A133 250fr multicolored 2.40 2.40
752 A133 270fr multicolored 2.50 2.50
Nos. 750-752 (3) 5.90 5.90

Christmas — A134

Various paintings of Madonna and Child.

1999, Jan. 19 *Perf. 11¾*

Frame color

753 A134 100fr green 1.40 1.40
754 A134 130fr yellow brown 2.00 2.00
755 A134 250fr rose 3.50 3.50
a. Souvenir sheet of 3, #753-755 9.00 9.00
Nos. 753-755 (3) 6.90 6.90

Nos. 753-755 are dated "1996," "1997," and "1998," respectively.

No. 755a sold for 580fr.

Diana, Princess of Wales (1961-97) A135

Denominations: a, 100fr. b, 250fr. c, 300fr.

1999, Sept. 30 *Perf. 13¾*
756 A135 Sheet of 6, 2 each #a.-c. 12.00 12.00

Fight Against Hunger — A136

2000, Feb. 28 Litho. *Perf. 14*
757 A136 350fr Danny Kaye 2.50 2.50

Issued in sheets of 5.

Second Republic, 10th Anniv. (in 1986) — A136a

Designs: 70fr, Coffee pickers, statue. 80fr, Pres. Jean-Baptiste Bagaza, arms of Burundi.

2000 ? Photo. *Perf. 13¾x14*
757C A136a 70fr multi —
757D A136a 80fr multi —

Two additional stamps were issued in this set. The editors would like to examine any examples.

Space — A137

No. 758, horiz.: a, Space plane (2003). b, Reuseable space plane. c, Future space ship. d, Galileo. e, Space telescope. f, Space platform. g, Satellite launched Feb. 17, 1996. h, Cassini. i, Solar probe. j, Vehicle without fenders. k, Vehicle with fenders. l, Spacecraft for Mars.

2000, July 24 Litho. *Perf. 14*
758 A137 165fr Sheet of 12, #a-l 20.00 20.00

Souvenir Sheet

759 A137 1500fr Newton's telescope 20.00 20.00

Flowers — A138

Design: 150fr, Dodecatheon. 200fr, Fremonto dendron. 250fr, Rudbeckia laciniata. 350fr, Helianthus amnus. 400fr, Lilium longiflorum.

2002, Apr. 4 Litho. *Perf. 13x12¾*
760 A138 150fr multi —
761 A138 200fr multi —
762 A138 250fr multi —
764 A138 350fr multi —
765 A138 400fr multi — —

One additional stamp was issued in this set. The editors would like to examine any examples.

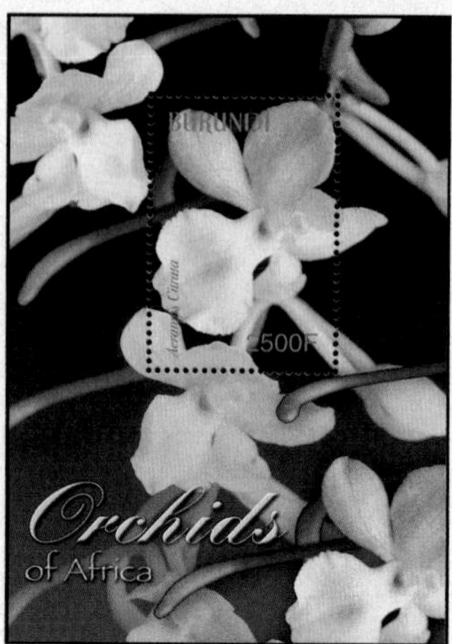

Orchids, Mushrooms, Birds and Butterflies — A139

No. 766, 650fr — Orchids: a, Angraceum eburnum. b, Disa cardinalis. c, Bulbophyllum guttulatum. d, Aerangis luteoalba. e, Disa diores. f, Disa kirstenbosch.

No. 767, 650fr, horiz. — Mushrooms: a, Stropharia aerugurosa. b, Inocybe rimosa. c, Cortinarius alboviolaceus. d, Hypholoma fasciculare. e, Cortinarius purpurascens. f, Hebeloma crustuliniforme.

No. 768, 650fr — Birds: a, Phalacrocorax carbo. b, Threskiornis aethiopicus. c, Nycticorax nycticorax. d, Phoeniconaias minor. e, Balaeniceps rex. f, Balearica regulorum.

No. 769, 650fr, horiz. — Butterflies: a, Papilio antenor. b, Graphium policenes. c, Papilio bromius. d, Graphium ridleyanus. e, Euritydes xanticles. f, Papilio gallienus.

No. 770, 2500fr, Aerangis citrata. No. 771, 2500fr, Coprinus picaceus. No. 772, 2500fr, Dendrocygna viduata. No. 773, 2500fr, Papilio dardanus, horiz.

2004, Nov. 8 Litho. *Perf. 14*

Sheets of 6, #a-f

766-769 A139 Set of 4 45.00 45.00

Souvenir Sheets

770-773 A139 Set of 4 30.00 30.00

Worldwide Fund for Nature (WWF) — A140

No. 774 — Sitatunga: a, Pair, both without horns. b, One, with horns. c, One, without horns. d, Pair, one with horns.

2004, Nov. 8 *Perf. 13¼*

774 A140 500fr Block or strip of 4, #a-d 13.00 13.00

e. Sheet, 2 each #774a-774d 25.00 25.00

Frames vary.

No. 774e exists imperf. Value $90.

Tourism A141

Designs: 150fr, Source of the Nile River (Luvironza River). 250fr, Monument to Burton and Speke, Nyanza. 500fr, Shanga Waterfall, Karera. 1000fr, Monument to Stanley and Livingstone, Mugere.

2007, May 8 Litho. *Perf. 13x13½*

775-778 A141 Set of 4 *15.00 15.00*

24th UPU Congress A142

2007, Oct. 16 Litho. *Perf. 13x13½*

779 A142 730fr multi 7.00 7.00

780 A142 730fr +20fr multi 8.00 8.00

The 24th UPU Congress was moved to Geneva from Nairobi because of political unrest.

No. 692 Surcharged in White and Black

Methods and Perfs As Before

2007

781 A114 1200fr on 120fr #692 12.00 12.00

782 A114 1300fr on 120fr #692 13.00 13.00

783 A114 2500fr on 120fr #692 25.00 25.00

Nos. 781-783 (3) 50.00 50.00

2008 Summer Olympics, Beijing — A144

2008, Aug. 1 Litho. *Perf. 13½x13*

787 A144 500fr multi *6.00 6.00*

Flowers and Birds A145

Designs: 90fr, Erythrina flowers. 150fr, Maracuja flower. 500fr, Werner flowers, vert. 810fr, Heron, vert. 1000fr, Aigle royal (golden eagle), vert.

2008, Dec. 24 *Perf. 13x13½, 13½x13*

788-792 A145 Set of 5 *25.00 25.00*

Birds A146

Designs: 290fr, Hieraaetus spilogaster. 295fr, Falco eleonorae. 505fr, Falco subbuteo. 515fr, Falco biarmicus. 555fr, Bubo africanus. 590fr, Milvus migrans aegyptius. 710fr, Haliaeetus vocifer. 730fr, Trigonoceps occipitalis. 810fr, Gypohierax angolensis.

2009, July 6 Litho. *Perf. 13x13½*

Granite Paper

793-801 A146 Set of 9 *50.00 50.00*

801a Sheet of 9, #793-801 *50.00 50.00*

Owls — A147

Various owls: 860fr, 1010fr, 1030fr, 1100fr.

2009, July 8 *Perf. 13½x13*

Granite Paper

802-805 A147 Set of 4 45.00 45.00

805a Souvenir sheet of 4, #802-805 *45.00 45.00*

A148

A149

A150

A151

A152

A153

A154

A155

Butterflies A156

2009, July 13 *Perf. 13x13½*

Granite Paper

806 A148 500fr multi *4.00 4.00*

807 A149 500fr multi *4.00 4.00*

808 A150 500fr multi *4.00 4.00*

809 A151 500fr multi *4.00 4.00*

810 A152 500fr multi *4.00 4.00*

811 A153 500fr multi *4.00 4.00*

812 A154 500fr multi *4.00 4.00*

813 A155 500fr multi *4.00 4.00*

814 A156 500fr multi *4.00 4.00*

a. Sheet of 9, #806-814 *40.00 40.00*

Nos. 806-814 (9) *36.00 36.00*

Miniature Sheet

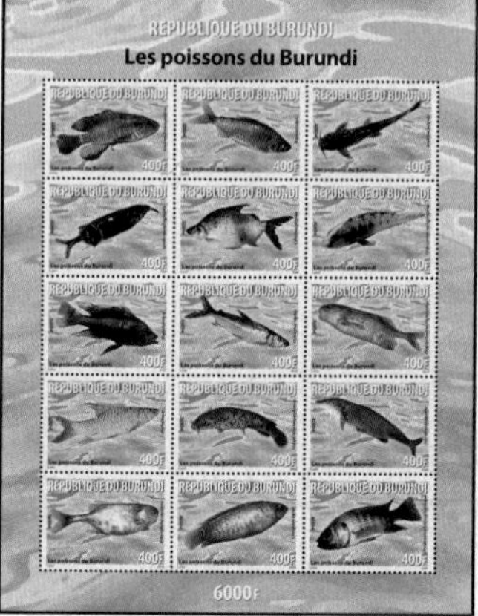

Fish — A157

No. 815: a, Astatoreochromis straeleni. b, Brycinus imberi. c, Amphilius jacksonii. d, Gnathonemus longibarbis. e, Citharinus gibbosus. f, Orthochromis malagaraziensis. g, Hapiochromis sp. h, Hydrocynus vittatus. i, Hippopotamyrus dischorhynchus. j, Labeobarbus sp. k, Malapterurus tanganyikaensis. l, Mormyrus longirostris. m, Petrocephalus catastoma. n, Ctenopoma muriei. o, Oreochromis niloticus eduardianus.

2009, Aug. 1

Granite Paper

815 A157 400fr Sheet of 15, #a-o *50.00 50.00*

Miniature Sheet

Traditional Hairstyles — A158

No. 816: a, Close-up of bearded man. b, Man with neckerchief and bag with letter "A." c, Bearded man, hand holding stick in background. d, Man with back of head shaved, with pipe in mouth, facing right. e, Man wearing patterned neckerchief with pipe in mouth, facing right. f, Man with necklace and bracelet.

2010, Jan. 1 *Perf. 13¾x13¼*

816 A158 500fr Sheet of 6, #a-f *18.00 18.00*

Souvenir Sheet

Traditional Houses — A159

No. 817: a, Family and house. b, House.

2010, Jan. 1 ***Perf. 13¼x13¾***
817 A159 500fr Sheet of 2, #a-b *6.50 6.50*

Miniature Sheet

Art and Culture — A160

No. 818: a, Dancers. b, Busts. c, Two women, spears, sculpture, flowers. d, Woman with bowls and containers. e, Large decorated pot. f, Man with stick and pot. g, Woman with head on hand, vert. h, Sculptures. i, Woman with necklace and headcovering, vert.

Perf. 13x13½, 13½x13 (#818g, 818i)
2010, June 1
Granite Paper
818 A160 500fr Sheet of 9, #a-i *24.00 24.00*

Pan-African Postal Union, 30th anniv.

Primates A161

Designs: 730fr, Chimpanzee. 1000fr, Baboons. 2500, Gorillas.

2011, Mar. 15 ***Perf. 13x13¼***
819-821 A161 Set of 3 *20.00 20.00*
821a Souvenir sheet of 3, #819-821 *20.00 20.00*

Animals A162

Hippopotamus amphibius: 1000fr, Three animals. 1020fr, Three animals, diff. No. 824, 3000fr, Three animals with open mouths. No. 825, 3000fr, Two animals.
No. 826: a, 1090fr, One animal facing right. b, 1090fr, One animal facing left. c, 3000fr, One animal facing forward. d, 3000fr, One animal facing left.

2011, Dec. 1 ***Perf. 13x13½***
822-825 A162 Set of 4 15.00 15.00
Miniature Sheet
Perf. 13½
826 A162 Sheet of 4, #a-d 15.00 15.00

Primates

Designs: 1020fr, Pan troglodytes. No. 828, 1090fr, Papio anubis. No. 829, 3000fr, Two Colobus angolensis. No. 830, 3000fr, Two Chlorocebus pygerythrus.
No. 831: a, 1090fr, Two Chlorocebus pygerythrus, diff. b, 1090fr, Pan troglodytes, diff. c, 3000fr, Papio anubis, diff. d, 3000fr, Adult, juvenile and head of Colobus angolensis.

Perf. 13x13½
827-830 A162 Set of 4 15.00 15.00
Miniature Sheet
Perf. 13½
831 A162 Sheet of 4, #a-d 15.00 15.00

Rhinoceroses

Designs: No. 832, 1090fr, Diceros bicornis. No. 833, 1090fr, Ceratotherium simum. No. 834, 3000fr, Diceros bicornis facing right. No. 835, 3000fr, Ceratotherium simum facing left.
No. 836: a, 1020fr, Ceratotherium simum, diff. b, 1120fr, Diceros bicornis, diff. c, 3000fr, Adult and juvenile Ceratotherium simum. d, 3000fr, Diceros bicornis facing left.

832-835 A162 Set of 4 15.00 15.00
Miniature Sheet
Perf. 13½
836 A162 Sheet of 4, #a-d 15.00 15.00

Bats

Designs: No. 837, 1020fr, Epomops franqueti. No. 838, 1020fr, Nyctalus noctula. No. 839, 3000fr, Desmodus rotundus. No. 840, 3000fr, Plecotus austriacus, name at LR.
No. 841: a, 1000fr, Nyctalus noctula, diff. b, 1120fr, Rhinolophus hipposideros. c, 3000fr, Plecotus austriacus, name at UL. d, 3000fr, Nyctophilus corbeni.

Perf. 13x13½
837-840 A162 Set of 4 15.00 15.00
Miniature Sheet
Perf. 13½
841 A162 Sheet of 4, #a-d 15.00 15.00

Cats

Designs: 1000fr, Acinonyx jubatus. No. 843, 1090fr, Leptailurus serval. No. 844, 3000fr, Panthera pardus facing left. No. 845, 3000fr, Panthera leo.
No. 846: a, 1020fr, Acinonyx jubatus, diff. b, 1090fr, Panthera leo, diff. c, 3000fr, Felis silvestris. d, 3000fr, Panthera pardus facing right.

Perf. 13x13½
842-845 A162 Set of 4 15.00 15.00
Miniature Sheet
Perf. 13½
846 A162 Sheet of 4, #a-d 15.00 15.00

Elephants

Loxodonta afrciana: No. 847, 1000fr, Adult and juvenile. 1120fr, Adult facing right. No. 849, 3000fr, Adult facing left, animal name at UR. No. 850, 3000fr, Adult and juvenile, diff.
No. 851: a, 1000fr, Adult, animal name at left. b, 1000fr, Adult, animal name at UR. c, 3000fr, Adult facing right, animal name at LR. d, 3000fr, Adult facing left, animal name at LL.

Perf. 13x13½
847-850 A162 Set of 4 15.00 15.00
Miniature Sheet
Perf. 13½
851 A162 Sheet of 4, #a-d 15.00 15.00

Dolphins

Designs: No. 852, 1020fr, Lagenorhynchus albirostris. 1090fr, Grampus griseus. No. 854, 3000fr, Delphinus delphis. No. 855, 3000fr, Lagenorhynchus cruciger.
No. 856: a, 1000fr, Tursiops truncatus. b, 1020fr, Stenella attenuata. c, 3000fr, Stenella longirostris. d, 3000fr, Stenella frontalis.

Perf. 13x13½
852-855 A162 Set of 4 15.00 15.00
Miniature Sheet
Perf. 13½
856 A162 Sheet of 4, #a-d 15.00 15.00

Whales

Designs: No. 857, 1020fr, Balaenoptera musculus. No. 858, 1020fr, Balaenoptera physalus. No. 859, 3000fr, Orcinus orca. No. 860, 3000fr, Eschrichtius robustus.
No. 861: a, 1000fr, Eschrichtius robustus, diff. b, 1000fr, Balaenoptera musculus, diff. c, 3000fr, Megaptera novaeangliae. d, 3000fr, Delphinopterus leucas.

Perf. 13x13½
857-860 A162 Set of 4 15.00 15.00
Miniature Sheet
Perf. 13½
861 A162 Sheet of 4, #a-d 15.00 15.00

Birds of Prey

Designs: 1000fr, Gypohierax angolensis. No. 863, 1090fr, Pandion haliaetus. No. 864, 3000fr, Torgos tracheliotos. No. 865, 3000fr, Aquila wahlbergi.
No. 866: a, 1020fr, Lophaetus occiptialis. b, 1090fr, Necrosyrtes monachus. c, 3000fr, Falco tinnunculus. d, 3000fr, Polemaetus bellicosus.

Perf. 13x13½
862-865 A162 Set of 4 15.00 15.00
Miniature Sheet
Perf. 13½
866 A162 Sheet of 4, #a-d 15.00 15.00

Birds

Designs: 1000fr, Pelecanus onocrotalus. 1090fr, Phalacrocorax carbo. No. 869, 3000fr, Podiceps cristatus. No. 870, 3000fr, Mycteria ibis.
No. 871: a, 1020fr, Microcarbo africanus. b, 1020fr, Nettapus auritus. c, 3000fr, Phoenicopterus minor. d, 3000fr, Balaeniceps rex.

Perf. 13x13½
867-870 A162 Set of 4 15.00 15.00
Miniature Sheet
Perf. 13½
871 A162 Sheet of 4, #a-d 15.00 15.00

Parrots

Designs: No. 872, 1000fr, Agapornis fischeri. No. 873, 1000fr, Poicephalus meyeri. No. 874, 3000fr, Psittacus erithacus, name at UL. No. 875, 3000fr, Poicephalus robustus, name at right.
No. 876: a, 1000fr, Agapornis pullarius. b, 1090fr, Agapornis fischeri, diff. c, 3000fr, Poicephalus robustus, name at left. d, 3000fr, Psittacus erithacus, name at right.

Perf. 13x13½
872-875 A162 Set of 4 15.00 15.00
Miniature Sheet
Perf. 13½
876 A162 Sheet of 4, #a-d 15.00 15.00

Owls

Designs: No. 877, 1090fr, Tyto alba. No. 878, 1090fr, Tyto capensis. No. 879, 3000fr, Asio capensis, name at top. No. 880, 3000fr, Bubo africanus.
No. 881: a, 1020fr, Tyto capensis, diff. b, 1090fr, Bubo africanus, diff. c, 3000fr, Asio capensis, name at LR. d, 3000fr, Otus scops.

Perf. 13x13½
877-880 A162 Set of 4 15.00 15.00
Miniature Sheet
Perf. 13½
881 A162 Sheet of 4, #a-d 15.00 15.00

Bees

Designs: 1000fr, Bombus mixtus. 1090fr, Xylocopa virginica. No. 884, 3000fr, Bombus lapidarius. No. 885, 3000fr, Thyreus nitidulus.
No. 886: a, 1020fr, Osmia ribifloris. b, 1020fr, Apis mellifera. c, 3000fr, Anthidium florentinum. d, 3000fr, Apis mellifera scutellata.

Perf. 13x13½
882-885 A162 Set of 4 15.00 15.00
Miniature Sheet
Perf. 13½
886 A162 Sheet of 4, #a-d 15.00 15.00

Butterflies

Designs: 1090fr, Papilio torquatus. No. 888, 1120fr, Boloria dia. No. 889, 3000fr, Lasiommata megera. No. 890, 3000fr, Papilio menatius.
No. 891: a, 1020fr, Salamis temora. b, 1120fr, Charaxes castor. c, 3000fr, Acraea acrita. d, 3000fr, Papilio demodocus.

Perf. 13x13½
887-890 A162 Set of 4 15.00 15.00
Miniature Sheet
Perf. 13½
891 A162 Sheet of 4, #a-d 15.00 15.00

Fish and Marine Life

Designs: No. 892, 1000fr, Rhinobatos lentiginosus. 1090fr, Anoplogaster cornuta. No. 894, 3000fr, Stegostoma fasciatum. No. 895, 3000fr, Ocypode quadrata.
No. 896: a, 1000fr, Carcharhinus limbatus. b, 1020fr, Myliobatis californica. c, 3000fr, Hippocampus ingens. d, 3000fr, Mola mola.

Perf. 13x13½
892-895 A162 Set of 4 15.00 15.00
Miniature Sheet
Perf. 13½
896 A162 Sheet of 4, #a-d 15.00 15.00

Turtles

Designs: No. 897, 1020fr, Pelusios sinuatus. 1120fr, Stigmochelys pardalis. No. 899, 3000fr, Pelusios subniger. No. 900, 3000fr, Pelomedusa subrufa, name at UL.
No. 901: a, 1000fr, Stigmochelys pardalis, diff. b, 1020fr, Pelusios subniger, diff. c, 3000fr, Pelomedusa subrufa, name at UR. d, 3000fr, Pelusios sinuatus, diff.

Perf. 13x13½
897-900 A162 Set of 4 15.00 15.00
Miniature Sheet
Perf. 13½
901 A162 Sheet of 4, #a-d 15.00 15.00

Frogs

Designs: 1020fr, Leptopelis kivuensis. 1090fr, Hyperolius discodactylus. No. 904, 3000fr, Phrynobatrachus versicolor. No. 905, 3000fr, Hyperolius castaneus.
No. 906: a, 1000fr, Hyperolius viridiflavus. b, 1120fr, Bubbling kassina. c, 3000fr, Common plantannia. d, 3000fr, Hyperolius marmoratus.

Perf. 13x13½
902-905 A162 Set of 4 15.00 15.00
Miniature Sheet
Perf. 13½
906 A162 Sheet of 4, #a-d 15.00 15.00

Prehistoric Crocodiles

Designs: No. 907, 1020fr, Shansisuchus. 1090fr, Desmatosuchus. No. 909, 3000fr, Luperosuchus. No. 910, 3000fr, Araripesuchus.
No. 911: a, 1020fr, Baurusuchus. b, 1120fr, Champsosaurus. c, 3000fr, Dokosaursus. d, 3000fr, Geosaurus.

Perf. 13x13½
907-910 A162 Set of 4 15.00 15.00
Miniature Sheet
Perf. 13½
911 A162 Sheet of 4, #a-d 15.00 15.00

Dinosaurs

Designs: No. 912, 1090fr, Giganotosaurus. No. 913, 1090fr, Ankylosaurus. No. 914, 3000fr, Temnodontosaurus. No. 915, 3000fr, Triceratops.
No. 916: a, 1000fr, Stegosaurus. b, 1120fr, Pterosaur. c, 3000fr, Chasmatosaursus. d, 3000fr, Scutosaurus.

Perf. 13x13½
912-915 A162 Set of 4 15.00 15.00
Miniature Sheet
Perf. 13½
916 A162 Sheet of 4, #a-d 15.00 15.00

1120F
POSTE 2011
Laniarius mufumbiri
WWF
République du BURUNDI

Worldwide Fund for Nature (WWF) A163

Laniarius mufumbiri: No. 917, 1120fr, Three birds. No. 918, 1120fr, One bird facing right. No. 919, 3000fr, One bird, facing left. No. 920, 3000fr, Two birds.

2011, Dec. 1 ***Perf. 13x13½***
917-920 A163 Set of 4 15.00 15.00
920a Souvenir sheet of 4, #917-920, perf. 13½ 15.00 15.00

Organizations, People and Events — A164

Scouting: No. 921, 1020fr, Six Scouts, purple emblem at LR. No. 922, 1020fr, Five scouts hunting and examining butterflies, green emblem at UR. No. 923, 3000fr, Scouts starting fire, green emblem at LR. No. 924, 3000fr, Kenyan Scouts, purple emblem at UL.

No. 925: a, 1000fr, Lord Robert Baden-Powell, scouts on rope bridge. b, 1090fr, Scout saluting, Scouts cooking, purple emblem at UL. c, 1090fr, Scouts around pile of sticks for campfire, green emblem at LR. d, 3000fr, Scout examining flower, Scouts in tower, purple emblem at LR.

2011, Dec. 30 Litho. *Perf. 13x13½*

921-924 A164 Set of 4 15.00 15.00

Miniature Sheet

Perf. 13½

925 A164 Sheet of 4, #a-d 15.00 15.00

Humanitarian Organizations

Designs: No. 926, 1020fr, International Red Cross emblem, relief efforts in Obo, Central African Republic. No. 927, 1020fr, Rotary International emblem, Rotary recruitment, Méru, Kenya. No. 928, 3000fr, Lions International emblem, planting of trees in China. No. 929, 3000fr, UNICEF emblem, relief efforts to Pakistan flood victims.

No. 930: a, 1020fr, Lions International emblem, food distribution to Philippine typhoon victims. b, 1120fr, UNICEF emblem, Vietnamese school children. c, 3000fr, International Red Cross emblem, first aid, Rio de Janeiro. d, 3000fr, Rotary International emblem, Saint Jude School, Tanzania.

Perf. 13x13½

926-929 A164 Set of 4 15.00 15.00

Miniature Sheet

Perf. 13½

930 A164 Sheet of 4, #a-d 15.00 15.00

Pope John Paul II

Pope John Paul II and: 1000fr, Sisters Marie Simon Pierre and Tobianna carrying relics of Pope John Paul II. 1020fr, Crowd holding banners. No. 933, 3000fr, Pope Benedict XVI holding infant. No. 929, 3000fr, Beatification ceremony for Pope John Paul II.

No. 935 — Pope John Paul II and: a, 1090fr, Pope Benedict XVI blessing crowd. b, 1090fr, Crowd holding banners, diff. c, 3000fr, Crowd holding banners and United States flag. d, 3000fr, Pope John Paul II waving to crowd.

Perf. 13x13½

931-934 A164 Set of 4 15.00 15.00

Miniature Sheet

Perf. 13½

935 A164 Sheet of 4, #a-d 15.00 15.00

Pope Benedict XVI

Pope Benedict XVI and works by Michelangelo: 1000fr, Ezekiel. 1120fr, Christ Carrying the Cross. No. 938, 3000fr, Zacharias. No. 939, 3000fr, Delphic Sybil.

No. 940 — Pope Benedict and works by Michelangelo: a, 1090fr, Libyan Sibyl. b, 1090fr, Joel. c, 3000fr, Creation of the Earth, Moon and Planets. d, 3000fr, Last Judgment.

Perf. 13x13½

936-939 A164 Set of 4 15.00 15.00

Miniature Sheet

Perf. 13½

940 A164 Sheet of 4, #a-d 15.00 15.00

Pierre-Auguste Renoir

Renoir and his works: No. 941, 1000fr, The Laundrywoman, 1891. No. 942, 1000fr, The Seine at Asnières, 1897. No. 943, 3000fr, Coucher de Soleil sur la Mer, 1879. No. 944, 3000fr, The Children of Monsieur Caillebotte, 1895.

No. 945 — Renoir and his works: a, 1000fr, Children on a Guernsey Beach, 1883. b, 1020fr, Oarsmen at Chatou, 1879. c, 1090fr, La Grenouillère, 1869. d, 3000fr, Luncheon of the Boating Party, 1880-81.

Perf. 13x13½

941-944 A164 Set of 4 15.00 15.00

Miniature Sheet

Perf. 13½

945 A164 Sheet of 4, #a-d 15.00 15.00

Pablo Picasso

Picasso and his works: No. 946, 1090fr, Child with a Dove, 1901. No. 947, 1090fr, Lecture, 1932. No. 948, 3000fr, Mother and Child, 1905. No. 949, 3000fr, Seated Woman in a Garden, 1938.

No. 950 — Picasso and his works: a, 1090fr, Guitar (I Love Eva), 1912. b, 1120fr, Head of a Woman, 1960. c, 3000fr, Jacqueline with Flowers, 1954. d, 3000fr, At the Lapin Agile, 1905.

Perf. 13x13½

946-949 A164 Set of 4 15.00 15.00

Miniature Sheet

Perf. 13½

950 A164 Sheet of 4, #a-d 15.00 15.00

Film Actors and Actresses

Designs: No. 951, 1000fr, James Dean. 1090fr, Marlene Dietrich. No. 953, 3000fr, Grace Kelly. No. 954, 3000fr, Clark Gable.

No. 955: a, 1000fr, John Wayne. b, 1120fr, Elizabeth Taylor. c, 3000fr, Romy Schneider. d, 3000fr, Marlon Brando.

Perf. 13x13½

951-954 A164 Set of 4 15.00 15.00

Miniature Sheet

Perf. 13½

955 A164 Sheet of 4, #a-d 15.00 15.00

Marilyn Monroe

Monroe: No. 956, 1020fr, With legs crossed. No. 957, 1020fr, With arms extended and leg raised. No. 958, 3000fr, With child on lap. No. 959, 3000fr, Holding drink.

No. 960: a, 1000fr, Seated, wearing gown . b, 1120fr, Seated on pilings, wearing bathing suit. c, 3000fr, Playing guitar. d, 3000fr, With skirt blowing up.

Perf. 13x13½

956-959 A164 Set of 4 15.00 15.00

Miniature Sheet

Perf. 13½

960 A164 Sheet of 4, #a-d 15.00 15.00

Elvis Presley

Presley: No. 961, 1090fr, Holding microphone, denomination at UL. No. 962, 1090fr, No microphone, denomination at UR. No. 963, 3000fr, Two images, microphone on stand, denomination at UR. No. 964, 3000fr, Two images, holding microphone, denomination at UR.

No. 965 — Presley: a, 1020fr, No microphone. b, 1120fr, Holding microphone. c, 3000fr, Three images, holding microphone, denomination at UR. d, 3000fr, Three images, no microphone, denomination at UL.

Perf. 13x13½

961-964 A164 Set of 4 15.00 15.00

Miniature Sheet

Perf. 13½

965 A164 Sheet of 4, #a-d 15.00 15.00

Singers

Designs: No. 966, 1090fr, Jimi Hendrix. No. 967, 1090fr, Paul McCartney. No. 968, 3000fr, Mick Jagger. No. 969, 3000fr, Ray Charles.

No. 970: a, 1020fr, Bob Marley. b, 1090fr, Tina Turner. c, 3000fr, Fats Domino. d, 3000fr, Stevie Wonder.

Perf. 13x13½

966-969 A164 Set of 4 15.00 15.00

Miniature Sheet

Perf. 13½

970 A164 Sheet of 4, #a-d 15.00 15.00

Composers

Designs: No. 971, 1000fr, Wolfgang Amadeus Mozart and memorial to Mozart, Vienna. 1090fr, Ludwig van Beethoven and Beethoven Monument, Bonn. No. 973, 3000fr, Antonio Vivaldi, and St. John the Baptist Church, Venice. No. 974, 3000fr, Frédéric Chopin, violin and bow.

No. 975: a, 1000fr, Mozart and keyboard. b, 1020fr, Beethoven and pipe organ. c, 3000fr, Vivaldi holding violin, churches. d, 3000fr, Chopin and piano.

Perf. 13x13½

971-974 A164 Set of 4 15.00 15.00

Miniature Sheet

Perf. 13½

975 A164 Sheet of 4, #a-d 15.00 15.00

Table Tennis Players

Designs: 1000fr, Wang Hao. 1120fr, Zhang Yining. No. 978, 3000fr, Guo Yue. No. 979, 3000fr, Werner Schlager.

No. 980: a, 1020fr, Ding Ning. b, 1090fr, Zhang Jike. c, 3000fr, Wang Liqin. d, 3000fr, Wang Nan.

Perf. 13x13½

976-979 A164 Set of 4 15.00 15.00

Miniature Sheet

Perf. 13½

980 A164 Sheet of 4, #a-d 15.00 15.00

Soccer Players

Designs: No. 981, 1000fr, Wayne Rooney, Municipal Stadium, Wroclaw, Poland. 1020fr, Bastian Schweinsteiger, National Stadium, Warsaw, Poland. No. 983, 3000fr, Samuel Eto'o, Poznan Stadium, Poznan, Poland. No. 984, 3000fr, Karim Benzema, Olympic Stadium, Kyiv, Ukraine.

No. 985: a, 1000fr, Cristiano Ronaldo, Olympic Stadium, Kyiv. b, 1090fr, Lionel Messi, Metalist Stadium, Kharkiv, Ukraine. c, 3000fr, Kaká, PGE Arena, Gdansk. d, 3000fr, Manuel Neuer, Donbass Arena, Donetsk, Ukraine.

Perf. 13x13½

981-984 A164 Set of 4 15.00 15.00

Miniature Sheet

Perf. 13½

985 A164 Sheet of 4, #a-d 15.00 15.00

Chess Players

Designs: 1020fr, Stan Vaughan. 1120fr, Emanuel Lasker. No. 988, 3000fr, Paul Morphy. No. 989, 3000fr, Alexandra Kosteniuk.

No. 990: a, 1090fr, François-André Danican Philidor. b, 1090fr, Domenico Ercole Del Rio. c, 3000fr, Howard Staunton. d, 3000fr, Johannes Zukertort.

Perf. 13x13½

986-989 A164 Set of 4 15.00 15.00

Miniature Sheet

Perf. 13½

990 A164 Sheet of 4, #a-d 15.00 15.00

Famous Africans

Designs: No. 991, 1020fr, Bishop Desmond Tutu. 1090fr, Wangari Maathai and Salamis temora butterfly. No. 993, 3000fr, Patrice Lumumba and Aerangis modesta flowers. No. 994, 3000fr, Kofi Annan.

No. 995: a, 1020fr, Nelson Mandela and Malachite. b, 1020fr, Léopold Sédar Senghor and Acraea acrita butterfly. c, 3000fr, Albert Lutuli and Precis sophia butterfly. d, 3000fr, Maathai and Fluorite.

Perf. 13x13½

991-994 A164 Set of 4 15.00 15.00

Miniature Sheet

Perf. 13½

995 A164 Sheet of 4, #a-d 15.00 15.00

Aviators

Designs: No. 996, 1020fr, Orville Wright and Wright biplane. No. 997, 1020fr, Adolphe Pégoud and Blériot monoplane. No. 998, 3000fr, Bert Hinkler and Puss Moth. No. 999, 3000fr, Richard E. Byrd and Curtiss-Wright biplane.

No. 1000: a, 1000fr, William Boeing, Boeing 787 and Boeing 80. b, 1090fr, Louis Blériot and Blériot XI. c, 3000fr, Charles Lindbergh and Spirit of St. Louis. d, 3000fr, Anthony Fokker and Fokker F-27 and Fokker Spin.

Perf. 13x13½

996-999 A164 Set of 4 15.00 15.00

Miniature Sheet

Perf. 13½

1000 A164 Sheet of 4, #a-d 15.00 15.00

Wedding of Prince William and Catherine Middleton

Prince William, Catherine Middleton and: 1090fr, Arms, British flag. No. 1002, 1120fr, Couple walking. No. 1003, 3000fr, Arms and Prince Harry. No. 1004, 3000fr, British flag, denomination at UR.

No. 1005 — Prince William, Catherine Middleton and: a, 1020fr, British flag, diff. b, 1120fr, British flag, diff. c, 3000fr, British flag, denomination at UL. d, 3000fr, British flag, denomination at UR, Prince wearing military cap.

Perf. 13x13½

1001-1004 A164 Set of 4 15.00 15.00

Miniature Sheet

Perf. 13½

1005 A164 Sheet of 4, #a-d 15.00 15.00

The Titanic

Titanic: No. 1006, 1000fr, At sea, denomination at UR in black. 1120fr, Near tugboats. No. 1008, 3000fr, Striking iceberg, denomination at UR in white, "Titanic" at UL in white. No. 1009, 3000fr, With Captain Edward Smith in ship's wheel, denomination at UR in black, "Titanic" at UL in black.

No. 1010 — Titanic: a, 1000fr, Sinking near lifeboat and iceberg. b, 1020fr, Sending up distress flares. c, 3000fr, At sea, denomination at UR in white, "Titanic" at UR in white. d, 3000fr, At sea, denomination at UR in black, "Titanic" at UR in black.

Perf. 13x13½

1006-1009 A164 Set of 4 12.50 12.50

Miniature Sheet

Perf. 13½

1010 A164 Sheet of 4, #a-d 12.00 12.00

Christmas

Paintings: No. 1011, 1020fr, Adoration of the Shepherds, by Gerrit van Honthorst. No. 1012, 1020fr, Adoration of the Shepherds, by Louis Le Nain. No. 1013, 3000fr, Nativity, by Georges de La Tour. No. 1014, 3000fr, Adoration of the Shepherds, by Bartolomé Esteban Murillo.

No. 1015: a, 1000fr, The Third Joyful Mystery, by Lorenzo Lotto. b, 1000fr, Adoration of the Child, by van Honthorst. c, 3000fr, Song of the Angels, by William Adolphe Bouguereau. d, 3000fr, Holy Family, by Lorenzo Costa.

Perf. 13x13½

1011-1014 A164 Set of 4 12.50 12.50

Miniature Sheet

Perf. 13½

1015 A164 Sheet of 4, #a-d 12.00 12.00

New Year 2012 (Year of the Dragon)

Dragon color: No. 1016, 1020fr, Red, tail at left. No. 1017, 1020fr, Green, tail at right. No. 1018, 3000fr, Blue, tail at UR. No. 1019, 3000fr, Brown, tail at LR.

No. 1020: a, 1090fr, Red, tail at left. b, 1090fr, Red and green, tail at right. c, 3000fr, Green and red, tail at right. d, 3000fr, Blue and red, tail at UL.

Perf. 13x13½

1016-1019 A164 Set of 4 12.50 12.50

Miniature Sheet

Perf. 13½

1020 A164 Sheet of 4, #a-d 12.50 12.50

A165

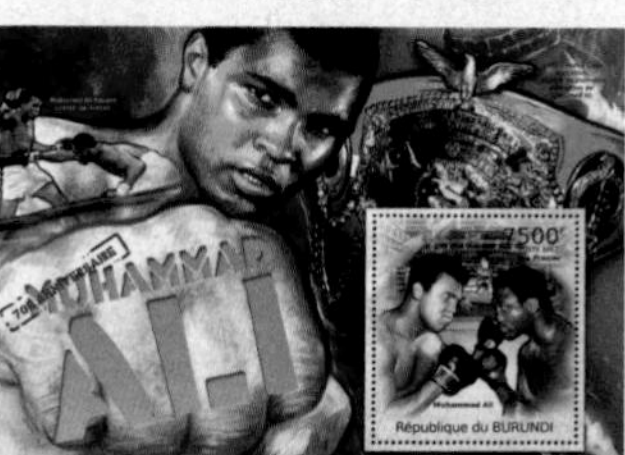

Sports Personalities — A166

No. 1021 — Muhammad Ali and scenes from fights with: a, 1070fr, Floyd Patterson. b, 1070fr, Doug Jones. c, 3000fr, Sonny Liston. d, 3000fr, Leon Spinks

No. 1022: a, 1070fr, He Chong, diving. b, 1070fr, Jordyn Marie Wieber, gymnastics. c, 1070fr, Olha Saladukha, triple jump. d, 5000fr, Pawel Wojciechowski, pole vault.

No. 1023: a, 1070fr, Lance Armstrong, cyclist. b, 1070fr, Martina Navratilova, tennis. c, 1070fr, Brian Lara, cricket. d, 5000fr, Pelé, soccer.

No. 1024: a, 1070fr, Lionel Messi, soccer. b, 1070fr, Novak Djokovic, tennis. c, 1070fr, Martin Kaymer, golf. d, 5000fr, Usain Bolt, track.

No. 1025, 7500fr, Muhammad Ali and Joe Frazier. No. 1026, 7500fr, Eric Guay, skiing. No. 1027, 7500fr, Carl Lewis, track. No. 1028, 7500fr, Magnus Carlsen, chess.

2012, Mar. 30 Litho. *Perf. 13¼*

Sheets of 4, #a-d

1021-1024 A165 Set of 4 50.00 50.00

Souvenir Sheets

1025-1028 A166 Set of 4 47.50 47.50

A167

Paintings — A168

No. 1029 — Paintings of Ivan Aivazovsky: a, 1070fr, Portrait of the Fleet on the Northern Sea, 1849. b, 1070fr, The Great Roads at Kronstadt, 1836, vert. c, 3000fr, Brig Mercury Attacked by Two Turkish Ships, 1892. d, 3000fr, The Battle in the Chios Channel, 1848, vert.

No. 1030 — Paintings of Camille Pissarro: a, 1070fr, Pont Boieldieu at Sunset, 1896. b, 1070fr, Woman Hanging Laundry, 1887, vert. c, 3000fr, Boulevard Montmartre on a Cloudy Morning, 1897. d, 3000fr, The Old Market in Rouen, 1898, vert.

No. 1031 — Paintings of Edgar Degas: a, 1070fr, Hall of the Opera Ballet, 1874. b, 1070fr, Dance Examination, 1880, vert. c, 3000fr, Dance School, 1873. d, 3000fr, Singer with a Glove, 1878, vert.

No. 1032 — Paintings of Paul Cézanne: a, 1070fr, Rideau, Couchon et Compotier, 1893-94. b, 1070fr, The Village of Gardanne, 1886, vert. c, 3000fr, The Card Players, 1893-96. d, 3000fr, Forest Near the Rocky Caves Above the Chateau Noir, 1904, vert.

No. 1033 — Paintings of Claude Monet: a, 1070fr, Arrival of the Normandy Train, Gare Saint-Lazare, 1877. b, 1070fr, The Boat Studio, 1876, vert. c, 3000fr, Impression, Sunrise, 1872. d, 3000fr, Woman with Parasol, 1875, vert.

No. 1034 — Paintings of Frédéric Bazille: a, 1070fr, Family Reunion, 1867. b, 1070fr, The Rose Dress, 1864, vert. c, 3000fr, The Banks of the Lez, 1870. d, 3000fr, La Diseuse de Bonne Aventure, 1869, vert.

No. 1035 — Paintings of Berthe Morisot: a, 1070fr, Interior, 1872. b, 1070fr, At the Ball, 1875, vert. c, 3000fr, Lady at her Toilette, 1875. d, 3000fr, Young Girl with Cage, 1885, vert.

No. 1036 — Paintings of Armand Guillaumin: a, 1070fr, Sunset at Ivry, 1873. b, 1070fr, Hollow in the Snow, 1869, vert. c, 3000fr, La Place Valhubert, 1875. d, 3000fr, Outskirts of Paris, 1875, vert.

No. 1037 — Paintings of Gustave Caillebotte: a, 1070fr, The Boating Party, 1877-78. b, 1070fr, Interior, 1880, vert. c, 3000fr, The Floor Scrapers, 1875. d, 3000fr, A Balcony, 1880, vert.

No. 1038 — Paintings of Edouard Manet: a, 1070fr, Racecourse in the Bois du Boulogne, 1872. b, 1070fr, Café Concert, 1878, vert. c, 3000fr, Bar at the Folies-Bergère, 1881-82. d, 3000fr, Portrait of Irma Brunner, 1882, vert.

No. 1039 — Paintings of Ivan Shishkin: a, 1070fr, Rye Field, 1869. b, 1070fr, Bratzevo, 1869, vert. c, 1070fr, Morning in a Pine Forest, 1886 (bears on trees, title incorrect on stamp). d, 5000fr, Birch Grove, 1896, vert.

No. 1040 — Paintings of Alfred Sisley: a, 1070fr, Flood at Port-Marly, 1876. b, 1070fr, Snow at Louveciennes, 1874, vert. c, 1070fr, The Seine at Port-Marly Sand Piles, 1875. d, 5000fr, Street in Ville d'Avray, 1873, vert.

No. 1041 — Paintings of Pierre-Auguste Renoir: a, 1070fr, Moulin de la Galette, 1876 (artist and title omitted on stamp). b, 1070fr, Two Sisters on the Terrace, 1881, vert. c, 1070fr, Madame Charpentier and Her Children, 1878. d, 5000fr, The Theater Box, 1874, vert.

No. 1042 — Paintings of Mary Cassatt: a, 1070fr, Cup of Tea, 1879 (title omitted on stamp). b, 1070fr, Portrait of a Lady of Seville, 1873, vert. c, 1070fr, A Woman and a Girl Driving, 1881. d, 5000fr, Spanish Dancer Wearing a Lace Mantilla Box, 1873, vert.

No. 1043 — Tingatina paintings by: a, 1070fr, Saidi Omary. b, 1070fr, Noel Kapanda, vert. c, 1070fr, George Lilanga. d, 5000fr, Iddi Issa, vert.

No. 1044 — Paintings depicting Joan of Arc: a, 1070fr, Joan of Arc Kissing the Sword of Deliverance, by Dante Gabriel Rossetti, 1863. b, 1070fr, Joan of Arc During the Siege of Orleans, by Jules Eugene Lenepveu, 1889, vert. c, 1070fr, Capture of Joan of Arc, by Adolphe Alexandre Dillens, 1850. d, 5000fr, Joan of Arc at the Coronation of Charles VII in the Cathedral of Reims, by Jean Auguste Dominique Ingres, 1854, vert.

No. 1045, 7500fr, A Ship in the Stormy Sea, 1887, by Aivazovsky. No. 1046, 7500fr, The Poultry Market at Pontoise, 1882, by Pissarro. No. 1047, 7500fr, The Green Dancer, 1879, by Degas. No. 1048, 7500fr, Harlequin, 1888-90, by Cézane. No. 1049, 7500fr, Rouen Cathedral, Magic in Blue, 1894, by Monet. No. 1050, 7500fr, Village View, 1868, by Bazille. No. 1051, 7500fr, In the Dining Room, 1875, by Morisot. No. 1052, 7500fr, Vase of Chrysanthemums, 1885, by Guillaumin. No. 1053, 7500fr, Young Man at His Window, 1876, by Caillebotte. No. 1054, 7500fr, Spring (Jeanne de Marsy), 1881, by Manet. No. 1055, 7500fr, Evening, 1892, by Shishkin. No. 1056, 7500fr, Grande Rue, Argenteuil, 1872, by Sisley. No. 1057, 7500fr, In the Garden, 1885, by Renoir. No. 1058, 7500fr, Woman with a Pearl Necklace in a Theater Box, 1879, by Cassatt. No. 1059, 7500fr, Paon sur un Baobab, 1972, by Edward Saidi Tingatinga. No. 1060, 7500fr, Joan of Arc in Battle, 1843, by Hermann Anton Stilke.

2012, Mar. 30 ***Perf. 13¼***

Sheets of 4, #a-d

1029-1044 A167 Set of 16 200.00 200.00

Souvenir Sheets

1045-1060 A168 Set of 16 190.00 190.00

Transportation and Space Flight — A169

No. 1061 — Boats: a, 1070fr, Anna Tunnicliffe sailing boat in 2008 Olympics. b, 1070fr, Yacht in Yarmouth Regatta. c, 3000fr, Europa, horiz. d, 3000fr, Colvin Gazelle, horiz.

No. 1062 — Steam trains: a, 1070fr, Venezia Santa Lucia. b, 1070fr, Class A4 Silver Fox. c, 3000fr, Flying Scotsman Express, horiz. d, 3000fr, Denver, Leadville and Gunnison train, horiz.

No. 1063 — French trains: a, 1070fr, TGV-PSE. b, 1070fr, Z-TER (Z 21561). c, 3000fr, Thalys PBKA, horiz. d, 3000fr, La Gironde and Joseph Eugène Schneider, horiz.

No. 1064 — German trains: a, 1070fr, ICE TD (Class 605). b, 1070fr, DB Class 614. c, 3000fr, RS-1 Regio Shuttle, horiz. d, 3000fr, Saxonia and Johann Andreas Schubert, horiz.

No. 1065 — Japanese trains: a, 1070fr, JRW Shinkansen Series 500 W1. b, 1070fr, Tobu 100. c, 3000fr, Shinkansen Superexpress Series 700, horiz. d, 3000fr, Shinkansen Series E5, horiz.

No. 1066 — Chinese trains: a, 1070fr, CRH5. b, 1070fr, CRH2. c, 3000fr, CRH2A, horiz. d, 3000fr, CRH3C, horiz.

No. 1067 — Bicycles: a, 1070fr, Mountain biker climbing hill. b, 1070fr, Mountain bikers descending hill. c, 3000fr, Road cycling (cyclisme sur route), horiz. d, 3000fr, Track cycling (cyclisme sur piste), horiz.

No. 1068 — Formula 1 race cars and drivers: a, 1070fr, AT&T Williams team car, Ayrton Senna, Brazilian flag. b, 1070fr, Mercedes GP Petronas team car, Michael Schumacher, German flag. c, 3000fr, Alfa Romeo 158, Giuseppe Farina, Italian flag, horiz. d, 3000fr, Mercedes-Benz W 196 R, Juan Manuel Fangio, Argentine flag, horiz.

No. 1069 — Helicopters: a, 1070fr, Boeing AH-64 Apache. b, 1070fr, Boeing CH-47 Chinook. c, 3000fr, Bell UH-1, horiz. d, 3000fr, MBB/Kawasaki BK 117 C2, horiz.

No. 1070 — Concorde: a, 1070fr, Two airplanes, line drawing of airplane's nose. b, 1070fr, Two airplanes, line drawing of airplane's tail. c, 3000fr, Denomination at UR, horiz. d, 3000fr, Denomination at UL, horiz.

No. 1071 — Ships and Amerigo Vespucci: a, 1070fr, Vespucci at right, horiz. b, 1070fr, Vespucci at left. c, 1070fr, Vespucci at right. d, 5000fr, Vespucci at right, horiz.

No. 1072 — Horses and carriages: a, 1070fr, Lewis Tompkins driving carriage, horiz. b, 1070fr, Queen Elizabeth II and Prince Philip in carriage. c, 1070fr, Horse's head and omnibus carriage. d, 5000fr, Horse-drawn ambulance, horiz.

No. 1073 — Balloons and their creators: a, 1070fr, Balloon of Francesco Lana de Terzi, horiz. b, 1070fr, Balloon of Jean-Pierre Blanchard. c, 1070fr, Balloon of André-Jacques Garnerin, ascending. d, 5000fr, Balloon of Garnerin descending, horiz.

No. 1074 — The Hindenburg and Ferdinand von Zeppelin: a, 1070fr, Hindenburg in flight, horiz. b, 1070fr, Hindenburg and Empire State Building. c, 1070fr, Hindenburg on fire. d, 5000fr, People around Hindenburg, horiz.

No. 1075 — Centenary of London to Paris flight of Henri Salmet: a, 1070fr, Salmet in cockpit of Blériot monoplane, plane in flight facing left, horiz. b, 1070fr, Salmet at left, post card depicting his plane in flight. c, 1070fr, Salmet at right, post card depicting his plane on ground. d, 5000fr, Salmet in cockpit, plane in flight facing right, horiz.

No. 1076 — Opel Automobile Company, 150th Anniv.: a, 1070fr, Adam Opel, Opel emblem, sewing machine, horiz. b, 1070fr, Fritz Opel on Opel bicycle, bicycle emblem. c, 1070fr, 1899 Opel automobile, automobile emblem. d, 5000fr, 1935 Opel Olympia and emblem, horiz.

No. 1077 — Fire-fighting vehicles: a, 1070fr, 1870 Tozer pumper, horiz. b, 1070fr, 1883 Valiant pumper. c, 1070fr, Ladder truck and motorcycle with sidecar. d, 5000fr, Ladder truck, horiz.

No. 1078 — Soviet space pioneers and vehicles: a, 1070fr, Dogs Belka and Strelka, horiz. b, 1070fr, Alexei Leonov. c, 1070fr, Valentina Tereshkova. d, 5000fr, Lunokhod 1, horiz.

No. 1079 — Sergei Krikalev and space vehicles: a, 1070fr, Space Shuttle Endeavour, horiz. b, 1070fr, Soyuz TM-7, denomination at UL. c, 1070fr, Soyuz TM-7, denomination at UR. d, 5000fr, Space Shuttle Flight STS-60 landing, horiz.

No. 1080, 7500fr, Viking drakkar, horiz. No. 1081, 7500fr, LNER Class A4 locomotive, Mallard commemorative plaque, horiz. No. 1082, 7500fr, TGV Duplex train, France, horiz. No. 1083, 7500fr, ICE 3 (Class 407), Germany, horiz. No. 1084, 7500fr, SL Yamaguchi C571 locomotive, Japan, horiz. No. 1085, 7500fr, CRH1 train, China, horiz. No. 1086, 7500fr, Arthur Zimmerman, world champion cyclist, 1893, horiz. No. 1087, 7500fr, Red Bull Formula 1 race cars, Sebastian Vettel, flag of Germany, horiz. No. 1088, 7500fr, Sikorsky S-70A Firehawk helicopter, horiz. No. 1089, 7500fr, Concorde, horiz. No. 1090, 7500fr, Ship and Vespucci, horiz. No. 1091, 7500fr, United States horse-drawn mail wagon, 1911, horiz. No. 1092, 7500fr, Balloon of Jacues Etienne Montgolfier, horiz. No. 1093, 7500fr, Zeppelin, Hindenburg in flight, horiz. No. 1094, 7500fr, Salmet in cockpit, plane in flight, horiz. No. 1095, 7500fr, 2011 Opel RAK e concept automobile, horiz. No. 1096, 7500fr, Firemen and pumper, 1903, horiz. No. 1097, 7500fr, Yuri Gagarin and Vostok 1, horiz. No. 1098, 7500fr, Krikalev and Mir Space Station, horiz.

2012, May 30 **Litho.**

Sheets of 4, #a-d

1061-1079 A169 Set of 19 225.00 225.00

Souvenir Sheets

1080-1098 A169 Set of 19 200.00 200.00

Miniature Sheets

Leaders of Burundi — A170

No. 1099 — King Mwambutsa IV Bangiricenge (1912-77): a, 270fr. b, 550fr. c, 1090fr. d, 2050fr.

No. 1100 — Prince Louis Rwagasore (1932-61), Prime Minister: a, 270fr. b, 550fr. c, 1090fr. d, 2050fr.

No. 1101 — Charles Ndizeye (King Ntare V) (1947-72): a, 270fr. b, 550fr. c, 1090fr. d, 2050fr.

No. 1102 — President Michel Micombero (1940-83): a, 270fr. b, 550fr. c, 1090fr. d, 2050fr.

No. 1103 — President Jean-Baptiste Bagaza: a, 270fr. b, 550fr. c, 1090fr. d, 2050fr.

No. 1104 — President Pierre Buyoya: a, 270fr. b, 550fr. c, 1090fr. d, 2050fr.

No. 1105 — President Melchior Ndadaye (1953-93): a, 270fr. b, 550fr. c, 1090fr. d, 2050fr.

No. 1106 — President Cyprien Ntaryamira (1955-94): a, 270fr. b, 550fr. c, 1090fr. d, 2050fr.

No. 1107 — President Sylvestre Ntibantunganya: a, 270fr. b, 550fr. c, 1090fr. d, 2050fr.

No. 1108 — President Domitien Ndayizeye: a, 270fr. b, 550fr. c, 1090fr. d, 2050fr.

No. 1109 — President Pierre Nkurunziza: a, 270fr. b, 550fr. c, 1090fr. d, 2050fr.

2012, Aug. 1 ***Perf. 13¼***

Sheets of 4, #a-d

1099-1109 A170 Set of 11 62.50 62.50

Nos. 1099c and 1099d lack king's name.

Nature Protection — A171

No. 1110 — Commerce in endangered wild animals: a, 1070fr, Two Panthera tigris in cage. b, 1070fr, Pongo pygmaeus abelii. c, 3000fr, Nycticebus sp. d, 3000fr, Gavialis gangeticus.

No. 1111 — Deforestation: a, 1070fr, Agalychnis callidryas. b, 1070fr, Harpia harpyja. c, 3000fr, Pongo pygmaeus. d, 3000fr, Ramphastos sulfuratus.

No. 1112 — Habitat fragmentation: a, 1070fr, Ceratotherium simum. b, 1070fr, Ursus arctos. c, 3000fr, Camelus dromedarius. d, 3000fr, Panthera leo and vans.

No. 1113 — Destruction of the Antarctic ozone layer: a, 1070fr, Orcinus orca, map of Antarctica. b, 1070fr, Balaenoptera musculus, scientific balloon launch. c, 3000fr, Megaleledone setebos, Antarctic research station. d, 3000fr, Leptonychotes weddellii, map of Antarctica.

No. 1114 — Warming of the climate: a, 1070fr, Bubo scandiacus. b, 1070fr, Sterna paradisaea. c, 3000fr, Pygoscelis adeliae. d, 3000fr, Odobenus rosmarus.

No. 1115 — Sea of plastic waste in North Pacific: a, 1070fr, Fish in net. b, 1070fr, Oceanographic vessel Kaisei and rubber raft. c, 3000fr, Map of Pacific Ocean, turtles ensnared in plastic packaging. d, 3000fr, Seals and plastic waste.

No. 1116 — Species extinct or threatened in the wild: a, 1070fr, Gallirallus owstoni. b, 1070fr, Nectophrynoides asperginis. c, 3000fr, Elaphurus davidianus. d, 3000fr, Brachylagus idahoensis.

No. 1117 — Endangered mammals: a, 1070fr, Panthera tigris facing right. b, 1070fr, Panthera leo on ground and in tree. c, 3000fr, Equus quagga. d, 3000fr, Adult and juvenile Ceratotherium simum.

No. 1118 — Sharks and pinnipeds: a, 1070fr, Carcharodon carcharias, Phocidae, "Phocidae" in black. b, 1070fr, Carcharodon carcharias, Phocidae, "Phocidae" in white. c, 3000fr, Carcharodon carcharias, name in black. d, 3000fr, Carcharodon carcharias, Phocidae, names in white.

No. 1119 — Dolphins: a, 1070fr, Stenella frontalis. b, 1070fr, Tursiops truncatus. c, 3000fr, Tursiops truncatus, denomination at UL. d, 3000fr, Tursiops truncatus, denomination at UR.

No. 1120 — Orcinus orca and Carcharodon carcharias with denomination in: a, 1070fr, White. b, 1070fr, Black. c, 3000fr, White. d, 3000fr, Black.

No. 1121 — Whales: a, 1070fr, Physeter macrocephalus. b, 1070fr, Megaptera novaeangliae. c, 3000fr, Eschrichtius robustus. d, 3000fr, Balaenoptera acutorostrata.

No. 1122 — Birds and air pollution: a, 1070fr, Cuculus canorus. b, 1070fr, Grus americana. c, 3000fr, Crax rubra. d, 3000fr, Carduelis cucullata.

No. 1123 — Endangered birds: a, 1070fr, Anodorhynchus hyacintinus, Ara militaris. b, 1070fr, Merops orientalis. c, 3000fr, Aquila rapax. d, 3000fr, Strix nebulosa.

No. 1124 — Endangered plants and insects: a, 1070fr, Lobelia bridgesii, Cerambyx dux. b, 1070fr, Begonia samhaensis, Chlorophorus aegyptiacus. c, 3000fr, Sarracenia flava, Ampedus cardinalis. d, 3000fr, Echinocactus grusonii, Magicicada cassini.

No. 1125 — Endangered butterflies: a, 1070fr, Papilio palinurus. b, 1070fr, Idea iasonia. c, 3000fr, Parides hahneli. d, 3000fr, Euphaedra themis.

No. 1126 — Endangered fish: a, 1070fr, Cheilochromis euchilus. b, 1070fr, Pomacanthus imperator. c, 3000fr, Apolemichthys xanthotis. d, 3000fr, Cephalopholis miniata.

No. 1127 — Endangered reptiles: a, 1070fr, Calumma tarzan. b, 1070fr, Astrochelys yniphora. c, 3000fr, Crotalus catalinensis. d, 3000fr, Acanthodactylus beershebensis.

No. 1128 — Dinosaurs: a, 1070fr, Pachyrhinosaurus. b, 1070fr, Tropeognathus. c, 3000fr, Lystrosaurus. d, 3000fr, Arrhinoceratops.

No. 1129 — Acid rain and mushrooms: a, 1070fr, Gyromitra esculenta. b, 1070fr, Calvatia gigantea. c, 3000fr, Chorioactis. d, 3000fr, Hydnellum peckii.

No. 1130, 7500fr, Nycticebus pygmaeus. No. 1131, 7500fr, Danaus plexippus. No. 1132, 7500fr, Odocoileus virginianus clavium. No. 1133, 7500fr, Aptenodytes forsteri, airplanes over iceberg, globe. No. 1134, 7500fr, Ursus maritimus. No. 1135, 7500fr, Zalophus californianus ensnared in net. No. 1136, 7500fr, Oryx dammah. No. 1137, 7500fr, Cebus flavius. No. 1138, 7500fr, Carcharodon carcharias, Otariidae, vert. No. 1139, 7500fr, Delphinus delphis. No. 1140, 7500fr, Orcinus orca and Carhcharodon carcharias, diff. No. 1141, 7500fr, Megaptera novaeangliae, diff. No. 1142, 7500fr, Cacatua sulphurea citrinocristata. No. 1143, 7500fr, Strix occidentalis. No. 1144, 7500fr, Latania loddegesii, Buprestis splendens. No. 1145, 7500fr, Diaethria eluina. No. 1146, 7500fr, Pomacanthus maculosus. No. 1147, 7500fr, Glyptemys insculpta. No. 1148, 7500fr, Compsognathus. No. 1149, 7500fr, Entoloma hochstetteri and acid rain.

2012, Aug. 31 Litho.

Sheets of 4, #a-d

1110-1129 A171 Set of 20 225.00 225.00

Souvenir Sheets

1130-1149 A171 Set of 20 210.00 210.00

Egg House, Moscow, and Fabergé Eggs — A172

No. 1150 — Egg House and: a, Red egg with three portraits of Emperor Nicholas II and two daughters at top. b, Jeweled frame with portraits of Emperor Nicholas II and Empress Alexandra. c, Egg with portrait of Emperor Nicholas II. d, Egg with portrait of Empress Alexandra at top. e, Egg with mounted horseman. f, Ship inside open egg.

No. 1151, 5000fr, Egg House, egg and coach. No. 1152, 5000fr, Egg House, blue egg, 12 pendants.

2012, Oct. 15 Litho. *Perf. 12¾x13¼*

1150 A172 1190fr Sheet of 6, #a-f 9.75 9.75

Souvenir Sheets

1151-1152 A172 Set of 2 13.50 13.50

Rossica 2013 Intl. Philatelic Exhibition, Moscow.

A173

No. 1153 — George Carlin (1937-2008), comedian, mask and text in French beginning with: a, 1180fr, "La seule bonne chose. . ." b, 1190fr, "J'ai finalement accepté Jésus. . ." c, 3000fr, "La religion est en quelque sorte. . ." d, 3000fr, "Nous avons créé Dieu. . ."

No. 1154 — Neil Armstrong (1930-2012), first man to walk on Moon, and: a, 1180fr, Apollo 11 emblem. b, 1190fr, Apollo command and service modules. c, 3000fr, Apollo 11 command, service and lunar modules. d, 3000fr, Astronaut and flag.

No. 1155 — Exploration of Mars: a, 1180fr, Artist's conception of Mars Exploration Rover. b, 1190fr, Curiosity rover. c, 3000fr, Satellite orbiting Mars. d, 3000fr, Sojourner rover.

No. 1156 — Impressionists and their paintings: a, 1180fr, The Soda Fountain, by William Glackens. b, 1190fr, In a Daisy Field, by Theodore Robinson. c, 3000fr, The Ballet Dancers, by William Metcalf. d, 3000fr, Portrait of a Woman, by Albert Henry Collings.

No. 1157 — Alexander Graham Bell (1847-1922), inventor of the telephone, and: a, 1180fr, AEA Silver Dart airplane. b, 1190fr, Examination of the wounded Pres. James A. Garfield. c, 3000fr, Magneto telephone. d, 3000fr, Columbia gramophone.

No. 1158 — Scenes from films adapted from works written by Ray Bradbury (1920-2012): a, 1180fr, *Moby Dick* (television play), 1956. b, 1190fr, *The Illustrated Man* (movie), 1969. c, 3000fr, *Something Wicked This Way Comes* (movie), 1983. d, 3000fr, *The Beast from 20,000 Fathoms* (movie), 1953.

No. 1159 — Marilyn Monroe (1926-62), actress, and: a, 1180fr, Arthur Miller (1915-2005), playwright and Monroe's husband. b, 1190fr, Second image of Monroe. c, 3000fr, Brooklyn Bridge, Pres. John F. Kennedy (1917-63). d, 3000fr, Frank Sinatra (1915-98), singer.

No. 1160 — Musicians: a, 1180fr, B.B. King. b, 1190fr, Stevie Ray Vaughan. c, 3000fr, Tina Turner. d, 3000fr, Cher.

No. 1161 — Khadja Nin, musician: a, 1180fr, Two images of Nin. b, 1190fr, One image of Nin. c, 3000fr, Stevie Wonder. d, 3000fr, Montserrat Caballe.

No. 1162 — Princess Diana (1961-97), and: a, 1180fr, Prince William. b, 1190fr, Land mine sign. c, 3000fr, Princes William and Harry. d, 3000fr, Princes Charles and William.

No. 1163 — Pope John Paul II (1920-2005): a, 1180fr, And dove flying to right. b, 1190fr, And dove flying to left. c, 3000fr, Praying, dove at LL . d, 3000fr, With hand raised.

No. 1164 — Sergio Pininfarina (1926-2012), automobile designer and: a, 1180fr, Peugeot 504 Cabriolet. b, 1190fr, Lancia Montecarlo. c, 3000fr, Rolls-Royce Hyperion. d, 3000fr, Ferrari F40.

No. 1165 — Sports of the 2012 Summer Olympics, London: a, 1180fr, Judo. b, 1190fr, Soccer. c, 3000fr, Table tennis. d, 3000fr, Cycling.

No. 1166 — Minerals: a, 1180fr, Tanzanite and Vanadinite. b, 1190fr, Diamond and Vanadinite. c, 3000fr, Liddicoatite tourmaline and Tanzanite. d, 3000fr, Liddicoatite tourmaline.

No. 1167 — Pigeons, with inscription: a, 1180fr, Pigeon Hirondelle. b, 1190fr, Le "Cravaté Africain." c, 3000fr, "Le Dragon." d, 3000fr, Le Pigeon Souabe.

No. 1168 — Somniosus microcephalus, with diagonal line running from: a, 1180fr, UL to LR. b, 1190fr, LL to UR. c, 3000fr, LL to UR. d, 3000fr, UL to LR.

No. 1169 — Festivals: a, 1180fr, Diwali, India. b, 1190fr, New Year, China. c, 3000fr, Octoberfest, Germany. d, 3000fr, Feast of San Fermin, Spain.

No. 1170 — Burundi coffee production: a, 1180fr, Hands holding coffee cherries, coffee bean sorters. b, 1190fr, Harvesters, bags of coffee beans. c, 3000fr, Women drinking coffee. d, 3000fr, Harvester with basket, hands holding coffee cherries.

No. 1171 — Royal Drummers and Dancers of Burundi, with diagonal line running from: a, 1180fr, UL to LR. b, 1190fr, LL to UR. c, 3000fr, LL to UR. d, 3000fr, UL to LR.

No. 1172, 7500fr, Carlin and mask. No. 1173, 7500fr, Armstrong and bald eagle from Apollo 11 emblem. No. 1174, 7500fr, Curiosity landing on Mars. No. 1175, 7500fr, Portrait of Miss Dora Wheeler, by William Merritt Chase. No. 1176, 7500fr, First telephone invented by Bell. No. 1177, 7500fr, Bradbury and scene from miniseries adapted from *The Martian Chronicles.* No. 1178, 7500fr, Monroe and Joe DiMaggio (1914-99), baseball player and Monroe's husband. No. 1179, 7500fr, Bob Marley (1945-81), musician. No. 1180, 7500fr, Nin and Wonder. No. 1181, 7500fr, Princess Diana and Red Cross flag. No. 1182, 7500fr, Pope John Paul II and dove, diff. No. 1183, 7500fr, Pininfarina and Maserati GranTurismo 5. No. 1184, 7500fr, Swimmer. No. 1185, 7500fr, Tanzanite and Vanadinite, diff. No. 1186, 7500fr, Two pigeons. No. 1187, 7500fr, Somniosus microcephalus, diff. No. 1188, 7500fr, Carnaval, Rio de Janeiro. No. 1189, 7500fr, Woman, coffee bush and beans. No. 1190, 7500fr, Royal Drummers and Dancers of Burundi, diff.

2012, Oct. 15 Litho. *Perf. 13¼*

Sheets of 4, #a-d

1153-1171 A173 Set of 19 220.00 220.00

Souvenir Sheets

1172-1190 A173 Set of 19 195.00 195.00

A174

No. 1191 — Hystrix africaeaustralis: a, 1180fr, Facing left. b, 1190fr, Facing right. c, 3000fr, Facing right, diff. d, 3000fr, Facing left, diff.

No. 1192 — Pangolins: a, 1180fr, Manis temminckii. b, 1190fr, Manis gigantea. c, 3000fr, Manis javanica. d, 3000fr, Manis temminckii, diff.

No. 1193 — Gorilla gorilla: a, 1180fr, Walking. b, 1190fr, Sitting. c, 3000fr, On back, denomination in black. d, 3000fr, Head, denomination in white.

No. 1194 — Pan troglodytes: a, 1180fr, On one tree branch. b, 1190fr, Holding two trees. c, 3000fr, Adult and juvenile. d, 3000fr, Adult.

No. 1195 — Lions International emblem and Panthera leo: a, 1180fr, Two females. b, 1190fr, Male running. c, 3000fr, Male walking. d, 3000fr, Male and female.

No. 1196 — Loxodonta africana: a, 1180fr, Adult and juvenile. b, 1190fr, Adult. c, 3000fr, Adults, animal name in black. d, 3000fr, Adult, animal name in white.

No. 1197 — Dolphins: a, 1180fr, Cephalorhynchus hectori maui. b, 1190fr, Lipotes vexillifer. c, 3000fr, Delphinus delphis . d, 3000fr, Orcaella brevirostris.

No. 1198 — Whales: a, 1180fr, Caperea marginata. b, 1190fr, Physeter catodon. c, 3000fr, Balaeniptera physalus. d, 3000fr, Balaenoptera musculus.

No. 1199 — Birds of prey: a, 1180fr, Elanus caeruleus. b, 1190fr, Milvus aegypticus. c, 3000fr, Haliaeetus vocifer. d, 3000fr, Milvus milvus.

No. 1200 — Owls: a, 1180fr, Bubo virginianus. b, 1190fr, Bubo africanus. c, 3000fr, Bubo bubo, Bubo africanus. d, 3000fr, Otus asio, Ptilopsis leucotis.

No. 1201 — Vultures: a, 1180fr, Vultur gryphus. b, 1190fr, Sarcogyps calvus. c, 3000fr, Necrosyrtes monachus. d, 3000fr, Gypaetus barbatus.

No. 1202 — Parrots: a, 1180fr, Psittacus erithacus. b, 1190fr, Agapornis fischeri. c, 3000fr, Poicephalus robustus. d, 3000fr, Agapornis personatus.

No. 1203 — Chrysolophus pictus: a, 1180fr, In flight. b, 1190fr, Two males. c, 3000fr, Male and female, denomination at LR. d, 3000fr, Two males and female, denomination at LL.

No. 1204 — Bees and wasps: a, 1180fr, Apis cerana. b, 1190fr, Vespula germanica. c, 3000fr, Apis mellifera. d, 3000fr, Vespa orientalis.

No. 1205 — Draogonflies: a, 1180fr, Trithemis arteriosa. b, 1190fr, Trithemis arteriosa, diff. c, 3000fr, Orthetrum chrysostigma. d, 3000fr, Schnura senegalensis.

No. 1206 — Butterflies: a, 1180fr, Belenois calypso. b, 1190fr, Graphium angolanus. c, 3000fr, Graphium ridleyanus. d, 3000fr, Papilio dardanus antinorii.

No. 1207 — Butterflies: a, 1180fr, Papilio demodocus. b, 1190fr, Cymothoe mabillei. c, 3000fr, Eurema hecabe. d, 3000fr, Euphaedra janetta.

No. 1208 — Goldfish breeds: a, 1180fr, Panda Moor. b, 1190fr, Celestial Eye. c, 3000fr, Bubble Eye. d, 3000fr, Black Moor.

No. 1209 — Fish: a, 1180fr, Pelvicachromis pulcher. b, 1190fr, Neochromis omnicaeruleus. c, 3000fr, Ptyochromis sp. d, 3000fr, Paralabidochromis sp.

No. 1210 — Shells: a, 1180fr, Chlamyis varia, Cardita calcyculata. b, 1190fr, Jujubinus exasperatus, Marmarostoma. c, 3000fr, Ovula ovum, Cymathium rubeculum. d, 3000fr, Epitonium commune, Solemya togata.

No. 1211 — Sea turtles: a, 1180fr, Dermochelys coriacea. b, 1190fr, Caretta caretta. c, 3000fr, Natator depressus. d, 3000fr, Eretmochelys imbricata.

No. 1212 — Cacti and animals: a, 1180fr, Euphorbia trigona, Varanus albigularis. b, 1190fr, Opuntia ficu-indica, hyaena hyaena. c, 3000fr, Euphorbia tortilis, Suricata suricatta. d, 3000fr, Euphorbia trigona var. rubra, Naja haje.

No. 1213 — Edible mushrooms: a, 1180fr, Amanita rubescens. b, 1190fr, Morchella conica. c, 3000fr, Cantharellus cibarius. d, 3000fr, Boletus edulis.

No. 1214 — Poisonous mushrooms: a, 1180fr, Entoloma sinuatum. b, 1190fr, Amanita verna, Amanita muscaria. c, 3000fr, Russula emetica. d, 3000fr, Amanita phalloides, Paxillus involutus.

No. 1215 — Minerals: a, 1180fr, Orthose. b, 1190fr, Agate. c, 3000fr, Galena. d, 3000fr, Topaz.

No. 1216, 7500fr, Hystrix africaeaustralis, diff. No. 1217, 7500fr, Manis tricuspis. No. 1218, 7500fr, Gorilla gorilla gorilla. No. 1219, 7500fr, Pan troglodytes, diff. No. 1220, 7500fr, Lions International emblem and Panthera leo, diff. No. 1221, 7500fr, Loxodonta africana, diff. No. 1222, 7500fr, Platanista gangetica. No. 1223, 7500fr, Delphinapterus leucas. No. 1224, 7500fr, Haliaeetus vocifer, diff. No. 1225, 7500fr, Tyto alba. No. 1226, 7500fr, Sarcoramphus papa. No. 1227, 7500fr, Poicephalus meyeri. No. 1228, 7500fr, Chrysolophus pictus, diff. No. 1229, 7500fr, Apis mellifera, diff. No. 1230, 7500fr, Crocothemis erythraea. No. 1231, 7500fr, Papilio dardanus cenea. No. 1232, 7500fr, Hypolycaena antifaunus. No. 1233, 7500fr, Pearlscale goldfish. No. 1234, 7500fr, Lithochromis rufus. No. 1235, 7500fr, Melo aethiopicus, Hippopus hippopus. No. 1236, 7500fr, Caretta caretta, diff. No. 1237, 7500fr, Opuntia robusta, Vulpes zerda. No. 1238, 7500fr, Amanita caesarea. No. 1239, 7500fr, Boletus satanas. No. 1240, 7500fr, Calcite.

2012, Dec. 21 Litho. *Perf. 13¼*

Sheets of 4, #a-d

1191-1215 A174 Set of 25 275.00 275.00

Souvenir Sheets

1216-1240 A174 Set of 25 245.00 245.00

Transportation and Space — A175

No. 1241 — Dog and sleds: a, 1180fr, Dogs, sled and driver. b, 1190fr, Dogs, sled and driver, diff. c, 3000fr, Sled dog, statue of Balto. d, 3000fr, Two dogs and sled.

No. 1242 — Paintings of horses and wagons by: a, 1180fr, Charles Cooper Henderson. b, 1190fr, James Pollard. c, 3000fr, Pollard, diff. d, 3000fr, John Nost Sartorius.

No. 1243 — Medieval ships: a, 1180fr, Norman ship, 11th cent. b, 1190fr, Venetian merchant ship, 1250. c, 3000fr, Galley, 1280. d, 3000fr, Nostra Senora, 1275.

No. 1244 — Discovery of America by Christopher Columbus, 520th anniv.: a, 1180fr, Columbus Before the Queen, painting by Emanuel Gottlieb Leutze. b, 1190fr, Columbus Landing at Guanahani, painting by John Vanderlyn. c, 3000fr, Columbus and ship, Santa Maria. d, 3000fr, The Death of Columbus, painting by Louis Prang.

No. 1245 — Steamboats, 225th anniv.: a, 1180fr, John Fitch and his steamboat. b, 1190fr, James Watt and steam engine. c, 3000fr, Robert Fulton and diagram of steamboat. d, 3000fr, Steamboat Washington.

No. 1246 — Warships: a, 1180fr, Prinz Eugen. b, 1190fr, Bismarck. c, 3000fr, Yamato. d, 3000fr, Georgy Pobedonosets.

No. 1247 — Invention of the locomotive: a, 1180fr, Limmat 4-2-2. b, 1190fr, The General 4-4-0. c, 3000fr, Statue of Richard Trevithick, Trevithick's 1804 locomotive. d, 3000fr, Statue of George Stephenson, Stockton & Darlington Railroad locomotive.

No. 1248 — Aerotrains: a, 1180fr, Prototype #02. b, 1190fr, Prototype Rohr. c, 3000fr, Experimental train 01. d, 3000fr, I-80 HV.

No. 1249 — Snowmobiles: a, 1180fr, BRP Ski-Doo Rev XP. b, 1190fr, Arctic Cat ProClimb M1100 Sno Pro Limited. c, 3000fr, Yamaha FX Nytro RMX. d, 3000fr, Polaris RMK 700.

No. 1250 — Fire trucks: a, 1180fr, 1915 American La France. b, 1190fr, 1985 Pierce Arrow. c, 3000fr, 2002 Pierce. d, 3000fr, 1946 Bickle Seagrave.

No. 1251 — Buses: a, 1180fr, 1940 Greyhound. b, 1190fr, 1954 Bristol double-decker. c, 3000fr, JCK 892. d, 3000fr, 1940 General American Autocoach.

No. 1252 — Automobiles: a, 1180fr, 1906 Mercedes-Benz race car. b, 1190fr, Mercedes-Benz W196 race car. c, 3000fr, 1935 Mercedes-Benz Roadster. d, 3000fr, 1923 Lancia Lambda Torpedo.

No. 1253 — Taxis: a, 1180fr, Coco taxi, Havana, Cuba. b, 1190fr, 1834 fiacre, England. c, 3000fr, 1912 Unic taxi, London. d, 3000fr, Maybach taxi, Moscow.

No. 1254 — Stock cars and NASCAR drivers: a, 1180fr, 2012 Chevrolet, Tony Stewart.

b, 1190fr, 1983 Ford, Dale Earnhardt. c, 3000fr, 2012 Dodge, Brad Keselowski. d, 3000fr, 1957 Oldsmobile, Richard Petty.

No. 1255 — Harley-Davidson motorcycles: a, 1180fr, 2012 FLTRX Road Glide Custom. b, 1190fr, 1942 WLA. c, 3000fr, 2010 CVO Fat Bob FXDFSE2. d, 3000fr, 2010 VRSCB V-Rod.

No. 1256 — Disappearance of Amelia Earhart (1897-1937), pilot: a, 1180fr, Earhart sitting on nose of plane. b, 1190fr, Earhart parachuting. c, 3000fr, Earhart in front of plane,denomination in white. d, Earhart in front of plane, denomination in black.

No. 1257 — Supersonic aircraft: a, 1180fr, Tupolev Tu-144, flying right. b, 1190fr, British Airways Concorde. c, 3000fr, Air France Concorde. d, 3000fr, Tupolev Tu-144, flying left.

No. 1258 — Air ambulances: a, 1180fr, Victoria Hawker Beechcraft B200C King Air. b, 1190fr, LAHAK MBB Bo-105CBS-4 helicopter. c, 3000fr, Eurocopter-Kawasaki EC-145 (BK-117C-2) helicopter. d, 3000fr, King Air B350.

No. 1259 — Military aircraft: a, 1180fr, Boeing B-52H Stratofortress. b, 1190fr, Boeing Bird of Prey, Boeing F/A-18E. c, 3000fr, Lockheed YF-117A Nighthawk, Lockheed F-117A Nighthawk. d, 3000fr, Northrop YB-35.

No. 1260 — American X-Planes: a, 1180fr, Northrup Grumman X-47A Pegasus. b, 1190fr, Boeing X-50 Dragonfly. c, 3000fr, McDonnell Douglas/Boeing X-36. d, 3000fr, Grumman X-29.

No. 1261 — Space tourism: a, 1180fr, White Knight One. b, 1190fr, Virgin Atlantic Global Flyer. c, 3000fr, Richard Branson and SpaceShip One. d, 3000fr, White Knight Two.

No. 1262 — Voyager 2, 35th anniv.: a, 1180fr, Voyager 2 and Neptune. b, 1190fr, Voyageer 2 and Saturn. c, 3000fr, Voyager 2 and Uranus. d, 3000fr, Storms on Jupiter, Jupiter's moons Callisto and Io.

No. 1263 — Mail transportation: a, 1180fr, Vespa scooter. b, 1190fr, Pacific Air Transport 840 biplane. c, 3000fr, Panhard Dyna van. d, 3000fr, 1931 Ford postal truck.

No. 1264 — Cargo transportation: a, 1180fr, Airbus Skylink A-300 B4-608ST Beluga. b, 1190fr, Cargo ship Irina Trader. c, 3000fr, Scania R620 trucks. d, 3000fr, Class 7100 electric locomotive.

No. 1265 — Electric vehicles: a, 1180fr, Heathrow Airport transport pods. b, 1190fr, Policeman on Segway personal transporter. c, 3000fr, Series 500 Shinkansen train. d, 3000fr, 2009 Nisan Denki concept vehicle.

No. 1266, 7500fr, Dogs, sled and driver, diff. No. 1267, 7500fr, Painting of Royal Mail coach by John Frederick Herring, Sr. No. 1268, 7500fr, Fortune, 1300 (ship). No. 1269, 7500fr, Santa Maria, statue of Columbus, Madrid. No. 1270, 7500fr, John Fitch and 1790 steamboat model. No. 1271, 7500fr, German battleship Scharnhorst. No. 1272, 7500fr, Stephenson's Rocket, 1829. No. 1273, 7500fr, Aerotrain I-80 HV on bridge. No. 1274, 7500fr, Arctic Cat Firecat F7 snowmobile. No. 1275, 7500fr, Pierce 105-foot rear mount ladder firetruck. No. 1276, 7500fr, 1951 Bristol Royal Blue LL6B bus. No. 1277, 7500fr, 1886 Benz automobile. No. 1278, 7500fr, London taxi, 1950-82. No. 1279, 7500fr, Chevrolet and Jimmie Johnson. No. 1280, 7500fr, 2008 Harley-Davidson VRSCA V-Rod motorcycle. No. 1281, 7500fr, Earhart airplane wing and compass rose, vert. No. 1282, 7500fr, Tupolev Tu-144, diff. No. 1283, 7500fr, Canadair CL-600-2B16 Challenger 604 air ambulance. No. 1284, 7500fr, Lockheed F-117A Nighthawk, diff. No. 1285, 7500fr, NASA X-38. No. 1286, 7500fr, SpaceShip Two. No. 1287, 7500fr, Antenna of Voyager 2. No. 1288, 7500fr, Royal Air Mail automobile. No. 1289, 7500fr, Cargo ship Angeln. No. 1290, 7500fr, Solar Impulse solar-powered airplane.

2012, Dec. 28 Litho. *Perf. 13¼*

Sheets of 4, #a-d

1241-1265 A175 Set of 25 275.00 275.00

Souvenir Sheets

1266-1290 A175 Set of 25 245.00 245.00

Famous People — A176

No. 1291 — Frank Sinatra (1915-98), singer: a, 90fr, Wearing hat. b, 1180fr, Holding microphone. c, 3000fr, Standing near microphone. d, 3000fr, Wearing hat, diff.

No. 1292 — Johann Sebastian Bach (1685-1750), composer: a, 90fr, Wearing blue cravat. b, 1190fr, Playing organ. c, 3000fr, With cello and bow. d, 3000fr, Wearing red cravat.

No. 1293 — Robert Schumann (1810-56), composer: a, 90fr, Wearing blue jacket. b, 1190fr, Reviewing score. c, 3000fr, At piano. d, 3000fr, Wearing blue jacket, diff.

No. 1294 — Georges Lemmen (1865-1916), painter: a, 90fr, Lemmen. b, 1190fr, The Carousel, by Lemmen, 1896. c, 3000fr, Houses at La Hulpe, by Lemmen, 1888. d, 3000fr, Plage à Heist, by Lemmen, 1891.

No. 1295 — Paul Signac (1863-1935), painter: a, 90fr, Signac. b, 1190fr, Woman at her Toilette Wearing a Purple Corset, by Signac, 1893. c, 3000fr, Lighthouse at Grox, by Signac, 1923. d, 3000fr, Portrait of Félix Fénéon, by Signac, 1890.

No. 1296 — Brigitte Bardot, actress: a, 90fr, Wearing hat. b, 1190fr, Holding mask. c, 3000fr, Without hat. d, 3000fr, Scene from *Viva Maria!*

No. 1297 — Ludwig van Beethoven (1770-1827), composer: a, 1020fr, Wearing red cravat. b, 1180fr, As conductor. c, 3000fr, Holding paper. d, 3000fr, Wearing white cravat.

No. 1298 — Wolfgang Amadeus Mozart (1756-91), composer: a, 1020fr, Playing harpsichord. b, 1180fr, Portrait. c, 3000fr, Playing violin. d, 3000fr, Playing harpsichord with woman.

No. 1299 — Franz Schubert (1797-1828), composer: a, 1020fr, Wearing blue shirt. b, 1180fr, Playing piano. c, 3000fr, Playing guitar. d, 3000fr, Wearing red cravat.

No. 1300 — Richard Wagner (1813-83), composer: a, 1020fr, Facing right, wearing red cravat. b, 1180fr, Playing piano. c, 3000fr, Writing at desk. d, 3000fr, Facing forward, wearing red cravat.

No. 1301 — Charlie Chaplin (1889-1977), actor: a, 1020fr, Wearing cap. b, 1180fr, With dog. c, 3000fr, Holding "Little Tramp" doll. d, 3000fr, Without hat.

No. 1302 — John Wayne (1907-79), actor: a, 1020fr, Wearing red neckerchief. b, 1180fr, On horse. c, 3000fr, Holding rifle, wearing badge. d, 3000fr, Wearing hat.

No. 1303 — Greta Garbo (1905-90), actress: a, 1020fr, With Herbert Marshall in *The Painted Veil*. b, 1180fr, Wearing blue dress. c, 3000fr, With Conrad Nagel in *The Mysterious Lady*. d, 3000fr, Wearing crown.

No. 1304 — Marilyn Monroe (1926-62), actress: a, 1020fr, Wearing yellow dress and red scarf. b, 1180fr, Wearing top hat. c, 3000fr, Seated, wearing blue dress. d, 3000fr, Holding money.

No. 1305 — Georges Seurat (1859-91), painter: a, 1020fr, Seurat. b, 1190fr, Chahut, by Seurat, 1889-90. c, 3000fr, The Eiffel Tower, by Seurat, 1889. d, 3000fr, Bathers at Asnières, by Seurat, 1884.

No. 1306 — Paul Sérusier (1864-1927), painter: a, 1020fr, Sérusier. b, 1190fr, The Flowered Barrier, by Sérusier, 1889. c, 3000fr, The Garland of Roses, by Sérusier, 1898. d, 3000fr, L'Averse, by Sérusier, 1893.

No. 1307 — Grace Kelly (1929-82), actress and princess: a, 1090fr, Wearing fur stole. b, 1180fr, Seated, wearing white gown. c, 3000fr, Wearing white blouse and blue pants. d, 3000fr, Wearing white dress.

No. 1308 — James Dean (1931-55), actor: a, 1090fr, With Julie Harris in *East of Eden*. b, 1180fr, Wearing dark shirt and jacket. c, 3000fr, Wearing t-shirt and jacket. d, 3000fr, With Elizabeth Taylor in *Giant*.

No. 1309 — Jane Fonda, actress: a, 1090fr, Holding weapon. b, 1180fr, Wearing striped blouse. c, 3000fr, Wearing nurse's cap. d, 3000fr, Saluting, holding space helmet.

No. 1310 — Paul Gauguin (1843-1903), painter: a, 1090fr, Gauguin. b, 1190fr, Agony in the Garden, by Gauguin, 1889. c, 3000fr, Picking Lemons, by Gauguin, 1891. d, 3000fr, Peasant Woman and Cows in a Landscape, by Gauguin, 1890.

No. 1311 — Vincent van Gogh (1853-90), painter: a, 1090fr, Van Gogh. b, 1190fr, Olive Picking, by van Gogh, 1889. c, 3000fr, The Good Samaritan, by van Gogh, 1890. d, 3000fr, Avenue of Poplars in Autumn, by van Gogh, 1884.

No. 1312 — Henri de Toulouse-Lautrec (1864-1901), painter: a, 1090fr, Toulouse-Lautrec. b, 1190fr, At the Circus Fernando - The Rider, by Toulouse-Lautrec, 1888. c, 3000fr, Woman with an Umbrella, by Toulouse-Lautrec, 1889. d, 3000fr, The Clowness Cha U Ka O at the Moulin Rouge, by Toulouse-Lautred, 1895.

No. 1313 — Félix Vallotton (1865-1925), painter: a, 1090fr, Vallotton. b, 1190fr, Woman Reading, by Vallotton, 1922. c, 3000fr, Still Life with Flowers, by Vallotton, 1925. d, 3000fr, Still Life with Marigolds and Tangerines, by Vallotton, 1924.

No. 1314 — Pierre Bonnard (1867-1947), painter: a, 1090fr, Bonnard. b, 1190fr, Woman with a Parrot, by Bonnard, 1910. c, 3000fr, View of Cannet, by Bonnard, 1927. d, 3000fr, Jeune Fillesà la Mouette, by Bonnard, 1917.

No. 1315 — Elvis Presley (1935-77), musician: a, 1090fr, With guitar. b, 1190fr, Wearing white shirt and blue jacket. c, 3000fr, Wearing striped jacket and green shirt. d, 3000fr, In Hawaiian shirt playing ukulele.

No. 1316, 7500fr, Sinatra, diff. No. 1317, 7500fr, Bach, diff. No. 1318, 7500fr, Schumann, diff. No. 1319, 7500fr, Lemmen, diff. No. 1320, 7500fr, Signac, diff. No. 1321, 7500fr, Bardot and Lino Ventura in *Rum Runners*. No. 1322, 7500fr, Beethoven, diff. No. 1323, 7500fr, Mozart, diff. No. 1324, 7500fr, Schubert, diff. No. 1325, 7500fr, Wagner, diff. No. 1326, 7500fr, Chaplin, diff. No. 1327, 7500fr, Wayne, diff. No. 1328, 7500fr, Garbo, diff. No. 1329, 7500fr, Monroe, diff. No. 1330, 7500fr, Seurat, diff. No. 1331, 7500fr, Sérusier, diff. No. 1332, 7500fr, Kelly, diff. No. 1333, 7500fr, Dean with Natalie Wood in *Rebel Without a Cause*. No. 1334, 7500fr, Fonda, diff. No. 1335, 7500fr, Gauguin, diff. No. 1336, 7500fr, Van Gogh, diff. No. 1337, 7500fr, Toulouse-Lautred, diff. No. 1338, 7500fr, Vallotton, diff. No. 1339, 7500fr, Bonnard, diff. No. 1340, 7500fr, Presley, diff.

2013, July 5 Litho. *Perf. 13¼*

Sheets of 4, #a-d

1291-1315 A176 Set of 25 260.00 260.00

Souvenir Sheets

1316-1340 A176 Set of 25 245.00 245.00

A177

No. 1341 — Intl. Red Cross, 150th anniv.: a, 90fr, Rescue dog. b, 1180fr, Red Cross doctor examining patient. c, 3000fr, Red Cross worker giving food box to child. d, 3000fr, Rescue dog, diff.

No. 1342 — Paul P. Harris (1868-1947), founder of Rotary International: a, 90fr, Rotary emblem, Harris, Laeliocattleya ridolfiana. b, 1180fr, Rotary and Rotary Foundation emblems, owl, books, mortarboard and diploma. c, 3000fr, Rotary emblem, needle with polio vaccine, brain of boy. d, 3000fr, Rotary emblem, Harris, Selenipedium grande.

No. 1343 — Edvard Munch (1863-1944), painter, and: a, 90fr, The Haymaker, 1917. b, 1180fr, The Scream, 1893. c, 3000fr, Red and White, 1899-1900. d, 3000fr, Self-portrait with a Wine Bottle, 1906.

No. 1344 — 50th anniv. of space flight of Valentina Tereshkova, first woman in space: a, 90fr, Tereshkova in space suit, space capsule. b, 1190fr, Tereshkova on wheel, Tereshkova in military uniform. c, 3000fr, Tereshkova in space suit, Tershkova in military uniform. d, 3000fr, Tereshkova being examined by technicians, Tereshkova in space suit.

No. 1345 — Haroun Tazieff (1914-88), geologist and vulcanologist: a, 90fr, Tazieff and Nyiragongo Volcano, Congo. b, 1190fr, Tyrannosaurus and Redoubt Volcano, Alaska. c, 3000fr, Compsognathus and Ulawun Volcano, Papua New Guinea. d, 3000fr, Tazieff and Mount Etna, Sicily.

No. 1346 — Magnus Carlsen, chess grand master: a, 1020fr, Wearing red suit. b, 1180fr, Playing against Garry Kasparov. c, 3000fr, Playing against Levon Aronian. d, 3000fr, Wearing red suit, diff.

No. 1347 — Shenzhou 10: a, 1020fr, Astronaut Nie Haisheng. b, 1180fr, Astronaut Wang Yaping. c, 3000fr, Astronaut Zhang Xiaoguang. d, 3000fr, Shenzhou 10 docking with Tiangong 1.

No. 1348 — Butterflies and Scouts: a, 1020fr, Ornithoptera paradisea, Lord Robert Baden-Powell (1857-1941), founder of Scouting movement. b, 1190fr, Chrysiridia rhipheus, Scout hiking. c, 3000fr, Appias nero, Scout leaning on walking stick. d, 3000fr, Rhetus periander, Baden-Powell.

No. 1349 — Campaign against malaria: a, 1020fr, Line of people, malaria detection test strip. b, 1190fr, Campaign emblem, man receiving package. c, 3000fr, Red Cross workers. d, 3000fr, World Malaria Day emblem, Anopheles stephensi.

No. 1350 — Joan Miró (1893-1983), painter, and: a, 1020fr, Still Life II - The Carbide Lamp, 1922-23. b, 1190fr, Vineyards and Olive Trees, 1919. c, 3000fr, Abstract painting, 1933. d, 3000fr, The Smile of the Flamboyant Wings, 1953.

No. 1351 — Paintings in Rijksmuseum, Amsterdam: a, 1020fr, The Windmill at Wijk-bij-Duurstede, by Jacob van Ruysdael. b, 1190fr, Children of the Sea, by Jozef Israels. c, 3000fr, The Damrak in Amsterdam, by George Hendrik Breitner. d, 3000fr, The Art Gallery of Jan Gildemeester, by Adriaan de Lelie.

No. 1352 — Resignation of Pope Benedict XVI: a, 1020fr, Pope Benedict XVI holding censer, statue of angel holding cross. b, 1190fr, Pope Benedict XVI with clasped hands, St. Peter's Basilica. c, 3000fr, Pope Benedict XVI waving, St. Peter's Basilica. d, 3000fr, Pope Benedict XVI wearing miter and holding cross, statue of angel.

No. 1353 — Election of Pope Francis: a, 1090fr, Pope Francis waving. b, 1180fr, Pope Francis consecrating host. c, 3000fr, Pope Francis with children. d, 3000fr, Popes Francis and Benedict XVI.

No. 1354 — Coronation of Queen Elizabeth II, 60th anniv: a, 1090fr, Queen Elizabeth II as young woman on throne. b, 1180fr, Queen Elizabeth II as older woman on throne. c, 3000fr, Queen Elizabeth II with attendant lifting cape. d, 3000fr, Queen Elizabeth II and Prince Philip.

No. 1355 — Miles Joseph Berkeley (1803-89), mycologist: a, 1090fr, Boletus appendiculatus, Uroglaux dimorpha. b, 1180fr, Berkeley, Cortinarius caperatus. c, 3000fr, Berkeley, Amanita muscaria. d, 3000fr, Hypholoma faciculare, Tyto alba.

No. 1356 — Pierre de Coubertin (1863-1937), founder of International Olympic Committee: a, 1090fr, Coubertin, cycling. b, 1180fr, Diving, running. c, 3000fr, Hurdling, women's gymnastics. d, 3000fr, Men's gymnastics, rhythmic gymnastics.

No. 1357 — New Year 2014 (Year of the Horse: a, 1090fr, Horse leaping. b, 1180fr, Head of horse. c, 3000fr, Head of horse, diff. d, 3000fr, Horse galloping.

No. 1358 — Airships: a, 1090fr, Early propellor-driven dirigible. b, 1190fr, 2005 dirigible concept. c, 3000fr, High-altitude dirigible. d, 3000fr, Hindenburg.

No. 1359 — Mohandas K. Gandhi (1869-1948), Indian nationalist leader, and butterflies: a, 1090fr, Troides aeacus. b, 1190fr, Teinopalpus imperialis. c, 3000fr, Papilio krishna. d, 3000fr, Junonia almana.

No. 1360 — Diplomatic relations between Burundi and the People's Republic of China, 50th anniv.: a, 1090fr, Flags of China and Burundi, Mao Zedong and King Mwambutsa IV. b, 1190fr, Jia Qinglin meeting with Gabriel Ntisezerana, 2012. c, 3000fr, Jia Qinglin and Pierre Nkurunziza shaking hands, 2006. d, 3000fr, Flags of China and Burundi, Mao Zedong and King Mwambutsa IV, diff.

No. 1361, 7500fr, Red Cross worker holding child, Henry Dunant, founder of Red Cross. No. 1362, 7500fr, Rotary emblems throughout the years. No. 1363, 7500fr, Munch and Evening on the Avenue Karl-Johan, 1892. No. 1364, 7500fr, Tereshkova and Yuri Gagarin. No. 1365, 7500fr, Tazieff, Mount Etna, Pteranodon. No. 1366, 7500fr, Carlsen playing Viswanathan Anand. No. 1367, 7500fr, Shenzhou 10 astronauts in capsule. No. 1368, 7500fr, Hebomoia leucippe, group of Scouts. No. 1369, 7500fr, Red Cross patient, Anopheles stephensi. No. 1370, 7500fr, Miró and Burnt Canvas I, 1973. No. 1371, 7500fr, Still Life, by Floris van Dyck. No. 1372, 7500fr, Pope Benedict XVI and his coat of arms. No. 1373, 7500fr, Pope Francis and his coat of arms, St. Peter's Basilica. No. 1374, 7500fr, Queen Elizabeth II, Buckingham Palace. No. 1375, 7500fr, Berkeley, Boletus regineus, Boletus edulis. No. 1376, 7500fr, Discus and high jump. No. 1377, 7500fr, Horse galloping, diff. No. 1378, 7500fr, Ferdinand von Zeppelin (1838-1917), airship manufacturer, and Graf Zeppelin. No. 1379, 7500fr, Gandhi and Parnassius maharaja. No. 1380, 7500fr, Hospital in Bubanza, Burundi, flags of Burundi and China.

2013, Aug. 5 Litho. *Perf. 13¼*

Sheets of 4, #a-d

1341-1360 A177 Set of 20 210.00 210.00

Souvenir Sheets

1361-1380 A177 Set of 20 195.00 195.00

Rossica 2013 Intl. Philatelic Exhibition, Moscow (#1344, 1364); 2013 China Intl. Collection Expo, Beijing (#1360, 1380).

A178

No. 1381 — African animals: a, 90fr, Loxodonta africana. b, 1180fr, Panthera onca. c, 3000fr, Giraffa camelopardalis. d, 3000fr, Gorilla gorilla gorilla.

No. 1382 — Wild dogs and cacti: a, 90fr, Lycaon pictus, Opuntia ovata. b, 1190fr, Canis lupus dingo, Ferocactus echidne. c, 3000fr, Canis lupus dingo, Ferocactus pileus. d, 3000fr, Cuon alpinus, Cylindropuntia fulgida.

No. 1383 — Fish: a, 90fr, Sphaeramia nematoptera. b, 1190fr, Pterapogon kauderni. c, 3000fr, Balistapus undulatus. d, 3000fr, Synchiropus splendidus.

No. 1384 — Snakes: a, 90fr, Elaphe obsoleta quadrivittata. b, 1190fr, Lampropeltis triangulum. c, 3000fr, Diadophis punctatus. d, 3000fr, Opheodrys vernalis.

No. 1385 — Minerals: a, 90fr, Brazilian carnelian agate. b, 1190fr, Malachite. c, 3000fr, Spirit quartz (amethyst). d, 3000fr, Blue azurite.

No. 1386 — Pope John Paul II (1920-2005), and: a, 90fr, His coat of arms. b, 1190fr, St. Peter's Basilica. c, 3000fr, Colonnades in St. Peter's Square. d, 3000fr, Doves.

No. 1387 — Cat breeds: a, 1020fr, Bambino. b, 1180fr, Persian. c, 3000fr, Sphynx. d, 3000fr, Abyssinian.

No. 1388 — Birds: a, 1020fr, Buteo augur. b, 1180fr, Gyps africnus. c, 3000fr, Aquila verreauxii. d, 3000fr, Aquila nipalensis.

No. 1389 — Dinosaurs: a, 1020fr, Tyrannosaurus rex. b, 1180fr, Nasutoceratops. c, 3000fr, Stegosaurus. d, 3000fr, Plateosaurus.

No. 1390 — Human ancestors: a, 1020fr, Homo erectus hunting. b, 1180fr, Homo neanderthalensis drawing on cave wall. c, 3000fr, Homo neanderthalensis, drawing of mammoth. d, 3000fr, Homo floresiensis hunting.

No. 1391 — Impressionist paintings: a, 1020fr, A Cloudy Day, by Julian Onderdonk. b, 1180fr, Woman Reading in the Garden, by Richard E. Miller. c, 3000fr, Summer Fragrance, by Edward Alfred Cucuel. d, 3000fr, Out to Sea, by Guy Rose.

No. 1392 — Giuseppe Verdi (1813-1901), composer, and costumes from: a, 1020fr, Aida. b, 1180fr, Rigoletto. c, 3000fr, Aida, diff. d, 3000fr, Don Carlos.

No. 1393 — Mao Zedong (1893-1976), Chinese communist leader: a, 1020fr, At desk. b, 1180fr, With arm raised. c, 3000fr, With hands together. d, 3000fr, Reading newspaper and giving speech.

No. 1394 — 95th birthday of Nelson Mandela, President of South Africa: a, 1020fr, Mandela with Mother Teresa. b, 1180fr, Mandela waving. c, 3000fr, Mandela with hands together. d, 3000fr, Mandela with Pope John Paul II.

No. 1395 — Turtles: a, 1020fr, Rhinoclemmys funerea, Leucocephalon yuwonoi. b, 1190fr, Heosemys spinosa. c, 3000fr, Eretmochelys imbricata. d, 3000fr, Chelonia mydas.

No. 1396 — Cricket players: a, 1020fr, Travis Birt. b, 1190fr, Graeme Swann. c, 3000fr, M. S. Dhoni. d, 3000fr, Misbah-ul-Haq.

No. 1397 — Dolphins: a, 1090fr, Sotalia fluviatilis. b, 1180fr, Stenella coeruleoalba. c, 3000fr, Steno bredanensis. d, 3000fr, Lagenorhynchus obscurus.

No. 1398 — Bees and flowers: a, 1090fr, Apis mellifera mellifera, Camellia japonica. b, 1180fr, Apis cerana, Primula sinensis. c, 3000fr, Apis mellifera, Rhododendron maximum. d, 3000fr, Apis florea, Syringa vulgaris.

No. 1399 — Fire trucks: a, 1090fr, Mercedes-Benz Atego LF 10/6 Ziegler. b, 1180fr, Ford F-350. c, 3000fr, Kronenburg MAC 11. d, 3000fr, Scania P270 FJ 07 ANP.

No. 1400 — Visit of Pope Francis to Brazil: a, 1090fr, Pope Francis, flag of Brazil, youth, World Youth Day emblem. b, 1180fr, Pope Francis, flag of Brazil, Aparecida Cathedral. c, 3000fr, Pope Francis, World Youth Day emblem and stage. d, 3000fr, Pope Francis, World Youth Day emblem, Christ the Redeemer statue, flags.

No. 1401 — Owls: a, 1090fr, Asio otus. b, 1190fr, Pseudoscops clamator. c, 3000fr, Asio flammeus. d, 3000fr, Strix aluco aluco.

No. 1402 — Endangered animals: a, 1090fr, Cercopithecus hamlyni. b, 1190fr, Eidolon helvum. c, 3000fr, Phataginus tricuspis. d, 3000fr, Felis margarita.

No. 1403 — Shells and lighthouses: a, 1090fr, Chicoreus palmarosae, Boca Chita Lighthouse, Florida. b, 1190fr, Lobatus gigas, Peggys Point Lighthouse, Nova Scotia. c, 3000fr, Cardium costatum, La Martre Lighthouse, Quebec. d, 3000fr, Columbarium pagoda pagoda, Maota Pagoda Lighthouse, China.

No. 1404 — Paintings by Pablo Picasso (1881-1973): a, 1090fr, Dying Bull, 1934. b, 1190fr, Mandolin and Guitar, 1924. c, 3000fr, Interior with a Girl Drawing, 1935. d, 3000fr, Les Demoiselles d'Avignon, 1907.

No. 1405 — High-speed trains: a, 1180fr, SNCF TGV Atlantique. b, 1190fr, BR Class 395 Javelin. c, 3000fr, NTV Alstom AGV ETR 575. d, 3000fr, Hitachi Super Express.

No. 1406, 7500fr, Ceratotherium simum. No. 1407, 7500fr, Cuon alpinus, Hylocereus undatus. No. 1408, 7500fr, Nemateleotris magnifica. No. 1409, 7500fr, Regina rigida sinicola. No. 1410, 7500fr, Variscite. No. 1411, 7500fr, Pope John Paul II, statue. No. 1412, 7500fr, Siberian cat. No. 1413, 7500fr, Terathopius ecaudatus. No. 1414, 7500fr, Dollodon. No. 1415, 7500fr, Homo neanderthalensis drawing on cave wall, diff. No. 1416, 7500fr, The Bowdoin, Monhegan Island, by Edward Willis Redfield. No. 1417, 7500fr, Verdi and scene from Aida. No. 1418, 7500fr, Mao Zedong and Chinese writing. No. 1419, 7500fr, Mandela, map of Africa. No. 1420, 7500fr, Psammobates geometricus. No. 1421, 7500fr, Adam Gilchrist. No. 1422, 7500fr, Cephalorhynchus commerssonii. No. 1423, 7500fr, Vespula germanica, Hydrangea macrophylla. No. 1424, 7500fr, Rosenbauer fire truck. No. 1425, 7500fr, Pope Francis, youths raising cross, flag of Brazil. No. 1426, 7500fr, Bubo virginianus. No. 1427, 7500fr, Varecia rubra. No. 1428, 7500fr, Charonia tritonis, Sambro Island Lighthouse, Nova Scotia. No. 1429, The Old Guitarist, by Picasso, 1903. No. 1430, 7500fr, Siemens Velaro ICE 3DB Class 407.

2013, Aug. 20 Litho. *Perf. 13¼*

Sheets of 4, #a-d

1381-1405 A178 Set of 25 260.00 260.00

Souvenir Sheets

1406-1430 A178 Set of 25 245.00 245.00

Brasiliana 2013 Intl. Philatelic Exhibition, Rio (#1400, 1425).

SEMI-POSTAL STAMPS

Prince Louis Rwagasore — SP1

Prince and Stadium SP2

Nos. B3, B6, Prince, memorial monument.

Perf. 14x13, 13x14

1963, Feb. 15 Photo. Unwmk.

B1 SP1 50c + 25c brt vio .25 .25
B2 SP2 1fr + 50c red org & dk bl .25 .25
B3 SP2 1.50fr + 75c lem & dk vio .25 .25
B4 SP1 3.50fr + 1.50fr lil rose .25 .25
B5 SP2 5fr + 2fr rose pink & dk bl .25 .25
B6 SP2 6.50fr + 3fr gray ol & dk vio .25 .25
Nos. B1-B6 (6) 1.50 1.50

Issued in memory of Prince Louis Rwagasore (1932-61), son of King Mwami Mwambutsa IV and Prime Minister. The surtax was for the stadium and monument in his honor.

Exist imperf. Value set, $18.

Red Cross Type of Regular Issue

Souvenir Sheet

1963, Sept. 26 Litho. *Imperf.*

B7 Sheet of 4 5.00 5.00
a. A5 4fr + 2fr fawn, red & black 1.00 1.00
b. A5 8fr + 2fr green, red & black 1.00 1.00
c. A5 10fr + 2fr gray, red & black 1.00 1.00
d. A5 20fr + 2fr ultra, red & black 1.00 1.00

Surtax for Red Cross work in Burundi.

Olympic Type of Regular Issue

Souvenir Sheet

Designs: 18fr+2fr, Hurdling, horiz. 20fr+5fr, Vaulting, horiz.

1964, Nov. 18 *Perf. 13½*

B8 Sheet of 2 12.00 12.00
a. A13 18fr + 2fr yel grn & multi 5.00 4.00
b. A13 20fr + 5fr brt pink & multi 5.00 4.00

Exists imperf. Value $12.

Scientist with Microscope and Map of Burundi — SP3

Lithographed and Photogravure

1965, Jan. 28 Unwmk. *Perf. 14½*

B9 SP3 2fr + 50c multi .25 .25
B10 SP3 4fr + 1.50fr multi .25 .25
B11 SP3 5fr + 2.50fr multi .30 .25
B12 SP3 8fr + 3fr multi .40 .25
B13 SP3 10fr + 5fr multi .65 .30
Nos. B9-B13 (5) 1.85 1.30

Souvenir Sheet

Perf. 13x13½

B14 SP3 10fr + 10fr multi 1.50 1.50

Issued for the fight against tuberculosis.

Exist imperf. Values: set $5; souvenir sheet $2.

Coat of Arms, 10fr Coin, Reverse SP4

Designs (Coins of Various Denominations): 4fr+50c, 8fr+50c, 15fr+50c, 40fr+50c, King Mwambutsa IV, obverse.

Lithographed; Embossed on Gilt Foil

1965, Aug. 9 *Imperf.*

Diameter: 39mm

B15 SP4 2fr + 50c crim & org .25 .25
B16 SP4 4fr + 50c ultra & ver .30 .30

Diameter: 45mm

B17 SP4 6fr + 50c org & gray .50 .50
B18 SP4 8fr + 50c bl & mag .65 .65

Diameter: 56mm

B19 SP4 12fr + 50c lt grn & red lil .95 .95
B20 SP4 15fr + 50c yel grn & lt lil 1.10 1.10

Diameter: 67mm

B21 SP4 25fr + 50c vio bl & buff 2.10 2.10
B22 SP4 40fr + 50c brt pink & red brn 4.00 4.00
Nos. B15-B22 (8) 9.85 9.85

Stamps are backed with patterned paper in blue, orange and pink engine-turned design.

Prince Louis Rwagasore and Pres. John F. Kennedy SP5

Designs: 4fr+1fr, 20fr+5fr, Prince Louis, memorial. 20fr+2fr, 40fr+5fr, Pres. John F. Kennedy, library shelves. 40fr+2fr, King Mwambutsa IV at Kennedy grave, Arlington, vert.

1966, Jan. 21 Photo. *Perf. 13½*

B23 SP5 4fr + 1fr gray bl & dk brn .25 .25
B24 SP5 10fr + 1fr pale grn, ind & brn .25 .25
B25 SP5 20fr + 2fr lil & dp grn .50 .25
B26 SP5 40fr + 2fr gray grn & dk brn 1.10 .55
Nos. B23-B26 (4) 2.10 1.30

Souvenir Sheet

B27 Sheet of 2 3.25 3.75
a. SP5 20fr + 5fr gray bl & dk brn 1.50 1.50
b. SP5 40fr + 5fr lilac & dp grn 1.50 1.50

Issued in memory of Prince Louis Rwagasore and President John F. Kennedy.

Exist imperf. Values: set $6; souvenir sheet $3.50.

Republic

Winston Churchill and St. Paul's, London SP6

Designs: 15fr+2fr, Tower of London and Churchill. 20fr+3fr, Big Ben and Churchill.

1967, Mar. 23 Photo. *Perf. 13½*

B28 SP6 4fr + 1fr multi .30 .25
B29 SP6 15fr + 2fr multi .50 .25
B30 SP6 20fr + 3fr multi .65 .40
Nos. B28-B30 (3) 1.45 .90

Issued in memory of Sir Winston Churchill (1874-1965), statesman and World War II leader.

Exist imperf. Value $4.50.

A souvenir sheet contains one airmail stamp, 50fr+5fr, with Churchill portrait centered. Size: 80x80mm. Exists perf and imperf. Value, each sheet, $2.

Nos. B28-B30 Overprinted

1967, July 14 Photo. *Perf. 13½*

B31 SP6 4fr + 1fr multi .70 .25
B32 SP6 15fr + 2fr multi 1.00 .40
B33 SP6 20fr + 3fr multi 1.25 .50
Nos. B31-B33 (3) 2.95 1.15

50th anniversary of Lions International.

Exist with dates transposed. Value, set $30.

Both the regular set imperf and the souvenir sheets described below No. B30 also received this Lions overprint. Value: set $8.50; souvenir sheet, each $3. Also exists imperf. Value, set $50.

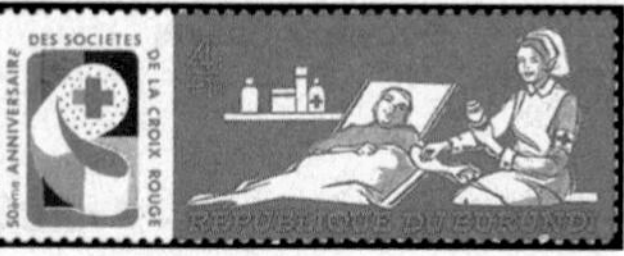

Blood Transfusion and Red Cross — SP7

Designs: 7fr+1fr, Stretcher bearers and wounded man. 11fr+1fr, Surgical team. 17fr+1fr, Nurses tending blood bank.

1969, June 26 Photo. *Perf. 13½*

B34 SP7 4fr + 1fr multi .25 .25
B35 SP7 7fr + 1fr multi .35 .25
B36 SP7 11fr + 1fr multi .40 .25
B37 SP7 17fr + 1fr multi .60 .25
Nos. B34-B37,CB9-CB11 (7) 5.55 2.25

League of Red Cross Societies, 50th anniv.

Exist imperf. Value set (7), $9.

Pope Paul VI and Map of Africa — SP8

3fr+2fr, 17fr+2fr, Pope Paul VI. 10fr+2fr, Flag made of flags of African Nations. 14fr+2fr, View of St. Peter's, Rome. 40fr+2fr, 40fr+5fr, Martyrs of Uganda. 50fr+2fr, 50fr+5fr, Pope on Throne.

1969, Sept. 12 Photo. *Perf. 13½*

B38 SP8 3fr + 2fr multi, vert. .25 .25
B39 SP8 5fr + 2fr multi .25 .25
B40 SP8 10fr + 2fr multi .35 .25
B41 SP8 14fr + 2fr multi .75 .25
B42 SP8 17fr + 2fr multi, vert. 1.25 .30
B43 SP8 40fr + 2fr multi 1.75 .60
B44 SP8 50fr + 2fr multi 2.00 .65
Nos. B38-B44 (7) 6.60 2.55

Souvenir Sheet

B45 Sheet of 2 4.50 4.50
a. SP8 40fr + 5fr multi 2.00 2.00
b. SP8 50fr + 5fr multi 2.00 2.00

Visit of Pope Paul VI to Uganda, 7/31-8/2.
Exist imperf. Values: set $11; souvenir sheet $4.50.

Virgin and Child, by Albrecht Dürer — SP9

Christmas (Paintings): 11fr+1fr, Madonna of the Eucharist, by Sandro Botticelli. 20fr+1fr, Holy Family, by El Greco.

1970, Dec. 14 Photo. *Perf. 13½*

Gold Frame

B46 SP9 6.50fr + 1fr multi .70 .25
B47 SP9 11fr + 1fr multi 1.00 .25
B48 SP9 20fr + 1fr multi 1.25 .35
a. Souv. sheet of 3, #B46-B48 3.50 3.50
Nos. B46-B48,CB12-CB14 (6) 6.95 2.15

Exist imperf. Values: set (6) $6.50; souvenir sheets $6.75.

Nos. 376-378 Surcharged in Gold and Black

1971, Nov. 27

B49 A51 3fr + 1fr multi .25 .25
B50 A51 5fr + 1fr multi .65 .25
B51 A51 6fr + 1fr multi .75 .25
a. Souvenir sheet of 3 4.00 4.00
Nos. B49-B51,CB19-CB21 (6) 5.45 1.80

UNICEF, 25th anniv. No. B51a contains 3 stamps similar to Nos. B49-B51 with 2fr surtax each.
Exist imperf. Values: set (6) $5.50; souvenir sheets $8.

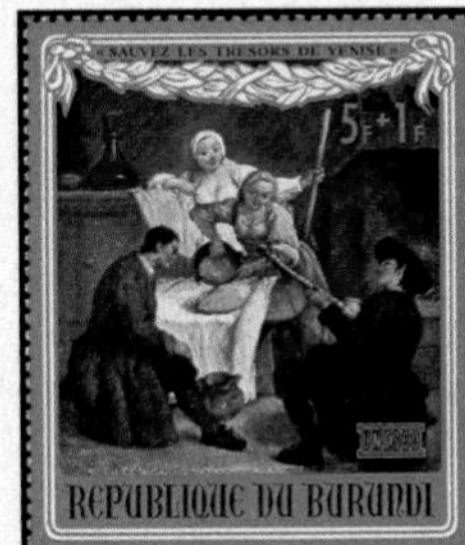

"La Polenta," by Pietro Longhi SP10

Designs: 3fr+1fr, Archangel Michael, Byzantine icon from St. Mark's 6fr+1fr, "Gossip," by Pietro Longhi. 11fr+1fr, "Diana's Bath," by Giovanni Batista Pittoni. All stamps inscribed UNESCO.

1971, Dec. 27

B52 SP10 3fr + 1fr gold & multi .25 .25
B53 SP10 5fr + 1fr gold & multi .35 .25
B54 SP10 6fr + 1fr gold & multi .45 .25
B55 SP10 11fr + 1fr gold & multi .70 .25
a. Souvenir sheet of 4 3.00 3.00
Nos. B52-B55,CB22-CB25 (8) 5.80 2.20

The surtax was for the UNESCO campaign to save the treasures of Venice. No. B55a contains 4 stamps similar to Nos. B52-B55, but with 2fr surtax.
Exist imperf. Values: set (8) $7.50; souvenir sheets $10.

Nos. 408-410 Surcharged in Silver

1972, Dec. 12 Photo. *Perf. 13½*

B56 A57 5fr + 1fr multi .55 .25
B57 A57 10fr + 1fr multi 1.00 .25
B58 A57 15fr + 1fr multi 1.60 .25
a. Souvenir sheet of 3 3.00 3.00
Nos. B56-B58,CB26-CB28 (6) 8.40 1.95

Christmas 1972. No. B58a contains 3 stamps similar to Nos. B56-B58, but with 2fr surtax.
Exist imperf. Values: set (6) $10; souvenir sheets $16.

Nos. 441-443 Surcharged "+1F" in Silver

1973, Dec. 14 Photo. *Perf. 13*

B59 A64 5fr + 1fr multi .70 .25
B60 A64 10fr + 1fr multi .90 .25
B61 A64 15fr + 1fr multi 1.10 .25
a. Souvenir sheet of 3 4.00 4.00
Nos. B59-B61,CB29-CB31 (6) 6.60 1.95

Christmas 1973. No. B61a contains 3 stamps similar to Nos. B59-B61 with 2fr surtax each.
Exist imperf. Values: set (6) $7.50; souvenir sheets $8.

Christmas Type of 1974

1974, Dec. 2 Photo. *Perf. 13*

B62 A70 5fr + 1fr multi 1.00 .25
B63 A70 10fr + 1fr multi 1.40 .30
B64 A70 15fr + 1fr multi 2.10 .40
a. Souvenir sheet of 3 5.50 5.50
Nos. B62-B64,CB32-CB34 (6) 10.10 2.85

No. B64a contains 3 stamps similar to Nos. B62-B64 with 2fr surtax each.
Exist imperf. Values: set (6) $11; souvenir sheets $17.

Nos. 485-487 Surcharged "+ 1F" in Silver and Black

1975, Dec. 22 Photo. *Perf. 13*

Pairs, #a.-b.

B65 A73 5fr + 1fr #485 3.25 .25
B66 A73 13fr + 1fr #486 6.50 .30
B67 A73 27fr + 1fr #487 10.00 .60
c. Souvenir sheet of 6 16.50 16.50
Nos. B65-B67,CB35-CB37 (6) 41.50 2.55

Michelangelo Buonarroti (1475-1564), 500th birth anniversary. No. B67c contains 6 stamps similar to Nos. B65a-B67b with 2fr surcharge each.

Exist imperf. Values: set (6) $28; souvenir sheets $26.

Nos. 504-506 Surcharged "+1f" in Silver and Black

1976, Nov. 25 Photo. *Perf. 13½*

B71 A76 5fr + 1fr multi .95 .25
B72 A76 13fr + 1fr multi 1.50 .25
B73 A76 27fr + 1fr multi 3.00 .60
a. Souvenir sheet of 3 5.50 5.50
Nos. B71-B73,CB41-CB43 (6) 12.55 2.35

Christmas 1976. No. B73a contains 3 stamps similar to Nos. B71-B73 with 2fr surtax each.
Exist imperf. Values: set (6) $11; souvenir sheets $10.

Nos. 531-533 Surcharged "+1fr" in Silver and Black

1977 Photo. *Perf. 14x13*

B74 A83 5fr + 1fr multi .90 .25
B75 A83 13fr + 1fr multi 2.50 .25
B76 A83 27fr + 1fr multi 3.00 .50
a. Souvenir sheet of 3 6.50 6.50
Nos. B74-B76,CB44-CB46 (6) 14.40 2.25

Christmas 1977. No. B76a contains 3 stamps similar to Nos. B74-B76 with 2fr surtax each.
Exist imperf. Values: set (6) $12; souvenir sheets $13.

Christmas Type of 1979

1979, Feb. Photo. *Perf. 14x13*

B77 A86 13fr + 1fr multi 1.50 1.25
B78 A86 17fr + 1fr multi 1.90 1.60
B79 A86 27fr + 1fr multi 3.50 2.50
B80 A86 31fr + 1fr multi 4.00 3.50
B81 A86 40fr + 1fr multi 5.25 4.50
Nos. B77-B81 (5) 16.15 13.35

Exist imperf. Value $12.

IYC Type of 1979

1979, July 19 Photo. *Perf. 14*

B82 Sheet of 4 11.00 11.00
a. A88 10fr + 2fr like #557 2.50 2.50
b. A88 20fr + 2fr like #558 2.50 2.50
c. A88 27fr + 2fr like #559 2.50 2.50
d. A88 50fr + 2fr like #560 2.50 2.50

Exist imperf. Value $12.50.

Christmas Type of 1979

1979, Dec. 10 Photo. *Perf. 13½*

B83 A89 20fr + 1fr like #561 2.50 1.00
B84 A89 27fr + 1fr like #562 4.75 2.00
B85 A89 31fr + 1fr like #563 6.50 2.50
B86 A89 50fr + 2fr like #564 8.25 2.75
Nos. B83-B86 (4) 17.50 8.25

Christmas Type of 1980

1981, Jan. 16 Photo. *Perf. 13½x13*

B87 A92 10fr + 1fr like #579 1.60 .65
B88 A92 30fr + 1fr like #580 3.25 1.25
B89 A92 40fr + 1fr like #581 7.25 3.00
B90 A92 50fr + 1fr like #582 10.00 4.00
Nos. B87-B90 (4) 20.00 8.90

Christmas Type of 1983

1983, Nov. 2 Litho. *Perf. 14½x13½*

B91 A97 10fr + 1fr like #607 5.50 1.25
B92 A97 25fr + 1fr like #608 8.00 1.75
B93 A97 30fr + 1fr like #609 15.00 3.50
B94 A97 50fr + 1fr like #610 21.00 9.00
Nos. B91-B94 (4) 40.00 15.50

Christmas Type of 1984

1984, Dec. 15 *Perf. 13½*

B95 A101 10fr + 1fr like #629 2.75 1.00
B96 A101 25fr + 1fr like #630 6.50 2.50
B97 A101 30fr + 1fr like #631 7.75 3.00
B98 A101 50fr + 1fr like #632 11.00 4.75
Nos. B95-B98 (4) 28.00 11.25

Multi-party Elections, 1st Anniv.
SP11 SP12

30fr+10fr, Pres. Buyoya handing Baton of Power to Pres. Ndadaye. 110fr+10fr, Pres. Ndadaye giving inauguration speech. 115fr+10fr, Arms, map of Burundi. 120fr+10fr, Warrior, flag of Burundi, trees, map of Burundi.

1994, Oct. 20 Litho. *Perf. 15*

B99 SP11 30fr +10fr multi 1.00 .75
B100 SP11 110fr +10fr multi 3.50 2.75
B101 SP12 115fr +10fr multi 4.00 2.75
B102 SP12 120fr +10fr multi 4.00 2.75
Nos. B99-B102 (4) 12.50 9.00

AIR POST STAMPS

Animal Type of Regular Issue

6fr, Zebra. 8fr, Cape buffalo (bubalis). 10fr, Impala. 14fr, Hippopotamus. 15fr, Defassa waterbuck. 20fr, Cheetah. 50fr, Elephant.

Unwmk.

1964, July 2 Litho. *Perf. 14*

Size: 42x21mm, 21x42mm

C1 A9 6fr multi .40 .25
C2 A9 8fr multi .50 .25
C3 A9 10fr multi, vert. .70 .25
C4 A9 14fr multi 1.05 .30
C5 A9 15fr multi, vert. 1.35 .40

Size: 53x32½mm

C6 A9 20fr multi 2.50 .50
C7 A9 50fr multi 6.00 .75
Nos. C1-C7 (7) 17.75 2.60

Bird Type of Regular Issue

Birds: 6fr, Secretary bird. 8fr, African anhinga. 10fr, African peacock. 14fr, Bee eater. 15fr, Yellow-billed stork. 20fr, Saddle-billed stork. 50fr, Abyssinian ground hornbill. 75fr, Martial eagle. 130fr, Lesser flamingo.

1965, June 10 Litho. *Perf. 14*

Size: 26x43mm

C8 A14 6fr multi .25 .25
C9 A14 8fr multi .35 .25
C10 A14 10fr multi .45 .25
C11 A14 14fr multi .75 .30
C12 A14 15fr multi .95 .40

Size: 33x53mm

C13 A14 20fr multi 1.90 .45
C14 A14 50fr multi 3.00 .65
C15 A14 75fr multi 4.50 1.00
C16 A14 130fr multi 7.75 1.60
Nos. C8-C16 (9) 19.90 5.15

For overprints see Nos. C35A-C35I.

Flower Type of Regular Issue

Flowers: 6fr, Dissotis. 8fr, Crossandra. 10fr, Ansellia. 14fr, Thunbergia. 15fr, Schizoglossum. 20fr, Gazania. 50fr, Protea. 75fr, Hibiscus. 130fr, Markhamia.

1966, Oct. 10 Unwmk. *Perf. 13½*

Size: 31x31mm

C17 A17 6fr multi .35 .25
C18 A17 8fr multi .50 .25
C19 A17 10fr multi .60 .25
C20 A17 14fr multi .75 .25
C21 A17 15fr multi 1.00 .25

Size: 39x39mm

C22 A17 20fr multi 1.25 .25
C23 A17 50fr multi 2.25 .35
C24 A17 75fr multi 3.50 .50
C25 A17 130fr multi 6.00 1.00
Nos. C17-C25 (9) 16.20 3.10

For overprints see Nos. C27-C35.

Tapestry Type of Regular Issue

Souvenir Sheet

1966, Nov. 4 Unwmk. *Perf. 13½*

C26 A18 Sheet of 7 (14fr) 9.00 6.50

See note after No. 158.

REPUBLIC

Nos. C17-C25 Overprinted

1967 Litho. *Perf. 13½*

Size: 31x31mm

C27 A17 6fr multi .25 .25
C28 A17 8fr multi .35 .25
C29 A17 10fr multi .50 .25
C30 A17 14fr multi .75 .25
C31 A17 15fr multi 1.00 .25

Size: 39x39mm

No.	Type	Description	Unused	Used
C32	A17	20fr multi	2.00	.35
C33	A17	50fr multi	5.00	.90
C34	A17	75fr multi	8.00	1.50
C35	A17	130fr multi	8.50	1.50
		Nos. C27-C35 (9)	26.35	5.25

Nos. C8-C16 Overprinted

1967 Litho. *Perf. 14*

Size: 26x43mm

No.	Type	Description	Unused	Used
C35A	A14	6fr multi	*.50*	.40
C35B	A14	8fr multi	*1.00*	.50
C35C	A14	10fr multi	*1.50*	.60
C35D	A14	14fr multi	*2.00*	.75
C35E	A14	15fr multi	*2.75*	.90

Size: 33x53mm

No.	Type	Description	Unused	Used
C35F	A14	20fr multi	*4.00*	2.00
C35G	A14	50fr multi	*8.50*	4.00
C35H	A14	75fr multi	*12.50*	5.00
C35I	A14	130fr multi	*18.00*	7.50
		Nos. C35A-C35I (9)	50.75	21.65

African Art Type of Regular Issue

10fr, Spirit of Bakutu figurine, Equatorial Africa. 14fr, Pearl throne of Sultan of the Bamum, Cameroun. 17fr, Bronze head of Mother Queen of Benin, Nigeria. 24fr, Statue of 109th Bakouba king, Kata-Mbula, Central Congo. 26fr, Baskets and lances, Burundi.

1967, June 5 Photo. *Perf. 13½*

No.	Type	Description	Unused	Used
C36	A20	10fr gold & multi	.25	.25
C37	A20	14fr gold & multi	.30	.25
C38	A20	17fr gold & multi	.45	.25
C39	A20	24fr gold & multi	.55	.30
C40	A20	26fr gold & multi	.90	.50
		Nos. C36-C40 (5)	3.05	1.45

Boy Scout Type of Regular Issue

10fr, Scouts on hiking trip. 14fr, Cooking at campfire. 17fr, Lord Baden-Powell. 24fr, Boy Scout & Cub Scout giving Scout sign. 26fr, First aid.

1967, Aug. 9 *Perf. 13½*

No.	Type	Description	Unused	Used
C41	A21	10fr gold & multi	1.25	.25
C42	A21	14fr gold & multi	1.50	.25
C43	A21	17fr gold & multi	1.75	.25
C44	A21	24fr gold & multi	2.75	.25
C45	A21	26fr gold & multi	3.00	.40
		Nos. C41-C45 (5)	10.25	1.20

A souvenir sheet of 2 contains one each of Nos. C44-C45 and 2 labels in the designs of Nos. 208-209 with commemorative inscriptions was issued 1/8/68. Size: 100x100mm. Value, $8 unused, $5 used.

Fish Type of Regular Issue

Designs: Various Tropical Fish

1967, Sept. 8 Photo. *Perf. 13½*

Size: 50x23mm

No.	Type	Description	Unused	Used
C46	A19	6fr multi	.95	.25
C47	A19	8fr multi	1.40	.25
C48	A19	10fr multi	1.90	.25
C49	A19	14fr multi	2.25	.25
C50	A19	15fr multi	2.00	.25

Size: 58x27mm

No.	Type	Description	Unused	Used
C51	A19	20fr multi	3.75	.25
C52	A19	50fr multi	7.75	.30
C53	A19	75fr multi	11.50	.35
C54	A19	130fr multi	18.00	.65
		Nos. C46-C54 (9)	39.10	2.55

Boeing 707 of Air Congo and ITY Emblem — AP1

Designs: 14fr, Boeing 727 of Sabena over lake. 17fr, Vickers VC10 of East African Airways over lake. 26fr, Boeing 727 of Sabena over airport.

1967, Nov. 3 Photo. *Perf. 13*

No.	Type	Description	Unused	Used
C55	AP1	10fr blk, yel brn & sil	.35	.25
C56	AP1	14fr blk, org & sil	.60	.25
C57	AP1	17fr blk, brt bl & sil	.70	.30
C58	AP1	26fr blk, brt rose lil & sil	1.40	.55
		Nos. C55-C58 (4)	3.05	1.35

Opening of the jet airport at Bujumbura and for International Tourist Year, 1967.
Exist imperf. Value set, $7.

Paintings Type of Regular Issue

Paintings: 17fr, Woman with Cat, by Renoir. 24fr, The Jewish Bride, by Rembrandt, horiz. 26fr, Pope Innocent X, by Velazquez.

1968, Mar. 29 Photo. *Perf. 13½*

No.	Type	Description	Unused	Used
C59	A26	17fr multi	.65	.30
C60	A26	24fr multi	1.00	.40
C61	A26	26fr multi	1.25	.90
		Nos. C59-C61 (3)	2.90	1.60

Issued in sheets of 6.

Space Type of Regular Issue

14fr, Moon Probe. 18fr, Russian astronaut walking in space. 25fr, Mariner satellite, Mars. 40fr, American astronaut walking in space.

1968, May 15 Photo. *Perf. 13½*

Size: 41x41mm

No.	Type	Description	Unused	Used
C62	A27	14fr sil & multi	.60	.25
C63	A27	18fr sil & multi	.80	.25
C64	A27	25fr sil & multi	.90	.25
C65	A27	40fr sil & multi	1.75	.60
		Nos. C62-C65 (4)	4.05	1.25

Butterfly Type of Regular Issue

Butterflies: 6fr, Teracolus annae. 8fr, Graphium ridleyanus. 10fr, Cymothoe. 14fr, Charaxes eupale. 15fr, Papilio bromius. 20fr, Papilio zenobia. 50fr, Salamis aethiops. 75fr, Danais chrysippus. 130fr, Salamis temora.

1968, Sept. 9 Photo. *Perf. 13½*

Size: 38x42mm

No.	Type	Description	Unused	Used
C66	A28	6fr gold & multi	1.10	.25
C67	A28	8fr gold & multi	2.00	.25
C68	A28	10fr gold & multi	2.25	.30
C69	A28	14fr gold & multi	2.75	.40
C70	A28	15fr gold & multi	3.00	.50

Size: 44x49mm

No.	Type	Description	Unused	Used
C71	A28	20fr gold & multi	4.25	.75
C72	A28	50fr gold & multi	7.50	1.00
C73	A28	75fr gold & multi	12.50	1.25
C74	A28	130fr gold & multi	20.00	1.50
		Nos. C66-C74 (9)	49.00	6.15

Painting Type of Regular Issue

Paintings: 17fr, The Letter, by Jean H. Fragonard. 26fr, Young Woman Reading Letter, by Jan Vermeer. 40fr, Lady Folding Letter, by Elisabeth Vigée-Lebrun. 50fr, Mademoiselle Lavergne, by Jean Etienne Liotard.

1968, Sept. 30 Photo. *Perf. 13½*

No.	Type	Description	Unused	Used
C84	A29	17fr multi	.65	.30
C85	A29	26fr multi	1.25	.30
C86	A29	40fr multi	2.00	.40
C87	A29	50fr multi	2.75	.40
		Nos. C84-C87 (4)	6.65	1.40

A souvenir sheet containing examples of Nos. C86-C87 with changed colors exists perf and imperf. Value, each $6.50.

Olympic Games Type

1968, Oct. 24

No.	Type	Description	Unused	Used
C88	A30	10fr Shot put	.25	.25
C89	A30	17fr Running	.45	.25
C90	A30	26fr Hammer throw	.90	.25
C91	A30	50fr Hurdling	1.75	.40
C92	A30	75fr Broad jump	3.25	.55
		Nos. C88-C92 (5)	6.55	1.60

Christmas Type of 1968

Paintings: 10fr, Virgin and Child, by Correggio. 14fr, Nativity, by Federigo Baroccio. 17fr, Holy Family, by El Greco. 26fr, Adoration of the Magi, by Maino.

1968, Nov. 26 Photo. *Perf. 13½*

No.	Type	Description	Unused	Used
C93	A31	10fr multi	.35	.25
C94	A31	14fr multi	.45	.25
C95	A31	17fr multi	.60	.25
C96	A31	26fr multi	1.25	.50
a.		Souv. sheet of 4, #C93-C96	3.00	2.25
		Nos. C93-C96 (4)	2.65	1.15

For overprints see Nos. C100-C103.

Human Rights Flame, Hand and Globe — AP2

1969, Jan. 22

No.	Type	Description	Unused	Used
C97	AP2	10fr multi	.35	.25
C98	AP2	14fr multi	.55	.25
C99	AP2	26fr lil & multi	.90	.25
		Nos. C97-C99 (3)	1.80	.75

International Human Rights Year, 1968.
Exist imperf. Value set, $4.50.

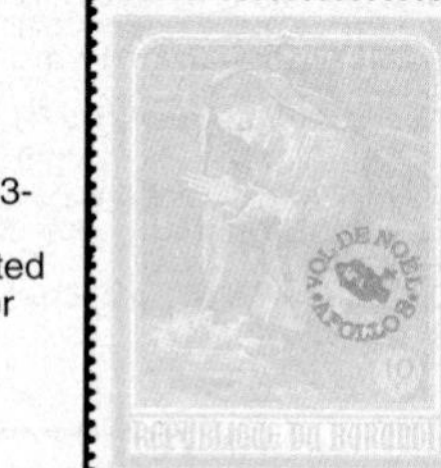

Nos. C93-C96 Overprinted in Silver

1969, Feb. 17 Photo. *Perf. 13½*

No.	Type	Description	Unused	Used
C100	A31	10fr multi	.45	.25
C101	A31	14fr multi	.60	.25
C102	A31	17fr multi	.70	.30
C103	A31	26fr multi	1.00	.50
		Nos. C100-C103 (4)	2.75	1.25

Man's 1st flight around the moon by the US spacecraft Apollo 8, Dec. 21-27, 1968.

Moon Landing Type of 1969

Designs: 26fr, Neil A. Armstrong leaving landing module. 40fr, Astronaut on moon. 50fr, Splashdown in the Pacific.

1969, Nov. 6 Photo. *Perf. 13½*

No.	Type	Description	Unused	Used
C104	A38	26fr gold & multi	1.75	.30
C105	A38	40fr gold & multi	2.50	.45
C106	A38	50fr gold & multi	4.00	.50
		Nos. C104-C106 (3)	8.25	1.25

Christmas Type of 1969

Paintings: 17fr, Madonna and Child, by Benvenuto da Garofalo. 26fr, Madonna and Child, by Jacopo Negretti. 50fr, Madonna and Child, by Il Giorgione. All horizontal.

1969, Dec. 2 Photo.

No.	Type	Description	Unused	Used
C107	A39	17fr gold & multi	.70	.25
C108	A39	26fr gold & multi	1.25	.25
C109	A39	50fr gold & multi	2.75	.35
a.		Souv. sheet of 3, #C107-C109	4.25	3.50
		Nos. C107-C109 (3)	4.70	.75

Insect Type of Regular Issue

Designs: Various Beetles and Weevils.

1970 Size: 46x32mm *Perf. 13½*

No.	Type	Description	Unused	Used
C110	A40	6fr gold & multi	.65	.25
C111	A40	8fr gold & multi	.80	.25
C112	A40	10fr gold & multi	1.00	.25
C113	A40	14fr gold & multi	1.25	.25
C114	A40	15fr gold & multi	1.50	.25

Size: 52x36mm

No.	Type	Description	Unused	Used
C115	A40	20fr gold & multi	3.00	.40
C116	A40	50fr gold & multi	5.75	.55
C117	A40	75fr gold & multi	8.50	.75
C118	A40	130fr gold & multi	13.50	1.25
		Nos. C110-C118 (9)	35.95	4.20

Issued: Nos. C110-C115, 1/20; Nos. C116-C118, 2/27.

Easter Type of 1970

Stations of the Cross, by Juan de Aranoa y Carredano: 8fr, Jesus meets the women of Jerusalem. 10fr, Jesus falls a third time. 14fr, Jesus stripped. 15fr, Jesus nailed to the cross. 18fr, Jesus dies on the cross. 20fr, Descent from the cross. 50fr, Jesus laid in the tomb.

1970, Mar. 16 Photo. *Perf. 13½*

No.	Type	Description	Unused	Used
C119	A41	8fr gold & multi	.30	.25
C120	A41	10fr gold & multi	.40	.25
C121	A41	14fr gold & multi	.55	.25
C122	A41	15fr gold & multi	.65	.25
C123	A41	18fr gold & multi	.90	.30
C124	A41	20fr gold & multi	1.00	.40
C125	A41	50fr gold & multi	2.10	.70
a.		Souv. sheet of 7, #C119-C125 + label	7.25	6.00
		Nos. C119-C125 (7)	5.90	2.25

EXPO '70 Type of Regular Issue

Souvenir Sheet

Designs: 40fr, Tower of the Sun, vert. 50fr, Flags of participating nations, vert.

1970, May 5 Photo. *Perf. 13½*

No.	Type	Description	Unused	Used
C126		Sheet of 2	3.00	3.00
a.	A42	40fr multi	1.00	1.00
b.	A42	50fr multi	1.25	1.25

Rhinoceros Type of Regular Issue

Fauna: a, i, Camel. c, d, Dromedary. g, r, Okapi. f, m, Addax. j, o, Rhinoceros. l, p, Burundi cow (each animal in 2 different poses).

Map of the Nile: b, Delta and pyramids. e, dhow. h, Falls. k, Blue Nile and crowned crane. n, Victoria Nile and secretary bird. q, Lake Victoria and source of Nile on Mt. Gikizi. Continuous design.

1970, July 8 Photo. *Perf. 13½*

No.	Type	Description	Unused	Used
C127		Sheet of 18	50.00	25.00
a.-r.	A43	14fr any single	2.00	.35

Publicizing the southernmost source of the Nile on Mt. Gikizi in Burundi.

UN Emblem and Headquarters, NYC — AP3

25th Anniv. of the UN (UN Emblem and): 11fr, Security Council and mural by Per Krohg. 26fr, Pope Paul VI and U Thant. 40fr, Flags in front of UN Headquarters, NYC.

1970, Oct. 23 Photo. *Perf. 13½*

No.	Type	Description	Unused	Used
C128	AP3	7fr gold & multi	.25	.25
C129	AP3	11fr gold & multi	.35	.25
C130	AP3	26fr gold & multi	.85	.25
C131	AP3	40fr gold & multi	1.10	.40
a.		Souvenir sheet of 2	3.75	3.75
		Nos. C128-C131 (4)	2.55	1.15

No. C131a contains 2 stamps similar to Nos. C130-C131 but without "Poste Aerienne."
Exist imperf. Values: set $4; souvenir sheet $7.

Bird Type of Regular Issue

8fr, 14fr, 30fr, vert.; 10fr, 20fr, 50fr, horiz.

1970 Photo. *Perf. 13½*

Stamp size: 52x44mm

No.	Type	Description	Unused	Used
C132	A44	Block of 4	13.50	1.50
a.		8fr Northern shrike	2.75	.25
b.		8fr European starling	2.75	.25
c.		8fr Yellow wagtail	2.75	.25
d.		8fr Bank swallow	2.75	.25
C133	A44	Block of 4	16.50	1.75
a.		10fr Winter wren	3.25	.30
b.		10fr Firecrest	3.25	.30
c.		10fr Skylark	3.25	.30
d.		10fr Crested lark	3.25	.30
C134	A44	Block of 4	20.00	2.00
a.		14fr Woodchat shrike	4.00	.35
b.		14fr Common rock thrush	4.00	.35
c.		14fr Black redstart	4.00	.35
d.		14fr Ring ouzel	4.00	.35
C135	A44	Block of 4	18.00	2.25
a.		20fr European redstart	3.75	.40
b.		20fr Hedge sparrow	3.75	.40
c.		20fr Gray wagtail	3.75	.40
d.		20fr Meadow pipit	3.75	.40
C136	A44	Block of 4	22.50	2.75
a.		30fr Eurasian hoopoe	4.50	.45
b.		30fr Pied flycatcher	4.50	.45
c.		30fr Great reed warbler	4.50	.45
d.		30fr Eurasian kingfisher	4.50	.45
C137	A44	Block of 4	32.50	3.50
a.		50fr House martin	7.00	.60
b.		50fr Sedge warbler	7.00	.60
c.		50fr Fieldfare	7.00	.60
d.		50fr European Golden oriole	7.00	.60
		Nos. C132-C137 (6)	123.00	13.75

Queen Fabiola and King Baudouin of Belgium
AP4

Designs: 20fr, Pres. Michel Micombero and King Baudouin. 40fr, Pres. Micombero and coats of arms of Burundi and Belgium.

1970, Nov. 28 Photo. *Perf. 13½*
C140 AP4 6fr multicolored 1.00 .25
C141 AP4 20fr multicolored 2.60 .65
C142 AP4 40fr multicolored 5.25 1.10
a. Souvenir sheet of 3 9.00 9.00
Nos. C140-C142 (3) 8.85 2.00

Visit of the King and Queen of Belgium. No. C142a contains 3 stamps similar to Nos. C140-C142, but without "Poste Aerienne."

Exist imperf. Values: set $10; souvenir sheet $9.

Easter Type of Regular Issue

Paintings of the Resurrection: 14fr, by Louis Borrassá. 17fr, Piero della Francesca. 26fr, Michel Wohlgemuth.

1971, Apr. 2 Photo. *Perf. 13½*
C143 A49 14fr gold & multi .95 .25
C144 A49 17fr gold & multi 1.25 .25
C145 A49 26fr gold & multi 2.40 .35
a. Souv. sheet of 3, #C143-C145 5.00 5.00
Nos. C143-C145 (3) 4.60 .80

Easter 1971.

Animal Type of Regular Issue

1971 Photo. *Perf. 13½*
Size: 44x44mm
C146 Strip of 4 8.50 .85
a. A48 10fr Lion 1.60 .25
b. A48 10fr Cape buffalo 1.60 .25
c. A48 10fr Hippopotamus 1.60 .25
d. A48 10fr Giraffe 1.60 .25
C147 Strip of 4 9.50 1.00
a. A48 14fr Hartebeest 1.90 .25
b. A48 14fr Black rhinoceros 1.90 .25
c. A48 14fr Zebra 1.90 .25
d. A48 14fr Leopard 1.90 .25
C148 Strip of 4 10.50 1.00
a. A48 17fr Grant's gazelles 2.10 .25
b. A48 17fr Cheetah 2.10 .25
c. A48 17fr African white-backed vultures 2.10 .25
d. A48 17fr Johnston's okapi 2.10 .25
C149 Strip of 4 12.00 1.50
a. A48 24fr Chimpanzee 2.25 .30
b. A48 24fr Elephant 2.25 .30
c. A48 24fr Spotted Hyenas 2.25 .30
d. A48 24fr Beisa 2.25 .30
C150 Strip of 4 13.50 1.90
a. A48 26fr Gorilla 2.50 .40
b. A48 26fr Gnu 2.50 .40
c. A48 26fr Warthog 2.50 .40
d. A48 26fr Cape hunting dog 2.50 .40
C151 Strip of 4 14.50 2.40
a. A48 31fr Sable antelope 3.00 .50
b. A48 31fr Caracal lynx 3.00 .50
c. A48 31fr Ostriches 3.00 .50
d. A48 31fr Bongo 3.00 .50
Nos. C146-C151 (6) 68.50 8.65

For overprint and surcharges see Nos. C152, CB15-C18.

No. C146 Overprinted in Gold and Black

1971, July 20 Photo. *Perf. 13½*
C152 Strip of 4 5.00 3.00
a. A48 10fr Lion 1.10 .25
b. A48 10fr Cape buffalo 1.10 .25
c. A48 10fr Hippopotamus 1.10 .25
d. A48 10fr Giraffe 1.10 .25

Intl. Year Against Racial Discrimination.

Christmas Type of Regular Issue

Paintings of the Madonna and Child by: 14fr, Cima de Conegliano. 17fr, Fra Filippo Lippi. 31fr, Leonardo da Vinci.

1971, Nov. 2 Photo. *Perf. 13½*
C153 A51 14fr red & multi .60 .25
C154 A51 17fr red & multi .80 .25
C155 A51 31fr red & multi 1.50 .35
a. Souv. sheet of 3, #C153-C155 3.00 3.00
Nos. C153-C155 (3) 2.90 .75

Christmas 1971.
For surcharges see Nos. CB19-CB21.

Spacecraft Type of Regular Issue
Souvenir Sheet

1972, Jan. 15 Photo. *Perf. 13½*
C156 Sheet of 6 7.00 7.00
a. A52 6fr Lunar Orbiter .75 .75
b. A52 11fr Vostok .75 .75
c. A52 14fr Luna I .75 .75
d. A52 17fr Apollo 11 astronaut on moon .75 .75
e. A52 26fr Soyuz 11 .75 .75
f. A52 40fr Lunar rover (Apollo 15) .75 .75

Sapporo '72 Type of Regular Issue
Souvenir Sheet

Emblem and: 26fr, Snow scooter. 31fr, Downhill skiing. 50fr, Bobsledding.

1972, Feb. 3
C157 Sheet of 3 6.00 5.00
a. A53 26fr silver & multi 1.50 1.25
b. A53 31fr silver & multi 1.50 1.25
c. A53 50fr silver & multi 1.50 1.25

Olympic Games Type of 1972

1972, July 24 Photo. *Perf. 13½*
C158 A55 24fr Weight lifting 1.60 .25
C159 A55 26fr Hurdles 1.75 .25
C160 A55 31fr Discus 2.10 .40
C161 A55 40fr Soccer 2.75 .45
Nos. C158-C161 (4) 8.20 1.25

Independence Type of 1972

Designs: 15fr, Prince Rwagasore, Pres. Micombero, Burundi flag, drummers. 18fr, Rwagasore, Micombero, flag, map of Africa, globe. 27fr, Micombero, flag, globe.

1972, Aug. 24 Photo. *Perf. 13½*
C162 A56 15fr gold & multi .40 .25
C163 A56 18fr gold & multi .50 .30
C164 A56 27fr gold & multi .80 .40
a. Souv. sheet of 3, #C162-C164 2.00 2.00
Nos. C162-C164 (3) 1.70 .95

Christmas Type of 1972

Paintings of the Madonna and Child by: 18fr, Sebastiano Mainardi. 27fr, Hans Memling. 40fr, Lorenzo Lotto.

1972, Nov. 2 Photo. *Perf. 13½*
C165 A57 18fr dk car & multi 1.50 .25
C166 A57 27fr dk car & multi 1.75 .25
C167 A57 40fr dk car & multi 2.75 .40
a. Souv. sheet of 3, #C165-C167 6.00 4.75
Nos. C165-C167 (3) 6.00 .80

For surcharges see Nos. CB26-CB28.

Orchid Type of Regular Issue

1973, Jan. 18 Photo. *Perf. 13½*
Size: 38x38mm
C168 A58 13fr Thelymitra pauciflora 2.50 .25
C169 A58 14fr Miltassia 2.75 .25
C170 A58 15fr Miltonia 3.00 .30
C171 A58 18fr Platycoryne crocea 3.50 .35
C172 A58 20fr Cattleya trinaei 4.00 .40
C173 A58 27fr Eulophia cucullata 5.00 .45
C174 A58 36fr Cymbidium hamsey 6.00 .60
Nos. C168-C174 (7) 26.75 2.60

African Exploration Type of 1973

Designs: 15fr, Livingstone writing his diary. 18fr, "Dr. Livingstone, I presume." 27fr, Livingstone and Stanley discussing expedition.

1973, Mar. 19 Photo. *Perf. 13½*
C175 A59 15fr gold & multi .85 .25
C176 A59 18fr gold & multi 1.00 .25
C177 A59 27fr gold & multi 1.50 .35
a. Souv. sheet of 3 4.00 4.00
Nos. C175-C177 (3) 3.35 .75

No. C177a contains 3 stamps similar to Nos. C175-C177, but without "Poste Aerienne."

Easter Type of 1973

Paintings: 15fr, Christ at the Pillar, by Guido Reni. 18fr, Crucifixion, by Mathias Grunewald. 27fr, Descent from the Cross, by Caravaggio.

1973, Apr. 10
C178 A60 15fr gold & multi 1.25 .25
C179 A60 18fr gold & multi 1.40 .30
C180 A60 27fr gold & multi 1.90 .35
a. Souv. sheet of 3, #C178-C180 4.75 3.75
Nos. C178-C180 (3) 4.55 .85

INTERPOL Type of Regular Issue

Designs: 27fr, INTERPOL emblem and flag. 40fr, INTERPOL flag and emblem.

1973, May 19 Photo. *Perf. 13½*
C181 A61 27fr gold & multi 1.25 .30
C182 A61 40fr gold & multi 1.60 .50

Copernicus Type of Regular Issue

Designs: 15fr, Copernicus (C183a), Earth, Pluto, and Jupiter. 18fr, Copernicus (No. C184a), Venus, Saturn, Mars. 27fr, Copernicus (No. C185a), Uranus, Neptune, Mercury. 36fr, Earth and various spacecraft.

a, UL. b, UR. c, LL. d, LR.

1973, July 27 Photo. *Perf. 13½*
C183 A62 15fr Block of 4, #a.-d. 3.50 1.75
C184 A62 18fr Block of 4, #a.-d. 4.25 .75
C185 A62 27fr Block of 4, #a.-d. 6.50 1.25
C186 A62 36fr Block of 4, #a.-d. 8.50 1.25
e. Souv. sheet, #C183-C186 25.00 25.00
Nos. C183-C186 (4) 22.75 5.00

Flower-Butterfly Type of 1973

Designs: Each block of 4 contains 2 flower and 2 butterfly designs. The 10fr, 14fr, 24fr and 31fr have flower designs listed as "a" and "d" numbers, butterflies as "b" and "c" numbers; the arrangement is reversed for the 17fr and 26fr.

1973, Sept. 28 Photo. *Perf. 13*
Stamp Size: 35x45mm
C187 A63 Block of 4 18.00 .40
a. 10fr Protea cynaroides 3.00 .25
b. 10fr Precis octavia 3.00 .25
c. 10fr Epiphora bauhiniae 3.00 .25
d. 10fr Gazania longiscapa 3.00 .25
C188 A63 Block of 4 12.50 .40
a. 14fr Kniphofia 2.00 .25
b. 14fr Cymothoe coccinata 2.00 .25
c. 14fr Nudaurelia zambesina 2.00 .25
d. 14fr Freesia refracta 2.00 .25
C189 A63 Block of 4 14.50 .75
a. 17fr Calotis eupompe 2.25 .25
b. 17fr Narcissus 2.25 .25
c. 17fr Cineraria hybrida 2.25 .25
d. 17fr Cyrestis camillus 2.25 .25
C190 A63 Block of 4 16.00 .75
a. 24fr Iris tingitana 2.50 .25
b. 24fr Papilio demodocus 2.50 .25
c. 24fr Catopsilia avelaneda 2.50 .25
d. 24fr Nerine sarniensis 2.50 .25
C191 A63 Block of 4 18.00 1.00
a. 26fr Hypolimnas dexithea 2.75 .25
b. 26fr Zantedeschia tropicalis 2.75 .25
c. 26fr Sandersonia aurantiaca 2.75 .25
d. 26fr Drurya antimachus 2.75 .25
C192 A63 Block of 4 20.00 1.25
a. 31fr Nymphaea capensis 3.00 .25
b. 31fr Pandoriana pandora 3.00 .25
c. 31fr Precis orythia 3.00 .25
d. 31fr Pelargonium domestica 3.00 .25
Nos. C187-C192 (6) 99.00 4.55

Christmas Type of 1973

Virgin and Child by: 18fr, Raphael. 27fr, Pietro Perugino. 40fr, Titian.

1973, Nov. 19
C193 A64 18fr gold & multi .85 .25
C194 A64 27fr gold & multi 1.50 .25
C195 A64 40fr gold & multi 2.40 .30
a. Souv. sheet of 3, #C193-C195 5.00 4.50
Nos. C193-C195 (3) 4.75 .75

For surcharges see Nos. CB239-CB31.

Soccer Type of Regular Issue

Designs: Various soccer scenes and cup.

1974, July 4 Photo. *Perf. 13*
C196 A67 20fr gold & multi 1.50 .30
C197 A67 26fr gold & multi 1.75 .45
C198 A67 40fr gold & multi 2.75 .55
Nos. C196-C198 (3) 6.00 1.30

For souvenir sheet see No. 459a.

UPU Type of 1974

No. C199a, Flags over UPU Headquarters, Bern. No. C199b, G.P.O., Bujumbura. No. C200a, Mailmen ("26F" in UR). No. C200b, Mailmen ("26F" in UL). No. C201a, UPU emblem. No. C201b, Means of transportation. No. C202a, Pigeon over globe showing Burundi. No. C202b, Swiss flag, pigeon over map showing Bern.

1974, July 23
C199 A68 24fr Pair, #a.-b. 2.75 .50
C200 A68 26fr Pair, #a.-b. 3.00 .50
C201 A68 31fr Pair, #a.-b. 3.25 .60
C202 A68 40fr Pair, #a.-b. 5.00 .75
c. Souv. sheet, #C199-C202 27.50 27.50
Nos. C199-C202 (4) 14.00 2.35

Fish Type of 1974

1974, Sept. 9 Photo. *Perf. 13*
Size: 35x35mm
C207 A66 Block of 4 4.75 .60
a. 10fr Haplochromis multicolor .90 .25
b. 10fr Pantodon buchholzi .90 .25
c. 10fr Tropheus duboisi .90 .25
d. 10fr Distichodus sexfasciatus .90 .25
C208 A66 Block of 4 7.75 .85
a. 14fr Pelmatochromis kribensis 1.50 .25
b. 14fr Nannaethiops tritaeniatus 1.50 .25
c. 14fr Polycentropsis abbreviata 1.50 .25
d. 14fr Hemichromis bimaculatus 1.50 .25
C209 A66 Block of 4 10.50 1.25
a. 17fr Ctenopoma acutirostre 1.90 .25
b. 17fr Synodontis angelicus 1.90 .25
c. 17fr Tilapia melanopleura 1.90 .25
d. 17fr Aphyosemion bivittatum 1.90 .25
C210 A66 Block of 4 14.50 1.50
a. 24fr Monodactylus argenteus 2.75 .30
b. 24fr Zanclus canescens 2.75 .30
c. 24fr Pygoplites diacanthus 2.75 .30
d. 24fr Cephalopholis argus 2.75 .30
C211 A66 Block of 4 18.00 1.90
a. 26fr Priacanthus arenatus 3.50 .35
b. 26fr Pomacanthus arcutus 3.50 .35
c. 26fr Scarus guacamaia 3.50 .35
d. 26fr Zeus faber 3.50 .35
C212 A66 Block of 4 24.00 2.10
a. 31fr Lactophrys quadricornis 4.50 .45
b. 31fr Balistes vetula 4.50 .45
c. 31fr Acanthurus bahianus 4.50 .45
d. 31fr Holocanthus ciliaris 4.50 .45
Nos. C207-C212 (6) 79.50 8.20

Christmas Type of 1974

Paintings of the Virgin and Child: 18fr, by Hans Memling. 27fr, by Filippino Lippi. 40fr, by Lorenzo di Gredi.

1974, Nov. 7 Photo. *Perf. 13*
C213 A70 18fr gold & multi 1.25 .25
C214 A70 27fr gold & multi 1.75 .30
C215 A70 40fr gold & multi 2.40 .45
a. Souv. sheet of 3, #C213-C215 5.00 4.00
Nos. C213-C215 (3) 5.40 1.00

Christmas 1974. Sheets of 20 stamps and one label.

Apollo-Soyuz Type of 1975

1975, July 10 Photo. *Perf. 13*
C216 A71 Block of 4 4.00 2.75
a. 27fr A.A. Leonov, V.N. Kubasov, Soviet flag .65
b. 27fr Soyuz and Soviet flag .65
c. 27fr Apollo and American flag .65
d. 27fr Slayton, Brand, Stafford, American flag .65
C217 A71 Block of 4 5.00 3.25
a. 40fr Apollo-Soyuz link-up .95
b. 40fr Apollo, blast-off .95
c. 40fr Soyuz, blast-off .95
d. 40fr Kubasov, Leonov, Slayton, Brand, Stafford .95

Nos. C216-C217 are printed in sheets of 32 containing 8 blocks of 4.

Animal Type of 1975

1975, Sept. 17 Photo. *Perf. 13½*
C218 Strip of 4 5.00 .35
a. A72 10fr Addax .90 .25
b. A72 10fr Roan antelope .90 .25
c. A72 10fr Nyala .90 .25
d. A72 10fr White rhinoceros .90 .25
C219 Strip of 4 6.75 .65
a. A72 14fr Mandrill 1.25 .25
b. A72 14fr Eland 1.25 .25
c. A72 14fr Salt's dik-dik 1.25 .25
d. A72 14fr Thomson's gazelles 1.25 .25
C220 Strip of 4 10.00 .65
a. A72 17fr African small-clawed otter 1.75 .25
b. A72 17fr Reed buck 1.75 .25
c. A72 17fr Indian civet 1.75 .25
d. A72 17fr Cape buffalo 1.75 .25
C221 Strip of 4 11.50 1.40
a. A72 24fr White-tailed gnu 2.00 .30
b. A72 24fr African wild asses 2.00 .30
c. A72 24fr Black-and-white colobus monkey 2.00 .30
d. A72 24fr Gerenuk 2.00 .30
C222 Strip of 4 13.00 1.40
a. A72 26fr Dama gazelle 2.25 .30
b. A72 26fr Black-backed jackal 2.25 .30
c. A72 26fr Sitatungas 2.25 .30
d. A72 26fr Zebra antelope 2.25 .30
C223 Strip of 4 14.00 1.60
a. A72 31fr Fennec 2.50 .35
b. A72 31fr Lesser kudus 2.50 .35
c. A72 31fr Blesbok 2.50 .35
d. A72 31fr Serval 2.50 .35
Nos. C218-C223 (6) 52.25 6.05

Nos. C218-C219 Ovptd. in Black & Silver

1975, Nov. 19 Photo. *Perf. 13½*

C224 Strip of 4 4.50 2.50
a. A72 10fr Addax .85 .40
b. A72 10fr Roan antelope .85 .40
c. A72 10fr Nyala .85 .40
d. A72 10fr White rhinoceros .85 .40
C225 Strip of 4 7.00 4.50
a. A72 14fr Mandrill 1.50 .75
b. A72 14fr Oryx 1.50 .75
c. A72 14fr Dik-dik 1.50 .75
d. A72 14fr Thomson's gazelles 1.50 .75

International Women's Year 1975.

Nos. C222-C223 Ovptd. in Black and Silver

1975, Nov. 19

C226 Strip of 4 13.00 12.00
a. A72 26fr Dama gazelle 2.25 2.00
b. A72 26fr Wild dog 2.25 2.00
c. A72 26fr Sitatungas 2.25 2.00
d. A72 26fr Striped duiker 2.25 2.00
C227 Strip of 4 17.00 15.00
a. A72 31fr Fennec 3.00 2.50
b. A72 31fr Lesser kudus 3.00 2.50
c. A72 31fr Blesbok 3.00 2.50
d. A72 31fr Serval 3.00 2.50

United Nations, 30th anniversary.

Michelangelo Type of 1975

Paintings from Sistine Chapel: No. C228a, Zachariah. No. C228b, Joel. No. C229a, Erythrean Sybil. No. C229b, Prophet Ezekiel. No. C230a, Persian Sybil. No. C230b, Prophet Jeremiah.

1975, Dec. 3 Photo. *Perf. 13*

C228 A73 18fr Pair, #a.-b. 4.50 .60
C229 A73 31fr Pair, #a.-b. 6.00 .90
C230 A73 40fr Pair, #a.-b. 9.00 1.00
c. Souv. sheet of 6, #C228-C230 16.00 12.00
Nos. C228-C230 (3) 24.00 1.65

Printed in sheets of 18 stamps + 2 labels.
For surcharges see Nos. CB35-CB37.

Olympic Games Type, 1976

Designs (Olympic Games Emblem and): 18fr, Ski jump. 36fr, Slalom. 50fr, Ice hockey.

1976, Jan. 23 Photo. *Perf. 14x13½*

C234 A74 18fr ol brn & multi .90 .25
C235 A74 36fr grn & multi 1.75 .50
C236 A74 50fr pur & multi 2.25 .65
a. Souvenir sheet of 4 5.00 4.00
Nos. C234-C236 (3) 4.90 1.35

No. C236a contains 4 stamps similar to Nos. 491-494, perf. 13½, inscribed "POSTE AERIENNE."

21st Olympic Games, Montreal, Canada, July 17-Aug. 1 — AP5

Montreal Games Emblem and: Nos. C237b, C239a, C240b, High jump. Nos. C238a, C239b, C240a, Athlete on rings. Nos. C237a, C238b, C240c, Hurdles.

1976, May 3 Litho. *Perf. 13½*

C237 AP5 27fr Pair, #a.-b. 3.75 2.40
C238 AP5 31fr Pair, #a.-b. 4.75 3.25
C239 AP5 50fr Pair, #a.-b. 9.50 6.50
Nos. C237-C239 (3) 18.00 12.15

Souvenir Sheet

C240 AP5 Sheet of 3, #a.-c. 13.50 13.50

Battle of Bunker Hill, by John Trumbull — AP6

Paintings: 26fr, Franklin, Jefferson and John Adams. 36fr, Declaration of Independence, by John Trumbull.

1976, July 16 Photo. *Perf. 13*

C244 AP6 18fr Pair, #a.-b. 2.00 .35
C245 AP6 26fr Pair, #a.-b. 3.00 .45
C246 AP6 36fr Pair, #a.-b. 3.75 .85
c. Souv. sheet of 6, #C244-C246 9.00 9.00
Nos. C244-C246 (3) 8.75 1.65

American Bicentennial.
Exist imperf. Values: set $11; souvenir sheet $10.

Christmas Type of 1976

Paintings: 18fr, Virgin and Child with St. Anne, by Leonardo da Vinci. 31fr, Holy Family with Lamb, by Raphael. 40fr, Madonna of the Basket, by Correggio.

1976, Oct. 18 Photo. *Perf. 13½*

C250 A76 18fr gold & multi 1.75 .25
C251 A76 31fr gold & multi 2.25 .30
C252 A76 40fr gold & multi 3.25 .45
a. Souv. sheet of 3, #C250-C252 7.50 5.00
Nos. C250-C252 (3) 7.25 .95

Christmas 1976. Sheets of 20 stamps and descriptive label.
For surcharges see Nos. CB41-CB43.

A.G. Bell Type of 1977

10fr, A.G. Bell and 1st telephone. No. C253a, 17fr, A.G. Bell speaking into microphone. Nos. C253a, C255e, Satellites around globe, videophone. No. C254a, Switchboard operator, c.1910, wall telephone. No. C254b, 26fr, Intelsat satellite, modern & old telephones. No. C255c, Intelsat, radar.

1977, May 17 Photo. *Perf. 13*

C253 A78 18fr Pair, #a.-b. 1.90 1.90
C254 A78 36fr Pair, #a.-b. 3.75 3.75
C255 Sheet of 5 7.00 7.00
a. A78 10fr multi 1.00 1.00
b. A78 17fr multi 1.00 1.00
c. A79 18fr multi 1.00 1.00
d. A79 26fr multi 1.00 1.00
e. A79 36fr multi 1.00 1.00

#C255c, C255e are air post stamps.

Animal Type of 1977

1977, Aug. 22 Photo. *Perf. 14x14½*

C258 Strip of 4 5.00 .35
a. A80 9fr Buffon's kob .95 .25
b. A80 9fr Marabous .95 .25
c. A80 9fr Brindled gnu .95 .25
d. A80 9fr River hog .95 .25
C259 Strip of 4 7.50 .80
a. A80 13fr Zebras 1.40 .25
b. A80 13fr Shoebill 1.40 .25
c. A80 13fr Striped hyenas 1.40 .25
d. A80 13fr Chimpanzee 1.40 .25
C260 Strip of 4 12.00 1.50
a. A80 30fr Flamingos 2.25 .25
b. A80 30fr Nile Crocodiles 2.25 .25
c. A80 30fr Green mamba 2.25 .25
d. A80 30fr Greater kudus 2.25 .25
C261 Strip of 4 21.00 1.75
a. A80 35fr Hyrax 4.00 .35
b. A80 35fr Cobra 4.00 .35
c. A80 35fr Jackals 4.00 .35
d. A80 35fr Verreaux's eagles 4.00 .35
C262 Strip of 4 30.00 2.00
a. A80 54fr Honey badger 6.00 .45
b. A80 54fr Harnessed antelopes 6.00 .45
c. A80 54fr Secretary bird 6.00 .45
d. A80 54fr Klipspringer 6.00 .45
C263 Strip of 4 45.00 2.50
a. A80 70fr African big-eared fox 8.50 .55
b. A80 70fr Elephants 8.50 .55
c. A80 70fr Vulturine guineafowl 8.50 .55
d. A80 70fr Impalas 8.50 .55
Nos. C258-C263 (6) 95.50 8.90

UN Type of 1977

Designs (UN Stamps and): 24fr, UN buildings by night. 27fr, UN buildings and view of Manhattan. 35fr, UN buildings by day.

1977, Oct. 10 Photo. *Perf. 13½*

C264 A82 Block of 4 6.00 6.00
a. 24fr No. 77 1.20 1.20
b. 24fr No. 78 1.20 1.20
c. 24fr No. 40 1.20 1.20
d. 24fr No. 32 1.20 1.20
C265 A82 Block of 4 7.00 7.00
a. 27fr No. 50 1.40 1.40
b. 27fr No. 21 1.40 1.40
c. 27fr No. 30 1.40 1.40
d. 27fr No. 44 1.40 1.40
C266 A82 Block of 4 10.50 10.50
a. 35fr No. C6 2.00 2.00
b. 35fr No. 105 2.00 2.00
c. 35fr No. 4 2.00 2.00
d. 35fr No. 1 2.00 2.00
e. Souvenir sheet of 3 1.40
Nos. C264-C266 (3) 33.75 33.75

No. C266e contains 24fr in design of No. C265b, 27fr in design of No. C266a, 35fr in design of No. C264c.

Christmas Type of 1977

Designs: Paintings of the Virgin and Child.

1977, Oct. 31 Photo. *Perf. 14x13*

C267 A83 18fr Master of Moulins 1.75 1.00
C268 A83 31fr Workshop of Lorenzo de Credi 2.75 1.75
C269 A83 40fr Palma Vecchio 3.50 2.25
a. Souv. sheet of 3, #C267-C269 6.00 6.00
Nos. C267-C269 (3) 5.75 5.00

Sheets of 24 stamps and descriptive label.
For surcharges see Nos. CB44-CB46.

Christmas 1978 Type of 1979

Souvenir Sheet

1979, Feb. Photo. *Perf. 14x13½*

C270 Sheet of 5 12.00 10.00
a. A86 13fr like #543 2.00 2.00
b. A86 17fr like #544 2.00 2.00
c. A86 27fr like #545 2.00 2.00
d. A86 31fr like #546 2.00 2.00
e. A86 40fr like #547 2.00 2.00

Christmas Type of 1979

Souvenir Sheet

1979, Oct. 12 *Perf. 13½*

C271 Sheet of 4 12.50 12.50
a. A89 20fr like #561 2.50 2.50
b. A89 27fr like #562 2.50 2.50
c. A89 31fr like #563 2.50 2.50
d. A89 50fr like #564 2.50 2.50

Hill Type of 1979

Souvenir Sheet

1979, Nov. 6

C272 Sheet of 5 11.00 8.00
a. A90 20fr like #565 2.00 1.40
b. A90 27fr like #566 2.00 1.40
c. A90 31fr like #567 2.00 1.40
d. A90 40fr like #568 2.00 1.40
e. A90 60fr like #569 2.00 1.40

Bird Type of 1979

1979 Photo. *Perf. 13½x3*

C273 A87 6fr like #548 1.25 .65
C274 A87 13fr like #549 2.25 1.50
C275 A87 18fr like #550 3.75 2.00
C276 A87 26fr like #551 5.00 3.00
C277 A87 31fr like #552 5.75 4.00
C278 A87 36fr like #553 7.25 5.00
C279 A87 40fr like #554 9.00 6.00
C280 A87 54fr like #555 13.00 7.50
C281 A87 70fr like #556 16.50 10.00
Nos. C273-C281 (9) 63.75 39.65

Olympic Type of 1980

Souvenir Sheet

1980, Oct. 24 Photo. *Perf. 13½*

C282 Sheet of 9 35.00 25.00
a. A91 20fr like #570 3.50 2.00
b. A91 20fr like #571 3.50 2.00
c. A91 20fr like #572 3.50 2.00
d. A91 30fr like #573 3.50 2.00
e. A91 30fr like #574 3.50 2.00
f. A91 30fr like #575 3.50 2.00
g. A91 40fr like #576 3.50 2.00
h. A91 40fr like #577 3.50 2.00
i. A91 40fr like #578 3.50 2.00

Christmas Type of 1980

Souvenir Sheet

1980, Dec. 12 Photo. *Perf. 13½x13*

C283 Sheet of 4 22.00 10.00
a. A92 10fr like #579 4.00 2.00
b. A92 30fr like #580 4.00 2.00
c. A92 40fr like #581 4.00 2.00
d. A92 45fr like #582 4.00 2.00

UPRONA Type of 1980

Souvenir Sheet

1980, Dec. 29 *Perf. 14½x13½*

C284 Sheet of 3 6.50 4.50
a. A93 10fr like #583 1.60 1.00
b. A93 40fr like #584 1.60 1.00
c. A93 45fr like #585 1.60 1.00

Christmas Type of 1983

Souvenir Sheet

1983, Oct. 3 Litho. *Perf. 14½x13½*

C285 Sheet of 4 75.00 75.00
a. A97 10fr like #607 15.00 15.00
b. A97 25fr like #608 15.00 15.00
c. A97 30fr like #609 15.00 15.00
d. A97 50fr like #610 15.00 15.00

UPU Congress Type of 1984

Souvenir Sheet

1984, July 14 *Perf. 13x13½*

C286 Sheet of 4 25.00 25.00
a. A99 10fr like #621 5.00 5.00
b. A99 30fr like #622 5.00 5.00
c. A99 35fr like #623 5.00 5.00
d. A99 65fr like #624 5.00 5.00

Summer Olympics Type of 1984

Souvenir Sheet

1984, Aug. 6 *Perf. 13½x13*

C287 Sheet of 4 30.00 30.00
a. A100 10fr like #625 6.25 6.25
b. A100 30fr like #626 6.25 6.25
c. A100 35fr like #627 6.25 6.25
d. A100 65fr like #628 6.25 6.25

Christmas Type of 1984

Souvenir Sheet

1984, Dec. 15 *Perf. 13½*

C288 Sheet of 4 30.00 12.00
a. A101 10fr like #629 6.00 2.40
b. A101 25fr like #630 6.00 2.40
c. A101 30fr like #631 6.00 2.40
d. A101 50fr like #632 6.00 2.40

Flower Type of 1986 with Dull Lilac Border

1986, July 31 Photo. *Perf. 13x13½*

C289 A102 70fr like #633 11.50 8.50
C290 A102 75fr like #634 13.00 9.00
C291 A102 80fr like #635 14.00 10.00
C292 A102 85fr like #636 15.50 11.00
C293 A102 100fr like #637 18.00 12.00
C294 A102 150fr like #638 26.00 14.00
Nos. C289-C294 (6) 98.00 64.50

Animals AP8

1992, June 2 Litho. *Perf. 14*

C298 AP8 100fr M. nemestrina 3.50 2.25
C299 AP8 115fr Equus grevyi 4.50 2.50
C300 AP8 200fr Long horn cattle 10.00 6.00
C301 AP8 220fr Pelecanus onocrotalus 12.00 7.00
a. Souvenir sheet of 4, #C298-C301, perf. 13½ 30.00
Nos. C298-C301 (4) 30.00 17.75

No. C301a exists imperf. Value, $30.

AIR POST SEMI-POSTAL STAMPS

Coin Type of Semi-Postal Issue

Designs (Coins of Various Denominations): 3fr+1fr, 11fr+1fr, 20fr+1fr, 50fr+1fr, Coat of Arms, reverse. 5fr+1fr, 14fr+1fr, 30fr+1fr, 100fr+1fr, King Mwambutsa IV, obverse.

Lithographed; Embossed on Gilt Foil

1965, Nov. 15 *Imperf.*

Diameter: 39mm

CB1 SP4 3fr + 1fr lt & dk vio .25 .25
CB2 SP4 5fr + 1fr pale grn & red .35 .35

Diameter: 45mm

CB3 SP4 11fr + 1fr org & lilac .55 .55
CB4 SP4 14fr + 1fr red & emer .70 .70

Diameter: 56mm

CB5 SP4 20fr + 1fr ultra & blk .90 .90
CB6 SP4 30fr + 1fr dp org & mar 1.25 1.25

Diameter: 67mm

CB7 SP4 50fr + 1fr bl & vio bl 2.50 2.50
CB8 SP4 100fr+ 1fr rose & dp cl 4.50 4.50
Nos. CB1-CB8 (8) 11.00 11.00

Stamps are backed with patterned paper in blue, orange, and pink engine-turned design.

Red Cross Type of Semi-Postal Issue

Designs: 26fr+3fr, Laboratory. 40fr+3fr, Ambulance and thatched huts. 50fr+3fr, Red Cross nurse with patient.

1969, June 26 Photo. *Perf. 13½*

CB9	SP7 26fr + 3fr multi	.95	.25
CB10	SP7 40fr + 3fr multi	1.25	.40
CB11	SP7 50fr + 3fr multi	1.75	.60
	Nos. CB9-CB11 (3)	3.95	1.25

Perf. and imperf. souvenir sheets exist containing 3 stamps similar to Nos. CB9-CB11, but without "Poste Aerienne." Size: 90½x97mm

Christmas Type of Semi-Postal Issue

Paintings: 14fr+3fr, Virgin and Child, by Velázquez. 26fr+3fr, Holy Family, by Joos van Cleve. 40fr+3fr, Virgin and Child, by Rogier van der Weyden.

1970, Dec. 14 Photo. *Perf. 13½*

CB12	SP9 14fr + 3fr multi	.75	.25
CB13	SP9 26fr + 3fr multi	1.25	.45
CB14	SP9 40fr + 3fr multi	2.00	.60
a.	Souv. sheet of 3, #CB12-CB14	4.00	4.00
	Nos. CB12-CB14 (3)	3.50	1.30

No. C147 Surcharged in Gold and Black

1971, Aug. 9 Photo. *Perf. 13½*

CB15	Strip of 4	11.00	4.00
a.	A48 14fr+2fr Hartebeest	2.40	.25
b.	A48 14fr+2fr Black rhinoceros	2.40	.25
c.	A48 14fr+2fr Zebra	2.40	.25
d.	A48 14fr+2fr Leopard	2.40	.25

UNESCO campaign against illiteracy.

No. C148 Surcharged in Gold and Black

1971, Aug. 9

CB16	Strip of 4	14.00	5.00
a.	A48 17fr+1fr Grant's gazelles	3.00	.25
b.	A48 17fr+1fr Cheetah	3.00	.25
c.	A48 17fr+1fr African white-backed vultures	3.00	.25
d.	A48 17fr+1fr Johnston's okapi	3.00	.25

International help for refugees.

Nos. C150-C151 Surcharged in Black and Gold

a

b

1971, Aug. 16

CB17	Strip of 4	14.00	4.00
a.	A48(a) 26fr+1fr Gorilla	3.00	.90
b.	A48(a) 26fr+1fr Gnu	3.00	.90
c.	A48(a) 26fr+1fr Warthog	3.00	.90
d.	A48(a) 26fr+1fr Cape hunting dog	3.00	.90
CB18	Strip of 4	17.50	5.00
a.	A48(b) 31fr+1fr Sable antelope	3.50	1.10
b.	A48(b) 31fr+1fr Caracal lynx	3.50	1.10
c.	A48(b) 31fr+1fr Ostriches	3.50	1.10
d.	A48(b) 31fr+1fr Bongo	3.50	1.10

75th anniv. of modern Olympic Games (#CB17); Olympic Games, Munich, 1972 (#CB18).

Nos. C153-C155 Surcharged

1971, Nov. 27 Photo. *Perf. 13½*

CB19	A51 14fr + 1fr multi	.80	.35
CB20	A51 17fr + 1fr multi	1.25	.35
CB21	A51 31fr + 1fr multi	1.75	.35
	Nos. CB19-CB21 (3)	3.80	1.05
a.	Souvenir Sheet of 3	4.00	3.25

25th anniv. of UNICEF.

No. CB21a contains 3 stamps similar to #CB19-CB21 with 2 fr surcharge each.

Casa D'Oro, Venice SPAP1

Views in Venice: 17fr+1fr, Doge's Palace. 24fr+1fr, Church of Sts. John and Paul. 31fr+1fr, Doge's Palace and Piazzetta at Feast of Ascension, by Canaletto.

1971, Dec. 27

CB22	SPAP1 10fr + 1fr multi	.45	.25
CB23	SPAP1 17fr + 1fr multi	.80	.25
CB24	SPAP1 24fr + 1fr multi	1.20	.35
CB25	SPAP1 31fr + 1fr multi	1.60	.35
a.	Souvenir sheet of 4	4.50	4.50
	Nos. CB22-CB25 (4)	5.40	1.20

Surtax for the UNESCO campaign to save the treasures of Venice. No. CB25a contains 4 stamps similar to Nos. CB22-CB25, but with 2fr surtax.

Nos. CB22-CB25a exist imperf. Value: set $6.50; souvenir sheet $8.

Nos. C165-C167, C193-C195 Srchd. in Silver

1972, Dec. 12 Photo. *Perf. 13½*

CB26	A57 18fr + 1fr multi	1.00	.25
CB27	A57 27fr + 1fr multi	1.75	.35
CB28	A57 40fr + 1fr multi	2.50	.60
a.	Souvenir sheet of 3	6.00	5.00
	Nos. CB26-CB28 (3)	5.25	1.20

Christmas 1972. No. CB28a contains 3 stamps similar to Nos. CB26-CB28 but with 2fr surtax.

1973, Dec. 14 Photo. *Perf. 13*

CB29	A64 18fr + 1fr multi	.90	.30
CB30	A64 27fr + 1fr multi	1.25	.40
CB31	A64 40fr + 1fr multi	1.75	.50
a.	Souvenir sheet of 3	4.50	4.00
	Nos. CB29-CB31 (3)	3.90	1.20

Christmas 1973. No. CB31a contains 3 stamps similar to Nos. CB29-CB31 with 2fr surtax each.

Christmas Type of 1974

1974, Dec. 2 Photo. *Perf. 13*

CB32	A70 18fr + 1fr multi	1.10	.30
CB33	A70 27fr + 1fr multi	1.75	.60
CB34	A70 40fr + 1fr multi	2.75	1.00
a.	Souvenir sheet of 3	6.00	6.00
	Nos. CB32-CB34 (3)	4.90	1.90

Christmas 1974. No. CB34a contains 3 stamps similar to Nos. CB32-CB34 with 2fr surtax.

Nos. C228-C230 Srchd. in Silver and Black

1975, Dec. 22 Photo. *Perf. 13*

CB35	A73 18fr +1fr Pair, #a-b	5.00	.30
CB36	A73 31fr +1fr Pair, #a-b	6.75	.50
CB37	A73 40fr +1fr Pair, #a-b	10.00	.60
c.	Souvenir sheet of 6	19.00	19.00
	Nos. CB35-CB37 (3)	15.25	1.40

Michelangelo Buonarroti (1475-1564). No. CB37c contains 6 stamps similar to Nos. CB35-CB37 with 2fr surtax each.

Nos. C250-C252 Surcharged "+1f" in Silver and Black

1976, Nov. 25 Photo. *Perf. 13½*

CB41	A76 18fr + 1fr multi	1.60	.25
CB42	A76 31fr + 1fr multi	2.25	.35
CB43	A76 40fr + 1fr multi	3.25	.65
a.	Souvenir sheet of 3	7.00	7.00
	Nos. CB41-CB43 (3)	6.15	1.25

Christmas 1976. No. CB43a contains 3 stamps similar to Nos. CB41-CB43 with 2fr surtax each.

Nos. C267-C269 Surcharged "+1fr" in Silver and Black

1977 Photo. *Perf. 14x13*

CB44	A83 18fr + 1fr multi	1.50	.30
CB45	A83 31fr + 1fr multi	2.75	.40
CB46	A83 40fr + 1fr multi	3.75	.55
a.	Souvenir sheet of 3	12.00	12.00
	Nos. CB44-CB46 (3)	6.50	1.25

Christmas 1977. No. CB46a contains 3 stamps similar to Nos. CB44-CB46 with 2fr surtax each.

Christmas 1978 Type
Souvenir Sheet

1979, Feb. Photo. *Perf. 14x13*

CB47	Sheet of 5	22.00	12.00
a.	A86 13fr + 2fr multi	3.75	1.75
b.	A86 17fr + 2fr multi	3.75	1.75
c.	A86 27fr + 2fr multi	3.75	1.75
d.	A86 31fr + 2fr multi	3.75	1.75
e.	A86 40fr + 2fr multi	3.75	1.75

Christmas Type of 1979
Souvenir Sheet

1979, Dec. 10 Photo. *Perf. 13½*

CB48	Sheet of 4	22.00	12.00
a.	A89 20fr + 2fr like #561	3.75	2.00
b.	A89 27fr + 2fr like #562	3.75	2.00
c.	A89 31fr + 2fr like #563	3.75	2.00
d.	A89 50fr + 2fr like #564	3.75	2.00

Exists imperf. Value $13.

Christmas Type of 1980
Souvenir Sheet

1981, Jan. 16 Photo. *Perf. 13½x13*

CB49	Sheet of 4	22.00	22.00
a.	A92 10fr + 2fr like #579	3.75	3.75
b.	A92 30fr + 2fr like #580	3.75	3.75
c.	A92 40fr + 2fr like #581	3.75	3.75
d.	A92 50fr + 2fr like #582	3.75	3.75

Exists imperf. Value $13.

Christmas Type of 1983
Souvenir Sheet

1983, Nov. 2 Litho. *Perf. 14½x13½*

CB50	Sheet of 4	16.00	16.00
a.	A97 10fr + 2fr like #607	1.25	1.00
b.	A97 25fr + 2fr like #608	2.00	1.75
c.	A97 30fr + 2fr like #609	4.00	3.50
d.	A97 50fr + 2fr like #610	5.50	5.00

Exists imperf. Value $13.

Christmas Type of 1984
Souvenir Sheet

1984, Dec. 15 *Perf. 13½*

CB51	Sheet of 4	15.00	15.00
a.	A101 10fr + 2fr like #629	3.00	3.00
b.	A101 25fr + 2fr like #630	3.00	3.00
c.	A101 30fr + 2fr like #631	3.00	3.00
d.	A101 50fr + 2fr like #632	3.00	3.00

BUSHIRE

bü-'shir

LOCATION — On Persian Gulf

Bushire is an Iranian port that British troops occupied Aug. 8, 1915.

20 Chahis (or Shahis) = 1 Kran
10 Krans = 1 Toman

Watermark

Wmk. 161 — Lion

ISSUED UNDER BRITISH OCCUPATION

Basic Iranian Designs

Ahmad Shah — A32

Imperial Crown — A33

King Darius, Farvahar overhead Overhead — A34

Ruins of Persepolis — A35

Iranian Stamps of 1911-13 Overprinted in Black

Perf. 11½, 11½x11
Typo. & Engr.

1915, Aug. 15 **Unwmk.**

No.	Design	Description	Unused	Used
N1	A32	1c green & org	120.00	*80.00*
N2	A32	2c red & sepia	120.00	80.00
N3	A32	3c gray brn & grn	150.00	*100.00*
N4	A32	5c brown & car	950.00	*800.00*
N5	A32	6c green & red brn	120.00	60.00
N6	A32	9c yel brn & vio	130.00	*100.00*
a.		Double overprint		
N7	A32	10c red & org brn	150.00	*120.00*
N8	A32	12c grn & ultra	150.00	*120.00*
N9	A32	1k ultra & car	200.00	150.00
a.		Double overprint	7,500.	
N10	A32	24c vio & grn	180.00	140.00
N11	A32	2k grn & red vio	475.00	350.00
N12	A32	3k vio & blk	500.00	*400.00*
N13	A32	5k red & ultra	400.00	325.00
N14	A32	10k ol bis & cl	400.00	350.00
		Nos. N1-N14 (14)	4,045.	3,175.

Nos. N1-N14, except No. N4, exist without period after "Occupation." This variety sells for more. See the *Scott Classic Catalogue of Stamps and Covers* for listings.

Forged overprints exist of Nos. N1-N29.

The Bushire overprint exists on Iran No. 537 but is considered a forgery.

On Iranian Stamps of 1915
Perf. 11, 11½

1915, Sept. **Wmk. 161**

No.	Design	Description	Unused	Used
N15	A33	1c car & indigo	800.	700.
N16	A33	2c blue & car	12,000.	*12,000.*
N17	A33	3c dk grn	950.	*950.*
N18	A33	5c red	11,000.	*11,000.*
N19	A33	6c ol grn & car	10,000.	*10,000.*
N20	A33	9c yel brn & vio	1,500.	*1,400.*
N21	A33	10c bl grn & yel brn	2,300.	*2,300.*
N22	A33	12c ultra	2,500.	*2,500.*
N23	A34	1k sil, yel brn & gray	1,600.	1,300.
N24	A33	24c yel brn & dk brn	1,300.	1,100.
N25	A34	2k sil, bl & rose	1,350.	1,200.
N26	A34	3k sil, vio & brn	1,350.	1,200.
N27	A34	5k sil, brn & grn	1,950.	1,400.
a.		Inverted overprint	—	*25,000.*
N28	A35	1t gold, pur & blk	2,300.	*1,700.*
N29	A35	3t gold, cl & red brn	6,500.	*6,500.*

Persia (Iran) resumed administration of Bushire post office Oct. 16, 1915.

album accessories

ADVANTAGE STOCK SHEETS

Advantage stock sheets fit directly in your 2-post or 3-ring National or Specialty album. Available with 1 to 8 pockets.

Sheets are sold in packages of 10.

- Stock sheets match album pages in every respect, including size, border, and color.
- Punched to fit perfectly in binder.
- Ideal for storing minor varieties and collateral material. A great place to keep new issues until the next supplement is available.
- Provides the protection of clear acetate pockets on heavyweight pages.

NATIONAL BORDER

Item			Retail	AA*
AD11	1 Pocket	242mm	$19.99	$17.99
AD12	2 Pockets	119mm	$19.99	$17.99
AD13	3 Pockets	79mm	$19.99	$17.99
AD14	4 Pockets	58mm	$19.99	$17.99
AD15	5 Pockets	45mm	$19.99	$17.99
AD16	6 Pockets	37mm	$19.99	$17.99
AD17	7 Pockets	34mm	$19.99	$17.99
AD18	8 Pockets	31mm	$19.99	$17.99

SPECIALTY BORDER

Item			Retail	AA*
AD21	1 Pocket	242mm	$19.99	$17.99
AD22	2 Pockets	119mm	$19.99	$17.99
AD23	3 Pockets	79mm	$19.99	$17.99
AD24	4 Pockets	58mm	$19.99	$17.99
AD25	5 Pockets	45mm	$19.99	$17.99
AD26	6 Pockets	37mm	$19.99	$17.99
AD27	7 Pockets	34mm	$19.99	$17.99
AD28	8 Pockets	31mm	$19.99	$17.99

BLANK PAGES

Ideal for developing your own album pages to be integrated with your album.

SPECIALTY SERIES PAGES (BORDER A)

(20 per pack)

Item		Retail	AA*
ACC110		$8.99	$6.99
ACC111	Quadrille*	$13.99	$11.99

** Graph pattern printed on page.*

SPECIALTY/NATIONAL SERIES BINDERS

National series pages are punched for 3-ring and 2-post binders. The 3-ring binder is available in two sizes. The 2-post binder comes in one size. All Scott binders are covered with a tough green leatherette material that is washable and reinforced at stress points for long wear.

3-RING BINDERS & SLIPCASES

With the three ring binder, pages lay flat and the rings make turning the pages easy. The locking mechanism insure that the rings won't pop open even when the binder is full.

Item			Retail	AA*
ACBR01	Small 3-Ring Binder	Holds up to 100 pages	$39.99	$32.99
ACBR03	Large 3-Ring Binder	Holds up to 250 pages	$39.99	$32.99
ACSR01	Small 3-Ring Slipcase.		$32.50	$26.99
ACSR03	Large 3-Ring Slipcase.		$37.50	$26.99

LARGE 2-POST BINDER & SLIPCASE

For the traditional Scott collector, we offer the standard hinge post binder. Scott album pages are punched with rectangular holes that fit on rectangular posts. The posts and pages are held by a rod that slides down from the top. With the post binder pages do not lie flat. However, filler strips are available for a minimal cost.

Item			Retail	AA*
ACBS03	Large 2-Post Binder	Holds up to 250 pages	$54.99	$46.99
ACSS03	Large 2-Post Slipcase		$37.50	$26.99

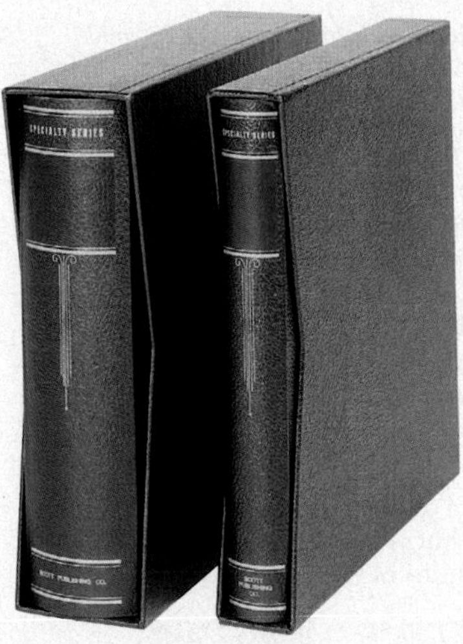

ALBUM PAGE DIVIDERS

Postage, air post, semi-postals; they're all right at your fingertips with Specialty Album Page Dividers. The dividers are a great way to keep your albums organized and save wear and tear on your pages.

Item		Retail	AA*
ACC145	Package of 10	$4.49	$3.49

NATIONAL SERIES PAGES (BORDER B)

(20 per pack)

Item		Retail	AA*
ACC120		$8.99	$6.99
ACC121	Quadrille*	$13.99	$11.99

PAGE PROTECTORS

Protect your stamps and album pages with a clear archival quality plastic sleeve. Sleeves fits over the entire page and protects pages from creases, fingerprints and tears. Scott Page protectors are pvc free and thin enough that they won't make your binder bulge. Page Protectors are available in two sizes. Sold in packages of 25.

2-Post Minuteman/International Pg Protectors

Item	Retail	AA*
ACC165	$13.99	$11.75

National/Specialty Series Pg Protectors*

Item	Retail	AA*
ACC166	$13.99	$11.75

*Punched to fit 2-post and 3-ring binder.

To Order Call 1-800-572-6885

AmosAdvantage.com

1. AA* prices apply to paid subscribers or orders placed online.
2. Prices, terms and product availability subject to change.
3. **Shipping & Handling:**
   United States: 10% of order total. Minimum charge $7.99 Maximum charge $45.00.
   Canada: 20% of order total. Minimum charge $19.99 Maximum charge $200.00.
   Foreign orders are shipped via FedEx Intl. and billed actual freight. Credit cards only.

Illustrated Identifier

This section pictures stamps or parts of stamp designs that will help identify postage stamps that do not have English words on them.

Many of the symbols that identify stamps of countries are shown here as well as typical examples of their stamps.

See the Index and Identifier on the previous pages for stamps with inscriptions such as "sen," "posta," "Baja Porto," "Helvetia," "K.S.A.", etc.

Linn's Stamp Identifier is now available. The 144 pages include more than 2,000 inscriptions and more than 500 large stamp illustrations. Available from Linn's Stamp News, P.O. Box 29, Sidney, OH 45365-0029.

1. HEADS, PICTURES AND NUMERALS

GREAT BRITAIN

Great Britain stamps never show the country name, but, except for postage dues, show a picture of the reigning monarch.

Victoria

Edward VII George V Edward VIII

George VI

Elizabeth II

Some George VI and Elizabeth II stamps are surcharged in annas, new paisa or rupees. These are listed under Oman.

Silhouette (sometimes facing right, generally at the top of stamp)

The silhouette indicates this is a British stamp. It is not a U.S. stamp.

VICTORIA

Queen Victoria

INDIA

Other stamps of India show this portrait of Queen Victoria and the words "Service" (or "Postage") and "Annas."

AUSTRIA

YUGOSLAVIA

(Also BOSNIA & HERZEGOVINA if imperf.)

BOSNIA & HERZEGOVINA

Denominations also appear in top corners instead of bottom corners.

HUNGARY

Another stamp has posthorn facing left

BRAZIL

AUSTRALIA

Kangaroo and Emu

GERMANY

Mecklenburg-Vorpommern

SWITZERLAND

PALAU

2. ORIENTAL INSCRIPTIONS

CHINA

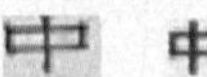

Any stamp with this one character is from China (Imperial, Republic or People's Republic). This character appears in a four-character overprint on stamps of Manchukuo. These stamps are local provisionals, which are unlisted. Other overprinted Manchukuo stamps show this character, but have more than four characters in the overprints. These are listed in People's Republic of China.

Some Chinese stamps show the Sun.

Most stamps of Republic of China show this series of characters.

Stamps with the China character and this character are from People's Republic of China. 人

Calligraphic form of People's Republic of China

(一)	(二)	(三)	(四)	(五)	(六)
1	2	3	4	5	6
(七)	(八)	(九)	(十)	(一十)	(二十)
7	8	9	10	11	12

Chinese stamps without China character

REPUBLIC OF CHINA

PEOPLE'S REPUBLIC OF CHINA

Mao Tse-tung

MANCHUKUO

Temple

Emperor Pu-Yi

The first 3 characters are common to many Manchukuo stamps.

The last 3 characters are common to other Manchukuo stamps.

Orchid Crest

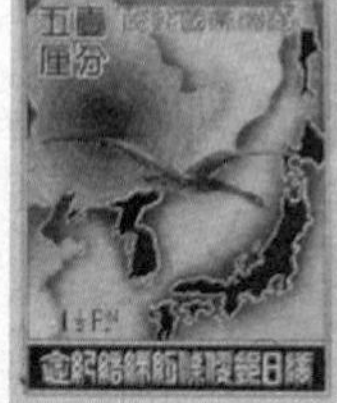

Manchukuo stamp without these elements

JAPAN

Chrysanthemum Crest

Country Name

Japanese stamps without these elements

The number of characters in the center and the design of dragons on the sides will vary.

RYUKYU ISLANDS

Country Name

PHILIPPINES (Japanese Occupation)

Country Name

NETHERLANDS INDIES (Japanese Occupation)

JAVA

SUMATRA

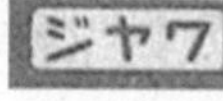

Java

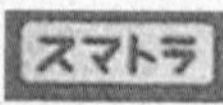

Sumatra

MOLUCCAS, CELEBES AND SOUTH BORNEO

NORTH BORNEO (Japanese Occupation)

Indicates Japanese Occupation

Country Name

MALAYA (Japanese Occupation)

Indicates Japanese Occupation

Country Name

BURMA

Union of Myanmar

ပြည်ထောင်စုမြန်မာနိုင်ငံတော်

Union of Myanmar

(Japanese Occupation)

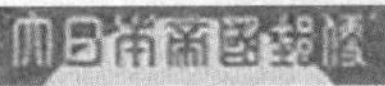

Indicates Japanese Occupation

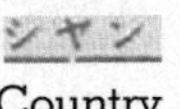

Country Name

Other Burma Japanese Occupation stamps without these elements

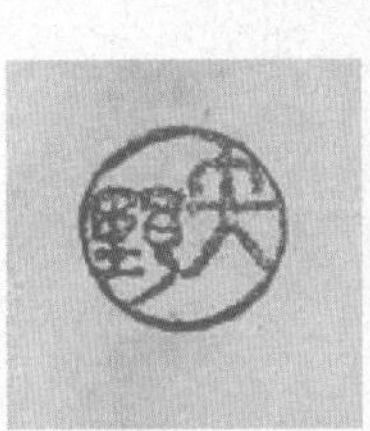

Burmese Script

KOREA

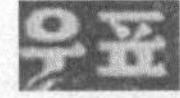

These two characters, in any order, are common to stamps from the Republic of Korea (South Korea) or of the People's Democratic Republic of Korea (North Korea).

조선 우표

This series of four characters can be found on the stamps of both Koreas. Most stamps of the Democratic People's Republic of Korea (North Korea) have just this inscription.

대한민국 우표

Indicates Republic of Korea (South Korea)

South Korean postage stamps issed after 1952 do not show currency expressed in Latin letters. Stamps wiith " HW," "HWAN," "WON," "WN," "W" or "W" with two lines through it, if not illustrated in listings of stamps before this date, are revenues. North Korean postage stamps do not have currency expressed in Latin letters.

Yin Yang appears on some stamps.

South Korean stamps show Yin Yang and starting in 1966, 'KOREA" in Latin letters

Example of South Korean stamps lacking Latin text, Yin Yang and standard Korean text of country name. North Korean stamps never show Yin Yang and starting in 1976 are inscribed "DPRK" or "DPR KOREA" in Latin letters.

THAILAND

Country Name

King Chulalongkorn

King Prajadhipok and Chao P'ya Chakri

3. CENTRAL AND EASTERN ASIAN INSCRIPTIONS

INDIA - FEUDATORY STATES

Alwar

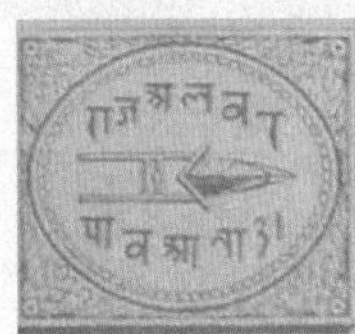

Bhor

Bundi

Similar stamps come with different designs in corners and differently drawn daggers (at center of circle).

Dhar

Duttia

Faridkot

Hyderabad

Similar stamps exist with different central design which is inscribed "Postage" or "Post & Receipt."

Indore

Jammu & Kashmir

Text varies.

Jasdan

Jhalawar

Kotah

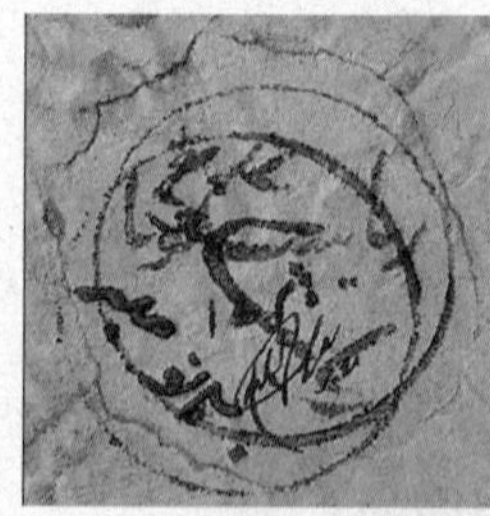

Size and text varies

Nandgaon

Nowanuggur

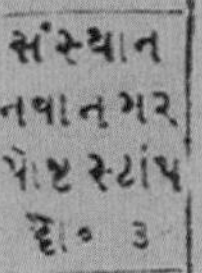

Poonch

Similar stamps exist in various sizes with different text

Rajasthan

Rajpeepla

Soruth

Tonk

BANGLADESH

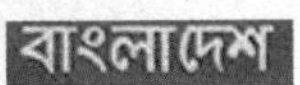

Country Name

NEPAL

Similar stamps are smaller, have squares in upper corners and have five or nine characters in central bottom panel.

TANNU TUVA

ISRAEL

GEORGIA

This inscription is found on other pictorial stamps.

Country Name

ARMENIA

The four characters are found somewhere on pictorial stamps. On some stamps only the middle two are found.

4. AFRICAN INSCRIPTIONS

ETHIOPIA

5. ARABIC INSCRIPTIONS

١ ٢ ٣ ٤ ٥
1 2 3 4 5

٦ ٧ ٨ ٩ ٠
6 7 8 9 0

AFGHANISTAN

Many early Afghanistan stamps show Tiger's head, many of these have ornaments protruding from outer ring, others show inscriptions in black.

Arabic Script

Crest of King Amanullah

Mosque Gate & Crossed Cannons

The four characters are found somewhere on pictorial stamps. On some stamps only the middle two are found.

BAHRAIN

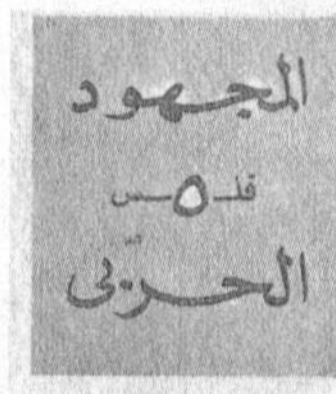

EGYPT

Postage

IRAN

Country Name

Royal Crown

Lion with Sword

Symbol

Emblem

IRAQ

JORDAN

LEBANON

Similar types have denominations at top and slightly different design.

LIBYA

Country Name in various styles

Other Libya stamps show Eagle and Shield (head facing either direction) or Red, White and Black Shield (with or without eagle in center).

Without Country Name

SAUDI ARABIA

Tughra (Central design)

Palm Tree and Swords

SYRIA

Arab Government Issues

THRACE

YEMEN

PAKISTAN

PAKISTAN - BAHAWALPUR

Country Name in top panel, star and crescent

TURKEY

Star & Crescent is a device found on many Turkish stamps, but is also found on stamps from other Arabic areas (see Pakistan-Bahawalpur)

Tughra (similar tughras can be found on stamps of Turkey in Asia, Afghanistan and Saudi Arabia)

Mohammed V

Mustafa Kemal

Plane, Star and Crescent

TURKEY IN ASIA

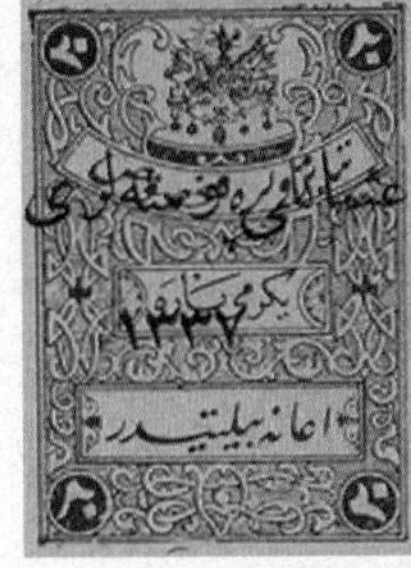

Other Turkey in Asia pictorials show star & crescent. Other stamps show tughra shown under Turkey.

6. GREEK INSCRIPTIONS

GREECE

Country Name in various styles (Some Crete stamps overprinted with the Greece country name are listed in Crete.)

Lepta

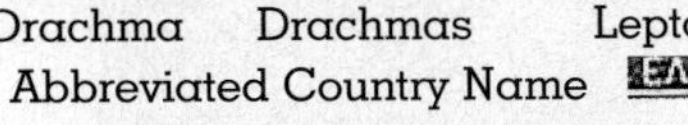

Drachma Drachmas Lepton

Abbreviated Country Name ΕΛΛ

Other forms of Country Name

No country name

CRETE

Country Name

Crete stamps with a surcharge that have the year "1922" are listed under Greece.

EPIRUS

Similar stamps have text above the eagle.

IONIAN IS.

7. CYRILLIC INSCRIPTIONS

RUSSIA

Postage Stamp Imperial Eagle

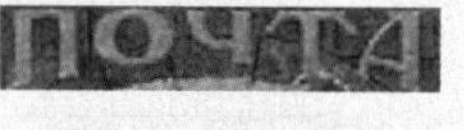

Postage in various styles

Abbreviation for Kopeck Abbreviation for Ruble Russia

Abbreviation for Russian Soviet Federated Socialist Republic RSFSR stamps were overprinted (see below)

Abbreviation for Union of Soviet Socialist Republics

This item is footnoted in Latvia

RUSSIA - Army of the North

"OKCA"

RUSSIA - Wenden

RUSSIAN OFFICES IN THE TURKISH EMPIRE

These letters appear on other stamps of the Russian offices.

The unoverprinted version of this stamp and a similar stamp were overprinted by various countries (see below).

ARMENIA

BELARUS

FAR EASTERN REPUBLIC

Country Name

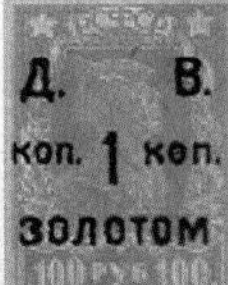

FINLAND

Circles and Dots on stamps similar to Imperial Russia issues

SOUTH RUSSIA

Country Name

BATUM

Forms of Country Name

TRANSCAUCASIAN FEDERATED REPUBLICS

Abbreviation for Country Name

KAZAKHSTAN

ҚАЗАҚСТАН

Country Name

KYRGYZSTAN

КЫРГЫЗСТАН

Country Name

ROMANIA

TAJIKISTAN

Country Name & Abbreviation

UKRAINE

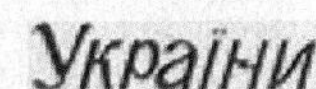
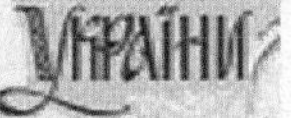

Country Name in various forms

The trident appears on many stamps, usually as an overprint.

Abbreviation for Ukrainian Soviet Socialist Republic

WESTERN UKRAINE

Abbreviation for Country Name

AZERBAIJAN

AZƏRBAYCAN

AZƏRBAYCAN

Country Name

A.C.C.P.

Abbreviation for Azerbaijan Soviet Socialist Republic

MONTENEGRO

ЦРНЕГОРЕ

ЦРНА ГОРА

Country Name in various forms

ЦР.ГОРЕ

Abbreviation for country name

No country name (A similar Montenegro stamp without country name has same vignette.)

SERBIA

СРПСКА СРБИЈА

Country Name in various forms

СРП. К.С.

Abbreviation for country name

No country name

MACEDONIA

МАКЕДОНИЈА

Country Name

МАКЕДОНСКИ

Different form of Country Name

SERBIA & MONTENEGRO

YUGOSLAVIA

ЈУГОСЛАВИЈА

Showing country name

No Country Name

BOSNIA & HERZEGOVINA (Serb Administration)

РЕПУБЛИКА СРПСКА

Country Name

РЕПУБЛИКЕ СРПСКЕ

Different form of Country Name

No Country Name

BULGARIA

Country Name Postage

Stotinka

Stotinki (plural) Abbreviation for Stotinki

Country Name in various forms and styles

No country name

Abbreviation for Lev, leva

MONGOLIA

Country name in one word Tugrik in Cyrillic

Country name in two words Mung in Cyrillic

Mung in Mongolian

Tugrik in Mongolian

Arms

No Country Name

National Album Series

The National series offers a panoramic view of our country's heritage through postage stamps. It is the most complete and comprehensive U.S. album series you can buy. There are spaces for every major U.S. stamp listed in the Scott Catalogue, including Special Printings, Newspaper stamps and much more.

- Pages printed on one side.
- All spaces identified by Scott numbers.
- All major variety of stamps are either illustrated or described.
- Chemically neutral paper protects stamps.
- Sold as page units only. Binders, slipcases and labels sold separately.

Item			*Retail*	*AA**
100NTL1	1845-1934	108 pgs	$64.99	$51.99
100NTL2	1935-1976	108 pgs	$64.99	$51.99
100NTL3	1977-1993	114 pgs	$64.99	$51.99
100NTL4	1994-1999	96 pgs	$64.99	$51.99
100NTL5	2000-2005	99 pgs	$69.99	$55.99
100NTL6	2006-2009	68 pgs	$55.00	$43.99
100S010	2010	14 pgs	$14.99	$11.99
100S011	2011	18 pgs	$15.99	$12.99
100S012	2012	18 pgs	$16.99	$13.99
100S013	2013	21 pgs	$16.99	$13.99

Supplemented in March.

U.S. National Kit

The most complete and comprehensive U.S. stamp album is now available in a money-saving complete kit package! The kit contains pages from 1848 to 2012, plus 4 large National Series 3-ring binders, slipcases, protector sheets and National album labels, pre-cut value pack of black ScottMounts and the *U.S. Specialized Catalogue.*

Item	*Retail*	*AA**
NATLKIT	$689.99	$479.99

What ever your collecting specialty Scott Publishing has an album for you. For more information on the entire line of Scott albums and products visit your local stamp dealer or online at:

AmosAdvantage.com

ORDERING INFORMATION

*AA prices apply to paid subscribers of Amos Hobby titles, or for orders placed online.
Prices, terms and product availability subject to change.

Shipping & Handling:
United States: 10% of order total. Minimum charge $6.99 Maximum charge $45.00.
Canada: 15% of order total. Minimum charge $19.99 Maximum charge $50.00.
Foreign orders are shipped via FedEx Economy Intl. and billed actual freight.

P.O. Box 828, Sidney OH 45365-0828

1-800-572-6885
P.O. BOX 828
Sidney OH 45365
AmosAdvantage.com

INDEX AND IDENTIFIER

All page numbers shown are those in this Volume 1.

Postage stamps that do not have English words on them are shown in the Illustrated Identifier.

Vol. 1 Number Additions, Deletions & Changes

United States

Number in 2014 Catalogue	Number in 2015 Catalogue
1035b	1035e
1035c	1035f
1035d	1035g
1036a	1036b
1036b	1036e
1036d	1036c
1036e	1036d
1054b	1054c
1055a	1055b
1055b	1055c
1055c	1055d
1057a	1057b
1057b	1057d
1058a	1058b
new	1757o
new	3436c
3436c	3436d
3436d	3436e
new	4640b

Revenues – Stock Transfer

Number in 2014 Catalogue	Number in 2015 Catalogue
RD71a	RD71b
new	RD67a
new	RD68a
new	RD70a
new	RD71a
new	RD73a
new	RD74a
new	RD75a
new	RD76a
new	RD77a
new	RD78a
new	RD80a
new	RD81a
new	RD82a
new	RD83a
new	RD84a
new	RD85a

Confederate States of America

Number in 2014 Catalogue	Number in 2015 Catalogue
new	148XU1

Alaouites

Number in 2014 Catalogue	Number in 2015 Catalogue
new	C5b
new	C6b
new	C7b
new	C8b
new	J9a

Algeria

Number in 2014 Catalogue	Number in 2015 Catalogue
new	C7a
new	C7b
new	C7c

Angola

Number in 2014 Catalogue	Number in 2015 Catalogue
70c	deleted
new	118
new	119
new	120
new	121
new	122
new	123
new	124
new	125
new	126
new	127
new	128
new	129
143	130
145	131
147	132
152	133
118	134
119	135
120	136
121	137
122	138
123	139
125	140
new	141
new	142
130	143
new	144
new	145
133	146
134	147
135	148
136	149
138	150
139	151
140	152
144	153
new	154
155	155
new	156
new	157
new	158
new	158C
new	158D
124	158E
new	158F
126	158G
127	158H
128	158I
new	158J
131	158K
132	158L
new	158M
new	158N
new	158O
new	158P
137	158Q
new	158R
new	158S
141	158T
142	158U
new	158V
new	158Va
146	158W
148	158X
149	158Y
150	158Z
151	159A
153	159B
new	159C
154	159D
new	159E
156	159F
157	159G
158	159H

Argentina

Number in 2014 Catalogue	Number in 2015 Catalogue
new	43b
44a	44
45a	45
new	45a
new	45b
44	44A
45	45A
new	92E
new	93E
new	94E
new	95E
new	96E
new	98E
new	99E
new	100E
101b	101E
102b	102E
104b	104E
new	92F
new	93F
new	94F
new	95F
new	96F
new	98F
new	99F
new	100F
new	102F
new	103F
new	104F
new	106E
new	107E
new	108E
new	109E
new	110E
new	111E
new	112E
new	113E
new	114E
new	115E
new	116E
new	117E
new	118E
new	119E
new	121E
new	106F
new	107F
new	108F
new	109F
new	110F
new	111F
new	112F
new	113F
new	115F
new	116F
new	117F
new	120F
new	122E
new	123E
new	124E
new	125E
new	126E
new	127E
new	128E
new	129E
new	130E
new	131E
new	132E
new	133E
new	134E
new	135E
new	136E
new	137E
new	137Ea
new	138E
139b	139E
new	122F
new	123F
new	124F
new	125F
new	127F
new	128F
new	129F
new	130F
new	131F
new	132F
new	134F
new	135F
new	136F
new	137F
new	138F
new	146A
new	147A
new	148A
new	149A
new	149c
new	151A
152	152A
new	153A
154	154A
new	156A
new	157A
159	159A
new	159Ab
new	231B
new	232B
new	233B
new	234B
new	235B
new	236B
new	237B
new	248B
new	249B
new	250B
new	251B
new	252B
new	253B
new	254B
new	264A
new	265A
new	266A
new	267A
new	269A
new	270A
new	290A
new	291A
new	294A
new	297A
new	298A
new	304B
new	305B
new	306B
new	307B
new	307C
new	308B
new	309B
new	310B
new	318A
new	319A
new	323A
new	324A
new	325A
new	326A
new	327A
new	328A
new	329A
new	330A
new	331A
new	332A
new	333A
new	334A
new	340B
new	345B
new	346B
new	349B
OD170a	OD170
OD174a	OD174

Argentina

Number in 2014 Catalogue	Number in 2015 Catalogue
OD170	OD170B
OD171a	OD171B
OD172	OD172B
new	OD172Bc
OD174	OD174B
new	OD174Bc
OD175	OD175B
new	OD175Bc
new	OD178D
new	OD178De
OD179	OD179D
new	OD179De
new	OD185a
new	DO193a
new	OD194a
new	OD195a
new	OD197a
new	OD198a
new	OD199a
new	OD204a
new	OD206a
new	OD208a
new	OD212a
new	OD213a
new	OD213b
new	OD214a
new	OD216a
new	OD219a
new	OD221a
OD222a	OD222
OD223a	OD223
OD224a	OD224
new	OD227a
OD217	OD217B
OD218a	OD218B
OD220a	OD220B
new	OD220Bc
OD221a	OD221B
OD222	OD222B
new	OD222Bc
OD223	OD223B
OD224	OD224B
new	OD224Bc
OD225	OD225B
new	OD225Bc
OD226	OD226B
new	OD232A
new	OD233a
new	OD235a
new	OD238a
new	OD244a
new	OD246a
new	OD247a
new	OD251a
new	OD253a
new	OD256a
new	OD257a
new	OD257b
new	OD258a
new	OD258b
new	OD258c
new	OD259a
new	OD260a
new	OD262a
new	OD264a
OD266a	OD266
OD263	OD263B
OD264	OD264B
OD265	OD265B
new	OD265Bc
OD266	OD266B
new	OD266Bc
OD267	OD267B
OD268	OD268B
new	OD273A

Argentina

Number in 2014 Catalogue	Number in 2015 Catalogue
new	OD273Ab
OD274	OD274A
new	OD274Ab
new	OD281a
new	OD284a
OD286	deleted
OD287	deleted
new	OD286
new	OD287
new	OD291a
new	OD292a
new	OD293a
new	OD294a
new	OD295a
new	OD297a
OD298a	OD298B
new	OD298Bc
new	OD299B
OD300a	OD300B
new	OD300Bc
new	OD301B
OD303	OD303B
OD304	OD304B
new	OD309A
new	OD309Ab
new	OD310Ba
new	OD322a
new	OD330A
new	OD331a
new	OD332a
new	OD333a
new	OD334a
new	OD338a
new	OD340a
OD341a	OD341
OD336	OD336B
OD341	OD341B
OD343a	OD343B
OD344a	OD344B
OD345	OD345B
new	OD350B
OD351	OD351B
new	OD351Bc

Azores

Number in 2014 Catalogue	Number in 2015 Catalogue
new	155
new	156
new	157
new	158
new	159
new	160
new	161
new	162
new	163
new	164
new	165
190	166
196	167
197	168
206	169
new	170
220	171
185	172
155	173
new	173a
156	174
157	175
new	175a
158	176
new	176a
159	177
new	177a
160	178
a.	178a
161	179

Azores

Number in 2014 Catalogue	Number in 2015 Catalogue
new	179a
162	180
new	180a
163	181
164	182
166	183
167	184
169	185
170	186
173	187
176	188
177	189
178	190
181	191
186	192
198	193
210	194
new	195
new	196
new	197
new	198
new	199
new	199a
new	200
165	201
new	202
new	202a
171	203
new	204A
new	204Ab
174	204
177a	205
179	206
180	207
new	208
182	209
183	210
new	210a
184	211
187	212
188	213
191	214
192	215
new	215a
193	216
194	217
195	218
196	219
199	220
200	221
201	222
202	223
204	224
207	225
210	226
211	227
213	228
215	229
216	230
218	231
219	232
221	233
224	234
225	235
231	236
222	237
226	237A
228	237B
229	237C
230	237D
232	237E
233	237F
234	237G
235	237H
236	237I

Azores

Number in 2014 Catalogue	Number in 2015 Catalogue
237	237J
168	313A
172	313B
175	313C
new	313D
189	313E
new	313F
203	313G
205	313H
208	313I
209	313J
212	313K
214	313L
217	313M
223	313N
227	313O

Bahamas

Number in 2014 Catalogue	Number in 2015 Catalogue
1022a	1022b

Barbados

Number in 2014 Catalogue	Number in 2015 Catalogue
new	132a
new	186a
new	187a
new	188a
new	189a
209a	deleted
new	209c

Bulgaria

Number in 2014 Catalogue	Number in 2015 Catalogue
new	3005

Cover Supplies

COVER SLEEVES

Protect your covers with clear polyethylene sleeves.
Sold in packages of 100.

U.S. POSTAL CARD

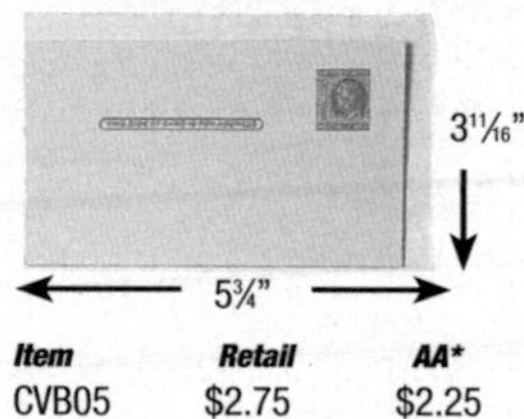

3 11/16"

5¾"

Item	*Retail*	*AA**
CVB05	$2.75	$2.25

U.S. FIRST DAY COVER #6

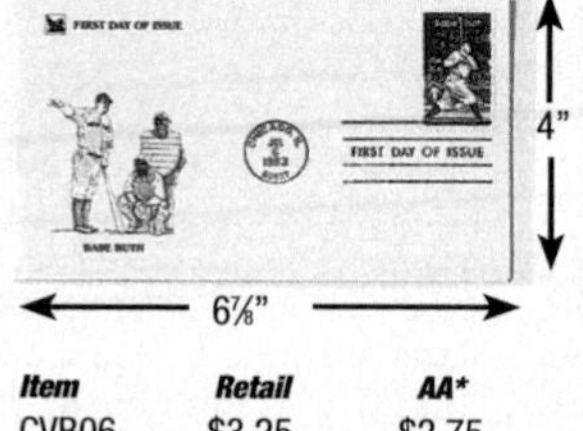

4"

6⅞"

Item	*Retail*	*AA**
CVB06	$3.25	$2.75

CONTINENTAL POSTCARD

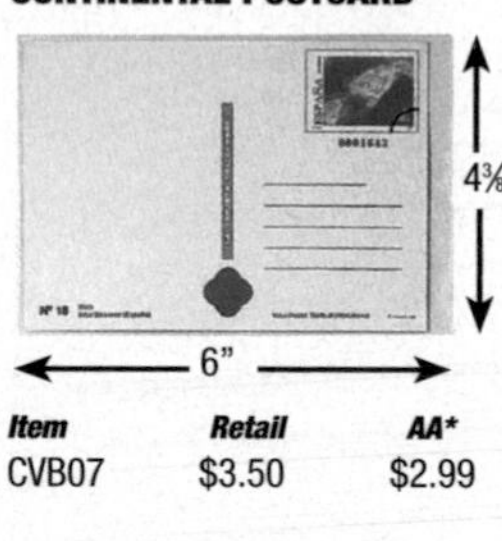

4⅜"

6"

Item	*Retail*	*AA**
CVB07	$3.50	$2.99

EUROPEAN FIRST DAY COVER

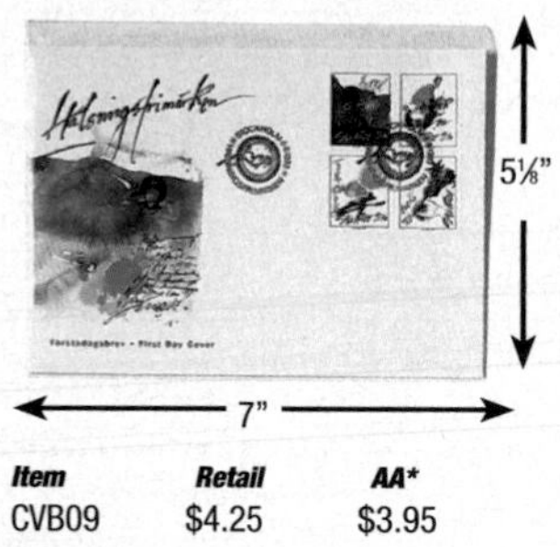

5⅛"

7"

Item	*Retail*	*AA**
CVB09	$4.25	$3.95

#10 BUSINESS ENVELOPE

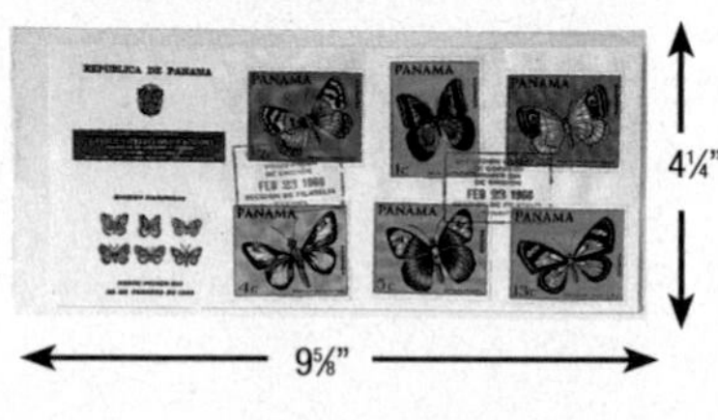

4¼"

9⅝"

Item	*Retail*	*AA**
CVB10	$5.75	$4.95

COVER BINDERS AND PAGES

Padded, durable, 3-ring binders will hold up to 100 covers. Features the "D" ring mechanism on the right hand side of album so you don't have to worry about creasing or wrinkling covers when opening or closing binder. Cover pages sold separately. Available in black with 1 or 2 pockets. Sold in packages of 10.

Item		*Retail*	*AA**
CBRD	Burgundy	$11.99	$9.59
CBBL	Blue	$11.99	$9.59
CBCA	Candy Apple	$11.99	$9.59
CBGY	Gray	$11.99	$9.59
CBBK	Black	$11.99	$9.59
SS2PGB	Pgs. 2-Pock.	$5.75	$4.75
SS2PG1B	Pgs. 1-Pock.	$5.75	$4.75

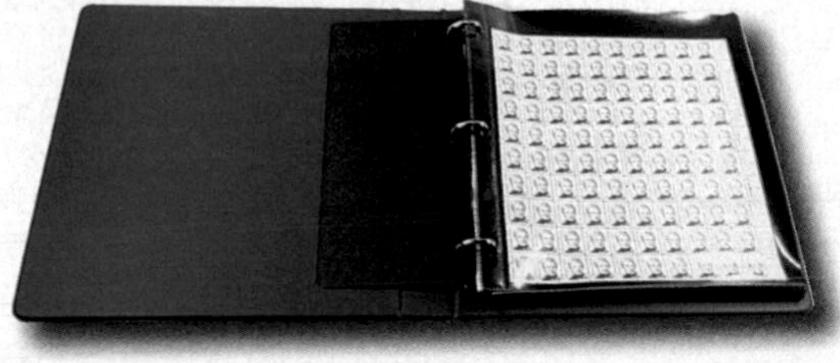

MINT SHEET BINDERS & PAGES

Keep those mint sheets intact in a handsome, 3-ring binder. Just like the cover album, the Mint Sheet album features the "D" ring mechanism on the right hand side of binder so you don't have to worry about damagaing your stamps when turning the pages.

Item			*Retail*	*AA**
MBRD	Red (Burgundy)		$18.99	$15.25
MBBL	Blue		$18.99	$15.25
MBGY	Gray		$18.99	$15.25
MBBK	Black		$18.99	$15.25
SSMP3B	Mint Sheet Pages	(Black 12 per pack)	$9.95	$8.95
SSMP3C	Mint Sheet Pages	(Clear 12 per pack)	$9.95	$8.95

PRINZ CORNER MOUNTS

Clear, self-adhesive corner mounts are ideal for postal cards and covers. Mounts measure ⅞" each side and are made from transparent glass foil. There are 250 mounts in each pack.

Item	*Retail*	*AA**
ACC176	$9.95	**$7.96**

1. AA* prices apply to paid subscribers of *Linn's and orders placed online.*
2. Prices, terms and product availability subject to change.
3. **Shipping & Handling:**
   United States: 10% of order total. Minimum charge $7.99 Maximum charge $45.00.
   Canada: 20% of order total. Minimum charge $19.99 Maximum charge $200.00.
   Foreign orders are shipped via FedEx Intl and billed actual freight. Credit cards only.

Call 1-800-572-6885

AmosAdvantage.com

Currency Conversion

Country	Dollar	Pound	S Franc	Yen	HK $	Euro	Cdn $	Aus $
Australia	1.1151	1.8239	1.2555	0.0108	0.1438	1.5338	1.0507	—
Canada	1.0613	1.7359	1.1949	0.0103	0.1369	1.4598	—	0.9518
European Union	0.7270	1.1891	0.8185	0.0071	0.0938	—	0.6850	0.6520
Hong Kong	7.7537	12.682	8.7297	0.0753	—	10.665	7.3059	6.9534
Japan	102.99	168.45	115.95	—	13.282	141.66	97.039	92.357
Switzerland	0.8882	1.4527	—	0.0086	0.1146	1.2217	0.8369	0.7965
United Kingdom	0.6114	—	0.6884	0.0059	0.0789	0.8410	0.5761	0.5483
United States	—	1.6356	1.1259	0.0097	0.1290	1.3755	0.9422	0.8968

Country	Currency	U.S. $ Equiv.
Afghanistan	afghani	.0184
Aitutaki	New Zealand dollar	.8275
Albania	lek	.0098
Algeria	dinar	.0128
Andorra (French)	euro	1.3755
Andorra (Spanish)	euro	1.3755
Angola	kwanza	.0103
Anguilla	East Caribbean dollar	.3704
Antigua	East Caribbean dollar	.3704
Argentina	peso	.1593
Armenia	dram	.0025
Aruba	guilder	.5587
Ascension	British pound	1.6356
Australia	dollar	.8968
Australian Antarctic Territory	dollar	.8968
Austria	euro	1.3755
Azerbaijan	manat	1.2750
Bahamas	dollar	1.00
Bahrain	dinar	2.6518
Bangladesh	taka	.0129
Barbados	dollar	.5000
Barbuda	East Caribbean dollar	.3704
Belarus	ruble	.0001
Belgium	euro	1.3755
Belize	dollar	.5025
Benin	Community of French Africa (CFA) franc	.0021
Bermuda	dollar	1.00
Bhutan	ngultrum	.0161
Bolivia	boliviano	.1447
Bosnia & Herzegovina	convertible mark	.7034
Botswana	pula	.1151
Brazil	real	.4275
British Antarctic Territory	British pound	1.6356
British Indian Ocean Territory	British pound	1.6356
Brunei	dollar	.7966
Bulgaria	lev	.7033
Burkina Faso	CFA franc	.0021
Burma	kyat	.0010
Burundi	franc	.0006
United Nations-New York	U.S. dollar	1.00
United Nations-Geneva	Swiss franc	1.1259
United Nations-Vienna	euro	1.3755
United States	dollar	1.00

Source: **xe.com** *Dec. 12, 2013. Figures reflect values as of Dec. 12, 2013.*

INDEX TO ADVERTISERS 2015 VOLUME 1

2015
VOLUME 1
DEALER DIRECTORY
YELLOW PAGE LISTINGS

This section of your Scott Catalogue contains advertisements to help you conveniently find what you need, when you need it...!

Accessories

BROOKLYN GALLERY COIN & STAMP, INC.
8725 4th Ave.
Brooklyn, NY 11209
PH: 718-745-5701
FAX: 718-745-2775
info@brooklyngallery.com
www.brooklyngallery.com

Asia

MICHAEL ROGERS, INC.
Suite 4-1
415 S. Orlando Ave.
Winter Park, FL 32789-3683
PH: 407-644-2290
PH: 800-843-3751
FAX: 407-645-4434
Stamps@michaelrogersinc.com
www.michaelrogersinc.com

THE STAMP ACT
PO Box 1136
Belmont, CA 94002
PH: 650-703-2342
PH: 650-592-3315
FAX: 650-508-8104
thestampact@sbcglobal.net

Auctions

DANIEL F. KELLEHER AUCTIONS LLC
PMB 44
60 Newtown Rd
Danbury, CT 06810
PH: 203-297-6056
FAX: 203-297-6059
info@kelleherauctions.com
www.kelleherauctions.com

DUTCH COUNTRY AUCTIONS
4115 Concord Pike
Wilmington, DE 19803
PH: 302-478-8740
FAX: 302-478-8779
auctions@dutchcountryauctions.com
www.dutchcountryauctions.com

MICHAEL ROGERS, INC.
Suite 4-1
415 S. Orlando Ave.
Winter Park, FL 32789-3683
PH: 407-644-2290
PH: 800-843-3751
FAX: 407-645-4434
Stamps@michaelrogersinc.com
www.michaelrogersinc.com

Auctions

R. MARESCH & SON LTD.
5th Floor - 6075 Yonge St.
Toronto, ON M2M 3W2
CANADA
PH: 416-363-7777
FAX: 416-363-6511
www.maresch.com

Auctions - Public

ALAN BLAIR AUCTIONS, L.L.C.
Suite 1
5405 Lakeside Ave.
Richmond, VA 23228-6060
PH: 800-689-5602
FAX: 804-262-9307
alanblair@verizon.net
www.alanblairstamps.com

Australia

ARON R. HALBERSTAM PHILATELISTS, LTD.
PO Box 150168
Van Brunt Station
Brooklyn, NY 11215-0168
PH: 718-788-397
arh@arhstamps.com
www.arhstamps.com

COLONIAL STAMP COMPANY
5757 Wilshire Blvd. PH #8
Los Angeles, CA 90036
PH: 323-933-9435
FAX: 323-939-9930
Toll Free in North America
PH: 877-272-6693
FAX: 877-272-6694
info@colonialstampcompany.com
www.colonialstampcompany.com

Austria

HENRY GITNER PHILATELISTS, INC.
PO Box 3077-S
Middletown, NY 10940
PH: 845-343-5151
PH: 800-947-8267
FAX: 845-343-0068
hgitner@hgitner.com
www.hgitner.com

Auctions

Bangkok

COLONIAL STAMP COMPANY
5757 Wilshire Blvd. PH #8
Los Angeles, CA 90036
PH: 323-933-9435
FAX: 323-939-9930
Toll Free in North America
PH: 877-272-6693
FAX: 877-272-6694
info@colonialstampcompany.com
www.colonialstampcompany.com

Bermuda

ARON R. HALBERSTAM PHILATELISTS, LTD.
PO Box 150168
Van Brunt Station
Brooklyn, NY 11215-0168
PH: 718-788-397
arh@arhstamps.com
www.arhstamps.com

COLONIAL STAMP COMPANY
5757 Wilshire Blvd. PH #8
Los Angeles, CA 90036
PH: 323-933-9435
FAX: 323-939-9930
Toll Free in North America
PH: 877-272-6693
FAX: 877-272-6694
info@colonialstampcompany.com
www.colonialstampcompany.com

British Asia

THE STAMP ACT
PO Box 1136
Belmont, CA 94002
PH: 650-703-2342
PH: 650-592-3315
FAX: 650-508-8104
thestampact@sbcglobal.net

British Commonwealth

ARON R. HALBERSTAM PHILATELISTS, LTD.
PO Box 150168
Van Brunt Station
Brooklyn, NY 11215-0168
PH: 718-788-397
arh@arhstamps.com
www.arhstamps.com

British E. Africa

COLONIAL STAMP COMPANY
5757 Wilshire Blvd. PH #8
Los Angeles, CA 90036
PH: 323-933-9435
FAX: 323-939-9930
Toll Free in North America
PH: 877-272-6693
FAX: 877-272-6694
info@colonialstampcompany.com
www.colonialstampcompany.com

British Guiana

COLONIAL STAMP COMPANY
5757 Wilshire Blvd. PH #8
Los Angeles, CA 90036
PH: 323-933-9435
FAX: 323-939-9930
Toll Free in North America
PH: 877-272-6693
FAX: 877-272-6694
info@colonialstampcompany.com
www.colonialstampcompany.com

Buying

DR. ROBERT FRIEDMAN & SONS
2029 W. 75th St.
Woodridge, IL 60517
PH: 800-588-8100
FAX: 630-985-1588
drbobstamps@comcast.net
www.drbobfriedmanstamps.com

Canada

CANADA STAMP FINDER
54 Soccavo Crescent
Brampton, ON L6Y 0W3
PH: 905-488-6109
Toll Free in North America
PH: 877-412-3106
FAX: 323-215-2635
info@canadastampfinder.com
www.canadastampfinder.com

Central America

GUY SHAW
PO Box 27138
San Diego, CA 92198
PH/FAX: 858-485-8269
guyshaw@guyshaw.com
www.guyshaw.com

China

MICHAEL ROGERS, INC.
Suite 4-1
415 S. Orlando Ave.
Winter Park, FL 32789-3683
PH: 407-644-2290
PH: 800-843-3751
FAX: 407-645-4434
Stamps@michaelrogersinc.com
www.michaelrogersinc.com

Classics

GARY POSNER, INC.
1407 Ave. Z, PMB #535
Brooklyn, NY 11235
PH: 800-323-4279
CELL PH: 917-538-8133
FAX: 718-241-2801
garyposnerinc@aol.com
www. garyposnerinc.com
www.gemstamps.com

J. NALBANDIAN, INC.
PO Box 71
East Greenwich, RI 02818
PH: 401-885-5020
FAX: 401-885-3040
nalbandianj@earthlink.net
www.nalbandstamp.com

Collections

GARY POSNER, INC.
1407 Ave. Z, PMB #535
Brooklyn, NY 11235
PH: 800-323-4279
CELL PH: 917-538-8133
FAX: 718-241-2801
garyposnerinc@aol.com
www. garyposnerinc.com
www.gemstamps.com

Confed. Stamps & Postal History

STANLEY M. PILLER & ASSOCIATES
(HOURS BY APPT. ONLY)
Suite 201
800 S. Broadway
Walnut Creek, CA 94596
PH: 925-938-8290
FAX: 925-938-8812
stmpdlr@aol.com
www.smpiller.com

Ducks

MICHAEL JAFFE
PO Box 61484
Vancouver, WA 98666
PH: 360-695-6161
PH: 800-782-6770
FAX: 360-695-1616
mjaffe@brookmanstamps.com
www.brookmanstamps.com

Errors, Freaks & Oddities

J. NALBANDIAN, INC.
PO Box 71
East Greenwich, RI 02818
PH: 401-885-5020
FAX: 401-885-3040
nalbandianj@earthlink.net
www.nalbandstamp.com

British Commonwealth

British Commonwealth

Europe-Western

HENRY GITNER PHILATELISTS, INC.
PO Box 3077-S
Middletown, NY 10940
PH: 845-343-5151
PH: 800-947-8267
FAX: 845-343-0068
hgitner@hgitner.com
www.hgitner.com

German Colonies

COLONIAL STAMP COMPANY
5757 Wilshire Blvd. PH #8
Los Angeles, CA 90036
PH: 323-933-9435
FAX: 323-939-9930
Toll Free in North America
PH: 877-272-6693
FAX: 877-272-6694
info@colonialstampcompany.com
www.colonialstampcompany.com

Great Britain

COLONIAL STAMP COMPANY
5757 Wilshire Blvd. PH #8
Los Angeles, CA 90036
PH: 323-933-9435
FAX: 323-939-9930
Toll Free in North America
PH: 877-272-6693
FAX: 877-272-6694
info@colonialstampcompany.com
www.colonialstampcompany.com

Hawaii Stamps & Postal History

STANLEY M. PILLER & ASSOCIATES
(HOURS BY APPT. ONLY)
Suite 201
800 S. Broadway
Walnut Creek, CA 94596
PH: 925-938-8290
FAX: 925-938-8812
stmpdlr@aol.com
www.smpiller.com

Japan

MICHAEL ROGERS, INC.
Suite 4-1
415 S. Orlando Ave.
Winter Park, FL 32789-3683
PH: 407-644-2290
PH: 800-843-3751
FAX: 407-645-4434
Stamps@michaelrogersinc.com
www.michaelrogersinc.com

Korea

MICHAEL ROGERS, INC.
Suite 4-1
415 S. Orlando Ave.
Winter Park, FL 32789-3683
PH: 407-644-2290
PH: 800-843-3751
FAX: 407-645-4434
Stamps@michaelrogersinc.com
www.michaelrogersinc.com

Manchukuo

MICHAEL ROGERS, INC.
Suite 4-1
415 S. Orlando Ave.
Winter Park, FL 32789-3683
PH: 407-644-2290
PH: 800-843-3751
FAX: 407-645-4434
Stamps@michaelrogersinc.com
www.michaelrogersinc.com

Middle East-Arab

MICHAEL ROGERS, INC.
Suite 4-1
415 S. Orlando Ave.
Winter Park, FL 32789-3683
PH: 407-644-2290
PH: 800-843-3751
FAX: 407-645-4434
Stamps@michaelrogersinc.com
www.michaelrogersinc.com

New Issues

DAVIDSON'S STAMP SERVICE
PO Box 36355
Indianapolis, IN 46236-0355
PH: 317-826-2620
ed-davidson@earthlink.net
www.newstampissues.com

Philatelic Literature

LEWIS KAUFMAN
PO Box 255
Kiamesha Lake, NY 12751
PH/FAX: 845-794-8013
kerik1@aol.com

South America

GUY SHAW
PO Box 27138
San Diego, CA 92198
PH/FAX: 858-485-8269
guyshaw@guyshaw.com
www.guyshaw.com

Stamp Stores

Arizona

A TO Z STAMPS & COINS
4950 E. Thomas Rd.
Phoenix, AZ 85018
OFFICE: 480-844-9878
CELL: 248-709-8939
michael@azstampcoin.com
www.WorldwideStamps.com

Stamp Stores

California

BROSIUS STAMP, COIN & SUPPLIES
2105 Main St.
Santa Monica, CA 90405
PH: 310-396-7480
FAX: 310-396-7455
brosius.stamp.coin@hotmail.com

COLONIAL STAMP COMPANY
5757 Wilshire Blvd. PH #8
Los Angeles, CA 90036
PH: 323-933-9435
FAX: 323-939-9930
Toll Free in North America
PH: 877-272-6693
FAX: 877-272-6694
info@colonialstampcompany.com
www.colonialstampcompany.com

FISCHER-WOLK PHILATELICS
Suite 211
22762 Aspan St.
Lake Forest, CA 92630
PH: 949-837-2932
fischerwolk@fw.occoxmail.com

Georgia

STAMPS UNLIMITED OF GEORGIA, INC.
Suite 1460
100 Peachtree St. NW
Atlanta, GA 30303
PH: 404-688-9161
tonyroozen@yahoo.com
www.stampsunlimitedofga.com

Illinois

DR. ROBERT FRIEDMAN & SONS
2029 W. 75th St.
Woodridge, IL 60517
PH: 800-588-8100
FAX: 630-985-1588
drbobstamps@comcast.net
www.drbobfriedmanstamps.com

Indiana

KNIGHT STAMP & COIN CO.
237 Main St.
Hobart, IN 46342
PH: 219-942-4341
PH: 800-634-2646
knight@knightcoin.com
www.knightcoin.com

Expertizing

EXPERTIZING
ANY U.S. STAMP, COVER, CANCEL, PROOF, etc.

Only $20.00 (plus shipping/insurance) for paper certificate with black & white photo ($25 with color photo).

WHY pay $50 or more only to find out the item isn't what you thought it was?

See all current service options on our website:
www.stampexpertizing.com

49 year APS member & 38 year *Linn's* advertiser.

Weiss Expertizing Service
William R. Weiss, Jr.
P.O.B. 5358-S, Bethlehem, PA 18015
Phone: (610) 691-6857
Email: weissauction@rcn.com
Website: www.stampexpertizing.com
APS USSS

Supplies

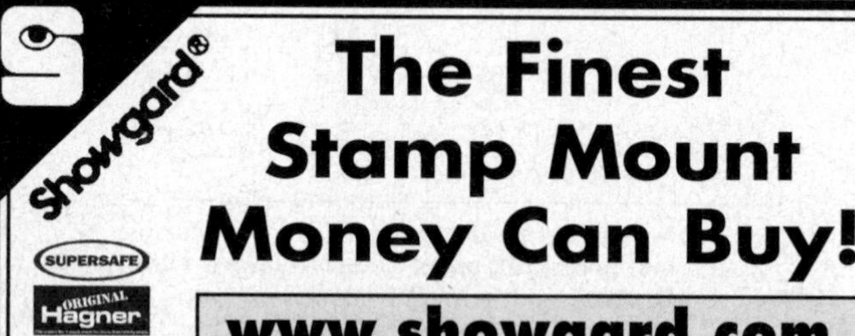

VIDIFORMS COMPANY, INC.
Showgard House
115 N. Rt. 9W, Congers, NY 10920
845-268-4005
Toll Free 877-507-5758

Stamp Stores

New Jersey

AALLSTAMPS
38 N. Main St.
PO Box 249
Milltown, NJ 08850
PH: 732-247-1093
FAX: 732-247-1094
mail@aallstamps.com
www.aallstamps.com

BERGEN STAMPS & COLLECTIBLES
306 Queen Anne Rd.
Teaneck, NJ 07666
PH: 201-836-8987

PHILLY STAMP & COIN CO., INC.
683 Haddon Ave.
Collingswood, NJ 08108
PH: 856-854-5333
FAX: 856-854-5377
phillysc@phillysc.net
www.phillystampandcoin.com

TRENTON STAMP & COIN CO
Thomas DeLuca
Store: Forest Glen Plaza
1804 Highway 33
Hamilton Square, NJ 08690
Mail: PO Box 8574
Trenton, NJ 08650
PH: 609-584-8100
PH: 800-446-8664
FAX: 609-587-8664
TOMD4TSC@aol.com

New York

CHAMPION STAMP CO., INC.
432 W. 54th St.
New York, NY 10019
PH: 212-489-8130
FAX: 212-581-8130
championstamp@aol.com
www.championstamp.com

Ohio

HILLTOP STAMP SERVICE
Richard A. Peterson
PO Box 626
Wooster, OH 44691
PH: 330-262-8907 (0)
PH: 330-262-5378
hilltop@bright.net
www.hilltopstamps.com

THE LINK STAMP CO.
3461 E. Livingston Ave.
Columbus, OH 43227
PH/FAX: 614-237-4125
PH/FAX: 800-546-5726

Virginia

LATHEROW & CO., INC.
5054 Lee Hwy.
Arlington, VA 22207
PH: 703-538-2727
PH: 800-647-4624
FAX: 703-538-5210
latherows@gmail.com

Supplies

BROOKLYN GALLERY COIN & STAMP, INC.
8725 4th Ave.
Brooklyn, NY 11209
PH: 718-745-5701
FAX: 718-745-2775
info@brooklyngallery.com
www.brooklyngallery.com

IHOBB.COM
PO Box 6502
Oceanside, CA 92052
PH: 800-978-5333
sales@ihobb.com
www.ihobb.com

Topicals

E. JOSEPH McCONNELL, INC.
PO Box 683
Monroe, NY 10949
PH: 845-783-9791
FAX: 845-782-0347
ejstamps@gmail.com
www.EJMcConnell.com

Topicals-Columbus

MR. COLUMBUS
PO Box 1492
Fennville, MI 49408
PH: 269-543-4755
David@MrColumbus1492.com
MrColumbus1492.com

United Nations

BRUCE M. MOYER
Box 99
East Texas, PA 18046
PH: 610-395-8410
FAX: 610-395-8537
moyer@unstamps.com
www.unstamps.com

United States

United States

ACS STAMP COMPANY
13650 Via Varra #210
Broomfield, CO 80020
PH: 303-841-8666
ACS@ACSStamp.com
www.acsstamp.com

BROOKMAN STAMP CO.
PO Box 90
Vancouver, WA 98666
PH: 360-695-1391
PH: 800-545-4871
FAX: 360-695-1616
info@brookmanstamps.com
www.brookmanstamps.com

GARY POSNER, INC.
1407 Ave. Z, PMB #535
Brooklyn, NY 11235
PH: 800-323-4279
CELL PH: 917-538-8133
FAX: 718-241-2801
garyposnerinc@aol.com
www. garyposnerinc.com
www.gemstamps.com

HENRY GITNER PHILATELISTS, INC.
PO Box 3077-S
Middletown, NY 10940
PH: 845-343-5151
PH: 800-947-8267
FAX: 845-343-0068
hgitner@hgitner.com
www.hgitner.com

U.S.-Classics

J. NALBANDIAN, INC.
PO Box 71
East Greenwich, RI 02818
PH: 401-885-5020
FAX: 401-885-3040
nalbandianj@earthlink.net
www.nalbandstamp.com

U.S.-Classics/Moderns

A TO Z STAMPS & COINS
4950 E. Thomas Rd.
Phoenix, AZ 85018
OFFICE: 480-844-9878
CELL: 248-709-8939
michael@azstampcoin.com
www.WorldwideStamps.com

U.S.-Collections Wanted

DR. ROBERT FRIEDMAN & SONS
2029 W. 75th St.
Woodridge, IL 60517
PH: 800-588-8100
FAX: 630-985-1588
drbobstamps@comcast.net
www.drbobfriedmanstamps.com

DUTCH COUNTRY AUCTIONS
4115 Concord Pike
Wilmington, DE 19803
PH: 302-478-8740
FAX: 302-478-8779
auctions@dutchcountryauctions.com
www.dutchcountryauctions.com

U.S.-Errors, Freaks & Oddities

GARY POSNER, INC.
1407 Ave. Z, PMB #535
Brooklyn, NY 11235
PH: 800-323-4279
CELL PH: 917-538-8133
FAX: 718-241-2801
garyposnerinc@aol.com
www. garyposnerinc.com
www.gemstamps.com

U.S.-Plate Blocks

GARY POSNER, INC.
1407 Ave. Z, PMB #535
Brooklyn, NY 11235
PH: 800-323-4279
CELL PH: 917-538-8133
FAX: 718-241-2801
garyposnerinc@aol.com
www. garyposnerinc.com
www.gemstamps.com

U.S.-Proofs & Essays

J. NALBANDIAN, INC.
PO Box 71
East Greenwich, RI 02818
PH: 401-885-5020
FAX: 401-885-3040
nalbandianj@earthlink.net
www.nalbandstamp.com

U.S.-Rare Stamps

GARY POSNER, INC.
1407 Ave. Z, PMB #535
Brooklyn, NY 11235
PH: 800-323-4279
CELL PH: 917-538-8133
FAX: 718-241-2801
garyposnerinc@aol.com
www. garyposnerinc.com
www.gemstamps.com

Want Lists-British Empire 1840-1935 German Cols./Offices

COLONIAL STAMP COMPANY
5757 Wilshire Blvd. PH #8
Los Angeles, CA 90036
PH: 323-933-9435
FAX: 323-939-9930
Toll Free in North America
PH: 877-272-6693
FAX: 877-272-6694
info@colonialstampcompany.com
www.colonialstampcompany.com

Want Lists-U.S.

GARY POSNER, INC.
1407 Ave. Z, PMB #535
Brooklyn, NY 11235
PH: 800-323-4279
CELL PH: 917-538-8133
FAX: 718-241-2801
garyposnerinc@aol.com
www. garyposnerinc.com
www.gemstamps.com

Wanted-Estates

A TO Z STAMPS & COINS
4950 E. Thomas Rd.
Phoenix, AZ 85018
OFFICE: 480-844-9878
CELL: 248-709-8939
michael@azstampcoin.com
www.WorldwideStamps.com

Wanted-U.S.

GARY POSNER, INC.
1407 Ave. Z, PMB #535
Brooklyn, NY 11235
PH: 800-323-4279
CELL PH: 917-538-8133
FAX: 718-241-2801
garyposnerinc@aol.com
www. garyposnerinc.com
www.gemstamps.com

Wanted-Worldwide Collections

DANIEL F. KELLEHER AUCTIONS LLC
PMB 44
60 Newtown Rd
Danbury, CT 06810
PH: 203-297-6056
FAX: 203-297-6059
info@kelleherauctions.com
www.kelleherauctions.com

DR. ROBERT FRIEDMAN & SONS
2029 W. 75th St.
Woodridge, IL 60517
PH: 800-588-8100
FAX: 630-985-1588
drbobstamps@comcast.net
www.drbobfriedmanstamps.com

DUTCH COUNTRY AUCTIONS
4115 Concord Pike
Wilmington, DE 19803
PH: 302-478-8740
FAX: 302-478-8779
auctions@dutchcountryauctions.com
www.dutchcountryauctions.com

Websites

ACS STAMP COMPANY
13650 Via Varra #210
Broomfield, CO 80020
PH: 303-841-8666
ACS@ACSStamp.com
www.acsstamp.com

J. NALBANDIAN, INC.
PO Box 71
East Greenwich, RI 02818
PH: 401-885-5020
FAX: 401-885-3040
nalbandianj@earthlink.net
www.nalbandstamp.com

Wholesale-Dealers

GARY POSNER, INC.
1407 Ave. Z, PMB #535
Brooklyn, NY 11235
PH: 800-323-4279
CELL PH: 917-538-8133
FAX: 718-241-2801
garyposnerinc@aol.com
www. garyposnerinc.com
www.gemstamps.com

Wholesale-Dealers

HENRY GITNER PHILATELISTS, INC.
PO Box 3077-S
Middletown, NY 10940
PH: 845-343-5151
PH: 800-947-8267
FAX: 845-343-0068
hgitner@hgitner.com
www.hgitner.com

Worldwide Stamps

A TO Z STAMPS & COINS
4950 E. Thomas Rd.
Phoenix, AZ 85018
OFFICE: 480-844-9878
CELL: 248-709-8939
michael@azstampcoin.com
www.WorldwideStamps.com

Worldwide